D0728224

# New American Bible

## REVISED EDITION

Printed for
Saint Mary's Press by

AMERICAN BIBLE SOCIETY

saint mary's press

# New American Bible

## REVISED EDITION

# New American Bible – Revised Edition

Scripture texts, prefaces, introductions, footnotes and cross references used in this work are taken from the *New American Bible*, revised edition © 2010, 1991, 1986, 1970 Confraternity of Christian Doctrine, Inc., Washington, D.C. All Rights Reserved. No part of this work may be reproduced or transmitted in any form or by any means, electronic or mechanical, including photocopying, recording, or by any information storage and retrieval system, without permission in writing from the copyright owner.

NEW TESTAMENT

| | |
|---|---|
| *Nihil Obstat* | Stephen J. Hartdegen, O.F.M., L.S.S.<br>Censor Deputatus |
| *Imprimatur* | + James A. Hickey, S.T.D., J.C.D.<br>Archbishop of Washington<br>August 27, 1986 |

OLD TESTAMENT

RESCRIPT

In accord with canon 825 §1 of the Code of Canon Law, the United States Conference of Catholic Bishops hereby approves for publication The New American Bible, Revised Old Testament, a translation of the Sacred Scriptures authorized by the Confraternity of Christian Doctrine, Inc.

The translation was approved by the Administrative Committee of the United States Conference of Catholic Bishops in November 2008 and September 2010. It is permitted by the undersigned for private use and study.

Given in the city of Washington, the District of Columbia, on the Feast of Saint Jerome, Priest and Doctor of the Church, the 30th day of September, in the year of our Lord 2010.

Francis Cardinal George, O.M.I.
Archbishop of Chicago
President, USCCB

This edition of the NAB Revised Edition published by
American Bible Society, 1865 Broadway, New York, NY 10023
www.bibles.com

Item 4136
ISBN 978-1-59982-170-2 Paperback

# CONTENTS

## THE OLD TESTAMENT

Preface to the Revised New American
Bible Old Testament ............................ 3

**The Pentateuch** Introduction ............................ 5
Genesis ............................ 7
Exodus ............................ 61
Leviticus ............................ 100
Numbers ............................ 131
Deuteronomy ............................ 169

**The Historical Books** Introduction ............ 204
Joshua ............................ 205
Judges ............................ 226
Ruth ............................ 248
1 Samuel ............................ 252
2 Samuel ............................ 281
1 Kings ............................ 303
2 Kings ............................ 333
1 Chronicles ............................ 359
2 Chronicles ............................ 384
Ezra ............................ 413
Nehemiah ............................ 423

**Biblical Novellas** Introduction ............ 436
Tobit ............................ 437
Judith ............................ 451
Esther ............................ 466

1 Maccabees ............................ 477
2 Maccabees ............................ 504

**The Wisdom Books** Introduction ............ 524
Job ............................ 526
Psalms ............................ 557
Proverbs ............................ 647
Ecclesiastes ............................ 684
Song of Songs ............................ 694
Wisdom ............................ 702
Ben Sira (Ecclesiasticus) ............................ 724

**The Prophetic Books** Introduction ............ 776
Isaiah ............................ 778
Jeremiah ............................ 847
Lamentations ............................ 905
Baruch ............................ 913
Ezekiel ............................ 921
Daniel ............................ 968
Hosea ............................ 987
Joel ............................ 999
Amos ............................ 1004
Obadiah ............................ 1014
Jonah ............................ 1016
Micah ............................ 1019
Nahum ............................ 1027
Habakkuk ............................ 1031
Zephaniah ............................ 1035
Haggai ............................ 1039
Zechariah ............................ 1042
Malachi ............................ 1053

## THE NEW TESTAMENT

Preface to the New American Bible
First Edition of the New Testament ............ 1059

Preface to the Revised Edition ............ 1060

**The Gospels** Introduction ............ 1064
Matthew ............................ 1065
Mark ............................ 1118
Luke ............................ 1142
John ............................ 1183

Acts of the Apostles ............................ 1214

**New Testament Letters** Introduction ............ 1249
Romans ............................ 1250
1 Corinthians ............................ 1269
2 Corinthians ............................ 1289
Galatians ............................ 1305
Ephesians ............................ 1314
Philippians ............................ 1321
Colossians ............................ 1328
1 Thessalonians ............................ 1334
2 Thessalonians ............................ 1338
1 Timothy ............................ 1342

2 Timothy ............................ 1348
Titus ............................ 1352
Philemon ............................ 1355
Hebrews ............................ 1357

**The Catholic Letters** Introduction ............ 1374
James ............................ 1375
1 Peter ............................ 1381
2 Peter ............................ 1387
1 John ............................ 1392
2 John ............................ 1397
3 John ............................ 1399
Jude ............................ 1401

Revelation ............................ 1404

The 3-Year Cycle of Readings
for Sunday Mass ............................ 1427

Readings for Major Feasts of the Year ............ 1434

Weekday Lectionary ............................ 1435

Maps ............................ 1441

# ALPHABETICAL LIST OF
# BIBLICAL BOOKS AND ABBREVIATIONS

| Book | Abbrev. | Page |
|---|---|---|
| Acts | Acts | 1214 |
| Amos | Am | 1004 |
| Baruch | Bar | 913 |
| 1 Chronicles | 1 Chr | 359 |
| 2 Chronicles | 2 Chr | 384 |
| Colossians | Col | 1328 |
| 1 Corinthians | 1 Cor | 1269 |
| 2 Corinthians | 2 Cor | 1289 |
| Daniel | Dn | 968 |
| Deuteronomy | Dt | 169 |
| Ecclesiastes | Eccl | 684 |
| Ephesians | Eph | 1314 |
| Esther | Est | 466 |
| Exodus | Ex | 61 |
| Ezekiel | Ez | 921 |
| Ezra | Ezr | 413 |
| Galatians | Gal | 1305 |
| Genesis | Gn | 7 |
| Habakkuk | Hb | 1031 |
| Haggai | Hg | 1039 |
| Hebrews | Heb | 1357 |
| Hosea | Hos | 987 |
| Isaiah | Is | 778 |
| James | Jas | 1375 |
| Jeremiah | Jer | 847 |
| Job | Jb | 526 |
| Joel | Jl | 999 |
| John | Jn | 1183 |
| 1 John | 1 Jn | 1392 |
| 2 John | 2 Jn | 1397 |
| 3 John | 3 Jn | 1399 |
| Jonah | Jon | 1016 |
| Joshua | Jos | 205 |
| Jude | Jude | 1401 |
| Judges | Jgs | 226 |
| Judith | Jdt | 451 |
| 1 Kings | 1 Kgs | 303 |

| Book | Abbrev. | Page |
|---|---|---|
| 2 Kings | 2 Kgs | 333 |
| Lamentations | Lam | 905 |
| Leviticus | Lv | 100 |
| Luke | Lk | 1142 |
| 1 Maccabees | 1 Mc | 477 |
| 2 Maccabees | 2 Mc | 504 |
| Malachi | Mal | 1053 |
| Mark | Mk | 1118 |
| Matthew | Mt | 1065 |
| Micah | Mi | 1019 |
| Nahum | Na | 1027 |
| Nehemiah | Neh | 423 |
| Numbers | Nu | 131 |
| Obadiah | Ob | 1014 |
| 1 Peter | 1 Pt | 1381 |
| 2 Peter | 2 Pt | 1387 |
| Philemon | Phlm | 1355 |
| Philippians | Phil | 1321 |
| Proverbs | Prv | 647 |
| Psalms | Ps(s) | 557 |
| Revelation | Rev | 1404 |
| Romans | Rom | 1250 |
| Ruth | Ru | 248 |
| 1 Samuel | 1 Sm | 252 |
| 2 Samuel | 2 Sm | 281 |
| Ben Sira (Ecclesiasticus) | Sir | 724 |
| Song of Songs | Sg | 694 |
| 1 Thessalonians | 1 Thes | 1334 |
| 2 Thessalonians | 2 Thes | 1338 |
| 1 Timothy | 1 Tim | 1342 |
| 2 Timothy | 2 Tim | 1348 |
| Titus | Ti | 1352 |
| Tobit | Tb | 437 |
| Wisdom | Wis | 702 |
| Zechariah | Zec | 1042 |
| Zephaniah | Zep | 1035 |

# COLLABORATORS ON THE OLD TESTAMENT OF THE NEW AMERICAN BIBLE 1970

## BISHOPS' COMMITTEE OF THE CONFRATERNITY OF CHRISTIAN DOCTRINE

Most Rev. Charles P. Greco, D.D., Chairman
Most Rev. Joseph T. McGucken, S.T.D.
Most Rev. Vincent S. Waters, D.D.

Most Rev. Romeo Blanchette, D.D.
Most Rev. Christopher J. Weldon, D.D.

## EDITORS IN CHIEF

Rev. Louis F. Hartman, C.SS.R., S.S.L., LING.
  OR. L., Chairman
Rev. Msgr. Patrick W. Skehan, S.T.D., LL.D.,
  Vice-Chairman

Rev. Stephen J. Hartdegen, O.F.M., S.S.L.,
  Secretary

## ASSOCIATE EDITORS AND TRANSLATORS

Rev. Edward P. Arbez, S.S., S.T.D.
Rev. Msgr. Edward J. Byrne, PH.D., S.T.D.
Rev. Edward A. Cerny, S.S., S.T.D.
Rev. James E. Coleran, S.J., S.T.L., S.S.L.
Rev. John J. Collins, S.J., M.A., S.S.L.
Sr. M. Emmanuel Collins, O.S.F., PH.D.
Prof. Frank M. Cross Jr., PH.D.
Rev. Patrick Cummins, O.S.B., S.T.D.
Rev. Antonine A. DeGuglielmo, O.F.M., S.T.D.,
  S.S.L., S.S.LECT. Gen.
Rev. Alexander A. Di Lella, O.F.M., S.T.L.,
  S.S.L., PH.D.
Most Rev. John J. Dougherty, S.T.L., S.S.D.
William A. Dowd, S.J., S.T.D., S.S.L.
Prof. David Noel Freedman, PH.D.
Rev. Michael J. Fruenthaner, S.J., S.T.D., S.S.D.
Rev. Msgr. Maurice A. Hofer, S.S.L.
Rev. Justin Krellner, O.S.B., S.T.D.
Rev. Joseph L. Lilly, C.M., S.T.D., S.S.L.
Rev. Roderick F. MacKenzie, S.J., M.A., S.S.D.
Rev. Edward A. Mangan, C.SS.R., S.S.L.

Rev. Daniel W. Martin, C.M., S.T.L., S.S.L.
Rev. William H. McClellan, S.J.
Rev. James McGlinchey, C.M., S.T.D.
Rev. Frederick Moriarty, S.J., S.S.L., S.T.D.
Rev. Richard T. Murphy, O.P., S.T.D., S.S.D.
Rev. Roland E. Murphy, O. Carm., M.A., S.T.D.,
  S.S.L.
Rev. Msgr. William R. Newton, M.S., S.S.D.
Rev. Everhard Olinger, O.S.B.
Rev. Charles H. Pickar, O.S.A., S.T.L., S.S.L.
Rev. Christopher Rehwinkel, O.F.M., S.T.D.,
  S.S. LECT. GEN.
Rev. Msgr. John R. Rowan, S.T.D., S.S.L.
Prof. J.A. Sanders, PH.D.
Rev. Edward F. Siegman, C.PP.S., S.T.D., S.S.L.
Rev. Msgr. Matthew P. Stapleton, S.T.D., S.S.L.
Rev. Msgr. John E. Steinmueller, S.T.D., S.S.L.
Rev. John Ujlaki, O.S.B., LITT.D.
Rev. Bruce Vawter, C.M., S.T.L., S.S.D.
Rev. John B. Weisengoff, S.T.D., S.S.L.

# COLLABORATORS ON THE REVISED NEW TESTAMENT OF THE NEW AMERICAN BIBLE 1986

## BISHOPS' AD HOC COMMITTEE

Most Rev. Theodore E. McCarrick, D.D.
Most Rev. Richard J. Sklba, D.D.

Most Rev. J. Francis Stafford, D.D.
Most Rev. John F. Whealon, D.D., Chairman

## BOARD OF EDITORS

Rev. Msgr. Myles M. Bourke
Rev. Francis T. Gignac, S.J., Chairman

Rev. Stephen J. Hartdegen, O.F.M., Secretary
Rev. John H. Reumann

## REVISERS

Rev. Msgr. Myles M. Bourke
Rev. Frederick W. Danker
Rev. Alexander A. Di Lella, O.F.M.
Rev. Charles H. Giblin, S.J.
Rev. Francis T. Gignac, S.J.
Rev. Stephen J. Hartdegen, O.F.M.
Dr. Maurya P. Horgan

Rev. John R. Keating, S.J.
Rev. John Knox
Dr. Paul J. Kobelski
Dr. J. Rebecca Lyman
Br. Elliott C. Maloney, O.S.B.
Dr. Janet A. Timbie

## CONSULTANTS

Rev. Joseph Jensen, O.S.B.
Rev. Aidan Kavanagh, O.S.B.

Dr. Marianne Sawicki

## BUSINESS MANAGER

Charles A. Buggé

## WORD PROCESSOR

Suzanna Jordan

# COLLABORATORS ON THE REVISED PSALMS OF THE NEW AMERICAN BIBLE 1991

## BISHOPS' AD HOC COMMITTEE

Most Rev. Enrique San Pedro, S.J.
Most Rev. Richard Sklba, D.D.
Most Rev. Donald W. Trautman, S.T.D., S.S.L.

Most Rev. Emil A. Wcela
Most Rev. John F. Whealon, S.S.L., Chairman

## BOARD OF EDITORS

Rev. Richard Clifford, S.J.
Br. Aloysius Fitzgerald, F.S.C.
Rev. Joseph Jensen, O.S.B.

Rev. Roland Murphy, O.Carm.
Sr. Irene Nowell, O.S.B.
Dr. Judith Sanderson

## REVISERS

Prof. Gary Anderson
Rev. Michael L. Barré, S.S.
Rev. Christopher T. Begg
Dr. Joseph Blenkinsopp
Rev. Anthony R. Ceresko, O.S.F.S.
Rev. Richard J. Clifford, S.J.
Rev. Aelred Cody, O.S.B.
Prof. Michael D. Coogan
Rev. Alexander A. Di Lella, O.F.M.
Dr. Robert A. Di Vito
Br. Aloysius Fitzgerald, F.S.C.
Rev. Michael D. Guinan, O.F.M.
Rev. William L. Holladay
Rev. William Irwin, C.S.B.
Rev. Joseph Jensen, O.S.B.

Rev. John S. Kselman
Rev. Leo Laberge, O.M.I.
Dr. Conrad E. L'Heureux
Dr. Paul G. Mosca
Rev. Dr. Roland E. Murphy, O.Carm.
Dr. Michael Patrick O'Connor
Rev. Brian J. Peckham, S.J.
Prof. Jimmy J. Roberts
Sr. Eileen M. Schuller, O.S.U.
Dr. Byron E. Shafer
Prof. Mark S. Smith
Prof. Matitiahu Tesvat
Dr. Eugene C. Ulrich
Prof. James C. VanderKam
Rev. Jerome T. Walsh

## ENGLISH CONSULTANTS

Dr. Catherine Dunn

Br. Daniel Burke, F.S.C.

## BUSINESS MANAGER

Charles A. Buggé

# COLLABORATORS ON THE OLD TESTAMENT OF THE NEW AMERICAN BIBLE 2010

## BISHOPS' COMMITTEE ON DOCTRINE

### SUBCOMMITTEE ON THE TRANSLATION OF SCRIPTURE TEXT

Most Rev. Arthur J. Serratelli, Chairman
Justin Cardinal Rigali
Most Rev. Blase J. Cupich

Most Rev. Richard J. Sklba
Most Rev. Anthony B. Taylor

### BOARD OF EDITORS

Dr. Deirdre A. Dempsey
Dr. Robert A. Di Vito
Rev. Francis T. Gignac, S.J.
Rev. Joseph Jensen, O.S.B., Chairman
Rev. Dale Launderville, O.S.B.

Rev. Roland E. Murphy, O.Carm. +
Dr. Kathleen S. Nash
Sr. Irene Nowell, O.S.B.
Rev. James P. M. Walsh, S.J.

### REVISERS

Dr. Gary A. Anderson
Reverend Michael L. Barré, S.S.
Reverend Christopher T. Begg
Dr. Joseph Blenkinsopp
Reverend Lawrence Boadt, C.S.P. +
Professor Edward F. Campbell
Professor Anthony Ceresko, OSFS +
Reverend Richard J. Clifford, S.J.
Reverend Aelred Cody, O.S.B.
Dr. John J. Collins
Professor Michael D. Coogan
Reverend T.J. Jeremy Corley
Dr. Toni Craven
Dr. James L. Crenshaw
Reverend Alexander A. Di Lella, O.F.M.
Dr. Robert A. Di Vito
Brother Aloysius Fitzgerald, F.S.C. +
Reverend Joseph A. Fitzmyer, S.J.
Dr. Carole R. Fontaine
Reverend Daniel J. Harrington, S.J.
Dr. Richard S. Hess

Dr. Theodore Hiebert
Dr. William L. Holladay
Dr. Tod Linafelt
Dr. P. Kyle McCarter, Jr.
Dr. Carol Meyers
Dr. Eric Meyers
Dr. Patrick D. Miller, Jr.
Reverend Craig E. Morrison, O. Carm.
Dr. Paul G. Mosca
Dr. Kathleen S. Nash
Professor Robert A. Oden, Jr.
Reverend Gregory J. Polan, O.S.B.
Dr. James J.M. Roberts
Dr. William M. Soll
Dr. Gene M. Tucker
Dr. Eugene C. Ulrich
Reverend Walter A. Vogels, W.F.
Reverend Jerome T. Walsh
Reverend Addison G. Wright, S.S.
Dr. David P. Wright

### BUSINESS MANAGERS

Charles Buggé

Mary Elizabeth Sperry

### WORD PROCESSORS

Ellen Coughlin

Nancy Hartnagel

# COLLABORATORS ON THE BOOK OF PSALMS OF THE NEW AMERICAN BIBLE 2010

## BISHOPS' COMMITTEE ON DOCTRINE

### SUBCOMMITTEE ON THE TRANSLATION OF SCRIPTURE TEXT

Most Rev. Arthur J. Serratelli, Chairman
Justin Cardinal Rigali
Most Rev. Blase J. Cupich

Most Rev. Richard J. Sklba
Most Rev. Anthony B. Taylor

### BOARD OF EDITORS

Rev. Joseph Mindling, OFM Cap.

Rev. J. Edward Owens, O.SS.T.

### REVISERS

Rev. Michael L. Barré, S.S.
Dr. Corrine L. Carvalho
Dr. Robert A. Di Vito
Dr. Robert D. Miller II, SFO

Rev. Joseph Mindling, OFM Cap.
Rev. J. Edward Owens, O.SS.T.
Dr. Eugene C. Ulrich

### BUSINESS MANAGER

Mary Elizabeth Sperry

# THE
# OLD TESTAMENT

# PREFACE TO THE
# REVISED
# NEW AMERICAN BIBLE
# OLD TESTAMENT

The first step in the genesis of the New American Bible was taken in 1936 when His Excellency, the Most Reverend Edwin V. O'Hara, D.D., chairman of the Episcopal Committee of the Confraternity of Christian Doctrine, invited a group of Catholic Scripture scholars to plan for a revised edition of the Challoner-Rheims New Testament, primarily on the basis of the Vulgate; the plans soon expanded to include the revision of the Old Testament. Archbishop O'Hara's initiative resulted in the formation of the Catholic Biblical Association, whose principal activity in its early years was this work of revision and translation. (For information on the work done on the New Testament, see the "Preface to the New American Bible: First Edition of the New Testament" and "Preface to the Revised Edition.") In 1943 His Holiness Pope Pius XII issued the encyclical *Divino afflante spiritu*, which encouraged Scripture scholars to translate the Scriptures from the original languages. He wrote: "We ought to explain the original text which was written by the inspired author himself and has more authority and greater weight than any, even the very best, translation whether ancient or modern. This can be done all the more easily and fruitfully if to the knowledge of languages be joined a real skill in literary criticism of the same text." Although at this point work on almost twenty of the Old Testament books was completed or near completion, that work was abandoned and the new project of translating from the Hebrew, Greek, and Aramaic was undertaken.

The completed books of the Old Testament were initially published, as they became available, in four volumes: Genesis–Ruth (1952), Job–Sirach (1955), Isaiah–Malachi (1961), and Samuel–Maccabees (1969). Some fifty scholars collaborated on this project; these were mainly Catholics, but, in accord with the suggestion of Vatican II that "with the approval of the church authority, these translations be produced in cooperation with separated brothers" so that "all Christians may be able to use them" (*Dei Verbum*, No. 22), non-Catholics also participated in the work. To this point the translation had been known under the name of the "Confraternity of Christian Doctrine" or CCD for short, but when these parts of the Old Testament were combined with the New Testament in a single volume, it was given the name "New American Bible," in part to reflect its ecumenical character. In producing the new volume certain changes were made from the original four volumes: a retranslation of the Book of Genesis, cross-references, new and expanded exegetical notes.

New translations and revision of existing translations are required from time to time for various reasons. For example, it is important to keep pace with the discovery and publication of new and better ancient manuscripts (e.g., the Dead Sea scrolls) so that the best possible textual tradition will be followed, as required by *Divino afflante spiritu*. There are advances in linguistics of the biblical languages which make possible a better understanding and more accurate translation of the original languages. And there are changes and developments in vocabulary and the cultural background of the receptor language. An obvious example of this is the abandonment in English of the second person singular (use of "thee," "thou," "sayest," "hearest"), which had a major impact on Bible translations. Other changes are less obvious but are nevertheless present. There have been changes in vocabulary; for example, the term "holocaust" is now normally reserved for the sacrilegious attempt to destroy the Jewish people by the Third Reich. Concerns such as these are reflected in what Pope John Paul II spoke of as the "three pillars" of good biblical translation: "A good translation is based on three pillars that must contemporaneously support the entire work. First, there must be a deep knowledge of the language and the cultural world at the point of origin. Next, there must be a good familiarity with the language and cultural context at the point where the work will arrive. Lastly, to crown the work with success, there must be an adequate mastery of the contents and meaning of what one is translating"—and he praised the translation that "utilizes the vocabulary and idioms of everyday speech" ("le parole e le forme della lingua di tutti i giorni"). (From an address to the United Bible Societies, November 26, 2001.)

This new edition is a thorough revision of the already excellent *New American Bible* Old Testament of 1970. Work on most books of the Old Testament, begun in 1994 and completed in 2001, was done by forty revisers and a board of eight editors. The 1991 revision of the Psalter, the work of thirty revisers and six editors, was further revised by seven revisers and two editors between 2009 and 2010. As suggested in the comments above, the revision aimed at making use of the best manuscript traditions available (see below), translating as accurately as possible, and rendering the result in good contemporary English. In many ways it is a more literal translation than the original *NAB* and has attempted to be more consistent in rendering Hebrew (or Greek) words and idioms, especially in technical contexts, such as regulations for sacrifices. In translating the Psalter special effort was made to provide a smooth, rhythmic translation for easy singing or recitation, and to retain the concrete imagery of the Hebrew.

Where the Old Testament translation supposes the received text—Hebrew, Aramaic, or Greek, as the case may be—ordinarily contained in the best-known editions, as the original or the oldest extant form, no additional remarks are necessary. Where the translators have departed from those received texts, e.g., by following the Septuagint rather than the Masoretic text, accepting a reading of what is judged to be a better textual tradition, as from a Qumran manuscript, or by emending a reading apparently corrupted in transmission, such changes are recorded in the revised edition of the *Textual Notes on the New American Bible*. Additional information on the textual tradition for some books may be found in the introduction to the book in the same *Textual Notes*.

In particular, important manuscripts from Cave 4 of Qumran, as well as the most useful recensions of the Septuagint, have been consulted in the preparation of 1 and 2 Samuel. Fragments of the lost Book of Tobit in Aramaic and in Hebrew, recovered from Cave 4 of Qumran, are in substantial agreement with the Sinaiticus Greek recension used for the translation of this book. The lost original Hebrew text of 1 Maccabees is replaced by its oldest extant form in Greek. Judith, 2 Maccabees, and parts of Esther are also translated from the Greek. The translation of The Wisdom of Ben Sira is based on the original Hebrew as far as it is preserved, with corrections from the ancient versions; otherwise, the Greek of the Septuagint is followed. In the Book of Baruch the basic text is the Greek of the Septuagint, with some readings derived from an underlying Hebrew form no longer extant. In the deuterocanonical sections of Daniel (3:24–90; 13:1–14:42), the basic text is the Greek text of so-called Theodotion, occasionally revised according to the Greek text of the Septuagint.

# THE
# PENTATEUCH

The Pentateuch (Greek for "five books") designates the first five books of the Jewish and Christian Bible (Genesis, Exodus, Leviticus, Numbers, and Deuteronomy). Jewish tradition calls the five books Torah (Teaching, Law) because of the centrality of the Sinai covenant and legislation mediated through Moses.

The unity of the Pentateuch comes from the single story it tells. God creates the world and destines human beings for the blessings of progeny and land possession (Gn 1–3). As the human race expands, its evil conduct provokes God to send the flood to wipe out all but righteous Noah's family. After the flood, the world is repopulated from his three sons, Ham, Shem, and Japheth (Gn 4–9). From them are descended the seventy nations of the civilized world whose offense this time (building a city rather than taking their assigned lands, Gn 10–11) provokes God to elect one family from the rest. Abraham and his wife, Sarah, landless and childless, are promised a child and the land of Canaan. Amid trials and fresh promises, a son (Isaac) is born to them and Abraham takes title to a sliver of Canaanite land, a kind of down payment for later possession (Gn 12–25). Gn 25–36 tells how their descendant Jacob becomes the father of twelve sons (because of which he is called "Israel"), and Gn 37–50 tells how the rejected brother Joseph saves the family from famine and brings them to Egypt.

In Egypt, a pharaoh who knew not Joseph subjects "the seventy sons of Jacob" ("the Hebrews") to hard labor, keeping them from their land and destroying their male progeny (Ex 1). Moses is commissioned to lead the people out of Egypt to their own land (Ex 2–6). In ten plagues, the Lord defeats Pharaoh. Free at last, the Hebrews leave Egypt and journey to Mount Sinai (Ex 7–18), where they enter into a covenant to be the people of the Lord and be shaped by the Ten Commandments and other laws (Ex 19–24). Though the people commit apostasy when Moses goes back to the mountain for the plans of the dwelling (tabernacle), Moses' intercession prevents the abrogation of the covenant by God (Ex 32–34). A principle has been established, however: even the people's apostasy need not end their relationship with God. The book ends with the cloud and the glory taking possession of the tent of meeting (Ex 36:34–38). "The sons of Israel" in Ex 1:1 are the actual sons of Jacob/Israel the patriarch, but at the end of the book they are the nation Israel, for all the elements of nationhood in antiquity have been granted: a god (and temple), a leader, a land, and an authoritative tradition.

Israel remains at the holy mountain for almost a year. The entire block of material from Ex 19:1 to Nm 10:11 is situated at Sinai. The rituals of Leviticus and Numbers are delivered to Moses at the holy mountain, showing that Israel's worship was instituted by God and part of the very fabric of the people's life. Priestly material in the Book of Exodus (chaps. 25–31, 35–40) describes the basic institutions of Israelite worship (the tabernacle, its furniture, and priestly vestments). Leviticus, aptly called in rabbinic tradition the Priests' Manual, lays down the role of priests to teach Israel the distinction between clean and unclean and to see to their holiness. In Nm 10:11–22:1, the journey is resumed, this time from Sinai through the wilderness to Transjordan; Nm 22:2–36:13 tells of events and laws in the plains of Moab.

The final book of the Pentateuch, Deuteronomy, consists of four speeches by Moses to the people who have arrived at the plains of Moab, ready to conquer the land: 1:1–4:43; 4:44–28:68; 29:1–32:52; 33:1–34:12. Each speech is introduced by the formula "This is the law/words/blessing."

The Priestly editor used literary formulas. The formula "These are the generations (the wording can vary) of . . . " occurs five times in the primordial history (Gn 2:4a; 5:1; 6:9; 10:1; 11:10) and five times in the ancestral history (11:27; 25:12; 25:19; 36:1 [v. 9 is secondary]; 37:2). In Exodus and Numbers the formula (with slight variations) "They departed from (place name) and encamped at (place name)" occurs in two groups of six: A. Ex 12:37a; 13:20; 14:1–2; 15:22a; 16:1; 17:1a; and B. 19:2; Nm 10:12; 20:1a; 20:22; 21:10–11; 22:1.

Who wrote the Pentateuch, and when? Up to the seventeenth century, the virtually unanimous answer of Jews and Christians was "Moses." Moses wrote the Pentateuch as David wrote the Psalter and Solomon wrote the wisdom literature. Though scholars had noted inconsistencies (compare Ishmael's age in Gn 16:16 and 21:5, 14) and duplications (Gn 12, 20, and 26), they assumed Mosaic authorship because of the prevalent theory of inspiration: God inspired authors while they wrote. With the rise of historical criticism, scholars began to use the doublets and inconsistencies as clues to different authors and traditions.

By the late nineteenth century, one theory of the sources of the Pentateuch had been worked out that proved acceptable in its main lines to the majority of scholars (apart from Christian and Jewish conservatives) then and now. It can be quickly sketched. In the premonarchic period of the Judges (ca. 1220–1020 B.C.), the twelve tribes had an oral form of their story from creation to the taking of the land. With the beginnings of monarchy in the late eleventh and tenth centuries, the oral material was written down, being known as the Yahwist account (from its use of the divine name Yhwh). Its abbreviation, "J," comes from the German spelling of the divine name. In the following century, another account took shape in the Northern Kingdom (called E after its use of Elohim as a divine name); some believe the E source is simply a supplement to J. After the fall of the Northern Kingdom in 722/721 B.C., the E version was taken to Jerusalem where it was combined with the J version to produce J-E. During the exile (conventionally dated 587–539 B.C.) or thereafter, an editor recast J-E to make it relevant for the exiled population. This editor is conventionally known as P (= Priestly) because of the chronological and ritual interests apparent in the work. P can also designate archival material and chronological notices. The audience for the Priestly edition no longer lived in the land and was deeply concerned about its survival and its claim on the land.

Deuteronomy (= D) stands alone in style, genre (preaching rather than narrative), and content. How did it come to be the fifth book of the Pentateuch? The J-E narrative actually ends in Numbers, when Israel arrives at the plains of Moab. Many scholars believe that Deuteronomy was secondarily attached to Numbers by moving the account of Moses' death from its original place in the J-E version in Numbers to the end of Deuteronomy (chap. 34). Deuteronomy was attached to Genesis–Numbers to link it to another great work, the Deuteronomistic History (Joshua to Kings). Deuteronomy is now the fifth book of the Pentateuch and the first book of the Deuteronomistic History.

In the last three decades, the above consensus on the composition of the Pentateuch has come under attack. Some critics are extremely skeptical about the historical value of the so-called early traditions, and a few doubt there ever was a preexilic monarchy of any substance. For such scholars, the Pentateuch is a retrojection from the fourth or third centuries B.C. Other scholars postulate a different sequence of sources, or understand the sources differently.

How should a modern religiously minded person read the Pentateuch? First, readers have before them the most significant thing, the text of the Pentateuch. It is accurately preserved, reasonably well understood, and capable of touching audiences of every age. Take and read! Second, the controversies are about the sources of the Pentateuch, especially their antiquity and character. Many details will never be known, for the evidence is scanty. Indeed, the origin of many great literary works is obscure.

The Pentateuch witnesses to a coherent story that begins with the creation of the world and ends with Israel taking its land. The same story is in the historical Ps 44, 77, 78, 80, 105, 114, and 149, and in the confessions Dt 26:5–9, Jos 24:2–13, and 1 Sm 12:7–13. Though the narrative enthralls and entertains, as all great literature does, it is well to remember that it is a theopolitical charter as well, meant to establish how and why descendants of the patriarchs are a uniquely holy people among the world's nations.

The destruction of the Jerusalem Temple and deportation of Israelites in the sixth century B.C. seemed to invalidate the charter, for Israel no longer possessed its land in any real sense. The last chapter of the ancient narrative—Israel dwelling securely in its land—no longer held true. The story had to be reinterpreted, and the Priestly editor is often credited with doing so. A preface (Gn 1) was added, emphasizing God's intent that human beings continue in existence through their progeny and possess their own land. Good news, surely, to a devastated people wondering whether they would survive and repossess their ancestral land. The ending of the old story was changed to depict Israel at the threshold of the promised land (the plains of Moab) rather than in it. Henceforth, Israel would be a people oriented toward the land rather than possessing it. The revised ending could not be more suitable for Jews and Christians alike. Both peoples can imagine themselves on the threshold of the promised land, listening to the word of God in order to be able to enter it in the future. For Christians particularly, the Pentateuch portrays the pilgrim people waiting for the full realization of the kingdom of God.

# THE BOOK OF
# GENESIS

⁓⁓

Genesis is the first book of the Pentateuch (Genesis, Exodus, Leviticus, Numbers, Deuteronomy), the first section of the Jewish and the Christian Scriptures. Its title in English, "Genesis," comes from the Greek of Gn 2:4, literally, "the book of the generation (*genesis*) of the heavens and earth." Its title in the Jewish Scriptures is the opening Hebrew word, *Bereshit*, "in the beginning."

The book has two major sections—the creation and expansion of the human race (2:4–11:9), and the story of Abraham and his descendants (11:10–50:26). The first section deals with God and the nations, and the second deals with God and a particular nation, Israel. The opening creation account (1:1–2:3) lifts up two themes that play major roles in each section—the divine command to the first couple (standing for the whole race) to produce offspring and to possess land (1:28). In the first section, progeny and land appear in the form of births and genealogies (chaps. 2–9) and allotment of land (chaps. 10–11), and in the second, progeny and land appear in the form of promises of descendants and land to the ancestors. Another indication of editing is the formulaic introduction, "this is the story; these are the descendants" (Hebrew *tôledôt*), which occurs five times in Section I (2:4; 5:1; 6:9; 10:1; 10:31) and five times in Section II (11:10; 25:12, 19; 36:1 [v. 9 is an addition]; 37:2).

**The Composition of the Book.** For the literary sources of Genesis, see Introduction to the Pentateuch. As far as the sources of Genesis are concerned, contemporary readers can reasonably assume that ancient traditions (J and E) were edited in the sixth or fifth century B.C. for a Jewish audience that had suffered the effects of the exile and was now largely living outside of Palestine. The editor highlighted themes of vital concern to this audience: God intends that every nation have posterity and land; the ancestors of Israel are models for their descendants who also live in hope rather than in full possession of what has been promised; the ancient covenant with God is eternal, remaining valid even when the human party has been unfaithful. By highlighting such concerns, the editor addressed the worries of exiled Israel and indeed of contemporary Jews and Christians.

**Genesis 1–11.** The seven-day creation account in Gn 1:1–2:3 tells of a God whose mere word creates a beautiful universe in which human beings are an integral and important part. Though Gn 2:4–3:24 is often regarded as "the second creation story," the text suggests that the whole of 2:4–11:9 tells one story. The plot of Gn 2–11 (creation, the flood, renewed creation) has been borrowed from creation-flood stories attested in Mesopotamian literature of the second and early first millennia. In the Mesopotamian creation-flood stories, the gods created the human race as slaves whose task it was to manage the universe for them—giving them food, clothing, and honor in temple ceremonies. In an unforeseen development, however, the human race grew so numerous and noisy that the gods could not sleep. Deeply angered, the gods decided to destroy the race by a universal flood. One man and his family, however, secretly warned of the flood by his patron god, built a boat and survived. Soon regretting their impetuous decision, the gods created a revised version of humankind. The new race was created mortal so they would never again grow numerous and bother the gods. The authors of Genesis adapted the creation-flood story in accord with their views of God and humanity. For example, they attributed the fault to human sin rather than to divine miscalculation (6:5–7) and had God reaffirm without change the original creation (9:1–7). In the biblical version God is just, powerful, and not needy.

How should modern readers interpret the creation-flood story in Gn 2–11? The stories are neither history nor myth. "Myth" is an unsuitable term, for it has several different meanings and connotes untruth in popular English. "History" is equally misleading, for it suggests that the events actually took place. The best term is creation-flood story. Ancient Near Eastern thinkers did not have our methods of exploring serious questions. Instead, they used narratives for issues that we would call philosophical and theological. They added and subtracted narrative details and varied the plot as they sought meaning in the ancient stories. Their stories reveal a privileged time, when divine decisions were made that determined the future of the human race. The origin of something was thought to explain its present meaning, e.g., how God acts with justice and generosity, why human beings are rebellious, the nature of sexual attraction and marriage, why there are many peoples and languages. Though the stories may initially strike us as primitive and naive, they are in fact told with skill, compression, and subtlety. They provide profound answers to perennial questions about God and human beings.

**Genesis 11–50.** One Jewish tradition suggests that God, having been rebuffed in the attempt to forge a relationship with the nations, decided to concentrate on one nation in the hope that it would eventually bring in all the nations. The migration of Abraham's family (11:26–31) is part of the general movement of the human race to take possession of their lands (see 10:32–11:9). Abraham, however, must come into possession of his land in a manner different from the nations, for he will not immediately possess it nor will he have descendants in the manner of the nations, for he is old and his wife is childless (12:1–9). Abraham and Sarah have to live with their God in trust and obedience until at last Isaac is born to them and they manage to buy a sliver of the land (the burial cave at Machpelah, chap. 23). Abraham's humanity and faith offer a wonderful example to the exilic generation.

The historicity of the ancestral stories has been much discussed. Scholars have traditionally dated them sometime in the first half of the second millennium, though a few regard them as late (sixth or fifth century B.C.) and purely fictional. There is unfortunately no direct extra-biblical evidence confirming (or disproving) the stories. The ancestral stories have affinities, however, to late second-millennium stories of childless ancestors, and their proper names fit linguistic patterns attested in the second millennium. Given the lack of decisive evidence, it is reasonable to accept the Bible's own chronology that the patriarchs were the ancestors of Israel and that they lived well before the exodus that is generally dated in the thirteenth century.

Gn 25:19–35:43 are about Jacob and his twelve sons. The stories are united by a geographical frame: Jacob lives in Canaan until his theft of the right of the firstborn from his brother Esau forces him to flee to Paddan-Aram (alternately Aram-Naharaim). There his uncle Laban tricks him as he earlier tricked his brother. But Jacob is blessed with wealth and sons. He returns to Canaan to receive the final blessing, land, and on the way is reconciled with his brother Esau. As the sons have reached the number of twelve, the patriarch can be given the name Israel (32:28; 35:10). The blessings given to Abraham are reaffirmed to Isaac and to Jacob.

The last cycle of ancestor stories is about Jacob's son Joseph (37:1–50:26, though in chaps. 48–49 the focus swings back to Jacob). The Joseph stories are sophisticated in theme, deftly plotted, and show keen interest in the psychology of the characters. Jacob's favoring of Joseph, the son of his beloved wife Rachel, provokes his brothers to kill him. Joseph escapes death through the intercession of Reuben, the eldest, and of Judah, but is sold into slavery in Egypt. In the immediately following chap. 38, Judah undergoes experiences similar to Joseph's. Joseph, endowed by God with wisdom, becomes second only to Pharaoh in Egypt. From that powerful position, he encounters his unsuspecting brothers who have come to Egypt because of the famine, and tests them to see if they have repented. Joseph learns that they have given up their hatred because of their love for Israel, their father. Judah, who seems to have inherited the mantle of the failed oldest brother Reuben, expresses the brothers' new and profound appreciation of their father and Joseph (chap. 44). At the end of Genesis, the entire family of Jacob/Israel is in Egypt, which prepares for the events in the Book of Exodus.

**Genesis in Later Biblical Books.** The historical and prophetic books constantly refer to the covenant with the ancestors Abraham, Isaac, and Jacob. Hos 10 sees the traits of Jacob in the behavior of the Israel of his own day. Is 51:2 cites Abraham and Sarah as a model for his dispirited community, for though only a couple, they became a great nation. Jn 1, "In the beginning was the word," alludes to Gn 1:1 (and Prv 8:22) to show that Jesus is creating a new world. St. Paul interprets Jesus as the New Adam in Rom 5:14 and 1 Cor 15:22, 24, whose obedience brings life just as the Old Adam's disobedience brought death. In Rom 4, Paul cites Abraham as someone who was righteous in God's eyes centuries before the Law was given at Sinai.

## Outline of Genesis

Preamble. The Creation of the World (1:1–2:3)
I. The Story of the Nations (2:4–11:26)
  A. The Creation of the Man and the Woman, Their Offspring, and the Spread of Civilization (2:4–4:26)
  B. The Pre-flood Generations (5:1–6:8)
  C. The Flood and the Renewed Blessing (6:9–9:29)
  D. The Populating of the World and the Prideful City (10:1–11:9)
  E. The Genealogy from Shem to Terah (11:10–26)
II. The Story of the Ancestors of Israel (11:27–50:26)
  A. The Story of Abraham and Sarah (11:27–25:18)
  B. The Story of Isaac and Jacob (25:19–36:43)
  C. The Story of Joseph (37:1–50:26)

## PREAMBLE.
## THE CREATION OF THE WORLD

### CHAPTER 1

**The Story of Creation.**[*] [1]In the beginning, when God created the heavens and the earth[a]— [2†]and the earth was without form or shape, with darkness over the abyss and a mighty wind sweeping over the waters—[b] [3]Then God said: Let there be light, and there was light.[c] [4]God saw that the light was good. God then separated the light from the darkness. [5]God called the light "day," and the darkness he called "night." Evening came, and morning followed—the first day.[‡]

[6]Then God said: Let there be a dome in the middle of the waters, to separate one body of water from the other. [7]God made the dome,[§] and it separated the water below the dome from the water above the dome. And so it happened.[d] [8]God called the dome "sky." Evening came, and morning followed—the second day.

[9]Then God said: Let the water under the sky be gathered into a single basin, so that the dry land may appear. And so it happened: the water under the sky was gathered into its basin, and the dry land appeared.[e] [10]God called the dry land "earth," and the basin of water he called "sea." God saw that it was good. [11f]Then God said: Let the earth bring forth vegetation: every kind of plant that bears seed and every kind of fruit tree on earth that bears fruit with its seed in it. And so it happened: [12]the earth brought forth vegetation: every kind of plant that bears seed and every kind of fruit tree that bears fruit with its

---

*[1:1–2:3] This section, from the Priestly source, functions as an introduction, as ancient stories of the origin of the world (cosmogonies) often did. It introduces the primordial story (2:4–11:26), the stories of the ancestors (11:27–50:26), and indeed the whole Pentateuch. The chapter highlights the goodness of creation and the divine desire that human beings share in that goodness. God brings an orderly universe out of primordial chaos merely by uttering a word. In the literary structure of six days, the creation events in the first three days are related to those in the second three.

| | | |
|---|---|---|
| 1. light (day)/darkness (night) | = | 4. sun/moon |
| 2. arrangement of water | = | 5. fish + birds from waters |
| 3. a) dry land b) vegetation | = | 6. a) animals b) human beings: male/female |

The seventh day, on which God rests, the climax of the account, falls outside the six-day structure.

Until modern times the first line was always translated, "In the beginning God created the heavens and the earth." Several comparable ancient cosmogonies, discovered in recent times, have a "when . . . then" construction, confirming the translation "when . . . then" here as well. "When" introduces the pre-creation state and "then" introduces the creative act affecting that state. The traditional translation, "In the beginning," does not reflect the Hebrew syntax of the clause.

†[1:2] This verse is parenthetical, describing in three phases the pre-creation state symbolized by the chaos out of which God brings order: "earth," hidden beneath the encompassing cosmic waters, could not be seen, and thus had no "form"; there was only darkness; turbulent wind swept over the waters. Commencing with the last-named elements (darkness and water), vv. 3–10 describe the rearrangement of this chaos: light is made (first day) and the water is divided into water above and water below the earth so that the earth appears and is no longer "without outline." **The abyss:** the primordial ocean according to the ancient Semitic cosmogony. After God's creative activity, part of this vast body forms the salt-water seas (vv. 9–10); part of it is the fresh water under the earth (Ps 33:7; Ez 31:4), which wells forth on the earth as springs and fountains (Gn 7:11; 8:2; Prv 3:20). Part of it, "the upper water" (Ps 148:4; Dn 3:60), is held up by the dome of the sky (vv. 6–7), from which rain descends on the earth (Gn 7:11; 2 Kgs 7:2, 19; Ps 104:13). **A mighty wind:** literally, "spirit or breath [*ruah*] of God"; cf. Gn 8:1.

‡[1:5] In ancient Israel a day was considered to begin at sunset.

§[1:7] **The dome:** the Hebrew word suggests a gigantic metal dome. It was inserted into the middle of the single body of water to form dry space within which the earth could emerge. The Latin Vulgate translation *firmamentum*, "means of support (for the upper waters); firmament," provided the traditional English rendering.

---

a. [1:1] Gn 2:1, 4; 2 Mc 7:28; Ps 8:4; 33:6; 89:12; 90:2; Wis 11:17; Sir 16:24; Jer 10:12; Acts 14:15; Col 1:16–17; Heb 1:2–3; 3:4; 11:3; Rev 4:11.

b. [1:2] Jer 4:23.  c. [1:3] 2 Cor 4:6.  d. [1:7] Prv 8:27–28; 2 Pt 3:5.  e. [1:9] Jb 38:8; Ps 33:7; Jer 5:22.  f. [1:11] Ps 104:14.

seed in it. God saw that it was good. ¹³Evening came, and morning followed—the third day.

¹⁴Then God said: Let there be lights in the dome of the sky, to separate day from night. Let them mark the seasons, the days and the years,ᵍ ¹⁵and serve as lights in the dome of the sky, to illuminate the earth. And so it happened: ¹⁶God made the two great lights, the greater one to govern the day, and the lesser one to govern the night, and the stars.ʰ ¹⁷God set them in the dome of the sky, to illuminate the earth, ¹⁸to govern the day and the night, and to separate the light from the darkness. God saw that it was good. ¹⁹Evening came, and morning followed—the fourth day.

²⁰ᶦThen God said: Let the water teem with an abundance of living creatures, and on the earth let birds fly beneath the dome of the sky. ²¹God created the great sea monsters and all kinds of crawling living creatures with which the water teems, and all kinds of winged birds. God saw that it was good, ²²and God blessed them, saying: Be fertile, multiply, and fill the water of the seas; and let the birds multiply on the earth.ʲ ²³Evening came, and morning followed—the fifth day.

²⁴ᵏThen God said: Let the earth bring forth every kind of living creature: tame animals, crawling things, and every kind of wild animal. And so it happened: ²⁵God made every kind of wild animal, every kind of tame animal, and every kind of thing that crawls on the ground. God saw that it was good. ²⁶ᶦThen God said: Let us make* human beings in our image, after our likeness. Let them have dominion over the fish of the sea, the birds of the air, the tame animals, all the wild animals, and all the creatures that crawl on the earth.

²⁷  God created mankind in his image;
        in the image of God he created
            them;
        male and female† he created them.

²⁸God blessed them and God said to them: Be fertile and multiply; fill the earth and subdue it.‡ Have dominion over the fish of the sea, the birds of the air, and all the living things that crawl on the earth.ᵐ ²⁹ⁿGod also said: See, I give you every seed-bearing plant on all the earth and every tree that has seed-bearing fruit on it to be your food; ³⁰and to all the wild animals, all the birds of the air, and all the living creatures that crawl on the earth, I give all the green plants for food. And so it happened. ³¹God looked at everything he had made, and found it very good. Evening came, and morning followed—the sixth day.ᵒ

## CHAPTER 2

¹Thus the heavens and the earth and all their array were completed.ᵖ ²ᵠOn the seventh day God completed the work he had been doing; he rested on the seventh day from all the work he had undertaken.ᵠ ³God blessed the seventh day and made it holy, because on it he rested from all the work he had done in creation.ʳ

## I. THE STORY OF THE NATIONS

**The Garden of Eden.** ⁴This is the story** of the heavens and the earth at their creation. When

‡[1:28] **Fill the earth and subdue it:** the object of the verb "subdue" may be not the earth as such but earth as the territory each nation must take for itself (chaps. 10–11), just as Israel will later do (see Nm 32:22, 29; Jos 18:1). The two divine commands define the basic tasks of the human race—to continue in existence through generation and to take possession of one's God-given territory. The dual command would have had special meaning when Israel was in exile and deeply anxious about whether they would continue as a nation and return to their ancient territory. **Have dominion:** the whole human race is made in the "image" and "likeness" of God and has "dominion." Comparable literature of the time used these words of kings rather than of human beings in general; human beings were invariably thought of as slaves of the gods created to provide menial service for the divine world. The royal language here does not, however, give human beings unlimited power, for kings in the Bible had limited dominion and were subject to prophetic critique.

§[1:29] According to the Priestly tradition, the human race was originally intended to live on plants and fruits as were the animals (see v. 30), an arrangement that God will later change (9:3) in view of the human inclination to violence.

¶[2:2] The mention of the seventh day, repeated in v. 3, is outside the series of six days and is thus the climax of the account. The focus of the account is God. The text does not actually institute the practice of keeping the Sabbath, for it would have been anachronistic to establish at this point a custom that was distinctively Israelite (Ex 31:13, 16, 17), but it lays the foundation for the later practice. Similarly, ancient creation accounts often ended with the construction of a temple where the newly created human race provided service to the gods who created them, but no temple is mentioned in this account. As was the case with the Sabbath, it would have been anachronistic to institute the temple at this point, for Israel did not yet exist. In Ex 25–31 and 35–40, Israel builds the tabernacle, which is the precursor of the Temple of Solomon.

**[2:4] This is the story:** the distinctive Priestly formula introduces older traditions, belonging to the tradition called Yahwist, and gives them a new setting. In the first part of Genesis, the formula "this is the story" (or a similar phrase)

*[1:26] **Let us make:** in the ancient Near East, and sometimes in the Bible, God was imagined as presiding over an assembly of heavenly beings who deliberated and decided about matters on earth (1 Kgs 22:19–22; Is 6:8; Ps 29:1–2; 82; 89:6–7; Jb 1:6; 2:1; 38:7). This scene accounts for the plural form here and in Gn 11:7 ("Let us then go down . . . "). Israel's God was always considered "Most High" over the heavenly beings. **Human beings:** Hebrew *ādām* is here the generic term for humankind; in the first five chapters of Genesis it is the proper name Adam only at 4:25 and 5:1–5. **In our image, after our likeness:** "image" and "likeness" (virtually synonyms) express the worth of human beings who have value in themselves (human blood may not be shed in 9:6 because of this image of God) and in their task, dominion (1:28), which promotes the rule of God over the universe.

†[1:27] **Male and female:** as God provided the plants with seeds (vv. 11, 12) and commanded the animals to be fertile and multiply (v. 22), so God gives sexuality to human beings as their means to continue in existence.

g. [1:14] Jb 26:10; Ps 19:2–3; Bar 3:33.   h. [1:16] Dt 4:19; Ps 136:7–9; Wis 13:2–4; Jer 31:35.   i. [1:20] Jb 12:7–10.   j. [1:22] Gn 8:17.   k. [1:24] Sir 16:27–28.   l. [1:26–27] Gn 5:1, 3; 9:6; Ps 8:5–6; Wis 2:23; 10:2; Sir 17:1, 3–4; Mt 19:4; Mk 10:6; Jas 3:7; Eph 4:24; Col 3:10.

m. [1:28] Gn 8:17; 9:1; Ps 8:6–9; 115:16; Wis 9:2.   n. [1:29–30] Gn 9:3; Ps 104:14–15.   o. [1:31] 1 Tm 4:4.   p. [2:1] Is 45:12; Jn 1:3.   q. [2:2] Ex 20:9–11; 31:17; Heb 4:4, 10.   r. [2:3] Ex 20:11; Dt 5:14; Neh 9:14.

the Lord God made the earth and the heavens— ⁵there was no field shrub on earth and no grass of the field had sprouted, for the Lord God had sent no rain upon the earth and there was no manʳ to till the ground, ⁶but a streamᵗ was welling up out of the earth and watering all the surface of the ground— ⁷then the Lord God formed the manᵗ out of the dust of the ground and blew into his nostrils the breath of life, and the man became a living being.ˢ

⁸The Lord God planted a garden in Eden, in the east,§ and placed there the man whom he had formed.ᵗ ⁹*Out of the ground the Lord God made grow every tree that was delightful to look at and good for food, with the tree of life in the middle of the garden and the tree of the knowledge of good and evil.ᵘ

¹⁰A river rises in Eden** to water the garden; beyond there it divides and becomes four branches. ¹¹The name of the first is the Pishon; it is the one that winds through the whole land of Havilah, where there is gold. ¹²The gold of that land is good; bdellium and lapis lazuli are also there. ¹³The name of the second river is the Gihon; it is the one that winds all through the land of Cush.ᵛ ¹⁴The name of the third river is the Tigris; it is the one that flows east of Asshur. The fourth river is the Euphrates.

¹⁵The Lord God then took the man and settled him in the garden of Eden, to cultivate and care for it.ʷ ¹⁶The Lord God gave the man this order: You are free to eat from any of the trees of the gardenˣ ¹⁷except the tree of knowledge of good and evil. From that tree you shall not eat; when you eat from it you shall die.††ʸ

¹⁸The Lord God said: It is not good for the man to be alone. I will make a helper suited to him.‡‡ᶻ ¹⁹So the Lord God formed out of the ground all the wild animals and all the birds of the air, and he brought them to the man to see what he would call them; whatever the man called each living creature was then its name.

occurs five times (2:4; 5:1; 6:9; 10:1; 11:10), which corresponds to the five occurrences of the formula in the second part of the book (11:27; 25:12, 19; 36:1[9]; 37:2). Some interpret the formula here as retrospective ("Such is the story"), referring back to chap. 1, but all its other occurrences introduce rather than summarize. It is introductory here; the Priestly source would hardly use the formula to introduce its own material in chap. 1.

The cosmogony that begins in v. 4 is concerned with the nature of human beings, narrating the story of the essential institutions and limits of the human race through their first ancestors. This cosmogony, like 1:1–3 (see note there), uses the "when . . . then" construction common in ancient cosmogonies. The account is generally attributed to the Yahwist, who prefers the divine name "Yhwh" (here rendered Lord) for God. God in this story is called "the Lord God" (except in 3:1–5); "Lord" is to be expected in a Yahwist account but the additional word "God" is puzzling.

*[2:5] **Man**: the Hebrew word *'adam* is a generic term meaning "human being." In chaps. 2–3, however, the archetypal human being is understood to be male (Adam), so the word *'adam* is translated "man" here.

†[2:6] **Stream**: the water wells up from the vast flood below the earth. The account seems to presuppose that only the garden of God was irrigated at this point. From this one source of all the fertilizing water on the earth, water will be channeled through the garden of God over the entire earth. It is the source of the four rivers mentioned in vv. 10–14. Later, with rain and cultivation, the fertility of the garden of God will appear in all parts of the world.

‡[2:7] God is portrayed as a potter molding the human body out of earth. There is a play on words in Hebrew between *'adam* ("human being," "man") and *'adama* ("ground"). It is not enough to make the body from earth; God must also breathe into the man's nostrils. A similar picture of divine breath imparted to human beings in order for them to live is found in Ez 37:5, 9–10; Jn 20:22. The Israelites did not think in the (Greek) categories of body and soul.

§[2:8] **Eden, in the east**: the place names in vv. 8–14 are mostly derived from Mesopotamian geography (see note on vv. 10–14). Eden may be the name of a region in southern Mesopotamia (modern Iraq), the term derived from the Sumerian word *eden*, "fertile plain." A similar-sounding Hebrew word means "delight," which may lie behind the Greek translation, "The Lord God planted a paradise [= pleasure park] in Eden." It should be noted, however, that the garden was not intended as a paradise for the human race, but as a pleasure park for God; the man tended it for God. The story is not about "paradise lost."

The garden in the precincts of Solomon's Temple in Jerusalem seems to symbolize the garden of God (like gardens in other temples); it is apparently alluded to in Ps 1:3; 80:10; 92:14; Ez 47:7–12; Rev 22:1–2.

¶[2:9] The second tree, the tree of life, is mentioned here and at the end of the story (3:22, 24). It is identified with Wisdom in Prv 3:18; 11:30; 13:12; 15:4, where the pursuit of wisdom gives back to human beings the life that is made inaccessible to them in Gn 3:24. In the new creation described in the Book of Revelation, the tree of life is once again made available to human beings (Rev 2:7; 22:2, 14, 19). **Knowledge of good and evil**: the meaning is disputed. According to some,

it signifies moral autonomy, control over morality (symbolized by "good and evil"), which would be inappropriate for mere human beings; the phrase would thus mean refusal to accept the human condition and finite freedom that God gives them. According to others, it is more broadly the knowledge of what is helpful and harmful to humankind, suggesting that the attainment of adult experience and responsibility inevitably means the loss of a life of simple subordination to God.

**[2:10–14] **A river rises in Eden**: the stream of water mentioned in v. 6, the source of all water upon earth, comes to the surface in the garden of God and from there flows out over the entire earth. In comparable religious literature, the dwelling of god is the source of fertilizing waters. The four rivers represent universality, as in the phrase "the four quarters of the earth." In Ez 47:1–12; Zec 14:8; Rev 22:1–2, the waters that irrigate the earth arise in the temple or city of God. The place names in vv. 11–14 are mainly from southern Mesopotamia (modern Iraq), where Mesopotamian literature placed the original garden of God. The Tigris and the Euphrates, the two great rivers in that part of the world, both emptied into the Persian Gulf. Gihon is the modest stream issuing from Jerusalem (2 Sm 5:8; 1 Kgs 1:9–10; 2 Chr 32:4), but is here regarded as one of the four great world rivers and linked to Mesopotamia, for Cush here seems to be the territory of the Kassites (a people of Mesopotamia) as in Gn 10:8. The word Pishon is otherwise unknown but is probably formed in imitation of Gihon. Havilah seems, according to Gn 10:7 and 1 Chr 1:9, to be in Cush in southern Mesopotamia though other locations have been suggested.

††[2:17] **You shall die**: since they do not die as soon as they eat from the forbidden tree, the meaning seems to be that human beings have become mortal, destined to die by virtue of being human.

‡‡[2:18] **Helper suited to him**: lit., "a helper in accord with him." "Helper" need not imply subordination, for God is called a helper (Dt 33:7; Ps 46:2). The language suggests a profound affinity between the man and the woman and a relationship that is supportive and nurturing.

s. [2:7] Gn 3:19; 18:27; Tb 8:6; Jb 34:15; Ps 103:14; 104:29; Eccl 3:20; 12:7; Wis 7:1; Sir 33:10; 1 Cor 15:45.　t. [2:8] Is 51:3; Ez 31:9.

u. [2:9] Gn 3:22; Prv 3:18; Rev 2:7; 22:2, 14.　v. [2:13] Sir 24:25. w. [2:15] Sir 7:15.　x. [2:16] Ps 104:14–15.　y. [2:17] Gn 3:2–3; Rom 6:23.　z. [2:18] Tb 8:6; Sir 36:24; 1 Cor 11:9; 1 Tm 2:13.

²⁰The man gave names to all the tame animals, all the birds of the air, and all the wild animals; but none proved to be a helper suited to the man. ²¹So the LORD God cast a deep sleep on the man, and while he was asleep, he took out one of his ribs and closed up its place with flesh.ᵃ ²²The LORD God then built the rib that he had taken from the man into a woman. When he brought her to the man, ²³the man said:

"This one, at last, is bone of my bones
    and flesh of my flesh;
This one shall be called 'woman,'
    for out of man this one has been
        taken."*

²⁴*That is why a man leaves his father and mother and clings to his wife, and the two of them become one body.†

²⁵The man and his wife were both naked, yet they felt no shame.‡

## CHAPTER 3

**Expulsion from Eden.** ¹Now the snake was the most cunning§ of all the wild animals that the LORD God had made. He asked the woman, "Did God really say, 'You shall not eat from any of the trees in the garden'?" ²The woman answered the snake: "We may eat of the fruit of the trees in the garden; ³it is only about the fruit of the tree in the middle of the garden that God said, 'You shall not eat it or even touch it, or else you will die.'" ⁴But the snake said to the woman: "You certainly will not die!ᵈ ⁵God knows well that when you eat of it your eyes will be opened and you will be like gods, who know¶ good and evil." ⁶The woman saw that the tree was good for food and pleasing to the eyes, and the tree was desirable for gaining wisdom. So she took some of its fruit and ate it; and she also gave some to her husband, who was with her, and he ate it.ᵉ ⁷Then the eyes of both of them were opened, and they knew that they were naked; so they sewed fig leaves together and made loincloths for themselves.

⁸When they heard the sound of the LORD God walking about in the garden at the breezy time of the day,** the man and his wife hid themselves from the LORD God among the trees of the garden.ᶠ ⁹The LORD God then called to the man and asked him: Where are you? ¹⁰He answered, "I heard you in the garden; but I was afraid, because I was naked, so I hid." ¹¹Then God asked: Who told you that you were naked? Have you eaten from the tree of which I had forbidden you to eat? ¹²The man replied, "The woman whom you put here with me—she gave me fruit from the tree, so I ate it." ¹³The LORD God then asked the woman: What is this you have done? The woman answered, "The snake tricked me, so I ate it."ᵍ

¹⁴Then the LORD God said to the snake:

Because you have done this,
    cursed are you
        among all the animals, tame or wild;
On your belly you shall crawl,
    and dust you shall eat
        all the days of your life.††ʰ
¹⁵ I will put enmity between you and the
        woman,
    and between your offspring and hers;
They will strike at your head,
    while you strike at their heel.‡‡ⁱ

¹⁶To the woman he said:

I will intensify your toil in childbearing;
    in pain§§ you shall bring forth
        children.

---

**[2:23]** The man recognizes an affinity with the woman God has brought him. Unlike the animals who were made from the ground, she is made from his very self. There is a play on the similar-sounding Hebrew words *'ishsha* ("woman," "wife") and *'ish* ("man," "husband").

†[2:24] **One body:** lit., "one flesh." The covenant of marriage establishes kinship bonds of the first rank between the partners.

‡[2:25] **They felt no shame:** marks a new stage in the drama, for the reader knows that only young children know no shame. This draws the reader into the next episode, where the couple's disobedience results in their loss of innocence.

§[3:1] **Cunning:** there is a play on the words for "naked" (2:25) and "cunning/wise" (Heb. *'arum*). The couple seek to be "wise" but end up knowing that they are "naked."

¶[3:5] **Like gods, who know:** or "like God who knows."

**[3:8] **The breezy time of the day:** lit., "the wind of the day." Probably shortly before sunset.

††[3:14] Each of the three punishments (the snake, the woman, the man) has a double aspect, one affecting the individual and the other affecting a basic relationship. The snake previously stood upright, enjoyed a reputation for being shrewder than other creatures, and could converse with human beings as in vv. 1–5. It must now move on its belly, is more cursed than any creature, and inspires revulsion in human beings (v. 15).

‡‡[3:15] **They will strike . . . at their heel:** the antecedent for "they" and "their" is the collective noun "offspring," i.e., all the descendants of the woman. Christian tradition has seen in this passage, however, more than unending hostility between snakes and human beings. The snake was identified with the devil (Wis 2:24; Jn 8:44; Rev 12:9; 20:2), whose eventual defeat seemed implied in the verse. Because "the Son of God was revealed to destroy the works of the devil" (1 Jn 3:8), the passage was understood as the first promise of a redeemer for fallen humankind, the protoevangelium. Irenaeus of Lyons (ca. A.D. 130–200), in his *Against Heresies* 5.21.1, followed by several other Fathers of the Church, interpreted the verse as referring to Christ, and cited Gal 3:19 and 4:4 to support the reference. Another interpretive translation is *ipsa*, "she," and is reflected in Jerome's Vulgate. "She" was thought to refer to Mary, the mother of the messiah. In Christian art Mary is sometimes depicted with her foot on the head of the serpent.

§§[3:16] **Toil . . . pain:** the punishment affects the woman directly by increasing the toil and pain of having children. **He shall rule over you:** the punishment also affects the woman's relationship with her husband. A tension is set up in which her urge (either sexual urge or, more generally, dependence

---

a. [2:21] Sir 17:1; 1 Cor 11:8–9; 1 Tm 2:13.   b. [2:24] Mt 19:5; Mk 10:7; 1 Cor 7:10–11; Eph 5:31.   c. [3:3] Gn 2:17; Rom 6:23.   d. [3:4–5] Wis 2:24; Sir 25:14; Is 14:14; Jn 8:44; 2 Cor 11:3.   e. [3:6] Gn 3:22; 1 Tm 2:14.

f. [3:8] Jer 23:24.   g. [3:13] 2 Cor 11:3.   h. [3:14] Is 65:25; Mi 7:17; Rev 12:9.   i. [3:15] Rom 16:20; 1 Jn 3:8; Rev 12:17.

Yet your urge shall be for your husband,
    and he shall rule over you.

¹⁷To the man he said: Because you listened to your wife and ate from the tree about which I commanded you, You shall not eat from it,

Cursed is the ground* because of you!
    In toil you shall eat its yield
    all the days of your life.ʲ
¹⁸ Thorns and thistles it shall bear for you,
    and you shall eat the grass of the
      field.
¹⁹ By the sweat of your brow
    you shall eat bread,
Until you return to the ground,
    from which you were taken;
For you are dust,
    and to dust you shall return.ᵏ

²⁰The man gave his wife the name "Eve," because she was the mother of all the living.† ²¹The LORD God made for the man and his wife garments of skin, with which he clothed them. ²²Then the LORD God said: See! The man has become like one of us, knowing good and evil! Now, what if he also reaches out his hand to take fruit from the tree of life, and eats of it and lives forever?ˡ ²³The LORD God therefore banished him from the garden of Eden, to till the ground from which he had been taken. ²⁴He expelled the man, stationing the cherubim and the fiery revolving sword east of the garden of Eden, to guard the way to the tree of life.

## CHAPTER 4

**Cain and Abel.** ¹The man had intercourse with his wife Eve, and she conceived and gave birth to Cain, saying, "I have produced a male child with the help of the LORD."‡ ²Next she gave birth to his brother Abel. Abel became a herder of flocks, and Cain a tiller of the ground.§ ³In the course of time Cain brought an offering to the LORD from the fruit of the ground, ⁴while Abel, for his part, brought the fatty portion⁵ of the firstlings of his flock.ᵐ The LORD looked with favor on Abel and his offering, ⁵but on Cain and his offering he did not look with favor. So Cain was very angry and dejected. ⁶Then the LORD said to Cain: Why are you angry? Why are you dejected? ⁷If you act rightly, you will be accepted;** but if not, sin lies in wait at the door: its urge is for you, yet you can rule over it.ⁿ

⁸Cain said to his brother Abel, "Let us go out in the field."†† When they were in the field, Cain attacked his brother Abel and killed him.ᵒ ⁹Then the LORD asked Cain, Where is your brother Abel? He answered, "I do not know. Am I my brother's keeper?" ¹⁰God then said: What have you done? Your brother's blood cries out to me from the ground! ¹¹Now you are banned from the ground‡‡ that opened its mouth to receive your brother's blood from your hand.ᵖ ¹²If you till the ground, it shall no longer give you its produce. You shall become a constant wanderer on the earth. ¹³Cain said to the LORD: "My punishment is too great to bear. ¹⁴Look, you have now banished me from the ground. I must avoid you and be a constant wanderer on the earth. Anyone may kill me at sight." ¹⁵Not so! the LORD said to him. If anyone kills Cain, Cain shall be avenged seven times. So the LORD put a mark§§ on Cain, so that no one would kill him at sight.

---

for sustenance) is for her husband but he rules over her. But see Sg 7:11.

*[3:17–19] **Cursed is the ground**: the punishment affects the man's relationship to the ground (*'adam* and *'adamah*). **You are dust**: the punishment also affects the man directly insofar as he is now mortal.

†[3:20] The man gives his wife a more specific name than "woman" (2:23). The Hebrew name *hawwa* ("Eve") is related to the Hebrew word *hay* ("living"); "mother of all the living" points forward to the next episode involving her sons Cain and Abel.

‡[4:1] The Hebrew name *qayin* ("Cain") and the term *qaniti* ("I have produced") present a wordplay that refers to metalworking; such wordplays are frequent in Genesis.

§[4:2] Some suggest the story reflects traditional strife between the farmer (Cain) and the nomad (Abel), with preference for the latter reflecting the alleged nomadic ideal of the Bible. But there is no disparagement of farming here, for Adam was created to till the soil. The story is about two brothers (the word "brother" occurs seven times) and God's unexplained preference for one, which provokes the first murder.

The motif of the preferred younger brother will occur time and again in the Bible, e.g., Isaac, Jacob, Joseph, and David (1 Sm 16:1–13).

¶[4:4] **Fatty portion**: it was standard practice to offer the fat portions of animals. Others render, less satisfactorily, "the choicest of the firstlings." The point is not that Abel gave a more valuable gift than Cain, but that God, for reasons not given in the text, accepts the offering of Abel and rejects that of Cain.

**[4:7] **You will be accepted**: the text is extraordinarily condensed and unclear. "You will be accepted" is a paraphrase of one Hebrew word, "lifting." God gives a friendly warning to Cain that his right conduct will bring "lifting," which could refer to acceptance (*lifting*) of his future offerings or of himself (as in the Hebrew idiom "*lifting* of the face") or *lifting* up of his head in honor (cf. note on 40:13), whereas wicked conduct will make him vulnerable to sin, which is personified as a force ready to attack. In any case, Cain has the ability to do the right thing. **Lies in wait**: sin is personified as a power that "lies in wait" (Heb. *robes*) at a place. In Mesopotamian religion, a related word (*rabisu*) refers to a malevolent god who attacks human beings in particular places like roofs or canals.

††[4:8] **Let us go out in the field**: to avoid detection. The verse presumes a sizeable population which Genesis does not otherwise explain.

‡‡[4:11] **Banned from the ground**: lit., "cursed." The verse refers back to 3:17 where the ground was cursed so that it yields its produce only with great effort. Cain has polluted the soil with his brother's blood and it will no longer yield any of its produce to him.

§§[4:15] **A mark**: probably a tattoo to mark Cain as protected by God. The use of tattooing for tribal marks has always been common among the Bedouin of the Near Eastern deserts.

---

j. [3:17] Gn 5:29; Rom 5:12; 8:20; Heb 6:8.   k. [3:19] Gn 2:7; Jb 10:9; 34:15; Ps 90:3; 103:14; Eccl 3:20; 12:7; Wis 15:8; Sir 10:9; 17:2; Rom 5:12; 1 Cor 15:21; Heb 9:27.   l. [3:22] Gn 2:9; Rev 22:2, 14.

m. [4:4] Ex 34:19; Heb 11:4.   n. [4:7] Sir 7:1; Jude 11.   o. [4:8] Wis 10:3; Mt 23:35; Lk 11:51; 1 Jn 3:12; Jude 11.   p. [4:11] Dt 27:24.

[16]Cain then left the LORD's presence and settled in the land of Nod,* east of Eden.

**Descendants of Cain and Seth.** [17†]Cain had intercourse with his wife, and she conceived and bore Enoch. Cain also became the founder of a city, which he named after his son Enoch. [18]To Enoch was born Irad, and Irad became the father of Mehujael; Mehujael became the father of Methusael, and Methusael became the father of Lamech. [19]Lamech took two wives; the name of the first was Adah, and the name of the second Zillah. [20]Adah gave birth to Jabal, who became the ancestor of those who dwell in tents and keep livestock. [21]His brother's name was Jubal, who became the ancestor of all who play the lyre and the reed pipe. [22]Zillah, on her part, gave birth to Tubalcain, the ancestor of all who forge instruments of bronze and iron. The sister of Tubalcain was Naamah. [23‡]Lamech said to his wives:

"Adah and Zillah, hear my voice;
  wives of Lamech, listen to my utterance:
I have killed a man for wounding me,
  a young man for bruising me.
[24] If Cain is avenged seven times,
  then Lamech seventy-seven times."

[25§]Adam again had intercourse with his wife, and she gave birth to a son whom she called Seth. "God has granted me another offspring in place of Abel," she said, "because Cain killed him." [26]To Seth, in turn, a son was born, and he named him Enosh.

At that time people began to invoke the LORD by name.[q]

---

*[4:16] **The land of Nod:** a symbolic name (derived from the verb *nûd,* to wander) rather than a definite geographic region.

†[4:17–24] Cain is the first in a seven-member linear genealogy ending in three individuals who initiate action (Jabal, Jubal, and Tubalcain). Other Genesis genealogies also end in three individuals initiating action (5:32 and 11:26). The purpose of this genealogy is to explain the origin of culture and crafts among human beings. The names in this genealogy are the same (some with different spellings) as those in the ten-member genealogy (ending with Noah), which has a slightly different function. See note on 5:1–32.

‡[4:23–24] Lamech's boast shows that the violence of Cain continues with his son and has actually increased. The question is posed to the reader: how will God's creation be renewed?

§[4:25–26] The third and climactic birth story in the chapter, showing that this birth, unlike the other two, will have good results. The name Seth (from the Hebrew verb *shat,* "to place, replace") shows that God has replaced Abel with a worthy successor. From this favored line Enosh ("human being/humankind"), a synonym of Adam, authentic religion began with the worship of Yhwh; this divine name is rendered as "the LORD" in this translation. The Yahwist source employs the name Yhwh long before the time of Moses. The Elohist source, the Elohist (from its use of the term *Elohim,* "God," instead of *Yhwh,* "LORD," for the pre-Mosaic period), makes Moses the first to use Yhwh as the proper name of Israel's God, previously known by other names as well; cf. Ex 3:13–15.

q. [4:26] 1 Chr 1:1; Lk 3:38.

---

# CHAPTER 5

**Generations: Adam to Noah.**[¶] [1r]This is the record of the descendants of Adam. When God created human beings, he made them in the likeness of God; [2]he created them male and female. When they were created, he blessed them and named them humankind.

[3s]Adam was one hundred and thirty years old when he begot a son in his likeness, after his image; and he named him Seth.[r] [4]Adam lived eight hundred years after he begot Seth, and he had other sons and daughters. [5]The whole lifetime of Adam was nine hundred and thirty years; then he died.

[6]When Seth was one hundred and five years old, he begot Enosh. [7]Seth lived eight hundred and seven years after he begot Enosh, and he had other sons and daughters. [8]The whole lifetime of Seth was nine hundred and twelve years; then he died.

[9]When Enosh was ninety years old, he begot Kenan. [10]Enosh lived eight hundred and fifteen years after he begot Kenan, and he had other sons and daughters. [11]The whole lifetime of Enosh was nine hundred and five years; then he died.

[12]When Kenan was seventy years old, he begot Mahalalel. [13]Kenan lived eight hundred and forty years after he begot Mahalalel, and he had other sons and daughters. [14]The whole lifetime of Kenan was nine hundred and ten years; then he died.

[15]When Mahalalel was sixty-five years old, he begot Jared. [16]Mahalalel lived eight hundred and thirty years after he begot Jared, and he had other sons and daughters. [17]The whole lifetime of Mahalalel was eight hundred and ninety-five years; then he died.

[18]When Jared was one hundred and sixty-two years old, he begot Enoch. [19]Jared lived eight

---

¶[5:1–32] The second of the five Priestly formulas in Part I ("This is the record of the descendants . . ."; see 2:4a; 6:9; 10:1; 11:10) introduces the second of the three linear genealogies in Gn 1–11 (4:17–24 and 11:10–26). In each, a list of individuals (six in 4:17–24, ten in 5:1–32, or nine in 11:10–26) ends in three people who initiate action. Linear genealogies (father to son) in ancient societies had a communicative function, grounding the authority or claim of the last-named individual in the first-named. Here, the genealogy has a literary function as well, advancing the story by showing the expansion of the human race after Adam, as well as the transmission to his descendant Noah of the divine image given to Adam. Correcting the impression one might get from the genealogy in 4:17–24, this genealogy traces the line through Seth rather than through Cain. Most of the names in the series are the same as the names in Cain's line in 4:17–19 (Enosh, Enoch, Lamech) or spelled with variant spellings (Mahalalel, Jared, Methuselah). The genealogy itself and its placement before the flood shows the influence of ancient Mesopotamian literature, which contains lists of cities and kings before and after the flood. Before the flood, the ages of the kings ranged from 18,600 to 36,000 years, but after it were reduced to between 140 and 1,200 years. The biblical numbers are much smaller. There are some differences in the numbers in the Hebrew and Greek manuscripts.

---

r. [5:1] Gn 1:27; Wis 2:23; Sir 17:1; Jas 3:9.  s. [5:3–32] 1 Chr 1:1–4; Lk 3:36–38.  t. [5:3] Gn 4:25.

hundred years after he begot Enoch, and he had other sons and daughters. [20]The whole lifetime of Jared was nine hundred and sixty-two years; then he died.

[21]When Enoch was sixty-five years old, he begot Methuselah. [22]Enoch walked with God after he begot Methuselah for three hundred years, and he had other sons and daughters. [23]The whole lifetime of Enoch was three hundred and sixty-five years. [24]Enoch walked with God,* and he was no longer here, for God took him.[u]

[25]When Methuselah was one hundred and eighty-seven years old, he begot Lamech. [26]Methuselah lived seven hundred and eighty-two years after he begot Lamech, and he had other sons and daughters. [27]The whole lifetime of Methuselah was nine hundred and sixty-nine years; then he died.

[28]When Lamech was one hundred and eighty-two years old, he begot a son [29]and named him Noah, saying, "This one shall bring us relief from our work and the toil of our hands, out of the very ground that the LORD has put under a curse."[†] [30]Lamech lived five hundred and ninety-five years after he begot Noah, and he had other sons and daughters. [31]The whole lifetime of Lamech was seven hundred and seventy-seven years; then he died.

[32]When Noah was five hundred years old, he begot Shem, Ham, and Japheth.[‡w]

## CHAPTER 6
## Origin of the Nephilim.[§] [1]When human beings began to grow numerous on the earth

and daughters were born to them, [2]the sons of God[ᶜ] saw how beautiful the daughters of human beings were, and so they took for their wives whomever they pleased.[x] [3]Then the LORD said: My spirit shall not remain in human beings forever, because they are only flesh. Their days shall comprise one hundred and twenty years.

[4]The Nephilim appeared on earth in those days, as well as later,** after the sons of God had intercourse with the daughters of human beings, who bore them sons. They were the heroes of old, the men of renown.[y]

**Warning of the Flood.** [5]††When the LORD saw how great the wickedness of human beings was on earth, and how every desire that their heart conceived was always nothing but evil,[z] [6]the LORD regretted making human beings on the earth, and his heart was grieved.[‡‡]

[7]So the LORD said: I will wipe out from the earth the human beings I have created, and not only the human beings, but also the animals and the crawling things and the birds of the air, for I regret that I made them.[§§] [8]But Noah found favor with the LORD.

[9]These are the descendants of Noah. Noah was a righteous man and blameless in his

---

*[5:24] Enoch is in the important seventh position in the ten-member genealogy. In place of the usual formula "then he died," the change to "Enoch walked with God" implies that he did not die, but like Elijah (2 Kgs 2:11–12) was taken alive to God's abode. This mysterious narrative spurred much speculation and writing (beginning as early as the third century B.C.) about Enoch the sage who knew the secrets of heaven and who could communicate them to human beings (see Sir 44:16; 49:14; Heb 11:5; Jude 14–15 and the apocryphal work 1 Enoch).

†[5:29] The sound of the Hebrew word *noah*, "Noah," is echoed in the word *yenahamenu*, "he will bring us relief"; the latter refers both to the curse put on the soil because of human disobedience (3:17–19) and to Noah's success in agriculture, especially in raising grapes for wine (9:20–21).

‡[5:32] **Shem, Ham, and Japheth**: like the genealogies in 4:17–24 and 11:10–26, the genealogy ends in three individuals who engage in important activity. Their descendants will be detailed in chap. 10, where it will be seen that the lineage is political-geographical as well as "ethnic."

§[6:1–4] These enigmatic verses are a transition between the expansion of the human race illustrated in the genealogy of chap. 5 and the flood depicted in chaps. 6–9. The text, apparently alluding to an old legend, shares a common ancient view that the heavenly world was populated by a multitude of beings, some of whom were wicked and rebellious. It is incorporated here, not only in order to account for the prehistoric giants, whom the Israelites called the Nephilim, but also to introduce the story of the flood with a moral orientation—the constantly increasing wickedness of humanity. This increasing wickedness leads God to reduce the human life span imposed on the first couple. As the ages in the preceding genealogy show, life spans had been exceptionally long in the

early period, but God further reduces them to something near the ordinary life span.

¶[6:2] **The sons of God**: other heavenly beings. See note on 1:26.

**[6:4] **As well as later**: the belief was common that human beings of gigantic stature once lived on earth. In some cultures, such heroes could make positive contributions, but the Bible generally regards them in a negative light (cf. Nm 13:33; Ez 32:27). The point here is that even these heroes, filled with vitality from their semi-divine origin, come under God's decree in v. 3.

††[6:5–8:22] The story of the great flood is commonly regarded as a composite narrative based on separate sources woven together. To the Yahwist source, with some later editorial additions, are usually assigned 6:5–8; 7:1–5, 7–10, 12, 16b, 17b, 22–23; 8:2b–3a, 6–12, 13b, 20–22. The other sections are usually attributed to the Priestly writer. There are differences between the two sources: the Priestly source has two pairs of every animal, whereas the Yahwist source has seven pairs of clean animals and two pairs of unclean; the floodwater in the Priestly source is the waters under and over the earth that burst forth, whereas in the Yahwist source the floodwater is the rain lasting forty days and nights. In spite of many obvious discrepancies in these two sources, one should read the story as a coherent narrative. The biblical story ultimately draws upon an ancient Mesopotamian tradition of a great flood, preserved in the Sumerian flood story, the eleventh tablet of the Gilgamesh Epic, and (embedded in a longer creation story) the Atrahasis Epic.

‡‡[6:6] **His heart was grieved**: the expression can be misleading in English, for "heart" in Hebrew is the seat of memory and judgment rather than emotion. The phrase is actually parallel to the first half of the sentence ("the LORD regretted . . .").

§§[6:7] Human beings are an essential part of their environment, which includes all living things. In the new beginning after the flood, God makes a covenant with human beings and every living creature (9:9–10). The same close link between human beings and nature is found elsewhere in the Bible; e.g., in Is 35, God's healing transforms human beings along with their physical environment, and in Rom 8:19–23, all creation, not merely human beings, groans in labor pains awaiting the salvation of God.

---

u. [5:24] Wis 4:10–11; Sir 44:16; 49:14; Heb 11:5.    v. [5:29] Gn 3:17–19.    w. [5:32] Gn 6:10; 10:1.

x. [6:2] Mt 24:38; Lk 17:26–27.    y. [6:4] Wis 14:6; Bar 3:26.    z. [6:5] Ps 14:2–3.

generation;[a] Noah walked with God. [10]Noah begot three sons: Shem, Ham, and Japheth.

[11]But the earth was corrupt* in the view of God and full of lawlessness.[b] [12]When God saw how corrupt the earth had become, since all mortals had corrupted their ways on earth,[c] [13]God said to Noah: I see that the end of all mortals has come, for the earth is full of lawlessness because of them. So I am going to destroy them with the earth.[d]

**Preparation for the Flood.** [14]Make yourself an ark of gopherwood,† equip the ark with various compartments, and cover it inside and out with pitch. [15]This is how you shall build it: the length of the ark will be three hundred cubits, its width fifty cubits, and its height thirty cubits.‡ [16]Make an opening for daylight§ and finish the ark a cubit above it. Put the ark's entrance on its side; you will make it with bottom, second and third decks. [17]I, on my part, am about to bring the flood waters on the earth, to destroy all creatures under the sky in which there is the breath of life; everything on earth shall perish.[e] [18]I will establish my covenant with you. You shall go into the ark, you and your sons, your wife and your sons' wives with you.[f] [19]Of all living creatures you shall bring two of every kind into the ark, one male and one female,¶ to keep them alive along with you. [20]Of every kind of bird, of every kind of animal, and of every kind of thing that crawls on the ground, two of each will come to you, that you may keep them alive. [21]Moreover, you are to provide yourself with all the food that is to be eaten, and store it away,

that it may serve as provisions for you and for them. [22]Noah complied; he did just as God had commanded him.**

## CHAPTER 7

[1]Then the LORD said to Noah: Go into the ark, you and all your household, for you alone in this generation have I found to be righteous before me.[g] [2]Of every clean animal, take with you seven pairs, a male and its mate; and of the unclean animals, one pair, a male and its mate; [3]likewise, of every bird of the air, seven pairs, a male and a female, to keep their progeny alive over all the earth. [4]For seven days from now I will bring rain down on the earth for forty days and forty nights, and so I will wipe out from the face of the earth every being that I have made.[h] [5]Noah complied, just as the LORD had commanded.

**The Great Flood.** [6]Noah was six hundred years old when the flood came upon the earth. [7]Together with his sons, his wife, and his sons' wives, Noah went into the ark because of the waters of the flood.[i] [8]Of the clean animals and the unclean, of the birds, and of everything that crawls on the ground, [9]two by two, male and female came to Noah into the ark, just as God had commanded him.[j] [10]When the seven days were over, the waters of the flood came upon the earth.

[11]In the six hundredth year of Noah's life, in the second month, on the seventeenth day of the month: on that day

All the fountains of the great abyss†† burst
        forth,
    and the floodgates of the sky were
        opened.

[12]For forty days and forty nights heavy rain poured down on the earth.

[13]On the very same day, Noah and his sons Shem, Ham, and Japheth, and Noah's wife, and the three wives of Noah's sons had entered the ark, [14]together with every kind of wild animal, every kind of tame animal, every kind of crawling thing that crawls on the earth, and every kind of bird. [15]Pairs of all creatures in which there was the breath of life came to Noah into the ark. [16]Those that entered were male and female; of all creatures they came, as God had commanded Noah. Then the LORD shut him in.

[17]The flood continued upon the earth for forty days. As the waters increased, they lifted

---

*[6:11] **Corrupt:** God does not punish arbitrarily but simply brings to its completion the corruption initiated by human beings.

†[6:14] **Gopherwood:** an unidentified wood mentioned only in connection with the ark. It may be the wood of the cypress, which in Hebrew sounds like "gopher" and was widely used in antiquity for shipbuilding.

‡[6:15] Hebrew "cubit," lit., "forearm," is the distance from the elbow to the tip of the middle finger, about eighteen inches (a foot and a half). The dimensions of Noah's ark were approximately 440 × 73 × 44 feet. The ark of the Babylonian flood story was an exact cube, 120 cubits (180 feet) in length, width, and height.

§[6:16] **Opening for daylight:** a conjectural rendering of the Hebrew word *sohar*, occurring only here. The reference is probably to an open space on all sides near the top of the ark to admit light and air. The ark also had a window or hatch, which could be opened and closed (8:6).

¶[6:19–21] **You shall bring two of every kind . . . , one male and one female:** For the Priestly source (P), there is no distinction between clean and unclean animals until Sinai (Lv 11), no altars or sacrifice until Sinai, and all diet is vegetarian (Gn 1:29–30); even after the flood P has no distinction between clean and unclean, since "any living creature that moves about" may be eaten (9:3). Thus P has Noah take the minimum to preserve all species, one pair of each, without distinction between clean and unclean, but he must also take on provisions for food (6:21). The Yahwist source (J), which assumes the clean-unclean distinction always existed but knows no other restriction on eating meat (Abel was a shepherd and offered meat as a sacrifice), requires additional clean animals ("seven pairs") for food and sacrifice (7:2–3; 8:20).

**[6:22] **Just as God had commanded him:** as in the creation of the world in chap. 1 and in the building of the tabernacle in Ex 25–31, 35–40 (all from the Priestly source), everything takes place by the command of God. In this passage and in Exodus, the commands of God are carried out to the letter by human agents, Noah and Moses. Divine speech is important. God speaks to Noah seven times in the flood story.

††[7:11] **Abyss:** the subterranean ocean; see note on 1:2.

---

a. [6:9] Wis 10:4; Sir 44:17.   b. [6:11] Jb 22:15–17.   c. [6:12] Ps 14:2.   d. [6:13] Sir 40:9–10; 44:17; Mt 24:37–39.   e. [6:17] Gn 7:4, 21; 2 Pt 2:5.   f. [6:18] Gn 9:9; Wis 14:6; Heb 11:7; 1 Pt 3:20.

g. [7:1] Wis 10:4; Sir 44:17; 2 Pt 2:5.   h. [7:4] Gn 6:17; 2 Pt 2:5.   i. [7:7] Wis 14:6; 1 Pt 3:20; 2 Pt 2:5.   j. [7:9] Gn 6:19.

the ark, so that it rose above the earth. [18]The waters swelled and increased greatly on the earth, but the ark floated on the surface of the waters. [19]Higher and higher on the earth the waters swelled, until all the highest mountains under the heavens were submerged. [20]The waters swelled fifteen cubits higher than the submerged mountains. [21]All creatures that moved on earth perished: birds, tame animals, wild animals, and all that teemed on the earth, as well as all humankind.[k] [22]Everything on dry land with the breath of life in its nostrils died. [23]The LORD wiped out every being on earth: human beings and animals, the crawling things and the birds of the air; all were wiped out from the earth. Only Noah and those with him in the ark were left.

[24]And when the waters had swelled on the earth for one hundred and fifty days,

## CHAPTER 8

[1]God remembered Noah and all the animals, wild and tame, that were with him in the ark. So God made a wind sweep over the earth, and the waters began to subside. [2]The fountains of the abyss and the floodgates of the sky were closed, and the downpour from the sky was held back. [3]Gradually the waters receded from the earth. At the end of one hundred and fifty days, the waters had so diminished [4]that, in the seventh month, on the seventeenth day of the month, the ark came to rest on the mountains of Ararat.* [5]The waters continued to diminish until the tenth month, and on the first day of the tenth month the tops of the mountains appeared.

[6]At the end of forty days Noah opened the hatch of the ark that he had made, [7†]and he released a raven. It flew back and forth until the waters dried from the earth. [8]Then he released a dove, to see if the waters had lessened on the earth. [9]But the dove could find no place to perch, and it returned to him in the ark, for there was water over all the earth. Putting out his hand, he caught the dove and drew it back to him inside the ark. [10]He waited yet seven days more and again released the dove from the ark. [11]In the evening the dove came back to him, and there in its bill was a plucked-off olive leaf! So Noah knew that the waters had diminished on the earth. [12]He waited yet another seven days and then released the dove; but this time it did not come back.

[13‡]In the six hundred and first year, in the first month, on the first day of the month, the water began to dry up on the earth. Noah then removed the covering of the ark and saw that the surface of the ground had dried. [14]In the second month, on the twenty-seventh day of the month, the earth was dry.

[15]Then God said to Noah: [16]Go out of the ark, together with your wife and your sons and your sons' wives. [17]Bring out with you every living thing that is with you—all creatures, be they birds or animals or crawling things that crawl on the earth—and let them abound on the earth, and be fertile and multiply on it.[l] [18]So Noah came out, together with his sons and his wife and his sons' wives; [19]and all the animals, all the birds, and all the crawling creatures that crawl on the earth went out of the ark by families.

[20]Then Noah built an altar to the LORD, and choosing from every clean animal and every clean bird, he offered burnt offerings on the altar. [21]When the LORD smelled the sweet odor, the LORD said to himself: Never again will I curse the ground because of human beings, since the desires of the human heart are evil from youth; nor will I ever again strike down every living being, as I have done.[m]

[22] All the days of the earth,
  seedtime and harvest,
   cold and heat,
 Summer and winter,
  and day and night
   shall not cease.[n]

## CHAPTER 9

**Covenant with Noah.** [1§]God blessed Noah and his sons and said to them: Be fertile and multiply and fill the earth.[o] [2¶]Fear and dread of you shall come upon all the animals of the earth and all the birds of the air, upon all the creatures that move about on the ground and all the fishes of the sea; into your power they are delivered. [3p]Any living creature that moves about shall be yours to eat; I give them all to you as I did the green plants. [4q]Only meat with its lifeblood still

---

‡[8:13–14] On the first day of the first month, the world was in the state it had been on the day of creation in chap. 1. Noah had to wait another month until the earth was properly dry as in 1:9.

§[9:1] God reaffirms without change the original blessing and mandate of 1:28. In the Mesopotamian epic Atrahasis, on which the Genesis story is partly modeled, the gods changed their original plan by restricting human population through such means as childhood diseases, birth demons, and mandating celibacy among certain groups of women.

¶[9:2–3] Pre-flood creatures, including human beings, are depicted as vegetarians (1:29–30). In view of the human propensity to violence, God changes the original prohibition against eating meat.

---

*[8:4] **The mountains of Ararat:** the mountain country of ancient Arartu in northwest Iraq, which was the highest part of the world to the biblical writer. There is no Mount Ararat in the Bible.

†[8:7–12] In the eleventh tablet of the Gilgamesh Epic, Utnapishtim (the equivalent of Noah) released in succession a dove, a swallow, and a raven. When the raven did not return, Utnapishtim knew it was safe to leave the ark. The first century A.D. Roman author Pliny tells of Indian sailors who release birds in order to follow them toward land.

---

k. [7:21–23] Jb 22:16; Mt 24:39; Lk 17:27; 2 Pt 3:6.

l. [8:17] Gn 1:22, 28. m. [8:21] Sir 44:18; Is 54:9; Rom 7:18.
n. [8:22] Jer 33:20, 25. o. [9:1] Gn 1:22, 28; 8:17. p. [9:3] Gn 1:29–30; Dt 12:15. q. [9:4] Lv 7:26–27; 17:4; Dt 12:16, 23; 1 Sm 14:33; Acts 15:20.

in it you shall not eat.` `[5]`Indeed for your own life-blood I will demand an accounting: from every animal I will demand it, and from a human being, each one for the blood of another, I will demand an accounting for human life.`[r]`

6    `†`Anyone who sheds the blood of a human
being,
by a human being shall that one's
blood be shed;
For in the image of God
have human beings been made.`[s]`

`[7]`Be fertile, then, and multiply; abound on earth and subdue it.`[t]`

`[8]``‡`God said to Noah and to his sons with him: `[9]`See, I am now establishing my covenant with you and your descendants after you`[u]` `[10]`and with every living creature that was with you: the birds, the tame animals, and all the wild animals that were with you—all that came out of the ark. `[11]`I will establish my covenant with you, that never again shall all creatures be destroyed by the waters of a flood; there shall not be another flood to devastate the earth.`[v]` `[12]`God said: This is the sign of the covenant that I am making between me and you and every living creature with you for all ages to come: `[13w]`I set my bow in the clouds to serve as a sign of the covenant between me and the earth. `[14]`When I bring clouds over the earth, and the bow appears in the clouds, `[15]`I will remember my covenant between me and you and every living crea-ture—every mortal being—so that the waters will never again become a flood to destroy every mortal being.`[x]` `[16]`When the bow appears in the clouds, I will see it and remember the everlast-ing covenant between God and every living creature—every mortal being that is on earth. `[17]`God told Noah: This is the sign of the covenant I have established between me and every mortal being that is on earth.

**Noah and His Sons.** `[18]``§`The sons of Noah who came out of the ark were Shem, Ham and

Japheth. Ham was the father of Canaan.`[y]` `[19]`These three were the sons of Noah, and from them the whole earth was populated.

`[20]`Noah, a man of the soil, was the first to plant a vineyard. `[21]`He drank some of the wine, became drunk, and lay naked inside his tent.`[z]` `[22]`Ham, the father of Canaan, saw his father's nakedness, and he told his two brothers outside. `[23]`Shem and Japheth, however, took a robe, and holding it on their shoulders, they walked back-ward and covered their father's nakedness; since their faces were turned the other way, they did not see their father's nakedness. `[24]`When Noah woke up from his wine and learned what his youngest son had done to him, `[25]`he said:

"Cursed be Caanan!
The lowest of slaves
shall he be to his brothers."`[a]`

`[26]`He also said:

"Blessed be the Lord, the God of Shem!
Let Canaan be his slave.
`[27]`  May God expand Japheth,`¶`
and may he dwell among the tents
of Shem;
and let Canaan be his slave."

`[28]`Noah lived three hundred and fifty years after the flood. `[29]`The whole lifetime of Noah was nine hundred and fifty years; then he died.

## CHAPTER 10

**Table of the Nations.**`**` `[1]`These are the descen-dants of Noah's sons, Shem, Ham and Japheth, to whom children were born after the flood.

know about the intoxicating effect of wine) but Ham's, who shames his father by looking on his nakedness, and then tells the other sons. Ham's conduct is meant to prefigure the later shameful sexual practices of the Canaanites, which are alleged in numerous biblical passages. The point of the story is revealed in Noah's curse of Ham's son Canaan and his blessing of Shem and Japheth.

¶[9:27] In the Hebrew text there is a play on the words *yapt* ("expand") and *yepet* ("Japheth").

**[10:1–32] Verse 1 is the fourth of the Priestly formulas (2:4; 5:1; 6:9; 11:10) that structure Part I of Genesis; it intro-duces 10:2–11:9, the populating of the world and the build-ing of the city. In a sense, chaps. 4–9 are concerned with the first of the two great commands given to the human race in 1:28, "Be fertile and multiply!" whereas chaps. 10–11 are concerned with the second command, "Fill the earth and subdue it!" ("Subdue it" refers to each nation's taking the land assigned to it by God.) Gn 9:19 already noted that all nations are descended from the three sons of Noah; the same senti-ment is repeated in 10:5, 18, 25, 32; 11:8. The presupposition of the chapter is that every nation has a land assigned to it by God (cf. Dt 32:8–9). The number of the nations is seventy (if one does not count Noah and his sons, and counts Sidon [vv. 15, 19] only once), which is a traditional biblical number (Jgs 8:30; Lk 10:1, 17). According to Gn 46:27 and Ex 1:5, Israel also numbered seventy persons, which shows that it in some sense represents the nations of the earth.

*[9:4] Because a living being dies when it loses most of its blood, the ancients regarded blood as the seat of life, and therefore as sacred. Jewish tradition considered the prohibi-tion against eating meat with blood to be binding on all, because it was given by God to Noah, the new ancestor of all humankind; therefore the early Christian Church retained it for a time (Acts 15:20, 29).

†[9:6] The image of God, given to the first man and woman and transmitted to every human being, is the reason that no violent attacks can be made upon human beings. That image is the basis of the dignity of every individual who, in some sense, "represents" God in the world.

‡[9:8–17] God makes a covenant with Noah and his descendants and, remarkably, with all the animals who come out of the ark: never again shall the world be destroyed by flood. The sign of this solemn promise is the appearance of a rainbow.

§[9:18–27] The character of the three sons is sketched here. The fault is not Noah's (for he could not be expected to

r. [9:5] Gn 4:10–11; Ex 21:12.   s. [9:6] Gn 1:26–27; Lv 24:17; Nm 35:33; Jas 3:9.   t. [9:7] Gn 1:28; 8:17; 9:2; Jas 3:7.   u. [9:9] Gn 6:18.   v. [9:11] Sir 44:18; Is 54:9.   w. [9:13] Sir 43:12.   x. [9:15] Is 54:9.

y. [9:18] Gn 5:32; 10:1.   z. [9:21] Lam 4:21; Hb 2:15.   a. [9:25] Dt 27:16; Wis 12:11.

²ᵇThe descendants of Japheth: Gomer,⁺ Magog, Madai, Javan, Tubal, Meshech and Tiras.ᶜ ³The descendants of Gomer: Ashkenaz,† Diphath and Togarmah. ⁴The descendants of Javan: Elishah,‡ Tarshish, the Kittim and the Rodanim. ⁵From these branched out the maritime nations.

These are the descendants of Japheth by their lands, each with its own language, according to their clans, by their nations.

⁶The descendants of Ham: Cush,§ Mizraim, Put and Canaan. ⁷The descendants of Cush: Seba, Havilah, Sabtah, Raamah and Sabteca. The descendants of Raamah: Sheba and Dedan.

⁸Cush§ became the father of Nimrod, who was the first to become a mighty warrior on earth. ⁹He was a mighty hunter in the eyes of the LORD; hence the saying, "Like Nimrod, a mighty hunter in the eyes of the LORD." ¹⁰His kingdom originated in Babylon, Erech and Accad, all of them in the land of Shinar.** ¹¹From that land he went forth to Assyria, where he built Nineveh, Rehoboth-Ir†† and Calah, ¹²as well as Resen, between Nineveh and Calah,‡‡ the latter being the principal city.

¹³ᵈMizraim became the father of the Ludim, the Anamim, the Lehabim, the Naphtuhim,

¹⁴the Pathrusim,§§ the Casluhim, and the Caphtorim from whom the Philistines came.

¹⁵Canaan became the father of Sidon, his firstborn, and of Heth;¶¶ ¹⁶also of the Jebusites, the Amorites, the Girgashites, ¹⁷the Hivites, the Arkites, the Sinites, ¹⁸the Arvadites, the Zemarites, and the Hamathites. Afterward, the clans of the Canaanites spread out, ¹⁹so that the Canaanite borders extended from Sidon all the way to Gerar, near Gaza, and all the way to Sodom, Gomorrah, Admah and Zeboiim, near Lasha.

²⁰These are the descendants of Ham, according to their clans, according to their languages, by their lands, by their nations.

²¹To Shem also, Japheth's oldest brother and the ancestor of all the children of Eber,*** children were born. ²²ᵉThe descendants of Shem: Elam, Asshur, Arpachshad, Lud and Aram. ²³The descendants of Aram: Uz, Hul, Gether and Mash.

²⁴Arpachshad became the father of Shelah, and Shelah became the father of Eber. ²⁵To Eber two sons were born: the name of the first was Peleg, for in his time the world was divided;††† and the name of his brother was Joktan.

²⁶Joktan became the father of Almodad, Sheleph, Hazarmaveth, Jerah, ²⁷Hadoram, Uzal, Diklah, ²⁸Obal, Abimael, Sheba, ²⁹Ophir, Havilah and Jobab. All these were descendants of Joktan. ³⁰Their settlements extended all the way from Mesha to Sephar, the eastern hill country.

³¹These are the descendants of Shem, according to their clans, according to their languages, by their lands, by their nations.

³²These are the clans of Noah's sons, according to their origins and by their nations. From these the nations of the earth branched out after the flood.

## CHAPTER 11

**Tower of Babel.**‡‡‡ ¹The whole world had the same language and the same words. ²When they were migrating from the east, they came to a valley in the land of Shinar§§§ and settled there. ³They said to one another, "Come, let us mold bricks and harden them with fire." They used bricks for stone, and bitumen for mortar. ⁴Then they said, "Come, let us build ourselves a city and a tower

---

This chapter classifies the various peoples known to the ancient Israelites; it is theologically important as stressing the basic family unity of all peoples on earth. It is sometimes called the Table of the Nations. The relationship between the various peoples is based on linguistic, geographic, or political grounds (v. 31). In general, the descendants of Japheth (vv. 2–5) are the peoples of the Indo-European languages to the north and west of Mesopotamia and Syria; the descendants of Ham (vv. 6–20) are the Hamitic-speaking peoples of northern Africa; and the descendants of Shem (vv. 21–31) are the Semitic-speaking peoples of Mesopotamia, Syria and Arabia. But there are many exceptions to this rule; the Semitic-speaking peoples of Canaan are considered descendants of Ham, because at one time they were subject to Hamitic Egypt (vv. 6, 15–19). This chapter is generally considered to be a composite from the Yahwist source (vv. 8–19, 21, 24–30) and the Priestly source (vv. 1–7, 20, 22–23, 31–32). Presumably that is why certain tribes of Arabia are listed under both Ham (v. 7) and Shem (vv. 26–28).

*[10:2] **Gomer:** the Cimmerians; **Madai:** the Medes; **Javan:** the Greeks.

†[10:3] **Ashkenaz:** an Indo-European people, which later became the medieval rabbinic name for Germany. It now designates one of the great divisions of Judaism, Eastern European Yiddish-speaking Jews.

‡[10:4] **Elishah:** Cyprus; **the Kittim:** certain inhabitants of Cyprus; **the Rodanim:** the inhabitants of Rhodes.

§[10:6] **Cush:** biblical Ethiopia, modern Nubia. **Mizraim:** Lower (i.e., northern) Egypt; **Put:** either Punt in East Africa or Libya.

¶[10:8] **Cush:** here seems to be Cossea, the country of the Kassites; see note on 2:10–14. **Nimrod:** possibly Tukulti-Ninurta I (thirteenth century B.C.), the first Assyrian conqueror of Babylonia and a famous city-builder at home.

**[10:10] **Shinar:** the land of ancient Babylonia, embracing Sumer and Akkad, present-day southern Iraq, mentioned also in 11:2; 14:1.

††[10:11] **Rehoboth-Ir:** lit., "wide-streets city," was probably not the name of another city, but an epithet of Nineveh; cf. Jon 3:3.

‡‡[10:12] **Calah:** Assyrian Kalhu, the capital of Assyria in the ninth century B.C.

§§[10:14] **The Pathrusim:** the people of Upper (southern) Egypt; cf. Is 11:11; Jer 44:1; Ez 29:14; 30:13. **Caphtorim:** Crete; for Caphtor as the place of origin of the Philistines, cf. Dt 2:23; Am 9:7; Jer 47:4.

¶¶[10:15] **Heth:** the biblical Hittites; see note on 23:3.

***[10:21] **Eber:** the eponymous ancestor of the Hebrews, that is, the one to whom they traced their name.

†††[10:25] In the Hebrew text there is a play on the name *Peleg* and the word *niplega*, "was divided."

‡‡‡[11:1–9] This story illustrates increasing human wickedness, shown here in the sinful pride that human beings take in their own achievements apart from God. Secondarily, the story explains the diversity of languages among the peoples of the earth.

§§§[11:2] **Shinar:** see note on 10:10.

---

b. [10:2–8] 1 Chr 1:5–10.   c. [10:2] Ez 38:2.   d. [10:13–18] 1 Chr 1:11–16.

e. [10:22–29] 1 Chr 1:17–23.

with its top in the sky,* and so make a name for ourselves; otherwise we shall be scattered all over the earth."

⁵The LORD came down to see the city and the tower that the people had built. ⁶Then the LORD said: If now, while they are one people and all have the same language, they have started to do this, nothing they presume to do will be out of their reach. ⁷Come, let us go down and there confuse their language, so that no one will understand the speech of another. ⁸So the LORD scattered them from there over all the earth, and they stopped building the city. ⁹That is why it was called Babel,† because there the LORD confused the speech of all the world. From there the LORD scattered them over all the earth.

**Descendants from Shem to Abraham.**‡ ¹⁰ᶠThese are the descendants of Shem. When Shem was one hundred years old, he begot Arpachshad, two years after the flood. ¹¹Shem lived five hundred years after he begot Arpachshad, and he had other sons and daughters. ¹²When Arpachshad was thirty-five years old, he begot Shelah.§ ¹³Arpachshad lived four hundred and three years after he begot Shelah, and he had other sons and daughters.

¹⁴When Shelah was thirty years old, he begot Eber. ¹⁵Shelah lived four hundred and three years after he begot Eber, and he had other sons and daughters.

¹⁶When Eber⁵ was thirty-four years old, he begot Peleg. ¹⁷Eber lived four hundred and thirty years after he begot Peleg, and he had other sons and daughters.

¹⁸When Peleg was thirty years old, he begot Reu. ¹⁹Peleg lived two hundred and nine years after he begot Reu, and he had other sons and daughters.

²⁰When Reu was thirty-two years old, he begot Serug. ²¹Reu lived two hundred and seven years after he begot Serug, and he had other sons and daughters.

²²When Serug was thirty years old, he begot Nahor. ²³Serug lived two hundred years after he begot Nahor, and he had other sons and daughters.

²⁴When Nahor was twenty-nine years old, he begot Terah. ²⁵Nahor lived one hundred and nineteen years after he begot Terah, and he had other sons and daughters.

²⁶When Terah was seventy years old, he begot Abram,** Nahor and Haran.ᵍ

## II. THE STORY OF THE ANCESTORS OF ISRAEL

**Terah.** ²⁷These are the descendants of Terah.†† Terah begot Abram, Nahor, and Haran, and Haran begot Lot. ²⁸Haran died before Terah his father, in his native land, in Ur of the Chaldeans.‡‡ ²⁹Abram and Nahor took wives; the name of Abram's wife was Sarai,§§ and the name of Nahor's wife was Milcah, daughter of Haran, the father of Milcah and Iscah.ʰ ³⁰Sarai was barren; she had no child.

³¹Terah took his son Abram, his grandson Lot, son of Haran, and his daughter-in-law Sarai, the wife of his son Abram, and brought them out of Ur of the Chaldeans, to go to the land of Canaan. But when they reached Haran, they settled there.ⁱ ³²The lifetime of Terah was two hundred and five years; then Terah died in Haran.¶¶

---

*[11:4] **Tower with its top in the sky**: possibly a reference to the chief ziggurat of Babylon, *E-sag-ila*, lit., "the house that raises high its head."

†[11:9] **Babel**: the Hebrew form of the name "Babylon"; the Babylonians interpreted their name for the city, *Bab-ili*, as "gate of god." The Hebrew word *balal*, "he confused," has a similar sound.

‡[11:10–26] The second Priestly genealogy goes from Shem to Terah and his three sons Abram, Nahor, and Haran, just as the genealogy in 5:3–32 went from Adam to Noah and his three sons Shem, Ham, and Japheth. This genealogy marks the important transition in Genesis between the story of the nations in 1:1–11:26 and the story of Israel in the person of its ancestors (11:27–50:26). As chaps. 1–11 showed the increase and spread of the nations, so chaps. 12–50 will show the increase and spread of Israel. The contrast between Israel and the nations is a persistent biblical theme. The ages given here are from the Hebrew text; the Samaritan and Greek texts have divergent sets of numbers in most cases. In comparable accounts of the pre-flood period, enormous life spans are attributed to human beings. It may be an attempt to show that the pre-flood generations were extraordinary and more vital than post-flood human beings.

§[11:12] The Greek text adds Kenan (cf. 5:9–10) between Arpachshad and Shelah. The Greek listing is followed in Lk 3:36.

⁵[11:16] **Eber**: the eponymous ancestor of the Hebrews, "descendants of Eber" (10:21, 24–30); see note on 14:13.

**[11:26] Abram is a dialectal variant of Abraham. God will change his name in view of his new task in 17:4.

††[11:27] **Descendants of Terah**: elsewhere in Genesis the story of the son is introduced by the name of the father (25:12, 19; 36:1; 37:2). The Abraham-Sarah stories begin (11:27–32) and end with genealogical notices (25:1–18), which concern, respectively, the families of Terah and of Abraham. Most of the traditions in the cycle are from the Yahwist source. The so-called Elohist source (E) is somewhat shadowy, denied by some scholars but recognized by others in passages that duplicate other narratives (20:1–18 and 21:22–34). The Priestly source consists mostly of brief editorial notices, except for chaps. 17 and 23.

‡‡[11:28] **Ur of the Chaldeans**: Ur was an extremely ancient city of the Sumerians (later, of the Babylonians) in southern Mesopotamia. The Greek text has "the land of the Chaldeans." After a millennium of relative unimportance, Ur underwent a revival during the Neo-Babylonian/Chaldean empire (625–539 B.C.). The sixth-century author here identified the place by its contemporary name. As chap. 24 shows, Haran in northern Mesopotamia is in fact the native place of Abraham. In the Genesis perspective, the human race originated in the East (3:24; 4:16) and migrated from there to their homelands (11:2). Terah's family moved from the East (Ur) and Abraham will complete the journey to the family's true homeland in the following chapters.

§§[11:29] **Sarai**: like Abram, a dialectal variant of the more usual form of the name Sarah. In 17:15, God will change it to Sarah in view of her new task.

¶¶[11:32] Since Terah was seventy years old when his son Abraham was born (v. 26), and Abraham was seventy-five when he left Haran (12:4), Terah lived in Haran for sixty

---

g. [11:26] Jos 24:2; 1 Chr 1:26–27. h. [11:29] Gn 17:15. i. [11:31] Jos 24:3; Neh 9:7; Jdt 5:6–9; Acts 7:4.

f. [11:10–26] 1 Chr 1:24–27; Lk 3:34–36.

## CHAPTER 12

**Abram's Call and Migration.** ¹The Lord said to Abram: Go forth* from your land, your relatives, and from your father's house to a land that I will show you.ʲ ²ᵏI will make of you a great nation, and I will bless you; I will make your name great, so that you will be a blessing.ᵏ ³I will bless those who bless you and curse those who curse you. All the families of the earth will find blessing in you.‡

⁴ᵐAbram went as the Lord directed him, and Lot went with him. Abram was seventy-five years old when he left Haran. ⁵§Abram took his wife Sarai, his brother's son Lot, all the possessions that they had accumulated, and the persons they had acquired in Haran, and they set out for the land of Canaan. When they came to the land of Canaan, ⁶§Abram passed through the land as far as the sacred place at Shechem, by the oak of Moreh. The Canaanites were then in the land.

⁷The Lord appeared to Abram and said: To your descendants I will give this land. So Abram built an altar there to the Lord who had appeared to him.ⁿ ⁸From there he moved on to the hill country east of Bethel, pitching his tent with Bethel to the west and Ai to the east. He built an altar there to the Lord and invoked the Lord by name. ⁹Then Abram journeyed on by stages to the Negeb."

**Abram and Sarai in Egypt.††** ¹⁰There was famine in the land; so Abram went down to Egypt to sojourn there, since the famine in the land was severe.ᵒ ¹¹When he was about to enter Egypt, he said to his wife Sarai: "I know that you are a beautiful woman. ¹²When the Egyptians see you, they will say, 'She is his wife'; then they will kill me, but let you live. ¹³Please say, therefore, that you are my sister,‡‡ so that I may fare well on your account and my life may be spared for your sake."ᵖ ¹⁴When Abram arrived in Egypt, the Egyptians saw that the woman was very beautiful. ¹⁵When Pharaoh's officials saw her they praised her to Pharaoh, and the woman was taken into Pharaoh's house. ¹⁶Abram fared well on her account, and he acquired sheep, oxen, male and female servants, male and female donkeys, and camels.§§

¹⁷But the Lord struck Pharaoh and his household with severe plagues because of Sarai, Abram's wife.�q ¹⁸Then Pharaoh summoned Abram and said to him: "How could you do this to me! Why did you not tell me she was your wife? ¹⁹Why did you say, 'She is my sister,' so that I took her for my wife? Now, here is your wife. Take her and leave!"

²⁰Then Pharaoh gave his men orders concerning Abram, and they sent him away, with his wife and all that belonged to him.

## CHAPTER 13

**Abram and Lot Part.** ¹From Egypt Abram went up to the Negeb with his wife and all that belonged to him, and Lot went with him.ʳ ²§§Now

---

years after Abraham's departure. According to the tradition in the Samaritan text, Terah died when he was one hundred and forty-five years old, therefore, in the same year in which Abraham left Haran. This is the tradition followed in Stephen's speech: Abraham left Haran "after his father died" (Acts 7:4).

*[12:1–3] **Go forth . . . find blessing in you**: the syntax of the Hebrew suggests that the blessings promised to Abraham are contingent on his going to Canaan.

†[12:2] The call of Abraham begins a new history of blessing (18:18; 22:15–18), which is passed on in each instance to the chosen successor (26:2–4; 28:14). This call evokes the last story in the primeval history (11:1–9) by reversing its themes: Abraham goes forth rather than settle down; it is God rather than Abraham who will make a name for him; the families of the earth will find blessing in him.

‡[12:3] **Will find blessing in you**: the Hebrew conjugation of the verb here and in 18:18 and 28:14 can be either reflexive ("shall bless themselves by you" = people will invoke Abraham as an example of someone blessed by God) or passive ("by you all the families of earth will be blessed" = the religious privileges of Abraham and his descendants ultimately will be extended to the nations). In 22:18 and 26:4, another conjugation of the same verb is used in a similar context that is undoubtedly reflexive ("bless themselves"). Many scholars suggest that the two passages in which the sense is clear should determine the interpretation of the three ambiguous passages: the privileged blessing enjoyed by Abraham and his descendants will awaken in all peoples the desire to enjoy those same blessings. Since the term is understood in a passive sense in the New Testament (Acts 3:25; Gal 3:8), it is rendered here by a neutral expression that admits of both meanings.

§[12:5] The ancestors appear in Genesis as pastoral nomads living at the edge of settled society, and having occasional dealings with the inhabitants, sometimes even moving into towns for brief periods. Unlike modern nomads such as the Bedouin, however, ancient pastoralists fluctuated between following the herds and sedentary life, depending on circumstances. Pastoralists could settle down and farm and later resume a pastoral way of life. Indeed, there was a symbiotic relationship between pastoralists and villagers, each providing goods to the other. **Persons**: servants and others who formed the larger household under the leadership of Abraham; cf. 14:14.

§[12:6] Abraham's journey to the center of the land, Shechem, then to Bethel, and then to the Negeb, is duplicated in Jacob's journeys (33:18; 35:1, 6, 27; 46:1) and in the general route of the conquest under Joshua (Jos 7:2; 8:9, 30). Abraham's journey is a symbolic "conquest" of the land he has been promised. In building altars here (vv. 7, 8) and elsewhere, Abraham acknowledges his God as Lord of the land.

**[12:9] **The Negeb**: the semidesert land south of Judah.

††[12:10–13:1] Abraham and Sarah's sojourn in Egypt and encounter with Pharaoh foreshadow their descendants' experience, suggesting a divine design in which they must learn to trust. The story of Sarah, the ancestor in danger, is told again in chap. 20, and also in 26:1–11 with Rebekah instead of Sarah. Repetition of similar events is not unusual in literature that has been orally shaped.

‡‡[12:13] **You are my sister**: the text does not try to excuse Abraham's deception, though in 20:12 a similar deception is somewhat excused.

§§[12:16] **Camels**: domesticated camels did not come into common use in the ancient Near East until the end of the second millennium B.C. Thus the mention of camels here (24:11–64; 30:43; 31:17, 34; 32:8, 16; 37:25) is seemingly an anachronism.

¶¶[13:2–18] In this story of Abraham and Lot going their separate ways, Abraham resolves a family dispute by an act that shows both trust in God and generosity toward his nephew. The story suggests Lot rather than Abraham is the natural choice to be the ancestor of a great family; he is young

---

j. [12:1] Acts 7:3; Heb 11:8.   k. [12:2] Gn 17:6; Sir 44:20–21; Rom 4:17–22.   l. [12:3] Gn 18:18; 22:18; Acts 3:25; Gal 3:8.   m. [12:4–5] Gn 11:31; Jos 24:3; Acts 7:4.

n. [12:7] Ex 33:1; Dt 34:4; Acts 7:5.   o. [12:10] Gn 26:1.   p. [12:13] Gn 20:12–13; 26:7.   q. [12:17] Ps 105:14.   r. [13:1] Gn 12:9.

Abram was very rich in livestock, silver, and gold.⁵ ³From the Negeb he traveled by stages toward Bethel, to the place between Bethel and Ai where his tent had formerly stood, ⁴the site where he had first built the altar; and there Abram invoked the LORD by name.ᵗ

⁵Lot, who went with Abram, also had flocks and herds and tents, ⁶so that the land could not support them if they stayed together; their possessions were so great that they could not live together. ⁷There were quarrels between the herders of Abram's livestock and the herders of Lot's livestock. At this time the Canaanites and the Perizzites were living in the land.

⁸So Abram said to Lot: "Let there be no strife between you and me, or between your herders and my herders, for we are kindred. ⁹Is not the whole land available? Please separate from me. If you prefer the left, I will go to the right; if you prefer the right, I will go to the left." ¹⁰Lot looked about and saw how abundantly watered the whole Jordan Plain was as far as Zoar, like the LORD's own garden, or like Egypt. This was before the LORD had destroyed Sodom and Gomorrah. ¹¹Lot, therefore, chose for himself the whole Jordan Plain and set out eastward. Thus they separated from each other. ¹²Abram settled in the land of Canaan, while Lot settled among the cities of the Plain, pitching his tents near Sodom. ¹³Now the inhabitants of Sodom were wicked, great sinners against the LORD.ᵘ

¹⁴After Lot had parted from him, the LORD said to Abram: Look about you, and from where you are, gaze to the north and south, east and west;ᵛ ¹⁵all the land that you see I will give to you and your descendants forever.ʷ ¹⁶I will make your descendants like the dust of the earth; if anyone could count the dust of the earth, your descendants too might be counted.ˣ ¹⁷Get up and walk through the land, across its length and breadth, for I give it to you. ¹⁸Abram moved his tents and went on to settle near the oak of Mamre, which is at Hebron. There he built an altar to the LORD.ʸ

## CHAPTER 14

**The Four Kings.** ¹When Amraphel king of Shinar, Arioch king of Ellasar, Chedorlaomer king of Elam, and Tidal king of Goiim ²made war on Bera king of Sodom, Birsha king of Gomorrah, Shinab king of Admah, Shemeber king of Zeboiim, and the king of Bela (that is, Zoar), ³all the latter kings joined forces in the Valley of Siddim (that is, the Salt Sea†). ⁴For twelve years they had served Chedorlaomer, but in the thirteenth year they rebelled. ⁵In the fourteenth year Chedorlaomer and the kings allied with him came and defeated the Rephaim in Ashteroth-karnaim, the Zuzim in Ham, the Emim in Shaveh-kiriathaim, ⁶and the Horites in the hill country of Seir, as far as El-paran, close by the wilderness.ᶻ ⁷They then turned back and came to En-mishpat (that is, Kadesh), and they subdued the whole country of both the Amalekites and the Amorites who lived in Hazazon-tamar. ⁸Thereupon the king of Sodom, the king of Gomorrah, the king of Admah, the king of Zeboiim, and the king of Bela (that is, Zoar) marched out, and in the Valley of Siddim they went into battle against them: ⁹against Chedorlaomer king of Elam, Tidal king of Goiim, Amraphel king of Shinar, and Arioch king of Ellasar—four kings against five. ¹⁰Now the Valley of Siddim was full of bitumen pits; and as the king of Sodom and the king of Gomorrah fled, they fell into these, while the rest fled to the mountains. ¹¹The victors seized all the possessions and food supplies of Sodom and Gomorrah and then went their way. ¹²They took with them Abram's nephew Lot, who had been living in Sodom, as well as his possessions, and departed.ᵃ

¹³A survivor came and brought the news to Abram the Hebrew,‡ who was camping at the oak of Mamre the Amorite, a kinsman of Eshcol and Aner; these were allies of Abram. ¹⁴When Abram heard that his kinsman had been captured, he mustered three hundred and eighteen of his retainers,§ born in his house, and went in pursuit as far as Dan. ¹⁵He and his servants deployed against them at night, defeated them, and pursued them as far as Hobah, which is north of Damascus. ¹⁶He recovered all the possessions. He also recovered his kinsman Lot and

and he takes the most fertile land (outside the land of Canaan). In contrast to Lot, who lifts his eyes to choose for himself (vv. 10–11), Abraham waits for God to tell him to lift his eyes and see the land he will receive (v. 14). Chaps. 18–19 continue the story of Abraham and Lot. Abraham's visionary possession of the land foreshadows that of Moses (Dt 3:27; 34:4).

*[14:1] Abraham plays a role with other world leaders. He defeats a coalition of five kings from the east (where, later, Israel's enemies lived) and is recognized by a Canaanite king as blessed by God Most High. The historicity of the events is controverted; apart from Shinar (Babylon), Tidal (Hittite Tudhaliya), and Elam, the names and places cannot be identified with certainty. The five cities were apparently at the southern end of the Dead Sea, and all but Bela (i.e., Zoar) were destined for destruction (19:20–24; Hos 11:8). The passage belongs to none of the traditional Genesis sources; it has some resemblance to reports of military campaigns in Babylonian and Assyrian royal annals.

†[14:3] **The Salt Sea:** the Dead Sea.

‡[14:13] **Abram the Hebrew:** "Hebrew" was used by biblical writers for the pre-Israelite ancestors. Linguistically, it is an ethnic term; it may be built on the root Eber, who is the eponymous ancestor of the Israelites, that is, the one to whom they traced their name (10:21, 24–25; 11:14–17), or it may reflect the tradition that the ancestors came from beyond (eber) the Euphrates. It is used only by non-Israelites, or by Israelites speaking to foreigners.

§[14:14] **Retainers:** the Hebrew word hanik is used only here in the Old Testament. Cognate words appear in Egyptian and Akkadian texts, signifying armed soldiers belonging to the household of a local leader.

s. [13:2] Ps 112:1–3; Prv 10:22.   t. [13:4] Gn 12:8.   u. [13:13] Gn 18:20; Ez 16:49; 2 Pt 2:6–8; Jude 7.   v. [13:14] Gn 28:14.   w. [13:15] Gn 12:7; Mt 5:5; Lk 1:55, 73; Acts 7:5; Rom 4:13; Gal 3:16.   x. [13:16] Gn 22:17; Nm 23:10.   y. [13:18] Gn 14:13.

z. [14:6] Dt 2:12.   a. [14:12] Gn 13:10–12.

his possessions, along with the women and the other people.

¹⁷When Abram returned from his defeat of Chedorlaomer and the kings who were allied with him, the king of Sodom went out to greet him in the Valley of Shaveh (that is, the King's Valley).

¹⁸Melchizedek, king of Salem,* brought out bread and wine. He was a priest of God Most High. ¹⁹He blessed Abram with these words:*b*

"Blessed be Abram by God Most High,
the creator of heaven and earth;
²⁰ And blessed be God Most High,
who delivered your foes into your
hand."

Then Abram gave him a tenth of everything.

²¹The king of Sodom said to Abram, "Give me the captives; the goods you may keep." ²²But Abram replied to the king of Sodom: "I have sworn to the LORD, God Most High,† the creator of heaven and earth, ²³that I would not take so much as a thread or a sandal strap from anything that is yours, so that you cannot say, 'I made Abram rich.' ²⁴Nothing for me except what my servants have consumed and the share that is due to the men who went with me—Aner, Eshcol and Mamre; let them take their share."

## CHAPTER 15
**The Covenant with Abram.**‡ ¹Some time afterward, the word of the LORD came to Abram in a

vision: Do not fear, Abram! I am your shield; I will make your reward very great.

²But Abram said, "Lord GOD, what can you give me, if I die childless and have only a servant of my household, Eliezer of Damascus?" ³Abram continued, "Look, you have given me no offspring, so a servant of my household will be my heir." ⁴Then the word of the LORD came to him: No, that one will not be your heir; your own offspring will be your heir.*c* ⁵He took him outside and said: Look up at the sky and count the stars, if you can. Just so, he added, will your descendants be.*d* ⁶"Abram put his faith in the LORD, who attributed it to him as an act of righteousness.§

⁷He then said to him: I am the LORD who brought you from Ur of the Chaldeans to give you this land as a possession.*f* ⁸"Lord GOD," he asked, "how will I know that I will possess it?" ⁹He answered him: Bring me a three-year-old heifer, a three-year-old female goat, a three-year-old ram, a turtledove, and a young pigeon.*g* ¹⁰He brought him all these, split them in two, and placed each half opposite the other; but the birds he did not cut up. ¹¹Birds of prey swooped down on the carcasses, but Abram scared them away. ¹²As the sun was about to set, a deep sleep fell upon Abram, and a great, dark dread descended upon him.

¹³**"**Then the LORD said to Abram: Know for certain that your descendants will reside as aliens in a land not their own, where they shall be enslaved and oppressed for four hundred years.*h* ¹⁴But I will bring judgment on the nation they must serve, and after this they will go out with great wealth.*i* ¹⁵You, however, will go to your ancestors in peace; you will be buried at a ripe old age. ¹⁶In the fourth generation†† your

---

*[14:18] Melchizedek, king of Salem (Jerusalem, cf. Ps 76:3), appears with majestic suddenness to recognize Abraham's great victory, which the five local kings were unable to achieve. He prepares a feast in his honor and declares him blessed or made powerful by God Most High, evidently the highest God in the Canaanite pantheon. Abraham acknowledges the blessing by giving a tenth of the recaptured spoils as a tithe to Melchizedek. The episode is one of several allusions to David, king at Jerusalem, who also exercised priestly functions (2 Sm 6:17). Heb 7 interprets Melchizedek as a prefiguration of Christ. **God Most High:** in Heb. *El Elyon*, one of several "El names" for God in Genesis, others being *El Olam* (21:33), *El* the God of Israel (33:20), *El Roi* (16:13), *El Bethel* (35:7), and *El Shaddai* (the usual P designation for God in Genesis). All the sources except the Yahwist use El as the proper name for God used by the ancestors. The god El was well-known across the ancient Near East and in comparable religious literature. The ancestors recognized this God as their own when they encountered him in their journeys and in the shrines they found in Canaan.

†[14:22] In vv. 22–24, Abraham refuses to let anyone but God enrich him. Portrayed with the traits of a later Israelite judge or tribal hero, Abraham acknowledges that his victory is from God alone.

‡[15:1–21] In the first section (vv. 1–6), Abraham is promised a son and heir, and in the second (vv. 7–21), he is promised a land. The structure is similar in both: each of the two promises is not immediately accepted; the first is met with a complaint (vv. 2–3) and the second with a request for a sign (v. 8). God's answer differs in each section—a sign in v. 5 and an oath in vv. 9–21. Some scholars believe that the Genesis promises of progeny and land were originally separate and only later combined, but progeny and land are persistent concerns especially of ancient peoples and it is hard to imagine one without the other.

§[15:6] Abraham's act of faith in God's promises was regarded as an act of righteousness, i.e., as fully expressive of his relationship with God. St. Paul (Rom 4:1–25; Gal 3:6–9) makes Abraham's faith a model for Christians.

¶[15:9–17] Cutting up animals was a well-attested way of making a treaty in antiquity. Jer 34:17–20 shows the rite is a form of self-imprecation in which violators invoke the fate of the animals upon themselves. The eighth-century B.C. Sefire treaty from Syria reads, "As this calf is cut up, thus Matti'el shall be cut up." The smoking fire pot and the flaming torch (v. 17), which represent God, pass between the pieces, making God a signatory to the covenant.

**[15:13–16] The verses clarify the promise of the land by providing a timetable of its possession: after four hundred years of servitude, your descendants will actually possess the land in the fourth generation (a patriarchal generation seems to be one hundred years). The iniquity of the current inhabitants (called here the Amorites) has not yet reached the point where God must intervene in punishment. Another table is given in Ex 12:40, which is not compatible with this one.

††[15:16] **Generation:** the Hebrew term *dor* is commonly rendered as "generation," but it may signify a period of varying length. A "generation" is the period between the birth of children and the birth of their parents, normally about twenty to twenty-five years. The actual length of a generation can

---

b. [14:19] Ps 110:4; Heb 5:6, 10; 7:1.

c. [15:4] Gn 17:16.　d. [15:5] Gn 22:17; 28:14; Ex 32:13; Dt 1:10; Sir 44:21; Rom 4:18; Heb 11:12.　e. [15:6] 1 Mc 2:52; Rom 4:3, 9, 22; Gal 3:6–7; Jas 2:23.　f. [15:7] Gn 11:31; 12:1; Ex 32:13; Neh 9:7–8; Acts 7:2–3.　g. [15:9] Lv 1:14.　h. [15:13] Ex 12:40; Nm 20:15; Jdt 5:9–10; Is 52:4; Acts 13:20; Gal 3:17.　i. [15:14] Ex 3:8, 21–22.

descendants will return here, for the wickedness of the Amorites is not yet complete.[j]

[17]When the sun had set and it was dark, there appeared a smoking fire pot and a flaming torch, which passed between those pieces. [18]On that day the LORD made a covenant with Abram, saying: To your descendants I give this land, from the Wadi of Egypt to the Great River, the Euphrates,[k] [19]the land of the Kenites, the Kenizzites, the Kadmonites, [20]the Hittites, the Perizzites, the Rephaim, [21]the Amorites, the Canaanites, the Girgashites, and the Jebusites.

## CHAPTER 16

**Birth of Ishmael.**[†] [1]Abram's wife Sarai had borne him no children. Now she had an Egyptian maidservant named Hagar.[m] [2]Sarai said to Abram: "The LORD has kept me from bearing children. Have intercourse with my maid; perhaps I will have sons through her." Abram obeyed Sarai.[‡n] [3]Thus, after Abram had lived ten years in the land of Canaan, his wife Sarai took her maid, Hagar the Egyptian, and gave her to her husband Abram to be his wife. [4]He had intercourse with her, and she became pregnant. As soon as Hagar knew she was pregnant, her mistress lost stature in her eyes.[§o] [5]So Sarai said to Abram: "This outrage against me is your fault. I myself gave my maid to your embrace; but ever since she knew she was pregnant, I have lost stature in her eyes. May the LORD decide between you and me!" [6]Abram told Sarai: "Your maid is in your power. Do to her what

you regard as right." Sarai then mistreated her so much that Hagar ran away from her.

[7]The LORD's angel[q] found her by a spring in the wilderness, the spring on the road to Shur,[q] [8]and he asked, "Hagar, maid of Sarai, where have you come from and where are you going?" She answered, "I am running away from my mistress, Sarai." [9]But the LORD's angel told her: "Go back to your mistress and submit to her authority. [10]I will make your descendants so numerous," added the LORD's angel, "that they will be too many to count."[r] [11]Then the LORD's angel said to her:

"You are now pregnant and shall bear a son;
     you shall name him Ishmael,"
For the LORD has heeded your affliction.
[12]   He shall be a wild ass of a man,
         his hand against everyone,
         and everyone's hand against him;
     Alongside[††] all his kindred
         shall he encamp."[s]

[13]To the LORD who spoke to her she gave a name, saying, "You are God who sees me";[‡‡] she meant, "Have I really seen God and remained alive after he saw me?"[t] [14]That is why the well is called Beer-lahai-roi.[§§] It is between Kadesh and Bered.

[15]Hagar bore Abram a son, and Abram named the son whom Hagar bore him Ishmael.[u] [16]Abram was eighty-six years old when Hagar bore him Ishmael.

## CHAPTER 17

**Covenant of Circumcision.**[¶¶] [1]When Abram was ninety-nine years old, the LORD appeared to

---

vary, however; in Jb 42:16 it is thirty-five and in Nm 32:13 it is forty. The meaning may be life spans, which in Gn 6:3 is one hundred twenty years and in Is 65:20 is one hundred years.

*[15:18–21] The **Wadi**, i.e., a gully or ravine, **of Egypt** is the Wadi-el-'Arish, which is the boundary between the settled land and the Sinai desert. Some scholars suggest that the boundaries are those of a Davidic empire at its greatest extent; others that they are idealized boundaries. Most lists of the ancient inhabitants of the promised land give three, six, or seven peoples, but vv. 19–21 give a grand total of ten.

†[16:1–16] In the previous chapter Abraham was given a timetable of possession of the land, but nothing was said about when the child was to be born. In this chapter, Sarah takes matters into her own hands, for she has been childless ten years since the promise (cf. 12:4 with 16:16). The story is about the two women, Sarah the infertile mistress and Hagar the fertile slave; Abraham has only a single sentence. In the course of the story, God intervenes directly on the side of Hagar, for she is otherwise without resources.

‡[16:2] The custom of an infertile wife providing her husband with a concubine to produce children is widely attested in ancient Near Eastern law; e.g., an Old Assyrian marriage contract states that the wife must provide her husband with a concubine if she does not bear children within two years.

§[16:4] Because barrenness was at that time normally blamed on the woman and regarded as a disgrace, it is not surprising that Hagar looks down on Sarah. Ancient Near Eastern legal practice addresses such cases of insolent slaves and allows disciplining of them. Prv 30:23 uses as an example of intolerable behavior "a maidservant when she ousts her mistress."

¶[16:7] The **LORD's angel**: a manifestation of God in human form; in v. 13 the messenger is identified with God. See note on Ex 3:2.

**[16:11] **Ishmael**: in the Hebrew the name means "God has heard." It is the same Hebrew verb that is translated "heeded" in the next clause. In other ancient Near Eastern texts, the name commemorated the divine answer to the parents' prayer to have a child, but here it is broadened to mean that God has "heard" Hagar's plight. In vv. 13–14, the verb "to see" is similarly broadened to describe God's special care for those in need.

††[16:12] **Alongside**: lit., "against the face of"; the same phrase is used of the lands of Ishmael's descendants in 25:18. It can be translated "in opposition to" (Dt 21:16; Jb 1:11; 6:28; 21:31), but here more likely means that Ishmael's settlement was near but not in the promised land.

‡‡[16:13] **God who sees me**: Hebrew el-ro'i is multivalent, meaning either "God of seeing," i.e., extends his protection to me, or "God sees," which can imply seeing human suffering (29:32; Ex 2:25; Is 57:18; 58:3). It is probable that Hagar means to express both of these aspects. **Remained alive**: for the ancient notion that a person died on seeing God, see Gn 32:31; Ex 20:19; Dt 4:33; Jgs 13:22.

§§[16:14] **Beer-lahai-roi**: possible translations of the name of the well include: "spring of the living one who sees me"; "the well of the living sight"; or "the one who sees me lives." See note on v. 13.

¶¶[17:1–27] The Priestly source gathers the major motifs of the story so far and sets them firmly within a covenant

---

j. [15:16] 1 Kgs 21:26.   k. [15:18] Ex 32:13; Neh 9:8; Ps 105:11; Sir 44:21.   l. [15:19–20] Dt 7:1.   m. [16:1] Gn 11:30.   n. [16:2] Gn 21:8–9; Gal 4:22.   o. [16:4] 1 Sm 1:6; Prv 30:23.   p. [16:5–16] Gn 21:10–19.

q. [16:7] Ex 15:22.   r. [16:10] Gn 17:20; 21:13, 18; 25:12–18.   s. [16:12] Gn 21:20; 25:18.   t. [16:13] Gn 24:62.   u. [16:15] Gn 16:2; Gal 4:22.

Abram and said: I am God the Almighty. Walk in my presence and be blameless.ᵛ ²Between you and me I will establish my covenant, and I will multiply you exceedingly.ʷ

³Abram fell face down and God said to him: ⁴For my part, here is my covenant with you: you are to become the father of a multitude of nations.ˣ ⁵No longer will you be called Abram; your name will be Abraham,* for I am making you the father of a multitude of nations.ʸ ⁶I will make you exceedingly fertile; I will make nations of you; kings will stem from you. ⁷I will maintain my covenant between me and you and your descendants after you throughout the ages as an everlasting covenant, to be your God and the God of your descendants after you.ᶻ ⁸I will give to you and to your descendants after you the land in which you are now residing as aliens, the whole land of Canaan, as a permanent possession; and I will be their God.ᵃ ⁹God said to Abraham: For your part, you and your descendants after you must keep my covenant throughout the ages. ¹⁰This is the covenant between me and you and your descendants after you that you must keep: every male among you shall be circumcised.†ᵇ ¹¹Circumcise the flesh of your foreskin. That will be the sign of the covenant between me and you.ᶜ ¹²Throughout the ages, every male among you, when he is eight days old, shall be circumcised, including houseborn slaves and those acquired with money from any foreigner who is not of your descendants.ᵈ ¹³Yes, both the houseborn slaves and those acquired with money must be circumcised. Thus my covenant will be in your flesh as an everlasting covenant. ¹⁴If a male is uncircumcised, that is, if the flesh of his foreskin has not been cut away, such a one will be cut off from his people; he has broken my covenant.

¹⁵God further said to Abraham: As for Sarai your wife, do not call her Sarai; her name will be Sarah.‡ ¹⁶I will bless her, and I will give you a son by her. Her also will I bless; she will give rise to nations, and rulers of peoples will issue from her.ᵉ ¹⁷Abraham fell face down and laughed§ as he said to himself, "Can a child be born to a man who is a hundred years old? Can Sarah give birth at ninety?"ᶠ ¹⁸So Abraham said to God, "If only Ishmael could live in your favor!" ¹⁹God replied: Even so, your wife Sarah is to bear you a son, and you shall call him Isaac. It is with him that I will maintain my covenant as an everlasting covenant and with his descendants after him.ᵍ ²⁰Now as for Ishmael, I will heed you: I hereby bless him. I will make him fertile and will multiply him exceedingly. He will become the father of twelve chieftains, and I will make of him a great nation.ʰ ²¹But my covenant I will maintain with Isaac, whom Sarah shall bear to you by this time next year.ⁱ ²²When he had finished speaking with Abraham, God departed from him.

²³Then Abraham took his son Ishmael and all his slaves, whether born in his house or acquired with his money—every male among the members of Abraham's household—and he circumcised the flesh of their foreskins on that same day, as God had told him to do. ²⁴Abraham was ninety-nine years old when the flesh of his foreskin was circumcised,ʲ ²⁵and his son Ishmael was thirteen years old when the flesh of his foreskin was circumcised. ²⁶Thus, on that same day Abraham and his son Ishmael were circumcised; ²⁷and all the males of his household, including the slaves born in his house or acquired with his money from foreigners, were circumcised with him.

## CHAPTER 18

**Abraham's Visitors.** ¹The Lᴏʀᴅ appeared to Abraham by the oak of Mamre, as he sat in the entrance of his tent, while the day was growing hot. ²Looking up, he saw three men standing near him. When he saw them, he ran from the entrance of the tent to greet them; and bowing

---

context; the word "covenant" occurs thirteen times. There are links to the covenant with Noah (v. 1 = 6:9; v. 7 = 9:9; v. 11 = 9:12–17). In this chapter, vv. 1–8 promise progeny and race; vv. 9–14 are instructions about circumcision; vv. 15–21 repeat the promise of a son to Sarah and distinguish this promise from that to Hagar; vv. 22–27 describe Abraham's carrying out the commands. **The Almighty:** traditional rendering of Hebrew *El Shaddai,* which is P's favorite designation of God in the period of the ancestors. Its etymology is uncertain, but its root meaning is probably "God, the One of the Mountains."

*[17:5] Abram and Abraham are merely two forms of the same name, both meaning, "the father is exalted"; another variant form is Abiram (Nm 16:1; 1 Kgs 16:34). The additional *-ha-* in the form Abraham is explained by popular etymology as coming from *ab-hamon goyim,* "father of a multitude of nations."

†[17:10] **Circumcised:** circumcision was widely practiced in the ancient world, usually as an initiation rite for males at puberty. By shifting the time of circumcision to the eighth day after birth, biblical religion made it no longer a "rite of passage" but the sign of the eternal covenant between God and the community descending from Abraham.

v. [17:1] Gn 35:11; Ex 6:3. w. [17:2] Gn 12:2; 13:16; Ex 32:13. x. [17:4] Sir 44:21; Rom 4:17. y. [17:5] Neh 9:7. z. [17:7] Ps 105:42; Lk 1:72–73; Gal 3:16. a. [17:8] Ex 32:13; Dt 1:8; 14:2; Lk 1:55; Acts 7:5. b. [17:10] Jn 7:22; Acts 7:8; Rom 4:11. c. [17:11] Sir 44:20. d. [17:12] Lv 12:3; Lk 1:59; 2:21.

‡[17:15] Sarai and Sarah are variant forms of the same name, both meaning "princess."

§[17:17] **Laughed:** *yishaq,* which is also the Hebrew form of the name "Isaac"; similar explanations of the name are given in Gn 18:12 and 21:6.

¶[18:1] Chapters 18 and 19 combined form a continuous narrative, concluding the story of Abraham and his nephew Lot that began in 13:2–18. The mysterious men visit Abraham in Mamre to promise him and Sarah a child the following year (18:1–15) and then visit Lot in Sodom to investigate and then to punish the corrupt city (19:1–29). Between the two visits, Abraham questions God about the justice of punishing Sodom (18:16–33). At the end of the destruction of Sodom, there is a short narrative about Lot as the ancestor of Moab and the Ammonites (19:30–38).

e. [17:16] Gn 18:10; Gal 4:23. f. [17:17] Rom 4:19; Heb 11:11–12. g. [17:19] Gn 11:30; 21:2; Ex 32:13; Sir 44:22. h. [17:20] Gn 16:10; 21:13, 18; 25:12–16. i. [17:21] Gn 18:14; 21:2; 26:2–5; Rom 9:7. j. [17:24] Gn 17:10; Rom 4:11.

to the ground,[k] [3]he said: "Sir,* if it please you, do not go on past your servant. [4]Let some water be brought, that you may bathe your feet, and then rest under the tree. [5]Now that you have come to your servant, let me bring you a little food, that you may refresh yourselves; and afterward you may go on your way." "Very well," they replied, "do as you have said."

[6]Abraham hurried into the tent to Sarah and said, "Quick, three measures† of bran flour! Knead it and make bread." [7]He ran to the herd, picked out a tender, choice calf, and gave it to a servant, who quickly prepared it. [8]Then he got some curds‡ and milk, as well as the calf that had been prepared, and set these before them, waiting on them under the tree while they ate.

[9]"Where is your wife Sarah?" they asked him. "There in the tent," he replied. [10]One of them§ said, "I will return to you about this time next year, and Sarah will then have a son." Sarah was listening at the entrance of the tent, just behind him.[l] [11]Now Abraham and Sarah were old, advanced in years, and Sarah had stopped having her menstrual periods.[m] [12]So Sarah laughed¶ to herself and said, "Now that I am worn out and my husband is old, am I still to have sexual pleasure?" [13]But the LORD said to Abraham: "Why did Sarah laugh and say, 'Will I really bear a child, old as I am?' [14]Is anything too marvelous for the LORD to do? At the appointed time, about this time next year, I will return to you, and Sarah will have a son."[n] [15]Sarah lied, saying, "I did not laugh," because she was afraid. But he said, "Yes, you did."

**Abraham Intercedes for Sodom.** [16]With Abraham walking with them to see them on their way, the men set out from there and looked down toward Sodom. [17]The LORD considered: Shall I hide from Abraham what I am about to do, [18]now that he is to become a great and mighty nation, and all the nations of the earth are to find blessing in him?[o] [19]Indeed, I have singled him out that he may direct his children and his household in the future to keep the way of the LORD by doing what is right and just, so that the LORD may put into effect for Abraham the promises he made about him. [20]So the LORD said: The outcry against Sodom and Gomorrah

is so great, and their sin so grave," [21]that I must go down to see whether or not their actions are as bad as the cry against them that comes to me. I mean to find out.

[22]As the men turned and walked on toward Sodom, Abraham remained standing before the LORD. [23]Then Abraham drew near and said: "Will you really sweep away the righteous with the wicked? [24]Suppose there were fifty righteous people in the city; would you really sweep away and not spare the place for the sake of the fifty righteous people within it? [25]Far be it from you to do such a thing, to kill the righteous with the wicked, so that the righteous and the wicked are treated alike! Far be it from you! Should not the judge of all the world do what is just?"[q] [26]The LORD replied: If I find fifty righteous people in the city of Sodom, I will spare the whole place for their sake. [27]Abraham spoke up again: "See how I am presuming to speak to my Lord, though I am only dust and ashes![r] [28]What if there are five less than fifty righteous people? Will you destroy the whole city because of those five?" I will not destroy it, he answered, if I find forty-five there. [29]But Abraham persisted, saying, "What if only forty are found there?" He replied: I will refrain from doing it for the sake of the forty. [30]Then he said, "Do not let my Lord be angry if I go on. What if only thirty are found there?" He replied: I will refrain from doing it if I can find thirty there. [31]Abraham went on, "Since I have thus presumed to speak to my Lord, what if there are no more than twenty?" I will not destroy it, he answered, for the sake of the twenty. [32]But he persisted: "Please, do not let my Lord be angry if I speak just this last time. What if ten are found there?" For the sake of the ten, he replied, I will not destroy it.[s]

[33]The LORD departed as soon as he had finished speaking with Abraham, and Abraham returned home.

# CHAPTER 19

**Destruction of Sodom and Gomorrah.**†† [1]The two angels reached Sodom in the evening, as Lot was sitting at the gate of Sodom. When Lot

---

*[18:3] Abraham addresses the leader of the group, whom he does not yet recognize as the Lord; in the next two verses he speaks to all three men. The other two are later (Gn 19:1) identified as angels. The shifting numbers and identification of the visitors is a narrative way of expressing the mysterious presence of God.

†[18:6] **Three measures:** Hebrew *seah*; three seahs equal one ephah, about half a bushel.

‡[18:8] **Curds:** a type of soft cheese or yogurt.

§[18:10] **One of them:** i.e., the Lord.

¶[18:12] **Sarah laughed:** a play on the verb "laugh," which prefigures the name of Isaac; see note on 17:17.

**[18:20] The immorality of the cities was already hinted at at 13:13, when Lot made his choice to live there. The "outcry" comes from the victims of the injustice and violence rampant in the city, which shortly be illustrated in the treatment of the visitors. The outcry of the Hebrews under the harsh treatment of Pharaoh (Ex 3:7) came up to God who reacts in anger at mistreatment of the poor (cf. Ex 22:21–23; Is 5:7). Sodom and Gomorrah became types of sinful cities in biblical literature. Is 1:9–10; 3:9 sees their sin as lack of social justice, Ez 16:46–51, as disregard for the poor, and Jer 23:14, as general immorality. In the Genesis story, the sin is violation of the sacred duty of hospitality by the threatened rape of Lot's guests.

††[19:1–29] The story takes place in one day (counting a day from the previous evening): evening (v. 1), dawn (v. 15), and sunrise (v. 23). The passage resembles Jgs 19:15–25, which suggests dependence of one story on the other.

k. [18:2] Heb 13:1–2. l. [18:10] Gn 17:19; 21:1; 2 Kgs 4:16; Rom 9:9. m. [18:11] Gn 17:17; Rom 4:19; Heb 11:11–12. n. [18:14] Mt 19:26; Mk 10:27; Lk 1:37; 18:27; Rom 4:21. o. [18:18] Lk 1:55. p. [18:20] Gn 19:13; Is 3:9; Lk 17:28; Jude 7.

q. [18:25] Dt 32:4; Jb 8:3, 20; Wis 12:15. r. [18:27] Sir 10:9; 17:27. s. [18:32] Jer 5:1; Ez 22:30.

saw them, he got up to greet them; and bowing down with his face to the ground, [2]he said, "Please, my lords,[*] come aside into your servant's house for the night, and bathe your feet; you can get up early to continue your journey." But they replied, "No, we will pass the night in the town square."[t] He urged them so strongly, however, that they turned aside to his place and entered his house. He prepared a banquet for them, baking unleavened bread, and they dined.

[4]"Before they went to bed, the townsmen of Sodom, both young and old—all the people to the last man—surrounded the house. [5]They called to Lot and said to him, "Where are the men who came to your house tonight? Bring them out to us that we may have sexual relations with them." [6]Lot went out to meet them at the entrance. When he had shut the door behind him, [7]he said, "I beg you, my brothers, do not do this wicked thing! [8]I have two daughters who have never had sexual relations with men. Let me bring them out to you,[†] and you may do to them as you please. But do not do anything to these men, for they have come under the shelter of my roof." [9]They replied, "Stand back! This man," they said, "came here as a resident alien, and now he dares to give orders! We will treat you worse than them!" With that, they pressed hard against Lot, moving in closer to break down the door.[v] [10]But his guests put out their hands, pulled Lot inside with them, and closed the door; [11]they struck the men at the entrance of the house, small and great, with such a blinding light[‡] that they were utterly unable to find the doorway.

[12]Then the guests said to Lot: "Who else belongs to you? Sons-in-law, your sons, your daughters, all who belong to you in the city—take them away from this place![w] [13]We are about to destroy this place, for the outcry reaching the LORD against those here is so great that the LORD has sent us to destroy it."[x] [14]So Lot went out and spoke to his sons-in-law, who had contracted marriage with his daughters.[§] "Come on, leave this place," he told them; "the LORD is about to destroy the city." But his sons-in-law thought he was joking.

[15]As dawn was breaking, the angels urged Lot on, saying, "Come on! Take your wife with you and your two daughters who are here, or you will be swept away in the punishment of the city." [16]When he hesitated, the men, because of the LORD's compassion for him, seized his hand and the hands of his wife and his two daughters and led them to safety outside the city. [17]As soon as they had brought them outside, they said: "Flee for your life! Do not look back or stop anywhere on the Plain. Flee to the hills at once, or you will be swept away."[y] [18]"Oh, no, my lords!" Lot replied to them. [19]"You have already shown favor to your servant, doing me the great kindness of saving my life. But I cannot flee to the hills, or the disaster will overtake and kill me. [20]Look, this town ahead is near enough to escape to. It is only a small place.[¶] Let me flee there—is it not a small place?—to save my life." [21]"Well, then," he replied, "I grant you this favor too. I will not overthrow the town you have mentioned. [22]Hurry, escape there! I cannot do anything until you arrive there." That is why the town is called Zoar.[z]

[23]The sun had risen over the earth when Lot arrived in Zoar, [24]and the LORD rained down sulfur upon Sodom and Gomorrah, fire from the LORD out of heaven.[a] [25]He overthrew[**] those cities and the whole Plain, together with the inhabitants of the cities and the produce of the soil.[b] [26]But Lot's wife looked back, and she was turned into a pillar of salt.[c]

[27]The next morning Abraham hurried to the place where he had stood before the LORD. [28]As he looked down toward Sodom and Gomorrah and the whole region of the Plain,[††] he saw smoke over the land rising like the smoke from a kiln.[d]

[29]When God destroyed the cities of the Plain, he remembered Abraham and sent Lot away from the upheaval that occurred when God overthrew the cities where Lot had been living.

**Moabites and Ammonites.**[‡‡] [30]Since Lot was afraid to stay in Zoar, he and his two daughters

---

*[19:2] **My lords:** Lot does not yet know that the men are God's messengers; cf. 18:3.

†[19:8] **Let me bring them out to you:** the authority of a patriarch within his house was virtually absolute. Lot's extreme response of offering his daughters to a violent mob seems to be motivated by the obligation of hospitality.

‡[19:11] **Blinding light:** an extraordinary flash that temporarily dazed the wicked men and revealed to Lot the true nature of his guests.

§[19:14] It is uncertain whether Lot's sons-in-law were fully married to his daughters or only "engaged" to them (Israelite "engagement" was the first part of the marriage ceremony), or even whether the daughters involved were the same as, or different from, the two daughters who were still in their father's house.

¶[19:20] **A small place:** the Hebrew word *misar*, lit., "a little thing," has the same root consonants as the name of the town Zoar in v. 22.

**[19:25] **Overthrew:** this term, lit., "turned upside down," is used consistently to describe the destruction of the cities of the Plain. The imagery of earthquake and subsequent fire fits the geology of this region.

††[19:28–29] In a deft narrative detail, Abraham looks down from the height east of Hebron, from which he could easily see the region at the southern end of the Dead Sea, where the cities of the Plain were probably located.

‡‡[19:30–38] This Israelite tale about the origin of Israel's neighbors east of the Jordan and the Dead Sea was told partly to ridicule these ethnically related but rival nations and partly to give popular etymologies for their names. The stylized nature of the story is seen in the names of the daughters ("the firstborn" and "the younger"), the ease with which they fool their father, and the identical descriptions of the encounters.

---

t. [19:2] Heb 13:1–2.  u. [19:4–9] Jgs 19:22–25; Jude 7.  v. [19:9] Gn 13:12; 2 Pt 2:7–8.  w. [19:12] 2 Pt 2:7–9.  x. [19:13] Is 1:7, 9; Ez 16:49–50; Zep 2:9.

y. [19:17] Wis 10:6.  z. [19:22] Wis 10:6.  a. [19:24] Ps 9:6; 11:6; 107:34; Wis 10:7; Sir 16:8; Is 1:9; Lk 17:29; 2 Pt 2:6.  b. [19:25] Dt 29:22; Is 13:19; Jer 50:40; Lam 4:6; Am 4:11.  c. [19:26] Wis 10:7; Lk 17:32.  d. [19:28] Rev 9:2; 14:10–11.

went up from Zoar and settled in the hill country, where he lived with his two daughters in a cave. ³¹The firstborn said to the younger: "Our father is getting old, and there is not a man in the land to have intercourse with us as is the custom everywhere. ³²Come, let us ply our father with wine and then lie with him, that we may ensure posterity by our father." ³³So that night they plied their father with wine, and the firstborn went in and lay with her father; but he was not aware of her lying down or getting up. ³⁴The next day the firstborn said to the younger: "Last night I lay with my father. Let us ply him with wine again tonight, and then you go in and lie with him, that we may ensure posterity by our father." ³⁵So that night, too, they plied their father with wine, and then the younger one went in and lay with him; but he was not aware of her lying down or getting up.

³⁶Thus the two daughters of Lot became pregnant by their father. ³⁷The firstborn gave birth to a son whom she named Moab, saying, "From my father." He is the ancestor of the Moabites of today.ᵉ ³⁸The younger one, too, gave birth to a son, and she named him Ammon, saying, "The son of my kin."ᶠ He is the ancestor of the Ammonites of today.ᶠ

## CHAPTER 20

**Abraham at Gerar.**‡ ¹From there Abraham journeyed on to the region of the Negeb, where he settled between Kadesh and Shur.§ While he resided in Gerar as an alien, ²Abraham said of his wife Sarah, "She is my sister." So Abimelech, king of Gerar, sent and took Sarah. ³But God came to Abimelech in a dream one night and said to him: You are about to die because of the woman you have taken, for she has a husband. ⁴Abimelech, who had not approached her, said: "O Lord, would you kill an innocent man? ⁵Was he not the one who told me, 'She is my sister'? She herself also stated, 'He is my brother.' I acted with pure heart and with clean hands." ⁶¶God answered him in the dream: Yes, I know you did it with a pure heart. In fact, it was I who kept

you from sinning against me; that is why I did not let you touch her. ⁷So now, return the man's wife so that he may intercede for you, since he is a prophet," that you may live. If you do not return her, you can be sure that you and all who are yours will die.

⁸Early the next morning Abimelech called all his servants and informed them of everything that had happened, and the men were filled with fear. ⁹Then Abimelech summoned Abraham and said to him: "What have you done to us! What wrong did I do to you that you would have brought such great guilt on me and my kingdom? You have treated me in an intolerable way. ¹⁰What did you have in mind," Abimelech asked him, "that you would do such a thing?" ¹¹Abraham answered, "I thought there would be no fear of God†† in this place, and so they would kill me on account of my wife. ¹²Besides, she really is my sister,‡‡ but only my father's daughter, not my mother's; and so she became my wife. ¹³When God sent me wandering from my father's house, I asked her: 'Would you do me this favor? In whatever place we come to, say: He is my brother.'ᵍ

¹⁴Then Abimelech took flocks and herds and male and female slaves and gave them to Abraham; and he restored his wife Sarah to him. ¹⁵Then Abimelech said, "Here, my land is at your disposal; settle wherever you please." ¹⁶To Sarah he said: "I hereby give your brother a thousand shekels of silver. This will preserve your honor before all who are with you and will exonerate you before everyone." ¹⁷Abraham then interceded with God, and God restored health to Abimelech, to his wife, and his maidservants, so that they bore children; ¹⁸for the LORD had closed every womb in Abimelech's household on account of Abraham's wife Sarah.

## CHAPTER 21

**Birth of Isaac.**§§ ¹The LORD took note of Sarah as he had said he would; the LORD did for her

---

*[19:37] **From my father**: in Hebrew, *me'abi*, similar in sound to the name "Moab."

†[19:38] **The son of my kin**: in Hebrew, *ben-ammi*, similar in sound to the name "Ammonites."

‡[20:1–18] Abraham again passes off his wife Sarah as his sister to escape trouble in a foreign land (cf. 12:10–13:1, the J source). The story appears to be from a different source (according to some, E) and deals with the ethical questions of the incident. Gn 26:6–11 is yet another retelling of the story, but with Isaac and Rebekah as characters instead of Abraham and Sarah.

§[20:1] **Kadesh and Shur**: Kadesh-barnea was a major oasis on the southernmost border of Canaan, and Shur was probably the "way to Shur," the road to Egypt. Gerar was a royal city in the area, but has not been identified with certainty.

¶[20:6] Abimelech is exonerated of blame, but by that fact not cleared of the consequences of his act. He is still under the sentence of death for abducting another man's wife; the consequences result from the deed not the intention.

**[20:7] **Prophet**: only here is Abraham explicitly called "prophet," Hebrew *nabi* (cf. Ps 105:15).

††[20:11] **Fear of God** is the traditional though unsatisfactory rendering of Hebrew *yir'at YHWH*, literally, "revering Yahweh." The phrase refers neither to the emotion of fear nor to religious reverence of a general kind. Rather it refers to adherence to a single deity (in a polytheistic culture), honoring that deity with prayers, rituals, and obedience. The phrase occurs again in 26:24; 43:23; and 50:19. It is very common in the wisdom literature of the Bible.

‡‡[20:12] **My sister**: marrying one's half sister was prohibited later in Israel's history.

§§[21:1–21] The long-awaited birth of Isaac parallels the birth of Ishmael in chap. 16, precipitating a rivalry and expulsion as in that chapter. Though this chapter is unified, the focus of vv. 1–7 is exclusively on Sarah and Isaac, and the focus of vv. 8–21 is exclusively on Hagar and Ishmael. The promise of a son to the barren Sarah and elderly Abraham has been central to the previous chapters and now that promise comes true with the birth of Isaac. The other great promise, that of land, will be resolved, at least in an anticipatory way, in Abraham's purchase of the cave at Machpelah in

---

e. [19:37] Dt 2:9.    f. [19:38] Dt 2:19.                              g. [20:13] Gn 12:13.

as he had promised.[h] [2]Sarah became pregnant and bore Abraham a son in his old age, at the set time that God had stated.[i] [3]Abraham gave the name Isaac to this son of his whom Sarah bore him.[j] [4]When his son Isaac was eight days old, Abraham circumcised him, as God had commanded.[k] [5]Abraham was a hundred years old when his son Isaac was born to him. [6]Sarah then said, "God has given me cause to laugh,' and all who hear of it will laugh with me.[l] [7]Who would ever have told Abraham," she added, "that Sarah would nurse children! Yet I have borne him a son in his old age." [8]The child grew and was weaned, and Abraham held a great banquet on the day of the child's weaning.

[9]Sarah noticed the son whom Hagar the Egyptian had borne to Abraham playing with her son Isaac; [10]so she demanded of Abraham: "Drive out that slave and her son! No son of that slave is going to share the inheritance with my son Isaac!"[m] [11]Abraham was greatly distressed because it concerned a son of his.[†] [12]But God said to Abraham: Do not be distressed about the boy or about your slave woman. Obey Sarah, no matter what she asks of you; for it is through Isaac that descendants will bear your name.[n] [13]As for the son of the slave woman, I will make a nation of him also,[‡] since he too is your offspring.

[14]Early the next morning Abraham got some bread and a skin of water and gave them to Hagar. Then, placing the child on her back,[§] he sent her away. As she roamed aimlessly in the wilderness of Beer-sheba, [15]the water in the skin was used up. So she put the child down under one of the bushes, [16]and then went and sat down opposite him, about a bowshot away; for she said to herself, "I cannot watch the child die." As she sat opposite him, she wept aloud. [17]God heard the boy's voice, and God's angel called to Hagar from heaven: "What is the matter, Hagar? Do not fear; God has heard the boy's voice in

this plight of his.[o] [18]Get up, lift up the boy and hold him by the hand; for I will make of him a great nation." [19]Then God opened her eyes, and she saw a well of water. She went and filled the skin with water, and then let the boy drink.

[20]God was with the boy as he grew up. He lived in the wilderness and became an expert bowman. [21]He lived in the wilderness of Paran. His mother got a wife for him from the land of Egypt.

**The Covenant at Beer-sheba.** [22]¶At that time Abimelech, accompanied by Phicol, the commander of his army, said to Abraham: "God is with you in everything you do. [23]So now, swear to me by God at this place" that you will not deal falsely with me or with my progeny and posterity, but will act as loyally toward me and the land in which you reside as I have acted toward you." [24]Abraham replied, "I so swear."

[25]Abraham, however, reproached Abimelech about a well that Abimelech's servants had seized by force. [26]"I have no idea who did that," Abimelech replied. "In fact, you never told me about it, nor did I ever hear of it until now." [27]Then Abraham took sheep and cattle and gave them to Abimelech and the two made a covenant. [28]Abraham also set apart seven ewe lambs of the flock, [29]and Abimelech asked him, "What is the purpose of these seven ewe lambs that you have set apart?" [30]Abraham answered, "The seven ewe lambs you shall accept from me that you may be my witness that I dug this well." [31]This is why the place is called Beer-sheba; the two of them took an oath there. [32]When they had thus made the covenant in Beer-sheba, Abimelech, along with Phicol, the commander of his army, left to return to the land of the Philistines.[††]

[33]Abraham planted a tamarisk at Beer-sheba, and there he invoked by name the LORD, God the Eternal.[‡‡] [34]Abraham resided in the land of the Philistines for a long time.

---

chap. 23. The parallel births of the two boys has influenced the Lucan birth narratives of John the Baptist and Jesus (Lk 1–2).

*[21:6] **Laugh:** for the third time (cf. 17:17 and 18:12) there is laughter, playing on the similarity in Hebrew between the pronunciation of the name Isaac and words associated with laughter.

†[21:11] **A son of his:** Abraham is the father of both boys, but Sarah is the mother only of Isaac. Abraham is very concerned that Ishmael have a sufficient inheritance.

‡[21:13] **I will make a nation of him also:** Ishmael's descendants are named in 25:12–18.

§[21:14] **Placing the child on her back:** a reading based on an emendation of the traditional Hebrew text. In the traditional Hebrew text, Abraham put the bread and the waterskin on Hagar's back, while her son apparently walked beside her. In this way the traditional Hebrew text harmonizes the data of the Priestly source, in which Ishmael would have been at least fourteen years old when Isaac was born; compare 16:16 with 21:5; cf. 17:25. But in the present Elohist (?) story, Ishmael is obviously a little boy, not much older than Isaac; cf. vv. 15, 18.

¶[21:22] Of the two related promises of progeny and land, that of progeny has been fulfilled in the previous chapter. Now the claim on the land begins to be solidified by Abimelech's recognition of Abraham's claim on the well at Beer-sheba; it will be furthered by Abraham's purchase of the cave at Machpelah in chap. 23. Two levels of editing are visible in the story: (1) vv. 22–24, 27, 32, the general covenant with Abimelech; (2) vv. 25–26, 28–30, 31, Abraham's claim on the well. Both versions play on the root of the Hebrew word *sheba'*, which means "seven" and "swear," and the place name Beer-sheba.

**[21:23] **This place:** Beer-sheba (v. 31). Abimelech had come from Gerar (20:2), about thirty miles west of Beer-sheba.

††[21:32] **Philistines:** one of the Sea Peoples, who migrated from Mycenaean Greece around 1200 B.C. and settled on the coastland of Canaan, becoming a principal rival of Israel. Non-biblical texts do not use the term "Philistine" before ca. 1200 B.C.; it is probable that this usage and those in chap. 26 are anachronistic, perhaps applying a later ethnic term for an earlier, less-known one.

‡‡[21:33] **God the Eternal:** in Hebrew, *'el 'olam*, perhaps the name of the deity of the pre-Israelite sanctuary at Beer-sheba, but used by Abraham as a title of God; cf. Is 40:28.

---

h. [21:1] Gn 17:19; 18:10.   i. [21:2] Gal 4:23; Heb 11:11.   j. [21:3] Mt 1:2; Lk 3:34.   k. [21:4] Gn 17:10–14; Acts 7:8.   l. [21:6] Gn 17:17.   m. [21:10] Jgs 11:2; Gal 4:30.   n. [21:12] Rom 9:7; Heb 11:18.

o. [21:17] Gn 16:7.

## CHAPTER 22

**The Testing of Abraham.** [*] ¹Some time afterward, God put Abraham to the test and said to him: Abraham! "Here I am!" he replied.[p] ²Then God said: Take your son Isaac, your only one, whom you love, and go to the land of Moriah. There offer him up as a burnt offering on one of the heights that I will point out to you.[q] ³Early the next morning Abraham saddled his donkey, took with him two of his servants and his son Isaac, and after cutting the wood for the burnt offering, set out for the place of which God had told him.

⁴On the third day Abraham caught sight of the place from a distance. ⁵Abraham said to his servants: "Stay here with the donkey, while the boy and I go on over there. We will worship and then come back to you." ⁶So Abraham took the wood for the burnt offering and laid it on his son Isaac, while he himself carried the fire and the knife. As the two walked on together, ⁷Isaac spoke to his father Abraham. "Father!" he said. "Here I am," he replied. Isaac continued, "Here are the fire and the wood, but where is the sheep for the burnt offering?" ⁸"My son," Abraham answered, "God will provide the sheep for the burnt offering." Then the two walked on together.

⁹When they came to the place of which God had told him, Abraham built an altar there and arranged the wood on it. Next he bound[†] his son Isaac, and put him on top of the wood on the altar.[r] ¹⁰Then Abraham reached out and took the knife to slaughter his son.[s] ¹¹But the angel of the LORD called to him from heaven, "Abraham, Abraham!" "Here I am," he answered. ¹²"Do not lay your hand on the boy," said the angel. "Do not do the least thing to him. For now I know that you fear God, since you did not withhold from me your son, your only one."[t] ¹³Abraham looked up and saw a single ram caught by its horns in the thicket. So Abraham went and took the ram and offered it up as a burnt offering in place of his son.[‡] ¹⁴Abraham named that place Yahweh-yireh;[§] hence people today say, "On the mountain the LORD will provide."

¹⁵A second time the angel of the LORD called to Abraham from heaven ¹⁶[u]and said: "I swear by my very self—oracle of the LORD—that because you acted as you did in not withholding from me your son, your only one, ¹⁷I will bless you and make your descendants as countless as the stars of the sky and the sands of the seashore; your descendants will take possession of the gates of their enemies,[v] ¹⁸and in your descendants all the nations of the earth will find blessing, because you obeyed my command."[w]

¹⁹Abraham then returned to his servants, and they set out together for Beer-sheba, where Abraham lived.

**Nahor's Descendants.** [*] ²⁰Some time afterward, the news came to Abraham: "Milcah too has borne sons to your brother Nahor: ²¹Uz, his firstborn, his brother Buz, Kemuel the father of Aram, ²²Chesed, Hazo, Pildash, Jidlaph, and Bethuel." ²³Bethuel became the father of Rebekah. These eight Milcah bore to Nahor, Abraham's brother. ²⁴His concubine, whose name was Reumah, also bore children: Tebah, Gaham, Tahash, and Maacah.

## CHAPTER 23

**Purchase of a Burial Plot.** [††] ¹The span of Sarah's life was one hundred and twenty-seven years.

---

[*] [22:1–19] The divine demand that Abraham sacrifice to God the son of promise is the greatest of the tests; after the successful completion of the test, he has only to buy a burial site for Sarah and find a wife for Isaac. The story is widely recognized as a literary masterpiece, depicting in a few lines God as the absolute Lord, inscrutable yet ultimately gracious, and Abraham, acting in moral grandeur as the great ancestor of Israel. Abraham speaks simply, with none of the wordy evasions of chaps. 13 and 21. The style is laconic; motivations and thoughts are not explained, and the reader cannot but wonder at the scene. In vv. 15–18, the angel repeats the seventh and climactic promise. **Moriah:** the mountain is not given a precise geographical location here, though 2 Chr 3:1 identifies Moriah as the mountain of Jerusalem where Solomon built the Temple; Abraham is thus the first to worship there. The word "Moriah" is a play on the verb "to see" (Heb. *ra'ah*); the wordplay is continued in v. 8, "God will provide (lit., "see")" and in v. 14, Yahweh-yireh, meaning "the Lord will see/provide."

[†] [22:9] **Bound:** the Hebrew verb is *'aqad*, from which is derived the noun Akedah, "the binding (of Isaac)," the traditional Jewish name for this incident.

[‡] [22:13] While the Bible recognizes that firstborn males belong to God (Ex 13:11–16; 34:19–20), and provides an alternate sacrifice to redeem firstborn sons, the focus here is on Abraham's being tested by God (v. 1). But the widely attested practice of child sacrifice underscores, for all its horror today, the realism of the test.

[§] [22:14] **Yahweh-yireh:** a Hebrew expression meaning "the Lord will see/provide." See note on vv. 1–19.

[¶] [22:15–19] The seventh and climactic statement of the blessings to Abraham. Unlike the other statements, which were purely promissory, this one is presented as a reward for Abraham's extraordinary trust.

[**] [22:20–24] The descendants to the second generation of Nahor, Abraham's brother, who married Milcah. Of Terah's three sons (11:27), the oldest, Abraham, fathered Isaac (21:1–7), and the youngest, Haran (who died in Ur), fathered Lot. Abraham is now told that Nahor had eight children by Milcah and four by his concubine Reumah. Apart from the notice about the children born to Abraham by his second wife, Keturah (25:1–6), all the information about Terah's family to the second generation is now complete. It is noteworthy that Jacob will, like Nahor, have eight children by his wives and four by his concubines.

[††] [23:1–20] The occasion for purchasing the land is the need for a burial site for Sarah, for it would be unthinkable to bury Sarah outside of the promised land. One of the two great promises to Abraham, that of progeny, has been fulfilled (21:1–7). And now the promise of land is to be fulfilled, through a kind of down payment on the full possession that will take place only with the conquest under Joshua and during the reign of David. This purchase has been prepared for by Abimelech's recognition of Abraham's claim to the well at Beer-sheba (21:22–34). Among the ancestral stories this narrative is one of two that are entirely from the P source (chap.

[p.] [22:1] Sir 44:20.    [q.] [22:2] 2 Chr 3:1; 1 Mc 2:52; Heb 11:17.    [r.] [22:9] Jas 2:21.    [s.] [22:10] Wis 10:5.    [t.] [22:12] Rom 8:32; 1 Jn 4:9.

[u.] [22:16–17] Gn 15:5; Ex 32:13; Lk 1:73; Rom 4:13; Heb 6:13–14; 11:12.    [v.] [22:17] Gn 24:60.    [w.] [22:18] Gn 12:3; 18:18; 26:4; Sir 44:21; Acts 3:25; Gal 3:16.

²She died in Kiriath-arba—now Hebron—in the land of Canaan, and Abraham proceeded to mourn and weep for her. ³Then he left the side of his deceased wife and addressed the Hittites:˙ ⁴"Although I am a resident alien† among you, sell me from your holdings a burial place, that I may bury my deceased wife."ˣ ⁵The Hittites answered Abraham: "Please, ⁶sir, listen to us! You are a mighty leader among us. Bury your dead in the choicest of our burial sites. None of us would deny you his burial ground for the burial of your dead." ⁷Abraham, however, proceeded to bow low before the people of the land, the Hittites, ⁸and said to them: "If you will allow me room for burial of my dead, listen to me! Intercede for me with Ephron, son of Zohar, ⁹so that he will sell me the cave of Machpelah that he owns; it is at the edge of his field. Let him sell it to me in your presence at its full price for a burial place."

¹⁰Now Ephron was sitting with the Hittites. So Ephron the Hittite replied to Abraham in the hearing of the Hittites, all who entered the gate of his city: ¹¹"Please, sir, listen to me! I give you both the field and the cave in it; in the presence of my people I give it to you. Bury your dead!" ¹²But Abraham, after bowing low before the people of the land, ¹³addressed Ephron in the hearing of these men: "If only you would please listen to me! I will pay you the price of the field. Accept it from me, that I may bury my dead there." ¹⁴Ephron replied to Abraham, "Please, ¹⁵sir, listen to me! A piece of land worth four hundred shekels‡ of silver—what is that between you and me? Bury your dead!" ¹⁶ʸAbraham accepted Ephron's terms; he weighed out to him the silver that Ephron had stipulated in the hearing of the Hittites, four hundred shekels of silver at the current market value.§

¹⁷ᶻThus Ephron's field in Machpelah, facing Mamre, together with its cave and all the trees anywhere within its limits, was conveyed ¹⁸to Abraham by purchase in the presence of the Hittites, all who entered the gate of Ephron's city. ¹⁹After this, Abraham buried his wife Sarah in the cave of the field of Machpelah, facing Mamre—now Hebron—in the land of Canaan. ²⁰Thus the field with its cave was transferred from the Hittites to Abraham as a burial place.

## CHAPTER 24

**Isaac and Rebekah.**¶ ¹Abraham was old, having seen many days, and the LORD had blessed him in every way. ²ᵃAbraham said to the senior servant of his household, who had charge of all his possessions: "Put your hand under my thigh,** ³and I will make you swear by the LORD, the God of heaven and the God of earth, that you will not take a wife for my son from the daughters of the Canaanites among whom I live,ᵇ ⁴but that you will go to my own land and to my relatives to get a wife for my son Isaac." ⁵The servant asked him: "What if the woman is unwilling to follow me to this land? Should I then take your son back to the land from which you came?" ⁶Abraham told him, "Never take my son back there for any reason! ⁷The LORD, the God of heaven, who took me from my father's house and the land of my relatives, and who confirmed by oath the promise he made to me, 'I will give this land to your descendants'—he will send his angel before you, and you will get a wife for my son there.ᶜ ⁸If the woman is unwilling to follow you, you will be released from this oath to me. But never take my son back there!" ⁹So the servant put his hand under the thigh of his master Abraham and swore to him concerning this matter.

¹⁰The servant then took ten of his master's camels, and bearing all kinds of gifts from his master, he made his way to the city of Nahor††

---

¶[24:1–67] The story of Abraham and Sarah is drawing to a close. The promises of progeny (21:1–7) and land (chap. 23) have been fulfilled and Sarah has died (23:1–2). Abraham's last duty is to ensure that his son Isaac shares in the promises. Isaac must take a wife from his own people (vv. 3–7), so the promises may be fulfilled. The extraordinary length of this story and its development of a single theme contrast strikingly with the spare style of the preceding Abraham and Sarah stories. It points ahead to the Jacob and Joseph stories.

The length of the story is partly caused by its meticulous attention to the sign (vv. 12–14), its fulfillment (vv. 15–20), and the servant's retelling of sign and fulfillment to Rebekah's family to win their consent (vv. 34–49).

**[24:2] Put your hand under my thigh:** the symbolism of this act was apparently connected with the Hebrew concept of children issuing from their father's "thigh" (the literal meaning of "direct descendants" in 46:26; Ex 1:5). Perhaps the man who took such an oath was thought to bring the curse of sterility on himself if he did not fulfill his sworn promise. Jacob made Joseph swear in the same way (Gn 47:29). In both these instances, the oath was taken to carry out the last request of a man upon his death.

††[24:10] Nahor: it is uncertain whether this is the place where Abraham's brother Nahor (11:27) had lived or whether it is the city Nahur, named in the Mari documents (nineteenth and eighteenth centuries B.C.), near the confluence of the Balikh and Middle Euphrates rivers. **Aram Naharaim:**

---

17 being the other). The Priestly writers may have intended to encourage the generation of the exile to a renewed hope of repossessing their land.

*[23:3] The Hittites: in the Bible the term is applied to several different groups—inhabitants of the second-millennium Hittite empire in Asia Minor and northern Syria, residents of the Neo-Hittite kingdoms in northern Syria in the first part of the first millennium, and (following Assyrian terminology) the inhabitants of Syria and Palestine. The third group is meant here.

†[23:4] A resident alien: such a one would normally not have the right to own property. The importance of Abraham's purchase of the field in Machpelah, which is worded in technical legal terms, lies in the fact that it gave his descendants their first, though small, land rights in the country that God had promised the patriarch they would one day inherit as their own. Abraham therefore insists on purchasing the field and not receiving it as a gift.

‡[23:15] Four hundred shekels: probably an exorbitant sum; Jeremiah (32:9) paid only seventeen shekels for his field in Anathoth, though the Babylonian invasion no doubt helped to reduce the price.

§[23:16] The current market value: the standard weight called a shekel varied according to time and place.

---

x. [23:4] Gn 33:19; Acts 7:16; Heb 11:9.  y. [23:16] Acts 7:16.
z. [23:17–18] Gn 49:29–30.

a. [24:2–3] Gn 47:29.  b. [24:3] Gn 24:37; 28:1–2; Jgs 14:3; Tb 4:12.  c. [24:7] Gn 12:7; Ex 6:8; Tb 5:17; Gal 3:16.

in Aram Naharaim. ¹¹Near evening, at the time when women go out to draw water, he made the camels kneel by the well outside the city. ¹²Then he said: "Lord, God of my master Abraham, let it turn out favorably for me˙ today and thus deal graciously with my master Abraham. ¹³While I stand here at the spring and the daughters of the townspeople are coming out to draw water, ¹⁴if I say to a young woman, 'Please lower your jug, that I may drink,' and she answers, 'Drink, and I will water your camels, too,' then she is the one whom you have decided upon for your servant Isaac. In this way I will know that you have dealt graciously with my master."

¹⁵ᵈHe had scarcely finished speaking when Rebekah—who was born to Bethuel, son of Milcah, the wife of Abraham's brother Nahor—came out with a jug on her shoulder. ¹⁶The young woman was very beautiful, a virgin, untouched by man. She went down to the spring and filled her jug. As she came up, ¹⁷the servant ran toward her and said, "Please give me a sip of water from your jug." ¹⁸"Drink, sir," she replied, and quickly lowering the jug into her hand, she gave him a drink. ¹⁹When she had finished giving him a drink, she said, "I will draw water for your camels, too, until they have finished drinking." ²⁰With that, she quickly emptied her jug into the drinking trough and ran back to the well to draw more water, until she had drawn enough for all the camels. ²¹The man watched her the whole time, silently waiting to learn whether or not the Lord had made his journey successful. ²²When the camels had finished drinking, the man took out a gold nose-ring weighing half a shekel, and two gold bracelets weighing ten shekels for her wrists. ²³Then he asked her: "Whose daughter are you? Tell me, please. And is there a place in your father's house for us to spend the night?" ²⁴She answered: "I am the daughter of Bethuel the son of Milcah, whom she bore to Nahor. ²⁵We have plenty of straw and fodder," she added, "and also a place to spend the night." ²⁶The man then knelt and bowed down to the Lord, ²⁷saying: "Blessed be the Lord, the God of my master Abraham, who has not let his kindness and fidelity toward my master fail. As for me, the Lord has led me straight to the house of my master's brother."

²⁸Then the young woman ran off and told her mother's household what had happened. ²⁹ᵉNow Rebekah had a brother named Laban. Laban rushed outside to the man at the spring. ³⁰†When he saw the nose-ring and the bracelets

on his sister's arms and when he heard Rebekah repeating what the man had said to her, he went to him while he was standing by the camels at the spring. ³¹He said: "Come, blessed of the Lord! Why are you standing outside when I have made the house ready, as well as a place for the camels?" ³²The man then went inside; and while the camels were being unloaded and provided with straw and fodder, water was brought to bathe his feet and the feet of the men who were with him. ³³But when food was set before him, he said, "I will not eat until I have told my story." "Go ahead," they replied.

³⁴"I am Abraham's servant," he began. ³⁵"The Lord has blessed my master so abundantly that he has become wealthy; he has given him flocks and herds, silver and gold, male and female slaves, and camels and donkeys. ³⁶My master's wife Sarah bore a son to my master in her old age, and he has given him everything he owns. ³⁷My master put me under oath, saying: 'You shall not take a wife for my son from the daughters of the Canaanites in whose land I live; ³⁸instead, you must go to my father's house, to my own family, to get a wife for my son.' ³⁹When I asked my master, 'What if the woman will not follow me?' ⁴⁰he replied: 'The Lord, in whose presence I have always walked, will send his angel with you and make your journey successful, and so you will get a wife for my son from my own family and my father's house.ᶠ ⁴¹Then you will be freed from my curse. If you go to my family and they refuse you, then, too, you will be free from my curse.‡

⁴²"When I came to the spring today, I said: 'Lord, God of my master Abraham, please make successful the journey I am on. ⁴³While I stand here at the spring, if I say to a young woman who comes out to draw water, 'Please give me a little water from your jug,' ⁴⁴and she answers, 'Drink, and I will draw water for your camels, too—then she is the woman whom the Lord has decided upon for my master's son.'

⁴⁵"I had scarcely finished saying this to myself when Rebekah came out with a jug on her shoulder. After she went down to the spring and drew water, I said to her, 'Please let me have a drink.' ⁴⁶She quickly lowered the jug she was carrying and said, 'Drink, and I will water your camels, too.' So I drank, and she watered the camels also. ⁴⁷When I asked her, 'Whose daughter are you?' she answered, 'The daughter of Bethuel, son of Nahor, borne to Nahor by Milcah.' So I put the ring on her nose and the bracelets on her wrists. ⁴⁸Then I knelt and bowed down to the Lord, blessing the Lord, the God

---

lit., "Aram between the two rivers," is the Yahwist designation for Terah's homeland. The two rivers are the Habur and the Euphrates. The Priestly designation for the area is Paddan-aram, which is from the Assyrian *padana*, "road or garden," and Aram, which refers to the people or land of the Arameans.

*[24:12] Let it turn out favorably for me: let me have a favorable sign; cf. end of v. 14.

†[24:30] Laban becomes hospitable only when he sees the servant's rich gifts, which is in humorous contrast to his

sister's spontaneous generosity toward the servant. Laban's opportunism points forward to his behavior in the Jacob stories (31:14–16).

‡[24:41] Curse: this would be the consequence of failing to carry out the oath referred to in v. 3.

d. [24:15] Gn 22:23.    e. [24:29] Gn 27:43.

f. [24:40] Tb 5:17; 10:13.

of my master Abraham, who had led me on the right road to obtain the daughter of my master's kinsman for his son. ⁴⁹Now, if you will act with kindness and fidelity toward my master, let me know; but if not, let me know that too. I can then proceed accordingly."

⁵⁰ᵍLaban and Bethuel said in reply: "This thing comes from the LORD; we can say nothing to you either for or against it. ⁵¹Here is Rebekah, right in front of you; take her and go, that she may become the wife of your master's son, as the LORD has said." ⁵²When Abraham's servant heard their answer, he bowed to the ground before the LORD. ⁵³Then he brought out objects of silver and gold and clothing and presented them to Rebekah; he also gave costly presents to her brother and mother. ⁵⁴After he and the men with him had eaten and drunk, they spent the night there.

When they got up the next morning, he said, "Allow me to return to my master."ʰ ⁵⁵Her brother and mother replied, "Let the young woman stay with us a short while, say ten days; after that she may go." ⁵⁶But he said to them, "Do not detain me, now that the LORD has made my journey successful; let me go back to my master." ⁵⁷They answered, "Let us call the young woman and see what she herself has to say about it." ⁵⁸So they called Rebekah and asked her, "Will you go with this man?" She answered, "I will." ⁵⁹At this they sent off their sister Rebekah and her nurse with Abraham's servant and his men. ⁶⁰They blessed Rebekah and said:

"Sister, may you grow
        into thousands of myriads;
And may your descendants gain
                possession
        of the gates of their enemies!"ⁱ

⁶¹Then Rebekah and her attendants started out; they mounted the camels and followed the man. So the servant took Rebekah and went on his way.

⁶²Meanwhile Isaac had gone from Beer-lahai-roi and was living in the region of the Negeb.ʲ ⁶³One day toward evening he went out to walk in the field, and caught sight of camels approaching. ⁶⁴Rebekah, too, caught sight of Isaac, and got down from her camel. ⁶⁵She asked the servant, "Who is the man over there, walking through the fields toward us?" "That is my master," replied the servant. Then she took her veil and covered herself.

⁶⁶The servant recounted to Isaac all the things he had done. ⁶⁷Then Isaac brought Rebekah into the tent of his mother Sarah. He took Rebekah as his wife. Isaac loved her and found solace after the death of his mother.

## CHAPTER 25

**Abraham's Sons by Keturah.** ¹†ᵏAbraham took another wife, whose name was Keturah. ²She bore him Zimran, Jokshan, Medan, Midian, Ishbak, and Shuah.‡ ³Jokshan became the father of Sheba and Dedan. The descendants of Dedan were the Asshurim, the Letushim, and the Leummim.ˡ ⁴The descendants of Midian were Ephah, Epher, Hanoch, Abida, and Eldaah. All of these were descendants of Keturah.

⁵Abraham gave everything that he owned to his son Isaac.§ ⁶To the sons of his concubines, however, he gave gifts while he was still living, as he sent them away eastward, to the land of Kedem,¶ away from his son Isaac.

**Death of Abraham.** ⁷The whole span of Abraham's life was one hundred and seventy-five years. ⁸Then he breathed his last, dying at a ripe old age, grown old after a full life; and he was gathered to his people. ⁹His sons Isaac and Ishmael buried him in the cave of Machpelah, in the field of Ephron, son of Zohar the Hittite, which faces Mamre,ᵐ ¹⁰the field that Abraham had bought from the Hittites; there he was buried next to his wife Sarah. ¹¹After the death of Abraham, God blessed his son Isaac, who lived near Beer-lahai-roi.

**Descendants of Ishmael.** ¹²**These are the descendants of Abraham's son Ishmael, whom Hagar the Egyptian, Sarah's slave, bore to Abraham. ¹³ⁿThese are the names of Ishmael's sons, listed in the order of their birth: Ishmael's firstborn Nebaioth, Kedar, Adbeel, Mibsam,ᵒ ¹⁴Mishma, Dumah, Massa, ¹⁵Hadad, Tema, Jetur, Naphish, and Kedemah. ¹⁶These are the

---

*[24:58] Marriages arranged by the woman's father did not require the woman's consent, but marriages arranged by the woman's brother did. Laban is the brother and Rebekah is therefore free to give her consent or not.

†[25:1–11] As with the story of Terah in 11:27–32, this section lists all the descendants of Abraham as a means of concluding the story. The Jacob story ends similarly with the listing of the twelve sons (35:22–26), the death of Isaac (35:27–29), and the descendants of Esau (chap. 36). **Abraham took another wife:** though mentioned here, Abraham's marriage to a "concubine," or wife of secondary rank, is not to be understood as happening chronologically after the events narrated in the preceding chapter.

‡[25:2] Three of the six names can be identified: the Midianites are a trading people, mentioned in the Bible as dwelling east of the Gulf of Aqaba in northwest Arabia; Ishbak is a north Syrian tribe; Shuah is a city on the right bank of the Middle Euphrates. The other names are probably towns or peoples on the international trade routes.

§[25:5] Amid so many descendants, Abraham takes steps that Isaac will be his favored heir.

¶[25:6] **The land of Kedem:** or "the country of the East," the region inhabited by the Kedemites or Easterners (29:1; Jgs 6:3, 33; Jb 1:3; Is 11:14). The names mentioned in vv. 2–4, as far as they can be identified, are those of tribes in the Arabian desert.

**[25:12] Like the conclusion of the Jacob story (chap. 36), where the numerous descendants of the rejected Esau are listed, the descendants of the rejected Ishmael conclude the story.

---

g. [24:50–51] Tb 7:11–12.   h. [24:54] Tb 7:14; 8:20.   i. [24:60] Gn 22:17.   j. [24:62] Gn 16:13–14; 25:11.

k. [25:1–4] 1 Chr 1:32–33.   l. [25:3] Is 21:13.   m. [25:9–10] Gn 23:3–20.   n. [25:13–16] 1 Chr 1:29–31.   o. [25:13] Is 60:7.

sons of Ishmael, their names by their villages and encampments; twelve chieftains of as many tribal groups.[p]

[17]The span of Ishmael's life was one hundred and thirty-seven years. After he had breathed his last and died, he was gathered to his people. [18]The Ishmaelites ranged from Havilah, by Shur, which is on the border of Egypt, all the way to Asshur; and they pitched camp[*] alongside their various kindred.[q]

**Birth of Esau and Jacob.** [19†]These are the descendants of Isaac, son of Abraham; Abraham begot Isaac. [20]Isaac was forty years old when he married Rebekah, the daughter of Bethuel the Aramean of Paddan-aram[‡] and the sister of Laban the Aramean.[r] [21]Isaac entreated the LORD on behalf of his wife, since she was sterile. The LORD heard his entreaty, and his wife Rebekah became pregnant. [22]But the children jostled each other in the womb so much that she exclaimed, "If it is like this,[§] why go on living!" She went to consult the LORD, [23]and the LORD answered her:

> Two nations are in your womb,
>      two peoples are separating while still
>          within you;
> But one will be stronger than the other,
>      and the older will serve the younger.[¶]

[24]When the time of her delivery came, there were twins in her womb.[t] [25]The first to emerge was reddish,[**] and his whole body was like a hairy mantle; so they named him Esau. [26]Next his brother came out, gripping Esau's heel;[††] so he was named Jacob. Isaac was sixty years old when they were born.[u]

[27]When the boys grew up, Esau became a skillful hunter, a man of the open country; whereas Jacob was a simple[‡‡] man, who stayed among the tents.[v] [28]Isaac preferred Esau, because he was fond of game; but Rebekah preferred Jacob. [29]Once, when Jacob was cooking a stew, Esau came in from the open country, famished. [30]He said to Jacob, "Let me gulp down some of that red stuff,[§§] I am famished." That is why he was called Edom. [31]But Jacob replied, "First sell me your right as firstborn."[¶¶][w] [32]"Look," said Esau, "I am on the point of dying. What good is the right as firstborn to me?" [33]But Jacob said, "Swear to me first!" So he sold Jacob his right as firstborn under oath.[x] [34]Jacob then gave him some bread and the lentil stew; and Esau ate, drank, got up, and went his way. So Esau treated his right as firstborn with disdain.

## CHAPTER 26

**Isaac and Abimelech.** [1***][y]There was a famine in the land, distinct from the earlier one that had occurred in the days of Abraham, and Isaac went down to Abimelech, king of the Philistines in Gerar.[z] [2]The LORD appeared to him and said: Do not go down to Egypt, but camp in this land wherever I tell you. [3]Sojourn in this land, and I will be with you and bless you; for to you and your descendants I will give all these lands, in fulfillment of the oath that I swore to your father Abraham.[a] [4]I will make your descendants as

---

[*][25:18] **Pitched camp:** lit., "fell"; the same Hebrew verb is used in Jgs 7:12 in regard to the hostile encampment of desert tribes. The present passage shows the fulfillment of the prediction contained in Gn 16:12.

[†][25:19–36:43] The Jacob cycle is introduced as the family history of Isaac (Jacob's father), just as the Abraham stories were introduced as the record of the descendants of Terah (Abraham's father, 11:27). The cycle, made up of varied stories, is given unity by several recurring themes: birth, blessing and inheritance, which are developed through the basic contrasts of barrenness/fertility, non-blessing/blessing, and inheritance/exile/homeland. The large story has an envelope structure in which Jacob's youth is spent in Canaan striving with his older brother Esau (25:19–28:22), his early adulthood in Paddan-aram building a family and striving with his brother-in-law Laban (chaps. 29–31), and his later years back in Canaan (chaps. 32–36).

[‡][25:20] **Paddan-aram:** the name used by the Priestly tradition for the northwest region of Mesopotamia, between the Habur and the Euphrates rivers. In Assyrian, *padana* is a road or a garden, and Aram refers to the people or the land of the Arameans. The equivalent geographical term in the Yahwist source is Aram Naharaim, "Aram between two rivers."

[§][25:22] **If it is like this:** in Hebrew, the phrase *lamah zeh* is capable of several meanings; it occurs again in v. 32 ("What good . . . ?"), 32:30 ("Why do you want . . . ?"), and 33:15 ("For what reason?"). It is one of several words and motifs that run through the story, suggesting that a divine pattern (unknown to the actors) is at work.

[¶][25:23] **The older will serve the younger:** Rebekah now knows something that no one else knows, that God favors Jacob over Esau. The text does not say if she shared this knowledge with anyone or kept it to herself, but, from their actions, it seems unlikely that either Isaac or Esau knew. That fact must be borne in mind in assessing Rebekah's role in chap. 27, the theft of Esau's blessing.

[**][25:25] **Reddish:** in Hebrew, *'admoni*, a reference to Edom, another name for Esau (v. 30; 36:1). Edom was also the name of the country south of Moab (southeast of the Dead Sea) where the descendants of Esau lived. It was called the "red" country because of its reddish sandstone. Moreover, "red" points ahead to the red stew in the next scene. **Hairy:** in Hebrew, *se'ar*, a reference to Seir, another name for Edom (36:8).

[††][25:26] **Heel:** in Hebrew *'aqeb*, a wordplay on the name Jacob; cf. 27:36. The first of three scenes of striving with Esau. The second is vv. 27–34, and the third, chap. 27. In all the scenes, Jacob values the blessing more than his ardent but unreflective brother Esau does.

[‡‡][25:27] **Simple:** the Hebrew word denotes soundness, integrity, health, none of which fit here. Whatever its precise meaning, it must be opposite to the qualities of Esau.

[§§][25:30] **Red stuff:** in Hebrew, *'adom*; another play on the word Edom, the "red" land.

[¶¶][25:31] **Right as firstborn:** the privilege that entitled the firstborn son to a position of honor in the family and to a double share in the possessions inherited from the father. There is a persistent wordplay between *bekorah*, "right of the firstborn," and *berakah*, "the blessing." Contrary to custom, the preference here is for the younger son, as it was in the choice of Isaac over Ishmael.

[***][26:1] The promise of land and numerous descendants given to Abraham (12:1–3; 15; 17; 22:17–18) is renewed for his son Isaac. The divine blessing to Isaac is mentioned also in vv. 12, 24, and 29.

---

p. [25:16] Gn 17:20.   q. [25:18] Gn 16:12.   r. [25:20] Gn 24:67. s. [25:23] Gn 27:29; Nm 24:18; Mal 1:2–5; Rom 9:10–13.   t. [25:24] Hos 12:4.

u. [25:26] Mt 1:2.   v. [25:27] Gn 27:6–7.   w. [25:31] Dt 21:17. x. [25:33] Heb 12:16.   y. [26:1–14] Gn 12:10–20.   z. [26:1] Gn 12:10. a. [26:3] Gn 12:7; 15:18; Ex 32:13; Ps 105:9; Sir 44:22; Heb 11:9.

numerous as the stars in the sky, and I will give them all these lands, and in your descendants all the nations of the earth will find blessing—[b] [5]this because Abraham obeyed me, keeping my mandate, my commandments, my ordinances, and my instructions.

[6]*So Isaac settled in Gerar. [7]When the men of the place asked questions about his wife, he answered, "She is my sister." He was afraid that, if he called her his wife, the men of the place would kill him on account of Rebekah, since she was beautiful. [8]But when they had been there for a long time, Abimelech, king of the Philistines, looked out of a window and saw Isaac fondling his wife Rebekah. [9]He called for Isaac and said: "She must certainly be your wife! How could you have said, 'She is my sister'?" Isaac replied, "I thought I might lose my life on her account." [10]"How could you have done this to us!" exclaimed Abimelech. "It would have taken very little for one of the people to lie with your wife, and so you would have brought guilt upon us!" [11]Abimelech then commanded all the people: "Anyone who maltreats this man or his wife shall be put to death."

[12]†Isaac sowed a crop in that region and reaped a hundredfold the same year. Since the LORD blessed him, [13]*he became richer and richer all the time, until he was very wealthy. [14]He acquired flocks and herds, and a great work force, and so the Philistines became envious of him. [15]*The Philistines had stopped up and filled with dirt all the wells that his father's servants had dug back in the days of his father Abraham. [16]So Abimelech said to Isaac, "Go away from us; you have become far too numerous for us." [17]Isaac left there and camped in the Wadi Gerar where he stayed. [18]Isaac reopened the wells which his father's servants had dug back in the days of his father Abraham and which the Philistines had stopped up after Abraham's death; he gave them names like those that his father had given them. [19]But when Isaac's servants dug in the wadi and reached spring water in their well, [20]the shepherds of Gerar argued with Isaac's shepherds, saying, "The water belongs to us!" So he named the well Esek,[‡] because they had quarreled there. [21]Then they dug another well, and they argued over that one too; so he named it Sitnah.[§] [22]So he moved on from there and dug still another well, but over this one they did not argue. He named it Rehoboth,[¶] and said, "Because the LORD has now given us ample room, we shall flourish in the land."

[23]From there Isaac went up to Beer-sheba. [24]The same night the LORD appeared to him and said: I am the God of Abraham, your father. Do not fear, for I am with you. I will bless you and multiply your descendants for the sake of Abraham, my servant.[e] [25]So Isaac built an altar there and invoked the LORD by name. After he pitched his tent there, Isaac's servants began to dig a well nearby.

[26]†Then Abimelech came to him from Gerar, with Ahuzzath, his councilor, and Phicol, the general of his army. [27]Isaac asked them, "Why have you come to me, since you hate me and have driven me away from you?" [28]They answered: "We clearly see that the LORD has been with you, so we thought: let there be a sworn agreement between our two sides—between you and us. Let us make a covenant with you: [29]you shall do no harm to us, just as we have not maltreated you, but have always acted kindly toward you and have let you depart in peace. So now, may you be blessed by the LORD!" [30]Isaac then made a feast for them, and they ate and drank. [31]Early the next morning they exchanged oaths. Then Isaac sent them on their way, and they departed from him in peace.

[32]That same day Isaac's servants came and informed him about the well they had been digging; they told him, "We have reached water!" [33]He called it Shibah;** hence the name of the city is Beer-sheba to this day. [34]††When Esau was forty years old, he married Judith, daughter of Beeri the Hittite, and Basemath, daughter of Elon the Hivite.[g] [35]But they became a source of bitterness to Isaac and Rebekah.

## CHAPTER 27

**Jacob's Deception.**‡‡ [1]When Isaac was so old that his eyesight had failed him, he called his older

---

*[26:6–11] This scene is the third version of the wife-in-danger story (cf. chaps. 12 and 20). The mention of the famine in 26:1 recalls the famine in 12:10; the name Abimelech, king of the Philistines in Gerar, recalls 20:2. The deception, according to all the stories, is the claim that the wife is a sister. This story (from the Yahwist source) departs from the two previous accounts in that the wife is not taken into the harem of the foreign king.

†[26:12–33] The dispute is over water rights. In a sparsely watered land, wells were precious and claims on water could function as a kind of claim on the land. Scholars generally judge the account of the dispute over water rights and its settlement by a legal agreement between Isaac and Abimelech to be a Yahwist version of the similar story about Abraham in 21:22–34. Here, Abimelech realizes that Isaac has brought blessing to his people and thus desires a covenant with him. The feast in v. 30 is part of the covenant ceremony.

b. [26:4] Gn 12:3; 22:17–18; 28:14; Ex 32:13.  c. [26:13–14] Jb 1:3.  d. [26:15–24] Gn 21:25–31.

‡[26:20] **Esek**: "quarrel."

§[26:21] **Sitnah**: "opposition."

¶[26:22] **Rehoboth**: "wide spaces," i.e., ample room to live; site is probably SW of modern day Beer-sheba.

**[26:33] **Shibah**: the place name Shibah is a play on two Hebrew words, *shebu'ah*, "oath," and *shwebaa'*, "seven." In v. 31, they exchanged oaths.

††[26:34–35] These verses from the Priestly source introduce the next section on Esau's loss of his right as firstborn by suggesting a motivation for this in Isaac's and Rebekah's dislike for Esau's Canaanite wives.

‡‡[27:1–45] The chapter, a literary masterpiece, is the third and climactic wresting away of the blessing of Esau. Rebekah manages the entire affair, using perhaps her privileged information about Jacob's status (25:23); Jacob's only qualm is that

e. [26:24] Gn 46:3.  f. [26:26–33] Gn 21:22–31; Prv 16:7.  g. [26:34–35] Gn 27:46.

son Esau and said to him, "My son!" "Here I am!" he replied. ²Isaac then said, "Now I have grown old. I do not know when I might die. ³So now take your hunting gear—your quiver and bow—and go out into the open country to hunt some game for me. ⁴Then prepare for me a dish in the way I like, and bring it to me to eat, so that I may bless you* before I die."

⁵Rebekah had been listening while Isaac was speaking to his son Esau. So when Esau went out into the open country to hunt some game for his father,ʰ ⁶Rebekah said to her son Jacob, "Listen! I heard your father tell your brother Esau, ⁷'Bring me some game and prepare a dish for me to eat, that I may bless you with the LORD's approval before I die.' ⁸Now, my son, obey me in what I am about to order you. ⁹Go to the flock and get me two choice young goats so that with these I might prepare a dish for your father in the way he likes. ¹⁰Then bring it to your father to eat, that he may bless you before he dies." ¹¹But Jacob said to his mother Rebekah, "But my brother Esau is a hairy man and I am smooth-skinned!ⁱ ¹²Suppose my father feels me? He will think I am making fun of him, and I will bring on myself a curse instead of a blessing." ¹³His mother, however, replied: "Let any curse against you, my son, fall on me! Just obey me. Go and get me the young goats."

¹⁴So Jacob went and got them and brought them to his mother, and she prepared a dish in the way his father liked. ¹⁵Rebekah then took the best clothes of her older son Esau that she had in the house, and gave them to her younger son Jacob to wear; ¹⁶and with the goatskins she covered up his hands and the hairless part of his neck. ¹⁷Then she gave her son Jacob the dish and the bread she had prepared.

¹⁸Going to his father, Jacob said, "Father!" "Yes?" replied Isaac. "Which of my sons are you?" ¹⁹Jacob answered his father: "I am Esau, your firstborn. I did as you told me. Please sit up and eat some of my game, so that you may bless me." ²⁰But Isaac said to his son, "How did you get it so quickly, my son?" He answered, "The LORD, your God, directed me." ²¹Isaac then said to Jacob, "Come closer, my son, that I may feel you, to learn whether you really are my son

Esau or not." ²²So Jacob moved up closer to his father. When Isaac felt him, he said, "Although the voice is Jacob's, the hands are Esau's." ²³(He failed to identify him because his hands were hairy, like those of his brother Esau; so he blessed him.) ²⁴Again Isaac said, "Are you really my son Esau?" And Jacob said, "I am." ²⁵Then Isaac said, "Serve me, my son, and let me eat of the game so that I may bless you." Jacob served it to him, and Isaac ate; he brought him wine, and he drank. ²⁶Finally his father Isaac said to him, "Come closer, my son, and kiss me." ²⁷As Jacob went up to kiss him, Isaac smelled the fragrance of his clothes. With that, he blessed him, saying,

"Ah, the fragrance of my son
    is like the fragrance of a field
    that the LORD has blessed!ʲ
²⁸ May God give to you
    of the dew of the heavens
And of the fertility of the earth
    abundance of grain and wine.
²⁹ ᵏMay peoples serve you,
    and nations bow down to you;
Be master of your brothers,
    and may your mother's sons bow
        down to you.
Cursed be those who curse you,
    and blessed be those who bless you."

³⁰Jacob had scarcely left his father after Isaac had finished blessing him, when his brother Esau came back from his hunt. ³¹Then he too prepared a dish, and bringing it to his father, he said, "Let my father sit up and eat some of his son's game, that you may then give me your blessing." ³²His father Isaac asked him, "Who are you?" He said, "I am your son, your first-born son, Esau." ³³Isaac trembled greatly. "Who was it, then," he asked, "that hunted game and brought it to me? I ate it all just before you came, and I blessed him. Now he is blessed!" ³⁴As he heard his father's words, Esau burst into loud, bitter sobbing and said, "Father, bless me too!" ³⁵When Isaac said, "Your brother came here by a ruse and carried off your blessing," ³⁶Esau exclaimed, "He is well named Jacob, is he not! He has supplanted me† twice! First he took away my right as firstborn, and now he has taken away my blessing." Then he said, "Have you not saved a blessing for me?"ⁱ ³⁷Isaac replied to Esau: "I have already appointed him your master, and I have assigned to him all his kindred as his servants; besides, I have sustained him with grain and wine. What then can I do for you, my son?" ³⁸But Esau said to his father, "Have you only one

---

if his father discovers the ruse, he will receive a curse instead of a blessing (vv. 11–12). Isaac is passive as he was in chaps. 22 and 24. The deception is effected through clothing (Jacob wears Esau's clothing), which points ahead to a similar deception of a patriarch by means of clothing in the Joseph story (37:21–33). Such recurrent acts and scenes let the reader know a divine purpose is moving the story forward even though the human characters are unaware of it.

* [27:4] **I may bless you:** Isaac's blessing confers fertility (vv. 27–28) and dominion (v. 29). The "dew of heaven" is rain that produces grain and wine, two of the principal foodstuffs of the ancient Near East. The "fertility of the earth" may allude to oil, the third basic foodstuff. The full agricultural year may be implied here: the fall rains are followed by the grain harvests of the spring and the grape harvest of late summer, and then the olive harvest of the fall (cf. Dt 11:14; Ps 104:13–15).

h. [27:5] Gn 25:28.  i. [27:11] Gn 25:25.

---

† [27:36] **He has supplanted me:** in Hebrew, *wayyaqebeni,* a wordplay on the name Jacob, *ya'aqob;* see Jer 9:3 and Gn 25:26. There is also a play between the Hebrew words *bekorah* ("right of the firstborn") and *berakah* ("blessing").

j. [27:27] Gn 22:17–18; Heb 11:20.  k. [27:29] Gn 25:23; 49:8; Nm 24:9.  l. [27:36] Gn 25:26, 29–34; Hos 12:4.

blessing, father? Bless me too, father!" and Esau wept aloud.[m] [39]His father Isaac said in response:

"See, far from the fertile earth
    will be your dwelling;
    far from the dew of the heavens
        above![n]
[40] By your sword you will live,
    and your brother you will serve;
But when you become restless,
    you will throw off his yoke from
        your neck."[o]

[41]Esau bore a grudge against Jacob because of the blessing his father had given him. Esau said to himself, "Let the time of mourning for my father come, so that I may kill my brother Jacob."[p] [42]When Rebekah got news of what her older son Esau had in mind, she summoned her younger son Jacob and said to him: "Listen! Your brother Esau intends to get his revenge by killing you. [43]So now, my son, obey me: flee at once to my brother Laban in Haran, [44]and stay with him a while until your brother's fury subsides— [45]until your brother's anger against you subsides and he forgets what you did to him. Then I will send for you and bring you back. Why should I lose both of you in a single day?" **Jacob Sent to Laban.** [46]Rebekah said to Isaac: "I am disgusted with life because of the Hittite women. If Jacob also should marry a Hittite woman, a native of the land, like these women, why should I live?"[q]

### CHAPTER 28

[1]Isaac therefore summoned Jacob and blessed him, charging him: "You shall not marry a Canaanite woman![r] [2]Go now to Paddan-aram, to the home of your mother's father Bethuel, and there choose a wife for yourself from among the daughters of Laban, your mother's brother.[s] [3]May God Almighty bless you and make you fertile, multiply you that you may become an assembly of peoples. [4]May God extend to you and your descendants the blessing of Abraham, so that you may gain possession of the land where you are residing, which he assigned to Abraham."[t] [5]Then Isaac sent Jacob on his way; he went to Paddan-aram, to Laban, son of Bethuel the Aramean, and brother of Rebekah, the mother of Jacob and Esau.[u]

[6]Esau noted that Isaac had blessed Jacob when he sent him to Paddan-aram to get himself a wife there, and that, as he gave him his blessing, he charged him, "You shall not marry a Canaanite woman," [7]and that Jacob had obeyed his father and mother and gone to Paddan-aram. [8]Esau realized how displeasing the Canaanite women were to his father Isaac, [9]so Esau went to Ishmael, and in addition to the wives he had, married Mahalath, the daughter of Abraham's son Ishmael and sister of Nebaioth.[v]

**Jacob's Dream at Bethel.**[†] [10]Jacob departed from Beer-sheba and proceeded toward Haran. [11]When he came upon a certain place,[‡] he stopped there for the night, since the sun had already set. Taking one of the stones at the place, he put it under his head and lay down in that place. [12]Then he had a dream: a stairway[§] rested on the ground, with its top reaching to the heavens; and God's angels were going up and down on it.[w] [13]And there was the LORD standing beside him and saying: I am the LORD, the God of Abraham your father and the God of Isaac; the land on which you are lying I will give to you and your descendants.[x] [14]Your descendants will be like the dust of the earth, and through them you will spread to the west and the east, to the north and the south. In you and your descendants all the families of the earth will find blessing.[y] [15]I am with you and will protect you wherever you go, and bring you back to this land. I will never leave you until I have done what I promised you.[z]

[16]When Jacob awoke from his sleep, he said, "Truly, the LORD is in this place and I did not

---

*[28:1–9] A glimpse of Rebekah's shrewdness is provided by 27:42–28:2. She is aware of Esau's murderous plot against Jacob (27:42–45) but realizes the episode of the stolen blessing is still painful to Isaac; she therefore uses another motive to persuade Isaac to send Jacob away—he must marry within the family (endogamy), unlike Esau. Esau, unreflective as usual, realizes too late he also should marry within the family but, significantly, marries from Abraham's rejected line. At this point in the story, Jacob (and his mother) have taken the blessing for themselves. Their actions have put Jacob in a precarious position: he must flee the land because of his brother's murderous intent and find a wife in a far country. One might ask how God's blessing can be given to such an unworthy schemer. There is a biblical pattern of preferring the younger brother over the older—Isaac over Ishmael, Jacob over Esau, Rachel over Leah, Joseph over his older brothers, Ephraim over Manasseh (Gn 48:14), David over his older brothers.

†[28:10–22] As Jacob is leaving the land on his way to an uncertain future in Paddan-aram, God appears to him at a sacred place that Jacob had visited only to take a night's rest. Jacob's unawareness of the holiness of the place underscores the graciousness of the gift. On his return to Canaan, he will again encounter a divine visitor in the form of the mysterious attacker (32:23–33) and, after his return and reconciliation with Esau, he will again go to Bethel (35:1–15).

‡[28:11] **Place:** the Hebrew word is often used specifically of a sacred site. The ambiguous word "place" is used here, for the text emphasizes that Jacob has no idea the place he has come upon is sacred; only when he wakes up does he realize it is sacred. The place was Bethel (v. 19), a sacred site as early as the time of Abraham (12:8).

§[28:12] **Stairway:** in Hebrew, *sullam,* traditionally but inaccurately translated as "ladder." The corresponding verb, *salal,* means "to heap up" something, such as dirt for a highway or a ramp. The imagery in Jacob's dream may be derived from the Babylonian ziggurat or temple tower, "with its top in the sky" (11:4), and with brick steps leading up to a small temple at the top.

---

m. [27:38] Heb 12:17.   n. [27:39] Heb 11:20.   o. [27:40] 2 Kgs 8:20, 22; 2 Chr 21:8.   p. [27:41] Wis 10:10; Ob 10.   q. [27:46] Gn 26:34–35.   r. [28:1] Gn 24:3–4; 26:35.   s. [28:2] Gn 22:22.

t. [28:4] Ex 32:13.   u. [28:5] Jdt 8:26.   v. [28:9] Gn 36:2–3.   w. [28:12] Jn 1:51.   x. [28:13] Dt 1:8; Mi 7:20.   y. [28:14] Gn 12:3; 13:14–15; 15:5–6; 18:18; 22:17–18; 26:4; Dt 19:8; Sir 44:21.   z. [28:15] Gn 31:3.

know it!" [17]He was afraid and said: "How awesome this place is! This is nothing else but the house of God, the gateway to heaven!" [18]Early the next morning Jacob took the stone that he had put under his head, set it up as a sacred pillar,* and poured oil on top of it.[a] [19]He named that place Bethel,† whereas the former name of the town had been Luz.[b]

[20]Jacob then made this vow:‡ "If God will be with me and protect me on this journey I am making and give me food to eat and clothes to wear, [21]and I come back safely to my father's house, the Lord will be my God. [22]This stone that I have set up as a sacred pillar will be the house of God. Of everything you give me, I will return a tenth part to you without fail."

## CHAPTER 29
**Arrival in Haran.**§ [1c]After Jacob resumed his journey, he came to the land of the Kedemites. [2]Looking about, he saw a well in the open country, with three flocks of sheep huddled near it, for flocks were watered from that well. A large stone covered the mouth of the well.[d] [3]When all the shepherds were assembled there they would roll the stone away from the mouth of the well and water the sheep. Then they would put the stone back again in its place over the mouth of the well.

[4]Jacob said to them, "My brothers, where are you from?" "We are from Haran," they replied. [5]Then he asked them, "Do you know Laban, son of Nahor?" "We do," they answered.[e] [6]He

inquired further, "Is he well?" "He is," they answered; "and here comes his daughter Rachel with the sheep." [7]Then he said: "There is still much daylight left; it is hardly the time to bring the animals home. Water the sheep, and then continue pasturing them." [8]They replied, "We cannot until all the shepherds are here to roll the stone away from the mouth of the well; then can we water the flocks."

[9]While he was still talking with them, Rachel arrived with her father's sheep, for she was the one who tended them. [10]As soon as Jacob saw Rachel, the daughter of his mother's brother Laban, and the sheep of Laban, he went up, rolled the stone away from the mouth of the well, and watered Laban's sheep. [11]Then Jacob kissed Rachel and wept aloud. [12]Jacob told Rachel that he was her father's relative, Rebekah's son. So she ran to tell her father. [13]When Laban heard the news about Jacob, his sister's son, he ran to meet him. After embracing and kissing him, he brought him to his house. Jacob then repeated to Laban all these things, [14]and Laban said to him, "You are indeed my bone and my flesh."¶

**Marriage to Leah and Rachel.** After Jacob had stayed with him a full month, [15]**Laban said to him: "Should you serve me for nothing just because you are a relative of mine? Tell me what your wages should be." [16]Now Laban had two daughters; the older was called Leah, the younger Rachel. [17]Leah had dull eyes,†† but Rachel was shapely and beautiful. [18]Because Jacob loved Rachel, he answered, "I will serve you seven years for your younger daughter Rachel."‡‡ [19]Laban replied, "It is better to give her to you than to another man. Stay with me." [20]So Jacob served seven years for Rachel, yet they seemed to him like a few days because of his love for her.[f]

[21]Then Jacob said to Laban, "Give me my wife, that I may consummate my marriage with her, for my term is now completed." [22]So Laban invited all the local inhabitants and gave a banquet. [23]At nightfall he took his daughter Leah and brought her to Jacob, and he consummated the marriage with her. [24]Laban assigned his maidservant Zilpah to his daughter Leah as her maidservant. [25]In the morning, there was

---

*[28:18] **Sacred pillar**: in Hebrew, *masseba*, a stone which might vary in shape and size, set upright and usually intended for some religious purpose. The custom of erecting such sacred pillars in Palestine went back to its pre-Israelite period; but since their polytheistic associations were often retained, later Israelite religion forbade their erection (Lv 26:1; Dt 16:22) and ordered the destruction of those that were associated with other religions (Ex 34:13; Dt 12:3).

†[28:19] **Bethel**: i.e., "house of God"; the reference is to the house of God in v. 17.

‡[28:20] **This vow**: knowing well that Esau's murderous wrath stands between him and the possession of the land promised him, Jacob makes his vow very precise. He vows to make the God who appeared to him his own if the God guides him safely to Paddan-aram and back to this land.

§[29:1–14] Jacob's arrival in Haran. The sight of Rachel inspires Jacob to the superhuman feat of rolling back the enormous stone by himself. The scene evokes the meeting of Abraham's steward and Jacob's mother Rebekah at a well (24:11–27).

The verse begins the story of Jacob's time in Mesopotamia (29:1–31:54), which is framed on either side by Jacob's time in Canaan, 25:19–28:22 and 32:1–36:43. In these chapters, Jacob suffers Laban's duplicity as Esau had to suffer his, though eventually Jacob outwits Laban and leaves Mesopotamia a wealthy man. An elaborate chiastic (or envelope) structure shapes the diverse material: (A) Jacob's arrival in Haran in 29:1–4; (B) contract with Laban in 29:15–20; (C) Laban's deception of Jacob in 29:21–30; (D) the center, the birth of Jacob's children in 29:31–30:24; (C′) Jacob's deception of Laban in 30:25–43; (B′) dispute with Laban in 31:17–42; (A′) departure from Laban in 31:43–54. As the chiasm reverses, so do the fortunes of Laban and Jacob. **Kedemites**: see note on 25:6.

¶[29:14] **Bone and . . . flesh**: the Hebrew idiom for English "flesh and blood" (cf. 2:23; Jgs 9:2; 2 Sm 5:1 = 1 Chr 11:1).

**[29:15–30] Laban's deception and Jacob's marriages. There are many ironies in the passage. Jacob's protest to Laban, "How could you do this to me?" echoes the question put to Abraham (20:9) and Isaac (26:10) when their deceptions about their wives were discovered. The major irony is that Jacob, the deceiver of his father and brother about the blessing (chap. 27), is deceived by his uncle (standing in for the father) about his wife.

††[29:17] **Dull eyes**: in the language of beauty used here, "dull" probably means lacking in the luster that was the sign of beautiful eyes, as in 1 Sm 16:12 and Sg 4:1.

‡‡[29:18] Jacob offers to render service (Jos 15:16–17; 1 Sm 17:25; 18:17) to pay off the customary bridal price (Ex 22:15–16; Dt 22:29).

a. [28:18] Gn 31:13; 35:14–15.   b. [28:19] Gn 35:6; 48:3; Jos 18:13; Jgs 1:23; Hos 12:5.   c. [29:1] Wis 10:10.   d. [29:2] Gn 24:11–12.   e. [29:5] Tb 7:4.

f. [29:20] Hos 12:13.

Leah! So Jacob said to Laban: "How could you do this to me! Was it not for Rachel that I served you? Why did you deceive me?" ²⁶Laban replied, "It is not the custom in our country to give the younger daughter before the firstborn. ²⁷Finish the bridal week⁎ for this one, and then the other will also be given to you in return for another seven years of service with me."ᵍ

²⁸Jacob did so. He finished the bridal week for the one, and then Laban gave him his daughter Rachel as a wife. ²⁹Laban assigned his maidservant Bilhah to his daughter Rachel as her maidservant. ³⁰Jacob consummated his marriage with Rachel also, and he loved her more than Leah. Thus he served Laban another seven years.ʰ

**Jacob's Children.†** ³¹When the Lᴏʀᴅ saw that Leah was unloved, he made her fruitful, while Rachel was barren. ³²Leah conceived and bore a son, and she named him Reuben;‡ for she said, "It means, 'The Lᴏʀᴅ saw my misery; surely now my husband will love me.'"ⁱ ³³She conceived again and bore a son, and said, "It means, 'The Lᴏʀᴅ heard that I was unloved,' and therefore he has given me this one also"; so she named him Simeon.§ ³⁴Again she conceived and bore a son, and she said, "Now at last my husband will become attached to me, since I have now borne him three sons"; that is why she named him Levi.¶ ³⁵Once more she conceived and bore a son, and she said, "This time I will give thanks to the Lᴏʀᴅ"; therefore she named him Judah.⁎⁎ Then she stopped bearing children.ʲ

## CHAPTER 30

¹When Rachel saw that she had not borne children to Jacob, she became envious of her sister.

She said to Jacob, "Give me children or I shall die!"ᵏ ²Jacob became angry with Rachel and said, "Can I take the place of God, who has denied you the fruit of the womb?"ˡ ³She replied, "Here is my maidservant Bilhah. Have intercourse with her, and let her give birth on my knees,†† so that I too may have children through her."ᵐ ⁴So she gave him her maidservant Bilhah as wife,‡‡ and Jacob had intercourse with her. ⁵When Bilhah conceived and bore a son for Jacob, ⁶Rachel said, "God has vindicated me; indeed he has heeded my plea and given me a son." Therefore she named him Dan.§§ ⁷Rachel's maidservant Bilhah conceived again and bore a second son for Jacob, ⁸and Rachel said, "I have wrestled strenuously with my sister, and I have prevailed." So she named him Naphtali.¶¶

⁹When Leah saw that she had ceased to bear children, she took her maidservant Zilpah and gave her to Jacob as wife. ¹⁰So Leah's maidservant Zilpah bore a son for Jacob. ¹¹Leah then said, "What good luck!" So she named him Gad.⁎⁎⁎ ¹²Then Leah's maidservant Zilpah bore a second son to Jacob; ¹³and Leah said, "What good fortune, because women will call me fortunate!" So she named him Asher.†††

¹⁴One day, during the wheat harvest, Reuben went out and came upon some mandrakes‡‡‡ in the field which he brought home to his mother Leah. Rachel said to Leah, "Please give me some of your son's mandrakes." ¹⁵Leah replied, "Was it not enough for you to take away my husband, that you must now take my son's mandrakes too?" Rachel answered, "In that case Jacob may lie with you tonight in exchange for your son's mandrakes." ¹⁶That evening, when Jacob came in from the field, Leah went out to meet him. She said, "You must have intercourse with me, because I have hired you with my son's mandrakes." So that night he lay with her, ¹⁷and God listened to Leah; she conceived and bore a fifth son to Jacob. ¹⁸Leah then said, "God has

---

⁎[29:27] **The bridal week:** an ancient wedding lasted for seven days; cf. Jgs 14:12, 17.

†[29:31–30:24] The note of strife, first sounded between Jacob and Esau in chaps. 25–27, continues between the two wives, since Jacob loved Rachel more than Leah (29:30). Jacob's neglect of Leah moves God to make her fruitful (29:31), Leah's fertility provokes Rachel. Leah bears Jacob four sons (Reuben, Levi, Simeon, and Judah) and her maidservant Zilpah, two (Gad and Asher). Rachel's maidservant Bilhah bears two (Dan and Naphtali). After the mandrakes (30:14–17), Leah bears Issachar and Zebulun and a daughter Dinah. Rachel then bears Joseph and, later in the land of Canaan, Benjamin (35:18).

‡[29:32] **Reuben:** the literal meaning of the Hebrew name is disputed. One interpretation is *re'u ben*, "look, a son!", but here in Genesis (as also with the names of all the other sons of Jacob), it is given a symbolic rather than an etymological interpretation. Name and person were regarded as closely interrelated. The symbolic interpretation of Reuben's name, according to the Yahwist source, is based on the similar-sounding *ra'a be'onyi*, "he saw my misery." In the Elohist source, the name is explained by the similar-sounding *ye'ehabani*, "he will love me."

§[29:33] **Simeon:** in popular etymology, related to *shama'*, "he heard."

¶[29:34] **Levi:** related to *yillaweh*, "he will become attached."

⁎⁎[29:35] **Judah:** related to *'odeh*, "I will give thanks, praise."

††[30:3] **On my knees:** in the ancient Near East, a father would take a newborn child in his lap to signify that he acknowledged it as his own; Rachel uses the ceremony in order to adopt the child and establish her legal rights to it.

‡‡[30:4] **As wife:** in 35:22 Bilhah is called a "concubine" (Heb. *pilegesh*). In v. 9, Zilpah is called "wife," and in 37:2 both women are called wives. The basic difference between a wife and a concubine was that no bride price was paid for the latter. The interchange of terminology shows that there was some blurring in social status between the wife and the concubine.

§§[30:6] **Dan:** explained by the term *dannanni*, "he has vindicated me."

¶¶[30:8] **Naphtali:** explained by the Hebrew term *naftulim*, lit., "contest" or "struggle."

⁎⁎⁎[30:11] **Gad:** explained by the Hebrew term *begad*, lit., "in luck," i.e., "what good luck!"

†††[30:13] **Asher:** explained by the term *be'oshri*, lit., "in my good fortune," i.e., "what good fortune," and by the term *yeashsheruni*, "they call me fortunate."

‡‡‡[30:14] **Mandrakes:** an herb whose root was thought to promote conception. The Hebrew word for mandrakes, *duda'im*, has erotic connotations, since it sounds like the words *daddayim* ("breasts") and *dodim* ("sexual pleasure").

---

g. [29:27] Hos 12:13.  h. [29:30] Dt 21:15–17.  i. [29:32] Gn 49:3.  j. [29:35] Mt 1:2; Lk 3:33.

k. [30:1] Prv 30:16.  l. [30:2] 2 Kgs 5:7.  m. [30:3] Gn 16:2–4.

given me my wages for giving my maidservant to my husband"; so she named him Issachar.* [19]Leah conceived again and bore a sixth son to Jacob; [20]and Leah said, "God has brought me a precious gift. This time my husband will honor me, because I have borne him six sons"; so she named him Zebulun.† [21]Afterwards she gave birth to a daughter, and she named her Dinah.

[22]Then God remembered Rachel. God listened to her and made her fruitful. [23]She conceived and bore a son, and she said, "God has removed my disgrace."[n] [24]She named him Joseph,‡ saying, "May the LORD add another son for me!"

**Jacob Outwits Laban.**§ [25]After Rachel gave birth to Joseph, Jacob said to Laban: "Allow me to go to my own region and land. [26]Give me my wives and my children for whom I served you and let me go, for you know the service that I rendered you." [27]Laban answered him: "If you will please! I have learned through divination that the LORD has blessed me because of you." [28]He continued, "State the wages I owe you, and I will pay them." [29]Jacob replied: "You know what work I did for you and how well your livestock fared under my care; [30]the little you had before I came has grown into an abundance, since the LORD has blessed you in my company. Now, when can I do something for my own household as well?" [31]Laban asked, "What should I give you?" Jacob answered: "You do not have to give me anything. If you do this thing for me, I will again pasture and tend your sheep. [32]Let me go through your whole flock today and remove from it every dark animal among the lambs and every spotted or speckled one among the goats.¶ These will be my wages. [33]In the future, whenever you check on my wages, my honesty will testify for me: any animal that is not speckled or spotted among the goats, or dark among the lambs, got into my

possession by theft!" [34]Laban said, "Very well. Let it be as you say."

[35]That same day Laban removed the streaked and spotted he-goats and all the speckled and spotted she-goats, all those with some white on them, as well as every dark lamb, and he put them in the care of his sons.** [36]Then he put a three days' journey between himself and Jacob, while Jacob was pasturing the rest of Laban's flock.

[37]Jacob, however, got some fresh shoots of poplar, almond and plane†† trees, and he peeled white stripes in them by laying bare the white core of the shoots. [38]The shoots that he had peeled he then set upright in the watering troughs where the animals came to drink, so that they would be in front of them. When the animals were in heat as they came to drink, [39]the goats mated by the shoots, and so they gave birth to streaked, speckled and spotted young. [40]The sheep, on the other hand, Jacob kept apart, and he made these animals face the streaked or completely dark animals of Laban. Thus he produced flocks of his own, which he did not put with Laban's flock. [41]Whenever the hardier animals were in heat, Jacob would set the shoots in the troughs in full view of these animals, so that they mated by the shoots; [42]but with the weaker animals he would not put the shoots there. So the feeble animals would go to Laban, but the hardy ones to Jacob. [43]So the man grew exceedingly prosperous, and he owned large flocks, male and female servants, camels, and donkeys.

## CHAPTER 31

**Flight from Laban.** [1]‡‡Jacob heard that Laban's sons were saying, "Jacob has taken everything that belonged to our father, and he has produced all this wealth from our father's property." [2]Jacob perceived, too, that Laban's attitude toward him was not what it had previously been. [3]Then the LORD said to Jacob: Return to the land of your ancestors, where you were born, and I will be with you.[o]

[4]So Jacob sent for Rachel and Leah to meet him in the field where his flock was. [5]There he said to them: "I have noticed that your father's attitude toward me is not as it was in the past; but the God of my father has been with me. [6]You know well that with all my strength I served your father; [7]yet your father cheated me and

---

*[30:18] **Issachar**: explained by the terms, *sekari*, "my reward," and in v. 16, *sakor sekartika*, "I have hired you."

†[30:20] **Zebulun**: explained by the terms, *zebadani . . . zebed tob*, "he has brought me a precious gift," and *yizbeleni*, "he will honor me."

‡[30:24] **Joseph**: explained by the words *yosep*, "may he add," and in v. 23, *'asap*, "he has removed."

§[30:25–43] Jacob's deception of Laban. Jacob has been living in Laban's household as an indentured worker paying off the bride price. Having paid off all his obligations, he wants to settle his accounts with Laban. His many children attest to the fulfillment of the Lord's promise of numerous progeny; the birth of Joseph to his beloved Rachel signals the fulfillment in a special way. To enter into the Lord's second promise, the land, he must now return to Canaan.

¶[30:32] **Dark . . . lambs . . . spotted or speckled . . . goats**: in the Near East the normal color of sheep is light gray, whereas that of goats is dark brown or black. A minority of sheep in that part of the world have dark patches, and a minority of goats, white markings. Laban is quick to agree to the offer, for Jacob would have received only a few animals. But Jacob gets the better of him, using two different means: (1) he separates out the weaker animals and then provides visual impressions to the stronger animals at mating time (a folkloric belief); (2) in 31:8–12, he transmits the preferred characteristics through controlled propagation. It should be noted that Jacob has been told what to do in a dream (31:10) and that God is behind the increase in his flocks.

n. [30:23] Lk 1:25.

**[30:35] By giving the abnormally colored animals to his sons, Laban not only deprived Jacob of his first small wages, but he also schemed to prevent the future breeding of such animals in the flock entrusted to Jacob.

††[30:37] **Plane**: also called the Oriental Plane, a deciduous tree found in riverine forests and marshes.

‡‡[31:1–54] Jacob flees with his family from Laban. The strife that has always accompanied Jacob continues as Laban's sons complain, "he has taken everything that belonged to our father"; the brothers' complaint echoes Esau's in 27:36. Rachel and Leah overcome their mutual hostility and are able to leave together, a harbinger of the reconciliation with Esau in chap. 33.

o. [31:3] Gn 26:3; 28:15; 32:10.

changed my wages ten times. God, however, did not let him do me any harm.[p] [8]Whenever your father said, 'The speckled animals will be your wages,' the entire flock would bear speckled young; whenever he said, 'The streaked animals will be your wages,' the entire flock would bear streaked young. [9]So God took away your father's livestock and gave it to me. [10]Once, during the flock's mating season, I had a dream in which I saw he-goats mating that were streaked, speckled and mottled. [11]In the dream God's angel said to me, 'Jacob!' and I replied, 'Here I am!' [12]Then he said: 'Look up and see. All the he-goats that are mating are streaked, speckled and mottled, for I have seen all the things that Laban has been doing to you. [13]I am the God of Bethel, where you anointed a sacred pillar and made a vow to me. Get up now! Leave this land and return to the land of your birth.'"[q]

[14]Rachel and Leah answered him: "Do we still have an heir's portion in our father's house? [15]Are we not regarded by him as outsiders?[*] He not only sold us; he has even used up the money that he got for us! [16]All the wealth that God took away from our father really belongs to us and our children. So do whatever God has told you."[r] [17]Jacob proceeded to put his children and wives on camels, [18]and he drove off all his livestock and all the property he had acquired in Paddan-aram, to go to his father Isaac in the land of Canaan.

[19]Now Laban was away shearing his sheep, and Rachel had stolen her father's household images.[†s] [20]Jacob hoodwinked[‡] Laban the Aramean by not telling him that he was going to flee. [21]Thus he fled with all that he had. Once he was across the Euphrates, he headed for the hill country of Gilead.

[22]On the third day, word came to Laban that Jacob had fled. [23]Taking his kinsmen with him, he pursued him for seven days[§] until he caught up with him in the hill country of Gilead. [24]But that night God appeared to Laban the Aramean in a dream and said to him: Take care not to say anything to Jacob.[t]

**Jacob and Laban in Gilead.** [25]When Laban overtook Jacob, Jacob's tents were pitched in the hill country; Laban also pitched his tents in the hill country of Gilead. [26]Laban said to Jacob, "How could you hoodwink me and carry off my daughters like prisoners of war?[¶] [27]Why did you dupe me by stealing away secretly? You did not tell me! I would have sent you off with joyful singing to the sound of tambourines and harps. [28]You did not even allow me a parting kiss to my daughters and grandchildren! Now what you have done makes no sense. [29]I have it in my power to harm all of you; but last night the God of your father said to me, 'Take care not to say anything to Jacob!' [30]Granted that you had to leave because you were longing for your father's house, why did you steal my gods?" [31]Jacob replied to Laban, "I was frightened at the thought that you might take your daughters away from me by force. [32]As for your gods, the one you find them with shall not remain alive! If, with our kinsmen looking on, you identify anything here as belonging to you, take it." Jacob had no idea that Rachel had stolen the household images.

[33]Laban then went in and searched Jacob's tent and Leah's tent, as well as the tents of the two maidservants; but he did not find them. Leaving Leah's tent, he went into Rachel's. [34]**Meanwhile Rachel had taken the household images, put them inside the camel's saddlebag, and seated herself upon them. When Laban had rummaged through her whole tent without finding them,[u] [35]she said to her father, "Do not let my lord be angry that I cannot rise in your presence; I am having my period." So, despite his search, he did not find the household images.

[36]Jacob, now angered, confronted Laban and demanded, "What crime or offense have I committed that you should hound me? [37]Now that you have rummaged through all my things, what have you found from your household belongings? Produce it here before your kinsmen and mine, and let them decide between the two of us.

[38]In the twenty years that I was under you, no ewe or she-goat of yours ever miscarried, and I have never eaten rams of your flock. [39]I never brought you an animal torn by wild beasts; I

---

*[31:15] **Outsiders**: lit., "foreign women"; they lacked the favored legal status of native women. **Used up**: lit., "eaten, consumed"; the bridal price that a man received for giving his daughter in marriage was legally reserved as her inalienable dowry. Perhaps this is the reason that Rachel took the household images belonging to Laban.

†[31:19] **Household images**: in Hebrew, *teraphim*, figurines used in divination (Ez 21:26; Zec 10:2). Laban calls them his "gods" (v. 30). The traditional translation "idols" is avoided because it suggests false gods, whereas Genesis seems to accept the fact that the ancestors did not always live according to later biblical religious standards and laws.

‡[31:20] **Hoodwinked**: lit., "stolen the heart of," i.e., lulled the mind of. **Aramean**: the earliest extra-biblical references to the Arameans date later than the time of Jacob, if Jacob is dated to the mid-second millennium; to call Laban an Aramean and to have him speak Aramaic (Jegar-sahadutha, v. 47) is an apparent anachronism. The word may have been chosen to underscore the growing estrangement between the two men and the fact that their descendants will be two different peoples.

§[31:23] **For seven days**: lit., "a way of seven days," a general term to designate a long distance; it would actually have taken a camel caravan many more days to travel from Haran

to Gilead, the region east of the northern half of the Jordan. The mention of camels in this passage is apparently anachronistic since camels were not domesticated until the late second millennium.

¶[31:26] **Prisoners of war**: lit., "women captured by the sword"; the women of a conquered people were treated as part of the victor's spoil; cf. 1 Sm 30:2; 2 Kgs 5:2.

**[31:34] As in chap. 27, a younger child (Rachel) deceives her father to gain what belongs to him.

---

p. [31:7] Jdt 8:26. q. [31:13] Gn 28:18. r. [31:16] Wis 10:10–11. s. [31:19] Gn 31:34; 1 Sm 19:13.

t. [31:24] Wis 10:12. u. [31:34] Gn 31:19. v. [31:39] Ex 22:12.

made good the loss myself. You held me responsible for anything stolen by day or night.* ⁴⁰Often the scorching heat devoured me by day, and the frost by night, while sleep fled from my eyes! ⁴¹Of the twenty years that I have now spent in your household, I served you fourteen years for your two daughters and six years for your flock, while you changed my wages ten times. ⁴²If the God of my father, the God of Abraham and the Fear of Isaac, had not been on my side, you would now have sent me away empty-handed. But God saw my plight and the fruits of my toil, and last night he reproached you."ʷ

⁴³†Laban replied to Jacob: "The daughters are mine, their children are mine, and the flocks are mine; everything you see belongs to me. What can I do now for my own daughters and for the children they have borne? ⁴⁴‡Come, now, let us make a covenant, you and I; and it will be a treaty between you and me."

⁴⁵Then Jacob took a stone and set it up as a sacred pillar.ˣ ⁴⁶Jacob said to his kinsmen, "Gather stones." So they got stones and made a mound; and they ate there at the mound. ⁴⁷Laban called it Jegar-sahadutha,§ but Jacob called it Galeed. ⁴⁸Laban said, "This mound will be a witness from now on between you and me." That is why it was named Galeed— ⁴⁹and also Mizpah,⁵ for he said: "May the LORD keep watch between you and me when we are out of each other's sight. ⁵⁰If you mistreat my daughters, or take other wives besides my daughters, know that even though no one else is there, God will be a witness between you and me."

⁵¹Laban said further to Jacob: "Here is this mound, and here is the sacred pillar that I have set up between you and me. ⁵²This mound will be a witness, and this sacred pillar will be a witness, that, with hostile intent, I may not pass beyond this mound into your territory, nor may you pass beyond it into mine. ⁵³May the God of Abraham and the God of Nahor, the God of

their father, judge between us!" Jacob took the oath by the Fear of his father Isaac.** ⁵⁴He then offered a sacrifice on the mountain and invited his kinsmen to share in the meal. When they had eaten, they passed the night on the mountain.

## CHAPTER 32

¹††Early the next morning, Laban kissed his grandchildren and his daughters and blessed them; then he set out on his journey back home. ²Meanwhile Jacob continued on his own way, and God's angels encountered him. ³When Jacob saw them he said, "This is God's encampment." So he named that place Mahanaim.‡‡

**Envoys to Esau.** ⁴Jacob sent messengers ahead to his brother Esau in the land of Seir, the country of Edom,ʸ ⁵ordering them: "Thus you shall say to my lord Esau: 'Thus says your servant Jacob: I have been residing with Laban and have been delayed until now. ⁶I own oxen, donkeys and sheep, as well as male and female servants. I have sent my lord this message in the hope of gaining your favor.'" ⁷When the messengers returned to Jacob, they said, "We found your brother Esau. He is now coming to meet you, and four hundred men are with him."

⁸Jacob was very much frightened. In his anxiety, he divided the people who were with him, as well as his flocks, herds and camels, into two camps. ⁹"If Esau should come and attack one camp," he reasoned, "the remaining camp may still escape." ¹⁰Then Jacob prayed: "God of my father Abraham and God of my father Isaac! You, LORD, who said to me, 'Go back to your land and your relatives, and I will be good to you.'ᶻ ¹¹I am unworthy of all the acts of kindness and faithfulness that you have performed for your servant: although I crossed the Jordan here with nothing but my staff, I have now grown into two camps. ¹²Save me from the hand of my brother, from the hand of Esau! Otherwise I fear that he will come and strike me down and the mothers with the children. ¹³You yourself said, 'I will be very good to you, and I will make your descendants like the sands of the sea, which are too numerous to count.'"ᵃ

¹⁴After passing the night there, Jacob selected from what he had with him a present for his brother Esau: ¹⁵two hundred she-goats and twenty he-goats; two hundred ewes and

---

*[31:39] Jacob's actions are more generous than the customs suggested in the Code of Hammurabi: "If in a sheepfold an act of god has occurred, or a lion has made a kill, the shepherd shall clear himself before the deity, and the owner of the fold must accept the loss" (par. 266); cf. Ex 22:12.

†[31:43–54] In this account of the non-aggression treaty between Laban and Jacob, the different objects that serve as witness (sacred pillar in v. 45, cairn of stones in v. 46), their different names (Jegar-sahadutha in v. 47, Mizpah in v. 49), and the two references to the covenant meal (vv. 46, 54) suggest that two versions have been fused. One version is the Yahwist source, and another source has been used to supplement it.

‡[31:44–54] The treaty is a typical covenant between two parties: Jacob was bound to treat his wives (Laban's daughters) well, and Laban was bound not to cross Jacob's boundaries with hostile intent.

§[31:47–48] **Jegar-sahadutha:** an Aramaic term meaning "mound of witness." **Galeed:** in Hebrew, "the mound of witness."

¶[31:49] **Mizpah:** a town in Gilead; cf. Jgs 10:17; 11:11, 34; Hos 5:1. The Hebrew name *mispa* ("lookout") is allied to *yisep yhwh* ("may the Lord keep watch"), and also echoes the word *masseba* ("sacred pillar").

w. [31:42] Gn 31:24, 29.  x. [31:45] Gn 28:18; 35:14.

**[31:53] **Fear of . . . Isaac:** an archaic title for Jacob's God of the Father.

††[32:1–22] Jacob's negotiations with Esau. Laban kisses his daughters and grandchildren good-bye but not Jacob. On leaving Mesopotamia, Jacob has an encounter with angels of God (vv. 2–3), which provokes him to exclaim, "This is God's encampment," just as he exclaimed upon leaving Canaan, "This is the house of God, the gateway to heaven" (28:11–17).

‡‡[32:3] **Mahanaim:** a town in Gilead (Jos 13:26, 30; 21:38; 2 Sm 2:8; etc.). The Hebrew name means "two camps." There are other allusions to the name in vv. 8, 11.

y. [32:4] Gn 36:6.  z. [32:10] Gn 31:3.  a. [32:13] Gn 28:14; 48:16; Ex 32:13; Heb 11:12.

twenty rams; [16]thirty female camels and their young; forty cows and ten bulls; twenty female donkeys and ten male donkeys. [17]He put these animals in the care of his servants, in separate herds, and he told the servants, "Go on ahead of me, but keep some space between the herds." [18]He ordered the servant in the lead, "When my brother Esau meets you and asks, 'To whom do you belong? Where are you going? To whom do these animals ahead of you belong?' [19]tell him, 'To your servant Jacob, but they have been sent as a gift to my lord Esau. Jacob himself is right behind us.'" [20]He also ordered the second servant and the third and all the others who followed behind the herds: "Thus and so you shall say to Esau, when you reach him; [21]and also tell him, 'Your servant Jacob is right behind us.'" For Jacob reasoned, "If I first appease him with a gift that precedes me, then later, when I face him, perhaps he will forgive me." [22]So the gifts went on ahead of him, while he stayed that night in the camp.

**Jacob's New Name.**[*] [23]That night, however, Jacob arose, took his two wives, with the two maidservants and his eleven children, and crossed the ford of the Jabbok. [24]After he got them and brought them across the wadi and brought over what belonged to him, [25]Jacob was left there alone. Then a man[†] wrestled with him until the break of dawn. [26]When the man saw that he could not prevail over him, he struck Jacob's hip at its socket, so that Jacob's socket was dislocated as he wrestled with him.[b] [27]The man then said, "Let me go, for it is daybreak." But Jacob said, "I will not let you go until you bless me." [28]"What is your name?" the man asked. He answered, "Jacob."[c] [29]Then the man said, "You shall no longer be named Jacob, but Israel,[‡] because you have contended with divine and human beings and have prevailed." [30]Jacob then asked him,

"Please tell me your name." He answered, "Why do you ask for my name?" With that, he blessed him. [31]Jacob named the place Peniel,[§] "because I have seen God face to face," he said, "yet my life has been spared."[d]

[32]At sunrise, as he left Penuel, Jacob limped along because of his hip. [33]That is why, to this day, the Israelites do not eat the sciatic muscle that is on the hip socket, because he had struck Jacob's hip socket at the sciatic muscle.

## CHAPTER 33

**Jacob and Esau Meet.**[¶] [1]Jacob looked up and saw Esau coming, and with him four hundred men. So he divided his children among Leah, Rachel, and the two maidservants, [2]putting the maidservants and their children first, Leah and her children next, and Rachel and Joseph last. [3]He himself went on ahead of them, bowing to the ground seven times, until he reached his brother. [4]Esau ran to meet him, embraced him, and flinging himself on his neck, kissed him as he wept.

[5]Then Esau looked up and saw the women and children and asked, "Who are these with you?" Jacob answered, "They are the children with whom God has graciously favored your servant." [6]Then the maidservants and their children came forward and bowed low; [7]next, Leah and her children came forward and bowed low; lastly, Joseph and Rachel came forward and bowed low. [8]Then Esau asked, "What did you intend with all those herds that I encountered?" Jacob answered, "It was to gain my lord's favor." [9]Esau replied, "I have plenty; my brother, you should keep what is yours." [10]"No, I beg you!" said Jacob. "If you will do me the favor, accept this gift from me, since to see your face is for me like seeing the face of God—and you have received me so kindly. [11]Accept the gift I have brought you. For God has been generous toward me, and I have an abundance." Since he urged him strongly, Esau accepted.

[12]Then Esau said, "Let us break camp and be on our way; I will travel in front of you." [13]But Jacob replied: "As my lord knows, the children are too young. And the flocks and herds that

---

*[32:23–33] As Jacob crosses over to the land promised him, worried about the impending meeting with Esau, he encounters a mysterious adversary in the night with whom he wrestles until morning. The cunning Jacob manages to wrest a blessing from the night stranger before he departs. There are folkloric elements in the tale—e.g., the trial of the hero before he can return home, the nocturnal demon's loss of strength at sunrise, the demon protecting its river, the power gained by knowledge of an opponent's name—but these have been worked into a coherent though elliptical narrative. The point of the tale seems to be that the ever-striving, ever-grasping Jacob must eventually strive with God to attain full possession of the blessing.

†[32:25] **A man**: as with Abraham's three visitors in chap. 18, who appear sometimes as three, two, and one (the latter being God), this figure is fluid; he loses the match but changes Jacob's name (v. 29), an act elsewhere done only by God (17:5, 15). A few deft narrative touches manage to express intimate contact with Jacob while preserving the transcendence proper to divinity.

‡[32:29] **Israel**: the first part of the Hebrew name *Yisrael* is given a popular explanation in the word *saritha*, "you contended"; the second part is the first syllable of *elohim*, "divine beings." The present incident, with a similar allusion to the name Israel, is referred to in Hos 12:5, where the mysterious wrestler is explicitly called an angel.

b. [32:26] Hos 12:5.   c. [32:28] Gn 35:10; 1 Kgs 18:31; 2 Kgs 17:34.

§[32:31] **Peniel**: a variant of the word Penuel (v. 32), the name of a town on the north bank of the Jabbok in Gilead (Jgs 8:8–9, 17; 1 Kgs 12:25). The name is explained as meaning "the face of God," *peni-'èl*. **Yet my life has been spared**: see note on 16:13.

¶[33:1–20] The truly frightening confrontation seems to have already occurred in Jacob's meeting the divine stranger in the previous chapter. In contrast, this meeting brings reconciliation. Esau, impulsive but largehearted, kisses the cunning Jacob and calls him brother (v. 9). Jacob in return asks Esau to accept his blessing (*berakah*, translated "gift," v. 11), giving back at least symbolically what he had taken many years before and responding to Esau's erstwhile complaint ("he has taken away my blessing," 27:36). Verses 12–17 show that the reconciliation is not total and, further, that Jacob does not intend to share the ancestral land with his brother.

d. [32:31] Jgs 13:22.

are nursing are a concern to me; if overdriven for even a single day, the whole flock will die. ¹⁴Let my lord, then, go before his servant, while I proceed more slowly at the pace of the livestock before me and at the pace of my children, until I join my lord in Seir." ¹⁵Esau replied, "Let me at least put at your disposal some of the people who are with me." But Jacob said, "Why is this that I am treated so kindly, my lord?" ¹⁶So on that day Esau went on his way back to Seir, ¹⁷and Jacob broke camp for Succoth.* There Jacob built a home for himself and made booths for his livestock. That is why the place was named Succoth.

¹⁸Jacob arrived safely at the city of Shechem, which is in the land of Canaan, when he came from Paddan-aram. He encamped in sight of the city.ᵉ ¹⁹The plot of ground on which he had pitched his tent he bought for a hundred pieces of money† from the descendants of Hamor, the father of Shechem.ᶠ ²⁰He set up an altar there and invoked "El, the God of Israel."ᵍ

## CHAPTER 34

**The Rape of Dinah.** ¹‡Dinah, the daughter whom Leah had borne to Jacob, went out to visit some of the women of the land. ²When Shechem, son of Hamor the Hivite,ˢ the leader of the region, saw her, he seized her and lay with her by force. ³He was strongly attracted to Dinah, daughter of Jacob, and was in love with the young woman. So he spoke affectionately to her. ⁴Shechem said to his father Hamor, "Get me this young woman for a wife."

⁵Meanwhile, Jacob heard that Shechem had defiled his daughter Dinah; but since his sons were out in the field with his livestock, Jacob kept quiet until they came home. ⁶Now Hamor, the father of Shechem, went out to discuss the matter with Jacob, ⁷just as Jacob's sons were coming in from the field. When they heard the news, the men were indignant and extremely angry.

Shechem had committed an outrage in Israel by lying with Jacob's daughter; such a thing is not done.ʰ ⁸Hamor appealed to them, saying: "My son Shechem has his heart set on your daughter. Please give her to him as a wife. ⁹Intermarry with us; give your daughters to us, and take our daughters for yourselves. ¹⁰Thus you can live among us. The land is open before you. Settle and move about freely in it and acquire holdings here."¶ ¹¹Then Shechem appealed to Dinah's father and brothers: "Do me this favor, and whatever you ask from me, I will give. ¹²No matter how high you set the bridal price and gift, I will give you whatever you ask from me; only give me the young woman as a wife."

**Revenge of Jacob's Sons.** ¹³Jacob's sons replied to Shechem and his father Hamor with guile, speaking as they did because he had defiled their sister Dinah. ¹⁴They said to them, "We are not able to do this thing: to give our sister to an uncircumcised man. For that would be a disgrace for us. ¹⁵Only on this condition will we agree to that: that you become like us by having every male among you circumcised. ¹⁶Then we will give you our daughters and take your daughters in marriage; we will settle among you and become one people. ¹⁷But if you do not listen to us and be circumcised, we will take our daughter and go."

¹⁸Their proposal pleased Hamor and his son Shechem. ¹⁹The young man lost no time in acting on the proposal, since he wanted Jacob's daughter. Now he was more highly regarded than anyone else in his father's house. ²⁰So Hamor and his son Shechem went to the gate of their city and said to the men of their city: ²¹"These men are friendly toward us. Let them settle in the land and move about in it freely; there is ample room in the land for them. We can take their daughters in marriage and give our daughters to them. ²²But only on this condition will the men agree to live with us and form one people with us: that every male among us be circumcised as they themselves are. ²³Would not their livestock, their property, and all their animals then be ours? Let us just agree with them, so that they will settle among us."

²⁴All who went out of the gate of the city listened to Hamor and his son Shechem, and all the males, all those who went out of the gate of the city,** were circumcised. ²⁵On the third day, while they were still in pain, two of Jacob's sons, Simeon and Levi, brothers of Dinah, each took his sword, advanced against the unsuspecting city and massacred all the males.ⁱ ²⁶After they

---

*[33:17] **Succoth:** an important town near the confluence of the Jabbok and the Jordan (Jos 13:27; Jgs 8:5–16; 1 Kgs 7:46). **Booths:** in Hebrew, *sukkot*, of the same sound as the name of the town.

†[33:19] **Pieces of money:** in Hebrew, *qesita*, a monetary unit of which the value is unknown. **Descendants of Hamor:** Hamorites, "the people of Hamor"; cf. Jgs 9:28. Hamor was regarded as the eponymous ancestor of the pre-Israelite inhabitants of Shechem.

‡[34:1–31] The story of the rape of Dinah and the revenge of Jacob's sons on the men of the city of Shechem may reflect the relations of the tribes of Simeon and Levi to their Canaanite neighbors around Shechem; the tribes are represented by their eponymous ancestors. Jacob's farewell testament (49:5–7) cites this incident as the reason for the decline of the tribes of Simeon and Levi. Ominously, vv. 30–31 leave the situation unresolved, with Jacob concerned about the welfare of the whole family, and Simeon and Levi concerned only about the honor of their full sister. The danger to the family from narrow self-interest will continue in the Joseph story.

§[34:2] **Hivite:** the Greek text has "Horite"; the terms were apparently used indiscriminately to designate the Hurrian or other non-Semitic elements in Palestine.

¶[34:10] Hamor seems to be making concessions to Jacob's family in the hope of avoiding warfare between the two families.

**[34:24] **All those who went out of the gate of the city:** apparently meaning all the residents. By temporarily crippling the men through circumcision, Jacob's sons deprived the city of its defenders.

---

e. [33:18] Gn 12:6; Jn 4:5.   f. [33:19] Jos 24:32; Jn 4:5; Acts 7:16.
g. [33:20] Jgs 6:24.

h. [34:7] 2 Sm 13:12.   i. [34:25] Gn 49:6.

had killed Hamor and his son Shechem with the sword, they took Dinah from Shechem's house and left.[j] [27]Then the other sons of Jacob followed up the slaughter and sacked the city because their sister had been defiled. [28]They took their sheep, cattle and donkeys, whatever was in the city and in the surrounding country. [29]They carried off all their wealth, their children, and their women, and looted whatever was in the houses.[k]

[30]Jacob said to Simeon and Levi: "You have brought trouble upon me by making me repugnant to the inhabitants of the land, the Canaanites and the Perizzites. I have so few men that, if these people unite against me and attack me, I and my household will be wiped out." [31]But they retorted, "Should our sister be treated like a prostitute?"

## CHAPTER 35

**Bethel Revisited.** [1]*God said to Jacob: Go up now to Bethel. Settle there and build an altar there to the God who appeared to you when you were fleeing from your brother Esau.[l] [2]So Jacob told his household and all who were with him: "Get rid of the foreign gods[†] among you; then purify yourselves and change your clothes. [3]Let us now go up to Bethel so that I might build an altar there to the God who answered me in the day of my distress and who has been with me wherever I have gone." [4]They gave Jacob all the foreign gods in their possession and also the rings they had in their ears[‡] and Jacob buried them under the oak that is near Shechem. [5]Then, as they set out, a great terror fell upon the surrounding towns, so that no one pursued the sons of Jacob.

[6]Thus Jacob and all the people who were with him arrived in Luz (now Bethel) in the land of Canaan.[m] [7]There he built an altar and called the place El-Bethel,[§] for it was there that God had revealed himself to him when he was fleeing from his brother.[n]

[8]Deborah, Rebekah's nurse, died. She was buried under the oak below Bethel, and so it was named Allon-bacuth.[¶]

[9]On Jacob's arrival from Paddan-aram, God appeared to him again and blessed him. [10]God said to him:

Your name is Jacob.
You will no longer be named Jacob,
    but Israel will be your name.[o]

So he was named Israel. [11]Then God said to him: I am God Almighty; be fruitful and multiply. A nation, indeed an assembly of nations, will stem from you, and kings will issue from your loins. [12]The land I gave to Abraham and Isaac I will give to you; and to your descendants after you I will give the land.[p]

[13]Then God departed from him. [14]In the place where God had spoken with him, Jacob set up a sacred pillar, a stone pillar, and upon it he made a libation and poured out oil.[q] [15]Jacob named the place where God spoke to him Bethel.

**Jacob's Family.** [16]Then they departed from Bethel; but while they still had some distance to go to Ephrath, Rachel went into labor and suffered great distress. [17]When her labor was most intense, the midwife said to her, "Do not fear, for now you have another son." [18]With her last breath—for she was at the point of death—she named him Ben-oni;[**] but his father named him Benjamin. [19]Thus Rachel died; and she was buried on the road to Ephrath (now Bethlehem).[††r] [20]Jacob set up a sacred pillar on her grave, and the same pillar marks Rachel's grave to this day.

[21]Israel moved on and pitched his tent beyond Migdal-eder. [22]While Israel was encamped in that region, Reuben went and lay with Bilhah, his father's concubine. When Israel heard of it, he was greatly offended.[‡‡s]

The sons of Jacob were now twelve. [23]The sons of Leah: Reuben, Jacob's firstborn, Simeon, Levi, Judah, Issachar, and Zebulun; [24]§§the sons of Rachel: Joseph and Benjamin; [25]the sons of Rachel's maidservant Bilhah: Dan and Naphtali; [26]the sons of Leah's maidservant Zilpah: Gad

---

*[35:1–7] Jacob returns to Bethel and founds the sanctuary, an event that forms a "bookend" to the first visit to Bethel in 28:10–22. To enter the Lord's sanctuary, one must purify oneself and get rid of all signs of allegiance to other gods (Jos 24:23; Jgs 10:16). Jacob also seems to initiate the custom of making a pilgrimage to Bethel (see Ps 122:1 and Is 2:3, 5).

†[35:2] **Foreign gods:** divine images, including those of household deities (see note on 31:19), that Jacob's people brought with them from Paddan-aram.

‡[35:4] **Rings . . . their ears:** the earrings may have belonged to the gods because earrings were often placed on statues.

§[35:7] **El-Bethel:** probably to be translated "the god of Bethel." This is one of several titles of God in Genesis that begin with *El* (= God), e.g., *El Olam* (21:33), *El Elyon* (14:18), *El* the God of Israel (33:20), and *El Shaddai*. Most of these (except *El Shaddai*) are tied to specific Israelite shrines.

¶[35:8] **Allon-bacuth:** the Hebrew name means "oak of weeping."

**[35:18] **Ben-oni:** means either "son of my vigor" or, more likely in the context, "son of affliction." **Benjamin:** "son of the right hand," meaning a son who is his father's help and support.

††[35:19] **Bethlehem:** the gloss comes from a later tradition that identified the site with Bethlehem, also called Ephrath or Ephratha (Jos 15:59; Ru 4:11; Mi 5:1). But Rachel's grave is actually near Ramah (Jer 31:15), a few miles north of Jerusalem, in the territory of Benjamin (1 Sm 10:2).

‡‡[35:22] The genealogy in vv. 23–29 is prefaced by a notice about Reuben's sleeping with Bilhah, his father's concubine. Such an act is a serious challenge to the authority of the father (cf. 2 Sm 3:7 and 16:21). In his final testament in chap. 49, Jacob cites this act of Reuben as the reason for Reuben's loss of the authority he had as firstborn son (49:4). Reuben's act is one more instance of strife in the family and of discord between father and son.

§§[35:24–26] Benjamin is here said to have been born in Paddan-aram, apparently because all twelve sons of Jacob are considered as a unit.

---

j. [34:26] Jdt 9:2.   k. [34:29] Jdt 9:3–4.   l. [35:1] Gn 28:12–13.
m. [35:6] Gn 28:19; Jos 18:13; Jgs 1:22–23.   n. [35:7] Gn 28:12–13.

o. [35:10] 1 Kgs 18:31; 2 Kgs 17:34.   p. [35:12] Ex 32:13; Heb 11:9.   q. [35:14] Gn 28:18; 31:45.   r. [35:19] Gn 48:7; 1 Sm 10:2; Mi 5:1.   s. [35:22] Gn 49:4; 1 Chr 5:1.

and Asher. These are the sons of Jacob who were born to him in Paddan-aram.

²⁷Jacob went home to his father Isaac at Mamre, in Kiriath-arba (now Hebron), where Abraham and Isaac had resided. ²⁸The length of Isaac's life was one hundred and eighty years; ²⁹then he breathed his last. He died as an old man and was gathered to his people. After a full life, his sons Esau and Jacob buried him.

## CHAPTER 36

**Edomite Lists.*** ¹These are the descendants of Esau (that is, Edom). ²ᵃEsau took his wives from among the Canaanite women: Adah, daughter of Elon the Hittite; Oholibamah, the daughter of Anah son of Zibeon the Hivite;ᵗ ³and Basemath, daughter of Ishmael and sister of Nebaioth. ⁴Adah bore Eliphaz to Esau; Basemath bore Reuel;ᵘ ⁵and Oholibamah bore Jeush, Jalam and Korah. These are the sons of Esau who were born to him in the land of Canaan.ᵛ

⁶Esau took his wives, his sons, his daughters, and all the members of his household, as well as his livestock, all his cattle, and all the property he had acquired in the land of Canaan, and went to the land of Seir, away from his brother Jacob.ʷ ⁷Their possessions had become too great for them to dwell together, and the land in which they were residing could not support them because of their livestock. ⁸So Esau settled in the highlands of Seir. (Esau is Edom.)ˣ ⁹These are the descendants of Esau,ᶻ ancestor of the Edomites, in the highlands of Seir.

¹⁰These are the names of the sons of Esau: Eliphaz, son of Adah, wife of Esau, and Reuel, son of Basemath, wife of Esau. ¹¹ʸThe sons of Eliphaz were Teman, Omar, Zepho, Gatam, and Kenaz. ¹²Timna was a concubine of Eliphaz, the son of Esau, and she bore Amalek to Eliphaz. Those were the sons of Adah, the wife of Esau. ¹³These were the sons of Reuel: Nahath, Zerah,

Shammah, and Mizzah. Those were the sons of Basemath, the wife of Esau.ᶻ ¹⁴These were the sons of Esau's wife Oholibamah—the daughter of Anah, son of Zibeon—whom she bore to Esau: Jeush, Jalam, and Korah.ᵃ

¹⁵These are the clans of the sons of Esau. The sons of Eliphaz, Esau's firstborn: the clans of Teman, Omar, Zepho, Kenaz, ¹⁶Korah, Gatam, and Amalek. These are the clans of Eliphaz in the land of Edom; they are the sons of Adah. ¹⁷These are the sons of Reuel, son of Esau: the clans of Nahath, Zerah, Shammah, and Mizzah. These are the clans of Reuel in the land of Edom; they are the sons of Basemath, wife of Esau. ¹⁸These were the sons of Oholibamah, wife of Esau: the clans of Jeush, Jalam, and Korah. These are the clans of Esau's wife Oholibamah, daughter of Anah. ¹⁹These are the sons of Esau—that is, Edom—according to their clans.

²⁰These are the sons of Seir the Horite,§ the inhabitants of the land: Lotan, Shobal, Zibeon, Anah,ᵇ ²¹Dishon, Ezer, and Dishan; those are the clans of the Horites, sons of Seir in the land of Edom. ²²ᶜThe sons of Lotan were Hori and Hemam, and Lotan's sister was Timna. ²³These are the sons of Shobal: Alvan, Mahanath, Ebal, Shepho, and Onam. ²⁴These are the sons of Zibeon: Aiah and Anah. He is the Anah who found water in the desert while he was pasturing the donkeys of his father Zibeon. ²⁵These are the children of Anah: Dishon and Oholibamah, daughter of Anah. ²⁶These are the sons of Dishon: Hemdan, Eshban, Ithran, and Cheran. ²⁷These are the sons of Ezer: Bilhan, Zaavan, and Akan. ²⁸These are the sons of Dishan: Uz and Aran. ²⁹These are the clans of the Horites: the clans of Lotan, Shobal, Zibeon, Anah, ³⁰Dishon, Ezer, and Dishan; those are the clans of the Horites, clan by clan, in the land of Seir.

³¹ᵈThese are the kings who reigned in the land of Edom before any king reigned over the Israelites.¶ ³²Bela, son of Beor, became king in Edom; the name of his city was Dinhabah. ³³When Bela died, Jobab, son of Zerah, from Bozrah, succeeded him as king. ³⁴When Jobab died, Husham, from the land of the Temanites, succeeded him as king. ³⁵When Husham died, Hadad, son of Bedad, succeeded him as king. He is the one who defeated Midian in the country of Moab; the name of his city was Avith. ³⁶When Hadad died, Samlah, from Masrekah, succeeded him as king.

---

*[36:1–43] The line of Esau. In the preceding chapter (35:22–26), the list of Jacob's children completes the narrative of Jacob; in this chapter, the narrative of Esau is complete when his descendants are listed. The notice of Abraham's death and burial in 25:7–10 was followed by a list of the line of his elder son Ishmael (25:12–18) and here Isaac's death and burial are followed by the line of Esau. The lines of both Ishmael and Esau are introduced by the same double formula, "These are the descendants of . . ." (25:12; 36:9) and "These are the names of the sons of . . ." (25:13; 36:10). The chapter consists of diverse material: vv. 1–3, Esau's wives; vv. 9–14, Esau's descendants; vv. 15–19, the clans of Esau; vv. 20–30, the Horites of Seir; vv. 31–39, the Edomite kings; vv. 40–43, the Edomites.

†[36:2–14] The names of Esau's wives and of their fathers given here differ considerably from their names cited from other old sources in 26:34 and 28:9. **Zibeon the Hivite**: in v. 20 he is called a "Horite"; see note on 34:2.

‡[36:9] **These are the descendants of Esau**: the original heading of the genealogy is preserved in v. 10 ("These are the names of the sons of Esau"). This use of the Priestly formula is secondary and should not be counted in the list of ten such formulas in Genesis.

§[36:20] **Seir the Horite**: according to Dt 2:12, the highlands of Seir were inhabited by Horites before they were occupied by the Edomites.

¶[36:31] **Before any king reigned over the Israelites**: obviously this statement was written after the time of Saul, Israel's first king. According to 1 Sm 14:47, Saul waged war against the Edomites; according to 2 Sm 8:2, 13–14 and 1 Kgs 11:14–17, David made Edom a vassal state and nearly wiped out the royal line. These events reflect the words of the Lord to Rebekah at the birth of the boys, "the older shall serve the younger" (25:23).

t. [36:2] Gn 26:34.   u. [36:4] 1 Chr 1:35.   v. [36:5] 1 Chr 1:35.   w. [36:6] Gn 32:4.   x. [36:8] Dt 2:4–5; Jos 24:4.   y. [36:11–12] 1 Chr 1:36.

z. [36:13] 1 Chr 1:37.   a. [36:14] 1 Chr 1:35.   b. [36:20–21] 1 Chr 1:38.   c. [36:22–28] 1 Chr 1:39–42.   d. [36:31–43] 1 Chr 1:43–54.

<sup>37</sup>When Samlah died, Shaul, from Rehoboth-on-the-River, succeeded him as king. <sup>38</sup>When Shaul died, Baal-hanan, son of Achbor, succeeded him as king. <sup>39</sup>When Baal-hanan, son of Achbor, died, Hadad succeeded him as king; the name of his city was Pau. His wife's name was Mehetabel, the daughter of Matred, son of Mezahab.

<sup>40</sup>These are the names of the clans of Esau identified according to their families and localities: the clans of Timna, Alvah, Jetheth, <sup>41</sup>Oholibamah, Elah, Pinon, <sup>42</sup>Kenaz, Teman, Mibzar, <sup>43</sup>Magdiel, and Iram. Those are the clans of the Edomites, according to their settlements in their territorial holdings—that is, of Esau, the ancestor of the Edomites.

## CHAPTER 37

**Joseph Sold into Egypt.** <sup>1</sup>Jacob settled in the land where his father had sojourned, the land of Canaan.* <sup>2</sup>This is the story of the family of Jacob.†

When Joseph was seventeen years old, he was tending the flocks with his brothers; he was an assistant to the sons of his father's wives Bilhah and Zilpah, and Joseph brought their father bad reports about them. <sup>3</sup>Israel loved Joseph best of all his sons, for he was the child of his old age; and he had made him a long ornamented tunic.‡ <sup>4</sup>When his brothers saw that their father loved him best of all his brothers, they hated him so much that they could not say a kind word to him.

<sup>5,6</sup>Once Joseph had a dream, and when he told his brothers, they hated him even more.<sup>e</sup>

<sup>6</sup>He said to them, "Listen to this dream I had. <sup>7</sup>There we were, binding sheaves in the field, when suddenly my sheaf rose to an upright position, and your sheaves formed a ring around my sheaf and bowed down to it." <sup>8</sup>His brothers said to him, "Are you really going to make yourself king over us? Will you rule over us?" So they hated him all the more because of his dreams and his reports.<sup>f</sup>

<sup>9</sup>Then he had another dream, and told it to his brothers. "Look, I had another dream," he said; "this time, the sun and the moon and eleven stars were bowing down to me." <sup>10</sup>When he told it to his father and his brothers, his father reproved him and asked, "What is the meaning of this dream of yours? Can it be that I and your mother and your brothers are to come and bow to the ground before you?" <sup>11</sup>So his brothers were furious at him but his father kept the matter in mind.

<sup>12</sup>One day, when his brothers had gone to pasture their father's flocks at Shechem, <sup>13</sup>Israel said to Joseph, "Are your brothers not tending our flocks at Shechem? Come and I will send you to them." "I am ready," Joseph answered. <sup>14</sup>"Go then," he replied; "see if all is well with your brothers and the flocks, and bring back word." So he sent him off from the valley of Hebron. When Joseph reached Shechem, <sup>15</sup>a man came upon him as he was wandering about in the fields. "What are you looking for?" the man asked him. <sup>16</sup>"I am looking for my brothers," he answered. "Please tell me where they are tending the flocks." <sup>17</sup>The man told him, "They have moved on from here; in fact, I heard them say, 'Let us go on to Dothan.'" So Joseph went after his brothers and found them in Dothan. <sup>18</sup>They saw him from a distance, and before he reached them, they plotted to kill him. <sup>19</sup>They said to one another: "Here comes that dreamer! <sup>20</sup>Come now, let us kill him and throw him into one of the cisterns here; we could say that a wild beast devoured him. We will see then what comes of his dreams."<sup>g</sup>

<sup>21</sup>‡But when Reuben heard this, he tried to save him from their hands, saying: "We must not take his life." <sup>22</sup>Then Reuben said, "Do not shed blood! Throw him into this cistern in the wilderness; but do not lay a hand on him." His purpose was to save him from their hands and restore him to his father.<sup>h</sup>

---

*[37:1] The statement points ahead to 47:27, "Thus Israel settled in the land of Egypt, in the region of Goshen." These two statements frame the Joseph narrative; the later material (47:28–49:33) is about Jacob; chap. 50 brings to a conclusion themes remaining from the earlier story. One aim of the Joseph story is to explain how Israel came to Egypt after sojourning so long in Canaan.

†[37:2] The Joseph story is great literature not only in its themes but in its art. The stories show an interest in the psychology of the characters; everyone acts "in character" yet there is never a doubt that a divine purpose is bringing events to their conclusion. According to a literary analysis, vv. 1–4 set the scene; vv. 5–36 introduce the dramatic tension in the form of a conflict within the family; chaps. 38–41 describe the journeys away from their family of the eponymous ancestors of the two great tribes of later times, Judah (chap. 38) and Joseph (chaps. 39–41) and their preliminary conclusions; chaps. 42–44 detail the famine and journeys for food (chaps. 42, 43) that bring the brothers and (indirectly) the father into fresh contact with a mature Joseph who now has the power of life and death over them; 45:1–47:27 is the resolution (reconciliation of Joseph to his brothers) and the salvation of the family.

‡[37:3] Jacob's favoring Joseph over his other sons is a cause of the brothers' attempt on his life. Throughout the story, Jacob is unaware of the impact of his favoritism on his other sons (cf. vv. 33–35; 42:36). **Long ornamented tunic:** the meaning of the Hebrew phrase is unclear. In 2 Sm 13:18–19, it is the distinctive dress of unmarried royal daughters. The "coat of many colors" in the Septuagint became the traditional translation. Ancient depictions of Semites in formal dress show them with long, ornamented robes and that is the most likely meaning here. Possibly, the young Joseph is given a coat that symbolizes honor beyond his years. Later, Pharaoh will clothe Joseph in a robe that symbolizes honor (41:42).

§[37:5–10] Joseph's dreams of ruling his brothers appear at first glance to be merely adolescent grandiosity, and they bring him only trouble. His later successes make it clear, however, that they were from God. Another confirmation of their divine source is the doubling of dreams (cf. 41:32).

¶[37:21–36] The chapter thus far is from the Yahwist source, as are also vv. 25–28a. But vv. 21–24 and 28b–36 are from another source (sometimes designated the Elohist source). In the latter, Reuben tries to rescue Joseph, who is taken in Reuben's absence by certain Midianites; in the Yahwist source, it is Judah who saves Joseph's life by having him sold to certain Ishmaelites. Although the two variant forms in which the story was handed down in early oral tradition differ in these minor points, they agree on the essential fact that Joseph was brought as a slave into Egypt because of the jealousy of his brothers.

---

e. [37:5] Gn 42:9.

f. [37:8] Gn 50:17–18.    g. [37:20] Gn 44:28.    h. [37:22] Gn 42:22.

²³So when Joseph came up to his brothers, they stripped him of his tunic, the long ornamented tunic he had on; ²⁴then they took him and threw him into the cistern. The cistern was empty; there was no water in it. ²⁵Then they sat down to eat. Looking up, they saw a caravan of Ishmaelites coming from Gilead, their camels laden with gum, balm, and resin to be taken down to Egypt.ⁱ ²⁶Judah said to his brothers: "What is to be gained by killing our brother and concealing his blood?ʲ ²⁷Come, let us sell him to these Ishmaelites, instead of doing away with him ourselves. After all, he is our brother, our own flesh." His brothers agreed. ²⁸Midianite traders passed by, and they pulled Joseph up out of the cistern. They sold Joseph for twenty pieces of silver* to the Ishmaelites, who took him to Egypt.ᵏ ²⁹When Reuben went back to the cistern and saw that Joseph was not in it, he tore his garments,† ³⁰and returning to his brothers, he exclaimed: "The boy is gone! And I—where can I turn?" ³¹They took Joseph's tunic, and after slaughtering a goat, dipped the tunic in its blood. ³²Then they sent someone to bring the long ornamented tunic to their father, with the message: "We found this. See whether it is your son's tunic or not." ³³He recognized it and exclaimed: "My son's tunic! A wild beast has devoured him! Joseph has been torn to pieces!"ˡ ³⁴Then Jacob tore his garments, put sackcloth on his loins, and mourned his son many days. ³⁵Though his sons and daughters tried to console him, he refused all consolation, saying, "No, I will go down mourning to my son in Sheol."‡ Thus did his father weep for him.ᵐ

³⁶The Midianites, meanwhile, sold Joseph in Egypt to Potiphar, an official of Pharaoh and his chief steward.ⁿ

## CHAPTER 38

**Judah and Tamar.**§ ¹About that time Judah went down, away from his brothers, and pitched his tent near a certain Adullamite named Hirah. ²There Judah saw the daughter of a Canaanite named Shua; he married her, and had intercourse with her.ᵒ ³She conceived and bore a son, whom she named Er. ⁴Again she conceived and bore a son, whom she named Onan. ⁵Then she bore still another son, whom she named Shelah. She was in Chezib¶ when she bore him.ᵖ

⁶Judah got a wife named Tamar for his firstborn, Er. ⁷But Er, Judah's firstborn, greatly offended the LORD; so the LORD took his life.�q ⁸Then Judah said to Onan, "Have intercourse with your brother's wife, in fulfillment of your duty as brother-in-law, and thus preserve your brother's line."** ⁹Onan, however, knew that the offspring would not be his; so whenever he had intercourse with his brother's wife, he wasted his seed on the ground, to avoid giving offspring to his brother. ¹⁰What he did greatly offended the LORD, and the LORD took his life too. ¹¹Then Judah said to his daughter-in-law Tamar, "Remain a widow in your father's house until my son Shelah grows up"—for he feared that Shelah also might die like his brothers. So Tamar went to live in her father's house.

¹²Time passed, and the daughter of Shua, Judah's wife, died. After Judah completed the period of mourning, he went up to Timnah, to those who were shearing his sheep, in company with his friend Hirah the Adullamite. ¹³Then Tamar was told, "Your father-in-law is on his way up to Timnah to shear his sheep." ¹⁴So she took off her widow's garments, covered herself with a shawl, and having wrapped herself sat down at the entrance to Enaim, which is on the way to Timnah; for she was aware that, although Shelah was now grown up, she had not been given to him in marriage.ʳ ¹⁵When Judah saw her, he thought she was a harlot, since she had covered her face. ¹⁶So he went over to her at the roadside and said, "Come, let me have intercourse with you," for he did not realize that she was his daughter-in-law. She replied, "What will you pay me for letting you have intercourse with me?" ¹⁷He answered, "I will send you a young goat from the flock." "Very well," she said, "provided you leave me a pledge until you send it." ¹⁸Judah asked, "What pledge should I leave

---

*[37:28] **They sold Joseph . . . silver**: editors tried to solve the confusion, created by different sources, by supposing that it was the Midianite traders who pulled Joseph out of the pit and sold him to Ishmaelites. In all probability, one source had the brothers selling Joseph to Ishmaelites, whereas the other had them cast him into the pit whence he was taken by Midianite traders.

†[37:29] **Tore his garments**: the traditional sign of mourning in the ancient Near East.

‡[37:35] **Sheol**: see note on Ps 6:6.

§[38:1–30] This chapter has subtle connections to the main Joseph story. It tells of the eponymous founder of the other great tribe of later times, Judah. Having already been introduced as one of the two good brothers in 37:26–27, he appears here as the father-in-law of the twice-widowed Tamar; he has reneged on his promise to provide his son Shelah to her in a levirate marriage. Unjustly treated, Tamar takes matters into her own hands and tricks Judah into becoming the father of her children, Perez and Zerah. Judah ultimately acknowledges that his daughter-in-law was right ("She is in the right rather than I," v. 26). In contrast to Judah's expectations, the family

line does not continue through his son Shelah, but through the children of Tamar. Similarities relate this little story to the main narrative: the deception involving an article of clothing (the widow's garments of Tamar, Judah's seal, cord, and staff) point back to the bloody tunic that deceives Jacob in 37:31–33; a woman attempts the seduction of a man separated from his family, for righteous purposes in chap. 38, for unrighteous purposes in chap. 39.

¶[38:5] **Chezib**: a variant form of Achzib (Jos 15:44; Mi 1:14), a town in the Judean Shephelah.

**[38:8] **Preserve your brother's line**: lit., "raise up seed for your brother": an allusion to the law of levirate, or "brother-in-law," marriage; see notes on Dt 25:5; Ru 2:20. Onan's violation of this law brought on him God's punishment (vv. 9–10).

---

i. [37:25] Gn 43:11.    j. [37:26] Jb 16:18.    k. [37:28] Ps 105:17; Wis 10:13; Acts 7:9.    l. [37:33] Gn 44:28.    m. [37:35] Gn 42:38. n. [37:36] Ps 105:17.

o. [38:2] 1 Chr 2:3.    p. [38:5] 1 Chr 4:21.    q. [38:7] 1 Chr 2:3. r. [38:8] Dt 25:5; Mt 22:24; Mk 12:19; Lk 20:28.    s. [38:14] Prv 7:10.

you?" She answered, "Your seal and cord,* and the staff in your hand." So he gave them to her and had intercourse with her, and she conceived by him. [19]After she got up and went away, she took off her shawl and put on her widow's garments again.

[20]Judah sent the young goat by his friend the Adullamite to recover the pledge from the woman; but he did not find her. [21]So he asked the men of that place, "Where is the prostitute,† the one by the roadside in Enaim?" But they answered, "No prostitute has been here." [22]He went back to Judah and told him, "I did not find her; and besides, the men of the place said, 'No prostitute has been here.'" [23]"Let her keep the things," Judah replied; "otherwise we will become a laughingstock. After all, I did send her this young goat, but you did not find her."

[24]About three months later, Judah was told, "Your daughter-in-law Tamar has acted like a harlot and now she is pregnant from her harlotry." Judah said, "Bring her out; let her be burned." [25]But as she was being brought out, she sent word to her father-in-law, "It is by the man to whom these things belong that I am pregnant." Then she said, "See whose seal and cord and staff these are." [26]Judah recognized them and said, "She is in the right rather than I, since I did not give her to my son Shelah." He had no further sexual relations with her.

[27]When the time of her delivery came, there were twins in her womb.[t] [28]While she was giving birth, one put out his hand; and the midwife took and tied a crimson thread on his hand, noting, "This one came out first." [29]But as he withdrew his hand, his brother came out; and she said, "What a breach you have made for yourself!" So he was called Perez.‡ [30]Afterward his brother, who had the crimson thread on his hand, came out; he was called Zerah.§[v]

## CHAPTER 39

**Joseph's Temptation.** [1]When Joseph was taken down to Egypt, an Egyptian, Potiphar, an official of Pharaoh and his chief steward, bought him from the Ishmaelites who had brought him there. [2]The LORD was with Joseph and

he enjoyed great success and was assigned to the household of his Egyptian master. [3]When his master saw that the LORD was with him and brought him success in whatever he did, [4]he favored Joseph and made him his personal attendant; he put him in charge of his household and entrusted to him all his possessions.[x] [5]From the moment that he put him in charge of his household and all his possessions, the LORD blessed the Egyptian's house for Joseph's sake; the LORD's blessing was on everything he owned, both inside the house and out. [6]Having left everything he owned in Joseph's charge, he gave no thought, with Joseph there, to anything but the food he ate.

Now Joseph was well-built and handsome. [7]After a time, his master's wife looked at him with longing and said, "Lie with me." [8]But he refused and said to his master's wife, "Look, as long as I am here, my master does not give a thought to anything in the house, but has entrusted to me all he owns. [9]He has no more authority in this house than I do. He has withheld from me nothing but you, since you are his wife. How, then, could I do this great wrong and sin against God?" [10]Although she spoke to him day after day, he would not agree to lie with her, or even be near her.[y]

[11]One such day, when Joseph came into the house to do his work, and none of the household servants were then in the house, [12]she laid hold of him by his cloak, saying, "Lie with me!" But leaving the cloak in her hand, he escaped and ran outside. [13]When she saw that he had left his cloak in her hand as he escaped outside, [14]she cried out to her household servants and told them, "Look! My husband has brought us a Hebrew man to mock us! He came in here to lie with me, but I cried out loudly. [15]When he heard me scream, he left his cloak beside me and escaped and ran outside."

[16]She kept the cloak with her until his master came home. [17]Then she told him the same story: "The Hebrew slave whom you brought us came to me to amuse himself at my expense. [18]But when I screamed, he left his cloak beside me and escaped outside." [19]When the master heard his wife's story in which she reported, "Thus and so your servant did to me," he became enraged. [20]Joseph's master seized him and put him into the jail where the king's prisoners were confined.[z] And there he sat, in jail.

[21]But the LORD was with Joseph, and showed him kindness by making the chief jailer well-disposed toward him.[a] [22]The chief jailer put Joseph in charge of all the prisoners in the jail. Everything that had to be done there, he was the one to do it. [23]The chief jailer did not have to look after anything that was in Joseph's charge,

---

*[38:18] **Seal and cord:** the cylinder seal, through which a hole was bored lengthwise so that it could be worn from the neck by a cord, was a distinctive means of identification. Apparently one's staff could also be marked with some sign of identification (cf. Nm 17:17–18).

†[38:21] **Prostitute:** the Hebrew term *qedesha*, lit., "consecrated woman," designates a woman associated with a sanctuary whose activities could include prostitution; cf. Dt 23:18; Hos 4:14, where the same Hebrew word is used. In 38:15 and 24 the common word for prostitute, *zona*, is used.

‡[38:29] **He was called Perez:** the Hebrew word means "breach."

§[38:30] **He was called Zerah:** a name connected here by popular etymology with a Hebrew word for the red light of dawn, alluding apparently to the crimson thread.

t. [38:27] 1 Chr 2:4.   u. [38:29] Ru 4:12; Mt 1:3; Lk 3:33.   v. [38:30] Nm 26:20; 1 Chr 2:4; Mt 1:3.   w. [39:2] 1 Sm 3:19; 10:7; 18:14; 2 Sm 5:10; 2 Kgs 18:7; Acts 7:9.

x. [39:4] Dn 1:9.   y. [39:10] 1 Mc 2:53.   z. [39:20] Ps 105:18.   a. [39:21] Acts 7:9–10.

since the LORD was with him and was bringing success to whatever he was doing.

## CHAPTER 40

**The Dreams Interpreted.** [1]*Some time afterward, the royal cupbearer and baker offended their lord, the king of Egypt. [2]Pharaoh was angry with his two officials, the chief cupbearer and the chief baker, [3]and he put them in custody in the house of the chief steward, the same jail where Joseph was confined. [4]The chief steward assigned Joseph to them, and he became their attendant.

After they had been in custody for some time, [5]the cupbearer and the baker of the king of Egypt who were confined in the jail both had dreams on the same night, each his own dream and each dream with its own meaning. [6]When Joseph came to them in the morning, he saw that they looked disturbed. [7]So he asked Pharaoh's officials who were with him in custody in his master's house, "Why do you look so troubled today?" [8]They answered him, "We have had dreams, but there is no one to interpret them." Joseph said to them, "Do interpretations not come from God? Please tell me the dreams."[b]

[9]Then the chief cupbearer told Joseph his dream. "In my dream," he said, "I saw a vine in front of me, [10]and on the vine were three branches. It had barely budded when its blossoms came out, and its clusters ripened into grapes. [11]Pharaoh's cup was in my hand; so I took the grapes, pressed them out into his cup, and put it in Pharaoh's hand." [12]Joseph said to him: "This is its interpretation. The three branches are three days; [13]within three days Pharaoh will single you out[†] and restore you to your post. You will be handing Pharaoh his cup as you formerly did when you were his cupbearer. [14]Only think of me when all is well with you, and please do me the great favor of mentioning me to Pharaoh, to get me out of this place. [15]The truth is that I was kidnapped from the land of the Hebrews, and I have not done anything here that they should have put me into a dungeon."

[16]When the chief baker saw that Joseph had given a favorable interpretation, he said to him: "I too had a dream. In it I had three bread baskets on my head; [17]in the top one were all kinds of bakery products for Pharaoh, but the birds were eating them out of the basket on my head." [18]Joseph said to him in reply: "This is its interpretation. The three baskets are three days; [19]within three days Pharaoh will single you out

and will impale you on a stake, and the birds will be eating your flesh."

[20]And so on the third day, which was Pharaoh's birthday, when he gave a banquet to all his servants, he singled out the chief cupbearer and chief baker in the midst of his servants. [21]He restored the chief cupbearer to his office, so that he again handed the cup to Pharaoh; [22]but the chief baker he impaled—just as Joseph had told them in his interpretation. [23]Yet the chief cupbearer did not think of Joseph; he forgot him.

## CHAPTER 41

**Pharaoh's Dream.** [1]‡After a lapse of two years, Pharaoh had a dream. He was standing by the Nile, [2]when up out of the Nile came seven cows, fine-looking and fat; they grazed in the reed grass. [3]Behind them seven other cows, poor-looking and gaunt, came up out of the Nile; and standing on the bank of the Nile beside the others, [4]the poor-looking, gaunt cows devoured the seven fine-looking, fat cows. Then Pharaoh woke up.

[5]He fell asleep again and had another dream. He saw seven ears of grain, fat and healthy, growing on a single stalk. [6]Behind them sprouted seven ears of grain, thin and scorched by the east wind; [7]and the thin ears swallowed up the seven fat, healthy ears. Then Pharaoh woke up—it was a dream!

[8]Next morning his mind was agitated. So Pharaoh had all the magicians[§] and sages of Egypt summoned and recounted his dream to them; but there was no one to interpret it for him. [9]Then the chief cupbearer said to Pharaoh: "Now I remember my negligence! [10]Once, when Pharaoh was angry with his servants, he put me and the chief baker in custody in the house of the chief steward. [11]Later, we both had dreams on the same night, and each of our dreams had its own meaning. [12]There was a Hebrew youth with us, a slave of the chief steward; and when we told him our dreams, he interpreted them for us and explained for each of us the meaning of his dream.[c] [13]Things turned out just as he had told us: I was restored to my post, but the other man was impaled."

[14]Pharaoh therefore had Joseph summoned, and they hurriedly brought him from the dungeon. After he shaved and changed his clothes,

---

*[40:1] Joseph interprets the dreams of the Pharaoh's two officials. His ability to interpret the dreams shows that God is still with him and points forward to his role of dream interpreter for Pharaoh in chap. 41.

†[40:13] **Single you out**: lit., "lift up your head" (see also vv. 19, 20).

b. [40:8] Gn 41:16.

‡[41:1–57] Joseph correctly interprets Pharaoh's dream and becomes second in command over all Egypt.

§[41:8] **Magicians**: one of the tasks of the "magicians" was interpreting dreams. The interpretation of dreams was a long-standing practice in Egypt. A manual of dream interpretation has been found, written in the early second millennium and re-published later in which typical dreams are given ("If a man sees himself in a dream . . .") followed by a judgment of "good" or "bad." Interpreters were still needed for dreams, however, and Pharaoh complains that none of his dream interpreters can interpret his unprecedented dream. The same term will be used of Pharaoh's magicians in Exodus.

c. [41:12] Dn 1:17.

he came to Pharaoh.*d* ¹⁵Pharaoh then said to Joseph: "I had a dream but there was no one to interpret it. But I hear it said of you, 'If he hears a dream he can interpret it.'" ¹⁶"It is not I," Joseph replied to Pharaoh, "but God who will respond for the well-being of Pharaoh."*e*

¹⁷Then Pharaoh said to Joseph: "In my dream, I was standing on the bank of the Nile, ¹⁸when up from the Nile came seven cows, fat and well-formed; they grazed in the reed grass. ¹⁹Behind them came seven other cows, scrawny, most ill-formed and gaunt. Never have I seen such bad specimens as these in all the land of Egypt! ²⁰The gaunt, bad cows devoured the first seven fat cows. ²¹But when they had consumed them, no one could tell that they had done so, because they looked as bad as before. Then I woke up. ²²In another dream I saw seven ears of grain, full and healthy, growing on a single stalk. ²³Behind them sprouted seven ears of grain, shriveled and thin and scorched by the east wind; ²⁴and the seven thin ears swallowed up the seven healthy ears. I have spoken to the magicians, but there is no one to explain it to me."

²⁵Joseph said to Pharaoh: "Pharaoh's dreams have the same meaning. God has made known to Pharaoh what he is about to do. ²⁶The seven healthy cows are seven years, and the seven healthy ears are seven years—the same in each dream. ²⁷The seven thin, bad cows that came up after them are seven years, as are the seven thin ears scorched by the east wind; they are seven years of famine. ²⁸Things are just as I told Pharaoh: God has revealed to Pharaoh what he is about to do. ²⁹Seven years of great abundance are now coming throughout the land of Egypt; ³⁰but seven years of famine will rise up after them, when all the abundance will be forgotten in the land of Egypt. When the famine has exhausted the land, ³¹no trace of the abundance will be found in the land because of the famine that follows it, for it will be very severe. ³²That Pharaoh had the same dream twice means that the matter has been confirmed by God and that God will soon bring it about.

³³"Therefore, let Pharaoh seek out a discerning and wise man and put him in charge of the land of Egypt. ³⁴Let Pharaoh act and appoint overseers for the land to organize it during the seven years of abundance. ³⁵They should collect all the food of these coming good years, gathering the grain under Pharaoh's authority, for food in the cities, and they should guard it. ³⁶This food will serve as a reserve for the country against the seven years of famine that will occur in the land of Egypt, so that the land may not perish in the famine."

³⁷This advice pleased Pharaoh and all his servants.*f* ³⁸"Could we find another like him," Pharaoh asked his servants, "a man so endowed with the spirit of God?" ³⁹So Pharaoh said to Joseph: "Since God has made all this known to you, there is no one as discerning and wise as you are. ⁴⁰You shall be in charge of my household, and all my people will obey your command. Only in respect to the throne will I outrank you."*g* ⁴¹Then Pharaoh said to Joseph, "Look, I put you in charge of the whole land of Egypt." ⁴²With that, Pharaoh took off his signet ring* and put it on Joseph's finger. He dressed him in robes of fine linen and put a gold chain around his neck. ⁴³He then had him ride in his second chariot, and they shouted "Abrek!"† before him.

Thus was Joseph installed over the whole land of Egypt. ⁴⁴"I am Pharaoh," he told Joseph, "but without your approval no one shall lift hand or foot in all the land of Egypt." ⁴⁵Pharaoh also bestowed the name of Zaphenath-paneah‡ on Joseph, and he gave him in marriage Asenath, the daughter of Potiphera, priest of Heliopolis. And Joseph went out over the land of Egypt. ⁴⁶Joseph was thirty years old when he entered the service of Pharaoh, king of Egypt.

After Joseph left Pharaoh, he went throughout the land of Egypt. ⁴⁷During the seven years of plenty, when the land produced abundant crops, ⁴⁸he collected all the food of these years of plenty that the land of Egypt was enjoying and stored it in the cities, placing in each city the crops of the fields around it. ⁴⁹Joseph collected grain like the sands of the sea, so much that at last he stopped measuring it, for it was beyond measure.

⁵⁰Before the famine years set in, Joseph became the father of two sons, borne to him by Asenath, daughter of Potiphera, priest of Heliopolis.*h* ⁵¹Joseph named his firstborn Manasseh,§ meaning, "God has made me forget entirely my troubles and my father's house"; ⁵²and the second he named Ephraim,¶ meaning, "God has made me fruitful in the land of my affliction."

---

*[41:42] **Signet ring**: a finger ring in which was set a stamp seal, different from the cylinder seal such as Judah wore; see note on 38:18. By receiving Pharaoh's signet ring, Joseph was made vizier of Egypt (v. 43); the vizier was known as "sealbearer of the king of Lower Egypt." The gold chain was a symbol of high office in ancient Egypt.

†[41:43] **Abrek**: apparently a cry of homage, though the word's derivation and actual meaning are uncertain.

‡[41:45] **Zaphenath-paneah**: a Hebrew transcription of an Egyptian name meaning "the god speaks and he (the newborn child) lives." **Asenath**: means "belonging to (the Egyptian goddess) Neith." **Potiphera**: means "he whom Ra (the Egyptian god) gave"; a shorter form of the same name was borne by Joseph's master (37:36). **Heliopolis**: in Hebrew, *On*, a city seven miles northeast of modern Cairo, site of the chief temple of the sun god; it is mentioned also in v. 50; 46:20; Ez 30:17.

§[41:51] **Manasseh**: an allusion to this name is in the Hebrew expression, *nishshani*, "he made me forget."

¶[41:52] **Ephraim**: related to the Hebrew expression *hiphrani*, "(God) has made me fruitful." The name originally meant something like "fertile land."

d. [41:14] Ps 105:20.    e. [41:16] Gn 40:8.    f. [41:37] Acts 7:10.

g. [41:40] 1 Mc 2:53; Ps 105:21; Wis 10:14; Acts 7:10.    h. [41:50] Gn 46:20; 48:5.

⁵³When the seven years of abundance enjoyed by the land of Egypt came to an end, ⁵⁴the seven years of famine set in, just as Joseph had said. Although there was famine in all the other countries, food was available throughout the land of Egypt.ⁱ ⁵⁵When all the land of Egypt became hungry and the people cried to Pharaoh for food, Pharaoh said to all the Egyptians: "Go to Joseph and do whatever he tells you." ⁵⁶When the famine had spread throughout the land, Joseph opened all the cities that had grain and rationed it to the Egyptians, since the famine had gripped the land of Egypt. ⁵⁷Indeed, the whole world came to Egypt to Joseph to buy grain, for famine had gripped the whole world.

## CHAPTER 42
### The Brothers' First Journey to Egypt.* ¹When Jacob learned that grain rations were for sale in Egypt, he said to his sons: "Why do you keep looking at one another?" ²He went on, "I hear that grain is for sale in Egypt. Go down there and buy some for us, that we may stay alive and not die."ʲ ³So ten of Joseph's brothers went down to buy grain from Egypt. ⁴But Jacob did not send Joseph's brother Benjamin with his brothers, for he thought some disaster might befall him. ⁵And so the sons of Israel were among those who came to buy grain, since there was famine in the land of Canaan.ᵏ

⁶Joseph, as governor of the country, was the one who sold grain to all the people of the land. When Joseph's brothers came, they bowed down to him with their faces to the ground.ˡ ⁷He recognized them as soon as he saw them. But he concealed his own identity from them and spoke harshly to them. "Where do you come from?" he asked them. They answered, "From the land of Canaan, to buy food."

⁸When Joseph recognized his brothers, although they did not recognize him, ⁹he was reminded of the dreams he had about them. He said to them: "You are spies.ᵐ You have come to see the weak points† of the land." ¹⁰"No, my lord," they replied. "On the contrary, your servants have come to buy food. ¹¹All of us are sons of the same man. We are honest men; your servants have never been spies." ¹²But he answered them: "Not so! It is the weak points of the land

that you have come to see." ¹³"We your servants," they said, "are twelve brothers, sons of a certain man in Canaan; but the youngest one is at present with our father, and the other one is no more."ⁿ ¹⁴"It is just as I said," Joseph persisted, "you are spies. ¹⁵This is how you shall be tested: I swear by the life of Pharaoh that you shall not leave here unless your youngest brother comes here. ¹⁶So send one of your number to get your brother, while the rest of you stay here under arrest. Thus will your words be tested for their truth; if they are untrue, as Pharaoh lives, you are spies!" ¹⁷With that, he locked them up in the guardhouse for three days.

¹⁸On the third day Joseph said to them: "Do this, and you shall live; for I am a God-fearing man. ¹⁹If you are honest men, let one of your brothers be confined in this prison, while the rest of you go and take home grain for your starving families. ²⁰But you must bring me your youngest brother. Your words will thus be verified, and you will not die." To this they agreed.ᵒ ²¹To one another, however, they said: "Truly we are being punished because of our brother. We saw the anguish of his heart when he pleaded with us, yet we would not listen. That is why this anguish has now come upon us."ᵖ ²²Then Reuben responded, "Did I not tell you, 'Do no wrong to the boy'? But you would not listen! Now comes the reckoning for his blood."�q ²³They did not know, of course, that Joseph understood what they said, since he spoke with them through an interpreter. ²⁴But turning away from them, he wept. When he was able to speak to them again, he took Simeon from among them and bound him before their eyes. ²⁵Then Joseph gave orders to have their containers filled with grain, their money replaced in each one's sack, and provisions given them for their journey. After this had been done for them, ²⁶they loaded their donkeys with the grain and departed.

²⁷At the night encampment, when one of them opened his bag to give his donkey some fodder, he saw his money there in the mouth of his bag. ²⁸He cried out to his brothers, "My money has been returned! Here it is in my bag!" At that their hearts sank. Trembling, they asked one another, "What is this that God has done to us?"

²⁹When they got back to their father Jacob in the land of Canaan, they told him all that had happened to them. ³⁰"The man who is lord of the land," they said, "spoke to us harshly and put us in custody on the grounds that we were spying on the land. ³¹But we said to him: 'We are honest men; we have never been spies. ³²We are twelve brothers, sons of the same father; but one is no more, and the youngest one is now with our father in the land of Canaan.' ³³Then the man who is lord of the land said to us: 'This is how

---

*[42:1–38] The first journey of the brothers to Egypt. Its cause is famine, which was also the reason Abraham and Sarah undertook their dangerous journey to Egypt. The brothers bow to Joseph in v. 6, which fulfills Joseph's dream in 37:5–11. Endowed with wisdom, Joseph begins a process of instruction or "discipline" for his brothers that eventually forces them to recognize the enormity of their sin against him and the family. He controls their experience of the first journey with the result that the second journey in chaps. 43–44 leads to full acknowledgment and reconciliation.

†[42:9, 12] **Weak points:** lit., "the nakedness of the land"; the military weakness of the land, like human nakedness, should not be seen by strangers.

---

i. [41:54] Ps 105:16; Acts 7:11.   j. [42:2] Acts 7:12.   k. [42:5] Jdt 5:10; Acts 7:11.   l. [42:6] Ps 105:21.   m. [42:9] Gn 37:5.

n. [42:13] Gn 44:20.   o. [42:20] Gn 43:5.   p. [42:21] Gn 37:18–27.   q. [42:22] Gn 37:22.

I will know if you are honest men: leave one of your brothers with me, then take grain for your starving families and go. [34]When you bring me your youngest brother, and I know that you are not spies but honest men, I will restore your brother to you, and you may move about freely in the land.'"

[35]When they were emptying their sacks, there in each one's sack was his moneybag! At the sight of their moneybags, they and their father were afraid. [36]Their father Jacob said to them: "Must you make me childless? Joseph is no more, Simeon is no more, and now you would take Benjamin away! All these things have happened to me!" [37]Then Reuben told his father: "You may kill my own two sons if I do not return him to you! Put him in my care, and I will bring him back to you." [38]But Jacob replied: "My son shall not go down with you. Now that his brother is dead, he is the only one left. If some disaster should befall him on the journey you must make, you would send my white head down to Sheol in grief."[r]

## CHAPTER 43

**The Second Journey to Egypt.**[*] [1]Now the famine in the land grew severe. [2]So when they had used up all the grain they had brought from Egypt, their father said to them, "Go back and buy us a little more food." [3]But Judah replied: "The man strictly warned us, 'You shall not see me unless your brother is with you.'[s] [4]If you are willing to let our brother go with us, we will go down to buy food for you. [5]But if you are not willing, we will not go down, because the man told us, 'You shall not see me unless your brother is with you.'"[t] [6]Israel demanded, "Why did you bring this trouble on me by telling the man that you had another brother?" [7]They answered: "The man kept asking about us and our family: 'Is your father still living? Do you have another brother?' We answered him accordingly. How could we know that he would say, 'Bring your brother down here'?"

[8]Then Judah urged his father Israel: "Let the boy go with me, that we may be off and on our way if you and we and our children are to keep from starving to death.[u] [9]I myself will serve as a guarantee for him. You can hold me responsible for him. If I fail to bring him back and set him before you, I will bear the blame before you forever.[v] [10]Had we not delayed, we could have been there and back twice by now!"

[11]Israel their father then told them: "If it must be so, then do this: Put some of the land's best products in your baggage and take them down to the man as gifts: some balm and honey, gum and resin, and pistachios and almonds.[w] [12]Also take double the money along, for you must return the amount that was put back in the mouths of your bags; it may have been a mistake. [13]Take your brother, too, and be off on your way back to the man. [14]May God Almighty grant you mercy in the presence of the man, so that he may let your other brother go, as well as Benjamin. As for me, if I am to suffer bereavement, I shall suffer it."

[15]So the men took those gifts and double the money and Benjamin. They made their way down to Egypt and presented themselves before Joseph. [16]When Joseph saw them and Benjamin, he told his steward, "Take the men into the house, and have an animal slaughtered and prepared, for they are to dine with me at noon." [17]Doing as Joseph had ordered, the steward conducted the men to Joseph's house. [18]But they became apprehensive when they were led to his house. "It must be," they thought, "on account of the money put back in our bags the first time, that we are taken inside—in order to attack us and take our donkeys and seize us as slaves." [19]So they went up to Joseph's steward and talked to him at the entrance of the house. [20]"If you please, sir," they said, "we came down here once before to buy food.[x] [21]But when we arrived at a night's encampment and opened our bags, there was each man's money in the mouth of his bag—our money in the full amount! We have now brought it back.[y] [22]We have brought other money to buy food. We do not know who put our money in our bags." [23]He replied, "Calm down! Do not fear! Your God and the God of your father must have put treasure in your bags for you. As for your money, I received it." With that, he led Simeon out to them.

[24]The steward then brought the men inside Joseph's house. He gave them water to wash their feet, and gave fodder to their donkeys. [25]Then they set out their gifts to await Joseph's arrival at noon, for they had heard that they were to dine there. [26]When Joseph came home, they presented him with the gifts they had brought inside, while they bowed down before him to the ground. [27]After inquiring how they were, he asked them, "And how is your aged father, of whom you spoke? Is he still alive?"[z] [28]"Your servant our father is still alive and doing well," they said, as they knelt and bowed down. [29]Then Joseph looked up and saw Benjamin, his brother, the son of his mother. He asked, "Is this your youngest brother, of whom you told me?" Then he said to him, "May God be gracious to you, my son!"[a] [30]With that, Joseph hurried out, for he was so overcome with affection for his

---

*[43:1–34] The second journey to Egypt. Joseph the sage has carefully prepared the brothers for a possible reconciliation. In this chapter and the following one Judah steps forward as the hero, in contrast to chaps. 37 and 42 where Reuben was the hero. Here Judah serves as guarantee for Benjamin.

r. [42:38] Gn 37:35.  s. [43:3] Gn 44:23.  t. [43:5] Gn 42:20.
u. [43:8] Gn 42:37.  v. [43:9] Gn 44:32.

w. [43:11] Gn 45:23.  x. [43:20] Gn 42:3.  y. [43:21] Gn 42:27–28.
z. [43:27] Tb 7:4.  a. [43:29] Gn 42:13.

brother that he was on the verge of tears. So he went into a private room and wept there.

³¹After washing his face, he reappeared and, now having collected himself, gave the order, "Serve the meal." ³²It was served separately to him,* to the brothers, and to the Egyptians who partook of his board. Egyptians may not eat with Hebrews; that is abhorrent to them. ³³When they were seated before him according to their age, from the oldest to the youngest, they looked at one another in amazement; ³⁴and as portions were brought to them from Joseph's table, Benjamin's portion was five times as large as† anyone else's. So they drank freely and made merry with him.

## CHAPTER 44

**Final Test.**‡ ¹Then Joseph commanded his steward: "Fill the men's bags with as much food as they can carry, and put each man's money in the mouth of his bag. ²In the mouth of the youngest one's bag put also my silver goblet, together with the money for his grain." The steward did as Joseph said. ³At daybreak the men and their donkeys were sent off. ⁴They had not gone far out of the city when Joseph said to his steward: "Go at once after the men! When you overtake them, say to them, 'Why did you repay good with evil? Why did you steal my silver goblet? ⁵Is it not the very one from which my master drinks and which he uses for divination?⁵ What you have done is wrong.'"

⁶When the steward overtook them and repeated these words to them, ⁷they said to him: "Why does my lord say such things? Far be it from your servants to do such a thing! ⁸We even brought back to you from the land of Canaan the money that we found in the mouths of our bags. How could we steal silver or gold from your master's house? ⁹If any of your servants is found to have the goblet, he shall die, and as for the rest of us, we shall become my lord's slaves." ¹⁰But he replied, "Now what you propose is fair

enough, but only the one who is found to have it shall become my slave, and the rest of you can go free." ¹¹Then each of them quickly lowered his bag to the ground and opened it; ¹²and when a search was made, starting with the oldest and ending with the youngest, the goblet turned up in Benjamin's bag. ¹³At this, they tore their garments. Then, when each man had loaded his donkey again, they returned to the city.

¹⁴When Judah and his brothers entered Joseph's house, he was still there; so they flung themselves on the ground before him. ¹⁵"How could you do such a thing?" Joseph asked them. "Did you not know that such a man as I could discern by divination what happened?" ¹⁶Judah replied: "What can we say to my lord? How can we plead or how try to prove our innocence? God has uncovered your servants' guilt.⁵ Here we are, then, the slaves of my lord—the rest of us no less than the one in whose possession the goblet was found." ¹⁷Joseph said, "Far be it from me to act thus! Only the one in whose possession the goblet was found shall become my slave; the rest of you may go back unharmed to your father."

¹⁸Judah then stepped up to him and said: "I beg you, my lord, let your servant appeal to my lord, and do not become angry with your servant, for you are the equal of Pharaoh. ¹⁹My lord asked his servants,** 'Have you a father, or another brother?' ²⁰So we said to my lord, 'We have an aged father, and a younger brother, the child of his old age. This one's full brother is dead, and since he is the only one by his mother who is left, his father is devoted to him.'ᵇ ²¹Then you told your servants, 'Bring him down to me that I might see him.' ²²We replied to my lord, 'The boy cannot leave his father; his father would die if he left him.' ²³But you told your servants, 'Unless your youngest brother comes down with you, you shall not see me again.'ᶜ ²⁴When we returned to your servant my father, we reported to him the words of my lord.

²⁵"Later, our father said, 'Go back and buy some food for us.' ²⁶So we reminded him, 'We cannot go down there; only if our youngest brother is with us can we go, for we may not see the man if our youngest brother is not with us.' ²⁷Then your servant my father said to us, 'As you know, my wife bore me two sons. ²⁸One of them, however, has gone away from me, and I said, "He must have been torn to pieces by wild beasts!" I have not seen him since.ᵈ ²⁹If you take this one away from me too, and a disaster befalls him, you will send my white head down to Sheol in grief.'

---

*[43:32] **Separately to him:** that Joseph did not eat with the other Egyptians was apparently a matter of rank.

†[43:34] **Five times as large as:** probably an idiomatic expression for "much larger than." Cf. 45:22.

‡[44:1–34] Joseph's pressure on his brothers and Judah's great speech. Judah has the longest speech in the Book of Genesis; it summarizes the recent past (vv. 18–29), shows the pain Joseph's actions have imposed on their aged father (vv. 30–32), and ends with the offer to take the place of Benjamin as servant of Joseph (vv. 33–34). The role of Judah in the entire story is exceedingly important and is easily underrated: he tries to rescue Joseph (37:26–27), his "going away down from the brothers" is parallel to Joseph's (chap. 38) and prepares him (as it prepares Joseph) for the reconciliation, his speech in chap. 44 persuades Joseph to reveal himself and be reconciled to his brothers. Here, Judah effectively replaces Reuben as a spokesman for the brothers. Jacob in his testament (chap. 49) devotes the most attention to Judah and Joseph. In one sense, the story can be called the story of Joseph and Judah.

§[44:5] **Divination:** seeking omens through liquids poured into a cup or bowl was a common practice in the ancient Near East; cf. v. 15. Even though divination was frowned on in later Israel (Lv 19:31), it is in this place an authentic touch which is ascribed to Joseph, the wisest man in Egypt.

⁵[44:16] **Guilt:** in trying to do away with Joseph when he was young.

**[44:19] **My lord asked his servants:** such frequently repeated expressions in Judah's speech show the formal court style used by a subject in speaking to a high official.

b. [44:20] Gn 42:13.   c. [44:23] Gn 43:3.   d. [44:28] Gn 37:20, 33.

30"So now, if the boy is not with us when I go back to your servant my father, whose very life is bound up with his, he will die as soon as he sees that the boy is missing; 31and your servants will thus send the white head of your servant our father down to Sheol in grief. 32Besides, I, your servant, have guaranteed the boy's safety for my father by saying, 'If I fail to bring him back to you, father, I will bear the blame before you forever.'ᵉ 33So now let me, your servant, remain in place of the boy as the slave of my lord, and let the boy go back with his brothers. 34How could I go back to my father if the boy were not with me? I could not bear to see the anguish that would overcome my father."

## CHAPTER 45

**The Truth Revealed.*** 1Joseph could no longer restrain himself in the presence of all his attendants, so he cried out, "Have everyone withdraw from me!" So no one attended him when he made himself known to his brothers. 2But his sobs were so loud that the Egyptians heard him, and so the news reached Pharaoh's house. 3/"I am Joseph," he said to his brothers. "Is my father still alive?" But his brothers could give him no answer, so dumbfounded were they at him.

4"Come closer to me," Joseph told his brothers. When they had done so, he said: "I am your brother Joseph, whom you sold into Egypt. 5But now do not be distressed, and do not be angry with yourselves for having sold me here. It was really for the sake of saving lives that God sent me here ahead of you.ᵍ 6The famine has been in the land for two years now, and for five more years cultivation will yield no harvest. 7God, therefore, sent me on ahead of you to ensure for you a remnant on earth and to save your lives in an extraordinary deliverance. 8So it was not really you but God who had me come here; and he has made me a father to Pharaoh,† lord of all his household, and ruler over the whole land of Egypt.

9‡"Hurry back, then, to my father and tell him: 'Thus says your son Joseph: God has made me lord of all Egypt; come down to me without delay.ʰ 10You can settle in the region of Goshen,§ where you will be near me—you and your children and children's children, your flocks and herds, and everything that you own. 11I will provide for you there in the five years of famine that lie ahead, so that you and your household and all that are yours will not suffer want.' 12Surely, you can see for yourselves, and Benjamin can see for himself, that it is I who am speaking to you. 13Tell my father all about my high position in Egypt and all that you have seen. But hurry and bring my father down here." 14Then he threw his arms around his brother Benjamin and wept on his shoulder. 15Joseph then kissed all his brothers and wept over them; and only then were his brothers able to talk with him.

16The news reached Pharaoh's house: "Joseph's brothers have come." Pharaoh and his officials were pleased. 17So Pharaoh told Joseph: "Say to your brothers: 'This is what you shall do: Load up your animals and go without delay to the land of Canaan. 18There get your father and your households, and then come to me; I will assign you the best land in Egypt, where you will live off the fat of the land.'ⁱ 19Instruct them further: 'Do this. Take wagons from the land of Egypt for your children and your wives and bring your father back here. 20Do not be concerned about your belongings, for the best in the whole land of Egypt shall be yours.'"

21The sons of Israel acted accordingly. Joseph gave them the wagons, as Pharaoh had ordered, and he supplied them with provisions for the journey. 22He also gave to each of them a set of clothes, but to Benjamin he gave three hundred shekels of silver and five sets of clothes. 23Moreover, what he sent to his father was ten donkeys loaded with the finest products of Egypt and another ten loaded with grain and bread and provisions for his father's journey. 24As he sent his brothers on their way, he told them, "Do not quarrel on the way."

25So they went up from Egypt and came to the land of Canaan, to their father Jacob. 26When they told him, "Joseph is still alive—in fact, it is he who is governing all the land of Egypt," he was unmoved, for he did not believe them. 27But when they recounted to him all that Joseph had told them, and when he saw the wagons that Joseph had sent to transport him, the spirit of their father Jacob came to life. 28"Enough," said Israel. "My son Joseph is still alive! I must go and see him before I die."

## CHAPTER 46

**Migration to Egypt.** 1§Israel set out with all that was his. When he arrived at Beer-sheba, he offered sacrifices to the God of his father Isaac. 2There God, speaking to Israel in a vision by night, called: Jacob! Jacob! He answered, "Here

---

*[45:1–28] Joseph reveals his identity and the family is reconciled.

†[45:8] **Father to Pharaoh**: a term applied to a vizier in ancient Egypt.

‡[45:9–15] In these verses, as in 46:31–47:5a, all from the Yahwist source, Joseph in his own name invites his father and brothers to come to Egypt. Only after their arrival is Pharaoh informed of the fact. On the other hand, in 45:16–20, which scholars have traditionally attributed to the Elohist source, it is Pharaoh himself who invites Joseph's family to migrate to his domain.

§[45:10] **The region of Goshen**: the meaning of the term is unknown. It is found in no Egyptian source. It is generally thought to be in the modern Wadi Tumilat in the eastern part of the Nile Delta.

e. [44:32] Gn 43:9.  f. [45:3–4] Acts 7:13.  g. [45:5] Gn 50:20.
h. [45:9] Acts 7:14.

§[46:1–47:26] Jacob and his family settle in Egypt. Joseph's economic policies.

i. [45:18] Acts 7:14.

I am." ³Then he said: I am God,* the God of your father. Do not be afraid to go down to Egypt, for there I will make you a great nation. ⁴I will go down to Egypt with you and I will also bring you back here, after Joseph has closed your eyes.

⁵So Jacob departed from Beer-sheba, and the sons of Israel put their father and their wives and children on the wagons that Pharaoh had sent to transport him. ⁶They took with them their livestock and the possessions they had acquired in the land of Canaan. So Jacob and all his descendants came to Egypt.ʲ ⁷His sons and his grandsons, his daughters and his granddaughters—all his descendants—he took with him to Egypt.

⁸These are the names of the Israelites, Jacob and his children, who came to Egypt.

Reuben, Jacob's firstborn,ᵏ ⁹†and the sons of Reuben: Hanoch, Pallu, Hezron, and Carmi.ˡ ¹⁰The sons of Simeon: Jemuel, Jamin, Ohad, Jachin, Zohar, and Shaul, son of a Canaanite woman.ᵐ ¹¹The sons of Levi: Gershon, Kohath, and Merari.ⁿ ¹²The sons of Judah: Er, Onan, Shelah, Perez, and Zerah—but Er and Onan had died in the land of Canaan; and the sons of Perez were Hezron and Hamul.ᵒ ¹³The sons of Issachar: Tola, Puah, Jashub, and Shimron.ᵖ ¹⁴The sons of Zebulun: Sered, Elon, and Jahleel.�q ¹⁵These were the sons whom Leah bore to Jacob in Paddan-aram, along with his daughter Dinah—thirty-three persons in all, sons and daughters.

¹⁶The sons of Gad: Zephon, Haggi, Shuni, Ezbon, Eri, Arod, and Areli.ʳ ¹⁷The sons of Asher: Imnah, Ishvah, Ishvi, and Beriah, with their sister Serah; and the sons of Beriah: Heber and Malchiel.ˢ ¹⁸These are the children of Zilpah, whom Laban had given to his daughter Leah; these she bore to Jacob—sixteen persons in all.

¹⁹The sons of Jacob's wife Rachel: Joseph and Benjamin. ²⁰In the land of Egypt Joseph became the father of Manasseh and Ephraim, whom Asenath, daughter of Potiphera, priest of Heliopolis, bore to him.ᵗ ²¹The sons of Benjamin: Bela, Becher, Ashbel, Gera, Naaman, Ahiram, Shupham, Hupham, and Ard.ᵘ ²²These are the sons whom Rachel bore to Jacob—fourteen persons in all.

²³The sons of Dan: Hushim.ᵛ ²⁴The sons of Naphtali: Jahzeel, Guni, Jezer, and Shillem.ʷ ²⁵These are the sons of Bilhah, whom Laban had

given to his daughter Rachel; these she bore to Jacob—seven persons in all.

²⁶Jacob's people who came to Egypt—his direct descendants, not counting the wives of Jacob's sons—numbered sixty-six persons in all.ˣ ²⁷Together with Joseph's sons who were born to him in Egypt—two persons—all the people comprising the household of Jacob who had come to Egypt amounted to seventy persons‡ in all.ʸ

²⁸Israel had sent Judah ahead to Joseph, so that he might meet him in Goshen. On his arrival in the region of Goshen, ²⁹Joseph prepared his chariot and went up to meet his father Israel in Goshen. As soon as Israel made his appearance, Joseph threw his arms around him and wept a long time on his shoulder. ³⁰And Israel said to Joseph, "At last I can die, now that I have seen for myself that you are still alive."

³¹Joseph then said to his brothers and his father's household: "I will go up and inform Pharaoh, telling him: 'My brothers and my father's household, whose home is in the land of Canaan, have come to me. ³²The men are shepherds, having been owners of livestock;§ and they have brought with them their flocks and herds, as well as everything else they own.' ³³So when Pharaoh summons you and asks what your occupation is, ³⁴you must answer, 'We your servants, like our ancestors, have been owners of livestock from our youth until now,' in order that you may stay in the region of Goshen, since all shepherds are abhorrent to the Egyptians."

## CHAPTER 47

**Settlement in Goshen.** ¹Joseph went and told Pharaoh, "My father and my brothers have come from the land of Canaan, with their flocks and herds and everything else they own; and they are now in the region of Goshen." ²He then presented to Pharaoh five of his brothers whom he had selected from their full number. ³When Pharaoh asked them, "What is your occupation?" they answered, "We, your servants, like our ancestors, are shepherds. ⁴We have come," they continued, "in order to sojourn in this land, for there is no pasture for your servants' flocks, because the famine has been severe in the land of Canaan. So now please let your servants settle in the region of Goshen."ᶻ ⁵Pharaoh

---

*[46:3] **I am God**: more precisely according to the Hebrew text, "I am El." "El" is here a divine name, not the common noun "god."

†[46:9–27] This genealogical list is based on the clan lists (Nm 26:5–50) from the Mosaic period.

‡[46:27] **Seventy persons**: it is difficult to get this exact number by adding up the persons mentioned in the preceding genealogies. One might assume it refers to Jacob and sixty-nine descendants, excluding Er and Onan but including Dinah. Ex 1:5 repeats the number but excludes Jacob. Dt 10:22 refers to seventy persons descending to Egypt. The best solution is to take the number as expressing totality. Since there are seventy nations in chap. 10, it is likely that the text is drawing a parallel between the two entities and suggesting that Israel "represents" the nations before God.

§[46:32] **Owners of livestock**: the phrase occurs only here and in v. 34. The difference between this term and "shepherds" is not clear, for the brothers do not mention it to Pharaoh in 47:3.

---

j. [46:6] Ex 1:1; Jos 24:4; Jdt 5:10; Acts 7:15.　k. [46:8] Ex 1:2.　l. [46:9] Ex 6:14; Nm 26:5; 1 Chr 5:3.　m. [46:10] Ex 6:15; Nm 26:12; 1 Chr 4:24.　n. [46:11] Ex 6:16; Nm 3:17; 26:57; 1 Chr 6:1.　o. [46:12] Gn 38:3–10, 29–30; Nm 26:19; Ru 4:12; 1 Chr 2:5.　p. [46:13] Nm 26:23–24; 1 Chr 7:1.　q. [46:14] Nm 26:26.　r. [46:16] Nm 26:15–16.　s. [46:17] Nm 26:44; 1 Chr 7:30–31.　t. [46:20] Gn 41:50; Nm 26:28, 35.　u. [46:21] Nm 26:38; 1 Chr 7:6; 8:1–4.　v. [46:23] Nm 26:42.　w. [46:24] Nm 26:48–49; 1 Chr 7:13.

x. [46:26] Ex 1:5.　y. [46:27] Ex 1:5; Dt 10:22; Acts 7:14.　z. [47:4] Ex 23:9; Dt 23:8.

said to Joseph, "Now that your father and your brothers have come to you, [6]the land of Egypt is at your disposal; settle your father and brothers in the pick of the land. Let them settle in the region of Goshen. And if you know of capable men among them, put them in charge of my livestock." [7]Then Joseph brought his father Jacob and presented him to Pharaoh. And Jacob blessed Pharaoh. [8]Then Pharaoh asked Jacob, "How many years have you lived?" [9]Jacob replied: "The years I have lived as a wayfarer amount to a hundred and thirty. Few and hard have been these years of my life, and they do not compare with the years that my ancestors lived as wayfarers." [10]Then Jacob blessed Pharaoh and withdrew from his presence.

[11]Joseph settled his father and brothers and gave them a holding in Egypt on the pick of the land, in the region of Rameses,[†] as Pharaoh had ordered. [12]And Joseph provided food for his father and brothers and his father's whole household, down to the youngest.

**Joseph's Land Policy.** [13]Since there was no food in all the land because of the extreme severity of the famine, and the lands of Egypt and Canaan were languishing from hunger, [14]Joseph gathered in, as payment for the grain that they were buying, all the money that was to be found in Egypt and Canaan, and he put it in Pharaoh's house. [15]When all the money in Egypt and Canaan was spent, all the Egyptians came to Joseph, pleading, "Give us food! Why should we perish in front of you? For our money is gone." [16]"Give me your livestock if your money is gone," replied Joseph. "I will give you food in return for your livestock." [17]So they brought their livestock to Joseph, and he gave them food in exchange for their horses, their flocks of sheep and herds of cattle, and their donkeys. Thus he supplied them with food in exchange for all their livestock in that year. [18]That year ended, and they came to him in the next one and said: "We cannot hide from my lord that, with our money spent and our livestock made over to my lord, there is nothing left to put at my lord's disposal except our bodies and our land. [19]Why should we and our land perish before your very eyes? Take us and our land in exchange for food, and we will become Pharaoh's slaves and our land his property; only give us seed, that we may survive and not perish, and that our land may not turn into a waste."

[20]So Joseph acquired all the land of Egypt for Pharaoh. Each of the Egyptians sold his field, since the famine weighed heavily upon them. Thus the land passed over to Pharaoh, [21]and the people were reduced to slavery, from one end of Egypt's territory to the other. [22]Only the priests'

lands Joseph did not acquire. Since the priests had a fixed allowance from Pharaoh and lived off the allowance Pharaoh had granted them, they did not have to sell their land.

[23]Joseph told the people: "Now that I have acquired you and your land for Pharaoh, here is your seed for sowing the land. [24]But when the harvest is in, you must give a fifth of it to Pharaoh, while you keep four-fifths as seed for your fields and as food for yourselves and your households and as food for your children." [25]"You have saved our lives!" they answered. "We have found favor with my lord; now we will be Pharaoh's slaves." [26]Thus Joseph made it a statute for the land of Egypt, which is still in force, that a fifth of its produce should go to Pharaoh. Only the land of the priests did not pass over to Pharaoh.

**Israel Blesses Ephraim and Manasseh.** [27]Thus Israel settled in the land of Egypt, in the region of Goshen. There they acquired holdings, were fertile, and multiplied greatly.[a] [28‡]Jacob lived in the land of Egypt for seventeen years; the span of his life came to a hundred and forty-seven years. [29]When the time approached for Israel to die, he called his son Joseph and said to him: "If it pleases you, put your hand under my thigh as a sign of your enduring fidelity to me; do not bury me in Egypt. [30]When I lie down with my ancestors, take me out of Egypt and bury me in their burial place."[b] "I will do as you say," he replied. [31]But his father demanded, "Swear it to me!" So Joseph swore to him. Then Israel bowed at the head of the bed.[§]

# CHAPTER 48

[1]Some time afterward, Joseph was informed, "Your father is failing." So he took along with him his two sons, Manasseh and Ephraim. [2]When Jacob was told, "Your son Joseph has

---

‡[47:28–50:26] Supplements to the Joseph story. Most of the material in this section centers on Jacob—his blessing of Joseph's sons, his farewell testament, and his death and burial in Canaan. Only the last verses (50:15–26) redirect attention to Jacob's sons, the twelve brothers; they are assured that the reconciliation will not collapse after the death of the patriarch.

§[47:31] **Israel bowed at the head of the bed:** meaning perhaps that he gave a nod of assent and appreciation as he lay on his bed. The oath and gesture are the same as Abraham's in 24:2. Israel's bowing here suggests the fulfillment of Joseph's dreams in 37:9–10, when parents and brothers bowed down to Joseph (cf. 42:6; 43:26). By using different vowels for the Hebrew word for "bed," the Greek version translated it as "staff," and understood the phrase to mean that he bowed in worship, leaning on the top of his staff; it is thus quoted in Heb 11:21.

¶[48:1–22] Jacob continues his preparations for death. In a scene that evokes the nearly blind Isaac blessing Jacob and Esau (chap. 27), Jacob blesses Joseph's two sons. He adopts them, elevating them to a status equal to that of Jacob's first sons Reuben and Simeon (cf. 1 Chr 5:1). The adoption is one more instance of Jacob's favoring Rachel and those born of her. The mention of Jacob's failing eyesight and his selection of the younger son over the older evokes the great deathbed scene in chap. 27. He reaffirms to Joseph the ancient divine promise of progeny and land.

---

*[47:9] **Wayfarer . . . wayfarers:** human beings are merely sojourners on earth; cf. Ps 39:13.

†[47:11] **The region of Rameses:** same as the region of Goshen; see note on 45:10.

---

a. [47:27] Ex 1:7.   b. [47:30] Gn 50:5.

come to you," Israel rallied his strength and sat up in bed.

³ᶜJacob then said to Joseph: "God Almighty appeared to me at Luz* in the land of Canaan, and blessing me, ⁴he said, 'I will make you fertile and multiply you and make you into an assembly of peoples, and I will give this land to your descendants after you as a permanent possession.' ⁵So now your two sons who were born to you in the land of Egypt before I joined you here, shall be mine; Ephraim and Manasseh shall be mine as much as Reuben and Simeon are mine. ⁶Progeny born to you after them shall remain yours; but their heritage shall be recorded in the names of their brothers. ⁷ᵈI do this because, when I was returning from Paddan, your mother Rachel died, to my sorrow, during the journey in Canaan, while we were still a short distance from Ephrath; and I buried her there on the way to Ephrath [now Bethlehem]."†

⁸When Israel saw Joseph's sons, he asked, "Who are these?" ⁹"They are my sons," Joseph answered his father, "whom God has given me here." "Bring them to me," said his father, "that I may bless them." ¹⁰Now Israel's eyes were dim from age; he could not see well. When Joseph brought his sons close to him, he kissed and embraced them. ¹¹Then Israel said to Joseph, "I never expected to see your face again, and now God has allowed me to see your descendants as well!"

¹²Joseph removed them from his father's knees and bowed down before him with his face to the ground. ¹³Then Joseph took the two, Ephraim with his right hand, to Israel's left, and Manasseh with his left hand, to Israel's right, and brought them up to him. ¹⁴But Israel, crossing his hands, put out his right hand and laid it on the head of Ephraim, although he was the younger, and his left hand on the head of Manasseh, although he was the firstborn. ¹⁵Then he blessed them with these words:

"May the God in whose presence
        my fathers Abraham and Isaac
        walked,
The God who has been my shepherd
        from my birth to this day,ᵉ
¹⁶The angel who has delivered me from
        all harm,
        bless these boys
That in them my name be recalled,
        and the names of my fathers,
        Abraham and Isaac,
And they may become teeming
        multitudes
        upon the earth!"

¹⁷When Joseph saw that his father had laid his right hand on Ephraim's head, this seemed wrong to him; so he took hold of his father's hand, to remove it from Ephraim's head to Manasseh's, ¹⁸saying, "That is not right, father; the other one is the firstborn; lay your right hand on his head!" ¹⁹But his father refused. "I know it, son," he said, "I know. That one too shall become a people, and he too shall be great. Nevertheless, his younger brother shall surpass him, and his descendants shall become a multitude of nations." ²⁰So he blessed them that day and said, "By you shall the people of Israel pronounce blessings, saying, 'God make you like Ephraim and Manasseh.'" Thus he placed Ephraim before Manasseh.ᶠ

²¹Then Israel said to Joseph: "I am about to die. But God will be with you and will restore you to the land of your ancestors. ²²ᵍAs for me, I give to you, as to the one above his brothers, Shechem, which I captured from the Amorites with my sword and bow."‡

## CHAPTER 49

**Jacob's Testament.**§ ¹Jacob called his sons and said: "Gather around, that I may tell you what is to happen to you in days to come.

²  "Assemble and listen, sons of Jacob,
        listen to Israel, your father.

³  "You, Reuben, my firstborn,
        my strength and the first fruit of my
        vigor,
        excelling in rank and excelling in
        power!
⁴  Turbulent as water, you shall no longer
        excel,
        for you climbed into your father's bed
        and defiled my couch to my sorrow.ʰ

---

* [48:3] **Luz:** an older name of Bethel (28:19).

† [48:7] Since her early death prevented Rachel from bearing more than two sons, Jacob feels justified in treating her two grandsons as if they were her own offspring.

‡ [48:22] Both the meaning of the Hebrew and the historical reference in this verse are obscure. By taking the Hebrew word for Shechem as a common noun meaning shoulder or mountain slope, some translators render the verse, "I give you one portion more than your brothers, which I captured . . ." The reference may be to the capture of Shechem by the sons of Jacob (34:24–29). Shechem lay near the border separating the tribal territory of Manasseh from that of Ephraim (Jos 16:4–9; 17:1–2, 7).

§ [49:1–27] The testament, or farewell discourse, of Jacob, which has its closest parallel in Moses' farewell in Dt 33:6–25. From his privileged position as a patriarch, he sees the future of his children (the eponymous ancestors of the tribes) and is able to describe how they will fare and so gives his blessing. The dense and archaic poetry is obscure in several places. The sayings often involve wordplays (explained in the notes). The poem begins with the six sons of Leah (vv. 2–15), then deals with the sons of the two secondary wives, and ends with Rachel's two sons, Joseph and Benjamin. Reuben, the oldest son, loses his position of leadership as a result of his intercourse with Bilhah (35:22), and the words about Simeon and Levi allude to their taking revenge for the rape of Dinah (chap. 34). The preeminence of Judah reflects his rise in the course of the narrative (mirroring the rise of Joseph). See note on 44:1–34.

---

c. [48:3–4] Gn 28:12–15; 35:6.   d. [48:7] Gn 35:19.   e. [48:15] Heb 11:21.   f. [48:20] Heb 11:21.   g. [48:22] Jos 17:14, 17–18; Jn 4:5.   h. [49:4] Gn 35:22; 1 Chr 5:1–2.

5 *"Simeon and Levi, brothers indeed,
    weapons of violence are their
        knives.†
6 Let not my person enter their council,
    or my honor be joined with their
        company;
For in their fury they killed men,
    at their whim they maimed oxen.ⁱ
7 Cursed be their fury so fierce,
    and their rage so cruel!
I will scatter them in Jacob,
    disperse them throughout Israel.

8 "You, Judah, shall your brothers praise
    —your hand on the neck of your
        enemies;
    the sons of your father shall bow
        down to you.
9 Judah is a lion's cub,
    you have grown up on prey, my son.
He crouches, lies down like a lion,
    like a lioness—who would dare
        rouse him?ʲ
10 The scepter shall never depart from
        Judah,
    or the mace from between his feet,
Until tribute comes to him,‡
    and he receives the people's
        obedience.
11 He tethers his donkey to the vine,
    his donkey's foal to the choicest
        stem.
In wine he washes his garments,
    his robe in the blood of grapes.§
12 His eyes are darker than wine,
    and his teeth are whiter than milk.

13 "Zebulun shall dwell by the seashore;
    he will be a haven for ships,
    and his flank shall rest on Sidon.

14 "Issachar is a rawboned donkey,
    crouching between the saddlebags.
15 When he saw how good a settled life was,
    and how pleasant the land,

He bent his shoulder to the burden
    and became a toiling serf.

16 "Dan shall achieve justice⁵ for his people
    as one of the tribes of Israel.
17 Let Dan be a serpent by the roadside,
    a horned viper by the path,
That bites the horse's heel,
    so that the rider tumbles backward.

18 "I long for your deliverance, O Lord!**

19 "Gad shall be raided by raiders,
    but he shall raid at their heels.††

20 "Asher's produce is rich,
    and he shall furnish delicacies for
        kings.

21 "Naphtali is a hind let loose,
    which brings forth lovely fawns.

22 "Joseph is a wild colt,
    a wild colt by a spring,
    wild colts on a hillside.
23 Harrying him and shooting,
    the archers opposed him;
24 But his bow remained taut,
    and his arms were nimble,
By the power of the Mighty One of Jacob,
    because of the Shepherd, the Rock
        of Israel,
25 The God of your father, who helps you,‡‡
    God Almighty, who blesses you,
With the blessings of the heavens above,
    the blessings of the abyss that
        crouches below,
The blessings of breasts and womb,
26     the blessings of fresh grain and
        blossoms,
    the blessings of the everlasting
        mountains,
    the delights of the eternal hills.
May they rest on the head of Joseph,
    on the brow of the prince among his
        brothers.

27 "Benjamin is a ravenous wolf;
    mornings he devours the prey,
    and evenings he distributes the
        spoils."

**Farewell and Death.** 28All these are the twelve tribes of Israel, and this is what their father said about them, as he blessed them. To each he

---

*[49:5–7] This passage probably refers to their attack on the city of Shechem (Gn 34). Because there is no indication that the warlike tribe of Levi will be commissioned as a priestly tribe (Ex 32:26–29; Dt 33:11), this passage reflects an early, independent tradition.

†[49:5] **Knives**: if this is the meaning of the obscure Hebrew word here, the reference may be to the knives used in circumcising the men of Shechem (34:24; cf. Jos 5:2).

‡[49:10] **Until tribute comes to him**: this translation is based on a slight change in the Hebrew text, which, as it stands, would seem to mean, "until he comes to Shiloh." A somewhat different reading of the Hebrew text would be, "until he comes to whom it belongs." This last has been traditionally understood in a messianic sense. In any case, the passage aims at the supremacy of the tribe of Judah and of the Davidic dynasty.

§[49:11] **In wine . . . the blood of grapes**: Judah's clothes are poetically pictured as soaked with grape juice from trampling in the wine press, the rich vintage of his land; cf. Is 63:2.

i. [49:6] Gn 34:25.    j. [49:9] 1 Chr 5:2.

⁵[49:16] In Hebrew the verb for "achieve justice" is from the same root as the name Dan.

**[49:18] This short plea for divine mercy has been inserted into the middle of Jacob's testament.

††[49:19] In Hebrew there is assonance between the name Gad and the words for "raided," "raiders," and "raid."

‡‡[49:25–26] A very similar description of the agricultural riches of the tribal land of Joseph is given in Dt 33:13–16.

gave a suitable blessing. [29]Then he gave them this charge: "Since I am about to be gathered to my people, bury me with my ancestors in the cave that lies in the field of Ephron the Hittite, [30]the cave in the field of Machpelah, facing on Mamre, in the land of Canaan, the field that Abraham bought from Ephron the Hittite for a burial ground.[k] [31]There Abraham and his wife Sarah are buried, and so are Isaac and his wife Rebekah, and there, too, I buried Leah— [32]the field and the cave in it that had been purchased from the Hittites."

[33]When Jacob had finished giving these instructions to his sons, he drew his feet into the bed, breathed his last, and was gathered to his people.

## CHAPTER 50

**Jacob's Funeral.** [1]Joseph flung himself upon his father and wept over him as he kissed him. [2]Then Joseph ordered the physicians in his service to embalm his father. When the physicians embalmed Israel, [3]they spent forty days at it, for that is the full period of embalming; and the Egyptians mourned him for seventy days. [4]When the period of mourning was over, Joseph spoke to Pharaoh's household. "If you please, appeal to Pharaoh, saying: [5]My father made me swear: 'I am dying. Bury me in my grave that I have prepared for myself in the land of Canaan.' So now let me go up to bury my father. Then I will come back."[l] [6]Pharaoh replied, "Go and bury your father, as he made you promise on oath."

[7]So Joseph went up to bury his father; and with him went all of Pharaoh's officials who were senior members of his household and all the other elders of the land of Egypt, [8]as well as Joseph's whole household, his brothers, and his father's household; only their children and their flocks and herds were left in the region of Goshen. [9]Chariots, too, and horsemen went up with him; it was a very imposing retinue.

[10]When they arrived at Goren-ha-atad,* which is beyond the Jordan, they held there a very great and solemn memorial service; and Joseph observed seven days of mourning for his father. [11]When the Canaanites who inhabited the land saw the mourning at Goren-ha-atad, they said, "This is a solemn funeral on the part

of the Egyptians!" That is why the place was named Abel-mizraim. It is beyond the Jordan.

[12]Thus Jacob's sons did for him as he had instructed them. [13]They carried him to the land of Canaan and buried him in the cave in the field of Machpelah, facing on Mamre, the field that Abraham had bought for a burial ground from Ephron the Hittite.[m]

[14]After Joseph had buried his father he returned to Egypt, together with his brothers and all who had gone up with him for the burial of his father.

**Plea for Forgiveness.** [15†]Now that their father was dead, Joseph's brothers became fearful and thought, "Suppose Joseph has been nursing a grudge against us and now most certainly will pay us back in full for all the wrong we did him!" [16]So they sent to Joseph and said: "Before your father died, he gave us these instructions: [17]'Thus you shall say to Joseph: Please forgive the criminal wrongdoing of your brothers, who treated you harmfully.' So now please forgive the crime that we, the servants of the God of your father, committed." When they said this to him, Joseph broke into tears. [18]Then his brothers also proceeded to fling themselves down before him and said, "We are your slaves!" [19]But Joseph replied to them: "Do not fear. Can I take the place of God? [20]Even though you meant harm to me, God meant it for good, to achieve this present end, the survival of many people.[n] [21]So now, do not fear. I will provide for you and for your children." By thus speaking kindly to them, he reassured them.[o]

[22]Joseph remained in Egypt, together with his father's household. He lived a hundred and ten years. [23]He saw Ephraim's children to the third generation, and the children of Manasseh's son Machir were also born on Joseph's knees.[p]

**Death of Joseph.** [24]Joseph said to his brothers: "I am about to die. God will surely take care of you and lead you up from this land to the land that he promised on oath to Abraham, Isaac and Jacob."[q] [25]Then, putting the sons of Israel under oath, he continued, "When God thus takes care of you, you must bring my bones up from this place."[r] [26]Joseph died at the age of a hundred and ten. He was embalmed and laid to rest in a coffin in Egypt.[s]

---

*[50:10–11] **Goren-ha-atad**: "Threshing Floor of the Brambles." **Abel-mizraim**: although the name really means "watercourse of the Egyptians," it is understood here, by a play on the first part of the term, to mean "mourning of the Egyptians." The site has not been identified through either reading of the name. But it is difficult to see why the mourning rites should have been held in the land beyond the Jordan when the burial was at Hebron. Perhaps an earlier form of the story placed the mourning rites beyond the Wadi of Egypt, the traditional boundary between Canaan and Egypt (Nm 34:5; Jos 15:4, 47).

†[50:15–26] The final reconciliation of the brothers. Fearful of what may happen after the death of their father, the brothers engage in a final deception, inventing the dying wish of Jacob. Again, Joseph weeps, and, again, his brothers fall down before him, offering to be his slaves (44:16, 33). Joseph's assurance is also a summation of the story: "Even though you meant harm to me, God meant it for good, to achieve this present end, the survival of many people" (v. 20). Joseph's adoption of the children of Manasseh's son Machir recalls Jacob's adoption of his grandchildren (48:5, 13–20); the adoptions reflect tribal history (cf. Jgs 5:14).

k. [49:30] Gn 23:17.  l. [50:5] Gn 47:30.

m. [50:13] Gn 23:16; Jos 24:32; Acts 7:16.  n. [50:20] Gn 45:5.  o. [50:21] Gn 47:12.  p. [50:23] Nm 32:39; Jos 17:1.  q. [50:24] Ex 3:8; Heb 11:22.  r. [50:25] Ex 13:19; Heb 11:22.  s. [50:26] Sir 49:15.

# THE BOOK OF
# EXODUS

The second book of the Pentateuch is called Exodus, from the Greek word for "departure," because its central event was understood by the Septuagint's translators to be the departure of the Israelites from Egypt. Its Hebrew title, *Shemoth* ("Names"), is from the book's opening phrase, "These are the names. . . ." Continuing the history of Israel from the point where the Book of Genesis leaves off, Exodus recounts the Egyptian oppression of Jacob's ever-increasing descendants and their miraculous deliverance by God through Moses, who led them across the Red Sea to Mount Sinai where they entered into a covenant with the Lord. Covenantal laws and detailed prescriptions for the tabernacle (a portable sanctuary foreshadowing the Jerusalem Temple) and its service are followed by a dramatic episode of rebellion, repentance, and divine mercy. After the broken covenant is renewed, the tabernacle is constructed, and the cloud signifying God's glorious presence descends to cover it.

These events made Israel a nation and confirmed their unique relationship with God. The "law" (Hebrew *torah*) given by God through Moses to the Israelites at Mount Sinai constitutes the moral, civil, and ritual legislation by which they were to become a holy people. Many elements of it were fundamental to the teaching of Jesus (Mt 5:21–30; 15:4) as well as to New Testament and Christian moral teaching (Rom 13:8–10; 1 Cor 10:1–5; 1 Pt 2:9).

The principal divisions of Exodus are:

I. Introduction: The Oppression of the Israelites in Egypt (1:1–2:22)
II. The Call and Commission of Moses (2:23–7:7)
III. The Contest with Pharaoh (7:8–13:16)
IV. The Deliverance of the Israelites from Pharaoh and Victory at the Sea (13:17–15:21)
V. The Journey in the Wilderness to Sinai (15:22–18:27)
VI. Covenant and Legislation at Mount Sinai (19:1–31:18)
VII. Israel's Apostasy and God's Renewal of the Covenant (32:1–34:35)
VIII. The Building of the Tabernacle and the Descent of God's Glory upon It (35:1–40:38)

## I. INTRODUCTION: THE OPPRESSION OF THE ISRAELITES IN EGYPT

### CHAPTER 1

**Jacob's Descendants in Egypt.** ¹These are the names of the sons of Israel* who, accompanied by their households, entered into Egypt with Jacob: ²†Reuben, Simeon, Levi and Judah; ³Issachar, Zebulun and Benjamin; ⁴Dan and Naphtali; Gad and Asher. ⁵The total number of Jacob's direct descendants‡ was seventy.ᵃ Joseph was already in Egypt.

⁶Now Joseph and all his brothers and that whole generation died.ᵇ ⁷But the Israelites were fruitful and prolific. They multiplied and became so very numerous that the land was filled with them.§

**The Oppression.** ⁸Then a new king, who knew nothing of Joseph,¶ rose to power in Egypt. ⁹He

---

*[1:1] **Sons of Israel**: here literally the first-generation sons of Jacob/Israel. Cf. v. 5. However, beginning with v. 7 the same Hebrew phrase refers to Jacob's more remote descendants; hence, from there on, it is ordinarily rendered "the Israelites." **Households**: the family in its fullest sense, including wives, children and servants.

†[1:2] Jacob's sons are listed here according to their respective mothers. Cf. Gn 29:31; 30:20; 35:16–26.

‡[1:5] **Direct descendants**: lit., "persons coming from Jacob's loins"; hence, wives of Jacob's sons and servants are

not included. Cf. Gn 46:26. **Seventy**: Gn 46:26, along with the Septuagint for the verse, agrees on a total of sixty-six coming down to Egypt with Jacob, but in v. 27 the Hebrew text adds the two sons born to Joseph in Egypt and presupposes Jacob himself and Joseph for a total of seventy; the Septuagint adds "nine sons" born to Joseph to get a total of seventy-five. This is the figure the Septuagint and 4QExᵃ have here in Ex 1:5.

§[1:7] **Fruitful . . . multiplied . . . the land was filled with them**: the language used here to indicate the fecundity of the Israelite population echoes the divine blessing bestowed upon humanity at creation (Gn 1:28) and after the flood (Gn 9:1) as well as suggesting fulfillment of the promises to the ancestors Abraham, Isaac, and Jacob (Gn 12:2; 13:16; 15:5; 28:14; passim).

¶[1:8] **Who knew nothing of Joseph**: the nuance intended by the Hebrew verb "know" here goes beyond precise

---

a. [1:5] Gn 46:26–27; Dt 10:22; Acts 7:14.  b. [1:6] Gn 50:26.  c. [1:8–10] Acts 7:18–19.

said to his people, "See! The Israelite people have multiplied and become more numerous than we are! [10]Come, let us deal shrewdly with them to stop their increase;[*] otherwise, in time of war they too may join our enemies to fight against us, and so leave the land."

[11]Accordingly, they set supervisors over the Israelites to oppress them with forced labor.[d] Thus they had to build for Pharaoh[†] the garrison cities of Pithom and Raamses. [12]Yet the more they were oppressed, the more they multiplied and spread, so that the Egyptians began to loathe the Israelites. [13]So the Egyptians reduced the Israelites to cruel slavery, [14]making life bitter for them with hard labor, at mortar[‡] and brick and all kinds of field work—cruelly oppressed in all their labor.

**Command to the Midwives.** [15]The king of Egypt told the Hebrew midwives, one of whom was called Shiphrah and the other Puah, [16]"When you act as midwives for the Hebrew women, look on the birthstool:[§] if it is a boy, kill him; but if it is a girl, she may live." [17]The midwives, however, feared God; they did not do as the king of Egypt had ordered them, but let the boys live. [18]So the king of Egypt summoned the midwives and asked them, "Why have you done this, allowing the boys to live?" [19]The midwives answered Pharaoh, "The Hebrew women are not like the Egyptian women. They are robust and give birth before the midwife arrives." [20]Therefore God dealt well with the midwives; and the people multiplied and grew very numerous. [21]And because the midwives feared God, God built up families for them. [22]Pharaoh then commanded all his people, "Throw into the Nile every boy that is born,[e] but you may let all the girls live."

## CHAPTER 2

**Birth and Adoption of Moses.** [1]Now a man[¶] of the house of Levi married a Levite woman,[f] [2]and the woman conceived and bore a son. Seeing what a fine child he was, she hid him for three months.[g] [3]But when she could no longer hide him, she took a papyrus basket,[**] daubed it with bitumen and pitch, and putting the child in it, placed it among the reeds on the bank of the Nile. [4]His sister stationed herself at a distance to find out what would happen to him.

[5]Then Pharaoh's daughter came down to bathe at the Nile, while her attendants walked along the bank of the Nile. Noticing the basket among the reeds, she sent her handmaid to fetch it. [6]On opening it, she looked, and there was a baby boy crying! She was moved with pity for him and said, "It is one of the Hebrews' children." [7]Then his sister asked Pharaoh's daughter, "Shall I go and summon a Hebrew woman to nurse the child for you?" [8]Pharaoh's daughter answered her, "Go." So the young woman went and called the child's own mother. [9]Pharaoh's daughter said to her, "Take this child and nurse him for me, and I will pay your wages."[††] So the woman took the child and nursed him. [10]When the child grew,[‡‡] she brought him to Pharaoh's daughter, and he became her son.[h] She named him Moses; for she said, "I drew him out of the water."

**Moses' Flight to Midian.** [11]On one occasion, after Moses had grown up,[§§] when he had gone out to his kinsmen and witnessed their forced labor, he saw an Egyptian striking a Hebrew,[i] one of his own kinsmen. [12]Looking about and seeing no one, he struck down the Egyptian

---

determination. The idea may be not simply that a new king came to power who had not heard of Joseph but that this king ignored the services that Joseph had rendered to Egypt, repudiating the special relationship that existed between Joseph and his predecessor on the throne.

[*] [1:10] **Increase:** Pharaoh's actions thereby immediately pit him against God's will for the Israelites to multiply; see note on v. 7 above.

[†] [1:11] **Pharaoh:** not a personal name, but a title common to all the kings of Egypt.

[‡] [1:14] **Mortar:** either the wet clay with which the bricks were made, as in Na 3:14, or the cement used between the bricks in building, as in Gn 11:3.

[§] [1:16] **Birthstool:** apparently a pair of stones on which the mother is seated for childbirth opposite the midwife. The Hebrew word elsewhere is used to refer to the stones of a potter's wheel.

[¶] [2:1] **Now a man:** the chapter begins abruptly, without names for the man or woman (in contrast to the midwives of 1:15), who in 6:20 are identified as Amram and Jochebed.

[**] [2:3] **Basket:** the same Hebrew word is used in Gn 6:14 and throughout the flood narrative for Noah's ark, but nowhere else in the Bible. Here, however, the "ark" or "chest" was made of papyrus stalks. Presumably the allusion to Genesis is intentional. Just as Noah and his family were preserved safe from the threatening waters of the flood in the ark he built, so now Moses is preserved from the threatening waters of the Nile in the ark prepared by his mother. **Among the reeds:** the Hebrew noun for "reed" is overwhelmingly used in the phrase "Reed Sea," traditionally translated "Red Sea."

[††] [2:9] **And I will pay your wages:** the idea that the child's mother will be paid for nursing her child—and by Pharaoh's own daughter—heightens the narrative's irony.

[‡‡] [2:10] **When the child grew:** while v. 9 implies that the boy's mother cared for him as long as he needed to be nursed (presumably between two and four years), the same verb appears in v. 11 to describe the attainment of adulthood. **And he became her son:** Pharaoh's daughter adopts Moses, thus adding to the irony of the account. The king of Egypt had ordered the killing of all the sons of the Hebrews, and one now becomes the son of his own daughter! **Moses:** in Hebrew, *mosheh*. There is a play on words here: *mosheh* echoes *meshithihu* ("I drew him out"). However, the name Moses actually has nothing to do with that Hebrew verb, but is probably derived from Egyptian "beloved" or "has been born," preserved in such Pharaonic names as Thutmoses (meaning approximately "Beloved of the god Thoth" or "The god Thoth is born, has given birth to [the child]"). The original meaning of Moses' name was no longer remembered (if it was Egyptian, it may have contained an Egyptian divine element as well, perhaps the name of the Nile god Hapi), or a secondary explanation was derived from this story (or gave rise to it, if the drawing from the water of the Nile was intended to foreshadow the Israelites' escape from Egypt through the Red Sea).

[§§] [2:11] **After Moses had grown up:** cf. 7:7, where Moses is said to be eighty years old at the time of his mission to Pharaoh. **Striking:** probably in the sense of "flogging"; in v. 12, however, the same verb is used in the sense of "killing."

---

d. [1:11] Dt 26:6.    e. [1:22] Acts 7:19.    f. [2:1] Ex 6:20; Nm 26:59.

g. [2:2] Acts 7:20; Heb 11:23.    h. [2:10] Acts 7:21; Heb 11:24. i. [2:11–14] Acts 7:23–28.

and hid him in the sand. [13]The next day he went out again, and now two Hebrews were fighting! So he asked the culprit, "Why are you striking your companion?" [14]But he replied, "Who has appointed you ruler and judge over us? Are you thinking of killing me as you killed the Egyptian?" Then Moses became afraid and thought, "The affair must certainly be known." [15]When Pharaoh heard of the affair, he sought to kill Moses. But Moses fled from Pharaoh and went to the land of Midian.[*j] There he sat down by a well.

[16]Now the priest of Midian had seven daughters, and they came to draw water and fill the troughs to water their father's flock. [17]But shepherds came and drove them away. So Moses rose up in their defense and watered their flock. [18]When they returned to their father Reuel,[†] he said to them, "How is it you have returned so soon today?" [19]They answered, "An Egyptian[‡] delivered us from the shepherds. He even drew water for us and watered the flock!" [20]"Where is he?" he asked his daughters. "Why did you leave the man there? Invite him to have something to eat." [21]Moses agreed to stay with him, and the man gave Moses his daughter Zipporah in marriage. [22]She conceived and bore a son, whom he named Gershom;[§] for he said, "I am a stranger residing in a foreign land."[k]

## II. THE CALL AND COMMISSION OF MOSES

**The Burning Bush.** [23]A long time passed, during which the king of Egypt died. The Israelites groaned under their bondage and cried out, and from their bondage their cry for help went up to God.[l] [24]God heard their moaning and God was mindful of his covenant[m] with Abraham, Isaac and Jacob. [25]God saw the Israelites, and God knew. . . .[*]

---

*[2:15] **Land of Midian:** the territory under the control of a confederation made up, according to Nm 31:8, of five Midianite tribes. According to Gn 25:1–2, Midian was a son of Abraham by Keturah. In view of the extreme hostility in later periods between Israel and Midian (cf. Nm 31; Jgs 6–8), the relationship is striking, as is the account here in Exodus of good relations between Moses and no less than a Midianite priest.

†[2:18] **Reuel:** also called Jethro. Cf. 3:1; 4:18; 18:1.

‡[2:19] **An Egyptian:** Moses was probably wearing Egyptian dress, or spoke Egyptian to Reuel's daughters.

§[2:22] **Gershom:** the name is explained unscientifically as if it came from the Hebrew word *ger,* "sojourner, resident alien," and the Hebrew word *sham,* "there." **Stranger residing:** Hebrew *ger,* one who seeks and finds shelter and a home away from his or her own people or land.

¶[2:25] **God knew:** in response to the people's cry, God, mindful of the covenant, looks on their plight and acknowledges firsthand the depth of their suffering (see 3:7). In vv. 23–25, traditionally attributed to the Priestly writer, God is mentioned five times, in contrast to the rest of chaps. 1–2, where God is rarely mentioned. These verses serve as a fitting transition to Moses' call in chap. 3.

j. [2:15] Acts 7:29; Heb 11:27.  k. [2:22] Ex 18:3.  l. [2:23] Ex 3:7, 9; Dt 26:7.  m. [2:24] Ex 6:5; Ps 105:8–9; 106:44–45.

## CHAPTER 3

[1]**Meanwhile Moses was tending the flock of his father-in-law Jethro, the priest of Midian. Leading the flock beyond the wilderness, he came to the mountain of God, Horeb.[††] [2]There the angel of the LORD[‡‡] appeared to him as fire flaming out of a bush.[n] When he looked, although the bush was on fire, it was not being consumed. [3]So Moses decided, "I must turn aside to look at this remarkable sight. Why does the bush not burn up?" [4]When the LORD saw that he had turned aside to look, God called out to him from the bush: Moses! Moses! He answered, "Here I am." [5]God said: Do not come near! Remove your sandals from your feet, for the place where you stand is holy ground.[o] [6]I am the God of your father,[§§] he continued, the God of Abraham, the

---

**[3:1–4:17] After the introduction to the narrative in 2:23–25, the commissioning itself falls into three sections: God's appearance under the aspect of a burning bush (3:1–6); the explicit commission (3:7–10); and an extended dialogue between Moses and God, in the course of which Moses receives the revelation of God's personal name. Although in the J source of the Pentateuch people have known and invoked God's personal name in worship since the time of Seth (Gn 4:26), for the E and P sources (see 6:2–4) God first makes this name publicly available here through Moses.

††[3:1] **The mountain of God, Horeb:** traditionally, "Horeb" is taken to be an alternate name in E source material and Deuteronomy (e.g., Dt 1:2) for what in J and P is known as Mount Sinai, the goal of the Israelites' journey after leaving Egypt and the site of the covenant God makes with Israel. However, it is not clear that originally the two names reflect the same mountain, nor even that "Horeb" refers originally to a mountain and not simply the dry, ruined region (from Hebrew *horeb,* "dryness, devastation") around the mountain. Additionally, the position of "Horeb" at the end of the verse may indicate that the identification of the "mountain of God" with Horeb (= Sinai?) represents a later stage in the evolution of the tradition about God's meeting with Moses. The phrase "mountain of God" simply anticipates the divine apparitions which would take place there, both on this occasion and after the Israelites' departure from Egypt; alternatively, it means that the place was already sacred or a place of pilgrimage in pre-Israelite times. In any case, the narrative offers no indications of its exact location.

‡‡[3:2] **The angel of the LORD:** Hebrew *mal'ak* or "messenger" is regularly translated *angelos* by the Septuagint, from which the English word "angel" is derived, but the Hebrew term lacks connotations now popularly associated with "angel" (such as wings). Although angels frequently assume human form (cf. Gn 18–19), the term is also used to indicate the visual form under which God occasionally appeared and spoke to people, referred to indifferently in some Old Testament texts either as God's "angel," *mal'ak,* or as God. Cf. Gn 16:7, 13; Ex 14:19, 24–25; Nm 22:22–35; Jgs 6:11–18. **The bush:** Hebrew *seneh,* perhaps "thorny bush," occurring only here in vv. 2–4 and in Dt 33:16. Its use here is most likely a wordplay on Sinai (Hebrew *sinay*), implying a popular etymology for the name of the sacred mountain.

§§[3:6] **God of your father:** a frequently used epithet in Genesis (along with the variants "my father" and "your father") for God as worshiped by the ancestors. As is known from its usage outside of the Bible in the ancient Near East, it suggests a close, personal relationship between the individual and the particular god in question, who is both a patron and a protector, a god traditionally revered by the individual's family and whose worship is passed on from father to son. **The God of Abraham . . . Jacob:** this precise phrase (only here and in v. 15; 4:5) stresses the continuity between the new revelation to Moses and the earlier religious experience of Israel's ancestors, identifying the God who is now addressing Moses with the God who promised land and numerous posterity to

n. [3:2–10] Acts 7:30–35.  o. [3:5] Jos 5:15.

God of Isaac, and the God of Jacob.[p] Moses hid his face, for he was afraid to look at God.

**The Call and Commission of Moses.** [7]But the LORD said: I have witnessed the affliction of my people in Egypt and have heard their cry against their taskmasters, so I know well what they are suffering. [8]Therefore I have come down[*] to rescue them from the power of the Egyptians and lead them up from that land into a good and spacious land, a land flowing with milk and honey, the country of the Canaanites, the Hittites, the Amorites, the Perizzites, the Girgashites, the Hivites and the Jebusites.[q] [9]Now indeed the outcry of the Israelites has reached me, and I have seen how the Egyptians are oppressing them. [10]Now, go! I am sending you to Pharaoh to bring my people, the Israelites, out of Egypt.

[11]But Moses said to God, "Who am I[†] that I should go to Pharaoh and bring the Israelites out of Egypt?" [12]God answered: I will be with you; and this will be your sign[‡] that I have sent you. When you have brought the people out of Egypt, you will serve God at this mountain. [13]"But," said Moses to God, "if I go to the Israelites and say to them, 'The God of your ancestors has sent me to you,' and they ask me, 'What is

his name?' what do I tell them?" [14]God replied to Moses: I am who I am.[§] Then he added: This is what you will tell the Israelites: I AM has sent me to you.

[15]God spoke further to Moses: This is what you will say to the Israelites: The LORD, the God of your ancestors, the God of Abraham, the God of Isaac, and the God of Jacob, has sent me to you.

This is my name forever;[r]
    this is my title for all generations.

[16]Go and gather the elders of the Israelites, and tell them, The LORD, the God of your ancestors, the God of Abraham, Isaac, and Jacob, has appeared to me and said: I have observed you and what is being done to you in Egypt; [17]so I have decided to lead you up out of your affliction in Egypt into the land of the Canaanites, the Hittites, the Amorites, the Perizzites, the Girgashites, the Hivites and the Jebusites, a land flowing with milk and honey. [18]They will listen to you. Then you and the elders of Israel will go to the king of Egypt and say to him:[s] The LORD, the God of the Hebrews, has come to meet us. So now, let us go a three days' journey in the wilderness to offer sacrifice to the LORD, our God. [19]Yet I know that the king of Egypt will not allow you to go unless his hand is forced. [20]So I will stretch out my hand and strike Egypt with all the wondrous deeds I will do in its midst. After that he will let you go. [21][t]I will even make the Egyptians so well-disposed toward this people that, when you go, you will not go empty-handed. [22]Every woman will ask her neighbor and the resident alien in her house for silver and gold articles[¶] and for clothing, and you will put

---

the ancestors. Cf. Mt 22:32; Mk 12:26; Lk 20:37. **Afraid to look at God:** the traditions about Moses are not uniform in regard to his beholding or not being able to look at God (cf. 24:11; 33:11, 18–23; 34:29–35). Here Moses' reaction is the natural and spontaneous gesture of a person suddenly confronted with a direct experience of God. Aware of his human frailty and the gulf that separates him from the God who is holy, he hides his face. To encounter the divine was to come before an awesome and mysterious power unlike any other a human being might experience and, as such, potentially threatening to one's very identity or existence (see Gn 32:30).

[*][3:8] **I have come down:** cf. Gn 11:5, 7; 18:21. **Flowing with milk and honey:** an expression denoting agricultural prosperity, which seems to have been proverbial in its application to the land of Canaan. Cf. Ex 13:5; Nm 13:27; Jos 5:6; Jer 11:5; 32:22; Ez 20:6, 15.

[†][3:11] **Who am I:** this question is always addressed by an inferior to a superior (to the ruler in 1 Sm 18:18; to God in 2 Sm 7:18 and its parallel, 1 Chr 17:16; 1 Chr 29:14; 2 Chr 2:5). In response to some special opportunity or invitation, the question expresses in a style typical of the ancient Near East the speaker's humility or gratitude or need of further assistance, but never unwillingness or an outright refusal to respond. Instead the question sets the stage for further support from the superior should that be needed (as here).

[‡][3:12] **Sign:** a visible display of the power of God. The ancient notion of a sign from God does not coincide with the modern understanding of "miracle," which suggests some disruption in the laws governing nature. While most any phenomenon can become a vehicle for displaying the purposes and providence of God, here the sign intended to confirm Moses' commission by God seems to be the burning bush itself. Since normally the giving of such a sign would follow the commission rather than precede it (see Jgs 6:11–24), some see Israel's service of God at Sinai after the exodus from Egypt as the confirmatory sign, albeit retroactively. It is more likely, however, that its mention here is intended to establish the present episode with Moses alone as a prefigurement of God's fiery theophany to all Israel on Mount Sinai. **Serve God:** Hebrew '-b-d, "serve," includes among its meanings both the notion of "serving or working for another" and the notion of "worship." The implication here is that the Israelites' service/worship of God is incompatible with their service to Pharaoh.

[p]. [3:6] Ex 4:5; Mt 22:32; Mk 12:26; Lk 20:37.   [q]. [3:8] Gn 15:19–21.

[§][3:14] **I am who I am:** Moses asks in v. 13 for the name of the One speaking to him, but God responds with a wordplay which preserves the utterly mysterious character of the divine being even as it appears to suggest something of the inner meaning of God's name: 'ehyeh "I am" or "I will be(come)" for "Yhwh," the personal name of the God of Israel. While the phrase "I am who I am" resists unraveling, it nevertheless suggests an etymological linking between the name "Yhwh" and an earlier form of the Hebrew verbal root h-y-h "to be." On that basis many have interpreted the name "Yhwh" as a third-person form of the verb meaning "He causes to be, creates," itself perhaps a shortened form of a longer liturgical name such as "(God who) creates (the heavenly armies)." Note in this connection the invocation of Israel's God as "LORD (Yhwh) of Hosts" (e.g., 1 Sm 17:45). In any case, out of reverence for God's proper name, the term Adonai, "my Lord," was later used as a substitute. The word LORD (in small capital letters) indicates that the Hebrew text has the sacred name (Yhwh), the tetragrammaton. The word "Jehovah" arose from a false reading of this name as it is written in the current Hebrew text. The Septuagint has egō eimi ho ōn, "I am the One who is" (ōn being the participle of the verb "to be"). This can be taken as an assertion of God's aseity or self-existence, and has been understood as such by the Church, since the time of the Fathers, as a true expression of God's being, even though it is not precisely the meaning of the Hebrew.

[¶][3:22] **Articles:** probably jewelry.

[r]. [3:15] Ps 135:13.   [s]. [3:18] Ex 5:3.   [t]. [3:21–22] Ex 11:2–3; 12:35–36.

them on your sons and daughters. So you will plunder the Egyptians.

## CHAPTER 4

¹"But," objected Moses, "suppose they do not believe me or listen to me? For they may say, 'The LORD did not appear to you.'" ²The LORD said to him: What is in your hand? "A staff," he answered. ³God said: Throw it on the ground. So he threw it on the ground and it became a snake," and Moses backed away from it. ⁴Then the LORD said to Moses: Now stretch out your hand and take hold of its tail. So he stretched out his hand and took hold of it, and it became a staff in his hand. ⁵That is so they will believe that the LORD, the God of their ancestors, the God of Abraham, the God of Isaac, and the God of Jacob, did appear to you.

⁶Again the LORD said to him: Put your hand into the fold of your garment. So he put his hand into the fold of his garment, and when he drew it out, there was his hand covered with scales, like snowflakes. ⁷Then God said: Put your hand back into the fold of your garment. So he put his hand back into the fold of his garment, and when he drew it out, there was it again like his own flesh. ⁸If they do not believe you or pay attention to the message of the first sign, they should believe the message of the second sign. ⁹And if they do not believe even these two signs and do not listen to you, take some water from the Nile and pour it on the dry land. The water you take from the Nile will become blood on the dry land.ᵛ

**Aaron's Office as Assistant.** ¹⁰Moses, however, said to the LORD, "If you please, my Lord, I have never been eloquent, neither in the past nor now that you have spoken to your servant; but I am slow of speech and tongue."ʷ ¹¹The LORD said to him: Who gives our person speech? Who makes another mute or deaf, seeing or blind? Is it not I, the LORD? ¹²Now go, I will assist you in speaking* and teach you what you are to say. ¹³But he said, "If you please, my Lord, send someone else!"† ¹⁴Then the LORD became angry with Moses and said: I know there is your brother, Aaron the Levite, who is a good speaker; even now he is on his way to meet you. When he sees you, he will truly be glad. ¹⁵You will speak to him and put the words in his mouth. I will assist both you and him in speaking and teach you both what you are to do. ¹⁶He will speak to the people for you: he will be your spokesman,‡ and you will be as

God to him.ˣ ¹⁷Take this staff§ in your hand; with it you are to perform the signs.

**Moses' Return to Egypt.** ¹⁸After this Moses returned to Jethro¶ his father-in-law and said to him, "Let me return to my kindred in Egypt, to see whether they are still living." Jethro replied to Moses, "Go in peace." ¹⁹Then the LORD said to Moses in Midian: Return to Egypt, for all those who sought your life are dead. ²⁰So Moses took his wife and his sons, mounted them on the donkey, and started back to the land of Egypt. Moses took the staff of God with him. ²¹The LORD said to Moses: On your return to Egypt, see that you perform before Pharaoh all the wonders I have put in your power. But I will harden his heart** and he will not let the people go. ²²ʸSo you will say to Pharaoh, Thus says the LORD: Israel is my son, my firstborn. ²³I said to you: Let my son go, that he may serve me. Since you refused to let him go, I will kill your son, your firstborn.ᶻ

²⁴††On the journey, at a place where they spent the night, the LORD came upon Moses and sought to put him to death. ²⁵ᵃBut Zipporah took a piece of flint and cut off her son's foreskin and, touching his feet,‡‡ she said, "Surely you are

---

§[4:17] **This staff**: probably the same as that of vv. 2–4; but some understand that a new staff is now given by God to Moses.

¶[4:18] **Jethro**: the Hebrew text has "Jether," apparently a variant form of "Jethro" found in the same verse. **To see whether they are still living**: Moses did not tell his father-in-law his main reason for returning to Egypt.

**[4:21] **Harden his heart**: in the biblical view, the heart, whose actual function in the circulation of blood was unknown, typically performs functions associated today more with the brain than with the emotions. Therefore, while it may be used in connection with various emotional states ranging from joy to sadness, it very commonly designates the seat of intellectual and volitional activities. For God to harden Pharaoh's heart is to harden his resolve against the Israelites' desire to leave. In the ancient world, actions which are out of character are routinely attributed not to the person but to some "outside" superhuman power acting upon the person (Jgs 14:16; 1 Sm 16:10). Uncharacteristically negative actions or states are explained in the same way (1 Sm 16:14). In this instance, the opposition of Pharaoh, in the face of God's displays of power, would be unintelligible to the ancient Israelites unless he is seen as under some divine constraint. But this does not diminish Pharaoh's own responsibility. In the anthropology of the ancient Israelites there is no opposition between individual responsibility and God's sovereignty over all of creation. Cf. Rom 9:17–18.

††[4:24–26] This story continues to perplex commentators and may have circulated in various forms before finding its place here in Exodus. Particularly troublesome is the unique phrase "spouse of blood." Nevertheless, v. 26, which apparently comes from the hand of a later commentator on the original story, is intended to offer some clarification. It asserts that when Zipporah used the problematic expression (addressing it either to Moses or her son), she did so with reference to the circumcision performed on her son—the only place in the Bible where this rite is performed by a woman. Whatever the precise meaning of the phrase "spouse of blood," circumcision is the key to understanding it as well as the entire incident. One may conclude, therefore, that God was angry with Moses for having failed to keep the divine command given to Abraham in Gn 17:10–12 and circumcise his son. Moses' life is spared when his wife circumcises their son.

‡‡[4:25] **Touching his feet**: a euphemism most probably for the male sexual organ (see 2 Kgs 18:27; Is 7:20); whether the

---

*[4:12] **Assist you in speaking**: lit., "be with your mouth"; cf. v. 15, lit., "be with your mouth and with his mouth."

†[4:13] **Send someone else**: lit., "send by means of him whom you will send," that is, "send whom you will."

‡[4:16] **Spokesman**: lit., "mouth"; Aaron was to serve as a mouthpiece for Moses, as a prophet does for God; hence the relation between Moses and Aaron is compared to that between God and his prophet: Moses "will be as God to," i.e., lit., "will become God for him." Cf. 7:1.

---

u. [4:3] Ex 7:10.   v. [4:9] Ex 7:17, 19–20.   w. [4:10] Ex 6:12.

x. [4:16] Ex 7:1.   y. [4:22] Sir 36:11.   z. [4:23] Ex 11:5; 12:29.
a. [4:25] Is 6:2; 7:20.

a spouse of blood to me." [26]So God let Moses alone. At that time she said, "A spouse of blood," in regard to the circumcision.

[27]The LORD said to Aaron: Go into the wilderness to meet Moses. So he went; when meeting him at the mountain of God, he kissed him. [28]Moses told Aaron everything the LORD had sent him to say, and all the signs he had commanded him to do. [29]Then Moses and Aaron went and gathered all the elders of the Israelites. [30]Aaron told them everything the LORD had said to Moses, and he performed the signs before the people. [31]The people believed, and when they heard that the LORD had observed the Israelites and had seen their affliction,* they knelt and bowed down.

## CHAPTER 5

**Pharaoh's Hardness of Heart.** [1]Afterwards, Moses and Aaron went to Pharaoh and said, "Thus says the LORD, the God of Israel: Let my people go, that they may hold a feast[†] for me in the wilderness." [2]Pharaoh answered, "Who is the LORD, that I should obey him and let Israel go? I do not know the LORD,[‡] and I will not let Israel go." [3]They replied, "The God of the Hebrews has come to meet us. Let us go a three days' journey in the wilderness, that we may offer sacrifice to the LORD, our God,[b] so that he does not strike us with the plague or the sword." [4]The king of Egypt answered them, "Why, Moses and Aaron, do you make the people neglect their work? Off to your labors!" [5]Pharaoh continued, "Look how they are already more numerous[§] than the people of the land, and yet you would give them rest from their labors!"

[6]That very day Pharaoh gave the taskmasters of the people and their foremen[¶] this order: [7]"You shall no longer supply the people with straw for their brickmaking** as before. Let them go and gather their own straw! [8]Yet you shall levy upon them the same quota of bricks as they made previously. Do not reduce it. They are lazy; that is why they are crying, 'Let us go to offer sacrifice to our God.' [9]Increase the work for the men, so that they attend to it and not to deceitful words."

[10]So the taskmasters of the people and their foremen went out and told the people, "Thus says Pharaoh,[††] 'I will not provide you with straw. [11]Go and get your own straw from wherever you can find it. But there will not be the slightest reduction in your work.'" [12]The people, then, scattered throughout the land of Egypt to gather stubble for straw, [13]while the taskmasters kept driving them on, saying, "Finish your work, the same daily amount as when the straw was supplied to you." [14]The Israelite foremen, whom the taskmasters of Pharaoh had placed over them, were beaten, and were asked, "Why have you not completed your prescribed amount of bricks yesterday and today, as before?"

**Complaint of the Foremen.** [15]Then the Israelite foremen came and cried out to Pharaoh:[‡‡] "Why do you treat your servants in this manner? [16]No straw is supplied to your servants, and still we are told, 'Make bricks!' Look how your servants are beaten! It is you who are at fault." [17]He answered, "Lazy! You are lazy! That is why you keep saying, 'Let us go and offer sacrifice to the LORD.' [18]Now off to work! No straw will be supplied to you, but you must supply your quota of bricks."

[19]The Israelite foremen realized they were in trouble, having been told, "Do not reduce your daily amount of bricks!" [20]So when they left Pharaoh they assailed Moses and Aaron, who were waiting to meet them, [21]and said to them, "The LORD look upon you and judge! You have made us offensive to Pharaoh and his servants, putting a sword into their hands to kill us."

**Renewal of God's Promise.** [22]Then Moses again had recourse to the LORD and said, "LORD, why have you treated this people badly? And why did you send me? [23]From the time I went to Pharaoh to speak in your name, he has treated this people badly, and you have done nothing to rescue your people."

## CHAPTER 6

[1]The LORD answered Moses: Now you will see what I will do to Pharaoh. For by a strong hand,

---

genitals of the child (after Zipporah circumcised him) or of Moses (after the circumcision of his son) is not clear.

\* [4:31] **Observed . . . their affliction:** the same phrases used in God's dialogue with Moses in 3:16–17.

† [5:1] **Hold a feast:** the Hebrew verb used here, *hagag* ("to celebrate a feast or a festival"; see 12:14; 23:14), refers to a community celebration marked above all by a procession to the sanctuary. It is used especially of three major feasts: Unleavened Bread, Pentecost (in 23:16, "the Feast of Harvest," but customarily "the Feast of Weeks" [*Shavuot*]), and Succoth/Sukkoth (in 34:16, "the Feast of Ingathering," as in Dt 16:13, 16; 31:10; Lv 23:34; Zec 14:16; passim) and—along with the related noun *hag*—the Passover in 12:14. See 23:14–18; 34:18–25.

‡ [5:2] **I do not know the LORD:** whether or not he had heard of the Lord, the God of Israel, Pharaoh refuses to acknowledge the Lord's authority. See note on 1:8.

§ [5:5] **They are already more numerous:** a recollection of Pharaoh's earlier words to his subjects in 1:9.

¶ [5:6] **The taskmasters of the people and their foremen:** the former were higher officials and probably Egyptians; the latter were lower officials (perhaps recordkeepers or clerks), chosen from the Israelites themselves. Cf. v. 14.

** [5:7] Straw was mixed with clay to give sun-dried bricks greater cohesion and durability.

†† [5:10] **Thus says Pharaoh:** the standard formula for prophetic oracles, but with Pharaoh rather than the Lord as the subject. This heightens the sense of personal conflict between Pharaoh, who acts as if he were God, and the Lord, whose claims are spurned by Pharaoh.

‡‡ [5:15] **Cried out to Pharaoh:** the Hebrew verb translated "cry out" and its related noun are normally used of appeals to God by Moses (8:8; 14:15; 15:25; 17:4), the people (3:7; 14:10), or an oppressed individual (22:22, 26). Here, by implication, these minor Israelite officials appeal to Pharaoh as if he were their God. See v. 10.

b. [5:3] Ex 3:18.

he will let them go; by a strong hand,* he will drive them from his land.

**Confirmation of the Promise to the Ancestors.** [2]Then God spoke to Moses, and said to him: I am the LORD. [3]As God the Almighty† I appeared‡ to Abraham, Isaac, and Jacob, but by my name, LORD, I did not make myself known to them. [4]I also established my covenant with them, to give them the land of Canaan, the land in which they were residing as aliens.d [5]Now that I have heard the groaning of the Israelites, whom the Egyptians have reduced to slavery, I am mindful of my covenant.e [6]Therefore, say to the Israelites: I am the LORD. I will free you from the burdens of the Egyptians and will deliver you from their slavery. I will redeem you by my outstretched arm and with mighty acts of judgment. [7]I will take you as my own people, and I will be your God;f and you will know that I, the LORD, am your God who has freed you from the burdens of the Egyptians [8]and I will bring you into the land which I swore to give to Abraham, Isaac, and Jacob. I will give it to you as your own possession—I, the LORD! [9]But when Moses told this to the Israelites, they would not listen to him because of their dejection and hard slavery.

[10]Then the LORD spoke to Moses: [11]Go, tell Pharaoh, king of Egypt, to let the Israelites leave his land. [12]However, Moses protested to the LORD, "If the Israelites did not listen to me, how is it possible that Pharaoh will listen to me, poor speaker§ that I am!" [13]But the LORD spoke to Moses and Aaron regarding the Israelites and Pharaoh, king of Egypt, and charged them to bring the Israelites out of the land of Egypt.

**Genealogy of Moses and Aaron.** [14]These are the heads of their ancestral houses.¶ The sons of Reuben,h the firstborn of Israel: Hanoch, Pallu, Hezron and Carmi; these are the clans of Reuben.

[15]The sons of Simeon:i Jemuel, Jamin, Ohad, Jachin, Zohar and Shaul, the son of a Canaanite woman; these are the clans of Simeon. [16]These are the names of the sons of Levi,j in their genealogical order: Gershon, Kohath and Merari. Levi lived one hundred and thirty-seven years.

[17]The sons of Gershon,k by their clans: Libni and Shimei. [18]The sons of Kohath:l Amram, Izhar, Hebron and Uzziel. Kohath lived one hundred and thirty-three years. [19]The sons of Merari:m Mahli and Mushi. These are the clans of Levi in their genealogical order.

[20]Amram married his aunt** Jochebed,n who bore him Aaron, Moses, and Miriam. Amram lived one hundred and thirty-seven years. [21]The sons of Izhar: Korah, Nepheg and Zichri. [22]The sons of Uzziel: Mishael, Elzaphan and Sithri. [23]Aaron married Elisheba, Amminadab'so daughter, the sister of Nahshon; she bore him Nadab, Abihu, Eleazar and Ithamar. [24]The sons of Korah: Assir, Elkanah and Abiasaph. These are the clans of the Korahites. [25]Eleazar, Aaron's son, married one of Putiel's daughters, who bore him Phinehas.†† These are the heads of the ancestral houses of the Levites by their clans. [26]These are the Aaron and the Moses to whom the LORD said, "Bring the Israelites out from the land of Egypt, company by company." [27]They are the ones who spoke to Pharaoh, king of Egypt, to bring the Israelites out of Egypt—the same Moses and Aaron.

[28]When the LORD spoke to Moses in the land of Egypt [29]the LORD said to Moses: I am the LORD. Say to Pharaoh, king of Egypt, all that I tell you. [30]But Moses protested to the LORD, "Since I am a poor speaker, how is it possible that Pharaoh will listen to me?"

## CHAPTER 7

[1]The LORD answered Moses: See! I have made you a god to Pharaoh,p and Aaron your brother will be your prophet.‡‡ [2]You will speak all that I command you. In turn, your brother Aaron will tell Pharaoh to let the Israelites go out of his land. [3]Yet I will make Pharaoh so headstrong that, despite the many signs and wonders that I work in the land of Egypt, [4]Pharaoh will not listen to you. Therefore I will lay my hand on

---

*[6:1] **By a strong hand:** by God's hand or Pharaoh's hand? The Hebrew is ambiguous; although it may be an allusion to God's hand of 3:19–20, both interpretations are possible.

†[6:2–7:7] According to the standard source criticism of the Pentateuch, 6:2–7:7 represents a Priestly version of the JE call narrative in 3:1–4:17. But in context the present account does more than simply repeat the earlier passage. See note below.

‡[6:3] **God the Almighty:** in Hebrew, El Shaddai. This traditional translation does not have a firm philological basis. **But by my name . . . I did not make myself known to them:** although the text implies that the name LORD was unknown previously, in context the emphasis in the passage falls on the understanding of God that comes with knowledge of the name. In this way God responds to the worsening plight of the Israelites and Moses' complaint in 5:23 that God has done nothing at all to rescue them.

§[6:12] **Poor speaker:** lit., "uncircumcised of lips": a metaphor expressing the hindrance of good communication expressed as "slow of speech and tongue" (4:10). Also used as a metaphor for impeded "heart" (Lv 26:41; Dt 10:16).

¶[6:14] The purpose of the genealogy here is to give the line from which Moses and Aaron sprang, with special emphasis placed on the line of Aaron. Reuben and Simeon are mentioned first because, as older brothers of Levi, their names occur before his in the genealogy.

**[6:20] **His aunt:** more exactly, "his father's sister." Later on such a marriage was forbidden. Cf. Lv 18:12. Hence, the Greek and Latin versions render here, "his cousin."

††[6:25] **Phinehas:** according to Nm 25:13, Phinehas was given by God "the covenant of an everlasting priesthood" because of his zeal for God when the Israelites committed apostasy by worshiping the Baal of Peor in the plains of Moab (see Nm 25:1–18).

‡‡[7:1] **Prophet:** Hebrew nabi, one who can legitimately speak for God and in God's name to another or others. Just as God spoke to Moses, so Moses will speak to Aaron, who will be a "prophet" to Pharaoh. Cf. 4:16.

---

c. [6:3] Gn 17:1; 35:11.   d. [6:4] Gn 15:18; 17:4–8.   e. [6:5] Ex 2:24.   f. [6:7] Lv 26:12.   g. [6:12] Ex 4:10.   h. [6:14] Nm 26:5–6; 1 Chr 5:3.

i. [6:15] Nm 26:12; 1 Chr 4:24.   j. [6:16] Nm 3:17; 1 Chr 6:1; 23:6.   k. [6:17] Nm 3:21; 1 Chr 6:2; 23:7.   l. [6:18] Nm 3:27; 1 Chr 6:3, 18.   m. [6:19] Nm 3:20; 1 Chr 6:4, 14; 23:21.   n. [6:20] Nm 26:59.   o. [6:23] Ru 4:19–20; 1 Chr 2:10.   p. [7:1] Ex 4:15–16.

Egypt and with mighty acts of judgment I will bring my armies, my people the Israelites, out of the land of Egypt. ⁵All Egyptians will know that I am the LORD, when I stretch out my hand against Egypt and bring the Israelites out of their midst.

⁶This, then, is what Moses and Aaron did. They did exactly as the LORD had commanded them. ⁷Moses was eighty years old, and Aaron eighty-three, when they spoke to Pharaoh.

### III. THE CONTEST WITH PHARAOH

**The Staff Turned into a Serpent.** ⁸The LORD spoke to Moses and Aaron: ⁹When Pharaoh demands of you, "Produce a sign or wonder," you will say to Aaron: "Take your staff and throw it down before Pharaoh, and it will turn into a serpent."�q ¹⁰Then Moses and Aaron went to Pharaoh and did just as the LORD had commanded. Aaron threw his staff down before Pharaoh and his servants, and it turned into a serpent. ¹¹Pharaoh, in turn, summoned the wise men and the sorcerers, and they also, the magiciansʳ of Egypt, did the same thing by their magic arts. ¹²Each one threw down his staff, and they turned into serpents. But Aaron's staff swallowed their staffs. ¹³Pharaoh, however, hardened his heart and would not listen to them, just as the LORD had foretold.

**First Plague: Water Turned into Blood.**ˢ ¹⁴Then the LORD said to Moses: Pharaoh is obstinate† in refusing to let the people go. ¹⁵In the morning, just when he sets out for the water, go to Pharaoh and present yourself by the bank of the Nile, holding in your hand the staff that turned into a snake.‡ ¹⁶Say to him: The LORD, the God of the Hebrews, sent me to you with the message: Let my people go to serve me in the wilderness. But as yet you have not listened. ¹⁷Thus says the LORD: This is how you will know that I am the LORD. With the staff here in my hand, I will strike the water in the Nile and it will be changed into blood.ᶦ ¹⁸The fish in the Nile will die, and the

Nile itself will stink so that the Egyptians will be unable to drink water from the Nile.

¹⁹The LORD then spoke to Moses: Speak to Aaron: Take your staff and stretch out your hand over the waters of Egypt—its streams, its canals, its ponds, and all its supplies of water—that they may become blood. There will be blood throughout the land of Egypt, even in the wooden pails and stone jars.

²⁰This, then, is what Moses and Aaron did, exactly as the LORD had commanded. Aaron raised his staff and struck the waters in the Nile in full view of Pharaoh and his servants, and all the water in the Nile was changed into blood. ²¹The fish in the Nile died, and the Nile itself stank so that the Egyptians could not drink water from it. There was blood throughout the land of Egypt. ²²But the Egyptian magicians did the same§ by their magic arts. So Pharaoh hardened his heart and would not listen to them, just as the LORD had said. ²³Pharaoh turned away and went into his house, with no concern even for this. ²⁴All the Egyptians had to dig round about the Nile for drinking water, since they could not drink any water from the Nile.

**Second Plague: The Frogs.** ²⁵Seven days passed after the LORD had struck the Nile. ²⁶Then the LORD said to Moses: Go to Pharaoh and tell him:ᵗ Thus says the LORD: Let my people go to serve me. ²⁷If you refuse to let them go, then I will send a plague of frogs over all your territory. ²⁸The Nile will teem with frogs. They will come up and enter into your palace and into your bedroom and onto your bed, into the houses of your servants, too, and among your people, even into your ovens and your kneading bowls. ²⁹The frogs will come up over you and your people and all your servants.

### CHAPTER 8

¹The LORD then spoke to Moses: Speak to Aaron: Stretch out your hand with your staff over the streams, the canals, and the ponds, and make frogs overrun the land of Egypt. ²So Aaron stretched out his hand over the waters of Egypt, and the frogs came up and covered the land of Egypt. ³But the magicians did the same by their magic arts and made frogs overrun the land of Egypt.

⁴Then Pharaoh summoned Moses and Aaron and said, "Pray to the LORD to remove the frogs from me and my people, and I will let the people go to sacrifice to the LORD." ⁵Moses answered Pharaoh, "Please designate for me the time when I am to pray for you and your

---

\* [7:14–12:30] After a brief preface (vv. 8–13) drawn from the Priestly source, a narrative depicting the series of ten disasters that God brings upon Pharaoh because of his stubbornness ensues. Although most of these disasters, known traditionally as the "ten plagues of Egypt," could be interpreted as naturally occurring phenomena, they are clearly represented by the biblical authors as extraordinary events indicative of God's intervention on behalf of Israel and as occurring exactly according to Moses' commands. See Ps 78:43–51 and 105:27–36 for poetic versions of these plagues, which also differ significantly from the account here.

† [7:14] **Pharaoh is obstinate**: lit., "Pharaoh's heart is heavy" (*kabed*); thus not precisely the same Hebrew idiom as found in vv. 13 and 22, "stubborn," lit., "Pharaoh's heart was hard(ened)" (*hazaq*) (cf. the related idiom with Pharaoh as the object, e.g., 4:21).

‡ [7:15] **The staff that turned into a snake**: the allusion is to 4:2–4 rather than 7:9–12. The latter comes from the hand of the Priestly writer and features Aaron—with his staff—as the principal actor.

§ [7:22] **The Egyptian magicians did the same**: this is an exaggeration, presumably influenced by the similar statement in v. 11; whereas the magicians could turn their staffs into snakes after Aaron had done so, after Aaron's sign there should not have been any water in Egypt still unchanged to blood for the magicians "to do the same" with it (cf. v. 24).

---

q. [7:9] Ex 4:3.　r. [7:11] 2 Tm 3:8.　s. [7:17–21] Ex 4:9; Ps 78:44; 105:29; Wis 11:5–7.

t. [7:26–29] Ps 78:45; 105:30.

servants and your people, to get rid of the frogs from you and your houses. They will be left only in the Nile." ⁶"Tomorrow," he said. Then Moses replied, "It will be as you have said, so that you may know that there is none like the LORD, our God. ⁷The frogs will leave you and your houses, your servants and your people; they will be left only in the Nile."

⁸After Moses and Aaron left Pharaoh's presence, Moses cried out to the LORD on account of the frogs that he had inflicted on Pharaoh; ⁹and the LORD did as Moses had asked. The frogs died off in the houses, the courtyards, and the fields. ¹⁰Heaps of them were piled up, and the land stank. ¹¹But when Pharaoh saw there was a respite, he became obstinate and would not listen to them, just as the LORD had said.

**Third Plague: The Gnats.** ¹²Thereupon the LORD spoke to Moses: Speak to Aaron: Stretch out your staff and strike the dust of the earth, and it will turn into gnats*ᵘ throughout the land of Egypt. ¹³They did so. Aaron stretched out his hand with his staff and struck the dust of the earth, and gnats came upon human being and beast alike. All the dust of the earth turned into gnats throughout the land of Egypt. ¹⁴Though the magicians did the same thing to produce gnats by their magic arts, they could not do so.ᵛ The gnats were on human being and beast alike, ¹⁵and the magicians said to Pharaoh, "This is the finger of God."† Yet Pharaoh hardened his heart and would not listen to them, just as the LORD had said.

**Fourth Plague: The Flies.** ¹⁶Then the LORD spoke to Moses: Early tomorrow morning present yourself to Pharaoh when he sets out toward the water, and say to him: Thus says the LORD: Let my people go to serve me. ¹⁷For if you do not let my people go, I will send swarms of flies upon you and your servants and your people and your houses. The houses of the Egyptians and the very ground on which they stand will be filled with swarms of flies. ¹⁸But on that day I will make an exception of the land of Goshen, where my people are, and no swarms of flies will be there, so that you may know that I the LORD am in the midst of the land. ¹⁹I will

make a distinction‡ between my people and your people. This sign will take place tomorrow. ²⁰This the LORD did. Thick swarms of flies entered the house of Pharaoh and the houses of his servants; throughout Egypt the land was devastated on account of the swarms of flies.ʷ

²¹Then Pharaoh summoned Moses and Aaron and said, "Go sacrifice to your God within the land." ²²But Moses replied, "It is not right to do so, for what we sacrifice to the LORD, our God, is abhorrent to the Egyptians.§ If we sacrifice what is abhorrent to the Egyptians before their very eyes, will they not stone us? ²³We must go a three days' journey in the wilderness and sacrifice to the LORD, our God, as he commands us." ²⁴Pharaoh said, "I will let you go to sacrifice to the LORD, your God, in the wilderness, provided that you do not go too far away. Pray for me." ²⁵Moses answered, "As soon as I leave you I will pray to the LORD that the swarms of flies may depart tomorrow from Pharaoh, his servants, and his people. Pharaoh, however, must not act deceitfully again and refuse to let the people go to sacrifice to the LORD." ²⁶When Moses left Pharaoh, he prayed to the LORD; ²⁷and the LORD did as Moses had asked, removing the swarms of flies from Pharaoh, his servants, and his people. Not one remained. ²⁸But once more Pharaoh became obstinate and would not let the people go.

## CHAPTER 9

**Fifth Plague: The Pestilence.** ¹Then the LORD said to Moses: Go to Pharaoh and tell him: Thus says the LORD, the God of the Hebrews: Let my people go to serve me. ²For if you refuse to let them go and persist in holding them, ³the hand of the LORD will strike your livestock in the field—your horses, donkeys, camels, herds and flocks—with a very severe pestilence. ⁴But the LORD will distinguish between the livestock of Israel and that of Egypt, so that nothing belonging to the Israelites will die. ⁵And the LORD set a definite time, saying: Tomorrow the LORD will do this in the land. ⁶And on the next day the LORD did it. All the livestock of the Egyptians died,ˣ but not one animal belonging to the Israelites died. ⁷But although Pharaoh found upon inquiry that not even so much as one of the

---

*[8:12, 17] **Gnats, flies:** it is uncertain what species of troublesome insects are meant here in vv. 12–14 and then in vv. 17–27, the identification as "gnat" (vv. 12–14) and as "fly" (vv. 17–27) being based on the rendering of the Septuagint. Others suggest "lice" in vv. 12–14, while rabbinic literature renders Hebrew *'arob* as a "mixture of wild animals." In the Hebrew of the Old Testament, the word occurs only in the context of the plagues (see also Ps 78:45 and 105:31).

†[8:15] **The finger of God:** previously the magicians had, for the most part, been able to replicate the signs and wonders Moses performed to manifest God's power—turning their staffs into snakes (7:11–12), turning water into blood (7:22), and producing frogs to overrun the land of Egypt (8:3). But now for the first time they are unable to compete, and confess a power greater than their own is at work. Cf. Lk 11:20.

‡[8:19] **A distinction:** while some uncertainty surrounds the Hebrew here rendered as "distinction," it is clear that now the Israelites begin to be set apart from the Egyptians, a separation that reaches a climax in the death of the Egyptian firstborn (11:7).

§[8:22] Perhaps Moses is deceiving the Pharaoh much like the "God-fearing" midwives (1:16–20), although ancient historians writing about Egypt some time after the period in which the exodus is set do note Egyptian prohibitions on sacrificing cattle or slaughtering sacred animals. As such, the Egyptians might well have fiercely resented certain sacrificial practices of the Israelites. Certain animals were held sacred in Egypt, as the representations of various deities.

---

u. [8:12–13] Ps 105:31.   v. [8:14] Wis 17:7.

w. [8:20] Ps 78:45; 105:31; Wis 16:9.   x. [9:6] Ps 78:48.

livestock of the Israelites had died, he remained obstinate and would not let the people go.

**Sixth Plague: The Boils.** [8]So the LORD said to Moses and Aaron: Each of you take handfuls of soot from a kiln, and in the presence of Pharaoh let Moses scatter it toward the sky. [9]It will turn into fine dust over the whole land of Egypt and cause festering boils* on human being and beast alike throughout the land of Egypt.

[10]So they took the soot from a kiln and appeared before Pharaoh. When Moses scattered it toward the sky, it caused festering boils on human being and beast alike. [11]Because of the boils the magicians could not stand in Moses' presence, for there were boils on the magicians as well as on the rest of the Egyptians. [12]But the LORD hardened Pharaoh's heart, and he would not listen to them, just as the LORD had said to Moses.

**Seventh Plague: The Hail.** [13]Then the LORD spoke to Moses: Early tomorrow morning present yourself to Pharaoh and say to him: Thus says the LORD, the God of the Hebrews: Let my people go to serve me, [14]for this time I will unleash all my blows upon you and your servants and your people, so that you may know that there is none like me anywhere on earth. [15]For by now I should have stretched out my hand and struck you and your people with such pestilence that you would have vanished from the earth. [16]But this is why I have let you survive: to show you† my power and to make my name resound throughout the earth!ʸ [17]Will you continue to exalt yourself over my people and not let them go? [18]At this time tomorrow, therefore, I am going to rain down such fierce hail as there has never been in Egypt from the day it was founded up to the present. [19]Therefore, order your livestock and whatever else you have in the open fields to be brought to a place of safety. Whatever human being or animal is found in the fields and is not brought to shelter will die when the hail comes down upon them. [20]Those of Pharaoh's servants who feared the word of the LORD hurried their servants and their livestock off to shelter. [21]But those who did not pay attention to the word of the LORD left their servants and their livestock in the fields.

[22]The LORD then said to Moses: Stretch out your hand toward the sky, that hail may fall upon the entire land of Egypt, on human being and beast alike and all the vegetation of the fields in the land of Egypt. [23]So Moses stretched out his staff toward the sky, and the LORD sent forth peals of thunder and hail.ᶻ Lightning flashed toward the earth, and the LORD rained down hail upon the land of Egypt. [24]There was hail and lightning flashing here and there through the hail, and the hail was so fierce that nothing like it had been seen in Egypt since it became a nation. [25]Throughout the land of Egypt the hail struck down everything in the fields, human being and beast alike; it struck down all the vegetation of the fields and splintered every tree in the fields. [26]Only in the land of Goshen, where the Israelites were, was there no hail.

[27]Then Pharaoh sent for Moses and Aaron and said to them, "I have sinned this time! The LORD is the just one, and I and my people are the ones at fault. [28]Pray to the LORD! Enough of the thunder‡ and hail! I will let you go; you need stay no longer." [29]Moses replied to him, "As soon as I leave the city I will extend my hands to the LORD; the thunder will cease, and there will be no more hail so that you may know that the earth belongs to the LORD. [30]But as for you and your servants, I know that you do not yet fear the LORD God."

[31]Now the flax and the barley were ruined, because the barley was in ear and the flax in bud. [32]But the wheat and the spelt were not ruined, for they grow later.

[33]When Moses had left Pharaoh and gone out of the city, he extended his hands to the LORD. The thunder and the hail ceased, and the rain no longer poured down upon the earth. [34]But Pharaoh, seeing that the rain and the hail and the thunder had ceased, sinned again and became obstinate, both he and his servants. [35]In the hardness of his heart, Pharaoh would not let the Israelites go, just as the LORD had said through Moses.

## CHAPTER 10

**Eighth Plague: The Locusts.** [1]Then the LORD said to Moses: Go to Pharaoh, for I have made him and his servants obstinate in order that I may perform these signs of mine among them [2]and that you may recount to your son and grandson how I made a fool of the Egyptians and what signs I did among them, so that you may know that I am the LORD.ᵃ

[3]So Moses and Aaron went to Pharaoh and told him, "Thus says the LORD, the God of the Hebrews: How long will you refuse to submit to me? Let my people go to serve me. [4]For if you refuse to let my people go, tomorrow I will bring locusts into your territory. [5]They will cover the surface of the earth, so that the earth itself will not be visible. They will eat up the remnant you saved undamaged from the hail, as well as all the trees that are growing in your fields. [6]They will

---

*[9:9] **Boils:** the exact nature of the disease is not clear. Semitic cognates, for example, suggest the Hebrew root means "to be hot" and thus point to some sort of inflammation. The fact that soot taken from the kiln is the agent of the disease would point in the same direction. See further Lv 13:18–23; Dt 28:35; 2 Kgs 20:7.

†[9:16] **To show you:** some ancient versions such as the Septuagint read, "to show through you." Cf. Rom 9:17.

‡[9:28] **Thunder:** lit., "divine voices," "voices of God," or the like.

y. [9:16] Rom 9:17.　　　　z. [9:23–24] Ps 78:47; 105:32–33.　　a. [10:2] Dt 6:20–25.

fill your houses and the houses of your servants and of all the Egyptians—something your parents and your grandparents have not seen from the day they appeared on this soil until today." With that he turned and left Pharaoh.

⁷But Pharaoh's servants said to him, "How long will he be a snare for us? Let the people go to serve the LORD, their God. Do you not yet realize that Egypt is being destroyed?" ⁸So Moses and Aaron were brought back to Pharaoh, who said to them, "Go, serve the LORD, your God. But who exactly will go?" ⁹Moses answered, "With our young and old we must go; with our sons and daughters, with our flocks and herds we must go. It is a pilgrimage feast of the LORD for us." ¹⁰"The LORD help you,"* Pharaoh replied, "if I let your little ones go with you! Clearly, you have some evil in mind. ¹¹By no means! Just you men go and serve the LORD.† After all, that is what you have been asking for." With that they were driven from Pharaoh's presence.

¹²ᵇThe LORD then said to Moses: Stretch out your hand over the land of Egypt for the locusts, that they may come upon it and eat up all the land's vegetation, whatever the hail has left. ¹³So Moses stretched out his staff over the land of Egypt, and the LORD drove an east wind‡ over the land all that day and all night. When it was morning, the east wind brought the locusts. ¹⁴The locusts came up over the whole land of Egypt and settled down over all its territory. Never before had there been such a fierce swarm of locusts, nor will there ever be again. ¹⁵They covered the surface of the whole land, so that it became black. They ate up all the vegetation in the land and all the fruit of the trees the hail had spared. Nothing green was left on any tree or plant in the fields throughout the land of Egypt.

¹⁶Pharaoh hurriedly summoned Moses and Aaron and said, "I have sinned against the LORD, your God, and against you. ¹⁷But now, do forgive me my sin only this once, and pray to the LORD, your God, only to take this death from me." ¹⁸When Moses left Pharaoh, he prayed to the LORD, ¹⁹and the LORD caused the wind to shift to a very strong west wind, which took up the locusts and hurled them into the Red Sea.§ Not a single locust remained within the whole territory

of Egypt. ²⁰Yet the LORD hardened Pharaoh's heart, and he would not let the Israelites go.

**Ninth Plague: The Darkness.** ²¹ᶜThen the LORD said to Moses: Stretch out your hand toward the sky, that over the land of Egypt there may be such darkness§ that one can feel it. ²²So Moses stretched out his hand toward the sky, and there was dense darkness throughout the land of Egypt for three days. ²³People could not see one another, nor could they get up from where they were, for three days. But all the Israelites had light where they lived.

²⁴Pharaoh then summoned Moses and Aaron and said, "Go, serve the LORD. Only your flocks and herds will be detained. Even your little ones may go with you." ²⁵But Moses replied, "You also must give us sacrifices and burnt offerings to make to the LORD, our God. ²⁶Our livestock also must go with us. Not an animal must be left behind, for some of them we will select for service** to the LORD, our God; but we will not know with which ones we are to serve the LORD until we arrive there." ²⁷But the LORD hardened Pharaoh's heart, and he was unwilling to let them go. ²⁸Pharaoh said to Moses, "Leave me, and see to it that you do not see my face again! For the day you do see my face you will die!" ²⁹Moses replied, "You are right! I will never see your face again."

## CHAPTER 11

**Tenth Plague: The Death of the Firstborn.** ¹Then the LORD spoke to Moses: One more plague I will bring upon Pharaoh and upon Egypt. After that he will let you depart. In fact, when he finally lets you go, he will drive you away. ²ᵈInstruct the people that every man is to ask his neighbor, and every woman her neighbor, for silver and gold articles and for clothing. ³The LORD indeed made the Egyptians well-disposed toward the people; Moses himself was very highly regarded by Pharaoh's servants and the people in the land of Egypt.

⁴Moses then said, "Thus says the LORD: About midnight I will go forth through Egypt.ᵉ ⁵Every firstborn in the land of Egypt will die, from the firstborn of Pharaoh who sits on his

---

*[10:10] **The LORD help you . . .** : lit., "May the Lord be with you in the same way as I let you . . ."; a sarcastic blessing intended as a curse.

†[10:11] Pharaoh realized that if the men alone went they would have to return to their families. He suspected that the Hebrews had no intention of returning.

‡[10:13] **East wind**: coming across the desert from Arabia, the strong east wind brings Egypt the burning sirocco and, at times, locusts. Cf. 14:21.

§[10:19] **The Red Sea**: the traditional translation, cf. Septuagint and other Versions; but the Hebrew literally means "sea of reeds" or "reedy sea," which could probably be applied to a number of bodies of shallow water, most likely somewhat to the north of the present deep Red Sea.

¶[10:21] **Darkness**: commentators note that at times a storm from the south, called the *khamsin*, blackens the sky of Egypt with sand from the Sahara; the dust in the air is then so thick that the darkness can, in a sense, "be felt." But such observations should not obscure the fact that for the biblical author what transpires in each of the plagues is clearly something extraordinary, an event which witnesses to the unrivaled power of Israel's God.

**[10:26] **Service**: as is obvious from v. 25, the service in question here is the offering of sacrifice. The continued use of the verb *'bd* "to serve" and related nouns for both the people's bondage in Egypt and their subsequent service to the Lord dramatizes the point of the conflict between Pharaoh and the God of Israel, who demands from the Israelites an attachment which is exclusive. See Lv 25:55.

b. [10:12–15] Ps 78:46; 105:34–35.

c. [10:21–22] Ps 105:28.   d. [11:2–3] Ex 3:21–22; 12:35–36.
e. [11:4] Ex 12:12.   f. [11:5–6] Ex 12:29–30.

throne to the firstborn of the slave-girl who is at the handmill,* as well as all the firstborn of the animals. [6]Then there will be loud wailing throughout the land of Egypt, such as has never been, nor will ever be again. [7]But among all the Israelites, among human beings and animals alike, not even a dog will growl, so that you may know that the LORD distinguishes between Egypt and Israel. [8]All these servants of yours will then come down to me and bow down before me, saying: Leave, you and all your followers![g] Then I will depart." With that he left Pharaoh's presence in hot anger.

[9]The LORD said to Moses: Pharaoh will not listen to you so that my wonders may be multiplied in the land of Egypt. [10]Thus, although Moses and Aaron performed all these wonders in Pharaoh's presence, the LORD hardened Pharaoh's heart, and he would not let the Israelites go from his land.

## CHAPTER 12

**The Passover Ritual Prescribed.**[†] [1]The LORD said to Moses and Aaron in the land of Egypt: [2]*This month will stand at the head of your calendar; you will reckon it the first month of the year.[h] [3]Tell the whole community of Israel: On the tenth of this month every family must procure for itself a lamb, one apiece for each household. [4]If a household is too small for a lamb, it along with its nearest neighbor will procure one, and apportion the lamb's cost[§] in proportion to the number of persons, according to what each household consumes. [5]Your lamb must be a year-old male and without blemish. You may take it from either the sheep or the goats. [6]You will keep it until the fourteenth day of this month, and then, with the whole community of Israel assembled, it will be slaughtered during the evening twilight. [7]They will take some of its blood and apply it to the two doorposts and the lintel of the houses in which they eat it. [8]They will consume its meat that same night, eating it roasted with unleavened bread and bitter herbs. [9]Do not eat any of it raw or even boiled in water, but roasted, with its head and shanks and inner organs. [10]You must not keep any of it beyond the

morning; whatever is left over in the morning must be burned up.

[11]This is how you are to eat it: with your loins girt, sandals on your feet and your staff in hand, you will eat it in a hurry. It is the LORD's Passover. [12]For on this same night I will go through Egypt, striking down every firstborn in the land, human being and beast alike, and executing judgment on all the gods of Egypt—I, the LORD![i] [13]But for you the blood will mark the houses where you are. Seeing the blood, I will pass over you; thereby, when I strike the land of Egypt, no destructive blow will come upon you.[j]

[14]This day will be a day of remembrance for you, which your future generations will celebrate with pilgrimage to the LORD; you will celebrate it as a statute forever. [15]For seven days you must eat unleavened bread. From the very first day you will have your houses clear of all leaven. For whoever eats leavened bread from the first day to the seventh will be cut off[¶] from Israel. [16]On the first day you will hold a sacred assembly, and likewise on the seventh. On these days no sort of work shall be done, except to prepare the food that everyone needs. [17]Keep, then, the custom of the unleavened bread,[k] since it was on this very day that I brought your armies out of the land of Egypt. You must observe this day throughout your generations as a statute forever. [18]From the evening of the fourteenth day of the first month until the evening of the twenty-first day of this month you will eat unleavened bread. [19]For seven days no leaven may be found in your houses; for anyone, a resident alien or a native, who eats leavened food will be cut off from the community of Israel. [20]You shall eat nothing leavened; wherever you dwell you may eat only unleavened bread.

**Promulgation of the Passover.** [21]Moses summoned all the elders of Israel and said to them, "Go and procure lambs for your families, and slaughter the Passover victims. [22]Then take a bunch of hyssop,** and dipping it in the blood that is in the basin, apply some of this blood to the lintel and the two doorposts. And none of you shall go outdoors until morning. [23]For when the LORD goes by to strike down the Egyptians, seeing the blood on the lintel and the two doorposts, the LORD will pass over that door and not let the destroyer come into your houses to strike you down.

---

*[11:5] **Handmill**: two pieces of stone were used to grind grain. A smaller upper stone was moved back and forth over a larger stationary stone. This menial work was done by slaves and captives.

†[12:1–20] This section, which interrupts the narrative of the exodus, contains later legislation concerning the celebration of Passover.

‡[12:2] As if to affirm victory over Pharaoh and sovereignty over the Israelites, the Lord proclaims a new calendar for Israel. **This month**: Abib, the month of "ripe grain." Cf. 13:4; 23:15; 34:18; Dt 16:1. It occurred near the vernal equinox, March–April. Later it was known by the Babylonian name of Nisan. Cf. Neh 2:1; Est 3:7.

§[12:4] **The lamb's cost**: some render the Hebrew, "reckon for the lamb the number of persons required to eat it." Cf. v. 10.

¶[12:15] **Cut off**: a common Priestly term, not easily reduced to a simple English equivalent, since its usage appears to involve a number of associated punishments, some or all of which may come into play in any instance of the term's use. These included the excommunication of the offender from the Israelite community, the premature death of the offender, the eventual eradication of the offender's posterity, and finally the loss by the offender of all ancestral holdings.

**[12:22] **Hyssop**: a plant with many small woody branches that was convenient for a sprinkling rite.

---

g. [11:8] Ex 12:31–33.　　h. [12:2–20] Lv 23:5–8; Nm 9:2–5; 28:16–25; Dt 16:1–8.

i. [12:12] Nm 33:4.　　j. [12:13] Heb 11:28.　　k. [12:17] Ex 13:3. l. [12:22–23] Ex 12:7, 13.

²⁴"You will keep this practice forever as a statute for yourselves and your descendants. ²⁵Thus, when you have entered the land which the LORD will give you as he promised, you must observe this rite. ²⁶ᵐWhen your children ask you, 'What does this rite of yours mean?' ²⁷you will reply, 'It is the Passover sacrifice for the LORD, who passed over the houses of the Israelites in Egypt; when he struck down the Egyptians, he delivered our houses.'"

Then the people knelt and bowed down, ²⁸and the Israelites went and did exactly as the LORD had commanded Moses and Aaron.

**Death of the Firstborn.** ²⁹ⁿAnd so at midnight the LORD struck down every firstborn in the land of Egypt, from the firstborn of Pharaoh sitting on his throne to the firstborn of the prisoner in the dungeon, as well as all the firstborn of the animals. ³⁰Pharaoh arose in the night, he and all his servants and all the Egyptians; and there was loud wailing throughout Egypt, for there was not a house without its dead.

**Permission to Depart.** ³¹During the night Pharaoh summoned Moses and Aaron and said, "Leave my people at once, you and the Israelites! Go and serve the LORD as you said. ³²Take your flocks, too, and your herds, as you said, and go; and bless me, too!'"

³³The Egyptians, in a hurry to send them away from the land, urged the people on, for they said, "All of us will die!" ³⁴The people, therefore, took their dough before it was leavened, in their kneading bowls wrapped in their cloaks on their shoulders. ³⁵ᵒAnd the Israelites did as Moses had commanded: they asked the Egyptians for articles of silver and gold and for clothing. ³⁶Indeed the LORD had made the Egyptians so well-disposed toward the people that they let them have whatever they asked for. And so they despoiled the Egyptians.

**Departure from Egypt.** ³⁷The Israelites set out from Rameses⁾ for Succoth, about six hundred thousand men on foot, not counting the children. ³⁸A crowd of mixed ancestry† also went up with them, with livestock in great abundance, both flocks and herds. ³⁹The dough they had brought out of Egypt they baked into unleavened loaves. It was not leavened, because they had been driven out of Egypt and could not wait. They did not even prepare food for the journey.

⁴⁰The time the Israelites had stayed in Egypt‡ was four hundred and thirty years.⁹ ⁴¹At the end of four hundred and thirty years, on this very date, all the armies of the LORD left the land of Egypt. ⁴²This was a night of vigil for the LORD, when he brought them out of the land of Egypt; so on this night all Israelites must keep a vigil for the LORD throughout their generations.

**Law of the Passover.** ⁴³The LORD said to Moses and Aaron: This is the Passover statute. No foreigner may eat of it. ⁴⁴However, every slave bought for money you will circumcise; then he may eat of it. ⁴⁵But no tenant or hired worker may eat of it. ⁴⁶It must be eaten in one house; you may not take any of its meat outside the house.ʳ You shall not break any of its bones.§ ⁴⁷The whole community of Israel must celebrate this feast. ⁴⁸If any alienˢ residing among you would celebrate the Passover for the LORD, all his males must be circumcised, and then he may join in its celebration just like the natives. But no one who is uncircumcised may eat of it. ⁴⁹There will be one lawᵗ for the native and for the alien residing among you.

⁵⁰All the Israelites did exactly as the LORD had commanded Moses and Aaron. ⁵¹On that same day the LORD brought the Israelites out of the land of Egypt company by company.

## CHAPTER 13

**Consecration of Firstborn.** ¹The LORD spoke to Moses and said: ²Consecrate to me every firstborn; whatever opens the womb among the Israelites,ᵘ whether of human being or beast, belongs to me.

³ᵘMoses said to the people, "Remember this day on which you came out of Egypt, out of a house of slavery. For it was with a strong hand that the LORD brought you out from there. Nothing made with leaven may be eaten. ⁴This day on which you are going out is in the month of Abib.** ⁵Therefore, when the LORD, your God, has brought you into the land of the Canaanites, the Hittites, the Amorites, the Perrizites, the Girgashites, the Hivites, and the Jebusites, which he swore to your ancestors to give you, a land flowing with milk and honey, you will perform the following service†† in this month.

---

*[12:32] **Bless me, too:** in a final and humiliating admission of defeat, once again Pharaoh asks Moses to intercede for him (cf. 8:24). However, Pharaoh may be speaking sarcastically.

†[12:38] **Mixed ancestry:** not simply descendants of Jacob; cf. Nm 11:4; Lv 24:10–11.

‡[12:40] **In Egypt:** according to the Septuagint and the Samaritan Pentateuch "in Canaan and Egypt," thus reckoning from the time of Abraham. Cf. Gal 3:17.

§[12:46] **You shall not break any of its bones:** the application of these words to Jesus on the cross (Jn 19:36) sees the Paschal lamb as a prophetic type of Christ, sacrificed to free men and women from the bondage of sin. Cf. also 1 Cor 5:7; 1 Pt 1:19.

¶[12:49] **One law:** the first appearance of the word torah, traditionally translated as "law," though it can have the broader meaning of "teaching" or "instruction." Elsewhere, too, it is said that the "alien" is to be accorded the same treatment as the Israelite (e.g., Lv 19:34).

**[13:4] **Abib:** lit., "ear (of grain)," the old Canaanite name for this month; Israel later called it "Nisan." It was the first month in their liturgical calendar (cf. Ex 12:2).

††[13:5] **The following service:** the celebration of the feast of Unleavened Bread now constitutes the Israelites' service, in contrast to the "service" they performed for Pharaoh as his slaves.

---

m. [12:26–27] Ex 13:8, 14–15; Dt 6:20–25.    n. [12:29–30] Ex 11:4–6; Nm 33:4; Ps 78:51; 105:36; 136:10; Wis 18:10–16.    o. [12:35–36] Ex 3:21–22; 11:2–3; Ps 105:37–38.    p. [12:37] Nm 33:3–5.    q. [12:40] Gn 15:13; Acts 7:6; Gal 3:17.    r. [12:46] Nm 9:12; Jn 19:36.    s. [12:48] Nm 9:14.    t. [13:2] Ex 13:12–15.    u. [13:3–10] Ex 12:2–20.

[6]"For seven days you will eat unleavened bread, and the seventh day will also be a festival to the LORD. [7]Unleavened bread may be eaten during the seven days, but nothing leavened and no leaven may be found in your possession in all your territory. [8]And on that day you will explain to your son, 'This is because of what the LORD did for me when I came out of Egypt.' [9]It will be like a sign° on your hand and a reminder on your forehead,ᵛ so that the teaching of the LORD will be on your lips: with a strong hand the LORD brought you out of Egypt. [10]You will keep this statute at its appointed time from year to year.

[11]"When the LORD, your God, has brought you into the land of the Canaanites, just as he swore to you and your ancestors, and gives it to you, [12]"you will dedicate to the LORD every newborn that opens the womb; and every firstborn male of your animals will belong to the LORD. [13]Every firstborn of a donkey you will ransom with a sheep. If you do not ransom it, you will break its neck. Every human firstborn of your sons you must ransom. [14]And when your son asks you later on, 'What does this mean?' you will tell him, 'With a strong hand the LORD brought us out of Egypt, out of a house of slavery. [15]When Pharaoh stubbornly refused to let us go, the LORD killed every firstborn in the land of Egypt, the firstborn of human being and beast alike. That is why I sacrifice to the LORD every male that opens the womb, and why I ransom every firstborn of my sons.' [16]It will be like a sign on your hand and a band on your forehead that with a strong hand the LORD brought us out of Egypt."ˣ

## IV. THE DELIVERANCE OF THE ISRAELITES FROM PHARAOH AND VICTORY AT THE SEA

**Toward the Red Sea.** [17]Now, when Pharaoh let the people go, God did not lead them by way of the Philistines' land,† though this was the nearest; for God said: If the people see that they have to fight, they might change their minds and return to Egypt. [18]Instead, God rerouted them toward the Red Sea by way of the wilderness road, and the Israelites went up out of the land of Egypt arrayed for battle. [19]Moses also took Joseph's bonesʸ with him, for Joseph had made the Israelites take a solemn oath, saying, "God will surely take care of you, and you must bring my bones up with you from here."

[20]Setting out from Succoth, they camped at Ethamᶻ near the edge of the wilderness. [21ᵃ]The LORD preceded them, in the daytime by means of a column of cloud to show them the way, and at night by means of a column of fire‡ to give them light. Thus they could travel both day and night. [22]Neither the column of cloud by day nor the column of fire by night ever left its place in front of the people.

## CHAPTER 14

[1]Then the LORD spoke to Moses: [2]Speak to the Israelites: Let them turn about and camp before Pi-hahiroth, between Migdol and the sea.ᵇ Camp in front of Baal-zephon,§ just opposite, by the sea. [3]Pharaoh will then say, "The Israelites are wandering about aimlessly in the land. The wilderness has closed in on them." [4]I will so harden Pharaoh's heart that he will pursue them. Thus I will receive glory through Pharaoh and all his army, and the Egyptians will know that I am the LORD.

This the Israelites did. [5ᶜ]When it was reported to the king of Egypt that the people had fled, Pharaoh and his servants had a change of heart about the people. "What in the world have we done!" they said. "We have released Israel from our service!" [6]So Pharaoh harnessed his chariots and took his army with him. [7]He took six hundred select chariots and all the chariots of Egypt, with officers¶ on all of them. [8]The LORD hardened the heart of Pharaoh, king of Egypt, so that he pursued the Israelites while they were going out in triumph. [9]The Egyptians pursued them— all Pharaoh's horses, his chariots, his horsemen,** and his army—and caught up with them as they lay encamped by the sea, at Pi-hahiroth, in front of Baal-zephon.

---

‡[13:21] **A column of cloud . . . a column of fire**: probably one and the same extraordinary phenomenon, a central nucleus of fire surrounded by smoke; only at night was its luminous nature visible; cf. 40:38.

§[14:2] **Pi-hahiroth . . . Migdol . . . Baal-zephon**: these places have not been definitively identified. Even the relative position of Pi-hahiroth and Baal-zephon is not clear; perhaps the former was on the west shore of the sea, where the Israelites were, and the latter on the opposite shore.

¶[14:7] **Officers**: cf. 1 Kgs 9:22; Ez 23:15. The Hebrew word *shalish*, rendered in 1 Kgs 9:22 as "adjutant," has yet to have its meaning convincingly established. Given the very possible etymological connection with the number "three," others suggest the translation "three-man crew" or, less likely, the "third man in the chariot" although Egyptian chariots carried two-man crews. The author of the text may have been describing the chariots of his experience without direct historical knowledge of Egyptian ways.

**[14:9] **Horsemen**: the usage here may be anachronistic, since horsemen, or cavalry, play a part in warfare only at the end of the second millennium B.C.

---

*[13:9] **Sign**: while here observance of the feast of Unleavened Bread is likened only metaphorically to a physical sign of one's piety that can be worn as a kind of badge in commemoration of the exodus, from ancient times Jews have seen in this verse also the basis for the wearing of phylacteries. These are small receptacles for copies of biblical verses which Jewish men bind to the arms and forehead as a kind of mnemonic device for the observance of the Law.

†[13:17] **By way of the Philistines' land**: the most direct route from Egypt to Palestine, along the shore of the Mediterranean.

---

v. [13:9] Ex 13:16; Dt 6:8; 11:18.   w. [13:12–15] Ex 13:2; 22:28–29; 34:19–20; Nm 3:12–13; 8:16–17; 18:15; Dt 15:19.   x. [13:16] Ex 13:9.   y. [13:19] Gn 50:25; Jos 24:32.

z. [13:20] Nm 33:6.   a. [13:21–22] Ex 40:38; Nm 9:15–22; Dt 1:33; Neh 9:19; Ps 78:14; 105:39; Wis 10:17.   b. [14:2] Nm 33:7–8.   c. [14:5–8] Wis 19:3; 1 Mc 4:9.

**Crossing the Red Sea.** ¹⁰Now Pharaoh was near when the Israelites looked up and saw that the Egyptians had set out after them. Greatly frightened, the Israelites cried out to the LORD. ¹¹To Moses they said, "Were there no burial places in Egypt that you brought us to die in the wilderness? What have you done to us, bringing us out of Egypt? ¹²Did we not tell you this in Egypt, when we said, 'Leave us alone that we may serve the Egyptians'? Far better for us to serve the Egyptians than to die in the wilderness." ¹³But Moses answered the people, "Do not fear! Stand your ground and see the victory the LORD will win for you today. For these Egyptians whom you see today you will never see again. ¹⁴The LORD will fight for you; you have only to keep still."

¹⁵Then the LORD said to Moses: Why are you crying out to me? Tell the Israelites to set out. ¹⁶And you, lift up your staff and stretch out your hand over the sea, and split it in two, that the Israelites may pass through the sea on dry land. ¹⁷But I will harden the hearts of the Egyptians so that they will go in after them, and I will receive glory through Pharaoh and all his army, his chariots and his horsemen. ¹⁸The Egyptians will know that I am the LORD, when I receive glory through Pharaoh, his chariots, and his horsemen.

¹⁹The angel of God,* who had been leading Israel's army, now moved and went around behind them. And the column of cloud, moving from in front of them, took up its place behind them, ²⁰so that it came between the Egyptian army and that of Israel. And when it became dark, the cloud illumined the night; and so the rival camps did not come any closer together all night long.† ²¹ᵈThen Moses stretched out his hand over the sea; and the LORD drove back the sea with a strong east wind all night long and turned the sea into dry ground. The waters were split, ²²so that the Israelites entered into the midst of the sea on dry land, with the water as a wall to their right and to their left.

**Rout of the Egyptians.** ²³The Egyptians followed in pursuit after them—all Pharaoh's horses and chariots and horsemen—into the midst of the sea. ²⁴But during the watch just before dawn, the LORD looked down from a column of fiery cloud upon the Egyptian army and threw it into a panic; ²⁵and he so clogged their chariot wheels that they could drive only with difficulty. With

that the Egyptians said, "Let us flee from Israel, because the LORD is fighting for them against Egypt."

²⁶Then the LORD spoke to Moses: Stretch out your hand over the sea, that the water may flow back upon the Egyptians, upon their chariots and their horsemen. ²⁷So Moses stretched out his hand over the sea, and at daybreak the sea returned to its normal flow. The Egyptians were fleeing head on toward it when the LORD cast the Egyptians into the midst of the sea. ²⁸ᵉAs the water flowed back, it covered the chariots and the horsemen. Of all Pharaoh's army which had followed the Israelites into the sea, not even one escaped. ²⁹But the Israelites had walked on dry land through the midst of the sea, with the water as a wall to their right and to their left. ³⁰Thus the LORD saved Israel on that day from the power of Egypt. When Israel saw the Egyptians lying dead on the seashore ³¹and saw the great power that the LORD had shown against Egypt, the people feared the LORD. They believed in the LORDᶠ and in Moses his servant.

## CHAPTER 15

¹Then Moses and the Israelites sangᵍ this song to the LORD:‡

> I will sing to the LORD, for he is gloriously
>     triumphant;
>         horse and chariot he has cast into
>             the sea.
> ² My strength and my refuge is the LORD,
>         and he has become my savior.ʰ
>     This is my God, I praise him;
>         the God of my father, I extol him.
> ³ The LORD is a warrior,
>         LORD is his name!
> ⁴ Pharaoh's chariots and army he hurled
>         into the sea;
>     the elite of his officers were drowned
>         in the Red Sea.§

---

‡[15:1–21] This poem, regarded by many scholars as one of the oldest compositions in the Bible, was once an independent work. It has been inserted at this important juncture in the large narrative of Exodus to celebrate God's saving power, having miraculously delivered the people from their enemies, and ultimately leading them to the promised land.

Although the victory it describes over the Egyptians at the sea bears a superficial resemblance in v. 8 to the preceding depiction of the water standing like a wall (14:22), the poem (as opposed to the following prose verse, v. 19) suggests a different version of the victory at sea than that found in chap. 14. There is no splitting of the sea in an act reminiscent of the Lord's combat at creation with the sea monsters Rahab and Leviathan (Jb 9:13; 26:12; Ps 74:13–14; 89:11; Is 51:9–10); nor is there mention of an east wind driving the waters back so that the Israelites can cross. In this version it is by means of a storm at sea, caused by a ferocious blast from his nostrils, that the Lord achieves a decisive victory against Pharaoh and his army (vv. 1–12). The second half of the poem (vv. 13–18) describes God's guidance into the promised land.

§[15:4] **Red Sea:** the traditional translation of the Hebrew *yam suph*, which actually means "Sea of Reeds" or "reedy sea."

---

*[14:19] **Angel of God:** Hebrew *mal'ak ha'elohim* (Septuagint *ho angelos tou theou*) here refers not to an independent spiritual being but to God's power at work in the world; corresponding to the column of cloud/fire, the expression more clearly preserves a sense of distance between God and God's creatures. The two halves of the verse are parallel and may come from different narrative sources.

†[14:20] The reading of the Hebrew text here is uncertain. The image is of a darkly glowing storm cloud, ominously bright, keeping the two camps apart.

d. [14:21–22] Ex 15:19; Ps 66:6; 78:13; 136:13–14; Wis 10:18; 19:7–8; Is 63:12–13; Heb 11:29.

e. [14:28–29] Dt 11:4; Ps 106:11.　f. [14:31] Ex 4:31; Ps 106:12; Wis 10:20.　g. [15:1] Ex 15:21.　h. [15:2] Ps 118:14; Is 12:2.

⁵ The flood waters covered them,
   they sank into the depths like a
      stone.ⁱ
⁶ Your right hand, O LORD, magnificent in
      power,
   your right hand, O LORD, shattered
      the enemy.
⁷ In your great majesty you overthrew your
      adversaries;
   you loosed your wrath to consume
      them like stubble.
⁸ At the blast of your nostrils the waters
      piled up,
   the flowing waters stood like a
      mound,
   the flood waters foamed in the midst
      of the sea.
⁹ The enemy boasted, "I will pursue and
      overtake them;
   I will divide the spoils and have my
      fill of them;
   I will draw my sword; my hand will
      despoil them!"
¹⁰ When you blew with your breath, the sea
      covered them;
   like lead they sank in the mighty
      waters.
¹¹ Who is like you among the gods, O LORD?
   Who is like you, magnificent among
      the holy ones?
   Awe-inspiring in deeds of renown, worker
      of wonders,
¹²     when you stretched out your right
      hand, the earth swallowed them!
¹³ In your love* you led the people you
      redeemed;
   in your strength you guided them to
      your holy dwelling.
¹⁴ The peoples heard and quaked,
   anguish gripped the dwellers in
      Philistia.
¹⁵ Then were the chieftains of Edom
      dismayed,
   the nobles of Moab seized by
      trembling;
   All the inhabitants of Canaan melted
      away;
¹⁶     ʲterror and dread fell upon them.
   By the might of your arm they became
      silent like stone,
   while your people, LORD, passed
      over,

while the people whom you created
      passed over.†
¹⁷ You brought them in, you planted them
   on the mountain that is your own—
   The place you made the base of your
      throne, LORD,
   the sanctuary, LORD, your hands
      established.
¹⁸ May the LORD reign forever and ever!

¹⁹When Pharaoh's horses and chariots and
horsemen entered the sea, the LORD made the
waters of the sea flow back upon them, though
the Israelites walked on dry land through the
midst of the sea.ᵏ ²⁰Then the prophet Miriam,
Aaron's sister, took a tambourine in her hand,
while all the women went out after her with tambourines, dancing; ²¹and she responded‡ to them:

Sing to the LORD, for he is gloriously
      triumphant;
   horse and chariot he has cast into
      the sea.ˡ

## V. THE JOURNEY IN THE WILDERNESS TO SINAI

**At Marah and Elim.** ²²ᵐThen Moses led Israel
forward from the Red Sea,§ and they marched
out to the wilderness of Shur. After traveling for
three days through the wilderness without finding water, ²³they arrived at Marah, where they
could not drink its water, because it was too bitter. Hence this place was called Marah. ²⁴As the
people grumbled against Moses, saying, "What
are we to drink?" ²⁵he cried out to the LORD, who
pointed out to him a piece of wood. When he
threw it into the water, the water became fresh.ⁿ

It was here that God, in making statutes
and ordinances for them, put them to the test.
²⁶He said: If you listen closely to the voice of the
LORD, your God, and do what is right in his eyes:
if you heed his commandments and keep all his
statutes, I will not afflict you with any of the diseases with which I afflicted the Egyptians;° for I,
the LORD, am your healer.

²⁷Then they came to Elim, where there were
twelve springs of water and seventy palm trees,
and they camped there near the water.ᵖ

---

The location is uncertain, though in view of the route taken
by the Israelites from Egypt to Sinai, it could not have been
the Red Sea, which is too far south. It was probably a smaller
body of water south of the Gulf of Suez. The term occurs also
in Exodus at 10:19; 13:18; and 23:31.

*[15:13] **Love:** the very important Hebrew term *hesed* carries a variety of nuances depending on context: love, kindness,
faithfulness. It is often rendered "steadfast love." It implies a
relationship that generates an obligation and therefore is at
home in a covenant context. Cf. 20:6.

i. [15:5] Neh 9:11.   j. [15:16–17] Ps 78:53–55.

†[15:16] **Passed over:** an allusion to the crossing of the Jordan River (cf. Jos 3–5), written as if the entry into the promised land had already occurred. This verse suggests that at one
time there was a ritual enactment of the conquest at a shrine
near the Jordan River which included also a celebration of the
victory at the sea.

‡[15:21] **She responded:** Miriam's refrain echoes the first
verse of this song and was probably sung as an antiphon after
each verse.

§[15:22] **Red Sea:** see note on Ex 15:4.

k. [15:19] Ex 14:21–29.   l. [15:21] Ex 15:1.   m. [15:22–23] Nm
33:8.   n. [15:25] Sir 38:5.   o. [15:26] Dt 7:15.   p. [15:27] Nm 33:9.

## CHAPTER 16

**The Wilderness of Sin.** [1]Having set out from Elim, the whole Israelite community came into the wilderness of Sin, which is between Elim and Sinai, on the fifteenth day of the second month* after their departure from the land of Egypt. [2]Here in the wilderness the whole Israelite community grumbled against Moses and Aaron. [3]The Israelites said to them, "If only we had died at the LORD's hand in the land of Egypt, as we sat by our kettles of meat and ate our fill of bread! But you have led us into this wilderness to make this whole assembly die of famine!"

**The Quail and the Manna.** [4]Then the LORD said to Moses:[q] I am going to rain down bread from heaven† for you. Each day the people are to go out and gather their daily portion; thus will I test them, to see whether they follow my instructions or not. [5]On the sixth day, however, when they prepare what they bring in, let it be twice as much as they gather on the other days. [6]So Moses and Aaron told all the Israelites,[r] "At evening you will know that it was the LORD who brought you out of the land of Egypt; [7]and in the morning you will see the glory of the LORD, when he hears your grumbling against him. But who are we that you should grumble against us?" [8]And Moses said, "When the LORD gives you meat to eat in the evening and in the morning your fill of bread, and hears the grumbling you utter against him, who then are we? Your grumbling is not against us, but against the LORD."

[9]Then Moses said to Aaron, "Tell the whole Israelite community: Approach the LORD, for he has heard your grumbling." [10]But while Aaron was speaking to the whole Israelite community, they turned in the direction of the wilderness, and there the glory of the LORD appeared in the cloud! [11]The LORD said to Moses: [12]I have heard the grumbling of the Israelites. Tell them: In the evening twilight you will eat meat, and in the morning you will have your fill of bread, and then you will know that I, the LORD, am your God.

[13]In the evening, quail[s] came up and covered the camp. In the morning there was a layer of dew all about the camp, [14]and when the layer of dew evaporated, fine flakes were on the surface of the wilderness, fine flakes like hoarfrost on the ground. [15]On seeing it, the Israelites asked one another, "What is this?"‡ for they did not know what it was. But Moses told them, "It is the bread which the LORD has given you to eat.[t]

**Regulations Regarding the Manna.** [16]"Now, this is what the LORD has commanded. Gather as much of it as each needs to eat, an omer§ for each person for as many of you as there are, each of you providing for those in your own tent." [17]The Israelites did so. Some gathered a large and some a small amount. [18]But when they measured it out by the omer, the one who had gathered a large amount did not have too much, and the one who had gathered a small amount did not have too little. They gathered as much as each needed to eat. [19]Moses said to them, "Let no one leave any of it over until morning." [20]But they did not listen to Moses, and some kept a part of it over until morning, and it became wormy and stank. Therefore Moses was angry with them.

[21]Morning after morning they gathered it, as much as each needed to eat; but when the sun grew hot, it melted away. [22]On the sixth day they gathered twice as much food, two omers for each person. When all the leaders of the community came and reported this to Moses, [23]he told them, "That is what the LORD has prescribed. Tomorrow is a day of rest, a holy sabbath of the LORD. Whatever you want to bake, bake; whatever you want to boil, boil; but whatever is left put away and keep until the morning." [24]When they put it away until the morning, as Moses commanded, it did not stink nor were there worms in it. [25]Moses then said, "Eat it today, for today is the sabbath of the LORD. Today you will not find any in the field. [26]Six days you will gather it, but on the seventh day, the sabbath, it will not be there." [27]Still, on the seventh day some of the people went out to gather it, but they did not find any. [28]Then the LORD said to Moses: How long will you refuse to keep my commandments and my instructions? [29]Take note! The LORD has given you the sabbath. That is why on the sixth day he gives you food for two days. Each of you stay where you are and let no one go out on the seventh day. [30]After that the people rested on the seventh day.

[31]The house of Israel named this food manna.[u] It was like coriander seed,** white, and it tasted like wafers made with honey.

---

*[16:1] **On the fifteenth day of the second month**: just one full month after their departure from Egypt. Cf. 12:2, 51; Nm 33:3–4. The Septuagint takes the date to be the beginning of the Israelites' grumbling.

†[16:4] **Bread from heaven**: as a gift from God, the manna is said to come down from the sky. Cf. Ps 78:24–25; Wis 16:20. Perhaps it was similar to a natural substance that is still found in small quantities on the Sinai peninsula—probably the honey-like resin from the tamarisk tree—but here it is, at least in part, clearly an extraordinary sign of God's providence. With reference to Jn 6:32, 49–52, the Christian tradition has regarded the manna as a type of the Eucharist. **Test**: as the text stands, it seems to leave open the question whether the test concerns trusting in God to provide them with the daily gift of food or observing the sabbath instructions.

‡[16:15] **What is this**: the Hebrew *man hu* is thus rendered by the ancient versions, which understood the phrase as a popular etymology of the Hebrew word *man*, "manna"; but some render *man hu*, "This is manna."

§[16:16] **Omer**: a dry measure of approximately two quarts.

¶[16:18] Paul cites this passage as an example of equitable sharing (2 Cor 8:15).

**[16:31] **Coriander seed**: small, round, aromatic seeds of bright brown color; the comparison, therefore, refers merely to the size and shape, not to the taste or color of the manna.

---

q. [16:4] Ps 78:24–25; 105:40; Jn 6:31–32; 1 Cor 10:3.    r. [16:6–7] Ex 16:12.    s. [16:13] Nm 11:31; Ps 27–28.

t. [16:15] Dt 8:3.    u. [16:31] Nm 11:7.

³²Moses said, "This is what the LORD has commanded. Keep a full omer of it for your future generations, so that they may see the food I gave you to eat in the wilderness when I brought you out of the land of Egypt." ³³Moses then told Aaron, "Take a jar* and put a full omer of manna in it. Then place it before the LORD to keep it for your future generations." ³⁴As the LORD had commanded Moses, Aaron placed it in front of the covenant† to keep it.

³⁵The Israelites ate the manna for forty years, until they came to settled land;ᵛ they ate the manna until they came to the borders of Canaan. ³⁶(An omer is one tenth of an ephah.)‡

## CHAPTER 17

**Water from the Rock.** ¹From the wilderness of Sin the whole Israelite community journeyed by stages, as the LORD directed, and encamped at Rephidim.ʷ

But there was no water for the people to drink, ²ᵃand so they quarreled with Moses and said, "Give us water to drink." Moses replied to them, "Why do you quarrel with me? Why do you put the LORD to a test?" ³Here, then, in their thirst for water, the people grumbled against Moses, saying, "Why then did you bring us up out of Egypt? To have us die of thirst with our children and our livestock?" ⁴So Moses cried out to the LORD, "What shall I do with this people? A little more and they will stone me!" ⁵The LORD answered Moses: Go on ahead of the people, and take along with you some of the elders of Israel, holding in your hand, as you go, the staff with which you struck the Nile. ⁶I will be standing there in front of you on the rock in Horeb. Strike the rock, and the water will flow from it for the people to drink.ʸ Moses did this, in the sight of the elders of Israel. ⁷The place was named Massah and Meribah,§ because the Israelites quarreled there and tested the LORD, saying, "Is the LORD in our midst or not?"ᶻ

**Battle with Amalek.** ⁸Then Amalek¶ came and waged war against Israel in Rephidim.ᵃ ⁹So Moses said to Joshua, "Choose some men for us, and tomorrow go out and engage Amalek in battle. I will be standing on top of the hill with the staff of God in my hand." ¹⁰Joshua did

as Moses told him: he engaged Amalek in battle while Moses, Aaron, and Hur climbed to the top of the hill. ¹¹As long as Moses kept his hands raised up, Israel had the better of the fight, but when he let his hands rest, Amalek had the better of the fight. ¹²Moses' hands, however, grew tired; so they took a rock and put it under him and he sat on it. Meanwhile Aaron and Hur supported his hands, one on one side and one on the other, so that his hands remained steady until sunset. ¹³And Joshua defeated Amalek and his people with the sword.

¹⁴Then the LORD said to Moses: Write this down in a book as something to be remembered, and recite it to Joshua:ᵇ I will completely blot out the memory of Amalek from under the heavens. ¹⁵Moses built an altar there, which he named Yahweh-nissi;** ¹⁶for he said, "Take up the banner of the LORD!"†† The LORD has a war against Amalek through the ages."

## CHAPTER 18

**Meeting with Jethro.** ¹Now Moses' father-in-law Jethro, the priest of Midian, heard of all that God had done for Moses and for his people Israel: how the LORD had brought Israel out of Egypt. ²So his father-in-law Jethro took along Zipporah, Moses' wife—now this was after Moses had sent her back—‡‡ ³and her two sons. One of these was named Gershom;ᶜ for he said, "I am a resident alien in a foreign land." ⁴The other was named Eliezer; for he said, "'The God of my father is my help; he has rescued me from Pharaoh's sword." ⁵Together with Moses' wife and sons, then, his father-in-law Jethro came to him in the wilderness where he was encamped at the mountain of God,§§ ⁶and he sent word to Moses, "I, your father-in-law Jethro, am coming to you, along with your wife and her two sons."

⁷Moses went out to meet his father-in-law, bowed down, and then kissed him. Having greeted each other, they went into the tent. ⁸Moses then told his father-in-law of all that the LORD had done to Pharaoh and the Egyptians for the sake of Israel, and of all the hardships that had beset them on their journey, and how the

---

*[16:33] **Jar**: according to the Greek translation, which is followed in Heb 9:4, this was a golden vessel.

†[16:34] **The covenant**: i.e., the ark of the covenant, in which were placed the two tablets of the Ten Commandments. Cf. 25:16, 21–22.

‡[16:36] **Omer . . . ephah**: see note on Is 5:10.

§[17:7] **Massah . . . Meribah**: Hebrew words meaning, respectively, "the place of the test" and "the place of strife, of quarreling."

¶[17:8] **Amalek**: the Amalekites appear in the Bible as early inhabitants of southern Palestine and the Sinai peninsula prior to the appearance of the Israelites in the region. Cf. Nm 24:20.

**[17:15] **Yahweh-nissi**: meaning, "the Lord is my banner."

††[17:16] **Take up the banner of the LORD**: lit., "a hand on the LORD's banner," apparently a war cry for the Israelite troops in the conduct of Holy War; however, the Hebrew text is difficult to interpret.

‡‡[18:2] **Moses had sent her back**: a later gloss which attempts to harmonize Zipporah's presence with Jethro here in this story and the account of Moses' return to Egypt with Zipporah in 4:20.

§§[18:5] The allusion to meeting Moses encamped at the mountain of God, prior to the arrival of the Israelites at Sinai in chap. 19, might well suggest a different narrative context for this story from an earlier stage of the biblical tradition's development. It is noteworthy that immediately after the Sinai pericope (Ex 19:1–Nm 10:28), recounting the theophany at Sinai and the giving of the law, the narrative of Israel's march through the wilderness resumes with an apparent doublet of the visit by Moses' father-in-law (Nm 10:29–32).

---

v. [16:35] Jos 5:12.   w. [17:1] Nm 33:12–14.   x. [17:2–7] Nm 20:2–13.
y. [17:5–6] Dt 8:15; Ps 78:15–16; 105:41; Wis 11:4; Is 43:20;
48:21.   z. [17:7] Ps 95:8–9.   a. [17:8] Dt 25:17–19; 1 Sm 15:2.

b. [17:14] Nm 24:20; 1 Sm 15:3, 20.   c. [18:3] Ex 2:22.

LORD had rescued them. [9]Jethro rejoiced over all the goodness that the LORD had shown Israel in rescuing them from the power of the Egyptians. [10]"Blessed be the LORD," he said, "who has rescued you from the power of the Egyptians and of Pharaoh. [11]Now I know that the LORD is greater than all the gods; for he rescued the people from the power of the Egyptians when they treated them arrogantly." [12]Then Jethro, the father-in-law of Moses, brought a burnt offering* and sacrifices for God, and Aaron came with all the elders of Israel to share with Moses' father-in-law in the meal before God.

**Appointment of Minor Judges.** [13]The next day Moses sat in judgment for the people, while they stood around him from morning until evening. [14]When Moses' father-in-law saw all that he was doing for the people, he asked, "What is this business that you are conducting for the people? Why do you sit alone while all the people have to stand about you from morning till evening?" [15]Moses answered his father-in-law, "The people come to me to consult God. [16]Whenever they have a disagreement, they come to me to have me settle the matter between them and make known to them God's statutes and instructions."

[17]"What you are doing is not wise," Moses' father-in-law replied. [18]"You will surely wear yourself out, both you and these people with you. The task is too heavy for you;[d] you cannot do it alone. [19]†Now, listen to me, and I will give you some advice, and may God be with you. Act as the people's representative before God, and bring their disputes to God. [20]Enlighten them in regard to the statutes and instructions, showing them how they are to conduct themselves and what they are to do. [21]But you should also look among all the people for able and God-fearing men, trustworthy men who hate dishonest gain, and set them over the people as commanders of thousands, of hundreds, of fifties, and of tens.[e] [22]Let these render decisions for the people in all routine cases. Every important case they should refer to you, but every lesser case they can settle themselves. Lighten your burden by letting them bear it with you! [23]If you do this, and God so commands you,‡ you will be able to

stand the strain, and all these people, too, will go home content."

[24]Moses listened to his father-in-law and did all that he had said. [25]He picked out able men from all Israel and put them in charge of the people as commanders of thousands, of hundreds, of fifties, and of tens. [26]They rendered decisions for the people in all routine cases. The more difficult cases they referred to Moses, but all the lesser cases they settled themselves. [27]Then Moses said farewell to his father-in-law, who went off to his own country.

## VI. COVENANT AND LEGISLATION AT MOUNT SINAI

### CHAPTER 19

**Arrival at Sinai.** [1]In the third month after the Israelites' departure from the land of Egypt, on the first day, they came to the wilderness of Sinai. [2]After they made the journey from Rephidim and entered the wilderness of Sinai, they then pitched camp in the wilderness.[§]

While Israel was encamped there in front of the mountain, [3]Moses went up to the mountain of God. Then the LORD called to him from the mountain, saying: This is what you will say to the house of Jacob; tell the Israelites: [4]You have seen how I treated the Egyptians and how I bore you up on eagles' wings and brought you to myself.[g] [5]Now, if you obey me completely and keep my covenant,¶ you will be my treasured possession among all peoples,[h] though all the earth is mine. [6]You will be to me a kingdom of priests,** a holy nation.[i] That is what you must tell the Israelites. [7]So Moses went and summoned the elders of the people. When he set before them all that the LORD had ordered him to tell them, [8]all the people answered together, "Everything the LORD

---

§[19:2] Apparently from a different source (P) than v. 1, which notes the date, v. 2 from the J source includes a second notice of the arrival in the wilderness of Sinai. The Israelites now will be camped at Sinai from this point on all the way to Nm 10:10. This is a striking indication of the centrality and importance of the Sinai narrative in the overall composition of the Pentateuch.

¶[19:5] **Covenant:** while covenants between individuals and between nations are ubiquitous in the ancient Near East, the adaptation of this concept to express the relationship that will henceforth characterize God's relationship to Israel represents an important innovation of biblical faith. Other gods might "choose" nations to fulfill a special destiny or role in the world; but only Israel's God is bound to a people by covenant. Thereby Israel's identity as a people is put upon a foundation that does not depend upon the vicissitudes of Israelite statehood or the normal trappings of national existence. Israel will be a covenant people.

**[19:6] **Kingdom of priests:** inasmuch as this phrase is parallel to "holy nation," it most likely means that the whole Israelite nation is set apart from other nations and so consecrated to God, or holy, in the way priests are among the people (cf. Is 61:6; 1 Pt 2:5, 9).

---

*[18:12] That a non-Israelite, such as Jethro, should bless Israel's God by way of acknowledging what God had done for Israel (v. 10) is not entirely surprising; but the Midianite priest's sacrifice to the God of Israel, including his presiding over a sacrificial meal with Aaron and the elders of Israel, is unusual, suggesting that he was himself already a worshiper of Yhwh, Israel's God. Note further in this connection the role Jethro takes in the following narrative (vv. 13–27) in instituting a permanent judiciary for the Israelites. **Burnt offering:** a sacrifice wholly burnt up as an offering to God.

†[18:19–20] By emphasizing Moses' mediatorial role for the people before God in regard to God's statutes and instructions, this story about the institution of Israel's judiciary prepares for Moses' role in the upcoming revelation of the law at Sinai.

‡[18:23] **And God so commands you:** i.e., and God approves.

---

d. [18:18] Nm 11:14.    e. [18:21, 25] Dt 1:15; 16:18.

f. [19:1–2] Nm 33:15.    g. [19:4] Dt 32:11–12.    h. [19:5] Dt 7:6; 14:2; 26:18–19; 32:8–9.    i. [19:6] 1 Pt 2:9.

has said, we will do." Then Moses brought back to the LORD the response of the people.

⁹The LORD said to Moses: I am coming to you now in a dense cloud,ʲ so that when the people hear me speaking with you, they will also remain faithful to you.

When Moses, then, had reported the response of the people to the LORD, ¹⁰the LORD said to Moses: Go to the people and have them sanctify themselves today and tomorrow. Have them wash their garments ¹¹and be ready for the third day; for on the third day the LORD will come down on Mount Sinai in the sight of all the people. ¹²Set limits for the people all around,ᵏ saying: Take care not to go up the mountain, or even to touch its edge. All who touch the mountain must be put to death. ¹³No hand shall touch them, but they must be stoned to death or killed with arrows. Whether human being or beast, they must not be allowed to live. Only when the ram's horn sounds may they go up on the mountain.ˣ ¹⁴Then Moses came down from the mountain to the people and had them sanctify themselves, and they washed their garments. ¹⁵He said to the people, "Be ready for the third day. Do not approach a woman."

**The Great Theophany.** ¹⁶On the morning of the third day there were peals of thunder and lightning, and a heavy cloud over the mountain, and a very loud blast of the shofar,† so that all the people in the camp trembled. ¹⁷But Moses led the people out of the camp to meet God, and they stationed themselves at the foot of the mountain. ¹⁸Now Mount Sinai was completely enveloped in smoke, because the LORD had come down upon it in fire. The smoke rose from it as though from a kiln, and the whole mountain trembled violently. ¹⁹The blast of the shofar grew louder and louder, while Moses was speaking and God was answering him with thunder.

²⁰ᶦWhen the LORD came down upon Mount Sinai, to the top of the mountain, the LORD summoned Moses to the top of the mountain, and Moses went up. ²¹Then the LORD told Moses: Go down and warn the people not to break through to the LORD in order to see him; otherwise many of them will be struck down. ²²For their part, the priests, who approach the LORD must sanctify themselves; else the LORD will break out in anger against them. ²³But Moses said to the LORD, "The people cannot go up to Mount Sinai, for you yourself warned us, saying: Set limits around the mountain to make it sacred." ²⁴So the LORD said to him: Go down and come up along with Aaron. But do not let the priests and people break through to come up to the LORD; else he will break out against them." ²⁵So Moses went down to the people and spoke to them.

## CHAPTER 20

**The Ten Commandments.**§ ¹Then God spoke all these words:

²ᵐI am the LORD your God, who brought you out of the land of Egypt,ⁿ out of the house of slavery. ³You shall not have other gods beside me.⁵ ⁴You shall not make for yourself an idolᵒ or a likeness of anything** in the heavens above or on the earth below or in the waters beneath the earth; ⁵you shall not bow down before them or serve them.ᵖ For I, the LORD, your God, am

---

§[20:1–17] The precise numbering and division of these precepts into "ten commandments" is somewhat uncertain. Traditionally among Catholics and Lutherans vv. 1–6 are considered as only one commandment, and v. 17 as two. The Anglican, Greek Orthodox, and Reformed churches count vv. 1–6 as two, and v. 17 as one. Cf. Dt 5:6–21. The traditional designation as "ten" is not found here but in 34:28 (and also Dt 4:13 and 10:4), where these precepts are alluded to literally as "the ten words." That they were originally written on two tablets appears in Ex 32:15–16; 34:28–29; Dt 4:13; 10:2–4.

The present form of the commands is a product of a long development, as is clear from the fact that the individual precepts vary considerably in length and from the slightly different formulation of Dt 5:6–21 (see especially vv. 12–15 and 21). Indeed they represent a mature formulation of a traditional morality. Why this specific selection of commands should be set apart is not entirely clear. None of them is unique in the Old Testament and all of the laws which follow are also from God and equally binding on the Israelites. Even so, this collection represents a privileged expression of God's moral demands on Israel and is here set apart from the others as a direct, unmediated communication of God to the Israelites and the basis of the covenant being concluded on Sinai.

¶[20:3] **Beside me**: this commandment is traditionally understood as an outright denial of the existence of other gods except the God of Israel; however, in the context of the more general prohibitions in vv. 4–5, v. 3 is more precisely, God's demand for Israel's exclusive worship and allegiance.

The Hebrew phrase underlying the translation "beside me" is, nonetheless, problematic and has been variously translated, e.g., "except me," "in addition to me," "in preference to me," "in defiance of me," and "in front of me" or "before my face." The latter translation, with its concrete, spatial nuances, has suggested to some that the prohibition once sought to exclude from the Lord's sanctuary the cult images or idols of other gods, such as the asherah, or stylized sacred tree of life, associated with the Canaanite goddess Asherah (34:13). Over the course of time, as vv. 4–5 suggest, the original scope of v. 3 was expanded.

**[20:4] **Or a likeness of anything**: compare this formulation to that found in Dt 5:8, which understands this phrase and the following phrases as specifications of the prohibited idol (Hebrew *pesel*), which usually refers to an image that is carved or hewn rather than cast.

---

*[19:13] **May they go up on the mountain**: in vv. 12–13a, a later Priestly reshaping of an earlier version of the instructions governing how the people are to prepare for the encounter with God (vv. 10–11, 13b), the people are to be restrained from ascending the mountain, which is suffused with the holiness of God and too dangerous for their approach. In the earlier version, as v. 13b suggests, the sanctified people must come near, in order to hear God speaking with Moses (v. 9) and in this way receive confirmation of his special relationship with God.

†[19:16] **Shofar**: a ram's horn used like a trumpet for signaling both for liturgical and military purposes.

‡[19:20–25] At this point the Priestly additions of vv. 12–13a are elaborated with further Priestly instructions, which include the priests' sanctifying themselves apart from the people (v. 22) and Aaron accompanying Moses to the top of the mountain (v. 24).

---

j. [19:9] Ex 20:21; 24:15–18.  k. [19:12–13] Ex 34:3; Heb 12:18–19. l. [19:16–19] Dt 4:10–12.

m. [20:2–17] Dt 5:6–21.  n. [20:2] Lv 26:13; Ps 81:11; Hos 13:4. o. [20:4] Ex 34:17; Lv 26:1; Dt 4:15–19; 27:15.  p. [20:5] Ex 34:7, 14; Nm 14:18; Dt 4:24; 6:15.

a jealous God, inflicting punishment for their ancestors' wickedness on the children of those who hate me, down to the third and fourth generation˙; ⁶but showing love down to the thousandth generation of those who love me and keep my commandments.

⁷You shall not invoke the name of the LORD, your God, in vain.†q For the LORD will not leave unpunished anyone who invokes his name in vain.

⁸Remember the sabbath day—keep it holy.‡ ⁹Six days you may labor and do all your work, ¹⁰but the seventh day is a sabbath of the LORD your God.ʳ You shall not do any work, either you, your son or your daughter, your male or female slave, your work animal, or the resident alien within your gates. ¹¹For in six days the LORD made the heavens and the earth, the sea and all that is in them; but on the seventh day he rested.ˢ That is why the LORD has blessed the sabbath day and made it holy.§

¹²¶Honor your father and your mother, that you may have a long life in the land the LORD your God is giving you.ᵘ

¹³You shall not kill.**ᵛ

¹⁴You shall not commit adultery.ʷ

¹⁵You shall not steal.ˣ

¹⁶You shall not bear false witness against your neighbor.ʸ

¹⁷You shall not covet your neighbor's house. You shall not covet your neighbor's wife, his male or female slave, his ox or donkey, or anything that belongs to your neighbor.ᶻ

**Moses Accepted as Mediator.** ¹⁸Now as all the people witnessed the thunder and lightning, the blast of the shofar and the mountain smoking, they became afraid and trembled.ᵃ So they took up a position farther away ¹⁹and said to Moses, "You speak to us, and we will listen; but do not let God speak to us, or we shall die." ²⁰Moses answered the people, "Do not be afraid, for God has come only to test you and put the fear of him upon you so you do not sin." ²¹So the people remained at a distance, while Moses approached the dark cloud where God was.

**The Covenant Code.** ²²††The LORD said to Moses: This is what you will say to the Israelites: You have seen for yourselves that I have spoken to you from heaven. ²³You shall not make alongside of me gods of silver, nor shall you make for yourselves gods of gold.ᵇ ²⁴An altar of earth make for me, and sacrifice upon it your burnt offerings and communion sacrifices, your sheep and your oxen.ᶜ In every place where I cause my name to be invoked‡‡ I will come to you and bless you. ²⁵But if you make an altar of stone for me,ᵈ do not build it of cut stone, for by putting a chisel to it you profane it. ²⁶You shall not ascend to my altar by steps, lest your nakedness be exposed.

## CHAPTER 21

**Laws Regarding Slaves.** ¹These are the ordinances§§ you shall lay before them. ²¶When you purchase a Hebrew slave,¶¶ he is to serve you for six years, but in the seventh year he shall leave as a free person without any payment. ³If he comes into service alone, he shall leave alone; if he comes with a wife, his wife shall leave with him. ⁴But if his master gives him a wife and she bears him sons or daughters, the woman and her

---

*[20:5] **Jealous:** demanding exclusive allegiance. **Inflicting punishment . . . the third and fourth generation:** the intended emphasis is on God's mercy by the contrast between punishment and mercy ("to the thousandth generation"—v. 6). Other Old Testament texts repudiate the idea of punishment devolving on later generations (cf. Dt 24:16; Jer 31:29–30; Ez 18:2–4). Yet it is known that later generations may suffer the punishing effects of sins of earlier generations, but not the guilt.

†[20:7] **In vain:** i.e., to no good purpose, a general framing of the prohibition which includes swearing falsely, especially in the context of a legal proceeding, but also goes beyond it (cf. Lv 24:16; Prv 30:8–9).

‡[20:8] **Keep it holy:** i.e., to set it apart from the other days of the week, in part, as the following verse explains, by not doing work that is ordinarily done in the course of a week. The special importance of this command can be seen in the fact that, together with vv. 9–11, it represents the longest of the Decalogue's precepts.

§[20:11] Here, in a formulation which reflects Priestly theology, the veneration of the sabbath is grounded in God's own hallowing of the sabbath in creation. Compare 31:13; Dt 5:15.

¶[20:12–17] The Decalogue falls into two parts: the preceding precepts refer to God, the following refer primarily to one's fellow Israelites.

**[20:13] **Kill:** as frequent instances of killing in the context of war or certain crimes (see vv. 12–18) demonstrate in the Old Testament, not all killing comes within the scope of the commandment. For this reason, the Hebrew verb translated here as "kill" is often understood as "murder," although it is in fact used in the Old Testament at times for unintentional acts of killing (e.g., Dt 4:41; Jos 20:3) and for legally sanctioned killing (Nm 35:30). The term may originally have designated any killing of another Israelite, including acts of manslaughter, for which the victim's kin could exact vengeance. In the present context, it denotes the killing of one Israelite by another, motivated by hatred or the like (Nm 35:20; cf. Hos 6:9).

††[20:22–23:33] This collection consists of the civil and religious laws, both apodictic (absolute) and casuistic (conditional), which were given to the people through the mediation of Moses. They will be written down by Moses in 24:4.

‡‡[20:24] **Where I cause my name to be invoked:** i.e., at the sacred site where God wishes to be worshiped. Dt 12 will demand the centralization of all sacrificial worship in one place chosen by God.

§§[21:1] **Ordinances:** judicial precedents to be used in settling questions of law and custom. More than half of the civil and religious laws in this collection (20:22–23:33), designated in 24:7 as "the book of the covenant," have parallels in the cuneiform laws of the ancient Near East. It is clear that Israel participated in a common legal culture with its neighbors.

¶¶[21:2] **Slave:** an Israelite could become a slave of another Israelite as a means of paying a debt, or an Israelite could be born into slavery due to a parent's status as a slave. Here a time limit is prescribed for such slavery; other stipulations (vv. 20–21, 26–27) tried to reduce the evils of slavery, but slavery itself is not condemned in the Old Testament.

---

q. [20:7] Lv 19:12; 24:16.  r. [20:8–11] Ex 23:12; 31:13–16; 34:21; 35:2; Lv 23:3.  s. [20:11] Ex 31:17; Gn 2:2–3.  t. [20:12–16] Mt 19:18–19; Mk 10:19; Lk 18:20; Rom 13:9.  u. [20:12] Lv 20:9; Mt 15:4; Mk 7:10; Eph 6:2–3.  v. [20:13] Mt 5:21.  w. [20:14] Lv 18:20; 20:10; Dt 22:22; Mt 5:27.  x. [20:15] Lv 19:11.  y. [20:16] Ex 23:1; Dt 19:16–19; Prv 19:5, 9; 24:28.

z. [20:17] Rom 7:7.  a. [20:18–21] Dt 4:11; 5:22–27; 18:16; Heb 12:18–19.  b. [20:23] Ex 20:3–4.  c. [20:24] Dt 12:5, 11; 14:23; 16:6.  d. [20:25] Dt 27:5; Jos 8:31.  e. [21:2–6] Lv 25:39–55; Dt 15:12–18; Jer 34:14.

children belong to her master and the man shall leave alone. ⁵If, however, the slave declares, 'I love my master and my wife and children; I will not leave as a free person,' ⁶his master shall bring him to God* and there, at the door or doorpost, he shall pierce his ear with an awl, thus keeping him as his slave forever.

⁷When a man sells his daughter as a slave, she shall not go free as male slaves do. ⁸But if she displeases her master, who had designated her† for himself, he shall let her be redeemed. He has no right to sell her to a foreign people, since he has broken faith with her. ⁹If he designates her for his son, he shall treat her according to the ordinance for daughters. ¹⁰If he takes another wife, he shall not withhold her food, her clothing, or her conjugal rights. ¹¹If he does not do these three things for her, she may leave without cost, without any payment.

**Personal Injury.** ¹²‡Whoever strikes someone a mortal blow must be put to death.ᶠ ¹³However, regarding the one who did not hunt another down, but God caused death to happen by his hand, I will set apart for you a place to which that one may flee. ¹⁴But when someone kills a neighbor after maliciously scheming to do so, you must take him even from my altar and put him to death. ¹⁵Whoever strikes father or mother must be put to death.§

¹⁶A kidnapper, whether he sells the person or the person is found in his possession, shall be put to death.ᵍ

¹⁷Whoever curses¶ father or mother shall be put to death.ʰ

¹⁸When men quarrel and one strikes the other with a stone or with his fist, not mortally, but enough to put him in bed, ¹⁹the one who struck the blow shall be acquitted, provided the other can get up and walk around with the help of his staff. Still, he must compensate him

for his recovery time and make provision for his complete healing.

²⁰When someone strikes his male or female slave with a rod so that the slave dies under his hand, the act shall certainly be avenged. ²¹If, however, the slave survives for a day or two, he is not to be punished, since the slave is his own property.

²²**When men have a fight and hurt a pregnant woman, so that she suffers a miscarriage, but no further injury, the guilty one shall be fined as much as the woman's husband demands of him, and he shall pay in the presence of the judges. ²³ᶦBut if injury ensues, you shall give life for life, ²⁴eye for eye, tooth for tooth, hand for hand, foot for foot, ²⁵burn for burn, wound for wound, stripe for stripe.

²⁶When someone strikes his male or female slave in the eye and destroys the use of the eye, he shall let the slave go free in compensation for the eye. ²⁷If he knocks out a tooth of his male or female slave, he shall let the slave go free in compensation for the tooth.

²⁸When an ox gores a man or a woman to death, the ox must be stoned; its meat may not be eaten. The owner of the ox, however, shall be free of blame. ²⁹But if an ox was previously in the habit of goring people and its owner, though warned, would not watch it; should it then kill a man or a woman, not only must the ox be stoned, but its owner also must be put to death. ³⁰If, however, a fine is imposed on him, he must pay in ransom†† for his life whatever amount is imposed on him. ³¹This ordinance applies if it is a boy or a girl that the ox gores. ³²But if it is a male or a female slave that it gores, he must pay the owner of the slave thirty shekels of silver, and the ox must be stoned.

**Property Damage.** ³³When someone uncovers or digs a cistern and does not cover it over again, should an ox or a donkey fall into it, ³⁴the owner of the cistern must make good by restoring the value of the animal to its owner, but the dead animal he may keep.

³⁵When one man's ox hurts another's ox and it dies, they shall sell the live ox and divide this money as well as the dead animal equally between them. ³⁶But if it was known that the

---

*[21:6] **To God**: the ritual of the piercing of the slave's ear, which signified a lifetime commitment to the master, probably took place at the door of the household, where God as protector of the household was called upon as a witness. Another possible location for the ritual would have been the door of the sanctuary, where God or judges would have witnessed the slave's promise of lifetime obedience to his master.

†[21:8] **Designated her**: intended her as a wife of second rank.

‡[21:12–14] Unintentional homicide is to be punished differently from premeditated, deliberate murder. One who kills unintentionally can seek asylum by grasping the horns of the altar at the local sanctuary. In later Israelite history, when worship was centralized in Jerusalem, cities throughout the realm were designated as places of refuge. Apparently the leaders of the local community were to determine whether or not the homicide was intentional.

§[21:15] The verb used most often signifies a violent, sometimes deadly, attack. The severe penalty assigned is intended to safeguard the integrity of the family.

¶[21:17] **Curses**: not merely an angrily uttered expletive at one's parents, but a solemn juridical formula of justifiable retribution which was considered to be legally binding and guaranteed by God.

**[21:22–25] This law of talion is applied here in the specific case of a pregnant woman who, as an innocent bystander, is injured by two fighting men. The law of talion is not held up as a general principle to be applied throughout the book of the covenant. (But see note on Lv 24:19–20.) Here this principle of rigorous accountability aimed to prevent injury to a woman about to give birth by apparently requiring the assailant to have his own wife injured as she was about to bring new life into his family. However, it is debatable whether talion was ever understood or applied literally in Israel. In his Sermon on the Mount, Jesus challenges his audience to find a deeper form of justice than the supposed equilibrium offered by talion (Mt 5:38–40).

††[21:30] **Ransom**: the amount of money or material goods required to restore the relationship between the relatives of the victim and the negligent owner of the goring ox.

---

f. [21:12] Lv 24:17; Nm 35:15–29; Dt 4:41–42; 19:2–5.    g. [21:16] Dt 24:7.    h. [21:17] Lv 20:9; Prv 20:20; Mt 15:4; Mk 7:10.      i. [21:23–25] Lv 24:18–21; Dt 19:21; Mt 5:38.

ox was previously in the habit of goring and its owner would not watch it, he must make full restitution, an ox for an ox; but the dead animal he may keep.

<sup> </sup>³⁷When someone steals an ox or a sheep and slaughters or sells it, he shall restore five oxen for the one ox, and four sheep for the one sheep.ʲ

## CHAPTER 22

¹[If a thief is caught* in the act of housebreaking and beaten to death, there is no bloodguilt involved. ²But if after sunrise he is thus beaten, there is bloodguilt.] He must make full restitution. If he has nothing, he shall be sold to pay for his theft. ³If what he stole is found alive in his possession, be it an ox, a donkey or a sheep, he shall make twofold restitution.

⁴When someone causes a field or a vineyard to be grazed over, by sending his cattle to graze in another's field, he must make restitution with the best produce of his own field or vineyard. ⁵If a fire breaks out, catches on to thorn bushes, and consumes shocked grain, standing grain, or the field itself, the one who started the fire must make full restitution.

**Trusts and Loans.** ⁶When someone gives money or articles to another for safekeeping and they are stolen from the latter's house, the thief, if caught, must make twofold restitution. ⁷If the thief is not caught, the owner of the house shall be brought to God,† to swear that he himself did not lay hands on his neighbor's property. ⁸In every case of dishonest appropriation, whether it be about an ox, or a donkey, or a sheep, or a garment, or anything else that has disappeared, where another claims that the thing is his, the claim of both parties shall be brought before God; the one whom God convicts must make twofold restitution to the other.

⁹When someone gives an ass, or an ox, or a sheep, or any other animal to another for safekeeping, if it dies, or is maimed or snatched away, without anyone witnessing the fact, ¹⁰there shall be an oath before the LORD between the two of them that the guardian did not lay hands on his neighbor's property; the owner must accept the oath, and no restitution is to be made. ¹¹But if the guardian has actually stolen from it, then he must make restitution to the owner. ¹²If it has been killed by a wild beast, let him bring it as evidence; he need not make restitution for the mangled animal.ᵏ

¹³When someone borrows an animal from a neighbor, if it is maimed or dies while the owner is not present, that one must make restitution. ¹⁴But if the owner is present, that one need not make restitution. If it was hired, this was covered by the price of its hire.

**Social Laws.** ¹⁵When a man seduces a virgin who is not betrothed, and lies with her, he shall make her his wife by paying the bride price. ¹⁶If her father refuses to give her to him, he must still pay him the bride price for virgins.‡

¹⁷You shall not let a woman who practices sorcery live.ᵐ

¹⁸Anyone who lies with an animal shall be put to death.ⁿ

¹⁹Whoever sacrifices to any god, except to the LORD alone, shall be put under the ban.ᵒ

²⁰You shall not oppress or afflict a resident alien, for you were once aliens residing in the land of Egypt.ᵖ ²¹You shall not wrong any widow or orphan. ²²If ever you wrong them and they cry out to me, I will surely listen to their cry. ²³My wrath will flare up, and I will kill you with the sword; then your own wives will be widows, and your children orphans.

²⁴If you lend money to my people, the poor among you, you must not be like a money lender; you must not demand interest from them. ²⁵If you take your neighbor's cloak as a pledge, you shall return it to him before sunset; ²⁶for this is his only covering; it is the cloak for his body. What will he sleep in? If he cries out to me, I will listen; for I am compassionate.ʳ

²⁷You shall not despise God,§ nor curse a leader of your people.ˢ

²⁸You shall not delay the offering of your harvest and your press. You shall give me the firstborn of your sons. ²⁹You must do the same with your oxen and your sheep; for seven days the firstling may stay with its mother, but on the eighth day you must give it to me.ᵗ

³⁰You shall be a people sacred to me. Flesh torn to pieces in the field you shall not eat; you must throw it to the dogs.ᵘ

## CHAPTER 23

¹You shall not repeat a false report. Do not join your hand with the wicked to be a witness supporting violence.ᵛ ²You shall not follow the crowd in doing wrong. When testifying in a lawsuit, you shall not follow the crowd in

---

*[22:1–2] **If a thief is caught**: this seems to be a fragment of what was once a longer law on housebreaking, which has been inserted here into the middle of a law on stealing animals. At night the householder would be justified in killing a burglar outright, but not so in the daytime, when the burglar could more easily be caught alive. **He must make full restitution**: this stood originally immediately after 21:37.

†[22:7] **Brought to God**: either within the household or at the sanctuary, the owner of the house is required to take an oath before God.

j. [21:37] 2 Sm 12:6.   k. [22:12] Gn 31:39.

‡[22:16] **The bride price for virgins**: fifty shekels according to Dt 22:29.

§[22:27] **Despise God**: a turning away from God's authority and so failing to honor God (cf. 1 Sm 2:30).

l. [22:15–16] Dt 22:28–29.   m. [22:17] Lv 19:26, 31; 20:6, 27; Dt 18:10–11.   n. [22:18] Lv 18:23; Dt 27:21.   o. [22:19] Dt 13; 17:2–7.   p. [22:20–23] Ex 23:9; Lv 19:33–34; Dt 10:18–19; 24:17–18; 27:19; Zec 7:10.   q. [22:24] Lv 25:35–38; Dt 23:19–20; 24:10–13; Ez 18:7–8, 17–18.   r. [22:25–26] Dt 24:10–13; Jb 22:6; Prv 20:16; 27:13; Am 2:8.   s. [22:27] Acts 23:5.   t. [22:29] Ex 13:2; 34:19; Lv 22:27; Dt 15:19.   u. [22:30] Lv 7:24; 17:15; 22:8.   v. [23:1–2] Dt 19:16–21.

perverting justice. ³You shall not favor the poor in a lawsuit.ʷ

⁴When you come upon your enemy's ox or donkey going astray, you must see to it that it is returned.ˣ ⁵When you notice the donkey of one who hates you lying down under its burden, you should not desert him; you must help him with it.

⁶You shall not pervert justice for the needy among you in a lawsuit. ⁷You shall keep away from anything dishonest. The innocent and the just you shall not put to death, for I will not acquit the guilty. ⁸Never take a bribe, for a bribe blinds the clear-sighted and distorts the words of the just.ʸ ⁹You shall not oppress a resident alien; you well know how it feels to be an alien, since you were once aliens yourselves in the land of Egypt.ᶻ

**Religious Laws.** ¹⁰ᵃFor six years you may sow your land and gather in its produce. ¹¹But the seventh year you shall let the land lie untilled and fallow, that the poor of your people may eat of it and their leftovers the wild animals may eat. So also shall you do in regard to your vineyard and your olive grove.

¹²For six days you may do your work, but on the seventh day you must rest,ᵇ that your ox and your donkey may have rest, and that the son of your maidservant and the resident alien may be refreshed. ¹³Give heed to all that I have told you.

You shall not mention the name of any other god; it shall not be heard from your lips.

¹⁴ᶜThree times a year you shall celebrate a pilgrim feast to me.* ¹⁵You shall keep the feast of Unleavened Bread. As I have commanded you, you must eat unleavened bread for seven days at the appointed time in the month of Abib, for it was then that you came out of Egypt. No one shall appear before me† empty-handed. ¹⁶You shall also keep the feast of the grain harvest with the first fruits of the crop that you sow in the field; and finally, the feast of Ingathering at the end of the year, when you collect your produce from the fields. ¹⁷Three times a year shall all your men appear before the LORD God.

¹⁸You shall not offer the blood of my sacrifice with anything leavened;ᵈ nor shall the fat of my feast be kept overnight till the next day. ¹⁹The choicest first fruits of your soil you shall bring to the house of the LORD, your God.

You shall not boil a young goat in its mother's milk.‡

**Reward of Fidelity.** ²⁰See, I am sending an angelᵉ before you, to guard you on the way and bring you to the place I have prepared. ²¹Be attentive to him and obey him. Do not rebel against him, for he will not forgive your sin. My authority is within him.§ ²²If you obey him and carry out all I tell you, I will be an enemy to your enemies and a foe to your foes.

²³My angel will go before you and bring you to the Amorites, Hittites, Perizzites, Canaanites, Hivites and Jebusites; and I will wipe them out. ²⁴Therefore, you shall not bow down to their gods and serve them, nor shall you act as they do; rather, you must demolish them and smash their sacred stones.¶ ²⁵You shall serve the LORD, your God; then he will bless your food and drink, and I will remove sickness from your midst; ²⁶no woman in your land will be barren or miscarry; and I will give you a full span of life.

²⁷I will have the terror of me precede you, so that I will throw into panic every nation you reach.ᵍ I will make all your enemies turn from you in flight, ²⁸and ahead of you I will send hornets** to drive the Hivites, Canaanites and Hittites out of your way. ²⁹But I will not drive them all out before you in one year, lest the land become desolate and the wild animals multiply against you. ³⁰Little by little I will drive them out before you, until you have grown numerous enough to take possession of the land. ³¹ʰI will set your boundaries from the Red Sea to the sea of the Philistines,†† and from the wilderness to the Euphrates; all who dwell in this land I will hand over to you and you shall drive them out before you. ³²You shall not make a covenant with them or their gods. ³³They must not live in your land. For if you serve their gods, this will become a snare to you.ᶦ

## CHAPTER 24

**Ratification of the Covenant.** ¹Moses himself was told: Come up to the LORD, you and Aaron, with Nadab, Abihu, and seventy of the elders of

---

understand. It may originate from a taboo that forbade killing the young that were still nursing from the mother, or that forbade the mixing of life and death: the slaughtered young goat with the milk that previously had nourished its life. The Jewish dietary custom of keeping meat and dairy products separate is based on this command.

§[23:21] **My authority is within him:** lit., "My name is within him."

¶[23:24] **Sacred stones:** objects that symbolized the presence of Canaanite deities. In general, standing stones served as memorials for deities, persons, or significant events such as military victories or covenant-making. See 24:4.

**[23:28] **Hornets:** the Hebrew *sirʿah* is a disputed term, but according to ancient interpreters it refers to hornets that were unleashed against the enemy to sting them and cause panic (cf. Dt 7:20; Jos 24:12; Wis 12:8). Others associate the word with plagues or troublesome afflictions.

††[23:31] **The sea of the Philistines:** the Mediterranean. Only in the time of David and Solomon did the territory of Israel come near to reaching such distant borders.

---

*[23:14] These three feasts—Passover/Unleavened Bread, Weeks (Pentecost), and Booths (Tabernacles or Succoth/Sukkoth)—are also listed in 34:18–26; Lv 23; Dt 16.

†[23:15] **Appear before me:** the original expression was "see my face"; so also in several other places, as 23:17; 34:23–24; Dt 16:16; 31:11.

‡[23:19] **Boil a young goat in its mother's milk:** this command, repeated in 34:26 and Dt 14:21, is difficult to

---

w. [23:3] Lv 19:15.   x. [23:4] Dt 22:1–4.   y. [23:8] Dt 16:19; 27:25; Sir 20:28.   z. [23:9] Ex 22:20.   a. [23:10–11] Lv 25:3–7.   b. [23:12] Ex 20:8–10.   c. [23:14–17] Ex 34:18, 22–24; Lv 23; Dt 16:1–17.   d. [23:18–19] Ex 34:25–26.

e. [23:20] Ex 14:19; 32:34; 33:2.   f. [23:23–24] Ex 34:10–16; Nm 33:51–52; Dt 7:24–26.   g. [23:27–30] Dt 2:25; 7:20–22.   h. [23:31] Gn 15:18; Dt 11:24; Jos 1:4.   i. [23:32–33] Ex 34:12–16; Dt 7:2–6.

Israel. You shall bow down at a distance. [2]Moses alone is to come close to the LORD; the others shall not come close, and the people shall not come up with them.

[3]When Moses came to the people and related all the words and ordinances of the LORD, they all answered with one voice, "We will do everything that the LORD has told us."[j] [4]Moses then wrote down all the words of the LORD and, rising early in the morning, he built at the foot of the mountain an altar and twelve sacred stones* for the twelve tribes of Israel. [5k]Then, having sent young men of the Israelites to offer burnt offerings and sacrifice young bulls as communion offerings to the LORD, [6]Moses took half of the blood and put it in large bowls; the other half he splashed on the altar. [7]Taking the book of the covenant, he read it aloud to the people, who answered, "All that the LORD has said, we will hear and do." [8]Then he took the blood and splashed it on the people, saying, "This is the blood of the covenant which the LORD has made with you according to all these words."

[9]Moses then went up with Aaron, Nadab, Abihu, and seventy elders of Israel, [10]and there beheld the God of Israel. Under his feet there appeared to be sapphire tilework, as clear as the sky itself. [11]Yet he did not lay a hand on these chosen Israelites. They saw God,[†] and they ate and drank.

**Moses on the Mountain.** [12]The LORD said to Moses: Come up to me on the mountain and, while you are there, I will give you the stone tablets[j] on which I have written the commandments intended for their instruction. [13]So Moses set out with Joshua, his assistant, and went up to the mountain of God. [14]He told the elders, "Wait here for us until we return to you. Aaron and Hur are with you. Anyone with a complaint should approach them." [15]Moses went up the mountain. Then the cloud covered the mountain. [16]The glory of the LORD settled upon Mount Sinai. The cloud covered it for six days, and on the seventh day he called to Moses from the midst of the cloud.[m] [17]To the Israelites the glory of the LORD was seen as a consuming fire on the top of the mountain.[n] [18]But Moses entered into the midst of the cloud and went up on the mountain. He was on the mountain for forty days and forty nights.[o]

# CHAPTER 25

**Collection of Materials.** [1]The LORD spoke to Moses:[p] [2]Speak to the Israelites: Let them receive contributions for me. From each you shall receive the contribution that their hearts prompt them to give me. [3]These are the contributions you shall accept from them: gold, silver, and bronze;[q] [4]violet, purple, and scarlet yarn; fine linen and goat hair; [5]rams' skins dyed red, and tahash[‡] skins; acacia wood; [6]oil for the light; spices for the anointing oil and for the fragrant incense; [7]onyx stones and other gems for mounting on the ephod and the breastpiece. [8]They are to make a sanctuary for me, that I may dwell in their midst.[r] [9]According to all that I show you regarding the pattern of the tabernacle and the pattern of its furnishings, so you are to make it.[s]

**Plan of the Ark.** [10]You shall make an ark of acacia wood,[t] two and a half cubits[§] long, one and a half cubits wide, and one and a half cubits high. [11]Plate it inside and outside with pure gold, and put a molding of gold around the top of it. [12]Cast four gold rings and put them on the four supports of the ark, two rings on one side and two on the opposite side. [13]Then make poles of acacia wood and plate them with gold. [14]These poles you are to put through the rings on the sides of the ark, for carrying it; [15]they must remain in the rings of the ark and never be withdrawn. [16]In the ark you are to put the covenant which I will give you.

[17]You shall then make a cover[¶] of pure gold, two and a half cubits long, and one and a half cubits wide. [18]Make two cherubim[**] of beaten gold for the two ends of the cover; [19]make one cherub at one end, and the other at the other end, of one piece with the cover, at each end. [20]The cherubim shall have their wings spread out above, sheltering the cover with them; they shall face each other, with their faces looking toward the cover. [21]This cover you shall then place on top of the ark. In the ark itself you are to put the covenant which I will give you. [22]There I will meet you and there, from above the cover, between the two cherubim on the ark of the covenant, I will tell you all that I command you regarding the Israelites.

**The Table.** [23]You shall also make a table of acacia[u] wood, two cubits long, a cubit wide, and a

---

‡[25:5] **Tahash:** perhaps a kind of specially finished leather. The Greek and Latin versions took it for the color hyacinth.

§[25:10] **Cubits:** the distance between the elbow and tip of the middle finger of an average-size person, about eighteen inches. The dimensions of the ark of the covenant were approximately 3 3/4 feet long, 2 1/4 feet wide, and 2 1/4 feet high.

¶[25:17] **Cover:** the Hebrew term, *kapporet*, has been connected with *kippur*, as in the feast of Yom Kippur or Day of Atonement (Lv 16; 23:26–32): hence, influenced by the Greek and Latin versions, and Luther's German, English translations have rendered it "propitiatory," "mercy seat," and the like.

**[25:18–20] **Cherubim:** probably in the form of human-headed winged lions. The cherubim over the ark formed the throne for the invisible Lord. Cf. Ps 80:2. For a more detailed description of the somewhat different cherubim in the Temple of Solomon, see 1 Kgs 6:23–28; 2 Chr 3:10–13.

---

*[24:4] **Sacred stones:** stone shafts or slabs, erected as symbols of the fact that each of the twelve tribes had entered into this covenant with God; see 23:24; Gn 28:18.

†[24:11] **They saw God:** the ancients thought that the sight of God would bring instantaneous death. Cf. 33:20; Gn 16:13; 32:31; Jgs 6:22–23; 13:22. **Ate and drank:** partook of the sacrificial meal.

---

j. [24:3] Ex 19:8.   k. [24:5–8] Heb 9:18–20.   l. [24:12] Ex 31:18; 32:15–16; Dt 5:22.   m. [24:16] Sir 45:5.   n. [24:17] Ex 19:18; Heb 12:18.   o. [24:18] Ex 34:28; Dt 9:9.   p. [25:1–7] Ex 35:4–9, 20–29.

q. [25:3] Ex 35:4–9.   r. [25:8–9] Ex 26:1–30; 36:8–38.   s. [25:9] Acts 7:44.   t. [25:10–22] Ex 37:1–9; Heb 9:1–5.   u. [25:23–30] Ex 37:10–16.

cubit and a half high. ²⁴Plate it with pure gold and make a molding of gold around it. ²⁵Make a frame* for it, a handbreadth high, and make a molding of gold around the frame. ²⁶You shall also make four rings of gold for it and fasten them at the four corners, one at each leg. ²⁷The rings shall be alongside the frame as holders for the poles to carry the table. ²⁸These poles for carrying the table you shall make of acacia wood and plate with gold. ²⁹You shall make its plates† and cups, as well as its pitchers and bowls for pouring libations; make them of pure gold. ³⁰On the table you shall always keep showbread set before me.ᵛ

**The Menorah.** ³¹You shall make a menorah‡ of pure beaten goldʷ—its shaft and branches—with its cups and knobs and petals springing directly from it. ³²Six branches are to extend from its sides, three branches on one side, and three on the other. ³³§On one branch there are to be three cups, shaped like almond blossoms, each with its knob and petals; on the opposite branch there are to be three cups, shaped like almond blossoms, each with its knob and petals; and so for the six branches that extend from the menorah. ³⁴On the menorah there are to be four cups,¶ shaped like almond blossoms, with their knobs and petals. ³⁵The six branches that go out from the menorah are to have a knob under each pair. ³⁶Their knobs and branches shall so spring from it that the whole will form a single piece of pure beaten gold. ³⁷**You shall then make seven lampsˣ for it and so set up the lamps that they give their light on the space in front of the menorah. ³⁸These, as well as the trimming shears and trays,†† must be of pure gold. ³⁹Use a talent‡‡ of pure gold for the menorah and all these utensils. ⁴⁰See that you make them according to the pattern shown you on the mountain.ʸ

---

*[25:25] **A frame**: probably placed near the bottom of the legs to keep them steady. The golden table of Herod's Temple is pictured thus on the Arch of Titus.

†[25:29–30] The plates held the showbread, that is, the holy bread which was placed upon the table every sabbath as an offering to God, and was later eaten by the priests. The cups held the incense which was strewn upon the bread. Cf. Lv 24:5–9. The libation wine was poured from the pitchers into the bowls. All these vessels were kept on the golden table.

‡[25:31] **Menorah**: this traditional lampstand is still used today in Jewish liturgy.

§[25:33] In keeping with the arrangement of the ornaments on the shaft, the three sets of ornaments on each branch were probably so placed that one was at the top and the other two equally spaced along the length of the branch. **Knob**: the cup-shaped seed capsule at the base of a flower.

¶[25:34–35] Of the four ornaments on the shaft, one was at the top and one was below each of the three sets of side branches.

**[25:37] The lamps were probably shaped like small boats, with the wick at one end; the end with the wick was turned toward the front of the menorah.

††[25:38] **Trays**: small receptacles for the burnt-out wicks.

‡‡[25:39] **Talent**: Heb. *kikkar*. The largest unit of weight used in the Bible, equivalent to 3,000 shekels (see 38:24). It is difficult to be precise about biblical weights; the Israelite talent may have weighed between 75–80 pounds.

v. [25:30] Lv 24:5–9.　w. [25:31–40] Ex 37:17–24.　x. [25:37] Lv 24:2–4; Nm 8:2.　y. [25:40] Heb 8:5.

---

# CHAPTER 26

**The Tent Cloth.** ¹The tabernacle itself you shall make out of ten sheets§§ woven of fine linen twined and of violet, purple, and scarlet yarn, with cherubim embroidered on them.ᶻ ²The length of each shall be twenty-eight cubits, and the width four cubits; all the sheets shall be of the same size. ³Five of the sheets are to be joined one to another; and the same for the other five. ⁴Make loops of violet yarn along the edge of the end sheet in one set, and the same along the edge of the end sheet in the other set. ⁵Make fifty loops along the edge of the end sheet in the first set, and fifty loops along the edge of the corresponding sheet in the second set, and so placed that the loops are directly opposite each other. ⁶Then make fifty clasps of gold and join the two sets of sheets, so that the tabernacle forms one whole.

⁷Also make sheets woven of goat hair for a tent¶¶ over the tabernacle. Make eleven such sheets; ⁸the length of each shall be thirty cubits, and the width four cubits: all eleven sheets shall be of the same size. ⁹Join five of the sheets into one set, and the other six sheets into another set. Use the sixth sheet double at the front of the tent.*** ¹⁰Make fifty loops along the edge of the end sheet in one set, and fifty loops along the edge of the end sheet in the second set. ¹¹Also make fifty bronze clasps and put them into the loops, to join the tent into one whole. ¹²There will be an extra half sheet of tent covering, which shall be allowed to hang down over the rear of the tabernacle. ¹³Likewise, the sheets of the tent will have an extra cubit's length to be left hanging down on either side of the tabernacle to cover it. ¹⁴Over the tent itself make a covering of rams' skins dyed red, and above that, a covering of tahash skins.

**The Framework.** ¹⁵ᵃYou shall make frames for the tabernacle, acacia-wood uprights. ¹⁶The length of each frame is to be ten cubits, and its width one and a half cubits. ¹⁷Each frame shall have two arms††† joined one to another; so you are to make all the frames of the tabernacle. ¹⁸Make the frames of the tabernacle as follows: twenty frames on the south side, ¹⁹with forty silver pedestals under the twenty frames, two pedestals under each frame for its two arms; ²⁰twenty frames on the other side of the tabernacle, the

---

§§[26:1] **Sheets**: strips of tapestry, woven of white linen, the colored threads being used for the cherubim which were embroidered on them. These sheets were stretched across the top of the tabernacle to form a roof, their free ends hanging down inside the framework that formed the walls.

¶¶[26:7] **Tent**: the cloth made of sheets of goat hair to cover the tabernacle.

***[26:9] Half the width of the end strip was folded back at the front of the tabernacle, thus leaving another half-strip to hang down at the rear. Cf. v. 12.

†††[26:17] **Arms**: lit., "hands." According to some, they served as "tongue and groove" to mortise the structural elements; according to others, they were pegs that fitted into sockets in the pedestals.

z. [26:1–14] Ex 36:8–19.　a. [26:15–30] Ex 36:20–34.

north side, [21]with their forty silver pedestals, two pedestals under each frame. [22]At the rear of the tabernacle, to the west, six frames, [23]and two frames for the corners of the tabernacle, at its rear. [24]These two shall be double at the bottom, and likewise double at the top, to the first ring. That is how both corner frames are to be made. [25]Thus, there shall be eight frames, with their sixteen silver pedestals, two pedestals under each frame. [26]Also make bars of acacia wood: five for the frames on one side of the tabernacle, [27]five for those on the other side, and five for those at the rear, to the west. [28]The center bar, at the middle of the frames, shall reach across from end to end. [29]Plate the frames with gold, and make gold rings on them as holders for the bars, which are also to be plated with gold. [30]You shall set up the tabernacle according to its plan, which you were shown on the mountain.

**The Veils.** [31]You shall make a veil woven of violet, purple, and scarlet yarn,[b] and of fine linen twined, with cherubim embroidered on it.[c] [32]It is to be hung on four gold-plated columns of acacia wood, which shall have gold hooks[*] and shall rest on four silver pedestals. [33]Hang the veil from clasps. The ark of the covenant you shall bring inside, behind this veil which divides the holy place from the holy of holies. [34]Set the cover on the ark of the covenant in the holy of holies.

[35]Outside the veil you shall place the table and the menorah, the latter on the south side of the tabernacle, opposite the table, which is to be put on the north side. [36]For the entrance of the tent make a variegated[†] curtain of violet, purple, and scarlet yarn and of fine linen twined. [37]Make five columns of acacia wood for this curtain; plate them with gold, with their hooks of gold; and cast five bronze pedestals for them.

# CHAPTER 27

**The Altar for Burnt Offerings.** [1]You shall make an altar[d] of acacia wood, on a square, five cubits long and five cubits wide; it shall be three cubits high. [2]At the four corners make horns[‡] that are of one piece with the altar. You shall then plate it with bronze. [3]Make pots for removing the ashes, as well as shovels, basins, forks, and fire pans; all these utensils you shall make of bronze. [4]Make for it a grating,[§] a bronze network; make four bronze rings for it, one at each of its four corners. [5]Put it down around the altar, on the ground. This network is to be half as high as the altar. [6]You shall also make poles of acacia wood for the altar, and plate them with bronze. [7]These poles are to be put through the rings, so that they are on either side of the altar when it is carried. [8]Make the altar itself in the form of a hollow[¶] box. Just as it was shown you on the mountain, so it is to be made.

**Court of the Tabernacle.** [9e]You shall also make a court for the tabernacle. On the south side the court shall have hangings, of fine linen twined, a hundred cubits long, [10]with twenty columns and twenty pedestals of bronze; the hooks and bands on the columns shall be of silver. [11]On the north side there shall be similar hangings, a hundred cubits long, with twenty columns and twenty pedestals of bronze; the hooks and bands on the columns shall be of silver. [12]On the west side, across the width of the court, there shall be hangings, fifty cubits long, with ten columns and ten pedestals. [13]The width of the court on the east side shall be fifty cubits. [14]On one side there shall be hangings to the extent of fifteen cubits, with three columns and three pedestals; [15]on the other side there shall be hangings to the extent of fifteen cubits, with three columns and three pedestals.

[16]At the gate of the court there shall be a variegated curtain, twenty cubits long, woven of violet, purple, and scarlet yarn and of fine linen twined. It shall have four columns and four pedestals.

[17]All the columns around the court shall have bands and hooks of silver, and pedestals of bronze. [18]The court is to be one hundred cubits long, fifty cubits wide, and five cubits high. Fine linen twined must be used, and the pedestals must be of bronze. [19]All the fittings of the tabernacle, whatever be their use, as well as all its tent pegs and all the tent pegs of the court, must be of bronze.

**Oil for the Lamps.** [20]You shall command the Israelites to bring you clear oil of crushed olives, to be used for the light, so that you may keep lamps burning always.[f] [21]From evening to morning Aaron and his sons shall maintain them before the LORD in the tent of meeting, outside the veil which hangs in front of the covenant. This shall be a perpetual statute for the Israelites throughout their generations.

# CHAPTER 28

**The Priestly Vestments.** [1g]Have your brother Aaron, and with him his sons, brought to you, from among the Israelites, that they may be my

---

*[26:32] **Hooks:** probably placed near the tops of the columns, to hold the rope from which the veils and curtains hung.

†[26:36] **Variegated:** without definite designs such as the cherubim on the inner veil.

‡[27:2] **Horns:** the horn of a ram, goat or ox is a common Old Testament figure for strength and dignity; they represent the divine character of the altar itself or the deity worshiped there.

§[27:4] **Grating:** it is not clear whether this was flush with the altar or at some small distance from it; in the latter case the space between the altar and the grating would be filled with

stones and serve as a platform around the altar, which would otherwise be too high for the priest to reach conveniently.

¶[27:8] **Hollow:** probably filled with earth or stones when in use. Cf. 20:24–25.

---

b. [26:31] 2 Chr 3:14.   c. [26:31] Ex 36:35–38.   d. [27:1–8] Ex 38:1–7.

e. [27:9–19] Ex 38:9–20.   f. [27:20–21] Lv 24:1–4.   g. [28:1–5] Ex 39:1; Sir 45:7.

priests: Nadab and Abihu, Eleazar and Ithamar, Aaron's sons. [2]For the glorious adornment of your brother Aaron you shall have sacred vestments made. [3]Therefore, tell the various artisans whom I have endowed with skill[*] to make vestments for Aaron to consecrate him as my priest. [4]These are the vestments they shall make: a breastpiece, an ephod, a robe, a brocade tunic, a turban, and a sash. In making these sacred vestments which your brother Aaron and his sons are to wear in serving as my priests, [5]they shall use gold, violet, purple, and scarlet yarn and fine linen.

**The Ephod and Breastpiece.** [6]The ephod[†] they shall make of gold thread and of violet, purple, and scarlet yarn, embroidered on cloth of fine linen twined.[h] [7]It shall have a pair of shoulder straps joined to its two upper ends. [8]The embroidered belt of the ephod shall extend out from it and, like it, be made of gold thread, of violet, purple, and scarlet yarn, and of fine linen twined.

[9]Get two onyx stones and engrave on them the names of the sons of Israel: [10]six of their names on one stone, and the names of the remaining six on the other stone, in the order of their birth. [11]As a gem-cutter engraves a seal, so shall you have the two stones engraved with the names of the sons of Israel and then mounted in gold filigree work. [12]Set these two stones on the shoulder straps of the ephod as memorial stones of the sons of Israel. Thus Aaron shall bear their names on his shoulders as a reminder before the LORD. [13]Make filigree rosettes of gold,[i] [14]as well as two chains of pure gold, twisted like cords, and fasten the cordlike chains to the filigree rosettes.

[15]The breastpiece[‡] of decision you shall also have made, embroidered like the ephod with gold thread and violet, purple, and scarlet yarn on cloth of fine linen twined. [16]It is to be square when folded double, a span high and a span wide. [17§]On it you shall mount four rows of precious stones: in the first row, a carnelian, a topaz, and an emerald; [18]in the second row, a garnet, a sapphire, and a beryl; [19]in the third row, a jacinth, an agate, and an amethyst; [20]in the

fourth row, a chrysolite, an onyx, and a jasper. These stones are to be mounted in gold filigree work, [21]twelve of them to match the names of the sons of Israel, each stone engraved like a seal with the name of one of the twelve tribes.

[22]When the chains of pure gold, twisted like cords, have been made for the breastpiece, [23]you shall then make two rings of gold for it and fasten them to the two upper ends of the breastpiece. [24]The gold cords are then to be fastened to the two rings at the upper ends of the breastpiece, [25]the other two ends of the cords being fastened in front to the two filigree rosettes which are attached to the shoulder straps of the ephod. [26]Make two other rings of gold and put them on the two lower ends of the breastpiece, on its edge that faces the ephod. [27]Then make two more rings of gold and fasten them to the bottom of the shoulder straps next to where they join the ephod in front, just above its embroidered belt. [28]Violet ribbons shall bind the rings of the breastpiece to the rings of the ephod, so that the breastpiece will stay right above the embroidered belt of the ephod and not swing loose from it.

[29]Whenever Aaron enters the sanctuary, he will thus bear the names of the sons of Israel on the breastpiece of decision over his heart as a constant reminder before the LORD. [30]In this breastpiece of decision[k] you shall put the Urim and Thummim,[¶] that they may be over Aaron's heart whenever he enters the presence of the LORD. Thus he shall always bear the decisions for the Israelites over his heart in the presence of the LORD.

**Other Vestments.** [31]The robe of the ephod[l] you shall make entirely of violet material. [32]It shall have an opening for the head in the center, and around this opening there shall be a selvage, woven as at the opening of a shirt, to keep it from being torn. [33]At the hem at the bottom you shall make pomegranates, woven of violet, purple, and scarlet yarn and fine linen twined, with gold bells between them; [34]a gold bell, a pomegranate, a gold bell, a pomegranate, all around the hem of the robe. [35]Aaron shall wear it when ministering, that its sound may be heard as he enters and leaves the LORD's presence in the sanctuary; else he will die.

[36]You shall also make a plate of pure gold and engrave on it, as on a seal engraving, "Sacred to the LORD." [37]This plate is to be tied over the turban with a violet ribbon in such a way that it rests on the front of the turban,[m] [38]over Aaron's forehead. Since Aaron bears whatever guilt the Israelites may incur in consecrating any of their sacred

---

[*][28:3] **Artisans . . . endowed with skill**: lit., "wise of heart," and "filled with a spirit of wisdom." In Hebrew wisdom includes practical skills. Cf. 35:35; 36:1–2.

[†][28:6] **Ephod**: this Hebrew word is retained in the translation because it is the technical term for a peculiar piece of the priestly vestments, the exact nature of which is uncertain. It seems to have been a sort of apron that hung from the shoulders of the priest by shoulder straps (v. 7) and was tied around his waist by the loose ends of the attached belt (v. 8).

[‡][28:15–30] **Breastpiece**: an approximately nine-inch square, pocketlike receptacle for holding the Urim and Thummim (v. 30). It formed an integral part of the ephod, to which it was attached by an elaborate system of rings and chains. Both the ephod and its breastpiece were made of brocaded linen. **Span**: Heb. zeret, the distance between the top of the little finger and the thumb; one half a cubit, approximately nine inches.

[§][28:17–20] The translation of the Hebrew names of some of these gems is quite conjectural.

[¶][28:30] **Urim and Thummim**: both the meaning of these Hebrew words and the exact nature of the objects so designated are uncertain. They were apparently lots of some kind which were drawn or cast by the priest to ascertain God's decision on particular questions. Hence, the pocket in which they were kept was called "the breastpiece of decision."

---

h. [28:6–12] Ex 39:2–7; Sir 45:8–14. i. [28:13–14] Ex 28:22, 25; 39:15, 18. j. [28:15–21] Ex 39:15–21.

k. [28:30] Lv 8:8; Sir 45:11. l. [28:31–35] Ex 39:20–25; Lv 8:9; Sir 45:10. m. [28:37] Ex 39:31; Lv 8:9.

gifts, this plate must always be over his forehead, so that they may find favor with the LORD.

<sup>39</sup>"The tunic of fine linen shall be brocaded. The turban shall be made of fine linen. The sash shall be of variegated work.

<sup>40</sup>Likewise, for the glorious adornment of Aaron's sons you shall have tunics and sashes and skullcaps made, for glorious splendor. <sup>41</sup>With these you shall clothe your brother Aaron and his sons. Anoint and install them,* consecrating them as my priests. <sup>42</sup>You must also make linen pants for them, to cover their naked flesh from their loins to their thighs.<sup>o</sup> <sup>43</sup>Aaron and his sons shall wear them whenever they go into the tent of meeting or approach the altar to minister in the sanctuary, lest they incur guilt and die. This shall be a perpetual ordinance for him and for his descendants.

## CHAPTER 29

**Consecration of the Priests.** <sup>1</sup>This is the rite you shall perform in consecrating them as my priests.<sup>p</sup> Procure a young bull and two unblemished rams. <sup>2</sup>With bran flour make unleavened cakes mixed with oil, and unleavened wafers spread with oil, <sup>3</sup>and put them in a basket. Take the basket of them along with the bull and the two rams. <sup>4</sup>Aaron and his sons you shall also bring to the entrance of the tent of meeting, and there wash them with water. <sup>5</sup>Take the vestments and clothe Aaron with the tunic, the robe of the ephod, the ephod itself, and the breastpiece, fastening the embroidered belt of the ephod around him. <sup>6</sup>Put the turban on his head, the sacred diadem on the turban. <sup>7</sup>Then take the anointing oil and pour it on his head, and anoint him. <sup>8</sup>Bring forward his sons also and clothe them with the tunics, <sup>9</sup>gird them with the sashes, and tie the skullcaps on them.<sup>q</sup> Thus shall the priesthood be theirs by a perpetual statute, and thus shall you install Aaron and his sons.

**Installation Sacrifices.** <sup>10</sup>"Now bring forward the bull in front of the tent of meeting. There Aaron and his sons shall lay their hands on its head. <sup>11</sup>Then slaughter the bull before the LORD, at the entrance of the tent of meeting. <sup>12</sup>Take some of its blood and with your finger put it on the horns of the altar. All the rest of the blood you shall pour out at the base of the altar. <sup>13</sup>All the fat that covers its inner organs, as well as the lobe of its liver and its two kidneys, together with the fat that is on them, you shall take and burn on the altar. <sup>14</sup>But the meat and hide and dung of the bull you must burn up outside the camp, since this is a purification offering.<sup>s</sup>

<sup>15</sup>Then take one of the rams, and after Aaron and his sons have laid their hands on its head, <sup>16</sup>slaughter it. The blood you shall take and splash on all the sides of the altar. <sup>17</sup>Cut the ram into pieces; you shall wash its inner organs and shanks and put them with the pieces and with the head. <sup>18</sup>Then you shall burn the entire ram on the altar, since it is a burnt offering, a sweet-smelling oblation to the LORD.

<sup>19</sup>After this take the other ram, and when Aaron and his sons have laid their hands on its head, <sup>20</sup>slaughter it. Some of its blood you shall take and put on the tip of Aaron's right ear and on the tips of his sons' right ears and on the thumbs of their right hands and the great toes of their right feet. Splash the rest of the blood on all the sides of the altar. <sup>21</sup>Then take some of the blood that is on the altar, together with some of the anointing oil, and sprinkle this on Aaron and his vestments, as well as on his sons and their vestments, that he and his sons and their vestments may be sacred.

<sup>22</sup>Now, from this ram you shall take its fat: its fatty tail,<sup>†</sup> the fat that covers its inner organs, the lobe of its liver, its two kidneys with the fat that is on them, and its right thigh, since this is the ram for installation; <sup>23</sup>then, out of the basket of unleavened food that you have set before the LORD, you shall take one of the loaves of bread, one of the cakes made with oil, and one of the wafers. <sup>24</sup>All these things you shall put into the hands of Aaron and his sons, so that they may raise them as an elevated offering<sup>‡</sup> before the LORD. <sup>25</sup>After you receive them back from their hands, you shall burn them on top of the burnt offering on the altar as a sweet-smelling oblation to the LORD. <sup>26</sup>Finally, take the brisket of Aaron's installation ram and raise it as an elevated offering before the LORD; this is to be your own portion.

<sup>27</sup>§Thus shall you set aside the brisket of whatever elevated offering is raised,<sup>t</sup> as well as the thigh of whatever contribution is raised up, whether this be the installation ram or anything else belonging to Aaron or to his sons. <sup>28</sup>Such things are due to Aaron and his sons from the Israelites by a perpetual statute as a contribution. From their communion offerings, too, the Israelites shall make a contribution, their contribution to the LORD.

<sup>29</sup>The sacred vestments<sup>u</sup> of Aaron shall be passed down to his sons after him, that in them they may be anointed and installed. <sup>30</sup>The son

---

*[28:41] **Install them**: lit., "fill their hands," a technical expression used for the installation of priests.

†[29:22] **Fatty tail**: the thick layer of fat surrounding the tails of sheep and rams bred in the Middle East. It is regarded as a choice food. Cf. Lv 3:9.

‡[29:24–26] **Elevated offering**: the portions of a communion offering, brisket and right thigh, which the officiating priest raised in the presence of the Lord. They were reserved for Aaron and his sons.

§[29:27–30] These verses are a parenthetical interruption of the installation ritual; v. 31 belongs logically immediately after v. 26.

---

n. [28:39–43] Ex 39:27–31.   o. [28:42] Ez 44:18.   p. [29:1–8] Lv 8:1–9.   q. [29:9] Lv 8:13.   r. [29:10–26] Lv 8:14–30.   s. [29:14] Heb 13:11.

t. [29:27–28] Lv 7:31–34; 10:14–15; Nm 18:18–19; Dt 18:3.
u. [29:29] Nm 20:26, 28.

who succeeds him as priest and who is to enter the tent of meeting to minister in the sanctuary shall be clothed with them for seven days.

³¹ʸYou shall take the installation ram and boil its meat in a holy place. ³²At the entrance of the tent of meeting Aaron and his sons shall eat the meat of the ram and the bread that is in the basket. ³³They themselves are to eat of these things by which atonement was made at their installation and consecration; but no unauthorized person may eat of them, since it is sacred. ³⁴If some of the meat of the installation sacrifice or some of the bread remains over on the next day, this remnant you must burn up; it is not to be eaten, since it is sacred.

³⁵Carry out all these commands in regard to Aaron and his sons just as I have given them to you.ʷ Seven days you shall spend installing them, ³⁶ˣsacrificing a bull each day as a purification offering, to make atonement. Thus you shall purify the altar* by purging it, and you shall anoint it in order to consecrate it. ³⁷Seven days you shall spend in purging the altar and in consecrating it. Then the altar will be most sacred, and whatever touches it will become sacred.

³⁸†Now, this is what you shall regularly offer on the altar: two yearling lambsʸ as the sacrifice established for each day; ³⁹one lamb in the morning and the other lamb at the evening twilight. ⁴⁰With the first lamb there shall be a tenth of an ephah of bran flour mixed with a fourth of a hin‡ of oil of crushed olives and, as its libation, a fourth of a hin of wine. ⁴¹The other lamb you shall offer at the evening twilight, with the same grain offering and libation as in the morning. You shall offer this as a sweet-smelling oblation to the LORD. ⁴²Throughout your generations this regular burnt offering shall be made before the LORD at the entrance of the tent of meeting, where I will meet you and speak to you.

⁴³There, at the altar, I will meet the Israelites; hence, it will be made sacred by my glory.ᶻ ⁴⁴Thus I will consecrate the tent of meeting and the altar, just as I also consecrate Aaron and his sons to be my priests. ⁴⁵I will dwell in the midst of the Israelites and will be their God. ⁴⁶They shall know that I, the LORD, am their God who brought them out of the land of Egypt, so that I, the LORD, their God, might dwell among them.

---

*[29:36–37] **Purify the altar**: the purpose of the purification offering here is to cleanse, or purify, the newly constructed altar of any defilement resulting from presumably minor and inadvertent sins, but the text is not explicit about what the offenses were or who committed them. So various theories have been proposed to explain the cause of the altar's contamination. Note, however, that the offering appears to be demanded of Aaron and his sons; they are the ones who lay hands upon it (v. 10).

†[29:38–42] A parenthesis inserted into the rubrics for consecrating the altar; v. 43 belongs directly after v. 37.

‡[29:40] **Hin**: see note on Ez 45:24.

v. [29:31–34] Lv 8:31–32.  w. [29:35] Lv 8:36.  x. [29:36–37] Lv 8:33–35.  y. [29:38–42] Nm 28:3–8.  z. [29:43] Ex 25:22.

---

# CHAPTER 30

**Altar of Incense.** ¹For burning incense you shall make an altar of acacia wood,ᵃ ²with a square surface, a cubit long, a cubit wide, and two cubits high, with horns that are of one piece with it. ³Its grate on top, its walls on all four sides, and its horns you shall plate with pure gold. Put a gold molding around it. ⁴Underneath the molding you shall put gold rings, two on one side and two on the opposite side, as holders for the poles used in carrying it. ⁵Make the poles, too, of acacia wood and plate them with gold. ⁶This altar you are to place in front of the veil that hangs before the ark of the covenant where I will meet you.ᵇ

⁷On it Aaron shall burn fragrant incense. Morning after morning, when he prepares the lamps, ⁸and again in the evening twilight, when he lights the lamps, he shall burn incense. Throughout your generations this shall be the regular incense offering before the LORD. ⁹On this altar you shall not offer up any profane incense, or any burnt offering or grain offering; nor shall you pour out a libation upon it. ¹⁰Once a year Aaron shall purge its horns.ᶜ Throughout your generations he is to purge it once a year with the blood of the atoning purification offering. This altar is most sacred to the LORD.

**Census Tax.** ¹¹The LORD also told Moses: ¹²When you take a censusᵈ of the Israelites who are to be enrolled, each one, as he is enrolled, shall give the LORD a ransom for his life, so that no plague may come upon them for being enrolled. ¹³This is what everyone who is enrolled must pay: a half-shekel, according to the standard of the sanctuary shekel—twenty gerahs to the shekel—a half-shekel contribution to the LORD.ᵉ ¹⁴Everyone who is enrolled, of twenty years or more, must give the contribution to the LORD. ¹⁵The rich need not give more, nor shall the poor give less, than a half-shekel in this contribution to the LORD to pay the ransom for their lives. ¹⁶ᶠWhen you receive this ransom money from the Israelites, you shall donate it to the service of the tent of meeting, that there it may be a reminder of the Israelites before the LORD of the ransom paid for their lives.

**The Basin.** ¹⁷The LORD told Moses: ¹⁸For ablutions you shall make a bronze basin with a bronze stand. Place it between the tent of meeting and the altar, and put water in it.ᵍ ¹⁹Aaron and his sons shall use it in washing their hands and feet.ʰ ²⁰When they are about to enter the tent of meeting, they must wash with water, lest they die. Likewise when they approach the altar to minister, to offer an oblation to the LORD, ²¹they must wash their hands and feet, lest they die. This shall be a perpetual statute for him and his descendants throughout their generations.

---

a. [30:1–5] Ex 37:25–28.  b. [30:6] Ex 40:26.  c. [30:10] Lv 16:18.  d. [30:12] Nm 1:2–3; 26:2.  e. [30:13] Mt 17:24–27.  f. [30:16] Ex 38:25.  g. [30:18] Ex 38:8; 40:7, 30.  h. [30:19–21] Ex 40:31–32.

**The Anointing Oil.** [22]The LORD told Moses: [23]Take the finest spices: five hundred shekels of free-flowing myrrh; half that amount, that is, two hundred and fifty shekels, of fragrant cinnamon; two hundred and fifty shekels of fragrant cane; [24]five hundred shekels of cassia—all according to the standard of the sanctuary shekel; together with a hin of olive oil; [25]and blend them into sacred anointing oil,[i] perfumed ointment expertly prepared.[j] With this sacred anointing oil [26]you shall anoint the tent of meeting and the ark of the covenant, [27]the table and all its utensils, the menorah and its utensils, the altar of incense [28]and the altar for burnt offerings with all its utensils, and the basin with its stand. [29]When you have consecrated them, they shall be most sacred; whatever touches them shall be sacred. [30]Aaron and his sons you shall also anoint and consecrate as my priests.[k] [31]Tell the Israelites: As sacred anointing oil this shall belong to me throughout your generations. [32]It may not be used in any ordinary anointing of the body, nor may you make any other oil of a like mixture. It is sacred, and shall be treated as sacred by you. [33]Whoever prepares a perfume like this, or whoever puts any of this on an unauthorized person, shall be cut off from his people.

**The Incense.** [34]The LORD told Moses: Take these aromatic substances: storax and onycha and galbanum, these and pure frankincense in equal parts; [35]and blend them into incense. This fragrant powder, expertly prepared, is to be salted and so kept pure and sacred. [36]Grind some of it into fine dust and put this before the covenant in the tent of meeting where I will meet you. This incense shall be treated as most sacred by you. [37]You may not make incense of a like mixture for yourselves; you must treat it as sacred to the LORD. [38]Whoever makes an incense like this for his own enjoyment of its fragrance, shall be cut off from his people.

### CHAPTER 31

**Choice of Artisans.** [1][m]The LORD said to Moses: [2]See, I have singled out* Bezalel, son of Uri, son of Hur, of the tribe of Judah, [3]and I have filled him with a divine spirit of skill and understanding and knowledge in every craft: [4]in the production of embroidery, in making things of gold, silver, or bronze, [5]in cutting and mounting precious stones, in carving wood, and in every other craft. [6]As his assistant I myself have appointed Oholiab, son of Ahisamach, of the tribe of Dan. I have also endowed all the experts with the necessary skill to make all the things I have commanded you: [7][n]the tent of meeting, the ark of the covenant with its cover, all the

furnishings of the tent, [8]the table with its utensils, the pure gold menorah with all its utensils, the altar of incense, [9]the altar for burnt offerings with all its utensils, the basin with its stand, [10]the service cloths,[†] the sacred vestments for Aaron the priest, the vestments for his sons in their ministry, [11]the anointing oil, and the fragrant incense for the sanctuary. According to all I have commanded you, so shall they do.

**Sabbath Laws.** [12][o]The LORD said to Moses: [13]You must also tell the Israelites: Keep my sabbaths, for that is to be the sign between you and me throughout the generations, to show that it is I, the LORD, who make you holy. [14][‡]Therefore, you must keep the sabbath for it is holiness for you. Whoever desecrates it shall be put to death. If anyone does work on that day, that person must be cut off from the people. [15]Six days there are for doing work, but the seventh day is the sabbath of complete rest, holy to the LORD. Anyone who does work on the sabbath day shall be put to death. [16]So shall the Israelites observe the sabbath, keeping it throughout their generations as an everlasting covenant. [17]Between me and the Israelites it is to be an everlasting sign; for in six days the LORD made the heavens and the earth, but on the seventh day he rested at his ease.

[18]When the LORD had finished speaking to Moses on Mount Sinai, he gave him the two tablets of the covenant, the stone tablets inscribed by God's own finger.[p]

## VII. ISRAEL'S APOSTASY AND GOD'S RENEWAL OF THE COVENANT

### CHAPTER 32

**The Golden Calf.** [1]When the people saw that Moses was delayed in coming down from the mountain, they gathered around Aaron and said to him, "Come, make us a god who will go before us; as for that man Moses who brought us out of the land of Egypt, we do not know what has happened to him."[q] [2]Aaron replied, "Take off the golden earrings that your wives, your sons, and your daughters are wearing, and bring them to me." [3]So all the people took off their earrings and brought them to Aaron. [4]He received their offering, and fashioning it with a tool, made a molten calf. Then they cried out, "These are your gods, Israel, who brought you[§] up from the land

---

*[31:2] **Singled out:** lit., "called by name"; cf. 35:30.

†[31:10] **The service cloths:** so the Greek. They were perhaps the colored cloths mentioned in Nm 4:4–15.

‡[31:14–15] For the distinction between work proscribed on certain festivals and weekly Sabbaths, see note on Lv 23:3.

§[32:4–5] **Who brought you . . . a feast of the LORD:** it seems that the golden calf was intended as an image, not of another god, but of the Lord, whose strength was symbolized by the strength of a young bull. The Israelites, however, had been forbidden to represent the Lord under any visible form.

---

i. [30:25] Ex 37:29.   j. [30:25–29] Ex 40:9–11; Lv 8:10; Nm 7:1.
k. [30:30] Ex 29:7; Lv 8:12.   l. [30:34–38] Ex 25:6; 37:29.
m. [31:1–6] Ex 35:30–35.   n. [31:7–11] Ex 35:10–19.

o. [31:12–17] Ex 20:8–11; 35:1–3.   p. [31:18] Ex 24:12; 32:15–16; Dt 5:22.   q. [32:1] Ex 32:23; Acts 7:40.

of Egypt."[r] [5]On seeing this, Aaron built an altar in front of the calf and proclaimed, "Tomorrow is a feast of the LORD." [6]Early the next day the people sacrificed burnt offerings and brought communion sacrifices. Then they sat down to eat and drink, and rose up to revel.[s]

[7r]Then the LORD said to Moses: Go down at once because your people, whom you brought out of the land of Egypt, have acted corruptly. [8]They have quickly turned aside from the way I commanded them, making for themselves a molten calf and bowing down to it, sacrificing to it and crying out, "These are your gods, Israel, who brought you up from the land of Egypt!" [9u]I have seen this people, how stiff-necked they are, continued the LORD to Moses. [10]Let me alone, then, that my anger may burn against them to consume them. Then I will make of you a great nation.

[11*]But Moses implored the LORD, his God, saying,[v] "Why, O LORD, should your anger burn against your people, whom you brought out of the land of Egypt with great power and with a strong hand? [12]Why should the Egyptians say, 'With evil intent he brought them out, that he might kill them in the mountains and wipe them off the face of the earth'? Turn from your burning wrath; change your mind about punishing your people. [13]Remember your servants Abraham, Isaac, and Israel, and how you swore to them by your own self, saying,[w] 'I will make your descendants as numerous as the stars in the sky; and all this land that I promised, I will give your descendants as their perpetual heritage.'" [14]So the LORD changed his mind about the punishment he had threatened to inflict on his people.

[15]Moses then turned and came down the mountain with the two tablets of the covenant in his hands,[x] tablets that were written on both sides, front and back. [16]The tablets were made by God; the writing was the writing of God, engraved on the tablets.[y] [17]Now, when Joshua heard the noise of the people shouting, he said to Moses, "That sounds like a battle in the camp." [18]But Moses answered,

"It is not the noise of victory,
    it is not the noise of defeat;
    the sound I hear is singing."

[19]As he drew near the camp, he saw the calf and the dancing. Then Moses' anger burned, and he threw the tablets down and broke them on the base of the mountain.[z] [20]Taking the calf they had made, he burned it in the fire and then ground it down to powder, which he scattered on the water[†] and made the Israelites drink.[a]

[21‡]Moses asked Aaron, "What did this people do to you that you should lead them into a grave sin?" [22]Aaron replied, "Do not let my lord be angry. You know how the people are prone to evil. [23]They said to me, 'Make us a god to go before us; as for this man Moses who brought us out of the land of Egypt, we do not know what has happened to him.' [24]So I told them, 'Whoever is wearing gold, take it off.' They gave it to me, and I threw it into the fire, and this calf came out."

[25]Moses saw that the people were running wild because Aaron had lost control—to the secret delight of their foes. [26]Moses stood at the gate of the camp and shouted, "Whoever is for the LORD, come to me!" All the Levites[b] then rallied to him, [27]and he told them, "Thus says the LORD, the God of Israel: Each of you put your sword on your hip! Go back and forth through the camp, from gate to gate, and kill your brothers, your friends, your neighbors!" [28]The Levites did as Moses had commanded, and that day about three thousand of the people fell. [29]Then Moses said, "Today you are installed as priests[§] for the LORD, for you went against your own sons and brothers, to bring a blessing upon yourselves this day."

**The Atonement.** [30]On the next day Moses said to the people,[c] "You have committed a grave sin. Now I will go up to the LORD; perhaps I may be able to make atonement for your sin." [31]So Moses returned to the LORD and said, "Ah, this people has committed a grave sin in making a god of gold for themselves! [32]Now if you would only forgive their sin! But if you will not, then blot me out of the book that you have written."[¶] [33]The LORD answered Moses: Only the one who has sinned against me will I blot out of my book. [34]Now, go and lead the people where I have told you. See, my angel will go before you. When it is time for me to punish, I will punish them for their sin.

---

Cf. 20:4. In the tenth century Jeroboam made golden calves for the shrines at Bethel and Dan, presumably to function as thrones for the Lord as the ark did in Jerusalem (see 1 Kgs 12:27–30).

*[32:11–13] Moses uses three arguments to persuade the Lord to remain faithful to the Sinai covenant even though the people have broken it: (1) they are God's own people, redeemed with God's great power; (2) God's reputation will suffer if they are destroyed; (3) the covenant with Abraham still stands. The Lord's change of mind is a testimony to Israel's belief in the power of intercessory prayer.

r. [32:4] Ex 32:8; 1 Kgs 12:28.   s. [32:6] 1 Cor 10:7.   t. [32:7–8] Dt 9:12, 16.   u. [32:9–10] Dt 9:13.   v. [32:11–12] Nm 14:13–19; Dt 9:28–29; Ps 106:23.   w. [32:13] Gn 22:16–17.   x. [32:15] Dt 9:15.   y. [32:16] Ex 31:18.

---

†[32:20] **The water:** according to Dt 9:21, this was the stream that flowed down Mount Sinai.

‡[32:21–24] Aaron attempts to persuade Moses not to act in anger, just as Moses persuaded the Lord. He also shifts the blame from himself to the people.

§[32:29] **Installed as priests:** lit., "fill your hands," a term for the ordination of priests (see 28:41; 29:9, 29, 33, 35; Nm 3:3). Because of their zeal for the true worship of the Lord, the Levites were chosen to be special ministers of the ritual service.

¶[32:32] **The book that you have written:** a symbolic reference to the list of God's faithful people.

z. [32:19] Dt 9:16–17.   a. [32:20] Dt 9:21.   b. [32:26–29] Dt 33:8–9.   c. [32:30–34] Dt 9:18–19.

³⁵Thus the Lᴏʀᴅ struck the people for making the calf, the one that Aaron made.

## CHAPTER 33

¹The Lᴏʀᴅ spoke to Moses: Go! You and the people whom you have brought up from the land of Egypt are to go up from here to the land about which I swore to Abraham, Isaac, and Jacob: I will give it to your descendants.ᵈ ²Driving out the Canaanites, Amorites, Hittites, Perizzites, Hivites and Jebusites, I will send an angel before youᵉ ³to a land flowing with milk and honey. But I myself will not go up in your company, because you are a stiff-necked people; otherwise I might consume you on the way. ⁴When the people heard this painful news, they mourned, and no one wore any ornaments.

⁵The Lᴏʀᴅ spoke to Moses: Speak to the Israelites: You are a stiff-necked people. Were I to go up in your company even for a moment, I would destroy you. Now off with your ornaments! Let me think what to do with you. ⁶So, from Mount Horeb onward, the Israelites stripped off their ornaments.

**Moses' Intimacy with God.** ⁷Moses used to pitch a tentᶠ outside the camp at some distance. It was called the tent of meeting. Anyone who wished to consult the Lᴏʀᴅ would go to the tent of meeting outside the camp. ⁸Whenever Moses went out to the tent, the people would all rise and stand at the entrance of their own tents, watching Moses until he entered the tent. ⁹As Moses entered the tent, the column of cloud would come down and stand at its entrance while the Lᴏʀᴅ spoke with Moses. ¹⁰On seeing the column of cloud stand at the entrance of the tent, all the people would rise and bow down at the entrance of their own tents. ¹¹The Lᴏʀᴅ used to speak to Moses face to face,ᵍ as a person speaks to a friend. Moses would then return to the camp, but his young assistant, Joshua, son of Nun, never left the tent. ¹²Moses said to the Lᴏʀᴅ, "See, you are telling me: Lead this people.ʰ But you have not let me know whom you will send with me. Yet you have said: You are my intimate friend;* You have found favor with me. ¹³Now, if I have found favor with you, please let me know your ways so that, in knowing you, I may continue to find favor with you. See, this nation is indeed your own people. ¹⁴The Lᴏʀᴅ answered: I myself† will go along, to give you rest. ¹⁵Moses replied, "If you are not going yourself, do not make us go up from here. ¹⁶For how can it be known that I and your people have

found favor with you, except by your going with us? Then we, your people and I, will be singled out from every other people on the surface of the earth." ¹⁷The Lᴏʀᴅ said to Moses: This request, too, which you have made, I will carry out, because you have found favor with me and you are my intimate friend.

¹⁸Then Moses said, "Please let me see your glory!" ¹⁹The Lᴏʀᴅ answered: I will make all my goodness pass before you, and I will proclaim my name, "Lᴏʀᴅ," before you; I who show favor to whom I will, I who grant mercy to whom I will.ⁱ ²⁰But you cannot see my face,ʲ for no one can see me and live.‡ ²¹Here, continued the Lᴏʀᴅ, is a place near me where you shall station yourself on the rock. ²²When my glory passes I will set you in the cleft of the rock and will cover you with my hand until I have passed by. ²³Then I will remove my hand, so that you may see my back; but my face may not be seen.

## CHAPTER 34

**Renewal of the Tablets.** ¹The Lᴏʀᴅ said to Moses: "Cut two stone tablets like the former,ᵏ that I may write on them the words§ which were on the former tablets that you broke. ²Get ready for tomorrow morning, when you are to go up Mount Sinai and there present yourself to me on the top of the mountain. ³No one shall come up with you, and let no one even be seen on any part of the mountain;ˡ even the sheep and the cattle are not to graze in front of this mountain." ⁴Moses then cut two stone tablets like the former, and early the next morning he went up Mount Sinai as the Lᴏʀᴅ had commanded him, taking in his hand the two stone tablets.

⁵The Lᴏʀᴅ came down in a cloud and stood with him there and proclaimed the name, "Lᴏʀᴅ." ⁶So the Lᴏʀᴅ passed before him and proclaimed: The Lᴏʀᴅ, the Lᴏʀᴅ, a God gracious and merciful, slow to anger and abounding in love and fidelity,¶ ⁷continuing his love for a thousand generations, and forgiving wickedness, rebellion, and sin; yet not declaring the guilty guiltless, but bringing punishment for their parents' wickedness on children and children's children to the third and fourth generation!ᵐ ⁸Moses at once knelt and bowed down to the ground. ⁹Then he said, "If I find

\*[33:12] **Intimate friend**: lit., "know by name." The root word meaning "know" or "make known" appears four times in vv. 12–13.

†[33:14] **I myself**: lit., "my face," that is, "my presence." The making of the calf (32:1–4) is an attempt to control the Lᴏʀᴅ's presence. In response the Lᴏʀᴅ refuses to accompany the people (33:3) until Moses persuades him.

‡[33:20] **No one can see me and live**: reflecting the tradition that to see God meant instant death. This is contradicted by the statements that Hagar (Gn 16:13), Jacob (Gn 32:31), and Manoah and his wife (Jgs 13:22) all "see God" and yet live (see also Ex 24:10–11).

§[34:1] **Words**: a common term for commandments, especially the Decalogue (see v. 28). In v. 27 "words" connotes the commands given in vv. 11–26.

¶[34:6] **Gracious . . . fidelity**: this succinct poetic description of God is an often-repeated statement of belief (see Nm 14:18; Ps 103:8; 145:8; Jl 2:13; Jon 4:2). All the terms describe God's relationship to the covenant people.

d. [33:1] Gn 12:7.  e. [33:2] Ex 23:23.  f. [33:7] Ex 29:42–43.  g. [33:11] Nm 12:8; Dt 34:10; Sir 45:4–5.  h. [33:12] Ex 32:34.

i. [33:19] Rom 9:15.  j. [33:20] Jn 1:18; 1 Tm 6:16.  k. [34:1] Dt 10:1–2.  l. [34:3] Ex 19:12–13, 21.  m. [34:6–7] Ex 20:5–6; Nm 14:18; Dt 5:9–10; Jer 32:18.

favor with you, Lord, please, Lord, come along in our company. This is indeed a stiff-necked people; yet pardon our wickedness and sins, and claim us as your own."

**Religious Laws.** ¹⁰The LORD said: Here is the covenant I will make. Before all your people I will perform marvels never before done* in any nation anywhere on earth, so that all the people among whom you live may see the work of the LORD. Awe-inspiring are the deeds I will perform with you! ¹¹As for you, observe what I am commanding you today.ⁿ

See, I am about to drive out before you the Amorites, Canaanites, Hittites, Perizzites, Hivites and Jebusites. ¹²₀"Take care not to make a covenant with the inhabitants of the land that you are to enter; lest they become a snare among you. ¹³Tear down their altars; smash their sacred stones, and cut down their asherahs.† ¹⁴You shall not bow down to any other god, for the LORD— "Jealous"‡ his name—is a jealous God. ¹⁵Do not make a covenant with the inhabitants of the land; else, when they prostitute themselves with their gods and sacrifice to them, one of them may invite you and you may partake of the sacrifice. ¹⁶And when you take their daughters as wives for your sons, and their daughters prostitute themselves with their gods, they will make your sons do the same.

¹⁷You shall not make for yourselves molten gods.ᵖ

¹⁸You shall keep the festival of Unleavened Bread.�q For seven days at the appointed time in the month of Abib you are to eat unleavened bread, as I commanded you; for in the month of Abib you came out of Egypt.

¹⁹To me belongs every male that opens the womb among all your livestock, whether in the herd or in the flock.ʳ ²⁰The firstling of a donkey you shall redeem with a lamb; if you do not redeem it, you must break its neck. The firstborn among your sons you shall redeem.

No one shall appear before me empty-handed. ²¹Six days you may labor,ˢ but on the seventh day you shall rest; even during the seasons of plowing and harvesting you must rest.

²²"You shall keep the feast of Weeks with the first fruits of the wheat harvest, likewise, the feast of the Ingathering at the close of the year.ˢ

²³Three times a year all your men shall appear before the Lord, the LORD God of Israel. ²⁴Since I will drive out the nations before you and enlarge your territory, no one will covet your land when you go up three times a year to appear before the LORD, your God.

²⁵You shall not offer me the blood of sacrifice with anything leavened, nor shall the sacrifice of the Passover feast be kept overnight for the next day.

²⁶The choicest first fruits of your soil you shall bring to the house of the LORD, your God.

You shall not boil a young goat in its mother's milk.ᵘ

**Radiance of Moses' Face.** ²⁷Then the LORD said to Moses: Write down these words, for in accordance with these words I have made a covenant with you and with Israel. ²⁸So Moses was there with the LORD for forty days and forty nights,ᵛ without eating any food or drinking any water, and he wrote on the tablets the words of the covenant, the ten words.

²⁹As Moses came down from Mount Sinai with the two tablets of the covenant in his hands, he did not know that the skin of his face had become radiant¶ while he spoke with the LORD. ³⁰When Aaron, then, and the other Israelites saw Moses and noticed how radiant the skin of his face had become, they were afraid to come near him. ³¹Only after Moses called to them did Aaron and all the leaders of the community come back to him. Moses then spoke to them. ³²Later, all the Israelites came up to him, and he enjoined on them all that the LORD had told him on Mount Sinai. ³³When Moses finished speaking with them, he put a veil over his face. ³⁴Whenever Moses entered the presence of the LORD to speak with him, he removed the veil until he came out again.ʷ On coming out, he would tell the Israelites all that he had been commanded. ³⁵Then the Israelites would see that the skin of Moses' face was radiant; so he would again put the veil over his face until he went in to speak with the LORD.

## VIII. THE BUILDING OF THE TABERNACLE AND THE DESCENT OF GOD'S GLORY UPON IT

### CHAPTER 35

**Sabbath Regulations.** ¹Moses assembled the whole Israelite community and said to them,ˣ

---

*[34:10] **Never before done**: lit., "created." The verb used here (Heb. *bara'*) is predicated only of God (see Gn 1:1, 21, 27; Ps 51:12). These wonders are a new creation and can be performed only by God.

†[34:13] Asherah was the name of a Canaanite goddess. In her honor wooden poles (*asherot*) were erected, just as stone pillars (*massebot*) were erected in honor of the god Baal. Both were placed near the altar in a Canaanite shrine.

‡[34:14] **Jealous**: see note on 20:5. Some, by a slight emendation, render, "The Lord is jealous for his name." Cf. Ez 39:25.

§[34:22] **Feast of Weeks**: the festival of thanksgiving for the harvest, celebrated seven weeks or fifty days after the

beginning of the harvest. It was also called Pentecost (fiftieth) and coincided with the giving of the law on Mount Sinai, fifty days after the offering of the first fruits; cf. Lv 23:10–11; Dt 16:9. **Feast of the Ingathering**: feast of Booths.

¶[34:29] **Radiant**: the Hebrew word translated "radiant" is spelled like the term for "horns." Thus the artistic tradition of portraying Moses with horns.

---

n. [34:11] Ex 13:5; 33:2.    o. [34:12–16] Ex 23:32–33; Dt 7:1–5; 12:2–3.
p. [34:17] Lv 19:4; Dt 5:8–9.    q. [34:18] Ex 12:15–20; 13:3–4.
r. [34:19–20] Ex 13:2, 12–13; 23:15.    s. [34:21] Ex 20:9–10.
t. [34:22–23] Ex 23:16–17; Dt 16:10, 13, 16.

u. [34:25–26] Ex 23:18–19.    v. [34:28] Ex 24:18; Dt 9:9, 18; 10:2, 4.
w. [34:33–34] 2 Cor 3:13, 16.    x. [35:1–3] Ex 31:13–17.

¹"These are the words the LORD has commanded to be observed. ²On six days work may be done, but the seventh day shall be holy to you as the sabbath of complete rest to the LORD. Anyone who does work on that day shall be put to death. ³You shall not even light a fire in any of your dwellings on the sabbath day."

**Collection of Materials.** ⁴Moses said to the whole Israelite community, "This is what the LORD has commanded: ⁵ʸReceive from among you contributions for the LORD. Everyone, as his heart prompts him, shall bring, as a contribution to the LORD, gold, silver, and bronze; ⁶violet, purple, and scarlet yarn; fine linen and goat hair; ⁷rams' skins dyed red, and tahash skins; acacia wood; ⁸oil for the light; spices for the anointing oil and for the fragrant incense; ⁹onyx stones and other gems for mounting on the ephod and on the breastpiece.

**Call for Artisans.** ¹⁰ᶻ"Let every artisan among you come and make all that the LORD has commanded: ¹¹the tabernacle, with its tent, its covering, its clasps, its frames, its bars, its columns, and its pedestals; ¹²the ark, with its poles, the cover, and the curtain veil; ¹³the table, with its poles and all its utensils, and the showbread; ¹⁴the menorah, with its utensils, the lamps, and the oil for the light; ¹⁵the altar of incense, with its poles; the anointing oil, and the fragrant incense; the entrance curtain for the entrance of the tabernacle; ¹⁶the altar for burnt offerings, with its bronze grating, its poles, and all its utensils; the basin, with its stand; ¹⁷the hangings of the court, with their columns and pedestals; the curtain for the gate of the court; ¹⁸the tent pegs for the tabernacle and for the court, with their ropes; ¹⁹the service cloths for use in the sanctuary; the sacred vestments for Aaron, the priest, and the vestments for his sons in their ministry."

**The Contribution.** ²⁰When the whole Israelite community left Moses' presence, ²¹all, as their hearts moved them and their spirit prompted, brought a contribution to the LORD for the work of the tent of meeting, for all its services, and for the sacred vestments. ²²Both the men and the women, all as their heart prompted them, brought brooches, earrings, rings, necklaces, and various other gold articles.ᵃ Everyone who could presented an offering of gold to the LORD. ²³Everyone who happened to have violet, purple, or scarlet yarn, fine linen or goat hair, rams' skins dyed red or tahash skins, brought them. ²⁴Whoever could make a contribution of silver or bronze offered it to the LORD; and everyone who happened to have acacia wood for any part of the work, brought it. ²⁵All the women who were expert spinners brought hand-spun violet, purple, and scarlet yarn and fine linen thread. ²⁶All the women, as their hearts and skills moved them, spun goat hair. ²⁷The tribal

leaders brought onyx stones and other gems for mounting on the ephod and on the breastpiece; ²⁸as well as spices, and oil for the light, anointing oil, and fragrant incense. ²⁹Every Israelite man and woman brought to the LORD such voluntary offerings as they thought best, for the various kinds of work which the LORD, through Moses, had commanded to be done.

**The Artisans.** ³⁰Moses said to the Israelites:ᵇ "See, the LORD has singled out Bezalel, son of Uri, son of Hur, of the tribe of Judah, ³¹and has filled him with a divine spirit of skill and understanding and knowledge in every craft: ³²in the production of embroidery, in making things of gold, silver, or bronze, ³³in cutting and mounting precious stones, in carving wood, and in every other craft. ³⁴He has also given both him and Oholiab, son of Ahisamach, of the tribe of Dan, the ability to teach others. ³⁵He has endowed them with skill to execute all types of work: engraving, embroidering, the making of variegated cloth of violet, purple, and scarlet yarn and fine linen thread, weaving, and all other arts and crafts.

### CHAPTER 36

¹"Bezalel, therefore, will set to work with Oholiab and with all the artisans whom the LORD has endowed with skill and understanding in knowing how to do all the work for the service of the sanctuary, just as the LORD has commanded."ᶜ

²Moses then called Bezalel and Oholiab and all the other artisans whom the LORD had endowed with skill, men whose hearts moved them to come and do the work. ³They received from Moses all the contributions which the Israelites had brought for the work to be done for the sanctuary service. Still, morning after morning the people continued to bring their voluntary offerings to Moses. ⁴Thereupon all the artisans who were doing the work for the sanctuary came from the work each was doing, ⁵and told Moses, "The people are bringing much more than is needed to carry out the work which the LORD has commanded us to do." ⁶Moses, therefore, ordered a proclamation to be made throughout the camp: "Let neither man nor woman make any more contributions for the sanctuary." So the people stopped bringing their offerings; ⁷there was already enough at hand, and more than enough, to complete the work to be done.

**The Tent Cloth and Coverings.** ⁸ᵈThe various artisans who were doing the work made the tabernacle with its ten sheets woven of fine linen twined, having cherubim embroidered on them with violet, purple, and scarlet yarn. ⁹The length of each sheet was twenty-eight cubits, and the width four cubits; all the sheets were the same size. ¹⁰Five of the sheets were joined together,

y. [35:5–9] Ex 25:2–7.   z. [35:10–19] Ex 31:6–11.   a. [35:22–28] Ex 25:3–7.

b. [35:30–35] Ex 31:1–6.   c. [36:1–2] Ex 31:1, 6.   d. [36:8–19] Ex 26:1–14.

edge to edge; and the other five sheets likewise, edge to edge. [11]Loops of violet yarn were made along the edge of the end sheet in the first set, and the same along the edge of the end sheet in the second set. [12]Fifty loops were thus put on one inner sheet, and fifty loops on the inner sheet in the other set, with the loops directly opposite each other. [13]Then fifty clasps of gold were made, with which the sheets were joined so that the tabernacle formed one whole.

[14]Sheets of goat hair were also woven as a tent over the tabernacle. Eleven such sheets were made. [15]The length of each sheet was thirty cubits and the width four cubits; all eleven sheets were the same size. [16]Five of these sheets were joined into one set, and the other six sheets into another set. [17]Fifty loops were made along the edge of the end sheet in one set, and fifty loops along the edge of the corresponding sheet in the other set. [18]Fifty bronze clasps were made with which the tent was joined so that it formed one whole. [19]A covering for the tent was made of rams' skins dyed red and, above that, a covering of tahash skins.

**The Framework.** [20]e Frames were made for the tabernacle, acacia-wood uprights. [21]The length of each frame was ten cubits, and the width one and a half cubits. [22]Each frame had two arms, fastening them one to another. In this way all the frames for the tabernacle were made. [23]The frames for the tabernacle were made as follows: twenty frames on the south side, [24]with forty silver pedestals under the twenty frames, two pedestals under each frame for its two arms; [25]twenty frames on the other side of the tabernacle, the north side, [26]with their forty silver pedestals, two pedestals under each frame. [27]At the rear of the tabernacle, to the west, six frames were made, [28]and two frames were made for the corners of the tabernacle, at its rear. [29]These were double at the bottom, and likewise double at the top, to the first ring. That is how both corner frames were made. [30]Thus, there were eight frames, with their sixteen silver pedestals, two pedestals under each frame. [31]Bars of acacia wood were also made, five for the frames on one side of the tabernacle, [32]five for those on the other side, and five for those at the rear, to the west. [33]The center bar, at the middle of the frames, was made to reach across from end to end. [34]The frames were plated with gold, and gold rings were made on them as holders for the bars, which were also plated with gold.

**The Veil.** [35]f The veil was made of violet, purple, and scarlet yarn, and of fine linen twined, with cherubim embroidered on it. [36]Four gold-plated columns of acacia wood, with gold hooks, were made for it, and four silver pedestals were cast for them.

[37]The curtain for the entrance of the tent was made of violet, purple, and scarlet yarn, and of fine linen twined, woven in a variegated manner. [38]Its five columns, with their hooks as well as their capitals and bands, were plated with gold; their five pedestals were of bronze.

## CHAPTER 37

**The Ark.** [1]Bezalel made the ark of acacia wood, two and a half cubits long, one and a half cubits wide, and one and a half cubits high. [2]The inside and outside were plated with gold, and a molding of gold was put around it. [3]Four gold rings were cast for its four supports, two rings on one side and two on the opposite side. [4]Poles of acacia wood were made and plated with gold; [5]these poles were put through the rings on the sides of the ark, for carrying it.

[6]The cover was made of pure gold, two and a half cubits long and one and a half cubits wide. [7]Two cherubim of beaten gold were made for the two ends of the cover; [8]one cherub was at one end, the other at the other end, made of one piece with the cover, at each end. [9]The cherubim had their wings spread out above, sheltering the cover. They faced each other, with their faces looking toward the cover.[g]

**The Table.** [10]h The table was made of acacia wood, two cubits long, a cubit wide, and a cubit and a half high. [11]It was plated with pure gold, and a molding of gold was put around it. [12]A frame a handbreadth high was also put around it, with a molding of gold around the frame. [13]Four rings of gold were cast for it and fastened at the four corners, one at each leg. [14]The rings were alongside the frame as holders for the poles to carry the table. [15]These poles for carrying the table were made of acacia wood and plated with gold. [16]The vessels that were set on the table, its plates and cups, as well as its pitchers and bowls for pouring libations, were made of pure gold.

**The Menorah.** [17]i The menorah was made of pure beaten gold—its shaft and branches—with its cups and knobs and petals springing directly from it. [18]Six branches extended from its sides, three branches on one side and three on the other. [19]On one branch there were three cups, shaped like almond blossoms, each with its knob and petals; on the opposite branch there were three cups, shaped like almond blossoms, each with its knob and petals; and so for the six branches that extended from the menorah. [20]On the menorah there were four cups, shaped like almond blossoms, with their knobs and petals. [21]The six branches that went out from the menorah had a knob under each pair. [22]The knobs and branches so sprang from it that the whole formed but a single piece of pure beaten gold. [23]Its seven lamps, as well as its trimming shears and trays, were made of pure gold. [24]A talent of pure gold was used for the menorah and its various utensils.

---

e. [36:20–34] Ex 26:15–29.    f. [36:35–38] Ex 26:31–37.

g. [37:1–9] Ex 25:10–22.    h. [37:10–16] Ex 25:23–30.    i. [37:17–24] Ex 25:31–39.

**The Altar of Incense.** [25j]The altar of incense was made of acacia wood, on a square, a cubit long, a cubit wide, and two cubits high, having horns that sprang directly from it. [26]Its grate on top, its walls on all four sides, and its horns were plated with pure gold; and a gold molding was put around it. [27]Underneath the molding gold rings were placed, two on one side and two on the opposite side, as holders for the poles used in carrying it. [28]The poles, too, were made of acacia wood and plated with gold.

[29]The sacred anointing oil and the fragrant incense were prepared in their pure form by a perfumer.[k]

## CHAPTER 38

**The Altar for Burnt Offerings.** [1]The altar for burnt offerings[l] was made of acacia wood, on a square, five cubits long and five cubits wide; its height was three cubits. [2]At the four corners horns were made that sprang directly from the altar. It was then plated with bronze. [3]All the utensils of the altar, the pots, shovels, basins, forks and fire pans, were likewise made of bronze. [4]A grating, a bronze network, was made for the altar and placed around it, on the ground, half as high as the altar itself. [5]Four rings were cast for the four corners of the bronze grating, as holders for the poles, [6]which were made of acacia wood and plated with bronze. [7]The poles were put through the rings on the sides of the altar for carrying it. The altar was made in the form of a hollow box.

[8]The bronze basin,[m] with its bronze stand, was made from the mirrors of the women who served* at the entrance of the tent of meeting.

**The Court of the Tabernacle.** [9n]The court was made as follows. On the south side the hangings of the court were of fine linen twined, a hundred cubits long, [10]with twenty columns and twenty pedestals of bronze, the hooks and bands of the columns being of silver. [11]On the north side there were similar hangings, a hundred cubits long, with twenty columns and twenty pedestals of bronze; the hooks and bands of the columns were of silver. [12]On the west side there were hangings, fifty cubits long, with ten columns and ten pedestals; the hooks and bands of the columns were of silver. [13]On the east side the court was fifty cubits. [14]On one side there were hangings to the extent of fifteen cubits, with three columns and three pedestals; [15]on the other side, beyond the gate of the court, there were likewise hangings to the extent of fifteen cubits, with three columns and three pedestals. [16]The hangings on all sides of the court were woven of fine linen twined. [17]The pedestals of the columns were of bronze, while the hooks and bands of the columns were of silver; the capitals were silver-plated, and all the columns of the court were banded with silver.

[18]At the gate of the court there was a variegated curtain, woven of violet, purple, and scarlet yarn and of fine linen twined, twenty cubits long and five cubits wide, in keeping with the hangings of the court. [19]There were four columns and four pedestals of bronze for it, while their hooks were of silver, and their capitals and their bands silver-plated. [20]All the tent pegs for the tabernacle and for the court around it were of bronze.

**Amount of Metal Used.** [21]The following is an account of the various amounts used on the tabernacle, the tabernacle of the covenant, drawn up at the command of Moses by the Levites under the direction of Ithamar, son of Aaron the priest. [22]However, it was Bezalel, son of Uri,[o] son of Hur, of the tribe of Judah, who made all that the LORD commanded Moses, [23]and he was assisted by Oholiab, son of Ahisamach, of the tribe of Dan, who was an engraver, an embroiderer, and a weaver of variegated cloth of violet, purple, and scarlet yarn and of fine linen.

[24]All the gold used in the entire construction of the sanctuary, having previously been given as an offering, amounted to twenty-nine talents and seven hundred and thirty shekels, according to the standard of the sanctuary shekel. [25]The silver of those of the community who were enrolled was one hundred talents and one thousand seven hundred and seventy-five shekels, according to the standard of the sanctuary shekel; [26]one bekah apiece, that is, a half-shekel, according to the standard of the sanctuary shekel, was received from everyone who was enrolled, of twenty years or more, namely, six hundred and three thousand five hundred and fifty men.[p] [27]One hundred talents of silver were used for casting the pedestals of the sanctuary and the pedestals of the veil, one talent for each pedestal, or one hundred talents for the one hundred pedestals. [28]The remaining one thousand seven hundred and seventy-five shekels were used for making the hooks on the columns, for plating the capitals, and for banding them with silver. [29]The bronze, given as an offering, amounted to seventy talents and two thousand four hundred shekels. [30]With this were made the pedestals at the entrance of the tent of meeting, the bronze altar with its bronze gratings, and all the utensils of the altar, [31]the pedestals around the court, the pedestals at the gate of the court, and all the tent pegs for the tabernacle and for the court around it.

## CHAPTER 39

**The Priestly Vestments.** [1]With violet, purple, and scarlet yarn were woven the service cloths for use in the sanctuary, as well as the sacred

---

*[38:8] The reflecting surface of ancient mirrors was usually of polished bronze. **The women who served:** cf. 1 Sm 2:22.

j. [37:25–28] Ex 30:1–5.   k. [37:29] Ex 30:23–25, 34–36.   l. [38:1–7] Ex 27:1–8; 2 Chr 1:5.   m. [38:8] Ex 30:18–21.   n. [38:9–20] Ex 27:9–19.

o. [38:22–23] Ex 31:2, 6; 35:30, 34; 36:1.   p. [38:26] Nm 1:46

vestments[q] for Aaron, as the LORD had commanded Moses.

[2r]The ephod was woven of gold thread and of violet, purple, and scarlet yarn and of fine linen twined. [3]Gold was first hammered into gold leaf and then cut up into threads, which were woven with the violet, purple, and scarlet yarn into an embroidered pattern on the fine linen. [4]Shoulder straps were made for it and joined to its two upper ends. [5]The embroidered belt on the ephod extended out from it, and like it, was made of gold thread, of violet, purple, and scarlet yarn, and of fine linen twined, as the LORD had commanded Moses. [6]The onyx stones were prepared and mounted in gold filigree work; they were engraved like seal engravings with the names of the sons of Israel. [7]These stones were set on the shoulder straps of the ephod as memorial stones of the sons of Israel, just as the LORD had commanded Moses.

[8s]The breastpiece was embroidered like the ephod, with gold thread and violet, purple, and scarlet yarn on cloth of fine linen twined. [9]It was square and folded double, a span high and a span wide in its folded form. [10]Four rows of precious stones were mounted on it: in the first row a carnelian, a topaz, and an emerald; [11]in the second row a garnet, a sapphire, and a beryl; [12]in the third row a jacinth, an agate, and an amethyst; [13]in the fourth row a chrysolite, an onyx, and a jasper. They were mounted in gold filigree work. [14]These stones were twelve, to match the names of the sons of Israel, and each stone was engraved like a seal with the name of one of the twelve tribes.

[15t]Chains of pure gold, twisted like cords, were made for the breastpiece, [16]together with two gold filigree rosettes and two gold rings. The two rings were fastened to the two upper ends of the breastpiece. [17]The two gold chains were then fastened to the two rings at the ends of the breastpiece. [18]The other two ends of the two chains were fastened in front to the two filigree rosettes, which were attached to the shoulder straps of the ephod. [19]Two other gold rings were made and put on the two lower ends of the breastpiece, on the edge facing the ephod. [20]Two more gold rings were made and fastened to the bottom of the two shoulder straps next to where they joined the ephod in front, just above its embroidered belt. [21]Violet ribbons bound the rings of the breastpiece to the rings of the ephod, so that the breastpiece stayed right above the embroidered belt of the ephod and did not swing loose from it. All this was just as the LORD had commanded Moses.

**Other Vestments.** [22]The robe of the ephod was woven entirely of violet yarn, [23]with an opening in its center like the opening of a shirt, with selvage around the opening to keep it from being

torn. [24]At the hem of the robe pomegranates were made of violet, purple, and scarlet yarn and of fine linen twined; [25]bells of pure gold were also made and put between the pomegranates all around the hem of the robe: [26]a bell, a pomegranate, a bell, a pomegranate, all around the hem of the robe which was to be worn in performing the ministry—all this, just as the LORD had commanded Moses.

[27]For Aaron and his sons there were also woven tunics of fine linen;[u] [28]the turban of fine linen; the ornate skullcaps of fine linen; linen pants of fine linen twined; [29]and sashes of variegated work made of fine linen twined and of violet, purple, and scarlet yarn, as the LORD had commanded Moses. [30v]The plate of the sacred diadem was made of pure gold and inscribed, as on a seal engraving: "Sacred to the LORD." [31]It was tied over the turban with a violet ribbon, as the LORD had commanded Moses.

**Presentation of the Work to Moses.** [32]Thus the entire work of the tabernacle of the tent of meeting was completed. The Israelites did the work just as the LORD had commanded Moses; so it was done. [33]They then brought to Moses the tabernacle, the tent with all its furnishings, the clasps, the frames, the bars, the columns, the pedestals, [34]the covering of rams' skins dyed red, the covering of tahash skins, the curtain veil; [35]the ark of the covenant with its poles, the cover, [36]the table with all its utensils and the showbread, [37]the pure gold menorah with its lamps set up on it and with all its utensils, the oil for the light, [38]the golden altar, the anointing oil, the fragrant incense; the curtain for the entrance of the tent, [39]the altar of bronze with its bronze grating, its poles and all its utensils, the basin with its stand, [40]the hangings of the court with their columns and pedestals, the curtain for the gate of the court with its ropes and tent pegs, all the equipment for the service of the tabernacle of the tent of meeting; [41]the service cloths for use in the sanctuary, the sacred vestments for Aaron the priest, and the vestments to be worn by his sons in their ministry. [42]Just as the LORD had commanded Moses, so the Israelites had carried out all the work. [43]So when Moses saw that all the work was done just as the LORD had commanded, he blessed them.

# CHAPTER 40

**Setting Up the Tabernacle.** [1]Then the LORD said to Moses: [2w]On the first day of the first month* you shall set up the tabernacle of the tent of meeting.[x] [3]Put the ark of the covenant in it, and screen off the ark with the veil.[y] [4]Bring in the table and set it. Then bring in the menorah and

---

* **[40:2] On the first day of the first month:** almost a year after the departure of the Israelites from Egypt. Cf. v. 17.

q. [39:1] Ex 31:10.   r. [39:2–10] Ex 28:6–12.   s. [39:8–14] Ex 28:15–21.   t. [39:15–21] Ex 28:31–35.

u. [39:27–29] Ex 28:39–42.   v. [39:30–31] Ex 28:36–37.   w. [40:2–8] Ex 40:16–33.   x. [40:2] Ex 26:30.   y. [40:3–8] Ex 26:33–37.

set up the lamps on it. ⁵Put the golden altar of incense in front of the ark of the covenant, and hang the curtain at the entrance of the tabernacle. ⁶Put the altar for burnt offerings in front of the entrance of the tabernacle of the tent of meeting. ⁷Place the basin between the tent of meeting and the altar, and put water in it. ⁸Set up the court round about, and put the curtain at the gate of the court.

⁹ᶻTake the anointing oil and anoint the tabernacle and everything in it, consecrating it and all its furnishings, so that it will be sacred. ¹⁰Anoint the altar for burnt offerings and all its utensils, consecrating it, so that it will be most sacred. ¹¹Likewise, anoint the basin with its stand, and thus consecrate it.

¹²ᵃThen bring Aaron and his sons to the entrance of the tent of meeting, and there wash them with water. ¹³Clothe Aaron with the sacred vestments and anoint him, thus consecrating him as my priest. ¹⁴Bring forward his sons also, and clothe them with the tunics. ¹⁵As you have anointed their father, anoint them also as my priests. Thus, by being anointed, shall they receive a perpetual priesthood throughout all future generations.

¹⁶Moses did just as the Lord had commanded him. ¹⁷On the first day of the first month of the second year the tabernacle was set up. ¹⁸It was Moses who set up the tabernacle. He placed its pedestals, set up its frames, put in its bars, and set up its columns. ¹⁹He spread the tent over the tabernacle and put the covering on top of the tent, as the Lord had commanded him. ²⁰ᵇHe took the covenant and put it in the ark; he placed poles alongside the ark and set the cover upon it. ²¹He brought the ark into the tabernacle and hung the curtain veil, thus screening off the ark of the covenant, as the Lord had commanded him. ²²He put the table in the tent of meeting, on the north side of the tabernacle, outside the veil, ²³and arranged the bread on it before the Lord, as the Lord had commanded him.ᶜ ²⁴He placed the menorah in the tent of meeting, opposite the table, on the south side of the tabernacle, ²⁵and he set up the lamps before the Lord, as the Lord had commanded him. ²⁶He placed the golden altar in the tent of meeting, in front of the veil, ²⁷and on it he burned fragrant incense, as the Lord had commanded him. ²⁸He hung the curtain at the entrance of the tabernacle. ²⁹He put the altar for burnt offerings in front of the entrance of the tabernacle of the tent of meeting, and sacrificed burnt offerings and grain offerings on it, as the Lord had commanded him. ³⁰ᵈHe placed the basin between the tent of meeting and the altar, and put water in it for washing. ³¹Moses and Aaron and his sons used to wash their hands and feet there, ³²for they washed themselves whenever they went into the tent of meeting or approached the altar, as the Lord had commanded Moses. ³³Finally, he set up the court around the tabernacle and the altar and hung the curtain at the gate of the court.

Thus Moses finished all the work.

**God's Presence in the Tabernacle.** ³⁴ᵉThen the cloud covered the tent of meeting, and the glory of the Lord filled the tabernacle. ³⁵Moses could not enter the tent of meeting, because the cloud settled down upon it and the glory of the Lord filled the tabernacle. ³⁶Whenever the cloud rose from the tabernacle, the Israelites would set out on their journey. ³⁷But if the cloud did not lift, they would not go forward; only when it lifted did they go forward. ³⁸The cloud of the Lord was over the tabernacle by day, and fire in the cloud at night, in the sight of the whole house of Israel in all the stages of their journey.

z. [40:9–11] Ex 30:26–29.   a. [40:12–15] Ex 28:41; 29:4–9; Lv 8:1–13.   b. [40:20–29] Ex 25:16, 21; 26:33–37.

c. [40:23] Ex 25:30.   d. [40:30–32] Ex 30:18–21.   e. [40:34–38] Nm 9:15–22.

# THE BOOK OF
# LEVITICUS

∿

The name "Leviticus" was given to the third book of the Pentateuch by the ancient Greek translators because a good part of this book deals with concerns of the priests, who are of the tribe of Levi.

The book mainly treats cultic matters (i.e., sacrifices and offerings, purity and holiness, the
priesthood, the operation of the sanctuary, and feast days) but is also interested in various behav-
ioral, ethical, and economic issues (e.g., sexual practices, idolatrous worship, treatment of others, the
sale of land, slavery). The goal of the laws is not merely legislative. For the most part they cohere as
a system and attempt to inculcate a way of life in the book's hearers and readers. In addition to these
concerns, Leviticus, comprising as it does the center of the Pentateuch, carries forward the narrative
of Exodus (cf. chaps. 1, 8–9, 10, 16, 24).

The book is part of the Priestly tradition (P) of the Pentateuch, to which belong various narratives
and legal passages (e.g., Gn 1:1–2:4; 9:1–17; 17:1–27; Ex 12:1–20, 40–50; 25:1–31:18; 35:1–40:38;
Nm 1:1–10:28; 15:1–14; 17:1–19:22; 25:6–31:54). Within the Priestly material itself there are signs of
variant traditions and development.

The main divisions of Leviticus are:

   I. Ritual of Sacrifices (1:1–7:38)
      A. Instructions for the Israelites (1:1–5:26)
      B. Instructions for the Priests (6:1–7:38)
  II. Ceremony of Ordination (8:1–10:20)
 III. Laws Regarding Ritual Purity (11:1–16:34)
 IV. Holiness Laws (17:1–26:46)
  V. Redemption of Offerings (27:1–34)

## I. RITUAL OF SACRIFICES

*A. Instructions for the Israelites*

### CHAPTER 1

**Burnt Offerings.** ¹The LORD called Moses, and
spoke to him from the tent of meeting:*ᵃ* ²Speak
to the Israelites and tell them: When any one of
you* brings an offering of livestock to the LORD,
you shall bring your offering from the herd or
from the flock.*ᵇ*

³*†If a person's offering is a burnt offering*‡
from the herd, the offering must be a male
without blemish.*ᵈ* The individual shall bring it
to the entrance of the tent of meeting to find
favor with the LORD, ⁴and shall lay a hand§
on the head*ᵉ* of the burnt offering, so that it
may be acceptable*ᶠ* to make atonement*ᵍ* for
the one who offers it. ⁵The bull shall then be

---

*[1:2] **Any one of you:** women as well as men bring sacrifices
(see 12:6–8; 15:28–30) and are explicitly obligated in other ritual
matters (e.g., 13:29, 38; Nm 5:6; 6:2; Lk 2:24). Thus, though the
Hebrew formulates sacrificial and other law with male reference,
the translation reflects the inclusion of women in ritual requirements. **From the herd or from the flock:** the only animals
which could be used as sacrificial victims were domestic animals
either of the bovine class (bulls, cows and calves) or the ovine
class (sheep and lambs, goats and kids). Excluded, therefore,
were not only all wild animals, but also such "unclean" domestic
animals as the camel and the donkey (cf. 11:1–47; 27:26–27).

a. [1:1] Ex 40.  b. [1:2] Lv 1:3, 10; 3:1, 6, 12.

---

†[1:3–5] **Entrance of the tent of meeting . . . before the
LORD:** probably the forecourt from the entrance of the court
to the entrance of the tent (cf. Ex 27). Thus the altar in front of
the tent was entirely accessible to the laity.

‡[1:3] The burnt offering is used for regular daily (6:1–6)
offerings, public festivals (Nm 28–29), purification rituals (Lv
12:6–8; 14:19–20; 15:15, 30), and individuals' vows and voluntary offerings (22:18–20).

§[1:4] **Lay a hand:** the imposition of a single hand for the
sacrifices in chaps. 1–5 may be a means of designating the animal as belonging to the offerer. See note on 16:21. **Atonement:**
see note on 16:6.

c. [1:3] Lv 6:1–6; 22:18–19.  d. [1:3] Lv 22:17–25; Ex 12:5.  e. [1:4]
Lv 3:2, 8, 13; 4:4, 15, 24, 29, 33; 8:14, 18, 22; Nm 8:12; 2 Chr 29:23; cf.
Lv 16:21; 24:14; Nm 27:18, 23; Dt 34:9.  f. [1:4] Lv 19:5; 22:19–29;
Gn 4:3–5; Mal 1:8–14.  g. [1:4] Lv 9:7; 14:20; Jb 1:5; 42:8; cf. Gn
32:21; Ex 29:36–37; 30:15; Lv 16:16–20; 17:11; Ez 43:20, 26.

slaughtered* before the LORD, and Aaron's sons, the priests, shall offer its blood by splashing it on all the sides of the altar which is at the entrance of the tent of meeting.[h] [6]Then the burnt offering shall be flayed and cut into pieces. [7]After Aaron's sons, the priests, have put burning embers on the altar and laid wood on them, [8]they shall lay the pieces of meat, together with the head and the suet, on top of the wood and the embers on the altar; [9]but the inner organs and the shanks shall be washed with water. The priest shall then burn all of it on the altar as a burnt offering, a sweet-smelling oblation to the LORD.[i]

[10]If a person's burnt offering is from the flock, that is, a sheep or a goat, the offering must be a male without blemish. [11]It shall be slaughtered on the north side of the altar before the LORD, and Aaron's sons, the priests, shall splash its blood on all the sides of the altar. [12]When it has been cut into pieces, the priest shall lay these, together with the head and suet, on top of the wood and the embers on the altar; [13]but the inner organs and the shanks shall be washed with water. The priest shall then offer all of it, burning it on the altar. It is a burnt offering, a sweet-smelling oblation to the LORD.

[14]If a person offers a bird as a burnt offering to the LORD, the offering brought must be a turtledove or a pigeon.[j] [15]Having brought it to the altar, the priest shall wring its head off and burn it on the altar. The blood shall be drained out against the side of the altar.[k] [16]He shall remove its crissum† by means of its feathers and throw it on the ash heap at the east side of the altar. [17]Then, having torn the bird open by its wings without separating the halves, the priest shall burn it on the altar, on the wood and the embers. It is a burnt offering, a sweet-smelling oblation to the LORD.

## CHAPTER 2
**Grain Offerings.** [1‡]When anyone brings a grain offering to the LORD, the offering must consist of bran flour. The offerer shall pour oil on it and put frankincense[m] over it, [2]and bring it to

Aaron's sons, the priests. A priest shall take a handful of the bran flour and oil, together with all the frankincense, and shall burn it on the altar as a token of the offering,[§] a sweet-smelling oblation to the LORD.[n] [3]The rest of the grain offering belongs to Aaron and his sons,[o] a most holy[p] portion from the oblations to the LORD.

[4]When you offer a grain offering baked in an oven, it must be in the form of unleavened cakes made of bran flour mixed with oil, or of unleavened wafers spread with oil.[q] [5]If your offering is a grain offering that is fried on a griddle,[r] it must be of bran flour mixed with oil and unleavened. [6]Break it into pieces, and pour oil over it. It is a grain offering. [7]If your offering is a grain offering that is prepared in a pan, it must be made of bran flour, fried in oil. [8]A grain offering that is made in any of these ways you shall bring to the LORD. It shall be presented to the priest, who shall take it to the altar. [9]The priest shall then remove from the grain offering a token and burn it on the altar as a sweet-smelling oblation to the LORD. [10]The rest of the grain offering belongs to Aaron and his sons, a most holy portion from the oblations to the LORD.

[11§]Every grain offering that you present to the LORD shall be unleavened, for you shall not burn any leaven or honey as an oblation to the LORD.[s] [12]Such you may present to the LORD in the offering of the first produce that is processed,[t] but they are not to be placed on the altar for a pleasing odor. [13]You shall season all your grain offerings with salt. Do not let the salt of the covenant with your God** be lacking from your grain offering. On every offering you shall offer salt.[u]

[14]If you offer a grain offering of first ripe fruits to the LORD, you shall offer it in the form of fresh early grain, roasted by fire and crushed as a grain offering of your first ripe fruits. [15]You shall put oil on it and set frankincense on it. It is a grain offering. [16]The priest shall then burn some of the groats and oil, together with all the frankincense, as a token of the offering, an oblation to the LORD.

## CHAPTER 3
**Communion Sacrifices.** [1††]If a person's offering is a communion sacrifice, if it is brought from

---

*[1:5] **Shall then be slaughtered**: lit., "he shall slaughter the bull." Slaughtering is not something the offerer must do (as opposed to, for example, hand placement [v. 4] or the presentation of sacrificial portions as an elevated offering [7:29–34]). Thus the verb is construed impersonally here.

†[1:16] **Crissum**: the area around the anus of the bird, lying beneath the bird's tail.

‡[2:1] Grain offerings are used as independent offerings (those in this chapter and cf. 6:12–16; 8:26–27; 23:10–11), as substitutes for other offerings in a case of poverty (5:11–13), and as accompaniments to animal offerings (cf. Nm 15:1–12; 28:1–29:39; Lv 14:20; 23:12, 18, 37). Chapter 2 describes two basic types of grain offering: uncooked (vv. 1–3) and cooked (vv. 4–10). The flour (*sōlet*) used was made of wheat (Ex 29:2) and Jewish tradition and Semitic cognates indicate that it is a coarse rather than a fine flour.

§[2:2] **Token of the offering**: lit., "reminder." Instead of burning the whole grain offering, only this part is burned on the altar.

¶[2:11–12] No grain offering that is leavened can be offered on the altar. Those in 7:13 and 23:17 are leavened but not offered on the altar. The Hebrew word for "honey" may refer to fruit syrup as well as to bee honey.

**[2:13] The salt of the covenant with your God**: partaking of salt in common was an ancient symbol of friendship and alliance. Cf. Mark 9:49–50 and Col 4:6.

††[3:1] The exact meaning of Hebrew *shelamim*, "communion sacrifice," is not clear. It has also been rendered "gift,"

---

h. [1:5] Lv 1:11, 15; 3:2, 8, 13; cf. Lv 4:5–7, 25.   i. [1:9] Lv 2:2; 3:5; 4:31; 26:31; Gn 8:20–21; Nm 28:2; cf. Lv 3:11; 21:6, 21; 22:25.   j. [1:14] Lv 5:7; 12:8; 15:14–15; Lk 2:24.   k. [1:15] Lv 5:8–9.   l. [2:1] Lv 5:11–13; 6:7–14; 7:9–14; 24:5–9; Nm 15:1–21; cf. Gn 4:3–5.   m. [2:2] Cf. Ex 30:1–10; Lv 16:11–13; Prv 27:9.

n. [2:2] Lv 1:9.   o. [2:3] Lv 6:9; 7:9–10.   p. [2:3] Lv 6:10, 18, 22; 10:12, 17; 24:9.   q. [2:4] 1 Chr 23:29.   r. [2:5] Lv 6:14.   s. [2:11] Mt 16:12; Mk 8:15; Lk 12:1; 1 Cor 5:7; Gal 5:9.   t. [2:12] Nm 18:12–13, 27; 15:20–21.   u. [2:13] Nm 18:19; Ezr 6:9; 7:22; Ez 43:24.   v. [3:1] Lv 7:11–36.

the herd, be it a male or a female animal, it must be presented without blemish[w] before the LORD. [2]The one offering it shall lay a hand on the head[x] of the offering. It shall then be slaughtered at the entrance of the tent of meeting. Aaron's sons, the priests, shall splash its blood on all the sides of the altar. [3y]From the communion sacrifice the individual shall offer as an oblation to the LORD the fat[*] that covers the inner organs, and all the fat that adheres to them, [4]as well as the two kidneys, with the fat on them near the loins, and the lobe of the liver, which is removed with the kidneys. [5]Aaron's sons shall burn this on the altar with the burnt offering that is on the wood and the embers, as a sweet-smelling oblation to the LORD.[z]

[6]If the communion sacrifice one offers to the LORD is from the flock, be it a male or a female animal, it must be presented without blemish. [7]If one presents a lamb as an offering, that person shall bring it before the LORD, [8]and after laying a hand on the head of the offering, it shall then be slaughtered before the tent of meeting. Aaron's sons shall splash its blood on all the sides of the altar. [9]From the communion sacrifice the individual shall present as an oblation to the LORD its fat: the whole fatty tail, which is removed close to the spine, the fat that covers the inner organs, and all the fat that adheres to them, [10]as well as the two kidneys, with the fat on them near the loins, and the lobe of the liver, which is removed with the kidneys. [11]The priest shall burn this on the altar as food,[a] an oblation to the LORD.

[12]If a person's offering is a goat, the individual shall bring it before the LORD, [13]and after laying a hand on its head, it shall then be slaughtered before the tent of meeting. Aaron's sons shall splash its blood on all the sides of the altar. [14]From this the one sacrificing shall present an offering as an oblation to the LORD: the fat that covers the inner organs, and all the fat that adheres to them, [15]as well as the two kidneys, with the fat on them near the loins, and the lobe of the liver, which is removed with the kidneys. [16]The priest shall burn these on the altar as food, a sweet-smelling oblation.

All the fat belongs to the LORD. [17]This shall be a perpetual ordinance for your descendants wherever they may dwell. You shall not eat any fat or any blood.[†b]

## CHAPTER 4

**Purification Offerings.** [1]The LORD said to Moses: [2]‘Tell the Israelites: When a person inadvertently[‡] does wrong by violating any one of the LORD's prohibitions—
**For the Anointed Priest.** [3]If it is the anointed priest[§] who thus does wrong and thereby makes the people guilty, he shall offer to the LORD an unblemished bull of the herd as a purification offering for the wrong he committed. [4]Bringing the bull to the entrance of the tent of meeting, before the LORD, he shall lay his hand on its head[d] and slaughter it before the LORD. [5]‘The anointed priest shall then take some of the bull's blood and bring it into the tent of meeting, [6]where, dipping his finger in the blood, he shall sprinkle some of it seven times before the LORD, toward the veil of the sanctuary.[¶] [7]The priest shall also put some of the blood on the horns of the altar of fragrant incense which stands before the LORD in the tent of meeting. The rest of the bull's blood he shall pour out at the base of the altar for burnt offerings which is at the entrance of the tent of meeting. [8]He shall remove all the fat of the bull of the purification offering: the fat that covers the inner organs, and all the fat that adheres to them, [9]as well as the two kidneys, with the fat on them near the loins, and the lobe of the liver, which is removed with the kidneys, [10]just as the fat pieces are removed from the ox of the communion sacrifice.[f] The priest shall burn these on the altar for burnt offerings. [11]‘‘But the hide of the bull and its meat, with its head, shanks, inner organs and dung, [12]that is, the whole bull, shall be brought outside the camp to a clean place[††] where the ashes are deposited and there be burned in a wood fire. At the place of the ash heap, there it must be burned.[g]

---

by lay Israelites, who may not be entirely familiar with the prohibition (cf. 7:22–27; 19:26). The fat prohibited is only the visceral fat mentioned in 3:9–10, 14–15, not muscular fat.

‡[4:2] **Inadvertently**: the concern in this chapter, and much of chap. 5, is wrongs done unintentionally. Intentional ("high-handed") sins are punished with being "cut off" from the people (Nm 15:30–31). See note on Lv 7:20. **LORD's prohibitions**: not included in the faults figured here is failure to perform positive commandments. Failing to perform positive commands, however, still renders the individual liable to other punishment (e.g., failing to observe the Passover, Nm 9:13). Cf. Nm 15:22–31.

§[4:3] **The anointed priest**: the chapter presents four cases of inadvertent wrong, arranged in descending order according to the status of the wrongdoer: high priest (vv. 3–12), entire community (vv. 13–21), tribal leader (vv. 22–26), and general populace (vv. 27–35). The higher one's position, the more deeply the sin affects the sanctuary (vv. 5–7, 17–18 versus vv. 25, 29, 34). See note on 16:6. **Purification offering**: the Hebrew verb *ḥiṭṭē'* means "remove sin, purify" (Lv 8:15; Ez 43:20–23; 45:18–19; cf. Ex 29:36). The offering cleansed the various places to which the blood was applied or the rooms in which it was sprinkled.

¶[4:5–7] On the structure of the sanctuary, see Ex 26–27.
**[4:11–12] See note on 6:17–23.
††[4:12] **Clean place**: i.e., ritually "clean" or pure. It has nothing to do with the presence of dirt or waste. See 6:4.

---

"(re)payment," "peace," "well-being," or "covenant" offering. This offering may be brought for a vow or voluntary offering (cf. 22:21). A distinct version of the communion sacrifice is the thanksgiving offering (7:11–15 vis-à-vis vv. 16–18).

*[3:3–5] **Fat**: only part of the offering is devoted to God, as opposed to the burnt offering (chap. 1), which is wholly burnt (except for the skin). The meat is distributed among the offerer (and the offerer's party) and the priests (cf. 7:11–36).

†[3:17] **Any fat or any blood**: this prohibition is mentioned here because portions of this offering could be eaten

---

w. [3:1] Lv 22:21.　x. [3:2] Lv 1:4.　y. [3:3–5] Lv 3:9–10, 14–16; 4:8–9, 31, 35; 6:5; 7:3–4, 30–31; 8:16, 25; 16:25; 17:6; Ex 29:13, 22; cf. Ez 44:15.　z. [3:5] Lv 1:9.　a. [3:11] Lv 9:19.　b. [3:17] Lv 17:10.

c. [4:2] Lv 6:17–23; Nm 15:22–31.　d. [4:4] Lv 1:4.　e. [4:6–7] Lv 4:17–18; 16:16; cf. 4:25.　f. [4:10] Lv 3:3.　g. [4:12] Lv 6:23.

**For the Community.** ¹³If the whole community of Israel errs* inadvertently and without even being aware of it violates any of the LORD's prohibitions, and thus are guilty, ¹⁴when the wrong that was committed becomes known, the community shall offer a bull of the herd as a purification offering. They shall bring it before the tent of meeting. ¹⁵The elders of the community shall lay their hands on the bull's head before the LORD. When the bull has been slaughtered before the LORD, ¹⁶the anointed priest shall bring some of its blood into the tent of meeting, ¹⁷and dipping his finger in the blood, he shall sprinkle it seven times before the LORD, toward the veil. ¹⁸He shall also put some of the blood on the horns of the altar which is before the LORD in the tent of meeting. The rest of the blood he shall pour out at the base of the altar for burnt offerings which is at the entrance of the tent of meeting. ¹⁹He shall remove all of its fat and burn it on the altar, ²⁰doing with this bull just as he did with the other bull of the purification offering; he will do the same thing. Thus the priest shall make atonement*ʰ* on their behalf, that they may be forgiven. ²¹This bull shall also be brought outside the camp and burned,*ⁱ* just as the first bull. It is a purification offering for the assembly.

**For the Tribal Leader.** ²²Should a tribal leader*ʲ* do wrong inadvertently by violating any one of the prohibitions of the LORD his God, and thus be guilty, ²³when he learns of the wrong he committed, he shall bring as his offering an unblemished male goat. ²⁴He shall lay his hand on its head and it shall be slaughtered in the place where the burnt offering is slaughtered, before the LORD. It is a purification offering. ²⁵The priest shall then take some of the blood of the purification offering on his finger and put it on the horns*ᵏ* of the altar for burnt offerings. The rest of the blood he shall pour out at the base of the altar. ²⁶All of its fat he shall burn on the altar like the fat of the communion sacrifice. Thus the priest shall make atonement on the tribal leader's behalf for his wrong, that he may be forgiven.

**For the General Populace.** ²⁷If anyone of the general populace does wrong inadvertently by violating one of the LORD's prohibitions, and thus is guilty, ²⁸upon learning of the wrong committed, that person shall bring an unblemished she-goat as the offering for the wrong committed. ²⁹The wrongdoer shall lay a hand on the head of the purification offering, and the purification offering shall be slaughtered at the place

of the burnt offerings. ³⁰The priest shall then take some of its blood on his finger and put it on the horns of the altar for burnt offerings. The rest of the blood he shall pour out at the base of the altar. ³¹He shall remove all the fat, just as the fat is removed from the communion sacrifice. The priest shall burn it on the altar for a sweet odor to the LORD. Thus the priest shall make atonement, so that the individual may be forgiven.

³²If, however, a person brings a lamb as a purification offering, that person shall bring an unblemished female, and ³³lay a hand on its head. It shall be slaughtered as a purification offering in the place where the burnt offering is slaughtered. ³⁴The priest shall then take some of the blood of the purification offering on his finger and put it on the horns of the altar for burnt offerings. The rest of the blood he shall pour out at the base of the altar. ³⁵He shall remove all its fat just as the fat is removed from the lamb of the communion sacrifice. The priest shall burn these on the altar with the other oblations for the LORD. Thus the priest shall make atonement on the person's behalf for the wrong committed, that the individual may be forgiven.

## CHAPTER 5

**Special Cases for Purification Offerings.**† ¹If a person, either having seen or come to know something, does wrong by refusing as a witness under oath to give information,*ˡ* that individual shall bear the penalty; ²or if someone, without being aware of it, touches any unclean thing, such as the carcass of an unclean wild animal, or an unclean domestic animal, or an unclean swarming creature,‡ and thus is unclean and guilty;*ᵐ* ³or if someone, without being aware of it, touches some human uncleanness,*ⁿ* whatever kind of uncleanness this may be, and then subsequently becomes aware of guilt; ⁴or if someone, without being aware of it, rashly utters an oath with bad or good intent,*ᵒ* whatever kind of oath this may be, and then subsequently becomes aware of guilt in regard to any of these matters— ⁵when someone is guilty in regard to any of these matters, that person shall confess the wrong committed, ⁶and make reparation to

---

†[5:1–13] This differs from the prescriptions for purification offerings in chap. 4 by listing four specific wrongs for which a purification offering is brought and allowing the substitution of birds and grain offerings in the case of poverty.

‡[5:2] **Swarming creature**: a rather imprecise categorization that includes various small creatures in the seas, such as fish that go about in large groups or swarms (Gn 1:20; Lv 11:10); or, similarly, various winged insects that mass in the skies (Lv 11:20; Dt 14:19); and, finally, various small creatures that move in swarms on land, whether crawlers, quadrupeds, or of the multilegged variety (Lv 11:41–42). According to 11:29–30, even various rodents and lizards can be included in this category.

l. [5:1] Jgs 17:2–3; Prv 29:24.   m. [5:2] Lv 11:1–45; 15:31; 17:15–16.   n. [5:3] Lv 12:4; 13:35–36; 15:2–12, 19–27; Nm 19:14–22. o. [5:4] Nm 30:3; Jgs 11:30–36; 1 Sm 14:24–30; Mk 6:23–26; Acts 23:12.

---

*[4:13] **Whole community . . . errs**: this case probably complements that of vv. 3–12. There the high priest sins so that the people become guilty. Those verses deal with his requirements for atonement; vv. 13–21 deal with the people's requirements.

h. [4:20] Lv 1:4.   i. [4:21] Lv 6:23.   j. [4:22] Nm 10:4; 25:14. k. [4:25] Lv 4:30, 34; 8:15; 9:9; 16:18; Ex 29:12; Ez 43:20; cf. Lv 4:7.

the LORD for the wrong committed: a female animal from the flock, a ewe lamb or a she-goat, as a purification offering. Thus the priest shall make atonement on the individual's behalf for the wrong.

⁷If, however, the person cannot afford an animal of the flock,ᵖ that person shall bring to the LORD as reparation for the wrong committed two turtledoves or two pigeons, one for a purification offering and the other for a burnt offering. ⁸The guilty party shall bring them to the priest, who shall offer the one for the purification offering first.�q Wringing its head at the neck, yet without breaking it off, ⁹he shall sprinkle some of the blood of the purification offering against the side of the altar. The rest of the blood shall be drained out against the base of the altar. It is a purification offering. ¹⁰The other bird he shall offer as a burnt offering according to procedure. Thus the priest shall make atonement on the person's behalf for the wrong committed, so that the individual may be forgiven.

¹¹If the person is unable to afford even two turtledoves or two pigeons, that person shall bring as an offering for the wrong committed one tenth of an ephah* of bran flour for a purification offering. The guilty party shall not put oil or place frankincense on it, because it is a purification offering.ʳ ¹²The individual shall bring it to the priest, who shall take a handful as a token of the offering and burn it on the altar with the other oblations for the LORD. It is a purification offering. ¹³Thus the priest shall make atonement on the person's behalf for the wrong committed in any of the above cases, so that the individual may be forgiven. The rest of the offering, like the grain offering, shall belong to the priest.

**Reparation Offerings.**† ¹⁴The LORD said to Moses: ¹⁵ˢWhen a person commits sacrilege by inadvertently misusing any of the LORD's sacred objects,ᵗ the wrongdoer shall bring to the LORD as reparation an unblemished ram from the flock, at the established value‡ in silver shekels according to the sanctuary shekel, as a reparation offering. ¹⁶The wrongdoer shall also restore what has been misused of the sacred objects, adding a fifth of its value,ᵘ and give this to the priest. Thus the priest shall make atonement

for the person with the ram of the reparation offering, so that the individual may be forgiven.

¹⁷If someone does wrong and violates one of the LORD's prohibitions without realizing it, that person is guiltyᵛ and shall bear the penalty. ¹⁸The individual shall bring to the priest an unblemished ram of the flock, at the established value, for a reparation offering. The priest shall then make atonement on the offerer's behalf for the error inadvertently and unknowingly committed so that the individual may be forgiven. ¹⁹It is a reparation offering. The individual must make reparation to the LORD.

²⁰The LORD said to Moses: ²¹When someone does wrong and commits sacrilege against the LORD by deceivingʷ a neighbor about a deposit or a pledge or a stolen article, or by otherwise retaining a neighbor's goods unjustly;ˣ ²²or if, having found a lost article, the person lies about it, swearing falsely about any of the things that a person may do wrong— ²³when someone has thus done wrong and is guilty, that person shall restore the thing that was stolen, the item unjustly retained, the item left as deposit, or the lost article that was found ²⁴or whatever else the individual swore falsely about. That person shall make full restitution of the thing itself, and add one fifth of its value to it, giving it to its owner at the time of reparation. ²⁵Then that person shall bring to the priest as reparation to the LORD an unblemished ram of the flock, at the established value, as a reparation offering. ²⁶The priest shall make atonement on the person's behalf before the LORD, so that the individual may be forgiven for whatever was done to incur guilt.

*B. Instructions for the Priests*

## CHAPTER 6

**The Daily Burnt Offering.** ¹The LORD said to Moses: ²ˣGive Aaron and his sons the following command: This is the ritual¶ for the burnt offering—the burnt offering that is to remain on the hearth of the altar all night until the next morning, while the fire is kept burning on the altar. ³The priest, clothed in his linen robe and wearing linen pants underneath, shall take away the ashes to which the fire has reduced the burnt offering on the altar, and lay them at the side of the altar. ⁴Then, having taken off these garments and put on other garments, he shall carry the ashes to a clean place outside the camp. ⁵The fire on the altar is to be kept burning; it must not go

---

*[5:11] **Ephah:** see note on Is 5:10.

†[5:14–26] This last half of the chapter deals with a distinct sacrifice, the reparation offering (Heb. *'asham*). The Hebrew root for this term has a basic meaning of "be guilty." The noun can have a consequential sense of "that which is due from guilt," i.e., "compensation, indemnification, reparation"; hence the translation "reparation offering," rather than the alternatives "guilt offering" or "trespass offering." This offering is brought most often in cases of sacrilege.

‡[5:15] **At the established value:** the Hebrew term *'erkĕkā*, which in context means "(established) value," may indicate that a person could bring the monetary equivalent of a ram instead of an actual animal. See vv. 18, 25.

---

p. [5:7] Cf. Lv 5:11; 12:8; 14:21.    q. [5:8] Lv 1:14–17.    r. [5:11] Lv 2:1–3; Nm 5:15.    s. [5:15] Lv 7:1–6; Nm 5:5–8.    t. [5:15] Lv 22:14.    u. [5:16] Lv 22:14; 27:13, 15, 19, 27.

---

§[6:2–6] This passage may have reference to the burnt offering that is offered in the morning and late afternoon each day (cf. Ex 29:38–42; Nm 28:3–8).

¶[6:2] **Ritual:** Hebrew *torah*, which also has the broader meaning of "instruction." The treatment of sacrifices in chaps. 6–7 recapitulates the offerings treated in 1–5 but now with more emphasis on priestly duties and prerogatives.

---

v. [5:17] Ps 19:13; Jb 1:5.    w. [5:21] Ps 59:13; Hos 4:2.    x. [5:21] Ex 22:6–12.    y. [6:2] Lv 1.

out. Every morning the priest shall put firewood on it. On this he shall lay out the burnt offering[z] and burn the fat of the communion offering. [6]The fire is to be kept burning continuously on the altar; it must not go out.

**The Grain Offering.**[*] [7]This is the ritual of the grain offering. Aaron's sons shall offer it before the LORD, in front of the altar. [8]A priest shall then take from the grain offering a handful of bran flour and oil, together with all the frankincense that is on it,[a] and this he shall burn on the altar as a token of the offering, a sweet aroma to the LORD. [9]The rest of it Aaron and his sons may eat; but it must be eaten unleavened in a sacred place;[b] in the court of the tent of meeting they shall eat it. [10]It shall not be baked with leaven. I have given it to them as their portion from the oblations for the LORD; it is most holy,[c] like the purification offering and the reparation offering. [11]Every male of Aaron's descendants may eat of it perpetually throughout your generations as their rightful due from the oblations for the LORD. Whatever touches the oblations becomes holy.

**High Priest's Daily Grain Offering.**[†] [12]The LORD said to Moses: [13]This is the offering that Aaron and his sons shall present to the LORD on the day he is anointed: one tenth of an ephah of bran flour for the regular grain offering, half of it in the morning and half of it in the evening. [14]You shall bring it well kneaded and fried in oil on a griddle.[d] Having broken the offering into pieces, you shall present it as a sweet aroma to the LORD. [15]The anointed priest descended from Aaron who succeeds him shall do likewise. This is the LORD's due forever. The offering shall be wholly burned.[e] [16]Every grain offering of a priest shall be a whole offering; it may not be eaten.

**Purification Offerings.**[‡] [17]The LORD said to Moses: [18]Tell Aaron and his sons: This is the ritual for the purification offering. At the place where the burnt offering is slaughtered, there also, before the LORD, shall the purification offering be slaughtered. It is most holy.[g] [19]The priest who offers the purification offering shall

eat of it; it shall be eaten in a sacred place,[h] in the court of the tent of meeting. [20]Whatever touches its flesh becomes holy. If any of its blood spatters on a garment, the stained part must be washed in a sacred place. [21]A clay vessel in which it has been boiled shall be broken; if it is boiled in a copper vessel, this shall be scoured afterward and rinsed with water.[i] [22]Every male of the priestly line may eat it. It is most holy. [23]But no purification offering of which some blood has been brought into the tent of meeting[j] to make atonement in the sanctuary shall be eaten; it must be burned with fire.[k]

## CHAPTER 7

**Reparation Offerings.**[§] [1]This is the ritual for the reparation offering. It is most holy. [2]At the place where the burnt offering is slaughtered, the reparation offering shall also be slaughtered.[m] Its blood shall be splashed on all the sides of the altar. [3]All of its fat shall be offered: the fatty tail, the fat that covers the inner organs, and all the fat that adheres to them, [4]as well as the two kidneys with the fat on them near the loins, and the lobe of the liver, which is removed with the kidneys. [5]The priest shall burn these on the altar as an oblation to the LORD. It is a reparation offering. [6]Every male of the priestly line may eat of it; but it must be eaten in a sacred place.[o] It is most holy.[p]

[7]Because the purification offering and the reparation offering are alike, both have the same ritual. The reparation offering belongs to the priest who makes atonement with it. [8]As for the priest who offers someone's burnt offering, to him belongs the hide of the burnt offering that is offered. [9][q]Also, every grain offering that is baked in an oven or made in a pan or on a griddle shall belong to the priest who offers it, [10]whereas all grain offerings[r] that are mixed with oil or are dry shall belong to all of Aaron's sons without distinction.

**Communion Sacrifices.**[**] [11][s]This is the ritual for the communion sacrifice that is offered to the

---

*[6:7–11] The passage is apparently concerned with the raw grain offering of 2:1–3.

†[6:12–16] This seems to refer to a grain offering offered twice daily by the high priest, perhaps identical to the regular grain offering in Nm 4:16 (cf. Neh 10:34). This offering is distinct from the grain offering that accompanies the daily burnt offering.

‡[6:17–23] There are two types of purification offering: one whose blood is used inside the tent sanctuary (4:1–12, 13–21) and another whose blood was only used at the outer sacrificial altar (4:22–26, 27–31, 32–35). The carcasses of the former, as well as of purification offerings brought by the priests themselves (cf. 8:14–17; 9:8–11), are not eaten by priests but disposed of at the ash heap outside the camp, which itself is set up around the sanctuary (Ex 29:14; Lv 4:11–12, 21; 6:23; 8:17; 9:11; 16:27). The Letter to the Hebrews compares Jesus' suffering "outside the gate" to the disposal of purification offering carcasses outside the camp (Heb 13:11–13).

§[7:1–6] These prescriptions may appear here rather than in 5:14–26 where this offering is first treated because the monetary equivalent of the offering might have been brought instead of an actual animal. See note on 5:15.

¶[7:9–10] For the distinction between uncooked and cooked grain offerings, see 2:1–10 and note on 2:1. The contradiction between v. 9 and 2:10 may reflect a development in custom, with the distribution in v. 9 coming from earlier times, when sanctuary personnel were more limited.

**[7:11–36] This section discusses three types of communion sacrifice: the thanksgiving offering (vv. 12–15), a votive offering, and a voluntary offering (vv. 16–18). The latter two are similar and are thus mentioned together. Verses 19–36 apply to all types of communion sacrifice.

z. [6:5] Lv 9:17.  a. [6:8] Lv 2:1–3.  b. [6:9] Lv 6:19; 7:6; 10:13, 17; 24:9.  c. [6:10] Lv 2:3.  d. [6:14] Lv 2:5.  e. [6:15] Lv 2:9.  f. [6:18] Lv 4:1–5:13.  g. [6:18] Lv 2:3.

h. [6:19] Lv 6:9.  i. [6:21] Lv 11:32–33; 15:12.  j. [6:23] Lv 4:5; Heb 13:11.  k. [6:23] Lv 4:11–12, 21; 8:17; 9:11; 16:27.  l. [7:1] Lv 5:14–26.  m. [7:2] Lv 6:18.  n. [7:3] Lv 3:4.  o. [7:6] Lv 6:9.  p. [7:6] Lv 2:3.  q. [7:9] Lv 2:3–10; Nm 18:9; Ez 44:29.  r. [7:10] Lv 2:14–15.  s. [7:11] Lv 3.

LORD. ¹²*If someone offers it for thanksgiving, that person shall offer it with unleavened cakes mixed with oil, unleavened wafers spread with oil, and cakes made of bran flour mixed with oil and well kneaded. ¹³One shall present this offering together with loaves of leavened bread along with the thanksgiving communion sacrifice. ¹⁴From this the individual shall offer one bread of each type of offering as a contribution† to the LORD; this shall belong to the priest who splashes the blood of the communion offering.

¹⁵‡The meat of the thanksgiving communion sacrifice shall be eaten on the day it is offered; none of it may be kept till the next morning.ᵘ ¹⁶However, if the sacrifice offered is a votive or a voluntary offering,§ it shall be eaten on the day the sacrifice is offered, and on the next day what is left over may be eaten.ᵛ ¹⁷But what is left over of the meat of the sacrifice on the third day must be burned in the fire. ¹⁸If indeed any of the flesh of the communion sacrifice is eaten on the third day, it shall not be accepted; it will not be reckoned to the credit of the one offering it. Rather it becomes a desecrated meat. Anyone who eats of it shall bear the penalty.¶

¹⁹**Should the meat touch anything unclean, it may not be eaten, but shall be burned in the fire.ʷ As for other meat, all who are clean may eat of it. ²⁰If, however, someone in a state of uncleanness eats the meat of a communion sacrifice belonging to the LORD, that person shall be cut off†ˣ from the people. ²¹Likewise, if someone touches anything unclean, whether it is human uncleanness or an unclean animal or an unclean loathsome creature, and then eats the meat of the communion sacrifice belonging to the LORD, that person, too, shall be cut off from the people.

**Prohibition Against Blood and Fat.** ²²The LORD said to Moses: ²³Tell the Israelites: You shall not eat the fat of any ox or sheep or goat.ʸ ²⁴Although the fat of an animal that has died a natural death or has been killed by wild beasts may be put to any other use, you may not eat it.ᶻ ²⁵If anyone eats the fat of an animal from which an oblation is made to the LORD, that person shall be cut off from the people. ²⁶ᵃWherever you dwell, you shall not eat any blood, whether of bird or of animal. ²⁷Every person who eats any blood shall be cut off from the people.

**Portions from the Communion Sacrifice for Priests.** ²⁸The LORD said to Moses: ²⁹Tell the Israelites: The person who offers a communion sacrifice to the LORD shall be the one to bring from it the offering to the LORD. ³⁰The offerer's own hands shall carry the oblations for the LORD: the person shall bring the fat together with the brisket, which is to be raised as an elevatedᵇ offering‡‡ before the LORD. ³¹The priest shall burn the fat on the altar,ᶜ but the brisket belongs to Aaron and his sons. ³²Moreover, from your communion sacrifices you shall give to the priest the right leg as a contribution. ³³The one among Aaron's sons who offers the blood and the fat of the communion offering shall have the right leg as his portion, ³⁴for from the communion sacrifices of the Israelites I have taken the brisket that is elevated and the leg that is a contribution, and I have given them to Aaron, the priest, and to his sons as their due from the Israelites forever.ᵈ

³⁵This is the priestly share from the oblations for the LORD, allotted to Aaron and his sons on the day they were brought forth to be the priests of the LORD, ³⁶which the LORD ordered to be given them from the Israelites on the day they were anointed, as their due throughout their generations forever.

**Summary.** ³⁷This is the ritual for the burnt offering, the grain offering, the purification offering, the reparation offering, the ordination offering,ᵉ and the communion sacrifice, ³⁸which the LORD enjoined on Moses at Mount Sinai at the time when he commanded the Israelites in the wilderness of Sinai to bring their offerings to the LORD.ᶠ

## II. CEREMONY OF ORDINATION

### CHAPTER 8

**Ordination of Aaron and His Sons.**§§ ¹ᵍThe LORD said to Moses: ²Take Aaron along with his

---

*[7:12–13] Four types of breads accompany the thanksgiving offering. Three types are cooked grain offerings comparable to those in 2:4–10. Also required are loaves of leavened bread (see 2:11).

†[7:14] **Contribution:** Hebrew *terumah*. This does not indicate a particular ritual action. The word simply means "gift, something set apart."

‡[7:15–18] Sacrifices must be properly consumed for them to be effective (cf. also 19:5–8; 22:30). Similar rules obtain for the Passover offering (Ex 12:10; Nm 9:12; cf. Ex 23:18; 34:25; Dt 16:4) and the ordination offering (Ex 29:34; Lv 8:32).

§[7:16] **Votive or a voluntary offering:** these are not specific types of offerings but rather motivations for bringing the communion sacrifice (cf. 22:18). A votive offering is brought as the consequence of a promise (vow) made to God. A voluntary offering is a spontaneous gift to God independent of a prior promise. See note on 27:2–13.

¶[7:18] **Bear the penalty:** this refers in many cases to punishment by God (cf. 17:16; 19:8; 20:17, 19; Nm 18:1, 23; 30:16).

**[7:19–21] For ritual impurity, see note on 11:1–15:33.

††[7:20] **Cut off:** a common term in the Priestly source that cannot always be reduced to a simple English equivalent, since its usage appears to involve a number of associated punishments, some or all of which may come into play in any one instance (see Ex 12:15 and note). All the same, as a punishment from God, to be "cut off" (from one's people) frequently appears to refer to termination of the offender's family line (and perhaps in some cases an early death); see Lv 20:2–3, 20–21; Ru 4:10; Ps 109:13; Mal 2:12.

‡‡[7:30] **Raised as an elevated offering:** these portions of the sacrifices were specially dedicated by lifting them in presentation before God's abode. The sanctifying effect of this action is clearly seen in 23:17–20; Nm 6:19–20.

§§[8:1–2] This chapter presents the fulfillment of the commands in Ex 28–29; 30:26–30; and 40:9–15.

---

t. [7:15] Lv 19:6–7.   u. [7:15] Lv 22:29–30.   v. [7:16] Lv 19:5–8. w. [7:19] Lv 12:4.   x. [7:20] Lv 17:4, 9–10, 14; 18:29; 20:3, 5–6, 17–18; Gn 17:14; Ex 30:33; Nm 15:31; Ps 37:9, 28, 34; 109:13.

y. [7:23] Lv 3:17.   z. [7:24] Lv 22:8.   a. [7:26] Lv 17:10.   b. [7:30] Lv 8:27, 29; 9:21; 10:15; 14:12, 21, 24; 23:17, 20; Nm 6:20; 8:13; 18:18.   c. [7:31] Lv 3:11, 16.   d. [7:34] Ex 29:27–28.   e. [7:37] Lv 8:22.   f. [7:38] Lv 26:46; 27:34.   g. [8:1] Cf. Ex 28–29; 30; 40:12–15.

sons, the vestments, the anointing oil, the bull for a purification offering, the two rams, and the basket of unleavened bread, [3]then assemble the whole community* at the entrance of the tent of meeting. [4]Moses did as the LORD had commanded. When the community[h] had assembled at the entrance of the tent of meeting, [5]Moses told them: "This is what the LORD has ordered to be done." [6]Bringing forward Aaron and his sons, Moses first washed them with water. [7†]Then he put the tunic on Aaron,[i] girded him with the sash, clothed him with the robe, placed the ephod on him, and girded him with the ephod's embroidered belt, fastening the ephod on him with it. [8]He then set the breastpiece on him, putting the Urim and Thummim[‡] in it. [9]He put the turban on his head, attaching the gold medallion, the sacred headband,[§] on the front of the turban, as the LORD had commanded Moses to do.

[10¶]Taking the anointing oil, Moses anointed and consecrated the tabernacle and all that was in it.[j] [11]Then he sprinkled some of the oil seven times on the altar, and anointed the altar, with all its utensils, and the laver, with its base, to consecrate them. [12]He also poured some of the anointing oil on Aaron's head and anointed him, to consecrate him.[k] [13]Moses likewise brought forward Aaron's sons, clothed them with tunics, girded them with sashes, and put skullcaps on them, as the LORD had commanded him to do.

**Ordination Sacrifices.** [14]He brought forward the bull for a purification offering, and Aaron and his sons laid their hands on its head. [15]When it was slaughtered, Moses took the blood** and with his finger he put it on the horns around the altar, thus purifying the altar.[l] He poured out the rest of the blood at the base of the altar. Thus he consecrated it so that atonement could be made on it. [16]Taking all the fat that was over the inner organs, as well as the lobe of the liver and

the two kidneys with their fat,[m] Moses burned them on the altar. [17]The bull, however, with its hide and flesh and dung he burned in the fire outside the camp, as the LORD had commanded Moses to do.[n]

[18]He next brought forward the ram of the burnt offering,[o] and Aaron and his sons laid their hands on its head. [19]When it was slaughtered, Moses splashed the blood on all sides of the altar. [20]After the ram was cut up into pieces, Moses burned the head, the cut-up pieces and the suet. [21]After the inner organs and the shanks were washed with water, Moses burned these remaining parts of the ram on the altar. It was a burnt offering for a sweet aroma, an oblation to the LORD, as the LORD had commanded Moses.

[22††]Then he brought forward the second ram, the ordination ram,[p] and Aaron and his sons laid their hands on its head. [23]When it was slaughtered, Moses took some of its blood and put it on the lobe of Aaron's right ear, on the thumb of his right hand, and on the big toe[‡‡] of his right foot.[q] [24]Moses had the sons of Aaron also come forward, and he put some of the blood on the lobes of their right ears, on the thumbs of their right hands, and on the big toes of their right feet. The rest of the blood he splashed on all the sides of the altar. [25]He then took the fat: the fatty tail and all the fat over the inner organs, the lobe of the liver and the two kidneys with their fat, and likewise the right thigh; [26]from the basket of unleavened bread that was set before the LORD he took one unleavened cake, one loaf of bread made with oil, and one wafer; these he placed on top of the portions of fat and the right thigh. [27]He then put all these things upon the palms of Aaron and his sons, whom he had raise them as an elevated offering before the LORD.[r] [28]When Moses had removed them from their palms, he burned them on the altar with the burnt offering. They were an ordination offering for a sweet aroma, an oblation to the LORD. [29]He then took the brisket and raised it as an elevated offering before the LORD; this was Moses' own portion of the ordination ram, as the LORD had commanded Moses. [30]Taking some of the anointing oil and some of the blood that was on the altar, Moses sprinkled it upon Aaron and his vestments, as well as his sons and their vestments, thus consecrating both Aaron and his vestments and his sons and their vestments.[s]

[31]Moses said to Aaron and his sons, "Boil the meat at the entrance of the tent of meeting, and

---

*[8:3–4] **Community**: this word (Heb. *'edah*) may refer to tribal leaders, all adult males, or the entire nation. The last is probably intended here.

†[8:7–9, 13] On the priestly clothing, see Ex 28–29. **Ephod**: according to Ex 28:6–14, the term for one of Aaron's special vestments made of gold thread, with multicolored woolen thread woven into it as well as fine linen. In appearance it resembled a kind of apron, hung on the priest by shoulder straps and secured by an embroidered belt. A somewhat simpler "apron" was presumably worn by other priests (1 Sm 22:18).

‡[8:8] **The Urim and Thummim**: see Ex 28:30 and note there. Although these terms and the object(s) they refer to are still unexplained, they appear to be small objects that functioned like dice or lots to render a decision for those making an inquiry of God, perhaps originally in legal cases where the guilt of the accused could not otherwise be determined (cf. Ex 28:30; Nm 27:21; Dt 33:8; 1 Sm 28:6; Ezr 2:63; Neh 7:65).

§[8:9] **Headband**: see Ex 39:30–31. The gold medallion, together with its cords, comprises the sacred headband.

¶[8:10–12] Anointing with the specially prepared oil (cf. Ex 30:22–33) is one of the means of making objects and persons holy by setting them apart for a special function or purpose.

**[8:15] **Moses took the blood**: Moses is acting as a priest in this chapter.

††[8:22–32] The priestly ordination offering is a unique type of sacrifice but similar in many respects to the communion sacrifice (chap. 3; 7:11–34).

‡‡[8:23–24] **Lobe...thumb...toe**: these parts of the body are meant to represent the body as a whole. The application of the blood symbolizes the priests' passing from a profane to a holy state. Cf. 14:14–17.

h. [8:4] Nm 27:19.   i. [8:7–9] Sir 45:8–13; Heb 5:1–4; 7:1–28. j. [8:10] Ex 30:26.   k. [8:12] Sir 45:15.   l. [8:15] Heb 9:22.

m. [8:16–17] Lv 3:4–5; 4:8–11.   n. [8:17] Lv 6:23.   o. [8:18] Lv 1:10–13.   p. [8:22] Lv 7:37.   q. [8:23] Lv 14:14, 17.   r. [8:27] Lv 7:30.   s. [8:30] Ex 40:15.

there eat it with the bread that is in the basket of the ordination offering, in keeping with the command I have received: 'Aaron and his sons shall eat of it.' ³²What is left over of the meat and the bread you shall burn in the fire. ³³Moreover, you are not to depart* from the entrance of the tent of meeting for seven days, until the days of your ordination are completed; for your ordination is to last for seven days. ³⁴What has been done today the Lord has commanded be done, to make atonement for you. ³⁵You must remain at the entrance of the tent of meeting day and night for seven days, carrying out the prescriptions of the Lord, so that you do not die, for this is the command I have received."[t] ³⁶So Aaron and his sons did all that the Lord had commanded through Moses.

## CHAPTER 9

**Octave of the Ordination.** ¹On the eighth day[†u] Moses summoned Aaron and his sons, together with the elders of Israel, ²and said to Aaron, "Take a calf of the herd for a purification offering and a ram for a burnt offering, both without blemish, and offer them before the Lord. ³[‡]Tell the Israelites, too: Take a he-goat for a purification offering, a calf and a lamb, both unblemished yearlings, for a burnt offering, ⁴and an ox and a ram for a communion sacrifice, to sacrifice before the Lord, along with a grain offering mixed with oil; for today the Lord will appear to you." ⁵So they brought what Moses had ordered before the tent of meeting. When the whole community had come forward and stood before the Lord, ⁶[§]Moses said, "This is what the Lord orders you to do, that the glory of the Lord may appear to you. ⁷Approach the altar," Moses then told Aaron, "and make your purification offering and your burnt offering in atonement for yourself and for your household;[¶] then make the offering of the people in atonement for them, as the Lord has commanded."[v]

⁸Approaching the altar, Aaron first slaughtered the calf of the purification offering that was his own offering. ⁹When his sons presented the blood to him, he dipped his finger in the blood and put it on the horns of the altar.[w] The rest of the blood he poured out at the base of the altar. ¹⁰He then burned on the altar the fat, the kidneys and the lobe of the liver from the purification offering, as the Lord had commanded Moses; ¹¹but the flesh and the hide he burned in the fire outside the camp.[x] ¹²Then Aaron slaughtered the burnt offering. When his sons brought him the blood, he splashed it on all sides of the altar. ¹³They then brought him the pieces and the head of the burnt offering, and he burned them on the altar. ¹⁴Having washed the inner organs and the shanks, he burned these also with the burnt offering on the altar.[y]

¹⁵Then he had the people's offering brought. Taking the goat that was for the people's purification offering, he slaughtered it and offered it as a purification offering as before. ¹⁶Then he brought forward the burnt offering and offered it according to procedure. ¹⁷He then presented the grain offering; taking a handful of it, he burned it on the altar, in addition to the morning burnt offering.[z] ¹⁸Finally he slaughtered the ox and the ram, the communion sacrifice of the people. When his sons brought him the blood, Aaron splashed it on all sides of the altar.[a] ¹⁹The portions of fat from the ox and from the ram, the fatty tail, the covering fat, the kidneys, and the lobe of the liver ²⁰they placed on top of the briskets. Aaron burned the fat pieces on the altar, ²¹but the briskets and the right thigh he raised as an elevated offering[b] before the Lord, as the Lord had commanded Moses.

**Revelation of the Lord's Glory.** ²²[**]Aaron then raised his hands over the people and blessed[c] them. When he came down from offering the purification offering, the burnt offering, and the communion offering, ²³Moses and Aaron went into the tent of meeting. On coming out they blessed the people. Then the glory of the Lord appeared to all the people. ²⁴[††]Fire came forth from the Lord's presence and consumed the burnt offering and the fat on the altar.[d] Seeing this, all the people shouted with joy and fell prostrate.

## CHAPTER 10

**Nadab and Abihu.** ¹[‡‡]Aaron's sons Nadab and Abihu took their censers and, putting incense on the fire they had set in them,[e] they offered

---

*[8:33–35] **You are not to depart**: the tenor and context of this requirement in vv. 33 and 35 seem to indicate that the priests are not to leave the sanctuary precincts for any reason. **Your ordination is to last for seven days . . . what has been done today . . . be done**: the consecration rites in Exodus are to be performed every day for seven days (cf. Ex 29:30, 35–37).

†[9:1] **Eighth day**: this is the conclusion of the priestly initiation ceremony.

‡[9:3–4] The seven-day consecration of the priests in chap. 8 did not require sacrifices from the community. Now communal sacrifices as well as priestly sacrifices are required.

§[9:6–21] Aaron and his sons now perform the offerings, instead of Moses (see note on 8:15).

¶[9:7] **For your household**: unlike the Septuagint, the Hebrew reads *be'ad ha'am*, "for the people."

**[9:22–23] The people are blessed twice. For the possible content of the blessing, compare the priestly blessing in Nm 6:22–27. Solomon offers a double blessing at the dedication of the Temple (1 Kgs 8:14–21, 55–61).

††[9:24] The theophany consists of a fire that apparently comes from the tent of meeting. God's fiery glory is also manifested in the pillar of cloud and fire that led the Israelites and rested over the tent of meeting (Ex 13:21; 40:38; Nm 9:15–23; 10:11). On God's fiery glory, see also Ex 24:17; Ez 1:27–28.

‡‡[10:1–2] Nadab and Abihu are the older sons of Aaron (Ex 6:23–24). Their sin apparently involves using embers from

---

t. [8:35] Lv 10:7.　u. [9:1] Lv 8:33.　v. [9:7] Lv 16:3–5.　w. [9:9] Lv 4:25, 30, 34.

x. [9:11] Lv 6:23.　y. [9:14] Lv 1:5–9.　z. [9:17] Nm 28:23; 2 Kgs 16:15; Ez 46:13–15.　a. [9:18] Lv 3:2.　b. [9:21] Lv 7:30–34. c. [9:22] Nm 6:22–27.　d. [9:24] 1 Kgs 18:38; 2 Chr 7:1; 2 Mc 2:10; cf. Ex 24:16–17.　e. [10:1] Lv 16:1; Nm 3:4; 26:61; 1 Chr 24:2.

before the LORD unauthorized fire, such as he had not commanded. ²Fire therefore came forth from the LORD's presence and consumed them,ᶠ so that they died in the LORD's presence. ³Moses then said to Aaron, "This is as the LORD said:

Through those near to me I will be
    sanctified;
in the sight of all the people I will
    obtain glory."*ᵍ

But Aaron said nothing. ⁴Then Moses summoned Mishael and Elzaphan, the sons of Aaron's uncle Uzziel, with the order, "Come, carry your kinsmen from before the sanctuary to a place outside the camp." ⁵So they drew near and carried them by means of their tunics outside the camp, as Moses had commanded.

**Conduct of the Priests.** ⁶Moses said to Aaron and his sons Eleazar and Ithamar, "Do not dishevel your hairʰ or tear your garments,ⁱ lest you die and bring God's wrath also on the whole community. While your kindred, the rest of the house of Israel, may mourn for those whom the LORD's fire has burned up, ⁷you shall not go beyond the entrance of the tent of meeting,ʲ else you shall die; for the anointing oil of the LORD is upon you." So they did as Moses told them.

⁸The LORD said to Aaron: ⁹When you are to go to the tent of meeting, you and your sons are forbidden, by a perpetual statute throughout your generations, to drink any wine or strong drink, lest you die.ᵏ ¹⁰You must be able to distinguish between what is sacred and what is profane, and between what is clean and what is unclean;†ˡ ¹¹and you must be able to teach the Israelites all the statutes that the LORD has given them through Moses.

**The Eating of the Priestly Portions.** ¹²Moses said to Aaron and his surviving sons, Eleazar and Ithamar, "Take the grain offering§ left over from the oblations to the LORD, and eat it beside the altar in the form of unleavened cakes, since it is most holy. ¹³You must eat it in a sacred place

because it is your and your sons' due from the oblations to the LORD; such is the command I have received. ¹⁴ᵐThe brisket of the elevated offering and the leg¶ of the contribution, however, you and your sons and daughters may eat, in a clean place; for these have been assigned to you and your children as your due from the communion sacrifices of the Israelites. ¹⁵The leg of the contribution and the brisket of the elevated offering shall be brought in with the oblations of fat to be raised as an elevated offering before the LORD. They shall belong to you and your children as your due forever, as the LORD has commanded."

¹⁶Moses inquired closely about the goat of the purification offering** and discovered that it had all been burned. So he was angry with the surviving sons of Aaron, Eleazar and Ithamar, and said, ¹⁷ⁿ"Why did you not eat the purification offering in the sacred place, since it is most holy? It has been given to you that you might remove the guilt of the community and make atonement for them before the LORD. ¹⁸Since its blood was not brought inside the sanctuary, you should certainly have eaten the offering in the sanctuary, as I was commanded." ¹⁹Aaron answered Moses, "Even though they presented their purification offering and burnt offering before the LORD today, still this misfortune has befallen me. Had I then eaten of the purification offering today, would it have been pleasing to the LORD?" ²⁰On hearing this, Moses was satisfied.

## III. LAWS REGARDING RITUAL PURITY††

### CHAPTER 11

**Clean and Unclean Meats.**‡‡ ¹ᵒThe LORD said to Moses and Aaron: ²Speak to the Israelites and

---

¶[10:14] **Brisket . . . leg:** these are from the Israelites' communion sacrifices in 9:4, 18–21.

**[10:16–20] **Goat of the purification offering:** this is the people's purification offering of 9:3, 15. Since its blood is not brought into the sanctuary, then, according to 6:17–23, this is the type of purification offering which is to be eaten by the priests in a holy place. **Eleazar and Ithamar:** they burned the entire goat of the people's purification offering (9:15) instead of eating it in a sacred place (6:19) to remove ritually the sin of the community by the ingestion of the meat of the offering. Aaron's defense of this action of his sons is somewhat vague: he merely alludes to the loss suffered in the death of Nadab and Abihu, without giving an explicit reason for Eleazar and Ithamar's not eating the people's purification offering, as required.

††[11:1–15:33] Priestly legislation manifests two types of impurity or uncleanness: tolerated and prohibited. Prohibited impurity arises from various sins (e.g., 4:1–5; 5:2–3; 18:6–23; 20:2–5; Nm 5:13–14; 6:6–7). Tolerated impurity has three main sources: certain dead bodies (animal and human; cf. Lv 11 and Nm 19), various regular and abnormal genital discharges (Lv 12; 15), and diseases (specifically "scaly infection," chaps. 13–14). An additional tolerated impurity is that generated by the cult in order to rectify the effect of these impurities or sins (cf. chap. 4; 16:26, 28).

‡‡[11:1–47] Apart from the introduction and conclusion (vv. 1–2a, 46–47), this chapter has three sections: (1) prohibitions against eating certain land, water, and air animals

---

an unapproved source instead of the altar (cf. 16:12). The fire that destroys them is the same type found in 9:24.

*[10:3] The explanation for the divine reaction indicates that improper cultic actions desecrate God and compromise God's glory. Desecration evokes divine punishment (cf. Ex 28:43; Nm 4:15, 19–20). **Those near to me:** i.e., cultic officials.

†[10:4–5] Moses has lay people remove the bodies so that the priests can continue their cultic activities free of contamination by a corpse (cf. Nm 19).

‡[10:10] **Sacred and . . . profane . . . clean and . . . unclean:** something or someone may be either sacred or profane (i.e., ordinary, not set apart), and at the same time clean or unclean. Priests would be particularly concerned about keeping what is unclean away from the sacred.

§[10:12–13] **Grain offering:** this is the grain offering of the people of 9:4, 17. Only the token offering had been offered; the rest was for the priests' consumption.

---

f. [10:2] Nm 16:35; cf. Lv 9:24.  g. [10:3] Lv 21:17, 21; Nm 20:12.  h. [10:6] Lv 13:45.  i. [10:6] Lv 21:5–6, 10–12.  j. [10:7] Lv 8:33–35; 21:12.  k. [10:9] Ez 44:21.  l. [10:10] Lv 11:47; 20:25; Ez 22:26; 44:23.

m. [10:14] Lv 7:34.  n. [10:17] Lv 6:18–19.  o. [11:1] Lv 27:11, 27; Gn 7:2–3, 8–9; Dt 14:3–21.

tell them: Of all land animals these are the ones you may eat: ³Any animal that has hoofs you may eat, provided it is cloven-footed and chews the cud. ⁴But you shall not eat[p] any of the following from among those that only chew the cud or only have hoofs: the camel, which indeed chews the cud, but does not have hoofs and is therefore unclean for you; ⁵the rock hyrax,* which indeed chews the cud, but does not have hoofs and is therefore unclean for you; ⁶the hare, which indeed chews the cud, but does not have hoofs and is therefore unclean for you; ⁷and the pig,[q] which does indeed have hoofs and is cloven-footed, but does not chew the cud and is therefore unclean for you. ⁸You shall not eat their meat, and you shall not touch their carcasses; they are unclean for you.

⁹Of the various creatures that live in the water, you may eat the following: whatever in the seas or in river waters that has both fins and scales you may eat.[r] ¹⁰But of the creatures that swarm in the water or of animals that otherwise live in the water, whether in the sea or in the rivers, all those that lack either fins or scales are loathsome for you, ¹¹and shall always be loathsome to you. Their meat you shall not eat, and their carcasses you shall loathe. ¹²Every water creature that lacks fins or scales is loathsome for you.

¹³Of the birds,† these you shall loathe; they shall not be eaten, they are loathsome: the griffon vulture, the bearded vulture, the black vulture, ¹⁴the kite, the various species of falcons, ¹⁵the various species of crows, ¹⁶the eagle owl, the kestrel, the long-eared owl, the various species of hawks, ¹⁷the little owl, the cormorant, the screech owl, ¹⁸the barn owl, the horned owl, the osprey, ¹⁹the stork, the various species of herons, the hoopoe, and the bat.

²⁰The various winged insects that walk on all fours are loathsome for you. ²¹But of the various winged insects that walk on all fours you may eat those that have legs jointed above their feet for leaping on the ground; ²²hence of these you may eat the following: the various kinds of locusts, the various kinds of bald locusts, the various kinds of crickets, and the various kinds of grasshoppers.[s] ²³All other winged insects that have four legs are loathsome for you.

²⁴You become unclean by the following—anyone who touches their carcasses shall be unclean until evening,[t] ²⁵and anyone who carries any part of their carcasses shall wash his garments and be unclean until evening— ²⁶by all hoofed animals that are not cloven-footed or do not chew the cud; they are unclean for you; anyone who touches them becomes unclean. ²⁷Also by the various quadrupeds that walk on paws; they are unclean for you; anyone who touches their carcasses shall be unclean until evening, ²⁸and anyone who carries their carcasses shall wash his garments and be unclean until evening. They are unclean for you.

²⁹Of the creatures that swarm on the ground, the following are unclean for you: the rat, the mouse, the various kinds of lizards, ³⁰the gecko, the spotted lizard, the agama, the skink, and the chameleon. ³¹Among the various swarming creatures, these are unclean for you. Everyone who touches them when they are dead shall be unclean until evening. ³²Everything on which one of them falls when dead becomes unclean, including any article of wood, cloth, leather or goat hair—any article of which use can be made. It must be immersed in water and remain unclean until evening, when it again becomes clean. ³³Should any of these creatures fall into a clay vessel, everything in it becomes unclean, and the vessel itself you must break. ³⁴Any food that can be eaten which makes contact with water, and any liquid that may be drunk, in any such vessel become unclean. ³⁵Any object on which any part of their carcasses falls becomes unclean; if it is an oven or stove, this must be broken to pieces; they are unclean and shall always be unclean to you. ³⁶However, a spring or a cistern for collecting water remains clean; but whoever touches such an animal's carcass becomes unclean. ³⁷If any part of their carcasses falls on any sort of grain that is to be sown, it remains clean; ³⁸but if the grain has become moistened, it becomes unclean to you when any part of their carcasses falls on it.

³⁹‡[u]When one of the animals that you could otherwise eat dies of itself, anyone who touches its carcass shall be unclean until evening; ⁴⁰and anyone who eats any part of its carcass shall wash his garments and be unclean until evening;[v] so also, anyone who carries its carcass shall wash his garments and be unclean until evening.

⁴¹All the creatures that swarm on the ground are loathsome and shall not be eaten. ⁴²Whether it crawls on its belly, goes on all fours, or has many legs—any creature that swarms on the earth—you shall not eat them; they are

---

(vv. 2b–23); (2) consequences of contact with various animals (vv. 24–41); (3) a prohibition against eating small land animals, which is motivated by the requirement that Israel be holy as God is holy (vv. 41–45). These animals are impure only when dead. Cf. Dt 14:3–21.

*[11:5–6] According to modern zoology, **the rock hyrax** (*Hyrax syriacus*) is classified as an ungulate, and **the hare** as a rodent; neither is a ruminant. They appear to chew their food as the true ruminants do, and it is upon this appearance that the classification in the text is based.

†[11:13–23, 30] **Birds:** the term is broader, including all animals that fly (including bats, v. 19, and flying insects, vv. 20–23). The identification of the various Hebrew names for these birds and reptiles is in many cases uncertain.

‡[11:39–40] These animals create uncleanness, but are not prohibited as food (cf. 17:15–16). Priests who have a higher degree of holiness than other Israelites may not eat these animals (22:8; cf. Ez 44:31). Cf. Ex 22:30; Dt 14:21.

p. [11:4] Jgs 13:4, 7; Is 66:17; Ez 4:12–14.   q. [11:7] Prv 11:22; Is 65:4; 66:17; Mt 7:6; 8:30–32; Mk 5:11–16; Lk 8:32–33; 15:15–16. r. [11:9] Jn 21:9–13.   s. [11:22] Mt 3:4; Mk 1:6.

t. [11:24] Lv 5:2; 7:21.   u. [11:39] Lv 17:15–16; 22:8; Ex 22:30; Ez 4:12–14; 44:31.   v. [11:40] Lv 17:15; 22:8.

loathsome. ⁴³Do not make yourselves loathsome by any swarming creature nor defile yourselves with them and so become unclean by them.ʷ ⁴⁴For I, the Lᴏʀᴅ, am your God. You shall make and keep yourselves holy,* because I am holy.ˣ You shall not make yourselves unclean, then, by any swarming creature that crawls on the ground. ⁴⁵Since I, the Lᴏʀᴅ, am the one who brought you up from the land of Egypt that I might be your God, you shall be holy, because I am holy.

⁴⁶This is the instruction for land animals, birds, and all the creatures that move about in the water, as well as any animal that swarms on the ground, ⁴⁷that you may distinguish between the clean and the unclean, and between creatures that may be eaten and those that may not be eaten.ʸ

## CHAPTER 12

**Uncleanness of Childbirth.** ¹The Lᴏʀᴅ said to Moses: ²Tell the Israelites: When a woman has a child, giving birth to a boy, she shall be unclean† for seven days, with the same uncleanness as during her menstrual period.ᶻ ³On the eighth day, the flesh of the boy's foreskin shall be circumcised,‡ᵃ ⁴and then she shall spend thirty-three days more in a state of blood purity; she shall not touch anything sacred nor enter the sanctuary till the days of her purification are fulfilled. ⁵If she gives birth to a girl, for fourteen days she shall be as unclean as during her menstrual period, after which she shall spend sixty-six days§ in a state of blood purity.

⁶When the days of her purification for a son or for a daughter are fulfilled,ᵇ she shall bring

to the priest at the entrance of the tent of meeting a yearling lamb for a burnt offering and a pigeon or a turtledove for a purification offering. ⁷The priest shall offer them before the Lᴏʀᴅ to make atonement for her, and thus she will be clean again after her flow of blood. Such is the ritual for the woman who gives birth to a child, male or female. ⁸If, however, she cannot afford a lamb,ᶜ she may take two turtledoves or two pigeons,ᵈ the one for a burnt offering and the other for a purification offering. The priest shall make atonement for her, and thus she will again be clean.

## CHAPTER 13

**Scaly Infection.**** ¹The Lᴏʀᴅ said to Moses and Aaron: ²ᵉWhen someone has on the skin a mark, lesion, or blotch which appears to develop into a scaly infection, the person shall be brought to Aaron, the priest, or to one of the priests among his sons. ³If the priest, upon examination of the skin's infection, finds that the hair on the infection has turned white and the infection itself appears to be deeper than the skin,†† it is indeed a scaly infection; the priest, on seeing this, shall declare the person unclean. ⁴‡‡If, however, the blotch on the skin is white, but does not seem to be deeper than the skin, nor has the hair turned white, the priest shall quarantine the afflicted person for seven days.§§ ⁵Should the priest, upon examination on the seventh day, find that the infection has remained unchanged in color and has not spread on the skin, the priest shall quarantine the person for another seven days. ⁶Should the priest, upon examination again on

---

*[11:44–45] **Keep yourselves holy . . . you shall be holy**: a similar idea is expressed in 20:25–26. There, distinguishing between the animals is compared to God's distinguishing between the peoples and choosing Israel.

†[12:2–5] The mother has two stages of uncleanness or impurity: the first where her uncleanness is as severe as during her menstrual period and is contagious to profane persons and objects (cf. 15:19–24), and the second where she does not contaminate persons and objects but is still impure to what is holy, such as the sanctuary (12:4) or sacrifices. The implication is that in the second stage she may resume sexual relations with her husband (which would be prohibited in the first stage according to 18:19).

‡[12:3] Circumcision is the sign of the covenant between God and Israel (Gn 17:1–27) and allows full participation in the religious community (Ex 12:43–49; Jos 5:2–10). This command was fulfilled after Jesus' birth (Lk 2:21).

§[12:5] **If she gives birth to a girl . . . sixty-six days**: while the longer period of uncleanness following the birth of a girl, compared to that following the birth of a boy, might reflect the relative disparity in social status between men and women in ancient Israel (and attested in other cultures), this is by no means certain. There is no simple correlation in the Bible between the worth of something and the degree of impurity it can occasion.

¶[12:6–8] Certain tolerated impurities (see note on 11:1–15:33) are strong enough to pollute the sanctuary and require purification offerings, including the parturient (see also 14:10–32; 15:13–15, 28–30). Cf. note on 4:3. Mary fulfilled

the command of bringing sacrifices after the birth of Jesus (Lk 2:22–24).

**[13:1–14:57] These chapters deal with scaly or fungal infections (Hebrew ṣāraʿat). The older translation "leprosy" is misleading because ṣāraʿat refers to not just one but several chronic and enduring skin diseases in human beings. The disease known as "leprosy" (Hansen's disease) is probably not included among the conditions described in the chapter. Also the term ṣāraʿat refers to fungal growths in fabrics and on the walls of houses. The reason why these conditions, and not other diseases, were considered unclean may be that they were quite visible, associated with death (cf. Nm 12:9–12), and traditionally connected with punishment by the deity (Lv 14:34; Dt 28:27, 35; 2 Sm 3:29; 2 Kgs 5:26–27; 2 Chr 26:16–21).

††[13:3] The symptoms of white hair and depth (perhaps a subcutaneous lesion) do not clearly correlate with known skin diseases or lesions. It may be that the symptoms are a hybrid ideal that do not reflect reality and are the result of priestly systematization. The same judgment applies to the conditions in vv. 10–11, 20, 25; cf. note on vv. 12–17.

‡‡[13:4–8] The symptoms here involve a flaky patch of skin that spreads after one week or stays the same after two. This correlates with many skin diseases, such as psoriasis, seborrheic dermatitis, certain mycotic infections, patchy eczema, and pityriasis rosea.

§§[13:4] **Quarantine . . . seven days**: unless lesions have unmistakable symptoms of scaly infection, time is needed to distinguish disease from a condition which is following the natural course of healing and remission. Cf. vv. 5, 21, 26, 27, 31, 33, 50, 54; 14:38.

---

w. [11:43–44] Lv 20:25–26.   x. [11:44] Lv 19:2; 20:7, 26; Mt 5:48; 1 Pt 1:16.   y. [11:47] Lv 10:10.   z. [12:2] Lv 15:19.   a. [12:3] Gn 17:12; Jn 7:22.   b. [12:6] Lk 2:22–24.

c. [12:8] Lv 14:21–22.   d. [12:8] Lv 1:14; Lk 2:24.   e. [13:2] Lv 22:4; Ex 4:6; Nm 5:2–3; Dt 24:8; 2 Sm 3:29; 2 Kgs 5:1, 3–7, 11, 27; Mk 1:40–45.

the seventh day, find that the infection is now faded and has not spread on the skin, the priest shall declare the person clean; it was merely a scab. The person shall wash his garments* and so become clean. [7]But if, after the person was examined by the priest and declared clean, the scab spreads at all on the skin, the person shall once more be examined by the priest. [8]Should the priest, upon examination, find that the scab has indeed spread on the skin, he shall declare the person unclean; it is a scaly infection.

[9]When someone is afflicted with a scaly infection, that person shall be brought to the priest. [10]Should the priest, upon examination, find that there is a white mark on the skin which has turned the hair white and that there is raw flesh in it, [11]it is a chronic scaly infection on the skin. The priest shall declare the person unclean without quarantine, since the individual is certainly unclean. [12]†If the scaly infection breaks out on the skin and, as far as the priest can see, covers all the skin of the afflicted person from head to foot, [13]should the priest then, upon examination, find that the scaly infection does cover the whole body, he shall declare the afflicted person clean; since the person has turned completely white; that individual is clean. [14]But as soon as raw flesh appears, the individual is unclean; [15]on observing the raw flesh, the priest shall declare the person unclean, because raw flesh is unclean; it is a scaly infection. [16]If, however, the raw flesh again turns white, the person shall return to the priest; [17]should the latter, upon examination, find that the infection has indeed turned white, he shall declare the afflicted person clean; the individual is clean.

[18]If a boil appeared on a person's skin which later healed, [19]should now in the place of the boil a white mark or a reddish white blotch develop, the person shall be examined by the priest. [20]If the latter, upon examination, finds that it is deeper than the skin and that the hair has turned white, he shall declare the person unclean; it is a scaly infection that has broken out in the boil. [21]But if the priest, upon examination, finds that there is no white hair in it and that it is not deeper than the skin and is faded, the priest shall quarantine the person for seven days. [22]If it has then spread on the skin, the priest shall declare the person unclean; it is an infection. [23]But if the blotch remains the same without spreading, it is merely the scar of the boil; the priest shall therefore declare the person clean.

[24]If there was a burn on a person's skin, and the burned area now becomes a reddish white or a white blotch, [25]when the priest, upon examination, finds that the hair has turned white in the blotch and this seems to be deeper than the skin, it is a scaly infection that has broken out in the burn; the priest shall therefore declare the person unclean; it is a scaly infection. [26]But if the priest, upon examination, finds that there is no white hair in the blotch and that this is not deeper than the skin and is faded, the priest shall quarantine the person for seven days. [27]Should the priest, upon examination on the seventh day, find that it has spread at all on the skin, he shall declare the person unclean; it is a scaly infection. [28]But if the blotch remains the same without spreading on the skin and is faded, it is merely the spot of the burn; the priest shall therefore declare the person clean, since it is only the scar of the burn.

[29]‡When a man or a woman has an infection on the head or in the beard, [30]should the priest, upon examination, find that the infection appears to be deeper than the skin and that there is fine yellow hair in it, the priest shall declare the person unclean; it is a scall. It is a scaly infection of the head or beard. [31]But if the priest, upon examining the scall infection, finds that it does not appear to be deeper than the skin, though the hair in it may not be black, the priest shall quarantine the scall-stricken person for seven days. [32]Should the priest, upon examining the infection on the seventh day find that the scall has not spread and has no yellow hair in it and does not seem to be deeper than the skin, [33]the person shall shave, but not the scall spot. Then the priest shall quarantine the scall-diseased person for another seven days. [34]If the priest, upon examining the scall on the seventh day, finds that it has not spread on the skin and that it does not appear to be deeper than the skin, he shall declare the person clean; the latter shall wash his garments, and will thus be clean. [35]But if the scall spreads at all on the skin after the person has been declared clean— [36]should the priest, upon examination, find that the scall has indeed spread on the skin, he need not look for yellow hair; the individual is unclean. [37]If, however, the scall has remained unchanged in color and black hair has grown in it, the disease has been healed; the person is clean, and the priest shall declare the individual clean.

[38]§When the skin of a man or a woman is spotted with several white blotches, [39]if the priest, upon examination, finds that the blotches on the skin are pale white, it is only tetter that

---

*[13:6] **Wash his garments**: even suspected scaly infections create some impurity, not just diagnosed infections (vv. 45–46).

†[13:12–17] This is not a paradox, namely where a limited lesion is impure but one that covers the whole body is pure. Rather, a white lesion that lacks ulcerated skin ("raw flesh") is pure, even if it covers the whole body. This formulation reflects priestly interest in systematization.

‡[13:29–37] The symptoms in this unit may include either favus (a mycotic infection) or a protein deficiency syndrome (Kwashiorkor) where the hair may be fine and copper-red to yellow.

§[13:38–39] This may refer to vitiligo, where patches of the skin and hair lose pigmentation.

has broken out on the skin, and the person therefore is clean.

⁴⁰When a man loses the hair of his head, he is simply bald on the crown and not unclean.ᶠ ⁴¹So too, if he loses the hair on the front of his head, he is simply bald on the forehead and not unclean. ⁴²But when there is a reddish white infection on his bald crown or bald forehead, it is a scaly infection that is breaking out there. ⁴³If the priest, upon examination, finds that the infection spot on the bald area on the crown or forehead has the same reddish white appearance as that of a scaly infection of the skin, ⁴⁴the man has a scaly infection and is unclean. The priest shall declare him unclean; his infection is on his head.

⁴⁵*The garments of one afflicted with a scaly infection shall be rent and the hair disheveled,ᵍ and the mustache covered.ʰ The individual shall cry out, "Unclean, unclean!" ⁴⁶As long as the infection is present, the person shall be unclean. Being unclean, that individual shall dwell apart, taking up residence outside the camp.ⁱ

**Fungal Infection of Fabrics and Leather.** ⁴⁷When a fungal infection is on a garment of wool or of linen, ⁴⁸or on the warp and woof† of linen or wool, or on a hide or anything made of leather, ⁴⁹if the infection on the garment or hide, or on the warp or woof, or on any leather article is greenish or reddish, the thing is indeed a fungal infection and must be examined by the priest. ⁵⁰Having examined the infection, the priest shall quarantine the infected article for seven days. ⁵¹If the priest, upon inspecting the infection on the seventh day, finds that it has spread on the garment, or on the warp or woof, or on the leather, whatever be its use, the infection is a harmful fungus; the article is unclean. ⁵²He shall therefore burn up the garment, or the warp or woof, be it of wool or linen, or any leather article which is infected; since it is a harmful fungus, it must be destroyed by fire. ⁵³But if the priest, upon examination, finds that it has not spread on the garment, or on the warp or woof, or on the leather article, ⁵⁴he shall give orders to have the infected article washed and then quarantined for another seven days. ⁵⁵If the priest, upon examination after the infection was washed, finds that it has not changed its color, even though it may not have spread, the article

is unclean. You shall burn it with fire. It is a fray, be it on its inner or outer side. ⁵⁶But if the priest, upon examination, finds that the infection has faded after the washing, he shall cut it out of the garment, or the leather, or the warp or woof. ⁵⁷If, however, the infection again appears on the garment, or on the warp or woof, or on the leather article, it is still virulent and you shall burn the thing infected with fire. ⁵⁸But if, after the washing, the infection has disappeared from the garment, or the warp or woof, or the leather article, the thing shall be washed a second time, and thus it will be clean. ⁵⁹This is the instruction for a fungalʲ infection on a garment of wool or linen, or on a warp or woof, or on any leather article, to determine whether it is clean or unclean.

## CHAPTER 14

**Purification After Scaly Infection.** ¹‡The LORD said to Moses: ²ᵏThis is the ritual for someone that had a scaly infection at the time of that person's purification.ˡ The individual shall be brought to the priest, ³who is to go outside the camp.ᵐ If the priest, upon inspection, finds that the scaly infection has healed in the afflicted person, ⁴he shall order that two live, clean birds,ⁿ as well as some cedar wood, scarlet yarn, and hyssop be obtained for the one who is to be purified.ⁿ ⁵*The priest shall then order that one of the birds be slaughtered over an earthen vessel with fresh water in it. ⁶Taking the living bird with the cedar wood, the scarlet yarn and the hyssop, the priest shall dip them, including the live bird, in the blood of the bird that was slaughtered over the fresh water, ⁷and then sprinkle seven times on the person to be purified from the scaly infection. When he has thus purified that person, he shall let the living bird fly away over the countryside.ᵒ ⁸The person being purified shall then wash his garments, shave off all hair, and bathe in water,** and so become clean. After this the person may come inside the camp, but shall still remain outside his or her tent for seven days.ᵖ ⁹On the seventh day this individual

---

\*[13:45–46] The symbolic association with death is found in the mourning activities in which those diagnosed with these afflictions engage: rending clothes, disheveling the hair, and covering the mouth. They are also excluded from the camp. Cf. examples of exclusion in Nm 5:1–4; 12:14–15; 2 Kgs 7:3–10; 15:5; 2 Chr 26:21. Persons with scaly infections must have been able to pollute others in the priestly system, though this is not stated. Hence, they must cry out "Unclean, unclean!" to warn others of their presence.

†[13:48] **Warp and woof**: it is possible that the nature of the weave allowed fungus to grow separately along warp or woof. Otherwise, this may refer to the yarns before they are woven together.

‡[14:1–32] The rites here are for purification from human scaly infections after recovery, not for healing (but cf. 2 Kgs 5:10–14).

§[14:4–7] The bird rite is also found for purifying a house from a fungus (vv. 49–53). The rite apparently removes impurity from the individual and, by means of the live bird, sends it away to unpopulated areas (v. 7). This is similar to the dispatch of a goat laden with sins on the Day of Atonement (16:21–22).

¶[14:5–7] The blood from the bird serves as a ritual detergent, much like the blood from the purification offering (see notes on 4:3). It is not a sacrifice, however, since it is not performed at the sanctuary. **Fresh water**: lit., "living water," taken from some source of running water, not from a cistern.

\*\*[14:8] **Bathe in water**: This phrase occurs frequently in Lv 14–16 and is imprecise. It can refer to both ordinary and cultic washing. The context will determine the meaning. At this early period in Israel's history it is probably not a reference to cultic immersion in a Mikveh—a Second Temple period ritual.

---

f. [13:40] 2 Kgs 2:23.   g. [13:45] Lv 10:6.   h. [13:45] Mi 3:7. i. [13:46] Lv 14:3; Nm 5:2; 12:14–15; 2 Kgs 7:3–10; 15:5; 2 Chr 26:21; Mt 26:6; Mk 14:3; Lk 17:11–19.

j. [13:59] Lv 14:54–57.   k. [14:2] 2 Kgs 5:10, 14; Mt 8:4; 10:8; Mk 1:44; Lk 4:27; 5:14.   l. [14:2] Lv 14:48–53.   m. [14:3] Lv 13:46. n. [14:4] Nm 19:6.   o. [14:7] Lv 16:21–22.   p. [14:8] Lv 15:13, 28.

shall again shave off all hair, of the head, beard, and eyebrows—all hair must be shaved—and also wash his garments and bathe the body in water, and so become clean.

¹⁰On the eighth day the individual shall take two unblemished male lambs, one unblemished yearling ewe lamb, three tenths of an ephah of bran flour mixed with oil for a grain offering, and one log* of oil. ¹¹The priest who performs the purification ceremony shall place the person who is being purified, as well as all these offerings, before the Lord at the entrance of the tent of meeting. ¹²Taking one of the male lambs, the priest shall present it as a reparation offering,�q along with the log of oil, raising them as an elevatedʳ offering before the Lord. ¹³This lamb shall be slaughtered in the sacred place where the purification offering and the burnt offering are slaughtered, because the reparation offering is like the purification offering; it belongs to the priest and is most holy. ¹⁴†ˢThen the priest shall take some of the blood of the reparation offering and put it on the lobe of the right ear, the thumb of the right hand, and the big toe of the right foot of the person being purified. ¹⁵The priest shall also take the log of oil and pour some of it into the palm of his own left hand; ¹⁶then, dipping his right finger in the oil on his left palm, he shall sprinkle some of it with his finger seven times before the Lord. ¹⁷Of the oil left in his hand the priest shall put some on the lobe of the right ear, the thumb of the right hand, and the big toe of the right foot of the person being purified, over the blood of the reparation offering. ¹⁸The rest of the oil in his hand the priest shall put on the headᵗ of the one being purified. Thus shall the priest make atonement for the individual before the Lord. ¹⁹The priest shall next offer the purification offering,ᵘ thus making atonement on behalf of the one being purified from the uncleanness. After this the burnt offering shall be slaughtered. ²⁰The priest shall offer the burnt offeringᵛ and the grain offering on the altar before the Lord. Thus shall the priest make atonement for the person, and the individual will become clean.

**Poor Person's Sacrifices.** ²¹If a person is poor and cannot afford so much,ʷ that person shall take one male lamb for a reparation offering, to be used as an elevated offering in atonement, one tenth of an ephah of bran flour mixed with oil for a grain offering, a log of oil, ²²and two turtledoves or pigeons, which the individual

can more easily afford, the one as a purification offering and the other as a burnt offering. ²³On the eighth day of purification the person shall bring them to the priest, at the entrance of the tent of meeting before the Lord. ²⁴Taking the lamb of the reparation offering, along with the log of oil, the priest shall raise them as an elevated offering before the Lord. ²⁵When the lamb of the reparation offering has been slaughtered, the priest shall take some of its blood, and put it on the lobe of the right ear, on the thumb of the right hand, and on the big toe of the right foot of the person being purified. ²⁶The priest shall then pour some of the oil into the palm of his own left hand ²⁷and with his right finger sprinkle some of the oil in his left palm seven times before the Lord. ²⁸Some of the oil in his hand the priest shall also put on the lobe of the right ear, the thumb of the right hand, and the big toe of the right foot of the person being purified, where he had sprinkled the blood of the reparation offering. ²⁹The rest of the oil in his hand the priest shall put on the head of the one being purified. Thus shall he make atonement for the individual before the Lord. ³⁰Then, of the turtledoves or pigeons, such as the person can afford, ³¹the priest shall offer one as a purification offering and the other as a burnt offering,ˣ along with the grain offering. Thus shall the priest make atonement before the Lord for the person who is being purified. ³²This is the ritual for one afflicted with a scaly infection who has insufficient means for purification.

**Fungal Infection of Houses.** ³³‡The Lord said to Moses and Aaron: ³⁴When you come into the land of Canaan, which I am giving you to possess, if I putʸ a fungal infection in any house of the land you occupy, ³⁵the owner of the house shall come and report to the priest, "Something like an infection has appeared in my house." ³⁶The priest shall then order the house to be cleared out before he goes in to examine the infection, lest everything in the house become unclean. Only after this is he to go in to examine the house. ³⁷If the priest, upon inspection, finds that the infection on the walls of the house consists of greenish or reddish spotsᶻ which seem to go deeper than the surface of the wall, ³⁸he shall go out of the house to the doorway and quarantine the house for seven days. ³⁹On the seventh day the priest shall return. If, upon inspection, he finds that the infection has spread on the walls, ⁴⁰he shall order the infected stones to be pulled out and cast in an unclean place outside the city. ⁴¹The whole inside of the house

---

*[14:10] **Log**: a liquid measure of capacity attested in the Bible only here. It is apparently equal in capacity to one-half liter.

†[14:14–17] The application of blood and oil here facilitates the movement of the person from the severely impure to the pure profane sphere; it reintegrates him or her into the community. Cf. 8:23–24.

q. [14:12] Lv 7:1–10.   r. [14:12] Lv 7:30.   s. [14:14] Lv 8:23–24.
t. [14:18] Lv 8:12, 30.   u. [14:19] Lv 4.   v. [14:20] Lv 1.   w. [14:21] Lv 5:7, 11; 12:8.

‡[14:33–53] Discussion of fungi in houses is probably delayed until here because it deals with a case pertaining to living in the land (v. 34) as opposed to the foregoing cases which apply even in the wilderness. The rules on fabrics (13:47–58) apply to the tent dwellings in the wilderness.

x. [14:31] Lv 1:14–17; 5:7–10.   y. [14:34] Nm 12:9–15; 2 Kgs 15:4–5; 2 Chr 26:16–21.   z. [14:37] Lv 13:49.

shall then be scraped, and the mortar that has been scraped off shall be dumped in an unclean place outside the city. ⁴²Then other stones shall be brought and put in the place of the old stones, and new mortar obtained and plastered on the house. ⁴³If the infection breaks out once more in the house after the stones have been pulled out and the house has been scraped and replastered, ⁴⁴the priest shall come; and if, upon inspection, he finds that the infection has spread in the house, it is a corrosive fungus in the house, and it is unclean. ⁴⁵It shall be pulled down, and all its stones, beams and mortar shall be hauled away to an unclean place outside the city. ⁴⁶ᵃWhoever enters a house while it is quarantined shall be unclean until evening. ⁴⁷Whoever sleeps or eats in such a house shall also wash his garments.

⁴⁸ᵇIf the priest finds, when he comes to the house, that the infection has in fact not spread in the house after the plastering, he shall declare the house clean, since the infection has been healed. ⁴⁹To purify the house, he shall take two birds, as well as cedar wood, scarlet yarn, and hyssop. ⁵⁰One of the birds he shall slaughter over an earthen vessel with fresh water in it. ⁵¹Then, taking the cedar wood, the hyssop and the scarlet yarn, together with the living bird, he shall dip them all in the blood of the slaughtered bird and the fresh water, and sprinkle the house seven times. ⁵²Thus he shall purify the house with the bird's blood and the fresh water, along with the living bird, the cedar wood, the hyssop, and the scarlet yarn. ⁵³He shall then let the living bird fly away over the countryside outside the city. Thus he shall make atonement for the house, and it will be clean.

⁵⁴This is the ritual for every kind of human scaly infection and scall, ⁵⁵and for fungus diseases in garments and houses— ⁵⁶for marks, lesions and blotches— ⁵⁷to give direction when there is a state of uncleanness and when a state of cleanness. This is the ritual for scaly infection.

## CHAPTER 15

**Sexual Uncleanness.*** ¹The Lord said to Moses and Aaron: ²ᵃSpeak to the Israelites and tell them: When any man has a genital discharge, he is thereby unclean.ᶜ ³Such is his uncleanness from this discharge, whether his body‡ drains freely with the discharge or is blocked up from the discharge. His uncleanness is on him all the days that his body discharges or is blocked up from his discharge; this is his uncleanness. ⁴Any bed on which the man with the discharge

lies is unclean, and any article on which he sits is unclean. ⁵Anyone who touches his bed shall wash his garments, bathe in water, and be unclean until evening. ⁶Whoever sits on an article on which the man with the discharge was sitting shall wash his garments, bathe in water, and be unclean until evening. ⁷Whoever touches the body of the man with the discharge shall wash his garments, bathe in water, and be unclean until evening. ⁸If the man with the discharge spits on a clean person, the latter shall wash his garments, bathe in water, and be unclean until evening. ⁹Any saddle on which the man with the discharge rides is unclean. ¹⁰Whoever touches anything that was under him shall be unclean until evening; whoever carries any such thing shall wash his garments, bathe in water, and be unclean until evening.ᵈ ¹¹Anyone whom the man with the discharge touches with his unrinsed hands shall wash his garments, bathe in water, and be unclean until evening. ¹²Earthenware touched by the man with the discharge shall be broken; and every wooden article shall be rinsed with water.

¹³When a man with a discharge becomes clean§ of his discharge, he shall count seven daysᵉ for his purification. Then he shall wash his garments and bathe his body in fresh water, and so he will be clean. ¹⁴On the eighth day he shall take two turtledoves or two pigeons,ᶠ and going before the Lord, to the entrance of the tent of meeting, he shall give them to the priest, ¹⁵who shall offer them up, the one as a purification offering and the other as a burnt offering. Thus shall the priest make atonement before the Lord for the man because of his discharge.

¹⁶¶When a man has an emission of semen, he shall bathe his whole body in water and be unclean until evening.ᵍ ¹⁷Any piece of cloth or leather with semen on it shall be washed with water and be unclean until evening.

¹⁸If a man has sexual relations with a woman, they shall both bathe in water and be unclean until evening.

¹⁹**When a woman has a flow of blood from her body, she shall be in a state of menstrual uncleanness for seven days. Anyone who touches her shall be unclean until evening.ʰ

---

*[15:1–33] Sexual discharges may be unclean partly because they involve the loss of life fluids or are otherwise involved with phenomena at the margins of life and death.

†[15:2–3] The uncleanness here is perhaps a discharge of pus because of urethritis (often but not solely associated with gonorrhea).

‡[15:3] **Body**: here a euphemism in the Hebrew for "penis."

§[15:13] **Becomes clean**: i.e., when his discharge ceases. The rite that follows is for purification, not a cure; see note on 14:1–32.

¶[15:16–18] Menstrual blood, semen, and other impurities in Lv 11–15 are considered "impure" either because they are force of life whose "loss" represents death or because, as uniquely human conditions, they are symbolically incompatible with the deity and the divine abode, the sanctuary. Lv 15:16 refers to a spontaneous nocturnal emission, and either because this marks life and death boundaries or because of its uniquely human (versus divine) character, any contact with it renders the object or person ritually unclean. Thus, in 15:18 it is not the marital act itself that is polluting, but only semen.

**[15:19–24] This is normal menstruation.

---

a. [14:46–47] cf. Lv 15:10.   b. [14:48] Lv 14:2–9.   c. [15:2] Nm 5:2.
d. [15:10] Lv 11:24–25, 27–28, 39–40; 14:46–47.   e. [15:13] Lv 14:8.   f. [15:14] Lv 12:8; 14:22.   g. [15:16] Ex 19:15; Dt 23:11–12; 1 Sm 21:6.   h. [15:19] Lv 12:2, 5; 2 Sm 11:4; Ez 36:17.

²⁰Anything on which she lies or sits during her menstrual period shall be unclean. ²¹Anyone who touches her bed shall wash his garments, bathe in water, and be unclean until evening. ²²Whoever touches any article on which she was sitting shall wash his garments, bathe in water, and be unclean until evening. ²³Whether an object* is on the bed or on something she sat upon, when the person touches it, that person shall be unclean until evening. ²⁴If a man lies with her, he contracts her menstrual uncleanness and shall be unclean for seven days;ᶦ every bed on which he then lies also becomes unclean.

²⁵†When a woman has a flow of blood for several days outside her menstrual period, or when her flow continues beyond the ordinary period, as long as she suffers this unclean flow she shall be unclean, just as during her menstrual period.ʲ ²⁶Any bed on which she lies during such a flow becomes unclean, as it would during her menstrual period, and any article on which she sits becomes unclean just as during her menstrual period. ²⁷Anyone who touches them becomes unclean; that person shall wash his garments, bathe in water, and be unclean until evening.

²⁸ᵏWhen she becomes clean from her flow, she shall count seven days; after this she becomes clean. ²⁹On the eighth day she shall take two turtledoves or two pigeons and bring them to the priest at the entrance of the tent of meeting. ³⁰The priest shall offer one of them as a purification offering and the other as a burnt offering. Thus shall the priest make atonement before the Lord for her because of her unclean flow.

³¹You shall warn the Israelites of their uncleanness, lest they die through their uncleanness by defiling my tabernacle,ˡ which is in their midst.

³²This is the ritual for the man with a discharge, or who has an emission of semen, and thereby becomes unclean; ³³as well as for the woman who has her menstrual period; or one who has a discharge, male or female; and also for the man who lies with an unclean woman.

## CHAPTER 16

**The Day of Atonement.** ¹‡After the death of Aaron's two sons,ᵐ who died when they encroached on the Lord's presence, the Lord spoke to Moses ²and said to him: Tell your brother Aaron that he is not to come whenever he pleases§ into the inner sanctuary, inside the veil,ⁿ in front of the cover on the ark, lest he die, for I reveal myself in a cloud above the ark's cover. ³Only in this way may Aaron enter the inner sanctuary. He shall bring a bull of the herd for a purification offering and a ram for a burnt offering. ⁴He shall wear the sacred linen tunic, with the linen pants underneath, gird himself with the linen sash and put on the linen turban.ᵒ But since these vestments are sacred, he shall not put them on until he has first bathed his body in water.ᵖ ⁵From the Israelite community he shall receive two male goats for a purification offering and one ram for a burnt offering.

⁶Aaron shall offer the bull, his purification offering, to make atonement¶ for himself and for his household. ⁷Taking the two male goats and setting them before the Lord at the entrance of the tent of meeting, ⁸he shall cast lots�q to determine which one is for the Lord and which for Azazel.**ʳ ⁹The goat that is determined by lot for the Lord, Aaron shall present and offer up as a purification offering. ¹⁰But the goat determined by lot for Azazel he shall place before the Lord alive, so that with it he may make atonement by sending it off to Azazel in the desert.

¹¹Thus shall Aaron offer his bull for the purification offering, to make atonement for himself and for his family. When he has slaughtered it, ¹²he shall take a censer full of glowing embers from the altar before the Lord, as well as a double handful of finely ground fragrant incense, and bringing them inside the veil, ¹³there before the Lord he shall put incense on the fire, so that a cloud of incense may shield the cover that is over the covenant, else he will die. ¹⁴Taking some of the bull's blood, he shall sprinkle it with his finger on the front of the ark's cover and likewise sprinkle some of the blood with his finger seven times in front of the cover.

---

*[15:23] **An object:** the Hebrew is unclear. This translation means that even an object on the woman's unclean bed or chair can mediate uncleanness to another, but only if all the object touched is still on the bed or article sat upon, thus forming a chain of simultaneous contact.

†[15:25–30] This is menstruation outside the normal cycle or for periods longer than normal. A woman with a chronic blood flow was healed by touching the tassel of Jesus' cloak (Mt 9:20–22; Mk 5:25–34; Lk 8:43–48).

‡[16:1–34] This is the narrative sequel of the story in chap. 10: The ritual in chapter 16 originally may have been an emergency rite in response to unexpected pollution of the sanctuary.

§[16:2] **Not to come whenever he pleases:** access to the various parts of the sanctuary is strictly controlled. Only the high priest can enter the most holy place, and only once a year. **The veil:** the Letter to the Hebrews makes use of the imagery of the Day of Atonement (in Hebrew *Yom Kippur*) to explain Jesus' sacrifice (Heb 9:1–14, 23–28). **Ark's cover:** the meaning of *kappōret* is not certain. It may be connected with the verb *kipper* "to atone, purge" (see note on v. 6) and thus refer to this part of the ark as a focus of atonement or purification.

¶[16:6] **Make atonement:** the Hebrew verb *kipper* refers specifically to the removal of sin and impurity (cf. Ex 30:10; Lv 6:23; 8:15; 16:16, 18, 20, 27, 33; Ez 43:20, 26; 45:20), thus "to purge" in vv. 16, 18, 20, and 33, and more generally to the consequence of the sacrificial procedure, which is atonement (cf. Lv 17:11). "Atonement" is preeminently a function of the purification sacrifice, but other sacrifices, except apparently for the communion sacrifice, achieve this as well.

**[16:8] **Azazel:** a name for a demon (meaning something like "angry/fierce god"). See note on 17:7.

---

i. [15:24] Lv 18:19; 20:18; Ez 18:6.   j. [15:25] Mt 9:20–22; Mk 5:25–34; Lk 8:43–48.   k. [15:28] Lv 15:13–15.   l. [15:31] Lv 5:2–3; 22:9; Nm 19:13, 20.   m. [16:1] Lv 10:1–5.

n. [16:2] Lv 23:26–32; Nm 29:7–11; Heb 9:6–28.   o. [16:4] Lv 8:7; Ex 28:1–40.   p. [16:4] Lv 8:6.   q. [16:8] Jos 7:14–20; Acts 1:26.   r. [16:8] Lv 17:7.

[15]Then he shall slaughter the goat of the people's purification offering, and bringing its blood inside the veil, he shall do with it as he did with the bull's blood, sprinkling it on the ark's cover and in front of it. [16]Thus he shall purge the inner sanctuary* of all the Israelites' impurities and trespasses, including all their sins. He shall do the same for the tent of meeting,† which is set up among them in the midst of their uncleanness. [17]No one else may be in the tent of meeting from the time he enters the inner sanctuary to make atonement until he departs. When he has made atonement for himself and his household, as well as for the whole Israelite assembly, [18†]he shall come out to the altar before the LORD and purge it also. Taking some of the bull's and the goat's blood, he shall put it on the horns around the altar, [19]and with his finger sprinkle some of the blood on it seven times.ᵗ Thus he shall purify it and sanctify it from the impurities of the Israelites.

**The Scapegoat.** [20]When he has finished purging the inner sanctuary, the tent of meeting and the altar, Aaron shall bring forward the live goat. [21]Laying both hands‡ on its head, he shall confess over it all the iniquities of the Israelites and their trespasses, including all their sins, and so put them on the goat's head.ᵘ He shall then have it led into the wilderness by an attendant. [22]The goat will carry off all their iniquities to an isolated region.ᵛ

When the goat is dispatched into the wilderness, [23]Aaron shall go into the tent of meeting, strip off the linen vestments he had put on when he entered the inner sanctuary, and leave them in the tent of meeting. [24]After bathing his body with water in a sacred place, he shall put on his regular vestments, and then come out and offer his own and the people's burnt offering, in atonement for himself and for the people, [25]and also burn the fat of the purification offering on the altar.

[26]The man who led away the goat for Azazel shall wash his garments and bathe his body in water; only then may he enter the camp. [27]The

bull and the goat of the purification offering whose blood was brought to make atonement in the inner sanctuary, shall be taken outside the camp,ʷ where their hides and flesh and dung shall be burned in the fire. [28]The one who burns them shall wash his garments and bathe his body in water; only then may he enter the camp.

**The Fast.** [29x]This shall be an everlasting statute for you: on the tenth day of the seventh month every one of you, whether a native or a resident alien, shall humble yourselves§ and shall do no work. [30]For on this day atonement is made for you to make you clean; of all your sins you will be cleansed before the LORD. [31]It shall be a sabbath of complete rest for you, on which you must humble yourselves—an everlasting statute.

[32]This atonement is to be made by the priest who has been anointed and ordained to the priesthood in succession to his father. He shall wear the linen garments, the sacred vestments, [33]and purge the most sacred part of the sanctuary, as well as the tent of meeting, and the altar. He shall also make atonement for the priests and all the people of the assembly. [34]This, then, shall be an everlasting statute for you: once a year atonement shall be made on behalf of the Israelites for all their sins. And Moses did as the LORD had commanded him.

# IV. HOLINESS LAWS

## CHAPTER 17

**Sacredness of Blood.** [1]The LORD said to Moses: [2]Speak to Aaron and his sons, as well as to all the Israelites, and tell them: This is what the LORD has commanded: [3¶]Any Israelite who slaughters an ox or a sheep or a goat, whether in the camp or outside of it, [4]without first bringing it to the entrance of the tent of meeting to present it as an offering to the LORD in front of the LORD's tabernacle, shall be judged guilty of bloodshed**ʸ— that individual has shed blood, and shall be cut off² from the people. [5]This is so that such sacrifices as they used to offer in the open field the Israelites shall henceforth bring to the LORD at the entrance of the tent of meeting, to the priest,

---

*[16:16] **Inner sanctuary**: this refers to the most holy room (vv. 2, 11–15). **Trespasses, including all their sins**: the term for "trespasses" (Heb. *pesha'im*), which has overtones of rebellion, and the phrase "all their sins" indicate that even sins committed intentionally are included (such as when the sinner "acts defiantly," as in Nm 15:30–31). This complements the scheme found in Lv 4 (see note on 4:3): intentional sins pollute the sanctuary more and penetrate even further than inadvertent sins; namely, to the most holy place. **The same for the tent of meeting**: this rite may be that found in 4:5–7, 16–18 where blood is sprinkled in the anterior room and blood is placed on the horns of the incense altar there. Cf. Ex 30:10.

†[16:18–19] Thus a third locale in the sanctuary complex, the open-air altar, is purified. See the summaries in 16:20, 33.

‡[16:21] **Both hands**: this gesture is for transferring sins to the head of the goat and is apparently different in meaning from the one-handed gesture that precedes the slaughtering of sacrificial animals (1:4; 3:2; 4:4; see note on 1:4).

§[16:29] **Humble yourselves**: also v. 31. The idiom used here (Heb. *'innâ nephesh*) involves mainly fasting (Ps 35:13), but probably prohibits other activities such as anointing (Dn 10:3) and sexual intercourse (2 Sm 12:15–24). Such acts of self-denial display the need for divine favor. Fasting is often undertaken in times of emergency and mourning (cf. 1 Sm 14:24; 2 Sm 1:12; 3:35; cf. Mk 2:18–22).

¶[17:3–4] Any animal slaughtered must be brought to the tent of meeting as an offering. This differs from Dt 12:15–28, which allows those living too far from the temple to slaughter an animal for food at home without offering it as a sacrifice.

**[17:4] **Guilty of bloodshed**: human beings and animals can incur blood guilt for killing human beings (cf. Gn 9:5–6); human beings can incur blood guilt for killing animals (see note on Lv 24:17–22).

---

s. [16:16] Lv 4:5–7, 16–18.   t. [16:19] Lv 4:25, 30, 34.   u. [16:21] Is 53:6; 2 Cor 5:21.   v. [16:22] Lv 14:7, 53; Is 53:11–12; Jn 1:29; 1 Pt 2:24.

w. [16:27] Lv 4:11–12; 6:23; Heb 13:11–13.   x. [16:29] Lv 23:27, 32; Nm 29:7.   y. [17:4] Lv 24:18.   z. [17:4] Lv 7:20.

and sacrifice them there as communion sacrifices to the LORD.$^a$ $^6$The priest will splash the
blood on the altar of the LORD at the entrance of
the tent of meeting and burn the fat for an odor
pleasing to the LORD. $^7$No longer shall they offer
their sacrifices to the demons* with whom they
prostituted themselves.$^b$ This shall be an everlasting statute for them and their descendants.

$^8$Tell them, therefore: Anyone, whether of the
house of Israel or of the aliens residing among
them, who offers a burnt offering or sacrifice
$^9$without bringing it to the entrance of the tent
of meeting to offer it to the LORD, shall be cut off
from the people. $^{10c}$As for anyone, whether of the
house of Israel or of the aliens residing among
them, who consumes any blood, I will set myself
against that individual and will cut that person
off from among the people, $^{11}$since the life of the
flesh is in the blood,$^d$ and I have given it to you
to make atonement† on the altar for yourselves,
because it is the blood as life that makes atonement. $^{12}$That is why I have told the Israelites: No
one among you, not even a resident alien, may
consume blood.

$^{13}$Anyone hunting,‡ whether of the Israelites or of the aliens residing among them, who
catches an animal or a bird that may be eaten,
shall pour out its blood and cover it with earth,$^e$
$^{14}$since the life of all flesh is its blood. I have told
the Israelites: You shall not consume the blood
of any flesh. Since the life of all flesh is its blood,
anyone who consumes it shall be cut off.

$^{15}$Everyone, whether a native or an alien,
who eats of an animal that died of itself or was
killed by a wild beast, shall wash his garments,
bathe in water, and be unclean until evening,
and then become clean.$^f$ $^{16}$If one does not wash
his garments and bathe, that person shall bear
the penalty.

## CHAPTER 18

**Laws Concerning Sexual Behavior.** $^1$The LORD
said to Moses: $^2$Speak to the Israelites and tell
them: I, the LORD, am your God.$^g$ $^3$You shall not
do as they do in the land of Egypt, where you
once lived, nor shall you do as they do in the

land of Canaan, where I am bringing you; do
not conform to their customs.$^g$ $^4$My decrees you
shall carry out, and my statutes you shall take
care to follow. I, the LORD, am your God. $^5$Keep,
then, my statutes and decrees, for the person
who carries them out will find life¶ through
them. I am the LORD.$^h$

$^6$"None of you shall approach a close rela-
tive†† to have sexual intercourse. I am the LORD.
$^{7‡‡}$You shall not disgrace your father by having
intercourse with your mother.$^i$ She is your own
mother; you shall not have intercourse with
her. $^8$You shall not have intercourse with your
father's wife, for that would be a disgrace to your
father. $^9$You shall not have intercourse with your
sister,$^{§§j}$ your father's daughter or your mother's
daughter, whether she was born in your own
household or born elsewhere. $^{10}$You shall not
have intercourse with your son's daughter or
with your daughter's daughter,¶¶ for that would
be a disgrace to you. $^{11}$You shall not have intercourse with the daughter whom your father's
wife bore to him in his household,$^k$ since she,
too, is your sister. $^{12}$You shall not have intercourse with your father's sister,$^l$ since she is your
father's relative. $^{13}$You shall not have intercourse
with your mother's sister, since she is your
mother's relative. $^{14}$You shall not disgrace your
father's brother by having sexual relations with
his wife,$^m$ since she, too, is your aunt. $^{15}$You shall
not have intercourse with your daughter-in-
law;***$^n$ she is your son's wife; you shall not have
intercourse with her. $^{16}$You shall not have intercourse with your brother's wife;†††$^o$ that would be
a disgrace to your brother. $^{17}$You shall not have
intercourse with a woman and also with her

---

¶ [18:5] **Find life**: in Dt 30:15–20 Moses sets before the
people life and death. The alternatives are set out in detail in
Lv 26 and Dt 28. Cf. Ez 20:11, 13, 21.

** [18:6–23] These laws deal with illicit sexual behavior. Lv
20:10–21 reiterates most of these cases, with penalties. Cf. also
Dt 27:15–26; Ez 22:7–12. The ordering of the cases in Lv 18
seems to be: blood relatives (vv. 6–13), those related by marriage (vv. 14–18), then other cases (vv. 19–23).

†† [18:6] **Close relative**: this refers to a blood relative and
includes those not specifically mentioned in the list, such as
one's own daughter and a full sister. **Have sexual intercourse**:
lit., "to uncover nakedness."

‡‡ [18:7–8] Cf. the story of Reuben lying with Bilhah, his
father's concubine and Rachel's maid (Gn 35:22; 49:4).

§§ [18:9, 11] Cf. actual or possible marriage to a half sister in
Gn 20:12 and 2 Sm 13:13.

¶¶ [18:10] Daughter incest is found in the story of Lot (Gn
19:30–38).

*** [18:15] Judah had intercourse with his daughter-in-law
Tamar (Gn 38), but did not know her true identity until her
pregnancy was discovered.

††† [18:16] This refers to cohabiting with one's sister-in-law
not only while the brother is alive, but also after he is dead. Dt
25:5–10 allows for the marriage to the wife of a brother when
that brother died without a male heir. Cf. Gn 38:6–14. It was
the violation of this law of Leviticus which aroused the wrath
of John the Baptist against Herod Antipas (Mt 14:4; Mk 6:18).

---

* [17:7] **Demons**: for Hebrew śe'îrîm, lit., "goats." Like the
demon Azazel (cf. 16:8, 10, 21–22), they dwell in the open
country (17:5). Cf. Is 13:21; 34:14.

† [17:11] **To make atonement**: this is probably to be understood in the context of liability for shedding animal blood (cf.
v. 4). Placing the blood on the altar exonerates the slaughterer
from guilt for the killing. See note on 16:6.

‡ [17:13] **Hunting**: game animals are not permitted as
offerings. One nonetheless has to treat the blood of these animals carefully by covering it with earth. Cf. Dt 12:16, 24.

§ [18:2] **I, the LORD, am your God**: this declaration
appears frequently elsewhere throughout chaps. 17–26, sometimes with a statement of God's holiness or his sanctifying
activity. It emphasizes the importance of the laws and the relationship of the divine lawgiver to the people.

---

a. [17:5] Lv 3:1–2, 7–8, 13.   b. [17:7] Ex 34:15; Dt 32:17; 2 Chr
11:15; 1 Cor 10:20.   c. [17:10–14] Lv 3:17; 7:26–27; Gn 9:4;
Dt 12:16, 23–24.   d. [17:11] Gn 9:4.   e. [17:13] Dt 12:15–16.
f. [17:15] Lv 11:39–40; 22:8.

g. [18:3] Lv 20:22–23.   h. [18:5] Ez 20:11, 13, 21; Gal 3:12.
i. [18:7] Lv 20:11; Dt 23:1; 27:20; 1 Cor 5:1.   j. [18:9] Lv 20:17; Dt
27:22.   k. [18:11] Lv 20:17.   l. [18:12] Lv 20:19.   m. [18:14] Lv
20:20.   n. [18:15] Lv 20:12.   o. [18:16] Lv 20:21; Dt 25:5–10; Mt
14:3–4; Mk 6:18.

daughter, nor shall you marry and have intercourse with her son's daughter or her daughter's daughter;*ᵖ* they are related to her. This would be shameful. ¹⁸While your wife is still living you shall not marry her sister as her rival and have intercourse with her.*�q*

¹⁹You shall not approach a woman to have intercourse with her while she is in her menstrual uncleanness.*ʳ* ²⁰You shall not have sexual relations with your neighbor's wife,*ˢ* defiling yourself with her. ²¹*ʳ*You shall not offer any of your offspring for immolation to Molech,† thus profaning the name of your God. I am the LORD. ²²You shall not lie with a male as with a woman;*ᵘ* such a thing is an abomination. ²³You shall not have sexual relations with an animal, defiling yourself with it; nor shall a woman set herself in front of an animal to mate with it; that is perverse.*ᵛ*

²⁴Do not defile yourselves by any of these things, because by them the nations whom I am driving out of your way have defiled themselves. ²⁵And so the land has become defiled, and I have punished it for its wickedness, and the land has vomited out its inhabitants.*ʷ* ²⁶You, however, must keep my statutes and decrees, avoiding all these abominations, both the natives and the aliens resident among you— ²⁷because the previous inhabitants did all these abominations and the land became defiled; ²⁸otherwise the land will vomit you out also for having defiled it, just as it vomited out the nations before you. ²⁹For whoever does any of these abominations shall be cut off from the people. ³⁰Heed my charge, then, not to observe the abominable customs that have been observed before your time, and thus become impure by them.*ˣ* I, the LORD, am your God.

## CHAPTER 19

**Various Rules of Conduct.** ¹The LORD said to Moses: ²Speak to the whole Israelite community and tell them: Be holy, for I, the LORD your God, am holy.*ᵗʸ* ³*§*Each of you revere your mother and father,*ᶻ* and keep my sabbaths.*ᵃ* I, the LORD, am your God.

⁴Do not turn aside to idols, nor make molten gods for yourselves.*ᵇ* I, the LORD, am your God.

⁵When you sacrifice your communion sacrifice to the LORD, you shall sacrifice it so that it is acceptable on your behalf. ⁶It must be eaten on the day of your sacrifice or on the following day. Whatever is left over until the third day shall be burned in fire. ⁷If any of it is eaten on the third day, it will be a desecrated offering and not be accepted;*ᶜ* ⁸whoever eats of it then shall bear the penalty for having profaned what is sacred to the LORD. Such a one shall be cut off*ᵈ* from the people.

⁹*§*When you reap the harvest of your land, you shall not be so thorough that you reap the field to its very edge, nor shall you gather the gleanings of your harvest.*ᵉ* ¹⁰Likewise, you shall not pick your vineyard bare, nor gather up the grapes that have fallen. These things you shall leave for the poor and the alien. I, the LORD, am your God.

¹¹**You shall not steal. You shall not deceive or speak falsely to one another.*ᶠ* ¹²You shall not swear falsely by my name, thus profaning the name of your God.*ᵍ* I am the LORD.

¹³You shall not exploit your neighbor. You shall not commit robbery. You shall not withhold overnight the wages of your laborer.*ʰ* ¹⁴†You shall not insult the deaf,*ⁱ* or put a stumbling block in front of the blind, but you shall fear your God. I am the LORD.

¹⁵You shall not act dishonestly in rendering judgment. Show neither partiality to the weak nor deference to the mighty, but judge your neighbor justly.*ⁱ* ¹⁶You shall not go about spreading slander among your people; nor shall you stand by idly when your neighbor's life is at stake. I am the LORD.

¹⁷‡‡You shall not hate any of your kindred in your heart. Reprove your neighbor openly so that you do not incur sin because of that person.*ⁱ*

---

*[18:20] Adultery in the Hebrew Bible and the ancient Near East is intercourse between a married or betrothed woman and any male. In the Bible it is generally punishable by the death of both individuals (20:10; cf. Dt 22:22–27). Intercourse with an unmarried or unbetrothed woman is not prohibited but carries responsibilities and fines (cf. Ex 22:15–16; Dt 22:28–29). Cf. Lv 19:20–22.

†[18:21] **Immolation to Molech**: the reference is to the custom of sacrificing children to the god Molech. Cf. Ez 16:20–21; 20:26, 31; 23:37. See note on Lv 20:1–5.

‡[19:2] **Be holy, for I . . . am holy**: in the writings commonly attributed to the Priestly collection, Israel is called to be holy through obeying God's precepts (11:44–45; 20:7–8, 24–26; Nm 15:40–41). Cf. Dt 14:2, 21; 26:19; and Ex 19:6.

§[19:3–4] Cf. the Decalogue laws on revering parents (Ex 20:12; Dt 5:16), keeping sabbaths (Ex 20:8–11; Dt 5:12–15), and not making or worshiping idols (Ex 20:2–6; Dt 5:7–10).

¶[19:9–10] The Israelites maintain the poor in part by letting them gather unharvested portions of fields and vineyards. Cf. 23:22; Ru 2:1–10.

**[19:11–13] Cf. the Decalogue commandments against stealing (Ex 20:15; Dt 5:19), wrongly using God's name (Ex 20:7; Dt 5:11), and swearing falsely against another (Ex 20:16; Dt 5:20).

††[19:14] In Dt 27:18 a curse falls on the head of the one who misleads the blind.

‡‡[19:17–18] These verses form a unit and describe different attitudes and actions towards one's fellow Israelites. A separate passage is necessary to advise a similar attitude toward aliens (vv. 33–34). Cf. 25:39–46. The admonition at the end of v. 18 came to be viewed in Judaism and Christianity as one of the central commandments. (See Mt 22:34–40; Mk 12:28–34; Lk 10:25–28; cf. Mt 19:19; Rom 13:8–10; Gal 5:14). The New Testament urges love for enemies as well as neighbors (Mt 5:43–48; Lk 6:27–36; cf. Prv 25:21–22).

---

p. [18:17] Lv 20:14; Dt 27:23.   q. [18:18] Gn 29:27–28.   r. [18:19] Lv 15:24, 33; 20:18; Ez 18:6; 22:10.   s. [18:20] Lv 20:10; Ex 20:14; Dt 5:18; 22:22; Mt 5:27–30; Jn 8:4–5.   t. [18:21] Lv 20:2–5; Dt 18:10; 1 Kgs 11:7; 2 Kgs 16:3.   u. [18:22] Lv 20:13; Gn 19:4–11; Jgs 19:22–30; Rom 1:27; 1 Cor 6:9.   v. [18:23] Lv 20:15–16; Ex 22:18; Dt 27:21.   w. [18:25] Lv 20:22.   x. [18:30] Lv 20:23; Dt 18:9.   y. [19:2] Lv 11:44.

z. [19:3] Lv 20:9; Ex 20:12.   a. [19:3] Lv 23:3.   b. [19:4] Lv 26:1; Ex 20:3–5; 34:17; Dt 5:8; 27:15.   c. [19:7] Lv 7:15–18.   d. [19:8] Lv 7:20.   e. [19:9] Lv 23:22; Dt 24:19–22.   f. [19:11] Ex 20:15–16.   g. [19:12] Ex 20:7; Mt 5:33–37.   h. [19:13] Dt 24:14–15.   i. [19:15] Ex 23:2–3; Dt 1:17; 16:19; Ps 82:2; Prv 24:23.   j. [19:17] Mt 18:15; Lk 17:3; Gal 6:1.

¹⁸Take no revenge and cherish no grudge against your own people. You shall love your neighbor as yourself. I am the Lord.ᵏ

¹⁹*Keep my statutes: do not breed any of your domestic animals with others of a different species; do not sow a field of yours with two different kinds of seed; and do not put on a garment woven with two different kinds of thread.ˡ

²⁰†ᵐIf a man has sexual relations with a female slave who has been acquired by another man but has not yet been redeemed or given her freedom, an investigation shall be made. They shall not be put to death, because she has not been freed. ²¹The man shall bring to the entrance of the tent of meeting as his reparation to the Lord a ram as a reparation offering.ⁿ ²²With the ram of the reparation offering the priest shall make atonement before the Lord for the wrong the man has committed, so that he will be forgiven for the wrong he has committed.

²³When you come into the land and plant any fruit tree there,ᵒ first look upon its fruit as if it were uncircumcised. For three years, it shall be uncircumcised for you; it may not be eaten. ²⁴In the fourth year, however, all of its fruit shall be dedicated to the Lord in joyous celebration. ²⁵Not until the fifth year may you eat its fruit, to increase the yield for you. I, the Lord, am your God.

²⁶Do not eat anything with the blood still in it.ᵖ Do not recite charms or practice soothsaying.‡�q ²⁷Do not clip your hair at the temples, nor spoil the edges of your beard. ²⁸Do not lacerate your bodies for the dead, and do not tattoo yourselves.§ʳ I am the Lord.

²⁹You shall not degrade your daughter by making a prostitute of her;ˢ otherwise the land will prostitute itself and become full of lewdness. ³⁰Keep my sabbaths, and reverence my sanctuary.ᵗ I am the Lord.

³¹Do not turn to ghosts or consult spirits, by which you will be defiled.ᵘ I, the Lord, am your God.

³²Stand up in the presence of the aged, show respect for the old, and fear your God. I am the Lord.

³³When an alien resides with you in your land, do not mistreat such a one.ᵛ ³⁴You shall treat the alien who resides with you no differently than the natives born among you; you shall love the alien as yourself; for you too were once aliens in the land of Egypt.ʷ I, the Lord, am your God.

³⁵Do not act dishonestly in using measures of length or weight or capacity. ³⁶You shall have a true scale and true weights, an honest ephah and an honest hin.¶ˣ I, the Lord, am your God, who brought you out of the land of Egypt. ³⁷Be careful, then, to observe all my statutes and decrees. I am the Lord.

## CHAPTER 20

**Penalties for Various Sins.** ¹**The Lord said to Moses: ²Tell the Israelites: Anyone, whether an Israelite or an alien residing in Israel, who gives offspring to Molech shall be put to death.ʸ The people of the land shall stone that person. ³ᵃI myself will turn against and cut offᵃ that individual from among the people; for in the giving of offspring to Molech, my sanctuary was defiledᵇ and my holy name was profaned. ⁴If the people of the land condone the giving of offspring to Molech, by failing to put the wrongdoer to death, ⁵I myself will turn against that individual and his or her family, and I will cut off from their people both the wrongdoer and all who follow this person by prostituting themselves with Molech.

⁶Should anyone turn to ghosts and spirits and prostitute oneself with them,ᶜ I will turn against that person and cut such a one off from among the people. ⁷Sanctify yourselves, then, and be holy; for I, the Lord, your God,ᵈ am holy. ⁸Be careful, therefore, to observe my statutes. I, the Lord, make you holy.

⁹Anyone who curses father or mother shall be put to death;††ᵉ and having cursed father or mother, such a one will bear the bloodguilt.‡‡

---

*[19:19] One reason why mixtures are prohibited seems to be that they are holy (see Dt 22:9, 10–11). Israelites are allowed mixtures in the wearing of fringes on the edges or corners of their clothing (Nm 15:37–41; Dt 22:12). Some mixtures are considered abominations (cf. Lv 18:23; Dt 22:5).

†[19:20–22] On adultery, see note on 18:20. Here it is not adultery in the technical sense since the woman is not free. A reparation offering is required as a penalty (see 5:14–26).

‡[19:26] **Recite charms . . . soothsaying**: methods of divination (cf. Gn 44:5, 15; Is 2:6; Ez 21:26–28). Legitimate means of learning the future or God's will were through the Urim and Thummim stones (see Lv 8:8), lots (see Lv 16:8) and prophets (cf. Dt 18:9–22; 1 Sm 28:6–7).

§[19:28] **Do not tattoo yourselves**: see note on Gn 4:15. This prohibition probably refers only to the common ancient Near Eastern practice of branding a slave with the owner's name as well as branding the devotees of a god with its name.

¶[19:36] **Ephah**: see note on Is 5:10; **hin**: see note on Ez 45:24.

**[20:1–5] The term Molech may refer to a deity, perhaps with an underworld association, and the activity forbidden here may be connected with divination. Cf. Dt 18:10; 2 Kgs 17:17; 21:6. In the kingdom of Judah the cult appears to have been practiced in the Valley of Hinnom, just outside Jerusalem on the west and south (2 Kgs 23:10; Jer 32:35).

††[20:9] **Curses father or mother . . . put to death**: this is more than a simple expletive uttered in anger against one's parents. See note on Ex 21:17.

‡‡[20:9–21] **Bloodguilt**: these penalties, beginning with cursing one's parents, reflect the concerns of a patriarchal society that the breakdown of one's relations with one's

---

k. [19:18] Mt 5:43; 19:19; 22:39; Mk 12:31; Rom 13:9; Gal 5:14; Jas 2:8; 1 Jn 3:14.  l. [19:19] Dt 22:9–12.  m. [19:20] Dt 22:22–29.  n. [19:21] Lv 5:14–26.  o. [19:23] Dt 20:19–20.  p. [19:26] Lv 17:10.  q. [19:26] Dt 18:10; 2 Kgs 17:17; 21:6; 2 Chr 33:6.  r. [19:28] Lv 21:5.  s. [19:29] Lv 21:7, 14.  t. [19:30] Lv 19:3.  u. [19:31] Lv 20:6, 27; Dt 18:11; Is 8:19.

v. [19:33] Ex 22:20; 23:9; Jer 22:3; Mal 3:5.  w. [19:34] Dt 10:19.  x. [19:36] Dt 25:13–16; Prv 16:11; Am 8:5; Mi 6:10–11.  y. [20:2] Lv 18:21; Dt 12:31; 18:10; 2 Kgs 16:3; 17:17; 21:6; 23:10; Jer 32:35.  z. [20:3] Ez 23:39.  a. [20:3] Lv 7:20.  b. [20:3] Lv 15:31.  c. [20:6] Lv 19:31.  d. [20:7] Lv 11:44.  e. [20:9] Lv 19:3; Ex 21:17; Dt 21:18–21; Prv 20:20; Mt 15:4; Mk 7:10.

¹⁰*If a man commits adultery with his neighbor's wife,ᶠ both the adulterer and the adulteress shall be put to death. ¹¹If a man disgraces his father by lying with his father's wife,ᵍ the two of them shall be put to death; their bloodguilt is upon them. ¹²If a man lies with his daughter-in-law,ʰ both of them shall be put to death; they have done what is perverse; their bloodguilt is upon them. ¹³If a man lies with a male as with a woman,ⁱ they have committed an abomination; the two of them shall be put to death; their bloodguilt is upon them. ¹⁴If a man marries a woman and her mother also,ʲ that is shameful conduct; the man and the two women as well shall be burned to death, so that shamefulness may not be found among you. ¹⁵If a man has sexual relations with an animal,ᵏ the man shall be put to death, and you shall kill the animal. ¹⁶If a woman goes up to any animal to mate with it,ˡ you shall kill the woman and the animal; they shall both be put to death; their bloodguilt is upon them. ¹⁷If a man marries his sister,ᵐ his father's daughter or his mother's daughter, and they have intercourse with each other, that is disgraceful; they shall be publicly cut off† from the people; the man shall bear the penalty of having had intercourse with his own sister. ¹⁸If a man lies with a woman during her menstrual period and has intercourse with her, he has laid bare the source of her flow and she has uncovered it.ⁿ The two of them shall be cut off from the people. ¹⁹You shall not have intercourse with your mother's sister or your father's sister,ᵒ because that dishonors one's own flesh; they shall bear their penalty. ²⁰If a man lies with his uncle's wife, he disgraces his uncle;ᵖ they shall bear the penalty; they shall die childless. ²¹If a man takes his brother's wife, it is severe defilement and he has disgraced his brother;�q they shall be childless.

²²Be careful to observe all my statutes and all my decrees; otherwise the land where I am bringing you to dwell will vomit you out.ʳ ²³Do not conform, therefore, to the customs of the nationsˢ whom I am driving out of your way, because all these things that they have done have filled me with disgust for them. ²⁴But to you I have said:ᵗ You shall take possession of their land. I am giving it to you to possess, a land flowing with milk and honey. I, the LORD, am

your God, who have set you apart from other peoples. ²⁵ᵘYou, too, must set apart, then, the clean animals from the unclean, and the clean birds from the unclean, so that you do not make yourselves detestable through any beast or bird or any creature which creeps on the ground that I have set apart for you as unclean. ²⁶To me, therefore, you shall be holy; for I, the LORD, am holy,ᵛ and I have set you apart from other peoples to be my own.

²⁷A man or a woman who acts as a medium or clairvoyantʷ shall be put to death. They shall be stoned to death; their bloodguilt is upon them.

## CHAPTER 21

**Sanctity of the Priesthood.** ¹ˣThe LORD said to Moses: Speak to the priests, Aaron's sons, and tell them: None of you shall make himself unclean for any dead person among his kindred,ˣ ²except for his nearest relatives, his mother or father, his son or daughter, his brotherʸ ³or his unmarried sister, who is of his own family while she remains single; for these he may make himself unclean. ⁴But as a husband among his kindred§ he shall not make himself unclean and thus profane himself.

⁵The priests shall not make bald the crown of their head, nor shave the edges of their beard, nor lacerate their body.ᶻ ⁶They shall be holy to their God, and shall not profane their God's name, since they offer the oblations of the LORD, the food of their God; so they must be holy.

⁷*A priest shall not marry a woman debased by prostitution, nor a woman who has been divorced by her husband; for the priest is holy to his God.ᵃ ⁸Honor him as holy for he offers the foodᵇ of your God; he shall be holy to you, because I, the LORD, am holy who make you holy.

⁹If a priest's daughter debases herself by prostitution, she thereby debases her father; she shall be burned with fire.ᶜ

¹⁰The most exalted of the priests, upon whose head the anointing oil has been poured and who has been ordained to wear the special

---

parents can lead to the breakdown of all other familial relationships, resulting in the breakdown of society.

*[20:10–21] See 18:6–23 and notes there. It appears that the inclusion of various penalties in 20:10–21 accounts for the different order of the cases here compared to the order found in 18:6–23. The reason why the offenses in 20:10–21 carry different penalties, however, is not clear. Perhaps the cases in vv. 17–21 were considered slightly less serious, being condemned but not criminally prosecuted.

†[20:17] **Cut off:** see note on 7:20.

‡[21:1–12] While off duty the regular priests are not to become corpse-contaminated except for the close relatives listed in vv. 2–3. While on duty they presumably could not become impure at all. The high priest is restricted from all corpse contamination, on or off duty (vv. 11–12). Lay Israelites are not restricted from corpse contamination, except when in contact with what is holy (cf. Dt 26:14). See note on Lv 11:39–40. Israelites who undertake a nazirite vow enter into a sanctified state and 'cannot contact corpses (Nm 6:6–12). Cf. Ez 44:25–27.

§[21:4] **Husband among his kindred:** this probably refers to relatives by marriage and may even include his wife.

¶[21:7] The ideal seems to be that a priest marry a virgin. This is explicitly stated for the high priest (cf. vv. 13–14; so also Ez 44:22, except there priests may marry widows of priests). The high priest has the added limitation that his wife must come from his kindred, i.e., the priestly family (cf. Ez 44:22).

---

f. [20:10] Lv 18:20.　g. [20:11] Lv 18:8.　h. [20:12] Lv 18:15.　i. [20:13] Lv 18:22.　j. [20:14] Lv 18:17.　k. [20:15] Lv 18:23.　l. [20:16] Lv 18:23.　m. [20:17] Lv 18:9.　n. [20:18] Lv 18:19.　o. [20:19] Lv 18:12–13.　p. [20:20] Lv 18:14.　q. [20:21] Lv 18:16.　r. [20:22] Lv 18:25, 28.　s. [20:23] Lv 18:30.　t. [20:24] Ex 3:8, 17.

u. [20:25] Lv 11:2–47; Dt 14:4–20.　v. [20:26] Lv 11:44.　w. [20:27] Lv 19:31; Ex 22:17; Dt 18:11.　x. [21:1] Ez 44:25–27.　y. [21:2] Lv 10:6–7.　z. [21:5] Lv 19:27–28; Ez 44:20.　a. [21:7] Lv 19:29; Ez 44:22.　b. [21:8] Lv 1:9.　c. [21:9] Gn 38:24.

vestments, shall not dishevel his hair or rend his garments, [11]nor shall he go near any dead person.[d] Not even for his father or mother may he thus become unclean; [12]nor shall he leave the sanctuary and profane the sanctuary of his God, for the consecration of the anointing oil of his God is upon him.[e] I am the LORD.

[13]He shall marry only a woman who is a virgin. [14]He shall not marry a widow or a woman who has been divorced or one who has been debased by prostitution, but only a virgin, taken from his kindred, he shall marry,[f] [15]so that he not profane his offspring among his kindred. I, the LORD, make him holy.

**Priestly Blemishes.**[*] [16]The LORD said to Moses: [17]Say to Aaron: None of your descendants, throughout their generations, who has any blemish shall come forward to offer the food of his God. [18]Anyone who has any of the following blemishes may not come forward:[g] he who is blind, or lame, or who has a split lip, or a limb too long, [19]or a broken leg or arm, [20]or who is a hunchback or dwarf or has a growth in the eye, or who is afflicted with sores, scabs, or crushed testicles. [21]No descendant of Aaron the priest who has any such blemish may draw near to offer the oblations of the LORD; on account of his blemish he may not draw near to offer the food of his God. [22]He may, however, eat the food of his God: of the most sacred as well as sacred offerings.[h] [23]Only, he may not enter through the veil nor draw near to the altar on account of his blemish; he shall not profane my sacred precincts, for it is I, the LORD, who make them holy.

[24]Moses, therefore, told this to Aaron and his sons and to all the Israelites.

## CHAPTER 22

**Priestly Purity.**[†] [1]The LORD said to Moses: [2]Tell Aaron and his sons to treat with respect the sacred offerings which the Israelites consecrate to me; otherwise they will profane my holy name. I am the LORD.

[3†]Tell them: If any one of you, or of your descendants in any future generation, dares, while he is in a state of uncleanness, to draw near the sacred offerings which the Israelites consecrate to the LORD, such a one shall be cut off from my presence.[i] I am the LORD.

[4]No descendant of Aaron who is stricken with a scaly infection,[j] or who suffers from a genital discharge,[k] may eat of the sacred offerings, until he again becomes clean. Moreover, if anyone touches a person who has become unclean by contact with a corpse,[l] or if anyone has had an emission of semen,[m] [5]or if anyone touches any swarming creature[n] whose uncleanness is contagious or any person whose uncleanness, of whatever kind it may be, is contagious—[o] [6]the one who touches such as these shall be unclean until evening and may not eat of the sacred portions until he has first bathed his body in water.[p] [7]Then, when the sun sets, he shall be clean.[q] Only then may he eat of the sacred offerings, for they are his food. [8]He shall not make himself unclean by eating of any animal that has died of itself or has been killed by wild beasts.[r] I am the LORD.

[9]They shall keep my charge so that they will not bear the punishment in this matter and die[s] for their profanation. I am the LORD who makes them holy.

[10]Neither an unauthorized person nor a priest's tenant or laborer may eat of any sacred offering.[t] [11]But a slave[§] whom a priest acquires by purchase or who is born in his house may eat of his food. [12**]A priest's daughter who is married to an unauthorized person may not eat of the sacred contributions. [13]But if a priest's daughter is widowed or divorced and, having no children, returns to her father's house, she may then eat of her father's food as in her youth. No unauthorized person, however, may eat of it. [14]If such a one eats of a sacred offering through inadvertence, that person shall make restitution to the priest for the sacred offering, with an increment of one fifth of the amount. [15]The priests shall not allow the sacred offerings which the Israelites contribute to the LORD to be profaned[v] [16]nor make them incur a penalty when they eat their sacred offerings. For I, the LORD, make them holy.

**Unacceptable Victims.** [17††]The LORD said to Moses: [18]Speak to Aaron and his sons and to all the Israelites, and tell them: When anyone of the house of Israel, or any alien residing in Israel, who presents an offering, brings a burnt offering[w] as a votive offering or as a voluntary offering to the LORD, [19]if it is to be acceptable

---

§[22:8] See note on 11:39–40.

¶[22:11] **Slave:** in contrast to the tenant or hired worker of v. 10, the slave, who is by definition a foreigner, is part of the priest's household and therefore may eat of sacrifices.

**[22:12–13] A priest's daughter, when a dependent of her father, may eat of the lesser holy offerings.

††[22:17–25] This passage complements the section on the bodily imperfections of priests in 21:16–23. The laws taken together indicate that whoever and whatever approaches and contacts the altar needs to be physically unimpaired.

---

*[21:16–23] Though priests with certain bodily imperfections cannot serve at the altar (vv. 18–20), they are not impure, since they may still eat of the offerings, which are holy, and do so within the sanctuary precincts since it is there the most holy offerings are to be eaten (v. 22).

†[22:1–16] While priests with bodily imperfections may eat the holy sacrifices (21:16–23), those impure and those not of the priestly household may not.

‡[22:3–8] On uncleanness, see chaps. 11–15 and notes there.

---

d. [21:11] Lv 10:4–7.   e. [21:12] Lv 10:7.   f. [21:14] Ez 44:22.   g. [21:18] Lv 22:19–25; Dt 23:2–9.   h. [21:22] Nm 2:3, 10; 6:29; 7:6, 34.   i. [22:3] Lv 7:20–21.

j. [22:4] Lv 13–14.   k. [22:4] Lv 15:2–18.   l. [22:4] Nm 19:14–22.   m. [22:4] Lv 15:16.   n. [22:5] Lv 11:29–31.   o. [22:5] Lv 15:2–12, 18–27.   p. [22:6] Lv 17:15; Nm 19:7–8, 19; Heb 10:22.   q. [22:7] Dt 23:12.   r. [22:8] Lv 11:39–40; Ez 44:31.   s. [22:9] Lv 15:31.   t. [22:10] Mt 12:4.   u. [22:14] Lv 5:15–16.   v. [22:15] Lv 19:8; Nm 18:32.   w. [22:18] Lv 1:3.

for you, it must be an unblemished male of the herd, of the sheep or of the goats.*ˣ* ²⁰You shall not offer one that has any blemish, for such a one would not be acceptable on your behalf.*ʸ* ²¹When anyone presents a communion sacrifice*ᶻ* to the Lᴏʀᴅ from the herd or the flock in fulfillment of a vow, or as a voluntary offering, if it is to find acceptance, it must be unblemished; it shall not have any blemish. ²²One that is blind or lame or maimed, or one that has running lesions or sores or scabs, you shall not offer to the Lᴏʀᴅ; do not put such an animal on the altar as an oblation to the Lᴏʀᴅ. ²³*An ox or a sheep that has a leg that is too long or is stunted you may indeed present as a voluntary offering, but it will not be acceptable as a votive offering. ²⁴One that has its testicles bruised or crushed or torn out or cut off you shall not offer to the Lᴏʀᴅ. You shall neither do this in your own land ²⁵nor receive from a foreigner any such animals to offer up as the food of your God; since they are deformed or blemished, they will not be acceptable on your behalf.

²⁶†The Lᴏʀᴅ said to Moses: ²⁷When an ox or a lamb or a goat is born, it shall remain with its mother for seven days; only from the eighth day onward will it be acceptable, to be offered as an oblation to the Lᴏʀᴅ.*ᵃ* ²⁸You shall not slaughter an ox or a sheep on one and the same day with its young. ²⁹Whenever you offer a thanksgiving sacrifice to the Lᴏʀᴅ, so offer it that it may be acceptable on your behalf; ³⁰it must be eaten on the same day; none of it shall be left over until morning.*ᵇ* I am the Lᴏʀᴅ.

³¹Be careful to observe my commandments. I am the Lᴏʀᴅ. ³²Do not profane my holy name, that in the midst of the Israelites I may be hallowed. I, the Lᴏʀᴅ, make you holy, ³³who led you out of the land of Egypt to be your God. I am the Lᴏʀᴅ.

## CHAPTER 23

**Holy Days.**‡ ¹The Lᴏʀᴅ said to Moses: ²Speak to the Israelites and tell them: The following are the festivals*ᶜ* of the Lᴏʀᴅ, which you shall declare holy days. These are my festivals:

³For six days work may be done; but the seventh day is a sabbath of complete rest,§ a declared holy day; you shall do no work. It is the Lᴏʀᴅ's sabbath wherever you dwell.*ᵈ*

**Passover.** ⁴These are the festivals of the Lᴏʀᴅ, holy days which you shall declare at their proper time.*ᵉ* ⁵The Passover of the Lᴏʀᴅ¶ falls on the fourteenth day of the first month, at the evening twilight.*ᶠ* ⁶The fifteenth day of this month is the Lᴏʀᴅ's feast of Unleavened Bread. For seven days you shall eat unleavened bread.*ᵍ* ⁷On the first of these days you will have a declared holy day; you shall do no heavy work. ⁸On each of the seven days you shall offer an oblation to the Lᴏʀᴅ. Then on the seventh day you will have a declared holy day; you shall do no heavy work.

⁹**The Lᴏʀᴅ said to Moses: ¹⁰Speak to the Israelites and tell them: When you come into the land which I am giving you, and reap its harvest, you shall bring the first sheaf of your harvest to the priest, ¹¹who shall elevate*ʰ* the sheaf before the Lᴏʀᴅ that it may be acceptable on your behalf.*ⁱ* On the day after the sabbath†† the priest shall do this. ¹²On this day, when your sheaf is elevated, you shall offer to the Lᴏʀᴅ for a burnt offering an unblemished yearling lamb. ¹³Its grain offering shall be two tenths of an ephah of bran flour mixed with oil, as a sweet-smelling oblation to the Lᴏʀᴅ; and its libation shall be a fourth of a hin of wine. ¹⁴You shall not eat any bread or roasted grain or fresh kernels until this day, when you bring the offering for your God. This shall be a perpetual statute throughout your generations wherever you dwell.

**Pentecost.** ¹⁵Beginning with the day after the sabbath, the day on which you bring the sheaf for elevation, you shall count seven full weeks;*ʲ* ¹⁶you shall count to the day after the seventh week, fifty days.‡‡*ᵏ* Then you shall present a new

---

§[23:3] **Sabbath of complete rest**: the sabbath and the Day of Atonement are called "sabbaths of complete rest" (Ex 16:23; 31:15; 35:2; Lv 16:31; 23:32). Work of any sort is prohibited on these days (Lv 23:3, 28; Nm 29:7) as opposed to other holy days where only laborious work is prohibited but light work, such as preparing food, is allowed (Ex 12:16; cf. Lv 23:7, 8, 21, 25, 35, 36; Nm 28:18, 25, 26; 29:1, 12, 35).

¶[23:5–6] **The Passover of the Lᴏʀᴅ . . . feast of Unleavened Bread**: the two occasions were probably separate originally. Combined they celebrate the exodus from Egypt. Cf. Ex 12:1–20, 43–49; Nm 28:16–25.

**[23:9–14] Around Passover a first fruits offering is to be brought (see 2:14), consisting of a sheaf of barley, the crop that matures at this time of year.

††[23:11] **Day after the sabbath**: the singular term *shabbat* "sabbath" may mean "week" here and refer to the seven-day period of the feast of Unleavened Bread. According to this interpretation, the barley sheaf is offered the day after the week of Unleavened Bread. Others understand it as referring to the first or last day of Unleavened Bread.

‡‡[23:16–21] **Fifty days**: Pentecost. This festival occurs on a single day, fifty days after the feast of Unleavened Bread, elsewhere called the "feast of the Harvest" (Ex 23:16), "Day of First Fruits" (Nm 28:26), and "feast of Weeks" (Ex 34:22;

---

*[22:23] Burnt offerings and communion sacrifices brought as voluntary offerings may have slight defects, probably because they are freely given and do not depend upon a prior promise as do votive offerings.

†[22:26–30] Other activities and procedures that would impair sacrifice are appended here. The rules in vv. 27–28 are reminiscent of the rule not to boil a young goat in its mother's milk (Ex 23:19; 34:26; Dt 14:21) and not to take a bird and its eggs (Dt 22:6–7), all of which have a humanitarian tenor.

‡[23:1–44] This is paralleled by another calendar from the Priestly tradition, in Nm 28–29. Non-Priestly resumes of festal and holy observances are found in Ex 23:10–17; 34:18–24 and Dt 16:1–17.

x. [22:19] Lv 21:16–23. y. [22:20] Dt 15:21; 17:1; Mal 1:7–14. z. [22:21] Lv 3:1; 7:11. a. [22:27] Ex 22:29; 23:19. b. [22:30] Lv 7:15. c. [23:2] Nm 28–29; Dt 16:1–17.

d. [23:3] Lv 19:3; 26:2; Ex 20:8–11; 23:12; 31:14–15; 34:21; Nm 28:9–10; Dt 5:12–15; Lk 13:14. e. [23:4] Ex 23:14–19. f. [23:5] Ex 12:1–51; Nm 9:1–8; 28:16–25; Dt 16:1–8. g. [23:6] Ex 12:18; 13:3–10; 23:15; 34:18. h. [23:11] Lv 7:30. i. [23:11] Dt 26:2. j. [23:15] Ex 23:16; 34:22; Nm 28:26–31; Dt 16:9–12. k. [23:16] Acts 2:1.

grain offering to the LORD. [17]For the elevated offering of your first-ripened fruits to the LORD, you shall bring with you from wherever you live two loaves of bread made of two tenths of an ephah of bran flour and baked with leaven. [18]Besides the bread, you shall offer to the LORD a burnt offering of seven unblemished yearling lambs, one bull of the herd, and two rams, along with their grain offering and libations, as a sweet-smelling oblation to the LORD. [19]One male goat shall be sacrificed as a purification offering, and two yearling lambs as a communion sacrifice. [20]The priest shall elevate them—that is, the two lambs—with the bread of the first-ripened fruits as an elevated offering before the LORD; these shall be sacred to the LORD and belong to the priest. [21]On this same day you shall make a proclamation: there shall be a declared holy day for you; no heavy work may be done. This shall be a perpetual statute through all your generations wherever you dwell.

[22]When you reap the harvest of your land, you shall not be so thorough that you reap the field to its very edge, nor shall you gather the gleanings of your harvest. These things you shall leave for the poor and the alien. I, the LORD, am your God.

**New Year's Day.** [23]The LORD said to Moses: [24]Tell the Israelites: On the first day of the seventh month[m] you will have a sabbath rest, with trumpet blasts as a reminder, a declared holy day; [25]you shall do no heavy work, and you shall offer an oblation to the LORD.

**The Day of Atonement.** [26]The LORD said to Moses: [27]Now the tenth day of this seventh month is the Day of Atonement.[n] You will have a declared holy day. You shall humble yourselves and offer an oblation to the LORD. [28]On this day you shall not do any work, because it is the Day of Atonement, when atonement is made for you before the LORD, your God. [29]Those who do not humble themselves on this day shall be cut off from the people. [30]If anyone does any work on this day, I will remove that person from the midst of the people. [31]You shall do no work; this is a perpetual statute throughout your generations wherever you dwell; [32]it is a sabbath of complete rest for you. You shall humble yourselves. Beginning on the evening of the ninth of the month, you shall keep your sabbath from evening to evening.

**The Feast of Booths.** [33]The LORD said to Moses: [34]Tell the Israelites: The fifteenth day of this seventh month is the LORD's feast of Booths,[‡o] which shall continue for seven days. [35]On the first day, a declared holy day, you shall do no heavy work. [36]For seven days you shall offer an oblation to the LORD, and on the eighth day you will have a declared holy day. You shall offer an oblation to the LORD. It is the festival closing. You shall do no heavy work.

[37§]These, therefore, are the festivals of the LORD which you shall declare holy days, in order to offer as an oblation to the LORD burnt offerings and grain offerings, sacrifices and libations, as prescribed for each day, [38]in addition to the LORD's sabbaths, your donations, your various votive offerings, and the voluntary offerings that you present to the LORD.

[39]On the fifteenth day, then, of the seventh month, when you have gathered in the produce of the land, you shall celebrate the feast of the LORD[¶] for a whole week. The first and the eighth day shall be days of rest. [40]On the first day you shall gather fruit of majestic trees, branches of palms, and boughs[**] of leafy trees and valley willows. Then for a week you shall make merry before the LORD, your God. [41]You shall keep this feast of the LORD for one whole week in the year. By perpetual statute throughout your generations in the seventh month of the year, you shall keep it. [42]You shall dwell in booths for seven days; every native-born Israelite shall dwell in booths, [43]that your descendants may realize that, when I led the Israelites out of the land of Egypt, I made them dwell in booths. I, the LORD, am your God.

[44]Thus did Moses announce to the Israelites the festivals of the LORD.

## CHAPTER 24

**The Sanctuary Light.**[††][1]The LORD said to Moses: [2]Order the Israelites to bring you clear oil of crushed olives for the light, so that you may

---

‡[23:34] **Feast of Booths**: this is the final harvest festival of the year celebrating the remaining harvest. It is called the "feast of Ingathering" (Ex 23:16; 34:22), the "feast of Booths" (Lv 23:34; Dt 16:13), or simply the "feast" (1 Kgs 8:65). It is a seven-day festival with an eighth closing day. The first and eighth days are rest days (see note on v. 3).

§[23:37–38] This appears to be the original conclusion of the chapter.

¶[23:39–43] **The feast of the LORD**: the feast of Booths, the preeminent festival. This section supplements vv. 33–36 by prescribing the popular activities for the festival.

**[23:40–43] Fruit ... branches ... boughs**: the fruit and/or foliage from these trees is to be gathered, but it is not said how they are used. The command to make merry suggests they may have been used in a procession or even circumambulation of the altar (cf. Ps 26:6). Later tradition understood these prescriptions as referring to making the booths out of the foliage (Neh 8:15).

††[24:1–4] On the lamp, see Ex 25:31–40; 26:35; 27:20–21; 37:17–24; 40:24–25; Nm 8:1–4. It occupies the south side of the anterior room of the sanctuary tent and provides light for that room.

---

Dt 16:10, 16). The name Pentecost comes from the later Greek term for the holy day (cf. Acts 2:1; 20:16; 1 Cor 16:8), referring to the fiftieth day. This is the occasion for bringing the first fruits of the wheat harvest.

*[23:24] **First day of the seventh month**: the seventh new moon is counted from a new year beginning in the spring (cf. v. 5). Like the seventh day in the week, it is preeminent among the new moon days (cf. Nm 28:11–15; 29:1–6).

†[23:27] **Day of Atonement**: see chap. 16 and notes there.

l. [23:22] Lv 19:9–10.   m. [23:24] Nm 29:1–6.   n. [23:27] Lv 16:1–34; 25:9; Nm 29:7–11.

o. [23:34] Ex 23:16; 34:22; Dt 16:13–15; 31:10; 2 Mc 1:9, 18; Jn 7:2.

keep the lamp burning regularly.[p] [3]In the tent of meeting, outside the veil that hangs in front of the covenant, Aaron shall set up the lamp to burn before the LORD regularly, from evening till morning, by a perpetual statute throughout your generations. [4]He shall set up the lamps on the pure gold menorah to burn regularly before the LORD.

**The Showbread.**[*] [5]You shall take bran flour and bake it into twelve cakes,[q] using two tenths of an ephah of flour for each cake. [6]These you shall place in two piles, six in each pile, on the pure gold table before the LORD. [7]With each pile put some pure frankincense, which shall serve as an oblation to the LORD, a token of the bread offering. [8]Regularly on each sabbath day the bread[r] shall be set out before the LORD on behalf of the Israelites by an everlasting covenant. [9]It shall belong to Aaron and his sons, who must eat it in a sacred place, since it is most sacred,[s] his as a perpetual due from the oblations to the LORD.

**Punishment of Blasphemy.**[†] [10]A man born of an Israelite mother and an Egyptian father went out among the Israelites, and in the camp a fight broke out between the son of the Israelite woman and an Israelite man. [11]The son of the Israelite woman uttered the LORD's name in a curse and blasphemed. So he was brought to Moses—now his mother's name was Shelomith, daughter of Dibri, of the tribe of Dan— [12]and he was kept in custody till a decision from the LORD should settle the case for them.[t] [13]The LORD then said to Moses: [14]Take the blasphemer outside the camp, and when all who heard him have laid their hands[‡] on his head,[u] let the whole community stone him. [15]Tell the Israelites: Anyone who blasphemes God shall bear the penalty; [16]whoever utters the name of the LORD in a curse shall be put to death.[v] The whole community shall stone that person; alien and native-born alike must be put to death for uttering the LORD's name in a curse.

[17]§Whoever takes the life of any human being shall be put to death;[w] [18]whoever takes the life of an animal shall make restitution of another animal, life for a life.[x] [19]¶Anyone who inflicts a permanent injury on his or her neighbor shall receive the same in return: [20]fracture for fracture, eye for eye, tooth for tooth. The same injury that one gives another shall be inflicted in return.[y] [21]Whoever takes the life of an animal shall make restitution, but whoever takes a human life shall be put to death. [22]You shall have but one rule, for alien and native-born alike.[z] I, the LORD, am your God.

[23]When Moses told this to the Israelites, they took the blasphemer outside the camp and stoned him;[a] they did just as the LORD commanded Moses.

## CHAPTER 25

**The Sabbatical Year.** [1]The LORD said to Moses on Mount Sinai: [2]*Speak to the Israelites and tell them: When you enter the land that I am giving you, let the land, too, keep a sabbath for the LORD. [3]For six years you may sow your field, and for six years prune your vineyard, gathering in their produce.[b] [4]But during the seventh year the land shall have a sabbath of complete rest, a sabbath for the LORD,[c] when you may neither sow your field nor prune your vineyard. [5]The aftergrowth of your harvest you shall not reap, nor shall you pick the grapes of your untrimmed vines. It shall be a year of rest for the land. [6]While the land has its sabbath, all its produce will be food to eat for you yourself and for your male and female slave, for your laborer and the tenant who live with you, [7]and likewise for your livestock and for the wild animals on your land.

**The Jubilee Year.** [8]†You shall count seven weeks of years—seven times seven years—such that the seven weeks of years amount to forty-nine years. [9]Then, on the tenth day of the seventh month‡‡ let the ram's horn resound; on this, the

---

*[24:5–9] On the bread table, see Ex 25:23–29; 26:35; 37:10–16; 40:22–23. It occupies the north side of the anterior room of the sanctuary tent. The bread is a type of grain offering (see note on 2:1).

†[24:10–22] This is a narrative where an offense leads to clarifying revelation similar to the cases in Lv 10:1–7 and 16:1–34; Nm 9:6–14 and 15:32–36.

‡[24:14] **Laid their hands**: see notes on 1:4 and 16:21. It may be that blasphemy generated a type of pollution which the hearers return to the culprit by this gesture.

§[24:17–22] A digression dealing with bodily injury follows the blasphemy rules. It may have been appended since the first case is another example of the death penalty. But the section develops according to its own logic. All legal traditions require death for homicide: Gn 9:5–6; Ex 21:12–14; Nm 35:9–34; Dt 19:1–13; cf. Ex 20:13 and Dt 5:17.

¶[24:19–20] The phrase "life for a life" in v. 18 leads to introducing the law of talion in vv. 19–20. Some have interpreted the law here and the similar expressions in Ex 21:23–25 and Dt 19:21 to mean that monetary compensation equal to the injury is to be paid, though the wording of the law here and the context of Dt 19:21 indicate an injury is to be inflicted upon the injurer.

**[25:2–7] As every seventh day is to be a day of rest (cf. 23:3), so every seventh year is a year of rest (cf. 26:34–35, 43). The rest consists in not doing agricultural work. The people are to live off what grows naturally in the fields (vv. 6–7). Verses 19–22 add insurance by saying that God will make the sixth-year crop abundant such that its excess will stretch over the seventh sabbatical year as well as the eighth year when new crops are not yet harvested (cf. 26:10). Cf. Ex 23:10–11.

††[25:8–17] The fiftieth year is the jubilee, determined by counting off "seven weeks of years." It is sacred, like the sabbath day. Specifically, in it indentured Israelites return to their own households and land that has been sold returns to its original owner. Different laws are found in Ex 21:1–6; Dt 15:1–3, 12–18 (cf. Jer 34:8–22).

‡‡[25:9] **Seventh month**: the priestly laws reflect the use of two calendars, one starting in the spring (cf. chap. 23) and one in the fall. The jubilee is calculated on the basis of the

---

p. [24:2] Ex 25:31–40; 27:20–21.   q. [24:5] Ex 25:23–30; 1 Kgs 7:48; 2 Chr 13:11; Heb 9:2.   r. [24:8] 1 Chr 9:32.   s. [24:9] 1 Sm 21:5.   t. [24:12] Nm 15:34.   u. [24:14] Lv 16:21.   v. [24:16] Ex 22:27; 1 Kgs 21:10, 13; Mt 26:65–66; Jn 10:33.   w. [24:17] Gn 9:5–6; Ex 21:12–14; Nm 35:9–34; Dt 19:11–13.

x. [24:18] Ex 21:33–34; cf. Lv 17:4.   y. [24:20] Ex 21:23–25; Dt 19:21; Mt 5:38.   z. [24:22] Lv 19:34; Ex 12:49; Nm 15:16.   a. [24:23] Acts 7:57–58.   b. [25:3] Ex 23:10–11.   c. [25:4] Lv 26:34; 1 Mc 6:49, 53.

Day of Atonement,[d] the ram's horn blast shall resound throughout your land. [10]You shall treat this fiftieth year as sacred. You shall proclaim liberty in the land for all its inhabitants.[e] It shall be a jubilee for you, when each of you shall return to your own property, each of you to your own family. [11]This fiftieth year is your year of jubilee; you shall not sow, nor shall you reap the aftergrowth or pick the untrimmed vines, [12]since this is the jubilee. It shall be sacred for you. You may only eat what the field yields of itself.

[13]In this year of jubilee, then, each of you shall return to your own property. [14]Therefore, when you sell any land to your neighbor or buy any from your neighbor, do not deal unfairly with one another. [15]On the basis of the number of years since the last jubilee you shall purchase the land from your neighbor;[f] and so also, on the basis of the number of years of harvest, that person shall sell it to you. [16]When the years are many, the price shall be so much the more; when the years are few, the price shall be so much the less. For it is really the number of harvests that the person sells you. [17]Do not deal unfairly with one another, then; but stand in fear of your God. I, the LORD, am your God.

[18]Observe my statutes and be careful to keep my ordinances, so that you will dwell securely in the land. [19]The land will yield its fruit and you will eat your fill, and live there securely.[g] [20]And if you say, "What shall we eat in the seventh year, if we do not sow or reap our crop?"[h] [21]I will command such a blessing for you in the sixth year that there will be crop enough for three years, [22]and when you sow in the eighth year, you will still be eating from the old crop; even into the ninth year, until the crop comes in, you will still be eating from the old crop.[i]

**Redemption of Property.**[*] [23]The land shall not be sold irrevocably; for the land is mine, and you are but resident aliens and under my authority. [24]Therefore, in every part of the country that you occupy, you must permit the land to be redeemed. [25]When one of your kindred is reduced to poverty and has to sell some property, that person's closest relative,[†] who has the duty to redeem it, shall come and redeem what the relative has sold.[j] [26]If, however, the person has no relative to redeem it, but later on acquires sufficient means to redeem it, [27]the person shall calculate the years since the sale, return the balance to the

one to whom it was sold, and thus regain the property.[k] [28]But if the person does not acquire sufficient means to buy back the land, what was sold shall remain in the possession of the purchaser until the year of the jubilee, when it must be released and returned to the original owner.[l]

[29‡]When someone sells a dwelling in a walled town, it can be redeemed up to a full year after its sale—the redemption period is one year. [30]But if such a house in a walled town has not been redeemed at the end of a full year, it shall belong irrevocably to the purchaser throughout the generations; it shall not be released in the jubilee. [31]However, houses in villages that are not encircled by walls shall be reckoned as part of the surrounding farm land; they may be redeemed, and in the jubilee they must be released.

[32§]In levitical cities[m] the Levites shall always have the right to redeem the houses in the cities that are in their possession. [33]As for levitical property that goes unredeemed—houses sold in cities of their possession shall be released in the jubilee; for the houses in levitical cities are their possession in the midst of the Israelites. [34]Moreover, the pasture land[n] belonging to their cities shall not be sold at all; it must always remain their possession.

[35]When one of your kindred is reduced to poverty and becomes indebted to you, you shall support that person like a resident alien; let your kindred live with you. [36]Do not exact interest in advance or accrued interest,[¶] but out of fear of God let your kindred live with you. [37o]Do not give your money at interest or your food at a profit. [38]I, the LORD, am your God, who brought you out of the land of Egypt to give you the land of Canaan and to be your God.

[39**]When your kindred with you, having been so reduced to poverty, sell themselves to you, do not make them work as slaves.[p] [40]Rather, let them be like laborers or like your tenants, working with you until the jubilee year, [41]when, together

‡[25:29–31] Not being able to redeem a house in a walled city after one year is probably due to the demographic and economic situation of large towns as opposed to small villages and open agricultural areas. The agricultural lands associated with the latter were the foundation for the economic viability of the Israelite family, and as such, God—who is the ultimate owner of the land (25:23)—has assigned them to the Israelites as permanent holdings.

§[25:32–34] An exception to the rule in vv. 29–31 is made for levitical cities (Nm 35:1–8), since the Levites have no broad land holdings. Their houses can be redeemed and are to be released in the jubilee year.

¶[25:36] **Interest in advance or accrued interest**: two types of interest are mentioned here. The former may refer to interest subtracted from the loaned amount in advance, and the latter, to interest or a payment in addition to the loaned amount.

**[25:39–43] Here the individual Israelite has no assets and must become indentured to another Israelite for economic survival. No provision is given for redemption before the jubilee year, though such is probably allowed.

latter. **Ram's horn**: Hebrew *shophar*. The name for the year, jubilee (Heb. *yobel*), also means "ram's horn" and comes from the horn blown to announce the occasion.

*[25:23–55] This is a series of laws dealing mainly with situations of poverty in which one has to sell land, obtain a loan, or become indentured. Many of the laws are connected with the release of debts in the jubilee year.

†[25:25] A close family member is responsible for redemption. Some of these are specified in v. 49.

d. [25:9] Lv 16:29.   e. [25:10] Nm 36:4; Is 61:2; Jer 34:8–22; Ez 46:17; Lk 4:19.   f. [25:15] Lv 27:18, 23.   g. [25:19] Lv 26:5–6.   h. [25:20] Mt 6:25, 31–34; Lk 12:22, 29.   i. [25:22] Lv 26:10.   j. [25:25] Ru 2:20; 4:4, 6; Jer 32:7–8.

k. [25:27] Lv 27:18, 23.   l. [25:28] Lv 27:24.   m. [25:32] Nm 35:1–8.   n. [25:34] Nm 35:3.   o. [25:37] Ex 22:24; Dt 23:20.   p. [25:39] Ex 21:2–11; Dt 15:12–18; 1 Kgs 9:22; Jer 34:8–22.

with any children, they shall be released from your service and return to their family and to their ancestral property. <sup>42</sup>Since they are my servants, whom I brought out of the land of Egypt, they shall not sell themselves as slaves are sold. <sup>43</sup>Do not lord it over them harshly, but stand in fear of your God.

<sup>44</sup>"The male and female slaves that you possess—these you shall acquire from the nations round about you.<sup>q</sup> <sup>45</sup>You may also acquire them from among the resident aliens who reside with you, and from their families who are with you, those whom they bore in your land. These you may possess, <sup>46</sup>and bequeath to your children as their hereditary possession forever. You may treat them as slaves. But none of you shall lord it harshly over any of your fellow Israelites.<sup>r</sup>

<sup>47</sup>When your kindred, having been so reduced to poverty, sell themselves to a resident alien who has become wealthy or to descendants of a resident alien's family, <sup>48</sup>even after having sold themselves, they still may be redeemed by one of their kindred, <sup>49</sup>by an uncle or cousin, or by some other relative from their family; or, having acquired the means, they may pay the redemption price themselves. <sup>50</sup>With the purchaser they shall compute the years from the sale to the jubilee, distributing the sale price over these years as though they had been hired as laborers. <sup>51</sup>The more years there are, the more of the sale price they shall pay back as the redemption price; <sup>52</sup>the fewer years there are before the jubilee year, the more they have as credit; in proportion to the years of service they shall pay the redemption price. <sup>53</sup>The tenant alien shall treat those who sold themselves as laborers hired on an annual basis, and the alien shall not lord it over them harshly before your very eyes. <sup>54</sup>And if they are not redeemed by these means, they shall nevertheless be released, together with any children, in the jubilee year. <sup>55</sup>For the Israelites belong to me as servants; they are my servants, whom I brought out of the land of Egypt, I, the LORD, your God.

## CHAPTER 26

**The Reward of Obedience.** <sup>1†</sup>Do not make idols for yourselves. You shall not erect a carved image or a sacred stone for yourselves, nor shall you set up a carved stone for worship in your land;<sup>s</sup> for

I, the LORD, am your God. <sup>2</sup>Keep my sabbaths,<sup>t</sup> and reverence my sanctuary. I am the LORD.

<sup>3‡u</sup>If you live in accordance with my statutes and are careful to observe my commandments, <sup>4</sup>I will give you your rains in due season, so that the land will yield its crops, and the trees their fruit;<sup>v</sup> <sup>5</sup>your threshing will last till vintage time, and your vintage till the time for sowing, and you will eat your fill of food, and live securely in your land.<sup>w</sup> <sup>6</sup>I will establish peace in the land, and you will lie down to rest with no one to cause you anxiety. I will rid the country of ravenous beasts, and no sword shall sweep across your land. <sup>7</sup>You will rout your enemies, and they shall fall before your sword. <sup>8</sup>Five of you will put a hundred of your foes to flight, and a hundred of you will put to flight ten thousand, till your enemies fall before your sword.<sup>x</sup> <sup>9</sup>I will look with favor upon you, and make you fruitful and numerous,<sup>y</sup> as I carry out my covenant with you. <sup>10</sup>You shall eat the oldest stored harvest, and have to discard it to make room for the new.<sup>z</sup> <sup>11a</sup>I will set my tabernacle in your midst, and will not loathe you. <sup>12</sup>Ever present in your midst, I will be your God, and you will be my people; <sup>13</sup>I, the LORD, am your God, who brought you out of the land of Egypt to be their slaves no more, breaking the bars of your yoke and making you walk erect.<sup>b</sup>

**The Punishment of Disobedience.**<sup>§</sup> <sup>14c</sup>But if you do not heed me and do not keep all these commandments, <sup>15</sup>if you reject my statutes and loathe my decrees, refusing to obey all my commandments and breaking my covenant, <sup>16</sup>then I, in turn, will do this to you: I will bring terror upon you—with consumption and fever to dim the eyes and sap the life. You will sow your seed in vain, for your enemies will consume the crop. <sup>17</sup>I will turn against you, and you will be beaten down before your enemies<sup>d</sup> and your foes will lord it over you. You will flee though no one pursues you.

<sup>18</sup>If even after this you do not obey me, I will increase the chastisement for your sins sevenfold,<sup>e</sup> <sup>19</sup>to break your proud strength. I will make the sky above you as hard as iron, and your soil as hard as bronze, <sup>20</sup>so that your strength will

---

‡[26:3–13] The blessings are concerned with the well-being of the nation and its land and involve agricultural bounty, national security, military success and population growth.

§[26:14–46] To encourage obedience, the list of punishments is longer than the blessings (cf. a similar proportion in Dt 28). The punishments are presented in waves (vv. 14–17, 18–20, 21–22, 23–26, 27–39), one group following another if the people do not return to obedience. Punishments involve sickness, pestilence, agricultural failure and famine, attack of wild animals, death of the people's children, destruction of illicit and even licit cults, military defeat, panic, and exile.

---

*[25:44–46] While Israelites may not be held as permanent slaves (vv. 39–43, 47–55), foreigners may be. They are not released in the jubilee, but may be bequeathed to one's children. They may be treated as "slaves," i.e., harshly (cf. Ex 21:20–21).

†[26:1–46] This chapter concludes the revelation of laws at Mount Sinai (cf. v. 46). Blessings and curses are also found at the end of Deuteronomy's law collection (Dt 28). Similar lists of blessings and curses appear in the conclusions of ancient Near Eastern treaties.

---

q. [25:44] Dt 21:10–14.  r. [25:46] Is 14:1–2.  s. [26:1] Lv 19:4; Nm 33:52.

t. [26:2] Lv 23:3.  u. [26:3] Dt 28:1–69.  v. [26:4] Dt 11:14; Ps 85:13; Ez 34:26–27.  w. [26:5] Lv 25:18–19; Dt 12:10.  x. [26:8] Dt 32:30; Jos 23:10.  y. [26:9] Gn 1:28; Ex 1:7.  z. [26:10] Lv 25:22.  a. [26:11–12] Ez 29:45; Ez 37:26–28; 2 Cor 6:16.  b. [26:13] Ez 34:27; Na 1:13.  c. [26:14] Dt 28:15–69.  d. [26:17] 2 Kgs 8:33–34.  e. [26:18] Ps 79:12; Prv 6:31.

be spent in vain; your land will bear no crops, and its trees no fruit.

²¹If then you continue hostile, unwilling to obey me, I will multiply my blows sevenfold, as your sins deserve. ²²I will unleash wild beasts against you, to rob you of your children and wipe out your livestock, till your population dwindles away and your roads become deserted.

²³If, with all this, you still do not accept my discipline and continue hostile to me, ²⁴ʲI, too, will continue to be hostile to you and I, for my part, will smite you for your sins sevenfold. ²⁵I will bring against you the sword, the avenger of my covenant. Though you then huddle together in your cities, I will send pestilence among you, till you are delivered to the enemy. ²⁶When I break your staff of bread, ten women will need but one oven for baking your bread, and they shall dole it out to you by weight;ᵍ and though you eat, you shall not be satisfied.

²⁷If, despite all this, you disobey and continue hostile to me, ²⁸I will continue in my hostile rage toward you, and I myself will discipline you for your sins sevenfold, ²⁹till you begin to eat the flesh of your own sons and daughters.ʰ ³⁰I will demolish your high places, overthrow your incense stands, and cast your corpses upon the corpses of your idols.ⁱ In my loathing of you, ³¹I will lay waste your cities and desolate your sanctuaries, refusing your sweet-smelling offerings. ³²So devastated will I leave the land that your enemies who come to live there will stand aghast at the sight of it.ʲ ³³And you I will scatter among the nationsᵏ at the point of my drawn sword, leaving your countryside desolate and your cities deserted. ³⁴Then shall the land, during the time it lies waste, make up its lost sabbaths, while you are in the land of your enemies; then shall the land have rest and make up for its sabbathsˡ ³⁵during all the time that it lies desolate, enjoying the rest that you would not let it have on your sabbaths when you lived there.

³⁶Those of you who survive in the lands of their enemies, I will make so fainthearted that the sound of a driven leaf will pursue them, and they shall run as if from the sword, and fall though no one pursues them; ³⁷stumbling over one another as if to escape a sword, while no one is after them—so helpless will you be to take a stand against your foes! ³⁸You shall perish among the nations, swallowed up in your enemies' country. ³⁹Those of you who survive will waste away in the lands of their enemies, for their own and their ancestors' guilt.ᵐ

⁴⁰*They will confessⁿ their iniquity and the iniquity of their ancestors in their treachery against me and in their continued hostility toward me, ⁴¹so that I, too, had to be hostile to them and bring them into their enemies' land. Then, when their uncircumcised hearts are humbled and they make amends for their iniquity, ⁴²I will remember my covenant with Jacob, and also my covenant with Isaac; and also my covenant with Abraham I will remember.ᵒ The land, too, I will remember. ⁴³The land will be forsaken by them, that in its desolation without them, it may make up its sabbaths, and that they, too, may make good the debt of their guilt for having spurned my decrees and loathed my statutes. ⁴⁴Yet even so, even while they are in their enemies' land, I will not reject or loathe them to the point of wiping them out, thus making void my covenant with them; for I, the LORD, am their God. ⁴⁵I will remember for them the covenant I made with their forebears, whom I brought out of the land of Egypt before the eyes of the nations,ᵖ that I might be their God. I am the LORD.

⁴⁶These are the statutes, decrees and laws which the LORD established between himself and the Israelites through Moses on Mount Sinai.�q

## V. REDEMPTION OF OFFERINGS

### CHAPTER 27

**Votive Offerings and Dedications.** ¹The LORD said to Moses: ²†Speak to the Israelites and tell them: When anyone makes a vow to the LORDʳ with respect to the value of a human being, ³the value for males between the ages of twenty and sixty shall be fifty silver shekels, by the sanctuary shekel; ⁴and for a female, the value shall be thirty shekels. ⁵For persons between the ages of five and twenty, the value for a male shall be twenty shekels, and for a female, ten shekels. ⁶For persons between the ages of one month and five years, the value for a male shall be five silver shekels, and for a female, three shekels. ⁷For persons of sixty or more, for a male the value shall

---

f. [26:24–25] Jer 2:30; Ez 5:17; 14:17.   g. [26:26] Is 9:19; Ez 4:16; 5:16; 14:13; Mi 6:14.   h. [26:29] Lam 2:20.   i. [26:30] 2 Chr 14:5; 34:3–4, 7; Ez 6:3–6.   j. [26:32] 1 Kgs 9:8; Jer 9:11; 18:16; 19:8; 25:18.   k. [26:33] Ps 44:12; Jer 15:7; Ez 6:8.   l. [26:34] Lv 25:2; 2 Chr 36:21.   m. [26:39] Ez 4:17; 24:23; 33:10.

*[26:40–45] Even though the people may be severely punished, God will remember the covenant when the people repent.

†[27:2–13] Vows are conditional promissory oaths. One covenants to do something for the benefit of God, usually to make a dedication, if God fulfills the individual's accompanying request (cf. Gn 28:20–21; Jgs 11:30–31; 1 Sm 1:11; 2 Sm 15:7–8; Ps 56:13–14). Vows must be fulfilled (Nm 30:3; Dt 23:22; cf. Ps 66:13–15). Verses 2–8 deal with votive offerings involving human beings. Actual dedication of human beings (cf. Jgs 11:30–31, 34–40; 1 Sm 1:11, 24–28) is obviated by payment of the person's value (mentioned in the temple income in 2 Kgs 12:5). The values reflect the different economic and administrative roles of people in different age and gender groups within ancient Israelite society. Verses 9–13 concern the bringing of animals for a vow.

n. [26:40] Lv 16:21; Nm 5:7; Neh 1:6.   o. [26:42] Ex 6:5; 2 Kgs 13:23; Ps 106:45; Ez 16:60.   p. [26:45] Ex 12:51.   q. [26:46] Lv 7:38; Nm 36:13.   r. [27:2] Dt 23:22–24; Jgs 11:30–31; Eccl 5:3–4.

be fifteen shekels, and ten shekels for a female. [8]However, if the one who made the vow is too poor to meet the sum,[s] the person must be set before the priest, who shall determine a value; the priest will do this in keeping with the means of the one who made the vow.

[9]If the offering vowed to the LORD is an animal that may be sacrificed, every such animal given to the LORD becomes sacred.[t] [10]The offerer shall not substitute or exchange another for it, either a worse or a better one. If the offerer exchanges one animal in place of another, both the original and its substitute shall become sacred. [11]If any unclean animal which is unfit for sacrifice[u] to the LORD is vowed, it must be set before the priest, [12]who shall determine its value* in keeping with its good or bad qualities, and the value set by the priest shall stand. [13]If the offerer wishes to redeem the animal, the person shall pay one fifth more than this valuation.[v]

[14†]When someone dedicates a house as sacred to the LORD,[‡] the priest shall determine its value in keeping with its good or bad qualities, and the value set by the priest shall stand. [15]A person dedicating a house who then wishes to redeem it shall pay one fifth more than the price thus established, and then it will again belong to that individual.[w]

[16]If someone dedicates to the LORD a portion of hereditary land, its valuation shall be made according to the amount of seed required to sow it, the acreage sown with a homer[§] of barley seed being valued at fifty silver shekels. [17]If the dedication of a field is made at the beginning of a jubilee period, the full valuation shall hold; [18]but if it is some time after this, the priest shall estimate its money value according to the number of years left until the next jubilee year, with a corresponding reduction on the valuation.[x] [19]A person dedicating a field who then wishes to redeem[*y] it shall pay one fifth more than the price thus established, and so reclaim it. [20]If,

instead of redeeming such a field, one sells it** to another, it may no longer be redeemed; [21]but at the jubilee it shall be released[z] as sacred[††] to the LORD; like a field that is put under the ban, it shall become priestly property.

[22]If someone dedicates to the LORD a field that was purchased and was not part of hereditary property, [23]the priest shall compute its value in proportion to the number of years until the next jubilee, and on the same day the person shall pay the price thus established, a sacred donation to the LORD; [24]at the jubilee the field shall revert to the hereditary owner of this land from whom it had been purchased.[‡‡]

[25]Every valuation shall be made according to the standard of the sanctuary shekel. There are twenty gerahs to the shekel.

**Irredeemable Offerings.** [26§§]Note that a firstborn animal,[a] which as such already belongs to the LORD, may not be dedicated. Whether an ox or a sheep, it is the LORD's. [27]But if it is an unclean animal,[¶] it may be redeemed by paying one fifth more than its value. If it is not redeemed, it shall be sold at its value.

[28]Note, also, that any possession which someone puts under the ban*** for the LORD, whether it is a human being, an animal, or a hereditary field, shall be neither sold nor redeemed; everything that is put under the ban becomes most holy to the LORD.[b] [29]All human beings that are put under the ban cannot be redeemed; they must be put to death.[c]

[30†††]All tithes of the land, whether in grain from the fields or in fruit from the trees, belong to the LORD; they are sacred to the LORD.[d] [31]If

---

*[27:12] **Determine its value**: in contrast to human beings (vv. 3–7) there are no set values for unclean animals, and the condition of the animal is taken into consideration (cf. vv. 14, 27).

†[27:14–24] These verses deal with dedications. They take effect when uttered and, unlike vows, they are not conditional. They are related to the jubilee year laws in 25:23–31.

‡[27:14] **House as sacred to the LORD**: the house becomes sanctuary property and presumably may be sold to another if the owner does not redeem it (cf. notes on vv. 20 and 21). While 25:31 requires that unredeemed houses in unwalled towns be returned to the original owners at the jubilee, in the laws here such houses apparently become the property of the sanctuary (cf. v. 21). It is likely that dedicated houses in a walled city needed to be redeemed within one year, following 25:29–30.

§[27:16] **Homer**: see note on Is 5:10.

¶[27:19] **Redeem**: the person apparently can redeem the land up to the jubilee year, following 25:23–28. See note on v. 21.

**[27:20] **If . . . one sells it**: the verse is difficult since the person should not be able to sell the land after it is dedicated. The verb "sells" may be construed impersonally here: "If . . . it is sold," i.e., by the sanctuary.

††[27:21] **Released as sacred**: the dedication changes the ownership of the land. It now belongs to the sanctuary. It returns to the sanctuary's possession after leasing it out (v. 20). Presumably if the land remained in the sanctuary's possession until the jubilee, and it was not redeemed, the land would belong permanently to the sanctuary and priests.

‡‡[27:24] In contrast to the cases in vv. 14–15 and 16–21, this land returns to the original owner since that individual did not personally make the dedication. The principle is that one cannot permanently dedicate what one does not own. Cf. 2 Sm 24:22–25.

§§[27:26] Firstborn animals and human beings already belong to God (cf. Ex 13:1–2, 12; 34:19); they cannot be vowed or dedicated. Cf. Nm 18:15–18; Dt 15:19–23.

¶[27:27] **An unclean animal**: such as the firstborn of a donkey, which was unfit for sacrifice. According to Ex 13:13; 34:20, a firstborn donkey was to be redeemed by offering a sheep in its stead, or was to have its neck broken.

***[27:28] **Puts under the ban**: this is a higher form of dedication to God than that found in vv. 14–24. Anything so dedicated is beyond redemption and cannot be sold by the sanctuary and priests (contrast vv. 15, 19, 20). This type of dedication is found mostly in contexts of war (e.g., Jos 6:17–21; 8:26; 10:1, 28). Lv 27:28 shows that the ban can apply to one's own property.

†††[27:30–33] On the regulation concerning the tithes see Dt 14:22–29.

---

s. [27:8] Lv 5:7, 11.   t. [27:9] Lv 27:11, 27.   u. [27:11] Lv 11:2–8; Ex 13:13; 34:20.   v. [27:13] Lv 5:16, 24.   w. [27:15] Lv 22:14.   x. [27:18] Lv 25:15–16, 26–27, 50–52.   y. [27:19] Lv 25:25.

z. [27:21] Lv 25:28, 31.   a. [27:26] Ex 13:2.   b. [27:28] Nm 18:14; Dt 7:26; Jos 7:1; 1 Sm 15:21; Ez 44:29.   c. [27:29] 1 Kgs 20:42.   d. [27:30] Nm 18:25–32; Dt 14:22–24; Mal 3:8, 10.

someone wishes to redeem any of the tithes, the person shall pay one fifth more than their value. <sup>32</sup>The tithes of the herd and the flock, every tenth animal that passes under the herdsman's rod, shall be sacred to the LORD. <sup>33</sup>It shall not matter whether good ones or bad ones are thus chosen, and no exchange may be made. If any exchange is made, both the original animal and its substitute become sacred and cannot be redeemed.

<sup>34</sup>These are the commandments which the LORD gave Moses on Mount Sinai for the Israelites.<sup>e</sup>

---

e. [27:34] Lv 7:38.

# THE BOOK OF

# NUMBERS

～～～

The Book of Numbers derives its name from the account of the two censuses taken of the Hebrew people, one near the beginning and the other toward the end of the journey in the wilderness (chaps. 1 and 26). It continues the story of that journey begun in Exodus, and describes briefly the experiences of the Israelites for a period of thirty-eight years, from the end of their encampment at Sinai to their arrival at the border of the promised land. Numerous legal ordinances are interspersed in the account, making the book a combination of law and history.

The book divides neatly into two parts. Each part begins with a census of the people (chaps. 1 and 26) and inaugurates a period of preparation prior to entering the promised land. In the first case these preparations come to a tragic end when scouts are sent forth to survey the promised land (chaps. 13–14). Upon their return, the people are so disheartened by the description of the native inhabitants and the seemingly impossible task that lies in front of them that they refuse to enter the land. This results in a decision to doom that entire generation to death and to allow another generation the chance to enter. After the death of the first generation, then, a second census is taken (chap. 26) and again preparations are made to enter the land. In this case, however, the birth of a new generation suggests these preparations will not be in vain. The book ends with the Israelites across the Jordan outside the land of Canaan, underscoring a chief theme of the Pentateuch as a whole: the people anticipating the fulfillment of God's promise of the land.

In the New Testament numerous allusions to incidents in the Book of Numbers appear: the bronze serpent (Jn 3:14–15), the sedition of Korah and its consequences (1 Cor 10:10), the prophecies of Balaam (2 Pt 2:15–16), and the water gushing from the rock (1 Cor 10:4).

The chief divisions of the Book of Numbers are as follows:

I.   Census and Preparation for the Departure from Sinai (1:1–10:10)
II.  Departure, Rebellion, and Wandering in the Wilderness for Forty Years (10:11–25:18)
III. Second Census of a New Generation and Preparation to Enter the Promised Land (25:19–36:13)

## I. CENSUS AND PREPARATION FOR THE DEPARTURE FROM SINAI

### CHAPTER 1

**The Census.** [1]In the second year after the Israelites' departure from the land of Egypt, on the first day of the second month, the LORD said to Moses at the tent of meeting in the wilderness of Sinai: [2]Take a census of the whole community of the Israelites,[a] by clans and ancestral houses, registering by name each male individually. [3]You and Aaron shall enroll in companies all the men in Israel of twenty years or more who are fit for military service.

---

*[1:2] All Israel was divided into tribes, each tribe into clans, and each clan into ancestral houses.

a. [1:2–3] Nm 14:29; 26:2–51.

**Moses' Assistants.** [4]With you there shall be a man from each tribe, each the head of his ancestral house. [5b]These are the names of those who are to assist you:

  from Reuben: Elizur, son of Shedeur;
[6] from Simeon: Shelumiel, son of Zurishaddai;
[7] from Judah:[c] Nahshon, son of Amminadab;
[8] from Issachar: Nethanel, son of Zuar;
[9] from Zebulun: Eliab, son of Helon;
[10] for the descendants of Joseph: from Ephraim: Elishama, son of Ammihud; and from Manasseh: Gamaliel, son of Pedahzur;
[11] from Benjamin: Abidan, son of Gideoni;

---

b. [1:5–15] Nm 10:14–28.   c. [1:7] Mt 1:4; Lk 3:32–33.

¹² from Dan: Ahiezer, son of Ammishaddai;
¹³ from Asher: Pagiel, son of Ochran;
¹⁴ from Gad: Eliasaph, son of Reuel;
¹⁵ from Naphtali: Ahira, son of Enan.

¹⁶ᵈThese were the elect of the community, leaders of their ancestral tribes, heads of the clans of Israel. ¹⁷So Moses and Aaron took these men who had been designated by name, ¹⁸and assembled the whole community on the first day of the second month. Every man of twenty years or more then registered individually his name and lineage according to clan and ancestral house, ¹⁹as the Lord had commanded Moses. So he enrolled them in the wilderness of Sinai.

**Count of the Twelve Tribes.** ²⁰Of the descendants of Reuben, the firstborn of Israel, registered individually by name and lineage according to their clans and ancestral houses, every male of twenty years or more, everyone fit for military service: ²¹those enrolled from the tribe of Reuben were forty-six thousand five hundred.

²²Of the descendants of Simeon, registered individually by name and lineage according to their clans and ancestral houses, every male of twenty years or more, everyone fit for military service: ²³those enrolled from the tribe of Simeon were fifty-nine thousand three hundred.

²⁴Of the descendants of Gad, registered by name and lineage according to their clans and ancestral houses, every male of twenty years or more, everyone fit for military service: ²⁵those enrolled from the tribe of Gad were forty-five thousand six hundred and fifty.

²⁶Of the descendants of Judah, registered by name and lineage according to their clans and ancestral houses, every male of twenty years or more, everyone fit for military service: ²⁷those enrolled from the tribe of Judah were seventy-four thousand six hundred.

²⁸Of the descendants of Issachar, registered by name and lineage according to their clans and ancestral houses, every male of twenty years or more, everyone fit for military service: ²⁹those enrolled from the tribe of Issachar were fifty-four thousand four hundred.

³⁰Of the descendants of Zebulun, registered by name and lineage according to their clans and ancestral houses, every male of twenty years or more, everyone fit for military service: ³¹those enrolled from the tribe of Zebulun were fifty-seven thousand four hundred.

³²Of the descendants of Joseph:

Of the descendants of Ephraim, registered by name and lineage according to their clans and ancestral houses, every male of twenty years or more, everyone fit for military service: ³³those enrolled from the tribe of Ephraim were forty thousand five hundred.

³⁴Of the descendants of Manasseh, registered by name and lineage according to their clans and ancestral houses, every male of twenty years or more, everyone fit for military service: ³⁵those enrolled from the tribe of Manasseh were thirty-two thousand two hundred.

³⁶Of the descendants of Benjamin, registered by name and lineage according to their clans and ancestral houses, every male of twenty years or more, everyone fit for military service: ³⁷those enrolled from the tribe of Benjamin were thirty-five thousand four hundred.

³⁸Of the descendants of Dan, registered by name and lineage according to their clans and ancestral houses, every male of twenty years or more, everyone fit for military service: ³⁹those enrolled from the tribe of Dan were sixty-two thousand seven hundred.

⁴⁰Of the descendants of Asher, registered by name and lineage according to their clans and ancestral houses, every male of twenty years or more, everyone fit for military service: ⁴¹those enrolled from the tribe of Asher were forty-one thousand five hundred.

⁴²Of the descendants of Naphtali, registered by name and lineage according to their clans and ancestral houses, every male of twenty years or more, everyone fit for military service: ⁴³those enrolled from the tribe of Naphtali were fifty-three thousand four hundred.

⁴⁴It was these who were enrolled, each according to his ancestral house, by Moses and Aaron and the twelve leaders of Israel. ⁴⁵The total enrollment of the Israelites of twenty years or more, according to their ancestral houses, everyone fit for military service in Israel— ⁴⁶the total enrollment was six hundred and three thousand, five hundred and fifty.

**Levites Omitted in the Census.** ⁴⁷Now the Levites were not enrolledᵉ by their ancestral tribe with the others.* ⁴⁸For the Lord had told Moses, ⁴⁹The tribe of Levi alone you shall not enroll nor include in the census along with the other Israelites. ⁵⁰You are to give the Levites charge of the tabernacle of the covenant with all its equipment and all that belongs to it. It is they who shall carry the tabernacle with all its equipment and who shall be its ministers;ᶠ and they shall camp all around the tabernacle. ⁵¹When the tabernacle is to move on, the Levites shall take it down; when the tabernacle is to be pitched, it is the Levites who shall set it up. Any unauthorized person who comes near† it shall be

---

*[1:47] The Levites were not enrolled in this census, which was principally for military purposes, but a separate census was made of them. Cf. 3:15–16, 39.

†[1:51] **Comes near**: here and in 3:10, 38; 17:5; 18:4, 7 the Hebrew word rendered "comes near" is very nearly a technical term for someone who intrudes upon or violates a space set apart as holy and for which they have not been qualified by priesthood.

---

e. [1:47] Nm 2:33; 3:14–39; 26:57–62.   f. [1:50] Nm 3:7–8; 4:2–49; 1 Chr 6:33.

d. [1:16] Ex 18:21, 25.

put to death.$^g$ $^{52}$The other Israelites shall camp according to their companies, each in their own divisional camps,$^h$ $^{53}$but the Levites shall camp around the tabernacle of the covenant to ensure that God's wrath will not fall upon the Israelite community. The Levites shall keep guard over the tabernacle of the covenant.$^i$ $^{54}$The Israelites complied; they did just as the LORD had commanded Moses.

## CHAPTER 2

**Arrangement of the Tribes.** $^1$The LORD said to Moses and Aaron: $^2$The Israelites shall camp, each in their own divisions, under the ensigns of their ancestral houses.$^j$ They shall camp at some distance all around the tent of meeting.

$^3$Encamped on the east side, toward the sunrise, shall be the divisional camp of Judah, arranged in companies. The leader of the Judahites is Nahshon, son of Amminadab, $^4$and the enrollment of his company is seventy-four thousand six hundred. $^5$Encamped beside it is the tribe of Issachar. The leader of the Issacharites is Nethanel, son of Zuar, $^6$and the enrollment of his company is fifty-four thousand four hundred. $^7$Also the tribe of Zebulun. The leader of the Zebulunites is Eliab, son of Helon, $^8$and the enrollment of his company is fifty-seven thousand four hundred. $^9$The total enrollment of the camp of Judah by companies is one hundred and eighty-six thousand four hundred. They shall be first on the march.

$^{10}$The divisional camp of Reuben shall be on the south side, by companies. The leader of the Reubenites is Elizur, son of Shedeur, $^{11}$and the enrollment of his company is forty-six thousand five hundred. $^{12}$Encamped beside it is the tribe of Simeon. The leader of the Simeonites is Shelumiel, son of Zurishaddai, $^{13}$and the enrollment of his company is fifty-nine thousand three hundred. $^{14}$Next is the tribe of Gad. The leader of the Gadites is Eliasaph, son of Reuel, $^{15}$and the enrollment of his company is forty-five thousand six hundred and fifty. $^{16}$The total enrollment of the camp of Reuben by companies is one hundred and fifty-one thousand four hundred and fifty. They shall be second on the march.

$^{17}$Then the tent of meeting and the camp of the Levites shall set out in the midst of the divisions. As they camp, so also they will march, each in place, by their divisions.

$^{18}$The divisional camp of Ephraim shall be on the west side, by companies. The leader of the Ephraimites is Elishama, son of Ammihud, $^{19}$and the enrollment of his company is forty thousand five hundred. $^{20}$Beside it shall be the tribe of Manasseh. The leader of the Manassites

is Gamaliel, son of Pedahzur, $^{21}$and the enrollment of his company is thirty-two thousand two hundred. $^{22}$Also the tribe of Benjamin. The leader of the Benjaminites is Abidan, son of Gideoni, $^{23}$and the enrollment of his company is thirty-five thousand four hundred. $^{24}$The total enrollment of the camp of Ephraim by companies is one hundred and eight thousand one hundred. They shall be third on the march.

$^{25}$The divisional camp of Dan shall be on the north side, by companies. The leader of the Danites is Ahiezer, son of Ammishaddai, $^{26}$and the enrollment of his company is sixty-two thousand seven hundred. $^{27}$Encamped beside it shall be the tribe of Asher. The leader of the Asherites is Pagiel, son of Ochran, $^{28}$and the enrollment of his company is forty-one thousand five hundred. $^{29}$Also the tribe of Naphtali. The leader of the Naphtalites is Ahira, son of Enan, $^{30}$and the enrollment of his company is fifty-three thousand four hundred. $^{31}$The total enrollment of the camp of Dan is one hundred and fifty-seven thousand six hundred. They shall be last on the march, by divisions.

$^{32k}$These are the enrollments of the Israelites according to their ancestral houses. The total enrollment of the camps by companies is six hundred and three thousand five hundred and fifty. $^{33}$The Levites, however, were not enrolled with the other Israelites, just as the LORD had commanded Moses. $^{34}$The Israelites did just as the LORD had commanded Moses; both in camp and on the march they were in their own divisions, everyone by clan and according to ancestral house.

## CHAPTER 3

**The Sons of Aaron.** $^1$These are the offspring of Aaron and Moses at the time the LORD spoke to Moses on Mount Sinai. $^2$These are the names of Aaron's sons: Nadab, the firstborn, Abihu, Eleazar, and Ithamar.$^l$ $^3$These are the names of Aaron's sons, the anointed priests whom he ordained to serve as priests. $^4$But Nadab and Abihu died$^m$ in the presence of the LORD when they offered unauthorized fire before the LORD in the wilderness of Sinai; and they left no sons. So only Eleazar and Ithamar served as priests during the lifetime of their father Aaron.

**Levites in Place of the Firstborn.** $^5$Now the LORD said to Moses: $^6$Summon the tribe of Levi and station them before Aaron the priest to serve him.$^n$ $^7$They shall discharge his obligations and those of the whole community before the tent of meeting$^o$ by maintaining the tabernacle. $^8$They shall have responsibility for all the furnishings of the tent of meeting and discharge the obligations of the Israelites by maintaining the tabernacle. $^9$You shall assign the Levites to

---

*[2:3–31] A similar arrangement of the tribes around the central sanctuary in the ideal Israel is given in Ez 48.

---

g. [1:51] Nm 3:10, 38; 18:7; 2 Sm 6:6–7; 1 Chr 13:10　h. [1:52] Nm 2:2, 34.　i. [1:53] Nm 3:7–8, 38; 8:19; 18:4–5..　j. [2:2] Nm 1:52.

k. [2:32–33] Nm 1:44–49.　l. [3:2] Ex 6:23; 1 Chr 24:1.　m. [3:4] Nm 26:61; Lv 10:1–2; 1 Chr 24:2.　n. [3:6] Nm 18:2.　o. [3:7] Nm 8:24.

Aaron and his sons;[p] they have been assigned unconditionally to him from among the Israelites. [10]But you will appoint only Aaron and his descendants to exercise the priesthood.[q] Any unauthorized person who comes near shall be put to death.

[11]The LORD said to Moses: [12]I hereby take the Levites from the Israelites in place of every firstborn that opens the womb among the Israelites.[r] The Levites, therefore, are mine, [13]because every firstborn is mine. When I struck down all the firstborn in the land of Egypt, I consecrated to me every firstborn in Israel, human being and beast alike. They belong to me; I am the LORD.

**Census of the Levites.** [14]The LORD said to Moses in the wilderness of Sinai: [15]Enroll the Levites by their ancestral houses and clans, enrolling every male of a month or more.[s] [16]Moses, therefore, enrolled them at the direction of the LORD, just as the LORD had charged.

[17r]These were the sons of Levi by name: Gershon, Kohath and Merari. [18]These were the names of the sons of Gershon, by their clans: Libni and Shimei. [19]The sons of Kohath, by their clans, were Amram, Izhar, Hebron and Uzziel. [20]The sons of Merari, by their clans, were Mahli and Mushi. These were the clans of the Levites by their ancestral houses.

**Duties of the Levitical Clans.** [21]To Gershon belonged the clan of the Libnites and the clan of the Shimeites; these were the clans of the Gershonites. [22]Their enrollment, registering every male of a month or more, was seven thousand five hundred. [23]The clans of the Gershonites camped behind the tabernacle, to the west. [24]The leader of the ancestral house of the Gershonites was Eliasaph, son of Lael. [25u]At the tent of meeting their responsibility was the tabernacle:[*] the tent and its covering, the curtain at the entrance of the tent of meeting, [26]the hangings of the court, the curtain at the entrance of the court enclosing both the tabernacle and the altar, and the ropes—whatever pertained to their maintenance.

[27]To Kohath belonged the clans of the Amramites, the Izharites, the Hebronites, and the Uzzielites; these were the clans of the Kohathites. [28]Their enrollment, registering every male of a month or more, was eight thousand three hundred. They were the ones who performed the duties of the sanctuary. [29]The clans of the Kohathites camped on the south side of the tabernacle. [30]And the leader of their ancestral

house of the clan of the Kohathites was Elizaphan, son of Uzziel. [31]Their responsibility was the ark, the table, the menorah, the altars, the utensils of the sanctuary with which the priests minister, the veil, and everything pertaining to their maintenance.[†] [32]The chief of the leaders of the Levites, however, was Eleazar, son of Aaron the priest; he was in charge of those who performed the duties of the sanctuary.

[33]To Merari belonged the clans of the Mahlites and the Mushites; these were the clans of Merari. [34]Their enrollment, registering every male of a month or more, was six thousand two hundred. [35]The leader of the ancestral house of the clans of Merari was Zuriel, son of Abihail. They camped at the north side of the tabernacle. [36‡]The Merarites were assigned responsibility for the boards of the tabernacle, its bars, columns, pedestals, and all its fittings—and everything pertaining to their maintenance, [37]as well as the columns of the surrounding court with their pedestals, pegs and ropes.

[38]East of the tabernacle, that is, in front of the tent of meeting, toward the sunrise, were camped Moses and Aaron and the latter's sons, performing the duties of the sanctuary incumbent upon the Israelites. Any unauthorized person who came near was to be put to death.

[39]The total enrollment of the Levites whom Moses and Aaron enrolled at the direction of the LORD, by clans, every male a month old or more, was twenty-two thousand.

**Census and Ransom of Firstborn.** [40]The LORD then said to Moses: Enroll every firstborn male of the Israelites a month old or more, and count the number of their names. [41]Then take the Levites for me—I am the LORD—in place of all the firstborn of the Israelites, as well as the Levites' cattle, in place of all the firstborn among the cattle of the Israelites. [42]So Moses enrolled all the firstborn of the Israelites, as the LORD had commanded him. [43]All the firstborn males, registered by name, of a month or more, numbered twenty-two thousand two hundred and seventy-three.

[44]The LORD said to Moses: [45]Take the Levites in place of all the firstborn of the Israelites, and the Levites' cattle in place of their cattle, that the Levites may belong to me. I am the LORD. [46]As a redemption-price for the two hundred and seventy-three firstborn of the Israelites over and above the number of the Levites, [47]you shall take five shekels for each individual, according to the sanctuary shekel, twenty gerahs to the shekel.[v] [48]Give this money to Aaron and his

---

*[3:25–26] The Gershonites had two wagons for transporting these things; cf. 7:7. For a description of the tabernacle, see Ex 26:1–6; the tent, Ex 26:7–13; its covering, Ex 26:14; the curtain at the entrance, Ex 26:36; the hangings of the court, Ex 27:9–15; the curtain at the entrance of the court, Ex 27:16; the ropes of the tabernacle, Ex 35:18.

p. [3:9] Nm 8:19.    q. [3:10] Nm 1:51; 18:7.    r. [3:12–13] Nm 3:41; 8:16–18; Ex 13:2, 12, 15.    s. [3:15] Nm 3:39; 26:62.    t. [3:17–20] Nm 26:57; Gn 46:11; Ex 6:16–19; 1 Chr 6:1–2, 16–19.    u. [3:25–26] Ex 26:7, 14, 36; 36:14.

†[3:31] The Kohathites had to carry these sacred objects on their shoulders; cf. 7:9. For a description of the ark, see Ex 25:10–22; the table, Ex 25:23–30; the menorah, Ex 25:31–40; the altars, Ex 27:1–8; 30:1–10.

‡[3:36–37] The Merarites had four wagons for transporting this heavy material; cf. 7:8. For a description of the boards, bars, etc., of the tabernacle, see Ex 26:15–30; the columns, pedestals, etc., of the court, Ex 27:9–19.

v. [3:47] Nm 18:16; Ex 30:13; Lv 27:25; Ez 45:12.

sons as a redemption-price for the extra number. [49]So Moses took the redemption money for those over and above the ones redeemed by the Levites. [50]From the firstborn of the Israelites he took the money, one thousand three hundred and sixty-five shekels according to the sanctuary shekel. [51]He then gave this redemption money to Aaron and his sons, at the direction of the LORD, just as the LORD had commanded Moses.

## CHAPTER 4

**Duties Further Defined.** [1]The LORD said to Moses and Aaron: [2]Take a census among the Levites of the Kohathites, by clans and ancestral houses, [3]all between thirty* and fifty years of age, who will join the personnel for doing tasks in the tent of meeting.[w]

[4]This is the task of the Kohathites in the tent of meeting: the most sacred objects. [5]In breaking camp, Aaron and his sons shall go in and take down the screening curtain† and cover the ark of the covenant with it. [6]Over these they shall put a cover of yellow-orange skin, and on top of this spread an all-violet cloth and put the poles in place. [7]On the table of the Presence they shall spread a violet cloth and put on it the plates and cups, as well as the bowls and pitchers for libations; the established bread offering shall remain on the table. [8]Over these they shall spread a scarlet cloth and cover it with a covering of yellow-orange skin, and put the poles in place. [9]They shall use a violet cloth to cover the menorah of the light with its lamps, tongs, and trays, as well as the various containers of oil from which it is supplied. [10]The menorah with all its utensils they shall then put in a covering of yellow-orange skin, and place on a litter. [11]Over the golden altar‡ they shall spread a violet cloth, and cover this also with a covering of yellow-orange skin, and put the poles in place. [12]Taking the utensils of the sanctuary service, they shall put them all in violet cloth and cover them with a covering of yellow-orange skin. They shall then place them on a litter. [13]After cleansing the altar§ of its ashes, they shall spread a purple cloth over it. [14]On this they shall put all the utensils with which it is served: the fire pans, forks,¶ shovels, basins, and all the utensils of the altar. They shall then spread a covering of yellow-orange skin over this, and put the poles in place.

[15]Only after Aaron and his sons have finished covering the sacred objects and all their utensils on breaking camp, can the Kohathites enter to carry them. But they shall not touch the sacred objects; if they do they will die.[x] These, then, are the objects in the tent of meeting that the Kohathites shall carry.

[16]Eleazar, son of Aaron the priest, shall be in charge of the oil for the light, the fragrant incense, the established grain offering, and the anointing oil. He shall be in charge of the whole tabernacle with all the sacred objects and utensils that are in it.

[17]The LORD said to Moses and Aaron: [18]Do not let the group of Kohathite clans perish from among the Levites. [19]That they may live and not die when they approach the most sacred objects, this is what you shall do for them: Aaron and his sons shall go in and assign to each of them his task and what he must carry; [20]but the Kohathites shall not go in to look upon the sacred objects even for an instant, or they will die.[y]

[21]The LORD said to Moses: [22]Take a census of the Gershonites also, by ancestral houses and clans, [23]enrolling all between thirty and fifty years of age who will join the personnel to do the work in the tent of meeting. [24]This is the task of the clans of the Gershonites, what they must do and what they must carry: [25]they shall carry the curtains of the tabernacle, the tent of meeting with its covering and the outer wrapping of yellow-orange skin, the curtain at the entrance of the tent of meeting, [26]the hangings of the court, the curtain at the entrance to the gate of the court that encloses both the tabernacle and the altar, together with their ropes and all other objects necessary for their use. Whatever is to be done to maintain these things, they shall do. [27]The service of the Gershonites shall be entirely under the direction of Aaron and his sons, with regard to what they must carry and what they must do; you shall list for them by name what they are to carry. [28]This, then, is the task of the clans of the Gershonites in the tent of meeting; and they shall be under the supervision of Ithamar, son of Aaron the priest.

[29]The Merarites, too, you shall enroll by clans and ancestral houses, [30]enrolling all between thirty and fifty years of age who will join the personnel to maintain the tent of meeting. [31]This is what they shall be responsible for carrying, with respect to all their service in the tent of meeting: the boards of the tabernacle with its bars, columns and pedestals, [32]and the columns of the surrounding court with their pedestals, pegs and ropes, including all their accessories and everything for their maintenance. You shall list by name the objects they shall be responsible for carrying. [33]This, then, is the task of the clans

---

*[4:3] **Thirty**: according to other passages the Levites began to serve when they were twenty-five (8:24) or even only twenty years old (1 Chr 23:24, 27; 2 Chr 31:17; Ezr 3:8; but cf. 1 Chr 23:3).

†[4:5] **The screening curtain**: the veil between the inner and the outer rooms of the sanctuary. Cf. Ex 26:31–33.

‡[4:11] **The golden altar**: the altar of incense. Cf. Ex 30:1–6.

§[4:13] **The altar**: the bronze altar for animal sacrifices. Cf. Ex 27:1–8.

¶[4:14] **Forks**: used in turning over the sacrificed animal on the fire of the altar. **Basins**: to receive the sacrificial blood; cf. Zec 9:15.

w. [4:3] Nm 8:24; 1 Chr 23:24–27.

x. [4:15] 2 Sm 6:6–7; 1 Chr 13:9–10.  y. [4:20] 1 Sm 6:19–20.
z. [4:31] Nm 3:36–37.

of the Merarites with respect to all their service in the tent of meeting under the supervision of Ithamar, son of Aaron the priest.

**Number of Adult Levites.** ³⁴So Moses and Aaron and the leaders of the community enrolled the Kohathites, by clans and ancestral houses, ³⁵all between thirty and fifty years of age who will join the personnel to work in the tent of meeting; ³⁶their enrollment by clans was two thousand seven hundred and fifty. ³⁷Such was the enrollment of the clans of the Kohathites, everyone who was to serve in the tent of meeting, whom Moses enrolled, together with Aaron, as the LORD directed through Moses.

³⁸As for the enrollment of the Gershonites, by clans and ancestral houses, ³⁹all between thirty and fifty years of age who will join the personnel to work in the tent of meeting—⁴⁰their enrollment by clans and ancestral houses was two thousand six hundred and thirty. ⁴¹Such was the enrollment of the clans of the Gershonites, everyone who was to serve in the tent of meeting, whom Moses enrolled, together with Aaron, as the LORD directed.

⁴²As for the enrollment of the clans of the Merarites, by clans and ancestral houses, ⁴³all from thirty up to fifty years of age who will join the personnel to work in the tent of meeting—⁴⁴their enrollment by clans was three thousand two hundred. ⁴⁵Such was the enrollment of the clans of the Merarites, whom Moses enrolled, together with Aaron, as the LORD directed through Moses.

⁴⁶As for the total enrollment of the Levites, which Moses and Aaron and the Israelite leaders had made, by clans and ancestral houses, ⁴⁷all between thirty and fifty years of age who were to undertake tasks of service or transport for the tent of meeting— ⁴⁸their total enrollment was eight thousand five hundred and eighty. ⁴⁹As the LORD directed through Moses, they gave each of them their assignments for service and for transport; just as the LORD had commanded Moses.

## CHAPTER 5

**The Unclean Expelled.** ¹The LORD said to Moses: ²Order the Israelites to expel from camp everyone with a scaly infection, and everyone suffering from a discharge, and everyone who has become unclean by contact with a corpse.*ᵃ ³Male and female alike, you shall expel them. You shall expel them from the camp so that they do not defile their camp, where I dwell in their midst.ᵇ ⁴This the Israelites did, expelling them from the camp; just as the LORD had commanded Moses, so the Israelites did.

**Unjust Possession.**† ⁵The LORD said to Moses: ⁶Tell the Israelites: If a man or a woman commits any offense against another person, thus breaking faith with the LORD, and thereby becomes guilty, ⁷that person shall confess the wrong that has been done, make restitution in full, and in addition give one fifth of its value to the one that has been wronged. ⁸However, if there is no next of kin,‡ one to whom restitution can be made, the restitution shall be made to the LORD and shall fall to the priest; this is apart from the ram of atonement with which the priest makes atonement for the guilty individual. ⁹Likewise, every contribution among the sacred offerings that the Israelites present to the priest will belong to him.ᵈ ¹⁰Each shall possess his own sacred offerings; what is given to a priest shall be his.ᵉ

**Ordeal for Suspected Adultery.** ¹¹The LORD said to Moses: ¹²Speak to the Israelites and tell them: If a man's wife goes astray and becomes unfaithful to a man having intercourse with herᶠ in secret from her husband and she is able to conceal the fact that she has defiled herself for lack of a witness who might have caught her in the act; ¹⁴or if a man is overcome by a feeling of jealousy that makes him suspect his wife, and she has defiled herself; or if a man is overcome by a feeling of jealousy that makes him suspect his wife and she has not defiled herself— ¹⁵then the man shall bring his wife to the priest as well as an offering on her behalf, a tenth of an ephah§ of barley meal. However, he shall not pour oil on it nor put frankincense over it, since it is a grain offering of jealousy, a grain offering of remembrance which recalls wrongdoing.

¹⁶The priest shall first have the woman come forward and stand before the LORD. ¹⁷In an earthen vessel he shall take holy water,¶ as well as some dust from the floor of the tabernacle and put it in the water.ᵍ ¹⁸Making the woman stand before the LORD, the priest shall uncover her head and place in her hands the grain offering of remembrance, that is, the grain offering of jealousy, while he himself shall hold the water of bitterness that brings a curse. ¹⁹Then the priest shall adjure the woman, saying to her, "If no other man has had intercourse with you, and you have not gone astray by defiling yourself while under the authority of your husband, be

---

*[5:2] For the laws regarding victims of skin disease, see Lv 13–14; those suffering from a discharge, Lv 15; those unclean by contact with a corpse, Nm 19:11–22; Lv 21:1–4.

a. [5:2] Nm 19:11, 13; Lv 13:46; 21:1; 22:4.   b. [5:3] Nm 35:34.

†[5:5–10] The basic law on unjust possession is given in Lv 5:14–26. The new item here concerns the case where the injured party has died and left no heirs, in which case the restitution must be made to the priest.

‡[5:8] **Next of kin:** Hebrew *goʾel* ("redeemer"), a technical term denoting the nearest relative, upon whom devolved the obligation of "redeeming" the family property, in order to keep it within the family. Cf. Lv 25:25; Ru 4:1–6.

§[5:15] **Ephah:** see note on Is 5:10.

¶[5:17] **Holy water:** water from the basin that stood in the court of the tabernacle.

c. [5:6–10] Lv 5:21–25.   d. [5:9] Dt 18:3–4; Ez 44:29–30.   e. [5:10] Lv 10:12–15.   f. [5:13] Lv 18:20; Jn 8:4.   g. [5:17] Nm 19:17.

immune to this water of bitterness that brings a curse. [20]But if you have gone astray while under the authority of your husband, and if you have defiled yourself and a man other than your husband has had intercourse with you"— [21]so shall the priest adjure the woman with this imprecation—"may the LORD make you a curse and malediction* among your people by causing your uterus to fall and your belly to swell! [22]May this water, then, that brings a curse, enter your bowels to make your belly swell and your uterus fall!"[h] And the woman shall say, "Amen, amen!"[†] [23]The priest shall put these curses in writing and shall then wash them off into the water of bitterness, [24]and he will have the woman drink the water of bitterness that brings a curse, so that the water that brings a curse may enter into her to her bitter hurt. [25]But first the priest shall take the grain offering of jealousy from the woman's hand, and having elevated the grain offering before the LORD, shall bring it to the altar, [26]where he shall take a handful of the grain offering as a token offering and burn it on the altar.[i] Only then shall he have the woman drink the water. [27]Once he has had her drink the water, if she has defiled herself and been unfaithful to her husband, the water that brings a curse will enter into her to her bitter hurt, and her belly will swell and her uterus will fall, so that she will become a curse among her people. [28]If, however, the woman has not defiled herself, but is still pure, she will be immune and will still be fertile.

[29]This, then, is the ritual for jealousy when a woman goes astray while under the authority of her husband and defiles herself, [30]or when such a feeling of jealousy comes over a man that he becomes suspicious of his wife; he shall have her stand before the LORD, and the priest shall perform this entire ritual for her. [31]The man shall be free from punishment,[‡] but the woman shall bear her punishment.

## CHAPTER 6

**Laws Concerning Nazirites.** [1]The LORD said to Moses: [2]Speak to the Israelites and tell them: When men or women solemnly take the nazirite[§] vow to dedicate themselves to the LORD, [3]they shall abstain from wine and strong drink;[j] they may neither drink wine vinegar, other vinegar, or any kind of grape juice, nor eat either fresh or dried grapes. [4]As long as they are nazirites they shall not eat anything of the produce of the grapevine; not even the seeds or the skins. [5]While they are under the nazirite vow, no razor shall touch their hair.[k] Until the period of their dedication to the LORD is over, they shall be holy, letting the hair of their heads grow freely. [6]As long as they are dedicated to the LORD, they shall not come near a dead person.[l] [7]Not even for their father or mother, sister or brother, should they defile themselves, when these die, since their heads bear their dedication to God. [8]As long as they are nazirites they are holy to the LORD.

[9]If someone dies very suddenly in their presence, defiling their dedicated heads, they shall shave their heads on the day of their purification, that is, on the seventh day. [10]On the eighth day they shall bring two turtledoves or two pigeons to the priest at the entrance of the tent of meeting. [11]The priest shall offer up the one as a purification offering and the other as a burnt offering, thus making atonement for them for the sin they committed with respect to the corpse. On the same day they shall reconsecrate their heads [12]and rededicate themselves to the LORD for the period of their dedication, bringing a yearling lamb as a reparation offering. The previous period is not valid, because they defiled their dedicated heads.

[13]This is the ritual for the nazirites:[m] When the period of their dedication is complete they shall go to the entrance of the tent of meeting, [14]bringing their offerings to the LORD, one unblemished yearling lamb for a burnt offering, one unblemished yearling ewe lamb for a purification offering, one unblemished ram as a communion offering, [15]and a basket of unleavened cakes of bran flour mixed with oil and of unleavened wafers spread with oil, along with their grain offerings and libations. [16]The priest shall present them before the LORD, and shall offer up the purification offering and the burnt offering for them. [17]He shall then offer up the ram as a communion sacrifice to the LORD, along with the basket of unleavened cakes, and the priest will offer the grain offering and libation. [18]Then at the entrance of the tent of meeting the nazirite shall shave his or her dedicated head, take the hair of the dedicated head, and put it in the fire under the communion sacrifice. [19]After the nazirite has shaved off the dedicated

---

*[5:21] **Curse and malediction**: the woman's name would be used in curses and oaths to invoke a similar misfortune on another person or on oneself. Cf. Is 65:15; Jer 29:22.

†[5:22] **Amen**: a Hebrew word meaning "certainly, truly," used to give assent to a statement, a curse, a blessing, a prayer, or the like, in the sense of "so be it."

‡[5:31] **Free from punishment**: the point is that a husband will not incur a harmful consequence if his accusation is not borne out by the ordeal; if he's right, his wife's punishment vindicates him. For her part, the woman (if guilty) must bear her punishment.

§[6:2–21] **Nazirite**: from the Hebrew word *nazir*, meaning "set apart as sacred, dedicated, vowed." The nazirite vow could be either for a limited period or for life. Those bound by this vow had to abstain from all the products of the grapevine, from cutting or shaving their hair, and from contact with a corpse. They were regarded as men and women of God like

the prophets; cf. Am 2:11–12. Examples of lifelong nazirites were Samson (Jgs 13:4–5, 7; 16:17), Samuel (1 Sm 1:11), and John the Baptist (Lk 1:15). At the time of Jesus the practice of taking the nazirite vow for a limited period seems to have been quite common, even among the early Christians; cf. Acts 18:18; 21:23–24, 26.

---

h. [5:22] Ps 109:18.   i. [5:26] Lv 5:12.

j. [6:3–4] Jgs 13:7, 14.   k. [6:5] Jgs 13:5; 16:17; 1 Sm 1:11.   l. [6:6] Nm 19:11, 16; Lv 21:11.   m. [6:13] Acts 21:24, 26.

hair, the priest shall take a boiled shoulder of the ram, as well as one unleavened cake from the basket and one unleavened wafer, and shall put them in the hands of the nazirite. [20]The priest shall then elevate them as an elevated offering before the LORD. They are an offering belonging to the priest, along with the brisket of the elevated offering and the leg of the contribution. Only after this may the nazirite drink wine.

[21]This, then, is the law for the nazirites, that is, what they vow as their offering to the LORD in accord with their dedication, apart from anything else which their means may allow. In keeping with the vow they take so shall they do, according to the law of their dedication.

**The Priestly Blessing.** [22]The LORD said to Moses: [23]Speak to Aaron and his sons and tell them: This is how you shall bless the Israelites. Say to them:

[24] The LORD bless you and keep you!
[25] The LORD let his face shine upon you, and
    be gracious to you!
[26] The LORD look upon you kindly and give
    you peace!*

[27]So shall they invoke my name upon the Israelites, and I will bless them.

## CHAPTER 7

**Offerings of the Tribal Leaders.** [1]Now, when Moses had completed the erection of the tabernacle, he anointed and consecrated it with all its equipment," as well as the altar with all its equipment. After he anointed and consecrated them, [2]an offering was made by the tribal leaders of Israel, who were heads of ancestral houses, the same leaders of the tribes who supervised those enrolled. [3]The offering they brought before the LORD consisted of six wagons for baggage and twelve oxen, that is, a wagon for every two tribal leaders, and an ox for each. These they presented before the tabernacle.

[4]The LORD then said to Moses: [5]Accept their offering, that these things may be put to use to maintain the tent of meeting. Assign them to the Levites, to each according to his duties. [6]So Moses accepted the wagons and oxen, and assigned them to the Levites. [7]He gave two wagons and four oxen to the Gershonites° according to their duties, [8]and four wagons and eight oxen to the Merarites according to their duties, under the supervision of Ithamar, son of Aaron the priest. [9]He gave none to the Kohathites, because they were responsible for maintenance of the sacred objects that had to be carried on their shoulders.ᵖ

[10]For the dedication of the altar also, the tribal leaders brought offerings when it was anointed;�q the leaders presented their offering before the altar. [11]But the LORD said to Moses: Let one leader each day present his offering for the dedication of the altar.

[12†]The one who presented his offering on the first day was Nahshon, son of Amminadab, of the tribe of Judah. [13]His offering consisted of one silver plate weighing a hundred and thirty shekels and one silver basin weighing seventy shekels according to the sanctuary shekel, both filled with bran flour mixed with oil for a grain offering; [14]one gold cup of ten shekels' weight filled with incense; [15]one bull from the herd, one ram, and one yearling lamb for a burnt offering; [16]one goat for a purification offering; [17]and two bulls, five rams, five he-goats, and five yearling lambs for a communion sacrifice. This was the offering of Nahshon, son of Amminadab.

[18]On the second day Nethanel, son of Zuar, tribal leader of Issachar, made his offering. [19]He presented as his offering one silver plate weighing a hundred and thirty shekels and one silver basin weighing seventy shekels according to the sanctuary shekel, both filled with bran flour mixed with oil for a grain offering; [20]one gold cup of ten shekels' weight filled with incense; [21]one bull from the herd, one ram, and one yearling lamb for a burnt offering; [22]one goat for a purification offering; [23]and two bulls, five rams, five he-goats, and five yearling lambs for a communion sacrifice. This was the offering of Nethanel, son of Zuar.

[24]On the third day it was the turn of the tribal leader of the Zebulunites, Eliab, son of Helon. [25]His offering consisted of one silver plate weighing a hundred and thirty shekels and one silver basin weighing seventy shekels according to the sanctuary shekel, both filled with bran flour mixed with oil for a grain offering; [26]one gold cup of ten shekels' weight filled with incense; [27]one bull from the herd, one ram, and one yearling lamb for a burnt offering; [28]one goat for a purification offering; [29]and two bulls, five rams, five he-goats, and five yearling lambs for a communion sacrifice. This was the offering of Eliab, son of Helon.

[30]On the fourth day it was the turn of the tribal leader of the Reubenites, Elizur, son of Shedeur. [31]His offering consisted of one silver plate weighing a hundred and thirty shekels and one silver basin weighing seventy shekels according to the sanctuary shekel, both filled with bran flour mixed with oil for a grain offering; [32]one gold cup of ten shekels' weight filled with incense; [33]one bull from the herd, one ram, and one yearling lamb for a burnt offering; [34]one

---

*[6:26] **Peace**: the Hebrew word *Shalom* includes the idea of happiness, good health, prosperity, friendship, and general well-being. To use this term as a greeting was to pray for all these things upon the one greeted.

ⁿ. [7:1] Ex 40:17.  o. [7:7–8] Nm 4:24–33.  p. [7:9] Nm 3:31; ʳ–15.

---

†[7:12–88] The repetitious account of the same offerings brought by each of the twelve tribal leaders and the summary of them are characteristic of an official registration.

q. [7:10] Nm 7:84.

goat for a purification offering; [35]and two bulls, five rams, five he-goats, and five yearling lambs for a communion sacrifice. This was the offering of Elizur, son of Shedeur.

[36]On the fifth day it was the turn of the tribal leader of the Simeonites, Shelumiel, son of Zurishaddai. [37]His offering consisted of one silver plate weighing a hundred and thirty shekels and one silver basin weighing seventy shekels according to the sanctuary shekel, both filled with bran flour mixed with oil for a grain offering; [38]one gold cup of ten shekels' weight filled with incense; [39]one bull from the herd, one ram, and one yearling lamb for a burnt offering; [40]one goat for a purification offering; [41]and two bulls, five rams, five he-goats, and five yearling lambs for a communion sacrifice. This was the offering of Shelumiel, son of Zurishaddai.

[42]On the sixth day it was the turn of the tribal leader of the Gadites, Eliasaph, son of Reuel. [43]His offering consisted of one silver plate weighing a hundred and thirty shekels and one silver basin weighing seventy shekels according to the sanctuary shekel, both filled with bran flour mixed with oil for a grain offering; [44]one gold cup of ten shekels' weight filled with incense; [45]one bull from the herd, one ram, and one yearling lamb for a burnt offering; [46]one goat for a purification offering; [47]and two bulls, five rams, five he-goats, and five yearling lambs for a communion sacrifice. This was the offering of Eliasaph, son of Reuel.

[48]On the seventh day it was the turn of the tribal leader of the Ephraimites, Elishama, son of Ammihud. [49]His offering consisted of one silver plate weighing a hundred and thirty shekels and one silver basin weighing seventy shekels according to the sanctuary shekel, both filled with bran flour mixed with oil for a grain offering; [50]one gold cup of ten shekels' weight filled with incense; [51]one bull from the herd, one ram, and one yearling lamb for a burnt offering; [52]one goat for a purification offering; [53]and two bulls, five rams, five he-goats, and five yearling lambs for a communion sacrifice. This was the offering of Elishama, son of Ammihud.

[54]On the eighth day it was the turn of the tribal leader of the Manassites, Gamaliel, son of Pedahzur. [55]His offering consisted of one silver plate weighing a hundred and thirty shekels and one silver basin weighing seventy shekels according to the sanctuary shekel, both filled with bran flour mixed with oil for a grain offering; [56]one gold cup of ten shekels' weight filled with incense; [57]one bull from the herd, one ram, and one yearling lamb for a burnt offering; [58]one goat for a purification offering; [59]and two bulls, five rams, five he-goats, and five yearling lambs for a communion sacrifice. This was the offering of Gamaliel, son of Pedahzur.

[60]On the ninth day it was the turn of the tribal leader of the Benjaminites, Abidan, son of Gideoni. [61]His offering consisted of one silver plate weighing a hundred and thirty shekels and one silver basin weighing seventy shekels according to the sanctuary shekel, both filled with bran flour mixed with oil for a grain offering; [62]one gold cup of ten shekels' weight filled with incense; [63]one bull from the herd, one ram, and one yearling lamb for a burnt offering; [64]one goat for a purification offering; [65]and two bulls, five rams, five he-goats, and five yearling lambs for a communion sacrifice. This was the offering of Abidan, son of Gideoni.

[66]On the tenth day it was the turn of the tribal leader of the Danites, Ahiezer, son of Ammishaddai. [67]His offering consisted of one silver plate weighing a hundred and thirty shekels and one silver basin weighing seventy shekels according to the sanctuary shekel, both filled with bran flour mixed with oil for a grain offering; [68]one gold cup of ten shekels' weight filled with incense; [69]one bull from the herd, one ram, and one yearling lamb for a burnt offering; [70]one goat for a purification offering; [71]and two bulls, five rams, five he-goats, and five yearling lambs for a communion sacrifice. This was the offering of Ahiezer, son of Ammishaddai.

[72]On the eleventh day it was the turn of the tribal leader of the Asherites, Pagiel, son of Ochran. [73]His offering consisted of one silver plate weighing one hundred and thirty shekels and one silver basin weighing seventy shekels according to the sanctuary shekel, both filled with bran flour mixed with oil for a grain offering; [74]one gold cup of ten shekels' weight filled with incense; [75]one bull from the herd, one ram, and one yearling lamb for a burnt offering; [76]one goat for a purification offering; [77]and two bulls, five rams, five he-goats, and five yearling lambs for a communion sacrifice. This was the offering of Pagiel, son of Ochran.

[78]On the twelfth day it was the turn of the tribal leader of the Naphtalites, Ahira, son of Enan. [79]His offering consisted of one silver plate weighing a hundred and thirty shekels and one silver basin weighing seventy shekels according to the sanctuary shekel, both filled with bran flour mixed with oil for a grain offering; [80]one gold cup of ten shekels' weight filled with incense; [81]one bull from the herd, one ram, and one yearling lamb for a burnt offering; [82]one goat for a purification offering; [83]and two bulls, five rams, five he-goats, and five yearling lambs for a communion sacrifice. This was the offering of Ahira, son of Enan.

[84]These were the offerings for the dedication of the altar, given by the tribal leaders of Israel on the occasion of its anointing: twelve silver plates, twelve silver basins, and twelve gold cups. [85]Each silver plate weighed a hundred and thirty shekels, and each silver basin seventy, so that all the silver of these vessels amounted to two thousand four hundred shekels, according

to the sanctuary shekel. [86]The twelve gold cups that were filled with incense weighed ten shekels apiece, according to the sanctuary shekel, so that all the gold of the cups amounted to one hundred and twenty shekels. [87]The animals for the burnt offerings were, in all, twelve bulls, twelve rams, and twelve yearling lambs, with their grain offerings; those for the purification offerings were twelve goats. [88]The animals for the communion sacrifices were, in all, twenty-four bulls, sixty rams, sixty he-goats, and sixty yearling lambs. These, then, were the offerings for the dedication of the altar after it was anointed.

**The Voice.** [89]When Moses entered the tent of meeting to speak with God, he heard the voice addressing him from above the cover[r] on the ark of the covenant, from between the two cherubim; and so it spoke to him.

## CHAPTER 8

**The Menorah.** [1]The LORD said to Moses: [2]Speak to Aaron and say: "When you set up the menorah-lamps,[s] have the seven lamps throw their light in front of the menorah."[*] [3]Aaron did so, setting up the menorah-lamps to face the area in front of the menorah, just as the LORD had commanded Moses. [4]This is the construction of the menorah: hammered gold,[t] from its base to its bowls[†] it was hammered; according to the pattern which the LORD had shown Moses, so he made the menorah.

**Purification of the Levites.** [5]The LORD said to Moses: [6]Take the Levites from among the Israelites and cleanse them.[‡] [7]This is what you shall do to them to cleanse them. Sprinkle them with the water of purification, have them shave their whole bodies and wash their garments, and so cleanse themselves. [8]Then they shall take a bull from the herd, along with its grain offering of bran flour mixed with oil; and you shall take another bull from the herd for a purification offering. [9]Bringing the Levites before the tent of meeting, you shall assemble also the whole community of the Israelites. [10]When you have brought the Levites before the LORD, the Israelites shall lay their hands upon them. [11]Aaron shall then present the Levites before the LORD as an elevated offering from the Israelites, that they may perform the service of the LORD. [12]The Levites in turn shall lay their hands on the heads of the bulls, offering one as a purification offering and the other as a burnt offering to the LORD, to make atonement for the Levites. [13]Then you

shall have the Levites stand before Aaron and his sons, and you shall present them as an elevated offering to the LORD; [14]thus you shall separate the Levites from the rest of the Israelites, and the Levites shall belong to me.[u]

[15]Only then shall the Levites enter upon their service in the tent of meeting, when you have cleansed them and presented them as an elevated offering. [16]For they, among the Israelites, are totally dedicated to me; I have taken them for myself in place of everyone that opens the womb, the firstborn of all the Israelites.[v] [17]Indeed, all the firstborn among the Israelites, human being and beast alike, belong to me; I consecrated them to myself on the day I killed all the firstborn in the land of Egypt.[w] [18]But I have taken the Levites in place of all the firstborn Israelites; [19]and from among the Israelites I have given to Aaron and his sons these Levites, who are to be dedicated,[x] to perform the service of the Israelites in the tent of meeting and to make atonement for them, so that no plague may strike among the Israelites should they come too near the sanctuary.

[20]This, then, is what Moses and Aaron and the whole community of the Israelites did with respect to the Levites; the Israelites did exactly as the LORD had commanded Moses concerning them. [21]When the Levites had purified themselves[§] and washed their garments, Aaron presented them as an elevated offering before the LORD, and made atonement for them to cleanse them. [22]Only then did they enter upon their service in the tent of meeting under the supervision of Aaron and his sons. Exactly as the LORD had commanded Moses concerning the Levites, so it was done with regard to them.

**Age Limits for Levitical Service.** [23]The LORD said to Moses: [24]This is the rule for the Levites. Everyone twenty-five years old or more shall join the personnel in the service of the tent of meeting.[y] [25]But everyone fifty on up shall retire from the work force and serve no more. [26]They shall assist their fellow Levites in the tent of meeting in performing their duties, but they shall not do the work. This, then, is how you are to regulate the duties of the Levites.

## CHAPTER 9

**Second Passover.** [1]The LORD said to Moses in the wilderness of Sinai, in the first month of the second year following their departure from the land of Egypt: [2]Tell the Israelites to celebrate the Passover at the prescribed time. [3]In the evening twilight of the fourteenth day of this month[z] you shall celebrate it at its prescribed time, in

---

*[8:2] **Menorah**: a seven-branched lampstand; see Ex 25:31–40; 37:17–24.

†[8:4] **Bowls**: lit., "blossom," a designation for the blossom-shaped cups holding the lamps of the menorah.

‡[8:6] **Cleanse them**: in the language of the Pentateuch only the priests were "consecrated," that is, made sacred or set aside for the Lord, in an elaborate ceremony described in Ex 29 and in this chapter. The Levites were "cleansed," that is, made ritually clean for their special work.

r. [7:89] Ex 25:22.   s. [8:2] Ex 25:37.   t. [8:4] Ex 25:31, 40.

§[8:21] **Purified themselves**: by having the "water of purification" sprinkled on them as prescribed in v. 7.

u. [8:14] Nm 3:45.   v. [8:16] Nm 3:12, 45.   w. [8:17] Nm 3:13; Lk 2:23.   x. [8:19] Nm 3:9–10.   y. [8:24] Nm 4:3, 23.   z. [9:3] Ex 12:6; Lv 23:5.

accord with all its statutes and regulations. <sup>4</sup>So Moses told the Israelites to celebrate the Passover, <sup>5</sup>and they did celebrate the Passover on the fourteenth day of the first month during the evening twilight in the wilderness of Sinai. Just as the LORD had commanded Moses, so the Israelites did.

<sup>6</sup>There were some, however, who were unclean because of a human corpse and so could not celebrate the Passover that day. These men came up to Moses and Aaron that same day <sup>7</sup>and they said to them, "Although we are unclean because of a human corpse, why should we be deprived of presenting the LORD's offering at its prescribed time along with other Israelites?" <sup>8</sup>Moses answered them, "Wait so that I can learn what the LORD will command in your regard."

<sup>9</sup>The LORD then said to Moses: <sup>10</sup>Speak to the Israelites: "If any one of you or of your descendants is unclean because of a human corpse, or is absent on a journey, you may still celebrate the LORD's Passover. <sup>11</sup>But you shall celebrate it in the second month,<sup>a</sup> on the fourteenth day of that month during the evening twilight, eating it with unleavened bread and bitter herbs, <sup>12</sup>and not leaving any of it over till morning, nor breaking any of its bones,<sup>b</sup> but observing all the statutes of the Passover. <sup>13</sup>However, anyone who is clean and not away on a journey, who yet fails to celebrate the Passover, shall be cut off from the people, for not presenting the LORD's offering at the prescribed time. That person shall bear the consequences of this sin.

<sup>14</sup>"If an alien* who lives among you would celebrate the LORD's Passover, it shall be celebrated according to the statutes and regulations for the Passover. You shall have the same law for the resident alien as for the native of the land."<sup>c</sup>

**The Fiery Cloud.** <sup>15</sup>On the day when the tabernacle was erected, the cloud<sup>†</sup> covered the tabernacle, the tent of the covenant; but from evening until morning it took on the appearance of fire over the tabernacle.<sup>d</sup> <sup>16</sup>It was always so: during the day the cloud covered the tabernacle and at night had the appearance of fire. <sup>17</sup>Whenever the cloud rose from the tent, the Israelites would break camp; wherever the cloud settled, the Israelites would pitch camp.<sup>e</sup> <sup>18</sup>At the direction of the LORD the Israelites broke camp, and at the LORD's direction they pitched camp.<sup>f</sup> As long as the cloud stayed over the tabernacle, they remained in camp.

<sup>19</sup>Even when the cloud lingered many days over the tabernacle, the Israelites kept the charge of the LORD and would not move on. <sup>20</sup>Yet if it

happened the cloud was over the tabernacle only for a few days, at the direction of the LORD they stayed in camp; and at the LORD's direction they broke camp. <sup>21</sup>If it happened the cloud remained there only from evening until morning, when the cloud rose in the morning, they would break camp. Whether the cloud lifted during the day or the night they would then break camp. <sup>22</sup>Whether the cloud lingered over the tabernacle for two days or for a month or longer, the Israelites remained in camp and did not break camp; but when it lifted, they broke camp. <sup>23</sup>At the direction of the LORD they pitched camp, and at the LORD's direction they broke camp; they kept the charge of the LORD, as the LORD directed them through Moses.

## CHAPTER 10

**The Silver Trumpets.** <sup>1</sup>The LORD said to Moses: <sup>2</sup>Make two trumpets of silver, making them of hammered silver, for you to use in summoning the community and in breaking camp. <sup>3</sup>When both are blown, the whole community shall gather round you at the entrance of the tent of meeting; <sup>4</sup>but when one of them is blown, only the tribal leaders, the heads of the clans of Israel, shall gather round you. <sup>5</sup>When you sound the signal, those encamped on the east side shall break camp; <sup>6</sup>when you sound a second signal, those encamped on the south side shall break camp; when you sound a third signal, those encamped on the west side shall break camp; when you sound a fourth signal, those encamped on the north side shall break camp. Thus shall the signal be sounded for them to break camp. <sup>7</sup>But in calling forth an assembly you are to blow a blast, without sounding the signal.

<sup>8</sup>The sons of Aaron, the priests, shall blow the trumpets; this is prescribed forever for you and your descendants. <sup>9g</sup>When in your own land you go to war against an enemy that is attacking you, you shall sound the alarm on the trumpets, and you shall be remembered before the LORD, your God, and be saved from your foes. <sup>10</sup>And when you rejoice<sup>‡</sup> on your festivals, and your new-moon feasts, you shall blow the trumpets over your burnt offerings and your communion sacrifices,<sup>h</sup> so that this serves as a reminder of you before your God. I, the LORD, am your God.

## II. DEPARTURE, REBELLION, AND WANDERING IN THE WILDERNESS FOR FORTY YEARS

**Departure from Sinai.** <sup>11</sup>In the second year, on the twentieth day of the second month, the cloud rose from the tabernacle of the covenant,

---

*[9:14] **An alien:** compare this passage with the Passover legislation in Ex 12:48, where circumcision is required of the alien who would celebrate the feast.

†[9:15] **The cloud:** already mentioned at the departure from Egypt; cf. Ex 13:21–22.

a. [9:11] 2 Chr 30:2–15.   b. [9:12] Ex 12:46; Jn 19:36.   c. [9:14] Ex 12:48–49.   d. [9:15] Ex 13:21.   e. [9:17] Wis 18:3.   f. [9:18] 1 Cor 10:1.

‡[10:10] **When you rejoice:** cf. Dt 16:14. **Festivals:** the great annual feasts of the Passover, Pentecost and Booths described in Lv 23; Nm 28–29.

g. [10:9] 2 Chr 13:14.   h. [10:10] Nm 29:1; 2 Chr 29:26–28.

¹²and the Israelites moved on from the wilderness of Sinai by stages, until the cloud came to rest in the wilderness of Paran.

¹³The first time that they broke camp at the direction of the LORD through Moses, ¹⁴the divisional camp of the Judahites, arranged in companies, was the first to set out. Over its whole company was Nahshon, son of Amminadab, ¹⁵with Nethanel, son of Zuar, over the company of the tribe of Issacharites, ¹⁶and Eliab, son of Helon, over the company of the tribe of Zebulunites. ¹⁷Then, after the tabernacle was dismantled, the Gershonites and Merarites who carried the tabernacle set out. ¹⁸The divisional camp of the Reubenites, arranged in companies, was the next to set out. Over its whole company was Elizur, son of Shedeur, ¹⁹with Shelumiel, son of Zurishaddai, over the company of the tribe of Simeonites, ²⁰and Eliasaph, son of Reuel, over the company of the tribe of Gadites. ²¹The Kohathites, who carried the sacred objects, then set out. Before their arrival the tabernacle would be erected. ²²The divisional camp of the Ephraimites set out next, arranged in companies. Over its whole company was Elishama, son of Ammihud, ²³with Gamaliel, son of Pedahzur, over the company of the tribe of Manassites, ²⁴and Abidan, son of Gideoni, over the company of the tribe of Benjaminites. ²⁵Finally, as rear guard for all the camps, the divisional camp of the Danites set out, arranged in companies. Over its whole company was Ahiezer, son of Ammishaddai, ²⁶with Pagiel, son of Ochran, over the company of the tribe of Asherites, ²⁷and Ahira, son of Enan, over the company of the tribe of Naphtalites. ²⁸This was the order of march for the Israelites, company by company, when they set out.

**Hobab as Guide.** ²⁹Moses said to Hobab,* son of Reuel the Midianite, Moses' father-in-law, "We are setting out for the place concerning which the LORD has said, 'I will give it to you.' Come with us, and we will be generous toward you, for the LORD has promised prosperity to Israel." ³⁰But he answered, "No, I will not come. I am going instead to the land of my birth." ³¹Moses said, "Please, do not leave us; you know where we can camp in the wilderness, and you can serve as our guide. ³²If you come with us, we will share with you the prosperity the LORD will bestow on us."

**Into the Wilderness.** ³³ʲFrom the mountain of the LORD† they made a journey of three days, and the ark of the covenant of the LORD went before them for the three-day journey to seek out a resting place for them. ³⁴And the cloud of the LORD was over them by day when they set out from camp.

³⁵Whenever the ark set out, Moses would say,

> "Arise, O LORD, may your enemies be
>     scattered,
>   and may those who hate you flee
>     before you."

³⁶And when it came to rest, he would say,

> "Bring back, O LORD, the myriads of
>     Israel's troops!"

## CHAPTER 11

**Discontent of the People.** ¹Now the people complained bitterly in the hearing of the LORD;ᵏ and when he heard it his wrath flared up, so that the LORD's fire burned among them and consumed the outskirts of the camp. ²But when the people cried out to Moses, he prayed to the LORD and the fire died out. ³Hence that place was called Taberah,‡ because there the fire of the LORD burned among them.

⁴The riffraff among them were so greedy for meat that even the Israelites lamented again,ˡ "If only we had meat for food! ⁵We remember the fish we used to eat without cost in Egypt, and the cucumbers, the melons, the leeks, the onions, and the garlic. ⁶But now we are famished; we have nothing to look forward to but this manna."ᵐ

⁷ⁿManna was like coriander seed§ and had the appearance of bdellium. ⁸When they had gone about and gathered it up, the people would grind it between millstones or pound it in a mortar, then cook it in a pot and make it into loaves, with a rich creamy taste. ⁹At night, when the dew fell upon the camp, the manna also fell.ᵒ

¹⁰When Moses heard the people, family after family, crying at the entrance of their tents, so that the LORD became very angry, he was grieved. ¹¹"Why do you treat your servant so badly?" Moses asked the LORD. "Why are you so displeased with me that you burden me with all this people? ¹²Was it I who conceived all this

---

*[10:29–32] **Hobab:** one of three names for the father-in-law of Moses (see Ex 2:18; 4:18; 18:6; Jgs 4:11). Here perhaps Hobab's initial refusal indicates he wished to be coaxed before granting the favor. From Jgs 1:16 it seems probable that he did accede to Moses' request. However, Ex 18:27 suggests Moses' father-in-law returned to his own land. Indeed, to the extent Nm 10:29–32 appears to repeat Ex 18:27, it may indicate a resumption of the narrative of Israel's march through the wilderness after the "digression" formed by the Israelite sojourn at Sinai, Ex 19:1–Nm 10:28.

i. [10:14–16] Nm 2:3, 5, 7.

†[10:33] **The mountain of the LORD:** Sinai (Horeb), elsewhere always called "the mountain of God."

‡[11:3] **Taberah:** means "the burning."

§[11:7] **Coriander seed:** see note on Ex 16:31. **Bdellium:** a transparent, amber-colored gum resin, which is also mentioned in Gn 2:12.

j. [10:33] Dt 1:33.   k. [11:1] Dt 9:22.   l. [11:4] Ps 78:18.   m. [11:5–6] Nm 21:5; Ex 16:3; Acts 7:39.   n. [11:7–8] Ex 16:14–15, 31; Ps 78:24; Wis 16:20; Jn 6:31.   o. [11:9] Ex 16:14–15.

people? or was it I who gave them birth, that you tell me to carry them at my breast, like a nurse carrying an infant, to the land you have promised under oath to their fathers? [13]Where can I get meat to give to all this people? For they are crying to me, 'Give us meat for our food.' [14]I cannot carry all this people by myself, for they are too heavy for me. [15]If this is the way you will deal with me, then please do me the favor of killing me at once, so that I need no longer face my distress."

**The Seventy Elders.** [16]Then the LORD said to Moses: Assemble for me seventy of the elders of Israel, whom you know to be elders and authorities among the people, and bring them to the tent of meeting. When they are in place beside you, [17]I will come down and speak with you there. I will also take some of the spirit that is on you and will confer it on them, that they may share the burden of the people with you. You will then not have to bear it by yourself.

[18]To the people, however, you shall say: "Sanctify yourselves for tomorrow, when you shall have meat to eat. For in the hearing of the LORD you have cried, 'If only we had meat for food! Oh, how well off we were in Egypt!' Therefore the LORD will give you meat to eat, [19]and you will eat it, not for one day, or two days, or five, or ten, or twenty days, [20]but for a whole month—until it comes out of your very nostrils and becomes loathsome to you. For you have rejected the LORD who is in your midst, and in his presence you have cried, 'Why did we ever leave Egypt?'"

[21]But Moses said, "The people around me include six hundred thousand soldiers; yet you say, 'I will give them meat to eat for a whole month.' [22]Can enough sheep and cattle be slaughtered for them? If all the fish of the sea were caught for them, would they have enough?" [23]The LORD answered Moses: Is this beyond the LORD's reach? You shall see now whether or not what I have said to you takes place.

**The Spirit on the Elders.** [24]So Moses went out and told the people what the LORD had said. Gathering seventy elders of the people, he had them stand around the tent. [25]The LORD then came down in the cloud and spoke to him. Taking some of the spirit that was on Moses, he bestowed it on the seventy elders; and as the spirit came to rest on them, they prophesied* but did not continue.

[26]Now two men, one named Eldad and the other Medad, had remained in the camp, yet the spirit came to rest on them also. They too had been on the list, but had not gone out to the tent; and so they prophesied in the camp. [27]So, when a young man ran and reported to Moses, "Eldad

and Medad are prophesying in the camp," [28]Joshua, son of Nun, who from his youth had been Moses' aide, said, "My lord, Moses, stop them." [29]But Moses answered him, "Are you jealous for my sake? If only all the people of the LORD were prophets! If only the LORD would bestow his spirit on them!" [30]Then Moses retired to the camp, along with the elders of Israel.

**The Quail.** [31]There arose a wind[p] from the LORD that drove in quail from the sea and left them all around the camp site, to a distance of a day's journey and at a depth of two cubits upon the ground.[†] [32]So all that day, all night, and all the next day the people set about to gather in the quail. Even the one who got the least gathered ten homers[‡] of them. Then they spread them out all around the camp. [33]But while the meat was still between their teeth, before it could be chewed, the LORD's wrath flared up against the people, and the LORD struck them with a very great plague. [34]So that place was named Kibroth-hattaavah,[§] because it was there that the greedy people were buried.

[35]From Kibroth-hattaavah the people set out for Hazeroth, where they stayed.

## CHAPTER 12

**Jealousy of Aaron and Miriam.** [1]Miriam and Aaron spoke against Moses on the pretext of the Cushite woman he had married; for he had in fact married a Cushite woman.[¶] [2]They complained,** "Is it through Moses alone that the LORD has spoken? Has he not spoken through us also?" And the LORD heard this. [3]Now the man Moses was very humble, more than anyone else on earth. [4]So at once the LORD said to Moses and Aaron and Miriam: Come out, you three, to the tent of meeting. And the three of them went. [5]Then the LORD came down in a column of cloud, and standing at the entrance of the tent, called, "Aaron and Miriam." When both came forward, [6]the LORD said: Now listen to my words:

If there are prophets among you,
    in visions I reveal myself to them,
    in dreams I speak to them;

---

*[11:25] **They prophesied:** in the sense, not of foretelling the future, but of speaking in enraptured enthusiasm. Such manifestations are mentioned in the early days of Hebrew prophecy (1 Sm 10:10–12; 19:20–21; Jl 3:1) and in the first years of the Church (Acts 2:6–11, 17; 19:6; 1 Cor 12–14).

†[11:31] The heaps of quail lying upon the ground all around the Israelites' camp suggest the ambiguity of God's response to the people's lament for meat in v. 4 and foreshadow the plague which God will now bring upon Israel (v. 33). Their request had been nothing less than a rejection of what God has done for them (v. 20).

‡[11:32] **Homers:** see note on Is 5:10. **They spread them out:** to cure by drying.

§[11:34] **Kibroth-hattaavah:** means "graves of greed."

¶[12:1] **Cushite woman:** apparently Zipporah, the Midianite, is meant; cf. Ex 2:21.

**[12:2] The apparent reason for Miriam's and Aaron's quarrel with their brother Moses was jealousy of his authority; his Cushite wife served only as an occasion for the dispute.

p. [11:31] Ps 78:26–28.   q. [11:32–33] Ps 78:26–31.   r. [12:3] Sir 45:1–2.

7 Not so with my servant Moses!
  Throughout my house he is worthy of
      trust:*ˢ
8     face to face I speak to him,ᵗ
      plainly and not in riddles.
  The likeness of the LORD he beholds.

Why, then, do you not fear to speak against my servant Moses? ⁹And so the LORD's wrath flared against them, and he departed.

**Miriam's Punishment.** ¹⁰Now the cloud withdrew from the tent, and there was Miriam,ᵘ stricken with a scaly infection, white as snow!† When Aaron turned toward Miriam and saw her stricken with snow-white scales, ¹¹he said to Moses, "Ah, my lord! Please do not charge us with the sin that we have foolishly committed! ¹²Do not let her be like the stillborn baby that comes forth from its mother's womb with its flesh half consumed." ¹³Then Moses cried to the LORD, "Please, not this! Please, heal her!" ¹⁴But the LORD answered Moses: Suppose her father had spit in her face, would she not bear her shame for seven days? Let her be confined outside the camp for seven days; afterwards she may be brought back. ¹⁵So Miriam was confined outside the camp for seven days, and the people did not start out again until she was brought back.

¹⁶After that the people set out from Hazeroth and encamped in the wilderness of Paran.

## CHAPTER 13

**The Twelve Scouts.** ¹The LORD said to Moses: ²Send men to reconnoiter the land of Canaan, which I am giving the Israelites. You shall send one man from each ancestral tribe, every one a leader among them. ³ᵛSo Moses sent them from the wilderness of Paran, at the direction of the LORD. All of them were leaders among the Israelites. ⁴These were their names:

from the tribe of Reuben, Shammua, son
    of Zaccur;
5 from the tribe of Simeon, Shaphat, son of
    Hori;
6 from the tribe of Judah, Caleb, son of
    Jephunneh;
7 from the tribe of Issachar, Igal;
8 for the Josephites, from the tribe of
    Ephraim, Hoshea, son of Nun;
9 from the tribe of Benjamin, Palti, son of
    Raphu;

10 from the tribe of Zebulun, Gaddiel, son of
    Sodi;
11 for the Josephites, from the tribe of
    Manasseh, Gaddi, son of Susi;
12 from the tribe of Dan, Ammiel, son of
    Gemalli;
13 from the tribe of Asher, Sethur, son of
    Michael;
14 from the tribe of Naphtali, Nahbi, son of
    Vophsi;
15 from the tribe of Gad, Geuel, son of Machi.

¹⁶These are the names of the men whom Moses sent to reconnoiter the land. But Hoshea, son of Nun, Moses called Joshua.‡

¹⁷In sending them to reconnoiter the land of Canaan, Moses said to them, "Go up there in the Negeb, up into the highlands, ¹⁸and see what kind of land it is and whether the people living there are strong or weak, few or many. ¹⁹Is the country in which they live good or bad? Are the towns in which they dwell open or fortified? ²⁰Is the soil fertile or barren, wooded or clear? And do your best to get some of the fruit of the land." It was then the season for early grapes.

²¹So they went up and reconnoitered the land from the wilderness of Zin§ as far as where Rehob adjoins Lebo-hamath. ²²Going up by way of the Negeb, they reached Hebron, where Ahiman, Sheshai and Talmai, descendants of the Anakim,¶ were. (Now Hebron had been built seven years before Zoan in Egypt.) ²³They also reached the Wadi Eshcol,** where they cut down a branch with a single cluster of grapes on it, which two of them carried on a pole, as well as some pomegranates and figs. ²⁴It was because of the cluster the Israelites cut there that they called the place Wadi Eshcol.ˣ

**Their Report.** ²⁵They returned from reconnoitering the land forty days later. ²⁶ʸProceeding directly to Moses and Aaron and the whole community of the Israelites in the wilderness of Paran at Kadesh, they made a report to them and to the whole community, showing them the fruit of the land. ²⁷They told Moses: "We came

---

*[12:7] **Worthy of trust**: the text is open to a variety of interpretations. Thus, the word of Moses may be relied upon by Israel because God speaks to him directly; or, Moses alone is worthy of God's trust in God's household (heavenly or earthly). An alternative translation, however, is: "with all my house he is entrusted."

†[12:10] **Stricken with a scaly infection, white as snow**: see note on Lv 13:1–14:47. The point of the simile lies either in the flakiness or the whiteness of snow.

‡[13:16] **Joshua**: in Hebrew, "Jehoshua," which was later modified to "Jeshua," the Hebrew name for "Jesus." Hoshea and Joshua are variants of one original name meaning "the LORD saves." Cf. Mt 1:21.

§[13:21] **The wilderness of Zin**: north of Paran and southwest of the Dead Sea. It is quite distinct from "the wilderness of Sin" near the border of Egypt (Ex 16:1; 17:1; Nm 33:11). **Lebo-hamath**: a town near Riblah (Jer 39:5–6) at the southern border of Hamath, an independent kingdom in southern Syria. David's conquests extended as far as Hamath (2 Sm 8:9–11), and Lebo-hamath thus formed the northern border of the ideal extent of Israel's possessions (Nm 34:7–9; Ez 47:15; 48:1). This may suggest that this verse was inserted precisely to extend the scope of the reconnaissance; cf. Dt 1:24.

¶[13:22, 28] **Anakim**: an aboriginal race in southern Palestine, largely absorbed by the Canaanites. Either because of their tall stature or because of the massive stone structures left by them, the Israelites regarded them as giants.

**[13:23] **Eshcol**: means "cluster."

---

s. [12:7] Heb 3:2, 5.   t. [12:8] Ex 33:1; Dt 34:10; Sir 45:3.   u. [12:10] Dt 24:9.   v. [13:3–33] Dt 1:22–28.

w. [13:22] Jos 11:21–22.   x. [13:24] Nm 32:9; Dt 1:24–25.   y. [13:26–27] Ex 3:8, 17.

to the land to which you sent us. It does indeed flow with milk and honey, and here is its fruit. [28]However, the people who are living in the land are powerful, and the towns are fortified and very large.[ε] Besides, we saw descendants of the Anakim there. [29]Amalekites live in the region of the Negeb; Hittites, Jebusites and Amorites dwell in the highlands, and Canaanites along the sea and the banks of the Jordan."

[30]Caleb, however, quieted the people before Moses and said, "We ought to go up and seize the land, for we can certainly prevail over it." [31]But the men who had gone up with him said, "We cannot attack these people; they are too strong for us." [32]They spread discouraging reports[d] among the Israelites about the land they had reconnoitered, saying, "The land that we went through and reconnoitered is a land that consumes its inhabitants. And all the people we saw there are huge. [33b]There we saw the Nephilim* (the Anakim are from the Nephilim); in our own eyes we seemed like mere grasshoppers, and so we must have seemed to them."

## CHAPTER 14

**Threats of Revolt.** [1]At this, the whole community broke out with loud cries, and the people wept into the night. [2c]All the Israelites grumbled against Moses and Aaron, the whole community saying to them, "If only we had died in the land of Egypt," or "If only we would die here in the wilderness! [3]Why is the LORD bringing us into this land only to have us fall by the sword? Our wives and little ones will be taken as spoil. Would it not be better for us to return to Egypt?" [4]So they said to one another, "Let us appoint a leader and go back to Egypt."

[5]But Moses and Aaron fell prostrate before the whole assembled community of the Israelites; [6]while Joshua, son of Nun, and Caleb, son of Jephunneh, who had been among those that reconnoitered the land, tore their garments [7]and said to the whole community of the Israelites,[d] "The land which we went through and reconnoitered is an exceedingly good land. [8]If the LORD is pleased with us, he will bring us in to this land and give it to us, a land which flows with milk and honey. [9e]Only do not rebel against the LORD! You need not be afraid of the people of the land, for they are but food for us![†] Their protection has left them, but the LORD is with us. Do not fear them." **The Lord's Sentence.** [10]The whole community threatened to stone them. But the glory of the

LORD appeared at the tent of meeting to all the Israelites. [11]And the LORD said to Moses: How long will this people spurn me? How long will they not trust me, despite all the signs I have performed among them?[f] [12]I will strike them with pestilence and disown them. Then I will make of you a nation greater and mightier than they.[g]

[13h]But Moses said to the LORD: "The Egyptians will hear of this, for by your power you brought out this people from among them. [14]They will tell the inhabitants of this land, who have heard that you, LORD, are in the midst of this people; you, LORD, who directly revealed yourself! Your cloud stands over them, and you go before them by day in a column of cloud and by night in a column of fire.[i] [15]If now you slay this people all at once, the nations who have heard such reports of you will say, [16]'The LORD was not able to bring this people into the land he swore to give them; that is why he slaughtered them in the wilderness.'[j] [17]Now then, may my Lord's forbearance be great, even as you have said, [18]'The LORD is slow to anger and abounding in kindness, forgiving iniquity and rebellion; yet certainly not declaring the guilty guiltless, but punishing children to the third and fourth generation for their parents' iniquity.' [19]Pardon, then, the iniquity of this people in keeping with your great kindness, even as you have forgiven them from Egypt until now."[l]

[20]The LORD answered: I pardon them as you have asked. [21]Yet, by my life and the LORD's glory that fills the whole earth, [22]of all the people who have seen my glory and the signs I did in Egypt and in the wilderness,[m] and who nevertheless have put me to the test ten times already and have not obeyed me, [23]not one shall see the land which I promised on oath to their ancestors. None of those who have spurned me shall see it. [24]But as for my servant Caleb, because he has a different spirit and follows me unreservedly,[n] I will bring him into the land which he entered, and his descendants shall possess it. [25]But now, since the Amalekites and Canaanites are living in the valleys,[‡] turn away tomorrow and set out into the wilderness by way of the Red Sea road.

[26]The LORD also said to Moses and Aaron: [27]How long will this wicked community grumble against me?[o] I have heard the grumblings of the Israelites against me. [28]Tell them:[§] "By my life"—oracle of the LORD—"I will do to you

---

[‡][14:25] **The valleys:** the low-lying plains in the Negeb and along the seacoast and in the Jordan depression, as well as the higher valleys in the mountains farther north: cf. v. 45.

[§][14:28–29] God punished the grumblers by giving them their wish; cf. v. 2. Their lack of trust in God is cited in 1 Cor 10:10 and Heb 3:12–18 as a warning for Christians.

---

*[13:33] **Nephilim:** i.e., "fallen ones" (in the Septuagint, "giants"), a reference to fallen heroes of old. Cf. Gn 6:4.

†[14:9] **They are but food for us:** lit., "for they are our bread." "Bread" (Heb. *lechem*) is here used in the sense of "prey, spoils" to be consumed by an invader. This is the answer to the pessimistic report that this land "consumes its inhabitants" (13:32).

z. [13:28–29] Dt 9:1–2.  a. [13:32] Nm 32:9; Jos 14:8.  b. [13:33] Dt 2:10.  c. [14:2] Ex 16:3; Ps 106:25.  d. [14:7–8] Dt 1:25. e. [14:9] Dt 7:18.

f. [14:11] Ps 78:22, 32.  g. [14:12] Ex 32:10.  h. [14:13–16] Ex 32:12; Dt 9:26–29; Ps 106:23.  i. [14:14] Ex 13:21; Jos 2:9–10. j. [14:16] Ex 32:12; Dt 9:28.  k. [14:18] Ex 20:5; 34:6–7; Ps 103:8; 145:8.  l. [14:19] Ps 78:38.  m. [14:22–23] Dt 1:35.  n. [14:24] Jos 14:8–9.  o. [14:27] Ex 16:7, 12.

just what I have heard you say. ²⁹Here in the wilderness*ᵖ* your dead bodies shall fall. Of all your men of twenty years or more, enrolled in your registration, who grumbled against me, ³⁰not one of you shall enter the land where I solemnly swore to settle you, except Caleb, son of Jephunneh, and Joshua, son of Nun. ³¹Your little ones, however, who you said would be taken as spoil, I will bring in, and they shall know the land you rejected.*ᵍ* ³²But as for you, your bodies shall fall here in the wilderness, ³³while your children will wander for forty years, suffering for your infidelity, till the last of you lies dead in the wilderness.*ʳ* ³⁴Corresponding to the number of days you spent reconnoitering the land—forty days—you shall bear your punishment one year for each day: forty years. Thus you will realize what it means to oppose me. ³⁵I, the LORD, have spoken; and I will surely do this to this entire wicked community that conspired against me: here in the wilderness they shall come to their end and there they will die."

³⁶And the men whom Moses had sent to reconnoiter the land*ˢ* and who on returning had set the whole community grumbling against him by spreading discouraging reports about the land— ³⁷these men who had spread discouraging reports about the land were struck down by the LORD and died. ³⁸Only Joshua, son of Nun, and Caleb, son of Jephunneh, survived of all the men who had gone to reconnoiter the land.*ᵗ*

**Unsuccessful Invasion.** ³⁹When Moses repeated these words to all the Israelites, the people mourned greatly. ⁴⁰Early the next morning they started up high into the hill country, saying, "Here we are, ready to go up to the place that the LORD spoke of:*ᵘ* for we did wrong." ⁴¹But Moses said, "Why are you now transgressing the LORD's order? This cannot succeed. ⁴²Do not go up, because the LORD is not in your midst; do not allow yourself to be struck down by your enemies.*ᵛ* ⁴³For there the Amalekites and Canaanites will face you, and you will fall by the sword. You have turned back from following the LORD; therefore the LORD will not be with you." ⁴⁴Yet they dared to go up high into the hill country,*ʷ* even though neither the ark of the covenant of the LORD nor Moses left the camp. ⁴⁵And the Amalekites and Canaanites who dwelt in that hill country came down and defeated them, beating them back as far as Hormah.*

---

\* [14:45] **Hormah**: one of the Canaanite royal cities in southern Judah, according to the tradition attested in Jos 12:14, although Nm 21:1–3 gives it as the new name for the city of Arad when it was destroyed by Israel. According to the list of conquered cities preserved in Jgs 1, the earlier name for the city of Hormah was Zephath. The precise location is unknown.

p. [14:29] Dt 1:35; Heb 3:17.  q. [14:31] Dt 1:39.  r. [14:33–34] Nm 13:26; 32:13; Ps 95:10; Ez 4:6.  s. [14:36–37] Nm 13:17, 32–33; 1 Cor 10:10.  t. [14:38] Nm 26:65.  u. [14:40] Nm 13:18; Dt 1:41.  v. [14:42] Dt 1:42.  w. [14:44] Dt 1:43.

---

## CHAPTER 15

**Secondary Offerings.** ¹The LORD spoke to Moses: ²Speak to the Israelites and say to them: When you enter the land that I am giving you for your settlements, ³if you make to the LORD an oblation from the herd or from the flock—either a burnt offering or a sacrifice, to fulfill a vow, or as a voluntary offering, or for one of your festivals—to produce a pleasing aroma for the LORD, ⁴the one presenting the offering shall also present to the LORD a grain offering, a tenth of a measure*‡* of bran flour mixed with a fourth of a hin of oil, ⁵as well as wine for a libation, a fourth of a hin. You will do this with the burnt offering or the sacrifice, for each lamb. ⁶Alternatively for a ram you shall make a grain offering of two tenths of a measure of bran flour mixed with a third of a hin of oil, ⁷and for a libation, a third of a hin of wine, thereby presenting a pleasing aroma to the LORD. ⁸If you make an offering from the herd—either a burnt offering, or a sacrifice, to fulfill a vow, or as a communion offering to the LORD, ⁹with it a grain offering of three tenths of a measure of bran flour mixed with half a hin of oil will be presented; ¹⁰and you will present for a libation, half a hin of wine—a sweet-smelling oblation to the LORD. ¹¹The same is to be done for each ox, ram, lamb or goat. ¹²Whatever the number you offer, do the same for each of them.

¹³All the native-born shall make these offerings in this way, whenever they present a sweet-smelling oblation to the LORD. ¹⁴Likewise, in any future generation, any alien residing with you or anyone else in your midst, who presents an oblation of pleasing aroma to the LORD, must do as you do. ¹⁵There is but one statute for you and for the resident alien, a perpetual statute throughout your generations. You and the resident alien will be alike before the LORD; ¹⁶you and the alien residing with you will have the same rule and the same application of it.

¹⁷The LORD spoke to Moses: ¹⁸Speak to the Israelites and say to them: When you enter the land into which I am bringing you ¹⁹and eat of the bread of the land, you shall offer the LORD a contribution. ²⁰A round loaf from your first batch of dough*§* you shall offer as a contribution. Just like a contribution from the threshing floor you shall offer it.*ˣ* ²¹Throughout your

---

† [15:2–16] These laws on sacrifice are complementary to those of Lv 1–3. Since the food of the Israelites consisted not only of meat but also of bread, oil and wine, they offered flour, wine and oil in sacrifice to the Lord besides the animal oblations.

‡ [15:4] **Measure**: the word, supplied from the context, does not appear in the Hebrew (as also in vv. 6, 9; 28:9, 12, 20, 28; 29:3, 9, 14). Probably the ephah (which is named in 5:15; 28:5) is intended. **Hin**: see note on Ez 45:24.

§ [15:20] **Dough**: the meaning of the Hebrew term is uncertain; some render, "baking utensils." This word is used elsewhere only in Ez 44:30 and Neh 10:33; a related Hebrew word is used in Lv 2:14.

x. [15:19–20] Ez 44:30.

generations you shall give a contribution to the LORD from your first batch of dough.

**Purification Offerings.** [*]²²If through inadvertence you fail to do any of these commandments which the LORD has given to Moses—[y] ²³anything the LORD commanded you through Moses from the time the LORD first gave the command down through your generations— ²⁴if it was done inadvertently without the community's knowledge, the whole community shall sacrifice one bull from the herd as a burnt offering of pleasing aroma to the LORD, along with its prescribed grain offering and libation, as well as one he-goat as a purification offering. ²⁵[z]Then the priest shall make atonement for the whole Israelite community; and they will be forgiven, since it was inadvertence, and for their inadvertence they have brought their offering: an oblation to the LORD as well as their purification offering before the LORD. ²⁶Not only the whole Israelite community but also the aliens residing among you shall be forgiven, since the inadvertent fault affects all the people.

²⁷If it is an individual who sins inadvertently,[a] this person shall bring a yearling she-goat as a purification offering. ²⁸And the priest shall make atonement before the LORD for the one who erred, since the sin was inadvertent, making atonement for the person to secure forgiveness. ²⁹You shall have but one rule for the person who sins inadvertently, whether a native-born Israelite or an alien residing among you.

³⁰But anyone who acts defiantly,[b] whether a native or an alien, reviles the LORD, and shall be cut off from among the people. ³¹[c]For having despised the word of the LORD and broken his commandment, he must be cut off entirely and bear the punishment.

**The Sabbath-breaker.** ³²While the Israelites were in the wilderness, a man was discovered gathering wood on the sabbath day. ³³Those who caught him at it brought him to Moses and Aaron and the whole community. ³⁴But they put him in custody, for there was no clear decision[†] as to what should be done with him.[d] ³⁵Then the LORD said to Moses: This man shall be put to death; let the whole community stone him outside the camp. ³⁶So the whole community led him outside the camp and stoned him to death, as the LORD had commanded Moses.

**Tassels on the Cloak.** ³⁷The LORD said to Moses: ³⁸Speak to the Israelites and tell them that throughout their generations they are to make tassels[‡] for the corners of their garments, fastening a violet cord to each corner.[e] ³⁹When you use these tassels, the sight of the cord will remind you of all the commandments of the LORD and you will do them, without prostituting yourself going after the desires of your hearts and your eyes. ⁴⁰Thus you will remember to do all my commandments and you will be holy to your God. ⁴¹I, the LORD, am your God who brought you out of the land of Egypt to be your God: I, the LORD your God.[f]

## CHAPTER 16

**Rebellion of Korah.** ¹[§]Korah, son of Izhar, son of Kohath, son of Levi, and the Reubenites Dathan and Abiram, sons of Eliab, and On, son of Peleth,[¶] son of Reuben took ²two hundred and fifty Israelites who were leaders in the community, members of the council and men of note, and confronted Moses. ³Holding an assembly against Moses and Aaron, they said,[g] "You go too far! The whole community, all of them, are holy; the LORD is in their midst. Why then should you set yourselves over the LORD's assembly?"

⁴When Moses heard this, he fell prostrate. ⁵Then he said to Korah and to all his faction, "May the LORD make known tomorrow morning who belongs to him and who is the holy one and whom he will have draw near to him! The one whom he chooses, he will have draw near to him. ⁶Do this: take your censers, Korah and all his faction, ⁷and put fire in them and place incense in them before the LORD tomorrow. He whom the LORD then chooses is the holy one. You Levites go too far!"

⁸Moses also said to Korah, "Hear, now, you Levites! ⁹ᵃAre you not satisfied that the God of Israel has singled you out from the community

---

[*][15:22–31] See note on Lv 4:2. Although Lv 4–5 and Nm 15:22–31 both concern inadvertent sins, the emphasis here, as opposed to Lv 4–5, is on the failure of the community to perform "positive commands" rather than on doing what is prohibited.

[†][15:34] **No clear decision:** either it was not clear that gathering wood constituted "work" and as such a willful violation of the sabbath and a capital offense; or they did not yet know how the death penalty was to be inflicted.

[‡][15:38] **Tassels:** at the time of Jesus these tassels were worn by all pious Jews, including Jesus (Mt 9:20–21; Mk 6:56); some Pharisees wore very large ones in a display of their zeal for the law (Mt 23:5).

[§][16:1–3] The evidence seems to show that accounts of two, if not more, distinct rebellions have been combined in this chapter. The most obvious are the rebellions of Korah and his faction (Nm 27:3) and of Dathan and Abiram (Dt 11:6); cf. Ps 106. The present account combines both events into one narrative; but even here it is rather easy to separate the two. The rebellion of the Reubenites, Dathan and Abiram, was more political in character, against Moses alone as the civil leader (cf. v. 13); these rebels were punished by being swallowed alive in an earthquake. The rebellion of Korah was more religious in character, directed primarily against the religious leadership of Aaron (though in vv. 19–22 it is Korah and the whole community against both Moses and Aaron). About two hundred and fifty Israelites joined Korah's faction, and they are punished by fire. The parts of the present section which refer to the rebellion of Dathan and Abiram are vv. 12–15 and vv. 25–34 of chap. 16; the rest of chap. 16 and all of chap. 17 chiefly concern the rebellion of Korah.

[¶][16:1] **The Reubenites . . . son of Peleth:** some suggest on the basis of 26:5, 8 and Gn 46:9 reading instead of the traditional Hebrew text: "son of Levi, and Dathan and Abiram, sons of Eliab, son of Pallu, son of Reuben."

y. [15:22–23] Lv 4:13–14.  z. [15:25] Lv 4:20.  a. [15:27–28] Lv 4:27–28.  b. [15:30] Dt 17:12.  c. [15:31] Prv 13:13.  d. [15:34] Lv 24:12.

e. [15:38] Dt 22:12.  f. [15:41] Lv 22:32–33.  g. [16:3] Ps 106:16–18; Sir 45:19.  h. [16:9] Dt 10:8.

of Israel, to have you draw near him to maintain the LORD's tabernacle, and to attend upon the community and to serve them? ¹⁰He has allowed you and your Levite kinsmen with you to approach him, and yet you seek the priesthood too. ¹¹It is therefore against the LORD that you and all your faction are conspiring. As for Aaron, what has he done that you should grumble against him?"

**Rebellion of Dathan and Abiram.** ¹²Moses summoned Dathan and Abiram, sons of Eliab, but they answered, "We will not go.' ¹³Are you not satisfied that you have brought us here from a land flowing with milk and honey to have us perish in the wilderness, that now you must also lord it over us? ¹⁴Far from bringing us to a land flowing with milk and honey, or giving us fields and vineyards for our inheritance, will you gouge out our eyes?† No, we will not go."

¹⁵Then Moses became very angry and said to the LORD, "Pay no attention to their offering. I have never taken a single donkey from them, nor have I wronged any one of them."ⁱ

**Korah.** ¹⁶Moses said to Korah, "You and all your faction shall appear before the LORD tomorrow—you and they and Aaron too. ¹⁷Then each of you take his own censer, put incense in it, and present it before the LORD, two hundred and fifty censers; and you and Aaron, each with his own censer, do the same." ¹⁸So each of them took their censers, and laying incense on the fire they had put in them, they took their stand by the entrance of the tent of meeting along with Moses and Aaron. ¹⁹Then, when Korah had assembled all the community against them at the entrance of the tent of meeting, the glory of the LORD appeared to the entire community, ²⁰and the LORD said to Moses and Aaron: ²¹Stand apart from this community, that I may consume them at once. ²²But they fell prostrate and exclaimed, "O God, God of the spirits of all living creatures, if one man sins will you be angry with the whole community?" ²³The LORD answered Moses: ²⁴Speak to the community and tell them: Withdraw from the area around the tent‡ of Korah, Dathan and Abiram.

**Punishment of Dathan and Abiram.** ²⁵Moses, followed by the elders of Israel, arose and went to Dathan and Abiram.§ ²⁶Then he spoke to the community, "Move away from the tents of

these wicked men and do not touch anything that is theirs: otherwise you too will be swept away because of all their sins." ²⁷So they withdrew from the area around the tents of Korah, Dathan and Abiram. When Dathan and Abiram had come out and were standing at the entrance of their tents with their wives, their children, and their little ones, ²⁸Moses said, "This is how you shall know that the LORD sent me to do all I have done, and that it was not of my own devising: ²⁹if these die an ordinary death, merely suffering the fate common to all humanity, the LORD has not sent me. ³⁰But if the LORD makes a chasm, and the ground opens its mouth and swallows them with all belonging to them, and they go down alive to Sheol,¶ then you will know that these men have spurned the LORD." ³¹No sooner had he finished saying all this than the ground beneath them split open, ³²and the earth opened its mouth and swallowed them and their families and all of Korah's people** with all their possessions. ³³They went down alive to Sheol with all belonging to them; the earth closed over them, and they disappeared from the assembly. ³⁴But all the Israelites near them fled at their shrieks, saying, "The earth might swallow us too!"

**Punishment of Korah.** ³⁵And fire from the LORD came forth which consumed the two hundred and fifty men who were offering the incense.

## CHAPTER 17

¹The LORD said to Moses: ²Tell Eleazar, son of Aaron the priest, to remove the censers from the embers; and scatter the fire some distance away, for they have become holy— ³††the censers of those who sinned at the cost of their lives. Have them hammered into plates to cover the altar, because in being presented before the LORD they have become holy. In this way they shall serve as a sign to the Israelites. ⁴So taking the bronze censers which had been presented by those who were burned, Eleazar the priest had them hammered into a covering for the altar, ⁵just as the LORD had directed him through Moses. This was to be a reminder to the Israelites that no unauthorized person, no one who was not a descendant of Aaron, should draw near to offer incense before the LORD, lest he meet the fate of Korah and his faction.

⁶The next day the whole Israelite community grumbled against Moses and Aaron, saying, "You have killed the people of the LORD." ⁷But

---

*[16:12] **We will not go:** to appear before Moses' "tribunal."
†[16:14] **Gouge out our eyes:** blind us to the real state of affairs.

‡[16:24] **Withdraw from the area around the tent:** the word for "tent," *mishkan*, here and in v. 27, is otherwise used in the singular only for the tent of meeting, suggesting possibly the erection of a rival sanctuary by the rebels. Note further, as an indication of the fact that various accounts of rebellion have been fused here, that in v. 19 the entire community had been assembled by Korah at the tent of meeting.

§[16:25] Since Dathan and Abiram had refused to go to Moses (vv. 12–14), he, with the elders as witnesses, was obliged to go to their tents.

¶[16:30] **Sheol:** see note on Ps 6:6.
**[16:32] **And all of Korah's people:** the implication of this secondary addition to the text is, on the one hand, that Korah met his death elsewhere, presumably with the two hundred and fifty offering incense (vv. 16–17, 35); or, on the other hand, he died along with Dathan and Abiram in the splitting of the earth.

††[17:3] Whatever was brought into intimate contact with something holy shared in its holiness. See note on 19:20.

i. [16:15] 1 Sm 12:3.

j. [16:31–34] Nm 26:10; Lv 10:2; Dt 11:6; Ps 106:17–18.

while the community was assembling against them, Moses and Aaron turned toward the tent of meeting, and the cloud now covered it and the glory of the LORD appeared. [8]Then Moses and Aaron came to the front of the tent of meeting, [9]and the LORD said to Moses: [10]Remove yourselves from this community, that I may consume them at once. But they fell prostrate.

[11]Then Moses said to Aaron, "Take your censer, put fire from the altar in it, lay incense on it, and bring it quickly to the community to make atonement for them; for wrath has come forth from the LORD and the plague has begun."[k] [12]Aaron took his censer just as Moses directed and ran in among the assembly, where the plague had already begun among the people. Then he offered the incense and made atonement for the people, [13]while standing there between the living and the dead. And so the scourge was checked. [14]There were fourteen thousand seven hundred dead from the scourge, in addition to those who died because of Korah. [15]When the scourge had been checked, Aaron returned to Moses at the entrance of the tent of meeting.

**Aaron's Staff.** [16]The LORD now said to Moses: [17]Speak to the Israelites and get from them a staff[*] for each ancestral house, twelve staffs in all, from all the leaders of their ancestral houses. Write each man's name on his staff; [18]and write Aaron's name on Levi's staff.[†] For each head of an ancestral house shall have a staff. [19]Then deposit them in the tent of meeting, in front of the covenant, where I meet you. [20]The staff of the man whom I choose shall sprout. Thus I will rid myself of the Israelites' grumbling against you.

[21]So Moses spoke to the Israelites, and all their leaders gave him staffs, twelve in all, one from each leader of their ancestral houses; and Aaron's staff was among them. [22]Moses deposited the staffs before the LORD in the tent of the covenant. [23]The next day, when Moses entered the tent of the covenant, Aaron's staff, representing the house of Levi, had sprouted. It had put forth sprouts, produced blossoms, and borne ripe almonds! [24]So Moses brought out all the staffs from the LORD's presence to all the Israelites, and each one identified his own staff and took it. [25]Then the LORD said to Moses: Put

back Aaron's staff in front of the covenant, for safe keeping as a sign to the rebellious, so that their grumbling against me may cease and they might not die. [26]Moses did this. Just as the LORD had commanded him, so he did.

**Charge of the Sacred Things.** [27‡]Then the Israelites exclaimed to Moses, "We will perish; we are lost, we are all lost! [28]Anyone who approaches the tabernacle of the LORD will die! Will there be no end to our perishing?"

## CHAPTER 18

[1]The LORD said to Aaron:[§] You and your sons as well as your ancestral house with you[¶] shall be responsible for any sin with respect to the sanctuary; but only you and your sons with you shall be responsible for any sin with respect to your priesthood. [2]You shall also present with you your kinsmen of the tribe of Levi, your ancestral tribe, that they may be joined to you[**] and assist you, while you and your sons with you are in front of the tent of the covenant. [3]They shall discharge your obligations and those with respect to the whole tent; however, they shall not come near the utensils of the sanctuary or the altar, or else both they and you will die. [4]They will be joined to you to perform the duties associated with the tent of meeting, all the labor pertaining to the tent. But no unauthorized person[††] shall come near you. [5]You shall perform the duties of the sanctuary and of the altar, that wrath may not fall again upon the Israelites.

[6]I hereby take your kinsmen, the Levites, from among the Israelites; they are a gift to you,[l] dedicated to the LORD for the labor they perform for the tent of meeting. [7m]But you and your sons with you must take care to exercise your priesthood in whatever concerns the altar and the area within the veil.[‡‡] I give you your priesthood as a gift. Any unauthorized person who comes near shall be put to death.

**The Priests' Share of the Sacrifices.** [8]The LORD said to Aaron:[§§] I hereby give to you charge of the contributions made to me, including the various holy offerings of the Israelites;[n] I assign them to you and to your sons as a perquisite, a

---

[*][17:17] The staff was not merely an article of practical use, but also a symbol of authority; cf. Gn 49:10; Nm 24:17; Jer 48:17. Therefore, the staff of a leader of a tribe was considered the emblem of the tribe; in fact, certain Hebrew words such as *matteh*, the word for "staff" here, also mean "tribe." Perhaps for this reason, to avoid confusion, the author here uses the term *bet'ab*, "ancestral house," for "tribe" instead of one of the ordinary words for "tribe."

[†][17:18] **Levi's staff:** it is not clear whether this is considered as one of the twelve mentioned in the preceding verse, or as a thirteenth staff. Sometimes Levi is reckoned as one of the twelve tribes (e.g., Dt 27:12–13), but more often the number twelve is arrived at by counting the two sub-tribes of Joseph, i.e., Ephraim and Manasseh, as distinct tribes. In this passage also it seems probable that the tribe of Levi is considered apart from the other twelve tribes.

[‡][17:27–28] The people's distress here echoes their panic in 16:34, and may be heightened further by the death of the two hundred and fifty leaders offering incense in 16:35.

[§][18:1–3] This law, which kept unqualified persons from contact with holy things, is in response to the Israelites' cry in 17:28. It is followed by other laws concerning priests and Levites.

[¶][18:1] **With you:** not only in the present but also those of his house in the future.

[**][18:2] **Be joined to you:** in Hebrew a pun on the popular etymology of the name "Levi." Cf. Gn 29:34.

[††][18:4] **Unauthorized person:** here, "one who is not a Levite"; in v. 7, "one who is not a priest."

[‡‡][18:7] **Veil:** the outer veil, or "curtain," is probably meant.

[§§][18:8–10] Two classes of offerings are here distinguished: the most holy offering, which only the male members of the priestly families could eat (vv. 8–10), and the other offerings, which the women of the priestly families could eat (vv. 11–19).

---

k. [17:11] Wis 18:20–21.

l. [18:6] Nm 3:9; 8:19.   m. [18:7] Nm 3:10.   n. [18:8] Nm 5:9.

perpetual due. ⁹This is what you shall have from the oblations that are most holy: every offering of theirs—namely, all their grain offerings, purification offerings, and reparation offerings which they must return to me—shall be most holy for you and for your sons. ¹⁰You shall eat them in a most holy place;* every male may partake of them. As holy, they belong to you.

¹¹This also you shall have: the contributions that are their gifts, including the elevated offering† of the Israelites; I assign them to you and to your sons and daughters with you as a perpetual due.ᵒ All in your household who are clean may eat them. ¹²I also assign to you all the bestᵖ of the new oil and of the new wine and grain that they give to the LORD as their first produce that has been processed. ¹³The first-ripened fruits of whatever is in their land, which they bring to the LORD, shall be yours; all of your household who are clean may eat them. ¹⁴Whatever is under the ban‡ in Israel shall be yours. ¹⁵Every living thing that opens the womb, human being and beast alike, such as are to be offered to the LORD, shall be yours;�q but you must redeem the firstborn of human beings, as well as redeem the firstborn of unclean animals. ¹⁶For the redemption price of a son, when he is a month old, you shall pay the equivalent of five silver shekels according to the sanctuary shekel, that is, twenty gerahs. ¹⁷But the firstborn of cattle, or the firstborn of sheep or the firstborn of goats you shall not redeem; they are holy. Their blood you must splash on the altar and their fat you must burn as an oblation of pleasing aroma to the LORD. ¹⁸Their meat, however, shall be yours, just as the brisket of the elevated offering and the right thigh belong to you. ¹⁹As a perpetual due I assign to you and to your sons and daughters with you all the contributions of holy things which the Israelites set aside for the LORD; this is a covenant of salt§ to last forever before the LORD, for you and for your descendants with you. ²⁰ˢThen the LORD said to Aaron:¶ You shall not have any heritage in their land nor hold any portion among them;

I will be your portion and your heritage among the Israelites.

**Tithes Due the Levites.** ²¹To the Levites, however, I hereby assign all tithes in Israel as their heritage in recompense for the labor they perform, the labor pertaining to the tent of meeting.ʳ ²²The Israelites may no longer approach the tent of meeting, thereby incurring the penalty of death. ²³Only the Levites are to perform the labor pertaining to the tent of meeting, and they shall incur the penalty for the Israelites' sin;** this is a permanent statute for all your generations. But they shall not have any heritage among the Israelites, ²⁴for I have assigned to the Levites as their heritage the tithes which the Israelites put aside as a contribution to the LORD. That is why I have said, they will not have any heritage among the Israelites.

**Tithes Paid by the Levites.** ²⁵The LORD said to Moses: ²⁶Speak to the Levites and say to them: When you take from the Israelites the tithes I have assigned you from them as your heritage, you are to make a contribution from them to the LORD, a tithe of the tithe; ²⁷and your contribution will be credited to you as if it were grain from the threshing floor or new wine from the vat. ²⁸Thus you too shall make a contribution to the LORD from all the tithes you take from the Israelites, handing over to Aaron the priest the contribution to the LORD. ²⁹From all the gifts to you, you shall make every contribution due to the LORD—from their best parts, that is the part to be consecrated from them.

³⁰Say to them also: Once you have made your contribution from the best part, the rest of the tithe will be credited to the Levites as if it were produce of the threshing floor or the produce of the vat. ³¹You and your households may eat it anywhere, since it is your recompense in exchange for labor in the tent of meeting. ³²You will incur no punishment when you contribute the best part of it. But do not profane the holy offerings of the Israelites or else you shall die.

## CHAPTER 19

**Ashes of the Red Heifer.** ¹The LORD spoke to Moses and Aaron: ²This is the statute for the ritual which the LORD has commanded. Tell the Israelites to procure for you a red heifer without defect and free from every blemish and on which no yoke has ever been laid. ³You will give it to Eleazar the priest, and it will be led outside the camp†† and slaughtered in his presence.

---

*[18:10] **In a most holy place**: in the court of the tabernacle, according to Lv 6:9, 19.

†[18:11] **Elevated offering**: this included the brisket and right thigh (v. 18), the shoulder of the peace offering (Lv 7:30–34), and portions of the nazirite sacrifice (Nm 6:19–20). **With you**: see note on v. 1. Aaron had no daughters; see also v. 19.

‡[18:14] **Under the ban**: in Hebrew, *herem*, which means here "set aside from profane use and made sacred to the Lord." Cf. Lv 27:21, 28.

§[18:19] **A covenant of salt**: cf. 2 Chr 13:5. The reference may perhaps be to the preservative power of salt (cf. Mt 5:13); but more likely the phrase refers to the custom of eating salt together to render a contract unbreakable. See note on Lv 2:13.

¶[18:20] The priests and Levites were forbidden to own hereditary land such as the other Israelites possessed; therefore in the allotment of the land (chap. 34) they did not receive any portion of it. Certain cities, however, were assigned to them for their residence; cf. 35:1–8.

**[18:23] **Incur the penalty for the Israelites' sin**: the Levites are responsible for protecting the sanctuary from illegitimate encroachment and in this sense pay the penalty for the Israelites' iniquity. This responds further to the fears of the people expressed in 17:27–28.

††[19:3] **Outside the camp**: several early Christian writers saw in this a prefiguring of the sacrificial death of Jesus outside the walls of Jerusalem; cf. Jn 19:20; Heb 13:12; in the

---

o. [18:11] Ex 29:27–28; Lv 7:34; 10:14.　p. [18:12–13] Dt 18:4; 26:2.　q. [18:15] Ex 13:2.　r. [18:18] Lv 7:31–34.　s. [18:20] Dt 10:9; 18:1–2; Jos 13:33; Ez 44:28.

t. [18:21] Heb 7:5.

⁴Eleazar the priest will take some of its blood on his finger and sprinkle it seven times toward the front of the tent of meeting.* ⁵Then the heifer will be burned in his sight; it will be burned with its hide and flesh, its blood and dung; ⁶and the priest will take cedar wood, hyssop and scarlet yarn and throw them into the fire in which the heifer is being burned. ⁷The priest shall then wash his garments and bathe his body in water, afterward he may enter the camp. The priest remains unclean until the evening. ⁸Likewise, the one who burned the heifer shall wash his garments in water, bathe his body in water, and be unclean until evening. ⁹Then somebody who is clean shall gather up the ashes of the heifer and deposit them in a clean place outside the camp. There they are to be kept to prepare purification water for the Israelite community. This is a purification offering. ¹⁰The one who has gathered up the ashes of the heifer shall also wash his garments and be unclean until evening. This is a permanent statute, both for the Israelites and for the alien residing among them. **Use of the Ashes.** ¹¹Those who touch the corpse of any human being will be unclean for seven days; ¹²they shall purify themselves with the water on the third and on the seventh day, and then be clean. But if they fail to purify themselves on the third and on the seventh day, they will not become clean. ¹³ᵘThose who touch the corpse of a human being who dies and who fail to purify themselves defile the tabernacle of the LORD and these persons shall be cut off from Israel. Since the purification water has not been splashed over them, they remain unclean: their uncleanness is still on them.

¹⁴This is the ritual: When someone dies in a tent, everyone who enters the tent, as well as everyone already in it, will be unclean for seven days; ¹⁵and every open vessel with its lid unfastened will be unclean. ¹⁶Moreover, everyone who in the open country touches a person who has been slain by the sword or who has died naturally, or who touches a human bone or a grave, will be unclean for seven days. ¹⁷For anyone who is thus unclean, ashes shall be taken from the burnt purification offering, and spring water will be poured on them from a vessel.ᵛ ¹⁸Then someone who is clean will take hyssop, dip it in this water, and sprinkle it on the tent and on all the vessels and persons that were in it, or on the one who touched the bone, the slain person or the other corpse, or the grave. ¹⁹The clean will sprinkle the unclean on the third and on the seventh day, and thus purify them on the

seventh day. Then they will wash their garments and bathe in water, and in the evening be clean. ²⁰†Those who become unclean and fail to purify themselves—those people will be cut off from the assembly, because they defile the sanctuary of the LORD. The purification water has not been splashed over them; they remain unclean. ²¹This will be a permanent statute for you.

Those who sprinkle the purification water will wash their garments, and those who come in contact with the purification water will be unclean until evening. ²²Moreover, anything that the unclean person touches becomes unclean itself, and the one who touches such a person becomes unclean until evening.

## CHAPTER 20‡

**Death of Miriam.** ¹The Israelites, the whole community, arrived in the wilderness of Zin§ in the first month, and the people stayed at Kadesh. It was here that Miriam died, and here that she was buried.

**Need for Water at Kadesh.** ²Since the community had no water, they held an assembly against Moses and Aaron. ³The people quarreled with Moses, exclaiming, "Would that we had perished when our kindred perished before the LORD! ⁴Why have you brought the LORD's assembly into this wilderness for us and our livestock to die here? ⁵Why have you brought us up out of Egypt, only to bring us to this wretched place? It is not a place for grain nor figs nor vines nor pomegranates! And there is no water to drink!" ⁶But Moses and Aaron went away from the assembly to the entrance of the tent of meeting, where they fell prostrate.

**Sin of Moses and Aaron.** Then the glory of the LORD appeared to them, ⁷and the LORD said to Moses: ⁸Take the staff and assemble the community, you and Aaron your brother, and in their presence command the rock to yield its waters. Thereby you will bring forth water from the rock for them, and supply the community and their livestock with water. ⁹So Moses took the staff from its place before the LORD, as he was ordered. ¹⁰Then Moses and Aaron gathered the assembly in front of the rock, where he said to them,ʷ "Just listen, you rebels! Are we to produce water for you out of this rock?" ¹¹ˣThen,

---

purifying water, into which the ashes of the red heifer were put, they saw a type of the water of Baptism.
*[19:4] **Toward the front of the tent of meeting:** since the tabernacle faced the east (Ex 26:15–30), the killing of the heifer would take place east of the camp; in later times it was done on the Mount of Olives, east of the Temple.

u. [19:13] Lv 15:31.   v. [19:17–19] Heb 9:13–14.

†[19:20] Ritual uncleanness is, as it were, contagious; so also sacredness; see note on 17:3.
‡[20:1–29] In this chapter the deaths of the three wilderness leaders are either intimated or explicitly reported: Miriam, v. 1; Moses, v. 12; Aaron, vv. 12, 22–29.
§[20:1] **The wilderness of Zin:** a barren region with a few good oases, southwest of the Dead Sea. See note on 13:21. **The first month:** we would expect the mention also of the day and of the year (after the exodus) when this took place; cf. similar dates in 1:1; 10:11; 33:38; Dt 1:3. Here the full date is left unspecified. According to one chronology, the Israelites arrived in Kadesh in the third year after the exodus (cf. Dt 1:46). But the itinerary in chap. 33 would suggest the fortieth year, the year in which Aaron died (33:38).

w. [20:10] Ex 17:5–6.   x. [20:11] Ps 78:15–16; Wis 11:4; 1 Cor 10:4.

raising his hand, Moses struck the rock twice[*] with his staff, and water came out in abundance, and the community and their livestock drank. [12†]But the LORD said to Moses and Aaron: Because you did not have confidence in me, to acknowledge my holiness before the Israelites, therefore you shall not lead this assembly into the land I have given them.

[13]These are the waters of Meribah,[y] where the Israelites quarreled with the LORD, and through which he displayed his holiness.

**Edom's Refusal.** [14]From Kadesh Moses sent messengers to the king of Edom: "Thus says your brother Israel:[‡] You know of all the hardships that have befallen us, [15]how our ancestors went down to Egypt, and we stayed in Egypt a long time, and the Egyptians treated us and our ancestors harshly. [16]When we cried to the LORD,[z] he heard our cry and sent an angel who led us out of Egypt. Now here we are at Kadesh, a town at the edge of your territory. [17]Please let us pass through your land. We will not cross any fields or vineyards, nor drink any well water, but we will go straight along the King's Highway[§] without turning to the right or to the left, until we have passed through your territory."

[18]But Edom answered him, "You shall not pass through here; if you do, I will advance against you with the sword." [19]The Israelites said to him, "We will go up along the highway. If we or our livestock drink any of your water, we will pay for it. It is nothing—just let us pass through on foot." [20]But Edom replied, "You shall not pass through,"[a] and advanced against them with a large and heavily armed force. [21]Therefore, since Edom refused to let Israel pass through their territory, Israel turned away from them.

**Death of Aaron.** [22b]Setting out from Kadesh, the Israelites, the whole community, came to Mount Hor.[¶] [23]There at Mount Hor, on the border of the land of Edom, the LORD said to Moses and Aaron: [24]Let Aaron be gathered to his people, for he shall not enter the land I have given to the Israelites, because you both rebelled against my directions at the waters of Meribah. [25]Take Aaron and Eleazar his son and bring them up on Mount Hor.[c] [26]Then strip Aaron of his garments and put them on Eleazar, his son; but there Aaron shall be gathered up in death.

[27]Moses did as the LORD commanded. When they had climbed Mount Hor in view of the whole community, [28]Moses stripped Aaron of his garments and put them on Eleazar his son. Then Aaron died there on top of the mountain.[d] When Moses and Eleazar came down from the mountain, [29]all the community understood that Aaron had breathed his last; and for thirty days the whole house of Israel mourned Aaron.

# CHAPTER 21

**Victory over Arad.** [1]When the Canaanite, the king of Arad,[**] who ruled over the Negeb,[e] heard that the Israelites were coming along the way of Atharim, he engaged Israel in battle and took some of them captive. [2]Israel then made this vow to the LORD: "If you deliver this people into my hand, I will put their cities under the ban."[f] [3]The LORD paid attention to Israel and delivered up the Canaanites,[g] and they put them and their cities under the ban. Hence that place was named Hormah.[††]

**The Bronze Serpent.** [4]From Mount Hor they set out by way of the Red Sea, to bypass the land of Edom, but the people's patience was worn out by the journey; [5]so the people complained[h] against God and Moses, "Why have you brought us up from Egypt to die in the wilderness, where there is no food or water? We are disgusted with this wretched food!"[‡‡]

[6]So the LORD sent among the people seraph[§§] serpents, which bit[i] the people so that many of the Israelites died. [7]Then the people came to Moses and said, "We have sinned in complaining against the LORD and you. Pray to the LORD to take the serpents from us." So Moses prayed for the people, [8]and the LORD said to Moses: Make a seraph and mount it on a pole, and everyone who has been bitten will look at it and recover.[¶¶] [9]Accordingly Moses made a bronze serpent[***] and

---

*[20:11] **Twice:** perhaps because he did not have sufficient faith to work the wonder with the first blow. Cf. v. 12.

†[20:12–13] What lay behind Moses and Aaron's lack of confidence is not made explicit in the text. **Holiness:** an allusion to the name of the place, Kadesh, which means "holy, sanctified, sacred." Meribah means "contention." Cf. Ex 17:7.

‡[20:14] **Your brother Israel:** according to biblical tradition, the Edomites were descended from Esau, the brother of Jacob. Their country, to the southeast of the Dead Sea, was also known as Seir; cf. Gn 25:24–26; 36:1, 8–9.

§[20:17] **The King's Highway:** an important highway, running north and south along the plateau east of the Dead Sea. In ancient times it was much used by caravans and armies; later it was improved by the Romans, and large stretches of it are still clearly recognizable.

¶[20:22] **Mount Hor:** not definitively identified, but probably to be sought in the vicinity of Kadesh. According to Dt 10:6, Aaron died at Moserah (cf. "Moseroth" in Nm 33:30–31), which is apparently the name of the region in which Mount Hor is situated.

**[21:1–3] The account of this episode seems to be a later insertion here, since logically v. 4 belongs immediately after 20:29. Perhaps this is the same event as that mentioned in Jgs 1:16–17.

††[21:3] **Hormah:** related to the Hebrew word *herem*, meaning "put under the ban." See notes on 14:45; 18:14.

‡‡[21:5] **This wretched food:** apparently the manna is meant.

§§[21:6] **Seraph:** the Hebrew name for a certain species of venomous snake; etymologically the word might signify "the fiery one." Compare the winged throne guardians in Is 6:2, 6; see also Is 14:29; 30:6.

¶¶[21:8] **Everyone who has been bitten will look at it and recover:** in the Gospel of John this scene is regarded as a type for the crucifixion of Jesus (Jn 3:14–15).

***[21:9] King Hezekiah, in his efforts to reform Israelite worship, "smashed the bronze serpent Moses had made" (2 Kgs 18:4).

---

y. [20:13] Nm 27:14; Ex 17:7.  z. [20:16] Ex 2:23.  a. [20:20] Jgs 11:17.  b. [20:21–22] Nm 33:37.

c. [20:25–26] Dt 32:50.  d. [20:28] Nm 33:38.  e. [21:1] Nm 33:40.  f. [21:2] Jos 6:17; Jgs 1:17.  g. [21:3] Nm 14:45.  h. [21:5] Nm 11:6; Ex 16:3.  i. [21:6] Dt 8:15; Wis 16:5; 1 Cor 10:9.

mounted it on a pole, and whenever the serpent bit someone, the person looked at the bronze serpent and recovered.[j]

**Journey Around Moab.** [10]The Israelites moved on and encamped in Oboth.[k] [11]Then they moved on from Oboth and encamped in Iye-abarim[*] in the wilderness facing Moab on the east. [12]Moving on from there, they encamped in the Wadi Zered. [13]Moving on from there, they encamped on the other side of the Arnon, in the wilderness that extends from the territory of the Amorites; for the Arnon forms Moab's boundary, between Moab and the Amorites. [14]Hence it is said in the "Book of the Wars of the LORD":[†]

"Waheb in Suphah and the wadies,
[15]     Arnon and the wadi gorges
That reach back toward the site of Ar[‡]
     and lean against the border of
     Moab."

[16]From there they went to Beer,[§] which is the well of which the LORD said to Moses, Gather the people together so that I may give them water. [17]Then Israel sang this song:

Spring up, O well!—so sing to it—
[18] The well that the princes sank,
     that the nobles of the people dug,
With their scepters and their staffs—
     from the wilderness, a gift.

[19]From Beer to Nahaliel, from Nahaliel to Bamoth, [20]from Bamoth to the valley in the country of Moab at the headland of Pisgah that overlooks Jeshimon.[¶]

**Victory over Sihon.** [21]Now Israel sent messengers to Sihon, king of the Amorites, with the message, [22]"Let us pass through your land. We will not turn aside into any field or vineyard, nor will we drink any well water, but we will go straight along the King's Highway until we have passed through your territory." [23]Sihon,[l] however, would not permit Israel to pass through his territory, but mustered all his forces and advanced against Israel into the wilderness. When he reached Jahaz, he engaged Israel in battle. [24]But Israel put him to the sword, and took possession of his land from the Arnon to the Jabbok and as far as Jazer of the Ammonites, for Jazer is the boundary of the Ammonites. [25m]Israel seized all the towns here, and Israel settled in all the towns of the Amorites, in Heshbon and all its dependencies. [26]For Heshbon was the city of Sihon, king of the Amorites, who had fought against the former king of Moab and had taken all his land from him as far as the Arnon. [27]That is why the poets say:

"Come to Heshbon, let it be rebuilt,
     let Sihon's city be firmly constructed.
[28] For fire went forth from Heshbon
     and a blaze from the city of Sihon;
It consumed Ar of Moab
     and swallowed up the high places of
     the Arnon.
[29] Woe to you, Moab!
     You are no more, people of
     Chemosh![**]
He let his sons become fugitives
     and his daughters be taken captive
     by the Amorite king Sihon.
[30] From Heshbon to Dibon their dominion
     is no more;
     Ar is laid waste; fires blaze as far as
     Medeba."

[31]So Israel settled in the land of the Amorites. [32]Moses sent spies to Jazer; and the Israelites captured it with its dependencies and dispossessed the Amorites who were there.

**Victory over Og.** [33n]Then they turned and went up along the road to Bashan. But Og, king of Bashan, advanced against them with all his forces to give battle at Edrei. [34]The LORD, however, said to Moses: Do not fear him; for into your hand I deliver him with all his forces and his land. You will do to him as you did to Sihon, king of the Amorites, who reigned in Heshbon.[o] [35]So they struck him down with his sons and all his forces, until not a survivor was left to him, and they took possession of his land.

## CHAPTER 22

[1]Then the Israelites moved on and encamped in the plains of Moab[††] on the other side of the Jordan opposite Jericho.

**Balaam Summoned.** [2]Now Balak, son of Zippor, saw all that Israel did to the Amorites, [3]and

---

*[21:11] **Iye-abarim:** probably means "the ruins in the Abarim (Mountains)." See note on 27:12.

†[21:14] **The "Book of the Wars of the LORD":** an ancient collection of Israelite songs, now lost. **Waheb in Suphah:** since neither place is mentioned elsewhere, it is uncertain whether these Hebrew words are to be considered as place names; some Hebrew words, now lost, must have preceded this phrase.

‡[21:15] **Ar:** a city or district in Moab, located on the Arnon; see v. 28; Dt 2:18.

§[21:16] **Beer:** "a well," here used as a place name.

¶[21:20] **Jeshimon:** "the wasteland"; in 1 Sm 23:19, 24 and 26:1, 3, this is the wilderness of Judah on the western side of the Dead Sea, but here and in Nm 23:28, it seems to refer to the southern end of the Jordan valley where Beth-jeshimoth was situated.

**[21:29] **Chemosh:** the chief god of the Moabites, mentioned in the famous inscription of Mesha, king of Moab, who ruled at the same time as the Omrides in Israel. Cf. 1 Kgs 11:7, 33; 2 Kgs 23:13; Jer 48:7, 13.

††[22:1] **The plains of Moab:** the lowlands to the northeast of the Dead Sea, between the Jordan and the foothills below Mount Nebo. Here the Israelites remained until they crossed the Jordan, according to Jos 1–4. Jericho lay to the west of the Jordan.

---

j. [21:9] Wis 16:6–7, 10; Jn 3:14–15.   k. [21:10] Nm 33:43–44. l. [21:23] Dt 2:32; Jgs 11:20.

m. [21:25–26] Jos 21:39; Jgs 11:26.   n. [21:33] Dt 3:1–7.   o. [21:34] Ps 136:17–22.

Moab feared the Israelites greatly because they were numerous. Moab was in dread of the Israelites. ⁴So Moab said to the elders of Midian, "Now this horde will devour everything around us as an ox devours the grass of the field." At that time Balak, son of Zippor, was king of Moab; ⁵and he sent messengers to Balaam, son of Beor, at Pethor on the river, in the land of the Ammonites,* to summon him with these words, "A people has come out of Egypt! They have covered up the earth and are settling down opposite me! ⁶Now come, curse this people for me,† since they are stronger than I am. Perhaps I may be able to defeat them and drive them out of the land. For I know that whoever you bless is blessed and whoever you curse is cursed." ⁷So the elders of Moab and the elders of Midian, themselves experts in divination,‡ left and went to Balaam, to whom they gave Balak's message. ⁸He said to them, "Stay here overnight, and I will give you whatever answer the LORD gives me." So the princes of Moab lodged with Balaam.

⁹Then God came to Balaam and said: Who are these men with you? ¹⁰Balaam answered God, "Balak, son of Zippor, king of Moab, sent me the message: ¹¹'This people that has come out of Egypt has covered up the earth. Now come, lay a curse on them for me; perhaps I may be able to fight them and drive them out.'" ¹²But God said to Balaam: Do not go with them and do not curse this people, for they are blessed. ¹³The next morning Balaam arose and told the princes of Balak, "Go back to your own country, for the LORD has refused to let me go with you." ¹⁴So the princes of Moab went back to Balak with the report, "Balaam refused to come with us."

**Second Appeal to Balaam.** ¹⁵Balak yet again sent princes, who were more numerous and more distinguished than the others. ¹⁶On coming to Balaam they told him, "Thus says Balak, son of Zippor: Please do not refuse to come to me. ¹⁷I will reward you very handsomely and will do anything you ask of me. Come, lay a curse on this people for me." ¹⁸ᵖBut Balaam replied to Balak's servants, "Even if Balak gave me his house full of silver and gold, I could not do anything, small or great, contrary to the command of the LORD, my God. ¹⁹But, you too stay here overnight, so that I may learn what else the LORD may say to me." ²⁰That night God came to Balaam and said to him: If these men

have come to summon you, go back with them; yet only on the condition that you do exactly as I tell you. ²¹So the next morning when Balaam arose, he saddled his donkey,§ and went off with the princes of Moab.

**The Talking Donkey.** ²²But now God's anger flared up¶ at him for going, and the angel of the LORD took up a position on the road as his adversary. As Balaam was riding along on his donkey, accompanied by two of his servants, ²³the donkey saw the angel of the LORD standing in the road with sword drawn. The donkey turned off the road and went into the field, and Balaam beat the donkey to bring her back on the road. ²⁴Then the angel of the LORD stood in a narrow lane between vineyards with a stone wall on each side. ²⁵When the donkey saw the angel of the LORD there, she pressed against the wall; and since she squeezed Balaam's leg against the wall, he beat her again. ²⁶Then the angel of the LORD again went ahead, and stood next in a passage so narrow that there was no room to move either to the right or to the left. ²⁷When the donkey saw the angel of the LORD there, she lay down under Balaam. Balaam's anger flared up and he beat the donkey with his stick.

²⁸�q Then the LORD opened the mouth of the donkey, and she asked Balaam, "What have I done to you that you beat me these three times?" ²⁹"You have acted so willfully against me," said Balaam to the donkey, "that if I only had a sword at hand, I would kill you here and now." ³⁰But the donkey said to Balaam, "Am I not your donkey, on which you have always ridden until now? Have I been in the habit of treating you this way before?" "No," he replied.

³¹Then the LORD opened Balaam's eyes, so that he saw the angel of the LORD standing on the road with sword drawn; and he knelt and bowed down to the ground. ³²But the angel of the LORD said to him: "Why have you beaten your donkey these three times? I have come as an adversary because this rash journey of yours is against my will. ³³When the donkey saw me, she turned away from me these three times. If she had not turned away from me, you are the one I would have killed, though I would have spared her." ³⁴Then Balaam said to the angel of the LORD, "I have sinned. Yet I did not know that you took up a position to oppose my journey. Since it has displeased you, I will go back home." ³⁵But the angel of the LORD said

---

*[22:5] **In the land of the Ammonites**: the translation rests on a slight emendation of the traditional Hebrew text in accordance with the tradition represented by the Vulgate. While Pethor remains unidentified, this verse supports an identification of Balaam's homeland in the Transjordan (cf. the Deir 'Alla Inscriptions), over against other traditions in the text which connect Balaam with Syria (23:7; Dt 23:5).

†[22:6] **Curse this people for me**: Balak believed that Balaam, known in the tradition as a diviner (cf. Jos 13:22), could utter a curse upon Israel which would come to pass.

‡[22:7] **Experts in divination**: lit., "divination was in their hand," i.e., "in their possession"; cf. Ezr 7:25.

p. [22:18] Nm 24:13.

§[22:21] **Donkey**: technically a she-donkey; Heb. *aton*.

¶[22:22] **God's anger flared up**: God's apparent change of mind became a source of much speculation in the tradition. So, for example, God was angry, not merely because Balaam was going to Balak, for he had God's permission for the journey (v. 20), but perhaps because he was tempted by greed to curse Israel against God's command (cf. 2 Pt 2:15; Jude 11; compare Nm 22:32). **Adversary**: Heb. *satan*; see also v. 32; cf. 1 Sm 29:4; 2 Sm 19:22; 1 Kgs 11; Jb 1–2; Ps 109:6; Zec 3:1–2; 1 Chr 21:1.

q. [22:28] 2 Pt 2:15–16.

to Balaam: "Go with the men; but you may say only what I tell you." So Balaam went on with the princes of Balak.

³⁶When Balak heard that Balaam was coming, he went out to meet him at Ar-Moab on the border formed by the Arnon, at its most distant point. ³⁷And Balak said to Balaam, "Did I not send an urgent summons to you? Why did you not come to me? Did you think I could not reward you?" ³⁸Balaam answered Balak, "Well, I have come to you after all. But what power have I to say anything? I can speak only what God puts in my mouth." ³⁹Then Balaam went with Balak, and they came to Kiriath-huzoth. ⁴⁰Here Balak sacrificed oxen and sheep, and sent portions to Balaam and to the princes who were with him.

**The First Oracle.** ⁴¹The next morning Balak took Balaam up on Bamoth-baal, and from there he could see some of the people.

## CHAPTER 23

¹Then Balaam said to Balak, "Build me seven altars here, and here prepare seven bulls and seven rams for me." ²So Balak did as Balaam had ordered, and Balak and Balaam offered a bull and a ram on each altar. ³Balaam said to Balak, "Stand here by your burnt offering while I go over there. Perhaps the LORD will meet me, and then I will tell you whatever he lets me see." And so he went out on the barren height. ⁴Then God met Balaam, and Balak said to him: "I have erected the seven altars, and have offered a bull and a ram on each altar." ⁵The LORD put an utterance in Balaam's mouth, and said: Go back to Balak, and speak accordingly. ⁶So he went back to Balak, who was still standing by his burnt offering together with all the princes of Moab. ⁷Then Balaam recited his poem:

From Aram* Balak has led me here,
    Moab's king, from the mountains of
        Qedem:ʳ
"Come, curse for me Jacob,
    come, denounce Israel."
⁸ How can I lay a curse on the one whom
        God has not cursed?
    How denounce the one whom the
        LORD has not denounced?
⁹ For from the top of the crags I see him,
    from the heights I behold him.
Here is a people that lives apart†
    and does not reckon itself among
        the nations.

¹⁰ Who has ever counted the dust of Jacob,
    who numbered Israel's dust-cloud?‡
May I die the death of the just,
    may my end be like theirs!

¹¹"What have you done to me?" cried Balak to Balaam. "It was to lay a curse on my foes that I brought you here; but instead, you have blessed them!" ¹²Balaam replied, "Is it not what the LORD puts in my mouth that I take care to repeat?"

**The Second Oracle.** ¹³Then Balak said to him, "Please come with me to another place§ from which you can see them; but you will see only some, not all of them, and from there lay a curse on them for me." ¹⁴So he brought him to a lookout post on the top of Pisgah, where he built seven altars and offered a bull and a ram on each of them. ¹⁵Balaam then said to Balak, "Stand here by your burnt offering, while I seek a meeting over there." ¹⁶Then the LORD met Balaam, and, having put an utterance in his mouth, said to him: Return to Balak, and speak accordingly. ¹⁷So he went to Balak, who was still standing by his burnt offering together with the princes of Moab. When Balak asked him, "What did the LORD say?" ¹⁸Balaam recited his poem:

Rise, Balak, and listen;
    give ear to my testimony, son of
        Zippor!
¹⁹ God is not a human being who speaks
        falsely,
    nor a mortal, who feels regret.
Is God one to speak and not act,
    to decree and not bring it to pass?
²⁰ I was summoned to bless;
    I will bless; I cannot revoke it!
²¹ Misfortune I do not see in Jacob,
    nor do I see misery¶ in Israel.
The LORD, their God, is with them;
    among them is the war-cry of their
        King.
²² They have the like of a wild ox's horns:**
    God who brought them out of
        Egypt.ˢ
²³ No, there is no augury against Jacob,
    nor divination against Israel.
Now it is said of Jacob,
    of Israel, "Look what God has
        done!"

‡[23:10] **The dust of Jacob . . . Israel's dust-cloud**: the Israelites will be as numerous as the dust kicked up by Israel in its march through the wilderness.

§[23:13] **To another place**: Balak thought that if Balaam would view Israel from a different site, he could deliver a different kind of omen.

¶[23:21] **Misfortune . . . misery**: Balaam states that he is unable to see any evils for Israel.

**[23:22] **A wild ox's horns**: Israel possesses the strength of a wild ox because of God's presence among them. Compare the claim by the psalmist, the Lord is "my rock . . . my saving horn" (Ps 18:3).

*[23:7] **Aram**: the ancient name of the region later known as Syria. **The mountains of Qedem**: Qedem is the name for a region in northern Syria. Qedem also means "eastern." Perhaps this designates the low ranges in the Syrian desert. The "mountains of old" is also a possible translation.

†[23:9] **A people that lives apart**: that is, "securely"; cf. Dt 33:28.

r. [23:7] Nm 22:6.

s. [23:22] Nm 24:8.

²⁴ Here is a people that rises up like a
                lioness,
        and gets up like a lion;
    It does not rest till it has devoured its prey
        and has drunk the blood of the
                slain.ᵗ

²⁵"Neither lay a curse on them nor bless them,"
said Balak to Balaam. ²⁶But Balaam answered
Balak, "Did I not tell you, 'Everything the LORD
tells me I must do'?"
**The Third Oracle.** ²⁷Then Balak said to Balaam,
"Come, let me bring you to another place; perhaps God will approve of your laying a curse on
them for me from there." ²⁸So he took Balaam
to the top of Peor, that overlooks Jeshimon.
²⁹Balaam then said to Balak, "Build me seven
altars here; and here prepare for me seven bulls
and seven rams." ³⁰And Balak did as Balaam had
ordered, offering a bull and a ram on each altar.

### CHAPTER 24

¹Balaam, however, perceiving that the LORD was
pleased to bless Israel, did not go aside as before
to seek omens, but turned his gaze toward the
wilderness. ²When Balaam looked up and saw
Israel encamped, tribe by tribe, the spirit of God
came upon him, ³and he recited his poem:

The oracle of Balaam, son of Beor,
        the oracle of the man whose eye is
                true,
⁴ The oracle of one who hears what God
                says,
        and knows what the Most High
                knows,
    Of one who sees what the Almighty sees,
        in rapture* and with eyes unveiled:
⁵ How pleasant are your tents, Jacob;
        your encampments, Israel!
⁶ Like palm trees spread out,
        like gardens beside a river,
    Like aloes the LORD planted,
        like cedars beside water;
⁷ Water will drip from their buckets,
        their seed will have plentiful water;
    Their king will rise higher than Agag†
        and their dominion will be
                exalted.
⁸ They have the like of a wild ox's horns:
        God who brought them out of
                Egypt.
    They will devour hostile nations,
        break their bones, and crush their
                loins.ᵘ

---

*[24:4] **In rapture**: lit., "falling," therefore possibly "in a
trance." However, this interpretation is uncertain.
†[24:7] **Agag**: during Saul's reign, king of Amalek (1 Sm
15:8), fierce enemy of Israel during the wilderness period; see
v. 20 (Ex 17:8–16).

t. [23:24] Nm 24:9; Gn 49:9.   u. [24:8] Nm 23:22.

⁹ Crouching, they lie like a lion,
        or like a lioness; who will arouse
                them?
    Blessed are those who bless you,
        and cursed are those who curse you!ᵛ

¹⁰In a blaze of anger at Balaam, Balak clapped
his hands‡ and said to him, "It was to lay a curse
on my foes that I summoned you here; yet three
times now you have actually blessed them!ʷ
¹¹Now flee to your home. I promised to reward
you richly, but the LORD has withheld the reward
from you!" ¹²Balaam replied to Balak, "Did I not
even tell the messengers whom you sent to me,
¹³'Even if Balak gave me his house full of silver
and gold, I could not of my own accord do anything, good or evil, contrary to the command of
the LORD'? Whatever the LORD says I must say.ˣ
**The Fourth Oracle.** ¹⁴"But now that I am about
to go to my own people, let me warn you what
this people will do to your people in the days to
come." ¹⁵Then he recited his poem:

The oracle of Balaam, son of Beor,
        the oracle of the man whose eye is
                true,
¹⁶ The oracle of one who hears what God
                says,
        and knows what the Most High
                knows,
    Of one who sees what the Almighty sees,
        in rapture and with eyes unveiled.
¹⁷ I see him, though not now;
        I observe him, though not near:
    A star shall advance from Jacob,
        and a scepter§ shall rise from Israel,

---

‡[24:10] **Balak clapped his hands**: a gesture suggesting
contempt or derision, apparently made in anger (cf. Jb 27:23;
Lam 2:15).

§[24:17] **A star . . . a scepter**: some early Christian writers,
as well as rabbinic interpreters, understood this prophecy in
messianic terms. So, for example, Rabbi Akiba designates Bar
Kosiba the messiah in the early second century A.D. by calling
him Bar Kokhba, i.e., son of the star, alluding to this passage.
Although this text is not referred to anywhere in the New Testament, in a Christian messianic interpretation the star would
refer to Jesus, as also the scepter from Israel; cf. Is 11:1. But it is
doubtful whether this passage is to be connected with the "star
of the Magi" in Mt 2:1–12. **The brows of Moab, and the skull
of all the Sethites**: under the figure of a human being, Moab
is specified as the object of conquest by a future leader of
Israel. The personification of peoples or toponyms is common
enough in the Old Testament; see, e.g., Hos 11:1; Ps 98:8. In
Jer 48:45, which paraphrases the latter part of our verse, Moab
is depicted as someone whose boasting warrants its ruin. In
view of the use of Heb. *pe'ah* (here "brows") in Nm 34:3 to
indicate a boundary, some see in the "brows" of Moab and the
"skull" of the Sethites a representation of features of Moab's
topography, i.e., the borderlands and the interior plateau. **The
Sethites**: cf. Gn 4:25; here probably a general designation for
nomadic/tribal groups on the borders of Palestine, unless they
are to be identified with the Shutu mentioned in Execration
texts of the early second millennium B.C. and the fourteenth
century Amarna tablets from Egypt; however, the Shutu are
not attested in Moab. On the basis of Gn 4:25 and Gn 25, one
might also think of a reference to humanity in general.

v. [24:9] Nm 23:24; Gn 12:3; 27:29; 49:9.   w. [24:10] Nm 23:11.
x. [24:13] Nm 22:18.

That will crush the brows of Moab,<sup>y</sup>
> and the skull of all the Sethites,
<sup>18</sup> Edom will be dispossessed,
> and no survivor is left in Seir.
Israel will act boldly,
<sup>19</sup>     and Jacob will rule his foes.

<sup>20</sup>Upon seeing Amalek, Balaam recited his poem:

> First<sup>*</sup> of the nations is Amalek,
> > but their end is to perish forever.<sup>z</sup>

<sup>21</sup>Upon seeing the Kenites,<sup>†</sup> he recited his poem:

> Though your dwelling is safe,
> > and your nest is set on a cliff;
> <sup>22</sup> Yet Kain will be destroyed
> > when Asshur<sup>‡</sup> takes you captive.

<sup>23</sup>Upon seeing<sup>§</sup> [the Ishmaelites?] he recited his poem:

> Alas, who shall survive of Ishmael,
> <sup>24</sup>     to deliver them from the hands of
> > the Kittim?
> When they have conquered Asshur and
> > conquered Eber,
> They too shall perish forever.

<sup>25</sup>Then Balaam set out on his journey home;
and Balak also went his way.

## CHAPTER 25

**Worship of Baal of Peor.** <sup>1</sup>While Israel was living at Shittim,<sup>¶</sup> the people profaned themselves
by prostituting themselves with the Moabite
women.<sup>a</sup> <sup>2</sup>These then invited the people to the
sacrifices of their god, and the people ate of the
sacrifices<sup>b</sup> and bowed down to their god. <sup>3</sup>Israel
thereby attached itself to the Baal of Peor,<sup>c</sup> and

the LORD's anger flared up against Israel. <sup>4d</sup>The
LORD said to Moses: Gather all the leaders of
the people, and publicly execute them<sup>**</sup> before
the LORD, that the blazing wrath of the LORD
may turn away from Israel. <sup>5</sup>So Moses told the
Israelite judges, "Each of you kill those of his
men who have attached themselves to the Baal
of Peor."<sup>††</sup>

**Zeal of Phinehas.** <sup>6</sup>At this a certain Israelite
came and brought in a Midianite woman<sup>‡‡</sup> to his
kindred in the view of Moses and of the whole
Israelite community, while they were weeping
at the entrance of the tent of meeting. <sup>7e</sup>When
Phinehas, son of Eleazar, son of Aaron the priest,
saw this, he rose up from the assembly, and taking a spear in his hand, <sup>8</sup>followed the Israelite
into the tent where he pierced the two of them,
the Israelite and the woman. Thus the plague
upon the Israelites was checked; <sup>9</sup>but the dead
from the plague were twenty-four thousand.

<sup>10</sup>Then the LORD said to Moses: <sup>11</sup>Phine-
has, son of Eleazar, son of Aaron the priest, has
turned my anger from the Israelites by his being
as jealous among them as I am; that is why I
did not put an end to the Israelites in my jeal-
ousy.<sup>§§</sup> <sup>12f</sup>Announce, therefore, that I hereby give
him my covenant of peace,<sup>¶¶</sup> <sup>13</sup>which shall be for
him and for his descendants after him the cov-
enant of an everlasting priesthood, because he
was jealous on behalf of his God and thus made
expiation for the Israelites.

<sup>14***</sup>The name of the slain Israelite, the one
slain with the Midianite woman, was Zimri, son
of Salu, prince of a Simeonite ancestral house.
<sup>15</sup>The name of the slain Midianite woman was
Cozbi, daughter of Zur, who was head of a clan,
an ancestral house, in Midian.

**Vengeance on the Midianites.** <sup>16†††</sup>The LORD
then said to Moses: <sup>17g</sup>Treat the Midianites as

---

*[24:20] **First:** lit., "the beginning." In the Bible, Amalek is
a people indigenous to Palestine and therefore considered as
of great antiquity. There is a deliberate contrast between
the words "first" and "end."

†[24:21] **The Kenites** lived in high strongholds in the
mountains of southern Palestine and the Sinai Peninsula, and
were skilled in working the various metals found in their territory. Their name is connected, at least by popular etymology,
with the Hebrew word for "smith"; of similar sound to *qayin*,
i.e., "Kain" or "smith," is the Hebrew word for "nest," *qen*—
hence the play on words in the present passage.

‡[24:22] **Asshur:** the mention of Asshur, i.e., Assyria, is not
likely before the ninth or eighth centuries B.C.

§[24:23–24] **Upon seeing:** this phrase, lacking the Hebrew
text, is found in the Septuagint, but without "the Ishmaelites"
designated as the subject of the oracle. The Hebrew text of
the oracle itself shows considerable disarray; the translation
therefore relies on reconstruction of the putative original and
is quite uncertain.

¶[25:1] **Shittim:** the full name was Abel-shittim, a locality
at the foot of the mountains in the northeastern corner of the
plains of Moab (33:49). **Prostituting themselves:** the application to men of such traditional language for apostasy clearly
suggests apostasy was taken to be an inevitable consequence
of intermarriage with the Midianite women.

**[25:4] **Publicly execute them:** the same phrase occurs
in 2 Sm 21:6–14, where the context shows that at least a part
of the penalty consisted in being denied honorable burial.
In both passages, dismemberment or impalement (perhaps
subsequent to the actual execution) as a punishment for the
breaking of covenant pledges, is a possible interpretation of
the Hebrew phrase.

††[25:5] Thereby Moses apparently alters the Lord's command to execute all the leaders.

‡‡[25:6] **Midianite woman:** according to 22:4, 7, the Midianites were allied with the Moabites in opposing Israel, while
31:16 claims that Balaam had induced the Midianite women
to lure the Israelites away from the Lord; cf. They were weeping:
on account of the plague that had struck them; cf. v. 8.

§§[25:11] **My jealousy:** God's desire to maintain an exclusive hold on the allegiance of the Israelites.

¶¶[25:12] **Covenant of peace:** by means of this covenant
between God and Phinehas, Phinehas can expect God's protection, especially from any threat of reprisal for his action; cf.
Is 54:10; Ez 34:25; 37:26.

***[25:14–15] The noble lineage of the slain couple is men-
tioned in order to stress the courage of Phinehas in punishing
them. The zeal of Phinehas became proverbial; cf. Ps 106:30;
Sir 45:23; 1 Mc 2:26, 54.

†††[25:16–18] The account of the execution of this command is given in 31:1–18.

---

y. [24:17] 2 Sm 8:2.    z. [24:20] Ex 17:14; 1 Sm 15:3.    a. [25:1] Nm
31:16.    b. [25:2] Ex 34:15–16.    c. [25:3] Ps 106:28; Hos 9:10.

d. [25:4] Dt 4:3.    e. [25:7] Ps 106:30.    f. [25:12–13] 1 Mc 2:26, 54;
Ps 106:31; Sir 45:23–24.    g. [25:17–18] Nm 31:2–12.

enemies and strike them, [18]for they have been your enemies by the deceitful dealings they had with you regarding Peor and their kinswoman Cozbi, the daughter of a Midianite prince, who was slain at the time of the plague because of Peor.

## III. SECOND CENSUS OF A NEW GENERATION AND PREPARATION TO ENTER THE PROMISED LAND

### CHAPTER 26

**The Second Census.** [19]After the plague [1]the LORD said to Moses and Eleazar, son of Aaron the priest: [2]Take a census, by ancestral houses, throughout the community of the Israelites of all those of twenty years or more who are eligible for military service in Israel.[h] [3]So on the plains of Moab along the Jordan at Jericho, Moses and Eleazar the priest enrolled them, [4]those of twenty years or more, as the LORD had commanded Moses.

The Israelites who came out of the land of Egypt were as follows:[*]

[5]Reuben, the firstborn of Israel. The descendants of Reuben by their clans were: through Hanoch, the clan of the Hanochites; through Pallu, the clan of the Palluites; [6]through Hezron, the clan of the Hezronites; through Carmi, the clan of the Carmites. [7]These were the clans of the Reubenites, and those enrolled numbered forty-three thousand seven hundred and thirty.

[8]From Pallu descended Eliab. [9]The sons of Eliab were Nemuel, Dathan, and Abiram[j]—the same Dathan and Abiram, ones designated by the community, who contended with Moses and Aaron as part of Korah's faction when they contended with the LORD. [10]The earth opened its mouth and swallowed them, along with Korah, as a warning. The faction was destroyed when the fire consumed two hundred and fifty men. [11]The descendants of Korah, however, did not die out.

[12]The descendants of Simeon by clans were: through Nemuel,[†] the clan of the Nemuelites; through Jamin, the clan of the Jaminites; through Jachin, the clan of the Jachinites; [13]through Zerah, the clan of the Zerahites; through Shaul, the clan of the Shaulites. [14]These were the clans of the Simeonites, twenty-two thousand two hundred.

[15]The descendants of Gad by clans were: through Zephon, the clan of the Zephonites; through Haggi, the clan of the Haggites; through Shuni, the clan of the Shunites; [16]through Ozni, the clan of the Oznites; through Eri, the clan of the Erites; [17]through Arod, the clan of the Arodites; through Areli, the clan of the Arelites. [18]These were the clans of the descendants of Gad, of whom there were enrolled forty thousand five hundred.

[19]The sons of Judah were Er and Onan. Er and Onan died in the land of Canaan.[k] [20]The descendants of Judah by their clans were: through Shelah, the clan of the Shelahites; through Perez, the clan of the Perezites; through Zerah, the clan of the Zerahites. [21]The descendants of Perez were: through Hezron, the clan of the Hezronites; through Hamul, the clan of the Hamulites. [22]These were the clans of Judah, of whom there were enrolled seventy-six thousand five hundred.

[23]The descendants of Issachar by their clans were: through Tola, the clan of the Tolaites; through Puvah, the clan of the Puvahites; [24]through Jashub, the clan of the Jashubites; through Shimron, the clan of the Shimronites. [25]These were the clans of Issachar, of whom there were enrolled sixty-four thousand three hundred.

[26]The descendants of Zebulun by their clans were: through Sered, the clan of the Seredites; through Elon, the clan of the Elonites; through Jahleel, the clan of the Jahleelites. [27]These were the clans of the Zebulunites, of whom there were enrolled sixty thousand five hundred.

[28]The sons of Joseph were Manasseh and Ephraim. [29]The descendants of Manasseh by clans were: through Machir, the clan of the Machirites. Now Machir begot Gilead: through Gilead, the clan of the Gileadites. [30]The descendants of Gilead were: through Iezer, the clan of the Iezrites; through Helek, the clan of the Helekites; [31]through Asriel, the clan of the Asrielites; through Shechem, the clan of the Shechemites; [32]through Shemida, the clan of the Shemidaites; through Hepher, the clan of the Hepherites. [33]As for Zelophehad, son of Hepher—he had no sons, but only daughters. The names of the daughters of Zelophehad were Mahlah, Noah, Hoglah, Milcah and Tirzah. [34]These were the clans of Manasseh, and those enrolled numbered fifty-two thousand seven hundred.

[35]These were the descendants of Ephraim by their clans: through Shuthelah, the clan of the Shuthelahites; through Becher, the clan of the Becherites; through Tahan, the clan of the Tahanites. [36]These were the descendants of Shuthelah: through Eran, the clan of the Eranites. [37]These were the clans of the Ephraimites, of

---

*[26:4] This introduction to the census seems to contradict vv. 64–65 by including those who came out of Egypt.

†[26:12] **Nemuel:** so also in 1 Chr 4:24. In Gn 46:10 and Ex 6:15, a son of Simeon with the same position in the genealogy bears the name "Jemuel"; it is uncertain which form is correct. See above, v. 9, where the name "Nemuel" occurs for a person descended from Pallu. Some speculate this name was inserted from v. 12 to provide a continuing line for Pallu.

---

h. [26:2] Nm 1:2–3.  i. [26:5–6] 1 Chr 5:3.  j. [26:9–10] Nm 16:1, 32.

k. [26:19] Gn 38:7, 10; 46:12; 1 Chr 2:3.  l. [26:33] Nm 27:1; 36:11; Jos 17:3.

whom there were enrolled thirty-two thousand five hundred.

These were the descendants of Joseph by their clans.

³⁸The descendants of Benjamin by their clans were: through Bela, the clan of the Belaites; through Ashbel, the clan of the Ashbelites; through Ahiram, the clan of the Ahiramites; ³⁹through Shupham, the clan of the Shuphamites; through Hupham, the clan of the Huphamites. ⁴⁰The sons of Bela were Ard and Naaman: through Ard, the clan of the Ardites; through Naaman, the clan of the Naamites. ⁴¹These were the descendants of Benjamin by their clans, of whom there were enrolled forty-five thousand six hundred.

⁴²These were the descendants of Dan by their clans: through Shuham the clan of the Shuhamites. These were the clans of Dan, ⁴³of whom there were enrolled sixty-four thousand four hundred.

⁴⁴The descendants of Asher by their clans were: through Imnah, the clan of the Imnites; through Ishvi, the clan of the Ishvites; through Beriah, the clan of the Beriites; ⁴⁵through Heber, the clan of the Heberites; through Malchiel, the clan of the Malchielites. ⁴⁶The name of Asher's daughter was Serah. ⁴⁷These were the clans of the descendants of Asher, of whom there were enrolled fifty-three thousand four hundred.

⁴⁸The descendants of Naphtali by their clans were: through Jahzeel, the clan of the Jahzeelites; through Guni, the clan of the Gunites; ⁴⁹through Jezer, the clan of the Jezerites; through Shillem, the clan of the Shillemites. ⁵⁰These were the clans of Naphtali, of whom there were enrolled forty-five thousand four hundred.

⁵¹These were the Israelites who were enrolled: six hundred and one thousand seven hundred and thirty.

**Allotment of the Land.**ᵐ ⁵²The LORD said to Moses: ⁵³ᵐAmong these the land shall be divided as their heritage in keeping with the number of people named. ⁵⁴ᵗTo a large tribe you shall assign a large heritage, to a small tribe a small heritage, each receiving its heritage in proportion to the number enrolled in it. ⁵⁵But the land shall be divided by lot, all inheriting according to the lists of their ancestral tribes. ⁵⁶As the lot falls the heritage of each tribe, large or small, will be assigned.

**Census of the Levites.** ⁵⁷These were the Levites enrolled by clans: through Gershon, the clan of the Gershonites; through Kohath, the clan of

the Kohathites; through Merari, the clan of the Merarites. ⁵⁸These were clans of Levi: the clan of the Libnites, the clan of the Hebronites, the clan of the Mahlites, the clan of the Mushites, the clan of the Korahites.ᵗ

Now Kohath begot Amram, ⁵⁹whose wife was named Jochebed. She was the daughter of Levi, born to Levi in Egypt. To Amram she bore Aaron and Moses and Miriam their sister. ⁶⁰To Aaron were born Nadab and Abihu, Eleazar and Ithamar. ⁶¹But Nadab and Abihu died when they offered unauthorized fire before the LORD. ⁶²The Levites enrolled were twenty-three thousand, every male one month or more of age.ᵒ They were not enrolled with the other Israelites, however, for no heritage was given them among the Israelites.

⁶³These, then, were those enrolled by Moses and Eleazar the priest, when they enrolled the Israelites on the plains of Moab along the Jordan at Jericho. ⁶⁴Among them there was not one of those who had been enrolled by Moses and Aaron the priest, when they enrolled the Israelites in the wilderness of Sinai. ⁶⁵ᵖFor the LORD had told them that they would surely die in the wilderness, and not one of them was left except Caleb, son of Jephunneh, and Joshua, son of Nun.

## CHAPTER 27

**Zelophehad's Daughters.** ¹The daughters of Zelophehad, son of Hepher, son of Gilead, son of Machir, son of Manasseh, came forward. (Zelophehad belonged to the clans of Manasseh, son of Joseph.) The names of his daughters were Mahlah, Noah, Hoglah, Milcah and Tirzah.�q ²Standing before Moses, Eleazar the priest, the princes, and the whole community at the entrance of the tent of meeting, they said: ³"Our father died in the wilderness. Although he did not join the faction of those who conspired against the LORD,‡ Korah's faction, he died for his own sin without leaving any sons. ⁴But why should our father's name be cut off from his clan merely because he had no son? Give us land among our father's kindred."

**Laws Concerning Heiresses.**§ ⁵So Moses laid their case before the LORD, ⁶and the LORD said to him: ⁷The plea of Zelophehad's daughters is just; you shall give them hereditary land among their father's kindred and transfer their father's heritage to them. ⁸Tell the Israelites: If a man

---

*[26:52–56] The division of Canaan among the various tribes and clans and families was determined not only by the size of each group but also by lot. Perhaps the lots determined the respective locality of each tribal land and the section reserved for each clan, while the relative size of the allotted locality and section depended on the numerical strength of each group. The Israelites considered the outcome of the drawing of lots as an expression of God's will; cf. Lv 16:8–10; Jos 14:2; 15:1; etc.; Acts 1:23–26.

†[26:58] Compare 3:18–20 for a different listing.

‡[27:3] **He did not join . . . against the LORD:** had he done so, he and his heirs could have been deprived of a portion in the promised land.

§[27:5–11] The purpose of this law, as also that of the related laws in 36:2–10 (marriage within the same tribe), Dt 25:5–10 (levirate marriage), and Lv 25:10 (return of property in the jubilee year), was to keep the landed property within the proper domain of each tribe.

---

m. [26:53] Jos 11:23.    n. [26:54] Nm 33:54; 35:8.

o. [26:62] Nm 3:39.    p. [26:65] Nm 14:22–24, 29.    q. [27:1] Nm 26:33; Jos 17:3.

dies without leaving a son, you shall transfer his heritage to his daughter; ⁹if he has no daughter, you shall give his heritage to his brothers; ¹⁰if he has no brothers, you shall give his heritage to his father's brothers; ¹¹if his father had no brothers, you shall give his heritage to his nearest relative in his clan, who shall then take possession of it.

This will be the statutory procedure for the Israelites, as the Lord commanded Moses.ʳ

**Joshua to Succeed Moses.** ¹²The Lord said to Moses: Go up into this mountain of the Abarim range* and view the land that I have given to the Israelites.ˢ ¹³When you have viewed it, you will be gathered to your people, as was Aaron your brother.ᵗ ¹⁴For in the rebellion of the community in the wilderness of Zin you both rebelled against my order to acknowledge my holiness before them by means of the water.ᵘ (These were the waters of Meribah of Kadesh in the wilderness of Zin.)

¹⁵Then Moses said to the Lord, ¹⁶"May the Lord, the God of the spirits of all humanity,† set over the community someone ¹⁷who will be their leader in battle and who will lead them out and bring them in, that the Lord's community may not be like sheep without a shepherd." ¹⁸And the Lord replied to Moses: Take Joshua, son of Nun,ᵛ a man of spirit,‡ and lay your hand upon him. ¹⁹Have him stand before Eleazar the priest and the whole community, and commission him in their sight. ²⁰Invest him with some of your own power, that the whole Israelite community may obey him. ²¹He shall present himself to Eleazar the priest, who will seek for him the decision of the Urim§ in the Lord's presence; and as it directs, Joshua, all the Israelites with him, and the whole community will go out for battle; and as it directs, they will come in.

²²Moses did as the Lord had commanded him. Taking Joshua and having him stand before Eleazar the priest and the whole community, ²³he laid his hands on him and commissioned him, as the Lord had directed through Moses.

---

\*[27:12] **The Abarim range**: the mountains on the eastern side of the Dead Sea. The peak of this chain is Mount Nebo where Moses views the promised land before he dies (Dt 32:49).

†[27:16] **The God of the spirits of all humanity**: the sense is that God knows the character and abilities of all people and therefore knows best whom to appoint (cf. Jgs 6:34; 11:29; 1 Sm 16:13); see the same phrase in Nm 16:22, where "spirit" evidently means the life principle.

‡[27:18] **A man of spirit**: lit., "a man in whom there is spirit," that is, probably one who is endowed with a courageous spirit (Jos 2:11); compare Gn 41:38; Dt 34:9.

§[27:21] **The Urim**: certain sacred objects which Israelite priests employed to discern the divine will, probably by obtaining a positive or negative answer to a given question. The full expression was "the Urim and Thummim"; cf. Ex 28:30; Lv 8:8; Dt 33:8; Ezr 2:63; Neh 7:65. Joshua ordinarily did not receive direct revelations from God as Moses had received them.

---

r. [27:11] Jer 32:6–9.   s. [27:12] Dt 3:27; 32:49; 34:1.   t. [27:13–14] Nm 20:12, 24.   u. [27:14] Dt 32:51.   v. [27:18] Dt 34:9.

# CHAPTER 28

**General Sacrifices.** ¹The Lord said to Moses: ²Give the Israelites this commandment: At their prescribed times, you will be careful to present to me the food offerings that are due me, oblations of pleasing aroma to me.

**Each Morning and Evening.** ³ʷYou will tell them therefore: This is the oblation which you will offer to the Lord: two unblemished yearling lambs each day as the regular burnt offering,¶ ⁴offering one lamb in the morning and the other during the evening twilight, ⁵each with a grain offering of one tenth of an ephah of bran flour mixed with a fourth of a hin of oil of crushed olives.** ⁶This is the regular burnt offering that was made at Mount Sinai for a pleasing aroma, an oblation to the Lord. ⁷And as the libation for the first lamb, you will make a libation to the Lord in the sanctuary†† of a fourth of a hin of strong drink. ⁸The other lamb you will offer during the evening twilight, making the same grain offering and the same libation as in the morning, as an oblation of pleasing aroma to the Lord.

**On the Sabbath.** ⁹On the sabbath day: two unblemished yearling lambs, with a grain offering of two tenths of an ephah of bran flour mixed with oil, and its libation. ¹⁰This is the sabbath burnt offering each sabbath, in addition to the regular burnt offering and its libation.

**At the New Moon Feast.** ¹¹On your new moons‡‡ you will offer as a burnt offering to the Lord two bulls of the herd, one ram, and seven unblemished yearling lambs, ¹²with three tenths of an ephah of bran flour mixed with oil as the grain offering for each bull, two tenths of an ephah of bran flour mixed with oil as the grain offering for the ram, ¹³and one tenth of an ephah of bran flour mixed with oil as the grain offering for each lamb, a burnt offering with a pleasing aroma, an oblation to the Lord. ¹⁴Their libations will consist of a half a hin of wine for each bull, a third of a hin for the ram, and a fourth of a hin for each lamb. This is the burnt offering for the new moon, for every new moon through the months of the year. ¹⁵Moreover, there will be one goat for a purification offering to the Lord; it will be offered in addition to the regular burnt offering and its libation.

---

¶[28:3] **The regular burnt offering**: "the *tamid* burnt offering," the technical term for the daily sacrifice. The lambs—as well as the goats for the purification offering (vv. 15, 22, 30)—are all specified as males.

**[28:5] **Oil of crushed olives**: this oil, probably made in a mortar, was purer and more expensive than oil extracted in the olive press.

††[28:7] **In the sanctuary**: i.e., the tent of meeting. But according to Sir 50:15, the libation was poured at the base of the outer altar.

‡‡[28:11] **On your new moons**: beginning on the evening when the crescent of the new moon first appeared. The beginning of the month is reckoned according to the new moon.

---

w. [28:3–8] Ex 29:38–42.

**At the Passover.** <sup>16</sup>The fourteenth day* of the first month is the Passover of the Lord,<sup>x 17</sup>and the fifteenth day of this month is the pilgrimage feast. For seven days unleavened bread is to be eaten. <sup>18</sup>On the first day you will declare a holy day, and you shall do no heavy work.†<sup>y</sup> <sup>19</sup>You will offer an oblation, a burnt offering to the Lord: two bulls of the herd, one ram, and seven yearling lambs that you are sure are unblemished. <sup>20</sup>Their grain offerings will be of bran flour mixed with oil; you will offer three tenths of an ephah for each bull and two tenths for the ram. <sup>21</sup>You will offer one tenth for each of the seven lambs; <sup>22</sup>and one goat as a purification offering to make atonement for yourselves. <sup>23</sup>These offerings you will make in addition to the morning burnt offering which is part of the regular burnt offering. <sup>24</sup>You will make exactly the same offerings each day for seven days as food offerings, oblations of pleasing aroma to the Lord; they will be offered in addition to the regular burnt offering with its libation. <sup>25</sup>On the seventh day you will declare a holy day: you shall do no heavy work.<sup>z</sup>

**At Pentecost.** <sup>26</sup>On the day of first fruits,<sup>‡</sup> on your Feast of Weeks,<sup>a</sup> when you present to the Lord an offering of new grain, you will declare a holy day: you shall do no heavy work. <sup>27</sup>You will offer burnt offering for a pleasing aroma to the Lord: two bulls of the herd, one ram, and seven yearling lambs that you are sure are unblemished. <sup>28</sup>Their grain offerings will be of bran flour mixed with oil: three tenths of an ephah for each bull, two tenths for the ram, <sup>29</sup>and one tenth for each of the seven lambs. <sup>30</sup>One goat will be for a purification offering to make atonement for yourselves. <sup>31</sup>You will make these offerings, together with their libations, in addition to the regular burnt offering with its grain offering.

## CHAPTER 29

**On New Year's Day.** <sup>1</sup>In the seventh month on the first day<sup>§</sup> you will declare a holy day, and do no heavy work; it shall be a day on which you sound the trumpet.<sup>b 2</sup>You will offer a burnt offering for a pleasing aroma to the Lord: one bull of the herd, one ram, and seven unblemished yearling lambs.

<sup>3</sup>Their grain offerings will be of bran flour mixed with oil: three tenths of an ephah for the bull, two tenths for the ram, <sup>4</sup>and one tenth for each of the seven lambs. <sup>5</sup>One goat will be a purification offering to make atonement for yourselves. <sup>6</sup>These are in addition to the burnt offering for the new moon with its grain offering, and in addition to the regular burnt offering with its grain offering, together with the libations prescribed for them, for a pleasing aroma, an oblation to the Lord.

**On the Day of Atonement.** <sup>7</sup>On the tenth day of this seventh month<sup>¶</sup> you will declare a holy day, humble yourselves, and do no sort of work.<sup>c</sup> <sup>8</sup>You will offer a burnt offering to the Lord, a pleasing aroma: one bull of the herd, one ram, and seven yearling lambs that you are sure are unblemished. <sup>9</sup>Their grain offerings of bran flour mixed with oil: three tenths of an ephah for the bull, two tenths for the one ram, <sup>10</sup>and one tenth for each of the seven lambs. <sup>11</sup>One goat will be a purification offering. These are in addition to the purification offering for purging,<sup>**</sup> the regular burnt offering with its grain offering, and their libations.

**On the Feast of Booths.** <sup>12††</sup>On the fifteenth day of the seventh month you will declare a holy day:<sup>d</sup> you shall do no heavy work. For the following seven days you will celebrate a pilgrimage feast to the Lord. <sup>13</sup>You will offer a burnt offering, an oblation of pleasing aroma to the Lord: thirteen bulls<sup>‡‡</sup> of the herd, two rams, and fourteen yearling lambs that are unblemished. <sup>14</sup>Their grain offerings will be of bran flour mixed with oil: three tenths of an ephah for each of the thirteen bulls, two tenths for each of the two rams, <sup>15</sup>and one tenth for each of the fourteen lambs. <sup>16</sup>One goat will be a purification offering. These are in addition to the regular burnt offering with its grain offering and libation.

<sup>17</sup>On the second day: twelve bulls of the herd, two rams, and fourteen unblemished yearling lambs, <sup>18</sup>with the grain offerings and libations for the bulls, rams and lambs in their prescribed number, <sup>19</sup>as well as one goat as a purification offering, besides the regular burnt offering with its grain offering and libation.

<sup>20</sup>On the third day: eleven bulls, two rams, and fourteen unblemished yearling lambs, <sup>21</sup>with the grain offerings and libations for the bulls, rams and lambs in their prescribed number,

---

*[28:16] **The fourteenth day:** toward evening at the end of this day; cf. Ex 12:6, 18.

†[28:18] **Heavy work:** apparently, some sorts of activity are permitted on a day such as this, whereas "any work" is prohibited by 29:7 on the Day of Atonement. See note on Lv 23:3.

‡[28:26] **The day of first fruits:** a unique term for this feast, which is usually called "the feast of Weeks"; it was celebrated as a thanksgiving for the wheat harvest seven weeks after the barley harvest (Passover). In the time of Jesus it was commonly known by the Greek word "Pentecost," that is, "fiftieth" (day after the Passover); see note on Lv 23:16–21.

§[29:1] **In the seventh month on the first day:** (about September–October) now the Jewish New Year's Day. In the older calendar the year began with the first of Nisan (March–April), which is still known as the first month; cf. Ex 12:2.

---

¶[29:7] **The tenth day of this seventh month:** the Day of Atonement. **Humble yourselves:** that is, with fasting.

**[29:11] **The purification offering for purging:** the bull prescribed in Lv 16:11–12 for the purging of the tent sanctuary.

††[29:12] This feast of Booths (Tabernacles or Sukkot) celebrating the vintage harvest was the most popular of all and therefore had the most elaborate ritual. See note on Lv 23:34.

‡‡[29:13] **Thirteen bulls:** the number of bulls sacrificed before the octave day was seventy, arranged on a descending scale so that the number on the seventh day was the sacred number seven.

---

x. [28:16] Ex 12:18; Lv 23:5; Dt 16:1.   y. [28:18] Ex 12:16; Lv 23:7.   z. [28:25] Ex 12:16; 13:6; Lv 23:8.   a. [28:26] Ex 34:22.   b. [29:1] Nm 10:10; Lv 23:24.

c. [29:7] Lv 16:29; 23:27–28, 32.   d. [29:12] Lv 23:34–35.

²²as well as one goat for a purification offering, besides the regular burnt offering with its grain offering and libation.

²³On the fourth day: ten bulls, two rams, and fourteen unblemished yearling lambs, ²⁴the grain offerings and libations for the bulls, rams and lambs in their prescribed number, ²⁵as well as one goat as a purification offering, besides the regular burnt offering, its grain offering and libation.

²⁶On the fifth day: nine bulls, two rams, and fourteen unblemished yearling lambs, ²⁷ᵉwith the grain offerings and libations for the bulls, rams and lambs in their prescribed number, ²⁸as well as one goat as a purification offering, besides the regular burnt offering with its grain offering and libation.

²⁹On the sixth day: eight bulls, two rams, and fourteen unblemished yearling lambs, ³⁰with the grain offerings and libations for the bulls, rams and lambs in their prescribed number, ³¹as well as one goat as a purification offering, besides the regular burnt offering, its grain offering and libation.

³²On the seventh day: seven bulls, two rams, and fourteen unblemished yearling lambs, ³³with the grain offerings and libations for the bulls, rams and lambs in their prescribed number, ³⁴as well as one goat as a purification offering, besides the regular burnt offering, its grain offering and libation.

³⁵On the eighth day$^f$ you will hold a public assembly:* you shall do no heavy work. ³⁶You will offer a burnt offering, an oblation of pleasing aroma to the LORD: one bull, one ram, and seven unblemished yearling lambs, ³⁷with the grain offerings and libations for the bulls, rams and lambs in their prescribed number, ³⁸as well as one goat as a purification offering, besides the regular burnt offering with its grain offering and libation.

³⁹These are the offerings you will make to the LORD on your festivals, besides your votive or voluntary offerings of burnt offerings, grain offerings, libations, and communion offerings.

## CHAPTER 30

¹So Moses instructed the Israelites exactly as the LORD had commanded him.

**Validity and Annulment of Vows.** ²Moses said to the heads of the Israelite tribes, "This is what the LORD has commanded: ³When a man makes a vow to the LORD or binds himself under oath to a pledge,† he shall not violate his word, but must fulfill exactly the promise he has uttered.$^g$

⁴"When a woman makes a vow to the LORD, or binds herself to a pledge, while still in her father's house in her youth, ⁵and her father learns of her vow or the pledge to which she bound herself and says nothing to her about it, then any vow or any pledge to which she bound herself remains valid. ⁶But if on the day he learns of it her father opposes her, then any vow or any pledge to which she bound herself becomes invalid; and the LORD will release her from it, since her father opposed her.

⁷"If she marries while under a vow or under a rash pledge to which she bound herself, ⁸and her husband learns of it, yet says nothing to her on the day he learns it, then the vows or the pledges to which she bound herself remain valid. ⁹But if on the day her husband learns of it he opposes her, he thereby annuls the vow she had made or the rash pledge to which she had bound herself, and the LORD will release her from it. ¹⁰(The vow of a widow or of a divorced woman, however, any pledge to which such a woman binds herself, is valid.)

¹¹"If it is in her husband's house‡ that she makes a vow or binds herself under oath to a pledge, ¹²and her husband learns of it yet says nothing to her to oppose her, then all her vows remain valid or any pledge to which she has bound herself. ¹³But if on the day he learns of them her husband annuls them, then whatever she has expressly promised in her vows or in her pledge becomes invalid; since her husband has annulled them, the LORD will release her from them.

¹⁴"Any vow or any pledge that she makes under oath to humble herself, her husband may either confirm or annul. ¹⁵But if her husband, day after day, says nothing at all to her, he thereby confirms all her vows or all the pledges incumbent upon her; he has confirmed them, because on the day he learned of them he said nothing to her. ¹⁶If, however, he annuls them§ some time after he first learned of them, he will be responsible for her guilt."

¹⁷These are the statutes which the LORD commanded Moses concerning a husband and his wife, as well as a father and his daughter while she is still in her youth in her father's house.

## CHAPTER 31

**Campaign Against the Midianites.** ¹The LORD said to Moses:¶ ²Avenge the Israelites on the Midianites, and then you will be gathered to

---

*[29:35] **A public assembly**: the Hebrew word is the technical term for the closing celebration of the three major feasts of the Passover, Pentecost and Booths, or of other special feasts that lasted for a week. Cf. Lv 23:36; Dt 16:8; 2 Chr 7:9; Neh 8:18.

†[30:3] **A vow . . . a pledge**: here the former signifies the promise to dedicate either a person, an animal, or a thing or their equivalent to the sanctuary upon the fulfillment of some specified conditions (Lv 27:1–13); the latter signifies the

assumption of either a positive or a negative obligation—that is, the promise either to do something or to abstain from something; cf. v. 14.

‡[30:11] **In her husband's house**: after her marriage. This contrasts with the case given in vv. 7–9.

§[30:16] **He annuls them**: he prevents their fulfillment. Since he has first allowed the vows to remain valid, he can no longer annul them.

¶[31:1–3] The narrative of Israel's campaign against Midian, which was interrupted after 25:18, is now resumed.

e. [29:27] Nm 29:30, 37.   f. [29:35] Lv 23:36; Jn 7:37.   g. [30:3] Dt 23:22; Eccl 5:3–4.

your people. ³So Moses told the people, "Arm some men among you for the campaign, to attack Midian and to execute the LORD's vengeance on Midian. ⁴From each of the tribes of Israel you will send a thousand men to the campaign." ⁵From the contingents of Israel, therefore, a thousand men of each tribe were levied, so that there were twelve thousand men armed for war. ⁶Moses sent them out on the campaign, a thousand from each tribe, with Phinehas, son of Eleazar, the priest for the campaign, who had with him the sacred vessels and the trumpets for sounding the alarm. ⁷They waged war against the Midianites, as the LORD had commanded Moses, and killed every male. ⁸Besides those slain in battle, they killed the kings of Midian: Evi, Rekem, Zur, Hur and Reba, the five kings of Midian;* and they also killed Balaam, son of Beor, with the sword. ⁹But the Israelites took captive the women of the Midianites with their children, and all their herds and flocks and wealth as loot, ¹⁰while they set on fire all the towns where they had settled and all their encampments. ¹¹Then they took all the plunder, with the people and animals they had captured, and brought the captives, together with the spoils and plunder, ¹²to Moses and Eleazar the priest and to the Israelite community at their camp on the plains of Moab by the Jordan opposite Jericho.

**Treatment of the Captives.** ¹³When Moses and Eleazar the priest, with all the leaders of the community, went outside the camp to meet them, ¹⁴Moses became angry with the officers of the army, the commanders of thousands and the commanders of hundreds, who were returning from the military campaign. ¹⁵"So you have spared all the women!" he exclaimed. ¹⁶"These are the very ones who on Balaam's advice were behind the Israelites' unfaithfulness to the LORD in the affair at Peor,ʰ so that plague struck the LORD's community. ¹⁷†Now kill, therefore, every male among the children and kill every woman who has had sexual relations with a man. ¹⁸But you may spare for yourselves all the girls who have not had sexual relations.

**Purification After Combat.** ¹⁹"Moreover, remain outside the camp for seven days; every one of you who has killed anyone or touched someone killed will purify yourselves on the third and on the seventh day—both you and your captives. ²⁰You will also purify every garment, every article of leather, everything made of goats' hair, and every article of wood."

²¹Eleazar the priest told the soldiers who had taken part in the battle: "This is the prescribed ritual which the LORD has commanded Moses: ²²gold, silver, bronze, iron, tin and lead— ²³whatever can stand fire—you shall put into the fire, that it may become clean; however, it must also be purified with water of purification.‡ But whatever cannot stand fire you must put into the water. ²⁴On the seventh day you will wash your garments, and then you will again be clean. After that you may enter the camp."

**Division of the Spoils.** ²⁵The LORD said to Moses: ²⁶With the help of Eleazar the priest and of the heads of the ancestral houses of the community, inventory all the spoils captured, human being and beast alike; ²⁷then divide the spoils§ between the warriors who went on the campaign and the whole community. ²⁸You will levy a tax for the LORD on the soldiers who went on the campaign: one out of every five hundred persons, oxen, donkeys, and sheep. ²⁹From their half you will take it and give it to Eleazar the priest as a contribution to the LORD. ³⁰From the Israelites' half you will take one captive from every fifty human beings, oxen, donkeys, and sheep—all the animals—and give them to the Levites, who perform the duties of the LORD's tabernacle. ³¹So Moses and Eleazar the priest did this, as the LORD had commanded Moses.

**Amount of the Plunder.** ³²This plunder, what was left of the loot which the troops had taken, amounted to six hundred and seventy-five thousand sheep, ³³seventy-two thousand oxen, ³⁴sixty-one thousand donkeys, ³⁵and thirty-two thousand women who had not had sexual relations.

³⁶The half-share that fell to those who had gone out on the campaign was in number: three hundred and thirty-seven thousand five hundred sheep, ³⁷of which six hundred and seventy-five fell as tax to the LORD; ³⁸thirty-six thousand oxen, of which seventy-two fell as tax to the LORD; ³⁹thirty thousand five hundred donkeys, of which sixty-one fell as tax to the LORD; ⁴⁰and sixteen thousand persons, of whom thirty-two persons fell as tax to the LORD. ⁴¹Moses gave the taxes contributed to the LORD to Eleazar the priest, exactly as the LORD had commanded Moses.

⁴²As for the Israelites' half, which Moses had taken from the men who had fought— ⁴³the community's half was three hundred and thirty-seven thousand five hundred sheep, ⁴⁴thirty-six thousand oxen, ⁴⁵thirty thousand five hundred donkeys, ⁴⁶and sixteen thousand persons. ⁴⁷From the Israelites' half, Moses took one captive from every fifty, from human being and beast alike, and gave them to the Levites, who

---

*[31:8] **The five kings of Midian:** they are called Midianite princes, Sihon's vassals, in Jos 13:21.

†[31:17] There are later references to Midian in Jgs 6–8; 1 Kgs 11:18; Is 60:6. The present raid was only against those Midianites who were dwelling at this time near the encampment of the Israelites.

h. [31:16] 2 Pt 2:15; Rev 2:14.

‡[31:23] **Water of purification:** water mixed with the ashes of the red heifer as prescribed in 19:9.

§[31:27] **Divide the spoils:** for a similar division of the plunder into two equal parts, between those who engaged in the battle and those who stayed with the baggage, cf. 1 Sm 30:24. But note that here the tax on the plunder of the noncombatants is ten times as much as that on the soldiers' plunder.

performed the duties of the LORD's tabernacle, exactly as the LORD had commanded Moses.

**Gifts of the Officers.** ⁴⁸Then those who were officers over the contingents of the army, commanders of thousands and commanders of hundreds, came up to Moses ⁴⁹and said to him, "Your servants have counted the soldiers under our command, and not one of us is missing. ⁵⁰So, we have brought as an offering to the LORD articles of gold that each of us has picked up— anklets, bracelets, rings, earrings, or pendants— to make atonement for ourselves before the LORD." ⁵¹Moses and Eleazar the priest accepted the gold from them, all fashioned pieces. ⁵²The gold that was given as a contribution to the LORD—from the commanders of thousands and the commanders of hundreds—amounted in all to sixteen thousand seven hundred and fifty shekels. ⁵³What the common soldiers had looted each one kept for himself.† ⁵⁴So Moses and Eleazar the priest accepted the gold from the commanders of thousands and of hundreds, and put it in the tent of meeting as a reminder on behalf of the Israelites before the LORD.

## CHAPTER 32

**Request of Gad and Reuben.** ¹Now the Reubenites and Gadites had a very large number of livestock. Noticing that the land of Jazer and of Gilead‡ was a place suited to livestock, ²the Gadites and Reubenites came to Moses and Eleazar the priest and to the leaders of the community and said, ³§"The region of Ataroth, Dibon, Jazer, Nimrah, Heshbon, Elealeh, Sebam, Nebo and Baal-meon— ⁴the land which the LORD has laid low before the community of Israel, is a land for livestock, and your servants have livestock." ⁵They continued, "If we find favor with you, let this land be given to your servants as their possession. Do not make us cross the Jordan."

**Moses' Rebuke.** ⁶But Moses answered the Gadites and Reubenites: "Are your kindred, then, to go to war, while you remain here? ⁷Why do you wish to discourage the Israelites from crossing to the land the LORD has given them? ⁸That is just what your ancestors did when I sent them from Kadesh-barnea to reconnoiter the land.ⁱ ⁹They went up to the Wadi Eshcol and reconnoitered the land, then so discouraged the

Israelites that they would not enter the land the LORD had given them. ¹⁰ʲAt that time the anger of the LORD flared up, and he swore: ¹¹None of the men twenty years old or more who have come up from Egypt will see the land I promised under oath to Abraham and Isaac and Jacob, because they have not followed me unreservedly— ¹²ᵏexcept the Kenizzite⁵ Caleb, son of Jephunneh, the Kenizzite, and Joshua, son of Nun, since they have followed the LORD unreservedly. ¹³So the anger of the LORD flared up against the Israelites and he made them wander in the wilderness forty years, until the whole generation that had done evil in the sight of the LORD had disappeared. ¹⁴And now here you are, offspring of sinful stock, rising up in your ancestors' place to add still more to the LORD's blazing anger against the Israelites. ¹⁵If you turn away from following him, he will again abandon them in the wilderness, and you will bring about the ruin of this entire people."

**Counter Proposal.** ¹⁶But they approached him and said: "We will only build sheepfolds here for our flocks and towns for our families; ¹⁷but we ourselves will march as troops in the vanguard before the Israelites,ˡ until we have led them to their destination. Meanwhile our families will remain in the fortified towns because of the land's inhabitants. ¹⁸We will not return to our homes until all the Israelites have taken possession of their heritage. ¹⁹ᵐBut we will not claim any heritage with them across the Jordan and beyond, because we have received a heritage for ourselves on the eastern side of the Jordan."

**Agreement Reached.** ²⁰**Moses said to them in reply: "If you do this—if you march as troops before the LORD into battle ²¹and cross the Jordan in full force before the LORD until he has driven his enemies out of his way ²²and the land is subdued before the LORD, then you may return here, free from every obligation to the LORD and to Israel, and this land will be your possession before the LORD.ⁿ ²³But if you do not do this, you will have sinned against the LORD, and you can be sure that the consequences of your sin will overtake you. ²⁴Build the towns, then, for your families, and the folds for your flocks, but fulfill what you have promised."

²⁵The Gadites and Reubenites answered Moses, "Your servants will do as my lord commands. ²⁶ᵒWhile our wives and children, our livestock and other animals remain there in the towns of Gilead, ²⁷all your servants will go across

---

*[31:50] The precise nature and use of some of these articles of gold is not certain.

†[31:53] Apparently because of the commanders' generosity the common troops were under no sort of obligation to make their own offerings and could keep their loot.

‡[32:1] **Gilead**: the name of the western part of the plateau east of the Jordan, sometimes signifying the whole region from the Yarmuk to the Jordan, sometimes only the northern part of this region, and sometimes, as here, only its southern part. Jazer lay to the east of southern Gilead.

§[32:3] The places named in this verse, as well as the additional ones given in vv. 34–38, were all in the former kingdom of Sihon, that is, in the region between the Jabbok and the Arnon. Cf. 21:23–24; Jos 13:19–21, 24–27.

i. [32:8–9] Nm 13:31–33; Dt 1:22.

¶[32:12] **Kenizzite**: a member of the clan of Kenaz, which, according to Gn 36:11, 15, 42, was Edomite; but, according to Nm 13:6; 34:19, Caleb belonged to the tribe of Judah; cf. also Jos 14:6, 14.

**[32:20–22] Since the ark of the Lord was carried into battle with the Israelite army, the vanguard was said to march before the Lord (see Jos 6:6–9).

j. [32:10–11] Dt 1:34–35.   k. [32:12] Nm 14:24; Dt 1:36.   l. [32:17] Jos 4:12–13.   m. [32:19] Jos 13:8.   n. [32:22] Jos 1:15.   o. [32:26] Jos 1:14.

as armed troops before the Lord to battle, just as my lord says."

²⁸So Moses gave this command in their regard to Eleazar the priest, to Joshua, son of Nun, and to the heads of the ancestral houses of the Israelite tribes: ²⁹He said to them, "If all the Gadites and Reubenites cross the Jordan with you in full force before the Lord into battle, the land will be subdued before you, and you will give them Gilead as a possession. ³⁰But if they will not go across in force with you before the Lord, you will bring their wives and children and livestock across before you into Canaan, and they will possess a holding among you in the land of Canaan."

³¹To this the Gadites and Reubenites replied, "We will do what the Lord has ordered your servants. ³²We ourselves will go across in force before the Lord into the land of Canaan, but we will retain our hereditary property on this side of the Jordan."* ³³So Moses gave them—†the Gadites and Reubenites, as well as half the tribe of Manasseh, son of Joseph—the kingdom of Sihon, king of the Amorites, and the kingdom of Og, king of Bashan, the land with its towns, and the districts of the surrounding towns.ᵖ

³⁴The Gadites rebuilt the cities of Dibon, Ataroth, Aroer, ³⁵Atroth-shophan, Jazer, Jogbehah, ³⁶Beth-nimrah and Beth-haran—fortified cities—and sheepfolds. ³⁷The Reubenites rebuilt Heshbon, Elealeh, Kiriathaim, ³⁸Nebo, Baal-meon (names to be changed!),‡ and Sibmah. These towns, which they rebuilt, they called by their old names.

**Other Conquests.** ³⁹The descendants of Machir, son of Manasseh, went to Gilead and captured it, dispossessing the Amorites who were there. ⁴⁰(Moses gave Gilead to Machir,�q son of Manasseh, and he settled there.) ⁴¹Jair,ʳ a descendant of Manasseh, went and captured their tent villages, and called them Havvoth-jair.§ ⁴²Nobah went and captured Kenath with its dependencies and called it Nobah after his own name.

## CHAPTER 33
**Stages of the Journey.** ¹The following are the stages by which the Israelites went out by companies from the land of Egypt under the guidance of Moses and Aaron.¶ ²Moses recorded the starting points of the various stages at the direction of the Lord. These are the stages according to their starting points: ³They set out from Rameses in the first month, on the fifteenth day of the first month. On the day after the Passover the Israelites went forth in triumph, in view of all Egypt, ⁴while the Egyptians buried those whom the Lord had struck down, every firstborn; on their gods, too, the Lord executed judgments.ˢ

**From Egypt to Sinai.** ⁵Setting out from Rameses, the Israelites camped at Succoth. ⁶Setting out from Succoth, they camped at Etham near the edge of the wilderness. ⁷Setting out from Etham, they turned back to Pi-hahiroth, which is opposite Baal-zephon, and they camped opposite Migdol.ᵗ ⁸Setting out from Pi-hahiroth, they crossed over through the sea into the wilderness,ᵘ and after they traveled a three days' journey in the wilderness of Etham, they camped at Marah. ⁹Setting out from Marah, they came to Elim; at Elim there were twelve springs of water and seventy palm trees, and they camped there.ᵛ ¹⁰Setting out from Elim, they camped beside the Red Sea. ¹¹Setting out from the Red Sea, they camped in the wilderness of Sin. ¹²Setting out from the wilderness of Sin, they camped at Dophkah. ¹³Setting out from Dophkah, they camped at Alush. ¹⁴Setting out from Alush, they camped at Rephidim, where there was no water for the people to drink.ʷ ¹⁵Setting out from Rephidim, they camped in the wilderness of Sinai.ˣ

**From Sinai to Kadesh.** ¹⁶Setting out from the wilderness of Sinai, they camped at Kibroth-hattaavah. ¹⁷Setting out from Kibroth-hattaavah, they camped at Hazeroth.ʸ ¹⁸Setting out from Hazeroth, they camped at Rithmah. ¹⁹Setting out from Rithmah, they camped at Rimmon-perez. ²⁰Setting out from Rimmon-perez, they camped at Libnah. ²¹Setting out from Libnah, they camped at Rissah. ²²Setting out from Rissah, they camped at Kehelathah. ²³Setting out from Kehelathah, they camped at Mount Shepher. ²⁴Setting out from Mount Shepher, they camped at Haradah. ²⁵Setting out from Haradah, they camped at Makheloth. ²⁶Setting out from Makheloth, they camped at Tahath. ²⁷Setting out

---

*[32:32] **This side of the Jordan:** lit., "beyond the Jordan"; the perspective in Hebrew is from the west bank looking toward the east bank where the Reubenites and Gadites finally settled.

†[32:33] The preceding is concerned solely with the two tribes of Gad and Reuben and with the land of the former kingdom of Sihon; it seems probable that the sudden reference here to the half-tribe of Manasseh and to their territory in Bashan, the former kingdom of Og, is a later addition to the text.

‡[32:38] The phrase in parentheses is probably a gloss, warning the reader perhaps to substitute some other word for Nebo and Baal, the names of foreign deities mentioned in the last two city names. **They called by their old names:** lit., "they called by their names"; however, some understand the current Hebrew text to mean, "they called by new names," or "their own names."

§[32:41] **Havvoth-jair:** that is, "villages of Jair."

¶[33:1–3] According to v. 2, this list of camping sites was drawn up by Moses as an itinerary recording Israel's trek through the wilderness. Comparison with the more detailed accounts of the journey as given elsewhere suggests that the list is not necessarily comprehensive. It records just forty camping sites, not counting the starting place, Rameses, and the terminus, the plains of Moab. This number, which corresponds exactly to the forty years of wandering in the wilderness, is probably a schematic device. Moreover, it seems that in its present form the order of some of the names here has been disturbed. Several names listed here are not recorded elsewhere.

p. [32:33] Dt 3:12; 29:7; Jos 12:6; 13:8. q. [32:40] Dt 3:15. r. [32:41] Dt 3:14.

s. [33:4–5] Ex 12:12, 29, 37. t. [33:7] Ex 14:2. u. [33:8] Ex 15:22. v. [33:9] Ex 15:27. w. [33:14] Ex 17:1. x. [33:15] Ex 19:2. y. [33:17–18] Nm 11:34–35.

from Tahath, they camped at Terah. [28]Setting out from Terah, they camped at Mithkah. [29]Setting out from Mithkah, they camped at Hashmonah. [30]Setting out from Hashmonah, they camped at Moseroth. [31]Setting out from Moseroth, they camped at Bene-jaakan. [32]Setting out from Bene-jaakan, they camped at Mount Gidgad. [33]Setting out from Mount Gidgad, they camped at Jotbathah. [34]Setting out from Jotbathah, they camped at Abronah. [35]Setting out from Abronah, they camped at Ezion-geber.[†] [36]Setting out from Ezion-geber, they camped in the wilderness of Zin, that is, Kadesh.[z]

**From Kadesh to the Plains of Moab.** [37]Setting out from Kadesh, they camped at Mount Hor on the border of the land of Edom.

[38]Aaron the priest ascended Mount Hor[a] at the LORD's direction, and there he died in the fortieth year after the departure of the Israelites from the land of Egypt, on the first day of the fifth month. [39]Aaron was a hundred and twenty-three years old when he died on Mount Hor.

[40][‡]When the Canaanite, the king of Arad, who ruled over the Negeb in the land of Canaan, heard that the Israelites were coming. . . .

[41][§]Setting out from Mount Hor, they camped at Zalmonah. [42]Setting out from Zalmonah, they camped at Punon. [43]Setting out from Punon, they camped at Oboth. [44]Setting out from Oboth, they camped at Iye-abarim on the border of Moab. [45]Setting out from Iye-abarim, they camped at Dibon-gad. [46]Setting out from Dibon-gad, they camped at Almon-diblathaim. [47]Setting out from Almon-diblathaim, they camped in the Abarim range opposite Nebo. [48]Setting out from the Abarim range, they camped on the plains of Moab by the Jordan opposite Jericho. [49]They camped by the Jordan on the plains of Moab extended from Beth-jeshimoth to Abel-shittim.

**Conquest and Division of Canaan.** [50]The LORD spoke to Moses on the plains of Moab by the Jordan opposite Jericho: [51]Speak to the Israelites and say to them: When you go across the Jordan into the land of Canaan, [52]dispossess all the inhabitants of the land before you; destroy all their stone figures, destroy all their molten images, and demolish all their high places.[b]

[53]You will take possession of the land and settle in it, for I have given you the land to possess. [54]You will apportion the land among yourselves by lot, clan by clan, assigning a large heritage to a large clan and a small heritage to a small clan.[c] Wherever anyone's lot falls, there will his possession be; you will apportion these shares within your ancestral tribe.

[55]But if you do not dispossess the inhabitants of the land before you, those whom you allow to remain will become barbs in your eyes and thorns in your sides, and they will harass you in the land where you live,[d] [56]and I will treat you as I had intended to treat them.

# CHAPTER 34

**The Boundaries.** [1]The LORD spoke to Moses: [2]Give the Israelites this order: When you enter the land of Canaan, this is the territory that shall fall to you as your heritage—the land of Canaan with its boundaries:

[3]Your southern boundary will be at the wilderness of Zin along the border of Edom;[e] on the east your southern boundary will begin at the end of the Salt Sea. [4]Then your boundary will turn south of the Akrabbim Pass and cross Zin. Terminating south of Kadesh-barnea, it extends to Hazar-addar and crosses to Azmon.[f] [5]Then the boundary will turn from Azmon to the Wadi of Egypt and terminate at the Sea.[g]

[6]For your western boundary you will have the Great Sea[¶] with its coast; this will be your western boundary.

[7]This will be your boundary on the north: from the Great Sea you will draw a line to Mount Hor,[**] [8]and draw it from Mount Hor to Lebo-hamath, with the boundary terminating at Zedad. [9]Then the boundary extends to Ziphron and terminates at Hazar-enan. This will be your northern boundary.

[10]For your eastern boundary you will draw a line from Hazar-enan to Shepham. [11]From Shepham the boundary will go down to Riblah, east of Ain, and descending further, the boundary will strike the ridge on the east side of the Sea of Chinnereth;[††] [12]then the boundary will descend along the Jordan and terminate at the Salt Sea.

This will be your land, with the boundaries that surround it.

[13]Moses also gave this order to the Israelites: "This is the land, to be apportioned among you by lot, which the LORD has commanded to be given to the nine and a half tribes. [14]For the tribe of the Reubenites according to their ancestral

---

*[33:30–36] Moseroth is mentioned in Dt 10:6 (in the form of "Moserah") as the place where Aaron died, apparently a variant of the tradition here in v. 38 regarding the place of Aaron's death; so also Nm 20:22–24 and Dt 32:50. Perhaps Moseroth was close to Mount Hor.

†[33:35] **Ezion-geber:** Solomon conducted sea trade with Ophir from this port (1 Kgs 9:26), today probably identified on the northern coast of the Gulf of Elath between the Jordanian city of Aqabah and the Israeli city of Elath.

‡[33:40] The verse repeats almost verbatim the same introduction to the account of the victory over Arad as is given in 21:1–3, where it also follows the account of Aaron's death. Perhaps the isolated verse here is intended by the editor(s) of Numbers to point the reader to the fuller account given there.

§[33:41b–49] It seems that this section stood originally immediately after v. 36a.

¶[34:6] **The Great Sea:** the Mediterranean.

**[34:7–8] **Mount Hor:** different from the one where Aaron died; cf. 20:22; 33:37–38.

††[34:11] **Sea of Chinnereth:** in the New Testament known as the Sea of Galilee; today called Lake Kinneret.

---

z. [33:36–37] Nm 20:1, 22. a. [33:38] Nm 20:25; Dt 32:50. b. [33:52] Ex 23:31; 34:13; Dt 7:5; 12:3.

c. [33:54] Nm 26:53–56. d. [33:55] Jos 23:13; Jgs 2:3. e. [34:3] Jos 15:1–2. f. [34:4] Jos 15:3. g. [34:5] Jos 15:4.

houses, and the tribe of the Gadites according to their ancestral houses, as well as half of the tribe of Manasseh, have already received their heritage; [15]these two and a half tribes have received their heritage across the Jordan opposite Jericho, in the east, toward the sunrise."

**Supervisors of the Allotment.** [16]The LORD spoke to Moses: [17]These are the names of the men who shall apportion the land among you: Eleazar the priest, and Joshua, son of Nun; [18h]and you will designate one leader from each of the tribes to apportion the land. [19]These are the names of the men:

from the tribe of Judah: Caleb, son of Jephunneh,
[20] from the tribe of the Simeonites: Samuel, son of Ammihud;
[21] from the tribe of Benjamin: Elidad, son of Chislon;
[22] from the tribe of the Danites: a leader, Bukki, son of Jogli;
[23] for the descendants of Joseph: from the tribe of the Manassites: a leader, Hanniel, son of Ephod; and
[24] from the tribe of the Ephraimites: a leader, Kemuel, son of Shiphtan;
[25] from the tribe of the Zebulunites: a leader, Elizaphan, son of Parnach;
[26] from the tribe of the Issacharites: a leader, Paltiel, son of Azzan;
[27] from the tribe of the Asherites: a leader, Ahihud, son of Shelomi;
[28] from the tribe of the Naphtalites: a leader, Pedahel, son of Ammihud.
[29] These are the ones whom the LORD commanded to apportion to the Israelites their heritage in the land of Canaan.

## CHAPTER 35

**Cities for the Levites.** [1]The LORD spoke to Moses on the plains of Moab by the Jordan opposite Jericho: [2i]Command the Israelites out of the heritage they possess to give the Levites cities to dwell in; you will also give the Levites the pasture lands around the cities. [3]The cities will be for them to dwell in, and the pasture lands will be for their cattle, their flocks, and all their other animals. [4]The pasture lands of the cities to be assigned the Levites shall extend a thousand cubits out from the city walls in every direction. [5]You will measure out two thousand cubits outside the city along the east side, two thousand cubits along the south side, two thousand cubits along the west side, and two thousand cubits along the north side, with the city lying in the center. These will be the pasture lands of their cities.
[6]Now these are the cities you will give to the Levites: the six cities of asylum which you

must establish for the homicide to run to, and in addition forty-two other cities— [7]a total of forty-eight cities with their pasture lands which you will assign to the Levites. [8*]In assigning the cities from what the Israelites possess, take more from a larger group and fewer from a smaller one, so that each will cede cities to the Levites in proportion to the heritage which it receives.

**Cities of Asylum.** [9k]The LORD spoke to Moses: [10]Speak to the Israelites and say to them: When you go across the Jordan into the land of Canaan, [11]select for yourselves cities to serve as cities of asylum, where a homicide who has killed someone inadvertently may flee. [12]These cities will serve you as places of asylum from the avenger of blood,[†] so that a homicide will not be put to death until tried before the community. [13]As for the cities you assign, you will have six cities of asylum: [14]you will designate three cities beyond the Jordan, and you will designate three cities in the land of Canaan. These will be cities of asylum. [15]These six cities will serve as places of asylum for the Israelites, and for the resident or transient aliens among them, so that anyone who has killed a person inadvertently may flee there.

**Murder and Manslaughter.** [16‡]If someone strikes another with an iron instrument and causes death, that person is a murderer, and the murderer must be put to death.[l] [17]If someone strikes another with a death-dealing stone in the hand and death results, that person is a murderer, and the murderer must be put to death. [18]Or if someone strikes another with a death-dealing club in the hand and death results, that person is a murderer, and the murderer must be put to death. [19]The avenger of blood is the one who will kill the murderer, putting the individual to death on sight.

[20]If someone pushes another out of hatred, or throws something from an ambush, and death results,[m] [21]or strikes another with the hand out of enmity and death results, the assailant must be put to death as a murderer. The avenger of blood will kill the murderer on sight.

[22n]However, if someone pushes another without malice aforethought, or without lying in ambush throws some object at another, [23]or without seeing drops upon another some death-dealing stone and death results, although there was neither enmity nor malice— [24]then the community will judge between the assailant and the avenger of blood in accordance with these norms. [25]The community will deliver the

---

*[35:8] This provision was hardly observed in the actual assignment of the levitical cities as narrated in Jos 21.

†[35:12] **The avenger of blood**: Hebrew, *go'el*, often translated as "redeemer," one who, as next of kin to the slain (2 Sm 14:7), and here, as executor of public justice, had the right and duty to take the life of the murderer; cf. Dt 19:6, 12; Jos 20:3, 5, 9.

‡[35:16–25] Here, as also in Ex 21:12–13, there is a casuistic development of the original law as stated in Ex 21:12–14.

---

h. [34:18] Nm 1:4.　i. [35:2] Jos 14:3–4; 21:2.　j. [35:6] Dt 4:41–42; Jos 20:2.

k. [35:9–15] Dt 19:2; Jos 20:2–6.　l. [35:16] Ex 21:12; Lv 24:17.　m. [35:20] Ex 21:14; Dt 19:11.　n. [35:22] Jos 20:3.

homicide from the avenger of blood and the community will return the homicide to the city of asylum where the latter had fled;[o] and the individual will stay there until the death of the high priest who has been anointed with sacred oil. [26]If the homicide leaves at all the bounds of the city of asylum to which flight had been made, [27]and is found by the avenger of blood beyond the bounds of the city of asylum, and the avenger of blood kills the homicide, the avenger incurs no bloodguilt; [28]for the homicide was required to stay in the city of asylum until the death of the high priest. Only after the death of the high priest may the homicide return to the land of the homicide's possession.

[29]This is the statute for you throughout all your generations, wherever you live, for rendering judgment.

**Judgment.** [30]Whenever someone kills another, the evidence of witnesses is required to kill the murderer.[p] A single witness does not suffice for putting a person to death.

**No Indemnity.** [31]You will not accept compensation in place of the life of a murderer who deserves to die, but that person must be put to death. [32]Nor will you accept compensation to allow one who has fled to a city of asylum to return to live in the land before the death of the high priest. [33]You will not pollute the land where you live. For bloodshed pollutes the land, and the land can have no expiation for the blood shed on it except through the blood of the one who shed it. [34]Do not defile the land in which you live and in the midst of which I dwell;[q] for I the LORD dwell in the midst of the Israelites.

## CHAPTER 36

**Inheritance of Daughters.** [1]The heads of the ancestral houses in a clan of the descendants of Gilead, son of Machir, son of Manasseh—one of the Josephite clans—came up and spoke before Moses and Eleazar the priest and before the leaders who were the heads of the ancestral houses of the Israelites. [2]They said: "The LORD commanded my lord to apportion the land by lot for a heritage among the Israelites;[r] and my lord was commanded by the LORD to give the heritage of Zelophehad our kinsman to his daughters. [3]But if they marry into one of the other Israelite tribes, their heritage will be withdrawn from our ancestral heritage and will be added to that of the tribe into which they marry; thus the heritage that fell to us by lot will be diminished. [4]When the Israelites celebrate the jubilee year,[*] the heritage of these women will be added to that of the tribe into which they marry and their heritage will be withdrawn from that of our ancestral tribe."

[5†]So Moses commanded the Israelites at the direction of the LORD: "The tribe of the Josephites are right in what they say. [6]This is what the LORD commands with regard to the daughters of Zelophehad: They may marry anyone they please, provided they marry into a clan of their ancestral tribe, [7]so that no heritage of the Israelites will pass from one tribe to another, but all the Israelites will retain their own ancestral heritage. [8]Every daughter who inherits property in any of the Israelite tribes will marry someone belonging to a clan of her own ancestral tribe, in order that all the Israelites may remain in possession of their own ancestral heritage. [9]Thus, no heritage will pass from one tribe to another, but all the Israelite tribes will retain their own ancestral heritage."

[10]The daughters of Zelophehad did exactly as the LORD commanded Moses. [11]Mahlah, Tirzah, Hoglah, Milcah and Noah, Zelophehad's daughters, married sons of their uncles on their father's side. [12]They married within the clans of the descendants of Manasseh, son of Joseph; hence their heritage remained in the tribe of their father's clan.

**Conclusion.** [13]These are the commandments and decisions which the LORD commanded the Israelites through Moses, on the plains of Moab beside the Jordan opposite Jericho.

---

*[36:4] Before the jubilee year various circumstances, such as divorce, could make such property revert to its original tribal owners; but in the jubilee year it became irrevocably attached to its new owners.

†[36:5–9] This is a supplement to the law given in 27:5–11.

o. [35:25] Jos 20:6.   p. [35:30] Dt 17:6; 19:15; Jn 8:17; 2 Cor 13:1; 1 Tm 5:19.   q. [35:34] Ex 29:45.

r. [36:2] Nm 26:55; 27:6; Jos 17:3–4.

# THE BOOK OF
# DEUTERONOMY

The title of Deuteronomy in Hebrew is *Debarim*, "words," from its opening phrase. The English title comes from the Septuagint of 17:18, *deuteronomion*, "copy of the law"; this title is appropriate because the book replicates much of the legal content of the previous books, serving as a "second law." It brings to a close the five books of the Torah or Pentateuch with a retrospective account of Israel's past—the exodus, the Sinai covenant, and the wilderness wanderings—and a look into Israel's future as they stand poised to enter the land of Canaan and begin their life as a people there.

The book consists of three long addresses by Moses. Each of these contains narrative, law, and exhortation, in varying proportions. In an expansion of the first commandment of the decalogue (Ex 20:5–6; Dt 5:9–10), Moses tells the Israelites how to make a success of their life as a people once they are settled in the land. The choice presented to Israel is to love the Lord and keep his commandments, or to serve "other gods." That choice will determine what kind of life they will make for themselves in the land. Whichever choice they make as a people carries consequences, which Deuteronomy terms "blessing" and "curse." Thus the book can be seen as a kind of survival manual for Israel in their life as a people: how to live and what to avoid. This gives the book its hortatory style and tone of life-or-death urgency.

One defining concern of the book is centralization of worship. As Israel's God is one (6:4–5), so its worship must be focused in one place, which the Lord "will choose from among your tribes"; there the Lord will "make his name dwell" (see note on 12:5). Thus the privileged status of the Jerusalem Temple is asserted; all other places and all other modes of worship of the God of Israel (the local shrines, the "high places," "under every green tree") are proscribed.

The book was probably composed over the course of three centuries, from the eighth century to the exile and beyond. It bears some relation to "the Book of the Law" discovered in the Jerusalem Temple around 622 B.C. during the reign of King Josiah (2 Kgs 22:8–13). It gives evidence of later editing: cf. the references to exile in 4:1–40; 28:63–68; 29:21–28; 30:1–10.

Over the book looms the disaster of 722/721, the fall of the Northern Kingdom, Israel. The detailed description of siege (28:49–57) especially echoes the fate the North suffered at the hands of the Assyrian invader. The book draws the minds of its intended readers back to a time before disastrous mistakes were made and their disastrous effects felt, and serves to explain the political and theological dynamics that led to the destruction of the North as well as to warn the surviving Southern Kingdom, Judah, to reform by keeping faith with Israel's covenant Lord.

The characteristic and highly recognizable language and theology of Deuteronomy are seen in editorial comments structuring the works that follow it in the Hebrew canon, the Books of Joshua, Judges, Samuel, and Kings. Together with Deuteronomy, these present a history of Israel from Moses to the time of the Babylonian exile. Conventionally this great multivolume work is termed the Deuteronomistic History. The Book of Deuteronomy itself was also incorporated into the Torah as its fifth volume.

The book presents three discourses by Moses, as follows:

I. First Address (1:1–4:43)
II. Second Address (4:44–28:69)
    A. The Lord's Covenant with Israel (4:44–11:32)
    B. The Deuteronomic Code (12:1–28:69)
III. Third Address (29:1–33:29)
IV. The Death of Moses (34:1–12)

## I. FIRST ADDRESS

## CHAPTER 1

**Introduction.** [1]These are the words that Moses spoke to all Israel beyond the Jordan in the wilderness, in the Arabah, opposite Suph, between Paran and Tophel, Laban, Hazeroth, and Dizahab. [2]It is a journey of eleven days from Horeb[†] to Kadesh-barnea by way of the highlands of Seir.

[3]In the fortieth year,[‡] on the first day of the eleventh month, Moses spoke to the Israelites according to all that the LORD had commanded him to speak to them, [4]after he had defeated Sihon, king of the Amorites, who reigned in Heshbon,[a] and Og, king of Bashan, who reigned in Ashtaroth and in Edrei. [5]Beyond the Jordan, in the land of Moab, Moses undertook to explain this law:

**Departure from Horeb.** [6]b[¶]The LORD, our God, said to us at Horeb:[¶] You have stayed long enough at this mountain. [7]Leave here and go to the hill country of the Amorites[**] and to all the surrounding regions, the Arabah, the mountains, the Shephelah, the Negeb and the seacoast—the land of the Canaanites and the Lebanon as far as the Great River, the Euphrates. [8]See, I have given that land over to you.[c] Go now and possess the land that the LORD swore to your ancestors, Abraham, Isaac, and Jacob, to give to them and to their descendants after them.

**Appointment of Elders.** [9]d[e]At that time I said to you, "I am unable to carry you by myself.[e] [10]The LORD, your God, has made you numerous, and now you are as numerous as the stars of the heavens.[f] [11]May the LORD, the God of your ancestors, increase you a thousand times over, and bless you as he promised! [12]But how can I, by myself, bear the weight, the contentiousness of you? [13]Provide wise, discerning, and reputable persons for each of your tribes, that I may appoint them as your leaders." [14]You answered me, "What you have proposed is good." [15]So I took the leaders of your tribes, wise and reputable, and set them as leaders over you, commanders over thousands, over hundreds, over fifties and over tens, and other tribal officers. [16]g[g]I charged your judges at that time, "Listen to complaints among your relatives, and administer true justice to both parties even if one of them is a resident alien. [17]In rendering judgment, do not consider who a person is; give ear to the lowly and to the great alike, fearing no one, for the judgment is God's. Any case that is too difficult for you bring to me and I will hear it." [18]Thus I charged you, at that time, with all the things you were to do.

**The Twelve Scouts.** [19]h[h]Then we set out from Horeb and journeyed through that whole vast and fearful wilderness that you have seen, in the direction of the hill country of the Amorites, as the LORD, our God, had commanded; and we came to Kadesh-barnea.[i] [20]I said to you, "You have come to the hill country of the Amorites, which the LORD, our God, is giving us. [21]See, the LORD, your God, has given this land over to you. Go up and take possession of it, as the LORD, the God of your ancestors, has promised you. Do not fear or be dismayed." [22]Then all of you approached me and said, "Let us send men ahead to spy out the land for us and report to us on the road we should follow and the cities we will come upon." [23]Agreeing with the proposal, I took twelve men from your number, one from each tribe. [24]They set out into the hill country as far as the Wadi Eshcol, and explored it. [25]Then, taking along some of the fruit of the land, they brought it down to us and reported, "The land the LORD, our God, is giving us is good."

**Threats of Revolt.** [26]j[j]But you refused to go up;[k] you defied the command of the LORD, your God. [27]You set to murmuring in your tents, "Out of hatred for us the LORD has brought us out of the land of Egypt,[l] to deliver us into the power of the Amorites and destroy us. [28]What shall we meet with up there? Our men have made our hearts melt by saying, 'The people are bigger and taller than we, and their cities are large and fortified to the sky; besides, we saw the Anakim[††] there.'"[m]

---

*[1:1] The entire book of Deuteronomy is set "beyond the Jordan," in the land of Moab (cf. v. 5; Nm 36:13), on the eve of the Israelites' crossing of the Jordan (Jos 3). **The Arabah**: the valley of the Jordan and the depression south of the Dead Sea.

†[1:2] **Horeb**: an alternative name for Mount Sinai, the wilderness mountain where the Israelites received revelation from God (cf. Ex 3; 19). **Kadesh-barnea**: the southern gateway to the land of Canaan, from which Moses sent spies to reconnoiter the land (cf. Nm 13:26; 32:8). **Seir**: Edom, the land just south of Moab.

‡[1:3] **Fortieth year**: counting from the exodus from Egypt (cf. Ex 12:2; 13:20–22).

§[1:6–3:29] Throughout this section Moses is reviewing the events following the departure from Horeb, as a basis for the exhortation beginning in 4:1. Most of these events are narrated with some variation in the Book of Numbers.

¶[1:6] **Horeb**: the name given to the mountain of revelation in the Elohist and Deuteronomic traditions; this mountain is called Sinai in the Yahwist and Priestly traditions.

**[1:7] **The hill country of the Amorites**: the central mountain range of Palestine. **The Negeb**: the arid land in southern Palestine. **The Lebanon**: the mountain range of Phoenicia, north of Palestine. This is an idealized presentation of the land the Israelites were to occupy; Israel never held power as far as the "Great River" (the Euphrates). The Amorites and the Canaanites were only two of several different peoples occupying the land (cf. 7:1).

---

††[1:28] **Anakim**: a people proverbially notable for height, mentioned in pre-Israelite Egyptian texts, and in the biblical tradition associated with the region of Hebron and the hill country of Judah (Nm 13:22, 28, 33; Jos 11:21; 14:12, 15).

---

a. [1:4] Dt 2:24–3:11; Nm 21:21–35. b. [1:6–8] Ex 32:34–33:3. c. [1:8] Dt 6:10, 23; 9:5, 27; 29:13; 30:20; 34:4; Gn 12:7; 13:14–15; 15:18–21; 17:8; 26:3–5; 28:13–14. d. [1:9–18] Ex 18:13–26; Nm 11:16–30. e. [1:9] Dt 1:31. f. [1:10] Dt 10:22; Gn 15:5; 22:17; 26:3–4; Ex 32:13.

g. [1:16–17] Dt 10:17–18; 16:18–20. h. [1:19–25] Nm 13:1–27. i. [1:19] Nm 11:11–36. j. [1:26–40] Nm 13:28–14:38. k. [1:26] Dt 9:23. l. [1:27] Dt 9:28. m. [1:28] Dt 1:28; 2:10–11, 21; 9:2; Nm 13:22, 28, 33; Jos 11:21–22; 14:12, 15; 15:13–14; 21:11; Jgs 1:20.

²⁹But I said to you, "Have no dread or fear of them. ³⁰ⁿThe LORD, your God, who goes before you, is the one who will fight for you, just as he acted with you before your very eyes in Egypt, ³¹as well as in the wilderness, where you saw how the LORD, your God, carried you, as one carries his own child, all along your journey until you arrived at this place." ³²Despite this, you would not trust the LORD, your God, ³³who journeys before you to find you a place to camp—by night in the fire, and by day in the cloud, to show you the way to go.ᵒ ³⁴When the LORD heard your words, he was angry, and took an oath: ³⁵Not a single one of this evil generation shall look upon the good land I swore to give to your ancestors, ³⁶except Caleb,˙ son of Jephunneh. He shall see it, for to him and to his descendants I will give the land he trod upon,ᵖ because he has fully followed the LORD.

³⁷The LORD was angered against me also on your account, and said, You shall not enter there either,�q ³⁸but Joshua,ʳ son of Nun, your attendant, shall enter. Encourage him, for he is the one who is to give Israel its possession. ³⁹Your little ones, who you said would become plunder, and your children, who as yet do not know good from evil—they shall enter there; to them I will give it, and they shall take possession of it. ⁴⁰But as for yourselves: turn back and proceed into the wilderness on the Red Sea road.
**Unsuccessful Invasion.** ⁴¹ˢIn reply you said to me, "We have sinned against the LORD. We will go up ourselves and fight, just as the LORD, our God, commanded us." And each of you girded on his weapons, making light of going up into the hill country. ⁴²But the LORD said to me, Warn them: Do not go up and fight—for I will not be in your midst—lest you be beaten down before your enemies. ⁴³I gave you this warning but you would not listen. You defied the LORD's command and arrogantly went off into the hill country. ⁴⁴Then the Amorites living in that hill country came out against you and put you to flight the way bees do, cutting you down in Seir as far as Hormah. ⁴⁵On your return you wept before the LORD, but the LORD did not listen to your voice or give ear to you. ⁴⁶That is why you had to stay as long as you did at Kadesh.

**CHAPTER 2**
**Northward Along Edom.** ¹ᵗThen we turned and proceeded into the wilderness on the Red Sea road,ᵘ as the LORD had told me, and circled around the highlands of Seir for a long time. ²Finally the LORD said to me, ³You have wandered round these highlands long enough;

turn and go north. ⁴Command the people: You are now about to pass through the territory of your relatives, the descendants of Esau, who live in Seir. Though they are afraid of you, be very careful ⁵not to come in conflict with them, for I will not give you so much as a foot of their land, since I have already given Esau possession of the highlands of Seir.ᵛ ⁶You shall purchase from them with money the food you eat; even the water you drink you shall buy from them with money. ⁷Surely, the LORD, your God, has blessed you in all your undertakings; he has been concerned† about your journey through this vast wilderness. It is now forty years that the LORD, your God, has been with you, and you have lacked nothing.ʷ ⁸So we passed by our relatives, the descendants of Esau who live in Seir, leaving behind us the Arabah route, Elath, and Ezion-geber.
**Along Moab.** Then we turned and passed on toward the wilderness of Moab. ⁹ˣAnd the LORD said to me, Do not show hostility to the Moabites or engage them in battle, for I will not give you possession of any of their land, since I have given Ar to the descendants of Lot as their possession.ʸ ¹⁰(Formerly the Emim lived there, a people great and numerous and as tall as the Anakim;ᶻ ¹¹like the Anakim they are considered Rephaim, though the Moabites call them Emim.ᵃ ¹²In Seir, however, the former inhabitants were the Horites;ᵇ the descendants of Esau dispossessed them, clearing them out of the way and dwelling in their place, just as Israel has done in the land of its possession which the LORD gave it.) ¹³Now get ready to cross the Wadi Zered.

So we crossed the Wadi Zered. ¹⁴ᶜNow thirty-eight years had elapsed between our departure from Kadesh-barnea and the crossing of the Wadi Zered; in the meantime the whole generation of soldiers had perished from the camp, as the LORD had sworn they should. ¹⁵Indeed the LORD's own hand was against them, to rout them from the camp completely.
**Along Ammon.** ¹⁶ᵈWhen at length death had put an end to all the soldiers among the people, ¹⁷the LORD said to me, ¹⁸You are now about to leave Ar and the territory of Moab behind. ¹⁹As you come opposite the Ammonites,ᵉ do not show hostility or come in conflict with them, for I will not give you possession of any land of the Ammonites, since I have given it to the descendants of Lot as their possession. ²⁰(This also is considered a country of the Rephaim; formerly the Rephaim dwelt there. The Ammonites call them Zamzummim,ᶠ ²¹a people great

†[2:7] **Concerned:** lit., "known"; cf. Ex 2:25.

n. [1:30–31] Dt 3:22; 8:15; 32:10; Ex 14:13–14.   o. [1:33] Ex 13:21; 40:38; Nm 9:15–16; 10:33–34; 14:14.   p. [1:36] Jos 14:6–14.   q. [1:37] Dt 4:21; 34:4; Nm 20:12.   r. [1:38] Dt 31:3, 7–8; Nm 27:18–23; 34:17; Jos 1:1–9.   s. [1:41–46] Nm 14:39–45.   t. [2:1–8] Nm 20:14–21; Jgs 11:15–17.   u. [2:1] Dt 1:40; Nm 14:25.

v. [2:5] Gn 36:6–8.   w. [2:7] Dt 8:2–5.   x. [2:9–13] Nm 21:12–15; Jgs 11:17–18.   y. [2:9] Gn 19:36–38.   z. [2:10] Dt 1:28.   a. [2:11] Dt 2:20; 3:11, 13; Gn 14:5; 15:20; Jos 12:4; 13:12; 17:15.   b. [2:12] Gn 14:6; 36:20–30.   c. [2:14–15] Nm 14:28–35.   d. [2:16–19] Nm 21:24.   e. [2:19] Gn 19:36–38.   f. [2:20] Dt 2:11; 3:11, 13; Gn 14:5; 15:20; Jos 12:4; 13:12; 17:15.

and numerous and as tall as the Anakim. But these, too, the Lord cleared out of the way for the Ammonites, so that they dispossessed them and dwelt in their place.[g] [22]He did the same for the descendants of Esau, who live in Seir, by clearing the Horites out of their way, so that they dispossessed them and dwelt in their place down to the present.[h] [23]As for the Avvim, who once lived in villages in the vicinity of Gaza,* the Caphtorim, migrating from Caphtor, cleared them away and dwelt in their place.)[i]

**Defeat of Sihon.** [24j]Advance now across the Wadi Arnon. I now deliver into your power Sihon, the Amorite king of Heshbon, and his land. Begin to take possession; engage him in battle.[k] [25]This day I will begin to put a fear and dread of you into the peoples everywhere under heaven, so that at the mention of your name they will quake and tremble before you.

[26]So I sent messengers from the wilderness of Kedemoth to Sihon, king of Heshbon, with this offer of peace: [27]"Let me pass through your country. I will travel only on the road. I will not turn aside either to the right or to the left. [28]The food I eat you will sell me for money, and the water I drink, you will give me for money. Only let me march through, [29]as the descendants of Esau who dwell in Seir and the Moabites who dwell in Ar have done, until I cross the Jordan into the land the Lord, our God, is about to give us."[l] [30]But Sihon, king of Heshbon, refused to let us pass through his land, because the Lord, your God, made him stubborn in mind and obstinate in heart that he might deliver him into your power, as indeed he has now done.

[31]Then the Lord said to me, Now that I have already begun to give over to you Sihon and his land, begin to take possession. [32]So Sihon and all his people advanced against us to join battle at Jahaz; [33]but since the Lord, our God, had given him over to us, we defeated him and his sons and all his people. [34m]At that time we captured all his cities and put every city under the ban,† men, women and children; we left no survivor. [35]Our only plunder was the livestock and the spoils of the captured cities. [36]From Aroer on the edge of the Wadi Arnon and from the town in the wadi itself, as far as Gilead,[n] no city was too well fortified for us. All of them the Lord, our God, gave over to us. [37]However, just as the Lord, our God, commanded us, you did not encroach upon any of the Ammonite land, neither the region bordering on the Wadi Jabbok, nor the cities of the highlands.[o]

# CHAPTER 3

**Defeat of Og.** [1]Then we turned and proceeded up the road to Bashan. But Og, king of Bashan,[p] came out against us with all his people to give battle at Edrei. [2]The Lord said to me, Do not be afraid of him, for I have delivered him into your power with all his people and his land. Do to him as you did to Sihon, king of the Amorites, who reigned in Heshbon. [3]And thus the Lord, our God, delivered into our power also Og, king of Bashan, with all his people. We defeated him so completely that we left him no survivor. [4]At that time we captured all his cities; there was no town we did not take: sixty cities in all, the whole region of Argob, the kingdom of Og in Bashan— [5]all these cities were fortified with high walls and gates and bars—besides a great number of unwalled towns. [6q]As we had done to Sihon, king of Heshbon, so also here we put all the towns under the ban, men, women and children; [7]but all the livestock and the spoils of each city we took as plunder for ourselves.

[8]And so at that time we took from the two kings of the Amorites beyond the Jordan territory from the Wadi Arnon to Mount Hermon [9](the Sidonians call Hermon Sirion and the Amorites call it Senir), [10]all the towns of the plateau, all of Gilead, and all of Bashan as far as Salecah and Edrei, towns of the kingdom of Og in Bashan. [11](Og, king of Bashan, was the last remaining survivor of the Rephaim. He had a bed of iron,‡ nine regular cubits long and four wide, which is still preserved in Rabbah of the Ammonites.)[r]

**Allotment of the Conquered Lands.** [12s]As for the land we took possession of at that time, I gave Reuben and Gad the territory from Aroer, on the edge of the Wadi Arnon, halfway up into the highlands of Gilead, with its cities. [13]The rest of Gilead and all of Bashan, the kingdom of Og, I gave to the half-tribe of Manasseh. (The whole Argob region, all that part of Bashan, was once called a land of the Rephaim.[t] [14]Jair, a Manassite,[u] took all the region of Argob as far as the border of the Geshurites and Maacathites, and named them—Bashan, that is—after himself, Havvoth-jair, the name it bears today.) [15]To Machir[s] I gave Gilead, [16]and to Reuben and Gad the territory from Gilead to the Wadi Arnon—the middle of

---

*[2:23] **Gaza**: later a stronghold of the Philistines (cf. Jos 13:3). **Caphtor**: the island of Crete.

†[2:34] **Under the ban**: in Hebrew, *herem*, which means to devote to the Lord (cf. 7:1–5; 20:10–18). The biblical text often presents *herem* as the total extermination of a population as a manifestation of the will of the Lord. It is historically doubtful that Israel ever literally carried out this theological program.

‡[3:11] **Bed of iron**: some translate, "a sarcophagus of basalt"; its dimensions would be approximately thirteen and a half feet by six feet.

§[3:15] **Machir**: a clan of the tribe of Manasseh (cf. Gn 50:23).

---

g. [2:21] Dt 1:28.   h. [2:22] Gn 14:6; 36:6–8, 20–30.   i. [2:23] Gn 10:14; Jos 13:3; 18:23; 1 Chr 1:12; Jer 47:4; Am 9:7.   j. [2:24–3:11] Dt 1:4; 29:7; 31:4; Jos 2:10; 9:10; 12:1–6; Neh 9:22; Ps 135:10–12; 136:17–22.   k. [2:24–37] Nm 21:21–32; Jgs 11:19–22.   l. [2:29] Dt 2:4–9.   m. [2:34–35] Dt 3:6; 7:2, 26; 13:16, 18; 20:16–18; Jos 10:40; 11:11–12.   n. [2:36] Dt 3:12–13; Jos 13:8–13, 15–23.

o. [2:37] Nm 21:24; Jos 12:2.   p. [3:1–11] Nm 21:33–35.   q. [3:6–7] Dt 2:34–35; 7:2, 26; 13:16, 18; 20:16–18; Jos 10:40; 11:11–12.   r. [3:11] Dt 2:11, 20; 3:13; Jos 14:5; 15:20; Jos 12:4; 13:12; 17:15.   s. [3:12–22] Nm 32:1–42; Jos 13:8–33.   t. [3:13] Dt 2:11, 20; 3:11; Gn 14:5; 15:20; Jos 12:4; 13:12; 17:15.   u. [3:14] Nm 32:41; Jgs 10:4; 1 Chr 2:23.

the wadi being its boundary—and to the Wadi Jabbok, which is the border of the Ammonites, [17]as well as the Arabah with the Jordan and its banks from Chinnereth* to the Salt Sea of the Arabah, under the slopes of Pisgah on the east.

[18v]At that time I charged you: The LORD, your God, has given you this land as your possession. But all your troops equipped for battle must cross over in the vanguard of your fellow Israelites. [19]But your wives and children, as well as your livestock, of which I know you have a large number, shall remain behind in the towns I have given you, [20]until the LORD has settled your relatives as well, and they too possess the land which the LORD, your God, will give them on the other side of the Jordan. Then you may all return to the possessions I have given you.

[21]And I charged Joshua as well, "Your own eyes have seen all that the LORD, your God, has done to both these kings; so, too, will the LORD do to all the kingdoms into which you will cross over. [22]Do not fear them, for it is the LORD, your God, who will fight for you."[w]

**Moses Excluded from the Promised Land.** [23x]It was then that I entreated the LORD, [24]"Lord GOD, you have begun to show to your servant your greatness and your mighty hand. What god in heaven or on earth can perform deeds and powerful acts like yours? [25]Ah, let me cross over and see the good land beyond the Jordan, that fine hill country, and the Lebanon!" [26]But the LORD was angry with me on your account[t] and would not hear me.[y] The LORD said to me, Enough! Speak to me no more of this. [27]Go up to the top of Pisgah and look out to the west, and to the north, and to the south, and to the east. Look well, for you shall not cross this Jordan.[z] [28]Commission Joshua,[a] and encourage and strengthen him, for it is he who will cross at the head of this people and he who will give them possession of the land you are to see.

[29]So we remained in the valley opposite Beth-peor.

## CHAPTER 4
**Advantages of Fidelity.** [1]Now therefore, Israel, hear the statutes and ordinances I am teaching you to observe, that you may live, and may enter in and take possession of the land which the LORD, the God of your ancestors, is giving you.[b]

[2]In your observance of the commandments of the LORD, your God,[c] which I am commanding you, you shall not add to what I command you nor subtract from it. [3]You have seen with your own eyes what the LORD did at Baal-peor:[d] the LORD, your God, destroyed from your midst everyone who followed the Baal of Peor; [4]but you, who held fast to the LORD, your God, are all alive today. [5]See, I am teaching you the statutes and ordinances as the LORD, my God, has commanded me, that you may observe them in the land you are entering to possess. [6]Observe them carefully, for this is your wisdom and discernment in the sight of the peoples, who will hear of all these statutes and say, "This great nation is truly a wise and discerning people."[e] [7]For what great nation is there that has gods so close to it as the LORD, our God, is to us whenever we call upon him? [8]Or what great nation has statutes and ordinances that are as just as this whole law which I am setting before you today?[g]

**Revelation at Horeb.** [9]However, be on your guard and be very careful not to forget the things your own eyes have seen, nor let them slip from your heart as long as you live, but make them known to your children[h] and to your children's children, [10]that day you stood before the LORD, your God, at Horeb, when the LORD said to me: Assemble the people for me, that I may let them hear my words, that they may learn to fear[t] me as long as they live in the land and may so teach their children. [11]You came near and stood at the foot of the mountain, while the mountain blazed to the heart of the heavens with fire and was enveloped in a dense black cloud. [12]Then the LORD spoke to you from the midst of the fire.[j] You heard the sound of the words, but saw no form; there was only a voice. [13]He proclaimed to you his covenant, which he commanded you to keep: the ten words,[s] which he wrote on two stone tablets.[k] [14]At that time the LORD charged me to teach you the statutes and ordinances for you to observe in the land you are about to cross into and possess.

**Danger of Idolatry.** [15]Because you saw no form at all on the day the LORD spoke to you at Horeb from the midst of the fire, be strictly on your guard [16]not to act corruptly by fashioning an idol for yourselves to represent any figure, whether it be the form of a man or of a woman,[l] [17]the form of any animal on the earth, the form of any bird that flies in the sky, [18]the form of anything that crawls on the ground, or the form

---

*[3:17] **Chinnereth**: later known as the Lake of Gennesaret and the Sea of Galilee. **The Salt Sea**: the Dead Sea. **Pisgah**: a mountain range to the northeast of the Salt Sea; Mount Nebo, from which Moses viewed the promised land, is in this range (cf. v. 27; 34:1).

†[3:26] **On your account**: that Moses saw but never entered the promised land is attested by every Pentateuchal tradition, but different reasons are given in different places. Nm 20:12 and Dt 32:51 present Moses as being at fault. Here, as in 1:37 and 4:21, the fault lies in the people but affects Moses.

‡[4:10] **Fear**: not in the sense of "be terrified," but rather "manifest reverence or awe."

§[4:13] **Ten words**: the ten commandments, or decalogue (cf. 5:22; Ex 34:28).

---

v. [3:18–20] Jos 1:12–15; 4:12; 22:1–4.   w. [3:22] Dt 1:30; Ex 14:13–14.   x. [3:23–29] Nm 27:12–23.   y. [3:26] Dt 4:21.   z. [3:27] Dt 3:17; 32:48–52; 34:1–4.   a. [3:28] Dt 1:38; 31:7–8.   b. [4:1] Dt 4:45; 5:1, 31; 6:1, 17, 20; 11:32; 12:1; 26:16.

c. [4:2] Dt 13:1.   d. [4:3] Nm 25:1–13; Ps 106:28; Hos 9:10.   e. [4:6] Dt 26:5; Gn 12:2; 18:18; 46:3; Ex 32:10.   f. [4:7–8] 2 Sm 7:23.   g. [4:8] Dt 4:44.   h. [4:9] Dt 6:7, 20–25; 11:19–21; 29:29; 31:12–13; Ps 78:3–6.   i. [4:11–13] Ex 19:7–20:21.   j. [4:12] Dt 4:33, 36; 5:4.   k. [4:13] Dt 5:6–21; 10:4; Ex 20:1–17; 24:12; 31:18; 34:27–28.   l. [4:16] Dt 5:8; Ex 20:4.

of any fish in the waters under the earth. [19]And when you look up to the heavens and behold the sun or the moon or the stars, the whole heavenly host, do not be led astray into bowing down to them and serving them.[m] These the LORD, your God, has apportioned to all the other nations under the heavens; [20]but you the LORD has taken and led out of that iron foundry, Egypt, that you might be his people, his heritage, as you are today.[n] [21]But the LORD was angry with me on your account[o] and swore that I should not cross the Jordan nor enter the good land which the LORD, your God, is giving you as a heritage. [22]I myself shall die in this country; I shall not cross the Jordan; but you are going to cross over and take possession of that good land.[p] [23]Be careful, therefore, lest you forget the covenant which the LORD, your God, has made with you, and fashion for yourselves against his command an idol in any form whatsoever.[q] [24]For the LORD, your God, is a consuming fire, a jealous God.*[r]

**God's Fidelity and Love.** [25]When you have children and children's children, and have grown old in the land, should you then act corruptly by fashioning an idol in the form of anything, and by this evil done in his sight provoke the LORD, your God, [26]I call heaven and earth this day to witness against you, that you shall all quickly perish from the land which you are crossing the Jordan to possess. You shall not live in it for any length of time but shall be utterly wiped out.[t] [27]The LORD will scatter you among the peoples, and there shall remain but a handful of you among the nations to which the LORD will drive you. [28]There you shall serve gods that are works of human hands, of wood and stone, gods which can neither see nor hear, neither eat nor smell.[u] [29]Yet when you seek the LORD, your God, from there, you shall indeed find him if you search after him with all your heart and soul.[v] [30]In your distress, when all these things shall have come upon you, you shall finally return to the LORD, your God, and listen to his voice. [31]Since the LORD, your God, is a merciful God, he will not abandon or destroy you, nor forget the covenant with your ancestors that he swore to them.[w]

[32]Ask now of the days of old, before your time, ever since God created humankind upon the earth; ask from one end of the sky to the other: Did anything so great ever happen before? Was it ever heard of? [33]Did a people ever hear the voice of God speaking from the midst of fire, as you did, and live?[x] [34]Or did any god venture to go and take a nation for himself from the midst of another nation, by testings, by signs and wonders,[y] by war, with strong hand and outstretched arm, and by great terrors, all of which the LORD, your God, did for you in Egypt before your very eyes? [35]All this you were allowed to see that you might know that the LORD is God; there is no other.[z] [36]Out of the heavens he let you hear his voice to discipline you; on earth he let you see his great fire, and you heard him speaking out of the fire. [37]For love of your ancestors he chose their descendants after them and by his presence and great power led you out of Egypt, [38]dispossessing before you nations greater and mightier than you, so as to bring you in and to give their land to you as a heritage, as it is today. [39]This is why you must now acknowledge, and fix in your heart, that the LORD is God in the heavens above and on earth below, and that there is no other.[a] [40]And you must keep his statutes and commandments which I command you today, that you and your children after you may prosper, and that you may have long life on the land which the LORD, your God, is giving you forever.[b]

**Cities of Refuge.** [41]Then Moses set apart three cities in the region east of the Jordan, [42]to which a homicide might flee who killed a neighbor unintentionally, where there had been no hatred previously, so that the killer might flee to one of these cities and live: [43]Bezer in the wilderness, in the region of the plateau, for the Reubenites; Ramoth in Gilead for the Gadites; and Golan in Bashan for the Manassites.

## II. SECOND ADDRESS

### A. The Lord's Covenant with Israel

**Introduction.** [44]This is the law[†] which Moses set before the Israelites.[d] [45]These are the decrees, and the statutes and ordinances[‡] which Moses proclaimed to the Israelites after they came

---

*[4:24] **A jealous God:** Hebrew *'el qanna*. The root of the adjective *qanna* expresses the idea of intense feeling focused on solicitude for someone or something; see, e.g., Ps 69:10; Sg 8:6; Is 9:6; 37:32; Ez 39:25. The Septuagint translated the adjective as *zelotes*, and the Vulgate followed suit; hence the traditional English rendering "jealous" (and sometimes "zealous") found in the Douai-Rheims and King James versions. In modern usage, however, "jealous" denotes unreasonable, petty possessiveness, a meaning, even as nuance, wanting in the Hebrew. In the first commandment (5:6–10; Ex 20:2–6) and passages derived from it (like 4:24; 6:15; Ex 34:14; Jos 24:19; Na 1:2), Israel's God is represented as totally committed to his purpose, and Israel is put on notice to take him and his directives for their life as a people with equal seriousness.

---

m. [4:19] Dt 17:3; Jb 31:26–28.   n. [4:20] 1 Kgs 8:51; Is 48:10; Jer 11:4.   o. [4:21] Dt 1:37; 3:26.   p. [4:22] Dt 3:27; 34:1–12; Jos 1–12.   q. [4:23] Dt 4:16; 9:12–14; Ex 32:1–10.   r. [4:24] Dt 5:9; 6:15; 9:3; Ex 24:17; 34:14.   s. [4:25–27] Dt 28:64–67.   t. [4:26] Dt 30:19; 31:28; 32:1; Is 1:2.   u. [4:28] Dt 28:64; 29:17; Lv 26:30–39; Ps 115:4–8; 135:15–18; Is 44:9–20.   v. [4:29] Dt 6:5; Jer 29:13–14.

---

†[4:44] **Law:** Hebrew *torah*, meaning "instruction," "law," "teaching"; the standard translation "law" comes from the influence of the Septuagint's *nomos*, "law," and the extensive legislation in Ex 20–Nm 10.

‡[4:45] **Statutes and ordinances:** terms referring to the legal corpus in 12:1–26:19.

---

w. [4:31] Dt 31:8; Gn 9:9–17; 15:18–21; 17:1–21; Ex 34:6–7.   x. [4:33] Dt 4:36; 5:24, 26; Ex 20:19.   y. [4:34] Dt 7:19; 26:8; 29:2; Ex 7:3; 15:3–10; Jer 32:21.   z. [4:35] Dt 4:39; 32:39; 1 Kgs 8:60; Is 43:10–13; Jl 2:27.   a. [4:39] Dt 4:35; 32:39; 1 Kgs 8:60; Is 43:10–13; Jl 2:27.   b. [4:40] Dt 6:3; 12:28.   c. [4:41–43] Dt 19:1–13; Nm 35:10–28; Jos 20:1–9.   d. [4:44] Dt 4:8; 17:18–19; 30:10; 31:11–12.

out of Egypt,*e 46*beyond the Jordan in the valley opposite Beth-peor, in the land of Sihon, king of the Amorites, who reigned in Heshbon, whom Moses and the Israelites defeated after they came out of Egypt.*g 47*They took possession of his land and the land of Og, king of Bashan, as well—the land of these two kings of the Amorites in the region beyond the Jordan to the east: 48*from Aroer on the edge of the Wadi Arnon to Mount Sion* (that is, Hermon) 49*and all the Arabah beyond the Jordan to the east, as far as the Arabah Sea† under the slopes of Pisgah.

## CHAPTER 5

**The Covenant at Horeb.** 1*Moses summoned all Israel and said to them, Hear, O Israel, the statutes and ordinances which I proclaim in your hearing this day, that you may learn them and take care to observe them.*h 2*The LORD, our God, made a covenant with us at Horeb; 3*not with our ancestors‡ did the LORD make this covenant, but with us, all of us who are alive here this day. 4*Face to face, the LORD spoke with you on the mountain from the midst of the fire,*j 5*while I was standing between the LORD and you at that time, to announce to you these words of the LORD, since you were afraid of the fire and would not go up the mountain:

**The Decalogue.** 6*I am the LORD your God, who brought you out of the land of Egypt,*i out of the house of slavery. 7*m*You shall not have other gods beside me. 8*You shall not make for yourself an idol or a likeness of anything in the heavens above or on the earth below or in the waters beneath the earth; 9*k*you shall not bow down before them or serve them. For I, the LORD, your God, am a jealous⁴ God, bringing punishment for their parents' wickedness on the children of those who hate me, down to the third and fourth generation, 10*but showing love down to

the thousandth generation of those who love me and keep my commandments. 11*You shall not invoke the name of the LORD, your God, in vain.*n For the LORD will not leave unpunished anyone who invokes his name in vain.

12*o*Observe the sabbath day—keep it holy, as the LORD, your God, commanded you. 13*Six days you may labor and do all your work, 14*but the seventh day is a sabbath of the LORD your God. You shall not do any work, either you, your son or your daughter, your male or female slave, your ox or donkey or any work animal, or the resident alien within your gates, so that your male and female slave may rest as you do. 15*Remember that you too were once slaves in the land of Egypt, and the LORD, your God, brought you out from there with a strong hand and outstretched arm. That is why the LORD, your God, has commanded you to observe the sabbath day.

16*p*Honor your father and your mother, as the LORD, your God, has commanded you, that you may have a long life and that you may prosper in the land the LORD your God is giving you.

17*q*You shall not kill.**

18*r*You shall not commit adultery.

19*s*You shall not steal.

20*t*You shall not bear dishonest witness against your neighbor.

21*u*You shall not covet your neighbor's wife.

You shall not desire your neighbor's house or field, his male or female slave, his ox or donkey, or anything that belongs to your neighbor.

**Moses as Mediator.** 22*These words the LORD spoke with a loud voice to your entire assembly on the mountain from the midst of the fire and the dense black cloud, and added no more. He inscribed them on two stone tablets and gave them to me.*v 23*But when you heard the voice from the midst of the darkness, while the mountain was ablaze with fire, you came near to me, all your tribal heads and elders, 24*and said, "The LORD, our God, has indeed let us see his glory and his greatness, and we have heard his voice from the midst of the fire."*w Today we have found

---

*[4:48] **Sion:** another name for Mount Hermon, besides those mentioned in 3:9 (to be distinguished from the Mount Zion of Jerusalem).

†[4:49] **The Arabah Sea:** the Dead Sea, cf. 3:17.

‡[5:3] **Not with our ancestors:** in fact, the covenant was made with the ancestors, but these had died out during the "forty" years. The covenant is considered to be ongoing—for Israel in Moab and beyond.

§[5:9–10] Israel is confronted with a choice, to "love" or to "hate" the Lord, and with the consequences of each choice. "Wickedness" works destruction not only on those who do it but also down the generations, in a sort of ripple effect. Yet, if Israel keeps the commandments, they will experience the Lord's *hesed* ("love") down to the thousandth generation. Thus the Lord's merciful love is disproportionate to the evil results of iniquity ("down to the third and fourth generation"). **To the thousandth generation:** lit., "to thousands"; cf. 7:9.

¶[5:9] **Jealous:** see note on 4:24.

---

**[5:17] Kill:** see note on Ex 20:13.

---

n. [5:11] Dt 6:13; 10:20; 18:20; 23:21–23; Ex 20:7; Lv 19:12; 24:10–23; Ps 24:4; Jer 29:23; Mt 5:33–37.  o. [5:12–15] Dt 14:22–16:17; 24:18, 22; Ex 20:8–11; 23:12; 31:12–17; 34:21; Is 58:13–14; Jer 17:21–27; Mt 12:1–14; Mk 2:23–3:6; Lk 6:1–11; 13:10–17; 14:1–6; Jn 5:2–18; 7:22–23.  p. [5:16] Dt 21:18–21; 27:16; Ex 20:12; 21:15, 17; Sir 3:1–16; Mt 10:34–39; 12:46–50; 15:4; 19:19; Mk 3:31–35; 7:10; 10:19; Lk 8:19–21; 14:26; 18:20, 28–30; Eph 6:1–4.  q. [5:17] Dt 4:41–43; 19:1–13; 20:1–21:9; 21:18–23; Gn 4:8–16; Ex 20:13; 21:12–14; Nm 35:16–34; Jer 7:9; Hos 4:2; Mt 5:21–26; 19:18; Mk 10:19; Lk 18:20; Jas 2:11.  r. [5:18] Dt 22:13–23:1; Gn 20:1–18; 39:7–20; Ex 20:14; Lv 18:20; 20:10; 2 Sm 11:1–12:25; Jer 7:9; Hos 4:2; Mt 5:27–30; 19:18; Mk 10:19; Lk 18:20; Jas 2:11.  s. [5:19] Dt 23:24; 24:7; Gn 40:15; Ex 20:15; 21:16, 37; 22:1–3, 12; Lv 19:11, 13; 1 Kgs 21:1–19; Jer 7:9; Hos 4:2; Mt 19:18; Mk 10:19; Lk 18:20.  t. [5:20] Dt 19:15–19; Ex 20:16; 23:1–3; Lv 19:11, 15–16; 1 Kgs 21:1–19; Ps 5:6–10; 10:7–9; 27:12; Prv 25:18; 30:8–10; Jer 7:9; Hos 4:2; Mt 19:18; 26:59–60; Mk 10:19; Lk 18:20.  u. [5:21] Dt 7:25; Ex 20:17; Jos 7:21; 2 Sm 11:1–12:25; 1 Kgs 21:1–19; Is 5:8; Mi 2:2; Mt 5:27–30; Lk 12:13–21; Eph 5:5; Col 3:5.  v. [5:22] Dt 4:13; 9:9–11, 17; 10:1–5; Ex 24:12; 31:18; 32:15–20; 34:1–5.  w. [5:24] Dt 4:33, 36; Ex 20:19.

out that God may speak to a mortal and that person may still live. [25]Now, why should we die? For this great fire will consume us. If we hear the voice of the LORD, our God, any more, we shall die.[x] [26]For what mortal has heard the voice of the living God speaking from the midst of fire, as we have, and lived? [27]You go closer and listen to all that the LORD, our God, will say, and then tell us what the LORD, our God, tells you; we will listen and obey."[y]

[28]The LORD heard your words as you were speaking to me and said to me, I have heard the words these people have spoken to you, which are all well said.[z] [29]Would that they might always be of such a mind, to fear me and to keep all my commandments! Then they and their descendants would prosper forever. [30]Go, tell them: Return to your tents. [31]Then you stand here near me and I will give you all the commandments, the statutes and the ordinances; you must teach them, that they may observe them in the land I am giving them to possess.[a]

[32]Be careful, therefore, to do as the LORD, your God, has commanded you, not turning aside to the right or to the left, [33]but following exactly the way that the LORD, your God, commanded you that you may live and prosper, and may have long life in the land which you are to possess.[b]

## CHAPTER 6

[1]This then is the commandment, the statutes and the ordinances,[c] which the LORD, your God, has commanded that you be taught to observe in the land you are about to cross into to possess, [2]so that you, that is, you, your child, and your grandchild, may fear the LORD, your God, by keeping, as long as you live, all his statutes and commandments[d] which I enjoin on you, and thus have long life. [3]Hear then, Israel, and be careful to observe them, that it may go well with you and that you may increase greatly; for the LORD, the God of your ancestors, promised you a land flowing with milk and honey.[e]

**The Great Commandment.**[*] [4]Hear, O Israel![†] The LORD is our God, the LORD alone![5]Therefore,

you shall love the LORD, your God, with your whole heart, and with your whole being, and with your whole strength.[g] [6h]Take to heart these words which I command you today.[i] [7]Keep repeating them to your children. Recite them when you are at home and when you are away, when you lie down and when you get up.[j] [8]Bind them on your arm as a sign[‡] and let them be as a pendant on your forehead.[k] [9]Write them on the doorposts of your houses and on your gates.[l]

**Fidelity in Prosperity.** [10m]When the LORD, your God, brings you into the land which he swore to your ancestors, to Abraham, Isaac, and Jacob, that he would give you, a land with fine, large cities that you did not build,[n] [11]with houses full of goods of all sorts that you did not garner, with cisterns that you did not dig, with vineyards and olive groves that you did not plant; and when, therefore, you eat and are satisfied,[o] [12p]be careful not to forget the LORD, who brought you out of the land of Egypt, that house of slavery. [13q]The LORD, your God, shall you fear; him shall you serve,[§] and by his name shall you swear. [14r]You shall not go after other gods, any of the gods of the surrounding peoples— [15]for the LORD, your God who is in your midst, is a passionate God—lest the anger of the LORD, your God, flare up against you and he destroy you from upon the land.

[16]You shall not put the LORD, your God, to the test, as you did at Massah.[s] [17]But keep the commandments of the LORD, your God, and the decrees and the statutes he has commanded you. [18]Do what is right and good in the sight of the LORD, that it may go well with you, and you may enter in and possess the good land which the LORD promised on oath to your ancestors, [19]driving all your enemies out of your way, as the LORD has promised.[t]

**Instruction to Children.** [20u]Later on, when your son asks you, "What do these decrees and statutes and ordinances mean?"[v] which the LORD, our God, has enjoined on you, [21w]you shall say to your son, "We were once slaves of Pharaoh in Egypt, but the LORD brought us out of Egypt

---

*[6:4–5] This passage, an expansion of the first commandment (5:6–10), contains the basic principle of the whole Mosaic law, the keynote of the Book of Deuteronomy: since the Lord alone is God, Israel must love him with an undivided heart. Jesus cited these words as "the greatest and the first commandment," embracing in itself the whole law of God (Mt 22:37–38; Mk 12:29–30; Lk 10:27).

†[6:4] Hear, O Israel!: in Hebrew, *shema yisra'el*; hence this passage (vv. 4–9), containing the Great Commandment, is called the Shema. In later Jewish tradition, 11:13–21 and Nm 15:37–41 were added to form a prayer recited every evening and morning. The LORD is our God, the LORD alone: other possible translations are "the Lord our God is one Lord";

"the Lord our God, the Lord is one"; "the Lord is our God, the Lord is one."

‡[6:8] Bind them . . . as a sign: these injunctions were probably meant merely in a figurative sense; cf. Ex 13:9, 16. In the late postexilic period, they were taken quite literally, and devout Jews tied on their arms and foreheads "phylacteries," boxes containing strips of parchment on which these words were inscribed; cf. Mt 23:5.

§[6:13] Him shall you serve: the verb could be translated as either "serve" or "worship" (cf. 5:9).

x. [5:25] Dt 18:16.y. [5:27] Ex 20:19. z. [5:28] Dt 18:17. a. [5:31] Dt 4:1, 45; 5:1; 6:1, 17, 20; 11:32; 12:1; 26:16. b. [5:33] Dt 4:40. c. [6:1] Dt 4:1, 45; 5:1, 31; 6:17, 20; 11:32; 12:1; 26:16. d. [6:2] Dt 4:10, 40; 5:29; 6:24; 10:12–13. e. [6:3] Ex 3:8. f. [6:4–5] Dt 4:35, 39; 5:6–10; 6:13–14; 10:17; 1 Kgs 8:60; 18:39; 2 Kgs 5:15; 19:15, 19; Is 44:6; 45:5–6; Mt 22:37–38; Mk 12:29–30; Lk 10:27.

g. [6:5] Dt 4:29; 10:12; 11:13; 13:4; 26:16; 30:2, 10; 1 Sm 7:3; 2 Kgs 23:3, 25. h. [6:6] Dt 11:18–21. i. [6:6] Dt 11:18; 30:14; 32:46; Ps 37:31; Prv 3:3; Is 51:7; Jer 31:33. j. [6:7] Dt 4:9–10; 6:20–25; 11:1–7, 19; 31:13; 32:46; Prv 6:22. k. [6:8] Dt 11:18; Ex 13:9, 16; Prv 3:3; 6:21. l. [6:9] Dt 11:20. m. [6:10–19] Dt 5:6–10. n. [6:10] Dt 1:8. o. [6:10–11] Dt 8:7–14; 32:11–14; Jos 24:13; Neh 9:25. p. [6:12] Dt 5:6. q. [6:13] Dt 10:20; Is 48:1; Jer 4:2; 12:16; Mt 4:10; Lk 4:8. r. [6:14–15] Dt 4:23–26; 8:19–20; 11:16–17, 28; 29:18–28; 30:17–18; 2 Kgs 17:7–18. s. [6:16] Ex 17:1–7; Ps 95:8–9; Mt 4:7; Lk 4:12. t. [6:19] Ex 23:27; 34:11; Jos 1–12. u. [6:20–25] Dt 6:6–9. v. [6:20] Ex 12:26; 13:14; Jos 4:6, 21. w. [6:21–23] Dt 26:5–10.

with a strong hand[x] [22]and wrought before our eyes signs and wonders, great and dire, against Egypt and against Pharaoh and his whole house. [23]He brought us from there to bring us in and give us the land he had promised on oath to our ancestors.[y] [24]The LORD commanded us to observe all these statutes in fear of the LORD, our God, that we may always have as good a life as we have today. [25]This is our justice before the LORD, our God: to observe carefully this whole commandment he has enjoined on us."

## CHAPTER 7

**Destruction of the Nations in the Land.** [1]When the LORD, your God, brings you into the land which you are about to enter to possess, and removes many nations before you—the Hittites, Girgashites, Amorites, Canaanites, Perizzites, Hivites, and Jebusites,[b] seven nations more numerous and powerful than you— [2]and when the LORD, your God, gives them over to you and you defeat them, you shall put them under the ban. Make no covenant with them[c] and do not be gracious to them. [3]You shall not intermarry with them, neither giving your daughters to their sons nor taking their daughters for your sons. [4]For they would turn your sons from following me to serving other gods, and then the anger of the LORD would flare up against you and he would quickly destroy you.

[5]But this is how you must deal with them:[e] Tear down their altars, smash their sacred pillars, chop down their asherahs,* and destroy their idols by fire. [6]For you are a people holy to the LORD, your God; the LORD, your God, has chosen you from all the peoples on the face of the earth to be a people specially his own.[f] [7]It was not because you are more numerous than all the peoples that the LORD set his heart on you and chose you; for you are really the smallest of all peoples.[g] [8]It was because the LORD loved you and because of his fidelity to the oath he had sworn to your ancestors, that the LORD brought you out with a strong hand and redeemed you from the house of slavery, from the hand of Pharaoh, king of Egypt.[h] [9]Know,

then, that the LORD, your God, is God: the faithful God who keeps covenant mercy to the thousandth generation toward those who love him and keep his commandments,[j] [10]but who repays with destruction those who hate him; he does not delay with those who hate him, but makes them pay for it. [11]Therefore carefully observe the commandment, the statutes and the ordinances which I command you today.

**Blessings of Obedience.** [12]As your reward for heeding these ordinances and keeping them carefully, the LORD, your God, will keep with you the covenant mercy he promised on oath to your ancestors. [13]He will love and bless and multiply you; he will bless the fruit of your womb and the produce of your soil, your grain and wine and oil, the young of your herds and the offspring of your flocks, in the land which he swore to your ancestors he would give you. [14]You will be blessed above all peoples; no man or woman among you shall be childless nor shall your livestock be barren. [15]The LORD will remove all sickness from you; he will not afflict you with any of the malignant diseases that you know from Egypt, but will leave them with all those who hate you.

[16]You shall consume all the peoples which the LORD, your God, is giving over to you. You are not to look on them with pity, nor serve their gods, for that would be a snare to you.[l] [17]If you say to yourselves, "These nations are more numerous than we. How can we dispossess them?" [18]do not be afraid of them. Rather, remember clearly what the LORD, your God, did to Pharaoh and to all Egypt: [19]the great testings which your own eyes have seen, the signs and wonders, the strong hand and outstretched arm with which the LORD, your God, brought you out. The same also will he do to all the peoples of whom you are now afraid. [20]Moreover, the LORD, your God, will send hornets among them, until those who are left and those who are hiding from you are destroyed.[n] [21]Therefore, do not be terrified by them, for the LORD, your God, who is in your midst, is a great and awesome God. [22]He will remove these nations before you little by little. You cannot finish with them quickly, lest the wild beasts become too numerous for you.[o] [23]The LORD, your God, will give them over to you and throw them into utter panic until they are destroyed.[p] [24]He will deliver their kings into your power, that you may make their names perish from under the heavens. No one will be able to stand up against you,[q] till you have destroyed them. [25]The images of their gods you shall destroy by fire. Do not covet the silver

---

*[7:5] **Sacred pillars . . . asherahs:** cut or uncut stones and wooden poles or trees (cf. 16:21) that had some cultic function. Fairly common religious artifacts, their association with the non-Israelite cults of Canaan and perhaps with Canaanite gods and goddesses, specifically the goddess Asherah, led to their condemnation in the Deuteronomic reform and possibly earlier.

x. [6:21] Dt 5:3, 6.   y. [6:23] Dt 1:8.   z. [6:24–25] Dt 4:1–4; 30:15–20.   a. [7:1–11] Ex 23:23–33; 34:11–16; Nm 33:51–56.   b. [7:1] Dt 1:7; Gn 10:16–17; 13:7; 15:19–21; 23:3–20; 34:2, 30; 49:29–30; Ex 3:8; 23:23; 33:2; Nm 13:29; Jos 1:4; 3:10; 9:1–7; 15:63; 17:15; 24:11; Jgs 1:4–5; 3:3, 5; 2 Sm 5:6–10; 1 Kgs 9:20; Ez 16:3, 45.   c. [7:2] Dt 2:34–35; 3:6; 7:26; 13:16, 18; 20:16–18; Ex 23:32–33; 34:12, 15; Jos 9:3–27; 10:40; 11:11–12; Jgs 2:2.   d. [7:3–4] Gn 34:9–10; Ex 34:16; Jos 23:12–13; Jgs 3:5–6; 1 Kgs 11:1–6.   e. [7:5] Dt 12:2–3, 29–31; 16:21–22; Ex 34:13; 2 Kgs 18:4; 23:4–24.   f. [7:6] Dt 14:2, 21; 26:18–19; 32:8–14; Ex 19:5–6; Ps 135:4; Mal 3:17.   g. [7:7] Dt 10:15.   h. [7:8] Dt 5:6; 9:26; 13:5; 15:15; 21:8; 24:18; Ps 78:42.   i. [7:9–10] Dt 4:31; 5:9–10; 24:16; Ex 20:5–6; 34:6–7; Nm 14:18; Jer 31:29–30; 32:18–19; Ez 18:1–24; Jn 9:1–3.   j. [7:9] Dt 5:9–10; 7:12; 32:4; 1 Kgs 8:23–24; Neh 1:5; 9:32; Ps 89:1–2, 24, 28, 33–34; 98:3; Is 49:7; 54:10; 55:3; Dn 9:4; Jon 4:2; Mi 7:20.   k. [7:12–15] Dt 15:6; 28:1–14; 30:1–10; Ex 23:22–33; Lv 26:3–13.   l. [7:16] Dt 5:7–10.   m. [7:17–19] Dt 1:30; 3:22; 4:34, 37–38; 9:1–3; 20:1; 29:2–3; Jos 23:3, 9–10.   n. [7:20] Ex 23:28.   o. [7:22] Ex 23:29–30; Jgs 3:1–6.   p. [7:23] Dt 7:2.   q. [7:24] Dt 11:25; Jos 12:7–24.   r. [7:25–26] Dt 5:8–9; 9:21; Jos 6:18–19; 7:1, 20–21; Jgs 8:24–27; 17:2–4; 1 Kgs 15:13; 2 Kgs 23:4.

or gold on them, nor take it for yourselves, lest you be ensnared by it; for it is an abomination to the LORD, your God.ˢ ²⁶You shall not bring any abominable thing into your house, so as to be, like it, under the ban; loathe and abhor it utterly for it is under the ban.˙

# CHAPTER 8

**God's Care.** ¹Be careful to observe this whole commandmentᵗ that I enjoin on you today, that you may live and increase, and may enter in and possess the land which the LORD promised on oath to your ancestors. ²Remember how for these forty years the LORD, your God, has directed all your journeying in the wilderness,ᵘ so as to test you by affliction, to know what was in your heart: to keep his commandments, or not. ³He therefore let you be afflicted with hunger, and then fed you with manna,ᵛ a food unknown to you and your ancestors, so you might know that it is not by bread alone† that people live, but by all that comes forth from the mouth of the LORD. ⁴The clothing did not fall from you in tatters, nor did your feet swell these forty years.ʷ ⁵So you must know in your heart that, even as a man disciplines his son, so the LORD, your God, disciplines you.ˣ ⁶Therefore, keep the commandments of the LORD, your God, by walking in his ways and fearing him.

**Cautions About Prosperity.** ⁷For the LORD, your God, is bringing you into a good country, a land with streams of water, with springs and fountains welling up in the hills and valleys, ⁸a land of wheat and barley, of vines and fig trees and pomegranates, of olive trees and of honey, ⁹a land where you will always have bread and where you will lack nothing, a land whose stones contain iron and in whose hills you can mine copper. ¹⁰But when you have eaten and are satisfied, you must bless the LORD, your God, for the good land he has given you. ¹¹Be careful not to forget the LORD, your God, by failing to keep his commandments and ordinances and statutes which I enjoin on you today: ¹²lest, when you have eaten and are satisfied, and have built fine houses and lived in them, ¹³and your herds and flocks have increased, your silver and gold has increased, and all your property has increased, ¹⁴you then become haughty of heart and forget the LORD, your God, who brought you out

of the land of Egypt, that house of slavery; ¹⁵he guided you through the vast and terrible wilderness with its saraph‡ serpents and scorpions, its parched and waterless ground; he brought forth water for you from the flinty rockᵃ ¹⁶and fed you in the wilderness with manna, a food unknown to your ancestors, that he might afflict you and test you, but also make you prosperous in the end. ¹⁷Otherwise, you might say in your heart,ᵇ "It is my own power and the strength of my own hand that has got me this wealth." ¹⁸Remember then the LORD, your God, for he is the one who gives you the power to get wealth, by fulfilling, as he has now done, the covenant he swore to your ancestors. ¹⁹But if you do forget the LORD, your God, and go after other gods, serving and bowing down to them,ᶜ I bear witness to you this day that you will perish utterly. ²⁰Like the nations which the LORD destroys before you, so shall you too perish for not listening to the voice of the LORD, your God.

# CHAPTER 9

**Unmerited Success.** ¹Hear, O Israel! You are now about to cross the Jordan to enter in and dispossess nations greater and stronger than yourselves, having large cities fortified to the heavens,ᵈ ²the Anakim, a people great and tall.ᵉ You yourselves know of them and have heard it said of them, "Who can stand up against the Anakim?" ³Know, then, today that it is the LORD, your God, who will cross over before you as a consuming fire; he it is who will destroy them and subdue them before you, so that you can dispossess and remove them quickly, as the LORD promised you.ᶠ ⁴After the LORD, your God, has driven them out of your way, do not say in your heart, "It is because of my justice the LORD has brought me in to possess this land,ᵍ and because of the wickedness of these nations the LORD is dispossessing them before me."§ ⁵No, it is not because of your justice or the integrity of your heart that you are going in to take possession of their land; but it is because of their wickedness that the LORD, your God, is dispossessing these nations before you and in order to fulfill the promise he made on oath to your ancestors, Abraham, Isaac, and Jacob.ʰ ⁶Know this, therefore: it is not because of your justice that the LORD, your God, is giving you this good land to possess, for you are a stiff-necked people.ⁱ

**The Golden Calf.** ⁷Remember and do not forget how you angered the LORD, your God, in

---

\*[7:26] **Under the ban**: and therefore doomed to destruction; see note on 2:34.
†[8:3] **Not by bread alone**: Deuteronomic theology puts the good things promised faithful Israel into the context of the Lord's gratuitous love. As in 6:10–12, the goods of life must be seen as gift. Israel is to seek what really matters; all else will be added (cf. Mt 6:33).

‡[8:15] **Saraph**: see note on Nm 21:6.
§[9:4] **Before me**: Hebrew reads "before you."

---

s. [7:25] Dt 12:31; 17:1; 18:12; 22:5; 23:18; 24:4; 25:16; Prv 6:16; 15:8–9, 26.   t. [8:1] Dt 4:1; 6:1.   u. [8:2] Dt 1:3; 2:7; 29:4; Ps 95:10; Am 2:10.   v. [8:3] Ex 16:11–36; Nm 11:5–9; Jos 5:12; Mt 4:4; Lk 4:4.   w. [8:4] Dt 29:4; Neh 9:21.   x. [8:5] Dt 4:36; 11:2; 21:18–21; Ps 94:12; Prv 3:11–12.   y. [8:7–9] Dt 1:25; 11:10–12; 32:13–14; 33:28.   z. [8:11–14] Dt 6:10–12.

a. [8:15] Dt 32:13; Ex 17:6; Nm 20:8–11; 21:6–9; Ps 114:8; Wis 11:4.   b. [8:17] Dt 9:4–5.   c. [8:19] Dt 4:25–26; 30:18; 2 Kgs 17:7–18.   d. [9:1] Dt 1:28; 4:38.   e. [9:2] Dt 1:28; 2:10–11, 21; Nm 13:22, 28, 33; Jos 11:21–22; 14:12, 15; 15:13–14; 21:11; Jgs 1:20.   f. [9:3] Dt 4:24; 31:3.   g. [9:4] Dt 8:17.   h. [9:5] Dt 1:8.   i. [9:6] Dt 9:13; 10:16; 31:27; Ex 32:9; 33:3; 34:9; Is 48:4; Jer 17:23; 19:15.

the wilderness. From the day you left the land of Egypt until you came to this place, you have been rebellious toward the LORD.$^j$ $^{8k}$At Horeb you so provoked the LORD that he was angry enough to destroy you,$^l$ $^9$when I had gone up the mountain to receive the stone tablets of the covenant which the LORD made with you.$^m$ Meanwhile I stayed on the mountain forty days and forty nights; I ate no food and drank no water. $^{10}$The LORD gave me the two stone tablets inscribed, by God's own finger,$^n$ with a copy of all the words that the LORD spoke to you on the mountain from the midst of the fire on the day of the assembly. $^{11}$Then, at the end of the forty days and forty nights, when the LORD had given me the two stone tablets, the tablets of the covenant, $^{12o}$the LORD said to me, Go down from here now, quickly, for your people whom you have brought out of Egypt are acting corruptly; they have already turned aside from the way I commanded them and have made for themselves a molten idol. $^{13}$I have seen now how stiff-necked this people is, the LORD said to me. $^{14}$Let me be, that I may destroy them and blot out their name from under the heavens. I will then make of you a nation mightier and greater than they.

$^{15}$When I had come down again from the blazing, fiery mountain, with the two tablets of the covenant in both my hands,$^p$ $^{16}$I saw how you had sinned against the LORD, your God, by making for yourselves a molten calf. You had already turned aside from the way which the LORD had commanded you.$^q$ $^{17}$I took hold of the two tablets and with both hands cast them from me and broke them before your eyes.$^r$ $^{18}$Then, as before, I lay prostrate before the LORD for forty days and forty nights; I ate no food, I drank no water, because of all the sin you had committed in the sight of the LORD, doing wrong and provoking him.$^s$ $^{19}$For I dreaded the fierce anger of the LORD against you: his wrath would destroy you.$^t$ Yet once again the LORD listened to me. $^{20}$With Aaron, too, the LORD was deeply angry, and would have destroyed him; but I prayed for Aaron also at that time.$^u$ $^{21}$Then, taking the calf, the sinful object you had made, I burnt it and ground it down to powder as fine as dust, which I threw into the wadi that went down the mountainside.$^v$

$^{22}$At Taberah, at Massah, and at Kibroth-hattaavah likewise, you enraged the LORD.$^w$ $^{23}$And when the LORD sent you up from Kadesh-barnea saying, Go up and take possession of the land I have given you, you rebelled against this command of the LORD, your God, and would not believe him or listen to his voice.$^x$ $^{24}$You have

been rebels against the LORD from the day I first knew you.

$^{25y}$Those forty days, then, and forty nights, I lay prostrate before the LORD, because he had threatened to destroy you. $^{26}$And I prayed to the Lord and said: O Lord GOD, do not destroy your people, the heritage you redeemed in your greatness and have brought out of Egypt with your strong hand.$^z$ $^{27}$Remember your servants, Abraham, Isaac, and Jacob. Do not look upon the stubbornness of this people nor upon their wickedness and sin,$^a$ $^{28}$lest the land from which you have brought us say, "The LORD was not able to bring them into the land he promised them, and out of hatred for them, he brought them out to let them die in the wilderness."$^b$ $^{29}$They are your people and your heritage, whom you have brought out by your great power and with your outstretched arm.$^c$

## CHAPTER 10

$^{1d}$At that time the LORD said to me, Cut two stone tablets like the first ones$^e$ and come up the mountain to me. Also make an ark out of wood. $^2$I will write upon the tablets the words that were on the tablets that you broke, and you shall place them in the ark. $^3$So I made an ark of acacia wood, and cut two stone tablets like the first ones, and went up the mountain with the two tablets in my hand.$^f$ $^{4g}$The LORD then wrote on the tablets, as he had written before, the ten words$^*$ that the LORD had spoken to you on the mountain from the midst of the fire on the day of the assembly; and the LORD gave them to me. $^5$Then I turned and came down from the mountain, and placed the tablets in the ark I had made.$^h$ There they have remained, as the LORD commanded me.

$^6$The Israelites set out from Beeroth Bene-jaakan for Moserah; Aaron died there and was buried. His son Eleazar succeeded him as priest.$^j$ $^7$From there they set out for Gudgodah, and from Gudgodah for Jotbathah, a region where there is water in the wadies. $^8$At that time the LORD set apart the tribe of Levi to carry the ark of the covenant of the LORD,$^k$ to stand before the LORD to minister to him, and to bless in his name, as they have done to this day. $^9$For this reason, Levi has no hereditary portion with his relatives;$^l$ the LORD himself is his portion, as the LORD, your God, promised him.

$^{10}$Meanwhile I stayed on the mountain as I did before, forty days and forty nights, and once again the LORD listened to me. The LORD was

---

$^*$[10:4] **Ten words**: the ten commandments (cf. 4:13).

j. [9:7] Dt 31:27; Ex 14:10–14; 2 Kgs 21:15; Jer 7:25–26. k. [9:8–21] Ex 32:1–34:29. l. [9:8] Ex 32:10. m. [9:9] Dt 4:13–14; 5:22; 9:11, 18, 25; 10:10; Ex 24:12–18; 34:28. n. [9:10] Dt 5:22; 10:4; Ex 31:18. o. [9:12–14] Ex 32:7–10. p. [9:15] Ex 32:15. q. [9:16] Dt 5:6–10; Ex 32:1–6; Ps 106:19–22. r. [9:17] Ex 32:19. s. [9:18] Dt 10:10; Ex 32:31; 34:28. t. [9:19] Dt 10:10; Ex 32:11–14. u. [9:20] Ex 32:1–6, 21–25, 35. v. [9:21] Ex 32:20. w. [9:22] Dt 6:16; Ex 17:1–7; Nm 11:1–34. x. [9:23] Dt 1:19–33.

y. [9:25–29] Ex 32:11–14. z. [9:26] Dt 4:20; 7:8. a. [9:27] Dt 7:8. b. [9:28] Dt 32:26–27; Nm 14:13–16. c. [9:29] Dt 4:20; Ex 6:6–7. d. [10:1–11] Ex 34:1–28. e. [10:1] Ex 34:1. f. [10:3] Ex 34:4. g. [10:4] Dt 4:13; 5:22; Ex 20:1–17; 34:1–4, 27–29. h. [10:5] Ex 40:20; 1 Kgs 8:9. i. [10:6–7] Nm 33:31–33. j. [10:6] Nm 3:1–4, 32; 20:22–29. k. [10:8] Dt 21:5; 33:8–11; Ex 32:25–29; Nm 3:6–10; 6:22–27; 8:23–26. l. [10:9] Dt 18:1–8; Nm 18:20.

unwilling to destroy you. [11]The LORD said to me, Go now and set out at the head of the people,[m] that they may enter in and possess the land that I swore to their ancestors I would give them.

**The Lord's Majesty and Compassion.** [12n]Now, therefore, Israel, what does the LORD, your God, ask of you but to fear the LORD, your God, to follow in all his ways, to love and serve the LORD, your God, with your whole heart and with your whole being,[o] [13]to keep the commandments and statutes of the LORD that I am commanding you today for your own well-being?[p] [14]Look, the heavens, even the highest heavens, belong to the LORD, your God, as well as the earth and everything on it.[q] [15]Yet only on your ancestors did the LORD set his heart to love them. He chose you, their descendants, from all the peoples, as it is today.[r] [16]Circumcise therefore the foreskins of your hearts,[*] and be stiff-necked no longer. [17]For the LORD, your God, is the God of gods, the Lord of lords, the great God, mighty and awesome, who has no favorites, accepts no bribes,[s] [18]who executes justice for the orphan and the widow, and loves the resident alien, giving them food and clothing.[t] [19]So you too should love the resident alien, for that is what you were in the land of Egypt.[u] [20]The LORD, your God, shall you fear, and him shall you serve; to him hold fast and by his name shall you swear.[v] [21]He is your praise; he is your God, who has done for you those great and awesome things that your own eyes have seen.[w] [22]Seventy strong your ancestors went down to Egypt,[x] and now the LORD, your God, has made you as numerous as the stars of heaven.

## CHAPTER 11

**Recalling the Wonders of the Lord.** [1]Love the LORD, your God, therefore, and keep his charge, statutes, ordinances, and commandments always.[y] [2]Recall today that it was not your children, who have neither known nor seen the discipline of the LORD, your God—his greatness, his strong hand and outstretched arm;[z] [3]the signs and deeds he wrought in the midst of Egypt, on Pharaoh, king of Egypt, and on all his land;[a] [4]what he did to the Egyptian army and to

their horses and chariots, engulfing them in the waters of the Red Sea[†] as they pursued you,[b] so that the LORD destroyed them even to this day; [5]what he did for you in the wilderness until you came to this place; [6]and what he did to the Reubenites Dathan and Abiram, sons of Eliab, when the earth opened its mouth and swallowed them up out of the midst of Israel, with their families and tents and every living thing that belonged to them—[c] [7]but it was you who saw with your own eyes all these great deeds that the LORD has done.

**The Gift of Rain.** [8d]So keep all the commandments I give you today, that you may be strong enough to enter in and take possession of the land that you are crossing over to possess, [9]and that you may have long life on the land which the LORD swore to your ancestors he would give to them and their descendants, a land flowing with milk and honey. [10]The land you are to enter and possess is not like the land of Egypt from which you have come, where you would sow your seed and then water it by hand,[‡] as in a vegetable garden. [11]No, the land into which you are crossing to take possession is a land of mountains and valleys that drinks in rain from the heavens, [12]a land which the LORD, your God, looks after; the eyes of the LORD, your God, are upon it continually through the year, from beginning to end.

[13§]If, then, you truly listen to my commandments which I give you today, loving and serving the LORD, your God, with your whole heart and your whole being, [14]I will give the seasonal rain to your land, the early rain¶ and the late rain, that you may have your grain, wine and oil to gather in; [15]and I will bring forth grass in your fields for your animals. Thus you may eat and be satisfied. [16g]But be careful lest your heart be so lured away that you serve other gods and bow down to them.[h] [17]For then the anger of the LORD will flare up against you and he will close up the heavens, so that no rain will fall, and the soil will not yield its crops, and you will soon perish from the good land the LORD is giving you.

**Need for Fidelity.** [18i]Therefore, take these words of mine into your heart and soul. Bind them on your arm as a sign, and let them be as a pendant

---

\*[10:16] **Circumcise therefore the foreskins of your hearts:** cf. 30:6; Jer 4:4; Rom 2:29. The "uncircumcised heart" (Lv 26:41; Jer 9:25; Ez 44:7, 9) is closed and unreceptive to God, just as "uncircumcised ears" (Jer 6:10) are closed to the word of the Lord, and "uncircumcised lips" (Ex 6:12, 30) are a hindrance to speaking on behalf of the Lord.

†[11:4] **The Red Sea:** Hebrew *yam suph*, that is, "sea of reeds" or "reedy sea."

‡[11:10] **By hand:** lit., "by foot," probably referring to a kind of mechanism for irrigation from the Nile.

§[11:13–15] Here as elsewhere Moses shifts between speaking of the Lord in the third person and speaking for the Lord in the first person.

¶[11:14] **The early rain:** the rains which begin in October or November and continue intermittently throughout the winter. **The late rain:** the heavy showers of March and April. In Palestine crops are sown in autumn and harvested in spring and summer.

---

m. [10:11] Dt 1:6; Ex 32:34; 33:1.   n. [10:12–13] Ps 15; 24:3–5; Mi 6:6–8.   o. [10:12] Dt 6:5, 13; 8:6; 11:13.   p. [10:13] Dt 4:1; 5:10, 29–33; 6:2; 7:9; 11:1, 13, 22.   q. [10:14] 1 Kgs 8:27; Neh 9:6; Ps 148:4.   r. [10:15] Dt 7:6–8; Ex 19:5–6.   s. [10:17] Dt 1:17; 16:19; Ex 15:11; 2 Chr 19:7; Jb 34:19; Ps 47:2; 136:2–3; Dn 2:47; Acts 10:34; Rom 2:11; Gal 2:6; 1 Tm 6:15; Rev 17:14; 19:16.   t. [10:18] Ps 68:5–6; 99:4; 146:7–9.   u. [10:19] Dt 24:17–22; Ex 22:21–24; 23:9; Lv 19:33–34.   v. [10:20] Dt 6:13; Mt 4:10; Lk 4:8.   w. [10:21] Ps 109:1; Jer 17:14.   x. [10:22] Dt 1:10; Gn 46:8–27; Ex 1:5; Acts 7:14.   y. [11:1] Gn 26:5; 1 Kgs 2:3.   z. [11:2] Dt 4:9; 6:20–25.   a. [11:3] Dt 6:22; 7:18–19; 26:8; 29:1–2; 34:11; Ps 78:42–51.

b. [11:4] Ex 14:26–31; 15:1–10; Jos 24:6–7; Ps 78:53; 106:9–11.   c. [11:6] Nm 16:1–35; Ps 106:16–17.   d. [11:8–9] Dt 5:33; 6:1–3.   e. [11:11–12] Dt 8:7–10.   f. [11:13–15] Dt 7:12–14; 10:12–13; 28:1–14; Lv 26:3–5; Ps 104:14; Jer 5:24.   g. [11:16–17] Dt 4:25–27; 6:14–15; 28:15–68.   h. [11:16] Dt 5:6–10; 7:1–6; 13:2–19; 1 Kgs 8:35–36.   i. [11:18–21] Dt 6:6–9.

on your forehead. [19]Teach them to your children, speaking of them when you are at home and when you are away, when you lie down and when you get up, [20]and write them on the doorposts of your houses and on your gates, [21]so that, as long as the heavens are above the earth, you and your children may live on in the land which the LORD swore to your ancestors he would give them.

[22]For if you are careful to observe this entire commandment I am giving you, loving the LORD, your God, following his ways exactly, and holding fast to him, [23]the LORD will dispossess all these nations before you, and you will dispossess nations greater and mightier than yourselves. [24a]Every place where you set foot shall be yours: from the wilderness and the Lebanon, from the Euphrates River to the Western Sea,* shall be your territory. [25]None shall stand up against you; the LORD, your God, will spread the fear and dread of you through any land where you set foot, as he promised you.[l]

**Blessing and Curse.** [26m]See, I set before you this day a blessing and a curse: [27]a blessing for obeying the commandments of the LORD, your God, which I give you today; [28]a curse if you do not obey the commandments of the LORD, your God, but turn aside from the way I command you today, to go after other gods, whom you do not know.[n] [29]When the LORD, your God, brings you into the land which you are to enter and possess, then on Mount Gerizim you shall pronounce the blessing,[o] on Mount Ebal, the curse.[†] [30](These are beyond the Jordan, on the other side of the western road in the land of the Canaanites who live in the Arabah, opposite Gilgal beside the oak of Moreh.)[p] [31]Now you are about to cross the Jordan to enter and possess the land which the LORD, your God, is giving you. When, therefore, you take possession of it and settle there, [32]be careful to observe all the statutes and ordinances that I set before you today.

*B. The Deuteronomic Code*

## CHAPTER 12

**One Center of Worship.** [1]These are the statutes and ordinances which you must be careful to observe in the land which the LORD, the God of your ancestors, has given you to possess, throughout the time you live on its soil.[q] [2]Destroy entirely all the places where the nations

you are to dispossess serve their gods, on the high mountains, on the hills, and under every green tree.[s] [3]Tear down their altars, smash their sacred pillars, burn up their asherahs, and chop down the idols of their gods, that you may destroy the very name of them from that place.

[4]That is not how you are to act toward the LORD, your God. [5]Instead,[t] you shall seek out the place which the LORD, your God, chooses out of all your tribes and designates as his dwelling to put his name there.[‡u] There you shall go, [6]bringing your burnt offerings and sacrifices, your tithes and personal contributions, your votive and voluntary offerings, and the firstlings of your herds and flocks.[v] [7]There, too, in the presence of the LORD, your God, you and your families shall eat and rejoice in all your undertakings, in which the LORD, your God, has blessed you.[w]

[8]You shall not do as we are doing here today, everyone doing what is right in their own sight,[x] [9]since you have not yet reached your resting place, the heritage which the LORD, your God, is giving you. [10]But after you have crossed the Jordan and dwell in the land which the LORD, your God, is giving you as a heritage, when he has given you rest from all your enemies round about and you live there in security,[y] [11§z]then to the place which the LORD, your God, chooses as the dwelling place for his name you shall bring all that I command you: your burnt offerings and sacrifices, your tithes and personal contributions, and every special offering you have vowed to the LORD. [12]You shall rejoice in the presence of the LORD, your God, with your sons and daughters, your male and female slaves, as well as with the Levite within your gates, who has no hereditary portion with you.

[13a]Be careful not to sacrifice your burnt offerings in any place you like, [14]but offer them in the place which the LORD chooses in one of

---

‡[12:5] **The place . . . to put his name there:** Moses thus designates Jerusalem (Mt. Zion), in accordance with the Deuteronomic doctrine that the Lord "chooses" Zion, as the place where eventually the Temple will be built, as he chooses the house of David to reign over Israel; see 2 Sm 7; 1 Kgs 8; Ps 132. But the Lord's presence in Jerusalem consists in putting his "name" there (12:11, 21; 14:23–24; 16:2, 6, 11; 26:2; 1 Kgs 8:44, 49; 9:3; 11:36; 14:21; 2 Kgs 17:34; 21:4, 7; 23:27). The Lord himself "cannot be contained" in an earthly dwelling (1 Kgs 8:27), but because he says of the Jerusalem Temple that "my name will be there" (1 Kgs 8:16, 29; 2 Kgs 23:27), he is present. This theology allows God in a way to dwell with Israel and at the same time preserves divine transcendence. See note on 1 Kgs 8:12–13.

§[12:11] Sacrifice is to be confined to the single place that the Lord has chosen; eventually this was Jerusalem.

---

*[11:24] **The Western Sea:** the Mediterranean.

†[11:29] For the full ceremony of blessing and curse, see chaps. 27–28. Gerizim and Ebal are mountains in Samaria, separated by a deep ravine.

j. [11:22–23] Dt 7:1; 9:1–3; 10:12–13.   k. [11:24] Dt 1:7; Ex 23:31; Jos 1:3.   l. [11:25] Dt 2:25; 7:23–24; Ex 23:27.   m. [11:26–28] Dt 28:1–68; 30:1, 15–20; Lv 26:3–45.   n. [11:28] Dt 32:16–18.   o. [11:29] Dt 27:12–13; Jos 8:30–35.   p. [11:30] Gn 12:6; 35:4.   q. [12:1] Dt 4:44–45.   r. [12:2–28] Dt 5:7–10; Ex 20:24–26; 2 Kgs 18:3–6, 22; 23:4–9.

s. [12:2–3] Dt 7:5, 24–25; Ex 23:23–24; 34:11–14; Nm 33:51–52; Jgs 17:3–5; 1 Kgs 12:28–30; 14:22–24; 2 Kgs 16:4; 17:7–12; Jer 2:20; 3:6–10; Hos 4:12–13.   t. [12:5–7] Dt 12:11–12; 14:22–26; 15:19–20; 16:2, 6, 10–11, 14–15; 26:2.   u. [12:5] 2 Sm 7:13; 1 Kgs 8:16–21, 27–30.   v. [12:6] Dt 14:22–27; 15:19–23; 23:21–23; 26:12–15; Lv 1:3–17; 3:1–17; 6:2–6; 7:29–36; 27:1–8; Nm 15:18–21; 28:2–8; 30:2–15; Am 4:4–5; 5:22.   w. [12:7] Dt 12:12, 18–19; 14:26–27; 15:20; 16:11, 14; 26:11.   x. [12:8] Dt 6:18; 12:28; Jgs 17:6; 21:25.   y. [12:10] Dt 3:18–20; 11:22–25; Jos 23:1; 2 Sm 7:1; 1 Kgs 5:17–18; 8:56.   z. [12:11–12] Dt 12:5–7; 14:22–26; 15:19–20; 16:2, 6, 10–11, 14–15; 26:2.   a. [12:13–14] Jos 22:10–34.

your tribal territories; there you shall do what I command you.

**Profane and Sacred Slaughter.** [15*]However, in any of your communities you may slaughter and eat meat freely, according to the blessing that the LORD, your God, has given you; the unclean as well as the clean may eat it, as they do the gazelle or the deer.[b] [16†]Only, you shall not eat of the blood, but must pour it out on the ground like water.[c] [17]Moreover, you may not, in your own communities, partake of your tithe of grain or wine or oil, of the firstborn of your herd or flock, of any offering you have vowed, of your voluntary offerings, or of your personal contributions. [18]These you must eat in the presence of the LORD, your God, in the place that the LORD, your God, chooses, along with your son and daughter, your male and female slave, and the Levite within your gates; and there, in the presence of the LORD, you shall rejoice in all your undertakings. [19]Be careful, also, that you do not neglect the Levite as long as you live in your land.[d]

[20e]After the LORD, your God, has enlarged your territory, as he promised you,[f] and you think, "I will eat meat," as it is your desire to eat meat, you may eat it freely; [21]and if the place where the LORD, your God, chooses to put his name is too far, you may slaughter in the manner I have commanded you any of your herd or flock that the LORD has given you, and eat it freely in your own community. [22]You may eat it as you would the gazelle or the deer: the unclean and the clean eating it together. [23g]But make sure that you do not eat of the blood; for blood is life; you shall not eat that life with the flesh. [24]Do not eat of the blood, therefore, but pour it out on the ground like water. [25]Do not eat of it, that you and your children after you may prosper for doing what is right in the sight of the LORD. [26]However, any sacred gifts or votive offerings that you may have, you shall bring with you to the place which the LORD chooses, [27]and there you must sacrifice your burnt offerings, both the flesh and the blood, on the altar of the LORD, your God; of your other sacrifices the blood indeed must be poured out against the altar of the LORD, your God,[h] but their flesh you may eat.

[28]Be careful to heed all these words I command you today, that you and your descendants after you may forever prosper for doing what is good and right in the sight of the LORD, your God.[i]

**Warning Against Abominable Practices.** [29j]When the LORD, your God, cuts down from before you the nations you are going in to dispossess, and you have dispossessed them and are settled in their land, [30]be careful that you not be trapped into following them after they have been destroyed before you. Do not inquire regarding their gods, "How did these nations serve their gods, so I might do the same." [31]You shall not worship the LORD, your God, that way, because they offered to their gods every abomination that the LORD detests, even burning their sons and daughters to their gods.[k]

## CHAPTER 13

**Penalties for Enticing to Idolatry.** [1]Every word that I command you, you shall be careful to observe, neither adding to it nor subtracting from it.

[2‡]If there arises in your midst a prophet or a dreamer[‡] who promises you a sign or wonder, [3]saying, "Let us go after other gods," whom you have not known, "and let us serve them," and the sign or wonder foretold to you comes to pass, [4]do not listen to the words of that prophet or that dreamer; for the LORD, your God, is testing you to know whether you really love the LORD, your God, with all your heart and soul.[m] [5]The LORD, your God, shall you follow, and him shall you fear; his commandments shall you observe, and to his voice shall you listen; him you shall serve, and to him you shall hold fast.[n] [6]But that prophet or that dreamer shall be put to death, because, in order to lead you astray from the way which the LORD, your God, has commanded you to take, the prophet or dreamer has spoken apostasy against the LORD, your God, who brought you out of the land of Egypt and redeemed you from the house of slavery. Thus shall you purge the evil from your midst.[o]

[7]If your brother, your father's child or your mother's child, your son or daughter, your beloved spouse, or your intimate friend entices you secretly, saying, "Come, let us serve other gods," whom you and your ancestors have not known, [8]any of the gods of the surrounding peoples, near to you or far away, from one end of the earth to the other: [9]do not yield or listen to any such person; show no pity or compassion and do not shield such a one,[p] [10q]but kill that person. Your hand shall be the first raised to put such a one to death; the hand of all the people shall

---

*[12:15] At this point a distinction is being made between cultic sacrifice and slaughter of animals for food. **In any of your communities:** lit., "within your gates."

†[12:16] The blood was understood to be the source or vehicle of life and so was not to be consumed. Cf. Gn 9:4.

‡[13:2, 4, 6] **Dreamer**: a false prophet who pretended to have received revelations from God in a dream; cf. Jer 23:25–32; 27:9; Zec 10:2. But dreams could also be a means of true prophecy (Nm 12:6; Jl 3:1) and of genuine revelations (Gn 20:3, 6; 31:11, 24; 37:5, 9; Mt 1:20; 2:12, 13, 19; etc.).

b. [12:15] Dt 12:20–22; 15:22; Lv 7:19–21.   c. [12:16] Dt 12:23–27; 15:23; Gn 9:4; Lv 3:17; 17:10–14; 19:26; 1 Sm 14:31–35.   d. [12:19] Dt 14:27.   e. [12:20–27] Lv 17:3–9.   f. [12:20] Dt 19:8; Gn 28:14; Ex 34:24.   g. [12:23–25] Dt 12:16; 15:23; Gn 9:4; Lv 3:17; 17:10–14; 19:26; 1 Sm 14:31–35.   h. [12:27] Lv 17:11.   i. [12:28] Dt 4:40; 5:29; 6:2–3, 17–18; 12:25.

j. [12:29–31] Dt 7:1–5, 25; Ex 23:33; 34:12; Jgs 2:2–3.   k. [12:31] Dt 18:10; Lv 18:21; 20:2–5; 2 Kgs 3:27; 16:3; 21:6; 23:10; Jer 7:31; 19:5.   l. [13:2–19] Dt 6:4, 14–15; 17:2–7.   m. [13:4] Dt 8:2, 16.   n. [13:5] Dt 6:4–5; 10:20; 11:22.   o. [13:6] Dt 17:7, 12; 19:19; 21:21; 22:21–22, 24; 24:7; Jer 28:16; 29:32.   p. [13:9] Dt 7:16; 19:13, 21; 25:12.   q. [13:10–11] Dt 17:5–7; 21:21; 22:20–24; Jos 7:25–26; 1 Kgs 21:13–14.

follow. ¹¹You shall stone that person to death, for seeking to lead you astray from the LORD, your God, who brought you out of the land of Egypt, out of the house of slavery. ¹²And all Israel shall hear of it and fear, and never again do such evil as this in your midst.ʳ

¹³If you hear it said concerning one of the cities which the LORD, your God, gives you to dwell in, ¹⁴that certain scoundrels have sprung up in your midst and have led astray the inhabitants of their city, saying, "Come, let us serve other gods," whom you have not known, ¹⁵you must inquire carefully into the matter and investigate it thoroughly. If you find that it is true and an established fact that this abomination has been committed in your midst,ˢ ¹⁶*you shall put the inhabitants of that city to the sword, placing the city and all that is in it, even its livestock, under the ban. ¹⁷Having heaped up all its spoils in the middle of its square, you shall burn the city with all its spoils as a whole burnt offering to the LORD, your God. Let it be a heap of ruins forever, never to be rebuilt. ¹⁸You shall not hold on to anything that is under the ban; then the LORD will turn from his burning anger and show you mercy, and in showing you mercy multiply you as he swore to your ancestors, ¹⁹because you have listened to the voice of the LORD, your God, keeping all his commandments, which I give you today, doing what is right in the sight of the LORD, your God.

## CHAPTER 14

**Improper Mourning Rites.** ¹You are children of the LORD, your God. You shall not gash yourselves nor shave the hair above your foreheads for the dead.ᵘ ²For you are a people holy to the LORD, your God; the LORD, your God, has chosen you from all the peoples on the face of the earth to be a people specially his own.ᵛ

**Clean and Unclean Animals.** ³You shall not eat any abominable thing.ʷ ⁴*These are the animals you may eat: the ox, the sheep, the goat, ⁵the deer, the gazelle, the roebuck, the wild goat, the ibex, the antelope, and the mountain sheep. ⁶Any among the animals that has divided hooves, with the foot cloven in two, and that chews the cud you may eat. ⁷But you shall not eat any of the following that chew the cud or have cloven hooves: the camel, the hare, and the rock badger, which indeed chew the cud, but do not have divided hooves; they are unclean for you. ⁸And the pig, which indeed has divided hooves, with cloven foot, but does not chew the cud, is unclean for you. Their flesh you shall not eat, and their dead bodies you shall not touch.

⁹These you may eat, of all that live in the water: whatever has both fins and scales you

may eat, ¹⁰but all those that lack either fins or scales you shall not eat; they are unclean for you.

¹¹You may eat all clean birds. ¹²*But you shall not eat any of the following: the griffon vulture, the bearded vulture, the black vulture, ¹³the various kites and falcons, ¹⁴all kinds of crows, ¹⁵the eagle owl, the kestrel, the long-eared owl, all species of hawks, ¹⁶the little owl, the screech owl, the barn owl, ¹⁷the horned owl, the osprey, the cormorant, ¹⁸the stork, any kind of heron, the hoopoe, and the bat. ¹⁹†All winged insects are also unclean for you and shall not be eaten. ²⁰Any clean winged creatures you may eat.

²¹You shall not eat the carcass of any animal that has died of itself; but you may give it to a resident alien within your gates to eat, or you may sell it to a foreigner. For you are a people holy to the LORD, your God.ʸ

You shall not boil a young goat in its mother's milk.‡

**Tithes.** ²²Each year you shall tithe all the produce of your seed that grows in the field;ᶻ ²³then in the place which the LORD, your God, chooses as the dwelling place of his nameᵃ you shall eat in his presence the tithe of your grain, wine and oil, as well as the firstlings of your herd and flock, that you may learn always to fear the LORD, your God. ²⁴ᵇBut if, when the LORD, your God, blesses you, the journey is too much for you and you are not able to bring your tithe, because the place which the LORD, your God, chooses to put his name is too far for you, ²⁵you may exchange the tithe for money, and with the money securely in hand, go to the place which the LORD, your God, chooses. ²⁶You may then exchange the money for whatever you desire, oxen or sheep, wine or beer, or anything else you want, and there in the presence of the LORD, your God, you shall consume it and rejoice, you and your household together.ᶜ ²⁷But do not neglect the Levite within your gates, for he has no hereditary portion with you.ᵈ

²⁸ᵉAt the end of every third year you shall bring out all the tithes of your produce for that year and deposit them within your own communities, ²⁹that the Levite who has no hereditary portion with you, and also the resident alien, the orphan and the widow within your

---

*[14:12–18] The identification of several of the birds in these verses is uncertain.

†[14:19–20] Lv 11:20–23 suggests that the unclean winged insects are those that walk on the ground; the clean winged creatures are those that leap on the ground, such as certain species of locusts.

‡[14:21] **Boil a young goat in its mother's milk**: the meaning of this regulation is obscure but it may have a humane concern similar to the prohibitions against slaughtering an animal and its young on the same day (Lv 22:27–28) and capturing a mother bird along with her fledgling or eggs (Dt 22:6–7). See note on Ex 23:19.

r. [13:12] Dt 17:13; 21:21.    s. [13:15] Dt 17:4; 19:18.    t. [13:16–17] Dt 20:16–18; Jos 6:17, 24; 7:25–26; 8:28.    u. [14:1] Dt 32:5–6, 18–20; Lv 19:27–28; 21:5; Ps 103:13; Is 1:2, 4; 30:1; Jer 3:14, 19, 22; 16:6; 31:9, 20; 41:4–5; Hos 2:1; 11:1–4.    v. [14:2] Dt 7:6; Ex 19:5–6.    w. [14:3] Acts 10:14.    x. [14:4–20] Lv 11:2–23.

y. [14:21] Ex 22:30; 23:19; 34:26; Lv 17:15; 22:8; Ez 44:31.    z. [14:22] Gn 14:20; 28:22; Lv 27:30–33; Nm 18:21–32; 1 Sm 8:15, 17; 2 Chr 31:2–19; Neh 12:44; Am 4:4.    a. [14:23] Dt 12:5–7, 11–12, 17–18; 15:19–20.    b. [14:24–26] Mk 11:15; Jn 2:13–14.    c. [14:26] Dt 12:7.    d. [14:27] Dt 12:12, 19.    e. [14:28–29] Dt 26:12–15.

gates, may come and eat and be satisfied; so that the LORD, your God, may bless you in all that you undertake.

## CHAPTER 15

**Debts and the Poor.** [1]At the end of every seven-year period* you shall have a remission of debts,[f] [2]and this is the manner of the remission. Creditors shall remit all claims on loans made to a neighbor, not pressing the neighbor, one who is kin, because the LORD's remission has been proclaimed. [3]You may press a foreigner, but you shall remit the claim on what your kin owes to you.[g] [4h]However, since the LORD, your God, will bless you abundantly in the land the LORD, your God, will give you to possess as a heritage, there shall be no one of you in need [5]if you but listen to the voice of the LORD, your God, and carefully observe this entire commandment which I enjoin on you today. [6]Since the LORD, your God, will bless you as he promised, you will lend to many nations, and borrow from none;[i] you will rule over many nations, and none will rule over you.

[7]If one of your kindred is in need in any community in the land which the LORD, your God, is giving you, you shall not harden your heart nor close your hand against your kin who is in need. [8]Instead, you shall freely open your hand and generously lend what suffices to meet that need.[k] [9]Be careful not to entertain the mean thought, "The seventh year, the year of remission, is near," so that you would begrudge your kin who is in need and give nothing, and your kin would cry to the LORD against you and you would be held guilty.[l] [10]When you give, give generously and not with a stingy heart; for that, the LORD, your God, will bless you in all your works and undertakings. [11]The land will never lack for needy persons; that is why I command you: "Open your hand freely to your poor and to your needy kin in your land."[m]

**Hebrew Slaves.** [12n]If your kin, a Hebrew man or woman, sells himself or herself to you, he or she is to serve you for six years, but in the seventh year you shall release him or her as a free person. [13o]When you release a male from your service, as a free person, you shall not send him away empty-handed, [14]but shall weigh him down with gifts from your flock and threshing floor and wine press; as the LORD, your God,

has blessed you, so you shall give to him. [15]For remember that you too were slaves in the land of Egypt, and the LORD, your God, redeemed you. That is why I am giving you this command today.[p] [16q]But if he says to you, "I do not wish to leave you," because he loves you and your household, since he is well off with you, [17]you shall take an awl and put it through his ear† into the door, and he shall be your slave forever. Your female slave, also, you shall treat in the same way. [18]Do not be reluctant when you let them go free, since the service they have given you for six years was worth twice a hired laborer's salary; and the LORD, your God, will bless you in everything you do.

**Firstlings.** [19r]You shall consecrate to the LORD, your God, every male firstling born in your herd and in your flock. You shall not work the firstlings of your cattle, nor shear the firstlings of your flock. [20]In the presence of the LORD, your God, you shall eat them year after year, you and your household, in the place that the LORD will choose.[s] [21t]But if a firstling has any defect, lameness or blindness, any such serious defect, you shall not sacrifice it to the LORD, your God, [22]but in your own communities you may eat it, the unclean and the clean eating it together, as you would a gazelle or a deer. [23]Only, you must not eat of its blood; you shall pour it out on the ground like water.

## CHAPTER 16

**Feast of the Passover.** [1]Observe the month of Abib‡ by keeping the Passover of the LORD, your God,[u] since it was in the month of Abib that the LORD, your God, brought you out of Egypt by night. [2]You shall offer the Passover sacrifice from your flock and your herd to the LORD, your God, in the place the LORD will choose as the dwelling place of his name.[v] [3w]You shall not eat leavened bread with it. For seven days you shall eat with it only unleavened bread, the bread of affliction, so that you may remember as long as you live the day you left the land of Egypt; for in hurried flight you left the land of Egypt. [4]No leaven is to be found with you in all your territory for seven days, and none of the meat which you sacrificed on the evening of the first day shall be kept overnight for the next day.

[5]You may not sacrifice the Passover in any of the communities which the LORD, your God,

---

*[15:1] **At the end of every seven-year period**: in every seventh, or sabbatical, year. Cf. 15:9; 31:10; and compare Jer 34:14 with Dt 15:12. **A remission of debts**: it is debated whether a full cancellation of debts is meant, or merely a suspension of payment on them or on their interest, but the former is more likely. Cf. Ex 23:11 where the same Hebrew root is used of a field that is "let lie fallow" in the sabbatical year.

†[15:17] **His ear**: cf. Ex 21:6 and note there.

‡[16:1] **Abib**: "ear of grain, ripe grain," the name of the month in which the barley harvest fell, corresponding to our March and April; at a later period this month received the Babylonian name of "Nisan."

f. [15:1] Dt 31:10; Lv 25:1–55; Neh 10:31.    g. [15:3] Dt 23:20.    h. [15:4–6] Dt 7:12–14; 28:1–14.    i. [15:6] Dt 28:12.    j. [15:7–11] Ex 22:25.    k. [15:8] Dt 24:19; Lv 25:35; Ps 37:21–22; Prv 19:17; Sir 29:1–2; Mt 5:42.    l. [15:9] Dt 24:15; Ex 22:23–24, 27.    m. [15:11] Dt 15:8; Mt 26:11.    n. [15:12–18] Ex 21:2–11; Jer 34:8–22.    o. [15:13–15] Ex 3:21–22; 12:35–36.

p. [15:15] Dt 5:15; 10:19; 16:12; 24:18, 22.    q. [15:16–17] Ex 21:5–6.    r. [15:19] Ex 13:2, 11–16; 22:29–30; 34:19–20; Lv 22:27; 27:26; Nm 18:15–18.    s. [15:20] Dt 12:6–7, 17–18; 14:23.    t. [15:21–23] Dt 12:15–16, 22–24; 17:1; Lv 22:17–25; Mal 1:8.    u. [16:1–8] Ex 12:2–13:10; 23:15; 34:18; Lv 23:5–8; Nm 28:16–25; Jos 5:10–12; 2 Kgs 23:21–23; 2 Chr 30:1–27; 35:1–19; Ez 45:21–24.    v. [16:2] Dt 12:5, 11; 16:6.    w. [16:3–4] Ex 12:34, 39; 13:6–7; 34:18.

gives you; [6]only at the place which the LORD, your God, will choose as the dwelling place of his name, and in the evening at sunset, at the very time when you left Egypt, shall you sacrifice the Passover.[x] [7]You shall cook and eat it at the place the LORD, your God, will choose; then in the morning you may return to your tents. [8]For six days you shall eat unleavened bread, and on the seventh day there shall be a solemn assembly for the LORD, your God; on that day you shall do no work.[y]

**Feast of Weeks.** [9z]You shall count off seven weeks; begin to count the seven weeks from the day when the sickle is first put to the standing grain. [10]You shall then keep the feast of Weeks[*] for the LORD, your God, and the measure of your own voluntary offering which you will give shall be in proportion to the blessing the LORD, your God, has given you. [11]You shall rejoice in the presence of the LORD, your God, together with your son and daughter, your male and female slave, and the Levite within your gates, as well as the resident alien, the orphan, and the widow among you, in the place which the LORD, your God, will choose as the dwelling place of his name.[a] [12]Remember that you too were slaves in Egypt, so carry out these statutes carefully.

**Feast of Booths.** [13b]You shall celebrate the feast of Booths[†] for seven days, when you have gathered in the produce from your threshing floor and wine press. [14]You shall rejoice at your feast,[c] together with your son and daughter, your male and female slave, and also the Levite, the resident alien, the orphan and the widow within your gates. [15]For seven days you shall celebrate this feast for the LORD, your God, in the place which the LORD will choose; since the LORD, your God, has blessed you in all your crops and in all your undertakings, you will be full of joy.

[16]Three times a year,[d] then, all your males shall appear before the LORD, your God, in the place which he will choose: at the feast of Unleavened Bread, at the feast of Weeks, and at the feast of Booths. They shall not appear before the LORD empty-handed, [17]but each with his own gift, in proportion to the blessing which the LORD, your God, has given you.

**Justice.** [18e]In all the communities which the LORD, your God, is giving you, you shall appoint judges and officials throughout your tribes to administer true justice for the people. [19]You must not distort justice: you shall not show partiality;[f] you shall not take a bribe, for a bribe blinds the eyes even of the wise and twists the words even of the just. [20]Justice, justice alone shall you pursue, so that you may live and possess the land the LORD, your God, is giving you.

**Illicit Worship.** [21g]You shall not plant an asherah[‡] of any kind of wood next to the altar of the LORD, your God, which you will build;[h] [22]nor shall you erect a sacred pillar, such as the LORD, your God, hates.

## CHAPTER 17

[1]You shall not sacrifice to the LORD, your God, an ox or a sheep with any serious defect;[i] that would be an abomination to the LORD, your God.

[2j]If there is found in your midst, in any one of the communities which the LORD, your God, gives you, a man or a woman who does evil in the sight of the LORD, your God, and transgresses his covenant,[k] [3]by going to serve other gods, by bowing down to them, to the sun or the moon or any of the host of heaven, contrary to my command;[l] [4]and if you are told or hear of it, you must investigate it thoroughly. If the truth of the matter is established that this abomination has been committed in Israel, [5]you shall bring the man or the woman who has done this evil deed out to your gates[§] and stone the man or the woman to death. [6]Only on the testimony of two or three witnesses shall a person be put to death;[m] no one shall be put to death on the testimony of only one witness. [7]The hands of the witnesses shall be the first raised to put the person to death, and afterward the hands of all the people.[n] Thus shall you purge the evil from your midst.

**Judges.** [8o]If there is a case for judgment which proves too baffling for you to decide, in a matter of bloodshed or of law or of injury, matters of dispute within your gates, you shall then go up to the place which the LORD, your God, will choose, [9]to the levitical priests or to the judge who is in office at that time. They shall investigate the case and then announce to you the decision.[p] [10]You shall act according to the decision they announce to you in the place which the LORD will choose, carefully observing everything as they instruct

---

*[16:10] **Feast of Weeks:** a celebration of the grain harvest, later known as "Pentecost"; cf. Acts 2:1.

†[16:13] **Feast of Booths:** also called Tabernacles; a harvest festival at the end of the agricultural year. In later times, during the seven days of the feast the Israelites camped in booths made of branches erected on the roofs of their houses or in the streets in commemoration of their wanderings in the wilderness, where they dwelt in such temporary shelters.

‡[16:21–22] **Asherah . . . sacred pillar:** see note on 7:5; Ex 34:13.

§[17:5] **Out to your gates:** outside the gates, so as not to defile the city; cf. Lv 24:14; Nm 15:36; Acts 7:58; Heb 13:12.

x. [16:6] Dt 12:5, 11; 16:2.   y. [16:8] Ex 13:6; Lv 23:36; Nm 29:35; Is 1:13; Am 5:21.   z. [16:9–12] Ex 23:16; 34:22; Lv 23:15–21; Nm 28:26–31.   a. [16:11] Dt 12:5–7, 11–12, 18.   b. [16:13–15] Dt 31:10–13; Ex 23:16; 34:22; Lv 23:34–43; Nm 29:12–38; 1 Kgs 8:2, 62–66; Ezr 3:4; Neh 8:14; Ez 45:25.   c. [16:14] Dt 16:11.   d. [16:16] Dt 12:7; 16:11, 14; Ex 23:14–15, 17; 34:23–24; 2 Chr 8:13.   e. [16:18–20] Dt 1:13–17; 17:8–13; 19:17; 21:5; Ex 18:13–26; 2 Chr 19:5–11.

f. [16:19] Dt 1:16–17; 10:17–18; Ex 23:2–3, 6–8; Lv 19:15; Prv 17:23; 18:5; 24:23; Is 1:23; Mi 7:3; Jn 7:24; Jas 2:9.   g. [16:21–17:7] Dt 5:7–10; 6:4–5; 12:29–14:2.   h. [16:21–22] Dt 7:5; Ex 34:13; 1 Kgs 14:15; 2 Kgs 23:6, 15; 2 Chr 33:3.   i. [17:1] Lv 22:20.   j. [17:2–7] Dt 13:2–19.   k. [17:2] Jos 7:11, 15; 23:16; Jgs 2:20; 2 Kgs 18:12; Jer 34:18; Hos 6:7; 8:1.   l. [17:3] Dt 4:19; 2 Kgs 17:16; 21:3; 23:5; Jer 8:2; Ez 8:16.   m. [17:6] Dt 19:15; Nm 35:30; Jn 8:17; 2 Cor 13:1.   n. [17:7] Dt 13:6, 10.   o. [17:8–9] Ex 18:13–26.   p. [17:9] Dt 21:5; 2 Chr 19:8; Ezr 7:25.

you. [11]You shall carry out the instruction they give you and the judgment they pronounce, without turning aside either to the right or left from the decision they announce to you. [12]Anyone who acts presumptuously and does not obey the priest* who officiates there in the ministry of the LORD, your God, or the judge, shall die. Thus shall you purge the evil from Israel. [13]And all the people, on hearing of it, shall fear, and will never again act presumptuously.[q]

**The King.** [14]"When you have come into the land which the LORD, your God, is giving you, and have taken possession of it and settled in it, should you then decide, "I will set a king over me, like all the surrounding nations,"[s] [15]you may indeed set over you a king whom the LORD, your God, will choose.[t] Someone from among your own kindred you may set over you as king; you may not set over you a foreigner, who is no kin of yours. [16]†But he shall not have a great number of horses; nor shall he make his people go back again to Egypt to acquire many horses, for the LORD said to you, Do not go back that way again.[u] [17]Neither shall he have a great number of wives, lest his heart turn away,[v] nor shall he accumulate a vast amount of silver and gold. [18]When he is sitting upon his royal throne, he shall write a copy of this law‡ upon a scroll from the one that is in the custody of the levitical priests.[w] [19]§It shall remain with him and he shall read it as long as he lives, so that he may learn to fear the LORD, his God, and to observe carefully all the words of this law and these statutes, [20]so that he does not exalt himself over his kindred or turn aside from this commandment to the right or to the left, and so that he and his descendants may reign long in Israel.

### CHAPTER 18

**Priests.** [1]The levitical priests, the whole tribe of Levi, shall have no hereditary portion with Israel; they shall eat the fire offerings of the LORD and the portions due to him.[y] [2]They shall

have no heritage among their kindred; the LORD himself is their heritage, as he has told them.[z] [3]This shall be the due of the priests from the people: those who are offering a sacrifice, whether an ox or a sheep, shall give the priest the shoulder, the jowls and the stomach. [4]The first fruits of your grain, your wine, and your oil,[a] as well as the first shearing of your flock, you shall also give him. [5]For the LORD, your God, has chosen him out of all your tribes to be in attendance to minister in the name of the LORD, him and his descendants for all time.[b]

[6]When a Levite goes from one of your communities anywhere in Israel in which he has been residing, to visit, as his heart may desire, the place which the LORD will choose, [7]and ministers there in the name of the LORD, his God, like all his fellow Levites who stand before the LORD there, [8]he shall receive the same portions to eat, along with his stipends and patrimony.¶

**Prophets.** [9]When you come into the land which the LORD, your God, is giving you, you shall not learn to imitate the abominations of the nations there.[c] [10]dLet there not be found among you anyone who causes their son or daughter to pass through the fire,** or practices divination, or is a soothsayer, augur, or sorcerer, [11]or who casts spells, consults ghosts and spirits, or seeks oracles from the dead. [12]Anyone who does such things is an abomination to the LORD, and because of such abominations the LORD, your God, is dispossessing them before you.[e] [13]You must be altogether sincere with the LORD, your God. [14]Although these nations whom you are about to dispossess listen to their soothsayers and diviners, the LORD, your God, will not permit you to do so.

[15]A prophet like me†† will the LORD, your God, raise up for you from among your own kindred; that is the one to whom you shall listen.[f] [16]This is exactly what you requested of the LORD, your God, at Horeb on the day of the assembly, when you said, "Let me not again hear the voice

---

*[17:12] **The priest:** the high priest; **the judge:** a layman. The court system here, involving lay and priestly officials, resembles the one whose establishment is attributed to King Jehoshaphat in 2 Chr 19:8–11 (cf. Ex 18:17–23 and Dt 1:17).

†[17:16–17] This restriction on royal acquisitions may have in mind the excesses of Solomon's reign mentioned in 1 Kgs 10:1–11:6. **Horses:** chariotry for war. Egypt engaged in horse trading, and the danger envisioned here is that some king might make Israel a vassal of Egypt for military aid.

‡[17:18] **A copy of this law:** the source of the name Deuteronomy, which in Hebrew is literally "double" or "copy"; in the Septuagint translated as *deuteronomion*, literally "a second law." In Jerome's Latin Vulgate as *deuteronomium*.

§[17:19] The only positive requirement imposed upon the king is strict adherence to the Mosaic or Deuteronomic law. In that respect, the king's primary task was to be a model Israelite.

¶[18:8] **His stipends and patrimony:** meaning of the Hebrew is uncertain.

**[18:10–11] **Causes their son or daughter to pass through the fire:** to Molech. See note on Lv 18:21. Such human sacrifices are classed here with various occult and magical practices because they were believed to possess powers for averting a calamity; cf. 2 Kgs 3:27. Three other categories of magic are listed here: divination of the future (by a soothsayer or augur); black magic (by a sorcerer or one who casts spells); and necromancy (by one who consults ghosts and spirits, or seeks oracles from the dead to divine the future).

††[18:15] **A prophet like me:** from the context (opposition to the practices described in vv. 10–11) it seems that Moses is referring in general to all the true prophets who succeed him. This passage came to be understood in a quasi-Messianic sense in the New Testament (Mt 17:5; Jn 6:14; 7:40; Acts 3:22; 7:37).

---

q. [17:13] Dt 13:12. r. [17:14–20] 1 Sm 10–25. s. [17:14] Dt 26:1; 1 Sm 8:5, 19–20. t. [17:15] 1 Sm 9:16; 10:24; 16:1–13; 1 Kgs 19:15–16; 2 Kgs 9:1–13. u. [17:16] Dt 28:68; 1 Sm 8:10–12; 1 Kgs 4:26; 10:26–29; Is 2:7. v. [17:17] 1 Kgs 10:10–25; 11:1–8; Neh 13:26; Is 2:7. w. [17:18] Dt 31:9, 24–26; Jos 8:32. x. [17:19–20] Dt 5:32–6:3; 2 Sm 7:12–16; 1 Kgs 2:4; Ps 132:11–18. y. [18:1] Nm 18:8–9, 20–24; Jos 13:14; 18:7; 2 Chr 31:2–19; 1 Cor 9:13.

z. [18:2] Nm 18:20; Jos 13:33. a. [18:4] Dt 26:1–11; Nm 18:12; 2 Chr 31:5; Neh 13:10–13. b. [18:5] Dt 10:8; Jer 33:18. c. [18:9] Dt 12:29–31; Lv 18:24–30. d. [18:10–11] Dt 12:31; Ex 22:18; Lv 18:21; 19:31; 20:6, 27; 1 Sm 28:7–19; 2 Kgs 17:17; 21:6; 23:10, 24; Is 8:19–20; Ez 21:21. e. [18:12] Dt 9:4. f. [18:15] Mt 17:5; Mk 9:7; Lk 9:35; Jn 1:45; 6:14; 7:40; Acts 3:22; 7:37.

of the Lord, my God, nor see this great fire any more, or I will die."[g] [17]And the Lord said to me, What they have said is good. [18]I will raise up for them a prophet like you from among their kindred, and will put my words into the mouth of the prophet; the prophet shall tell them all that I command.[h] [19]Anyone who will not listen to my words which the prophet speaks in my name, I myself will hold accountable for it.[i] [20]But if a prophet presumes to speak a word in my name[j] that I have not commanded, or speaks in the name of other gods, that prophet shall die.

[21]Should you say to yourselves, "How can we recognize that a word is one the Lord has not spoken?", [22]if a prophet speaks in the name of the Lord but the word does not come true, it is a word the Lord did not speak. The prophet has spoken it presumptuously; do not fear him.

## CHAPTER 19

**Cities of Refuge.** [1k]When the Lord, your God, cuts down the nations whose land the Lord, your God, is giving you, and you have dispossessed them and settled in their cities and houses,[l] [2]you shall set apart three cities* in the land the Lord, your God, is giving you to possess. [3]You shall measure the distances and divide into three regions the land of which the Lord, your God, is giving you possession, so that every homicide will be able to find a refuge.

[4]This is the case of a homicide who may take refuge there and live: when someone strikes down a neighbor unintentionally and not out of previous hatred. [5]For example, if someone goes with a neighbor to a forest to cut wood, wielding an ax to cut down a tree, and its head flies off the handle and hits the neighbor a mortal blow, such a person may take refuge in one of these cities and live. [6]Should the distance be too great, the avenger of blood[†] might in hot anger pursue, overtake, and strike the killer dead, even though that one does not deserve the death penalty since there had been no previous hatred; [7]for this reason I command you: Set apart three cities.

[8m]But if the Lord, your God, enlarges your territory, as he swore to your ancestors, and gives you all the land he promised your ancestors he would give, [9]because you carefully observe this whole commandment which I give you today, loving the Lord, your God, and ever walking in his ways, then add three more cities to these three. [10]Thus, in the land which the Lord, your God, is giving you as a heritage, innocent blood will not be shed and you will not become guilty of bloodshed.[n]

[11]However, if someone, hating a neighbor, lies in wait, attacks, and strikes the neighbor dead, and then flees to one of these cities, [12]the elders of the killer's own city shall send and have the killer taken from there, to be handed over to the avenger of blood and slain. [13]Do not show pity, but purge from Israel the innocent blood, so that it may go well with you.[o]

**Removal of Landmarks.** [14]You shall not move your neighbor's boundary markers[‡] erected by your forebears in the heritage that will be allotted to you in the land the Lord, your God, is giving you to possess.[p]

**False Witnesses.** [15q]One witness alone shall not stand against someone in regard to any crime or any offense that may have been committed; a charge shall stand only on the testimony of two or three witnesses.[r]

[16]If a hostile witness rises against someone to accuse that person of wrongdoing, [17]the two parties in the dispute shall appear in the presence of the Lord, in the presence of the priests and judges in office at that time,[s] [18]and the judges must investigate it thoroughly. If the witness is a false witness and has falsely accused the other,[u] [19]you shall do to the false witness just as that false witness planned to do to the other. Thus shall you purge the evil from your midst. [20]The rest shall hear and be afraid, and never again do such an evil thing as this in your midst.[v] [21]Do not show pity. Life for life,[§] eye for eye, tooth for tooth, hand for hand, and foot for foot![w]

## CHAPTER 20

**Courage in War.** [1]When you go out to war against your enemies and you see horses and chariots and an army greater than your own, you shall not be afraid of them, for the Lord, your God, who brought you up from the land of Egypt, will be with you.

[2]When you are drawing near to battle, the priest shall come forward and speak to the army, [3]and say to them, "Hear, O Israel! Today you are drawing near for battle against your enemies. Do not be weakhearted or afraid, alarmed or frightened by them. [4]For it is the Lord, your

---

*[19:2] **Set apart three cities**: the Israelites were to have at least six cities of refuge, three in the land east of the Jordan and three in the land of Canaan west of the Jordan (Nm 35:9–34); but since the three cities east of the Jordan had now been appointed (Dt 4:41–43), reference is made here only to the three west of the Jordan. The execution of this command is narrated in Jos 20.

†[19:6] **The avenger of blood**: see note on Nm 35:12.

‡[19:14] **Move your neighbor's boundary markers**: a prohibition against furtively extending one's property by moving a neighbor's boundary stone.

§[19:21] **Life for life . . .** : this phrasing of the *lex talionis* may seem exaggerated, but the law itself is meant to ensure equity and proportional punishment; cf. note on Ex 21:22–25.

---

g. [18:16] Ex 20:19.   h. [18:18] Ex 4:10–16; Jer 1:9; 15:19; Ez 3:1–4.   i. [18:19] Jer 11:21–23; Am 7:10–17; Acts 3:23.   j. [18:20, 22] Dt 13:2–6; 1 Kgs 22:1–40; Jer 14:13–16; 23:9–40; 28:1–17; Ez 13:1–23.   k. [19:1–13] Dt 4:41–43; Ex 21:12–14; Nm 35:9–34; Jos 20:1–9.   l. [19:1] Dt 6:10–11; 12:29.   m. [19:8] Dt 11:22–25; 12:20; Gn 15:18–21; 28:14; Ex 23:31.

n. [19:10] Dt 21:8–9.   o. [19:13] Dt 13:6, 9.   p. [19:14] Dt 27:17; Jb 24:2; Prv 22:28; 23:10; Hos 5:10.   q. [19:15–21] Dt 5:20; Ex 20:16; 23:1.   r. [19:15] Dt 17:6; Nm 35:30; Mt 18:16; Jn 8:17; 2 Cor 13:1.   s. [19:17] Dt 1:17; 17:8–12.   t. [19:18–19] Dn 13:61–62.   u. [19:18] Dt 13:15; 17:4.   v. [19:20] Dt 3:11.   w. [19:21] Ex 21:23–25; Lv 24:19–20; Mt 5:38.

God, who goes with you to fight for you against your enemies and give you victory."[x]

[5]Then the officials shall speak to the army:[y] "Is there anyone who has built a new house and not yet dedicated it? Let him return home, lest he die in battle and another dedicate it. [6]Is there anyone who has planted a vineyard and not yet plucked its fruit? Let him return home, lest he die in battle and another pluck its fruit. [7]Is there anyone who has betrothed a woman and not yet married her? Let him return home, lest he die in battle and another marry her."[z] [8]The officials shall continue to speak to the army: "Is there anyone who is afraid and weakhearted?[a] Let him return home, or else he might make the hearts of his fellows melt as his does."

[9]When the officials have finished speaking to the army, military commanders shall be appointed over them.

**Cities of the Enemy.** [10b]When you draw near a city to attack it, offer it terms of peace. [11]If it agrees to your terms of peace and lets you in, all the people to be found in it shall serve you in forced labor. [12]But if it refuses to make peace with you and instead joins battle with you, lay siege to it, [13]and when the LORD, your God, delivers it into your power, put every male in it to the sword; [14]but the women and children and livestock and anything else in the city—all its spoil—you may take as plunder for yourselves, and you may enjoy this spoil of your enemies, which the LORD, your God, has given you.

[15]That is how you shall deal with any city at a considerable distance from you, which does not belong to these nations here. [16d]But in the cities of these peoples that the LORD, your God, is giving you as a heritage, you shall not leave a single soul alive. [17]You must put them all under the ban—the Hittites, Amorites, Canaanites, Perizzites, Hivites, and Jebusites—just as the LORD, your God, has commanded you, [18]so that they do not teach you to do all the abominations that they do for their gods, and you thus sin against the LORD, your God.

**Trees of a Besieged City.** [19e]When you are at war with a city and have to lay siege to it for a long time before you capture it, you shall not destroy its trees by putting an ax to them. You may eat of them, but you must not cut them down. Are the trees of the field human beings, that they should be included in your siege? [20]However, those trees which you know are not fruit trees you may destroy. You may cut them down to build siegeworks against the city that is waging war with you, until it falls.

# CHAPTER 21

**Absolution of Untraced Murder.**[†] [1]If the corpse of someone who has been slain is found lying in the open, in the land the LORD, your God, is giving you to possess, and it is not known who killed the person, [2]your elders and judges shall go out and measure the distances to the cities that are in the neighborhood of the corpse. [3]When it is established which city is nearest the corpse, the elders of that city shall take a heifer that has never been put to work or worn a yoke; [4]the elders of that city shall bring the heifer down to a wadi with an everflowing stream at a place that has not been plowed or sown, and shall break the heifer's neck there in the wadi. [5]The priests, the descendants of Levi, shall come forward, for the LORD, your God, has chosen them to minister to him and to bless in the name of the LORD, and every case of dispute or assault shall be for them to decide. [6]Then all the elders of that city nearest the corpse shall wash their hands[‡] over the heifer whose neck was broken in the wadi, [7]and shall declare, "Our hands did not shed this blood,[§] and our eyes did not see the deed. [8]Absolve, O LORD, your people Israel, whom you have redeemed, and do not let the guilt of shedding innocent blood remain in the midst of your people Israel." Thus they shall be absolved from the guilt of bloodshed, [9]and you shall purge the innocent blood from your midst, and do what is right in the eyes of the LORD.[g]

**Marriage with a Female Captive.** [10h]When you go out to war against your enemies and the LORD, your God, delivers them into your power, so that you take captives, [11]if you see a beautiful woman among the captives and become so enamored of her that you wish to have her as a wife, [12]and so you take her home to your house, she must shave her head,[¶] cut her nails, [13]lay aside her captive's garb, and stay in your house, mourning her father and mother for a full month. After that, you may come to her, and you shall be her husband and she shall be your wife. [14]If later on you lose your liking for her, you shall give her her freedom, if she wishes it; you must not sell her for money. Do not enslave her, since you have violated her.[i]

---

*[20:15] Deuteronomy makes a distinction between treatment of nations far away and those close at hand whose abhorrent religious practices might, or did, influence Israel's worship. This harsh policy was to make sure the nations nearby did not pass their practices on to Israel (cf. chap. 7).

†[21:1–9] This law has to do with absolving the community of bloodguilt that accrues to it and to the land when a homicide occurs and the murderer cannot be identified and punished.

‡[21:6] **Wash their hands**: a symbolic gesture in protestation of one's own innocence when human blood is unjustly shed; cf. Mt 27:24.

§[21:7] **This blood**: the blood of the slain, or the bloodguilt effected by the killing.

¶[21:12–13] **Shave her head . . .** : these symbolic actions probably signified the transition or change of status of the woman or perhaps the end of her period of mourning for her previous husband or family.

x. [20:4] Dt 1:30; 3:22; Ex 14:14; 15:3; Jos 23:10; Jgs 4:14.   y. [20:5–8] 1 Mc 3:56.   z. [20:7] Dt 24:5.   a. [20:8] Jgs 7:3.   b. [20:10–11] Jos 9:23–27; 11:19; 2 Sm 10:19.   c. [20:12–14] Nm 31:7, 9, 11; Jos 22:8.   d. [20:16–18] Dt 7:1–2; 12:29–31; Jos 10:40; 11:11, 14.   e. [20:19–20] 2 Kgs 3:18, 25.

f. [21:3–4] Nm 19:2–3.   g. [21:9] Dt 19:13.   h. [21:10–14] Dt 20:14.   i. [21:14] Dt 15:12–18; 22:13–19, 28–29; 24:1–3; Jer 34:15–16.

**Rights of the Firstborn.** [15]If a man has two wives, one loved and the other unloved, and if both the loved and the unloved bear him sons, but the firstborn is the son of the unloved wife: [16]when he comes to bequeath his property to his sons he may not consider as his firstborn the son of the wife he loves, in preference to the son of the wife he does not love, the firstborn. [17]On the contrary, he shall recognize as his firstborn the son of the unloved wife, giving him a double share of whatever he happens to own, since he is the first fruits of his manhood, and to him belong the rights of the firstborn.[k]

**The Stubborn and Rebellious Son.** [18]If someone has a stubborn and rebellious son who will not listen to his father or mother, and will not listen to them even though they discipline him,[m] [19]his father and mother shall take hold of him and bring him out to the elders at the gate* of his home city, [20]where they shall say to the elders of the city, "This son of ours is a stubborn and rebellious fellow who will not listen to us; he is a glutton and a drunkard."[n] [21]Then all his fellow citizens shall stone him to death. Thus shall you purge the evil from your midst, and all Israel will hear and be afraid.[o]

**Corpse of a Criminal.** [22]If a man guilty of a capital offense is put to death and you hang him on a tree,[†] [23]his corpse shall not remain on the tree overnight.[q] You must bury it the same day; anyone who is hanged is a curse of God.[‡] You shall not defile the land which the LORD, your God, is giving you as a heritage.

## CHAPTER 22

**Concern for the Neighbor.** [1]You shall not see your neighbor's ox or sheep going astray and ignore it; you must bring it back. [2]If this neighbor does not live near you, or you do not know who the owner may be, take it to your own house and keep it with you until your neighbor claims it; then return it. [3]You shall do the same with a donkey; you shall do the same with a garment; and you shall do the same with anything else which your neighbor loses and you happen to find. You may not ignore them.

[4]You shall not see your neighbor's donkey or ox fallen on the road and ignore it; you must help in lifting it up.

**Various Precepts.** [5]A woman shall not wear a man's garment, nor shall a man put on a woman's clothing; for anyone who does such things is an abomination to the LORD, your God.[s]

[6]If, while walking along, you come across a bird's nest with young birds or eggs in it, in any tree or on the ground, and the mother bird is sitting on them, you shall not take away the mother bird along with her brood. [7]You must let the mother go, taking only her brood, in order that you shall prosper and have a long life.

[8]When you build a new house, put a parapet around the roof, so that you do not bring bloodguilt upon your house if someone falls off.[u]

[9]§You shall not sow your vineyard with two different kinds of seed, or else its produce shall become forfeit, both the crop you have sown and the yield of the vineyard. [10]You shall not plow with an ox and a donkey harnessed together. [11]You shall not wear cloth made from wool and linen woven together.

[12]You shall put tassels on the four corners of the cloak that you wrap around yourself.[w]

**Marriage Legislation.** [13]If a man, after marrying a woman and having relations with her, comes to dislike her,[x] [14]and accuses her of misconduct and slanders her by saying, "I married this woman, but when I approached her I did not find evidence of her virginity," [15]the father and mother of the young woman shall take the evidence of her virginity¶ and bring it to the elders at the city gate. [16]There the father of the young woman shall say to the elders, "I gave my daughter to this man in marriage, but he has come to dislike her, [17]and now accuses her of misconduct, saying: 'I did not find evidence of your daughter's virginity.' But here is the evidence of my daughter's virginity!" And they shall spread out the cloth before the elders of the city. [18]Then these city elders shall take the man and discipline him,** [19]and fine him one hundred silver shekels, which they shall give to the young woman's father, because the man slandered a virgin in Israel. She shall remain his wife, and he may not divorce her as long as he lives. [20]But if this charge is true, and evidence of the young woman's virginity is not found, [21]they shall bring the young woman to the entrance of her father's house and there the men of her town shall stone her to death, because she committed

---

*[21:19] **The gate:** in the city walls. This open space served as the forum for the administration of justice. Cf. 22:15; 25:7; Ru 4:1, 2, 11; Is 29:21; Am 5:10, 12, 15.

†[21:22] **You hang him on a tree:** some understand, "impaled on a stake." In any case the hanging or impaling was not the means used to execute the criminal; he was first put to death by the ordinary means, stoning, and his corpse was then exposed on high as a warning for others. Cf. Jos 8:29; 10:26; 1 Sm 31:10; 2 Sm 21:9.

‡[21:23] Gal 3:13 applies these words to the crucifixion of Jesus, who "redeemed us from the curse of the law, becoming a curse for us."

j. [21:15–17] Gn 21:9–13; 1 Kgs 1:5–21.  k. [21:17] Gn 49:3–4.
l. [21:18–21] Dt 5:16; 27:16; Ex 20:12; 21:15, 17; Lv 20:9.  m. [21:18] Ps 78:8; Jer 5:23.  n. [21:20] Prv 23:20–21; 28:7; Mt 11:19; Lk 7:34.  o. [21:21] Dt 13:6, 11–12; 22:21, 24; Lv 20:2; 24:14–16.
p. [21:22–23] Jos 8:29; 10:26–27; 1 Sm 31:8–13; 2 Sm 4:12.
q. [21:23] Gal 3:13.  r. [22:1–4] Ex 23:4–5.

§[22:9–11] Some understand these laws as serving to preserve distinctions set by God in the creation. **Become forfeit:** to the sanctuary; lit., "be holy"; cf. Lv 19:19; Jos 6:19.

¶[22:15] **The evidence of her virginity:** the bridal garment or sheet stained with blood from the first nuptial relations.

**[22:18] **Discipline him:** whip him, as prescribed in 25:1–3.

---

s. [22:5] Dt 7:25–26.  t. [22:6–7] Lv 22:28.  u. [22:8] Dt 19:10.
v. [22:9–11] Lv 19:19.  w. [22:12] Nm 15:38–41; Mt 23:5.
x. [22:13] Dt 24:1.

a shameful crime in Israel by prostituting herself in her father's house. Thus shall you purge the evil from your midst.[y]

²²If a man is discovered lying with a woman who is married to another, they both shall die, the man who was lying with the woman as well as the woman.[z] Thus shall you purge the evil from Israel.

²³If there is a young woman, a virgin who is betrothed,* and a man comes upon her in the city and lies with her, ²⁴you shall bring them both out to the gate of the city and there stone them to death: the young woman because she did not cry out though she was in the city, and the man because he violated his neighbor's wife. Thus shall you purge the evil from your midst. ²⁵But if it is in the open fields that a man comes upon the betrothed young woman, seizes her and lies with her, only the man who lay with her shall die. ²⁶You shall do nothing to the young woman, since the young woman is not guilty of a capital offense. As when a man rises up against his neighbor and murders him, so in this case:[†a] ²⁷it was in the open fields that he came upon her, and though the betrothed young woman may have cried out, there was no one to save her.

²⁸[b]If a man comes upon a young woman, a virgin who is not betrothed, seizes her and lies with her, and they are discovered, ²⁹the man who lay with her shall give the young woman's father fifty silver shekels and she will be his wife, because he has violated her. He may not divorce her as long as he lives.

### CHAPTER 23

¹A man shall not marry his father's wife,[‡] nor shall he dishonor his father's bed.[c]

**Membership in the Assembly.** ²[d]No one whose testicles have been crushed or whose penis has been cut off may come into the assembly of the Lord.[d] ³No one born of an illicit union may come into the assembly of the Lord, nor any descendant of such even to the tenth generation may come into the assembly of the Lord.[e] ⁴No Ammonite or Moabite may ever come into the assembly of the Lord, nor may any of their descendants even to the tenth generation

come into the assembly of the Lord, ⁵because they would not come to meet you with food and water on your journey after you left Egypt, and because they hired Balaam, son of Beor, from Pethor in Aram Naharaim, to curse you. ⁶The Lord, your God, would not listen to Balaam but turned his curse into a blessing for you, because the Lord, your God, loves you. ⁷Never seek their welfare or prosperity as long as you live.[g] ⁸[h]Do not abhor the Edomite: he is your brother. Do not abhor the Egyptian: you were a resident alien in his country. ⁹Children born to them may come into the assembly of the Lord in the third generation.

**Cleanliness in Camp.** ¹⁰When in camp during an expedition against your enemies, you shall keep yourselves from anything bad. ¹¹If one of you becomes unclean because of a nocturnal emission, he shall go outside the camp; he shall not come back into the camp. ¹²Toward evening, he shall bathe in water; then, when the sun has set, he may come back into the camp. ¹³Outside the camp you shall have a place set aside where you shall go. ¹⁴You shall keep a trowel in your equipment and, when you go outside to relieve yourself, you shall dig a hole with it and then cover up your excrement. ¹⁵Since the Lord, your God, journeys along in the midst of your camp to deliver you and to give your enemies over to you, your camp must be holy, so that he does not see anything indecent in your midst and turn away from you.[j]

**Various Precepts.** ¹⁶[k]You shall not hand over to their master any slaves who have taken refuge with you from their master. ¹⁷Let them live among you in any place they choose, in any one of your communities[¶] that seems good to them. Do not oppress them.

¹⁸There shall be no temple prostitute** among the Israelite women, nor a temple prostitute among the Israelite men.[l] ¹⁹You shall not offer a prostitute's fee or a dog's pay[††] as any kind of votive offering in the house of the Lord, your God; both these things are an abomination to the Lord, your God.[m]

²⁰[n]You shall not demand interest from your kindred on a loan of money or of food or of anything else which is loaned. ²¹From a foreigner you

---

*[22:23] **A young woman, a virgin who is betrothed:** a girl who is married but not yet brought to her husband's home and whose marriage is therefore still unconsummated.

†[22:26] **So in this case:** in the absence of witnesses ("in the open field"), the presumption must be that the woman is the victim, and so guiltless.

‡[23:1] **Father's wife:** stepmother.

§[23:2] Exclusion of an emasculated male may have had to do with association of emasculation with the practices of other peoples, or it may have been rejection of someone with a significant blemish who was thus not suitable for participation in the sacral assembly.

¶[23:17] **In any one of your communities:** from this it would seem that the slave in question is a fugitive from a foreign country.

**[23:18–19] **Temple prostitute:** Heb. *qedesha*, lit., "holy one," a title of the goddess of fertility. The role or function of the *qedesha* is debated; some see this as simply a term for a prostitute (Heb. *zona*). Others see it as designating a cultic role but not necessarily one involving sexual activity. The evidence is insufficient to give a final answer.

††[23:19] **Dog's pay:** "dog" is a derogatory term for a male temple prostitute.

---

y. [22:21] Dt 13:6; Gn 34:7; 2 Sm 13:12.    z. [22:22] Dt 5:18; Ex 20:14; Lv 20:10; Ez 16:38–40; Jn 8:3–5.    a. [22:26] Dt 19:4–6.
b. [22:28–29] Dt 22:19; Ex 22:16–17.    c. [23:1] Dt 27:20; Gn 9:20–27; 49:4; Lv 18:6–19; 20:11; Ez 22:10.    d. [23:2] Lv 21:16–24.
e. [23:3] Gn 19:30–38; Lv 18:6–18.    f. [23:4–6] Nm 22:1–24:25; Ru 4:9–17; Ezr 10:10–44; Neh 13:1–3, 23–27.

g. [23:7] Ezr 9:12.    h. [23:8] Dt 2:2–8; 26:5; Gn 12:10–20; 25:19–26; 36:6–9; 46:5–7; 47:27.    i. [23:11–12] Lv 15:16–17.    j. [23:15] Dt 1:30; 20:4; 31:6, 8; 2 Sm 7:6.    k. [23:16–17] 1 Kgs 2:39–40.
l. [23:18] Gn 38:21–22; 1 Kgs 14:24; 15:12; 22:46; 2 Kgs 23:7; Hos 4:14.
m. [23:19] Dt 7:25–26; Is 23:17–18.    n. [23:20–21] Dt 15:1–11; 24:10–13; Ex 22:25; Lv 25:35–38; Ez 18:8, 13, 17; 22:12; Lk 6:34–35.

may demand interest, but you may not demand interest from your kindred, so that the LORD, your God, may bless you in all your undertakings on the land you are to enter and possess. [22o]When you make a vow to the LORD, your God, you shall not delay in fulfilling it; for the LORD, your God, will surely require it of you and you will be held guilty. [23]Should you refrain from making a vow, you will not be held guilty. [24]But whatever your tongue utters you must be careful to do, just as you freely vowed to the LORD, your God, with your own mouth.

[25]When you go through your neighbor's vineyard, you may eat as many grapes as you wish, until you are satisfied, but do not put them in your basket. [26]When you go through your neighbor's grainfield, you may pluck some of the ears with your hand, but do not put a sickle to your neighbor's grain.

## CHAPTER 24

**Marriage Legislation.**[*] [1p]When a man, after marrying a woman, is later displeased with her because he finds in her something indecent, and he writes out a bill of divorce and hands it to her, thus dismissing her from his house, [2]if on leaving his house she goes and becomes the wife of another man, [3]and the second husband, too, comes to dislike her and he writes out a bill of divorce and hands it to her, thus dismissing her from his house, or if this second man who has married her dies, [4]then her former husband, who dismissed her, may not again take her as his wife after she has become defiled. That would be an abomination before the LORD, and you shall not bring such guilt upon the land the LORD, your God, is giving you as a heritage.[q]

[5r]When a man is newly wed, he shall not go out on a military expedition, nor shall any duty be imposed on him. He shall be exempt for one year for the sake of his family, to bring joy to the wife he has married.

**Pledges and Kidnappings.** [6†]No one shall take a hand mill or even its upper stone as a pledge for debt, for that would be taking as a pledge the debtor's life.

[7]If anyone is caught kidnapping a fellow Israelite, enslaving or selling the victim, that kidnapper shall be put to death.[s] Thus shall you purge the evil from your midst.

**Skin Diseases.** [8‡]In an attack of scaly infection[‡] you shall be careful to observe exactly and to carry out all the instructions the levitical priests give you, as I have commanded them: observe them carefully. [9u]Remember what the LORD, your God, did to Miriam on the journey after you left Egypt.

**Loans and Wages.** [10]When you make a loan of any kind to your neighbor, you shall not enter the neighbor's house to receive the pledge, [11]but shall wait outside until the person to whom you are making the loan brings the pledge outside to you. [12]If the person is poor, you shall not sleep in the pledged garment, [13]but shall definitely return it at sunset, so that your neighbor may sleep in the garment[v] and bless you. That will be your justice before the LORD, your God.

[14w]You shall not exploit a poor and needy hired servant, whether one of your own kindred or one of the resident aliens who live in your land, within your gates.[x] [15]On each day you shall pay the servant's wages before the sun goes down, since the servant is poor and is counting on them. Otherwise the servant will cry to the LORD against you, and you will be held guilty.[y]

**Individual Responsibility.** [16]Parents shall not be put to death for their children, nor shall children be put to death for their parents; only for one's own crime shall a person be put to death.[z]

**Rights of the Unprotected.** [17a]You shall not deprive the resident alien or the orphan of justice, nor take the clothing of a widow as pledge. [18]For, remember, you were slaves in Egypt, and the LORD, your God, redeemed you from there; that is why I command you to do this.

[19b]When you reap the harvest in your field and overlook a sheaf in the field, you shall not go back to get it; let it be for the resident alien, the orphan, and the widow, so that the LORD, your God, may bless you in all your undertakings. [20]When you knock down the fruit of your olive trees, you shall not go over the branches a second time; let what remains be for the resident alien, the orphan, and the widow. [21]When you pick your grapes, you shall not go over the vineyard a second time; let what remains be for the resident alien, the orphan, and the widow.

---

*[24:1–4] This law is directly concerned only with forbidding a divorced man from remarrying his former wife, and indirectly with checking hasty divorces, by demanding sufficient cause and certain legal formalities. Divorce itself is taken for granted and tolerated as an existing custom whose potential evils this law seeks to lessen. Cf. 22:19, 29; Mal 2:14–16. **Something indecent**: a rather indefinite phrase, meaning perhaps "immodest conduct," but possibly including any kind of objectionable conduct. By New Testament times Jewish opinion differed concerning what was sufficient ground for divorce; cf. Mt 19:3.

†[24:6] Since the Israelites ground their grain into flour only in sufficient quantity for their current need, to deprive a debtor of his hand mill was equivalent to condemning him to starvation.

‡[24:8] **Scaly infection**: the Hebrew word seems to have to do with one or more skin diseases that produce scales, such as psoriasis. Its precise meaning is uncertain. See note on Lv 13:1–14:57.

o. [23:22–24] Gn 28:20–22; Nm 21:2–3; 30:1–15; Jgs 11:30–40; 1 Sm 1:11; Ps 56:12–13; 66:13–15; 132:1–5; Eccl 5:3–5.  p. [24:1–4] Dt 22:13–19, 28–29; Sir 7:26; Jer 3:1; Mt 5:31–32; 19:3–9.  q. [24:4] Dt 7:25–26.  r. [24:5] Dt 20:7.

s. [24:7] Dt 13:6; Ex 21:16.  t. [24:8] Lv 13:1–14:57.  u. [24:9] Nm 12:10–15.  v. [24:13] Dt 6:25; Ex 22:25–26; Am 2:8.  w. [24:14–15] Lv 19:13; Sir 34:26–27; Jer 22:13.  x. [24:14] Dt 1:16.  y. [24:15] Dt 15:9; Mt 20:1–16.  z. [24:16] Dt 7:10; 2 Kgs 14:6; 2 Chr 25:4; Jer 31:29–30; Ez 18:20.  a. [24:17–18] Dt 10:17–19; 15:15; 24:22; 27:19; Ex 22:21–24; 23:9.  b. [24:19–22] Ex 23:10–11; Lv 19:9–10; 23:22; Ru 2:1–23.

²²For remember that you were slaves in the land of Egypt; that is why I command you to do this.

## CHAPTER 25

**Limits on Punishments.** ¹When there is a dispute and the parties draw near for judgment, and a decision is given, declaring one party in the right and the other in the wrong, ²if the one in the wrong deserves whipping, the judge shall have him lie down and in the presence of the judge receive the number of lashes the crime warrants. ³Forty lashes* may be given, but no more;ᶜ or else, if more lashes are added to these many blows, your brother will be degraded in your sight.

**Treatment of Oxen.†** ⁴You shall not muzzle an ox when it treads out grain.ᵈ

**Levirate Marriage.** ⁵ᵉWhen brothers live together‡ and one of them dies without a son, the widow of the deceased shall not marry anyone outside the family; but her husband's brother shall come to her, marrying her and performing the duty of a brother-in-law.ᶠ ⁶The firstborn son she bears shall continue the name of the deceased brother, that his name may not be blotted out from Israel. ⁷But if a man does not want to marry his brother's wife, she shall go up to the elders at the gate and say, "My brother-in-law refuses to perpetuate his brother's name in Israel and does not intend to perform his duty toward me." ⁸Thereupon the elders of his city shall summon him and speak to him. If he persists in saying, "I do not want to marry her," ⁹ᵍhis sister-in-law, in the presence of the elders, shall go up to him and strip his sandal from his foot and spit in his face, declaring, "This is how one should be treated who will not build up his brother's family!" ¹⁰And his name shall be called in Israel, "the house of the man stripped of his sandal."

**Various Precepts.** ¹¹When two men are fighting and the wife of one intervenes to save her husband from the blows of his opponent, if she stretches out her hand and seizes the latter by his genitals, ¹²you shall chop off her hand; show no pity.

¹³ᵍYou shall not keep two differing weights in your bag, one heavy and the other light; ¹⁴nor shall you keep two different ephahs⁵ in your house, one large and the other small. ¹⁵But use a full and just weight, a full and just ephah, so that you may have a long life on the land the LORD, your God, is giving you. ¹⁶For everyone who does these things, everyone who does what is dishonest, is an abomination to the LORD, your God.ʰ

¹⁷**`Bear in mind what Amalek did to you on the journey after you left Egypt, ¹⁸how he surprised you along the way, weak and weary as you were, and struck down at the rear all those who lagged behind; he did not fear God. ¹⁹Therefore, when the LORD, your God, gives you rest from all your enemies round about in the land which the LORD, your God, is giving you to possess as a heritage, you shall blot out the memory of Amalek from under the heavens. Do not forget!

## CHAPTER 26

**Thanksgiving for the Harvest.** ¹ʲWhen you have come into the land which the LORD, your God, is giving you as a heritage, and have taken possession and settled in it, ²you shall take some first fruitsᵏ of the various products of the soil which you harvest from the land the LORD, your God, is giving you; put them in a basket and go to the place which the LORD, your God, will choose as the dwelling place for his name. ³There you shall go to the priest in office at that time and say to him, "Today I acknowledge to the LORD, my God, that I have indeed come into the land which the LORD swore to our ancestors to give us."ⁱ ⁴The priest shall take the basket from your hands and set it in front of the altar of the LORD, your God. ⁵Then you shall declare in the presence of the LORD, your God, "My father was a refugee Aramean†† who went down to Egypt with a small household and lived there as a resident alien.ᵐ But there he became a nation great, strong and numerous. ⁶ⁿWhen the Egyptians maltreated and oppressed us, imposing harsh servitude upon us, ⁷we cried to the LORD, the God of our ancestors, and the LORD heard our cry and saw our affliction, our toil

---

*[25:3] **Forty lashes**: while the punishment is severe, the law seeks to limit it from being overly harsh and inhumane. Later Jewish practice limited the number to thirty-nine; cf. 2 Cor 11:24.

†[25:4] This is comparable in spirit to 22:6–7; Israelites are not to be grasping and calculating. St. Paul argues from this verse that laborers have the right to live on the fruits of their labor; cf. 1 Cor 9:9; 1 Tm 5:18.

‡[25:5] **When brothers live together**: when relatives of the same clan, though married, hold their property in common. It was only in this case that the present law was to be observed, since one of its purposes was to keep the property of the deceased within the same clan. Such a marriage of a widow with her brother-in-law is known as a "levirate" marriage from the Latin word *levir*, meaning "a husband's brother."

§[25:9–10] The penalty decreed for a man who refuses to comply with this law of family loyalty is public disgrace; the widow is to spit in his face. Some commentators connect this symbolic act with the ceremony mentioned in Ru 4:7, 8.

⁵[25:14] **Ephahs**: see note on Is 5:10.

**[25:17–19] This attack on Israel by Amalek is not mentioned elsewhere in the Old Testament, although it probably was connected with the battle mentioned in Ex 17:8. A campaign against Amalek was carried out by Saul; cf. 1 Sm 15.

††[26:5] **Aramean**: probably in reference to the origin of the patriarchs from Aram Naharaim (cf. Gn 24:10; 25:20; 28:5; 31:20, 24).

---

c. [25:3] 2 Cor 11:24.   d. [25:4] Prv 12:10; 1 Cor 9:9; 1 Tm 5:18.   e. [25:5–10] Gn 38:1–30; Ru 4:5–10; Lk 20:27–33.   f. [25:5] Mt 22:24; Mk 12:19; Lk 20:28.

g. [25:13–16] Lv 19:35–36; Prv 16:11; 20:23; Ez 45:10; Hos 12:7; Mi 6:11.   h. [25:16] Dt 7:25–26.   i. [25:17–19] Ex 17:8–16; 1 Sm 15:2–33.   j. [26:1–11] Dt 14:22–29; 16:1–17; Ex 22:29; Lv 23:9–21; Nm 28:26–31.   k. [26:2] Dt 12:5, 11; 18:4; Ex 23:19; 34:26; Tb 1:6–7.   l. [26:3] Dt 1:8, 20–21.   m. [26:5] Gn 46:5–7, 26–27; Ex 1:7, 9; Acts 7:14–15.   n. [26:6–7] Ex 1:8–22; 2:23–25; 3:7–10; 6:9; Nm 20:15–16; 1 Kgs 12:4.

and our oppression. [8]Then the LORD brought us out of Egypt with a strong hand and outstretched arm, with terrifying power, with signs and wonders,[o] [9]and brought us to this place, and gave us this land, a land flowing with milk and honey.[p] [10]Now, therefore, I have brought the first fruits of the products of the soil which you, LORD, have given me." You shall set them before the LORD, your God, and you shall bow down before the LORD, your God. [11]Then you and your household, together with the Levite and the resident aliens who live among you, shall celebrate with all these good things which the LORD, your God, has given you.[q]

**Declaration Concerning Tithes.** [12]When you have finished setting aside all the tithes of your produce in the third year,[r] the year of the tithes, and have given them to the Levite, the resident alien, the orphan and the widow, that they may eat and be satisfied in your own communities, [13]you shall declare before the LORD, your God, "I have purged my house of the sacred portion and I have given it to the Levite, the resident alien, the orphan and the widow, just as you have commanded me. I have not transgressed any of your commandments, nor forgotten any. [14]*I have not eaten any of the tithe while in mourning; I have not brought any of it while unclean; I have not offered any of it to the dead. I have thus obeyed the voice of the LORD, my God, and done just as you have commanded me.[s] [15]Look down, then, from heaven, your holy abode, and bless your people Israel and the fields you have given us, as you promised on oath to our ancestors, a land flowing with milk and honey."[t]

**The Covenant.** [16]*This day the LORD, your God, is commanding you to observe these statutes and ordinances. Be careful, then, to observe them with your whole heart and with your whole being. [17]Today you have accepted the LORD's agreement: he will be your God, and you will walk in his ways, observe his statutes, commandments, and ordinances, and obey his voice. [18]And today the LORD has accepted your agreement: you will be a people specially his own, as he promised you, you will keep all his commandments, [19]and he will set you high in praise and renown and glory above all nations he has made, and you will be a people holy to the LORD, your God, as he promised.

# CHAPTER 27

**The Altar on Mount Ebal.** [1]Then Moses, with the elders of Israel, commanded the people,

saying: Keep this whole commandment which I give you today. [2]On the day you cross the Jordan into the land which the LORD, your God, is giving you, set up some large stones and coat them with plaster. [3]Write on them,[v] at the time you cross, all the words of this law, so that you may enter the land which the LORD, your God, is giving you, a land flowing with milk and honey, just as the LORD, the God of your ancestors, promised you. [4]When you cross the Jordan, on Mount Ebal you shall set up these stones concerning which I command you today, and coat them with plaster, [5w]and you shall build there an altar to the LORD, your God, an altar made of stones that no iron tool has touched. [6]You shall build this altar of the LORD, your God, with unhewn stones, and shall offer on it burnt offerings to the LORD, your God. [7]You shall also offer communion sacrifices[†] and eat them there, rejoicing in the presence of the LORD, your God. [8]On the stones you shall inscribe all the words of this law very clearly.

[9]Moses, with the levitical priests, then said to all Israel: Be silent, Israel, and listen! This day you have become the people of the LORD, your God.[x] [10]You shall obey the voice of the LORD, your God, and keep his commandments and statutes which I am giving you today.

**Preparation for Blessings and Curses.** [11]That same day Moses commanded the people, saying: [12y]When you cross the Jordan, these shall stand on Mount Gerizim to bless the people: Simeon, Levi, Judah, Issachar, Joseph and Benjamin. [13]And these shall stand on Mount Ebal for the curse: Reuben, Gad, Asher, Zebulun, Dan and Naphtali.

**The Twelve Curses.** [14]The Levites shall proclaim in a loud voice to all the Israelites: [15‡]"Cursed be anyone who makes a carved or molten idol,[z] an abomination to the LORD, the work of a craftsman's hands, and sets it up in secret!" And all the people shall answer, "Amen!"

[16]"Cursed be anyone who dishonors father or mother!"[a] And all the people shall answer, "Amen!"

[17]"Cursed be anyone who moves a neighbor's boundary markers!"[b] And all the people shall answer, "Amen!"

---

†[27:7] **Communion sacrifices:** The principal feature of this ritual (see Lv 3:1–17) is the sharing of the sacrifice with God, the priest and the person offering the sacrifice, who eat it as a holy thing (cf. Ex 24:5).

‡[27:15–26] The ceremony described here reflects the structure of covenant. The people assent to the directives their covenant Lord sets forth; their "Amen" ratifies the proscription of idolatry, injustice, incest, murder, and infidelity in general. Thus the "love" of the Lord which is at the heart of Israel's existence as his covenant people (6:4–5) is spelled out in terms of particular actions. The "Amen" is an acceptance of the curses or sanctions entailed by breaking faith with the Lord. Cf. 30:15–20, a concise statement of covenant theology.

---

*[26:14] These are allusions to foreign religious practices. **To the dead:** to feed the spirits of the dead, or perhaps to worship Baal.

---

o. [26:8] Dt 4:34; 6:21–22; Ex 12:51.    p. [26:9] Ex 3:8.    q. [26:11] Dt 12:7, 12.    r. [26:12] Dt 14:28–29.    s. [26:14] Dt 14:1; Lv 11:24–25; 22:3; Jer 16:7.    t. [26:15] 1 Kgs 8:39, 43, 49; Ps 102:19.    u. [26:16–19] Dt 7:6; 8:6; 10:12–13; 11:22; 14:2; 27:9; 28:1, 9; 29:12–13; Ex 6:7; 19:5–6; 24:7; Lv 26:12; 2 Sm 7:24; Jer 7:23; 31:33; Ez 11:20; Hos 2:23.

v. [27:3] Jos 8:32.    w. [27:5–7] Ex 20:24–25; Jos 8:30–31.    x. [27:9] Dt 26:17–19.    y. [27:12–13] Dt 11:26–29; Jos 8:33–35.    z. [27:15] Dt 4:15–20; 5:8–9; Ex 20:4, 23; 34:17; Lv 19:4; 26:1; Ps 115:4–8; Wis 14:8.    a. [27:16] Dt 5:16; 21:18–21; Ex 20:12; 21:17; Lv 20:9.    b. [27:17] Dt 19:14.

<sup>18</sup>"Cursed be anyone who misleads the blind on their way!"<sup>c</sup> And all the people shall answer, "Amen!"

<sup>19</sup>"Cursed be anyone who deprives the resident alien, the orphan or the widow of justice!"<sup>d</sup> And all the people shall answer, "Amen!"

<sup>20</sup>"Cursed be anyone who has relations with his father's wife, for he dishonors his father's bed!"<sup>e</sup> And all the people shall answer, "Amen!"

<sup>21</sup>"Cursed be anyone who has relations with any animal!"<sup>f</sup> And all the people shall answer, "Amen!"

<sup>22</sup>"Cursed be anyone who has relations with his sister, whether his father's daughter or his mother's daughter!"<sup>g</sup> And all the people shall answer, "Amen!"

<sup>23</sup>"Cursed be anyone who has relations with his mother-in-law!"<sup>h</sup> And all the people shall answer, "Amen!"

<sup>24</sup>"Cursed be anyone who strikes down a neighbor in secret!"<sup>i</sup> And all the people shall answer, "Amen!"

<sup>25</sup>"Cursed be anyone who accepts payment to kill an innocent person!"<sup>j</sup> And all the people shall answer, "Amen!"

<sup>26</sup>"Cursed be anyone whose actions do not uphold the words of this law!"<sup>k</sup> And all the people shall answer, "Amen!"

## CHAPTER 28

**Blessings for Obedience.** <sup>1</sup>Now,<sup>lm</sup> if you diligently obey the voice of the LORD, your God, carefully observing all his commandments which I give you today, the LORD, your God, will set you high above all the nations of the earth.<sup>n</sup> <sup>2</sup>All these blessings will come upon you and overwhelm you when you obey the voice of the LORD, your God:

<sup>3</sup>   <sup>o</sup>May you be blessed in the city,
        and blessed in the country!

<sup>4</sup>   Blessed be the fruit of your womb,
        the produce of your soil and the
            offspring of your livestock,
        the issue of your herds and the
            young of your flocks!<sup>p</sup>

<sup>5</sup>   Blessed be your grain basket and your
        kneading bowl!

<sup>6</sup>   May you be blessed in your coming in,
        and blessed in your going out!*<sup>q</sup>

**Victory and Prosperity.** <sup>7</sup>The LORD will beat down before you the enemies that rise up against you; they will come out against you from one direction, and flee before you in seven.†<sup>r</sup> <sup>8</sup>The LORD will affirm the blessing upon you, on your barns and on all your undertakings; he will bless you in the land that the LORD, your God, is giving you. <sup>9</sup>The LORD will establish you as a holy people, as he swore to you,<sup>s</sup> if you keep the commandments of the LORD, your God, and walk in his ways. <sup>10</sup>All the peoples of the earth will see that the name of the LORD is proclaimed over you,‡ and they will be afraid of you.<sup>t</sup> <sup>11</sup>The LORD will generously increase the fruit of your womb, the offspring of your livestock, and the produce of your soil, upon the land which the LORD swore to your ancestors he would give you.<sup>u</sup> <sup>12</sup>The LORD will open up for you his rich storehouse, the heavens, to give your land rain in due season and to bless all the works of your hands. You will lend to many nations but borrow from none.<sup>v</sup> <sup>13</sup>The LORD will make you the head not the tail, the top not the bottom, if you obey the commandments of the LORD, your God, which I am giving you today, observing them carefully, <sup>14</sup>not turning aside, either to the right or to the left, from any of the words which I am giving you today, following other gods and serving them.<sup>w</sup>

**Curses for Disobedience.** <sup>15</sup>But if you do not obey the voice of the LORD, your God,<sup>x</sup> carefully observing all his commandments and statutes which I give you today, all these curses shall come upon you and overwhelm you:

<sup>16y</sup>May you be cursed in the city, and cursed in the country! <sup>17</sup>Cursed be your grain basket and your kneading bowl! <sup>18</sup>Cursed be the fruit of your womb, the produce of your soil and the offspring of your livestock, the issue of your herds and the young of your flocks! <sup>19</sup>May you be cursed in your coming in, and cursed in your going out!

**Sickness and Defeat.** <sup>20</sup>The LORD will send on you a curse, panic, and frustration in everything you set your hand to, until you are speedily destroyed and perish for the evil you have done in forsaking me. <sup>21z</sup>The LORD will make disease cling to you until he has made an end of you from the land you are entering to possess. <sup>22</sup>The LORD will strike you with consumption, fever, and inflammation, with fiery heat and drought, with blight and mildew, that will pursue you

---

*[28:6] **In your coming in . . . in your going out:** at the beginning and end of every action, or in all actions in general. The rhetorical figure is called merismus. See also 6:7.

†[28:7] **From one direction . . . in seven:** in one disciplined body, contrasted with many scattered groups.

‡[28:10] **The name of the LORD is proclaimed over you:** an expression signifying ownership and protection. Cf. 2 Sm 12:28; 1 Kgs 8:43; Is 4:1; 63:19; Jer 7:10–11; 14:9; 15:16; 25:29; Am 9:12.

c. [27:18] Lv 19:14.   d. [27:19] Dt 24:17–18; Ex 22:21–24; 23:9; Lv 19:33–34.   e. [27:20] Dt 23:1; Lv 18:7–8; 20:11.   f. [27:21] Ex 22:18; Lv 18:23; 20:15–16.   g. [27:22] Lv 18:9; 20:17.   h. [27:23] Lv 18:17; 20:14.   i. [27:24] Dt 5:17; 21:1; Ex 20:13; 21:12; Nm 35:20–21.   j. [27:25] Dt 16:19; Ex 23:7–8.   k. [27:26] Jer 11:3; Gal 3:10.   l. [28:1–68] Lv 26:3–45.   m. [28:1–14] Dt 7:12–16; 11:13–15.   n. [28:1] Dt 26:19; Ps 89:27; Is 55:3–5.   o. [28:3–6] Dt 28:16–19.   p. [28:4] Dt 7:13–14; 30:9; Ex 23:26; Lv 26:9.   q. [28:6] Ps 121:8.

r. [28:7] Dt 9:1–3; Ex 23:27–28; Lv 26:6–8.   s. [28:9] Dt 26:18–19; Ex 19:5–6.   t. [28:10] Dt 2:25; 11:25; Is 61:9.   u. [28:11] Dt 28:4.   v. [28:12] Dt 15:6.   w. [28:14] Dt 5:32.   x. [28:15] Bar 1:20; Dn 9:11; Mal 2:2.   y. [28:16–19] Dt 28:3–6.   z. [28:21–22] Lv 26:16, 25; Jer 14:12; Am 4:9–10; Hg 2:17.

until you perish. <sup>23</sup>The heavens over your heads will be like bronze and the earth under your feet like iron.<sup>a</sup> <sup>24</sup>For rain the LORD will give your land powdery dust, which will come down upon you from the heavens until you are destroyed. <sup>25</sup>The LORD will let you be beaten down before your enemies; though you advance against them from one direction, you will flee before them in seven,<sup>*</sup> so that you will become an object of horror to all the kingdoms of the earth.<sup>b</sup> <sup>26</sup>Your corpses will become food for all the birds of the air and for the beasts of the field, with no one to frighten them off.<sup>c</sup> <sup>27</sup>The LORD will strike you with Egyptian boils<sup>d</sup> and with tumors, skin diseases and the itch, from none of which you can be cured.<sup>f</sup> <sup>28e</sup>And the LORD will strike you with madness, blindness and panic, <sup>29</sup>so that even at midday you will grope in the dark as though blind, unable to find your way.

**Despoilment.** You will be oppressed and robbed continually, with no one to come to your aid. <sup>30</sup>Though you betroth a wife, another will have her. Though you build a house, you will not live in it. Though you plant a vineyard, you will not pluck its fruits.<sup>f</sup> <sup>31g</sup>Your ox will be slaughtered before your eyes, but you will not eat its flesh. Your donkey will be stolen in your presence, but you will never get it back. Your flocks will be given to your enemies, with no one to come to your aid. <sup>32</sup>Your sons and daughters will be given to another people while you strain your eyes looking for them every day, having no power to do anything. <sup>33</sup>A people you do not know will consume the fruit of your soil and of all your labor, and you will be thoroughly oppressed and continually crushed, <sup>34</sup>until you are driven mad by what your eyes must look upon. <sup>35</sup>The LORD will strike you with malignant boils of which you cannot be cured, on your knees and legs, and from the soles of your feet to the crown of your head.

**Exile.** <sup>36h</sup>The LORD will bring you, and your king whom you have set over you, to a nation which you and your ancestors have not known, and there you will serve other gods, of wood and stone, <sup>37</sup>and you will be a horror, a byword, a taunt among all the peoples to which the LORD will drive you.

**Fruitless Labors.** <sup>38i</sup>Though you take out seed to your field, you will harvest but little, for the locusts will devour it. <sup>39</sup>Though you plant and cultivate vineyards, you will not drink or store up the wine, for the worms will eat them. <sup>40</sup>Though you have olive trees throughout your country, you will have no oil for ointment, for your olives will drop off. <sup>41</sup>Though you beget sons and daughters, they will not remain with you, for they will go into captivity. <sup>42</sup>Buzzing insects will take possession of all your trees and the crops of your soil. <sup>43j</sup>The resident aliens among you will rise above you higher and higher, while you sink lower and lower. <sup>44</sup>They will lend to you, not you to them. They will become the head, you the tail.

<sup>45</sup>All these curses will come upon you, pursuing you and overwhelming you, until you are destroyed, because you would not obey the voice of the LORD, your God, by keeping his commandments and statutes which he gave you.<sup>k</sup> <sup>46</sup>They will be a sign and a wonder<sup>†</sup> for you and your descendants for all time. <sup>47</sup>Since you would not serve the LORD, your God, with heartfelt joy for abundance of every kind, <sup>48</sup>in hunger and thirst, in nakedness and utter want, you will serve the enemies whom the LORD will send against you. He will put an iron yoke on your neck, until he destroys you.<sup>l</sup>

**Invasion and Siege.** <sup>49m</sup>The LORD will raise up against you a nation from afar, from the end of the earth, that swoops down like an eagle, a nation whose language you do not understand, <sup>50</sup>a nation of fierce appearance, that shows neither respect for the aged nor mercy for the young. <sup>51</sup>They will consume the offspring of your livestock and the produce of your soil, until you are destroyed; they will leave you no grain or wine or oil, no issue of herd, no young of flock, until they have brought about your ruin. <sup>52</sup>They will besiege you in each of your communities, until the great, fortified walls, in which you trust, come tumbling down all over your land. They will besiege you in every community throughout the land which the LORD, your God, has given you, <sup>53n</sup>and because of the siege and the distress to which your enemy subjects you, you will eat the fruit of your womb, the flesh of your own sons and daughters whom the LORD, your God, has given you. <sup>54</sup>The most refined and fastidious man among you will begrudge his brother and his beloved wife and his surviving children, <sup>55</sup>any share in the flesh of his children that he himself is using for food because nothing else is left him—such the siege and distress to which your enemy will subject you in all your communities. <sup>56</sup>The most fastidious woman among you, who would not venture to set the sole of her foot on the ground, so refined and fastidious is she, will begrudge her beloved husband and her son and daughter <sup>57</sup>the afterbirth that issues from her womb and the infants she brings forth because she secretly eats them for want of anything else—such the siege and

---

<sup>*</sup>[28:25] **From one direction . . . in seven:** see note on v. 7.

a. [28:23] Lv 26:19.  b. [28:25] Dt 1:44; 28:7; Lv 26:17, 37.  c. [28:26] Ps 79:2; Jer 7:33; 34:20.  d. [28:27] Dt 7:15; 28:60; Ex 9:8–12.  e. [28:28–29] Is 59:10.  f. [28:30] Dt 20:5–7; Am 5:11.  g. [28:31–34] Jer 5:17; Lam 5:1–18; Am 7:17.  h. [28:36–37] Dt 4:27–28; 1 Kgs 9:6–9; 2 Kgs 25:6–7, 11; 2 Chr 7:19–22; 33:11; 36:6, 20; Jer 16:13; 24:8–9; 25:8–11; Ez 17:12.  i. [28:38–42] Dt 28:18; Lv 26:20; Lam 1:5; Mi 6:15; Zep 1:13; Hg 1:6.

<sup>†</sup>[28:46] **A sign and a wonder:** an ominous example, attracting attention; cf. 29:21–28.

j. [28:43–44] Dt 15:6; 28:12–13.  k. [28:45] Dt 28:15.  l. [28:48] Jer 28:14.  m. [28:49–52] Jer 5:15–17; 6:22–26; Bar 4:15–16.  n. [28:53–57] Lv 26:29; 2 Kgs 6:28–29; Jer 19:9; Lam 2:20; 4:10; Bar 2:3.

distress to which your enemy will subject you in your communities.

**Plagues.** [58]If you are not careful to observe all the words of this law which is written in this book, and to fear this glorious and awesome name, the LORD, your God,[o] [59p]the LORD will bring upon you and your descendants wondrous calamities, severe and constant calamities, and malignant and constant sicknesses. [60]He will bring back upon you all the diseases of Egypt* which you dread, and they will cling to you. [61]Even any sickness or calamity not written in this book of the law, that too the LORD will bring upon you until you are destroyed. [62]You who were numerous as the stars of the heavens[q] will be left few in number, because you would not obey the voice of the LORD, your God.

**Exile.** [63r]Just as the LORD once took delight in making you prosper and grow, so will the LORD now take delight in ruining and destroying you, and you will be plucked out of the land you are now entering to possess. [64]The LORD will scatter you among all the peoples from one end of the earth to the other, and there you will serve other gods, of wood and stone, which you and your ancestors have not known. [65]Among these nations you will find no rest, not even a resting place for the sole of your foot, for there the LORD will give you an anguished heart and wearied eyes[†] and a trembling spirit. [66]Your life will hang in suspense and you will stand in dread both day and night, never sure of your life. [67]In the morning you will say, "Would that it were evening!" and in the evening you will say, "Would that it were morning!" because of the dread that your heart must feel and the sight that your eyes must see. [68]The LORD will send you back in ships to Egypt, by a route which I told you that you would never see again;[s] and there you will offer yourselves for sale to your enemies as male and female slaves, but there will be no buyer.

[69]These are the words of the covenant which the LORD commanded Moses to make with the Israelites in the land of Moab, in addition to the covenant he made with them at Horeb.

## III. THIRD ADDRESS

### CHAPTER 29

**Past Favors Recalled.** [1]Moses summoned all Israel and said to them, You have seen with your own eyes all that the LORD did in the land of Egypt to Pharaoh and all his servants and to all his land, [2]the great testings your own eyes have

seen, and those great signs and wonders.[t] [3]But the LORD has not given you a heart to understand, or eyes to see, or ears to hear until this day.[u] [4v]I led you for forty years in the wilderness. Your clothes did not fall from you in tatters nor your sandals from your feet; [5]it was not bread that you ate, nor wine or beer that you drank—so that you might know that I, the LORD, am your God. [6w]When you came to this place, Sihon, king of Heshbon, and Og, king of Bashan, came out to engage us in battle, but we defeated them [7]and took their land, and gave it as a heritage to the Reubenites, Gadites, and the half-tribe of Manasseh.[x] [8]Observe carefully the words of this covenant, therefore, in order that you may succeed in whatever you do.[y]

**All Israel Bound by Covenant.** [9]You are standing today, all of you, in the presence of the LORD, your God—your tribal heads, elders, and officials, all of the men of Israel, [10]your children, your wives, and the resident alien who lives in your camp, from those who cut wood to those who draw water for you— [11]to enter into the covenant of the LORD, your God, which the LORD, your God, is making with you today, with its curse, [12]so that he may establish you today as his people and he may be your God, as he promised you and as he swore to your ancestors, to Abraham, Isaac and Jacob. [13z]But it is not with you alone that I am making this covenant, with its curse, [14]but with those who are standing here with us today in the presence of the LORD, our God, and with those who are not here with us[‡] today.

**Warning Against Idolatry.** [15]You know that we lived in the land of Egypt and that we passed through the nations, that you too passed through [16]and saw the loathsome things and idols of wood and stone, of gold and silver, that they possess. [17]There may be among you a man or woman, or a clan or tribe, whose heart is now turning away from the LORD, our God, to go and serve the gods of these nations; there may be among you a root bearing poison and wormwood; [18]if any such persons, after hearing the words of this curse, should congratulate themselves, saying in their hearts, "I am safe, even though I walk in stubbornness of heart," thereby sweeping away moist and dry alike,[§a] [19]the LORD will never consent to pardon them. Instead, the LORD's burning wrath will flare up against them; every curse written in this book will pounce on

---

*[28:60] **He will bring back upon you all the diseases of Egypt:** such as the Lord had promised to remove from the people (7:15); cf. v. 27.
†[28:65] **Wearied eyes:** cf. v. 32.

‡[29:14] **Not here with us:** this includes future generations. This attitude appears also in 5:3.
§[29:18] **Sweeping away moist and dry alike:** possibly a proverbial expression: because of Israel's infidelity the Lord will punish the just with the wicked (cf. Gn 18:25), rooting out good plants in irrigated soil, together with worthless plants growing in dry ground.

o. [28:58] Dt 6:13; Jos 24:14.   p. [28:59–61] Dt 7:15; 28:21–22, 27.   q. [28:62] Dt 1:10; 10:22; 26:5; Jer 42:2.   r. [28:63–67] Dt 4:26–28; 30:9; Lv 26:33–39.   s. [28:68] Jer 42–44; Hos 8:13; 9:3; 6; 11:5.

t. [29:1–2] Dt 4:34, 37–38; 6:21–23; 7:19; 26:5–9.   u. [29:3] Is 6:9–10; Jer 5:21; Ez 12:2; Mt 13:14–15; Mk 4:12; Lk 8:10; Jn 12:40; Acts 28:26–27.   v. [29:4–5] Dt 8:2–4.   w. [29:6] Dt 1:4; 2:31–33; 3:1–3; Nm 21:23–24, 33–35.   x. [29:7] Dt 3:16–17; Nm 32:33.   y. [29:8] Jos 1:7–8; 1 Kgs 2:3.   z. [29:13–14] Dt 5:3.   a. [29:18] Jer 7:10.

them, and the LORD will blot out their names from under the heavens.[b] [20]The LORD will single them out from all the tribes of Israel for doom, in keeping with all the curses of the covenant written in this book of the law.

**Punishment for Idolatry.** [21c]Future generations, your descendants who will rise up after you, as well as the foreigners who will come here from distant lands, when they see the calamities of this land and the ills the LORD has inflicted upon it— [22]all its soil burned out by sulphur and salt, unsown and unfruitful, without a blade of grass, like the catastrophe of Sodom and Gomorrah,[d] Admah and Zeboiim,* which the LORD overthrew in his furious wrath— [23e]they and all the nations will ask, "Why has the LORD dealt thus with this land? Why this great outburst of wrath?" [24]And they will say, "Because they abandoned the covenant of the LORD, the God of their ancestors, which he had made with them when he brought them out of the land of Egypt, [25]and they went and served other gods and bowed down to them, gods whom they did not know and whom he had not apportioned to them.[f] [26g]So the anger of the LORD flared up against this land and brought on it every curse written in this book. [27]The LORD uprooted them from their soil in anger, fury, and great wrath, and cast them out into another land, as they are today." [28]The hidden things[†] belong to the LORD our God, but the revealed things are for us and for our children forever, to observe all the words of this law.

## CHAPTER 30

**Compassion for the Repentant.** [1‡h]When all these things, the blessing and the curse which I have set before you, come upon you,[i] and you take them to heart in any of the nations where the LORD, your God, has dispersed you, [2j]and return to the LORD, your God, obeying his voice, according to all that I am commanding you today, you and your children, with your whole heart and your whole being, [3]the LORD, your God, will restore your fortunes and will have compassion on you; he will again gather you from all the peoples where the LORD, your God, has scattered you. [4]Though you may have been

dispersed to the farthest corner of the heavens, even from there will the LORD, your God, gather you; even from there will he bring you back.[k] [5]The LORD, your God, will then bring you into the land your ancestors once possessed, that you may possess it; and he will make you more prosperous and numerous than your ancestors.[l] [6]The LORD, your God, will circumcise your hearts[§] and the hearts of your descendants,[m] so that you will love the LORD, your God, with your whole heart and your whole being, in order that you may live. [7]The LORD, your God, will put all those curses on your enemies and the foes who pursued you.[n] [8]You, however, shall again obey the voice of the LORD and observe all his commandments which I am giving you today. [9]Then the LORD, your God, will generously increase your undertakings, the fruit of your womb, the offspring of your livestock, and the produce of your soil;[o] for the LORD, your God, will again take delight in your prosperity, just as he took delight in your ancestors', [10]because you will obey the voice of the LORD, your God, keeping the commandments and statutes that are written in this book of the law, when you return to the LORD, your God, with your whole heart and your whole being.

[11p]For this command which I am giving you today is not too wondrous or remote for you. [12]It is not in the heavens, that you should say, "Who will go up to the heavens to get it for us and tell us of it, that we may do it?" [13]Nor is it across the sea, that you should say, "Who will cross the sea to get it for us and tell us of it, that we may do it?" [14]No, it is something very near to you, in your mouth[¶] and in your heart, to do it.

**The Choice Before Israel.** [15]See, I have today set before you life and good, death and evil.[q] [16]If you obey the commandments of the LORD, your God, which I am giving you today, loving the LORD, your God, and walking in his ways, and keeping his commandments, statutes and ordinances, you will live and grow numerous, and the LORD, your God, will bless you in the land you are entering to possess.[r] [17s]If, however, your heart turns away and you do not obey, but are led astray and bow down to other gods and serve them, [18]I tell you today that you will certainly perish; you will not have a long life on the land which you are crossing the Jordan to enter and possess. [19]I call heaven and earth today to witness against you:[t] I have set before you life and death, the blessing and the curse. Choose

---

*[29:22] **Admah and Zeboiim**: neighboring cities of Sodom and Gomorrah in the Jordan Plain and identified in the tradition as destroyed with them. Cf. Hos 11:8; Jer 50:40.

†[29:28] **The hidden things**: probably the events of the future. **The revealed things**: the covenant and its provisions, including the sanctions of blessing and curse. This aphorism may mean: leave "hidden things" to God; what matters is to keep the law.

‡[30:1–5] Text such as this suggests a postexilic perspective; cf. also chaps. 31–32.

§[30:6] **Circumcise your hearts**: see note on 10:16.

¶[30:14] **In your mouth**: that is, memorized and recited; cf. 6:7; 11:19. **And in your heart**: internalized and appropriated; cf. 6:6; 11:18.

---

b. [29:19] Dt 9:14; 25:19.   c. [29:21–27] Dt 4:25–28.   d. [29:22] Gn 19:24–25; Hos 11:8.   e. [29:23–24] 1 Kgs 9:8–9; Jer 5:19; 9:12–16; 16:10–13; 22:8–9.   f. [29:25] Dt 4:19; 32:8–9.   g. [29:26–27] Dt 29:20–21; Dn 9:11–14.   h. [30:1–10] Dt 4:29–31; Lv 26:40–45. i. [30:1] Dt 11:26–28; 27:11–28:69.   j. [30:2–3] Dt 4:29–30; 6:5; 30:10; 1 Kgs 8:47–48; Jer 24:7; 29:14; 33:26; Ez 39:25; Am 9:14; Zep 3:20.

k. [30:4] Neh 1:9; Is 43:5–7; Jer 31:10; 32:37; Ez 36:24; 37:21. l. [30:5] Jer 23:3.   m. [30:6] Dt 6:5; 10:16; Ez 11:19–20; 36:26–28. n. [30:7] Dt 7:15.   o. [30:9] Dt 28:4, 11; 30:2.   p. [30:11–14] Dt 6:6; 11:18; Jer 1:9; Bar 3:29–31; Rom 10:6–8.   q. [30:15] Dt 11:26–28; Jer 21:8.   r. [30:16] Dt 4:1; 8:1; 11:22.   s. [30:17–18] Dt 5:7; 6:4; 8:19–20.   t. [30:19] Dt 4:26; 11:26–28; 28:2, 15; 31:28.

life, then, that you and your descendants may live, [20]by loving the LORD, your God, obeying his voice, and holding fast to him. For that will mean life for you, a long life for you to live on the land which the LORD swore to your ancestors, to Abraham, Isaac, and Jacob, to give to them.[u]

## CHAPTER 31

**The Lord's Leadership.** [1]When Moses had finished speaking these words to all Israel, [2]he said to them, I am now one hundred and twenty years old[v] and am no longer able to go out and come in; besides, the LORD has said to me, Do not cross this Jordan. [3]It is the LORD, your God, who will cross before you; he will destroy these nations before you, that you may dispossess them.[w] (It is Joshua who will cross before you, as the LORD promised.) [4]*The LORD* will deal with them just as he dealt with Sihon and Og, the kings of the Amorites, and with their country, when he destroyed them. [5]When, therefore, the LORD delivers them up to you, you shall deal with them according to the whole commandment which I have given you.[y] [6]Be strong and steadfast; have no fear or dread of them, for it is the LORD, your God, who marches with you; he will never fail you or forsake you.[z]

**Call of Joshua.** [7]Then Moses summoned Joshua and in the presence of all Israel said to him,[a] "Be strong and steadfast, for you shall bring this people into the land which the LORD swore to their ancestors he would give it; it is you who will give them possession of it. [8]It is the LORD who goes before you; he will be with you and will never fail you or forsake you. So do not fear or be dismayed."[b]

**The Reading of the Law.** [9]*When Moses had written down this law, he gave it to the levitical priests who carry the ark of the covenant of the LORD, and to all the elders of Israel.[d] [10]Moses commanded them, saying, On the feast of Booths,[e] at the prescribed time in the year for remission* which comes at the end of every seven-year period, [11]when all Israel goes to appear before the LORD, your God, in the place which he will choose, you shall read this law aloud in the presence of all Israel. [12]Assemble the people—men, women and children, as well as the resident aliens who live in your communities—that they may hear and so learn to fear the LORD, your God, and to observe carefully all the words of this law. [13]Their children also, who do not know it yet, shall hear and learn to fear the LORD, your God, as long as you live on

the land which you are about to cross the Jordan to possess.

**Commission to Joshua.** [14]*The LORD said to Moses, The time is now approaching for you to die. Summon Joshua, and present yourselves at the tent of meeting that I may commission him. So Moses and Joshua went and presented themselves at the tent of meeting. [15]And the LORD appeared at the tent in a column of cloud; the column of cloud stood at the entrance of the tent.

**A Command to Moses.** [16]The LORD said to Moses, Soon you will be at rest with your ancestors, and then this people will prostitute themselves[†] by following the foreign gods among whom they will live in the land they are about to enter.[g] They will forsake me and break the covenant which I have made with them. [17h]At that time my anger will flare up against them; I will forsake them and hide my face from them; they will become a prey to be devoured, and much evil and distress will befall them. At that time they will indeed say, "Is it not because our God is not in our midst that these evils have befallen us?" [18]Yet I will surely hide my face at that time because of all the evil they have done in turning to other gods. [19]Now, write out this song[i] for yourselves. Teach it to the Israelites and have them recite it, so that this song may be a witness for me against the Israelites. [20]For when I have brought them into the land flowing with milk and honey which I promised on oath to their ancestors, and they have eaten and are satisfied and have grown fat, if they turn to other gods and serve them, despising me and breaking my covenant, [21]then, when great evil and distress befall them, this song will speak to them as a witness, for it will not be forgotten if their descendants recite it. For I know what they are inclined to do even at the present time, before I have brought them into the land which I promised on oath. [22]So Moses wrote this song that same day, and he taught it to the Israelites.

**Commission of Joshua.** [23]Then he commissioned Joshua, son of Nun, and said to him, Be strong and steadfast, for it is you who will bring the Israelites into the land which I promised them on oath.[j] I myself will be with you.

**The Law Placed in the Ark.** [24]When Moses had finished writing out on a scroll the words of this law in their entirety, [25]Moses gave the Levites[k] who carry the ark of the covenant of the LORD this order: [26]Take this book of the law and put it beside the ark of the covenant of the LORD, your God, that there it may be a witness against

---

*[31:10] **The year for remission:** cf. 15:1–3 and note there.

u. [30:20] Dt 1:8; 4:1, 40.   v. [31:2] Dt 1:37; 3:23–28; 4:21–24; 34:7; Gn 6:3; Ex 7:7; Nm 20:12; Acts 7:23, 30.   w. [31:3] Dt 1:30–33; 3:22, 28; 9:3.   x. [31:4] Dt 2:26–3:7; 3:21–22; Nm 21:21–35.   y. [31:5] Dt 7:1–5; 20:16–18.   z. [31:6] Dt 1:29; 20:3–4.   a. [31:7–8] Dt 1:21; 31:23; Jos 1:6–9; 10:25.   b. [31:8] Ex 3:12; Jos 1:5, 17; 3:7; 2 Sm 7:9.   c. [31:9–13] Dt 31:24–27.   d. [31:9] Dt 10:1–5, 8.   e. [31:10–12] Dt 12:5; 15:1–11; 16:13–15; 2 Kgs 23:2; Neh 8:1–8.

†[31:16] **Prostitute themselves:** lit., "whore after," a play on the phrase "go after," viz. after other gods.

f. [31:14–15] Ex 33:7–11; Nm 12:5.   g. [31:16] Dt 32:16–17; Ex 34:15–16; Jgs 2:11–23; 8:27, 33; 1 Kgs 11:1–10; 2 Kgs 17:7–41; Jer 11:9–10; Hos 4:12; 9:1.   h. [31:17–18] Dt 1:42; 32:19–25; Nm 14:42.   i. [31:19] Dt 6:6–9; 31:21; 32:1–43.   j. [31:23] Dt 3:7–8; Nm 27:15–23; Jos 1:1–9.   k. [31:24–25] Dt 31:9.

you.[l] [27]For I already know how rebellious and stiff-necked you will be. Why, even now, while I am alive among you, you have been rebels against the LORD! How much more, then, after I am dead![m] [28n]Assemble all your tribal elders and your officials before me, that I may speak these words for them to hear and so may call heaven and earth to witness against them. [29o]For I know that after my death you are sure to act corruptly and to turn aside from the way along which I commanded you, so that evil will befall you in time to come because you have done what is evil in the LORD's sight, and provoked him by your deeds.
**The Song of Moses.** [30]Then Moses recited the words of this song in their entirety, for the whole assembly of Israel to hear:

## CHAPTER 32

[1]    'Give ear, O heavens, and let me speak;
         let the earth hear the words of my
             mouth![p]
[2]    May my teaching soak in like the rain,
         and my utterance drench like the
             dew,
       Like a downpour upon the grass,
         like a shower upon the crops.
[3]    For I will proclaim the name of the LORD,
         praise the greatness of our God!

[4]    The Rock—how faultless are his deeds,
         how right all his ways!
       A faithful God, without deceit,
         just and upright is he![q]

[5]    Yet his degenerate children have treated
             him basely,
         a twisted and crooked generation![r]
[6]    Is this how you repay the LORD,
         so foolish and unwise a people?
       Is he not your father who begot you,
         the one who made and established
             you?[s]

[7]    Remember the days of old,
         consider the years of generations
             past.
       Ask your father, he will inform you,
         your elders, they will tell you:[t]

[8]    When the Most High allotted each nation
             its heritage,
         when he separated out human
             beings,[u]
       He set up the boundaries of the peoples
         after the number of the divine
             beings;[†]
[9]    But the LORD's portion was his people;
         his allotted share was Jacob.[v]

[10]   He found them in a wilderness,
         a wasteland of howling desert.
       He shielded them, cared for them,
         guarded them as the apple of his eye.[w]
[11]   As an eagle incites its nestlings,
         hovering over its young,
       So he spread his wings, took them,
         bore them upon his pinions.[x]
[12]   The LORD alone guided them,
         no foreign god was with them.[y]

[13]   [z]He had them mount the summits of the
             land,[‡]
         fed them the produce of its fields;
       He suckled them with honey from the
             crags
         and olive oil from the flinty rock;
[14]   Butter from cows and milk from sheep,
         with the best of lambs;
       Bashan[§] bulls and goats,
         with the cream of finest wheat;
         and the foaming blood of grapes you
             drank.

[15]   So Jacob ate and was satisfied,
         Jeshurun[¶] grew fat and kicked;
         you became fat and gross and gorged.
       They forsook the God who made them
         and scorned the Rock of their
             salvation.[a]
[16]   With strange gods they incited him,
         with abominations provoked him
             to anger.[b]
[17]   They sacrificed to demons, to "no-gods,"
         to gods they had never known,
       Newcomers from afar,
         before whom your ancestors had
             never trembled.

---

[†][32:8] **Divine beings:** lit., "sons of God" (see also v. 43); members of the divine assembly; cf. 1 Kgs 22:19; Jb 1:6; 2:1; 38:7; Ps 82; 89:6–7. The nations are portrayed as having their respective tutelary deities.
[‡][32:13] **The land:** Canaan.
[§][32:14] **Bashan:** a fertile grazing land east of the Jordan, famous for its sleek, strong cattle. Cf. Ps 22:13; Ez 39:18; Am 4:1.
[¶][32:15] **Jeshurun:** a term for Israel from *yashar*, meaning "upright"; its use here is possibly ironic.

---

*[32:1–43] The whole song is a poetic sermon, having for its theme the Lord's benefits to Israel (vv. 1–14) and Israel's ingratitude and idolatry in turning to the gods of the nations; these sins will be punished by the nations themselves (vv. 15–29); in turn, the foolish pride of the nations will be punished, and the Lord's honor will be vindicated (vv. 30–43).

---

.l. [31:26] Dt 10:1–5; Ex 40:20; 1 Kgs 8:9.    m. [31:27] Dt 9:6–7, 22–24.    n. [31:28] Dt 31:12–13, 19–22; 30:19; 32:1–43.    o. [31:29] Jgs 2:11–23.    p. [32:1] Dt 4:26; 30:19; 31:28.    q. [32:4] Dt 7:9; 32:15, 18, 30–31; 2 Sm 22:3; Ps 18:2, 31, 46; 92:15; Is 17:10; Hb 1:12; Rev 15:3.    r. [32:5] Dt 9:12; 14:1; 31:29; Ps 78:8; Is 1:2–4; Lk 9:41.    s. [32:6] Ex 4:22–23; Is 63:16; 64:8; Jer 31:9; Hos 11:1–4.    t. [32:7] Dt 4:32–34.

u. [32:8] Gn 14:18–22; Nm 24:16; Jb 1:6; 2:1; Ps 29:1; 47:2; 82:6; 83:18; 89:5–7; Is 14:14; Acts 17:26.    v. [32:9] Dt 7:6; Ex 19:5–6; Ps 33:12; Sir 17:17; Jer 10:16; Zec 2:16.    w. [32:10] Dt 1:31; 2:7; 8:15; Ps 17:8; Prv 7:2; Jer 2:2–3, 6; Hos 2:15; 13:5–6; Zec 2:12.    x. [32:11] Ex 19:4.    y. [32:12] Ex 15:13; Is 43:12; Hos 13:4.    z. [32:13–14] Dt 8:7–10; Ps 81:16.    a. [32:15] Dt 8:12–18; 31:20; 33:5, 26; Neh 9:25; Is 44:2.    b. [32:16–17] Dt 31:16; Ps 78:58; 81:9; 106:34–39.

18 You were unmindful of the Rock that
        begot you,
    you forgot the God who gave you
        birth.<sup>c</sup>

19 The LORD saw and was filled with
        loathing,
    provoked by his sons and
        daughters.<sup>d</sup>
20 He said, I will hide my face from them,
        and see what becomes of them.
    For they are a fickle generation,
        children with no loyalty in them!<sup>e</sup>
21 Since they have incited me with a
        "no-god,"
        and provoked me with their empty
            idols,
    I will incite them with a "no-people";*
        with a foolish nation I will provoke
            them.<sup>f</sup>
22 For by my wrath a fire is kindled
        that has raged to the depths of Sheol,
    It has consumed the earth with its yield,
        and set on fire the foundations of
            the mountains.<sup>g</sup>
23 I will heap evils upon them
        and exhaust all my arrows against
            them:<sup>h</sup>
24 Emaciating hunger and consuming fever
        and bitter pestilence,
    And the teeth of wild beasts I will send
        among them,
        with the venom of reptiles gliding in
            the dust.<sup>i</sup>
25 Out in the street the sword shall bereave,
        and at home the terror
    For the young man and the young woman
        alike,
        the nursing babe as well as the gray
            beard.<sup>j</sup>
26 I said: I will make an end of them
        and blot out their name from human
            memory,
27 Had I not feared the provocation by the
        enemy,
        that their foes might misunderstand,
    And say, "Our own hand won the victory;
        the LORD had nothing to do with
            any of it."<sup>k</sup>

28 For they are a nation devoid of reason,†
        having no understanding.
29 If they had insight they would realize
        this,
        they would understand their end:
30 "How could one rout a thousand,
        or two put ten thousand to flight,
    Unless it was because their Rock sold
        them,
        the LORD delivered them up?"

31 Indeed, their "rock" is not like our Rock;
        our enemies are fools.
32 For their vine is from the vine of Sodom,
        from the vineyards of Gomorrah.
    Their grapes are grapes of poison,
        and their clusters are bitter.<sup>l</sup>
33 Their wine is the venom of serpents,
        the cruel poison of vipers.
34 Is not this stored up with me,
        sealed up in my storehouses?
35 Vengeance is mine and recompense,
        for the time they lose their footing;
    Because the day of their disaster is at hand
        and their doom is rushing upon
            them!<sup>m</sup>

36 Surely, the LORD will do justice for his
        people;
        on his servants he will have pity.
    When he sees their strength is gone,
        and neither bond nor free‡ is left,<sup>n</sup>
37 He will say, Where are their gods,<sup>o</sup>
        the rock in whom they took refuge,
38 Who ate the fat of their sacrifices
        and drank the wine of their
            libations?
    Let them rise up now and help you!
        Let them be your protection!
39 See now that I, I alone, am he,
        and there is no god besides me.
    It is I who bring both death and life,
        I who inflict wounds and heal them,
        and from my hand no one can
            deliver.<sup>p</sup>
40 For I raise my hand to the heavens
        and will say: As surely as I live
            forever,
41 When I sharpen my flashing sword,
        and my hand lays hold of judgment,
    With vengeance I will repay my foes
        and requite those who hate me.<sup>q</sup>
42 I will make my arrows drunk with
        blood,
        and my sword shall devour flesh—

---

*[32:21] **"No-god"** . . . **"no-people"**: worship of the gods
of the nations brings destruction at the hands of a foreign
invader. A false god cannot sustain or protect (cf. Jer 14:22);
and though the nations seem "foolish" (see their characterization in such passages as Ps 114:1; Is 28:11; 33:19), they will
prove to be anything but nonentities when the Lord stirs them
up against Israel (Is 9:10–12). For the "no-" or "not-" construction, see Hos 1:6, 9; 2:1, 25.

†[32:28–35] The reference is to the nations, not to Israel.
‡[32:36] **Neither bond nor free**: an all-inclusive expression; cf. 1 Kgs 14:10; 2 Kgs 9:8.

c. [32:18] Is 49:15; Jer 2:32.  d. [32:19] Dt 4:24.  e. [32:20] Dt
31:17–18; Nm 6:25–26.  f. [32:21] Dt 28:49–50; Jgs 2:14–15; Is
9:11–12; Rom 10:19.  g. [32:22] Dt 4:24; Ps 18:7–8; 50:3; Lam
4:11.  h. [32:23] Dt 32:42; Ps 7:12–13; 18:14; Ez 5:16.  i. [32:24]
Dt 28:21–22.  j. [32:25] Lv 26:25; Jer 6:11; Lam 1:20; 2:21; Ez 7:15.
k. [32:27] Dt 9:26–29; Ex 32:11–14; Ps 74:18.

l. [32:32] Dt 29:23.  m. [32:35] Ps 94:1; Is 59:18; 61:2; Hos 9:7.
n. [32:36] 2 Mc 7:6; Ps 9:8; 135:14.  o. [32:37–38] Jgs 10:14; 1 Kgs
18:27; Jer 2:28.  p. [32:39] Dt 4:35; 6:4; 1 Sm 2:6–8; Tb 13:2; Jb 5:18;
Wis 16:13; Is 30:26; 43:10–13; 44:6; Hos 6:1–2.  q. [32:41] Is 1:24;
Na 1:2.

With the blood of the slain and the
        captured,
    from the long-haired heads of the
        enemy.

43  Exult with him, you heavens,
        bow to him, all you divine beings!
    For he will avenge the blood of his
        servants,
        take vengeance on his foes;
    He will requite those who hate him,
        and purge his people's land.[r]

44So Moses, together with Hoshea,* son of
Nun, went and spoke all the words of this song
in the hearing of the people.[s]
**Final Appeal.** 45When Moses had finished
speaking all these words to all Israel, 46he said
to them,[t] Take to heart all the words that I am
giving in witness against you today, words you
should command your children, that they may
observe carefully every word of this law. 47For
this is no trivial matter for you, but rather your
very life; by this word you will enjoy a long life on
the land you are crossing the Jordan to possess.[u]
**Moses Looks upon Canaan.** 48On that very
day the LORD said to Moses, 49Ascend this
mountain of the Abarim,† Mount Nebo in the
land of Moab facing Jericho, and view the land
of Canaan, which I am giving to the Israelites
as a possession.[v] 50Then you shall die on the
mountain you are about to ascend, and shall
be gathered to your people, just as your brother
Aaron died on Mount Hor‡ and there was gathered to his people,[w] 51because both of you broke
faith with me among the Israelites at the waters
of Meribath-kadesh in the wilderness of Zin:
you did not manifest my holiness among the
Israelites.§x 52You may indeed see the land from a
distance, but you shall not enter that land which
I am giving to the Israelites.[y]

## CHAPTER 33
**Blessing upon the Tribes.**¶ 1This is the blessing
with which Moses, the man of God, blessed the
Israelites before he died.[z]

2aHe said:

    The LORD came from Sinai
        and dawned on his people from Seir;
        he shone forth from Mount Paran.
    With him were myriads of holy ones;
        at his right hand advanced the gods.**
3   Indeed, lover of the peoples,
        all the holy ones are at your side;
    They follow at your heels,
        carry out your decisions.
4   Moses charged us with the law,
        as a possession for the assembly of
            Jacob.[b]
5   A king arose†† in Jeshurun
        when the chiefs of the people
            assembled,
        and the tribes of Israel united.[c]

6   May Reuben live and not die out,[d]
        but let his numbers be few.

7Of Judah he said this:

    Hear, LORD, the voice of Judah,
        and bring him to his people.‡‡
    His own hands defend his cause;
        be a help against his foes.[e]

8Of Levi he said:[f]

    Give to Levi your Thummim,
        your Urim§§ to your faithful one;
    Him you tested at Massah,
        contended against him at the waters
            of Meribah.[g]
9   "He said of his father and mother,
        'I have no regard for them'";
    His brothers he would not acknowledge,
        and his own children he did not
            recognize.

---

resembles the Blessing of Jacob (Gn 49) and the Song of Deborah (Jgs 5, especially vv. 14–18); all three poems seem to date
from the early premonarchic period.
    **[33:2] **Gods:** the divine beings who constitute the armies
of the Lord, the heavenly hosts (Sabaoth); see note on 32:8.
These "holy ones" (v. 3) are the retinue of the Lord, the warrior God, in his march from the southern mountains (Sinai,
Seir, Paran).
    ††[33:5] **A king arose:** it is unclear whether this refers to
divine kingship or the beginning of the monarchy in Israel.
**Jeshurun:** see note on 32:15.
    ‡‡[33:7] **Bring him to his people:** this probably refers to
the isolated position of the tribe of Judah (cf. Jgs 1:17–19);
according to some commentators the reference is to the
divided kingdom.
    §§[33:8] **Thummim . . . Urim:** devices priests used for divi-
nation (cf. note on Ex 28:30).
    ¶¶[33:9] The reference is probably to the Levites' slaughter
of other Israelites after the incident of the golden calf; cf. Ex
32:27–29.

---

    *[32:44] **Hoshea:** a variant of "Joshua." Cf. note on Nm
13:16.
    †[32:49] **Abarim:** probably the mountain range to the east
of the Dead Sea.
    ‡[32:50] **Mount Hor:** on the western border of Seir or
Edom; cf. Nm 20:23–28; 33:37–38. Dt 10:6 locates elsewhere
the place of Aaron's death.
    §[32:51] Cf. note on 3:26.
    ¶[33:1–29] This poem, called the Blessing of Moses, con-
sists of a series of poetic characterizations of each of the tribes
of Israel (vv. 6–25), introduced (vv. 2–3) and concluded (vv.
26–27) by a theophany; vv. 4–5 lead into the blessing proper;
and the poem ends with a blessing on Israel as a whole (vv.
28–29). This catalog of the tribal units of the people Israel

---

r. [32:43] Dt 32:1, 8; Is 49:13.   s. [32:44] Dt 31:14–15, 23.
t. [32:46] Dt 4:9.   u. [32:47] Dt 4:40; 6:1–2.   v. [32:49] Dt 34:1;
Nm 27:12.   w. [32:50] Dt 10:6; Nm 20:23–29; 27:13; 33:38–39.
x. [32:51] Ex 17:1–7; Nm 20:1–13; 27:14; Ps 106:32–33.   y. [32:52]
Dt 3:27; 34:4.   z. [33:1] Jos 14:6; Ps 90:1.

a. [33:2–3] Ex 15:14–17; 19:18–20; Nm 10:36; Jgs 5:4–5; Ps 68:7–8,
17; 89:7; Hb 3:3–6.   b. [33:4] Dt 4:44; Jn 1:17; 7:19.   c. [33:5] Dt
32:15.   d. [33:6] Gn 49:3–4.   e. [33:7] Gn 49:8–12.   f. [33:8–11]
Gn 49:5–7.   g. [33:8] Dt 6:16; 9:22; 32:51; Ex 17:1–7; 28:30; Lv 8:8;
Nm 20:1–13; 1 Sm 14:41–42.

For they kept your words,
 and your covenant they upheld.[h]
10 [i]They teach your ordinances to Jacob,
 your law to Israel.
They bring incense to your nostrils,
 and burnt offerings to your altar.
11 Bless, LORD, his strength,
 be pleased with the work of his
  hands.
Crush the loins of his adversaries
 and of his foes, that they may not rise.

12Of Benjamin he said:

The beloved of the LORD,
 he abides in safety beside him;
He shelters him all day long;
 the beloved abides at his breast.*[j]

13Of Joseph he said:[k]

Blessed by the LORD is his land
 with the best of heaven above
 and of the abyss crouching beneath;
14 With the best of the produce of the sun,
 and the choicest yield of the months;
15 With the finest gifts of the ancient
  mountains
 and the best from the everlasting hills;
16 With the best of the earth and its fullness,
 and the favor of the one who dwells
  on Sinai.
Let these come upon the head of Joseph
 and upon the brow of the prince
  among his brothers.[l]
17 His firstborn bull, majesty is his!
 His horns are the horns of a wild ox;
With them he gores the peoples,
 attacks the ends of the earth.
These are the myriads of Ephraim,
 and these the thousands of
  Manasseh.

18Of Zebulun he said:[m]

Rejoice, Zebulun, in your expeditions,
 exult, Issachar, in your tents!
19 They invite peoples to the mountain
 where they offer right sacrifices,
Because they suck up the abundance of
  the seas†
 and the hidden treasures of the sand.

20Of Gad he said:[n]

Blessed be the one who has made Gad
  so vast!
He lies there like a lion;
 he tears the arm, the head as well.
21 He saw that the best should be his,
 for there the commander's portion
  was assigned;
 he came at the head of the people.
He carried out the justice of the LORD
 and his ordinances for Israel.[o]

22Of Dan he said:

Dan is a lion's cub,[p]
 that springs away from a viper!

23Of Naphtali he said:

Naphtali, abounding with favor,
 filled with the blessing of the LORD,
 take possession of the west and
  south.[q]

24Of Asher he said:[r]

Most blessed‡ of sons be Asher!
 May he be the favorite among his
  brothers,
 and may he dip his foot in oil!
25 May the bolts of your gates be iron and
  bronze;
 may your strength endure through
  all your days!

26 There is none like the God of Jeshurun,
 who rides the heavens in his power,
 who rides the clouds in his majesty;[s]
27 The God of old is a refuge;
 a support are the arms of the
  Everlasting.
He drove the enemy out of your way
 and he said, "Destroy!"[t]
28 Israel abides securely,
 Jacob dwells apart,
In a land of grain and wine,
 where the heavens drip with dew.[u]
29 Happy are you, Israel! Who is like you,
 a people delivered by the LORD,
Your help and shield,
 and the sword of your glory.

---

*[33:12] **Abides at his breast**: an image of security under
divine protection.
†[33:19] **The abundance of the seas**: perhaps the wealth
that comes from sea trade or from fishing. **The hidden treasures of the sand**: possibly an allusion to the valuable purple
dye extracted from certain marine shells found on the coast
of northern Palestine.

h. [33:9] Lk 14:26.   i. [33:10–11] Dt 10:8; 17:9–11; 18:1–8; Ex
30:7–8; Lv 10:11; 2 Kgs 17:27–28; Mal 2:4–9.   j. [33:12] Gn 49:27.
k. [33:13–17] Gn 49:22–26.   l. [33:16] Ex 3:1–6; Jgs 5:6.
m. [33:18–19] Gn 49:13–15.

‡[33:24] **Most blessed**: Hebrew *baruk*; but the name Asher
may suggest a play on the Hebrew *'ashre*, "happy"; cf., e.g., v.
29; Ps 1:1. **Oil**: the land of the tribe of Asher was covered with
olive groves.

n. [33:20–21] Gn 49:19.   o. [33:21] Nm 32:1–32; Jos 1:12–15; 1 Chr
5:18–22; 12:8–15.   p. [33:22] Gn 49:16–17.   q. [33:23] Gn 49:21;
Jos 19:32–39.   r. [33:24–25] Gn 49:20.   s. [33:26] Dt 32:15; Ps
18:10; 68:4, 33; 104:3; Is 19:1.   t. [33:27] Dt 7:1, 17–24.   u. [33:28]
Dt 7:12–16; Gn 27:28; Nm 23:9.

Your enemies cringe before you;
 you stride upon their backs.[v]

## IV. THE DEATH OF MOSES

### CHAPTER 34

[1]Then Moses went up from the plains of Moab to Mount Nebo,[w] the peak of Pisgah which faces Jericho, and the LORD showed him all the land— Gilead, and as far as Dan, [2]all Naphtali, the land of Ephraim and Manasseh, all the land of Judah as far as the Western Sea,[x] [3]the Negeb, the plain (the valley of Jericho, the City of Palms), and as far as Zoar. [4]The LORD then said to him, This is the land[y] about which I promised on oath to Abraham, Isaac, and Jacob, "I will give it to your descendants." I have let you see it with your own eyes, but you shall not cross over. [5]So there, in the land of Moab, Moses, the servant of the LORD, died[z] as the LORD had said; [6]and he was buried in a valley in the land of Moab, opposite Beth-peor; to this day no one knows the place of his burial.[a] [7]Moses was one hundred and twenty years old[b] when he died, yet his eyes were undimmed and his vigor unabated. [8]The Israelites wept for Moses in the plains of Moab for thirty days, till they had completed the period of grief and mourning for Moses.

[9]Now Joshua, son of Nun,[c] was filled with the spirit of wisdom, since Moses had laid his hands upon him; and so the Israelites gave him their obedience, just as the LORD had commanded Moses.

[10d]Since then no prophet has arisen in Israel like Moses, whom the LORD knew face to face, [11c]in all the signs and wonders the LORD sent him to perform in the land of Egypt against Pharaoh and all his servants and against all his land, [12]and all the great might and the awesome power that Moses displayed in the sight of all Israel.

---

v. [33:29] Dt 4:7–8; Gn 15:1; 2 Sm 22:3; Ps 28:7; 119:114.   w. [34:1] Dt 3:27; 32:49.   x. [34:2] Dt 11:24.   y. [34:4] Dt 1:8; 3:27; 32:52; Gn 12:7; 15:18–21.   z. [34:5] Dt 32:50; Ex 14:31; Nm 12:7–8; Jos 1:1–2, 7, 13, 15; 1 Kgs 8:53, 56; Mal 3:22.

a. [34:6] Dt 3:29.   b. [34:7] Dt 31:2.   c. [34:9] Nm 27:18–23; Jos 1:17.   d. [34:10] Dt 5:4; 18:15; Ex 33:11; Nm 12:8; Sir 45:5.   e. [34:11–12] Dt 4:34; Ex 4:21; 7:1, 8–12.

# THE
# HISTORICAL BOOKS

Where the Hebrew Bible comprises three sections—Torah or Pentateuch; Prophetic Books, both the Former and the Latter Prophets; and the Writings, including everything else in the Hebrew Canon—the Christian Old Testament has traditionally been arranged along different lines. After the Pentateuch comes a series of books that continue, in roughly chronological order, the history of Israel. The Book of Joshua depicts Israel taking possession of the land of Canaan. Judges collects stories about the leaders of early Israel in the two hundred years before the emergence of the monarchy. After the tale of Ruth, a sort of interlude in the narrative sweep of these books, 1 and 2 Samuel tell of the rise and fall of Saul, Israel's first king, and the succession and successes of David. The Books of Kings take us from the death of David and the enthronement of Solomon, through the division of the people into the two kingdoms of Israel and Judah, to the destruction of the Northern Kingdom, Israel, at the hands of the Assyrian invader (722/721 B.C.), and the fall of Judah, the Southern Kingdom, to the Babylonians (587 B.C.) and its ensuing exile, the Babylonian captivity.

Except for Ruth, these writings bear the marks of a specific theological outlook, that of the Book of Deuteronomy, and together with that book as its introductory volume constitute what is called the Deuteronomistic History. In this theology, what has characterized Israel's history, in the six hundred years from Moses to the Babylonian exile, has been a dynamic of fidelity or infidelity to Israel's covenant Lord, and the consequent destiny Israel forges for itself of covenant blessing or covenant curse. This dynamic of choice and consequences serves to explain the disasters Israel incurs throughout its history, from the so-called conquest and the days of the Judges to the fall of the North. In its preexilic edition, the Deuteronomistic History would have stood also as warning and wake-up call to the surviving Southern Kingdom.

The Books of Chronicles recycle much of the material found in the previous works, but the author ("the Chronicler") treats it selectively, with a characteristic theological point of view; its focus is the Jerusalem Temple and its cultic arrangements, which by way of legitimation are attributed to David, the ideal king. The Chronicler's interests carry through the Books of Ezra and Nehemiah, which recount the restoration of Jewish worship and life in the period of Persian rule following release from exile in Babylon.

The Books of Maccabees give us two overlapping but somewhat differing accounts of Jewish resistance to Seleucid persecution in the early second century B.C., and the assumption of power by the leaders of the resistance, the Maccabees or Hasmoneans.

The traditional designation of these books as "historical" describes their scope and contents, and is not meant to assert factual verifiability; while they contain much valuable historical information, in the narrow sense, their purpose is theological rather than historiographic.

The Books of Tobit, Judith, and Esther are sometimes reckoned among the historical books, but they differ from the writings sketched above, and call for special treatment; see the introduction to those books.

# THE BOOK OF
# JOSHUA

ও৵৶৹

The Book of Joshua presents a narrative of the way Israel took possession of the land of Canaan, making it the land of Israel. This process is swift and inexorable, and is followed by an orderly division and disposition of the land among the twelve tribes, with a concluding ceremony of covenant renewal.

The theological message of the book is unmistakable. God has been faithful to the promise of the land. If Israel relies totally on the Lord for victory; if Israel is united as a people; if the law of *herem* is kept and no one grows rich from victory in war—then and only then will Israel possess the land.

The Israelites are led by Joshua, the successor of Moses, and the book is at pains to show not only how Joshua carries on the work of Moses but how the "conquest" of Canaan is continuous with the exodus from Egypt. This is seen in the repeated insistence that, as the Lord was with Moses, so he is with Joshua; and, especially, in the crossing of the Jordan River, which is patterned after the crossing of the Red Sea.

The book preserves older traditions of Israel's settlement in the land, especially in the division of the land among the tribes. As with Deuteronomy and the whole Deuteronomistic History (see introduction to Deuteronomy), the fall of the Northern Kingdom in 722/721 B.C. shows its influence throughout. As addressed to the needs of a late preexilic audience, then, the book should be read not so much as imparting information about how Israel took over the land of Canaan, many centuries before the composition of the book, as teaching a lesson about how Israel is to avoid losing the land.

Modern readers may be put off by the description of battles and their aftermath, the destruction of everyone and everything in the cities taken under the "ban" (*herem*). The ban was practiced in the ancient Near East, in Israel and elsewhere, but in Joshua the wholesale destruction of the Canaanites is an idealization of the deuteronomic idea that pagans are to be wiped out so they will not be an occasion for apostasy from the Lord (cf. Dt 7:1–6); note in particular the artificial, formalized description of destruction of towns in Jos 10:28–39. It should be remembered that by the time the book was written, the Canaanites were long gone. Progressive revelation throughout Israel's history produced far more lofty ideals, as when the prophets see all the nations embracing faith in Yahweh, being joined to Israel, and living in peace with one another (Is 2:2–4; 19:23–25; 45:22–25; Zec 8:22–23), and the New Testament teaches us to love even our enemies (Mt 5:43–45).

A comparison of Joshua with the account of Israel's early history found in the first chapter of the Book of Judges shows that Israel's emergence as the dominant presence in the land was a slow and piecemeal affair, not achieved at one stroke and with great ease: the Book of Joshua, with its highly idealized depiction of the "conquest," is a theologically programmatic cautionary tale about what the people are to do and not do in order to avoid the fate of the Northern Kingdom in losing the land.

The Book of Joshua may be divided as follows:

  I. Conquest of Canaan (1:1–12:24)
 II. Division of the Land (13:1–21:45)
III. Return of the Transjordan Tribes and Joshua's Farewell (22:1–24:33)

# I. CONQUEST OF CANAAN

## CHAPTER 1

**Divine Promise of Assistance.** [1]After Moses, the servant of the LORD, had died, the LORD said to Moses' aide Joshua, son of Nun: [2]*"Moses my servant is dead. So now, you and the whole people with you, prepare to cross the Jordan to the land that I will give the Israelites. [3a]Every place where you set foot I have given you, as I promised Moses. [4†]All the land of the Hittites, from the wilderness and the Lebanon east to the great river Euphrates and west to the Great Sea, will be your territory.[b] [5]No one can withstand you as long as you live. As I was with Moses, I will be with you:[c] I will not leave you nor forsake you. [6]Be strong and steadfast, so that you may give this people possession of the land I swore to their ancestors that I would give them. [7d]Only be strong and steadfast, being careful to observe the entire law which Moses my servant enjoined on you. Do not swerve from it either to the right or to the left, that you may succeed wherever you go. [8]Do not let this book of the law depart from your lips. Recite it by day and by night,[e] that you may carefully observe all that is written in it; then you will attain your goal; then you will succeed. [9]I command you: be strong and steadfast! Do not fear nor be dismayed, for the LORD, your God, is with you wherever you go.

[10]So Joshua commanded the officers of the people: [11]"Go through the camp and command the people, 'Prepare your provisions, for three days from now you shall cross the Jordan here, to march in and possess the land the LORD, your God, is giving as your possession.'"

**The Transjordan Tribes.** [12g]Joshua addressed the Reubenites, the Gadites, and the half-tribe of Manasseh, [13]"Remember what Moses, the servant of the LORD, commanded you when he said, 'The LORD, your God, is about to give you rest; he will give you this land.' [14]Your wives, your children, and your livestock may remain in the land Moses gave you here beyond the Jordan. But all the warriors among you must cross over armed, ahead of your kindred, and you must help them [15]until the LORD has settled your kindred, and they like you possess the land the LORD, your God, is giving them. Afterward you may return and possess your own land, which Moses, the servant of the LORD, has given you east of the Jordan."[h] [16]They answered Joshua, "We will do all you have commanded us, and we will go wherever you send us. [17]As completely as we obeyed Moses, we will obey you. Only, may the LORD, your God, be with you as God was with Moses. [18]Anyone who rebels against your orders and does not obey all your commands shall be put to death. Only be strong and steadfast."

## CHAPTER 2

**Spies Saved by Rahab.** [1]Then Joshua, son of Nun, secretly sent out two spies from Shittim, saying, "Go, reconnoiter the land and Jericho." When the two reached Jericho, they went into the house of a prostitute named Rahab,[i] where they lodged. [2]But a report was brought to the king of Jericho: "Some men came here last night, Israelites, to spy out the land." [3]So the king of Jericho sent Rahab the order, "Bring out the men who have come to you and entered your house, for they have come to spy out the entire land." [4]The woman[j] had taken the two men and hidden them, so she said, "True, the men you speak of came to me, but I did not know where they came from. [5]At dark, when it was time to close the gate, they left, and I do not know where they went. You will have to pursue them quickly to overtake them." [6]Now, she had led them to the roof, and hidden them among her stalks of flax spread out‡ there. [7]But the pursuers set out along the way to the fords of the Jordan. As soon as they had left to pursue them, the gate was shut.

[8]Before the spies lay down, Rahab went up to them on the roof [9]and said:[§] "I know that the LORD has given you the land, that a dread of you has come upon us, and that all the inhabitants of the land tremble with fear because of you.[k] [10]For we have heard how the LORD dried up the waters of the Red Sea before you when you came out of Egypt,[l] and what you did to Sihon and Og, the two kings of the Amorites beyond the Jordan, whom you destroyed under the ban. [11]We heard, and our hearts melted within us; everyone is

---

*[1:2–9] The beginning of the Book of Joshua strongly emphasizes the credentials of Joshua as Moses' worthy successor (vv. 2, 3, 4, 7; cf. v. 17; 3:7; 4:14; 5:15). The movement Joshua leads, whereby the Israelites take possession of the land of Canaan, is thus made continuous with the exodus from Egypt, even though (except for Joshua and Caleb) the generation that left Egypt under Moses' leadership has died out (5:4, 6), and the people who will make the land of Canaan the land of Israel are a new generation. Thus the book is at pains to establish the continuity between exodus and conquest.

†[1:4] The frontiers are as follows: in the south the wilderness of Sinai, in the north the Lebanon range, in the east the Euphrates, and in the west the Great Sea, the Mediterranean. These boundaries are ideal rather than actual.

‡[2:6] **Stalks of flax spread out:** to dry in the sun, after they had been soaked in water, according to the ancient process of preparing flax for linen-making. In the Near East the flax harvest occurs near the time of the feast of the Passover (4:19; 5:10); cf. Ex 9:31.

§[2:9–11] Rahab's speech is Deuteronomic in content and style. Through her, the author expresses a theological conviction: the Lord, the God of Israel, is God above all gods; the formation of the people Israel and its success is the Lord's doing; and all the rulers of the neighboring nations do well to panic at what the Lord is doing (cf. 5:1). Rahab the prostitute is pointedly mentioned in the Matthean genealogy of Jesus (Mt 1:5) and in Jas 2:25.

---

a. [1:3–4] Jos 14:9; Gn 15:18; Dt 11:24–25; 34:4.   b. [1:4] Gn 10:19; Nm 13:17, 21–22; 34:3–12.   c. [1:5] Dt 3:21–22; 31:8, 23; Heb 13:5.   d. [1:7–8] Dt 2:27; 5:29; 17:11, 20; 28:14; Ps 1:1–3.   e. [1:8] Ps 1:2.   f. [1:10–11] Dt 20:5–9.   g. [1:12–18] Nm 32; Dt 3:12–20.

h. [1:15] Jos 22:4; Dt 3:20.   i. [2:1] Dt 1:22; Mt 1:5; Jas 2:25.   j. [2:4] Jos 6:17; Heb 11:31.   k. [2:9] Ex 15:15–16; 23:27.   l. [2:10] Jos 4:23; Ex 14:21; Nm 21:23–26, 33–35.

utterly dispirited because of you, since the LORD, your God, is God in heaven above and on earth below.*m* 12*n*Now then, swear to me by the LORD that, since I am showing kindness to you, you in turn will show kindness to my family.*o* Give me a reliable sign 13that you will allow my father and mother, brothers and sisters, and my whole family to live, and that you will deliver us from death." 14"We pledge our lives for yours," they answered her. "If you do not betray our mission, we will be faithful in showing kindness to you when the LORD gives us the land."

15Then she let them down through the window with a rope; for she lived in a house built into the city wall.* 16"Go up into the hill country," she said, "that your pursuers may not come upon you. Hide there for three days, until they return; then you may go on your way." 17They answered her, "We are free of this oath that you made us take, unless, 18when we come into the land, you tie this scarlet cord in the window through which you are letting us down. Gather your father and mother, your brothers, and all your family into your house. 19Should any of them pass outside the doors of your house, their blood will be on their own heads, and we will be guiltless. But if anyone in your house is harmed, their blood will be on our heads. 20If, however, you betray our mission, we will be free of the oath you have made us take." 21"Let it be as you say," she replied, and sent them away. When they were gone, she tied the scarlet cord in the window.

22They went up into the hill country, where they stayed three days until their pursuers, who had sought them all along the road without finding them, returned. 23Then the two came back down from the hills, crossed the Jordan to Joshua, son of Nun, and told him all that had happened to them. 24They assured Joshua, "The LORD has given all this land into our power; indeed, all the inhabitants of the land tremble with fear because of us."

## CHAPTER 3

**Preparations for Crossing the Jordan.** 1Early the next morning, Joshua and all the Israelites moved from Shittim and came to the Jordan, where they stayed before crossing over. 2*p*Three days later the officers went through the camp 3*q*and issued these commands to the people: "When you see the ark of the covenant of the LORD, your God, which the levitical priests will carry, you must break camp and follow it, 4that you may know the way to take, for you have

not gone over this road before. But let there be a space of two thousand cubits between you and the ark: do not come nearer to it." 5Joshua also said to the people, "Sanctify yourselves, for tomorrow the LORD will perform wonders among you." 6And he told the priests, "Take up the ark of the covenant and cross ahead of the people"; so they took up the ark of the covenant and went before the people.

7Then the LORD said to Joshua: Today I will begin to exalt you in the sight of all Israel, that they may know that, as I was with Moses, so I will be with you.*r* 8Now command the priests carrying the ark of the covenant, "When you come to the edge of the waters of the Jordan, there take your stand."

9So Joshua said to the Israelites, "Come here and listen to the words of the LORD, your God." 10He continued: "By this you will know that there is a living God in your midst: he will certainly dispossess before you the Canaanites, Hittites, Hivites, Perizzites, Girgashites, Amorites, and Jebusites.*s* 11The ark of the covenant of the Lord of the whole earth will cross the Jordan before you. 12Now choose twelve men,*t* one from each of the tribes of Israel. 13When the soles of the feet of the priests carrying the ark of the LORD, the Lord of the whole earth, touch the waters of the Jordan, it will cease to flow; the water flowing down from upstream will halt in a single heap."†

**The Crossing Begun.** 14The people set out from their tents to cross the Jordan, with the priests carrying the ark of the covenant ahead of them. 15When those bearing the ark came to the Jordan and the feet of the priests bearing the ark were immersed in the waters of the Jordan—which overflows all its banks during the entire season of the harvest—‡ 16the waters flowing from upstream halted, standing up in a single heap*v* for a very great distance indeed, from Adam, a city in the direction of Zarethan; those flowing downstream toward the Salt Sea of the Arabah disappeared entirely.§ Thus the people crossed over opposite Jericho. 17The priests carrying the ark of the covenant of the LORD stood on dry ground in the Jordan riverbed*w* while all Israel

---

†[3:13] **Heap:** Heb. *nēd*, the same word found in Ex 15:8; the narrative echoes the ancient Song of Miriam (Ex 15:1–18), which celebrates the crossing of the Red Sea. Thus the language provides another parallel between Joshua and Moses, conquest and exodus.

‡[3:15] **Season of the harvest:** toward the end of March and the beginning of April, when the barley and other crops that grew during the rainy season of winter were reaped. The crossing took place "on the tenth day of the first month" of the Hebrew year, which began with the first new moon after the spring equinox; cf. 4:19. At this time of the year the Jordan would be swollen as a result of the winter rains and the melting snow of Mount Hermon.

§[3:16] Some scholars have suggested that this account may reflect an annual ritual reenactment of the event near the sanctuary of Gilgal.

---

*[2:15] **A house built into the city wall:** the city wall formed the back wall of the house; remains of such houses have been found at ancient sites. The upper story of Rahab's house was evidently higher than the city wall. It was through the window of such a house that St. Paul escaped from Damascus; cf. Acts 9:25; 2 Cor 11:33.

---

m. [2:11] Jos 5:1; Dt 4:39; Rom 10:9.   n. [2:12–13] Jgs 1:22–26.
o. [2:12] Jos 2:18; 6:23, 25.   p. [3:2] Jos 2:1.   q. [3:3] Nm 10:33.

r. [3:7] Jos 1:5; Dt 31:23.   s. [3:7] Jos 1:5; 4:14.   t. [3:10] Ex 32:2; Dt 7:1.   u. [3:12] Jos 4:2, 4.   v. [3:16] Ps 114:3.   w. [3:17] Jos 4:7, 22.

crossed on dry ground, until the whole nation had completed the crossing of the Jordan.

## CHAPTER 4

**Memorial Stones.** [1]After the entire nation had completed the crossing of the Jordan, [2]the LORD said to Joshua: Choose twelve men[x] from the people, one from each tribe, [3]and command them, "Take up twelve stones from this spot in the Jordan riverbed where the priests have been standing.[y] Carry them over with you, and place them where you are to stay tonight." 

[4]Summoning the twelve men he had selected from among the Israelites, one from each tribe, [5]Joshua said to them: "Go to the Jordan riverbed in front of the ark of the LORD, your God; lift to your shoulders one stone apiece, so that they will equal in number the tribes of the Israelites. [6]In the future, these are to be a sign among you. When your children ask you,* 'What do these stones mean to you?'[z] [7]you shall answer them, 'The waters of the Jordan ceased to flow before the ark of the covenant of the LORD when it crossed the Jordan.'[a] Thus these stones are to serve as a perpetual memorial to the Israelites." [8]The twelve Israelites did as Joshua had commanded: they took up twelve stones from the Jordan riverbed as the LORD had said to Joshua, one for each of the tribes of the Israelites. They carried them along to the camp site, and there they placed them. [9]Joshua set up the twelve stones that had been in the Jordan riverbed on the spot where the priests stood who were carrying the ark of the covenant. They are there to this day.

[10]†The priests carrying the ark stood in the Jordan riverbed until everything had been done that the LORD had commanded Joshua to tell the people, just as Moses had commanded Joshua. The people crossed over quickly, [11]and when all the people had completed the crossing, the ark of the LORD also crossed; and the priests were now in front of them. [12]The Reubenites, Gadites, and half-tribe of Manasseh, armed, marched in the vanguard of the Israelites, as Moses had ordered. [13]About forty thousand troops, equipped for battle, crossed over before the LORD to the plains of Jericho for war.

[14]That day the LORD exalted Joshua in the sight of all Israel,[b] and so during his whole life they feared him as they feared Moses.

[15]Then the LORD said to Joshua: [16]Command the priests carrying the ark of the covenant to come up from the Jordan. [17]Joshua commanded the priests, "Come up from the Jordan," [18]and

when the priests carrying the ark of the covenant of the LORD had come up from the Jordan riverbed, as the soles of their feet regained the dry ground, the waters of the Jordan resumed their course and as before overflowed all its banks.

[19]The people came up from the Jordan on the tenth day of the first month, and camped in Gilgal on the eastern limits of Jericho.[c] [20]At Gilgal Joshua set up the twelve stones that had been taken from the Jordan, [21]saying to the Israelites, "In the future, when your children ask their parents, 'What do these stones mean?' [22]you shall inform them, 'Israel crossed the Jordan here on dry ground.' [23]For the LORD, your God, dried up the waters of the Jordan in front of you until you crossed over, just as the LORD, your God, had done at the Red Sea, drying it up in front of us until we crossed over,[d] [24]in order that all the peoples of the earth may know that the hand of the LORD is mighty, and that you may fear the LORD, your God, forever."[e]

## CHAPTER 5

**Rites at Gilgal.** [1]When all the kings of the Amorites to the west of the Jordan and all the kings of the Canaanites by the sea heard that the LORD had dried up the waters of the Jordan before the Israelites until they crossed over, their hearts melted and they were utterly dispirited because of the Israelites.

[2]On this occasion the LORD said to Joshua: Make flint knives and circumcise Israel for the second time. [3]So Joshua made flint knives and circumcised the Israelites at Gibeath-haaraloth.‡ [4]This was the reason for the circumcision: Of all the people who had come out of Egypt, every male of military age had died in the wilderness[f] during the journey after they came out of Egypt. [5]Though all the men who came out were circumcised, none of those born in the wilderness during the journey after the departure from Egypt were circumcised. [6]Now the Israelites wandered forty years in the wilderness, until all the warriors among the people that came forth from Egypt died off because they had not listened to the voice of the LORD. For the LORD swore[h] that he would not let them see the land he had sworn to their ancestors to give us, a land flowing with milk and honey. [7]It was the children God raised up in their stead whom Joshua circumcised, for these were yet with foreskins, not having been circumcised on the journey. [8]When the circumcision of the entire nation was complete, they remained in camp where they were, until they recovered. [9]Then the LORD said to Joshua: Today I have removed the reproach

---

*[4:6] **When your children ask you:** reminiscent of the question and response at the Passover meal, Ex 12:26–27.

†[4:10–18] After the digression about the memorial stones, the author resumes the narrative by briefly repeating the story of the crossing, which had already been told in 3:14–17.

‡[5:3] **Gibeath-haaraloth:** "Hill of the Foreskins."

x. [4:2] Jos 3:12.   y. [4:3] Jos 3:13; 4:8–9; Dt 27:2.   z. [4:6] Ex 12:26–27; Dt 6:7, 20–25.   a. [4:7] Jos 3:13, 16.   b. [4:14] Jos 3:7.

c. [4:19] Ex 12:2–3.   d. [4:23] Ex 14:21.   e. [4:24] Ex 9:3; 14:31; 16:3.   f. [5:2] Gn 17; 34; Ex 4:24–26.   g. [5:4] Nm 14:29; 26:64–65; 1 Cor 10:5.   h. [5:6] Nm 14:33–34; Heb 3:11, 17.   i. [5:7] Gn 17:8–14.

of Egypt from you.[j] Therefore the place is called Gilgal[*] to the present day.

[10k]While the Israelites were encamped at Gilgal on the plains of Jericho, they celebrated the Passover on the evening of the fourteenth day of the month.[†] [11]On the day after the Passover they ate of the produce of the land in the form of unleavened cakes and parched grain. On that same day [12]after they ate of the produce of the land, the manna ceased. No longer was there manna for the Israelites, who that year ate of the yield of the land of Canaan.[l]

**Siege at Jericho.** [13‡]While Joshua was near Jericho, he raised his eyes and saw one who stood facing him, drawn sword in hand.[m] Joshua went up to him and asked, "Are you one of us or one of our[*] enemies?" [14]He replied, "Neither. I am the commander[§] of the army of the LORD: now I have come." Then Joshua fell down to the ground in worship, and said to him, "What has my lord to say to his servant?" [15]The commander of the army of the LORD replied to Joshua, "Remove your sandals from your feet, for the place on which you are standing is holy."[n] And Joshua did so.

## CHAPTER 6

[1]Now Jericho was in a state of siege because of the presence of the Israelites. No one left or entered. [2]And to Joshua the LORD said: I have delivered Jericho, its king, and its warriors into your power. [3o]Have all the soldiers circle the city, marching once around it. Do this for six days, [4]with seven priests carrying ram's horns ahead of the ark. On the seventh day march around the city seven times, and have the priests blow the horns. [5]When they give a long blast on the ram's horns and you hear the sound of the horn, all the people shall shout aloud. The wall of the city will collapse, and the people shall attack straight ahead.

[6]Summoning the priests, Joshua, son of Nun, said to them, "Take up the ark of the covenant with seven of the priests carrying ram's horns in front of the ark of the LORD." [7]And he ordered the people, "Proceed and surround the city, with the picked troops marching ahead of the ark of the LORD." [8]When Joshua spoke to the people, the seven priests who carried the ram's horns before the LORD marched and blew their horns, and the ark of the covenant of the LORD followed them. [9]In front of the priests with the horns marched the picked troops; the rear guard followed the ark, and the blowing of horns was kept up continually as they marched. [10]But Joshua had commanded the people, "Do not shout or make any noise or outcry until I tell you, 'Shout!' Then you must shout." [11]So he had the ark of the LORD circle the city, going once around it, after which they returned to camp for the night.

[12]Early the next morning, Joshua had the priests take up the ark of the LORD. [13]The seven priests bearing the ram's horns marched in front of the ark of the LORD, blowing their horns. Ahead of these marched the picked troops, while the rear guard followed the ark of the LORD, and the blowing of horns was kept up continually. [14]On this second day they again marched around the city once before returning to camp; and for six days in all they did the same.

[15]On the seventh day, beginning at daybreak, they marched around the city seven times in the same manner; on that day only did they march around the city seven times. [16]The seventh time around, the priests blew the horns and Joshua said to the people, "Now shout, for the LORD has given you the city. [17p]The city and everything in it is under the ban. Only Rahab the prostitute and all who are in the house with her are to live, because she hid the messengers we sent. [18q]But be careful not to covet or take anything that is under the ban;[¶] otherwise you will bring upon the camp of Israel this ban and the misery of it. [19]All silver and gold, and the articles of bronze or iron, are holy to the LORD. They shall be put in the treasury of the LORD."

**The Fall of Jericho.** [20]As the horns blew, the people began to shout. When they heard the sound of the horn, they raised a tremendous shout. The wall collapsed,[**] and the people attacked the city straight ahead and took it.[r] [21]They observed the ban by putting to the sword all living creatures[s] in the city: men and women, young and old, as well as oxen, sheep and donkeys.

---

*[5:9] **The place is called Gilgal:** by popular etymology, because of the similarity of sound with the Hebrew word *gallothi*, "I have removed." Gilgal probably means "circle," i.e., the place of the circle of standing stones. Cf. 4:4–8.

†[5:10] **The month:** the first month of the year, later called Nisan; see note on 3:15. The crossing of the Jordan occurred, therefore, about the same time of the year as did the crossing of the Red Sea; cf. Ex 12–14.

‡[5:13–6:26] The account of the siege of Jericho embraces: (1) the command of the Lord to Joshua (5:13–6:5); (2) Joshua's instructions to the Israelites, with a brief summary of how these orders were carried out (6:6–11); (3) a description of the action on each of the first six days (6:12–14); (4) the events on the seventh day (6:15–26).

§[5:14] **Commander:** the leader of the heavenly army of the Lord of hosts is either the Lord or an angelic warrior; if the latter, he is a messenger who speaks in the person of the one who sent him. **I have come:** the solemn language of theophany; cf., e.g., Ps 50:3; 96:13.

¶[6:18] **Under the ban:** doomed to destruction; see notes on Lv 27:28; Nm 18:14; 21:3.

**[6:20] The blowing of the horns and the shouting, features of the ritual procession with the ark of the covenant (cf. 1 Chr 15:28; 2 Chr 5:11–14), are the people's counterpart of the Lord's theophany; cf. note on Jgs 5:4–5; and Jgs 7:15–22; 2 Chr 13:15. The Lord gives the victory; this is the theological point of the story.

j. [5:9] Jos 4:19; Eph 2:11–22.   k. [5:10] Ex 12:6; Nm 9:3–5. l. [5:12] Ex 16:35.   m. [5:13] Ex 23:20.   n. [5:15] Ex 3:5; Acts 7:33.   o. [6:3–5] Nm 10:2–9; 2 Sm 6:15–16.

p. [6:17] Jos 2:4; Dt 20:17; Heb 11:31.   q. [6:18] Jos 7:12, 25; Dt 13:18.   r. [6:20] 2 Mc 12:15; Heb 11:30.   s. [6:21] Gn 15:16; Dt 7:2.

²²ʳTo the two men who had spied out the land, Joshua said, "Go into the prostitute's house and bring out the woman with all her family, as you swore to her you would do." ²³The spies entered and brought out Rahab, with her father, mother, brothers, and all her family; her entire family they led forth and placed outside the camp of Israel. ²⁴The city itself they burned with all that was in it;ᵘ but the silver, gold, and articles of bronze and iron they placed in the treasury of the house of the LORD. ²⁵ˣBecause Rahab the prostitute had hidden the messengers whom Joshua had sent to reconnoiter Jericho, Joshua let her live, along with her father's house and all her family, who dwell in the midst of Israel to this day.

²⁶ᵛOn that occasion Joshua imposed the oath: Cursed before the LORD be the man who attempts to rebuild this city, Jericho. At the cost of his firstborn will he lay its foundation, and at the cost of his youngest son will he set up its gates.†

²⁷Thus the LORD was with Joshua so that his fame spread throughout the land.ʷ

## CHAPTER 7

**Defeat at Ai.** ¹But the Israelites acted treacherously with regard to the ban; Achan, son of Carmi, son of Zabdi, son of Zerah of the tribe of Judah, took goods that were under the ban,ˣ and the anger of the LORD flared up against the Israelites.

²ʸJoshua next sent men from Jericho to Ai, which is near Beth-aven and east of Bethel, with the order, "Go up and reconnoiter the land." When they had explored Ai, ³they returned to Joshua and advised, "Do not send all the people up; if only about two or three thousand go up, they can attack and overcome Ai. You need not tire all the people: the enemy there are few." ⁴About three thousand of the people made the attack, but they fled before the army at Ai, ⁵who killed some thirty-six of them. They pursued them from the city gate to the Shebarim, and defeated them on the descent, so that the confidence of the people melted away like water.

⁶Joshua, together with the elders of Israel, tore their garments and fell face down before the ark of the LORD until evening; and they threw dust on their heads. ⁷"Alas, Lord GOD," Joshua prayed, "why did you ever allow this people to cross over the Jordan, delivering us into the power of the Amorites, that they might destroy

us? Would that we had been content to dwell on the other side of the Jordan. ⁸Please, Lord, what can I say, now that Israel has turned its back to its enemies? ⁹When the Canaanites and the other inhabitants of the land hear of it, they will close in around us and efface our name from the earth. What will you do for your great name?"ᶻ

¹⁰The LORD replied to Joshua: Stand up. Why are you lying there? ¹¹ᵃIsrael has sinned: they have transgressed the covenant‡ which I enjoined on them. They have taken goods subject to the ban. They have stolen and lied, placing the goods in their baggage. ¹²If the Israelites cannot stand up to their enemies, but must turn their back to them, it is because they are under the ban. I will not continue to be with you unless you remove that which is banned from among you. ¹³Get up, sanctify the people.ᵇ Tell them, "Sanctify yourselves before tomorrow, for thus says the LORD, the God of Israel: That which is banned is in your midst, Israel. You cannot stand up to your enemies until you remove it from among you. ¹⁴In the morning you must come forward by tribes. The tribe which the LORD designates shall come forward by clans; the clan which the LORD designates shall come forward by families; the family which the LORD designates shall come forward one by one. ¹⁵Whoever is designated as having incurred the ban shall be destroyed by fire, with all that is his, because he has transgressed the covenant of the LORD and has committed a shameful crime in Israel."ᶜ

**Achan's Guilt and Punishment.** ¹⁶Early the next morning Joshua had Israel come forward by tribes, and the tribe of Judah was designated.ˢ ¹⁷Then he had the clans of Judah come forward, and the clan of Zerah was designated. He had the clan of Zerahᵈ come forward by families, and Zabdi was designated. ¹⁸Finally he had that family come forward one by one, and Achan, son of Carmi, son of Zabdi, son of Zerah of the tribe of Judah, was designated. ¹⁹Joshua said to Achan, "My son, give glory to the LORD, the God of Israel, and praise him by telling me what you have done; do not hide it from me." ²⁰Achan answered Joshua, "I have indeed sinned against the LORD, the God of Israel. This is what I have done: ²¹Among the spoils, I saw a beautiful Babylonian mantle, two hundred shekels of silver, and a bar of gold fifty shekels in weight; I coveted them and I took them. They are now hidden in the ground inside my tent, with the silver underneath." ²²Joshua sent messengers

---

*[6:25] The genealogy of Jesus in Matthew (1:2–16) presents Rahab the prostitute as the wife of Salmon (1:5) and so the ancestor of David (Ru 4:18–22) and of Jesus.

†[6:26] **At the cost of his firstborn . . . its gates:** this curse was fulfilled when Hiel rebuilt Jericho as a fortified city during the reign of Ahab, king of Israel; cf. 1 Kgs 16:34.

‡[7:11] **Transgressed the covenant:** the Hebrew word translated "transgressed" appears frequently in the first five chapters where it is used to describe how Israel "crossed" the Jordan River. There is a wordplay here to emphasize Israel's responsibility to follow God to the promised land and so to obey and not transgress the divine command.

§[7:16–18] **Was designated:** probably by means of the Urim and Thummim; cf. 1 Sm 14:38–42. See note on Ex 28:30.

---

t. [6:22–23] Jos 2:13–14.  u. [6:24] Jos 8:2.  v. [6:26] Jos 9:23; 1 Kgs 16:34.  w. [6:27] Jos 1:5.  x. [7:1] Jos 6:18; 22:20; 1 Chr 2:7, y. [7:2] Nm 13:17–20.

z. [7:9] Nm 14:13–19.  a. [7:11–12] Jos 6:17–19.  b. [7:13] Jos 3:5; Lv 20:7; 1 Sm 16:5.  c. [7:15] Dt 13:15–16.  d. [7:17] Nm 26:20.

and they ran to the tent and there they were, hidden in the tent, with the silver underneath. [23]They took them from the tent, brought them to Joshua and all the Israelites, and spread them out before the LORD.

[24]Then Joshua and all Israel took Achan, son of Zerah, with the silver, the mantle, and the bar of gold, and with his sons and daughters, his ox, his donkey and his sheep, his tent, and all his possessions, and led them off to the Valley of Achor. [25]Joshua said, "What misery have you caused us? May the LORD bring misery upon you today!"[e] And all Israel stoned him to death. They burnt them with fire and they stoned them. [26]Over Achan they piled a great heap of stones, which remains to the present day.[f] Then the LORD turned from his anger. That is why the place is called the Valley of Achor[*] to this day.

## CHAPTER 8

**Capture of Ai.** [1]The LORD then said to Joshua: Do not be afraid or dismayed. Take all the army with you and prepare to attack Ai.[h] I have delivered the king of Ai into your power, with his people, city, and land. [2]Do to Ai and its king what you did to Jericho and its king—except that you may take its spoil and livestock as plunder.[i] Set an ambush behind the city. [3]So Joshua and all the soldiers prepared to attack Ai. Picking out thirty thousand warriors,[†] Joshua sent them off by night [4]with these orders: "See that you ambush the city from the rear. Do not be very far from the city. All of you must be ready. [5]The rest of the people and I will come up to the city, and when they make a sortie against us as they did the last time, we will flee from them. [6]They will keep coming out after us until we have drawn them away from the city, for they will think, 'They are fleeing from us as they did the last time.' When we flee, [7]then you rise from ambush and take possession of the city, which the LORD, your God, will deliver into your power. [8]When you have taken the city, set it on fire in obedience to the LORD's command. These are my orders to you."[j] [9]Then Joshua sent them away. They went to the place of ambush, taking up their position to the west of Ai, toward Bethel. Joshua, however, spent that night with the army.

[10]Early the next morning Joshua mustered the army and went up to Ai at its head, with the elders of Israel. [11]When all the troops he led were drawn up in position before the city, they pitched camp north of Ai, on the other side of the ravine. [12]He took about five thousand warriors and set them in ambush between Bethel and Ai, west of the city. [13]Thus the people took up their stations, with the main body north of the city and the ambush west of it, and Joshua waited overnight in the valley. [14]The king of Ai saw this, and he and all his army came out very early in the morning to engage Israel in battle at the place in front of the Arabah, not knowing that there was an ambush behind the city. [15]Joshua and the main body of the Israelites fled toward the wilderness, pretending defeat, [16]until the last of the soldiers in the city had been called out to pursue them. Since they were drawn away from the city, with everyone pursuing Joshua, [17]not a soldier remained in Ai or Bethel. They abandoned the city, leaving it open, as they pursued Israel.

[18]Then the LORD directed Joshua: Stretch out the javelin in your hand toward Ai, for I will deliver it into your power. Joshua stretched out the javelin in his hand toward the city, [19]and as soon as he did so, the men in ambush rose from their post, rushed in, captured the city, and immediately set it on fire. [20]By the time the army of Ai looked back, the smoke from the city was going up to the heavens. Escape in any direction was impossible, because the Israelites retreating toward the wilderness now turned on their pursuers; [21]for when Joshua and the main body of Israelites saw that the city had been taken by ambush and was going up in smoke, they struck back at the forces of Ai. [22]Since those in the city came out to intercept them, Ai's army was hemmed in by Israelites on both sides, who cut them down without any fugitives or survivors[k] [23]except the king, whom they took alive and brought to Joshua.

[24]When Israel finished killing all the inhabitants of Ai in the open, who had pursued them into the wilderness, and all of them to the last man fell by the sword, then all Israel returned and put to the sword those inside the city. [25]There fell that day a total of twelve thousand men and women, the entire population of Ai. [26]Joshua kept the javelin in his hand stretched out until he had carried out the ban on all the inhabitants of Ai. [27]However, the Israelites took for themselves as plunder the livestock and the spoil of that city, according to the command of the LORD issued to Joshua. [28]Then Joshua destroyed Ai by fire, reducing it to an everlasting mound of ruins, as it remains today.[m] [29]He had the king of Ai hanged on a tree until evening;[n] then at sunset Joshua ordered the body removed

---

*[7:26] **Achor:** "misery," or "disaster." The reference is to the saying of Joshua in v. 25, with an allusion also to the similar-sounding name of Achan.

†[8:3] **Thirty thousand warriors:** this figure of the Hebrew text, which seems extremely high, may be due to a copyist's error; some manuscripts of the Septuagint have "three thousand," which is the number of the whole army in the first, unsuccessful attack (7:4); the variant reading in v. 12 mentions "five thousand." More likely, the word for "thousand" here and in other military contexts may designate a squad or fighting unit, itself composed of significantly fewer warriors.

---

e. [7:25] Jos 6:18; 22:20; Dt 13:15–16; 1 Chr 2:7.   f. [7:26] Jos 8:29; Dt 13:18.   g. [8:1–26] Jgs 20:20–38.   h. [8:1] Jos 2:24; Dt 1:21. i. [8:2] Jos 6:21, 24; Dt 20:14.   j. [8:8] Jos 6:24.

k. [8:22] Dt 7:2.   l. [8:26] Ex 17:11–13.   m. [8:28] Dt 13:16. n. [8:29] Jos 10:26–27; Dt 21:22–23; Jn 19:31.

from the tree and cast at the entrance of the city gate, where a great heap of stones was piled up over it, which remains to the present day.

**Altar on Mount Ebal.** [30]*Later, on Mount Ebal, Joshua built to the LORD, the God of Israel, an altar [31]of unhewn stones on which no iron tool had been used,[p] just as Moses, the servant of the LORD, had commanded the Israelites, as recorded in the book of the law. On this altar they sacrificed burnt offerings to the LORD and made communion sacrifices. [32]There, in the presence of the Israelites, Joshua inscribed upon the stones a copy of the law written by Moses. [33]And all Israel, resident alien and native alike, with their elders, officers, and judges, stood on either side of the ark facing the levitical priests who were carrying the ark of the covenant of the LORD.[q] Half of them were facing Mount Gerizim and half Mount Ebal, just as Moses, the servant of the LORD, had first commanded for the blessing of the people of Israel. [34]rThen were read aloud all the words of the law, the blessings and the curses, exactly as written in the book of the law. [35]sEvery single word that Moses had commanded, Joshua read aloud to the entire assembly, including the women and children, and the resident aliens among them.

## CHAPTER 9

**Confederacy Against Israel.** [1]When the news reached all the kings west of the Jordan, in the mountain regions and in the Shephelah, and all along the coast of the Great Sea as far as the Lebanon: Hittites, Amorites, Canaanites, Perizzites, Hivites, and Jebusites,[t] [2]they gathered together to launch a common attack against Joshua and Israel.

**The Gibeonite Deception.** [3]On hearing what Joshua had done to Jericho and Ai, the inhabitants of Gibeon[u] [4]formed their own scheme. They chose provisions for a journey, making use of old sacks for their donkeys, and old wineskins, torn and mended. [5]They wore old, patched sandals and shabby garments; and all the bread they took was dry and crumbly. [6]Thus they journeyed to Joshua in the camp at Gilgal, where they said to him and to the Israelites, "We have come from a far-off land; now, make a covenant with us."[v] [7]But the Israelites replied to the Hivites,[†] "You may be living in land that is ours. How, then, can we make a covenant with you?" [8]But they answered Joshua, "We are your servants."

Then Joshua asked them, "Who are you? Where do you come from?" [9]They answered him, "Your servants have come from a far-off land, because of the fame of the LORD, your God. For we have heard reports of all that he did in Egypt[w] [10]and all that he did to the two kings of the Amorites beyond the Jordan,[x] Sihon, king of Heshbon, and Og, king of Bashan, who lived in Ashtaroth. [11]So our elders and all the inhabitants of our land said to us, 'Take along provisions for the journey and go to meet them. Say to them: "We are your servants; now make a covenant with us."' [12]This bread of ours was still warm when we brought it from home as provisions the day we left to come to you, but now it is dry and crumbly. [13]Here are our wineskins, which were new when we filled them, but now they are torn. Look at our garments and sandals; they are worn out from the very long journey." [14]Then the Israelite leaders partook of their provisions, without inquiring of the LORD.[y] [15]So Joshua made peace with them and made a covenant to let them live,[z] which the leaders of the community sealed with an oath.

**Gibeonites Made Vassals.** [16]Three days after the covenant was made, the Israelites heard that these people were from nearby, and would be living in Israel. [17]The third day on the road, the Israelites came to their cities of Gibeon, Chephirah, Beeroth, and Kiriath-jearim, [18]but did not attack them, because the leaders of the community had sworn to them by the LORD, the God of Israel. When the entire community grumbled against the leaders, [19]these all remonstrated with the community, "We have sworn to them by the LORD, the God of Israel, and so we cannot harm them. [20]Let us therefore let them live, and so deal with them that no wrath fall upon us because of the oath we have sworn to them."[a] [21]Thus the leaders said to them, "Let them live, and become hewers of wood and drawers of water[‡] for the entire community." So the community did as the leaders advised them.[b]

[22]Joshua summoned the Gibeonites and said to them, "Why did you deceive us and say, 'We live far off from you'?—You live among us! [23]Now are you accursed: every one of you shall always be a slave, hewers of wood and drawers of water, for the house of my God." [24]They answered Joshua, "Your servants were fully informed of how the LORD, your God, commanded Moses his servant that you be given the entire land and that all its inhabitants be destroyed before you. Since, therefore, at your advance, we were in great fear for our lives, we acted as we did.[c] [25]And now that we are in your power, do with us what is good and right in your

---

*[8:30–35] These ceremonies were prescribed in Dt 11:29 and 27:2–26.

†[9:7] **The Hivites:** apparently the Gibeonites belonged to this larger ethnic group (cf. also 11:19), although in 2 Sm 21:2 they are classed as Amorites; both groups are listed among the seven nations of Canaan whom, according to Dt 7:1–2, the Israelites were to dispossess.

‡[9:21] **Hewers of wood and drawers of water:** proverbial terms for those who do menial work; cf. Dt 29:10–11.

---

o. [8:30–35] Dt 27:1–8, 12–13.   p. [8:31] Ex 20:24–25.   q. [8:33] Jos 3:3; Dt 11:27; 31:9, 12.   r. [8:34] Dt 28:2–68; 30:19; 31:11; Neh 8:2–3.   s. [8:35] Dt 31:12.   t. [9:1] Jos 3:10; 5:1; Ex 3:8, 17; 23:23; Dt 1:7.   u. [9:3] Jos 6:21, 24.   v. [9:6] Ex 23:32; Dt 7:2.

w. [9:9–10] Jos 2:10–11.   x. [9:10] Nm 21:25, 33–35; Dt 1:4.   y. [9:14] Nm 27:21.   z. [9:15] Jos 11:19; 2 Sm 21:2.   a. [9:20] Jos 22:20.   b. [9:21] Dt 29:11.   c. [9:24] Ex 23:27–28; Dt 7:1–2.

eyes." ²⁶*Joshua did what he had decided: while he saved them from being killed by the Israelites, ²⁷on that day he made them, as they still are, hewers of wood and drawers of water for the community and for the altar of the LORD, in the place the LORD would choose.

## CHAPTER 10

**The Siege of Gibeon.** ¹Now when Adonizedek, king of Jerusalem, heard that Joshua had captured Ai and put it under the ban, and had done to that city and its king as he had done to Jericho and its king,ᵈ and that the inhabitants of Gibeon had made their peace with Israel, remaining among them, ²there was great fear abroad, because Gibeon was a great city, like one of the royal cities, greater even than Ai, and all its men were warriors. ³So Adonizedek, king of Jerusalem, sent to Hoham, king of Hebron, Piram, king of Jarmuth, Japhia, king of Lachish, and Debir, king of Eglon, with this message: ⁴"Come and help me attack Gibeon, for it has made peace with Joshua and the Israelites."ᵉ ⁵The five Amorite kings, of Jerusalem, Hebron, Jarmuth, Lachish, and Eglon,† gathered with all their forces, and marched against Gibeon to make war on it. ⁶Thereupon, the Gibeonites sent an appeal to Joshua in his camp at Gilgal: "Do not abandon your servants. Come up here quickly and save us. Help us, because all the Amorite kings of the mountain country have joined together against us."ᶠ
**Joshua's Victory.** ⁷So Joshua marched up from Gilgal with all his army and all his warriors. ⁸The LORD said to Joshua: Do not fear them, for I have delivered them into your power. Not one of them will be able to withstand you. ⁹After an all-night march from Gilgal, Joshua made a surprise attack upon them, ¹⁰and the LORD threw them into disorder before Israel. The Israelites inflicted a great slaughter on them at Gibeon and pursued them down the Beth-horon slope, attacking them as far as Azekah and Makkedah.

¹¹While they fled before Israel along the descent of Beth-horon, the LORD hurled great stones from the heavens‡ above them all the way to Azekah, killing many.ᵍ More died from these hailstones than the Israelites killed with the sword. ¹²It was then, when the LORD delivered up the Amorites to the Israelites, that Joshua prayed to the LORD, and said in the presence of Israel:

Sun, stand still at Gibeon,
    Moon, in the valley of Aijalon!

¹³ The sun stood still,
        the moon stayed,
    while the nation took vengeance on
        its foes.ʰ

This is recorded§ in the Book of Jashar. The sun halted halfway across the heavens; not for an entire day did it press on. ¹⁴Never before or since was there a day like this, when the LORD obeyed the voice of a man; for the LORD fought for Israel. ¹⁵Then Joshua and all Israel returned to the camp at Gilgal.

**Execution of Amorite Kings.** ¹⁶The five kings who had fled hid in the cave at Makkedah. ¹⁷When Joshua was told, "The five kings have been found, hiding in the cave at Makkedah," ¹⁸he said, "Roll large stones to the mouth of the cave and post guards over it. ¹⁹But do not remain there yourselves. Pursue your enemies, and harry them in the rear. Do not allow them to reach their cities, for the LORD, your God, has delivered them into your power."

²⁰Once Joshua and the Israelites had finally inflicted the last blows in this very great slaughter, and the survivors had escaped from them into the fortified cities, ²¹all the army returned to Joshua and the camp at Makkedah in victory; no one uttered a sound against the Israelites. ²²Then Joshua said, "Open the mouth of the cave and bring me those five kings from the cave." ²³They did so; they brought out to him from the cave the five kings, of Jerusalem, Hebron, Jarmuth, Lachish, and Eglon. ²⁴When they brought the five kings out to Joshua, he summoned all the army of Israel and said to the commanders of the soldiers who had marched with him, "Come forward and put your feet on the necks of these kings." They came forward and put their feet upon their necks. ²⁵ⁱThen Joshua said to them, "Do not be afraid or dismayed, be firm and steadfast. This is what the LORD will do to all the enemies against whom you fight." ²⁶ʲThereupon Joshua struck and killed the kings, and hanged them on five trees, where they remained hanging until evening. ²⁷At sunset Joshua commanded that they be taken down from the trees and be thrown into the cave where they had hidden; over the mouth of the cave large stones were placed, which remain until this very day.
**Conquest of Southern Canaan.** ²⁸ᵏMakkedah, too, Joshua captured and put to the sword at that time. He put the city, its king, and every

---

§[10:13] **This is recorded**: the reference is to the preceding poetic passage. Evidently the *Book of Jashar*, like the *Book of the Wars of the Lord* (Nm 21:14), recounted in epic style the exploits of Israel's early heroes. **The sun halted**: lit., "the sun stood"; this obscure passage may suppose a longer than natural day caused when the sun stopped moving across the sky, or it may refer to the sun stopping its light-giving function, perhaps through an eclipse. In any case it was seen as a sign that God fought Israel's battle (v. 42; cf. Ex 14:14).

---

*[9:26–27] Later on, Saul violated the immunity of the Gibeonites, but David vindicated it; cf. 2 Sm 21:1–9.
†[10:5] **Hebron . . . Eglon**: these four cities were to the south and southwest of Jerusalem.
‡[10:11] **Great stones from the heavens**: the hailstones mentioned in the next sentence.

---

d. [10:1] Jos 6:21, 24; 8:26–29.   e. [10:4] Jos 9:15.   f. [10:6] Jos 9:6.   g. [10:11] Jb 38:22–23.

h. [10:13] Sir 46:4; Is 28:21.   i. [10:25] Jos 1:9.   j. [10:26–27] Jos 8:29; Dt 21:22–23.   k. [10:28] Jos 6:21.

person in it under the ban, leaving no survivors. Thus he did to the king of Makkedah what he had done to the king of Jericho. [29]Joshua then passed on with all Israel from Makkedah to Libnah, and attacked it, [30]and the LORD delivered it, with its king, into the power of Israel. He put it to the sword with every person there, leaving no survivors. Thus he did to its king what he had done to the king of Jericho. [31]Joshua next passed on with all Israel from Libnah to Lachish, where they set up a camp during the attack. [32]The LORD delivered Lachish into the power of Israel, so that on the second day Joshua captured it and put it to the sword with every person in it, just as he had done to Libnah. [33]At that time Horam, king of Gezer, came up to help Lachish, but Joshua defeated him and his people, leaving him no survivors. [34]From Lachish, Joshua passed on with all Israel to Eglon; encamping near it, they attacked it [35]and captured it the same day, putting it to the sword. On that day he put under the ban every person in it, just as he had done at Lachish. [36]From Eglon, Joshua went up with all Israel to Hebron, which they attacked [37]and captured. They put it to the sword with its king, all its cities, and every person there, leaving no survivors, just as Joshua had done to Eglon. He put it under the ban and every person in it. [38]Then Joshua and all Israel turned back to Debir and attacked it, [39]capturing it with its king and all its cities. They put them to the sword and put under the ban every person in it, leaving no survivors. Thus he did to Debir and its king what he had done to Hebron, as well as to Libnah and its king.

[40]lJoshua conquered the entire land; the mountain regions, the Negeb, the Shephelah, and the mountain slopes, with all their kings. He left no survivors, but put under the ban every living being, just as the LORD, the God of Israel, had commanded. [41]Joshua conquered them from Kadesh-barnea to Gaza, and all the land of Goshen* to Gibeon. [42]All these kings and their lands Joshua captured all at once, for the LORD, the God of Israel, fought for Israel. [43]Thereupon Joshua with all Israel returned to the camp at Gilgal.

## CHAPTER 11

**Northern Confederacy.** [1]When Jabin, king of Hazor,† learned of this, he sent a message to Jobab, king of Madon, to the king of Shimron, to the king of Achshaph, [2]and to the northern kings in the mountain regions and in the Arabah near Chinneroth, in the Shephelah, and in Naphath-dor to the west.[m] [3]These were Canaanites to the east and west, Amorites, Hittites, Perizzites, and Jebusites in the mountain regions, and Hivites at the foot of Hermon in the land of Mizpah.[n] [4]They came out with all their troops, an army numerous as the sands on the seashore, and with a multitude of horses and chariots.[o] [5]All these kings made a pact and together they marched to the waters of Merom,‡ where they encamped to fight against Israel.

[6]The LORD said to Joshua, "Do not fear them, for by this time tomorrow I will present them slain to Israel. You must hamstring their horses and burn their chariots." [7]Joshua with his whole army came upon them suddenly at the waters of Merom and fell upon them. [8]The LORD delivered them into the power of the Israelites, who defeated them and pursued them to Greater Sidon, to Misrephoth-maim,[p] and eastward to the valley of Mizpah. They struck them all down, leaving no survivors. [9]Joshua did to them as the LORD had commanded: he hamstrung their horses and burned their chariots.

**Conquest of Northern Canaan.** [10]At that time Joshua, turning back, captured Hazor and struck down its king with the sword; for Hazor formerly was the chief of all those kingdoms. [11]He also struck down with the sword every person there, carrying out the ban, till none was left alive. Hazor itself he burned. [12]All the cities of those kings, and the kings themselves, Joshua captured and put to the sword, carrying out the ban on them, as Moses, the servant of the LORD, had commanded.[q] [13]However, Israel did not destroy by fire any of the cities built on their mounds, except Hazor, which Joshua burned. [14]All the spoil and livestock of these cities the Israelites took as plunder; but the people they put to the sword, until they had destroyed the last of them, leaving none alive. [15]As the LORD had commanded his servant Moses, so Moses commanded Joshua, and Joshua acted accordingly.[r] He left nothing undone that the LORD had commanded Moses should be done.

**Survey of the Conquest.** [16]So Joshua took all this land: the mountain regions, the entire Negeb, all the land of Goshen, the Shephelah, the Arabah, as well as the mountain regions and Shephelah of Israel,[s] [17]from Mount Halak that rises toward Seir[t] as far as Baal-gad in the Lebanon valley at the foot of Mount Hermon. All their kings he captured and put to death. [18]Joshua waged war against all these kings for a long time. [19]With the exception of the Hivites who lived in Gibeon,

---

*[10:41] **Goshen**: a town and its surrounding district at the southern end of the Judean mountains (cf. 11:16; 15:51); not to be confused with the land of Goshen in northeastern Egypt (Gn 45:10).

†[11:1-3] **Hazor, Madon, Shimron,** and **Chinneroth**: cities and their surrounding districts in eastern Galilee. **Achshaph** and **Naphath-dor**: southwest of Galilee. The **mountain regions**: in central and northern Galilee.

l. [10:40] Dt 20:16–17.

‡[11:5] **The waters of Merom**: of uncertain identification, perhaps Tel Qarnei Hittin, about seven and a half kilometers west of modern Tiberias.

m. [11:2] Jos 12:3.   n. [11:3] Jos 3:10.   o. [11:4] Ex 15:1, 21.   p. [11:8] Jos 13:6.   q. [11:12] Dt 7:2; 20:16–17.   r. [11:15] Dt 7:2; 31:7–8.   s. [11:16] Jos 10:41; 12:8.   t. [11:17] Jos 12:7; Dt 7:24.

no city made peace with the Israelites; all were taken in battle.[u] [20]For it was the LORD's doing to make their hearts obstinate to meet Israel in battle, that they might be put under the ban without mercy, and be destroyed as the LORD had commanded Moses.[v]

[21]*At that time Joshua penetrated the mountain regions and exterminated the Anakim in Hebron,[w] Debir, Anab, the entire mountain region of Judah, and the entire mountain region of Israel. Joshua put them and their cities under the ban, [22]so that no Anakim were left in the land of the Israelites. However, some survived in Gaza, in Gath, and in Ashdod. [23]*Thus Joshua took the whole land, just as the LORD had said to Moses. Joshua gave it to Israel as their heritage, apportioning it among the tribes. And the land had rest from war.[†]

## CHAPTER 12[‡]
**Lists of Conquered Kings.** [1]These are the kings of the land whom the Israelites conquered and whose lands they occupied, east of the Jordan, from the River Arnon to Mount Hermon, including all the eastern section of the Arabah: [2]yFirst, Sihon, king of the Amorites, who lived in Heshbon. His domain extended from Aroer, which is on the bank of the Wadi Arnon, to include the wadi itself, and the land northward through half of Gilead to the Wadi Jabbok at the border with the Ammonites, [3]as well as the Arabah from the eastern side of the Sea of Chinnereth, as far south as the eastern side of the Salt Sea of the Arabah in the direction of Beth-jeshimoth,[z] southward under the slopes of Pisgah. [4]Secondly, the border of Og, king of Bashan, a survivor of the Rephaim, who lived at Ashtaroth and Edrei.[a] [5]He ruled over Mount Hermon, Salecah, and all Bashan as far as the boundary of the Geshurites and Maacathites, and over half of Gilead as far as the territory of Sihon, king of Heshbon. [6]It was Moses, the servant of the LORD, and the Israelites who conquered them; Moses, the servant of the LORD, gave possession of their land to the Reubenites, the Gadites, and the half-tribe of Manasseh.[b]

[7]This is a list of the kings of the land whom Joshua and the Israelites conquered west of the Jordan, from Baal-gad in the Lebanon valley to Mount Halak which rises toward Seir; Joshua apportioned their land and gave possession of it to the tribes of Israel; [8]it included the mountain regions and Shephelah, the Arabah, the slopes, the wilderness, and the Negeb, belonging to the Hittites, Amorites, Canaanites, Perizzites, Hivites, and Jebusites: [9]The king of Jericho, one;[c] the king of Ai, which is near Bethel, one; [10]the king of Jerusalem, one; the king of Hebron, one; [11]the king of Jarmuth, one; the king of Lachish, one;[d] [12]the king of Eglon, one; the king of Gezer, one;[e] [13]the king of Debir, one; the king of Geder, one;[f] [14]the king of Hormah, one; the king of Arad, one; [15]the king of Libnah, one; the king of Adullam, one;[g] [16]the king of Makkedah, one; the king of Bethel, one;[h] [17]the king of Tappuah, one; the king of Hepher, one;[i] [18]the king of Aphek, one; the king of Lasharon, one;[j] [19]the king of Madon, one; the king of Hazor, one;[k] [20]the king of Shimron, one; the king of Achshaph, one;[l] [21]the king of Taanach, one; the king of Megiddo, one;[m] [22]the king of Kedesh, one; the king of Jokneam, at Carmel, one;[n] [23]the king of Dor, in Naphath-dor, one; the king of Goyim at Gilgal, one;[o] [24]and the king of Tirzah, one—thirty-one kings in all.

## II. DIVISION OF THE LAND

## CHAPTER 13
**Division of Land Commanded.** [1]When Joshua was old and advanced in years, the LORD said to him:[p] Though now you are old and advanced in years, a very large part of the land still remains to be possessed. [2]This is the remaining land: all Geshur[§] and all the districts of the Philistines [3](from the stream adjoining Egypt to the boundary of Ekron in the north is reckoned Canaanite territory, though held by the five lords of the Philistines in Gaza, Ashdod, Ashkelon, Gath, and Ekron); [4]also where the Avvim are in the south;[q] all the land of the Canaanites from Mearah of the Sidonians to Aphek, and the boundaries of the Amorites;[r] [5]and the Gebalite territory; and all the Lebanon on the east, from Baal-gad at the foot of Mount Hermon to Lebo-hamath. [6]All the inhabitants of the mountain regions between Lebanon and Misrephoth-maim, all Sidonians, I will drive out before the

---

*[11:21–23] Most of the land assigned to the tribe of Judah was not conquered by it until the early period of the Judges. See note on Jgs 1:1–36.

†[11:23] **The land had rest from war:** later passages (15:13–17; 17:12–13) show individual tribes still fighting against the remaining Canaanites. This verse forms the conclusion to the first part of the book.

‡[12:1–24] This chapter, inserted between the two principal parts of the book (chaps. 1–11 and 13–21), resembles the lists of conquered cities which are inscribed on monuments of Egyptian and Assyrian rulers. Perhaps this list was copied here from some such public Israelite record.

§[13:2] **Geshur:** not to be confused with the large Aramean district of the same name in Bashan (vv. 11–13; Dt 3:14); here it is a region to the south of the Philistine country, since vv. 2–5 list the unconquered lands along the coast from south to north; cf. also 1 Sm 27:8.

---

u. [11:19] Jos 9:3, 7, 15.   v. [11:20] Dt 2:30; 20:16–17.   w. [11:21] Jos 15:13–14; Nm 13:22; Dt 1:28; 9:1–3.   x. [11:23] Jos 14:1–19:51; Nm 34:2–12; Dt 1:5–10.   y. [12:2–5] Nm 21:21–35; Dt 1:4; 2:24–37.   z. [12:3] Jos 13:20.   a. [12:4] Nm 34:11–12.   b. [12:6] Nm 32:33; Dt 3:12–13.

c. [12:9] Jos 6:2; 8:23.   d. [12:10–11] Jos 10:23.   e. [12:12] Jos 10:23, 33.   f. [12:13] Jos 10:38–39; 15:36.   g. [12:15] Jos 10:29–30; 15:35.   h. [12:16] Jos 8:17; 10:28.   i. [12:17] Jos 15:34.   j. [12:18] Jos 15:53.   k. [12:19] Jos 11:1, 10.   l. [12:20] Jos 11:1.   m. [12:21] Jos 17:11.   n. [12:22] Jos 19:37.   o. [12:23] Jos 11:2.   p. [13:1] Jos 23:1.   q. [13:4] Jgs 3:3.   r. [13:4] Jos 1:4.

Israelites;[s] at least include these areas in the division of the Israelite heritage, just as I have commanded you. [7]Now, therefore, apportion among the nine tribes and the half-tribe of Manasseh the land which is to be their heritage.

**The Eastern Tribes.** [8]Now the other half of the tribe of Manasseh, as well as the Reubenites and Gadites, had taken as their heritage what Moses, the servant of the LORD, had given them east of the Jordan: [9]from Aroer on the bank of the Wadi Arnon and the city in the wadi itself, through the tableland of Medeba and Dibon, [10]with the rest of the cities of Sihon, king of the Amorites, who reigned in Heshbon, to the boundary of the Ammonites; [11]also Gilead and the territory of the Geshurites and Maacathites, all Mount Hermon, and all Bashan as far as Salecah, [12]the entire kingdom in Bashan of Og, who was king at Ashtaroth and Edrei (he was a holdover from the remnant of the Rephaim). These Moses defeated and dispossessed. [13]But the Israelites did not dispossess the Geshurites and Maacathites, so that Geshur and Maacath dwell in the midst of Israel to this day. [14]However, Moses assigned no heritage to the tribe of Levi; the LORD, the God of Israel, is their heritage, as the LORD had promised them.

**Reuben.** [15]This is what Moses gave to the tribe of the Reubenites by their clans:[w] [16]Their territory reached from Aroer, on the bank of the Wadi Arnon, and the city in the wadi itself, through the tableland about Medeba, [17]to include Heshbon and all its towns on the tableland, Dibon, Bamoth-baal, Beth-baal-meon, [18]Jahaz, Kedemoth, Mephaath, [19]Kiriathaim, Sibmah, Zereth-shahar on the knoll within the valley, [20]Beth-peor, the slopes of Pisgah, Beth-jeshimoth, [21]and the other cities of the tableland and of the whole kingdom of Sihon. This Amorite king, who reigned in Heshbon, Moses had defeated, with the princes of Midian, vassals of Sihon who were settled in the land: Evi, Rekem, Zur, Hur, and Reba;[x] [22]Balaam, son of Beor, the diviner, the Israelites killed with the sword, together with those they struck down.[y] [23]The boundary of the Reubenites was the Jordan. These cities and their villages were the heritage of the Reubenites by their clans.

**Gad.** [24]This is what Moses gave to the tribe of the Gadites by their clans: [25]Their territory included Jazer, all the cities of Gilead, and half the land of the Ammonites as far as Aroer, toward Rabbah [26](that is, from Heshbon to Ramath-mizpeh and Betonim, and from Mahanaim to the boundary of Lo-debar); [27]and in the Jordan valley: Beth-haram, Beth-nimrah, Succoth, Zaphon, the other part of the kingdom of Sihon, king of Heshbon, with the bank of the Jordan to the southeastern tip of the Sea of Chinnereth. [28]These cities and their villages were the heritage of the clans of the Gadites.

**Manasseh.** [29]This is what Moses gave to the half-tribe of Manasseh; the half-tribe of the Manassites, by their clans, had [30]territory including Mahanaim, all of Bashan, the entire kingdom of Og, king of Bashan, and all the villages of Jair, which are sixty cities in Bashan. [31]Half of Gilead, with Ashtaroth and Edrei, royal cities of Og in Bashan, fell to the descendants of Machir, son of Manasseh, to half the Machirites, by their clans.

[32]These are the heritages which Moses gave when he was in the plains of Moab, beyond the Jordan east of Jericho. [33]But Moses gave no heritage to the tribe of Levi: the LORD, the God of Israel, is their heritage, as he had promised them.[b]

# CHAPTER 14

**The Western Tribes.** [1]These are the portions which the Israelites received as heritage in the land of Canaan.[c] Eleazar the priest, Joshua, son of Nun, and the heads of families in the tribes of the Israelites determined [2]their heritage by lot, as the LORD had commanded through Moses concerning the remaining nine and a half tribes.[d] [3]To two and a half tribes Moses had already given a heritage beyond the Jordan; to the Levites he had given no heritage among them:[e] [4]the descendants of Joseph formed two tribes, Manasseh and Ephraim. But the Levites were given no share of the land except cities to live in, with their pasture lands for the herds and flocks.[f]

[5]As the LORD had commanded Moses, so the Israelites did: they apportioned the land.

**Caleb's Portion.** [6]When the Judahites approached Joshua in Gilgal, the Kenizzite Caleb, son of Jephunneh, said to him: "You know the word the LORD spoke to Moses, the man of God, concerning you and concerning me in Kadesh-barnea. [7]I was forty years old when Moses, the servant of the LORD, sent me from Kadesh-barnea to reconnoiter the land; and I brought back to him a frank report. [8]My fellow scouts who went up with me made the people's confidence melt away, but I was completely loyal to the LORD, my God. [9]On that occasion Moses swore this oath, 'The land where you have set foot shall become your heritage and that of your descendants forever, because you have been completely loyal to the LORD, my God.' [10]Now, as he promised, the LORD has preserved me these forty-five years since the LORD spoke thus to Moses while Israel journeyed in the wilderness; and now I am eighty-five years old,[j] [11]but I am still as strong today as I was the day Moses sent me

s. [13:6] Nm 11:8.   t. [13:8] Jos 12:6; Nm 32:33.   u. [13:14] Jos 14:3–4; Nm 18:20–24.   v. [13:15–31] Dt 3:12–17.   w. [13:15–23] Nm 21:25–31; 32:37–38.   x. [13:21] Nm 21:24; 31:8; Dt 3:10.   y. [13:22] Nm 31:8.   z. [13:24–28] Nm 32:34–36.

a. [13:29–31] Nm 32:39–42.   b. [13:33] Jos 18:7; Nm 18:20.   c. [14:1] Jos 17:4; 21:1; Nm 27:19–22; 34:17–18.   d. [14:2] Nm 26:55; 33:54; 34:13.   e. [14:3] Jos 13:8, 14, 33.   f. [14:4] Jos 21:3–40; Gn 48:5.   g. [14:6] Nm 14:24, 30; 32:12; Dt 1:36, 38.   h. [14:7] Nm 14:6–9.   i. [14:8] Nm 13:31–33; 14:24; 32:12; Dt 1:36.   j. [14:10] Nm 14:30.

forth, with no less vigor whether it be for war or for any other tasks."*k 12Now give me this mountain region which the Lord promised me that day, as you yourself heard. True, the Anakim are there, with large fortified cities, but if the Lord is with me I shall be able to dispossess them, as the Lord promised."*l 13Joshua blessed Caleb, son of Jephunneh, and gave him Hebron as his heritage.m 14Therefore Hebron remains the heritage of the Kenizzite Caleb, son of Jephunneh, to the present day, because he was completely loyal to the Lord, the God of Israel. 15Hebron was formerly called Kiriath-arba, for Arba, the greatest among the Anakim.n And the land had rest from war.

## CHAPTER 15

**Boundaries of Judah.** 1The lot for the tribe of Judah by their clans fell toward the boundary of Edom, the wilderness of Zin in the Negeb, in the extreme south.o 2Their southern boundary ran from the end of the Salt Sea,† from the tongue of land that faces the Negeb, 3and went southward below the pass of Akrabbim, across through Zin, up to a point south of Kadesh-barnea, across to Hezron, and up to Addar; from there, looping around Karka, 4it crossed to Azmon and then joined the Wadi of Egypt‡ before coming out at the sea. (This is your southern boundary.) 5The eastern boundary was the Salt Sea as far as the mouth of the Jordan.

The northern boundary climbed northward from the tongue of the sea, toward the mouth of the Jordan, 6up to Beth-hoglah, and ran north of Beth-arabah, up to Eben-Bohan-ben-Reuben. 7Thence the boundary climbed to Debir, north of the Valley of Achor,r in the direction of the Gilgal that faces the pass of Adummim, on the south side of the wadi; from there it crossed to the waters of En-shemesh and emerged at En-rogel. 8Climbing again to the Valley of Ben-hinnom§ on the southern flank of the Jebusites (that is, Jerusalem), the boundary rose to the top of the mountain at the northern end of the Valley of Rephaim,s which bounds the Valley of Hinnom on the west. 9From the top of the mountain it ran to the fountain of waters

of Nephtoah,t extended to the cities of Mount Ephron, and continued to Baalah, or Kiriath-jearim. 10From Baalah the boundary curved westward to Mount Seir and passed north of the ridge of Mount Jearim (that is, Chesalon); it descended to Beth-shemesh, and ran across to Timnah. 11It then extended along the northern flank of Ekron, continued through Shikkeron, and across to Mount Baalah, from there to include Jabneel, before it came out at the sea. 12The western boundary was the Great Sea¶ and its coast. This was the complete boundary of the Judahites by their clans.

**Conquest by Caleb.** 13uAs the Lord had commanded, Joshua gave Caleb, son of Jephunneh,v a portion among the Judahites, namely, Kiriath-arba (Arba was the father of Anak), that is, Hebron. 14wAnd Caleb dispossessed from there the three Anakim, the descendants of Anak: Sheshai, Ahiman, and Talmai. 15From there he marched up against the inhabitants of Debir,x which was formerly called Kiriath-sepher. 16Caleb said, "To the man who attacks Kiriath-sepher and captures it, I will give my daughter Achsah in marriage." 17**Othniel captured it, the son of Caleb's brother Kenaz; so Caleb gave him his daughter Achsah in marriage. 18When she came to him, she induced him to ask her father for some land. Then, as she alighted from the donkey, Caleb asked her, "What do you want?" 19She answered, "Give me a present! Since you have assigned to me land in the Negeb, give me also pools of water." So he gave her the upper and the lower pools.

**Cities of Judah.**†† 20This is the heritage of the tribe of Judahites by their clans: 21The cities of the tribe of the Judahites in the extreme southern district toward Edom were: Kabzeel, Eder, Jagur, 22Kinah, Dimonah, Adadah, 23Kedesh, Hazor, and Ithnan; 24Ziph, Telem, Bealoth, 25Hazor-hadattah, and Kerioth-hezron (that is, Hazor); 26Amam, Shema, Moladah, 27Hazar-gaddah, Heshmon, Beth-pelet, 28Hazar-shual, Beer-sheba, and Biziothiah; 29Baalah, Iim, Ezem, 30Eltolad, Chesil, Hormah, 31Ziklag, Madmannah, Sansannah, 32Lebaoth, Shilhim, and Ain and Rimmon; a total of twenty-nine cities with their villages.

33In the Shephelah: Eshtaol, Zorah, Ashnah, 34Zanoah, Engannim, Tappuah, Enam, 35Jarmuth, Adullam, Socoh, Azekah, 36Shaaraim, Adithaim, Gederah, and Gederothaim; fourteen cities and their villages. 37Zenan, Hadashah, Migdal-gad,

---

*[14:11] **War . . . other tasks:** lit., "to go forth and to come in," i.e., to conduct military expeditions and to return after victory; cf. 1 Sm 18:16; 2 Sm 5:2.

†[15:2] **Salt Sea:** the Dead Sea. The "tongue," a prominent feature of the landscape, is a spit of land thrusting into the Dead Sea from its eastern shore; it is now called by its Arabic name, *el lisân,* "tongue."

‡[15:4] **Wadi of Egypt:** the natural boundary between Gaza and the Sinai Peninsula.

§[15:8] **The Valley of Ben-hinnom:** the southern limit of Jerusalem. *Ben-hinnom* means "son of Hinnom." The place was also called Valley of Hinnom, in Hebrew *ge-hinnom,* whence the word "Gehenna" is derived.

¶[15:12] **Great Sea:** the Mediterranean.

**[15:17–19] The story of Othniel is told again in Jgs 1:13–15; cf. also Jgs 3:9–11.

††[15:20–62] This elaborate list of the cities of Judah was probably taken from a document made originally for administrative purposes; the cities are divided into four provincial districts, some of which have further subdivisions. For similar lists of the cities of Judah, cf. 19:2–7; 1 Chr 4:28–32; Neh 11:25–30. This list has suffered in transmission, so that the totals given in vv. 32 and 36 are not exact; many of the cities cannot be identified.

k. [14:11] Sir 46:1–10. l. [14:12] Jos 11:21–22. m. [14:13] Jos 10:36–37; 15:13–19; 21:11–12. n. [14:15] Jgs 1:10. o. [15:1] Nm 34:3. p. [15:2–4] Nm 34:3–12. q. [15:6] Jos 18:18–19, 22. r. [15:7] Jos 7:26; 18:16–18. s. [15:8] Jos 18:16.

t. [15:9] Jos 18:15. u. [15:13–19] Jgs 1:10–15. v. [15:13] Jos 14:13–15. w. [15:14] Nm 13:22; Jgs 1:20. x. [15:15] Jos 10:38.

³⁸Dilean, Mizpeh, Joktheel, ³⁹Lachish, Bozkath, Eglon, ⁴⁰Cabbon, Lahmas, Chitlish, ⁴¹Gederoth, Beth-dagon, Naamah, and Makkedah; sixteen cities and their villages. ⁴²Libnah, Ether, Ashan, ⁴³Iphtah, Ashnah, Nezib, ⁴⁴Keilah, Achzib, and Mareshah; nine cities and their villages. ⁴⁵Ekron and its towns and villages; ⁴⁶from Ekron to the sea, all the towns that lie alongside Ashdod, and their villages; ⁴⁷Ashdod and its towns and villages; Gaza and its towns and villages, as far as the Wadi of Egypt and the coast of the Great Sea.

⁴⁸In the mountain regions: Shamir, Jattir, Socoh, ⁴⁹Dannah, Kiriath-sannah (that is, Debir), ⁵⁰Anab, Eshtemoh, Anim, ⁵¹Goshen, Holon, and Giloh; eleven cities and their villages. ⁵²Arab, Dumah, Eshan, ⁵³Janim, Beth-tappuah, Aphekah, ⁵⁴Humtah, Kiriath-arba (that is, Hebron), and Zior; nine cities and their villages. ⁵⁵Maon, Carmel, Ziph, Juttah, ⁵⁶Jezreel, Jokdeam, Zanoah, ⁵⁷Kain, Gibbeah, and Timnah; ten cities and their villages. ⁵⁸Halhul, Beth-zur, Gedor, ⁵⁹Maarath, Beth-anoth, and Eltekon; six cities and their villages. Tekoa, Ephrathah (that is, Bethlehem), Peor, Etam, Kulom, Tatam, Zores, Karim, Gallim, Bether, and Manoko; eleven cities and their villages. ⁶⁰Kiriath-baal (that is, Kiriath-jearim) and Rabbah; two cities and their villages.ʸ

⁶¹In the wilderness:* Beth-arabah, Middin, Secacah, ⁶²Nibshan, Ir-hamelah, and En-gedi; six cities and their villages. ⁶³But the Jebusites who lived in Jerusalem the Judahites could not dispossess; so the Jebusites dwell in Jerusalem beside the Judahites to the present day.ᶻ

## CHAPTER 16

**The Joseph Tribes.**† ¹The lot that fell to the Josephites extended from the Jordan at Jericho to the waters of Jericho east of the wilderness; then the boundary went up from Jericho to the heights at Bethel.‡ ²Leaving Bethel for Luz, it crossed the ridge to the border of the Archites at Ataroth, ³and descended westward to the border of the Japhletites, to that of the Lower Beth-horon, and to Gezer, and from there to the sea.ᵃ **Ephraim.** ⁴Within the heritage of Manasseh and Ephraim, sons of Joseph, ⁵the dividing line§ for the heritage of the Ephraimites by their clans ran from east of Ataroth-addar to Upper Beth-horonᵇ ⁶and thence to the sea. From

Michmethathᶜ on the north, their boundary curved eastward around Taanath-shiloh, and continued east of it to Janoah; ⁷from there it descended to Ataroth and Naarah, and reaching Jericho, it ended at the Jordan. ⁸From Tappuah the boundary ran westward to the Wadi Kanah and ended at the sea. This was the heritage of the Ephraimites by their clans, ⁹including the villages that belonged to each city set aside for the Ephraimites within the heritage of the Manassites. ¹⁰But they did not dispossess the Canaanites living in Gezer;ᵈ they live within Ephraim to the present day, though they have been put to forced labor.

## CHAPTER 17

**Manasseh.** ¹ᵉNow as for the lot that fell to the tribe of Manassehᶠ as the firstborn of Joseph: since Manasseh's eldest son, Machir, the father of Gilead, was a warrior, who had already obtained Gilead and Bashan, ²the allotment was now made to the rest of the Manassites by their clans: the descendants of Abiezer, Helek, Asriel, Shechem, Hepher, and Shemida; these are the other male children of Manasseh, son of Joseph, by their clans.

³ᵍFurthermore, Zelophehad, son of Hepher, son of Gilead, son of Machir, son of Manasseh, had no sons, but only daughters, whose names were Mahlah, Noah, Hoglah, Milcah, and Tirzah. ⁴These presented themselves to Eleazar the priest, to Joshua, son of Nun, and to the leaders, saying, "The LORD commanded Moses to give us a heritage among our relatives." So in accordance with the command of the LORD a heritage was given them among their father's relatives. ⁵Thus ten shares fell to Manasseh apart from the land of Gilead and Bashan beyond the Jordan,ʰ ⁶since these female descendants of Manasseh received each a portion among his sons. The land of Gilead fell to the rest of the Manassites.

⁷Manasseh bordered on Asher.¶ From Michmethath, near Shechem, another boundary ran southward to include the inhabitants of En-Tappuah, ⁸because the district of Tappuah belonged to Manasseh, although Tappuah itself was an Ephraimite city on the border of Manasseh. ⁹This same boundary continued down to the Wadi Kanah.ⁱ The cities that belonged to Ephraim from among the cities in Manasseh were those to the south of that wadi; thus the territory of Manasseh ran north of the wadi and ended at the sea. ¹⁰The land on the south belonged to Ephraim and that on the north to Manasseh; with the sea

---

*[15:61] **In the wilderness**: in the Jordan rift near the Dead Sea.

†[16:1–17:18] After the boundaries and cities of Judah, the most important tribe, are given, the land of the next most important group, the two Joseph tribes of Ephraim and Manasseh, is described, though it was separated from Judah by the territories of Benjamin (18:11–20) and Dan (19:40–48).

‡[16:1–3] This line formed the southern boundary of Ephraim and the northern boundaries of Benjamin and of Dan.

§[16:5] **The dividing line**: separating Ephraim from Manasseh. Ephraim's northern border (v. 5) is given in an east-to-west direction; its eastern border (vv. 6–7) in a north-to-south direction.

¶[17:7] **Manasseh bordered on Asher**: only at the extreme northwestern section of Manasseh's territory. The boundary given in the following sentences (vv. 7–10) is a more detailed description of the one already mentioned in 16:5–7, as separating Manasseh from Ephraim.

y. [15:60] Jos 18:14.   z. [15:63] Jgs 1:21; 2 Sm 5:6.   a. [16:3] Jos 10:10, 33.   b. [16:5] Jos 18:13.

c. [16:6–9] Jos 17:7–9.   d. [16:10] Jgs 1:29.   e. [17:1–3] Nm 26:29–33.   f. [17:1] Gn 41:51; 46:20; 48:18; 50:23; Dt 3:13, 15.   g. [17:3–6] Nm 27:1–7; 36:2.   h. [17:5] Nm 13:30–31.   i. [17:9] Jos 16:8–9.

as their common boundary, they reached Asher on the north and Issachar on the east.

[11]¡Moreover, in Issachar and in Asher Manasseh was awarded Beth-shean and its towns, Ibleam and its towns, the inhabitants of Dor and its towns, the inhabitants of Endor and its towns, the inhabitants of Taanach and its towns, the inhabitants of Megiddo and its towns (the third is Naphath-dor). [12]Since the Manassites were not able to dispossess these cities, the Canaanites continued to inhabit this region. [13]When the Israelites grew stronger they put the Canaanites to forced labor, but they did not dispossess them.

**Protest of Joseph Tribes.** [14]The descendants of Joseph said to Joshua, "Why have you given us only one lot and one share as our heritage?[k] Our people are too many, because of the extent to which the LORD has blessed us." [15]Joshua answered them, "If you are too many, go up to the forest and clear out a place for yourselves there in the land of the Perizzites and Rephaim, since the mountain regions of Ephraim are so narrow." [16]For the Josephites said, "Our mountain regions are not enough for us; on the other hand, the Canaanites living in the valley region all have iron chariots, in particular those in Beth-shean and its towns, and those in the valley of Jezreel." [17]Joshua therefore said to Ephraim and Manasseh, the house of Joseph, "You are a numerous people and very strong. You shall not have merely one share, [18]for the mountain region which is now forest shall be yours when you clear it. Its adjacent land shall also be yours if, despite their strength and iron chariots, you dispossess the Canaanites."

## CHAPTER 18

[1]The whole community of the Israelites assembled at Shiloh, where they set up the tent of meeting; and the land was subdued before them.[l]

**The Seven Remaining Portions.** [2]There remained seven tribes among the Israelites that had not yet received their heritage. [3]Joshua therefore said to the Israelites, "How much longer will you put off taking steps to possess the land which the LORD, the God of your ancestors, has given you? [4]Choose three representatives from each of your tribes; I will send them to go throughout the land and describe it for purposes of acquiring their heritage. When they return to me [5]you shall divide it into seven parts. Judah is to retain its territory in the south,[m] and the house of Joseph its territory in the north. [6]You shall bring to me here the description of the land in seven sections. I will then cast lots for you here before the LORD, our God. [7]For the Levites have no share among you,[n] because the priesthood of the LORD is their heritage; while

Gad, Reuben, and the half-tribe of Manasseh have already received the heritage east of the Jordan which Moses, the servant of the LORD, gave them."

[8]When those who were to describe the land were ready for their journey, Joshua commanded them, "Go throughout the land and describe it; return to me and I will cast lots for you here before the LORD in Shiloh." [9]So they went through the land, described its cities in writing in seven sections, and returned to Joshua in the camp at Shiloh. [10]Joshua then cast lots for them before the LORD in Shiloh, and divided up the land for the Israelites into their separate shares.

**Benjamin.** [11]One lot fell to the tribe of Benjaminites by their clans. The territory allotted them lay between the descendants of Judah and those of Joseph. [12]°Their northern boundary* began at the Jordan and went over the northern flank of Jericho, up westward into the mountains, until it reached the wilderness of Beth-aven. [13]From there it crossed over to the southern flank of Luz (that is, Bethel). Then it ran down to Ataroth-addar, on the mountaintop south of Lower Beth-horon.[p] [14]For the western border, the boundary line swung south from the mountaintop opposite Beth-horon until it reached Kiriath-baal (that is, Kiriath-jearim; this city belonged to the Judahites). This was the western boundary. [15]The southern boundary began at the limits of Kiriath-jearim and projected to the spring at Nephtoah. [16q]It went down to the edge of the mountain on the north of the Valley of Rephaim, where it faces the Valley of Ben-hinnom; and continuing down the Valley of Hinnom along the southern flank of the Jebusites, reached En-rogel. [17]Inclining to the north, it extended to En-shemesh, and thence to Geliloth, opposite the pass of Adummim. Then it dropped to Eben-Bohan-ben-Reuben, [18]across the northern flank of the Arabah overlook, down into the Arabah. [19]From there the boundary continued across the northern flank of Beth-hoglah and extended northward to the tongue of the Salt Sea, toward the southern end of the Jordan. This was the southern boundary. [20]The Jordan bounded it on the east. This was how the heritage of the Benjaminites by their clans was bounded on all sides.

[21]Now the cities belonging to the tribe of the Benjaminites by their clans were: Jericho, Beth-hoglah, Emek-keziz, [22]Beth-arabah, Zemaraim, Bethel, [23]Avvim, Parah, Ophra, [24]Chephar-ammoni, Ophni, and Geba; twelve cities and

---

j. [17:11] 1 Chr 7:29.   k. [17:14] Jos 16:4; Gn 48:19–22.   l. [18:1] Jos 11:23; 14:15; 19:51.   m. [18:5] Jos 15:1–17:18.   n. [18:7] Jos 13:8, 33.

*[18:12–20] Benjamin's northern boundary (vv. 12–13) corresponded to part of the southern boundary of Ephraim (16:1–2). Their western border (v. 14) was the eastern border of Dan (cf. 19:40–47). Their southern boundary (vv. 15–19) corresponded to part of the northern boundary of Judah (15:5–9).

o. [18:12–13] Jos 16:1–5.   p. [18:13] Gn 28:19.   q. [18:16–18] Jos 15:6–8.

their villages. ²⁵Also Gibeon, Ramah, Beeroth, ²⁶Mizpeh, Chephirah, Mozah, ²⁷Rekem, Irpeel, Taralah, ²⁸Zela, Haeleph, the Jebusite city (that is, Jerusalem), Gibeah, and Kiriath; fourteen cities and their villages. This was the heritage of the clans of Benjaminites.

## CHAPTER 19

**Simeon.** ¹The second lot fell to Simeon. The heritage of the tribe of Simeonites by their clans lay within that of the Judahites. ²ʳFor their heritage they received Beer-sheba, Shema, Moladah, ³Hazar-shual, Balah, Ezem, ⁴Eltolad, Bethul, Hormah, ⁵Ziklag, Bethmar-caboth, Hazar-susah, ⁶Beth-lebaoth, and Sharuhen; thirteen cities and their villages. ⁷Also Ain, Rimmon, Ether, and Ashan; four cities and their villages, ⁸besides all the villages around these cities as far as Baalath-beer (that is, Ramoth-negeb). This was the heritage of the tribe of the Simeonites by their clans. ⁹This heritage of the Simeonites was within the confines of the Judahites; for since the portion of the latter was too large for them, the Simeonites obtained their heritage within it.
**Zebulun.** ¹⁰The third lot fell to the Zebulunites by their clans. The boundary of their heritage was at Sarid. ¹¹Their boundary went up west and through Mareal, reaching Dabbesheth and the wadi that is near Jokneam. ¹²From Sarid eastward it ran to the district of Chisloth-tabor, on to Daberath, and up to Japhia. ¹³From there it continued eastward to Gath-hepher and to Eth-kazin, extended to Rimmon, and turned to Neah. ¹⁴Skirting north of Hannathon, the boundary ended at the valley of Iphtahel. ¹⁵Thus, with Kattath, Nahalal, Shimron, Idalah, and Bethlehem, there were twelve cities and their villages. ¹⁶This was the heritage of the Zebulunites by their clans, these cities and their villages.
**Issachar.** ¹⁷ᵗThe fourth lot fell to Issachar. The territory of the Issacharites by their clans ¹⁸included Jezreel, Chesulloth, Shunem, ¹⁹Hapharaim, Shion, Anaharath, ²⁰Rabbith, Kishion, Ebez, ²¹Remeth, En-gannim, En-haddah, and Beth-pazzez. ²²The boundary reached Tabor, Shahazumah, and Beth-shemesh, ending at the Jordan: sixteen cities and their villages. ²³This

was the heritage of the Issacharites by their clans, these cities and their villages.
**Asher.** ²⁴ᵗThe fifth lot fell to the Asherites by their clans. ²⁵Their territory included Helkath, Hali, Beten, Achshaph, ²⁶Allammelech, Amad, and Mishal, and reached Carmel on the west, and Shihor-libnath. ²⁷In the other direction, it ran eastward of Beth-dagon, reached Zebulun and the valley of Iphtahel; then north of Beth-emek and Neiel, it extended northward to Cabul, ²⁸Ebron, Rehob,ᵗ Hammon, and Kanah, near Greater Sidon. ²⁹Then the boundary turned back to Ramah and to the fortress city of Tyre; thence it cut back to Hosah and ended at the sea. Thus, with Mahalab, Achzib, ³⁰Ummah, Acco, Aphek, and Rehob, there were twenty-two cities and their villages. ³¹This was the heritage of the tribe of the Asherites by their clans, these cities and their villages.
**Naphtali.** ³²ᵍThe sixth lot fell to the Naphtalites. ³³Their boundary extended from Heleph, from the oak at Zaanannim, including Adami-nekeb and Jabneel, to Lakkum, and ended at the Jordan. ³⁴In the opposite direction, westerly, it ran through Aznoth-tabor and from there extended to Hukkok; it reached Zebulun on the south, Asher on the west, and the Jordan on the east. ³⁵The fortified cities were Ziddim, Zer, Hammath, Rakkath, Chinnereth, ³⁶Adamah, Ramah, Hazor, ³⁷Kedesh, Edrei, En-hazor, ³⁸Yiron, Migdal-el, Horem, Beth-anath, and Beth-shemesh;ᶠ nineteen cities and their villages. ³⁹This was the heritage of the tribe of the Naphtalites by their clans, these cities and their villages.
**Dan.** ⁴⁰ˢThe seventh lot fell to the tribe of Danites by their clans. ⁴¹Their heritage was the territory of Zorah, Eshtaol, Ir-shemesh, ⁴²Shaalabbin, Aijalon, Ithlah,ᵘ ⁴³Elon, Timnah, Ekron, ⁴⁴Eltekoh, Gibbethon, Baalath, ⁴⁵Jehud, Beneberak, Gath-rimmon, ⁴⁶Me-jarkon, and Rakkon, with the coast at Joppa. ⁴⁷ᵛBut the territory of the Danites was too small for them; so the Danites marched up and attacked Leshem,** which they captured and put to the sword. Once they had taken possession of Leshem, they dwelt there and named it after their ancestor Dan. ⁴⁸This was the heritage of the tribe of the Danites by their clans, these cities and their villages.

---

*[19:10–16] Zebulun's territory was in the central section of the Jezreel Valley and of southern Galilee; it was bounded on the south by Manasseh, on the southeast by Issachar, on the northeast and north by Naphtali, and on the west by Asher. The site of the later city of Nazareth was within its borders. Bethlehem of Zebulun was, of course, distinct from the city of the same name in Judah. **Twelve cities:** apparently seven of the names are missing from v. 15, unless some of the places mentioned in vv. 12–14 are to be included in the number.

†[19:17–23] Issachar's land was on the eastern watershed of the Jezreel Valley, but also included the southeastern end of the Galilean mountains. It was surrounded by Manasseh on the south and east, by Naphtali on the north, and by Zebulun on the west. Jezreel (v. 18) dominated the valley to which it gave its name, the later form of which was Esdraelon.

r. [19:2–8] 1 Chr 4:28–33.

‡[19:24–31] Asher inherited the western slope of the Galilean hills as far as the Mediterranean, with Manasseh to the south, Zebulun and Naphtali to the east, and Phoenicia to the north.

§[19:32–39] Naphtali received eastern Galilee; Asher was to the west and Zebulun and Issachar were to the south, while the upper Jordan and Mount Hermon formed the eastern border. Part of the tribe of Dan later on occupied the northern extremity of Naphtali's lands, at the sources of the Jordan (v. 47).

¶[19:40–46] The original territory of Dan was a small enclave between Judah, Benjamin, Ephraim, and the Philistines.

**[19:47] **Leshem:** called Laish in Jgs 18, where the story of the migration of the Danites is told at greater length.

s. [19:28–30] Jgs 1:31.  t. [19:38] Jgs 1:33.  u. [19:42] Jgs 1:35.
v. [19:47] Jgs 18:27–29.

**Joshua's City.** [49]When the last of them had received the portions of the land they were to inherit, the Israelites assigned a heritage in their midst to Joshua, son of Nun. [50]According to the command of the Lord, they gave him the city he requested, Timnah-serah[w] in the mountain region of Ephraim. He rebuilt the city and made it his home.

[51]These are the heritages which Eleazar the priest, Joshua, son of Nun, and the heads of families in the tribes of the Israelites apportioned by lot in the presence of the Lord, at the door of the tent of meeting in Shiloh. Thus they finished dividing the land.

## CHAPTER 20

**Cities of Refuge.** [1*]The Lord said to Joshua:[*] [2]Tell the Israelites: Designate for yourselves the cities of refuge of which I spoke to you through Moses, [3]to which anyone guilty of inadvertent and unintentional homicide may flee for asylum from the avenger of blood. [4]To one of these cities the killer shall flee, and standing at the entrance of the city gate, shall plead his case in the hearing of the elders of the city, who must receive him and assign him a place in which to live among them. [5]Though the avenger of blood pursues him, they shall not deliver up to him the one who killed a neighbor unintentionally, when there had been no hatred previously. [6]Once he has stood judgment before the community, he shall live on in that city until the death of the high priest who is in office at the time. Then the killer may return home to the city from where he originally fled.

**List of Cities.** [7]So they set apart Kedesh in Galilee in the mountain region of Naphtali, Shechem in the mountain region of Ephraim, and Kiriath-arba (that is, Hebron) in the mountain region of Judah.[y] [8]And beyond the Jordan east of Jericho they designated Bezer in the wilderness on the tableland in the tribe of Reuben, Ramoth in Gilead in the tribe of Gad, and Golan in Bashan in the tribe of Manasseh.[z] [9]These are the designated cities to which any Israelite or alien residing among them who had killed a person unintentionally might flee to escape death at the hand of the avenger of blood, until the killer could appear before the community.

## CHAPTER 21

**Levitical Cities.** [1]The heads of the Levite families[†] approached Eleazar the priest, Joshua,

son of Nun, and the heads of families of the other tribes of the Israelites[d] [2]at Shiloh in the land of Canaan, and said to them, "The Lord commanded, through Moses, that cities be given us to dwell in, with pasture lands for our livestock."[b] [3]Out of their own heritage, according to the command of the Lord, the Israelites gave the Levites the following cities with their pasture lands.

[4]When the first lot among the Levites fell to the clans of the Kohathites, the descendants of Aaron the priest obtained by lot from the tribes of Judah, Simeon, and Benjamin, thirteen cities. [5]From the clans of the tribe of Ephraim, from the tribe of Dan, and from the half-tribe of Manasseh, the rest of the Kohathites obtained by lot ten cities.[c] [6]From the clans of the tribe of Issachar, from the tribe of Asher, from the tribe of Naphtali, and from the half-tribe of Manasseh, the Gershonites obtained by lot thirteen cities. [7]From the tribes of Reuben, Gad, and Zebulun, the clans of the Merarites obtained by lot twelve cities. [8]These cities with their pasture lands the Israelites gave by lot to the Levites, as the Lord had commanded through Moses.

**Cities of the Priests.** [9d]From the tribes of the Judahites and Simeonites they gave the following cities [10]and assigned them to the descendants of Aaron in the Kohathite clan of the Levites, since the first lot fell to them: [11]first, Kiriath-arba (Arba was the father of Anak), that is, Hebron, in the mountain region of Judah, with the adjacent pasture lands, [12]although the open country and villages belonging to the city had been given to Caleb, son of Jephunneh, as his holding.[e] [13]Thus to the descendants of Aaron the priest were given the city of refuge for homicides at Hebron, with its pasture lands; also, Libnah with its pasture lands, [14]Jattir with its pasture lands, Eshtemoa with its pasture lands, [15]Holon with its pasture lands, Debir with its pasture lands, [16]Ain with its pasture lands, Juttah with its pasture lands, and Beth-shemesh with its pasture lands: nine cities from these two tribes. [17]From the tribe of Benjamin they obtained Gibeon with its pasture lands, Geba with its pasture lands, [18]Anathoth[f] with its pasture lands, and Almon with its pasture lands: four cities. [19]These cities which with their pasture lands belonged to the priestly descendants of Aaron, were thirteen in all.

**Cities of the Other Kohathites.** [20g]The rest of the Kohathite clans among the Levites obtained by lot, from the tribe of Ephraim, four cities. [21]They were assigned, with its pasture lands, the

---

*[20:1–9] The laws concerning the cities of refuge are given in Nm 35:9–28; Dt 19:1–13; see notes on Nm 35:16–25; Dt 19:2.

†[21:1] The order to establish special cities for the Levites is given in Nm 35:1–8. The forty-eight cities listed here were hardly the exclusive possession of the Levites; at least the more

important of them, such as Hebron, Shechem, and Ramoth in Gilead, were certainly peopled for the most part by the tribe in whose territory they were situated. But in all these cities the Levites had special property rights which they did not possess in other cities; cf. Lv 25:32–34.

---

w. [19:50] Jos 24:30; Jgs 2:9.    x. [20:1–9] Ex 21:12–14; Nm 35:9–15; Dt 4:41–43; 19:1–10.    y. [20:7] Jos 15:13; 19:37; 21:21.    z. [20:8] Jos 21:27, 36.

a. [21:1] Ex 6:16–19; Nm 3:17–20.    b. [21:2–3, 8] Nm 35:1–8.    c. [21:5] Gn 46:11.    d. [21:9–19] 1 Chr 6:39–66.    e. [21:12] Jos 14:14; 15:13.    f. [21:18] Jer 1:1.    g. [21:20–26] 1 Chr 6:51–55.

city of refuge for homicides at Shechem in the mountain region of Ephraim; also Gezer with its pasture lands, [22]Kibzaim with its pasture lands, and Beth-horon with its pasture lands. [23]From the tribe of Dan they obtained Elteke with its pasture lands, Gibbethon with its pasture lands, [24]Aijalon with its pasture lands, and Gath-rimmon with its pasture lands: four cities. [25]From the half-tribe of Manasseh, Taanach with its pasture lands, and Gath-rimmon with its pasture lands: two cities. [26]These cities which with their pasture lands belonged to the rest of the Kohathite clans were ten in all.

**Cities of the Gershonites.** [27h]The Gershonite clan of the Levites received from the half-tribe of Manasseh the city of refuge for homicides at Golan in Bashan, with its pasture lands; and also Beth-Astharoth with its pasture lands: two cities. [28]From the tribe of Issachar they obtained Kishion with its pasture lands, Daberath with its pasture lands, [29]Jarmuth with its pasture lands, and En-gannim with its pasture lands: four cities. [30]From the tribe of Asher, Mishal with its pasture lands, Abdon with its pasture lands, [31]Helkath with its pasture lands, and Rehob with its pasture lands: four cities. [32]From the tribe of Naphtali, the city of refuge for homicides at Kedesh in Galilee, with its pasture lands; also Hammath with its pasture lands, and Kartan with its pasture lands: three cities. [33]The cities which belonged to the Gershonite clans, with their pasture lands, were thirteen in all.

**Cities of the Merarites.** [34i]The Merarite clans, the last of the Levites, received, from the tribe of Zebulun, Jokneam with its pasture lands, Kartah with its pasture lands, [35]Dimnah with its pasture lands, and Nahalal with its pasture lands: four cities. [36]Also, across the Jordan, from the tribe of Reuben, the city of refuge for homicides at Bezer with its pasture lands, Jahaz with its pasture lands, [37]Kedemoth with its pasture lands, and Mephaath with its pasture lands: four cities. [38]From the tribe of Gad, the city of refuge for homicides at Ramoth in Gilead with its pasture lands, Mahanaim with its pasture lands, [39]Heshbon with its pasture lands, and Jazer with its pasture lands: four cities in all. [40]The cities allotted to the Merarite clans, the last of the Levites, were therefore twelve in all.

[41]Thus the total number of cities[j] within the territory of the Israelites which, with their pasture lands, belonged to the Levites, was forty-eight. [42]With each and every one of these cities went the pasture lands round about it.

[43]And so the LORD gave Israel the entire land he had sworn to their ancestors he would give them.[k] Once they had taken possession of it, and dwelt in it, [44]the LORD gave them peace on every side, just as he had promised their ancestors. Not one of their enemies could withstand

them; the LORD gave all their enemies into their power. [45]Not a single word of the blessing[l] that the LORD had promised to the house of Israel failed; it all came true.

## III. RETURN OF THE TRANSJORDAN TRIBES AND JOSHUA'S FAREWELL

### CHAPTER 22

**The Eastern Tribes Dismissed.** [1]At that time Joshua summoned the Reubenites, the Gadites, and the half-tribe of Manasseh [2]and said to them:[m] "You have observed all that Moses, the servant of the LORD, commanded you, and have listened to my voice in everything I commanded you. [3]For many years now, even until today, you have not abandoned your allies, but have taken care to observe the commands of the LORD, your God. [4]Now that the LORD, your God, has settled your allies as he promised them, you may return to your own land, which Moses, the servant of the LORD, gave you, across the Jordan.[n] [5]But be very careful to observe the commandment and the law which Moses, the servant of the LORD, commanded you: love the LORD, your God,[o] follow him in all his ways, keep his commandments, hold fast to him, and serve him with your whole heart and your whole self." [6]Joshua then blessed them and sent them away, and they went to their tents.

[7](For, to half of the tribe of Manasseh Moses had assigned land in Bashan;[p] and to the other half Joshua had given a portion along with their allies west of the Jordan.) When Joshua sent them away to their tents and blessed them, [8]he said, "Now that you are returning to your own tents with great wealth, with abundant livestock, with silver, gold, bronze and iron, and with a very large supply of clothing, divide these spoils of your enemies with your allies there."[q] [9]So the Reubenites, the Gadites, and the half-tribe of Manasseh left the other Israelites at Shiloh in the land of Canaan and returned to the land of Gilead, their own land, which they had received according to the LORD's command through Moses.[r]

**The Altar Beside the Jordan.** [10]When the Reubenites, the Gadites, and the half-tribe of Manasseh came to the region of the Jordan in the land of Canaan, they built an altar there at the Jordan, an impressively large altar. [11]The other Israelites heard the report:[s] "The Reubenites, the Gadites, and the half-tribe of Manasseh have built an altar" in the region of the Jordan facing the land of Canaan, across from the Israelites.

---

*[22:11] **In the region of the Jordan facing the land of Canaan:** on the eastern side of the Jordan valley. The river itself formed the boundary between these eastern tribes and the rest of the tribes who lived in what was formerly

h. [21:27–33] 1 Chr 6:56–61.   i. [21:34–38] 1 Chr 6:62–66.
j. [21:41] Nm 35:7.   k. [21:43] Gn 12:7; 13:15; 15:18; 26:3; 28:4, 13.

l. [21:45] Jos 23:14–15.   m. [22:2–6] Jos 1:12–17; Nm 32:20–32; Dt 3:18–20.   n. [22:4] Jos 13:8.   o. [22:5] Dt 6:5–6, 17; 10:12; 11:1, 13, 22.   p. [22:7] Jos 17:5.   q. [22:8] Nm 31:27.   r. [22:9] Jos 18:1; Nm 32:1, 26, 29.   s. [22:11] Dt 12:5, 11–14; 13:13–17.

¹²When the Israelites heard this, they assembled at Shiloh, as the entire Israelite community to take military action against them.*

**Accusation of the Western Tribes.** ¹³The Israelites sent Phinehas, son of Eleazar the priest, to the Reubenites, the Gadites, and the half-tribe of Manasseh in the land of Gilead,ᵗ ¹⁴and with him ten leaders, one from each tribe of Israel, each one the head of an ancestral house among the clans of Israel. ¹⁵When these came to the Reubenites, the Gadites, and the half-tribe of Manasseh in the land of Gilead, they said to them: ¹⁶"Thus says the whole community of the LORD: What act of treachery is this you have committed against the God of Israel? This day you have turned from following the LORD; by building an altar of your own you have rebelled against the LORD this day. ¹⁷Is the iniquity of Peor not enough, by which we made ourselves impure, even to this day, and a plague came upon the community of the LORD?ᵘ ¹⁸If today you turn away from following the LORD, and rebel against the LORD, tomorrow he will be angry with the whole community of Israel! ¹⁹If you consider the land you now possess unclean,† cross over to the land the LORD possesses, where the tabernacle of the LORD stands, and share that with us. But do not rebel against the LORD, nor involve us in rebellion, by building an altar of your own in addition to the altar of the LORD, our God. ²⁰When Achan, son of Zerah,ᵛ acted treacherously by violating the ban, was it not upon the entire community of Israel that wrath fell? Though he was but a single man, he did not perish alone‡ for his guilt!"

**Reply of the Eastern Tribes.** ²¹The Reubenites, the Gadites, and the half-tribe of Manasseh replied to the heads of the Israelite clans: ²²"The LORD is the God of gods. The LORD, the God of gods,§ knows and Israel shall know. If now we have acted out of rebellion or treachery against the LORD, our God, do not try to save us this day, ²³and if we have built an altar of our own to turn from following the LORD, or to sacrifice burnt offerings, grain offerings, or communion

sacrifices upon it, the LORD himself will exact the penalty. ²⁴We did it rather out of our anxious concern lest in the future your children should say to our children: 'What have you to do with the LORD, the God of Israel? ²⁵For the LORD has placed the Jordan as a boundary between you and us, you Reubenites and Gadites. You have no share in the LORD.' Thus your children would prevent ours from revering the LORD. ²⁶So we thought, 'Let us act for ourselves by building this altar of our own'—not for burnt offerings or sacrifice, ²⁷but as witness between us and you and our descendants, that we have the right to provide for the service of the LORD in his presence with our burnt offerings, sacrifices, and communion sacrifices. Now in the future your children cannot say to our children, 'You have no share in the LORD.' ²⁸Our thought was that, if in the future they should speak thus to us or to our descendants, we could answer: 'Look at the copy of the altar of the LORD which our ancestors made, not for burnt offerings or for sacrifices, but to witness§ between you and us.' ²⁹Far be it from us to rebel against the LORD or to turn now from following the LORD by building an altar for burnt offering, grain offering, or sacrifice in addition to the altar of the LORD, our God, which stands before his tabernacle."

³⁰When Phinehas the priest and the leaders of the community, the heads of the Israelite clans, heard what the Reubenites, the Gadites, and the Manassites had to say, they were satisfied. ³¹Phinehas, son of Eleazar the priest, said to the Reubenites, the Gadites, and the Manassites, "Today we know that the LORD is in our midst. Since you have not rebelled against the LORD by this act of treachery, you have delivered the Israelites from the hand of the LORD."

³²Phinehas, son of Eleazar the priest, and the leaders returned from the Reubenites and the Gadites in the land of Gilead to the Israelites in the land of Canaan, and reported the matter to them. ³³The report satisfied the Israelites, who blessed God and decided not to take military action against the Reubenites and Gadites nor to ravage the land where they lived.

³⁴The Reubenites and the Gadites gave the altar its name** as a witness among them that the LORD is God.

## CHAPTER 23

**Joshua's Final Plea.** ¹Many years later, after the LORD had given the Israelites rest from all their enemies round about them, and when Joshua was old and advanced in years,ˣ ²he summoned all

---

Canaan—though the term "Canaan" could also be used of both sides of the Jordan valley (cf. v. 10). The Transjordan tribes naturally built their altar in their own territory.

*[22:12] **To take military action against them**: the western Israelites considered this altar, which seemed to violate the customary unity of the sanctuary (cf. Lv 17:1–9; Dt 12:4–14), as constituting rebellion against the Lord and compromising national unity.

†[22:19] **Unclean**: not sanctified by the tabernacle.

‡[22:20] **Achan . . . did not perish alone**: his guilt caused the failure of the first attack on Ai (7:4–23); this fact is adduced as an argument for the solidarity and mutual responsibility of all the Israelites.

§[22:22] **The LORD, the God of gods**: the Hebrew, which cannot be adequately rendered in English here, adds to the divine name Yhwh ("the LORD") two synonymous words for "God," *'el* and *'elohim*. The repetition of these three sacred words adds force to the protestations of fidelity and innocence.

¶[22:28] **To witness**: far from being destined to form a rival sanctuary, the copy of the altar is intended by the eastern tribes solely as a means of teaching their children to be faithful to the one true sanctuary beyond the Jordan.

**[22:34] The name of this altar was the Hebrew word for "witness," *'ed.*

---

t. [22:13] Ex 6:25; Sir 45:23–24.   u. [22:17] Nm 25:3–4; Dt 4:3.
v. [22:20] Jos 7:1, 5.

w. [22:27] Ex 27:1–8; Dt 12:5–6, 11–14.   x. [23:1] Jos 13:1.

Israel, including their elders, leaders, judges, and officers, and said to them: "I am old and advanced in years.$^y$ $^3$You have seen all that the LORD, your God, has done for you against all these nations; for it has been the LORD, your God, who fought for you. $^4$See, I have apportioned among your tribes as their heritage the nations that survive, as well as those I destroyed, between the Jordan and the Great Sea in the west. $^5$The LORD, your God, will drive them out and dispossess them at your approach, so that you will take possession of their land as the LORD, your God, promised you. $^6$Therefore be strong and be careful to observe all that is written in the book of the law of Moses, never turning from it right or left,$^a$ $^7$or mingling with these nations that survive among you. You must not invoke their gods by name, or swear by them, or serve them, or bow down to them,$^b$ $^8$but you must hold fast to the LORD, your God, as you have done up to this day. $^9$At your approach the LORD has dispossessed great and strong nations; not one has withstood you up to this day. $^{10}$One of you puts to flight a thousand, because it is the LORD, your God, himself who fights for you,$^c$ as he promised you. $^{11}$As for you, take great care to love the LORD, your God. $^{12}$For if you ever turn away from him and join with the remnant of these nations that survive among you, by intermarrying and intermingling with them,$^d$ $^{13}$know for certain that the LORD, your God, will no longer dispossess these nations at your approach. Instead they will be a snare and a trap for you, a scourge for your sides and thorns for your eyes, until you perish from this good land which the LORD, your God, has given you.$^e$

$^{14}$"Today, as you see, I am going the way of all the earth.$^*$ So now acknowledge with your whole heart and soul that not one of all the promises the LORD, your God, made concerning you has failed. Every one has come true for you; not one has failed. $^{15}$But just as every promise the LORD, your God, made to you has come true for you, so will he bring upon you every threat,$^†$ even so far as to exterminate you from this good land which the LORD, your God, has given you. $^{16}$If you transgress the covenant of the LORD, your God, which he enjoined on you, to go and serve other gods and bow down to them, the anger of the LORD will flare up against you and you will quickly perish from the good land he has given you."

## CHAPTER 24

**Covenant Ceremony.** $^1$Joshua gathered together all the tribes of Israel at Shechem, summoning

the elders, leaders, judges, and officers of Israel. When they stood in ranks before God, $^2$Joshua addressed all the people: "Thus says the LORD, the God of Israel: In times past your ancestors, down to Terah,$^h$ father of Abraham and Nahor, lived beyond the River$^‡$ and served other gods. $^3$But I brought your father Abraham from the region beyond the River and led him through the entire land of Canaan.$^i$ I made his descendants numerous, and gave him Isaac. $^4$To Isaac I gave Jacob and Esau.$^j$ To Esau I assigned the mountain region of Seir to possess, while Jacob and his children went down to Egypt.

$^5$"Then I sent Moses and Aaron, and struck Egypt with the plagues and wonders that I wrought in her midst.$^k$ Afterward I led you out. $^6$And when I led your ancestors out of Egypt, you came to the sea, and the Egyptians pursued your ancestors to the Red Sea with chariots and charioteers.$^l$ $^7$When they cried out to the LORD,$^m$ he put darkness between you and the Egyptians, upon whom he brought the sea so that it covered them. Your eyes saw what I did to Egypt. After you dwelt a long time in the wilderness, $^8$I brought you into the land of the Amorites who lived east of the Jordan. They fought against you, but I delivered them into your power. You took possession of their land, and I destroyed them at your approach. $^9$Then Balak, son of Zippor, king of Moab, prepared to war against Israel. He summoned Balaam, son of Beor, to curse you, $^{10}$but I would not listen to Balaam. Instead, he had to bless you, and I delivered you from his power. $^{11}$Once you crossed the Jordan$^q$ and came to Jericho, the citizens of Jericho fought against you, but I delivered them also into your power. $^{12}$And I sent the hornets$^§$ ahead of you which drove them—the Amorites, Perizzites, Canaanites, Hittites, Girgashites, Hivites, and Jebusites—out of your way; it was not your sword or your bow.$^r$ $^{13}$I gave you a land you did not till and cities you did not build, to dwell in; you ate of vineyards and olive groves you did not plant.$^s$

$^{14}$"Now, therefore, fear the LORD and serve him completely and sincerely. Cast out the gods your ancestors served beyond the River and in Egypt, and serve the LORD. $^{15}$If it is displeasing to you to serve the LORD, choose today whom you will serve, the gods your ancestors served beyond the River or the gods of the Amorites in whose country you are dwelling. As for me and my household, we will serve the LORD."

---

$^*$[23:14] **Going the way of all the earth:** drawing near to death, the inevitable end of all; cf. 1 Kgs 2:1–2.

$^†$[23:15] **Every threat:** mentioned especially in the list of curses in Dt 28:15–68.

$^‡$[24:2] **Beyond the River:** east of the Euphrates; cf. Gn 11:28–31.

$^§$[24:12] **The hornets:** see note on Ex 23:28.

y. [23:2] Dt 29:10.   z. [23:4] Jos 13:2–7; 14:2; 18:10; Ps 78:55. a. [23:6] Jos 1:7.   b. [23:7] Ex 20:3–6; Dt 5:7–10; 7:2–11.   c. [23:10] Ex 14:14; Lv 26:8; Dt 3:22.   d. [23:12] Ex 34:16; Dt 7:3.   e. [23:13] Nm 33:55.   f. [23:15] Lv 26:14–39; Dt 28:15–68.   g. [24:1] Ex 19:17.

h. [24:2] Gn 11:26, 31; 31:53.   i. [24:3] Gn 12:1; Acts 7:2–4. j. [24:4] Gn 36:8; 46:1, 6; Acts 7:15.   k. [24:5] Ex 3:10; 7:14; 12:30. l. [24:6] Ex 12:37; 14:9.   m. [24:7] Ex 14:10, 20, 27–28. n. [24:8] Nm 21:21–35.   o. [24:9] Nm 22:2–5.   p. [24:10] Nm 23:1–24:25.   q. [24:11] Jos 3:14; 6:1.   r. [24:12] Jos 3:10; 11:20; Ex 23:28; Dt 7:20; Ps 44:3.   s. [24:13] Dt 6:10–11.   t. [24:14] Dt 10:12; 1 Sm 7:3; 12:24; Tb 14:9.   u. [24:15] Dt 30:15–19; Jgs 2:11–13.

[16]But the people answered, "Far be it from us to forsake the LORD to serve other gods. [17]For it was the LORD, our God, who brought us and our ancestors up out of the land of Egypt, out of the house of slavery. He performed those great signs before our very eyes and protected us along our entire journey and among all the peoples through whom we passed. [18]At our approach the LORD drove out all the peoples, including the Amorites who dwelt in the land. Therefore we also will serve the LORD, for he is our God."

[19]Joshua in turn said to the people, "You may not be able to serve the LORD, for he is a holy God; he is a passionate God[v] who will not forgive your transgressions or your sins. [20]If you forsake the LORD and serve strange gods, he will then do evil to you and destroy you, after having done you good."

[21]But the people answered Joshua, "No! We will serve the LORD." [22]Joshua therefore said to the people, "You are witnesses against yourselves that you have chosen to serve the LORD." They replied, "We are witnesses!" [23]"Now, therefore, put away the foreign gods that are among you and turn your hearts to the LORD, the God of Israel." [24]Then the people promised Joshua, "We will serve the LORD, our God, and will listen to his voice."

[25]So Joshua made a covenant with the people that day and made statutes and ordinances for them at Shechem. [26]Joshua wrote these words in the book of the law of God. Then he took a large stone and set it up there under the terebinth that was in the sanctuary of the LORD.[w] [27]And Joshua said to all the people, "This stone shall be our witness,[x] for it has heard all the words which the LORD spoke to us. It shall be a witness against you, should you wish to deny your God." [28]Then Joshua dismissed the people, each to their own heritage.[y]

**Death of Joshua.** [29z]After these events, Joshua, son of Nun, servant of the LORD, died at the age of a hundred and ten, [30]and they buried him within the borders of his heritage at Timnath-serah[a] in the mountain region of Ephraim north of Mount Gaash.[*] [31]Israel served the LORD during the entire lifetime of Joshua, and of those elders who outlived Joshua and who knew all the work the LORD had done for Israel. [32b]The bones of Joseph,[†] which the Israelites had brought up from Egypt, were buried in Shechem in the plot of ground Jacob had bought from the sons of Hamor, father of Shechem, for a hundred pieces of money. This was a heritage of the descendants of Joseph. [33]When Eleazar, son of Aaron, also died, he was buried on the hill which had been given to his son Phinehas[c] in the mountain region of Ephraim.

---

*[24:30] Following this verse the Greek translation of the Bible (the Septuagint) adds: "They laid with him there, in the tomb where they buried him, the flint knives with which he had circumcised the Israelites at Gilgal, when he brought them out of Egypt, as Yhwh commanded them. There they are to this very day."

†[24:32] Joseph's bones (Gn 50:24–26) and Jacob's purchase of the burial ground (Gn 33:18–20) relate Joshua with Genesis. **A hundred pieces of money**: see note on Gn 33:19.

w. [24:26] Gn 28:18; 31:45; Jgs 9:6.   x. [24:27] Jos 4:1–9; Gn 31:48, 52; Dt 31:19, 21, 26.   y. [24:28] Jgs 2:6.   z. [24:29–31] Jgs 2:7–9.   a. [24:30] Jos 19:50.   b. [24:32] Gn 33:19; 50:24; Ex 13:19.   c. [24:33] Jos 22:13.

v. [24:19] Ex 20:5; 23:21; 34:14; Lv 19:2; Dt 5:9.

# THE BOOK OF
# JUDGES

❧

The Hebrew word translated "Judges" in the English title of the book refers not to specialized judicial officers or magistrates but to leaders in general. According to the biblical narrative these judges led Israel from the end of the conquest of Canaan until the beginning of the monarchy. The period of the Judges, therefore, extended from the death of Joshua (Jos 24:29–31; cf. Jgs 1:1) until the installation of Saul as Israel's first king by the prophet Samuel, who was also the last judge (see 1 Sm 7:15–17).

The Book of Judges begins with two introductory passages. The first (chap. 1) gives a description of the situation in Canaan after the Israelite conquest. It emphasizes the continued existence of the indigenous inhabitants of Canaan in many parts of the land because of Israel's inability to drive them out completely. The second passage (2:1–3:6) is a thematic introduction to the period of the Judges, describing a cyclical pattern of infidelity, oppression, "crying out," and deliverance (see note on 2:10–19).

The main part of the book (3:7–16:31) consists of a series of stories about thirteen leaders whose careers are described in greater or lesser detail. The exploits of six of these—Othniel, Ehud, Deborah, Gideon, Jephthah, and Samson—are related at length, and all are shown to have delivered Israel from oppression or danger. They are customarily called "major judges," whereas the other six—Shamgar, Tola, Jair, Ibzan, Elon, and Abdon—who appear only in brief notices, are designated "minor judges." The thirteenth, Abimelech, is included in neither group, since his story is essentially a continuation of that of Gideon and his career is presented as deplorable, a cautionary tale of royal ambition.

The final section of the book consists of two episodes, one about the migration of the tribe of Dan (chaps. 17–18) and the other about an intertribal war directed against the tribe of Benjamin (chaps. 19–21). These stories illustrate the religious and political disorder that prevailed at the time when, as yet, "there was no king in Israel" (see note on 17:6).

The principal contribution of the Deuteronomistic historian to the Book of Judges is the thematic introduction to—and theological evaluation of—the period of the Judges in 2:1–3:6, as well as editorial comments structuring the narrative throughout, e.g., 3:7; 4:1; etc. The historian drew the stories of the judges themselves from older sources, which could have existed in written form but derive ultimately from oral tradition.

Thus the principal divisions of the book in outline are as follows:

I.  The Situation in Canaan Following the Israelite Conquest (1:1–3:6)
II. Stories of the Judges (3:7–16:31)
III. Further Stories of the Tribes of Dan and Benjamin (17:1–21:25)

## I. THE SITUATION IN CANAAN FOLLOWING THE ISRAELITE CONQUEST

### CHAPTER 1

**Canaanites in Palestine.** ¹*After the death of Joshua the Israelites consulted the LORD,

asking, "Who shall be first among us to attack the Canaanites and to do battle with them?" ²The LORD answered: Judah shall attack: I have

*[1:1–36] The chapter depicts the Israelite settlement of Canaan as a gradual and incomplete process (cf. Ex 23:29–30; Dt 7:22). This picture contrasts sharply with that found in

Joshua, where the conquest is rapid and total. Accordingly, some scholars believe that Jgs 1 derives from an early account, which is less idealized and more realistic than that on which Joshua is based. Others, noting that Judah is presented as the only tribe that was completely successful in driving foreigners from its territory, think that the account was written at a late date and reflects suspicion in Judah about foreign elements in the Israelite populations of outlying areas (cf. 2 Kgs 17:24–33).

delivered the land into his power.[a] [3]Judah then said to his brother Simeon, "Come up with me into the territory allotted to me, and let us do battle with the Canaanites. I will likewise go with you into the territory allotted to you." So Simeon went with him.[b]

[4]When Judah attacked, the LORD delivered the Canaanites and Perizzites into their power, and they struck down ten thousand of them in Bezek. [5c]They came upon Adonibezek in Bezek and fought against him. When they struck down the Canaanites and Perizzites, [6]Adonibezek fled. They pursued him, and when they caught him, they cut off his thumbs and big toes. [7]"Seventy kings," said Adonibezek, "used to pick up scraps under my table with their thumbs and big toes cut off. As I have done, so has God repaid me." He was brought to Jerusalem, and he died there. [8]The Judahites fought against Jerusalem, captured it, and put it to the sword, setting the city itself on fire.[d]

[9]Afterward the Judahites went down to fight against the Canaanites who lived in the mountain region, in the Negeb, and in the foothills.[e] [10]Judah also marched against the Canaanites who lived in Hebron, which was formerly called Kiriath-arba, and defeated Sheshai, Ahiman, and Talmai.[f] [11]They marched from there against the inhabitants of Debir, which was formerly called Kiriath-sepher. [12]Caleb said, "To the man who attacks Kiriath-sepher and captures it, I will give my daughter Achsah in marriage." [13g]Othniel captured it, the son of Caleb's younger brother Kenaz; so Caleb gave him his daughter Achsah in marriage. [14]When she came to him, she induced him to ask her father for some land. Then, as she alighted from the donkey, Caleb asked her, "What do you want?" [15]She answered, "Give me a present. Since you have put me in the land of the Negeb, give me pools of water." So Caleb gave her what she wanted, both the upper and the lower pool.

[16h]The descendants of Hobab the Kenite, Moses' father-in-law,[†] came up with the Judahites from the City of Palms to the wilderness of Arad, which is in the Negeb, and they settled among the Amalekites. [17r]Then Judah went with his brother Simeon, and they defeated the Canaanites who lived in Zephath. They put the

city under the ban and renamed it Hormah.[‡j] [18]Judah captured Gaza with its territory, Ashkelon with its territory, Ekron with its territory, and Ashdod[§] with its territory.[k] [19]The LORD was with Judah, so they gained possession of the mountain region. But they could not dispossess those who lived on the plain, because they had iron chariots. [20l]As Moses had commanded, they gave Hebron to Caleb, who then drove the three sons of Anak away from there.

[21¶]As for the Jebusites dwelling in Jerusalem, the Benjaminites did not dispossess them, so that the Jebusites live with the Benjaminites in Jerusalem to the present day.[m]

[22]The house of Joseph, too, went up against Bethel, and the LORD was with them. [23]The house of Joseph reconnoitered Bethel, which formerly was called Luz.[n] [24]The scouts saw a man coming out of the city and said to him, "Tell us the way into the city, and we will show you mercy." [25]He showed them the way into the city, and they put the city to the sword; but they let the man and his whole clan go free. [26]The man then went to the land of the Hittites, where he built a city and called it Luz, which is its name to this day.

[27o]Manasseh did not take possession of Beth-shean with its towns or of Taanach with its towns. Nor did they dispossess the inhabitants of Dor and its towns, those of Ibleam and its towns, or those of Megiddo and its towns. The Canaanites continued to live in this district. [28]When Israel grew stronger, they conscripted the Canaanites as laborers, but did not actually drive them out. [29p]Ephraim did not drive out the Canaanites living in Gezer, and so the Canaanites lived among them in Gezer.

[30q]Nor did Zebulun dispossess the inhabitants of Kitron or those of Nahalol; the Canaanites lived among them and became forced laborers.

[31r]Nor did Asher dispossess the inhabitants of Acco or those of Sidon, or take possession of Mahaleb, Achzib, Helbah, Aphik, or Rehob. [32]So the Asherites settled among the Canaanite

---

‡[1:17] **The ban . . . Hormah**: the narrator relates the city-name "Hormah" to "the ban" (Hebrew *herem*), which commanded the Israelites to devote to the Lord—and thus to destroy—whatever was captured within the land (cf. Dt 20:10–18).

§[1:18] **Gaza . . . Ashkelon . . . Ekron . . . Ashdod**: four of the five major cities of the Philistines (see note on 3:3). Since these cities were on the coastal plain, the statement that Judah captured them is contrary to v. 19, which notes Judah's failure to drive out the inhabitants of the lowlands. In the Septuagint the problem is removed by changing the beginning of this verse to read "Judah did not dispossess. . . ."

¶[1:21] According to Jos 18:16, Jerusalem was assigned to the tribe of Benjamin. According to the notice in 1:8 above, the city was burned by the Judahites, but elsewhere (2 Sm 5:6–9) we learn that it was not actually taken from the Jebusites until David captured it and made it his capital.

---

*[1:8] See note on 1:21 below.

†[1:16] **Hobab the Kenite, Moses' father-in-law**: as in 4:11. However, in Nm 10:29 Hobab is identified as Moses' brother-in-law, while Reuel is identified as Moses' father-in-law (see also Ex 2:18). The more common name of Moses' father-in-law is Jethro, also a Midianite (e.g., Ex 3:1). It is impossible to sort out the relationships among these three men in the ancient traditions. **City of Palms**: Jericho (cf. Dt 34:3) or a town in the Negeb.

---

a. [1:2] Jgs 20:18.  b. [1:3] Jgs 1:17.  c. [1:5] Jos 10:1.  d. [1:8] Jos 10:1–27; 2 Sm 5:6–9.  e. [1:9] Jos 10:40; 11:16; 12:8.  f. [1:10] Jos 15:13–19; Nm 13:22; Jos 14:15.  g. [1:13] Jgs 3:9.  h. [1:16] Jgs 4:11; Nm 10:29–32.  i. [1:17] Jos 1:3.

j. [1:17] Nm 21:3; Jos 12:14.  k. [1:18] Jos 11:22.  l. [1:20] Jos 14:6–15.  m. [1:21] Jos 15:63; 18:16; 2 Sm 5:6–9.  n. [1:23] Gn 28:19; Jos 18:13.  o. [1:27–28] Jos 17:11–13.  p. [1:29] Jos 16:10.  q. [1:30] Jos 19:10–16.  r. [1:31–32] Jos 19:24–31.

inhabitants of the land, for they had not dispossessed them.

³³ᵃNor did Naphtali drive out the inhabitants of Beth-shemesh or those of Beth-anath. They settled among the Canaanite inhabitants of the land and the inhabitants of Beth-shemesh and Beth-anath became forced laborers for them.

³⁴The Amorites hemmed in the Danites in the mountain region, not permitting them to come down onto the plain. ³⁵So the Amorites continued to live in Harheres, Aijalon, and Shaalbim, but as the power of the house of Joseph grew, they were conscripted as laborers. ³⁶The territory of the Amorites extended from the Akrabbim pass, from Sela and upward.

## CHAPTER 2

**Infidelities of the Israelites.** ¹A messenger of the LORD went up from Gilgal to Bochim and said, I brought you up from Egypt and led you into the land which I promised on oath to your ancestors. I said, I will never break my covenant with you, ²but you must not make a covenant with the inhabitants of this land; you must pull down their altars.ᵗ But you did not listen to me. Look what you have done! ³For I also said,* I will not clear them out of your way; they will become traps for you, and their gods a snare for you.ᵘ

⁴When the messenger of the LORD had spoken these things to all the Israelites, the people wept aloud. ⁵They named that place Bochim,† and they offered sacrifice there to the LORD.

⁶ᵛThen Joshua dismissed the people, and the Israelites went, each to their own heritage, to take possession of the land. ⁷The people served the LORD during the entire lifetime of Joshua, and of those elders who outlived Joshua and who had seen all the great work the LORD had done for Israel. ⁸Joshua, son of Nun, the servant of the LORD, died at the age of a hundred and ten, ⁹and they buried him within the borders of his heritage at Timnath-heres in the mountain region of Ephraim north of Mount Gaash.ʷ

¹⁰ᵗWhen the rest of that generation were also gathered to their ancestors, and a later generation arose that did not know the LORD or the work he had done for Israel, ¹¹ˣthe Israelites

did what was evil in the sight of the LORD. They served the Baals,§ ¹²and abandoned·the LORD, the God of their ancestors, the one who had brought them out of the land of Egypt. They followed other gods, the gods of the peoples around them, and bowed down to them, and provoked the LORD.

¹³Because they had abandoned the LORD and served Baal and the Astartes,⁵ ¹⁴the anger of the LORD flared up against Israel, and he delivered them into the power of plunderers who despoiled them. He sold them into the power of the enemies around them, and they were no longer able to withstand their enemies. ¹⁵Whenever they marched out, the hand of the LORD turned against them, as the LORD had said, and as the LORD had sworn to them;ʸ and they were in great distress. ¹⁶But the LORD raised up judges to save them from the power of their plunderers; ¹⁷but they did not listen to their judges either, for they prostituted themselves by following other gods, bowing down to them. They were quick to stray from the way their ancestors had taken, who obeyed the commandments of the LORD; but these did not. ¹⁸When the LORD raised up judges for them, he would be with the judge and save them from the power of their enemies as long as the judge lived. The LORD would change his mind when they groaned in their affliction under their oppressors. ¹⁹But when the judge died, they would again do worse than their ancestors, following other gods, serving and bowing down to them, relinquishing none of their evil practices or stubborn ways.ᶻ

²⁰ᵃThe anger of the LORD flared up against Israel, and he said: Because this nation has transgressed my covenant, which I enjoined on their ancestors, and has not listened to me, ²¹I for my part will not clear away for them any more of the nations Joshua left when he died. ²²ᵇThey will be made to test Israel, to see whether or not they will keep to the way of the LORD and continue in it as their ancestors did. ²³Therefore the LORD allowed these nations to remain instead of expelling them immediately. He had not delivered them into the power of Joshua.

## CHAPTER 3

¹These are the nations the LORD allowed to remain, so that through them he might test Israel, all those who had not experienced any of the Canaanite wars— ²to teach warfare to

---

*[2:3] **I also said**: the Lord explicitly warned the Israelites of the consequences of disobedience; see Nm 33:55 and especially Jos 23:13.

†[2:5] **Bochim**: Hebrew for "weepers."

‡[2:10–19] This long thematic passage establishes the cyclical pattern for the stories found in the rest of the book. When the Israelites are secure, they forsake the Lord and worship other gods. In punishment the Lord places them in the power of a foreign oppressor. But when they cry out in distress, the Lord takes pity on them and raises up a judge, who delivers them from the oppressor. The Israelites remain faithful to the Lord during the lifetime of the judge, but when the judge dies they again abandon the Lord, and the cycle begins anew.

§[2:11] **The Baals**: the title "Baal," meaning "lord" or "master," belonged to a large number of Canaanite, Phoenician, and Syrian deities, including especially the great storm god Hadad Baal, widely revered as lord of the earth. The plural form, which occurs here, was used by the biblical writers to refer to foreign gods in general.

⁵[2:13] **The Astartes**: Ashtoreth, or Astarte, was an important Canaanite and Phoenician goddess. The plural form used here probably refers to foreign goddesses in general.

---

s. [1:33] Jos 19:32–39.    t. [2:2] Ex 23:32; 34:12–13; Dt 7:2, 5; 12:2–3.    u. [2:3] Ex 23:33; Dt 7:16; Jos 23:13.    v. [2:6–9] Jos 24:28–31.    w. [2:9] Jos 19:49–50.    x. [2:11–14] Jgs 3:7–8, 12; 4:1–2; 6:1; 10:6–8; 13:1.

y. [2:15] Lv 26:14–39; Dt 28:15–68.    z. [2:19] Jgs 3:12; 4:1; 8:33–34.    a. [2:20–21] Jos 23:13; Jgs 2:2–3.    b. [2:22] Jgs 3:1, 4 those generations of Israelites who had never experienced it: ³*the five lords of the Philistines,* and all the Canaanites, the Sidonians, and the Hivites who lived in the mountain region of the Lebanon between Baal-hermon and Lebo-hamath. ⁴These served as a test for Israel, to know whether they would obey the commandments the LORD had enjoined on their ancestors through Moses. ⁵So the Israelites settled among the Canaanites, Hittites, Amorites, Perizzites, Hivites, and Jebusites.ᵈ ⁶They took their daughters in marriage, and gave their own daughters to their sons in marriage,ᵉ and served their gods.

## II. STORIES OF THE JUDGES

**Othniel.** ⁷Then the Israelites did what was evil in the sight of the LORD; they forgot the LORD, their God, and served the Baals and the Asherahs,† ⁸and the anger of the LORD flared up against them. He sold them into the power of Cushan-rishathaim,‡ king of Aram Naha-raim; and the Israelites served Cushan-risha-thaim for eight years. ⁹But when the Israelites cried out to the LORD,ᵍ he raised up a savior for them, to save them. It was Othniel, son of Caleb's younger brother Kenaz.ʰ ¹⁰The spirit of the LORD came upon him,ⁱ and he judged Israel. When he marched out to war, the LORD delivered Cushan-rishathaim, king of Aram into his power, and his hold on Cushan-rishathaim was firm. ¹¹So the land was at rest for forty years,ʲ until Othniel, son of Kenaz, died.

**Ehud.** ¹²Again the Israelites did what was evil in the sight of the LORD, so he strengthened Eglon, king of Moab, against Israel because they did what was evil in the sight of the LORD. ¹³Taking the Ammonites and Amalek as allies, he went and defeated Israel, taking possession of the City of Palms. ¹⁴So the Israelites served Eglon, king of Moab, for eighteen years.

¹⁵But when the Israelites cried out to the LORD, he raised up for them a savior, Ehud, son of Gera, a Benjaminite who was left-handed.§ The Israelites would send their tribute to Eglon, king of Moab, by him. ¹⁶Ehud made himself a two-edged dagger a foot long, and strapped it under his clothes on his right thigh. ¹⁷He presented the tribute to Eglon, king of Moab; now Eglon was a very fat man. ¹⁸When he had finished presenting the tribute, he dismissed the troops who had carried the tribute. ¹⁹But he himself turned back at the sculptured stones near Gilgal, and said, "I have a secret message for you, O king." And the king said, "Silence!" Then when all his attendants had left his presence, ²⁰Ehud went in to him where he sat alone in his cool upper room. Ehud said, "I have a word from God for you." So the king rose from his throne. ²¹Then Ehud with his left hand drew the dagger from his right thigh, and thrust it into Eglon's belly. ²²The hilt also went in after the blade, and the fat closed over the blade because he did not withdraw the dagger from the body.

²³Then Ehud went out onto the porch, shutting the doors of the upper room on Eglon and locking them. ²⁴When Ehud had left and the servants had come, they saw that the doors of the upper room were locked, and thought, "He must be easing himself in the cool chamber." ²⁵They waited until they were at a loss when he did not open the doors of the upper room. So they took the key and opened them, and there was their lord lying on the floor, dead.

²⁶During their delay Ehud escaped and, passing the sculptured stones, took refuge in Seirah. ²⁷On his arrival he sounded the horn in the mountain region of Ephraim, and the Israelites went down from the mountains with him as their leader. ²⁸"Follow me," he said to them, "for the LORD has delivered your enemies the Moabites into your power."ᵏ So they followed him down and seized the fords of the Jordan against the Moabites, permitting no one to cross. ²⁹On that occasion they slew about ten thousand Moabites, all of them strong warriors. Not one escaped. ³⁰So Moab was brought under the power of Israelˡ at that time; and the land had rest for eighty years.ᵐ

**Shamgar.** ³¹After him there was Shamgar,¶ son of Anath,ⁿ who slew six hundred Philistines with an oxgoad.ᵒ He, too, was a savior for Israel.

## CHAPTER 4

**Deborah and Barak.** ¹*The Israelites again did what was evil in the sight of the LORD; Ehud was dead. ²So the LORD sold them into the power of the Canaanite king, Jabin, who reigned in Hazor. The general of his army was Sisera, who lived in Harosheth-ha-goiim.ᵖ ³*But the Israelites cried

---

*[3:3] **The Philistines**: a people of Aegean origin who settled on the coastal plain of southern Canaan in the twelfth century B.C.; from their name derives the geographic designation Palestine. Israel competed for control of the country against a group of their cities: Gaza, Ashkelon, Ashdod, Gath, and Ekron.

†[3:7] **The Asherahs**: Asherah was an important goddess, whose presence in the cult was represented by a wooden pole, also called an "asherah"; see notes on Ex 34:13 and Dt 7:5. Here the plural is used to refer to goddesses in general.

‡[3:8] **Cushan-rishathaim**: this king is not known from other biblical or extrabiblical sources. His title, "king of Aram Naharaim," indicates that he was a Mesopotamian ruler.

§[3:15] **Left-handed**: this detail is important because it shows why Ehud is able to conceal a weapon on his right thigh (3:16). There is also a wordplay involved, since "Benjaminite" in Hebrew could also mean "right-handed man."

¶[3:31] Shamgar is the first of the so-called minor judges; cf. Introduction.

---

c. [3:3] Jos 13:2–5. d. [3:5] Ex 3:8, 17; 23:23; 33:2; 34:11; Dt 7:1; 20:17; Jos 3:10; 24:11. e. [3:6] Ex 34:16; Dt 7:3; Jos 23:12. f. [3:7–8] Jgs 2:11–14. g. [3:9] Jgs 3:15; 4:3; 6:6, 7; 10:10; 1 Sm 12:8, 10. h. [3:9] Jgs 1:13. i. [3:10] Jgs 6:34; 11:29; 13:25; 14:6, 19; 15:14; 1 Sm 11:6. j. [3:11] Jgs 3:30; 5:31; 8:28.

k. [3:28] Nm 21:34; Dt 2:24; Jos 2:24; Jgs 4:7, 14; 7:7, 9, 15. l. [3:30] Jgs 8:28; 11:23; 1 Sm 7:13. m. [3:30] Jgs 3:11; 5:31; 8:28. n. [3:31] Jgs 5:6. o. [3:31] Jgs 15:15; 2 Sm 23:8, 18. p. [4:1] Jgs 2:19; 3:12; 8:33–34. q. [4:2] Jos 11:1–15; Ps 83:10; 1 Sm 12:9. r. [4:3] Jgs 3:9, 15; 6:6, 7; 10:10; 1 Sm 12:8, 10.

out to the LORD; for with his nine hundred iron chariots Jabin harshly oppressed the Israelites for twenty years.

⁴At that time the prophet Deborah, wife of Lappidoth, was judging Israel. ⁵She used to sit under Deborah's palm tree, between Ramah and Bethel in the mountain region of Ephraim, where the Israelites came up to her for judgment. ⁶She had Barak, son of Abinoam,ˢ summoned from Kedesh of Naphtali. She said to him, "This is what the LORD, the God of Israel, commands: Go, march against Mount Tabor, and take with you ten thousand men from Naphtali and Zebulun. ⁷I will draw Sisera, the general of Jabin's army, out to you at the Wadi Kishon,ᵗ together with his chariots and troops, and I will deliver them into your power." ⁸But Barak answered her, "If you come with me, I will go; if you do not come with me, I will not go." ⁹"I will certainly go with you," she replied, "but you will not gain glory for the expedition on which you are setting out, for it is into a woman's power that the LORD is going to sell Sisera." So Deborah arose and went with Barak and journeyed with him to Kedesh.

¹⁰Barak summoned Zebulun and Naphtali to Kedesh, and ten thousand men followed him.ᵘ Deborah also went up with him. ¹¹Now Heber the Kenite had detached himself from Cain, the descendants of Hobab, Moses' father-in-law,ᵛ and had pitched his tent by the terebinth of Zaanannim, which was near Kedesh.

¹²It was reported to Sisera that Barak, son of Abinoam, had gone up to Mount Tabor. ¹³So Sisera called out all nine hundred of his iron chariots and all his forces from Harosheth-ha-goiim to the Wadi Kishon. ¹⁴Deborah then said to Barak, "Up! This is the day on which the LORD has delivered Sisera into your power. The LORD marches before you." So Barak went down Mount Tabor, followed by his ten thousand men. ¹⁵And the LORD threw Sisera and all his chariots and forces into a panic before Barak.ʷ Sisera himself dismounted from his chariot and fled on foot, ¹⁶but Barak pursued the chariots and the army as far as Harosheth-ha-goiim. The entire army of Sisera fell beneath the sword, not even one man surviving.

¹⁷Sisera fled on foot to the tent of Jael, wife of Heber the Kenite, for there was peace between Jabin, king of Hazor, and the family of Heber the Kenite. ¹⁸Jael went out to meet Sisera and said to him, "Turn aside, my lord, turn aside with me; do not be afraid." So he went into her tent,

and she covered him with a rug. ¹⁹He said to her, "Please give me a little water to drink. I am thirsty." So she opened a skin of milk, gave him a drink, and then covered him.ˣ ²⁰"Stand at the entrance of the tent," he said to her. "If anyone comes and asks, 'Is there someone here?' say, 'No!'" ²¹Jael, wife of Heber, got a tent peg and took a mallet in her hand. When Sisera was in a deep sleep from exhaustion, she approached him stealthily and drove the peg through his temple and down into the ground, and he died.ʸ ²²Then when Barak came in pursuit of Sisera, Jael went out to meet him and said to him, "Come, I will show you the man you are looking for." So he went in with her, and there lay Sisera dead, with the tent peg through his temple.

²³Thus on that day God humbled the Canaanite king, Jabin, before the Israelites; ²⁴their power weighed ever more heavily on him, until at length they finished off the Canaanite king, Jabin.

## CHAPTER 5

**Song of Deborah.** ¹ᵃOn that day Deborah sang this song—and Barak, son of Abinoam:

2   ᵇWhen uprising broke out in Israel,
         when the people rallied for duty—
                 bless the LORD!

3   Hear, O kings! Give ear, O princes!
         I will sing, I will sing to the LORD,
         I will make music to the LORD, the
                 God of Israel.

4   ᶜLORD, when you went out from Seir,
         when you marched from the plains
                 of Edom,
     The earth shook, the heavens poured,
         the clouds poured rain,

5   The mountains streamed,
         before the LORD, the One of Sinai,
         before the LORD, the God of Israel.

6   In the days of Shamgar, son of Anath,ᵇ
         in the days of Jael, caravans ceased:
     Those who traveled the roads
         now traveled by roundabout paths.ᶜ

7   Gone was freedom beyond the walls,
         gone indeed from Israel.
     When I, Deborah, arose,
         when I arose, a mother in Israel.ˢ

8   New gods were their choice;
         then war was at the gates.
     No shield was to be found, no spear,
         among forty thousand in Israel!

---

*[4:11] It was characteristic of the Kenites that they encamped alongside or among other nomadic groups, such as the Amalekites (cf. 1:16; 1 Sm 15:6). They are most often mentioned in connection with tribes living in the southern part of Judah, but Heber's group seems to have moved north and pitched its tents in the lower Galilee. **Cain**: in this case a collective term for the Kenites. For Hobab, see 1:16.

†[5:2–31] This canticle is an excellent example of early Hebrew poetry, even though some of its verses are now obscure. ‡[5:4–5] The Lord himself marches to war in support of Israel. Storm and earthquake are part of the traditional imagery of theophany; cf. Ex 19:16, 18–20; Dt 33:2–3; Ps 18:7–15; 77:17–20; 144:5–7.

§[5:7] **A mother in Israel**: the precise meaning of the term "mother" is unclear, except that it seems to indicate Deborah's position of leadership, and so may be a title (cf. 2 Sm 20:19).

s. [4:6] Heb 11:32.   t. [4:7] Jgs 5:21; Ps 83:10.   u. [4:10] Jgs 5:18.   v. [4:11] Nm 10:29; Jgs 1:16.   w. [4:15] Ex 14:24; Jos 10:10; 1 Sm 7:10.

x. [4:19] Jgs 5:25.   y. [4:21] Jgs 5:26.   z. [5:1] Ex 15:1.   a. [5:4–5] Dt 33:2; Ps 68:8–9; Hb 3:3–15.   b. [5:6] Jgs 3:31.   c. [5:6] Is 33:8.

9 My heart is with the leaders of Israel,
    with the dedicated ones of the
        people—bless the LORD;
10 Those who ride on white donkeys,
    seated on saddle rugs,
    and those who travel the road,
Sing of them
11   to the sounds of musicians at the
        wells.
There they recount the just deeds of the
        LORD,
    his just deeds bringing freedom to
        Israel.
12 Awake, awake, Deborah!
    Awake, awake, strike up a song!
Arise, Barak!
    Take captive your captors, son of
        Abinoam!
13 Then down went Israel against the
        mighty,
    the army of the LORD went down for
        him against the warriors.
14 *From Ephraim, their base in the valley;
    behind you, Benjamin, among your
        troops.
From Machir came down commanders,
    from Zebulun wielders of the mar-
        shal's staff.
15 The princes of Issachar were with
        Deborah,
    Issachar, faithful to Barak;
    in the valley they followed at his
        heels.
Among the clans of Reuben
    great were the searchings of heart!
16 Why did you stay beside your hearths
    listening to the lowing of the herds?
Among the clans of Reuben
    great were the searchings of heart!
17 Gilead stayed beyond the Jordan;
    Why did Dan spend his time in
        ships?
Asher remained along the shore,
    he stayed in his havens.
18 Zebulun was a people who defied
        death,
    Naphtali, too, on the open heights!^d
19 The kings came and fought;
    then they fought, those kings of
        Canaan,
At Taanach by the waters of Megiddo;
    no spoil of silver did they take.

20 †From the heavens the stars fought;
    from their courses they fought
        against Sisera.^e
21 The Wadi Kishon swept them away;
    the wadi overwhelmed them, the
        Wadi Kishon.^f
    Trample down the strong!^‡
22 Then the hoofs of the horses
        hammered,
    the galloping, galloping of steeds.
23 "Curse Meroz,"^§ says the messenger of
        the LORD,
    "curse, curse its inhabitants!
For they did not come when the LORD
        helped,
    the help of the LORD against the
        warriors."
24 Most blessed of women is Jael,^g
    the wife of Heber the Kenite,
    blessed among tent-dwelling
        women!
25 He asked for water, she gave him milk,
    in a princely bowl she brought him
        curds.^h
26 ^iWith her hand she reached for the peg,
    with her right hand, the workman's
        hammer.
She hammered Sisera, crushed his head;
    she smashed, pierced his temple.
27 At her feet he sank down, fell, lay still;
    down at her feet he sank and fell;
    where he sank down, there he fell,
        slain.

28 ¶From the window she looked down,
    the mother of Sisera peered through
        the lattice:
"Why is his chariot so long in coming?
    why are the hoofbeats of his chariots
        delayed?"
29 The wisest of her princesses answers her;
    she even replies to herself,
30 "They must be dividing the spoil they
        took:
    a slave woman or two for each man,
Spoil of dyed cloth for Sisera,
    spoil of ornate dyed cloth,
    a pair of ornate dyed cloths for my
        neck in the spoil."

---

† [5:20–21] **Stars:** the heavenly host, or angelic army. The roles played by the stars and the flash floods underscore the divine involvement in the battle (cf. 5:4–5).

‡ [5:21] **Trample down the strong!:** the meaning of these words is obscure. If this interpretation is correct, Deborah is the one addressed.

§ [5:23] **Meroz:** an unknown locality in which Israelites probably resided, since its inhabitants are cursed for their failure to participate in the battle.

¶ [5:28–30] The scene shifts to the household of the slain Canaanite general, where the anxious foreboding of Sisera's mother is countered by the assurances of the noblewomen.

---

* [5:14–22] The poet praises the tribes that participated in the war against Sisera: Ephraim, Benjamin, Machir (later regarded as a clan of Manasseh), Zebulun, Issachar, and Naphtali, the tribe of Barak (cf. 4:6). By contrast, the tribes of Reuben, Gilead (elsewhere a region occupied by Reubenites and Gadites), Dan, and Asher are chided for their lack of participation. The more distant tribes of Judah and Simeon are not mentioned, and some historians believe they were not part of Israel at this time.

d. [5:18] Jgs 4:10.

e. [5:20] Jgs 4:15.   f. [5:21] Jgs 4:7, 13; Ps 83:10.   g. [5:24] Jgs 4:17; Jdt 13:18; Lk 1:42.   h. [5:25] Jgs 4:19.   i. [5:26–27] Jgs 4:21.

³¹ So perish all your enemies, O LORD!ʲ
But may those who love you be like
the sun rising in its might!

And the land was at rest for forty years.ᵏ

## CHAPTER 6

**The Call of Gideon.** ¹The Israelites did what
was evil in the sight of the LORD, who therefore
delivered them into the power of Midian for
seven years, ²so that Midian held Israel subject.
From fear of Midian the Israelites made dens in
the mountains, the caves, and the strongholds.ˡ
³For it used to be that whenever the Israelites had
completed sowing their crops, Midian, Amalek,
and the Kedemites* would come up, ⁴encamp
against them, and lay waste the produce of the
land as far as the outskirts of Gaza, leaving no
sustenance in Israel, and no sheep, ox, or donkey. ⁵For they would come up with their livestock, and their tents would appear as thick as
locusts. They would be too many to count when
they came into the land to lay it waste. ⁶ᵐIsrael
was reduced to utter poverty by Midian, and so
the Israelites cried out to the LORD.

⁷When Israel cried out to the LORD because
of Midian, ⁸ⁿthe LORD sent a prophet to the Israelites who said to them: Thus says the LORD, the
God of Israel: I am the one who brought you up
from Egypt; I brought you out of the house of
slavery. ⁹I rescued you from the power of Egypt
and all your oppressors. I drove them out before
you and gave you their land. ¹⁰And I said to you:
I, the LORD, am your God; you shall not fear
the gods of the Amorites in whose land you are
dwelling. But you did not listen to me.

¹¹Then the messenger of the LORD came and
sat under the terebinth in Ophrah that belonged
to Joash the Abiezrite. Joash's son Gideonᵒ was
beating out wheat in the wine press to save it
from the Midianites, ¹²and the messenger of
the LORD appeared to him and said: The LORD
is with you, you mighty warrior! ¹³"My lord,"
Gideon said to him, "if the LORD is with us,
why has all this happened to us? Where are his
wondrous deeds about which our ancestors told
us when they said, 'Did not the LORD bring us
up from Egypt?' For now the LORD has abandoned us and has delivered us into the power
of Midian." ¹⁴ᵖThe LORD turned to him and said:
Go with the strength you have, and save Israel
from the power of Midian. Is it not I who send
you? ¹⁵But he answered him, "Please, my Lord,
how can I save Israel? My family is the poorest
in Manasseh, and I am the most insignificant
in my father's house."�q ¹⁶The LORD said to him:

I will be with you,† and you will cut down Midian to the last man. ¹⁷He answered him, "If
you look on me with favor, give me a sign that
you are the one speaking with me. ¹⁸Please do
not depart from here until I come to you and
bring out my offering and set it before you." He
answered: I will await your return.

¹⁹So Gideon went off and prepared a young
goat and an ephah‡ of flour in the form of
unleavened cakes. Putting the meat in a basket
and the broth in a pot, he brought them out to
him under the terebinth and presented them.
²⁰ʳThe messenger of God said to him: Take the
meat and unleavened cakes and lay them on
this rock; then pour out the broth. When he had
done so, ²¹the messenger of the LORD stretched
out the tip of the staff he held. When he touched
the meat and unleavened cakes, a fire came
up from the rock and consumed the meat and
unleavened cakes. Then the messenger of the
LORD disappeared from sight. ²²§Gideon, now
aware that it had been the messenger of the
LORD, said, "Alas, Lord GOD, that I have seen
the messenger of the LORD face to face!"ˢ ²³The
LORD answered him: You are safe. Do not fear.
You shall not die. ²⁴So Gideon built there an
altar to the LORD and called it Yahweh-shalom.¶ᵗ
To this day it is still in Ophrah of the Abiezrites.

²⁵That same night the LORD said to him: Take
your father's bull, the bull fattened for seven
years, and pull down your father's altar to Baal.
As for the asherah** beside it, cut it down ²⁶and
build an altar to the LORD, your God, on top of
this stronghold with the pile of wood. Then take
the fattened bull and offer it as a whole-burnt
sacrifice on the wood from the asherah you have
cut down. ²⁷So Gideon took ten of his servants
and did as the LORD had commanded him. But
he was too afraid of his family and of the townspeople to do it by day; he did it at night. ²⁸Early
the next morning the townspeople found that
the altar of Baal had been dismantled, the asherah beside it cut down, and the fattened bull
offered on the altar that was built. ²⁹They asked
one another, "Who did this?" They inquired and
searched until they were told, "Gideon, son of
Joash, did it." ³⁰So the townspeople said to Joash,
"Bring out your son that he may die, for he has

---

†[6:16] **I will be with you:** narratives telling how the Lord
commissions someone for a task depict the person's reactions
of reluctance, confusion, or sense of inadequacy, and the
Lord's reassurance ("I will be with you"), sometimes accompanied by a sign (cf. Ex 3:12; Jer 1:8). Lk 1:28–37 is modeled
on this pattern.
‡[6:19] **Ephah:** see note on Is 5:10.
§[6:22] Ancient Israel thought that seeing God face to face
meant mortal danger, as Ex 33:20 indicates and as Gideon's
reaction here shows. Compare the reaction of Samson's parents (13:22–23) when they realize they have been conversing
with the Lord.
¶[6:24] **Yahweh-shalom:** a reference to the Lord's words,
"You are safe" (v. 23), lit., "Peace be to you!"
**[6:25] **The asherah:** see note on Ex 34:13.

---

*[6:3] **Midian, Amalek, and the Kedemites:** three groups
of camel nomads, whose raids were a constant threat to settled
peoples like the Israelites during the period of the Judges.

---

j. [5:31] Ps 83.   k. [5:31] Jgs 3:11, 30; 8:28.   l. [6:2] 1 Sm 13:6.   m. [6:6–
7] Jgs 3:9, 15; 4:3; 10:10; 1 Sm 12:8, 10.   n. [6:8–10] Jgs 2:1–3; 10:11–
14.   o. [6:11] Heb 11:32.   p. [6:14] Ex 3:10–12.   q. [6:15] 1 Sm 9:21.

r. [6:20–22] Jgs 13:19–22.   s. [6:22] Gn 32:31; Dt 5:24–26; Jgs
13:22.   t. [6:24] Gn 33:20; 35:7; Ex 7:15.

dismantled the altar of Baal and cut down the asherah that was beside it." ³¹But Joash replied to all who were standing around him, "Is it for you to take action for Baal, or be his savior? Anyone who takes action for him shall be put to death by morning. If he is a god, let him act for himself," since his altar has been dismantled!" ³²So on that day Gideon was called Jerubbaal,ᵛ because of the words, "Let Baal take action against him, since he dismantled his altar."

³³Then all Midian and Amalek and the Kedemites mustered and crossed over into the valley of Jezreel, where they encamped. ³⁴And Gideon was clothed with the spirit of the LORD,†ʷ and he blew the horn summoning Abiezer to follow him. ³⁵He sent messengers throughout Manasseh, and they, too, were summoned to follow him; he also sent messengers throughout Asher, Zebulun, and Naphtali, and they advanced to meet the others. ³⁶Gideon said to God, "If indeed you are going to save Israel through me, as you have said, ³⁷I am putting this woolen fleece on the threshing floor, and if dew is on the fleece alone, while all the ground is dry, I shall know that you will save Israel through me, as you have said." ³⁸That is what happened. Early the next morning when he wrung out the fleece, he squeezed enough dew from it to fill a bowl. ³⁹Gideon then said to God, "Do not be angry with me if I speak once more. Let me make just one more test with the fleece. Let the fleece alone be dry, but let there be dew on all the ground." ⁴⁰That is what God did that night: the fleece alone was dry, but there was dew on all the ground.

## CHAPTER 7

**Defeat of Midian.** ¹Early the next morning Jerubbaalˣ (that is, Gideon) encamped by the spring of Harod with all his soldiers. The camp of Midian was north of him, beside the hill of Moreh in the valley. ²The LORD said to Gideon: You have too many soldiers with you for me to deliver Midian into their power, lest Israel vaunt itself against me and say, "My own power saved me."†ʸ ³So announce in the hearing of the soldiers, "If anyone is afraid or fearful, let him

leave!ᶻ Let him depart from Mount Gilead!"§ Twenty-two thousand of the soldiers left, but ten thousand remained. ⁴The LORD said to Gideon: There are still too many soldiers. Lead them down to the water and I will test them for you there. If I tell you that a certain man is to go with you, he must go with you. But no one is to go if I tell you he must not. ⁵When Gideon led the soldiers down to the water, the LORD said to him: Everyone who laps up the water with his tongue as a dog does with its tongue you shall set aside by himself; and everyone who kneels down to drink raising his hand to his mouth you shall set aside by himself. ⁶Those who lapped up the water with their tongues numbered three hundred, but all the rest of the soldiers knelt down to drink the water. ⁷The LORD said to Gideon: By means of the three hundred who lapped up the water I will save you and deliver Midian into your power. So let all the other soldiers go home. ⁸They took up such supplies as the soldiers had with them, as well as their horns, and Gideon sent the rest of the Israelites to their tents, but kept the three hundred men. Now the camp of Midian was below him in the valley.

⁹That night the LORD said to Gideon: Go, descend on the camp, for I have delivered it into your power. ¹⁰If you are afraid to attack, go down to the camp with your aide Purah ¹¹and listen to what they are saying. After that you will have the courage to descend on the camp. So he went down with his aide Purah to the outposts of the armed men in the camp. ¹²ᵃThe Midianites, Amalekites, and all the Kedemites were lying in the valley, thick as locusts. Their camels could not be counted, for they were as many as the sands on the seashore. ¹³When Gideon arrived, one man was telling another about a dream. "I had a dream," he said, "that a round loaf of barley bread was rolling into the camp of Midian. It came to a certain tent and struck it and turned it upside down, and the tent collapsed." ¹⁴"This can only be the sword of the Israelite Gideon, son of Joash," the other replied. "God has delivered Midian and all the camp into his power." ¹⁵When Gideon heard the account of the dream and its explanation, he bowed down. Then returning to the camp of Israel, he said, "Arise, for the LORD has delivered the camp of Midian into your power."

---

*[6:32] **Jerubbaal**: similar in sound to the Hebrew words meaning, "Let Baal take action."

†[6:34] **Clothed with the spirit of the LORD**: narratives about the selection of leaders in early Israel typically attribute their prowess to "the spirit of the Lord," not to their own qualities (cf. v. 15). The Lord's spirit "comes upon" them (3:10; 11:29; 13:25) or "rushes upon" them (14:6, 19; 15:14; 1 Sm 11:6), and they are transformed into effective leaders. Here, Gideon is "clothed" with the Lord's spirit; cf. the clothing or vesture imagery in Is 59:17; 61:10; Ez 16:10–14; Jb 29:14.

‡[7:2] **My own power saved me**: Deuteronomic theology constantly warns Israel against attributing success to their own efforts; cf. Dt 6:10–12; 8:17.

§[7:3] **Mount Gilead**: since the well-known highlands of Gilead were east of the Jordan River, some other hill of Gilead must be intended here. Perhaps its name is preserved in Ain Jalud (or Galud), the modern Arabic name of the spring of Harod, where Gideon's army is encamped (v. 1). The narrator plays on the Hebrew word "fearful" (*hared*) and the name of the spring, *harod*.

¶[7:5] The point of this selection process is clear: the battle against the nomadic raiders is going to be won not because of the numerical superiority of the Israelite troops but because of the power of the Lord.

**[7:13] The dream seems to foretell the victory of the agricultural Israelites (the barley loaf) over the nomadic Midianites (the tent).

---

u. [6:31] 1 Kgs 18:27.   v. [6:32] 1 Sm 12:11.   w. [6:34] Jgs 3:10; 11:29; 13:25; 14:6, 19; 15:14; 1 Sm 11:6.   x. [7:1] Jgs 6:32.   y. [7:2] Dt 8:17; 9:4.

z. [7:3] Dt 20:8.   a. [7:12] Jgs 6:3.

[16]He divided the three hundred men into three companies, and provided them all with horns and with empty jars and torches inside the jars. [17]"Watch me and follow my lead," he told them. "I shall go to the edge of the camp, and as I do, you must do also. [18]When I and those with me blow horns, you too must blow horns all around the camp and cry out, 'For the LORD and for Gideon!'" [19]So Gideon and the hundred men who were with him came to the edge of the camp at the beginning of the middle watch,* just after the posting of the guards. They blew the horns and broke the jars they were holding. [20]When the three companies had blown their horns and broken their jars, they took the torches in their left hands, and in their right the horns they had been blowing, and cried out, "A sword for the LORD and for Gideon!" [21]They all remained standing in place around the camp, while the whole camp began to run and shout and flee. [22]When they blew the three hundred horns, the LORD set the sword of one against another throughout the camp, and they fled as far as Beth-shittah in the direction of Zeredah, near the border of Abel-meholah at Tabbath.

[23]*b*The Israelites were called to arms from Naphtali, from Asher, and from all Manasseh, and they pursued Midian. [24]Gideon also sent messengers throughout the mountain region of Ephraim to say, "Go down to intercept Midian, and seize the water courses against them as far as Beth-barah, as well as the Jordan." So all the Ephraimites were called to arms, and they seized the water courses as far as Beth-barah, and the Jordan as well. [25]*c*They captured the two princes of Midian, Oreb and Zeeb, killing Oreb at the rock of Oreb and Zeeb at the wine press of Zeeb. Then they pursued Midian, but they had the heads of Oreb and Zeeb brought to Gideon beyond the Jordan.

## CHAPTER 8

[1]*d*But the Ephraimites said to him, "What have you done to us, not summoning us when you went to fight against Midian?" And they quarreled bitterly with him. [2]But he answered them, "What have I done in comparison with you? Is not the gleaning of Ephraim better than the vintage of Abiezer?*e* [3]It was into your power God delivered the princes of Midian, Oreb and Zeeb.*f* What have I been able to do in comparison with you?" When he said this, their anger against him subsided.

[4]When Gideon reached the Jordan and crossed it, he and his three hundred men were exhausted and famished. [5]So he said to the people of Succoth, "Will you give my followers some loaves of bread? They are exhausted, and I am pursuing Zebah and Zalmunna, kings of Midian." [6]But the princes of Succoth replied, "Are the hands of Zebah and Zalmunna already in your possession, that we should give food to your army?"† [7]Gideon said, "Very well; when the LORD has delivered Zebah and Zalmunna into my power, I will thrash your bodies with desert thorns and briers." [8]He went up from there to Penuel and made the same request of them, but the people of Penuel answered him as had the people of Succoth. [9]So to the people of Penuel, too, he said, "When I return in peace, I will demolish this tower."

[10]Now Zebah and Zalmunna were in Karkor with their force of about fifteen thousand men; these were all who were left of the whole Kedemite army, a hundred and twenty thousand swordsmen having fallen. [11]Gideon went up by the route of the tent-dwellers east of Nobah and Jogbehah, and attacked the force when it felt secure. [12]Zebah and Zalmunna fled and Gideon pursued them. He captured the two kings of Midian, Zebah and Zalmunna, terrifying the entire force.

[13]Then Gideon, son of Joash, returned from battle by the pass of Heres. [14]He captured a young man of Succoth and questioned him, and he wrote down for him the seventy-seven princes and elders of Succoth. [15]So he went to the princes of Succoth and said, "Here are Zebah and Zalmunna, with whom you taunted me, 'Are the hands of Zebah and Zalmunna already in your possession, that we should give food to your weary men?'" [16]He seized the elders of the city, and with desert thorns and briers he thrashed the people of Succoth. [17]He also demolished the tower of Penuel and killed the people of the city.

[18]Then he said to Zebah and Zalmunna, "What about the men you killed at Tabor?" "They were all like you," they replied. "They appeared to be princes." [19]"They were my brothers, my mother's sons," he said. "As the LORD lives, if you had spared their lives, I would not kill you." [20]Then he said to his firstborn, Jether, "Go, kill them." But the boy did not draw his sword, for he was afraid, for he was still a boy. [21]*g*Zebah and Zalmunna said, "Come, kill us yourself, for as a man is, so is his strength." So Gideon stepped forward and killed Zebah and Zalmunna. He also took the crescents that were on the necks of their camels.

[22]*h*The Israelites then said to Gideon, "Rule over us—you, your son, and your son's son—for you saved us from the power of Midian." [23]But Gideon answered them, "I will not rule over

---

*[7:19] **At the beginning of the middle watch:** at the start of the second of the three watches into which the night was divided. The sentinels were changed at the beginning of a watch, thus making the camp momentarily vulnerable.

b. [7:23] Jgs 6:35.    c. [7:25] Ps 83:12; Is 10:26.    d. [8:1] Jgs 12:1.
e. [8:2] Jgs 6:34.    f. [8:3] Jgs 7:25.

†[8:6] **Are the hands . . . already in your possession . . . ?:** i.e., can you already boast of victory? The hands of slain enemies were sometimes cut off and counted as trophies.

g. [8:21] Ps 83:12.    h. [8:22] 1 Sm 8:5; Hos 13:10.

you, nor shall my son rule over you. The LORD must rule over you."[i]

²⁴Gideon went on to say, "Let me make a request of you. Give me, each of you, a ring from his spoils." (Since they were Ishmaelites,* the enemy had gold rings.) ²⁵"We will certainly give them," they replied, and they spread out a cloak into which everyone threw a ring from his spoils. ²⁶The gold rings he had requested weighed seventeen hundred gold shekels, apart from the crescents and pendants, the purple garments worn by the kings of Midian, and apart from the trappings that were on the necks of their camels. ²⁷Gideon made an ephod out of the gold and placed it in his city, Ophrah. All Israel prostituted themselves there, and it became a snare to Gideon and his household.

²⁸Midian was brought into subjection by the Israelites; they no longer held their heads high, and the land had rest for forty years,[k] during the lifetime of Gideon.

**Gideon's Son Abimelech.** ²⁹Then Jerubbaal, son of Joash, went to live in his house. ³⁰Now Gideon had seventy sons, his own offspring, for he had many wives. ³¹His concubine† who lived in Shechem also bore him a son, whom he named Abimelech. ³²At a good old age Gideon, son of Joash, died and was buried in the tomb of Joash his father in Ophrah of the Abiezrites. ³³ᵐBut after Gideon was dead, the Israelites again prostituted themselves by following the Baals, making Baal-berith‡ their god. ³⁴The Israelites did not remember the LORD, their God, who had delivered them from the power of their enemies all around them. ³⁵Nor were they loyal to the house of Jerubbaal (Gideon) for all the good he had done for Israel.

## CHAPTER 9

¹Abimelech, son of Jerubbaal, went to his mother's kin in Shechem,[n] and said to them and to the whole clan to which his mother's family belonged, ²"Put this question to all the lords of Shechem: 'Which is better for you: that seventy men, all Jerubbaal's sons, rule over you, or that one man rule over you?' You must remember that I am your own flesh and bone."[o] ³When his mother's kin repeated these words on his behalf to all the lords of Shechem, they set their hearts on Abimelech, thinking, "He is our kin." ⁴They

also gave him seventy pieces of silver from the temple of Baal-berith, with which Abimelech hired worthless men and outlaws as his followers. ⁵He then went to his father's house in Ophrah, and killed his brothers, the seventy sons of Jerubbaal, on one stone. Only the youngest son of Jerubbaal, Jotham, escaped, for he was hidden. ⁶Then all the lords of Shechem and all Beth-millo came together and made Abimelech king by the terebinth at the memorial pillar in Shechem.

⁷When this was reported to Jotham, he went and stood at the top of Mount Gerizim and cried out in a loud voice:

"Hear me, lords of Shechem,
    and may God hear you!
⁸ One day the trees went out
    to anoint a king over themselves.
So they said to the olive tree,
    'Reign over us.'
⁹ But the olive tree answered them,
    'Must I give up my rich oil,
    whereby gods and human beings are
        honored,§
    and go off to hold sway over the
        trees?'
¹⁰ Then the trees said to the fig tree,
    'Come; you reign over us!'
¹¹ But the fig tree answered them,
    'Must I give up my sweetness
    and my sweet fruit,
    and go off to hold sway over the
        trees?'
¹² Then the trees said to the vine,
    'Come you, reign over us.'
¹³ But the vine answered them,
    'Must I give up my wine
    that cheers gods¶ and human beings,
    and go off to hold sway over the
        trees?'
¹⁴ Then all the trees said to the buckthorn,
    'Come you, reign over us!'
¹⁵ The buckthorn answered the trees,
    'If you are anointing me in good
        faith,
    to make me king over you,
    come, and take refuge in my shadow.
    But if not, let fire come from the
        buckthorn
    and devour the cedars of Lebanon.'[p]

¹⁶"Now then, if you have acted in good faith and integrity in appointing Abimelech your

---

*[8:24] **Ishmaelites**: evidently used here as a general term for nomads, whose wealth was in the form of gold and flocks. The genealogies in Genesis place the Midianites as descendants of Abraham and his wife Keturah (Gn 25:1–2), and the Ishmaelites as the descendants of Ishmael, son of Abraham and Hagar, Sarah's Egyptian slave (Gn 25:12–16).

†[8:31] **Concubine**: a wife of secondary rank.

‡[8:33] **Baal-berith**: a divine epithet meaning "lord of the covenant." The same deity is called El-berith, "god of the covenant," in 9:46.

i. [8:23] 1 Sm 8:7; 10:19; 12:12.   j. [8:27] Jgs 17:5; 18:14.   k. [8:28] Jgs 3:11, 30; 5:31.   l. [8:30] Jgs 9:2, 5; 10:4; 12:9, 14.   m. [8:33–34] Jgs 2:19; 3:12; 4:1.   n. [9:1] Jgs 8:31.   o. [9:2] 2 Sm 5:1; 19:12, 13.

§[9:9] **Whereby gods and human beings are honored**: olive oil had a variety of cultic uses (e.g., Lv 2:1, 6, 15; 24:2), and it was also used in the consecration of priests and kings for office (e.g., Ex 30:25, 30; 1 Sm 10:1; 16:13).

¶[9:13] **Cheers gods**: wine was part of a number of types of offerings in the Israelite cult (cf. Ex 29:40; Lv 23:13; Nm 15:7, 10), and it was also used widely in the worship of foreign gods (cf. Dt 32:37–38; Is 65:11).

p. [9:15] 2 Kgs 14:9.

king, if you have acted with good will toward Jerubbaal and his house, and if you have treated him as he deserved— [17]for my father fought for you at the risk of his life when he delivered you from the power of Midian, [18]but you have risen against my father's house today and killed his seventy sons upon one stone and made Abimelech, the son of his maidservant,[q] king over the lords of Shechem, because he is your kin— [19]if, then, you have acted in good faith and integrity toward Jerubbaal and his house today, then rejoice in Abimelech and may he in turn rejoice in you! [20]But if not, let fire come forth from Abimelech and devour the lords of Shechem and Beth-millo, and let fire come forth from the lords of Shechem and Beth-millo and devour Abimelech." [21]Then Jotham fled and escaped to Beer, where he remained for fear of his brother Abimelech.

[22]When Abimelech had ruled Israel for three years, [23]God put an evil spirit[r] between Abimelech and the lords of Shechem, and the lords of Shechem broke faith with the house of Abimelech. [24]This was to repay the violence done to the seventy sons of Jerubbaal and to avenge their blood upon their brother Abimelech, who killed them, and upon the lords of Shechem, who encouraged him to kill his brothers. [25]The lords of Shechem then set men in ambush for him on the mountaintops, and they robbed all who passed them on the road. It was reported to Abimelech.

[26]Now Gaal, son of Ebed, and his kin came, and when they passed through Shechem, the lords of Shechem put their trust in him. [27]They went out into the fields, harvested the grapes from their vineyards, trod them out, and held a festival. Then they went to the temple of their god, where they ate and drank and cursed Abimelech. [28]Gaal, son of Ebed, said, "Who is Abimelech? And who is Shechem that we should serve him? Did not the son of Jerubbaal and his lieutenant Zebul serve the men of Hamor, father of Shechem?[s] So why should we serve him? [29]Would that these troops were entrusted to my command! I would depose Abimelech. I would say to Abimelech, 'Get a larger army and come out!'"

[30]When Zebul, the ruler of the city, heard what Gaal, son of Ebed, had said, he was angry [31]and sent messengers to Abimelech in Arumah to say, "Gaal, son of Ebed, and his kin have come to Shechem and are stirring up the city against you. [32]So take action tonight, you and the troops who are with you, and set an ambush in the fields. [33]Promptly at sunrise tomorrow morning, make a raid on the city. When he and the troops who are with him come out against you, deal with him as best you can."

[34]During the night Abimelech went into action with all his soldiers and set up an ambush outside of Shechem in four companies. [35]Gaal, son of Ebed, went out and stood at the entrance of the city gate. When Abimelech and his soldiers rose from their place of ambush, [36]Gaal saw the soldiers and said to Zebul, "There are soldiers coming down from the mountaintops!" But Zebul answered him, "It is the shadow of the hills that you see as men." [37]But Gaal went on to say, "Soldiers are coming down from the region of Tabbur-haarez, and one company is coming by way of Elon-meonenim." [38]Zebul said to him, "Where now is your boast, when you said, 'Who is Abimelech that we should serve him?' Are these not the troops for whom you expressed contempt? Go out now and fight with them." [39]So Gaal went out at the head of the lords of Shechem to fight against Abimelech; [40]but when Abimelech went after him, he fled from him. Many fell slain right up to the entrance of the gate. [41]Abimelech returned to Arumah, and Zebul drove Gaal and his kin away so that they could no longer remain at Shechem.

[42]The next day, the army marched out into the field, and it was reported to Abimelech. [43]He divided the troops he had into three companies, and set up an ambush in the fields. He watched until he saw the army leave the city and then went on the attack against them. [44]Abimelech and the company with him rushed in and stood by the entrance of the city gate, while the other two companies rushed upon all who were in the field and attacked them. [45]That entire day Abimelech fought against the city. He captured it, killed the people who were in it, and demolished the city itself, sowing it with salt.*[u]

[46]When they heard of this, all the lords of the Migdal-shechem went into the crypt of the temple of El-berith. [47]It was reported to Abimelech that all the lords of the Migdal-shechem were gathered together. [48]So he went up Mount Zalmon with all his soldiers, took his ax in his hand, and cut down some brushwood. This he lifted to his shoulder, then said to the troops with him, "Hurry! Do just as you have seen me do." [49]So all the soldiers likewise cut down brushwood and, following Abimelech, placed it against the crypt. Then they set the crypt on fire over them, so that every one of the people of the Migdal-shechem, about a thousand men and women, perished.

[50]Abimelech proceeded to Thebez, encamped, and captured it. [51]Now there was a strong tower in the middle of the city, and all the men and women and all the lords of the city fled there, shutting themselves in and going up to the roof of the tower. [52]Abimelech came up to the tower

---

*[9:45] **Sowing it with salt**: a severe measure, since it rendered the soil barren and useless.

q. [9:18] Jgs 8:31.   r. [9:23] 1 Sm 16:14; 18:10; 19:9; 1 Kgs 22:19–23.   s. [9:28] 1 Sm 25:10.   t. [9:28] Gn 33:19; 34:2.

u. [9:45] Dt 29:23; Jer 17:6; Ps 107:34.

and fought against it. When he came close to the entrance of the tower to set it on fire, [53]a certain woman cast the upper part of a millstone* down on Abimelech's head, and it fractured his skull.[v] [54]He immediately called his armor-bearer and said to him, "Draw your sword and put me to death so they will not say about me, 'A woman killed him.'"[w] So his attendant ran him through and he died. [55]When the Israelites saw that Abimelech was dead, they all left for their homes.

[56]Thus did God repay the evil that Abimelech had done to his father in killing his seventy brothers. [57]God also brought all the wickedness of the people of Shechem back on their heads, for the curse of Jotham, son of Jerubbaal, overtook them.

### CHAPTER 10

**Tola.** [1]After Abimelech, Tola,[†] son of Puah, son of Dodo, a man of Issachar, rose up to save Israel; he lived in Shamir in the mountain region of Ephraim. [2]When he had judged Israel twenty-three years, he died and was buried in Shamir. **Jair.** [3]Jair the Gileadite came after him and judged Israel twenty-two years. [4a]He had thirty sons who rode on thirty donkeys[‡] and possessed thirty cities in the land of Gilead (these are called Havvoth-jair to the present day).[y] [5]Jair died and was buried in Kamon.

**Oppression by the Ammonites.** [6z]The Israelites again did what was evil in the sight of the LORD, serving the Baals and Ashtarts, the gods of Aram, the gods of Sidon, the gods of Moab, the gods of the Ammonites, and the gods of the Philistines. Since they had abandoned the LORD and would not serve him, [7]the LORD became angry with Israel and he sold them into the power of the Philistines and the Ammonites. [8]For eighteen years they afflicted and oppressed the Israelites in Bashan, and all the Israelites in the Amorite land beyond the Jordan in Gilead. [9]The Ammonites also crossed the Jordan to fight against Judah, Benjamin and the house of Ephraim, so that Israel was in great distress. [10a]Then the Israelites cried out to the LORD, "We have sinned against you, for we have abandoned our God and served the Baals." [11b]The LORD answered the Israelites: Did not the Egyptians, the Amorites,[c] the Ammonites, the Philistines, [12]the Sidonians, the Amalekites, and the

Midianites[d] oppress you? Yet when you cried out to me, and I saved you from their power, [13]you still abandoned me and served other gods. Therefore I will save you no more.[e] [14]Go and cry out to the gods you have chosen; let them save you in your time of distress. [15]But the Israelites said to the LORD, "We have sinned. Do to us whatever is good in your sight. Only deliver us this day!" [16]And they cast out the foreign gods from their midst and served the LORD, so that he grieved over the misery of Israel.

[17]The Ammonites were called out for war and encamped in Gilead, while the Israelites assembled and encamped at Mizpah. [18]The captains of the army of Gilead said to one another, "The one who begins the war against the Ammonites shall be leader of all the inhabitants of Gilead."[f]

### CHAPTER 11

**Jephthah.** [1]Jephthah[g] the Gileadite was a warrior. He was the son of a prostitute, fathered by Gilead. [2]Gilead's wife had also borne him sons. When they grew up the sons of the wife had driven Jephthah away, saying to him, "You shall inherit nothing in our father's house, for you are the son of another woman." [3]So Jephthah had fled from his brothers and taken up residence in the land of Tob.[h] Worthless men had joined company with him, and went out with him on raids.[i]

[4]Some time later, the Ammonites went to war with Israel. [5]As soon as the Ammonites were at war with Israel, the elders of Gilead went to bring Jephthah from the land of Tob. [6]"Come," they said to Jephthah, "be our commander so that we can fight the Ammonites." [7]"Are you not the ones who hated me and drove me from my father's house?" Jephthah replied to the elders of Gilead, "Why do you come to me now, when you are in distress?" [8]The elders of Gilead said to Jephthah, "This is the reason we have come back to you now: if you go with us to fight against the Ammonites, you shall be the leader of all of the inhabitants of Gilead." [9]Jephthah answered the elders of Gilead, "If you bring me back to fight against the Ammonites and the LORD delivers them up to me, I will be your leader." [10]The elders of Gilead said to Jephthah, "The LORD is witness between us that we will do as you say." [11]So Jephthah went with the elders of Gilead, and the army made him their leader and commander. Jephthah gave all his orders in the presence of the LORD in Mizpah.

[12]Then he sent messengers to the king of the Ammonites to say, "What do you have against me that you come to fight with me in my land?" [13]The king of the Ammonites answered the messengers of Jephthah, "Israel took away my land from the Arnon to the Jabbok and the Jordan

---

*[9:53] **The upper part of a millstone**: a common hand mill consisted of a large flat stone base and a smaller upper stone (cf. Dt 24:6) shaped so that it could be held in the hands and rolled or ground against the lower stone. It is an upper stone that the woman hurls over the wall to kill Abimelech.

†[10:1–5] **Tola . . . Jair**: two more of the so-called "minor judges"; see Introduction.

‡[10:4] **Donkeys**: mounts signifying rank and wealth; cf. 5:10; 12:14.

---

v. [9:53] 2 Sm 11:21.   w. [9:54] 1 Sm 31:4; 2 Sm 1:9; 1 Chr 10:4.
x. [10:4] Jgs 8:30; 9:2, 5; 12:9, 14.   y. [10:4] Dt 3:14.   z. [10:6–8]
Jgs 2:11–14; 3:7–8, 12; 4:1–2; 6:1; 13:1.   a. [10:10] Jgs 3:9, 15; 4:3;
6:6, 7; 1 Sm 12:8, 10.   b. [10:11–14] Jgs 2:1–3; 6:8–10.   c. [10:11]
Nm 21:21–32.

d. [10:12] Jgs 6:1–6.   e. [10:13] Jgs 2:21.   f. [10:18] Jgs 11:5–
11.   g. [11:1] Heb 11:32.   h. [11:3] 2 Sm 10:6, 8.   i. [11:3] Jgs 9:4;
1 Sm 22:2.   j. [11:8–11] Jgs 10:18.

when they came up from Egypt.ᵏ Now restore it peaceably."

¹⁴Again Jephthah sent messengers to the king of the Ammonites, ¹⁵saying to him, "This is what Jephthah says: 'Israel did not take the land of Moab or the land of the Ammonites.ˡ ¹⁶For when they came up from Egypt, Israel went through the wilderness to the Red Sea and came to Kadesh. ¹⁷Israel then sent messengers to the king of Edom saying, "Let me pass through your land." But the king of Edom did not give consent.ᵐ They also sent to the king of Moab, but he too was unwilling. So Israel remained in Kadesh.ⁿ ¹⁸Then they went through the wilderness, and bypassing the land of Edom and the land of Moab, they arrived east of the land of Moab and encamped across the Arnon.ᵒ Thus they did not enter the territory of Moab, for the Arnon is the boundary of Moab.ᵖ ¹⁹qThen Israel sent messengers to the Amorite king Sihon, who was king of Heshbon. Israel said to him, "Let me pass through your land to my own place." ²⁰But Sihon refused to let Israel pass through his territory. He gathered all his soldiers, and they encamped at Jahaz and fought Israel. ²¹But the Lord, the God of Israel, delivered Sihon and his entire army into the power of Israel, who defeated them and occupied all the land of the Amorites who lived in that region. ²²They occupied all of the Amorite territory from the Arnon to the Jabbok and the wilderness to the Jordan.ʳ ²³Now, then, it was the Lord, the God of Israel, who dispossessed the Amorites for his people, Israel. And you are going to dispossess them? ²⁴Should you not take possession of that which your god Chemosh* gave you to possess, and should we not take possession of all that the Lord, our God, has dispossessed for us? ²⁵Now, then, are you any better than Balak, son of Zippor, king of Moab? Did he ever quarrel with Israel or make war against them?ˢ ²⁶Israel has dwelt in Heshbon and its villages, Aroer and its villages, and all the cities on the banks of the Arnon for three hundred years.ᵗ Why did you not recover them during that time? ²⁷As for me, I have not sinned against you, but you wrong me by making war against me. Let the Lord, who is judge, decide this day between the Israelites and the Ammonites!'" ²⁸But the king of the Ammonites paid no heed to the message Jephthah sent him.

**Jephthah's Vow.** ²⁹The spirit of the Lord came upon Jephthah.ᵘ He passed through Gilead

and Manasseh, and through Mizpah of Gilead as well, and from Mizpah of Gilead he crossed over against the Ammonites. ³⁰ᵛJephthah made a vow to the Lord.ᵛ "If you deliver the Ammonites into my power," he said, ³¹"whoever comes out of the doors of my house to meet me when I return from the Ammonites in peace shall belong to the Lord. I shall offer him up as a burnt offering."

³²Jephthah then crossed over against the Ammonites to fight against them, and the Lord delivered them into his power. ³³He inflicted a very severe defeat on them from Aroer to the approach of Minnith—twenty cities in all—and as far as Abel-keramin. So the Ammonites were brought into subjection by the Israelites. ³⁴When Jephthah returned to his house in Mizpah, it was his daughter who came out to meet him, with tambourine-playing and dancing. She was his only child: he had neither son nor daughter besides her. ³⁵When he saw her, he tore his garments and said, "Ah, my daughter! You have struck me down and brought calamity upon me. For I have made a vow‡ to the Lord and I cannot take it back."ʷ ³⁶"Father," she replied, "you have made a vow to the Lord. Do with me as you have vowed, because the Lord has taken vengeance for you against your enemies the Ammonites." ³⁷Then she said to her father, "Let me have this favor. Do nothing for two months, that I and my companions may go wander in the mountains to weep for my virginity." ³⁸"Go," he replied, and sent her away for two months. So she departed with her companions and wept for her virginity in the mountains. ³⁹At the end of the two months she returned to her father, and he did to her as he had vowed. She had not had relations with any man.

It became a custom in Israel ⁴⁰for Israelite women to go yearly to mourn the daughter of Jephthah the Gileadite for four days of the year.

## CHAPTER 12

**The Shibboleth Incident.** ¹The men of Ephraim were called out, and they crossed over to Zaphon. They said to Jephthah, "Why did you go to fight with the Ammonites without calling us to go with you?ˣ We will burn your house on top of you." ²Jephthah answered them, "My

---

*[11:24] **Chemosh**: the god of the Moabites (1 Kgs 11:7; 2 Kgs 23:13) not the Ammonites, whose god was Milcom (1 Kgs 11:5; 2 Kgs 23:13). Much of the disputed land, which lay between the Jabbok and Arnon Rivers, was actually in Moab, and many of the details of this passage (vv. 12–28) seem more applicable to a quarrel with the king of the Moabites than with the king of the Ammonites.

†[11:30–40] Jephthah's rash vow and its tragic consequences reflect a widespread folklore motif, most familiar in the Greek story of Iphigenia and her father, Agamemnon. The sacrifice of children was strictly forbidden by Mosaic law (Lv 18:21; 20:2–5), and when the biblical writers report its occurrence, they usually condemn it in strong terms (2 Kgs 16:3; 21:6; Jer 7:31; 19:5). In this case, however, the narrator simply records the old story, offering no comment on the acceptability of Jephthah's extreme gesture. The story may have been preserved because it provided an explanation of the custom described in vv. 39–40 according to which Israelite women mourned Jephthah's daughter annually in a four-day ceremony.

‡[11:35] **Made a vow**: lit., "opened my mouth"; so in v. 36.

---

k. [11:13] Nm 21:24.  l. [11:15] Dt 2:9, 19.  m. [11:17] Nm 21:14–21.  n. [11:17] Dt 1:46.  o. [11:18] Nm 20:21; 21:4, 10–12; Dt 2:8.  p. [11:18] Nm 21:13; 22:36.  q. [11:19–21] Nm 21:21–26; Dt 2:26–36.  r. [11:22] Jgs 11:13.  s. [11:25] Nm 22–24; Jos 24:9–10; Mi 6:5.  t. [11:26] Nm 21:25; Dt 2:36.  u. [11:29] Jgs 3:10; 6:34; 13:25; 14:6, 19; 15:14; 1 Sm 11:6.

v. [11:30] Gn 28:20–22; 1 Sm 1:11; 2 Sm 15:7–8.  w. [11:35] Nm 30:3; Dt 23:22; Eccl 5:4.  x. [12:1] Jgs 8:1.

soldiers and I were engaged in a contest with the Ammonites. They were pressing us hard, and I cried out to you, but you did not come to save me from their power. ³When I saw that you were not coming to save me, I took my life in my own hand and crossed over against the Ammonites, and the LORD delivered them into my power. Why, then, should you come up against me this day to fight with me?"

⁴Then Jephthah gathered together all the men of Gilead and fought against Ephraim. The men of Gilead defeated Ephraim, ⁵and Gilead seized the fords of the Jordan against Ephraim. When any of the fleeing Ephraimites said, "Let me pass," the men of Gilead would say to him, "Are you an Ephraimite?" If he answered, "No!" ⁶they would ask him to say "Shibboleth."* If he said "Sibboleth," not pronouncing it exactly right, they would seize him and kill him at the fords of the Jordan. Forty-two thousand Ephraimites fell at that time.

⁷Jephthah judged Israel for six years, and Jephthah the Gileadite died and was buried in his city in Gilead.ʸ

**Ibzan.** ⁸After him Ibzan† of Bethlehem judged Israel. ⁹ᶻHe had thirty sons and thirty daughters whom he gave in marriage outside the family, while bringing in thirty wives for his sons from outside the family. He judged Israel for seven years. ¹⁰Ibzan died and was buried in Bethlehem. **Elon.** ¹¹After him Elon the Zebulunite judged Israel; he judged Israel for ten years. ¹²Elon the Zebulunite died and was buried at Aijalon in the land of Zebulun.

**Abdon.** ¹³After him Abdon, son of Hillel, the Pirathonite, judged Israel. ¹⁴ᵃHe had forty sons and thirty grandsons, who rode on seventy donkeys. He judged Israel for eight years. ¹⁵Abdon, son of Hillel, the Pirathonite, died and was buried in Pirathon in the land of Ephraim in the mountain region of the Amalekites.

# CHAPTER 13

**The Birth of Samson.** ¹ᵇThe Israelites again did what was evil in the sight of the LORD, who therefore delivered them into the power of the Philistines for forty years.

²There was a certain man from Zorah, of the clan of the Danites,‡ whose name was Manoah. His wife was barren and had borne no children.ᶜ

³ᵈAn angel of the LORD appeared to the woman and said to her: Though you are barren and have had no children, you will conceive and bear a son. ⁴ᵉNow, then, be careful to drink no wine or beer and to eat nothing unclean, ⁵for you will conceive and bear a son. No razor shall touch his head, for the boy is to be a nazirite for God§ from the womb. It is he who will begin to save Israel from the power of the Philistines.

⁶The woman went and told her husband, "A man of God came to me; he had the appearance of an angel of God, fearsome indeed. I did not ask him where he came from, nor did he tell me his name. ⁷But he said to me, 'You will conceive and bear a son. So drink no wine or beer, and eat nothing unclean. For the boy shall be a nazirite for God from the womb, until the day of his death.'" ⁸Manoah then prayed to the LORD. "Please, my Lord," he said, "may the man of God whom you sent return to us to teach us what to do for the boy who is to be born."

⁹God heard the prayer of Manoah, and the angel of God came again to the woman as she was sitting in the field; but her husband Manoah was not with her. ¹⁰The woman ran quickly and told her husband. "The man who came to me the other day has appeared to me," she said to him; ¹¹so Manoah got up and followed his wife. When he reached the man, he said to him, "Are you the one who spoke to my wife?" I am, he answered. ¹²Then Manoah asked, "Now, when what you say comes true, what rules must the boy follow? What must he do?" ¹³The angel of the LORD answered Manoah: Your wife must be careful about all the things of which I spoke to her. ¹⁴She must not eat anything that comes from the vine, she must not drink wine or beer, and she must not eat anything unclean. Let her observe all that I have commanded her. ¹⁵Then Manoah said to the angel of the LORD, "Permit us to detain you, so that we may prepare a young goat for you." ¹⁶But the angel of the LORD answered Manoah: Though you detained me, I would not eat your food. But if you want to prepare a burnt offering, then offer it up to the LORD. For Manoah did not know that he was the angel of the LORD. ¹⁷ᶠThen Manoah said to the angel of the LORD, "What is your name, that we may honor you when your words come true?" ¹⁸ᵍThe angel of the LORD answered him: Why do you ask my name? It is wondrous. ¹⁹ᵍThen Manoah took a young goat with a grain offering and offered it on the

---

*[12:6] **Shibboleth:** Hebrew meaning "ear of grain" or "torrent of water." Though the Ephraimites probably spoke the same dialect of Hebrew as their Gileadite neighbors, there was enough regional variation in their pronunciation of the initial sound of this word to betray them to their enemies.

†[12:8–15] **Ibzan . . . Elon . . . Abdon:** three more of the so-called "minor judges"; see Introduction.

‡[13:2] **The clan of the Danites:** before the migration described in chap. 18 the tribe of Dan occupied a small territory west of Benjamin, adjacent to the Philistine plain; see note on 3:3.

§[13:5] **A nazirite for God:** according to the rules for nazirites set forth in Nm 6:2–8, Samson's vows would have obliged him to abstain from wine and other products of the vine and to keep his hair uncut. As the story that follows shows, the last requirement proved especially fateful in Samson's life.

¶[13:17–19] Manoah asks for a name so that he will know how to acknowledge the help of the visitor, but the angel will say only that his name is "wondrous," i.e., beyond human comprehension. Manoah's response is to dedicate his offering to "the Lord, who works wonders."

y. [12:7] Jgs 10:2, 5; 12:10, 12, 15; 15:20.    z. [12:9] Jgs 8:30; 9:2, 5; 10:4; 12:14.    a. [12:14] Jgs 9:2, 5; 10:4; 12:9.    b. [13:1] Jgs 2:11–14; 3:7–8, 12; 4:1–2; 6:1; 10:6–8.    c. [13:2] 1 Sm 1:2; Lk 1:7.

d. [13:3] 1 Sm 1:20; Lk 1:13, 31.    e. [13:4–5] Nm 6:1–5; 1 Sm 1:11; Lk 1:15.    f. [13:18] Gn 32:30.    g. [13:19–20] Jgs 6:19–21.

rock to the LORD, who works wonders. While Manoah and his wife were looking on, ²⁰as the flame rose to the heavens from the altar, the angel of the LORD ascended in the flame of the altar. When Manoah and his wife saw this, they fell on their faces to the ground; ²¹but the angel of the LORD was seen no more by Manoah and his wife.ʰ Then Manoah, realizing that it was the angel of the LORD, ²²said to his wife, "We will certainly die,* for we have seen God." ²³But his wife said to him, "If the LORD had meant to kill us, he would not have accepted a burnt offering and grain offering from our hands! Nor would he have let us see all this, or hear what we have heard."

²⁴The woman bore a son and named him Samson, and when the boy grew up the LORD blessed him. ²⁵The spirit of the LORD came upon him for the first timeⁱ in Mahaneh-dan, between Zorah and Eshtaol.

## CHAPTER 14

**Marriage of Samson.** ¹Samson went down to Timnah where he saw one of the Philistine women. ²On his return he told his father and mother, "I saw in Timnah a woman, a Philistine. Get her for me as a wife." ³ʲHis father and mother said to him, "Is there no woman among your kinsfolk or among all your people, that you must go and take a woman from the uncircumcised Philistines?" But Samson answered his father, "Get her for me, for she is the one I want." ⁴ᵏNow his father and mother did not know that this had been brought about by the LORD, who was seeking an opportunity against the Philistines;† for at that time they ruled over Israel.ˡ

⁵So Samson went down to Timnah with his father and mother. When he turned aside to the vineyards of Timnah, a young lion came roaring out toward him. ⁶ᵐBut the spirit of the LORD rushed upon Samson, and he tore the lion apart barehanded,ⁿ as one tears a young goat. Without telling his father or mother what he had done, ⁷he went down and spoke to the woman. He liked her. ⁸Later, when he came back to marry her, he turned aside to look at the remains of the lion, and there was a swarm of bees in the lion's carcass, and honey. ⁹So he scooped the honey out into his hands and ate it as he went along. When he came to his father and mother,

he gave them some to eat, but he did not tell them that he had scooped the honey from the lion's carcass.

¹⁰His father also went down to the woman, and Samson gave a feast there, since it was customary for the young men to do this. ¹¹Out of their fear of him, they brought thirty men to be his companions. ¹²Samson said to them, "Let me propose a riddle to you. If within the seven days of the feast you solve it for me, I will give you thirty linen tunics and thirty sets of garments. ¹³But if you cannot answer it for me, you must give me thirty tunics and thirty sets of garments." "Propose your riddle," they responded, "and we will listen to it." ¹⁴So he said to them,

"Out of the eater came food,
　　out of the strong came sweetness."

For three days they were unable to answer the riddle, ¹⁵and on the fourth day they said to Samson's wife,ᵒ "Trick your husband into solving the riddle for us, or we will burn you and your family.ᵖ Did you invite us here to reduce us to poverty?" ¹⁶‡�q So Samson's wife wept at his side and said, "You just hate me! You do not love me! You proposed a riddle to my people, but did not tell me the answer." He said to her, "If I did not tell even my father or my mother, must I tell you?" ¹⁷But she wept beside him during the seven days the feast lasted, and on the seventh day, he told her the answer, because she pressed him, and she explained the riddle to her people.ʳ

¹⁸On the seventh day, before the sun set, the men of the city said to him,

"What is sweeter than honey,
　　what is stronger than a lion?"

He replied to them,

"If you had not plowed with my heifer,
　　you would not have solved my riddle."

¹⁹ˢThe spirit of the LORD rushed upon him, and he went down to Ashkelon, where he killed thirty of their men and stripped them; he gave their garments to those who had answered the riddle. Then he went off to his own family in anger, ²⁰and Samson's wife was married to the companion who had been his best man.ᵗ

---

*[13:22] **We will certainly die**: seeing God face to face was believed to be fatal, as explained in note on 6:22, where Gideon's reaction is similar to that of Manoah here.

†[14:4] **An opportunity against the Philistines**: although the story of Samson's first love might be taken as an illustration of the danger of foreign marriages, the narrator explains it differently. Samson's infatuation with the Timnite woman was the Lord's way of creating an opportunity to punish the Philistines for their oppression of Israel.

‡[14:16] The story of Samson and the Timnite woman is very similar in its narrative structure to the better-known story of Samson and Delilah (16:1–22). In both, Samson's success in his conflict with the Philistines depends on keeping a secret. In both stories Samson is betrayed by the Philistine woman he loves when she importunes him to reveal the secret to her and then, when he gives in, divulges it to her people.

h. [13:21–23] Jgs 6:22–23. i. [13:25] Jgs 3:10; 6:34; 11:29; 14:6, 19; 15:14; 1 Sm 11:6. j. [14:3] Gn 24:3–4; 26:34–35; 28:1–2, 6–9. k. [14:4] 1 Sm 10:14–16; Lk 2:41–51. l. [14:4] 2 Kgs 5:7. m. [14:6] Jgs 3:10; 6:34; 11:29; 13:25; 14:19; 15:14; 1 Sm 11:6. n. [14:6] 1 Sm 17:34–36; 2 Sm 23:20.

o. [14:15] Jgs 16:5. p. [14:15] Jgs 15:6. q. [14:16] Jgs 16:15. r. [14:17] Jgs 16:16–18. s. [14:19] Jgs 3:10; 6:34; 11:29; 13:25; 14:6; 15:14; 1 Sm 11:6. t. [14:20] Jgs 15:2, 6.

## CHAPTER 15

**Samson Defeats the Philistines.** ¹After some time, in the season of the wheat harvest, Samson visited his wife, bringing a young goat. But when he said, "Let me go into my wife's room," her father would not let him go in. ²He said, "I thought you hated her, so I gave her to your best man. Her younger sister is better; you may have her instead." ³Samson said to him, "This time I am guiltless if I harm the Philistines." ⁴So Samson went and caught three hundred jackals, and turning them tail to tail, he took some torches and tied one between each pair of tails. ⁵He then kindled the torches and set the jackals loose in the standing grain of the Philistines, thus burning both the shocks and standing grain, the vineyards and olive groves.

⁶"When the Philistines asked, "Who has done this?" they were told, "Samson, the son-in-law of the Timnite, because his wife was taken and given to his best man." So the Philistines went up and destroyed her and her family by fire.ᵛ ⁷Samson said to them, "If this is how you act, I will not stop until I have taken revenge on you." ⁸And he struck them hip and thigh—a great slaughter. Then he went down and stayed in a cleft of the crag of Etam.

⁹The Philistines went up and encamped in Judah, deploying themselves against Lehi.ʷ ¹⁰When the men of Judah asked, "Why have you come up against us?" they answered, "To take Samson prisoner; to do to him as he has done to us." ¹¹Three thousand men of Judah went down to the cleft of the crag of Etam and said to Samson, "Do you not know that the Philistines are our rulers? Why, then, have you done this to us?" He answered them, "As they have done to me, so have I done to them." ¹²They said to him, "We have come down to bind you and deliver you to the Philistines." Samson said to them, "Swear to me that you will not attack me yourselves." ¹³"No," they replied, "we will only bind you and hand you over to them. We will certainly not kill you." So they bound him with two new ropes and brought him up from the crag. ¹⁴When he reached Lehi, and the Philistines came shouting to meet him,ˣ the spirit of the Lᴏʀᴅ rushed upon him: the ropes around his arms became like flax that is consumed by fire, and his bonds melted away from his hands. ¹⁵Coming upon the fresh jawbone of an ass, he reached out, grasped it, and with it killed a thousand men.ʸ ¹⁶Then Samson said,

"With the jawbone of an ass
    I have piled them in a heap;
With the jawbone of an ass
    I have slain a thousand men."

¹⁷As he finished speaking he threw the jawbone from him; and so that place was named Ramath-lehi.* ¹⁸Being very thirsty, he cried to the Lᴏʀᴅ and said, "You have put this great victory into the hand of your servant. Must I now die of thirst and fall into the hands of the uncircumcised?" ¹⁹Then God split the cavity in Lehi, and water issued from it, and Samson drank till his spirit returned and he revived. Hence it is called En-hakkore† in Lehi to this day.

²⁰Samson judged Israel for twenty years in the days of the Philistines.ᶻ

## CHAPTER 16

¹Once Samson went to Gaza, where he saw a prostitute and visited her. ²The people of Gaza were told, "Samson has come here," and they surrounded him with an ambush at the city gate all night long. And all the night they waited, saying, "At morning light we will kill him." ³Samson lay there until midnight. Then he rose at midnight, seized the doors of the city gate and the two gateposts, and tore them loose, bar and all. He hoisted them on his shoulders and carried them to the top of the ridge opposite Hebron.

**Samson and Delilah.** ⁴After that he fell in love with a woman in the Wadi Sorek whose name was Delilah. ⁵The lords of the Philistines came up to her and said, "Trick him and find out where he gets his great strength, and how we may overcome and bind him so as to make him helpless. Then for our part, we will each give you eleven hundred pieces of silver."

⁶So Delilah said to Samson, "Tell me where you get your great strength and how you may be bound so as to be made helpless." ⁷"If they bind me with seven fresh bowstrings that have not dried," Samson answered her, "I shall grow weaker and be like anyone else." ⁸So the lords of the Philistines brought her seven fresh bowstrings that had not dried, and she bound him with them. ⁹She had men lying in wait in the room, and she said to him, "The Philistines are upon you, Samson!" But he snapped the bowstrings as a thread of tow is snapped by a whiff of flame; and his strength remained unexplained.

¹⁰Delilah said to Samson, "You have mocked me and told me lies. Now tell me how you may be bound." ¹¹"If they bind me tight with new ropes, with which no work has been done," he answered her, "I shall grow weaker and be like anyone else." ¹²So Delilah took new ropes and bound him with them. Then she said to him, "The Philistines are upon you, Samson!" For

---

*[15:17] **Ramath-lehi:** "Jawbone Height"; in Hebrew *lehi* means "jawbone."

†[15:19] **En-hakkore:** understood as "the spring of the crier," an allusion to Samson's cry in v. 18. The story is used to explain the name of a well-known spring in Lehi. The Hebrew also means "Partridge Spring."

u. [15:6] Jgs 14:20.   v. [15:6] Jgs 14:15.   w. [15:9] 2 Sm 23:11–12.   x. [15:14] Jgs 3:10; 6:34; 11:29; 13:25; 14:6, 19; 1 Sm 11:6.   y. [15:15] Jgs 3:31; 2 Sm 23:12.

z. [15:20] Jgs 10:2, 5; 12:7, 10, 12, 15; 16:31.   a. [16:5] Jgs 14:15.

there were men lying in wait in the room. But he snapped the ropes off his arms like thread.

[13]Delilah said to Samson again, "Up to now you have mocked me and told me lies. Tell me how you may be bound." He said to her, "If you weave the seven locks of my hair into the web and fasten them with the pin, I shall grow weaker and be like anyone else." [14]So when he went to bed, Delilah took the seven locks of his hair and wove them into the web, and fastened them with the pin. Then she said, "The Philistines are upon you, Samson!" Awakening from his sleep, he pulled out both the loom and the web.

[15b]Then she said to him, "How can you say 'I love you' when your heart is not mine? Three times already you have mocked me, and not told me where you get your great strength!" [16c]She pressed him continually and pestered him till he was deathly weary of it. [17]So he told her all that was in his heart and said, "No razor has touched my head, for I have been a nazirite for God from my mother's womb.[d] If I am shaved, my strength will leave me, and I shall grow weaker and be like anyone else." [18]When Delilah realized that he had told her all that was in his heart, she summoned the lords of the Philistines, saying, "Come up this time, for he has told me all that is in his heart." So the lords of the Philistines came to her and brought the money with them.[e] [19]She put him to sleep on her lap, and called for a man who shaved off the seven locks of his hair. He immediately became helpless, for his strength had left him.[*] [20]When she said "The Philistines are upon you, Samson!" he woke from his sleep and thought, "I will go out as I have done time and again and shake myself free." He did not realize that the LORD had left him. [21]But the Philistines seized him and gouged out his eyes. Then they brought him down to Gaza and bound him with bronze fetters, and he was put to grinding grain in the prison. [22]But the hair of his head began to grow as soon as it was shaved.

**The Death of Samson.** [23f]The lords of the Philistines assembled to offer a great sacrifice to their god Dagon[†] and to celebrate. They said, "Our god has delivered Samson our enemy into our power." [24]When the people saw him, they praised their god. For they said,

> "Our god has delivered into our power
> our enemy, the ravager of our land,
> the one who has multiplied our slain."

[25]When their spirits were high, they said, "Call Samson that he may amuse us." So they called Samson from the prison, and he provided amusement for them. They made him stand between the columns, [26]and Samson said to the attendant who was holding his hand, "Put me where I may touch the columns that support the temple, so that I may lean against them." [27]The temple was full of men and women: all the lords of the Philistines were there, and from the roof about three thousand men and women looked on as Samson provided amusement. [28]Samson cried out to the LORD and said, "Lord GOD, remember me! Strengthen me only this once that I may avenge myself on the Philistines at one blow for my two eyes." [29]Samson grasped the two middle columns on which the temple rested and braced himself against them, one at his right, the other at his left. [30]Then saying, "Let me die with the Philistines!" Samson pushed hard, and the temple fell upon the lords and all the people who were in it. Those he killed by his dying were more than those he had killed during his lifetime.

[31]His kinsmen and all his father's house went down and bore him up for burial in the grave of Manoah his father between Zorah and Eshtaol. He had judged Israel for twenty years.[g]

## III. FURTHER STORIES OF THE TRIBES OF DAN AND BENJAMIN

### CHAPTER 17

**Micah and the Levite.** [1]There was a man from the mountain region of Ephraim whose name was Micah. [2]He said to his mother, "The eleven hundred pieces of silver that were taken from you, about which you pronounced a curse and even said it in my hearing—I have that silver. I took it. So now I will restore it to you." Then his mother said, "May my son be blessed by the LORD!" [3]When he restored the eleven hundred pieces of silver to his mother, she said, "I consecrate the silver to the LORD from my own hand on behalf of my son to make an idol overlaid with silver."[§h] [4]So when he restored the silver to his mother, she took two hundred pieces and gave them to the silversmith, who made of them an idol overlaid with silver. So it remained in the house of Micah. [5]The man Micah had a shrine, and he made an ephod and teraphim,[¶i] and

---

‡[17:2] The narrator picks up the story after a number of events, including a theft and a mother's curse, have already taken place.

§[17:3] **An idol overlaid with silver:** two nouns in Hebrew, one indicating a wooden image and the other denoting an image cast from metal. The probable interpretation is that the woman intends for her silver to be recast as a covering for an image of a god, possibly the Lord. This was forbidden in Mosaic law (cf. Ex 20:4 and Dt 5:8).

¶[17:5] **An ephod and teraphim:** cultic paraphernalia. An ephod was a priestly garment, especially that worn by the high priest (cf. Ex 28 and 39), which contained a pocket for objects used for divination. Teraphim were household idols

---

*[16:19] See note on 13:5.

†[16:23] **Dagon:** an ancient Syrian grain deity (cf. Hebrew *dagan*, "grain") whom the Philistines adopted as their national god after their arrival on the coast of Canaan.

b. [16:15] Jgs 14:16.   c. [16:16–18] Jgs 14:17.   d. [16:17] Jgs 13:5.   e. [16:18] Jgs 16:5.   f. [16:23] 1 Sm 5:2–5.

g. [16:31] Jgs 10:2, 5; 12:7, 10, 12, 15; 15:20.   h. [17:3] Ex 20:4; Lv 19:4; Dt 5:8.   i. [17:5] Jgs 18:14, 18.

installed one of his sons, who became his priest.[j] [6]In those days there was no king in Israel; everyone did what was right in their own eyes.[k]

[7]There was a young man from Bethlehem of Judah, from the clan of Judah; he was a Levite residing there.[l] [8]The man set out from the city, Bethlehem of Judah, to take up residence wherever he could find a place. On his journey he came into the mountain region of Ephraim as far as the house of Micah. [9]"Where do you come from?" Micah asked him. He answered him, "I am a Levite, from Bethlehem in Judah, and I am on my way to take up residence wherever I can find a place." [10]"Stay with me," Micah said to him. "Be father and priest to me,"[m] and I will give you ten silver pieces a year, a set of garments, and your living." He pressed the Levite, [11]and he agreed to stay with the man. The young man became like one of his own sons. [12]Micah installed the Levite, and the young man became his priest, remaining in the house of Micah. [13]Then Micah said, "Now I know that the LORD will prosper me, since I have the Levite as my priest."

## CHAPTER 18

**Migration of the Danites.** [1]In those days there was no king in Israel.[n] In those days the tribe of the Danites were in search of a heritage to dwell in, for up to that time no heritage had been allotted[‡] to them among the tribes of Israel.[o]

[2]So the Danites sent from their clans five powerful men of Zorah and Eshtaol, to reconnoiter the land and scout it. "Go, scout the land," they were told. They went into the mountain region of Ephraim, and they spent the night there. [3]While they were near the house of Micah,[p] they recognized the voice[§] of the young Levite,[q]

so they turned aside. They asked him, "Who brought you here? What are you doing here? What is your interest here?" [4]"This is what Micah has done for me," he replied to them. "He has hired me and I have become his priest."[r] [5]They said to him, "Consult God, that we may know whether the journey we are making will lead to success."[s] [6]The priest said to them, "Go in peace! The journey you are making is under the eye of the LORD."

[7]So the five men went on and came to Laish. They saw the people there living securely after the manner of the Sidonians, quiet and trusting, with no lack of any natural resource. They were distant from the Sidonians and had no dealings with the Arameans.[¶] [8]When the five returned to their kin in Zorah and Eshtaol, they were asked, "What do you have to report?" [9]They replied, "Come, let us attack them, for we have seen the land and it is very good. Are you going to hesitate? Do not be slow to go in and take possession of the land! [10]When you go you will come to a trusting people. The land stretches out in both directions, and God has indeed given it into your power—a place where no natural resource is lacking."[t]

[11]So six hundred of the clan of the Danites, men armed with weapons of war, set out from Zorah and Eshtaol. [12]They marched up into Judah and encamped near Kiriath-jearim; for this reason the place is called Mahaneh-dan[**] to this day (it lies west of Kiriath-jearim).[u]

[13]From there they passed on into the mountain region of Ephraim and came to the house of Micah. [14]Then the five men who had gone to reconnoiter the land spoke up and said to their kindred, "Do you know that in these houses there are an ephod, teraphim, and an idol overlaid with silver?[v] Now decide what you must do!" [15]So turning in that direction, they went to the house of the young Levite at the home of Micah and greeted him. [16]The six hundred Danites stationed themselves at the entrance of the gate armed with weapons of war. [17]The five men who had gone to reconnoiter the land went up [18]and entered the house of Micah with the priest standing there. They took the idol, the ephod, the teraphim and the metal image. When the priest said to them, "What are you doing?" [19]they said to him, "Be still! Put your hand over your mouth! Come with us and be our father and priest.[w] Is it better for you to be priest for the family of one man or to be priest for a tribe and a clan in Israel?" [20]The priest, agreeing,

---

(Gn 31:19, 34–35; 1 Sm 19:13), which may also have had a divinatory function.

*[17:6] This refrain, which will be repeated fully or in part three more times (18:1; 19:1; 21:25), calls attention to the disorder and lawlessness that prevailed before the establishment of kingship in Israel. In this case the problem is cultic impropriety, seen not only in the making of an idol but in the establishment of a local temple, complete with an ephod and teraphim.

†[17:12–13] Previously one of Micah's sons served as priest (v. 5). But Micah's family were probably Ephraimites (cf. v. 1) rather than Levites, and the story reflects a sense that only Levites were to be consecrated as priests; cf. Nm 18:7, where descent from Aaron is further specified as a requirement to be a priest. Thus Micah believes it will be to his advantage to retain the itinerant Levite.

‡[18:1] **No heritage . . . allotted:** according to Jos 19:40–48, the Danites received an allotment in the central part of the country (cf. note on 13:2 above). The point here may be that since they were unable to take full possession of that original allotment, as indicated by the notice in Jgs 1:34, they are now seeking territory elsewhere.

§[18:3] **Recognized the voice:** this might indicate that the Danite scouts were personally acquainted with the young Levite, but it is more likely to mean that, being originally from Judah, his dialect or accent was noticeably different from others in Micah's household.

¶[18:7] **The Sidonians . . . the Arameans:** the people of Laish were not in regular contact with their neighbors, including the Sidonians or Phoenicians in the coastal district to the west and the Arameans in the regions to the north and east. This isolation is mentioned to underscore the vulnerability of the peaceful and unfortified city.

**[18:12] **Mahaneh-dan:** Hebrew, "camp of Dan."

---

j. [17:5] 1 Sm 7:1.   k. [17:6] Jgs 18:1; 19:1; 21:25.   l. [17:7] Jgs 19:1.   m. [17:10] Jgs 18:19.   n. [18:1] Jgs 17:6; 19:1; 21:25.   o. [18:1] Jgs 1:34; Jos 19:40–48.   p. [18:3] Jgs 17:1.   q. [18:3] Jgs 17:7–12.

r. [18:4] Jgs 17:10.   s. [18:5] Jgs 1:1; 1 Sm 14:18–19, 36–44; 23:2, 4, 9–12; 30:7–8.   t. [18:10] 1 Chr 5:40.   u. [18:12] Jgs 13:25.   v. [18:14] Jgs 17:4–5.   w. [18:19] Jgs 17:10.

took the ephod, the teraphim, and the idol, and went along with the troops. [21]As they turned to depart, they placed their little ones, their livestock, and their goods at the head of the column.

[22x]When the Danites had gone some distance from the house of Micah, Micah and the men in the houses nearby mustered and overtook them. [23]They called to the Danites, who turned and said to Micah, "What do you want that you have called this muster?" [24]"You have taken my god, which I made for myself, and you have gone off with my priest as well," he answered. "What is left for me? How, then, can you ask me, 'What do you want?'" [25]The Danites said to him, "Do not let your voice be heard near us, or aggravated men will attack you, and you will have forfeited your life and the lives of your family!" [26]Then the Danites went on their way, and Micah, seeing that they were too strong for him, turned back and went home.

[27y]Having taken what Micah had made and his priest, they marched against Laish, a quiet and trusting people; they put them to the sword and destroyed the city by fire. [28]No one came to their aid, since the city was far from Sidon and they had no dealings with the Arameans; the city was in the valley that belongs to Beth-rehob. The Danites then rebuilt the city and occupied it. [29]They named it Dan after their ancestor Dan, who was born to Israel.[z] But Laish was the name of the city formerly. [30]*The Danites set up the idol for themselves, and Jonathan, son of Gershom, son of Moses,[a] and his descendants were priests for the tribe of the Danites until the time the land went into captivity. [31]They maintained the idol Micah had made as long as the house of God was in Shiloh.[†]

## CHAPTER 19

**The Levite from Ephraim.** [1]In those days, when there was no king in Israel,[‡b] there was a Levite

---

*[18:30] Micah's shrine is now reinstalled at Laish-Dan. In the time of the kings of Israel and Judah, Dan was the site of one of the two national sanctuaries of the Northern Kingdom, both of which are strongly condemned by the editors of the Books of Kings, who regarded Jerusalem as the only acceptable place for a temple (1 Kgs 12:26–30). This verse draws a direct connection between Micah's temple and the later royal sanctuary at Dan. Seen in this light the account of the establishment of Micah's shrine, with its idol cast from stolen silver, becomes a highly polemical foundation story for the temple at Dan. **Jonathan, son of Gershom, son of Moses:** Micah's Levite is now identified as the son or descendant of Gershom, Moses' eldest son (Ex 2:22; 18:3). In the traditional Hebrew text an additional letter has been suspended over the name "Moses" to alter it to "Manasseh," thus protecting Moses from association with idol worship. **Captivity:** although Samaria fell in 722/721 B.C., much of the northern part of the country, probably including Dan, had been subjugated about a decade earlier by the Assyrian emperor Tilgath-pileser III.

†[18:31] **Shiloh:** a major sanctuary which has a role in the final episode of Judges (21:12, 21).

‡[19:1] **No king in Israel:** see note on 17:6. The violent story that follows is offered as another example of the disorder that prevailed before the inauguration of the monarchy.

---

x. [18:22–26] Gn 31:22–32:1.   y. [18:27–29] Jos 19:47.   z. [18:29] Gn 30:5–6.   a. [18:30] Ex 2:22; 18:3.   b. [19:1] Jgs 17:6; 18:1; 21:25.

residing in remote parts of the mountain region of Ephraim[c] who had taken for himself a concubine from Bethlehem of Judah. [2]But his concubine spurned him and left him for her father's house in Bethlehem of Judah, where she stayed for some four months. [3]Her husband then set out with his servant and a pair of donkeys, and went after her to soothe her and bring her back. He arrived at her father's house, and when the young woman's father saw him, he came out joyfully to meet him. [4]His father-in-law, the young woman's father, urged him to stay, and so he spent three days eating and drinking and passing the night there. [5]On the fourth day they rose early in the morning and he prepared to go. But the young woman's father said to his son-in-law, "Fortify yourself with a little food; you can go later on." [6]So they stayed and the two men ate and drank together. Then the young woman's father said to the husband, "Why not decide to spend the night here and enjoy yourself?" [7]The man made a move to go, but when his father-in-law pressed him he went back and spent the night there.

[8]On the fifth morning he rose early to depart, but the young woman's father said, "Fortify yourself!" He coaxed him, and he tarried until the afternoon, and the two of them ate. [9]Then when the husband was ready to go with his concubine and servant, the young woman's father said to him, "See, the day is wearing on toward evening. Stay for the night. See, the day is coming to an end. Spend the night here and enjoy yourself. Early tomorrow you can start your journey home." [10]The man, however, refused to stay another night; he and his concubine set out with a pair of saddled donkeys, and traveled until they came opposite Jebus, which is Jerusalem. [11]Since they were near Jebus with the day far gone, the servant said to his master, "Come, let us turn off to this city of the Jebusites and spend the night in it." [12]But his master said to him, "We will not turn off to a foreigner's city,[d] where there are no Israelites. We will go on to Gibeah. [13]Come," he said to his servant, "let us make for some other place and spend the night in either Gibeah or Ramah."[e] [14]So they continued on their way until the sun set on them when they were opposite Gibeah of Benjamin.

[15§]There they turned off to enter Gibeah for the night.[f] The man went in and sat down in the town square, but no one took them inside to spend the night. [16]In the evening, however, an old man came from his work in the field; he was from the mountain region of Ephraim,

---

§[19:15–21] The narrative casts a very unfavorable light on Gibeah of Benjamin, the town from which Israel's first king would come (cf. 1 Sm 9:1–2). No Benjaminite offers hospitality to the Levite and his travel party, who are obliged to wait at night in the town square until an Ephraimite residing in Gibeah welcomes them into his home.

---

c. [19:1] Jgs 17:7.   d. [19:12] Jgs 1:21; 2 Sm 5:6.   e. [19:13] Jos 18:25.   f. [19:15] Jgs 20:4.

though he was living in Gibeah where the local people were Benjaminites. [17g]When he noticed the traveler in the town square, the old man asked, "Where are you going, and where have you come from?" [18]He said to him, "We are traveling from Bethlehem of Judah far up into the mountain region of Ephraim, where I am from. I have been to Bethlehem of Judah, and now I am going home; but no one has taken me into his house. [19]We have straw and fodder for our donkeys, and bread and wine for myself and for your maidservant and the young man who is with your servant; there is nothing else we need." [20]"Rest assured," the old man said to him, "I will provide for all your needs, but do not spend the night in the public square." [21]So he led them to his house and mixed fodder for the donkeys. Then they washed their feet, and ate and drank.[h]

**The Outrage at Gibeah.** [22*i]While they were enjoying themselves, the men of the city, a bunch of scoundrels, surrounded the house and beat on the door. They said to the old man who was the owner of the house, "Bring out the man who has come into your house, so that we may get intimate with him." [23]The man who was the owner of the house went out to them and said, "No, my brothers; do not be so wicked. This man has come into my house; do not commit this terrible crime. [24]Instead, let me bring out my virgin daughter and this man's concubine. Humiliate them, or do whatever you want; but against him do not commit such a terrible crime." [25]But the men would not listen to him. So the man seized his concubine and thrust her outside to them. They raped her and abused her all night until morning, and let her go as the sun was coming up. [26]At the approach of morning the woman came and collapsed at the entrance of the house in which her husband was, and lay there until morning. [27]When her husband rose in the morning and opened the door of the house to start out again on his journey, there was the woman, his concubine, collapsed at the entrance of the house with her hands on the threshold. [28]"Come, let us go," he said to her, but there was no answer. So the man placed her on a donkey and started out again for home.

[29†]On reaching home, he got a knife and took hold of the body of his concubine. He cut her up limb by limb into twelve pieces and sent them throughout the territory of Israel.[j] [30]He instructed the men whom he sent, "Thus you shall say to all the men of Israel: 'Has such a thing ever happened from the day the Israelites

came up from the land of Egypt to this day?[‡k] Take note of it; form a plan and give orders.'"

## CHAPTER 20

**Assembly of Israelites.** [1]So all the Israelites came out as one, from Dan to Beer-sheba[§l] including the land of Gilead, and the assembly gathered to the LORD at Mizpah. [2]The leaders of all the people, all the staff-bearers of Israel,[¶] presented themselves in the assembly of the people of God—four hundred thousand foot soldiers who carried swords. [3]Meanwhile, the Benjaminites heard that the Israelites had gone up to Mizpah. The Israelites asked, "How did this evil thing happen?" [4]and the Levite, the husband of the murdered woman, testified: "It was at Gibeah of Benjamin, which my concubine and I had entered for the night.[m] [5]The lords of Gibeah rose up against me and surrounded me in the house at night. I was the one they intended to kill, but they abused my concubine and she died. [6]So I took my concubine and cut her up and sent her through every part of the territory of Israel, because of the terrible thing they had done in Israel. [7]So now, all you Israelites, give your judgment and counsel in this matter."[p] [8]All the people rose as one to say, "None of us will leave for our tents or return to our homes. [9]Now as for Gibeah, this is what we will do: We will go up against it by lot, [10]taking from all the tribes of Israel ten men for every hundred, a hundred for every thousand, a thousand for every ten thousand, and procuring supplies for the soldiers who will go to exact from Gibeah of Benjamin the full measure of the terrible thing it committed in Israel."

[11]So all the men of Israel gathered against the city, united as one. [12]The tribes of Israel sent men throughout the tribe of Benjamin to say, "What is this evil that has occurred among you? [13]Now give up the men, the scoundrels who are in Gibeah, that we may put them to death and thus purge the evil from Israel." But the Benjaminites refused to listen to their kindred, the Israelites. [14]Instead, the Benjaminites assembled from their cities at Gibeah, to march out to battle with the Israelites. [15]On that day the Benjaminites mustered from their cities twenty-six thousand swordsmen, in addition to the inhabitants of Gibeah, who mustered seven hundred

---

*[19:22–25] This part of the grim story closely parallels that of the assault on Lot's angelic visitors in Gn 19:4–8.

†[19:29] The Levite's gruesome way of summoning the tribes is a drastic version of that used by Saul in 1 Sm 11:7, where he dismembers a yoke of oxen.

‡[19:30] **Has such a thing ever happened . . . ?**: the outrage became a byword in Israel, so that in the eighth century the prophet Hosea could invoke "the days of Gibeah" (Hos 9:9; cf. 10:9) to signify corruption and wrongdoing.

§[20:1] **From Dan to Beer-sheba**: the entire country, from north to south. **The land of Gilead**: Israelite territory east of the Jordan.

¶[20:2] **The staff-bearers of Israel**: the tribal leaders.

---

g. [19:17–21] Gn 19:1–3.  h. [19:21] Gn 18:4; 24:32; 43:24.  i. [19:22–25] Gn 19:4–9.  j. [19:29] 1 Sm 11:7.

k. [19:30] Hos 9:9; 10:9.  l. [20:1] 1 Sm 3:20; 2 Sm 3:10; 17:11; 24:2, 15; 1 Kgs 5:5.  m. [20:4] Jgs 19:15.  n. [20:5] Jgs 19:22–28.  o. [20:6] Jgs 19:29.  p. [20:7] Jgs 19:30.

picked men [16*]who were left-handed, every one of them able to sling a stone at a hair without missing. [17]The men of Israel, without Benjamin, mustered four hundred thousand swordsmen, all of them warriors. [18]They went up to Bethel and consulted God. When the Israelites asked, "Who shall go up first for us to do battle with the Benjaminites?" the LORD said: Judah first.[†q] [19‡]The Israelites rose in the morning and encamped against Gibeah.

**War with Benjamin.** [20]The men of Israel marched out to do battle with Benjamin and drew up in battle array against them at Gibeah. [21]The Benjaminites marched out of Gibeah that day and felled twenty-two thousand men of Israel. [22§]But the army of the men of Israel took courage and again drew up for battle in the place where they had drawn up on the previous day. [23]Then the Israelites went up and wept before the LORD until evening. "Shall I again engage my brother Benjamin in battle?" they asked the LORD; and the LORD answered: Attack! [24]When the Israelites drew near to the Benjaminites on the second day, [25]Benjamin marched out of Gibeah against them again and felled eighteen thousand Israelites, all of them swordsmen. [26]So the entire Israelite army went up and entered Bethel, where they sat weeping before the LORD. They fasted that day until evening and presented burnt offerings and communion offerings before the LORD. [27]The Israelites consulted the LORD (for the ark of the covenant of the LORD was there in those days, [28]and Phinehas, son of Eleazar, son of Aaron,[¶] was standing in his presence in those days), and asked, "Shall I again go out to battle with my brother Benjamin, or shall I stop?" The LORD said: Attack! For tomorrow I will deliver him into your power. [29**r]So Israel set men in ambush around Gibeah.

[30]When the Israelites went up against the Benjaminites on the third day, they drew up against Gibeah as on other occasions. [31]When the Benjaminites marched out to meet the army, they began, as on other occasions, to strike down some of the troops along the highways, one of which goes up to Bethel and one to Gibeah in the open country; about thirty Israelites were slain. [32]The Benjaminites thought, "They are routed before us as previously." The Israelites, however, were thinking, "We will flee and draw them out from the city onto the highways." [33]And then all the men of Israel rose from their places, forming up at Baal-tamar, and the Israelites in ambush rushed from their place west of Gibeah [34]and advanced against Gibeah with ten thousand picked men from all Israel. The fighting was severe, but no one knew that a disaster was closing in. [35]The LORD defeated Benjamin before Israel; and on that day the Israelites killed twenty-five thousand one hundred men of Benjamin, all of them swordsmen.

[36]Then the Benjaminites saw that they were defeated. The men of Israel gave ground to Benjamin, trusting in the ambush they had set at Gibeah. [37]Then the men in ambush, having made a sudden dash against Gibeah, marched in and put the whole city to the sword. [38]The arrangement the men of Israel had with the men in ambush was that they would send up a smoke signal from the city, [39]and the men of Israel would then wheel about in the battle. Benjamin, having begun by killing off some thirty of the men of Israel, thought, "Surely they are completely routed before us, as in the earlier fighting." [40]But when the signal, the column of smoke, began to rise up from the city, Benjamin looked back and there was the whole city going up in smoke toward heaven. [41]Then when the men of Israel wheeled about, the men of Benjamin were thrown into confusion, for they realized that disaster was closing in on them. [42]They retreated before the men of Israel in the direction of the wilderness, but the fighting kept pace with them, and those who had been in the city were spreading destruction in between. [43]They surrounded the men of Benjamin, pursued them from Nohah and drove them along to a point east of Gibeah. [44]Eighteen thousand from Benjamin fell, all of them warriors. [45]They turned and fled into the wilderness to the crag of Rimmon. The Israelites picked off five thousand men on the highways and kept pace with them as far as Gidom, where they struck down another two thousand of them. [46]The total of those from Benjamin who fell that day was twenty-five thousand swordsmen, all of them warriors. [47]Six hundred men turned and fled into the wilderness to the crag of Rimmon, where they remained for four months.[s]

---

*[20:16] The strange notice that the Gibeahite warriors were left-handed was probably added here under the influence of the Ehud story; cf. 3:15 and the note there.

†[20:18] **Judah first**: as in 1:2, where the enemy is the Canaanites. This time the attack is against fellow Israelites, an indication of how far things have deteriorated in these days when as yet "there was no king in Israel"; see note on 17:6.

‡[20:19–25] The Israelites are defeated twice by the Benjaminites.

§[20:22–23] These two verses seem to be transposed. The day of supplication described in v. 23 must have preceded the assembly for battle reported in v. 22.

¶[20:28] **Phinehas, son of Eleazar, son of Aaron**: the main line of the priesthood was traced through a grandson of Aaron by this name; see Ex 6:25 and Nm 25:10–13. Whether the priest identified here is the same man or his lineal descendant, the mention of his name adds authority to the sanctuary at Bethel. The reference to the ark of the covenant in the preceding verse has the same effect.

**[20:29–46] The Israelites are successful in their third attempt to defeat Benjamin. Leaving an ambush behind, they decoy the enemy troops out of the city by pretending to be routed as on the two previous occasions. The stratagem is strongly reminiscent of that employed in the conquest of Ai (Jos 8). Two accounts of the present battle against Gibeah are preserved, one in 20:29–36a and another in 20:36b–46.

q. [20:18] Jgs 1:1–2.   r. [20:29–46] Jos 8:3–24.

s. [20:47] Jgs 21:13.

⁴⁸Then the men of Israel turned back against the Benjaminites, putting them to the sword—the inhabitants of the cities, the livestock, and all they came upon.ᵗ Moreover they destroyed by fire all the cities they came upon.

## CHAPTER 21

**Ensuring a Future for Benjamin.** ¹ˑThe men of Israel took an oath at Mizpah: "None of us will give his daughter in marriage to anyone from Benjamin." ²So the people went to Bethel and remained there before God until evening, raising their voices in bitter weeping.ᵘ ³They said, "Lᴏʀᴅ, God of Israel, why has this happened in Israel that today one tribe of Israel should be lacking?" ⁴Early the next day the people built an altar there and offered burnt offerings and communion offerings. ⁵Then the Israelites asked, "Are there any among all the tribes of Israel who did not come up to the Lᴏʀᴅ for the assembly?" For there was a solemn oath that anyone who did not go up to the Lᴏʀᴅ at Mizpah should be put to death.ᵛ

⁶The Israelites were disconsolate over their brother Benjamin and said, "Today one tribe has been cut off from Israel. ⁷What can we do about wives for the survivors, since we have sworn by the Lᴏʀᴅ not to give them any of our daughters in marriage?" ⁸And when they asked, "Is there one among the tribes of Israel who did not come up to the Lᴏʀᴅ in Mizpah?" they found that none of the men of Jabesh-gilead had come to the encampment for the assembly. ⁹A roll call of the people was taken, and none of the inhabitants of Jabesh-gileadʷ was present. ¹⁰So the assembly sent twelve thousand warriors there with orders, "Go put the inhabitants of Jabesh-gilead to the sword. ¹¹This is what you are to do: Every male and every woman who has had relations with a male you shall put under the ban."†ˣ ¹²Finding among the inhabitants of Jabesh-gilead four hundred young virgin women, who had not had relations with a man, they brought them to the camp at Shiloh, in the land of Canaan.ʸ ¹³Then the whole assembly

sent word to the Benjaminites at the crag of Rimmon,ᶻ offering them peace. ¹⁴ˑSo Benjamin returned at that time, and they were given as wives the women of Jabesh-gilead who had been spared; but these proved to be not enough for them.

¹⁵The people had regrets about Benjamin because the Lᴏʀᴅ had made a breach among the tribes of Israel.ᵃ ¹⁶The elders of the assembly said, "What shall we do for wives for the survivors? For the women of Benjamin have been annihilated."ᵇ ¹⁷They said, "There must be heirs for the survivors of Benjamin, so that a tribe will not be wiped out from Israel. ¹⁸Yet we cannot give them any of our daughters in marriage." For the Israelites had taken an oath, "Cursed be he who gives a wife to Benjamin!" ¹⁹Then they thought of the yearly feast of the Lᴏʀᴅ at Shiloh,ᶜ north of Bethel, east of the highway that goes up from Bethel to Shechem, and south of Lebonah. ²⁰And they instructed the Benjaminites, "Go and set an ambush in the vineyards. ²¹When you see the women of Shiloh come out to join in the dances, come out of the vineyards and catch a wife for each of you from the women of Shiloh; then go on to the land of Benjamin. ²²When their fathers or their brothers come to complain to us, we shall say to them, 'Release them to us as a kindness, since we did not take a woman for every man in battle. Nor did you yourselves give your daughters to them, thus incurring guilt.'"§

²³The Benjaminites did this; they carried off wives for each of them from the dancers they had seized, and they went back each to his own heritage, where they rebuilt the cities and settled them. ²⁴At that time the Israelites dispersed from there for their own tribes and clans; they set out from there each to his own heritage.

²⁵In those days there was no king in Israel; everyone did what was right in their own sight.ᵈ

---

*[21:1–7] The victorious Israelites now become concerned about the survival of the tribe they have defeated. Despite the large number of Benjaminites killed in the final battle (20:46) and the general carnage that followed (20:48), there does not seem to be a shortage of men. The problem is rather a shortage of wives for the surviving men, the result of a previously unmentioned vow the Israelites took not to permit their daughters to marry Benjaminites.

†[21:11] **Under the ban:** see note on 1:17. In this case the sanction is imposed not because of the rules for the conquest of the promised land (cf. Dt 20:10–18) but because of the failure of the men of Jabesh-gilead to honor their oath and report for the assembly.

‡[21:14] Very strong political ties existed between the people of Jabesh-gilead and the Benjaminites, especially those involving Saul, the Benjaminite king of Israel. See 1 Sm 11, where Saul rescues Jabesh from an Ammonite siege, and 1 Sm 31:11–13, where the people of Jabesh exert themselves to ensure that the bodies of Saul and his sons should receive honorable burial.

§[21:22] **Release them . . . guilt:** this verse is difficult. Evidently the elders intend to make two arguments in support of their request that the men of Shiloh release their claims on the abducted women. The first argument seems to be that an insufficient number of women were taken "in battle"—i.e., the raid on Jabesh-gilead—to provide "a woman for every man"—i.e., a wife for every Benjaminite. The second argument is that since the women have been kidnapped, the men of Shiloh will not be guilty of having violated the oath mentioned above in 21:1, 7, and 18.

¶[21:25] See note on 17:6. This final editorial comment calls attention to the chaos that followed the Benjaminite civil war and the near anarchy that characterized the various efforts to meet the need for wives for the Benjaminites.

---

t. [20:48] Dt 13:15–17.  u. [21:2] Jgs 20:26.  v. [21:5] Jgs 20:8–10.  w. [21:9] 1 Sm 11:1–11; 31:11–13; 2 Sm 2:4–7; 21:11–14.  x. [21:11] Nm 31:17.  y. [21:12] Jos 21:2; 22:9.

z. [21:13] Jgs 20:47.  a. [21:15] 2 Sm 6:8.  b. [21:16] Jgs 20:48.  c. [21:19] 1 Sm 1:3, 21.  d. [21:25] Jgs 17:6; 18:1; 19:1.

# THE BOOK OF
# RUTH

❧

The Book of Ruth is named for the Moabite woman who commits herself to the Israelite people by an oath to her mother-in-law Naomi and becomes the great-grandmother of David by marriage to Boaz of Bethlehem. Thus she is an ancestor in the messianic line that leads to Jesus (Mt 1:5).

The book portrays the love and loyalty of human beings in working their way through tragic circumstances to participation in the community of the faithful people of God. The key is responsible and loving decision-making: Ruth's loyalty (2:11), her generosity (1:15–17; 2:2, 7) and her willingness to take risks for the sake of righteousness set in motion a chain of beneficial events, while behind the scenes God blesses each step in the developing drama. Ruth is so frequently designated "the Moabite" in the book that the audience of the story is constantly reminded of the universality of the embrace of salvation.

In the Greek and Latin canons, Ruth follows Judges, to which it is related by its opening time reference ("Once back in the time of the judges . . ."), and precedes Samuel, serving as transition from Israel as tribal union to monarchy. In the present sequence of the Hebrew canon it is placed among the "Writings" immediately after the Book of Proverbs, which ends with a powerful portrayal of "the woman of worth" (Prv 31:10–31; cf. Ru 3:11). Ruth is the primary liturgical text in Judaism for the celebration of the feast of Weeks (Shabuot).

The beauty of the story's construction, its use of dialogue (nearly two thirds of the text), and the sheer drama of its content mark it as one of the classic short stories of world literature. Based on the recollection of an historical figure, a story is developed which grips its audience with profound insight into divine and human relationships. The story is presented from a point some time after the course of events, as is indicated by the explanation of an obscure custom in 4:7. Wherever and whenever it was told, its claim of God's universal concern for humankind and the attractiveness of caring human responsibility shines forth.

The date of composition is disputed. Many authors date it early in the monarchy, and valid arguments can be presented for that position. Others argue for a postexilic date; they see the favorable presentation of a Moabite woman who became David's grandmother as a counter to the stringent measures of Ezra and Nehemiah against marriage with Moabites and other non-Jews (Ezr 9–10; Neh 13:23–29).

## CHAPTER 1

**Naomi in Moab.** ¹Once back in the time of the judges* there was a famine in the land; so a man from Bethlehem of Judah left home with his wife and two sons to reside on the plateau of Moab. ²The man was named Elimelech, his wife Naomi, and his sons Mahlon and Chilion; they were Ephrathites from Bethlehem of Judah. Some time after their arrival on the plateau of Moab, ³Elimelech, the husband of Naomi, died, and she was left with her two sons. ⁴They married Moabite women, one named Orpah, the other Ruth. When they had lived there about ten years, ⁵both Mahlon and Chilion died also, and the woman was left with neither her two boys† nor her husband.

⁶She and her daughters-in-law then prepared to go back from the plateau of Moab because word had reached her there that the

---

*[1:1–2] **Back in the time of the judges**: the story looks back three generations before King David (4:17) into the time of the tribal confederation described in the Book of Judges. David's Moabite connections are implied in 1 Sm 22:3–4. **Bethlehem of Judah**: Bethlehem, a town in which part of the Judean clan-division called Ephrathah lived; cf. 1 Chr 2:50–51; 4:4; Mi 5:1. Jos 19:15 mentions a different Bethlehem in the north. **The plateau of Moab**: on the east side of the Jordan valley rift, where the hills facing west get more rain, and where agricultural conditions differ from those in Judah. **Ephrathites**: a reminder of David's origins; cf. Mi 5:1.

†[1:5] **Boys**: the way the storyteller chooses certain words as guides is shown here; "boy" will not appear again until 4:16.

LORD had seen to his people's needs* and given them food. ⁷She and her two daughters-in-law left the place where they had been living. On the road back to the land of Judah, ⁸Naomi said to her daughters-in-law, "Go back, each of you to your mother's house.† May the LORD show you the same kindness as you have shown to the deceased and to me. ⁹ᵃMay the LORD guide each of you to find a husband and a home in which you will be at rest." She kissed them good-bye, but they wept aloud, ¹⁰crying, "No! We will go back with you, to your people." ¹¹Naomi replied, "Go back, my daughters. Why come with me? Have I other sons in my womb who could become your husbands?‡ ¹²Go, my daughters, for I am too old to marry again. Even if I had any such hope, or if tonight I had a husband and were to bear sons, ¹³would you wait for them and deprive yourselves of husbands until those sons grew up? No, my daughters, my lot is too bitter for you, because the LORD has extended his hand against me." ¹⁴Again they wept aloud; then Orpah kissed her mother-in-law good-bye, but Ruth clung to her.

¹⁵"See now," she said, "your sister-in-law has gone back to her people and her god. Go back after your sister-in-law!" ¹⁶§But Ruth said, "Do not press me to go back and abandon you!

Wherever you go I will go,
        wherever you lodge I will lodge.
Your people shall be my people
        and your God, my God.
¹⁷ Where you die I will die,
        and there be buried.

May the LORD do thus to me, and more, if even death separates me from you!" ¹⁸Naomi then ceased to urge her, for she saw she was determined to go with her.

**The Return to Bethlehem.** ¹⁹So they went on together until they reached Bethlehem. On their arrival there, the whole town was excited about them, and the women asked: "Can this be Naomi?" ²⁰ᵇBut she said to them, "Do not call me Naomi ['Sweet']. Call me Mara ['Bitter'], for the Almighty has made my life very bitter. ²¹ᶜI went away full, but the LORD has brought me back empty. Why should you call me 'Sweet,' since the LORD has brought me to trial, and the Almighty has pronounced evil sentence on me." ²²Thus it was that Naomi came back with her Moabite daughter-in-law Ruth, who accompanied her back from the plateau of Moab. They arrived in Bethlehem at the beginning of the barley harvest.**

## CHAPTER 2

**The Meeting.** ¹††Naomi had a powerful relative named Boaz,ᵈ through the clan of her husband Elimelech. ²‡‡Ruth the Moabite said to Naomi, "I would like to go and glean grain in the field of anyone who will allow me." Naomi said to her, "Go ahead, my daughter." ³So she went. The field she entered to glean after the harvesters happened to be the section belonging to Boaz, of the clan of Elimelech. ⁴§§Soon, along came Boaz from Bethlehem and said to the harvesters, "The LORD be with you," and they replied, "The LORD bless you." ⁵Boaz asked the young man overseeing his harvesters, "Whose young woman is this?" ⁶The young man overseeing the harvesters answered, "She is the young Moabite who came back with Naomi from the plateau of Moab.ᵉ ⁷¶¶She said, 'I would like to gather the gleanings into sheaves after the harvesters.' Ever since she

¶[1:21] Naomi's despair is made clear by her play on the meaning of her name in v. 20 and now by her accusation, like that in many psalms and in Job, that God has acted harshly toward her. The language belongs to the realm of judicial proceedings. By crying out in this way, the faithful Israelite opens the door to change, since the cry assumes that God hears and will do something about such seemingly unjust circumstances.

**[1:22] Barley and wheat harvests come in succession, from as early as April–May into June–July; Dt 16:9–12 suggests that the grain harvest lasts about seven weeks. The time reference leads effectively to the next episode.

††[2:1] Kinship ties and responsibilities now become very important. Boaz is introduced as one of a group surrounding Naomi through her husband's kin who are expected to extend care. The particular term used here (*moda'*, "relative") is picked up in 3:2; otherwise, most of the terminology about this responsibility to care will use the vocabulary of redeeming (*go'el*, "redeemer").

‡‡[2:2] Israelite custom made provision for the poor, the widow, the stranger and the orphan to gather what was left behind by the harvesters, and instructed farmers not to cut to the edges of their fields, for the sake of these marginalized; Lv 19:9–10; 23:22; Dt 24:19–22.

§§[2:4] The story brings Boaz upon the scene quickly, but he moves among his workers with the grace of a man of prominence, greeting them and being received with courtesy. The Hebrew blessing formulas used are frequent in Jewish and Christian liturgies.

¶¶[2:7] The verse is somewhat garbled, but the points are clear that Ruth has been appropriately deferential in seeking permission to glean, and has worked steadily since arriving. Or perhaps she has waited patiently until Boaz arrives to gain permission.

---

*[1:6] **Had seen to his people's needs**: lit., "had visited his people."

†[1:8] **Mother's house**: the women's part of the home, but also perhaps the proper location for arranging marriage; Sg 3:4; 8:2; Gn 24:28. **Kindness**: Hebrew *hesed*. The powerful relationship term used here will recur in 2:20 and 3:10; kindness operates on both the divine-human and human-human level in Ruth.

‡[1:11] **Other sons . . . husbands**: a reference to a customary practice known from Dt 25:5–10, levirate marriage, which assigns responsibility to the brother-in-law to produce heirs in order to perpetuate the name and hold the patrimonial land of a man who died childless. How far the responsibility extended beyond blood brothers is unclear; cf. Gn 38:8 and the upcoming scene in Ru 4:5–6. Naomi imagines the impossible: were she to have more sons they could take Ruth and Orpah as wives.

§[1:16–17] Ruth's adherence to her mother-in-law in 1:14 is now expressed in a profound oath of loyalty, culminating in a formulary found frequently in Samuel and Kings; cf. especially 1 Sm 20:13. **Even death**: burial in Naomi's family tomb means that not even death will separate them.

a. [1:9] Ru 3:1.

b. [1:20] Ex 15:23.   c. [1:21] Ru 3:17; 1 Kgs 17:20.   d. [2:1] Ru 3:2, 12; Mt 1:5.   e. [2:6] Ru 1:22.

came this morning she has remained here until now, with scarcely a moment's rest."

⁸Boaz then spoke to Ruth, "Listen, my daughter. Do not go to glean in anyone else's field; you are not to leave here. Stay here with my young women. ⁹Watch to see which field is to be harvested, and follow them. Have I not commanded the young men to do you no harm? When you are thirsty, go and drink from the vessels the young people have filled." ¹⁰Casting herself prostrate upon the ground, she said to him, "Why should I, a foreigner, be favored with your attention?" ¹¹ᶠBoaz answered her: "I have had a complete account of what you have done for your mother-in-law after your husband's death; you have left your father and your mother and the land of your birth, and have come to a people whom previously you did not know. ¹²ᵍMay the LORD reward what you have done! May you receive a full reward from the LORD, the God of Israel, under whose wings you have come for refuge." ¹³She said, "May I prove worthy of your favor, my lord. You have comforted me. You have spoken to the heart of your servant*—and I am not even one of your servants!" ¹⁴At mealtime Boaz said to her, "Come here and have something to eat; dip your bread in the sauce." Then as she sat near the harvesters, he handed her some roasted grain and she ate her fill and had some left over. ¹⁵As she rose to glean, Boaz instructed his young people: "Let her glean among the sheaves themselves without scolding her, ¹⁶and even drop some handfuls and leave them for her to glean; do not rebuke her."

¹⁷She gleaned in the field until evening, and when she beat out what she had gleaned it came to about an ephah† of barley, ¹⁸which she took into the town and showed to her mother-in-law. Next she brought out what she had left over from the meal and gave it to her. ¹⁹So her mother-in-law said to her, "Where did you glean today? Where did you go to work? May the one who took notice of you be blessed!" Then she told her mother-in-law with whom she had worked. "The man at whose place I worked today is named Boaz," she said. ²⁰ʰ"May he be blessed by the LORD, who never fails to show kindness to the living and to the dead," Naomi exclaimed to her daughter-in-law. She continued, "This man is a near relative of ours, one of our redeemers."‡ ²¹"He even told me," added Ruth the Moabite, "Stay with my young people until they complete my entire harvest." ²²"You would do well, my daughter," Naomi rejoined, "to work with his young women; in someone else's field you might be insulted." ²³So she stayed gleaning with Boaz's young women until the end of the barley and wheat harvests.

## CHAPTER 3

**Ruth Again Presents Herself.** When Ruth was back with her mother-in-law, ¹Naomi said to her, "My daughter, should I not be seeking a pleasing home for you?ⁱ ²Now! Is not Boaz,ʲ whose young women you were working with, a relative of ours? This very night he will be winnowing barley at the threshing floor. ³Now, go bathe and anoint yourself; then put on your best attire and go down to the threshing floor. Do not make yourself known to the man before he has finished eating and drinking. ⁴But when he lies down, take note of the place where he lies; then go uncover a place at his feet¶ and you lie down. He will then tell you what to do." ⁵"I will do whatever you say," Ruth replied. ⁶She went down to the threshing floor and did just as her mother-in-law had instructed her.

⁷Boaz ate and drank to his heart's content, and went to lie down at the edge of the pile of grain. She crept up, uncovered a place at his feet, and lay down. ⁸Midway through the night, the man gave a start and groped about, only to find a woman lying at his feet. ⁹"Who are you?" he asked. She replied, "I am your servant Ruth. Spread the wing of your cloak** over your servant, for you are a redeemer." ¹⁰He said, "May the LORD bless you, my daughter! You have been even more loyal now than before in not going after the young men, whether poor or rich. ¹¹Now rest assured, my daughter, I will do for you whatever you say; all my townspeople know you to be a worthy woman.†† ¹²ᵏNow, I am in fact a redeemer, but there is another redeemer closer than I.‡‡ ¹³Stay where you are for tonight,

---

*[2:13] **Servant**: only here is the language of servanthood used. Ruth has spoken with very deferential words to Boaz, but then seems to think that she has assumed too much.

†[2:17] **Ephah**: see note on Is 5:10.

‡[2:20] For the first time, the story uses the Hebrew word *goʾel*, "redeemer," for the responsibilities of the circle of kinship surrounding Naomi and Ruth and their deceased relatives. Involved are the recovery or retention of family land (Lv 25:25; 27:9–33; Jer 32:6–25), release of a relative from voluntary servitude to pay debts (Lv 25:47–55), and "redeeming blood" or vengeance, attested in passages which regulate such

vengeance. No explicit connection is made elsewhere in the Bible between marriage responsibilities and redeeming.

§[3:2] Ruth's determined action to bring relief to Naomi's and her own circumstances now impels Naomi to move, using means available in Israelite custom which no one in the story has up to this point brought into play.

¶[3:4] **Uncover a place at his feet**: Naomi advocates a course of action that will lead Boaz to act. Israelite custom and moral expectations strongly suggest that there is no loss of virtue involved in the scene.

**[3:9] **Spread the wing of your cloak**: Ez 16:8 makes it clear that this is a request for marriage. Ruth connects it to "redeemer" responsibility. A wordplay on "wing" links what Boaz is asked to do to what he has asked God to do for Ruth in 2:12.

††[3:11] **Worthy woman**: the language corresponds to the description of Boaz in 2:1 (lit., "strong and worthy"); the two worthy people are linked in character to one another, as they have already proven to be in their generous behavior toward the ones in need of their care. The townspeople, lit., "all the gate of my people," will ratify this at the gate in the sequel.

‡‡[3:12] **Another redeemer closer than I**: Boaz knows of a closer relative who would have a prior right to buy the field and marry Ruth.

---

f. [2:11] Ru 1:14–17.   g. [2:12] Ru 3:9; Dt 32:37; Ps 91:4.   h. [2:20] Gn 24:27; Lv 25:25; 27:9–33.

i. [3:1] Ru 1:9.   j. [3:2] Ru 2:1.   k. [3:12] Ru 4:1.

and tomorrow, if he will act as redeemer for you, good. But if he will not, as the LORD lives, I will do it myself. Lie there until morning."[l] [14]So she lay at his feet until morning, but rose before anyone could recognize another, for Boaz had said, "Let it not be known that this woman came to the threshing floor." [15]Then he said to her, "Take off the shawl you are wearing; hold it firmly." When she did so, he poured out six measures of barley and helped her lift the bundle; then he himself left for the town.

[16]She, meanwhile, went home to her mother-in-law, who asked, "How did things go, my daughter?" So she told her all the man had done for her, [17]and concluded, "He gave me these six measures of barley and said, 'Do not go back to your mother-in-law empty.'"[m] [18]Naomi then said, "Wait here, my daughter, until you learn what happens, for the man will not rest, but will settle the matter today."

## CHAPTER 4

**Boaz Marries Ruth.** [1]Boaz went to the gate* and took a seat there. Along came the other redeemer[n] of whom he had spoken. Boaz called to him by name, "Come, sit here." And he did so. [2]Then Boaz picked out ten of the elders[†] of the town and asked them to sit nearby. When they had done this, [3]he said to the other redeemer: "Naomi, who has come back from the plateau of Moab, is putting up for sale the piece of land that belonged to our kinsman Elimelech. [4‡]So I thought I would inform you. Before those here present, including the elders of my people, purchase the field; act as redeemer.[o] But if you do not want to do it, tell me so, that I may know, for no one has a right of redemption prior to yours, and mine is next." He answered, "I will act as redeemer."

[5§]Boaz continued, "When you acquire the field from Naomi, you also acquire responsibility for Ruth the Moabite,[p] the widow of the late heir, to raise up a family for the deceased on his estate." [6]The redeemer replied, "I cannot exercise my right of redemption for that would endanger my own estate. You do it in my place, for I cannot." [7q]Now it used to be the custom in Israel that, to make binding a contract of redemption or exchange, one party would take off a sandal[¶] and give it to the other. This was the form of attestation in Israel. [8]So the other redeemer, in saying to Boaz, "Acquire it for yourself," drew off his sandal. [9]Boaz then said to the elders and to all the people, "You are witnesses today that I have acquired from Naomi all the holdings of Elimelech, Chilion and Mahlon. [10]I also acquire Ruth the Moabite, the widow of Mahlon, as my wife, in order to raise up a family for her late husband on his estate, so that the name of the deceased may not perish from his people and his place. Do you witness this today?" [11r]All those at the gate, including the elders, said, "We do. May the LORD make this woman come into your house like Rachel and Leah, who between them built up the house of Israel. Prosper in Ephrathah! Bestow a name in Bethlehem! [12]With the offspring the LORD will give you from this young woman, may your house become like the house of Perez, whom Tamar bore to Judah."**

[13]Boaz took Ruth. When they came together as husband and wife, the LORD enabled her to conceive and she bore a son. [14]Then the women said to Naomi, "Blessed is the LORD who has not failed to provide you today with a redeemer. May he become famous in Israel! [15]He will restore your life and be the support of your old age, for his mother is the daughter-in-law who loves you. She is worth more to you than seven sons!" [16]Naomi took the boy, cradled him[††] against her breast, and cared for him. [17]The neighbor women joined the celebration: "A son has been born to Naomi!"[s] They named him Obed. He was the father of Jesse, the father of David.

[18t]These are the descendants of Perez: Perez was the father of Hezron,[u] [19]Hezron was the father of Ram, Ram was the father of Amminadab, [20v]Amminadab was the father of Nahshon, Nahshon was the father of Salma, [21]Salma was the father of Boaz, Boaz was the father of Obed, [22w]Obed was the father of Jesse, and Jesse became the father of David.

---

*[4:1] The gate of an Israelite town was the place where commercial and other legal matters were dealt with in publicly witnessed fashion.

†[4:2] **Ten of the elders**: to serve as judges in legal matters as well as witnesses of the settlement of business affairs; cf. Dt 25:7–9.

‡[4:4] Although the laws governing inheritance by Israelite widows are not specified in the Bible, Naomi seems to have the right of disposal of a piece of Elimelech's land. The redemption custom in Lv 25:25 would then guide the procedure.

§[4:5–6] Although redemption and levirate practices are not otherwise linked in the Bible, they belong in the same area of need. Boaz claims that buying Elimelech's field obligates the other redeemer to produce an heir for Mahlon, who would then inherit the land. That would jeopardize this redeemer's overall holdings, since he would lose the land he had paid for. He can afford the first step but not the second, and cedes his responsibility to Boaz, who is willing to do both.

¶[4:7] **Take off a sandal**: the legislation in Dt 25:8–10 provides that if a "redeemer" refuses to carry out the obligation of marrying his brother's wife, the woman shall strip off his sandal as a gesture of insult. In later years, when the obligation of carrying out this function of the "redeemer" was no longer keenly felt, the removal of the sandal may have become a formalized way of renouncing the rights/obligations of the "redeemer," as in this text.

**[4:12] Gn 38 contains a story about Tamar similar to Ruth's in levirate marriage. Judah, under less laudable circumstances, fulfills the same role as Boaz will, and Perez, son of Judah and Tamar, perpetuates the line. Thus two non-Israelite women, Tamar and Ruth, are important links in David's genealogy.

††[4:16] **Cradled him**: the child belongs to Naomi in the sense that he now becomes the redeemer in the family, as stated in 4:14. This tender act by Naomi is not necessarily adoptive and differs from the relationship in Nm 11:12. Naomi now has a "boy" to replace her two lost "boys" in 1:5.

---

l. [3:13] Ru 1:16; 4:5.   m. [3:17] Ru 1:21.   n. [4:1] Ru 3:12. o. [4:4] Lv 25:25.   p. [4:5] Ru 3:13.

q. [4:7] Dt 25:9.   r. [4:11] Gn 29:31–30:24; 35:16–19.   s. [4:17] Lk 1:58.   t. [4:18–22] 1 Chr 2:4–15; Mt 1:3–6.   u. [4:18] Gn 46:12; Nm 26:21; 1 Chr 4:1.   v. [4:20] Ex 6:23; Nm 1:7; 2:3; 7:12–17; 10:14.   w. [4:22] 1 Sm 16:2–13.

# THE BOOKS OF
# SAMUEL

These books describe the rise and development of kingship in Israel. Samuel is a pivotal figure. He bridges the gap between the period of the Judges and the monarchy, and guides Israel's transition to kingship. A Deuteronomistic editor presents both positive and negative traditions about the monarchy, portraying it both as evidence of Israel's rejection of the Lord as their sovereign (1 Sm 8:6–22; 12:1–25) and as part of God's plan to deliver the people (1 Sm 9:16; 10:17–27; 2 Sm 7:8–17). Samuel's misgivings about abuse of royal power foreshadow the failures and misdeeds of Saul and David and the failures of subsequent Israelite kings.

Although the events described in 1 and 2 Samuel move from the last of the judges to the decline of David's reign and the beginning of a legendary "Golden Age" under Solomon's rule, this material does not present either a continuous history or a systematic account of this period. The author/editor developed a narrative timeline around freely composed speeches, delivered by prophets like Samuel (e.g., 1 Sm 15:10–31; 28:15–19) and Nathan (2 Sm 12:1–12), who endorse Deuteronomistic perspectives regarding the establishment of the monarchy, the relationship between worship and obedience, and the divine covenant established with the house of David.

These books include independent blocks (e.g., the Ark Narrative [1 Sm 4:1–7:1], Saul's rise to power [1 Sm 9:1–11:15], David's ascendancy over Saul [1 Sm 16–31], the Succession Narrative [2 Sm 9–20; 1 Kgs 1–2]), which the editor shaped into three narrative cycles, the last two marked by transitional passages in 1 Sm 13:1 and 2 Sm 1:1. Each section focuses on a major figure in the development of the monarchy: Samuel, the reluctant king maker (1 Sm 1–12); Saul, the king whom the Lord rejects (1 Sm 13–31); David, the king after the Lord's own heart (2 Sm 1–24). A common theme unites these narratives: Israel's God acts justly, prospering those who remain faithful and destroying those who reject his ways (1 Sm 2:9). Along with the rest of the Deuteronomistic History, the Books of Samuel become an object lesson for biblical Israel as it tries to re-establish its religious identity after the destruction of Jerusalem and the loss of its homeland (587/586 B.C.).

The contents of the Books of Samuel may be divided as follows:

I. The Last Judges, Eli and Samuel (1 Sm 1:1–7:17)
II. Establishment of the Monarchy (1 Sm 8:1–12:25)
III. Saul and David (1 Sm 13:1–2 Sm 2:7)
IV. The Reign of David (2 Sm 2:8–20:26)
V. Appendixes (2 Sm 21:1–24:25)

# THE FIRST BOOK OF
# SAMUEL

༄

## I. THE LAST JUDGES, ELI AND SAMUEL

### CHAPTER 1

**Elkanah and His Family at Shiloh.** ¹There was a certain man from Ramathaim, a Zuphite from the hill country of Ephraim. His name was Elkanah, the son of Jeroham, son of Elihu, son of Tohu, son of Zuph, an Ephraimite.ᵃ ²He had two wives, one named Hannah, the other Peninnah; Peninnah had children, but Hannah had no children. ³Each year this man went up from his city to worship and offer sacrifice to the Lord of hosts at Shiloh, where the two sons of Eli, Hophni and Phinehas, were ministering as priests of the Lord.ᵇ ⁴When the day came for Elkanah to offer sacrifice, he used to give portions to his wife Peninnah and to all her sons and daughters, ⁵but he would give a double portion to Hannah because he loved her, though the Lord had closed her womb.ᶜ ⁶Her rival,* to upset her, would torment her constantly, since the Lord had closed her womb.ᵈ ⁷Year after year, when she went up to the house of the Lord, Peninnah would provoke her, and Hannah would weep and refuse to eat.† ⁸Elkanah, her husband, would say to her: "Hannah, why are you weeping? Why are you not eating? Why are you so miserable? Am I not better for you than ten sons?"ᵉ

**Hannah's Prayer.** ⁹Hannah rose after one such meal at Shiloh, and presented herself before the Lord; at the time Eli the priest was sitting on a chair near the doorpost of the Lord's temple. ¹⁰In her bitterness she prayed to the Lord, weeping freely, ¹¹and made this vow: "O Lord of hosts, if you look with pity on the hardship of your servant, if you remember me and do not forget me, if you give your handmaid a male child, I will give him to the Lord all the days of his life. No razor shall ever touch his head."*ᶠ ¹²As she continued praying before

the Lord, Eli watched her mouth, ¹³for Hannah was praying silently; though her lips were moving, her voice could not be heard. Eli, thinking she was drunk, ¹⁴said to her, "How long will you make a drunken spectacle of yourself? Sober up from your wine!" ¹⁵"No, my lord!" Hannah answered. "I am an unhappy woman. I have had neither wine nor liquor; I was only pouring out my heart to the Lord. ¹⁶Do not think your servant a worthless woman; my prayer has been prompted by my deep sorrow and misery." ¹⁷Eli said, "Go in peace, and may the God of Israel grant you what you have requested." ¹⁸She replied, "Let your servant find favor in your eyes," and left. She went to her quarters, ate and drank with her husband, and no longer appeared downhearted. ¹⁹Early the next morning they worshiped before the Lord, and then returned to their home in Ramah. When they returned Elkanah had intercourse with his wife Hannah, and the Lord remembered her.

**Hannah Bears a Son.** ²⁰She conceived and, at the end of her pregnancy, bore a son whom she named Samuel.§ "Because I asked the Lord for him." ²¹The next time her husband Elkanah was going up with the rest of his household to offer the customary sacrifice to the Lord and to fulfill his vows, ²²Hannah did not go, explaining to her husband, "Once the child is weaned, I will take him to appear before the Lord and leave him there forever."¶ ²³Her husband Elkanah answered her: "Do what you think best; wait until you have weaned him. Only may the Lord fulfill his word!" And so she remained at home and nursed her son until she had weaned him.ᵍ

**Hannah Presents Samuel to the Lord.** ²⁴Once he was weaned, she brought him up with her,

---

\* [1:6] **Her rival:** Hebrew *sara*, "rival wife, co-wife"; in the Talmud, a technical term for a second or co-wife.

† [1:7] In biblical narrative, the social status gained by producing children, especially males, often set woman against woman; cf. e.g., Gn 16, 21, 30. Peninnah's provocations may be the arrogant boasting mentioned in 2:3.

‡ [1:11] **No razor . . . :** the Septuagint adds "he shall drink neither wine nor liquor." This addition is a further suggestion

---

that Samuel is dedicated to God under a nazirite vow (Nm 6:4–5); see note on v. 22.

§ [1:20] **Samuel:** Hannah's explanation associates her son's name with the narrative's wordplay on the Hebrew verbs *s'l* ("ask," vv. 17, 27), *his'il* ("hand over, dedicate," v. 28), *sa'ul* ("dedicated," v. 28), and the noun *se'elah* ("request," vv. 17, 27). The name, however, is related to the Hebrew root *s'l* only through assonance. It means "his name is El/God," not "the one requested or dedicated (*sa'ul*) to God" (v. 28), which is the meaning of the name Saul. The author may have lifted the *s'l* wordplay from a narrative about Saul to portray Samuel as God's gracious answer to Hannah's request.

¶ [1:22] **Leave him there forever:** a Qumran manuscript adds "I will give him as a nazirite forever"; it interprets v. 11 to mean that Hannah dedicates Samuel under a nazirite vow (cf. Nm 6:4–5).

---

a. [1:1] 1 Chr 6:19–20.   b. [1:3] Ex 23:14–17; 34:23; Dt 16:16; Jgs 21:19.   c. [1:5] Dt 21:15–17.   d. [1:6] Gn 16:4–5; 29:31; Jgs 13:2; Lk 1:7.   e. [1:8] Ru 4:15.   f. [1:11] Nm 6:1–5; Jgs 13:2–5; 16:17; Lk 1:15.

g. [1:23] Dt 9:5; 2 Sm 7:25; 1 Kgs 2:4.

along with a three-year-old bull, an ephah* of flour, and a skin of wine, and presented him at the house of the LORD in Shiloh. ²⁵After they had slaughtered the bull, they brought the child to Eli. ²⁶Then Hannah spoke up: "Excuse me, my lord! As you live, my lord, I am the woman who stood here near you, praying to the LORD. ²⁷I prayed for this child, and the LORD granted my request. ²⁸Now I, in turn, give him to the LORD; as long as he lives, he shall be dedicated to the LORD." Then they worshiped there before the LORD.

## CHAPTER 2

¹And Hannah prayed:†

"My heart exults in the LORD,
    my horn is exalted by my God.
I have swallowed up my enemies;
    I rejoice in your victory.ʰ
²  There is no Holy One like the LORD;
    there is no Rock like our God.ⁱ
³  Speak boastfully no longer,
        Do not let arrogance issue from
            your mouths.‡
    For an all-knowing God is the LORD,
        a God who weighs actions.ʲ

⁴  "The bows of the mighty are broken,
        while the tottering gird on strength.ᵏ
⁵  The well-fed hire themselves out for
            bread,
        while the hungry no longer have
            to toil.
    The barren wife bears seven sons,
        while the mother of many
            languishes.ˡ

⁶  "The LORD puts to death and gives life,
        casts down to Sheol and brings up
            again.ᵐ
⁷  The LORD makes poor and makes rich,
    humbles, and also exalts.
⁸  He raises the needy from the dust;
        from the ash heap lifts up the poor,
    To seat them with nobles
        and make a glorious throne their
            heritage.

"For the pillars of the earth are the
        LORD's,
    and he has set the world upon
        them.ⁿ
⁹  He guards the footsteps of his faithful
        ones,
    but the wicked shall perish in the
        darkness;
    for not by strength does one prevail.
¹⁰ The LORD's foes shall be shattered;
    the Most High in heaven thunders;
    the LORD judges the ends of the
        earth.
May he give strength to his king,
    and exalt the horn of his anointed!"ᵒ

¹¹When Elkanah returned home to Ramah, the child remained in the service of the LORD under the priest Eli.

**Wickedness of Eli's Sons.** ¹²Now the sons of Eli were wicked; they had respect neither for the LORD ¹³nor for the priests' duties toward the people. When someone offered a sacrifice, the priest's servant would come with a three-pronged fork, while the meat was still boiling,ᵖ ¹⁴and would thrust it into the basin, kettle, caldron, or pot. Whatever the fork brought up, the priest would take for himself. They treated all the Israelites who came to the sanctuary at Shiloh in this way. ¹⁵In fact, even before the fat was burned, the priest's servant would come and say to the one offering the sacrifice, "Give me some meat to roast for the priest. He will not accept boiled meat from you, only raw meat." ¹⁶And if this one protested, "Let the fat be burned first, then take whatever you wish," he would reply, "No, give it to me now, or else I will take it by force."�q ¹⁷Thus the young men sinned grievously in the presence of the LORD, treating the offerings to the LORD with disdain.

**The Lord Rewards Hannah.** ¹⁸Meanwhile the boy Samuel, wearing a linen ephod,§ was serving in the presence of the LORD. ¹⁹His mother used to make a little garment for him, which she would bring him each time she went up with her husband to offer the customary sacrifice. ²⁰And Eli would bless Elkanah and his wife, as they were leaving for home. He would say, "May the LORD repay you with children from this woman for the gift she has made to the LORD!" ²¹The LORD favored Hannah so that she conceived and gave birth to three more sons and two daughters, while young Samuel grew up in the service of the LORD.ʳ

---

*[1:24] **Ephah**: see note on Is 5:10.

†[2:1–10] Hannah appeals to a God who maintains order by keeping human affairs in balance, reversing the fortunes of the arrogant, who, like Peninnah, boast of their good fortune (vv. 1, 3, 9) at the expense of those like Hannah who receive less from the Lord. Hannah's admission places her among the faithful who trust that God will execute justice on their behalf. The reference "his king . . . his anointed" (v. 10) recalls the final sentence of the Book of Judges and introduces the kingship theme that dominates the Books of Samuel.

‡[2:3] **Speak . . . mouths**: addressed to the enemies mentioned in v. 1.

§[2:18] **Linen ephod**: not the same as the high priest's ephod (Ex 28:6–14) or the ephod used in divination (v. 28). Samuel wore the same kind of a ceremonial garment as the priests did (1 Sm 22:18). David also wore an ephod when he danced before the ark (2 Sm 6:14).

h. [2:1] Dt 33:17; 2 Sm 22:3; Ps 18:2; 89:18; Is 61:10; Lk 1:47, 69. i. [2:2] 2 Sm 22:3; Ps 18:2. j. [2:3] Ps 75:5–6. k. [2:4] Is 40:29. l. [2:5] Ru 4:15; Jer 15:9. m. [2:6] Dt 32:39; Tb 4:19; Jb 5:11; Ps 30:4; Wis 16:13; Lk 1:52.

n. [2:8] Jb 9:6; 38:6; Ps 75:4; 104:5; 113:8; 121:3. o. [2:10] Ps 98:9. p. [2:13–15] Ex 29:27–28; Lv 7:29–36; Dt 18:3. q. [2:16] Lv 3:3–5; Nm 18:17. r. [2:21] 1 Sm 3:19.

**Eli's Futile Rebuke.** ²²When Eli was very old, he kept hearing how his sons were treating all Israel, and that they were behaving promiscuously* with the women serving at the entry of the meeting tent. ²³So he said to them: "Why are you doing such things? I hear from everyone that your behavior is depraved. ²⁴Stop this, my sons! The report that I hear the LORD's people spreading is not good. ²⁵If someone sins against another, anyone can intercede for the sinner with the LORD; but if anyone sins against the LORD, who can intercede† for the sinner?" But they disregarded their father's warning, since the LORD wanted them dead. ²⁶Meanwhile, young Samuel was growing in stature and in worth in the estimation of the LORD and the people.ˢ

**The Fate of Eli's House.**‡ ²⁷A man of God came to Eli and said to him: "Thus says the LORD: I went so far as to reveal myself to your father's house when they were in Egypt as slaves to the house of Pharaoh. ²⁸I chose them out of all the tribes of Israel to be my priests, to go up to my altar, to burn incense, and to wear the ephod§ in my presence; and I assigned all the fire offerings of the Israelites to your father's house.ᵗ ²⁹Why do you stare greedily at my sacrifices and at the offerings that I have prescribed? Why do you honor your sons more than you honor me, fattening yourselves with the choicest part of every offering of my people Israel? ³⁰ᵘThis, therefore, is the oracle of the LORD, the God of Israel: I said in the past that your family and your father's house should minister in my presence forever. But now—oracle of the LORD: Far be it from me! I will honor those who honor me, but those who despise me shall be cursed. ³¹Yes, the days are coming when I will break your strength and the strength of your father's house, so that no one in your family lives to old age. ³²You shall witness, like a disappointed rival, all the benefits enjoyed by Israel, but no member of your household shall ever grow old. ³³I will leave you one man at my altar to wear out his eyes and waste his

strength, but the rest of your family shall die by the sword. ³⁴This is a sign for you—what happens to your two sons, Hophni and Phinehas. Both of them will die on the same day.ᵛ ³⁵I will choose a faithful priest who shall do what I have in heart and mind. I will establish a lasting house for him and he shall serve in the presence of my anointed forever. ³⁶Then whoever is left of your family will grovel before him for a piece of silver or a loaf of bread, saying: Please assign me a priestly function, that I may have a crust of bread to eat."ʷ

## CHAPTER 3

**Revelation to Samuel.** ¹During the time young Samuel was minister to the LORD under Eli, the word of the LORD was scarce and vision infrequent. ²¶One day Eli was asleep in his usual place. His eyes had lately grown so weak that he could not see. ³The lamp of God was not yet extinguished,** and Samuel was sleeping in the temple of the LORD where the ark of God was.ˣ ⁴The LORD called to Samuel, who answered, "Here I am." ⁵He ran to Eli and said, "Here I am. You called me." "I did not call you," Eli answered. "Go back to sleep." So he went back to sleep. ⁶Again the LORD called Samuel, who rose and went to Eli. "Here I am," he said. "You called me." But he answered, "I did not call you, my son. Go back to sleep."

⁷Samuel did not yet recognize the LORD, since the word of the LORD had not yet been revealed to him. ⁸The LORD called Samuel again, for the third time. Getting up and going to Eli, he said, "Here I am. You called me." Then Eli understood that the LORD was calling the youth. ⁹So he said to Samuel, "Go to sleep, and if you are called, reply, 'Speak, LORD, for your servant is listening.'" When Samuel went to sleep in his place, ¹⁰the LORD came and stood there, calling out as before: Samuel, Samuel! Samuel answered, "Speak, for your servant is listening." ¹¹The LORD said to Samuel: I am about to do something in Israel that will make the ears of everyone who hears it ring.ʸ ¹²On that day I will carry out against Eli everything I have said about his house, beginning to end. ¹³I announce to him that I am condemning his house once and for all, because of this crime: though he knew his sons were blaspheming God, he did not reprove them.ᶻ ¹⁴Therefore, I swear to Eli's house: No sacrifice or offering will ever expiate

---

* [2:22] **Behaving promiscuously**: this part of the verse, which recalls Ex 38:8, is a gloss; it is lacking in the oldest Greek translation, and in 4QSamᵃ.

† [2:25] **Who can intercede**: Eli's sons fail to understand that their crime is directly against God and that God will punish them for it. Their behavior is set in sharp contrast to Samuel's, which meets with God's approval.

‡ [2:27–36] These verses describe the punishment of Eli from a point of view contemporary with the reform of Josiah (2 Kgs 23:9; cf. v. 36); they hint at the events recorded in 1 Sm 22:18–23 and 1 Kgs 2:27. The older story of this divine warning occurs in 1 Sm 3:11–14. **A man of God**: often an anonymous figure whose speech foreshadows events in the near future. Cf. 1 Sm 9:6; 1 Kgs 13:1; 2 Kgs 23:16–17.

§ [2:28] **Ephod**: a portable container, presumably of cloth, for the lots used in ritual consultation of God during the days of the Judges (Jgs 17:5; 18:14–15) and into the time of David (1 Sm 14:3; 23:6–9; 30:7–8). Attached to the ephod of the high priest described in Ex 28:6–8 is a "breastpiece of decision" which symbolized, but did not facilitate, such consultation. The Exodus text codifies a later form of the tradition.

¶ [3:2–18] The call of Samuel: This section may be divided as follows: 1. the triple summons (vv. 2–9); 2. God's revelation (vv. 10–14); 3. Samuel informs Eli (vv. 15–18).

** [3:3] **Not yet extinguished**: referring to the nighttime setting of this narrative (cf. Ex 27:20–21) and foreshadowing a permanently extinguished lamp when the ark is captured and Shiloh destroyed.

---

s. [2:26] Lk 2:52.    t. [2:28] 1 Sm 23:9; 30:7–8; Jgs 17:5.    u. [2:30–31] 2 Sm 22:26; 1 Kgs 2:27; Ps 18:25.

v. [2:34] 1 Sm 4:11.    w. [2:36] 2 Kgs 23:9.    x. [3:3] Ex 27:20–22.    y. [3:11] 2 Kgs 21:12.    z. [3:13] 1 Sm 2:27–36.

its crime.* ¹⁵Samuel then slept until morning, when he got up early and opened the doors of the temple of the LORD. He was afraid to tell Eli the vision, ¹⁶but Eli called to him, "Samuel, my son!" He replied, "Here I am." ¹⁷Then Eli asked, "What did he say to you? Hide nothing from me! May God do thus to you, and more,† if you hide from me a single thing he told you." ¹⁸So Samuel told him everything, and held nothing back. Eli answered, "It is the LORD. What is pleasing in the LORD's sight, the LORD will do."

**Samuel Acknowledged as Prophet.** ¹⁹Samuel grew up, and the LORD was with him, not permitting any word of his to go unfulfilled.ᵃ ²⁰ᵇThus all Israel from Dan to Beer-sheba came to know that Samuel was a trustworthy prophet of the LORD. ²¹The LORD continued to appear at Shiloh, manifesting himself to Samuel at Shiloh through his word. Samuel's word spread throughout Israel.

### CHAPTER 4

**Defeat of the Israelites.**‡ ¹At that time, the Philistines gathered for an attack on Israel. Israel went out to engage them in battle and camped at Ebenezer, while the Philistines camped at Aphek. ²The Philistines then drew up in battle formation against Israel. After a fierce struggle Israel was defeated by the Philistines, who killed about four thousand men on the battlefield. ³When the troops retired to the camp, the elders of Israel said, "Why has the LORD permitted us to be defeated today by the Philistines? Let us fetch the ark of the LORD from Shiloh that it may go into battle among us and save us from the grasp of our enemies."ᶜ

**Loss of the Ark.** ⁴So the people sent to Shiloh and brought from there the ark of the LORD of hosts, who is enthroned upon the cherubim.§ The two sons of Eli, Hophni and Phinehas, accompanied the ark of God.ᵈ ⁵When the ark of the LORD arrived in the camp, all Israel shouted so loudly that the earth shook. ⁶The Philistines, hearing the uproar, asked, "What does this loud shouting in the camp of the Hebrews mean?" On learning that the ark of the LORD had come into the camp, ⁷the Philistines were frightened,

crying out, "Gods have come to their camp. Woe to us! This has never happened before. ⁸Woe to us! Who can deliver us from the power of these mighty gods?¶ These are the gods who struck the Egyptians with various plagues in the desert. ⁹Take courage and act like soldiers, Philistines; otherwise you will become slaves to the Hebrews, as they were your slaves. Fight like soldiers!" ¹⁰The Philistines fought and Israel was defeated; everyone fled to their own tents.** It was a disastrous defeat; Israel lost thirty thousand foot soldiers. ¹¹The ark of God was captured, and Eli's two sons, Hophni and Phinehas, were dead.ᵉ

**Death of Eli.** ¹²A Benjaminite fled from the battlefield and reached Shiloh that same day, with his clothes torn and his head covered with dirt.ᶠ ¹³When he arrived, Eli was sitting in his chair beside the gate, watching the road, for he was troubled at heart about the ark of God. The man, however, went into the city to announce his news; then the whole city cried out. ¹⁴When Eli heard the uproar, he wondered why there was such commotion. Just then the man rushed up to inform him. ¹⁵Eli was ninety-eight years old, and his eyes would not focus. So he could not see. ¹⁶The man said to Eli: "I have come from the battlefield; today I fled from there." He asked, "What happened, my son?" ¹⁷And the messenger answered: "Israel fled from the Philistines; in fact, the troops suffered heavy losses. Your two sons, Hophni and Phinehas, are dead, and the ark of God has been captured." ¹⁸At this mention of the ark of God, Eli fell backward from his chair into the gateway; he died of a broken neck since he was an old man and heavy. He had judged Israel for forty years.

¹⁹His daughter-in-law, the wife of Phinehas, was pregnant and about to give birth. When she heard the news about the capture of the ark of God and the deaths of her father-in-law and her husband, she crouched down in labor, and gave birth. ²⁰She was about to die when the women standing around her said to her, "Do not be afraid, you have given birth to a son." Yet she neither answered nor paid any attention.ᵍ ²¹She named the child Ichabod, saying, "Gone is the glory from Israel," referring to the capture of the ark of God and to her father-in-law and her husband. ²²She said, "Gone is the glory from Israel," because the ark of God had been captured.ʰ

### CHAPTER 5

**The Ark in the Temple of Dagon.** ¹††The Philistines, having captured the ark of God, transferred

---

*[3:14] Lv 4:3–12 presents another view: the offering of a bull can expiate priestly sin.

†[3:17] **May God do thus to you, and more:** an oath formula which strengthens Eli's demand by threatening divine punishment if Samuel does not obey. Cf. 14:44; 20:13; 25:22; 2 Sm 3:9, 35; 19:14.

‡[4:1–7:1] The Ark Narrative: A striking indication that this is an independent narrative is the absence of any mention of Samuel. **The Philistines:** one of the Sea Peoples, of Aegean origin, who occupied the coastal plain of Palestine and threatened the Israelites who settled the inland hills.

§[4:4] **Enthroned upon the cherubim:** this divine title first occurs in the Old Testament at the sanctuary at Shiloh (cf. 2 Sm 6:2); God is represented seated upon a throne borne through the heavens by cherubim, creatures partly human being, partly beast (cf. Ez 1 and 10).

¶[4:8] **These mighty gods:** the Philistines, who were polytheists, presume that the Israelites also honored several gods.

**[4:10] **To their own tents:** the defeat is so catastrophic that the soldiers abandon the army for home; cf. 2 Sm 18:17.

††[5:1–12] The Philistines take the ark to Dagon's temple in Ashdod to confirm their victory. Their action, however,

---

a. [3:19] 1 Sm 2:21.　b. [3:20] Jgs 20:1; 2 Sm 3:10; 17:11; 24:2.　c. [4:3] Nm 10:35; 14:42–44. . d. [4:4] Ex 25:21–22.

e. [4:11] 1 Sm 2:34.　f. [4:12] Jos 7:6; 2 Sm 1:2; Jer 7:12.　g. [4:20] 1 Sm 14:3; Gn 35:16–20.　h. [4:22] Ps 78:61.　i. [5:1–5] Jgs 16:23–30; Is 45:5–6, 20–21.

it from Ebenezer to Ashdod.[j] [2]They then took the ark of God and brought it into the temple of Dagon, placing it beside Dagon. [3]When the people of Ashdod rose early the next morning, Dagon was lying face down on the ground before the ark of the LORD. So they picked Dagon up and put him back in his place. [4]But early the next morning, when they arose, Dagon lay face down on the ground before the ark of the LORD, his head and hands broken off and lying on the threshold, his trunk alone intact. [5]For this reason, neither the priests of Dagon nor any others who enter the temple of Dagon tread on the threshold of Dagon in Ashdod to this very day.

**The Ark Is Carried About.** [6]Now the hand of the LORD weighed heavily on the people of Ashdod, ravaging the city and afflicting the city and its vicinity with tumors.[*k] [7]On seeing how matters stood, the people of Ashdod decided, "The ark of the God of Israel must not remain with us, for his hand weighs heavily on us and Dagon our god." [8]So they summoned all the Philistine leaders and inquired of them, "What shall we do with the ark of the God of Israel?" The people of Gath replied, "Let them move the ark of the God of Israel to us." So they moved the ark of the God of Israel to Gath. [9]But after it had been brought there, the hand of the LORD was against the city, resulting in utter turmoil: the LORD afflicted its inhabitants, young and old, and tumors broke out on them. [10]The ark of God was next sent to Ekron; but as it entered that city, the people there cried out, "Why have they brought the ark of the God of Israel here to kill us and our kindred?" [11]Then they, too, sent a summons to all the Philistine leaders and pleaded: "Send away the ark of the God of Israel. Send it back to its place so it does not kill us and our kindred." A deadly panic had seized the whole city, since the hand of God lay heavy upon it. [12]Those who escaped death were afflicted with tumors. Thus the outcry from the city went up to the heavens.

## CHAPTER 6

**The Ark Is Returned.** [1]The ark of the LORD had been in the land of the Philistines seven months [2]when they summoned priests and diviners to ask, "What shall we do with the ark of the LORD? Tell us what we should send back with it." [3]They replied: "If you intend to send back the ark of

the God of Israel, you must not send it alone, but must, by all means, make amends to God through a reparation offering.[†] Then you will be healed, and will learn why God continues to afflict you." [4]When asked further, "What reparation offering should be our amends to God?" they replied: "Five golden tumors and five golden mice to correspond to the number of Philistine leaders, since the same plague has struck all of you and your leaders. [5]Therefore, make images of the tumors and of the mice that are devastating your land and so give glory to the God of Israel. Perhaps then God will lift his hand from you, your gods, and your land. [6]Why should you become stubborn, the way the Egyptians and Pharaoh were stubborn? Was it not after he had dealt ruthlessly with them that the Israelites were released and departed?[l] [7]So now set to work and make a new cart. Then take two milk cows that have not borne the yoke; hitch them to the cart, but drive their calves indoors away from them.[‡m] [8]You shall next take the ark of the LORD and place it on the cart, putting the golden articles that you are offering as reparation for your guilt in a box beside it. Start it on its way, and let it go. [9]Then watch! If it goes up to Beth-shemesh[§] along the route to the LORD's territory, then it was the LORD who brought this great calamity upon us; if not, we will know that it was not the LORD's hand, but a bad turn, that struck us."

**The Ark in Beth-shemesh.** [10]They acted upon this advice. Taking two milk cows, they hitched them to the cart but shut up their calves indoors. [11]Then they placed the ark of the LORD on the cart, along with the box containing the golden mice and the images of the tumors. [12]The cows went straight for the route to Beth-shemesh and continued along this road, mooing as they went, turning neither right nor left. The Philistine leaders followed them as far as the border of Beth-shemesh. [13]The people of Beth-shemesh were harvesting the wheat in the valley. They looked up and rejoiced when they saw the ark. [14]The cart came to the field of Joshua the Beth-shemite and stopped there. At a large stone in the field, the wood of the cart was split up and the cows were offered as a burnt offering to the LORD.[n] [15]The Levites, meanwhile, had taken down the ark of God and the box beside it, with the golden articles, and had placed them on the great stone. The people of Beth-shemesh also

---

underscores Dagon's impotence and the Lord's power. The narrator relates the transfer of the ark from Ashdod to Gath and then Ekron as the progress of a conquering warrior king through the Philistine cities along the central plain. The Philistines' humiliation recalls the climax of the Samson story (Jgs 16:13–21).

*[5:6] **Tumors:** the Septuagint adds that mice, suggestive of bubonic plague, infested their fields, thus anticipating the golden mice in 6:4–5. One symptom of bubonic plague is swollen lymph nodes ("tumors").

†[6:3] **A reparation offering:** an offering to make amends for unwitting transgressions against holy things or property rights; cf. Lv 6:1–3.

‡[6:7] **But drive their calves indoors away from them:** a test to confirm the source of the Philistines' trouble. Left to their instincts, milk cows would remain near their calves rather than head for the road to Beth-shemesh.

§[6:9] **Beth-shemesh:** a border city (about twenty-four miles west of Jerusalem) between Philistine and Israelite territory.

---

j. [5:1] Jos 13:3.   k. [5:6] Ps 32:4.

l. [6:6] Ex 7:14; 8:15; 9:34.   m. [6:7] Nm 19:2; Dt 21:3; 2 Sm 6:3.
n. [6:14] 2 Sm 24:21–25.

offered other burnt offerings and sacrifices to the LORD that day.[o] [16]After witnessing this, the five Philistine leaders returned to Ekron the same day.

[17]The golden tumors the Philistines sent back as a reparation offering to the LORD were as follows: one for Ashdod, one for Gaza, one for Ashkelon, one for Gath, and one for Ekron. [18]The golden mice, however, corresponded to the number of all the cities of the Philistines belonging to the five leaders, including fortified cities and open villages.[*] The large stone on which the ark of the LORD was placed is still in the field of Joshua the Beth-shemite at the present time.[p]

**Penalty for Irreverence.** [19]The descendants of Jeconiah did not join in the celebration with the inhabitants of Beth-shemesh when they saw the ark of the LORD, and seventy of them were struck down. The people mourned over this great calamity which the LORD had inflicted upon them. [20]The men of Beth-shemesh asked, "Who can stand in the presence of the LORD, this Holy God? To whom can the ark go so that we are rid of it?" [21]They then sent messengers to the inhabitants of Kiriath-jearim, saying, "The Philistines have returned the ark of the LORD; come down and get it."

### CHAPTER 7

[1]So the inhabitants of Kiriath-jearim came for the ark of the LORD and brought it into the house of Abinadab on the hill, appointing his son Eleazar as guardian of the ark of the LORD.

**Samuel the Judge.** [2]From the day the ark came to rest in Kiriath-jearim, a long time, twenty years, elapsed, and the whole house of Israel turned to the LORD. [3]Then Samuel addressed the whole house of Israel: "If you would return to the LORD with your whole heart, remove your foreign gods and your Astartes, fix your hearts on the LORD, and serve him alone, then the LORD will deliver you from the hand of the Philistines."[q] [4]So the Israelites removed their Baals and Astartes,[†] and served the LORD alone. [5]Samuel then gave orders, "Gather all Israel to Mizpah, that I may pray to the LORD for you."[r] [6]When they had gathered at Mizpah, they drew water and poured it out[‡] on the ground before the LORD, and they fasted that day, saying, "We

have sinned against the LORD." It was at Mizpah that Samuel began to judge the Israelites.[s]

**Rout of the Philistines.** [7]When the Philistines heard that the Israelites had gathered at Mizpah, their leaders went up against Israel. Hearing this, the Israelites became afraid of the Philistines [8]and appealed to Samuel, "Do not stop crying out to the LORD our God for us, to save us from the hand of the Philistines."[t] [9]Samuel therefore took an unweaned lamb and offered it whole as a burnt offering to the LORD.[u] He cried out to the LORD for Israel, and the LORD answered him. [10]While Samuel was sacrificing the burnt offering, the Philistines drew near for battle with Israel. That day, however, the LORD thundered loudly against the Philistines, and threw them into such confusion that they were defeated by Israel.[v] [11]Thereupon the Israelites rushed out from Mizpah and pursued the Philistines, striking them down even beyond Beth-car. [12]Samuel then took a stone and placed it between Mizpah and Jeshanah; he named it Ebenezer,[§] explaining, "As far as this place the LORD has been our help." [13]Thus were the Philistines subdued, never again to enter the territory of Israel, for the hand of the LORD was against them as long as Samuel lived.[w] [14]The cities from Ekron to Gath which the Philistines had taken from Israel were restored to them. Israel also freed the territory of these cities from Philistine domination. There was also peace between Israel and the Amorites.[¶]

[15]Samuel judged Israel as long as he lived. [16]He made a yearly circuit, passing through Bethel, Gilgal and Mizpah[**] and judging Israel at each of these places. [17]Then he used to return to Ramah, for that was his home. There, too, he judged Israel and built an altar to the LORD.[x]

## II. ESTABLISHMENT OF THE MONARCHY

### CHAPTER 8

**Request for a King.** [††][1]In his old age Samuel appointed his sons judges over Israel.[y] [2]His firstborn was named Joel, his second son, Abijah;

---

*[6:18] **Open villages:** the plague devastated both fortified cities and villages, an indication of the Lord's power over the Philistines.

†[7:4] **Baals and Astartes:** a Deuteronomistic phrase; cf. Jgs 2:13; 10:6; 1 Sm 12:10. Baal and Astarte were Canaanite divinities.

‡[7:6] **Drew water and poured it out:** this ritual act does not appear elsewhere in the Old Testament. Linked with fasting and admission of sin, it seems to function as a purification ritual that washes away the guilt incurred by worshiping the Canaanite Baal and his consort Astarte. Its effectiveness is

immediately evident when the Lord thunders a response to Samuel's offering.

§[7:12] **Ebenezer:** "stone of the helper," i.e., the Lord.

¶[7:14] **The Amorites:** enemies in Transjordan. Israel is now secure, safe from external and internal threat.

**[7:16] **Bethel, Gilgal and Mizpah:** Bethel and Mizpah are located about five and eight miles north of Jerusalem respectively, in the district around Ramah, Samuel's home. Perhaps Gilgal, which has not been definitively located, was also in this area.

††[8:1–22] From this chapter on, the editors of 1 Samuel provide two and sometimes three perspectives on the same event: e.g., the selection of Saul as king is recounted in chap. 8; 10:17–24; chap. 12.

---

o. [6:15] Dt 31:25; 1 Chr 15:2.    p. [6:18] 1 Sm 7:12; Gn 31:52; Jos 24:27.    q. [7:3] 1 Sm 12:10, 20, 24; Jos 24:23; Jgs 6:6–10; 10:10–16.    r. [7:5] 1 Sm 10:17; Jgs 20:1.

s. [7:6] Jgs 20:26; Ps 22:14; Lam 2:19.    t. [7:8] Jos 24:7; Jgs 3:9, 15; 6:6; 10:15.    u. [7:9–10] 2 Sm 22:14–15; Sir 46:16–18.    v. [7:10] Ex 9:23; 2 Sm 22:14.    w. [7:13] Jgs 3:20; 8:28; 11:33.    x. [7:17] 1 Sm 9:12; 14:35.    y. [8:1] 1 Chr 6:13.

they judged at Beer-sheba. ³His sons did not follow his example, but looked to their own gain, accepting bribes and perverting justice.ᶻ ⁴Therefore all the elders of Israel assembled and went to Samuel at Ramah ⁵and said to him, "Now that you are old, and your sons do not follow your example, appoint a king over us, like all the nations, to rule us."ᵃ

⁶Samuel was displeased when they said, "Give us a king to rule us." But he prayed to the Lord. ⁷The Lord said: Listen to whatever the people say. You are not the one they are rejecting. They are rejecting me as their king.ᵇ ⁸They are acting toward you just as they have acted from the day I brought them up from Egypt to this very day, deserting me to serve other gods. ⁹Now listen to them; but at the same time, give them a solemn warning and inform them of the rights of the king who will rule them.

**The Governance of the King.** ¹⁰Samuel delivered the message of the Lord in full to those who were asking him for a king. ¹¹He told them: "The governance of the king who will rule you will be as follows: He will take your sons and assign them to his chariots and horses, and they will run before his chariot.ᶜ ¹²He will appoint from among them his commanders of thousands and of hundreds. He will make them do his plowing and harvesting and produce his weapons of war and chariotry.ᵈ ¹³He will use your daughters as perfumers, cooks, and bakers. ¹⁴He will take your best fields, vineyards, and olive groves, and give them to his servants.ᵉ ¹⁵He will tithe your crops and grape harvests to give to his officials* and his servants.ᶠ ¹⁶He will take your male and female slaves, as well as your best oxen and donkeys, and use them to do his work. ¹⁷He will also tithe your flocks. As for you, you will become his slaves.ᵍ ¹⁸On that day you will cry out because of the king whom you have chosen, but the Lord will not answer you on that day."

**Persistent Demand.** ¹⁹The people, however, refused to listen to Samuel's warning and said, "No! There must be a king over us.ʰ ²⁰We too must be like all the nations, with a king to rule us, lead us in warfare, and fight our battles." ²¹Samuel listened to all the concerns of the people and then repeated them to the Lord. ²²The Lord said: Listen to them! Appoint a king to rule over them. Then Samuel said to the people of Israel, "Return, each one of you, to your own city."†

**CHAPTER 9**

**Saul.** ¹There was a powerful man from Benjamin named Kish, who was the son of Abiel, son of Zeror, son of Becorath, son of Aphiah, a Benjaminite.ⁱ ²He had a son named Saul, who was a handsome young man. There was no other Israelite more handsome than Saul; he stood head and shoulders above the people.ʲ

**The Lost Donkeys.** ³Now the donkeys of Saul's father, Kish, had wandered off. Kish said to his son Saul, "Take one of the servants with you and go out and hunt for the donkeys." ⁴So they went through the hill country of Ephraim, and through the land of Shalishah. Not finding them there, they continued through the land of Shaalim without success. They also went through the land of Benjamin, but they failed to find the animals. ⁵When they came to the land of Zuph, Saul said to the servant who was with him, "Come, let us turn back, lest my father forget about the donkeys and become anxious about us." ⁶The servant replied, "Listen! There is a man of God in this city, a man held in high esteem; everything he says comes true. Let us go there now! Perhaps he can advise us about the journey we have undertaken." ⁷ᵏBut Saul said to his servant, "If we go, what can we offer the man? The food in our bags has run out; we have no present to give the man of God. What else do we have?" ⁸Again the servant answered Saul, "I have a quarter shekel of silver.‡ If I give that to the man of God, he will advise us about the journey." ⁹ˡ(In former times in Israel, anyone who went to consult God used to say, "Come, let us go to the seer." For the one who is now called prophet was formerly called seer.) ¹⁰Saul then said to his servant, "You are right! Come on, let us go!" So they headed toward the city where the man of God lived.

**Meeting the Young Women.** ¹¹ᵐAs they were going up the path to the city, they met some young women coming out to draw water and they asked them, "Is the seer in town?" ¹²ⁿThe young women answered, "Yes, there—straight ahead. Hurry now; just today he came to the city, because the people have a sacrifice today on the high place.§ ¹³When you enter the city, you may reach him before he goes up to the high place to eat. The people will not eat until he arrives; only after he blesses the sacrifice will the invited guests eat. Go up immediately, for you should find him right now."

**Saul Meets Samuel.** ¹⁴So they went up to the city. As they entered it—there was Samuel coming

---

*[8:15] **Officials**: lit., eunuchs. These high-ranking administrators were not necessarily emasculated.

†[8:22] **To your own city**: Samuel will later reassemble the people at Mizpah (10:17) to acclaim Saul as their king.

‡[9:8] **A quarter shekel of silver**: about a tenth of an ounce of silver.

§[9:12] **On the high place**: the local sanctuary on the top of a hill, where the sacrifice was offered and the sacrificial meal eaten.

z. [8:3] 1 Sm 2:12–17; Ex 23:8; Dt 16:19; Prv 17:23.   a. [8:5–6] Dt 17:14–15; Hos 13:10; Acts 13:21.   b. [8:7–8] 1 Sm 12:1, 12–13; Jgs 8:22–23; 10:13; 1 Kgs 9:9.   c. [8:11] 1 Sm 10:25; Dt 17:14–20; 1 Kgs 12.   d. [8:12] 2 Sm 15:1; 1 Kgs 1:5.   e. [8:14] Dt 14:22–23.   f. [8:15] 1 Sm 22:7; 1 Kgs 21:1–24; Ez 46:18.   g. [8:17] 1 Kgs 12:4.   h. [8:19] 1 Sm 10:19.

i. [9:1] 1 Sm 14:51; 1 Chr 8:33.   j. [9:2] 1 Sm 10:23; 16:12.   k. [9:7–8] Nm 22:7; 1 Kgs 14:3; 2 Kgs 4:42; 5:15; 8:8–9.   l. [9:9] Sir 46:15.   m. [9:11] Gn 24:11–14; Ex 2:16.   n. [9:12] 1 Sm 7:17; 16:2, 5; 20:6, 29; Dt 12:13; 1 Kgs 3:2, 4.

toward them on his way to the high place. [15]The day before Saul's arrival, the LORD had revealed to Samuel:[o] [16]At this time tomorrow I will send you a man from the land of Benjamin whom you are to anoint as ruler of my people Israel. He shall save my people from the hand of the Philistines. I have looked upon my people; their cry has come to me.[p] [17]When Samuel caught sight of Saul, the LORD assured him: This is the man I told you about; he shall govern my people. [18]Saul met Samuel in the gateway and said, "Please tell me where the seer lives." [19]Samuel answered Saul: "I am the seer. Go up ahead of me to the high place and eat with me today. In the morning, before letting you go, I will tell you everything on your mind. [20]As for your donkeys that were lost three days ago, do not worry about them, for they have been found. Whom should Israel want if not you and your father's family?" [21]Saul replied: "Am I not a Benjaminite, from the smallest of the tribes of Israel,[*] and is not my clan the least among the clans of the tribe of Benjamin? Why say such things to me?"[q]

**The Meal.**[†] [22]Samuel then took Saul and his servant and brought them into the room. He seated them at the head of the guests, of whom there were about thirty. [23]He said to the cook, "Bring the portion I gave you and told you to put aside." [24]So the cook took up the leg and what went with it, and placed it before Saul. Samuel said: "This is a reserved portion that is set before you. Eat, for it was kept for you until this time; I explained that I was inviting some guests." Thus Saul dined with Samuel that day. [25]When they came down from the high place into the city, a mattress was spread for Saul on the roof, [26]and he slept there.

**Saul's Anointing.** At daybreak Samuel called to Saul on the roof, "Get up, and I will send you on your way." Saul got up, and he and Samuel went outside the city together. [27]As they were approaching the edge of the town, Samuel said to Saul, "Tell the servant to go on ahead of us, but you stay here for a moment, that I may give you a word from God."

## CHAPTER 10

[1]Then, from a flask he had with him, Samuel poured oil on Saul's head and kissed him, saying: "The LORD anoints you ruler over his people Israel. You are the one who will govern the

LORD's people and save them from the power of their enemies all around them.[r]

**The Signs Foretold.** "This will be the sign[‡] for you that the LORD has anointed you ruler over his heritage: [2]When you leave me today, you will meet two men near Rachel's tomb[§] at Zelzah in the territory of Benjamin. They will say to you, 'The donkeys you went to look for have been found. Now your father is no longer worried about the donkeys, but is anxious about you and says: What shall I do about my son?'[s] [3]Farther on, when you arrive at the oak of Tabor,[¶] three men will meet you as they go up to God at Bethel; one will be bringing three young goats, another three loaves of bread, and the third a skin of wine. [4]They will greet you and offer you two elevated offerings of bread, which you should accept from them. [5]After that you will come to Gibeath-elohim, where the Philistine garrison[**] is located. As you enter that city, you will meet a band of prophets coming down from the high place. They will be preceded by lyres, tambourines, flutes, and harps, and will be in prophetic ecstasy. [6]The spirit of the LORD will rush upon you, and you will join them in their prophetic ecstasy and will become a changed man.[u] [7]When these signs have come to pass, do whatever lies to hand, because God is with you. [8]Now go down ahead of me to Gilgal, for I shall come down to you, to offer burnt offerings and to sacrifice communion offerings. Wait seven days until I come to you; I shall then tell you what you must do."[††]

**The Signs Come to Pass.** [9]As Saul turned to leave Samuel, God changed his heart. That very day all these signs came to pass.... [10][‡‡]From there they arrived at Gibeah, where a band of prophets met Saul, and the spirit of God rushed upon him, so that he joined them in their prophetic ecstasy.[w] [11]When all who had known him previously saw him in a prophetic state among the

‡[10:1] **The sign:** the role of the new ruler is confirmed by specific signs; cf. Ex 7:9.

§[10:2] Here, as in Jer 31:15, Rachel's tomb is placed at Ramah, north of Jerusalem. Later tradition understood Ephrath (Gn 35:19–20) as Bethlehem and placed the tomb farther south (Mt 2:16–18).

¶[10:3] **Oak of Tabor:** or terebinth. Such a tree often indicates a shrine.

**[10:5] **The Philistine garrison:** the Hebrew word for "garrison" has been explained alternatively to mean a stele established to mark the Philistine occupation, or an inspector or officer for the collection of taxes. **Prophetic ecstasy:** a condition of religious enthusiasm often induced by communal rituals of music and dancing.

††[10:8] By inserting this verse, with its seven days, an editor has named in the very context of Saul's anointing the condition which in a later narrative will be the grounds for the rejection of the dynastic character of Saul's kingship (13:8–15).

‡‡[10:10] An editor has abridged a longer version of this story by omitting mention of the first two signs Samuel has given (vv. 2–4).

---

*[9:21] **Smallest of the tribes of Israel:** Saul's objection is a common element in call narrative, e.g., Ex 3:11; 4:10; Jgs 6:15.

†[9:22–24] At this ritual meal, Samuel treats the youthful Saul as if he were already king. Saul receives the part of the sacrificed animal reserved for the priest and his family, perhaps the sheep's fat tail. Legal texts (Ex 29:22; Lv 3:9; 7:3–4) require the priest to burn this portion of the sheep on the altar.

---

o. [9:15] Acts 13:21.  p. [9:16] 1 Sm 10:1; Jgs 6:14.  q. [9:21] 1 Sm 15:17.

r. [10:1] 1 Sm 9:16–17; 16:13; 24:7; Jgs 9:9; 1 Kgs 1:39; Acts 13:21.
s. [10:2] Jer 31:15; Mk 14:13.  t. [10:5–6] 1 Sm 13:3; 16:13; 19:20–21.  u. [10:6] 1 Sm 11:6; 16:13; Jgs 14:6, 19; 15:14; 2 Kgs 3:15.
v. [10:8] 1 Sm 13:8; Lv 3:1.  w. [10:10] 1 Sm 19:20–24; Nm 11:25.

prophets, they said to one another, "What has happened to the son of Kish? Is Saul also among the prophets?"ˣ ¹²And someone from that district responded, "And who is their father?" Thus the saying arose, "Is Saul also among the prophets?" ¹³When he came out of the prophetic ecstasy, he went home.

**Silence About the Kingship.** ¹⁴Saul's uncle asked him and his servant, "Where have you been?" Saul replied, "Looking for the donkeys. When we could not find them, we went to Samuel." ¹⁵Saul's uncle said, "Tell me, then, what Samuel said to you." ¹⁶Saul said to his uncle, "He assured us that the donkeys had been found." But Saul told him nothing about what Samuel had said about the kingship.

**Saul Chosen King.** ¹⁷Samuel called the people together to the Lᴏʀᴅ at Mizpah.ʸ ¹⁸and addressed the Israelites: "Thus says the Lᴏʀᴅ, the God of Israel: It was I who brought Israel up from Egypt and delivered you from the power of the Egyptians and from the power of all the kingdoms that oppressed you.ᶻ ¹⁹But today you have rejected your God, who saves you from all your evils and calamities, by saying, 'No! You must appoint a king over us.' Now, therefore, take your stand before the Lᴏʀᴅ according to your tribes and families."ᵃ ²⁰So Samuel had all the tribes of Israel come forward, and the tribe of Benjamin was chosen.* ²¹Next he had the tribe of Benjamin come forward by clans, and the clan of Matri was chosen, and finally Saul, son of Kish, was chosen. But when they went to look for him, he was nowhere to be found. ²²ᵇAgain they consulted the Lᴏʀᴅ, "Is there still someone else to come forward?" The Lᴏʀᴅ answered: He is hiding among the baggage. ²³They ran to bring him from there; when he took his place among the people, he stood head and shoulders above all the people.ᶜ ²⁴Then Samuel addressed all the people, "Do you see the man whom the Lᴏʀᴅ has chosen? There is no one like him among all the people!" Then all the people shouted out, "Long live the king!"ᵈ

²⁵Samuel next explained to the people the rules of the monarchy,† wrote them in a book, and placed them before the presence of the Lᴏʀᴅ. Samuel then sent the people back to their own homes.ᵉ ²⁶Saul also went home to Gibeah, accompanied by warriors whose hearts the Lᴏʀᴅ had touched. ²⁷But some worthless people said, "How can this fellow save us?" They despised him and brought him no tribute.‡ᶠ

## CHAPTER 11

**Defeat of the Ammonites.** ¹ᵍAbout a month later, Nahash the Ammonite went up and besieged Jabesh-gilead. All the people of Jabesh begged Nahash, "Make a treaty with us, and we will serve you."ᵍ ²But Nahash the Ammonite replied, "This is my condition for making a treaty with you: I will gouge out the right eye of every man,¶ and thus bring shame on all Israel." ³The elders of Jabesh said to him: "Give us seven days to send messengers throughout the territory of Israel. If there is no one to save us, we will surrender to you." ⁴When the messengers arrived at Gibeah of Saul and reported the news in the people's hearing, they all wept aloud. ⁵Just then Saul came in from the field, behind his oxen. "Why are the people weeping?" he asked. They repeated the message of the inhabitants of Jabesh for him. ⁶As he listened to this report, the spirit of God rushed upon him and he became very angry.ʰ ⁷Taking a yoke of oxen, he cut them into pieces and sent them throughout the territory of Israel** by messengers saying, "If anyone does not come out to follow Saul and Samuel, the same thing will be done to his oxen!" The dread of the Lᴏʀᴅ came upon the people and they went forth as one.ⁱ ⁸When Saul reviewed them in Bezek,†† there were three hundred thousand Israelites and seventy thousand Judahites.

⁹To the messengers who had come he said, "Tell the inhabitants of Jabesh-gilead that tomorrow, when the sun grows hot, they will be saved." The messengers went and reported this to the inhabitants of Jabesh, and they rejoiced. ¹⁰The men of Jabesh said to Nahash, "Tomorrow we will surrender to you, and you may do with us whatever you want." ¹¹The next day, Saul arranged his troops in three companies and invaded the camp during the dawn watch. They slaughtered Ammonites until the day had gotten hot; by then the survivors were so scattered that no two of them were left together.

---

§[11:1] A text from Qumran (1QSamᵃ) introduces this chapter with the report that Nahash, king of the Ammonites, had attacked the Gadites and the Reubenites, gouging out their right eyes. Seven thousand of them had fled to Jabesh-gilead. This additional information would explain why Nahash besieged Jabesh-gilead. There is no consensus among scholars whether the Qumran text represents an original reading or a secondary expansion.

¶[11:2] **Right eye of every man:** thus rendering them incapable of military action.

**[11:7] **Throughout the territory of Israel:** Saul's gesture summons the Israelite confederacy to a coordinated response against Nahash; cf. Jgs 19:29 for a similar action. **Dread of the Lᴏʀᴅ:** often a panic that immobilizes Israel's enemies; here, however, it has the opposite effect and incites the Israelites to battle.

††[11:8] **Bezek:** probably modern Khirbet Ibziq, northeast of Shechem, on the west slope of the Jordan valley, opposite Jabesh-gilead.

---

*[10:20] **Was chosen:** probably by casting lots; cf. 14:40–42; Jos 7:14, 17.

†[10:25] **Rules of the monarchy:** a charter describing the relationship between the king and the people.

‡[10:27] **Tribute:** a gift to honor a new ruler as a pledge of one's loyalty; see Gn 32:14; Jgs 3:15; 2 Sm 8:2.

x. [10:11] 1 Sm 19:24.   y. [10:17] 1 Sm 7:5.   z. [10:18] Ex 20:2; Lv 11:45; 25:38; Nm 15:41; Dt 5:6; Jgs 6:8–9.   a. [10:19] 1 Sm 8:19.   b. [10:22] 1 Sm 30:24.   c. [10:23] 1 Sm 9:2; 16:7.   d. [10:24] 2 Sm 16:16; 1 Kgs 1:25; 2 Kgs 11:12.   e. [10:25] 1 Sm 8:11; Dt 17:14–20.   f. [10:27] 1 Sm 11:12.

g. [11:1] 1 Sm 12:12; 31:11; 2 Sm 10:2.   h. [11:6] 1 Sm 16:13; Jgs 14:6, 19; 15:14.   i. [11:7] 1 Kgs 11:30; 2 Kgs 13:18.

**Saul Accepted as King.** <sup>12</sup>The people then said to Samuel: "Who questioned whether Saul should rule over us? Hand them over and we will put them to death."<sup>j</sup> <sup>13</sup>But Saul objected, "No one will be put to death this day, for today the LORD has rescued Israel."<sup>k</sup> <sup>14</sup>Samuel said to the people, "Come, let us go to Gilgal to renew the kingship there." <sup>15</sup>So all the people went to Gilgal, and there they made Saul king in the LORD's presence. They also sacrificed communion offerings there before the LORD, and Saul and all the Israelites rejoiced greatly.

## CHAPTER 12†

**Samuel's Integrity.** <sup>1</sup>Samuel addressed all Israel: "I have granted your request in every respect," he said. "I have set a king over you<sup>l</sup> <sup>2</sup>and now the king will lead you. As for me, I am old and gray, and my sons are among you. I was your leader from my youth to the present day. <sup>3</sup>Here I stand! Answer me in the presence of the LORD and the LORD's anointed. Whose ox have I taken? Whose donkey have I taken? Whom have I cheated? Whom have I wronged? From whom have I accepted a bribe and shut my eyes because of it? I will make restitution to you."<sup>m</sup> <sup>4</sup>They replied, "You have neither cheated us, nor oppressed us, nor accepted anything from anyone." <sup>5</sup>So he said to them, "The LORD is witness against you this day, and the LORD's anointed is witness, that you have found nothing in my possession." "The LORD is witness," they said.

**Samuel Admonishes the People.** <sup>6</sup>Samuel continued: "The LORD is witness, who appointed Moses and Aaron and brought your ancestors up from the land of Egypt.<sup>n</sup> <sup>7</sup>Now take your stand, that I may judge you in the presence of the LORD according to all the gracious acts that the LORD has done for you and your ancestors. <sup>8</sup>When Jacob and his sons went to Egypt and the Egyptians oppressed them, your ancestors cried out to the LORD. The LORD then sent Moses and Aaron to bring them out of Egypt and settled them in this place.<sup>o</sup> <sup>9</sup>But they forgot the LORD their God; and so the LORD sold them into the power of Sisera, the captain of the army of Hazor, the power of the Philistines, and

the power of the king of Moab, who made war against them.<sup>p</sup> <sup>10</sup>They cried out to the LORD and said, 'We have sinned because we abandoned the LORD and served the Baals and Astartes. Now deliver us from the power of our enemies, and we will serve you.'<sup>q</sup> <sup>11</sup>The LORD sent Jerubbaal, Barak, Jephthah, and Samuel; he delivered you from the power of your enemies on every side, so that you could live in security.<sup>r</sup> <sup>12</sup>Yet, when you saw Nahash, king of the Ammonites, advancing against you, you said to me, 'No! A king must rule us,' even though the LORD your God is your king.<sup>s</sup>

**Warnings for People and King.** <sup>13</sup>"Now here is the king you chose. See! The LORD has given you a king.<sup>t</sup> <sup>14</sup>If you fear and serve the LORD, if you listen to the voice of the LORD and do not rebel against the LORD's command, if both you and the king, who rules over you, follow the LORD your God—well and good. <sup>15</sup>But if you do not listen to the voice of the LORD and if you rebel against the LORD's command, the hand of the LORD will be against you and your king. <sup>16</sup>Now then, stand ready to witness the great marvel the LORD is about to accomplish before your eyes. <sup>17</sup>Are we not in the harvest time for wheat?<sup>§</sup> Yet I will call upon the LORD, and he will send thunder and rain. Thus you will see and understand how great an evil it is in the eyes of the LORD that you have asked for a king."<sup>u</sup> <sup>18</sup>Samuel called upon the LORD, and the LORD sent thunder and rain that day.

**Assistance Promised.** Then all the people feared the LORD and Samuel. <sup>19</sup>They said to Samuel, "Pray to the LORD your God for us, your servants, that we may not die for having added to all our other sins the evil of asking for a king." <sup>20</sup>"Do not fear," Samuel answered them. "You have indeed committed all this evil! Yet do not turn from the LORD, but serve him with your whole heart. <sup>21</sup>Do not turn aside to gods who are nothing,<sup>¶</sup> who cannot act and deliver. They are nothing." <sup>22</sup>For the sake of his own great name** the LORD will not abandon his people, since the LORD has decided to make you his people.<sup>w</sup> <sup>23</sup>As for me, far be it from me to sin against the LORD by ceasing to pray for you and to teach you the good and right way.<sup>x</sup> <sup>24</sup>But you must

---

*[11:12–14] With the defeat of the Ammonites, Saul demonstrates his ability to command Israel's army and defend the land. At Gilgal, Saul's kingship is ratified; ironically, he loses his kingship at the same place (13:7).

†[12:1–25] This chapter narrates the transition from the leadership of the judges to the rule of the king. The Deuteronomistic redactor has Samuel contrast the wickedness of Israel's ancestors with the Lord's gracious deliverance (vv. 6–12). The people realize that their demand for a king has compounded that wickedness. Now that the Lord has given them a king, Samuel urges the people and their king to serve the Lord wholeheartedly (vv. 13–25).

‡[12:1–5] Samuel's upright leadership is set in sharp contrast to the despotic powers of the king described in chap. 8. By their testimony, the people witness to Samuel's righteousness.

§[12:17] **Harvest time for wheat**: in May–June. Since this is a period of little or no rainfall in Israel, the people will not mistake the sign for a natural phenomenon.

¶[12:21] **Gods who are nothing**: Hebrew *tohu*, lit., "emptiness," cf. Gn 1:2 (. . . *webohu*); here, idols without power or substance, as in Is 41:29.

**[12:22] **His own great name**: were the Lord to abandon his people, even if they abandon him, he would diminish his stature or reputation in the divine council or among the nations (e.g., Ez 20:9). Throughout the Old Testament the Lord is encouraged to deliver Israel, despite its evil, "for the sake of his name."

j. [11:12] 1 Sm 10:27.   k. [11:13] 2 Sm 19:23.   l. [12:1] 1 Sm 8:7, 9, 22.   m. [12:3] Ex 20:17; 23:8; Nm 16:15; Dt 16:19; Sir 46:19.   n. [12:6] Mi 6:4.   o. [12:8] Gn 46:5; Ex 1:11; 2:23–25.

p. [12:9] Jgs 3:12–15; 4:2–3; 10:7; 13:1.   q. [12:10] 1 Sm 7:3–4; Jgs 10:10.   r. [12:11] Jgs 6:14, 32; 11:1.   s. [12:12] 1 Sm 8:6–7, 19; 11:1–2; Jgs 8:23.   t. [12:13] 1 Sm 8:7.   u. [12:17] Ex 9:23, 28–30; 1 Kgs 18:1.   v. [12:21] Dt 32:37–39; Is 41:29; 44:9–10.   w. [12:22] Ex 18:10; Dt 4:34; Jos 7:9; Is 48:9; Jer 14:21; Dn 3:34.   x. [12:23] Ex 32:11.

fear the Lord and serve him faithfully with all your heart, for you have seen the great things the Lord has done among you. [25]If instead you continue to do evil, both you and your king shall be swept away."

## III. SAUL AND DAVID

### CHAPTER 13

[1][Saul was . . . years old when he became king and he reigned . . . -two years over Israel.][*]

**Saul Offers Sacrifice.** [2]Saul chose three thousand of Israel, of whom two thousand remained with him in Michmash and in the hill country of Bethel, and one thousand were with Jonathan in Gibeah of Benjamin. He sent the rest of the army back to their tents. [3]Now Jonathan struck the Philistine garrison[†] in Gibeah, and the Philistines got word of it. Then Saul sounded the horn throughout the land, saying, "Let the Hebrews hear!"[y] [4]Then all Israel heard the report, "Saul has struck the garrison of the Philistines! Israel has become odious to the Philistines!" Then the army was called up to Saul in Gilgal. [5]The Philistines also assembled for battle against Israel, with thirty thousand chariots,[‡] six thousand horsemen, and foot soldiers as numerous as the sand on the seashore.[z] They came up and encamped in Michmash, east of Beth-aven.[a] [6]When the soldiers saw they were in danger because the army was hardpressed, they hid themselves in caves, thickets, rocks, caverns, and cisterns. [7]Other Hebrews crossed the Jordan into the land of Gad and Gilead. Saul, however, held out in Gilgal, all his army trembling in fear behind him.[b] [8]He waited seven days, until the appointed time Samuel had set, but Samuel did not come, and the army deserted Saul.[b] [9]He then said, "Bring me the burnt offering and communion offerings!" Then he sacrificed the burnt offering.

**King Saul Reproved.** [10]As he finished sacrificing the burnt offering, there came Samuel! So Saul went out toward him in order to greet him. [11]Samuel asked him, "What have you done?" Saul explained: "When I saw that the army was deserting me and you did not come

on the appointed day, and that the Philistines were assembling at Michmash, [12]I said to myself, 'Now the Philistines will come down against me at Gilgal, and I have not yet sought the Lord's blessing.' So I thought I should sacrifice the burnt offering." [13]Samuel replied to Saul: "You have acted foolishly! Had you kept the command the Lord your God gave you, the Lord would now establish your kingship in Israel forever; [14]but now your kingship shall not endure. The Lord has sought out a man after his own heart[*] to appoint as ruler over his people because you did not observe what the Lord commanded you."[c]

**Philistine Invasion.** [15]Then Samuel set out from Gilgal and went his own way; but what was left of the army went up after Saul to meet the soldiers, going from Gilgal to Gibeah of Benjamin. Saul then counted the soldiers he had with him, about six hundred.[d] [16]Saul, his son Jonathan, and the soldiers they had with them were now occupying Geba of Benjamin, and the Philistines were encamped at Michmash. [17]Meanwhile, raiders left the camp of the Philistines in three bands.[e] One band took the Ophrah road toward the district of Shual; [18]another turned in the direction of Beth-horon; and the third took the road for Geba that overlooks the Valley of the Hyenas toward the desert.

**Disarmament of Israel.**[**] [19]Not a single smith was to be found anywhere in Israel, for the Philistines had said, "Otherwise the Hebrews will make swords or spears."[f] [20]All Israel, therefore, had to go down to the Philistines to sharpen their plowshares, mattocks, axes, and sickles. [21]The price for the plowshares and mattocks was two thirds of a shekel, and a third of a shekel for sharpening the axes and for setting the oxgoads. [22]And so on the day of battle neither sword nor spear could be found in the hand of any of the soldiers with Saul or Jonathan. Only Saul and his son Jonathan had them.

**Jonathan's Exploit.** [23]An outpost of the Philistines had pushed forward to the pass of Michmash.[g]

### CHAPTER 14

[1]One day Jonathan, son of Saul, said to his armor-bearer, "Come, let us go over to the Philistine outpost on the other side." But he did not inform his father—[h] [2]Saul was sitting under the pomegranate tree in Migron on the outskirts of Gibeah; with him were about six hundred men.

---

*[13:1] A formula like that of 2 Sm 5:4 was introduced here at some time; but the age of Saul when he became king remains a blank, and the two years assigned for his reign in the Masoretic text cannot be correct. Acts 13:21 offers the round number of forty years.

†[13:3–4] **The Philistine garrison**: see note on 10:5. **Let the Hebrews hear**: a different reading of these verses, based on the Greek, would read: "And the Philistines heard that the Hebrews (or: the slaves) had revolted. Saul in the meantime sounded the trumpet throughout all the land (v. 4), and all Israel heard that Saul. . . ."

‡[13:5] **Thirty thousand chariots**: some Greek manuscripts read "three thousand chariots."

§[13:7–15] These verses, like 10:8, anticipate the rejection of Saul; a different occasion and motivation for this are given in chap. 15 and 28:17–18.

¶[13:14] **After his own heart**: i.e., of his choosing, for his purpose. While the verse undoubtedly refers to David, it concerns the Lord's decision to continue the kingship, even though he has rejected Saul, by selecting the heir to Saul's throne.

**[13:19–22] These details emphasize the Philistines' military power and superior technology, a reminder that an Israelite victory depends on God.

---

y. [13:3] 1 Sm 14:1–15; Jgs 3:27; 6:34; 2 Sm 20:1–2.    z. [13:5] Gn 22:17; 41:49; Jgs 7:12.    a. [13:5] 1 Sm 14:22.    b. [13:8] 1 Sm 10:8.
c. [13:14] 1 Sm 15:28; 25:30; 2 Sm 7:15–16; Ps 78:70; Acts 13:22.
d. [13:15] 1 Sm 14:2.    e. [13:17] 1 Sm 14:15.    f. [13:19] Jgs 5:8.
g. [13:23] 1 Sm 14:15.    h. [14:1] 1 Sm 13:3.

[3]Ahijah, son of Ahitub, brother of Ichabod, the son of Phinehas, son of Eli, the priest of the LORD at Shiloh, was wearing the ephod—nor did the soldiers know that Jonathan had gone.[i] [4]Flanking the ravine through which Jonathan intended to cross to the Philistine outpost were rocky crags on each side, one named Bozez and the other Seneh. [5]One crag was to the north, toward Michmash; the other to the south, toward Geba. [6]Jonathan said to his armor-bearer: "Come, let us go over to that outpost of the uncircumcised. Perhaps the LORD will help us, because it is no more difficult for the LORD to grant victory by means of a few than it is by means of many."[j] [7]His armor-bearer replied, "Do whatever you think best; I am with you in whatever you decide." [8]Jonathan continued: "When we cross over to those men, we will be visible to them. [9]If they say to us, 'Stay there until we can come to you,' we will stop where we are; we will not go up to them. [10]But if they say, 'Come up to us,' we will go up, because the LORD has delivered them into our hand. That will be our sign."[k] [11]When the two of them came into the view of the Philistine outpost, the Philistines remarked, "Look, some Hebrews[†] are coming out of the holes where they have been hiding." [12]The men of the outpost called to Jonathan and his armor-bearer. "Come up here," they said, "and we will teach you a lesson." So Jonathan said to his armor-bearer, "Climb up after me, for the LORD has delivered them into the hand of Israel." [13]Jonathan clambered up with his armor-bearer behind him. As the Philistines fell before Jonathan, his armor-bearer, who followed him, would finish them off. [14]In this first attack Jonathan and his armor-bearer killed about twenty men within half a furlong. [15]Then terror spread through the camp and the countryside; all the soldiers in the outpost and in the raiding parties shuddered in terror. The earth shook with an awesome shuddering.[‡l]

**Rout of the Philistines.** [16]Saul's sentinels in Gibeah of Benjamin saw that the enemy camp had scattered and were running in all directions. [17]Saul said to those around him, "Count the troops and find out if any of us are missing." When they had taken the count, they found Jonathan and his armor-bearer missing. [18]Saul then said to Ahijah, "Bring the ephod here." (Ahijah was wearing the ephod before the Israelites at that time.) [19]While Saul was speaking to the priest, the uproar in the Philistine camp kept increasing. So he said to the priest, "Withdraw your hand." [20]And Saul and all his men rallied and rushed into the fight, where the Philistines, wholly confused, were thrusting swords at one another.[m] [21]The Hebrews who had previously sided with the Philistines and had gone up with them to their camp turned to join the Israelites under Saul and Jonathan.[n] [22]Likewise, all the Israelites who were hiding in the hill country of Ephraim, hearing that the Philistines were fleeing, kept after them in the battle.[o] [23§]Thus the LORD saved Israel that day.

**Saul's Oath.** The battle continued past Bethaven. [24]Even though the Israelites were exhausted that day, Saul laid an oath on them, saying, "Cursed be the one who takes food before evening, before I am able to avenge myself on my enemies." So none of the people tasted food. [25]Now there was a honeycomb lying on the ground, [26]and when the soldiers came to the comb the honey was flowing; yet no one raised a hand from it to his mouth, because the people feared the oath.

**Violation of the Oath.** [27]Jonathan, who had not heard that his father had put the people under oath, thrust out the end of the staff he was holding and dipped it into the honeycomb. Then he raised it to his mouth and his eyes brightened. [28]At this, one of the soldiers spoke up: "Your father put the people under a strict oath, saying, 'Cursed be the one who takes food today!' As a result the people are weakened." [29p]Jonathan replied: "My father brings trouble to the land. Look how bright my eyes are because I had this little taste of honey. [30]What is more, if the army had eaten freely of the enemy's plunder when they came across it today, surely the slaughter of the Philistines would have been the greater by now!"

**Consuming the Blood.** [31]After the Philistines were routed that day from Michmash to Aijalon, the people were completely exhausted. [32]So the army pounced upon the plunder and took sheep, oxen, and calves, slaughtering them on the ground and eating the meat with the blood in it.[q] [33]Informed that the army was sinning against the LORD by eating the meat with blood in it, Saul said: "You have broken faith. Roll a large stone here for me." [34]He continued: "Mingle with the people and tell each of them, 'Bring an ox or sheep to me. Slaughter them here and then eat. But you must not sin against the LORD by eating meat with blood in it.'" So that night they all brought whatever oxen they had seized, and they slaughtered them there; [35]and

---

*[14:10] **That will be our sign:** Jonathan acknowledges that the battle is in God's hands.

†[14:11] **Hebrews:** while this term is often used by foreigners of Israelites, in this verse it seems to be a derogatory epithet for soldiers who deserted Saul's army while he was waiting for Samuel to arrive in Gilgal.

‡[14:15] **Awesome shuddering:** lit., "shuddering caused by God"; the panic in the Philistine camp is the work of Israel's warrior God.

§[14:23] The victory apparently cleared the Philistines off the main ridge of mountains in the territories of Benjamin and Ephraim.

i. [14:3] 1 Sm 2:28; 4:21; 14:18; 23:9; 30:7.    j. [14:6] 1 Sm 17:26, 36, 47; Jgs 14:3; Sir 39:18; 1 Mc 3:19.    k. [14:10] Jos 8:1; 10:8; Jgs 12:3.    l. [14:15] 2 Sm 22:8; Jl 2:10–11.

m. [14:20] Jgs 7:22.    n. [14:21] 1 Sm 29:4.    o. [14:22] 1 Sm 13:6.    p. [14:29] Jos 7:25; 1 Kgs 18:17–18.    q. [14:32] 1 Sm 15:19, 21; Gn 4:9; Lv 3:17; 7:26–27; 17:10–14; Acts 15:20, 29.

Saul built an altar to the LORD—this was the first time he built an altar to the LORD.[r]

**Jonathan in Danger of Death.** [36]Then Saul said, "Let us go down in pursuit of the Philistines by night, to plunder them until daybreak and leave no one alive." They replied, "Do what you think best." But the priest said, "Let us consult God." [37]So Saul inquired of God: "Shall I go down in pursuit of the Philistines? Will you deliver them into the hand of Israel?" But he received no answer on this occasion.[s] [38]"All officers of the army," Saul announced, "come forward. Find out how this sin was committed today. [39]As the LORD lives who has given victory to Israel, even if my son Jonathan has committed it, he shall surely die!" But none of the people answered him. [40]So he said to all Israel, "Stand on one side, and my son Jonathan and I will stand on the other." The people responded, "Do what you think best."[t] [41]And Saul said to the LORD, the God of Israel: "Why did you not answer your servant this time? If the blame for this resides in me or my son Jonathan, LORD, God of Israel, respond with Urim; but if this guilt is in your people Israel, respond with Thummim.*" Jonathan and Saul were designated, and the people went free.[u] [42]Saul then said, "Cast lots between me and my son Jonathan." And Jonathan was designated. [43]Saul said to Jonathan, "Tell me what you have done." Jonathan replied, "I only tasted a little honey from the end of the staff I was holding. Am I to die for this?" [44]Saul declared, "May God do thus to me, and more, if you do not indeed die, Jonathan!"[v]

**Rescue of Jonathan.** [45]But the soldiers protested to Saul: "Is Jonathan to die, the man who won this great victory for Israel? This must not be! As the LORD lives, not a single hair of his head shall fall to the ground, for God was with him in what he did today!" Thus the soldiers rescued† Jonathan and he did not die.[w] [46]After that Saul gave up the pursuit of the Philistines, who returned to their own territory.

**Saul's Victories.** [47]After taking possession of the kingship over Israel, Saul waged war on its enemies all around—Moab, the Ammonites, Edom, the kings of Zobah, and the Philistines. Wherever he turned, he was successful[x] [48]and fought bravely. He defeated Amalek and delivered Israel from the hand of those who were plundering them.[y]

**Saul's Family.** [49]The sons of Saul were Jonathan, Ishvi, and Malchishua; the name of his firstborn daughter was Merob; the name of the younger was Michal.[z] [50]The name of Saul's wife was Ahinoam, daughter of Ahimaaz. The name of his general was Abner, son of Ner, Saul's uncle; [51]Kish, Saul's father, and Ner, Abner's father, were sons of Abiel.[a]

[52]There was heavy fighting with the Philistines during Saul's lifetime. Whenever Saul saw any strong or brave man, he took him into his service.

## CHAPTER 15‡

**Disobedience of Saul.** [1]Samuel said to Saul: "It was I the LORD sent to anoint you king over his people Israel. Now, therefore, listen to the message of the LORD.[b] [2]Thus says the LORD of hosts: I will punish what Amalek did to the Israelites when he barred their way as they came up from Egypt.[c] [3]Go, now, attack Amalek, and put under the ban§ everything he has. Do not spare him; kill men and women, children and infants, oxen and sheep, camels and donkeys."[d]

[4]Saul alerted the army, and at Telaim reviewed two hundred thousand foot soldiers and ten thousand men of Judah.¶ [5]Saul went to the city of Amalek and set up an ambush in the wadi. [6]He warned the Kenites: "Leave Amalek, turn aside and come down so I will not have to destroy you with them, for you were loyal to the Israelites when they came up from Egypt."** After the Kenites left, [7]Saul routed Amalek from Havilah to the approaches of Shur, on the frontier of Egypt.[f] [8]He took Agag, king of Amalek, alive, but the rest of the people he destroyed by the sword, putting them under the ban. [9]He and his troops spared Agag and the best of the fat sheep and oxen, and the lambs. They refused to put under the ban anything that was worthwhile, destroying only what was worthless and of no account.

**Samuel Rebukes Saul.** [10]Then the word of the LORD came to Samuel: [11]I regret having made Saul king, for he has turned from me and has not kept my command. At this Samuel grew angry and cried out to the LORD all night.[g] [12]Early

---

‡[15:1–35] The rejection of Saul sets the stage for the remainder of 1 Samuel. The audience knows that, in the ensuing struggle between David and Saul, David will triumph as king.

§[15:3] **Put under the ban:** this terminology mandates that all traces of the Amalekites (people, cities, animals, etc.) be exterminated. No plunder could be seized for personal use. In the light of Dt 20:16–18, this injunction would eliminate any tendency toward syncretism. The focus of this chapter is that Saul fails to execute this order.

¶[15:4] The numbers here are not realistic; compare 14:2.

**[15:6] The Kenites honored the terms of an alliance with Israel.

---

*[14:41] **Urim . . . Thummim:** objects, one representing a positive response and the other a negative response, kept in the front pocket of the priest's ephod, a garment worn as a breastplate, and used to ascertain God's will in certain instances, e.g., whether Saul should help rout the Philistines. Saul consults the priest but is too impatient to finish the consultation and hurries impulsively into battle.

†[14:45] **Rescued:** the Hebrew word used is that for the "redemption" of the firstborn (Ex 13:13–15).

---

r. [14:35] 1 Sm 7:17; Jgs 6:24.   s. [14:37] 1 Sm 28:6, 15.   t. [14:40] Jos 7:13–15.   u. [14:41] 1 Sm 10:20; 28:6; Ex 28:30; Dt 33:8.   v. [14:44] 1 Sm 3:17; Ru 1:17.   w. [14:45] 2 Sm 14:11; 1 Kgs 1:52.   x. [14:47] 2 Sm 1:22; 8:2–5.   y. [14:48] 1 Sm 15:7.

z. [14:49] 1 Sm 18:20, 25; 31:2; 1 Chr 8:33; 9:39; 10:2.   a. [14:51] 1 Sm 9:1.   b. [15:1] Jos 3:9; 2 Kgs 20:16; Is 28:14.   c. [15:2] Ex 17:8–10, 16; Dt 25:17–19.   d. [15:3] 1 Sm 27:8; 30:17; Ex 17:16; Nm 24:20; Jos 6:17.   e. [15:6] Nm 24:21.   f. [15:7] 1 Sm 27:8.   g. [15:11] 1 Sm 15:35; Gn 6:6–7.

in the morning he went to meet Saul, but was informed that Saul had gone to Carmel, where he set up a monument in his own honor, and that on his return he had gone down to Gilgal. [13]When Samuel came to him, Saul greeted him: "The LORD bless you! I have kept the command of the LORD." [14]But Samuel asked, "What, then, is this bleating of sheep that comes to my ears, the lowing of oxen that I hear?" [15]Saul replied: "They were brought from Amalek. The people spared the best sheep and oxen to sacrifice to the LORD, your God; but the rest we destroyed, putting them under the ban." [16]Samuel said to Saul: "Stop! Let me tell you what the LORD said to me last night." "Speak!" he replied. [17]Samuel then said: "Though little in your own eyes, are you not chief of the tribes of Israel? The LORD anointed you king of Israel[h] [18]and sent you on a mission, saying: Go and put the sinful Amalekites under a ban of destruction. Fight against them until you have exterminated them.[i] [19]Why then have you disobeyed the LORD? You have pounced on the spoil, thus doing what was evil in the LORD's sight."[j] [20]Saul explained to Samuel: "I did indeed obey the LORD and fulfill the mission on which the LORD sent me. I have brought back Agag, the king of Amalek, and, carrying out the ban, I have destroyed the Amalekites. [21]But from the spoil the army took sheep and oxen, the best of what had been banned, to sacrifice to the LORD your God in Gilgal."[k] [22]But Samuel said:

"Does the LORD delight in burnt offerings
    and sacrifices
        as much as in obedience to the
            LORD's command?
Obedience is better than sacrifice,
    to listen, better than the fat of rams.[*]
[23] For a sin of divination is rebellion,
    and arrogance, the crime of idolatry.
Because you have rejected the word of the
        LORD,
    the LORD in turn has rejected you
        as king."[m]

**Rejection of Saul.** [24]Saul admitted to Samuel: "I have sinned, for I have transgressed the command of the LORD and your instructions. I feared the people and obeyed them.[n] [25]Now forgive my sin, and return with me, that I may worship the LORD." [26]But Samuel said to Saul, "I will not return with you, because you rejected the word of the LORD and the LORD has rejected you as king of Israel."[o] [27]As Samuel turned to

go, Saul seized a loose end of his garment, and it tore off.[p] [28]So Samuel said to him: "The LORD has torn the kingdom of Israel from you this day, and has given it to a neighbor of yours, who is better than you.[q] [29]The Glory of Israel neither deceives nor repents,[†] for he is not a mortal who repents."[r] [30]But Saul answered: "I have sinned, yet honor me now before the elders of my people and before Israel. Return with me that I may worship the LORD your God." [31]And so Samuel returned with him, and Saul worshiped the LORD.

**Samuel Executes Agag.** [32]Afterward Samuel commanded, "Bring Agag, king of Amalek, to me." Agag came to him struggling and saying, "So it is bitter death!" [33]And Samuel said,

"As your sword has made women
        childless,
    so shall your mother be childless
        among women."

Then he cut Agag to pieces before the LORD in Gilgal.[s] [34]Samuel departed for Ramah, while Saul went up to his home in Gibeah of Saul. [35]Never again, as long as he lived, did Samuel see Saul. Yet he grieved over Saul, because the LORD repented that he had made him king of Israel.[t]

## CHAPTER 16

**Samuel Is Sent to Bethlehem.** [1][u]The LORD said to Samuel: How long will you grieve for Saul, whom I have rejected as king of Israel? Fill your horn with oil, and be on your way. I am sending you to Jesse of Bethlehem, for from among his sons I have decided on a king.[‡] [2]But Samuel replied: "How can I go? Saul will hear of it and kill me." To this the LORD answered: Take a heifer along and say, "I have come to sacrifice to the LORD." [3]Invite Jesse to the sacrifice, and I myself will tell you what to do; you are to anoint for me the one I point out to you.[v]

**Samuel Anoints David.** [4]Samuel did as the LORD had commanded him. When he entered Bethlehem, the elders of the city came trembling to meet him and asked, "Is your visit peaceful, O seer?" [5]He replied: "Yes! I have come to sacrifice to the LORD. So purify yourselves and celebrate with me today." He also had Jesse and his sons purify themselves and invited them to

---

†[15:29] **Nor repents:** the apparent contradiction between this verse and vv. 11, 35 leads some scholars to consider it a gloss (cf. Nm 23:19). However, this phrase can be understood to underscore the definitive character of Samuel's declaration that Saul has lost the kingship.

‡[16:1] David is anointed two more times after Saul's death (2 Sm 2:4; 5:3). In 17:28, his brother Eliab is not aware of David's selection. These repetitions and inconsistencies reflect the final editor's use of multiple sources.

---

*[15:22] Samuel's reprimand echoes that of the prophets. Cultic practice is meaningless, even hypocritical, unless accompanied by an attentiveness to God's will.

---

h. [15:17] 1 Sm 9:21.  i. [15:18] 1 Sm 28:18.  j. [15:19] 1 Sm 14:32.  k. [15:21] Lv 27:28.  l. [15:22] Prv 21:3; Hos 6:6; Am 5:21–25; Zec 10:2; Mt 9:13; 12:7; Heb 10:9.  m. [15:23] Dt 18:10.  n. [15:24] 1 Sm 26:21.  o. [15:26] 1 Kgs 11:11, 30–31.

p. [15:27] 1 Sm 24:6; 1 Kgs 11:29–31.  q. [15:28] 1 Sm 28:17; 2 Sm 7:15–16.  r. [15:29] Nm 23:19.  s. [15:33] Ex 21:23; Jgs 8:21.  t. [15:35] 1 Sm 28:15.  u. [16:1] Ru 4:17–22; 1 Kgs 1:39; 1 Chr 11:3; Is 11:1; Mt 2:6; Lk 2:4.  v. [16:3] 1 Sm 9:13, 22, 24.

the sacrifice.[w] [6]As they came, he looked at Eliab and thought, "Surely the anointed is here before the LORD." [7]But the LORD said to Samuel: Do not judge from his appearance or from his lofty stature, because I have rejected him. God does not see as a mortal, who sees the appearance. The LORD looks into the heart.[x] [8]Then Jesse called Abinadab and presented him before Samuel, who said, "The LORD has not chosen him." [9]Next Jesse presented Shammah, but Samuel said, "The LORD has not chosen this one either." [10]In the same way Jesse presented seven sons before Samuel, but Samuel said to Jesse, "The LORD has not chosen any one of these." [11]Then Samuel asked Jesse, "Are these all the sons you have?" Jesse replied, "There is still the youngest, but he is tending the sheep." Samuel said to Jesse, "Send for him; we will not sit down to eat until he arrives here."[z] [12]Jesse had the young man brought to them. He was ruddy, a youth with beautiful eyes, and good looking. The LORD said: There—anoint him, for this is the one![a] [13]Then Samuel, with the horn of oil in hand, anointed him in the midst of his brothers, and from that day on, the spirit of the LORD rushed upon David. Then Samuel set out for Ramah.[b]

**David Wins Saul's Approval.** [14] *c*The spirit of the LORD had departed from Saul, and he was tormented by an evil spirit from the LORD. [15]So the servants of Saul said to him: "Look! An evil spirit from God is tormenting you. [16]If your lordship will order it, we, your servants here attending to you, will look for a man skilled in playing the harp. When the evil spirit from God comes upon you, he will play and you will feel better." [17]Saul then told his servants, "Find me a good harpist and bring him to me." [18]*d*One of the servants spoke up: "I have observed that a son of Jesse of Bethlehem is a skillful harpist. He is also a brave warrior, an able speaker, and a handsome young man. The LORD is certainly with him."

**David Made Armor-Bearer.** [19]Accordingly, Saul dispatched messengers to ask Jesse to send him his son David, who was with the flock. [20]Then Jesse took five loaves of bread, a skin of wine, and a young goat, and sent them to Saul with his son David.[e] [21]Thus David came to Saul and entered his service. Saul became very fond of him and made him his armor-bearer.[f] [22]Saul sent Jesse the message, "Let David stay in my service, for he meets with my approval." [23]Whenever the spirit from God came upon Saul, David would take the harp and play, and Saul would be relieved and feel better, for the evil spirit would leave him.

## CHAPTER 17

**The Challenge of Goliath.** [1]The Philistines rallied their forces for battle at Socoh in Judah and camped between Socoh and Azekah at Ephes-dammim. [2]Saul and the Israelites rallied and camped in the valley of the Elah, drawing up their battle line to meet the Philistines. [3]The Philistines were stationed on one hill and the Israelites on an opposite hill, with a valley between them.

[4]A champion named Goliath of Gath came out from the Philistine camp; he was six cubits and a span[†] tall. [5]He had a bronze helmet on his head and wore a bronze breastplate of scale armor weighing five thousand shekels, [6]bronze greaves, and had a bronze scimitar slung from his shoulders. [7]The shaft of his javelin was like a weaver's beam, and its iron head weighed six hundred shekels.[‡] His shield-bearer went ahead of him.[g] [8]He stood and shouted to the ranks of Israel: "Why come out in battle formation? I am a Philistine, and you are Saul's servants. Choose one of your men, and have him come down to me. [9]If he beats me in combat and kills me, we will be your vassals; but if I beat him and kill him, you shall be our vassals and serve us." [10]The Philistine continued: "I defy the ranks of Israel today. Give me a man and let us fight together." [11]When Saul and all Israel heard this challenge of the Philistine, they were stunned and terrified.

**David Comes to the Camp.** [§] [12]David was the son of an Ephrathite named Jesse from Bethlehem in Judah who had eight sons. In the days of Saul Jesse was old and well on in years.[h] [13]The three oldest sons of Jesse had followed Saul to war; the names of these three sons who had gone off to war were Eliab the firstborn; Abinadab the second; and Shammah the third. [14]David was the youngest. While the three oldest had joined Saul, [15]David would come and go from Saul's presence to tend his father's sheep at Bethlehem.[i]

---

*[16:14–23] These verses explain Saul's loss of divine favor and David's rise to power. By approving the young man, Saul identifies David as his legitimate successor. Of the two traditions in the Hebrew text about David's entry into Saul's service, 14–23; 17:1–11, 32–54. **An evil spirit from the LORD:** Saul's erratic behavior is attributed to a change in the Lord's relationship with him. Cf. Jgs 9:23, where the Lord puts an evil spirit between Abimelech and the citizens of Shechem.

w. [16:5] 1 Sm 9:12–13; 20:26; Ex 19:10; Jb 1:5.   x. [16:7] 1 Sm 10:23–24; 1 Kgs 11:4; 1 Chr 28:9; Prv 15:11; Jer 17:10; 20:12; Lk 16:15; Acts 1:24.   y. [16:8–11] 1 Sm 17:12–13; 1 Chr 2:13–15.   z. [16:11] 1 Sm 17:15, 28, 34; 2 Sm 7:8; Ps 78:70–71.   a. [16:12] 1 Sm 9:2.   b. [16:13] 1 Sm 10:6; 11:6; Jgs 3:10; 9:9; Sir 46:13.   c. [16:14] 1 Sm 18:10–11.   d. [16:18] 1 Sm 18:12, 14, 28; 2 Sm 5:10; 17:8; Jn 3:2.   e. [16:20] 1 Sm 9:7–8; 10:3–4; 16:1; 17:17–19.

†[17:4] **Six cubits and a span:** about nine feet nine inches (a cubit equals about eighteen inches; a span equals about eight inches). The Greek text and 4QSam[a] read: "four cubits and a span" (six feet nine inches). The description of the Philistine's might and his powerful weapons contrasts with the picture of the youthful David who trusts in God.

‡[17:7] **Six hundred shekels:** over fifteen pounds.

§[17:12–31] Here the final editor begins an alternative account of David's encounter with the Philistine hero, which continues in vv. 50–51 and concludes in 17:55–18:5.

f. [16:21] 1 Sm 18:2.   g. [17:7] 2 Sm 21:19; 1 Chr 11:23; 20:5.   h. [17:12] 1 Sm 16:1, 10; Ru 1:2.   i. [17:15] 1 Sm 16:11; 18:2; 2 Sm 7:8; Ps 78:70–71.

¹⁶Meanwhile the Philistine came forward and took his stand morning and evening for forty days.

¹⁷Now Jesse said to his son David: "Take this ephah of roasted grain and these ten loaves for your brothers, and bring them quickly to your brothers in the camp. ¹⁸Also take these ten cheeses for the field officer. Greet your brothers and bring home some token from them. ¹⁹Saul and your brothers, together with all Israel, are at war with the Philistines in the valley of the Elah." ²⁰Early the next morning, having left the flock with a shepherd, David packed up and set out, as Jesse had commanded him. He reached the barricade of the camp just as the army, on their way to the battleground, were shouting their battle cry.ʲ ²¹The Israelites and the Philistines drew up opposite each other in battle array. ²²David entrusted what he had brought to the keeper of the baggage and hastened to the battle line, where he greeted his brothers.ᵏ ²³While he was talking with them, the Philistine champion, by name Goliath of Gath, came up from the ranks of the Philistines and spoke as before, and David listened. ²⁴When the Israelites saw the man, they all retreated before him, terrified. ²⁵The Israelites had been saying: "Do you see this man coming up? He comes up to insult Israel. The king will make whoever kills him a very wealthy man. He will give his daughter to him and declare his father's family exempt from taxes in Israel."ˡ ²⁶David now said to the men standing near him: "How will the man who kills this Philistine and frees Israel from disgrace be rewarded? Who is this uncircumcised Philistine that he should insult the armies of the living God?"ᵐ ²⁷They repeated the same words to him and said, "That is how the man who kills him will be rewarded." ²⁸When Eliab, his oldest brother, heard him speaking with the men, he grew angry with David and said: "Why did you come down? With whom have you left those sheep in the wilderness? I know your arrogance and dishonest heart. You came down to enjoy the battle!"ⁿ ²⁹David protested, "What have I done now? I was only talking." ³⁰He turned from him to another and asked the same question; and everyone gave him the same answer as before. ³¹The words that David had spoken were overheard and reported to Saul, who sent for him.

**David Challenges Goliath.** ³²Then David spoke to Saul: "My lord should not lose heart. Let your servant go and fight this Philistine." ³³But Saul answered David, "You cannot go up against this Philistine and fight with him, for you are only a youth, while he has been a warrior from his youth." ³⁴Then David told Saul: "Your servant used to tend his father's sheep, and whenever

a lion or bear came to carry off a sheep from the flock, ³⁵I would chase after it, attack it, and snatch the prey from its mouth. If it attacked me, I would seize it by the throat, strike it, and kill it. ³⁶Your servant has killed both a lion and a bear. This uncircumcised Philistine will be as one of them, because he has insulted the armies of the living God."

³⁷David continued: "The same LORD who delivered me from the claws of the lion and the bear will deliver me from the hand of this Philistine." Saul answered David, "Go! the LORD will be with you."ᵖ

**Preparation for the Encounter.** ³⁸Then Saul dressed David in his own tunic, putting a bronze helmet on his head and arming him with a coat of mail. ³⁹David also fastened Saul's sword over the tunic. He walked with difficulty, however, since he had never worn armor before. He said to Saul, "I cannot go in these, because I am not used to them." So he took them off. ⁴⁰Then, staff in hand, David selected five smooth stones from the wadi and put them in the pocket of his shepherd's bag. With his sling in hand, he approached the Philistine.

**David's Victory.** ⁴¹With his shield-bearer marching before him, the Philistine advanced closer and closer to David. ⁴²When he sized David up and saw that he was youthful, ruddy, and handsome in appearance, he began to deride him. ⁴³He said to David, "Am I a dog that you come against me with a staff?" Then the Philistine cursed David by his gods ⁴⁴and said to him, "Come here to me, and I will feed your flesh to the birds of the air and the beasts of the field."�q ⁴⁵David answered him: "You come against me with sword and spear and scimitar, but I come against you in the name of the LORD of hosts, the God of the armies of Israel whom you have insulted. ⁴⁶Today the LORD shall deliver you into my hand; I will strike you down and cut off your head. This very day I will feed your dead body and the dead bodies of the Philistine army to the birds of the air and the beasts of the field; thus the whole land shall learn that Israel has a God. ⁴⁷All this multitude, too, shall learn that it is not by sword or spear that the LORD saves. For the battle belongs to the LORD, who shall deliver you into our hands."ʳ

⁴⁸The Philistine then moved to meet David at close quarters, while David ran quickly toward the battle line to meet the Philistine. ⁴⁹David put his hand into the bag and took out a stone, hurled it with the sling, and struck the Philistine on the forehead. The stone embedded itself in his brow, and he fell on his face to the ground. ⁵⁰Thus David triumphed over the Philistine with sling and stone; he struck the Philistine dead,

---

j. [17:20] 1 Sm 26:5.   k. [17:22] 1 Sm 25:13.   l. [17:25] 1 Sm 18:17; Jos 15:16.   m. [17:26] 1 Sm 18:25; Dt 5:26; Jgs 15:18; 2 Kgs 19:4; Is 37:4; Jer 10:10.   n. [17:28] 1 Sm 16:6.   o. [17:34–35] Jgs 14:6; Sir 47:3.

*[17:41–47] The two combatants trade theological taunts. God uses the most unlikely opponent to destroy Goliath.

p. [17:37] Prv 28:1.   q. [17:44] Dt 28:26; Ps 79:2–3; Is 18:6; Jer 7:33; 15:3.   r. [17:47] 1 Sm 14:6, 10; Ps 33:16.

and did it without a sword in his hand.[s] [51]Then David ran and stood over him; with the Philistine's own sword which he drew from its sheath he killed him, and cut off his head.[t]

**Flight of the Philistines.** When the Philistines saw that their hero was dead, they fled. [52]Then the men of Israel and Judah sprang up with a battle cry and pursued them to the approaches of Gath and to the gates of Ekron, and Philistines fell wounded along the road from Shaaraim as far as Gath and Ekron. [53]When they returned from their pursuit of the Philistines, the Israelites looted their camp. [54]*David took the head of the Philistine and brought it to Jerusalem; but he kept Goliath's armor in his own tent.*

**David Presented to Saul.** [55]As Saul watched David go out to meet the Philistine, he asked his general Abner, "Abner, whose son is that young man?" Abner replied, "On your life, O king, I have no idea."[v] [56]And the king said, "Find out whose son the lad is." [57]So when David returned from slaying the Philistine, Abner escorted him into Saul's presence. David was still holding the Philistine's head. [58]Saul then asked him, "Whose son are you, young man?" David replied, "I am the son of your servant Jesse of Bethlehem."

## CHAPTER 18

**David and Jonathan.** [1]By the time David finished speaking with Saul, Jonathan's life became bound up with David's life; he loved him as his very self.[w] [2]Saul retained David on that day and did not allow him to return to his father's house.[x] [3]Jonathan and David made a covenant, because Jonathan loved him as his very self. [4]Jonathan took off[†] the cloak he was wearing and handed it over to David, along with his military dress, even his sword, bow, and belt.[y] [5]David then carried out successfully every mission on which Saul sent him. So Saul put him in charge of his soldiers; this met with the approval of the whole army, even Saul's officers.

**Saul's Jealousy.** [6]At the approach of Saul and David, on David's return after striking down the Philistine, women came out from all the cities of Israel to meet Saul the king, singing and dancing, with tambourines, joyful songs, and stringed instruments.[‡z] [7]The women played and sang:

"Saul has slain his thousands,
    David his tens of thousands."[a]

[8]Saul was very angry and resentful of the song, for he thought: "They give David tens of thousands, but only thousands to me. All that remains for him is the kingship." [9]From that day on, Saul kept a jealous eye on David.

[10b]The next day[*] an evil spirit from God rushed upon Saul, and he raged in his house. David was in attendance, playing the harp as at other times, while Saul was holding his spear. [11]Saul poised the spear, thinking, "I will nail David to the wall!" But twice David escaped him. [12]Saul then began to fear David because the LORD was with him but had turned away from Saul. [13]Saul sent him out of his presence and appointed him a field officer. So David led the people on their military expeditions [14]and prospered in all his ways, for the LORD was with him. [15]Seeing how he prospered, Saul feared David. [16]But all Israel and Judah loved David, since he led them on their expeditions.[§c]

**Saul Plots Against David.** [17]Saul said to David, "Look, I will give you my older daughter, Merob, in marriage if you become my warrior and fight the battles of the LORD." Saul thought, "I will not lay a hand on him. Let the hand of the Philistines strike him."[d] [18]But David answered Saul: "Who am I? And who are my kindred or my father's clan in Israel that I should become the king's son-in-law?" [19]But when the time came for Saul's daughter Merob to be given to David, she was given as wife to Adriel the Meholathite instead.[e]

[20]Now Saul's daughter Michal loved David. When this was reported to Saul, he was pleased.[f] [21]He thought, "I will offer her to him as a trap, so that the hand of the Philistines may strike him." So for the second time Saul said to David, "You shall become my son-in-law today." [22]Saul then ordered his servants, "Speak to David privately and say: The king favors you, and all his officers love you. You should become son-in-law to the king." [23]But when Saul's servants mentioned this to David, he said: "Is becoming the king's son-in-law a trivial matter in your eyes? I am poor and insignificant." [24]When his servants reported David's answer to him, [25]Saul commanded them, "Say this to David: The king desires no other price for the bride than the foreskins of one hundred Philistines, that he may thus take vengeance on his enemies." Saul intended to have David fall into the hands of the Philistines.[g] [26]When the servants reported this

---

*[17:54] Jerusalem was a Jebusite city; it came under Israelite control only at the beginning of David's rule. As a young shepherd, David would not have had a military tent. In 21:10, Goliath's sword is in the Nob temple.

†[18:4] **Jonathan took off:** with the details in this verse, the narrator identifies David as Jonathan's replacement and Saul's heir to the throne. Cf. 23:17 and Gn 41:39–43.

‡[18:6] **Stringed instruments:** perhaps a lute-like instrument with three strings; the Hebrew word, *shalshim*, perhaps related to the root *shlsh* ("three"), occurs only here in the Old Testament.

§[18:16] **Led them on their expeditions:** lit., "go out and come in," i.e., through the city gates; an idiom for military victory.

---

s. [17:50] 1 Mc 4:30; Sir 47:4.   t. [17:51] 1 Sm 21:10.   u. [17:54] 1 Sm 31:9.   v. [17:55] 1 Sm 14:50.   w. [18:1] 1 Sm 19:1–7; 20:17; 23:16; 2 Sm 1:26; 9:1.   x. [18:2] 1 Sm 16:21; 17:15.   y. [18:4] 2 Sm 1:22.   z. [18:6] Ex 15:20–21; Jgs 11:34; Jdt 15:12.

a. [18:7] 1 Sm 21:12; 29:5; Ps 91:7; Sir 47:6–7.   b. [18:10–11] 1 Sm 16:14; 19:9–10; 20:33; 22:6; 26:8.   c. [18:16] 2 Sm 5:2.   d. [18:17] 1 Sm 14:49; 17:25.   e. [18:19] 1 Sm 21:8; 24:16.   f. [18:20] 1 Sm 14:49; 25:44; 26:23; 2 Sm 3:13.   g. [18:25] 1 Sm 17:26; Gn 34:12.

offer to David, he was pleased with the prospect of becoming the king's son-in-law. Before the year was up, ²⁷David arose and went with his men and slew two hundred Philistines. He brought back their foreskins and counted them out before the king that he might become the king's son-in-law. So Saul gave him his daughter Michal as wife. ²⁸Then Saul realized that the LORD was with David and that his own daughter Michal loved David. ²⁹So Saul feared David all the more and was his enemy ever after.

³⁰The Philistine chiefs continued to make forays, but each time they took the field, David was more successful against them than any of Saul's other officers, and his name was held in great esteem.

## CHAPTER 19

**Persecution of David.** ¹Saul discussed his intention to kill David with his son Jonathan and with all his servants. But Saul's son Jonathan, who was very fond of David,ʰ ²told him: "My father Saul is trying to kill you. Therefore, please be on your guard tomorrow morning; stay out of sight and remain in hiding. ³I, however, will go out and stand beside my father in the countryside where you are, and will speak to him about you. If I learn anything, I will let you know."

⁴Jonathan then spoke well of David to his father Saul, telling him: "The king should not harm his servant David. He has not harmed you, but has helped you very much by his deeds.* ⁵When he took his life in his hands and killed the Philistine, and the LORD won a great victory for all Israel, you were glad to see it. Why, then, should you become guilty of shedding innocent blood by killing David without cause?"ⁱ ⁶Saul heeded Jonathan's plea and swore, "As the LORD lives, he shall not be killed." ⁷So Jonathan summoned David and repeated the whole conversation to him. He then brought David to Saul, and David served him as before.

**David Escapes from Saul.** ⁸When war broke out again, David went out to fight against the Philistines and inflicted such a great defeat upon them that they fled from him. ⁹Then an evil spirit from the LORD came upon Saul as he was sitting in his house with spear in hand while David was playing the harp nearby. ¹⁰Saul tried to pin David to the wall with the spear, but David eluded Saul, and the spear struck only the wall, while David got away safely.

¹¹The same night, Saul sent messengers to David's house to guard it, planning to kill him in the morning. David's wife Michal informed him, "Unless you run for your life tonight,

tomorrow you will be killed."† ¹²Then Michal let David down through a window, and he made his escape in safety.ᵏ ¹³Michal took the teraphim‡ and laid it in the bed, putting a tangle of goat's hair at its head and covering it with a blanket.ˡ ¹⁴When Saul sent officers to arrest David, she said, "He is sick." ¹⁵Saul, however, sent the officers back to see David and commanded them, "Bring him up to me in his bed, that I may kill him." ¹⁶But when the messengers entered, they found the teraphim in the bed, with the tangle of goat's hair at its head. ¹⁷Saul asked Michal: "Why did you lie to me like this? You have helped my enemy to get away!" Michal explained to Saul: "He threatened me, saying 'Let me go or I will kill you.'"

**David and Saul in Ramah.** ¹⁸When David got safely away, he went to Samuel in Ramah, informing him of all that Saul had done to him. Then he and Samuel went to stay in Naioth.§ ¹⁹When Saul was told that David was at Naioth in Ramah, ²⁰he sent officers to arrest David. But when they saw the band of prophets presided over by Samuel in a prophetic state, the spirit of God came upon them and they too fell into the prophetic ecstasy.ᵐ ²¹Informed of this, Saul sent other messengers, who also fell into the prophetic ecstasy. For the third time Saul sent messengers, but they too fell into a prophetic ecstasy. **Saul Among the Prophets.** ²²Finally Saul went to Ramah himself. Arriving at the large cistern in Secu, he asked, "Where are Samuel and David?" Someone answered, "At Naioth in Ramah." ²³As he walked from there to Naioth in Ramah, the spirit of God came upon him also, and he continued on, acting like a prophet until he reached Naioth in Ramah. ²⁴Then he, too, stripped himself of his garments and remained in a prophetic state in the presence of Samuel;¶ all that day and night he lay naked. That is why they say, "Is Saul also among the prophets?"ⁿ

## CHAPTER 20

**David Consults with Jonathan.** ¹David fled from Naioth in Ramah, and went to Jonathan. "What have I done?" he asked him. "What crime or what offense does your father hold against me

---

*[19:4] Jonathan reminds Saul that David has served him loyally and done nothing to earn a traitor's death. Cf. 24:18–20.

†[19:11] This story may have originally followed 18:29, placing the episode of David's escape on the night of his marriage with Michal.

‡[19:13] **Teraphim**: a life-sized image of a household god in human form; cf. also note on Gn 31:19. Elsewhere in the Deuteronomistic History, use of teraphim is condemned (15:23; 2 Kgs 23:24).

§[19:18] **Naioth**: meaning "the pastures." This place appears only in chaps. 19–20 and is associated with Ramah.

¶[19:24] **In the presence of Samuel**: this verse, which disagrees with 15:35, is further evidence of the diverse origins of these accounts. **"Is Saul also among the prophets?"**: although similar to the story of Saul's prophetic ecstasy in 10:10–13, this account offers a more disparaging portrait of Saul.

h. [19:1] 1 Sm 18:1; 20:1–3.    i. [19:5] 1 Sm 17:55–56; Dt 19:10; Ps 119:109.    j. [19:9–10] 1 Sm 16:14; 18:10–11.

k. [19:12] Jos 2:15; Acts 9:25; 2 Cor 11:33.    l. [19:13] Gn 31:19; Jgs 17:5; 18:14, 18, 20; Ez 21:26.    m. [19:20] 1 Sm 10:5–6, 10; Nm 11:25.    n. [19:24] 1 Sm 10:10–12; 2 Sm 6:20.

that he seeks my life?"[o] [2]Jonathan answered him: "Heaven forbid that you should die! My father does nothing, great or small, without telling me. Why, then, should my father conceal this from me? It cannot be true!" [3]But David replied: "Your father is well aware that I am favored with your friendship, so he has decided, 'Jonathan must not know about this or he will be grieved.' Nevertheless, as the LORD lives and as you live, there is only a step between me and death." [4]Jonathan then said to David, "I will do whatever you say." [5]David answered: "Tomorrow is the new moon, when I should in fact dine with the king. Let me go and hide in the open country until evening.[p] [6]If it turns out that your father misses me, say, 'David urged me to let him go on short notice to his city Bethlehem, because his whole clan is holding its seasonal sacrifice there.'[q] [7]If he says, 'Very well,' your servant is safe. But if he becomes quite angry, you can be sure he has planned some harm. [8]Do this kindness for your servant because of the LORD's covenant into which you brought us: if I am guilty, kill me yourself! Why should you give me up to your father?" [9]But Jonathan answered: "Not I! If ever I find out that my father is determined to harm you, I will certainly let you know." [10]David then asked Jonathan, "Who will tell me if your father gives you a harsh answer?"

**Mutual Agreement.** [11]Jonathan replied to David, "Come, let us go out into the field." When they were out in the open country together, [12]Jonathan said to David: "As the LORD, the God of Israel, lives, I will sound out my father about this time tomorrow. Whether he is well disposed toward David or not, I will inform you. [13]Should it please my father to bring any harm upon you, may the LORD do thus to Jonathan and more,* if I do not inform you of it and send you on your way in peace. May the LORD be with you even as he was with my father. [14]Only this: if I am still alive, may you show me the kindness of the LORD. But if I die, [15]never cut off your kindness from my house. And when the LORD cuts off all the enemies of David from the face of the land, [16]the name of Jonathan must never be cut off from the family of David, or the LORD will make you answer for it." [17]And in his love for David, Jonathan renewed his oath to him, because he loved him as he loved himself.

[18]Jonathan then said to him: "Tomorrow is the new moon; you will be missed, since your place will be vacant. [19]On the third day you will be missed all the more. Go to the spot where you hid on the other occasion and wait near the mound there.[r] [20]On the third day of the month I will shoot arrows to the side of it, as though aiming at a target. [21]I will then send my attendant to recover the arrows. If in fact I say to him, 'Look, the arrow is this side of you; pick it up,' come, for you are safe. As the LORD lives, there will be nothing to fear. [22]But if I say to the boy, 'Look, the arrow is beyond you,' go, for the LORD sends you away. [23]However, in the matter which you and I have discussed, the LORD shall be between you and me forever." [24]So David hid in the open country.

**David's Absence.** On the day of the new moon, when the king sat down at the feast to dine, [25]he took his usual place against the wall. Jonathan sat facing him, while Abner sat at the king's side. David's place was vacant. [26u]Saul, however, said nothing that day, for he thought, "He must have become unclean by accident."[†] [27]On the next day, the second day of the month, David's place was still vacant. So Saul asked his son Jonathan, "Why has the son of Jesse not come to table yesterday or today?" [28]Jonathan explained to Saul: "David pleaded with me to let him go to Bethlehem. [29]'Please let me go,' he begged, 'for we are having a clan sacrifice in our city, and my brothers insist on my presence. Now then, if you think well of me, give me leave to visit my brothers.' That is why he has not come to the king's table." [30]But Saul grew angry with Jonathan and said to him: "Son of a rebellious woman, do I not know that, to your own disgrace and to the disgrace of your mother's nakedness, you are the companion of Jesse's son? [31]For as long as the son of Jesse lives upon the earth, you cannot make good your claim to the kingship![‡] Now send for him, and bring him to me, for he must die."[v] [32]But Jonathan argued with his father Saul: "Why should he die? What has he done?" [33]At this Saul brandished his spear to strike him, and thus Jonathan learned that his father was determined to kill David.[w] [34]Jonathan sprang up from the table in a rage and ate nothing that second day of the month, because he was grieved on David's account, and because his father had humiliated him.

**Jonathan's Farewell.** [35]The next morning Jonathan, accompanied by a young boy, went out into the field for his appointment with David. [36]There he said to the boy, "Run and find the arrows." And as the boy ran, he shot an arrow past him. [37]When the boy made for the spot where Jonathan had shot the arrow, Jonathan called after him, "The arrow is farther on!" [38]Again he called to the boy, "Hurry, be quick, don't delay!"

---

[†][20:26] The meal on the first day of the month would have had religious overtones, and a ritual impurity (Lv 15:16; Dt 23:10–12) would have barred David from sharing in it.

[‡][20:31] **Your claim to the kingship:** Saul admits his intention that Jonathan should succeed him and that David is a threat to his lineage (cf. 23:17). However Jonathan has already acknowledged David's kingship (18:3–4) and his own subservient role (20:13–16).

---

*[20:13] See note on 3:17.

---

o. [20:1] 1 Sm 19:1–7, 11–17; 21:11; 27:4; Gn 31:36.  p. [20:5] Nm 10:10; 28:11–15; Ezr 3:5; Neh 10:34.  q. [20:6] 1 Sm 17:12. r. [20:8–9] 1 Sm 18:3; 23:17–18.  s. [20:13–16] 1 Sm 10:7; 17:37; 18:12, 14; 24:22–23; 2 Sm 9:1–13; 21:7.  t. [20:19] 1 Sm 1:9–7.

u. [20:26] 1 Sm 16:5; Lv 7:20–21; 15:1–3.  v. [20:31] 2 Sm 12:5. w. [20:33] 1 Sm 18:11.

Jonathan's boy picked up the arrow and brought it to his master. ³⁹The boy suspected nothing; only Jonathan and David knew what was meant. ⁴⁰Then Jonathan gave his weapons to his boy and said to him, "Go, take them to the city." ⁴¹When the boy had gone, David rose from beside the mound and fell on his face to the ground three times in homage. They kissed each other and wept aloud together. ⁴²ˣAt length Jonathan said to David, "Go in peace, in keeping with what the two of us have sworn by the name of the LORD: 'The LORD shall be between you and me, and between your offspring and mine forever.'"

## CHAPTER 21

¹Then David departed on his way, while Jonathan went back into the city.

**The Holy Bread.** ²David went to Ahimelech, the priest of Nob, who came trembling to meet him. He asked, "Why are you alone? Is there no one with you?"ʸ ³David answered the priest: "The king gave me a commission and told me, 'Do not let anyone know anything about the business on which I have sent you or the commission I have given you.' For that reason I have arranged a particular meeting place with my men. ⁴ᶻNow what do you have on hand? Give me five loaves, or whatever you can find." ⁵†But the priest replied to David, "I have no ordinary bread on hand, only holy bread; if the men have abstained from women, you may eat some of that." ⁶David answered the priest: "We have indeed stayed away from women. In the past whenever I went out on a campaign, all the young men were consecrated—even for an ordinary campaign. All the more so are they consecrated with their weapons today!" ⁷So the priest gave him holy bread, for no other bread was on hand except the showbread which had been removed from before the LORD and replaced by fresh bread when it was taken away.ᵈ ⁸One of Saul's servants was there that day, detained before the LORD;‡ his name was Doeg the Edomite, the chief of Saul's shepherds.ᵇ

**The Sword of Goliath.** ⁹David then asked Ahimelech: "Do you have a spear or a sword on hand? I brought along neither my sword nor my weapons, because the king's business was urgent." ¹⁰The priest replied: "The sword of Goliath the Philistine, whom you killed in the Valley of Elah, is here wrapped in a garment behind an ephod.§ If you wish to take it, do so; there is no sword here except that one." "There is none like it," David cried, "give it to me!"ᶜ

**David a Fugitive.** ¹¹That same day David fled from Saul, going to Achish, king of Gath.ᵈ ¹²But the servants of Achish said to him, "Is this not David, the king of the land? Is it not for him that during their dances they sing out,

'Saul has slain his thousands,
    David his tens of thousands'?"ᵉ

¹³David took note of these remarks and became very much afraid of Achish, king of Gath.ᶠ ¹⁴So, he feigned insanity in front of them and acted like a madman in their custody, drumming on the doors of the gate and drooling onto his beard. ¹⁵Finally Achish said to his servants: "You see the man is mad. Why did you bring him to me? ¹⁶Do I not have enough madmen, that you bring this one to rant in my presence? Should this fellow come into my house?"

## CHAPTER 22

¹David left Gath and escaped to the cave of Adullam. When his brothers and the rest of his family heard about it, they came down to him there.ᶠ ²He was joined by all those in difficulties or in debt, or embittered,** and became their leader. About four hundred men were with him.

³From there David went to Mizpeh of Moab and said to the king of Moab, "Let my father and mother stay with you, until I learn what God will do for me." ⁴He left them with the king of Moab; they stayed with him as long as David remained in the stronghold.††

⁵But Gad the prophet said to David: "Do not remain in the stronghold! Leave! Go to the land of Judah." And so David left and went to the forest of Hereth.ᵍ

**Doeg Betrays Ahimelech.** ⁶Now Saul heard that David and his men had been located. At the time he was sitting in Gibeah under a tamarisk tree on the high place, holding his spear, while all his servants stood by him.ʰ ⁷So he said to

---

*[21:2] Ahimelech realizes that he risks incurring Saul's anger if David has come to Nob as a fugitive.

†[21:5–6] According to Lv 24:5–9, the showbread consisted of twelve loaves that were replaced each sabbath. Since the old bread was to be consumed by the priests, Ahimelech questions David regarding the ritual purity of his men (see 2 Sm 11:11). David's answer supposes the discipline of a military campaign under the conditions of "holy war" (Dt 23:10–15).

‡[21:8] **Detained before the LORD:** perhaps to fulfill a ritual obligation. David's arrival at Nob seems to coincide with a festival day, since the showbread has recently been replaced with fresh bread. **Shepherds:** i.e., Saul's palace guard. Cf. 22:9–10, where Doeg has easy access to Saul.

§[21:10] **Ephod:** here an object or image large enough to conceal Goliath's sword. Cf. Gideon's ephod in Jgs 8:27.

¶[21:13] **Gath:** a Philistine city (see note on 5:1–12), the home of Goliath.

**[22:2] **Embittered:** Hebrew *mar-nephesh*, "bitter of spirit," used of Hannah, deprived of a child, in 1:10, and of David's soldiers, whose women and children the Amalekites had seized (30:6). Cf. also 2 Sm 17:8. David becomes a hero for those who have endured loss or deprivation.

††[22:4–5] **Stronghold:** seemingly connected with the cave complex in v. 1.

---

x. [20:42] 2 Sm 9:1; 21:7.   y. [21:2] 1 Sm 16:4; Is 10:32; Mk 2:26.   z. [21:4] Lv 24:5, 9.   a. [21:7] Lv 24:5–9; Mt 12:3–4; Mk 2:26; Lk 6:3–5.   b. [21:8] 1 Sm 22:9.

c. [21:10] 1 Sm 17:51, 54.   d. [21:11] 1 Sm 27:2; 29:5.   e. [21:12] 1 Sm 18:7; 29:5.   f. [22:1] 2 Sm 23:13; Ps 63; Mi 1:15.   g. [22:5] 2 Sm 24:11–13.   h. [22:6] 1 Sm 14:2; Jgs 4:5.

them: "Listen, men of Benjamin! Will the son of Jesse give all of you fields and vineyards? Will he appoint any of you an officer over a thousand or a hundred men?[i] [8]Is that why you have all conspired against me? Why no one told me that my son had made a pact with the son of Jesse? None of you has shown compassion for me by revealing to me that my son has incited my servant to ambush me, as is the case today."[j] [9k]Then Doeg the Edomite, who was standing with Saul's officers, spoke up: "I saw the son of Jesse come to Ahimelech, son of Ahitub, in Nob. [10]He consulted the LORD for him, furnished him with provisions, and gave him the sword of Goliath the Philistine."

**Slaughter of the Priests.** [11]So the king summoned Ahimelech the priest, son of Ahitub, and all his family, the priests in Nob. They all came to the king. [12]"Listen, son of Ahitub!" Saul declared. "Yes, my lord," he replied. [13]Saul questioned him, "Why have you conspired against me with the son of Jesse by giving him food and a sword and by consulting God for him, that he might rise up against me in ambush, as is the case today?" [14]Ahimelech answered the king: "Who among all your servants is as loyal as David, the king's son-in-law, captain of your bodyguard, and honored in your own house? [15]Is this the first time I have consulted God for him? No indeed! Let not the king accuse his servant or anyone in my family of such a thing. Your servant knows nothing at all, great or small, about the whole matter." [16]But the king said, "You shall certainly die, Ahimelech, with all your family." [17]The king then commanded his guards standing by him: "Turn and kill the priests of the LORD, for they gave David a hand. They knew he was a fugitive and yet failed to inform me." But the king's servants refused to raise a hand to strike the priests of the LORD.[l]

[18]The king therefore commanded Doeg, "You, turn and kill the priests!" So Doeg the Edomite himself turned and killed the priests that day—eighty-five who wore the linen ephod. [19]Saul also put the priestly city of Nob to the sword, including men and women, children and infants, and oxen, donkeys and sheep.

**Abiathar Escapes.** [20]One son of Ahimelech, son of Ahitub, named Abiathar,* escaped and fled to David.[m] [21]When Abiathar told David that Saul had slain the priests of the LORD, [22]David said to him: "I knew that day, when Doeg the Edomite was there, that he would certainly tell Saul. I am

responsible for the slaughter of all your family. [23]Stay with me. Do not be afraid; whoever seeks your life must seek my life also. You are under my protection."[†]

## CHAPTER 23

**Keilah Liberated.** [1]David was informed that the Philistines were attacking Keilah and plundering the threshing floors.[n] [2]So he consulted the LORD, asking, "Shall I go and attack these Philistines?" The LORD answered, Go, attack them, and free Keilah.[o] [3]But David's men said to him: "Even in Judah we have reason to fear. How much more so if we go to Keilah against the forces of the Philistines!" [4]Again David consulted the LORD, who answered: Go down to Keilah, for I will deliver the Philistines into your power.[p] [5]So David went with his men to Keilah and fought against the Philistines. He drove off their cattle and inflicted a severe defeat on them, and freed the inhabitants of Keilah.

[6]Abiathar, son of Ahimelech, who had fled to David, went down with David to Keilah, taking the ephod with him.[q]

**Flight from Keilah.** [7]When Saul was told that David had entered Keilah, he thought: "God has put him in my hand, for he has boxed himself in by entering a city with gates and bars." [8]Saul then called all the army to war, in order to go down to Keilah and besiege David and his men. [9]When David found out that Saul was planning to harm him, he said to the priest Abiathar, "Bring the ephod here."[r] [10]"LORD God of Israel," David prayed, "your servant has heard that Saul plans to come to Keilah, to destroy the city on my account. [11]Will they hand me over? Will Saul come down as your servant has heard? LORD God of Israel, tell your servant." The LORD answered: He will come down. [12]David then asked, "Will the citizens of Keilah deliver me and my men into the hand of Saul?" The LORD answered: They will deliver you. [13]So David and his men, about six hundred in number, left Keilah and wandered from place to place. When Saul was informed that David had fled from Keilah, he did not go forth.

**David and Jonathan in Horesh.** [14]David now lived in the strongholds in the wilderness, or in the barren hill country near Ziph. Though Saul sought him continually, the LORD did not deliver David into his hand. [15]While David was in the wilderness of Ziph at Horesh he was afraid that Saul had come out to seek his life. [16]Then Saul's son, Jonathan, came down to David at Horesh and encouraged him in the LORD.[s] [17]He said to him: "Have no fear, my father Saul shall not lay

---

*[22:20] **Abiathar**: the sole survivor of Eli's household (2:27–36). David now has in his service the only priest of the Lord left in the land and exclusive access to the ephod for consulting the Lord (cf. 23:9–13). David later appoints Abiathar co-high priest with Zadok in Jerusalem (2 Sm 20:25), but Solomon exiles Abiathar to Anathoth when the priest does not support his bid for the throne. Cf. 1 Kgs 2:26–27.

†[22:23] **You are under my protection**: once again a sharp contrast is drawn between Saul, who kills the Lord's priests, and David, who protects the lone survivor.

i. [22:7] 1 Sm 8:14.    j. [22:8] 1 Sm 18:3; 20:8; 23:18.    k. [22:9–10] 1 Sm 21:2–10; Ps 52.    l. [22:17] 1 Sm 2:31, 33; 21:7.    m. [22:20] 1 Sm 23:6; 30:7; 2 Sm 20:25; 1 Kgs 2:26–27.

n. [23:1] Jos 15:44.    o. [23:2] 1 Sm 28:6.    p. [23:4] 1 Sm 17:47.    q. [23:6] 1 Sm 22:20; 30:7.    r. [23:9] 1 Sm 2:28.    s. [23:16] 1 Sm 18:1.

a hand to you. You shall be king of Israel* and I shall be second to you. Even my father Saul knows this."[t] [18]The two of them made a covenant before the LORD in Horesh, where David remained, while Jonathan returned to his home.[u]

**Treachery of the Ziphites.** [19]Some of the Ziphites went up to Saul in Gibeah and said, "David is hiding among us in the strongholds at Horesh on the hill of Hachilah, south of Jeshimon.[v] [20]Therefore, whenever the king wishes to come down, let him do so. It will be our task to deliver him into the king's hand." [21]Saul replied: "The LORD bless you for your compassion toward me."[w] [22]Go now and make sure once more! Take note of the place where he sets foot for I am told that he is very cunning. [23]Look around and learn in which of all the various hiding places he is holding out. Then come back to me with reliable information, and I will go with you. If he is in the region, I will track him down out of all the families of Judah." [24]So they went off to Ziph ahead of Saul. At this time David and his men were in the wilderness below Maon, in the Arabah south of the wasteland.[x]

**Escape from Saul.** [25]When Saul and his men came looking for him, David got word of it and went down to the gorge in the wilderness below Maon. Saul heard of this and pursued David into the wilderness below Maon. [26]As Saul moved along one side of the gorge, David and his men took to the other. David was anxious to escape Saul, while Saul and his men were trying to outflank David and his men in order to capture them. [27]Then a messenger came to Saul, saying, "Come quickly, because the Philistines have invaded the land." [28]Saul interrupted his pursuit of David and went to meet the Philistines. This is how that place came to be called the Rock of Divisions.

## CHAPTER 24

**David Spares Saul.**[†] [1]David then went up from there and stayed in the strongholds of Engedi. [2]When Saul returned from the pursuit of the Philistines, he was told that David was in the desert near Engedi. [3]So Saul took three thousand of the best men from all Israel and went in search of David and his men in the direction of the wild goat crags. [4]When he came to the sheepfolds along the way, he found a cave, which he entered to relieve himself. David and his men were occupying the inmost recesses of the cave.[y]

[5]David's servants said to him, "This is the day about which the LORD said to you: I will deliver your enemy into your hand; do with him as you see fit." So David moved up and stealthily cut off an end of Saul's robe. [6]Afterward, however, David regretted that he had cut off an end of Saul's robe.[z] [7]He said to his men, "The LORD forbid that I should do such a thing to my master, the LORD's anointed, to lay a hand on him, for he is the LORD's anointed."[a] [8]With these words David restrained his men and would not permit them to attack Saul. Saul then left the cave and went on his way. [9]David also stepped out of the cave, calling to Saul, "My lord the king!" When Saul looked back, David bowed, his face to the ground in homage, [10]and asked Saul: "Why do you listen to those who say, 'David is trying to harm you'? [11]You see for yourself today that the LORD just now delivered you into my hand in the cave. I was told to kill you, but I took pity on you instead. I decided, 'I will not raise a hand against my master, for he is the LORD's anointed.' [12]Look here, my father. See the end of your robe which I hold. I cut off an end of your robe and did not kill you. Now see and be convinced that I plan no harm and no rebellion. I have done you no wrong, though you are hunting me down to take my life.[b] [13]May the LORD judge between me and you. May the LORD exact justice from you in my case. I shall not lay a hand on you. [14]As the old proverb says, 'From the wicked comes wickedness.' Thus I will not lay a hand on you. [15]What is the king of Israel attacking? What are you pursuing? A dead dog! A single flea![c] [16]The LORD will be the judge to decide between us. May the LORD see this, defend my cause, and give me justice against you!"[d]

**Saul's Remorse.** [17]When David finished saying these things to Saul, Saul answered, "Is that your voice, my son David?" And he wept freely. [18]Saul then admitted to David: "You are more in the right than I am. You have treated me graciously, while I have treated you badly. [19]You have declared this day how you treated me graciously: the LORD delivered me into your hand and you did not kill me. [20]For if someone comes upon an enemy, do they send them graciously on their way? So may the LORD reward you graciously for what you have done this day. [21]And now, since I know that you will certainly become king and that the kingship over Israel shall come into your possession,[e] [22]swear to me by the LORD that you will not cut off my descendants and that you will not blot out my name from my father's house."[f] [23]David gave Saul his oath and Saul returned home, while David and his men went up to the stronghold.

---

*[23:17] **King of Israel**: to emphasize the inevitability of the Lord's plan, the narrator frames Jonathan's statement with two accounts of David's mercy toward Saul.

†[24:1] The first of two accounts (see chap. 26) in which David spares Saul's life. The two accounts, which do not make reference to each other, are probably alternative versions of the same story.

---

t. [23:17] 1 Sm 20:14–16.   u. [23:18] 1 Sm 18:3; 20:8.   v. [23:19] 1 Sm 26:1–3; Ps 54.   w. [23:21] 2 Sm 2:5.   x. [23:24] 1 Sm 25:2.   y. [24:4] Ps 57.

z. [24:6] 1 Sm 15:27.   a. [24:7] 1 Sm 10:1; 26:9; 31:4; 2 Sm 1:14.   b. [24:12] Rom 12:19.   c. [24:15] 2 Sm 9:8; 16:9.   d. [24:16] 1 Sm 18:19, 31; 26:19; Ps 35:1–3; 43:1.   e. [24:21] 1 Sm 26:25.   f. [24:22] 2 Sm 9:1–3.

## CHAPTER 25

**Death of Samuel.** ¹Samuel died, and all Israel gathered to mourn him; they buried him at his home in Ramah.ᵍ Then David went down to the wilderness of Paran.

**Nabal and Abigail.** ²There was a man of Maon who had property in Carmel; he was very wealthy, owning three thousand sheep and a thousand goats. At the time, he was present for the shearing of his flock in Carmel.ʰ ³The man's name was Nabal and his wife was Abigail. The woman was intelligent and attractive, but Nabal, a Calebite, was harsh and bad-mannered.ⁱ ⁴While in the wilderness, David heard that Nabal was shearing his flock, ⁵so he sent ten young men, instructing them: "Go up to Carmel. Pay Nabal a visit and greet him in my name. ⁶Say to him, 'Peace be with you, my brother, and with your family, and with all who belong to you. ⁷I have just heard that shearers are with you. Now, when your shepherds were with us, we did them no injury, neither did they miss anything while they were in Carmel. ⁸Ask your servants and they will tell you. Look kindly on these young men, since we come at a festival time. Please give your servants and your son David* whatever you can.'"

⁹When David's young men arrived, they delivered the entire message to Nabal in David's name, and then waited. ¹⁰But Nabal answered the servants of David: "Who is David? Who is the son of Jesse? Nowadays there are many servants who run away from their masters. ¹¹Must I take my bread, my wine, my meat that I have slaughtered for my own shearers, and give them to men who come from who knows where?" ¹²So David's young men retraced their steps and on their return reported to him all that had been said. ¹³Thereupon David said to his men, "Let everyone strap on his sword." And everyone did so, and David put on his own sword. About four hundred men went up after David, while two hundred remained with the baggage.

¹⁴Abigail, Nabal's wife, was informed of this by one of the servants, who said: "From the wilderness David sent messengers to greet our master, but he screamed at them. ¹⁵Yet these men were very good to us. We were not harmed, neither did we miss anything all the while we were living among them during our stay in the open country. ¹⁶Day and night they were a wall of protection for us, the whole time we were pasturing the sheep near them. ¹⁷Now, see what you can do, for you must realize that otherwise disaster is in store for our master and for his whole house. He is such a scoundrel that no one can talk to him." ¹⁸Abigail quickly got

together two hundred loaves, two skins of wine, five dressed sheep, five seahs of roasted grain, a hundred cakes of pressed raisins, and two hundred cakes of pressed figs, and loaded them on donkeys. ¹⁹She then said to her servants, "Go on ahead; I will follow you." But to her husband Nabal she said nothing.

²⁰Hidden by the mountain, she came down riding on a donkey, as David and his men were coming down from the opposite direction. When she met them, ²¹David had just been saying: "Indeed, it was in vain that I guarded all this man's possessions in the wilderness, so that nothing of his was missing. He has repaid good with evil. ²²May God do thus to David, and more, if by morning I leave a single male alive among all those who belong to him."ʲ ²³As soon as Abigail saw David, she dismounted quickly from the donkey, and, falling down, bowed low to the ground before David in homage.

²⁴As she fell at his feet she said: "My lord, let the blame be mine. Please let your maidservant speak to you; listen to the words of your maidservant.ᵏ ²⁵My lord, do not pay any attention to that scoundrel Nabal, for he is just like his name. His name means fool,† and he acts the fool. I, your maidservant, did not see the young men whom my lord sent. ²⁶Now, therefore, my lord, as the LORD lives, and as you live, the LORD has kept you from shedding blood and from avenging yourself by your own hand. May your enemies and those who seek to harm my lord become as Nabal!‡ˡ ²⁷Accept this gift, then, which your maidservant has brought for my lord, and let it be given to the young men who follow my lord. ²⁸Please forgive the offense of your maidservant, for the LORD shall certainly establish a lasting house for my lord, because my lord fights the battles of the LORD. Let no evil be found in you your whole life long.ᵐ ²⁹If any adversary pursues you to seek your life, may the life of my lord be bound in the bundle of the living§ in the care of the LORD your God; may God hurl out the lives of your enemies as from the hollow of a sling.ⁿ ³⁰And when the LORD fulfills for my lord the promise of success he has made concerning you, and appoints you as ruler over Israel,ᵒ ³¹you shall not have any regrets or burdens on your conscience, my lord, for having shed innocent

†[25:25] Hebrew *nabal* means "fool" (cf. Is 32:5–7). Abigail, on the other hand, acts wisely to save herself and her household by offering prudent counsel to the future king of Israel.

‡[25:26] Abigail, encouraging David to trust in God's promise, anticipates that some misfortune will shortly overtake Nabal, as in fact it does (vv. 37–38).

§[25:29] **The bundle of the living**: the figure is perhaps taken from the practice of tying up valuables in a kerchief or bag for safekeeping. Abigail desires that David enjoy permanent peace and security, but that his enemies be subject to constant agitation and humiliation like a stone whirled about, cast out of the sling, and thereafter disregarded.

*[25:8] **Your son David**: this kinship language may reflect a political or social relationship between Nabal and David. Nabal, however, does not acknowledge it.

g. [25:1] 1 Sm 28:3; Sir 46:13–20.  h. [25:2] 1 Sm 23:24; Jos 15:55.  i. [25:3] 1 Sm 27:3; Dt 1:35–36; Jos 14:6–15; 1 Chr 2:42, 45.

j. [25:22] 1 Kgs 16:11; 21:21; 2 Kgs 9:8.  k. [25:24] 2 Sm 14:9.  l. [25:26] Dt 20:4; Jgs 7:2.  m. [25:28] 1 Kgs 11:38.  n. [25:29] Ps 69:28.  o. [25:30] 1 Sm 13:14; 2 Sm 3:10.

blood or for having rescued yourself. When the LORD bestows good on my lord, remember your maidservant." [32]David said to Abigail: "Blessed is the LORD, the God of Israel, who sent you to meet me today. [33]Blessed is your good judgment and blessed are you yourself. Today you have prevented me from shedding blood and rescuing myself with my own hand. [34]Otherwise, as the LORD, the God of Israel, lives, who has kept me from harming you, if you had not come so promptly to meet me, by dawn Nabal would not have had so much as one male left alive." [35]David then took from her what she had brought him and said to her: "Go to your home in peace! See, I have listened to your appeal and have granted your request."

**Nabal's Death.** [36]When Abigail came to Nabal, he was hosting a banquet in his house like that of a king, and Nabal was in a festive mood and very drunk. So she said not a word to him until daybreak the next morning. [37]But then, when Nabal was sober, his wife told him what had happened. At this his heart died within him, and he became like a stone. [38]About ten days later the LORD struck Nabal and he died. [39]Hearing that Nabal was dead, David said: "Blessed be the LORD, who has defended my cause against the insult from Nabal, and who restrained his servant from doing evil, but has repaid Nabal for his evil deeds."

**David Marries Abigail and Ahinoam.** David then sent a proposal of marriage to Abigail.[p] [40]When David's servants came to Abigail in Carmel, they said to her, "David has sent us to make his proposal of marriage to you." [41]Rising and bowing to the ground, she answered, "Let your maidservant be the slave who washes the feet of my lord's servants." [42]She got up immediately, mounted a donkey, and followed David's messengers, with her five maids attending her. She became his wife. [43q]David also married Ahinoam of Jezreel. Thus both of them were his wives. [44]But Saul gave David's wife Michal, Saul's own daughter, to Palti, son of Laish, who was from Gallim.[r]

## CHAPTER 26

**David Spares Saul Again.**[*] [1a]Men from Ziph came to Saul in Gibeah, reporting that David was hiding on the hill of Hachilah at the edge of Jeshimon. [2]So Saul went down to the wilderness of Ziph with three thousand of the best warriors of Israel, to search for David in the wilderness of Ziph. [3]Saul camped beside the road on the hill of Hachilah, at the edge of Jeshimon. David, who was living in the wilderness, saw that Saul had come into the wilderness after him [4]and

sent out scouts, who confirmed Saul's arrival. [5]David then went to the place where Saul was encamped and saw the spot where Saul and his general, Abner, son of Ner, had their sleeping quarters. Saul was lying within the camp, and all his soldiers were bivouacked around him.[t] [6]David asked Ahimelech the Hittite, and Abishai, son of Zeruiah and brother of Joab, "Who will go down into the camp with me to Saul?" Abishai replied, "I will."[u] [7]So David and Abishai reached Saul's soldiers by night, and there was Saul lying asleep within the camp, his spear thrust into the ground at his head and Abner and his troops sleeping around him.

[8]Abishai whispered to David: "God has delivered your enemy into your hand today. Let me nail him to the ground with one thrust of the spear; I will not need to strike him twice!"[v] [9]But David said to Abishai, "Do not harm him, for who can lay a hand on the LORD's anointed and remain innocent? [10]As the LORD lives," David declared, "only the LORD can strike him: either when the time comes for him to die, or when he goes out and perishes in battle.[tw] [11]But the LORD forbid that I lay a hand on the LORD's anointed! Now take the spear at his head and the water jug, and let us be on our way." [12]So David took the spear and the water jug from their place at Saul's head, and they withdrew without anyone seeing or knowing or awakening. All remained asleep, because a deep slumber‡ from the LORD had fallen upon them.[x]

**David Taunts Abner.** [13]Crossing over to an opposite slope, David stood on a distant hilltop. With a great distance between them [14]David called to the army and to Abner, son of Ner, "Will you not answer, Abner?" Then Abner shouted back, "Who is it that calls me?" [15]David said to Abner: "Are you not a man? Who in Israel is your equal? Why were you not guarding your lord the king when one of his subjects came to assassinate the king, your lord? [16]What you have done is not right. As the LORD lives, you people deserve death because you have not guarded your lord, the anointed of the LORD. Go, look: where are the king's spear and the water jug that was at his head?"

**Saul Admits His Guilt.** [17]Saul recognized David's voice and asked, "Is that your voice, David my son?"§ David answered, "Yes, my lord the king."

---

† [26:10] **Perishes in battle:** David's words foreshadow how Saul will die (31:3–4). They also emphasize that David, unlike Saul, knows his proper place before God. David comes to the kingship innocent of Saul's blood, although the king pursues him like an enemy and David has had two opportunities to kill him.

‡ [26:12] **Deep slumber:** as in Gn 2:21; 15:12; Is 29:10. The Lord aids David's foray into Saul's camp and allows David to come and go undetected.

§ [26:17] **David my son:** Saul's reference to David as his son, which appears three times in this chapter (vv. 17, 21, 25), alludes to David's role as his successor.

* [26:1] The second account of David sparing Saul's life; cf. note on 24:1.

p. [25:39] 1 Kgs 2:44.   q. [25:43] 1 Sm 27:3.   r. [25:44] 1 Sm 18:20; 27:3; 30:5; 2 Sm 2:2, 13–16; 1 Chr 3:1.   s. [26:1–2] 1 Sm 23:19–20; Ps 54.

t. [26:5] 1 Sm 17:20.   u. [26:6] 2 Sm 3:30; 1 Chr 2:16.   v. [26:8] 1 Sm 18:11; 19:10; 20:33.   w. [26:10] Ps 37:13.   x. [26:12] Gn 2:21; 15:12.

[18]He continued: "Why does my lord pursue his servant? What have I done? What evil am I planning? [19]Please, now, let my lord the king listen to the words of his servant. If the LORD has incited you against me, may an offering please the LORD. But if it is the people who have done so, may they be cursed before the LORD. They have driven me away so that today I have no share in the LORD's heritage,[*] but am told: 'Go serve other gods!'[y] [20]Do not let my blood spill on the ground far from the presence of the LORD. For the king of Israel has come out to seek a single flea as if he were hunting partridge[†] in the mountains." [21]Then Saul said: "I have done wrong. Come back, David, my son! I will not harm you again, because you considered my life precious today even though I have been a fool and have made a serious mistake." [22]But David answered: "Here is the king's spear. Let an attendant come over to get it. [23]The LORD repays everyone's righteousness and faithfulness. Although the LORD delivered you into my hands today, I could not lay a hand on the LORD's anointed.[z] [24]Just as I regarded your life as precious today, so may the LORD regard my life as precious and deliver me from all dangers." [25]Then Saul said to David: "Blessed are you, my son David! You shall certainly succeed in whatever you undertake." David went his way, and Saul returned to his place.[a]

### CHAPTER 27

**David Flees to the Philistines.** [1]David said to himself: "I shall perish some day at the hand of Saul. I have no choice but to escape to the land of the Philistines; then Saul will give up his continual search for me throughout the land of Israel, and I will be out of his reach." [2]Accordingly, David departed with his six hundred soldiers and went over to Achish, son of Maoch, king of Gath.[b] [3]David and his men lived in Gath with Achish; each one had his family, and David had his two wives, Ahinoam from Jezreel and Abigail, the widow of Nabal from Carmel.[c] [4]When Saul learned that David had fled to Gath, he no longer searched for him.

[5]David said to Achish: "If I meet with your approval, let me have a place to live in one of the country towns. Why should your servant live with you in the royal city?" [6]That same day Achish gave him Ziklag, which has, therefore,

belonged to the kings of Judah[‡] up to the present time.[d] [7]In all, David lived a year and four months in Philistine territory.[e]

**David Raids Israel's Foes.** [8]David and his men went out on raids against the Geshurites, Girzites, and Amalekites—peoples living in the land between Telam, on the approach to Shur, and the land of Egypt.[f] [9]In attacking the land David would not leave a man or woman alive, but would carry off sheep, oxen, donkeys, camels, and clothes. Then he would return to Achish, [10]who would ask, "Against whom did you raid this time?" David would reply, "Against the Negeb of Judah,"[§] or "Against the Negeb of Jerahmeel," or "Against the Negeb of the Kenites."[g] [11]David never left a man or woman alive to be brought to Gath. He thought, "They will betray us and say, 'This is what David did.'" This was his custom as long as he lived in Philistine territory. [12]Achish trusted David, thinking, "His people Israel must certainly detest him. I shall have him as my vassal forever."

### CHAPTER 28

[1]In those days the Philistines mustered their military forces to fight against Israel. So Achish said to David, "You realize, of course, that you and your warriors[¶] must march out for battle with me." [2]David answered Achish, "Good! Now you shall learn what your servant can do." Then Achish said to David, "I shall appoint you as my permanent bodyguard."

[3]Now, Samuel was dead. All Israel had mourned him and buried him in his city, Ramah. Meanwhile Saul had driven mediums and diviners out of the land.[h]

**Saul in Despair.** [4]The Philistines rallied and, coming to Shunem, they encamped. Saul, too, mustered all Israel; they camped on Gilboa. [5]When Saul saw the Philistine camp, he grew afraid and lost heart completely. [6]He consulted the LORD; but the LORD gave no answer, neither in dreams nor by Urim nor through prophets.[i] [7]Then Saul said to his servants, "Find me a medium[**] through whom I can seek counsel." His servants answered him, "There is a woman in Endor who is a medium."[j]

---

*[26:19] **The LORD's heritage:** the land and people of Israel (Dt 32:8–9; Ps 33:12). If driven from the land, David could not take part in worship of Israel's God; nonetheless, God has blessed David (cf. v. 25).

†[26:20] **Partridge:** lit., "the caller." The metaphor is built on clever wordplay: in v. 14, David calls out to the army and Abner asks the caller's identity. David calls out the answer: "the caller" is the object of the king's pursuit.

‡[27:6] Ziklag was a royal city and not part of Israel's tribal land holdings. Jerusalem later enjoyed a similar status (2 Sm 5:7–9).

§[27:10] **The Negeb of Judah:** David deceives Achish by assuring him that he has attacked Israelite territory.

¶[28:1] **You and your warriors:** David is faced with a potentially dangerous dilemma: either to reveal his continuing loyalty to his own people or to obey Achish and fight against his own people.

**[28:7] **A medium:** Saul's own prohibition of necromancy and divination (v. 3) was in keeping with the consistent teaching of the Old Testament (cf. Lv 19:31; 20:6, 27; Dt 18:10).

---

y. [26:19] 1 Sm 24:16.  z. [26:23] 1 Sm 18:20.  a. [26:25] 1 Sm 18:14; 24:21.  b. [27:2] 1 Sm 21:11–16.  c. [27:3] 1 Sm 25:3, 44; 30:3–5; 2 Sm 2:3.

d. [27:6] 1 Sm 30:1.  e. [27:7] 1 Sm 29:3.  f. [27:8] 1 Sm 15:3, 7; Jos 13:2–3.  g. [27:10] 1 Sm 30:14, 29; 1 Chr 2:9, 25, 42.  h. [28:3] 1 Sm 25:1; Sir 46:20.  i. [28:6] 1 Sm 14:37, 41; Ex 28:30; Lv 8:8.  j. [28:7] Lv 19:31; 20:27; Dt 18:10–12; 2 Kgs 21:6; 1 Chr 10:13–14; Acts 16:16.

**The Medium at Endor.** [8]So he disguised himself, putting on other clothes, and set out with two companions. They came to the woman at night, and Saul said to her, "Divine for me; conjure up the spirit I tell you."[k] [9]But the woman answered him, "You know what Saul has done, how he expelled the mediums and diviners from the land. Then why are you trying to entrap me and get me killed?" [10]But Saul swore to her by the Lord, "As the Lord lives, you shall incur no blame for this." [11]"Whom do you want me to conjure up?" the woman asked him. "Conjure up Samuel for me," he replied.

**Samuel Appears.** [12]When the woman saw Samuel, she shrieked at the top of her voice and said to Saul, "Why have you deceived me? You are Saul!" [13]But the king said to her, "Do not be afraid. What do you see?" "I see a god rising from the earth," she replied. [14]"What does he look like?" asked Saul. "An old man is coming up wrapped in a robe," she replied. Saul knew that it was Samuel, and so he bowed his face to the ground in homage.

**Saul's Doom.** [15]*Samuel then said to Saul, "Why do you disturb me by conjuring me up?" Saul replied: "I am in great distress, for the Philistines are waging war against me and God has turned away from me. Since God no longer answers me through prophets or in dreams, I have called upon you to tell me what I should do."[l] [16]To this Samuel said: "But why do you ask me, if the Lord has abandoned you for your neighbor?[m] [17]The Lord has done to you what he declared through me: he has torn the kingdom from your hand and has given it to your neighbor David. [18]"Because you disobeyed the Lord's directive and would not carry out his fierce anger against Amalek, the Lord has done this to you today.[n] [19]Moreover, the Lord will deliver Israel, and you as well, into the hands of the Philistines. By tomorrow you and your sons will be with me, and the Lord will have delivered the army of Israel into the hands of the Philistines."[o]

[20]Immediately Saul fell full length on the ground, in great fear because of Samuel's message. He had no strength left, since he had eaten nothing all that day and night. [21]Then the woman came to Saul, and seeing that he was quite terror-stricken, said to him: "Remember, your maidservant obeyed you: I took my life in my hands and carried out the request you made of me. [22]Now you, in turn, please listen to your maidservant. Let me set out a bit of food for you to eat, so that you are strong enough to go on your way." [23]But he refused, saying, "I

will not eat." However, when his servants joined the woman in urging him, he listened to their entreaties, got up from the ground, and sat on a couch. [24]The woman had a stall-fed calf in the house, which she now quickly slaughtered. Then taking flour, she kneaded it and baked unleavened bread. [25]She set the meal before Saul and his servants, and they ate. Then they got up and left the same night.

## CHAPTER 29

**David's Aid Rejected.** [1]Now the Philistines had mustered all their forces in Aphek, and the Israelites were encamped at the spring in Jezreel.[p] [2]As the Philistine lords were marching their units of a hundred and a thousand, David and his warriors were marching in the rear guard with Achish. [3]The Philistine commanders asked, "What are those Hebrews doing here?" Achish answered them: "Why, that is David, the officer of Saul, king of Israel. He has been with me for a year or two, and from the day he came over to me until now I have never found fault in him."[q] [4]But the Philistine commanders were angered at this and said to him: "Send that man back! Let him return to the place you picked out for him. He must not go down into battle with us; during the battle he might become our enemy. For how else can he win back his master's favor, if not at the expense of our soldiers?" [5]Is this not the David for whom they sing during their dances,

'Saul has slain his thousands,
    David his tens of thousands'?"[s]

[6]So Achish summoned David and said to him: "As the Lord lives, you are honest, and I would want you with me in all my battles. To this day I have found nothing wrong with you since you came to me. But in the view of the chiefs you are not welcome. [7]Leave peacefully, now, and do nothing that might displease the Philistine chiefs." [8]But David said to Achish: "What have I done? What fault have you found in your servant from the day I entered your service until today, that I cannot go to fight against the enemies of my lord the king?" [9]"I recognize," Achish answered David, "that you are trustworthy, like an angel of God. But the Philistine commanders are saying, 'He must not go with us into battle.' [10]So the first thing tomorrow, you and your lord's servants who came with you, go to the place I picked out for you. Do not take to heart their worthless remarks; for you have been valuable in my service. But make an early morning start, as soon as it grows light, and be on your way." [11]So David and his warriors left early in the morning to return to the land of the Philistines, and the Philistines went on up to Jezreel.

---

*[28:15–19] The consultation with the medium serves to remind the reader that the Lord's plan for David marches onward; no sorcery can thwart it.

---

k. [28:8] 1 Sm 15:23; 1 Kgs 14:2.  l. [28:15] 1 Sm 14:37; Sir 46:20.  m. [28:16] 1 Sm 15:27–28.  n. [28:18] 1 Sm 15:18–19, 26.  o. [28:19] 1 Sm 31:2–6; Sir 46:20.

p. [29:1] 1 Sm 4:1.  q. [29:3] 1 Sm 27:7.  r. [29:4] 1 Chr 12:19–20.  s. [29:5] 1 Sm 18:6–7; 21:12.

## CHAPTER 30

**Ziklag in Ruins.** [1]Before David and his men reached Ziklag on the third day, the Amalekites had raided the Negeb and Ziklag. They stormed Ziklag, and set it on fire.[t] [2]They took captive the women and all who were in the city, young and old, killing no one, and they herded them off when they left. [3]David and his men arrived at the city to find it burned to the ground and their wives, sons, and daughters taken captive. [4]Then David and those who were with him wept aloud until they could weep no more. [5]David's two wives, Ahinoam of Jezreel and Abigail, the widow of Nabal from Carmel, had also been carried off.[u] [6]Now David found himself in great danger, for the soldiers spoke of stoning him, so bitter were they over the fate of their sons and daughters. David took courage in the LORD his God [7]and said to Abiathar, the priest, son of Ahimelech, "Bring me the ephod!" When Abiathar brought him the ephod, [8]David inquired of the LORD, "Shall I pursue these raiders? Can I overtake them?" The LORD answered him: Go in pursuit, for you will certainly overtake them and bring about a rescue.

**Raid on the Amalekites.** [9]So David went off with his six hundred as far as the Wadi Besor, where those who were to remain behind halted. [10]David continued the pursuit with four hundred, but two hundred were too exhausted to cross the Wadi Besor and remained behind. [11]An Egyptian was found in the open country and brought to David. They gave him food to eat and water to drink; [12]they also offered a cake of pressed figs and two cakes of pressed raisins. When he had eaten, he revived, for he had not taken food nor drunk water for three days and three nights. [13]Then David asked him, "To whom do you belong? Where did you come from?" "I am an Egyptian, the slave of an Amalekite," he replied. "My master abandoned me three days ago because I fell sick. [14]We raided the Negeb of the Cherethites, the territory of Judah, and the Negeb of Caleb; and we set Ziklag on fire."[w] [15]David then asked him, "Will you lead me down to these raiders?" He answered, "Swear to me by God that you will not kill me or hand me over to my master, and I will lead you down to the raiders." [16]So he led them down, and there were the Amalekites lounging all over the ground, eating, drinking, and celebrating because of all the rich plunder they had taken from the land of the Philistines and from the land of Judah.

**The Plunder Recovered.** [17]From dawn to sundown the next day David attacked them, allowing no one to escape except four hundred young men, who mounted their camels and fled.[x] [18]David recovered everything the Amalekites had taken, and he rescued his two wives. [19]Nothing was missing, small or great, plunder or sons or daughters, of all that the Amalekites had taken. David brought back everything. [20]Moreover, David took all the sheep and oxen, and as they drove these before him, they shouted, "This is David's plunder!"

**Division of the Plunder.** [21]When David came to the two hundred men who had been too exhausted to follow him, whom he had left behind at the Wadi Besor, they came out to meet David and the men with him. As David approached, he greeted them. [22]But all the greedy and worthless among those who had accompanied David said, "Since they did not accompany us, we will not give them anything from the plunder, except for each man's wife and children." [23]But David said: "You must not do this, my brothers, after what the LORD has given us. The LORD has protected us and delivered into our hands the raiders that came against us.[y] [24]Who could agree with this proposal of yours? Rather, the share of the one who goes down to battle shall be the same as that of the one who remains with the baggage—they share alike."[z] [25]And from that day forward he made this a law and a custom in Israel, as it still is today.[a]

**David's Gifts to Judah.** [26]When David came to Ziklag, he sent part of the plunder to his friends, the elders of Judah,[*] saying, "This is a gift to you from the plunder of the enemies of the LORD," namely, [27]to those in Bethel, Ramoth-negeb, Jattir, [28]Aroer, Siphmoth, Eshtemoa, [29]Racal, Jerahmeelite cities and Kenite cities,[b] [30]Hormah, Borashan, Athach, [31]Hebron, and to all the places that David and his men had frequented.[c]

## CHAPTER 31

**Death of Saul and His Sons.** [1][d]Now the Philistines went to war against Israel, and the Israelites fled before them, and fell, slain on Mount Gilboa. [2]The Philistines pressed hard after Saul and his sons. When the Philistines had struck down Jonathan, Abinadab, and Malchishua, sons of Saul,[e] [3]the fury of the battle converged on Saul. Then the archers hit him, and he was severely wounded. [4]Saul said to his armor-bearer, "Draw your sword and run me through; otherwise these uncircumcised will come and abuse me." But the armor-bearer, badly frightened, refused, so Saul took his own sword and fell upon it.[f] [5]When the armor-bearer saw that Saul was dead, he too fell upon his sword and died with him. [6]Thus Saul, his three sons, and his armor-bearer died together on that same day. [7]When the Israelites on the slope of the valley and those

---

[*][30:26] **Elders of Judah:** David consolidates his power in southern Judah in preparation for his anointing at Hebron (2 Sm 5:3).

---

t. [30:1] 1 Sm 15:2; 27:6, 10; 1 Chr 12:21.   u. [30:5] 1 Sm 25:42; 27:3; 30:5.   v. [30:7–8] 1 Sm 2:28; 23:6; Ex 28:30.   w. [30:14] 1 Sm 27:10; Ez 25:16.   x. [30:17] 1 Sm 15:3; Jos 6:17; Jgs 7:12.

y. [30:23] Dt 20:4, 14.   z. [30:24] 1 Sm 17:22; 25:13.   a. [30:25] Nm 31:27.   b. [30:29] 1 Sm 27:10.   c. [30:31] 2 Sm 2:1–4.   d. [31:1–13] 2 Sm 1:1–16; 4:4; 1 Chr 10:1–12.   e. [31:2] 1 Sm 14:49; 28:19; 1 Chr 10:2–3.   f. [31:4] 1 Sm 24:6; Jgs 9:54; 1 Chr 10:4.   g. [31:5] 1 Sm 10:1; 26:9; 2 Mc 14:42.

along the Jordan saw that the men of Israel had fled and that Saul and his sons were dead, they abandoned their cities and fled. Then the Philistines came and lived in those cities.

⁸On the following day, when the Philistines came to strip the slain, they found Saul and his three sons fallen on Mount Gilboa. ⁹They cut off Saul's head and stripped him of his armor; these they sent throughout the land of the Philistines to bring the good news to the temple of their idols and to the people.ʰ ¹⁰They put his armor in the temple of Astarte but impaled his body on the wall of Beth-shan.

**Burial of Saul.** ¹¹When the inhabitants of Jabesh-gilead heard what the Philistines had done to Saul, ¹²all their warriors set out and traveled through the night; they removed the bodies of Saul and his sons from the wall of Beth-shan, and, returning to Jabesh, burned them.* ¹³Then they took their bones and buried them under the tamarisk tree in Jabesh, and fasted for seven days.

---

\*[31:12] **Burned them**: cremation was not an Israelite custom. The people of Jabesh-gilead repay Saul's victory over the Ammonites on their behalf (chap. 11) by providing burial and funeral rites for him and his sons. Probably the damaged state of the corpus necessitated cremation.

---

h. [31:9] 1 Sm 17:54; 2 Sm 1:20; 2 Mc 15:35.

i. [31:11–13] 1 Sm 11:1–11; 2 Sm 2:4–7; 21:12–14.

# THE SECOND BOOK OF
# SAMUEL

ೲ

## CHAPTER 1

**Report of Saul's Death.** ¹After the death of Saul, David returned from his victory over the Amalekites and stayed in Ziklag two days.ᵃ ²On the third day a man came from the field of battle, one of Saul's people, with his garments torn and his head covered with dirt. Going to David, he fell to the ground in homage. ³David asked him, "Where have you come from?" He replied, "From the Israelite camp: I have escaped." ⁴"What happened?" David said. "Tell me." He answered that the soldiers had fled the battle and many of them had fallen and were dead; and that Saul and his son Jonathan were dead. ⁵Then David said to the youth who was reporting to him, "How do you know that Saul and his son Jonathan are dead?" ⁶ᵇThe youth reporting to him replied: "I happened to find myself on Mount Gilboa and saw Saul leaning on his spear, with chariots and horsemen closing in on him. ⁷He turned around and saw me, and called me to him. When I said, 'Here I am,' ⁸he asked me, 'Who are you?' and I replied, 'An Amalekite.' ⁹Then he said to me, 'Stand over me, please, and put me to death, for I am in great suffering, but still alive.' ¹⁰So I stood over him and put him to death, for I knew that he could not survive his wound. I removed the crown from his head and the armlet from his arm and brought them here to my lord."

¹¹David seized his garments and tore them, and so did all the men who were with him.ᶜ ¹²They mourned and wept and fasted until evening for Saul and his son Jonathan, and for the people of the LORD and the house of Israel, because they had fallen by the sword.ᵈ ¹³David said to the youth who had reported to him, "Where are you from?" He replied, "I am the son of a resident alien, an Amalekite." ¹⁴David said to him, "How is it that you were not afraid to put forth your hand to desecrate the LORD's anointed?"ᵉ ¹⁵David then called one of the attendants and said to him, "Come, strike him down"; so he struck him and he died. ¹⁶David said to him, "Your blood is on your head, for you testified against yourself when you said, 'I put the LORD's anointed to death.'"

**Lament for Saul and Jonathan.** ¹⁷Then David chanted this lament for Saul and his son Jonathan ¹⁸(he commanded that it be taught to the Judahites; it is recorded in the Book of Jashar):ᶠ

¹⁹ Alas! the glory of Israel,
     slain upon your heights!
  How can the warriors have fallen!
²⁰ Do not report it in Gath,
     as good news in Ashkelon's streets,
  Lest Philistine women rejoice,
     lest the women of the
        uncircumcised exult!ᵍ
²¹ O mountains of Gilboa,
     upon you be neither dew nor rain,
     nor surging from the deeps!*
  Defiled there the warriors' shields,
     the shield of Saul—no longer
        anointed with oil!ʰ
²² From the blood of the slain,
     from the bodies of the warriors,
  The bow of Jonathan did not turn back,
     nor the sword of Saul return
        unstained.†ⁱ
²³ Saul and Jonathan, beloved and dear,
     separated neither in life nor death,
     swifter than eagles, stronger than
        lions!
²⁴ Women of Israel, weep over Saul,
     who clothed you in scarlet and in
        finery,
     covered your clothing with
        ornaments of gold.
²⁵ How can the warriors have fallen
     in the thick of battle!
     Jonathan—slain upon your heights!
²⁶ I grieve for you, Jonathan my brother!
     Most dear have you been to me;
  More wondrous your love to me
     than the love of women.ʲ
²⁷ How can the warriors have fallen,
     the weapons of war have perished!

## CHAPTER 2

**David Is Anointed King.** ¹After this, David inquired of the LORD, "Shall I go up into one of the cities of Judah?" The LORD replied to him: Go up. Then David asked, "Where shall I go?"

---

*[1:21] **Surging from the deeps**: this conjectural reading of the Hebrew yields a parallelism with dew and rain: the mountains where the warriors have fallen in battle are to be desiccated, deprived of water from above (rain, dew) and below (the primordial deeps).

†[1:22] **Unstained**: lit., "empty." The sword was conceived as a devouring mouth; see, e.g., 2:26.

---

a. [1:1] 1 Sm 30:17–20; 31:1–13.    b. [1:6–10] 2 Sm 4:10; 1 Sm 31:1–4; 1 Chr 10:1–4.    c. [1:11] 2 Sm 13:31.    d. [1:12] 1 Sm 31:13.    e. [1:14] 1 Sm 10:1; 24:7; Ps 105:15.    f. [1:18] Jos 10:13.

g. [1:20] Jgs 16:23; 1 Sm 31:9; Mi 1:10.    h. [1:21] Gn 27:28.    i. [1:22] 1 Sm 14:47.    j. [1:26] 1 Sm 18:1–4.

He replied: To Hebron. [2]So David went up there, with his two wives, Ahinoam of Jezreel and Abigail, the wife of Nabal of Carmel.[k] [3]David also brought up his men with their families, and they dwelt in the towns of Hebron. [4]Then the men of Judah came there and anointed David king over the house of Judah.

A report reached David that the people of Jabesh-gilead had buried Saul.[l] [5]So David sent messengers to the people of Jabesh-gilead and said to them: "May you be blessed by the LORD for having done this kindness to your lord Saul in burying him. [6]And now may the LORD show you kindness and fidelity. For my part, I will show generosity to you for having done this. [7]So take courage and prove yourselves valiant, for though your lord Saul is dead, the house of Judah has anointed me king over them."

## IV. THE REIGN OF DAVID

**Ishbaal King of Israel.** [8]Abner, son of Ner, captain of Saul's army, took Ishbaal,[*] son of Saul, and brought him over to Mahanaim,[m] [9]where he made him king over Gilead, the Asherites, Jezreel, Ephraim, Benjamin, and the rest of Israel. [10]Ishbaal, son of Saul, was forty years old when he became king over Israel, and he reigned two years; but the house of Judah followed David. [11]In all, David was king in Hebron over the house of Judah seven years and six months.[n]

**Combat near Gibeon.** [12]Now Abner, son of Ner, and the servants of Ishbaal, Saul's son, set out from Mahanaim for Gibeon. [13]Joab, son of Zeruiah, and the servants of David also set out and encountered them at the pool of Gibeon. And they sat down, one group on one side of the pool and the other on the opposite side. [14]Then Abner said to Joab, "Let the young men rise and perform for us."[†] Joab replied, "All right." [15]So they rose and were counted off: twelve of the Benjaminites of Ishbaal, son of Saul, and twelve of David's servants. [16]Then each one grasped his opponent's head and thrust his sword into his opponent's side, and they all fell down together.[‡] And so that place was named the Field of the Sides; it is in Gibeon.

**Death of Asahel.** [17]The battle that day was very fierce, and Abner and the men of Israel were defeated by David's servants. [18]The three sons of Zeruiah were there—Joab, Abishai, and Asahel.[o] Asahel, who was as fleet of foot as a gazelle in the open field, [19]set out after Abner, turning

neither right nor left in his pursuit. [20]Abner turned around and said, "Is that you, Asahel?" He replied, "Yes." [21]Abner said to him, "Turn right or left; seize one of the young men and take what you can strip from him." But Asahel would not stop pursuing him. [22]Once more Abner said to Asahel: "Stop pursuing me! Why must I strike you to the ground? How could I show my face to your brother Joab?"[p] [23]Still he refused to stop. So Abner struck him in the abdomen with the heel of his spear, and the weapon protruded from his back. He fell there and died on the spot. All who came to the place where Asahel had fallen and died, halted. [24]But Joab and Abishai continued the pursuit of Abner. The sun had gone down when they came to the hill of Ammah which lies east of the valley toward the wilderness near Geba.

**Truce Between Joab and Abner.** [25]Here the Benjaminites rallied around Abner, forming a single group, and made a stand on a hilltop. [26]Then Abner called to Joab and said: "Must the sword devour forever? Do you not know that afterward there will be bitterness? How long before you tell the people to stop pursuing their brothers?" [27]Joab replied, "As God lives, if you had not spoken, it would be morning before the people would be stopped from pursuing their brothers." [28]Joab then sounded the horn, and all the people came to a halt, pursuing Israel no farther and fighting no more. [29]Abner and his men marched all night long through the Arabah, crossed the Jordan, marched all through the morning, and came to Mahanaim. [30]Joab, coming from the pursuit of Abner, assembled all the men. Nineteen other servants of David were missing, besides Asahel. [31]But David's servants had struck down and killed three hundred and sixty men of Benjamin, followers of Abner. [32]They took up Asahel and buried him in his father's tomb in Bethlehem. Joab and his men made an all-night march, and dawn found them in Hebron.

## CHAPTER 3

[1]There followed a long war between the house of Saul and the house of David, in which David grew ever stronger, but the house of Saul ever weaker.

**Sons Born in Hebron.** [2][q]Sons were born to David in Hebron: his firstborn, Amnon, of Ahinoam from Jezreel; [3]the second, Chileab, of Abigail the wife of Nabal of Carmel; the third, Absalom, son of Maacah, who was the daughter of Talmai, king of Geshur;[r] [4]the fourth, Adonijah, son of Haggith; the fifth, Shephatiah, son of Abital;[s] [5]and the sixth, Ithream, by David's wife Eglah. These were born to David in Hebron.

**Ishbaal and Abner Quarrel.** [6]During the war between the house of Saul and the house of

---

*[2:8] **Ishbaal:** here and elsewhere in the Hebrew text, his name appears as "Ishbosheth"; the second part of Ishbaal, -baal, refers to the Canaanite god Baal, and is therefore suppressed, replaced by bosheth, "shame."

†[2:14] **Perform:** lit., "play."

‡[2:16] The nature of this gruesome game is not clear, and the place name is variously given in the older texts.

k. [2:2] 1 Sm 25:42–43.  l. [2:4] 1 Sm 31:11–13.  m. [2:8] 1 Sm 14:50.  n. [2:11] 2 Sm 5:5; 1 Kgs 2:11.  o. [2:18] 2 Sm 23:24; 1 Chr 2:16; 27:7.

p. [2:22] 2 Sm 3:27–28, 30.  q. [3:2–5] 1 Chr 3:1–4.  r. [3:3] 2 Sm 13:37; 15:8.  s. [3:4] 1 Kgs 1:5.

David, Abner was gaining power in the house of Saul. [7]Now Saul had had a concubine, Rizpah, the daughter of Aiah. And Ishbaal, son of Saul, said to Abner, "Why have you slept with my father's concubine?"*[8]Enraged at the words of Ishbaal, Abner said, "Am I a dog's head from Judah? As of today, I have been loyal to the house of Saul your father, to his brothers and his friends, and I have kept you out of David's clutches; and today you charge me with a crime involving a woman! [9]May God do thus to Abner, and more, if I do not carry out for David what the LORD swore to him—[u] [10]that is, take away the kingdom from the house of Saul and establish the throne of David over Israel as well as Judah, from Dan to Beer-sheba."[v] [11]Ishbaal was no longer able to say a word to Abner, he feared him so.

**Abner and David Reconciled.** [12]Then Abner sent messengers to David in Telam, where he was at the moment, to say, "Make a covenant with me, and you have me on your side, to bring all Israel over to you." [13]He replied, "Good, I will make a covenant with you. But one thing I require of you. You must not appear before me unless you bring back Michal, Saul's daughter, when you come to present yourself to me."[w] [14]At the same time David sent messengers to Ishbaal, son of Saul, to say, "Give me my wife Michal, whom I betrothed by paying a hundred Philistine foreskins." [15]Ishbaal sent for her and took her away from her husband Paltiel, son of Laish,[x] [16]who followed her weeping as far as Bahurim. But Abner said to him, "Go back!" So he turned back.

[17]Abner then had a word with the elders of Israel: "For some time you have been wanting David as your king. [18]Now take action, for the LORD has said of David: By David my servant I will save my people Israel from the power of the Philistines and from the power of all their enemies." [19]Abner also spoke with Benjamin, and then went to speak with David in Hebron concerning all that would be agreeable to Israel and to the whole house of Benjamin. [20]When Abner, accompanied by twenty men, came to David in Hebron, David prepared a feast for Abner and for the men who were with him. [21]Then Abner said to David, "I will now go to assemble all Israel for my lord the king, that they may make a covenant with you; you will then be king over all whom you wish to rule." So David let Abner go on his way in peace.

**Death of Abner.** [22]Just then David's servants and Joab were coming in from an expedition, bringing much plunder with them. Abner, having been dismissed by David, was no longer with him in Hebron but had gone on his way in peace. [23]When Joab and the whole force he had with him arrived, he was informed, "Abner, son of Ner, came to David, and he let him go on his way in peace." [24]So Joab went to the king and said: "What have you done? Abner came to you! Why did you let him get away? [25]Don't you know Abner? He came to trick you, to learn your comings and goings, to learn everything you do." [26]Joab then left David and sent messengers after Abner to bring him back from the cistern of Sirah; but David did not know. [27]When Abner returned to Hebron, Joab took him aside within the city gate to speak with him privately. There he stabbed him in the abdomen, and he died for the blood of Asahel, Joab's brother.[y] [28]Later David heard of it and said: "Before the LORD, I and my kingdom are forever innocent.[z] [29]May the blood of Abner, son of Ner, be on the head of Joab and all his family. May Joab's family never be without one suffering from a discharge, or one with a skin disease, or a man who holds the distaff, or one falling by the sword, or one in need of food!"†[30]Joab and Abishai his brother had been lying in wait for Abner because he killed Asahel their brother in battle at Gibeon.

**David Mourns Abner.** [31]Then David said to Joab and to all the people who were with him, "Tear your garments, put on sackcloth, and mourn over Abner." King David himself followed the bier.[a] [32]When they had buried Abner in Hebron, the king wept aloud at the grave of Abner, and all the people wept. [33]And the king sang this lament over Abner:

Should Abner have died like a fool?
[34] Your hands were not bound with chains,
nor your feet placed in fetters;
As one falls before the wicked, you fell.

And all the people continued to weep for him. [35]Then they went to console David with food while it was still day. But David swore, "May God do thus to me, and more, if before the sun goes down I eat bread or anything else."[b] [36]All the people noted this with approval, just as everything the king did met with their approval. [37]So on that day all the people and all Israel came to know that it was not the king's doing that Abner, son of Ner, was put to death. [38]The king then said to his servants: "Do you not know that a prince, a great man, has fallen today in Israel. [39]Although I am the anointed king, I am weak this day, and these men, the sons of Zeruiah, are too ruthless for me. May the LORD repay the evildoer in accordance with his evil deed."[c]

*[3:7] Asserting a right to the late king's harem was tantamount to claiming his kingship; cf. 16:21–22; 1 Kgs 2:21–22.

†[3:29] An assortment of imprecations, consisting of physical ailments, weakness, violent death, and poverty.

t. [3:7] 2 Sm 16:21–22; 21:8–10; 1 Kgs 2:21–22.   u. [3:9] Ru 1:17.   v. [3:10] 2 Sm 5:2; 1 Sm 25:30.   w. [3:13] 1 Sm 18:20–27.   x. [3:15] 1 Sm 25:44.

y. [3:27] 2 Sm 2:17–23; 1 Kgs 2:5, 31–33.z. [3:28, 30] 2 Sm 2:22–23.   a. [3:31] 2 Sm 21:10.   b. [3:35] Ru 1:17.   c. [3:39] Ps 28:4; Is 3:11.

## CHAPTER 4

**Death of Ishbaal.** ¹When Ishbaal, son of Saul, heard that Abner was dead in Hebron, he lost his resolve and all Israel was alarmed. ²Ishbaal, son of Saul, had two company leaders named Baanah and Rechab, sons of Rimmon the Beerothite, of the tribe of Benjamin—Beeroth, too, was ascribed to Benjamin:ᵈ ³the Beerothites fled to Gittaim, where they have been resident aliens to this day.ᵉ ⁴(Jonathan, son of Saul, had a son with crippled feet. He was five years old when the news about Saul and Jonathan came from Jezreel; his nurse took him and fled, but in their hasty flight, he fell and became lame. His name was Meribbaal.)*ᶠ ⁵The sons of Rimmon the Beerothite, Rechab and Baanah, came into the house of Ishbaal during the heat of the day, while he was lying on his bed in the afternoon. ⁶The gatekeeper of the house had dozed off while sifting wheat, and was asleep. So Rechab and his brother Baanah slipped past her ⁷and entered the house while Ishbaal was lying asleep in his bedroom. They struck and killed him, and cut off his head. Then, taking the head, they traveled on the Arabah road all night long.

**The Murder Avenged.** ⁸They brought the head of Ishbaal to David in Hebron and said to the king: "This is the head of Ishbaal, son of your enemy Saul, who sought your life. Thus has the LORD this day avenged my lord the king on Saul and his posterity." ⁹But David replied to Rechab and his brother Baanah, sons of Rimmon the Beerothite: "As the LORD lives, who rescued me from every distress: ¹⁰the man who reported to me, 'Saul is dead,' and thought he was bringing good news, that man I seized and killed in Ziglag: that was the reward I gave him.ᵍ ¹¹How much more now, when wicked men have slain an innocent man in bed at home, must I require his blood from you and purge you from the land!" ¹²So at David's command, the young men killed them and cut off their hands and feet, hanging them up near the pool in Hebron. But he took the head of Ishbaal and buried it in Abner's grave in Hebron.ʰ

## CHAPTER 5

**David King of Israel.** ¹ᵃAll the tribes of Israel came to David in Hebron, and they said: "Look! We are your bone and your flesh. ²In days past, when Saul was still our king, you were the one who led Israel out in all its battles and brought it back. And the LORD said to you: You shall

shepherd my people Israel; you shall be ruler over Israel."ⁱʲ ³Then all the elders of Israel came to the king in Hebron, and at Hebron King David made a covenant with them in the presence of the LORD; and they anointed David king over Israel. ⁴David was thirty years old when he became king, and he reigned forty years: ⁵in Hebron he was king over Judah seven years and six months, and in Jerusalem he was king thirty-three years over all Israel and Judah.ᵏ

**Capture of Zion.**† ⁶Then the king and his men went to Jerusalem against the Jebusites who inhabited the land. They told David, "You shall not enter here: the blind and the lame will drive you away!" which was their way of saying, "David shall not enter here."ᵐ ⁷David nevertheless captured the fortress of Zion, which is the City of David. ⁸On that day David said: "All who wish to strike at the Jebusites must attack through the water shaft. The lame and the blind shall be the personal enemies of David." That is why it is said, "The blind and the lame shall not enter the palace."ⁿ ⁹David took up residence in the fortress which he called the City of David. David built up the city on all sides, from the Millo toward the center.ᵒ ¹⁰David became ever more powerful, for the LORD of hosts was with him.ᵖ ¹¹ᵃHiram, king of Tyre, sent envoys to David along with cedar wood, and carpenters and masons, who built a house for David.ʳ ¹²David now knew‡ that the LORD had truly established him as king over Israel and had exalted his kingdom for the sake of his people Israel.

**David's Family in Jerusalem.** ¹³ᵃDavid took more concubines and wives in Jerusalem after he had come from Hebron, and more sons and daughters were born to him. ¹⁴These are the names of those who were born to him in Jerusalem: Shammua, Shobab, Nathan, Solomon, ¹⁵Ibhar, Elishua, Nepheg, Japhia, ¹⁶Elishama, Beeliada, and Eliphelet.

**Rout of the Philistines.** ¹⁷When the Philistines had heard that David was anointed king over Israel, they marched out in force to come after him. When David heard this, he went down

---

† [5:6–12] David's most important military exploit, the taking of Jerusalem, is here presented before his battles with the Philistines, vv. 17–25, which took place earlier. The sense of vv. 6 and 8 is in doubt. Perhaps the Jebusites boasted that Jerusalem was impregnable, using a metaphorical or proverbial expression that claimed the city was defensible even by people not suited for military action. The saying then received a different sense (v. 8), to the effect that "the blind and the lame" were David's enemies. Mt 21:14 and Lk 14:13 seem to play off, and transform, this saying.

‡ [5:12] **David now knew:** Hiram's carpenters and masons built David a house of cedar, the very model of a Canaanite king's palace. This house then represented the consolidation of David's royal power, in the Canaanite mode, with Jerusalem as David's personal fiefdom and capital city.

---

* [4:4] **Meribbaal:** Hebrew has *mephiboseth*; see note on 2:8. His name, in fact, is Meribbaal; cf. 1 Chr 8:34; 9:40. He is the subject of chap. 9 below. The text of this verse may owe its present place to the fact that ancient copies of the Books of Samuel tended to confuse his name with that of his uncle Ishbaal, Saul's son and successor, a principal figure in chaps. 2–4.

---

d. [4:2] 2 Sm 9:3; Jos 9:17–18.   e. [4:3] Jos 18:25.   f. [4:4] 2 Sm 9:3; 19:25.   g. [4:10] 2 Sm 1:6–10, 14, 16.   h. [4:12] Dt 21:22–23; 1 Sm 31:10.   i. [5:1–5] 1 Chr 11:1–3.

j. [5:2] 2 Sm 3:10; Dt 17:15; 1 Sm 18:16.   k. [5:5] 2 Sm 2:11; 1 Kgs 2:11; 1 Chr 3:4.   l. [5:6–10] 1 Chr 11:4–9.   m. [5:6] Jos 15:63; Jgs 1:19, 21; Is 29:3.   n. [5:8] Lv 21:18; Mt 21:14–15.   o. [5:9] 1 Kgs 3:1; 9:15; 11:27.   p. [5:10] Ps 78:70–72; 89; 132:13.   q. [5:11–25] 1 Chr 14:1–16.   r. [5:11–12] 1 Kgs 5:15; 1 Chr 14:1–2.   s. [5:13–16] 1 Chr 3:5–8; 14:3–7.

to the refuge.* [18]Meanwhile the Philistines had come and deployed themselves in the valley of Rephaim.† [19]David inquired of the LORD, "Shall I attack the Philistines, and will you deliver them into my power?" The LORD answered David: Attack, for I will surely deliver the Philistines into your power. [20]So David went to Baal-perazim,‡ and he defeated them there. He said, "The LORD has broken through my enemies before me just as water breaks through a dam." Therefore that place was called Baal-perazim. [21]The Philistines abandoned their gods there, and David and his men carried them away. [22]Once again the Philistines came up and deployed themselves in the valley of Rephaim, [23]and again David inquired of the LORD, who replied: Do not attack the front—circle behind them and come against them near the balsam trees. [24]When you hear the sound of marching§ in the tops of the balsam trees, act decisively, for then the LORD has already gone before you to strike the army of the Philistines. [25]David did as the LORD commanded him, and routed the Philistines from Gibeon as far as Gezer.

## CHAPTER 6

**The Ark Brought to Jerusalem.** [1]David again assembled all the picked men of Israel, thirty thousand in number. [2]Then David and all the people who were with him set out for Baala of Judah to bring up from there the ark of God, which bears the name "the LORD of hosts enthroned above the cherubim."ᵘ [3]They transported the ark of God on a new cart and took it away from the house of Abinadab on the hill. Uzzah and Ahio, sons of Abinadab, were guiding the cart,ᵛ [4]with Ahio walking before it, [5]while David and all the house of Israel danced before the LORD with all their might, with singing, and with lyres, harps, tambourines, sistrums, and cymbals.ʷ [6]As they reached the threshing floor of Nodan, Uzzah stretched out his hand to the ark of God and steadied it, for the oxen were tipping it. [7]Then the LORD became angry with Uzzah; God struck him on that spot, and he died there in God's presence. [8]David was angry because the LORD's wrath had broken out against Uzzah. Therefore that place has been

called Perez-uzzah¶ even to this day. [9]David became frightened of the LORD that day, and he said, "How can the ark of the LORD come to me?" [10]So David was unwilling to take the ark of the LORD with him into the City of David. David deposited it instead at the house of Obed-edom the Gittite.

[11]The ark of the LORD remained in the house of Obed-edom the Gittite for three months, and the LORD blessed Obed-edom and all his household.ˣ [12]When it was reported to King David that the LORD had blessed the household of Obed-edom and all that he possessed because of the ark of God, David went to bring up the ark of God from the house of Obed-edom into the City of David with joy.ᶻ [13]As soon as the bearers of the ark of the LORD had advanced six steps, he sacrificed an ox and a fatling. [14]Then David came dancing before the LORD with abandon, girt with a linen ephod."ᵃ [15]David and all the house of Israel were bringing up the ark of the LORD with shouts of joy and sound of horn. [16]As the ark of the LORD was entering the City of David, Michal, daughter of Saul, looked down from her window, and when she saw King David jumping and dancing before the LORD, she despised him in her heart. [17]They brought in the ark of the LORD and set it in its place within the tent which David had pitched for it. Then David sacrificed burnt offerings and communion offerings before the LORD. [18]When David had finished sacrificing burnt offerings and communion offerings, he blessed the people in the name of the LORD of hosts, [19]and distributed among all the people, the entire multitude of Israel, to every man and every woman, one loaf of bread, one piece of meat, and one raisin cake. Then all the people returned to their homes.

[20]When David went home to bless his own house,ᶜ Michal, the daughter of Saul, came out to meet him and said, "How well the king of Israel has honored himself today, exposing himself to the view of the slave girls of his followers, as a commoner might expose himself!" [21]But David replied to Michal: "I was dancing before the LORD. As the LORD lives, who chose me over your father and all his house when he appointed me ruler over the LORD's people, Israel, not only will I make merry before the LORD,ᵈ [22]but I will demean myself even more. I will be lowly in

---

*[5:17] **Refuge**: probably near Adullam (1 Sm 22:1–5).

†[5:18–25] The successive defeats of the Philistines in the valley of Rephaim southwest of Jerusalem had the effect of blocking their access to the mountain ridge near Gibeon, and confining them to their holdings on the coast and in the foothills beyond Gezer to the west and south.

‡[5:20] **Baal-perazim**: here the title *ba'al*, "master, lord," refers to the Lord; *perazim* is the plural of *perez*, which means "breaking" or "bursting," as in 6:8.

§[5:24] **Sound of marching**: the wind in the treetops suggestive of the footsteps of the Lord and the heavenly host.

¶[6:8] **Perez-uzzah**: this Hebrew phrase means "the breaking out against Uzzah"; see note on 5:20.

**[6:14] **Girt with a linen ephod**: the ephod was some sort of priestly vestment (probably like an apron); cf. Ex 28:4; Jgs 17:5; 1 Sm 2:18, 28; 14:3; 22:18; 23:6. The cultic procession that accompanies the ark to the holy mountain, Zion, is led by King David, dancing ecstatically and wearing a priestly vestment.

††[6:20–23] Michal's reaction to David's dancing comes from her conception of how a king should comport himself. David rejects this understanding, saying he needs no instruction from the House of the failed king, Saul.

---

t. [6:1–11] 1 Chr 13:1–14.   u. [6:2] Ex 25:10; Jos 15:9; 1 Chr 13:6; Ps 132:8–10.   v. [6:3] 1 Sm 4:3–4; 6:7–8; 7:1; Dn 3:55.   w. [6:5] Ps 68:24–25; 150:3–5.

x. [6:11] 1 Chr 26:4.   y. [6:12–23] 1 Chr 15:1–29; Ps 24:7–10.   z. [6:12] 1 Kgs 8:1.   a. [6:14] 1 Sm 2:18.   b. [6:17–19] Lv 1:1–17; 3:1–17; 1 Chr 16:1–3.   c. [6:20] 1 Chr 16:43.   d. [6:21] 1 Sm 13:14; 15:28.

your eyes, but in the eyes of the slave girls you spoke of I will be somebody." [23]Saul's daughter Michal was childless to the day she died.

## CHAPTER 7

**The Oracle of Nathan.** [1]eAfter the king had taken up residence in his house, and the Lord had given him rest from his enemies on every side,[f] [2]the king said to Nathan the prophet, "Here I am living in a house of cedar, but the ark of God dwells in a tent!"[g] [3]Nathan answered the king, "Whatever is in your heart, go and do, for the Lord is with you."[h] [4]But that same night the word of the Lord came to Nathan: [5]Go and tell David my servant, Thus says the Lord: Is it you who would build me a house to dwell in?[i] [6]I have never dwelt in a house from the day I brought Israel up from Egypt to this day, but I have been going about in a tent or a tabernacle. [7]As long as I have wandered about among the Israelites, did I ever say a word to any of the judges whom I commanded to shepherd my people Israel: Why have you not built me a house of cedar?

[8]Now then, speak thus to my servant David, Thus says the Lord of hosts:[*] I took you from the pasture, from following the flock, to become ruler over my people Israel.[j] [9]I was with you wherever you went, and I cut down all your enemies before you. And I will make your name like that of the greatest on earth.[k] [10]I will assign a place for my people Israel and I will plant them in it to dwell there; they will never again be disturbed, nor shall the wicked ever again oppress them, as they did at the beginning, [11]and from the day when I appointed judges over my people Israel. I will give you rest from all your enemies. Moreover, the Lord also declares to you that the Lord will make a house for you:[l] [12]mwhen your days have been completed and you rest with your ancestors, I will raise up your offspring after you, sprung from your loins, and I will establish his kingdom. [13]He it is[†] who shall build a house for my name, and I will establish

his royal throne forever. [14]I will be a father to him, and he shall be a son to me. If he does wrong, I will reprove him with a human rod and with human punishments;[n] [15]but I will not withdraw my favor from him as I withdrew it from Saul who was before you.[o] [16]Your house and your kingdom are firm forever before me; your throne shall be firmly established forever.[‡p] [17]In accordance with all these words and this whole vision Nathan spoke to David.

**David's Thanksgiving.** [18]Then King David went in and sat in the Lord's presence and said, "Who am I, Lord God, and what is my house, that you should have brought me so far?[q] [19]And yet even this is too little in your sight, Lord God! For you have made a promise regarding your servant's house reaching into the future, and giving guidance to the people, Lord God! [20]What more can David say to you? You know[§] your servant, Lord God! [21]For your servant's sake and as you have had at heart, you have brought about this whole magnificent disclosure to your servant. [22]Therefore, great are you, Lord God! There is no one like you, no God but you, as we have always heard.[r] [23]What other nation on earth is there like your people Israel? What god has ever led a nation, redeeming it as his people and making a name by great and awesome deeds, as you drove out the nations and their gods before your people, whom you redeemed for yourself from Egypt?[s] [24]You have established for yourself your people Israel as your people forever, and you, Lord, have become their God. [25]Now, Lord God, confirm the promise that you have spoken concerning your servant and his house forever. Bring about what you have promised [26]so that your name may be forever great. People will say: 'The Lord of hosts is God over Israel,' when the house of your servant David is established in your presence. [27]Because you, Lord of hosts, God of Israel, have revealed to your servant, 'I will build you a house,' your servant now finds the courage to make this prayer before you. [28]Since you, Lord God, are truly God and your words are truth and you have made this generous promise to your servant,[u] [29]do, then, bless the house of your servant, that it may be in your presence forever—since you, Lord God, have promised, and by your blessing the house of your servant shall be blessed forever."

---

*[7:8–16] The message Nathan delivers to David, called the Dynastic Oracle, is prompted by David's intention to build a house (i.e., a temple) for the Lord, like David's own house (i.e., palace) of cedar. David is told, in effect, not to bother building a house for the Lord; rather, the Lord will make a house for him—a dynasty, the House of David. Not only will he have descendants (v. 12) who will sit upon the throne of Israel (v. 13), their rule will last forever (vv. 13, 16); and even if they transgress the Lord's commands, the line of David will never be removed from kingship as Saul was (cf. 1 Sm 13; 15). The oracle establishes the Davidic king as standing in relationship to the Lord as a son to a father (v. 14; cf. Ps 2:7; 89:27). The Dynastic Oracle, with cognate texts in the Scriptures, is the basis for Jewish expectations of an anointed king (1 Sm 12:3, 5), son of David (Mt 21:9); cf. Acts 2:30; Heb 1:5.

†[7:13] **He it is:** Solomon, in the event.

‡[7:16] The unconditional promise made here, and reflected in Ps 89:34–35, stands in contrast to the tradition in Ps 132:12, where the continuation of the line of David depends on their fidelity to the Lord; cf. also 1 Kgs 2:4; 6:12; 8:25.

§[7:20] **Know:** give recognition, choose, single out: cf. Gn 18:19; Ex 33:12; Am 3:2.

---

e. [7:1–29] 1 Chr 17:1–27.　f. [7:1] Dt 12:10; 25:19; 1 Kgs 5:4.　g. [7:2] Ex 39:32.　h. [7:3] Ps 132:1–5.　i. [7:5] 1 Kgs 5:3; 8:16, 27; 1 Chr 22:8; 28:3; Is 66:1; Acts 7:48–49.　j. [7:8] 1 Sm 16:13; 17:15–20; Ps 78:70–71; Am 7:14–15.　k. [7:9] Ps 89:27.　l. [7:11] 2 Sm 23:5; 1 Kgs 2:4–24.　m. [7:12–15] 1 Kgs 5:19; 8:19; 1 Chr 22:10; 2 Chr 7:18; Ps 89:4, 26–29, 36–37; Lk 1:32; Heb 1:5.

n. [7:14] Ps 2:7; 89:26; Prv 3:12.　o. [7:15] 2 Sm 23:5; 1 Sm 13:14; 15:26, 28; 2 Kgs 19:34; 1 Chr 17:11–14; Ps 89:33–34.　p. [7:16] 2 Sm 23:5; Dn 2:44; 1 Mc 2:57; Mk 11:10; Lk 1:32–33; Heb 1:8.　q. [7:18] 1 Chr 17:16.　r. [7:22] Ex 15:11; Is 45:5.　s. [7:23] Dt 4:7, 34.　t. [7:24–25] Ex 6:7; Dt 7:6; 26:17; 29:13.　u. [7:28] Nm 23:19; Jn 17:17.

## CHAPTER 8

**Summary of David's Wars.** [1v]After this, David defeated the Philistines and subdued them; and David took . . . ˙ from the Philistines. [2]He also defeated Moab and measured them with a line. Making them lie down on the ground, he measured two lengths of line for death, and a full length for life.[†] Thus the Moabites became subject to David, paying tribute. [3w]David then defeated Hadadezer, son of Rehob, king of Zobah, when he went to re-establish his dominion at the River.[x] [4]David captured from him one thousand seven hundred horsemen and twenty thousand foot soldiers. David hamstrung all the chariot horses, but left one hundred for his chariots.[y] [5]The Arameans of Damascus came to help Hadadezer, king of Zobah, but David also defeated twenty-two thousand of them in Aram. [6]David then placed garrisons in the Damascus region of Aram, and the Arameans became David's subjects, paying tribute. The LORD brought David victory in all his undertakings. [7]David took the golden shields that were carried by Hadadezer's attendants and brought them to Jerusalem. (These Shishak, king of Egypt, took away when he came to Jerusalem in the days of Rehoboam, son of Solomon.) [8]From Tebah and Berothai, cities of Hadadezer, King David removed a very large quantity of bronze. [9]When Toi, king of Hamath, heard that David had defeated the entire army of Hadadezer, [10]Toi sent his son Hadoram to wish King David well and to congratulate him on having waged a victorious war against Hadadezer; for Hadadezer had been at war with Toi. Hadoram also brought with him articles of silver, gold, and bronze. [11]These also King David consecrated to the LORD along with the silver and gold that he had taken for this purpose from all the nations he had subdued: [12]from Edom, Moab, the Ammonites, the Philistines, and Amalek, and from the spoils of Hadadezer, son of Rehob, king of Zobah. [13]On his return,[‡] David made a name for himself by defeating eighteen thousand Edomites in the Valley of Salt.[z] [14]He set up garrisons in Edom, and all the Edomites became David's subjects. Thus the LORD brought David victory in all his undertakings.

**David's Officials.** [15a]David was king over all Israel; he dispensed justice and right to all his people. [16]Joab, son of Zeruiah, was in command of the army. Jehoshaphat, son of Ahilud, was chancellor. [17]Zadok, son of Ahitub, and Ahimelech, son of Abiathar, were priests.[§] Shavsha was scribe. [18]Benaiah, son of Jehoiada, was in command of the Cherethites and the Pelethites; and David's sons were priests.[b]

## CHAPTER 9

**David and Meribbaal.** [1]David asked, "Is there any survivor of Saul's house to whom I may show kindness for the sake of Jonathan?"[c] [2]Now there was an official of the house of Saul named Ziba. He was summoned to David, and the king asked him, "Are you Ziba?" He replied, "Your servant."[d] [3]Then the king asked, "Is there any survivor of Saul's house to whom I may show God's kindness?" Ziba answered the king, "There is still Jonathan's son, the one whose feet are crippled."[e] [4]The king asked him, "Where is he?" and Ziba answered the king, "He is in the house of Machir, son of Ammiel, in Lodebar."[f] [5]So King David sent for him and had him brought from the house of Machir, son of Ammiel, from Lodebar. [6]When Meribbaal, son of Jonathan, son of Saul, came to David, he fell face down in homage. David said, "Meribbaal," and he answered, "Your servant." [7]"Do not be afraid," David said to him, "I will surely be kind to you for the sake of Jonathan your father. I will restore to you all the lands of Saul your grandfather, and you shall eat at my table always." [8]Bowing low, he answered, "What am I, your servant, that you should pay attention to a dead dog like me?"[g] [9]The king then called Ziba, Saul's attendant, and said to him: "All that belonged to Saul and to his entire house, I am giving to your lord's son. [10]You and your sons and servants must till the land for him. You shall bring in the produce, which shall be food for your lord's household to eat. But Meribbaal, your lord's son, shall always eat at my table." Now Ziba had fifteen sons and twenty servants. [11]Ziba answered the king, "Whatever my lord the king commands his servant, so shall your servant do." And so Meribbaal ate at David's table like one of the king's sons.[h] [12]Meribbaal had a young son whose name was Mica; and all the tenants of Ziba's household

---

*[8:1] **David took . . .** : the original Hebrew seems irretrievable. The transmitted text gives "the bridle of the cubit"; 1 Chr 18:1 understood "Gath and its towns"; others implausibly read "dominion of the capital city."

†[8:2] **Two lengths . . . a full length for life**: usually taken to mean that two-thirds of them were executed; but it could mean that two-thirds were spared, if the line was used full length in their case but doubled on itself to make "two lines" for those to be put to death. Note the contrasting good relations in 1 Sm 22:3–4.

‡[8:13] **On his return**: possibly to Jerusalem, after the revolt of Absalom (chaps. 15–18), which this catalogue of victories would avoid mentioning. 1 Chr 18:12 attributes the defeat of the Edomites to Abishai, while the superscription of Ps 60 attributes it to Joab.

§[8:17] **Zadok . . . Ahimelech, son of Abiathar, were priests**: the names of Abiathar and Ahimelech are frequently associated with David (1 Sm 22:20; 23:6; 30:7; 2 Sm 15:24, 29, 35; 17:15; 19:12; 20:25), but they show Abiathar acting as priest, not Ahimelech: Abiathar shared the priestly office with Zadok in David's reign and even during Solomon's early years (1 Kgs 2:26; 4:4). Ahimelech was the name of Abiathar's father. This verse and 1 Chr 18:16 may indicate that Abiathar had a son named Ahimelech who also acted as a priest, like his father and his namesake grandfather, in the last years of David.

---

a. [8:15–18] 2 Sm 20:23–26; 1 Kgs 4:1–6; 1 Chr 18:14–17.
b. [8:18] 2 Sm 15:18; 20:7, 23; 23:20.   c. [9:1] 2 Sm 21:7; 1 Sm 18:1–4; 20:8–10, 15–17, 42.   d. [9:2] 2 Sm 16:1–4; 19:27.   e. [9:3] 2 Sm 4:4.
f. [9:4] 2 Sm 17:27.   g. [9:8] 1 Sm 24:15.   h. [9:11] 2 Sm 19:29.

---

v. [8:1–18] 1 Chr 18:1–17.   w. [8:3–8] 2 Sm 10:15–19.   x. [8:3] 2 Sm 10:6; 1 Kgs 11:23.   y. [8:4] Jos 11:6, 9.   z. [8:13] 2 Kgs 14:7.

worked for Meribbaal.[i] [13]But Meribbaal lived in Jerusalem, because he always ate at the king's table. He was lame in both feet.[j]

## CHAPTER 10

**Campaigns Against Ammon.** [1k]After this,[*] the king of the Ammonites died, and Hanun his son succeeded him as king. [2]David said, "I will show kindness to Hanun, the son of Nahash, as his father showed kindness to me." Therefore David sent his servants to Hanun to console him concerning his father. But when David's servants had entered the land of the Ammonites, [3]the Ammonite princes said to their lord Hanun, "Do you think David is doing this—sending you these consolers—to honor your father? Is it not rather to explore the city, to spy on it, and to overthrow it, that David has sent his servants to you?" [4]So Hanun seized David's servants, shaved off half their beards, cut away the lower halves of their garments at the buttocks, and sent them away.[l] [5]David was told of it and he sent word for them to be intercepted, for the men had been greatly disgraced. "Remain at Jericho," the king told them, "until your beards have grown again; then come back here."

[6†]When the Ammonites realized that they were in bad odor with David, they sent for and hired twenty thousand Aramean foot soldiers from Beth-rehob and Zobah, as well as the king of Maacah with one thousand men, and twelve thousand men from Tob.[m]

[7]When David heard of this, he sent Joab and his whole army of warriors against them.[n] [8]The Ammonites marched out and lined up for battle at the entrance of their city gate, while the Arameans of Zobah and Rehob and the men of Tob and Maacah remained apart in the open field. [9]When Joab saw that there was a battle line both in front of and behind him, he chose some of the best fighters of Israel and lined them up against the Arameans; [10]the rest of the army he placed under the command of his brother Abishai and lined up to oppose the Ammonites. [11]And he said, "If the Arameans prove too strong for me, you must come and save me; and if the Ammonites prove too strong for you, I will come to save you. [12]Hold firm and let us show ourselves courageous for the sake of our people and the cities of our God; and may the Lord do what is good in his sight." [13]Joab

therefore advanced with his men for battle with the Arameans, but they fled before him. [14]And when the Ammonites saw that the Arameans had fled, they too fled before Abishai, and reentered their city. Joab then ceased his attack on the Ammonites and came to Jerusalem. [15o]Seeing themselves vanquished by Israel, the Arameans held a full muster of troops. [16]Hadadezer sent for and brought Arameans from beyond the River. They came to Helam, with Shobach, the captain of Hadadezer's army, at their head. [17]When this was reported to David, he gathered all Israel together, crossed the Jordan, and went to Helam. The Arameans drew up in formation against David and gave battle. [18]But the Arameans fled before Israel, and David killed seven hundred of their chariot fighters and forty thousand of their foot soldiers. He struck down Shobach, commander of the army, and he died on the field. [19]When Hadadezer's vassal kings saw themselves vanquished by Israel, they made peace with the Israelites and became their subjects. After this, the Arameans were afraid to give further aid to the Ammonites.

## CHAPTER 11

**David's Sin.** [1]At the turn of the year,[‡] the time when kings go to war, David sent out Joab along with his officers and all Israel, and they laid waste the Ammonites and besieged Rabbah. David himself remained in Jerusalem.[p] [2]One evening David rose from his bed and strolled about on the roof of the king's house. From the roof he saw a woman bathing; she was very beautiful. [3]David sent people to inquire about the woman and was told, "She is Bathsheba, daughter of Eliam, and wife of Uriah the Hittite, Joab's armor-bearer."[q] [4]Then David sent messengers and took her. When she came to him, he took her to bed, at a time when she was just purified after her period; and she returned to her house.[r] [5]But the woman had become pregnant; she sent a message to inform David, "I am pregnant."

[6]So David sent a message to Joab, "Send me Uriah the Hittite." Joab sent Uriah to David. [7]And when he came, David asked him how Joab was, how the army was, and how the war was going, and Uriah answered that all was well. [8]David then said to Uriah, "Go down to your house and bathe your feet." Uriah left the king's house, and a portion from the king's table was sent after him. [9]But Uriah slept at the entrance of the king's house with the other officers of his lord, and did not go down to his own house. [10]David was told, "Uriah has not gone down to his house." So he said to Uriah, "Have you not come from a journey? Why, then, did you not go

---

*[10:1] **After this:** early in the reign of David, since Hanun's father Nahash (1 Chr 19:1) had been ruling in Ammon at the beginning of Saul's reign (1 Sm 11) and Solomon was not yet born (2 Sm 11:1; 12:24).

†[10:6–9] A Hebrew text from Qumran (4QSam[a]) comes closer in these verses to what is given in 1 Chr 19:6–9. The scene of the conflict is more likely the Ammonite capital, Rabbath-Ammon (v. 8; cf. Josephus *Antiquities* 7:123), than Medeba (1 Chr 19:7).

i. [9:12] 1 Chr 8:34.    j. [9:13] 2 Sm 21:7.    k. [10:1–19] 1 Chr 19:1–19.    l. [10:4] Is 20:4.    m. [10:6] 2 Sm 8:3; 1 Sm 14:47.    n. [10:7] 2 Sm 11:1.

‡[11:1] **At the turn of the year:** in the spring.

o. [10:15–19] 2 Sm 8:3–8; 1 Chr 9:16–19.    p. [11:1] 2 Sm 10:7; 1 Chr 20:1.    q. [11:3] 2 Sm 23:39.    r. [11:4] Lv 15:19.

down to your house?" ¹¹Uriah answered David, "The ark and Israel and Judah are staying in tents, and my lord Joab and my lord's servants are encamped in the open field. Can I go home to eat and to drink and to sleep with my wife? As the LORD lives and as you live, I will do no such thing."ₛ ¹²Then David said to Uriah, "Stay here today also, and tomorrow I will send you back." So Uriah stayed in Jerusalem that day. On the following day, ¹³David summoned him, and he ate and drank with David, who got him drunk. But in the evening he went out to sleep on his bed among his lord's servants, and did not go down to his house. ¹⁴The next morning David wrote a letter to Joab which he sent by Uriah. ¹⁵This is what he wrote in the letter: "Place Uriah up front, where the fighting is fierce. Then pull back and leave him to be struck down dead." ¹⁶So while Joab was besieging the city, he assigned Uriah to a place where he knew the defenders were strong. ¹⁷When the men of the city made a sortie against Joab, some officers of David's army fell, and Uriah the Hittite also died.

¹⁸Then Joab sent David a report of all the details of the battle, ¹⁹instructing the messenger, "When you have finished giving the king all the details of the battle, ²⁰the king may become angry and say to you: 'Why did you go near the city to fight? Did you not know that they would shoot from the wall above? ²¹Who killed Abimelech, son of Jerubbaal? Was it not a woman who threw a millstone down on him from the wall above, so that he died in Thebez? Why did you go near the wall?' Then you in turn are to say, 'Your servant Uriah the Hittite is also dead.'"ₜ ²²The messenger set out, and on his arrival he reported to David everything Joab had sent him to tell.' ²³He told David: "The men had the advantage over us and came out into the open against us, but we pushed them back to the entrance of the city gate. ²⁴Then the archers shot at your servants from the wall above, and some of the king's servants died; and your servant Uriah the Hittite is also dead." ²⁵David said to the messenger: "This is what you shall say to Joab: 'Do not let this be a great evil in your sight, for the sword devours now here and now there. Strengthen your attack on the city and destroy it.' Encourage him."

²⁶When the wife of Uriah heard that her husband had died, she mourned her lord. ²⁷But once the mourning was over, David sent for her and brought her into his house. She became his wife and bore him a son. But in the sight of the LORD what David had done was evil.

## CHAPTER 12

**Nathan's Parable.**† ¹The LORD sent Nathan to David, and when he came to him, he said: "Tell me how you judge this case: In a certain town there were two men, one rich, the other poor.ᵘ ²The rich man had flocks and herds in great numbers. ³But the poor man had nothing at all except one little ewe lamb that he had bought. He nourished her, and she grew up with him and his children. Of what little he had she ate; from his own cup she drank; in his bosom she slept; she was like a daughter to him. ⁴Now, a visitor came to the rich man, but he spared his own flocks and herds to prepare a meal for the traveler who had come to him: he took the poor man's ewe lamb and prepared it for the one who had come to him." ⁵David grew very angry with that man and said to Nathan: "As the LORD lives, the man who has done this deserves death! ⁶He shall make fourfold restitution‡ for the lamb because he has done this and was unsparing."ᵛ ⁷Then Nathan said to David: "You are the man!

**Nathan's Indictment.** "Thus says the LORD God of Israel: I anointed you king over Israel. I delivered you from the hand of Saul.ʷ ⁸I gave you your lord's house and your lord's wives for your own. I gave you the house of Israel and of Judah. And if this were not enough, I could count up for you still more. ⁹Why have you despised the LORD and done what is evil in his sight? You have cut down Uriah the Hittite with the sword; his wife you took as your own, and him you killed with the sword of the Ammonites. ¹⁰Now, therefore, the sword shall never depart from your house, because you have despised me and have taken the wife of Uriah the Hittite to be your wife.ˣ ¹¹Thus says the LORD: I will bring evil upon you out of your own house. I will take your wives before your very eyes, and will give them to your neighbor: he shall lie with your wives in broad daylight.§ʸ ¹²You have acted in secret, but I will do this in the presence of all Israel, in the presence of the sun itself."

**David's Repentance.** ¹³Then David said to Nathan, "I have sinned against the LORD." Nathan answered David: "For his part, the LORD

---

*[11:22–24] In these verses the Greek text has David, angry with Joab, repeat exactly the questions Joab had foreseen in vv. 20–21. In v. 24 of our oldest Greek text, the messenger specifies that about eighteen men were killed. The Greek is considerably longer than the transmitted Hebrew text, suggesting that the Hebrew may have lost some sentences.

†[12:1–7] David has committed adultery with Bathsheba and arranged the death of her husband. Instead of directly indicting the king for this criminal abuse of his royal authority, the prophet Nathan tells David a story. In the story, a parable of David's own actions, a powerful man takes cruel advantage of his vulnerable neighbor. Hearing the story, David is outraged and denounces the rich man—thus unwittingly pronouncing judgment on himself ("You are the man," v. 7).

‡[12:6] **Fourfold restitution:** David's judgment foreshadows the deaths of four of his own sons: the child born of his adulterous union with Bathsheba (v. 18); Amnon (13:28–29); Absalom (18:15; 19:1); and Adonijah (1 Kgs 2:24–25).

§[12:11] **In broad daylight:** lit., "before the eyes of the sun"; the phrase echoes "before your very eyes" and anticipates "in the presence of the sun itself" (v. 12). The reference is to Absalom's action in appropriating his father's harem (16:22).

---

s. [11:11] 1 Sm 4:3–4.  t. [11:21] Jgs 9:50–54.

u. [12:1] Sir 47:1.  v. [12:6] Ex 21:37; Lk 19:8.  w. [12:7] 1 Sm 16:13.  x. [12:10] 2 Sm 13:28–29; 18:14.  y. [12:11] 2 Sm 16:21–22.

has removed your sin. You shall not die,$^z$ $^{14}$but since you have utterly spurned the LORD by this deed, the child born to you will surely die." $^{15}$Then Nathan returned to his house.

The LORD struck the child that the wife of Uriah had borne to David, and it became desperately ill. $^{16}$David pleaded with God on behalf of the child. He kept a total fast, and spent the night lying on the ground clothed in sackcloth. $^{17}$The elders of his house stood beside him to get him to rise from the ground; but he would not, nor would he take food with them. $^{18}$On the seventh day, the child died. David's servants were afraid to tell him that the child was dead, for they said: "When the child was alive, we spoke to him, but he would not listen to what we said. How can we tell him the child is dead? He may do some harm!" $^{19}$But David noticed his servants whispering among themselves and realized that the child was dead. He asked his servants, "Is the child dead?" They said, "Yes." $^{20}$Rising from the ground, David washed and anointed himself, and changed his clothes. Then he went to the house of the LORD and worshiped. He returned to his own house and asked for food; they set it before him, and he ate. $^{21}$His servants said to him: "What is this you are doing? While the child was living, you fasted and wept and kept vigil; now that the child is dead, you rise and take food." $^{22}$He replied: "While the child was living, I fasted and wept, thinking, 'Who knows? The LORD may grant me the child's life.' $^{23}$But now he is dead. Why should I fast? Can I bring him back again? I shall go to him, but he will not return to me."$^a$ $^{24}$Then David consoled Bathsheba his wife. He went and slept with her; and she conceived and bore him a son, who was named Solomon. The LORD loved him $^{25}$and sent the prophet Nathan to name him Jedidiah,$^*$ on behalf of the LORD.

**End of the Ammonite War.** $^{26b}$Joab fought against Rabbah of the Ammonites and captured that royal city. $^{27}$He sent messengers to David to say: "I have fought against Rabbah and have taken the water-city. $^{28}$Therefore, assemble the rest of the soldiers, join the siege against the city, and capture it, lest I be the one to capture the city and mine be the name people mention, not yours." $^{29}$So David assembled the rest of the soldiers, went to Rabbah, fought against it, and captured it. $^{30}$He took the crown of Milcom from the idol's head, a talent$^†$ of gold in weight, with precious stones; this crown David wore on his own head. He also brought out a great amount of spoil from the city. $^{31}$He deported the people of the city and set them to work with saws, iron picks, and iron axes, or put them to work at the

brickmold. He dealt thus with all the cities of the Ammonites. Then David and his whole army returned to Jerusalem.

## CHAPTER 13

**Amnon's Rape of Tamar.** $^1$After this, the following occurred. David's son Absalom had a beautiful sister named Tamar, and David's son Amnon loved her.$^c$ $^2$He was in such anguish over his sister Tamar that he became sick; she was a virgin, and Amnon thought it impossible to do anything to her. $^3$Now Amnon had a friend named Jonadab, son of David's brother Shimeah, who was very clever.$^{†d}$ $^4$He asked him, "Prince, why are you so dejected morning after morning? Why not tell me?" So Amnon said to him, "I am in love with Tamar, my brother Absalom's sister." $^5$Then Jonadab replied, "Lie down on your bed and pretend to be sick. When your father comes to visit you, say to him, 'Please let my sister Tamar come and encourage me to take food. If she prepares something in my presence, for me to see, I will eat it from her hand.'" $^6$So Amnon lay down and pretended to be sick. When the king came to visit him, Amnon said to the king, "Please let my sister Tamar come and prepare some fried cakes before my eyes, that I may take food from her hand."

$^7$David then sent home a message to Tamar, "Please go to the house of your brother Amnon and prepare some food for him." $^8$Tamar went to the house of her brother Amnon, who was in bed. Taking dough and kneading it, she twisted it into cakes before his eyes and fried the cakes. $^9$Then she took the pan and set out the cakes before him. But Amnon would not eat; he said, "Have everyone leave me." When they had all left him, $^{10}$Amnon said to Tamar, "Bring the food into the bedroom, that I may have it from your hand." So Tamar picked up the cakes she had prepared and brought them to her brother Amnon in the bedroom. $^{11}$But when she brought them close to him so he could eat, he seized her and said to her, "Come! Lie with me, my sister!" $^{12}$But she answered him, "No, my brother! Do not force me! This is not done in Israel. Do not commit this terrible crime.$^e$ $^{13}$Where would I take my shame? And you would be labeled a fool in Israel.$^§$ So please, speak to the king; he will not keep me from you."$^f$ $^{14}$But he would not listen to her; he was too strong for her: he forced her down and raped her. $^{15}$Then Amnon felt intense hatred for her; the hatred he felt for her far surpassed the love he had had for her.

---

* [12:25] **Jedidiah:** the name means "beloved of Yhwh."
† [12:30] **A talent:** since this would normally be more than seventy-five pounds, the report may have been embellished.

‡ [13:3] **Clever:** lit., "wise." Jonadab's "wisdom" extends only to sly cleverness in getting things done; he devises the plan that will enable Amnon to pursue his infatuation. In the categories of the Old Testament wisdom tradition, Jonadab is a fool.
§ [13:13] **A fool in Israel:** a play on *nebala* (v. 12), "terrible crime," lit., "folly."

---

z. [12:13] 1 Kgs 21:29; Ps 32:5; 51:4; Sir 47:11.    a. [12:23] Jb 7:9–10.    b. [12:26–31] 1 Chr 20:1–3.

c. [13:1] 2 Sm 3:2–3; 1 Chr 3:9.    d. [13:3] 2 Sm 21:21.    e. [13:12] Lv 18:9; 20:17; Dt 22:21; 27:22.    f. [13:13] Gn 34:7–8.

Amnon said to her, "Get up, leave." [16]She replied, "No, brother, because sending me away would be far worse than this evil thing you have done to me." He would not listen to her, [17]but called the youth who was his attendant and said, "Send this girl outside, away from me, and bar the door after her." [18]Now she had on a long tunic, for that is how virgin princesses dressed in olden days. When his attendant put her out and barred the door after her, [19]Tamar put ashes on her head and tore the long tunic in which she was clothed. Then, putting her hands to her head, she went away crying loudly. [20]Her brother Absalom said to her: "Has your brother Amnon been with you? Keep still now, my sister; he is your brother. Do not take this so to heart." So Tamar remained, devastated, in the house of her brother Absalom. [21]King David, when he heard of the whole affair, became very angry. He would not, however, antagonize Amnon, his high-spirited son; he loved him, because he was his firstborn. [22]And Absalom said nothing, good or bad, to Amnon; but Absalom hated Amnon for having humiliated his sister Tamar.

**Absalom's Plot.** [23]Two years went by. It was sheep-shearing time for Absalom in Baal-hazor near Ephraim, and Absalom invited all the king's sons. [24]Absalom went to the king and said: "Your servant has hired the shearers. Please, may the king come with all his servants to your servant." [25]But the king said to Absalom, "No, my son, all of us should not go lest we be a burden to you." And though Absalom urged him, he would not go but began to bid him good-bye. [26]Absalom then said, "If not you, then please let my brother Amnon come with us." The king asked him, "Why should he go with you?" [27]But at Absalom's urging, the king sent Amnon and with him all his other sons. Absalom prepared a banquet fit for a king. [28]gBut Absalom had instructed his attendants: "Now watch! When Amnon is merry with wine and I say to you, 'Kill Amnon,' put him to death. Do not be afraid, for it is I who order you to do it. Be strong and act like warriors."

**Death of Amnon.** [29]When the attendants did to Amnon as Absalom had commanded, all the king's other sons rose up, mounted their mules, and fled. [30]While they were still on the road, a report reached David: "Absalom has killed all the king's sons and not one of them is left." [31]The king stood up, tore his garments, and lay on the ground. All his servants standing by him also tore their garments.[h] [32]But Jonadab, son of David's brother Shimeah, spoke up: "Let not my lord think that all the young men, the king's sons, have been killed! Amnon alone is dead, for Absalom was set on this ever since Amnon humiliated his sister Tamar. [33]Now let my lord the king not take so to heart that report, 'All the king's sons are dead.' Amnon alone is dead."

[34]Meanwhile, Absalom had taken flight. Then the servant on watch looked out and saw a large group coming down the slope from the direction of Bahurim. He came in and reported this to the king: "I saw some men coming down the mountainside from the direction of Bahurim." [35]So Jonadab said to the king: "There! The king's sons have come. It is as your servant said." [36]No sooner had he finished speaking than the king's sons came in, weeping aloud. The king, too, and all his servants wept very bitterly. [37]But Absalom, who had taken flight, went to Talmai, son of Ammihud, king of Geshur,[i] [38]and stayed in Geshur for three years. [39]All that time the king continued to mourn his son; but his intention of going out against Absalom abated as he was consoled over the death of Amnon.

## CHAPTER 14

**The Wise Woman of Tekoa.** [1]Now Joab, son of Zeruiah, knew how the king felt toward Absalom. [2]Joab sent to Tekoa and brought from there a wise woman, to whom he said: "Pretend to be in mourning. Put on mourning apparel and do not anoint yourself with oil, that you may appear to be a woman who has long been mourning someone dead. [3]Then go to the king and speak to him in this manner." And Joab told her what to say.

[4]So the woman of Tekoa went to the king and fell to the ground in homage, saying, "Help, O king!" [5]The king said to her, "What do you want?" She replied: "Alas, I am a widow; my husband is dead. [6]Your servant had two sons, who quarreled in the field, with no one to part them, and one of them struck his brother and killed him. [7]Then the whole clan confronted your servant and demanded: 'Give up the one who struck down his brother. We must put him to death for the life of his brother whom he has killed; we must do away with the heir also.' Thus they will quench my remaining hope' and leave my husband neither name nor posterity upon the earth."[k] [8]The king then said to the woman: "Go home. I will issue a command on your behalf." [9]The woman of Tekoa answered him, "Upon me and my family be the blame, my lord king; the king and his throne are innocent." [10]Then the king said, "If anyone says a word to you, have him brought to me, and he shall not touch you again." [11]But she said, "Please, let the king remember the LORD your God, that the avenger of blood may not go too far in destruction and that my son may not be done away with." He replied, "As the LORD lives, not a hair of your son shall fall to the ground."

---

* [14:7] **Hope:** lit., "glowing coal." The image is similar to that of a lighted lamp, cf. Ps 132:17, or small hearth fire, to keep alive the ancestral name.

g. [13:28–29] 2 Sm 12:10.    h. [13:31] 2 Sm 1:11.

i. [13:37] 2 Sm 3:3; 15:8.    j. [14:5–7] 2 Kgs 6:26–28.    k. [14:7] Nm 35:19.

[12]But the woman continued, "Please let your servant say still another word to my lord the king." He replied, "Speak." [13]So the woman said: "Why, then, do you think the way you do against the people of God? In pronouncing as he has, the king shows himself guilty, in not bringing back his own banished son. [14]We must indeed die; we are then like water that is poured out on the ground and cannot be gathered up. Yet, though God does not bring back to life, he does devise means so as not to banish* anyone from him.[l] [15]And now, if I have presumed to speak to the king of this matter, it is because the people have given me cause to fear. And so your servant thought: 'Let me speak to the king. Perhaps he will grant the petition of his servant. [16]For the king must surely listen and rescue his servant from the grasp of one who would destroy both me and my son from the heritage of God.' [17]And your servant says, 'Let the word of my lord the king lead to rest;† indeed, my lord the king is like an angel of God, discerning good and evil. The LORD your God be with you.'"[m]

[18]The king answered the woman, "Now do not conceal from me anything I may ask you!" The woman said, "Let my lord the king speak." [19]So the king asked, "Is the hand of Joab with you in all this?" And the woman answered: "As you live, my lord the king, it is just as my lord has said, and not otherwise. It was your servant Joab who instructed me and told your servant all these things she was to say. [20]Your servant Joab did this in order to approach the matter in a roundabout way. But my lord is wise with the wisdom of an angel of God, knowing all things on earth."

**Absalom's Return.** [21]Then the king said to Joab: "I am granting this request. Go and bring back young Absalom." [22]Falling to the ground in homage and blessing the king, Joab said, "This day your servant knows that I am in good favor with you, my lord king, since the king has granted the request of your servant." [23]Joab then went off to Geshur and brought Absalom to Jerusalem. [24]But the king said, "Let him go off to his own house; he shall not appear before‡ me." So Absalom went off to his house and did not appear before the king.

[25]In all Israel there was no man more praised for his beauty than Absalom, flawless from the sole of his foot to the crown of his head. [26]When he shaved his head—as he used to do at the end of every year, because his hair became too heavy for him—the hair weighed two hundred shekels according to the royal standard. [27]Absalom

had three sons born to him, besides a daughter named Tamar, who was a beautiful woman.[n]

**Absalom Is Pardoned.** [28]Absalom lived in Jerusalem for two years without appearing before the king. [29]Then he sent a message asking Joab to send him to the king, but Joab would not come to him. Although he asked him a second time, Joab would not come. [30]He therefore instructed his servants: "You see Joab's field that borders mine, where he has barley. Go, set it on fire." And so Absalom's servants set the field on fire.[o] Joab's farmhands came to him with torn garments and told him, "Absalom's servants set your field on fire." [31]Joab went to Absalom in his house and asked him, "Why have your servants set my field on fire?" [32]Absalom answered Joab: "I sent you a message: Come here, that I may send you to the king to say: 'Why did I come back from Geshur? I would be better off if I were still there!' Now, let me appear before the king. If I am guilty, let him put me to death." [33]Joab went to the king and reported this. The king then called Absalom; he came to him and in homage fell on his face to the ground before the king. Then the king kissed Absalom.

## CHAPTER 15

**Absalom's Ambition.** [1]After this, Absalom provided himself with chariots, horses, and a retinue of fifty.[p] [2]Moreover, Absalom used to rise early and stand alongside the road leading to the gate. If someone had a lawsuit to be decided by the king, Absalom would call to him and say, "From what city are you?" And when he replied, "Your servant is of such and such a tribe of Israel," [3]Absalom would say to him, "Your case is good and just, but there is no one to hear you in the king's name." [4]And he would continue: "If only I could be appointed judge in the land! Then everyone who has a lawsuit to be decided might come to me and I would render him justice." [5]Whenever a man approached him to show homage, he would extend his hand, hold him, and kiss him. [6]By behaving in this way toward all the Israelites who came to the king for judgment, Absalom was stealing the heart of Israel.

**Conspiracy in Hebron.** [7]After a period of four years, Absalom said to the king: "Please let me go to Hebron and fulfill a vow I made to the LORD. [8]For while living in Geshur in Aram, your servant made this vow: 'If the LORD ever brings me back to Jerusalem, I will worship him in Hebron.'"[q] [9]The king said to him, "Go in peace," and he went off to Hebron. [10]Then Absalom sent agents throughout the tribes of Israel to say, "When you hear the sound of the horn, say, 'Absalom is king in Hebron!'" [11]Two hundred men had accompanied Absalom from Jerusalem. They had been invited and went in all innocence, knowing nothing. [12]Absalom

---

*[14:14] **Not to banish**: a possible allusion to the religious institution of cities of refuge for involuntary murderers; see Nm 35:9–15.

†[14:17] **Rest**: cf. Ru 1:9; Ps 95:11; Mi 2:10. The reference here is to a return home for Absalom.

‡[14:24] **Appear before**: lit., "see the face of," a term from court etiquette; so also in vv. 28, 32.

l. [14:14] Jb 7:9; 14:7–12; Ps 88:4, 10–12.    m. [14:17, 20] 1 Sm 29:9.

n. [14:27] 2 Sm 18:18.    o. [14:30] Jgs 15:4–5.    p. [15:1] 1 Sm 8:11; 1 Kgs 1:5.    q. [15:8] 2 Sm 3:3; 13:37.

also sent to Ahithophel the Gilonite, David's counselor, an invitation to come from his town, Giloh, for the sacrifices he was about to offer. So the conspiracy gained strength, and the people with Absalom increased in numbers.[r]

**David Flees Jerusalem.** [13]An informant came to David with the report, "The Israelites have given their hearts to Absalom,[s] and they are following him." [14]At this, David said to all his servants who were with him in Jerusalem: "Get up, let us flee, or none of us will escape from Absalom. Leave at once, or he will quickly overtake us, and then bring disaster upon us, and put the city to the sword." [15]The king's servants answered him, "Whatever our lord the king chooses to do, we are your servants." [16]Then the king set out, accompanied by his entire household, except for ten concubines whom he left behind to care for the palace.[t] [17]As the king left the city, with all his officers accompanying him, they halted opposite the ascent of the Mount of Olives, at a distance, [18]while the whole army marched past him.

**David and Ittai.** As all the Cherethites and Pelethites, and the six hundred Gittites who had entered his service from that city, were passing in review before the king,[u] [19]the king said to Ittai the Gittite: "Why should you also go with us? Go back and stay with the king, for you are a foreigner and you, too, are an exile from your own country. [20]You came only yesterday, and today shall I have you wander off with us wherever I have to go? Return and take your brothers with you, and may the LORD show you kindness and fidelity." [21]But Ittai answered the king, "As the LORD lives, and as my lord the king lives, your servant shall be wherever my lord the king is, whether for death or for life."[v] [22]So the king said to Ittai, "Go, then, march on." And Ittai the Gittite, with all his men and all the dependents that were with him, marched on. [23]The whole land wept aloud as the last of the soldiers went by, and the king crossed the Wadi Kidron with all the soldiers moving on ahead of him by way of the ascent of the Mount of Olives, toward the wilderness.

**David and the Priests.** [24]Zadok, too, and all the Levites bearing the ark of the covenant of God set down the ark of God until the whole army had finished marching out of the city; and Abiathar came up. [25]Then the king said to Zadok: "Take the ark of God back to the city. If I find favor with the LORD, he will bring me back and permit me to see it and its lodging place. [26]But if he should say, 'I am not pleased with you,' I am ready; let him do to me as he sees fit."[w] [27]The king also said to Zadok the priest: "Look, you and Abiathar return to the city in peace, and both your sons with you, your own son Ahimaaz, and Abiathar's son Jonathan. [28]Remember, I shall be

waiting at the fords near the wilderness until a report from you comes to me." [29]So Zadok and Abiathar took the ark of God back to Jerusalem and remained there.

[30]As David went up the ascent of the Mount of Olives, he wept without ceasing. His head was covered, and he was walking barefoot. All those who were with him also had their heads covered and were weeping as they went.[x] [31]When David was told, "Ahithophel is among the conspirators with Absalom," he said, "O LORD, turn the counsel of Ahithophel to folly!"[y]

**David and Hushai.** [32]When David reached the top, where God was worshiped, Hushai the Archite was there to meet him, with garments torn and dirt upon his head.[z] [33]David said to him: "If you come with me, you will be a burden to me; [34]but if you return to the city and say to Absalom, 'Let me be your servant, O king; I was formerly your father's servant, but now I will be yours,' you will thwart for me the counsel of Ahithophel.[a] [35]You will have the priests Zadok and Abiathar there with you. If you hear anything from the king's house, you shall report it to the priests Zadok and Abiathar, [36]who have there with them their two sons, Zadok's son Ahimaaz and Abiathar's son Jonathan. Through them you shall send on to me whatever you hear." [37]So David's friend Hushai went into the city, Jerusalem, as Absalom was about to enter it.

## CHAPTER 16

**David and Ziba.** [1]David went a little beyond the top and Ziba, the servant of Meribbaal, was there to meet him with saddled donkeys laden with two hundred loaves of bread, an ephah of cakes of pressed raisins, an ephah of summer fruits, and a skin of wine.[b] [2]The king said to Ziba, "What are you doing with all this?" Ziba replied: "The donkeys are for the king's household to ride on. The bread and summer fruits are for your servants to eat, and the wine to drink when they grow weary in the wilderness." [3]Then the king said, "And where is your lord's son?" Ziba answered the king, "He is staying in Jerusalem, for he said, 'Today the house of Israel will restore to me my father's kingdom.'"[c] [4]The king therefore said to Ziba, "So! Everything Meribbaal had is yours." Then Ziba said: "I pay you homage, my lord the king. May I find favor with you!"[d]

**David and Shimei.** [5]As King David was approaching Bahurim, there was a man coming out; he was of the same clan as the house of Saul, and his name was Shimei, son of Gera. He kept cursing as he came out,[e] [6]and throwing stones at David and at all King David's officers, even though all the soldiers, including the royal guard,

r. [15:12] 2 Sm 16:23.    s. [15:13] Ps 3.    t. [15:16] 2 Sm 16:21–22; 20:3.    u. [15:18] 2 Sm 8:18.    v. [15:21] Ru 1:16–17.    w. [15:26] 2 Sm 16:10.

x. [15:30] 2 Sm 19:5; Mi 1:8.    y. [15:31] 2 Sm 16:23; 17:14, 23.    z. [15:32] 2 Sm 16:16.    a. [15:34] 2 Sm 16:19.    b. [16:1] 2 Sm 4:4; 9:1–13; 19:18, 25.    c. [16:3] 2 Sm 19:26–27.    d. [16:4] 2 Sm 19:30.    e. [16:5] 2 Sm 3:16; 19:17, 22–23; 1 Kgs 2:8.

were on David's right and on his left. [7]Shimei was saying as he cursed: "Get out! Get out! You man of blood, you scoundrel! [8]The LORD has paid you back for all the blood shed from the family of Saul,* whom you replaced as king, and the LORD has handed over the kingdom to your son Absalom. And now look at you: you suffer ruin because you are a man of blood." [9]Abishai, son of Zeruiah, said to the king: "Why should this dead dog curse my lord the king? Let me go over and take off his head."[f] [10]But the king replied: "What business is it of mine or of yours, sons of Zeruiah, that he curses? Suppose the LORD has told him to curse David; who then will dare to say, 'Why are you doing this?'"[g] [11]Then David said to Abishai and to all his servants: "If my own son, who came forth from my loins, is seeking my life, how much more might this Benjaminite do so! Let him alone and let him curse, for the LORD has told him to.[h] [12]Perhaps the LORD will look upon my affliction and repay me with good for the curses he is uttering this day." [13]David and his men continued on the road, while Shimei kept up with them on the hillside, all the while cursing and throwing stones and dirt as he went.[i] [14]The king and all the soldiers with him arrived at the Jordan tired out, and stopped there to rest.

**Absalom's Counselors.** [15]In the meantime Absalom, with all the Israelites, entered Jerusalem, and Ahithophel was with him. [16]When David's friend Hushai the Archite came to Absalom, he said to him: "Long live the king! Long live the king!"[j] [17]But Absalom asked Hushai: "Is this your devotion to your friend? Why did you not go with your friend?" [18]Hushai replied to Absalom: "On the contrary, I am his whom the LORD and all this people and all Israel have chosen, and with him I will stay. [19]Furthermore, as I was in attendance upon your father, so will I be before you. Whom should I serve, if not his son?"[k]

[20]Then Absalom said to Ahithophel, "Offer your counsel on what we should do." [21]Ahithophel replied to Absalom: "Go to your father's concubines, whom he left behind to take care of the palace. When all Israel hears how odious you have made yourself to your father, all those on your side will take courage."[l] [22]So a tent was pitched on the roof for Absalom, and Absalom went to his father's concubines in view of all Israel.[m]

**Counsel of Ahithophel.** [23]Now the counsel given by Ahithophel at that time was as though one sought the word of God. Such was all the counsel of Ahithophel both to David and to Absalom.[n]

## CHAPTER 17

[1]Ahithophel went on to say to Absalom: "Let me choose twelve thousand men and be off in pursuit of David tonight. [2]If I come upon him when he is weary and discouraged, I shall cause him panic, and all the people with him will flee, and I shall strike down the king alone. [3]Then I can bring back the rest of the people to you, as a bride returns to her husband. It is the death of only one man you are seeking; then all the people will be at peace." [4]This plan sounded good to Absalom and to all the elders of Israel.

**Counsel of Hushai.** [5]Then Absalom said, "Now call Hushai the Archite also; let us hear what he too has to say." [6]When Hushai came to Absalom, Absalom said to him: "This is Ahithophel's plan. Shall we follow his plan? If not, give your own." [7]Hushai replied to Absalom, "This time Ahithophel has not given good counsel." [8]And he went on to say: "You know that your father and his men are warriors, and that they are as fierce as a bear in the wild robbed of her cubs. Moreover, since your father is a skilled fighter, he will not spend the night with the army.[o] [9]Even now he lies hidden in one of the caves or in one of his other places. And if some of our soldiers should fall at the first attack, whoever hears of it will say, 'Absalom's followers have been slaughtered.' [10]Then even the brave man with the heart of a lion—his heart will melt. For all Israel knows that your father is a fighter and those who are with him are brave. [11]This is what I counsel: Let all Israel be assembled, from Dan to Beer-sheba, as numerous as the sands by the sea, and you yourself go with them. [12]We can then attack him wherever we find him, settling down upon him as dew alights on the ground. None shall survive—neither he nor any of his followers. [13]And if he retires into a city, all Israel shall bring ropes to that city and we can drag it into the gorge, so that not even a pebble of it can be found." [14]Then Absalom and all the Israelites said, "The counsel of Hushai the Archite is better than the counsel of Ahithophel." For the LORD had commanded that Ahithophel's good counsel should be thwarted, so that he might bring Absalom to ruin.[p]

**David Told of the Plan.** [15]Then Hushai said to the priests Zadok and Abiathar: "This is the counsel Ahithophel gave Absalom and the elders of Israel, and this is what I counseled. [16]So send a warning to David immediately: 'Do not spend the night at the fords near the wilderness, but cross over without fail. Otherwise the king and all the people with him will be destroyed.'" [17]Now Jonathan and Ahimaaz were staying at En-rogel. A maidservant was to come with information for them, and they in turn were to go and report to King David. They could not risk being seen entering the city, [18]but an attendant did see them and informed Absalom. They

---

*[16:8] **Blood shed . . . Saul:** probably refers to the episode recounted in 21:1–14.

f. [16:9] 2 Sm 19:22; 1 Sm 24:15; 26:6.   g. [16:10] 2 Sm 15:25–26; 19:23.   h. [16:11] 2 Sm 12:11.   i. [16:13] 2 Sm 19:19–24.   j. [16:16] 2 Sm 15:32–37.   k. [16:19] 2 Sm 15:34.   l. [16:21] 2 Sm 15:16; 20:3.   m. [16:22] 2 Sm 12:11–12.   n. [16:23] 2 Sm 15:12, 31; 17:23.

o. [17:8] Hos 13:8.   p. [17:14] 2 Sm 15:31, 34.

hurried on their way and reached the house of a man in Bahurim who had a cistern in his courtyard. They let themselves down into it, ¹⁹and the woman took the cover and spread it over the mouth of the cistern, strewing crushed grain on the cover so that nothing could be noticed. ²⁰When Absalom's servants came to the woman at the house, they asked, "Where are Ahimaaz and Jonathan?" The woman replied, "They went by a short while ago toward the water." They searched, but found no one, and so returned to Jerusalem. ²¹As soon as they left, Ahimaaz and Jonathan came up out of the cistern and went on to report to King David. They said to him: "Leave! Cross the water at once, for Ahithophel has given such and such counsel in regard to you." ²²So David and all his people moved on and crossed the Jordan. By daybreak, there was no one left who had not crossed.

²³When Ahithophel saw that his counsel was not acted upon, he saddled his donkey and departed, going to his home in his own city. Then, having left orders concerning his household, he hanged himself. And so he died and was buried in his father's tomb.⁹

²⁴Now David had arrived at Mahanaim while Absalom crossed the Jordan accompanied by all the Israelites. ²⁵Absalom had put Amasa in command of the army in Joab's place. Amasa was the son of an Ishmaelite named Ithra, who had married Abigail, daughter of Jesse and sister of Joab's mother Zeruiah.ʳ ²⁶Israel and Absalom encamped in the land of Gilead.

²⁷When David came to Mahanaim, Shobi, son of Nahash from Rabbah of the Ammonites, Machir, son of Ammiel from Lodebar, and Barzillai, the Gileadite from Rogelim,ˢ ²⁸brought beds and covers, basins and pottery, as well as wheat, barley, flour, roasted grain, beans, lentils, ²⁹honey, and butter and cheese from the flocks and herds, for David and those who were with him to eat; for they said, "The people will be hungry and tired and thirsty in the wilderness."

## CHAPTER 18

**Preparation for Battle.** ¹After mustering the troops he had with him, David placed officers in command of units of a thousand and units of a hundred. ²David then divided the troops three ways, a third under Joab, a third under Abishai, son of Zeruiah and brother of Joab, and a third under Ittai the Gittite. The king said to the troops, "I intend to go out with you myself." ³But they replied: "You must not come out with us. For if we flee, no one will care; even if half of us die, no one will care. But you are worth ten thousand of us. Therefore it is better that we have you to help us from the city." ⁴The king said to them, "I will do what you think best." So the king stood by the gate as all the soldiers

marched out in units of a hundred and a thousand. ⁵But the king gave this command to Joab, Abishai, and Ittai: "Be gentle with young Absalom for my sake." All the soldiers heard as the king gave commands to the various leaders with regard to Absalom.

**Defeat of Absalom's Forces.** ⁶David's army then took the field against Israel, and a battle was fought in the forest near Mahanaim. ⁷The forces of Israel were defeated by David's servants, and the casualties there that day were heavy—twenty thousand men. ⁸The battle spread out over that entire region, and the forest consumed more combatants that day than did the sword.

**Death of Absalom.** ⁹Absalom unexpectedly came up against David's servants. He was mounted on a mule, and, as the mule passed under the branches of a large oak tree, his hair caught fast in the tree. He hung between heaven and earth while the mule under him kept going. ¹⁰Someone saw this and reported to Joab, "I saw Absalom hanging from an oak tree." ¹¹Joab said to the man who told him this: "If you saw him, why did you not strike him to the ground on the spot? Then it would have been my duty to give you fifty pieces of silver and a belt." ¹²But the man replied to Joab: "Even if I already held a thousand pieces of silver in my two hands, I would not lay a hand on the king's son, for in our hearing the king gave you and Abishai and Ittai a command: 'Protect the youth Absalom for my sake.' ¹³Had I been disloyal and killed him, it would all have come out before the king, and you would stand aloof." ¹⁴Joab replied, "I will not waste time with you in this way." And taking three pikes in hand, he thrust for the heart of Absalom. He was still alive in the tree.ᵗ ¹⁵When ten of Joab's young armor-bearers closed in on Absalom, and killed him with further blows, ¹⁶Joab then sounded the horn, and the soldiers turned back from the pursuit of the Israelites, because Joab called them to halt. ¹⁷They took Absalom and cast him into a deep pit in the forest, and built up a very large mound of stones over him. And all the Israelites fled to their own tents.ᵘ

¹⁸During his lifetime Absalom had taken a pillar and set it up for himself in the King's Valley, for he said, "I have no son to perpetuate my name." The pillar which he named for himself is called Absalom's Monument to the present day.ᵛ

**David Told of Absalom's Death.** ¹⁹Then Ahimaaz, son of Zadok, said, "Let me run to take the good news to the king that the LORD has set him free from the power of his enemies." ²⁰But Joab said to him: "You are not the man to bring the news today. On some other day you may take the good news, but today you would not be bringing good news, for in fact the king's son is dead." ²¹Then Joab said to a Cushite, "Go, tell the king what you have seen." The Cushite

---

q. [17:23] 2 Sm 15:31; 16:23.   r. [17:25] 2 Sm 19:14; 20:4–13.
s. [17:27] 2 Sm 9:4; 19:32; 1 Kgs 2:7; Ezr 2:61.

t. [18:14] 2 Sm 12:10; 13:28–29.   u. [18:17] Jos 7:26; 8:29; 10:27.
v. [18:18] 2 Sm 14:27.

bowed to Joab and ran off. ²²But Ahimaaz, son of Zadok, said to Joab again, "Come what may, permit me also to run after the Cushite." Joab replied: "Why do you want to run, my son? You will receive no reward." ²³But he insisted, "Come what may, I want to run." Joab said to him, "Run." Ahimaaz took the way of the Jordan plain and outran the Cushite.

²⁴Now David was sitting between the two gates, and a lookout mounted to the roof of the gate above the city wall, where he looked out and saw a man running all alone. ²⁵The lookout shouted to inform the king, who said, "If he is alone, he has good news to report." As he kept coming nearer, ²⁶the lookout spied another runner. From his place atop the gate he cried out, "There is another man running by himself." And the king responded, "He, too, is bringing good news." ²⁷Then the lookout said, "I notice that the first one runs like Ahimaaz, son of Zadok." The king replied, "He is a good man; he comes with good news."ʷ ²⁸Then Ahimaaz called out and greeted the king. With face to the ground he paid homage to the king and said, "Blessed be the Lᴏʀᴅ your God, who has delivered up the men who rebelled against my lord the king." ²⁹But the king asked, "Is young Absalom safe?" And Ahimaaz replied, "I saw a great disturbance when the king's servant Joab sent your servant on, but I do not know what it was." ³⁰The king said, "Step aside and remain in attendance here." So he stepped aside and remained there. ³¹When the Cushite came in, he said, "Let my lord the king receive the good news that this day the Lᴏʀᴅ has freed you from the power of all who rose up against you." ³²But the king asked the Cushite, "Is young Absalom all right?" The Cushite replied, "May the enemies of my lord the king and all who rebel against you with evil intent be as that young man!"

## CHAPTER 19

¹The king was shaken, and went up to the room over the city gate and wept. He said as he wept, "My son Absalom! My son, my son Absalom! If only I had died instead of you, Absalom, my son, my son!"

**Joab Reproves David.** ²Joab was told, "The king is weeping and mourning for Absalom," ³and that day's victory was turned into mourning for the whole army when they heard, "The king is grieving for his son." ⁴The soldiers stole into the city that day like men shamed by flight in battle. ⁵Meanwhile the king covered his face and cried out in a loud voice, "My son Absalom! Absalom! My son, my son!"ˣ ⁶So Joab went to the king's residence and said: "Though they saved your life and your sons' and daughters' lives, and the lives of your wives and your concubines, you have put all your servants to shame today ⁷by loving those who hate you and hating those who love

you. For you have announced today that officers and servants are nothing to you. Indeed I am now certain that if Absalom were alive today and all of us dead, that would be fine with you. ⁸Now then, get up! Go out and speak kindly to your servants. I swear by the Lᴏʀᴅ that if you do not go out, not a single man will remain with you overnight, and this will be a far greater disaster for you than any that has come upon you from your youth until now." ⁹So the king got up and sat at the gate. When all the people were told, "The king is sitting at the gate," they came into his presence.

**The Reconciliation.** Now the Israelites had fled to their separate tents, ¹⁰but throughout the tribes of Israel all the people were arguing among themselves, saying to one another: "The king delivered us from the grasp of our enemies, and it was he who rescued us from the grasp of the Philistines. Now, he has fled the country before Absalom, ¹¹but Absalom, whom we anointed over us, has died in battle. Why, then, should you remain silent about restoring the king to his palace?" When the talk of all Israel reached the king, ¹²David sent word to the priests Zadok and Abiathar: "Say to the elders of Judah: 'Why should you be last to restore the king to his palace? ¹³You are my brothers, you are my bone and flesh. Why should you be last to restore the king?' ¹⁴Also say to Amasa: 'Are you not my bone and flesh? May God do thus to me, and more, if you do not become commander of my army permanently in place of Joab.'"ʸ ¹⁵He won the hearts of the Judahites all together, and so they sent a message to the king: "Return, with all your servants."

**David and Shimei.** ¹⁶So the king returned, and when he reached the Jordan, Judah had come to Gilgal to meet him and to bring him across the Jordan. ¹⁷Shimei, son of Gera, the Benjaminite from Bahurim, hurried down with the Judahites to meet King David,ᶻ ¹⁸accompanied by a thousand men from Benjamin. Ziba, too, the servant of the house of Saul, accompanied by his fifteen sons and twenty servants, hastened to the Jordan before the king.ᵃ ¹⁹ᵇThey crossed over the ford to bring the king's household over and to do whatever he wished. When Shimei, son of Gera, crossed the Jordan, he fell down before the king ²⁰and said to him: "May my lord not hold me guilty; do not remember or take to heart the wrong that your servant did the day my lord the king left Jerusalem. ²¹For your servant knows that I have done wrong. But I now am the first of the whole house of Joseph to come down today to meet my lord the king." ²²But Abishai, son of Zeruiah, countered: "Shimei must be put to death for this. He cursed the anointed of the Lᴏʀᴅ." ²³David replied: "What has come between you and me, sons of Zeruiah, that you

---

w. [18:27] 2 Kgs 9:20.   x. [19:5] 2 Sm 15:30.

y. [19:14] 2 Sm 17:25; 20:4.   z. [19:17] 2 Sm 16:5–13.   a. [19:18] 2 Sm 16:1–4; 19:25–31.   b. [19:19–24] 2 Sm 16:13; Ex 22:27; 1 Kgs 2:8–9.

would become my adversaries this day? Should anyone die today in Israel? Am I not aware that today I am king over Israel?"[c] [24]Then the king said to Shimei, "You shall not die." And the king gave him his oath.

**David and Meribbaal.** [25]Meribbaal, son of Saul, also went down to meet the king. He had not cared for his feet nor trimmed his mustache nor washed his clothes from the day the king left until he returned safely. [26]When he came from Jerusalem to meet the king, the king asked him, "Why did you not go with me, Meribbaal?"[d] [27]He replied: "My lord king, my servant deceived me. For your servant said to him, 'Saddle the donkey for me, that I may ride on it and go with the king'; your servant is lame.[e] [28]But he slandered your servant before my lord the king. But my lord the king is like an angel of God. Do whatever seems good to you. [29]For though my father's entire house deserved only death from my lord the king, yet you placed your servant among those who eat at your table. What right do I still have to make further appeal to the king?"[f] [30]But the king said to him: "Why do you go on talking? I say, 'You and Ziba shall divide the property.'"[g] [31]Meribbaal answered the king, "Indeed let him take it all, now that my lord the king has returned safely to his house."

**David and Barzillai.** [32]Barzillai the Gileadite also came down from Rogelim and escorted the king to the Jordan for his crossing, taking leave of him at the Jordan.[h] [33]It was Barzillai, a very old man of eighty, who had provided for the king during his stay in Mahanaim; he was a very great man. [34]The king said to Barzillai, "Cross over with me, and I will provide for your old age as my guest in Jerusalem." [35]But Barzillai answered the king: "How much longer have I to live, that I should go up to Jerusalem with the king? [36]I am now eighty years old. Can I distinguish between good and evil? Can your servant taste what he eats and drinks, or still hear the voices of men and women singers? Why should your servant be any further burden to my lord the king? [37]In escorting the king across the Jordan, your servant is doing little enough! Why should the king give me this reward? [38]Please let your servant go back to die in my own city by the tomb of my father and mother. Here is your servant Chimham. Let him cross over with my lord the king. Do for him whatever seems good to you." [39]Then the king said to him, "Chimham shall cross over with me, and for him I will do whatever seems good to you. And anything else you would like me to do for you, I will do." [40]Then all the people crossed over the Jordan but the king remained; he kissed Barzillai and bade him farewell as he returned to his own place. [41]Finally the king crossed over to Gilgal, accompanied by Chimham.

**Israel and Judah Quarrel.** All of the people of Judah and half of the people of Israel had escorted the king across. [42]But then all these Israelites began coming to the king and saying, "Why did our brothers the Judahites steal you away and bring the king and his household across the Jordan, along with all David's men?" [43]All the Judahites replied to the men of Israel: "Because the king is our relative. Why are you angry over this? Have we had anything to eat at the king's expense? Or have portions from his table been given to us?" [44]The Israelites answered the Judahites: "We have ten shares in the king. Also, we are the firstborn[*] rather than you. Why do you slight us? Were we not first to speak of restoring our king?" Then the Judahites in turn spoke even more fiercely than the Israelites.[i]

## CHAPTER 20

**Sheba's Rebellion.** [1]Now a scoundrel named Sheba, the son of Bichri, a Benjaminite, happened to be there. He sounded the horn and cried out,

> "We have no share in David,
>      nor any heritage in the son of Jesse.
>      Everyone to your tents, O Israel!"[j]

[2]So all the Israelites left David to follow Sheba, son of Bichri. But the Judahites, from the Jordan to Jerusalem, remained loyal to their king. [3]David came to his house in Jerusalem, and the king took the ten concubines whom he had left behind to care for the palace and placed them under guard. He provided for them, but never again saw them. And so they remained shut away to the day of their death, lifelong widows.[k]

**Amasa's Death.** [4]Then the king said to Amasa: "Summon the Judahites for me within three days. Then present yourself here."[l] [5]Accordingly Amasa set out to summon Judah, but delayed beyond the time set for him. [6]Then David said to Abishai: "Sheba, son of Bichri, may now do us more harm than Absalom did. Take your lord's servants and pursue him, lest he find fortified cities and take shelter while we look on." [7]So Joab and the Cherethites and Pelethites and all the warriors marched out behind Abishai from Jerusalem to campaign in pursuit of Sheba, son of Bichri.[m] [8][†]They were at the great stone in Gibeon when Amasa met them. Now Joab had a belt over his tunic, from which was slung a sword in its sheath at his thigh; the sword would slide out downwards.[n] [9]Joab asked Amasa, "Is everything all right, my brother?" and with his right hand held

---

[*] [19:44] The firstborn had special rights over the other siblings.

[†] [20:8] The text of this verse is quite uncertain.

---

c. [19:23] 2 Sm 16:9–10; 1 Sm 11:13; 1 Kgs 2:8–9, 36–46.   d. [19:26] 2 Sm 16:3.   e. [19:27] 2 Sm 9:2–13.   f. [19:29] 2 Sm 9:9–11.   g. [19:30] 2 Sm 16:4.   h. [19:32] 2 Sm 17:27–29; 1 Kgs 2:7; Ezr 2:61.

i. [19:44] 1 Kgs 11:31.   j. [20:1] 1 Kgs 12:16.   k. [20:3] 2 Sm 15:16; 16:20–22.   l. [20:4] 2 Sm 17:25; 19:14.   m. [20:7] 2 Sm 8:18.   n. [20:8] 2 Sm 2:13.

Amasa's beard as if to kiss him. ¹⁰And since Amasa was not on his guard against the sword in Joab's other hand, Joab stabbed him in the abdomen with it, so that his entrails burst forth to the ground, and he died; there was no second thrust. Then Joab and Abishai his brother pursued Sheba, son of Bichri.ᵒ ¹¹One of Joab's attendants stood by Amasa and said, "Let him who favors Joab and is for David follow Joab." ¹²Amasa lay covered with blood in the middle of the highroad, and the man noticed that all the soldiers were stopping. So he rolled Amasa away from the road to the field and spread a garment over him, because he saw how all who came upon him were stopping. ¹³When he had been removed from the road, everyone went on after Joab in pursuit of Sheba, son of Bichri.

**Joab Pursues Sheba.** ¹⁴Sheba had passed through all the tribes of Israel to Abel Beth-maacah. Then all the Bichrites assembled and they too entered the city after him. ¹⁵So all Joab's troops came and besieged him in Abel Beth-maacah. They built up a mound against the city, so that it stood against the rampart, and were battering the wall to knock it down. ¹⁶Then a wise woman from the city called out, "Listen, listen! Tell Joab, 'Come here, so I can speak with you.'" ¹⁷When Joab had come near her, the woman said, "Are you Joab?" And he replied, "Yes." She said to him, "Listen to what your servant has to say." He replied, "I am listening." ¹⁸Then she went on to say: "There is a saying from long ago,∗ 'Let them ask if they will in Abel or in Dan whether loyalty is finished ¹⁹or ended in Israel.' You are seeking to batter down a city that is a mother in Israel. Why do you wish to swallow up the heritage of the LORD?"ᵖ ²⁰Joab answered, "Not at all, not at all! I do not wish to swallow or batter anything. ²¹That is not the case at all. A man from the hill country of Ephraim, whose name is Sheba, son of Bichri, has rebelled against King David. Give him up, just him, and I will withdraw from the city." Then the woman said to Joab, "His head shall be thrown to you across the wall." ²²In her wisdom, the woman went to all the people, and they cut off the head of Sheba, son of Bichri, and threw it out to Joab. He then sounded the horn, and they scattered from the city to their own tents, while Joab returned to Jerusalem to the king.

**David's Officials.** ²³Joab was in command of the whole army of Israel. Benaiah, son of Jehoiada, was in command of the Cherethites and Pelethites.�q ²⁴Adoram was in charge of the forced labor. Jehoshaphat, son of Ahilud, was the chancellor. ²⁵Shawsha was the scribe. Zadok

and Abiathar were priests.ʳ ²⁶Ira the Jairite was also David's priest.

## V. APPENDIXES

### CHAPTER 21

**Gibeonite Vengeance.** ¹In David's time there was a famine for three years, year after year. David sought the presence of the LORD, who said: There is bloodguilt on Saul and his family because he put the Gibeonites to death.ˢ ²So the king called the Gibeonites and spoke to them. (Now the Gibeonites were not Israelites, but survivors of the Amorites; and although the Israelites had given them their oath, Saul had sought to kill them off in his zeal for the Israelites and for Judah.)ᵗ ³David said to the Gibeonites, "What must I do for you and how must I make atonement, that you may bless the heritage of the LORD?" ⁴The Gibeonites answered him, "We have no claim against Saul and his house for silver or gold, nor is it our place to put anyone to death in Israel." Then he said, "I will do for you whatever you propose." ⁵They said to the king, "As for the man who was exterminating us and who intended to destroy us that we might have no place in all the territory of Israel, ⁶let seven men from among his descendants be given to us, that we may execute them before the LORD in Gibeon, on the LORD's mountain." The king replied, "I will give them up." ⁷The king, however, spared Meribbaal, son of Jonathan, son of Saul, because of the LORD's oath that formed a bond between David and Saul's son Jonathan.ᵘ ⁸But the king took Armoni and Meribbaal, the two sons that Aiah's daughter Rizpah had borne to Saul, and the five sons of Saul's daughter Merob that she had borne to Adriel, son of Barzillai the Meholathite,ᵛ ⁹and delivered them into the power of the Gibeonites, who then executed them on the mountain before the LORD. The seven fell at the one time; they were put to death during the first days of the harvest—that is, at the beginning of the barley harvest.

¹⁰Then Rizpah, Aiah's daughter, took sackcloth and spread it out for herself on the rock from the beginning of the harvest until rain came down on them from the heavens, fending off the birds of the heavens from settling on them by day, and the wild animals by night.ʷ ¹¹When David was informed of what Rizpah, Aiah's daughter, the concubine of Saul, had done, ¹²he went and obtained the bones of Saul and of his son Jonathan from the citizens of Jabesh-gilead, who had stolen them away secretly from the public square of Beth-shan, where the Philistines had hanged them at the time they defeated Saul on Gilboa.ˣ ¹³When he

---

∗[20:18–19] This proverbial expression is obscure but seems to reflect a tradition that this Danite town was associated with oracles or other sorts of revelation. Cf. Mt 16:13–17; and the intertestamental *Testament of Levi* 2:3.

---

o. [20:10] 1 Kgs 2:5.  p. [20:19] Gn 49:16.  q. [20:23] 2 Sm 8:16–18; 23:20.

r. [20:25] 2 Sm 8:17–18.  s. [21:1] 2 Sm 24:13.  t. [21:2] Jos 9:3–27.  u. [21:7] 2 Sm 9:13; 1 Sm 18:3; 20:8–10, 15–16, 42.  v. [21:8] 2 Sm 3:7.  w. [21:10] 2 Sm 3:31; 12:16.  x. [21:12] 1 Sm 31:10–13.

had brought up from there the bones of Saul and of his son Jonathan, the bones of those who had been executed were also gathered up. [14]Then the bones of Saul and of his son Jonathan were buried in the land of Benjamin, at Zela, in the tomb of his father Kish. After all that the king commanded had been carried out, God granted relief to the land.[y]

**Exploits in Philistine Wars.** [15]There was another battle between the Philistines and Israel. David went down with his servants and fought the Philistines, but David grew tired. [16]Dadu, a descendant of the Rephaim, whose bronze spear weighed three hundred shekels, was about to take him captive. Dadu was girt with a new sword and thought he would kill David, [17]but Abishai, son of Zeruiah, came to help him, and struck and killed the Philistine. Then David's men swore to him, "You must not go out to battle with us again, lest you quench the lamp of Israel."[z]

[18a]After this, there was another battle with the Philistines, in Gob. On that occasion Sibbecai the Hushathite struck down Saph, a descendant of the Rephaim.[b] [19c]There was another battle with the Philistines, in Gob, and Elhanan, son of Jair from Bethlehem, killed Goliath of Gath, whose spear shaft was like a weaver's beam. [20]There was another battle, at Gath, and there was a giant, who had six fingers on each hand and six toes on each foot—twenty-four in all. He too was descended from the Rephaim. [21]And when he insulted Israel, Jonathan, son of David's brother Shimei, struck him down.[d] [22]These four were descended from the Rephaim in Gath, and they fell at the hands of David and his servants.

## CHAPTER 22

**Song of Thanksgiving.**[*] [1]David proclaimed the words of this song to the Lord when the Lord had rescued him from the grasp of all his enemies and from the grasp of Saul.[e] [2]He said:[f]

O Lord, my rock, my fortress, my
            deliverer,
[3]      my God, my rock of refuge!

My shield, my saving horn,[†]
      my stronghold, my refuge,
      my savior, from violence you keep
            me safe.[g]
[4]  Praised be the Lord, I exclaim!
      I have been delivered from my
            enemies.

[5]  The breakers of death surged round about
            me,
      the menacing floods[‡] terrified me;
[6]  The cords of Sheol tightened;
      the snares of death lay in wait for me.
[7]  In my distress I called out: Lord!
      I cried out to my God;
From his temple[§] he heard my voice,
      my cry reached his ears.

[8]  The earth rocked and shook;[¶]
      the foundations of the heavens
            trembled;
      they shook as his wrath flared up.
[9]  Smoke rose in his nostrils,
      a devouring fire from his mouth;
      it kindled coals into flame.
[10] He parted the heavens and came down,
      a dark cloud under his feet.[h]
[11] Mounted on a cherub[**] he flew,
      borne along on the wings of the
            wind.[i]
[12] He made darkness the cover about him,
      a mass of water, heavy
            thunderheads.
[13] From the brightness of his presence
      coals were kindled to flame.
[14] The Lord thundered from heaven;
      the Most High made his voice
            resound.
[15] He let fly arrows and scattered them;
      lightning, and dispersed them.[j]
[16] Then the bed of the sea appeared;
      the world's foundations lay bare,
At the roar of the Lord,
      at the storming breath of his
            nostrils.[k]

---

[*][22:1–51] This psalm of thanksgiving also appears in the Psalter, with a few small variants, as Ps 18. In both places it is attributed to David. Two main sections can be distinguished. In the first part, after an introductory stanza of praise to God (vv. 2–4), the writer describes the peril he was in (vv. 5–7), and then poetically depicts, under the form of a theophany, God's intervention in his behalf (vv. 8–20), concluding with an acknowledgment of God's justice (vv. 21–31). In the second part, God is praised for having prepared the psalmist for war (vv. 32–35), given him victory over his enemies (vv. 36–39), whom he put to flight (vv. 40–43), and bestowed on him dominion over many peoples (vv. 44–46). The entire song ends with an expression of grateful praise (vv. 47–51).

---

y. [21:14] 2 Sm 24:25.   z. [21:17] 1 Kgs 11:36; 15:4; 2 Kgs 8:19.   a. [21:18–22] 1 Chr 20:4–8.   b. [21:18] 2 Sm 23:27.   c. [21:19–20] 1 Sm 17:4, 7.   d. [21:21] 2 Sm 13:3.   e. [22:1] Ps 18:1.   f. [22:2–51] Ps 18:3–51.

---

†[22:3] **My saving horn:** my strong savior. The horn, such as that of an enraged bull, was a symbol of strength; cf. Lk 1:69.

‡[22:5–6] **Breakers . . . floods:** traditional Old Testament imagery for lethal danger, from which the Lord is uniquely able to rescue; cf. Ps 69:2, 15–16; 89:10–11; Jon 2:3–6.

§[22:7] **His temple:** his heavenly abode.

¶[22:8–10] The Lord's coming is depicted by means of a storm theophany, including earthquake (vv. 8, 16) and thunderstorm (vv. 9–15); cf. Jgs 5:4–5; Ps 29; 97:2–6; Hb 3.

**[22:11] **Mounted on a cherub:** in the traditional storm theophany, as here, the Lord appears with thunder, lightning, earthquake, rain, darkness, cloud, and wind. Sometimes these are represented as his retinue; sometimes he is said to ride upon the clouds or "the wings of the wind" (Ps 104:3). The parallelism in v. 11 suggests that the winged creatures called cherubim are imagined as bearing the Lord aloft. In the iconography of the ark of the covenant, the Lord was "enthroned upon the cherubim"; cf. Ex 37:7–9; 1 Sm 4:4; 2 Sm 6:2; 2 Kgs 19:15; Ps 80:2; 99:1.

---

g. [22:3] 1 Sm 2:1–2.   h. [22:10] Ps 144:5.   i. [22:11] Ex 25:18–22.   j. [22:15] Ps 144:6.   k. [22:16] Ex 15:8.

¹⁷ He reached down from on high and
        seized me,
        drew me out of the deep waters.ˡ
¹⁸ He rescued me from my mighty enemy,
        from foes too powerful for me.
¹⁹ They attacked me on a day of distress,
        but the LORD came to my support.
²⁰ He set me free in the open;
        he rescued me because he loves me.

²¹ The LORD acknowledged my
        righteousness;
        rewarded my clean hands.
²² For I kept the ways of the LORD;
        I was not disloyal to my God.
²³ His laws were all before me,
        his decrees I did not cast aside.
²⁴ I was honest toward him;
        I was on guard against sin.
²⁵ So the LORD rewarded my righteousness,
        the cleanness of my hands in his
        sight.
²⁶ ᵐ"Toward the faithful you are faithful;"
        to the honest you are honest;
²⁷ Toward the sincere you are sincere;
        but to the perverse you are devious.
²⁸ Humble people you save,
        though on the haughty your eyes
        look down.
²⁹ You are my lamp, O LORD!
        My God brightens the darkness
        about me.
³⁰ With you I can rush an armed band,
        with my God to help I can leap a wall.
³¹ God's way is unerring;
        the LORD's promise is tried and true;
        he is a shield for all who trust in
        him."

³² Truly, who is God except the LORD?
        Who but our God is the rock?
³³ This God who girded me with might,
        kept my way unerring,
³⁴ Who made my feet swift as a deer's,
        set me safe on the heights,ᵒ
³⁵ Who trained my hands for war,
        my arms to bend even a bow of
        bronze.

³⁶ You have given me your protecting
        shield,
        and your help has made me great.
³⁷ You gave me room to stride;
        my feet never stumbled.
³⁸ I pursued my enemies and overtook
        them;
        I did not turn back till I destroyed
        them.

³⁹ I struck them down, and they did not rise;
        they fell dead at my feet.
⁴⁰ You girded me with strength for war;
        subdued adversaries at my feet.
⁴¹ My foes you put to flight before me;
        those who hated me I destroyed.
⁴² They cried for help, but no one saved
        them,
        cried to the LORD but got no answer.
⁴³ I ground them fine as the dust of the
        earth;
        like mud in the streets I trod them
        down.
⁴⁴ You rescued me from the strife of my
        people;
        you made me head over nations.
    A people I had not known became my
        slaves;
⁴⁵ Foreigners cringed before me;
        as soon as they heard of me they
        obeyed.
⁴⁶ Their courage failed;
        they came trembling from their
        fortresses.
⁴⁷ The LORD lives! Blessed be my rock!
        Exalted be God, the rock of my
        salvation.
⁴⁸ O God who granted me vindication,
        subdued peoples under me,
⁴⁹ and helped me escape from my
        enemies,
    Truly you have exalted me above my
        adversaries,
        from the violent you have rescued
        me.
⁵⁰ Thus I will proclaim you, LORD, among
        the nations;
        I will sing the praises of your name.ᵖ
⁵¹ You have given great victories to your
        king,
        and shown kindness to your
        anointed,
        to David and his posterity forever.

## CHAPTER 23

**The Last Words of David.**† ¹These are the last
words of David:

    The oracle of David, son of Jesse;
        the oracle of the man God raised up,
    Anointed of the God of Jacob,
        favorite of the Mighty One of Israel.�q
² The spirit of the LORD spoke through me;
        his word was on my tongue.ʳ
³ The God of Israel spoke;
        of me the Rock of Israel said,

---

*[22:26–27] People are treated by God in the same way
they treat him and other people.

†[23:1–7] **The last words of David:** the text of this short
composition is difficult in places; it views David's career in
retrospect.

l. [22:17] Ps 144:7.   m. [22:26–27] 1 Sm 2:30.   n. [22:31] Prv
30:5.   o. [22:34] Ps 62:3; Hb 3:19.

p. [22:50] Ps 22:23; Rom 15:9.   q. [23:1] 1 Kgs 2:1–9; Sir 47:8.
r. [23:2] Is 59:21; Jer 1:9.

"One who rules over humankind with
     justice,
     who rules in the fear of God,"[s]
4 Is like the light at sunrise
     on a cloudless morning,
     making the land's vegetation glisten
        after rain."[t]
5 Is not my house firm before God?
     He has made an eternal covenant
        with me,
     set forth in detail and secured."[u]
     Will he not bring to fruition
        all my salvation and my every
        desire?
6 But the wicked are all like thorns to be
        cast away;
     they cannot be taken up by hand."[v]
7 One wishing to touch them
     must be armed with iron or the shaft
        of a spear.
     They must be utterly consumed by
        fire.

**David's Warriors.** [8]These are the names of
David's warriors.[*] Ishbaal, the son of Hachamoni, chief of the Three. He brandished his spear
over eight hundred whom he had slain in a
single encounter.[w] [9]Next to him was Eleazar, the
son of Dodo the Ahohite, one of the Three warriors with David at Ephes-dammim, when they
insulted the Philistines who had massed there
for battle. The Israelites had retreated,[x] [10]but he
stood there and struck down the Philistines until
his hand grew tired from clutching the sword.
The LORD brought about a great victory on that
day; the army turned back to rejoin Eleazar, but
only to strip the slain. [11]Next to him was Shammah, son of Agee the Hararite. The Philistines
had assembled at Lehi, where there was a plot
of land full of lentils. The people were fleeing
before the Philistines,[y] [12]but he took his stand in
the middle of the plot, kept it safe, and cut down
the Philistines. Thus the LORD brought about a
great victory. Such deeds as these the Three warriors performed.

[13]Three of the Thirty chiefs went down to
David in the cave of Adullam during the harvest, while a Philistine clan was encamped in
the Valley of Rephaim.[z] [14]David was then in the
stronghold, and there was a garrison of Philistines in Bethlehem. [15]Now David had a craving and said, "If only someone would give me

a drink of water from the cistern by the gate
of Bethlehem!" [16]Thereupon the three warriors
broke through the encampment of the Philistines, drew water from the cistern by the gate of
Bethlehem, and carried it back to David. But he
refused to drink it, and instead poured it out[†] to
the LORD, [17]saying: "The LORD forbid that I do
such a thing! Could I drink the blood of these
men who went at the risk of their lives?" So he
refused to drink it.

[18]Abishai, the brother of Joab, son of Zeruiah, was the chief of the Thirty; he brandished
his spear over three hundred whom he had
slain. He made a name among the Thirty, [19]but
was more famous than any of the Thirty, becoming their leader. However, he did not attain to
the Three.

[20]Benaiah, son of Jehoiada, a valiant man of
mighty deeds, from Kabzeel, killed the two sons
of Ariel of Moab. Also, he went down and killed
the lion in the cistern on a snowy day.[a] [21]He likewise slew an Egyptian, a huge man. The Egyptian
carried a spear, but Benaiah came against him
with a staff; he wrested the spear from the Egyptian's hand, and killed him with that spear. [22]Such
deeds as these Benaiah, the son of Jehoiada, performed; and he made a name among the Thirty
warriors [23]but was more famous than any of the
Thirty. However, he did not attain to the Three.
David put him in charge of his bodyguard.[b]
[24]Asahel,[c] brother of Joab, was among the Thirty;
Elhanan, son of Dodo, from Bethlehem; [25]Sham-
mah, from En-harod; Elika, from En-harod;
[26]Helez, from Beth-pelet; Ira, son of Ikkesh,
from Tekoa; [27]Abiezer, from Anathoth; Sibbecai,
from Husha;[d] [28]Zalmon, from Ahoh; Maharai,
from Netophah; [29]Heled, son of Baanah, from
Netophah; Ittai, son of Ribai, from Gibeah of
Benjamin; [30]Benaiah, from Pirathon; Hiddai,
from the valley of Gaash; [31]Abibaal, from Beth-
arabah; Azmaveth, from Bahurim; [32]Eliahba,
from Shaalbon; Jashen the Gunite; Jonathan,
[33]son of Shammah the Hararite; Ahiam, son of
Sharar the Hararite; [34]Eliphelet, son of Ahasbai,
from Beth-maacah; Eliam, son of Ahithophel,
from Gilo; [35]Hezrai, from Carmel; Paarai the
Arbite; [36]Igal, son of Nathan, from Zobah; Bani
the Gadite; [37]Zelek the Ammonite; Naharai,
from Beeroth, the armor-bearer of Joab, son of
Zeruiah; [38]Ira, from Jattir; Gareb, from Jattir;
[39]Uriah the Hittite—thirty-seven in all.[e]

## CHAPTER 24

**David's Census; the Plague.** [1]The LORD's anger
against Israel flared again,[f] and he incited David
against them: "Go, take a census of Israel and
Judah." [2]The king therefore said to Joab and the

---

[*][23:8–39] There are thirty-seven warriors in all named
in this list. First there are the Three warriors most noted for
single-handed exploits (vv. 8–12). Then comes the story of a
daring adventure by three unnamed members of the larger
group of the Thirty (vv. 13–17). Next come the commanders
of the king's bodyguard, Abishai (vv. 18–19) and Benaiah (vv.
20–23), with whom must be counted Asahel (v. 24) and Joab
(vv. 18, 24, 37), and finally the group of the Thirty (vv. 24–39).

s. [23:3] Ps 72:1–4.   t. [23:4] Jgs 5:31; Ps 72:6.   u. [23:5] 2 Sm
7:11, 15–16; Ps 89:30; Is 55:3.   v. [23:6] Dt 13:14.   w. [23:8–39]
1 Chr 11:11–41; 27:1–15.   x. [23:9] 1 Sm 17:1.   y. [23:11] Jgs 15:9.
z. [23:13] 1 Sm 22:1; Mi 1:15.

---

†[23:16] **Poured it out**: as a libation.

---

a. [23:20] 2 Sm 8:18; 20:23; Jgs 14:6; 1 Kgs 2:29–30.   b. [23:23]
1 Sm 22:14.   c. [23:24] 2 Sm 2:18–23.   d. [23:27] 2 Sm 21:18.
e. [23:39] 2 Sm 11:3.   f. [24:1–25] 1 Chr 21:1–27.

leaders of the army who were with him, "Tour all the tribes of Israel from Dan to Beer-sheba and register the people, that I may know their number." [3]But Joab replied to the king: "May the LORD your God increase the number of people a hundredfold for my lord the king to see it with his own eyes. But why does it please my lord to do a thing of this kind?" [4]However, the king's command prevailed over Joab and the leaders of the army, so they left the king's presence in order to register the people of Israel. [5]Crossing the Jordan, they began near Aroer, south of the city in the wadi, and turned in the direction of Gad toward Jazer. [6]They continued on to Gilead and to the district below Mount Hermon. Then they proceeded to Dan; from there they turned toward Sidon, [7]going to the fortress of Tyre and to all the cities of the Hivites and Canaanites, and ending up in the Negeb of Judah, at Beer-sheba. [8]Thus they toured the whole land, reaching Jerusalem again after nine months and twenty days. [9]Joab then reported the census figures to the king: of men capable of wielding a sword, there were in Israel eight hundred thousand, and in Judah five hundred thousand.

[10]Afterward, however, David regretted having numbered the people. David said to the LORD: "I have sinned grievously in what I have done.[g] Take away, LORD, your servant's guilt, for I have acted very foolishly." [11]When David rose in the morning, the word of the LORD came to the prophet Gad, David's seer, saying: [12]Go, tell David: Thus says the LORD: I am offering you three options; choose one of them, and I will give you that. [13]Gad then went to David to inform him. He asked: "Should three years of famine come upon your land; or three months of fleeing from your enemy while he pursues you; or is it to be three days of plague in your land? Now consider well: what answer am I to give to him who sent me?"[h] [14]David answered Gad: "I am greatly distressed. But let us fall into the hand of God, whose mercy is great, rather than into human hands." [15]Thus David chose the plague. At the time of the wheat harvest it broke out among the people. The LORD sent plague over Israel from morning until the time appointed, and from Dan to Beer-sheba seventy thousand of the people died. [16]But when the angel stretched forth his hand toward Jerusalem to destroy it, the LORD changed his mind about the calamity, and said to the angel causing the destruction among the people: Enough now! Stay your hand.[i] The angel of the LORD was then standing at the threshing floor of Araunah the Jebusite.[j] [17]When David saw the angel who was striking the people, he said to the LORD: "It is I who have sinned; it is I, the shepherd, who have done wrong. But these sheep, what have they done? Strike me and my father's family!"

**David Offers Sacrifices.** [18]On the same day Gad went to David and said to him, "Go and set up an altar to the LORD on the threshing floor of Araunah the Jebusite." [19]According to Gad's word, David went up as the LORD had commanded. [20]Now Araunah looked down and saw the king and his servants coming toward him while he was threshing wheat. So he went out and bowed down before the king, his face to the ground. [21]Then Araunah asked, "Why does my lord the king come to his servant?" David replied, "To buy the threshing floor from you, to build an altar to the LORD, that the plague may be withdrawn from the people." [22]But Araunah said to David: "Let my lord the king take it and offer up what is good in his sight. See, here are the oxen for burnt offerings, and the threshing sledges and the yokes of oxen for wood. [23]All this does Araunah give to the king." Araunah then said to the king, "May the LORD your God accept your offering." [24]The king, however, replied to Araunah, "No, I will buy it from you at the proper price, for I cannot sacrifice to the LORD my God burnt offerings that cost me nothing." So David bought the threshing floor and the oxen for fifty silver shekels. [25]Then David built an altar to the LORD there, and sacrificed burnt offerings and communion offerings. The LORD granted relief to the land, and the plague was withdrawn from Israel.

---

*[24:10] The narrative supposes that since the people belonged to the Lord rather than to the king, only the Lord should know their exact number. Further, since such an exact numbering of the people would make it possible for the king to exercise centralized power, imposing taxation, conscription, and expropriation upon Israel, the story shares the view of monarchy found in 1 Sm 8:4–18. See also Nm 3:44–51, where census taking requires an apotropaic offering.

g. [24:10] 1 Sm 24:6; 1 Chr 21:7–8.    h. [24:13] 2 Sm 21:1.

i. [24:16] Gn 6:6; Ex 32:14; 1 Chr 21:15; Jon 3:10.    j. [24:16] Ex 12:23; 2 Kgs 19:35.    k. [24:22–23] 1 Sm 6:14; 1 Kgs 19:21.

# THE BOOKS OF
# KINGS

~ৎ৯~

The two Books of Kings are regarded by many as the last part of a work commonly known as the Deuteronomistic History. The latter tells the story of Israel from its settlement in the land (Joshua and Judges) through the transition from judgeship to monarchy under Samuel, Saul, and David (1 and 2 Samuel) to the reign of Solomon, the disintegration of the united kingdom into the kingdoms of Israel and Judah and the eventual downfall of both kingdoms (1 and 2 Kings). The Deuteronomistic History along with the Pentateuch forms a single historical narrative stretching from creation to exile.

The Books of Kings can be approached in several ways. They contain history and are an important source of information about the Israelite kingdoms. They are also narrative that calls for careful reading; historical accuracy is sometimes sacrificed to the demands of compelling characterization and dramatic tension. Most importantly, both historical presentation and narrative creativity are shaped by a particular religious worldview.

The multifaceted character of the work means that it has a variety of focal points. The historical events themselves, of course, are important, but the patterns according to which the author organizes those events give a unity to the author's historical reconstruction. The northern kings are condemned without exception, and the royal line degenerates from the divine election of Jeroboam I through a succession of short-lived dynasties to the bloodbath of Jehu's coup d'état, and finally dies out in a series of assassinations. (It must be admitted that the author at times skews the story to preserve the pattern: the relatively prosperous forty-one-year reign of Jeroboam II is dismissed in seven verses!) Judah's kings, on the other hand, follow a cyclic pattern of infidelity followed by reform, with each reformer king (Asa, Joash, Hezekiah, Josiah) greater than the last. Unfortunately the apostate kings also progress in wickedness, until the evil of Manasseh is so great that even Josiah's fidelity cannot turn away the Lord's wrath (2 Kgs 23:26).

As a literary work, the Books of Kings are admirable. Some of the brilliance is accessible only in Hebrew: wordplays, the sounds and rhythms of poetic passages, verbal allusions to other passages of the Hebrew Bible. Scenes are drawn with a vibrancy and immediacy that English cannot reproduce without sounding overdone. But other literary techniques survive translation: symmetrical structures for narrative units (and the disruptions of symmetry at significant points), rich ambiguities (see 1 Kgs 3:26), foreshadowings (such as the way the prophet of Bethel and the man of God of Judah in 1 Kgs 13 portend the destinies of their respective kingdoms). Characterization is rich and complex (Solomon, Jeroboam, Elijah, Ahab, Elisha, Jehu, etc.), revealing deep insight into human nature.

In offering a theological interpretation of history, 1–2 Kings upholds a double principle: the justification of the political disintegration of the Davidic empire, and the necessity of the religious unity of the Lord's people. This double principle is, practically speaking, unrealistic; see Jeroboam I's reasonable assessment in 1 Kgs 12:26–27. But for the Deuteronomistic historian, that is irrelevant. Just as the separation of the kingdoms is the Lord's will (1 Kgs 12:22–24), so too is the centralization of worship at the Temple in Jerusalem (1 Kgs 9:3; see Dt 12). 1–2 Kings reflects that double principle in its organization. The story of each king is told integrally, whether the king is of Israel or Judah: both lines of kings are legitimate. But the stories of the two lines are recounted in the order in which each king came to the throne, irrespective of which kingdom he ruled: there is only one people of God, though they are under two different royal jurisdictions. Moreover, each king is evaluated on theological grounds, with no allowance made for political or economic successes or failures. All Israelite kings are condemned because they did not reverse Jeroboam I's sin of setting up sanctuaries outside Jerusalem. Judahite kings are condemned for apostasy or praised for reform, as the case may be; but a continuing source of irritation to the Deuteronomistic historian is the failure of even the praiseworthy kings to do anything about local shrines outside Jerusalem (the "high places").

Into the stories of the kings, almost as a counterpoint, are woven numerous stories of prophets, named and great (Elijah, Elisha, Isaiah), and less known or anonymous (1 Kgs 13; 22). Many of the stories are anecdotal, reflecting the everyday life of prophets and prophetic guilds (1 Kgs 17; 2 Kgs 4). But the volatile dynamics of prophetic involvement in the political realm are prominent: prophets in opposition to kings (1 Kgs 14; 21; 2 Kgs 9), prophets in support of kings (1 Kgs 20:1–34; 2 Kgs 19–20; 22:14–20). This too is part of the theological worldview of the Deuteronomistic historian. The destiny of Israel is in God's hand. Through prophets, the divine will is made known on earth to kings and people and the future consequences of their response to God's will are spelled out. It is perhaps indicative of the importance prophets have in 1 and 2 Kings that the structural center of the two books is the story of Elisha's succession to Elijah's prophetic ministry (2 Kgs 2), and that this is one of the few passages in Kings that occurs outside the account of any king's reign. Behind the temporal realm of kings and reigns lies the continuing realm of the divine word and its servants, the prophets.

1–2 Kings draws on older sources (perhaps on archival records, certainly on works called "The Book of the Chronicles of the Kings"; see, for example, 1 Kgs 14:19, 29), which it uses for its own theological purpose. The so-called Deuteronomistic History itself underwent a complex process of editorial revision whose stages are disputed by scholars. There may have been an edition sometime late in the reign of Josiah (640–609 B.C.), but in the form we have it the work comes from the time of the exile (see 2 Kgs 25:27–30). In its turn the Deuteronomistic History was one of the sources used by the Chronicler in postexilic times to compile the history presented in 1 and 2 Chronicles. Though Chronicles has little interest in the Northern Kingdom, much of the material in Kings about the kingdom of Judah reappears, sometimes in altered form, in Chronicles.

The Books of Kings may be divided as follows:

    I. The Reign of Solomon (1 Kgs 1:1–11:43)
   II. The Reign of Jeroboam (1 Kgs 12:1–14:20)
  III. Kings of Judah and Israel (1 Kgs 14:21–16:34)
  IV. The Story of Elijah (1 Kgs 17:1–19:21)
   V. The Story of Ahab (1 Kgs 20:1–2 Kgs 1:18)
  VI. Elisha Succeeds Elijah (2 Kgs 2:1–25)
 VII. Stories of Elisha and Joram (2 Kgs 3:1–9:13)
VIII. The End of the Omrid Dynasty (2 Kgs 9:14–11:20)
  IX. Kings of Judah and Israel (2 Kgs 12:1–17:5)
   X. The End of Israel (2 Kgs 17:6–41)
  XI. The End of Judah (2 Kgs 18:1–25:30)

# THE FIRST BOOK OF

# KINGS

~~~

## I. THE REIGN OF SOLOMON*

### CHAPTER 1

**David's Old Age.** ¹¹When King David was old and advanced in years, though they covered him with blankets he could not get warm. ²His servants therefore said to him, "Let a young virgin be sought to attend my lord the king,‡ and to nurse him. If she sleeps with you, my lord the king will be warm." ³So they sought for a beautiful girl throughout the territory of Israel, and found Abishag the Shunamite. So they brought her to the king. ⁴The girl was very beautiful indeed, and she nursed the king and took care of him. But the king did not have relations with her.
**Adonijah's Ambition.** ⁵Adonijah, son of Haggith, boasted, "I shall be king!" and he provided himself with chariots, horses, and a retinue of fifty to go before him.ª ⁶Yet his father would never antagonize him by asking, "Why are you doing this?" Adonijah was also very handsome, and next in age to Absalom by the same mother. ⁷He consulted with Joab, son of Zeruiah, and with Abiathar the priest, and they became Adonijah's supporters. ⁸However, Zadok the priest, Benaiah, son of Jehoiada, Nathan the prophet, Shimei and Rei, and David's warriors did not support Adonijah.

⁹Adonijah slaughtered sheep, oxen, and fatlings at the stone Zoheleth near En-rogel§

and invited all his brothers, the king's sons, and all the royal officials of Judah; ¹⁰but he did not invite Nathan the prophet, or Benaiah, or the warriors, or Solomon his brother.
**Solomon Proclaimed King.** ¹¹Then Nathan said to Bathsheba, Solomon's mother: "Have you not heard that Adonijah, son of Haggith, has become king, and our lord David does not know? ¹²Come now, let me advise you so that you may save your life and the life of your son Solomon. ¹³Go, visit King David, and say to him, 'Did you not, my lord king, swear to your handmaid: Your son Solomon shall be king after me; it is he who shall sit upon my throne? Why, then, has Adonijah become king?' ¹⁴And while you are still there speaking to the king, I will come in after you and confirm your words."

¹⁵So Bathsheba visited the king in his room. The king was very old, and Abishag the Shunamite was caring for the king.¶ ¹⁶Bathsheba bowed in homage to the king. The king said to her, "What do you wish?"** ¹⁷She answered him: "My lord, you swore to your servant by the LORD, your God, 'Solomon your son will be king after me; it is he who shall sit upon my throne.' ¹⁸But now Adonijah has become king, and you, my lord king, do not know it.†† ¹⁹He has sacrificed bulls, fatlings, and sheep in great numbers; he has invited all the king's sons, Abiathar the priest, and Joab, the commander of the army, but not your servant Solomon. ²⁰‡‡Now, my lord king, all Israel is looking to you to declare to them who is to sit upon the throne of my lord the king after him. ²¹If this is not done, when my lord the king rests with his ancestors, I and my son Solomon will be considered criminals."

---

*[1:1–11:43] The story of the reign of Solomon comprises twelve major units, organized concentrically. That is, the first unit (1:1–2:12a) balances the last (11:26–43), the second (2:12b–46) balances the second last (11:14–25), and so forth. (See the structural notes at the beginning of each major unit.) The center of the whole story is a diptych that narrates the construction of the Temple (6:1–7:51) and its dedication (8:1–9:10).

†[1:1–2:12a] The first major unit of the Solomon story concludes the so-called Succession Narrative (2 Sm 9–20; 1 Kgs 1–2). This unit tells how Solomon, a younger son, came to succeed David on the throne of Israel through the intervention of the prophet Nathan. Compare the last unit of the Solomon story, 11:26–43, where the prophet Ahijah begins the process whereby Jeroboam becomes king of the northern tribes after Solomon's death. The story of Solomon's accession is itself concentrically arranged: David's decline, Adonijah's rise, Solomon's supporters, David's decision, Solomon's inauguration, Adonijah's fall, David's death. Chronicles has no developed parallel to this story (see 1 Chr 23:1).

‡[1:2] The fulsome use of royal titles and the elaborate etiquette in the Succession Narrative suggest the raw ambition of the contending parties and the oppressive atmosphere of the court.

§[1:9] En-rogel: the modern Job's Well just southeast of Jerusalem. It marked the ancient boundary between the tribes of Benjamin and Judah (Jos 15:7; 18:16).

a. [1:5] 2 Sm 15:1.

¶[1:15] Entering the king's chambers, Bathsheba confronts two realities: he is very old; and she herself, the woman for whom David once committed adultery and murder, has been replaced at the king's side and in his bed.

**[1:16] Throughout 1 Kgs 1 the key question is "Who shall be king (*malak*)?" David's feeble, two-syllable question to Bathsheba is an ironic echo of that key word: "What do you wish?" renders the Heb. *mahlak*?

††[1:18] Bathsheba uses a clever wordplay to conceal the rivalry between Solomon and Adonijah and imply that the real rivalry is between David and Adonijah. She repeatedly addresses David as "my lord king" (*'adoni melek*), but claims that "Adonijah has become king" (*'adoniya malak*). Know: the term means both "be aware of" and "recognize, acknowledge, ratify."

‡‡[1:20] There was no precedent for determining succession to the throne of Israel. Adonijah and his supporters assumed that primogeniture would assure the succession as it did in the monarchies of the surrounding nations. But Bathsheba persuades David that he is free to name anyone he chooses.

²²While she was still speaking to the king, Nathan the prophet came in. ²³They told the king, "Nathan the prophet is here." He entered the king's presence and did him homage, bowing to the floor. ²⁴Then Nathan said: "My lord king, did you say, 'Adonijah shall be king after me and shall sit upon my throne'? ²⁵For today he went down and sacrificed bulls, fatlings, and sheep in great numbers; he invited all the king's sons, the commanders of the army, and Abiathar the priest, and even now they are eating and drinking in his company and saying, 'Long live King Adonijah!' ²⁶But me, your servant, he did not invite; nor Zadok the priest, nor Benaiah, son of Jehoiada, nor your servant Solomon. ²⁷If this was done by order of my lord the king, you did not tell me, your servant, who is to sit upon the throne of my lord the king after him."

²⁸King David answered, "Call Bathsheba here." When she entered the king's presence and stood before him, ²⁹the king swore, "As the LORD lives, who has redeemed my life from all distress, ³⁰this very day I will fulfill the oath I swore to you by the LORD, the God of Israel, 'Your son Solomon shall be king after me and shall sit upon my throne in my place.'" ³¹Bowing to the floor in homage to the king, Bathsheba said, "May my lord, King David, live forever!"

³²Then King David said, "Call Zadok the priest, Nathan the prophet, and Benaiah, son of Jehoiada." When they had entered the king's presence, ³³he said to them: "Take with you the royal officials. Mount my son Solomon upon my own mule and escort him down to Gihon. ³⁴There Zadok the priest and Nathan the prophet shall anoint him king over Israel, and you shall blow the ram's horn and cry, 'Long live King Solomon!' ³⁵When you come back up with him, he is to go in and sit upon my throne. It is he that shall be king in my place: him I designate ruler of Israel and of Judah." ³⁶Benaiah, son of Jehoiada, answered the king: "So be it! May the LORD, the God of my lord the king, so decree! ³⁷As the LORD has been with my lord the king, so may he be with Solomon, and make his throne even greater than that of my lord, King David!"

³⁸So Zadok the priest, Nathan the prophet, Benaiah, son of Jehoiada, and the Cherethites and Pelethites* went down, and mounting Solomon on King David's mule, escorted him to Gihon. ³⁹Then Zadok the priest took the horn of oil from the tent and anointed Solomon. They blew the ram's horn and all the people shouted, "Long live King Solomon!" ⁴⁰Then all the people went up after him, playing flutes and rejoicing so much the earth split with their shouting.

**Adonijah Submits to Solomon.** ⁴¹Adonijah and all the guests who were with him heard it, just as they ended their banquet. When Joab heard the sound of the ram's horn, he asked, "Why this uproar in the city?" ⁴²As he was speaking, Jonathan, son of Abiathar the priest, arrived. Adonijah said, "Come, you are a man of worth and must bring good news." ⁴³Jonathan answered Adonijah, "Hardly!† Our lord, King David, has made Solomon king. ⁴⁴The king sent with him Zadok the priest, Nathan the prophet, Benaiah, son of Jehoiada, and the Cherethites and Pelethites, and they mounted him upon the king's own mule. ⁴⁵Zadok the priest and Nathan the prophet anointed him king at Gihon, and they went up from there rejoicing, so that the city is in an uproar. That is the noise you hear. ⁴⁶Moreover, Solomon has taken his seat on the royal throne, ⁴⁷and moreover the king's servants have come to pay their respects to our lord, King David, saying, 'May your God make Solomon's name more famous than your name, his throne greater than your throne!' And the king in his bed did homage. ⁴⁸This is what the king said: 'Blessed be the LORD, the God of Israel, who has this day provided one to sit upon my throne, so that I see it with my own eyes.'" ⁴⁹All the guests of Adonijah got up trembling, and went each their way; ⁵⁰but Adonijah, in fear of Solomon, got up and went to grasp the horns of the altar.‡

⁵¹It was reported to Solomon: "Adonijah, in fear of King Solomon, is clinging to the horns of the altar and saying, 'Let King Solomon first swear that he will not kill me, his servant, with the sword.'" ⁵²Solomon answered, "If he proves worthy, not a hair of his shall fall to the ground. But if evil is found in him, he shall die." ⁵³King Solomon sent to have him brought down from the altar, and he came and paid homage to King Solomon. Solomon then said to him, "Go to your house."

## CHAPTER 2

**David's Last Instructions and Death.** ¹When the time of David's death drew near, he gave these instructions to Solomon his son: ²"I am going the way of all the earth. Be strong and be a man! ³ᵇKeep the mandate of the LORD, your God, walking in his ways and keeping his statutes, commands, ordinances, and decrees as they are written in the law of Moses, that you may succeed in whatever you do, and wherever you turn, ⁴ᶜand that the LORD may fulfill the word he spoke concerning me: If your sons so

---

*[1:38] **Cherethites and Pelethites**: mercenaries in David's bodyguard. They became part of his retinue after he defeated the Philistines and established himself in Jerusalem; cf. 2 Sm 8:18; 15:18; 20:23.

†[1:43] **Hardly**: Jonathan's first word, *'abal*, whose meaning (such as "indeed," "on the contrary") must be discerned from the context, may be ironic. This irony is deepened by an untranslatable wordplay in Hebrew: a very similar word means "to mourn," which is an appropriate comment about the death of Adonijah's hopes for the throne.

‡[1:50] **Horns of the altar**: the protuberances on each of the four corners of the altar (Ex 27:2; 29:12). By grasping the horns of the altar Adonijah is claiming asylum (Ex 21:13–14; 1 Kgs 2:28).

b. [2:3] Dt 17:18–19.   c. [2:4] 2 Sm 7:11–16; Ps 132:11–12.

conduct themselves that they walk before me in faithfulness with their whole heart and soul, there shall never be wanting someone of your line on the throne of Israel.

⁵*ᵈ"You yourself know what Joab, son of Zeruiah, did to me—what he did to the two commanders of Israel's armies, Abner, son of Ner, and Amasa, son of Jether: he killed them and brought the blood of war into a time of peace, and put the blood of war on the belt about his waist and the sandal on his foot. ⁶Act with all the wisdom you possess; do not let his gray head go down to Sheol in peace. ⁷ᵉBut be true to the sons of Barzillai the Gileadite, and have them among those who eat at your table. For they were loyal to me when I was fleeing from your brother Absalom. ⁸ᶠYou also have with you Shimei, son of Gera, the Benjaminite of Bahurim, who cursed me bitterly the day I was going to Mahanaim. When he came down to meet me at the Jordan, I swore to him by the LORD: 'I will not kill you by the sword.' ⁹But you must not let him go unpunished. You are wise; you will know what to do to send his gray head down to Sheol in blood."

¹⁰ᵍDavid rested with his ancestors and was buried in the City of David. ¹¹ʰDavid was king over Israel for forty years: he was king seven years in Hebron and thirty-three years in Jerusalem.

**The Kingdom Made Secure.**† ¹²Then Solomon sat on the throne of David his father, and his kingship was established.

¹³Adonijah, son of Haggith, came to Bathsheba, the mother of Solomon. "Do you come in peace?" she asked. "In peace," he answered, ¹⁴and he added, "I have something to say to you." She replied, "Speak." ¹⁵So he said: "You know that the kingship was mine, and all Israel expected me to be king. But the kingship passed me by and went to my brother; by the LORD's will it went to him. ¹⁶But now there is one favor I would ask of you. Do not refuse me." And she said, "Speak on."

¹⁷‡He said, "Please ask King Solomon, who will not refuse you, to give me Abishag the Shunamite to be my wife." ¹⁸Bathsheba replied, "Very well, I will speak to the king for you."

¹⁹Then Bathsheba went to King Solomon to speak to him for Adonijah, and the king stood up to meet her and paid her homage. Then he sat down upon his throne, and a throne was provided for the king's mother, who sat at his right. ²⁰She said, "There is one small favor I would ask of you. Do not refuse me." The king said to her, "Ask it, my mother, for I will not refuse you." ²¹So she said, "Let Abishag the Shunamite be given to your brother Adonijah to be his wife." ²²King Solomon answered his mother, "And why do you ask that Abishag the Shunamite be given to Adonijah? Ask the kingship for him as well, for he is my older brother! Ask for him, for Abiathar the priest, for Joab, son of Zeruiah!" ²³And King Solomon swore by the LORD: "May God do thus to me and more, if Adonijah has not spoken this word at the cost of his life. ²⁴ⁱAnd now, as the LORD lives, who has established me and set me on the throne of David my father and made for me a house as he promised, this day shall Adonijah be put to death." ²⁵Then King Solomon sent Benaiah, son of Jehoiada, who struck him dead.

²⁶ʲThe king said to Abiathar the priest: "Go to your estate in Anathoth. Though you deserve to die, I will not put you to death at this time, because you carried the ark of the Lord GOD before David my father and shared in all the hardships my father endured."§ ²⁷ᵏSo Solomon dismissed Abiathar from the office of priest of the LORD, thus fulfilling the word the LORD had spoken in Shiloh against the house of Eli.

²⁸When the news came to Joab, since he had sided with Adonijah, though not with Absalom, he fled to the tent of the LORD and clung to the horns of the altar. ²⁹King Solomon was told, "Joab has fled to the tent of the LORD and is by the altar." He sent Benaiah, son of Jehoiada, with the order, "Go, strike him down." ³⁰Benaiah went to the tent of the LORD and said to him, "The king says, 'Come out.'" But he answered, "No! I will die here." Benaiah reported to the king, "This is what Joab said to me in reply." ³¹The king answered him: "Do as he has said. Strike him down and bury him, and remove from me and from my father's house the blood which Joab shed without provocation. ³²The LORD will bring blood upon his own head, because he struck down two men better and more just than

---

*[2:5–9] David urges Solomon to purge Joab and Shimei and supplies him with justification for doing so. Joab had killed Abner (2 Sm 3:22–30) and Amasa (2 Sm 20:4–12), thereby bringing blood guilt upon himself and perhaps upon his master David. Shimei had cursed David (2 Sm 16:5–8), though David pledged that Shimei would not be killed for it (2 Sm 19:16–24). David's motives, however, may have been more personal. Joab also killed David's son Absalom and chided David for his untimely public display of grief (2 Sm 18:9–19:8), and David may have felt himself free of the promise he made to Shimei because that promise was coerced by the presence of Shimei's thousand partisans backing him at the time.

†[2:12–46] The second major unit of the Solomon story shows how Solomon eliminated people he considered threats to the security of his throne. It is marked by a device called "inclusion," where the text repeats a word, phrase, or idea at the beginning and end of a literary unit (see vv. 12b, 46b). Compare 11:14–25, where Solomon is unable to eliminate other threats to his security.

d. [2:5] 2 Sm 3:22–30; 20:8–10.   e. [2:7] 2 Sm 17:27–29; 19:32–41.   f. [2:8] 2 Sm 16:5–13; 19:17–24.   g. [2:10] Acts 2:29.   h. [2:11] 2 Sm 2:1–4; 5:1–5.

‡[2:17–25] Abishag had belonged to David's harem (1:3–4), which Solomon inherited. Adonijah's request could imply a challenge to Solomon's accession and so exposes Adonijah to the suspicion of insurrection that will cost him his life; cf. 2 Sm 3:6–11; 16:21–22.

§[2:26] The narrator indulges in a subtle wordplay: Abiathar's exile to Anathoth ('anatot) continues the series of hardships he has endured (hit'annita).

i. [2:24] 2 Sm 7:11–16.   j. [2:26] 1 Sm 22:20–23.   k. [2:27] 1 Sm 2:27–33.   l. [2:32] 2 Sm 3:22–30; 20:8–10.

himself, and slew them with the sword without my father David's knowledge: Abner, son of Ner, commander of Israel's army, and Amasa, son of Jether, commander of Judah's army. 33Their blood will be upon the head of Joab and his descendants. But upon David and his descendants, upon his house and his throne, there shall be peace forever from the LORD." 34Benaiah, son of Jehoiada, went back, struck him down and killed him; he was buried in his house in the wilderness. 35The king appointed Benaiah, son of Jehoiada, over the army in his place; Zadok the priest the king put in place of Abiathar.

36Then the king summoned Shimei and said to him: "Build yourself a house in Jerusalem and stay there. Do not go anywhere else. 37For the day you leave, and cross the Wadi Kidron, be certain you shall surely die. Your blood shall be upon your own head." 38Shimei answered the king: "I accept. Your servant will do just as my lord the king has said." So Shimei stayed in Jerusalem for a long time. 39But three years later, two of Shimei's servants ran away to Achish, son of Maacah, king of Gath, and Shimei was told, "Your servants are in Gath." 40So Shimei rose, saddled his donkey, and went to Achish in Gath in search of his servants; and Shimei returned from Gath with his servants. 41When Solomon was told that Shimei had gone from Jerusalem to Gath, and had returned, 42the king summoned Shimei and said to him: "Did I not have you swear by the LORD and warn you clearly, 'The day you leave and go anywhere else, be certain you shall surely die'? And you answered, 'I accept and obey.'" 43Why, then, have you not kept the oath of the LORD and the command that I gave you?" 44mAnd the king said to Shimei: "In your heart you know very well the evil that you did to David my father. Now the LORD is bringing your own evil upon your head. 45But King Solomon shall be blessed, and David's throne shall be established before the LORD forever." 46The king then gave the order to Benaiah, son of Jehoiada, who went out and struck him dead.

And the royal power was established in Solomon's hand.

## CHAPTER 3

**Early Promise of Solomon's Reign.**† 1nSolomon allied himself by marriage with Pharaoh, king of Egypt. He married the daughter of Pharaoh and brought her to the City of David, until he should finish building his own house, and the house of the LORD, and the wall around Jerusalem. 2The people were sacrificing on the high places, however, for up to that time no house had been built for the name of the LORD. 3Although Solomon loved the LORD, walking in the statutes of David his father, he offered sacrifice and burned incense on the high places.

4The king went to Gibeon to sacrifice there, because that was the great high place. Upon its altar Solomon sacrificed a thousand burnt offerings. 5In Gibeon the LORD appeared to Solomon in a dream at night. God said: Whatever you ask I shall give you. 6Solomon answered: "You have shown great kindness to your servant, David my father, because he walked before you with fidelity, justice, and an upright heart; and you have continued this great kindness toward him today, giving him a son to sit upon his throne. 7Now, LORD, my God, you have made me, your servant, king to succeed David my father; but I am a mere youth, not knowing at all how to act— 8I, your servant, among the people you have chosen, a people so vast that it cannot be numbered or counted. 9Give your servant, therefore, a listening heart to judge your people and to distinguish between good and evil. For who is able to give judgment for this vast people of yours?"

10The Lord was pleased by Solomon's request. 11So God said to him: Because you asked for this—you did not ask for a long life for yourself, nor for riches, nor for the life of your enemies— but you asked for discernment to know what is right— 12I now do as you request. I give you a heart so wise and discerning that there has never been anyone like you until now, nor after you will there be anyone to equal you. 13oIn addition, I give you what you have not asked for: I give you such riches and glory that among kings there will be no one like you all your days. 14And if you walk in my ways, keeping my statutes and commandments, as David your father did, I will give you a long life. 15Solomon awoke; it was a dream! He went to Jerusalem, stood before the ark of the covenant of the Lord, sacrificed burnt offerings and communion offerings, and gave a feast for all his servants.

**Solomon's Listening Heart.**‡ 16Later, two prostitutes came to the king and stood before him. 17One woman said: "By your leave, my lord, this

---

*[2:42–44] In his charge against Shimei, Solomon misrepresents the truth in two ways. He did not make Shimei take an oath. And he imposed capital punishment only on crossing the Wadi Kidron, to the east of Jerusalem. This was presumably to prevent Shimei from returning to his home, Bahurim, which lay in that direction; Gath, however, is southwest of Jerusalem. Solomon's next words to Shimei reveal that he is really being punished for cursing David, not for violating Solomon's command.

†[3:1–15] The third major unit of the Solomon story depicts the bright beginning of his reign. It includes the narrator's remarks about Solomon's marriage and his building projects, and a divine appearance to Solomon. Compare 11:1–13,

where the same themes recur, but in negative fashion. The story of the divine appearance is told also in 2 Chr 1:1–13.

‡[3:16–5:14] The fourth major unit of the Solomon story shows how Solomon used the three gifts that the Lord gave him in 3:12–13: a listening heart (3:16–28), riches (4:1–5:8), universal renown (5:9–14). In each case his gifts benefited the populace, from the lowest classes (3:16–28) to his whole people (4:20; 5:5) to the whole world (5:9–14). Compare 9:26–10:29, where the same three gifts all redound to the benefit of Solomon himself.

---

m. [2:44] 2 Sm 16:5–13; 19:17–24.　n. [3:1] 1 Kgs 7:8; 9:24.

o. [3:13] Eccl 1:12–13; Wis 7:7–11; Mt 6:29.

woman and I live in the same house, and I gave birth in the house while she was present. ¹⁸On the third day after I gave birth, this woman also gave birth. We were alone; no one else was in the house with us; only the two of us were in the house. ¹⁹This woman's son died during the night when she lay on top of him. ²⁰So in the middle of the night she got up and took my son from my side, as your servant was sleeping. Then she laid him at her bosom and laid her dead son in my bosom. ²¹I rose in the morning to nurse my son, and he was dead! But when I examined him in the morning light, I saw it was not the son I had borne." ²²The other woman answered, "No! The living one is my son, the dead one is yours." But the first kept saying, "No! the dead one is your son, the living one is mine!" Thus they argued before the king. ²³Then the king said: "One woman claims, 'This, the living one, is my son, the dead one is yours.' The other answers, 'No! The dead one is your son, the living one is mine.'" ²⁴The king continued, "Get me a sword." When they brought the sword before the king, ²⁵he said, "Cut the living child in two, and give half to one woman and half to the other." ²⁶The woman whose son was alive, because she was stirred with compassion for her son, said to the king, "Please, my lord, give her the living baby—do not kill it!" But the other said, "It shall be neither mine nor yours. Cut it in two!" ²⁷The king then answered, "Give her the living baby! Do not kill it! She is the mother." ²⁸When all Israel heard the judgment the king had given, they were in awe of him, because they saw that the king had in him the wisdom of God for giving right judgment.

## CHAPTER 4

**Solomon's Riches: Domestic Affairs.†** ¹Solomon was king over all Israel, ²and these were the officials he had in his service:

Azariah, son of Zadok, the priest;
³ Elihoreph and Ahijah, sons of Shisha, scribes;
Jehoshaphat, son of Ahilud, the chancellor;
⁴ Benaiah, son of Jehoiada, in charge of the army;
Zadok and Abiathar, priests;
⁵ Azariah, son of Nathan, in charge of the governors;
Zabud, son of Nathan, priest and companion to the king;
⁶ Ahishar, master of the palace; and

Adoniram, son of Abda, in charge of the forced labor.

⁷‡Solomon had twelve governors over all Israel who supplied food for the king and his household, each having to provide for one month in the year. ⁸Their names were:§

the son of Hur in the hill country of Ephraim;
⁹ the son of Deker in Makaz, Shaalbim, Beth-shemesh, and Elon Beth-hanan;
¹⁰ the son of Hesed in Arubboth, as well as in Socoh and the whole region of Hepher;
¹¹ the son of Abinadab, in all Naphath-dor; he was married to Taphath, Solomon's daughter;
¹² Baana, son of Ahilud, in Taanach and Megiddo and all Beth-shean near Zarethan below Jezreel, from Beth-shean to Abel-meholah to beyond Jokmeam;
¹³ the son of Geber in Ramoth-gilead, having charge of the villages of Jair, son of Manasseh, in Gilead; and of the district of Argob in Bashan—sixty large walled cities with gates barred with bronze;
¹⁴ Ahinadab, son of Iddo, in Mahanaim;
¹⁵ Ahimaaz, in Naphtali; he was married to Basemath, another daughter of Solomon;
¹⁶ Baana, son of Hushai, in Asher and Aloth;
¹⁷ Jehoshaphat, son of Paruah, in Issachar;
¹⁸ Shimei, son of Ela, in Benjamin;
¹⁹ Geber, son of Uri, in the land of Gilead, the land of Sihon, king of the Amorites, and of Og, king of Bashan.

There was one governor besides, in the land of Judah.¶ ²⁰Judah and Israel were as numerous as the sands by the sea; they ate and drank and rejoiced.

## CHAPTER 5

**Solomon's Riches: International Affairs.** ¹**Solomon ruled over all the kingdoms from

---

*[3:26–27] The true mother reveals herself by an uncommon and tender word for the child, "baby." With this, and the woman's willingness to give up her child, Solomon realizes that she is the true mother, and quotes her words exactly in rendering his judgment.

†[4:1–5:8] The sub-unit on Solomon's riches is organized around domestic affairs (4:1–20) and international affairs (5:1–5), with a short appendix on Solomon's horses and chariots (5:6–8). Compare 9:26–10:29, where comparable elements reappear.

‡[4:7–19] The administration of the kingdom thus initiated by Solomon continued in its main features for the duration of the monarchy in Israel and Judah. Note the use of "all Israel" to mean only the northern tribes (see also 5:27). Solomon's exactions did not fall evenly on the whole people, but favored his own southern tribe of Judah. Eventually this inequity would lead to the dissolution of the union of Israel and Judah (12:1–19).

§[4:8–19] Several of the governors are identified only by their fathers' names.

¶[4:19] One governor . . . land of Judah: the royal territory of Judah had its own peculiar administration different from that of the twelve northern districts, each of which had to supply the king and his household with a month's provisions of food each year (v. 7).

**[5:1–32] This translation follows the numeration of the Hebrew Bible, rather than the Vulgate; in many English

p. [4:20] Gn 22:17; 32:13; Dn 3:36; Hos 1:10; Heb 11:12.

the River* to the land of the Philistines, down to the border of Egypt; they paid Solomon tribute and served him as long as he lived. ²¹Solomon's provisions for each day were thirty kors of fine flour, sixty kors of meal, ³ten fatted oxen, twenty pasture-fed oxen, and a hundred sheep, not counting harts, gazelles, roebucks, and fatted fowl. ⁴He had dominion over all the land west of the River, from Tiphsah to Gaza, and all its kings, and he had peace on all his borders round about. ⁵ᵠThus Judah and Israel lived in security, everyone under their own vine and fig tree from Dan to Beer-sheba, as long as Solomon lived.

**Solomon's Riches: Chariots and Horses.** ⁶ʳSolomon had forty thousand stalls for horses for chariots and twelve thousand horsemen. ⁷ᵗThe governors, one for each month, provided food for King Solomon and for all the guests at King Solomon's table. They left nothing unprovided. ⁸For the chariot horses and draft animals also, each brought his quota of barley and straw to the required place.

**Solomon's Renown.** ⁹ˢMoreover, God gave Solomon wisdom, exceptional understanding, and knowledge, as vast as the sand on the seashore. ¹⁰Solomon's wisdom surpassed that of all the peoples of the East and all the wisdom of Egypt. ¹¹He was wiser than anyone else—wiser than Ethan the Ezrahite, or Heman, Chalcol, and Darda, the musicians—and his fame spread throughout the neighboring peoples. ¹²Solomon also uttered three thousand proverbs, and his songs numbered a thousand and five. ¹³He spoke of plants, from the cedar on Lebanon to the hyssop growing out of the wall, and he spoke about beasts, birds, reptiles, and fishes. ¹⁴ᵗPeople from all nations came to hear Solomon's wisdom, sent by all the kings of the earth who had heard of his wisdom.

**Preparations for the Temple.**§ ¹⁵When Hiram, king of Tyre, heard that Solomon had been anointed king in place of his father, he sent an embassy to him; for Hiram had always been

David's friend.⁵ ¹⁶Solomon sent back this message to Hiram: ¹⁷ᵘ"You know that David my father, because of the wars that beset him, could not build a house for the name of the LORD his God until such time as the LORD should put his enemies under the soles of his feet. ¹⁸But now the LORD, my God, has given me rest on all sides, without adversary or misfortune. ¹⁹ᵛSo I intend to build a house for the name of the LORD, my God, as the LORD said to David my father: Your son whom I will put upon your throne in your place shall build the house for my name. ²⁰Give orders, then, to have cedars from the Lebanon cut down for me. My servants shall accompany yours, and I will pay you whatever you say for your servants' wages. For you know that there is no one among us who is skilled in cutting timber like the Sidonians." ²¹When Hiram had heard the words of Solomon, he was overjoyed, and said, "Blessed be the LORD this day, who has given David a wise son over this numerous people." ²²"Hiram then sent word to Solomon, "I have heard the proposal you sent me, and I will provide all the cedars and fir trees you desire. ²³My servants shall bring them down from the Lebanon to the sea, and I will arrange them into rafts in the sea and bring them wherever you say. There I will break up the rafts, and you shall take the lumber. You, for your part, shall furnish the provisions I desire for my household." ²⁴So Hiram continued to provide Solomon with all the cedars and fir trees he desired, ²⁵while Solomon gave Hiram twenty thousand kors of wheat to provide for his household, and twenty kors†† of hand-pressed oil. Solomon gave Hiram all this every year. ²⁶The LORD gave Solomon wisdom as he promised him. So there was peace between Hiram and Solomon, and the two of them made‡‡ a covenant.

²⁷King Solomon raised thirty thousand forced laborers from all Israel.§§ ²⁸He sent them to the Lebanon for a month in relays of ten

---

*[5:1] **The River:** that is, the Euphrates. This claim may be exaggerated, but "from the Euphrates to the border of Egypt" was the traditional description of the extent of the Davidic holdings.

†[5:2] The list of Solomon's supplies may have originally belonged with the list of governors in 4:7–19, but the author has placed it here to imply that Solomon's vassal kingdoms, not his own citizenry, supplied his vast daily needs. The daily provisions listed could have supported several thousand people. **Kors:** see note on Ez 45:14.

‡[5:7] This verse suggests that the governors also saw to the provender for Solomon's animals (v. 8).

§[5:15–32] The fifth major unit of the Solomon story explains the preparations Solomon made for the construction of the Temple. He negotiates with Hiram of Tyre for materiel (5:15–26), and conscripts a labor force for personnel (5:27–32). Compare 9:11–23, which returns to the same two themes after the Temple has been built and dedicated. 2 Chr 2:1–17 presents another version of the same material.

¶[5:15] **David's friend:** the term "to be a friend," lit., "to love," is political, and means that David and Hiram had been allies. The purpose of Hiram's embassy is to determine whether Solomon is willing to continue the alliance. This unspoken agenda lies behind the negotiations about materials for the Temple, as the concluding v. 26 makes clear.

**[5:22–23] Although his reply is couched in polite, diplomatic language, Hiram renegotiates Solomon's terms in his own favor. No Israelites are to enter Tyrian territory, and Solomon is not to pay the salary of Hiram's laborers but rather to furnish "provisions" for his household—the same language used of the tribute Solomon received from his own vassals in v. 2.

††[5:25] **Twenty kors:** this means about two thousand gallons of the finest olive oil available, hand-pressed rather than produced in large olive presses, so that no debris (such as crushed olive pits, powder from the grinding stones) would contaminate the oil. Also see note on 2 Chr 2:9.

‡‡[5:26] **Made:** lit., "cut." The story of Solomon's arrangements with Hiram is framed by references to political alliance between Israel and Tyre (vv. 15, 26). Since, in Hebrew idiom, Hiram and Solomon "cut" a covenant, this suggests that the agreement they reach for "cutting" wood (which clearly favors Hiram) reflects the terms of the larger treaty.

§§[5:27] **All Israel:** see note on 4:7–19.

---

translations, 5:1–14 is 4:21–34, and 5:15 is 5:1.

q. [5:5] Sir 47:13.   r. [5:6] 1 Kgs 10:26; Dt 17:16; 2 Chr 1:14; 9:25.   s. [5:9–14] Sir 47:15–17.   t. [5:14] 1 Kgs 10:1.

u. [5:17] 2 Sm 7:5–7; 1 Chr 22:7–8.   v. [5:19] 2 Sm 7:12–13.

thousand, so that they spent one month in the Lebanon and two months at home. Adoniram was in charge of the forced labor. [29]Solomon had seventy thousand carriers and eighty thousand stonecutters in the mountain, [30]in addition to three thousand three hundred overseers answerable to Solomon, who were in charge of the work and directed the people engaged in the work. [31]By order of the king, fine, large blocks of stone were quarried to give the house a foundation of hewn stone. [32]Solomon's and Hiram's builders, along with others from Gebal,* shaped them, and prepared the wood and stones for building the house.

## CHAPTER 6

**Building of the Temple.**[†] [1]In the four hundred and eightieth year after the Israelites went forth from the land of Egypt, in the fourth year of Solomon's reign over Israel, in the month of Ziv (the second month), he began to build the house of the LORD.[‡]

[2]The house which King Solomon built for the LORD was sixty cubits long, twenty wide, and thirty high. [3]The porch in front of the nave of the house was twenty cubits from side to side along the width of the house, and ten cubits deep in front of the house. [4]Windows with closed lattices were made for the house, [5]and adjoining the wall of the house he built a substructure around its walls that enclosed the nave and the

---

* [5:32] **Gebal**: Byblos.

[†] [6:1–7:51] The central units of the Solomon story describe the building of the Temple (6:1–7:51) and its dedication ceremony (8:1–9:10). The account of the construction of the Temple ("the house") is organized to give the reader a guided tour. Approaching from a distance, we see ground plans (6:2–3) and structural work in stone (6:4–8) and wood (6:9–10). After a brief interruption that recounts a divine word to Solomon (6:11–13), we enter the Temple to view the paneling and ornamentation of the nave (6:14–18), the gilded walls and golden entrance of the inner sanctuary or holy of holies (6:19–22), with its priceless interior decoration and furnishings (6:23–28). As we leave, we admire the interior carvings and gilded floor of the inner sanctuary (6:29–30), return to the nave through carved and gilded doors (6:31–32), and exit from the nave through another set of carved and gilded doors (6:33–35) to the courtyard (6:36). Our guide briefly points out the nearby palace complex (7:1–12); then we walk around the courtyard to marvel at Hiram's heroic works in bronze: the two columns (7:15–22), the "sea" (7:23–26), and the ten stands and basins set along either side of the Temple buildings (7:27–39). The account ends with the smaller bronze vessels Hiram made for the Temple services (7:40–47) and the gold vessels that Solomon made (7:48–50). Unfortunately, several factors make it impossible to use the account to produce a satisfactory model of Solomon's Temple. Throughout the account there are numerous technical architectural terms whose meaning is lost to us; and it is moreover likely that the author is describing the Temple as it stood in his own time, centuries after Solomon's day. The Chronicler also describes the construction of the Temple in 2 Chr 3:1–4:22 and its dedication in 2 Chr 5:1–7:22.

[‡] [6:1] Construction of the Temple is here dated in relation to the traditional date of the exodus from Egypt, rounded off to a conventional twelve generations of forty years each. This chronology means that the Temple was built approximately midway between Israel's two foundational deliverances, the exodus and the return from the Babylonian exile. The schematization of history implied in these figures recommends caution in using them for historical reconstruction.

---

inner sanctuary, and he made side chambers all around. [6]The lowest story was five cubits wide, the middle one six cubits wide, the third seven cubits wide, because he put recesses along the outside of the house to avoid fastening anything into the walls of the house. [7]The house was built of stone dressed at the quarry, so that no hammer or ax, no iron tool, was to be heard in the house during its construction. [8]The entrance to the middle story was on the south side of the house; stairs led up to the middle story and from the middle story to the third. [9]When he had finished building the house, it was roofed in with rafters and boards of cedar. [10]He built the substructure five cubits high all along the outside of the house, to which it was joined by cedar beams.

[11]The word of the LORD came to Solomon: [12w]As to this house you are building—if you walk in my statutes, carry out my ordinances, and observe all my commands, walking in them, I will fulfill toward you my word which I spoke to David your father. [13]I will dwell in the midst of the Israelites and will not forsake my people Israel.

[14]When Solomon finished building the house, [15]its inside walls were lined with cedar paneling: he covered the interior with wood from floor to ceiling, and he covered its floor with fir planking. [16]At the rear of the house a space of twenty cubits was set off by cedar panels from the floor to the ceiling, enclosing the inner sanctuary, the holy of holies. [17]The house was forty cubits long, that is, the nave, the part in front. [18]The cedar in the interior of the house was carved in the form of gourds and open flowers; all was of cedar, and no stone was to be seen.

[19]In the innermost part of the house[§] he set up the inner sanctuary to house the ark of the LORD's covenant. [20]In front of the inner sanctuary (it was twenty cubits long, twenty wide, and twenty high, and he covered it with pure gold), he made an altar of cedar. [21]Solomon covered the interior of the house with pure gold, and he drew golden chains across in front of the inner sanctuary, and covered it with gold. [22]He covered the whole house with gold, until the whole house was done, and the whole altar that belonged to the inner sanctuary he covered with gold. [23]In the inner sanctuary he made two cherubim, each ten cubits high, made of pine. [24]Each wing of a cherub was five cubits so that the span from wing tip to wing tip was ten cubits. [25]The second cherub was also ten cubits: the two cherubim were identical in size and shape; [26]the first cherub was ten cubits high, and so was the second. [27]He placed the cherubim in the inmost part of the house; the wings of the cherubim

---

[§] [6:19] **The innermost part of the house**: the inner sanctuary or holy of holies reserved exclusively for the Lord, enthroned upon the cherubim over the ark of the covenant (2 Chr 3:10–13). See note on Ex 25:18–20.

w. [6:12] 2 Sm 7:13–16.

were spread wide, so that one wing of the first touched the side wall and the wing of the second touched the other wall; the wings pointing to the middle of the room touched each other. [28]He overlaid the cherubim with gold.

[29]The walls of the house on all sides of both the inner and the outer rooms had carved figures of cherubim, palm trees, and open flowers. [30]The floor of the house of both the inner and the outer rooms was overlaid with gold. [31]At the entrance of the inner sanctuary, doors of pine were made; the doorframes had five-sided posts. [32]The two doors were of pine, with carved figures of cherubim, palm trees, and open flowers. The doors were overlaid with gold, and the cherubim and the palm trees were also covered with beaten gold. [33]He did the same at the entrance to the nave, where the doorposts were of pine and were four-sided. [34]The two doors were of fir wood, each door consisting of two panels hinged together; [35]and he carved cherubim, palm trees, and open flowers, and plated them with gold. [36]He walled off the inner court with three courses of hewn stones and one course of cedar beams.

[37]The foundations of the LORD's house were laid in the month of Ziv in the fourth year, [38]and it was finished, in all particulars, exactly according to plan, in the month of Bul, the eighth month, in the eleventh year. Thus Solomon built it in seven years.

## CHAPTER 7

[1]*To finish the building of his own house Solomon took thirteen years. [2]He built the House of the Forest of Lebanon one hundred cubits long, fifty wide, and thirty high; it was supported by four rows of cedar columns, with cedar beams upon the columns. [3]Moreover, it had a ceiling of cedar above the rafters resting on the columns; these rafters numbered forty-five, fifteen to a row. [4]There were lattices in three rows, each row facing the next, [5]and all the openings and doorposts were squared with lintels, each facing across from the next. [6]He also made the Porch of Columns, fifty cubits long and thirty wide. The porch extended across the front, and there were columns with a canopy in front of them. [7]He also made the Porch of the Throne where he gave judgment—that is, the Porch of Judgment; it was paneled with cedar from floor to ceiling beams. [8]yThe house in which he lived was in another court, set in deeper than the Porch

and of the same construction. (Solomon made a house like this Porch for Pharaoh's daughter, whom he had married.)[†] [9]All these buildings were of fine stones, hewn to size and trimmed front and back with a saw, from the foundation to the bonding course and outside as far as the great court. [10]The foundation was made of fine, large blocks, some ten cubits and some eight cubits. [11]Above were fine stones hewn to size, and cedar wood. [12]The great court had three courses of hewn stones all around and a course of cedar beams. So also were the inner court of the house of the LORD and its porch.

[13]King Solomon brought Hiram[‡] from Tyre. [14]He was a bronze worker, the son of a widow from the tribe of Naphtali; his father had been from Tyre. He was endowed with wisdom, understanding, and knowledge for doing any work in bronze. He came to King Solomon and did all his metal work.

[15]§He fashioned two bronze columns, each eighteen cubits high and twelve cubits in circumference. [16]He also made two capitals cast in bronze, to be placed on top of the columns, each of them five cubits high. [17]There were meshes made like netting and braid made like chains for the capitals on top of the columns, seven for each capital. [18]¶He also cast pomegranates, two rows around each netting to cover the capital on top of the columns. [19]The capitals on top of the columns (in the porch) were made like lilies, four cubits high. [20]And the capitals on the two columns, both above and adjoining the bulge where it crossed out of the netting, had two hundred pomegranates in rows around each capital. [21]He set up the columns at the temple porch; one he set up to the south, and called it Jachin, and the other to the north, and called it Boaz.** [22]The top of the columns was made like a lily. Thus the work on the columns was completed.

---

†[7:8] Solomon did not build the house for Pharaoh's daughter until Temple and palace were finished (3:1). By mentioning this marriage, the narrator keeps before the reader a developing theme in the Solomon story: the king's building activities for his foreign wives, which eventually implicate him in idolatry (3:1; 7:8; 9:24; 11:1–8).

‡[7:13] Hiram: a craftsman, not the king of Tyre (5:15–26).

§[7:15] The two bronze columns were called Jachin and Boaz (v. 21; also 2 Chr 3:17); the significance of the names is unclear. The columns stood to the right and left of the Temple porch, and may have been intended to mark the entrance to the building as the entrance to God's private dwelling. Their extraordinary size and elaborate decoration would have made them the most impressive parts of the Temple visible to the ordinary viewer, who was not permitted into the nave, let alone into the innermost sanctuary. According to Jer 52:21, the columns were hollow, the bronze exterior being "four fingers thick."

¶[7:18–20] The Hebrew text is corrupt in many places here, and alternative readings attested in the ancient versions are secondary attempts to make sense of the text. A clearer description of the columns and their decoration is found in vv. 41–42.

**[7:21] Jachin . . . Boaz: see note on 7:15.

---

*[7:1–12] The account of Solomon's building of the Temple (the Lord's "house") is interrupted by an account of his building of the palace (Solomon's "house"), which contained also the main buildings of public administration. The passage is anachronistic, since 6:38–7:1 and 9:10 imply that the palace was not begun until the Temple was completed. By placing the account here, the narrator highlights the fact that Solomon spent almost twice as long on his own "house" as on the Lord's.

---

x. [7:1] 1 Kgs 9:10.    y. [7:8] 1 Kgs 3:1; 9:24.          z. [7:15–18] Jer 52:21–23.

²³Then he made the molten sea;* it was made with a circular rim, and measured ten cubits across, five in height, and thirty in circumference. ²⁴Under the brim, gourds encircled it for ten cubits around the compass of the sea; the gourds were in two rows and were cast in one mold with the sea. ²⁵This rested on twelve oxen, three facing north, three facing west, three facing south, and three facing east, with their haunches all toward the center; upon them was set the sea. ²⁶It was a handbreadth thick, and its brim resembled that of a cup, being lily-shaped. Its capacity was two thousand baths.†

²⁷He also made ten stands of bronze, each four cubits long, four wide, and three high. ²⁸When these stands were constructed, panels were set within the framework. ²⁹On the panels within the frames there were lions, oxen, and cherubim; and on the frames likewise, above and below the lions and oxen, there were wreaths in hammered relief. ³⁰Each stand had four bronze wheels and bronze axles. The four legs of each stand had cast braces, which were under the basin; they had wreaths on each side. ³¹The mouth of the basin was inside, and a cubit above, the crown, whose opening was round, made like a receptacle, a cubit and a half in depth. There was carved work at the opening, on panels that were square, not circular. ³²The four wheels were below the paneling, and the axletrees of the wheels and the stand were of one piece. Each wheel was a cubit and a half high. ³³The wheels were constructed like chariot wheels; their axletrees, rims, spokes, and hubs were all cast. ³⁴The four braces reached the four corners of each stand, and formed part of the stand. ³⁵At the top of the stand there was a raised collar half a cubit high, and the handles and panels on top of the stand formed part of it. ³⁶On the flat ends of the handles and on the panels, wherever there was a bare space, cherubim, lions, and palm trees were carved, as well as wreaths all around. ³⁷This was how he made the ten stands, all of the same casting, the same size, the same shape. ³⁸He made ten bronze basins, each four cubits in diameter with a capacity of forty baths, one basin atop each of the ten stands.

³⁹He placed the stands, five on the south side of the house and five on the north. The sea he placed off to the southeast from the south side of the house.

⁴⁰When Hiram had made the pots, shovels, and bowls, he finished all his work for King Solomon in the house of the LORD: ⁴¹two columns; two nodes for the capitals on top of the columns; two pieces of netting covering the two nodes for the capitals on top of the columns; ⁴²four hundred pomegranates in double rows on both pieces of netting that covered the two nodes of the capitals on top of the columns; ⁴³ten stands; ten basins on the stands; ⁴⁴one sea; twelve oxen supporting the sea; ⁴⁵pots, shovels, and bowls. All these articles which Hiram made for King Solomon in the house of the LORD were of burnished bronze. ⁴⁶The king had them cast in the neighborhood of the Jordan, between Succoth and Zarethan, in thick clay molds. ⁴⁷Solomon did not weigh all the articles because they were so numerous; the weight of the bronze, therefore, was not determined.

⁴⁸Solomon made all the articles that were for the house of the LORD: the golden altar; the table on which the showbread lay; ⁴⁹the lampstands of pure gold, five to the right and five to the left before the inner sanctuary; their flowers, lamps, and tongs of gold; ⁵⁰basins, snuffers, bowls, cups, and firepans of pure gold; hinges of gold for the doors of the innermost part of the house, or holy of holies, and for the doors of the outer room, the nave. ⁵¹ᵃWhen all the work undertaken by King Solomon in the house of the LORD was completed,‡ he brought in the votive offerings of his father David, and put the silver, gold, and other articles in the treasuries of the house of the LORD.

## CHAPTER 8

**Dedication of the Temple.**§ ¹Then Solomon assembled the elders of Israel and all the heads of the tribes, the princes in the ancestral houses of the Israelites. They came to King Solomon in Jerusalem, to bring up the ark of the LORD's covenant from the city of David (which is Zion). ²All the people of Israel assembled before King Solomon during the festival in the month of Ethanim (the seventh month).¶ ³When all the elders of Israel had arrived, the priests took up the ark; ⁴and they brought up the ark of the LORD and the tent of meeting with all the sacred vessels that were in the tent. The priests and Levites brought them up. ⁵King Solomon and the entire community of Israel, gathered for the occasion before the ark, sacrificed sheep and oxen too

---

*[7:23–26] **The molten sea**: this was a large circular tank containing about twelve thousand gallons of water.

†[7:26] **Baths**: see note on Is 5:10.

‡[7:51] The account of the Temple's construction has been punctuated by references to "building" (*banah*) or "finishing" (*killah*) it (6:1b, 9a, 14, 38; 7:40). Here, at the end of the account, the narrator uses a different verb for its "completion," *shillem*, which allows him to play on the name of Solomon (*shelomo*).

§[8:1–66] The account of the Temple's dedication ceremony is organized concentrically: Solomon gathers the assembly (vv. 1–13), blesses it (vv. 14–21), utters a long dedicatory prayer (vv. 22–53), blesses the assembly again (vv. 54–61), and dismisses it (vv. 62–66). To this account is appended an appearance of the Lord to Solomon (9:2–9) that balances the divine word to Solomon in the account of the Temple's construction (6:11–13).

¶[8:2] "The seventh month" ("Ethanim" in the Canaanite calendar) corresponded to late September/early October. The great festival at that time of year is the feast of Booths, or Succoth/Sukkoth (see Lv 23:33–43; Dt 16:13–15). The feast was important enough to warrant holding the dedication ceremony either a month before or eleven months after the Temple was completed in the eighth month (6:38).

a. [7:51] 2 Sm 8:9–12.

many to number or count. ⁶The priests brought the ark of the covenant of the LORD to its place, the inner sanctuary of the house, the holy of holies, beneath the wings of the cherubim. ⁷The cherubim had their wings spread out over the place of the ark, sheltering the ark and its poles from above. ⁸ᵇThe poles were so long that their ends could be seen from the holy place in front of the inner sanctuary. They cannot be seen from outside, but they remain there to this day. ⁹ᶜThere was nothing in the ark but the two stone tablets which Moses had put there at Horeb, when the LORD made a covenant with the Israelites after they went forth from the land of Egypt. ¹⁰ᵈWhen the priests left the holy place, the cloud filled the house of the LORD ¹¹so that the priests could no longer minister because of the cloud, since the glory of the LORD had filled the house of the LORD. ¹²ᵗᵉThen Solomon said,

"The LORD intends to dwell in the dark cloud;
¹³  I have indeed built you a princely house,
the base for your enthronement forever."

¹⁴The king turned and blessed the whole assembly of Israel, while the whole assembly of Israel stood. ¹⁵He said: "Blessed be the LORD, the God of Israel, who with his own mouth spoke a promise to David my father and by his hand fulfilled it, saying: ¹⁶Since the day I brought my people Israel out of Egypt, I have not chosen a city out of any tribe of Israel for the building of a house, that my name might be there; but I have chosen David to rule my people Israel. ¹⁷When David my father wished to build a house for the name of the LORD, the God of Israel, ¹⁸the LORD said to him: In wishing to build a house for my

name, you did well. ¹⁹But it is not you who will build the house, but your son, who comes from your loins; he shall build the house for my name. ²⁰Now the LORD has fulfilled the word he spoke: I have succeeded David my father, and I sit on the throne of Israel, as the LORD has spoken, and I have built this house for the name of the LORD, the God of Israel. ²¹I have provided there a place for the ark in which is the covenant of the LORD that he made with our ancestors when he brought them out of the land of Egypt."

**Solomon's Prayer.** ²²Solomon stood before the altar of the LORD in the presence of the whole assembly of Israel, and stretching forth his hands toward heaven, ²³he said, "LORD, God of Israel, there is no God like you in heaven above or on earth below; you keep covenant and love toward your servants who walk before you with their whole heart, ²⁴the covenant that you kept toward your servant, David my father, what you promised him; your mouth has spoken and your hand has fulfilled this very day. ²⁵ᵍAnd now, LORD, God of Israel, keep toward your servant, David my father, what you promised: There shall never be wanting someone from your line to sit before me on the throne of Israel, provided that your descendants keep to their way, walking before me as you have. ²⁶Now, God of Israel, may the words you spoke to your servant, David my father, be confirmed.

²⁷"Is God indeed to dwell on earth? If the heavens and the highest heavens cannot contain you, how much less this house which I have built! ²⁸Regard kindly the prayer and petition of your servant, LORD, my God, and listen to the cry of supplication which I, your servant, utter before you this day. ²⁹May your eyes be open night and day toward this house, the place of which you said, My name shall be there; listen to the prayer your servant makes toward this place. ³⁰Listen to the petition of your servant and of your people Israel which they offer toward this place. Listen, from the place of your enthronement, heaven, listen and forgive.

³¹ʰ"If someone sins in some way against a neighbor and is required to take an oath sanctioned by a curse, and comes and takes the oath before your altar in this house, ³²listen in heaven; act and judge your servants. Condemn the wicked, requiting their ways; acquit the just, rewarding their justice.

³³"When your people Israel are defeated by an enemy because they sinned against you, and then they return to you, praise your name, pray to you, and entreat you in this house, ³⁴listen in heaven and forgive the sin of your people Israel, and bring them back to the land you gave their ancestors.

³⁵"When the heavens are closed, so that there is no rain, because they have sinned against you,

---

*[8:6–9] The transfer of the ark of the covenant into the newly constructed Temple building, God's act of possession (8:10–13), and Solomon's dedicatory prayer and sacrifices constituted the Temple's solemn dedication and made of it the place of God's presence in the midst of Israel for which David had hoped (2 Sm 6:12–15; 7:1–3). Later God expresses approval of the Temple with an oracle (1 Kgs 9:3–9).

†[8:12–13] This brief poem is rich in layered meanings. The "dark cloud" in which the Lord intends to dwell refers not only to the cloud that filled the Temple (v. 10) but to the darkness of the windowless holy of holies and to the mystery of the God enthroned invisibly upon the cherubim as well. Solomon calls the Temple he offers God a firm base, using terminology similar to that used for God's firm establishment of Solomon's own kingdom (2:12, 46). Finally, Solomon intends this as a place for God to *yashab*, but the Hebrew word *yashab* can mean "to dwell" or "to sit." In other words, the Temple can be understood both as a place where God resides and as the earthly foundation of God's heavenly throne. The double meaning allows an understanding of the divine presence as both transcendent and graciously immanent. See Solomon's sentiments in 8:27, and the frequent reference in 8:30–52 to God's hearing in heaven prayers that were offered in or toward the Temple.

---

b. [8:8] Ex 25:13–15.  c. [8:9] Ex 25:16; 34:27–28; Dt 10:5; Heb 9:4.  d. [8:10] Ex 13:21; 40:34–38.  e. [8:12] Ex 20:21; Dt 4:11; 5:22; Ps 97:2.  f. [8:16–19] 2 Sm 7:5–8, 12–13.

g. [8:25] 1 Kgs 2:4; 9:5; 2 Sm 7:14–16; Jer 33:17.  h. [8:31] Ex 22:6–10.

but they pray toward this place and praise your name, and turn from their sin because you have afflicted them, <sup>36</sup>listen in heaven and forgive the sin of your servants, your people Israel (for you teach them the good way in which they should walk). Give rain to this land of yours which you have given to your people as their heritage.

<sup>37</sup>"If there is famine in the land or pestilence; or if blight comes, or mildew, or locusts, or caterpillars; if an enemy of your people presses upon them in the land and at their gates; whatever plague or sickness there may be; <sup>38</sup>whatever prayer or petition any may make, any of your people Israel, who know heartfelt remorse and stretch out their hands toward this house, <sup>39</sup>listen in heaven, the place of your enthronement; forgive and take action. Render to each and all according to their ways, you who know every heart; for it is you alone who know the heart of every human being. <sup>40</sup>So may they revere you as long as they live on the land you gave our ancestors.

<sup>41</sup>"To the foreigners, likewise, who are not of your people Israel, but who come from a distant land for the sake of your name <sup>42</sup>(since people will hear of your great name and your mighty hand and your outstretched arm), when they come and pray toward this house, <sup>43</sup>listen in heaven, the place of your enthronement. Do all that the foreigner asks of you, that all the peoples of the earth may know your name, may revere you as do your people Israel, and may know that your name has been invoked upon this house that I have built.

<sup>44</sup>"When your people go out to war against their enemies, by whatever way you send them, and they pray to the LORD toward the city you have chosen and the house I have built for your name, <sup>45</sup>listen in heaven to their prayer and petition, and uphold their cause.

<sup>46</sup><sup>i</sup>"When they sin against you (for there is no one who does not sin), and in your anger against them you deliver them to an enemy, so that their captors carry them off to the land of the enemy, far or near, <sup>47</sup>and they have a change of heart in the land of their captivity and they turn and entreat you in the land of their captors and say, 'We have sinned and done wrong; we have been wicked'; <sup>48</sup>if with their whole heart and soul they turn back to you in the land of their enemies who took them captive, and pray to you toward the land you gave their ancestors, the city you have chosen, and the house I have built for your name, <sup>49</sup>listen in heaven, your dwelling place, to their prayer and petition, and uphold their cause. <sup>50</sup>Forgive your people who have sinned against you and all the offenses they have committed against you, and grant them mercy in the sight of their captors, so that these will be merciful to them. <sup>51</sup>For they are your people and your

heritage, whom you brought out of Egypt, from the midst of the iron furnace.

<sup>52</sup>"Thus may your eyes be open to the petition of your servant and to the petition of your people Israel; thus may you listen to them whenever they call upon you. <sup>53</sup>For you have set them apart from all the peoples of the earth to be your heritage, as you declared through Moses your servant when you brought our ancestors out of Egypt, Lord my GOD."

<sup>54</sup>After Solomon finished offering this entire prayer and petition to the LORD, he rose from before the altar of the LORD, where he had been kneeling, hands outstretched toward heaven. <sup>55</sup>He stood and blessed the whole assembly of Israel, saying in a loud voice: <sup>56</sup>"Blessed be the LORD who has given rest to his people Israel, just as he promised. Not a single word has gone unfulfilled of the entire gracious promise he made through Moses his servant. <sup>57</sup>May the LORD, our God, be with us as he was with our ancestors and may he not forsake us nor cast us off. <sup>58</sup>May he draw our hearts to himself, that we may walk in his ways and keep the commands, statutes, and ordinances that he enjoined on our ancestors. <sup>59</sup>May these words of mine, the petition I have offered before the LORD, our God, be present to the LORD our God day and night, that he may uphold the cause of his servant and the cause of his people Israel as each day requires, <sup>60</sup>so that all the peoples of the earth may know that the LORD is God and there is no other. <sup>61</sup>Your heart must be wholly devoted to the LORD, our God, observing his statutes and keeping his commandments, as on this day."

<sup>62</sup>The king and all Israel with him offered sacrifices before the LORD. <sup>63</sup>†Solomon offered as communion offerings to the LORD twenty-two thousand oxen and one hundred twenty thousand sheep. Thus the king and all the Israelites dedicated the house of the LORD. <sup>64</sup>On that day the king consecrated the middle of the court facing the house of the LORD; he offered there the burnt offerings, the grain offerings, and the fat of the communion offerings, because the bronze altar before the LORD was too small to hold the burnt offering, the grain offering, and the fat of the communion offering. <sup>65</sup>On this occasion Solomon and all Israel with him, a great assembly from Lebo-hamath to the Wadi of Egypt, celebrated the festival before the LORD, our God, for seven days. <sup>66</sup>On the eighth day he dismissed the people, who blessed the king and went to their tents, rejoicing and glad of heart because of all the blessings the LORD had given to David his servant and to his people Israel.

---

*[8:61] In urging the people to be "wholly devoted" (*shalem*), Solomon plays on his own name (*shelomo*), as if to imply that he himself exemplifies perfect fidelity to God.

†[8:63] "Communion offerings" (*shelamim*) is another wordplay on the name of Solomon.

i. [8:46] Eccl 7:20; 1 Jn 1:8.

## CHAPTER 9

**Promise and Warning to Solomon.** [1]After Solomon finished building the house of the LORD, the house of the king, and everything else that he wanted to do, [2]the LORD appeared to Solomon a second time, as he had appeared to him in Gibeon. [3]The LORD said to him: I have heard the prayer of petition which you offered in my presence. I have consecrated this house which you have built and I set my name there forever; my eyes and my heart shall be there always. [4]As for you, if you walk before me as David your father did, wholeheartedly and uprightly, doing all that I have commanded you, keeping my statutes and ordinances, [5k]I will establish your royal throne over Israel forever, as I promised David your father: There shall never be wanting someone from your line on the throne of Israel. [6]But if ever you and your descendants turn from following me, fail to keep my commandments and statutes which I set before you, and proceed to serve other gods and bow down to them, [7]I will cut off Israel from the land I gave them and repudiate the house I have consecrated for my name. Israel shall become a proverb and a byword among all nations, [8l]and this house shall become a heap of ruins. Every passerby shall gasp in horror and ask, "Why has the LORD done such things to this land and to this house?" [9]And the answer will come: "Because they abandoned the LORD, their God, who brought their ancestors out of the land of Egypt, and they embraced other gods, bowing down to them and serving them. That is why the LORD has brought upon them all this evil."

**After Building the Temple.** [*] [10m]After the twenty years during which Solomon built the two houses, the house of the LORD and the house of the king—[11]Hiram, king of Tyre, supplying Solomon with all the cedar wood, fir wood, and gold he wished, and King Solomon giving Hiram in return twenty cities in the land of Galilee— [12]Hiram left Tyre to see the cities Solomon had given him, but he was not satisfied with them. [13]So he said, "What are these cities you have given me, my brother?"[†] And he called them the land of Cabul, as they are called to this day. [14]Hiram, however, had sent King Solomon one hundred and twenty talents of gold.[‡]

[15]This is an account of the conscript labor force King Solomon raised in order to build the house of the LORD, his own house, Millo,[§] the wall of Jerusalem, Hazor, Megiddo, Gezer [16](Pharaoh, king of Egypt, had come up and taken Gezer and, after destroying it by fire and slaying all the Canaanites living in the city, had given it as a farewell gift to his daughter, Solomon's wife; [17]Solomon then rebuilt Gezer), Lower Beth-horon, [18]Baalath, Tamar in the desert of Judah, [19]all his cities for supplies, cities for chariots and cities for cavalry, and whatever Solomon desired to build in Jerusalem, in Lebanon, and in the entire land under his dominion. [20]All the people who were left of the Amorites, Hittites, Perizzites, Hivites, and Jebusites, who were not Israelites— [21]those of their descendants who were left in the land and whom the Israelites had not been able to destroy under the ban—these Solomon conscripted as forced laborers, as they are to this day. [22]But Solomon made none of the Israelites forced laborers, for they were his fighting force, his ministers, commanders, adjutants, chariot officers, and cavalry. [23]There were five hundred fifty overseers answerable to Solomon's governors for the work, directing the people engaged in the work.

[24n]As soon as Pharaoh's daughter went up from the City of David to her house, which he had built for her, Solomon built Millo. [25]Three times a year Solomon used to offer burnt offerings and communion offerings on the altar which he had built to the LORD, and to burn incense before the LORD.

Thus he completed the temple.[¶]

**Solomon's Gifts.** [**] [26]King Solomon also built a fleet at Ezion-geber, which is near Elath on the shore of the Red Sea in the land of Edom.[††] [27]To this fleet Hiram sent his own servants, expert sailors, with the servants of Solomon. [28]They went to Ophir, and obtained four hundred and twenty talents of gold and brought it to King Solomon.

---

*[9:10–25] This unit of the Solomon story corresponds to 5:15–32. It comprises the same two themes, negotiations with Hiram of Tyre (vv. 10–14) and use of conscripted labor (vv. 15–23); the last two verses mark the end of the account of Solomon's building projects (vv. 24–25). Chronicles has an incomplete parallel in 2 Chr 8:1–13.

†[9:13] **Brother**: a term for a treaty partner; cf. 20:32–33. **Cabul**: the meaning is uncertain; perhaps "of no value."

‡[9:14] The talent was a measure of weight that varied in the course of ancient Israel's history from forty-five to one hundred thirty pounds. This would mean that, at the least, Hiram sent five thousand pounds of gold to Solomon, and the figure may be as much as three times that amount.

§[9:15] **Millo**: probably means ground fill, and may refer to an artificial earthwork or platform of stamped ground south of the Temple area. It was begun by David (2 Sm 5:9); cf. 1 Kgs 9:24; 11:27.

¶[9:25] With these words the account of the construction and dedication of the Temple, which began in 6:1, comes to a close. The verb "complete" (*shillem*) is a play on Solomon's name (*shelomo*); see also the note on 7:51.

**[9:26–10:29] The next major unit of the Solomon story returns to the theme of the three gifts the Lord gave Solomon in 3:12–13: a listening heart (10:1–13), riches (9:26–27; 10:14–22, 26–29), universal renown (10:23–25). In 3:16–5:14, where the same three themes structure the passage, the emphasis was on the benefits these gifts brought to the whole nation; here it is on the luxury they afford to Solomon's own court. The material in 9:26–28; 10:11–12, 22 dealing with Solomon's commercial fleet corresponds to the material on Solomon's international affairs in 5:1–5. Chronicles has a partial parallel to this material in 2 Chr 9:17–28; see also 2 Chr 1:14–17.

††[9:26] **Ezion-geber . . . Edom**: the first mention of maritime commerce in the Israelite kingdom; Edom was subject after David conquered it; cf. 2 Sm 8:13–14.

---

j. [9:2] 1 Kgs 3:4–15; 6:11–13; 11:9–13.  k. [9:5] 2 Sm 7:16.  l. [9:8] Dt 29:23; Jer 22:8.  m. [9:10] 1 Kgs 6:38–7:1.

n. [9:24] 1 Kgs 3:1; 7:8.

## CHAPTER 10

### Solomon's Listening Heart: The Queen of Sheba.° ¹°The queen of Sheba,† having heard a report of Solomon's fame, came to test him with subtle questions. ²She arrived in Jerusalem with a very numerous retinue, and with camels bearing spices, a large amount of gold, and precious stones. She came to Solomon and spoke to him about everything that she had on her mind. ³King Solomon explained everything she asked about, and there was nothing so obscure that the king could not explain it to her. ⁴When the queen of Sheba witnessed Solomon's great wisdom, the house he had built, ⁵the food at his table, the seating of his ministers, the attendance and dress of his waiters, his servers, and the burnt offerings he offered in the house of the LORD, it took her breath away. ⁶"The report I heard in my country about your deeds and your wisdom is true," she told the king. ⁷"I did not believe the report until I came and saw with my own eyes that not even the half had been told me. Your wisdom and prosperity surpass the report I heard. ⁸Happy are your servants, happy these ministers of yours, who stand before you always and listen to your wisdom. ⁹Blessed be the LORD, your God, who has been pleased to place you on the throne of Israel. In his enduring love for Israel, the LORD has made you king to carry out judgment and justice." ¹⁰Then she gave the king one hundred and twenty gold talents, a very large quantity of spices, and precious stones. Never again did anyone bring such an abundance of spices as the queen of Sheba gave to King Solomon.

¹¹Hiram's fleet, which used to bring gold from Ophir, also brought from there a very large quantity of almug‡ wood and precious stones. ¹²With this wood the king made supports for the house of the LORD and for the house of the king, and harps and lyres for the singers. Never again was any such almug wood brought or seen to the present day.

¹³King Solomon gave the queen of Sheba everything she desired and asked for, besides what King Solomon gave her from Solomon's royal bounty. Then she returned with her servants to her own country.

### Solomon's Riches: Domestic Affairs.§ ¹⁴ᵖThe gold that came to Solomon in one year weighed six hundred and sixty-six gold talents, ¹⁵in addition to what came from the tolls on travelers, from the traffic of merchants, and from all the kings of Arabia and the governors of the country. ¹⁶ᵠKing Solomon made two hundred shields of beaten gold (six hundred shekels of gold went into each shield) ¹⁷and three hundred bucklers of beaten gold (three minas of gold went into each buckler); and the king put them in the house of the Forest of Lebanon. ¹⁸The king made a large ivory throne, and overlaid it with refined gold. ¹⁹The throne had six steps, a back with a round top, and an arm on each side of the seat, with two lions standing next to the arms, ²⁰and twelve other lions standing there on the steps, two to a step, one on either side of each step. Nothing like this was made in any other kingdom. ²¹All King Solomon's drinking vessels were gold, and all the utensils in the house of the Forest of Lebanon were pure gold. There was no silver, for in Solomon's time silver was reckoned as nothing. ²²For the king had a fleet of Tarshish ships⁵ at sea with Hiram's fleet. Once every three years the fleet of Tarshish ships would come with a cargo of gold, silver, ivory, apes, and peacocks.

### Solomon's Renown. ²³Thus King Solomon surpassed all the kings of the earth in riches and wisdom. ²⁴And the whole world sought audience with Solomon, to hear the wisdom God had put into his heart. ²⁵They all brought their yearly tribute: vessels of silver and gold, garments, weapons, spices, horses and mules—what was due each year.

### Solomon's Riches: Chariots and Horses. ²⁶ʳSolomon amassed chariots and horses; he had one thousand four hundred chariots and twelve thousand horses; these he allocated among the chariot cities and to the king's service in Jerusalem. ²⁷ˢThe king made silver as common in Jerusalem as stones, and cedars as numerous as the sycamores of the Shephelah. ²⁸Solomon's horses were imported from Egypt and from Cilicia, where the king's merchants purchased them. ²⁹A chariot imported from Egypt cost six hundred shekels of silver, a horse one hundred and fifty shekels; they were exported at these rates to all the Hittite and Aramean kings.

---

\*[10:1–13] The sub-unit on Solomon's wisdom contrasts with 3:16–28. There Solomon's gifts led him to listen to the humblest of his subjects; he accomplished justice and was revered by all his people. Here the emphasis is on his clever speech to a foreign monarch. She is duly impressed by the glory of his court, but it is she, not Solomon, who recalls the monarch's duty of establishing justice (v. 9). The unit is interrupted briefly by a remark about Solomon's maritime commerce (10:11–12).

†[10:1] **Queen of Sheba**: women rulers among the Arabs are recorded in eighth-century B.C. Assyrian inscriptions. Sheba was for centuries the leading principality in what is now Yemen.

‡[10:11–12] **Almug**: the identification of this wood is unknown.

§[10:14–29] The material on Solomon's riches, like that in 4:1–5:8, is organized around domestic affairs, international affairs, and chariots and horses (see note on 4:1–5:8), but contrasts with that earlier passage. There, Solomon's domestic administration produced prosperity for all Judah and Israel (4:20); here the focus is on the wealth and luxury of Solomon's own palace (10:14–21). There his international hegemony assured peace for all Judah and Israel (5:5); here his maritime ventures simply bring him more and more wealth (9:26–28; 10:11–12, 22). There even his livestock benefited from his prudent administration; here chariotry and horses are just another commodity to be traded (10:26–29).

¶[10:22] **Tarshish ships**: large, strong vessels for long voyages. Tarshish was probably the ancient Tartessus, a Phoenician colony in southern Spain. **Ivory, apes, and peacocks**: the Hebrew words are obscure and the translations conjectural; however, the reference is certainly to exotic luxury items.

---

o. [10:1] Mt 12:42; Lk 11:31.   p. [10:14] Dt 17:17; Sir 47:18.

q. [10:16] 1 Kgs 14:26–28; 2 Sm 8:7.   r. [10:26] 1 Kgs 5:6; Dt 17:16; 2 Chr 1:14; 9:25.   s. [10:27] Dt 17:17; Sir 47:18.

## CHAPTER 11

**The End of Solomon's Reign.**[*] [11]King Solomon loved many foreign women besides the daughter of Pharaoh—Moabites, Ammonites, Edomites, Sidonians, Hittites—[2]from nations of which the LORD had said to the Israelites: You shall not join with them and they shall not join with you, lest they turn your hearts to their gods. But Solomon held them[†] close in love. [3]He had as wives seven hundred princesses and three hundred concubines, and they turned his heart.

[4]When Solomon was old his wives had turned his heart to follow other gods, and his heart was not entirely with the LORD, his God, as the heart of David his father had been. [5]Solomon followed Astarte, the goddess of the Sidonians, and Milcom, the abomination of the Ammonites. [6]Solomon did what was evil in the sight of the LORD, and he did not follow the LORD unreservedly as David his father had done. [7]Solomon then built a high place to Chemosh, the abomination of Moab, and to Molech, the abomination of the Ammonites, on the mountain opposite Jerusalem. [8]He did the same for all his foreign wives who burned incense and sacrificed to their gods.

[9]The LORD became angry with Solomon, because his heart turned away from the LORD, the God of Israel, who had appeared to him twice [10]and commanded him not to do this very thing, not to follow other gods. But he did not observe what the LORD commanded. [11]So the LORD said to Solomon: Since this is what you want, and you have not kept my covenant and the statutes which I enjoined on you, I will surely tear the kingdom away from you and give it to your servant. [12]But I will not do this during your lifetime, for the sake of David your father; I will tear it away from your son's hand. [13]Nor will I tear away the whole kingdom. I will give your son one tribe for the sake of David my servant and for the sake of Jerusalem, which I have chosen.

**Threats to Solomon's Kingdom.**[‡] [14]The LORD then raised up an adversary[§] against Solomon:

Hadad the Edomite, who was of the royal line in Edom. [15x]Earlier, when David had conquered Edom, Joab, the commander of the army, while going to bury the slain, killed every male in Edom. [16]Joab and all Israel remained there six months until they had killed off every male in Edom. [17]But Hadad, with some Edomite servants of his father, fled toward Egypt. Hadad was then a young boy. [18]They left Midian and came to Paran; they gathered men from Paran and came to Egypt, to Pharaoh, king of Egypt; he gave Hadad a house, appointed him rations, and assigned him land. [19]Hadad won great favor with Pharaoh, so that he gave him in marriage his sister-in-law, the sister of Queen Tahpenes, his own wife. [20]Tahpenes' sister bore Hadad a son, Genubath. Tahpenes weaned him in Pharaoh's palace. And Genubath lived in Pharaoh's house, with Pharaoh's own sons. [21]When Hadad in Egypt heard that David rested with his ancestors and that Joab, the commander of the army, was dead, he said to Pharaoh, "Give me leave to return to my own land." [22]Pharaoh said to him, "What do you lack with me, that you are seeking to return to your own land?" He answered, "Nothing, but please let me go!"

[23]God raised up against Solomon another adversary, Rezon, the son of Eliada, who had fled from his lord, Hadadezer, king of Zobah, [24]when David was slaughtering them. Rezon gathered men about him and became leader of a marauding band. They went to Damascus, settled there, and made him king in Damascus. [25]Rezon was an adversary of Israel as long as Solomon lived, in addition to the harm done by Hadad, and he felt contempt for Israel. He became king over Aram.

**Ahijah Announces Jeroboam's Kingship.**[¶] [26]Solomon had a servant, Jeroboam, son of Nebat, an Ephraimite from Zeredah with a widowed mother named Zeruah. He rebelled against the king. [27]This is how he came to rebel. King Solomon was building Millo, closing up the breach of the City of David, his father. [28]Jeroboam was a very able man, and when Solomon saw that the young man was also a good worker, he put him in charge of all the carriers conscripted from the house of Joseph.

[29]At that time Jeroboam left Jerusalem, and the prophet Ahijah the Shilonite met him on the road. The prophet was wearing a new cloak,[**]

---

[*] [11:1–13] The next major unit of the Solomon story corresponds to 3:1–15. Like the earlier passage it includes the narrator's remarks about Solomon's foreign wives and his building projects, and a divine word commenting on Solomon's conduct. However, where 3:1–15 is generally positive toward Solomon, the present passage is unrelievedly negative. Chronicles has no parallel to this material.

[†] [11:2] **Them:** both the nations and their gods.

[‡] [11:14–25] This unit of the Solomon story corresponds to 2:12b–46, where Solomon secured his kingdom by eliminating three men he perceived as threats. In this passage, we learn of two foreigners the Lord raised up as "adversaries" to Solomon as early as the beginning of his reign (despite Solomon's complacent claim to Hiram in 5:18 that he had no adversary). In the next section we will learn of a third opponent, Israelite rather than foreign, who turns out to be the "servant of Solomon" announced by the Lord in 11:11. Chronicles has no parallel to this material.

[§] [11:14] **Adversary:** Hebrew *śatan*, one who stands in opposition; in this context a political opponent.

[¶] [11:26–43] The last major unit of the Solomon story tells how the prophet Ahijah announces the divine intention to take the larger part of Solomon's kingdom from his control and give it to Jeroboam, Solomon's servant. This counterbalances the first unit of the story, 1:1–2:12a, where another prophet, Nathan, managed to influence the royal succession and obtain the throne for Solomon. The unit is also the first part of the story of Jeroboam (11:26–14:20). It thus acts as a literary hinge connecting the two stories. Chronicles contains a death notice for Solomon in 2 Chr 9:29–31.

[**] [11:29] The narrator uses a powerful wordplay here. In the Hebrew consonantal text, Ahijah's cloak (*slmh*) is

---

t. [11:1–3] Dt 17:17; Sir 47:19–20.   u. [11:2] Ex 34:16.   v. [11:9] 1 Kgs 3:4–15; 6:11–13; 9:2–9.   w. [11:12–13] 1 Kgs 11:34–36.

x. [11:15] 2 Sm 8:13–14.   y. [11:24] 2 Sm 8:3–6.

and when the two were alone in the open country, [30z]Ahijah took off his new cloak, tore it into twelve pieces, [31a]and said to Jeroboam: "Take ten pieces for yourself. Thus says the LORD, the God of Israel: I am about to tear the kingdom out of Solomon's hand and will give you ten of the tribes. [32]He shall have one tribe for the sake of my servant David, and for the sake of Jerusalem, the city I have chosen out of all the tribes of Israel. [33]For they have forsaken me and have bowed down to Astarte, goddess of the Sidonians, Chemosh, god of Moab, and Milcom, god of the Ammonites. They have not walked in my ways or done what is right in my eyes, according to my statutes and my ordinances, as David his father did. [34]Yet I will not take any of the kingdom from Solomon himself, but will keep him a prince as long as he lives, for the sake of David my servant, whom I have chosen, who kept my commandments and statutes.

[35]But I will take the kingdom from his son's hand and give it to you—that is, the ten tribes. [36]I will give his son one tribe, that David my servant may always have a holding before me in Jerusalem, the city I have chosen, to set my name there. [37]You I will take and you shall reign over all that you desire and shall become king of Israel. [38]If, then, you heed all that I command you, walking in my ways, and do what is right in my eyes by keeping my statutes and my commandments like David my servant, I will be with you. I will build a lasting house for you, just as I did for David; I will give Israel to you. [39]I will humble David's line for this, but not forever."

[40]When Solomon tried to have Jeroboam killed, Jeroboam fled to Shishak, king of Egypt. He remained in Egypt until Solomon's death.

[41]The rest of the acts of Solomon, with all that he did and his wisdom, are recorded in the book of the acts of Solomon. [42]Solomon was king in Jerusalem over all Israel for forty years. [43]Solomon rested with his ancestors and was buried in the City of David, his father, and Rehoboam his son succeeded him as king.

## II. THE REIGN OF JEROBOAM[*]

### CHAPTER 12

**Political Disunity.**[†] [1]Rehoboam went to Shechem,[‡] where all Israel had come to make

him king. [2]When Jeroboam, son of Nebat, heard about it, he was still in Egypt. He had fled from King Solomon and remained in Egypt, [3]and they sent for him.

Then Jeroboam and the whole assembly of Israel came and said to Rehoboam, [4]"Your father put a heavy yoke on us. If you now lighten the harsh servitude and the heavy yoke your father imposed on us, we will be your servants." [5]He answered them, "Come back to me in three days," and the people went away.

[6]King Rehoboam asked advice of the elders who had been in his father Solomon's service while he was alive, and asked, "How do you advise me to answer this people?" [7]They replied, "If today you become the servant of this people and serve them, and give them a favorable answer, they will be your servants forever." [8]But he ignored the advice the elders had given him, and asked advice of the young men who had grown up with him and were in his service. [9]He said to them, "What answer do you advise that we should give this people, who have told me, 'Lighten the yoke your father imposed on us'?" [10]The young men who had grown up with him replied, "This is what you must say to this people who have told you, 'Your father made our yoke heavy; you lighten it for us.' You must say, 'My little finger is thicker than my father's loins. [11]My father put a heavy yoke on you, but I will make it heavier. My father beat you with whips, but I will beat you with scorpions.'" [12]Jeroboam and the whole people came back to King Rehoboam on the third day, as the king had instructed them: "Come back to me in three days." [13]Ignoring the advice the elders had given him, the king gave the people a harsh answer. [14]He spoke to them as the young men had advised: "My father made your yoke heavy, but I will make it heavier. My father beat you with whips, but I will beat you with scorpions." [15b]The king did not listen to the people, for this turn of events was from the LORD: he fulfilled the word the LORD

---

indistinguishable from Solomon's name (*slmh*). Since a prophetic gesture such as Ahijah's was understood as effecting the event it announced, Ahijah's tearing of his cloak embodies the divine action that will tear Solomon's kingdom apart (cf. vv. 11–13).

[*][12:1–14:20] Like the story of the reign of Solomon, the story of the reign of Jeroboam is concentrically organized. Ahijah's oracle of promise to Jeroboam (11:26–43) belongs to both stories, ending that of Solomon (see note on 1:1–11:43) and beginning that of Jeroboam; it corresponds to Ahijah's

oracle of condemnation in 14:1–20. Within those literary boundaries are accounts of political (12:1–20) and religious (13:11–34) disunity between Israel and Judah. The center of the story is the account of Jeroboam's heterodox cultic innovations (12:26–31).

[†][12:1–20] The first major unit of the Jeroboam story was Ahijah's oracle (11:26–40), followed by the notice of Solomon's death (11:41–43). This is the second major unit. It tells how Jeroboam came to the throne of Israel after the intransigence of Solomon's son Rehoboam provoked the northern tribes to secede from Jerusalem. The political disunity of the two kingdoms fulfills the word spoken by Ahijah. Compare 13:11–32, where Jeroboam's improper cultic innovations produce religious disunity as well. The scene is concentrically arranged: narrative introduction, first interview, first consultation, second consultation, second interview, narrative conclusion. Chronicles has a parallel version of this story in 2 Chr 10:1–19.

[‡][12:1] **Shechem:** chief city of the northern tribes, where a covenant had previously been made between the Lord and his people and a stone of witness had been erected in memory of the event (Jos 24:25–27). **All Israel:** see note on 4:7–19.

---

z. [11:30] 1 Sm 15:27–28.    a. [11:31–32] 1 Kgs 12:20.

b. [12:15] 1 Kgs 11:26–39.

had spoken through Ahijah the Shilonite to Jeroboam, son of Nebat. [16c]When all Israel saw that the king did not listen to them, the people answered the king:

"What share have we in David?[*]
 We have no heritage in the son of Jesse.
To your tents, Israel!
 Now look to your own house, David."

So Israel went off to their tents. [17]But Rehoboam continued to reign over the Israelites who lived in the cities of Judah.

[18]King Rehoboam then sent out Adoram,[†] who was in charge of the forced labor, but all Israel stoned him to death. King Rehoboam then managed to mount his chariot and flee to Jerusalem. [19]And so Israel has been in rebellion against the house of David to this day. [20]When all Israel heard that Jeroboam had returned, they summoned him to an assembly and made him king over all Israel. None remained loyal to the house of David except the tribe of Judah alone. **Divine Approval.**[‡] [21]On his arrival in Jerusalem, Rehoboam assembled all the house of Judah and the tribe of Benjamin—one hundred and eighty thousand elite warriors—to wage war against the house of Israel, to restore the kingdom to Rehoboam, son of Solomon. [22]However, the word of God came to Shemaiah, a man of God: [23]Say to Rehoboam, son of Solomon, king of Judah, and to all the house of Judah and to Benjamin, and to the rest of the people: [24]Thus says the LORD: You must not go out to war against your fellow Israelites. Return home, each of you, for it is I who have brought this about. They obeyed the word of the LORD and turned back, according to the word of the LORD.

[25]Jeroboam built up Shechem in the hill country of Ephraim and lived there. Then he left it and built up Penuel.
**Jeroboam's Cultic Innovations.**[§] [26]Jeroboam thought to himself: "Now the kingdom will

return to the house of David. [27]If this people go up to offer sacrifices in the house of the LORD in Jerusalem, the hearts of this people will return to their master, Rehoboam, king of Judah, and they will kill me and return to Rehoboam, king of Judah." [28d]The king took counsel, made two calves of gold, and said to the people: "You have been going up to Jerusalem long enough. Here are your gods, O Israel, who brought you up from the land of Egypt." [29e]And he put one in Bethel, the other in Dan.[f] [30]This led to sin, because the people frequented these calves in Bethel and in Dan. [31]He also built temples on the high places and made priests from among the common people who were not Levites.
**Divine Disapproval.**[**] [32]Jeroboam established a feast in the eighth month on the fifteenth day of the month like the pilgrimage feast in Judah, and he went up to the altar. He did this in Bethel, sacrificing to the calves he had made. He stationed in Bethel the priests of the high places he had built. [33]Jeroboam went up to the altar he built in Bethel on the fifteenth day of the eighth month, the month he arbitrarily chose. He established a feast for the Israelites, and he went up to the altar to burn incense.

## CHAPTER 13

[1]A man of God came from Judah to Bethel by the word of the LORD, while Jeroboam was standing at the altar to burn incense. [2]He cried out against the altar by the word of the LORD: "Altar, altar, thus says the LORD: A child shall be born to the house of David, Josiah by name, who shall slaughter upon you the priests of the high places who burn incense upon you, and they shall burn human bones upon you."[g] [3]He also

---

[*][12:16] **What share have we in David?:** even in David's time the northern tribes seemed ready to withdraw from the union with Judah (2 Sm 20:1). The unreasonable attitude of Rehoboam toward them intensified the discontent caused by the oppression of Solomon (v. 4) and thus precipitated the political separation of the two kingdoms. In the view of the Deuteronomistic historian (1 Kgs 11:35–36; 12:24), this was by the Lord's decree.

[†][12:18] **Adoram:** the name is a shortened form of "Adoniram" (see 4:6; 5:28). If this is the same Adoram who held the position in David's day (2 Sm 20:24), he would have been a very old man.

[‡][12:21–25] The center of this unit is a divine oracle delivered by a man of God of the Southern Kingdom in which the Lord affirms his approval of the secession of the northern tribes. Compare 13:1–10, where another man of God from Judah proclaims the Lord's condemnation of Jeroboam's religious separatism. Chronicles has a very similar version of Shemaiah's oracle in 2 Chr 11:1–4.

[§][12:26–31] At the center of the story of Jeroboam the narrator describes how the king went beyond the political

separation of Israel from Judah to create a separatist religious system as well. Jeroboam feared that continued worship in the single Temple in Jerusalem would threaten the political independence of his kingdom. To prevent this he established sanctuaries with non-levitical clergy in his own territory. At two of the sanctuaries he set up golden calves, which the narrator depicts as idols. Thus begins what will later be called "the sin of Jeroboam" (13:34), a theme that will be echoed throughout 1–2 Kings in the condemnations of almost every king of the Northern Kingdom. Historically, Jeroboam's innovations were not as heterodox as our narrator portrays them. Bethel was an ancient and traditional site for worship of the Lord; and the calves were probably intended to be a dais for the deity invisibly enthroned upon them, rather like the cherubim atop the ark of the covenant.

[¶][12:29] **Bethel . . . Dan:** at the southern and northern boundaries of the separate kingdom of Israel, where sanctuaries had existed in the past (Gn 12:8; 13:3–4; 28:10–22; 35:1–15; Jgs 18:1–31).

[**][12:32–13:10] This unit of the Jeroboam story corresponds to 12:21–25. Before Jeroboam's cultic innovations, a man of God from Judah proclaimed the Lord's approval of the political separation of the kingdoms. After Jeroboam's cultic innovations, a man of God from Judah proclaims the Lord's disapproval of Israel's religious separatism. The unit begins with a long, detailed introduction about the dedication festival Jeroboam holds at Bethel (12:32–33); then follows the scene of the ceremony disrupted by the oracle of the man of God (13:1–10).

---

c. [12:16] 2 Sm 20:1.

d. [12:28] Ex 32:1–10.　e. [12:29] Tb 1:5.　f. [13:2] 2 Kgs 23:16.
g. [13:3] 2 Kgs 23:15.

gave a sign that same day and said: "This is the sign that the LORD has spoken: The altar shall be torn apart and the ashes on it shall be scattered." [4]When the king heard the word of the man of God which he was crying out against the altar in Bethel, Jeroboam stretched forth his hand from the altar and said, "Seize him!" But the hand he stretched forth against him withered, so that he could not draw it back. [5](The altar was torn apart and the ashes from the altar were scattered, in accordance with the sign the man of God gave by the word of the LORD.)

[6]Then the king said to the man of God, "Entreat the LORD, your God, and intercede for me that my hand may be restored." So the man of God entreated the LORD, and the king's hand was restored as it was before. [7]The king told the man of God, "Come with me to the house for some refreshment so that I may give you a present." [8]The man of God said to the king, "If you gave me half your palace, I would not go with you, nor eat bread or drink water in this place. [9]For I was instructed by the word of the LORD: Do not eat bread or drink water, and do not return by the way you came." [10]So he departed by another road and did not go back the way he had come to Bethel.

**Prophetic Disunity.**[*] [11]There was an old prophet living in Bethel, whose son came and told him all that the man of God had done that day in Bethel. When his sons repeated to their father the words the man of God had spoken to the king, [12]the father asked them, "Which way did he go?" So his sons pointed out to him the road taken by the man of God who had come from Judah. [13]Then he said to his sons, "Saddle the donkey for me." When they had saddled it, he mounted [14]and followed the man of God, whom he found seated under a terebinth. When he asked him, "Are you the man of God who came from Judah?" he answered, "Yes." [15]Then he said, "Come home with me and have some bread." [16]"I cannot return with you or go with you, and I cannot eat bread or drink water with you in this place," he answered, [17]"for I was told by the word of the LORD: You shall not eat bread or drink water there, and do not go back the way you came." [18]But he said to him, "I, too, am a prophet like you, and an angel told me by the word of the LORD: Bring him back with you to your house to eat bread and drink water." But he was lying to him. [19]So he went back with him, and ate bread and drank water in his house. [20]But while they were sitting at table, the word of the LORD came to the prophet who had brought him back, [21]and he cried out to the man of God who had come from Judah: "Thus says the LORD: Because you rebelled against the charge of the LORD and did not keep the command which the LORD, your God, gave you, [22]but returned and ate bread and drank water in the place where he told you, Do not eat bread or drink water, your corpse shall not be brought to the grave of your ancestors." [23]After he had eaten bread and drunk, they saddled for him the donkey that belonged to the prophet who had brought him back, [24]and he set out. But a lion met him on the road, and killed him. His body lay sprawled on the road, and the donkey remained standing by it, and so did the lion.

[25]Some passersby saw the body lying in the road, with the lion standing beside it, and carried the news to the city where the old prophet lived. [26]On hearing it, the prophet who had brought him back from his journey said: "It is the man of God who rebelled against the charge of the LORD. The LORD has delivered him to a lion, which mangled and killed him, according to the word which the LORD had spoken to him." [27]Then he said to his sons, "Saddle the donkey for me," and they saddled it. [28]He went off and found the body sprawled on the road with the donkey and the lion standing beside it. The lion had not eaten the body nor had it harmed the donkey. [29]The prophet lifted up the body of the man of God and put it on the donkey, and brought him back to the city to mourn and to bury him. [30]He laid the man's body in his own grave, and they mourned over it: "Alas, my brother!" [31h]After he had buried him, he said to his sons, "When I die, bury me in the grave where the man of God is buried. Lay my bones beside his. [32i]For the word which he proclaimed by the word of the LORD against the altar in Bethel and against all the temples on the high places in the cities of Samaria shall certainly come to pass."

[33]Even after this, Jeroboam did not turn from his evil way, but again made priests for the high places from among the common people. Whoever desired it was installed as a priest of the high places. [34]This is the account of the sin of the house of Jeroboam for which it was to be cut off and destroyed from the face of the earth.

## CHAPTER 14

**Ahijah Announces Jeroboam's Downfall.**[†] [1]At that time Abijah, son of Jeroboam, took sick.

---

*[13:1–34] The next major unit illustrates how Jeroboam's cultic innovations begin to alienate prophetic figures of the two kingdoms. Nevertheless, the Lord's word is stronger than any human attempt to thwart it. The two prophets also foreshadow the destinies of their respective kingdoms. Israel's experiment with idolatry can tempt Judah to abandon its faithfulness to the Lord. If Judah succumbs, and no longer speaks the word that can call Israel back to the true God, then the only hope for reuniting the two kingdoms will be when they have both died the death of exile.

†[14:1–20] The last major unit of the Jeroboam story recounts the story of Ahijah of Shiloh's oracle condemning the entire house of Jeroboam; this is followed by a formulaic notice of Jeroboam's death and the succession of his son. Compare the first unit of the Jeroboam story, 11:26–43, which recounted Ahijah's oracle proclaiming Jeroboam's kingship, followed by the formulaic notice of the death of Solomon.

h. [13:31] 2 Kgs 23:17–18.   i. [13:32] 2 Kgs 23:19–20.

2)So Jeroboam said to his wife, "Go and disguise yourself so that no one will recognize you as Jeroboam's wife. Then go to Shiloh, where you will find Ahijah the prophet. It was he who spoke the word that made me king over this people. ³Take along ten loaves, some cakes, and a jar of honey, and go to him. He will tell you what will happen to the child." ⁴The wife of Jeroboam did so. She left and went to Shiloh and came to the house of Ahijah.

Now Ahijah could not see because age had dimmed his sight. ⁵But the LORD said to Ahijah: Jeroboam's wife is coming to consult you about her son, for he is sick. Thus and so you must tell her. When she comes, she will be in disguise. ⁶So Ahijah, hearing the sound of her footsteps as she entered the door, said, "Come in, wife of Jeroboam. Why are you in disguise? For my part, I have been commissioned to give you bitter news. ⁷Go, tell Jeroboam, 'Thus says the LORD, the God of Israel: I exalted you from among the people and made you ruler of my people Israel. ⁸I tore the kingdom away from the house of David and gave it to you. Yet you have not been like my servant David, who kept my commandments and followed me with his whole heart, doing only what is right in my sight. ⁹You have done more evil than all who were before you: you have gone and made for yourself other gods and molten images to provoke me; but me you have cast behind your back. ¹⁰ᵏTherefore, I am bringing evil upon the house of Jeroboam:

I will cut off from Jeroboam's line every
        male
    —bond or free—in Israel;
I will burn up what is left of the house of
        Jeroboam
    as dung is burned, completely.
¹¹ ˡAnyone of Jeroboam's line who dies in the
        city,
    dogs will devour;
anyone who dies in the field,
    the birds of the sky will devour.

For the LORD has spoken!' ¹²As for you, leave, and go home! As you step inside the city, the child will die, ¹³and all Israel will mourn him and bury him, for he alone of Jeroboam's line will be laid in the grave, since in him alone of Jeroboam's house has something pleasing to the LORD, the God of Israel, been found. ¹⁴The LORD will raise up for himself a king over Israel who will cut off the house of Jeroboam—today, at this very moment! ¹⁵The LORD will strike Israel like a reed tossed about in the water and will pluck out Israel from this good land which he gave their ancestors, and will scatter them beyond the

River,* because they made asherahs for themselves, provoking the LORD. ¹⁶He will give up Israel because of the sins Jeroboam has committed and caused Israel to commit." ¹⁷So Jeroboam's wife left and went back; when she came to Tirzah and crossed the threshold of her house, the child died. ¹⁸He was buried and all Israel mourned him, according to the word of the LORD spoken through his servant Ahijah the prophet.

¹⁹The rest of the acts of Jeroboam, how he fought and how he reigned, these are recorded in the book of the chronicles of the kings of Israel. ²⁰The length of Jeroboam's reign was twenty-two years. He rested with his ancestors, and Nadab his son succeeded him as king.

## III. KINGS OF JUDAH AND ISRAEL†

**Reign of Rehoboam.** ²¹‡Rehoboam, son of Solomon, became king in Judah. Rehoboam was forty-one years old when he became king, and he reigned seventeen years in Jerusalem, the city in which, out of all the tribes of Israel, the LORD chose to set his name. His mother's name was Naamah the Ammonite.

²²Judah did evil in the LORD's sight and they angered him even more than their ancestors had done. ²³They, too, built for themselves high places, sacred pillars, and asherahs,§ upon every high hill and under every green tree. ²⁴There were also pagan priests in the land. Judah imitated all the abominable practices of the nations whom the LORD had driven out of the Israelites' way. ²⁵•In the fifth year of King Rehoboam, Shishak, king of Egypt, attacked Jerusalem. ²⁶ᵐHe took everything, including the treasures of the house of the LORD and the treasures of the house of the king, even the gold shields Solomon had made. ²⁷To replace them, King Rehoboam made bronze shields, which

---

*[14:15] **The River**: the Euphrates; see note on 5:1.

†[14:21–16:34] The treatment of the events of Jeroboam's reign shows that the author believes that the political division of the kingdoms embodies the Lord's will, but that their religious separation is undesirable. The Israelites are, in effect, one people of God under two royal administrations. This complex arrangement is reflected in the way 1–2 Kings organizes the history of the divided kingdoms. Each reign is treated as a unity: the kings, whether of Israel or Judah, are legitimate rulers. But the accounts of northern and southern kings are interwoven in the order in which each came to the throne, without regard to which kingdom they ruled: the people of God is one.

‡[14:21] The account of each king's reign follows the same basic pattern: a formulaic introduction, a theological evaluation based on religious fidelity, a brief account of an event from the king's reign, and a formulaic conclusion.

§[14:23] **Asherahs**: see note on Ex 34:13.

¶[14:25–28, 30] The narrator recounts Shishak's campaign here to imply that it was punishment for Judah's evil, and perhaps to cast him as supporting Jeroboam in his constant warfare with Rehoboam. (Shishak was named as Jeroboam's protector and patron in 11:40.) Egyptian records of the campaign list one hundred fifty cities conquered in Israel as well as Judah, but Jerusalem is not one of them. Chronicles has a parallel version of this account in 2 Chr 12:9–11.

j. [14:2] 1 Kgs 11:29–39.  k. [14:10] 1 Kgs 15:29–30.  l. [14:11] 1 Kgs 16:4; 21:22.

m. [14:26] 1 Kgs 10:16–17.

he entrusted to the officers of the guard on duty at the entrance of the royal house. ²⁸Whenever the king visited the house of the LORD, those on duty would carry the shields, and then return them to the guardroom.

²⁹The rest of the acts of Rehoboam, with all that he did, are recorded in the book of the chronicles of the kings of Judah. ³⁰There was war between Rehoboam and Jeroboam all their days. ³¹Rehoboam rested with his ancestors; he was buried with his ancestors in the City of David. His mother's name was Naamah the Ammonite. His son Abijam succeeded him as king.

## CHAPTER 15

**Reign of Abijam.** ¹In the eighteenth year of King Jeroboam, son of Nebat, Abijam became king of Judah; ²he reigned three years in Jerusalem. His mother's name was Maacah, daughter of Abishalom.

³He followed all the sins his father had committed before him, and his heart was not entirely with the LORD, his God, as was the heart of David his father. ⁴Yet for David's sake the LORD, his God, gave him a holding in Jerusalem, raising up his son after him and permitting Jerusalem to endure, ⁵*because David had done what was right in the sight of the LORD and did not disobey any of his commands as long as he lived, except in the case of Uriah the Hittite.

⁶There was war between Rehoboam and Jeroboam all their days. ⁷The rest of the acts of Abijam, with all that he did, are recorded in the book of the chronicles of the kings of Judah. There was war between Abijam and Jeroboam. ⁸Abijam rested with his ancestors; they buried him in the City of David, and his son Asa succeeded him as king.

**Reign of Asa.** ⁹In the twentieth year of Jeroboam, king of Israel, Asa, king of Judah, became king; ¹⁰he reigned forty-one years in Jerusalem. His mother's name was Maacah, daughter of Abishalom. ¹¹Asa did what was right in the sight of the LORD like David his father, ¹²banishing the pagan priests from the land and removing all the idols his ancestors had made. ¹³He also deposed his grandmother Maacah from her position as queen mother, because she had made an outrageous object for Asherah. Asa cut down this object and burned it in the Wadi Kidron. ¹⁴The high places did not disappear; yet Asa's heart was entirely with the LORD as long as he lived. ¹⁵He brought into the house of the LORD his father's and his own votive offerings of silver and gold and various vessels.

¹⁶There was war between Asa and Baasha, king of Israel, all their days. ¹⁷Baasha, king of Israel, attacked Judah and fortified Ramah to blockade Asa, king of Judah. ¹⁸Asa then took all the silver and gold remaining in the treasuries of the house of the LORD and the house of the king. Entrusting them to his ministers, King Asa sent them to Ben-hadad, son of Tabrimmon, son of Hezion, king of Aram,† who ruled in Damascus. He said: ¹⁹"There is a treaty between you and me, as there was between your father and my father. I am sending you a present of silver and gold. Go, break your treaty with Baasha, king of Israel, that he may withdraw from me." ²⁰Ben-hadad agreed with King Asa and sent the leaders of his troops against the cities of Israel. They attacked Ijon, Dan, Abel-beth-maacah, and all Chinnereth, besides all the land of Naphtali. ²¹When Baasha heard of it, he left off fortifying Ramah, and stayed in Tirzah. ²²Then King Asa summoned all Judah without exception, and they carried away the stones and beams with which Baasha was fortifying Ramah. With them King Asa built Geba of Benjamin and Mizpah. ²³All the rest of the acts of Asa, with all his valor and all that he did, and the cities he built, are recorded in the book of the chronicles of the kings of Judah. But in his old age, Asa had an infirmity in his feet. ²⁴Asa rested with his ancestors; he was buried with his ancestors in the City of David his father, and his son Jehoshaphat succeeded him as king.

**Reign of Nadab.** ²⁵Nadab, son of Jeroboam, became king of Israel in the second year of Asa, king of Judah. For two years he reigned over Israel.

²⁶He did what was evil in the LORD's sight, walking in the way of his father and the sin he had caused Israel to commit. ²⁷Baasha, son of Ahijah, of the house of Issachar, plotted against him and struck him down at Gibbethon of the Philistines, which Nadab and all Israel were besieging. ²⁸Baasha killed him in the third year of Asa, king of Judah, and succeeded him as king. ²⁹⁰Once he was king, he killed the entire house of Jeroboam, not leaving a single soul but destroying Jeroboam utterly, according to the word of the LORD spoken through his servant, Ahijah the Shilonite, ³⁰because of the sins Jeroboam committed and caused Israel to commit, by which he provoked the LORD, the God of Israel, to anger.

³¹The rest of the acts of Nadab, with all that he did, are recorded in the book of the chronicles of

---

*[15:10] Maacah was in fact Asa's grandmother (see v. 2), but "king's mother" was perhaps a title for the *gebira*, the "Great Lady" or "queen mother" (see, for instance, 2:19). This influential position was usually held by the king's biological mother, but Maacah may have retained it after the early death of her son Abijam.

†[15:18] **Ben-hadad . . . king of Aram**: Ben-hadad I, third successor of Rezon, who had thrown off the yoke of the Israelites during the reign of Solomon and become king of Aram (11:23–24). Chronicles has a parallel version of this account in 2 Chr 16:1–6. **Who ruled**: lit., "sitting," i.e., enthroned, possibly also meaning "resident" or "residing."

n. [15:5] 2 Sm 11:1–27.

o. [15:29] 1 Kgs 14:10–11.

the kings of Israel. ³²There was war between Asa and Baasha, king of Israel, all their days.

**Reign of Baasha.** ³³In the third year of Asa, king of Judah, Baasha, son of Ahijah, became king of all Israel in Tirzah for twenty-four years.

³⁴He did what was evil in the LORD's sight, walking in the way of Jeroboam and the sin he had caused Israel to commit.

## CHAPTER 16

¹The word of the LORD came to Jehu, son of Hanani, against Baasha: ²Inasmuch as I exalted you from the dust and made you ruler of my people Israel, but you have walked in the way of Jeroboam and have caused my people Israel to sin, provoking me to anger by their sins, ³I will burn up what is left of Baasha and his house; I will make your house like that of Jeroboam, son of Nebat:

4    ��۹One of Baasha's line who dies in the city,
         dogs will devour;
    One who dies in the field,
         the birds of the sky will devour.

⁵The rest of the acts of Baasha, what he did and his valor, are recorded in the book of the chronicles of the kings of Israel. ⁶Baasha rested with his ancestors; he was buried in Tirzah, and his son Elah succeeded him as king. ⁷(Through the prophet Jehu, son of Hanani, the word of the LORD came against Baasha and his house, because of all the evil Baasha did in the sight of the LORD, provoking him to anger by his deeds so that he became like the house of Jeroboam, and because of what he destroyed.)

**Reign of Elah.** ⁸In the twenty-sixth year of Asa, king of Judah, Elah, son of Baasha, became king of Israel in Tirzah for two years.

⁹His servant Zimri, commander of half his chariots, plotted against him. As he was in Tirzah, drinking to excess in the house of Arza, master of his palace in Tirzah, ¹⁰ʳZimri entered; he struck and killed him in the twenty-seventh year of Asa, king of Judah, and succeeded him as king. ¹¹Once he was king, seated on the throne, he killed the whole house of Baasha, not sparing a single male relative or friend of his. ¹²ˢZimri destroyed the entire house of Baasha, according to the word the LORD spoke against Baasha through Jehu the prophet, ¹³because of all the sins which Baasha and his son Elah committed and caused Israel to commit, provoking the LORD, the God of Israel, to anger by their idols.

¹⁴The rest of the acts of Elah, with all that he did, are recorded in the book of the chronicles of the kings of Israel.

**Reign of Zimri.** ¹⁵In the twenty-seventh year of Asa, king of Judah, Zimri became king for seven days in Tirzah.

The army was encamped at Gibbethon of the Philistines ¹⁶when they heard, "Zimri has formed a conspiracy and has killed the king." So that day in the camp all Israel made Omri, commander of the army, king of Israel. ¹⁷Omri and all Israel with him marched up from Gibbethon and besieged Tirzah. ¹⁸When Zimri saw that the city was captured, he entered the citadel of the king's house and burned it down over him. He died ¹⁹because of the sins he had committed, doing what was evil in the LORD's sight by walking in the way of Jeroboam and the sin he had caused Israel to commit.

²⁰The rest of the acts of Zimri, with the conspiracy he carried out, are recorded in the book of the chronicles of the kings of Israel.

**Civil War.** ²¹At that time the people of Israel were divided in two, half following Tibni, son of Ginath, to make him king, and half for Omri. ²²The partisans of Omri prevailed over those of Tibni, son of Ginath. Tibni died and Omri became king.

**Reign of Omri.** ²³In the thirty-first year of Asa, king of Judah, Omri became king of Israel for twelve years; the first six of them he reigned in Tirzah.

²⁴He then bought the mountain of Samaria from Shemer for two silver talents and built upon the mountain the city he named Samaria, after Shemer, the former owner. ²⁵But Omri did what was evil in the LORD's sight, more than any of his predecessors. ²⁶In every way he imitated the sinful conduct of Jeroboam, son of Nebat, and the sin he had caused Israel to commit, thus provoking the LORD, the God of Israel, to anger by their idols.

²⁷The rest of the acts of Omri, what he did and his valor, are recorded in the book of the chronicles of the kings of Israel. ²⁸Omri rested with his ancestors; he was buried in Samaria, and Ahab his son succeeded him as king.

**Reign of Ahab.** ²⁹Ahab, son of Omri, became king of Israel in the thirty-eighth year of Asa, king of Judah. Ahab, son of Omri, reigned over Israel in Samaria for twenty-two years.

³⁰Ahab, son of Omri, did what was evil in the LORD's sight more than any of his predecessors. ³¹It was not enough for him to follow the sins of Jeroboam, son of Nebat. He even married Jezebel, daughter of Ethbaal, king of the Sidonians, and began to serve Baal, and worship him. ³²Ahab set up an altar to Baal in the house of Baal which he built in Samaria, ³³and also made an asherah. Ahab did more to provoke the LORD, the God of Israel, to anger than any of the kings of Israel before him. ³⁴During his reign, Hiel from Bethel rebuilt Jericho. At the cost of Abiram, his firstborn son, he laid the foundation, and at the cost of Segub, his youngest son,

p. [16:3] 1 Kgs 16:11; 21:22.    q. [16:4] 1 Kgs 14:11.    r. [16:10] 2 Kgs 9:31.    s. [16:12] 1 Kgs 16:2–4.

t. [16:34] Jos 6:26.

he set up the gates, according to the word of the Lord spoken through Joshua, son of Nun.*

## IV. THE STORY OF ELIJAH†

### CHAPTER 17

**Elijah Proclaims a Drought.**‡ ¹Elijah the Tishbite,§ᵘ from Tishbe in Gilead, said to Ahab: "As the Lord, the God of Israel, lives, whom I serve, during these years there shall be no dew or rain except at my word." ²The word of the Lord came to Elijah: ³Leave here, go east and hide in the Wadi Cherith, east of the Jordan. ⁴You shall drink of the wadi, and I have commanded ravens to feed you there. ⁵So he left and did as the Lord had commanded. He left and remained by the Wadi Cherith, east of the Jordan. ⁶ᵛRavens brought him bread and meat in the morning, and bread and meat in the evening, and he drank from the wadi.

⁷After some time, however, the wadi ran dry, because no rain had fallen in the land. ⁸ʷSo the word of the Lord came to him: ⁹Arise, go to Zarephath of Sidon and stay there. I have commanded a widow there to feed you. ¹⁰He arose and went to Zarephath. When he arrived at the entrance of the city, a widow was there gathering sticks; he called out to her, "Please bring me a small cupful of water to drink." ¹¹She left to get it, and he called out after her, "Please bring along a crust of bread." ¹²She said, "As the Lord, your God, lives, I have nothing baked; there is only a handful of flour in my jar and a little oil in my jug. Just now I was collecting a few sticks, to go in and prepare something for myself and my son; when we have eaten it, we shall die." ¹³Elijah said to her, "Do not be afraid. Go and do as you have said. But first make me a little cake and bring it to me. Afterwards you can prepare something for yourself and your son. ¹⁴For the Lord, the God of Israel, says: The jar of flour shall not go empty, nor the jug of oil run dry, until the day when the Lord sends rain upon the earth." ¹⁵She left and did as Elijah had said. She had enough to eat for a long time—he and she and her household. ¹⁶The jar of flour did not go empty, nor the jug of oil run dry, according to the word of the Lord spoken through Elijah.

¹⁷ˣSome time later the son of the woman, the owner of the house, fell sick, and his sickness grew more severe until he stopped breathing. ¹⁸So she said to Elijah, "Why have you done this to me, man of God? Have you come to me to call attention to my guilt and to kill my son?" ¹⁹Elijah said to her, "Give me your son." Taking him from her lap, he carried him to the upper room where he was staying, and laid him on his own bed. ²⁰He called out to the Lord: "Lord, my God, will you afflict even the widow with whom I am staying by killing her son?" ²¹Then he stretched himself out upon the child three times and he called out to the Lord: "Lord, my God, let the life breath return to the body of this child." ²²The Lord heard the prayer of Elijah; the life breath returned to the child's body and he lived. ²³Taking the child, Elijah carried him down into the house from the upper room and gave him to his mother. Elijah said, "See! Your son is alive." ²⁴The woman said to Elijah, "Now indeed I know that you are a man of God, and it is truly the word of the Lord that you speak."

### CHAPTER 18

**Elijah Ends the Drought.**¶ ¹Long afterward, in the third year, the word of the Lord came to Elijah: Go, present yourself to Ahab, that I may

---

*[16:34] See note on Jos 6:26.

†[17:1–19:21] The central section of 1–2 Kings tells the story of the dynasty of Omri. That dynasty begins and ends in civil war (1 Kgs 16:21–22; 2 Kgs 9–11). Most of the story is set during the reigns of Ahab of Israel (1 Kgs 16:29–22:40) and his son Joram (2 Kgs 3:1–9:26) and focuses particularly on the interaction of the king with various prophets, especially Ahab with Elijah and Elisha. The story of Ahab itself contains two large complexes, a series of narratives about Elijah (1 Kgs 17:1–19:21) and a series about hostility between Ahab and the prophets (1 Kgs 20:1–22:38).

‡[17:1–24] The story of Elijah is in three parts. The first (chap. 17) describes how Elijah proclaimed a drought on God's authority and how he survived during the drought. The second (chap. 18) describes how he ends the drought by bringing the populace back to exclusive worship of the Lord. The third (chap. 19) describes Elijah's despair at the failure of his prophetic mission and his consequent attempt to resign from the prophetic office.

§[17:1] This verse introduces the enigmatic figure of Elijah the Tishbite. (The name "Elijah" means "the Lord is my God." The meaning of "Tishbite" is unknown; it may refer to a place or to a social class.) His appearance before Ahab is abrupt and involves several matters that will unify the whole Elijah story. His claim to "serve the Lord" (lit., to "stand before the Lord") points forward to 19:13, where he refuses to do so; the center of narrative tension on this level is the question of the prophet's autonomy in God's service. His proclamation of a drought points forward to 18:41–45 where he announces the drought's end; the center of narrative tension on this level is the struggle between the Lord and the Canaanite fertility god Baal for the loyalties of Israel. His claim that the drought is due to his own word of power ("except at my word") points forward to 17:24 where the widow acknowledges the divine source of the word Elijah speaks; the center of narrative tension on this level is the gradual characterization of the prophet as one who receives a divine word (vv. 2, 8), obeys it (v. 5), conveys an effective divine word of threat (v. 1) or promise (vv. 14, 16), and even speaks an effective human word of entreaty to God (vv. 20, 22).

¶[18:1–45] The story of the conflict with the prophets of Baal (vv. 21–40) is embedded in the story of the drought and its ending (vv. 1–20, 41–45). The connection between the two stories is found in Canaanite theology, in whose pantheon Baal, "the Cloud Rider," the god of rain and storm, was recognized as the one who brings fertility. Worship of many gods was virtually universal in the ancient world; the Israelite requirement of exclusive worship of the Lord (Ex 20:3) was unique. The people of Israel had apparently become comfortable worshiping both Baal and the Lord, perhaps assigning mutually exclusive spheres of influence to each. By claiming authority over the rain (17:1; 18:1), the Lord was challenging Baal's power in Baal's own domain. The entire drought story in chaps. 17–18 implies what becomes explicit in 18:21–40: this

u. [17:1] Sir 48:1–12; Jas 5:17–18.   v. [17:6] Ex 16:8, 12.   w. [17:8–16] 2 Kgs 4:1–7; Lk 4:25–26.

x. [17:17–24] 2 Kgs 4:18–37; Lk 7:11–16.

send rain upon the earth. ²So Elijah went to present himself to Ahab.

Now the famine in Samaria was severe, ³and Ahab had summoned Obadiah, master of his palace, who greatly revered the LORD. ⁴When Jezebel was slaughtering the prophets of the LORD, Obadiah took a hundred prophets, hid them away by fifties in caves, and supplied them with food and water. ⁵Ahab said to Obadiah, "Go through the land to all sources of water and to all the wadies. We may find grass and keep the horses and mules alive, so that we shall not have to slaughter any of the beasts." ⁶Dividing the land to explore between them, Ahab went one way by himself, Obadiah another way by himself. ⁷As Obadiah was on his way, Elijah met him. Recognizing him, Obadiah fell prostrate and asked, "Is it you, my lord Elijah?" ⁸He said to him, "Yes. Go tell your lord, 'Elijah is here!'"* ⁹But Obadiah said, "What sin has your servant committed, that you are handing me over to Ahab to be killed? ¹⁰As the LORD, your God, lives, there is no nation or kingdom where my lord has not sent in search of you. When they replied, 'He is not here,' he made each kingdom and nation swear they could not find you. ¹¹And now you say, 'Go tell your lord: Elijah is here!' ¹²After I leave you, the spirit of the LORD will carry you to some place I do not know, and when I go to inform Ahab and he does not find you, he will kill me—though your servant has revered the LORD from his youth! ¹³Have you not been told, my lord, what I did when Jezebel was murdering the prophets of the LORD—that I hid a hundred of the prophets of the LORD, fifty each in caves, and supplied them with food and water? ¹⁴And now you say, 'Go tell your lord: Elijah is here!' He will kill me!" ¹⁵Elijah answered, "As the LORD of hosts lives, whom I serve, I will present myself to him today."

¹⁶So Obadiah went to meet Ahab and informed him, and Ahab came to meet Elijah. ¹⁷When Ahab saw Elijah, he said to him, "Is it you, you disturber of Israel?" ¹⁸He answered, "It is not I who disturb Israel, but you and your father's house, by forsaking the commands of the LORD and you by following the Baals. ¹⁹Now summon all Israel to me on Mount Carmel, as well as the four hundred and fifty prophets of Baal and the four hundred prophets of Asherah who eat at Jezebel's table." ²⁰So Ahab summoned all the Israelites and had the prophets gather on Mount Carmel.

²¹Elijah approached all the people and said, "How long will you straddle the issue? If the LORD is God, follow him; if Baal, follow him." But the people did not answer him. ²²So Elijah said to the people, "I am the only remaining prophet of the LORD, and there are four hundred and fifty prophets of Baal. ²³Give us two young bulls. Let them choose one, cut it into pieces, and place it on the wood, but start no fire. I shall prepare the other and place it on the wood, but shall start no fire. ²⁴You shall call upon the name of your gods, and I will call upon the name of the LORD. The God who answers with fire is God." All the people answered, "We agree!"

²⁵Elijah then said to the prophets of Baal, "Choose one young bull and prepare it first, for there are more of you. Call upon your gods, but do not start the fire." ²⁶Taking the young bull that was turned over to them, they prepared it and called upon Baal from morning to noon, saying, "Baal, answer us!" But there was no sound, and no one answering. And they hopped around the altar they had prepared. ²⁷When it was noon, Elijah taunted them: "Call louder, for he is a god; he may be busy doing his business, or may be on a journey. Perhaps he is asleep and must be awakened." ²⁸They called out louder and slashed themselves with swords and spears according to their ritual until blood gushed over them. ²⁹Noon passed and they remained in a prophetic state until the time for offering sacrifice. But there was no sound, no one answering, no one listening.

³⁰Then Elijah said to all the people, "Come here to me." When they drew near to him, he repaired the altar of the LORD which had been destroyed. ³¹He took twelve stones, for the number of tribes of the sons of Jacob, to whom the LORD had said: Israel shall be your name. ³²He built the stones into an altar to the name of the LORD, and made a trench around the altar large enough for two measures of grain. ³³When he had arranged the wood, he cut up the young bull and laid it on the wood. ³⁴He said, "Fill four jars with water and pour it over the burnt offering and over the wood." "Do it again," he said, and they did it again. "Do it a third time," he said, and they did it a third time. ³⁵The water flowed around the altar; even the trench was filled with the water. ³⁶At the time for offering sacrifice, Elijah the prophet came forward and said, "LORD, God of Abraham, Isaac, and Israel, let it be known this day that you are God in Israel and that I am your servant and have done all these things at your command. ³⁷ʸAnswer me, LORD! Answer me, that this people may know that you, LORD, are God and that you have turned their hearts back to you." ³⁸The LORD's fire came down and devoured the burnt offering, wood, stones, and dust, and lapped up the water in the trench. ³⁹Seeing this, all the people fell prostrate and said, "The LORD is God! The LORD is God!" ⁴⁰ᶻThen Elijah said to them, "Seize the prophets of Baal. Let none of them escape!" They seized them, and Elijah brought them down to the

---

is a struggle between the Lord and Baal for the loyalties of the people of Israel.

* [18:8] **Elijah is here:** the Hebrew *hinneh ʾeliyahu* involves a pun. The sentence means both "Elijah is here," informing Ahab that the prophet has been found, and "Behold, Yhwh is my God" (the meaning of the name "Elijah").

y. [18:37] Ex 32:13.   z. [18:40] Ex 32:26–28.

Wadi Kishon and there he slaughtered them. [41]Elijah then said to Ahab, "Go up, eat and drink, for there is the sound of a heavy rain." [42]So Ahab went up to eat and drink, while Elijah went up to the top of Carmel, crouched down to the earth, and put his head between his knees. [43]He said to his servant, "Go up and look out to sea." He went up and looked, but reported, "There is nothing." Seven times he said, "Go look again!" [44]And the seventh time the youth reported, "There is a cloud as small as a man's hand rising from the sea." Elijah said, "Go and say to Ahab, 'Harness up and go down the mountain before the rain stops you.'" [45]All at once the sky grew dark with clouds and wind, and a heavy rain fell. Ahab mounted his chariot and headed for Jezreel. [46]But the hand of the LORD was on Elijah. He girded up his clothing and ran before Ahab as far as the approaches to Jezreel.

## CHAPTER 19

**Flight to Horeb.**[*] [1]Ahab told Jezebel all that Elijah had done—that he had murdered all the prophets by the sword. [2]Jezebel then sent a messenger to Elijah and said, "May the gods do thus to me and more, if by this time tomorrow I have not done with your life what was done to each of them." [3]Elijah was afraid and fled for his life, going to Beer-sheba of Judah. He left his servant there [4a]and went a day's journey into the wilderness, until he came to a solitary broom tree and sat beneath it. He prayed for death: "Enough, LORD! Take my life, for I am no better than my ancestors." [5]He lay down and fell asleep under the solitary broom tree, but suddenly a messenger[†] touched him and said, "Get up and eat!" [6]He looked and there at his head was a hearth cake and a jug of water. After he ate and drank, he lay down again, [7]but the angel of the LORD came back a second time, touched him, and said, "Get up and eat or the journey will be too much for you!" [8b]He got up, ate, and drank; then strengthened by that food, he walked forty days and forty nights to the mountain of God, Horeb.

[9]There he came to a cave, where he took shelter. But the word of the LORD came to him: Why are you here, Elijah? [10]He answered: "I have been most zealous for the LORD, the God of hosts, but the Israelites have forsaken your covenant. They have destroyed your altars and murdered your prophets by the sword. I alone remain, and they seek to take my life." [11c]Then the LORD said: Go

out and stand on the mountain before the LORD;[‡] the LORD will pass by. There was a strong and violent wind rending the mountains and crushing rocks before the LORD—but the LORD was not in the wind; after the wind, an earthquake—but the LORD was not in the earthquake; [12]after the earthquake, fire—but the LORD was not in the fire; after the fire, a light silent sound.[§]

[13]When he heard this, Elijah hid his face in his cloak and went out and stood at the entrance of the cave. A voice said to him, Why are you here, Elijah? [14d]He replied, "I have been most zealous for the LORD, the God of hosts, but the Israelites have forsaken your covenant. They have destroyed your altars and murdered your prophets by the sword. I alone remain, and they seek to take my life." [15e]The LORD said to him: Go back! Take the desert road to Damascus. When you arrive, you shall anoint Hazael as king of Aram. [16]You shall also anoint Jehu, son of Nimshi, as king of Israel, and Elisha, son of Shaphat of Abel-meholah, as prophet to succeed you. [17]Anyone who escapes the sword of Hazael, Jehu will kill. Anyone who escapes the sword of Jehu, Elisha will kill. [18g]But I will spare seven thousand in Israel—every knee that has not bent to Baal, every mouth that has not kissed him.

[19]**Elijah set out, and came upon Elisha, son of Shaphat, as he was plowing with twelve yoke of oxen; he was following the twelfth. Elijah went over to him and threw his cloak on him. [20h]Elisha left the oxen, ran after Elijah, and said, "Please, let me kiss my father and mother goodbye, and I will follow you." Elijah answered, "Go back! What have I done to you?" [21]Elisha left him and, taking the yoke of oxen, slaughtered them; he used the plowing equipment for fuel to

---

‡[19:11–13] To "stand before the Lord" is a literal translation of a Hebrew idiom meaning "to serve the Lord"; Elijah has used this idiom twice before to describe himself as the Lord's servant (17:1; 18:15). The Lord's command, then, means that Elijah is to take up once again the prophetic service to which he has been appointed. The Lord's question, "Why are you here?" (v. 9, repeated in v. 13), could imply an accusation that he is abandoning his prophetic office. In v. 15, the Lord tells him to go back.

§[19:12] Compare these divine manifestations to Elijah with those to Moses on the same mountain (Ex 19:16–19; 33:18–23; 34:5–6; Dt 4:10–15). Though various phenomena, such as wind, storms, earthquakes, fire, accompany the divine presence, they do not constitute the presence itself which, like the "silent sound," is mysterious and ultimately ungraspable. Moses and Elijah, the two figures who experienced God's theophany on this mountain, reappear with Jesus on another mountain at his transfiguration (Mt 17:1–9; Mk 9:2–9; Lk 9:28–36).

¶[19:15–17] Elijah himself carried out only the last of the three commissions entrusted to him (vv. 19–21); Elisha performed the first himself (2 Kgs 8:7–19), and the second, the anointing of Jehu, through one of his followers (2 Kgs 9:1–10).

**[19:19–21] Elijah's act of throwing his mantle over the shoulders of Elisha associates him with Elijah as a servant (v. 21). Elisha will later succeed to Elijah's position and prophetic power (2 Kgs 2:1–15). Elisha's prompt response, destroying his plow and oxen, signifies a radical change from his former manner of living.

---

*[19:1–21] The story of Elijah's journey to Mount Horeb begins as a flight from danger, but takes a surprising turn. The prophet makes his solitary way to the mountain where the Lord had appeared to Moses and the Israelites ("Horeb" is an alternate name for "Sinai"). Like Moses on the holy mountain, Elijah experiences a theophany and receives a commission.

†[19:5–7] Sound asleep, Elijah is startled awake by an unspecified "messenger." Only in v. 7 is the figure identified as a messenger (or "angel") of the Lord.

a. [19:4] Jon 4:6–9.   b. [19:8] Ex 34:28.   c. [19:11–13] Ex 33:18–23; 34:5–6.

d. [19:14] Rom 11:3.   e. [19:15] 2 Kgs 8:7–15.   f. [19:16] 2 Kgs 2:1–15; 9:1–10.   g. [19:18] Rom 11:4.   h. [19:20] Lk 9:61–62.

boil their flesh, and gave it to the people to eat. Then he left and followed Elijah to serve him.

# V. THE STORY OF AHAB*

## CHAPTER 20

**Ahab's Victories over Aram.**† ¹Ben-hadad, king of Aram, gathered all his forces and, accompanied by thirty-two kings with horses and chariotry, set out to besiege and attack Samaria. ²He sent messengers to Ahab, king of Israel, within the city, ³and said to him, "This is Ben-hadad's message: 'Your silver and gold are mine, and your wives and your fine children are mine.'" ⁴The king of Israel answered, "Just as you say, my lord king, I and all I have are yours." ⁵But the messengers came again and said, "This is Ben-hadad's message: 'I sent you word: Give me your silver and gold, your wives and your children. ⁶But now I say: At this time tomorrow I will send my servants to you, and they shall ransack your house and the houses of your servants. They shall seize and take away whatever you consider valuable.'" ⁷The king of Israel then summoned all the elders of the land and said: "Understand clearly that this man is intent on evil. When he sent to me for my wives and children, my silver and my gold, I did not refuse him." ⁸All the elders and all the people said to him, "Do not listen. Do not give in." ⁹Accordingly he directed the messengers of Ben-hadad, "Say this: 'To my lord the king: I will do all that you demanded of your servant the first time. But this I cannot do.'" The messengers left and reported this. ¹⁰Ben-hadad then responded, "May the gods do thus to me and more, if there will remain enough dust in Samaria to make handfuls for all my followers." ¹¹The king of Israel replied, "Tell him, 'Let not one who puts on armor boast like one who takes it off.'" ¹²Ben-hadad was drinking in the pavilions with the kings when he heard this reply. He commanded his servants, "Get ready!"; and they got ready to storm the city.

¹³Then a prophet came up to Ahab, king of Israel, and said: "The Lord says, Do you see all this vast army? Today I am giving it into your power, that you may know that I am the Lord." ¹⁴But Ahab asked, "Through whom will it be given over?" He answered, "The Lord says, Through the aides of the provincial governors." Then Ahab asked, "Who is to attack?" He replied, "You are." ¹⁵So Ahab mustered the aides of the provincial governors, two hundred thirty-two of them. Behind them he mustered all the Israelite soldiery, who numbered seven thousand in all. ¹⁶‡They marched out at noon, while Ben-hadad was drinking heavily in the pavilions with the thirty-two kings who were his allies. ¹⁷When the aides of the provincial governors marched out first, Ben-hadad received word, "Some men have marched out of Samaria." ¹⁸He answered, "Whether they have come out for peace or for war, take them alive." ¹⁹But when these had come out of the city—the aides of the provincial governors with the army following them— ²⁰each of them struck down his man. The Arameans fled with Israel pursuing them, while Ben-hadad, king of Aram, escaped on a chariot horse. ²¹Then the king of Israel went out and destroyed the horses and chariots. Thus he inflicted a severe defeat on Aram.

²²Then the prophet approached the king of Israel and said to him: "Go, regroup your forces. Understand clearly what you must do, for at the turning of the year§ the king of Aram will attack you." ²³Meanwhile the servants of the king of Aram said to him: "Their gods are mountain gods. That is why they defeated us. But if we fight them on level ground, we shall be sure to defeat them. ²⁴This is what you must do: Take the kings from their posts and put prefects in their places. ²⁵Raise an army as large as the army you have lost, horse for horse, chariot for chariot. Let us fight them on level ground, and we shall surely defeat them." He took their advice and did this. ²⁶At the turning of the year, Ben-hadad mustered Aram and went up to Aphek to fight against Israel. ²⁷The Israelites, too, were mustered and supplied with provisions; then they went out to meet the enemy. The Israelites, encamped opposite, looked like little flocks of goats, while Aram covered the land. ²⁸A man of God approached and said to the king of Israel: "The Lord says, Because Aram has said the Lord is a god of mountains, not a god of plains, I will give all this vast army into your power that you may know I am the Lord." ²⁹They were encamped opposite each other for seven days. On the seventh day battle was joined, and the Israelites struck down one hundred thousand

---

*[20:1–22:54] Although coverage of Ahab's reign began in 16:29, he was only a secondary character in the chapters about Elijah. Now attention focuses on Ahab. Each of these chapters tells a story of the king (20:1–34; 21:1–16; 22:1–4, 29–38), to which is attached a scene of prophetic condemnation (20:30–42; 21:17–29; 22:5–28). As relations between Ahab and the prophets of the Lord deteriorate, the scenes of prophetic condemnation get longer and the condemnations themselves become more pointed. Some historians doubt that the stories of hostility between Israel and Aram (chaps. 20 and 22) originally pertained to the reign of Ahab. If this is correct, their original setting may have been several decades later.

†[20:1–34] This story recounts two battles through which Ahab won freedom for Israel from vassalage to Ben-hadad of Syria. The story is chiastically arranged: negotiations (vv. 1–12), battle (vv. 13–21), battle (vv. 22–30), negotiations (vv. 31–34). The ensuing prophetic condemnation is surprising, since the portrait of Ahab in vv. 1–34 is apparently quite positive.

‡[20:16–19] The narrator uses a sort of verbal split-screen technique to show us two separate and simultaneous scenes. At the gates of Samaria, the Israelite forces are coming out to battle (v. 16a): first the aides (lit., "young men"; v. 17a), then the whole army (v. 19). Meanwhile in the Aramean camp Ben-hadad is getting drunk (v. 16b), receiving reports (v. 17b) and issuing commands (v. 18).

§[20:22] **At the turning of the year:** the idiom may mean "next year about this time" or "at the beginning of the year," i.e., the spring (cf. 2 Sm 11:1).

foot soldiers of Aram in one day. ³⁰The survivors fled into the city of Aphek, where the wall collapsed on twenty-seven thousand of them. Benhadad, too, fled, and took refuge within the city, in an inner room.

³¹His servants said to him: "We have heard that the kings of the house of Israel are merciful kings. Allow us, therefore, to garb ourselves in sackcloth, with cords around our heads, and go out to the king of Israel. Perhaps he will spare your life." ³²Dressed in sackcloth girded at the waist and wearing cords around their heads, they went to the king of Israel and said, "Your servant Ben-hadad says, 'Spare my life!'" He asked, "Is he still alive? He is my brother.'"* ³³Hearing this as a good omen, the men quickly took him at his word and said, "Ben-hadad is your brother." He answered, "Go and get him." When Ben-hadad came out to him, the king had him mount his chariot. ³⁴Ben-hadad said to him, "The cities my father took from your father I will restore, and you may set up bazaars for yourself in Damascus, as my father did in Samaria." Ahab replied, "For my part, I will set you free on those terms." So he made a covenant with him and then set him free.

**Prophetic Condemnation.** ³⁵Acting on the word of the LORD, one of the guild prophets said to his companion, "Strike me." But he refused to strike him. ³⁶Then he said to him, "Since you did not obey the voice of the LORD, a lion will attack you when you leave me." When he left him, a lion came upon him and attacked him.ⁱ ³⁷Then the prophet met another man and said, "Strike me." The man struck him a blow and wounded him. ³⁸The prophet went on and waited for the king on the road, disguising himself with a bandage over his eyes. ³⁹As the king was passing, he called out to the king and said: "Your servant went into the thick of the battle, and suddenly someone turned and brought me a man and said, 'Guard this man. If he is missing, you shall have to pay for his life with your life or pay out a talent of silver.'† ⁴⁰But while your servant was occupied here and there, the man disappeared." The king of Israel said to him, "That is your sentence. You have decided it yourself." ⁴¹He quickly removed the bandage from his eyes, and the king of Israel recognized

him as one of the prophets. ⁴²ʲHe said to him: "The LORD says, Because you have set free the man I put under the ban,‡ your life shall pay for his life, your people for his people." ⁴³ᵏDisturbed and angry, the king of Israel set off for home and entered Samaria.

## CHAPTER 21

**Seizure of Naboth's Vineyard.**§ ¹Naboth the Jezreelite had a vineyard in Jezreel next to the palace of Ahab, king of Samaria. Some time later, ²Ahab said to Naboth, "Give me your vineyard to be my vegetable garden, since it is close by, next to my house. I will give you a better vineyard in exchange, or, if you prefer, I will give you its value in money." ³Naboth said to Ahab, "The LORD forbid that I should give you my ancestral heritage."¶ ⁴Ahab went home disturbed and angry at the answer Naboth the Jezreelite had given him: "I will not give you my ancestral heritage." Lying down on his bed, he turned away and would not eat. ⁵His wife Jezebel came to him and said to him, "Why are you so sullen that you will not eat?" ⁶He answered her, "Because I spoke to Naboth the Jezreelite and said to him, 'Sell me your vineyard, or, if you prefer, I will give you a vineyard in exchange.' But he said, 'I will not give you my vineyard.'" ⁷Jezebel his wife said to him, "What a king of Israel you are! Get up! Eat and be cheerful. I will give you the vineyard of Naboth the Jezreelite."

⁸So she wrote letters in Ahab's name and, having sealed them with his seal, sent them to the elders and to the nobles who lived in the same city with Naboth. ⁹This is what she wrote in the letters: "Proclaim a fast and set Naboth at the head of the people. ¹⁰Next, set two scoundrels opposite him to accuse him: 'You have cursed God and king.' Then take him out and stone him to death."

¹¹His fellow citizens—the elders and the nobles who dwelt in his city—did as Jezebel had ordered in the letters she sent them. ¹²They proclaimed a fast and set Naboth at the head of the people. ¹³Two scoundrels came in and sat opposite Naboth, and the scoundrels accused him in the presence of the people, "Naboth has cursed God and king." And they led him out of the city and stoned him to death. ¹⁴Then they sent word to Jezebel: "Naboth has been stoned to death."

¹⁵When Jezebel learned that Naboth had been stoned to death, she said to Ahab, "Go,

---

*[20:32] **He is my brother:** cf. note on 9:13.

†[20:39] The "man" is ostensibly a prisoner of war, to be kept or sold as a slave. In the event he escapes, the one charged with guarding him would be obliged either to pay a fine or to take his place as a slave. The fine, however, is exorbitant: a talent of silver is roughly one hundred times the price of an ordinary slave (see Ex 21:32). This is the only clue Ahab will get that he is being set up and that the story is really about himself in his dealings with Ben-hadad. In 2 Sm 14:1–20, the wise woman of Tekoa uses the same technique with King David: she tells a story that elicits a reaction from the king; David is tricked into pronouncing judgment on himself, as the story parallels his own situation. The prophet Nathan (2 Sm 12:1–7) likewise uses a story that leads David to see his sin for what it is.

‡[20:42] **Under the ban:** cf. note on Dt 2:34.

§[21:1–16] The story tells how Jezebel manipulates important structures of Israelite social order, law, and religious observance to eliminate a faithful Israelite landowner who frustrates Ahab's will.

¶[21:3] **Heritage:** Hebrew *naḥalah*. Naboth is unwilling to sell or exchange his vineyard. According to the Israelite system of land tenure and distribution, land was held in common within a social unit. The ancestral *naḥalah* was not private property, to be alienated at will.

---

i. [20:36] 1 Kgs 13:24.

j. [20:42] 1 Kgs 22:35.   k. [20:43] 1 Kgs 21:4.

take possession of the vineyard of Naboth the Jezreelite which he refused to sell you, because Naboth is not alive, but dead." ¹⁶When Ahab heard that Naboth was dead, he started on his way down to the vineyard of Naboth the Jezreelite, to take possession of it.

**Prophetic Condemnation.** ¹⁷Then the word of the LORD came to Elijah the Tishbite: ¹⁸Go down to meet Ahab, king of Israel, who is in Samaria. He will be in the vineyard of Naboth, where he has gone to take possession. ¹⁹Tell him: "Thus says the LORD: After murdering, do you also take possession?" And tell him, "Thus says the LORD: In the place where the dogs licked up the blood of Naboth, the dogs shall lick up your blood, too."

²⁰*Ahab said to Elijah, "Have you found me out, my enemy?" He said, "I have found you. Because you have given yourself up to doing evil in the LORD's sight, ²¹ᵐI am bringing evil upon you: I will consume you and will cut off every male belonging to Ahab, whether bond or free, in Israel. ²²I will make your house like that of Jeroboam, ·son of Nebat, and like the house of Baasha, son of Ahijah, because you have provoked me by leading Israel into sin."

²³Against Jezebel, too, the LORD declared: The dogs shall devour Jezebel in the confines of Jezreel.

²⁴ Anyone of Ahab's line who dies in the city,
       dogs will devour;
   Anyone who dies in the field,
       the birds of the sky will devour.

²⁵Indeed, no one gave himself up to the doing of evil in the sight of the LORD as did Ahab, urged on by his wife Jezebel. ²⁶He became completely abominable by going after idols, just as the Amorites had done, whom the LORD drove out of the Israelites' way.

²⁷When Ahab heard these words, he tore his garments and put on sackcloth over his bare flesh. He fasted, slept in the sackcloth, and went about subdued. ²⁸Then the word of the LORD came to Elijah the Tishbite, ²⁹"Have you seen how Ahab has humbled himself before me? Since he has humbled himself before me, I will not bring the evil in his time. I will bring the evil upon his house in his son's time.

# CHAPTER 22

**Ahab's Defeat by Aram.**† ¹Three years passed without war between Aram and Israel. ²In the third year, however, King Jehoshaphat of Judah came down to the king of Israel. ³The king of Israel said to his servants, "Do you not know that Ramoth-gilead is ours and we are doing nothing to take it from the king of Aram?" ⁴He asked Jehoshaphat, "Will you come with me to fight against Ramoth-gilead?" Jehoshaphat answered the king of Israel, "You and I are as one, and your people and my people, your horses and my horses as well."

**Prophetic Condemnation.** ⁵Jehoshaphat also said to the king of Israel, "Seek the word of the LORD at once." ⁶The king of Israel assembled the prophets, about four hundred of them, and asked, "Shall I go to fight against Ramoth-gilead or shall I refrain?" They said, "Attack. The Lord will give it into the power of the king."‡ ⁷But Jehoshaphat said, "Is there no other prophet of the LORD here we might consult?" ⁸The king of Israel answered, "There is one other man through whom we might consult the LORD; but I hate him because he prophesies not good but evil about me. He is Micaiah, son of Imlah." Jehoshaphat said, "Let not the king say that." ⁹So the king of Israel called an official and said to him, "Get Micaiah, son of Imlah, at once."

¹⁰The king of Israel and Jehoshaphat, king of Judah, were seated, each on his throne, clothed in their robes of state in the square at the entrance of the gate of Samaria, and all the prophets were prophesying before them. ¹¹ᵒZedekiah, son of Chenaanah, made himself two horns of iron§ and said, "The LORD says, With these you shall gore Aram until you have destroyed them." ¹²The other prophets prophesied in a similar vein, saying: "Attack Ramoth-gilead and conquer! The LORD will give it into the power of the king."

¹³Meanwhile, the messenger who had gone to call Micaiah said to him, "Look now, the prophets are unanimously predicting good for the king. Let your word be the same as any of theirs; speak a good word." ¹⁴Micaiah said, "As

---

*[21:20–26] In these verses the narrator uses against the third Israelite dynasty the same condemnation formula that was uttered against the first two dynasties, those of Jeroboam (14:9–11) and Baasha (16:2–4). Part of the formula is put in Elijah's mouth, in an oracle against Ahab and his descendants (vv. 21–22), and part of it in an aside to the reader that extends the condemnation to Ahab's wife, Jezebel, and his whole household (vv. 23–24). The oracle against Jezebel will be fulfilled in 2 Kgs 9:36; the obliteration of the dynasty will be recounted in the bloody stories of 2 Kgs 9–11.

†[22:1–40] This chapter presents a contrasting parallel to chap. 20, where Ahab enjoyed victories over Aram's aggression. Here Ahab is the aggressor, but falls in battle against Aram. Like the preceding chapters, it contains a story of Ahab plus an episode of prophetic condemnation. The story ends with the formulaic conclusion to Ahab's reign (vv. 39–40). Chronicles has a parallel version of this account in 2 Chr 18:1–34. After the story of Ahab's death come accounts of the reign of Jehoshaphat (paralleled in 2 Chr 20:31–37) and of the beginning of the reign of Ahaziah.

‡[22:6] Though Ahab is clearly intended to understand the oracle as prophesying his success, the prophets' words are ambiguous. "The lord" (not "the LORD," i.e., the proper name of Israel's God) who will give victory is unidentified, as is the king to whom it will be given.

§[22:11] The "two" horns probably symbolize the coalition of two kings, Ahab and Jehoshaphat.

---

l. [21:19] 1 Kgs 22:38; 2 Kgs 9:26.   m. [21:21–23] 1 Kgs 14:10–11; 15:29; 16:3–4, 11; 2 Kgs 9:8–10, 36.   n. [21:29] 2 Kgs 9:25–26.

o. [22:11] Dt 33:17.

the LORD lives, I shall speak whatever the LORD tells me."

¹⁵When he came to the king, the king said to him, "Micaiah, shall we go to fight at Ramoth-gilead, or shall we refrain?" He said, "Attack and conquer! The LORD will give it into the power of the king." ¹⁶But the king answered him, "How many times must I adjure you to tell me nothing but the truth in the name of the LORD?" ¹⁷*So Micaiah said:

"I see all Israel
    scattered on the mountains,
    like sheep without a shepherd,
And the LORD saying,
    These have no master!
    Let each of them go back home in peace."

¹⁸The king of Israel said to Jehoshaphat, "Did I not tell you, he does not prophesy good about me, but only evil?" ¹⁹†Micaiah continued: "Therefore hear the word of the LORD: I saw the LORD seated on his throne, with the whole host of heaven standing to his right and to his left. ²⁰The LORD asked: Who will deceive Ahab, so that he will go up and fall on Ramoth-gilead?‡ And one said this, another that, ²¹until this spirit came forth and stood before the LORD, saying, 'I will deceive him.' The LORD asked: How? ²²He answered, 'I will go forth and become a lying spirit in the mouths of all his prophets.' The LORD replied: You shall succeed in deceiving him. Go forth and do this. ²³So now, the LORD has put a lying spirit in the mouths of all these prophets of yours; the LORD himself has decreed evil against you."

²⁴Thereupon Zedekiah, son of Chenaanah, came up and struck Micaiah on the cheek, saying, "Has the spirit of the LORD, then, left me to speak with you?" ²⁵Micaiah said, "You shall find out on the day you go into an inner room to hide." ²⁶The king of Israel then said, "Seize Micaiah and take him back to Amon, prefect of the city, and to Joash, the king's son, ²⁷and say, 'This is the king's order: Put this man in prison and feed him scanty rations of bread and water until I come back in safety.'" ²⁸ᵖBut Micaiah said, "If

you return in safety, the LORD has not spoken through me." (He also said, "Hear, O peoples, all of you.")§

**Ahab at Ramoth-gilead.** ²⁹The king of Israel and Jehoshaphat, king of Judah, went up to Ramoth-gilead, ³⁰and the king of Israel said to Jehoshaphat, "I will disguise myself and go into battle, but you put on your own robes." So the king of Israel disguised himself and entered the battle. ³¹In the meantime the king of Aram had given his thirty-two chariot commanders the order, "Do not fight with anyone, great or small, except the king of Israel alone."

³²When the chariot commanders saw Jehoshaphat, they cried out, "There is the king of Israel!" and wheeled to fight him. But Jehoshaphat cried out, ³³and the chariot commanders, seeing that he was not the king of Israel, turned away from him. ³⁴But someone drew his bow at random, and hit the king of Israel between the joints of his breastplate. He ordered his charioteer, "Rein about and take me out of the ranks, for I am wounded."

³⁵�q The battle grew fierce during the day, and the king, who was propped up in his chariot facing the Arameans, died in the evening. The blood from his wound flowed to the bottom of the chariot. ³⁶At sunset a cry went through the army, "Every man to his city, every man to his land!"

³⁷And so the king died, and came back to Samaria, and they buried him there. ³⁸ʳWhen they washed out the chariot at the pool of Samaria, the dogs licked up his blood and prostitutes bathed there, as the LORD had prophesied.

³⁹The rest of the acts of Ahab, with all that he did, including the ivory house he built and all the cities he built, are recorded in the book of the chronicles of the kings of Israel. ⁴⁰Ahab rested with his ancestors, and his son Ahaziah succeeded him as king.

**Reign of Jehoshaphat.** ⁴¹Jehoshaphat, son of Asa, became king of Judah in the fourth year of Ahab, king of Israel. ⁴²Jehoshaphat was thirty-five years old when he became king, and he reigned twenty-five years in Jerusalem. His mother's name was Azubah, daughter of Shilhi. ⁴³He walked in the way of Asa his father unceasingly, doing what was right in the LORD's sight. ⁴⁴Nevertheless, the high places did not disappear, and the people still sacrificed on the high places and burned incense there. ⁴⁵Jehoshaphat also made peace with the king of Israel.

⁴⁶The rest of the acts of Jehoshaphat, with his valor, what he did and how he fought, are recorded in the book of the chronicles of the

---

*[22:17] Micaiah's oracle uses the common ancient metaphor of "shepherd" for the king. It means that the Israelite forces will be left leaderless because the king (or perhaps both kings: the word "master" could be singular or plural in Hebrew) will die in battle.

†[22:19–23] Since Ahab's intention to attack Ramoth-gilead is unshaken, Micaiah reveals God's plan to trick Ahab to his death, and thus virtually dares Ahab to walk into the trap with his eyes open. The work of the "lying spirit" explains the ambiguities of the prophets' original oracle in v. 6. Prophets "stand in the council of the Lord" and are privy to its deliberations; cf. Jer 23:22.

‡[22:20] **Fall on Ramoth-gilead**: lit., "heights of Gilead"; even the Lord's words are double-meaning. God wants Ahab to "fall on" (that is, attack) Ramoth-gilead so that he will "fall on" (that is, die on) Ramoth-gilead.

§[22:28] The last words of the verse are a scribal gloss attributing to Micaiah, son of Imlah, the opening words of the book of a different Micaiah (Micah), the prophet of Moresheth, the sixth of the twelve minor prophets of the Old Testament canon.

---

p. [22:28] Mi 1:2.

q. [22:35] 1 Kgs 20:42.   r. [22:38] 1 Kgs 21:19.

kings of Judah. ⁴⁷He removed from the land the rest of the pagan priests who had remained in the reign of Asa his father. ⁴⁸There was no king in Edom, but an appointed regent. ⁴⁹Jehoshaphat made Tarshish ships to go to Ophir for gold; but in fact the ships did not go, because they were wrecked at Ezion-geber. ⁵⁰That was the time when Ahaziah, son of Ahab, had said to Jehoshaphat, "Let my servants accompany your servants in the ships." But Jehoshaphat would not agree. ⁵¹Jehoshaphat rested with his ancestors; he was buried with his ancestors in the City of David his father, and his son Jehoram succeeded him as king.

**Reign of Ahaziah.**[*] ⁵²Ahaziah, son of Ahab, became king over Israel in Samaria in the seventeenth year[†] of Jehoshaphat, king of Judah; he reigned two years over Israel.

⁵³He did what was evil in the sight of the LORD, walking in the way of his father, his mother, and Jeroboam, son of Nebat, who caused Israel to sin. ⁵⁴He served Baal and worshiped him, thus provoking the LORD, the God of Israel, just as his father had done.

---

*[22:52–54] The account of Ahaziah's reign continues in 2 Kings.

†[22:52] **Seventeenth year**: so the present Hebrew text. This is consistent with the figures in 2 Kgs 3:1, but together those figures conflict with information in 1 Kgs 22:42 and 2 Kgs 1:17. The problem of the chronology of the kings of Israel and Judah has never been convincingly resolved; it is complicated by the fact that the ancient Greek translation sometimes has different lengths of reign and different accession dates. See further note on 2 Kgs 3:1.

# THE SECOND BOOK OF
# KINGS

~&~

## CHAPTER 1

**Reign of Ahaziah, Continued.** ¹After Ahab's death, Moab rebelled against Israel.ᵃ

²Ahaziah fell through the lattice of his roof terrace at Samaria and was injured. So he sent out messengers with the instructions: "Go and inquire of Baalzebub,* the god of Ekron, whether I shall recover from this injury."

³Meanwhile, the messenger of the LORD said to Elijah the Tishbite: Go and meet the messengers of Samaria's king, and tell them: "Is it because there is no God in Israel that you are going to inquire of Baalzebub, the god of Ekron?" ⁴For this, the LORD says: You shall not leave the bed upon which you lie; instead, you shall die. And Elijah departed. ⁵The messengers then returned to Ahaziah, who asked them, "Why have you returned?" ⁶They answered, "A man met us and said to us, 'Go back to the king who sent you and tell him: The LORD says: Is it because there is no God in Israel that you are sending to inquire of Baalzebub, the god of Ekron? For this you shall not leave the bed upon which you lie; instead, you shall die.'" ⁷The king asked them, "What was the man like who met you and said these things to you?" ⁸They replied, "He wore a hairy garment† with a leather belt around his waist." "It is Elijah the Tishbite!" he exclaimed.

⁹Then the king sent a captain with his company of fifty men after Elijah. The prophet was seated on a hilltop when he found him. He said, "Man of God, the king commands you, 'Come down.'" ¹⁰Elijah answered the captain, "Well, if I am a man of God, may fire come down from heaven and consume you and your fifty men." And fire came down from heaven and consumed him and his fifty men.ᵇ ¹¹The king sent another captain with his company of fifty men after Elijah. He shouted up and said, "Man of God, the king says, 'Come down immediately!'" ¹²Elijah answered them, "If I am a man of God, may fire come down from heaven and consume you and your fifty men." And divine fire‡ came down from heaven and consumed him

and his fifty men. ¹³The king sent a third captain with his company of fifty men. When the third captain had climbed the hill, he fell to his knees before Elijah, pleading with him. He said, "Man of God, let my life and the lives of these fifty men, your servants, count for something in your sight! ¹⁴Already fire has come down from heaven, consuming the first two captains with their companies of fifty men. But now, let my life count for something in your sight!" ¹⁵Then the messenger of the LORD said to Elijah: Go down with him; you need not be afraid of him. So Elijah left and went down with him to the king. ¹⁶He declared to the king: "Thus says the LORD: Because you sent messengers to inquire of Baalzebub, the god of Ekron—do you think there is no God in Israel to inquire of?—you shall not leave the bed upon which you lie; instead you shall die."ᶜ

¹⁷Ahaziah died according to the word of the LORD spoken by Elijah. Since he had no son, Joram§ succeeded him as king, in the second year of Joram, son of Jehoshaphat, king of Judah.

¹⁸The rest of the acts of Ahaziah, which he did, are recorded in the book of chronicles of the kings of Israel.

## VI. ELISHA SUCCEEDS ELIJAH¶

## CHAPTER 2

**Elijah's Journey.** ¹When the LORD was about to take Elijah up to heaven in a whirlwind, he and Elisha were on their way from Gilgal.**

described the miraculous divine fire that fell from a cloudless sky to consume Elijah's offering in 1 Kgs 18:38.

§[1:17] **Joram**: in 2 Kings the name "Joram" (*yoram*) and its variant "Jehoram" (*yehoram*) are used interchangeably. To avoid the impression that they are different names and designate different people, both forms are rendered "Joram" in this translation. Confusion arises, however, because the king of Israel whose reign is recounted beginning in 3:1 and the contemporary king of Judah whose reign is recounted beginning in 8:16 share this name. On the relationship of Joram of Israel to Joram of Judah, see note on 3:1.

¶[2:1–25] The story of Elisha's succession to Elijah's prophetic office is oddly set between the death of Ahaziah (1:17) and the accession of his successor (3:1). The effect is to place this scene, which is the central scene in the whole of 1–2 Kings, outside of time. It thereby becomes almost mythic in its import and reminds us that, behind the transitory flow of kings and kingdoms, stand the eternal word of God and the prophets who give it voice. Just as 1–2 Kings pivots on this chapter, so this scene too is concentrically constructed. Together Elijah and Elisha journey to Bethel, thence to Jericho, and thence across the Jordan. There Elijah is taken up in the whirlwind and Elijah's mantle of power comes to Elisha. Now alone, Elisha crosses the Jordan again, returns to Jericho and thence back to Bethel.

**[2:1] **Gilgal**: there are several places in the Hebrew Bible named Gilgal; the word probably means "circle," viz. of stones.

---

*[1:2] **Baalzebub**: in this form, "Baal of flies." The name in the Hebrew text is a derisive alteration of Baalzebul, "Prince Baal." The best New Testament evidence supports the latter form in Mt 10:25; Lk 11:15.

†[1:8] **Hairy garment**: a sign of prophetic calling; see Zec 13:4. John the Baptizer wore a similarly distinctive mantle; see Mt 3:4; Mk 1:6.

‡[1:12] **Divine fire**: lit., "fire of God," which in Hebrew sounds quite like "man of God." The play on words is the basis for Elijah's retort. This story was told among the people to enhance the dignity of the prophet and to reflect the power of God whom he served. A similar phrase, "the LORD's fire,"

---

a. [1:1] 2 Kgs 3:4–27.  b. [1:10] Lv 10:1–2; Sir 48:3; Lk 9:51–55.    c. [1:16] Sir 48:6.

²Elijah said to Elisha, "Stay here, please. The LORD has sent me on to Bethel." Elisha replied, "As the LORD lives, and as you yourself live, I will not leave you." So they went down to Bethel. ³The guild prophets who were in Bethel went out to Elisha and asked him, "Do you know that today the LORD will take your master from you?" He replied, "Yes, I know that. Be still."

⁴Elijah said to him, "Elisha, stay here, please. The LORD has sent me on to Jericho." Elisha replied, "As the LORD lives, and as you yourself live, I will not leave you." So they came to Jericho. ⁵The guild prophets who were in Jericho approached Elisha and asked him, "Do you know that today the LORD will take your master from you?" He replied, "Yes, I know that. Be still."

⁶Elijah said to him, "Stay here, please. The LORD has sent me on to the Jordan." Elisha replied, "As the LORD lives, and as you yourself live, I will not leave you." So the two went on together. ⁷Fifty of the guild prophets followed and stood facing them at a distance, while the two of them stood next to the Jordan.

**Elisha Succeeds Elijah.** ⁸Elijah took his mantle, rolled it up and struck the water: it divided, and the two of them crossed over on dry ground.ᵈ

⁹ᵉWhen they had crossed over, Elijah said to Elisha, "Request whatever I might do for you, before I am taken from you." Elisha answered, "May I receive a double portion of your spirit." ¹⁰He replied, "You have asked something that is not easy. Still, if you see me taken up from you, your wish will be granted; otherwise not." ¹¹As they walked on still conversing, a fiery chariot and fiery horses came between the two of them, and Elijah went up to heaven in a whirlwind.ᶠ ¹²and Elisha saw it happen. He cried out,ᵍ "My father! my father!† Israel's chariot and steeds!" Then he saw him no longer.

He gripped his own garment, tore it into two pieces, ¹³and picked up the mantle which had fallen from Elijah. Then he went back and stood at the bank of the Jordan. ¹⁴Wielding the mantle which had fallen from Elijah, he struck the water and said, "The LORD, the God of Elijah—where is he now?"‡ He struck the water: it divided, and he crossed over.

**Elisha's Journey.** ¹⁵The guild prophets in Jericho, who were on the other side, saw him and said, "The spirit of Elijah rests on Elisha." They went to meet him, bowing to the ground before him.ᵍ ¹⁶They said, "Among your servants are fifty brave men. Let them go in search of your master. Perhaps the spirit of the LORD has lifted him up and left him on some mountain or in some valley." He answered, "Do not send them."ʰ ¹⁷But they kept urging him, until he was embarrassed and said, "Send them." So they sent the fifty men, who searched for three days without finding him.ⁱ ¹⁸When they returned to Elisha in Jericho, where he was staying, he said to them, "Did I not tell you not to go?"

¹⁹ʲThe inhabitants of the city complained to Elisha, "The site of the city is fine indeed, as my lord can see, but the water is bad and the land sterile." ²⁰Elisha said, "Bring me a new bowl and put salt into it." When they had brought it to him, ²¹he went out to the spring and threw salt into it, saying, "Thus says the LORD: I have purified this water. Never again shall death or sterility come from it." ²²And the water has stayed pure even to this day, according to the word Elisha had spoken.

²³§From there Elisha went up to Bethel. While he was on the way, some little boys came out of the city and jeered at him: "Go away, baldy; go away, baldy!" ²⁴The prophet turned and saw them, and he cursed them in the name of the LORD. Then two she-bears came out of the woods and tore forty-two of the children to pieces.

²⁵From there he went to Mount Carmel, and returned to Samaria from there.

# VII. STORIES OF ELISHA AND JORAM¶

## CHAPTER 3

**Reign of Joram of Israel.** ¹Joram, son of Ahab, became king over Israel in Samaria in the

---

Here the route of the prophets' journey rules out the most famous Gilgal (Jos 4–5), the one near Jericho. This Gilgal may have been located in the area of modern Jiljulieh, approximately seven miles north of Bethel, which seems to preserve the ancient name.

*[2:9] **Double portion of your spirit:** as the firstborn son inherited a double portion of his father's property (Dt 21:17), so Elisha asks to inherit from Elijah his spirit of prophecy in the degree befitting his principal disciple. In Nm 11:17–25, God bestows some of the spirit of Moses on others.

†[2:12] **My father:** a religious title accorded prophetic leaders; cf. 6:21; 8:9; and 13:14, where King Joash of Israel reacts to Elisha's own impending death with the same words Elisha uses here.

‡[2:14] **The LORD, the God of Elijah—where is he now?:** the words in Hebrew have an incantatory quality, as if Elisha is invoking both the divine name and the name of his departed master in an attempt to duplicate Elijah's miracle.

§[2:23–24] This story probably was told to warn children of the importance of respect for prophets.

¶[3:1–9:13] After the formulaic introduction to the reign of Joram of Israel, this section falls into two parts. The first contains several stories about the prophet Elisha, both in private and in public life. There are four longer stories, arranged in an ABBA pattern: drought during war with Moab (vv. 4–27), restoration of the Shunammite's son (4:8–37), healing of Naaman (5:1–27), famine during war with Aram (6:24–7:20). The last three of these stories are each preceded and followed by short anecdotal tales about Elisha. The second part of this section turns to the political realm. Elisha carries out the Lord's commissions to Elijah (1 Kgs 19:15–17) to anoint Hazael king of Aram (2 Kgs 8:7–15) and Jehu king of Israel (9:1–13). To prepare for the story of Jehu's insurrection (9:14–11:20), the narrator places between those two narratives notices about the royal succession in Judah (8:16–24, 25–29). The formulaic conclusions to the reigns of Joram of Israel and Ahaziah of Judah (8:25–29) are missing, since the deaths of both will be recounted in the story of Jehu's insurrection.

---

d. [2:8] Ex 14:15–22; Jos 3:14–17.    e. [2:9–15] Nm 11:16–17, 24–29.    f. [2:11] Gn 5:24; 1 Mc 2:58; Sir 48:9–12; Acts 1:9.

g. [2:15] 1 Kgs 19:19; Sir 48:12.    h. [2:16] 1 Kgs 18:12.    i. [2:17] 1 Kgs 17:2; 18:10.    j. [2:19–22] 2 Kgs 4:38–41.

eighteenth year of Jehoshaphat, king of Judah, and he reigned twelve years.*

²⁴He did what was evil in the LORD's sight, though not like his father and mother. He did away with the pillar of Baal that his father had made, ³but he still held fast unceasingly to the sins which Jeroboam, son of Nebat, caused Israel to commit.

**War Against Moab: Drought.** ⁴†Now Mesha, king of Moab, who raised sheep, used to pay the king of Israel as tribute a hundred thousand lambs and the wool of a hundred thousand rams. ⁵But when Ahab died, the king of Moab rebelled against the king of Israel. ⁶King Joram set out from Samaria and mustered all Israel. ⁷Then he sent Jehoshaphat, the king of Judah, the message: "The king of Moab has rebelled against me. Will you come with me to Moab to fight?" He replied, "I will. You and I are as one, your people and my people, and your horses and my horses as well." ⁸He said, "By what route shall we attack?" and the other said, "By way of the wilderness of Edom."

⁹So the king of Israel set out, accompanied by the king of Judah and the king of Edom. After a roundabout journey of seven days the water gave out for the army and for the animals with them. ¹⁰The king of Israel exclaimed, "Alas! The LORD has called three kings together only to deliver us into the power of Moab." ¹¹But Jehoshaphat asked, "Is there no prophet of the LORD here through whom we may inquire of the LORD?" One of the servants of the king of Israel replied, "Elisha, son of Shaphat, who poured water on the hands of Elijah,‡ is here." ¹²Jehoshaphat agreed, "He has the word of

the LORD." So the king of Israel, along with Jehoshaphat and the king of Edom, went down to Elisha. ¹³Elisha asked the king of Israel, "What do you want with me? Go to the prophets of your father and to the prophets of your mother." The king of Israel replied, "No, the LORD has called these three kings together only to deliver us into the power of Moab." ¹⁴Then Elisha said, "As the LORD of hosts lives, whom I serve, were it not that I respect Jehoshaphat, the king of Judah, I should neither look at you nor notice you at all. ¹⁵Now get me a minstrel." When the minstrel played, the hand of the LORD came upon Elisha, ¹⁶and he announced: "Thus says the LORD: Provide many catch basins in this wadi. ¹⁷For the LORD says: Though you will see neither wind nor rain, yet this wadi will be filled with water for you to drink, and for your livestock and pack animals. ¹⁸And since the LORD does not consider this enough, he will also deliver Moab into your power. ¹⁹You shall destroy every fortified city and every choice city, fell every fruit tree, stop up all the springs, and ruin every fertile field with stones."ᵐ

²⁰In the morning, at the time of the sacrifice, water came from the direction of Edom and filled the land.

²¹Meanwhile, all Moab had heard that the kings had come to war against them; troops from the youngest on up were mobilized and stationed at the border. ²²When they rose early that morning, the sun was shining across the water. The Moabites saw the water as red as blood, ²³and said, "This is blood! The kings have fought among themselves and killed one another. Quick! To the spoils, Moab!" ²⁴But when they reached the camp of Israel, the Israelites rose up and attacked the Moabites, who fled from them. They ranged through the countryside destroying Moab— ²⁵leveling the cities, each one casting the stones onto every fertile field and filling it, stopping up every spring, felling every fruit tree, until only the stones of Kir-hareseth§ remained. Then the slingers surrounded and attacked it. ²⁶When he saw that the battle was going against him, the king of Moab took seven hundred swordsmen to break through to the king of Edom, but he failed. ²⁷So he took his firstborn, who was to succeed him as king, and offered him as a burnt offering upon the wall. The wrath against Israel¶ was so great that they gave up the siege and returned to their own land.ⁿ

---

**CHAPTER 4**

**The Widow's Oil.** ¹ᵒA certain woman, the widow of one of the guild prophets, cried out

---

*[3:1] The contradiction between 1:17 and v. 1 regarding the year when Joram succeeded Ahaziah of Israel makes any reconstruction of the chronology of Israel's and Judah's kings uncertain. Some scholars think that one or the other notice is simply incorrect. Others propose to explain the discrepancy by a co-regency: Jehoshaphat of Judah would have shared the throne with his son Joram from Jehoshaphat's seventeenth year until he died in the twenty-fifth year of his reign (1 Kgs 22:42; see also 2 Kgs 8:16). The issue is further complicated by the speculation of some historians that "Joram of Israel" ("son" of Ahab of Israel: v. 1) and "Joram of Judah" ("son-in-law" of Ahab of Israel: 8:18) were in fact the same person, in whom the royal houses and separate realms of Israel and Judah were briefly reunited.

†[3:4] In the period of oral tradition, it seems that stories of kings were often told without identifying the kings by name. (Vestiges of this anonymity are still visible in 1 Kgs 3:16–28; 20:1–43; 22:1–38; 2 Kgs 6:8–7:20.) Names (such as "Ahab" in 1 Kgs 20:13–14; 22:20) were added later. As a consequence, the historical attachment of such stories to the kings about whom they are told is open to question. (See note on 1 Kgs 20:1–22:54.) The present story about a campaign against Moab by Joram and Jehoshaphat has several striking similarities to the campaign against Ramoth-gilead by Ahab and Jehoshaphat in 1 Kgs 22:1–38. There exists a Moabite inscription that contains Mesha's self-aggrandizing account of his successful rebellion against Israel, but the times and places it mentions are different from those implied in vv. 4–27.

‡[3:11] **Poured water on the hands of Elijah:** possibly a metaphor for "was Elijah's servant." But the phrase occurs nowhere else in the Old Testament and its meaning is not certain.

§[3:25] **Kir-hareseth:** a major city of Moab, identified with modern Kerak, east of the Dead Sea; cf. Is 16:7, 11; Jer 48:31, 36.

¶[3:27] **The wrath against Israel:** probably the wrath of Chemosh, the Moabite god to whom the child was offered. The Israelites, intimidated by this wrath, retreat.

---

k. [3:2] 1 Kgs 16:32.    l. [3:7–11] 1 Kgs 22:3–8.

m. [3:19] Dt 20:19.    n. [3:27] Jgs 11:30–31.    o. [4:1–7] 1 Kgs 17:8–16.

to Elisha: "My husband, your servant, is dead. You know that he revered the LORD, yet now his creditor has come to take my two children into servitude." [2]Elisha answered her, "What am I to do for you? Tell me what you have in the house." She replied, "This servant of yours has nothing in the house but a jug of oil." [3]He said, "Go out, borrow vessels from all your neighbors—as many empty vessels as you can. [4]Then come back and close the door on yourself and your children; pour the oil into all the vessels, and as each is filled, set it aside." [5]So she went out. She closed the door on herself and her children and, as they handed her the vessels, she would pour in oil. [6]When all the vessels were filled, she said to her son, "Bring me another vessel." He answered, "There is none left." And then the oil stopped. [7]She went and told the man of God, who said, "Go sell the oil to pay off your creditor; with what remains, you and your children can live."

**Elisha Raises the Shunammite's Son.** [8]One day Elisha came to Shunem, where there was a woman of influence, who pressed him to dine with her. Afterward, whenever he passed by, he would stop there to dine. [9]So she said to her husband, "I know that he is a holy man of God. Since he visits us often, [10]let us arrange a little room on the roof and furnish it for him with a bed, table, chair, and lamp, so that when he comes to us he can stay there."*p*

[11]One day Elisha arrived and stayed in the room overnight. [12]Then he said to his servant Gehazi, "Call this Shunammite woman." He did so, and when she stood before Elisha, [13]he told Gehazi, "Say to her, 'You have troubled yourself greatly for us; what can we do for you? Can we say a good word for you to the king or to the commander of the army?'" She replied, "I am living among my own people."† [14]Later Elisha asked, "What can we do for her?" Gehazi answered, "She has no son, and her husband is old." [15]Elisha said, "Call her." He did so, and when she stood at the door, [16]Elisha promised, "This time next year you will be cradling a baby son." She said, "My lord, you are a man of God; do not deceive your servant."*q* [17]Yet the woman conceived, and by the same time the following year she had given birth to a son, as Elisha had promised; [18]and the child grew up healthy.*r*

One day the boy went out to his father among the reapers. [19]He said to his father, "My head! My head!" And his father said to the servant, "Carry him to his mother." [20]The servant picked him up and carried him to his mother; he sat in her lap until noon, and then died. [21]She went upstairs and laid him on the bed of the man of God. Closing the door on him, she went out [22]and called to her husband, "Let me have one of the servants and a donkey. I must go quickly to the man of God, and I will be back." [23]He asked, "Why are you going to him today? It is neither the new moon nor the sabbath." But she said, "It is all right." [24]When the donkey was saddled, she said to her servant, "Lead on! Do not stop my donkey unless I tell you." [25]She kept going till she reached the man of God on Mount Carmel. When he saw her at a distance, the man of God said to his servant Gehazi: "There is the Shunammite! [26]Hurry to meet her, and ask if everything is all right with her, with her husband, and with the boy." "Everything is all right," she replied. [27]But when she reached the man of God on the mountain, she clasped his feet. Gehazi came near to push her away, but the man of God said: "Let her alone, she is in bitter anguish; the LORD hid it from me and did not let me know." [28]She said, "Did I ask my lord for a son? Did I not say, 'Do not mislead me'?" [29]He said to Gehazi, "Get ready for a journey. Take my staff with you and be off; if you meet anyone, give no greeting,‡ and if anyone greets you, do not answer. Lay my staff upon the boy." [30]But the boy's mother cried out: "As the LORD lives and as you yourself live, I will not release you." So he started back with her.

[31]Meanwhile, Gehazi had gone on ahead and had laid the staff upon the boy, but there was no sound, no response. He returned to meet Elisha and told him, "The boy has not awakened." [32]When Elisha reached the house, he found the boy dead, lying on the bed. [33]He went in, closed the door on them both, and prayed to the LORD. [34]Then he lay upon the child on the bed, placing his mouth upon the child's mouth, his eyes upon the eyes, and his hands upon the hands. As Elisha stretched himself over the child, the boy's flesh became warm.*s* [35]He arose, paced up and down the room, and then once more stretched himself over him, and the boy sneezed seven times and opened his eyes.*t* [36]Elisha summoned Gehazi and said, "Call the Shunammite." He called her, and she came to him, and Elisha said to her, "Take your son." [37]She came in and fell at his feet in homage; then she took her son and left.

**The Poisoned Stew.** [38u]When Elisha returned to Gilgal, there was a famine in the land. Once, when the guild prophets were seated before

---

\*[4:1] **His creditor . . . into servitude:** Israelite law permitted the selling of wife and children into slavery for debt; cf. Ex 21:7; Am 2:6; 8:6; Is 50:1.

†[4:13] **I am living among my own people:** the Shunammite woman declines Elisha's offer. Surrounded by the support of her family and her clan, she is secure. Ironically, at some point in the future Elisha's advice will send her to live among foreigners (see 8:1–2).

‡[4:29] **Give no greeting:** a profuse exchange of greetings and compliments would normally surround the chance encounter of acquaintances on the road. This would, however, take time, and Gehazi's mission was urgent. Compare Lk 10:4.

p. [4:10] 1 Kgs 17:9.   q. [4:16] Gn 18:9–15.   r. [4:18–37] 1 Kgs 17:17–24; Lk 7:11–16; Acts 20:10–12.

s. [4:34–37] Sir 48:13.   t. [4:35] Heb 11:35.   u. [4:38–41] 2 Kgs 2:19–22.

him, he said to his servant, "Put the large pot on, and make some vegetable stew for the guild prophets." ³⁹Someone went out into the field to gather herbs and found a wild vine, from which he picked a sackful of poisonous wild gourds. On his return he cut them up into the pot of vegetable stew without anybody's knowing it. ⁴⁰The stew was served, but when they began to eat it, they cried, "Man of God, there is death in the pot!" And they could not eat it. ⁴¹He said, "Bring some meal." He threw it into the pot and said, "Serve it to the people to eat." And there was no longer anything harmful in the pot.

**The Barley Loaves.** ⁴²ᵛA man came from Baal-shalishah bringing the man of God twenty barley loaves made from the first fruits, and fresh grain in the ear. Elisha said, "Give it to the people to eat." ⁴³But his servant objected, "How can I set this before a hundred?" Elisha again said, "Give it to the people to eat, for thus says the LORD: You will eat and have some left over." ⁴⁴He set it before them, and when they had eaten, they had some left over, according to the word of the LORD.

### CHAPTER 5

**Elisha Cures Naaman's Leprosy.** ¹Naaman, the army commander of the king of Aram, was highly esteemed and respected by his master, for through him the LORD had brought victory to Aram. But valiant as he was, the man was a leper.* ²Now the Arameans had captured from the land of Israel in a raid a little girl, who became the servant of Naaman's wife. ³She said to her mistress, "If only my master would present himself to the prophet in Samaria! He would cure him of his leprosy." ⁴Naaman went and told his master, "This is what the girl from the land of Israel said." ⁵The king of Aram said, "Go. I will send along a letter to the king of Israel." So Naaman set out, taking along ten silver talents, six thousand gold pieces, and ten festal garments.

⁶He brought the king of Israel the letter, which read: "With this letter I am sending my servant Naaman to you, that you may cure him of his leprosy." ⁷When he read the letter, the king of Israel tore his garments and exclaimed: "Am I a god with power over life and death, that this man should send someone for me to cure him of leprosy? Take note! You can see he is only looking for a quarrel with me!"ʷ ⁸When Elisha, the man of God, heard that the king of Israel had torn his garments, he sent word to the king: "Why have you torn your garments? Let him

come to me and find out that there is a prophet in Israel."

⁹Naaman came with his horses and chariot and stopped at the door of Elisha's house. ¹⁰Elisha sent him the message: "Go and wash seven times in the Jordan, and your flesh will heal, and you will be clean."ˣ ¹¹But Naaman went away angry, saying, "I thought that he would surely come out to me and stand there to call on the name of the LORD his God, and would move his hand over the place, and thus cure the leprous spot. ¹²Are not the rivers of Damascus, the Abana and the Pharpar, better than all the waters of Israel? Could I not wash in them and be cleansed?"† With this, he turned about in anger and left.

¹³But his servants came up and reasoned with him: "My father, if the prophet told you to do something extraordinary, would you not do it? All the more since he told you, 'Wash, and be clean'?" ¹⁴So Naaman went down and plunged into the Jordan seven times, according to the word of the man of God. His flesh became again like the flesh of a little child, and he was clean.ʸ

¹⁵He returned with his whole retinue to the man of God. On his arrival he stood before him and said, "Now I know that there is no God in all the earth, except in Israel. Please accept a gift from your servant."ᶻ ¹⁶Elisha replied, "As the LORD lives whom I serve, I will not take it." And despite Naaman's urging, he still refused. ¹⁷Naaman said: "If you will not accept, please let me, your servant, have two mule-loads of earth,‡ for your servant will no longer make burnt offerings or sacrifices to any other god except the LORD. ¹⁸But may the LORD forgive your servant this: when my master enters the temple of Rimmon to bow down there, as he leans upon my arm, I too must bow down in the temple of Rimmon. When I bow down in the temple of Rimmon, may the LORD please forgive your servant this." ¹⁹Elisha said to him, "Go in peace."§

Naaman had gone some distance ²⁰when Gehazi, the servant of Elisha, the man of God, thought to himself: "My master was too easy on this Aramean Naaman, not accepting what he brought. As the LORD lives, I will run after him and get something out of him." ²¹So Gehazi hurried after Naaman. Seeing that someone was running after him, Naaman alighted from his chariot to wait for him. He asked, "Is everything all right?" ²²Gehazi replied, "Yes, but my master

---

†[5:12] **Wash in them and be cleansed:** typical of the ambiguity in ritual healing or cleanliness. The muddy waters of the Jordan are no match hygienically for the mountain spring waters of Damascus; ritually, it is the other way around.

‡[5:17] **Two mule-loads of earth:** worship of the Lord is associated with the soil of the Holy Land, where he is present.

§[5:19] **Go in peace:** Elisha understands and approves the situation of Naaman who, though now a worshiper of the God of Israel, is required by his courtly office to assist his master, the king ("leans upon my arm," v. 18), worshiping in the temple of the Canaanite god Baal-Rimmon.

---

*[5:1] **Leper:** the terms traditionally translated "leper" and "leprosy" covered a wide variety of skin disorders like psoriasis, eczema, and seborrhea, but probably not Hansen's disease (modern "leprosy"); there is no clear evidence of its existence in biblical times.

v. [4:42–44] Mt 14:13–21; 15:32–38; Mk 6:34–44; 8:1–9; Lk 9:10–17; Jn 6:1–13.   w. [5:7] 1 Sm 2:6; Jn 5:21.

x. [5:10] Jn 9:7.   y. [5:14] Lk 4:27.   z. [5:15] Lk 17:17–19.

sent me to say, 'Two young men have just come to me, guild prophets from the hill country of Ephraim. Please give them a talent of silver and two festal garments.'" ²³Naaman said, "I insist! Take two talents," and he pressed him. He tied up two silver talents in bags and gave them, with two festal garments, to two of his servants, who carried them before Gehazi. ²⁴When he reached the hill, Gehazi received these things, appropriated them for his house, and sent the men on their way.

²⁵He went in and stood by Elisha his master, who asked him, "Where have you been, Gehazi?" He answered, "Your servant has not gone anywhere." ²⁶But Elisha said to him: "Was I not present in spirit when someone got down from his chariot to wait for you? Is this a time to take money or to take garments, olive orchards or vineyards, sheep or cattle, male or female servants? ²⁷The leprosy of Naaman shall cling to you and your descendants forever." And Gehazi went out, a leper with skin like snow.*

## CHAPTER 6

**The Lost Ax.** ¹The guild prophets once said to Elisha: "This place where we live with you is too cramped for us. ²Let us go to the Jordan, where by getting one beam apiece we can build ourselves a place to live." Elisha said, "Go." ³One of them requested, "Please agree to accompany your servants." He replied, "Yes, I will come."

⁴So he went with them, and when they arrived at the Jordan they began to cut down trees. ⁵While one of them was felling a tree trunk, the iron ax blade slipped into the water. He cried out, "Oh, no, master! It was borrowed!" ⁶"Where did it fall?" asked the man of God. When he pointed out the spot, Elisha cut off a stick, threw it into the water, and brought the iron to the surface. ⁷He said, "Pick it up." And the man stretched out his hand and grasped it.

**The Aramean Ambush.** ⁸When the king of Aram was waging war on Israel, he would make plans with his servants: "I will bivouac at such and such a place." ⁹But the man of God would send word to the king of Israel, "Be careful! Do not pass by this place, for Aram will attack there." ¹⁰So the king of Israel would send word to the place which the man of God had indicated, and alert it; then they would be on guard. This happened several times.

¹¹Greatly disturbed over this, the king of Aram called together his officers and asked them, "Will you not tell me who among us is for the king of Israel?" ¹²"No one, my lord king," answered one of the officers. "The Israelite prophet Elisha can tell the king of Israel the very

words you speak in your bedroom." ¹³He said, "Go, find out where he is, so that I may take him captive."

Informed that Elisha was in Dothan, ¹⁴he sent there a strong force with horses and chariots. They arrived by night and encircled the city. ¹⁵Early the next morning, when the servant of the man of God arose and went out, he saw the force with its horses and chariots surrounding the city. "Alas!" he said to Elisha. "What shall we do, my lord?" ¹⁶Elisha answered, "Do not be afraid. Our side outnumbers theirs." ¹⁷Then he prayed, "O LORD, open his eyes, that he may see." And the LORD opened the eyes of the servant, and he saw that the mountainside was filled with fiery chariots and horses around Elisha.ᵃ

¹⁸When the Arameans came down to get him, Elisha prayed to the LORD, "Strike this people blind, I pray you." And the LORD struck them blind, according to Elisha's word. ¹⁹Then Elisha said to them: "This is the wrong road, and this is the wrong city. Follow me! I will take you to the man you want." And he led them to Samaria. ²⁰When they entered Samaria, Elisha prayed, "O LORD, open their eyes that they may see." The LORD opened their eyes, and they saw that they were inside Samaria. ²¹When the king of Israel saw them, he asked, "Shall I kill them, my father? Shall I kill them?" ²²Elisha replied, "You must not kill them. Do you slay those whom you have taken captive with your sword or bow?† Serve them a meal. Let them eat and drink, and then go back to their master." ²³The king spread a great feast for them. When they had eaten and drunk he sent them away, and they went back to their master. No more Aramean raiders came into the land of Israel.

**War Against Aram: Famine.** ²⁴After this, Benhadad, king of Aram, mustered his whole army and laid siege to Samaria. ²⁵Because of the siege the famine in Samaria was so severe that a donkey's head sold for eighty pieces of silver, and a fourth of a kab of "dove droppings"‡ for five pieces of silver.

²⁶ᵇOne day, as the king of Israel was walking on the city wall, a woman cried out to him, "Save us, my lord king!" ²⁷He replied, "If the LORD does not save you, where could I find means to save you? On the threshing floor? In the wine press?" ²⁸Then the king asked her, "What is your trouble?" She replied: "This woman said to me, 'Give up your son that we may eat him

---

†[6:22] **With your sword or bow:** since the king would not slay prisoners who had surrendered to his power, much less should he slay prisoners captured by God's power. This wartime practice stands in contrast to that of holy war, where prisoners were placed under the ban and so devoted to destruction (see 1 Kgs 20:35–43).

‡[6:25] **"Dove droppings":** it is unclear whether this phrase is to be read literally (e.g., dung used as fuel) or as the nickname of a type of edible plant, as attested in Arabic. A kab was probably around a quart.

---

*[5:27] **With skin like snow:** "snow" is often used to describe the skin conditions covered by the term "leprosy" (Ex 4:6; Nm 12:10; see note on 5:1). It is unclear whether the comparison is with the white color, dry flakes, or moist shine, any of which can occur in the relevant skin diseases.

a. [6:17] 2 Kgs 2:11; 7:6; Ps 68:18.    b. [6:26–29] Dt 28:53–57.

today; then tomorrow we will eat my son.' ²⁹So we boiled my son and ate him. The next day I said to her, 'Now give up your son that we may eat him.' But she hid her son." ³⁰When the king heard the woman's words, he tore his garments. And as he was walking on the wall, the people saw that he was wearing sackcloth underneath, next to his skin.

³¹The king exclaimed, "May God do thus to me, and more, if the head of Elisha, son of Shaphat, stays on him today!"

³²Meanwhile, Elisha was sitting in his house in conference with the elders. The king had sent one of his courtiers; but before the messenger reached him, Elisha said to the elders: "Do you know that this murderer is sending someone to cut off my head? When the messenger comes, see that you close the door and hold it fast against him. His master's footsteps are echoing behind him." ³³While Elisha was still speaking, the messenger came down to him and said, "This evil is from the LORD. Why should I trust in the LORD any longer?"

## CHAPTER 7

¹Elisha replied: "Hear the word of the LORD! Thus says the LORD: At this time tomorrow a seah of fine flour will sell for a shekel, and two seahs of barley for a shekel, in the market† of Samaria." ²But the adjutant, upon whose arm the king leaned, answered the man of God, "Even if the LORD were to make windows in heaven, how could this happen?" Elisha said, "You shall see it with your own eyes, but you shall not eat of it."

³At the city gate four lepers were asking one another, "Why should we sit here until we die?ᶜ ⁴If we decide to go into the city, we shall die there, for there is famine in the city. If we remain here, we shall die too. So come, let us desert to the camp of the Arameans. If they let us live, we live; if they kill us, we die." ⁵At twilight they left for the Arameans; but when they reached the edge of the camp, no one was there. ⁶ᵈThe Lord had caused the army of the Arameans to hear the sound of chariots and horses, the sound of a large army, and they had reasoned among themselves, "The king of Israel has hired the kings of the Hittites and the kings of Egypt to fight us." ⁷Then in the twilight they had fled, abandoning their tents, their horses, and their donkeys, the whole camp just as it was, and fleeing for their lives.

⁸After the lepers reached the edge of the camp, they went first into one tent, ate and drank, and took silver, gold, and clothing from it, and went out and hid them. Back they came into another tent, took things from it, and again went out and hid them. ⁹Then they said to one another: "We are not doing right. This is a day of good news, and we are keeping silent. If we wait until morning breaks, we will be blamed. So come, let us go and inform the palace." ¹⁰They came and summoned the city gatekeepers. They said, "We went to the camp of the Arameans, but no one was there—not a human voice, only the horses and donkeys tethered, and the tents just as they were left." ¹¹The gatekeepers announced this and it was reported within the palace.

¹²Though it was night, the king got up; he said to his servants, "Let me tell you what the Arameans have done to us. Knowing that we are starving, they have left their camp to hide in the field. They are thinking, 'The Israelites will leave the city and we will take them alive and enter it.'" ¹³ᵗOne of his servants, however, suggested: "Let some of us take five of the horses remaining in the city—they are just like the whole throng of Israel that has reached its limit—and let us send scouts to investigate." ¹⁴They took two chariots, and horses, and the king sent them to reconnoiter the Aramean army with the order, "Go and find out." ¹⁵They followed the Arameans as far as the Jordan, and the whole route was strewn with garments and other objects that the Arameans had thrown away in their haste. The messengers returned and told the king. ¹⁶The people went out and plundered the camp of the Arameans.

Then a seah of fine flour sold for a shekel and two seahs of barley for a shekel, according to the word of the LORD. ¹⁷The king had put in charge of the gate the officer upon whose arm he leaned; but the people trampled him to death at the gate, just as the man of God had predicted when the messenger came down to him. ¹⁸This was in accordance with the word the man of God spoke to the king: "Two seahs of barley will sell for a shekel, and a seah of fine flour for a shekel at this time tomorrow in the market of Samaria." ¹⁹The adjutant had answered the man of God, "Even if the LORD were to make windows in heaven, how could this happen?" And Elisha had replied, "You shall see it with your own eyes, but you shall not eat of it." ²⁰And that is what happened to him, for the people trampled him to death at the gate.

## CHAPTER 8

**The Shunammite's Return.** ¹Elisha once said to the woman whose son he had restored to life: "Get ready! Leave with your household and live wherever you can, because the LORD has decreed a seven-year famine which is coming upon the land."ᵉ ²The woman got ready and did as the man of God said, setting out with her

---

*[6:33] The messenger speaks in the king's name. Similarly, Elisha's response in the next verse can be spoken of as delivered to the king (7:18).

†[7:1] **Market**: lit., "gate," the principal place of trading in ancient walled cities in time of peace.

‡[7:13] The Hebrew of this verse is difficult and its meaning is uncertain.

c. [7:3] Lv 13:46.   d. [7:6–7] 2 Kgs 6:17; 2 Sm 5:24.

e. [8:1] 2 Kgs 4:18–37.

household, and living in the land of the Philistines for seven years.

³At the end of the seven years, the woman returned from the land of the Philistines and went out to the king to appeal for her house and her field. ⁴The king was talking with Gehazi, the servant of the man of God: "Tell me all the great things that Elisha has done." ⁵Just as he was telling the king how his master had restored a dead person to life, the very woman whose son Elisha had restored to life came to the king appealing for her house and field. Gehazi said, "My lord king, this is the woman, and this is that son of hers whom Elisha restored to life." ⁶The king questioned the woman, and she told him her story. With that the king placed an official* at her disposal, saying, "Restore all her property to her, with all that the field produced from the day she left the land until now."

**Elisha and Hazael of Aram.**† ⁷Elisha came to Damascus at a time when Ben-hadad, king of Aram, lay sick. When he was told, "The man of God has come here," ⁸the king said to Hazael, "Take a gift with you and go call on the man of God. Consult the LORD through him, 'Will I recover from this sickness?'"ᵍ ⁹Hazael went to visit him, carrying a present, and with forty camel loads of the best goods of Damascus. On his arrival, he stood before Elisha and said, "Your son Ben-hadad, king of Aram, has sent me to you to ask, 'Will I recover from my sickness?'" ¹⁰Elisha answered, "Go and tell him, 'You will surely recover.' But the LORD has showed me that he will surely die." ¹¹Then he stared him down until he became ill at ease. The man of God wept, ¹²and Hazael asked, "Why are you weeping, my lord?" Elisha replied, "Because I know the evil that you will inflict upon the Israelites. You will burn their fortresses, you will slay their youth with the sword, you will dash their little children to pieces, you will rip open their pregnant women."ʰ ¹³Hazael exclaimed, "How can your servant, a dog‡ like me, do anything so important?" Elisha replied, "The LORD has showed you to me as king over Aram." ¹⁴Hazael left Elisha and returned to his master, who asked, "What did Elisha tell you?" Hazael replied, "He said, 'You will surely recover.'" ¹⁵The next day, however, Hazael took a cloth, dipped it in water, and spread it over the king's face, so that he died. And Hazael succeeded him as king.

**Reign of Joram of Judah.** ¹⁶§In the fifth year of Joram, son of Ahab, king of Israel, Joram, son of Jehoshaphat, king of Judah, became king. ¹⁷He was thirty-two years old when he became king, and he reigned eight years in Jerusalem.

¹⁸He walked in the way of the kings of Israel as the house of Ahab had done, since the daughter of Ahab was his wife; and he did what was evil in the LORD's sight. ¹⁹Even so, the LORD was unwilling to destroy Judah, for the sake of his servant David. For he had promised David that he would leave him a holding in the LORD's presence for all time.ⁱ ²⁰During Joram's reign, Edom revolted against the rule of Judah and installed a king of its own. ²¹Thereupon Joram with all his chariots crossed over to Zair. He arose by night and broke through the Edomites when they had surrounded him and the commanders of his chariots. Then his army fled homeward. ²²To this day Edom has been in revolt against the rule of Judah. Libnah also revolted at that time.ʲ

²³The rest of the acts of Joram, with all that he did, are recorded in the book of the chronicles of the kings of Judah. ²⁴Joram rested with his ancestors; he was buried with his ancestors in the City of David, and his son Ahaziah succeeded him as king.

**Reign of Ahaziah of Judah.**ᶜ ²⁵In the twelfth year of Joram, son of Ahab, king of Israel, Ahaziah, son of Joram, king of Judah, became king. ²⁶Ahaziah was twenty-two years old when he became king, and he reigned one year in Jerusalem. His mother's name was Athaliah, daughter of Omri, king of Israel.**

²⁷He walked in the way of the house of Ahab and did what was evil in the LORD's sight like the house of Ahab, since he was related to them by marriage. ²⁸He joined Joram, son of Ahab, in battle against Hazael, king of Aram, at Ramoth-gilead, where the Arameans wounded Joram.ᵏ ²⁹King Joram returned to Jezreel to be healed of the wounds which the Arameans had inflicted on him at Ramah in his battle against Hazael, king of Aram. Then Ahaziah, son of Joram, king of Judah, went down to Jezreel to visit Joram, son of Ahab, for he was sick.

# CHAPTER 9

**Elisha and Jehu of Israel.**†† ¹Elisha the prophet called one of the guild prophets and said to him:

---

§[8:16] On the apparent contradictions among 1:17, 3:1, and this verse, see note on 3:1.

¶[8:25–29] The narrative of Ahaziah's reign, like that of Joram of Israel, lacks the standard formulaic conclusion. The deaths of both kings, and indeed the obliteration of the whole house of Omri, will be recounted in the story of Jehu's insurrection.

**[8:26] It is unclear whether Athaliah was Omri's daughter (v. 26) or his granddaughter (v. 18). Perhaps "daughter" here is being used loosely for "female descendant."

††[9:1–13] Elisha carries out the commission the Lord gave Elijah in 1 Kgs 19:16. See note on 2 Kgs 3:1–9:13.

---

*[8:6] **An official**: lit., "eunuch," and perhaps actually so in this instance.

†[8:7–15] Elisha carries out the commission the Lord gave Elijah in 1 Kgs 19:15. See note on 2 Kgs 3:1–9:13.

‡[8:13] To call oneself a "dog" is to admit one's insignificance (1 Sm 24:15; 2 Sm 9:8); it is not necessarily a term of contempt, as in English. Hazael focuses on the question of his power, making no comment on the atrocities Elisha predicts he will commit.

---

f. [8:7–15] 1 Kgs 19:15.    g. [8:8] 1 Kgs 14:1–3.    h. [8:12] 2 Kgs 13:3–7.

i. [8:19] 2 Sm 7:12–16; 1 Kgs 11:36; 15:4.    j. [8:22] Gn 27:40.    k. [8:28–29] 2 Kgs 9:14–15.    l. [9:1–13] 1 Kgs 19:16.

"Get ready for a journey. Take this flask of oil with you, and go to Ramoth-gilead. ²When you get there, look for Jehu, son of Jehoshaphat, son of Nimshi. Enter and take him away from his companions and bring him into an inner chamber. ³From the flask you have, pour oil on his head, and say, 'Thus says the LORD: I anoint you king over Israel.' Then open the door and flee without delay."

⁴The aide (the prophet's aide) went to Ramoth-gilead. ⁵When he arrived, the commanders of the army were in session. He said, "I have a message for you, commander." Jehu asked, "For which one of us?" "For you, commander," he answered. ⁶Jehu got up and went into the house. Then the prophet's aide poured the oil on his head and said, "Thus says the LORD, the God of Israel: I anoint you king over the people of the LORD, over Israel. ⁷*You shall destroy the house of Ahab your master; thus will I avenge the blood of my servants the prophets, and the blood of all the other servants of the LORD shed by Jezebel. ⁸ᵐThe whole house of Ahab shall perish:

> I will cut off from Ahab's line every male,
> whether bond or free in Israel.

⁹I will make the house of Ahab like that of Jeroboam, son of Nebat, and like that of Baasha, son of Ahijah. ¹⁰In the confines of Jezreel, the dogs shall devour Jezebel so that no one can bury her." Then he opened the door and fled.

¹¹When Jehu rejoined his master's servants, they asked him, "Is all well? Why did that madman come to you?" He replied, "You know that kind of man and his talk." ¹²But they said, "Tell us another lie!" So he told them, "This is what the prophet's aide said to me, 'Thus says the LORD: I anoint you king over Israel.'" ¹³At once each took his garment, spread it under Jehu on the bare steps, blew the horn, and cried out, "Jehu is king!"

## VIII. THE END OF THE OMRID DYNASTY†

**Death of Joram of Israel.** ¹⁴ⁿJehu, son of Jehoshaphat, son of Nimshi, formed a conspiracy

against Joram. (Joram, with all Israel, had been besieging Ramoth-gilead against Hazael, king of Aram, ¹⁵but had returned to Jezreel to be healed of the wounds the Arameans had inflicted on him in the battle against Hazael, king of Aram.)

Jehu said to them, "If this is what you really want, see that no one escapes from the city to report in Jezreel."

¹⁶Then Jehu mounted his chariot and drove to Jezreel, where Joram lay ill and Ahaziah, king of Judah, had come to visit him. ¹⁷The watchman standing on the tower in Jezreel saw the troop of Jehu coming and reported, "I see chariots." Joram said, "Get a driver and send him to meet them and to ask whether all is well." ¹⁸So a horseman went out to meet him and said, "The king asks, 'Is everything all right?'" Jehu said, "What does it matter to you how things are? Get behind me." The watchman reported to the king, "The messenger has reached them, but is not returning." ¹⁹Joram sent a second horseman, who went to them and said, "The king asks, 'Is everything all right?'" "What does it matter to you how things are?" Jehu replied. "Get behind me." ²⁰The watchman reported, "He has reached them, but is not returning. The driving is like that of Jehu, son of Nimshi; he drives like a madman." ²¹ᵒ"Hitch up my chariot," said Joram, and they hitched up his chariot. Then Joram, king of Israel, and Ahaziah, king of Judah, set out, each in his own chariot, to meet Jehu. They reached him near the plot of ground of Naboth the Jezreelite.

²²When Joram recognized Jehu, he asked, "Is everything all right, Jehu?" Jehu replied, "How could everything be all right as long as all the harlotry and sorcery‡ of your mother Jezebel continues?" ²³Joram reined about and fled, crying to Ahaziah, "Treason, Ahaziah!" ²⁴But Jehu had drawn his bow and he shot Joram between the shoulders, so that the arrow went through his heart and he collapsed in his chariot. ²⁵Then Jehu said to his adjutant Bidkar, "Take him and throw him into the plot of ground in the field of Naboth the Jezreelite. For remember when you and I were driving teams behind Ahab his father, the LORD delivered this oracle against him: ²⁶As surely as I saw yesterday the blood of Naboth and the blood of his sons—oracle of the LORD—I will repay you for it in that very plot of ground—oracle of the LORD. So now take him and throw him into this plot of ground, in keeping with the word of the LORD."

**Death of Ahaziah of Judah.** ²⁷ᵖSeeing what was happening, Ahaziah, king of Judah, fled toward Beth-haggan. Jehu pursued him, shouting, "Him too!" They struck him as he rode through the pass of Gur near Ibleam, but he continued

---

*[9:7–10] The author has Elisha's emissary expand considerably the speech Elisha told him to deliver by adding the same type of prophetic indictments and sanctions as were invoked on previous occasions against the dynasties of Jeroboam (1 Kgs 14:10–11), of Baasha (1 Kgs 16:3–4), and of Ahab himself (1 Kgs 21:21–24).

†[9:14–11:20] Death pervades this section. The dynasty founded by Omri (1 Kgs 16:23) drowns in a bloodbath, taking numberless others along with it. The scenes are in three parallel sets of three: death comes (1) to Joram of Israel, Ahab's son; to Ahaziah of Judah, his son-in-law; and to Jezebel, the Baalist queen mother of Israel; (2) then to seventy descendants of Ahab; to forty-two relatives of Ahaziah of Judah; and to numerous Baal worshipers; (3) finally to Jehu of Israel; to the blood royal of Judah; and to Athaliah, the Baalist queen mother of Judah and last of the Omrids.

m. [9:8–10] 1 Kgs 14:10–11; 16:3–4; 21:21–24.    n. [9:14–15] 2 Kgs 8:28–29.

‡[9:22] **Harlotry and sorcery**: both terms are metaphors referring to Jezebel's worship of the foreign god Baal.

o. [9:21–26] 1 Kgs 21:1–24.    p. [9:27–28] 2 Chr 22:7–9.

his flight as far as Megiddo and died there. ²⁸His servants brought him in a chariot to Jerusalem and they buried him in his grave with his ancestors in the City of David. ²⁹In the eleventh year of Joram, son of Ahab, Ahaziah became king over Judah.

**Death of Jezebel.** ³⁰Jehu came to Jezreel, and when Jezebel heard of it, she shadowed her eyes, adorned her hair, and looked down from her window. ³¹As Jehu came through the gate, she cried out, "Is all well, you Zimri, murderer of your master?"�q ³²Jehu looked up to the window and shouted, "Who is on my side? Who?" At this, two or three eunuchs looked down toward him. ³³"Throw her down," he ordered. They threw her down, and some of her blood spurted against the wall and against the horses. Jehu trod over her body ³⁴and, after eating and drinking, he said: "Attend to that accursed woman and bury her; for she was the daughter of a king." ³⁵But when they went to bury her, they found nothing of her but the skull, the feet, and the hands. ³⁶They returned to Jehu, and when they told him, he said, "This is the word the LORD spoke through his servant Elijah the Tishbite: In the confines of Jezreel the dogs shall devour the flesh of Jezebel.ʳ ³⁷The corpse of Jezebel shall be like dung in the field in the confines of Jezreel, so that no one can say: This was Jezebel."

## CHAPTER 10

**Death of the Sons of Ahab of Israel.** ¹ʹAhab had seventy sons in Samaria. Jehu wrote letters and sent them to Samaria, to the elders who were rulers of Jezreel and to Ahab's guardians. Jehu wrote: ²"Since your master's sons are with you, as well as his chariots, horses, fortified city, and weaponry, when this letter reaches you ³decide which is the best and the fittest of your master's sons, place him on his father's throne, and fight for your master's house." ⁴They were overcome with fright and said, "If the two kings could not withstand him, how can we?" ⁵So the master of the palace and the chief of the city, along with the elders and the guardians, sent this message to Jehu: "We are your servants, and we will do everything you tell us. We will proclaim no one king; do whatever you think best." ⁶So Jehu wrote them a second letter: "If you are on my side and will obey me, bring along the heads of your master's sons* and come to me in Jezreel at this time tomorrow." (The seventy princes were in the care of prominent men of the city, who were rearing them.)

⁷When the letter arrived, they took the princes and slew all seventy of them, put their heads in baskets, and sent them to Jehu in Jezreel. ⁸A messenger came in and told him, "They have brought the heads of the princes." He said, "Pile them in two heaps at the gate of the city until morning."

⁹In the morning he came outside, stood there, and said to all the people: "You are guiltless, for it was I who conspired against my lord and slew him. But who killed all these? ¹⁰Know that not a single word which the LORD has spoken against the house of Ahab shall fail. The LORD has accomplished what he decreed through his servant Elijah."ᵗ ¹¹(And so Jehu slew all who were left of the house of Ahab in Jezreel, as well as all his powerful supporters, intimates, and priests, leaving him no survivor.)ᵘ ¹²Then he went back inside.

**Death of the Relatives of Ahaziah of Judah.** He set out for Samaria and, at Beth-eked-haroim on the way, ¹³Jehu came across relatives of Ahaziah, king of Judah. "Who are you?" he asked, and they said, "We are relatives of Ahaziah. We are going down to visit the princes and the family of the queen mother."† ¹⁴"Take them alive," Jehu ordered. They were taken alive, forty-two in number, then slain at the pit of Beth-eked. Not one of them survived.

¹⁵When he set out from there, Jehu met Jehonadab, son of Rechab, on the road. He greeted him and asked, "Are you with me wholeheartedly, as I am with you?" "Yes," he replied. "If you are, give me your hand." He gave him his hand, and he had him mount his chariot,ᵛ ¹⁶and said, "Come with me and see my zeal for the LORD." And they took him along in his chariot. **Slaughter of the Worshipers of Baal.** ¹⁷When he arrived in Samaria, Jehu slew all who were left of Ahab's line in Samaria, doing away with them completely, according to the word the LORD spoke to Elijah.

¹⁸Jehu gathered all the people together and said to them: "Ahab served Baal to some extent, but Jehu will serve him yet more.ʷ ¹⁹Now summon for me all Baal's prophets, all his servants, and all his priests. See that no one is absent, for I have a great sacrifice for Baal. Whoever is absent shall not live." This Jehu did as a ruse, so that he might destroy the servants of Baal.ˣ

²⁰Jehu said further, "Proclaim a solemn assembly in honor of Baal." They did so, ²¹and

---

*[10:6] **Heads of your master's sons:** Jehu's command is cleverly ambiguous. He allows the Samarian leaders to understand "heads" either literally or metaphorically as "most important individuals." Then, when the leaders decapitate Ahab's potential successors, Jehu can claim to be innocent of their blood (v. 9).

†[10:13] Since Athaliah, the queen mother in Judah, was of the Israelite royal house (8:18, 26), both the "princes" (lit., the "king's sons") and the queen mother's "family" (lit., her "sons") would belong to the royal houses of both kingdoms. They may thus be numbered among the seventy "sons of Ahab" killed in vv. 1–7. Because "sons" can refer to more remote offspring, the queen mother's "sons" may include Ahaziah's brothers, sons, nephews, as well as the "relatives" (lit., the "brothers") of Ahaziah who are speaking in this scene.

q. [9:31] 1 Kgs 16:8–13.   r. [9:36] 1 Kgs 21:23.   s. [10:1–11] Jgs 9:5; 1 Kgs 15:29; 16:11–12; 21:8.

t. [10:10] 1 Kgs 21:17–29.   u. [10:11] Hos 1:4.   v. [10:15] 1 Kgs 20:33; 1 Chr 2:55; Jer 35:1–19.   w. [10:18] 1 Kgs 16:30–33.   x. [10:19] 1 Kgs 18:19, 40.

Jehu sent word of it throughout all Israel. All the servants of Baal came; there was no one who did not come; they came to the temple of Baal, and it was filled from wall to wall. ²²Then Jehu said to the custodian of the wardrobe, "Bring out garments for all the servants of Baal." When he had brought out the garments for them, ²³Jehu, with Jehonadab, son of Rechab, entered the temple of Baal and said to the servants of Baal, "Search and be sure that there is no one who serves the LORD here with you, but only servants of Baal." ²⁴Then they proceeded to offer sacrifices and burnt offerings. Now Jehu had stationed eighty troops outside with this warning, "Any of you who lets someone escape of those whom I shall deliver into your hands shall pay life for life."

²⁵As soon as he finished offering the burnt offering, Jehu said to the guards and aides, "Go in and slay them. Let no one escape." So the guards and aides put them to the sword and cast them out. Afterward they went into the inner shrine of the temple of Baal, ²⁶and took out the pillars of the temple of Baal. They burned the shrine, ²⁷tore down the pillar of Baal, tore down the temple of Baal, and turned it into a latrine, as it remains today.

²⁸Thus Jehu destroyed Baal in Israel.

**Death of Jehu of Israel.** ²⁹However, Jehu did not desist from the sins which Jeroboam, son of Nebat, had caused Israel to commit, the golden calves at Bethel and at Dan.ʸ

³⁰The LORD said to Jehu: Because you have done well what is right in my eyes, and have done to the house of Ahab all that was in my heart, your sons to the fourth generation shall sit upon the throne of Israel.ᶻ ³¹But Jehu was not careful to walk in the law of the LORD, the God of Israel, with all his heart, since he did not desist from the sins which Jeroboam had caused Israel to commit. ³²ᵃAt that time the LORD began to dismember Israel. Hazael defeated the Israelites throughout their territory ³³east of Jordan (all the land of Gilead, of the Gadites, Reubenites, and Manassites), from Aroer on the wadi Arnon up through Gilead and Bashan.

³⁴The rest of the acts of Jehu, with all that he did and all his valor, are recorded in the book of the chronicles of the kings of Israel. ³⁵Jehu rested with his ancestors and was buried in Samaria, and his son Jehoahaz succeeded him as king. ³⁶The length of Jehu's reign over Israel was twenty-eight years in Samaria.

## CHAPTER 11

**Death of the Heirs of Ahaziah of Judah.** ¹ᵇWhen Athaliah, the mother of Ahaziah, saw that her son was dead, she began to kill off the whole royal family. ²But Jehosheba,* daughter of King Joram and sister of Ahaziah, took Joash, Ahaziah's son, and spirited him away, along with his nurse, from the bedroom where the princes were about to be slain. He was concealed from Athaliah, and so he did not die. ³For six years he remained hidden with her in the house of the LORD, while Athaliah ruled as queen over the land.

**Death of Athaliah.** ⁴But in the seventh year, Jehoiada summoned the captains of the Cariansᵗ and of the guards. He had them come to him in the house of the LORD, made a covenant with them, exacted an oath from them in the house of the LORD, and then showed them the king's son. ⁵He gave them these orders: "This is what you must do: one third of you who come on duty on the sabbath shall guard the king's house; ⁶another third shall be at the gate Sur; and the last third shall be at the gate behind the guards. You shall guard the palace on all sides, ⁷while the two of your divisions who are going off duty that week shall keep guard over the house of the LORD for the king. ⁸You shall surround the king, each with drawn weapons, and anyone who tries to approach the guard detail is to be killed; stay with the king, wherever he goes."

⁹The captains did just as Jehoiada the priest commanded. Each took his troops, both those going on duty for the week and those going off duty that week, and came to Jehoiada the priest. ¹⁰ᶜHe gave the captains King David's spear and quivers, which were in the house of the LORD. ¹¹And the guards, with drawn weapons, lined up from the southern to the northern limit of the enclosure, surrounding the altar and the temple on the king's behalf. ¹²Then Jehoiada brought out the king's son and put the crown and the testimonyᵗ upon him. They proclaimed him king and anointed him, clapping their hands and shouting, "Long live the king!"

¹³When Athaliah heard the noise made by the people, she came before them in the house of the LORD. ¹⁴When she saw the king standing by the column,§ as was the custom, and the captains and trumpeters near the king, and all the people of the land rejoicing and blowing trumpets, Athaliah tore her garments and cried out, "Treason, treason!" ¹⁵Then Jehoiada the priest

---

*[11:2] According to 2 Chr 22:11, Jehosheba was the wife of Jehoiada, the high priest. If this is historical, it would explain her access to the Temple's residential precincts.

†[11:4] **Carians:** foreign mercenaries serving as the royal bodyguard. Compare "Cherethites and Pelethites" in 1 Kgs 1:38.

‡[11:12] **Testimony:** that is, the two tablets of the law preserved in the ark in the Temple. Presumably they were placed upon the king during his installation ceremony as a reminder of the law he was to uphold.

§[11:14] **By the column:** the king's special place in the Temple court; cf. 23:3; 2 Chr 23:13. **People of the land:** in this period, the phrase referred to the important citizenry, whose influence sometimes extended to the selection of royal successors (cf. 2 Kgs 11:14–20; 15:5; 16:15; 21:24; 23:6, 30–35; 24:14; 25:3, 19). In postexilic times, by contrast, the phrase was used of the poor.

y. [10:29] 1 Kgs 12:28–30.  z. [10:30] 2 Kgs 15:12.  a. [10:32] 2 Kgs 8:12; Am 1:3.  b. [11:1–2] Jgs 9:5.

c. [11:10] 2 Sm 8:7.

instructed the captains in command of the force: "Escort her with a guard detail. If anyone follows her, let him die by the sword." For the priest had said, "She must not die in the house of the LORD." [16]So they seized her, and when she reached the Horse Gate of the king's house, she was put to death.

[17d]Then Jehoiada made a covenant between the LORD and the king and the people,* by which they would be the LORD's people; and another between the king and the people. [18]Thereupon all the people of the land went to the temple of Baal and demolished it. They shattered its altars and images completely, and slew Mattan, the priest of Baal, before the altars. Jehoiada the priest appointed a detachment for the house of the LORD, [19]and took the captains, the Carians, the guards, and all the people of the land, and they led the king down from the house of the LORD; they came through the guards' gate to the king's house, and Joash took his seat on the royal throne. [20]All the people of the land rejoiced and the city was quiet, now that Athaliah had been slain with the sword at the king's house.

## IX. KINGS OF JUDAH AND ISRAEL[†]

### CHAPTER 12

**Reign of Joash of Judah.** [1]Joash was seven years old when he became king. [2]In the seventh year of Jehu, Joash became king, and he reigned forty years in Jerusalem. His mother's name was Zibiah, from Beer-sheba.

[3]Joash did what was right in the LORD's sight as long as he lived, because Jehoiada the priest guided him, [4]though the high places did not disappear; the people continued to sacrifice and to burn incense on the high places.

[5]Joash said to the priests: "All the funds for sacred purposes that are brought to the house of the LORD—the census tax, personal redemption money—and all funds that are freely brought to the house of the LORD, [6]the priests may take for themselves, each from his own vendor. However, they must make whatever repairs on the temple may prove necessary." [7]Nevertheless, as late as the twenty-third year of the reign of King Joash, the priests had not made needed repairs on the temple. [8]Accordingly, King Joash summoned the priest Jehoiada and the other priests.

He asked, "Why do you not repair the temple? You must no longer take funds from your vendors, but you shall turn them over for the repairs." [9]So the priests agreed that they would neither take funds from the people nor make the repairs on the temple.

[10]Jehoiada the priest then took a chest, bored a hole in its lid, and set it beside the altar, on the right as one entered the house of the LORD. The priests who kept the doors would put into it all the silver that was brought to the house of the LORD. [11e]When they noticed that there was a large amount of silver in the chest, the royal scribe would come up with the high priest, and they would gather up and weigh all the silver that was in the house of the LORD. [12]The amount thus realized they turned over to the workers assigned to the house of the LORD. They in turn would pay it to the carpenters and builders working in the house of the LORD, [13]and to the masons and stone cutters, and for the purchase of the wood and hewn stone used in repairing the breaches, and for any other expenses that were necessary to repair the house of the LORD. [14]None of the valuables brought to the house of the LORD were used there to make silver basins, snuffers, bowls, trumpets, or any gold or silver article. [15]Instead, they were given to the workers, and with them they repaired the house of the LORD. [16]Moreover, no reckoning was asked of those who were provided with the funds to give to the workers, because they held positions of trust. [17]The funds from reparation offerings and from purification offerings, however, were not brought to the house of the LORD; they belonged to the priests.

[18]Then Hazael, king of Aram, came up and attacked Gath. When he had taken it, Hazael resolved to go on to attack Jerusalem. [19]Joash,[‡] king of Judah, took all the sacred offerings presented by his forebears, Jehoshaphat, Jehoram, and Ahaziah, kings of Judah, as well as his own, and all the gold there was in the treasuries of the house of the LORD and the king's house, and sent them to King Hazael of Aram, who then turned away from Jerusalem.

[20]The rest of the acts of Joash, with all that he did, are recorded in the book of the chronicles of the kings of Judah. [21]Certain of his officials[§] entered into a conspiracy and struck Joash down at Beth-millo. [22]Jozacar, son of Shimeath, and Jehozabad, son of Shomer, were the officials who struck and killed him. He was buried with

---

*[11:17] There are two covenants. One is between the Lord as one party and the people, headed by the king, as the other. The second covenant, between king and people, is comparable to that made between David and the elders of Israel at Hebron (2 Sm 5:3).

†[12:1–17:5] This section recounts briefly the reigns of the last several kings of Israel and the kings of Judah contemporary with them. As always, the accounts of the kings are given in the order in which each came to the throne, without regard to which kingdom they ruled. See note on the similar section that begins in 1 Kgs 14:21.

‡[12:19] **Joash:** in 2 Kings the name "Joash" and its variant "Jehoash" are interchangeable (see note on "Joram" and "Jehoram" at 1:17), whether in reference to the king of Judah (vv. 1–22) or his slightly later contemporary, Joash of Israel (13:10–25). Both forms are rendered "Joash" in this translation.

§[12:21] **Officials:** lit., "servants." The Hebrew *ebed* ("servant") has a wide range of meanings, always including service to another.

---

d. [11:17] 2 Kgs 23:3.

e. [12:11–16] 2 Kgs 22:3–7.

his ancestors in the City of David, and his son Amaziah succeeded him as king.

## CHAPTER 13

**Reign of Jehoahaz of Israel.** ¹In the twenty-third year of Joash, son of Ahaziah, king of Judah, Jehoahaz, son of Jehu, became king over Israel in Samaria for seventeen years.

²He did what was evil in the LORD's sight: he did not depart from following the sins that Jeroboam, son of Nebat, had caused Israel to commit. ³The LORD was angry with Israel and for a long time gave them into the power of Hazael, king of Aram, and of Ben-hadad, son of Hazael. ⁴Then Jehoahaz entreated the LORD, who heard him, since he saw the oppression to which the king of Aram had subjected Israel.ᶠ ⁵So the LORD gave Israel a savior,* and the Israelites, freed from the power of Aram, dwelt in their own tents as formerly. ⁶Nevertheless, they did not desist from the sins the house of Jeroboam had caused Israel to commit, but persisted in them. The Asherah† remained even in Samaria.ᵍ ⁷No army was left to Jehoahaz, except fifty horses with ten chariots and ten thousand foot soldiers, since the king of Aram had destroyed them and trampled them like dust.

⁸The rest of the acts of Jehoahaz, with all that he did and his valor, are recorded in the book of the chronicles of the kings of Israel. ⁹Jehoahaz rested with his ancestors; he was buried in Samaria and his son Joash succeeded him as king. **Reign of Joash of Israel.** ¹⁰In the thirty-seventh year of Joash, king of Judah, Joash, son of Jehoahaz, became king over Israel in Samaria sixteen years.

¹¹He did what was evil in the LORD's sight; he did not desist from any of the sins Jeroboam, son of Nebat, had caused Israel to commit, but persisted in them.

¹²‡The rest of the acts of Joash, with all that he did and his valor, and how he fought with Amaziah, king of Judah, are recorded in the book of the chronicles of the kings of Israel. ¹³Joash rested with his ancestors. Then Jeroboam

sat on his throne. Joash was buried in Samaria with the kings of Israel.

**Elisha's Deathbed Prophecy.** ¹⁴When Elisha was suffering from the sickness of which he was to die, Joash, king of Israel, went down to weep over him. "My father, my father!"ʰ he exclaimed, "Israel's chariot and steeds!"ʰ ¹⁵Elisha said to him, "Take bow and arrows," and he took bow and arrows. ¹⁶¶Elisha said to the king of Israel, "Rest your hand on the bow," and he rested his hand on it. Elisha placed his hands over the king's hands ¹⁷and said, "Open the window toward the east." He opened it. Elisha said, "Shoot," and he shot. He said,

> "An arrow of victory for the LORD!
>  An arrow of victory over Aram!
> You will beat Aram at Aphek and finish
>  him!"

¹⁸Then he said to the king of Israel, "Take the arrows," which he did. Elisha said to the king of Israel, "Beat the ground!" He beat the ground three times and stopped. ¹⁹The man of God became angry with him and said, "You should have beat five or six times. You would have beaten Aram and finished him. Now you will beat Aram only three times."

²⁰And so Elisha died and was buried.

At that time of year, bands of Moabites used to raid the land. ²¹Once some people were burying a man, when suddenly they saw such a raiding band. So they cast the man into the grave of Elisha, and everyone went off. But when the man came in contact with the bones of Elisha, he came back to life and got to his feet.ⁱ

²²King Hazael of Aram oppressed Israel all the days of Jehoahaz. ²³But the LORD was gracious with Israel and looked on them with compassion because of his covenant with Abraham, Isaac, and Jacob. He was unwilling to destroy them or to cast them out from his presence even up to now. ²⁴So when King Hazael of Aram died and his son Ben-hadad succeeded him as king, ²⁵Joash, son of Jehoahaz, took back from Ben-hadad, son of Hazael, the cities Hazael had taken in battle from Jehoahaz, his father. Three times Joash beat him, and thus recovered the cities of Israel.

## CHAPTER 14

**Reign of Amaziah of Judah.** ¹In the second year** of Joash, son of Jehoahaz, king of Israel,

---

*[13:5] **A savior**: i.e., a military leader (cf. Jgs 3:9, 15). Here the identity of the savior is unclear, but the reappearance of a militant Elisha in this chapter after an absence of several chapters and nearly thirty years suggests the narrator may have had him in mind. Two generations later Joash's grandson, Jeroboam II, will also "save" Israel (14:27).

†[13:6] **Asherah**: see note on Ex 34:13.

‡[13:12–13] The conclusion to the reign of Joash is given again in 14:15–16. In both places it disrupts the standard pattern followed in the Books of Kings. The account of Joash's reign ends in vv. 12–13; this leaves the story of Elisha's last illness (in which Joash figures prominently) suspended between regnal accounts, much as the story of Elisha's succession to Elijah's prophetic office (chap. 2) was suspended between the accounts of Ahaziah and Joram. In 14:15–16 the concluding formula for Joash's reign interrupts the account of the reign of Amaziah of Judah (14:1–22), much as Joash himself invaded Amaziah's kingdom (14:11–14).

§[13:14] **My father, my father**: the way the king addresses the dying Elisha echoes Elisha's address to Elijah in 2:12.

¶[13:16–19] Symbolic acts, like prophetic oracles, were understood to unleash the power they expressed. Similar symbolic acts are seen in Ex 17:8–13; Jos 8:18–20; Ez 4:1–3.

**[14:1–2] **In the second year . . . twenty-nine years in Jerusalem**: as they stand, the chronological data in the introductions to the reigns of the kings of Judah and Israel are incompatible with one another. The kings of Judah between

---

f. [13:4] 2 Kgs 14:26–27.    g. [13:6] Ex 34:13; 1 Kgs 16:33.

h. [13:14] 2 Kgs 2:12.    i. [13:21] Sir 48:14.

Amaziah, son of Joash, king of Judah, became king. ²He was twenty-five years old when he became king, and he reigned twenty-nine years in Jerusalem. His mother's name was Jehoaddin, from Jerusalem.

³He did what was right in the LORD's eyes, though not like David his father. He did just as his father Joash had done, ⁴though the high places did not disappear, and the people continued to sacrifice and to burn incense on the high places.

⁵When Amaziah had the kingdom firmly in hand, he struck down the officials who had struck down the king, his father. ⁶But their children he did not put to death, according to what is written in the book of the law of Moses, which the LORD commanded: "Parents shall not be put to death for their children, nor shall children be put to death for their parents; only for one's own crimes shall a person be put to death."ʲ

⁷Amaziah struck down ten thousand Edomites in the Salt Valley. He took Sela in battle and renamed it Joktheel, the name it has to this day.ᵏ

⁸Then Amaziah sent messengers to Joash, son of Jehoahaz, son of Jehu, king of Israel, with this message: "Come, let us meet face to face." ⁹Joash, king of Israel, sent this reply to Amaziah, king of Judah: "A thistle of Lebanon sent word to a cedar of Lebanon, 'Give your daughter to my son in marriage,' but an animal of Lebanon passed by and trampled the thistle underfoot.ˡ ¹⁰You have indeed struck down Edom, and your heart is lifted up; enjoy your glory, but stay home! Why bring misfortune and failure on yourself and on Judah with you?" ¹¹But Amaziah did not listen. So Joash, king of Israel, advanced, and he and Amaziah, king of Judah, met face to face at Beth-shemesh of Judah, ¹²and Judah was defeated by Israel, and all fled to their tents. ¹³But Amaziah, king of Judah, son of Joash, son of Ahaziah, was captured by Joash, king of Israel, at Beth-shemesh. When they came to Jerusalem Joash tore down the wall of Jerusalem, from the Gate of Ephraim to the Corner Gate, four hundred cubits. ¹⁴He took all the gold and silver and all the vessels found in the house of the LORD and in the treasuries of the king's house, and hostages as well. Then he returned to Samaria.

¹⁵The rest of the acts of Joash, what he did and his valor, and how he made war against Amaziah, king of Judah, are recorded in the book of the chronicles of the kings of Israel. ¹⁶Joash rested with his ancestors; he was buried in Samaria with the kings of Israel, and his son Jeroboam succeeded him as king.

¹⁷Amaziah, son of Joash, king of Judah, survived Joash, son of Jehoahaz, king of Israel, by fifteen years. ¹⁸The rest of the acts of Amaziah are recorded in the book of the chronicles of the kings of Judah. ¹⁹When a conspiracy was formed against him in Jerusalem, he fled to Lachish. But he was pursued to Lachish and killed there. ²⁰He was brought back on horses and was buried in Jerusalem with his ancestors in the City of David. ²¹Thereupon all the people of Judah‡ took Azariah, who was only sixteen years old, and made him king to succeed Amaziah, his father. ²²It was he who rebuilt Elath and restored it to Judah, after the king rested with his ancestors.

**Reign of Jeroboam II of Israel.** ²³In the fifteenth year of Amaziah, son of Joash, king of Judah, Jeroboam, son of Joash, king of Israel, became king in Samaria for forty-one years.

²⁴He did evil in the LORD's sight; he did not desist from any of the sins that Jeroboam, son of Nebat, had caused Israel to commit. ²⁵He restored the boundaries of Israel from Lebo-hamath to the sea of the Arabah,§ as the LORD, the God of Israel, had foretold through his servant, the prophet Jonah, son of Amittai, from Gath-hepher. ²⁶For the LORD saw the very bitter affliction of Israel, where there was neither bond nor free, no one at all to help Israel. ²⁷Since the LORD had not resolved to wipe out the name of Israel from under the heavens, he saved them through Jeroboam, son of Joash.

²⁸The rest of the acts of Jeroboam, with all that he did and his valor, how he fought, and how he regained Damascus and Hamath for Israel, are recorded in the book of the chronicles of the kings of Israel. ²⁹Jeroboam rested with his ancestors, the kings of Israel, and his son Zechariah succeeded him as king.

## CHAPTER 15

**Reign of Azariah of Judah.** ¹In the twenty-seventh year¶ of Jeroboam, king of Israel, Azariah, son of Amaziah, king of Judah, became king. ²He was sixteen years old when he became king, and he reigned fifty-two years in Jerusalem. His mother's name was Jecholiah, from Jerusalem.

³He did what was right in the LORD's sight, just as his father Amaziah had done, ⁴though the high places did not disappear, and the people continued to sacrifice and to burn incense on the high places. ⁵The LORD afflicted the king, and he was a leper until the day he died. He lived

---

Athaliah and Ahaz are assigned too many years in all to correspond to the reigns in Israel from Jehu to the fall of Samaria. Various theories have been proposed in an attempt to explain the discrepancy, such as co-regencies, or textual corruption in the process of transmission.
*[14:15–16] See note on 13:12–13.

j. [14:6] Dt 24:16; Ez 18:20.    k. [14:7] 2 Sm 8:13–14.    l. [14:9] Jgs 9:8–15.

†[14:17] See note on vv. 1–2.
‡[14:21] **All the people of Judah:** this phrase may refer to the army (compare, for example, "all Israel" in 1 Kgs 16:16–17). If this is its meaning here, then Amaziah's assassination and Azariah's succession are owing to a military coup. **Azariah:** also called Uzziah in many texts.
§[14:25] **Sea of the Arabah:** the Dead Sea. **Jonah, son of Amittai:** see note on Jon 1:1.
¶[15:1] **Twenty-seventh year:** see note on 14:1–2.

in a house apart, while Jotham, the king's son, was master of the palace and ruled the people of the land.*

⁶The rest of the acts of Azariah, and all that he did, are recorded in the book of the chronicles of the kings of Judah. ⁷Azariah rested with his ancestors, and was buried with them in the City of David, and his son Jotham succeeded him as king.

**Reign of Zechariah of Israel.** ⁸In the thirty-eighth year of Azariah, king of Judah, Zechariah, son of Jeroboam, became king over Israel in Samaria for six months.

⁹He did what was evil in the LORD's sight, as his ancestors had done, and did not desist from the sins that Jeroboam, son of Nebat, had caused Israel to commit. ¹⁰Shallum, son of Jabesh, plotted against him and struck him down at Ibleam. He killed him and reigned in his place.

¹¹As for the rest of the acts of Zechariah, these are recorded in the book of the chronicles of the kings of Israel. ¹²This was the word the LORD had spoken to Jehu: Sons of your line to the fourth generation shall sit upon the throne of Israel; and so it was.ᵐ

**Reign of Shallum of Israel.** ¹³Shallum, son of Jabesh, became king in the thirty-ninth year of Uzziah, king of Judah; he reigned one month in Samaria.

¹⁴Menahem, son of Gadi, came up from Tirzah to Samaria, and struck down Shallum, son of Jabesh, in Samaria. He killed him and reigned in his place.

¹⁵As for the rest of the acts of Shallum, with the conspiracy he carried out, these are recorded in the book of the chronicles of the kings of Israel. ¹⁶At that time, Menahem attacked Tappuah, all its inhabitants, and its whole district as far as Tirzah, because they did not let him in. He attacked them; he even ripped open all their pregnant women.

**Reign of Menahem of Israel.** ¹⁷In the thirty-ninth year of Azariah, king of Judah, Menahem, son of Gadi, became king over Israel for ten years in Samaria. ¹⁸He did what was evil in the LORD's sight as long as he lived, not desisting from the sins that Jeroboam, son of Nebat, had caused Israel to commit. ¹⁹Pul,† king of Assyria, came against the land. But Menahem gave Pul a thousand talents of silver to have his help in holding onto his kingdom. ²⁰Menahem paid out silver on behalf of Israel, that is, for all the people of substance, by giving the king of Assyria fifty shekels of silver for each one. So the king of Assyria went home and did not stay in the land.

²¹The rest of the acts of Menahem, with all that he did, are recorded in the book of the chronicles of the kings of Israel. ²²Menahem

rested with his ancestors, and his son Pekahiah succeeded him as king.

**Reign of Pekahiah of Israel.** ²³In the fiftieth year of Azariah, king of Judah, Pekahiah, son of Menahem, became king over Israel in Samaria for two years.

²⁴He did what was evil in the LORD's sight, not desisting from the sins that Jeroboam, son of Nebat, had caused Israel to commit. ²⁵His adjutant Pekah, son of Remaliah, conspired against him, and struck him down at Samaria within the palace stronghold; he had with him fifty men from Gilead. He killed him and reigned in his place. ²⁶As for the rest of the acts of Pekahiah, with all that he did, these are recorded in the book of the chronicles of the kings of Israel.

**Reign of Pekah of Israel.** ²⁷‡In the fifty-second year of Azariah, king of Judah, Pekah, son of Remaliah, became king over Israel in Samaria for twenty years.

²⁸He did what was evil in the LORD's sight, not desisting from the sins that Jeroboam, son of Nebat, had caused Israel to commit. ²⁹In the days of Pekah, king of Israel, Tiglath-pileser, king of Assyria, came and took Ijon, Abel-beth-maacah, Janoah, Kedesh, Hazor, Gilead, and Galilee—all the land of Naphtali—deporting the inhabitants to Assyria. ³⁰§Hoshea, son of Elah, carried out a conspiracy against Pekah, son of Remaliah; he struck and killed him, and succeeded him as king in the twentieth year of Jotham, son of Uzziah.

³¹As for the rest of the acts of Pekah, with all that he did, these are recorded in the book of the chronicles of the kings of Israel.

**Reign of Jotham of Judah.** ³²In the second year of Pekah, son of Remaliah, king of Israel, Jotham, son of Uzziah, king of Judah, became king. ³³He was twenty-five years old when he became king, and he reigned sixteen years in Jerusalem. His mother's name was Jerusha, daughter of Zadok.

³⁴He did what was right in the LORD's sight, just as his father Uzziah had done, ³⁵though the high places did not disappear, and the people continued to sacrifice and to burn incense on the high places. It was he who built the Upper Gate⁵ of the LORD's house.

³⁶The rest of the acts of Jotham, with what he did, are recorded in the book of the chronicles

---

*[15:5] **People of the land**: see note on 11:14.

†[15:19] **Pul**: the Babylonian throne name of the Assyrian Tiglath-pileser III; cf. v. 29.

m. [15:12] 2 Kgs 10:30.

‡[15:27] The twenty years here ascribed to Pekah are difficult to reconcile with other chronological notices about the kings. One theory would see Pekah and Menahem as rival kings over parts of a divided Israelite territory; this could explain Menahem's concern for Assyrian support (vv. 19–20) and Assyria's attack on Pekah (v. 29). See 16:1 and note on 14:1–2.

§[15:30] The twenty years here reckoned to Jotham of Judah may include his co-regency with Azariah (v. 5); otherwise they are impossible to reconcile with v. 33, which ascribes him only sixteen years. The verse also appears to contradict 16:1, which has Jotham's son and successor, Ahaz, coming to the throne while Pekah still reigns in Israel, and 17:1, which dates Hoshea's accession to the throne to the twelfth year of Ahaz.

⁵[15:35] **The Upper Gate**: also called the Gate of Benjamin; cf. Jer 20:2; Ez 9:2.

of the kings of Judah. [37]It was at that time that the LORD began to unleash Rezin, king of Aram, and Pekah, son of Remaliah, against Judah." [38]Jotham rested with his ancestors; he was buried with his ancestors in the City of David his father, and his son Ahaz succeeded him as king.

## CHAPTER 16

**Reign of Ahaz of Judah.**[*] [1]In the seventeenth year of Pekah, son of Remaliah, Ahaz, son of Jotham, king of Judah, became king. [2]Ahaz was twenty years old when he became king, and he reigned sixteen years in Jerusalem.

He did not do what was right in the sight of the LORD his God, as David his father had done. [3]He walked in the way of the kings of Israel; he even immolated his child by fire, in accordance with the abominable practices of the nations whom the LORD had dispossessed before the Israelites.[o] [4]Further, he sacrificed and burned incense on the high places, on hills, and under every green tree.[p]

[5]Then Rezin, king of Aram, and Pekah, son of Remaliah, king of Israel, came up to Jerusalem to attack it. Although they besieged Ahaz, they were unable to do battle. [6](In those days Rezin, king of Aram, recovered Elath for Aram, and drove the Judahites out of it. The Edomites then entered Elath, which they have occupied until the present.)

[7]Meanwhile, Ahaz sent messengers to Tiglath-pileser, king of Assyria, with the plea: "I am your servant and your son. Come up and rescue me from the power of the king of Aram and the king of Israel, who are attacking me." [8]Ahaz took the silver and gold that were in the house of the LORD and in the treasuries of the king's house and sent them as a present to the king of Assyria. [9]The king of Assyria listened to him and moved against Damascus, captured it, deported its inhabitants to Kir, and put Rezin to death.

[10]King Ahaz went to Damascus to meet Tiglath-pileser, king of Assyria. When he saw the altar in Damascus, King Ahaz sent to Uriah the priest a model of the altar and a detailed design of its construction. [11]Uriah the priest built an altar according to the plans which King Ahaz sent him from Damascus, and had it completed by the time King Ahaz returned from Damascus. [12]On his arrival from Damascus, the king inspected the altar; the king approached the

altar, went up [13]and sacrificed his burnt offering and grain offering, pouring out his libation, and sprinkling the blood of his communion offerings on the altar. [14]The bronze altar that stood before the LORD he brought from the front of the temple—that is, from the space between the new altar and the house of the LORD—and set it on the north side of his altar. [15]qKing Ahaz commanded Uriah the priest, "Upon the large altar sacrifice the morning burnt offering and the evening grain offering, the king's burnt offering and grain offering, and the burnt offering and grain offering of the people of the land.[†] Their libations you must sprinkle on it along with all the blood of burnt offerings and sacrifices. But the old bronze altar shall be mine for consultation." [16]Uriah the priest did just as King Ahaz had commanded. [17]King Ahaz detached the panels from the stands and removed the basins from them; he also took down the bronze sea from the bronze oxen that supported it, and set it on a stone pavement. [18]In deference to the king of Assyria he removed the sabbath canopy that had been set up in the house of the LORD and the king's outside entrance[‡] to the temple.

[19]The rest of the acts of Ahaz, with what he did, are recorded in the book of the chronicles of the kings of Judah. [20]Ahaz rested with his ancestors; he was buried with his ancestors in the City of David, and his son Hezekiah succeeded him as king.

## CHAPTER 17

**Reign of Hoshea of Israel.** [1]In the twelfth year of Ahaz, king of Judah, Hoshea, son of Elah, became king in Samaria over Israel for nine years.

[2]He did what was evil in the LORD's sight, yet not to the extent of the kings of Israel before him. [3]Shalmaneser,[§] king of Assyria, advanced against him, and Hoshea became his vassal and paid him tribute.[r] [4]But the king of Assyria found Hoshea guilty of conspiracy for sending messengers to the king of Egypt at Sais, and for failure to pay the annual tribute to the king of Assyria. So the king of Assyria arrested and imprisoned him. [5]Then the king of Assyria[¶] occupied the whole land and attacked Samaria, which he besieged for three years.

---

*[16:1–20] Firmly dated events bearing on chaps. 16–20 are: the fall of Damascus (16:9) in 732 B.C., the fall of Samaria (18:9–11) in 722/721 B.C., and Sennacherib's invasion of Judah (18:13) in 701 B.C., which both in Kings and in Is 36:1 occurs in the fourteenth year of Hezekiah. These data make it possible to connect the chronology of Israel and Judah to the larger chronology of ancient Near Eastern history, but they also complicate further the already vexed problem of inconsistencies in the biblical data about accession years and lengths of reign.

†[16:15] **People of the land:** see note on 11:14. **For consultation:** perhaps the introduction into Judah of the Babylonian practice of reading omens from animal sacrifices; cf. Ez 21:26.

‡[16:18] **Sabbath canopy . . . outside entrance:** the Hebrew is obscure, but as a vassal Ahaz must have had to divest himself of signs of sovereignty.

§[17:3] **Shalmaneser:** son and successor of the Assyrian king Tiglath-pileser III. **Vassal:** lit., "servant"; cf. 16:7; so also in 24:1.

¶[17:5] **The king of Assyria:** Shalmaneser was succeeded by Sargon II, who usurped the Assyrian throne in 722/721 B.C. In his inscriptions, Sargon claims to have captured Samaria during the first year of his reign.

---

n. [15:37] Is 7:1–16.   o. [16:3] Lv 18:21; Dt 18:10.   p. [16:4] Dt 12:2.

q. [16:15] Ex 29:38–41; Nm 28:3–8.   r. [17:3] 2 Kgs 18:9.

## X. THE END OF ISRAEL*

**Israelites Deported.** [6]In Hoshea's ninth year, the king of Assyria took Samaria, deported the Israelites to Assyria, and settled them in Halah, and at the Habor, a river of Gozan, and in the cities of the Medes.[s] [7]This came about because the Israelites sinned against the Lord, their God, who had brought them up from the land of Egypt, from under the hand of Pharaoh, king of Egypt. They venerated other gods, [8]they followed the rites of the nations whom the Lord had dispossessed before the Israelites and those that the kings of Israel had practiced. [9]They adopted unlawful practices toward the Lord, their God. They built high places in all their cities, from guard post to garrisoned town. [10]They set up pillars and asherahs[†] for themselves on every high hill and under every green tree. [11]They burned incense there, on all the high places, like the nations whom the Lord had sent into exile at their coming. They did evil things that provoked the Lord, [12]and served idols, although the Lord had told them: You must not do this.

[13]The Lord warned Israel and Judah by every prophet and seer: Give up your evil ways and keep my commandments and statutes, in accordance with the entire law which I enjoined on your ancestors and which I sent you by my servants the prophets. [14]But they did not listen. They grew as stiff-necked as their ancestors, who had not believed in the Lord, their God.[v] [15]They rejected his statutes, the covenant he had made with their ancestors, and the warnings he had given them. They followed emptiness and became empty; they followed the surrounding nations whom the Lord had commanded them not to imitate.[w] [16]They abandoned all the commandments of the Lord, their God: they made for themselves two molten calves; they made an asherah; they bowed down to all the host of heaven; they served Baal.[x] [17]They immolated their sons and daughters by fire. They practiced augury and divination. They surrendered themselves to doing what was evil in the Lord's sight, and provoked him.

[18]The Lord became enraged, and removed them from his presence. Only the tribe of Judah was left. [19]Even the people of Judah did not keep the commandments of the Lord, their God, but followed the rites practiced by Israel. [20]So the Lord rejected the entire people of Israel: he afflicted them and delivered them over to plunderers, finally casting them from his presence.[a] [21]When he tore Israel away from the house of David, they made Jeroboam, son of Nebat, king; but Jeroboam lured the Israelites away from the Lord, causing them to commit a great sin.[b] [22]The Israelites imitated Jeroboam in all the sins he committed; they would not depart from them. [23]Finally, the Lord removed Israel from his presence, just as he had declared through all his servants, the prophets. Thus Israel went into exile from their native soil to Assyria until this very day.

**Foreigners Deported to Israel.** [24]The king of Assyria brought people from Babylon, Cuthah, Avva, Hamath, and Sepharvaim, and settled them in the cities of Samaria in place of the Israelites. They took possession of Samaria and dwelt in its cities. [25]When they first settled there, they did not venerate the Lord, so he sent lions among them that killed some of them. [26]A report reached the king of Assyria: "The nations you deported and settled in the cities of Samaria do not know the proper worship of the god of the land, so he has sent lions among them that are killing them, since they do not know the law of the god of the land." [27]The king of Assyria gave the order, "Send back some of the priests you deported, to go there and settle, to teach them the proper worship of the god of the land." [28]So one of the priests who had been deported from Samaria returned and settled in Bethel, and began to teach them how to venerate the Lord.

[29]Thus each of these nations continued to make its own gods, setting them up in the shrines of the high places the Samarians had made: each nation in the cities in which they dwelt. [30]The Babylonians made Sukkot-Benot;[‡] the people of Cuth made Nergal; those from Hamath made Ashima; [31]those from Avva made Nibhaz and Tartak; and those from Sepharvaim immolated their children by fire to their city gods, King Hadad and King Anu. [32]At the same time, they were venerating the Lord, appointing from their own number priests for the high places to officiate for them in the shrines on the high places. [33]They were both venerating the Lord and serving their own gods. They followed the custom of the nations from among whom they had been deported.

---

*[17:6–41] This brief section is the Deuteronomistic historian's theological reflection on the causes and aftermath of Assyria's conquest of the Northern Kingdom. The text contrasts the Israelites, who were deported (v. 6) because they abandoned the worship of the Lord (vv. 7–23), with the foreigners who were brought into the land (v. 24) and undertook, however imperfectly, to worship the Lord alongside their own traditional deities (vv. 25–34a). The last verses recapitulate the apostasy of the Israelites (vv. 34b–40) and the syncretism of the foreigners (v. 41). This is a deliberately disparaging, and not wholly accurate, account of the origin of the Samaritans; it reflects the hostility the Judahites continued to hold toward the inhabitants of the northern territories.

†[17:10] **Asherahs:** see note on Ex 34:13.

s. [17:6] 2 Kgs 18:10–11; Tb 1:2.   t. [17:8–12] Ex 23:24; 34:13; Dt 12:2.   u. [17:13] Jer 25:5.   v. [17:14] Dt 9:13.   w. [17:15] Jer 2:5.   x. [17:16] Ex 34:13; Dt 4:19; 17:2–3; 1 Kgs 12:28; 16:33.   y. [17:17] Lv 18:21; Dt 18:10.

---

‡[17:30] **Sukkot-Benot:** several of the divine names in vv. 30–31 are problematic or conjectural. Sukkot-Benot is unknown, but the name may have been corrupted from that of Sarpanitu, the consort of the Babylonian god Marduk.

z. [17:18] Sir 48:15.   a. [17:20] Jer 25:9.   b. [17:21] 1 Kgs 12:20, 26–33; 13:34.

³⁴To this very day they continue to act according to their former customs, not venerating the LORD nor observing the statutes and regulations, the law and commandment, that the LORD enjoined on the descendants of Jacob, whom he had named Israel.ᶜ ³⁵When the LORD made a covenant with them, he commanded them: You must not venerate other gods, nor bow down to them, nor serve them, nor offer sacrifice to them,ᵈ ³⁶but only to the LORD, who brought you up from the land of Egypt with great power and outstretched arm. Him shall you venerate, to him shall you bow down, and to him shall you offer sacrifice. ³⁷You must be careful always to observe the statutes and ordinances, the law and commandment, which he wrote for you; you must not venerate other gods. ³⁸The covenant I made with you, you must not forget; you must not venerate other gods. ³⁹You must venerate only the LORD, your God; it is he who will deliver you from the power of all your enemies. ⁴⁰But they did not listen; they continued to act according to their former customs.

⁴¹But these nations were both venerating the LORD and serving their own idols. Their children and children's children are still acting like their ancestors, to this very day.

## XI. THE END OF JUDAH*

### CHAPTER 18

**Reign of Hezekiah.** ¹In the third year of Hoshea, son of Elah, king of Israel, Hezekiah, son of Ahaz, king of Judah, became king. ²He was twenty-five years old when he became king, and he reigned twenty-nine years in Jerusalem. His mother's name was Abi, daughter of Zechariah.

³He did what was right in the LORD's sight, just as David his father had done. ⁴It was he who removed the high places, shattered the pillars, cut down the asherah,† and smashed the bronze serpent Moses had made, because up to that time the Israelites were burning incense to it. (It was called Nehushtan.)ᵉ ⁵He put his trust in the LORD, the God of Israel; and neither before

nor after him was there anyone like him among all the kings of Judah. ⁶Hezekiah held fast to the LORD and never turned away from following him, but observed the commandments the LORD had given Moses. ⁷The LORD was with him, and he succeeded in all he set out to do. He rebelled against the king of Assyria and did not serve him. ⁸It was he who struck the Philistines as far as Gaza, and all its territory from guard post to garrisoned town.

⁹‡In the fourth year of King Hezekiah, which was the seventh year of Hoshea, son of Elah, king of Israel, Shalmaneser, king of Assyria, attacked Samaria and laid siege to it, ¹⁰and after three years they captured it. In the sixth year of Hezekiah, the ninth year of Hoshea, king of Israel, Samaria was taken. ¹¹The king of Assyria then deported the Israelites to Assyria and led them off to Halah, and the Habor, a river of Gozan, and the cities of the Medes. ¹²This happened because they did not obey the LORD, their God, but violated his covenant; they did not obey nor do all that Moses, the servant of the LORD, commanded.ᵍ

**Sennacherib and Hezekiah.** ¹³§In the fourteenth year of King Hezekiah, Sennacherib, king of Assyria,ᶠ attacked all the fortified cities of Judah and captured them.ʰ ¹⁴Hezekiah, king of Judah, sent this message to the king of Assyria at Lachish: "I have done wrong. Leave me, and whatever you impose on me I will bear." The king of Assyria exacted three hundred talents of silver and thirty talents of gold from Hezekiah, king of Judah. ¹⁵Hezekiah gave him all the funds there were in the house of the LORD and in the treasuries of the king's house. ¹⁶At the same time, Hezekiah removed the nave doors and the uprights of the house of the LORD, which the king of Judah had ordered to be overlaid with gold, and gave them to the king of Assyria.ᶦ

¹⁷The king of Assyria sent the general, the lord chamberlain, and the commander** from Lachish with a great army to King Hezekiah at Jerusalem. They went up and came to Jerusalem, to the conduit of the upper pool on the highway

---

*[18:1–25:30] The Books of Kings end, as they began, with the people of the Lord in a single kingdom, Judah, centered on the capital, Jerusalem, and the Solomonic Temple. The reigns of two reformer kings, both praised, are recounted at length: Hezekiah (chaps. 18–20) and Josiah (22:1–23:30). Each is followed by shorter accounts of two kings who are condemned: Manasseh and Amon (chap. 21) and Jehoahaz and Jehoiakim (23:31–24:7). The book ends with the last days of Judah under Jehoiachin and Zedekiah and the beginning of the Babylonian exile.

†[18:4] **Asherah:** see note on Ex 34:13. **Nehushtan:** the name *nehushtan* contains several wordplays in Hebrew. It recalls the word "serpent" (*nahash*), the word "bronze" (*nehoshet*), and the word "to read omens" (*nihesh*). The sentence is also unclear about who named the bronze serpent "Nehushtan"—whether Moses when he made it, or the people when they venerated it, or Hezekiah when he destroyed it.

‡[18:9] The correlations between the reigns of Hezekiah and Hoshea in vv. 9–10 conflict with other biblical data and with the date for the fall of Samaria, 722/721 B.C. (see note on 16:1–20). Since Sennacherib's invasion in the fourteenth year of Hezekiah (v. 13) took place in 701, Hezekiah cannot have been on the throne twenty years earlier. Various solutions have been proposed: scribal errors in writing the numbers; a Hezekian co-regency with his father Ahaz beginning in 729; etc. None of the solutions has won a consensus among historians.

§[18:13–20:19] This material is found also in Is 36–39, with one long addition (Is 38:9–20) and only a few other changes.

¶[18:13] Sennacherib succeeded Sargon II as king of Assyria. His Judean campaign was waged in 701 B.C. See notes on 16:1–20 and 18:9.

**[18:17] **General, the lord chamberlain . . . commander:** the text lists three major functionaries by their Assyrian titles, of which only the first, more nearly "lord lieutenant," is military in origin; the commander was technically the king's chief butler.

---

c. [17:34] Gn 32:29; 35:10.   d. [17:35–38] Ex 20:3–6.   e. [18:4] Ex 23:24; 34:13; Nm 21:4–9; Dt 12:2; Wis 16:5–7; Jn 3:14.

f. [18:10–11] 2 Kgs 17:5–6; Tb 1:2.   g. [18:12] 2 Kgs 17:6–23; Ex 24:7.   h. [18:13–19:36] Sir 48:18–21.   i. [18:16] 1 Kgs 6:31–35.

of the fuller's field, where they took their stand. [18]They called for the king, but Eliakim, son of Hilkiah, the master of the palace, came out, along with Shebnah the scribe and the chancellor Joah, son of Asaph.[j]

[19]The commander said to them, "Tell Hezekiah, 'Thus says the great king, the king of Assyria: On what do you base this trust of yours? [20]Do you think mere words substitute for strategy and might in war? In whom, then, do you place your trust, that you rebel against me? [21]Do you trust in Egypt, that broken reed of a staff, which pierces the hand of anyone who leans on it? That is what Pharaoh, king of Egypt, is to all who trust in him.[k] [22]Or do you people say to me, "It is in the LORD our God we trust!"? Is it not he whose high places and altars Hezekiah has removed, commanding Judah and Jerusalem, "Worship before this altar in Jerusalem"?'

[23]"Now, make a wager with my lord, the king of Assyria: I will give you two thousand horses if you are able to put riders on them. [24]How then can you turn back even a captain, one of the least servants of my lord, trusting, as you do, in Egypt for chariots and horses? [25]Did I come up to destroy this place without the LORD? The LORD himself said to me: Go up and destroy that land!"

[26]Then Eliakim, son of Hilkiah, and Shebnah and Joah said to the commander: "Please speak to your servants in Aramaic; we understand it. Do not speak to us in the language of Judah within earshot of the people who are on the wall." [27]But the commander replied: "Was it to your lord and to you that my lord sent me to speak these words? Was it not rather to those sitting on the wall, who, with you, will have to eat their own excrement and drink their urine?"*

[28]Then the commander stepped forward and cried out in a loud voice in the language of Judah, "Listen to the words of the great king, the king of Assyria. [29]Thus says the king: Do not let Hezekiah deceive you, for he cannot rescue you from my hand. [30]And do not let Hezekiah induce you to trust in the LORD, saying, 'The LORD will surely rescue us, and this city will not be handed over to the king of Assyria.' [31]Do not listen to Hezekiah, for thus says the king of Assyria: Make peace with me, and surrender to me! Eat, each of you, from your vine, each from your own fig tree. Drink water, each from your own well, [32]until I arrive and take you to a land like your own, a land of grain and wine, a land of bread and vineyards, a land of rich olives and honey. Live, and do not die! And do not listen to Hezekiah when he would incite you by saying, 'The LORD will rescue us.' [33]Has any of the

gods of the nations ever rescued his land from the power of the king of Assyria? [34]Where are the gods of Hamath and Arpad? Where are the gods of Sepharvaim, Hena, and Ivvah? Did they indeed rescue Samaria from my power?[†] [35]Which of the gods for all these lands ever rescued his land from my power? Will the LORD then rescue Jerusalem from my power?" [36]But the people remained silent and did not answer at all, for the king's command was, "Do not answer him."

[37]Then the master of the palace, Eliakim, son of Hilkiah, Shebnah the scribe, and the chancellor Joah, son of Asaph, came to Hezekiah with their garments torn, and reported to him the words of the commander.

## CHAPTER 19

**Hezekiah and Isaiah.** [1]When King Hezekiah heard this, he tore his garments, covered himself with sackcloth, and went into the house of the LORD. [2]He sent Eliakim, the master of the palace, Shebnah the scribe, and the elders of the priests, covered with sackcloth, to tell the prophet Isaiah, son of Amoz, [3]"Thus says Hezekiah:

A day of distress and rebuke,
    a day of disgrace is this day!
Children are due to come forth,
    but the strength to give birth is
        lacking.[‡]

[4]Perhaps the LORD, your God, will hear all the words of the commander, whom his lord, the king of Assyria, sent to taunt the living God, and will rebuke him for the words which the LORD, your God, has heard. So lift up a prayer for the remnant that is here." [5]When the servants of King Hezekiah had come to Isaiah, [6]he said to them, "Tell this to your lord: Thus says the LORD: Do not be frightened by the words you have heard, by which the deputies of the king of Assyria have blasphemed me.[l] [7]I am putting in him such a spirit that when he hears a report he will return to his land. I will make him fall by the sword in his land."

[8]When the commander, on his return, heard that the king of Assyria had withdrawn from Lachish, he found him besieging Libnah. **Sennacherib, Hezekiah, and Isaiah.** [9]The king of Assyria heard a report: "Tirhakah, king of Ethiopia, has come out to fight against you." Again he sent messengers to Hezekiah to say:

---

*[18:27] **Excrement . . . urine**: the reference is to the famine that results from a prolonged siege (compare 6:24–25; Dt 28:53–57). For public hearing, ancient tradition (e.g., the Qere reading of the Masoretic text) softened the terms to "eat their own waste and drink their own bodies' water."

j. [18:18] Is 22:15–25.　k. [18:21] Is 30:1–7; 31:1–3; Ez 29:6–7.

†[18:34] **Did they indeed . . . power?**: some time after the fall of Samaria in 722/721 B.C., Hamath, Arpad, and other small states in the region formed an anti-Assyrian coalition. If the coalition had succeeded, it could have broken Assyrian control over the whole region, including Samaria, and allowed the kingdom of Israel to free itself. When Assyria crushed the coalition, it also crushed Israel's hopes for liberation.

‡[19:3] See note on Is 37:3.

l. [19:6] Is 10:5–14.

10"Thus shall you say to Hezekiah, king of Judah: Do not let your God in whom you trust deceive you by saying, 'Jerusalem will not be handed over to the king of Assyria.' 11You, certainly, have heard what the kings of Assyria have done to all the lands: they put them under the ban! And are you to be rescued? 12mDid the gods of the nations whom my fathers destroyed deliver them—Gozan, Haran, Rezeph, or the Edenites in Telassar? 13Where are the king of Hamath, the king of Arpad, or the kings of the cities Sepharvaim, Hena and Ivvah?"

14Hezekiah took the letter from the hand of the messengers and read it; then he went up to the house of the LORD, and spreading it out before the LORD, 15Hezekiah prayed in the LORD's presence: "LORD, God of Israel, enthroned on the cherubim! You alone are God over all the kingdoms of the earth. It is you who made the heavens and the earth.n 16Incline your ear, LORD, and listen! Open your eyes, LORD, and see! Hear the words Sennacherib has sent to taunt the living God. 17Truly, O LORD, the kings of Assyria have laid waste the nations and their lands. 18They gave their gods to the fire— they were not gods at all, but the work of human hands—wood and stone, they destroyed them. 19Therefore, LORD, our God, save us from this man's power, that all the kingdoms of the earth may know that you alone, LORD, are God."o

20Then Isaiah, son of Amoz, sent this message to Hezekiah: "Thus says the LORD, the God of Israel, to whom you have prayed concerning Sennacherib, king of Assyria: I have listened! 21This is the word the LORD has spoken concerning him:

> She despises you, laughs you to scorn,
>     the virgin daughter Zion!
> Behind you she wags her head,
>     daughter Jerusalem.
> 22 Whom have you insulted and
>       blasphemed,
>     at whom have you raised your voice
> And lifted up your eyes on high?
>     At the Holy One of Israel!
> 23 Through the mouths of your messengers
>       you insulted the Lord when you
>       said,
> 'With my many chariots I went up
>     to the tops of the peaks,
>     to the recesses of Lebanon,
> To cut down its lofty cedars,
>     its choice cypresses;
> I reached to the farthest shelter,
>     the forest ranges.
> 24 I myself dug wells
>     and drank foreign waters,

> Drying up all the rivers of Egypt
>     beneath the soles of my feet.'
> 25 "Have you not heard?
>     A long time ago I prepared it,
>     from days of old I planned it.
> Now I have brought it about:
> You are here to reduce
>     fortified cities to heaps of ruins,
> 26 Their people powerless,
>     dismayed and distraught.
> They are plants of the field,
>     green growth,
>     thatch on the rooftops,
> Grain scorched by the east wind.
> 27 I know when you stand or sit,
>     when you come or gop
>     and how you rage against me.
> 28 Because you rage against me,
>     and your smugness has reached my
>       ears,
> I will put my hook in your nose
>     and my bit in your mouth,
> And make you leave by the way you came.

> 29 "This shall be a sign for you:
> This year you shall eat the aftergrowth,
>     next year, what grows of itself;
> But in the third year, sow and reap,
>     plant vineyards and eat their fruit!
> 30 The remaining survivors of the house of
>       Judah
>     shall again strike root below
>     and bear fruit above.
> 31 For out of Jerusalem shall come a
>       remnant,
>     and from Mount Zion, survivors.
> The zeal of the LORD of hosts shall do this.

32"Therefore, thus says the LORD about the king:

> He shall not come as far as this city,
>     nor shoot there an arrow,
>     nor confront it with a shield,
> Nor cast up a siege-work against it.
> 33 By the way he came he shall leave,
>     never coming as far as this city,
>     oracle of the LORD.
> 34 I will shield and save this city
>     for my own sake and the sake of
>       David my servant."q

35That night the angel of the LORD went forth and struck down one hundred and eighty-five thousand men in the Assyrian camp. Early the next morning, there they were, dead, all those corpses!r 36So Sennacherib, the king of Assyria, broke camp, departed, returned home, and stayed in Nineveh.

---

*[19:21–31] Verses 21–28 are addressed to Sennacherib, vv. 29–31 to Judah.

m. [19:12–13] 2 Kgs 17:6, 24; 18:34.   n. [19:15] Ex 25:17–22; 1 Kgs 6:23–28; 8:6–7.   o. [19:19] 1 Kgs 18:36.

p. [19:27] Ps 139:2–3.   q. [19:34] 2 Sm 7:12.   r. [19:35] 1 Mc 7:41; 2 Mc 8:19.

[37]When he was worshiping in the temple of his god Nisroch, his sons Adrammelech and Sharezer struck him down with the sword and fled into the land of Ararat. His son Esarhaddon reigned in his place.

## CHAPTER 20

**End of Hezekiah's Reign.** [1]In those days, when Hezekiah was mortally ill, the prophet Isaiah, son of Amoz, came and said to him: "Thus says the LORD: Put your house in order, for you are about to die; you shall not recover." [2]He turned his face to the wall and prayed to the LORD: [3]"Ah, LORD, remember how faithfully and wholeheartedly I conducted myself in your presence, doing what was good in your sight!" And Hezekiah wept bitterly. [4]Before Isaiah had left the central courtyard, the word of the LORD came to him: [5]Go back and tell Hezekiah, the leader of my people: "Thus says the LORD, the God of David your father:

I have heard your prayer;
I have seen your tears.
Now I am healing you.
On the third day you shall go up
    to the house of the LORD.
[6] I will add to your life fifteen years.
I will rescue you and this city
    from the hand of the king of Assyria;
I will be a shield to this city
    for my own sake and the sake of
        David my servant."

[7]Then Isaiah said, "Bring a poultice of figs and apply it to the boil for his recovery." [8]Hezekiah asked Isaiah, "What is the sign that the LORD will heal me and that I shall go up to the house of the LORD on the third day?" [9]Isaiah replied, "This will be the sign for you from the LORD that he will carry out the word he has spoken: Shall the shadow go forward or back ten steps?" [10]"It is easy for the shadow to advance ten steps," Hezekiah answered. "Rather, let it go back ten steps." [11]So Isaiah the prophet invoked the LORD. He made the shadow go back the ten steps it had descended on the staircase to the terrace of Ahaz.

[12]At that time, Berodach-baladan,* son of Baladan, king of Babylon, sent letters and gifts to Hezekiah when he heard that he had been ill. [13]Hezekiah listened to the envoys and then showed off his whole treasury: his silver, gold, spices and perfumed oil, his armory, and everything in his storerooms; there was nothing in his house or in all his realm that Hezekiah did not

show them. [14]Then Isaiah the prophet came to King Hezekiah and asked him: "What did these men say to you? Where did they come from?" Hezekiah replied, "They came from a distant land, from Babylon." [15]He asked, "What did they see in your house?" Hezekiah answered, "They saw everything in my house. There is nothing in my storerooms that I did not show them." [16]Then Isaiah said to Hezekiah: "Hear the word of the LORD: [17]The time is coming when all that is in your house, everything that your ancestors have stored up until this day, shall be carried off to Babylon; nothing shall be left, says the LORD. [18]Some of your own descendants, your offspring, your progeny, shall be taken and made attendants in the palace of the king of Babylon." [19]Hezekiah replied to Isaiah, "The word of the LORD which you have spoken is good." For he thought, "There will be peace and stability in my lifetime."

[20]The rest of the acts of Hezekiah, with all his valor, and how he constructed the pool and conduit[†] and brought water into the city, are recorded in the book of the chronicles of the kings of Judah.[t] [21]Hezekiah rested with his ancestors, and his son Manasseh succeeded him as king.

## CHAPTER 21

**Reign of Manasseh.** [1]Manasseh was twelve years old when he became king, and he reigned fifty-five years in Jerusalem. His mother's name was Hephzibah.

[2]He did what was evil in the LORD's sight, following the abominable practices of the nations whom the LORD had dispossessed before the Israelites. [3]He rebuilt the high places which Hezekiah his father had destroyed. He set up altars to Baal and also made an asherah, as Ahab, king of Israel, had done. He bowed down to the whole host of heaven and served them.[u] [4]He built altars in the house of the LORD, of which the LORD had said: In Jerusalem I will set my name. [5]And he built altars for the whole host of heaven in the two courts of the house of the LORD. [6]He immolated his child by fire. He practiced soothsaying and divination, and reintroduced the consulting of ghosts and spirits.

He did much evil in the LORD's sight and provoked him to anger.[v] [7]The Asherah idol he had made, he placed in the LORD's house, of which the Lord had said to David and to his son Solomon: In this house and in Jerusalem, which I have chosen out of all the tribes of Israel, I shall set my name forever.[w] [8]I will no longer make Israel step out of the land I gave their ancestors, provided that they are careful to observe

---

*[20:12] **Berodach-baladan**: this famous king's name is more correctly recorded in Is 39:1 as "Merodach-baladan." The Babylonian form, Marduk-apal-idinna, means "Marduk has granted a son." Historically, any embassy from him to Hezekiah must have been aimed at establishing an anti-Assyrian strategy of cooperation.

†[20:20] **Pool and conduit**: Hezekiah's tunnel is described in more detail in 2 Chr 32:30.

s. [20:1–11] Sir 48:23.

t. [20:20] Sir 48:17.   u. [21:3] 2 Kgs 17:16; 1 Kgs 16:31–33.   v. [21:6] Lv 18:21; 19:26; Dt 18:10–14; 1 Sm 28:3.   w. [21:7] 2 Sm 7:13; 1 Kgs 8:16; 9:3.

all I have commanded them and the entire law which Moses my servant enjoined upon them. ⁹But they did not listen.

Manasseh misled them into doing even greater evil than the nations the LORD had destroyed at the coming of the Israelites. ¹⁰Then the LORD spoke through his servants the prophets: ¹¹"Because Manasseh, king of Judah, has practiced these abominations, and has done greater evil than all that was done by the Amorites before him, and has led Judah into sin by his idols,ˣ ¹²therefore, thus says the LORD, the God of Israel: I am about to bring such evil on Jerusalem and Judah that, when any hear of it, their ears shall ring: ¹³I will measure Jerusalem with the same cord as I did Samaria, and with the plummet I used for the house of Ahab. I will wipe Jerusalem clean as one wipes a dish, wiping it inside and out.ʸ ¹⁴I will cast off the survivors of my inheritance. I will deliver them into enemy hands, to become prey and booty for all their enemies, ¹⁵because they have done what is evil in my sight and provoked me from the day their ancestors came forth from Egypt until this very day." ¹⁶Manasseh shed so much innocent blood that it filled the length and breadth of Jerusalem, in addition to the sin he caused Judah to commit by doing what was evil in the LORD's sight.

¹⁷The rest of the acts of Manasseh, with all that he did and the sin he committed, are recorded in the book of the chronicles of the kings of Judah. ¹⁸Manasseh rested with his ancestors; he was buried in his palace garden, the garden of Uzza, and his son Amon succeeded him as king.

**Reign of Amon.** ¹⁹Amon was twenty-two years old when he became king, and he reigned two years in Jerusalem. His mother's name was Meshullemeth, daughter of Haruz, from Jotbah.

²⁰He did what was evil in the LORD's sight, as his father Manasseh had done. ²¹He walked in all the ways of his father; he served the idols his father had served, and bowed down to them. ²²He abandoned the LORD, the God of his ancestors, and did not walk in the way of the LORD.

²³Officials of Amon plotted against him and killed the king in his palace, ²⁴but the people of the land* then slew all who had plotted against King Amon, and the people of the land made his son Josiah king in his stead. ²⁵The rest of the acts of Amon, which he did, are recorded in the book of the chronicles of the kings of Judah. ²⁶He was buried in his own grave in the garden of Uzza, and his son Josiah succeeded him as king.

## CHAPTER 22

**Reign of Josiah.** ¹Josiah was eight years old when he became king, and he reigned thirty-one years in Jerusalem. His mother's name was Jedidah, daughter of Adaiah, from Bozkath.

²He did what was right in the LORD's sight, walking in the way of David his father, not turning right or left.

**The Book of the Law.** ³ᶻIn his eighteenth year, King Josiah sent the scribe Shaphan,† son of Azaliah, son of Meshullam, to the house of the LORD with these orders: ⁴"Go to the high priest Hilkiah and have him calculate the valuables that have been brought to the house of the LORD, which the doorkeepers have collected from the people. ⁵Then have him turn them over to the master workers in the house of the LORD, and have them give them to the ordinary workers who are in the house of the LORD to repair its breaches: ⁶to the carpenters, the builders, and the masons, and to purchase wood and hewn stone. ⁷No reckoning shall be asked of them regarding the funds provided to them, because they hold positions of trust."

⁸The high priest Hilkiah informed the scribe Shaphan, "I have found the book of the law‡ in the temple of the LORD." Hilkiah gave the book to Shaphan, who read it. ⁹Then the scribe Shaphan went to the king and reported, "Your servants have smelted down the silver deposited in the temple and have turned it over to the master workers in the house of the LORD." ¹⁰The scribe Shaphan also informed the king, "Hilkiah the priest has given me a book," and then Shaphan read it in the presence of the king. ¹¹When the king heard the words of the book of the law, he tore his garments.

¹²The king then issued this command to Hilkiah the priest, Ahikam, son of Shaphan, Achbor, son of Micaiah, Shaphan the scribe, and Asaiah the king's servant: ¹³"Go, consult the LORD for me, for the people, and for all Judah, about the words of this book that has been found, for the rage of the LORD has been set furiously ablaze against us, because our ancestors did not obey the words of this book, nor do what is written for us." ¹⁴So Hilkiah the priest, Ahikam, Achbor, Shaphan, and Asaiah went to Huldah the prophet, wife of Shallum, son of Tikvah, son of Harhas, keeper of the wardrobe; she lived in Jerusalem, in the Second Quarter. When they had spoken to her, ¹⁵she said to them, "Thus says the LORD, the God of Israel: Say to the man who sent you to me, ¹⁶Thus says the LORD: I am about to bring evil upon this place and upon its inhabitants—all the words of the book which the king of Judah has read. ¹⁷Because they have abandoned me and have

---

†[22:3] **Shaphan:** head of a prominent family in the reign of Josiah, secretary to the king, bearer and reader of the newly found book of the law (vv. 3–13; 25:22). He and his sons favored the reform of King Josiah and supported the prophet Jeremiah; cf. Jer 26:24; 29:1–3; 36:10–12; 39:14.

‡[22:8] **Book of the law:** probably an early edition of material now found in the Book of Deuteronomy.

---

*[21:24] **People of the land:** see note on 11:14.

x. [21:11] Jer 15:4.　　y. [21:13] Is 34:11; Lam 2:8; Am 7:7–9.

z. [22:3–7] 2 Kgs 12:11–16.

burned incense to other gods, provoking me by all the works of their hands, my rage is ablaze against this place and it cannot be extinguished. [18]"But to the king of Judah who sent you to consult the LORD, give this response: Thus says the LORD, the God of Israel: As for the words you have heard, [19]because you were heartsick and have humbled yourself before the LORD when you heard what I have spoken concerning this place and its inhabitants, that they would become a desolation and a curse; and because you tore your garments and wept before me, I in turn have heard, oracle of the LORD. [20]I will therefore gather you to your ancestors; you shall go to your grave in peace, and your eyes shall not see all the evil I am about to bring upon this place." This they reported to the king.

## CHAPTER 23

[1]The king then had all the elders of Judah and of Jerusalem summoned before him. [2]The king went up to the house of the LORD with all the people of Judah and all the inhabitants of Jerusalem: priests, prophets, and all the people, great and small. He read aloud to them all the words of the book of the covenant that had been found in the house of the LORD.[a] [3]The king stood by the column and made a covenant in the presence of the LORD to follow the LORD and to observe his commandments, statutes, and decrees with his whole heart and soul, and to re-establish the words of the covenant written in this book. And all the people stood by the covenant.

**Josiah's Religious Reform.** [4]Then the king commanded the high priest Hilkiah, his assistant priests, and the doorkeepers to remove from the temple of the LORD all the objects that had been made for Baal, Asherah, and the whole host of heaven. These he burned outside Jerusalem on the slopes of the Kidron; their ashes were carried to Bethel.[b] [5]He also put an end to the idolatrous priests whom the kings of Judah had appointed to burn incense on the high places in the cities of Judah and in the vicinity of Jerusalem, as well as those who burned incense to Baal, to the sun, moon, and signs of the zodiac, and to the whole host of heaven.[c] [6]From the house of the LORD he also removed the Asherah to the Wadi Kidron, outside Jerusalem; he burned it and beat it to dust, in the Wadi Kidron, and scattered its dust over the graveyard of the people of the land.[d] [7]He tore down the apartments of the cult prostitutes in the house of the LORD, where the women wove garments for the Asherah.[e] [8]He brought in all the priests from the cities of Judah, and then defiled, from Geba to Beer-sheba, the high places where they had offered incense. He also tore down the high places of the gates, which were at the entrance of the Gate of Joshua, governor of the city, north of the city gate. [9](The priests of the high places could not function at the altar of the LORD in Jerusalem; but they, along with their relatives, ate the unleavened bread.)

[10]The king also defiled Topheth in the Valley of Ben-hinnom, so that there would no longer be any immolation of sons or daughters by fire[†] in honor of Molech.[f] [11]He did away with the horses which the kings of Judah had dedicated to the sun; these were at the entrance of the house of the LORD, near the chamber of Nathan-melech the official, which was in the large building. The chariots of the sun he destroyed by fire. [12]He also demolished the altars made by the kings of Judah on the roof (the roof terrace of Ahaz), and the altars made by Manasseh in the two courts of the LORD's house. He pulverized them and threw the dust into the Wadi Kidron.[g] [13]The king defiled the high places east of Jerusalem, south of the Mount of the Destroyer,[‡] which Solomon, king of Israel, had built in honor of Astarte, the Sidonian horror, of Chemosh, the Moabite horror, and of Milcom, the Ammonites' abomination.[h] [14]He broke to pieces the pillars, cut down the asherahs, and filled the places where they had been with human bones.[i]

[15]Likewise the altar which was at Bethel, the high place built by Jeroboam, son of Nebat, who caused Israel to sin—this same altar and high place he tore down and burned, grinding the high place to powder and burning the asherah.[j] [16]When Josiah turned and saw the graves there on the mountainside, he ordered the bones taken from the graves and burned on the altar, and thus defiled it, according to the LORD's word proclaimed by the man of God as Jeroboam stood by the altar on the feast day. When the king looked up and saw the grave of the man of God who had proclaimed these words, [17]he asked, "What is that marker I see?" The people of the city replied, "The grave of the man of

---

*[23:6] **People of the land:** see note on 11:14.

a. [23:2] Dt 17:18–19.   b. [23:4] Sir 49:3.   c. [23:5] Dt 4:19; 17:2–7.   d. [23:6] Dt 16:21.   e. [23:7] Dt 23:18–19.

---

†[23:10] **Topheth . . . by fire**: Topheth was a cultic site probably in the Hinnom Valley just west of Jerusalem where, apparently, children were immolated to the god Molech (Hebrew *melek*, "king," deformed in the biblical tradition to "Molech"). The practice was condemned by Deuteronomic law and denounced by Jeremiah (Dt 12:31; Jer 7:29–31). In Jer 19 the deity is identified as the Canaanite god Baal.

‡[23:13] **Mount of the Destroyer**: the name of the mountain in Hebrew is a wordplay. "The Mount of the *mashchit*" means "the Mount of the Destroyer" or perhaps "the Mount of Destruction." The word plays on *mishchah*, "anointment," and on *mashiach*, "anointed one," both of which are references to the ceremony that consecrated the king. The mountain in question was the Mount of Olives, whose trees produced oil for the royal anointing. In the present context, both sides of the wordplay allude to Solomon, the anointed king (*mashiach*), whose building of non-Yahwistic shrines on this very mountain resulted in the destruction (*mashchit*) of the Davidic realm (see 1 Kgs 11:4–13). **Horror . . . abomination**: all three idols are described with pejorative terms.

f. [23:10] Lv 18:21; Dt 18:10–12.   g. [23:12] 2 Kgs 20:11; 21:5.   h. [23:13] 1 Kgs 11:4–8.   i. [23:14] Dt 16:21; 1 Kgs 14:23.   j. [23:15–20] 1 Kgs 12:26–13:34.

God who came from Judah and proclaimed the very things you have done to the altar in Bethel." [18]"Let him be," he said, "let no one move his bones." So they left his bones undisturbed together with the bones of the prophet who had come from Samaria.* [19]Josiah also removed all the temples on the high places in the cities of Samaria which the kings of Israel had built, provoking the LORD; he did the very same to them as he had done in Bethel. [20]He slaughtered upon the altars all the priests of the high places that were there, and burned human bones upon them. Then he returned to Jerusalem.

[21]The king issued a command to all the people: "Observe the Passover of the LORD, your God, as it is written in this book of the covenant."[k] [22]No Passover such as this had been observed during the period when the judges ruled Israel, or during the entire period of the kings of Israel and the kings of Judah, [23]until the eighteenth year of King Josiah, when this Passover of the LORD was kept in Jerusalem.

[24]Further, Josiah purged the consultation of ghosts and spirits, with the household gods, idols,† and all the other horrors to be seen in the land of Judah and in Jerusalem, so that he might carry out the words of the law that were written in the book that Hilkiah the priest had found in the house of the LORD.[l]

[25]Before him there had been no king who turned to the LORD as he did, with his whole heart, his whole being, and his whole strength, in accord with the entire law of Moses; nor did any king like him arise after him.[m] [26]Yet the LORD did not turn from his fiercely burning anger against Judah, because of all the provocations that Manasseh had given. [27]The LORD said: Even Judah will I put out of my sight as I did Israel. I will reject this city, Jerusalem, which I chose, and the house of which I said: There shall my name be.

[28]The rest of the acts of Josiah, with all that he did, are recorded in the book of the chronicles of the kings of Judah. [29]In his time Pharaoh Neco, king of Egypt, went up toward the Euphrates River against the king of Assyria.‡ King Josiah set out to meet him, but was slain at Megiddo at the first encounter. [30]His servants brought his body on a chariot from Megiddo to Jerusalem, where they buried him in his own grave. Then

the people of the land took Jehoahaz, son of Josiah, anointed him, and proclaimed him king to succeed his father.

**Reign of Jehoahaz.** [31]Jehoahaz was twenty-three years old when he became king, and he reigned three months in Jerusalem. His mother's name was Hamutal, daughter of Jeremiah, from Libnah.[n]

[32]He did what was evil in the LORD's sight, just as his ancestors had done. [33]Pharaoh Neco took him prisoner at Riblah in the land of Hamath, thus ending his reign in Jerusalem. He imposed a fine upon the land of a hundred talents of silver and a talent of gold.§ [34]Pharaoh Neco then made Eliakim, son of Josiah, king in place of Josiah his father; he changed his name to Jehoiakim. Jehoahaz he took away with him to Egypt, where he died. [35]Jehoiakim gave the silver and gold to Pharaoh, but taxed the land to raise the amount Pharaoh demanded. He exacted the silver and gold from the people of the land, from each proportionately, to pay Pharaoh Neco.

**Reign of Jehoiakim.** [36]Jehoiakim was twenty-five years old when he became king, and he reigned eleven years in Jerusalem. His mother's name was Zebidah, daughter of Pedaiah, from Rumah.

[37]He did what was evil in the LORD's sight, just as his ancestors had done.

## CHAPTER 24

[1]During Jehoiakim's reign Nebuchadnezzar, king of Babylon, attacked, and Jehoiakim became his vassal for three years. Then Jehoiakim turned and rebelled against him. [2]The LORD loosed against him bands of Chaldeans, Arameans, Moabites, and Ammonites; he unleashed them against Judah to destroy him, according to the LORD's word spoken through his servants the prophets. [3]This befell Judah because the LORD had stated that he would put them out of his sight for the sins Manasseh had committed in all that he did, [4]and especially because of the innocent blood he shed; he filled Jerusalem with innocent blood, and the LORD would not forgive.[o]

[5]The rest of the acts of Jehoiakim, with all that he did, are recorded in the book of the chronicles of the kings of Judah. [6]Jehoiakim rested with his ancestors, and his son Jehoiachin succeeded him as king. [7]The king of Egypt did not again leave his own land, for the king of Babylon had taken all that belonged to the king of Egypt from the wadi of Egypt to the Euphrates River.

---

*[23:18] **From Samaria:** an anachronistic use of the name of the later capital city for the whole region. The prophet was from Bethel; cf. 1 Kgs 13:11.

†[23:24] **Household gods, idols:** teraphim. See note on Gn 31:19.

‡[23:29] **Against the king of Assyria:** the narrator depicts Neco's advance as an attack on Assyrian forces. The Babylonian record of the event, however, implies that Neco intended to support the remnant of Assyrian forces against a Babylonian onslaught in order to prop up a buffer state between Egypt and Babylon and assure Egyptian control of the Syro-Palestinian region.

§[23:33] **A talent of gold:** unless the fine imposed was a mere token, this figure seems too low; cf. 18:14. A number may have dropped from the Hebrew text; various ancient translations read "ten" or "one hundred" here.

---

k. [23:21] Dt 16:1–8.   l. [23:24] 2 Kgs 21:6; Gn 31:19; Dt 18:10–14; Jgs 18:14.   m. [23:25] Dt 6:5; Sir 49:1–3.

n. [23:31] 2 Kgs 24:18.   o. [24:4] 2 Kgs 21:16.

**Reign of Jehoiachin.** [8]Jehoiachin was eighteen years old when he became king, and he reigned three months in Jerusalem. His mother's name was Nehushta, daughter of Elnathan, from Jerusalem.

[9]He did what was evil in the LORD's sight, just as his father had done.

[10p]At that time officers of Nebuchadnezzar, king of Babylon, attacked Jerusalem, and the city came under siege. [11]Nebuchadnezzar, king of Babylon, himself arrived at the city while his officers were besieging it. [12]Then Jehoiachin, king of Judah, together with his mother, his ministers, officers, and functionaries, surrendered to the king of Babylon, who, in the eighth year of his reign,* took him captive. [13]He carried off all the treasures of the house of the LORD and the treasures of the king's house, and broke up all the gold utensils that Solomon, king of Israel, had provided in the house of the LORD, as the LORD had decreed.[q] [14]He deported all Jerusalem: all the officers and warriors of the army, ten thousand in number, and all the artisans and smiths. Only the lowliest of the people of the land† were left. [15]He deported Jehoiachin to Babylon, and the king's mother, his wives, his functionaries, and the chiefs of the land he led captive from Jerusalem to Babylon.[r] [16]All seven thousand soldiers of the army, and a thousand artisans and smiths, all of them trained warriors, these too the king of Babylon brought captive to Babylon. [17]In place of Jehoiachin the king of Babylon made Mattaniah, Jehoiachin's uncle, king; he changed his name to Zedekiah.

**Reign of Zedekiah.** [18‡]Zedekiah was twenty-one years old when he became king, and he reigned eleven years in Jerusalem. His mother's name was Hamutal, daughter of Jeremiah, from Libnah.[s]

[19]He did what was evil in the sight of the LORD, just as Jehoiakim had done. [20]This befell Jerusalem and Judah because the LORD was so angry that he cast them out of his sight.

Zedekiah rebelled against the king of Babylon.

## CHAPTER 25

[1]In the tenth month of the ninth year of Zedekiah's reign, on the tenth day of the month, Nebuchadnezzar, king of Babylon, and his whole army advanced against Jerusalem, encamped around it, and built siege walls on every side. [2]The siege of the city continued until the eleventh year of Zedekiah. [3]On the ninth day of the month,§ when famine had gripped the city, and the people of the land had no more food, [4]the city walls were breached. That night, all the soldiers came to the gate between the two walls near the king's garden (the Chaldeans had the city surrounded), while the king went toward the Arabah.¶ [5]But the Chaldean army pursued the king and overtook him in the desert near Jericho, abandoned by his whole army. [6]The king was therefore arrested and brought to Riblah to the king of Babylon, who pronounced sentence on him. [7]They slew Zedekiah's sons before his eyes; then they put out his eyes, bound him with fetters, and brought him to Babylon.

[8]On the seventh day of the fifth month (this was in the nineteenth year of Nebuchadnezzar, king of Babylon), Nebuzaradan, captain of the bodyguard, came to Jerusalem as the agent of the king of Babylon. [9]He burned the house of the LORD, the house of the king, and all the houses of Jerusalem (every noble house); he destroyed them by fire.[u] [10]The Chaldean troops who were with the captain of the guard tore down the walls that surrounded Jerusalem, [11]and Nebuzaradan, captain of the guard, led into exile the last of the army remaining in the city, and those who had deserted** to the king of Babylon, and the last of the commoners. [12]But some of the country's poor the captain of the guard left behind as vinedressers and farmers.

[13]The bronze columns that belonged to the house of the LORD, and the stands and the bronze sea in the house of the LORD, the Chaldeans broke into pieces; they carried away the bronze to Babylon.[v] [14]They took also the pots, the shovels, the snuffers, the cups and all the bronze articles used for service.[w] [15]The fire pans and the bowls that were of solid gold or silver the captain of the guard also carried off.[x] [16]The two columns, the one bronze sea, and the stands, which Solomon had made for the house of the LORD—the weight in bronze of all these articles was never calculated.[y] [17]Each of the columns was eighteen cubits high; a bronze capital three cubits high surmounted each column, and a netting with pomegranates encircled the capital, all of bronze; and they were duplicated on the other column, on the netting.[z]

[18]The captain of the guard also took Seraiah, the chief priest, Zephaniah, an assistant priest,

---

*[24:12] **The eighth year of his reign:** that is, of Nebuchadnezzar's reign, not Jehoiachin's. The year was 597 B.C.

†[24:14] **People of the land:** see note on 11:14.

‡[24:18–25:30] Much of this material closely parallels Jer 52; some of the events are also recounted in Jer 39.

§[25:3] **Ninth day of the month:** the text does not say which month, but Jer 39:2 and 52:6 set the breaching of the city walls in the fourth month; in later times that was the date of a fast commemorating the event (cf. Zec 8:19). **People of the land:** the influential citizens (see note on 11:14); even they, whose resources went beyond those of the ordinary people, were starving.

¶[25:4] The Hebrew text of this verse is missing some words. The present translation is based on a likely reconstruction.

**[25:11] **Those who had deserted:** perhaps on the advice of Jeremiah; cf. Jer 38:2–3.

---

p. [24:10–17] Dn 1:1–2.  q. [24:13] 2 Kgs 20:17.  r. [24:15] Est A:3; 2:6.  s. [24:17] Jer 37:1.  t. [24:18] 2 Kgs 23:31.

u. [25:9] Ps 74:2–7.  v. [25:13] 2 Kgs 16:17; 1 Kgs 7:15–39; Jer 27:19–23.  w. [25:14] 1 Kgs 7:40–45.  x. [25:15] 1 Kgs 7:50. y. [25:16] 1 Kgs 7:47.  z. [25:17] 1 Kgs 7:15–20; Jer 52:21–23.

and the three doorkeepers. ¹⁹And from the city he took one officer who was a commander of soldiers, five courtiers in the personal service of the king who were still in the city, the scribe in charge of the army who mustered the people of the land,* and sixty of the people of the land still remaining in the city. ²⁰The captain of the guard, Nebuzaradan, arrested these and brought them to the king of Babylon at Riblah, and ²¹the king of Babylon struck them down and put them to death in Riblah, in the land of Hamath. And thus Judah went into exile from their native soil.

**Governorship of Gedaliah.** ²²ªAs for the people whom he had allowed to remain in the land of Judah, Nebuchadnezzar, king of Babylon, appointed Gedaliah, son of Ahikam, son of Shaphan, over them. ²³Hearing that the king of Babylon had appointed Gedaliah over them, all the army commanders and the troops came to him at Mizpah: Ishmael, son of Nethaniah, Johanan, son of Kareah, Seraiah, son of Tanhumeth the Netophathite, and Jaazaniah, son of the Maakite, each with his troops. ²⁴Gedaliah gave the commanders and their troops his oath. He said to them, "Do not be afraid of the Chaldean officials. Remain in the country and serve the king of Babylon, so that all will be well with you."

²⁵But in the seventh month Ishmael, son of Nethaniah, son of Elishama, of royal descent, came with ten others, attacked Gedaliah and killed him, along with the Judahites and Chaldeans who were in Mizpah with him. ²⁶Then all the people, great and small, left with the army commanders and went to Egypt for fear of the Chaldeans.

**Release of Jehoiachin.** ²⁷In the thirty-seventh year of the exile of Jehoiachin, king of Judah, on the twenty-seventh day of the twelfth month, Evil-merodach, king of Babylon, in the inaugural year of his own reign, raised up Jehoiachin, king of Judah, from prison. ²⁸He spoke kindly to him and gave him a throne higher than that of the other kings who were with him in Babylon. ²⁹Jehoiachin took off his prison garb; he ate regularly in the king's presence as long as he lived; ³⁰and for his allowance the king granted him a regular allowance, in fixed daily amounts, for as long as he lived.

---

*[25:19] **People of the land**: see note on 11:14.

a. [25:22–26] Jer 40:7–41:18.

# THE FIRST BOOK OF
# CHRONICLES

❧

The Greek title, *paraleipomena*, means "things omitted," or "passed over" (i.e., in the accounts found in Samuel and Kings). The Books of Chronicles, however, are much more than a supplement to Samuel and Kings; a comparison of the two histories discloses striking differences of scope and purpose. The Books of Chronicles record in some detail the lengthy span (some five hundred fifty years) from the death of King Saul to the return from the exile. Unlike today's history writing, wherein factual accuracy and impartiality of judgment are the norm, biblical history, with rare exceptions, was less concerned with reporting in precise detail all the facts of a situation than with drawing out the meaning of those facts. Biblical history was thus primarily interpretative, and its purpose was to disclose the action of the living God in human affairs. For this reason we speak of it as "sacred history."

These characteristics are apparent when we examine the primary objective of the Chronicler (the conventional designation for the anonymous author) in compiling his work. Given the situation which confronted the Jewish people at this time (the end of the fifth century B.C.), the Chronicler realized that Israel's political greatness was a thing of the past. Yet, for the Chronicler, Israel's past held the key to the people's future. In particular, the Chronicler aimed to establish and defend the legitimate claims of the Davidic monarchy in Israel's history, and to underscore the status of Jerusalem and its divinely established Temple worship as the center of religious life for the Jewish people. If Judaism was to survive and prosper, it would have to heed the lessons of the past and devoutly serve its God in the place where he had chosen to dwell, the Temple in Jerusalem. From the Chronicler's point of view, the reigns of David and Solomon were the ideal to which all subsequent rule in Judah must aspire. The Chronicler was much more interested in David's religious and cultic influence than in his political power, however. He saw David's (and Solomon's) primary importance as deriving rather from their roles in the establishment of Jerusalem and its Temple as the center of the true worship of the Lord. Furthermore, he presents David as the one who prescribed the Temple's elaborate ritual (which, in point of fact, only gradually evolved in the Second Temple period) and who appointed the Levites to supervise the liturgical services there.

The Chronicler used a variety of sources in writing his history. Besides the canonical Books of Genesis, Exodus, Numbers, Joshua, and Ruth, and especially the Books of Samuel and Kings (specifically 1 Sm 31–2 Kings 25), he cites the titles of many other works which have not come down to us, e.g., "The Books of the Kings of Israel," or "The Books of the Kings of Israel and Judah," and "The History of Gad the Seer." In addition, the Chronicler's work contains early preexilic material not found in the Books of Kings.

The principal divisions of 1 Chronicles are as follows:

  I. Genealogical Tables (1:1–9:34)
 II. The History of David (9:35–29:30)

## I. GENEALOGICAL TABLES*

### CHAPTER 1

**From Adam to Abraham.** ¹Adam, Seth, Enosh,ᵃ ²Kenan, Mahalalel, Jared,ᵇ ³Enoch, Methuselah, Lamech,ᶜ ⁴Noah, Shem, Ham, and Japheth.ᵈ ⁵The sons of Japheth were Gomer, Magog, Madai, Javan, Tubal, Meshech, and Tiras.ᵉ ⁶The sons of Gomer were Ashkenaz, Riphath, and Togarmah. ⁷The sons of Javan were Elishah, Tarshish, the Kittim, and the Rodanim.

⁸The sons of Ham were Cush, Mizraim, Put, and Canaan. ⁹The sons of Cush were Seba, Havilah, Sabta, Raama, and Sabteca. The sons of Raama were Sheba and Dedan. ¹⁰Cush became the father of Nimrod, who was the first to be a warrior on the earth.ᶠ ¹¹ᵍMizraim became the father of the Ludim, Anamim, Lehabim, Naphtuhim, ¹²Pathrusim, Casluhim, and Caphtorim, from whom the Philistines sprang. ¹³Canaan became the father of Sidon, his firstborn, and Heth, ¹⁴and the Jebusites, the Amorites, the Girgashites, ¹⁵the Hivites, the Arkites, the Sinites, ¹⁶the Arvadites, the Zemarites, and the Hamathites.

¹⁷ʰThe sons of Shem were Elam, Asshur, Arpachshad, Lud, and Aram. The sons of Aram were Uz, Hul, Gether, and Mash. ¹⁸Arpachshad became the father of Shelah, and Shelah became the father of Eber. ¹⁹Two sons were born to Eber; the first was named Peleg (for in his time the world was divided),† and his brother was named Joktan. ²⁰Joktan became the father of Almodad, Sheleph, Hazarmaveth, Jerah, ²¹Hadoram, Uzal, Diklah, ²²Ebal, Abimael, Sheba, ²³Ophir, Havilah, and Jobab; all these were the sons of Joktan.

²⁴ⁱShem, Arpachshad, Shelah, ²⁵Eber, Peleg, Reu, ²⁶Serug, Nahor, Terah, ²⁷Abram, that is, Abraham.ʲ
**From Abraham to Jacob.** ²⁸The sons of Abraham were Isaac and Ishmael.ᵏ ²⁹These were their generations:

Nebaioth, the firstborn of Ishmael, then Kedar, Adbeel, Mibsam, ³⁰Mishma, Dumah, Massa, Hadad, Tema, ³¹Jetur, Naphish, and Kedemah. These were the sons of Ishmael.ˡ

³²The sons of Keturah, Abraham's concubine: she bore Zimran, Jokshan, Medan, Midian, Ishbak, and Shuah. The sons of Jokshan were Sheba and Dedan. ³³The sons of Midian were Ephah, Epher, Hanoch, Abida, and Eldaah. All these were the sons of Keturah.ᵐ

³⁴Abraham begot Isaac. The sons of Isaac were Esau and Israel.ⁿ

³⁵The descendants of Esau were Eliphaz, Reuel, Jeush, Jalam, and Korah. ³⁶The descendants of Eliphaz were Teman, Omar, Zephi, Gatam, Kenaz, Timna, and Amalek. ³⁷The descendants of Reuel were Nahath, Zerah, Shammah, and Mizzah.ᵒ

³⁸The sons of Seir‡ were Lotan, Shobal, Zibeon, Anah, Dishon, Ezer, and Dishan. ³⁹The sons of Lotan were Hori and Homam; Timna was the sister of Lotan. ⁴⁰The sons of Shobal were Alian, Manahath, Ebal, Shephi, and Onam. The sons of Zibeon were Aiah and Anah. ⁴¹The sons of Anah: Dishon. The sons of Dishon were Hemdan, Eshban, Ithran, and Cheran. ⁴²The sons of Ezer were Bilhan, Zaavan, and Jaakan. The sons of Dishan were Uz and Aran.ᵖ

⁴³ᵠThe kings who reigned in the land of Edom before the Israelites had kings were the following: Bela, son of Beor, the name of whose city was Dinhabah. ⁴⁴When Bela died, Jobab, son of Zerah, from Bozrah, succeeded him as king.ʳ ⁴⁵When Jobab died, Husham, from the land of the Temanites, succeeded him as king.ˢ ⁴⁶Husham died and Hadad, son of Bedad, succeeded him as king. He overthrew the Midianites on the Moabite plateau, and the name of his city was Avith. ⁴⁷Hadad died and Samlah of Masrekah succeeded him as king. ⁴⁸Samlah died and Shaul from Rehoboth on the Euphrates succeeded him as king. ⁴⁹When Shaul died, Baalhanan, son of Achbor, succeeded him as king. ⁵⁰Baalhanan died and Hadad succeeded him as king. The name of his city was Pai, and his wife's name was Mehetabel. She was the daughter of Matred, who was the daughter of Mezahab. ⁵¹ᵗAfter Hadad died, there were chiefs in Edom: the chiefs of Timna, Aliah, Jetheth, ⁵²Oholibamah, Elah, Pinon, ⁵³Kenaz, Teman, Mibzar, ⁵⁴Magdiel, and Iram were the chiefs of Edom.

### CHAPTER 2

¹These were the sons of Israel: Reuben, Simeon, Levi, Judah, Issachar, Zebulun,ᵘ ²Dan, Joseph, Benjamin, Naphtali, Gad, and Asher.ᵛ
**Judah.** ³The sons of Judah§ were: Er, Onan, and Shelah; these three Bathshua, a Canaanite

---

*[1:1–9:34] The Chronicler's intention seems to have been to retell, from his particular viewpoint, the story of God's people from creation down to his own day. Since his primary interest was the history of David and the Davidic dynasty of Judah, he hurries through everything that preceded the death of Saul, David's predecessor as king, by the use of genealogical lists. The sources for these genealogies are mostly the books, already largely in their present form in the Chronicler's time, that eventually formed the Hebrew canon. For any given portion of these chapters, see the cross-references to their scriptural sources.
†[1:19] Divided: see note on Gn 10:25.

‡[1:38] Seir: another name for Esau (v. 35) or Edom (v. 43).
§[2:3–4:23] The Chronicler had two reasons for placing his genealogy of the tribe of Judah before those of the other tribes, and for making it longer than all the others: his interest

---

a. [1:1] Gn 5:3, 6, 9.   b. [1:2–4] Gn 5:9–32; 10:2–32.   c. [1:3] Gn 4:24.   d. [1:4] Gn 5:32; 6:10; 9:18.   e. [1:5–7] Gn 10:2–4.   f. [1:10] Gn 10:8.   g. [1:11–16] Gn 10:13–18.   h. [1:17–23] Gn 10:22–29; 11:10–18.   i. [1:24–27] Gn 11:10–26; Lk 3:34–36.   j. [1:27] Gn 17:5; Neh 9:7.   k. [1:28] Gn 16:11, 15; 21:2–3; Gal 4:22–23; Heb 11:11.   l. [1:29–31] Gn 25:13–16.

m. [1:32–33] Gn 25:1–4.   n. [1:34] Gn 21:2–3; 25:19, 25–26; 32:28–29; Mt 1:2; Lk 3:34.   o. [1:35–37] Gn 36:4–5, 10–13, 15–19.   p. [1:38–42] Gn 36:20–28.   q. [1:43–54] Gn 36:31–43.   r. [1:44] Is 34:6; 63:1; Jer 49:13, 22.   s. [1:45] Gn 36:11; Jb 2:11; Jer 49:7, 20.   t. [1:51–54] Gn 36:40–43.   u. [2:1] Gn 29:32–35; 30:18, 20; 35:23.   v. [2:2] Gn 30:6, 8, 11, 13, 24; 35:18, 24–26.

woman, bore to him. But Judah's firstborn, Er, was wicked in the sight of the Lord, so he took his life.<sup>w</sup> ⁴Judah's daughter-in-law Tamar bore him Perez and Zerah, so that he had five sons in all.<sup>x</sup>

⁵The sons of Perez were Hezron and Hamul.<sup>y</sup> ⁶The sons of Zerah were Zimri, Ethan, Heman, Calcol, and Darda—five in all.<sup>z</sup> ⁷The sons of Zimri: Carmi. The sons of Carmi: Achar, who brought trouble upon Israel by violating the ban.<sup>a</sup> ⁸The sons of Ethan: Azariah. ⁹The sons born to Hezron were Jerahmeel, Ram, and Chelubai.*<sup>b</sup>

¹⁰†Ram became the father of Amminadab, and Amminadab became the father of Nahshon, a prince of the Judahites.<sup>c</sup> ¹¹ᵈNahshon became the father of Salmah. Salmah became the father of Boaz. ¹²Boaz became the father of Obed. Obed became the father of Jesse. ¹³ᵉJesse became the father of Eliab, his firstborn, the second son, Shimea, the third,<sup>f</sup> ¹⁴Nethanel, the fourth, Raddai, the fifth, ¹⁵Ozem, the sixth, and David, the seventh. ¹⁶Their sisters were Zeruiah and Abigail. Zeruiah had three sons: Abishai, Joab, and Asahel.<sup>g</sup> ¹⁷Abigail bore Amasa, whose father was Jether the Ishmaelite.<sup>h</sup>

¹⁸‡By his wife Azubah, Caleb, son of Hezron, became the father of a daughter, Jerioth. Her sons were Jesher, Shobab, and Ardon.<sup>i</sup> ¹⁹When Azubah died, Caleb married Ephrath, who bore him Hur.<sup>j</sup> ²⁰Hur became the father of Uri, and Uri became the father of Bezalel.<sup>k</sup> ²¹Then Hezron had relations with the daughter of Machir, the father of Gilead, whom he married when he was sixty years old. She bore him Segub.<sup>l</sup> ²²Segub became the father of Jair, who possessed twenty-three cities in the land of Gilead.<sup>m</sup> ²³Geshur and Aram took from them the villages of Jair, that is, Kenath and its towns, sixty cities in all, which had belonged to the sons of Machir, the father of Gilead.<sup>n</sup> ²⁴After the death of Hezron, Caleb had relations with Ephrathah, the widow of his father Hezron, and she bore him Ashhur, the father of Tekoa.<sup>o</sup>

²⁵The sons of Jerahmeel,<sup>§</sup> the firstborn of Hezron, were Ram, the firstborn, then Bunah, Oren, and Ozem, his brothers.<sup>p</sup> ²⁶Jerahmeel also had another wife, named Atarah, who was the mother of Onam. ²⁷The sons of Ram, the firstborn of Jerahmeel, were Maaz, Jamin, and Eker. ²⁸The sons of Onam were Shammai and Jada. The sons of Shammai were Nadab and Abishur. ²⁹Abishur's wife, who was named Abihail, bore him Ahban and Molid. ³⁰The sons of Nadab were Seled and Appaim. Seled died childless. ³¹The sons of Appaim: Ishi. The sons of Ishi: Sheshan. The sons of Sheshan: Ahlai.<sup>q</sup> ³²The sons of Jada, the brother of Shammai, were Jether and Jonathan. Jether died childless. ³³The sons of Jonathan were Peleth and Zaza. These were the sons of Jerahmeel. ³⁴Sheshan had no sons, only daughters; he had an Egyptian slave named Jarha. ³⁵Sheshan gave his daughter in marriage to his slave Jarha, and she bore him Attai. ³⁶Attai became the father of Nathan. Nathan became the father of Zabad. ³⁷Zabad became the father of Ephlal. Ephlal became the father of Obed. ³⁸Obed became the father of Jehu. Jehu became the father of Azariah. ³⁹Azariah became the father of Helez. Helez became the father of Eleasah. ⁴⁰Eleasah became the father of Sismai. Sismai became the father of Shallum. ⁴¹Shallum became the father of Jekamiah. Jekamiah became the father of Elishama.

⁴²The sons of Caleb,<sup>¶</sup> the brother of Jerahmeel: Mesha his firstborn, who was the father of Ziph. Then the sons of Mareshah, who was the father of Hebron. ⁴³The sons of Hebron were Korah, Tappuah, Rekem, and Shema. ⁴⁴Shema became the father of Raham, who was the father of Jorkeam. Rekem became the father of Shammai. ⁴⁵The son of Shammai: Maon, who was the father of Beth-zur. ⁴⁶Ephah, Caleb's concubine, bore Haran, Moza, and Gazez. Haran became the father of Gazez. ⁴⁷The sons of Jahdai were Regem, Jotham, Geshan, Pelet, Ephah, and Shaaph. ⁴⁸Maacah, Caleb's concubine, bore Sheber and Tirhanah. ⁴⁹She also bore Shaaph, the father of Madmannah, Sheva, the father of Machbenah, and the father of Gibea. Achsah was Caleb's daughter.<sup>r</sup>

⁵⁰These were sons of Caleb, sons of Hur,** the firstborn of Ephrathah: Shobal, the father of Kiriath-jearim, ⁵¹Salma, the father of Bethlehem, and Hareph, the father of Bethgader. ⁵²The sons of Shobal, the father of Kiriath-jearim, were Reaiah, half of the Manahathites, ⁵³and the clans of Kiriath-jearim: the Ithrites, the Puthites, the Shumathites, and the Mishraites. From these the Zorahites and the Eshtaolites

in David, who was of the tribe of Judah; and the prominence of descendants of that tribe among the Jews of the Chronicler's time.

*[2:9] **Chelubai**: a variant form of the name Caleb (vv. 18, 42), a different person from the Chelub mentioned in 4:11.

†[2:10–17] These verses list the immediate ancestors of David. A similar list appears in Ru 4:18–22.

‡[2:18–24] These verses record the descendants of Caleb. In 4:15 as well as frequently in the Pentateuch (see Nm 13:6; 14:6, 30; 26:65; etc.), Caleb is called the son of Jephunneh. Here his father is called Hezron, perhaps because the Calebites were reckoned as part of the clan of the Hezronites.

w. [2:3] 1 Chr 4:21; Gn 38:1–5; 46:12.   x. [2:4] Gn 38:7, 13–30; 46:12; Mt 1:3.   y. [2:5] Gn 46:12.   z. [2:6] 1 Kgs 5:11.   a. [2:7] Jos 7:1, 18–21, 24–25; 22:20.   b. [2:9] Mt 1:3.   c. [2:10] Mt 1:4.   d. [2:11–12] Nm 1:7; Mt 1:4–5.   e. [2:13–15] 1 Sm 16:6–13; 17:13–14.   f. [2:13] 2 Chr 11:18.   g. [2:16] 2 Sm 2:18.   h. [2:17] 2 Sm 17:25; 19:14; 20:4–13.   i. [2:18] 1 Chr 2:24.   j. [2:19] 1 Chr 2:24.   k. [2:20] Ex 24:14; 31:2; 35:30; 2 Chr 1:5.   l. [2:21] Nm 26:29; 27:1; 32:39; Jos 13:31; Jgs 5:14.   m. [2:22] Nm 32:41; 1 Kgs 4:13.   n. [2:23] Dt 3:14; Jos 13:30.   o. [2:24] 1 Chr 2:19; 2 Sm 14:2; 2 Chr 11:6.

§[2:25–41] The Jerahmeelites were a clan living in the Negeb of Judah.

¶[2:42–49] Another list (see vv. 18–24) of the Calebites, a clan inhabiting the south of Judah.

**[2:50–55] The Hurites were a clan dwelling to the south and west of Jerusalem and related to the Calebites.

p. [2:25] 1 Sm 27:10; 30:29; Jb 32:2.   q. [2:31] 1 Chr 4:20.   r. [2:49] Jos 15:16; Jgs 1:12.

derived.[s] [54]The sons of Salma were Bethlehem, the Netophathites, Atroth-beth-Joab, half of the Manahathites, and the Zorites. [55]The clans of the Sopherim dwelling in Jabez were the Tirathites, the Shimeathites, and the Sucathites. They were the Kenites, who descended from Hammath, the ancestor of the Rechabites.[t]

## CHAPTER 3

[1*][u]These were the sons of David born to him in Hebron: the firstborn, Amnon, by Ahinoam of Jezreel; the second, Daniel,[†] by Abigail of Carmel; [2]the third, Absalom, son of Maacah, who was the daughter of Talmai, king of Geshur; the fourth, Adonijah, son of Haggith; [3]the fifth, Shephatiah, by Abital; the sixth, Ithream, by his wife Eglah. [4]Six in all were born to him in Hebron, where he reigned seven years and six months. Then he reigned thirty-three years in Jerusalem.[v] [5w]In Jerusalem the following were born to him: Shimea,[‡] Shobab, Nathan, Solomon—four by Bathsheba, the daughter of Ammiel;[x] [6]Ibhar, Elishua, Eliphelet, [7]Nogah, Nepheg, Japhia, [8]Elishama, Eliada, and Eliphelet—nine. [9]All these were sons of David, in addition to other sons by concubines; and Tamar was their sister.[y]

[10§z]The son of Solomon was Rehoboam, whose son was Abijah, whose son was Asa, whose son was Jehoshaphat,[a] [11]whose son was Joram, whose son was Ahaziah, whose son was Joash,[b] [12]whose son was Amaziah, whose son was Azariah, whose son was Jotham,[c] [13]whose son was Ahaz, whose son was Hezekiah, whose son was Manasseh,[d] [14]whose son was Amon, whose son was Josiah.[e] [15]The sons of Josiah were: the firstborn Johanan; the second, Jehoiakim; the third, Zedekiah; the fourth, Shallum.[¶f] [16]The sons of Jehoiakim were: Jeconiah, his son; Zedekiah, his son.[g] [17]The sons of Jeconiah** the captive were: Shealtiel,[h] [18]Malchiram, Pedaiah, Shenazzar,[††]

---

*[3:1–9] A list of David's sons.

†[3:1] **Daniel**: he is called Chileab in 2 Sm 3:3.

‡[3:5] **Shimea**: he bears the name Shammua in 2 Sm 5:14. **Ammiel**: Bathsheba's father is called Eliam in 2 Sm 11:3.

§[3:10–16] The kings of Judah from Solomon down to the destruction of Jerusalem by the Babylonians.

¶[3:15] **Shallum**: another name for Jehoahaz, Josiah's immediate successor; cf. Jer 22:11.

**[3:17–24] The descendants of King Jeconiah down to the time of the Chronicler. If twenty-five years are allowed for each generation, the ten generations between Jeconiah and Anani (the last name on the list) would put the birth of the latter at about 405 B.C.—an important item in establishing the approximate date of the Chronicler's work in its final form.

††[3:18] **Shenazar**: presumably he is the same as Sheshbazzar (Ezr 1:8; 11; 5:14–16), the prince of Judah who was the first Jewish governor of Judah after the exile. Both forms of the

s. [2:53] Jgs 18:2.    t. [2:55] Nm 24:21; Jgs 1:16; 4:11; 1 Sm 15:6; Jer 35.    u. [3:1–4] 2 Sm 3:2–5.    v. [3:4] 2 Sm 2:11; 5:5.    w. [3:5–8] 2 Sm 5:14–16.    x. [3:5] 2 Sm 11:3.    y. [3:9] 2 Sm 13:1–2.    z. [3:10–17] Mt 1:7–12.    a. [3:10] 1 Kgs 11:43; 14:31; 15:1, 8, 24; 2 Chr 9:31; 12:16; 13:23; 17:1.    b. [3:11] 1 Kgs 22:51; 2 Chr 21:1; 22:1; 24:1, 27.    c. [3:12] 2 Kgs 12:21; 14:21; 15:7; 2 Chr 26:1, 23; 27:1.    d. [3:13] 2 Kgs 15:38; 16:20; 20:21; 2 Chr 28:1, 27; 32:33.    e. [3:14] 2 Kgs 21:18, 26; 2 Chr 33:20, 25.    f. [3:15] 2 Kgs 23:34; 24:17; 2 Chr 36:4, 10.    g. [3:16] 2 Kgs 24:6, 17; 2 Chr 36:8, 10.    h. [3:17, 19] Ezr 2:2; 3:2, 8; 5:2; Sir 49:11; Hg 1:1, 12, 14; Mt 1:12–13; Lk 3:27.

---

Jekamiah, Hoshama, and Nedabiah. [19]The sons of Pedaiah were Zerubbabel[‡‡] and Shimei. The sons of Zerubbabel were Meshullam and Hananiah; Shelomith was their sister. [20]The sons of Meshullam were Hashubah, Ohel, Berechiah, Hasadiah, Jushabhesed—five. [21]The sons of Hananiah were Pelatiah, Jeshaiah, Rephaiah, Arnan, Obadiah, and Shecaniah. [22]The sons of Shecaniah were Shemaiah, Hattush, Igal, Bariah, Neariah, Shaphat—six.[i] [23]The sons of Neariah were Elioenai, Hizkiah, and Azrikam—three. [24]The sons of Elioenai were Hodaviah, Eliashib, Pelaiah, Akkub, Johanan, Delaiah, and Anani—seven.

## CHAPTER 4

[1§§]The sons of Judah were: Perez, Hezron, Carmi, Hur, and Shobal.[j] [2]Reaiah, the son of Shobal, became the father of Jahath, and Jahath became the father of Ahumai and Lahad. These were the clans of the Zorathites.

[3]These were the sons of Hareph, the father of Etam: Jezreel, Ishma, and Idbash; their sister was named Hazzelelponi. [4]Penuel was the father of Gedor, and Ezer the father of Hushah. These were the sons of Hur, the firstborn of Ephrathah, the father of Bethlehem.

[5]Ashhur, the father of Tekoa, had two wives, Helah and Naarah.[k] [6]Naarah bore him Ahuzzam, Hepher, the Temenites, and the Ahashtarites. These were the sons of Naarah. [7]The sons of Helah were Zereth, Izhar, Ethnan, and Koz. [8]Koz became the father of Anub and Zobebah, as well as of the clans of Aharhel, son of Harum. [9]Jabez was the most distinguished of his brothers. His mother had named him Jabez, saying, "I bore him with pain." [10]Jabez prayed to the God of Israel: "Oh, that you may truly bless me and extend my boundaries! May your hand be with me and make me free of misfortune, without pain!" And God granted his prayer.

[11]Chelub, the brother of Shuhah, became the father of Mehir, who was the father of Eshton. [12]Eshton became the father of Bethrapha, Paseah, and Tehinnah, the father of the city of Nahash. These were the men of Recah. [13]The sons of Kenaz were Othniel and Seraiah. The sons of Othniel were Hathath and Meonothai;[l] [14]Meonothai became the father of Ophrah. Seraiah became the father of Joab, the father of Geharashim, so called because they were artisans. [15]The sons of Caleb, son of

---

name probably go back to the Babylonian name Sin-ab-ussar, meaning "O [god] Sin, protect [our] father!"

‡‡[3:19] **Zerubbabel**: here called the son of Pedaiah, though elsewhere (Hg 1:12, 14; 2:2, 23; Ezr 3:2, 8; 5:2; Neh 12:1) his father's name is given as Shealtiel. The latter indication may merely point to the fact that Zerubbabel succeeded Shealtiel as head of the house of David.

§§[4:1–43] Genealogies of the southern tribes, Judah and Simeon.

i. [3:22] Neh 3:29.    j. [4:1] 1 Chr 2:4–5, 7, 9, 50; Gn 38:29; 46:12; Mt 1:3.    k. [4:5] 1 Chr 2:24.    l. [4:13] Jos 15:17; Jgs 1:13; 3:9, 11.

Jephunneh, were Ir, Elah, and Naam. The sons of Elah: Kenaz.*[m] [16]The sons of Jehallelel were Ziph, Ziphah, Tiria, and Asarel. [17]The sons of Ezrah were Jether, Mered, Epher, and Jalon. Jether became the father of Miriam, Shammai, and Ishbah, the father of Eshtemoa.[n] [18]Mered's Egyptian wife bore Jered, the father of Gedor, Heber, the father of Soco, and Jekuthiel, the father of Zanoah. These were the sons of Bithiah, the daughter of Pharaoh, whom Mered married. [19]The sons of his Jewish wife, the sister of Naham, the father of Keilah, were Shimon the Garmite and Ishi the Maacathite. [20]The sons of Shimon were Amnon, Rinnah, Benhanan, and Tilon. The son of Ishi was Zoheth and the son of Zoheth. . . .

[21]The sons of Shelah, son of Judah, were: Er, the father of Lecah; Laadah, the father of Mareshah; the clans of the linen weavers' guild in Bethashbea;[o] [22]Jokim; the people of Cozeba; and Joash and Saraph, who held property in Moab, but returned to Bethlehem. (These are events of old.) [23]They were potters and inhabitants of Netaim and Gederah, where they lived in the king's service.

**Simeon.** [24]The sons of Simeon were Nemuel, Jamin, Jachin, Zerah, and Shaul,[p] [25]whose son was Shallum, whose son was Mibsam, whose son was Mishma. [26]The sons of Mishma were his son Hammuel, whose son was Zaccur, whose son was Shimei. [27]Shimei had sixteen sons and six daughters. His brothers, however, did not have many sons, and as a result all their clans did not equal the number of the Judahites.

[28]They dwelt in Beer-sheba, Moladah, Hazar-shual, [29]Bilhah, Ezem, Tolad, [30]Bethuel, Hormah, Ziklag, [31]Beth-marcaboth, Hazarsusim, Bethbiri, and Shaaraim. Until the reign of David, these were their cities [32]and their villages. Etam, also, and Ain, Rimmon, Tochen, and Ashan—five cities,[q] [33]together with all their outlying villages as far as Baal. Here is where they dwelt, and so it was inscribed of them in their family records.

[34]Meshobab, Jamlech, Joshah, son of Amaziah, [35]Joel, Jehu, son of Joshibiah, son of Seraiah, son of Asiel, [36]Elioenai, Jaakobah, Jeshohaiah, Asaiah, Adiel, Jesimiel, Benaiah, [37]Ziza, son of Shiphi, son of Allon, son of Jedaiah, son of Shimri, son of Shemaiah— [38]these just named were princes in their clans, and their ancestral houses spread out to such an extent[r] [39]that they went to the approaches of Gedor,* east of the valley, seeking pasture for their flocks. [40]They found abundant and good pastures, and the land was spacious, quiet, and peaceful—for the Hamites dwelt there formerly. [41]They who have

just been listed by name set out during the reign of Hezekiah, king of Judah, and attacked their tents and also the Meunites who were there. They put them under the ban that is still in force to this day and dwelt in their place because they found pasture there for their flocks.[s]

[42]Five hundred of them (the Simeonites) went to Mount Seir, with Pelatiah, Neariah, Rephaiah, and Uzziel, sons of Ishi, at their head. [43]They attacked the surviving Amalekites who had escaped, and have lived there to the present day.[t]

## CHAPTER 5

**Reuben.** [1][1]The sons of Reuben, the firstborn of Israel. (He was indeed the firstborn, but because he defiled the couch of his father his birthright was given to the sons of Joseph, son of Israel, so that he is not listed in the family records according to his birthright.[u] [2]Judah, in fact, became powerful among his brothers, so that the ruler came from him, though the birthright had been Joseph's.)[v] [3]The sons of Reuben, the firstborn of Israel, were Hanoch, Pallu, Hezron, and Carmi.[w] [4]His son was Joel, whose son was Shemaiah, whose son was Gog, whose son was Shimei, [5]whose son was Micah, whose son was Reaiah, whose son was Baal, [6]whose son was Beerah, whom Tilgath-pileser, the king of Assyria, took into exile; he was a prince of the Reubenites.[x] [7]His brothers who belonged to his clans, when they were listed in the family records according to their descendants, were: Jeiel, the chief, and Zechariah, [8]and Bela, son of Azaz, son of Shema, son of Joel. The Reubenites lived in Aroer and as far as Nebo and Baal-meon;[y] [9]toward the east they dwelt as far as the wilderness which extends from the Euphrates River, for they had much livestock in the land of Gilead.[z] [10]In Saul's time they waged war with the Hagrites, and when they had defeated them they dwelt in their tents throughout the region east of Gilead.[a]

**Gad.** [11]The Gadites lived alongside them in the land of Bashan as far as Salecah.[b] [12]Joel was chief, Shapham was second in command, and Janai was judge in Bashan.[c] [13]Their brothers, according to their ancestral houses, were: Michael, Meshullam, Sheba, Jorai, Jacan, Zia, and Eber—seven. [14]These were the sons of Abihail, son of Huri, son of Jaroah, son of Gilead, son of Michael, son of Jeshishai, son of Jahdo, son of Buz. [15]Ahi, son of Abdiel, son of Guni, was the head of their ancestral houses. [16]They dwelt in Gilead, in Bashan and its towns, and in all the pasture lands of

---

†[5:1–26] Genealogies of the Transjordanian tribes, Reuben, Gad, and the half-tribe of Manasseh.

---

*[4:39] **Gedor:** the Greek reads Gerar, probably correctly.

---

m. [4:15] Nm 13:6; 14:6; 32:12; Jos 14:6, 14.  n. [4:17] 1 Sm 30:28.  o. [4:21] 1 Chr 2:3; Gn 38:5; 46:12; Nm 26:20.  p. [4:24] Gn 46:10; Ex 6:15; Nm 26:12–13.  q. [4:28–32] Jos 19:2–8.  r. [4:38] Nm 1:2.

s. [4:41] 2 Kgs 18:1–2; 2 Chr 29:1.  t. [4:43] Ex 17:8, 14; Dt 25:17–19; 1 Sm 14:48; 15:3, 7–8; 2 Sm 8:12.  u. [5:1] Gn 35:22; 48:5, 15–22; 49:3–4; Dt 33:6.  v. [5:2] 1 Chr 28:4; Gn 49:8–12.  w. [5:3] Gn 46:9; Ex 6:14; Nm 26:5–6.  x. [5:6] 2 Kgs 15:29.  y. [5:8] Jos 13:9, 16–17; Nm 32:3, 38.  z. [5:9] Jos 22:9.  a. [5:10] Ps 83:6–7.  b. [5:11] Jos 13:11, 24–28.  c. [5:12] Gn 46:16.

Sirion to the borders. [17]All were listed in the family records in the time of Jotham, king of Judah, and of Jeroboam, king of Israel.

[18]The Reubenites, Gadites, and the half-tribe of Manasseh were warriors, men who bore shield and sword and who drew the bow, trained in warfare—forty-four thousand seven hundred and sixty men fit for military service. [19]When they waged war against the Hagrites and against Jetur, Naphish, and Nodab,[d] [20]they received help so that the Hagrites and all who were with them were delivered into their power. For during the battle they cried out to God, and he heard them because they had put their trust in him.[e] [21]Along with one hundred thousand persons they also captured their livestock: fifty thousand camels, two hundred fifty thousand sheep, and two thousand donkeys. [22]Many were slain and fell; for "From God the victory." They dwelt in their place until the time of the exile.[f]

**The Half-tribe of Manasseh.** [23]The half-tribe of Manasseh lived in the land of Bashan as far as Baal-hermon, Senir, and Mount Hermon; they were numerous. [24]The following were the heads of their ancestral houses: Epher, Ishi, Eliel, Azriel, Jeremiah, Hodaviah, and Jahdiel—men who were warriors, famous men, and heads over their ancestral houses.

[25]However, they acted treacherously toward the God of their ancestors by prostituting themselves to follow the gods of the peoples of the land, whom God had destroyed before them.[g] [26]Therefore the God of Israel stirred up against them the anger of Pul,* king of Assyria, and the anger of Tilgath-pilneser [sic], king of Assyria, who deported the Reubenites, the Gadites, and the half-tribe of Manasseh and brought them to Halah, Habor, and Hara, and to the river Gozan, where they have remained to this day.[h]

**Levi.**[†] [27]The sons of Levi were Gershon, Kohath, and Merari.[i] [28]The sons of Kohath were Amram, Izhar, Hebron, and Uzziel.[j] [29]The children of Amram were Aaron, Moses, and Miriam. The sons of Aaron were Nadab, Abihu, Eleazar, and Ithamar.[k] [30†]Eleazar became the father of Phinehas. Phinehas became the father of Abishua. [31]Abishua became the father of Bukki. Bukki became the father of Uzzi. [32]Uzzi became the father of Zerahiah. Zerahiah became the father

of Meraioth. [33]Meraioth became the father of Amariah. Amariah became the father of Ahitub. [34]Ahitub became the father of Zadok. Zadok became the father of Ahimaaz. [35]Ahimaaz became the father of Azariah. Azariah became the father of Johanan. [36]Johanan became the father of Azariah, who served as priest in the temple Solomon built in Jerusalem. [37]Azariah became the father of Amariah. Amariah became the father of Ahitub. [38]Ahitub became the father of Zadok. Zadok became the father of Shallum. [39]Shallum became the father of Hilkiah. Hilkiah became the father of Azariah. [40]Azariah became the father of Seraiah. Seraiah became the father of Jehozadak. [41]Jehozadak was one of those who went into the exile which the LORD inflicted on Judah and Jerusalem through Nebuchadnezzar.

## CHAPTER 6

[1]The sons of Levi were Gershon, Kohath, and Merari.[l] [2]The sons of Gershon were named Libni and Shimei.[m] [3]The sons of Kohath were Amram, Izhar, Hebron, and Uzziel.[n] [4]The sons of Merari were Mahli and Mushi.[o]

These were the clans of Levi, according to their ancestors. [5]Of Gershon: his son Libni, whose son was Jahath, whose son was Zimmah, [6]whose son was Joah, whose son was Iddo, whose son was Zerah, whose son was Jetherai.

[7]The sons of Kohath: his son Amminadab, whose son was Korah, whose son was Assir, [8]whose son was Elkanah, whose son was Ebiasaph, whose son was Assir, [9]whose son was Tahath, whose son was Uriel, whose son was Uzziah, whose son was Shaul. [10]The sons of Elkanah were Amasai and Ahimoth, [11]whose son was Elkanah, whose son was Zophai, whose son was Nahath, [12]whose son was Eliab, whose son was Jeroham, whose son was Elkanah, whose son was Samuel. [13]The sons of Samuel were Joel, the firstborn, and Abijah, the second.

[14]The sons of Merari: Mahli, whose son was Libni, whose son was Shimei, whose son was Uzzah,[p] [15]whose son was Shimea, whose son was Haggiah, whose son was Asaiah.

[16]The following were established by David for the service of song[§] in the LORD's house at the time when the ark had a resting place. [17]They served as singers before the tabernacle of the tent of meeting until Solomon built the house of the LORD in Jerusalem, and they performed their services according to the order prescribed for them. [18]Those who so performed are the following, together with their sons.

---

*[5:26] **Pul:** the Chronicler seems to speak of two different kings here, but Pul was the name which the Assyrian king Tilgath-pileser III (745–727 B.C.) adopted as king of Babylon.

†[5:27–6:66] The tribe of Levi. The Chronicler's list gives special prominence to Levi's son Kohath, from whom were descended both the Aaronite priests (vv. 28–41) and the leading group of Temple singers (6:18–23).

‡[5:30–41] The line of preexilic high priests. The list seems to become confused in vv. 36–38, which repeat the same names, mostly in inverse order, that occur in vv. 34–36. A similar but shorter list occurs, with variations, in Ezr 7:1–5.

§[6:16–32] The cultic functions performed by the levitical families in the postexilic Temple at the time of the Chronicler are here traced back to David, in a way analogous to that in which all the laws in the Pentateuch are attributed to Moses.

---

d. [5:19] 1 Chr 1:31; 5:10; Gn 25:15; Ps 83:6–7.   e. [5:20] Dt 33:20–21.   f. [5:22] Nm 32:39; Dt 3:8–10; Jgs 3:3.   g. [5:25] Ex 34:14–16; 2 Kgs 17:7.   h. [5:26] 2 Kgs 15:9, 29; 17:6.   i. [5:27] 1 Chr 6:1; 23:6; Gn 46:11; Ex 6:16; Nm 26:57.   j. [5:28] 1 Chr 6:3; Ex 6:18.   k. [5:29] Ex 6:20; Nm 26:59–60.

l. [6:1] 1 Chr 5:27; 23:6; Gn 46:11; Ex 6:16; Nm 26:57.   m. [6:2] Ex 6:17.   n. [6:3] Ex 6:18; Nm 3:19; 26:59.   o. [6:4] 1 Chr 6:14; Ex 6:19; Nm 3:20; 26:58.   p. [6:14] 1 Chr 6:4; Ex 6:19; Nm 3:20; 26:58.

Among the Kohathites: Heman, the chanter, son of Joel, son of Samuel, [19]son of Elkanah, son of Jeroham, son of Eliel, son of Toah, [20]son of Zuph, son of Elkanah, son of Mahath, son of Amasi, [21]son of Elkanah, son of Joel, son of Azariah, son of Zephaniah, [22]son of Tahath, son of Assir, son of Ebiasaph, son of Korah,[q] [23]son of Izhar, son of Kohath, son of Levi, son of Israel.

[24]His brother Asaph stood at his right hand. Asaph was the son of Berechiah, son of Shimea, [25]son of Michael, son of Baaseiah, son of Malchijah, [26]son of Ethni, son of Zerah, son of Adaiah, [27]son of Ethan, son of Zimmah,[r] son of Shimei, [28]son of Jahath, son of Gershon, son of Levi.

[29]Their brothers, the Merarites, stood at the left: Ethan, son of Kishi, son of Abdi, son of Malluch, [30]son of Hashabiah, son of Amaziah, son of Hilkiah, [31]son of Amzi, son of Bani, son of Shemer, [32]son of Mahli, son of Mushi, son of Merari, son of Levi.[s]

[33]Their brother Levites were appointed to all the other services of the tabernacle of the house of God.[t] [34]However, it was Aaron and his sons who made the sacrifice on the altar for burnt offerings and on the altar of incense; they alone had charge of the holy of holies and of making atonement for Israel, as Moses, the servant of God, had commanded.[u]

[35]These were the sons of Aaron: his son Eleazar, whose son was Phinehas, whose son was Abishua, [36]whose son was Bukki, whose son was Uzzi, whose son was Zerahiah, [37]whose son was Meraioth, whose son was Amariah, whose son was Ahitub, [38]whose son was Zadok, whose son was Ahimaaz.

[39]*The following were their dwelling places, by encampments in their territories. To the sons of Aaron who belonged to the clan of the Kohathites, since the lot fell to them, [40]was assigned Hebron in the land of Judah, with its adjacent pasture lands. [41]However, the open country and the villages belonging to the city had been given to Caleb, the son of Jephunneh. [42]There were assigned to the sons of Aaron: Hebron a city of refuge, Libnah with its pasture lands, Jattir with its pasture lands, Eshtemoa with its pasture lands, [43]Holon with its pasture lands, Debir with its pasture lands, [44]Ashan with its pasture lands, Jetta with its pasture lands, and Beth-shemesh with its pasture lands. [45]Also from the tribe of Benjamin: Gibeon with its pasture lands, Geba with its pasture lands, Almon with its pasture lands, Anathoth with its pasture lands. In all, they had thirteen cities with their pasture lands. [49]The Israelites assigned these cities with their pasture lands to the Levites, [50]designating them by name

and assigning them by lot from the tribes of the Judahites, Simeonites, and Benjaminites.

[46]The other Kohathites obtained ten cities by lot for their clans from the tribe of Ephraim, from the tribe of Dan, and from the half-tribe of Manasseh. [47]The clans of the Gershonites obtained thirteen cities from the tribes of Issachar, Asher, and Naphtali, and from the half-tribe of Manasseh in Bashan. [48]The clans of the Merarites obtained twelve cities by lot from the tribes of Reuben, Gad, and Zebulun.

[51]The clans of the Kohathites obtained cities by lot from the tribe of Ephraim. [52]They were assigned cities of refuge: Shechem in the mountain region of Ephraim, with its pasture lands, Gezer with its pasture lands, [53]Kibzaim with its pasture lands, and Beth-horon with its pasture lands. [54]From the tribe of Dan: Elteke with its pasture lands, Gibbethon with its pasture lands, Aijalon with its pasture lands, and Gath-rimmon with its pasture lands. [55]From the half-tribe of Manasseh: Taanach with its pasture lands and Ibleam with its pasture lands. These belonged to the rest of the Kohathite clan.

[56]The clans of the Gershonites received from the half-tribe of Manasseh: Golan in Bashan with its pasture lands and Ashtaroth with its pasture lands. [57]From the tribe of Issachar: Kedesh with its pasture lands, Daberath with its pasture lands, [58]Ramoth with its pasture lands, and Engannim with its pasture lands. [59]From the tribe of Asher: Mashal with its pasture lands, Abdon with its pasture lands, [60]Hilkath with its pasture lands, and Rehob with its pasture lands. [61]From the tribe of Naphtali: Kedesh in Galilee with its pasture lands, Hammon with its pasture lands, and Kiriathaim with its pasture lands.

[62]The rest of the Merarites received from the tribe of Zebulun: Jokneam with its pasture lands, Kartah with its pasture lands, Rimmon with its pasture lands, and Tabor with its pasture lands. [63]Across the Jordan at Jericho (that is, east of the Jordan) they received from the tribe of Reuben: Bezer in the desert with its pasture lands, Jahzah with its pasture lands, [64]Kedemoth with its pasture lands, and Mephaath with its pasture lands. [65]From the tribe of Gad: Ramoth in Gilead with its pasture lands, Mahanaim with its pasture lands, [66]Heshbon with its pasture lands, and Jazer with its pasture lands.

## CHAPTER 7

**Issachar.** [1]†The sons of Issachar were Tola, Puah, Jashub, and Shimron: four.[v] [2]The sons of Tola were Uzzi, Rephaiah, Jeriel, Jahmai, Ibsam, and Shemuel, heads of the ancestral houses of Tola, mighty warriors in their generations. In the time of David they numbered twenty-two thousand six hundred.[w] [3]The sons of Uzzi: Izarahiah. The

---

*[6:39–66] For the rights of the Levites in the cities assigned to them, see note on Jos 21:1.

q. [6:22] Ex 6:24.   r. [6:27] 1 Chr 6:2, 5.   s. [6:32] Ex 6:19; Nm 26:58.   t. [6:33] 1 Chr 15:17, 19; 16:41–42; 2 Chr 5:12.   u. [6:34] 1 Chr 16:39–40.

†[7:1–40] The seven northern tribes.

v. [7:1] Gn 46:13.   w. [7:2] Nm 26:23–24; Jgs 10:1.

sons of Izarahiah were Michael, Obadiah, Joel, and Isshiah. All five of these were chiefs. [4]Along with them, in their generations, according to ancestral houses, were thirty-six thousand men in organized military troops, since they had more wives and children [5]than their fellow tribesmen. In all the clans of Issachar there was a total of eighty-seven thousand warriors listed in their family records.

**Benjamin.** [6]The sons of Benjamin were Bela, Becher, and Jediael—three.[x] [7]The sons of Bela were Ezbon, Uzzi, Uzziel, Jerimoth, and Iri—five. They were heads of their ancestral houses and warriors. Their family records listed twenty-two thousand and thirty-four. [8]The sons of Becher were Zemirah, Joash, Eliezer, Elioenai, Omri, Jeremoth, Abijah, Anathoth, and Alemeth—all these were sons of Becher.[y] [9]Their family records listed twenty thousand two hundred of their kindred who were heads of their ancestral houses and warriors. [10]The sons of Jediael: Bilhan. The sons of Bilhan were Jeush, Benjamin, Ehud, Chenaanah, Zethan, Tarshish, and Ahishahar. [11]All these were sons of Jediael, heads of ancestral houses and warriors. They numbered seventeen thousand two hundred men fit for military service . . .' [12]Shupham and Hupham.[z]

**Dan, Naphtali and Manasseh.** The sons of Dan: Hushim. [13]The sons of Naphtali were Jahziel, Guni, Jezer, and Shallum. These were sons of Bilhah.[a] [14]The sons of Manasseh, whom his Aramean concubine bore:[b] she bore Machir, the father of Gilead.[c] [15]Machir took a wife whose name was Maacah; his sister's name was Molecheth. Manasseh's second son was named Zelophehad, who had only daughters.[d] [16]Maacah, Machir's wife, bore a son whom she named Peresh. He had a brother named Sheresh, whose sons were Ulam and Rakem. [17]The sons of Ulam: Bedan. These were the sons of Gilead, the son of Machir, the son of Manasseh. [18]His sister Molecheth bore Ishhod, Abiezer, and Mahlah. [19]The sons of Shemida were Ahian, Shechem, Likhi, and Aniam.

**Ephraim.** [20e]The sons of Ephraim: Shuthelah, whose son was Bered, whose son was Tahath, whose son was Eleadah, whose son was Tahath, [21]whose son was Zabad. Ephraim's son Shuthelah, and Ezer and Elead, who were born in the land, were killed by the inhabitants of Gath because they had gone down to take away their livestock. [22]Their father Ephraim mourned a long time, but after his relatives had come and comforted him, [23]he had relations with his wife, who conceived and bore a son whom he named Beriah,

since evil[†] had befallen his house./ [24]He had a daughter, Sheerah, who built Lower and Upper Beth-horon and Uzzen-sheerah. [25]Zabad's son was Rephah, whose son was Resheph, whose son was Telah, whose son was Tahan, [26]whose son was Ladan, whose son was Ammihud, whose son was Elishama,[g] [27]whose son was Nun, whose son was Joshua.

[28]Their property and their dwellings were in Bethel and its towns, Naaran to the east, Gezer and its towns to the west, and also Shechem and its towns as far as Ayyah and its towns.[h] [29]Manasseh, however, had possession of Beth-shean and its towns, Taanach and its towns, Megiddo and its towns, and Dor and its towns. In these dwelt the sons of Joseph, the son of Israel.[i]

**Asher.** [30]The sons of Asher were Imnah, Ishvah, Ishvi, and Beriah; their sister was Serah.[j] [31]Beriah's sons were Heber and Malchiel, who was the father of Birzaith. [32]Heber became the father of Japhlet, Shomer, Hotham, and their sister Shua. [33]The sons of Japhlet were Pasach, Bimhal, and Ashvath; these were the sons of Japhlet. [34]The sons of Shomer were Ahi, Rohgah, Jehubbah, and Aram. [35]The sons of his brother Hotham were Zophah, Imna, Shelesh, and Amal. [36]The sons of Zophah were Suah, Harnepher, Shual, Beri, Imrah, [37]Bezer, Hod, Shamma, Shilshah, Ithran, and Beera. [38]The sons of Jether were Jephunneh, Pispa, and Ara. [39]The sons of Ulla were Arah, Hanniel, and Rizia. [40]All these were sons of Asher, heads of ancestral houses, distinguished men, warriors, and chiefs among the princes. Their family records numbered twenty-six thousand men fit for military service.

## CHAPTER 8

**Benjamin.** [1#]Benjamin became the father of Bela, his firstborn, Ashbel, the second son, Aharah, the third,[k] [2]Nohah, the fourth, and Rapha, the fifth. [3]The sons of Bela were Addar and Gera, the father of Ehud. [4]The sons of Ehud were Abishua, Naaman, Ahoah,[l] [5]Gera, Shephuphan, and Huram. [6]These were the sons of Ehud, family heads over those who dwelt in Geba and were deported to Manahath. [7]Also Naaman, Ahijah, and Gera. The last, who led them into exile, became the father of Uzza and Ahihud. [8]Shaharaim became a father on the Moabite plateau after he had put away his wives Hushim and Baara. [9]By his wife Hodesh he begot Jobab, Zibia, Mesha, Malcam, [10]Jeuz, Sachia, and Mirmah. These were his sons, family heads. [11]By Hushim he begot Abitub and Elpaal. [12]The sons of Elpaal

---

†[7:23] **Beriah . . . evil:** the name sounds like the Hebrew word for "evil," with the preposition *be.*

‡[8:1–40] A second, variant list (cf. 7:6–11) of the Benjaminites, highlighting the family of Saul (vv. 33–40).

---

x. [7:6] Gn 46:21; Nm 26:38.   y. [7:8] Gn 46:21.   z. [7:12] Nm 26:39.   a. [7:12–13] Gn 46:24; Nm 26:48–49.   b. [7:14–19] Nm 26:29–32.   c. [7:14] Nm 26:29; Jos 17:1.   d. [7:15] Nm 26:33; Jos 17:3.   e. [7:20] Nm 26:35.   f. [7:23] 1 Chr 8:13.   g. [7:26] Nm 1:10; 2:18; 7:48; 10:22.   h. [7:28] Gn 12:8; 1 Kgs 9:16.   i. [7:29] Jos 17:11.   j. [7:30] Gn 46:17; Nm 26:44–46.   k. [8:1] 1 Chr 7:6; Gn 46:21; Nm 26:38–44.   l. [8:4] Jgs 3:15.

were Eber, Misham, Shemed (who built Ono and Lod with its nearby towns),^m ^13and Beriah, and Shema. They were family heads of those who dwelt in Aijalon, and they put the inhabitants of Gath to flight. ^14Their relatives were Elpaal, Shashak, and Jeremoth. ^15Zebadiah, Arad, Eder, ^16Michael, Ishpah, and Joha were the sons of Beriah. ^17Zebadiah, Meshullam, Hizki, Heber, ^18Ishmerai, Izliah, and Jobab were the sons of Elpaal. ^19Jakim, Zichri, Zabdi, ^20Elienai, Zillethai, Eliel, ^21Adaiah, Beraiah, and Shimrath were the sons of Shimei. ^22Ishpan, Eber, Eliel, ^23Abdon, Zichri, Hanan, ^24Hananiah, Elam, Anthothijah, ^25Iphdeiah, and Penuel were the sons of Shashak. ^26Shamsherai, Sheariah, Athaliah, ^27Jaareshiah, Elijah, and Zichri were the sons of Jeroham. ^28These were family heads in their generations, chiefs who dwelt in Jerusalem.

^29nIn Gibeon dwelt Jeiel, the founder of Gibeon, whose wife's name was Maacah; ^30also his firstborn son, Abdon, and Zur, Kish, Baal, Ner, Nadab, ^31Gedor, Ahio, Zecher, and Mikloth. ^32Mikloth became the father of Shimeah. These, too, dwelt with their relatives in Jerusalem, opposite their fellow tribesmen. ^33oNer became the father of Kish, and Kish became the father of Saul. Saul became the father of Jonathan, Malchishua, Abinadab, and Eshbaal.^p ^34The son of Jonathan was Meribbaal, and Meribbaal became the father of Micah.^q ^35The sons of Micah were Pithon, Melech, Tarea, and Ahaz. ^36Ahaz became the father of Jehoaddah, and Jehoaddah became the father of Alemeth, Azmaveth, and Zimri. Zimri became the father of Moza.^r ^37Moza became the father of Binea, whose son was Raphah, whose son was Eleasah, whose son was Azel. ^38Azel had six sons, whose names were Azrikam, his firstborn, Ishmael, Sheariah, Azariah, Obadiah, and Hanan; all these were the sons of Azel.^s ^39The sons of Eshek, his brother, were Ulam, his firstborn, Jeush, the second son, and Eliphelet, the third. ^40The sons of Ulam were warriors, skilled with the bow, and they had many sons and grandsons: one hundred and fifty. All these were the sons of Benjamin.

## CHAPTER 9

^1Thus all Israel was listed in family lists, and these are recorded in the book of the kings of Israel.^t

Now Judah had been exiled to Babylon because of its treachery. ^2*uThe first to settle again in their cities and dwell there were certain Israelites, the priests, the Levites, and the temple servants.^v

**Jerusalemites.** ^3In Jerusalem lived Judahites and Benjaminites; also Ephraimites and Manassites. ^4Among the Judahites was Uthai, son of Ammihud, son of Omri, son of Imri, son of Bani, one of the sons of Perez, son of Judah. ^5Among the Shelanites were Asaiah, the firstborn, and his sons. ^6Among the Zerahites were Jeuel and six hundred and ninety of their relatives. ^7Among the Benjaminites were Sallu, son of Meshullam, son of Hodaviah, son of Hassenuah, ^8as well as Ibneiah, son of Jeroham; Elah, son of Uzzi, son of Michri; Meshullam, son of Shephatiah, son of Reuel, son of Ibnijah. ^9Their kindred of various families were nine hundred and fifty-six. All those named were heads of their ancestral houses.

^10Among the priests were Jedaiah; Jehoiarib; Jachin; ^11Azariah, son of Hilkiah, son of Meshullam, son of Zadok, son of Meraioth, son of Ahitub, the ruler of the house of God; ^12Adaiah, son of Jeroham, son of Pashhur, son of Malchijah; Maasai, son of Adiel, son of Jahzerah, son of Meshullam, son of Meshillemith, son of Immer. ^13Their brothers, heads of their ancestral houses, were one thousand seven hundred and sixty, valiant in the work of the service of the house of God.

^14Among the Levites were Shemaiah, son of Hasshub, son of Azrikam, son of Hashabiah, one of the sons of Merari; ^15Bakbakkar; Heresh; Galal; Mattaniah, son of Mica, son of Zichri, a descendant of Asaph; ^16Obadiah, son of Shemaiah, son of Galal, a descendant of Jeduthun; and Berechiah, son of Asa, son of Elkanah, whose family lived in the villages of the Netophathites.

^17The gatekeepers were Shallum, Akkub, Talmon, Ahiman, and their brothers; Shallum was the chief. ^18Previously they had stood guard at the king's gate on the east side; now they became gatekeepers for the encampments of the Levites. ^19Shallum, son of Kore, son of Ebiasaph, a descendant of Korah, and his brothers of the same ancestral house of the Korahites had as their assigned task the guarding of the threshold of the tent, just as their fathers had guarded the entrance to the encampment of the LORD. ^20Phinehas, son of Eleazar, had been their chief in times past; the LORD was with him.^w ^21Zechariah, son of Meshelemiah, guarded the gate of the tent of meeting.^x ^22In all, those who were chosen for gatekeepers at the threshold were two hundred and twelve. They were inscribed in the family records of their villages. David and Samuel the seer had established them in their position of trust. ^23Thus they and their sons kept guard over the gates of the house of the LORD, the house which was then a tent. ^24The gatekeepers were stationed at the four sides, to the east, the west, the north, and the south.^y ^25Their brothers who lived in their own villages took

---

*[9:2–34] The inhabitants of Jerusalem after the exile. A similar list, though with many variants in the names, occurs in Neh 11:3–24.

m. [8:12] Neh 11:35.   n. [8:29–32] 1 Chr 9:35–38.   o. [8:33–38] 1 Chr 9:39–44.   p. [8:33] 1 Chr 10:2; 1 Sm 9:1; 14:49, 51; 31:2.   q. [8:34] 2 Sm 4:4; 9:6; 10:12.   r. [8:36] 1 Chr 9:42.   s. [8:38] 1 Chr 9:43.   t. [9:1] 2 Chr 16:11; 20:34; 25:26; 27:7; 33:18; 36:8.   u. [9:2–34] Neh 11:3–24.   v. [9:2] Ezr 2:70; 7:7; Neh 11:3.

w. [9:20] Ex 6:25; Nm 25:7, 11; Jgs 20:28.   x. [9:21] 1 Chr 26:2, 14.   y. [9:24] 1 Chr 26:13.

turns in assisting them for seven-day periods,[z] [26]while the four chief gatekeepers were on permanent duty. These were the Levites who also had charge of the chambers and treasures of the house of God. [27]They would spend the night near the house of God, for it was in their charge and they had the duty of opening it each morning.

[28]Some of them had charge of the vessels used there, tallying them as they were brought in and taken out. [29]Others were appointed to take care of the utensils and all the sacred vessels, as well as the fine flour, the wine, the oil, the frankincense, and the spices. [30]It was the sons of priests, however, who mixed the spiced ointments.[a] [31b]Mattithiah, one of the Levites, the firstborn of Shallum the Korahite, was entrusted with preparing the cakes. [32]Benaiah the Kohathite, one of their brothers, was in charge of setting out the showbread each sabbath.[c]

[33]These were the singers and the gatekeepers, family heads over the Levites. They stayed in the chambers when free of duty, for day and night they had to be ready for service. [34]These were the levitical family heads by their generations, chiefs who dwelt in Jerusalem.

## II. THE HISTORY OF DAVID

**Genealogy of Saul.** [35d]Jeiel, the founder of Gibeon, dwelt in Gibeon; his wife's name was Maacah. [36]His firstborn son was Abdon; then came Zur, Kish, Baal, Ner, Nadab, [37]Gedor, Ahio, Zechariah, and Mikloth. [38]Mikloth became the father of Shimeam. These, too, with their relatives, dwelt opposite their relatives in Jerusalem. [39]Ner became the father of Kish, and Kish became the father of Saul. Saul became the father of Jonathan, Malchishua, Abinadab, and Eshbaal. [40]The son of Jonathan was Meribbaal, and Meribbaal became the father of Micah. [41]The sons of Micah were Pithon, Melech, Tahrea, and Ahaz. [42]Ahaz became the father of Jehoaddah, and Jehoaddah became the father of Alemeth, Azmaveth, and Zimri. Zimri became the father of Moza. [43]Moza became the father of Binea, whose son was Rephaiah, whose son was Eleasah, whose son was Azel. [44]Azel had six sons, whose names were Azrikam, his firstborn, Ishmael, Sheariah, Azariah, Obadiah, and Hanan; these were the sons of Azel.

## CHAPTER 10

**Death of Saul and His Sons.** [1e]Now the Philistines went to war against Israel, and Israel fled before them, and they fell, slain on Mount Gilboa. [2]The Philistines pressed hard after Saul and his sons. When the Philistines had struck down Jonathan, Abinadab, and Malchishua, sons of Saul, [3]the fury of the battle converged on Saul.

Then the archers hit him, and he was severely wounded.

[4]Saul said to his armor-bearer, "Draw your sword and run me through; otherwise these uncircumcised will come and abuse me." But the armor-bearer, badly frightened, refused, so Saul took his own sword and fell upon it. [5]When the armor-bearer saw that Saul was dead, he too fell upon his sword and died. [6]Thus Saul, and his three sons, his whole house, died together. [7]When all the Israelites in the valley saw that Saul and his sons had fled and that they had died, they abandoned their cities and fled. Then the Philistines came and lived in those cities.

[8]On the following day, when the Philistines came to strip the slain, they found Saul and his sons fallen on Mount Gilboa. [9]They stripped him, and took his head and his armor; these they sent throughout the land of the Philistines to bring the good news to their idols and to the people. [10]They put his armor in the temple of their gods, but his skull they impaled at the temple of Dagon.

**Burial of Saul.** [11]When all the inhabitants of Jabesh-gilead heard all that the Philistines had done to Saul, [12]all their warriors set out, recovered the corpses of Saul and his sons, and brought them to Jabesh. They buried their bones under the oak of Jabesh, and fasted for seven days.[f]

[13]Thus Saul died because of his treason against the LORD in disobeying his word, and also because he had sought counsel from a ghost,[g] [14]rather than from the LORD. Therefore the LORD took his life, and turned his kingdom over to David, the son of Jesse.[h]

## CHAPTER 11

**David Is Made King.** [1]Then all Israel gathered around David in Hebron, and they said: "Look! We are your bone and your flesh. [2]In days past, when Saul was still the king, it was you who led Israel in all its battles. And now the LORD, your God, has said to you: You shall shepherd my people Israel; you shall be ruler over my people Israel."[j] [3]Then all the elders of Israel came to the king at Hebron, and at Hebron David made a covenant with them in the presence of the LORD; and they anointed David king over Israel, in accordance with the word of the LORD given through Samuel.[k]

**Jerusalem Captured.** [4]Then David and all Israel went to Jerusalem, that is, Jebus, where the inhabitants of the land were called Jebusites.[l]

---

*[10:13–14] The Chronicler explains why Saul met his tragic end: he had disobeyed the Lord's command given through the prophet Samuel (1 Sm 15:3–9), and had consulted a necromancer (1 Sm 28:6–19), contrary to the Mosaic law (Dt 18:10–11).

z. [9:25] 2 Chr 23:4–5.   a. [9:30] Ex 30:20–33.   b. [9:31–32] 1 Chr 23:29; Lv 2:1–15; 6:13–16; 7:11.   c. [9:32] Ex 25:30; Lv 24:5–8.   d. [9:35–44] 1 Chr 8:29–38.   e. [10:1–12] 1 Sm 31:1–13.

f. [10:12] 2 Sm 2:5.   g. [10:13] Dt 18:10–14; 1 Sm, 13:13–14; 15:3, 11, 26.   h. [10:14] 1 Sm 15:28; 2 Sm 3:9–10.   i. [11:1–9] 2 Sm 5:1–10.   j. [11:2] 1 Sm 18:5, 13–16, 30; 19:8.   k. [11:3] 1 Sm 16:1, 13; 2 Sm 2:4.   l. [11:4] Jos 15:8; Jgs 1:21; 19:10–11.

⁵The inhabitants of Jebus said to David, "You shall not enter here." David nevertheless captured the fortress of Zion, which is the City of David. ⁶David said, "Whoever strikes the Jebusites first shall be made chief and captain." Joab, the son of Zeruiah, was the first to attack; and so he became chief.ᵐ ⁷David took up residence in the fortress, which therefore was called the City of David. ⁸He built up the city on all sides, from the Millo all the way around, while Joab restored the rest of the city.ⁿ ⁹David became ever more powerful, for the LORD of hosts was with him.

**David's Warriors.** ¹⁰°These were David's chief warriors who, together with all Israel, supported him in his reign in order to make him king, according to the LORD's word concerning Israel. ¹¹Here is the list of David's warriors:

Ishbaal, the son of Hachamoni, chief of the Three.* He brandished his spear over three hundred, whom he had slain in a single encounter. ¹²Next to him was Eleazar, the son of Dodo the Ahohite, one of the Three warriors.ᵖ ¹³He was with David at Pas-dammim, where the Philistines had massed for battle. There was a plot of land full of barley. The people were fleeing before the Philistines,�q ¹⁴but he took his stand in the middle of the plot, kept it safe, and cut down the Philistines. Thus the LORD brought about a great victory.

¹⁵Three of the Thirty chiefs went down to the rock, to David, who was in the cave of Adullam while the Philistines were encamped in the valley of Rephaim.ʳ ¹⁶David was then in the stronghold, and a Philistine garrison was at Bethlehem. ¹⁷David had a strong craving, and said, "If only someone would give me a drink of water from the cistern by the gate of Bethlehem!" ¹⁸Thereupon the Three broke through the encampment of the Philistines, drew water from the cistern by the gate of Bethlehem, and carried it back to David. But David refused to drink it. Instead, he poured it out† to the LORD, ¹⁹saying, "God forbid that I should do such a thing! Could I drink the blood of these men who risked their lives? For at the risk of their lives they brought it." So he refused to drink it. Such deeds as these the Three warriors performed.

²⁰ˢAbishai, the brother of Joab, was the chief of the Thirty;‡ he brandished his spear over three hundred, whom he had slain. He made a name beside the Three,ᵗ ²¹but was twice as famous as

any of the Thirty, becoming their leader. However, he did not attain to the Three.

²²Benaiah, son of Jehoiada, a valiant man of mighty deeds, from Kabzeel, killed the two sons of Ariel of Moab. Also, he went down and killed the lion in the cistern on a snowy day. ²³He likewise slew the Egyptian, a huge man five cubits tall. The Egyptian carried a spear that was like a weaver's beam, but Benaiah came against him with a staff; he wrested the spear from the Egyptian's hand, and killed him with that spear. ²⁴Such deeds as these Benaiah, the son of Jehoiada, performed, and he made a name beside the Three warriors, ²⁵but was more famous than any of the Thirty. However, he did not attain to the Three. David put him in charge of his bodyguard.ᵘ

²⁶Also these warriors: Asahel, the brother of Joab; Elhanan, son of Dodo, from Bethlehem;ᵛ ²⁷Shammoth, from En-harod; Helez, from Bethpelet; ²⁸Ira, son of Ikkesh, from Tekoa; Abiezer, from Anathoth; ²⁹Sibbecai, from Husha; Ilai, from Ahoh;ʷ ³⁰Maharai, from Netophah; Heled, son of Baanah, from Netophah;ˣ ³¹Ithai, son of Ribai, from Gibeah of Benjamin; Benaiah, from Pirathon;ʸ ³²Hurai, from Nahale-gaash; Abiel, from Beth-arabah; ³³Azmaveth, from Bahurim; Eliahba, from Shaalbon; ³⁴Jashen the Gunite; Jonathan, son of Shagee the Hararite; ³⁵Ahiam, son of Sachar the Hararite; Elipheleth, son of ³⁶Ahasbai, from Beth-maacah; Ahijah, from Gilo; ³⁷Hezro, from Carmel; Naarai, the son of Ezbai; ³⁸Joel, brother of Nathan, from Rehob, the Gadite; ³⁹Zelek the Ammonite; Naharai, from Beeroth, the armor-bearer of Joab, son of Zeruiah; ⁴⁰Ira, from Jattir; Gareb, from Jattir; ⁴¹Uriah the Hittite; Zabad, son of Ahlai, ⁴²and, in addition to the Thirty, Adina, son of Shiza, the Reubenite, chief of the tribe of Reuben; ⁴³Hanan, son of Maacah; Joshaphat the Mithnite; ⁴⁴Uzzia, the Ashterathite; Shama and Jeiel, sons of Hotham, from Aroer; ⁴⁵Jediael, son of Shimri, and Joha, his brother, the Tizite; ⁴⁶Eliel the Mahavite; Jeribai and Joshaviah, sons of Elnaam; Ithmah, from Moab; ⁴⁷Eliel, Obed, and Jaasiel the Mezobian.

## CHAPTER 12

**David's Early Followers.** ¹The following men came to David in Ziklag while he was still under banishment from Saul, son of Kish; they, too, were among the warriors who helped him in his battles.ᶻ ²They were archers who could use either the right or the left hand, both in slinging stones and in shooting arrows with the bow. They were some of Saul's kinsmen, from Benjamin. ³Ahiezer was their chief, along with Joash, both sons of Shemaah of Gibeah; also Jeziel and Pelet, sons of Azmaveth; Beracah; Jehu, from Anathoth;ᵃ ⁴Ishmaiah the Gibeonite, a warrior

---

*[11:11] **The Three**: the Chronicler actually names only two of these figures, Ishbaal and Eleazar. According to 2 Sm 23:11, the third member of the Three was Shammah.

†[11:18] **Poured it out**: as a libation.

‡[11:20] **The Thirty**: they are listed by name in vv. 26–47. The parallel list in 2 Sm 23:8–39 often differs in names and spellings; for the numbers, see note on 2 Sm 23:8–39.

m. [11:6] 2 Sm 8:16.   n. [11:8] 1 Kgs 9:15, 24; 11:27; 2 Chr 32:5.   o. [11:10–41] 2 Sm 23:8–39.   p. [11:12] 1 Chr 27:4.   q. [11:13] 1 Sm 17:1.   r. [11:15] 1 Chr 14:9; 2 Sm 5:18, 22.   s. [11:20–21] 2 Sm 23:18–19.   t. [11:20] 1 Chr 18:12; 1 Sm 26:6–10; 2 Sm 16:9; 18:2; 21:17.

u. [11:25] 2 Sm 8:18; 20:23.   v. [11:26] 1 Chr 2:16; 27:7.   w. [11:29] 1 Chr 27:11.   x. [11:30] 1 Chr 27:13.   y. [11:31] 1 Chr 27:14.   z. [12:1] 1 Sm 27:1–7.   a. [12:3] 1 Chr 27:12.

among the Thirty, and over the Thirty; [5]Jeremiah; Jahaziel; Johanan; Jozabad from Gederah; [6]Eluzai; Jerimoth; Bealiah; Shemariah; Shephatiah the Haruphite; [7]Elkanah, Isshiah, Azarel, Joezer, and Jashobeam, who were Korahites; [8]Joelah and Zebadiah, sons of Jeroham, from Gedor.

[9]Some of the Gadites also went over to David when he was at the stronghold in the wilderness. They were valiant warriors, experienced soldiers equipped with shield and spear, fearsome as lions, swift as gazelles on the mountains.[b] [10]Ezer was their chief, Obadiah was second, Eliab third, [11]Mishmannah fourth, Jeremiah fifth, [12]Attai sixth, Eliel seventh, [13]Johanan eighth, Elzabad ninth, [14]Jeremiah tenth, and Machbannai eleventh. [15]These Gadites were army commanders, the lesser over hundreds and the greater over thousands. [16]It was they who crossed over the Jordan in the first month, when it was overflowing both its banks, and chased away all who were in the valleys to the east and to the west.

[17]Some Benjaminites and Judahites also came to David at the stronghold. [18]David went out to meet them and addressed them in these words: "If you come peacefully, to help me, I am of a mind to have you join me. But if you have come to betray me to my enemies though my hands have done no wrong, may the God of our ancestors see and punish you."

[19]Then a spirit clothed Amasai, the chief of the Thirty, and he answered David:

"We are yours, O David,
    we are with you, son of Jesse.
Peace, peace to you,
    and peace to him who helps you;
    may your God be your helper!"

So David received them and placed them among the leaders of his troops.

[20]Men from Manasseh also deserted to David when he came with the Philistines to battle against Saul. However, he did not help the Philistines, for their lords took counsel and sent him home, saying, "At the cost of our heads he will desert to his master Saul." [21]As he was returning to Ziklag, therefore, these deserted to him from Manasseh: Adnah, Jozabad, Jediael, Michael, Jozabad, Elihu, and Zillethai, chiefs of thousands of Manasseh.[*] [22]They helped David by taking charge of his troops, for they were all warriors and became commanders of his army. [23]And from day to day men kept coming to David's help until there was a vast encampment, like God's own encampment.

**The Assembly at Hebron.** [24]This is the muster of the detachments of armed troops that came to David at Hebron to bring Saul's kingdom over to him, as the LORD had ordained. [25]†Judahites bearing shields and spears: six thousand eight hundred armed troops. [26]Of the Simeonites, warriors fit for battle: seven thousand one hundred. [27]Of the Levites: four thousand six hundred, [28]along with Jehoiada, leader of the line of Aaron, with another three thousand seven hundred, [29]and Zadok, a young warrior, with twenty-two princes of his father's house. [30]Of the Benjaminites, the kinsmen of Saul: three thousand—until this time, most of them had kept their allegiance to the house of Saul. [31]Of the Ephraimites: twenty thousand eight hundred warriors, men renowned in their ancestral houses. [32]Of the half-tribe of Manasseh: eighteen thousand, designated by name to come and make David king. [33]Of the Issacharites, their chiefs who were endowed with an understanding of the times and who knew what Israel had to do: two hundred chiefs, together with all their kinsmen under their command. [34]From Zebulun, men fit for military service, set in battle array with every kind of weapon for war: fifty thousand men rallying with a single purpose. [35]From Naphtali: one thousand captains, and with them, armed with shield and lance, thirty-seven thousand men. [36]Of the Danites, set in battle array: twenty-eight thousand six hundred. [37]From Asher, fit for military service and set in battle array: forty thousand. [38]From the other side of the Jordan, of the Reubenites, Gadites, and the half-tribe of Manasseh, men equipped with every kind of weapon of war: one hundred and twenty thousand.

[39]All these soldiers, drawn up in battle order, came to Hebron with the resolute intention of making David king over all Israel. The rest of Israel was likewise of one mind to make David king. [40]They remained with David for three days, eating and drinking, for their relatives had prepared for them. [41]Moreover, their neighbors from as far as Issachar, Zebulun, and Naphtali came bringing food on donkeys, camels, mules, and oxen—provisions in great quantity of meal, pressed figs, raisins, wine, oil, oxen, and sheep. For there was rejoicing in Israel.

## CHAPTER 13

**Transfer of the Ark.** [1c]After David had taken counsel with his commanders of thousands and of hundreds, that is, with every leader, [2]he said to the whole assembly of Israel: "If it seems good to you, and is so decreed by the LORD our God, let us send to the rest of our kindred from all the districts of Israel, and also the priests and the Levites from their cities with pasture lands, that they may join us;[d] [3]and let us bring the ark of

---

†[12:25–38] The Chronicler here takes the brief account of David's installation as king in 2 Sm 5:1–3 (= 1 Chr 11:1–3) and expands it in line with his exaltation of David and his dynasty.

our God here among us, for in the days of Saul we did not consult it." [4]And the whole assembly agreed to do it, for it seemed right in the eyes of all the people.

[5]Then David assembled all Israel, from Shihor of Egypt* to Lebo-hamath, to bring the ark of God from Kiriath-jearim.[e] [6]David and all Israel went up to Baalah, that is, to Kiriath-jearim, of Judah, to bring up from there the ark of God, which was known by the name "LORD enthroned upon the cherubim."[f] [7]They transported the ark of God on a new cart from the house of Abinadab; Uzzah and Ahio were guiding the cart, [8]while David and all Israel danced before God with all their might, with singing, and with lyres, harps, tambourines, cymbals, and trumpets.

[9]As they reached the threshing floor of Chidon,† Uzzah stretched out his hand to steady the ark, for the oxen were tipping it. [10]Then the LORD became angry with Uzzah and struck him, because he had laid his hand on the ark; he died there in God's presence. [11]David was angry because the LORD's anger had broken out against Uzzah. Therefore that place has been called Perez-uzzah‡ even to this day.

[12]David was afraid of God that day, and he said, "How can I bring in the ark of God to me?" [13]Therefore he did not take the ark with him into the City of David, but deposited it instead at the house of Obed-edom the Gittite. [14]The ark of God remained in the house of Obed-edom with his family for three months, and the LORD blessed Obed-edom's household and all that he possessed.[g]

## CHAPTER 14

**David in Jerusalem.** [1h]Hiram, king of Tyre, sent envoys to David along with cedar wood, and masons and carpenters to build him a house.[§i] [2]David now knew§ that the LORD had truly established him as king over Israel, for his kingdom was greatly exalted for the sake of his people Israel. [3]David took other wives in Jerusalem and became the father of more sons and daughters. [4]These are the names of those who were born to him in Jerusalem: Shammua, Shobab, Nathan, Solomon, [5]Ibhar, Elishua, Elpelet, [6]Nogah, Nepheg, Japhia, [7]Elishama, Beeliada, and Eliphelet.[j]

**The Philistine Wars.** [8]When the Philistines had heard that David was anointed king over all Israel, they marched out in force looking for him. But when David heard of this, he went out against them. [9]Meanwhile the Philistines had come and raided the valley of Rephaim.[k] [10]David inquired of God, "Shall I attack the Philistines, and will you deliver them into my power?" The LORD answered him, "Attack, for I have delivered them into your power." [11]So they attacked, at Baal-perazim, and David defeated them there. Then David said, "By my hand God has broken through my enemies just as water breaks through a dam." Therefore that place was called Baal-perazim.** [12]The Philistines abandoned their gods there, and David ordered them to be burnt.[l]

[13]Once again the Philistines raided the valley, [14]and again David inquired of God. But God answered him: Do not try to pursue them, but go around them and come against them near the balsam trees. [15]When you hear the sound of marching in the tops of the balsam trees, then go forth to battle, for God has already gone before you to strike the army of the Philistines. [16]David did as God commanded him, and they routed the Philistine army from Gibeon to Gezer.

[17]Thus David's fame was spread abroad through every land, and the LORD put the fear of him on all the nations.

## CHAPTER 15

**Preparations for Moving the Ark.** [1]David built houses for himself in the City of David and prepared a place for the ark of God, pitching a tent for it there. [2]At that time he said, "No one may carry the ark of God except the Levites, for the LORD chose them to carry the ark of the LORD and to minister to him forever."[m] [3]Then David assembled all Israel to Jerusalem to bring up the ark of the LORD to its place, which he had prepared for it.[n] [4]David also convened the sons of Aaron and the Levites: [5]of the sons of Kohath, Uriel, their chief, and one hundred and twenty of his brothers; [6]of the sons of Merari, Asaiah, their chief, and two hundred and twenty of his brothers; [7]of the sons of Gershon, Joel, their chief, and one hundred and thirty of his brothers; [8]of the sons of Elizaphan, Shemaiah, their chief, and two hundred of his brothers; [9]of the sons of Hebron, Eliel, their chief, and eighty of his brothers; [10]of the sons of Uzziel, Amminadab, their chief, and one hundred and twelve of his brothers.

[11]David summoned the priests Zadok and Abiathar, and the Levites Uriel, Asaiah, Joel, Shemaiah, Eliel, and Amminadab,[o] [12]and said to them: "You heads of the levitical houses, sanctify yourselves along with your brothers to bring

---

*[13:5] **Shihor of Egypt:** the eastern branch of the Nile delta. **Lebo-hamath:** in southern Syria.

†[13:9] **Chidon:** in 2 Sm 6:6 the name is Nodan (variant: Nacon).

‡[13:11] **Perez-uzzah:** this Hebrew phrase means "the breaking out against Uzza."

§[14:1] The Chronicler's account of David's establishment as king and his victories over the Philistines follows 2 Sm 5:11–25, but makes David's rule even more prominent.

§[14:2] **David now knew:** see note on 2 Sm 5:12.

**[14:11] See note on 2 Sm 5:20.

---

e. [13:5] 1 Chr 15:3; Jos 13:3, 5; 1 Sm 6:21; 7:1–2; 2 Sm 6:1–11. f. [13:6] Jos 15:9; 18:14; 1 Sm 4:4; 7:1. g. [13:14] 1 Chr 26:4–5. h. [14:1–16] 2 Sm 5:11–25. i. [14:1] 2 Sm 5:11; 2 Chr 2:4. j. [14:3–7] 1 Chr 3:5–8; 2 Sm 5:13–16.

k. [14:9] 1 Chr 11:15. l. [14:12] Dt 7:5, 25. m. [15:2] Nm 1:50; 7:9; Dt 10:8; 31:25; 1 Sm 6:15; Jos 3:8. n. [15:3] 1 Chr 13:5; 2 Sm 6:15, 17. o. [15:11] 1 Chr 16:39; 2 Sm 8:17; 15:29, 35.

up the ark of the LORD, the God of Israel, to the place which I have prepared for it.*p* ¹³Because you were not with us the first time, the LORD our God broke out against us, for we did not seek him aright."*q* ¹⁴Accordingly, the priests and the Levites sanctified themselves to bring up the ark of the LORD, the God of Israel. ¹⁵The Levites carried the ark of God on their shoulders with poles, as Moses had commanded according to the word of the LORD.*r*

¹⁶David commanded the commanders of the Levites to appoint their brothers as singers and to play on musical instruments, harps, lyres, and cymbals, to make a loud sound of rejoicing.*s* ¹⁷Therefore the Levites appointed Heman, son of Joel, and, among his brothers, Asaph, son of Berechiah; and among the sons of Merari, their brothers, Ethan, son of Kushaiah;*t* ¹⁸and, together with these, their brothers of the second rank: the gatekeepers Zechariah, Uzziel, Shemiramoth, Jehiel, Unni, Eliab, Benaiah, Maaseiah, Mattithiah, Eliphelehu, Mikneiah, Obed-edom, and Jeiel. ¹⁹The singers, Heman, Asaph, and Ethan, sounded brass cymbals. ²⁰Zechariah, Uzziel, Shemiramoth, Jehiel, Unni, Eliab, Maaseiah, and Benaiah played on harps set to "Alamoth."* ²¹But Mattithiah, Eliphelehu, Mikneiah, Obed-edom, and Jeiel led the song on lyres set to "sheminith." ²²Chenaniah was the chief of the Levites in the singing; he directed the singing, for he was skillful.*u* ²³Berechiah and Elkanah were gatekeepers before the ark. ²⁴The priests, Shebaniah, Joshaphat, Nethanel, Amasai, Zechariah, Benaiah, and Eliezer, sounded the trumpets before the ark of God.*v* Obed-edom and Jeiel were also gatekeepers before the ark.

**The Ark Comes to Jerusalem.** ²⁵ʷThus David, the elders of Israel, and the commanders of thousands went to bring up the ark of the covenant of the LORD with joy from the house of Obed-edom. ²⁶While God helped the Levites to carry the ark of the covenant of the LORD, they sacrificed seven bulls and seven rams.*x* ²⁷David was vested in a robe of fine linen, as were all the Levites who carried the ark, the singers, and Chenaniah, the leader of song; David was also wearing a linen ephod.*y* ²⁸Thus all Israel brought up the ark of the covenant of the LORD with joyful shouting, to the sound of horns, trumpets, and cymbals, and the music of harps and lyres. ²⁹But as the ark of the covenant of the LORD was entering the City of David, Michal, daughter of Saul, looked down from her window, and when

she saw King David leaping and dancing, she despised him in her heart.*z*

## CHAPTER 16

¹ᵃThey brought in the ark of God and set it within the tent which David had pitched for it.*b* Then they sacrificed burnt offerings and communion offerings to God. ²When David had finished sacrificing the burnt offerings and communion offerings, he blessed the people in the name of the LORD, ³and distributed to every Israelite, to every man and every woman, a loaf of bread, a piece of meat, and a raisin cake.

**David's Directives for the Levites.** ⁴He then appointed certain Levites to minister before the ark of the LORD, to celebrate, thank, and praise the LORD, the God of Israel.*c* ⁵Asaph was their chief, and second to him were Zechariah, Uzziel, Shemiramoth, Jehiel, Mattithiah, Eliab, Benaiah, Obed-edom, and Jeiel. These were to play on harps and lyres, while Asaph was to sound the cymbals, ⁶and the priests Benaiah and Jahaziel were to be the regular trumpeters before the ark of the covenant of God.

⁷On that same day, David appointed Asaph and his brothers to sing for the first time these praises of the LORD:

8     †Give thanks to the LORD, invoke his
          name;*d*
        make known among the peoples his
          deeds.
9     Sing praise, play music;
        proclaim all his wondrous deeds.
10    Glory in his holy name;
        rejoice, O hearts that seek the LORD!
11    Rely on the mighty LORD;
        constantly seek his face.
12    Recall the wondrous deeds he has done,
        his signs, and his words of
          judgment,
13    You sons of Israel, his servants,
        offspring of Jacob, the chosen ones!
14    The LORD is our God;
        who rules the whole earth.
15    He remembers forever his covenant
        the pact imposed for a thousand
          generations—
16    Which was made with Abraham,
        confirmed by oath to Isaac,
17    And ratified as binding for Jacob,
        an everlasting covenant for Israel:
18    "To you will I give the land of Canaan,
        your own allotted heritage."
19    When they were few in number,
        a handful, and strangers there,

---

*[15:20–21] Alamoth . . . sheminith:* musical terms of uncertain meaning. *Alamoth,* lit., "young women," occurs in the superscription to Ps 46. The term *sheminith,* in v. 21, might mean "bass" or "octave"; cf. Ps 6:1; 12:1.

p. [15:12] 2 Chr 29:5, 15, 34; 30:3, 15, 24.    q. [15:13] 1 Chr 13:3.    r. [15:15] Ex 25:10–22; Nm 1:50; 7:9; 2 Chr 35:3.    s. [15:16] 1 Chr 13:8; 16:5; 2 Chr 5:12; 29:25; Neh 12:27.    t. [15:17] 1 Chr 6:31–47; 25:1–8.    u. [15:22] 1 Chr 26:29.    v. [15:24] Nm 10:8; Jos 6:4–8.    w. [15:25–29] 2 Sm 6:12–16.    x. [15:26] 2 Sm 6:17; 2 Chr 29:21.    y. [15:27] 1 Sm 2:18; 2 Sm 6:14.

---

†[16:8–36] A hymn composed of parts of several psalms: vv. 8–22 = Ps 105:1–15; vv. 23–33 = Ps 96:1–13; vv. 34–36 = Ps 106:1, 47–48. There are minor textual variants between this hymn and the psalms it is drawn from.

z. [15:29] 2 Sm 6:20–23.    a. [16:1–3] 2 Sm 6:17–19.    b. [16:1] 1 Chr 15:1.    c. [16:4] Sir 47:9.    d. [16:8–22] Ps 105:1–15.

²⁰ Wandering from nation to nation,
    from one kingdom to another,
²¹ He let no one oppress them;
    for their sake he rebuked kings:
²² "Do not touch my anointed,
    to my prophets do no harm."
²³ ᵉSing to the LORD, all the earth,
    announce his salvation, day after
        day.
²⁴ Tell his glory among the nations;
    among all peoples, his wondrous
        deeds.
²⁵ For great is the LORD and highly to be
        praised;
    to be feared above all gods.
²⁶ For the gods of the nations all do nothing,
    but the LORD made the heavens.
²⁷ Splendor and majesty go before him;
    power and rejoicing are in his holy
        place.
²⁸ Give to the LORD, you families of
        nations,
    give to the LORD glory and might;
²⁹ Give to the LORD the glory due his
        name!
    Bring gifts, and come before him;
    bow down to the LORD, splendid in
        holiness.
³⁰ Tremble before him, all the earth;
    the world will surely stand fast,
        never to be moved.
³¹ Let the heavens be glad and the earth
        rejoice;
    let them say among the nations: The
        LORD is king.
³² Let the sea and what fills it resound;
    let the plains be joyful and all that is
        in them!
³³ Then let all the trees of the forest exult
    before the LORD, who comes,
    who comes to rule the earth.
³⁴ᶠ Give thanks to the LORD, who is good,
    whose love endures forever;
³⁵ And say, "Save us, O God, our savior,
    gather us and deliver us from among
        the nations,
    That we may give thanks to your holy
        name
    and glory in praising you."
³⁶ Blessed be the LORD, the God of Israel,
    from everlasting to everlasting!
    Let all the people say, Amen! Hallelujah.

³⁷Then David left Asaph and his brothers there before the ark of the covenant of the LORD to minister before the ark regularly according to the daily ritual; ³⁸he also left there Obed-edom and sixty-eight of his brothers, including Obed-edom, son of Jeduthun, and Hosah, to be gatekeepers.ᵍ

³⁹But the priest Zadok and his priestly brothers he left before the tabernacle of the LORD on the high place at Gibeon,ʰ ⁴⁰to make burnt offerings to the LORD on the altar for burnt offerings regularly, morning and evening, and to do all that is written in the law of the LORD which he commanded Israel.ⁱ ⁴¹With them were Heman and Jeduthun and the others who were chosen and designated by name to give thanks to the LORD, "whose love endures forever,"ʲ ⁴²with trumpets and cymbals for accompaniment, and instruments for sacred song. The sons of Jeduthun kept the gate.ᵏ

⁴³Then all the people departed, each to their own homes, and David returned to bless his household.ˡ

## CHAPTER 17

**The Oracle of Nathan.** ¹ᵐAfter David had taken up residence in his house, he said to Nathan the prophet, "See, I am living in a house of cedar, but the ark of the covenant of the LORD is under tentcloth."ⁿ ²Nathan replied to David, "Whatever is in your heart, go and do, for God is with you."

³But that same night the word of God came to Nathan: ⁴Go and tell David my servant, Thus says the LORD: It is not you who are to build the house for me to dwell in.ᵒ ⁵For I have never dwelt in a house, from the day I brought Israel up, even to this day, but I have been lodging in tent or tabernacle. ⁶As long as I have wandered about with all Israel, did I ever say a word to any of the judges of Israel whom I commanded to shepherd my people, Why have you not built me a house of cedar? ⁷Now then, speak thus to my servant David, Thus says the LORD of hosts: I took you from the pasture, from following the flock, to become ruler over my people Israel.ᵖ ⁸I was with you wherever you went, and I cut down all your enemies before you. I will make your name like that of the greatest on the earth. ⁹I will assign a place for my people Israel and I will plant them in it to dwell there; they will never again be disturbed, nor shall the wicked ever again oppress them, as they did at the beginning, ¹⁰and during all the time when I appointed judges over my people Israel. And I will subdue all your enemies. Moreover, I declare to you that the LORD will build you a house: ¹¹when your days have been completed and you must join your ancestors, I will raise up your offspring after you who will be one of your own sons, and I will establish his kingdom.�q ¹²He it is who shall build me a house, and I will establish his throne forever.ʳ ¹³I will be a father to him, and he shall be a son to me, and I will not withdraw my favor from him as I withdrew it from the one

---

e. [16:23–33] Ps 96:1–13.  f. [16:34–36] Ps 106:1, 47–48.
g. [16:38] 1 Chr 15:24.
h. [16:39] 1 Kgs 3:4.  i. [16:40] Ex 29:38–42; Lv 6:9; Nm 28:3, 6; 2 Chr 13:11.  j. [16:41] 2 Chr 5:12; 7:3, 6; 20:21; Ezr 3:11.
k. [16:42] 2 Chr 29:27.  l. [16:43] 2 Sm 6:19–20.  m. [17:1–27] 2 Sm 7:1–29.  n. [17:1] 1 Chr 15:1; 2 Sm 5:11.  o. [17:4] 1 Chr 28:3; 1 Kgs 8:19.  p. [17:7] 1 Sm 16:11.  q. [17:11] 2 Sm 7:12–13.
r. [17:12] 1 Chr 22:10; 28:6, 10.

who was before you;[*] [14]but I will maintain him in my house and in my kingdom forever, and his throne shall be firmly established forever.

[15]In accordance with all these words and this whole vision Nathan spoke to David.

**David's Thanksgiving.** [16]Then King David came in and sat in the LORD's presence, and said: "Who am I, LORD God, and what is my house, that you should have brought me so far? [17]And yet, even this is too little in your sight, O God! For you have made a promise regarding your servant's house reaching into the future, and you have looked on me as henceforth the most notable of men, LORD God.[t] [18]What more can David say to you? You have known[*] your servant. [19]LORD, for your servant's sake and in keeping with your purpose, you have done this great thing. [20]LORD, there is no one like you, no God but you, just as we have always heard.[u]

[21]"Is there, like your people Israel, whom you redeemed from Egypt, another nation on earth whom a god went to redeem as his people? You won for yourself a name for great and awesome deeds by driving out the nations before your people.[v] [22]You made your people Israel your own forever, and you, LORD, became their God. [23]Now, LORD, may the promise that you have spoken concerning your servant and his house remain firm forever. Bring about what you have promised, [24]that your name, LORD of hosts, God of Israel, may be great and abide forever, while the house of your servant is established in your presence.

[25]"Because you, my God, have revealed to your servant that you will build him a house, your servant dares to pray before you.[w] [26]Since you, LORD, are truly God and have made this generous promise to your servant, [27]do, then, bless the house of your servant, that it may be in your presence forever—since it is you, LORD, who blessed it, it is blessed forever."[x]

### CHAPTER 18

**David's Victories.** [1y]After this, David defeated the Philistines and subdued them; and he took Gath and its towns away from the Philistines. [2]He also defeated Moab, and the Moabites became David's subjects, paying tribute.

[3]David then defeated Hadadezer, king of Zobah, toward Hamath, who was on his way to set up his victory stele at the river Euphrates. [4]David captured from him one thousand chariots, seven thousand horsemen, and twenty thousand foot soldiers. David hamstrung all the chariot horses, but left one hundred for his chariots.[z] [5]The Arameans of Damascus came to help Hadadezer,

king of Zobah, but David also defeated twenty-two thousand of their men in Aram. [6]Then David set up garrisons in the Damascus region of Aram, and the Arameans became David's subjects, paying tribute. Thus the LORD made David victorious in all his campaigns.

[7]David took the golden shields that were carried by Hadadezer's attendants and brought them to Jerusalem. [8]David likewise took away from Tibhath and Cun, cities of Hadadezer, large quantities of bronze; Solomon later used it to make the bronze sea and the pillars and the vessels of bronze.[a]

[9]When Tou, king of Hamath, heard that David had defeated the entire army of Hadadezer, king of Zobah, [10]he sent his son Hadoram to wish King David well and to congratulate him on having waged a victorious war against Hadadezer; for Hadadezer had been at war with Tou. He also brought gold, silver and bronze articles of every sort.[b] [11]These also King David consecrated to the LORD along with all the silver and gold that he had taken from the nations: from Edom, Moab, the Ammonites, the Philistines, and Amalek.

[12]Abishai, the son of Zeruiah, also defeated eighteen thousand Edomites in the Valley of Salt.[c] [13]He set up garrisons in Edom, and all the Edomites became David's subjects. Thus the LORD brought David victory in all his undertakings.

**David's Officials.** [14d]David was king over all Israel; he dispensed justice and right to all his people. [15]Joab, son of Zeruiah, was in command of the army; Jehoshaphat, son of Ahilud, was chancellor;[e] [16]Zadok, son of Ahitub, and Ahimelech, son of Abiathar, were priests;[†] Shavsha was scribe;[f] [17]Benaiah, son of Jehoiada, was in command of the Cherethites and the Pelethites; and David's sons were the chief assistants to the king.[‡g]

### CHAPTER 19

**Campaigns Against Ammon.** [1h]Afterward Nahash, king of the Ammonites, died and his son succeeded him as king. [2]David said, "I will show kindness to Hanun, the son of Nahash, for his father showed kindness to me." Therefore he sent envoys to console him over his father. But when David's servants had entered the land of the Ammonites to console Hanun, [3]the Ammonite princes said to Hanun, "Do you think David

---

†[18:16] **Zadok . . . and Ahimelech, son of Abiathar, were priests**: emendation—the Masoretic text here reads "Abimelech," not "Ahimelech"; but 2 Sm 8:17, the Chronicler's source, has "Ahimelech." See note there.

‡[18:17] **Chief assistants to the king**: according to 2 Sm 8:18, the Chronicler's source here, David's sons were priests. The Chronicler's modification reflects his conviction that only Aaron's descendants could be priests.

---

*[17:18] **Known**: given David recognition, chosen him, singled him out; cf. Gn 18:19; Ex 33:12; Am 3:2.

---

s. [17:13] 2 Sm 7:14.  t. [17:17] 2 Sm 7:19.  u. [17:20] Sir 36:4.  v. [17:21] Dt 4:7; 2 Sm 7:23.  w. [17:25] 2 Sm 7:27.  x. [17:27] Nm 22:6.  y. [18:1–13] 2 Sm 8:1–14.  z. [18:4] 2 Sm 8:14; Jos 11:6, 9.

a. [18:8] 2 Sm 8:8; 1 Kgs 7:15, 23, 27.  b. [18:10] 2 Sm 8:10.  c. [18:12] 2 Sm 8:13; 2 Kgs 14:7.  d. [18:14–17] 2 Sm 8:15–18.  e. [18:15] 1 Chr 11:6; 2 Sm 8:16; 1 Kgs 4:3.  f. [18:16] 1 Chr 24:3, 6, 31; 2 Sm 8:17.  g. [18:17] 1 Chr 11:22; 2 Sm 8:18; 1 Kgs 1:38, 44.  h. [19:1–19] 2 Sm 10:1–19.

is doing this—sending you these consolers—to honor your father? Have not his servants rather come to you to explore the land, spying it out for its overthrow?" ⁴So Hanun seized David's servants and had them shaved and their garments cut off halfway at the hips. Then he sent them away. ⁵David was told about the men, and he sent word for them to be intercepted, for the men had been greatly disgraced. "Remain at Jericho," the king told them, "until your beards have grown again; then come back here."

⁶When the Ammonites realized that they had put themselves in bad odor with David, Hanun and the Ammonites sent a thousand talents of silver to hire chariots and horsemen from Aram Naharaim, from Aram-maacah, and from Zobah. ⁷They hired thirty-two thousand chariots along with the king of Maacah and his army, who came and encamped before Medeba. The Ammonites also assembled from their cities and came out for war.

⁸When David heard of this, he sent Joab and his whole army of warriors against them. ⁹The Ammonites marched out and lined up for battle at the entrance of the city, while the kings who had come to their help remained apart in the open field. ¹⁰When Joab saw that there was a battle line both in front of and behind him, he chose some of the best fighters among the Israelites and lined them up against the Arameans; ¹¹the rest of the army, which he placed under the command of his brother Abishai, then lined up to oppose the Ammonites. ¹²And he said: "If the Arameans prove too strong for me, you must come and save me; and if the Ammonites prove too strong for you, I will save you. ¹³Hold firm and let us show ourselves courageous for the sake of our people and the cities of our God; and may the Lord do what is good in his sight." ¹⁴Joab therefore advanced with his men to engage the Arameans in battle; but they fled before him. ¹⁵And when the Ammonites saw that the Arameans had fled, they too fled before his brother Abishai, and entered their city. Joab then came to Jerusalem.

¹⁶Seeing themselves vanquished by Israel, the Arameans sent messengers to bring out the Arameans from beyond the Euphrates, with Shophach, the commander of Hadadezer's army, at their head. ¹⁷When this was reported to David, he gathered all Israel together, crossed the Jordan, and met them. With the army of David drawn up to fight the Arameans, they gave battle. ¹⁸But the Arameans fled before Israel, and David killed seven thousand of their chariot fighters and forty thousand of their foot soldiers; he also put to death Shophach, the commander of the army. ¹⁹When the vassals of Hadadezer saw themselves vanquished by Israel, they made peace with David and became his subjects. After this, the Arameans refused to come to the aid of the Ammonites.

## CHAPTER 20

¹At the turn of the year,* the time when kings go to war, Joab led the army out in force, laid waste the land of the Ammonites, and went on to besiege Rabbah; David himself remained in Jerusalem. When Joab had attacked Rabbah and destroyed it, ²David took the crown of Milcom from the idol's head. It was found to weigh a talent of gold, with precious stones on it; this crown David wore on his own head. He also brought out a great amount of spoil from the city. ³He deported the people of the city and set them to work with saws, iron picks, and axes. David dealt thus with all the cities of the Ammonites. Then David and his whole army returned to Jerusalem.ⁱ

**Victories over the Philistines.** ⁴ʲAfterward there was another battle with the Philistines, at Gezer. At that time, Sibbecai the Hushathite struck down Sippai, one of the descendants of the Rephaim, and the Philistines were subdued.ᵏ

⁵There was another battle with the Philistines, and Elhanan, the son of Jair, slew Lahmi, the brother of Goliath† of Gath, whose spear shaft was like a weaver's beam.ˡ

⁶There was another battle, at Gath, and there was a giant, who had six fingers to each hand and six toes to each foot; twenty-four in all. He too was descended from the Rephaim. ⁷He defied Israel, and Jonathan, the son of Shimea, David's brother, slew him. ⁸These were the descendants of the Rephaim of Gath who died at the hands of David and his servants.

## CHAPTER 21

**David's Census; the Plague.** ¹ᵐA satan‡ rose up against Israel, and he incited David to take a census of Israel.ⁿ ²David therefore said to Joab and to the other generals of the army, "Go, number the Israelites from Beer-sheba to Dan, and report back to me that I may know their number." ³But Joab replied: "May the Lord increase his people a hundredfold! My lord king, are not all of them my lord's subjects? Why does

---

*[20:1] **At the turn of the year:** thus in 2 Sm 11 begins the story of David's adultery with Bathsheba and his murder of her husband Uriah, but the Chronicler omits it.

†[20:5] **Elhanan . . . slew Lahmi, the brother of Goliath:** with this notice the Chronicler solves the difficulty of the apparent contradiction between 1 Sm 17:49, 51 (David killed Goliath) and 2 Sm 21:19 (Elhanan killed Goliath).

‡[21:1] **A satan:** in the parallel passage (2 Sm 24:1) David is led astray because of the Lord's anger. The Chronicler's modification reflects the changed theological outlook of postexilic Israel, when evil was no longer attributed directly to God. At an earlier period the Hebrew word *satan* ("adversary," or, especially in a court of law, "accuser") designated both human beings (1 Kgs 11:14) and a "son of God" who accused people before God (Jb 1:6–12; 2:1–7; Zec 3:1–2). In later Judaism (cf. Wis 2:24) and in the New Testament, *satan*, or the "devil" (from *diablos*, the Greek translation of the Hebrew word), designates an evil spirit who tempts people to do wrong.

---

i. [20:2–3] 2 Sm 12:30–31.   j. [20:4–8] 2 Sm 21:18–22.   k. [20:4] 1 Chr 11:29; 27:11.   l. [20:5] 1 Chr 11:26; 1 Sm 17:4, 23.   m. [21:1–27] 2 Sm 24:1–25.   n. [21:1] Zec 3:1–2.

my lord seek to do this thing? Why should he bring guilt upon Israel?" [4]However, the king's command prevailed over Joab, who departed and traversed all of Israel, and then returned to Jerusalem. [5]Joab reported the census figures to David: of men capable of wielding a sword, there were in all Israel one million one hundred thousand, and in Judah four hundred and seventy thousand. [6]Levi and Benjamin, however, he did not include in the census, for the king's command was repugnant to Joab.[o] [7]This command was evil in the sight of God, and he struck Israel. [8]Then David said to God, "I have sinned greatly in doing this thing. Take away your servant's guilt, for I have acted very foolishly."

[9]Then the LORD spoke to Gad, David's seer, in these words:[p] [10]Go, tell David: Thus says the LORD: I am laying out three options; choose one of them, and I will inflict it on you. [11]Accordingly, Gad went to David and said to him: "Thus says the LORD: Decide now— [12]will it be three years of famine; or three months of fleeing your enemies, with the sword of your foes ever at your back; or three days of the LORD's own sword, a plague in the land, with the LORD's destroying angel in every part of Israel? Now consider: What answer am I to give him who sent me?" [13]Then David said to Gad: "I am in serious trouble. But let me fall into the hand of the LORD, whose mercy is very great, rather than into hands of men."

[14]Therefore the LORD sent a plague upon Israel, and seventy thousand Israelites died. [15]God also sent an angel to Jerusalem to destroy it; but as the angel was on the point of destroying it, the LORD saw and changed his mind about the calamity, and said to the destroying angel, "Enough now! Stay your hand!"[q]

**Ornan's Threshing Floor.** The angel of the LORD was then standing by the threshing floor of Ornan the Jebusite. [16]When David raised his eyes, he saw the angel of the LORD standing between earth and heaven, drawn sword in hand stretched out against Jerusalem.[r] David and the elders, clothed in sackcloth, fell face down, [17]and David prayed to God: "Was it not I who ordered the census of the people? I am the one who sinned, I did this wicked thing. But these sheep, what have they done? O LORD, my God, strike me and my father's family, but do not afflict your people with this plague!"

[18]Then the angel of the LORD commanded Gad to tell David to go up and set up an altar to the LORD on the threshing floor of Ornan the Jebusite.[s] [19]David went up at the word of Gad, which he spoke in the name of the LORD. [20]Ornan turned around and saw the king; his four sons who were with him hid themselves, but Ornan kept on threshing wheat. [21]But as David came toward Ornan, he looked up and

saw that it was David, and left the threshing floor and bowed down before David, his face to the ground. [22]David said to Ornan: "Sell me the site of this threshing floor, that I may build on it an altar to the LORD. Sell it to me at its full price, that the plague may be withdrawn from the people." [23]But Ornan said to David: "Take it as your own, and let my lord the king do what is good in his sight. See, I also give you the oxen for the burnt offerings, the threshing sledges for the wood, and the wheat for the grain offering. I give it all to you." [24]But King David replied to Ornan: "No! I will buy it from you properly, at its full price. I will not take what is yours for the LORD, nor bring burnt offerings that cost me nothing." [25]So David paid Ornan six hundred shekels of gold* for the place.

**Altar for Burnt Offerings.** [26]David then built an altar there to the LORD, and sacrificed burnt offerings and communion offerings. He called upon the LORD, who answered him by sending down fire from heaven upon the altar for burnt offerings.[t] [27]Then the LORD gave orders to the angel to return his sword to its sheath.

[28]Once David saw that the LORD had answered him at the threshing floor of Ornan the Jebusite, he continued to offer sacrifices there. [29]The tabernacle of the LORD, which Moses had made in the wilderness, and the altar for burnt offerings were at that time on the high place at Gibeon.[u] [30]But David could not go into his presence to inquire of God, for he was fearful of the sword of the angel of the LORD.

## CHAPTER 22

[1]Thus David said, "This is the house of the LORD God, and this is the altar for burnt offerings for Israel."[v] [2]David then ordered that the resident aliens in the land of Israel should be brought together, and he appointed them stonecutters to hew out stone blocks for building the house of God.[w] [3]David also laid up large stores of iron to make nails for the doors of the gates, and clamps, together with so much bronze that it could not be weighed,[x] [4]and cedar trees without number. The Sidonians and Tyrians brought great stores of cedar logs to David.[y] [5]David said: "My son Solomon is young and inexperienced; but the house that is to be built for the LORD must be made so magnificent that it will be renowned

---

*[21:25] **Six hundred shekels of gold:** according to 2 Sm 24:24, David paid only fifty shekels of silver for Ornan's threshing floor; the Chronicler's higher figure reflects the value the site of the future Temple had in his eyes.

†[22:2–4] According to 1 Kgs 5:15–32, Solomon himself made the material preparations for building the Temple, even though David had wished to do so (1 Kgs 5:17–19). The Chronicler, however, seeks to enhance David's role in the building of the Temple.

---

o. [21:6] 1 Chr 27:24; Nm 1:49.   p. [21:9] 1 Chr 29:29; 1 Sm 9:9; 2 Chr 29:25.   q. [21:15] Gn 6:6; Ex 32:14; 2 Sm 24:16; Jon 3:10. r. [21:16] Jos 5:13.   s. [21:18] 2 Chr 3:1.   t. [21:26] Lv 9:24; Jgs 6:21; 1 Kgs 18:38; 2 Chr 7:1; 2 Mc 2:10–12. u. [21:29] 1 Chr 16:39; 1 Kgs 8:4; 2 Chr 1:3.   v. [22:1] 1 Chr 21:18, 26, 28; 2 Chr 3:1.   w. [22:2] 1 Kgs 5:31–32; 9:20–21; 2 Chr 2:16–17.   x. [22:3] 1 Chr 18:8; 1 Kgs 7:47.   y. [22:4] Ezr 3:7; 2 Chr 2:9.

and glorious in all lands. Therefore I will make preparations for it." Thus before his death David laid up materials in abundance.[z]

**Charge to Solomon.** [6]Then he summoned his son Solomon and commanded him to build a house for the LORD, the God of Israel. [7a]David said to Solomon: "My son, it was my purpose to build a house myself for the name of the LORD, my God. [8]But this word of the LORD came to me: You have shed much blood, and you have waged great wars. You may not build a house for my name, because you have shed too much blood upon the earth in my sight. [9]However, a son will be born to you. He will be a peaceful man, and I will give him rest from all his enemies on every side. For Solomon shall be his name, and in his time I will bestow peace[*] and tranquility on Israel.[b] [10]It is he who shall build a house for my name; he shall be a son to me, and I will be a father to him,[c] and I will establish the throne of his kingship over Israel forever.

[11]"Now, my son, the LORD be with you, and may you succeed in building the house of the LORD your God, as he has said you shall. [12]But may the LORD give you prudence and discernment when he gives you command over Israel, so that you keep the law of the LORD, your God. [13]Only then shall you succeed, if you are careful to observe the statutes and ordinances which the LORD commanded Moses for Israel. Be strong and steadfast; do not fear or be dismayed.[d] [14]See, with great effort I have laid up for the house of the LORD a hundred thousand talents of gold,[†] a million talents of silver, and bronze and iron in such great quantities that they cannot be weighed. I have also laid up wood and stones, to which you must add.[e] [15]Moreover, you have available workers, stonecutters, masons, carpenters, and experts in every craft, [16]without number, skilled with gold, silver, bronze, and iron. Set to work, therefore, and the LORD be with you!"

**Charge to the Officials.** [17]David also commanded all of the officials of Israel to help his son Solomon: [18]"Is not the LORD your God with you? Has he not given you rest on every side? Indeed, he has delivered the inhabitants of the land into my power, and the land is subdued before the LORD and his people.[f] [19]Therefore, devote your hearts and souls to seeking the LORD your God. Proceed to build the sanctuary of the LORD God, that the ark of the covenant of the LORD and God's sacred vessels may be brought into the house built for the name of the LORD."[g]

## CHAPTER 23

**The Levitical Divisions.** [1]When David had grown old and was near the end of his days, he made his son Solomon king over Israel.[h] [2]He then gathered together all the officials of Israel, along with the priests and the Levites.

[3]The Levites thirty years old and above were counted, and their total number was found to be thirty-eight thousand.[i] [4]Of these, twenty-four thousand were to direct the service of the house of the LORD, six thousand were to be officials and judges, [5]four thousand were to be gatekeepers,[j] and four thousand were to praise the LORD with the instruments which [David] had devised for praise. [6]David apportioned them into divisions according to the sons of Levi: Gershon, Kohath, and Merari.[k]

[7]To the Gershonites belonged Ladan and Shimei. [8]The sons of Ladan: Jehiel the chief, then Zetham and Joel; three in all.[l] [9]The sons of Shimei were Shelomoth, Haziel, and Haran; three. These were the heads of the families of Ladan. [10]The sons of Shimei were Jahath, Zizah, Jeush, and Beriah; these were the sons of Shimei, four in all. [11]Jahath was the chief and Zizah was second to him; but Jeush and Beriah had few sons, and therefore they were classed as a single family, exercising a single office.

[12]The sons of Kohath: Amram, Izhar, Hebron, and Uzziel; four in all.[m] [13]The sons of Amram were Aaron and Moses. Aaron was set apart to be consecrated as most holy, he and his sons forever, to offer sacrifice before the LORD, to minister to him, and to bless in his name forever.[n] [14]As for Moses, however, the man of God, his sons were counted as part of the tribe of Levi. [15]The sons of Moses were Gershom and Eliezer.[o] [16]The sons of Gershom: Shubael the chief.[p] [17]The sons of Eliezer were Rehabiah the chief—Eliezer had no other sons, but the sons of Rehabiah were very numerous. [18]The sons of Izhar: Shelomith the chief. [19]The sons of Hebron: Jeriah, the chief, Amariah, the second, Jahaziel, the third, and Jekameam, the fourth.[q] [20]The sons of Uzziel: Micah, the chief, and Isshiah, the second.[r]

[21]The sons of Merari: Mahli and Mushi. The sons of Mahli: Eleazar and Kish.[s] [22]Eleazar died

---

*[22:9] The Hebrew word for peace, *shalom*, is reflected in the name Solomon, in Hebrew, *Shelomo*. The Chronicler draws a contrast here between Solomon, the "peaceful man," and David, who "waged great wars" (v. 8). David was prevented from building the Temple, not only because his time was taken up in waging war (1 Kgs 5:17), but also because he shed much blood (1 Chr 22:8), thereby making himself, in the Chronicler's view, ritually unfit for the task.

†[22:14] **A hundred thousand talents of gold**: about 3,775 tons of gold. **A million talents of silver**: about 37,750 tons of silver. These highly exaggerated figures are intended to stress the inestimable value of the Temple as the center of Israelite worship. More modest figures are given in 1 Kgs 9:14, 28; 10:10, 14.

z. [22:5] 1 Chr 29:1.　a. [22:7–10] 1 Chr 17:1–14; 28:2–7; 2 Sm 7:1–16; 1 Kgs 5:17–19; 8:17–21.　b. [22:9] 2 Sm 12:24.　c. [22:10] Heb 1:5.　d. [22:13] 1 Chr 28:7, 20; Dt 31:6, 23; Jos 1:6–7, 9; 1 Kgs 2:2–3.　e. [22:14] 1 Chr 29:2–5.

f. [22:18] 1 Chr 23:25; Jos 21:44; 23:1; 2 Sm 7:1.　g. [22:19] 1 Kgs 8:6, 21; 2 Chr 5:7; 6:11.　h. [23:1] 1 Chr 28:5; 1 Kgs 1:30.　i. [23:3] Nm 4:3, 23, 30, 35, 39, 43, 47; 8:23–26; 2 Chr 31:17.　j. [23:5] 1 Chr 9:22.　k. [23:6] 1 Chr 6:1, 16–30; 26:1–19; Ex 6:16; Nm 3:17; 26:57.　l. [23:8] 1 Chr 26:21–22; 29:8.　m. [23:12] 1 Chr 26:23; Ex 6:18; Nm 3:19; 26:58–61.　n. [23:13] 1 Chr 6:49; Ex 6:20; 28:1; Nm 6:23.　o. [23:15] Ex 2:22; 18:3–4.　p. [23:16] 1 Chr 26:24.　q. [23:19] 1 Chr 24:23.　r. [23:20] 1 Chr 24:24–25.　s. [23:21] 1 Chr 6:29; 24:26, 28–29; Ex 6:19; Nm 3:20, 33.

leaving no sons, only daughters; the sons of Kish, their kinsmen, married them.[t] [23]The sons of Mushi: Mahli, Eder, and Jeremoth; three in all.[u]

[24]These were the sons of Levi according to their ancestral houses, the family heads as they were enrolled one by one according to their names. They performed the work of the service of the house of the LORD beginning at twenty years of age.[v] [25]David said: "The LORD, the God of Israel, has given rest to his people, and has taken up his dwelling in Jerusalem forever.[w] [26]Henceforth the Levites need not carry the tabernacle or any of the equipment for its service."[x] [27]For by David's last words the Levites were enlisted from the time they were twenty years old. [28]Their duty is to assist the sons of Aaron in the service of the house of the LORD, having charge of the courts, the chambers, and the preservation of everything holy: they take part in the service of the house of God. [29]They also have charge of the showbread, of the fine flour for the grain offering, of the wafers of unleavened bread, and of the baking and mixing, and of all measures of quantity and size.[y] [30]They are to be present every morning to offer thanks and to praise the LORD, and likewise in the evening;[z] [31]and at every sacrifice of burnt offerings to the LORD on sabbaths, new moons, and feast days, in such numbers as are prescribed, they must always be present before the LORD[a] [32]and observe what is prescribed for them concerning the tent of meeting, the sanctuary, and the sons of Aaron, their kinsmen, in the service of the house of the LORD.[b]

## CHAPTER 24

**The Priestly Divisions.** [1]There were also divisions for the sons of Aaron. The sons of Aaron were Nadab, Abihu, Eleazar, and Ithamar.[c] [2]Nadab and Abihu died before their father, leaving no sons; therefore only Eleazar and Ithamar served as priests.[d] [3]David, with Zadok, a descendant of Eleazar, and Ahimelech, a descendant of Ithamar, apportioned them their offices in the priestly service.[e] [4]But since the sons of Eleazar were found to be more numerous by male heads than those of Ithamar, the former were divided into sixteen groups, and the latter into eight groups, each under its family heads. [5]Their functions were assigned impartially by lot, for there were officers of the holy place, and officers of God, descended both from Eleazar and from Ithamar. [6]The scribe Shemaiah, son of Nethanel, a Levite, recorded them in the presence of the king, and of the officials, of Zadok the priest, and

of Ahimelech, son of Abiathar,* and of the heads of the ancestral houses of the priests and of the Levites, listing two successive family groups from Eleazar before each one from Ithamar.[f]

[7f]The first lot fell to Jehoiarib, the second to Jedaiah, [8]the third to Harim, the fourth to Seorim, [9]the fifth to Malchijah, the sixth to Mijamin, [10]the seventh to Hakkoz, the eighth to Abijah,[h] [11]the ninth to Jeshua, the tenth to Shecaniah, [12]the eleventh to Eliashib, the twelfth to Jakim, [13]the thirteenth to Huppah, the fourteenth to Ishbaal, [14]the fifteenth to Bilgah, the sixteenth to Immer, [15]the seventeenth to Hezir, the eighteenth to Happizzez, [16]the nineteenth to Pethahiah, the twentieth to Jehezkel, [17]the twenty-first to Jachin, the twenty-second to Gamul, [18]the twenty-third to Delaiah, the twenty-fourth to Maaziah. [19]This was the appointed order of their service when they functioned in the house of the LORD according to the precepts given them by Aaron, their father, as the LORD, the God of Israel, had commanded him.[i]

**Other Levites.** [20]Of the remaining Levites, there were Shubael, of the sons of Amram, and Jehdeiah, of the sons of Shubael; [21]Isshiah, the chief, of the sons of Rehabiah; [22]Shelomith of the Izharites, and Jahath of the sons of Shelomith. [23]The sons of Hebron were Jeriah, the chief, Amariah, the second, Jahaziel, the third, Jekameam, the fourth. [24]The sons of Uzziel were Micah; Shamir, of the sons of Micah; [25]Isshiah, the brother of Micah; and Zechariah, a descendant of Isshiah. [26]The sons of Merari were Mahli, Mushi, and the sons of his son Uzziah. [27]The sons of Merari through his son Uzziah: Shoham, Zaccur, and Ibri. [28]The sons of Mahli were Eleazar, who had no sons, [29]and Jerahmeel, of the sons of Kish. [30]The sons of Mushi were Mahli, Eder, and Jerimoth.

These were the sons of the Levites according to their ancestral houses. [31]They too, in the same manner as their kinsmen, the sons of Aaron, cast lots in the presence of King David, Zadok, Ahimelech, and the heads of the priestly and levitical families; the more important family did so in the same way as the less important one.[k]

## CHAPTER 25

**The Singers.** [1]David and the leaders of the liturgy set apart for the service the sons of Asaph, Heman, and Jeduthun, who prophesied[†] to the accompaniment of lyres and harps and cymbals.[l]

*[24:6] **Ahimelech, son of Abiathar:** see note on 18:16.

†[25:1] This list of twenty-four classes of Temple singers balances the list of the twenty-four classes of priests (24:4–19). The last nine names in v. 4, which seem to form a special group, were perhaps originally fragments or incipits (the opening words) of hymns. With some slight changes in the vocalization, these names would mean: "Have mercy on me,

---

t. [23:22] 1 Chr 24:28–29.   u. [23:23] 1 Chr 6:47; 24:30.   v. [23:24] 2 Chr 31:17; Ezr 3:8.   w. [23:25] 1 Chr 22:18; Ps 132:13.   x. [23:26] 1 Chr 15:15; 2 Chr 35:3.   y. [23:29] 1 Chr 9:29, 31–32; Lv 2:1, 4–5; 24:5–8.   z. [23:30] Nm 28:3–8.   a. [23:31] Nm 28:2–29:39.   b. [23:32] Nm 3:6–9; 18:2–5.   c. [24:1] Ex 6:23; Nm 3:2–4; 26:60.   d. [24:2] Lv 10:1–7, 12; Nm 3:2, 4.   e. [24:3] 1 Chr 18:16; 2 Sm 8:17; 2 Chr 8:14.

f. [24:6] 1 Chr 18:16; 2 Sm 8:17.   g. [24:7–10] 1 Chr 9:10–13; Ezr 2:36–38; Neh 7:39–42; 11:10–14.   h. [24:10] Lk 1:5.   i. [24:19] 2 Chr 23:8.   j. [24:20–31] 1 Chr 23:7–23.   k. [24:31] 1 Chr 25:8; 26:13.   l. [25:1] 1 Chr 6:16–32; 15:16–17, 19; 16:37; 2 Chr 5:12; 35:15; Neh 12:27, 45.

This is the list of those who performed this service: [2]Of the sons of Asaph: Zaccur, Joseph, Nethaniah, and Asharelah, sons of Asaph, under the direction of Asaph, who prophesied under the guidance of the king. [3]Of Jeduthun, these sons of Jeduthun: Gedaliah, Zeri, Jeshaiah, Shimei, Hashabiah, and Mattithiah; six, under the direction of their father Jeduthun, who prophesied to the accompaniment of a lyre, to give thanks and praise to the Lord. [4]Of Heman, these sons of Heman: Bukkiah, Mattaniah, Uzziel, Shubael, and Jerimoth; Hananiah, Hanani, Eliathah, Giddalti, Romamti-ezer, Joshbekashah, Mallothi, Hothir, and Mahazioth. [5]All these were the sons of Heman, the king's seer for divine matters; to exalt him God gave Heman fourteen sons and three daughters.[m] [6]All these, whether of Asaph, Jeduthun, or Heman, were under their fathers' direction in the singing in the house of the Lord to the accompaniment of cymbals, harps and lyres, serving in the house of God, under the guidance of the king.[n] [7]Their number, together with that of their kinsmen who were trained in singing to the Lord, all of them skilled men, was two hundred and eighty-eight. [8]They cast lots for their functions equally, young and old, master and pupil alike.[o]

[9]The first lot fell to Asaph, to the family of Joseph; he and his sons and his kinsmen were twelve. Gedaliah was the second; he and his kinsmen and his sons were twelve. [10]The third was Zaccur, his sons, and his kinsmen: twelve. [11]The fourth fell to Izri, his sons, and his kinsmen: twelve. [12]The fifth was Nethaniah, his sons, and his kinsmen: twelve. [13]The sixth was Bukkiah, his sons, and his kinsmen: twelve. [14]The seventh was Jesarelah, his sons, and his kinsmen: twelve. [15]The eighth was Jeshaiah, his sons, and his kinsmen: twelve. [16]The ninth was Mattaniah, his sons, and his kinsmen: twelve. [17]The tenth was Shimei, his sons, and his kinsmen: twelve. [18]The eleventh was Uzziel, his sons, and his kinsmen: twelve. [19]The twelfth fell to Hashabiah, his sons, and his kinsmen: twelve. [20]The thirteenth was Shubael, his sons, and his kinsmen: twelve. [21]The fourteenth was Mattithiah, his sons, and his kinsmen: twelve. [22]The fifteenth fell to Jeremoth, his sons, and his kinsmen: twelve. [23]The sixteenth fell to Hananiah, his sons, and his kinsmen: twelve. [24]The seventeenth fell to Joshbekashah, his sons, and his kinsmen: twelve. [25]The eighteenth fell to Hanani, his sons, and his kinsmen: twelve. [26]The nineteenth fell to Mallothi, his sons, and his kinsmen: twelve. [27]The twentieth fell to Eliathah, his sons, and his kinsmen: twelve. [28]The twenty-first fell to Hothir, his sons, and his kinsmen: twelve.

[29]The twenty-second fell to Giddalti, his sons, and his kinsmen: twelve. [30]The twenty-third fell to Mahazioth, his sons, and his kinsmen: twelve. [31]The twenty-fourth fell to Romamti-ezer, his sons, and his kinsmen: twelve.

## CHAPTER 26

**Divisions of Gatekeepers.** [1]As for the divisions of gatekeepers: Of the Korahites was Meshelemiah, the son of Kore, one of the sons of Abiasaph. [2]Meshelemiah's sons: Zechariah, the firstborn, Jediael, the second son, Zebadiah, the third, Jathniel, the fourth, [3]Elam, the fifth, Jehohanan, the sixth, Eliehoenai, the seventh. [4]Obed-edom's sons: Shemaiah, the firstborn, Jehozabad, a second son, Joah, the third, Sachar, the fourth, Nethanel, the fifth, [5]Ammiel, the sixth, Issachar, the seventh, Peullethai, the eighth, for God blessed him. [6]To his son Shemaiah were born sons who ruled over their family, for they were warriors. [7]The sons of Shemaiah were Othni, Rephael, Obed, and Elzabad; also his kinsmen who were men of substance, Elihu and Semachiah. [8]All these were the sons of Obed-edom, who, together with their sons and their kinsmen, were men of substance, fit for the service. Of Obed-edom, sixty-two. [9]Of Meshelemiah, eighteen sons and kinsmen, men of substance.

[10]Hosah, a descendant of Merari, had these sons: Shimri, the chief (for though he was not the firstborn, his father made him chief),[q] [11]Hilkiah, the second son, Tebaliah, the third, Zechariah, the fourth. All the sons and kinsmen of Hosah were thirteen.

[12]To these divisions of the gatekeepers, by their chief men, were assigned watches for them to minister in the house of the Lord, for each group in the same way. [13]They cast lots for each gate, small and large families alike. [14]When the lot was cast for the east side, it fell to Meshelemiah. Then they cast lots for his son Zechariah, a prudent counselor, and the north side fell to his lot.[r] [15]To Obed-edom fell the south side, and to his sons the storehouse. [16]To Hosah fell the west side with the Shallecheth gate at the ascending highway. For each family, watches were established. [17]On the east, six watched each day, on the north, four each day, on the south, four each day, and at the storehouse they were two and two; [18]as for the large building[*] on the west, there were four at the highway and two at the large building. [19]These were the classes of the gatekeepers, sons of Korah and Merari.

**Treasurers.** [20]Their brother Levites had oversight of the treasuries of the house of God and the treasuries of votive offerings.[s] [21]Among the

---

O Lord," "Have mercy on me," "You are my God," "I magnify," "I extol the help of . . .," "Sitting in adversity," "I have fulfilled," "He made abundant," and "Visions."

m. [25:5] 2 Chr 35:15.   n. [25:6] 1 Chr 15:16.   o. [25:8] 1 Chr 24:31.

*[26:18] **The large building**: *parbar*, mentioned also in 2 Kgs 23:11; the meaning of the word is unclear.

p. [26:1] 1 Chr 9:19; 2 Chr 8:14; 23:19; 35:15; Neh 12:45.   q. [26:10] 1 Chr 16:38.   r. [26:14] 1 Chr 9:21.   s. [26:20] 1 Chr 28:12; 1 Kgs 7:51.

sons of Ladan the Gershonite, the family heads were sons of Jehiel:[t] [22u]the sons of Jehiel, Zetham and his brother Joel, who oversaw the treasures of the house of the LORD. [23]Of the Amramites, Izharites, Hebronites, and Uzzielites, [24]Shubael, son of Gershom, son of Moses, was principal overseer of the treasures. [25v]His associate was of the line of Eliezer, whose son was Rehabiah, whose son was Jeshaiah, whose son was Joram, whose son was Zichri, whose son was Shelomith. [26]This Shelomith and his kinsmen oversaw all the treasures of the votive offerings dedicated by King David, the heads of the families, the commanders of thousands and of hundreds, and the commanders of the army;[w] [27]what came from wars and from spoils, they dedicated for the support of the house of the LORD. [28]Also, whatever Samuel the seer, Saul, son of Kish, Abner, son of Ner, Joab, son of Zeruiah, and all others had consecrated, was under the charge of Shelomith and his kinsmen.

**Magistrates.** [29]Among the Izharites, Chenaniah and his sons were in charge of Israel's civil affairs* as officials and judges.[x] [30]Among the Hebronites, Hashabiah[y] and his kinsmen, one thousand seven hundred men of substance, had the administration of Israel on the western side of the Jordan for all the work of the LORD and the service of the king. [31]Among the Hebronites, Jerijah was their chief according to their family records. In the fortieth year of David's reign search was made, and there were found among them warriors at Jazer of Gilead.[z] [32]His kinsmen were also men of substance, two thousand seven hundred heads of families. King David appointed them to the administration of the Reubenites, the Gadites, and the half-tribe of Manasseh for everything pertaining to God and to the king.

### CHAPTER 27

**Army Commanders.**[†] [1]This is the list of the Israelite family heads, commanders of thousands and of hundreds, and other officers who served the king in all that pertained to the divisions, of twenty-four thousand men each, that came and went month by month throughout the year.

[2]Over the first division for the first month was Ishbaal, son of Zabdiel, and in his division were twenty-four thousand men; [3]a descendant of Perez, he was chief over all the commanders

of the army for the first month. [4]Over the division of the second month was Eleazar, son of Dodo, from Ahoh, and in his division were twenty-four thousand men.[a] [5b]The third army commander, for the third month, was Benaiah, son of Jehoiada the chief priest, and in his division were twenty-four thousand men. [6]This Benaiah was a warrior among the Thirty and over the Thirty. His son Ammizabad was over his division. [7]Fourth, for the fourth month, was Asahel, brother of Joab, and after him his son Zebadiah, and in his division were twenty-four thousand men.[c] [8]Fifth, for the fifth month, was the commander Shamhuth, a descendant of Zerah, and in his division were twenty-four thousand men. [9]Sixth, for the sixth month, was Ira, son of Ikkesh, from Tekoa, and in his division were twenty-four thousand men. [10]Seventh, for the seventh month, was Hellez, from Bethpelet, of the Ephraimites, and in his division were twenty-four thousand men. [11]Eighth, for the eighth month, was Sibbecai the Hushathite, a descendant of Zerah, and in his division were twenty-four thousand men.[d] [12]Ninth, for the ninth month, was Abiezer from Anathoth, of Benjamin, and in his division were twenty-four thousand men. [13]Tenth, for the tenth month, was Maharai from Netophah, a descendant of Zerah, and in his division were twenty-four thousand men. [14]Eleventh, for the eleventh month, was Benaiah the Pirathonite, of the Ephraimites, and in his division were twenty-four thousand men. [15]Twelfth, for the twelfth month, was Heldai the Netophathite, of the family of Othniel, and in his division were twenty-four thousand men.

**Tribal Leaders.** [16]Over the tribes of Israel, for the Reubenites the leader was Eliezer, son of Zichri; for the Simeonites, Shephatiah, son of Maacah; [17]for Levi, Hashabiah, son of Kemuel; for Aaron, Zadok; [18]for Judah, Eliab,[e] one of David's brothers; for Issachar, Omri, son of Michael; [19]for Zebulun, Ishmaiah, son of Obadiah; for Naphtali, Jeremoth, son of Azriel; [20]for the Ephraimites, Hoshea, son of Azaziah; for the half-tribe of Manasseh, Joel, son of Pedaiah; [21]for the half-tribe of Manasseh in Gilead, Iddo, son of Zechariah; for Benjamin, Jaasiel, son of Abner; [22]for Dan, Azarel, son of Jeroham. These were the commanders of the tribes of Israel.

[23]David did not count those who were twenty years of age or younger, for the LORD had promised to multiply Israel like the stars of the heavens.[f] [24]Joab, son of Zeruiah, began to take the census, but he did not complete it, for because of it wrath fell upon Israel. Therefore the number was not recorded in the book of chronicles of King David.[g]

**Overseers.** [25]Over the treasuries of the king was Azmaveth,[h] the son of Adiel. Over the treasuries

---

*[26:29] **Civil affairs:** lit., "external work," i.e., conduct of affairs external to the Temple.

†[27:1–15] This list of army commanders is similar to, but distinct from, the list of David's warriors given in 11:10–47. The schematic enumeration of the soldiers presented here appears artificial and exaggerated (12 x 24,000 = 288,000 men!). However, the Hebrew word (*'eleph*) translated "thousand" might also designate a military unit of much smaller size.

---

t. [26:21] 1 Chr 23:7–8; 29:8.  u. [26:22–24] 1 Chr 23:8, 12, 16.
v. [26:25] 1 Chr 23:17–18; 24:21.  w. [26:26] 2 Sm 8:11.  x. [26:29] 1 Chr 23:4.  y. [26:30] 1 Chr 27:17; Neh 11:15–16.  z. [26:31] 1 Chr 23:19; 29:27; Jos 13:25.

a. [27:4] 1 Chr 11:12; 2 Sm 23:9.  b. [27:5–6] 1 Chr 11:22–25; 18:17; 2 Sm 23:20–23.  c. [27:7] 2 Sm 2:18; 23:24.  d. [27:11] 1 Chr 11:29; 20:4; 2 Sm 21:18.  e. [27:18] 1 Chr 2:13.  f. [27:23] Gn 22:17. g. [27:24] 2 Sm 24:10.  h. [27:25] 2 Sm 23:31.

in the country, the cities, the villages, and the towers was Jonathan, son of Uzziah. ²⁶Over the farm workers who tilled the soil was Ezri, son of Chelub. ²⁷Over the vineyards was Shimei from Ramah, and over their produce for the wine cellars was Zabdi the Shiphmite. ²⁸Over the olive trees and sycamores of the Shephelah was Baalhanan the Gederite, and over the stores of oil was Joash. ²⁹Over the cattle that grazed in Sharon was Shitrai the Sharonite, and over the cattle in the valleys was Shaphat, the son of Adlai; ³⁰over the camels was Obil the Ishmaelite; over the donkeys was Jehdeiah the Meronothite; ³¹and over the flocks was Jaziz the Hagrite. All these were the overseers of King David's possessions.

**David's Court.** ³²Jonathan, David's uncle and a man of intelligence, was counselor and scribe; he and Jehiel, the son of Hachmoni, attended the king's sons. ³³Ahithophel was also the king's counselor, and Hushai the Archite was the king's friend.ⁱ ³⁴After Ahithophel* came Jehoiada, the son of Benaiah, and Abiathar. The commander of the king's army was Joab.

### CHAPTER 28

**The Assembly at Jerusalem.** ¹David assembled at Jerusalem all the commanders of Israel, the tribal commanders, the commanders of the divisions who were in the service of the king, the commanders of thousands and of hundreds, those in command of all the king's estates and possessions, and his sons, together with the courtiers, the warriors, and every person of substance.ʲ ²ᵏKing David rose to his feet and said: "Hear me, my kinsmen and my people. It was my purpose to build a house of repose myself for the ark of the covenant of the LORD, the footstool for the feet of our God;† and I was preparing to build it. ³But God said to me, You may not build a house for my name, for you are a man who waged wars and shed blood. ⁴However, the LORD, the God of Israel, chose me from all my father's family to be king over Israel forever. For he chose Judah as leader, then one family of Judah, that of my father; and finally, among all the sons of my father, it pleased him to make me king over all Israel.ˡ ⁵And of all my sons—for the LORD has given me many sons—he has chosen my son Solomon to sit on the throne of the LORD's kingship over Israel.ᵐ ⁶For

he said to me: It is your son Solomon who shall build my house and my courts, for I have chosen him for my son, and I will be a father to him.ⁿ ⁷I will establish his kingdom forever, if he perseveres in carrying out my commandments and ordinances as he does now. ⁸Therefore, in the sight of all Israel, the assembly of the LORD, and in the hearing of our God: keep and carry out all the commandments of the LORD, your God, that you may continue to possess this good land and afterward leave it as an inheritance to your children forever.ᵒ

⁹"As for you, Solomon, my son, know the God of your father and serve him with a whole heart and a willing soul, for the LORD searches all hearts and understands all the mind's thoughts. If you search for him, he will be found; but if you abandon him, he will cast you off forever.ᵖ ¹⁰See, then! The LORD has chosen you to build a house as his sanctuary. Be strong and set to work."

**Temple Plans Given to Solomon.** ¹¹Then David gave to his son Solomon the design of the portico and of the house itself, with its storerooms, its upper rooms and inner chambers, and the shrine containing the cover of the ark.�q ¹²He provided also the design for all else that he had in mind by way of courts for the house of the LORD, with the surrounding compartments for the treasuries of the house of God and the treasuries for the votive offerings, ¹³as well as for the divisions of the priests and Levites, for all the work of the service of the house of the LORD, and for all the liturgical vessels of the house of the LORD. ¹⁴He specified the weight of gold to be used in the golden vessels for the various services and the weight of silver to be used in the silver vessels for the various services; ¹⁵likewise for the golden menorahs and their lamps he specified the weight of gold for each menorah and its lamps, and for the silver menorahs he specified the weight of silver for each menorah and its lamps, depending on the use to which each menorah was to be put.ʳ ¹⁶He specified the weight of gold for each table that was to hold the showbread, and the silver for the silver tables; ¹⁷the pure gold for the forks, basins, and pitchers; the weight of gold for each golden bowl and the weight of silver for each silver bowl; ¹⁸the refined gold, and its weight, to be used for the altar of incense; and, finally, gold to fashion the chariot:‡ the cherubim spreading their wings and covering the ark of the covenant of the LORD.ˢ ¹⁹All this he wrote down, by the hand of the LORD, to make him understand it—the working out of the whole design.

---

*[27:34] **After Ahithophel**: after Ahithophel's suicide (2 Sm 17:23), Jehoiada succeeded him as the king's counselor. **Abiathar**: David's priest, along with Zadok. See note on 18:16.

†[28:2] **The ark . . . the footstool . . . of our God**: the Lord, who was invisibly enthroned upon the cherubim associated with the ark of the covenant at Shiloh and later in the Jerusalem Temple, had the ark as his footstool; cf. Ps 99:5; 132:7. There was no ark in the postexilic Temple. Cf. note on 2 Chr 5:9.

‡[28:18] **Chariot**: this reference is probably inspired by the vision account in Ez 1:4–24; 10:1–22.

---

i. [27:33] 2 Sm 15:12, 32–37; 16:16–19, 23; 17:5–16, 23.   j. [28:1] 1 Chr 27:2–22, 25–31; 11:10–47.   k. [28:2–3] 1 Chr 17:4; 22:7–10; 2 Sm 7:5; 1 Kgs 5:3; Ps 132:3–7.   l. [28:4] 1 Chr 17:23; Gn 49:8–12; 1 Sm 16:6–13.   m. [28:5] 1 Chr 3:1–9; 14:3–7; 22:9; 23:1; Wis 9:7.

n. [28:6] 1 Chr 17:11–14; 22:9–10; 2 Sm 7:12–13.   o. [28:8] Dt 4:5.   p. [28:9] 1 Chr 29:17; 2 Chr 15:2; 1 Kgs 8:61.   q. [28:11] Ex 25:9, 40; 26:30.   r. [28:15] Ex 25:31–37.   s. [28:18] Ex 25:18–22; 30:1–10; 1 Kgs 6:23–28.

[20]Then David said to his son Solomon: "Be strong and steadfast, and go to work; do not fear or be dismayed, for the LORD God, my God, is with you. He will not fail you or abandon you before you have completed all the work for the service of the house of the LORD.[t] [21]The divisions of the priests and Levites are ready for all the service of the house of God; they will be with you in all the work with all those who are eager to show their skill in every kind of craftsmanship. Also the commanders and all the people will do everything that you command."[u]

## CHAPTER 29

**Offerings for the Temple.** [1]King David then said to the whole assembly: "My son Solomon, whom alone God has chosen, is still young and inexperienced; the work, however, is great, for this palace is not meant for human beings, but for the LORD God.[v] [2]For this reason I have stored up for the house of my God, as far as I was able, gold for what will be made of gold, silver for what will be made of silver, bronze for what will be made of bronze, iron for what will be made of iron, wood for what will be made of wood, onyx stones and settings for them, carnelian and mosaic stones, every other kind of precious stone, and great quantities of marble.[w] [3]But now, because of the delight I take in the house of my God, in addition to all that I stored up for the holy house, I give to the house of my God my personal fortune in gold and silver: [4]three thousand talents of Ophir gold, and seven thousand talents of refined silver, for overlaying the walls of the rooms,[x] [5]for the various utensils to be made of gold and silver, and for every work that is to be done by artisans. Now, who else will contribute generously and consecrate themselves this day to the LORD?"[y]

[6]Then the heads of the families, the tribal commanders of Israel, the commanders of thousands and of hundreds, and those who had command of the king's affairs came forward willingly[z] [7]and contributed for the service of the house of God five thousand talents and ten thousand darics of gold, ten thousand talents of silver, eighteen thousand talents of bronze, and one hundred thousand talents of iron.[a] [8]Those who had precious stones gave them into the keeping of Jehiel the Gershonite for the treasury of the house of the LORD.[b] [9]The people rejoiced over these free-will offerings, for they had been contributed to the LORD wholeheartedly. King David also rejoiced greatly.[c]

**David's Prayer.** [10]Then David blessed the LORD in the sight of the whole assembly. David said:

"Blessed are you, LORD,
  God of Israel our father,
  from eternity to eternity.
[11] Yours, LORD, are greatness and might,
  majesty, victory, and splendor.
For all in heaven and on earth is yours;
  yours, LORD, is kingship;
  you are exalted as head over all.
[12] Riches and glory are from you,
  and you have dominion over all.
In your hand are power and might;
  it is yours to give greatness and
  strength to all.[d]
[13] Therefore, our God, we give you thanks
  and we praise the majesty of your
  name.

[14]"But who am I, and who are my people, that we should have the means to contribute so freely? For everything is from you, and what we give is what we have from you. [15]For before you we are strangers and travelers, like all our ancestors. Our days on earth are like a shadow, without a future.[e] [16]LORD our God, all this wealth that we have brought together to build you a house for your holy name comes from you and is entirely yours. [17]I know, my God, that you put hearts to the test and that you take pleasure in integrity. With a whole heart I have willingly given all these things, and now with joy I have seen your people here present also giving to you generously. [18]LORD, God of our ancestors Abraham, Isaac, and Israel,[f] keep such thoughts in the hearts and minds of your people forever, and direct their hearts toward you. [19]Give to my son Solomon a wholehearted desire to keep your commandments, precepts, and statutes, that he may carry out all these plans and build the palace for which I have made preparation."

[20]Then David told the whole assembly, "Now bless the LORD your God!" And the whole assembly blessed the LORD, the God of their ancestors, bowing down in homage before the LORD and before the king. [21]On the following day they brought sacrifices and burnt offerings to the LORD, a thousand bulls, a thousand rams, and a thousand lambs, together with their libations and many other sacrifices for all Israel; [22]and on that day they ate and drank in the LORD's presence with great rejoicing.

**Solomon Anointed.** Then for a second time[*] they proclaimed David's son Solomon king, and they anointed him for the LORD as ruler, and Zadok as priest. [23]Thereafter Solomon sat on the throne of the LORD as king succeeding his father David; he prospered, and all Israel obeyed him.[g]

---

*[29:22] **For a second time:** the first time is in 23:1 where David appoints Solomon his successor. Now there is a solemn public ratification of that appointment.

---

t. [28:20] 1 Chr 22:13; Jos 1:5.  u. [28:21] Ex 36:1–5.  v. [29:1] 1 Chr 22:5; 28:5.  w. [29:2] 1 Chr 22:14.  x. [29:4] 2 Chr 9:10; 1 Kgs 9:28; 10:11.  y. [29:5] Ezr 25:2; 35:5–6.  z. [29:6] 1 Chr 27:1, 25–31; 28:1.  a. [29:7] Ezr 2:69; 8:27; Neh 7:70–71.  b. [29:8] 1 Chr 23:8; 26:21.  c. [29:9] 2 Kgs 12:4.

d. [29:12] 2 Chr 20:6; Wis 6:3.  e. [29:15] Lv 25:23; Wis 2:5; 5:9.  f. [29:18] Ex 3:6, 15; 4:5; 1 Kgs 18:36.  g. [29:23] 1 Chr 28:5; 2 Chr 9:8; 1 Kgs 2:12.

²⁴All the commanders and warriors, and also all the other sons of King David, swore allegiance to King Solomon. ²⁵And the LORD exalted Solomon greatly in the eyes of all Israel, giving him a glorious reign such as had not been enjoyed by any king over Israel before him.*ʰ*

**David's Death.** ²⁶Thus David, the son of Jesse, had reigned over all Israel. ²⁷He was king over Israel for forty years: he was king seven years in Hebron and thirty-three years in Jerusalem.*ⁱ*

²⁸He died at a ripe old age, rich in years and wealth and glory, and his son Solomon succeeded him as king.*ʲ*

²⁹Now the deeds of King David, first and last, are recorded in the history of Samuel the seer, the history of Nathan the prophet, and the history of Gad the seer,*ᵏ* ³⁰together with the particulars of his reign and valor, and of the events that affected him and all Israel and all the kingdoms of the earth.

h. [29:25] 2 Chr 1:12; 1 Kgs 3:13.   i. [29:27] 2 Sm 5:5; 1 Kgs 2:11.   j. [29:28] 1 Chr 23:1.   k. [29:29] 1 Chr 21:9; 1 Sm 22:5.

# THE SECOND BOOK OF
# CHRONICLES

⁓ ❧ ⁓

The Second Book of Chronicles takes up the history of the monarchy where the First Book leaves off. It begins with the account of the reign of Solomon (chaps. 1–9) from the special viewpoint of the Chronicler. The portrait of Solomon is an idealized one; he appears as second only to David. Solomon's building of the Temple and the magnificence of his court are described in detail while the serious defects of his reign as cited in 1 Kings are simply not mentioned. This procedure is in keeping with the Chronicler's purpose of stressing the supreme importance of the Temple and its worship. He wishes to impress on his readers the splendor of God's dwelling and the magnificence of the liturgy of sacrifice, prayer, and praise offered there. Judah's kings are judged by their attitude toward the Temple and its cult. To this ideal of one people, united in the worship of the one true God at the Temple of Jerusalem founded by David and Solomon, the restored community is to conform.

In treating the period of divided monarchy (chaps. 10–36), the Chronicler gives practically all his attention to the kingdom of Judah. His virtual omission of the northern Israelite kings is significant. In his view, the northern tribes of Israel were guilty of religious schism as long as they worshiped the Lord in a place other than the Temple of Jerusalem. The Chronicler makes no mention of the important sanctuaries of Yhwh at Dan and Bethel—as though they had never existed. Nevertheless, he retains the ancient ideal of "all Israel" (a phrase occurring forty-one times in Chronicles) as the people of God. This unity, however, can exist only if the worship of "the whole congregation of Israel" takes place exclusively in the Jerusalem Temple. This requirement explains the Chronicler's praise of Kings Hezekiah and Josiah for striving, after the fall of Samaria, to unite the remnants of the northern tribes of Israel with the kingdom of Judah. Nevertheless, after Josiah's death, Judah quickly careens toward its demise at the hands of the Babylonians. That catastrophe is reversed by the edict of Cyrus allowing a return to Jerusalem and rebuilding of the Temple. Thus 2 Chronicles ends.

The Second Book of Chronicles can be divided into two major segments as follows:

I. The Reign of Solomon (1:1–9:31)
II. The Post-Solomonic Monarchy of Judah (10:1–36:23)

## I. THE REIGN OF SOLOMON

### CHAPTER 1

**Solomon at Gibeon.** ¹Solomon, son of David, strengthened his hold on the kingdom, for the LORD, his God, was with him, making him ever greater. ²Solomon summoned all Israel, the commanders of thousands and of hundreds, the judges, the princes of all Israel, and the family heads; ³ᵃand, accompanied by the whole assembly, Solomon went to the high place at Gibeon, because the tent of meeting of God, made in the wilderness by Moses, the LORD's servant, was there. ⁴David had, however, brought up the ark of God from Kiriath-jearim to Jerusalem, where he had provided a place and pitched a tent for

it; ⁵the bronze altar made by Bezalel, son of Uri, son of Hur, he put in front of the tabernacle of the LORD.* There Solomon and the assembly sought out the LORD,ᵇ ⁶and Solomon offered sacrifice in the LORD's presence on the bronze altar at the tent of meeting; he sacrificed a thousand burnt offerings upon it.

⁷That night God appeared to Solomon and said to him: Whatever you ask, I will give you.

---

*[1:5] **The bronze altar . . . the tabernacle of the LORD:** by this notice, the Chronicler justifies Solomon's worship at the high place of Gibeon. He pictures the tabernacle, i.e., the Mosaic meeting tent, and the bronze altar made at Moses' command (Ex 31:1–9) as remaining at Gibeon after David had installed the ark of the covenant in another tent in Jerusalem (1 Chr 15:1, 25; 16:1). Bezalel's altar was made of acacia wood plated with bronze (Ex 27:1–2). Later, Solomon made an all-bronze altar for the Temple in Jerusalem (2 Chr 4:1).

---

a. [1:3–12] 1 Kgs 3:4–15; 1 Chr 21:29.

b. [1:5] Ex 27:1–2; 31:2; 1 Chr 2:20.

[8]Solomon answered God: "You have shown great favor to David my father, and you have made me king to succeed him. [9]Now, LORD God, may your word to David my father be confirmed, for you have made me king over a people as numerous as the dust of the earth.[c] [10]Give me, therefore, wisdom and knowledge to govern this people, for otherwise who could rule this vast people of yours?" [11]God then replied to Solomon: Because this has been your wish—you did not ask for riches, treasures, and glory, or the life of those who hate you, or even for a long life for yourself, but you have asked for wisdom and knowledge in order to rule my people over whom I have made you king— [12]wisdom and knowledge are given you. I will also give you riches, treasures, and glory, such as kings before you never had, nor will those who come after you.

**Solomon's Wealth.** [13]Solomon returned to Jerusalem from the high place at Gibeon, from before the tent of meeting, and became king over Israel. [14]Solomon amassed chariots and horses: he had one thousand four hundred chariots and twelve thousand horses; these he allocated among the chariot cities and to the king's service in Jerusalem.[d] [15]The king made silver and gold as common in Jerusalem as stones, and cedars as numerous as the sycamores of the Shephelah.[e] [16]Solomon's horses were imported from Egypt and Cilicia,* where the king's agents purchased them at the prevailing price.[f] [17]A chariot imported from Egypt cost six hundred shekels of silver, a horse one hundred and fifty shekels; so they were exported to all the Hittite and Aramean kings.[g]

**Preparations for the Temple.** [18]Solomon gave orders for the building of a house for the name of the LORD and also a king's house for himself.

## CHAPTER 2

[1]Solomon conscripted seventy thousand men to carry stones and eighty thousand to cut the stones in the mountains, and over these he placed three thousand six hundred overseers.[h] [2]Moreover, Solomon sent this message to Huram, king of Tyre: "As you dealt with David my father, and sent him cedars to build a house for his dwelling— [3]now I am going to build a house for the name of the LORD, my God, and to consecrate it to him, for the burning of fragrant incense in his presence, for the perpetual display of the showbread, for burnt offerings morning and evening, and for the sabbaths,

new moons, and festivals of the LORD, our God: such is Israel's perpetual obligation.[j] [4]And the house I am going to build must be great, for our God is greater than all other gods. [5]Yet who is really able to build him a house, since the heavens and even the highest heavens cannot contain him? And who am I that I should build him a house,[k] unless it be to offer incense in his presence? [6]Now, send me men skilled at work in gold, silver, bronze, and iron, in purple, crimson, and violet fabrics, and who know how to do engraved work, to join the skilled craftsmen who are with me in Judah and Jerusalem, whom David my father appointed. [7]Also send me boards of cedar, cypress and cabinet wood from Lebanon, for I realize that your servants know how to cut the wood of Lebanon. My servants will work with yours [8]in order to prepare for me a great quantity of wood, since the house I intend to build must be great and wonderful. [9]I will furnish as food for your servants, the woodcutters, twenty thousand kors of wheat, twenty thousand kors of barley, twenty thousand baths of wine, and twenty thousand baths of oil."[†j]

[10]Huram, king of Tyre, wrote an answer which he sent to Solomon: "Because the LORD loves his people, he has placed you over them as king." [11]He added: "Blessed be the LORD, the God of Israel, who made heaven and earth, for having given King David a wise son of intelligence and understanding, who will build a house for the LORD and also his own royal house.[m] [12n]I am now sending you a craftsman of great skill, Huram-abi, [13]son of a Danite woman[‡] and of a father from Tyre; he knows how to work with gold, silver, bronze, and iron, with stone and wood, with purple, violet, fine linen, and crimson, and also how to do all kinds of engraved work and to devise every type of design that may be given him and your craftsmen and the craftsmen of my lord David your father. [14o]And now, let my lord send to his servants the wheat, barley, oil, and wine which he has promised. [15]For our part, we will cut trees on Lebanon, as many as you need, and send them down to you in rafts to the port of Joppa, whence you may take them up to Jerusalem."[p]

[16q]Thereupon Solomon took a census of all the alien men resident in the land of Israel

---

† [2:9] There is probably some exaggeration here. The parallel passage in 1 Kgs 5:25 does not list the barley or the wine, and mentions only twenty kors of olive oil. **Kors**: see note on Ez 45:14; **baths**: see note on Is 5:10. The amount given in Chronicles would be one hundred times as much (20,000 baths equals 2,000 kors).

‡ [2:13] **A Danite woman**: in 1 Kgs 7:14 she is called a widow of the tribe of Naphtali. The Danites had settled in the northern section of Naphtali's territory (Jgs 18:27–29). Bezalel, the head artisan in the time of Moses, had as his assistant a member of the tribe of Dan (Ex 31:6).

---

\* [1:16–17] **Egypt and Cilicia**: it seems likely that the horses came from Cilicia and the chariots from Egypt. Some scholars find a reference in Musur, a mountain district north of Cilicia, rather than to Egypt (Misrayim) in 1 Kgs 10:28–29, the Chronicler's source for this notice. The Chronicler himself probably understood the source to be speaking of Egypt; cf. 2 Chr 9:28.

c. [1:9] Gn 13:16; 28:14.   d. [1:14] 2 Chr 9:25; 1 Kgs 10:26–29.
e. [1:15] 1 Kgs 10:27.   f. [1:16] 1 Kgs 10:28.   g. [1:17] 1 Kgs 10:29.   h. [2:1] 2 Chr 2:17; 5:29–30.   i. [2:2–9] 1 Kgs 5:15–20; 1 Chr 14:1.
j. [2:3] Lv 24:5–8; Nm 28–29.   k. [2:5] 2 Chr 6:18.   l. [2:9] 1 Kgs 5:25; Ezr 3:7.   m. [2:11] 1 Kgs 5:21.   n. [2:12–13] Ex 31:1–5; 1 Kgs 7:13–14.   o. [2:14–15] 1 Kgs 5:22–26.   p. [2:15] Ezr 3:7.
q. [2:16–17] 1 Chr 22:2.

(following the census David his father had taken of them); they were found to number one hundred fifty-three thousand six hundred. [17]Of these he made seventy thousand carriers and eighty thousand cutters in the mountains, and three thousand six hundred overseers to keep the people working.[r]

## CHAPTER 3

**Building of the Temple.** [1]Then Solomon began to build the house of the LORD in Jerusalem on Mount Moriah,[*] which had been shown to David his father, in the place David had prepared, the threshing floor of Ornan the Jebusite. [2]He began to build in the second month of the fourth year of his reign. [3]These were the specifications laid down by Solomon for building the house of God: the length was sixty cubits according to the old measure, and the width was twenty cubits;[s] [4]the front porch along the width of the house was also twenty cubits, and it was twenty cubits high.[†] He covered its interior with pure gold.[u] [5]The nave he overlaid with cypress wood and overlaid that with fine gold, embossing on it palms and chains.[v] [6]He also covered the house with precious stones for splendor; the gold was from Parvaim. [7]The house, its beams and thresholds, as well as its walls and its doors, he overlaid with gold, and he engraved cherubim upon the walls. [8]He also made the room of the holy of holies. Its length corresponded to the width of the house, twenty cubits, and its width was also twenty cubits. He overlaid it with fine gold to the amount of six hundred talents.[w] [9]The weight of the nails was fifty gold shekels. The upper chambers he likewise overlaid with gold.

[10x]For the room of the holy of holies he made two cherubim of carved workmanship, which were then covered with gold. [11]The wings of the cherubim spanned twenty cubits: one wing of each cherub, five cubits in length, extended to a wall of the house, while the other wing, also five cubits in length, touched the corresponding wing of the other cherub. [12]The wing of the cherub, five cubits, touched the wall of the house, and the other wing, five cubits, was joined to the wing of the other cherub. [13]The combined wingspread of the two cherubim was thus twenty cubits. They stood upon their own feet, facing toward the nave. [14]He made the veil[‡] of violet, purple, crimson, and fine linen, and had cherubim embroidered upon it.[y]

[15z]In front of the house he set two columns thirty-five cubits high; the capital of each was five cubits. [16]He devised chains in the form of a collar with which he encircled the capitals of the columns, and he made a hundred pomegranates which he set on the chains. [17]He set up the columns to correspond with the nave, one for the right side and the other for the left, and he called the one to the right Jachin and the one to the left Boaz.

## CHAPTER 4

[1]Then he made a bronze altar twenty cubits long, twenty cubits wide and ten cubits high.[a] [2b]He also made the molten sea. It was made with a circular rim, and measured ten cubits across, five in height, and thirty in circumference. [3]Under the brim a ring of figures of oxen[§] encircled it for ten cubits, all the way around the compass of the sea; there were two rows of oxen cast in one mold with the sea. [4]This rested on twelve oxen, three facing north, three facing west, three facing south, and three facing east, with their haunches all toward the center; upon them was set the sea. [5]It was a handbreadth thick, and its brim resembled that of a cup, being lily-shaped. It had a capacity of three thousand baths.[¶]

[6]Then he made ten basins for washing, placing five of them to the right and five to the left. In these the victims for the burnt offerings were washed; but the sea was for the priests to wash in.[c]

[7]He made the menorahs of gold, ten of them as was prescribed, and placed them in the nave, five to the right and five to the left.[d] [8]He made ten tables and had them set in the nave, five to the right and five to the left; and he made a hundred golden bowls.[e] [9]He made the court of the priests and the great courtyard[f] and the gates of the courtyard; the gates he covered with bronze. [10]The sea he placed off to the southeast from the south side of the house.[g]

[11h]When Huram had made the pots, shovels, and bowls, he finished all his work for King Solomon in the house of God: [12]two columns; two

---

*[3:1] **Mount Moriah**: Gn 22:2 speaks of a "height in the land of Moriah." This is the only place in the Bible where the Temple mount is identified with the site where Abraham was to have sacrificed Isaac.

†[3:4] **The front porch . . . twenty cubits high**: this figure, not given in 1 Kgs 7, is based on a variant Greek text that may be due to a later revision. The Hebrew text itself has "one hundred and twenty cubits high." The Chronicler nearly doubles the height of the two free-standing columns adjacent to the porch in 2 Chr 3:15 as compared with the source, 1 Kgs 7:15–16.

‡[3:14] **The veil**: this was suspended at the entrance of the holy of holies, in imitation of the veil of the Mosaic meeting tent (Ex 26:31–32). Solomon's Temple had doors at this point, according to 1 Kgs 6:31. Apparently the Temple of the Chronicler's time did have a veil, just as did Herod's Temple (Mt 27:51; Mk 15:38; Lk 23:45).

§[4:3] **Oxen**: in 1 Kgs 7:24 this double row of ornaments is described as consisting of gourds. The text of Kings available to the Chronicler may have been corrupt at this point since the two words sound similar in Hebrew. In 4:16 the Chronicler speaks of forks while 1 Kgs 7:40 refers to bowls.

¶[4:5] **Three thousand baths**: two thousand baths according to 1 Kgs 7:26; see note on 1 Kgs 7:23–26.

r. [2:17] 2 Chr 2:1.　s. [3:1–2] Gn 22:2; 1 Kgs 6:1; 1 Chr 21:22–26; 22:1.　t. [3:3] 1 Kgs 6:2.　u. [3:4] 1 Kgs 6:3.　v. [3:5] 1 Kgs 6:15; Ez 41:1.　w. [3:8] 1 Kgs 6:16–17, 20.　x. [3:10–13] 1 Kgs 6:23–27.

y. [3:14] Mt 27:51.　z. [3:15–17] 1 Kgs 7:15–20; Ez 40:49.　a. [4:1] Ez 43:13–17.　b. [4:2–5] 1 Kgs 7:23–26.　c. [4:6] 1 Kgs 7:38–39; Ez 40:38.　d. [4:7] 1 Kgs 7:49.　e. [4:8] 1 Kgs 7:50; 1 Chr 28:16.　f. [4:9] 1 Kgs 7:12.　g. [4:10] 1 Kgs 7:39.　h. [4:11–22] 1 Kgs 7:40–51.

nodes for the capitals on top of the columns; and two pieces of netting covering the two nodes for the capitals on top of the columns; [13]four hundred pomegranates in double rows on both pieces of netting that covered the two nodes of the capitals on top of the columns. [14]He made the stands, and the basins on the stands; [15]one sea, and the twelve oxen under it; [16]pots, shovels, forks, and all the articles Huram-abi made for King Solomon for the house of the LORD; they were of burnished bronze. [17]The king had them cast in the neighborhood of the Jordan, between Succoth and Zeredah, in thick clay molds. [18]Solomon made all these vessels, so many in number that the weight of the bronze could not be determined.

[19]Solomon made all the articles that were for the house of God: the golden altar, the tables on which the showbread lay, [20]the menorahs and their lamps of pure gold which were to burn as prescribed before the inner sanctuary, [21]flowers, lamps, and gold tongs (this was of purest gold), [22]snuffers, bowls, cups, and firepans of pure gold. As for the entrance to the house, its inner doors to the holy of holies, as well as the doors to the nave of the temple, were of gold.

## CHAPTER 5

**Dedication of the Temple.** [1]When all the work undertaken by Solomon for the house of the LORD was completed, he brought in the votive offerings of David his father, putting the silver, the gold, and other articles in the treasuries of the house of God. [2]Then Solomon assembled the elders of Israel and all the heads of the tribes, the princes in the ancestral houses of the Israelites, to Jerusalem to bring up the ark of the LORD's covenant from the City of David, which is Zion. [3]All the people of Israel assembled before the king during the festival of the seventh month.* [4]When all the elders of Israel had arrived, the Levites† took up the ark; [5]and they brought up the ark and the tent of meeting with all the sacred vessels that were in the tent. The levitical priests brought them up.

[6]King Solomon and the entire community of Israel, gathered for the occasion before the ark, sacrificed sheep and oxen too many to number or count. [7]The priests brought the ark of the covenant of the LORD to its place: the inner sanctuary of the house, the holy of holies, beneath the wings of the cherubim. [8]The cherubim had their wings spread out over the place of the ark, covering the ark and its poles from above. [9]The poles were so long that their ends could be seen from the holy place in front of the inner

sanctuary. (They cannot be seen from outside, but they remain there to this day.)‡ [10]There was nothing in the ark but the two tablets which Moses had put there at Horeb when the LORD made a covenant with the Israelites after they went forth from Egypt.

[11]When the priests left the holy place (all the priests who were present had purified themselves regardless of the rotation of their various divisions), [12]the Levites who were singers, all who belonged to Asaph, Heman, Jeduthun, and their sons and brothers, clothed in fine linen, with cymbals, harps, and lyres, stood east of the altar, and with them a hundred and twenty priests blowing trumpets. [13]When the trumpeters and singers were heard as a single voice praising and giving thanks to the LORD, and when they raised the sound of the trumpets, cymbals, and other musical instruments to "Praise the LORD, who is so good, whose love endures forever," the cloud filled the house of the LORD.[k] [14]The priests could no longer minister because of the cloud, since the glory of the LORD had filled the house of God.[l]

## CHAPTER 6

[1][m]Then Solomon said:

> "The LORD intends to dwell in the dark
>     cloud;
> [2]    I have built you a princely house,
>     the base for your enthronement
>         forever."

[3][n]The king turned and blessed the whole assembly of Israel, while the whole assembly of Israel stood. [4]He said: "Blessed be the LORD, the God of Israel, who with his own mouth spoke a promise to David my father and by his hand fulfilled it, saying: [5]Since the day I brought my people out of the land of Egypt, I have not chosen a city out of any tribe of Israel for the building of a house, that my name might be there; nor have I chosen any man to be ruler of my people Israel; [6]but now I have chosen Jerusalem, that my name may be there, and I have chosen David§ to rule my people Israel. [7]When David my father wished to build a house for the name of the LORD, the God of Israel, [8]the LORD said to him: In wishing to build a house for my name, you did well. [9]But it is not you who will build

---

*[5:3] **Festival of the seventh month**: feast of Booths (Tabernacles); cf. notes on 7:9–10; 1 Kgs 8:2.

†[5:4] **The Levites**: the parallel passage in 1 Kgs 8:3 reads "the priests"; but in 2 Chr 5:5 the Deuteronomic expression "levitical priests" is used, as it is in 23:18; 30:27.

i. [5:1–14] 1 Kgs 7:51–8:13.  j. [5:4–5] 2 Chr 35:3.

‡[5:9] **They remain there to this day**: the Chronicler must have copied this notice from his source (1 Kgs 8:8), losing sight of the fact that there was no ark in the Temple of his own day. (According to 2 Mc 2:4–8, the ark of Solomon's Temple was concealed by Jeremiah at the time of the Babylonian destruction of Jerusalem.)

§[6:6] **Jerusalem . . . David**: Ps 132:11, 13 puts in parallel the Lord's choice of Zion, the royal house of David and the mountain in Jerusalem as the site for the Lord's house.

k. [5:13] Ps 136; Jer 33:11.  l. [5:14] 2 Chr 7:2; 1 Kgs 8:10–11.
m. [6:1–2] 1 Kgs 8:12–13.  n. [6:3–11] 1 Kgs 8:14–21.

the house, but your son, who comes from your loins: he shall build the house for my name."

¹⁰"Now the Lord has fulfilled the word he spoke. I have succeeded David my father, and I sit on the throne of Israel, as the Lord has said, and I have built this house for the name of the Lord, the God of Israel. ¹¹I have placed there the ark, in which is the covenant of the Lord that he made with the Israelites."

**Solomon's Prayer.** ¹²*°Then he stood before the altar of the Lord in the presence of the whole assembly of Israel and stretched forth his hands. ¹³*Solomon had made a bronze platform five cubits long, five cubits wide, and three cubits high, which he had placed in the middle of the courtyard. Having ascended it, Solomon knelt in the presence of the whole assembly of Israel and stretched forth his hands toward heaven. ¹⁴He said: "Lord, God of Israel, there is no God like you in heaven or on earth; you keep the covenant and love toward your servants who walk before you with their whole heart, ¹⁵the covenant that you kept toward your servant, David my father. That which you promised him, your mouth has spoken and your hand has fulfilled this very day. ¹⁶And now, Lord, God of Israel, keep toward your servant, David my father, what you promised: There shall never be wanting someone from your line to sit before me on the throne of Israel, provided that your descendants keep to their way, walking by my law, as you have. ¹⁷Now, Lord, God of Israel, may the words which you spoke to David your servant be confirmed.

¹⁸"Is God indeed to dwell with human beings on earth? If the heavens and the highest heavens cannot contain you, how much less this house which I have built! ¹⁹Regard kindly the prayer and petition of your servant, Lord, my God, and listen to the cry of supplication which I, your servant, utter before you. ²⁰May your eyes be open day and night toward this house, the place where you have decreed your name shall be; listen to the prayer your servant makes toward this place. ²¹Listen to the petition of your servant and of your people Israel which they offer toward this place. Listen, from the place of your enthronement, heaven, and listen and forgive.

²²"If someone sins against a neighbor and is required to take an oath sanctioned by a curse, and comes and takes the oath before your altar in this house, ²³listen in heaven: act and judge your servants. Condemn the wicked, requiting their ways; acquit the just, rewarding their justice. ²⁴When your people Israel are defeated by an enemy because they have sinned against

you, and then they turn, praise your name, pray to you, and entreat you in this house, ²⁵listen from heaven and forgive the sin of your people Israel, and bring them back to the land you gave them and their ancestors. ²⁶When the heavens are closed so that there is no rain, because they have sinned against you, but they pray toward this place and praise your name, and turn from their sin because you have afflicted them, ²⁷listen in heaven and forgive the sin of your servants, your people Israel. (For you teach them the good way in which they should walk.) Give rain upon this land of yours which you have given to your people as their heritage.

²⁸"If there is famine in the land or pestilence; or if blight comes, or mildew, or locusts swarm, or caterpillars; when their enemies besiege them at any of their gates; whatever plague or sickness there may be; ²⁹whatever prayer of petition any may make, any of your people Israel, who know affliction and pain and stretch out their hands toward this house, ³⁰listen from heaven, the place of your enthronement, and forgive. Render to each and all according to their ways, you who know every heart; for it is you alone who know the heart of every human being. ³¹So may they revere you and walk in your ways as long as they live on the land you gave our ancestors.

³²"To the foreigners, likewise, who are not of your people Israel, but who come from a distant land for the sake of your great name, your mighty hand and outstretched arm, and come in prayer to this house, ³³listen from heaven, the place of your enthronement. Do all that the foreigner asks of you, that all the peoples of the earth may know your name, may revere you as do your people Israel, and may know that your name has been invoked upon this house that I have built.

³⁴"When your people go out to war against their enemies, by whatever way you send them, and they pray to you toward the city you have chosen and the house I have built for your name, ³⁵listen from heaven to their prayer and petition, and uphold their cause. ³⁶When they sin against you (for there is no one who does not sin), and in your anger against them you deliver them to an enemy, so that their captors carry them off to another land, far or near, ³⁷and they have a change of heart in the land of their captivity and they turn and entreat you in the land of their captors and say, 'We have sinned and done wrong; we have been wicked,' ³⁸if with all their heart and soul they turn back to you in the land of those who took them captive, and pray toward their land which you gave their ancestors, the city you have chosen, and the house which I have built for your name, ³⁹listen from heaven, the place of your enthronement, to their prayer and petitions, and uphold their cause. Forgive your people who have sinned against you. ⁴⁰Now, my God, may your eyes be

---

*[6:13] This verse has no equivalent in 1 Kgs 8:22–23, the Chronicler's source. Solomon is depicted as praying on "a bronze platform . . . in the middle of the courtyard" because in the time of the Chronicler only priests were permitted to pray before the altar.

o. [6:12–40] 1 Kgs 8:22–53.

open and your ears be attentive to the prayer of this place. [41]And now:

"Arise, LORD God, come to your resting place,
> you and your majestic ark.
Your priests, LORD God, will be clothed with salvation,
> your faithful ones rejoice in good things.
[42] LORD God, do not reject the plea of your anointed,
> remember the devotion of David, your servant."[p]

## CHAPTER 7

[1q]When Solomon had ended his prayer, fire came down from heaven and consumed the burnt offerings and the sacrifices, and the glory of the LORD filled the house. [2]But the priests could not enter the house of the LORD, for the glory of the LORD filled the house of the LORD.[r] [3]All the Israelites looked on while the fire came down and the glory of the LORD was upon the house, and they fell down upon the pavement with their faces to the earth and worshiped, praising the LORD, "who is so good, whose love endures forever." [4]The king and all the people offered sacrifices before the LORD.[s] [5]King Solomon offered as sacrifice twenty-two thousand oxen, and one hundred twenty thousand sheep.[t]
**End of the Dedication.** Thus the king and all the people dedicated the house of God. [6]The priests were standing at their stations, as were the Levites, with the musical instruments of the LORD which King David had made to give thanks to the LORD, "whose love endures forever," when David offered praise through them. The priests opposite them blew the trumpets and all Israel stood.[u]

[7]Then Solomon consecrated the middle of the court facing the house of the LORD; he offered there the burnt offerings and the fat of the communion offerings, since the bronze altar which Solomon had made could not hold the burnt offering, the grain offering, and the fat.[v]

[8]On this occasion Solomon and with him all Israel, a great assembly from Lebo-hamath to the Wadi of Egypt, celebrated the festival for seven days.[w] [9x]On the eighth day they held a solemn assembly, for they had celebrated the dedication of the altar for seven days and the feast[*]

for seven days. [10]On the twenty-third day of the seventh month he dismissed the people to their tents, rejoicing and glad of heart because of all the blessings the LORD had given to David, to Solomon, and to his people Israel. [11y]Solomon finished building the house of the LORD, the house of the king, and everything else he wanted to do in regard to the house of the LORD and his own house.
**God's Promise to Solomon.** [12]The LORD appeared to Solomon during the night and said to him: I have heard your prayer, and I have chosen this place for my house of sacrifice. [13]If I close heaven so that there is no rain, if I command the locust to devour the land, if I send pestilence among my people, [14]if then my people, upon whom my name has been pronounced, humble themselves and pray, and seek my face and turn from their evil ways, I will hear them from heaven and pardon their sins and heal their land. [15]Now, therefore, my eyes shall be open and my ears attentive to the prayer of this place; [16]now I have chosen and consecrated this house that my name may be there forever; my eyes and my heart shall be there always.

[17]As for you, if you walk before me as David your father did, doing all that I have commanded you and keeping my statutes and ordinances, [18]I will establish the throne of your kingship as I covenanted with David your father when I said, There shall never be wanting someone from your line as ruler in Israel. [19]But if ever you turn away and forsake my commandments and statutes which I set before you, and proceed to serve other gods, and bow down to them, [20]I will uproot the people from the land I gave and repudiate the house I have consecrated for my name. I will make it a proverb and a byword among all nations. [21]And this house which is so exalted—every passerby shall be horrified and ask: "Why has the LORD done such things to this land and to this house?" [22]And the answer will come: "Because they abandoned the LORD, the God of their ancestors, who brought them out of the land of Egypt, and they embraced other gods, bowing down to them and serving them. That is why he has brought upon them all this evil."

## CHAPTER 8

**Public Works.** [1z]After the twenty years during which Solomon built the house of the LORD and his own house, [2]he built up the cities which Huram had given him,[†] and settled Israelites

---

*[7:9–10] **The feast:** Booths, celebrated on the fifteenth day of the seventh month and followed by a solemn octave lasting through the twenty-second day (Lv 23:33–36; Nm 29:12–35); the people are therefore sent home on the twenty-third day of the month (v. 10). The festival (v. 8) marking the dedication of the altar and of the Temple was held during the

seven days prior to the feast of Booths, i.e., from the seventh to the fourteenth day of the seventh month. According to 1 Kgs 8:3, 65–66 the dedication of the Temple was celebrated concomitantly with the seven days of the feast of Booths, after which the people were dismissed on the eighth day.

†[8:2] **The cities which Huram had given him:** according to 1 Kgs 9:10–14, it was Solomon who ceded the cities to the king of Tyre as payment for the timber and gold received from him. Since, however, 1 Kgs 9:12 states that Hiram was

---

p. [6:41–42] Ps 132:8–10.   q. [7:1–10] Jgs 6:21; 1 Kgs 8:54–66; 1 Chr 21:26; 2 Mc 2:10.   r. [7:2] 2 Chr 5:14; Ex 24:16; 1 Kgs 8:10–11.   s. [7:4] 2 Chr 5:13; 1 Kgs 8:62; Ps 136:1.   t. [7:5] 1 Kgs 8:63.   u. [7:6] Nm 10:8, 10; Ps 136:1.   v. [7:7] 1 Kgs 8:64.   w. [7:8] 1 Kgs 8:65.   x. [7:9–10] 1 Kgs 8:66.

y. [7:11–22] 1 Kgs 9:1–9.   z. [8:1–2] 1 Kgs 9:10–11.

there. ³Then Solomon went to Hamath of Zoba and conquered it. ⁴He built Tadmor˙ in the wilderness and all the supply cities, which he built in Hamath. ⁵ᵃHe built Upper Beth-horon and Lower Beth-horon, fortified cities with walls, gates, and bars; ⁶also Baalath, all the supply cities belonging to Solomon, and all the cities for the chariots, the cities for horses, and whatever else Solomon desired to build in Jerusalem, in Lebanon, and in the entire land under his dominion. ⁷All the people who were left of the Hittites, Amorites, Perizzites, Hivites, and Jebusites who were not Israelites— ⁸those of their descendants who were left in the land and whom the Israelites had not destroyed—Solomon conscripted as forced laborers, as they are to this day. ⁹But Solomon made none of the Israelites forced laborers for his works, for they were his fighting force, commanders, adjutants, chariot officers, and cavalry. ¹⁰They were also King Solomon's two hundred and fifty overseers who directed the people.

**Solomon's Piety.** ¹¹Solomon brought the daughter of Pharaoh up from the City of David to the house which he had built for her, for he said, "No wife of mine shall dwell in the house of David, king of Israel, for the places where the ark of the LORD has come are holy."

¹²In those times Solomon sacrificed burnt offerings to the LORD upon the altar of the LORD which he had built in front of the porch, ¹³as was required to be done day by day according to the command of Moses, especially on the sabbaths, at the new moons, and on the fixed festivals three times a year: on the feast of the Unleavened Bread, the feast of Weeks, and the feast of Booths.ᵇ

¹⁴And according to the ordinance of David his father he appointed the various divisions of the priests for their service, and the Levites according to their functions of praise and attendance upon the priests, as the daily duty required. The gatekeepers by their divisions stood guard at each gate, since such was the command of David, the man of God.ᶜ ¹⁵There was no deviation from the king's command in whatever related to the priests and Levites or the treasuries. ¹⁶All of Solomon's work was carried out successfully from the day the foundation of the house of the LORD was laid until its completion. The house of the LORD was finished.

**Glories of the Court.** ¹⁷In those times Solomon went to Ezion-geber and to Elath on the seashore of the land of Edom.ᵈ ¹⁸Huram had his servants send him ships and his own servants, expert seamen; they went with Solomon's servants to Ophir, and obtained there four hundred and fifty talents of gold and brought it to King Solomon.ᵉ

## CHAPTER 9

**The Queen of Sheba.** ¹ᶠThe queen of Sheba, having heard a report of Solomon's fame, came to Jerusalem to test him with subtle questions, accompanied by a very numerous retinue and by camels bearing spices, a large amount of gold, and precious stones. She came to Solomon and spoke to him about everything that she had on her mind. ²Solomon explained to her everything she asked about, and there was nothing so obscure that Solomon could not explain it to her.ᵍ

³ʰWhen the queen of Sheba witnessed Solomon's great wisdom, the house he had built, ⁴the food at his table, the seating of his ministers, the attendance and dress of his waiters, his cupbearers and their dress, and the burnt offerings he sacrificed in the house of the LORD, it took her breath away. ⁵"The report I heard in my country about your deeds and your wisdom is true," she told the king. ⁶"I did not believe the report until I came and saw with my own eyes that not even the half of your great wisdom had been told me. You have surpassed the report I heard. ⁷Happy your servants, happy these ministers of yours, who stand before you always and listen to your wisdom. ⁸Blessed be the LORD, your God, who was pleased to set you on his throne as king for the LORD, your God. In the love your God has for Israel, to establish them forever, he has made you king over them to carry out judgment and justice." ⁹Then she gave the king one hundred and twenty gold talents, a very large quantity of spices, and precious stones. Never again did anyone bring such an abundance of spices as the queen of Sheba gave to King Solomon.

¹⁰The servants of Huram and of Solomon who brought gold from Ophir also brought cabinet wood and precious stones. ¹¹With the cabinet wood the king made stairs for the house of the LORD and the house of the king, and harps and lyres for the chanters. The like of these had not been seen before in the land of Judah.ⁱ

¹²King Solomon gave the queen of Sheba everything she desired and asked for, more than she had brought to the king. Then she returned with her servants to her own country.ʲ

¹³ᵏThe gold that came to Solomon in one year weighed six hundred and sixty-six gold talents, ¹⁴in addition to what came from the tolls on travelers and what the merchants brought. All the kings of Arabia also, and the governors of the country, brought gold and silver to Solomon.

¹⁵King Solomon made two hundred large shields of beaten gold (six hundred shekels of

---

not satisfied with the cities, the Chronicler may have inferred that he gave them back to Solomon.

*[8:4] **Tadmor:** later known as Palmyra, an important caravan city in the Syrian desert. The parallel passage in 1 Kgs 9:18 has "Tamar," in southern Judah; cf. Ez 47:19; 48:28. But Solomon may well have fortified Tadmor against the Arameans.

a. [8:5–12] 1 Kgs 9:17–25.   b. [8:13] Ex 23:14; Nm 28–29; 1 Kgs 9:25.   c. [8:14] 1 Chr 23–26; Neh 12:46.   d. [8:17] 1 Kgs 9:26.

e. [8:18] 1 Kgs 9:27–28.   f. [9:1] 1 Kgs 10:1–2.   g. [9:2] 1 Kgs 10:3.   h. [9:3–9] 1 Kgs 10:4–9.   i. [9:10–11] 1 Kgs 10:11–12.   j. [9:12] 1 Kgs 10:13.   k. [9:13–28] 1 Kgs 10:14–28.

gold went into each shield) [16]and three hundred bucklers of beaten gold (three hundred shekels of gold went into each buckler); and the king put them in the house of the Forest of Lebanon.

[17]The king made a large ivory throne, and overlaid it with fine gold. [18]The throne had six steps; a footstool of gold was fastened to the throne, and there was an arm on each side of the seat, with two lions standing next to the arms, [19]and twelve other lions standing there on the steps, two to a step. Nothing like this was made in any other kingdom. [20]All King Solomon's drinking vessels were gold, and all the utensils in the house of the Forest of Lebanon were pure gold. There was no silver, for in Solomon's time silver was reckoned as nothing. [21]For the king had ships that went to Tarshish with the servants of Huram. Once every three years the fleet of Tarshish ships would come with a cargo of gold, silver, ivory, apes, and monkeys.

**Solomon's Renown.** [22]Thus King Solomon surpassed all the kings of the earth in riches and wisdom.

[23]All the kings of the earth sought audience with Solomon, to hear the wisdom God had put into his heart. [24]They all brought their tribute: vessels of silver and gold, garments, weapons, spices, horses, and mules—what was due each year. [25]Solomon had four thousand stalls for horses, chariots, and twelve thousand horses; these he allocated among the chariot cities and to the king's service in Jerusalem. [26]He was ruler over all the kings from the River to the land of the Philistines and down to the border of Egypt. [27]The king made silver as common in Jerusalem as stones, and cedars as numerous as the sycamores of the Shephelah. [28]*Solomon's horses were imported from Egypt and from all the lands.

**The Death of Solomon.** [29]The remainder of the acts of Solomon, first and last, are recorded in the acts of Nathan the prophet, in the prophecy of Ahijah the Shilonite, and in the visions of Iddo the seer concerning Jeroboam, son of Nebat. [30]Solomon was king in Jerusalem over all Israel for forty years. [31]Solomon rested with his ancestors and was buried in the City of David, his father, and Rehoboam his son succeeded him as king.

## II. THE POST-SOLOMONIC MONARCHY OF JUDAH

### CHAPTER 10

**Division of the Kingdom.** [1]*m*Rehoboam went to Shechem, where all Israel[†] had come to make

him king. [2]When Jeroboam, son of Nebat, heard about it, he was in Egypt where he had fled from King Solomon; and he returned from Egypt. [3]They sent for him; Jeroboam and all Israel came and said to Rehoboam: [4]"Your father put on us a heavy yoke. If you now lighten the harsh servitude and the heavy yoke your father imposed on us, we will be your servants." [5]He answered them, "Come back to me in three days," and the people went away.

[6]King Rehoboam asked advice of the elders who had been in his father Solomon's service while he was still alive, and asked, "How do you advise me to answer this people?" [7]They replied, "If you will deal kindly with this people and please them, giving them a favorable reply, they will be your servants forever." [8]But he ignored the advice the elders had given him and asked advice of the young men who had grown up with him and were in his service. [9]He said to them, "What answer do you advise us to give this people, who have told me, 'Lighten the yoke your father imposed on us'?" [10]The young men who had grown up with him replied: "This is what you must say to this people who have told you, 'Your father laid a heavy yoke on us; lighten it for us.' You must say, 'My little finger is thicker than my father's loins. [11]My father put a heavy yoke on you; I will make it heavier. My father beat you with whips; I will use scorpions!'"

[12]On the third day, Jeroboam and the whole people came back to King Rehoboam as the king had instructed them: "Come back to me in three days." [13]Ignoring the advice the elders had given him, King Rehoboam gave the people a harsh answer. [14]He spoke to them as the young men had advised: "My father laid a heavy yoke on you; I will make it heavier. My father beat you with whips; I will use scorpions." [15]The king did not listen to the people, for this turn of events was from God: the LORD fulfilled the word he had spoken through Ahijah the Shilonite to Jeroboam, the son of Nebat.[*n*]

[16]*When all Israel saw that the king did not listen to them, the people answered the king:

> "What share have we in David?
>     We have no heritage in the son of
>     Jesse.
> Everyone to your tents, Israel!
>     Now look to your own house,
>     David!"

So all Israel went off to their tents, [17]but the Israelites who lived in the cities of Judah had Rehoboam as their king. [18]King Rehoboam then sent out Hadoram, who was in charge of the forced labor, but the Israelites stoned him to

---

*[9:28] See note on 1:16–17.

†[10:1] **All Israel:** as in the source (1 Kgs 12:1), this term designates the northern tribes, as distinct from Judah and Benjamin. Elsewhere the Chronicler, writing on his own,

speaks comprehensively of "those Israelites who lived in the cities of Judah" (10:17), and "all the Israelites [lit., all Israel] in Judah and Benjamin" (11:3).

---

l. [9:29–31] 1 Kgs 11:41–43.   m. [10:1–14] 1 Kgs 12:1–14.

n. [10:15] 1 Kgs 11:29–39; 12:15.   o. [10:16–19] 1 Kgs 12:16–19.

death. King Rehoboam, however, managed to mount his chariot and flee to Jerusalem. [19]And so Israel has been in rebellion against the house of David to this day.

## CHAPTER 11

[1p]On his arrival in Jerusalem, Rehoboam assembled the house of Judah and Benjamin—one hundred and eighty thousand elite warriors—to wage war against Israel and restore the kingdom to Rehoboam. [2]However, the word of the LORD came to Shemaiah, a man of God: [3]Say to Rehoboam, son of Solomon, king of Judah, and to all the Israelites in Judah and Benjamin: [4]"Thus says the LORD: You must not go out to war against your kinsmen. Return home, each of you, for it is I who have brought this about." They obeyed the word of the LORD and turned back from going against Jeroboam.

**Rehoboam's Works.** [5]Rehoboam took up residence in Jerusalem and built fortified cities in Judah. [6]He built up Bethlehem, Etam, Tekoa, [7]Beth-zur, Soco, Adullam, [8]Gath, Mareshah, Ziph, [9]Adoraim, Lachish, Azekah, [10]Zorah, Aijalon, and Hebron; these were fortified cities in Judah and Benjamin. [11]Then he strengthened the fortifications and put commanders in them, along with supplies of food, oil, and wine. [12]In every city were shields and spears, and he made them very strong. Thus Judah and Benjamin remained his.

**Refugees from the North.** [13]Now the priests and Levites throughout Israel presented themselves to him from all parts of their land, [14]for the Levites left their assigned pasture lands and their holdings and came to Judah and Jerusalem, because Jeroboam and his sons rejected them as priests of the LORD.[q] [15]In their place, he himself appointed priests for the high places as well as for the satyrs and calves he had made.[r] [16]After them, all those, of every tribe of Israel, who set their hearts to seek the LORD, the God of Israel, came to Jerusalem to sacrifice to the LORD, the God of their ancestors. [17]Thus they strengthened the kingdom of Judah and made Rehoboam, son of Solomon, prevail for three years; for they walked in the way of David and Solomon three years.

**Rehoboam's Family.** [18]Rehoboam married Mahalath, daughter of Jerimoth, son of David and of Abihail, daughter of Eliab, son of Jesse. [19]She bore him sons: Jehush, Shemariah, and Zaham. [20]After her, he married Maacah, daughter of Absalom, who bore him Abijah,[s] Attai, Ziza, and Shelomith. [21]Rehoboam loved Maacah, daughter of Absalom, more than all his other wives and concubines; he had taken eighteen wives and sixty concubines, and he

fathered twenty-eight sons and sixty daughters. [22]Rehoboam put Abijah, son of Maacah, first among his brothers, as leader, for he intended to make him king. [23]He acted prudently, distributing his various sons throughout all the districts of Judah and Benjamin, in all the fortified cities; and he gave them generous provisions and sought an abundance of wives for them.

## CHAPTER 12

**Rehoboam's Apostasy.** [1]Once Rehoboam had established himself as king and was firmly in charge, he abandoned the law of the LORD, and so did all Israel with him.[t] [2]So in the fifth year of King Rehoboam, Shishak, king of Egypt, attacked Jerusalem, for they had acted treacherously toward the LORD.[u] [3]He had twelve hundred chariots and sixty thousand horsemen, and there was no counting the army that came with him from Egypt—Libyans, Sukkites,[†] and Ethiopians. [4]They captured the fortified cities of Judah and came as far as Jerusalem. [5]Then Shemaiah[v] the prophet came to Rehoboam and the commanders of Judah who had gathered at Jerusalem because of Shishak, and said to them: "Thus says the LORD: You have abandoned me, and so I have abandoned you to the power of Shishak."

[6]Then the commanders of Israel and the king humbled themselves saying, "The LORD is in the right." [7]When the LORD saw that they had humbled themselves, the word of the LORD came to Shemaiah: Because they have humbled themselves, I will not destroy them; I will give them some deliverance, and my wrath shall not be poured out upon Jerusalem through Shishak. [8]But they shall be his servants. Then they will know what it is to serve me and what it is to serve the kingdoms of the earth. [9w]Thereupon Shishak, king of Egypt, attacked Jerusalem and took away the treasures of the house of the LORD and the treasures of the house of the king. He took everything, including the gold shields that Solomon had made. [10]To replace them, King Rehoboam made bronze shields, which he entrusted to the officers of the attendants on duty at the entrance of the king's house. [11]Whenever the king visited the house of the LORD, the attendants would carry them, and then return them to the guardroom. [12]Because he had humbled himself, the anger of the LORD turned from him so as not to destroy him completely; in Judah, moreover, there was some good.

[13]King Rehoboam was firmly in power in Jerusalem and continued to rule. Rehoboam was forty-one years old when he became king, and he reigned seventeen years in Jerusalem, the city in which, out of all the tribes of Israel, the

---

*[11:5–12] These verses have no parallel in 1 Kings; they are apparently based on a separate source.

†[12:3] **Sukkites:** foreign mercenaries in the Egyptian army.

p. [11:1–4] 1 Kgs 12:21–24.   q. [11:14] 1 Kgs 12:32.   r. [11:15] Lv 17:7; 1 Kgs 12:32.   s. [11:20] 1 Kgs 15:2.

t. [12:1] 1 Kgs 11:4; 14:22.   u. [12:2] 1 Kgs 14:25.   v. [12:5] 2 Chr 11:2.   w. [12:9–11] 1 Kgs 14:25–28.

LORD chose to set his name. His mother's name was Naamah, the Ammonite.ˣ ¹⁴He did evil, for he had not set his heart to seek the LORD. ¹⁵ʸThe acts of Rehoboam, first and last, are recorded in the history of Shemaiah the prophet and of Iddo the seer (his family record). There were wars between Rehoboam and Jeroboam all their days. ¹⁶Rehoboam rested with his ancestors; he was buried in the City of David. His son Abijah* succeeded him as king.

## CHAPTER 13

**War Between Abijah and Jeroboam.** ¹ᶜIn the eighteenth year of King Jeroboam, Abijah became king of Judah; ²he reigned three years in Jerusalem. His mother was named Micaiah, daughter of Uriel of Gibeah. There was war between Abijah and Jeroboam.

³†Abijah joined battle with a force of four hundred thousand picked warriors, while Jeroboam lined up against him in battle with eight hundred thousand picked and valiant warriors. ⁴Abijah stood on Mount Zemaraim, which is in the highlands of Ephraim, and said: "Listen to me, Jeroboam and all Israel! ⁵Do you not know that the LORD, the God of Israel, has given David kingship over Israel forever, to him and to his sons, by a covenant of salt?‡ ⁶Yet Jeroboam, son of Nebat, the servant of Solomon, son of David, arose and rebelled against his lord!ᵃ ⁷Worthless men, scoundrels, joined him and overcame Rehoboam, son of Solomon, when Rehoboam was young and inexperienced, and no match for them. ⁸But now, do you think you are a match for the kingdom of the LORD led by the descendants of David, simply because you are a huge multitude and have with you the golden calves which Jeroboam made you for gods? ⁹Have you not expelled the priests of the LORD, the sons of Aaron, and the Levites, and made for yourselves priests like the peoples of other lands? Everyone who comes to consecrate himself with a young bull and seven rams becomes a priest of no-gods. ¹⁰But as for us, the LORD is our God, and we have not abandoned him. The priests ministering to the LORD are sons of Aaron, and the Levites also have their offices. ¹¹They sacrifice burnt offerings to the LORD and fragrant incense morning after morning and evening after evening; they set out the showbread on the pure table, and the lamps of the golden menorah burn evening after evening; for we observe our duties to the LORD, our God,

but you have abandoned him. ¹²See, God is with us, at our head, and his priests are here with trumpets to sound the attack against you. Israelites, do not fight against the LORD, the God of your ancestors, for you will not succeed!"

¹³But Jeroboam had an ambush go around them to come at them from the rear; so that while his army faced Judah, his ambush lay behind them. ¹⁴When Judah turned and saw that they had to battle on both fronts, they cried out to the LORD and the priests sounded the trumpets. ¹⁵Then the Judahites shouted; and when they shouted, God struck down Jeroboam and all Israel before Abijah and Judah. ¹⁶The Israelites fled before Judah, and God delivered them into their power. ¹⁷Abijah and his people inflicted a severe defeat upon them; five hundred thousand picked men of Israel fell slain. ¹⁸The Israelites were humbled on that occasion, while the Judahites were victorious because they relied on the LORD, the God of their ancestors. ¹⁹Abijah pursued Jeroboam and seized cities from him: Bethel and its dependencies, Jeshanah and its dependencies, and Ephron and its dependencies. ²⁰Jeroboam did not regain power during Abijah's time; the LORD struck him down and he died, ²¹while Abijah continued to grow stronger. He married fourteen wives and fathered twenty-two sons and sixteen daughters. **Death of Abijah.** ²²ᵇThe rest of the acts of Abijah, his deeds and his words, are recorded in the midrash of the prophet Iddo. ²³Abijah rested with his ancestors; they buried him in the City of David and his son Asa succeeded him as king. During his time, the land had ten years of peace.

## CHAPTER 14

**Asa's Initial Reforms.** ¹ᶜAsa did what was good and right in the sight of the LORD, his God. ²He removed the illicit altars and the high places, smashed the sacred pillars, and cut down the asherahs. ³He told Judah to seek the LORD, the God of their ancestors, and to observe the law and the commandment. ⁴He removed the high places and incense stands from all the cities of Judah, and under him the kingdom had peace. ⁵He built fortified cities in Judah, for the land had peace and no war was waged against him during these years, because the LORD had given him rest. ⁶He said to Judah: "Let us build these cities and surround them with walls, towers, gates and bars. The land is still ours, for we have sought the LORD, our God; we sought him, and he has given us rest on every side." So they built and prospered.

**The Ethiopian Invasion.**§ ⁷Asa had an army of three hundred thousand shield- and lance-bearers

---

*[12:16] **Abijah:** in 1 Kgs 14:31–15:8 this king is called Abijam.

†[13:3–21] This passage is a free composition of the Chronicler based on the reference in 1 Kgs 15:6 to the war between Abijam (so in Kings, "Abijah" in Chronicles) and Jeroboam.

‡[13:5] **Covenant of salt:** see note on Nm 18:19.

§[14:7–14] This Ethiopian invasion of Judah is not mentioned in 1 Kings. The account is likely a legend intended to

---

x. [12:13] 1 Kgs 14:21.   y. [12:15–16] 1 Kgs 14:29–31.   z. [13:1–2] 1 Kgs 15:1–2.   a. [13:6] 1 Kgs 11:26.

b. [13:22–23] 2 Chr 12:15–16; 1 Kgs 15:7–8.   c. [14:1–2] 2 Chr 33:15; Ex 23:24; 34:13; 1 Kgs 15:11–12.

from Judah, and from Benjamin two hundred and eighty thousand who carried bucklers and were archers, all of them valiant warriors. [8]Zerah the Ethiopian advanced against them with a force of one million men and three hundred chariots, and he came as far as Mareshah.[d] [9]Asa went out to meet him and they drew up for battle in the valley of Zephathah, near Mareshah. [10]Asa called upon the LORD, his God: "LORD, there is none like you to help the powerless against the strong. Help us, LORD, our God, for we rely on you, and in your name we have come against this multitude. You are the LORD, our God; do not let men prevail against you."[e] [11]And so the LORD defeated the Ethiopians before Asa and Judah, and the Ethiopians fled. [12]Asa and those with him pursued them as far as Gerar, and the Ethiopians fell until there were no survivors, for they were crushed before the LORD and his army, which carried away enormous spoils. [13]Then the Judahites conquered all the cities around Gerar, for the fear of the LORD was upon them; they plundered all the cities, for there was much plunder in them. [14]They also attacked the tents of the cattle-herders and carried off a great number of sheep and camels. Then they returned to Jerusalem.

## CHAPTER 15

**Further Reforms.** [1]The spirit of God came upon Azariah, son of Oded. [2]He went forth to meet Asa and said to him: "Hear me, Asa and all Judah and Benjamin! The LORD is with you when you are with him, and if you seek him he will be found; but if you abandon him, he will abandon you.[f] [3]For a long time Israel was without a true God, without a priest-teacher, without instruction, [4]but when in their distress they turned to the LORD, the God of Israel, and sought him, he was found by them.[g] [5]At that time there was no peace for anyone to go or come; rather, there were many terrors upon the inhabitants of the lands. [6]Nation crushed nation and city crushed city,[h] for God overwhelmed them with every kind of distress. [7]But as for you, be strong and do not slack off, for there shall be a reward for what you do."[i]

[8]When Asa heard these words and the prophecy (Oded the prophet), he was encouraged to remove the detestable idols from the whole land of Judah and Benjamin and from the cities he had taken in the highlands of Ephraim, and to restore the altar of the LORD which was before the vestibule of the LORD. [9]Then he gathered all Judah and Benjamin, together with those of Ephraim, Manasseh, and Simeon who

were resident with them; for many had defected to him from Israel when they saw that the LORD, his God, was with him. [10]They gathered at Jerusalem in the third month* of the fifteenth year of Asa's reign, [11]and sacrificed to the LORD on that day seven hundred oxen and seven thousand sheep from the spoils they had brought. [12]They entered into a covenant to seek the LORD, the God of their ancestors, with all their heart and soul; [13]and everyone who would not seek the LORD, the God of Israel, was to be put to death, from least to greatest, man or woman. [14]They swore an oath to the LORD with a loud voice, with shouting and with trumpets and horns. [15]All Judah rejoiced over the oath, for they had sworn it with their whole heart and sought him with complete desire. The LORD was found by them,[k] and gave them rest on every side.

[16]He also deposed Maacah, the mother[†] of King Asa, from her position as queen mother because she had made an obscene object for Asherah; Asa cut down this object, smashed it, and burnt it in the Wadi Kidron. [17]The high places did not disappear from Israel, yet Asa's heart was undivided as long as he lived. [18]He brought into the house of God his father's and his own votive offerings: silver, gold, and vessels. [19]There was no war until the thirty-fifth year of Asa's reign.

## CHAPTER 16

**Asa's Infidelity.** [1m]In the thirty-sixth year of Asa's reign, Baasha, king of Israel, attacked Judah and fortified Ramah to block all movement for Asa, king of Judah. [2]Asa then brought out silver and gold from the treasuries of the house of the LORD and the house of the king and sent them to Ben-hadad, king of Aram, who ruled in Damascus. He said: [3]"There is a treaty between you and me, as there was between your father and my father. I am sending you silver and gold. Go, break your treaty with Baasha, king of Israel, that he may withdraw from me." [4]Ben-hadad agreed with King Asa and sent the leaders of his troops against the cities of Israel. They attacked Ijon, Dan, Abel-maim, besides all the store cities of Naphtali. [5]When Baasha heard of it, he left off fortifying Ramah, putting an end to his work. [6]Then King Asa commandeered all Judah and they carried away the stones and

---

*[15:10–12] With this description of a covenant ceremony in "the third month" of a year beginning in the spring, the Chronicler provides a basis for the later understanding of the ancient Jewish spring feast of Weeks as a commemoration of the covenant on Mount Sinai; see Ex 19:1–3; Lv 23:16 and note on Lv 23:16–21. In the Greek period the feast came to be called Pentecost, from the Greek word for "fifty," i.e., fifty days or seven weeks after Passover. The Chronicler's presentation here has also influenced the celebration of Christian Pentecost as the "birthday of the Church"; cf. Acts 2.

†[15:16] **Mother:** see note on 1 Kgs 15:10.

---

show the pious King Asa being rewarded with divine assistance. It could, however, reflect an incursion by nomads from the Negeb in Asa's time.

---

d. [14:8] 2 Chr 16:8. e. [14:10] 2 Chr 32:8. f. [15:2] Jer 29:13–14; Hos 3:4–5. g. [15:4] Dt 4:29–30. h. [15:6] Is 19:2. i. [15:7] Is 7:4; Jer 31:16.

j. [15:12–13] Neh 10:29–30. k. [15:15] Dt 4:29. l. [15:16–18] 1 Kgs 15:13–15. m. [16:1–6] 1 Kgs 15:16–21.

beams with which Baasha was fortifying Ramah. With them he fortified Geba and Mizpah.

⁷At that time Hanani the seer came to Asa, king of Judah, and said to him: "Because you relied on the king of Aram and did not rely on the Lord, your God, the army of the king of Aram has escaped* your power. ⁸ⁿWere not the Ethiopians and Libyans a vast army, with great numbers of chariots and horses? And yet, because you relied on the Lord, he delivered them into your power. ⁹The eyes of the Lord roam over the whole earth,ᵒ to encourage those who are devoted to him wholeheartedly. You have acted foolishly in this matter, for from now on you will have wars." ¹⁰But Asa became angry with the seer and imprisoned him in the stocks, so greatly was he enraged at him over this. Asa also oppressed some of his people at this time.

¹¹ᵖNow the acts of Asa, first and last, are recorded in the book of the kings of Judah and Israel. ¹²In the thirty-ninth year of his reign, Asa contracted disease in his feet; it became worse, but even with this disease he did not seek the Lord, only physicians. ¹³Asa rested with his ancestors; he died in the forty-first year of his reign. ¹⁴They buried him in the tomb he had hewn for himself in the City of David, after laying him on a couch that was filled with spices and various kinds of aromatics compounded into an ointment; and they kindled a huge fire for him.

## CHAPTER 17

**Jehoshaphat's Zeal for the Law.** ¹His son Jehoshaphat succeeded him as king and strengthened his position against Israel.�q ²He placed armed forces in all the fortified cities of Judah, and set garrisons in the land of Judah and in the cities of Ephraim which Asa his father had taken. ³The Lord was with Jehoshaphat,† for he walked in the earlier ways of David his father, and did not seek the Baals. ⁴Rather, he sought the God of his father and walked in his commands, and not the practices of Israel. ⁵Through him, the Lord made the kingdom secure, and all Judah gave Jehoshaphat gifts, so that great wealth and glory was his. ⁶Thus he was encouraged‡ to follow the Lord's ways, and once again he removed the high places and the asherahs from Judah.ʳ

⁷In the third year of his reign he sent his officials, Ben-hail, Obadiah, Zechariah, Nethanel, and Micaiah, to teach in the cities of Judah. ⁸With them he sent the Levites Shemaiah, Nethaniah, Zebadiah, Asahel, Shemiramoth, Jehonathan, Adonijah, and Tobijah, together with Elishama and Jehoram the priests.ˢ ⁹They taught in Judah, having with them the book of the law of the Lord; they traveled through all the cities of Judah and taught among the people.ᵗ

**His Power.** ¹⁰Now the fear of the Lord was upon all the kingdoms of the countries surrounding Judah, so that they did not war against Jehoshaphat. ¹¹Some of the Philistines brought Jehoshaphat gifts and a tribute of silver; the Arabians also brought him a flock of seven thousand seven hundred rams and seven thousand seven hundred he-goats.

¹²Jehoshaphat grew ever greater. He built strongholds and store cities in Judah. ¹³He carried out many works in the cities of Judah, and he had soldiers, valiant warriors, in Jerusalem. ¹⁴This was their mustering according to their ancestral houses. From Judah, the commanders of thousands: Adnah the commander, and with him three hundred thousand valiant warriors. ¹⁵Next to him, Jehohanan the commander, and with him two hundred eighty thousand. ¹⁶Next to him, Amasiah, son of Zichri, who offered himself to the Lord, and with him two hundred thousand valiant warriors. ¹⁷From Benjamin: Eliada, a valiant warrior, and with him two hundred thousand armed with bow and buckler. ¹⁸Next to him, Jehozabad, and with him one hundred and eighty thousand equipped for war. ¹⁹These attended the king; in addition to those whom the king had stationed in the fortified cities throughout all Judah.

## CHAPTER 18

**Alliance with Israel.** ¹ᵘJehoshaphat therefore had wealth and glory in abundance; but he became related to Ahab by marriage. ²After some years he went down to Ahab at Samaria; Ahab slaughtered numerous sheep and oxen for him and for the people with him, and incited him to go up against Ramoth-gilead. ³Ahab, king of Israel, asked Jehoshaphat, king of Judah, "Will you come with me to Ramoth-gilead?" He answered, "You and I are as one, and your people and my people as well. We will be with you in the battle." ⁴Jehoshaphat also said to the king of Israel, "Seek the word of the Lord at once."

**Prophets in Conflict.** ⁵The king of Israel assembled the prophets, four hundred of them, and asked, "Shall we go to fight against Ramoth-gilead, or shall I refrain?" They said, "Attack. God will give it into the power of the king." ⁶But Jehoshaphat said, "Is there no other prophet of the Lord here we might consult?" ⁷The king

---

*[16:7] **The king of Aram has escaped:** the Lucianic recension of the Septuagint reads, "the king of Israel escaped." This may well be the original reading, since according to the story Asa hired the king of Aram as an ally against Israel.

†[17:3] **The Lord was with Jehoshaphat:** along with his successors Hezekiah and Josiah, Jehoshaphat is one of the Chronicler's exemplary kings.

‡[17:6] **Thus he was encouraged:** lit., "his heart was high," a phrase that ordinarily describes arrogance and rebelliousness; in this case, however, it introduces a notice of Jehoshaphat's fidelity to the Lord.

n. [16:8] 2 Chr 14:8–14. o. [16:9] Ps 33:13–15. p. [16:11–14] 1 Kgs 15:23–24. q. [17:1] 1 Kgs 15:24. r. [17:6] 2 Chr 20:33; Ex 34:13.

s. [17:8] 2 Chr 19:8. t. [17:9] Ezr 7:25. u. [18:1–34] 1 Kgs 22:1–35.

of Israel answered, "There is one other man through whom we may consult the LORD; but I hate him, because he prophesies not good but always evil about me. He is Micaiah, son of Imlah." Jehoshaphat said, "Let not the king say that." ⁸So the king of Israel called an official, and said to him, "Get Micaiah, son of Imlah, at once." ⁹The king of Israel and Jehoshaphat, king of Judah, were seated, each on his throne, clothed in their robes of state in the square at the entrance of the gate of Samaria, and all the prophets were prophesying before them.

¹⁰Zedekiah, son of Chenaanah, made himself two horns of iron and said: "The LORD says: With these you shall gore Aram until you have destroyed them." ¹¹The other prophets prophesied in the same vein, saying: "Attack Ramoth-gilead, and conquer! The LORD will give it into the power of the king." ¹²Meanwhile the messenger who had gone to call Micaiah said to him: "Look now, the words of the prophets are as one in speaking good for the king. Let your word be at one with theirs; speak a good word." ¹³Micaiah said, "As the LORD lives, I shall speak whatever my God says."

¹⁴When he came to the king, the king said to him, "Micah, shall we go to fight at Ramoth-gilead, or shall I refrain?" He said, "Attack and conquer! They will be delivered into your power." ¹⁵But the king answered him, "How many times must I adjure you to tell me nothing but the truth in the name of the LORD?" ¹⁶So Micaiah said:

> "I see all Israel
>     scattered on the mountains,
>     like sheep without a shepherd,
> And the LORD saying,
>     These have no masters!
>     Let each of them go back home in
>         peace."

¹⁷The king of Israel said to Jehoshaphat, "Did I not tell you, he does not prophesy good about me, but only evil?" ¹⁸Micaiah continued: "Therefore hear the word of the LORD. I saw the LORD seated on his throne, with the whole host of heaven standing to his right and to his left. ¹⁹The LORD asked: Who will deceive Ahab, king of Israel, so that he will go up and fall on Ramoth-gilead? And one said this, another that, ²⁰until this spirit came forth and stood before the LORD, saying, 'I will deceive him.' The LORD asked: How? ²¹He answered, 'I will go forth and become a lying spirit in the mouths of all his prophets.' The LORD replied: You shall succeed in deceiving him. Go forth and do this. ²²So now the LORD has put a lying spirit in the mouths of these prophets of yours; but the LORD himself has decreed evil against you."

²³Thereupon Zedekiah, son of Chenaanah, came up and struck Micaiah on the cheek,

saying, "Has the spirit of the LORD, then, passed from me to speak with you?" ²⁴Micaiah said, "You shall find out on the day you go into an innermost room to hide." ²⁵The king of Israel then said: "Seize Micaiah and take him back to Amon, prefect of the city, and to Joash the king's son, ²⁶and say, 'This is the king's order: Put this man in prison and feed him scanty rations of bread and water until I come back in safety!'" ²⁷But Micaiah said, "If ever you return in safety, the LORD has not spoken through me." (He also said, "Hear, O peoples, all of you!")†

**Ahab's Death.** ²⁸The king of Israel and Jehoshaphat, king of Judah, went up to Ramoth-gilead, ²⁹and the king of Israel said to Jehoshaphat, "I will disguise myself and go into battle. But you, put on your own robes." So the king of Israel disguised himself and they entered the battle. ³⁰In the meantime, the king of Aram had given his chariot commanders the order, "Fight with no one, great or small, except the king of Israel alone." ³¹When the chariot commanders saw Jehoshaphat, they thought, "There is the king of Israel!" and wheeled to fight him. But Jehoshaphat cried out and the LORD helped him; God induced them to leave him alone. ³²The chariot commanders, seeing that he was not the king of Israel, turned away from him. ³³But someone drew his bow at random and hit the king of Israel between the joints of his breastplate. He ordered his charioteer, "Rein about and take me out of the ranks, for I am wounded."ᵛ ³⁴The battle grew fierce during the day, and the king of Israel braced himself up in his chariot facing the Arameans until evening. He died as the sun was setting.

## CHAPTER 19

**Jehoshaphat Rebuked.** ¹Jehoshaphat king of Judah returned in safety to his house in Jerusalem. ²Jehu the seer, son of Hanani,‡ went out to meet King Jehoshaphat and said to him: "Should you help the wicked and love those who hate the LORD? For this reason, wrath is upon you from the LORD. ³Yet some good has been found§ in you, since you have removed the asherahs from the land and have set your heart to seek God."

**Judges Appointed.** ⁴Jehoshaphat dwelt in Jerusalem; but he went out again among the people from Beer-sheba to the highlands of Ephraim and brought them back to the LORD, the God of their ancestors. ⁵He appointed judges in the

---

† [18:27] **"Hear, O peoples, all of you!":** this quotation, which also appears in 1 Kgs 22:28, ascribes to the prophet Micaiah ben Imlah the opening words of the book of the prophet Micah of Moresheth (Mi 1:2), who was active a century later.

‡ [19:2] **Jehu the seer, son of Hanani:** probably not the Jehu, son of Hanani, who prophesied against Baasha of Israel almost fifty years earlier (1 Kgs 16:1).

§ [19:3] **Has been found:** theological passive, i.e., God is the implied agent.

*[18:12–22] See note on 1 Kgs 22:19–23.

v. [18:33] 2 Chr 35:23; 1 Kgs 22:34.

land, in all the fortified cities of Judah, city by city, [6]and he said to them: "Take care what you do, for the judgment you give is not human but divine; for when it comes to judgment God will be with you.[w] [7]And now, let the fear of the LORD be upon you. Act carefully, for with the LORD, our God, there is no injustice, no partiality, no bribe-taking."[x] [8]In Jerusalem also, Jehoshaphat appointed some Levites and priests and some of the family heads of Israel for the LORD's judgment and the disputes of those who dwell in Jerusalem.[y] [9]He gave them this command: "Thus you shall act: in the fear of the LORD, with fidelity and with an undivided heart. [10]And in every dispute that comes to you from your kin living in their cities, whether it concerns bloodguilt or questions of law, command, statutes, or ordinances, warn them lest they incur guilt before the LORD and his wrath come upon you and your kin. Do that and you shall not incur guilt.[z] [11]See now, Amariah is chief priest over you for everything that pertains to the LORD, and Zebadiah, son of Ishmael, is leader of the house of Judah in all that pertains to the king; and the Levites will be your officials. Take firm action, and the LORD will be with the good."

## CHAPTER 20

**Invasion from Edom.** [1]*After this the Moabites, the Ammonites, and with them some Meunites came to fight against Jehoshaphat. [2]Jehoshaphat was told: "A great multitude is coming against you from across the sea, from Edom; they are already in Hazazon-tamar" (which is En-gedi). [3]Frightened, Jehoshaphat resolved to consult the LORD. He proclaimed a fast throughout all Judah. [4]Then Judah gathered to seek the LORD's help; from every one of the cities of Judah they came to seek the LORD.[a]

**Jehoshaphat's Prayer.** [5]Jehoshaphat stood up in the assembly of Judah and Jerusalem in the house of the LORD before the new court, [6]and he said: "LORD, God of our ancestors, are you not God in heaven, and do you not rule over all the kingdoms of the nations? In your hand is power and might, and no one can withstand you.[b] [7]Was it not you, our God, who dispossessed the inhabitants of this land before your people Israel and gave it forever to the descendants of Abraham, your friend? [8]They have dwelt in it and they built in it a sanctuary for your name. They have said: [9]If evil comes upon us, the sword of judgment, or pestilence, or famine, we will

stand before this house and before you, for your name is in this house, and we will cry out to you in our affliction, and you will hear and save!'[c] [10]And now, see the Ammonites, Moabites, and those of Mount Seir whom you did not allow Israel to invade when they came from the land of Egypt, but instead they passed them by and did not destroy them:[d] [11]See how they are now repaying us by coming to drive us out of the possession you have given us. [12]O our God, will you not bring judgment on them? We are powerless before this vast multitude that is coming against us. We ourselves do not know what to do, so our eyes are turned toward you."

**Victory Prophesied.** [13]All Judah was standing before the LORD, with their little ones, their wives, and their children. [14]And the spirit of the LORD came upon Jahaziel, son of Zechariah, son of Benaiah, son of Jeiel, son of Mattaniah, a Levite of the clan of Asaph, in the midst of the assembly, [15]and he said: "Pay attention, all of Judah, inhabitants of Jerusalem, and King Jehoshaphat! The LORD says to you: Do not fear or be dismayed at the sight of this vast multitude, for the battle is not yours but God's. [16]Go down against them tomorrow. You will see them coming up by the ascent of Ziz, and you will come upon them at the end of the wadi which opens on the wilderness of Jeruel. [17]You will not have to fight in this encounter. Take your places, stand firm, and see the salvation of the LORD; he will be with you, Judah and Jerusalem. Do not fear or be dismayed. Tomorrow go out to meet them, and the LORD will be with you."[e] [18]Then Jehoshaphat knelt down with his face to the ground, and all Judah and the inhabitants of Jerusalem fell down before the LORD in worship. [19]Levites from among the Kohathites and Korahites stood up to sing the praises of the LORD, the God of Israel, their voices ever louder.

**The Invaders Destroyed.** [20]Early in the morning they went out to the wilderness of Tekoa. As they were going out, Jehoshaphat halted and said: "Listen to me, Judah and inhabitants of Jerusalem! Let your faith in the LORD, your God, be firm, and you will be firm.[f] Have faith in his prophets and you will succeed." [21]†After taking counsel with the people, he appointed some to sing to the LORD and some to praise the holy

---

*[20:1–30] This account seems to be a free composition of the Chronicler. However, there could well have been a raid of nomads against Judah in the reign of Jehoshaphat, similar to the one that occurred under Asa (14:8–14). The story may also be connected in some way with the campaign of Israel and Judah against Moab launched through the territory of Edom (2 Kgs 3:4–27).

†[20:21] In accordance with Israelite conceptions of Holy War (cf. Ex 14:13–14), this highly stylized narrative presents the Lord as active in battle, while the people have only to sing hymns of praise; the enemy, in panic, fight among themselves to their mutual destruction (v. 23). **Splendor**: the Lord "goes before," i.e., leads, the army of Israel (cf. 2 Sm 5:24) with the heavenly hosts. Israel's God is depicted as present "enthroned upon the cherubim" atop the ark of the covenant. By postexilic times, the ark had disappeared, but the Lord was still present to his people. Here that presence is described as "holy Splendor," a phrase found in Ps 29:2; 96:9. Cf. the cognate image of cloud and fire that led Israel in the wilderness (Ex 13:21–22), or the cloud of the Lord's glory that fills the sanctuary (Ex 40:34; 1 Kgs 8:10–11).

---

w. [19:6] Dt 1:16–18; 16:19–20.  x. [19:7] Dt 10:17.  y. [19:8] 2 Chr 17:8–9; Dt 7:8–13; Ps 122:3–5.  z. [19:10] Dt 7:8–13. a. [20:4] Jer 36:6.  b. [20:6] 2 Chr 32:7; Dt 4:39.

c. [20:9] 2 Chr 6:28–31; 7:13–14; 1 Kgs 8:37–40.  d. [20:10] Dt 2:4–5, 9–10, 18–19.  e. [20:17] Ex 14:13–14; Is 8:10.  f. [20:20] Is 7:9.

Splendor as it went forth at the head of the army. They sang: "Give thanks to the LORD, whose love endures forever."[g] [22]At the moment they began their jubilant praise, the LORD laid an ambush against the Ammonites, Moabites, and those of Mount Seir who were coming against Judah, so that they were defeated. [23]For the Ammonites and Moabites set upon the inhabitants of Mount Seir and exterminated them according to the ban.[h] And when they had finished with the inhabitants of Seir, each helped to destroy the other.

[24]When Judah came to the watchtower of the wilderness and looked toward the throng, there were only corpses fallen on the ground, with no survivors. [25]Jehoshaphat and his people came to gather the spoils, and they found an abundance of cattle and personal property, garments and precious vessels. They took so much that they were unable to carry it all; it took them three days to gather the spoils, there was so much of it. [26]On the fourth day they held an assembly in the Valley of Berakah*—for there they blessed the LORD; that is why the place is called the Valley of Berakah to this day. [27]Then all the men of Judah and Jerusalem, with Jehoshaphat at their head, returned to Jerusalem with joy; for the LORD had given them joy over their enemies. [28]They came to Jerusalem, with harps, lyres, and trumpets, to the house of the LORD. [29]And the fear of God came upon all the kingdoms of the surrounding lands when they heard how the LORD had fought against the enemies of Israel. [30]Thereafter Jehoshaphat's kingdom had peace, for his God gave him rest on every side.

**Jehoshaphat's Other Deeds.** [31i]Thus Jehoshaphat reigned over Judah. He was thirty-five years old when he became king, and he reigned twenty-five years in Jerusalem. His mother's name was Azubah, daughter of Shilhi. [32]He walked in the way of Asa his father unceasingly, doing what was right in the LORD's sight. [33]Nevertheless, the high places did not disappear and the people had not yet set their hearts on the God of their ancestors.

[34]The rest of the acts of Jehoshaphat, first and last, are recorded in the chronicle of Jehu, son of Hanani, which was incorporated into the book of the kings of Israel. [35]After this, Jehoshaphat king of Judah joined with Ahaziah king of Israel—he acted wickedly. [36j]He joined with him in building ships to go to Tarshish; the fleet was built at Ezion-geber. [37]But Eliezer, son of Dodavahu from Mareshah, prophesied against Jehoshaphat. He said: "Because you have joined with Ahaziah, the LORD will shatter your work."

And the ships were wrecked and were unable to sail to Tarshish.

## CHAPTER 21

[1]Jehoshaphat rested with his ancestors; he was buried with them in the City of David. Jehoram, his son, succeeded him as king.[k] [2]He had brothers, Jehoshaphat's sons: Azariah, Jehiel, Zechariah, Azariah, Michael, and Shephatiah; all these were sons of King Jehoshaphat of Judah. [3]Their father gave them many gifts of silver, gold, and precious objects, together with fortified cities in Judah, but the kingship he gave to Jehoram because he was the firstborn.

**Jehoram's Evil Deeds.** [4]When Jehoram had acceded to his father's kingdom and was firmly in power, he killed all his brothers with the sword, and also some of the princes of Israel. [5l]Jehoram was thirty-two years old when he became king, and he reigned eight years in Jerusalem. [6]He walked in the way of the kings of Israel as the house of Ahab had done, since the daughter of Ahab[†] was his wife; and he did what was evil in the LORD's sight. [7]Even so, the LORD was unwilling to destroy the house of David because of the covenant he had made with David and because of his promise to leave him and his sons a holding for all time.[m]

[8n]During his time Edom revolted against the rule of Judah and installed its own king. [9]Thereupon Jehoram with his officers and all his chariots crossed over. He arose by night and broke through the Edomites when they had surrounded him and the commanders of his chariots. [10]To this day Edom has been in revolt against the rule of Judah. Libnah also revolted at that time against his rule because he had abandoned the LORD, the God of his ancestors. [11]He also set up high places in the mountains of Judah, prostituting the inhabitants of Jerusalem, leading Judah astray.

**Jehoram Punished.** [12]A letter came to him from Elijah[‡] the prophet with this message: "Thus says the LORD, the God of David your father: Because you have not walked in the way of your father Jehoshaphat, nor of Asa, king of Judah, [13]but instead have walked in the way of the kings of Israel, leading Judah and the inhabitants of Jerusalem into prostitution, like the harlotries of the house of Ahab, and because you have killed your brothers of your father's house, who were better than you, [14]the LORD will strike your people, your children, your wives, and all that is

†[21:6] **The daughter of Ahab**: her name was Athaliah. In 22:2 (and its source, 2 Kgs 8:26) she is called the daughter of Ahab's father Omri, but this should probably be understood in the sense of granddaughter.

‡[21:12] **Elijah**: this is the Chronicler's only mention of this prophet of the Northern Kingdom. It is doubtful that Elijah was still living in the reign of Jehoram of Judah; in any case, the attribution of the letter to him has a folkloristic quality.

*[20:26] **Berakah**: the Hebrew word for "blessing."

g. [20:21] Ps 136:1.  h. [20:23] Jos 6:17.  i. [20:31–34] 1 Kgs 22:41–45.  j. [20:36–37] 1 Kgs 22:48–49.

k. [21:1] 1 Kgs 22:51.  l. [21:5–7] 1 Kgs 8:17–19.  m. [21:7] 1 Kgs 11:36; 2 Kgs 8:19.  n. [21:8–10] Gn 27:40; 2 Kgs 8:20–22.

yours with a great plague. [15]You shall have severe pains from a disease in your bowels, which will fall out because of the disease, day after day."

[16]Then the LORD stirred up against Jehoram the animosity of the Philistines and of the Arabians who were neighbors of the Ethiopians. [17]They came up against Judah, breached it, and carried away all the wealth found in the king's house, along with his sons and his wives. He was left with only one son, Jehoahaz, his youngest. [18]After these events, the LORD afflicted him with a disease of the bowels for which there was no cure. [19]Some time later, after a period of two years had elapsed, his bowels fell out because of the disease and he died in great pain. His people did not make a fire for him as they had for his ancestors.[o] [20]He was thirty-two years old when he became king, and he reigned eight years in Jerusalem. He departed unloved; and they buried him in the City of David, though not in the tombs of the kings.[p]

## CHAPTER 22

**Ahaziah.** [1a]Then the inhabitants of Jerusalem made Ahaziah, his youngest son, king to succeed him, since all the older sons had been killed by the band that had come into the camp with the Arabians. Thus Ahaziah, son of Jehoram, reigned as the king of Judah. [2]Ahaziah was twenty-two years old when he became king, and he reigned one year in Jerusalem. His mother's name was Athaliah, daughter of Omri. [3]He, too, walked in the ways of the house of Ahab, because his mother was his counselor in doing evil. [4]To his own destruction, he did what was evil in the sight of the LORD, like the house of Ahab, since they were his counselors after the death of his father.

[5]He was also following their counsel when he joined Jehoram, son of Ahab, king of Israel, in battle against Hazael, king of Aram, at Ramoth-gilead, where the Arameans wounded Jehoram. [6]He returned to Jezreel to be healed of the wounds that had been inflicted on him at Ramah in his battle against Hazael, king of Aram. Then Ahaziah, son of Jehoram, king of Judah, went down to Jezreel to visit Jehoram, son of Ahab, for he was sick. [7]Now from God came Ahaziah's downfall, that he should join Jehoram; for after his arrival he rode out with Jehoram to Jehu, son of Nimshi, whom the LORD had anointed to cut down the house of Ahab.[r] [8]While Jehu was executing judgment on the house of Ahab, he also came upon the princes of Judah and the nephews of Ahaziah who were his attendants, and he killed them.[s] [9]Then he looked for Ahaziah himself. They caught him hiding in Samaria and brought him to Jehu, who put him to death. They buried him, for they said, "He was the grandson of Jehoshaphat, who sought

the LORD with his whole heart."[t] Now the house of Ahaziah did not retain the power of kingship.*

**Usurpation of Athaliah.** [10u]When Athaliah, the mother of Ahaziah, saw that her son was dead, she began to kill off the whole royal family of the house of Judah. [11]But Jehosheba, a daughter of the king, took Joash, Ahaziah's son, and spirited him away from among the king's sons who were about to be slain, and put him and his nurse in a bedroom. In this way Jehosheba, the daughter of King Jehoram, a sister of Ahaziah and wife of Jehoiada the priest, concealed the child from Athaliah, so that she did not put him to death. [12]For six years he remained hidden with them in the house of God, while Athaliah ruled as queen over the land.

## CHAPTER 23

**Athaliah Overthrown.** [1v]In the seventh year, Jehoiada took courage and brought into covenant with himself the captains: Azariah, son of Jehoram; Ishmael, son of Jehohanan; Azariah, son of Obed; Maaseiah, son of Adaiah; and Elishaphat, son of Zichri. [2]They journeyed about Judah, gathering the Levites from all the cities of Judah and also the heads of the Israelite families, and they came to Jerusalem. [3]The whole assembly made a covenant with the king in the house of God. Jehoiada said to them: "Here is the king's son who must reign, as the LORD promised concerning the sons of David. [4]This is what you must do: a third of your number, both priests and Levites, who come on duty on the sabbath must guard the thresholds, [5]another third must be at the king's house, and the final third at the Foundation Gate, when all the people will be in the courts of the LORD's house. [6]Let no one enter the LORD's house except the priests and those Levites who are ministering. They may enter because they are holy; but all the other people must observe the prescriptions of the LORD. [7]The Levites shall surround the king on all sides, each with drawn weapon. Whoever tries to enter the house is to be killed. Stay with the king wherever he goes."

[8]The Levites and all Judah did just as Jehoiada the priest commanded. Each took his troops, both those going on duty for the week and those going off duty that week, since Jehoiada the priest had not dismissed any of the divisions.[w] [9]Jehoiada the priest gave to the captains the spears, shields, and bucklers of King David which were in the house of God. [10]He stationed all the people, each with spear in hand, from the southern to the northern limit of the enclosure, surrounding the altar and the temple on the king's behalf. [11]Then they brought out the

---

\*[22:9] This account of the death of Ahaziah of Judah does not agree with that given in 2 Kgs 9:27–28.

o. [21:19] 2 Chr 16:14.   p. [21:20] 2 Kgs 8:24.   q. [22:1–6] 2 Kgs 8:24–29.   r. [22:7] 2 Kgs 9:21.   s. [22:8] 2 Kgs 10:12–14.

t. [22:9] 2 Kgs 9:27–28.   u. [22:10–12] 2 Kgs 11:1–3.   v. [23:1–17, 19–21] 2 Kgs 11:4–20.   w. [23:8] 2 Kgs 11:9; 1 Chr 24:19.

king's son and put the crown and the testimony upon him, and proclaimed him king. Jehoiada and his sons anointed him, and they cried, "Long live the king!"

¹²When Athaliah heard the noise of the people running and acclaiming the king, she came before them in the house of the LORD. ¹³When she saw the king standing by his column* at the entrance, the captains and the trumpeters near the king, and all the people of the land rejoicing and blowing trumpets, while the singers with their musical instruments were leading the acclaim, Athaliah tore her garments, saying, "Treason! treason!" ¹⁴Then Jehoiada the priest brought out the captains in command of the force: "Escort her with a guard detail. If anyone follows her, let him die by the sword." For the priest had said, "You must not put her to death in the house of the LORD." ¹⁵So they seized her, and when she reached the Horse Gate of the royal palace, they put her to death.

¹⁶Then Jehoiada made a covenant between himself and all the people and the king, that they should be the LORD's people. ¹⁷Thereupon all the people went to the temple of Baal and demolished it. They shattered its altars and images completely, and killed Mattan, the priest of Baal, before the altars. ¹⁸Then Jehoiada gave the charge of the LORD's house into the hands of the levitical priests, to whom David had assigned turns in the LORD's house for sacrificing the burnt offerings of the LORD, as is written in the law of Moses, with rejoicing and song, as David had provided.ˣ ¹⁹Moreover, he stationed guards at the gates of the LORD's house so that no one unclean in any respect might enter. ²⁰Then he took the captains, the nobles, the rulers among the people, and all the people of the land, and led the king out of the LORD's house; they came within the upper gate of the king's house, and seated the king upon the royal throne. ²¹All the people of the land rejoiced and the city was quiet, now that Athaliah had been slain with the sword.

## CHAPTER 24

**The Temple Restored.** ¹ʸJoash was seven years old when he became king, and he reigned forty years in Jerusalem. His mother's name was Zibiah, from Beer-sheba. ²Joash did what was right in the LORD's sight as long as Jehoiada the priest lived. ³Jehoiada provided him with two wives, and he became the father of sons and daughters.

⁴After some time, Joash decided to restore the house of the LORD. ⁵He gathered together the priests and Levites and said to them: "Go out to all the cities of Judah and gather money† from all Israel that you may repair the house of your God over the years. You must hurry this project." But the Levites did not. ⁶Then the king summoned Jehoiada, who was in charge, and said to him: "Why have you not required the Levites to bring in from Judah and Jerusalem the tax levied by Moses, the servant of the LORD, and by the assembly of Israel, for the tent of the testimony?"ᶻ ⁷For the wicked Athaliah and her sons had damaged the house of God and had even turned over to the Baals the holy things of the LORD's house.

⁸At the king's command, therefore, they made a chest, which they put outside the gate of the LORD's house.ᵃ ⁹They had it proclaimed throughout Judah and Jerusalem that the tax which Moses, the servant of God, had imposed on Israel in the wilderness should be brought to the LORD.ᵇ ¹⁰All the princes and the people rejoiced; they brought what was asked and cast it into the chest until it was filled. ¹¹Whenever the chest was brought to the royal officials by the Levites and they noticed that there was a large amount of money, the royal scribe and an overseer for the chief priest would come up, empty the chest, and then take it back and return it to its place. This they did day after day until they had collected a large sum of money. ¹²Then the king and Jehoiada gave it to the workers in charge of the labor on the LORD's house, who hired masons and carpenters to restore the LORD's house, and also iron- and bronze-smiths to repair it. ¹³The workers labored, and the task of restoration progressed under their hands. They restored the house of God according to its original form, and reinforced it. ¹⁴After they had finished, they brought the rest of the money to the king and to Jehoiada, who had it made into utensils for the house of the LORD, utensils for the service and the burnt offerings, and basins and other gold and silver utensils.‡ They sacrificed burnt offerings in the LORD's house continually all the days of Jehoiada. ¹⁵Jehoiada grew old, full of years, and died; he was a hundred and thirty years old. ¹⁶They buried him in the City of David with the kings, because of the good he had done in Israel, especially for God and his house.

**Joash's Apostasy.** ¹⁷After the death of Jehoiada, the princes of Judah came and paid homage to the king; then the king listened to them. ¹⁸They

---

*[23:13] **By his column:** there was a special place reserved for the king in the eastern gateway of the Temple court where the altar for burnt offerings stood. The king occupied this place on feasts and sabbaths at the time of the prescribed offerings, or when he came to make voluntary offerings of his own; cf. 2 Kgs 11:14 and Ez 46:1–8.

x. [23:18] 1 Chr 23:13.    y. [24:1–14] 2 Kgs 12:1–13.

†[24:5] **Gather money:** according to 2 Kgs 12:5 the people themselves brought the money, consisting at least in part of voluntary contributions, to the Temple. By the time of the Chronicler, a fixed head tax for the upkeep of the Temple had been introduced; see 2 Chr 34:9; Neh 10:32; Ex 30:12–16. This was still in force in New Testament times (Mt 17:24–25).

‡[24:14] See the parallel in 2 Kgs 12:14–15; the passages are difficult to reconcile.

z. [24:6] Ex 25:1–9; Neh 10:33.    a. [24:8] 2 Chr 34:9.    b. [24:9] Ex 30:13.

abandoned the house of the LORD, the God of their ancestors, and began to serve the asherahs and the idols;*c* and because of this crime of theirs, wrath came upon Judah and Jerusalem. [19]Although prophets were sent to them to turn them back to the LORD and to warn them, the people would not listen. [20d]Then the spirit of God clothed Zechariah, son of Jehoiada the priest. He took his stand above the people and said to them: "Thus says God, Why are you transgressing the LORD's commands, so that you cannot prosper? Because you have abandoned the LORD, he has abandoned you." [21]But they conspired against him, and at the king's command they stoned him in the court of the house of the LORD. [22]Thus King Joash was unmindful of the devotion shown him by Jehoiada, Zechariah's father, and killed the son. As he was dying, he said, "May the LORD see and avenge."

**Joash Punished.** [23]At the turn of the year a force of Arameans came up against Joash. They invaded Judah and Jerusalem, killed all the princes of the people, and sent all their spoil to the king of Damascus.*e* [24]Though the Aramean force was small, the LORD handed over a very large force into their power,*f* because Judah had abandoned the LORD, the God of their ancestors. So judgment was meted out to Joash. [25g]After the Arameans had departed from him, abandoning him to his many injuries, his servants conspired against him because of the murder of the son of Jehoiada the priest. They killed him on his sickbed. He was buried in the City of David, but not in the tombs of the kings.

[26]Those who conspired against him were Zabad, son of Shimeath from Ammon, and Jehozabad, son of Shimrith from Moab. [27]An account of his sons, the great tribute imposed on him, and his rebuilding of the house of God is written in the midrash of the book of the kings. His son Amaziah succeeded him as king.*h*

## CHAPTER 25

**Amaziah's Good Start.** [1]Amaziah was twenty-five years old when he became king, and he reigned twenty-nine years in Jerusalem. His mother's name was Jehoaddan, from Jerusalem. [2]He did what was right in the LORD's sight, though not wholeheartedly. [3]When he had the kingdom firmly in hand, he struck down the officials who had struck down the king, his father. [4]But their children he did not put to death, for he acted according to what is written in the law, in the Book of Moses, which the LORD commanded: "Parents shall not be put to death for their children, nor shall children be put to death for their parents; they shall each die for their own sin."*j*

[5]Amaziah gathered Judah and placed them, out of all Judah and Benjamin according to their ancestral houses, under leaders of thousands and of hundreds. When he made a count of those twenty years old and over, he found that there were three hundred thousand picked men fit for war, capable of handling lance and shield. [6]He also hired a hundred thousand valiant warriors from Israel for a hundred talents of silver. [7]But a man of God came to him and said: "O king, let not the army of Israel go with you, for the LORD is not with Israel—with any Ephraimite. [8]Instead, go on your own, strongly prepared for the battle; why should the LORD hinder you in the face of the enemy: for with God is power to help or to hinder." [9]Amaziah answered the man of God, "But what is to be done about the hundred talents that I paid for the troops of Israel?" The man of God replied, "The LORD can give you much more than that." [10]Amaziah then disbanded the troops that had come to him from Ephraim, and sent them home. But they became furiously angry with Judah, and returned home blazing with anger.

[11]Amaziah now assumed command of his army. They proceeded to the Valley of Salt, where they killed ten thousand men of Seir.*k* [12]The Judahites also brought back another ten thousand alive, led them to the summit of Sela, and then threw them down from that rock* so that their bodies split open. [13]Meanwhile, the troops Amaziah had dismissed from going into battle with him raided the cities of Judah from Samaria to Beth-horon. They struck down three thousand of the inhabitants and carried off much plunder.

**Amaziah's Apostasy.** [14]When Amaziah returned from his conquest of the Edomites he brought back with him the gods of the people of Seir. He set these up as his own gods; he bowed down before them and offered sacrifice to them. [15]Then the anger of the LORD blazed out against Amaziah, and he sent a prophet to him who said: "Why have you sought this people's gods that could not deliver their own people from your power?" [16]While he was still speaking, however, the king said to him: "Have you been appointed the king's counselor? Stop! Why should you have to be killed?" Therefore the prophet stopped. But he said, "I know that God's counsel is your destruction, for by doing this you have refused to listen to my counsel."

**Amaziah Punished.** [17l]Having taken counsel, Amaziah, king of Judah, sent word to Joash, son of Jehoahaz, son of Jehu, the king of Israel, saying, "Come, let us meet face to face." [18]Joash, king of Israel, sent this reply to Amaziah, king of Judah: "A thistle of Lebanon sent word to a

---

c. [24:18] Ex 34:13.  d. [24:20] Jgs 6:34.  e. [24:23] 2 Kgs 12:17–18.  f. [24:24] Dt 32:30.  g. [24:25–26] 2 Kgs 12:21–22.  h. [24:27] 2 Kgs 12:19, 22.  i. [25:1–4] 2 Kgs 14:1–6.  j. [25:4] Dt 24:16; 2 Kgs 14:5–6; Ez 18:20.

\*[25:12] **Sela . . . rock:** a pun—the name of the city, Sela, in Hebrew means "rock."

k. [25:11] 2 Kgs 14:7.  l. [25:17–24] 2 Kgs 14:8–14.

cedar of Lebanon, 'Give your daughter to my son in marriage,' but an animal of Lebanon passed by and trampled the thistle underfoot.[m] [19]You are thinking,

'See, I have struck down Edom!'
Your heart is lifted up,
And glories in it. Stay home!
Why bring misfortune and failure
        on yourself and on Judah with you?"

[20]But Amaziah did not listen; for it was God's doing that they be handed over because they sought the gods of Edom. [21]So Joash, king of Israel, advanced, and he and Amaziah, king of Judah, met face to face at Beth-shemesh of Judah, [22]and Judah was defeated by Israel, and all fled to their tents. [23]But Amaziah, king of Judah, son of Joash, son of Jehoahaz, was captured by Joash, king of Israel, at Beth-shemesh. Joash brought him to Jerusalem and tore down the wall of Jerusalem from the Gate of Ephraim to the Corner Gate, four hundred cubits. [24]He took all the gold and silver and all the vessels found in the house of God with Obed-edom,* and in the treasuries of the king's house, and hostages as well. Then he returned to Samaria.

[25n]Amaziah, son of Joash, king of Judah, survived Joash, son of Jehoahaz, king of Israel, by fifteen years. [26]The rest of the acts of Amaziah, first and last, are recorded in the book of the kings of Judah and Israel. [27]Now from the time that Amaziah turned away from the LORD, a conspiracy was formed against him in Jerusalem, and he fled to Lachish. But he was pursued to Lachish and killed there. [28]He was brought back on horses and was buried with his ancestors in the City of Judah.[†]

## CHAPTER 26

**Uzziah's Projects.** [1o]All the people of Judah took Uzziah, who was only sixteen years old, and made him king to succeed Amaziah his father. [2]It was he who rebuilt Elath and restored it to Judah, after the king rested with his ancestors. [3]Uzziah was sixteen years old when he became king, and he reigned fifty-two years in Jerusalem. His mother's name was Jecoliah, from Jerusalem. [4]He did what was right in the LORD's sight, just as his father Amaziah had done. [5]He was prepared to seek God as long as Zechariah[‡] lived,[p] who taught him to fear God;

and as long as he sought the LORD, God made him prosper. [6]He went out and fought the Philistines and razed the walls of Gath, Jabneh, and Ashdod, and built cities in the district of Ashdod and in Philistia.[q] [7]God helped him against the Philistines, against the Arabians who dwelt in Gurbaal, and against the Meunites. [8]The Ammonites paid tribute to Uzziah and his fame spread as far as Egypt, for he grew stronger and stronger. [9]Moreover, Uzziah built towers in Jerusalem at the Corner Gate, at the Valley Gate, and at the Angle, and he fortified them. [10]He built towers in the wilderness and dug numerous cisterns, for he had many cattle. He had plowmen in the Shephelah and the plains, farmers and vinedressers in the highlands and the garden land. He was a lover of the soil.

[11]Uzziah also had a standing army of fit soldiers divided into bands according to the number in which they were mustered by Jeiel the scribe and Maaseiah the recorder, under the command of Hananiah, one of the king's officials. [12]The entire number of family heads over these valiant warriors was two thousand six hundred, [13]and at their disposal was a mighty army of three hundred seven thousand five hundred fighting men of great valor to help the king against his enemies. [14]Uzziah provided for them—for the entire army—bucklers, lances, helmets, breastplates, bows, and slingstones. [15]He also built machines in Jerusalem, devices designed to stand on the towers and at the angles of the walls to shoot arrows and cast large stones. His name spread far and wide; the help he received was wondrous, so strong did he become.

**Pride and Fall.** [16]But after he had become strong, he became arrogant to his own destruction and acted treacherously with the LORD, his God. He entered the temple of the LORD to make an offering on the altar of incense. [17]But Azariah the priest, and with him eighty other priests of the LORD, courageous men, followed him. [18]They stood up to King Uzziah, saying to him: "It is not for you, Uzziah, to burn incense to the LORD, but for the priests, the sons of Aaron, who have been consecrated for this purpose.[r] Leave the sanctuary, for you have acted treacherously and no longer have a part in the glory that comes from the LORD God." [19]Uzziah, who was holding a censer for burning the incense, became angry. But at the very moment he showed his anger to the priests, while they were looking at him in the house of the LORD beside the altar of incense, leprosy broke out on his forehead.[s] [20]Azariah the chief priest and all the other priests examined him, and when they saw that his forehead was leprous, they rushed him out. He let himself be expelled, for the LORD had afflicted him. [21r]King Uzziah remained a leper till the day he died. As a leper he lived in a house apart, for he was

---

*[25:24] **With Obed-edom:** perhaps an Edomite priest (cf. v. 14), or possibly a member of a levitical family or gatekeepers; cf. 1 Chr 15:18; 26:12–15.

†[25:28] **The City of Judah:** i.e., Jerusalem, the capital of Judah; the parallel passage (2 Kgs 14:20) reads "the City of David."

‡[26:5] **Zechariah:** not otherwise identified, but cf. 29:1.

m. [25:18] Jgs 9:7–15; 2 Kgs 14:9.    n. [25:25–28] 2 Kgs 14:17–20. o. [26:1–4] 2 Kgs 14:21–22; 15:1–3.    p. [26:5] 2 Chr 24:2.

q. [26:6] Am 1:8.    r. [26:18] Ex 30:7.    s. [26:19] Nm 12:10. t. [26:21–23] 2 Kgs 15:5–7; Lv 13:46; Nm 19:20.

excluded from the house of the LORD. Therefore his son Jotham was master of the palace and ruled the people of the land.

²²The rest of the acts of Uzziah, first and last, were written by Isaiah the prophet, son of Amoz. ²³Uzziah rested with his ancestors and was buried with them in the field adjoining the royal cemetery, for they said, "He was a leper." His son Jotham succeeded him as king.

## CHAPTER 27

**Jotham.** ¹ᵘJotham was twenty-five years old when he became king, and he reigned sixteen years in Jerusalem. His mother's name was Jerusha, daughter of Zadok. ²He did what was right in the LORD's sight, just as his father Uzziah had done, though he did not enter the temple of the LORD. The people, however, continued to act corruptly.

³It was he who built the Upper Gate of the LORD's house and did much construction on the wall of Ophel. ⁴Moreover, he built cities in the hill country of Judah, and in the wooded areas he set up fortresses and towers. ⁵He fought with the king of the Ammonites and conquered them. That year the Ammonites paid him one hundred talents of silver, together with ten thousand kors of wheat and ten thousand of barley. They brought the same to him also in the second and in the third year. ⁶Thus Jotham continued to grow strong because he made sure to walk before the LORD, his God. ⁷ᵛThe rest of the acts of Jotham, his wars and his activities, are recorded in the book of the kings of Israel and Judah. ⁸He was twenty-five years old when he became king, and he reigned sixteen years in Jerusalem. ⁹Jotham rested with his ancestors and was buried in the City of David, and his son Ahaz succeeded him as king.

## CHAPTER 28

**Ahaz's Misdeeds.** ¹ʷAhaz was twenty years old when he became king, and he reigned sixteen years in Jerusalem. He did not do what was right in the sight of the LORD as David his father had done. ²He walked in the ways of the kings of Israel and even made molten idols for the Baals. ³Moreover, he offered sacrifice in the Valley of Ben-hinnom, and immolated his children by fire in accordance with the abominable practices of the nations whom the LORD had dispossessed before the Israelites.ˣ ⁴He sacrificed and burned incense on the high places, on hills, and under every green tree.

**Ahaz Punished.** ⁵Therefore the LORD, his God, delivered him into the power of the king of Aram. The Arameans defeated him and carried away captive a large number of his people, whom they brought to Damascus. He was also delivered into the power of the king of Israel, who defeated him with great slaughter.ʸ ⁶For Pekah, son of Remaliah, killed one hundred and twenty thousand of Judah in a single day, all of them valiant men, because they had abandoned the LORD, the God of their ancestors. ⁷Zichri, an Ephraimite warrior, killed Maaseiah, the king's son, and Azrikam, the master of the palace, and also Elkanah, who was second to the king. ⁸The Israelites took away as captives two hundred thousand of their kinfolk's wives, sons, and daughters; they also took from them much plunder, which they brought to Samaria.

**Oded's Prophecy.** ⁹In Samaria there was a prophet of the LORD by the name of Oded. He went out to meet the army returning to Samaria and said to them: "It was because the LORD, the God of your ancestors, was angry with Judah that he delivered them into your power. You, however, have killed them with a fury that has reached up to heaven. ¹⁰And now you are planning to subjugate the people of Judah and Jerusalem as your slaves and bondwomen. Are not you yourselves, therefore, guilty of a crime against the LORD, your God? ¹¹Now listen to me: send back the captives you have carried off from among your kin, for the burning anger of the LORD is upon you."

¹²At this, some of the Ephraimite leaders, Azariah, son of Johanan, Berechiah, son of Meshillemoth, Jehizkiah, son of Shallum, and Amasa, son of Hadlai, themselves stood up in opposition to those who had returned from the war. ¹³They said to them: "Do not bring the captives here, for what you are planning will make us guilty before the LORD and increase our sins and our guilt. Great is our guilt, and there is burning anger upon Israel." ¹⁴Therefore the soldiers left their captives and the plunder before the princes and the whole assembly. ¹⁵Then the men just named proceeded to help the captives. All of them who were naked they clothed from the spoils; they clothed them, put sandals on their feet, gave them food and drink, anointed them, and all who were weak they set on donkeys. They brought them to Jericho, the City of Palms, to their kinfolk. Then they returned to Samaria.ᶻ

**Further Sins of Ahaz.** ¹⁶At that time King Ahaz sent an appeal for help to the kings of Assyria.ᵃ ¹⁷The Edomites had returned, attacked Judah,

---

*[28:5–8, 16–23] The account of Ahaz's reign in 2 Kings refers to hostilities of Syria (Aram) and Israel against Judah, the revolt of the Edomites, submission to Tilgath-pilneser, king of Assyria, the stripping of Temple treasures to pay him tribute, and, in deference to him, shaping the cult of the Jerusalem Temple according to patterns seen in Damascus (2 Kgs 16:5–18; cf. Is 7:1–2). The account in Kings relates all this to an attack of Syria and Israel on Judah (735 B.C.), as they attempted to force Judah into an anti-Assyrian coalition; but the Chronicler, who does not mention the attack, depicts these troubles as the result of, or examples of, Ahaz's infidelity.

u. [27:1–3] 2 Kgs 15:32–35.   v. [27:7–9] 2 Kgs 15:36–38.   w. [28:1–4] 2 Kgs 16:1–4.   x. [28:3] Lv 18:21; 2 Kgs 16:3.

y. [28:5] 2 Kgs 16:5; Is 7:1–9.   z. [28:15] Lk 10:25–37.   a. [28:16] 2 Kgs 16:7.

and carried off captives.$^b$ $^{18}$The Philistines too had raided the cities of the Shephelah and the Negeb of Judah; they captured Beth-shemesh, Aijalon, Gederoth, Soco and its dependencies, Timnah and its dependencies, and Gimzo and its dependencies, and settled there. $^{19}$For the LORD had brought Judah low because of Ahaz, king of Israel,* who let Judah go its own way and committed treachery against the LORD. $^{20}$Tilgath-pilneser, king of Assyria, did indeed come to him, but to oppress him rather than to lend strength.$^c$ $^{21}$Though Ahaz plundered the LORD's house and the houses of the king and the princes to pay off the king of Assyria, it was no help to him.$^d$

$^{22}$While he was already in distress, the same King Ahaz increased his treachery to the LORD. $^{23}$He sacrificed to the gods of Damascus who had defeated him, saying, "Since it was the gods of the kings of Aram who helped them, I will sacrifice to them that they may help me also." However, they only furthered his downfall and that of all Israel.$^e$ $^{24}$Ahaz gathered up the utensils of God's house and broke them in pieces. He closed the doors of the LORD's house and made altars for himself in every corner of Jerusalem.$^f$ $^{25}$In every city throughout Judah he set up high places to offer sacrifice to other gods. Thus he provoked the LORD, the God of his ancestors, to anger.

$^{26}$The rest of his words and his deeds, first and last, are recorded in the book of the kings of Judah and Israel. $^{27}$Ahaz rested with his ancestors and was buried in Jerusalem—in the city, for they did not bring him to the tombs of the kings of Israel. His son Hezekiah succeeded him as king.

## CHAPTER 29

**Hezekiah's Reforms.** $^{1h}$Hezekiah was twenty-five years old when he became king, and he reigned twenty-nine years in Jerusalem. His mother's name was Abijah, daughter of Zechariah. $^2$He did what was right in the LORD's sight, just as David his father had done. $^3$In the first month of the first year of his reign, he opened the doors of the LORD's house and repaired them.$^i$ $^4$He summoned the priests and Levites, gathering them in the open space to the east, $^5$and said to them: "Listen to me, you Levites! Sanctify yourselves now and sanctify the house of the LORD, the God of your ancestors, and clean out the filth from the sanctuary. $^6$Our ancestors acted treacherously and did what was evil in the eyes of the LORD, our God. They abandoned

him, turned away their faces from the LORD's dwelling, and turned their backs on him. $^7$They also closed the doors of the vestibule, extinguished the lamps, and failed to burn incense and sacrifice burnt offerings in the sanctuary to the God of Israel.$^j$ $^{8k}$Therefore the anger of the LORD has come upon Judah and Jerusalem; he has made them an object of terror, horror, and hissing, as you see with your own eyes. $^9$For our ancestors fell by the sword, and our sons, our daughters, and our wives have been taken captive because of this. $^{10}$Now, I intend to make a covenant with the LORD, the God of Israel, that his burning anger may turn away from us. $^{11}$My sons, do not be negligent any longer, for it is you whom the LORD has chosen to stand before him, to minister to him, to be his ministers and to offer incense."

$^{12}$Then the Levites arose: Mahath, son of Amasai, and Joel, son of Azariah, of the Kohathites; of the descendants of Merari: Kish, son of Abdi, and Azariah, son of Jehallel; of the Gershonites: Joah, son of Zimmah, and Eden, son of Joah; $^{13}$of the sons of Elizaphan: Shimri and Jeuel; of the sons of Asaph: Zechariah and Mattaniah; $^{14}$of the sons of Heman: Jehuel and Shimei; of the sons of Jeduthun: Shemiah and Uzziel. $^{15}$They gathered their kinfolk together and sanctified themselves; then they came as the king had ordered, in keeping with the words of the LORD, to cleanse the LORD's house.

$^{16}$The priests entered the interior of the LORD's house to cleanse it. Whatever they found in the LORD's temple that was unclean they brought out to the court of the LORD's house, where the Levites took it from them and carried it out to the Wadi Kidron. $^{17}$They began the work of consecration on the first day of the first month, and on the eighth day of the month they reached the vestibule of the LORD; they consecrated the LORD's house over an eight-day period, and on the sixteenth day of the first month, they had finished.

$^{18}$Then they went inside to King Hezekiah and said: "We have cleansed the entire house of the LORD, the altar for burnt offerings with all its utensils, and the table for the showbread with all its utensils. $^{19}$We have restored and consecrated all the articles which King Ahaz had thrown away during his reign because of his treachery; they are now before the LORD's altar."

**The Rite of Expiation.** $^{20}$Then King Hezekiah hastened to convoke the princes of the city and went up to the LORD's house. $^{21}$Seven bulls, seven rams, seven lambs, and seven he-goats were presented as a purification offering for the kingdom, for the sanctuary, and for Judah. Hezekiah ordered the sons of Aaron, the priests, to offer them on the altar of the LORD. $^{22}$They slaughtered the bulls, and the priests collected the blood and splashed it on the altar. Then they

---

*[28:19] **Ahaz, king of Israel**: in his account of the period of the divided monarchy, the Chronicler regularly uses the term "Israel" as here to designate, not the Northern Kingdom, but the entire people. See note on 10:1.

b. [28:17] 2 Kgs 16:6.   c. [28:20] 2 Kgs 16:10; Is 7:17–20; 8:5–8.
d. [28:21] 2 Kgs 16:8.   e. [28:23] 2 Kgs 16:12–13; Is 10:20.
f. [28:24] 2 Chr 29:3; 30:14; 2 Kgs 16:17.   g. [28:26–27] 2 Kgs 16:19–20.   h. [29:1–2] 2 Kgs 18:2–3.   i. [29:3] 2 Chr 28:24.

j. [29:7] 2 Kgs 16:15.   k. [29:8–9] Lv 26:32–33; Dt 28:25; Jer 25:18.

slaughtered the rams and splashed the blood on the altar; then they slaughtered the lambs and splashed the blood on the altar. [23]Then the he-goats for the purification offering were led before the king and the assembly, who laid their hands upon them. [24]The priests then slaughtered them and offered their blood on the altar to atone for the sin of all Israel. For the king had said, "The burnt offering and the purification offering are for all Israel."

[25]He stationed the Levites in the LORD's house with cymbals, harps, and lyres, according to the command of David, of Gad the king's seer, and of Nathan the prophet; for this command was from the LORD through his prophets. [26]The Levites were stationed with the instruments of David, and the priests with the trumpets. [27]Then Hezekiah ordered the burnt offering to be sacrificed on the altar. At the very moment the burnt offering began, they also began the song of the LORD, to the accompaniment of the trumpets and the instruments of David, king of Israel. [28]The entire assembly bowed down, and the song was sung and the trumpets sounded until the burnt offering had been completed. [29]Once the burnt offering was completed, the king and all who were with him knelt and worshiped. [30]King Hezekiah and the princes then told the Levites to sing the praises of the LORD in the words of David and of Asaph the seer. They sang praises till their joy was full, then fell down and worshiped.

[31]Hezekiah then said: "You have dedicated yourselves to the LORD. Approach, and bring forward the sacrifices and thank offerings for the house of the LORD." Then the assembly brought forward the sacrifices and thank offerings and all their voluntary burnt offerings. [32]The number of burnt offerings that the assembly brought forward was seventy oxen, one hundred rams, and two hundred lambs: all of these as a burnt offering to the LORD. [33]As consecrated gifts there were six hundred oxen and three thousand sheep. [34]Since there were too few priests to skin all the victims for the burnt offerings, their fellow Levites assisted them until the task was completed and the priests had sanctified themselves. The Levites, in fact, were more careful than the priests to sanctify themselves.[l] [35]The burnt offerings were indeed many, along with the fat of the communion offerings and the libations for the burnt offerings. Thus the service of the house of the LORD was re-established. [36]Hezekiah and all the people rejoiced over what God had re-established for the people, and at how suddenly this had been done.

## CHAPTER 30

**Invitation to Passover.** [1]Hezekiah sent word to all Israel and Judah, and even wrote letters to Ephraim and Manasseh, saying that they should come to the house of the LORD in Jerusalem to celebrate the Passover to the LORD, the God of Israel.[m] [2]The king, his princes, and the entire assembly in Jerusalem had agreed to celebrate the Passover during the second month. [3]They could not celebrate it at the regular time because the priests had not sanctified themselves in sufficient numbers, and the people were not gathered at Jerusalem. [4]This seemed right to the king and the entire assembly, [5]and they issued a decree to be proclaimed throughout all Israel from Beersheba to Dan, that everyone should come to celebrate the Passover to the LORD, the God of Israel, in Jerusalem; for not many had kept it in the prescribed manner. [6]By the king's command, the couriers, with the letters written by the king and his princes, went through all Israel and Judah. They said: "Israelites, return to the LORD, the God of Abraham, Isaac, and Israel, that he may return to you, the remnant left from the hands of the Assyrian kings. [7]Do not be like your ancestors and your kin who acted treacherously toward the LORD, the God of their ancestors, so that he handed them over to desolation, as you yourselves now see.[o] [8]Do not be stiff-necked, as your ancestors were; stretch out your hands to the LORD and come to his sanctuary that he has consecrated forever, and serve the LORD, your God, that he may turn his burning anger from you. [9]If you return to the LORD, your kinfolk and your children will find mercy with their captors and return to this land. The LORD, your God, is gracious and merciful and he will not turn away his face from you if you return to him."[p]

[10]So the couriers passed from city to city in the land of Ephraim and Manasseh and as far as Zebulun, but they were derided and scoffed at. [11]Nevertheless, some from Asher, Manasseh, and Zebulun humbled themselves and came to Jerusalem. [12]In Judah, however, the hand of God brought it about that the people were of one heart to carry out the command of the king and the princes by the word of the LORD. [13]Thus many people gathered in Jerusalem to celebrate the feast of Unleavened Bread in the second month; it was a very great assembly.

**Passover Celebrated.** [14]They proceeded to remove the altars that were in Jerusalem as well as all the altars of incense, and cast them into the Wadi Kidron.[q] [15]They slaughtered the Passover on the fourteenth day of the second month. The priests and Levites were shamed into sanctifying themselves and brought burnt offerings into the house of the LORD. [16]They stood in the places prescribed for them according to the law of Moses, the man of God. The priests splashed the blood given them by the Levites; [17]for many in the assembly had not sanctified themselves, and the Levites were in charge of slaughtering the Passover victims for all who were unclean so

---

l. [29:34] 1 Chr 15:12.

m. [30:1] Ex 12:1–28.   n. [30:2–3] Nm 9:6–13.   o. [30:7] Acts 7:51.   p. [30:9] 1 Kgs 8:50.   q. [30:14] 2 Chr 28:24–25.

as to consecrate them to the Lord.[r] [18]The greater part of the people, in fact, chiefly from Ephraim, Manasseh, Issachar, and Zebulun, had not cleansed themselves. Nevertheless they ate the Passover, contrary to the prescription; because Hezekiah prayed for them, saying, "May the good Lord grant pardon to [19]all who have set their heart to seek God, the Lord, the God of their ancestors, even though they are not clean as holiness requires." [20]The Lord heard Hezekiah and healed the people.

[21]Thus the Israelites who were in Jerusalem celebrated the feast of Unleavened Bread with great rejoicing for seven days, and the Levites and the priests sang the praises of the Lord day after day with all their strength. [22]Hezekiah spoke encouragingly to all the Levites who had shown themselves well skilled in the service of the Lord. And when they had completed the seven days of festival, sacrificing communion offerings and singing praises to the Lord, the God of their ancestors, [23]the whole assembly agreed to celebrate another seven days. So with joy they celebrated seven days more. [24]King Hezekiah of Judah had contributed a thousand bulls and seven thousand sheep to the assembly, and the princes a thousand bulls and ten thousand sheep. The priests sanctified themselves in great numbers, [25]and the whole assembly of Judah rejoiced, together with the priests and Levites and the rest of the assembly that had come from Israel, as well as the resident aliens from the land of Israel and those that lived in Judah. [26]There was great rejoicing in Jerusalem, for since the days of Solomon, son of David, king of Israel, there had been nothing like it in the city. [27]Then the levitical priests rose and blessed the people; their voice was heard and their prayer reached heaven, God's holy dwelling.

## CHAPTER 31

**Liturgical Reforms.** [1]After all this was over, those Israelites who had been present went forth to the cities of Judah and smashed the sacred pillars, cut down the asherahs, and tore down the high places and altars throughout Judah, Benjamin, Ephraim, and Manasseh, until they were all destroyed.[s] Then the Israelites returned to their cities, each to his own possession.

[2]Hezekiah re-established the divisions of the priests and the Levites according to their former divisions, assigning to each priest and Levite his proper service, whether in regard to burnt offerings or communion offerings, thanksgiving or praise, or ministering in the gates of the encampment of the Lord. [3]From his own wealth the king allotted a portion for burnt offerings, those of morning and evening and those on sabbaths, new moons, and festivals, as is written in the law of the Lord.[t] [4]He also commanded

the people living in Jerusalem to provide for the support of the priests and Levites, that they might firmly adhere to the law of the Lord.

[5]As soon as the order was promulgated, the Israelites brought, in great quantities, the best of their grain, wine, oil, and honey, and all the produce of the fields; they gave a generous tithe of everything.[u] [6]Israelites and Judahites living in other cities of Judah also brought in tithes of oxen, sheep, and votive offerings consecrated to the Lord, their God; these they brought in and heaped up in piles.[v] [7]It was in the third month that they began to establish these heaps, and they completed them in the seventh month.[*] [8]When Hezekiah and the princes had come and seen the piles, they blessed the Lord and his people Israel. [9]Then Hezekiah questioned the priests and the Levites concerning the piles, [10]and the priest Azariah, head of the house of Zadok, answered him, "Since they began to bring the offerings to the house of the Lord, we have eaten, been satisfied, and had much left over, for the Lord has blessed his people. This great supply is what was left over."[w]

[11]Hezekiah then gave orders that chambers be constructed in the house of the Lord. When this had been done, [12]they deposited the offerings, tithes, and votive offerings there for safekeeping. The overseer of these things was Conaniah the Levite, and his brother Shimei was second in command. [13]Jehiel, Azaziah, Nahath, Asahel, Jerimoth, Jozabad, Eliel, Ismachiah, Mahath, and Benaiah were supervisors subject to Conaniah the Levite and his brother Shimei by appointment of King Hezekiah and of Azariah, the prefect of the house of God. [14]Kore, the son of Imnah, a Levite and the keeper of the eastern gate, was in charge of the voluntary offerings made to God; he distributed the offerings made to the Lord and the most holy of the votive offerings. [15]Under him in the priestly cities were Eden, Miniamin, Jeshua, Shemaiah, Amariah, and Shecaniah, who faithfully made the distribution to their brothers, great and small alike, according to their divisions.

[16]There was also a register by ancestral houses of males three years of age[†] and over, for all priests who were eligible to enter the house of the Lord according to the daily schedule to fulfill their service in the order of their divisions.[x] [17]The priests were inscribed in their family records according to their ancestral houses, as were the Levites twenty years of age and over

---

*[31:7] **Third month . . . seventh month:** between the late spring feast of Weeks or Pentecost and the fall feast of Booths or Tabernacles, there is seldom any rain in Palestine; at the end of this dry period the problem of storage (v. 11) would become acute.

†[31:16] **Three years of age:** this may be a textual error for "thirty years." According to Nm 4:3, 23, 30, men of the priestly clans served from the ages of thirty to fifty.

r. [30:17] 2 Chr 35:6.   s. [31:1] 2 Chr 34:3–4; 2 Kgs 18:4.   t. [31:3] Nm 28–29; 1 Chr 29:3; Ez 45:17.

u. [31:5] Nm 18:18–24; Dt 14:22–23.   v. [31:6] Neh 12:44–47; 13:10–13.   w. [31:10] Lv 25:19–22.   x. [31:16] 1 Chr 23:3–4.

according to their various offices and divisions.^y ^18A distribution was also made to all who were inscribed in the family records, for their little ones, wives, sons and daughters—thus for the entire assembly, since they were to sanctify themselves by sharing faithfully in the votive offerings. ^19The sons of Aaron, the priests who lived on the lands attached to their cities, had in every city men designated by name to distribute portions to every male of the priests and to every Levite listed in the family records.

^20Hezekiah did this in all Judah. He did what was good, upright, and faithful before the LORD, his God. ^21Everything that he undertook, for the service of the house of God or for the law and the commandment, was to seek his God. He did this with all his heart, and he prospered.^z

## CHAPTER 32

**Sennacherib's Invasion.** ^1But after all this and all Hezekiah's fidelity, there came Sennacherib, king of Assyria. He invaded Judah and besieged the fortified cities, intending to breach and take them.^a ^2When Hezekiah saw that Sennacherib was coming with the intention of attacking Jerusalem, ^3he took the advice of his princes and warriors to stop the waters of the springs outside the city; they promised their help. ^4bA large force was gathered and stopped all the springs and also the stream running nearby. For they said, "Why should the kings of Assyria come and find an abundance of water?" ^5He then looked to his defenses: he rebuilt the wall where it was broken down, raised towers upon it, and built another wall outside.^c He strengthened the Millo of the City of David and made a great number of spears and shields. ^6Then he appointed army commanders over the people. He gathered them together in his presence in the open space at the gate of the city and encouraged them with these words: ^7"Be strong and steadfast; do not be afraid or dismayed because of the king of Assyria and all the horde coming with him, for there is more with us than with him.^d ^8He has only an arm of flesh, but we have the LORD, our God, to help us and to fight our battles."^e And the people took confidence from the words of Hezekiah, king of Judah.

**Threat of Sennacherib.** ^9fAfter this, while Sennacherib, king of Assyria, himself remained at Lachish with all his forces, he sent his officials to Jerusalem with this message for Hezekiah, king of Judah, and all the Judahites who were in Jerusalem: ^10"Thus says Sennacherib, king of Assyria: In what are you trusting, now that you are under siege in Jerusalem? ^11Is not Hezekiah deceiving you, delivering you over to a death of famine and thirst, by his claim that 'the LORD,

our God, will rescue us from the grasp of the king of Assyria'? ^12Has not this same Hezekiah removed the Lord's own high places and altars and commanded Judah and Jerusalem, 'You shall bow down before one altar only, and on it alone you shall offer incense'? ^13Do you not know what my fathers and I have done to all the peoples of other lands? Were the gods of the nations in those lands able to rescue their lands from my hand? ^14Who among all the gods of those nations which my fathers put under the ban was able to rescue their people from my hand? Will your god, then, be able to rescue you from my hand? ^15Let not Hezekiah mislead you further and deceive you in any such way. Do not believe him! Since no other god of any other nation or kingdom has been able to rescue his people from my hand or the hands of my fathers, how much the less shall your god rescue you from my hand!"

^16His officials said still more against the LORD God and against his servant Hezekiah, ^17for he had written letters to deride the LORD, the God of Israel, speaking of him in these terms: "As the gods of the nations in other lands have not rescued their people from my hand, neither shall Hezekiah's god rescue his people from my hand."^g ^18In a loud voice they shouted in the language of Judah to the people of Jerusalem who were on the wall, to frighten and terrify them so that they might capture their city. ^19They spoke of the God of Israel as though he were one of the gods of the other peoples of the earth, a work of human hands. ^20But because of this, King Hezekiah and Isaiah the prophet, son of Amoz, prayed and cried out to heaven.^h

**Sennacherib's Defeat.** ^21Then the LORD sent an angel, who destroyed every warrior, leader, and commander in the camp of the Assyrian king, so that he had to return shamefaced to his own country. And when he entered the temple of his god, some of his own offspring struck him down there with the sword.^i ^22Thus the LORD saved Hezekiah and the inhabitants of Jerusalem from the hand of Sennacherib, king of Assyria, as from every other power; he gave them rest on every side. ^23Many brought gifts for the LORD to Jerusalem and costly objects for Hezekiah, king of Judah, who thereafter was exalted in the eyes of all the nations.^j

**Hezekiah's Later Reign.** ^24In those days Hezekiah became mortally ill. He prayed to the LORD, who answered him by giving him a sign.^k ^25Hezekiah, however, did not respond with like generosity, for he had become arrogant. Therefore wrath descended upon him and upon Judah and Jerusalem. ^26But then Hezekiah humbled himself for his pride—both he and the inhabitants of Jerusalem; and therefore the wrath of

---

y. [31:17] 1 Chr 23:6–24.   z. [31:21] Ps 119:2.   a. [32:1] 2 Kgs 18:13.   b. [32:4] Is 22:9, 11.   c. [32:5] Neh 2:17–18.   d. [32:7] 2 Chr 14:10; 20:6–12.   e. [32:8] Is 31:3.   f. [32:9–20] 2 Kgs 18:17–37; Is 36:1–22.

g. [32:17] 2 Kgs 19:9–13; Is 37:9–13.   h. [32:20] 2 Kgs 19:14–19; Is 37:14–20.   i. [32:21] 2 Kgs 19:35–37; Is 37:36–38.   j. [32:23] 2 Chr 17:10–11.   k. [32:24] 2 Kgs 20:1–11; Is 38:1–8.   l. [32:26, 31] 2 Kgs 20:12–19; Is 39:1–8.

the Lord did not come upon them during the time of Hezekiah.

²⁷ᵐHezekiah possessed very great wealth and glory. He made treasuries for his silver, gold, precious stones, spices, jewels, and other precious things of all kinds; ²⁸also storehouses for the harvest of grain, for wine and oil, and barns for the various kinds of cattle and flocks. ²⁹He built cities for himself, and he acquired sheep and oxen in great numbers, for God gave him very great riches. ³⁰This same Hezekiah stopped the upper outlet for water from Gihon and redirected it underground westward to the City of David. Hezekiah prospered in all his works.ⁿ ³¹Nevertheless, in respect to the ambassadors of the Babylonian officials who were sent to him to investigate the sign that had occurred in the land, God abandoned him as a test, to know all that was in his heart.

³²The rest of Hezekiah's acts, including his good deeds, are recorded in the vision of Isaiah the prophet, son of Amoz, and in the book of the kings of Judah and Israel. ³³Hezekiah rested with his ancestors; he was buried at the approach to the tombs* of the descendants of David. All Judah and the inhabitants of Jerusalem paid him honor at his death. His son Manasseh succeeded him as king.

## CHAPTER 33

**Manasseh's Impiety.** ¹ᵒManasseh was twelve years old when he became king, and he reigned fifty-five years in Jerusalem. ²He did what was evil in the Lord's sight, following the abominable practices of the nations whom the Lord dispossessed before the Israelites. ³He rebuilt the high places which Hezekiah his father had torn down. He set up altars to the Baals, and also made asherahs. He bowed down to the whole host of heaven and served them. ⁴He built altars in the house of the Lord, of which the Lord had said: In Jerusalem shall my name be forever; ⁵and he built altars to the whole host of heaven in the two courts of the house of the Lord. ⁶It was he, too, who immolated his children by fire in the Valley of Ben-hinnom. He practiced soothsaying and divination, and reintroduced the consulting of ghosts and spirits.

He did much evil in the Lord's sight and provoked him to anger. ⁷An idol he had made he placed in the house of God, of which God had said to David and to his son Solomon: In this house and in Jerusalem, which I have chosen out of all the tribes of Israel, I shall set my name forever. ⁸I will no longer make Israel step out of the land I assigned to your ancestors, provided

that they are careful to observe all I commanded them, the entire law, the statutes, and the ordinances given by Moses.

⁹Manasseh misled Judah and the inhabitants of Jerusalem into doing even greater evil than the nations the Lord had destroyed at the coming of the Israelites. ¹⁰The Lord spoke to Manasseh and his people, but they paid no attention.

**Manasseh's Conversion.** ¹¹ᵖTherefore the Lord brought against them the army commanders of the Assyrian king; they captured Manasseh with hooks, shackled him with chains, and transported him to Babylon.† ¹²In his distress, he began to appease the Lord, his God. He humbled himself abjectly before the God of his ancestors, ¹³and prayed to him.‡ The Lord let himself be won over: he heard his prayer and restored him to his kingdom in Jerusalem. Then Manasseh knew that the Lord is indeed God.

¹⁴Afterward he built an outer wall for the City of David to the west of Gihon in the valley, extending to the Fish Gate and encircling Ophel; he built it very high. He stationed army officers in all the fortified cities of Judah. ¹⁵He removed the foreign gods and the idol from the Lord's house and all the altars he had built on the mount of the Lord's house and in Jerusalem, and cast them outside the city.�q ¹⁶He restored the altar of the Lord, and sacrificed on it communion offerings and thank offerings, and commanded Judah to serve the Lord, the God of Israel. ¹⁷Though the people continued to sacrifice on the high places, they now did so to the Lord, their God.

¹⁸ʳThe rest of the acts of Manasseh, his prayer to his God, and the words of the seers who spoke to him in the name of the Lord, the God of Israel, are written in the chronicles of the kings of Israel. ¹⁹His prayer and how his supplication was heard, all his sins and his treachery, the sites where he built high places and set up asherahs and carved images before he humbled himself, all this is recorded in the chronicles of his seers. ²⁰Manasseh rested with his ancestors and was buried in his own palace. His son Amon succeeded him as king.

**Reign of Amon.** ²¹ˢAmon was twenty-two years old when he became king, and he reigned two

---

† [33:11] There is no evidence elsewhere for such an imprisonment of King Manasseh in Babylon. According to the Assyrian inscriptions, however, Manasseh did pay tribute to the Assyrian kings Esarhaddon (680–669 B.C.) and Asshurbanipal (668–627 B.C.). He may well then have been obliged to go to Nineveh, Assyria's capital (rather than to Babylon as the Chronicler has it), to take his oath of allegiance as vassal to the king of Assyria.

‡ [33:13] **And prayed to him:** these words inspired an unknown writer to compose the apocryphal "Prayer of Manasseh," which since the Council of Trent appears as an appendix to many editions of the Vulgate Bible and is used in the Church's liturgy.

---

\* [32:33] **The approach to the tombs:** lit., "the ascent of the tombs," perhaps "the upper section of the tombs," i.e., their most prominent and honored place.

---

m. [32:27–28] 2 Kgs 20:13; Is 39:2.   n. [32:30] 2 Kgs 20:20–21.
o. [33:1–10] 2 Kgs 21:1–9.

p. [33:11] Jb 36:8; Ez 19:9.   q. [33:15] 2 Chr 14:2.   r. [33:18, 20] 2 Kgs 21:17–18.   s. [33:21–25] 2 Kgs 21:19–26.

years in Jerusalem. ²²He did what was evil in the LORD's sight, as his father Manasseh had done. Amon offered sacrifice to all the idols his father Manasseh had made, and served them. ²³Moreover, he did not humble himself before the LORD as his father Manasseh had humbled himself; on the contrary, Amon only increased his guilt. ²⁴His officials plotted against him and put him to death in his palace, ²⁵but the people of the land then slew all who had plotted against King Amon, and the people of the land made his son Josiah king in his stead.

## CHAPTER 34

**Josiah's Reforms.** ¹ᵗJosiah was eight years old when he became king, and he reigned thirty-one years in Jerusalem. ²He did what was right in the LORD's sight, walking in the way of David his father, not turning right or left. ³ᵘIn the eighth year of his reign, while he was still a youth, he began to seek after the God of David his father. Then in his twelfth year* he began to purify Judah and Jerusalem of the high places, the asherahs, and the carved and molten images. ⁴In his presence, the altars of the Baals were torn down; the incense stands erected above them he broke down; the asherahs and the carved and molten images he smashed and beat into dust, which he scattered over the tombs of those who had sacrificed to them; ⁵and the bones of the priests he burned upon their altars. Thus he purified Judah and Jerusalem. ⁶He did likewise in the cities of Manasseh, Ephraim, Simeon, and in the ruined villages of the surrounding country as far as Naphtali; ⁷he tore down the altars and asherahs, and the carved images he beat into dust, and broke down the incense stands throughout the land of Israel. Then he returned to Jerusalem.

**The Temple Restored.** ⁸ᵛIn the eighteenth year of his reign, in order to purify the land and the temple, he sent Shaphan, son of Azaliah, Maaseiah, the ruler of the city, and Joah, son of Joahaz, the chancellor, to restore the house of the LORD, his God. ⁹They came to Hilkiah the high priest and turned over the money brought to the house of God which the Levites, the guardians of the threshold, had collected from Manasseh, Ephraim, and all the remnant of Israel, as well as from all of Judah, Benjamin, and the inhabitants of Jerusalem.ʷ ¹⁰They turned it over to the master workers in the house of

the LORD, and these in turn used it to pay the workers in the LORD's house who were restoring and repairing it. ¹¹They also gave it to the carpenters and the masons to buy hewn stone and timber for the tie beams and rafters of the buildings which the kings of Judah had allowed to fall into ruin. ¹²The men worked faithfully at their task; their overseers were Jahath and Obadiah, Levites of the line of Merari, and Zechariah and Meshullam, of the Kohathites, who directed them. All those Levites who were skillful with musical instruments ¹³were in charge of the men who carried the burdens, and they directed all the workers in every kind of labor. Some of the other Levites were scribes, officials, and gatekeepers.

**The Finding of the Law.** ¹⁴ˣWhen they brought out the money that had been deposited in the house of the LORD, Hilkiah the priest found the book of the law of the LORD given through Moses. ¹⁵He reported this to Shaphan the scribe, saying, "I have found the book of the law in the house of the LORD." Hilkiah gave the book to Shaphan, ¹⁶who brought it to the king at the same time that he made his report to him. He said, "Your servants are doing everything that has been entrusted to them; ¹⁷they have smelted down the silver deposited in the LORD's house and have turned it over to the overseers and the workers." ¹⁸Then Shaphan the scribe also informed the king, "Hilkiah the priest has given me a book," and then Shaphan read it in the presence of the king.

¹⁹When the king heard the words of the law, he tore his garments. ²⁰The king then issued this command to Hilkiah, to Ahikam, son of Shaphan, to Abdon, son of Michah, to Shaphan the scribe, and to Asaiah, the king's servant: ²¹"Go, consult the LORD for me and for those who are left in Israel and Judah, about the words of the book that has been found, for the anger of the LORD burns furiously against us, because our ancestors did not keep the word of the LORD and have not done all that is written in this book." ²²Then Hilkiah and others from the king went to Huldah the prophet, wife of Shallum, son of Tokhath, son of Hasrah, keeper of the wardrobe; she lived in Jerusalem, in the Second Quarter. They spoke to her as they had been instructed, ²³and she said to them: "Thus says the LORD, the God of Israel: Say to the man who sent you to me, ²⁴Thus says the LORD: I am about to bring evil upon this place and upon its inhabitants, all the curses written in the book that was read before the king of Judah. ²⁵Because they have abandoned me and have burned incense to other gods, provoking me by all the works of their hands, my anger burns against this place and it cannot be extinguished.

²⁶"But to the king of Judah who sent you to consult the LORD, give this response: Thus says

*[34:3] **In his twelfth year:** ca. 628 B.C., i.e., around the time of the Assyrian emperor Asshurbanipal's death, which enabled Judah to free itself from Assyrian domination. On the basis of 2 Kgs 22:1–23:25 alone, one might suppose that Josiah's reform began only after and as a result of the discovery of the book of the law in the Temple, in the eighteenth year of his reign (622 B.C.). But the Chronicler is no doubt right in placing the beginning of the reform at an earlier period. The repair of the Temple itself, which led to the finding of the book of the law, was likely part of a cultic reform initiated by Josiah.

t. [34:1–2] 2 Kgs 22:1–2. u. [34:3–7] 2 Chr 14:1–4; 31:1; 2 Kgs 23:4–20. v. [34:8–13] 2 Kgs 22:3–7. w. [34:9] 2 Chr 24:8–9.

x. [34:14–28] 2 Kgs 22:8–20.

the LORD, the God of Israel: As for the words you have heard, [27]because you were heartsick and have humbled yourself before God when you heard his words concerning this place and its inhabitants; because you humbled yourself before me, tore your garments, and wept before me, I in turn have heard—oracle of the LORD. [28]I will gather you to your ancestors and you shall go to your grave in peace, and your eyes shall not see all the evil I am about to bring upon this place and upon its inhabitants."

This they reported to the king.

**Covenant Renewal.** [29]The king then had all the elders of Judah and of Jerusalem summoned before him. [30]The king went up to the house of the LORD with all the people of Judah and the inhabitants of Jerusalem: priests, Levites, and all the people, great and small. He read aloud to them all the words of the book of the covenant that had been found in the house of the LORD. [31]The king stood by the column[*] and made a covenant in the presence of the LORD to follow the LORD and to observe his commandments, statutes, and decrees with his whole heart and soul, carrying out the words of the covenant written in this book. [32]He thereby committed all who were in Jerusalem and Benjamin, and the inhabitants of Jerusalem acted according to the covenant of God, the God of their ancestors. [33]Josiah removed every abomination from all the territories belonging to the Israelites, and he obliged all who were in Israel to serve the LORD, their God. During his lifetime they did not turn away from following the LORD, the God of their ancestors.[z]

## CHAPTER 35

**The Passover.** [1a]Josiah celebrated in Jerusalem a Passover to honor the LORD; the Passover sacrifice was slaughtered on the fourteenth day of the first month.[b] [2]He reappointed the priests to their duties and confirmed them in the service of the LORD's house. [3]He said to the Levites who were to instruct all Israel, and who were consecrated to the LORD: "Put the holy ark in the house built by Solomon, son of David, king of Israel. It shall no longer be a burden on your shoulders. Serve now the LORD, your God, and his people Israel.[c] [4]Prepare yourselves by your ancestral houses and your divisions according to the prescriptions of David, king of Israel, and the prescriptions of his son Solomon. [5]Stand in the sanctuary according to the branches of the ancestral houses of your kin, the common people, so that the distribution of the Levites and the families may be the same.[d] [6]Slaughter the Passover sacrifice, sanctify yourselves, and be at the disposition of your kin,

that all may be done according to the word of the LORD given through Moses."[e]

[7]Josiah contributed to the common people a flock of lambs and young goats,[f] thirty thousand in number, each to serve as a Passover victim for all who were present, and also three thousand oxen; these were from the king's property. [8]His princes also gave a voluntary offering to the people, the priests, and the Levites. Hilkiah, Zechariah, and Jehiel, prefects of the house of God, gave to the priests two thousand six hundred Passover victims along with three hundred oxen.[g] [9]Conaniah and his brothers Shemaiah, Nethanel, Hashabiah, Jehiel, and Jozabad, the rulers of the Levites, contributed to the Levites five thousand Passover victims, together with five hundred oxen.

[10]When the service had been arranged, the priests took their places, as did the Levites in their divisions according to the king's command. [11]The Passover sacrifice was slaughtered, whereupon the priests splashed some of the blood and the Levites proceeded with the skinning. [12]They separated out what was destined for the burnt offering and gave it to various groups of the ancestral houses of the common people to offer to the LORD, as is written in the book of Moses. They did the same with the oxen. [13]They cooked the Passover on the fire as prescribed, and also cooked the sacred portions in pots, caldrons, and pans, then brought them quickly to all the common people.[h] [14]Afterward they prepared the Passover for themselves and for the priests. Indeed the priests, the sons of Aaron, were busy sacrificing burnt offerings and the fatty portions until night; therefore the Levites prepared for themselves and for the priests, the sons of Aaron. [15]The singers, the sons of Asaph, were at their posts as commanded by David and by Asaph, Heman, and Jeduthun, the king's seer. The gatekeepers were at every gate; there was no need for them to leave their stations, for their fellow Levites prepared for them. [16]Thus the entire service of the LORD was arranged that day so that the Passover could be celebrated and the burnt offerings sacrificed on the altar of the LORD, as King Josiah had commanded. [17]The Israelites who were present on that occasion kept the Passover and the feast of the Unleavened Bread for seven days. [18]No such Passover had been observed in Israel since the time of Samuel the prophet; no king of Israel had observed a Passover like that celebrated by Josiah, the priests, and Levites, all of Judah and Israel that were present, and the inhabitants of Jerusalem. [19]It was in the eighteenth year of Josiah's reign that this Passover was observed.

**Josiah's End.** [20]After Josiah had done all this to restore the temple, Neco, king of Egypt, came up to fight at Carchemish on the Euphrates, and

---

[*][34:31] **The column:** see note on 23:13.

y. [34:29–31] 2 Kgs 23:1–3.   z. [34:33] 2 Kgs 23:4–20.   a. [35:1–19] 2 Kgs 23:21–23.   b. [35:1] Ex 12:1–28; 2 Kgs 23:21.   c. [35:3] 2 Chr 5:4; 1 Chr 15:12, 15.   d. [35:5] 1 Chr 24–26.

e. [35:6] 2 Chr 30:17.   f. [35:7] Ex 12:5.   g. [35:8] Nm 7:1–83.   h. [35:13] Ex 12:8–9.   i. [35:18–19] 2 Kgs 23:22–23.

Josiah went out to meet him. ²¹Neco sent messengers to him, saying: "What quarrel is between us, king of Judah? I have not come against you this day, for my war is with another kingdom, and God has told me to hasten. Do not interfere with God who is with me; let him not destroy you." ²²But Josiah would not withdraw from him, for he was seeking a pretext to fight with him. Therefore he would not listen to the words of Neco that came from the mouth of God, but went out to fight in the plain of Megiddo. ²³Then the archers shot King Josiah, who said to his servants, "Take me away, I am seriously wounded."ʲ ²⁴His servants took him from his own chariot, placed him in the one he had in reserve, and brought him to Jerusalem, where he died. He was buried in the tombs of his ancestors, and all Judah and Jerusalem mourned him. ²⁵Jeremiah also composed a lamentation for Josiah, which is recited to this day by all the male and female singers in their lamentations for Josiah. These have been made an ordinance for Israel, and can be found written in the Lamentations.*

²⁶ᵏThe rest of the acts of Josiah, his good deeds in accord with what is written in the law of the Lord, ²⁷and his words, first and last, are recorded in the book of the kings of Israel and Judah.

## CHAPTER 36

**Jehoahaz.** ¹ˡThe people of the land took Jehoahaz, son of Josiah, and made him king in Jerusalem to succeed his father. ²Jehoahaz was twenty-three years old when he became king, and he reigned three months in Jerusalem. ³The king of Egypt deposed him in Jerusalem and fined the land one hundred talents of silver and a talent of gold. ⁴Then the king of Egypt made Eliakim, the brother of Jehoahaz, king over Judah and Jerusalem, changing his name to Jehoiakim. Neco took Jehoahaz his brother away and brought him to Egypt.

**Jehoiakim.** ⁵Jehoiakim was twenty-five years old when he became king, and he reigned eleven years in Jerusalem. He did what was evil in the sight of the Lord, his God.ᵐ ⁶ⁿNebuchadnezzar, king of Babylon, attacked and bound him in chains to take him to Babylon.† ⁷Nebuchadnezzar also carried away to Babylon some of the vessels of the house of the Lord and put

them in his palace in Babylon. ⁸The rest of the acts of Jehoiakim, the abominable things that he did, and what therefore happened to him, are recorded in the book of the kings of Israel and Judah. His son Jehoiachin succeeded him as king.ᵒ

**Jehoiachin.** ⁹Jehoiachin was eighteen years old when he became king, and he reigned three months and ten days in Jerusalem. He did what was evil in the Lord's sight.ᵖ ¹⁰At the turn of the year, King Nebuchadnezzar sent for him and had him brought to Babylon, along with precious vessels from the house of the Lord. He made his brother Zedekiah‡ king over Judah and Jerusalem.�q

**Zedekiah.** ¹¹Zedekiah was twenty-one years old when he became king, and he reigned eleven years in Jerusalem.ʳ ¹²He did what was evil in the sight of the Lord, his God, and he did not humble himself before Jeremiah the prophet, who spoke for the Lord.ˢ ¹³He also rebelled against King Nebuchadnezzar, who had made him swear by God. He became stiff-necked and hardened his heart rather than return to the Lord, the God of Israel.ᵗ ¹⁴Likewise all the princes of Judah, the priests, and the people added treachery to treachery, practicing all the abominations of the nations and defiling the Lord's house which he had consecrated in Jerusalem.

**The Fall of Judah.** ¹⁵Early and often the Lord, the God of their ancestors, sent his messengers to them, for he had compassion on his people and his dwelling place.ᵘ ¹⁶But they mocked God's messengers, despised his words, and scoffed at his prophets, until the Lord's anger against his people blazed up beyond remedy.ᵛ ¹⁷Then he brought up against them the king of the Chaldeans, who killed their young men with the sword in their own sanctuary, with compassion for neither young men nor young women, neither the old nor the infirm; all of them he delivered into his power.ʷ ¹⁸All the utensils of the house of God, large and small, the treasures of the Lord's house, and the treasures of the king and his princes, all these he brought to Babylon.ˣ ¹⁹They burnt the house of God, tore down the walls of Jerusalem, burnt down all its palaces, and destroyed all its precious objects.ʸ ²⁰Those who escaped the sword he carried captive to Babylon, where they became servants to him and his sons until the Persian kingdom came to power. ²¹All this was to fulfill the word

---

*[35:25] There is no mention of such a lamentation for Josiah composed by Jeremiah in either 2 Kings or Jeremiah; but see note on Zec 12:11. **Lamentations:** probably a reference to the Book of Lamentations.

†[36:6] **Nebuchadnezzar . . . bound him in chains to take him to Babylon:** the Chronicler does not state that Jehoiakim was actually taken to Babylon. According to 2 Kgs 24:1–6, Jehoiakim revolted after being Nebuchadnezzar's vassal for three years; he died in Jerusalem before the city surrendered to the Babylonians. Dn 1:1–2, apparently based on 2 Chr 36:6–7, does speak of Jehoiakim's deportation to Babylon.

‡[36:10] **His brother Zedekiah:** Zedekiah was actually the brother of Jehoiakim and the uncle of Jehoiachin (2 Kgs 24:17; Jer 37:1), though scarcely older than his nephew (2 Kgs 24:8, 18; 2 Chr 36:9, 11).

j. [35:23] 2 Chr 18:33–34.   k. [35:26] 2 Kgs 23:28.   l. [36:1–4] 2 Kgs 23:30–34; 1 Chr 3:15–16.   m. [36:5] 2 Kgs 23:36–37; Jer 22:18–19.   n. [36:6] 2 Kgs 24:1–2.

o. [36:8] 2 Kgs 24:5.   p. [36:9] 2 Kgs 24:8–9.   q. [36:10] 2 Kgs 24:10–17.   r. [36:11] 2 Kgs 24:18–19; Jer 52:1.   s. [36:12] Jer 37:1–2.   t. [36:13] 2 Kgs 24:20; Jer 52:4; Ez 17:13–16.   u. [36:15] Jer 7:25; Heb 1:1.   v. [36:16] Mt 23:34–37.   w. [36:17] Lam 1:15; 5:11–14.   x. [36:18] 2 Kgs 25:14–15.   y. [36:19] 2 Kgs 25:9–10; Lam 2:8.

of the LORD spoken by Jeremiah: Until the land has retrieved its lost sabbaths, during all the time it lies waste it shall have rest while seventy years are fulfilled.

**Decree of Cyrus.** [22]*In the first year of Cyrus, king of Persia, in order to realize the word of the LORD spoken by Jeremiah, the LORD roused the spirit of Cyrus, King of Persia, to spread this proclamation throughout his kingdom, both by word of mouth and in writing: [23]z"Thus says Cyrus, king of Persia: The LORD, the God of heaven, has given to me all the kingdoms of the earth. He has also charged me to build him a house in Jerusalem, which is in Judah. All among you, therefore, who belong to his people, may their God be with them; let them go up."

---

*[36:22–23] These verses are identical with those of Ezr 1:1–3a and were to prevent the work from ending on a note of doom.

z. [36:22] Ezr 1:1–4.

# THE BOOK OF
# EZRA

The last four books of the Hebrew canon are Ezra, Nehemiah, and 1 and 2 Chronicles, in that order. At one time, however, Ezra and Nehemiah followed 1 and 2 Chronicles and were generally considered to be the work of one and the same author known as "the Chronicler." In recent years, however, the question of the authorship of Ezra and Nehemiah is seen to be more complex. While some scholars still maintain unity of authorship, others prefer to speak of the influence of a "Chronistic school" on the formation of Ezra-Nehemiah as a single book. The treatment of Ezra-Nehemiah as a single book by the earliest editors was undoubtedly due to the fact that in ancient times the two books were put under the one name, Ezra. The combined work Ezra-Nehemiah is our most important literary source for the formation of the Jewish religious community in the province of Judah after the Babylonian exile. This is known as the period of the Restoration, and the two men most responsible for the reorganization of Jewish life at this time were Ezra and Nehemiah.

In the present state of the Ezra-Nehemiah text, there are several dislocations of large sections so that the chronological or logical sequence is disrupted. The major instance is Ezra's public reading of the law in Neh 8; others will be pointed out in the footnotes. Since arguments in favor of the chronological priority of Nehemiah to Ezra are indecisive, we accept the order in the text according to which Ezra's activity preceded that of Nehemiah.

What is known of Ezra and his work is derived almost exclusively from Ezr 7–10 (the "Ezra Memoirs") and Neh 8–9. Strictly speaking, the term "Ezra Memoirs" should be used only of that section in which Ezra speaks in the first person, i.e., Ezr 7:27–9:15. Compare the "Nehemiah Memoirs" in Neh 1:1–7:72a; 11:1, 2; 12:27–43; 13:4–31. The author combined this material with other sources at his disposal. The personality of Ezra is not so well-known as that of Nehemiah. Ben Sira, in his praise of the fathers (Sir 44–49), omits mention of Ezra, perhaps for polemical reasons. The genealogy of Ezra (7:1–5) traces his priesthood back to Aaron, brother of Moses. This was the accepted way of establishing the legality of one's priestly office. He is also called a scribe, well-versed in the law of Moses (7:6), indicating Ezra's dedication to the study of the Torah, which he sought to make the basic rule of life in the restored community. It was in religious and cultic reform rather than in political affairs that Ezra made his mark as a postexilic leader. Jewish tradition holds him in great esteem. The apocryphal 2 Esdras, sometimes included as an appendix to the Vulgate, where it is known as 4 Esdras, transforms him into a prophet and visionary. The Talmud regards him as a second Moses, claiming that the Torah would have been given to Israel through Ezra had not Moses preceded him.

Ezra is sometimes accused of having been a legalist who gave excessive attention to the letter of the law. His work, however, should be seen and judged within a specific historical context. He gave to his people a cohesion and spiritual unity which helped to prevent the disintegration of the small Jewish community settled in the province of Judah. Had it not been for the intransigence of Ezra and of those who adopted his ideal, it is doubtful that Judaism would have so effectively resisted Hellenism in later centuries. Ezra set the tone of the postexilic community, and it was characterized by fidelity to the Torah, Judaism's authentic way of life. It is in this light that we can judge most fairly the work of Ezra during the Restoration.

The Book of Ezra is divided as follows:

I. The Return from Exile (1:1–6:22)
II. The Work of Ezra (7:1–10:44)

The following list of the kings of Persia, with the dates of their reigns, will be useful for dating the events mentioned in Ezra-Nehemiah:

| Cyrus | 539–530 B.C. |
| Cambyses | 530–522 B.C. |
| Darius I | 522–486 B.C. |
| Xerxes I | 486–465 B.C. |
| Artaxerxes I | 465–424 B.C. |
| Darius II | 423–404 B.C. |
| Artaxerxes II | 404–358 B.C. |
| Artaxerxes III | 358–337 B.C. |
| End of the Persian Empire (Defeat of Darius III) | 331 B.C. |

## I. THE RETURN FROM EXILE

### CHAPTER 1

**The Decree of Cyrus.** [1a]In the first year of Cyrus,* king of Persia, in order to fulfill the word of the LORD spoken by Jeremiah, the LORD stirred up the spirit of Cyrus king of Persia to issue a proclamation throughout his entire kingdom, both by word of mouth and in writing: [2]"Thus says Cyrus, king of Persia: 'All the kingdoms of the earth the LORD, the God of heaven,† has given to me, and he has charged me to build him a house in Jerusalem, which is in Judah. [3]Those among you who belong to any part of his people, may their God be with them! Let them go up to Jerusalem in Judah to build the house of the LORD the God of Israel, that is, the God who is in Jerusalem. [4]Let all those who have survived, in whatever place they may have lived, be assisted by the people of that place with silver, gold, goods, and livestock, together with voluntary offerings for the house of God in Jerusalem.'"

[5]Then the heads of ancestral houses‡ of Judah and Benjamin and the priests and Levites—everyone, that is, whose spirit had been stirred up by God—prepared to go up to build the house of the LORD in Jerusalem. [6b]All their neighbors gave them help in every way, with silver, gold, goods, livestock, and many precious gifts, besides all their voluntary offerings. [7c]King Cyrus, too, had the vessels of the house of the LORD brought forth that Nebuchadnezzar had taken from Jerusalem and placed in the house of his god. [8]Cyrus, king of Persia, had them brought forth by the treasurer Mithredath, who counted them out to Sheshbazzar, prince of Judah.§ [9]This was the inventory: baskets of goldware, thirty; baskets of silverware, one thousand and twenty-nine; [10]golden bowls, thirty; silver bowls, four hundred and ten; other vessels, one thousand. [11]Total of the gold and silver vessels: five thousand four hundred.¶ All these Sheshbazzar took with him when the exiles were brought up from Babylon to Jerusalem.

### CHAPTER 2

**A Census of the Returned Exiles.** [1**d]These are the inhabitants of the province who returned from the captivity of the exiles, whom Nebuchadnezzar, king of Babylon, had carried away to Babylon, and who came back to Jerusalem and Judah, to their various cities [2](those who returned with Zerubbabel, Jeshua, Nehemiah,

---

*[1:1] **In the first year of Cyrus**: the first regnal year of Cyrus was 539 B.C., but his first year as ruler of Babylon, after the conquest of that city, was 538 B.C., the year in which he issued an edict, replicated on the famous Cyrus cylinder, permitting the repatriation of peoples deported by the Babylonians.

†[1:2] **The God of heaven**: this title, used as in 7:12, 21, 23, corresponds to a title of the Zoroastrian supreme deity Ahura Mazda, though it is not certain that Cyrus was a Zoroastrian.

‡[1:5] **Heads of ancestral houses**: the ancestral house was the basic organizational unit of the postexilic community, consisting of an extended kinship group claiming descent from a common ancestor. The patriarchs of these units played an important role in civic government.

a. [1:1] Ezr 6:3–5; 2 Chr 36:22–23; Jer 25:11–12; 29:10; Zec 1:12.

§[1:8] **Sheshbazzar, prince of Judah**: often identified with Shenassar, fourth son of Jehoiachin, king of Judah, exiled in 598 B.C. (see 1 Chr 3:17–18), and therefore the uncle of Zerubbabel (Ezr 3:2–4). This identification is uncertain.

¶[1:11] **Five thousand four hundred**: either this figure or the figures given for one or more of the items listed have been corrupted in the transmission of the text.

**[2:1–67] As it now stands, this list, which also appears at Neh 7:6–72, is an expanded form of lists of Babylonian repatriates from the sixth century B.C. It served to establish membership in the reconstituted Temple community; civic status and perhaps also title to property depended on this membership.

b. [1:6] Ex 3:21–22; 11:2; 12:35.   c. [1:7] 2 Kgs 25:14–15.   d. [2:1] Neh 7:6–72.

Seraiah, Reelaiah, Mordecai, Bilshan, Mispar, Bigvai, Rehum, and Baanah):

The census of the people of Israel: ³descendants of Parosh, two thousand one hundred and seventy-two; ⁴descendants of Shephatiah, three hundred and seventy-two; ⁵descendants of Arah, seven hundred and seventy-five; ⁶descendants of Pahath-moab, who were descendants of Jeshua and Joab, two thousand eight hundred and twelve; ⁷descendants of Elam, one thousand two hundred and fifty-four; ⁸descendants of Zattu, nine hundred and forty-five; ⁹descendants of Zaccai, seven hundred and sixty; ¹⁰descendants of Bani, six hundred and forty-two; ¹¹descendants of Bebai, six hundred and twenty-three; ¹²descendants of Azgad, one thousand two hundred and twenty-two; ¹³descendants of Adonikam, six hundred and sixty-six; ¹⁴descendants of Bigvai, two thousand and fifty-six; ¹⁵descendants of Adin, four hundred and fifty-four; ¹⁶descendants of Ater, who were descendants of Hezekiah, ninety-eight; ¹⁷descendants of Bezai, three hundred and twenty-three; ¹⁸descendants of Jorah, one hundred and twelve; ¹⁹descendants of Hashum, two hundred and twenty-three; ²⁰descendants of Gibeon, ninety-five; ²¹descendants of Bethlehem, one hundred and twenty-three; ²²people of Netophah, fifty-six; ²³people of Anathoth, one hundred and twenty-eight; ²⁴people of Beth-azmaveth, forty-two; ²⁵people of Kiriath-jearim, Chephirah, and Beeroth, seven hundred and forty-three; ²⁶people of Ramah and Geba, six hundred and twenty-one; ²⁷people of Michmas, one hundred and twenty-two; ²⁸people of Bethel and Ai, two hundred and twenty-three; ²⁹descendants of Nebo, fifty-two; ³⁰descendants of Magbish, one hundred and fifty-six; ³¹descendants of the other Elam, one thousand two hundred and fifty-four; ³²descendants of Harim, three hundred and twenty; ³³descendants of Lod, Hadid, and Ono, seven hundred and twenty-five; ³⁴descendants of Jericho, three hundred and forty-five; ³⁵descendants of Senaah, three thousand six hundred and thirty.

³⁶The priests: descendants of Jedaiah, of the house of Jeshua, nine hundred and seventy-three; ³⁷descendants of Immer, one thousand and fifty-two; ³⁸descendants of Pashhur, one thousand two hundred and forty-seven; ³⁹descendants of Harim, one thousand and seventeen.

⁴⁰ᵉThe Levites: descendants of Jeshua and Kadmiel, of the descendants of Hodaviah, seventy-four.

⁴¹The singers:* descendants of Asaph, one hundred and twenty-eight.

⁴²The gatekeepers:† descendants of Shallum, descendants of Ater, descendants of Talmon, descendants of Akkub, descendants of Hatita, descendants of Shobai, one hundred and thirty-nine in all.

⁴³The temple servants: descendants of Ziha, descendants of Hasupha, descendants of Tabbaoth, ⁴⁴descendants of Keros, descendants of Siaha, descendants of Padon, ⁴⁵descendants of Lebanah, descendants of Hagabah, descendants of Akkub, ⁴⁶descendants of Hagab, descendants of Shamlai, descendants of Hanan, ⁴⁷descendants of Giddel, descendants of Gahar, descendants of Reaiah, ⁴⁸descendants of Rezin, descendants of Nekoda, descendants of Gazzam, ⁴⁹descendants of Uzza, descendants of Paseah, descendants of Besai, ⁵⁰descendants of Asnah, descendants of the Meunites, descendants of the Nephusites, ⁵¹descendants of Bakbuk, descendants of Hakupha, descendants of Harhur, ⁵²descendants of Bazluth, descendants of Mehida, descendants of Harsha, ⁵³descendants of Barkos, descendants of Sisera, descendants of Temah, ⁵⁴descendants of Neziah, descendants of Hatipha.

⁵⁵Descendants of Solomon's servants: descendants of Sotai, descendants of Hassophereth, descendants of Peruda, ⁵⁶descendants of Jaalah, descendants of Darkon, descendants of Giddel, ⁵⁷descendants of Shephatiah, descendants of Hattil, descendants of Pochereth-hazzebaim, descendants of Ami. ⁵⁸The total of the temple servants together with the descendants of Solomon's servants was three hundred and ninety-two.

⁵⁹The following who returned from Telmelah, Tel-harsha, Cherub, Addan, and Immer were unable to prove that their ancestral houses and their descent were Israelite: ⁶⁰descendants of Delaiah, descendants of Tobiah, descendants of Nekoda, six hundred and fifty-two. ⁶¹ᶠAlso, of the priests: descendants of Habaiah, descendants of Hakkoz, descendants of Barzillai (he had married one of the daughters of Barzillai the Gileadite and was named after him). ⁶²These searched their family records, but their names could not be found there, and they were excluded from the priesthood. ⁶³ᵍThe governor‡ ordered them not to partake of the most holy foods until there should be a priest to consult the Urim and Thummim.

---

*[2:41] **The singers**: the term covers the composition as well as the rendition of liturgical music. Since they are listed as distinct from Levites (2:40), they had not yet attained levitical status, as in Chronicles (e.g., 1 Chr 9:33–34; 23:3–6).

e. [2:40] Neh 12:23.

†[2:42] **The gatekeepers**: their principal task was to protect the ritual purity of the temple area (e.g., 2 Chr 23:19). The author assumes that they were established by David as a distinct levitical category (1 Chr 15:18; 26:1–19).

‡[2:63] **The governor**: the honorific title was also held by Nehemiah (Neh 8:9; 10:2). The identity of the governor is unknown; both Sheshbazzar (Ezr 5:14) and Zerubbabel (Hg 1:1, 14; 2:2, 21) are identified as governors of Judah in the early Persian period. Mal 1:8 refers to an unnamed governor, and the names of other occupants of the office (Yehoezer, Ahzai, Elnathan) occur on seal impressions, though their date is uncertain. **Urim and Thummim**: cf. Ex 28:30.

f. [2:61] 2 Sm 17:27; 19:32–33; 1 Kgs 2:7.   g. [2:63] Nm 27:21; Dt 33:8; 1 Sm 14:41–42; 28:6.

[64]The entire assembly taken together came to forty-two thousand three hundred and sixty, [65]not counting their male and female servants, who numbered seven thousand three hundred and thirty-seven. They also had two hundred male and female singers. [66]Their horses numbered seven hundred and thirty-six, their mules two hundred and forty-five, [67]their camels four hundred and thirty-five, their donkeys six thousand seven hundred and twenty.

[68]When they arrived at the house of the LORD in Jerusalem, some of the heads of ancestral houses made voluntary offerings for the house of God, to rebuild it in its place. [69]According to their means they contributed to the treasury for the temple service: sixty-one thousand drachmas of gold, five thousand minas of silver, and one hundred priestly robes. [70]The priests, the Levites, and some of the people took up residence in Jerusalem; the singers, the gatekeepers, and the temple servants settled in their cities. Thus all the Israelites settled in their cities.

## CHAPTER 3

**Restoration of Worship.** [1h]Now when the seventh month* came, after the Israelites had settled in their cities, the people gathered as one in Jerusalem. [2]Then Jeshua, son of Jozadak, together with his kinsmen the priests, and Zerubbabel, son of Shealtiel, together with his kinsmen, began building the altar of the God of Israel in order to offer on it the burnt offerings prescribed in the law of Moses, the man of God. [3i]They set the altar on its foundations, for they lived in fear of the peoples of the lands,† and offered burnt offerings to the LORD on it, both morning and evening. [4j]They also kept the feast of Booths in the manner prescribed, and they offered the daily burnt offerings in the proper number required for each day. [5]Thereafter they offered regular burnt offerings, the sacrifices prescribed for the new moons and all the festivals sacred to the LORD, and those which anyone might bring as a voluntary offering to the LORD. **Laying the Foundations of the Temple.** [6]From the first day of the seventh month they reinstituted the burnt offering to the LORD, though

the foundation of the LORD's temple had not yet been laid. [7k]Then they hired stonecutters and carpenters, and sent food and drink and oil to the Sidonians and Tyrians that they might ship cedar trees from the Lebanon to the port of Joppa, as Cyrus, king of Persia, had authorized. [8]In the year after their coming to the house of God in Jerusalem, in the second month, Zerubbabel, son of Shealtiel, and Jeshua, son of Jozadak, together with the rest of their kinsmen, the priests and Levites and all who had come from the captivity to Jerusalem, began by appointing the Levites twenty years of age and over to supervise the work on the house of the LORD. [9]Jeshua and his sons and kinsmen, with Kadmiel and Binnui, son of Hodaviah, and their sons and their kindred, the Levites, together undertook to supervise those who were engaged in the work on the house of God. [10l]While the builders were laying the foundation of the LORD's temple, the priests in their vestments were stationed with trumpets and the Levites, sons of Asaph, with cymbals to praise the LORD in the manner laid down by David, king of Israel. [11m]They alternated in songs of praise and thanksgiving to the LORD, "for he is good, for his love for Israel endures forever";‡ and all the people raised a great shout of joy, praising the LORD because the foundation of the LORD's house had been laid. [12n]Many of the priests, Levites, and heads of ancestral houses, who were old enough to have seen the former house, cried out in sorrow as they watched the foundation of the present house being laid. Many others, however, lifted up their voices in shouts of joy. [13]No one could distinguish the sound of the joyful shouting from the sound of those who were weeping; for the people raised a mighty clamor which was heard far away.

## CHAPTER 4

**Outside Interference.** [1]When the enemies of Judah and Benjamin heard that the exiles were building a temple for the LORD, the God of Israel, [2o]they approached Zerubbabel and the heads of ancestral houses and said to them, "Let us build with you, for we seek your God just as you do, and we have sacrificed to him since the days of Esarhaddon, king of Assyria,§ who brought us here." [3]But Zerubbabel, Jeshua, and the rest of the heads of ancestral houses of

---

*[3:1–2] **The seventh month:** Tishri (September–October), apparently of the first year of the return (538 B.C.), followed by events in the second year (v. 8). In that case it was Sheshbazzar who laid the foundations of the Temple (5:16), and it was in the second year of Darius I (520 B.C.) that Jeshua and Zerubbabel resumed work on the Temple that had been temporarily interrupted (Ezr 4:24–5:1; Hg 1:1; 2:1). The author, or a later editor, has set the construction and dedication of the Temple under Darius I back into the earliest period of the return. Shealtiel was the oldest son of King Jehoiachin (1 Chr 3:17–19); Zerubbabel was therefore Jehoiachin's grandson; see note on Ezr 1:8.

†[3:3] **Peoples of the lands:** referring either to those who had never left Judah or to neighboring peoples—Edomites, Arabs, inhabitants of Samaria—who opposed those who returned.

‡[3:11] **"For he is good . . . forever":** a refrain occurring frequently in liturgies of ancient Israel (cf. Ps 136).

§[4:2] **Esarhaddon, king of Assyria:** the enemies represent themselves as descendants of foreigners forcibly resettled in the Samaria region after the incorporation of the Northern Kingdom into the Assyrian empire (722 B.C.; cf. 2 Kgs 17:24). We have no record of a settlement under Esarhaddon (681–669 B.C.); the Aramaic source (Ezr 4:10) refers to a different resettlement under Osnappar/Ashurbanipal (668–627 B.C.).

---

h. [3:1] Neh 7:7–78.    i. [3:3] Dt 9:25; 1 Kgs 8:64.    j. [3:4] Ex 23:16; Nm 28:3–8; Dt 16:13–15.

k. [3:7] 1 Chr 22:4; 2 Chr 2:9.    l. [3:10] Ezr 2:41.    m. [3:11] 1 Chr 16:34; 2 Chr 5:13; 7:3; Ps 106:1; 136:1; Jer 33:11.    n. [3:12] Hg 2:3.    o. [4:2] Ezr 4:10.

Israel answered them, "It is not your responsibility to build with us a house for our God, but we alone must build it for the LORD, the God of Israel, as Cyrus king of Persia has commanded us." ⁴Thereupon the local inhabitants* discouraged the people of Judah and frightened them off from building. ⁵They also bribed counselors to work against them and to frustrate their plans during all the years of Cyrus, king of Persia, and even into the reign of Darius,† king of Persia.

**Later Hostility.** ⁶In the reign of Ahasuerus,‡ at the beginning of his reign, they prepared a written accusation against the inhabitants of Judah and Jerusalem.

⁷§Again, in the time of Artaxerxes, Tabeel and the rest of his fellow officials, in concert with Mithredath, wrote to Artaxerxes, king of Persia. The document was written in Aramaic and was accompanied by a translation.

⁸¶Then Rehum, the governor, and Shimshai, the scribe, wrote the following letter against Jerusalem to King Artaxerxes: ⁹"Rehum, the governor, Shimshai, the scribe, and their fellow officials, judges, legates, and agents from among the Persians, Urukians, Babylonians, Susians (that is, Elamites), ¹⁰and the other peoples whom the great and illustrious Osnappar** transported and settled in the city of Samaria and elsewhere in the province West-of-Euphrates, as follows. . . ." ¹¹This is a copy of the letter that they sent to him:

"To King Artaxerxes, your servants, the men of West-of-Euphrates, as follows: ¹²Let it be known to the king that the Jews who came up from you to us have arrived at Jerusalem and are now rebuilding this rebellious and evil city. They are completing its walls, and the foundations have already been laid. ¹³Now let it be known to the king that if this city is rebuilt and its walls completed, they will no longer pay taxes, tributes, or tolls; eventually the throne will be harmed. ¹⁴Now, since we eat the salt of the palace†† and it is not fitting for us to look on while the king is being dishonored, we have sent this message to inform the king, ¹⁵so that

inquiry may be made in the historical records of your fathers. In the historical records you will discover and verify that this is a rebellious city, harmful to kings and provinces; its people have been acting seditiously there since ancient times. That is why this city was destroyed. ¹⁶We therefore inform the king, that if this city is rebuilt and its walls completed again, you will thereupon not have a portion in the province West-of-Euphrates."

¹⁷The king sent this answer: "To Rehum, the governor, Shimshai, the scribe, and their fellow officials living in Samaria and elsewhere in the province West-of-Euphrates, greetings: ¹⁸The communication which you sent us has been read in translation in my presence. ¹⁹When at my command inquiry was made, it was verified that from ancient times this city has risen up against kings and that rebellion and sedition have been fostered there. ²⁰Powerful kings once ruled in Jerusalem who controlled all West-of-Euphrates, and taxes, tributes, and tolls were paid to them. ²¹Give orders, therefore, to stop these men. This city may not be rebuilt until a further decree has been issued by me. ²²Take care that you do not neglect this matter. Why should evil increase to harm the throne?"

²³ᵖAs soon as a copy of King Artaxerxes' letter had been read before Rehum, the governor, Shimshai, the scribe, and their fellow officials, they immediately went to the Jews in Jerusalem and stopped their work by force of arms. ²⁴As a result, work on the house of God in Jerusalem ceased. This interruption lasted until the second year of the reign of Darius,‡‡ king of Persia.

## CHAPTER 5

**The Work Resumed Under Darius; Further Problems.** ¹ᑫThen the prophets Haggai and Zechariah,§§ son of Iddo, began to prophesy to the Jews in Judah and Jerusalem in the name of the God of Israel. ²Thereupon Zerubbabel, son of Shealtiel, and Jeshua, son of Jozadak, began again to build the house of God in Jerusalem, with the prophets of God giving them support. ³At that time Tattenai, governor of West-of-Euphrates, came to them, along with Shethar-bozenai, and their fellow officials, and asked of them: "Who issued the decree for you to build this house and complete this edifice? ⁴What are the names of the men who are building this structure?" ⁵But the eye of their God was upon the elders of the Jews, and they were not delayed

---

*[4:4] **Local inhabitants:** lit., "the people of the land."

†[4:5] **Darius:** Darius I (522–486 B.C.). The Temple-building narrative continues in v. 24. In between (vv. 6–23) is a series of notices about opposition to the returned exiles voiced at the Persian court in the early fifth century B.C., after the Temple had been built.

‡[4:6] **Ahasuerus:** Xerxes (486–465 B.C.); the early years of his reign were occupied with revolts in several parts of the empire.

§[4:7] There is a note placed in the original text to indicate a change from Hebrew to Aramaic. The Aramaic section beginning here ends with 6:18; in 7:12–26 a royal letter is cited in Aramaic.

¶[4:8–23] The letter to Artaxerxes I (465–424 B.C.) deals with the building of the fortification walls of Jerusalem, not the building of the Temple. The interruption of the work on the city wall some time before 445 B.C. was the occasion for the arrival of Nehemiah in the province (Neh 1:1–4; 2:1–5).

**[4:10] **Osnappar:** probably Ashurbanipal; see note on 4:2.

††[4:14] **Eat the salt of the palace:** the idiom signifies sharing in the benefits of the palace.

‡‡[4:24] **The second year . . . of Darius:** that is, 520 B.C.; it marks the beginning of the successful restoration of the Temple, completed within the five years following (5:1–6:18).

§§[5:1] **The prophets Haggai and Zechariah:** Haggai and Zechariah were active during the early years of Darius I. They decreed the rebuilding of the Temple and the messianic expectations associated with the Davidic descendant Zerubbabel.

p. [4:23] Neh 1:3.   q. [5:1] Hg 1:14–2:9; Zec 4:9.

during the time a report went to Darius and a written order came back concerning this matter.

⁶A copy of the letter which Tattenai, governor of West-of-Euphrates, along with Shethar-bozenai and their fellow officials from West-of-Euphrates, sent to King Darius; ⁷they sent him a report in which was written the following:

"To King Darius, all good wishes! ⁸Let it be known to the king that we have visited the province of Judah and the house of the great God: it is being rebuilt of cut stone and the walls are being reinforced with timber; the work is being carried out diligently, prospering under their hands. ⁹We then questioned the elders, addressing to them the following words: 'Who issued the decree for you to build this house and complete this edifice?' ¹⁰We also asked them their names, in order to give you a list of the men who are their leaders. ¹¹This was their answer to us: 'We are the servants of the God of heaven and earth, and we are rebuilding the house built here many years ago, which a great king of Israel built and completed. ¹²But because our ancestors provoked the wrath of the God of heaven, he delivered them into the power of the Chaldean, Nebuchadnezzar, king of Babylon, who destroyed this house and exiled the people to Babylon. ¹³ʳHowever, in the first year of Cyrus, king of Babylon, King Cyrus issued a decree for the rebuilding of this house of God. ¹⁴Moreover, the gold and silver vessels of the house of God, which Nebuchadnezzar had taken from the temple in Jerusalem and carried off to the temple in Babylon, King Cyrus ordered to be removed from the temple in Babylon, and they were given to a certain Sheshbazzar, whom he named governor. ¹⁵He commanded him: Take these vessels and deposit them in the temple of Jerusalem, and let the house of God be rebuilt on its former site. ¹⁶Then this same Sheshbazzar came and laid the foundations of the house of God in Jerusalem. Since that time to the present the building has been going on, and is not yet completed.' ¹⁷Now, if it please the king, let a search be made in the royal archives of Babylon to discover whether a decree really was issued by King Cyrus for the rebuilding of this house of God in Jerusalem. And may the king's decision in this matter be communicated to us."

## CHAPTER 6

**The Decree of Darius.** ¹ˢThereupon King Darius issued an order to search the archives in which the treasures were stored in Babylon. ²However, a scroll was found in Ecbatana, the stronghold

in the province of Media, containing the following text: "Memorandum. ³In the first year of his reign, King Cyrus issued a decree: With regard to the house of God in Jerusalem: the house is to be rebuilt as a place for offering sacrifices and bringing burnt offerings. Its height is to be sixty cubits and its width sixty cubits. ⁴It shall have three courses of cut stone for each one of timber. The costs are to be borne by the royal house. ⁵Also, let the gold and silver vessels of the house of God which Nebuchadnezzar took from the temple of Jerusalem and brought to Babylon be sent back; let them be returned to their place in the temple of Jerusalem and deposited in the house of God."

⁶"Now, therefore, Tattenai, governor of West-of-Euphrates, and Shethar-bozenai, and you, their fellow officials in West-of-Euphrates, stay away from there. ⁷Let the governor and the elders of the Jews continue the work on that house of God; they are to rebuild it on its former site. ⁸I also issue this decree concerning your dealing with these elders of the Jews in the rebuilding of that house of God: Let these men be repaid for their expenses, in full and without delay from the royal revenue, deriving from the taxes of West-of-Euphrates, so that the work not be interrupted. ⁹Whatever else is required—young bulls, rams, and lambs for burnt offerings to the God of heaven, wheat, salt, wine, and oil, according to the requirements of the priests who are in Jerusalem—let that be delivered to them day by day without fail, ¹⁰that they may continue to offer sacrifices of pleasing odor to the God of heaven and pray for the life of the king and his sons. ¹¹I also issue this decree: if any man alters this edict, a beam is to be taken from his house, and he is to be lifted up and impaled on it; and his house is to be reduced to rubble for this offense. ¹²And may the God who causes his name to dwell there overthrow every king or people who may undertake to alter this decree or to destroy this house of God in Jerusalem. I, Darius, have issued this decree; let it be diligently executed."

**The Task Finally Completed.** ¹³Then Tattenai, the governor of West-of-Euphrates, and Shethar-bozenai, and their fellow officials carried out with all diligence the instructions King Darius had sent them. ¹⁴The elders of the Jews continued to make progress in the building, supported by the message of the prophets, Haggai and Zechariah, son of Iddo. They finished the building according to the command of the God of Israel and the decrees of Cyrus and Darius, and of Artaxerxes, king of Persia. ¹⁵They completed this house on the third day of the month Adar, in the sixth year of the reign of King Darius. ¹⁶The Israelites—priests, Levites, and the other returned exiles—celebrated the dedication of this house of God with joy. ¹⁷For the dedication of this house of God, they offered

---

*[6:1–2] Babylon was the capital city of the satrapy to which Judah belonged; it was therefore the natural place to look. The decree was discovered eventually, however, in Ecbatana (Hamadan), the former capital of the Medes and summer residence of the Persian kings. Cf. the Hebrew version of the decree (1:2–4).

r. [5:13] Ezr 1:1–5.   s. [6:2] Ezr 1:4–11.

one hundred bulls, two hundred rams, and four hundred lambs, together with twelve he-goats as a sin offering for all Israel, in keeping with the number of the tribes of Israel. [18]Finally, they set up the priests in their classes and the Levites in their divisions for the service of God in Jerusalem, as is prescribed in the book of Moses.

**The Passover.** [19]ʳThe returned exiles kept the Passover on the fourteenth day of the first month. [20]The Levites, every one of whom had purified himself for the occasion, sacrificed the Passover for all the exiles, for their colleagues the priests, and for themselves. [21]The Israelites who had returned from the exile and all those who had separated themselves from the uncleanness of the Gentiles in the land shared in it, seeking the LORD, the God of Israel. [22]ᵘThey joyfully kept the feast of Unleavened Bread for seven days, for the LORD had filled them with joy by making the king of Assyria* favorable to them, so that he gave them help in their work on the house of God, the God of Israel.

## II. THE WORK OF EZRA

### CHAPTER 7

**Ezra, Priest and Scribe.** [1]ᵛAfter these events, during the reign of Artaxerxes, king of Persia, Ezra, son of Seraiah, son of Azariah, son of Hilkiah, [2]son of Shallum, son of Zadok, son of Ahitub, [3]son of Amariah, son of Azariah, son of Meraioth, [4]son of Zerahiah, son of Uzzi, son of Bukki, [5]son of Abishua, son of Phinehas, son of Eleazar, son of Aaron, the high priest— [6]ʷthis Ezra came up from Babylon. He was a scribe, well-versed in the law of Moses given by the LORD, the God of Israel. The king granted him all that he requested, because the hand of the LORD, his God, was over him.

[7]Some of the Israelites and some priests, Levites, singers, gatekeepers, and temple servants also came up to Jerusalem in the seventh year of King Artaxerxes. [8]Ezra came to Jerusalem in the fifth month of that seventh year of the king. [9]On the first day of the first month he began the journey up from Babylon, and on the first day of the fifth month he arrived at Jerusalem, for the

favoring hand of his God was over him. [10]ˣEzra had set his heart on the study and practice of the law of the LORD and on teaching statutes and ordinances in Israel.

**The Decree of Artaxerxes.** [11]This is a copy of the rescript which King Artaxerxes gave to Ezra the priest-scribe, the scribe versed in matters concerning the LORD's commandments and statutes for Israel:

[12]ʸ"Artaxerxes, king of kings, to Ezra the priest, scribe of the law of the God of heaven, greetings! And now, [13]I have issued this decree, that anyone in my kingdom belonging to the people of Israel, its priests or Levites, who is willing to go up to Jerusalem with you, may go, [14]for you are the one sent by the king and his seven counselors to supervise Judah and Jerusalem with regard to the law of your God which is in your possession, [15]and to bring the silver and gold which the king and his counselors have freely contributed to the God of Israel, whose dwelling is in Jerusalem, [16]as well as all the silver and gold which you may receive throughout the province of Babylon, together with the voluntary offerings the people and priests freely contribute for the house of their God in Jerusalem. [17]Therefore, you must use this money with all diligence to buy bulls, rams, lambs, and the grain offerings and libations proper to these, and offer them on the altar of the house of your God in Jerusalem. [18]You and your kinsmen may do whatever seems best to you with the remainder of the silver and gold, as your God wills. [19]The vessels given to you for the service of the house of your God you are to deposit before the God of Jerusalem. [20]Whatever else you may be required to supply for the needs of the house of your God, you may draw from the royal treasury. [21]I, Artaxerxes the king, issue this decree to all the treasurers of West-of-Euphrates: Whatever Ezra the priest, scribe of the law of the God of heaven, requests of you, let it be done with all diligence, [22]within these limits: silver, one hundred talents; wheat, one hundred kors;‡ wine, one hundred baths; oil, one hundred baths; salt, without limit. [23]Let everything that is decreed by the God of heaven be carried out exactly for the house of the God of heaven, that wrath may not come upon the realm of the king and his sons. [24]We also inform you that it is not permitted to impose taxes, tributes, or tolls on any priest, Levite, singer, gatekeeper, temple servant, or any other servant of that house of God.

[25]ᶻ"As for you, Ezra, in accordance with the wisdom of your God§ which is in your possession,

---

*[6:22] **The king of Assyria:** "Assyria" is perhaps used in a broad sense for the Persian empire; or the editor may have in mind the account of Hezekiah's Passover which refers to those who had escaped the hand of the king of Assyria (2 Chr 30:6).

†[7:1-10] The editor's introduction to Ezra's autobiographical narrative. The context suggests the seventh year of Artaxerxes I, therefore, 458 B.C., as the date of Ezra's arrival in Jerusalem. The arguments often advanced for 398 B.C., the seventh year of Artaxerxes II, or less often for the thirty-seventh year of Artaxerxes I, that is, 428 B.C., are inconclusive. For Ezra's descent from Aaron, the editor has drawn selectively on 1 Chr 5:27-41. Seraiah, the chief priest executed by the Babylonians after the fall of Jerusalem (2 Kgs 25:18-21), cannot be Ezra's father in a literal sense, and Ezra was not himself high priest.

‡[7:22] **Kors:** see note on Ez 45:14; **baths:** see note on Is 5:10.

§[7:25] **The wisdom of your God:** with reference to the law (cf. Dt 4:6). The law in question was certainly not new, since it was assumed to be known by Jews in Judah and else-

---

t. [6:19] Ex 12:1-20; 2 Chr 30:14-27; 35:1-19.   u. [6:22] 2 Chr 30:6.   v. [7:1] 1 Chr 5:27-41.   w. [7:6] Ezr 7:28; 8:18; Neh 2:8, 18.

x. [7:10] Ps 119:45.   y. [7:12] Ezr 1:2-4.   z. [7:25] Dt 4:6; 2 Chr 17:7-9; Ps 37:30-31; 119:98.

appoint magistrates and judges to administer justice to all the people in West-of-Euphrates, to all, that is, who know the laws of your God. Instruct those who do not know these laws. ²⁶All who will not obey the law of your God and the law of the king, let judgment be executed upon them with all diligence, whether death, or corporal punishment, or confiscation of goods, or imprisonment."

**Ezra Prepares for the Journey.** ²⁷Blessed be the LORD, the God of our ancestors, who put it into the heart of the king thus to glorify the house of the LORD in Jerusalem, ²⁸ᵃand who let me find favor with the king, with his counselors, and with all the most influential royal officials. I therefore took courage and, with the hand of the LORD, my God, over me, I gathered together Israelite leaders to make the return journey with me.

## CHAPTER 8

**Ezra's Caravan.** ¹These are the heads of the ancestral houses and the genealogies of those who returned with me from Babylon during the reign of King Artaxerxes:

²Of the descendants of Phinehas, Gershon; of the descendants of Ithamar, Daniel; of the descendants of David, Hattush, ³son of Shecaniah; of the descendants of Parosh, Zechariah, and with him one hundred and fifty males were enrolled; ⁴of the descendants of Pahath-moab, Eliehoenai, son of Zerahiah, and with him two hundred males; ⁵of the descendants of Zattu, Shecaniah, son of Jahaziel, and with him three hundred males; ⁶of the descendants of Adin, Ebed, son of Jonathan, and with him fifty males; ⁷of the descendants of Elam, Jeshaiah, son of Athaliah, and with him seventy males; ⁸of the descendants of Shephatiah, Zebadiah, son of Michael, and with him eighty males; ⁹of the descendants of Joab, Obadiah, son of Jehiel, and with him two hundred and eighteen males; ¹⁰of the descendants of Bani, Shelomoth, son of Josiphiah, and with him one hundred and sixty males; ¹¹of the descendants of Bebai, Zechariah, son of Bebai, and with him twenty-eight males; ¹²of the descendants of Azgad, Johanan, son of Hakkatan, and with him one hundred and ten males; ¹³of the descendants of Adonikam, younger sons, whose names were Eliphelet, Jeiel, and Shemaiah, and with him sixty males; ¹⁴of the descendants of Bigvai, Uthai, son of Zakkur, and with him seventy males.

**Final Preparations for the Journey.** ¹⁵I assembled them by the river that flows toward Ahava,* where we camped for three days. There

I perceived that both laymen and priests were present, but I could not discover a single Levite. ¹⁶So I sent for discerning leaders, Eliezer, Ariel, Shemaiah, Jarib, Elnathan, Nathan, Zechariah, and Meshullam, ¹⁷with a command for Iddo, the leader in the place Casiphia, instructing them what to say to Iddo and his kinsmen, and to the temple servants in Casiphia, in order to procure for us ministers for the house of our God. ¹⁸ᵇSince the favoring hand of our God was over us, they sent to us a well-instructed man, one of the descendants of Mahli, son of Levi, son of Israel, namely Sherebiah, with his sons and kinsmen, eighteen men. ¹⁹They also sent us Hashabiah, and with him Jeshaiah, descendants of Merari, and their kinsmen and their sons, twenty men. ²⁰ᶜOf the temple servants, those whom David and the princes appointed to serve the Levites, there were two hundred and twenty. All these were enrolled by name.

²¹Then I proclaimed a fast, there by the river of Ahava, that we might humble ourselves before our God to seek from him a safe journey for ourselves, our children, and all our possessions. ²²ᵈFor I was ashamed to ask the king for troops and horsemen to protect us against enemies along the way, since we had said to the king, "The favoring hand of our God is over all who seek him, but his fierce anger is against all who forsake him." ²³So we fasted, seeking this from our God, and it was granted. ²⁴Next I selected twelve of the priestly leaders along with Sherebiah, Hashabiah, and ten of their kinsmen, ²⁵and I weighed out before them the silver and the gold and the vessels offered for the house of our God by the king, his counselors, his officials, and all the Israelites of that region. ²⁶I weighed out into their hands these amounts: silver, six hundred and fifty talents; silver vessels, one hundred; gold, one hundred talents; ²⁷twenty golden bowls valued at a thousand darics; two vases of excellent polished bronze, as precious as gold. ²⁸I addressed them in these words: "You are consecrated to the LORD, and the vessels are also consecrated; the silver and the gold are a voluntary offering to the LORD, the God of your ancestors. ²⁹Watch over them carefully until you weigh them out in Jerusalem in the presence of the chief priests and Levites and the leaders of ancestral houses of Israel, in the chambers of the house of the LORD." ³⁰The priests and the Levites then took over the silver, the gold, and the vessels that had been weighed out, to bring them to Jerusalem, to the house of our God.

**Arrival in Jerusalem.** ³¹We set out from the river of Ahava on the twelfth day of the first month to go to Jerusalem. The hand of our God remained over us, and he protected us from enemies and robbers along the way. ³²We arrived in Jerusalem, where we rested for three days. ³³On the fourth day, the silver, the gold, and the vessels

---

where. It corresponded to Pentateuchal law, though perhaps this had not yet been given in this final form.

*[8:15] **Ahava:** an unidentified location near Babylon; also the name of the river or canal on which it stood (vv. 21, 31). A location near water was dictated by ritual as well as practical reasons (cf. Ps 137:1; Ez 1:1, 3; 3:15).

---

a. [7:28] Ezr 7:6.                    b. [8:18] Ezr 7:6.   c. [8:20] Ezr 2:43.   d. [8:22] Neh 2:9.

were weighed out in the house of our God and given to the priest Meremoth, son of Uriah, with whom was Eleazar, son of Phinehas; they were assisted by the Levites Jozabad, son of Jeshua, and Noadiah, son of Binnui. ³⁴Everything was in order as to number and weight, and the total weight was registered. At that same time, ³⁵those who had returned from the captivity, the exiles, offered as burnt offerings to the God of Israel twelve bulls for all Israel, ninety-six rams, seventy-seven lambs, and twelve goats as sin offerings: all these as a burnt offering to the LORD. ³⁶*Finally, the orders of the king were presented to the king's satraps and to the governors in West-of-Euphrates, who gave their support to the people and to the house of God.

## CHAPTER 9

**The Crisis of Mixed Marriages.** ¹ᵉWhen these matters had been concluded, the leaders approached me with this report: "Neither the Israelite laymen nor the priests nor the Levites have kept themselves separate from the peoples of the lands and their abominations—Canaanites, Hittites, Perizzites, Jebusites, Ammonites, Moabites, Egyptians, and Amorites— ²for they have taken some of their daughters as wives for themselves and their sons, thus intermingling the holy seed with the peoples of the lands. Furthermore, the leaders and rulers have taken a prominent part in this apostasy!"

**Ezra's Reaction.** ³ᶠWhen I had heard this, I tore my cloak and my mantle, plucked hair from my head and beard, and sat there devastated. ⁴ᵍAround me gathered all who were in dread of the sentence of the God of Israel† on the apostasy of the exiles, while I remained devastated until the evening sacrifice. ⁵Then, at the time of the evening sacrifice, I rose in my wretchedness, and with cloak and mantle torn I fell on my knees, stretching out my hands to the LORD, my God.

**A Penitential Prayer.** ⁶ᵗʰI said: "My God, I am too ashamed and humiliated to raise my face to you, my God, for our wicked deeds are heaped up above our heads and our guilt reaches up to heaven. ⁷From the time of our ancestors even to this day our guilt has been great, and for our wicked deeds we have been delivered, we and

our kings and our priests, into the hands of the kings of foreign lands, to the sword, to captivity, to pillage, and to disgrace, as is the case today. ⁸ⁱAnd now, only a short time ago, mercy came to us from the LORD, our God, who left us a remnant and gave us a stake in his holy place; thus our God has brightened our eyes and given us relief in our slavery. ⁹ʲFor slaves we are, but in our slavery our God has not abandoned us; rather, he has turned the good will of the kings of Persia toward us. Thus he has given us new life to raise again the house of our God and restore its ruins, and has granted us a protective wall in Judah and Jerusalem. ¹⁰But now, our God, what can we say after all this? For we have abandoned your commandments, ¹¹ᵏwhich you gave through your servants the prophets: The land which you are entering to take as your possession is a land unclean with the filth of the peoples of the lands, with the abominations with which they have filled it from one end to the other by their uncleanness. ¹²ˡDo not, then, give your daughters to their sons in marriage, and do not take their daughters for your sons. Never promote their welfare and prosperity; thus you will grow strong, enjoy the produce of the land, and leave it as an inheritance to your children forever.

¹³After all that has come upon us for our evil deeds and our great guilt—though you, our God, have made less of our sinfulness than it deserved and have allowed us to survive as we do— ¹⁴shall we again violate your commandments by intermarrying with these abominable peoples? Would you not become so angered with us as to destroy us without remnant or survivor? ¹⁵LORD, God of Israel, you are just; yet we have been spared, the remnant we are today. Here we are before you in our sins. Because of all this, we can no longer stand in your presence."

## CHAPTER 10

**Response to the Crisis.** ¹While Ezra prayed and acknowledged their guilt, weeping and prostrate before the house of God, a very large assembly of Israelites gathered about him, men, women, and children; and the people wept profusely. ²Then Shecaniah, the son of Jehiel, one of the descendants of Elam, made this appeal to Ezra: "We have indeed betrayed our God by taking as wives foreign women of the peoples of the land. Yet in spite of this there still remains a hope for Israel. ³Let us therefore enter into a covenant before our God to dismiss all our foreign wives and the children born of them, in keeping with what you, my lord, advise, and those who are in dread of the commandments of our God. Let it be done according to the law! ⁴Rise, then, for this is your duty! We are with you, so have courage and act!"

---

* [8:36] The story of Ezra's mission is apparently continued from this point by Neh 7:72b–8:18, which may be read before Ezr 9:1.

† [9:4] **All who were in dread . . . God of Israel**: lit., "all who trembled"; these people are also mentioned at 10:3, and a similar designation occurs in Is 66:2, 5, a text more or less contemporary with this passage. The allusion may be to a distinct social group of rigorist tendencies who supported Ezra's marriage reform.

‡ [9:6–15] The prayer attributed to Ezra is a communal confession of sin, of a kind characteristic of the Second Temple period (cf. Neh 9:6–37; Dn 9:4–19; 1QS 1:4–2:1), but adapted to the present situation.

---

e. [9:1] Dt 7:1; Neh 9:2.    f. [9:3] Ps 119:136.    g. [9:4] Ezr 10:3; Is 66:2, 5.    h. [9:6] Neh 9:6–37; Ps 38:4; Dn 9:4–19.

i. [9:8] Is 4:3.    j. [9:9] Ps 106:46.    k. [9:11] Lv 18:24–25; Ez 36:17.    l. [9:12] Dt 7:3.

[5]Ezra stood and demanded an oath from the leaders of the priests, from the Levites and from all Israel that they would do as had been proposed; and they swore it. [6]Then Ezra left his place before the house of God and entered the chamber of Johanan, son of Eliashib,* where he spent the night neither eating food nor drinking water, for he was in mourning over the apostasy of the exiles. [7]A proclamation was made throughout Judah and Jerusalem that all the exiles should gather together in Jerusalem, [8]and that whoever failed to appear within three days would, according to the judgment of the leaders and elders, suffer the confiscation of all his possessions, and would be excluded from the assembly of the exiles.

[9]All the men of Judah and Benjamin gathered together in Jerusalem within the three-day period: it was in the ninth month,† on the twentieth day of the month. All the people, sitting in the open place before the house of God, were trembling both over the matter at hand and because it was raining. [10m]Then Ezra, the priest, stood up and said to them: "Your apostasy in taking foreign women as wives has added to Israel's guilt. [11]But now, give praise to the LORD, the God of your ancestors, and do his will: separate yourselves from the peoples of the land and from the foreign women." [12]In answer, the whole assembly cried out with a loud voice: "Yes, it is our duty to do as you say! [13]But the people are numerous and it is the rainy season, so that we cannot remain outside; besides, this is not a task that can be performed in a single day or even two, for those of us who have sinned in this regard are many. [14]Let our leaders represent the whole assembly; then let all those in our cities who have taken foreign women for wives appear at appointed times, accompanied by the elders and magistrates of each city in question, till we have turned away from us our God's burning anger over this affair." [15]Only Jonathan, son of Asahel, and Jahzeiah, son of Tikvah, were against this proposal, with Meshullam and Shabbethai the Levite supporting them.

[16‡]The exiles did as agreed. Ezra the priest appointed as his assistants men who were heads of ancestral houses, one for each ancestral house, all of them designated by name. They held sessions to examine the matter, beginning with the first day of the tenth month. [17]By the first day of the first month they had finished dealing with all the men who had taken foreign women for wives.

**The List of Transgressors.** [18]Among the priests, the following were found to have taken foreign women for wives: Of the descendants of Jeshua, son of Jozadak, and his kinsmen: Maaseiah, Eliezer, Jarib, and Gedaliah. [19]They pledged themselves to dismiss their wives, and as a guilt offering for their guilt they gave a ram from the flock. [20]Of the descendants of Immer: Hanani and Zebadiah; [21]of the descendants of Harim: Maaseiah, Elijah, Shemaiah, Jehiel, and Uzziah; [22]of the descendants of Pashhur: Elioenai, Maaseiah, Ishmael, Nethanel, Jozabad, and Elasah.

[23n]Of the Levites: Jozabad, Shimei, Kelaiah (also called Kelita), Pethahiah, Judah, and Eliezer. [24]Of the singers: Eliashib; of the gatekeepers: Shallum, Telem, and Uri.

[25]Of the people of Israel: Of the descendants of Parosh: Ramiah, Izziah, Malchijah, Mijamin, Eleazar, Malchijah, and Benaiah; [26]of the descendants of Elam: Mattaniah, Zechariah, Jehiel, Abdi, Jeremoth, and Elijah; [27]of the descendants of Zattu: Elioenai, Eliashib, Mattaniah, Jeremoth, Zabad, and Aziza; [28]of the descendants of Bebai: Jehohanan, Hananiah, Zabbai, and Athlai; [29]of the descendants of Bani: Meshullam, Malluch, Adaiah, Jashub, Sheal, and Jeremoth; [30]of the descendants of Pahath-moab: Adna, Chelal, Benaiah, Maaseiah, Mattaniah, Bezalel, Binnui, and Manasseh; [31]of the descendants of Harim: Eliezer, Isshijah, Malchijah, Shemaiah, Shimeon, [32]Benjamin, Malluch, Shemariah; [33]of the descendants of Hashum: Mattenai, Mattattah, Zabad, Eliphelet, Jeremai, Manasseh, Shimei; [34]of the descendants of Begui: Maadai, Amram, Uel, [35]Benaiah, Bedeiah, Cheluhi, [36]Vaniah, Meremoth, Eliashib, [37]Mattaniah, Mattenai, and Jaasu; [38]of the descendants of Binnui: Shimei, [39]Shelemiah, Nathan, and Adaiah; [40]of the descendants of Zachai: Shashai, Sharai, [41]Azarel, Shelemiah, Shemariah, [42]Shallum, Amariah, Joseph; [43]of the descendants of Nebo: Jeiel, Mattithiah, Zabad, Zebina, Jaddai, Joel, Benaiah.

[44§]All these had taken foreign wives; but they sent them away, both the women and their children.

---

*[10:6] **Johanan, son of Eliashib**: if this Eliashib is identical with the high priest of that name during Nehemiah's mission (Neh 3:1), it would be difficult to avoid the conclusion that Ezra followed Nehemiah. But Eliashib is a common name, and, on the hypothesis of Nehemiah's chronological priority, it would be unlikely that Ezra would consort with a family which had "defiled the priesthood" (Neh 13:28–29).

†[10:9] **The ninth month**: Kislev (November–December), during the first of two rainy seasons in Palestine.

‡[10:16–17] The work of the committee lasted three months, from the first day of the tenth month, Tebeth (December–January), to the first day of the first month, Nisan (March–April), of the following year.

m. [10:10] Neh 9:2.

§[10:44] Some scholars find the continuation of the account of the marriage reform in Neh 9:1–5, though the date given at Neh 9:1 would fit better after Ezr 10:15; cf. Hg 2:10–14. The abrupt conclusion to Ezr 9–10 suggests that the policy of forced separation from foreign wives, not mandated by any law known to us, did not succeed. Assuming the chronological priority of Ezra, marriage outside the community was still prevalent during Nehemiah's administration, and the remarkable demographic expansion of Judaism in the following centuries would be difficult to explain if Ezra's measures had been put into effect.

n. [10:23] Neh 8:7; 10:11.

# THE BOOK OF
# NEHEMIAH

✺

Problems common to the combined books Ezra-Nehemiah have been pointed out in the Introduction to the Book of Ezra. The achievements of the two men were complementary; each helped to make it possible for Judaism to maintain its identity during the difficult days of the Restoration. Ezra was the great religious reformer who succeeded in establishing the Torah as the constitution of the returned community. Nehemiah, governor of the province of Judah, was the man of action who rebuilt the walls of Jerusalem and introduced necessary administrative reforms.

The biblical sources for Nehemiah's life and work are the autobiographical portions scattered through the book. They are called the "Memoirs of Nehemiah," and have been used more effectively by the editor than the "Memoirs of Ezra." The substantial authenticity of Nehemiah's memoirs is widely accepted. From these and other sources, the picture emerges of a man dedicated to the single purpose of the welfare of his people. While serving as cupbearer to the king at the Persian court in Susa, Nehemiah received permission from Artaxerxes I to fortify Jerusalem, and served as governor of Judah for two terms, the first lasting twelve years (445–432 B.C.), the second of unknown length (Neh 5:14; 13:6). Despite temperamental shortcomings, Nehemiah was a man of good practical sense combined with deep faith in God. He used his influence as governor of Judah to serve God and the fledgling Jewish community in Jerusalem.

The Book of Nehemiah is divided as follows:

I. The Deeds of Nehemiah (1:1–7:72)
II. Promulgation of the Law (8:1–10:40)
III. Dedication of the Wall; Other Reforms (11:1–13:31)

## I. THE DEEDS OF NEHEMIAH

### CHAPTER 1

**Nehemiah Hears Bad News.** [1]*The words of Nehemiah, son of Hacaliah.

In the month Kislev of the twentieth year, I was in the citadel of Susa [2]when Hanani, one of my brothers, came with other men from Judah. I asked them about the Jews, the remnant preserved after the captivity, and about Jerusalem. [3]They answered me: "The survivors of the captivity there in the province are in great distress and under reproach. The wall of Jerusalem has been breached, its gates gutted by fire." [4]When I heard this report, I began to weep and continued mourning for several days, fasting and praying before the God of heaven.

[5]†*aI prayed: "Lord, God of heaven, great and awesome God, you preserve your covenant of mercy with those who love you and keep your commandments. [6]*bMay your ears be attentive, and your eyes open, to hear the prayer that I, your servant, now offer in your presence day and night for your servants the Israelites, confessing the sins we have committed against you, I and my ancestral house included. [7]*cWe have greatly offended you, not keeping the commandments, the statutes, and the ordinances you entrusted to your servant Moses. [8]*dBut remember the admonition which you addressed to Moses, your servant, when you said: If you prove faithless, I will scatter you among the peoples; [9]but if you return to me and carefully keep my commandments, even though your outcasts have been driven to the farthest corner of the world, I will gather them

---

*[1:1] The first mission of Nehemiah, from the twentieth year of Artaxerxes I, lasted from the spring (2:1) of 445 B.C. until 433 B.C. (5:14). It is recounted in 1:1–6:15; 12:27–43; 6:16–7:5; 11:1–21; in terms of chronology, these texts may usefully be read in that order. **Kislev**: the ninth month (November–December). **Susa**: the winter residence of the Persian kings, in southwest Iran.

†[1:5] Nehemiah's prayer is a communal confession of sin, characteristic of Second Temple piety; cf. Ezr 9:6–15; Neh 9:6–37; Dn 9:4–19.

a. [1:5] Dt 7:9, 12; Dn 9:4.  b. [1:6] 2 Chr 6:40.  c. [1:7] Dn 3:29–30.  d. [1:8] Dt 30:1–5.

from there, and bring them back to the place I have chosen as the dwelling place for my name. [10e]They are your servants, your people, whom you freed by your great might and strong hand. [11]Lord, may your ears be attentive to the prayer of your servant and that of all your servants who willingly revere your name. Grant success to your servant this day, and let him find favor with this man"—for I was cupbearer to the king.[*]

## CHAPTER 2

**Appointment by the King.** [1]In the month Nisan of the twentieth year of King Artaxerxes, when the wine was in my charge, I took some and offered it to the king. Because I had never before been sad in his presence, [2]the king asked me, "Why do you look sad? If you are not sick, you must be sad at heart." Though I was seized with great fear, [3]I answered the king: "May the king live forever! How could I not look sad when the city where my ancestors are buried lies in ruins, and its gates consumed by fire?" [4]The king asked me, "What is it, then, that you wish?" I prayed to the God of heaven [5]and then answered the king: "If it please the king, and if your servant is deserving of your favor, send me to Judah, to the city where my ancestors are buried, that I may rebuild it." [6]Then the king, with the queen seated beside him, asked me, "How long will your journey take and when will you return?" My answer was acceptable to the king and he agreed to let me go; I set a date for my return.

[7]I asked the king further: "If it please the king, let letters be given to me for the governors of West-of-Euphrates, that they may give me safe-conduct till I arrive in Judah; [8g]also a letter for Asaph, the keeper of the royal woods, that he may give me timber to make beams for the gates of the temple citadel, for the city wall and the house that I will occupy." Since I enjoyed the good favor of my God, the king granted my requests. [9h]Thus I proceeded to the governors of West-of-Euphrates and presented the king's letters to them. The king also sent with me army officers and cavalry.

[10]When Sanballat the Horonite[†] and Tobiah the Ammonite official had heard of this, they were very much displeased that someone had come to improve the lot of the Israelites.

**Circuit of the City.** [11]When I arrived in Jerusalem, and had been there three days, [12]I set out by night with only a few other men and with no other animals but my own mount (for I had not told anyone what my God had inspired me to do for Jerusalem). [13i]I rode out at night by the Valley Gate, passed by the Dragon Spring, and came to the Dung Gate, observing that the walls of Jerusalem were breached and its gates consumed by fire. [14]Then I passed over to the Fountain Gate and to the King's Pool. Since there was no room here for my mount to pass with me astride, [15]I continued on foot up the wadi by night, inspecting the wall all the while, until I once more reached the Valley Gate, by which I went back in. [16]The magistrates knew nothing of where I had gone or what I was doing, for as yet I had disclosed nothing to the Jews, neither to the priests, nor to the nobles, nor to the magistrates, nor to the others who were to do the work.

**Decision to Rebuild the City Wall.** [17]Afterward I said to them: "You see the trouble we are in: how Jerusalem lies in ruins and its gates have been gutted by fire. Come, let us rebuild the wall of Jerusalem, so that we may no longer be a reproach!" [18j]Then I explained to them how God had shown his gracious favor to me, and what the king had said to me. They replied, "Let us begin building!" And they undertook the work with vigor.

[19]When they heard about this, Sanballat the Horonite, Tobiah the Ammonite official, and Geshem the Arab[§] mocked and ridiculed us. "What are you doing?" they asked. "Are you rebelling against the king?" [20]My answer to them was this: "It is the God of heaven who will grant us success. We, his servants, shall set about the rebuilding; but you have neither share nor claim nor memorial[¶] in Jerusalem."

---

*[1:11] **Cupbearer to the king:** an important official in the royal household.

†[2:10] **Sanballat the Horonite:** the governor of the province of Samaria (3:33–34), apparently a native of one of the Beth-horons. A letter from the Jews living at Elephantine in southern Egypt, dated 408–407 B.C., mentions "Delayah and Shelemyah, the sons of Sanballat, the governor of Samaria," and papyri discovered in the Wadi ed-Dâliyeh in the Jordan Valley refer to a Sanballat, governor of Samaria, during the last years of Persian rule. Although his own name was Babylonian—Sin-uballit, i.e., "Sin (the moon god) has given life"—his two sons had names based on the divine name Yhwh. **Tobiah the Ammonite official:** the governor of the province of Ammon in Transjordan. His title, "official," lit., "servant" (in Hebrew, 'ebed), could also be understood as "slave," and Nehemiah perhaps meant it in this derogatory sense. The Tobiads

remained a powerful family even in Maccabean times, and something of their history is known from 2 Maccabees (3:11; 12:17), Josephus (Antiquities 12:160–236), the Zeno papyri of the third century B.C., and excavation at 'Araq el-'Emir in Jordan. Sanballat and Tobiah, together with Geshem the Arab (Neh 2:19; 6:1–2), who was probably in charge of Edom and the regions to the south and southeast of Judah, opposed the rebuilding of Jerusalem's walls on political grounds; the city was the capital of a rival province.

‡[2:13–15] Nehemiah left Jerusalem by the Valley Gate near the northwestern end of the old City of David and went south down the Tyropoean Valley toward the Dragon Spring (or the En-rogel [Jos 15:7; 18:16; 2 Sm 17:17; 1 Kgs 1:9], now known as Job's Well) at the juncture of the Valley of Hinnom and the Kidron Valley. He then turned north at the Dung Gate (or the Potsherd Gate of Jer 19:2) at the southern end of the city and proceeded up the wadi, that is, the Kidron Valley, passing the Fountain Gate (at the Spring of Gihon) and the King's Pool (unidentified); finally he turned west and then south to his starting point.

§[2:19] **Geshem the Arab:** see also 6:1–2; in 6:6 the name occurs as Gashmu. He is known from a contemporary inscription as ruler of the Kedarite Arabs, who were threatening Judah from the south and east.

¶[2:20] **Neither share nor claim nor memorial:** although Sanballat and Tobiah worshiped Yhwh, Nehemiah would not

---

e. [1:10] Dt 9:29.  f. [1:11] Ps 118:25.  g. [2:8] Ezr 7:6.  h. [2:9] Ezr 8:22.

i. [2:11] Ezr 8:32.  j. [2:18] Ezr 7:6.

## CHAPTER 3

**List of Workers.** [1][k]Eliashib the high priest and his priestly kinsmen took up the task of rebuilding the Sheep Gate. They consecrated it and set up its doors, its bolts, and its bars, then continued the rebuilding to the Tower of the Hundred, the Tower of Hananel. [2]At their side the men of Jericho were rebuilding, and next to them was Zaccur, son of Imri. [3][l]The Fish Gate was rebuilt by the people of Hassenaah; they timbered it and set up its doors, its bolts, and its bars. [4]At their side Meremoth, son of Uriah, son of Hakkoz, carried out the work of repair; next to him was Meshullam, son of Berechiah, son of Meshezabel; and next to him was Zadok, son of Baana. [5]Next to him the Tekoites carried out the work of repair; however, some of their most powerful men would not submit to the labor asked by their masters. [6]The Mishneh Gate[†] was repaired by Joiada, son of Paseah; and Meshullam, son of Besodeiah; they timbered it and set up its doors, its bolts, and its bars. [7]At their side Melatiah the Gibeonite did the repairing, together with Jadon the Meronothite, and the men of Gibeon and of Mizpah, who were under the jurisdiction of the governor of West-of-Euphrates. [8]Next to them the work of repair was carried out by Uzziel, son of Harhaiah, a member of the goldsmiths' guild, and at his side was Hananiah, one of the perfumers' guild. They restored Jerusalem as far as the Broad Wall.[‡] [9]Next to them the work of repair was carried out by Rephaiah, son of Hur, administrator of half the district of Jerusalem, [10]and at his side was Jedaiah, son of Harumaph, who repaired opposite his own house. Next to him Hattush, son of Hashabneiah, carried out the work of repair. [11]The adjoining sector, as far as the Oven Tower, was repaired by Malchijah, son of Harim, and Hasshub, son of Pahath-moab. [12]At their side the work of repair was carried out by Shallum, son of Hallohesh, administrator of half the district of Jerusalem, together with his daughters. [13]The Valley Gate was repaired by Hanun and the inhabitants of Zanoah; they rebuilt it and set up its doors, its bolts, and its bars. They also repaired a thousand cubits of the wall up to the Dung Gate. [14]The Dung Gate was repaired by Malchijah, son of Rechab, administrator of the district of Beth-haccherem; he rebuilt it and set up its doors, its bolts, and its bars. [15]The Fountain Gate was

repaired by Shallum, son of Colhozeh, administrator of the district of Mizpah; he rebuilt it, roofed it, and set up its doors, its bolts, and its bars. He also repaired the wall of the Aqueduct Pool near the King's Garden as far as the steps that lead down from the City of David. [16]After him, the work of repair was carried out by Nehemiah, son of Azbuk, administrator of half the district of Beth-zur, to a place opposite the tombs of David, as far as the Artificial Pool and the barracks.

[17]After him, these Levites carried out the work of repair: Rehum, son of Bani, and next to him, for his own district, was Hashabiah, administrator of half the district of Keilah. [18]After him, their kinsmen carried out the work of repair: Binnui, son of Henadad, administrator of half the district of Keilah; [19]next to him Ezer, son of Jeshua, administrator of Mizpah, who repaired the adjoining sector, the Corner, opposite the ascent to the arsenal. [20]After him, Baruch, son of Zabbai, repaired the adjoining sector from the Corner to the entrance of the house of Eliashib, the high priest. [21]After him, Meremoth, son of Uriah, son of Hakkoz, repaired the adjoining sector from the entrance of Eliashib's house to its end.

[22]After him, the work of repair was carried out by the priests, men of the surrounding country. [23]After them, Benjamin and Hasshub carried out the repair in front of their houses; after them, Azariah, son of Maaseiah, son of Ananiah, made the repairs alongside his house. [24]After him, Binnui, son of Henadad, repaired the adjoining sector from the house of Azariah to the Corner (that is, to the Angle). [25]After him, Palal, son of Uzai, carried out the work of repair opposite the Corner and the tower projecting from the Upper Palace at the quarters of the guard. After him, Pedaiah, son of Parosh, carried out the work of repair [26]to a point opposite the Water Gate on the east, and the projecting tower. [27]After him, the Tekoites repaired the adjoining sector opposite the great projecting tower, to the wall of Ophel.

[28]Above the Horse Gate the priests carried out the work of repair, each opposite his own house. [29][m]After them Zadok, son of Immer, carried out the repair opposite his house, and after him the repair was carried out by Shemaiah, son of Shecaniah, keeper of the East Gate. [30]After him, Hananiah, son of Shelemiah, and Hanun, the sixth son of Zalaph, repaired the adjoining sector; after them, Meshullam, son of Berechiah, repaired the place opposite his own lodging. [31]After him, Malchijah, a member of the goldsmiths' guild, carried out the work of repair as far as the quarters of the temple servants and the merchants, in front of the Gate of Inspection and as far as the upper chamber of the Angle. [32]Between the upper chamber of the Angle and

---

let them participate in any of the activities of the religious community in Jerusalem.

\*[3:1–32] The construction work on the gates and walls of the city is described in counterclockwise direction, beginning and ending at the Sheep Gate (to the north of the Temple). The exact locations of many of the topographical points mentioned are uncertain.

†[3:6] **The Mishneh Gate**: the gate leading into the second, expanded quarter of the city; cf. 2 Kgs 22:14; Zep 1:10.

‡[3:8] **The Broad Wall**: perhaps identical with the wall, seven meters thick, discovered in the Jewish quarter of the Old City.

k. [3:1] Jer 31:38.   l. [3:3] Ezr 2:35; Zep 1:10.   m. [3:29] Ez 40:6.

the Sheep Gate, the goldsmiths and the merchants carried out the work of repair.

**Opposition from Judah's Enemies.** [33]When Sanballat heard that we were rebuilding the wall, he became angry and very much incensed. He ridiculed the Jews, [34]saying in the presence of his associates and the troops of Samaria: "What are these miserable Jews trying to do? Will they complete their restoration in a single day? Will they recover these stones, burnt as they are, from the heaps of dust?" [35]Tobiah the Ammonite was beside him, and he said: "Whatever they are building—if a fox attacks it, it will breach their wall of stones!" [36]Hear, our God, how we were mocked! Turn back their reproach upon their own heads and deliver them up as plunder in a land of captivity! [37n]Do not hide their crime and do not let their sin be blotted out in your sight, for they insulted the builders to their faces! [38]We, however, continued to build the wall, and soon it was completed up to half its height. The people worked enthusiastically.

## CHAPTER 4

[1]When Sanballat, Tobiah, the Arabs, the Ammonites, and the Ashdodites heard that the restoration of the walls of Jerusalem was progressing—for the gaps were beginning to be closed up—they became extremely angry. [2]They all plotted together to come and fight against Jerusalem and to throw us into confusion. [3]We prayed to our God and posted a watch against them day and night for fear of what they might do. [4]Meanwhile the Judahites were saying:

> "Slackened is the bearers' strength,
>     there is no end to the rubbish;
> Never will we be able
>     to rebuild the wall."

[5]Our enemies thought, "Before they are aware of it or see us, we will come into their midst, kill them, and put an end to the work." [6]When the Jews who lived near them had come to us from one place after another, and had told us ten times over that they were about to attack us, [7]I stationed guards down below, behind the wall, near the exposed points, assigning them by family groups with their swords, spears, and bows. [8]I made an inspection, then addressed these words to the nobles, the magistrates, and the rest of the people: "Do not fear them! Keep in mind the LORD, who is great and to be feared, and fight for your kindred, your sons and daughters, your wives and your homes." [9]When our enemies realized that we had been warned and that God had upset their plan, we all went back, each to our own task at the wall. [10o]From that time on, however, only half my work force took a hand in the work, while the

other half, armed with spears, bucklers, bows, and breastplates, stood guard behind the whole house of Judah [11]as they rebuilt the wall. The load carriers, too, were armed; each worked with one hand and held a weapon with the other. [12]Every builder, while working, had a sword tied at his side. A trumpeter stood beside me, [13]for I had said to the nobles, the magistrates, and the rest of the people: "Our work is scattered and extensive, and we are widely separated from one another along the wall; [14]wherever you hear the trumpet sound, join us there; our God will fight with us." [15]Thus we went on with the work, half with spears in hand, from daybreak till the stars came out.

[16]At the same time I told the people to spend the nights inside Jerusalem, each with an attendant, so that they might serve as a guard by night and a working force by day. [17]Neither I, nor my kindred, nor any of my attendants, nor any of the bodyguard that accompanied me took off our clothes; everyone kept a weapon at hand.

## CHAPTER 5

**Social and Economic Problems.** [1p]Then there rose a great outcry of the people and their wives against certain of their Jewish kindred.* [2]Some said: "We are forced to pawn our sons and daughters in order to get grain to eat that we may live." [3]Others said: "We are forced to pawn our fields, our vineyards, and our houses, that we may have grain during the famine." [4]Still others said: "To pay the king's tax we have borrowed money on our fields and vineyards. [5q]And though these are our own kindred, and our children are as good as theirs, we have had to reduce our sons and daughters to slavery, and violence has been done to some of our daughters! Yet we can do nothing about it, for our fields and vineyards belong to others."

[6]I was extremely angry when I heard the reasons for their complaint. [7r]After some deliberation, I called the nobles and magistrates to account, saying to them, "You are exacting interest from your own kindred!"† I then rebuked them severely, [8s]saying to them: "As far as we were able, we bought back our Jewish kindred who had been sold to Gentiles; you, however, are selling your own kindred, to have them bought back by us." They remained silent, for they could find no answer. [9]I continued: "What you are doing is not good. Should you not conduct yourselves out of fear of our God rather than fear of the reproach of our Gentile enemies? [10]I myself, my kindred, and my attendants have lent the

---

* [5:1] **Certain of their Jewish kindred:** probably Jews who had returned from Babylonia who formed the social and economic elite in the province.

† [5:7] **You are exacting interest from your own kindred!:** contrary to the Mosaic law (Dt 23:20).

p. [5:1] Jer 34:8–22.  q. [5:5] Ex 21:7; Lv 25:39.  r. [5:7] Dt 23:20.  s. [5:8] Lv 25:48.

n. [3:37] Neh 6:14; 13:29; Jer 18:23.  o. [4:10] Ps 149:6.

people money and grain without charge. Let us put an end to this usury! ¹¹Return to them this very day their fields, vineyards, olive groves, and houses, together with the interest on the money, the grain, the wine, and the oil that you have lent them." ¹²They answered: "We will return everything and exact nothing further from them. We will do just what you ask." Then I called for the priests to administer an oath to them that they would do as they had promised. ¹³I shook out the folds of my garment, saying, "Thus may God shake from home and fortune every man who fails to keep this promise, and may he thus be shaken out and emptied!" And the whole assembly answered, "Amen," and praised the LORD. Then the people did as they had promised.

**Nehemiah's Record.** ¹⁴Moreover, from the time that King Artaxerxes appointed me governor in the land of Judah, from his twentieth to his thirty-second year—during these twelve years neither I nor my kindred lived off the governor's food allowance. ¹⁵The earlier governors,* my predecessors, had laid a heavy burden on the people, taking from them each day forty silver shekels for their food; then, too, their attendants oppressed the people. But I, because I feared God, did not do this. ¹⁶In addition, though I had acquired no land of my own, I did my part in this work on the wall, and all my attendants were gathered there for the work. ¹⁷Though I set my table for a hundred and fifty persons, Jews and magistrates, as well as the neighboring Gentiles who came to us, ¹⁸and though the daily preparations were made at my expense—one ox, six choice sheep, poultry—besides all kinds of wine in abundance every ten days, despite this I did not claim the governor's allowance, for the labor lay heavy upon this people. ¹⁹Keep in mind, my God, to my credit all that I did for this people.

### CHAPTER 6

**Plots Against Nehemiah.** ¹When it had been reported to Sanballat, Tobiah, Geshem the Arab, and our other enemies that I had rebuilt the wall and that there was no breach left in it (though up to that time I had not yet set up the doors in the gates), ²Sanballat and Geshem sent me this message: "Come, let us hold council together at Chephirim in the plain of Ono." They were planning to do me harm. ³I sent messengers to them with this reply: "I am engaged in a great enterprise and am unable to come down. Why should the work stop, while I leave it to come down to you?" ⁴Four times they sent me this same proposal, and each time I gave the same reply. ⁵Then, the fifth time, Sanballat sent me the same message by one of his servants, who bore an unsealed letter ⁶containing this text: "Among

the nations it has been reported—Gashmu† is witness to this—that you and the Jews are planning a rebellion; that for this reason you are rebuilding the wall; and that you are to be their king. ⁷Also, that you have set up prophets in Jerusalem to proclaim you king of Judah. Now, since matters like these will reach the ear of the king, come, let us hold council together." ⁸I sent him this answer: "Nothing of what you report is happening; rather, it is the invention of your own mind." ⁹They were all trying to intimidate us, thinking, "They will be discouraged from continuing with the work, and it will never be completed." But instead, I then redoubled my efforts.

¹⁰I went to the house of Shemaiah, son of Delaiah, son of Mehetabel, who was confined to his house, and he said: "Let us meet in the house of God, inside the temple building; let us lock the doors of the temple. For they are coming to kill you—by night they are coming to kill you." ¹¹My answer was: "A man like me take flight? Should a man like me enter the temple to save his life? I will not go!" ¹²For on consideration, it was plain to me that God had not sent him; rather, because Tobiah and Sanballat had bribed him, he voiced this prophecy concerning me, ¹³that I might act on it out of fear and commit this sin. Then they would have had a shameful story with which to discredit me. ¹⁴ᵗKeep in mind Tobiah and Sanballat, my God, because of these things they did; keep in mind as well Noadiah the woman prophet and the other prophets who were trying to intimidate me.

**Completion of the Work.** ¹⁵The wall was finished on the twenty-fifth day of Elul;‡ the work had taken fifty-two days. ¹⁶ᵘWhen all our enemies had heard of this, and all the neighboring Gentiles round about had taken note of it, they were very discouraged, for they knew that it was with our God's help that this work had been completed. ¹⁷At that same time, however, many letters were going to Tobiah from the nobles of Judah, and Tobiah's letters were reaching them, ¹⁸for many in Judah were in league with him, since he was the son-in-law of Shecaniah, son of Arah, and his son Jehohanan had married the daughter of Meshullam, son of Berechiah. ¹⁹They would praise his good deeds in my presence and relate to him whatever I said; and Tobiah sent letters trying to intimidate me.

### CHAPTER 7

¹Now that the wall had been rebuilt, I had the doors set up, and the gatekeepers, the singers, and the Levites were put in charge of them.

---

*[5:15] **The earlier governors**: both Sheshbazzar (Ezr 5:14) and Zerubbabel (Hg 1:1, 14; 2:2, 21) are said to be governors, and Mal 1:8 mentions a governor but does not name him. Other names are known from seal impressions of uncertain date.

†[6:6] **Gashmu**: elsewhere (vv. 1–2; 2:19) the name is given as Geshem.

‡[6:15] **Elul**: the sixth month (August–September). **Fifty-two days**: according to Josephus (*Ant.* 11:174–183), the rebuilding of the walls of Jerusalem by Nehemiah took two years and four months.

t. [6:14] Jer 23:9–40; Zec 13:3.   u. [6:16] Ps 118:22–23; 127:1.

²Over Jerusalem I placed Hanani, my brother, and Hananiah, the commander of the citadel, who was more trustworthy and God-fearing than most. ³I said to them: "The gates of Jerusalem are not to be opened until the sun is hot, and while the sun is still shining they shall shut and bar the doors. Appoint as sentinels the inhabitants of Jerusalem, some at their watch posts, and others in front of their own houses." **Census of the Province.** ⁴Now, the city was quite wide and spacious, but its population was small, and none of the houses had been rebuilt. ⁵When my God had inspired me to gather together the nobles, the magistrates, and the people, and to examine their family records, I came upon the family list of those who had returned in the earliest period. There I found the following written:

⁶*These are the inhabitants of the province who returned from the captivity of the exiles whom Nebuchadnezzar, king of Babylon, had carried away, and who came back to Jerusalem and Judah, to their own cities: ⁷They returned with Zerubbabel, Jeshua, Nehemiah, Azariah, Raamiah, Nahamani, Mordecai, Bilshan, Mispereth, Bigvai, Nehum, and Baanah.

The census of the people of Israel: ⁸descendants of Parosh, two thousand one hundred and seventy-two; ⁹descendants of Shephatiah, three hundred and seventy-two; ¹⁰descendants of Arah, six hundred and fifty-two; ¹¹descendants of Pahath-moab who were descendants of Jeshua and Joab, two thousand eight hundred and eighteen; ¹²descendants of Elam, one thousand two hundred and fifty-four; ¹³descendants of Zattu, eight hundred and forty-five; ¹⁴descendants of Zaccai, seven hundred and sixty; ¹⁵descendants of Binnui, six hundred and forty-eight; ¹⁶descendants of Bebai, six hundred and twenty-eight; ¹⁷descendants of Azgad, two thousand three hundred and twenty-two; ¹⁸descendants of Adonikam, six hundred and sixty-seven; ¹⁹descendants of Bigvai, two thousand and sixty-seven; ²⁰descendants of Adin, six hundred and fifty-five; ²¹descendants of Ater who were descendants of Hezekiah, ninety-eight; ²²descendants of Hashum, three hundred and twenty-eight; ²³descendants of Bezai, three hundred and twenty-four; ²⁴descendants of Hariph, one hundred and twelve; ²⁵descendants of Gibeon, ninety-five; ²⁶people of Bethlehem and Netophah, one hundred and eighty-eight; ²⁷people of Anathoth, one hundred and twenty-eight; ²⁸people of Beth-azmaveth, forty-two; ²⁹people of Kiriath-jearim, Chephirah, and Beeroth, seven hundred and forty-three; ³⁰people of Ramah and Geba, six hundred and twenty-one; ³¹people of Michmas, one hundred and twenty-two; ³²people of Bethel and Ai, one hundred and twenty-three; ³³people of Nebo, fifty-two; ³⁴descendants

of the other Elam, one thousand two hundred and fifty-four; ³⁵descendants of Harim, three hundred and twenty; ³⁶descendants of Jericho, three hundred and forty-five; ³⁷descendants of Lod, Hadid, and Ono, seven hundred and twenty-one; ³⁸descendants of Senaah, three thousand nine hundred and thirty.

³⁹The priests: descendants of Jedaiah of the house of Jeshua, nine hundred and seventy-three; ⁴⁰descendants of Immer, one thousand and fifty-two; ⁴¹descendants of Pashhur, one thousand two hundred and forty-seven; ⁴²descendants of Harim, one thousand and seventeen.

⁴³The Levites: descendants of Jeshua, Kadmiel of the descendants of Hodeviah, seventy-four.

⁴⁴The singers: descendants of Asaph, one hundred and forty-eight.

⁴⁵The gatekeepers: descendants of Shallum, descendants of Ater, descendants of Talmon, descendants of Akkub, descendants of Hatita, descendants of Shobai, one hundred and thirty-eight.

⁴⁶The temple servants: descendants of Ziha, descendants of Hasupha, descendants of Tabbaoth, ⁴⁷descendants of Keros, descendants of Sia, descendants of Padon, ⁴⁸descendants of Lebana, descendants of Hagaba, descendants of Shalmai, ⁴⁹descendants of Hanan, descendants of Giddel, descendants of Gahar, ⁵⁰descendants of Reaiah, descendants of Rezin, descendants of Nekoda, ⁵¹descendants of Gazzam, descendants of Uzza, descendants of Paseah, ⁵²descendants of Besai, descendants of the Meunites, descendants of the Nephusites, ⁵³descendants of Bakbuk, descendants of Hakupha, descendants of Harhur, ⁵⁴descendants of Bazlith, descendants of Mehida, descendants of Harsha, ⁵⁵descendants of Barkos, descendants of Sisera, descendants of Temah, ⁵⁶descendants of Neziah, descendants of Hatipha.

⁵⁷Descendants of Solomon's servants: descendants of Sotai, descendants of Sophereth, descendants of Perida, ⁵⁸descendants of Jaala, descendants of Darkon, descendants of Giddel, ⁵⁹descendants of Shephatiah, descendants of Hattil, descendants of Pochereth-hazzebaim, descendants of Amon. ⁶⁰The total of the temple servants and the descendants of Solomon's servants was three hundred and ninety-two.

⁶¹The following who returned from Telmelah, Tel-harsha, Cherub, Addon, and Immer were unable to prove that their ancestral houses and their descent were Israelite: ⁶²descendants of Delaiah, descendants of Tobiah, descendants of Nekoda, six hundred and forty-two. ⁶³Also, of the priests: descendants of Hobaiah, descendants of Hakkoz, descendants of Barzillai (he had married one of the daughters of Barzillai the Gileadite and was named after him). ⁶⁴These men searched their family records, but their names could not be found written there; hence they were disqualified from the priesthood, ⁶⁵and the governor† ordered them not to partake

---

*[7:6–72] See note on Ezr 2:1–67.

†[7:65, 69] **The governor:** see note on Ezr 2:63.

of the most holy foods until there should be a priest to consult the Urim and Thummim.

⁶⁶The entire assembly taken together came to forty-two thousand three hundred and sixty, ⁶⁷not counting their male and female servants, who were seven thousand three hundred and thirty-seven. They also had two hundred male and female singers. Their horses were seven hundred and thirty-six, their mules two hundred and forty-five, ⁶⁸their camels four hundred and thirty-five, their donkeys six thousand seven hundred and twenty.

⁶⁹Certain of the heads of ancestral houses contributed to the temple service. The governor put into the treasury one thousand drachmas of gold, fifty basins, thirty vestments for priests, and five hundred minas of silver. ⁷⁰Some of the heads of ancestral houses contributed to the treasury for the temple service: twenty thousand drachmas of gold and two thousand two hundred minas of silver. ⁷¹The contributions of the rest of the people amounted to twenty thousand drachmas of gold, two thousand minas of silver, and sixty-seven vestments for priests.

⁷²The priests, the Levites, the gatekeepers, the singers, the temple servants, and all Israel took up residence in their cities.

## II. PROMULGATION OF THE LAW

### CHAPTER 8

**Ezra Reads the Law.** ¹*ʷNow when the seventh month came, the whole people gathered as one in the square in front of the Water Gate, and they called upon Ezra the scribe to bring forth the book of the law of Moses which the LORD had commanded for Israel. ²ˣOn the first day of the seventh month, therefore, Ezra the priest brought the law before the assembly, which consisted of men, women, and those children old enough to understand. ³In the square in front of the Water Gate, Ezra read out of the book from daybreak till midday, in the presence of the men, the women, and those children old enough to understand; and all the people listened attentively to the book of the law. ⁴Ezra the scribe stood on a wooden platform that had been made for the occasion; at his right side stood Mattithiah, Shema, Anaiah, Uriah, Hilkiah, and Maaseiah, and on his left Pedaiah, Mishael, Malchijah, Hashum, Hashbaddanah, Zechariah, Meshullam. ⁵Ezra opened the scroll so that all the people might see it, for he was standing higher than any of the people. When he opened it, all the people stood. ⁶Ezra blessed the LORD, the great God, and all the people, their hands raised high, answered, "Amen, amen!" Then they knelt down and bowed before the LORD, their faces to the ground. ⁷ʸThe Levites Jeshua, Bani, Sherebiah, Jamin, Akkub, Shabbethai, Hodiah, Maaseiah, Kelita, Azariah, Jozabad, Hanan, and Pelaiah explained the law to the people, who remained in their places. ⁸ᶻEzra read clearly from the book of the law of God, interpreting it so that all could understand what was read. ⁹Then Nehemiah, that is, the governor, and Ezra the priest-scribe, and the Levites who were instructing the people said to all the people: "Today is holy to the LORD your God. Do not lament, do not weep!"—for all the people were weeping as they heard the words of the law. ¹⁰ᵃHe continued: "Go, eat rich foods and drink sweet drinks, and allot portions to those who had nothing prepared; for today is holy to our LORD. Do not be saddened this day, for rejoicing in the LORD is your strength!" ¹¹And the Levites quieted all the people, saying, "Silence! Today is holy, do not be saddened." ¹²Then all the people began to eat and drink, to distribute portions, and to celebrate with great joy, for they understood the words that had been explained to them.

**The Feast of Booths.** ¹³On the second day, the heads of ancestral houses of the whole people, and also the priests and the Levites, gathered around Ezra the scribe to study the words of the law. ¹⁴ᵇThey found it written in the law commanded by the LORD through Moses that the Israelites should dwell in booths during the feast of the seventh month; ¹⁵ᶜand that they should have this proclamation made throughout their cities and in Jerusalem: "Go out into the hill country and bring in branches of olive, oleaster, myrtle, palm, and other trees in leaf, to make booths, as it is written." ¹⁶The people went out and brought in branches with which they made booths for themselves, on the roof of their houses, in their courtyards, in the courts of the house of God, and in the squares of the Water Gate and the Gate of Ephraim. ¹⁷ᵈSo the entire assembly of the returned exiles made booths and dwelt in them. Now the Israelites had done nothing of this sort from the days of Jeshua, son of Nun, until this occasion; therefore there was very great joy. ¹⁸Ezra read from the book of the law of God day after day, from the first day to the last. They kept the feast for seven days, and the solemn assembly on the eighth day, as was required.

### CHAPTER 9

**Public Confession of Sin.** ¹ᵉOn the twenty-fourth day of this month, the Israelites gathered together while fasting and wearing sackcloth,

---

*[8:1–18] Chronologically this belongs after Ezr 8:36. The gloss mentioning Nehemiah in Neh 8:9 was inserted in this Ezra section after the dislocation of several parts of Ezra-Nehemiah had occurred. There is no clear evidence of a simultaneous presence of Nehemiah and Ezra in Jerusalem; Neh 12:26, 36 are also scribal glosses.

w. [8:1] Ezr 3:1.   x. [8:2] Lv 23:23–25; Nm 29:1–6.

†[9:1–5] The feast of Booths is followed by a penitential liturgy. Since it includes separation from foreigners, some read it as a sequel to Ezr 9–10.

y. [8:7] Neh 10:10–13.   z. [8:8] Ezr 7:6.   a. [8:10] Est 9:19.
b. [8:14] Ex 23:14–16; Lv 23:33–36; Nm 29:1–38; Ez 45:25.
c. [8:15] Ps 118:27.   d. [8:17] 2 Chr 30:26; 35:18.   e. [9:1] Dn 9:3.

their heads covered with dust. ²ᶠThose of Israelite descent separated themselves from all who were of foreign extraction, then stood forward and confessed their sins and the guilty deeds of their ancestors. ³When they had taken their places, they read from the book of the law of the Lᴏʀᴅ their God, for a fourth of the day, and during another fourth they made their confession and bowed down before the Lᴏʀᴅ their God. ⁴Standing on the platform of the Levites were Jeshua, Binnui, Kadmiel, Shebaniah, Bunni, Sherebiah, Bani, and Chenani, who cried out to the Lᴏʀᴅ their God, with a loud voice. ⁵ᵍThe Levites Jeshua, Kadmiel, Bani, Hashabneiah, Sherebiah, Hodiah, Shebaniah, and Pethahiah said,

"Arise, bless the Lᴏʀᴅ, your God,
    from eternity to eternity!"
"And may they bless your glorious name,
    which is exalted above all blessing
      and praise."
⁶ ᵍ"You are the Lᴏʀᴅ, you alone;
You made the heavens,
    the highest heavens and all their host,
The earth and all that is upon it,
    the seas and all that is in them.
To all of them you give life,
    the heavenly hosts bow down before
      you.
⁷ ʰYou are the Lᴏʀᴅ God
    who chose Abram,
Who brought him from Ur of the
      Chaldees,
    who named him Abraham.
⁸ ⁱYou found his heart faithful in your sight,
    you made the covenant with him
To give the land of the Canaanites,
      Hittites, Amorites,
Perizzites, Jebusites, and Girgashites
    to him and his descendants.
You fulfilled your promises,
    for you are just.
⁹ ʲYou saw the affliction of our ancestors in
      Egypt,
    you heard their cry by the Red Sea;
¹⁰ ᵏYou worked signs and wonders against
      Pharaoh,
    against all his servants and the
      people of his land,
Because you knew of their insolence
      toward them;
    thus you made for yourself a name
      even to this day.
¹¹ ˡThe sea you divided before them,
    on dry ground they passed through
      the midst of the sea;

Their pursuers you hurled into the depths,
    like a stone into the mighty waters.
¹² ᵐWith a column of cloud you led them by
      day,
    and by night with a column of fire,
To light the way of their journey,
    the way in which they must travel.
¹³ ⁿOn Mount Sinai you came down,
    you spoke with them from heaven;
You gave them just ordinances, true laws,
    good statutes and commandments;
¹⁴ ᵒYour holy sabbath you made known to
      them,
    commandments, statutes, and law
      you prescribed for them,
    by the hand of Moses your servant.
¹⁵ ᵖFood from heaven you gave them in their
      hunger,
    water from a rock you sent them in
      their thirst.
You told them to enter and occupy the land
    which you had sworn to give them.
¹⁶ But they, our ancestors, proved to be
      insolent;
    they were obdurate† and did not
      obey your commandments.
¹⁷ �q They refused to obey and no longer
      remembered
    the wonders you had worked for
      them.
They were obdurate and appointed a leader
    in order to return to their slavery in
      Egypt.
But you are a forgiving God, gracious and
      merciful,
    slow to anger and rich in mercy;
    you did not forsake them.
¹⁸ ʳThough they made for themselves a
      molten calf,
    and proclaimed, 'Here is your God
      who brought you up from
      Egypt,'
    and were guilty of great insults,
¹⁹ Yet in your great mercy
    you did not forsake them in the
      desert.
By day the column of cloud did not cease
      to lead them on their journey,
    by night the column of fire did not
      cease to light the way they
      were to travel.
²⁰ ˢYour good spirit you bestowed on them,
    to give them understanding;
Your manna you did not withhold from
      their mouths,
    and you gave them water in their
      thirst.

---

*[9:6–37] The Septuagint attributes the prayer to Ezra; cf. Ezr 9:6–15.

†[9:16] **They were obdurate**: lit., "they stiffened their necks."

---

f. [9:2] Ezr 9:1–2; 10:11.   g. [9:5] Ps 41:14; 106:48; Dn 2:20; 3:52.   h. [9:7] Gn 12:1; 17:5.   i. [9:8] Gn 15:18–19.   j. [9:9] Ex 2:23–24.   k. [9:10] Ex 7–11; 14.   l. [9:11] Ex 15:5, 10.

m. [9:12] Ex 13:21–22.   n. [9:13] Ex 19–24.   o. [9:14] Ex 20:8.   p. [9:15] Ex 16:4; 17:1–2.   q. [9:17] Ex 34:6; Nm 14:1–4; Dt 9:9.   r. [9:18] Ex 32:4, 8.   s. [9:20] Dt 2:7.

<sup>21</sup> <sup>t</sup>Forty years in the desert you sustained
them:
they did not want;
Their garments did not become worn,
and their feet did not swell.
<sup>22</sup> <sup>u</sup>You gave them kingdoms and peoples,
which you divided among them as
border lands.
They possessed the land of Sihon, king of
Heshbon,
and the land of Og, king of Bashan.
<sup>23</sup> <sup>v</sup>You made their children as numerous as
the stars of the heavens,
and you brought them into the land
which you had commanded their
ancestors to enter and possess.
<sup>24</sup> The children went in to possess the land;
you humbled before them the
Canaanite inhabitants
and gave them into their power,
Their kings and the peoples of the land,
to do with them as they wished.
<sup>25</sup> <sup>w</sup>They captured fortified cities and fertile
land;
they took possession of houses filled
with all good things,
Cisterns already dug, vineyards, olive
groves,
and fruit trees in abundance.
They ate and had their fill,
fattened and feasted on your great
goodness.
<sup>26</sup> <sup>x</sup>But they were contemptuous and rebelled
against you:
they cast your law behind their backs.
They murdered your prophets
who bore witness against them to
bring them back to you:
they were guilty of great insults.
<sup>27</sup> <sup>y</sup>Therefore you gave them into the power
of their enemies,
who oppressed them.
But in the time of their oppression they
would cry out to you,
and you would hear them from
heaven,
And according to your great mercy give
them saviors
to deliver them from the power of
their enemies.
<sup>28</sup> As soon as they had relief,
they would go back to doing evil in
your sight.
Again you abandoned them to the power
of their enemies,
who crushed them.
Once again they cried out to you, and you
heard them from heaven
and delivered them according to
your mercy, many times over.

<sup>29</sup> <sup>z</sup>You bore witness against them,
to bring them back to your law.
But they were insolent
and would not obey your
commandments;
They sinned against your ordinances,
which give life to those who keep
them.
They turned stubborn backs, stiffened
their necks,
and would not obey.
<sup>30</sup> You were patient with them for many years,
bearing witness against them
through your spirit, by means
of your prophets;
Still they would not listen.
Therefore you delivered them into
the power of the peoples of the
lands.
<sup>31</sup> Yet in your great mercy you did not
completely destroy them
and did not forsake them, for you
are a gracious and merciful God.
<sup>32</sup> <sup>a</sup>Now, our God, great, mighty, and
awesome God,
who preserves the covenant of
mercy,
do not discount all the hardship that
has befallen us,
Our kings, our princes, our priests,
our prophets, our ancestors, and
your entire people,
from the time of the kings of Assyria
until this day!
<sup>33</sup> <sup>b</sup>In all that has come upon us you have
been just,
for you kept faith while we have
done evil.
<sup>34</sup> Yes, our kings, our princes, our priests,
and our ancestors
have not kept your law;
They paid no attention to your
commandments
and the warnings which you gave
them.
<sup>35</sup> While they were still in their kingdom,
in the midst of the many good
things that you had given them
And in the wide, fertile land
that you had spread out before them,
They did not serve you
nor turn away from their evil deeds.
<sup>36</sup> Today we are slaves!
As for the land which you gave our
ancestors
That they might eat its fruits and good
things—
see, we have become slaves upon it!
<sup>37</sup> Its rich produce goes to the kings
you set over us because of our sins,

t. [9:21] Dt 8:4.   u. [9:22] Nm 21:21–35; Dt 1:4; 2:26–3:11.
v. [9:23] Dt 1:10.   w. [9:25] Dt 3:5; 6:10–11; 11:11; 32:15.   x. [9:26]
Wis 2:10–20.   y. [9:27] Dn 9:19.

z. [9:29] Lv 18:5; Dt 30:16; 32:47.   a. [9:32] Lam 5.   b. [9:33] Dn
3:27; 9:14.

Who rule over our bodies and our cattle
       as they please.
       We are in great distress!"

## CHAPTER 10

**Signatories to the Pact.** [1]*In view of all this,
we are entering into a firm pact, which we are
putting into writing. On the sealed document
appear the names of our princes, our Levites,
and our priests.

[2]On the sealed document: the governor
Nehemiah, son of Hacaliah, and Zedekiah.

[3c]Seraiah, Azariah, Jeremiah, [4]Pashhur, Amariah, Malchijah, [5]Hattush, Shebaniah, Malluch,
[6]Harim, Meremoth, Obadiah, [7]Daniel, Ginnethon, Baruch, [8]Meshullam, Abijah, Mijamin,
[9]Maaziah, Bilgai, Shemaiah: these are the priests.

[10]The Levites: Jeshua, son of Azaniah; Binnui, of the descendants of Henadad; Kadmiel;
[11d]and their kinsmen Shebaniah, Hodiah, Kelita, Pelaiah, Hanan, [12]Mica, Rehob, Hashabiah,
[13]Zaccur, Sherebiah, Shebaniah, [14]Hodiah, Bani,
Beninu.

[15]The leaders of the people: Parosh, Pahath-
moab, Elam, Zattu, Bani, [16]Bunni, Azgad, Bebai,
[17]Adonijah, Bigvai, Adin, [18]Ater, Hezekiah,
Azzur, [19]Hodiah, Hashum, Bezai, [20]Hariph, Anathoth, Nebai, [21]Magpiash, Meshullam, Hezir,
[22]Meshezabel, Zadok, Jaddua, [23]Pelatiah, Hanan,
Anaiah, [24]Hoshea, Hananiah, Hasshub, [25]Hall-
hohesh, Pilha, Shobek, [26]Rehum, Hashabnah,
Maaseiah, [27]Ahiah, Hanan, Anan, [28]Malluch,
Harim, Baanah.

**Provisions of the Pact.** [29]The rest of the people,
priests, Levites, gatekeepers, singers, temple servants, and all others who have separated themselves from the local inhabitants in favor of the
law of God, with their wives, their sons, their
daughters, all who are of the age of discretion,
[30e]join their influential kindred, and with the
sanction of a curse take this oath to follow the
law of God given through Moses, the servant of
God, and to observe carefully all the commandments of the LORD, our Lord, his ordinances and
his statutes.

[31f]We will not marry our daughters to the
local inhabitants, and we will not accept their
daughters for our sons.

[32g]When the local inhabitants bring in merchandise or any kind of grain for sale on the
sabbath day, we will not buy from them on the
sabbath or on any other holy day. In the seventh year we will forgo the produce, and forgive
every kind of debt.

[33h]We impose these commandments on ourselves: to give a third of a shekel each year for
the service of the house of our God, [34]for the
showbread, the daily grain offering, the daily
burnt offering, for the sabbaths, new moons,
and festivals, for the holy offerings and sin offerings to make atonement for Israel, for every
service of the house of our God. [35i]We, priests,
Levites, and people, have determined by lot
concerning the procurement of wood: it is to be
brought to the house of our God by each of our
ancestral houses at stated times each year, to be
burnt on the altar of the LORD, our God, as the
law prescribes. [36j]We have agreed to bring each
year to the house of the LORD the first fruits of
our fields and of our fruit trees, of every kind;
[37]also, as is prescribed in the law, to bring to the
house of our God, to the priests who serve in
the house of our God, the firstborn of our children and our animals, including the firstborn
of our flocks and herds. [38k]The first batch of our
dough, and our offerings of the fruit of every
tree, of wine and oil, we will bring to the priests,
to the chambers of the house of our God. The
tithe of our fields we will bring to the Levites;
they, the Levites, shall take the tithe in all the
cities of our service. [39]An Aaronite priest shall
be with the Levites when they take the tithe, and
the Levites shall bring the tithe of the tithes to
the house of our God, to the chambers of the
treasury. [40]For to these chambers the Israelites
and Levites bring the offerings of grain, wine,
and oil; there also are housed the vessels of the
sanctuary, and the ministering priests, the gatekeepers, and the singers. We will not neglect the
house of our God.

## III. DEDICATION OF THE WALL; OTHER REFORMS

## CHAPTER 11

**Resettlement of Jerusalem.** [1†]The administrators took up residence in Jerusalem, and the rest
of the people cast lots to bring one man in ten
to reside in Jerusalem, the holy city, while the
other nine would remain in the other cities. [2]The
people blessed all those who willingly agreed to
take up residence in Jerusalem.

[3m]These are the heads of the province who
took up residence in Jerusalem. In the cities of
Judah dwelt Israelites, priests, Levites, temple
servants, and the descendants of Solomon's
servants, each on the property they owned in their
own cities.

---

*[10:1–39] This section belongs to the Nehemiah narrative
rather than to that of Ezra. It is best read after Neh 13:31, since
the stipulations of the pact seem to presuppose Nehemiah's
measures recorded in Neh 13. **In view of all this**: considering
the situation described in Neh 13:4–31.

c. [10:3] Neh 12:1–7, 12–26.   d. [10:11] Ezr 10:23.   e. [10:30]
Neh 13:23–27.   f. [10:31] Dt 7:2–4; Ezr 9:2, 12; Neh 13:15–22.
g. [10:32] Neh 5:1–13; 13:15–22; Ex 20:8; Lv 25:2–7.

†[11:1–19] This list of the family heads who lived in Jerusalem at the time of Nehemiah is best read after Neh 7:72.
It parallels at many points the list of early settlers in 1 Chr
9:2–17.

h. [10:33] Lv 24:5–9; 2 Chr 24:6, 9–10.   i. [10:35] Neh 13:31.
j. [10:36] Ex 13:1, 11–16; Dt 26:1.   k. [10:38] Neh 13:10–14; Nm
18:21–32.   l. [11:1] Neh 7:4.   m. [11:3] 1 Chr 9:2–34.

[4]In Jerusalem dwelt both Judahites and Benjaminites. Of the Judahites: Athaiah, son of Uzziah, son of Zechariah, son of Amariah, son of Shephatiah, son of Mehallalel, of the sons of Perez; [5]Maaseiah, son of Baruch, son of Colhozeh, son of Hazaiah, son of Adaiah, son of Joiarib, son of Zechariah, a son of the Shelanites. [6]The total of the descendants of Perez who dwelt in Jerusalem was four hundred and sixty-eight people of substance.

[7]These were the Benjaminites: Sallu, son of Meshullam, son of Joed, son of Pedaiah, son of Kolaiah, son of Maaseiah, son of Ithiel, son of Jeshaiah, [8]and his kinsmen, warriors, nine hundred and twenty-eight in number. [9]Joel, son of Zichri, was their commander, and Judah, son of Hassenuah, was second in command of the city.

[10]Among the priests were: Jedaiah; Joiarib; Jachin; [11]Seraiah, son of Hilkiah, son of Meshullam, son of Zadok, son of Meraioth, son of Ahitub, the ruler of the house of God, [12]and their kinsmen who carried out the temple service, eight hundred and twenty-two; Adaiah, son of Jeroham, son of Pelaliah, son of Amzi, son of Zechariah, son of Pashhur, son of Malchijah, [13]and his kinsmen, heads of ancestral houses, two hundred and forty-two; and Amasai, son of Azarel, son of Ahzai, son of Meshillemoth, son of Immer, [14]and his kinsmen, warriors, one hundred and twenty-eight. Their commander was Zabdiel, son of Haggadol.

[15]Among the Levites were Shemaiah, son of Hasshub, son of Azrikam, son of Hashabiah, son of Bunni; [16]Shabbethai and Jozabad, levitical chiefs who were placed over the external affairs of the house of God; [17]Mattaniah, son of Micah, son of Zabdi, son of Asaph, director of the psalms, who led the thanksgiving at prayer; Bakbukiah, second in rank among his kinsmen; and Abda, son of Shammua, son of Galal, son of Jeduthun. [18]The total of the Levites in the holy city was two hundred and eighty-four.

[19]The gatekeepers were Akkub, Talmon, and their kinsmen, who kept watch over the gates; one hundred and seventy-two in number.

[20]The rest of Israel, including priests and Levites, were in all the other cities of Judah in their own inheritances.

[21]The temple servants lived on Ophel. Ziha and Gishpa were in charge of the temple servants.

[22]n The prefect of the Levites in Jerusalem was Uzzi, son of Bani, son of Hashabiah, son of Mattaniah, son of Micah; he was one of the descendants of Asaph, the singers appointed to the service of the house of God—[23]for they had been appointed by royal decree, and there was a fixed schedule for the singers assigning them their daily duties.

[24]Pethahiah, son of Meshezabel, a descendant of Zerah, son of Judah, was royal deputy in all affairs that concerned the people.

**Other Settlements.** [25]As concerns their villages with their fields: Judahites lived in Kiriath-arba and its dependencies, in Dibon and its dependencies, in Jekabzeel and its villages, [26]in Jeshua, Moladah, Beth-pelet, [27]in Hazarshual, in Beersheba and its dependencies, [28]in Ziklag, in Meconah and its dependencies, [29]in En-rimmon, Zorah, Jarmuth, [30]Zanoah, Adullam, and their villages, Lachish and its fields, Azekah and its dependencies. They were settled from Beersheba to Ge-hinnom.

[31]Benjaminites were in Geba, Michmash, Aija, Bethel and its dependencies, [32]Anathoth, Nob, Ananiah, [33]Hazor, Ramah, Gittaim, [34]Hadid, Zeboim, Neballat, [35]Lod, Ono, and the Valley of the Artisans.

[36]Some divisions of the Levites from Judah were attached to Benjamin.

## CHAPTER 12

**Priests and Levites at the Time of Zerubbabel.**
[1]o The following are the priests and Levites who returned with Zerubbabel, son of Shealtiel, and Jeshua: Seraiah, Jeremiah, Ezra, [2]Amariah, Malluch, Hattush, [3]Shecaniah, Rehum, Meremoth, [4]Iddo, Ginnethon, Abijah, [5]Mijamin, Maadiah, Bilgah, [6]Shemaiah, and Joiarib, Jedaiah, [7]Sallu, Amok, Hilkiah, Jedaiah. These were the priestly heads and their kinsmen in the days of Jeshua.

[8]The Levites were Jeshua, Binnui, Kadmiel, Sherebiah, Judah, Mattaniah, who, together with his kinsmen, was in charge of the thanksgiving hymns, [9]while Bakbukiah and Unno and their kinsmen ministered opposite them by turns.

**High Priests.** [10]*Jeshua became the father of Joiakim, Joiakim the father of Eliashib, and Eliashib the father of Joiada; [11]Joiada the father of Johanan, and Johanan the father of Jaddua.

**Priests and Levites Under Joiakim.** [12]p In the days of Joiakim these were the priestly family heads: for Seraiah, Meraiah; for Jeremiah, Hananiah; [13]for Ezra, Meshullam; for Amariah, Jehohanan; [14]for Malluchi, Jonathan; for Shebaniah, Joseph; [15]for Harim, Adna; for Meremoth, Helkai; [16]for Iddo, Zechariah; for Ginnethon, Meshullam; [17]for Abijah, Zichri; for Miamin, . . .; for Moadiah, Piltai; [18]for Bilgah, Shammua; for Shemaiah, Jehonathan; [19]and for Joiarib, Mattenai; for Jedaiah, Uzzi; [20]for Sallu, Kallai;

---

*[12:10–11] Jeshua was the high priest when Zerubbabel was governor, in the last decades of the sixth century B.C. (Hg 1:1, 12, 14; 2:2, 4). He was the grandfather of Eliashib, the high priest early in Nehemiah's governorship (445–433 B.C.; Neh 3:1, 20, 21) and perhaps later. Eliashib, the grandfather of Johanan, was a grown man, if not yet a high priest, at the time of Ezra, ca. 400 B.C. (Ezr 10:6; and note). According to Josephus (*Ant.* 11:120–183), whose testimony here is doubtful, Jaddua, son of Johanan, died as an old man about the time that Alexander the Great died, 323 B.C. If, as seems probable, this list of the postexilic high priests, at least as far as Johanan, comes from the author himself (cf. Neh 12:23) and not from a later scribe, it is of prime importance for dating the author's work in the first decades of the fourth century B.C.

---

n. [11:22] 2 Chr 20:14.               o. [12:1] Neh 12:12–22.   p. [12:12] Neh 10:3–9; 12:1–6.

for Amok, Eber; [21]for Hilkiah, Hashabiah; for Jedaiah, Nethanel.

[22]In the time of Eliashib, Joiada, Johanan, and Jaddua, the heads of ancestral houses of the priests were written down in the Book of Chronicles, up until the reign of Darius the Persian. [23]The sons of Levi: the family heads were written down in the Book of Chronicles, up until the time of Johanan, the son of Eliashib.

[24q]The heads of the Levites were Hashabiah, Sherebiah, Jeshua, Binnui, Kadmiel. Their kinsmen who stood opposite them to sing praises and thanksgiving in fulfillment of the command of David, the man of God, one section opposite the other, [25r]were Mattaniah, Bakbukiah, Obadiah.

Meshullam, Talmon, and Akkub were gatekeepers. They guarded the storerooms at the gates. [26]All these lived in the time of Joiakim, son of Jeshua, son of Jozadak (and in the time of Nehemiah the governor and of Ezra the priest-scribe).

**Dedication of the Wall.** [27*]At the dedication of the wall of Jerusalem, the Levites were sought out wherever they lived and were brought to Jerusalem to celebrate a joyful dedication with thanksgiving hymns and the music of cymbals, harps, and lyres. [28]The levitical singers gathered together from the region about Jerusalem, from the villages of the Netophathites, [29]from Beth-gilgal, and from the plains of Geba and Azmaveth (for the singers had built themselves settlements about Jerusalem). [30]The priests and Levites first purified themselves, then they purified the people, the gates, and the wall.

[31]I had the administrators of Judah go up on the wall, and I arranged two great choirs. The first of these proceeded to the right, along the top of the wall, in the direction of the Dung Gate, [32]followed by Hoshaiah and half the administrators of Judah, [33]along with Azariah, Ezra, Meshullam, [34]Judah, Benjamin, Shemaiah, and Jeremiah, [35]priests with the trumpets, and also Zechariah, son of Jonathan, son of Shemaiah, son of Mattaniah, son of Micaiah, son of Zaccur, son of Asaph, [36]and his kinsmen Shemaiah, Azarel, Milalai, Gilalai, Maai, Nethanel, Judah, and Hanani, with the musical instruments of David, the man of God. Ezra the scribe was at their head. [37]At the Fountain Gate they went straight up by the steps of the City of David and continued along the top of the wall above the house of David until they came to the Water Gate on the east.

[38]The second choir proceeded to the left, followed by myself and the other half of the administrators, along the top of the wall past the Oven Tower as far as the Broad Wall, [39]then past the Ephraim Gate to the Mishneh Gate, the Fish Gate, the Tower of Hananel, and the Hundred Tower, as far as the Sheep Gate. They came to a halt at the Prison Gate.

[40]Both choirs took up a position in the house of God; I, too, and half the magistrates with me, [41]together with the priests Eliakim, Maaseiah, Minjamin, Micaiah, Elioenai, Zechariah, Hananiah, with the trumpets, [42]and Maaseiah, Shemaiah, Eleazar, Uzzi, Jehohanan, Malchijah, Elam, and Ezer. The singers were heard under the leadership of Jezrahiah. [43]Great sacrifices were offered on that day, and they rejoiced, for God had given them cause for great rejoicing. The women and the children joined in, and the rejoicing at Jerusalem could be heard from far off.

[44ts]At that time men were appointed over the chambers set aside for stores, offerings, first fruits, and tithes; in them they were to collect from the fields of the various cities the portions legally assigned to the priests and Levites. For Judah rejoiced in its appointed priests and Levites [45]who carried out the ministry of their God and the ministry of purification (as did the singers and the gatekeepers) in accordance with the prescriptions of David and Solomon, his son. [46t]For in the days of David and Asaph, long ago, there were leaders of singers for songs of praise and thanksgiving to God. [47u]All Israel, in the days of Zerubbabel and in the days of Nehemiah, gave the singers and the gatekeepers their portions, according to their daily needs. They made their consecrated offering to the Levites, and the Levites made theirs to the descendants of Aaron.

## CHAPTER 13

[1‡v]At that time, when the book of Moses was being read in the hearing of the people, it was found written there: "No Ammonite or Moabite may ever be admitted into the assembly of God; [2w]for they did not meet the Israelites with food and water, but they hired Balaam to curse them, though our God turned the curse into a blessing." [3x]When they had heard the law, they separated all those of mixed descent from Israel.

**Reform in the Temple.** [4§]Before this, the priest Eliashib, who had been placed in charge of the chambers of the house of our God and who was an associate of Tobiah, [5y]had set aside for

---

*[12:27–43] The dedication of the wall of Jerusalem took place, no doubt, soon after the restoration of the wall and its gates had been completed. This section, therefore, is best read after Neh 6:15.

---

q. [12:24] Ezr 2:40.   r. [12:25] Neh 11:17.

---

†[12:44–47] This account of the provisions made for the Temple services is a composition either of the author or of a later scribe. The gloss mentioning Nehemiah is not in the Septuagint.

‡[13:1–3] These verses serve as an introduction to the reforms Nehemiah instituted during his second mission in Jerusalem (vv. 4–31). The part of the Book of Moses read to the people is freely quoted here from Dt 23:3–6.

§[13:4–31] This is part of the "Memoirs of Nehemiah"; it is continued in 10:1–40.

---

s. [12:44] 1 Chr 23–26; 2 Chr 8:14.   t. [12:46] 2 Chr 29:30; 35:15.   u. [12:47] Neh 10:39; 13:10–11; Nm 18:26.   v. [13:1] Dt 23:3–6.   w. [13:2] Nm 22–24.   x. [13:3] Neh 13:23–28.   y. [13:5] Neh 12:44.

the latter's use a large chamber in which had previously been stored the grain offerings, incense and vessels, the tithes in grain, wine, and oil allotted to the Levites, singers, and gatekeepers, and the offerings due the priests. ⁶During all this time I had not been in Jerusalem, for in the thirty-second year of Artaxerxes,* king of Babylon, I had gone back to the king. After a suitable period of time, however, I asked leave of the king ⁷and returned to Jerusalem, where I discovered the evil thing that Eliashib had done for Tobiah, in setting aside for him a chamber in the courts of the house of God. ⁸This displeased me very much, so I had all of Tobiah's household goods thrown outside the chamber. ⁹Then I gave orders to purify the chambers, and I brought back the vessels of the house of God, the grain offerings, and the incense.

¹⁰I learned, too, that the portions due the Levites were no longer being given, so that the Levites and the singers who should have been carrying out the services had deserted to their own fields. ¹¹I reprimanded the magistrates, demanding, "Why is the house of God neglected?" Then I brought the Levites together and had them resume their stations. ¹²ᶻAll Judah once more brought in the tithes of grain, wine, and oil to the storerooms. ¹³In charge of the storerooms I appointed Shelemiah the priest, Zadok the scribe, and Pedaiah, one of the Levites, together with Hanan, son of Zaccur, son of Mattaniah, as their assistant; for they were considered trustworthy. It was their duty to make the distribution to their kinsmen. ¹⁴Remember this to my credit, my God! Do not forget the good deeds I have done for the house of my God and its services!

**Sabbath Observance.** ¹⁵ᵃIn those days I perceived that people in Judah were treading the wine presses on the sabbath; that they were bringing in sheaves of grain, loading them on their donkeys, together with wine, grapes, figs, and every other kind of load, and bringing them to Jerusalem on the sabbath day. I warned them to sell none of these provisions. ¹⁶In Jerusalem itself the Tyrians residing there were importing fish and every other kind of merchandise and selling it to the Judahites on the sabbath. ¹⁷I reprimanded the nobles of Judah, demanding: "What is this evil thing you are doing, profaning the sabbath day? ¹⁸Did not your ancestors act in this same way, with the result that our God has

brought all this evil upon us and upon this city? Would you add to the wrath against Israel by once more profaning the sabbath?"

¹⁹When the shadows were falling on the gates of Jerusalem before the sabbath, I ordered the doors to be closed and prohibited their reopening until after the sabbath. I posted some of my own people at the gates so that no load might enter on the sabbath day. ²⁰The merchants and sellers of various kinds of merchandise spent the night once or twice outside Jerusalem, ²¹but then I warned them: "Why do you spend the night alongside the wall? If you keep this up, I will beat you!" From that time on, they did not return on the sabbath. ²²Then I ordered the Levites to purify themselves and to watch the gates, so that the sabbath day might be kept holy. This, too, remember in my favor, my God, and have mercy on me in accordance with your great mercy!

**Mixed Marriages.** ²³ᵇAlso in those days I saw Jews who had married women of Ashdod, Ammon, or Moab. ²⁴Of their children, half spoke the language of Ashdod,† or of one of the other peoples, and none of them knew how to speak the language of Judah. ²⁵So I reprimanded and cursed them; I beat some of their men and pulled out their hair; and I adjured them by God: "You shall not marry your daughters to their sons nor accept any of their daughters for your sons or for yourselves! ²⁶ᶜDid not Solomon, the king of Israel, sin because of them? Though among the many nations there was no king like him, and though he was beloved of his God and God had made him king over all Israel, yet even he was led into sin by foreign women. ²⁷Must it also be heard of you that you have done this same terrible evil, betraying our God by marrying foreign women?"

²⁸ᵈOne of the sons of Joiada, son of Eliashib the high priest, was the son-in-law of Sanballat the Horonite! I drove him from my presence. ²⁹Remember against them, my God, how they defiled the priesthood and the covenant of the priesthood and the Levites!

³⁰So I cleansed them of all foreign contamination. I established the various functions for the priests and Levites, so that each had an appointed task. ³¹ᵉI also provided for the procurement of wood at stated times and for the first fruits. Remember this in my favor, my God!

*[13:6] **In the thirty-second year of Artaxerxes**: Artaxerxes I, therefore 433 B.C. **After . . . time**: it is not known when Nehemiah returned to Jerusalem or how long his second period of activity there lasted.

z. [13:12] Neh 10:38–39; 12:44–45, 47; 2 Chr 31:6.   a. [13:15] Neh 10:32; Ex 20:8.

†[13:24] **Language of Ashdod**: more likely an Aramaic rather than a Philistine dialect. **The language of Judah**: probably Hebrew.

b. [13:23] Neh 10:31; 13:1–3; Dt 23:3; Ezr 9–10.   c. [13:26] 1 Kgs 11:1–13.   d. [13:28] Neh 2:10; 13:4–5, 7–9.   e. [13:31] Neh 10:35–36.

# BIBLICAL NOVELLAS

❧

The Bible conveys the Word of God in many literary forms: historical narrative, poetry, prophetic exhortation, wisdom sayings, and novellas (edifying stories). In the Constitution on Divine Revelation from Vatican II (*Dei Verbum*), the council fathers give instruction on how to approach this variety: "Attention must be paid to literary forms, for the fact is that truth is differently presented and expressed in the various types of historical writing, in prophetical and poetical texts, and in other forms of literary expression. Hence the interpreter must look for that meaning which the sacred writer intended to express and did in fact express through the medium of a contemporary literary form" (DV 12).

The Books of Tobit, Judith, and Esther are often grouped together. They are stories told to instruct the people concerning the ways of God, to encourage them in critical times, and to entertain. They are aids to the imagination. While they may contain kernels of historical fact, these stories are told primarily to illustrate truths that transcend history.

The author of the Book of Tobit, writing in the second century B.C., tells a story about the life of a devout family in seventh-century Assyria. He gives the people of his own time an example to follow as they struggle with the tensions of living a faithful Jewish life in the midst of a non-Jewish civilization. Tobit, suffering from the affliction of blindness, perseveres in good works and prayer, as do the other characters in the story. God sends an angel who, while hidden from them, leads them to health and happiness. The conclusion demonstrates that God does answer prayer and that perseverance in good works does not go unrewarded.

The author of the Book of Judith gives many clues that this story is beyond history. All the worst enemies of the people—the Assyrians of the eighth and seventh centuries, the sixth-century Babylonian king Nebuchadnezzar—are rolled into one terror. The hero, Judith, is modeled on the heroes of the Book of Judges, yet her story is also reminiscent of a second-century hero, Judas Maccabeus (1–2 Maccabees). Even the conflation of time indications—the eighteenth year of Nebuchadnezzar (2:1; the year 587 B.C., when he destroyed Jerusalem and took the Jews into exile) with the return from exile and rededication of the Temple (4:3; the events of 538 and 515 respectively)—suggests God's deliverance from the most terrible circumstances. The story may be set in a time long past, but it is meant to encourage the people of the late second century to trust in God when their way of life is threatened. God can use even the most unlikely means, such as a widow, a biblical figure of powerlessness and vulnerability, to deliver them from their enemies.

The Book of Esther includes several historical elements. The Persian king Xerxes (486–465 B.C.), the city of Susa, a court official named Marduka, are all known from other sources. But further investigation shows this is not meant to be a historical account. There is no record of Xerxes having any other queen than Amestris and no mention of such a massacre during his reign. The book has a different purpose: to suggest a historical basis to the festival of Purim, perhaps originally a Persian feast. Through the story of Esther, Purim becomes a celebration of God's rescue of the people from persecution and certain death.

The message conveyed in these stories is not confined to one geographic place or historical period. It remains a valid expression of God's care for faithful people in every time and place.

# THE BOOK OF
# TOBIT

❧

The Book of Tobit, named after its principal character, combines Jewish piety and morality with folklore in a fascinating story that has enjoyed wide popularity in both Jewish and Christian circles. Prayers, psalms, and words of wisdom, as well as the skillfully constructed story itself, provide valuable insights into the faith and the religious milieu of its unknown author. The book was probably written early in the second century B.C.; it is not known where.

Tobit, a devout and wealthy Israelite living among the captives deported to Nineveh from the Northern Kingdom of Israel in 722/721 B.C., suffers severe reverses and is finally blinded. Because of his misfortunes he begs the Lord to let him die. But recalling the large sum he had formerly deposited in far-off Media, he sends his son Tobiah there to bring back the money. In Media, at this same time, a young woman, Sarah, also prays for death, because she has lost seven husbands, each killed in turn on her wedding night by the demon Asmodeus. God hears the prayers of Tobit and Sarah and sends the angel Raphael in human form to aid them both.

Raphael makes the trip to Media with Tobiah. When Tobiah is attacked by a large fish as he bathes in the Tigris River, Raphael orders him to seize it and to remove its gall, heart, and liver because they are useful for medicine. Later, at Raphael's urging, Tobiah marries Sarah, and uses the fish's heart and liver to drive Asmodeus from the bridal chamber. Returning to Nineveh with his wife and his father's money, Tobiah rubs the fish's gall into his father's eyes and cures him. Finally, Raphael reveals his true identity and returns to heaven. Tobit then utters his beautiful hymn of praise. Before dying, Tobit tells his son to leave Nineveh because God will destroy that wicked city. After Tobiah buries his father and mother, he and his family depart for Media, where he later learns that the destruction of Nineveh has taken place.

The inspired author of the book used the literary form of religious novel (as in Esther and Judith) for the purpose of instruction and edification. The seemingly historical data, names of kings, cities, etc., are used as vivid details not only to create interest and charm, but also to illustrate the negative side of the theory of retribution: the wicked are indeed punished.

Although the Book of Tobit is usually listed with the historical books, it more correctly stands midway between them and the wisdom literature. It contains numerous maxims like those found in the wisdom books (cf. 4:3–19, 21; 12:6–10; 14:7, 9) as well as standard wisdom themes: fidelity to the law, intercessory function of angels, piety toward parents, purity of marriage, reverence for the dead, and the value of almsgiving, prayer, and fasting. The book makes Tobit a relative of Ahiqar, a noted hero of ancient Near Eastern wisdom literature and folklore.

Written most likely in Aramaic, the original of the book was lost for centuries. Fragments of four Aramaic texts and of one Hebrew text were discovered in Qumran Cave 4 in 1952 and have only recently been published. These Semitic forms of the book are in substantial agreement with the long Greek recension of Tobit found in Codex Sinaiticus, which had been recovered from St. Catherine's Monastery (Mount Sinai) only in 1844, and in mss. 319 and 910. Two other Greek forms of Tobit have long been known: the short recension, found mainly in the mss. Alexandrinus, Vaticanus, Venetus, and numerous cursive mss.; and an intermediate Greek recension, found in mss. 44, 106, 107. The Book of Tobit has also been known from two Latin versions: the long recension in the Vetus Latina, which is closely related to the long Greek recension and sometimes is even closer to the Aramaic and Hebrew texts than the Greek is; and the short recension in the Vulgate, related to the short Greek recension. The present English translation has been based mainly on Sinaiticus, which is the most complete form of the long Greek recension, despite two lacunae (4:7–19b and 13:6i–10b) and some missing phrases, which make succeeding verses difficult to understand and make it necessary to supplement Sinaiticus from the Vetus Latina or from the short Greek recension. Occasionally, phrases or words have been introduced from the Aramaic or Hebrew texts, when they are significantly different. Forms of the Book of Tobit are also extant in ancient Arabic, Armenian, Coptic (Sahidic), Ethiopic, and Syriac, but these are almost all secondarily derived from the short Greek recension.

The divisions of the Book of Tobit are:

    I. Tobit's Ordeals (1:3–3:6)

   II. Sarah's Plight (3:7–17)

  III. Preparation for the Journey (4:1–6:1)

  IV. Tobiah's Journey to Media (6:2–18)

   V. Marriage and Healing of Sarah (7:1–9:6)

  VI. Tobiah's Return Journey to Nineveh and the Healing of Tobit (10:1–11:18)

 VII. Raphael Reveals His Identity (12:1–22)

VIII. Tobit's Song of Praise (13:1–18)

  IX. Epilogue (14:1–15)

## CHAPTER 1

**Tobit.** ¹This book tells the story of Tobit,* son of Tobiel, son of Hananiel, son of Aduel, son of Gabael, son of Raphael, son of Raguel, of the family of Asiel and the tribe of Naphtali. ²During the days of Shalmaneser,† king of the Assyrians, he was taken captive from Thisbe, which is south of Kedesh Naphtali in upper Galilee, above and to the west of Asher, north of Phogor.ᵃ

### I. TOBIT'S ORDEALS

**His Virtue.** ³I, Tobit, have walked all the days of my life on paths of fidelity and righteousness. I performed many charitable deeds for my kindred and my people who had been taken captive with me to Nineveh, in the land of the Assyrians. ⁴When I lived as a young man in my own country, in the land of Israel, the entire tribe of my ancestor Naphtali broke away from the house of David, my ancestor, and from Jerusalem, the city that had been singled out of all Israel's tribes that all Israel might offer sacrifice there. It was the place where the temple, God's dwelling, had been built and consecrated for all generations to come. ⁵ᵇAll my kindred, as well as the house of Naphtali, my ancestor, used to offer

sacrifice on every hilltop in Galilee to the calf that Jeroboam, king of Israel, had made in Dan.‡

⁶But I alone used to go often to Jerusalem for the festivals, as was prescribed for all Israel by longstanding decree.§ Bringing with me the first fruits of crops, the firstlings of the flock, the tithes of livestock, and the first shearings of sheep,ᵈ I used to hasten to Jerusalem ⁷ᵉand present them to the priests, Aaron's sons, at the altar. To the Levites ministering in Jerusalem I used to give the tithe of grain, wine, olive oil, pomegranates, figs, and other fruits. Six years in a row, I used to give a second tithe in money, which each year I would go to pay in Jerusalem. ⁸The third-year tithe I gave to orphans, widows, and converts who had joined the Israelites. Every third year I would bring them this offering, and we ate it in keeping with the decree laid down in the Mosaic law concerning it, and according to the commands of Deborah, the mother of my father Tobiel; for my father had died and left me an orphan.

⁹When I reached manhood, I married Anna, a woman of our ancestral family. By her I had a son whom I named Tobiah. ¹⁰Now, after I had been deported to the Assyrians and came

---

*[1:1] **Tobit:** in the Aramaic text the name is given as Tobi, an abbreviated form of Tobiyah (Ezr 2:60) or of Tobiyahu (2 Chr 17:8), a name that means "Yhwh is my welfare." **Tobiel:** "El [God] is my welfare." **Hananiel:** "El [God] has shown mercy." The book abounds in theophoric names.

†[1:2] **Shalmaneser** (V) (727–722 B.C.): began the siege of Samaria; the inhabitants of the Northern Kingdom were taken into captivity by his successor, Sargon II (722–705); cf. 2 Kgs 17:1–6. **Thisbe** and **Phogor:** unidentified towns of Galilee. **Kedesh Naphtali:** cf. Jos 20:7; 2 Kgs 15:29. **Asher:** probably Hazor (Jos 11:1).

‡[1:5] Jeroboam established sanctuaries in Dan and Bethel so that the people would no longer have to go to Jerusalem for the festivals. The gold statues of calves that he placed in the sanctuaries were considered the throne of Yhwh; but the people may have tended to worship the images themselves. Jeroboam also encouraged high places or hilltop shrines (1 Kgs 12:26–33).

§[1:6–8] **Longstanding decree:** Dt 12:11, 13–14. Refusing to worship at Jeroboam's shrines, the faithful Tobit continued to bring his offerings to Jerusalem; see 2 Chr 11:16. For the various tithes, cf. Lv 27:30–33; Nm 18:20–32; 2 Chr 31:4–6; Dt 14:22–29; 26:12–13.

a. [1:2] 2 Kgs 17:3; 18:9–12.  b. [1:5] 1 Kgs 12:26–32.    c. [1:6] Ex 23:14–15, 17; 34:23.  d. [1:6] Dt 16:16.  e. [1:7–8] Nm 18:12–13, 24; Dt 14:22–29; 18:4–5.

as a captive to Nineveh, all my kindred and my people used to eat the food of the Gentiles,[f] [11]but I refrained from eating that Gentile food. [12]Because I was mindful of God with all my heart, [13]the Most High granted me favor and status with Shalmaneser, so that I became purchasing agent for all his needs.[g] [14]Until he died, I would go to Media to buy goods for him there. I also deposited pouches of silver worth ten talents* in trust with my kinsman Gabael, son of Gabri, who lived at Rages, in the land of Media. [15]When Shalmaneser died and his son Sennacherib[†] came to rule in his stead, the roads to Media became unsafe, so I could no longer go to Media.

**Courage in Burying the Dead.** [16]In the days of Shalmaneser I had performed many charitable deeds for my kindred, members of my people. [17h]I would give my bread to the hungry and clothing to the naked. If I saw one of my people who had died and been thrown behind the wall of Nineveh, I used to bury him.[‡] [18]Sennacherib returned from Judea, having fled during the days of the judgment enacted against him by the King of Heaven because of the blasphemies he had uttered; whomever he killed I buried. For in his rage he killed many Israelites, but I used to take their bodies away by stealth and bury them. So when Sennacherib looked for them, he could not find them. [19]But a certain Ninevite went and informed the king about me, that I was burying them, and I went into hiding. When I realized that the king knew about me and that I was being hunted to be put to death, I became afraid and took flight. [20]All my property was confiscated; I was left with nothing. All that I had was taken to the king's palace, except for my wife Anna and my son Tobiah.[§]

[21]But forty days did not pass before two of the king's sons assassinated him and fled to the mountains of Ararat. A son of his, Esarhaddon,[¶] succeeded him as king. He put Ahiqar, my kinsman Anael's son, in charge of all the credit accounts of his kingdom, and he took control over the entire administration.[i] [22]Then Ahiqar interceded on my behalf, and I returned to Nineveh. Ahiqar had been chief cupbearer, keeper of the signet ring, treasury accountant, and credit accountant under Sennacherib, king of the Assyrians; and Esarhaddon appointed him as Second to himself. He was, in fact, my nephew, of my father's house, and of my own family.

## CHAPTER 2

[1]Thus under King Esarhaddon I returned to my home, and my wife Anna and my son Tobiah were restored to me. Then on our festival of Pentecost, the holy feast of Weeks,** a fine dinner was prepared for me, and I reclined to eat.[j] [2]The table was set for me, and the dishes placed before me were many. So I said to my son Tobiah: "Son, go out and bring in whatever poor person you find among our kindred exiled here in Nineveh who may be a sincere worshiper of God to share this meal with me. Indeed, son, I shall wait for you to come back."[††]

[3]Tobiah went out to look for some poor person among our kindred, but he came back and cried, "Father!" I said to him, "Here I am, son." He answered, "Father, one of our people has been murdered! He has been thrown out into the market place, and there he lies strangled." [4]I sprang to my feet, leaving the dinner untouched, carried the dead man from the square, and put him in one of the rooms until sundown, so that I might bury him. [5]I returned and washed[‡‡] and in sorrow ate my food.[k] [6]I remembered the oracle pronounced by the prophet Amos against Bethel:[l]

> "I will turn your feasts into mourning,
>     and all your songs into dirges."

[7]Then I wept. At sunset I went out, dug a grave, and buried him.

[8]My neighbors mocked me, saying: "Does he have no fear? Once before he was hunted, to be executed for this sort of deed, and he ran away; yet here he is again burying the dead!"

**Tobit's Blindness.** [9]That same night I washed and went into my courtyard, where I lay down to sleep beside the wall. Because of the heat I left my face uncovered. [10]I did not know that sparrows were perched on the wall above me; their warm droppings settled in my eyes, causing

---

*[1:14] **Silver worth ten talents:** a great sum of money; about ten thousand dollars, at least. **Rages:** modern Rai, about five miles southeast of Tehran. **Media:** the northwestern part of modern Iran.

†[1:15] **Sennacherib** (705–681 B.C.): the son of Sargon II; neither was descended from Shalmaneser. On such historical inconsistencies, see Introduction; also notes on 5:6; 6:2; 9:2; 14:15.

‡[1:17–18] Tobit risked his own life to bury the dead. Deprivation of burial was viewed with horror by the Jews. Cf. 4:3–4; 6:15; 14:12–13.

§[1:20] **Tobiah:** the son bears the fuller form of his father's name; see note on 1:1.

¶[1:21] **Esarhaddon:** 681–669 B.C. **Ahiqar:** a hero of ancient folklore, known for his outstanding wisdom. *The Story (or Wisdom) of Ahiqar* was very popular in antiquity and is extant in many different forms: Aramaic, Syriac, Armenian, Arabic (*Arabian Nights*), Greek (*Aesop's Fables*), Slavonic, Ethiopic, and Romanian. The sacred author makes Tobit the uncle of the famous Ahiqar in order to enhance Tobit's own prestige. See note on 14:10.

**[2:1] **Feast of Weeks:** also called by its Greek name, Pentecost, was celebrated fifty days after the Passover. Cf. Lv 23:15–21; Dt 16:9–12.

††[2:2] Almsgiving and charity to the poor are important virtues taught by the book (4:7–11, 16–17; 12:8–9; 14:10–11). **A sincere worshiper of God:** lit., "who is mindful of God with the whole heart."

‡‡[2:5] **Washed:** because of ritual defilement from touching a corpse (Nm 19:11–13).

---

f. [1:10] Lv 11; Dt 14:3–21; Acts 15:29; 1 Cor 8:7–13.   g. [1:13] Dn 2:48–49.   h. [1:17] Jb 31:16–20.

i. [1:21] 2 Kgs 19:37; 2 Chr 32:21; 2 Mc 8:19; Sir 48:21; Is 37:38.   j. [2:1] Lv 23:15–21; Nm 28:26–31; Dt 16:9–12.   k. [2:5] Nm 19:11–22.   l. [2:6] 1 Mc 1:39; Am 8:10.

white scales* on them. I went to doctors for a cure, but the more they applied ointments, the more my vision was obscured by the white scales, until I was totally blind. For four years I was unable to see, and all my kindred were distressed at my condition. Ahiqar, however, took care of me for two years, until he left for Elam.

¹¹At that time my wife Anna worked for hire at weaving cloth, doing the kind of work women do. ¹²When she delivered the material to her employers, they would pay her a wage. On the seventh day of the month of Dystrus,† she finished the woven cloth and delivered it to her employers. They paid her the full salary and also gave her a young goat for a meal. ¹³On entering my house, the goat began to bleat. So I called to my wife and said: "Where did this goat come from? It was not stolen, was it? Give it back to its owners; we have no right to eat anything stolen!" ¹⁴ᵐBut she said to me, "It was given to me as a bonus over and above my wages." Yet I would not believe her and told her to give it back to its owners. I flushed with anger at her over this. So she retorted: "Where are your charitable deeds now? Where are your righteous acts? Look! All that has happened to you is well known!"‡

## CHAPTER 3

¹Then sad at heart, I groaned and wept aloud. With sobs I began to pray:§

### Tobit's Prayer for Death

² "You are righteous, Lord,
      and all your deeds are just;
   All your ways are mercy and fidelity;
      you are judge of the world.ⁿ
³ And now, Lord, be mindful of me
      and look with favor upon me.
   Do not punish me for my sins,
      or for my inadvertent offenses,
      or for those of my ancestors.ᵒ

   "They sinned against you,
⁴      and disobeyed your
         commandments.
   So you handed us over to plunder,
      captivity, and death,

to become an object lesson, a
      byword, and a reproach
   in all the nations among whom you
      scattered us.ᵖ

⁵ "Yes, your many judgments are right
      in dealing with me as my sins,
      and those of my ancestors, deserve.
   For we have neither kept your
         commandments,
      nor walked in fidelity before you.

⁶ "So now, deal with me as you please;
      command my life breath to be taken
         from me,
   that I may depart from the face of
      the earth and become dust.
   It is better for me to die than to live,ˢ
      because I have listened to
         undeserved reproaches,
      and great is the grief within me.�q

   "Lord, command that I be released from
         such anguish;
      let me go to my everlasting abode;
   Do not turn your face away from
      me, Lord.
   For it is better for me to die
      than to endure so much misery in
         life,
      and to listen to such reproaches!"

## II. SARAH'S PLIGHT

**Sarah Falsely Accused.** ⁷**On that very day, at
Ecbatana in Media, it so happened that Raguel's
daughter Sarah also had to listen to reproaches
from one of her father's maids. ⁸For she had
been given in marriage to seven husbands, but
the wicked demon Asmodeus†† kept killing them
off before they could have intercourse with her,
as is prescribed for wives. The maid said to her:
"You are the one who kills your husbands! Look!
You have already been given in marriage to
seven husbands, but you do not bear the name

---

*[2:10] **White scales**: or white films. A primitive way of describing an eye ailment that results in blindness. **Elam**: or in Greek, *Elymais*, an ancient district northeast of the head of the Persian Gulf.

†[2:12] **Seventh day of the month of Dystrus**: late in winter. The Macedonian month Dystros corresponds to the Jewish month of Shebat (January–February). **A meal**: lit., "for the hearth"; the gift had probably been made in view of some springtime festival like the Jewish Purim.

‡[2:14] Anna's sharp rebuke calls to mind the words of Job's wife (Jb 2:9).

§[3:1] **Pray**: prayer is a significant theme, occurring at six major turning points in the story (3:2–6, 11–15; 8:5–8, 15–17; 11:14–15; 13:1–18).

¶[3:6] **It is better for me to die than to live**: in his distress Tobit uses the words of the petulant Jonah (Jon 4:3, 8), who wished to die because God did not destroy the hated Ninevites. In similar circumstances, Moses (Nm 11:15), Elijah (1 Kgs 19:4), and Job (Jb 7:15) also prayed for death. **Everlasting abode**: a reference to Sheol, the dismal abode of the dead from which no one returns (Jb 7:9–10; 14:12; Is 26:14). See note on Tb 4:6.

**[3:7] From here on, the story is told in the third person. Verse 7 relates one of the several marvelous coincidences that the storyteller uses to suggest divine providence; see also vv. 16–17; 4:1; 5:4. **Ecbatana**: Hamadan in modern Iran; this was the capital of ancient Media. **Raguel**: the Greek form of the Hebrew name *Re'u'el*, "friend of God."

††[3:8] **Asmodeus**: in Persian *aeshma daeva*, "demon of wrath," adopted into Aramaic with the sense of "the Destroyer." It will be subdued (8:3) by Raphael (v. 17), whose name means "God has healed."

---

m. [2:14] Jb 2:9.   n. [3:2] Ps 25:10; 119:137; Dn 3:27.   o. [3:3] Ex 34:7.

p. [3:4] Dt 28:15; Bar 1:16–22; 2:4–5; 3:8; Dn 9:5–6.   q. [3:6] Nm 11:15; 1 Kgs 19:4; Jb 7:15; Jon 4:3, 8.

of a single one of them. ⁹Why do you beat us? Because your husbands are dead? Go, join them! May we never see son or daughter of yours!"

¹⁰That day Sarah was sad at heart. She went in tears to an upstairs room in her father's house and wanted to hang herself. But she reconsidered, saying to herself: "No! May people never reproach my father and say to him, 'You had only one beloved daughter, but she hanged herself because of her misfortune.' And thus would I bring my father laden with sorrow in his old age to Hades. It is far better for me not to hang myself, but to beg the Lord that I might die, and no longer have to listen to such reproaches in my lifetime."ʳ

¹¹At that same time, with hands outstretched toward the window,* she implored favor:

### Sarah's Prayer for Death

"Blessed are you, merciful God!
　　Blessed be your holy and honorable
　　　　name forever!
　　May all your works forever bless you.ˢ
¹²　Now to you, Lord, I have turned my face
　　　　and have lifted up my eyes.
¹³　Bid me to depart from the earth,
　　　　never again to listen to such
　　　　　　reproaches.

¹⁴ "You know, Master, that I am clean
　　　　of any defilement with a man.
¹⁵　I have never sullied my own name
　　　　or my father's name in the land of
　　　　　　my captivity.

　　"I am my father's only daughter,
　　　　and he has no other child to be his
　　　　　　heir,
　　Nor does he have a kinsman or close
　　　　relative
　　　　whose wife I should wait to become.
　　Seven husbands of mine have already died.
　　　　Why then should I live any longer?
　　But if it does not please you, Lord, to take
　　　　my life,
　　　　look favorably upon me and have
　　　　　　pity on me,
　　　　that I may never again listen to such
　　　　　　reproaches!"

**An Answer to Prayer.** ¹⁶At that very time, the prayer of both of them was heard in the glorious presence of God. ¹⁷ᵗSo Raphael was sent to heal them both: to remove the white scales from

Tobit's eyes, so that he might again see with his own eyes God's light; and to give Sarah, the daughter of Raguel, as a wife to Tobiah, the son of Tobit, and to rid her of the wicked demon Asmodeus. For it fell to Tobiah's lot† to claim her before any others who might wish to marry her.

At that very moment Tobit turned from the courtyard to his house, and Raguel's daughter Sarah came down from the upstairs room.

## III. PREPARATION FOR THE JOURNEY

### CHAPTER 4

**A Father's Instruction.** ¹That same day Tobit remembered the money he had deposited in trust with Gabael at Rages in Media. ²He thought to himself, "Now that I have asked for death, why should I not call my son Tobiah and let him know about this money before I die?" ³So he called his son Tobiah; and when he came, he said to him:‡ "Son, when I die, give me a decent burial. Honor your mother, and do not abandon her as long as she lives. Do whatever pleases her, and do not grieve her spirit in any way.ᵘ ⁴Remember, son, how she went through many dangers for you while you were in her womb. When she dies, bury her in the same grave with me.

⁵"Through all your days, son, keep the Lord in mind, and do not seek to sin or to transgress the commandments. Perform righteous deeds all the days of your life, and do not tread the paths of wickedness. ⁶ᵛFor those who act with fidelity, all who practice righteousness, will prosper in their affairs.§

⁷"Give alms from your possessions. Do not turn your face away from any of the poor, so that God's face will not be turned away from you.ʷ ⁸Give in proportion to what you own. If you have great wealth, give alms out of your abundance; if you have but little, do not be afraid to give alms even of that little. ⁹You will be storing up a goodly treasure for yourself against the day of adversity.ˣ ¹⁰For almsgiving delivers from death and keeps one from entering into Darkness.

---

*[3:11] **Toward the window:** that is, looking in prayer toward Jerusalem; cf. Dn 6:11. "Blessed are you" and "Blessed be God" are traditional openings of Jewish prayers (Tb 8:5, 15; 11:14; 13:1).

†[3:17] **It fell to Tobiah's lot:** according to the patriarchal custom of marriage within the family group. Tobiah was Sarah's closest eligible relative (6:12). Cf. 4:12–13; Gn 24:4; 28:2; Ru 3:9–12; 4:1–12.

‡[4:3–19] A collection of maxims that parallel those in the wisdom literature, especially Proverbs and Sirach (see Introduction): duties toward parents (vv. 3–4; cf. also 14:13); perseverance in virtue and avoidance of evil (vv. 5–6, 14b); necessity and value of almsgiving and charity (vv. 7–11, 16–17); marriage within the clan (vv. 12–13a); industry (v. 13b); prompt payment of wages (v. 14a); the golden rule (v. 15a); temperance (v. 15b); docility (v. 18); prayer (v. 19).

§[4:6] It was commonly thought in the Old Testament that virtue guaranteed earthly prosperity, and sin earthly disaster (Prv 10:2; cf. Dt 28).

r. [3:10] Tb 6:15; Gn 37:35; 42:38; 44:29, 31.　s. [3:11] 1 Kgs 8:44, 48; Ps 28:2; 134:2; Dn 6:11.　t. [3:17] Tb 4:12–13; 6:12–13; Gn 24:3–4.

u. [4:3] Ex 20:12; Prv 23:22; Sir 7:27.　v. [4:6] Tb 13:6; Jn 3:21; Eph 4:15.　w. [4:7–8] Tb 12:8–10; Dt 15:7–8, 11; Prv 19:17; Sir 4:1–6; 14:13; Lk 14:13; 1 Jn 3:17.　x. [4:9] Mt 6:20–21.

¹¹Almsgiving is a worthy offering in the sight of the Most High for all who practice it.ʸ

¹²"Be on your guard, son, against every kind of fornication, and above all, marry a woman of your own ancestral family. Do not marry a foreign woman, one who is not of your father's tribe, because we are descendants of the prophets, who were the first to speak the truth. Noah prophesied first, then Abraham, Isaac, and Jacob, our ancestors from the beginning of time. Son, remember that all of them took wives from among their own kindred and were blessed in their children, and that their posterity would inherit the land.ᶻ ¹³Therefore, son, love your kindred. Do not act arrogantly toward any of them, the sons and daughters of your people, by refusing to take a wife for yourself from among them. For in arrogance there is ruin and great instability. In idleness there is loss and dire poverty, for idleness is the mother of famine.

¹⁴"Do not keep with you overnight the wages of those who have worked for you, but pay them at once. If you serve God thus, you will receive your reward. Be on your guard, son, in everything you do; be wise in all that you say and discipline yourself in all your conduct.ᵃ ¹⁵Do to no one what you yourself hate. Do not drink wine till you become drunk or let drunkenness accompany you on your way.ᵇ

¹⁶"Give to the hungry some of your food, and to the naked some of your clothing. Whatever you have left over, give away as alms; and do not let your eye begrudge the alms that you give. ¹⁷ᵈPour out your wine and your bread on the grave of the righteous, but do not share them with sinners.*

¹⁸"Seek counsel from every wise person, and do not think lightly of any useful advice. ¹⁹ᵉAt all times bless the Lord, your God, and ask him that all your paths may be straight and all your endeavors and plans may prosper. For no other nation possesses good counsel, but it is the Lord who gives all good things. Whomever the Lord chooses to raise is raised; and whomever the Lord chooses to cast down is cast down to the recesses of Hades. So now, son, keep in mind these my commandments, and never let them be erased from your heart.

²⁰"Now, I must tell you, son, that I have deposited in trust ten talents of silver with Gabael, the son of Gabri, at Rages in Media. ²¹Do not fear, son, that we have lived in poverty. You will have great wealth, if you fear God, avoid all sin, and do what is good before the Lord your God.ᶠ

## CHAPTER 5

**The Angel Raphael.** ¹Then Tobiah replied to his father Tobit: "Everything that you have commanded me, father, I shall do. ²But how will I be able to get that money from him, since he does not know me, and I do not know him? What sign can I give him so that he will recognize and trust me, and give me the money? I do not even know the roads to Media, in order to go there." ³Tobit answered his son Tobiah: "He gave me his bond,† and I gave him mine; I divided his into two parts, and each of us took one part; I put one part with the money. It is twenty years since I deposited that money! So, son, find yourself a trustworthy person who will make the journey with you, and we will give him wages when you return; but bring back that money from Gabael while I am still alive."

⁴Tobiah went out to look for someone who would travel with him to Media, someone who knew the way. He went out and found the angel Raphael standing before him (though he did not know‡ that this was an angel of God).ᵍ ⁵Tobiah said to him, "Where do you come from, young man?" He replied, "I am an Israelite, one of your kindred. I have come here to work." Tobiah said to him, "Do you know the way to Media?" ⁶"Yes," he replied, "I have been there many times. I know the place well and am acquainted with all the routes. I have often traveled to Media; I used to stay with our kinsman Gabael, who lives at Rages in Media. It is a good two days' journey from Ecbatana to Rages,§ for Rages is situated in the mountains, but Ecbatana is in the middle of the plain." ⁷Tobiah said to him, "Wait for me, young man, till I go in and tell my father; for I need you to make the journey with me. I will pay you your wages."ʰ ⁸He replied, "Very well, I will wait; but do not be long."

⁹Tobiah went in and informed his father Tobit: "I have found someone of our own Israelite kindred who will go with me!" Tobit said, "Call the man in, so that I may find out from what family and tribe he comes, and whether he is trustworthy enough to travel with you, son."

¹⁰Tobiah went out to summon him, saying, "Young man, my father is calling for you."

---

*[4:17] Tobit counsels his son to give alms in honor of the dead or, more probably, to give the "bread of consolation" to the family of the deceased. Cf. Jer 16:7; Ez 24:17.

y. [4:11] Sir 3:30; 29:12.   z. [4:12] Tb 3:15, 17; 6:12; Gn 11:29, 31; 25:20; 28:1–4; 29:15–30; Ex 34:16; Dt 7:3; Jgs 14:3.   a. [4:14] Lv 19:3; Dt 24:15.   b. [4:15] Mt 7:12; Lk 6:31.   c. [4:16] Dt 15:10; Is 58:7; Mt 25:35–36; 2 Cor 9:7.   d. [4:17] Jer 16:7; Lk 14:13.   e. [4:19] Dt 4:6; Ps 119:10.   f. [4:21] 1 Tm 6:6–10.

---

†[5:3] **Bond**: a document called in Greek *cheirographon*. In the Middle Ages, notably in England, a deed and its duplicate were written on one piece of parchment, with the Latin word *chirographum* inscribed across the top of the sheet or between the two copies of the text. The document was then cut in two in either a straight or a wavy line, the parts being given to the persons concerned. Perhaps this procedure was derived from the present verse of Tobit. Duplicate documents, usually one part open and the other sealed, are well known from the ancient Near East.

‡[5:4] **He did not know**: the theme of an angel in disguise occurs frequently in folklore as well as in the Old Testament (Gn 18; cf. Heb 13:2).

§[5:6] **It is a good two days' journey from Ecbatana to Rages**: Alexander's army took eleven days in forced marches to cover this distance, about 180 miles. (See notes on 1:15; 3:7 and Introduction.)

g. [5:4] Heb 13:2.   h. [5:7] Tb 12:2.

When Raphael entered the house, Tobit greeted him first. He replied, "Joyful greetings to you!" Tobit answered, "What joy is left for me? Here I am, a blind man who cannot see the light of heaven, but must remain in darkness, like the dead who no longer see the light! Though alive, I am among the dead. I can hear people's voices, but I do not see them." The young man said, "Take courage! God's healing is near; so take courage!" Tobit then said: "My son Tobiah wants to go to Media. Can you go with him to show him the way? I will pay you your wages, brother." He answered: "Yes, I will go with him, and I know all the routes. I have often traveled to Media and crossed all its plains so I know well the mountains and all its roads." ¹¹Tobit asked him, "Brother, tell me, please, from what family and tribe are you?" ¹²He replied, "Why? What need do you have for a tribe? Aren't you looking for a hired man?" Tobit replied, "I only want to know, brother, whose son you truly are and what your name is."ⁱ

¹³He answered, "I am Azariah,* son of the great Hananiah, one of your own kindred." ¹⁴Tobit exclaimed: "Welcome! God save you, brother! Do not be provoked with me, brother, for wanting to learn the truth about your family. It turns out that you are a kinsman, from a noble and good line! I knew Hananiah and Nathan, the two sons of the great Shemeliah. They used to go to Jerusalem with me, where we would worship together. They were not led astray; your kindred are good people. You are certainly of good lineage. So welcome!"

¹⁵Then he added: "For each day I will give you a drachma as wages,† as well as expenses for you and for my son. So go with my son ¹⁶I will even add a bonus to your wages!" The young man replied: "I will go with him. Do not fear. In good health we will leave you, and in good health we will return to you, for the way is safe." ¹⁷Tobit said, "Blessing be upon you, brother." Then he called his son and said to him: "Son, prepare whatever you need for the journey, and set out with your kinsman. May God in heaven protect you on the way and bring you back to me safe and sound; may his angel accompany you for your safety, son."

Tobiah left to set out on his journey, and he kissed his father and mother. Tobit said to him, "Have a safe journey." ¹⁸But his mother began to weep and she said to Tobit: "Why have you sent my child away? Is he not the staff of our hands, as he goes in and out before us? ¹⁹Do not heap money upon money! Rather relinquish it

in exchange for our child! ²⁰What the Lord has given us to live on is certainly enough for us." ²¹Tobit reassured her: "Do not worry! Our son will leave in good health and come back to us in good health. Your own eyes will see the day when he returns to you safe and sound. So, do not worry; do not fear for them, my sister.‡ ²²For a good angel§ will go with him, his journey will be successful, and he will return in good health." ¹Then she stopped weeping.

## IV. TOBIAH'S JOURNEY TO MEDIA

### CHAPTER 6

**On the Way to Rages.** ²When the young man left home, accompanied by the angel, the dog followed Tobiah out and went along with them. Both journeyed along, and when the first night came, they camped beside the Tigris River.¶ ³When the young man went down to wash his feet in the Tigris River, a large fish leaped out of the water and tried to swallow his foot. He shouted in alarm. ⁴But the angel said to the young man, "Grab the fish and hold on to it!" He seized the fish and hauled it up on dry land. ⁵The angel then told him: "Slit the fish open and take out its gall, heart, and liver, and keep them with you; but throw away the other entrails. Its gall, heart, and liver are useful for medicine."** ⁶After Tobiah had slit the fish open, he put aside the gall, heart, and liver. Then he roasted and ate part of the fish; the rest he salted and kept for the journey.

**Raphael's Instructions.** Afterward the two of them traveled on together till they drew near to Media. ⁷Then the young man asked the angel this question: "Brother Azariah, what medicine is in the fish's heart, liver, and gall?" ⁸He answered: "As for the fish's heart and liver, if you burn them to make smoke in the presence of a man or a woman who is afflicted by a demon or evil spirit, any affliction will flee and never return. ⁹As for the gall, if you apply it to the eyes of one who has white scales, blowing right into them, sight will be restored."

¹⁰When they had entered Media and were getting close to Ecbatana, ¹¹Raphael said to the young man, "Brother Tobiah!" He answered, "Here I am!" Raphael continued, "Tonight we must stay in the house of Raguel, who is a relative of yours. He has a beautiful daughter named Sarah, ¹²but no other son or daughter apart from

---

*[5:13–14] Azariah, "Yhwh has helped"; Hananiah, "Yhwh has shown mercy"; Nathan is a shortened form of Nathaniah, "Yhwh has given"; Shemeliah may be a Greek corruption of the Hebrew name, Shemaiah, "Yhwh has heard."

†[5:15] **A drachma as wages:** the normal wages, about seventeen cents, a day's wage for a laborer.

ⁱ. [5:12] Jgs 13:17–18.

‡[5:21] **My sister:** "sister" was a term of endearment used in antiquity even for one's wife; similarly "brother" for one's husband. Cf. 7:11, 15; 8:4, 21; 10:6, 13; Sg 4:9–10, 12; 5:1–2.

§[5:22] **A good angel:** a reference to a guardian angel, though Tobit does not know, of course, that Raphael himself, disguised as Azariah, is the good angel in this case.

¶[6:2] **Tigris River:** this river is actually west of Nineveh, so they would not have come to it on their way to Media. See note on 1:15 and the Introduction.

**[6:5] **Its gall . . . medicine:** belief in the healing power of these organs was common among the physicians of antiquity.

Sarah. Since you are Sarah's closest relative, you more than any other have the right to marry her. Moreover, her father's estate is rightfully yours to inherit. The girl is wise, courageous, and very beautiful; and her father is a good man who loves her dearly."[j] [13]He continued: "You have the right to marry her. So listen to me, brother. Tonight I will speak to her father about the girl so that we may take her as your bride. When we return from Rages, we will have the wedding feast for her. For I know that Raguel cannot keep her from you or promise her to another man; he would incur the death penalty as decreed in the Book of Moses.[*] For he knows that you, more than anyone else, have the right to marry his daughter. Now listen to me, brother; we will speak about this girl tonight, so that we may arrange her engagement to you. Then when we return from Rages, we will take her and bring her back with us to your house."

[14]But Tobiah said to Raphael in reply, "Brother Azariah, I have heard that she has already been given in marriage to seven husbands, and that they have died in the bridal chamber. On the very night they approached her, they would die. I have also heard it said that it was a demon that killed them. [15]So now I too am afraid of this demon, because it is in love with her and does not harm her; but it kills any man who wishes to come close to her. I am my father's only child. If I should die, I would bring the life of my father and mother down to their grave in sorrow over me; they have no other son to bury them!"[k]

[16]Raphael said to him: "Do you not remember your father's commands? He ordered you to marry a woman from your own ancestral family. Now listen to me, brother; do not worry about that demon. Take Sarah. I know that tonight she will be given to you as your wife! [17]When you go into the bridal chamber, take some of the fish's liver and the heart, and place them on the embers intended for incense, and an odor will be given off. [18]As soon as the demon smells the odor, it will flee and never again show itself near her. Then when you are about to have intercourse with her, both of you must first get up to pray.[†] Beg the Lord of heaven that mercy and protection be granted you. Do not be afraid, for she was set apart for you before the world existed. You will save her, and she will go with you. And I assume that you will have children by her, and they will be like brothers for you. So do not worry."

---

[*][6:13] Raguel . . . Book of Moses: Nm 36:6–8 prescribed marriage within the ancestral tribe for daughters who had no brothers who might inherit the ancestral property, but no death penalty is mentioned.

[†][6:18] Get up to pray: prayer, combined with ritual action, drives out the demon.

j. [6:12] Tb 4:12–13; Nm 36:8.    k. [6:15] Tb 3:10.

---

When Tobiah heard Raphael's words that she was his kinswoman, and of the lineage of his ancestral house, he loved her deeply, and his heart was truly set on her.

## V. MARRIAGE AND HEALING OF SARAH

### CHAPTER 7

**At the House of Raguel.** [1]When they entered Ecbatana, Tobiah said, "Brother Azariah, bring me straight to the house of our kinsman Raguel." So he did, and they came to the house of Raguel, whom they found seated by his courtyard gate. They greeted him first, and he answered, "Many greetings to you, brothers! Welcome! You have come in peace! Now enter in peace!" And he brought them into his house. [2]He said to his wife Edna, "How this young man resembles Tobit, the son of my uncle!" [3]So Edna asked them, saying, "Where are you from, brothers?" They answered, "We are descendants of Naphtali, now captives in Nineveh." [4]She said to them, "Do you know our kinsman Tobit?" They answered her, "Indeed, we do know him!" She asked, "Is he well?" [5]They answered, "Yes, he is alive and well." Then Tobiah said, "He is my father!" [6]Raguel jumped up, kissed him, and broke into tears. [7]Then, finding words, he said, "A blessing upon you, son! You are the son of a good and noble father. What a terrible misfortune that a man so righteous and charitable has been afflicted with blindness!" He embraced his kinsman Tobiah and continued to weep. [8]His wife Edna also wept for Tobit; and their daughter Sarah also began to weep.

**Marriage of Tobiah and Sarah.** [9]Afterward, Raguel slaughtered a ram from the flock and gave them a warm reception. When they had washed, bathed, and reclined to eat and drink, Tobiah said to Raphael, "Brother Azariah, ask Raguel to give me my kinswoman Sarah." [10]Raguel overheard the words; so he said to the young man: "Eat and drink and be merry tonight, for no man has a greater right to marry my daughter Sarah than you, brother. Besides, not even I have the right to give her to anyone but you, because you are my closest relative. However, son, I must frankly tell you the truth. [11]I have given her in marriage to seven husbands who were kinsmen of ours, and all died on the very night they approached her. But now, son, eat and drink. The Lord will look after you both." Tobiah answered, "I will neither eat nor drink anything here until you settle what concerns me."

Raguel said to him: "I will do it. She is yours as decreed by the Book of Moses. It has been decided in heaven that she be given to you! Take your kinswoman; from now on you are her brother, and she is your sister.[‡] She is given to

---

[‡][7:11] You are her brother, and she is your sister: the marriage formula is similar to a marriage contract from the

you today and here ever after. May the Lord of heaven prosper you both tonight, son, and grant you mercy and peace." [12]Then Raguel called his daughter Sarah, and she came to him. He took her by the hand and gave her to Tobiah with these words: "Take her according to the law. According to the decree written in the Book of Moses I give her to be your wife. Take her and bring her safely to your father. And may the God of heaven grant both of you a safe journey in peace!"[l] [13]He then called her mother and told her to bring writing materials. He wrote out a copy of a marriage contract stating that he gave Sarah to Tobiah as his wife as decreed by the law of Moses. Her mother brought the material, and he drew up the contract, to which he affixed his seal.[m]

[14]Afterward they began to eat and drink. [15]Later Raguel called his wife Edna and said, "My sister, prepare the other bedroom and bring Sarah there." [16]She went, made the bed in the room, as he had told her, and brought Sarah there. After she had cried over her, she wiped away her tears and said, [17]"Take courage, my daughter! May the Lord of heaven grant you joy in place of your grief! Courage, my daughter!" Then she left.

## CHAPTER 8

**Expulsion of the Demon.** [1]When they had finished eating and drinking, they wanted to retire. So they brought the young man out and led him to the bedroom. [2]Tobiah, mindful of Raphael's instructions, took the fish's liver and heart from the bag where he had them, and put them on the embers intended for incense.[*] [3]The odor of the fish repulsed the demon, and it fled to the upper regions of Egypt;[†] Raphael went in pursuit of it and there bound it hand and foot. Then Raphael returned immediately.

[4]When Sarah's parents left the bedroom and closed the door behind them, Tobiah rose from bed and said to his wife, "My sister, come, let us pray and beg our Lord to grant us mercy and protection." [5]She got up, and they started to pray and beg that they might be protected. He began with these words:

> "Blessed are you, O God of our ancestors;
> blessed be your name forever and
> ever!
> Let the heavens and all your creation bless
> you forever.[n]

[6]  You made Adam, and you made his wife
  Eve
> to be his helper and support;
> and from these two the human race
> has come.
> You said, 'It is not good for the man to be
> alone;
> let us make him a helper like
> himself.'[o]
[7]  Now, not with lust,
> but with fidelity I take this
> kinswoman as my wife.
> Send down your mercy on me and on her,
> and grant that we may grow old
> together.
> Bless us with children."

[8]They said together, "Amen, amen!" [9]Then they went to bed for the night.

But Raguel got up and summoned his servants. They went out with him and dug a grave, [10]for he said, "Perhaps Tobiah will die; then we would be a laughingstock and an object of mockery." [11]When they had finished digging the grave, Raguel went back into the house and called his wife, [12]saying, "Send one of the maids in to see whether he is alive. If he has died, let us bury him without anyone knowing about it." [13]They sent the maid, lit a lamp, and opened the bedroom door; she went in and found them sleeping together. [14]The maid came out and told them that Tobiah was alive, and that nothing was wrong. [15]Then they praised the God of heaven in these words:

> "Blessed are you, God, with every pure
> blessing!
> Let all your chosen ones bless you
> forever!
[16]  Blessed are you, for you have made me
> happy;
> what I feared did not happen.
> Rather you have dealt with us
> according to your abundant mercy.
[17]  Blessed are you, for you have shown
> mercy
> toward two only children.
> Grant them, Master, mercy and
> protection,
> and bring their lives to fulfillment
> with happiness and mercy."

[18]Then Raguel told his servants to fill in the grave before dawn. **Wedding Feast.** [19]He asked his wife to bake many loaves of bread; he himself went out to the herd and brought two steers and four rams, which he ordered to be slaughtered. So they began to prepare the feast. [20]He summoned Tobiah and said

---

fifth century B.C. found at Elephantine in Egypt: "She is my wife and I am her husband from this day forever."

\*[8:2–3] The manner of coping with demonic influences among the ancients seems strange to us. However, the fish here is a folktale element, suggesting the hero's fight with a dragon, and not a recipe for exorcism. It is clear that the author places primary emphasis on the value of prayer to God (6:18; 8:4–8), on the role of the angel as God's agent, and on the pious disposition of Tobiah.

†[8:3] The desert was considered the dwelling place of demons. Cf. Is 13:21; 34:14; Mt 4:1; 12:43.

l. [7:12] Gn 24:50–51.  m. [7:13] Tb 6:12.  n. [8:5] Dn 3:26.

o. [8:6] Gn 2:18–23.

to him, "For fourteen days* you shall not stir from here, but shall remain here eating and drinking with me; you shall bring joy to my daughter's afflicted spirit. ²¹Now take half of what I own here; go back in good health to your father. The other half will be yours when I and my wife die. Take courage, son! I am your father, and Edna is your mother; we belong to you and to your sister both now and forever. So take courage, son!"

## CHAPTER 9

**The Money Recovered.** ¹Then Tobiah called Raphael and said to him: ²"Brother Azariah, take along with you from here four servants and two camels and travel to Rages.† Go to Gabael's house and give him this bond. Get the money and then bring him along with you to the wedding celebration. ³For you know that my father will be counting the days. If I should delay even by a single day, I would cause him intense grief. ⁴You have witnessed the oath that Raguel has sworn; I cannot violate his oath." ⁵So Raphael, together with the four servants and two camels, traveled to Rages in Media, where they stayed at Gabael's house. Raphael gave Gabael his bond and told him about Tobit's son Tobiah, that he had married and was inviting him to the wedding celebration. Gabael got up and counted out for him the moneybags with their seals, and they packed them on the camels.

⁶The following morning they both got an early start and traveled to the wedding celebration. When they entered Raguel's house, they found Tobiah reclining at table. He jumped up and greeted Gabael, who wept and blessed him, exclaiming: "Good and noble child, son of a good and noble, righteous and charitable man, may the Lord bestow a heavenly blessing on you and on your wife, and on your wife's father and mother. Blessed be God, because I have seen the very image of my cousin Tobit!"

## VI. TOBIAH'S RETURN JOURNEY TO NINEVEH AND THE HEALING OF TOBIT

## CHAPTER 10

**Anxiety of the Parents.** ¹Meanwhile, day by day, Tobit was keeping track of the time Tobiah would need to go and to return. When the number of days was reached and his son did not appear, ²he said, "Could it be that he has been detained there? Or perhaps Gabael has died, and there is no one to give him the money?" ³And he began to grieve. ⁴His wife Anna said, "My son has perished and is no longer among the living!" And she began to weep aloud and

to wail over her son: ⁵"Alas, child, light of my eyes, that I have let you make this journey!" ⁶But Tobit kept telling her: "Be still, do not worry, my sister; he is safe! Probably they have to take care of some unexpected business there. The man who is traveling with him is trustworthy and one of our kindred. So do not grieve over him, my sister. He will be here soon." ⁷But she retorted, "You be still, and do not try to deceive me! My son has perished!" She would rush out and keep watch every day at the road her son had taken. She ate nothing. After the sun had set, she would go back home to wail and cry the whole night through, getting no sleep at all.ᵖ

**Departure from Ecbatana.** Now when the fourteen days of the wedding celebration, which Raguel had sworn to hold for his daughter, had come to an end, Tobiah went to him and said: "Send me off, now, since I know that my father and mother do not believe they will ever see me again. So I beg you, father, let me depart and go back to my own father. I have already told you how I left him." ⁸Raguel said to Tobiah: "Stay, son, stay with me. I am sending messengers to your father Tobit, and they will give him news of you." ⁹But Tobiah insisted, "No, I beg you to send me back to my father."

¹⁰Raguel then promptly handed over to Tobiah his wife Sarah, together with half of all his property: male and female slaves, oxen and sheep, donkeys and camels, clothing, money, and household goods. ¹¹He saw them safely off. Embracing Tobiah, he said to him: "Farewell, son. Have a safe journey. May the Lord of heaven grant prosperity to you and to your wife Sarah. And may I see children of yours before I die!" ¹²Then he said to his daughter Sarah, "My daughter, honor your father-in-law and your mother-in-law, because from now on they are as much your parents as the ones who brought you into the world. Go in peace, daughter; let me hear a good report about you as long as I live." Finally he said good-bye to them and let them go.

Edna also said to Tobiah: "My child and beloved kinsman, may the Lord bring you back safely, and may I live long enough to see children of you and of my daughter Sarah before I die. Before the Lord, I entrust my daughter to your care. Never cause her grief all the days of your life. Go in peace, son. From now on I am your mother, and Sarah is your sister. Together may we all prosper throughout the days of our lives." She kissed them both and saw them safely off.

¹³Tobiah left Raguel, full of happiness and joy, and he blessed the Lord of heaven and earth, the King of all, for making his journey so successful. Finally he blessed Raguel and his wife Edna, and added, "I have been commanded by the Lord to honor you all the days of your life!"

---

*[8:20] **For fourteen days:** because of the happy, and unexpected, turn of events, Raguel doubles the time of the wedding feast. When Tobiah returns home, the usual seven-day feast is held (11:18). Cf. Jgs 14:12.

†[9:2] **To Rages:** see note on 5:6.

p. [10:7] Gn 45:26.

## CHAPTER 11

**Homeward Journey.** [1]As they drew near to Kaserin, which is opposite Nineveh, [2]Raphael said: "You know how we left your father. [3]Let us hurry on ahead of your wife to prepare the house while they are still on the way." [4]So both went on ahead together, and Raphael said to him, "Take the gall in your hand!" And the dog ran along behind them.

[5]Meanwhile, Anna sat watching the road by which her son was to come. [6]When she saw him coming, she called to his father, "Look, your son is coming, and the man who traveled with him!"

[7]Raphael said to Tobiah before he came near to his father: "I know that his eyes will be opened. [8]Apply the fish gall to his eyes, and the medicine will make the white scales shrink and peel off from his eyes; then your father will have sight again and will see the light of day."

**Sight Restored.** [9]Then Anna ran up to her son, embraced him, and said to him, "Now that I have seen you again, son, I am ready to die!" And she sobbed aloud.[q] [10]Tobit got up and stumbled out through the courtyard gate to meet his son. Tobiah went up to him [11]with the fish gall in his hand and blew into his eyes. Holding him firmly, he said, "Courage, father." Then he applied the medicine to his eyes, and it made them sting. [12, 13]Tobiah used both hands to peel the white scales from the corners of his eyes. Tobit saw his son and threw his arms around him. [14]Weeping, he exclaimed, "I can see you, son, the light of my eyes!" Then he prayed,

"Blessed be God,
> blessed be his great name,
> and blessed be all his holy angels.
May his great name be with us,
> and blessed be all the angels
> > throughout all the ages.
[15] God it was who afflicted me,
> and God who has had mercy on me.
Now I see my son Tobiah!"

Then Tobit went back in, rejoicing and praising God with full voice. Tobiah related to his father how his journey had been a success; that he had brought back the money; and that he had married Raguel's daughter Sarah, who was about to arrive, for she was near the gate of Nineveh.[r]

[16]Rejoicing and blessing God, Tobit went out to the gate of Nineveh to meet his daughter-in-law. When the people of Nineveh saw him coming, walking along briskly, with no one leading him by the hand, they were amazed. [17]Before them all Tobit proclaimed how God had shown mercy to him and opened his eyes. When Tobit came up to Sarah, the wife of his son Tobiah, he blessed her and said: "Welcome, my daughter! Blessed be your God for bringing you to us, daughter! Blessed are your father and your mother. Blessed be my son Tobiah, and blessed be you, daughter! Welcome to your home with blessing and joy. Come in, daughter!" That day there was joy for all the Jews who lived in Nineveh. [18]Ahiqar and his nephew Nadin[*] were also on hand to rejoice with Tobit. Tobiah's wedding feast was celebrated with joy for seven days, and many gifts were given to him.

## VII. RAPHAEL REVEALS HIS IDENTITY

## CHAPTER 12

**Raphael's Wages.**[†] [1]When the wedding celebration came to an end, Tobit called his son Tobiah and said to him, "Son, see to it that you pay his wages to the man who made the journey with you and give him a bonus too." [2]Tobiah said: "Father, how much shall I pay him? It would not hurt to give him half the wealth he brought back with me.[s] [3]He led me back safe and sound, healed my wife, brought the money back with me, and healed you. How much should I pay him?" [4]Tobit answered, "It is only fair, son, that he should receive half of all that he brought back." [5]So Tobiah called Raphael and said, "Take as your wages half of all that you have brought back, and farewell!"

**Exhortation.**[‡] [6]Raphael called the two of them aside privately and said to them: "Bless God and give him thanks before all the living for the good things he has done for you, by blessing and extolling his name in song. Proclaim before all with due honor the deeds of God, and do not be slack in thanking him.[§] [7]A king's secret should be kept secret, but one must declare the works of God and give thanks with due honor. Do good, and evil will not overtake you. [8]Prayer with fasting is good. Almsgiving with righteousness is better than wealth with wickedness. It is better to give alms than to store up gold,[t] [9]for almsgiving saves from death, and purges all sin. Those who give alms will enjoy a full life,[u] [10]but those who commit sin and do evil are their own worst enemies.

**Raphael's Identity.** [11]"I shall now tell you the whole truth and conceal nothing at all from you. I have already said to you, 'A king's secret should be kept secret, but one must declare the works of God with due honor.' [12]Now when you, Tobit, and Sarah prayed, it was I who presented the record of your prayer before the Glory of the

---

*[11:18] **Nadin**: see note on 14:10.

†[12:1–5] Tobit and his son generously agree to give Raphael far more than the wages agreed upon in 5:15–16.

‡[12:6–10] In the fashion of a wisdom teacher, Raphael gives the two men a short exhortation similar to the one Tobit gave his son in 4:3–19.

§[12:6–7] The faithful considered the praise of God their most esteemed privilege. Without it, life was meaningless; cf. Is 38:16–20.

---

q. [11:9] Gn 33:4; 45:14; 46:29–30; Lk 15:20.    r. [11:15] Tb 13:2; Dt 32:39; 1 Sm 2:6.

s. [12:2]  Tb  5:3,  7,  15–16.    t. [12:8]  Tb  4:7–11; Sir  29:8–13.
u. [12:9] Dn 4:24.    v. [12:12] Jb 33:23–24; Acts 10:4; Rev 8:3–4.

Lord; and likewise whenever you used to bury the dead.* ¹³When you did not hesitate to get up and leave your dinner in order to go and bury that dead man, ¹⁴I was sent to put you to the test. At the same time, however, God sent me to heal you and your daughter-in-law Sarah. ¹⁵I am Raphael, one of the seven angels who stand and serve before the Glory of the Lord."ʷ

¹⁶Greatly shaken, the two of them fell prostrate in fear. ¹⁷But Raphael said to them: "Do not fear; peace be with you! Bless God now and forever. ¹⁸As for me, when I was with you, I was not acting out of any favor on my part, but by God's will. So bless God every day; give praise with song. ¹⁹Even though you saw me eat and drink, I did not eat or drink anything; what you were seeing was a vision. ²⁰So now bless the Lord on earth and give thanks to God. Look, I am ascending to the one who sent me. Write down all that has happened to you."ˣ And he ascended. ²¹They stood up but were no longer able to see him. ²²They kept blessing God and singing his praises, and they continued to give thanks for these marvelous works that God had done, because an angel of God appeared to them.

## VIII. TOBIT'S SONG OF PRAISE

### CHAPTER 13

¹†Then Tobit spoke and composed a song of joyful praise; he said:

Blessed be God who lives forever,
    because his kingship lasts for all ages.ʸ
² For he afflicts and shows mercy,
    casts down to the depths of Hades,
    brings up from the great abyss.
What is there that can snatch from his hand?ᶻ

³ Give thanks to him, you Israelites, in the presence of the nations,
    for though he has scattered you among them,
⁴     even there recount his greatness.
Exalt him before every living being,
    because he is your Lord, and he is your God,

our Father and God forever and ever!
⁵ He will afflict you for your iniquities,
    but will have mercy on all of you.
He will gather you from all the nations
    among whom you have been scattered.ᵃ

⁶ When you turn back to him with all your heart,
    and with all your soul do what is right before him,
Then he will turn to you,
    and will hide his face from you no longer.ᵇ

Now consider what he has done for you,
    and give thanks with full voice.
Bless the Lord of righteousness,
    and exalt the King of the ages.

In the land of my captivity I give thanks,
    and declare his power and majesty to a sinful nation.
According to your heart do what is right before him:
    perhaps there will be pardon for you.

⁷ As for me, I exalt my God,
    my soul exalts the King of heaven,
    and rejoices all the days of my life.
Let all sing praise to his greatness,
⁸     let all speak and give thanks in Jerusalem.

⁹ Jerusalem, holy city,
    he will afflict you for the works of your hands,‡
    but will again pity the children of the righteous.ᶜ
¹⁰ Give thanks to the Lord with righteousness,
    and bless the King of the ages,
    so that your tabernacle may be rebuilt in you with joy.
May he gladden within you all who are captives;
    may he cherish within you all who are distressed
    for all generations to come.ᵈ

¹¹ A bright light will shine to the limits of the earth.
    Many nations will come to you from afar,
And inhabitants of all the ends of the earth to your holy name,
    Bearing in their hands gifts for the King of heaven.
Generation after generation will offer

---

*[12:12] Raphael is one of the seven Angels of the Presence, specially designated intercessors who present prayers to God. Angelology was developing in this period. The names of two other of these seven angels are given in the Bible: Gabriel (Dn 8:16; 9:21; Lk 1:19, 26) and Michael (Dn 10:13, 21; 12:1; Jude 9; Rev 12:7). See 1 Enoch for the names of the rest.

†[13:1–18] Tobit's hymn of praise is divided into two parts. The first part (vv. 1–8) is a song of praise that echoes themes from the psalms; the second (vv. 9–18) is addressed to Jerusalem in the style of those prophets who spoke of a new and ideal Jerusalem (Is 60; cf. Rev 21). **Joyful praise**: words for joy and gladness occur throughout this prayer (vv. 1, 7, 10, 11, 13, 14, 16, 18).

w. [12:15] Lk 1:19; Rev 8:2.    x. [12:20] Jgs 13:20.    y. [13:1] Tb 3:11; 8:5, 15; 1 Chr 29:10; Dn 3:26.    z. [13:2] Tb 11:15; 13:9; Dt 32:39; 1 Sm 2:6; Wis 16:13.

‡[13:9] **Works of your hands**: idols.

a. [13:5] Dt 30:3; Neh 1:9.    b. [13:6] Dt 30:2.    c. [13:9] Tb 11:15; Mi 7:19; Rev 21.    d. [13:10] Is 44:26, 28; Am 9:11; Zec 1:16.

joyful worship in you;
>    your name will be great forever and
>        ever.[e]

12 Cursed be all who despise you and revile
>        you;
>    cursed be all who hate you and
>        speak a harsh word against you;
>    cursed be all who destroy you
>    and pull down your walls,
> And all who overthrow your towers
>    and set fire to your homes.
>    But blessed forever be all those who
>        respect you.[f]

13 Go, then, rejoice and exult over the
>        children of the righteous,
>    for they will all be gathered together
>    and will bless the Lord of the ages.

14 Happy are those who love you,
>    and happy are those who rejoice in
>        your peace.
> Happy too are all who grieve
>    over all your afflictions,
> For they will rejoice over you
>    and behold all your joy forever.[g]

15 My soul, bless the Lord, the great King;
16   for Jerusalem will be rebuilt as his
>        house forever.
> Happy too will I be if a remnant of my
>        offspring survives
>    to see your glory and to give thanks
>        to the King of heaven!

> The gates of Jerusalem will be built with
>        sapphire and emerald,
>    and all your walls with precious
>        stones.
> The towers of Jerusalem will be built with
>        gold,
>    and their battlements with purest
>        gold.[h]

17 The streets of Jerusalem will be paved
>        with rubies and stones of Ophir;

18 The gates of Jerusalem will sing hymns of
>        gladness,
>    and all its houses will cry out,
>        Hallelujah!
> Blessed be the God of Israel for all ages!
> For in you the blessed will bless the holy
>        name forever and ever.

## IX. EPILOGUE

## CHAPTER 14

**Parting Advice.** [1]So the words of Tobit's hymn of praise came to an end. Tobit died in peace at the age of a hundred and twelve and was buried with honor in Nineveh. [2]He was fifty-eight years old when he lost his eyesight, and after he recovered it he lived in prosperity, giving alms; he continued to fear God and give thanks to the divine Majesty.

[3]As he was dying, he summoned his son Tobiah and Tobiah's seven sons, and commanded him, "Son, take your children[i] [4]and flee into Media, for I believe God's word that Nahum[*] spoke against Nineveh. It will all happen and will overtake Assyria and Nineveh; indeed all that was said by Israel's prophets whom God sent will come to pass. Not one of all their words will remain unfulfilled, but everything will take place in the time appointed for it. So it will be safer in Media than in Assyria or Babylon. For I know and believe that whatever God has said will be accomplished. It will happen, and not a single word of the prophecies will fail.

As for our kindred who dwell in the land of Israel, they will all be scattered and taken into captivity from the good land. All the land of Israel will become a wilderness; even Samaria and Jerusalem will be a wilderness! For a time, the house of God will be desolate and will be burned.[j] [5]But God will again have mercy on them and bring them back to the land of Israel. They will build the house again, but it will not be like the first until the era when the appointed times will be completed.[†] Afterward all of them will return from their captivity, and they will rebuild Jerusalem with due honor. In it the house of God will also be rebuilt, just as the prophets of Israel said of it.[k] [6]All the nations of the world will turn and reverence God in truth; all will cast away their idols, which have deceitfully led them into error.[‡] [7]They will bless the God of the ages in righteousness. All the Israelites truly mindful of God, who are to be saved in those days, will be gathered together and will come to Jerusalem; in security will they dwell forever in the land of Abraham, which will be given to them. Those who love God sincerely will rejoice, but those who commit sin and wickedness will disappear completely from the land.[m]

[8, 9]"Now, my children, I give you this command: serve God sincerely and do what is pleasing in his sight; you must instruct your children

---

*[14:4–5] **Nahum**: one of the minor prophets, whose book contains oracles of doom against Nineveh. Here, in keeping with the period in which the story is set, the author makes Tobit speak as if the punishment of Nineveh, the destruction of Jerusalem (587 B.C.), the exile from Judah and the return, would all take place in the future. The technique of using the facts of past history as seemingly future predictions is a frequent device of apocalyptic writers. **The good land**: a favorite name for the promised land. Cf. Dt 1:35; 3:25; 4:21–22.

†[14:5] **Until the era . . . completed**: a reference to the coming of the day of the Lord, when a new, more perfect temple was to be expected. Cf. Heb 9:1–14.

‡[14:6] Conversion of the nations is also to come with the day of the Lord.

e. [13:11] Is 2:3–4; 9:1; 49:6; 60:1; Mi 4:2; Zec 8:22.  f. [13:12] Bar 4:31–32.  g. [13:14] Ps 122:6; Is 66:10.  h. [13:16] Tb 14:5; Is 54:11–13; 62:2; Rev 21:10–21.

i. [14:3] Gn 47:29–30.  j. [14:4] Na 2:2–3:19.  k. [14:5] Neh 12:27; Jer 31:38.  l. [14:6] Is 60:1–4.  m. [14:7] Is 60:21; Jer 32:37; Ez 34:28; 37:25; 39:26.

to do what is right and to give alms, to be mindful of God and at all times to bless his name sincerely and with all their strength. Now, as for you, son, leave Nineveh; do not stay here. ¹⁰The day you bury your mother next to me, do not even stay overnight within the confines of the city. For I see that there is much wickedness in it, and much treachery is practiced in it, and people are not ashamed. See, my son, all that Nadin* did to Ahiqar, the very one who reared him. Was not Ahiqar brought down alive into the earth? Yet God made Nadin's disgraceful crime rebound against him. Ahiqar came out again into the light, but Nadin went into the everlasting darkness, for he had tried to kill Ahiqar. Because Ahiqar had given alms he escaped from the deadly trap Nadin had set for him. But Nadin

---

*[14:10] **Nadin**: in the *Story of Ahiqar*, the hero Ahiqar, chancellor under the Assyrian kings Sennacherib and Esarhaddon, adopts his nephew Nadin and prepares him to become his successor. But Nadin treacherously plots to have his uncle put to death. Ahiqar hides in a friend's house and is finally vindicated when Nadin's scheme is discovered. Thereupon Nadin is thrown into a dungeon where he dies. It was Ahiqar's almsgiving that delivered him from death; see note on 2:2. The Greek and Latin versions of the Book of Tobit read the name as Nadab, but the Aramaic form has the ancient name Nadin, which is also found in the fifth-century B.C. Aramaic *Story of Ahiqar*.

fell into the deadly trap himself, and it destroyed him." ¹¹So, my children, see what almsgiving does, and also what wickedness does—it kills! But now my spirit is about to leave me."

**Death of Tobit and Tobiah.** They laid him on his bed, and he died; and he was buried with honor. ¹²When Tobiah's mother died, he buried her next to his father. He then departed with his wife and children for Media, where he settled in Ecbatana with his father-in-law Raguel.° ¹³He took respectful care of his aging father-in-law and mother-in-law; and he buried them at Ecbatana in Media. Then he inherited Raguel's estate as well as that of his father Tobit. ¹⁴He died highly respected at the age of one hundred seventeen. ¹⁵But before he died, he saw and heard of the destruction of Nineveh. He saw the inhabitants of the city being led captive into Media by Cyaxares,† the king of Media. Tobiah blessed God for all that he had done against the Ninevites and Assyrians. Before dying he rejoiced over Nineveh, and he blessed the Lord God forever and ever.

---

†[14:15] **Cyaxares**: Nabopolassar, king of Babylon, and Cyaxares conquered and destroyed Nineveh in 612 B.C.; see note on 1:15.

n. [14:10] Tb 1:21–22.   o. [14:12] Tb 4:4.

# THE BOOK OF
# JUDITH

～∞～

The Book of Judith relates the story of God's deliverance of the Jewish people. This was accomplished "by the hand of a female"—a constant motif (cf. 8:33; 9:9, 10; 12:4; 13:4, 14, 15; 15:10; 16:5) meant to recall the "hand" of God in the Exodus narrative (cf. Ex 15:6). The work may have been written around 100 B.C., but its historical range is extraordinary. Within the reign of Nebuchadnezzar (1:1; 2:1), it telescopes five centuries of historical and geographical information with imaginary details. There are references to Nineveh, the Assyrian capital destroyed in 612 B.C., to Nebuchadnezzar, the ruler not of Assyria but of Babylon (605/604–562), and to the second Temple, built around 515. The postexilic period is presumed (e.g., governance by the High Priest). The Persian period is represented by two characters, Holofernes and Bagoas, who appear together in the military campaigns of Artaxerxes III Ochus (358–338); there seem to be allusions to the second-century Seleucid ruler Antiochus IV Epiphanes. Several mysteries remain: Judith herself, Arphaxad, and others are otherwise unknown. The geographical details, such as the narrow defile into Bethulia (an unidentified town which gives access to the heart of the land), are fanciful. The simple conclusion from these and other details is that the work is historical fiction, written to exalt God as Israel's deliverer from foreign might, not by an army, but by means of a simple widow.

There are four Greek recensions of Judith (Septuagint codices Vaticanus, Sinaiticus, Alexandrinus, and Basiliano-Vaticanus), four ancient translations (Old Latin, Syriac, Sahidic, and Ethiopic), and some late Hebrew versions, apparently translated from the Vulgate. Despite Jerome's claim to have translated an Aramaic text, no ancient Aramaic or Hebrew manuscripts have been found. The oldest extant text of Judith is the preservation of 15:1–7 inscribed on a third-century A.D. potsherd. Whatever the reasons, the rabbis did not count Judith among their scriptures, and the Reformation adopted that position. The early Church, however, held this book in high honor. The first-century Pope, St. Clement of Rome, proposes Judith as an example of courageous love (1 Corinthians 55). St. Jerome holds her up as an example of a holy widow and a type of the Church (To Salvina: Letter 79, par. 10; see also To Furia: Letter 54, par. 16) and, in another place, describes Mary as a new Judith (To Eustochium: Letter 22, par. 21). The Council of Trent (1546) included Judith in the canon; thus it is one of the seven deuterocanonical books.

Inner-biblical references are noteworthy: as God acted through Moses' hand (Ex 10:21–22; 14:27–30), so God delivers "by the hand of a female," Judith. Like Jael, who drove a tent peg through the head of Sisera (Jgs 4), Judith kills an enemy general. Like Deborah (Jgs 4–5), Judith "judges" Israel in the time of military crisis. Like Sarah, the mother of Israel's future (Gn 17:6), Judith's beauty deceives foreigners, with the result that blessings redound to Israel (Gn 12:11–20). Her Hebrew name means "Jewish woman." Her exploits captured the imagination of liturgists, artists, and writers through the centuries. The book is filled with double entendres and ironic situations, e.g., Judith's conversation with Holofernes in 11:5–8, 19, where "my lord" is ambiguous, and her declaration to Holofernes that she will lead him through Judea to Jerusalem (his head goes on such a journey).

The book can be divided into five parts:

I. Assyrian Threat (1:1–3:10)
II. Siege of Bethulia (4:1–7:32)
III. Judith, Instrument of the Lord (8:1–10:10)
IV. Judith Goes Out to War (10:11–13:20)
V. Victory and Thanksgiving (14:1–16:25)

# I. ASSYRIAN THREAT*

## CHAPTER 1

**Nebuchadnezzar Against Arphaxad.**[†] [1]It was the twelfth year[‡] of the reign of Nebuchadnezzar, who ruled over the Assyrians in the great city of Nineveh. At that time Arphaxad was ruling over the Medes in Ecbatana.[a] [2a]Around Ecbatana he built a wall of hewn stones, three cubits thick and six cubits long. He made the walls seventy cubits high and fifty cubits wide. [3]At its gates he raised towers one hundred cubits high with foundations sixty cubits wide. [4]He made its gates seventy cubits high and forty cubits wide to allow passage of his mighty forces, with his infantry in formation. [5]At that time King Nebuchadnezzar waged war against King Arphaxad in the vast plain that borders Ragau.[¶] [6]Rallying to him were all who lived in the hill country, all who lived along the Euphrates, the Tigris, and the Hydaspes, as well as Arioch, king of the Elamites, in the plains. Thus many nations joined the ranks of the Chelodites."[b]

[7]Then Nebuchadnezzar, king of the Assyrians, contacted all the inhabitants of Persia[††] and all who lived in the west, the inhabitants of Cilicia and Damascus, Lebanon and Antilebanon, and all who lived along the seacoast, [8]the peoples of Carmel, Gilead, Upper Galilee, and the vast plain of Esdraelon, [9]and all in Samaria and its cities, and west of the Jordan as far as Jerusalem, Bethany, Chelous, Kadesh,[c] and the river

of Egypt; Tahpanhes,[d] Raamses, all the land of Goshen, [10]Tanis, Memphis[e] and beyond, and all the inhabitants of Egypt as far as the borders of Ethiopia.

[11]But all the inhabitants of the whole land[‡‡] made light of the summons of Nebuchadnezzar, king of the Assyrians, and would not join him in the war. They were not afraid of him, since he was only a single opponent. So they sent back his envoys empty-handed and disgraced.[f] [12]Then Nebuchadnezzar fell into a violent rage against all the land, and swore by his throne and his kingdom that he would take revenge on all the territories of Cilicia, Damascus, and Syria, and would destroy with his sword all the inhabitants of Moab, Ammon, the whole of Judea, and all those living in Egypt as far as the coasts of the two seas.[§§]

**Defeat of Arphaxad.** [13]In the seventeenth year[¶¶] he mustered his forces against King Arphaxad and was victorious in his campaign. He routed the whole force of Arphaxad, his entire cavalry, and all his chariots, [14]and took possession of his cities. He pressed on to Ecbatana, took its towers, sacked its marketplaces, and turned its glory into shame. [15]He captured Arphaxad in the mountains of Ragau, ran him through with spears, and utterly destroyed him once and for all. [16]Then he returned to Nineveh with all his consolidated forces, a very great multitude of warriors; and there he and his forces relaxed and feasted for one hundred and twenty days.[g]

## CHAPTER 2

**Revenge Planned Against the Western Nations.**[***] [1]In the eighteenth year,[†††] on the twenty-second day of the first month, there was a discussion in the palace of Nebuchadnezzar, king of the Assyrians, about taking revenge on all the land, as he had threatened.[h] [2]He summoned all his attendants and officers, laid before them his secret plan, and with his own lips recounted in full detail the wickedness of all

---

*[1:1–3:10] This section consists of an introduction to Nebuchadnezzar (1:1–16), his commissioning of Holofernes (2:1–13), and a description of the campaigns Holofernes leads against the disobedient vassal nations of the west (2:14–3:10).

†[1:1–16] Introduction to Nebuchadnezzar and his campaign against Arphaxad. Nebuchadnezzar (605/4–562 B.C.), the most famous Neo-Babylonian king, destroyed Jerusalem in 587 B.C., the eighteenth year of his reign (see Jer 32:1). His depiction here as an Assyrian is an invention of the author, as is the description of Arphaxad, an otherwise unknown king of the Medes, in Ecbatana.

‡[1:1] **Twelfth year**: in the twelfth year of Nebuchadnezzar (593 B.C.) Zedekiah, king of Judah, refused to join a revolt against him (see Jer 27:3; 28:1). **Nineveh**: capital of Assyria, destroyed in 612 B.C.

§[1:2–4] Since a cubit was the distance from the elbow to the fingertip (approximately eighteen inches), these dimensions are prodigious. The massive wall around Ecbatana is described as 105 feet high and 75 feet thick, with each stone measuring four and a half feet thick and nine feet long. The tower gates are 150 feet high and 60 feet wide. Such unlikely massive structures have never been found at Ecbatana, which lies beneath the modern city of Hamadan, located in the Zagros mountains of northwest Iran. Ecbatana is mentioned in vv. 1, 2, 14 as Arphaxad's headquarters. Tradition claims Esther and Mordecai are buried there.

¶[1:5] Ragau, the place where Arphaxad is slain (v. 15), one of the oldest settlements in Iran, is located on a plain one hundred miles northeast of Ecbatana. In the Book of Tobit it is the home of Gabael (Tb 1:14; 4:1, 20; 5:6; 6:13; 9:2, 5).

**[1:6] **Chelodites**: Greek *Cheleoud*, probably a corruption of "Chaldeans," i.e., the Neo-Babylonians.

††[1:7] Mention of Persia suggests a postexilic setting for the book, since this area would have been designated Media before the middle of the fifth century B.C.

‡‡[1:11] References to "the whole land," "all the land" are used ten times in the first two chapters (vv. 11, 12; 2:1, 2, 5, 6, 7, 9, 10, 19). This signifies all the nations west of Persia as far as Egypt that were subject to Nebuchadnezzar, i.e., the whole earth or world (esp. 2:9). These and similar formulations throughout the book build the case that the "God of heaven" (5:8; 6:19; 11:17) is the true "Master of heaven and earth" (9:12).

§§[1:12] **The two seas**: probably the Mediterranean to the Persian Gulf, though possibly the Red Sea and Mediterranean.

¶¶[1:13] **Seventeenth year**: 588 B.C. Without help from the vassal nations, Nebuchadnezzar defeats Arphaxad.

***[2:1–13] Nebuchadnezzar commissions Holofernes to take vengeance on the vassal nations that refused him auxiliary military support (see 1:7–12).

†††[2:1] **Eighteenth year**: 587 B.C. Most of the story is set in the catastrophic year when the historical Nebuchadnezzar, king of Babylon, destroyed Jerusalem.

---

a. [1:1] Gn 10:22; Ezr 6:2; Tb 3:7; 5:6; 6:10; 7:1; 14:12–13; 2 Mc 9:3; Jon 1:2; 3:2–3.  b. [1:6] Gn 14:1, 9.  c. [1:9] Nm 34:4; Dt 32:51; Jos 15:23.  d. [1:9] Jer 2:16; 43:7–9; 44:1; 46:14.  e. [1:10] Is 19:13; Jer 2:16; 44:1; 46:14, 19; Ez 30:13, 15; Hos 9:6.  f. [1:11] 2 Sm 17:3; Ez 33:24.  g. [1:16] Est 1:3–4.  h. [2:1] Jer 32:1; 52:29.

the land. ³They decided to destroy all who had refused to obey the order he had issued.

⁴When he had fully recounted his plan, Nebuchadnezzar, king of the Assyrians, summoned Holofernes, the ranking general* of his forces, second only to himself in command, and said to him: ⁵"Thus says the great king, the lord of all the earth: Go forth from my presence, take with you men of proven valor, one hundred and twenty thousand infantry and twelve thousand cavalry;ⁱ ⁶and proceed against all the land of the west, because they disobeyed the order I issued. ⁷Tell them to have earth and water† ready, for I will come against them in my wrath; I will cover all the land with the feet of my soldiers, to whom I will deliver them as spoils. ⁸Their wounded will fill their ravines and wadies, the swelling river will be choked with their dead; ⁹and I will deport them as exiles to the very ends of the earth.

¹⁰"Go before me and take possession of all their territories for me. If they surrender to you, guard them for me until the day of their sentencing. ¹¹As for those who disobey, show them no mercy, but deliver them up to slaughter and plunder in all the land you occupy.ʲ ¹²For as I live,‡ and by the strength of my kingdom, what I have spoken I will accomplish by my own hand.ᵏ ¹³Do not disobey a single one of the orders of your lord; fulfill them exactly as I have commanded you, and do it without delay."

**Campaigns of Holofernes.**§ ¹⁴So Holofernes left the presence of his lord, and summoned all the commanders, generals, and officers of the Assyrian forces. ¹⁵He mustered one hundred and twenty thousand picked troops, and twelve thousand mounted archers, ¹⁶and drew them up as a vast force organized for battle. ¹⁷He took along a very large number of camels, donkeys, and mules for carrying their supplies; innumerable sheep, cattle, and goats for their food;ˡ ¹⁸abundant provisions for each man, and much gold and silver from the royal palace.

¹⁹Then he and all his forces set out on their expedition in advance of King Nebuchadnezzar, to overrun all the lands of the western region with their chariots, cavalry, and picked infantry. ²⁰A huge, irregular force, too many to count, like locusts, like the dust of the earth, went along with them.ᵐ

²¹After a three-day marchˢ from Nineveh, they reached the plain of Bectileth, and camped opposite Bectileth near the mountains to the north of Upper Cilicia. ²²From there Holofernes took all his forces, the infantry, cavalry, and chariots, and marched into the hill country. ²³He devastated Put and Lud,** and plundered all the Rassisites and the Ishmaelites on the border of the wilderness toward the south of the Chelleans.ⁿ

²⁴Then, following the Euphrates, he went through Mesopotamia, and battered down every fortified city along the Wadi Abron, until he reached the sea. ²⁵He seized the territory of Cilicia, and cut down everyone who resisted him. Then he proceeded to the southern borders of Japheth, toward Arabia. ²⁶He surrounded all the Midianites, burned their tents, and sacked their encampments.ᵒ ²⁷Descending to the plain of Damascus at the time of the wheat harvest, he set fire to all their fields, destroyed their flocks and herds, looted their cities, devastated their plains, and put all their young men to the sword.ᵖ

²⁸ᵍFear and dread of him fell upon all the inhabitants of the coastland, upon those in Sidon and Tyre,ʳ and those who dwelt in Sur and Ocina, and the inhabitants of Jamnia. Those in Azotus and Ascalon also feared him greatly.††

**CHAPTER 3**

**Submission of the Vassal Nations.** ¹So they sent messengers to him to sue for peace in these words: ²"We, the servants of Nebuchadnezzar the great king, lie prostrate before you; do with us as you will. ³See, our dwellings and all our land and every wheat field, our flocks and herds, and all our encampments are at your disposal; make use of them as you please. ⁴Our cities and their inhabitants are also at your service; come and deal with them as you see fit."

⁵After the spokesmen had reached Holofernes and given him this message, ⁶he went down with his forces to the seacoast, stationed garrisons in

---

* [2:4] **The ranking general**: Holofernes is so identified six times in Judith. See also 4:1; 5:1; 6:1; 10:13; 13:15. Holofernes and Bagoas (12:11) are Persian names; two officers of Artaxerxes III Ochos (358–338 B.C.) were so named.

† [2:7] **Earth and water**: in the Persian period, offering these to a conqueror was a symbolic gesture signifying humble submission of one asking for a treaty.

‡ [2:12] **As I live**: an oath proper to God; see the promissory oath of God the divine warrior in Dt 32:39–42; cf. Is 49:18; Jer 22:24; Ez 5:11. **By my own hand**: in his pride, Nebuchadnezzar claims to do this by his own hand (cf. Is 10:13). In contrast, Judith claims that God will deliver Israel "by my hand" (8:33; 12:4).

§ [2:14–3:10] As Holofernes attacks the western nations, terror sweeps across the empire at large (2:28), then Judea (4:1–2), and finally Bethulia (7:1). In these verses, the line of advance is from Nineveh to Damascus and all who submit are nonetheless devastated and forced to worship Nebuchadnezzar.

§ [2:21] **A three-day march**: no ancient army could have traveled three hundred miles from Nineveh to Cilicia in three days.

** [2:23] **Put and Lud**: mentioned together in Jer 46:9; Ez 27:10; 30:5. Put is thought to be in Libya in Africa; Lud is usually identified with Lydia in Asia Minor. Rather than indicating definite localities here, Put and Lud add assonance and prophetic overtones to the narrative.

†† [2:28] Symbolic of the completeness of the terror that descended on the area, seven towns are listed: Tyre, Sidon, Sur, Ocina, Jamnia, Ashdod, and Ashkelon.

i. [2:5] 2 Kgs 18:19, 28; 1 Mc 15:13; Is 36:4, 13; Hos 5:13; 10:6. j. [2:11] Dt 7:2; Jos 11:20; Is 13:18. k. [2:12] Dt 32:39–41. l. [2:17] Gn 41:49.

m. [2:20] Ex 10:4, 13, 14; Jgs 6:5; 7:12; Ps 105:34; Jl 1:4. n. [2:23] Gn 2:2; 10:6, 22; Is 66:19; Ez 30:5. o. [2:26] Gn 37:36; Ex 2:15; Jgs 6–8. p. [2:27] Gn 34:26; Jos 6:21; 1 Sm 15:8. q. [2:28] Ex 15:16; Ps 55:6. r. [2:28] Ez 26:7–14; 29:17–20.

the fortified cities, and took selected men from them as auxiliaries. ⁷The people of these cities and all the inhabitants of the countryside received him with garlands and dancing to the sound of timbrels. ⁸But he devastated their whole territory and cut down their sacred groves, for he was allowed to destroy all the gods of the land, so that every nation might worship only Nebuchadnezzar, and all their tongues and tribes should invoke him as a god.*ˢ ⁹At length Holofernes reached Esdraelon in the neighborhood of Dothan,† the approach to the main ridge of the Judean mountains; ¹⁰he set up his camp between Geba‡ and Scythopolis, and stayed there a whole month to replenish all the supplies of his forces.

## II. SIEGE OF BETHULIA§

### CHAPTER 4

**Israel Prepares for War.¶** ¹When the Israelites who lived in Judea heard of all that Holofernes, the ranking general of Nebuchadnezzar king of the Assyrians, had done to the nations, and how he had looted all their shrines** and utterly destroyed them, ²they were in very great fear of him, and greatly alarmed for Jerusalem and the temple of the Lord, their God. ³Now, they had only recently returned from exile, and all the people of Judea were just now reunited, and the vessels, the altar, and the temple had been purified from profanation.†† ⁴So they sent word to the whole region of Samaria, to Kona,

Beth-horon, Belmain, and Jericho, to Choba and Aesora, and to the valley of Salem.‡‡ ⁵The people there secured all the high hilltops, fortified the villages on them, and since their fields had recently been harvested, stored up provisions in preparation for war.

⁶Joakim, who was high priest§§ in Jerusalem in those days, wrote to the inhabitants of Bethulia and Betomesthaim, which is opposite Esdraelon, facing the plain near Dothan,ᵘ ⁷and instructed them to keep firm hold of the mountain passes, since these offered access to Judea. It would be easy to stop those advancing, as the approach was only wide enough for two at a time.¶¶ ⁸The Israelites carried out the orders given them by Joakim, the high priest, and the senate of the whole people of Israel, in session in Jerusalem.ᵛ

**Israel at Prayer.** ⁹All the men of Israel cried to God with great fervor and humbled themselves. ¹⁰They, along with their wives, and children, and domestic animals, every resident alien, hired worker, and purchased slave, girded themselves with sackcloth.***ʷ ¹¹And all the Israelite men, women, and children who lived in Jerusalem fell prostrate in front of the temple†††ˣ and sprinkled ashes on their heads, spreading out their sackcloth before the Lord.ʸ ¹²The altar, too, they draped in sackcloth;††† and with one accord they cried out fervently to the God of Israel not to allow their children to be seized, their wives to be taken captive, the cities of their inheritance to be ruined, or the sanctuary to be profaned and mocked for the nations to gloat over.

¹³The Lord heard their cry§§§ and saw their distress. The people continued fasting for many days throughout Judea and before the sanctuary of the Lord Almighty in Jerusalem.ᶻ ¹⁴Also girded with sackcloth, Joakim, the high priest, and all the priests in attendance before the Lord, and those who ministered to the Lord offered the daily burnt offering, the votive offerings, and the voluntary offerings of the people.ᵃ ¹⁵With

---

*[3:8] **Invoke him as a god:** Holofernes violates Nebuchadnezzar's instructions (see 2:5–13). No Assyrian, Neo-Babylonian, or Persian king is known to have claimed divinity. During Hellenistic times, Ptolemy V (203–181 B.C.) and the Seleucid Antiochus IV made claims to divinity. In Dn 3 and 6, divinity is ascribed to Nebuchadnezzar and Darius, respectively.

†[3:9] **Dothan:** a town in Ephraimite territory fourteen miles north of Shechem, mentioned elsewhere only twice (Gn 37:17 and 2 Kgs 6:13), but five times in Judith (3:9; 4:6; 7:3, 18; 8:3). Destroyed in 810 B.C. by Aramean invasions, Dothan was deserted until the Hellenistic period when a small settlement was constructed. Because it is mentioned so often, Dothan is sometimes thought to be the author's home.

‡[3:10] **Geba:** location uncertain. Scythopolis, the Greek name for ancient Beth-shean (Jos 17:11), the only city in Judith given its Greek name, strategically guarded the eastern end of the Valley of Jezreel.

§[4:1–7:32] In this section the focus narrows to Judea and specifically the little town of Bethulia. The scenes alternate between the Assyrian camp (5:1–6:13; 7:1–3, 6–18) and Judea/Bethulia (4:1–15; 6:14–21; 7:4–5, 19–32).

¶[4:1–15] Here the scene shifts to Judea where Israel hears and is greatly terrified about Holofernes' destruction of the neighboring places of worship. At Joakim's instruction they take defensive measures and then pray fervently that God will not allow their sanctuary to be destroyed.

**[4:3] **Shrines:** the Greek word *hiera* is used only here and may mean holy places or things. By contrast, the sanctuary in Jerusalem is *naos*, "temple" (v. 2); *oikos*, "house" (v. 3); and *hagia*, lit., "holy things" (v. 12).

††[4:3] **Returned from exile . . . purified from profanation:** conflated historical references associated with events in 538 B.C. (return from exile) and 515 B.C. (dedication of the Second Temple) or perhaps even 164 B.C. (the rededication of the Second Temple in the Maccabean period).

‡‡[4:4] Of the eight cities listed, only the locations of Beth-horon, Jericho, and Samaria are known. Salem, mentioned in Gn 17:17, is thought to be an ancient name of Jerusalem.

§§[4:6] **Joakim, who was high priest:** see also vv. 8, 14; 15:8. Joakim exercises religious and military authority comparable to that of Jonathan in Maccabean times (cf. 1 Mc 10:18–21). **Bethulia and Betomesthaim:** unknown locations mentioned only in Judith. Bethulia may mean "House of God" (*byt 'l/yh*) or "House of Ascent" (*byt 'lyh*), perhaps a reference to either Bethel or Shechem.

¶¶[4:7] **Only wide enough for two at a time:** such a narrow pass near Esdraelon cannot be identified.

***[4:10] **Sackcloth:** traditional sign of penitence and supplication is here taken to the extreme. Cf. Jon 3:8.

†††[4:11] **Fell prostrate in front of the temple:** for a parallel to this ceremony of entreaty see Jl 1:13, 14; 2:15–17.

‡‡‡[4:12] **The altar . . . draped in sackcloth:** attested nowhere else in the Bible.

§§§[4:13] **The Lord heard their cry:** this anticipates the role of Judith, the instrument of deliverance (chap. 16), though the people believe God has abandoned them (7:25).

---

s. [3:8] Ex 34:13; 2 Kgs 18:4; 23:14–15; 2 Chr 14:2; 17:6; 31:1; 34:4.   t. [4:3] 1 Mc 4:36–61; 2 Mc 10:3–5.

u. [4:6] Dn 13:1, 4, 28, 29, 63.   v. [4:8] 2 Mc 11:27.   w. [4:10] Neh 9:1; Est 4:1–4; Jl 1:13, 14; Jon 3:5, 6, 8.   x. [4:11] 1 Chr 29:20; 2 Mc 3:15.   y. [4:11] 2 Sm 21:10.   z. [4:13] Est 4:16; Jl 2:15.   a. [4:14] Ex 29:38–46; Nm 28:1–8; Ezr 3:4.

ashes upon their turbans, they cried to the Lord with all their strength to look with favor on the whole house of Israel.[b]

## CHAPTER 5

**Achior in the Assyrian War Council.**[*] [1]It was reported to Holofernes, the ranking general of the Assyrian forces, that the Israelites were ready for battle, had blocked the mountain passes, fortified the high hilltops, and placed roadblocks in the plains. [2]In great anger he summoned all the rulers of Moab, the governors of Ammon, and all the satraps of the coastland[c] [3]and said to them: "Now tell me, you Canaanites, what sort of people is this that lives in the hill country? Which cities do they inhabit? How large is their force? In what does their power and strength consist? Who has set himself up as their king and the leader of their army? [4]Why have they alone of all the inhabitants of the west refused to come out to meet me?"

[5][†]Then Achior, the leader of all the Ammonites, said to him: "My lord, please listen to a report from your servant. I will tell you the truth about this people that lives in the hill country near here. No lie shall escape your servant's lips.

[6]"These people are descendants of the Chaldeans. [7]They formerly lived in Mesopotamia, for they did not wish to follow the gods of their ancestors who were in the land of the Chaldeans.[d] [8]Since they abandoned the way of their ancestors, and worshiped the God of heaven,[‡] the God whom they had come to know, their ancestors expelled them from the presence of their gods. So they fled to Mesopotamia and lived there a long time. [9]Their God told them to leave the place where they were living and go to the land of Canaan. Here they settled, and grew very rich in gold, silver, and a great abundance of livestock.[e] [10]Later, when famine had gripped the land of Canaan, they went down into Egypt. They stayed there as long as they found sustenance and there they grew into such a great multitude that the number of their people could not be counted.[f] [11][g]The king of Egypt, however, rose up against them, and shrewdly forced them to labor at brickmaking; they were oppressed and made into slaves. [12]But they cried to their God, and he

struck the whole land of Egypt with plagues for which there was no remedy. So the Egyptians drove them out. [13]Then God dried up the Red Sea before them[h] [14]and led them along the route to Sinai and Kadesh-barnea. They drove out all the inhabitants of the wilderness [15]and settled in the land of the Amorites. By their strength they destroyed all the Heshbonites,[i] crossed the Jordan, and took possession of all the hill country.[j] [16]They drove out before them the Canaanites, the Perizzites, the Jebusites, the Shechemites,[§] and all the Gergesites,[k] and they lived there a long time.

[17]"As long as the Israelites did not sin in the sight of their God, they prospered, for their God, who hates wickedness, was with them. [18]But when they abandoned the way he had prescribed for them, they were utterly destroyed by frequent wars, and finally taken as captives into foreign lands. The temple of their God was razed to the ground, and their cities were occupied by their enemies.[m] [19]But now they have returned to their God, and they have come back from the Diaspora where they were scattered. They have reclaimed Jerusalem, where their sanctuary is, and have settled again in the hill country, because it was unoccupied.

[20][n]"So now, my master[**] and lord, if these people are inadvertently at fault, or if they are sinning against their God, and if we verify this offense of theirs, then we will be able to go up and conquer them. [21]But if they are not a guilty nation, then let my lord keep his distance; otherwise their Lord and God will shield them, and we will be mocked in the eyes of all the earth."

[22]Now when Achior had finished saying these things, all the people standing round about the tent murmured; and the officers of Holofernes and all the inhabitants of the seacoast and of Moab alike said he should be cut to pieces. [23]"We are not afraid of the Israelites," they said, "for they are a powerless people, incapable of a strong defense. [24]Therefore let us attack, master Holofernes. They will become fodder for your great army."

## CHAPTER 6

[1]When the noise of the crowd surrounding the council had subsided, Holofernes, the ranking general of the Assyrian forces, said to Achior, in the presence of the whole throng of foreigners,

---

*[5:1–6:13] The scene shifts to the Assyrian camp below Bethulia where Holofernes talks with Achior and then expels him to the foot of the hill below the little town.

†[5:5–21] Achior (Heb. "brother of light") traces the covenant of Israel from Abraham to the exile and defends the inviolability of the people because their powerful God will defend them if they do not sin. He later identifies the head Judith displays as that of Holofernes (14:6–10). He may be modeled on the famous sage, Ahiqar (see note on Tb 1:21). Achior is wise, but the wisdom granted Judith by God is more effective than his.

‡[5:8] **God of heaven:** a common expression in Persian times; see also 6:19; 11:17 (cf. 7:28; 9:12; 13:18).

§[5:16] **Shechemites:** perhaps anticipates the allusion in Judith's prayer (9:2) to Simeon's revenge on these people.

¶[5:18–19] Knowledge of the Babylonian exile is presupposed; cf. also 4:3.

**[5:20] **Master:** the Greek word *despota*, usually applied to God in the Septuagint, is applied to Holofernes five times in the Book of Judith (vv. 20, 24; 7:9, 11; 11:10), and only once to God (9:12).

---

b. [4:15] Lv 16:4; Ez 24:23; 44:18; Zec 3:5.   c. [5:2] Dt 2:21; 2 Kgs 24:2.   d. [5:7] Gn 11:31.   e. [5:9] Gn 11:31–12:5; 13:2.   f. [5:10] Gn 42:1–5; 46:1–7; Ex 1:7.   g. [5:11–12] Ex 1:10–14; 5:1–21; 7:1–11:10.

h. [5:13] Ex 14:21; Jos 2:10; 4:23; Ps 106:9; Wis 9:7; Heb 11:29.   i. [5:15] Nm 21:25–28, 30, 34; Dt 1:4; 2:24, 26, 30; 3:2, 6; 4:46.   j. [5:15] Jos 3.   k. [5:16] Gn 10:16; 15:20; Dt 7:1; Jos 3:10; 24:12; 1 Chr 1:14.   l. [5:17–18] Dt 28–30; Jgs 2:11–15; Ps 106:40–46.   m. [5:18] 2 Kgs 25.   n. [5:20–21] Jdt 8:12–23; 11:10; Tb 3:3.   o. [5:23–24] Jdt 6:2; 9:7–8; 16:2.

of the Moabites, and of the Ammonite mercenaries: [2]"Who are you,* Achior and the mercenaries of Ephraim, to prophesy among us as you have done today, and to tell us not to fight against the people of Israel because their God shields them? Who is God beside Nebuchadnezzar? He will send his force and destroy them from the face of the earth. Their God will not save them;[p] [3]but we, the servants of Nebuchadnezzar, will strike them down with one blow, for they will be unable to withstand the force of our cavalry. [4]We will overwhelm them with it, and their mountains shall be drunk with their blood, and their plains filled with their corpses. Not a trace of them shall survive our attack; they will utterly perish. So says King Nebuchadnezzar, lord of all the earth. For he has spoken, and his words will not be in vain. [5]As for you, Achior, you Ammonite mercenary, for saying these things in a moment of perversity, you will not see my face after today, until I have taken revenge on this people that came out of Egypt. [6]Then at my return, the sword of my army or the spear of my attendants will pierce your sides, and you will fall among their wounded. [7]My servants will now conduct you to the hill country, and leave you at one of the cities beside the passes. [8]You will not die until you are destroyed together with them. [9]If you still harbor the hope that they will not be taken, then there is no need for you to be downcast.[q] I have spoken, and not one of my words will fail to be fulfilled."

[10]Then Holofernes ordered the servants who were standing by in his tent to seize Achior, conduct him to Bethulia, and hand him over to the Israelites. [11]So the servants seized him and took him out of the camp into the plain. From the plain they led him up into the hill country until they reached the springs below Bethulia. [12]When the men of the city saw them, they seized their weapons and ran out of the city to the top of the hill, and all the slingers kept them from coming up by hurling stones at them. [13]So, taking cover below the hill, they bound Achior and left him lying at the foot of the hill; then they returned to their lord.

**Achior in Bethulia.**[†] [14]The Israelites came down from their city and found him, untied him, and brought him into Bethulia. They placed him before the rulers of the city, [15]who in those days were Uzziah,[‡] son of Micah of the tribe of Simeon, and Chabris, son of Gothoniel, and

Charmis, son of Melchiel.[r] [16]They then convened all the elders of the city, and all their young men, as well as the women, gathered in haste at the place of assembly. They placed Achior in the center of the people, and Uzziah questioned him about what had happened. [17]He replied by giving them an account of what was said in the council of Holofernes, and of all his own words among the Assyrian rulers, and of all the boasting threats of Holofernes against the house of Israel. [18]At this the people fell prostrate and worshiped God,[§] and they cried out: [19]"Lord, God of heaven, look at their arrogance! Have mercy on our people in their abject state, and look with favor this day on the faces of those who are consecrated to you." [20]Then they reassured Achior and praised him highly. [21]Uzziah brought him from the place of assembly to his home, where he gave a banquet for the elders. That whole night they called upon the God of Israel for help.

## CHAPTER 7

**The Campaign Against Israel.**[¶] [1]The following day Holofernes ordered his whole army, and all the troops who had come to join him, to break camp and move against Bethulia, seize the passes into the hills, and make war on the Israelites. [2]That same day all their fighting men went into action. Their forces numbered a hundred and seventy thousand infantry and twelve thousand cavalry, not counting the baggage train or the men who accompanied it on foot, a very great army. [3]They encamped at the spring in the valley near Bethulia, and spread crosswise toward Dothan as far as Balbaim, and lengthwise from Bethulia to Cyamon, which faces Esdraelon.

[4]When the Israelites saw how many there were, they were greatly distressed and said to one another, "Soon they will strip the whole land bare. Neither the high mountains nor the valleys nor the hills will bear their weight." [5]Yet they all seized their weapons, lighted fires on their towers, and kept watch throughout the night.[s]

**The Siege of Bethulia.**[**] [6]On the second day Holofernes led out all his cavalry in the sight of the Israelites who were in Bethulia. [7]He reconnoitered the ascents to their city and located their springs of water; these he seized, stationing armed detachments around them, while he himself returned to his troops.

---

7:30 highlights the irony of his name. **Chabris . . . Charmis:** unknown outside Judith.

[§][6:18] **The people fell prostrate and worshiped God:** here in response to Achior's report, the people properly turn to God in their distress. See 4:12.

[¶][7:1–5] The scene returns to the Assyrian camp (vv. 1–3) and then shifts back to Bethulia (vv. 4–5). Holofernes orders war preparations; Israel sees and is greatly terrified.

[**][7:6–32] The scene is set first in the Assyrian camp where Holofernes moves against Bethulia (vv. 6–18), and then in Bethulia where the people cry out to God and, when their courage fails, determine it is time to surrender (vv. 19–32).

---

*[6:2] **Who are you:** repeated by Judith in 8:12 to the officials of Bethulia and modified in 12:14 in her response to Bagoas' invitation on Holofernes' behalf. The question, "Who is God?" motivates the entire narrative. Holofernes defends Nebuchadnezzar; Judith defends the Lord.

†[6:14–21] The scene shifts back to Bethulia where Achior tells the town leaders and citizens all that Holofernes has planned against them. The people cry out to God for help.

‡[6:15] **Uzziah:** *Ozeias* is the Greek equivalent of the Hebrew *'uzziyyah,* "Yah-is-my-strength." His compromise in

p. [6:2] Jdt 3:8; 9:7–8; 1 Kgs 22:15–17; 2 Kgs 18:32–35; Is 36:18–20; Dn 3:14–18.  q. [6:9] Gn 4:5; 40:7.

r. [6:15] Gn 29:33; 34:25, 30; 35:23.  s. [7:5] 1 Mc 12:28–29; 2 Mc 10:36.

[8]All the rulers of the Edomites, all the leaders of the Moabites, together with the generals of the coastal region, came to Holofernes and said:[t] [9]"Master, please listen to what we have to say, that there may be no losses among your forces. [10]These Israelite troops do not rely on their spears, but on the height of the mountains where they dwell, for it is not easy to reach the summit of their mountains.[u] [11]Therefore, master, do not attack them in regular formation, and not a single one of your troops will fall. [12]Stay in your camp, and spare every man of your force. Have some of your servants keep control of the spring of water that flows out at the base of the mountain, [13]for that is where the inhabitants of Bethulia get their water. Then thirst will destroy them, and they will surrender their city. Meanwhile, we and our troops will go up to the nearby hilltops and encamp there to guard against anyone's leaving the city. [14]They and their wives and children will languish with hunger, and even before the sword strikes them they will be laid low in the streets where they live. [15]Thus you will render them dire punishment for their rebellion and their refusal to meet you peacefully."

[16]Their words pleased Holofernes and all his attendants, and he ordered their proposal to be carried out. [17]So the Ammonites moved camp, together with five thousand Assyrians. They encamped in the valley and held the water supply and the springs of the Israelites. [18]The Edomites and the Ammonites went up and encamped in the hill country opposite Dothan; and they sent some of their men to the southeast opposite Egrebel, near Chusi, which is on Wadi Mochmur. The rest of the Assyrian army was encamped in the plain, covering all the land. Their tents and equipment were spread out in profusion everywhere, and they formed a vast multitude.

**The Distress of the Israelites.** [19]The Israelites cried to the Lord, their God, for they were disheartened, since all their enemies had them surrounded, and there was no way of escaping from them.[*] [20]The whole Assyrian army, infantry, chariots, and cavalry, kept them thus surrounded for thirty-four days.[†] All the reservoirs of water failed the inhabitants of Bethulia, [21]and the cisterns ran dry, so that on no day did they have enough water to drink, for their drinking water was rationed. [22]Their children were listless, and the women and youths were fainting from thirst and were collapsing in the streets

and gateways of the city, with no strength left in them.

[23]So all the people, including youths, women, and children, went in a crowd to Uzziah and the rulers of the city. They cried out loudly and said before all the elders: [24]"May God judge between you and us! You have done us grave injustice in not making peace with the Assyrians.[v] [25]There is no one to help us now! God has sold us into their hands by laying us prostrate before them in thirst and utter exhaustion.[w] [26]So now, summon them and deliver the whole city as plunder to the troops of Holofernes and to all his forces; [27]we would be better off to become their prey. Although we would be made slaves, at least we would live, and not have to see our little ones dying before our eyes, and our wives and children breathing their last.[x] [28]We adjure you by heaven and earth and by our God, the Lord of our ancestors, who is punishing us for our sins and the sins of our ancestors,[‡] that this very day you do as we have proposed."[y]

[29]All in the assembly with one accord broke into shrill wailing and cried loudly to the Lord their God. [30]But Uzziah said to them, "Courage, my brothers and sisters! Let us endure patiently five days more for the Lord our God to show mercy toward us; for God will not utterly forsake us. [31]But if these days pass and help does not come to us, I will do as you say." [32]Then he dismissed the people. The men returned to their posts on the walls and towers of the city, the women and children went back to their homes. Throughout the city they were in great misery.

## III. JUDITH, INSTRUMENT OF THE LORD[§]

### CHAPTER 8

**Description of Judith.** [1][*]Now in those days Judith, daughter of Merari,[a] son of Ox, son of Joseph, son of Oziel, son of Elkiah, son of Ananias, son of Gideon, son of Raphain, son of Ahitub, son of Elijah, son of Hilkiah, son of Eliab, son of Nathanael, son of Salamiel, son of Sarasadai, son of Simeon, son of Israel, heard of this. [2]Her husband, Manasseh,[**] of her own tribe and clan, had died at the time of the barley harvest. [3]While he was supervising those who bound the

---

*[7:19] The prayers of the Israelites shift focus from concern for the Temple and Jerusalem (4:12), to concern that God see the arrogance of the enemy and show pity on the covenant people (6:18), to expression of fear and loss of courage regarding their own safety (7:19).

†[7:20] **Thirty-four days:** the Bethulians lose heart after being without water; Judith will spend four days in the enemy camp (12:10) and the Israelites will plunder the enemy camp for thirty days (15:11).

‡[7:28] In keeping with the deuteronomic theme of retribution, the Bethulians interpret their persecution as punishment for their sins and the sins of their ancestors (see Ex 20:5; 34:7; Ez 18). In 8:18–27, Judith argues that they are being tested.

§[8:1–10:10] In this section the hero is introduced (8:1–8) and prepares to deliver Israel (8:9–10:10).

¶[8:1] Judith has the longest genealogy accorded any biblical woman, with family ties back to Israel/Jacob.

**[8:2] Manasseh:** Judith's marriage was endogamous, within her own tribe. The tribe and clan are identified as hers, though usually it is the husband's tribe and clan that are noted.

---

t. [7:8] Gn 36:1; 1 Mc 5:3.  u. [7:10] 1 Kgs 20:23, 28; 2 Kgs 19:23; Ps 95:4; Is 37:24.

v. [7:24] Ex 5:21.  w. [7:25] Est 7:4.  x. [7:27] Ex 14:12; 16:3; 1 Mc 1:62–63.  y. [7:28] Ps 106:6; Lam 5:7.  z. [8:1] Gn 26:34; Jer 36:14, 21, 23.  a. [8:1] Gn 46:11; Ex 6:16; Nm 3:17.

sheaves in the field, he was overcome by the heat; and he collapsed on his bed and died in Bethulia, his native city. He was buried with his ancestors in the field between Dothan and Balamon. <sup>4b</sup>Judith was living as a widow* in her home for three years and four months. <sup>5</sup>She set up a tent for herself on the roof of her house, put sackcloth about her waist, and wore widow's clothing.<sup>c</sup> <sup>6</sup>She fasted all the days of her widowhood, except sabbath eves and sabbaths, new moon eves and new moons, feastdays and holidays of the house of Israel.<sup>d</sup> <sup>7</sup>She was beautiful in appearance and very lovely to behold.<sup>e</sup> Her husband, Manasseh, had left her gold and silver, male and female servants, livestock and fields, which she was maintaining. <sup>8</sup>No one had a bad word to say about her, for she feared God greatly.

**Judith and the Elders.**† <sup>9</sup>So when Judith heard of the harsh words that the people, discouraged by their lack of water, had spoken against their ruler, and of all that Uzziah had said to them in reply, swearing that he would hand over the city to the Assyrians at the end of five days, <sup>10</sup>she sent her maid who was in charge of all her things‡ to summon Uzziah, Chabris, and Charmis, the elders of her city. <sup>11</sup>When they came, she said to them: "Listen to me, you rulers of the people of Bethulia. What you said to the people today is not right. You pronounced this oath, made between God and yourselves, and promised to hand over the city to our enemies unless within a certain time the Lord comes to our aid. <sup>12</sup>Who are you to put God to the test today, setting yourselves in the place of God in human affairs?<sup>§f</sup> <sup>13</sup>And now it is the Lord Almighty you are putting to the test, but you will never understand anything! <sup>14</sup>You cannot plumb the depths of the human heart or grasp the workings of the human mind; how then can you fathom God,

who has made all these things, or discern his mind, or understand his plan?<sup>g</sup>

"No, my brothers, do not anger the Lord our God. <sup>15</sup>For if he does not plan to come to our aid within the five days, he has it equally within his power to protect us at such time as he pleases, or to destroy us in the sight of our enemies. <sup>16</sup>Do not impose conditions on the plans of the Lord our God. God is not like a human being to be moved by threats, nor like a mortal to be cajoled.

<sup>17</sup>"So while we wait for the salvation that comes from him, let us call upon him to help us, and he will hear our cry if it pleases him. <sup>18</sup>For there has not risen among us in recent generations, nor does there exist today, any tribe, or clan, or district, or city of ours that worships gods made by hands, as happened in former days.<sup>h</sup> <sup>19</sup>It was for such conduct that our ancestors were handed over to the sword and to pillage, and fell with great destruction before our enemies.<sup>i</sup> <sup>20</sup>But since we acknowledge no other god but the Lord, we hope that he will not disdain us or any of our people. <sup>21</sup>If we are taken, then all Judea will fall, our sanctuary will be plundered, and God will demand an account from us for their profanation. <sup>22</sup>For the slaughter of our kindred, for the taking of exiles from the land, and for the devastation of our inheritance, he will hold us responsible among the nations. Wherever we are enslaved, we will be a scandal and a reproach in the eyes of our masters. <sup>23</sup>Our servitude will not work to our advantage, but the Lord our God will turn it to disgrace.

<sup>24</sup>"Therefore, my brothers, let us set an example** for our kindred. Their lives depend on us, and the defense of the sanctuary, the temple, and the altar rests with us. <sup>25</sup>Besides all this, let us give thanks to the Lord our God for putting us to the test as he did our ancestors.<sup>k</sup> <sup>26</sup>Recall how he dealt with Abraham, and how he tested Isaac, and all that happened to Jacob in Syrian Mesopotamia while he was tending the flocks of Laban, his mother's brother. <sup>27</sup>He has not tested us with fire, as he did them, to try their hearts, nor is he taking vengeance on us. But the Lord chastises those who are close to him in order to admonish them."

<sup>28</sup>Then Uzziah said to her: "All that you have said you have spoken truthfully, and no one can

---

*[8:4] **Widow**: in a reversal of traditional property law, Judith holds title to her husband's estate (see v. 7). However, she will give a part of her inheritance to her late husband's family before her death (16:24); she chooses not to remarry (16:22).

†[8:9–10:10] This section opens with a repetition of the information that Judith heard about the discouragement of the people and about Uzziah's vow (cf. v. 1). Judith's plan to save Israel then takes shape. In her own home, she meets with the elders of Bethulia (vv. 9–36), prays (9:1–14), prepares herself and the food she will need in the Assyrian camp (10:1–5), goes out to meet the elders again at the gate of Bethulia (10:6–8), and sets out with her maid for the Assyrian camp (10:9–10).

‡[8:10] **Her maid who was in charge of all her things**: cf. Gn 15:2; 24:2; 39:4. Judith's first act in the story is to send this unnamed maid (*habra*, lit., "graceful one" or "favorite slave," v. 33; 10:2, 5, 17; 13:9; 16:23) to summon the town officials (see also other terms for female servants, *paidiske* in 10:10 and *doule* in 12:15; 13:3). Her last act in the story will be to give this woman her freedom (16:23).

§[8:12] Judith reprimands the leaders for putting God to the test (cf. Dt 6:16). She will argue that the right to test belongs to God (vv. 25–27).

¶[8:15–16] God's plans are in opposition to Nebuchadnezzar's plans (2:2, 4). **To protect . . . or to destroy**: Judith defends God's freedom (cf. Jb 1:21; 2:10).

**[8:24] **Let us set an example**: when Judith says "us," she includes herself. She proposes that she together with Uzziah, Chabris, and Charmis model a faithful response to God's test for the wavering people. "Let us give thanks to the Lord our God for putting us to the test" (v. 25) repeats her intention. "Us" for Uzziah does not include her (see vv. 30, 31).

b. [8:4] 1 Sm 25:39–42; 2 Sm 11:27; Is 54:4; Lam 1:1; 5:3.    c. [8:5] Jos 2:6, 8; Jgs 3:20–25; 1 Sm 9:25–26; 2 Sm 11:2; 16:22; 2 Kgs 4:10; 23:12; Ps 102:8; Acts 10:9.    d. [8:6] Lk 2:37.    e. [8:7] Gn 12:11; 29:17; Est 2:7.    f. [8:12] Dt 6:16; Jb 38:2; 40:2, 7–8; Ps 106:14; Mal 3:15.

g. [8:14] Ps 139:17–18; Wis 9:13; Is 40:13; Rom 11:33–34; 1 Cor 2:11.    h. [8:18] Jdt 5:20–21; 11:10.    i. [8:19] Ps 78:56–57; 106:13–14; Jer 7:16–20.    j. [8:25] Dt 8:5; Tb 12:14; Ps 94:12; Prv 3:11–12; Wis 3:4–6; Sir 2:1–6; Heb 12:5–6.    k. [8:25] Gn 22:1–19; 32:22–32; Ex 20:20; Dt 8:16.

deny your words. ²⁹For today is not the first time your wisdom has been evident, but from your earliest days all the people have recognized your understanding, for your heart's disposition is right. ³⁰The people, however, were so thirsty that they forced us to do for them as we have promised, and to bind ourselves by an oath that we cannot break."*¹ ³¹But now, since you are a devout woman, pray for us that the Lord may send rain to fill up our cisterns. Then we will no longer be fainting from thirst."

³²Then Judith said to them: "Listen to me! I will perform a deed that will go down from generation to generation among our descendants. ³³Stand at the city gate tonight to let me pass through with my maid; and within the days you have specified before you will surrender the city to our enemies, the Lord will deliver Israel by my hand. ³⁴You must not inquire into the affair, for I will not tell you what I am doing until it has been accomplished." ³⁵Uzziah and the rulers said to her, "Go in peace, and may the Lord God go before you to take vengeance upon our enemies!" ³⁶Then they withdrew from the tent and returned to their posts.

## CHAPTER 9

**The Prayer of Judith.**† ¹Judith fell prostrate, put ashes upon her head, and uncovered the sackcloth she was wearing. Just as the evening incense was being offered in the temple of God in Jerusalem, Judith cried loudly to the Lord:ᵐ ²"Lord, God of my father Simeon, into whose hand you put a sword to take revenge upon the foreigners‡ who had defiled a virgin by violating her, shaming her by uncovering her thighs, and dishonoring her by polluting her womb. You said, 'This shall not be done!' Yet they did it. ³Therefore you handed over their rulers to slaughter; and you handed over to bloodshed the bed in which they lay deceived, the same bed that had felt the shame of their own deceiving. You struck down the slaves together with their masters, and the masters upon their thrones.§

⁴Their wives you handed over to plunder, and their daughters to captivity, and all the spoils you divided among your favored children, who burned with zeal for you and in their abhorrence of the defilement of their blood called on you for help. O God, my God, hear me also, a widow.

⁵"It is you who were the author of those events and of what preceded and followed them. The present and the future you have also planned.ⁿ Whatever you devise comes into being. ⁶The things you decide come forward and say, 'Here we are!' All your ways are in readiness, and your judgment is made with foreknowledge.ᵒ

⁷"Here are the Assyrians, a vast force, priding themselves on horse and chariot, boasting of the power of their infantry, trusting in shield and spear, bow and sling.ᵖ They do not know that you are the Lord who crushes wars;¶ ⁸Lord is your name. Shatter their strength in your might, and crush their force in your wrath.�q For they have resolved to profane your sanctuary, to defile the tent where your glorious name resides, and to break off the horns of your altar with the sword. ⁹"See their pride, and send forth your fury upon their heads.ʳ Give me, a widow, a strong hand to execute my plan.ˢ ¹⁰By the deceit of my lips, strike down slave together with ruler, and ruler together with attendant. Crush their arrogance by the hand of a female.ᵗ

¹¹**⁺*"Your strength is not in numbers, nor does your might depend upon the powerful.ᵛ You are God of the lowly, helper of those of little account, supporter of the weak, protector of those in despair, savior of those without hope.

¹²"Please, please, God of my father, God of the heritage of Israel, Master of heaven and earth, Creator of the waters, King of all you have created, hear my prayer! ¹³Let my deceitful words‡‡ʷ wound and bruise those who have planned dire things against your covenant, your

---

¶[9:7–8] **You are the Lord who crushes wars; Lord is your name**: cf. Ex 15:3, "The Lord is a warrior; Lord is his name" and Jdt 16:2, "The Lord is a God who crushes wars."

**[9:9–10] In a five-fold petition, Judith asks that God see their pride, send fury on their heads, give her a strong hand, strike down the enemy through her deceit, and crush their pride by the hand of a female (*theleia*, see also 13:15 and 16:5, rather than the more usual *gyne*, woman). In an androcentric society, there was no greater dishonor for a male than that he die at the hand of a female (see Jgs 9:53–54). Nine verses emphasize that by her hand God's deliverance is accomplished: 8:33; 9:9, 10; 12:4; 13:4, 14, 15; 15:10; and 16:5.

††[9:11–12] Ten titles for God are arranged in two groups of five on either side of the repeated Greek particle, *nai nai* ("verily" or "please"). The title "Master of heaven and earth" (v. 12; see notes on 1:11 and 5:20) is unique to Judith in the Septuagint, as are also "God of the heritage of Israel" and "Creator of the waters."

‡‡[9:13] **Deceitful words**: twice Judith asks God to make her a successful liar in order to preserve her people (vv. 10, 13).

---

*[8:30–31] **An oath that we cannot break**: Uzziah's request that Judith pray for rain underscores his lack of imagination concerning how God's deliverance might come.

†[9:1–14] Judith prepares to confront the enemy by turning to God, the source of her strength. Her prayer, an individual lament, moves from a remembrance of God's saving deeds of the past to an appeal to God to exercise the same power in the present. Judith contrasts the empty pride of the Assyrians with God's surpassing might, powerful enough to be exercised in unlikely ways, even through the hand of a woman.

‡[9:2] **The foreigners**: Shechem, the Hivite, violated Dinah, Jacob and Leah's daughter (Gn 34:2). **Defiled a virgin by violating her**: meaning of the Greek is unclear; lit., "who loosened the virgin's womb (*metran*) to defilement." Some read "headdress" or "girdle" (*mitran*) instead of "womb" (*metran*).

§[9:3] Because Shechem had deceived and violated Dinah, her brothers, Simeon and Levi, tricked Shechem and the men of his city into being circumcised, and then killed them while they were recovering from the circumcision (Gn 34:13–29).

---

l. [8:30] Ex 32:22; 1 Sm 15:20–24.   m. [9:1] Ex 30:7–8; 1 Chr 28:18; Ezr 9:5; Ps 141:2; Dn 9:21.

---

n. [9:5] Is 41:22–23; 42:9; 43:9; 44:7; 46:10.   o. [9:6] Jb 38:35; Is 46:9–13; Bar 3:35.   p. [9:7] Ex 15:1, 21.   q. [9:8] Ex 15:3; Ps 46:9–10; 76:4–5.   r. [9:9] Ex 15:7.   s. [9:9] Ex 15:1–20; 4:2, 4, 6, 7, 17, 20; 5:21; 6:1; 7:4, 5, 15, 17, 19; 8:1, 2, 12, 13; 9:3, 22; 10:12, 21, 22; 12:11; 13:3, 9, 14, 16; 14:16, 21, 26, 27; 15:6, 9, 12, 20; Jgs 5:26.   t. [9:10] Jgs 4:9.   u. [9:11] Ps 33:16–17.   v. [9:11] Ex 15:2; Jgs 7:2; 1 Sm 17:45–47; 2 Chr 16:8–9.   w. [9:13] Jdt 10:4; 11:20, 23; 16:6, 9; Est C:24.

holy temple, Mount Zion, and the house your children possess.ˣ ¹⁴Make every nation and every tribe know clearly that you are God, the God of all power and might, and that there is no other who shields the people of Israel but you alone."

## CHAPTER 10

**Judith Prepares to Depart.** ¹As soon as Judith had ceased her prayer to the God of Israel and finished all these words, ²she rose from the ground. She called her maid and they went down into the house, which she used only on sabbaths and feast days. ³She took off the sackcloth she had on, laid aside the garments of her widowhood, washed her body with water, and anointed herself with rich ointment. She arranged her hair, put on a diadem, and dressed in the festive attire she had worn while her husband, Manasseh, was living.ʸ ⁴She chose sandals for her feet, and put on her anklets, bracelets, rings, earrings, and all her other jewelry.ᶻ Thus she made herself very beautiful, to entice the eyes of all the men who should see her.*

⁵She gave her maid a skin of wine and a jug of oil. She filled a bag with roasted grain, dried fig cakes, and pure bread.†ᵃ She wrapped all her dishes and gave them to the maid to carry.ᵇ

⁶Then they went out to the gate of the city of Bethulia and found Uzziah and the elders of the city, Chabris and Charmis, standing there. ⁷When they saw Judith transformed in looks and differently dressed, they were very much astounded at her beauty and said to her, ⁸"'May the God of our ancestors grant you favor and make your design successful, for the glory of the Israelites and the exaltation of Jerusalem." ⁹Judith bowed down to God.

**Judith and Her Maid Leave Bethulia.** Then she said to them, "Order the gate of the city opened for me, that I may go to accomplish the matters we discussed." So they ordered the young men to open the gate for her, as she had requested, ¹⁰and they did so. Then Judith and her maidservant went out. The men of the city kept her in view as she went down the mountain and crossed the valley; then they lost sight of her.

## IV. JUDITH GOES OUT TO WAR‡

¹¹As Judith and her maid walked directly across the valley, they encountered the Assyrian patrol.

¹²The men took her in custody and asked her, "To what people do you belong? Where do you come from, and where are you going?"ᶜ She replied: "I am a daughter of the Hebrews, and I am fleeing from them, because they are about to be delivered up to you as prey. ¹³I have come to see Holofernes, the ranking general of your forces, to give him a trustworthy report; in his presence I will show him the way by which he can ascend and take possession of the whole hill country without a single one of his men suffering injury or loss of life."ᵈ

¹⁴When the men heard her words and gazed upon her face, which appeared marvelously beautiful to them, they said to her, ¹⁵"By hastening down to see our master, you have saved your life. Now go to his tent; some of us will accompany you to hand you over to him. ¹⁶When you stand before him, have no fear in your heart; give him the report you have given us, and he will treat you well." ¹⁷So they selected a hundred of their men as an escort for her and her maid, and these conducted them to the tent of Holofernes.

¹⁸As the news of her arrival spread among the tents, a crowd gathered in the camp. They came and stood around her as she waited outside the tent of Holofernes, while he was being informed about her. ¹⁹They marveled at her beauty, regarding the Israelites with wonder because of her, and they said to one another, "Who can despise this people who have such women among them? It is not good to leave one of their men alive, for if any were to be spared they could beguile the whole earth."

**Judith Meets Holofernes.** ²⁰Then the guards of Holofernes and all his attendants came out and ushered her into the tent. ²¹Holofernes was reclining on his bed under a canopy§ woven of purple, gold, emeralds, and other precious stones. ²²When they announced her to him, he came out to the front part of the tent, preceded by silver lamps. ²³When Judith came before Holofernes and his attendants, they all marveled at the beauty of her face. She fell prostrate and paid homage to him, but his servants raised her up.ᵉ

## CHAPTER 11

¹Then Holofernes said to her: "Take courage, woman! Have no fear in your heart! I have never harmed anyone who chose to serve Nebuchadnezzar, king of all the earth. ²As for your people who live in the hill country, I would never have raised my spear against them, had they not insulted me. They have brought this upon themselves. ³But now tell me why you have fled from them and come to us? In any case, you have

---

*[10:4] Judith's beauty overcomes all who meet her (8:7; 10:7, 14, 19, 23; 11:21, 23; 12:13).

†[10:5] Concern for Israel's dietary laws, reflected in her selection of wine, roasted grain, and bread, emphasizes Judith's religious fidelity (cf. 1 Sm 25:18 and Dn 1:8–16).

‡[10:11–13:20] In this section Judith and her maid arrive in the Assyrian camp (10:11–19), where Judith meets (10:20–12:9) and triumphs over Holofernes (12:10–13:10a). Then she and her maid return to Bethulia and announce the victory (13:10b–20).

x. [9:13] Dn 11:28.   y. [10:3] Gn 43:24; Lv 8:6; 22:6; Tb 6:3; Ez 16:4, 9.   z. [10:4] Gn 24:47, 53; 35:4; Ex 3:22; 12:35; 32:3; 35:22; Nm 31:50; Is 3:18, 21; Hos 2:15.   a. [10:5] 1 Sm 25:18.   b. [10:5] Jdt 12:2; Est C:28.

§[10:21] **Canopy:** netting for protection against insects. A prized possession in this story (cf. 13:15; 16:19).

c. [10:12] Gn 16:8.   d. [10:13] Jdt 11:5–6.   e. [10:23] Ru 2:10; 1 Sm 25:41; 2 Sm 14:4.

come to safety. Take courage! Your life is spared tonight and for the future.ʲ ⁴No one at all will harm you. Rather, you will be well treated, as are the servants of my lord, King Nebuchadnezzar."

⁵Judith answered him: "Listen to the words of your servant, and let your maidservant speak in your presence! I will say nothing false to my lord* this night. ⁶If you follow the words of your maidservant, God will successfully perform a deed through you, and my lord will not fail to achieve his designs.† ⁷I swear by the life of Nebuchadnezzar, king of all the earth, and by the power of him who has sent you to guide all living things, that not only do human beings serve him through you; but even the wild animals, and the cattle, and the birds of the air, because of your strength, will live for Nebuchadnezzar and his whole house.ᵍ ⁸Indeed, we have heard of your wisdom and cleverness.ʰ The whole earth is aware that you above all others in the kingdom are able, rich in experience, and distinguished in military strategy.

⁹"As for Achior's speech in your council, we have heard it. When the men of Bethulia rescued him, he told them all he had said to you. ¹⁰So then, my lord and master, do not disregard his word, but bear it in mind, for it is true. Indeed our people are not punished, nor does the sword prevail against them, except when they sin against their God.ʲ ¹¹But now their sin‡ has caught up with them, by which they will bring the wrath of their God upon them when they do wrong; so that my lord will not be repulsed and fail, but death will overtake them. ¹²Because their food has given out and all their water is running low, they have decided to kill their animals, and are determined to consume all the things which God in his laws has forbidden them to eat. ¹³They have decided that they would use the first fruits of grain and the tithes of wine and oil, which they had consecrated and reserved for the priests who minister in the presence of our God in Jerusalem—things which the people should not so much as touch with their hands.ᵏ ¹⁴They have sent messengers to Jerusalem to bring back permission from the senate, for even there people have done these things.ˡ ¹⁵On the very day when the response reaches them and they act upon it, they will be handed over to you for destruction.

¹⁶"As soon as I, your servant, learned all this, I fled from them. God has sent me to perform with you such deeds as will astonish people throughout the whole earth who hear of them. ¹⁷Your servant is, indeed, a God-fearing woman, serving the God of heaven night and day. Now I will remain with you, my lord; but each night your servant will go out into the valley and pray to God. He will tell me when they have committed their offenses. ¹⁸Then I will come and let you know, so that you may march out with all your forces, and not one of them will be able to withstand you. ¹⁹I will lead you through the heart of Judea until you come to Jerusalem, and there in its center I will set up your throne. You will drive them like sheep that have no shepherd, and not even a dog will growl at you.ᵐ This was told to me in advance and announced to me, and I have been sent to tell you."

²⁰Her words pleased Holofernes and all his attendants. They marveled at her wisdom and exclaimed, ²¹"No other woman from one end of the earth to the other looks so beautiful and speaks so wisely!" ²²Then Holofernes said to her: "God has done well in sending you ahead of your people, to bring victory to our hands, and destruction to those who have despised my lord. ²³You are not only beautiful in appearance, but you are also eloquent. If you do as you have said, your God will be my God;§ you will live in the palace of King Nebuchadnezzar and be renowned throughout the whole earth."

## CHAPTER 12

¹Then he ordered them to lead her into the room where his silver dinnerware was kept, and ordered them to set a table for her with his own delicacies to eat and his own wine to drink. ²But Judith said, "I cannot eat any¶ of them, because it would be a scandal.ⁿ Besides, I will have enough with the things I brought with me." ³Holofernes asked her, "But if your provisions give out, where can we get more of the same to provide for you? None of your people are with us." ⁴Judith answered him, "As surely as you live, my lord, your servant will not use up her supplies before the Lord accomplishes by my hand what he has determined."

⁵Then the attendants of Holofernes led her to her tent, where she slept until the middle of the night. Toward the early morning watch, she roseᵒ ⁶and sent this message to Holofernes, "Give orders, my lord, to let your servant go out for

---

*[11:5–6] Here the word "lord" has a double meaning, indicating both Holofernes and God. Much irony is evident in Judith's conversation with Holofernes (e.g., 12:4).

†[11:6] **Designs:** cf. 10:8; 11:6; 13:5 where this word is used as a synonym for Judith's "affair" (8:34), which she kept secret as she carried out the plan of her God (8:15, 16), unlike her counterpart Nebuchadnezzar, who told all the details of his plan (2:2, 4).

‡[11:11] **Sin:** but in 8:18–20 Judith asserts that the people have not committed idolatry in recent generations.

f. [11:3] 2 Mc 11:19.    g. [11:7] Jgs 8:19; 1 Sm 14:45; 25:26; 28:10; 2 Sm 11:11; Ez 17:16; Dn 2:38.    h. [11:8] Sir 1:6; 42:18.    i. [11:9–10] Jdt 5:5.    j. [11:10] Jdt 5:21; 8:18.    k. [11:13] Nm 18:8–9.    l. [11:14] 1 Mc 2:31–41.

§[11:23] **Your God will be my God:** in 3:8, Holofernes insisted that Nebuchadnezzar alone is god.

¶[12:2] **Cannot eat any:** the food of Gentiles was avoided by pious Jews (see Dn 1:8, 13, 15; Tb 1:10–11) because it might have been prohibited as unclean (see Lv 11:13–44), sacrificed to idols (see Ex 34:15; Dt 32:37–38), or contaminated with blood (see Lv 7:26–27). In addition, eating together symbolized the sharing of life.

m. [11:19] Ex 11:7.    n. [12:2] Tb 1:10–11; Est C:28; 1 Mc 1:62–63; 2 Mc 5:27; 6:18–7:2; Dn 1:8.    o. [12:5] Ex 14:24; 1 Sm 11:11.

prayer." ⁷So Holofernes ordered his guards not to hinder her. Thus she stayed in the camp three days. Each night she went out to the valley of Bethulia, where she bathed herself* at the spring of the camp.ᵖ ⁸After bathing, she prayed to the Lord, the God of Israel, to direct her way for the triumph of her people. ⁹Then she returned purified to the tent and remained there until her food was brought to her toward evening.ᵍ

**Judith at the Banquet of Holofernes.** ¹⁰On the fourth day Holofernes gave a banquet for his servants alone, to which he did not invite any of the officers. ¹¹And he said to Bagoas, the eunuch in charge of his personal affairs, "Go and persuade the Hebrew woman in your care to come and to eat and drink with us. ¹²It would bring shame on us to be with such a woman without enjoying her. If we do not seduce her, she will laugh at us."ʳ

¹³So Bagoas left the presence of Holofernes, and came to Judith and said, "So lovely a maidservant should not be reluctant to come to my lord to be honored by him, to enjoy drinking wine with us, and to act today like one of the Assyrian women who serve in the palace of Nebuchadnezzar." ¹⁴Judith replied, "Who am I to refuse my lord? Whatever is pleasing to him I will promptly do. This will be a joy† for me until the day of my death."

¹⁵So she proceeded to put on her festive garments and all her finery. Meanwhile her servant went ahead and spread out on the ground opposite Holofernes the fleece Bagoas had furnished for her daily use in reclining while eating.ˢ ¹⁶Then Judith came in and reclined. The heart of Holofernes was in rapture over her and his passion was aroused. He was burning with the desire to possess her, for he had been biding his time to seduce her from the day he saw her.ᵗ ¹⁷Holofernes said to her, "Drink and be happy with us!" ¹⁸Judith replied, "I will gladly drink, my lord, for today is the greatest day of my whole life." ¹⁹She then took the things her servant had prepared and ate and drank in his presence. ²⁰Holofernes, charmed by her, drank a great quantity of wine, more than he had ever drunk on any day since he was born.

**CHAPTER 13**

**Judith Beheads Holofernes.** ¹When it grew late, his servants quickly withdrew. Bagoas closed the tent from the outside and dismissed the attendants from their master's presence. They went off to their beds, for they were all tired because the banquet had lasted so long. ²Judith was left alone in the tent with Holofernes, who lay sprawled on his bed, for he was drunk with wine. ³Judith had ordered her maidservant to stand outside the bedchamber and to wait, as on the other days, for her to come out; she had said she would be going out for her prayer. She had also said this same thing to Bagoas.

⁴When all had departed, and no one, small or great, was left in the bedchamber, Judith stood by Holofernes' bed and prayed silently, "O Lord, God of all might, in this hour look graciously on the work of my hands for the exaltation of Jerusalem. ⁵Now is the time for aiding your heritage and for carrying out my design to shatter the enemies who have risen against us."ᵘ ⁶She went to the bedpost near the head of Holofernes, and taking his sword from it, ⁷she drew close to the bed, grasped the hair of his head, and said, "Strengthen me this day, Lord, God of Israel!" ⁸Then with all her might she struck his neck twice and cut off his head.ᵛ ⁹She rolled his body off the bed and took the canopy from its posts. Soon afterward, she came out and handed over the head of Holofernes to her maid, ¹⁰who put it into her food bag. Then the two went out together for prayer as they were accustomed to do.

**Judith and Her Maid Return to Bethulia.** They passed through the camp, and skirting that valley, went up the mountain to Bethulia, and approached its gates. ¹¹From a distance, Judith shouted to the guards at the gates: "Open! Open the gate! God, our God, is with us. Once more he has shown his strength in Israel and his power against the enemy, as he has today!"

**Judith Displays the Head of Holofernes.** ¹²‡When the citizens heard her voice, they hurried down to their city gate and summoned the elders of the city. ¹³All the people, from the least to the greatest, hurriedly assembled, for her return seemed unbelievable. They opened the gate and welcomed the two women. They made a fire for light and gathered around the two. ¹⁴Judith urged them with a loud voice: "Praise God, give praise! Praise God, who has not withdrawn his mercy from the house of Israel, but has shattered our enemies by my hand this very night!" ¹⁵Then she took the head out of the bag, showed it to them, and said: "Here is the head of Holofernes, the ranking general of the Assyrian forces, and here is the canopy under which he lay in his drunkenness. The Lord struck him down by the hand of a female!§ ¹⁶Yet I swear by the Lord, who has protected me in the way I have walked, that it was my face that seduced

---

*[12:7] **Bathed herself**: she bathes to purify herself after contact with the Gentiles. Her nightly departure from the camp provides for her escape (cf. 13:10).

†[12:14] **Joy**: the irony of this response is obvious; see also the joy of 14:9 and Judith's "new song" in chap. 16.

‡[13:12–20] Elements from chaps. 8–9 are echoed here. The assembly of the people at Judith's return parallels the meeting of the town officials summoned by Judith in 8:10. Uzziah blesses Judith in 8:5 and again in 13:18–20.

§[13:15] **By the hand of a female**: cf. 16:5 and note on 9:9–10.

p. [12:7] Tb 7:9.   q. [12:9] 2 Sm 3:35.   r. [12:12] Dn 13:37, 54, 57–58.   s. [12:15] Tb 9:6; Ez 23:41.   t. [12:16] Dn 13:20, 39.

u. [13:5] Gn 24:45; 1 Sm 1:13.   v. [13:8] Jgs 4:21; 1 Sm 17:51; 31:9.

Holofernes to his ruin, and that he did not defile me with sin or shame."

<sup>17</sup>All the people were greatly astonished. They bowed down and worshiped God, saying with one accord, "Blessed are you, our God, who today have humiliated the enemies of your people." <sup>18</sup>Then Uzziah said to her, "Blessed are you, daughter, by the Most High God, above all the women on earth; and blessed be the Lord God, the creator of heaven and earth, who guided your blow at the head of the leader of our enemies.<sup>w</sup> <sup>19</sup>Your deed of hope will never be forgotten by those who recall the might of God.<sup>x</sup> <sup>20</sup>May God make this redound to your everlasting honor, rewarding you with blessings, because you risked your life when our people were being oppressed, and you averted our disaster, walking in the straight path before our God." And all the people answered, "Amen! Amen!"<sup>y</sup>

# V. VICTORY AND THANKSGIVING*

## CHAPTER 14

**Judith's Plan of Attack.** <sup>1</sup>Then Judith said to them: "Listen to me,<sup>†</sup> my brothers and sisters. Take this head and hang it on the parapet of your wall.<sup>z</sup> <sup>2</sup>At daybreak, when the sun rises on the earth, each of you seize your weapons, and let all the able-bodied men rush out of the city under command of a captain, as if about to go down into the valley against the Assyrian patrol, but without going down. <sup>3</sup>The Assyrians will seize their weapons and hurry to their camp to awaken the generals of the army. When they run to the tent of Holofernes and do not find him, panic will seize them, and they will flee before you.<sup>a</sup> <sup>4</sup>Then you and all the other inhabitants of the whole territory of Israel will pursue them and strike them down in their tracks. <sup>5</sup>But before doing this, summon for me Achior the Ammonite, that he may see and recognize the one who despised the house of Israel and sent him here to meet his death."

---

*[14:1–16:25] This section describes Judith's plan to attack the Assyrian camp (14:1–5) and its execution (14:11–15:7). Between the plan and its execution, Achior identifies the head of Holofernes and is converted to Judaism. The book concludes with the victory celebration (15:8–14), hymn of thanksgiving (16:1–20), and a description of Judith's final days (16:21–25). Elements from chaps. 8–9 recur here: Judith, widow of Manasseh (8:2; 16:22), lived alone in Bethulia on her estate (8:4; 16:22), with servants and property (8:7; 16:21). Judith's instructions begin with the words "listen to me" (8:11; 14:1). Her prayer for success (9:1–14) is balanced by a prayer and display of success in 14:14–16.

†[14:1–5] Listen to me: an imperative (used also in 8:11, 32) opens Judith's instruction that the people display the head of Holofernes on the parapet and themselves in ranks before the enemy at daybreak. The strategy is to throw the Assyrians into panic and strike them down in their confusion; cf. 15:1–3.

w. [13:18] Jgs 5:24; Lk 1:42.   x. [13:19] Sir 35:9.   y. [13:20] Dt 27:15–26; Ps 41:14; 72:19; 89:53.   z. [14:1] 1 Sm 17:54; 31:9–10; 2 Sm 20:21; 2 Kgs 10:7–8; 1 Mc 7:47; 2 Mc 15:30; Mt 14:8.   a. [14:3] 1 Mc 7:44.

**Achior's Conversion.**<sup>‡</sup> <sup>6</sup>So they called Achior from the house of Uzziah. When he came and saw the head of Holofernes in the hand of one of the men in the assembly of the people, he collapsed in a faint. <sup>7</sup>Then, after they lifted him up, he threw himself at the feet of Judith in homage, saying: "Blessed are you in every tent of Judah! In every nation, all who hear your name will be struck with terror.<sup>b</sup> <sup>8</sup>But now, tell me all that you did during these days." So Judith told him, in the midst of the people, all that she had done, from the day she left until the time she began speaking to them. <sup>9</sup>When she had finished her account, the people cheered loudly, so that the city resounded with shouts of joy. <sup>10</sup>Now Achior, seeing all that the God of Israel had done, believed firmly in God. He circumcised the flesh of his foreskin and he has been united with the house of Israel to the present day.<sup>c</sup>

**Panic in the Assyrian Camp.** <sup>11</sup>At daybreak they hung the head of Holofernes on the wall. Then all the Israelite men took up their weapons and went out by groups to the mountain passes.<sup>d</sup> <sup>12</sup>When the Assyrians saw them, they notified their commanders, who, in turn, went to their generals, their division leaders, and all their other leaders. <sup>13</sup>They came to the tent of Holofernes and said to the one in charge of all his things, "Awaken our lord, for the slaves have dared come down against us in battle, to their utter destruction." <sup>14</sup>So Bagoas went in and knocked at the entry of the tent, presuming that Holofernes was sleeping with Judith. <sup>15</sup>When no one answered, he parted the curtains, entered the bedchamber, and found him thrown on the floor dead, with his head gone! <sup>16</sup>He cried out loudly, weeping, groaning, and howling, and tore his garments. <sup>17</sup>Then he entered the tent where Judith had her quarters; and, not finding her, he rushed out to the troops and cried: <sup>18</sup>"The slaves have duped us! One Hebrew woman has brought shame on the house of King Nebuchadnezzar. Look! Holofernes on the ground—without a head!"<sup>e</sup>

<sup>19</sup>When the leaders of the Assyrian forces heard these words, they tore their tunics and were overcome with great distress. Their loud cries and shouts were heard throughout the camp.

## CHAPTER 15

<sup>1</sup>On hearing what had happened, those still in their tents were horrified. <sup>2</sup>Overcome with fear and dread, no one kept ranks any longer.

---

‡[14:6–10] Recognizing the head of Holofernes, Achior faints. Then he throws himself down before Judith, acclaiming her blessed in Judah and every nation. After listening to all she had done, Achior is circumcised and joins the house of Israel. Since this violates the prohibition of Dt 23:4 that no Ammonite or Moabite shall enter the assembly, even to the tenth generation, some suggest that the book was not included in the Hebrew scriptures for this reason. However, see Is 56:3–6.

b. [14:7] Jgs 5:24.   c. [14:10] Dt 23:4.   d. [14:11] 2 Mc 8:23; 12:20.   e. [14:18] Jgs 9:54.

They scattered in all directions, and fled along every path, both through the valley and in the hill country.[f] [3]Those who were stationed in the hill country around Bethulia also took to flight. Then the Israelites, every warrior among them, came charging down upon them.

[4]Uzziah sent messengers to Betomasthaim, to Choba and Kona, and to the whole territory of Israel to report what had happened and to urge them all to attack the enemy and destroy them. [5]On hearing this, all the Israelites, with one accord, attacked them and cut them down as far as Choba. Even those from Jerusalem and the rest of the hill country took part in this, for they too had been notified of the happenings in the camp of their enemy. The Gileadites and the Galileans struck the enemy's flanks with great slaughter, even beyond Damascus and its borders. [6]The remaining people of Bethulia swept down on the camp of the Assyrians, plundered it, and acquired great riches. [7]The Israelites, when they returned from the slaughter, took possession of what was left. Even the towns and villages in the hill country and on the plain got an enormous quantity of spoils, for there was a tremendous amount of it.

**Israel Celebrates Judith's Victory.** [8]Then the high priest Joakim and the senate of the Israelites who lived in Jerusalem came to see for themselves the good things that the Lord had done for Israel, and to meet and congratulate Judith. [9]When they came to her, all with one accord blessed her, saying:

"You are the glory of Jerusalem![*]
    You are the great pride of Israel!
    You are the great boast of our
        nation!
[10] By your own hand you have done all
        this.
    You have done good things for
        Israel,
    and God is pleased with them.
    May the Almighty Lord bless you
        forever!"

And all the people said, "Amen!"
[11]For thirty days[†] all the people plundered the camp, giving Judith the tent of Holofernes, with all his silver, his beds, his dishes, and all his furniture. She took them and loaded her mule, hitched her carts, and loaded these things on them.

[12]All the women of Israel gathered to see her, and they blessed her and performed a dance in her honor.[g] She took branches in her hands and distributed them to the women around her, [13]and she and the other women crowned themselves with olive leaves. Then, at the head of all the people, she led the women in the dance, while the men of Israel followed, bearing their weapons, wearing garlands and singing songs of praise. [14]Judith led all Israel in this song of thanksgiving, and the people loudly sang this hymn of praise:

## CHAPTER 16

### Judith's Hymn of Deliverance

[1]And Judith sang:

"Strike up a song to my God with
        tambourines,[h]
    sing to the Lord with cymbals;
Improvise for him a new song,
    exalt and acclaim his name.
[2] For the Lord is a God who crushes wars;[i]
    he sets his encampment among his
        people;
    he delivered me from the hands of
        my pursuers.

[3] "The Assyrian came from the mountains
        of the north,
    with myriads of his forces he came;
Their numbers blocked the wadies,
    their cavalry covered the hills.
[4] He threatened to burn my territory,
    put my youths to the sword,
Dash my infants to the ground,
    seize my children as plunder.
    And carry off my virgins as spoil.

[5] "But the Lord Almighty thwarted them,
    by the hand of a female!
[6] Not by youths was their champion struck
        down,[j]
    nor did Titans bring him low,
    nor did tall giants attack him;[k]
But Judith, the daughter of Merari,
    by the beauty of her face brought
        him down.
[7] She took off her widow's garb
    to raise up the afflicted in Israel.
She anointed her face with fragrant oil;
[8]    fixed her hair with a diadem,
    and put on a linen robe to beguile
        him.

---

*[15:9] In the Lectionary of the Catholic Church, this passage is one of several choices for feasts of Mary (e.g., the Presentation of Mary). These words of praise are also echoed in antiphons for the Liturgy of the Hours on Marian feasts.

†[15:11] **Thirty days**: the central actions in each half of the book are accomplished in a total of thirty-four days. Bethulia was without water for thirty-four days (7:20). Judith spent four days in the enemy camp and the Israelites plunder the Assyrian camp for thirty days.

f. [15:2] Gn 9:2; Dt 11:25; 1 Mc 7:18; Sir 4:17.

‡[15:14–16:17] Judith's hymn of deliverance is patterned on the Song of Miriam (Ex 15:20–21).

g. [15:12] Ex 15:20; Jgs 11:34; 1 Sm 18:6; Jer 31:4.  h. [16:1] Gn 31:27; Ex 15:20; 1 Sm 18:6; 2 Sm 6:5; 1 Chr 13:8; Ps 68:26; 81:3; 149:3; Jer 31:4.  i. [16:2] Ex 15:3; Ps 46:10.  j. [16:6] 1 Sm 17:4, 51.  k. [16:6] Gn 6:1–4; Dt 2:10, 21; 2 Sm 21:16–22; 1 Chr 20:4–8.

⁹ Her sandals ravished his eyes,ˡ
  her beauty captivated his mind,
  the sword cut through his neck!ᵐ

¹⁰ "The Persians trembled at her boldness,
  the Medes were daunted at her
  daring.
¹¹ When my lowly ones shouted,
  and my weak ones cried out,
  The enemy was terrified,
  screamed and took to flight.
¹² Sons of maidservants pierced them
  through;
  wounded them like deserters'
  children.
  They perished before the ranks of
  my Lord.

¹³ "I will sing a new song to my God.ⁿ
  O Lord, great are you and glorious,
  marvelous in power and
  unsurpassable.
¹⁴ Let your every creature serve you;
  for you spoke, and they were made.
  You sent forth your spirit, and it created
  them;ᵒ
  no one can resist your voice.ᵖ
¹⁵ For the mountains to their bases
  are tossed with the waters;
  the rocks, like wax, melt before your
  glance.�q

"But to those who fear you,
  you will show mercy.
¹⁶ Though the sweet fragrance of every
  sacrifice is a trifle,
  and the fat of all burnt offerings but
  little in your sight,
  one who fears the Lord is forever
  great.

¹⁷ "Woe to the nations that rise against my
  people!
  the Lord Almighty will requite
  them;

in the day of judgment he will
  punish them:
He will send fire and worms into their
  flesh,ʳ
  and they will weep and suffer
  forever."

¹⁸When they arrived at Jerusalem, they worshiped God. As soon as the people were purified, they offered their burnt offerings, voluntary offerings, and donations.ˢ ¹⁹Judith dedicated to God all the things of Holofernes that the people had given her, putting under the ban the canopy that she herself had taken from his bedchamber.ᵗ ²⁰For three months the people continued their celebration in Jerusalem before the sanctuary, and Judith remained with them.

**The Renown and Death of Judith.** ²¹When those days were over, all of them returned to their inheritance. Judith went back to Bethulia and remained on her estate. For the rest of her life she was renowned throughout the land. ²²Many wished to marry her, but she gave herself to no man all the days of her life from the time her husband, Manasseh, died and was gathered to his people. ²³Her fame continued to increase, and she lived in the house of her husband, reaching the advanced age of one hundred and five.*ᵘ She set her maid free. And when she died in Bethulia, they buried her in the cave of her husband, Manasseh;ᵛ ²⁴and the house of Israel mourned her for seven days.†ʷ Before she died, she distributed her property to the relatives of her husband, Manasseh, and to her own relatives.ˣ

²⁵ʸDuring the lifetime of Judith and for a long time after her death, no one ever again spread terror‡ among the Israelites.

---

*[16:23] **One hundred and five**: long life was a sign of blessing (see Jb 42:16; Prv 16:31; 20:29). The fact that the Maccabean period was one hundred and five years long (168–63 B.C.) may account for assigning this age to Judith.

†[16:24] **Seven days**: the customary period for mourning the dead (1 Sm 31:13).

‡[16:25] **Spread terror**: Judith is compared to the heroes of the Book of Judges (cf. Jgs 3:11, 30).

l. [16:9] Sg 7:2; Ez 16:10.   m. [16:9] Jgs 5:26.   n. [16:13] Ps 33:3; 40:4; 96:1; 98:1; 144:9; 149:1; Is 42:10.   o. [16:14] Gn 1; Ps 104:30; 148:5.   p. [16:14] Est C:3–4; Ps 33:9; Is 55:11.   q. [16:15] Ps 97:5; Mi 1:4; Na 1:5.

r. [16:17] Sir 7:17; Is 66:24; Mk 9:48.   s. [16:18] Nm 19:11–22; 34:19.   t. [16:19] Lv 7:16.   u. [16:23] Jb 42:16; Prv 16:31; 20:29; Sir 18:9; Lk 2:36.   v. [16:23] Gn 23:19; 25:9; 49:29–32; 50:13.   w. [16:24] Gn 50:3; 1 Sm 31:13; 1 Chr 10:12; Sir 22:12.   x. [16:24] Nm 27:6–11.   y. [16:25] Jgs 3:11, 30; 5:31; 8:28.

# THE BOOK OF
# ESTHER

⁂

The Book of Esther tells a story of the deliverance of the Jewish people. We are shown a Persian emperor, Ahasuerus (loosely based on Xerxes, 485–464 B.C.), who makes momentous decisions for trivial reasons, and his wicked minister, Haman, who takes advantage of the king's compliance to pursue a personal vendetta against the Jews by having a royal decree issued ordering their destruction. The threat is averted by two Jews, Esther and Mordecai. Their influence and intervention allow the Jews to turn the tables on their enemies and rout their attackers. This deliverance is commemorated by the inauguration of the Jewish festival of Purim on the fourteenth and fifteenth of Adar (mid-February through mid-March). The book confronts the modern reader with important themes, the evils of genocide and racism.

Esther's character matures over the course of the narrative. As a girl she is recruited for the king's harem because of her physical beauty. But at a key moment in the book (chap. 4), she rises to the challenge to risk her life for the salvation of her people. At that point, she transforms her status as queen from a position of personal privilege to one of power and public responsibility.

Esther's uncle, Mordecai, appears first as an adoptive father, whose solicitude for Esther leads him to the king's gate, where he foils a plot to assassinate the king. When he learns of the edict against the Jews, he encourages Esther to confront the king. The book ends with Mordecai as the king's chief minister.

The book is a free composition, not a historical document. Its fictional character can be illustrated by many examples of literary motifs: the use of extensive conversation to move the plot along; the motif of concealment (Esther is a Jew, related to Mordecai, but Haman does not know it, even as he comes to her banquet in chap. 7). A whole series of banquets structure the work: two by the king, one by Vashti, three by Esther, and the joyful banqueting that ends the book. Further artificialities are clear in the way characters are paired (e.g., Mordecai and Esther) and in the delays and the speed of the action (Esther delays the banquet in 5:3–8, but the tempo of chaps. 5–6 is particularly fast); Mordecai passes from the threat of death (5:9–14) to royal honors (6:10–11) within twenty-four hours. There are many exaggerations, and even sarcastic implausibilities (cf. the effect of Vashti's disobedience in 1:17–18), and huge ironies (e.g., Haman in 6:6, 10). The work is a composite of reversals (cf. 9:1) in the lives of individuals and communities.

The book was probably written in the third or second century B.C. It has come down to us in two versions: an older Hebrew version, and a Greek version based on a text similar to the Hebrew, but with additions and alterations as described below.

One striking feature of the Hebrew version of the Book of Esther is that no divine names or titles are employed here; God is not mentioned at all. This would not be unusual in a book whose subject matter or outlook was more secular, but Esther is a book in which the religious element is prominent: the Jews fast in order to be delivered from imminent peril, experience deliverance at the eleventh hour, and commemorate their deliverance with an annual festival. Moreover, there are indirect references to divine activity (for example, in 4:14).

The Greek additions to Esther have many explicit references to God, as well as explicit descriptions of the beliefs and emotional states of Esther and Mordecai. They also elaborate on the content of the edicts from Ahasuerus as illustrations of Gentile attitudes toward Jews. While there are only a few contradictions between these Greek additions and the older Hebrew text, reading the book with these additions is a very different experience from reading the book without them. The additions to Esther are an excellent example of a process that occurs throughout the Bible: further reflections on the story become part of the story itself. Although the Book of Esther was questioned by some early Christians, even St. Jerome, the whole book, including the Greek additions, was included in the canon of Scripture by the Council of Trent.

The Greek version of the book dates from ca. 116 to 48 B.C. (see note on F:11). In the present translation, the Greek additions are indicated by the letters A through F. The regular chapter numbers apply to the Hebrew text.

The book may be divided as follows:

I.   Prologue (A:1–17)
II.  Esther Becomes Queen (1:1–2:23)
III. Haman's Plot Against the Jews (3:1–13; B:1–7; 3:14–15)
IV.  Esther and Mordecai Plead for Help (4:1–17; C:1–D:16; 5:1–5)
V.   Haman's Downfall (5:6–8:2)
VI.  The Jewish Victory and the Feast of Purim (8:3–12; E:1–24; 8:13–9:23)
VII. Epilogue: The Rise of Mordecai (9:24–10:3; F:1–11)

The order of the Vulgate text in relation to the order of the Greek text is as follows:

| Vulg. 11:2–12:6 | = | A:1–17 at the beginning of the book. |
| 13:1–7 | = | B:1–7 after 3:13. |
| 13:8—15:3–19 | = | C:1–D:16 after 4:17. |
| 15:1–2 | = | B:8, 9 after 4:8. |
| 16:1–24 | = | E:1–24 after 8:12. |
| 10:4–13 | = | F:1–10 after 10:3. |

## I. PROLOGUE

### CHAPTER A

**Dream of Mordecai.** [1]In the second year of the reign of Ahasuerus the great, on the first day of Nisan, Mordecai, son of Jair, son of Shimei, son of Kish, of the tribe of Benjamin, had a dream.[*a] [2†]He was a Jew residing in the city of Susa, a prominent man who served at the king's court, [3]and one of the captives whom Nebuchadnezzar, king of Babylon, had taken from Jerusalem with Jeconiah, king of Judah.[b]

[4‡]This was his dream.[‡] There was noise and tumult, thunder and earthquake—confusion upon the earth. [5]Two great dragons advanced, both poised for combat. They uttered a mighty cry, [6]and at their cry every nation prepared for war, to fight against the nation of the just. [7]It was a dark and gloomy day. Tribulation and distress, evil and great confusion, lay upon the earth. [8]The whole nation of the just was shaken with fear at the evils to come upon them, and they expected

to perish. [9d]Then they cried out to God, and from their crying there arose, as though from a tiny spring, a mighty river, a flood of water. [10]The light of the sun broke forth; the lowly were exalted and they devoured the boastful.

[11]Having seen this dream and what God intended to do, Mordecai awoke. He kept it in mind, and tried in every way, until night, to understand its meaning.

**Mordecai Thwarts an Assassination.**[§] [12e]Mordecai lodged in the courtyard with Bigthan and Teresh, two eunuchs of the king who guarded the courtyard. [13]He overheard them plotting, investigated their plans, and discovered that they were preparing to assassinate King Ahasuerus. So he informed the king about them. [14]The king had the two eunuchs questioned and, upon their confession, put to death. [15]Then the king had these things recorded; Mordecai, too, put them into writing. [16]The king also appointed Mordecai to serve at the court, and rewarded him for his actions.[f]

---

*[A:1] The genealogy of Mordecai is designed to reflect opposition to Israel's enemy Haman, an Agagite (v. 17). In 1 Sm 15:1–9, Saul (whose father's name was Kish, of the tribe of Benjamin) conquered Agag the Amalekite.

†[A:2–3] Repeats information from 2:5–6, on which see note, but states that Mordecai is already a court official. In the Hebrew text, Mordecai is not given this rank until 7:10–8:2.

‡[A:4] An interpretation of the dream that relates its features to the plot of the book is given in F:1–6.

§[A:12–17] Retells the story in 2:21–23, but with several differences. Addition A has Mordecai inform the king directly, whereas in 2:22 Mordecai informs the king through Esther after she has become queen. A:16 has Mordecai rewarded immediately after his service, whereas the Hebrew text defers the reward of Mordecai to 6:3–13. In A:17, the failure of the eunuchs' plot becomes Haman's reason for seeking the destruction of Mordecai and his people, something which the Hebrew text attributes to Mordecai's refusal to bow to Haman (see note on 3:2).

---

a. [A:1] Est 2:5.   b. [A:3] Est 2:6; 2 Kgs 24:15; 2 Chr 36:9–10; Jer 22:24–30; 24:1; 29:1–2.   c. [A:4–10] Est F:2, 4–6.

d. [A:9–10] Est F:3.   e. [A:12–15] Est 2:21–23; 6:1–3.   f. [A:16] Est 6:3.

[17]Haman, however, son of Hammedatha, a Bougean,[*] who was held in high honor by the king, sought to harm Mordecai and his people because of the two eunuchs of the king.[g]

## II. ESTHER BECOMES QUEEN

### CHAPTER 1

**The Banquet of Ahasuerus.** [1][1]During the reign of Ahasuerus—the same Ahasuerus who ruled over a hundred and twenty-seven provinces from India to Ethiopia— [2]while he was occupying the royal throne in the royal precinct of Susa,[‡] [3]in the third year of his reign, he gave a feast for all his officials and ministers: the Persian and Median army officers, the nobles, and the governors of the provinces.[h] [4]For as many as a hundred and eighty days, he displayed the glorious riches of his kingdom and the resplendent wealth of his royal estate.

[5]At the end of this time the king gave a feast of seven days in the garden court of the royal palace for all the people, great and small, who were in the royal precinct of Susa. [6]There were white cotton draperies and violet hangings, held by cords of fine crimson linen from silver rings on marble pillars. Gold and silver couches were on a mosaic pavement, which was of porphyry, marble, mother-of-pearl, and colored stones. [7]Drinks were served in a variety of golden cups, and the royal wine flowed freely, as befitted the king's liberality. [8]By ordinance of the king the drinking was unstinted, for he had instructed all the stewards of his household to comply with the good pleasure of everyone. [9]Queen Vashti also gave a feast for the women in the royal palace of King Ahasuerus.

**Refusal of Vashti.** [10]On the seventh day, when the king was merry with wine, he instructed Mehuman, Biztha, Harbona, Bigtha, Abagtha, Zethar, and Carkas, the seven eunuchs who attended King Ahasuerus,[i] [11]to bring Queen Vashti into his presence wearing the royal crown, that he might display her beauty to the populace and the officials, for she was lovely to behold. [12]But Queen Vashti refused to come at the royal order issued through the eunuchs. At this the king's wrath flared up, and he burned with fury. [13]He conferred with the sages who understood the times, because the king's business was conducted in general consultation with lawyers and jurists. [14]He summoned Carshena, Shethar, Admatha, Tarshish, Meres, Marsena, and Memucan, the seven Persian and Median officials who were in the king's personal service and held first rank in the realm,[j] [15]and asked them, "What is to be done by law with Queen Vashti for disobeying the order of King Ahasuerus issued through the eunuchs?"

[16]In the presence of the king and of the officials, Memucan answered: "Queen Vashti has not wronged the king alone, but all the officials and the populace throughout the provinces of King Ahasuerus. [17]For the queen's conduct will become known to all the women, and they will look with disdain upon their husbands when it is reported, 'King Ahasuerus commanded that Queen Vashti be ushered into his presence, but she would not come.' [18]This very day the Persian and Median noblewomen who hear of the queen's conduct will recount it to all the royal officials, and disdain and rancor will abound. [19]If it please the king, let an irrevocable royal decree[§] be issued by him and inscribed among the laws of the Persians and Medes, forbidding Vashti to come into the presence of King Ahasuerus and authorizing the king to give her royal dignity to one more worthy than she.[k] [20]Thus, when the decree that the king will issue is published throughout his realm, vast as it is, all wives will honor their husbands, from the greatest to the least."

[21]This proposal pleased the king and the officials, and the king acted on the advice of Memucan. [22]He sent letters to all the royal provinces, to each province in its own script and to each people in its own language, to the effect that every man should be lord in his own home.

### CHAPTER 2

**The Search for a New Queen.** [1]After this, when King Ahasuerus' wrath had cooled, he thought over what Vashti had done and what had been decreed against her. [2]Then the king's personal attendants suggested: "Let beautiful young virgins be sought for the king. [3]Let the king appoint emissaries in all the provinces of his realm to gather all beautiful young virgins into the harem in the royal precinct of Susa. Under the care of the royal eunuch Hegai, guardian of the women, let cosmetics be given them. [4]Then the young woman who pleases the king shall reign in place of Vashti." This suggestion pleased the king, and he acted accordingly.

---

*[A:17] **A Bougean:** the origin of this term is unknown; it may represent a garbled attempt to render the Hebrew "Agagite" (3:1). In the Greek additions Haman not only knows the plot to assassinate the king, but is apparently a co-conspirator.

†[1:1] The Hebrew text opens with a portrait of the power and luxury of the Persian king Ahasuerus (Xerxes I, whose empire consisted of only about thirty provinces).

‡[1:2] Susa was the winter capital of the Persian empire. The "royal precinct" (sometimes translated "stronghold" or "citadel") was a well-fortified section of the city that included the king's residence. The Book of Esther depicts other citizens living in this section as well.

§[1:19] **An irrevocable royal decree:** the first of several in the book. In a satiric portrayal, even a minor domestic disagreement is resolved through a sweeping international edict. The irrevocable nature of the decree is intended to increase its force, but creates problems if the king needs to adapt to new information or conditions. See note on 8:8.

---

g. [A:17] Est 3:1–15; B:1–7; E:13.    h. [1:3] Jdt 1:16.    i. [1:10] Dn 5:1.

j. [1:14] 1 Chr 12:32; Ezr 7:14.    k. [1:19] Est 8:5, 8; Dn 6:8–9.

⁵There was in the royal precinct of Susa a certain Jew named Mordecai,* son of Jair, son of Shimei, son of Kish, a Benjaminite, ⁶who had been exiled from Jerusalem with the captives taken with Jeconiah, king of Judah, whom Nebuchadnezzar, king of Babylon, had deported.¹ ⁷He became foster father to his cousin Hadassah, that is, Esther,† when she lost both father and mother. The young woman was beautifully formed and lovely to behold. On the death of her father and mother, Mordecai adopted her as his own daughter.ᵐ

⁸When the king's order and decree had been proclaimed and many young women brought together to the royal precinct of Susa under the care of Hegai, Esther also was brought in to the royal palace under the care of Hegai, guardian of the women. ⁹The young woman pleased him and won his favor. So he promptly furnished her with cosmetics and provisions. Then choosing seven maids for her from the royal palace, he transferred both her and her maids to the best place in the harem. ¹⁰Esther did not reveal her nationality or family, for Mordecai had commanded her not to do so.

¹¹Day by day Mordecai would walk about in front of the court of the harem to learn how Esther was faring and what was to become of her.

¹²After the twelve months' preparation decreed for the women, each one went in turn to visit King Ahasuerus. During this period of beautifying treatment, six months were spent with oil of myrrh, and the other six months with perfumes and cosmetics. ¹³Then, when each one was to visit the king, she was allowed to take with her from the harem to the royal palace whatever she chose. ¹⁴She would go in the evening and return in the morning to a second harem under the care of the royal eunuch Shaashgaz, guardian of the concubines. She could not return to the king unless he was pleased with her and had her summoned by name.ⁿ ¹⁵As for Esther, daughter of Abihail and adopted daughter of his nephew Mordecai, when her turn came to visit the king, she did not ask for anything but what the royal eunuch Hegai, guardian of the women, suggested. And she won the admiration of all who saw her.

**Ahasuerus Chooses Esther.** ¹⁶Esther was led to King Ahasuerus in his palace in the tenth month, Tebeth, in the seventh year of his reign. ¹⁷The king loved Esther more than all other women, and of all the virgins she won his favor and good will. So he placed the royal crown on her head and made her queen in place of Vashti. ¹⁸Then the king gave a great feast in honor of Esther to all his officials and servants, granting a holiday to the provinces and bestowing gifts with royal generosity.

**Mordecai Thwarts an Assassination.**‡ ¹⁹ᵒAs was said, from the time the virgins had been brought together, and while Mordecai was passing his time at the king's gate, ²⁰Esther had not revealed her family or nationality, because Mordecai had told her not to; and Esther continued to follow Mordecai's instructions, just as she had when she was being brought up by him. ²¹ᵖDuring the time that Mordecai spent at the king's gate, Bigthan and Teresh, two of the royal eunuchs who guarded the entrance, became angry and plotted to assassinate King Ahasuerus. ²²When the plot became known to Mordecai, he told Queen Esther, who in turn informed the king in Mordecai's name. ²³The matter was investigated and verified, and both of them were impaled on stakes.§ This was written in the annals in the king's presence.

## III. HAMAN'S PLOT AGAINST THE JEWS

### CHAPTER 3

**Mordecai Refuses to Honor Haman.** ¹After these events King Ahasuerus promoted Haman, son of Hammedatha the Agagite, to high rank, seating him above all his fellow officials.�q ²All the king's servants who were at the royal gate would kneel and bow down to Haman; for that is what the king had ordered in his regard.ʳ Mordecai, however, would not kneel and bow down.ˢ ³The king's servants who were at the royal gate said to Mordecai, "Why do you disobey the king's order?"ˢ ⁴When they had reminded him day after day and he would not listen to them, they informed Haman, to see whether Mordecai's explanation would prevail, since he had told them that he was a Jew.

**Haman's Reprisal.** ⁵When Haman observed that Mordecai would not kneel and bow down to him, he was filled with anger. ⁶But he thought it was beneath him to attack only Mordecai. Since they had told Haman of Mordecai's nationality, he sought to destroy all the Jews, Mordecai's

---

*[2:5] **Mordecai**: a Babylonian name, deriving from the god Marduk. Like Esther, Mordecai may have had a Jewish name as well, although in his case we do not know what it is. The chronology of the book makes him well over one hundred years old, since he was deported with Jehoiachin about 598 B.C.; cf. A:1.

†[2:7] **Esther**: a Babylonian name, deriving from the goddess Ishtar. She is given a Hebrew name as well, "Hadassah," which means "myrtle."

‡[2:19–23] This story is retold and placed at the beginning of the book in Greek addition A:12–17, with significant differences (see note). The Greek also has a translation of the account in 2:19–23 at this point in the narrative.

§[2:23] **Impaled on stakes**: a method of execution used by the Persians, known from ancient records and reliefs.

¶[3:2] We are not told the reasons for Mordecai's refusal to bow. It may be the result of a form of Jewish piety that refuses to offer such homage to any mortal; see also Greek addition C:5–7.

l. [2:6] Est A:3; 2 Kgs 24:15; 2 Chr 36:9–10; Jer 22:24–30; 24:1; 29:1–2. m. [2:7] Est 2:15.  n. [2:14] Est 2:19–20; 4:11, 16.

o. [2:19–20] Est 2:14.  p. [2:21–23] Est A:12–15; 6:1–3.  q. [3:1] Est B:3; 5:11; E:11.  r. [3:2] Est C:5; 5:9, 13; 6:10, 12.  s. [3:3] Est 4:16.

people, throughout the realm of King Ahasuerus. [7]In the first month, Nisan, in the twelfth year of King Ahasuerus, the *pur*, or lot,* was cast in Haman's presence to determine the day and the month for the destruction of Mordecai's people on a single day, and the lot fell on the thirteenth day of the twelfth month, Adar.[t]

**Decree Against the Jews.** [8]Then Haman said to King Ahasuerus: "Dispersed among the nations throughout the provinces of your kingdom, there is a certain people living apart. Their laws differ from those of every other people and they do not obey the laws of the king; so it is not proper for the king to tolerate them.[u] [9]If it please the king, let a decree be issued to destroy them; and I will deliver to the procurators ten thousand silver talents for deposit in the royal treasury."[v] [10]The king took the signet ring[†] from his hand and gave it to Haman, son of Hammedatha the Agagite, the enemy of the Jews.[w] [11]The king said to Haman, "The silver is yours, as well as the people, to do with as you please."[‡]

[12]So the royal scribes were summoned on the thirteenth day of the first month, and they wrote, at the dictation of Haman, an order to the royal satraps, the governors of every province, and the officials of every people, to each province in its own script and to each people in its own language. It was written in the name of King Ahasuerus and sealed with the royal signet ring. [13]Letters were sent by couriers to all the royal provinces, to destroy, kill and annihilate all the Jews, young and old, including women and children in one day, the thirteenth day of the twelfth month, Adar, and to seize their goods as spoil.[x]

### CHAPTER B

[1]This is a copy of the letter:

"The great King Ahasuerus writes to the satraps of the hundred and twenty-seven provinces from India to Ethiopia, and the governors subordinate to them, as follows: [2]When I came to rule many peoples and to hold sway over the whole world, not being carried away by a sense of my own authority but always acting fairly and with mildness, I determined to provide for my subjects a life of lasting tranquility; and, by making my kingdom civilized and safe for travel to its farthest borders, to restore the peace desired by all people.[y] [3]When I consulted my counselors as to how this might be accomplished, Haman, who excels among us in discretion, who is outstanding for constant good will and steadfast loyalty, and who has gained a place in the kingdom second only to me,[z] [4]brought it to our attention that, mixed among all the nations throughout the world, there is one people of ill will, which by its laws is opposed to every other people and continually disregards the decrees of kings, so that the unity of empire blamelessly designed by us cannot be established.[a]

[5]"Having noted, therefore, that this nation, and it alone, is continually at variance with all people, lives by divergent and alien laws, is inimical to our government, and does all the harm it can to undermine the stability of the kingdom, [6]we hereby decree that all those who are indicated to you in the letters of Haman, who is in charge of the administration and is a second father to us, shall, together with their wives and children, be utterly destroyed by the swords of their enemies, without any pity or mercy, on the fourteenth day[§] of the twelfth month, Adar, of the current year;[b] [7]so that when these people, whose present ill will is of long standing, have gone down into Hades by a violent death on a single day, they may leave our government completely stable and undisturbed for the future."

### (CHAPTER 3)

[14]A copy of the decree to be promulgated as law in every province was published to all the peoples, that they might be prepared for that day. [15]The couriers set out in haste at the king's command; meanwhile, the decree was promulgated in the royal precinct of Susa. The king and Haman then sat down to drink, but the city of Susa was thrown into confusion.

## IV. ESTHER AND MORDECAI PLEAD FOR HELP

### CHAPTER 4

**Mordecai Exhorts Esther.** [1]When Mordecai learned all that was happening, he tore his garments, put on sackcloth and ashes, and went through the city crying out loudly and bitterly,[c] [2]till he came before the royal gate, which no one clothed in sackcloth might enter. [3]Likewise in each of the provinces, wherever the king's

---

*[3:7] **The pur, or lot**: the Hebrew text preserves the Akkadian word *pur* because its plural, *purim*, became the name of the feast of Purim commemorating the deliverance of the Jews; cf. 9:24, 26. The lot functions as a kind of horoscope to determine the most favorable day for the pogrom.

†[3:10] **Signet ring**: a ring containing a seal that was impressed on documents to authenticate them. With this ring, Haman can issue decrees in the king's name.

‡[3:11] Although Ahasuerus seems to refuse the bribe, this is probably a polite way of accepting it that makes him appear munificent (compare Gn 23:11–15, where Ephron tells Abraham that he "gives" him the field and, after a few more pleasantries, sets a very high price for it). Both 4:7 and 7:4 seem to assume Ahasuerus has accepted the money.

§[B:6] **Fourteenth day**: only the Greek text here names the fourteenth of Adar as the day set aside for the destruction of the Jews. The Hebrew text consistently gives the date as the thirteenth of Adar (e.g., 3:13) as does Greek addition E:20; see note on 9:17–19.

---

t. [3:7] Est 9:24–32; F:10. u. [3:8] Est 3:13; B:4; E:24; Wis 2:14–15; Dn 3:8–12. v. [3:9] Est 7:4. w. [3:10] Gn 41:42. x. [3:13] Est B:6; 7:4.

y. [B:2] Est E:8–9. z. [B:3] Est 3:1; 5:11; E:11. a. [B:4] Est 3:8; E:24. b. [B:6] Est 3:13; 7:4; E:11. c. [4:1] Jdt 4:12.

decree and law reached, the Jews went into deep mourning, with fasting, weeping, and lament; most of them lay on sackcloth and ashes.

[4]Esther's maids and eunuchs came and told her. Overwhelmed with anguish, the queen sent garments for Mordecai to put on, so that he might take off his sackcloth; but he refused. [5]Esther then summoned Hathach, one of the king's eunuchs whom he had placed at her service, and commanded him to find out what this action of Mordecai meant and the reason for it. [6]So Hathach went out to Mordecai in the public square in front of the royal gate, [7]and Mordecai recounted all that had happened to him, as well as the exact amount of silver Haman had promised to pay to the royal treasury for the slaughter of the Jews. [8]He also gave him a copy of the written decree for their destruction that had been promulgated in Susa, to show and explain to Esther. Hathach was to instruct her to go to the king and to plead and intercede with him on behalf of her people.*

[9]Hathach returned to Esther and told her what Mordecai had said. [10]Then Esther replied to Hathach and gave him this message for Mordecai: [11]"All the servants of the king and the people of his provinces know that any man or woman who goes to the king in the inner court without being summoned is subject to the same law—death. Only if the king extends the golden scepter will such a person live. Now as for me, I have not been summoned to the king for thirty days."[d]

[12]When Esther's words were reported to Mordecai, [13]he had this reply brought to her: "Do not imagine that you are safe in the king's palace, you alone of all the Jews. [14]Even if you now remain silent, relief and deliverance will come to the Jews from another source;[†] but you and your father's house will perish. Who knows—perhaps it was for a time like this that you became queen?"

[15]Esther sent back to Mordecai the response: [16]"Go and assemble all the Jews who are in Susa; fast on my behalf, all of you, not eating or drinking night or day for three days. I and my maids will also fast in the same way. Thus prepared, I will go to the king, contrary to the law. If I perish, I perish!"[e] [17]Mordecai went away and did exactly as Esther had commanded.

## CHAPTER C

**Prayer of Mordecai.** [1]Recalling all that the Lord had done, Mordecai prayed to the Lord [2]and said: "Lord, Lord, King and Ruler of all, everything is in your power, and there is no one to oppose you when it is your will to save Israel. [3]You made heaven and earth and every wonderful thing under heaven. [4]You are Lord of all, and there is no one who can resist you, the Lord. [5]You know all things. You know, Lord, that it was not out of insolence or arrogance or desire for glory that I acted thus in not bowing down to the arrogant Haman. [6]I would have gladly kissed the soles of his feet for the salvation of Israel. [7]But I acted as I did so as not to place the honor of a mortal above that of God. I will not bow down to anyone but you, my Lord. It is not out of arrogance that I am acting thus. [8]And now, Lord God, King, God of Abraham, spare your people, for our enemies regard us with deadly envy and are bent upon destroying the inheritance that was yours from the beginning. [9]Do not spurn your portion, which you redeemed for yourself out of the land of Egypt. [10]Hear my prayer; have pity on your inheritance and turn our mourning into feasting, that we may live to sing praise to your name, Lord. Do not silence the mouths of those who praise you."

[11]All Israel, too, cried out with all their strength, for death was staring them in the face. **Prayer of Esther.** [12g]Queen Esther, seized with mortal anguish, fled to the Lord for refuge. [13]Taking off her splendid garments, she put on garments of distress and mourning. In place of her precious ointments she covered her head with dung and ashes. She afflicted her body severely and in place of her festive adornments, her tangled hair covered her.

[14]Then she prayed to the Lord, the God of Israel, saying: "My Lord, you alone are our King. Help me, who am alone and have no help but you, [15]for I am taking my life in my hand.[h] [16]From birth, I have heard among my people that you, Lord, chose Israel from among all nations, and our ancestors from among all their forebears, as a lasting inheritance, and that you fulfilled all your promises to them.[i] [17]But now we have sinned in your sight, and you have delivered us into the hands of our enemies, [18]because we worshiped their gods. You are just, O Lord. [19]But now they are not satisfied with our bitter servitude, but have sworn an oath to their idols [20]to do away with the decree you have pronounced, to destroy your inheritance, to close the mouths of those who praise you, to extinguish the glory of your house and your altar, [21]to open the mouths of the nations to acclaim their worthless gods, and to extol a mortal king forever.

[22]"Lord, do not relinquish your scepter to those who are nothing. Do not let our foes gloat over our ruin, but turn their own counsel against them and make an example of the one who began this against us. [23]Be mindful of us,

---

*[4:8] The Greek text adds the following to Mordecai's message to Esther: "Remember the days of your lowly estate, when you were brought up in my charge; for Haman, who is second to the king, has asked for our death. Invoke the Lord and speak to the king for us: save us from death."

†[4:14] **From another source:** probably Mordecai refers to divine aid; the Greek additions (C) are explicit about this.

d. [4:11] Est 2:14; 4:12; D:12.   e. [4:16] Est C:12–13.

f. [C:5–7] Est 3:2; 5:9.   g. [C:12–13] Est 4:16.   h. [C:15] Est 4:16.   i. [C:16] Dt 4:20; 7:6; 9:29; 14:2; 26:18; 32:9.

Lord. Make yourself known in the time of our distress and give me courage, King of gods and Ruler of every power. ²⁴Put in my mouth persuasive words in the presence of the lion, and turn his heart to hatred for our enemy, so that he and his co-conspirators may perish. ²⁵Save us by your power, and help me, who am alone and have no one but you, Lord.

²⁶"You know all things. You know that I hate the pomp of the lawless, and abhor the bed of the uncircumcised or of any foreigner. ²⁷You know that I am under constraint, that I abhor the sign of grandeur that rests on my head when I appear in public. I abhor it like a polluted rag, and do not wear it in private. ²⁸I, your servant, have never eaten at the table of Haman, nor have I graced the banquet of the king or drunk the wine of libations.* ²⁹From the day I was brought here till now, your servant has had no joy except in you, Lord, God of Abraham. ³⁰O God, whose power is over all, hear the voice of those in despair. Save us from the power of the wicked, and deliver me from my fear."

### CHAPTER D
**Esther Goes to Ahasuerus.**† ¹On the third day, ending her prayers, she took off her prayer garments and arrayed herself in her splendid attire. ²In making her appearance, after invoking the all-seeing God and savior, she took with her two maids; ³on the one she leaned gently for support, ⁴while the other followed her, bearing her train. ⁵She glowed with perfect beauty and her face was as joyous as it was lovely, though her heart was pounding with fear. ⁶She passed through all the portals till she stood before the king, who was seated on his royal throne, clothed in full robes of state, and covered with gold and precious stones, so that he inspired great awe. ⁷As he looked up in extreme anger, his features fiery and majestic, the queen staggered, turned pale and fainted, collapsing against the maid in front of her. ⁸But God changed the king's anger to gentleness. In great anxiety he sprang from his throne, held her in his arms until she recovered, and comforted her with reassuring words. ⁹"What is it, Esther?" he said to her. "I am your brother.‡ Take courage! ¹⁰You shall not die; this order of ours applies only to our subjects. ¹¹Come near!" ¹²Raising the golden scepter, he touched her neck with it, embraced her, and said, "Speak to me."ʲ

¹³She replied: "I saw you, my lord, as an angel of God, and my heart was shaken by fear of your majesty. ¹⁴For you are awesome, my lord, though your countenance is full of mercy." ¹⁵As she said

this, she fainted. ¹⁶The king was shaken and all his attendants tried to revive her.

### CHAPTER 5
¹§[Now on the third day, Esther put on her royal garments and stood in the inner courtyard, looking toward the royal palace, while the king was seated on his royal throne in the audience chamber, facing the palace doorway. ²When he saw Queen Esther standing in the courtyard, she won his favor and he extended toward her the golden scepter he held. She came up to him, and touched the top of the scepter.]

³Then the king said to her, "What is it, Queen Esther? What is your request? Even if it is half of my kingdom, it shall be granted you."ᵏ ⁴Esther replied, "If it please your majesty, come today with Haman to a banquet I have prepared." ⁵The king ordered, "Have Haman make haste to fulfill the wish of Esther."

### V. HAMAN'S DOWNFALL
**First Banquet of Esther.** So the king went with Haman to the banquet Esther had prepared. ⁶During the drinking of the wine, the king said to Esther, "Whatever you ask for shall be granted, and whatever request you make shall be honored, even if it is for half my kingdom."ˡ ⁷Esther replied: "This is my petition and request: ⁸if I have found favor with the king and if it pleases your majesty to grant my petition and honor my request, let the king come with Haman tomorrow to a banquet I will prepare; and tomorrow I will do as the king asks."

**Haman's Plot Against Mordecai.** ⁹That day Haman left happy and in good spirits. But when he saw that Mordecai at the royal gate did not rise, and showed no fear of him, he was filled with anger toward him.ᵐ ¹⁰Haman restrained himself, however, and went home, where he summoned his friends and his wife Zeresh. ¹¹He recounted the greatness of his riches, the large number of his sons, and how the king had promoted him and placed him above the officials and royal servants.ⁿ ¹²"Moreover," Haman added, "Queen Esther invited no one but me to come with the king to the banquet she prepared; again tomorrow I am to be her guest with the king. ¹³Yet none of this satisfies me as long as I continue to see the Jew Mordecai sitting at the royal gate."ᵒ ¹⁴His wife Zeresh and all his friends said to him, "Have a stake set up, fifty cubits in height, and in the morning ask the king to have Mordecai impaled on it. Then go to the banquet with the king in good spirits." This suggestion pleased Haman, and he had the stake erected.ᵖ

---

*[C:28] **Wine of libations**: offered in sacrifice to the gods.
†[D:1–16] Addition D expands on and replaces 5:1–2 of the Hebrew text.
‡[D:9] **Brother**: along with "sister," a common term of affection between lovers or husband and wife. See, e.g., Sg 4:9–12; 8:1; Tb 5:22; 7:11.

j. [D:12] Est 4:11.

§[5:1–2] The Hebrew text translated here is a short form of the account which is in Greek addition D.

k. [5:3] Est 5:6; 7:2; 9:12.   l. [5:6] Est 5:3.   m. [5:9] Est 3:2–3; C:5–7; 6:10, 12.   n. [5:11] Est 3:1; B:3; E:11; 9:6–10.   o. [5:13] Est 3:2–3; 6:10, 12.   p. [5:14] Est 6:4; 7:9–10.

## CHAPTER 6

**Mordecai's Reward from the King.** [1]That night the king, unable to sleep, asked that the chronicle of notable events be brought in. While this was being read to him, [2]the passage occurred in which Mordecai reported Bigthan and Teresh, two of the royal eunuchs who guarded the entrance, for seeking to assassinate King Ahasuerus.[q] [3]The king asked, "What was done to honor and exalt Mordecai for this?" The king's attendants replied, "Nothing was done for him."[r]

[4]"Who is in the court?" the king asked. Now Haman had entered the outer court of the king's palace to suggest to the king that Mordecai should be impaled on the stake he had raised for him.[s] [5]The king's attendants answered him, "Haman is waiting in the court." The king said, "Let him come in." [6]When Haman entered, the king said to him, "What should be done for the man whom the king wishes to reward?" Now Haman thought to himself, "Whom would the king wish to honor more than me?" [7]So he replied to the king: "For the man whom the king wishes to honor [8]there should be brought the royal robe the king wore and the horse the king rode with the royal crest placed on its head. [9]The robe and the horse should be given to one of the noblest of the king's officials, who must clothe the man the king wishes to reward, have him ride on the horse in the public square of the city, and cry out before him, 'This is what is done for the man whom the king wishes to honor!'"[t] [10]Then the king said to Haman: "Hurry! Take the robe and horse as you have proposed, and do this for the Jew Mordecai, who is sitting at the royal gate. Do not omit anything you proposed."[u] [11]So Haman took the robe and horse, clothed Mordecai, had him ride in the public square of the city, and cried out before him, "This is what is done for the man whom the king wishes to honor!"

[12]Mordecai then returned to the royal gate, while Haman hurried home grieving, with his head covered.[v] [13]When he told his wife Zeresh and all his friends everything that had happened to him, his advisers and his wife Zeresh said to him, "If Mordecai, before whom you are beginning to fall, is of Jewish ancestry, you will not prevail against him, but will surely be defeated by him."

**Esther's Second Banquet.** [14]While they were speaking with him, the king's eunuchs arrived and hurried Haman off to the banquet Esther had prepared.

---

*[6:4–13] Haman's presumption that the king wants to honor him creates the irony that Haman himself prescribes and fulfills the elaborate terms of Mordecai's reward. This comic reversal mirrors the fatal reversal to come: Haman and those who hate the Jews find that their plot to destroy them recoils on their own head.

q. [6:2] Est A:12–14; 2:21–23.  r. [6:3] Est A:16.  s. [6:4] Est 5:14; 7:9–10.  t. [6:9] Gn 41:42–43; 1 Kgs 1:33; Dn 5:29.  u. [6:10] Est 2:21; 3:2–3; 5:9, 13.  v. [6:12] Est 2:21; 3:2–3; 5:9, 13.

## CHAPTER 7

[1]So the king and Haman went to the banquet with Queen Esther. [2]Again, on this second day, as they were drinking wine, the king said to Esther, "Whatever you ask, Queen Esther, shall be granted you. Whatever request you make, even for half the kingdom, shall be honored."[w] [3]Queen Esther replied: "If I have found favor with you, O king, and if it pleases your majesty, I ask that my life be spared, and I beg that you spare the lives of my people. [4]For we have been sold, I and my people, to be destroyed, killed, and annihilated. If we were only to be sold into slavery I would remain silent, for then our distress would not have been worth troubling the king."[x] [5]King Ahasuerus said to Queen Esther, "Who and where is the man who has dared to do this?"[y] Esther replied, "The enemy oppressing us is this wicked Haman." At this, Haman was seized with dread of the king and queen.

[7]The king left the banquet in anger and went into the garden of the palace, but Haman stayed to beg Queen Esther for his life, since he saw that the king had decided on his doom. [8]When the king returned from the palace garden to the banquet hall, Haman had thrown himself on the couch on which Esther was reclining; and the king exclaimed, "Will he also violate the queen while she is with me in my own house!" Scarcely had the king spoken when the face of Haman was covered over.

**Punishment of Haman.** [9]Harbona, one of the eunuchs who attended the king, said, "At the house of Haman stands a stake fifty cubits high. Haman made it for Mordecai, who gave the report that benefited the king." The king answered, "Impale him on it." [10]So they impaled Haman on the stake he had set up for Mordecai, and the anger of the king abated.

## CHAPTER 8

[1]That day King Ahasuerus gave the house of Haman, enemy of the Jews, to Queen Esther; and Mordecai was admitted to the king's presence, for Esther had revealed his relationship to her.[a] [2]The king removed his signet ring that he had taken away from Haman, and gave it to Mordecai; and Esther put Mordecai in charge of the house of Haman.[b]

### VI. THE JEWISH VICTORY AND THE FEAST OF PURIM

**The Second Royal Decree.** [3]Esther again spoke to the king. She fell at his feet and tearfully implored him to revoke the harm done by Haman the Agagite and the plan he had devised against the Jews. [4]The king stretched forth the golden scepter to Esther. So she rose

w. [7:2] Est 5:3.  x. [7:4] Est 3:13; B:6.  y. [7:5] Est 3:8–9.  z. [7:9–10] Est 5:14; 6:4.  a. [8:1] Est 9:1; Prv 11:8; 26:27; Mt 7:2.  b. [8:2] Prv 13:22; Dn 2:48–49.

and, standing before him, [5]said: "If it seems
good to the king and if I have found favor
with him, if the thing seems right to the king
and I am pleasing in his eyes, let a document
be issued to revoke the letters that the schemer
Haman, son of Hammedatha the Agagite, wrote
for the destruction of the Jews in all the royal
provinces.[c] [6]For how can I witness the evil that
is to befall my people, and how can I behold the
destruction of my kindred?"

[7]King Ahasuerus then said to Queen Esther
and to the Jew Mordecai: "Now that I have
given Esther the house of Haman, and they
have impaled him on the stake because he was
going to attack the Jews, [8d]you in turn may write
in the king's name what you see fit concerning
the Jews and seal the letter with the royal signet
ring." For a decree written in the name of the
king and sealed with the royal signet ring cannot be revoked.[*]

[9]At that time, on the twenty-third day of
the third month, Sivan, the royal scribes were
summoned. Exactly as Mordecai dictated, they
wrote to the Jews and to the satraps, governors,
and officials of the hundred and twenty-seven
provinces from India to Ethiopia: to each province in its own script and to each people in its
own language, and to the Jews in their own
script and language. [10]These letters, which he
wrote in the name of King Ahasuerus and sealed
with the royal signet ring, he sent by mounted
couriers riding thoroughbred royal steeds. [11e]In
these letters the king authorized the Jews in each
and every city to gather and defend their lives, to
destroy, kill, and annihilate every armed group
of any nation or province that might attack
them, along with their wives and children, and
to seize their goods as spoil [12]on a single day
throughout the provinces of King Ahasuerus,
the thirteenth day of the twelfth month, Adar.

## CHAPTER E

[1]The following is a copy of the letter:
"The great King Ahasuerus to the governors of the provinces in the hundred and
twenty-seven satrapies from India to Ethiopia,
and to those who are loyal to our government:
Greetings!

[2]"Many have become more ambitious the
more they were showered with honors through
the bountiful generosity of their patrons. [3]Not

only do they seek to do harm to our subjects
but, incapable of dealing with such greatness,
they even begin plotting against their own benefactors. [4]Not only do they drive out gratitude
from among humankind but, with the arrogant
boastfulness of those to whom goodness has
no meaning, they suppose they will escape the
stern judgment of the all-seeing God.

[5]"Often, too, the fair speech of friends
entrusted with the administration of affairs has
induced many placed in authority to become
accomplices in the shedding of innocent blood,
and has involved them in irreparable calamities
[6]by deceiving with malicious slander the sincere
good will of rulers. [7]This can be verified in the
ancient stories that have been handed down to
us, but more fully when you consider the wicked
deeds perpetrated in your midst by the pestilen-
tial influence of those undeserving of authority.
[8]We must provide for the future, so as to render
the kingdom undisturbed and peaceful for all
people, [9]taking advantage of changing conditions and always deciding matters coming to
our attention with equitable treatment.

[10]"For instance, Haman, son of Hammedatha, a Macedonian,[†] certainly not of Persian
blood, and very different from us in generosity,
was hospitably received by us. [11]He benefited
so much from the good will we have toward
all peoples that he was proclaimed 'our father,'
before whom everyone was to bow down; and
he attained a position second only to the royal
throne.[g] [12]But, unable to control his arrogance,
he strove to deprive us of kingdom and of life,
[13]and by weaving intricate webs of deceit he
demanded the destruction of Mordecai, our
savior and constant benefactor, and of Esther,
our blameless royal consort, together with their
whole nation.[h] [14]For by such measures he hoped
to catch us defenseless and to transfer the rule of
the Persians to the Macedonians. [15]But we find
that the Jews, who were doomed to extinction by
this archcriminal, are not evildoers, but rather
are governed by very just laws [16]and are the children of the Most High, the living God of majesty,
who has maintained the kingdom in a flourishing condition for us and for our forebears.

[17]"You will do well, then, to ignore the letter sent by Haman, son of Hammedatha, [18]for
he who composed it has been impaled, together
with his entire household, before the gates of
Susa. Thus swiftly has God, who governs all,
brought just punishment upon him.[i]

---

*[8:8] **A decree written . . . cannot be revoked:** the king
cannot directly grant Esther's request (v. 5) to revoke the
previous decree against the Jews because of the irrevocable
character of the laws of the Medes and Persians (see 1:19 and
note). He can, however, empower Esther to issue another
decree in his name to counteract the earlier one. The second
decree authorizes the Jews to defend themselves against those
who would kill them, which is what they do in 9:2. This is
why the outcome of the two decrees is that the attackers are
killed instead of the Jews, rather than a simple cancellation
of all hostilities.

c. [8:5] Est 1:19.   d. [8:8] Est 1:19.   e. [8:11–12] Est 9:1–4.

†[E:10] **Macedonian:** throughout the book Haman is
identified with terms of contempt—in the Hebrew text as an
Agagite (3:1, 10; 8:3, 5; 9:24; cf. note on A:17), thus making
him a descendant of Agag, king of the Amalekites, a group
hated by the Israelites; in the Greek additions Haman is identified as a Macedonian, reflecting the enmity between the
Persians and the Macedonians after Macedonia's conquest of
Persia in the fourth century B.C.

f. [E:8–9] Est B:2.   g. [E:11] Est B:3,6.   h. [E:13] Est A:17.   i. [E:18]
Est 7:10; 9:14.

[19]"You shall exhibit a copy of this letter publicly in every place to certify that the Jews may follow their own laws [20]and that you may help them on the day set for their ruin, the thirteenth day of the twelfth month, Adar, to defend themselves against those who attack them. [21]For God, the ruler of all, has turned that day from one of destruction of the chosen people into one of joy for them. [22]Therefore, you too must celebrate this memorable day among your designated feasts with all rejoicing, [23]so that both now and in the future it may be a celebration of deliverance for us and for Persians of good will, but for those who plot against us a reminder of destruction.

[24]"Every city and province without exception that does not observe this decree shall be ruthlessly destroyed with fire and sword, so that it will be left not merely untrodden by people, but even shunned by wild beasts and birds forever."[j]

## (CHAPTER 8)

[13]A copy of the letter to be promulgated as law in each and every province was published among all the peoples, so that the Jews might be prepared on that day to avenge themselves on their enemies. [14]Couriers mounted on royal steeds sped forth in haste at the king's order, and the decree was promulgated in the royal precinct of Susa.

[15]Mordecai left the king's presence clothed in a royal robe of violet and of white cotton, with a large crown of gold and a mantle of fine crimson linen. The city of Susa shouted with joy,[k] [16]and for the Jews there was splendor and gladness, joy and triumph. [17]In each and every province and in each and every city, wherever the king's order arrived, there was merriment and joy, banqueting and feasting for the Jews. And many of the peoples of the land identified themselves as Jews, for fear of the Jews fell upon them.[l]

## CHAPTER 9

**The Massacre Reversed.** [1m]When the day arrived on which the order decreed by the king was to be carried out, the thirteenth day of the twelfth month, Adar, on which the enemies of the Jews had expected to overpower them, the situation was reversed: the Jews overpowered those who hated them. [2]The Jews mustered in their cities throughout the provinces of King Ahasuerus to attack those who sought to do them harm, and no one could withstand them, for fear of them fell upon all the peoples. [3]Moreover, all the officials of the provinces, the satraps, governors, and royal procurators supported the Jews out of fear of Mordecai; [4]for Mordecai was powerful in the royal palace, and the report was spreading through all the provinces that he was continually growing in power.

[5]The Jews struck down all their enemies with the sword, killing and destroying them; they did to those who hated them as they pleased.[n] [6]In the royal precinct of Susa, the Jews killed and destroyed five hundred people. [7]They also killed Parshandatha, Dalphon, Aspatha, [8]Poratha, Adalia, Aridatha, [9]Parmashta, Arisai, Aridai, and Vaizatha, [10p]the ten sons of Haman, son of Hammedatha, the foe of the Jews. However, they did not engage in plundering.

[11]On the same day, when the number of those killed in the royal precinct of Susa was reported to the king, [12]he said to Queen Esther: "In the royal precinct of Susa the Jews have killed and destroyed five hundred people, as well as the ten sons of Haman. What must they have done in the other royal provinces! You shall again be granted whatever you ask, and whatever you request shall be honored." [13]So Esther said, "If it pleases your majesty, let the Jews in Susa be permitted again tomorrow to act according to today's decree, and let the ten sons of Haman be impaled on stakes." [14]The king then gave an order that this be done, and the decree was published in Susa. So the ten sons of Haman were impaled,[q] [15]and the Jews in Susa mustered again on the fourteenth of the month of Adar and killed three hundred people in Susa. However, they did not engage in plundering.[r]

[16]The other Jews, who dwelt in the royal provinces, also mustered and defended themselves, and obtained rest from their enemies. They killed seventy-five thousand of those who hated them, but they did not engage in plunder.[s] [17]This happened on the thirteenth day of the month of Adar.

**The Feast of Purim.*** On the fourteenth of the month they rested, and made it a day of feasting and rejoicing.

[18]The Jews in Susa, however, mustered on the thirteenth and fourteenth of the month. But on the fifteenth they rested, and made it a day of joyful banqueting. [19]That is why the rural Jews, who dwell in villages, celebrate the fourteenth of the month of Adar as a day of joyful banqueting, a holiday on which they send food to one another.

[20]Mordecai recorded these events and sent letters to all the Jews, both near and far, in all the provinces of King Ahasuerus. [21]He ordered them to celebrate every year both the fourteenth

---

*[9:17–19] According to Esther, Jewish feasting on the day after the defeat of their enemies establishes the date of the holiday. Since in Susa the fighting lasts for two days, the Jews of that community initially celebrate Purim a day later than Jews elsewhere.

†[9:21] Mordecai creates a compromise among the Jews by making Purim a two-day festival.

---

j. [E:24] Est 3:8–9; B:4.   k. [8:15] Dn 5:7.   l. [8:17] Est 9:27.
m. [9:1–2] Est 8:11–12.

n. [9:5] Jdt 15:6.   o. [9:6–10] Est 5:11; B:3; E:11.   p. [9:10] Est 9:15; Jdt 15:7, 11.   q. [9:14] Est 7:10; E:18.   r. [9:15] Est 9:10.   s. [9:16] Jdt 15:6.

and the fifteenth of the month of Adar [22]as the days on which the Jews obtained rest from their enemies and as the month which was turned for them from sorrow into joy, from mourning into celebration. They were to observe these days with joyful banqueting, sending food to one another and gifts to the poor. [23]*The Jews adopted as a custom what they had begun doing and what Mordecai had written to them.[t]

## VII. EPILOGUE: THE RISE OF MORDECAI

**Summary of the Story.** [24u]Haman, son of Hammedatha the Agagite, the foe of all the Jews, had planned to destroy them and had cast the *pur*, or lot, for the time of their defeat and destruction. [25]Yet, when the plot became known to the king, the king ordered in writing that the wicked plan Haman had devised against the Jews should instead be turned against Haman and that he and his sons should be impaled on stakes.[v] [26]And so these days have been named Purim after the word *pur*.

Thus, because of all that was contained in this letter, and because of what they had witnessed and experienced in this event, [27]the Jews established and adopted as a custom for themselves, their descendants, and all who should join them, the perpetual obligation of celebrating these two days every year in the manner prescribed by this letter, and at the time appointed.[w] [28]These days were to be commemorated and kept in every generation, by every clan, in every province, and in every city. These days of Purim were never to be neglected among the Jews, nor forgotten by their descendants.
**Esther and Mordecai Act in Concert.**[†] [29]Queen Esther, daughter of Abihail, and Mordecai the Jew, wrote to confirm with full authority this second letter about Purim, [30]and Mordecai sent documents concerning peace and security to all the Jews in the hundred and twenty-seven provinces of Ahasuerus' kingdom.[x] [31]Thus were established, for their appointed time, these days of Purim which Mordecai the Jew and Queen Esther had designated for the Jews, just as they had previously enjoined upon themselves and upon their descendants the duty of fasting and

supplication. [32]The command of Esther confirmed these prescriptions for Purim and was recorded in the book.

## CHAPTER 10
**The Rise of Mordecai Completed.** [1]King Ahasuerus levied a tax on the land and on the islands of the sea. [2]All the acts of his power and valor, as well as a detailed account of the greatness of Mordecai, whom the king promoted, are recorded in the chronicles of the kings of Media and Persia. [3]The Jew Mordecai was next in rank to King Ahasuerus, in high standing among the Jews, popular with many of his kindred, seeking the good of his people and speaking out on behalf of the welfare of all its descendants.[y]

## CHAPTER F
**Mordecai's Dream Fulfilled.** [1z]Then Mordecai said: "This is the work of God. [2]I recall the dream I had about these very things, and not a single detail has been left unfulfilled— [3]the tiny spring that grew into a river, and there was light, and sun, and many waters. The river is Esther, whom the king married and made queen. [4]The two dragons are myself and Haman. [5]The nations are those who assembled to destroy the name of the Jews, [6]but my people is Israel, who cried to God and was saved.

"The Lord saved his people and delivered us from all these evils. God worked signs and great wonders, such as have not occurred among the nations. [7]For this purpose he arranged two lots:[‡] one for the people of God, the second for all the other nations. [8]These two lots were fulfilled in the hour, the time, and the day of judgment before God and among all the nations. [9]God remembered his people and rendered justice to his inheritance.
[10a]"Gathering together with joy and happiness before God, they shall celebrate these days on the fourteenth and fifteenth of the month Adar throughout all future generations of his people Israel."
**Colophon.**[§] [11]In the fourth year of the reign of Ptolemy and Cleopatra, Dositheus, who said he was a priest and Levite, and his son Ptolemy brought the present letter of Purim, saying that it was genuine and that Lysimachus, son of Ptolemy, of the community of Jerusalem, had translated it.

---

*[9:23] According to the story, the two-day celebration has its roots in popular observance, which Mordecai's leadership reinforces and regularizes.

†[9:29–32] In attempting to give the impression of concerted action between Esther and Mordecai, the Hebrew text here presents several unresolved difficulties. Verse 29 makes Mordecai and Esther joint authors of a letter that is ascribed in v. 32 to Esther alone. Verse 31 makes Mordecai and Esther joint authors of a letter that is ascribed in vv. 20–22 to Mordecai alone. Finally, it is difficult to see the purpose of confirming a second letter in the second letter itself.

‡[F:7] **Two lots:** this passage of the Greek text gives an additional interpretation of the feast. The two lots are drawn by God to determine, respectively, the destiny of Israel and that of the nations; contrast with 3:7 of the Hebrew text.

§[F:11] Several "Ptolemies" (Greek kings reigning in Egypt) had wives named Cleopatra. This postscript dates the Greek version somewhere between 116 B.C. and 48 B.C.

---

t. [9:23] Est 9:29.   u. [9:24–26] Est 3:7; F:10.   v. [9:25] Est 6:5–13.   w. [9:27] Est 8:12, 17.   x. [9:30] Est 9:23–26.

y. [10:3] 2 Mc 15:14.   z. [F:1–6] Est A:4–10.   a. [F:10] Est 3:7; 9:17–18, 21, 24–28.

# THE FIRST BOOK OF
# MACCABEES

The name Maccabee, probably meaning "hammer," is actually applied in the Books of Maccabees to only one man, Judas, third son of the priest Mattathias and first leader of the revolt against the Seleucid kings who persecuted the Jews (1 Mc 2:4, 66; 2 Mc 8:5, 16; 10:1, 16). Traditionally the name has come to be extended to the brothers of Judas, his supporters, and even to other Jewish heroes of the period, such as the seven brothers (2 Mc 7).

The two Books of Maccabees contain independent accounts of events (in part identical) that accompanied the attempted suppression of Judaism in Palestine in the second century B.C. The vigorous reaction to this attempt established for a time the religious and political independence of the Jews.

First Maccabees was written about 100 B.C., in Hebrew, but the original has not come down to us. Instead, we have an early, pre-Christian, Greek translation full of Hebrew idioms. The author, probably a Palestinian Jew, is unknown. He was familiar with the traditions and sacred books of his people and had access to much reliable information on their recent history (from 175 to 134 B.C.). He may well have played some part in it himself in his youth. His purpose in writing is to record the deliverance of Israel that God worked through the family of Mattathias (5:62)—especially through his three sons, Judas, Jonathan, and Simon, and his grandson, John Hyrcanus. The writer compares their virtues and their exploits with those of Israel's ancient heroes, the Judges, Samuel, and David.

There are seven poetic sections in the book that imitate the style of classical Hebrew poetry: four laments (1:25–28, 36–40; 2:7–13; 3:45), and three hymns of praise of "our fathers" (2:51–64), of Judas (3:3–9), and of Simon (14:4–15). The doctrine expressed in the book is the customary belief of Israel, without the new developments which appear in 2 Maccabees and Daniel. The people of Israel have been specially chosen by the one true God as covenant-partner, and they alone are privileged to know and worship God, their eternal benefactor and unfailing source of help. The people, in turn, must worship the Lord alone and observe exactly the precepts of the law given to them. The rededication of the Jerusalem Temple described in 4:36–59 (see 2 Mc 10:1–8) is the origin of the Jewish feast of Hanukkah.

Unlike the Second Book of Maccabees, there is no doctrine of individual immortality except in the survival of one's name and fame, nor does the book express any messianic expectation, though messianic images are applied historically to "the days of Simon" (1 Mc 14:4–17). In true Deuteronomic tradition, the author insists on fidelity to the law as the expression of Israel's love for God. The contest which he describes is a struggle, not simply between Jew and Gentile, but between those who would uphold the law and those, Jews or Gentiles, who would destroy it. His severest condemnation goes, not to the Seleucid politicians, but to the lawless apostates among his own people, adversaries of Judas and his brothers, who are models of faith and loyalty.

The first and second Books of Maccabees, though regarded by Jews and Protestants as apocryphal, i.e., not inspired Scripture, because not contained in the Jewish list of books drawn up at the end of the first century A.D., have always been accepted by the Catholic Church as inspired and are called "deuterocanonical" to indicate that they are canonical even though disputed by some.

First Maccabees can be divided as follows:

I. Crisis and Response (1:1–2:70)
II. Leadership of Judas Maccabeus (3:1–9:22)
III. Leadership of Jonathan (9:23–12:53)
IV. Leadership of Simon (13:1–16:24)

## I. CRISIS AND RESPONSE

### CHAPTER 1

**From Alexander to Antiochus.** ¹ªAfter Alexander the Macedonian, Philip's son, who came from the land of Kittim,* had defeated Darius, king of the Persians and Medes, he became king in his place, having first ruled in Greece. ²He fought many battles, captured fortresses, and put the kings of the earth to death. ³He advanced to the ends of the earth, gathering plunder from many nations; the earth fell silent before him, and his heart became proud and arrogant. ⁴He collected a very strong army and won dominion over provinces, nations, and rulers, and they paid him tribute.

⁵But after all this he took to his bed, realizing that he was going to die. ⁶So he summoned his noblest officers, who had been brought up with him from his youth, and divided his kingdom among them while he was still alive. ⁷Alexander had reigned twelve years† when he died.

⁸So his officers took over his kingdom, each in his own territory, ⁹and after his death they all put on diadems,‡ and so did their sons after them for many years, multiplying evils on the earth.

¹⁰There sprang from these a sinful offshoot, Antiochus Epiphanes, son of King Antiochus, once a hostage at Rome. He became king in the one hundred and thirty-seventh year⁵ of the kingdom of the Greeks.

**Lawless Jews.** ¹¹bIn those days there appeared in Israel transgressors of the law who seduced many, saying: "Let us go and make a covenant with the Gentiles all around us; since we separated from them, many evils have come upon us." ¹²The proposal was agreeable; ¹³some from among the people promptly went to the king, and he authorized them to introduce the ordinances of the Gentiles. ¹⁴Thereupon they built a gymnasium⁵ in Jerusalem

according to the Gentile custom. ¹⁵They disguised their circumcision and abandoned the holy covenant; they allied themselves with the Gentiles and sold themselves to wrongdoing.

**Antiochus in Egypt.** ¹⁶ᶜWhen his kingdom seemed secure, Antiochus undertook to become king of the land of Egypt and to rule over both kingdoms. ¹⁷He invaded Egypt with a strong force, with chariots, elephants** and cavalry, and with a large fleet, ¹⁸to make war on Ptolemy,†† king of Egypt. Ptolemy was frightened at his presence and fled, and many were wounded and fell dead. ¹⁹The fortified cities in the land of Egypt were captured, and Antiochus plundered the land of Egypt.

**Robbery of the Temple.** ²⁰ᵈAfter Antiochus had defeated Egypt in the one hundred and forty-third year,‡‡ he returned and went up against Israel and against Jerusalem with a strong force. ²¹He insolently entered the sanctuary⁵⁵ and took away the golden altar, the lampstand for the light with all its utensils, ²²the offering table, the cups and bowls, the golden censers, and the curtain. The cornices and the golden ornament on the facade of the temple—he stripped it all off. ²³And he took away the silver and gold and the precious vessels; he also took all the hidden treasures he could find. ²⁴Taking all this, he went back to his own country. He shed much blood and spoke with great arrogance.

²⁵ And there was great mourning
        throughout all Israel,
²⁶     and the rulers and the elders
        groaned.
  Young women and men languished,
        and the beauty of the women faded.
²⁷ Every bridegroom took up lamentation,
        while the bride sitting in her
        chamber mourned,
²⁸ And the land quaked on account of its
        inhabitants,
        and all the house of Jacob was
        clothed with shame.

**Attack and Occupation.** ²⁹ᵉTwo years later, the king sent the Mysian commander⁵⁵ to the cities of Judah, and he came to Jerusalem with a

---

*[1:1] **Land of Kittim:** Greece. The name referred originally to inhabitants of Kiti, capital of the isle of Cyprus, then to any Cypriots (Is 23:1; Jer 2:10), later to Greeks in general, and finally even to Romans. See note on Dn 11:30. **Darius:** Darius III, Codoman (336–331 B.C.).

†[1:7] **Twelve years:** 336–323 B.C. The division of the empire was not fully settled until 305 B.C.

‡[1:9] **Diadems:** decorated bands of white cloth worn around the head, symbolizing kingship. The Ptolemies, based in Egypt, controlled Judea until 198 B.C., when they were replaced by the Seleucids, based in Syria.

§[1:10] **The one hundred and thirty-seventh year:** Antiochus IV seized the throne in September, 175 B.C. Dates are given in this book according to the beginning of the Seleucid era, which however was reckoned in two different ways. Antiochians considered this date to be October, 312 B.C. (Syrian calendar), while Babylonians and Jewish priests accepted April, 311 B.C. as the commencement of the era (Temple calendar). The author of 1 Maccabees dates political events by the Syrian calendar but religious events by the Temple calendar. Accordingly, the civil New Year occurred variously in September or October, the religious New Year in March or April.

¶[1:14] **Gymnasium:** symbol and center of Greek athletic and intellectual life, it was the chief instrument of Hellenistic culture. Jewish youth were attracted by sports and encouraged to join youth clubs. They received training in military skills

and in the duties of citizens. Many were won over to paganism, and some even sought surgical correction of their circumcision (since physical exercise was carried out in nudity).

**[1:17] **Elephants:** an important part of Seleucid armament (cf. 6:34–37).

††[1:18] Ptolemy VI Philometer, a nephew of Antiochus.

‡‡[1:20] **Defeated Egypt in the one hundred and forty-third year:** 169 B.C. No mention is made in 1 Maccabees of the second expedition to Egypt a year later, described in 2 Mc 5:1, 11; Dn 11:25, 29 records both.

§§[1:21] **Entered the sanctuary:** to pay his soldiers, Antiochus seized the sacred vessels and the money deposited at the Temple (see 2 Mc 3:10–11).

¶¶[1:29] **Mysian commander:** in 2 Mc 5:24 he is identified as "Apollonius, commander of the Mysians" (mercenaries from

---

a. [1:1–10] Dn 8:20–22; 11:3–4, 21.   b. [1:11–15] 2 Mc 4:12–17.

c. [1:16–19] 2 Mc 5:1–10; Dn 11:25–30.   d. [1:20–24] 2 Mc 5:11–21.   e. [1:29–40] 2 Mc 5:24–26.

strong force. ³⁰He spoke to them deceitfully in peaceful terms, and they believed him. Then he attacked the city suddenly, in a great onslaught, and destroyed many of the people in Israel. ³¹He plundered the city and set fire to it, demolished its houses and its surrounding walls. ³²And they took captive the women and children, and seized the animals. ³³Then they built up the City of David with a high, strong wall and strong towers, and it became their citadel.* ³⁴There they installed a sinful race, transgressors of the law, who fortified themselves inside it. ³⁵They stored up weapons and provisions, depositing there the plunder they had collected from Jerusalem, and they became a great snare.

³⁶ The citadel became an ambush against the
      sanctuary,
      and a wicked adversary to Israel at
      all times.
³⁷ They shed innocent blood around the
      sanctuary;
      they defiled the sanctuary.
³⁸ Because of them the inhabitants of
      Jerusalem fled away,
      she became the abode of strangers.
    She became a stranger to her own
      offspring,
      and her children forsook her.
³⁹ ʲHer sanctuary became desolate as a
      wilderness,
      her feasts were turned into
      mourning,
    Her sabbaths to shame,
      her honor to contempt.
⁴⁰ As her glory had been, so great was her
      dishonor;
      her exaltation was turned into
      mourning.

**Religious Persecution.** ⁴¹ᵍThen the king wrote to his whole kingdom that all should be one people, ⁴²and abandon their particular customs. All the Gentiles conformed to the command of the king, ⁴³and many Israelites delighted in his religion; they sacrificed to idols and profaned the sabbath.

⁴⁴The king sent letters by messenger to Jerusalem and to the cities of Judah, ordering them to follow customs foreign to their land; ⁴⁵to prohibit burnt offerings, sacrifices, and libations in the sanctuary, to profane the sabbaths and feast days, ⁴⁶to desecrate the sanctuary and the sacred ministers, ⁴⁷to build pagan altars and temples and shrines, to sacrifice swine and unclean animals, ⁴⁸to leave their sons uncircumcised, and to defile themselves with every kind of impurity and abomination; ⁴⁹so that they might forget the law and change all its ordinances. ⁵⁰Whoever refused to act according to the command of the king was to be put to death.ʰ

⁵¹In words such as these he wrote to his whole kingdom. He appointed inspectors over all the people, and he ordered the cities of Judah to offer sacrifices, each city in turn. ⁵²Many of the people, those who abandoned the law, joined them and committed evil in the land. ⁵³They drove Israel into hiding, wherever places of refuge could be found.

⁵⁴On the fifteenth day of the month Kislev, in the year one hundred and forty-five,† the king erected the desolating abomination upon the altar of burnt offerings, and in the surrounding cities of Judah they built pagan altars.ⁱ ⁵⁵They also burned incense at the doors of houses and in the streets. ⁵⁶Any scrolls of the law‡ that they found they tore up and burned. ⁵⁷Whoever was found with a scroll of the covenant, and whoever observed the law, was condemned to death by royal decree. ⁵⁸So they used their power against Israel, against those who were caught, each month, in the cities. ⁵⁹On the twenty-fifth day of each month they sacrificed on the pagan altar that was over the altar of burnt offerings. ⁶⁰In keeping with the decree, they put to death women who had their children circumcised, ⁶¹and they hung their babies from their necks; their families also and those who had circumcised them were killed.

⁶²But many in Israel were determined and resolved in their hearts not to eat anything unclean; ⁶³they preferred to die rather than to be defiled with food or to profane the holy covenant; and they did die. ⁶⁴And very great wrath came upon Israel.

## CHAPTER 2

**Mattathias and His Sons.** ¹In those days Mattathias, son of John, son of Simeon, a priest of the family of Joarib,ʲ left Jerusalem and settled in Modein.§ ²He had five sons: John, who was called Gaddi; ³Simon, who was called Thassi; ⁴Judas, who was called Maccabeus; ⁵Eleazar, who was called Avaran; and Jonathan, who was called Apphus. ⁶When he saw the sacrileges

---

†[1:54] **Fifteenth day of the month Kislev, in the year one hundred and forty-five**: December 6, 167 B.C. **Desolating abomination**: in the original Hebrew, a contemptuous pun on the title "Lord of heaven" given to the god to whom an image or perhaps an altar was erected upon the altar of burnt offerings in the Temple of Jerusalem; cf. Dn 9:27; 11:31.

‡[1:56] **Scrolls of the law**: one or more of the first five books of the Old Testament, the traditional law of Israel.

§[2:1] **Modein**: a village about twenty miles northwest of Jerusalem, the family's ancestral home (see 2:70; 9:19).

---

Asia Minor). The Greek text of 1 Mc 1:29 ("chief collector of tribute") reflects a misreading of the Hebrew original.

*[1:33] **Citadel**: literally, *akra* means fortress. This was a garrison for foreign troops and renegade Jews that was established near the Temple area and fell to Simon only in 141 B.C. (13:49–50).

f. [1:39–40] Am 8:10; Tb 2:6.   g. [1:41–64] 2 Mc 6:1–11.

h. [1:50] 1 Mc 2:29–38; 2 Mc 6:18–7:42.   i. [1:54] Dn 9:27; 11:31; Mk 13:14.   j. [2:1] 1 Chr 9:10; 24:7.

that were being committed in Judah and in Jerusalem, [7]he said:

"Woe is me! Why was I born
　　to see the ruin of my people,
　　the ruin of the holy city—
To dwell there
　　as it was given into the hands of
　　　enemies,
　　the sanctuary into the hands of
　　　strangers?
[8]　Her temple has become like a man
　　　disgraced,
[9]　　her glorious vessels carried off as
　　　spoils,
Her infants murdered in her streets,
　　her youths by the sword of the
　　　enemy.[k]
[10]　What nation has not taken its share of her
　　　realm,
　　and laid its hand on her spoils?
[11]　All her adornment has been taken away.
　　Once free, she has become a slave.
[12]　We see our sanctuary laid waste,
　　our beauty, our glory.
　　The Gentiles have defiled them!
[13]　　Why are we still alive?"

[14]Then Mattathias and his sons tore their garments, put on sackcloth, and mourned bitterly. **Pagan Worship Refused and Resisted.** [15]The officers of the king in charge of enforcing the apostasy came to the city of Modein to make them sacrifice. [16]Many of Israel joined them, but Mattathias and his sons drew together. [17]Then the officers of the king addressed Mattathias: "You are a leader, an honorable and great man in this city, supported by sons and kindred. [18]Come now, be the first to obey the king's command, as all the Gentiles and Judeans and those who are left in Jerusalem have done. Then you and your sons shall be numbered among the King's Friends,[*] and you and your sons shall be honored with silver and gold and many gifts."

[19]But Mattathias answered in a loud voice: "Although all the Gentiles in the king's realm obey him, so that they forsake the religion of their ancestors and consent to the king's orders, [20]yet I and my sons and my kindred will keep to the covenant of our ancestors. [21]Heaven forbid that we should forsake the law and the commandments. [22]We will not obey the words of the king by departing from our religion in the slightest degree."

[23]As he finished saying these words, a certain Jew came forward in the sight of all to offer sacrifice on the altar in Modein according to the king's order. [24]When Mattathias saw him, he was filled with zeal; his heart was moved and his just fury was aroused; he sprang forward and killed him upon the altar. [25]At the same time, he also killed the messenger of the king who was forcing them to sacrifice, and he tore down the altar. [26]Thus he showed his zeal for the law, just as Phinehas did with Zimri, son of Salu.[l]

[27]Then Mattathias cried out in the city, "Let everyone who is zealous for the law and who stands by the covenant follow me!" [28]Then he and his sons fled to the mountains, leaving behind in the city all their possessions.[m]

[29]At that time many who sought righteousness and justice went out into the wilderness[†] to settle there, [30]they and their children, their wives and their animals, because misfortunes pressed so hard on them. [31]It was reported to the officers and soldiers of the king who were in the City of David, in Jerusalem, that those who had flouted the king's order had gone out to secret refuges in the wilderness. [32][n]Many hurried out after them, and having caught up with them, camped opposite and prepared to attack them on the sabbath. [33]The pursuers said to them, "Enough of this! Come out and obey the king's command, and you will live." [34]But they replied, "We will not come out, nor will we obey the king's command to profane the sabbath." [35]Then the enemy attacked them at once. [36]But they did not retaliate; they neither threw stones, nor blocked up their secret refuges. [37]They said, "Let us all die in innocence; heaven and earth are our witnesses that you destroy us unjustly." [38]So the officers and soldiers attacked them on the sabbath, and they died with their wives, their children and their animals, to the number of a thousand persons.

[39]When Mattathias and his friends heard of it, they mourned deeply for them. [40]They said to one another, "If we all do as our kindred have done, and do not fight against the Gentiles for our lives and our laws, they will soon destroy us from the earth." [41]So on that day they came to this decision: "Let us fight against anyone who attacks us on the sabbath, so that we may not all die as our kindred died in their secret refuges."

[42]Then they were joined by a group of Hasideans,[‡] mighty warriors of Israel, all of them devoted to the law. [43]And all those who were fleeing from the persecutions joined them and supported them. [44]They gathered an army and struck down sinners in their wrath and the lawless in their anger, and the survivors fled to the Gentiles for safety. [45]Mattathias and his friends

---

[*][2:18] **The King's Friends:** a regular order of nobility at Hellenistic courts (see 10:65; 11:27).

k. [2:9] Lam 2:11, 21.

[†][2:29] **The wilderness:** the sparsely inhabited mountain country southward from Jerusalem and west of the Dead Sea, in the region where the Dead Sea Scrolls were found.

[‡][2:42] **Hasideans:** in Hebrew *hasidim,* "pious ones," a militant religious group devoted to the strict observance of the law. They first supported the Maccabean movement, but subsequently opposed it, regarding it as too political (see 7:12–18).

l. [2:26] Nm 25:6–15; Ps 106:28–31; Sir 45:23–24; 1 Mc 2:54. m. [2:28] 2 Mc 5:27. n. [2:32–38] 2 Mc 6:11.

went about and tore down the pagan altars; ⁴⁶they also forcibly circumcised any uncircumcised boys whom they found in the territory of Israel. ⁴⁷They put to flight the arrogant, and the work prospered in their hands. ⁴⁸They saved the law from the hands of the Gentiles and of the kings and did not let the sinner triumph.

**Farewell of Mattathias.** ⁴⁹When the time came for Mattathias to die, he said to his sons: "Arrogance and scorn have now grown strong; it is a time of disaster and violent wrath. ⁵⁰Therefore, my children, be zealous for the law and give your lives for the covenant of our ancestors.

⁵¹ "Remember the deeds that our ancestors
       did in their times,
   and you shall win great honor and
       an everlasting name.
⁵² Was not Abraham found faithful in trial,
   and it was credited to him as
       righteousness?ᵒ
⁵³ Joseph, when in distress, kept the
       commandment,
   and he became master of Egypt.ᵖ
⁵⁴ Phinehas our ancestor, for his burning
       zeal,
   received the covenant of an
       everlasting priesthood.�q
⁵⁵ Joshua, for executing his commission,
   became a judge in Israel.ʳ
⁵⁶ Caleb, for bearing witness before the
       assembly,
   received an inheritance in the land.ˢ
⁵⁷ David, for his loyalty,
   received as a heritage a throne of
       eternal kingship.ᵗ
⁵⁸ Elijah, for his burning zeal for the law,
   was taken up to heaven.ᵘ
⁵⁹ Hananiah, Azariah and Mishael, for their
       faith,
   were saved from the fire.ᵛ
⁶⁰ Daniel, for his innocence,
   was delivered from the mouths of
       lions.ʷ
⁶¹ And so, consider this from generation to
       generation,
   that none who hope in Heaven shall
       fail in strength.
⁶² Do not fear the words of sinners,
   for their glory ends in corruption
       and worms.ˣ
⁶³ Today exalted, tomorrow not to be
       found,
   they have returned to dust,
   their schemes have perished.
⁶⁴ Children! be courageous and strong in
       keeping the law,
   for by it you shall be honored.

⁶⁵"Here is your brother Simeon who I know is a wise counselor; listen to him always, and he will be a father to you. ⁶⁶And Judas Maccabeus, a mighty warrior from his youth, shall be the leader of your army and wage the war against the nations. ⁶⁷Gather about you all who observe the law, and avenge your people. ⁶⁸Pay back the Gentiles what they deserve, and observe the precepts of the law."

⁶⁹Then he blessed them, and he was gathered to his ancestors. ⁷⁰He died in the year one hundred and forty-six,* and was buried in the tombs of his ancestors in Modein, and all Israel mourned him greatly.

## II. LEADERSHIP OF JUDAS MACCABEUS

### CHAPTER 3

**Judas and His Early Victories.** ¹Then his son Judas, who was called Maccabeus, took his place. ²All his brothers and all who had joined his father supported him, and they gladly carried on Israel's war.

³  He spread abroad the glory of his people,
       and put on his breastplate like a
           giant.
   He armed himself with weapons of war;
       he fought battles and protected the
           camp with his sword.
⁴  In his deeds he was like a lion,
       like a young lion roaring for prey.
⁵  He pursued the lawless, hunting them
           out,
       and those who troubled his people
           he destroyed by fire.
⁶  The lawless were cowed by fear of him,
       and all evildoers were dismayed.
   By his hand deliverance was happily
           achieved,
⁷      and he afflicted many kings.
   He gave joy to Jacob by his deeds,
       and his memory is blessed forever.
⁸  He went about the cities of Judah
       destroying the renegades there.
   He turned away wrath from Israel,
⁹      was renowned to the ends of the
           earth;
       and gathered together those who
           were perishing.

¹⁰Then Apollonius† gathered together the Gentiles, along with a large army from Samaria, to fight against Israel. ¹¹When Judas learned of it, he went out to meet him and struck and killed him. Many fell wounded, and the rest fled. ¹²They took their spoils, and Judas took the

---

o. [2:52] Gn 15:6; 22:1–18.  p. [2:53] Gn 39:7–10; 41:39–43.  q. [2:54] Nm 25:6–15.  r. [2:55] Jos 1, 2, 5.  s. [2:56] Nm 13:30; 14:6–9, 24; Jos 14:14.  t. [2:57] 2 Sm 2:4; 7:16.  u. [2:58] 1 Kgs 19:10, 14; 2 Kgs 2:11.  v. [2:59] Dn 3:26.  w. [2:60] Dn 6:23.  x. [2:62] 2 Mc 9:5–10, 28.

*[2:70] **In the year one hundred and forty-six:** 166 B.C.
†[3:10] **Apollonius:** the Mysian commander mentioned in 1 Mc 1:29; 2 Mc 5:24.

sword of Apollonius and fought with it the rest of his life.

¹³But Seron, commander of the Syrian army, heard that Judas had mustered an assembly of faithful men ready for war. ¹⁴So he said, "I will make a name for myself and win honor in the kingdom. I will wage war against Judas and his followers, who have despised the king's command." ¹⁵And again a large company of renegades advanced with him to help him take revenge on the Israelites.

¹⁶When he reached the ascent of Beth-horon,* Judas went out to meet him with a few men. ¹⁷But when they saw the army coming against them, they said to Judas: "How can we, few as we are, fight such a strong host as this? Besides, we are weak since we have not eaten today." ¹⁸But Judas said: "Many are easily hemmed in by a few; in the sight of Heaven there is no difference between deliverance by many or by few; ¹⁹for victory in war does not depend upon the size of the army, but on strength that comes from Heaven.ʸ ²⁰With great presumption and lawlessness they come against us to destroy us and our wives and children and to despoil us; ²¹but we are fighting for our lives and our laws. ²²Heᵗ will crush them before us; so do not fear them." ²³When he finished speaking, he rushed suddenly upon Seron and his army, who were crushed before him. ²⁴He pursued Seron down the descent of Beth-horon into the plain. About eight hundred‡ of their men fell, and the rest fled to the land of the Philistines. ²⁵Then Judas and his brothers began to be feared, and dread fell upon the Gentiles about them. ²⁶His fame reached the king, and the Gentiles talked about the battles of Judas.

**The King's Strategy.** ²⁷When King Antiochus heard these reports, he was filled with rage; so he ordered that all the forces of his kingdom be gathered, a very strong army. ²⁸He opened his treasury, gave his soldiers a year's pay, and commanded them to be prepared for anything. ²⁹But then he saw that this exhausted the money in his treasury; moreover the tribute from the province was small because of the dissension and distress he had brought upon the land by abolishing the laws which had been in effect from of old. ³⁰He feared that, as had happened once or twice, he would not have enough for his expenses and for the gifts that he was accustomed to give with a lavish hand—more so than all previous kings.

³¹Greatly perplexed, he decided to go to Persia and levy tribute on those provinces, and so raise a large sum of money.

³²He left Lysias, a noble of royal descent, in charge of the king's affairs from the Euphrates River to the frontier of Egypt, ³³and commissioned him to take care of his son Antiochus until his return. ³⁴He entrusted to him half of his forces, and the elephants, and gave him instructions concerning everything he wanted done. As for the inhabitants of Judea and Jerusalem, ³⁵Lysias was to send an army against them to crush and destroy the power of Israel and the remnant of Jerusalem and efface their memory from the place. ³⁶He was to settle foreigners in all their territory and distribute their land by lot. ³⁷§The king took the remaining half of the army and set out from Antioch, his capital, in the year one hundred and forty-seven; he crossed the Euphrates River and went through the provinces beyond.

**Preparations for Battle.** ³⁸ᶻLysias chose Ptolemy, son of Dorymenes, and Nicanor¶ and Gorgias, powerful men among the King's Friends, ³⁹and with them he sent forty thousand foot soldiers and seven thousand cavalry to invade and ravage the land of Judah according to the king's orders. ⁴⁰Setting out with their whole force, they came and pitched their camp near Emmaus** in the plain. ⁴¹When the merchants of the region heard of their prowess, they came to the camp, bringing a huge sum of silver and gold, along with fetters, to buy the Israelites as slaves. A force from Edom and from Philistia joined with them.

⁴²Judas and his brothers saw that evils had multiplied and that armies were encamped within their territory. They learned of the orders which the king had given to destroy and utterly wipe out the people. ⁴³So they said to one another, "Let us raise our people from their ruin and fight for them and for our sanctuary!" ⁴⁴The assembly gathered together to prepare for battle and to pray and ask for mercy and compassion.

⁴⁵ Jerusalem was uninhabited, like a
              wilderness;
       not one of her children came in or
              went out.
   The sanctuary was trampled on,
          and foreigners were in the citadel;
       it was a habitation for Gentiles.
   Joy had disappeared from Jacob,
          and the flute and the harp were
              silent.

---

*[3:16] **Beth-horon**: the famous pass leading up from the coastal plain to the Judean hill country. Here Joshua won an important battle (Jos 10:10–11), and in A.D. 66 a Roman force under Cestius was trapped and massacred.

†[3:22] **He**: out of reverence for God, the author of 1 Maccabees prefers to use the pronoun and other expressions, such as "Heaven," instead of the divine name. Cf. v. 50.

‡[3:24] **About eight hundred**: the figures given in this book for strength of armies and number of casualties are not always to be taken literally. In accordance with biblical usage, they indicate rather the importance of the battle described or the greatness of the victory.

y. [3:19] 1 Sm 14:6.

§[3:37] This expedition, in the spring of 165 B.C., resulted in failure; cf. chap. 6.

¶[3:38] **Nicanor**: perhaps the leader of another attack against the Jews four years later; he was finally killed by Judas; cf. 7:26–46.

**[3:40] **Emmaus**: probably not the village mentioned in Lk 24:13 but a settlement about twenty miles west of Jerusalem at the edge of the hill country.

z. [3:38–60] 2 Mc 8:9–23.

⁴⁶*Thus they assembled and went to Mizpah near Jerusalem, because formerly at Mizpah there was a place of prayer for Israel.ᵃ ⁴⁷That day they fasted and wore sackcloth; they sprinkled ashes on their heads and tore their garments. ⁴⁸They unrolled the scroll of the law, to learn about the things for which the Gentiles consulted the images of their idols.† ⁴⁹They brought with them the priestly garments, the first fruits, and the tithes; and they brought forward the nazirites‡ᵇ who had completed the time of their vows. ⁵⁰And they cried aloud to Heaven: "What shall we do with these, and where shall we take them? ⁵¹For your sanctuary has been trampled on and profaned, and your priests are in mourning and humbled. ⁵²Now the Gentiles are gathered together against us to destroy us. You know what they plot against us. ⁵³How shall we be able to resist them unless you help us?" ⁵⁴Then they blew the trumpets and cried out loudly.

⁵⁵After this Judas appointed officers for the people, over thousands, over hundreds, over fifties, and over tens. ⁵⁶He proclaimed that those who were building houses, or were just married, or were planting vineyards, and those who were afraid, could each return home, according to the law.ᶜ ⁵⁷Then the army moved off, and they camped to the south of Emmaus. ⁵⁸Judas said: "Arm yourselves and be brave; in the morning be ready to fight these Gentiles who have assembled against us to destroy us and our sanctuary. ⁵⁹It is better for us to die in battle than to witness the evils befalling our nation and our sanctuary. ⁶⁰Whatever is willed in heaven will be done."

## CHAPTER 4

**Victory over Gorgias.** ¹Now Gorgias took five thousand infantry and a thousand picked cavalry, and this detachment set out at night ²in order to fall upon the camp of the Jews in a surprise attack. Some from the citadel were his guides. ³Judas heard of it and himself set out with his soldiers to attack the king's army at Emmaus ⁴while these forces were still scattered away from the camp. ⁵During the night Gorgias came into the camp of Judas, and found no one there; so he sought them in the mountains, saying, "They are fleeing from us."

⁶But at daybreak Judas appeared in the plain with three thousand men; furthermore they lacked the helmets and swords they wanted.

⁷They saw the army of the Gentiles,§ strong, breastplated, and flanked with cavalry, and made up of experienced soldiers. ⁸ᵈJudas said to the men with him: "Do not fear their numbers or dread their attack. ⁹Remember how our ancestors were saved in the Red Sea, when Pharaoh pursued them with an army.ᵉ ¹⁰So now let us cry to Heaven in the hope that he will favor us, remember the covenant with our ancestors, and destroy this army before us today. ¹¹All the Gentiles shall know that there is One who redeems and delivers Israel."

¹²When the foreigners looked up and saw them marching toward them, ¹³they came out of their camp for battle. The men with Judas blew the trumpet, and ¹⁴joined the battle. They crushed the Gentiles, who fled toward the plain. ¹⁵Their whole rear guard fell by the sword, and they were pursued as far as Gazaraˢ and the plains of Idumaea, to Azotus and Jamnia. About three thousand of their men fell.

¹⁶When Judas and the army returned from the pursuit, ¹⁷he said to the people: "Do not be greedy for plunder; for there is a fight ahead of us, ¹⁸and Gorgias and his army are near us on the mountain. But now stand firm against our enemies and fight them. Afterward you can freely take the plunder."

¹⁹As Judas was finishing this speech, a detachment** appeared, looking down from the mountain. ²⁰They saw that their army had been put to flight and their camp was burning. The smoke they saw revealed what had happened. ²¹When they realized this, they completely lost heart; and when they also saw the army of Judas in the plain ready to attack, ²²they all fled to the land of the foreigners.††

²³Then Judas went back to plunder the camp, and they took much gold and silver, cloth dyed blue and marine purple, and great treasure. ²⁴As they returned, they were singing hymns and glorifying Heaven, "who is good, whose mercy endures forever."ᶠ ²⁵Thus Israel experienced a great deliverance that day.

**Victory over Lysias.** ²⁶ᵍBut those of the foreigners who had escaped went and told Lysias all that had occurred. ²⁷When he heard it he was disturbed and discouraged, because things had not turned out in Israel as he intended and as the king had ordered:

---

*[3:46] **Mizpah . . . a place of prayer for Israel:** a holy place of great antiquity eight miles north and slightly west of Jerusalem. It was here that Samuel began to judge the Israelites (1 Sm 7:5–11; 10:17).

†[3:48] **To learn . . . idols:** favorable omens for the coming battle. A contrast is intended between the idol worship of the pagans and the consultation of the word of God by the Jews; cf. 2 Mc 8:23.

‡[3:49] **Nazirites:** see note on Nm 6:2–21.

§[4:7] **Army of the Gentiles:** the main force; cf. 3:39–40; 4:1–2.

¶[4:15] **Gazara:** Gezer of the Hebrew Bible, five miles northwest of Emmaus; **Azotus,** Hebrew Ashdod, lay to the southwest; **and Jamnia,** Hebrew Jabneel (Jos 15:11) or Jabneh (2 Chr 26:6), to the west of Gazara.

**[4:19] **A detachment:** i.e., Gorgias' force; cf. vv. 1–5.

††[4:22] **The land of the foreigners:** territory controlled by the Syrians. The Greek term used here is the same as that used throughout 1–2 Samuel in Greek for Philistine territory and intends to compare Maccabean victories to those of Saul and David.

a. [3:46] Jgs 20:1; 1 Sm 7:5–9; 10:17.   b. [3:49] Nm 6:1–21.   c. [3:56] Dt 20:5–8.

d. [4:8–11] Dt 20:3–4; Jgs 7:2–3.   e. [4:9] Ex 14:21–31.   f. [4:24] Ps 118:1–4, 29; 136.   g. [4:26–35] 2 Mc 11:1–15.

[28]So the following year he gathered together sixty thousand picked men and five thousand cavalry, to fight them. [29]They came into Idumea and camped at Beth-zur,* and Judas met them with ten thousand men. [30]Seeing that the army was strong, he prayed thus:

"Blessed are you, Savior of Israel, who crushed the attack of the mighty one by the hand of your servant David and delivered the foreign camp into the hand of Jonathan, the son of Saul, and his armor-bearer.[h] [31]Give this army into the hands of your people Israel; make them ashamed of their troops and their cavalry. [32]Strike them with cowardice, weaken the boldness of their strength, and let them tremble at their own destruction. [33]Strike them down by the sword of those who love you, that all who know your name may sing your praise."

[34]Then they engaged in battle, and about five thousand of Lysias' army fell in hand-to-hand fighting. [35]When Lysias saw the tide of the battle turning, and the increased boldness of Judas, whose men were ready either to live or to die nobly, he withdrew to Antioch and began to recruit mercenaries so as to return to Judea with greater numbers.[i]

**Purification and Rededication of the Temple.** [36]Then Judas and his brothers said, "Now that our enemies have been crushed, let us go up to purify the sanctuary‡ and rededicate it." [37]So the whole army assembled, and went up to Mount Zion. [38]They found the sanctuary desolate, the altar desecrated, the gates burnt, weeds growing in the courts as in a thicket or on some mountain, and the priests' chambers demolished.[k] [39]Then they tore their garments and made great lamentation; they sprinkled their heads with ashes [40]and prostrated themselves. And when the signal was given with trumpets, they cried out to Heaven.

[41]Judas appointed men to attack those in the citadel, while he purified the sanctuary. [42]He chose blameless priests, devoted to the law; [43]these purified the sanctuary and carried away the stones of the defilement to an unclean place. [44]They deliberated what ought to be done with the altar for burnt offerings that had been desecrated.[l] [45]They decided it best to tear it down, lest it be a lasting shame to them that the Gentiles had defiled it; so they tore down the altar. [46]They stored the stones in a suitable place on the temple mount, until the coming of

a prophet who could determine what to do with them.[m] [47]Then they took uncut stones, according to the law, and built a new altar like the former one.[n] [48]They also repaired the sanctuary and the interior of the temple and consecrated the courts. [49]They made new sacred vessels and brought the lampstand, the altar of incense, and the table into the temple.[o] [50]Then they burned incense on the altar and lighted the lamps on the lampstand, and these illuminated the temple. [51]They also put loaves on the table and hung up the curtains. Thus they finished all the work they had undertaken.

[52]They rose early on the morning of the twenty-fifth day of the ninth month, that is, the month of Kislev, in the year one hundred and forty-eight,§ [53]and offered sacrifice according to the law on the new altar for burnt offerings that they had made.[p] [54]On the anniversary of the day on which the Gentiles had desecrated it, on that very day it was rededicated with songs, harps, lyres, and cymbals. [55]All the people prostrated themselves and adored and praised Heaven, who had given them success.

[56]For eight days they celebrated the dedication of the altar and joyfully offered burnt offerings and sacrifices of deliverance and praise. [57]They ornamented the facade of the temple with gold crowns and shields; they repaired the gates and the priests' chambers and furnished them with doors. [58]There was great joy among the people now that the disgrace brought by the Gentiles was removed. [59]Then Judas and his brothers and the entire assembly of Israel decreed that every year for eight days, from the twenty-fifth day of the month Kislev,[q] the days of the dedication¶ of the altar should be observed with joy and gladness on the anniversary.

[60]At that time they built high walls and strong towers around Mount Zion, to prevent the Gentiles from coming and trampling it as they had done before. [61]Judas also placed a garrison there to protect it, and likewise fortified Beth-zur, that the people might have a stronghold facing Idumea.

## CHAPTER 5

**Victories over Hostile Neighbors.**** [1]When the nations round about heard that the altar had been rebuilt and the sanctuary restored as before, they were enraged. [2]So they decided to destroy the descendants of Jacob who were among them, and they began to kill and eradicate the people.

---

*[4:29] **Beth-zur:** an important frontier city (between Judea and Idumea) in the mountain area, fifteen miles south of Jerusalem.

†[4:35] According to 2 Mc 11:13–15, peace negotiations followed between Lysias and Judas.

‡[4:36] **The sanctuary:** the whole Temple area with its walls, courts and outbuildings, to be distinguished from the Temple proper, the oblong edifice with porch, main room and inner shrine.

§[4:52] **Twenty-fifth day of the ninth month . . . in the year one hundred and forty-eight:** December 14, 164 B.C.

¶[4:59] **Days of the dedication:** institution of the feast of Hanukkah, also called the feast of Dedication (Jn 10:22). Josephus calls it the feast of Lights (*Antiquities* 12:325).

**[5:1] The events of this chapter occurred within the year 163 B.C.

h. [4:30] 1 Sm 17:48–58. i. [4:35] 1 Mc 6:28–31. j. [4:36–61] 2 Mc 10:1–8. k. [4:38] Ps 74:2–7. l. [4:44] 1 Kgs 8:64.

m. [4:46] 1 Mc 14:41; Dt 18:15. n. [4:47] Ex 20:25. o. [4:49] Ex 25:23–39; 30:1–6. p. [4:53] Ex 30:10; Ez 43:18–27. q. [4:59] Jn 10:22. r. [5:1–2] 1 Mc 13:6.

³ᵉThen Judas attacked the Edomites* at Akrabattene in Idumea, because they were blockading Israel; he dealt them a heavy blow, humbled and despoiled them. ⁴He also remembered the malice of the Baeanites,† who had become a snare and a stumbling block to the people by ambushing them along the roads. ⁵He forced them to take refuge in towers, which he besieged; he put them under the ban and burned down their towers along with all who were in them. ⁶ᵗThen he crossed over to the Ammonites, where he found a strong army and a large body of people with Timothy as their leader. ⁷He fought many battles with them, routed them, and struck them down. ⁸After seizing Jazer and its villages, he returned to Judea.

**Liberation of Jews in Galilee and Gilead.** ⁹The Gentiles in Gilead assembled to destroy the Israelites who were in their territory; these then fled to the stronghold of Dathema.§ ¹⁰They sent a letter to Judas and his brothers saying: "The Gentiles around us have assembled against us to destroy us, ¹¹and they are preparing to come and seize this stronghold to which we have fled. Timothy is the leader of their army. ¹²Come at once to rescue us from them, for many of us have fallen. ¹³All our kindred who were in the territory of the Tobiads¶ have been killed; the Gentiles have captured their wives, their children and their goods, and they have slain there about a thousand men."ᵘ

¹⁴While they were reading this letter, suddenly other messengers, with garments torn, arrived from Galilee to deliver a similar message: ¹⁵that "the inhabitants of Ptolemais,** Tyre, and Sidon, and the whole of Gentile Galilee have joined forces to destroy us." ¹⁶When Judas and the people heard this, a great assembly convened to consider what they should do for their kindred who were in distress and being attacked by enemies.

¹⁷Judas said to his brother Simon: "Choose men for yourself, and go, rescue your kindred in Galilee; my brother Jonathan and I will go to Gilead."

¹⁸He left Joseph, son of Zechariah, and Azariah, leader of the people, with the rest of the army in Judea to guard it. ¹⁹He commanded them, "Take charge of these people, but do not join battle against the Gentiles until we return." ²⁰Three thousand men were allotted to Simon to go into Galilee, and eight thousand men to Judas, for Gilead.

²¹Simon went into Galilee and fought many battles with the Gentiles. They were crushed before him, ²²and he pursued them to the very gate of Ptolemais. About three thousand of the Gentiles fell, and he gathered their spoils. ²³He took with him the Jews who were in Galilee and in Arbatta,†† with their wives and children and all that they had, and brought them to Judea with great rejoicing.

²⁴ᵛJudas Maccabeus and his brother Jonathan crossed the Jordan and marched for three days through the wilderness. ²⁵There they met some Nabateans,‡‡ who received them peaceably and told them all that had happened to their kindred in Gilead: ²⁶"Many of them are shut up in Bozrah, in Bosor near Alema, in Chaspho, Maked, and Carnaim"—all of these are large, fortified cities— ²⁷"and some are shut up in other cities of Gilead. Tomorrow their enemies plan to attack the strongholds and to seize and destroy all these people in one day."

²⁸Thereupon Judas suddenly changed direction with his army, marched across the wilderness to Bozrah, and captured the city. He put every male to the sword, took all their spoils, and set fire to the city. ²⁹§§He led his army from that place by night, and they marched toward the stronghold. ³⁰When morning came, they looked ahead and saw a countless multitude, with ladders and machines for capturing the stronghold, beginning to attack. ³¹When Judas perceived that the struggle had begun and that the noise of the battle was resounding to heaven with trumpet blasts and loud shouting, ³²he said to the men of his army, "Fight for our kindred today." ³³He came up behind them with three columns blowing their trumpets and crying out in prayer. ³⁴When the army of Timothy realized that it was Maccabeus, they fled before him, and he inflicted on them a great defeat. About eight thousand of their men fell that day.

³⁵Then he turned toward Alema¶¶ and attacked and captured it; he killed every male, took spoils, and burned it down. ³⁶From there

---

*[5:3] **Edomites:** lit., "sons of Esau"; here a pejorative term for the Idumeans. Cf. also 5:65. **Akrabattene:** either a district southwest of the Dead Sea or on the eastern border of Judea and Samaria.

†[5:4] **Baeanites:** 2 Mc 10:15–23 calls them simply Idumeans.

‡[5:6–8] This summary anticipates the order of events and would fit better between vv. 36 and 37. It corresponds to 2 Mc 12:17–23. The action was probably a reprisal for the massacre referred to in 1 Mc 5:13. Timothy may have been a local ruler, or the Seleucid governor of Transjordan. **Jazer:** a town on the road from the Jordan to Amman.

§[5:9] **Dathema:** the exact location is uncertain; it was east of the Jordan (in Gilead) and a night's journey from Bozrah (v. 29).

¶[5:13] **Tobiads:** a prominent Jewish family that settled east of the Jordan.

**[5:15] **Ptolemais:** Hebrew *Acco* (Jgs 1:31), modern Acre, on the coast north of Haifa.

††[5:23] **Arbatta:** (or, Narbatta), probably south of Mount Carmel.

‡‡[5:25] **Nabateans:** an Arab people who acquired wealth and power as caravan merchants in the final two centuries B.C. They established Petra as their capital and for a time controlled all of Transjordan, even as far as Damascus. It was from a Nabatean governor of Damascus that Paul escaped (2 Cor 11:32–33).

§§[5:29] Cf. v. 9.

¶¶[5:35] **Alema:** see v. 26; other manuscripts read Maapha, which may be Mizpah of Gilead (Jgs 11:29).

---

s. [5:3–5] 2 Mc 10:15–23.   t. [5:6–7] 2 Mc 8:30–33.   u. [5:13] 2 Mc 12:17.

v. [5:24–36] 2 Mc 12:10–16.

he moved on and took Chaspho, Maked, Bosor, and the other cities of Gilead.

[37w]After these events Timothy assembled another army and camped opposite Raphon, on the other side of the wadi. [38]Judas sent men to spy on the camp, and they reported to him: "All the Gentiles around us have rallied to him, making a very large force; [39]they have also hired Arabians to help them, and have camped beyond the wadi, ready to attack you." So Judas went forward to meet them.

[40]As Judas and his army were approaching the flowing wadi, Timothy said to the officers of his army: "If he crosses over to us first, we shall not be able to resist him; he will certainly defeat us.[x] [41]But if he is hesitant and camps on the other side of the river, we will cross over to him and defeat him." [42]But when Judas reached the flowing wadi, he stationed the officers of the people beside it and gave them this order: "Do not allow anyone to encamp; all must go into battle." [43]He was the first to cross to the attack, with all the people behind him, and all the Gentiles were crushed before them. They threw away their arms and fled to the temple enclosure at Carnaim. [44]But Judas' troops captured the city and burnt the temple enclosure with all who were in it. So Carnaim was subdued, and Judas met with no more resistance.

**Return to Jerusalem.** [45y]Then Judas assembled all the Israelites, great and small, who were in Gilead, with their wives and children and their goods, a very large company, to go into the land of Judah. [46]When they reached Ephron,[*] a large and strongly fortified city along the way, they found it impossible to go around it on either the right or the left; they would have to march right through it.[z] [47]But the people in the city shut them out and blocked up the gates with stones. [48]Then Judas sent them this peaceful message: "Let us cross your territory in order to reach our own; no one will harm you; we will only march through." But they would not open to him. [49]So Judas ordered a proclamation to be made in the camp that everyone should take up positions where they were. [50]When the men of the army took up their positions, he assaulted the city all that day and night, and it was delivered into his hand. [51]He put every male to the sword, leveled the city, took spoils and passed through it over the slain.

[52]Then they crossed the Jordan to the great plain in front of Beth-shan; [53]and Judas kept gathering the stragglers and encouraging the people the whole way, until he reached the land of Judah. [54]They ascended Mount Zion in joy and gladness and sacrificed burnt offerings, because not one of them had fallen; they had returned in safety.

**Joseph and Azariah Defeated.** [55]In those days when Judas and Jonathan were in the land of Gilead, and Simon his brother was in Galilee opposite Ptolemais, [56]Joseph, son of Zechariah, and Azariah, the leaders of the army, heard about the brave deeds and the fighting that they were doing. [57]They said, "Let us also make a name for ourselves by going out and fighting against the Gentiles around us." [58]They gave orders to those of their army who were with them, and marched against Jamnia.[†] [59]But Gorgias and his men came out of the city to meet them in battle. [60]Joseph and Azariah were routed and were pursued to the frontiers of Judea, and about two thousand Israelites fell that day. [61]It was a great setback for the people, because they had not obeyed Judas and his brothers, thinking that they would do brave deeds. [62]But they were not of the family through whom Israel's deliverance was given.

**Victories at Hebron and Azotus.** [63]The valiant Judas and his brothers were greatly honored in all Israel and among all the Gentiles, wherever their name was heard; [64]and people gathered about them and praised them.

[65a]Then Judas and his brothers went out and attacked the Edomites in the land toward the south; he took Hebron and its villages, and he destroyed its strongholds and burned the towers around it. [66]He then set out for the land of the foreigners and passed through Marisa. [67]On that day some priests fell in battle who had gone out rashly to fight in their desire to do brave deeds. [68]Judas then turned toward Azotus in the land of the foreigners. He destroyed their altars and burned the carved images of their gods; and after plundering their cities he returned to the land of Judah.

## CHAPTER 6

[1b]As King Antiochus passed through the eastern provinces, he heard that in Persia there was a city, Elam,[‡] famous for its wealth in silver and gold, [2]and that its temple was very rich, containing gold helmets, breastplates, and weapons left there by the first king of the Greeks, Alexander, son of Philip, king of Macedon. [3]He went therefore and tried to capture and loot the city. But he could not do so, because his plan became known to the people of the city [4]who rose up in battle against him. So he fled and in great dismay withdrew from there to return to Babylon.

---

[*] [5:46] **Ephron:** a city in Transjordan opposite Beth-shan (v. 52), about nine miles east of the Jordan River. Situated on a height, it dominated the valleys of the two tributaries of the Jordan.

[†] [5:58] **Jamnia:** Yavneh (see 10:69), the capital of the province of Azotus (Ashdod).

[‡] [6:1] **Elam:** in fact, the mountainous region north of the Persian Gulf, rather than a city. The city may have been Persepolis. This section continues the story from 3:37 and pertains to events preceding those in 4:37–39.

---

w. [5:37–44] 2 Mc 12:17–25.   x. [5:40] 1 Sm 14:9–10.   y. [5:45–54] 2 Mc 12:26–31.   z. [5:46] Nm 20:17–21; 21:21–25.

a. [5:65–68] 2 Mc 12:36–46.   b. [6:1–13] 2 Mc 1:13–17; 9:1–29; Dn 11:40–45.

⁵While he was in Persia, a messenger brought him news that the armies that had gone into the land of Judah had been routed; ⁶that Lysias had gone at first with a strong army and been driven back; that the people of Judah had grown strong by reason of the arms, wealth, and abundant spoils taken from the armies they had cut down; ⁷that they had pulled down the abomination which he had built upon the altar in Jerusalem; and that they had surrounded with high walls both the sanctuary, as it had been before, and his city of Beth-zur.ᶜ

⁸When the king heard this news, he was astonished and very much shaken. Sick with grief because his designs had failed, he took to his bed. ⁹There he remained many days, assailed by waves of grief, for he thought he was going to die. ¹⁰So he called in all his Friends and said to them: "Sleep has departed from my eyes, and my heart sinks from anxiety. ¹¹I said to myself: 'Into what tribulation have I come, and in what floods of sorrow am I now! Yet I was kindly and beloved in my rule.' ¹²But I now recall the evils I did in Jerusalem, when I carried away all the vessels of silver and gold that were in it, and for no cause gave orders that the inhabitants of Judah be destroyed. ¹³I know that this is why these evils have overtaken me; and now I am dying, in bitter grief, in a foreign land."

¹⁴Then he summoned Philip, one of his Friends, and put him in charge of his whole kingdom. ¹⁵He gave him his diadem, his robe, and his signet ring, so that he might guide the king's son Antiochus and bring him up to be king. ¹⁶So King Antiochus died there in the one hundred and forty-ninth year.* ¹⁷When Lysias learned that the king was dead, he set up the king's son Antiochus,† whom he had reared as a child, to be king in his place; and he gave him the title Eupator.ᵈ

**Siege of the Citadel.** ¹⁸Those in the citadel were hemming Israel in around the sanctuary, continually trying to harm them and to strengthen the Gentiles.ᵉ ¹⁹And so Judas planned to destroy them, and assembled the people to besiege them. ²⁰So in the one hundred and fiftieth year‡ they assembled and besieged the citadel, for which purpose he constructed platforms and siege engines. ²¹But some of the besieged

escaped, and some renegade Israelites joined them. ²²They went to the king and said: "How long will you fail to do justice and to avenge our kindred? ²³We agreed to serve your father and to follow his orders and obey his edicts. ²⁴And for this our own people have become our enemies; they have put to death as many of us as they could find and have seized our inheritances. ²⁵They have acted aggressively not only against us, but throughout their whole territory. ²⁶Look! Today they have besieged the citadel in Jerusalem in order to capture it, and they have fortified the sanctuary and Beth-zur. ²⁷Unless you act quickly to prevent them, they will do even worse things than these, and you will not be able to stop them."

²⁸When the king heard this he was enraged, and he called together all his Friends, the officers of his army, and the commanders of the cavalry. ²⁹Mercenary forces also came to him from other kingdoms and from the islands of the seas. ³⁰His army numbered a hundred thousand footsoldiers, twenty thousand cavalry, and thirty-two elephants trained for war. ³¹They passed through Idumea and camped before Beth-zur. For many days they attacked it; they constructed siege engines, but the besieged made a sortie and burned these, and they fought bravely.

**Battle of Beth-zechariah.** ³²Then Judas marched away from the citadel and moved his camp to Beth-zechariah,§ opposite the king's camp. ³³The king, rising before dawn, moved his force hastily along the road to Beth-zechariah; and the troops prepared for battle and sounded the trumpet. ³⁴They made the elephants drunk on the juice of grapes and mulberries to get them ready to fight. ³⁵The beasts were distributed along the phalanxes, each elephant having assigned to it a thousand men in coats of mail, with bronze helmets on their heads, and five hundred picked cavalry. ³⁶These accompanied the beast wherever it was; wherever it moved, they moved too and never left it. ³⁷Each elephant was outfitted with a strong wooden tower, fastened to it by a harness; each tower held three soldiers who fought from it, besides the Indian driver. ³⁸The remaining cavalry were stationed on one or the other of the two flanks of the army, to harass the enemy and to be protected by the phalanxes. ³⁹When the sun shone on the gold and bronze shields, the mountains gleamed with their brightness and blazed like flaming torches. ⁴⁰Part of the king's army spread out along the heights, while some were on low ground, and they marched forward steadily in good order. ⁴¹All who heard the noise of their numbers, the tramp of their marching, and the clanging of the arms, trembled; for the army was very great and strong.

---

*[6:16] **The one hundred and forty-ninth year:** September 22, 164, to October 9, 163 B.C. A Babylonian list of the Seleucid kings indicates that Antiochus died in November or early December of 164, about the same time as the rededication of the Temple.

†[6:17] **The king's son Antiochus:** Antiochus V Eupator ("of a good father"), then about nine years old. He was in Antioch, still in the charge of Lysias, who proceeded to govern and wage wars in his name. Both were put to death two years later, when Demetrius, brother of Antiochus IV, arrived to claim the kingship; cf. 7:1–3.

‡[6:20] **The one hundred and fiftieth year:** October, 163, to September, 162 B.C.

§[6:32] **Beth-zechariah:** south of Jerusalem, and six miles north of Beth-zur.

---

c. [6:7] 1 Mc 1:54; 4:41–61.   d. [6:17] 2 Mc 10:10–11.   e. [6:18] 1 Mc 1:33–36.

f. [6:28–54] 2 Mc 13:1–26.

⁴²Judas with his army advanced to fight, and six hundred men of the king's army fell. ⁴³Eleazar, called Avaran, saw one of the beasts covered with royal armor and bigger than any of the others, and so he thought the king was on it.ᵍ ⁴⁴He gave up his life to save his people and win an everlasting name for himself. ⁴⁵He dashed courageously up to it in the middle of the phalanx, killing men right and left, so that they parted before him. ⁴⁶He ran under the elephant, stabbed it and killed it. The beast fell to the ground on top of him, and he died there. ⁴⁷But when Judas' troops saw the strength of the royal army and the ardor of its forces, they retreated from them.
**The Siege of Jerusalem.** ⁴⁸Some of the king's army went up to Jerusalem to attack them, and the king established camps in Judea and at Mount Zion. ⁴⁹He made peace with the people of Beth-zur, and they evacuated the city, because they had no food there to enable them to withstand a siege, for that was a sabbath year in the land.*ʰ ⁵⁰The king took Beth-zur and stationed a garrison there to hold it. ⁵¹For many days he besieged the sanctuary, setting up platforms and siege engines, fire-throwers, catapults and mechanical bows for shooting arrows and projectiles. ⁵²The defenders countered by setting up siege engines of their own, and kept up the fight a long time. ⁵³But there were no provisions in the storerooms, because it was the seventh year, and the reserves had been eaten up by those who had been rescued from the Gentiles and brought to Judea. ⁵⁴Few men remained in the sanctuary because the famine was too much for them; the rest scattered, each to his own home.
**Peace Treaty.** ⁵⁵Lysias heard that Philip, whom King Antiochus, before his death, had appointed to train his son Antiochus to be king, ⁵⁶had returned from Persia and Media with the army that accompanied the king, and that he was seeking to take over the government. ⁵⁷So he hastily decided to withdraw. He said to the king, the leaders of the army, and the soldiers: "We are growing weaker every day, our provisions are scanty, the place we are besieging is strong, and it is our duty to take care of the affairs of the kingdom.ʲ ⁵⁸Therefore let us now come to terms with these people and make peace with them and all their nation. ⁵⁹Let us grant them freedom to live according to their own laws as formerly; it was on account of their laws, which we abolished, that they became enraged and did all these things."
⁶⁰The proposal pleased the king and the leaders; he sent peace terms to the Jews, and they accepted. ⁶¹So the king and the leaders

swore an oath to them, and on these terms the Jews evacuated the fortification. ⁶²But when the king entered Mount Zion and saw how the place was fortified, he broke the oath he had sworn and gave orders to tear down the encircling wall. ⁶³Then he departed in haste and returned to Antioch, where he found Philip in control of the city. He fought against him and took the city by force.

# CHAPTER 7
**Expedition of Bacchides and Alcimus.** ¹ᵏIn the one hundred and fifty-first year,† Demetrius, son of Seleucus, set out from Rome, arrived with a few men at a coastal city, and began to rule there. ²As he was entering the royal palace of his ancestors, the soldiers seized Antiochus and Lysias to bring them to him. ³When he was informed of this, he said, "Do not show me their faces." ⁴So the soldiers killed them, and Demetrius assumed the royal throne.
⁵Then all the lawless men and renegades of Israel came to him. They were led by Alcimus,‡ who desired to be high priest. ⁶They made this accusation to the king against the people: "Judas and his brothers have destroyed all your friends and have driven us out of our land. ⁷So now, send a man whom you trust to go and see all the destruction Judas has wrought on us and on the king's territory, and let him punish them and all their supporters."
⁸So the king chose Bacchides, one of the King's Friends, who ruled the province of West-of-Euphrates, a great man in the kingdom, and faithful to the king. ⁹He sent him and the renegade Alcimus, to whom he granted the high priesthood, with orders to take revenge on the Israelites. ¹⁰They set out and, on arriving in the land of Judah with a great army, sent messengers who spoke deceitfully to Judas and his brothers in peaceful terms. ¹¹But these paid no attention to their words, seeing that they had come with a great army.
¹²A group of scribes, however, gathered about Alcimus and Bacchides to ask for a just agreement. ¹³ˡThe Hasideans were the first among the Israelites to seek peace with them, ¹⁴for they said, "A priest of the line of Aaron has come with the army, and he will not do us any wrong." ¹⁵He spoke with them peacefully and swore to them,

---

*[6:49] **A sabbath year in the land:** when sowing and reaping were prohibited (Ex 23:10–11; Lv 25:2–7). The year without a harvest (autumn of 164 to autumn of 163) was followed by a food shortage.

g. [6:43] 2 Mc 13:15.   h. [6:49] Lv 25:1–7.   i. [6:55–63] 2 Mc 13:23–26.   j. [6:57] 2 Mc 11:13–15.

---

†[7:1–3] **The one hundred and fifty-first year:** the spring of 161 B.C. Demetrius, son of Seleucus, was the lawful heir to the kingdom; but when only nine years old, he was taken as a hostage to Rome in place of his uncle, who ruled as Antiochus IV Epiphanes. At the age of twenty-five Demetrius fled secretly from Rome and, with the support of the Syrians, overcame his rival Antiochus V and put him to death. **The royal palace:** at Antioch.
‡[7:5–6] **Alcimus:** a Jew hostile to the Maccabees, who became high priest after the death of Menelaus (2 Mc 14:3). He received confirmation in his office from the new king Demetrius (1 Mc 7:9), and brought malicious charges against Judas and his brothers and the people (1 Mc 7:6).

k. [7:1–7] 2 Mc 14:1–11.   l. [7:13–14] 1 Mc 2:42.

"We will not seek to injure you or your friends." [16]So they trusted him. But he arrested sixty of them and killed them in one day, according to the words that he wrote:[*]

[17]  "The flesh of your faithful,
        and their blood they have spilled all
            around about Jerusalem,
        and no one was left to bury them."[m]

[18]Then fear and dread of them came upon all the people, who said: "There is no truth or justice among them; they violated the agreement and the oath that they swore."

[19]Bacchides withdrew from Jerusalem and camped in Beth-zaith.[†] He had many of the men who deserted to him arrested and some of the people. He killed them and threw them into a great cistern. [20]He handed the province over to Alcimus, leaving troops to help him, while he himself returned to the king.

[21]Alcimus struggled to maintain his high priesthood, [22]and all those who were troubling the people gathered about him. They took possession of the land of Judah and caused great distress in Israel. [23]When Judas saw all the evils that Alcimus and those with him were bringing upon the Israelites, even more than the Gentiles had, [24]he went about all the borders of Judea and took revenge on the men who had deserted, preventing them from going out into the country. [25]But when Alcimus saw that Judas and his followers were gaining strength and realized that he could not resist them, he returned to the king and accused them of grave crimes.

**Defeat of Nicanor.** [26]nThen the king sent Nicanor, one of his honored officers, who was a bitter enemy of Israel, with orders to destroy the people. [27]Nicanor came to Jerusalem with a large force and deceitfully sent to Judas[‡] and his brothers this peaceable message: [28]"Let there be no fight between me and you. I will come with a few men to meet you face to face in peace."

[29]So he came to Judas, and they greeted one another peaceably. But Judas' enemies were prepared to seize him. [30]When he became aware that Nicanor had come to him with deceit in mind, Judas was afraid of him and would not meet him again.[o] [31]When Nicanor saw that his plan had been discovered, he went out to fight Judas near Capharsalama.[§] [32]About five hundred

men of Nicanor's army fell; the rest fled to the City of David.[¶]

[33]pAfter this, Nicanor went up to Mount Zion. Some of the priests from the sanctuary and some of the elders of the people came out to greet him peaceably and to show him the burnt offering that was being sacrificed for the king. [34]But he mocked and ridiculed them, defiled them,[**] and spoke arrogantly. [35]In a rage he swore: "If Judas and his army are not delivered to me at once, when I return victorious I will burn this temple down." He went away in great anger. [36]qThe priests, however, went in and stood before the altar and the sanctuary. They wept and said: [37]"You have chosen this house to bear your name, to be a house of prayer and supplication for your people. [38]Take revenge on this man and his army, and let them fall by the sword. Remember their blasphemies, and do not let them continue."

[39]Nicanor left Jerusalem and camped at Beth-horon, where the Syrian army joined him. [40]But Judas camped in Adasa[††] with three thousand men. Here Judas uttered this prayer: [41]r"When they who were sent by the king[‡‡] blasphemed, your angel went out and killed a hundred and eighty-five thousand of them.[s] [42]In the same way, crush this army before us today, and let the rest know that Nicanor spoke wickedly against your sanctuary; judge him according to his wickedness."

[43]The armies met in battle on the thirteenth day of the month Adar. Nicanor's army was crushed, and he himself was the first to fall in the battle.[t] [44]When his army saw that Nicanor had fallen, they threw down their weapons and fled. [45]The Jews pursued them a day's journey from Adasa to near Gazara, blowing the trumpets behind them as signals. [46]From all the surrounding villages of Judea people came out and outflanked them. They turned them back, and all the enemies fell by the sword; not a single one escaped.

[47]Then the Jews collected the spoils and the plunder; they cut off Nicanor's head and his right arm, which he had lifted up so arrogantly. These they brought and displayed in the sight of Jerusalem. [48]The people rejoiced greatly, and observed that day as a day of much joy. [49]They

---

*[7:16] **The words that he wrote:** based on Ps 79:2–3. But who is "he"—David, Alcimus, Judas, or someone else?

†[7:19] **Beth-zaith:** about three miles north of Beth-zur and twelve miles south of Jerusalem.

‡[7:27] **Nicanor . . . deceitfully sent to Judas:** a more favorable picture of Nicanor, as an honest man who became a personal friend of Judas, is given in 2 Mc 14:17–25. Their friendship was broken by the intrigues of Alcimus (2 Mc 14:26–30).

§[7:31] **Capharsalama:** a village north of Jerusalem whose precise location is disputed.

¶[7:32] **City of David:** the citadel occupied by the Seleucid garrison in Jerusalem.

**[7:34] **Defiled them:** spitting on the priests caused them to become legally defiled.

††[7:40] **Adasa:** a village between Jerusalem and Beth-horon.

‡‡[7:41] **They who were sent by the king:** 2 Kgs 18:19–25, 29–35; 19:10–13 recount in detail the boastful threats made by Sennacherib, the Assyrian king, through his emissaries. **Your angel:** a reference to 2 Kgs 19:35, which describes the fate of the Assyrian army which besieged Jerusalem in the days of Hezekiah, king of Judah.

---

m. [7:17] Ps 79:2–3.   n. [7:26–27] 1 Mc 3:38; 2 Mc 8:9; 14:12–13.   o. [7:30] 2 Mc 14:30.

p. [7:33–38] 2 Mc 14:31–36.   q. [7:36–38] 1 Kgs 8:29–30, 33–34, 43.   r. [7:41–42] 2 Mc 8:19; 15:22–24.   s. [7:41] 2 Kgs 19:35–36; Is 37:36–37.   t. [7:43] 2 Mc 15:25–36.

decreed that it should be observed every year on the thirteenth of Adar.* ⁵⁰And so for a few days† the land of Judah was at rest.

## CHAPTER 8

**Eulogy of the Romans.** ¹†Judas had heard of the reputation of the Romans. They were valiant fighters and acted amiably to all who took their side. They established a friendly alliance with all who applied to them. ²He was also told of their battles and the brave deeds that they performed against the Gauls,§ conquering them and forcing them to pay tribute; ³and what they did in Spain to get possession of the silver and gold mines there. ⁴By planning and persistence they subjugated the whole region, although it was very remote from their own. They also subjugated the kings who had come against them from the far corners of the earth until they crushed them and inflicted on them severe defeat. The rest paid tribute to them every year. ⁵Philip§ and Perseus, king of the Macedonians, and the others who opposed them in battle they overwhelmed and subjugated. ⁶Antiochus** the Great, king of Asia, who fought against them with a hundred and twenty elephants and with cavalry and chariots and a very great army, was defeated by them. ⁷They took him alive and obliged him and the kings who succeeded him to pay a heavy tribute, to give hostages and to cede ⁸Lycia, Mysia, and Lydia†† from among their best provinces. The Romans took these from him and gave them to King Eumenes. ⁹‡‡When the Greeks planned to come and destroy them, ¹⁰the Romans discovered it, and sent against the Greeks a single general who made war on them. Many were wounded and fell, and the Romans took their wives and children captive. They plundered them, took possession of their land, tore down their strongholds and reduced them to slavery even to this day. ¹¹All the other kingdoms and islands that had ever opposed them they destroyed and enslaved; with their friends, however, and those who relied on them, they maintained friendship. ¹²They subjugated kings both near and far, and all who heard of their fame were afraid of them. ¹³Those whom they wish to help and to make kings, they make kings; and those whom they wish, they depose; and they were greatly exalted. ¹⁴Yet with all this, none of them put on a diadem or wore purple as a display of grandeur. ¹⁵But they made for themselves a senate chamber, and every day three hundred and twenty men took counsel, deliberating on all that concerned the people and their well-being. ¹⁶They entrust their government to one man§§ every year, to rule over their entire land, and they all obey this one, and there is no envy or jealousy among them.

**Treaty with the Romans.** ¹⁷So Judas chose Eupolemus, son of John, son of Accos, and Jason, son of Eleazar, and sent them to Rome to establish friendship and alliance with them.ᵘ ¹⁸He did this to lift the yoke from Israel, for it was obvious that the kingdom of the Greeks was subjecting them to slavery. ¹⁹After making a very long journey to Rome, the envoys entered the senate chamber and spoke as follows: ²⁰"Judas, called Maccabeus, and his brothers, with the Jewish people, have sent us to you to establish alliance and peace with you, and to be enrolled among your allies and friends." ²¹The proposal pleased the Romans, ²²and this is a copy of the reply they inscribed on bronze tablets and sent to Jerusalem,⁹⁹ to remain there with the Jews as a record of peace and alliance:ᵛ

²³"May it be well with the Romans and the Jewish nation at sea and on land forever; may sword and enemy be far from them. ²⁴But if war is first made on Rome, or any of its allies in any

---

*[7:49] **The thirteenth of Adar:** March 27, 160 B.C. This day in the Jewish calendar was called the "Day of Nicanor" (2 Mc 15:36), but it was not long celebrated by the Jews.

†[7:50] **For a few days:** about one month following the death of Nicanor. After that began the attack of Bacchides resulting in the death of Judas (9:1–18).

‡[8:1] This chapter contains the account of the embassy which Judas sent to Rome, probably before the death of Nicanor, to conclude a treaty of alliance between Rome and the Jewish nation. Without precise chronology, the pertinent data are gathered into a unified account.

The image of the Roman Republic greatly impressed the smaller Eastern peoples seeking support against their overlords (vv. 1+16), because of Roman success in war (vv. 2–11) and effective aid to their allies (vv. 12–13). Numerous interventions by Rome in the politics of the Near East bear witness to its power and prestige in the second century B.C. See 1:10; 7:2; 12:3; 15:15–24; 2 Mc 11:34. With the increased Roman control of Palestine after 63 B.C., the Republic and later the Empire became heartily detested. The eulogy of Rome in this chapter is one of the reasons why 1 Maccabees was not preserved by the Palestinian Jews of the century that followed.

§[8:2] **Gauls:** probably the Celts of northern Italy and southern France, subdued by the Romans in 222 B.C., and again in 200–191 B.C.; but also those in Asia Minor (the Galatians), whom the Romans defeated in 189 B.C.

¶[8:5] **Philip:** Philip V of Macedonia, defeated by a Graeco-Roman alliance at Cynoscephalae in 197 B.C. Perseus, his son, was defeated at Pydna in 168 B.C., and died a prisoner. With this, the kingdom of Macedonia came to an end.

**[8:6] **Antiochus:** Antiochus III, greatest of the Seleucid kings. He was defeated at Magnesia in 190 B.C. By the Treaty of Apamea in 189 B.C., he was obliged to pay Rome a crushing indemnity of 15,000 talents. The weakening of Antiochene power and the growing military and economic influence of Rome may have led Antiochus IV to adopt the policy of political, religious, and cultural unification of Syria and Palestine.

††[8:8] **Lycia, Mysia, and Lydia:** regions in western Asia Minor. "Lycia" and "Mysia" are restored here by conjectural

emendation; the Greek text has "India, Media," most likely through scribal error. **Eumenes:** Eumenes II (197–158 B.C.), king of Pergamum, an ally of Rome who benefited greatly from Antiochus' losses.

‡‡[8:9–10] The revolt of the Achaean League, inserted here, occurred in 146 B.C., after Judas' time. It was crushed by the Roman consul Lucius Mummius and marked the end of Greek independence.

§§[8:16] **They entrust their government to one man:** actually the Roman Republic had two consuls chosen yearly as joint heads of the government.

¶¶[8:22] **The reply . . . on bronze tablets and sent to Jerusalem:** the decree of the Senate would be inscribed on bronze and kept in the Roman Capitol, with only a copy in letter form sent to Jerusalem.

---

u. [8:17] 1 Mc 12:1–4; 15:15–22.    v. [8:22] 1 Mc 14:17–18.

of their dominions, <sup>25</sup>the Jewish nation will fight along with them wholeheartedly, as the occasion shall demand; <sup>26</sup>and to those who wage war they shall not give or provide grain, weapons, money, or ships, as seems best to Rome. They shall fulfill their obligations without receiving any recompense. <sup>27</sup>In the same way, if war is made first on the Jewish nation, the Romans will fight along with them willingly, as the occasion shall demand, <sup>28</sup>and to those who attack them there shall not be given grain, weapons, money, or ships, as seems best to Rome. They shall fulfill their obligations without deception. <sup>29</sup>On these terms the Romans have made an agreement with the Jewish people. <sup>30</sup>But if both parties hereafter agree to add or take away anything, they shall do as they choose, and whatever they shall add or take away shall be valid.

<sup>31</sup>"Moreover, concerning the wrongs that King Demetrius is doing to them, we have written to him thus: 'Why have you made your yoke heavy upon our friends and allies the Jews? <sup>32</sup>If they petition against you again, we will enforce justice and make war on you by sea and land.'"

## CHAPTER 9

**Death of Judas.** <sup>1</sup>When Demetrius heard that Nicanor and his army had fallen in battle, he again sent Bacchides and Alcimus into the land of Judah, along with the right wing of his army. <sup>2</sup>They took the road to Galilee, and camping opposite the ascent at Arbela, they captured it* and killed many people. <sup>3</sup>In the first month of the one hundred and fifty-second year,† they encamped against Jerusalem. <sup>4</sup>Then they set out for Berea with twenty thousand men and two thousand cavalry. <sup>5</sup>Judas, with three thousand picked men, had camped at Elasa. <sup>6</sup>When they saw the great number of the troops, they were very much afraid, and many slipped away from the camp, until only eight hundred of them remained.

<sup>7</sup>When Judas saw that his army was melting away just as the battle was imminent, he was brokenhearted, because he had no time to gather them together. <sup>8</sup>In spite of his discouragement he said to those who remained: "Let us go forward to meet our enemies; perhaps we can put up a good fight against them." <sup>9</sup>They tried to dissuade him, saying: "We certainly cannot. Let us save our own lives now, and come back with our kindred, and then fight against them.

Now we are too few." <sup>10</sup>But Judas said: "Far be it from me to do such a thing as to flee from them! If our time has come, let us die bravely for our kindred and not leave a stain upon our honor!"

<sup>11</sup>Then the army of Bacchides moved out of camp and took its position for combat. The cavalry were divided into two squadrons, and the slingers and the archers came on ahead of the army, and in the front line were all the best warriors. Bacchides was on the right wing. <sup>12</sup>Flanked by the two squadrons, the phalanx attacked as they blew their trumpets. Those who were on Judas' side also blew their trumpets. <sup>13</sup>The earth shook with the noise of the armies, and the battle raged from morning until evening.

<sup>14</sup>When Judas saw that Bacchides was on the right, with the main force of his army, all the most stouthearted rallied to him, <sup>15</sup>and the right wing was crushed; Judas pursued them as far as the mountain slopes.‡ <sup>16</sup>But when those on the left wing saw that the right wing was crushed, they closed in behind Judas and those with him. <sup>17</sup>The battle became intense, and many on both sides fell wounded. <sup>18</sup>Then Judas fell, and the rest fled.

<sup>19</sup>Jonathan and Simon took their brother Judas and buried him in the tomb of their ancestors at Modein. <sup>20</sup>All Israel wept for him with great lamentation. They mourned for him many days, and they said, <sup>21</sup>"How the mighty one has fallen, the savior of Israel!"ʷ <sup>22</sup>The other acts of Judas, his battles, the brave deeds he performed, and his greatness have not been recorded; but they were very many.

## III. LEADERSHIP OF JONATHAN

**Jonathan Succeeds Judas.** <sup>23</sup>After the death of Judas, the lawless raised their heads in every part of Israel, and all kinds of evildoers appeared. <sup>24</sup>In those days there was a very great famine, and the country deserted to them. <sup>25</sup>Bacchides chose renegades and made them masters of the country. <sup>26</sup>These sought out and hunted down the friends of Judas and brought them to Bacchides, who punished and derided them. <sup>27</sup>There was great tribulation in Israel, the like of which had not been since the time prophets ceased to appear among them.

<sup>28</sup>Then all the friends of Judas came together and said to Jonathan: <sup>29</sup>"Ever since your brother Judas died, there has been no one like him to lead us against our enemies, both Bacchides and those of our nation who are hostile to us. <sup>30</sup>Now therefore we have chosen you today to be our ruler and leader in his place, to fight our battle." <sup>31</sup>From that moment Jonathan accepted the leadership, and took the place of Judas his brother.

---

*[9:2] **They took the road . . . Arbela, they captured it:** this passage is restored, in part, by conjectural emendation. The present Greek text could be translated, "They took the road to Gilgal, and camping opposite Mesaloth at Arbela, they captured it." But Arbela (modern Khirbet Irbid) was in Galilee, on a high hill overlooking the western shore of the Sea of Galilee. Gilgal, on the contrary, was in the Jordan valley near Jericho. "Mesaloth" is probably a corrupt form of a Hebrew word meaning "steps, ascent." It is possible, however, that all these terms referred to places in the Judean hills.

†[9:3] **The first month of the one hundred and fifty-second year:** April/May 160 B.C., by the Temple calendar.

‡[9:15] **As far as the mountain slopes:** conjectural emendation. The Greek text has "as far as Mount Azotus"; this is most unlikely. Apparently the Greek translator mistook the Hebrew word *ashdot*, "slopes," for *ashdod*, "Azotus."

w. [9:21] 2 Sm 1:19, 25, 27; Jgs 3:9.

**Bacchides Pursues Jonathan.** ³²When Bacchides learned of it, he sought to kill him. ³³But Jonathan and his brother Simon and all who were with him discovered this, and they fled to the wilderness of Tekoa* and camped by the waters of the pool of Asphar.[³⁴]†

³⁵Jonathan sent his brother‡ as leader of the convoy to implore his friends, the Nabateans, to let them deposit with them their great quantity of baggage.ˣ ³⁶But the tribe of Jambri from Medaba§ made a raid and seized and carried off John and everything he had.

³⁷After this, word was brought to Jonathan and his brother Simon: "The tribe of Jambri are celebrating a great wedding, and with a large escort they are bringing the bride, the daughter of one of the great princes of Canaan, from Nadabath." ³⁸Remembering the blood of John their brother, they went up and hid themselves under cover of the mountain. ³⁹As they watched there appeared a noisy throng with much baggage; then the bridegroom and his friends and kinsmen came out to meet them with tambourines and musicians with their instruments. ⁴⁰Jonathan and his party rose up against them from their ambush and killed them. Many fell wounded; the rest fled toward the mountain; all their spoils were taken. ⁴¹Thus the wedding was turned into mourning, and the sound of their music into lamentation. ⁴²Having taken their revenge for the blood of their brother, they returned to the marshes of the Jordan.

⁴³When Bacchides heard of it, he came on the sabbath to the banks of the Jordan with a large force. ⁴⁴Then Jonathan said to his companions, "Let us rise up now and fight for our lives, for today is not like yesterday and the day before. ⁴⁵The battle is before us, behind us are the waters of the Jordan, on either side of us, marsh and thickets; there is no way of escape.¶ ⁴⁶Cry out now to Heaven so that you may be delivered from the hand of our enemies." ⁴⁷When they joined battle, Jonathan raised his hand to strike Bacchides, but Bacchides backed away from him. ⁴⁸Jonathan and those with him jumped into the Jordan and swam across to the other side, but the enemy did not pursue them across the Jordan. ⁴⁹About a thousand men on Bacchides' side fell that day.

⁵⁰On returning to Jerusalem, Bacchides built strongholds in Judea: the Jericho fortress, as well as Emmaus, Beth-horon, Bethel, Timnath, Pharathon, and Tephon, with high walls and gates and bars." ⁵¹In each he put a garrison to harass Israel. ⁵²He fortified the city of Beth-zur, Gazara and the citadel, and put troops in them and stores of provisions. ⁵³He took as hostages the sons of the leading people of the country and put them in custody in the citadel at Jerusalem.ʸ

⁵⁴In the one hundred and fifty-third year, in the second month,†† Alcimus ordered the wall of the inner court of the sanctuary to be torn down, thus destroying the work of the prophets. But he only began to tear it down. ⁵⁵Just at that time Alcimus was stricken, and his work was interrupted; his mouth was closed and he was paralyzed, so that he could no longer utter a word or give orders concerning his household. ⁵⁶Alcimus died in great agony at that time. ⁵⁷Seeing that Alcimus was dead, Bacchides returned to the king, and the land of Judah was at rest for two years.

⁵⁸Then all the lawless took counsel and said: "Jonathan and those with him are living in peace and security. Now then, let us have Bacchides return, and he will capture all of them in a single night." ⁵⁹So they went and took counsel with him. ⁶⁰When Bacchides was setting out with a large force, he sent letters secretly to all his allies in Judea, telling them to seize Jonathan and his companions. They were not able to do this, however, because their plan became known. ⁶¹In fact, Jonathan's men seized about fifty of the men of the country who were leaders in the conspiracy and put them to death.

⁶²Then Jonathan and those with him, along with Simon, withdrew to Bethbasi‡‡ in the wilderness; he rebuilt its ruins and fortified it. ⁶³When Bacchides learned of this, he gathered together his whole force and sent word to those who were in Judea. ⁶⁴He came and camped before Bethbasi, and constructing siege engines, he fought against it for many days.

⁶⁵Leaving his brother Simon in the city, Jonathan, accompanied by a small group of men, went out into the countryside. ⁶⁶He struck down Odomera and his kindred and the tribe of Phasiron in their encampment; these men had begun to attack and they were going up with their forces. ⁶⁷Simon and those with him then sallied forth from the city and set fire to the siege engines. ⁶⁸They fought against Bacchides, and he was crushed. They caused him great distress, because the enterprise he had planned was in vain. ⁶⁹He was enraged with the lawless men who had advised him to invade the province. He

---

*[9:33] **Tekoa**: home of the prophet Amos in the wild country above the Dead Sea, southeast of Jerusalem.

†[9:34] Omitted, it is a dittography of v. 43.

‡[9:35] **Jonathan sent his brother**: this was John who was called Gaddi (2:2; cf. 9:36, 38).

§[9:36] **Medaba**: northeast of the Dead Sea.

¶[9:45] Jonathan's force may have been trapped in one of the many oxbows of the lower Jordan. Bacchides had crossed and caught them still on the east bank.

x. [9:35] 1 Mc 5:25.

**[9:50] These sites constitute a ring on the edges of the province of Judea.

††[9:54] **In the one hundred and fifty-third year, in the second month**: May, 159 B.C. **The work of the prophets**: probably Haggai and Zechariah, who were instrumental in building the Second Temple after the Babylonian exile; cf. Hg 1:12–14; Zec 4:8–10; Ezr 5:1–2.

‡‡[9:62] **Bethbasi**: two miles east of Bethlehem and six miles north of Tekoa.

y. [9:53] 1 Mc 10:9.

killed many of them and resolved to return to his own country.

⁷⁰Jonathan learned of this and sent ambassadors to agree on peace with him and to obtain the release of the prisoners. ⁷¹He agreed to do as Jonathan asked. He swore an oath to him that he would never try to do him any harm for the rest of his life; ⁷²and he released to him the prisoners he had previously taken from the land of Judah. Thereupon he returned to his own land and never came into their territory again. ⁷³Then the sword ceased from Israel. Jonathan settled in Michmash;ᵃ he began to judge the people and he eliminated the renegades from Israel.

## CHAPTER 10

**Jonathan Becomes High Priest.** ¹In the one hundred and sixtieth year,† Alexander Epiphanes, son of Antiochus, came up and took Ptolemais. They accepted him as king and he began to reign there. ²When King Demetrius heard of it, he mustered a very large army and marched out to engage him in battle. ³Demetrius sent a letter to Jonathan written in peaceful terms, to exalt him; ⁴for he said: "Let us be the first to make peace with him, before he makes peace with Alexander against us, ⁵since he will remember all the wrongs we have done to him, his brothers, and his nation."

⁶So Demetrius authorized him to gather an army and procure arms as his ally; and he ordered that the hostages in the citadel be released to him. ⁷Accordingly Jonathan went to Jerusalem and read the letter to all the people and to those who were in the citadel. ⁸They were struck with fear when they heard that the king had given him authority to gather an army. ⁹Those in the citadel released the hostages to Jonathan, and he gave them back to their parents.ᶻ ¹⁰Thereafter Jonathan dwelt in Jerusalem, and began to build and restore the city. ¹¹He ordered those doing the work to build the walls and to encircle Mount Zion with square stones for its fortification, and they did so. ¹²The foreigners in the strongholds that Bacchides had built took flight; ¹³all of them left their places and returned to their own lands. ¹⁴Only in Beth-zur did some remain of those who had abandoned the law and the commandments, for it was a place of refuge.

¹⁵King Alexander heard of the promises that Demetrius had made to Jonathan; he was also told of the battles and brave deeds of Jonathan and his brothers and of the troubles that they had endured. ¹⁶He said, "Shall we ever find another man like him? Let us now make him our friend and ally." ¹⁷So he sent Jonathan a letter written in these terms: ¹⁸"King Alexander sends greetings to his brother Jonathan. ¹⁹We have heard of you, that you are a mighty warrior and worthy to be our friend. ²⁰We have therefore appointed you today to be high priest of your nation; you are to be called the King's Friend, and you are to look after our interests and preserve friendship with us." He also sent him a purple robe and a crown of gold.ᵃ ²¹Jonathan put on the sacred vestments in the seventh month of the one hundred and sixtieth year at the feast of Booths,‡ and he gathered an army and procured many weapons.

**A Letter from Demetrius to Jonathan.** ²²When Demetrius heard of these things, he was distressed and said: ²³"Why have we allowed Alexander to get ahead of us by gaining the friendship of the Jews and thus strengthening himself? ²⁴I too will write them encouraging words and offer honors and gifts, so that they may support me." ²⁵So he sent them this message: "King Demetrius sends greetings to the Jewish nation. ²⁶We have heard how you have kept the treaty with us and continued in our friendship and not gone over to our enemies, and we are glad. ²⁷Continue, therefore, to keep faith with us, and we will reward you with favors in return for what you do in our behalf. ²⁸We will grant you many exemptions and will bestow gifts on you.

²⁹"I now free you and exempt all the Jews from the tribute, the salt tax, and the crown levies. ³⁰Instead of collecting the third of the grain and the half of the fruit of the trees that should be my share, I renounce the right from this day forward. Neither now nor in the future will I collect them from the land of Judah or from the three districts annexed from Samaria.§ ³¹Let Jerusalem and her territory, her tithes and her tolls, be sacred and free from tax. ³²I also yield my authority over the citadel in Jerusalem, and I transfer it to the high priest, that he may put in it such men as he shall choose to guard it. ³³Every Jew who has been carried into captivity from the land of Judah into any part of my kingdom I set

---

*[9:73] **Michmash**, southeast of Bethel, famous for the exploits of Jonathan, son of Saul; see 1 Sm 14. It was Jonathan's base from 157 to 152 B.C. **Began to judge**: exercise the governing authority as in the Book of Judges. With Jerusalem and the garrison towns (v. 50) firmly in Seleucid hands, Jonathan's freedom of action was greatly restricted.

†[10:1] **The one hundred and sixtieth year**: 152 B.C. **Alexander . . . Antiochus**: Alexander Balas claimed to be a son of Antiochus IV. He had the backing of the Romans, who had never forgiven Demetrius for becoming king without their permission. The latter meanwhile had become unpopular with his own people as well as with the Jews.

‡[10:21] **Jonathan . . . feast of Booths**: Jonathan began to discharge the office of high priest in October 152 B.C. For seven years after the death of Alcimus there had been no high priest in Jerusalem. It was taken for granted that the king, though a Gentile, had the power to appoint one (2 Mc 4:7, 23–24). The Maccabees, though a priestly family (1 Mc 2:1), were not of the line of Zadok, and some in Israel (perhaps the Qumran community) regarded Jonathan's tenure as a usurpation.

§[10:30] **The three districts annexed from Samaria**: mentioned by name in 11:34. The present Greek text, by a scribal error, has added "and Galilee" after "Samaria."

z. [10:9] 1 Mc 9:53.          a. [10:20] 1 Mc 2:18.    b. [10:29–30] 1 Mc 11:28, 34.

at liberty without ransom; and let all their taxes, even those on their cattle, be canceled.

³⁴Let all feast days, sabbaths, new moon festivals, appointed days, and the three days that precede each feast day, and the three days that follow, be days of immunity and exemption for all Jews in my kingdom. ³⁵No one will have authority to exact payment from them or to harass any of them in any matter.

³⁶"Let thirty thousand Jews be enrolled in the king's army and allowances be given them, as is due to all the king's soldiers. ³⁷Let some of them be stationed in the king's principal strongholds, and of these let some be given positions of trust in the affairs of the kingdom. Let their superiors and their rulers be chosen from among them, and let them follow their own laws, as the king has commanded in the land of Judah.

³⁸"Let the three districts that have been added to Judea from the province of Samaria be annexed to Judea so that they may be under one rule and obey no other authority than the high priest. ³⁹Ptolemais and its confines I give as a present to the sanctuary in Jerusalem for the necessary expenses of the sanctuary. ⁴⁰I make a yearly personal grant of fifteen thousand silver shekels out of the royal revenues, taken from appropriate places. ⁴¹All the additional funds that the officials did not hand over as they had done in the first years shall henceforth be handed over for the services of the temple. ⁴²Moreover, the dues of five thousand silver shekels that used to be taken from the revenue of the sanctuary every year shall be canceled, since these funds belong to the priests who perform the services. ⁴³All who take refuge in the temple of Jerusalem or in any of its precincts, because of money they owe the king, or because of any other debt, shall be released, together with all the goods they possess in my kingdom. ⁴⁴The cost of rebuilding and restoring the structures of the sanctuary shall be covered out of the royal revenue. ⁴⁵Likewise the cost of building the walls of Jerusalem and fortifying it all around, and of building walls in Judea, shall be donated from the royal revenue."

⁴⁶When Jonathan and the people heard these words, they neither believed nor accepted them, for they remembered the great evil that Demetrius had done in Israel, and the great tribulation he had brought upon them. ⁴⁷They therefore decided in favor of Alexander, for he had been the first to address them peaceably, and they remained his allies for the rest of his life.

⁴⁸Then King Alexander gathered together a large army and encamped opposite Demetrius. ⁴⁹The two kings joined battle, and when the army of Demetrius fled, Alexander pursued him, and overpowered his soldiers. ⁵⁰He pressed the battle hard until sunset, and Demetrius fell that day.

**Treaty of Ptolemy and Alexander.** ⁵¹Alexander sent ambassadors to Ptolemy, king of Egypt, with this message: ⁵²"Now that I have returned to my realm, taken my seat on the throne of my ancestors, and established my rule by crushing Demetrius and gaining control of my country— ⁵³for I engaged him in battle, he and his army were crushed by us, and we assumed his royal throne— ⁵⁴let us now establish friendship with each other. Give me now your daughter for my wife; and as your son-in-law, I will give to you and to her gifts worthy of you."

⁵⁵King Ptolemy answered in these words: "Happy the day on which you returned to the land of your ancestors and took your seat on their royal throne! ⁵⁶I will do for you what you have written; but meet me in Ptolemais, so that we may see each other, and I will become your father-in-law as you have proposed."

⁵⁷So Ptolemy with his daughter Cleopatra* set out from Egypt and came to Ptolemais in the one hundred and sixty-second year. ⁵⁸There King Alexander met him, and Ptolemy gave him his daughter Cleopatra in marriage. Their wedding was celebrated at Ptolemais with great splendor according to the custom of kings.

⁵⁹King Alexander also wrote to Jonathan to come and meet him. ⁶⁰So he went with pomp to Ptolemais, where he met the two kings and gave them and their friends silver and gold and many gifts and thus won their favor.ᶜ ⁶¹Some villainous men of Israel, transgressors of the law, united against him to accuse him, but the king paid no heed to them. ⁶²The king ordered Jonathan to be divested of his garments and to be clothed in royal purple; and so it was done. ⁶³The king also had him seated at his side. He said to his magistrates: "Go with him to the center of the city and make a proclamation that no one is to bring charges against him on any grounds or be troublesome to him for any reason." ⁶⁴ᵈWhen his accusers saw the honor paid to him according to the king's proclamation, and him clothed in purple, they all fled. ⁶⁵And so the king honored him, enrolling him among his Chief Friends, and he made him governor and chief of the province. ⁶⁶So Jonathan returned in peace and happiness to Jerusalem.

**Jonathan Defeats Apollonius.** ⁶⁷In the one hundred and sixty-fifth year,† Demetrius, son of Demetrius, came from Crete to the land of his ancestors. ⁶⁸When King Alexander heard of it he was greatly troubled, and returned to Antioch.

---

*[10:57] **Cleopatra:** Cleopatra Thea, then about fifteen years old. She later married Demetrius II, and later still, his brother Antiochus VII. Ptolemais (Acco) on the coast of Palestine was a neutral site. **The one hundred and sixty-second year:** 151/150 B.C.

†[10:67] **The one hundred and sixty-fifth year:** 147 B.C. **Demetrius:** Demetrius II Nicator.

c. [10:60] 1 Mc 2:18.    d. [10:64–65] 1 Mc 2:18; 11:27.

⁶⁹Demetrius set Apollonius over Coelesyria.* Having gathered a large army, Apollonius encamped at Jamnia. From there he sent this message to Jonathan the high priest: ⁷⁰"You are the only one who resists us. I am laughed at and put to shame on your account. Why are you exercising authority against us in the mountains? ⁷¹If you have confidence in your forces, come down now to us in the plain, and let us test each other's strength there; for the forces of the cities are on my side. ⁷²Inquire and find out who I am and who the others are who are helping me. People are saying that you cannot make a stand against us because your ancestors were twice put to flight† in their own land. ⁷³Now you too will be unable to withstand our cavalry and such a force as this in the plain, where there is not a stone or a pebble or a place to flee."

⁷⁴When Jonathan heard the message of Apollonius, he was provoked. Choosing ten thousand men, he set out from Jerusalem, and Simon his brother joined him to help him. ⁷⁵He encamped near Joppa, but the people of the city shut him out because Apollonius had a garrison in Joppa. When they attacked it, ⁷⁶the people of the city became afraid and opened the gates, and so Jonathan took possession of Joppa.‡

⁷⁷When Apollonius heard of it, he drew up three thousand cavalry and a large force of infantry. He marched toward Azotus as though he were going on through, but at the same time he was advancing into the plain, because he had such a large number of cavalry to rely on. ⁷⁸Jonathan pursued him toward Azotus, and the armies engaged in battle. ⁷⁹Apollonius, however, had left a thousand cavalry in hiding behind them. ⁸⁰Jonathan discovered that there was an ambush behind him; his army was surrounded. From morning until evening they showered his troops with arrows. ⁸¹But his troops held their ground, as Jonathan had commanded, while the enemy's horses became tired out.

⁸²Then Simon brought forward his force, and engaged the phalanx in battle. Since the cavalry were exhausted, the phalanx was crushed by him and fled, ⁸³while the cavalry too were scattered over the plain. They fled to Azotus and entered Beth-dagon, the temple of their idol, to save themselves. ⁸⁴But Jonathan burned and plundered Azotus with its neighboring towns, and destroyed by fire both the temple of Dagon and those who had taken refuge in it.ᵉ ⁸⁵Those who fell by the sword, together with those who were burned alive, came to about eight thousand.

⁸⁶Then Jonathan left there and encamped at Askalon, and the people of that city came out to meet him with great pomp. ⁸⁷Jonathan and those with him then returned to Jerusalem, with much spoil. ⁸⁸When King Alexander heard of these events, he accorded new honors to Jonathan. ⁸⁹He sent him a gold buckle, such as is usually given to King's Kinsmen;§ he also gave him Ekron and all its territory as a possession.

## CHAPTER 11

### Alliance of Ptolemy and Demetrius II.
¹Then the king of Egypt gathered forces as numerous as the sands of the seashore, and many ships; and he sought by deceit to take Alexander's kingdom and add it to his own. ²He set out for Syria with peaceful words, and the people in the cities opened their gates to welcome him, as King Alexander had ordered them to do, since Ptolemy was his father-in-law. ³But when Ptolemy entered the cities, he stationed a garrison of troops in each one.

⁴As they neared Azotus, they showed him the temple of Dagon destroyed by fire, Azotus and its suburbs demolished, corpses lying about, and the charred bodies of those burned in the war, for they had heaped them up along his route.ᶠ ⁵They told the king what Jonathan had done in order to denigrate him; but the king said nothing. ⁶Jonathan met the king with pomp at Joppa, and they greeted each other and spent the night there. ⁷Jonathan accompanied the king as far as the river called Eleutherus¶ and then returned to Jerusalem.

⁸And so King Ptolemy took possession of the cities along the seacoast as far as Seleucia by the sea,** plotting evil schemes against Alexander all the while. ⁹He sent ambassadors to King Demetrius, saying: "Come, let us make a covenant with each other; I will give you my daughter whom Alexander has married, and you shall reign over your father's kingdom. ¹⁰I regret that I gave him my daughter, for he has sought to kill me."†† ¹¹He was criticizing Alexander, however, because he coveted his kingdom. ¹²After taking his daughter away, Ptolemy gave her to Demetrius and broke with Alexander; the enmity between them was now evident. ¹³Then Ptolemy entered Antioch and assumed the crown‡‡ of Asia; thus he set upon his head two crowns, that of Egypt and that of Asia.

---

*[10:69] **Coelesyria:** originally the region between the Lebanon and anti-Lebanon mountains, it came later to refer to Palestine also. **Jamnia:** on the coast, also known as Yavneh (5:58).

†[10:72] **Twice put to flight:** the reference is unclear.

‡[10:76] **Joppa:** about forty miles northwest of Jerusalem. For the first time the Maccabees took possession of a seaport, though nominally it was on behalf of King Alexander.

e. [10:84] 1 Mc 11:4; 1 Sm 5:2–5.

§[10:89] **Kinsmen:** a rank higher than Chief Friends.

¶[11:7] **Eleutherus:** two hundred miles north of Joppa, in the second century B.C. the northern limit of Coelesyria.

**[11:8] **Seleucia by the sea:** at the mouth of the Orontes, the port city of Antioch.

††[11:10] **I regret . . . to kill me:** according to Josephus, Ammonius, a friend of Alexander, had tried to assassinate Ptolemy, and the latter claimed that Alexander was the instigator, thus calumniating him to gain his kingdom (v. 11).

‡‡[11:13] **Crown:** lit., diadem.

f. [11:4] 1 Mc 10:84.

¹⁴Now King Alexander was in Cilicia at that time, because the people of that region had revolted. ¹⁵When Alexander heard the news, he came against Ptolemy in battle. Ptolemy marched out and met him with a strong force and routed him. ¹⁶When Alexander fled to Arabia to seek protection, King Ptolemy was triumphant. ¹⁷Zabdiel the Arabian cut off Alexander's head and sent it to Ptolemy. ¹⁸But three days later King Ptolemy himself died, and his troops in the strongholds were killed by the inhabitants of the strongholds. ¹⁹Thus Demetrius became king in the one hundred and sixty-seventh year.*

**Alliance of Jonathan and Demetrius II.** ²⁰In those days Jonathan gathered together the people of Judea to attack the citadel in Jerusalem, and they set up many siege engines against it. ²¹But some transgressors of the law, enemies of their own nation, went to the king and informed him that Jonathan was besieging the citadel. ²²When Demetrius heard this, he was enraged; and as soon as he heard it, he set out and came to Ptolemais. He wrote to Jonathan to discontinue the siege and to meet him for a conference at Ptolemais as soon as possible.

²³On hearing this, Jonathan ordered the siege to continue. He selected some elders and priests of Israel and put himself at risk. ²⁴Taking with him silver, gold and apparel, and many other presents, he went to the king at Ptolemais, and found favor with him. ²⁵Although certain renegades of his own nation kept on bringing charges against him, ²⁶the king treated him just as his predecessors had done and exalted him in the presence of all his Friends. ²⁷He confirmed him in the high priesthood and in the other honors he had previously held, and had him enrolled among his Chief Friends.

²⁸Jonathan asked the king to exempt Judea and the three districts of Samaria from tribute, promising him in return three hundred talents.ᵍ ²⁹The king agreed and wrote a letter to Jonathan about all these matters as follows:

³⁰ʰ"King Demetrius sends greetings to his brother† Jonathan and to the Jewish nation. ³¹We are sending you, for your information, a copy of the letter that we wrote to Lasthenes‡ our Kinsman concerning you. ³²King Demetrius sends greetings to his father Lasthenes. ³³Upon the Jewish nation, who are our friends and observe their obligations to us, we have decided to bestow benefits because of the good will they show us. ³⁴Therefore we confirm their possession, not only of the territory of Judea, but also of the three districts of Aphairema,§ Lydda, and Ramathaim. These districts, together with all their dependencies, are hereby transferred from Samaria to Judea for those who offer sacrifices in Jerusalem in lieu of the royal taxes the king used to receive yearly from the produce of earth and trees. ³⁵From payment of the other things that would henceforth be due to us, namely, the tithes and taxes, as well as the salt tax, and the crown tax—from all these we grant them release. ³⁶Henceforth and forever not one of these provisions shall ever be revoked. ³⁷See to it, therefore, that a copy of these instructions be made and given to Jonathan. Let it be displayed on the holy mountain in a conspicuous place.'"

**The Intrigue of Trypho.** ³⁸When King Demetrius saw that the land was peaceful under his rule and that he had no opposition, he dismissed his entire army, each to his own home, except the foreign troops which he had hired from the islands of the nations. So all the soldiers who had served under his predecessors became hostile to him. ³⁹When a certain Trypho, who had previously supported Alexander, saw that all the troops were grumbling against Demetrius, he went to Imalkue the Arabian, who was raising Alexander's young son Antiochus.ʲ ⁴⁰Trypho kept urging Imalkue to hand over the boy to him, so that he might succeed his father as king. He told him of all that Demetrius had done and of the hostility his soldiers had for him; and he remained there for many days.

**Jonathan Aids Demetrius II.** ⁴¹Meanwhile Jonathan sent the request to King Demetrius to withdraw the troops in the citadel from Jerusalem and from the other strongholds, for they were constantly waging war on Israel. ⁴²Demetrius, in turn, sent this word to Jonathan: "I will do not only this for you and your nation, but I will greatly honor you and your nation when I find the opportunity. ⁴³Now, therefore, you will do well to send men to fight for me, because all my troops have revolted."

⁴⁴So Jonathan sent three thousand good fighting men to him at Antioch. When they came to the king, he was delighted over their arrival. ⁴⁵The populace, one hundred and twenty thousand strong, massed in the center of the city in an attempt to kill the king. ⁴⁶So the king took refuge in the palace, while the populace gained control of the main streets of the city and prepared for battle. ⁴⁷Then the king called the

---

*[11:19] **The one hundred and sixty-seventh year:** 146/145 B.C. The two deaths (vv. 17–18) occurred in the summer of 145 B.C.

†[11:30] **Brother:** this term and "father" in v. 32 are honorific expressions used of the Kinsmen.

‡[11:31] **Lasthenes:** leader of the mercenary troops who had come with Demetrius from Crete. He was now the young king's chief minister and was apparently responsible for the disastrous policy (v. 38) of disbanding the national army.

§[11:34] **Aphairema:** the Ophrah of Jos 18:23; 1 Sm 13:17; the Ephron of 2 Chr 13:19; and the Ephraim of Jn 11:54—modern et-Taiyibeh, five miles northeast of Bethel. **Lydda:** the Lod of the postexilic Jews (Ezr 2:33; Neh 11:35) and the hometown of Aeneas, who was cured by Peter (Acts 9:32–34). It is ten miles southeast of Joppa. **Ramathaim:** the Ramathaim-zophim of 1 Sm 1:1, and the Arimathea of Mt 27:57, modern Rentis, nine miles northeast of Lydda.

g. [11:28] 1 Mc 10:29; 11:34–35. h. [11:30–37] 1 Mc 10:25–45. i. [11:34–35] 1 Mc 10:29; 11:28.

j. [11:39] 1 Mc 12:39.

Jewish force to his aid. They all rallied around him and spread out through the city. On that day they killed about a hundred thousand in the city. ⁴⁸At the same time, they set the city on fire and took much spoil. Thus they saved the king. ⁴⁹When the populace saw that the Jewish force controlled the city, they lost courage and cried out to the king in supplication, ⁵⁰"Extend the hand of friendship to us, and make the Jews stop attacking us and the city." ⁵¹So they threw down their weapons and made peace. The Jews thus gained honor in the eyes of the king and all his subjects, and they became renowned throughout his kingdom. Finally they returned to Jerusalem with much plunder.

⁵²But when King Demetrius was sure of his royal throne, and the land was peaceful under his rule, ⁵³he broke all his promises and became estranged from Jonathan. Instead of repaying Jonathan for all the favors he had received from him, he caused him much distress.

**Alliance of Jonathan and Antiochus VI.** ⁵⁴After this, Trypho returned and brought with him the young boy Antiochus, who became king and put on the diadem.ᵏ ⁵⁵All the soldiers whom Demetrius had discharged rallied around Antiochus and fought against Demetrius, who was routed and fled. ⁵⁶Trypho captured the elephants and occupied Antioch. ⁵⁷Then young Antiochus wrote to Jonathan: "I confirm you in the high priesthood and appoint you ruler over the four districts, and to be one of the King's Friends." ⁵⁸He also sent him gold dishes and a table service, gave him the right to drink from gold cups, to dress in royal purple, and to wear a gold buckle.ˡ ⁵⁹Likewise, he made Jonathan's brother Simon governor of the region from the Ladder of Tyre* to the borders of Egypt.

**Campaigns of Jonathan and Simon.** ⁶⁰Jonathan set out and traveled through the province of West-of-Euphrates† and its cities, and all the forces of Syria espoused his cause as allies. When he arrived at Askalon, the citizens welcomed him with pomp. ⁶¹But when he set out for Gaza, the people of Gaza shut him out. So he besieged it, and burned and plundered its suburbs. ⁶²Then the people of Gaza appealed to Jonathan, and he granted them terms of peace. He took the sons of their leaders as hostages and sent them to Jerusalem. He then traveled on through the province as far as Damascus.

⁶³Jonathan heard that the generals of Demetrius had come with a strong force to Kadesh in Galilee, intending to remove him from office. ⁶⁴So he went to meet them, leaving his brother

Simon in the province. ⁶⁵ᵐSimon encamped against Beth-zur, attacked it for many days, and shut in the inhabitants. ⁶⁶They appealed to him, and he granted them terms of peace. He expelled them from the city, took possession of it, and put a garrison there.

⁶⁷Meanwhile, Jonathan and his army pitched their camp near the waters of Gennesaret, and at daybreak they went to the plain of Hazor.‡ ⁶⁸There the army of the foreigners met him on the plain. Having first detached an ambush in the mountains, this army mounted a frontal attack. ⁶⁹Then those in ambush rose out of their places and joined in the battle. ⁷⁰All of Jonathan's men fled; no one stayed except the army commanders Mattathias, son of Absalom, and Judas, son of Chalphi. ⁷¹Jonathan tore his clothes, threw dust on his head, and prayed. ⁷²Then he went back to the battle and routed them, and they fled. ⁷³Those of his men who were running away saw it and returned to him; and with him they pursued the enemy as far as their camp in Kadesh, and there they encamped. ⁷⁴About three thousand of the foreign troops fell on that day. Then Jonathan returned to Jerusalem.

## CHAPTER 12

**Alliances with Rome and Sparta.** ¹When Jonathan saw that the time was right, he chose men and sent them to Rome to confirm and renew the friendship with the Romans.ⁿ ²He also sent letters to the Spartans and other places to the same effect.

³After reaching Rome, the men entered the senate chamber and said, "The high priest Jonathan and the Jewish people have sent us to renew the friendship and alliance of earlier times with them." ⁴The Romans gave them letters addressed to authorities in various places, with the request to provide them with safe conduct to the land of Judah.

⁵This is a copy of the letter that Jonathan wrote to the Spartans: ⁶"Jonathan the high priest, the senate of the nation, the priests, and the rest of the Jewish people send greetings to their brothers the Spartans. ⁷Long ago a letter was sent§ to the high priest Onias from Arius, who then reigned over you, stating that you are our brothers, as the attached copy shows.ᵒ ⁸Onias welcomed the envoy with honor and received the letter, which spoke clearly of alliance and friendship. ⁹Though we have no need of these things, since we have for our encouragement the holy books that are in our possession,¶ᵖ ¹⁰we have ventured to send word to

---

*[11:59] **Ladder of Tyre**: modern Ras en-Naqurah, where the mountains reach the sea, so that the coastal road must ascend in a series of steps. Thus the Maccabees controlled the coastal area from Syria to Egypt.

†[11:60] **The province of West-of-Euphrates**: refers here to the territory of Palestine and Coelesyria, but not Upper Syria; cf. 7:8.

‡[11:67] **Plain of Hazor**: the site of the ancient Canaanite city (Jos 11:10), ten miles north of the Lake of Gennesaret.

§[12:7] **Long ago a letter was sent**: i.e., a century and a half before. **Onias**: Onias I, high priest from 323 to 300 or 290 B.C. **Arius**: Arius I, king from 309 to 265 B.C.

¶[12:9] **The holy books . . . in our possession**: a reference to "the law, the prophets and other books," as mentioned in the Prologue to Sirach.

k. [11:54] 1 Mc 11:39; 12:39.   l. [11:58] 1 Mc 2:18.

m. [11:65–66] 1 Mc 9:52; 10:14.   n. [12:1] 1 Mc 8:17.   o. [12:7] 1 Mc 12:20–23.   p. [12:9] 2 Mc 2:14.

you for the renewal of brotherhood and friendship, lest we become strangers to you; a long time has passed since you sent your message to us. ¹¹We, on our part, have unceasingly remembered you in the sacrifices and prayers that we offer on our feasts and other appropriate days, as it is right and proper to remember brothers. ¹²We likewise rejoice in your renown. ¹³But many tribulations and many wars have beset us, and the kings around us have attacked us. ¹⁴We did not wish to be troublesome to you and to the rest of our allies and friends in these wars. ¹⁵For we have the help of Heaven for our support, and we have been saved from our enemies, and our enemies have been humbled. ¹⁶So we have chosen Numenius, son of Antiochus, and Antipater, son of Jason, and we have sent them to the Romans to renew with them the friendship and alliance of earlier times.�q ¹⁷We have also ordered them to come to you and greet you, and to deliver to you our letter concerning the renewal of our brotherhood. ¹⁸Therefore kindly send us an answer on this matter."

¹⁹This is a copy of the letter that they sent to Onias: ²⁰"Arius, king of the Spartans, sends greetings to Onias the high priest. ²¹A document has been found stating that the Spartans and the Jews are brothers and that they are of the family of Abraham. ²²Now that we have learned this, kindly write to us about your welfare. ²³We, for our part, declare to you that your animals and your possessions are ours, and ours are yours. We have, therefore, given orders that you should be told of this."

**More Campaigns of Jonathan and Simon.** ²⁴Then Jonathan heard that the officers of Demetrius had returned to attack him with a stronger army than before. ²⁵So he set out from Jerusalem and met them in the territory of Hamath,* giving them no opportunity to enter his province. ²⁶The spies he had sent into their camp came back and reported to him that the enemy were preparing to attack them that night. ²⁷Therefore, when the sun set, Jonathan ordered his men to keep watch, with their weapons at the ready for battle, throughout the night; and he set outposts around the camp. ²⁸When the enemy heard that Jonathan and his men were ready for battle, their hearts sank with fear and dread. They lighted fires in their camp and then withdrew. ²⁹But because Jonathan and his men were watching the campfires burning, they did not know until the morning what had happened. ³⁰Then Jonathan pursued them, but he could not overtake them, for they had crossed the river Eleutherus. ³¹So Jonathan turned aside against the Arabians who are called Zabadeans, and he

struck them down and plundered them. ³²Then he broke camp, marched on toward Damascus and traveled through the whole region.

³³Simon also set out and traveled as far as Askalon and its neighboring strongholds. He then turned to Joppa and took it by surprise, ³⁴for he heard that its people intended to hand over the stronghold to the supporters of Demetrius. He left a garrison there to guard it.

³⁵When Jonathan returned, he assembled the elders of the people, and with them he made plans for building strongholds in Judea, ³⁶for making the walls of Jerusalem still higher, and for erecting a high barrier between the citadel and the city, to separate it from the city and isolate it, so that its garrison could neither buy nor sell. ³⁷The people therefore gathered together to build up the city, for part of the wall of the eastern valley had collapsed. And Jonathan repaired the quarter called Chaphenatha. ³⁸Simon likewise built up Adida in the Shephelah, and fortified it by installing gates and bars.

**Capture of Jonathan.** ³⁹Then Trypho sought to become king of Asia, assume the diadem, and do violence to King Antiochus.s ⁴⁰But he was afraid that Jonathan would not permit him, but would fight against him. Looking for a way to seize and kill him, he set out and came to Bethshan. ⁴¹Jonathan marched out to meet him with forty thousand picked fighting men and came to Beth-shan. ⁴²But when Trypho saw that Jonathan had arrived with a large army he was afraid to do him violence. ⁴³Instead, he received him with honor, introduced him to all his friends, and gave him presents. He also ordered his friends and soldiers to obey him as they would himself. ⁴⁴Then he said to Jonathan: "Why have you put all these people to so much trouble when we are not at war? ⁴⁵Now pick out a few men to stay with you, send the rest to their homes, and then come with me to Ptolemais. I will hand it over to you together with other strongholds and the remaining troops, as well as all the officials; then I will turn back and go home. That is why I came here."

⁴⁶Jonathan trusted him and did as he said. He dismissed his troops, and they returned to the land of Judah. ⁴⁷But he kept with him three thousand men, of whom he left two thousand in Galilee while one thousand accompanied him. ⁴⁸Then as soon as Jonathan entered Ptolemais, the people of Ptolemais closed the gates and seized him; all who had entered with him, they killed with the sword.t

⁴⁹Then Trypho sent soldiers and cavalry to Galilee and the Great Plain† to destroy all Jonathan's men. ⁵⁰These, upon learning that Jonathan had been captured and killed along with

---

\*[12:25] **Territory of Hamath:** the Seleucid territory of Upper Syria northeast of Coelesyria and separated from it by the Eleutherus River. The latter territory was under the command of Jonathan (11:59–60).

---

†[12:49] **The Great Plain:** of Beth-shan (v. 41), where Jonathan's disbanded troops remained.

q. [12:16] 1 Mc 14:22; 15:15.   r. [12:20–23] 1 Mc 12:7.            s. [12:39] 1 Mc 11:39–40, 54–55.   t. [12:48] 1 Mc 5:15, 22; 55.

his companions, encouraged one another and went out in close formation, ready to fight. ⁵¹As their pursuers saw that they were ready to fight for their lives, they turned back. ⁵²Thus all Jonathan's men came safely into the land of Judah. They mourned Jonathan and those who were with him. They were in great fear, and all Israel fell into deep mourning. ⁵³All the nations round about sought to crush them. They said, "Now that they have no leader or helper, let us make war on them and wipe out their memory from the earth."ᵘ

## IV. LEADERSHIP OF SIMON

### CHAPTER 13

**Simon as Leader.** ¹When Simon heard that Trypho was gathering a large army to invade and ravage the land of Judah, ²and saw that the people were trembling with terror, he went up to Jerusalem. There he assembled the people ³and exhorted them in these words: "You know what I, my brothers, and my father's house have done for the laws and the sanctuary; what battles and hardships we have seen. ⁴For the sake of this, for the sake of Israel, all my brothers have perished, and I alone am left. ⁵Far be it from me, then, to save my own life in any time of distress, for I am not better than my brothers. ⁶But I will avenge my nation and the sanctuary, as well as your wives and children, for out of hatred all the Gentiles have united to crush us."ᵛ

⁷As the people heard these words, their spirit was rekindled. ⁸They shouted in reply: "You are our leader in place of your brothers Judas and Jonathan. ⁹Fight our battles, and we will do everything that you tell us." ¹⁰So Simon mustered all the men able to fight, and hastening to complete the walls of Jerusalem, fortified it on every side. ¹¹He sent Jonathan, son of Absalom, to Joppa with a strong force; Jonathan drove out the occupants and remained there.

**Trypho's Deceit.** ¹²Then Trypho moved from Ptolemais with a large army to invade the land of Judah, bringing Jonathan with him as a prisoner. ¹³Simon encamped at Adida, facing the plain. ¹⁴When Trypho learned that Simon had succeeded his brother Jonathan, and that he intended to fight him, he sent ambassadors to him with this message: ¹⁵"It was on account of the money your brother Jonathan owed the royal treasury in connection with the offices that he held, that we have detained him. ¹⁶Now send a hundred talents of silver, and two of his sons as hostages to guarantee that when he is set free he will not revolt against us, and we will release him."

¹⁷Simon knew that they were speaking deceitfully to him. Nevertheless, for fear of provoking much hostility among the people, he sent for the money and the boys, ¹⁸lest the people say "Jonathan perished because I would not send Trypho the money and the boys." ¹⁹So he sent the boys and the hundred talents; but Trypho broke his promise and would not release Jonathan.

²⁰Next Trypho moved to invade and ravage the country. His troops went around by the road that leads to Adora, but Simon and his army moved along opposite him everywhere he went. ²¹The people in the citadel kept sending emissaries to Trypho, pressing him to come to them by way of the wilderness, and to send them provisions. ²²Although Trypho got all his cavalry ready to go, there was a very heavy snowfall that night, and he could not go on account of the snow. So he left for Gilead. ²³When he was approaching Baskama,† he had Jonathan killed and buried him there. ²⁴Then Trypho returned to his own land.

**Jonathan's Tomb.** ²⁵Simon sent for the remains of his brother Jonathan, and buried him in Modein, the city of his ancestors. ²⁶All Israel bewailed him with solemn lamentation, mourning over him for many days. ²⁷Then Simon erected over the tomb of his father and his brothers a monument of stones, polished front and back, and raised high enough to be seen at a distance. ²⁸He set up seven pyramids facing one another for his father and his mother and his four brothers.ʷ ²⁹For the pyramids he devised a setting of massive columns, which he adorned with suits of armor as a perpetual memorial, and next to the armor carved ships, which could be seen by all who sailed the sea. ³⁰This tomb which he built at Modein is there to the present day.

**Alliance of Simon and Demetrius II.** ³¹Trypho dealt treacherously with the young King Antiochus. He killed him ³²and became king in his place, putting on the crown of Asia. Thus he brought much evil on the land.ˣ ³³Simon, for his part, built up the strongholds of Judea, fortifying them all around with high towers, thick walls, and gates with bars, and he stored up provisions in the strongholds. ³⁴Simon also chose men and sent them to King Demetrius to obtain for the land an exemption from taxation, since Trypho did nothing but plunder. ³⁵King Demetrius replied favorably and sent him the following letter:

³⁶"King Demetrius sends greetings to Simon, high priest and friend of kings, and to the elders and the Jewish people. ³⁷We have received the gold crown and the palm branch that you sent. We are ready to make a lasting peace with you and to write to our officials to grant you exemption.

---

* [13:20–21] The invaders made a wide flanking movement to invade Judea from the south (see 4:29; 6:31). Adora was a few miles southwest of Beth-zur. They would avoid Beth-zur itself and other strongholds of the Maccabees by following the way of the wilderness.

† [13:23] **Baskama**: perhaps northeast of the Sea of Galilee.

---

u. [12:53] 1 Mc 5:2; 13:6.    v. [13:6] 1 Mc 5:2; 12:53.    w. [13:28] 2 Sm 18:18.    x. [13:32] 1 Mc 8:6.

³⁸Whatever decrees we have made in your regard remain in force, and the strongholds that you have built you may keep. ³⁹We pardon any oversights and offenses committed up to now, as well as the crown tax that you owe. Any other tax that used to be collected in Jerusalem shall no longer be collected there. ⁴⁰Any of you qualified for enrollment in our service may be enrolled. Let there be peace between us."

⁴¹Thus in the one hundred and seventieth year,* the yoke of the Gentiles was removed from Israel, ⁴²and the people began to write in their records and contracts, "In the first year of Simon, great high priest, governor, and leader of the Jews."

**Simon Captures Gazara.** ⁴³ʸIn those days Simon besieged Gazara† and surrounded it with troops. He made a siege machine, brought it up against the city, and attacked and captured one of the towers. ⁴⁴Those in the siege machine leaped down into the city and a great tumult arose there. ⁴⁵Those in the city, together with their wives and children, went up on the wall, with their garments rent, and cried out in loud voices, begging Simon to grant them terms of peace. ⁴⁶They said, "Treat us not according to our evil deeds but according to your mercy." ⁴⁷So Simon came to terms with them and did not attack them. He expelled them from the city, however, and he purified the houses in which there were idols. Then he entered the city with hymns and songs of praise. ⁴⁸After removing from it everything that was impure, he settled there people who observed the law. He improved its fortifications and built himself a residence.

**Simon Captures the Citadel.** ⁴⁹The people in the citadel in Jerusalem were prevented from going out into the country and back to buy or sell; they suffered greatly from hunger, and many of them died of starvation. ⁵⁰They finally cried out to Simon, and he gave them terms of peace. He expelled them from the citadel and cleansed it of impurities. ⁵¹On the twenty-third day of the second month,‡ in the one hundred and seventy-first year, the Jews entered the citadel with shouts of praise, the waving of palm branches, the playing of harps and cymbals and lyres, and the singing of hymns and canticles, because a great enemy of Israel had been crushed.ᶻ ⁵²Simon decreed that this day should be celebrated every year with rejoicing. He also strengthened the fortifications of the temple mount alongside the citadel, and he and his people dwelt there. ⁵³Seeing that his son John§ was now a grown man,

Simon made him commander of all his soldiers, and he dwelt in Gazara.

## CHAPTER 14

**Capture of Demetrius II.** ¹In the one hundred and seventy-second year,¶ King Demetrius assembled his army and marched into Media to obtain help so that he could fight Trypho. ²When Arsaces,** king of Persia and Media, heard that Demetrius had entered his territory, he sent one of his generals to take him alive. ³The general went forth and attacked the army of Demetrius; he captured him and brought him to Arsaces, who put him under guard.

### Praise of Simon

⁴ The land was at rest all the days of Simon,
    who sought the good of his nation.
  His rule delighted his people
    and his glory all his days.ᵃ
⁵ As his crowning glory he took Joppa for a port
    and made it a gateway to the isles of the sea.ᵇ
⁶ He enlarged the borders of his nation
    and gained control of the country.
⁷ He took many prisoners of war
    and made himself master of Gazara,
      Beth-zur, and the citadel.
  He cleansed the citadel of its impurities;
    there was no one to withstand him.
⁸ The people cultivated their land in peace;
    the land yielded its produce,
    the trees of the field their fruit.ᶜ
⁹ Old men sat in the squares,
    all talking about the good times,
  while the young men put on the
      glorious raiment of war.ᵈ
¹⁰ He supplied the cities with food
    and equipped them with means of defense,
  till his glorious name reached the
      ends of the earth.
¹¹ He brought peace to the land,
    and Israel was filled with great joy.ᵉ
¹² Every one sat under his vine and fig tree,
    with no one to disturb them.ᶠ
¹³ No attacker was left in the land;
    the kings in those days were crushed.
¹⁴ He strengthened all the lowly among his people

---

*[13:41] **The one hundred and seventieth year:** March, 142, to April, 141 B.C., by the Temple calendar.

†[13:43] **Gazara:** ancient Gezer, a key position in the Shephelah, fortified by Bacchides in 160 B.C.; cf. 9:52.

‡[13:51] **The twenty-third day of the second month:** June 3, 141 B.C.

§[13:53] **John:** John Hyrcanus, who was to succeed his father as ruler and high priest; cf. 16:23–24.

¶[14:1] **The one hundred and seventy-second year:** 141/140 B.C. The expedition began most probably in the spring of 140.

**[14:2] **Arsaces:** Arsaces VI, also called Mithridates I, the Parthian king (171–138 B.C.). Parthians had overrun Persia and now held Babylonia, both of which had hitherto belonged to the Seleucid empire. The Greeks and Macedonians in these countries had appealed to Demetrius for help.

y. [13:43–48] 2 Mc 10:32–38.    z. [13:51] 1 Mc 1:36.

a. [14:4] 1 Mc 3:3–9.    b. [14:5] 1 Mc 12:33;13:11.    c. [14:8]Lv 26:3–4; Zec 8:12.    d. [14:9] Zec 8:4–5.    e. [14:11] Lv 26:6.    f. [14:12] Mi 4:4; Zec 3:10.

and was zealous for the law;
  he destroyed the lawless and the
  wicked.
¹⁵ The sanctuary he made splendid
  and multiplied its furnishings.

**Alliance with Rome and Sparta.** ¹⁶When people in Rome and even in Sparta heard that Jonathan had died, they were deeply grieved.* ¹⁷But when they heard that his brother Simon had become high priest in his place and was master of the territory and its cities, ¹⁸they sent him inscribed tablets of bronze to renew with him the friendship and alliance that they had established with his brothers Judas and Jonathan.ᵍ ¹⁹These were read before the assembly in Jerusalem.

²⁰This is a copy of the letter that the Spartans sent: "The rulers and the city of the Spartans send greetings to Simon the high priest, the elders, the priests, and the rest of the Jewish people, our brothers. ²¹The ambassadors sent to our people have informed us of your glory and renown, and we rejoiced at their coming. ²²In accordance with what they said we have recorded the following in the public decrees: Numenius, son of Antiochus, and Antipater, son of Jason, ambassadors of the Jews, have come to us to renew their friendship with us.ʰ ²³The people have resolved to receive these men with honor, and to deposit a copy of their words in the public archives, so that the people of Sparta may have a record of them. A copy of this decree has been made for Simon the high priest."

²⁴After this, Simon sent Numenius to Rome with a large gold shield weighing a thousand minas, to confirm the alliance with the Romans.
**Official Honors for Simon.** ²⁵When the people heard of these things, they said, "How shall we thank Simon and his sons? ²⁶He and his brothers and his father's house have stood firm and repulsed Israel's enemies, and so have established its freedom." So they made an inscription on bronze tablets, which they affixed to pillars on Mount Zion.

²⁷The following is a copy of the inscription: "On the eighteenth day of Elul,† in the one hundred and seventy-second year, that is, the third year under Simon the great high priest in Asaramel, ²⁸in a great assembly of priests, people, rulers of the nation, and elders of the region, the following proclamation was made to us:

²⁹"Since there have often been wars in our country, Simon, son of the priest Mattathias, descendant of Joarib, and his brothers have put themselves in danger and resisted the enemies

of their nation, so that their sanctuary and law might be maintained, and they have thus brought great glory to their nation. ³⁰Jonathan rallied the nation, became their high priest, and was gathered to his people. ³¹When their enemies sought to invade and ravage their country and to violate their sanctuary, ³²Simon rose up and fought for his nation, spending large sums of his own money to equip his nation's forces and give them their pay. ³³He fortified the cities of Judea, especially the border city of Beth-zur, formerly the site of the enemy's weaponry, and he stationed there a garrison of Jewish soldiers. ³⁴He also fortified Joppa by the sea and Gazara on the border of Azotus, a place previously occupied by the enemy; these cities he settled with Jews and furnished them with all that was necessary for their restoration. ³⁵When the people saw Simon's fidelity and the glory he planned to bring to his nation, they made him their leader and high priest because of all he had accomplished and the justice and fidelity he had shown his nation. In every way he sought to exalt his people.

³⁶"In his time and under his guidance they succeeded in driving the Gentiles out of their country and those in the City of David in Jerusalem, who had built for themselves a citadel from which they used to sally forth to defile the environs of the sanctuary and inflict grave injury on its purity. ³⁷In this citadel he stationed Jewish soldiers, and he strengthened its fortifications for the security of the land and the city, while he also built up the wall of Jerusalem to a greater height. ³⁸Consequently, King Demetrius confirmed him in the high priesthood, ³⁹made him one of his Friends, and conferred great honor on him.ⁱ ⁴⁰This was because he had heard that the Romans had addressed the Jews as friends, allies, and brothers, that they had received Simon's envoys with honor, ⁴¹and that the Jewish people and their priests had decided the following: Simon shall be their leader and high priest forever until a trustworthy prophet arises.ʲ ⁴²He shall act as governor over them, and shall have charge of the sanctuary, to make regulations concerning its functions and concerning the country, its weapons and strongholds. ⁴³He shall be obeyed by all. All contracts in the country shall be written in his name, and he shall be clothed in purple and gold.ᵏ ⁴⁴It shall not be lawful for any of the people or priests to nullify any of these decisions, or to contradict the orders given by him, or to convene an assembly in the country without his consent, to be clothed in purple or wear a gold buckle. ⁴⁵Whoever acts otherwise or violates any of these prescriptions shall be liable to punishment.

⁴⁶"Thus all the people approved of granting Simon the right to act in accord with these decisions, ⁴⁷and Simon accepted and agreed to

---

* [14:16] The embassy to Rome and Sparta was sent soon after Simon's accession to power, and the replies were received before Demetrius' expedition (vv. 1–3), probably in 142 B.C.

† [14:27] **Eighteenth day of Elul:** September 13, 140 B.C. **Asaramel:** perhaps a Hebrew name meaning "court of the people of God."

g. [14:18] 1 Mc 8:22.   h. [14:22] 1 Mc 12:16; 15:15.

i. [14:39] 1 Mc 2:18.   j. [14:41] 1 Mc 4:46; 9:27.   k. [14:43] 1 Mc 10:20, 89.

be high priest, governor, and ethnarch˙ of the Jewish people and priests, and to have authority over all.'"

⁴⁸It was decreed that this inscription should be engraved on bronze tablets, to be set up in a conspicuous place in the precincts of the sanctuary, ⁴⁹and that copies of it should be deposited in the treasury, where they would be available to Simon and his sons.

## CHAPTER 15
**Letter of Antiochus VII.** ¹Antiochus,† son of King Demetrius, sent a letter from the islands of the sea to Simon, the priest and ethnarch of the Jews, and to all the nation, ²which read as follows:

"King Antiochus sends greetings to Simon, the high priest and ethnarch, and to the Jewish nation. ³Whereas certain villains have gained control of the kingdom of our ancestors, I intend to reclaim it, that I may restore it to its former state. I have recruited a large number of mercenary troops and equipped warships. ⁴I intend to make a landing in the country so that I may take revenge on those who have ruined our country and laid waste many cities in my kingdom. ⁵Now, therefore, I confirm to you all the tax exemptions that the kings before me granted you and whatever other privileges they conceded to you. ⁶I authorize you to coin your own money, as legal tender in your country. ⁷Jerusalem and its sanctuary shall be free. All the weapons you have prepared and all the strongholds you have built and now occupy shall remain in your possession. ⁸All debts, present or future, due to the royal treasury shall be canceled for you, now and for all time. ⁹When we establish our kingdom, we will greatly honor you and your nation and the temple, so that your glory will be manifest in all the earth."

¹⁰In the one hundred and seventy-fourth year‡ Antiochus invaded the land of his ancestors, and all the troops rallied to him, so that few were left with Trypho. ¹¹Pursued by Antiochus, Trypho fled to Dor, by the sea,§ ¹²realizing what troubles had come upon him now that his soldiers had deserted him. ¹³Antiochus encamped before Dor with a hundred and twenty thousand infantry and eight thousand cavalry. ¹⁴While he surrounded the city, his ships closed from the sea, so that he pressed it hard by land and sea and let no one go in or out.

**Roman Alliance Renewed.** ¹⁵Meanwhile, Numenius and his companions came from Rome with letters containing this message to various kings and countries:ˡ ¹⁶"Lucius,¶ Consul of the Romans, sends greetings to King Ptolemy. ¹⁷Ambassadors of the Jews, our friends and allies, have come to us to renew their earlier friendship and alliance. They had been sent by Simon the high priest and the Jewish people, ¹⁸and they brought with them a gold shield of a thousand minas.ᵐ ¹⁹Therefore we have decided to write to various kings and countries, that they are not to venture to harm them, or wage war against them or their cities or their country, and are not to assist those who fight against them. ²⁰We have also decided to accept the shield from them. ²¹If, then, any troublemakers from their country take refuge with you, hand them over to Simon the high priest, so that he may punish them according to their law."

²²The consul sent identical letters to Kings Demetrius, Attalus,˙˙ Ariarthes and Arsaces; ²³to all the countries—Sampsames, the Spartans, Delos, Myndos, Sicyon, Caria, Samos, Pamphylia, Lycia, Halicarnassus, Rhodes, Phaselis, Cos, Side, Aradus, Gortyna, Cnidus, Cyprus, and Cyrene. ²⁴A copy of the letter was also sent to Simon the high priest.

**Hostility from Antiochus VII.** ²⁵When King Antiochus encamped before Dor, he assaulted it continuously both with troops and with the siege engines he had made. He blockaded Trypho by preventing anyone from going in or out. ²⁶Simon sent to Antiochus' support two thousand elite troops, together with silver and gold and much equipment. ²⁷But he refused to accept the aid; in fact, he broke all the agreements he had previously made with Simon and became hostile toward him.ⁿ

²⁸He sent Athenobius, one of his Friends, to confer with Simon and say: "You are occupying Joppa and Gazara and the citadel of Jerusalem; these are cities of my kingdom. ²⁹You have laid waste their territories, done great harm to the land, and taken possession of many districts in my kingdom. ³⁰Now, therefore, give up the cities you have seized and the tribute money of the districts you control outside the territory of Judea; ³¹or instead, pay me five hundred talents of silver for the devastation you have caused and five hundred talents more for the tribute money of the cities. If you do not do this, we will come and make war on you."

³²So Athenobius, the king's Friend, came to Jerusalem and on seeing the splendor of

---

*[14:47] **Ethnarch:** a subordinate ruler over an ethnic group whose office needed confirmation by a higher authority within the empire.

†[15:1] **Antiochus:** Antiochus VII Sidetes, son of Demetrius I, and younger brother of Demetrius II (now a prisoner of the Parthians). At the age of twenty he set out from the island of Rhodes to take his brother's place and drive out the usurper Trypho.

‡[15:10] **The one hundred and seventy-fourth year:** 138 B.C.

§[15:11] **Dor, by the sea:** a fortress on the Palestinian coast, fifteen miles south of Carmel.

¶[15:16] **Lucius:** perhaps Lucius Caecilius Metellus, consul in 142 B.C., or Lucius Calpurnicus Piso, consul in 140–139 B.C. This document pertains to Simon's first years as leader.

**[15:22] **Attalus:** Attalus II of Pergamum, reigned 159–138 B.C. **Ariarthes:** Ariarthes V of Cappadocia, reigned 162–130 B.C. **Arsaces:** see note on 14:2.

l. [15:15] 1 Mc 8:17; 12:16; 14:22, 24.   m. [15:18] 1 Mc 14:24.
n. [15:27] 1 Mc 15:5–9.

Simon's court, the gold and silver plate on the sideboard, and his rich display, he was amazed. When he gave him the king's message, ³³Simon said to him in reply: "It is not foreign land we have taken nor have we seized the property of others, but only our ancestral heritage which for a time had been unjustly held by our enemies. ³⁴Now that we have the opportunity, we are holding on to the heritage of our ancestors. ³⁵As for Joppa and Gazara, which you demand, those cities were doing great harm to our people and our country. For these we will give you a hundred talents." Athenobius made no reply, ³⁶but returned to the king in anger. When he told him of Simon's words, of his splendor, and of all he had seen, the king fell into a violent rage.

**Victory over Cendebeus.** ³⁷Trypho had boarded a ship and escaped to Orthosia.* ³⁸Then the king appointed Cendebeus commander-in-chief of the seacoast, and gave him infantry and cavalry forces. ³⁹He ordered him to encamp against Judea and to fortify Kedron† and strengthen its gates, so that he could wage war on the people. Meanwhile the king went in pursuit of Trypho. ⁴⁰When Cendebeus came to Jamnia, he began to harass the people and to make incursions into Judea, where he took people captive and massacred them. ⁴¹As the king ordered, he fortified Kedron and stationed cavalry and infantry there, so that they could go out and patrol the roads of Judea.

## CHAPTER 16

¹John then went up from Gazara and told his father Simon what Cendebeus was doing.° ²Simon called his two oldest sons, Judas and John, and said to them: "I and my brothers and my father's house have fought the wars of Israel from our youth until today, and many times we succeeded in saving Israel. ³I have now grown old, but you, by the mercy of Heaven, have come to maturity. Take my place and my brother's, and go out and fight for our nation; and may the help of Heaven be with you!"

⁴John then mustered in the land twenty thousand warriors and cavalry. Setting out against Cendebeus, they spent the night at Modein, ⁵rose early, and marched into the plain. There, facing them, was an immense army of foot soldiers and cavalry, and between the two armies was a wadi. ⁶John and his people took their position against the enemy. Seeing that his people were afraid to cross the wadi, John crossed first. When his men saw this, they crossed over after him.ᵖ ⁷Then he divided his infantry and put his cavalry in the center, for

the enemy's cavalry were very numerous. ⁸They blew the trumpets, and Cendebeus and his army were routed; many of them fell wounded, and the rest fled toward the stronghold. ⁹It was then that John's brother Judas fell wounded; but John pursued them until Cendebeus reached Kedron, which he had fortified. ¹⁰Some took refuge in the towers on the plain of Azotus, but John set fire to these, and about two thousand of the enemy perished. He then returned to Judea in peace.�q

**Murder of Simon and His Sons.** ¹¹Ptolemy, son of Abubus, had been appointed governor of the plain of Jericho, and he had much silver and gold, ¹²being the son-in-law of the high priest. ¹³But his heart became proud and he was determined to get control of the country. So he made treacherous plans to do away with Simon and his sons. ¹⁴As Simon was inspecting the cities of the country and providing for their needs, he and his sons Mattathias and Judas went down to Jericho in the one hundred and seventy-seventh year, in the eleventh month‡ (that is, the month Shebat). ¹⁵The son of Abubus gave them a deceitful welcome in the little stronghold called Dok§ which he had built. He served them a sumptuous banquet, but he had his men hidden there. ¹⁶Then, when Simon and his sons were drunk, Ptolemy and his men sprang up, weapons in hand, rushed upon Simon in the banquet hall, and killed him, his two sons, and some of his servants. ¹⁷By this vicious act of treachery he repaid good with evil.

¹⁸Then Ptolemy wrote a report and sent it to the king, asking him to send troops to help him and to turn over to him their country and its cities. ¹⁹He sent other men to Gazara to do away with John. To the army officers he sent letters inviting them to come to him so that he might present them with silver, gold, and gifts. ²⁰He also sent others to seize Jerusalem and the temple mount. ²¹But someone ran ahead and brought word to John at Gazara that his father and his brothers had perished, and "Ptolemy has sent men to kill you also." ²²On hearing this, John was utterly astounded. When the men came to kill him, he seized them and put them to death, for he knew that they sought to kill him.

²³¶Now the rest of the acts of John, his wars and the brave deeds he performed, his rebuilding of the walls, and all his achievements—ʳ ²⁴these are recorded in the chronicle of his high priesthood, from the time that he succeeded his father as high priest.

---

‡[16:14] **In the one hundred and seventy-seventh year, in the eleventh month**: January–February, 134 B.C., by the Temple calendar.

§[16:15] **Dok**: a fortress built on a cliff three miles northwest of Jericho, near modern Ain Duq.

¶[16:23–24] John Hyrcanus was ruler and high priest from 134 B.C. till his death in 104 B.C. These verses suggest that the book was written, or at least completed, only after he died.

---

*[15:37] **Orthosia**: a port between Tripoli and the Eleutherus River.

†[15:39] **Kedron**: a few miles southeast of Jamnia and facing the fortress of Gazara held by John Hyrcanus (13:53; 16:1).

---

o. [16:1] 1 Mc 13:53.    p. [16:6] 1 Mc 5:40–43.

q. [16:10] 1 Mc 10:84.    r. [16:23] 1 Mc 9:22.

# THE SECOND BOOK OF
# MACCABEES

～ᦉ～

Although this book, like the preceding one, receives its title from its protagonist, Judas Maccabee (or Maccabeus), it is not a sequel to 1 Maccabees. The two differ in many respects. Whereas the first covers the period from the beginning of the reign of Antiochus IV (175 B.C.) to the accession of John Hyrcanus I (134 B.C.), this book treats of the events in Jewish history from the time of the high priest Onias III and King Seleucus IV (ca. 180 B.C.) to the defeat of Nicanor's army (161 B.C.).

The author of 2 Maccabees states (2:23) that this one-volume work is an abridgment of a five-volume work by Jason of Cyrene; but since this latter has not survived, it is difficult to determine its relationship to the present epitome. One does not know how freely the anonymous epitomizer may have rewritten the original composition or how closely the abridgment follows the wording of the original. Some parts of the text here clearly not derived from Jason's work are the preface (2:19–32), the epilogue (15:37–39), and probably also certain moralizing reflections (e.g., 5:17–20; 6:12–17). It is certain, however, that both works were written in Greek, which explains in part why 2 Maccabees was not included in the canon of the Hebrew Bible.

The book is not without genuine historical value in supplementing 1 Maccabees, and it contains some apparently authentic official documents (11:16–38). Its purpose, whether intended by Jason himself or read into it by the compiler, is to give a theological interpretation to the history of the period. The major concern is the Jerusalem Temple, whose defender is the God of Israel. There is less interest, therefore, in the military exploits of Judas Maccabeus and more in God's marvelous interventions on behalf of the Jews and their Temple. These divine actions direct the course of events, both to punish the sacrilegious and blasphemous pagans and to purify and restore the Temple. The author sometimes effects this purpose by transferring events from their proper chronological order, by giving exaggerated figures for the size of armies and the numbers killed in battle, by placing long, edifying discourses and prayers in the mouths of heroes, and by describing elaborate celestial apparitions (3:24–34; 5:2–4; 10:29–30; 15:11–16). The book is the earliest known source of stories that glorify God's holy martyrs (6:18–7:42; 14:37–46).

Of theological importance are the author's teachings on Israel's sufferings (5:17–20; 6:12–17), the resurrection of the just on the last day (7:9, 11, 14, 23; 14:46), the intercession of the saints in heaven for people living on earth (15:11–16), and the power of the living to offer prayers and sacrifices for the dead (12:39–46).

The beginning of 2 Maccabees consists of two letters sent by the Jews of Jerusalem to their coreligionists in Egypt. They deal with the observance of the feast commemorating the central event of the book, the purification of the Temple (Hanukkah). It is uncertain whether the author or a later scribe prefixed these letters to the narrative proper. If the author is responsible for their insertion, the book must have been written some time after 124 B.C., the date of the more recent of the two letters. A date of composition in the late second century B.C. is likely.

The main divisions of 2 Maccabees are:

I. Letters to the Jews in Egypt (1:1–2:18)
II. Compiler's Preface (2:19–32)
III. Heliodorus' Attempt to Profane the Temple (3:1–40)
IV. Profanation and Persecution (4:1–7:42)
V. Victories of Judas and Purification of the Temple (8:1–10:9)
VI. Renewed Persecution (10:10–15:36)
VII. Epilogue (15:37–39)

# I. LETTERS TO THE JEWS IN EGYPT

## CHAPTER 1

**Letter 1: 124 B.C.** [1]The Jews in Jerusalem and in the land of Judea send greetings to their kindred, the Jews in Egypt, and wish them true peace! [2]May God do good to you and remember his covenant with his faithful servants, Abraham, Isaac and Jacob, [3]give to all of you a heart to worship him and to do his will wholeheartedly and with a willing spirit, [4]open your heart to his law and commandments and grant you peace, [5]hear your prayers, and be reconciled to you, and never forsake you in time of adversity. [6]Even now we are praying for you here.

[7]In the reign of Demetrius,* the one hundred and sixty-ninth year, we Jews wrote to you during the height of the distress that overtook us in those years after Jason and his followers revolted against the holy land and the kingdom,[a] [8]set fire to the gatehouse and shed innocent blood. But we prayed to the Lord, and our prayer was heard;† we offered sacrifices and fine flour; we lighted the lamps and set out the loaves of bread.[b] [9]We are now reminding you to celebrate the feast of Booths in the month of Kislev.‡ [10]Dated in the one hundred and eighty-eighth year.§

**Letter 2: 164 B.C.** The people of Jerusalem and Judea, the senate, and Judas send greetings and good wishes to Aristobulus, teacher of King Ptolemy and member of the family of the anointed priests, and to the Jews in Egypt. [11]Since we have been saved by God from grave dangers, we give him great thanks as befits those who fought against the king;¶ [12c]for it was God who drove out those who fought against the holy city. [13]When their leader arrived in Persia with his seemingly irresistible army, they were cut to pieces in the temple of the goddess Nanea** through a deceitful stratagem employed by Nanea's priests. [14††]On the pretext of marrying the goddess, Antiochus with his Friends had come to the place to get its great treasures as a dowry. [15]When the priests of Nanea's temple had displayed the treasures and Antiochus with a few attendants had come inside the wall of the temple precincts, the priests locked the temple as soon as he entered. [16]Then they opened a hidden trapdoor in the ceiling, and hurling stones at the leader and his companions, struck them down. They dismembered the bodies, cut off their heads and tossed them to the people outside. [17]Forever blessed be our God, who has thus punished the impious!

[18‡‡]Since we shall be celebrating the purification of the temple on the twenty-fifth day of the month Kislev,[d] we thought it right to inform you, that you too may celebrate the feast of Booths and of the fire that appeared when Nehemiah, the rebuilder of the temple§§ and the altar, offered sacrifices. [19]For when our ancestors were being led into captivity in Persia,¶¶ devout priests at the time took some of the fire from the altar and hid it secretly in the hollow of a dry cistern, making sure that the place would be unknown to anyone. [20]Many years later, when it so pleased God, Nehemiah, commissioned by the king of Persia, sent the descendants of the priests who had hidden the fire to look for it. [21]When they informed us that they could not find any fire, but only a thick liquid, he ordered them to scoop some out and bring it. After the material for the sacrifices had been prepared, Nehemiah ordered the priests to sprinkle the wood and what lay on it with the liquid. [22]This was done, and when at length the sun, which had been clouded over, began to shine, a great fire blazed up, so that everyone marveled. [23]While the sacrifice was being burned, the priests recited a prayer, and all present joined in with them. Jonathan led and the rest responded with Nehemiah.

[24]The prayer was as follows: "Lord, Lord God, creator of all things, awesome and strong, just and merciful, the only king and benefactor, [25]who alone are gracious, just, almighty, and eternal, Israel's savior from all evil, who chose our ancestors and sanctified them: [26]accept this sacrifice on behalf of all your people Israel and guard and sanctify your portion. [27]Gather together our

---

*[1:7] **Demetrius**: Demetrius II, king of Syria (145–139, 129–125 B.C.). **The one hundred and sixty-ninth year**: i.e., of the Seleucid era, 143 B.C. Regarding the dates in 1 and 2 Maccabees, see note on 1 Mc 1:10. On the troubles caused by Jason and his revolt against the kingdom, i.e., the rule of the legitimate high priest, see 2 Mc 4:7–22.

†[1:8] **Our prayer was heard**: in the victory of the Maccabees.

‡[1:9] **Feast of Booths in the month of Kislev**: really the feast of the Dedication of the Temple, Hanukkah (2 Mc 10:1–8), celebrated on the twenty-fifth of Kislev (Nov.–Dec.). Its solemnity resembles that of the actual feast of Booths (Lv 23:33–43), celebrated on the fifteenth of Tishri (Sept.–Oct.); cf. 2 Mc 1:18.

§[1:10] **The one hundred and eighty-eighth year**: 124 B.C. The date pertains to the preceding, not the following letter. **Senate**: the council of Jewish elders of Jerusalem; cf. 1 Mc 12:6. **King Ptolemy**: Ptolemy VI Philometor, ruler of Egypt from 180 to 145 B.C.; he is mentioned also in 1 Mc 1:18; 10:51–59.

¶[1:11–12] **The king**: Antiochus IV of Syria, the bitter persecutor of the Jews, who, as leader of the Syrian army that invaded Persia, perished there in 164 B.C.

**[1:13] **Nanea**: an oriental goddess comparable to Artemis of the Greeks.

††[1:14–17] Differing accounts of the death of Antiochus IV are found in 2 Mc 9:1–29 and in 1 Mc 6:1–16 (see also Dn 11:40–45). The writer of this letter had probably heard a distorted rumor of the king's death. This and other indications suggest that the letter was written very soon after Antiochus IV died, perhaps in 164 B.C.

‡‡[1:18–36] This legendary account of Nehemiah's miraculous fire is incorporated in the letter because of its connection with the Temple and its rededication. **Booths**: see note on v. 9.

§§[1:18] **Nehemiah, the rebuilder of the temple**: he rebuilt the walls of Jerusalem, but the Temple had been rebuilt by Zerubbabel almost a century before.

¶¶[1:19] **Persia**: actually Babylonia, which later became part of the Persian empire.

---

a. [1:7] 2 Mc 4:7–20.   b. [1:8] 1 Mc 4:50–51.   c. [1:12–17] 2 Mc 9:1–29; 1 Mc 6:1–13; Dn 11:40–45.

d. [1:18] 2 Mc 6:7; 10:5; 1 Mc 1:59; 4:59.

scattered people, free those who are slaves among the Gentiles, look kindly on those who are despised and detested, and let the Gentiles know that you are our God. [28]Punish those who lord it over us and in their arrogance oppress us. [29]Plant your people in your holy place, as Moses said."[e]

[30]Then the priests sang hymns. [31]After the sacrifice was consumed, Nehemiah ordered the rest of the liquid to be poured upon large stones. [32]As soon as this was done, a flame blazed up, but its light was lost in the brilliance coming from the altar. [33]When the event became known and the king of the Persians was told that, in the very place where the exiled priests had hidden the fire, a liquid was found with which Nehemiah and his people had burned the sacrifices, [34]the king, after verifying the fact, fenced the place off and declared it sacred. [35]To those whom the king favored, he distributed many benefits he received. [36]Nehemiah and his companions called the liquid nephthar, meaning purification, but most people named it naphtha.[*f]

## CHAPTER 2

[1]In the records it will be found that Jeremiah the prophet ordered the deportees to take some of the fire with them as indicated, [2]and that the prophet, in giving them the law, directed the deportees not to forget the commandments of the Lord or be led astray in their thoughts, when seeing the gold and silver idols and their adornments.[g] [3]With other similar words he exhorted them that the law should not depart from their hearts.

[4†]The same document also tells how the prophet, in virtue of an oracle, ordered that the tent and the ark should accompany him, and how he went to the very mountain that Moses climbed to behold God's inheritance.[h] [5]When Jeremiah arrived there, he found a chamber in a cave in which he put the tent, the ark, and the altar of incense; then he sealed the entrance. [6]Some of those who followed him came up intending to mark the path, but they could not find it. [7]When Jeremiah heard of this, he reproved them: "The place is to remain unknown until God gathers his people together again and shows them mercy. [8]Then the Lord will disclose these things, and the glory of the Lord and the cloud will be seen, just as they appeared in the time of Moses and of Solomon when he prayed that the place[‡] might be greatly sanctified."[i]

[9]It is also related how Solomon in his wisdom offered a sacrifice for the dedication and the completion of the temple. [10]Just as Moses prayed to the Lord and fire descended from the sky and consumed the sacrifices, so also Solomon prayed and fire came down and consumed the burnt offerings.[j] [11§]Moses had said, "Because it had not been eaten, the purification offering was consumed."[k] [12]Solomon also celebrated the feast in the same way for eight days.

[13]These same things are also told in the records and in Nehemiah's memoirs,[¶] as well as how he founded a library and collected the books about the kings and the prophets, the books of David, and the royal letters about votive offerings. [14]In like manner Judas also collected for us all the books that had been scattered because of the war, and we now have them in our possession.[l] [15]If you need them, send messengers to get them for you.

[16]As we are about to celebrate the purification, we are writing: you should celebrate the feast days. [17]It is God who has saved all his people and has restored to all of them their inheritance, the kingdom, the priesthood, and the sacred rites, [18]as he promised through the law. For we hope in God, that he will soon have mercy on us and gather us together from everywhere under the heavens to his holy place, for he has rescued us from great perils and has purified the place.[m]

## II. COMPILER'S PREFACE

[19]This is the story of Judas Maccabeus and his brothers, of the purification of the great temple, the dedication of the altar, [20]the campaigns against Antiochus Epiphanes and his son Eupator,[**] [21]and of the heavenly manifestations accorded to the heroes who fought bravely for the Jewish people. Few as they were, they plundered the whole land, put to flight the barbarian hordes, [22]regained possession of the temple renowned throughout the world, and liberated the city. They re-established the laws that were in danger of being abolished, while the Lord favored them with every kindness. [23]All this, detailed by Jason of Cyrene in five volumes, we will try to condense into a single book.

[24]For in view of the flood of data, and the difficulties encountered, given such abundant material, by those who wish to plunge into accounts of the history, [25]we have aimed to please those who prefer simply to read, to make it easy for the studious who wish to commit things to

---

*[1:36] By a play on words, the Greek term *naphtha* (petroleum) is assimilated to some Semitic word, perhaps *nephthar*, meaning "loosened."

†[2:4–5] This legendary account is given for the purpose of explaining why the postexilic Temple was the legitimate place of worship even without these sacred objects. **The very mountain:** Nebo; cf. Dt 32:49; 34:1.

‡[2:8] **The place:** the Temple of Jerusalem.

§[2:11] The statement attributed here to Moses seems to be based on Lv 10:16–20.

¶[2:13] **Nehemiah's memoirs:** a lost apocryphal work, or perhaps Neh 1–7, 11–13.

**[2:20] For the account of the campaigns against Antiochus IV Epiphanes, see 4:7–10:9; and for the account of those against his son Antiochus V Eupator, see 10:10–13:26.

---

e. [1:29] 2 Mc 2:18; Ex 15:17; Dt 30:3–5.  f. [1:36] 2 Mc 2:18; 10:3; 14:36.  g. [2:2] Bar 6:1–72.  h. [2:4] Dt 32:49; 34:1; Rev 11:19.  i. [2:8] Ex 40:34–35; 1 Kgs 8:11.

j. [2:10] Lv 9:23–24; 2 Chr 7:1.  k. [2:11] Lv 10:16–20.  l. [2:14] 1 Mc 1:57.  m. [2:18] Dt 30:3–5.

memory, and to be helpful to all. [26]For us who have undertaken the labor of making this digest, the task, far from being easy, is one of sweat and of sleepless nights. [27]Just so, the preparation of a festive banquet is no light matter for one who seeks to give enjoyment to others. Similarly, to win the gratitude of many we will gladly endure this labor, [28]leaving the responsibility for exact details to the historian, and confining our efforts to presenting only a summary outline. [29]As the architect of a new house must pay attention to the whole structure, while the one who undertakes the decoration and the frescoes has to be concerned only with what is needed for ornamentation, so I think it is with us.[n] [30]To enter into questions and examine them from all sides and to be busy about details is the task of the historian; [31]but one who is making an adaptation should be allowed to aim at brevity of expression and to forgo complete treatment of the matter. [32]Here, then, let us begin our account without adding to what has already been said; it would be silly to lengthen the preface to the history and then cut short the history itself.

### III. HELIODORUS' ATTEMPT TO PROFANE THE TEMPLE*

#### CHAPTER 3

**Heliodorus' Arrival in Jerusalem.** [1]While the holy city lived in perfect peace and the laws were strictly observed because of the piety of the high priest Onias[†] and his hatred of evil,[o] [2]the kings themselves honored the place and glorified the temple with the most magnificent gifts. [3]Thus Seleucus,[‡] king of Asia, defrayed from his own revenues all the expenses necessary for the liturgy of sacrifice.

[4]But a certain Simon, of the priestly clan of Bilgah,[§] who had been appointed superintendent of the temple, had a quarrel with the high priest about the administration of the city market.[p] [5]Since he could not prevail against Onias, he went to Apollonius of Tarsus, who at that time was governor of Coelesyria and Phoenicia, [6]and reported to him that the treasury in Jerusalem was full of such untold riches that the sum total of the assets was past counting and that since they did not belong to the account of

the sacrifices, it would be possible for them to fall under the authority of the king.

[7]When Apollonius had an audience with the king, he informed him about the riches that had been reported to him. The king chose his chief minister Heliodorus and sent him with instructions to seize those riches. [8]So Heliodorus immediately set out on his journey, ostensibly to visit the cities of Coelesyria and Phoenicia, but in reality to carry out the king's purpose.

[9]When he arrived in Jerusalem and had been graciously received by the high priest of the city, he told him about the information that had been given, and explained the reason for his presence, and he inquired if these things were really true. [10]The high priest explained that there were deposits for widows and orphans,[q] [11]and some was the property of Hyrcanus, son of Tobias,[¶] a man who occupied a very high position. Contrary to the misrepresentations of the impious Simon, the total amounted only to four hundred talents of silver and two hundred of gold. [12]It was utterly unthinkable to defraud those who had placed their trust in the sanctity of the place and in the sacred inviolability of a temple venerated all over the world.

**Heliodorus' Plan to Rob the Temple.** [13]But Heliodorus, because of the orders he had from the king, said that in any case this money must be confiscated for the royal treasury. [14]So on the day he had set he went in to take an inventory of the funds. There was no little anguish throughout the city. [15]Priests prostrated themselves before the altar in their priestly robes, and called toward heaven for the one who had given the law about deposits to keep the deposits safe for those who had made them.[r] [16]Whoever saw the appearance of the high priest was pierced to the heart, for the changed complexion of his face revealed his mental anguish. [17]The terror and bodily trembling that had come over the man clearly showed those who saw him the pain that lodged in his heart. [18]People rushed out of their houses and crowded together making common supplication, because the place was in danger of being profaned. [19]Women, girded with sackcloth below their breasts, filled the streets. Young women secluded indoors all ran, some to the gates, some to the walls, others peered through the windows— [20]all of them with hands raised toward heaven, making supplication. [21]It was pitiful to see the populace prostrate everywhere and the high priest full of dread and anguish. [22]While they were imploring the almighty Lord to keep the deposits safe and secure for those who had placed them in trust, [23]Heliodorus went on with his plan.

---

*[3:1–40] This legendary episode about Heliodorus is recounted here for the purpose of stressing the inviolability of the Temple of Jerusalem; its later profanation was interpreted as owing to the sins of the people; cf. 5:17–18.

†[3:1] **Onias:** Onias III was high priest from 196 to 175 B.C. and died in 171 B.C. He was the son of Simon, whose praises are sung in Sir 50:1–21.

‡[3:3] **Seleucus:** Seleucus IV Philopator, who reigned from 187 to 175 B.C.

§[3:4] **Bilgah:** a priestly family mentioned in 1 Chr 24:14; Neh 12:5, 18.

¶[3:11] **Hyrcanus, son of Tobias:** a member of the Tobiad family of Transjordan (Neh 2:10; 6:17–19; 13:4–8). Hyrcanus' father was Joseph, whose mother was the sister of the high priest Onias II.

---

n. [2:29] 2 Mc 15:38–39.   o. [3:1] 2 Mc 5:19–20; 15:12.   p. [3:4] 2 Mc 4:23.

q. [3:10] Dt 14:29; 26:12.   r. [3:15] Ex 22:6–14.

**God Protects the Temple.** [24]But just as Heliodorus was arriving at the treasury with his bodyguards, the Lord of spirits and all authority produced an apparition so great that those who had been bold enough to accompany Heliodorus were panic-stricken at God's power and fainted away in terror. [25]There appeared to them a richly caparisoned horse, mounted by a fearsome rider. Charging furiously, the horse attacked Heliodorus with its front hooves. The rider was seen wearing golden armor. [26]Then two other young men, remarkably strong, strikingly handsome, and splendidly attired, appeared before him. Standing on each side of him, they flogged him unceasingly, inflicting innumerable blows. [27]Suddenly he fell to the ground, enveloped in great darkness. His men picked him up and laid him on a stretcher. [28]They carried away helpless the man who a moment before had entered that treasury under arms with a great retinue and his whole bodyguard. They clearly recognized the sovereign power of God.

**The Restoration and Testimony of Heliodorus.** [29]As Heliodorus lay speechless because of God's action and deprived of any hope of recovery, [30]the people praised the Lord who had marvelously glorified his own place; and the temple, charged so shortly before with fear and commotion, was filled with joy and gladness, now that the almighty Lord had appeared. [31]Quickly some of the companions of Heliodorus begged Onias to call upon the Most High to spare the life of one who was about to breathe his last. [32]The high priest, suspecting that the king might think that Heliodorus had suffered some foul play at the hands of the Jews, offered a sacrifice for the man's recovery. [33]While the high priest was offering the sacrifice of atonement, the same young men dressed in the same clothing again appeared and stood before Heliodorus. "Be very grateful to the high priest Onias," they told him. "It is for his sake that the Lord has spared your life. [34]Since you have been scourged by Heaven, proclaim to all God's great power." When they had said this, they disappeared.

[35]After Heliodorus had offered a sacrifice to the Lord and made most solemn vows to the one who had spared his life, he bade Onias farewell, and returned with his soldiers to the king. [36]Before all he gave witness to the deeds of the most high God that he had seen with his own eyes. [37]When the king asked Heliodorus what sort of person would be suitable to be sent to Jerusalem next, he answered: [38]"If you have an enemy or one who is plotting against the government, send him there, and you will get him back with a flogging, if indeed he survives at all; for there is certainly some divine power about the place. [39]The one whose dwelling is in heaven watches over that place and protects it, and strikes down and destroys those who come to harm it." [40]This was how the matter concerning Heliodorus and the preservation of the treasury turned out.

## IV. PROFANATION AND PERSECUTION

### CHAPTER 4

**Simon Accuses Onias.** [1]The Simon mentioned above as the informer about the funds against his own country slandered Onias as the one who incited Heliodorus and instigated the whole miserable affair. [2]He dared to brand as a schemer against the government the man who was the benefactor of the city, the protector of his compatriots, and a zealous defender of the laws. [3]When Simon's hostility reached such a pitch that murders were being committed by one of his henchmen, [4]Onias saw that the opposition was serious and that Apollonius, son of Menestheus, was the governor of Coelesyria and Phoenicia, was abetting Simon's wickedness. [5]So he had recourse to the king, not as an accuser of his compatriots, but as one looking to the general and particular good of all the people. [6]He saw that without royal attention it would be impossible to have a peaceful government, and that Simon would not desist from his folly.

**Jason as High Priest.** [7]But Seleucus died,[*] and when Antiochus surnamed Epiphanes succeeded him on the throne, Onias' brother Jason obtained the high priesthood by corrupt means:[s] [8]in an interview, he promised the king three hundred and sixty talents of silver, as well as eighty talents from another source of income. [9]Besides this he would undertake to pay a hundred and fifty more, if he was given authority to establish a gymnasium and a youth center[†] for it and to enroll Jerusalemites as citizens of Antioch.

[10]When Jason received the king's approval and came into office, he immediately initiated his compatriots into the Greek way of life. [11]He set aside the royal concessions granted to the Jews through the mediation of John, father of Eupolemus[‡] (that Eupolemus who would later go on an embassy to the Romans to establish friendship and alliance with them); he set aside the lawful practices and introduced customs contrary to the law.[t] [12]uWith perverse delight

---

*[4:7] **Seleucus died:** he was murdered by Heliodorus. Antiochus Epiphanes was his younger brother. Onias' brother showed his enthusiasm for the Greek way of life (v. 10) by changing his Hebrew name Joshua, or Jesus, to the Greek name Jason.

†[4:9] **Youth center:** an educational institution in which young men were trained both in Greek intellectual culture and in physical fitness. **Citizens of Antioch:** honorary citizens of Antioch, a Hellenistic city of the Seleucid Kingdom that had a corporation of such Antiochians, who enjoyed certain political and commercial privileges.

‡[4:11] **Eupolemus:** one of the two envoys sent to Rome by Judas Maccabeus (1 Mc 8:17).

s. [4:7] 2 Mc 1:7; 1 Mc 1:10.    t. [4:11] 1 Mc 8:17.    u. [4:12–17] 1 Mc 1:11–15.

he established a gymnasium* at the very foot of the citadel, where he induced the noblest young men to wear the Greek hat. [13]The craze for Hellenism and the adoption of foreign customs reached such a pitch, through the outrageous wickedness of Jason, the renegade and would-be high priest, [14]that the priests no longer cared about the service of the altar. Disdaining the temple and neglecting the sacrifices, they hastened, at the signal for the games, to take part in the unlawful exercises at the arena. [15]What their ancestors had regarded as honors they despised; what the Greeks esteemed as glory they prized highly. [16]For this reason they found themselves in serious trouble: the very people whose manner of life they emulated, and whom they desired to imitate in everything, became their enemies and oppressors. [17]It is no light matter to flout the laws of God, as subsequent events will show.

[18]When the quinquennial games were held at Tyre in the presence of the king, [19]the vile Jason sent representatives of the Antiochians of Jerusalem, to bring three hundred silver drachmas for the sacrifice to Hercules. But the bearers themselves decided that the money should not be spent on a sacrifice, as that was not right, but should be used for some other purpose. [20]So the contribution meant for the sacrifice to Hercules by the sender, was in fact applied to the construction of triremes† by those who brought it.

[21]When Apollonius, son of Menestheus, was sent to Egypt for the coronation of King Philometor,‡ Antiochus learned from him that the king was opposed to his policies. He took measures for his own security; so after going to Joppa, he proceeded to Jerusalem. [22]There he was received with great pomp by Jason and the people of the city, who escorted him with torchlights and acclamations; following this, he led his army into Phoenicia.

**Menelaus as High Priest.** [23]Three years later Jason sent Menelaus,§ brother of the aforementioned Simon, to deliver the money to the king, and to complete negotiations on urgent matters. [24]But after his introduction to the king, he flattered him with such an air of authority that he secured the high priesthood for himself, outbidding Jason by three hundred talents of silver. [25]He returned with the royal commission, but with nothing that made him worthy of the high priesthood; he had the temper of a cruel tyrant and the rage of a wild beast. [26]So Jason, who had cheated

his own brother and now saw himself cheated by another man, was driven out as a fugitive to the country of the Ammonites. [27]But Menelaus, who obtained the office, paid nothing of the money he had promised to the king, [28]in spite of the demand of Sostratus, the commandant of the citadel, whose duty it was to collect the taxes. For this reason, both were summoned before the king. [29]Menelaus left his brother Lysimachus as his deputy in the high priesthood, while Sostratus left Crates, commander of the Cypriots.ᵛ

**Murder of Onias.** [30]While these things were taking place, the people of Tarsus and Mallus¶ rose in revolt, because their cities had been given as a gift to Antiochis, the king's concubine. [31]So the king hastened off to settle the affair, leaving Andronicus, one of his nobles, as his deputy. [32]Menelaus, for his part, thinking this a good opportunity, stole some gold vessels from the temple and presented them to Andronicus; he had already sold other vessels in Tyre and in the neighboring cities. [33]When Onias had clear evidence, he accused Menelaus publicly, after withdrawing to the inviolable sanctuary at Daphne, near Antioch. [34]Thereupon Menelaus approached Andronicus privately and urged him to seize Onias. So Andronicus went to Onias, treacherously reassuring him by offering his right hand in oath, and persuaded him, in spite of his suspicions, to leave the sanctuary. Then, with no regard for justice, he immediately put him to death.

[35]As a result, not only the Jews, but many people of other nations as well, were indignant and angry over the unjust murder of the man. [36]When the king returned from the region of Cilicia, the Jews of the city,** together with the Greeks who detested the crime, went to see him about the murder of Onias. [37]Antiochus was deeply grieved and full of pity; he wept as he recalled the prudence and noble conduct of the deceased. [38]Inflamed with anger, he immediately stripped Andronicus of his purple robe, tore off his garments, and had him led through the whole city to the very place where he had committed the outrage against Onias; and there he put the murderer to death. Thus the Lord rendered him the punishment he deserved.

**More Outrages.** [39]Many acts of sacrilege had been committed by Lysimachus in the city†† with the connivance of Menelaus. When word spread, the people assembled in protest against Lysimachus, because a large number of gold vessels had been stolen. [40]As the crowds, now thoroughly enraged, began to riot, Lysimachus launched an unjustified attack against them with about three

---

*[4:12] Since the **gymnasium**, where the youth exercised naked (Greek *gymnos*), lay in the Tyropoeon Valley to the east of the citadel, it was directly next to the Temple on its eastern side. **The Greek hat**: a wide-brimmed hat, traditional headgear of Hermes, the patron god of athletic contests; it formed part of the distinctive costume of the members of the "youth center."

†[4:20] **Triremes**: war vessels with three banks of oars.

‡[4:21] **Philometor**: Ptolemy VI, king of Egypt, ca. 172 to ca. 145 B.C.

§[4:23] **Menelaus**: Jewish high priest from ca. 172 to his execution in 162 B.C. (13:3–8).

¶[4:30] **Mallus**: a city of Cilicia (v. 36) in southeastern Asia Minor, about thirty miles east of Tarsus.

**[4:36] **The city**: Antioch. But some understand the Greek to mean "each city."

††[4:39] **The city**: Jerusalem. Menelaus was still in Syria.

v. [4:29] 2 Mc 4:39–42.

thousand armed men under the leadership of a certain Auranus, a man as advanced in folly as he was in years. ⁴¹Seeing Lysimachus' attack, people picked up stones, pieces of wood or handfuls of the ashes lying there and threw them in wild confusion at Lysimachus and his men. ⁴²As a result, they wounded many of them and even killed a few, while they put all to flight. The temple robber himself they killed near the treasury.

⁴³Charges about this affair were brought against Menelaus. ⁴⁴When the king came to Tyre, three men sent by the senate pleaded the case before him. ⁴⁵But Menelaus, seeing himself on the losing side, promised Ptolemy, son of Dorymenes, a substantial sum of money if he would win the king over.ʷ ⁴⁶So Ptolemy took the king aside into a colonnade, as if to get some fresh air, and persuaded him to change his mind. ⁴⁷Menelaus, who was the cause of all the trouble, the king acquitted of the charges, while he condemned to death those poor men who would have been declared innocent even if they had pleaded their case before Scythians. ⁴⁸Thus, those who had prosecuted the case on behalf of the city, the people, and the sacred vessels, quickly suffered unjust punishment. ⁴⁹For this reason, even Tyrians, detesting the crime, provided sumptuously for their burial. ⁵⁰But Menelaus, thanks to the greed of those in power, remained in office, where he grew in wickedness, scheming greatly against his fellow citizens.

## CHAPTER 5

**Jason's Revolt.** ¹About this time Antiochus sent his second expedition* into Egypt.ˣ ²⁹It then happened that all over the city, for nearly forty days, there appeared horsemen, clothed in garments of a golden weave, charging in midair—companies fully armed with lances and drawn swords; ³squadrons of cavalry in battle array, charges and countercharges on this side and that, with brandished shields and bristling spears, flights of arrows and flashes of gold ornaments, together with armor of every sort. ⁴Therefore all prayed that this vision might be a good omen.

⁵But when a false rumor circulated that Antiochus was dead, Jason† gathered at least a thousand men and suddenly attacked the city. As the defenders on the walls were forced back

and the city was finally being taken, Menelaus took refuge in the citadel. ⁶For his part, Jason continued the merciless slaughter of his fellow citizens, not realizing that triumph over one's own kindred is the greatest calamity; he thought he was winning a victory over his enemies, not over his own people. ⁷Even so, he did not gain control of the government, but in the end received only disgrace for his treachery, and once again took refuge in the country of the Ammonites. ⁸At length he met a miserable end. Called to account before Aretas,‡ ruler of the Arabians, he fled from city to city, hunted by all, hated as an apostate from the laws, abhorred as the executioner of his country and his compatriots. Driven into Egypt, ⁹he set out by sea for the Lacedaemonians, among whom he hoped to find protection because of his relations with them. He who had exiled so many from their country perished in exile; ¹⁰and he who had cast out so many to lie unburied went unmourned and without a funeral of any kind, nor any place in the tomb of his ancestors.

**Revenge by Antiochus.** ¹¹ᵉWhen these happenings were reported to the king, he thought that Judea was in revolt. Raging like a wild animal, he set out from Egypt and took Jerusalem by storm. ¹²He ordered his soldiers to cut down without mercy those whom they met and to slay those who took refuge in their houses. ¹³There was a massacre of young and old, a killing of women and children, a slaughter of young women and infants. ¹⁴In the space of three days, eighty thousand were lost, forty thousand meeting a violent death, and the same number being sold into slavery.

¹⁵Not satisfied with this, the king dared to enter the holiest temple in the world; Menelaus, that traitor both to the laws and to his country, served as guide. ¹⁶He laid his impure hands on the sacred vessels and swept up with profane hands the votive offerings made by other kings for the advancement, the glory, and the honor of the place. ¹⁷Antiochus became puffed up in spirit, not realizing that it was because of the sins of the city's inhabitants that the Sovereign Lord was angry for a little while: hence the disregard of the place.ᵃ ¹⁸If they had not become entangled in so many sins, this man, like that Heliodorus sent by King Seleucus to inspect the treasury, would have been flogged and turned back from his presumptuous act as soon as he approached. ¹⁹The Lord, however, had not chosen the nation for the sake of the place, but the place for the sake of the nation. ²⁰Therefore, the place itself, having shared in the nation's misfortunes, afterward participated in their good fortune; and what the Almighty had forsaken in

---

*[5:1] **Second expedition**: the first invasion of Egypt by Antiochus IV in 169 B.C. (1 Mc 1:16–20) is not mentioned in 2 Maccabees, unless the coming of the Syrian army to Palestine (2 Mc 4:21–22) is regarded as the first invasion. The author of 2 Maccabees apparently combines the first pillage of Jerusalem in 169 B.C. after Antiochus' first invasion of Egypt (1 Mc 1:20–28; cf. 2 Mc 5:5–7) with the second pillage of the city two years later (167 B.C.), following the king's second invasion of Egypt in 168 B.C. (1 Mc 1:29–35; cf. 2 Mc 5:24–26).

†[5:5] **Jason**: brother of Onias III, claimant of the high priesthood (4:7–10). Later he was supplanted by Menelaus, who drove him into Transjordan (4:26).

‡[5:8] **Aretas**: King Aretas I of the Nabateans; cf. 1 Mc 5:25.

---

w. [4:45] 2 Mc 8:8; 1 Mc 3:38.   x. [5:1–10] 1 Mc 1:16–19; Dn 11:25–30.   y. [5:2–3] 2 Mc 3:24–26; 10:29–30; 11:8.

z. [5:11–21] 1 Mc 1:20–24.   a. [5:17] 2 Mc 6:12–16; 7:16–19, 32–38.

wrath was restored in all its glory, once the great Sovereign Lord became reconciled.

[21b]Antiochus carried off eighteen hundred talents from the temple and hurried back to Antioch, thinking in his arrogance that he could make the land navigable and the sea passable on foot, so carried away was he with pride. [22]He left governors to harass the nation: at Jerusalem, Philip, a Phrygian by birth,* and in character more barbarous than the man who appointed him;[c] [23]at Mount Gerizim,† Andronicus; and besides these, Menelaus, who lorded it over his fellow citizens more than the others. Out of hatred for the Jewish citizens, [24d]the king sent Apollonius,‡ commander of the Mysians, at the head of an army of twenty-two thousand, with orders to kill all the grown men and sell the women and children into slavery. [25]When this man arrived in Jerusalem, he pretended to be peacefully disposed and waited until the holy day of the sabbath; then, finding the Jews refraining from work, he ordered his men to parade fully armed. [26]All those who came out to watch, he massacred, and running through the city with armed men, he cut down a large number of people.

[27]But Judas Maccabeus and about nine others withdrew to the wilderness to avoid sharing in defilement; there he and his companions lived like the animals in the hills, eating what grew wild.[e]

## CHAPTER 6

**Abolition of Judaism.** [1]Not long after this the king sent an Athenian senator§ to force the Jews to abandon the laws of their ancestors and live no longer by the laws of God, [2]also to profane the temple in Jerusalem and dedicate it to Olympian Zeus,¶ and the one on Mount Gerizim to Zeus the Host to Strangers, as the local inhabitants were wont to be.[g] [3]This was a harsh and utterly intolerable evil. [4]The Gentiles filled the temple with debauchery and revelry; they amused themselves with prostitutes and had intercourse with women even in the sacred courts. They also brought forbidden things into the temple,[h] [5]so that the altar was covered with abominable offerings prohibited by the laws.

[6]No one could keep the sabbath or celebrate the traditional feasts, nor even admit to being a Jew. [7]Moreover, at the monthly celebration of the king's birthday the Jews, from bitter necessity, had to partake of the sacrifices, and when the festival of Dionysus** was celebrated, they were compelled to march in his procession, wearing wreaths of ivy.[i]

[8]Following upon a vote of the citizens of Ptolemais, a decree was issued ordering the neighboring Greek cities to adopt the same measures, obliging the Jews to partake of the sacrifices, [9]and putting to death those who would not consent to adopt the customs of the Greeks. It was obvious, therefore, that disaster had come upon them. [10]Thus, two women who were arrested for having circumcised their children were publicly paraded about the city with their babies hanging at their breasts and then thrown down from the top of the city wall.[j] [11]Others, who had assembled in nearby caves to observe the seventh day in secret, were betrayed to Philip and all burned to death. In their respect for the holiness of that day, they refrained from defending themselves.[k]

**God's Purpose.** [12]Now I urge those who read this book not to be disheartened by these misfortunes, but to consider that these punishments were meant not for the ruin but for the correction of our nation. [13]It is, in fact, a sign of great kindness to punish the impious promptly instead of letting them go for long. [14m]Thus, in dealing with other nations, the Sovereign Lord patiently waits until they reach the full measure of their sins before punishing them; but with us he has decided to deal differently, [15]in order that he may not have to punish us later, when our sins have reached their fullness. [16]Therefore he never withdraws his mercy from us. Although he disciplines us with misfortunes, he does not abandon his own people. [17]Let these words suffice for recalling this truth. Without further ado we must go on with our story.

**Martyrdom of Eleazar.** [18††]Eleazar, one of the foremost scribes, a man advanced in age and of noble appearance, was being forced to open his mouth to eat pork." [19]But preferring a glorious death to a life of defilement, he went forward of his own accord to the instrument of torture, [20]spitting out the meat as they should do who have the courage to reject food unlawful to taste even for love of life.

---

*[5:22] **Philip, a Phrygian by birth:** the Philip of 2 Mc 6:11 and 8:8, but probably not the same as Philip the regent of 2 Mc 9:29 and 1 Mc 6:14.

†[5:23] **Mount Gerizim:** the sacred mountain of the Samaritans at Shechem; cf. 2 Mc 6:2.

‡[5:24] **Apollonius:** the Mysian commander of 1 Mc 1:29; mentioned also in 2 Mc 3:5; 4:4.

§[6:1] **Athenian senator:** or, Geron the Athenian, since *geron* can also be a proper name.

¶[6:2] **Olympian Zeus:** equated with the Syrian Baal Shamen ("the lord of the heavens"), a term which the Jews mockingly rendered as *shiqquṣ shomem*, "desolating abomination" (Dn 9:27; 11:31; 12:11; 1 Mc 1:54).

**[6:7] **Dionysus:** also called Bacchus, the god of the grape harvest and of wine; ivy was one of his symbols.

††[6:18–7:42] The stories of Eleazar and of the mother and her seven sons, among the earliest models of "martyrology," were understandably popular. Written to encourage God's people in times of persecution, they add gruesome details to the record of tortures, and place long speeches in the mouths of the martyrs.

b. [5:21] 1 Mc 1:23–24.   c. [5:22] 2 Mc 6:11; 8:8.   d. [5:24–26] 1 Mc 1:29–40.   e. [5:27] 2 Mc 8:1; 1 Mc 2:28.   f. [6:1] 1 Mc 1:41–63.   g. [6:2] 1 Mc 1:46, 54; Dn 9:27; 11:31; 12:11.   h. [6:4] Ez 23:36–49; Dn 11:31; Am 2:7.

i. [6:7] 1 Mc 1:58–59.   j. [6:10] 1 Mc 1:60–61.   k. [6:11] 1 Mc 2:32–38.   l. [6:12–16] 2 Mc 5:17; 7:16–19, 32–38.   m. [6:14] Wis 11:9–10; 12:2, 22.   n. [6:18] Lv 11:6–8.

²¹Those in charge of that unlawful sacrifice took the man aside, because of their long acquaintance with him, and privately urged him to bring his own provisions that he could legitimately eat, and only to pretend to eat the sacrificial meat prescribed by the king. ²²Thus he would escape death, and be treated kindly because of his old friendship with them. ²³But he made up his mind in a noble manner, worthy of his years, the dignity of his advanced age, the merited distinction of his gray hair, and of the admirable life he had lived from childhood. Above all loyal to the holy laws given by God, he swiftly declared, "Send me to Hades!"

²⁴"At our age it would be unbecoming to make such a pretense; many of the young would think the ninety-year-old Eleazar had gone over to an alien religion. ²⁵If I dissemble to gain a brief moment of life, they would be led astray by me, while I would bring defilement and dishonor on my old age. ²⁶Even if, for the time being, I avoid human punishment, I shall never, whether alive or dead, escape the hand of the Almighty. ²⁷Therefore, by bravely giving up life now, I will prove myself worthy of my old age, ²⁸and I will leave to the young a noble example of how to die willingly and nobly for the revered and holy laws."

He spoke thus, and went immediately to the instrument of torture. ²⁹Those who shortly before had been kindly disposed, now became hostile toward him because what he had said seemed to them utter madness.° ³⁰When he was about to die under the blows, he groaned, saying: "The Lord in his holy knowledge knows full well that, although I could have escaped death, I am not only enduring terrible pain in my body from this scourging, but also suffering it with joy in my soul because of my devotion to him." ³¹This is how he died, leaving in his death a model of nobility and an unforgettable example of virtue not only for the young but for the whole nation.

## CHAPTER 7

**Martyrdom of a Mother and Her Seven Sons.** ¹It also happened that seven brothers with their mother were arrested and tortured with whips and scourges by the king to force them to eat pork in violation of God's law.ᵖ ²One of the brothers, speaking for the others, said: "What do you expect to learn by questioning us? We are ready to die rather than transgress the laws of our ancestors."

³At that the king, in a fury, gave orders to have pans and caldrons heated. ⁴These were quickly heated, and he gave the order to cut out the tongue of the one who had spoken for the others, to scalp him and cut off his hands and feet, while the rest of his brothers and his mother looked on. ⁵When he was completely

maimed but still breathing, the king ordered them to carry him to the fire and fry him. As a cloud of smoke spread from the pan, the brothers and their mother encouraged one another to die nobly, with these words: ⁶"The Lord God is looking on and truly has compassion on us, as Moses declared in his song, when he openly bore witness, saying, 'And God will have compassion on his servants.'"�q

⁷After the first brother had died in this manner, they brought the second to be made sport of. After tearing off the skin and hair of his head, they asked him, "Will you eat the pork rather than have your body tortured limb by limb?" ⁸Answering in the language of his ancestors, he said, "Never!" So he in turn suffered the same tortures as the first. ⁹With his last breath he said: "You accursed fiend, you are depriving us of this present life, but the King of the universe will raise us up* to live again forever, because we are dying for his laws."ʳ

¹⁰After him the third suffered their cruel sport. He put forth his tongue at once when told to do so, and bravely stretched out his hands, ¹¹as he spoke these noble words: "It was from Heaven that I received these; for the sake of his laws I disregard them; from him I hope to receive them again." ¹²Even the king and his attendants marveled at the young man's spirit, because he regarded his sufferings as nothing.

¹³After he had died, they tortured and maltreated the fourth brother in the same way. ¹⁴When he was near death, he said, "It is my choice to die at the hands of mortals with the hope that God will restore me to life; but for you, there will be no resurrection to life."

¹⁵They next brought forward the fifth brother and maltreated him. ¹⁶Looking at the king, he said:ˢ "Mortal though you are, you have power over human beings, so you do what you please. But do not think that our nation is forsaken by God. ¹⁷Only wait, and you will see how his great power will torment you and your descendants."

¹⁸After him they brought the sixth brother. When he was about to die, he said: "Have no vain illusions. We suffer these things on our own account, because we have sinned against our God; that is why such shocking things have happened. ¹⁹Do not think, then, that you will go unpunished for having dared to fight against God."

²⁰Most admirable and worthy of everlasting remembrance was the mother who, seeing her seven sons perish in a single day, bore it courageously because of her hope in the Lord. ²¹Filled with a noble spirit that stirred her womanly

---

*[7:6] **The King of the universe will raise us up**: here, and in vv. 11, 14, 23, 29, 36, belief in the future resurrection of the body, at least for the just, is clearly stated; cf. also 12:44; 14:46; Dn 12:2.

q. [7:6] Dt 32:36–38.   r. [7:9] 2 Mc 12:44; 14:46; Dn 12:1–3.
s. [7:16–19] 2 Mc 5:17; 6:12–16; 7:32.

o. [6:29] Wis 3:1–4; 5:4.   p. [7:1] Jer 15:9.

reason with manly emotion, she exhorted each of them in the language of their ancestors with these words: ²²"I do not know how you came to be in my womb; it was not I who gave you breath and life, nor was it I who arranged the elements you are made of. ²³Therefore, since it is the Creator of the universe who shaped the beginning of humankind and brought about the origin of everything, he, in his mercy, will give you back both breath and life, because you now disregard yourselves for the sake of his law."

²⁴Antiochus, suspecting insult in her words, thought he was being ridiculed. As the youngest brother was still alive, the king appealed to him, not with mere words, but with promises on oath, to make him rich and happy if he would abandon his ancestral customs: he would make him his Friend and entrust him with high office. ²⁵When the youth paid no attention to him at all, the king appealed to the mother, urging her to advise her boy to save his life. ²⁶After he had urged her for a long time, she agreed to persuade her son. ²⁷She leaned over close to him and, in derision of the cruel tyrant, said in their native language: "Son, have pity on me, who carried you in my womb for nine months, nursed you for three years, brought you up, educated and supported you to your present age. ²⁸I beg you, child, to look at the heavens and the earth and see all that is in them; then you will know that God did not make them out of existing things.* In the same way humankind came into existence. ²⁹Do not be afraid of this executioner, but be worthy of your brothers and accept death, so that in the time of mercy I may receive you again with your brothers."

³⁰She had scarcely finished speaking when the youth said: "What is the delay? I will not obey the king's command. I obey the command of the law given to our ancestors through Moses. ³¹But you, who have contrived every kind of evil for the Hebrews, will not escape the hands of God. ³²We, indeed, are suffering because of our sins.ᵘ ³³Though for a little while our living Lord has been angry, correcting and chastising us, he will again be reconciled with his servants. ³⁴But you, wretch, most vile of mortals, do not, in your insolence, buoy yourself up with unfounded hopes, as you raise your hand against the children of heaven. ³⁵You have not yet escaped the judgment of the almighty and all-seeing God. ³⁶Our brothers, after enduring brief pain, have drunk of never-failing life, under God's covenant. But you, by the judgment of God, shall receive just punishments for your arrogance.

³⁷Like my brothers, I offer up my body and my life for our ancestral laws, imploring God to show mercy soon to our nation, and by afflictions and blows to make you confess that he alone is God. ³⁸Through me and my brothers, may there be an end to the wrath of the Almighty that has justly fallen on our whole nation."

³⁹At that, the king became enraged and treated him even worse than the others, since he bitterly resented the boy's contempt. ⁴⁰Thus he too died undefiled, putting all his trust in the Lord. ⁴¹Last of all, after her sons, the mother was put to death. ⁴²Enough has been said about the sacrificial meals and the excessive cruelties.

## V. VICTORIES OF JUDAS AND PURIFICATION OF THE TEMPLE

### CHAPTER 8

**Resistance from Judas Maccabeus.** ¹ᵛJudas Maccabeus and his companions entered the villages secretly, summoned their kindred, and enlisted others who had remained faithful to Judaism. Thus they assembled about six thousand men. ²They implored the Lord to look kindly upon this people, who were being oppressed by all; to have pity on the sanctuary, which was profaned by renegades; ³to have mercy on the city, which was being destroyed and was about to be leveled to the ground; to listen to the blood that cried out to him; ⁴to remember the criminal slaughter of innocent children and the blasphemies uttered against his name; and to manifest his hatred of evil.

⁵ʷOnce Maccabeus got his men organized, the Gentiles could not withstand him, for the Lord's wrath had now changed to mercy. ⁶Coming by surprise upon towns and villages, he set them on fire. He captured strategic positions, and put to flight not a few of the enemy. ⁷He preferred the nights as being especially favorable for such attacks. Soon talk of his valor spread everywhere.

**First Victory over Nicanor.†** ⁸When Philip saw that Judas was gaining ground little by little and that his successful advances were becoming more frequent, he wrote to Ptolemy, governor of Coelesyria and Phoenicia, to come to the aid of the king's interests.ˣ ⁹ʸPtolemy promptly selected Nicanor, son of Patroclus, one of the Chief Friends, and sent him at the head of at least twenty thousand armed men of various nations to wipe out the entire Jewish nation. With him he associated Gorgias, a general, experienced in the art of war.ᶻ ¹⁰Nicanor planned to raise the two thousand talents of tribute owed by the

---

*[7:28] **God did not make them out of existing things:** that is, all things were made solely by God's omnipotent will and creative word; cf. Heb 11:3. This statement has often been taken as a basis for "creation out of nothing" (Latin *creatio ex nihilo*).

t. [7:22–23] 2 Mc 7:11, 28; Jb 1:10–12; Ps 139:13–16; Eccl 11:5.
u. [7:32] 2 Mc 5:17; 6:12–16; 7:16–19.

---

†[8:8–29, 34–35] This account of the campaign of Nicanor and Gorgias against Judas is paralleled, with certain differences, in 1 Mc 3:38–4:24.

v. [8:1–7] 2 Mc 5:27; 1 Mc 3:10–26.   w. [8:5–7] 1 Mc 3:3–9.   x. [8:8] 2 Mc 4:45; 1 Mc 3:38.   y. [8:9–23] 1 Mc 3:38–59.   z. [8:9] 1 Mc 7:26.

king to the Romans[*] by selling captured Jews into slavery. [11]So he immediately sent word to the coastal cities, inviting them to buy Jewish slaves and promising to deliver ninety slaves for a talent[†]—little anticipating the punishment that was to fall upon him from the Almighty.

[12]When Judas learned of Nicanor's advance and informed his companions about the approach of the army, [13]those who were fearful and those who lacked faith in God's justice deserted and got away. [14]But the others sold everything they had left, and at the same time entreated the Lord to deliver those whom the ungodly Nicanor had sold before even capturing them. [15]They entreated the Lord to do this, if not for their sake, at least for the sake of the covenants made with their ancestors, and because they themselves invoked his holy and glorious name. [16]Maccabeus assembled his forces, six thousand strong, and exhorted them not to be panic-stricken before the enemy, nor to fear the very large number of Gentiles unjustly attacking them, but to fight nobly. [17]They were to keep before their eyes the lawless outrage perpetrated by the Gentiles against the holy place and the affliction of the humiliated city, as well as the subversion of their ancestral way of life. [18]He said, "They trust in weapons and acts of daring, but we trust in almighty God, who can by a mere nod destroy not only those who attack us but even the whole world." [19]He went on to tell them of the times when help had been given their ancestors: both the time of Sennacherib, when a hundred and eighty-five thousand of his men perished,[a] [20]and the time of the battle in Babylonia against the Galatians,[‡] when only eight thousand Jews fought along with four thousand Macedonians; yet when the Macedonians were hard pressed, the eight thousand, by the help they received from Heaven, destroyed one hundred and twenty thousand and took a great quantity of spoils. [21b]With these words he encouraged them and made them ready to die for their laws and their country.

Then Judas divided his army into four, [22]placing his brothers, Simon, Joseph,[§] and Jonathan, each over a division, assigning them fifteen hundred men apiece.[c] [23]There was also Eleazar.[¶] After reading to them from the holy book and giving them the watchword, "The help of God," Judas himself took charge of the first division and joined in battle with Nicanor.[d] [24]With the Almighty as their ally, they killed more than nine thousand of the enemy, wounded and disabled the greater part of Nicanor's army, and put all of them to flight. [25]They also seized the money of those who had come to buy them as slaves. When they had pursued the enemy for some time, they were obliged to return by reason of the late hour. [26]It was the day before the sabbath, and for that reason they could not continue the pursuit. [27]They collected the enemy's weapons and stripped them of their spoils, and then observed the sabbath with fervent praise and thanks to the Lord who kept them safe for that day on which he allotted them the beginning of his mercy. [28]After the sabbath, they gave a share of the spoils to those who were tortured and to widows and orphans; the rest they divided among themselves and their children.[e] [29]When this was done, they made supplication in common, imploring the merciful Lord to be completely reconciled with his servants.

**Other Victories.** [30]They also challenged the forces of Timothy and Bacchides, killed more than twenty thousand of them, and captured some very high fortresses. They divided the considerable plunder, allotting half to themselves and the rest to victims of torture, orphans, widows, and the aged. [31]They collected the enemies' weapons and carefully stored them in strategic places; the rest of the spoils they carried to Jerusalem. [32]They also killed the commander of Timothy's forces, a most wicked man, who had done great harm to the Jews. [33]While celebrating the victory in their ancestral city, they burned both those who had set fire to the sacred gates and Callisthenes, who had taken refuge in a little house; so he received the reward his wicked deeds deserved.

[34]The thrice-accursed Nicanor, who had brought the thousand slave dealers to buy the Jews, [35]after being humbled through the Lord's help by those whom he had thought of no account, laid aside his fine clothes and fled alone across country like a runaway slave, until he reached Antioch. He was eminently successful in destroying his own army. [36]So he who had promised to provide tribute for the Romans by the capture of the people of Jerusalem proclaimed that the Jews had a champion, and that because they followed the laws laid down by him, they were unharmed.

---

*[8:10] **Tribute owed by the king to the Romans:** the payment imposed on Antiochus III in 188 B.C. by the treaty of Apamea.

†[8:11] **Ninety slaves for a talent:** a low price for so many slaves, thus expressing the opponents' contempt for the Jews.

‡[8:20] **Galatians:** a mercenary force, defeated by Jews and Macedonians in Babylon. Nothing else is known about this battle.

§[8:22] **Joseph:** called John in 1 Mc 2:2; 9:36, 38. This paragraph interrupts the story of Nicanor's defeat, which is resumed in v. 34. The purpose of the author apparently is to group together the defeats suffered by the Syrians on various occasions. Battles against Timothy are recounted in 1 Mc 5:37–44 and 2 Mc 12:10–25; against Bacchides, in 1 Mc 7:8–20.

¶[8:23] **Eleazar:** this parenthetical reference notes the existence of a fifth brother; cf. 1 Mc 2:5.

a. [8:19] 2 Mc 15:22; 2 Kgs 19:35–36; 1 Mc 7:41–42; Is 37:36–37.  b. [8:21–29] 1 Mc 4:1–25.

c. [8:22] 1 Mc 2:2–5; 5:18, 55–62.    d. [8:23] 1 Mc 3:48.    e. [8:28] Nm 31:25–47; Dt 26:12–13; 1 Sm 30:21–25.    f. [8:34–35] 2 Mc 8:23–24; 1 Mc 7:26.

## CHAPTER 9

**Punishment and Death of Antiochus IV.***

¹ᵍAbout that time Antiochus retreated in disgrace from the region of Persia. ²He had entered the city called Persepolis and attempted to rob the temples and gain control of the city. Thereupon the people had swift recourse to arms, and Antiochus' forces were routed, so that in the end Antiochus was put to flight by the people of that region and forced to beat a shameful retreat. ³On his arrival in Ecbatana, he learned what had happened to Nicanor and to Timothy's forces. ⁴Overcome with anger, he planned to make the Jews suffer for the injury done by those who had put him to flight. Therefore he ordered his charioteer to drive without stopping until he finished the journey. Yet the condemnation of Heaven rode with him, because he said in his arrogance, "I will make Jerusalem the common graveyard of Jews as soon as I arrive there."

⁵So the all-seeing Lord, the God of Israel, struck him down with an incurable and invisible blow; for scarcely had he uttered those words when he was seized with excruciating pains in his bowels and sharp internal torment,ʰ ⁶a fit punishment for him who had tortured the bowels of others with many barbarous torments. ⁷Far from giving up his insolence, he was all the more filled with arrogance. Breathing fire in his rage against the Jews, he gave orders to drive even faster. As a result he hurtled from the speeding chariot, and every part of his body was racked by the violent fall. ⁸Thus he who previously, in his superhuman presumption, thought he could command the waves of the sea, and imagined he could weigh the mountaintops in his scales, was now thrown to the ground and had to be carried on a litter, clearly manifesting to all the power of God.ⁱ ⁹The body of this impious man swarmed with worms, and while he was still alive in hideous torments, his flesh rotted off, so that the entire army was sickened by the stench of his corruption.ʲ ¹⁰Shortly before, he had thought that he could reach the stars of heaven, and now, no one could endure to transport the man because of this intolerable stench.

¹¹At last, broken in spirit, he began to give up his excessive arrogance, and to gain some understanding, under the scourge of God, for he was racked with pain unceasingly. ¹²When he could no longer bear his own stench, he said, "It is right to be subject to God, and not to think

one's mortal self equal to God."ᵏ ¹³Then this vile man vowed to him who would never again show him mercy, the Sovereign Lord, ¹⁴that the holy city, toward which he had been hurrying with the intention of leveling it to the ground and making it a common graveyard, he would now set free; ¹⁵that the Jews, whom he had judged not even worthy of burial, but fit only to be thrown out with their children to be eaten by vultures and wild animals—all of them he would make equal to the Athenians; ¹⁶that he would adorn with the finest offerings the holy temple which he had previously despoiled, restore all the sacred vessels many times over, and provide from his own revenues the expenses required for the sacrifices. ¹⁷Besides all this, he would become a Jew himself and visit every inhabited place to proclaim there the power of God. ¹⁸But since his sufferings were not lessened, for God's just judgment had come upon him, he lost hope for himself and wrote the following letter to the Jews in the form of a supplication. It read thus:

¹⁹†"To the worthy Jewish citizens, Antiochus, king and general, sends hearty greetings and best wishes for their health and prosperity. ²⁰If you and your children are well and your affairs are going as you wish, I thank God very much, for my hopes are in heaven. ²¹Now that I am ill, I recall with affection your esteem and goodwill. On returning from the regions of Persia, I fell victim to a troublesome illness; so I thought it necessary to form plans for the general security of all. ²²I do not despair about my health, since I have much hope of recovering from my illness. ²³Nevertheless, I know that my father, whenever he went on campaigns in the hinterland, would name his successor, ²⁴so that, if anything unexpected happened or any unwelcome news came, the people throughout the realm would know to whom the government had been entrusted, and so not be disturbed. ²⁵I am also bearing in mind that the neighboring rulers, especially those on the borders of our kingdom, are on the watch for opportunities and waiting to see what will happen. I have therefore appointed as king my son Antiochus, whom I have often before entrusted and commended to most of you, when I made hurried visits to the outlying provinces. I have written to him what is written here. ²⁶Therefore I beg and entreat each of you to remember the general and individual benefits you have received, and to continue to show goodwill toward me and my son. ²⁷I am confident that, following my policy, he will treat

---

*[9:1–29] In order to keep together the various accounts of God's punishment of the persecutors of his people, the author places here the stories of Antiochus' illness and death (in actuality the king died about the same time as the purification of the Temple, i.e., 164 B.C.; cf. 1 Mc 4:36–59; 6:1–16; 2 Mc 10:1–8); of Judas' campaigns in Idumea and Transjordan; cf. 1 Mc 5:1–51; 2 Mc 10:14–38; and of the first expedition of Lysias (1 Mc 4:26–35; 2 Mc 11:1–15).

g. [9:1–29] 2 Mc 1:12–17; 1 Mc 6:1–13; Dn 11:40–45.  h. [9:5] Acts 12:20–23.  i. [9:8] Jb 38:8–11; Ps 65:6–7; Is 40:12.  j. [9:9] Jdt 16:17; Sir 7:17; Is 14:11; 66:24; Acts 12:23.

†[9:19–27] Despite the statement in v. 18 this letter is not really a supplication. It is rather a notification to all the king's subjects of the appointment of his son as his successor and a request that they be loyal to the new king. Apparently the same letter, which has every appearance of being authentic, was sent to the various peoples throughout the kingdom, with only a few words of address changed for each group.

k. [9:12] Dn 4:31–34.

you with equity and kindness in his relations with you."

²⁸So this murderer and blasphemer, after extreme sufferings, such as he had inflicted on others, died a miserable death in the mountains of a foreign land. ²⁹His foster brother* Philip brought the body home; but fearing Antiochus' son, he later withdrew into Egypt, to Ptolemy Philometor.ˡ

## CHAPTER 10

**Purification of the Temple.** ¹ᵐWhen Maccabeus and his companions, under the Lord's leadership, had recovered the temple and the city, ²they destroyed the altars erected by the foreigners in the marketplace and the sacred shrines. ³After purifying the temple, they made another altar. Then, with fire struck from flint, they offered sacrifice for the first time in two years,† burned incense, and lighted lamps. They also set out the showbread. ⁴When they had done this, they prostrated themselves and begged the Lord that they might never again fall into such misfortunes, and that if they should sin at any time, he might chastise them with moderation and not hand them over to blasphemous and barbarous Gentiles. ⁵On the anniversary of the day on which the temple had been profaned by the foreigners, that is, the twenty-fifth of the same month Kislev, the purification of the temple took place. ⁶The Jews celebrated joyfully for eight days as on the feast of Booths, remembering how, a little while before, they had spent the feast of Booths living like wild animals in the mountains and in caves. ⁷Carrying rods entwined with leaves,‡ beautiful branches and palms, they sang hymns of grateful praise to him who had successfully brought about the purification of his own place. ⁸By public decree and vote they prescribed that the whole Jewish nation should celebrate these days every year. ⁹Such was the end of Antiochus surnamed Epiphanes.

## VI. RENEWED PERSECUTION

**Accession of Antiochus V.** ¹⁰Now we shall relate what happened under Antiochus Eupator, the son of that godless man, and shall give a summary of the chief evils caused by the wars. ¹¹When Eupator succeeded to the kingdom, he put a certain Lysias in charge of the government as commander-in-chief of Coelesyria and Phoenicia. ¹²Ptolemy, called Macron,§ had taken the lead in treating the Jews fairly because of the previous injustice that had been done them, and he endeavored to have peaceful relations with them. ¹³As a result, he was accused before Eupator by the King's Friends. In fact, on all sides he heard himself called a traitor for having abandoned Cyprus, which Philometor had entrusted to him, and for having gone over to Antiochus Epiphanes. Since he could not command the respect due to his high office, he ended his life by taking poison.

**Victory over the Idumeans.**⁵ ¹⁴ⁿWhen Gorgias became governor of the region, he employed foreign troops and used every opportunity to attack the Jews. ¹⁵At the same time the Idumeans, who held some strategic strongholds, were harassing the Jews; they welcomed fugitives from Jerusalem and endeavored to continue the war. ¹⁶Maccabeus and his companions, after public prayers asking God to be their ally, moved quickly against the strongholds of the Idumeans. ¹⁷Attacking vigorously, they gained control of the places, drove back all who were fighting on the walls, and cut down those who opposed them, killing no fewer than twenty thousand. ¹⁸When at least nine thousand took refuge in two very strong towers, well equipped to sustain a siege, ¹⁹Maccabeus left Simon and Joseph, along with Zacchaeus and his forces, in sufficient numbers to besiege them, while he himself went off to places where he was more urgently needed. ²⁰But some of those in Simon's force who were lovers of money let themselves be bribed by some of those in the towers; on receiving seventy thousand drachmas, they allowed a number of them to escape. ²¹When Maccabeus was told what had happened, he assembled the rulers of the people and accused those men of having sold their kindred for money by setting their enemies free to fight against them. ²²So he put them to death as traitors, and without delay captured the two towers. ²³As he was successful at arms in all his undertakings, he destroyed more than twenty thousand in the two strongholds.

**Victory over Timothy.** ²⁴Timothy, who had previously been defeated by the Jews,** gathered a tremendous force of foreign troops and collected a large number of cavalry from Asia; then he appeared in Judea, ready to conquer it by force. ²⁵At his approach, Maccabeus and his companions made supplication to God, sprinkling earth upon their heads and girding their loins in sackcloth. ²⁶Lying prostrate at the foot

---

*[9:29] **Foster brother**: an honorary title conferred by the king on prominent courtiers, whether or not they had been raised with him. Philip tried to seize control of Antioch from the young Antiochus V (1 Mc 6:55–56, 63) and fled to Egypt when he failed.

†[10:3] **Two years**: three years according to 1 Mc 1:54 and 4:52.

‡[10:7] **Rods entwined with leaves**: the wreathed wands (*thyrsoi*) carried in processions honoring Dionysus (6:7) were apparently not regarded as distinctively pagan.

§[10:12] **Ptolemy, called Macron**: son of Dorymenes (4:45); he supported Antiochus IV in 168 B.C. during his invasion of Cyprus.

⁵[10:14–23] Probably the same campaign of Judas against the Idumeans that is mentioned in 1 Mc 5:1–3.

**[10:24] **Timothy, who had previously been defeated by the Jews**: as recounted in 8:30–33.

---

l. [9:29] 1 Mc 6:55–56, 63.   m. [10:1–8] 1 Mc 4:36–61.

n. [10:14] 1 Mc 5:3–5.

of the altar, they begged him to be gracious to them, and to be an enemy to their enemies, and a foe to their foes, as the law declares.[o] [27]After the prayer, they took up their weapons and advanced a considerable distance from the city, halting when they were close to the enemy. [28]As soon as dawn broke,* the armies joined battle, the one having as pledge of success and victory not only their valor but also their reliance on the Lord, and the other taking fury as their leader in the fight.

[29p]In the midst of the fierce battle, there appeared to the enemy five majestic men from the heavens riding on golden-bridled horses, leading the Jews. [30]They surrounded Maccabeus, and shielding him with their own armor, kept him from being wounded. They shot arrows and hurled thunderbolts at the enemy, who were bewildered and blinded, routed in utter confusion. [31]Twenty thousand five hundred of their foot soldiers and six hundred cavalry were slain.

[32]Timothy, however, fled to a well-fortified stronghold called Gazara, where Chaereas was in command.[q] [33]For four days Maccabeus and his forces eagerly besieged the fortress. [34]Those inside, relying on the strength of the place, kept repeating outrageous blasphemies and uttering abominable words. [35]When the fifth day dawned, twenty young men in the army of Maccabeus, angered over such blasphemies, bravely stormed the wall and with savage fury cut down everyone they encountered. [36]Similarly, others climbed up and swung around on the defenders; they put the towers to the torch, spread the fire and burned the blasphemers alive. Still others broke down the gates and let in the rest of the troops, who took possession of the city. [37]Timothy had hidden in a cistern, but they killed[†] him, along with his brother Chaereas, and Apollophanes. [38]On completing these exploits, they blessed, with hymns of grateful praise, the Lord who shows great kindness to Israel and grants them victory.

## CHAPTER 11

**Defeat of Lysias.**[‡] [1r]Very soon afterward, Lysias, guardian and kinsman of the king and head of the government, being greatly displeased at what had happened, [2]mustered about eighty thousand infantry and all his cavalry and marched against the Jews. His plan was to make their city a Greek settlement; [3]to levy tribute on the temple, as he did on the shrines of the other nations; and to put the high priesthood up for sale every year.[s] [4]He did not take God's power into account at all, but felt exultant confidence in his myriads of foot soldiers, his thousands of cavalry, and his eighty elephants.[t] [5]So he invaded Judea, and when he reached Beth-zur, a fortified place about five stadia[§] from Jerusalem, launched a strong attack against it.

[6]When Maccabeus and his companions learned that Lysias was besieging the strongholds, they and all the people begged the Lord with lamentations and tears to send a good angel to save Israel.[u] [7]Maccabeus himself was the first to take up arms, and he exhorted the others to join him in risking their lives to help their kindred. Then they resolutely set out together. [8]Suddenly, while they were still near Jerusalem, a horseman appeared at their head, clothed in white garments and brandishing gold weapons.[v] [9]Then all of them together thanked the merciful God, and their hearts were filled with such courage that they were ready to assault not only human beings but even the most savage beasts, or even walls of iron. [10]Now that the Lord had shown mercy toward them, they advanced in battle order with the aid of their heavenly ally. [11]Hurling themselves upon the enemy like lions, they laid low eleven thousand foot soldiers and sixteen hundred cavalry, and put all the rest to flight. [12]Most of those who survived were wounded and disarmed, while Lysias himself escaped only by shameful flight.

**Peace Negotiations.** [13w]But Lysias was not a stupid man. He reflected on the defeat he had suffered, and came to realize that the Hebrews were invincible because the mighty God was their ally. He therefore sent a message [14]persuading them to settle everything on just terms, and promising to persuade the king also, and to induce him to become their friend. [15]Maccabeus, solicitous for the common good, agreed to all that Lysias proposed; and the king granted on behalf of the Jews all the written requests of Maccabeus to Lysias.

[16]These are the terms of the letter which Lysias wrote to the Jews: "Lysias sends greetings to the Jewish people. [17]John and Absalom, your envoys, have presented your signed communication and asked about the matters contained in it. [18]Whatever had to be referred to the king I called to his attention, and the things that were acceptable he has granted. [19]If you maintain your loyalty to the government, I will endeavor

---

*[10:28] **As soon as dawn broke:** the same battle at dawn as in 1 Mc 5:30–34.

†[10:37] **Timothy . . . they killed:** apparently Timothy is still alive in 12:2, 18–25. Perhaps there was more than one Timothy. Or the present passage is not in chronological order. Gazara, v. 32 (Gezer), was not captured by the Jews until much later (cf. 1 Mc 9:50–52; 13:53). See 1 Mc 5:8 for the capture of Jazer.

‡[11:1–12] The defeat of Lysias at Beth-zur probably occurred before the purification of the Temple; cf. 1 Mc 4:26–35.

§[11:5] **Five stadia:** one stadium is equal to about six hundred six feet. The actual distance to Beth-zur is about twenty miles.

---

o. [10:26] Ex 23:22.   p. [10:29–30] 2 Mc 3:24–26; 5:2–3; 11:8.
q. [10:32] 1 Mc 13:43–48.   r. [11:1–15] 1 Mc 4:26–35.

s. [11:3] 2 Mc 4:7–8, 23–24.   t. [11:4] 1 Mc 3:34.   u. [11:6] Ex 23:20.   v. [11:8] 2 Mc 3:24–26; 5:2–3; 10:29–30.   w. [11:13–33] 1 Mc 6:57–61.

to further, your interests in the future. ²⁰On the details of these matters I have authorized my representatives, as well as your envoys, to confer with you. ²¹Farewell." The one hundred and forty-eighth year,ʳ the twenty-fourth of Dioscorinthius.

²²The king's letter read thus: "King Antiochus sends greetings to his brother Lysias. ²³Now that our father has taken his place among the gods, we wish the subjects of our kingdom to be undisturbed in conducting their own affairs. ²⁴We have heard that the Jews do not agree with our father's change to Greek customs but prefer their own way of life. They are petitioning us to let them retain their own customs. ²⁵Since we desire that this people too should be undisturbed, our decision is that their temple be restored to them and that they live in keeping with the customs of their ancestors. ²⁶Accordingly, please send them messengers to give them our assurances of friendship, so that, when they learn of our decision, they may have nothing to worry about but may contentedly go about their own business."

²⁷The king's letter to the people was as follows: "King Antiochus sends greetings to the Jewish senate and to the rest of the Jews. ²⁸If you are well, it is what we desire. We too are in good health. ²⁹Menelaus has told us of your wish to return home and attend to your own affairs. ³⁰Therefore, those who return by the thirtieth of Xanthicus will have our assurance of full permission ³¹to observe their dietary and other laws, just as before, and none of the Jews shall be molested in any way for faults committed through ignorance. ³²I have also sent Menelaus to reassure you. ³³Farewell." In the one hundred and forty-eighth year, the fifteenth of Xanthicus.†

³⁴The Romans also sent them a letter as follows: "Quintus Memmius and Titus Manius, legates of the Romans, send greetings to the Jewish people. ³⁵What Lysias, kinsman of the king, has granted you, we also approve. ³⁶But for the matters that he decided should be submitted to the king, send someone to us immediately with your decisions so that we may present them to your advantage, for we are on our way to Antioch. ³⁷Make haste, then, to send us those who can inform us of your preference. ³⁸Farewell." In the one hundred and forty-eighth year, the fifteenth of Xanthicus.‡

---

*[11:21] **The one hundred and forty-eighth year:** 164 B.C. The reading of the name of the month and its position in the calendar are uncertain. The most likely chronological sequence of the four letters is vv. 16–21; vv. 34–38; vv. 27–33; vv. 22–26.

†[11:33] The date, which is the same as the date of the Romans' letter (v. 38), cannot be correct. The king's letter must be connected with the peace treaty of the one hundred forty-ninth year of the Seleucid era, i.e., 163 B.C. Perhaps the mention of the month of Xanthicus in the body of the letter (v. 30) caused the date of the Romans' letter to be transferred to this one.

‡[11:38] The date is March 12, 164 B.C.

---

# CHAPTER 12

**Incidents at Joppa and Jamnia.** ¹After these agreements were made, Lysias returned to the king, and the Jews went about their farming. ²But some of the local governors, Timothy and Apollonius, son of Gennaeus,§ as also Hieronymus and Demophon, to say nothing of Nicanor, the commander of the Cyprians, would not allow them to live in peace and quiet.

³Some people of Joppa also committed this outrage: they invited the Jews who lived among them, together with their wives and children, to embark on boats which they had provided. There was no hint of enmity toward them. ⁴This was done by public vote of the city. When the Jews, wishing to live on friendly terms and not suspecting anything, accepted the invitation, the people of Joppa took them out to sea and drowned at least two hundred of them.

⁵As soon as Judas heard of the barbarous deed perpetrated against his compatriots, he summoned his men; ⁶and after calling upon God, the just judge, he marched against the murderers of his kindred. In a night attack he set the harbor on fire, burned the boats, and put to the sword those who had taken refuge there. ⁷Because the gates of the town were shut, he withdrew, intending to come back later and wipe out the entire population of Joppa.

⁸On hearing that the people of Jamnia planned in the same way to wipe out the Jews who lived among them, ⁹he attacked the Jamnians by night, setting fire to the harbor and the fleet, so that the glow of the flames was visible as far as Jerusalem, thirty miles away.

**More Victories by Judas.** ¹⁰ˣWhen the Jews had gone about a mile from thereʳ in the march against Timothy, they were attacked by Arabians numbering at least five thousand foot soldiers and five hundred cavalry. ¹¹After a hard fight, Judas and his companions, with God's help, were victorious. The defeated nomads begged Judas to give pledges of friendship, and they promised to supply the Jews with livestock and to be of service to them in any other way. ¹²Realizing that they could indeed be useful in many respects, Judas agreed to make peace with them. After the pledges of friendship had been exchanged, the Arabians withdrew to their tents.

¹³He also attacked a certain city called Caspin, fortified with earthworks and walls and inhabited by a mixed population of Gentiles. ¹⁴Relying on the strength of their walls and their supply of provisions, the besieged treated Judas and his men with contempt, insulting them

---

§[12:2] **Apollonius, son of Gennaeus:** not the Apollonius who was the son of Menestheus (4:21). **Nicanor:** probably distinct from the Nicanor of 14:2.

¶[12:10] **From there:** not from Jamnia (vv. 8–9) or Joppa (vv. 3–7), but from a place in Transjordan; vv. 10–26 parallel the account given in 1 Mc 5:9–13, 24–54 of Judas' campaign in northern Transjordan.

x. [12:10–16] 1 Mc 5:24–36.

and even uttering blasphemies and profanity. [15]But Judas and his men invoked the aid of the great Sovereign of the world, who, in the days of Joshua, overthrew Jericho without battering rams or siege engines; then they furiously stormed the walls.[y] [16]Capturing the city by the will of God, they inflicted such indescribable slaughter on it that the adjacent pool, which was about a quarter of a mile wide, seemed to be filled with the blood that flowed into it.

[17z]When they had gone on some ninety miles, they reached Charax, where there were certain Jews known as Toubians.[*a] [18]But they did not find Timothy in that region, for he had already departed from there without having done anything except to leave behind in one place a very strong garrison. [19]But Dositheus and Sosipater, two of Maccabeus' captains, marched out and destroyed the force of more than ten thousand men that Timothy had left in the stronghold. [20]Meanwhile, Maccabeus divided his army into cohorts, with a commander over each cohort, and went in pursuit of Timothy, who had a force of a hundred and twenty thousand foot soldiers and twenty-five hundred cavalry. [21]When Timothy learned of the approach of Judas, he sent on ahead of him the women and children, as well as the baggage, to a place called Karnion, which was hard to besiege and even hard to reach because of the difficult terrain of that region. [22]But when Judas' first cohort appeared, the enemy was overwhelmed with fear and terror at the manifestation of the all-seeing One. Scattering in every direction, they rushed away in such headlong flight that in many cases they wounded one another, pierced by the points of their own swords. [23]Judas pressed the pursuit vigorously, putting the sinners to the sword and destroying as many as thirty thousand men.

[24]Timothy himself fell into the hands of those under Dositheus and Sosipater; but with great cunning, he begged them to spare his life and let him go, because he had in his power the parents and relatives of many of them, and would show them no consideration. [25]When he had fully confirmed his solemn pledge to restore them unharmed, they let him go for the sake of saving their relatives.

[26b]Judas then marched to Karnion and the shrine of Atargatis,[†] where he killed twenty-five thousand people. [27]After the defeat and destruction of these, he moved his army to Ephron, a fortified city inhabited by Lysias and people of many nationalities. Robust young men took up their posts in defense of the walls, from which

they fought valiantly; inside were large supplies of war machines and missiles. [28]But the Jews, invoking the Sovereign who powerfully shatters the might of enemies, got possession of the city and slaughtered twenty-five thousand of the people in it.

[29]Then they set out from there and hastened on to Scythopolis,[‡] seventy-five miles from Jerusalem. [30]But when the Jews who lived there testified to the goodwill shown by the Scythopolitans and to their kind treatment even in times of adversity, [31]Judas and his men thanked them and exhorted them to be well disposed to their nation in the future also. Finally they arrived in Jerusalem, shortly before the feast of Weeks.

[32]After this feast, also called Pentecost, they lost no time in marching against Gorgias, governor of Idumea, [33]who opposed them with three thousand foot soldiers and four hundred cavalry. [34]In the ensuing battle, a few of the Jews were slain. [35]A man called Dositheus, a powerful horseman and one of Bacenor's men,[§] caught hold of Gorgias, grasped his military cloak and dragged him along by brute strength, intending to capture the vile wretch alive, when a Thracian horseman attacked Dositheus and cut off his arm at the shoulder. Then Gorgias fled to Marisa.

[36]After Esdris and his men had been fighting for a long time and were weary, Judas called upon the Lord to show himself their ally and leader in the battle. [37]Then, raising a battle cry in his ancestral language, and with hymns, he charged Gorgias' men when they were not expecting it and put them to flight.

**Expiation for the Dead.** [38]Judas rallied his army and went to the city of Adullam. As the seventh day was approaching, they purified themselves according to custom and kept the sabbath there. [39]On the following day, since the task had now become urgent, Judas and his companions went to gather up the bodies of the fallen and bury them with their kindred in their ancestral tombs. [40]But under the tunic of each of the dead they found amulets sacred to the idols of Jamnia, which the law forbids the Jews to wear. So it was clear to all that this was why these men had fallen.[c] [41]They all therefore praised the ways of the Lord, the just judge who brings to light the things that are hidden. [42¶]Turning to supplication, they prayed that the sinful deed might

---

*[12:17] **Certain Jews known as Toubians**: because they lived "in the land of Tob" (1 Mc 5:13).

†[12:26] **Atargatis**: a Syrian goddess, represented by the body of a fish, who in Hellenistic times was identified with Astarte and Artemis.

y. [12:15] Jos 6:1–21.  z. [12:17–26] 1 Mc 5:37–44.  a. [12:17] 1 Mc 5:13.  b. [12:26–31] 1 Mc 5:45–54.

‡[12:29] **Scythopolis**: the Greek name of the city of Beth-shan; cf. 1 Mc 5:52.

§[12:35] **One of Bacenor's men**: certain ancient witnesses to the text have "one of the Toubians"; cf. v. 17.

¶[12:42–45] This is the earliest statement of the doctrine that prayers (v. 42) and sacrifices (v. 43) for the dead are efficacious. Judas probably intended his purification offering to ward off punishment from the living. The author, however, uses the story to demonstrate belief in the resurrection of the just (7:9, 14, 23, 36), and in the possibility of expiation for the sins of otherwise good people who have died. This belief is similar to, but not quite the same as, the Catholic doctrine of purgatory.

c. [12:40] Dt 7:25–26.

be fully blotted out. The noble Judas exhorted the people to keep themselves free from sin, for they had seen with their own eyes what had happened because of the sin of those who had fallen.<sup>d</sup> <sup>43</sup>He then took up a collection among all his soldiers, amounting to two thousand silver drachmas, which he sent to Jerusalem to provide for an expiatory sacrifice. In doing this he acted in a very excellent and noble way, inasmuch as he had the resurrection in mind; <sup>44</sup>for if he were not expecting the fallen to rise again, it would have been superfluous and foolish to pray for the dead. <sup>45</sup>But if he did this with a view to the splendid reward that awaits those who had gone to rest in godliness, it was a holy and pious thought. <sup>46</sup>Thus he made atonement for the dead that they might be absolved from their sin.

## CHAPTER 13

**Death of Menelaus.** <sup>1</sup><sup>e</sup>In the one hundred and forty-ninth year,* Judas and his men learned that Antiochus Eupator was invading Judea with a large force, <sup>2</sup>and that with him was Lysias, his guardian, who was in charge of the government. They led<sup>†</sup> a Greek army of one hundred and ten thousand foot soldiers, fifty-three hundred cavalry, twenty-two elephants, and three hundred chariots armed with scythes.

<sup>3</sup>Menelaus also joined them, and with great duplicity kept urging Antiochus on, not for the welfare of his country, but in the hope of being established in office. <sup>4</sup>But the King of kings<sup>f</sup> aroused the anger of Antiochus against the scoundrel. When the king was shown by Lysias that Menelaus was to blame for all the trouble, he ordered him to be taken to Beroea<sup>‡</sup> and executed there in the customary local method. <sup>5</sup>There is at that place a tower seventy-five feet high, full of ashes,<sup>§</sup> with a circular rim sloping down steeply on all sides toward the ashes. <sup>6</sup>Anyone guilty of sacrilege or notorious for certain other crimes is brought up there and then hurled down to destruction. <sup>7</sup>In such a manner was Menelaus, that transgressor of the law, fated to die, deprived even of burial. <sup>8</sup>It was altogether just that he who had committed so many sins against the altar with its pure fire and ashes, in ashes should meet his death.

**Battle near Modein.** <sup>9</sup>The king was advancing, his mind full of savage plans for inflicting on the Jews things worse than those they suffered in his father's time. <sup>10</sup>When Judas learned of this,

he urged the people to call upon the Lord day and night, now more than ever, to help them when they were about to be deprived of their law, their country, and their holy temple; <sup>11</sup>and not to allow this people, which had just begun to revive, to be subjected again to blasphemous Gentiles. <sup>12</sup>When they had all joined in doing this, and had implored the merciful Lord continuously with weeping and fasting and prostrations for three days, Judas encouraged them and told them to stand ready.

<sup>13</sup>After a private meeting with the elders, he decided that, before the king's army could invade Judea and take possession of the city, the Jews should march out and settle the matter with God's help. <sup>14</sup>Leaving the outcome to the Creator of the world, and exhorting his followers to fight nobly to death for the laws, the temple, the city, the country, and the government, he encamped near Modein. <sup>15</sup>Giving his troops the battle cry "God's Victory," he made a night attack on the king's pavilion with a picked force of the bravest young men and killed about two thousand in the camp. He also stabbed the lead elephant and its rider.<sup>g</sup> <sup>16</sup>Finally they withdrew in triumph,<sup>¶</sup> having filled the camp with terror and confusion. <sup>17</sup>Day was just breaking when this was accomplished with the help and protection of the Lord.

**Treaty with Antiochus V.** <sup>18</sup><sup>h</sup>The king, having had a taste of the Jews' boldness, tried to take their positions by a stratagem. <sup>19</sup>So he marched against Beth-zur, a strong fortress of the Jews; but he was driven back, checked, and defeated. <sup>20</sup>Judas sent supplies to the men inside, <sup>21</sup>but Rhodocus, of the Jewish army, betrayed military secrets** to the enemy. He was found out, arrested, and imprisoned. <sup>22</sup>The king made a second attempt by negotiating with the people of Beth-zur. After giving them his pledge and receiving theirs, he withdrew <sup>23</sup>and attacked Judas' men. But he was defeated. Next he heard that Philip, who was left in charge of the government in Antioch, had rebelled. Dismayed, he negotiated with the Jews, submitted to their terms, and swore to observe all their rights. Having come to this agreement, he offered a sacrifice, and honored the sanctuary and the place with a generous donation. <sup>24</sup>He received Maccabeus, and left Hegemonides as governor of the territory from Ptolemais to the region of the Gerrhenes.<sup>††</sup> <sup>25</sup>When he came to Ptolemais, the people of Ptolemais were angered by the peace treaty; in fact they were so indignant that they wanted to annul its provisions. <sup>26</sup>But Lysias

---

*[13:1] **In the one hundred and forty-ninth year:** 163/162 B.C.

†[13:2] **They led:** the Greek means literally "each (of them) led," but it is unlikely that the author meant the already immense numbers to be doubled; the numbers are similar to those in 1 Mc 6:30.

‡[13:4] **Beroea:** the Greek name of Aleppo in Syria.

§[13:5] **Ashes:** probably smoldering ashes; the tower resembles the ancient Persian fire towers.

---

d. [12:42] Jos 7:1–26.    e. [13:1–26] 1 Mc 6:28–54.    f. [13:4] 1 Tm 6:15; Rev 17:14; 19:16.

---

¶[13:16] **They withdrew in triumph:** according to 1 Mc 6:47 they fled.

**[13:21] **Military secrets:** probably about the lack of provisions in the besieged city; cf. 1 Mc 6:49.

††[13:24] **Gerrhenes:** probably the inhabitants of Gerar, southeast of Gaza.

---

g. [13:15] 1 Mc 6:43–46.    h. [13:18–23] 1 Mc 6:48–53.

took the platform, defended the treaty as well as he could and won them over by persuasion. After calming them and gaining their goodwill, he returned to Antioch. That is the story of the king's attack and withdrawal.

## CHAPTER 14

[1]*Three years later,* Judas and his companions learned that Demetrius, son of Seleucus, had sailed into the port of Tripolis with a powerful army and a fleet, [2]and that he had occupied the country, after doing away with Antiochus and his guardian Lysias.

[3]A certain Alcimus, a former high priest,† who had willfully incurred defilement before the time of the revolt, realized that there was no way for him to be safe and regain access to the holy altar. [4]So he went to King Demetrius around the one hundred and fifty-first year and presented him with a gold crown and a palm branch, as well as some of the customary olive branches from the temple. On that day he kept quiet.ʲ [5]But he found an opportunity to further his mad scheme when he was invited to the council by Demetrius and questioned about the dispositions and intentions of the Jews. He replied: [6]"Those Jews called Hasideans, led by Judas Maccabeus,‡ are warmongers, who stir up sedition and keep the kingdom from enjoying peace.ᵏ [7]For this reason, now that I am deprived of my ancestral dignity, that is to say, the high priesthood, I have come here, [8]first, out of my genuine concern for the king's interests, and second, out of consideration for my own compatriots, since our entire nation is suffering no little affliction from the rash conduct of the people just mentioned. [9]When you have informed yourself in detail on these matters, O king, provide for our country and its hard-pressed people with the same gracious consideration that you show toward all. [10]As long as Judas is around, it is impossible for the government to enjoy peace." [11]When he had said this, the other Friends who were hostile to Judas quickly added fuel to Demetrius' indignation.

**Dealings with Nicanor.** [12]The king immediately chose Nicanor, who had been in command of the elephants, and appointed him governor of Judea. He sent him off [13]with orders to put Judas to death, to disperse his followers, and to set up Alcimus as high priest of the great temple. [14]The Gentiles from Judea, who had fled before Judas, flocked to Nicanor, thinking that the misfortunes and calamities of the Jews would mean prosperity for themselves.

[15]ᵐWhen the Jews heard of Nicanor's coming, and that the Gentiles were rallying to him, they sprinkled themselves with earth and prayed to him who established his people forever, and who always comes to the aid of his heritage by manifesting himself. [16]At their leader's command, they set out at once from there and came upon the enemy at the village of Adasa. [17]Judas' brother Simon had engaged Nicanor, but he suffered a slight setback because of the sudden appearance of the enemy.

[18]However, when Nicanor heard of the valor of Judas and his companions, and the great courage with which they fought for their country, he shrank from deciding the issue by bloodshed. [19]So he sent Posidonius, Theodotus and Mattathias to exchange pledges of friendship. [20]After a long discussion of the terms, each leader communicated them to his troops; and when general agreement was expressed, they assented to the treaty. [21]A day was set on which the leaders would meet by themselves. From each side a chariot came forward, and thrones were set in place. [22]Judas had posted armed men in readiness at strategic points for fear that the enemy might suddenly commit some treachery. But the conference was held in the proper way.

[23]Nicanor stayed on in Jerusalem, where he did nothing out of place. He disbanded the throngs of people who gathered around him; [24]and he always kept Judas in his company, for he felt affection§ for the man. [25]He urged him to marry and have children; so Judas married and settled into an ordinary life.

**Nicanor's Threat Against Judas.** [26]When Alcimus saw their mutual goodwill, he took the treaty that had been made, went to Demetrius, and said that Nicanor was plotting against the government, for he had appointed Judas, that conspirator against the kingdom, as his successor. [27]Stirred up by the villain's slander, the king became enraged. He wrote to Nicanor, stating that he was displeased with the treaty, and ordering him to send Maccabeus at once as a prisoner to Antioch. [28]When this message reached Nicanor he was dismayed and troubled at the thought of annulling his agreement with a man who had done no wrong. [29]However, there was no way of opposing the king, so he watched for an opportunity to carry out this order by a stratagem. [30]But Maccabeus, noticing that Nicanor was more harsh in his dealings with him, and acting with unaccustomed rudeness when they met, concluded that this harshness was not

---

*[14:1] **Three years later:** actually, Demetrius (I Soter), son of Seleucus (IV), landed at Tripolis in the year 151 of the Seleucid era (cf. 1 Mc 14:4), i.e., 162/161 B.C.; cf. 1 Mc 7:1–7.

†[14:3] **Alcimus, a former high priest:** he was apparently appointed high priest by Antiochus V after Menelaus was executed, and then deposed for collaborating with the Seleucids.

‡[14:6] **Hasideans, led by Judas Maccabeus:** according to 1 Mc 2:42 and 7:12–17, the Hasideans were a party separate from the Maccabees.

§[14:24] **Affection:** compare 1 Mc 7:26–32, where there is no hint of this cordial relationship between Nicanor and Judas.

i. [14:1–11] 1 Mc 7:1–7.   j. [14:4] 1 Mc 7:5–7, 25.   k. [14:6] 1 Mc 2:42; 7:12–17.   l. [14:12–13] 2 Mc 8:9; 1 Mc 3:38; 7:26–27.

m. [14:15–19] 1 Mc 7:26–32.

a good sign. So he gathered together not a few of his men, and went into hiding from Nicanor.

[31n]When Nicanor realized that he had been cleverly outwitted by the man, he went to the great and holy temple, at a time when the priests were offering the customary sacrifices, and ordered them to surrender Judas. [32]As they declared under oath that they did not know where the man they sought was, [33]he stretched out his right arm toward the temple and swore this oath: "If you do not hand Judas over to me as prisoner, I will level this shrine of God to the ground; I will tear down the altar, and erect here a splendid temple to Dionysus."

[34]With these words he went away. The priests stretched out their hands toward heaven, calling upon the unfailing defender of our nation in these words: [35]"Lord of all, though you are in need of nothing, you were pleased to have a temple for your dwelling place among us. [36]Therefore, Holy One, Lord of all holiness, preserve forever undefiled this house, which has been so recently purified."[o]

**Martyrdom of Razis.**[*] [37]A certain Razis, one of the elders of Jerusalem, was denounced to Nicanor as a patriot. A man highly regarded, he was called a father of the Jews because of his goodwill toward them. [38]In the days before the revolt, he had been convicted of being a Jew, and had risked body and soul in his ardent zeal for Judaism. [39]Nicanor, to show his disdain for the Jews, sent more than five hundred soldiers to arrest him. [40]He thought that by arresting that man he would deal the Jews a hard blow.

[41]But when the troops, on the point of capturing the tower, were forcing the outer gate and calling for fire to set the door ablaze, Razis, now caught on all sides, turned his sword against himself, [42]preferring to die nobly[†] rather than fall into the hands of vile men and suffer outrages unworthy of his noble birth. [43]In the excitement of the struggle he failed to strike exactly. So while the troops rushed in through the doors, he gallantly ran up to the top of the wall and courageously threw himself down into the crowd. [44]But as they quickly drew back and left an opening, he fell into the middle of the empty space. [45]Still breathing, and inflamed with anger, he got up and ran through the crowd, with blood gushing from his frightful wounds. Then, standing on a steep rock, [46]as he lost the last of his blood, he tore out his entrails and flung them with both hands into the crowd, calling upon the Lord of life and of spirit to give

these back to him again. Such was the manner of his death.[p]

# CHAPTER 15

**Nicanor's Arrogance.** [1]When Nicanor learned that Judas and his companions were in the territory of Samaria, he decided he could attack them in complete safety on the day of rest. [2]The Jews who were forced to accompany him pleaded, "Do not massacre them so savagely and barbarously, but show respect for the day which the All-seeing has exalted with holiness above all other days." [3]At this the thrice-accursed wretch asked if there was a ruler in heaven who prescribed the keeping of the sabbath day.[q] [4]They replied, "It is the living Lord, the ruler in heaven, who commands the observance of the sabbath day." [5]Then he said, "I, the ruler on earth, command you to take up arms and carry out the king's business." Nevertheless he did not succeed in carrying out his cruel plan.

[6]In his utter boastfulness and arrogance Nicanor had determined to erect a public victory monument[‡] over Judas and his companions. [7]But Maccabeus remained confident, fully convinced that he would receive help from the Lord. [8]He urged his men not to fear the attack of the Gentiles, but mindful of the help they had received in the past from Heaven, to expect now the victory that would be given them by the Almighty. [9]By encouraging them with words from the law and the prophets,[§] and by reminding them of the battles they had already won, he filled them with fresh enthusiasm. [10]Having stirred up their courage, he gave his orders and pointed out at the same time the perfidy of the Gentiles and their violation of oaths. [11]When he had armed each of them, not so much with the security of shield and spear as with the encouragement of noble words, he cheered them all by relating a dream, a kind of waking vision, worthy of belief.

[12]What he saw was this: Onias, the former high priest,[¶] a noble and good man, modest in bearing, gentle in manner, distinguished in speech, and trained from childhood in all that belongs to excellence, was praying with outstretched arms for the whole Jewish community.[r] [13]Then in the same way another man appeared, distinguished by his white hair and dignity, and with an air of wondrous and majestic authority. [14]Onias then said of him, "This is a man"[**] who

---

‡[15:6] **Public victory monument:** a heap of stones covered with the arms and armor of the fallen enemy.

§[15:9] **The law and the prophets:** the first of the three parts of the Hebrew Scriptures, called the sacred books (1 Mc 12:9; 2 Mc 2:14).

¶[15:12] **Onias, the former high priest:** Onias III (3:1–40). Evidently the author believed that departed just persons were in some way alive even before their resurrection.

**[15:14] **A man:** regarded by the postexilic Jews as one of the greatest figures in their history; cf. 2:1; Mt 16:14.

---

*[14:37–46] The story of Razis belongs to the "martyrology" class of literature; it is similar to the stories in 6:18–7:42.

†[14:42] **Die nobly:** Razis's willingness to die nobly rather than to fall into enemy hands had a precedent in Saul (1 Sm 31:4). Razis took his life because he was convinced that God would restore his body in the resurrection of the dead (see 7:11, 22–23; 14:46).

---

n. [14:31–36] 1 Mc 7:30–38.   o. [14:36] 2 Mc 15:34.

p. [14:46] 2 Mc 7:9–11.   q. [15:3] 1 Mc 7:34.   r. [15:12] 2 Mc 3:1–40.

loves his fellow Jews and fervently prays for the people and the holy city—the prophet of God, Jeremiah." <sup>15</sup>Stretching out his right hand, Jeremiah presented a gold sword to Judas. As he gave it to him he said, <sup>16</sup>"Accept this holy sword as a gift from God; with it you shall shatter your adversaries."

<sup>17</sup>Encouraged by Judas' words, so noble and capable of instilling valor and stirring young hearts to courage, they determined not merely to march, but to charge gallantly and decide the issue by hand-to-hand combat with the utmost courage, since city, sanctuary and temple were in danger. <sup>18</sup>They were not so much concerned about wives and children, or family and relations; their first and foremost fear was for the consecrated sanctuary.<sup>s</sup> <sup>19</sup>Those who were left in the city suffered no less an agony, anxious as they were about the battle in the open country. <sup>20</sup>Everyone now awaited the decisive moment. The enemy were already drawing near with their troops drawn up in battle line, their beasts placed in strategic positions, and their cavalry stationed on the flanks.

**Defeat of Nicanor.** <sup>21</sup>Maccabeus, surveying the hosts before him, the variety of weaponry, and the fierceness of their beasts, stretched out his hands toward heaven and called upon the Lord who works wonders; for he knew that it is not weapons but the Lord's decision that brings victory to those who deserve it. <sup>22</sup>Calling upon God, he spoke in this manner: "You, master, sent your angel in the days of King Hezekiah of Judea, and he slew a hundred and eighty-five thousand men of Sennacherib's camp.<sup>t</sup> <sup>23</sup>And now, Sovereign of the heavens, send a good angel to spread fear and trembling ahead of us. <sup>24</sup>By the might of your arm may those be struck down who have blasphemously come against your holy people!" With these words he ended his prayer.

<sup>25</sup>"Nicanor and his troops advanced to the sound of trumpets and battle songs. <sup>26</sup>But Judas and his troops met the enemy with supplication and prayers. <sup>27</sup>Fighting with their hands and praying to God with their hearts, they laid low at least thirty-five thousand, and rejoiced greatly over this manifestation of God's power.

<sup>28</sup>When the battle was over and they were joyfully departing, they discovered Nicanor fallen there in all his armor; <sup>29</sup>so they raised tumultuous shouts in their ancestral language in praise of the divine Sovereign.

<sup>30</sup>Then Judas, that man who was ever in body and soul the chief defender of his fellow citizens, and had maintained from youth his affection for his compatriots, ordered Nicanor's head and right arm up to the shoulder to be cut off and taken to Jerusalem. <sup>31</sup>When he arrived there, he assembled his compatriots, stationed the priests before the altar, and sent for those in the citadel.<sup>*</sup> <sup>32</sup>He showed them the vile Nicanor's head and the wretched blasphemer's arm that had been boastfully stretched out against the holy dwelling of the Almighty. <sup>33</sup>He cut out the tongue of the godless Nicanor, saying he would feed it piecemeal to the birds and would hang up the other wages of his folly opposite the temple. <sup>34</sup>At this, everyone looked toward heaven and praised the Lord who manifests himself: "Blessed be the one who has preserved undefiled his own place!" <sup>35</sup>Judas hung Nicanor's head and arm on the wall of the citadel, a clear and evident sign to all of the Lord's help.<sup>v</sup> <sup>36</sup>By public vote it was unanimously decreed never to let this day pass unobserved, but to celebrate the thirteenth day of the twelfth month, called Adar in Aramaic, the eve of Mordecai's Day.<sup>†w</sup>

## VII. EPILOGUE

**Compiler's Apology.** <sup>37</sup>Since Nicanor's doings ended in this way, with the city remaining in the possession of the Hebrews from that time on, I will bring my story to an end here too. <sup>38</sup>If it is well written and to the point, that is what I wanted; if it is poorly done and mediocre, that is the best I could do. <sup>39</sup>Just as it is unpleasant to drink wine by itself or just water, whereas wine mixed with water makes a delightful and pleasing drink, so a skillfully composed story delights the ears of those who read the work. Let this, then, be the end.

---

*[15:31] **Those in the citadel**: presumably Jewish soldiers; actually, the citadel was still in the possession of the Syrians (1 Mc 13:50).

†[15:36] **Mordecai's Day**: the feast of Purim, celebrated on the fourteenth and fifteenth days of Adar (Est 3:7; 9:20–23; F:10).

---

**Who . . . prays for the people:** Jeremiah's prayer in heaven has been taken in the Roman Catholic tradition as a biblical witness to the intercession of the saints.

---

s. [15:18] 1 Mc 4:36.   t. [15:22–23] 2 Mc 8:19; 2 Kgs 19:35–36; 1 Mc 7:41–42; Is 37:36–37.   u. [15:25–36] 1 Mc 7:43.

v. [15:35] 1 Sm 31:9–10.   w. [15:36] 1 Mc 7:49.   x. [15:38–39] 2 Mc 2:19–32.

# THE
# WISDOM BOOKS

❧

"Wisdom" is a convenient umbrella term to designate the Books of Job, Proverbs, Ecclesiastes (Qoheleth), Wisdom, and Sirach (Ecclesiasticus). Two other books are often associated with them: Psalms, a collection of mostly devotional lyrics, and the Song of Songs, a collection of love poems. All are marked by a skillful use of parallelism, or verses of balanced and symmetrical phrases. These works have been classified as wisdom or didactic literature, so called because their general purpose is instruction.

A striking feature of the wisdom books is the absence of references to the promises made to the patriarchs or to Moses, or to Sinai or typical items in Israelite tradition; Sirach (chaps. 44–50) and Wisdom (chaps. 10–19) are the exception. Biblical wisdom literature concentrates on daily human experience: how is life to be lived? In this respect it is comparable to other ancient Near Eastern compositions from Mesopotamia and Egypt that also reflect on the problems of everyday life. The literary style is wide-ranging: aphorisms, numerical sayings, paradoxes, instructions, alphabetical and acrostic poems, lively speeches, and so forth. Wisdom itself is an art: how to deal with various situations and achieve a good life. And it is also a teaching: the lessons garnered from experience were transmitted at various levels, from education in the home all the way to training in the court. Belief in the Lord and acceptance of the prevailing codes of conduct were presupposed; they fed into the training of youths. The task of wisdom is character formation: what is the wise path to follow? The lessons are conveyed by observations that challenge as well as by admonitions that warn. Although the need of discipline is underlined, the general approach is persuasion. The pursuit of wisdom demands more than human industry. Paradoxically, it remains also the gift of God (Prv 2:6). Its religious character is indicated by the steady identification of wisdom and virtue (e.g., Prv 10–15).

But wisdom is far more than a practical guide. The strongest personification in the Bible is Woman Wisdom, and she speaks somewhat mysteriously in divine accents about her origins and identity. Her appeal to humanity is sounded in several books: Prv 8; Sir 24; Wis 7–9; Bar 3:9–4:4. She offers "life" to her followers (Prv 8:35, "whoever finds me finds life"). This image of personified Wisdom is reflected in the Logos poem of Jn 1:1–18 and in Paul's reference to Jesus as "the wisdom of God" (1 Cor 1:24, 30). The bearing of wisdom literature on the New Testament is also exemplified in the sayings and parables of Jesus and in the practical admonitions in the Letter of James.

Each book has a distinctive character. Proverbs consists of long poems dealing with moral conduct (chaps. 1–9), which introduce collections of aphorisms (chaps. 10–29) reflecting on the experiences of life. The Book of Job is a literary presentation of the problem of the suffering of the innocent and god-fearing Job. Psalms, the book of prayer par excellence, derives from varied origins, especially liturgical celebrations; it contains personal cries of agony as well as of praise and thanksgiving. Some betray a wisdom influence (e.g., Ps 37), and the very first Psalm serves as an invitation to learn about the ways of the just and wicked in the rest of the psalter. Ecclesiastes examines the hard questions of life, and has become famous for the expressive phrase "vanity of vanities." The Song of Songs is a collection of poems that give meaning to human and divine love (Sg 8:6; Prv 30:18–19). Ben Sira is the only author who identifies himself (Sir 50:27), and circa 200 B.C. he writes a compendium of Jewish wisdom and creation theology. The Wisdom of Solomon was written in Greek against a Hellenistic background, affirming human immortality in terms of a continuing relationship with God. Except for Psalms (of which almost half are attributed to David), Job, and Sirach, the books are attributed to Solomon, but he is not the author. The Solomonic claim is doubtless due to his fame as a wise man, according to 1 Kgs 5:9–14; 10:1–10. Who were the sages? Some were found in ordinary families (father, mother, Prv 1:8; 10:1); others were scribes at court. All contributed, both men (the counselors of Absalom, 2 Sm 16–17; the men of King Hezekiah, Prv 25:1) and also women (the "wise woman" of Abel Beth-maacah, 2 Sm 20:16). The wisdom literature is predominantly a postexilic composition, but the dating is only approximate.

In Jewish tradition, *Megillot* (Scrolls) came to be the accepted term for the five books of Ruth, Song of Songs, Ecclesiastes, Lamentations, and Esther. In the Protestant tradition, Sirach and Wisdom are classified as apocrypha and not printed as a part of Scripture. The Orthodox tradition does accept them, along with other works, such as 3–4 Maccabees and the Prayer of Manasseh.

# THE BOOK OF
# JOB

The Book of Job, named after its protagonist (apparently not an Israelite; cf. Ez 14:14, 20), is an exquisite dramatic treatment of the problem of the suffering of the innocent. The contents of the book, together with its artistic structure and elegant style, place it among the literary masterpieces of all time. This is a literary composition, and not a transcript of historical events and conversations.

The prologue (chaps. 1–2) provides the setting for Job's testing. When challenged by the satan's questioning of Job's sincerity, the Lord gives leave for a series of catastrophes to afflict Job. Three friends come to console him. Job breaks out in complaint (chap. 3), and a cycle of speeches begins. Job's friends insist that his plight can only be a punishment for personal wrongdoing and an invitation from God to repent. Job rejects their inadequate explanation and challenges God to respond (chaps. 3–31). A young bystander, Elihu, now delivers four speeches in support of the views of the three friends (chaps. 32–37). In response to Job's plea that he be allowed to see God and hear directly the reason for his suffering, the Lord answers (38:1–42:6), not by explaining divine justice, but by cataloguing the wonders of creation. Job is apparently content with this, and, in an epilogue (42:7–17), the Lord restores Job's fortune.

The author or authors of the book are unknown; it was probably composed some time between the seventh and fifth centuries B.C. Its literary pattern, with speeches, prologue and epilogue disposed according to a studied plan, indicates that the purpose of the writing is didactic. But the lessons that the book teaches are not transparent, and different interpretations of the divine speeches and of the final chapter are possible. The Book of Job does not definitively answer the problem of the suffering of the innocent, but challenges readers to come to their own understanding.

The Book of Job can be divided as follows:

   I. Prologue (1:1–2:13)
  II. First Cycle of Speeches (3:1–14:22)
 III. Second Cycle of Speeches (15:1–21:34)
 IV. Third Cycle of Speeches (22:1–27:21)
  V. The Poem on Wisdom (28:1–28)
 VI. Job's Final Summary of His Cause (29:1–31:37)
VII. Elihu's Speeches (32:1–37:24)
VIII. The Lord and Job Meet (38:1–42:6)
 IX. Epilogue (42:7–17)

## I. PROLOGUE

### CHAPTER 1

**Job's Piety.** ¹In the land of Uz* there was a blameless and upright man named Job,ᵃ who feared God and avoided evil. ²Seven sons and three daughters were born to him; ³and he had seven thousand sheep, three thousand camels, five hundred yoke of oxen, five hundred she-donkeys, and a very large household, so that he was greater than anyone in the East.† ⁴His sons used to take turns giving feasts, sending invitations to their three sisters to eat and drink with them. ⁵And when each feast had run its course, Job would send for them and sanctify them, rising early and offering sacrifices for every one of them. For Job said, "It may be that my children

---

*[1:1] **Uz**: somewhere in Edom or Arabia; see Lam 4:21. **Job**: the name probably means "Where is the (divine) father?" In Hebrew it is almost a homonym with the word for "enemy" (see note on 13:24; cf. 33:10).

a. [1:1] Jb 2:3.

†[1:3] **The East**: that is, east of Palestine.

have sinned and cursed* God in their hearts." Job did this habitually.

**The Interview Between the Lord and the Satan.** [6b]One day, when the sons of God† came to present themselves before the LORD, the satan also came among them.[c] [7]The LORD said to the satan, "Where have you been?" Then the satan answered the LORD and said,[d] "Roaming the earth and patrolling it." [8]The LORD said to the satan, "Have you noticed my servant Job? There is no one on earth like him, blameless and upright, fearing God and avoiding evil." [9]The satan answered the LORD and said, "Is it for nothing that Job is God-fearing? [10]Have you not surrounded him and his family and all that he has with your protection? You have blessed the work of his hands, and his livestock are spread over the land. [11c]But now put forth your hand and touch all that he has, and surely he will curse you to your face." [12]The LORD said to the satan, "Very well, all that he has is in your power; only do not lay a hand on him." So the satan went forth from the presence of the LORD.

**The First Trial.** [13]One day, while his sons and daughters were eating and drinking wine in the house of their eldest brother, [14]a messenger came to Job and said, "The oxen were plowing and the donkeys grazing beside them, [15]and the Sabeans‡ carried them off in a raid. They put the servants to the sword, and I alone have escaped to tell you." [16]He was still speaking when another came and said, "God's fire has fallen from heaven and struck the sheep and the servants and consumed them; I alone have escaped to tell you." [17]He was still speaking when another came and said, "The Chaldeans§ formed three columns, seized the camels, carried them off, and put the servants to the sword; I alone have escaped to tell you." [18]He was still speaking when another came and said, "Your sons and daughters were eating and drinking wine in the house of their eldest brother, [19]and suddenly a great wind came from across the desert and smashed the four corners of the house. It fell upon the young people and they are dead; I alone have escaped to tell you."

**Job's Reaction.** [20]Then Job arose and tore his cloak and cut off his hair. He fell to the ground and worshiped. [21]He said,

> "Naked I came forth from my mother's
>    womb,[f]

and naked shall I go back there.[s]
The LORD gave and the LORD has taken
    away;
    blessed be the name of the LORD!"

[22]In all this Job did not sin,[g] nor did he charge God with wrong.

## CHAPTER 2

**The Second Interview.** [1]One day, when the sons of God[h] came to present themselves before the LORD, the satan also came with them. [2]The LORD said to the satan, "Where have you been?" Then the satan answered the LORD and said, "Roaming the earth and patrolling it." [3]The LORD said to the satan, "Have you noticed my servant Job? There is no one on earth like him, blameless and upright, fearing God and avoiding evil.[i] He still holds fast to his innocence although you incited me against him to ruin him for nothing." [4]The satan answered the LORD and said, "Skin for skin!* All that a man has he will give for his life. [5]But put forth your hand and touch his bone and his flesh. Then surely he will curse you to your face." [6]And the LORD said to the satan, "He is in your power; only spare his life."

**The Second Trial.** [7]So the satan went forth from the presence of the LORD and struck Job with severe boils from the soles of his feet to the crown of his head.

**Job's Reaction.** [8]He took a potsherd to scrape himself, as he sat among the ashes. [9]Then his wife said to him,[k] "Are you still holding to your innocence? Curse God and die!"†† [10]But he said to her, "You speak as foolish women do. We accept good things from God; should we not accept evil?" Through all this, Job did not sin in what he said.[l]

**Job's Three Friends.** [11]Now when three of Job's friends heard of all the misfortune that had come upon him, they set out each one from his own place: Eliphaz from Teman,‡‡ Bildad from Shuh, and Zophar from Naamath. They met and journeyed together to give him sympathy and comfort. [12]But when, at a distance, they lifted up their eyes and did not recognize him, they began to weep aloud; they tore their cloaks and threw dust into the air over their heads. [13]Then they sat down upon the ground with him seven days and seven nights, but none of them spoke a word to him; for they saw how great was his suffering.

---

*[1:5] **Cursed:** lit., "blessed." So also in v. 11; 2:5, 9.

†[1:6] **Sons of God:** members of the divine council; see Gn 6:1–4; Dt 32:8; Ps 82:1. **The satan:** lit., "adversary" (as in 1 Kgs 11:14). Here a member of the heavenly court, "the accuser" (Zec 3:1). In later biblical traditions this character will be developed as the devil (Gk. *diabolos*, "adversary").

‡[1:15] **Sabeans:** from southern Arabia.

§[1:17] **Chaldeans:** from southern Mesopotamia; in the mid-first millennium B.C., synonymous with "Babylonians."

**[2:4] **Skin for skin:** a proverbial expression derived perhaps from bartering; the precise meaning is unclear.

††[2:9] **Curse God and die:** the presupposition is that such blasphemy would be met with immediate death.

‡‡[2:11] **Teman:** in Edom (see Gn 36:9–11). The Temanites (Jer 49:7; cf. Ob 8) enjoyed a reputation for wisdom. **Shuh** and **Naamath:** locations unknown.

b. [1:6–8] Jb 2:1–3.  c. [1:6] Gn 6:2, 4; Zec 3:1; Lk 22:31; Rev 12:9.  d. [1:7] 1 Pt 5:8.  e. [1:11] Jb 2:5.  f. [1:21] Eccl 5:14; 1 Tm 6:7.

g. [1:22] Jb 2:10; Jas 5:11.  h. [2:1] Jb 1:6.  i. [2:3] Jb 1:1.  j. [2:5] Jb 1:11.  k. [2:9] Jb 19:17.  l. [2:10] Jb 1:22; Sir 2:4.

## II. FIRST CYCLE OF SPEECHES

### CHAPTER 3

**Job's Complaint.** ¹After this, Job opened his mouth and cursed his day.* ²Job spoke out and said:

³ Perish the day on which I was born,ᵐ
  the night when they said, "The child is a boy!"
⁴ May that day be darkness:
  may God† above not care for it,
  may light not shine upon it!
⁵ May darkness and gloom claim it,
  clouds settle upon it,
  blackness of day‡ affright it!
⁶ May obscurity seize that night;
  may it not be counted among the days of the year,
  nor enter into the number of the months!
⁷ May that night be barren;
  let no joyful outcry greet it!
⁸ Let them curse it who curse the Sea,
  those skilled at disturbing Leviathan!§
⁹ May the stars of its twilight be darkened;
  may it look for daylight, but have none,
  nor gaze on the eyes of the dawn,
¹⁰ Because it did not keep shut the doors of the womb
  to shield my eyes from trouble!
¹¹ Why did I not die at birth,ⁿ
  come forth from the womb and expire?
¹² Why did knees receive me,
  or breasts nurse me?
¹³ For then I should have lain down and been tranquil;
  had I slept, I should then have been at rest.
¹⁴ With kings and counselors of the earth
  who rebuilt what were ruins
¹⁵ Or with princes who had gold
  and filled their houses with silver.
¹⁶ Or why was I not buried away like a stillborn child,
  like babies that have never seen the light?
¹⁷ There⁵ the wicked cease from troubling,
  there the weary are at rest.
¹⁸ The captives are at ease together,
  and hear no overseer's voice.

¹⁹ Small and great are there;
  the servant is free from the master.
²⁰ Why is light given to the toilers,
  life to the bitter in spirit?
²¹ They wait for death and it does not come;
  they search for it more than for hidden treasures.
²² They rejoice in it exultingly,
  and are glad when they find the grave:
²³ A man whose path is hidden from him,
  one whom God has hemmed in!**
²⁴ For to me sighing comes more readily than food;
  my groans well forth like water.
²⁵ For what I feared overtakes me;
  what I dreaded comes upon me.
²⁶ I have no peace nor ease;
  I have no rest, for trouble has come!

### CHAPTER 4

**Eliphaz's First Speech.** ¹Then Eliphaz the Temanite answered and said:

² If someone attempts a word with you,
  would you mind?
  How can anyone refrain from speaking?
³ Look, you have instructed many,
  and made firm their feeble hands.
⁴ Your words have upheld the stumbler;
  you have strengthened faltering knees.
⁵ But now that it comes to you, you are impatient;
  when it touches you, you are dismayed.
⁶ Is not your piety a source of confidence,
  and your integrity of life your hope?
⁷ Reflect now, what innocent person perishes?ᵒ
  Where are the upright destroyed?
⁸ As I see it, those who plow mischief
  and sow trouble will reap them.
⁹ By the breath of God they perish,ᵖ
  and by the blast of his wrath they are consumed.
¹⁰ Though the lion†† roars, though the king of beasts cries out,
  yet the teeth of the young lions are broken;
¹¹ The old lion perishes for lack of prey,
  and the cubs of the lioness are scattered.

---

*[3:1] **His day:** that is, the day of his birth.
†[3:4] **God:** in Heb. *'Eloah,* another name for the divinity, used frequently in Job.
‡[3:5] **Blackness of day:** that is, an eclipse.
§[3:8] **Leviathan:** a mythological sea monster symbolizing primeval chaos. It is parallel to Sea, which was the opponent of Baal in the Ugaritic legends. Cf. 9:13; 26:13; 40:25–41:26; Ps 74:13–14; 104:26; Is 27:1.
⁵[3:17] **There:** in death.

m. [3:3] Jer 20:14.    n. [3:11] Jb 10:18–19.

---

**[3:23] **Hemmed in:** contrast the same verb as used in 1:10.
††[4:10] **The lion:** used figuratively here for the violent, rapacious sinner who cannot prevail against God.

o. [4:7] Ps 37:25.    p. [4:9] Ps 18:16; Is 11:4; 2 Thes 2:8.

¹² A word was stealthily brought to me,*
    my ear caught a whisper of it.
¹³ In my thoughts during visions of the
        night,�q
    when deep sleep falls on mortals,
¹⁴ Fear came upon me, and shuddering,
    that terrified me to the bone.
¹⁵ Then a spirit passed before me,
    and the hair of my body stood on
        end.
¹⁶ It paused, but its likeness I could not
        recognize;
    a figure was before my eyes,
    in silence I heard a voice:ʳ
¹⁷ "Can anyone be more in the right than
        God?ˢ
    Can mortals be more blameless than
        their Maker?
¹⁸ Look, he puts no trust in his servants,ᵗ
    and even with his messengers he
        finds fault.
¹⁹ How much more with those who dwell in
        houses of clay,
    whose foundation is in the dust,
    who are crushed more easily than
        a moth!
²⁰ Morning or evening they may be
        shattered;
    unnoticed, they perish forever.
²¹ The pegs of their tent are plucked up;
    they die without knowing wisdom."

## CHAPTER 5

¹ Call now! Will anyone respond to you?
    To which of the holy ones† will you
        turn?
² Surely impatience kills the fool
    and indignation slays the simpleton.
³ I have seen a fool spreading his roots,ᵘ
    but I cursed his household suddenly:
⁴ May his children be far from safety;
    may they be crushed at the gate‡
        without a rescuer.
⁵ What they have reaped may the hungry
        eat up,
    or God take away by blight,
    or the thirsty swallow their
        substance.
⁶ For not from dust does mischief come,
    nor from the soil does trouble
        sprout.

⁷ Human beings beget mischief
    as sparks§ fly upward.
⁸ In your place, I would appeal to God,
    and to God I would state my plea.
⁹ ¶He does things great and unsearchable,
    things marvelous and innumerable.
¹⁰ He gives rain upon the earth
    and sends water upon the fields;
¹¹ ᵛHe sets up the lowly on high,
    and those who mourn are raised to
        safety.
¹² He frustrates the plans of the cunning,
    so that their hands achieve no
        success;
¹³ He catches the wise in their own ruses,ʷ
    and the designs of the crafty are
        routed.
¹⁴ They meet with darkness in the daytime,
    at noonday they grope as though it
        were night.
¹⁵ But he saves the poor from the sword of
        their mouth,**
    from the hand of the mighty.
¹⁶ Thus the needy have hope,
    and iniquity closes its mouth.
¹⁷ Happy the one whom God reproves!
    The Almighty's†† discipline do not
        reject.
¹⁸ For he wounds, but he binds up;ˣ
    he strikes, but his hands give healing.
¹⁹ Out of six troubles he will deliver you,
    and at the seventh‡‡ no evil shall
        touch you.
²⁰ In famine he will deliver you from death,
    and in war from the power of the
        sword;
²¹ From the scourge of the tongue you shall
        be hidden,
    and you shall not fear approaching
        ruin.
²² At ruin and want you shall laugh;
    the beasts of the earth, do not fear.
²³ With the stones of the field shall your
        covenant be,
    and the wild beasts shall be at peace
        with you.
²⁴ And you shall know that your tent is
        secure;
    taking stock of your household, you
        shall miss nothing.
²⁵ You shall know that your descendants are
        many,

---

*[4:12–21] A dramatic presentation of the idea of human nothingness in contrast to God's greatness (v. 17). The message of the "private revelation" that stirs Eliphaz so deeply is in reality expressed countless times in the Bible. The statements of the friends are often "truths" that are insensitive or irrelevant to Job's questioning.

†[5:1] **Holy ones**: members of the heavenly court; cf. 1:6 and note. They were viewed as heavenly intercessors.

‡[5:4] **At the gate**: of the city, where justice was administered.

q. [4:13] Jb 33:15.    r. [4:16] 1 Kgs 19:12.    s. [4:17] Jb 9:2; 15:14–16; 25:4; Ps 130:3; 143:2.    t. [4:18] Jb 15:15; 2 Pt 2:4; Jude 6.    u. [5:3] Ps 37:35–36.

§[5:7] **Sparks**: in Hebrew, "sons of resheph," which the ancient versions took as the name of a bird. Resheph was an underworld deity of plague, but the word also means "flames" in Sg 8:6.

¶[5:9] Perhaps to be omitted here; it is a duplicate of 9:10.

**[5:15] **From the sword of their mouth**: the Hebrew is obscure.

††[5:17] **Almighty**: standard translation of Heb. *Shaddai*.

‡‡[5:19] **Six . . . the seventh**: proverbial expression for any large number; cf. Prv 24:16; Lk 17:4.

v. [5:11] 1 Sm 2:7–8; Ps 113:7; Lk 1:52.    w. [5:13] 1 Cor 3:19.    x. [5:18] Hos 6:1–2.

and your offspring like the grass of
the earth.

²⁶ You shall approach the grave in full
vigor,
as a shock of grain comes in at its
season.

²⁷ See, this we have searched out; so it is!
This we have heard, and you should
know.

## CHAPTER 6

**Job's First Reply.** ¹Then Job answered and said:

² Ah, could my anguish but be measured
and my calamity laid with it in the
scales,

³ They would now outweigh the sands of
the sea!
Because of this I speak without
restraint.

⁴ For the arrows of the Almighty are in
me,ʸ
and my spirit drinks in their poison;
the terrors of God are arrayed
against me.

⁵ Does the wild donkey bray when it has
grass?*
Does the ox low over its fodder?

⁶ Can anything insipid be eaten without
salt?
Is there flavor in the white of an egg?

⁷ I refuse to touch them;
they are like loathsome food to me.

⁸ Oh, that I might have my request,
and that God would grant what I
long for:

⁹ Even that God would decide to crush me,
that he would put forth his hand and
cut me off!

¹⁰ Then I should still have consolation
and could exult through
unremitting pain,
because I have not transgressed the
commands of the Holy One.

¹¹ What strength have I that I should
endure,
and what is my limit that I should be
patient?

¹² Have I the strength of stones,
or is my flesh of bronze?

¹³ Have I no helper,ᶻ
and has my good sense deserted me?

¹⁴ A friend owes kindness to one in
despair,
though he has forsaken the fear of
the Almighty.

¹⁵ My companions are undependable as a
wadi,
as watercourses that run dry in the
wadies;

¹⁶ Though they may be black with ice,
and with snow heaped upon them,

¹⁷ Yet once they flow, they cease to be;
in the heat, they disappear from
their place.

¹⁸ Caravans wander from their routes;
they go into the wasteland and
perish.

¹⁹ The caravans of Tema† search,
the companies of Sheba have hopes;

²⁰ They are disappointed, though they were
confident;
they come there and are frustrated.

²¹ It is thus that you have now become for
me;‡
you see a terrifying thing and are
afraid.

²² Have I said, "Give me something,
make a bribe on my behalf from
your possessions"?

²³ Or "Deliver me from the hand of the
enemy,
redeem me from oppressors"?

²⁴ Teach me, and I will be silent;
make me understand how I have
erred.

²⁵ How painful honest words can be;
yet how unconvincing is your
argument!

²⁶ Do you consider your words as proof,
but the sayings of a desperate man
as wind?

²⁷ You would even cast lots for the orphan,
and would barter over your friend!

²⁸ Come, now, give me your attention;
surely I will not lie to your face.

²⁹ Think it over; let there be no injustice.
Think it over; I still am right.

³⁰ Is there insincerity on my tongue,
or cannot my taste discern falsehood?

## CHAPTER 7

¹ ªIs not life on earth a drudgery,§
its days like those of a hireling?

² Like a slave who longs for the shade,
a hireling who waits for wages,

³ So I have been assigned months of
futility,

---

*[6:5–6] Job would not complain if his life were as pleasant to him as fodder to a hungry animal; but his life is as disagreeable as insipid food. **White of an egg**: thus the obscure Hebrew has been understood in Jewish tradition; some render it "mallow juice."

---

y. [6:4] Ps 88:17.   z. [6:13] Jb 19:14–15.

---

†[6:19] **Tema**: in northwest Arabia. **Sheba**: home of the Sabeans; see note on 1:15.

‡[6:21] It is only at this point that the previous lines (vv. 1–20) are clearly directed to the three friends. The style of replying in these chapters (3–31) is often indirect. Job and the friends become mouthpieces through which the author presents current views on divine retribution in dramatic fashion. In chap. 7, Job will not even speak directly to the friends.

§[7:1] **Drudgery**: taken by some to refer to military service; cf. also 14:14.

---

a. [7:1] Jb 14:14.

and troubled nights have been
counted off for me.
4 When I lie down I say, "When shall I
arise?"
then the night drags on;
I am filled with restlessness until the
dawn.
5 My flesh is clothed with worms and
scabs;[b]
my skin cracks and festers;
6 My days are swifter than a weaver's
shuttle;
they come to an end without hope.
7 Remember that my life is like the wind;[c]
my eye will not see happiness again.
8 The eye that now sees me shall no more
behold me;
when your eye is on me, I shall be
gone.
9 As a cloud dissolves and vanishes,[d]
so whoever goes down to Sheol shall
not come up.
10 They shall not return home again;
their place shall know them no
more.
11 My own utterance I will not restrain;
I will speak in the anguish of my
spirit;
I will complain in the bitterness of
my soul.
12 *Am I the Sea, or the dragon,
that you place a watch over me?[†]
13 When I say, "My bed shall comfort me,
my couch shall ease my complaint,"
14 Then you frighten me with dreams
and terrify me with visions,
15 So that I should prefer strangulation
and death rather than my existence.[‡]
16 I waste away: I will not live forever;[e]
let me alone, for my days are but a
breath.
17 §What are human beings, that you make
much of them,
or pay them any heed?
18 You observe them every morning[f]
and try them at every moment!
19 How long before you look away from me,
and let me alone till I swallow my
spit?
20 If I sin, what do I do to you,
O watcher of mortals?
Why have you made me your target?
Why should I be a burden for you?

21 Why do you not pardon my offense,
or take away my guilt?
For soon I shall lie down in the dust;
and should you seek me I shall be
gone.

## CHAPTER 8

**Bildad's First Speech.** ¹Bildad the Shuhite
answered and said:

2 How long will you utter such things?
The words from your mouth are a
mighty wind!
3 Does God pervert judgment,[g]
does the Almighty pervert justice?
4 If your children have sinned against him
and he has left them in the grip of
their guilt,
5 Still, if you yourself have recourse to God
and make supplication to the
Almighty,
6 Should you be blameless and upright,
surely now he will rouse himself
for you
and restore your rightful home.
7 Though your beginning was small,
your future will flourish indeed.
8 Inquire of the former generations,
pay attention to the experience of
their ancestors—[h]
9 As we are but of yesterday and have no
knowledge,
because our days on earth are but a
shadow—[i]
10 Will they not teach you and tell you
and utter their words of
understanding?
11 ¶Can the papyrus grow up without
mire?
Can the reed grass flourish without
water?
12 While it is yet green and uncut,
it withers quicker than any grass.
13 So is the end of everyone who forgets
God,
and so shall the hope of the godless
perish.
14 His confidence is but a gossamer thread,
his trust is a spider's house.
15 He shall lean upon his house, but it shall
not stand;
he shall cling to it, but it shall not
endure.
16 He thrives in full sun,
and over his garden his shoots go
forth;

---

*[7:12–21] Job now speaks not to his friends (who never
speak to God), but to God. He does this frequently; cf. 9:28;
10:2–22; 13:20–28; 14:13–22.

†[7:12] An allusion to the personification of primeval chaos
as a monstrous ocean vanquished by God; see note on 3:8.

‡[7:15] **Existence:** lit., bones; the Hebrew is unclear.

§[7:17–18] An ironic allusion to Ps 8:5.

b. [7:5] Jb 2:7–8.   c. [7:7] Ps 144:4.   d. [7:9–10] Jb 10:21; 14:10–12;
2 Sm 12:23; 14:14; Wis 2:1.   e. [7:16] Jb 14:1–2, 5.   f. [7:18] Ps
17:3.

---

¶[8:11–13] As marsh plants need water, so human beings
need God. These verses may be a quotation from the teaching
of the ancestors; cf. v. 10.

g. [8:3] Jb 34:10–12.   h. [8:8] Dt 4:32; 32:7.   i. [8:9] Jb 14:2; Ps
102:12; 109:23; 144:4; Wis 2:5.

17 About a heap of stones his roots are
      entwined;
         among the rocks he takes hold.
18 Yet if one tears him from his place,
      it will disown him: "I have never
         seen you!"
19 There he lies rotting beside the road,
      and out of the soil another sprouts.
20 Behold, God will not cast away the
      upright;
         neither will he take the hand of the
            wicked.
21 Once more will he fill your mouth with
      laughter
         and your lips with rejoicing.
22 Those who hate you shall be clothed with
      shame,
         and the tent of the wicked shall be
            no more.

## CHAPTER 9

**Job's Second Reply.** ¹Then Job answered and
said:

2 I know well that it is so;
      but how can anyone be in the right
         before God?
3 Should one wish to contend with him,*
      he could not answer him once in a
         thousand times.
4 God is wise in heart and mighty in
      strength;
         who has withstood him and
            remained whole?
5 He removes the mountains before they
      know it;
         he overturns them in his anger.
6 He shakes the earth out of its place,ʲ
      and the pillars beneath it tremble.
7 He commands the sun, and it does not
      rise;
         he seals up the stars.
8 He alone stretches out the heavensᵏ
      and treads upon the back of the sea.
9 He made the Bear and Orion,
      the Pleiades and the constellations
         of the south;
10 He does things great and unsearchable,
      things marvelous and innumerable.
11 Should he come near me, I do not see
      him;
         should he pass by, I am not aware
            of him;
12 Should he seize me forcibly, who can
      resist?
         Who can say to him, "What are you
            doing?"

13 He is God and he does not relent;
      the helpers of Rahab† bow beneath
         him.
14 How then could I give him any answer,
      or choose out arguments against
         him!
15 Even though I were right, I could not
      answer,ˡ
         but should rather beg for what was
            due me.
16 If I appealed to him and he answered
      me,
         I could not believe that he would
            listen to me;
17 With a storm he might overwhelm me,
      and multiply my wounds for
         nothing;
18 He would not allow me to draw breath,
      but might fill me with bitter griefs.
19 If it be a question of strength, he is
      mighty;
         or of judgment, who will call him to
            account?
20 Though I were right, my own mouth
      might condemn me;ᵐ
         were I innocent, it might put me in
            the wrong.
21 I am innocent, but I cannot know it;
      I despise my life.
22 It is all one! therefore I say:
      Both the innocent and the wicked
         he destroys.ⁿ
23 When the scourge slays suddenly,
      he scoffs at the despair of the
         innocent.
24 The earth is given into the hands of the
      wicked;
         he covers the faces of its judges.
         If it is not he, who then is it?
25 My days are swifter than a runner,
      they flee away; they see no
         happiness;ᵒ
26 They shoot by like skiffs of reed,
      like an eagle swooping upon its prey.
27 If I say: I will forget my complaining,
      I will lay aside my sadness and be of
         good cheer,
28 Then I am in dread of all my pains;
      I know that you‡ will not hold me
         innocent.
29 It is I who will be accounted guilty;
      why then should I strive in vain?
30 If I should wash myself with soap
      and cleanse my hands with lye,
31 Yet you would plunge me in the ditch,
      so that my garments would abhor
         me.

---

*[9:3] Job begins to explore the possibility of challenging
God in a lawsuit, a theme that will recur (10:2), but he knows
the odds are against him (vv. 12–20).

j. [9:6] Jb 26:11.   k. [9:8] Ps 104:2; Is 40:22.

†[9:13] **Rahab**: another name for the primeval sea-monster; see notes on 3:8 and Ps 89:11; cf. Jb 7:12; 26:12.
‡[9:28–31] **You**: refers to God.

l. [9:15] Jb 10:15.   m. [9:20] Jb 15:6.   n. [9:22] Eccl 9:2.   o. [9:25]
Jb 7:6.

³² For he is not a man like myself, that I
            should answer him,
        that we should come together in
            judgment.
³³ Would that there were an arbiter
            between us,
        who could lay his hand upon us both
³⁴     and withdraw his rod from me,
    So that his terrors did not frighten me;
³⁵     that I might speak without being
            afraid of him.
    Since this is not the case with me,
¹⁰:¹     *I loathe my life.*ᵖ

## CHAPTER 10

    I will give myself up to complaint;
        I will speak from the bitterness of
            my soul.
² I will say to God: Do not put me in the
            wrong!
        Let me know why you oppose me.
³ †Is it a pleasure for you to oppress,
        to spurn the work of your hands,
        and shine on the plan of the wicked?
⁴ Have you eyes of flesh?
        Do you see as mortals see?
⁵ Are your days like the days of a mortal,�q
        and are your years like a human
            lifetime,
⁶ That you seek for guilt in me
        and search after my sins,
⁷ Even though you know that I am not
            wicked,ʳ
        and that none can deliver me out of
            your hand?
⁸ Your hands have formed me and
            fashioned me;
        will you then turn and destroy me?
⁹ Oh, remember that you fashioned me
            from clay!ˢ
        Will you then bring me down to
            dust again?
¹⁰ Did you not pour me out like milk,
        and thicken me like cheese?
¹¹ With skin and flesh you clothed me,
        with bones and sinews knit me
            together.
¹² Life and love you granted me,
        and your providence has preserved
            my spirit.
¹³ Yet these things you have hidden in your
            heart;
        I know they are your purpose:
¹⁴ If I should sin, you would keep a watch on
            me,

and from my guilt you would not
            absolve me.
¹⁵ If I should be wicked, alas for me!
        even if righteous, I dare not hold up
            my head,
        sated with shame, drenched in
            affliction!
¹⁶ Should it lift up, you hunt me like a lion:
        repeatedly you show your wondrous
            power against me,
¹⁷ You renew your attackᵗ upon me
        and multiply your harassment of me;
        in waves your troops come against
            me.
¹⁸ Why then did you bring me forth from
            the womb?ᵗ
        I should have died and no eye have
            seen me.
¹⁹ I should be as though I had never lived;
        I should have been taken from the
            womb to the grave.
²⁰ Are not my days few? Stop!
        Let me alone, that I may recover a
            little
²¹ Before I go whence I shall not return,ᵘ
        to the land of darkness and of
            gloom,
²² The dark, disordered land
        where darkness is the only light.

## CHAPTER 11

**Zophar's First Speech.** ¹And Zophar the
Naamathite answered and said:

² Should not many words be answered,
        or must the garrulous man
            necessarily be right?
³ Shall your babblings keep others silent,
        and shall you deride and no one give
            rebuke?
⁴ Shall you say: "My teaching is pure,
        and I am clean in your sight"?
⁵ But oh, that God would speak,ˢ
        and open his lips against you,
⁶ And tell you the secrets of wisdom,
        for good sense has two sides;
    So you might learn that God
        overlooks some of your sinfulness.
⁷ Can you find out the depths of God?ᵛ
        or find out the perfection of the
            Almighty?
⁸ It is higher than the heavens; what can
            you do?
        It is deeper than Sheol; what can you
            know?

---

*[10:1] **I loathe my life**: these words complete the thought
of 9:35.

†[10:3–12] These lines are a delicate mixture of sarcasm
and prayer; Job "reminds" God, challenging the divine providence. Note the piteous tone of the final request in vv. 20–22.

‡[10:17] **Attack**: or "witnesses," continuing the metaphor
of lawsuit used in these chapters.

§[11:5] This is another of many ironies (e.g., cf. 11:16–19)
that occur throughout the book. Zophar does not know that
God will speak (chaps. 38–42), but contrary to what he thinks.

---

p. [10:1] Jb 9:21.   q. [10:5] Jb 36:26.   r. [10:7] Jb 2:3, 9; Dt 32:39;
Wis 16:15.   s. [10:9] Jb 4:19; 33:6; Gn 2:7; 3:19; Ps 146:4.

t. [10:18] Jb 3:3, 11.   u. [10:21] Jb 7:9–10; 16:22.   v. [11:7] Rom
11:33.

9 It is longer than the earth in measure,
     and broader than the sea.
10 If he should seize and imprison
       or call to judgment, who then could
         turn him back?
11 For he knows the worthless
       and sees iniquity; will he then ignore
         it?
12 An empty head will gain understanding,
       when a colt of a wild jackass[w] is born
         human.*
13 If you set your heart aright
       and stretch out your hands toward
         him,
14 If iniquity is in your hand, remove it,
       and do not let injustice dwell in your
         tent,
15 Surely then you may lift up your face in
       innocence;
       you may stand firm and unafraid.
16 For then you shall forget your misery,
       like water that has ebbed away you
         shall regard it.
17 Then your life shall be brighter than the
       noonday;
       its gloom shall become like the
         morning,
18 And you shall be secure, because there is
       hope;
       you shall look round you and lie
         down in safety;[x]
19      you shall lie down and no one will
         disturb you.
     Many shall entreat your favor,
20      but the wicked, looking on, shall be
         consumed with envy.
     Escape shall be cut off from them,
       their only hope their last breath.

## CHAPTER 12

**Job's Third Reply.** 1†Then Job answered and said:

2 No doubt you are the people
     with whom wisdom shall die!
3 But I have intelligence as well as you;[y]
     I do not fall short of you;
       for who does not know such things
         as these?
4 I have become the sport of my
     neighbors:‡

"The one whom God answers when
     he calls upon him,
The just, the perfect man," is a
     laughingstock;[z]
5 The undisturbed esteem my downfall a
     disgrace
     such as awaits unsteady feet;
6 Yet the tents of robbers are prosperous,
     and those who provoke God are
       secure,
     whom God has in his power.§
7 But now ask the beasts to teach you,
     the birds of the air to tell you;
8 Or speak to the earth to instruct you,
     and the fish of the sea to inform you.
9 Which of all these does not know
     that the hand of God has done this?
10 In his hand is the soul of every living
     thing,[a]
     and the life breath of all mortal flesh.
11 Does not the ear judge words
     as the mouth tastes food?[b]
12 So with old age is wisdom,[c]
     and with length of days
       understanding.
13 With him are wisdom and might;
     his are counsel and understanding.
14 If he knocks a thing down, there is no
     rebuilding;[d]
     if he imprisons, there is no release.
15 He holds back the waters and there is
     drought;[e]
     he sends them forth and they
       overwhelm the land.
16 With him are strength and prudence;
     the misled and the misleaders are
       his.
17 He sends counselors away barefoot,
     makes fools of judges.
18 He loosens the belt of kings,
     ties a waistcloth on their loins.¶
19 He sends priests away barefoot,
     leads the powerful astray.
20 He silences the trusted adviser,
     takes discretion from the elders.
21 He pours shame on nobles,[f]
     the waistband of the strong he
       loosens.
22 He uncovers deep things from the
     darkness,
     brings the gloom into the light.
23 He makes nations great and destroys
     them,
     spreads peoples abroad and
       abandons them.

---

*[11:12] **A colt . . . is born human**: the Hebrew is obscure. As translated, it seems to be a proverb referring to an impossible event.

†[12:1] Job begins his third and longest speech to the friends with sarcasm, and eventually he accuses them of falsehood (13:4–11). The dialogue between them becomes increasingly sharp. With the appeal to learning from beasts and birds (12:7), Job launches into what seems to be a bitter parody of the power of God.

‡[12:4–5] The Hebrew is somewhat obscure, but the general sense is that the wicked mock the pious when the latter appear to be abandoned by God; cf. Ps 22:7–9; Mt 27:39–43.

§[12:6] **Whom God has in his power**: the Hebrew is obscure. The line may be a scribal error; some of the phrases occur in vv. 9, 10.

¶[12:18] He reduces kings to the condition of slaves, who wear only a cloth wrapped about the waist.

---

w. [11:12] Jb 39:5–8.   x. [11:18] Lv 26:6; Ps 4:9.   y. [12:3] Jb 13:2; 15:9.

z. [12:4] Jb 21:3; 30:1.   a. [12:10] Acts 17:28.   b. [12:11] Jb 34:3.   c. [12:12] Jb 32:7.   d. [12:14] Jer 1:10; Rev 3:7.   e. [12:15] Gn 7:11–24.   f. [12:21] Ps 107:40.

²⁴ He takes understanding from the leaders
   of the land,
      makes them wander in a pathless
      desert.
²⁵ They grope in the darkness without
   light;
      he makes them wander like
      drunkards.

## CHAPTER 13

¹ All this my eye has seen;
      my ear has heard and perceived it.
² What you know, I also know;ᵍ
      I do not fall short of you.
³ But I would speak with the Almighty;ʰ
      I want to argue with God.
⁴ But you gloss over falsehoods,
      you are worthless physicians, every
      one of you!
⁵ Oh, that you would be altogether silent;
      that for you would be wisdom!
⁶ Hear now my argument
      and listen to the accusations from
      my lips.
⁷ Is it for God that you speak falsehood?
      Is it for him that you utter deceit?
⁸ Is it for him that you show partiality?
      Do you make accusations on behalf
      of God?
⁹ Will it be well when he shall search you
   out?
      Can you deceive him as you do a
      mere human being?
¹⁰ He will openly rebuke you
      if in secret you show partiality.
¹¹ Surely his majesty will frighten you
      and dread of him fall upon you.
¹² Your reminders are ashy maxims,
      your fabrications mounds of clay.
¹³ Be silent! Let me alone that I may speak,
      no matter what happens to me.
¹⁴ I will carry my flesh between my teeth,
      and take my life in my hand.*
¹⁵ Slay me though he might,ⁱ I will wait for
   him;†
      I will defend my conduct before
      him.
¹⁶ This shall be my salvation:
      no impious man can come into his
      presence.
¹⁷ Pay close attention to my speech,
      give my statement a hearing.
¹⁸ Behold, I have prepared my case,ʲ

      I know that I am in the right.
¹⁹ If anyone can make a case against me,
      then I shall be silent and expire.
²⁰ Two things only do not use against me,‡
      then from your presence I need not
      hide:
²¹ Withdraw your hand far from me,
      do not let the terror of you frighten
      me.
²² Then call me, and I will respond;
      or let me speak first, and answer me.
²³ What are my faults and my sins?
      My misdeed, my sin make known
      to me!
²⁴ Why do you hide your face
      and consider me your enemy?§ᵏ
²⁵ Will you harass a wind-driven leaf
      or pursue a withered straw?
²⁶ For you draw up bitter indictments
      against me,
      and punish in me the faults of my
      youth.
²⁷ You put my feet in the stocks;
      you watch all my paths
      and trace out all my footsteps,
²⁸ Though I wear out like a leather bottle,
      like a garment the moth has
      consumed.

## CHAPTER 14

¹ Man born of woman
      is short-lived and full of trouble,¶ˡ
² Like a flower that springs up and fades,ᵐ
      swift as a shadow that does not
      abide.
³ Upon such a one will you set your eyes,
      bringing me into judgment before
      you?
⁴ Can anyone make the unclean clean?ⁿ
      No one can.
⁵ Since his days are determined—
      you know the number of his
      months;
      you have fixed the limit which he
      cannot pass—
⁶ Look away from him and let him be,
      while, like a hireling, he completes
      his day.

‡[13:20] In 13:20–14:22, Job directs his address to God; cf. 7:8–21; 9:28–10:22. His three friends never do this.

§[13:24] The Hebrew word for "enemy" (*'ōyeb*) is very close to the Hebrew form of Job's name (*'iyyôb*). The play on the word implies that God has confused the two.

¶[14:1] The sorrowful lament of Job is that God should relent in view of the limited life of human beings. When compared to plant life, which dies but can revive, the death of human beings is final. Job's wild and "unthinkable" wish in vv. 13–17 is a bold stroke of imagination and desire: if only in Sheol he were protected till God would remember him! Were he to live again (v. 14), things would be different, but alas, God destroys "the hope of mortals" (v. 19).

---

*[13:14] The second half of the verse is a common biblical expression for risking one's life; cf. Jgs 12:3; 1 Sm 19:5; 28:21; Ps 119:109; the first half of the verse must have a similar meaning. Job is so confident of his innocence that he is willing to risk his life by going to judgment with God.

†[13:15] Many translations adopt the Ketib reading, "I have no hope."

---

g. [13:2] Jb 12:3; 15:9.   h. [13:3] Jb 23:4.   i. [13:15] Jb 27:5.
j. [13:18] Jb 33:9.

k. [13:24] Jb 19:11; 33:10.   l. [14:1] Jb 10:20; 15:14; Ps 39:5–6; 89:46;
Wis 2:1.   m. [14:2] Jb 8:9; Ps 90:6; 102:12; 103:15; 109:23; 144:4; Is
40:6–7; Jas 1:10.   n. [14:4] Ps 51:4, 7.

7 For a tree there is hope;
    if it is cut down, it will sprout again,
        its tender shoots will not cease.
8 Even though its root grow old in the earth
        and its stump die in the dust,
9 Yet at the first whiff of water it sprouts
        and puts forth branches like a young
            plant.
10 But when a man dies, all vigor leaves
        him;[o]
    when a mortal expires, where then
        is he?
11 As when the waters of a lake fail,
        or a stream shrivels and dries up,
12 So mortals lie down, never to rise.
        Until the heavens are no more, they
            shall not awake,
        nor be roused out of their sleep.[p]
13 Oh, that you would hide me in Sheol,
        shelter me till your wrath is past,
        fix a time to remember me!
14 If a man were to die, and live again,
        all the days of my drudgery I would
            wait[q]
        for my relief to come.
15 You would call, and I would answer you;
        you would long for the work of your
            hands.
16 Surely then you would count my steps,[r]
        and not keep watch for sin in me.
17 My misdeeds would be sealed up in a
            pouch,[*]
        and you would cover over my guilt.
18 Mountains fall and crumble,
        rocks move from their place,
19 And water wears away stone,
        and floods wash away the soil of the
            land—
        so you destroy the hope of mortals!
20 You prevail once for all against them and
            they pass on;
        you dismiss them with changed
            appearance.
21 If their children are honored, they are not
            aware of it;
        or if disgraced, they do not know
            about them.
22 Only for themselves, their pain;
        only for themselves, their mourning.

## III. SECOND CYCLE OF SPEECHES

### CHAPTER 15

**Second Speech of Eliphaz.** [1†]Then Eliphaz the
Temanite answered and said:

2 Does a wise man answer with windy
            opinions,
        or puff himself up with the east
            wind?
3 Does he argue in speech that does not
            avail,
        and in words that are to no profit?
4 You in fact do away with piety,
        you lessen devotion toward God,
5 Because your wickedness instructs your
            mouth,
        and you choose to speak like the
            crafty.
6 Your own mouth condemns you, not I;[s]
        your own lips refute you.
7 Were you the first to be born?
        Were you brought forth before the
            hills?
8 Do you listen in on God's council[t]
        and restrict wisdom to yourself?
9 What do you know that we do not know,[u]
        or understand that we do not?
10 There are gray-haired old men among us,
        more advanced in years than your
            father.
11 Are the consolations of God not enough
            for you,
        and speech that deals gently with you?
12 Why does your heart carry you away,
        and why do your eyes flash,
13 So that you turn your anger against God
        and let such words escape your
            mouth!
14 How can any mortal be blameless,[v]
        anyone born of woman be
            righteous?[w]
15 If in his holy ones God places no
            confidence,[x]
        and if the heavens are not without
            blame in his sight,
16 How much less so is the abominable and
            corrupt:
        people who drink in iniquity like
            water!
17 I will show you, if you listen to me;
        what I have seen I will tell—
18 What the wise relate
        and have not contradicted since the
            days of their ancestors,
19 To whom alone the land was given,
        when no foreigner moved among
            them:
20 The wicked is in torment all his days,
        and limited years are in store for the
            ruthless;

---

*[14:17] **Sealed up in a pouch**: hidden away and forgotten.
†[15:1] The tone of Eliphaz's speech is now much rougher.
In vv. 7–9 he ridicules Job's knowledge with a sarcastic question about whether he was a member of the divine council

before creation and thus had unique wisdom (according to
Prv 8:22–31, only Woman Wisdom existed before creation).
Verses 20–35 are a typical description of the fate of the wicked.

o. [14:10] Jb 20:7.    p. [14:12] Jb 7:10.    q. [14:14] Jb 7:1.    r. [14:16]
Jb 31:4; 34:21.

s. [15:6] Jb 9:20.    t. [15:8] Jb 11:7; Wis 9:13; Jer 23:18; Rom 11:34;
1 Cor 2:11, 16.    u. [15:9] Jb 12:3; 13:2.    v. [15:14–16] Jb 25:4–6.
w. [15:14] Jb 14:4.    x. [15:15] Jb 4:18–19.

²¹ The sound of terrors is in his ears;
        when all is prosperous, a spoiler
            comes upon him.
²² He despairs of escaping the darkness,
        and looks ever for the sword;
²³ A wanderer, food for vultures,
        he knows destruction is imminent.
²⁴ A day of darkness fills him with dread;
        distress and anguish overpower him,
        like a king expecting an attack.
²⁵ Because he has stretched out his hand
            against God
        and arrogantly challenged the
            Almighty,
²⁶ Rushing defiantly against him,
        with the stout bosses of his shields.
²⁷ Although he has covered his face with his
            crassness,
        padded his loins with blubber,
²⁸ He shall dwell in ruined cities,
        in houses that are deserted,
        crumbling into rubble.
²⁹ He shall not be rich, his possessions shall
            not endure;
        his property shall not spread over
            the land.
³⁰ A flame shall sear his early growth,
        and with the wind his blossoms shall
            disappear.
³¹ Let him not trust in his height, misled,
        even though his height be like the
            palm tree.*
³² He shall wither before his time,
        his branches no longer green.
³³ He shall be like a vine that sheds its
            grapes unripened,
        like an olive tree casting off its
            blossom.
³⁴ For the breed of the impious shall be
            sterile,ʸ
        and fire shall consume the tents of
            extortioners.
³⁵ They conceive malice, bring forth deceit,ᶻ
        give birth to fraud.†

## CHAPTER 16
**Job's Fourth Reply.** ¹Then Job answered and said:

² I have heard this sort of thing many
            times.ᵃ
        Troublesome comforters, all of you!
³ Is there no end to windy words?
        What sickness makes you rattle on?
⁴ I also could talk as you do,
        were you in my place.

I could declaim over you,
        or wag my head at you;
⁵ I could strengthen you with talk,
        with mere chatter give relief.
⁶ If I speak, my pain is not relieved;
        if I stop speaking, nothing changes.
⁷ But now he has exhausted me;
        you have stunned all my companions.
⁸ You‡ have shriveled me up; it is a witness,
        my gauntness rises up to testify
            against me;
⁹ His wrath tears and assails me,
        he gnashes his teeth against me;
My enemy looks daggers at me.
¹⁰       They gape at me with their mouths;
They strike me on the cheek with insults;
        they are all enlisted against me.
¹¹ God has given me over to the impious;
        into the hands of the wicked he has
            cast me.
¹² I was in peace, but he dislodged me,
        seized me by the neck, dashed me
            to pieces.
He has set me up for a target;
¹³       his arrows strike me from all
            directions.
He pierces my sides without mercy,
        pours out my gall upon the ground.
¹⁴ He pierces me, thrust upon thrust,
        rushes at me like a warrior.
¹⁵ I have sewn sackcloth on my skin,
        laid my horn low in the dust.
¹⁶ My face is inflamed with weeping,
        darkness covers my eyes,
¹⁷ Although my hands are free from
            violence,
        and my prayer sincere.
¹⁸ O earth, do not cover my blood,
        nor let my outcry come to rest!§
¹⁹ Even now my witness¶ is in heaven,
        my advocate is on high.
²⁰ My friends it is who wrong me;
        before God my eyes shed tears,
²¹ That justice may be done for a mortal
            with God:
        as for a man with his neighbor.
²² For my years are numbered,
        and I go the road of no return.

## CHAPTER 17
¹ My spirit is broken, my days finished,
        my burial at hand.
² Surely mockers surround me,
        at their provocation, my eyes grow
            dim.

---

*[15:31] The translation is uncertain.
†[15:35] The plans of the wicked yield nothing but futile results. Cf. Ps 7:15; Is 59:4.

y. [15:34] Wis 3:11, 18.   z. [15:35] Ps 7:15; Is 59:4.   a. [16:2] Jb 12:3.

‡[16:8] **You:** God. Job then describes in vv. 9–17 the savage treatment that he has received from God.
§[16:18] As the exposed blood of those who were unjustly slain cries to heaven for vengeance (Gn 4:10; Ez 24:6–9), so Job's sufferings demand redress.
¶[16:19] **Witness:** refers perhaps to God (is Job appealing to God against God?), or to a mediator (cf. 9:33), or to a personification of Job's prayer.

³ Put up a pledge for me with you:*
  who is there to give surety for me?
⁴ You darken their minds to knowledge;
  therefore you will not exalt them.
⁵ For a share of property he informs on
    friends,
  while the eyes of his children grow
    dim.
⁶ I am made a byword of the people;ᵇ
  I am one at whom people spit.
⁷ My eyes are blind with anguish,
  and my whole frame is like a shadow.
⁸ The upright are astonished at this,
  the innocent aroused against the
    wicked.
⁹ The righteous holds to his way,
  the one with clean hands increases
    in strength.
¹⁰ But turn now, and come on again;
  I do not find a wise man among you!
¹¹ My days pass by, my plans are at an end,
  the yearning of my heart.
¹² They would change the night into day;
  where there is darkness they talk of
    approaching light.
¹³ †If my only hope is dwelling in Sheol,
  and spreading my couch in
    darkness,
¹⁴ If I am to say to the pit, "You are my
    father,"
  and to the worm "my mother," "my
    sister,"
¹⁵ Where then is my hope,
  my happiness, who can see it?
¹⁶ Will they descend with me into Sheol?
  Shall we go down together into the
    dust?

## CHAPTER 18

**Bildad's Second Speech.** ¹Then Bildad the
Shuhite answered and said:

² When will you put an end to words?
  Reflect, and then we can have
    discussion.
³ Why are we accounted like beasts,
  equal to them in your sight?
⁴ You who tear yourself in your anger—
  shall the earth be neglected on your
    account
  or the rock be moved out of its
    place?
⁵ Truly, the light of the wicked is
    extinguished;
  the flame of his fire casts no light.
⁶ In his tent light is darkness;
  the lamp above him goes out.ᶜ

⁷ His vigorous steps are hemmed in,
  his own counsel casts him down.
⁸ A net catches him by the feet,
  he wanders into a pitfall.
⁹ A trap seizes him by the heel,
  a snare lays hold of him.
¹⁰ A noose is hidden for him on the
    ground,
  a netting for him on the path.
¹¹ On every side terrors frighten him;ᵈ
  they harry him at each step.
¹² His strength is famished,
  disaster is ready at his side,
¹³ His skin is eaten to the limbs,
  the firstborn of Death‡ eats his
    limbs.
¹⁴ He is plucked from the security of his
    tent,
  and marched off to the king of
    terrors.§
¹⁵ Fire lodges in his tent,
  over his abode brimstone is
    scattered.
¹⁶ Below, his roots dry up,
  and above, his branches wither.
¹⁷ His memory perishes from the earth,ᵉ
  and he has no name in the
    countryside.
¹⁸ He is driven from light into darkness,
  and banished from the world.
¹⁹ He has neither offshoot nor offspring
    among his people,
  no survivor where once he dwelt.
²⁰ Those who come after shall be appalled at
    his fate;
  those who went before are seized
    with horror.
²¹ So is it then with the dwelling of the
    impious;
  such is the place of the one who
    does not know God!

## CHAPTER 19

**Job's Fifth Reply.** ¹¶Then Job answered and said:

² How long will you afflict my spirit,
  grind me down with words?
³ These ten times you have humiliated me,
  have assailed me without shame!
⁴ Even if it were true that I am at fault,
  my fault would remain with me;
⁵ If truly you exalt yourselves at my
    expense,
  and use my shame as an argument
    against me,

---

*[17:3] Addressed to God; v. 10 to Job's friends.
†[17:13–16] Job elaborates another of the vivid descriptions of "life" in Sheol; cf. 3:13–23; 10:21–22.

b. [17:6] Jb 30:9.   c. [18:6] Jb 21:17; Prv 13:9; 24:20.

---

‡[18:13] **Firstborn of Death**: that is, disease, plague.
§[18:14] **The king of terrors**: of Sheol, of Death (cf. the "terrors" in v. 11). However, the Hebrew of this verse is obscure.

¶[19:1] Job continues railing against his friends (vv. 2–5),
and describing God's savage attack in words reminiscent of
16:9–17.

d. [18:11] Jb 15:20–24; 27:20.   e. [18:17] Ps 34:17; Prv 2:22; 10:7.

⁶ Know then that it is God who has dealt
    unfairly with me,
    and compassed me round with his
    net.
⁷ If I cry out "Violence!" I am not
    answered.ᶠ
    I shout for help, but there is no
    justice.
⁸ He has barred my way and I cannot pass;
    veiled my path in darkness;
⁹ He has stripped me of my glory,
    taken the diadem from my brow.
¹⁰ He breaks me down on every side, and I
    am gone;
    he has uprooted my hope like a tree.
¹¹ He has kindled his wrath against me;
    he counts me one of his enemies.ᵍ
¹² His troops advance as one;
    they build up their road to attack me,
    encamp around my tent.
¹³ My family has withdrawn from me,ʰ
    my friends are wholly estranged.
¹⁴ My relatives and companions neglect me,
    my guests have forgotten me.
¹⁵ Even my maidservants consider me a
    stranger;
    I am a foreigner in their sight.
¹⁶ I call my servant, but he gives no answer,
    though I plead aloud with him.
¹⁷ My breath is abhorrent to my wife;ⁱ
    I am loathsome to my very children.
¹⁸ Even young children despise me;
    when I appear, they speak against
    me.
¹⁹ All my intimate friends hold me in
    horror;
    those whom I loved have turned
    against me!ʲ
²⁰ My bones cling to my skin,
    and I have escaped by the skin of
    my teeth.*
²¹ Pity me, pity me, you my friends,
    for the hand of God has struck me!
²² Why do you pursue me like God,
    and prey insatiably upon me?
²³ Oh, would that my words were written
    down!ᵏ
    Would that they were inscribed in a
    record:†
²⁴ That with an iron chisel and with lead
    they were cut in the rock forever!
²⁵ As for me, I know that my vindicator
    lives,‡

and that he will at last stand forth
    upon the dust.ˡ
²⁶ This will happen when my skin has been
    stripped off,
    and from my flesh I will see God:
²⁷ I will see for myself,
    my own eyes, not another's, will
    behold him:
    my inmost being is consumed with
    longing.
²⁸ But you who say, "How shall we persecute
    him,
    seeing that the root of the matter is
    found in him?"
²⁹ Be afraid of the sword for yourselves,
    for your anger is a crime deserving
    the sword;
    that you may know that there is a
    judgment.

## CHAPTER 20

**Zophar's Second Speech.** ¹Then Zophar the
Naamathite answered and said:

² So now my thoughts provide an answer
    for me,
    because of the feelings within me.
³ A rebuke that puts me to shame I hear,
    and from my understanding a spirit
    gives me a reply.
⁴ Do you not know this: from of old,
    since human beings were placed
    upon the earth,
⁵ The triumph of the wicked is short
    and the joy of the impious but for a
    moment?ᵐ
⁶ Though his pride mount up to the
    heavens
    and his head reach to the clouds,
⁷ Yet he perishes forever like the dung he
    uses for fuel,
    and onlookers say, "Where is he?"ⁿ
⁸ Like a dream he takes flight and cannot be
    found;
    he fades away like a vision of the
    night.
⁹ The eye which saw him does so no more;
    nor shall his dwelling again behold
    him.
¹⁰ His sons will restore to the poor,
    and his hands will yield up his
    riches.ᵒ
¹¹ Though his bones are full of youthful
    vigor,

---

*[19:20] **Skin of my teeth**: although the metaphor is not
clear, this has become a proverbial expression for a narrow
escape. It does not fit Job's situation here.

†[19:23–24] What Job is about to say is so important that
he wants it recorded in a permanent manner.

‡[19:25–27] The meaning of this passage is obscure
because the original text has been poorly preserved and the
ancient versions do not agree among themselves. Job asserts

three times that he shall see a future vindicator (Hebrew *goel*),
but he leaves the time and manner of this vindication unde-
fined. The Vulgate translation has Job indicating a belief in
resurrection after death, but the Hebrew and the other ancient
versions are less specific.

---

f. [19:7] Jb 30:20.   g. [19:11] Jb 13:24; 33:10.   h. [19:13] Jb
6:13.   i. [19:17] Jb 2:9.   j. [19:19] Sir 6:8.   k. [19:23] Jb 31:35.

l. [19:25–26] Phil 3:20; Ti 2:13.   m. [20:5] Jb 21:13; Ps 37:35–36.
n. [20:7] Jb 14:10; Ps 37:10, 36.   o. [20:10] Jb 27:14.

12 Though wickedness is sweet in his mouth,
     and he hides it under his tongue,
13 Though he retains it and will not let it go
     but keeps it still within his mouth,
14 Yet in his stomach the food shall turn;
     it shall be venom of asps inside him.
15 The riches he swallowed he shall vomit
     up;
     God shall make his belly disgorge
     them.
16 The poison of asps he shall drink in;
     the viper's fangs shall slay him.
17 He shall see no streams of oil,*
     no torrents of honey or milk.
18 He shall give back his gains, never used;
     like his profit from trade, never
     enjoyed.
19 Because he has oppressed and neglected
     the poor,
     and stolen a house he did not build;
20 For he has known no quiet in his greed,
     in his treasure he cannot save
     himself.ᵖ
21 None of his survivors will consume it,
     therefore his prosperity shall not
     endure.
22 ᑫWhen he has more than enough, distress
     shall be his,
     every sort of trouble shall come
     upon him.
23 When he has filled his belly,
     God shall send against him the fury
     of his wrath
     and rain down his missiles upon
     him.
24 Should he escape an iron weapon,
     a bronze bow shall pierce him
     through;
25 The dart shall come out of his back,
     a shining point out of his
     gall-bladder:
     terrors fall upon him.
26 Complete darkness is in store for his
     treasured ones;
     a fire unfanned shall consume him;ʳ
     any survivor in his tent shall be
     destroyed.
27 The heavens shall reveal his guilt,
     and the earth rise up against him.
28 The flood shall sweep away his house,
     torrents in the day of God's anger.
29 This is the portion of the wicked,
     the heritage appointed him by God.†ˢ

**CHAPTER 21**

**Job's Sixth Reply.** ¹Then Job answered and said:

2    At least listen to my words,ᵗ
       and let that be the consolation you
       offer.
3    Bear with me while I speak;
       and after I have spoken, you can
       mock!
4    Is my complaint toward any human being?
       Why should I not be impatient?
5    Look at me and be appalled,
       put your hands over your mouths.
6    When I think of it, I am dismayed,
       and shuddering seizes my flesh.
7    ‡Why do the wicked keep on living,
       grow old, become mighty in power?ᵘ
8    Their progeny is secure in their sight;
       their offspring are before their eyes.
9    Their homes are safe, without fear,
       and the rod of God is not upon
       them.
10   Their bulls breed without fail;
       their cows calve and do not
       miscarry.
11   They let their young run free like sheep,
       their children skip about.
12   They sing along with drum and lyre,
       and make merry to the sound of
       the pipe.
13   They live out their days in prosperity,
       and tranquilly go down to Sheol.ᵛ
14   Yet they say to God, "Depart from us,ʷ
       for we have no desire to know your
       ways!
15   What is the Almighty that we should
       serve him?
       And what do we gain by praying to
       him?"ˣ
16   Their happiness is not in their own hands.
       The designs of the wicked are far
       from me!ʸ
17   How often is the lamp of the wicked put
       out?
       How often does destruction come
       upon them,
       the portion God allots in his anger?
18   Let them be like straw before the wind,
       like chaff the storm carries away!
19   "God is storing up the man's misery for
       his children"?—
       let him requite the man himself so
       that he knows it!
20   Let his own eyes behold his calamity,
       and the wrath of the Almighty let
       him drink!

---

*[20:17] **Oil**: olive oil, one of the main agricultural products of ancient Palestine, a land proverbially rich in honey and milk; see Ex 3:8; etc.
†[20:29] Zophar ends his lecture in the style of Bildad (cf. 18:19) with a summary appraisal of what he has been saying about the fate of the wicked.

‡[21:7] In vv. 7–29 Job launches into a realistic description of the fate of the wicked, contrary to the claims made by the friends.

---

p. [20:20] Eccl 5:9; Lk 12:20.   q. [20:22] Jb 15:20–35.   r. [20:26] Dt 32:22.   s. [20:29] Jb 27:13.

t. [21:2] Jb 13:17.   u. [21:7] Jb 12:6; Ps 37:35; 73:3; Eccl 8:14; Jer 12:1–2; Mal 3:14–15.   v. [21:13] Jb 34:20.   w. [21:14] Jb 22:17.   x. [21:15] Mal 3:14.   y. [21:16] Jb 22:18.

<sup>21</sup> For what interest has he in his family after
　　him,
　　　　when the number of his months is
　　　　　finished?
<sup>22</sup> Can anyone teach God knowledge,
　　　　seeing that he judges those on high?*
<sup>23</sup> One dies in his full vigor,
　　　　wholly at ease and content;
<sup>24</sup> His figure is full and nourished,
　　　　his bones are moist with marrow.
<sup>25</sup> Another dies with a bitter spirit,
　　　　never having tasted happiness.
<sup>26</sup> Alike they lie down in the dust,
　　　　and worms cover them both.
<sup>27</sup> See, I know your thoughts,
　　　　and the arguments you plot against
　　　　　me.
<sup>28</sup> For you say, "Where is the house of the
　　great,
　　　　and where the dwelling place of the
　　　　　wicked?"
<sup>29</sup> Have you not asked the wayfarers
　　　　and do you not acknowledge the
　　　　　witness they give?
<sup>30</sup> On the day of calamity the evil man is
　　spared,
　　　　on the day that wrath is released.
<sup>31</sup> Who will charge him to his face about his
　　conduct,
　　　　and for what he has done who will
　　　　　repay him?
<sup>32</sup> He is carried to the grave
　　　　and at his tomb they keep watch.
<sup>33</sup> Sweet to him are the clods of the valley.
　　All humankind will follow after him,
　　　　and countless others before him.
<sup>34</sup> How empty the consolation you offer
　　me!
　　　　Your arguments remain a fraud.

## IV. THIRD CYCLE OF SPEECHES†

### CHAPTER 22
**Eliphaz's Third Speech.** <sup>1</sup>Then Eliphaz the
Temanite answered and said:

<sup>2</sup>Can a man be profitable to God?<sup>z</sup>
　　Can a wise man be profitable to
　　　him?
<sup>3</sup> Does it please the Almighty that you are
　　just?<sup>a</sup>

Does he gain if your ways are
　　perfect?<sup>‡</sup>
<sup>4</sup> Is it because of your piety that he reproves
　　you—
　　　　that he enters into judgment with
　　　　　you?
<sup>5</sup> Is not your wickedness great,
　　　　your iniquity endless?
<sup>6</sup> You keep your relatives' goods in pledge
　　unjustly,<sup>§</sup>
　　　　leave them stripped naked of their
　　　　　clothing.<sup>b</sup>
<sup>7</sup> To the thirsty you give no water to drink,
　　　　and from the hungry you withhold
　　　　　bread;
<sup>8</sup> As if the land belonged to the powerful,
　　　　and only the privileged could dwell
　　　　　in it!
<sup>9</sup> You sent widows away empty-handed,
　　　　and the resources of orphans are
　　　　　destroyed.<sup>c</sup>
<sup>10</sup> Therefore snares are round about you,<sup>d</sup>
　　　　sudden terror makes you panic,
<sup>11</sup> Or darkness—you cannot see!
　　　　A deluge of waters covers you.
<sup>12</sup> Does not God, in the heights of the
　　heavens,<sup>e</sup>
　　　　behold the top of the stars, high
　　　　　though they are?
<sup>13</sup> Yet you say, "What does God know?<sup>f</sup>
　　　　Can he judge through the thick
　　　　　darkness?
<sup>14</sup> Clouds hide him so that he cannot see
　　　　as he walks around the circuit of the
　　　　　heavens!"
<sup>15</sup> Do you indeed keep to the ancient way
　　　　trodden by the worthless?
<sup>16</sup> They were snatched before their time;
　　　　their foundations a river swept
　　　　　away.
<sup>17</sup> They said to God, "Let us alone!"
　　　　and, "What can the Almighty do
　　　　　to us?"
<sup>18</sup> Yet he had filled their houses with good
　　things.
　　　　The designs of the wicked are far
　　　　　from me!<sup>§g</sup>
<sup>19</sup> The just look on and are glad,
　　　　and the innocent deride them:**<sup>h</sup>

---

‡[22:3] Another irony: God will "gain," because he will have
been proved right in his claim to the satan that Job is "perfect."

§[22:6–9] This criticism of Job by Eliphaz is untrue (cf.
31:19), but he is driven to it by his belief that God always acts
justly, even when he causes someone to suffer; suffering is due
to wrongdoing (cf. v. 29).

¶[22:18] The second part of the verse repeats 21:16.

**[22:19] Them: the wicked. Eliphaz obviously thinks that
the just can be pleased by God's punishment of the wicked.
Such pleasure at the downfall of the wicked is expressed elsewhere, e.g., Ps 58:11; 63:12.

b. [22:6] Jb 24:3; Dt 24:6, 17; Ez 18:12, 16.　c. [22:9] Jb 29:12–13; Dt
24:17; 27:19.　d. [22:10] Jb 18:8–10.　e. [22:12] Jb 11:8.　f. [22:13–
14] Ps 10:11; 73:11; 94:7; Is 29:15; Ez 8:12; 9:9.　g. [22:18] Jb
21:16.　h. [22:19] Ps 107:42.

---

*[21:22] **Those on high**: the heavenly beings; cf. 1:6; Ps
82:1–8.

†[22:1–27:23] The traditional three cycles of speeches
breaks down in chaps. 22–27, because Zophar does not
appear. This may be interpreted as a sign that the three friends
see no point in further dialogue, or that Job's replies have
reduced them to silence, or that there has been a mistake in
the transmission of the text (hence various transferrals of
verses have been proposed to include Zophar, but without any
textual evidence).

z. [22:2] Jb 9:2.　a. [22:3] Jb 35:7.

<sup>20</sup> "Truly our enemies are destroyed,
      and what was left to them, fire has
          consumed!"
<sup>21</sup> Settle with him and have peace.
      That way good shall come to you:
<sup>22</sup> Receive instruction from his mouth,
      and place his words in your heart.
<sup>23</sup> If you return to the Almighty, you will be
        restored;
      if you put iniquity far from your tent,
<sup>24</sup> And treat raw gold as dust,
      the fine gold of Ophir* as pebbles in
          the wadi,
<sup>25</sup> Then the Almighty himself shall be your
        gold
      and your sparkling silver.
<sup>26</sup> For then you shall delight in the
        Almighty,
      you shall lift up your face toward
         God.
<sup>27</sup> Entreat him and he will hear you,<sup>i</sup>
      and your vows you shall fulfill.
<sup>28</sup> What you decide shall succeed for you,
      and upon your ways light shall
         shine.
<sup>29</sup> For when they are brought low, you will
        say, "It is pride!"
      But downcast eyes he saves.<sup>j</sup>
<sup>30</sup> He will deliver whoever is innocent;
      you shall be delivered if your hands
         are clean.<sup>k</sup>

## CHAPTER 23

**Job's Seventh Reply.** <sup>1</sup>Then Job answered and
said:

<sup>2</sup> Today especially my complaint is bitter,
      his hand is heavy upon me in my
         groanings.
<sup>3</sup> Would that I knew how to find him,
      that I might come to his dwelling!
<sup>4</sup> I would set out my case before him,
      fill my mouth with arguments;
<sup>5</sup> I would learn the words he would answer
        me,
      understand what he would say to me.
<sup>6</sup> Would he contend against me with his
        great power?
      No, he himself would heed me!
<sup>7</sup> There an upright man might argue with
        him,
      and I would once and for all be
         delivered from my judge.
<sup>8</sup> But if I go east, he is not there;<sup>†</sup>
      or west, I cannot perceive him;

<sup>9</sup> The north enfolds him, and I cannot catch
        sight of him;
      The south hides him, and I cannot
        see him.
<sup>10</sup> Yet he knows my way;
      if he tested me, I should come forth
        like gold.<sup>l</sup>
<sup>11</sup> My foot has always walked in his steps;
      I have kept his way and not turned
        aside.
<sup>12</sup> From the commands of his lips I have not
        departed;
      the words of his mouth I have
        treasured in my heart.
<sup>13</sup> But once he decides, who can contradict
        him?
      What he desires, that he does.<sup>m</sup>
<sup>14</sup> For he will carry out what is appointed for
        me,
      and many such things he has in
        store.
<sup>15</sup> Therefore I am terrified before him;
      when I take thought, I dread him.
<sup>16</sup> For it is God who has made my heart
        faint,
      the Almighty who has terrified me.
<sup>17</sup> Yes, would that I had vanished in
        darkness,
      hidden by the thick gloom before me.

## CHAPTER 24

<sup>1</sup> Why are times not set by the Almighty,
      and why do his friends not see his
        days?<sup>‡</sup>
<sup>2</sup> People remove landmarks;
      they steal herds and pasture them.
<sup>3</sup> The donkeys of orphans they drive away;
      they take the widow's ox for a
        pledge.
<sup>4</sup> They force the needy off the road;
      all the poor of the land are driven
        into hiding.
<sup>5</sup> Like wild donkeys in the wilderness,
      they go forth to their task of seeking
        prey;
      the steppe provides food for their
        young;
<sup>6</sup> They harvest fodder in the field,
      and glean in the vineyard of the
        wicked.
<sup>7</sup> They pass the night naked, without
        clothing;
      they have no covering against the
        cold;
<sup>8</sup> They are drenched with rain from the
        mountains,

---

*[22:24] **Ophir**: see note on Ps 45:10.

†[23:8] Job's confident desire to confront God (vv. 2–7,
contrary to his fears in 9:14–20 and 13:21–27) gives way to
his dark night: God's absence (vv. 8–9), which also terrifies
(vv. 13–17).

‡[24:1] After his failure to find God, Job takes up the question: Why does God not favor his friends by the speedy punishment of his enemies?

---

i. [22:27] Jb 33:26.    j. [22:29] Ps 138:6; Prv 29:23; Mt 23:12; Lk 1:52;
Jas 4:10; 1 Pt 5:5.    k. [22:30] Jb 17:9; Ps 18:21, 25; 24:4.

l. [23:10] Ps 66:10; Prv 17:3; Mal 3:3; 1 Pt 1:7.    m. [23:13] Jb 42:2;
Ps 115:3; 135:6.

and for want of shelter they cling to
  the rock.

9 Orphans are snatched from the breast,
  infants of the needy are taken in
    pledge.*

10 They go about naked, without clothing,
  and famished, they carry the
    sheaves.†

11 Between the rows they press out the oil;
  they tread the wine presses, yet are
    thirsty.

12 In the city the dying groan,
  and the souls of the wounded cry
    out.
  Yet God does not treat it as a
    disgrace!

13 They are rebels against the light:ⁿ
  they do not recognize its ways;
  they do not stay in its paths.

14 When there is no light the murderer
    rises,
  to kill the poor and needy;
  in the night he acts like a thief.

15 The eye of the adulterer watches for the
    twilight;ᵒ
  he says, "No eye will see me."
  He puts a mask over his face;

16   in the dark he breaks into houses;
  By day they shut themselves in;
  they do not know the light.

17 Indeed, for all of them morning is deep
    darkness;
  then they recognize the terrors of
    deep darkness.

18 He is swift on the surface of the water:‡
  their portion in the land is accursed,
  they do not turn aside by way of the
    vineyards.

19 Drought and heat snatch away the snow
    waters,
  Sheol, those who have sinned.

20 May the womb forget him,
  may the worm find him sweet,
  may he no longer be remembered;
  And may wickedness be broken like a
    tree.

21 May his companion be barren, unable to
    give birth,
  may his widow not prosper!

22 He§ sustains the mighty by his strength,
  to him who rises without assurance
    of his life

23   he gives safety and support,
  and his eyes are on their ways.

24 They are exalted for a while, and then are
    no more;
  laid low, like everyone else they are
    gathered up;
  like ears of grain they shrivel.

25 If this be not so, who can make me a liar,
  and reduce my words to nothing?

## CHAPTER 25

**Bildad's Third Speech.** ¹*Then Bildad the
Shuhite answered and said:

2   Dominion and dread are his
  who brings about harmony in his
    heavens.

3   Is there any numbering of his troops?**
  Yet on which of them does his light
    not rise?

4   How can anyone be in the right against
    God,ᵖ
  or how can any born of woman be
    innocent?

5   Even the moon is not bright
  and the stars are not clean in his eyes.

6   How much less a human being, who is but
    a worm,
  a mortal, who is only a maggot?�q

## CHAPTER 26

**Job's Reply.** ¹Then Job answered and said:††

2   What help you give to the powerless,
  what strength to the feeble arm!

3   How you give counsel to one without
    wisdom;
  how profuse is the advice you offer!

4   With whose help have you uttered those
    words,
  whose breath comes forth from you?ʳ

5   The shades‡‡ beneath writhe in terror,ˢ
  the waters, and their inhabitants.

6   Naked before him is Sheol,§§
  and Abaddon has no covering.ᵗ

7   He stretches out Zaphon⁵⁵ over the void,
  and suspends the earth over nothing
    at all;

---

*[24:9] This verse continues the description of the plight of
the poor in vv. 2–4, and may belong there.

†[24:10] This verse is a variant of v. 7, and may be an erroneous scribal repetition.

‡[24:18–24] These verses are inconsistent with Job's views
elsewhere. Moreover, they are in general poorly preserved,
and in some cases obscure.

§[24:22] **He**: God.

¶[25:1] At this point any structure in the dialogues disappears. Bildad's speech is very short, and there follow two
speeches attributed to Job, with significantly different introductions in 27:1 and 29:1, and with no intervening third speech
of Zophar.

**[25:3] **His troops**: the heavenly host, or army, the stars
(cf. Jgs 5:20), later understood as angels.

††[26:1–14] Perhaps to be read as Job's reply to Bildad's
short speech.

‡‡[26:5] **Shades**: the dead in Sheol, the nether world; cf. Ps
88:11; Is 26:14.

§§[26:6] **Sheol**: cf. note on Ps 6:6. **Abaddon**: Hebrew for
"(place of) destruction," a synonym for nether world; cf. Jb
28:22; Rev 9:11.

¶¶[26:7] **Zaphon**: lit., "the north," used here as a synonym
for the firmament, the heavens; cf. Is 14:13.

n. [24:13] Jn 3:19–20.  o. [24:15] Prv 7:9–10.

p. [25:4] Jb 4:17; 9:2; 35:2.   q. [25:6] Jb 4:19; 15:16.   r. [26:4] Gn
2:7.   s. [26:5] Prv 9:18.   t. [26:6] Ps 139:7–12.

8 He binds up the waters in his clouds,
    yet the cloud is not split by their
      weight;
9 He holds back the appearance of the full
    moon
    by spreading his clouds before it.
10 He has marked out a circle* on the surface
    of the deep<sup>u</sup>
    as the boundary of light and
      darkness.
11 The pillars of the heavens tremble
    and are stunned at his thunderous
      rebuke;<sup>v</sup>
12 By his power he stilled Sea,
    by his skill he crushed Rahab;<sup>†</sup>
13 By his wind the heavens were made clear,
    his hand pierced the fleeing
      serpent.<sup>‡w</sup>
14 Lo, these are but the outlines of his ways,
    and what a whisper of a word we
      hear of him:
    Who can comprehend the thunder
      of his power?

## CHAPTER 27

**Job's Reply.** [1]Job took up his theme again and said:

2 As God lives,<sup>§</sup> who takes away my right,<sup>x</sup>
    the Almighty, who has made my life
      bitter,
3 So long as I still have life breath in me,
    the breath of God in my nostrils,
4 My lips shall not speak falsehood,
    nor my tongue utter deceit!
5 Far be it from me to account you right;
    till I die I will not renounce my
      innocence.<sup>y</sup>
6 My justice I maintain and I will not
    relinquish it;
    my heart does not reproach me for
      any of my days.
7 'Let my enemy be as the wicked
    and my adversary as the unjust!
8 For what hope has the impious when he is
    cut off,
    when God requires his life?

9 Will God then listen to his cry
    when distress comes upon him,
10 If he delights in the Almighty
    and calls upon God constantly?
11 I will teach you what is in God's hand,
    and the way of the Almighty I will
      not conceal.
12 Look, you yourselves have all seen it;
    why do you spend yourselves in
      empty words!
13 This is the portion of the wicked with God,
    the heritage oppressors receive from
      the Almighty:<sup>z</sup>
14 Though his children be many, the sword
    awaits them.
    His descendants shall want for bread.
15 His survivors shall be buried in death;
    their widows shall not weep.
16 Though he heap up silver like dust
    and store away mounds of clothing,
17 What he has stored the righteous shall
    wear,
    and the innocent shall divide the
      silver.
18 He builds his house as of cobwebs,
    or like a booth put up by a watchman.
19 He lies down a rich man, one last time;
    he opens his eyes—nothing is there.<sup>a</sup>
20 Terrors flood over him like water,
    at night the tempest carries him off.
21 The east wind seizes him and he is gone;
    it sweeps him from his place;
22 It hurls itself at him without pity,
    as he tries to flee from its power.
23 It claps its hands at him,
    and whistles at him from its place.

## V. THE POEM ON WISDOM

## CHAPTER 28

### Where Is Wisdom to Be Found?

1 There is indeed a mine for silver,<sup>**</sup>
    and a place for refining gold.
2 Iron is taken from the earth,
    and copper smelted out of stone.
3 <sup>††</sup>He sets a boundary for the darkness;
    the farthest confines he explores.

---

*[26:10] **Circle**: the horizon of the ocean which serves as the boundary for the activity of light and darkness; cf. Prv 8:27.

†[26:12] **Rahab**: another name for the primeval sea-monster; see notes on Jb 3:8 and Ps 89:11; cf. also Jb 7:12; 9:13.

‡[26:13] **The fleeing serpent**: the same term occurs in Is 27:1 in apposition to Leviathan; see note on Jb 3:8.

§[27:2–6] **As God lives . . . far be it**: Job affirms two oaths about his innocence by the very God whom he has accused of violating his right. Such is the paradoxical situation of a tortured person who cannot give the lie to his personal justice, but also refuses to renounce God. He dares God to be "just" as he, Job, understands this.

¶[27:7–23] These verses are inconsistent with Job's views elsewhere, and may be part of a missing speech of Zophar; cf. notes on 24:18–24 and 25:1. Or possibly they are an ironic description of the fate of the three friends.

u. [26:10] Jb 38:8–11; Prv 8:29.  v. [26:11] Jb 9:6; Ps 18:16; 104:7.  w. [26:13] Is 27:1.  x. [27:2] Jb 34:5.  y. [27:5] Jb 2:3, 9; 13:15; 33:9.

---

**[28:1–28] This chapter contains a beautifully vivid description of that Wisdom which is beyond the attainment of creatures and known only to God. The pronouns referring to Wisdom may be translated as either feminine or neuter; in view of Wisdom's role as God's companion and partner in creation (see Prv 8:22–30; Sir 24:1–21; Wis 9:9; Bar 3:9–4:4), the feminine is used here. There is no consensus about the authorship of this poem; it may originally have been an independent composition incorporated into the Book of Job.

††[28:3–4] The subject of the verbs in these verses has no clear antecedent; the context of vv. 2–6 suggests miners. The Hebrew of v. 4 is especially difficult. The general sense of vv. 1–11 is that one can find minerals in the earth; in contrast, where is Wisdom to be found (vv. 12, 20)?

z. [27:13] Jb 20:4–29.  a. [27:19] Ps 49:18; 76:6.

4 He breaks open a shaft far from
    habitation,
        unknown to human feet;
        suspended, far from people, they
            sway.
5 The earth, though out of it comes forth
        bread,
    is in fiery upheaval underneath.
6 Its stones are the source of lapis lazuli,
    and there is gold in its dust.
7 The path no bird of prey knows,
    nor has the hawk's eye seen it.
8 The proud beasts have not trodden it,
    nor has the lion gone that way.
9 He sets his hand to the flinty rock,
    and overturns the mountains at
        their root.
10 He splits channels in the rocks;
    his eyes behold all that is precious.
11 He dams up the sources of the streams,
    and brings hidden things to light.
12 As for wisdom—where can she be found?
        Where is the place of
            understanding?[b]
13 Mortals do not know her path,
    nor is she to be found in the land of
        the living.
14 The Deep says, "She is not in me";
    and the Sea says, "She is not with
        me."
15 Solid gold cannot purchase her,
    nor can her price be paid with
        silver.[c]
16 She cannot be bought with gold of Ophir,*
    with precious onyx or lapis lazuli,
17 Gold or crystal cannot equal her,
    nor can golden vessels be exchanged
        for her.
18 Neither coral nor crystal should be
        thought of;
    the value of wisdom surpasses
        pearls.
19 Ethiopian topaz does not equal her,
    nor can she be weighed out for pure
        gold.
20 As for wisdom, where does she come
        from?
        Where is the place of
            understanding?
21 She is hidden from the eyes of every living
        thing;
    even from the birds of the air she is
        concealed.
22 Abaddon[†] and Death say,
    "Only by rumor have we heard of
        her."

23 ‡But God understands the way to her;[d]
    it is he who knows her place.[e]
24 For he beholds the ends of the earth
    and sees all that is under the
        heavens.
25 When he weighed out the wind,
    and measured out the waters;
26 When he made a rule for the rain
    and a path for the thunderbolts,[f]
27 Then he saw wisdom and appraised her,
    established her, and searched her
        out.
28 §And to mortals he said:
    See: the fear of the Lord is wisdom;
    and avoiding evil is understanding.[g]

### VI. JOB'S FINAL SUMMARY
### OF HIS CAUSE

### CHAPTER 29

1 Job took up his theme again and said:

2 Oh, that I were as in the months past,
    as in the days when God watched
        over me:[h]
3 While he kept his lamp shining above my
        head,
    and by his light I walked through
        darkness;
4 As I was in my flourishing days,
    when God sheltered my tent;
5 When the Almighty was still with me,
    and my children were round about
        me;
6 When my footsteps were bathed in cream,
    and the rock flowed with streams
        of oil.**
7 Whenever I went out to the gate of the
        city
    and took my seat in the square,
8 The young men saw me and withdrew,
    and the elders rose up and stood;
9 Officials refrained from speaking
    and covered their mouths with their
        hands;[i]

---

‡[28:23–27] In reply to the question of vv. 12, 20, these
verses indicate that the creator (vv. 24–26) knows the "place"
of wisdom and even "established" her, but the specifics are not
given. For further development of this theme, cf. Sir 1:1–10
and Bar 3:9–4:4.

§[28:28] This verse may be a later addition expressing a
commonplace of the wisdom tradition; see cross-references.
The addition seems to tie the poem in with the description of
Job as fearing God and avoiding evil (1:1; 8; 2:3).

¶[29:1] This chapter begins Job's soliloquy, which will end
in 31:40. He describes in florid and exaggerated terms his former lifestyle with all its blessings, a deliberate contrast to his
current plight, which will be further described in chap. 30.

**[29:6] Hyperbole to express abundance; see note on
20:17.

---

*[28:16] **Ophir:** cf. note on Ps 45:10.
†[28:22] **Abaddon:** cf. note on Jb 26:6.

b. [28:12] Eccl 7:24–25; Bar 3:14–15, 29–33.    c. [28:15] Prv 3:14;
8:10–11, 19; 16:16; Wis 7:7–11.

d. [28:23–27] Prv 8:22–31.    e. [28:23] Prv 2:6; Sir 1:1; Jas
1:5.    f. [28:26] Jb 38:25; Prv 3:20.    g. [28:28] Ps 111:10; Prv 1:7;
9:10; Sir 1:13–21.    h. [29:2] Jb 1:10.    i. [29:9] Wis 8:10–12.

<sup>10</sup> The voice of the princes was silenced,
  and their tongues stuck to the roofs
    of their mouths.
<sup>11</sup> The ear that heard blessed me;
  the eye that saw acclaimed me.
<sup>12</sup> For I rescued the poor who cried out for
    help,
  the orphans, and the unassisted;
<sup>13</sup> The blessing of those in extremity came
    upon me,
  and the heart of the widow I made
    joyful.
<sup>14</sup> I wore my righteousness like a garment;
  justice was my robe and my turban.
<sup>15</sup> I was eyes to the blind,
  and feet to the lame was I.
<sup>16</sup> I was a father to the poor;
  the complaint of the stranger I
    pursued.
<sup>17</sup> And I broke the jaws of the wicked man;
  from his teeth I forced the prey.
<sup>18</sup> I said: "In my own nest I shall grow old;
  I shall multiply years like the
    phoenix.*
<sup>19</sup> My root is spread out to the waters;
  the dew rests by night on my
    branches.
<sup>20</sup> My glory is fresh within me,
  and my bow is renewed in my hand!"
<sup>21</sup> For me they listened and waited;
  they were silent for my counsel.
<sup>22</sup> Once I spoke, they said no more,
  but received my pronouncement
    drop by drop.
<sup>23</sup> They waited for me as for the rain;
  they drank in my words like the
    spring rains.
<sup>24</sup> When I smiled on them they could not
    believe it;
  they would not let the light of my
    face be dimmed.
<sup>25</sup> I decided their course and sat at their
    head,
  I lived like a king among the troops,
  like one who comforts mourners.

### CHAPTER 30

<sup>1</sup> But now they hold me in derision
  who are younger than I,<sup>j</sup>
  Whose fathers I should have disdained
    to rank with the dogs of my flock.
<sup>2</sup> Such strength as they had meant nothing
    to me;
  their vigor had perished.
<sup>3</sup> In want and emaciating hunger<sup>k</sup>
  they fled to the parched lands:
  to the desolate wasteland by night.

<sup>4</sup> They plucked saltwort<sup>†</sup> and shrubs;
  the roots of the broom plant were
    their food.
<sup>5</sup> They were banished from the community,
  with an outcry like that against a
    thief—
<sup>6</sup> To dwell on the slopes of the wadies,
  in caves of sand and stone;
<sup>7</sup> Among the bushes they brayed;
  under the nettles they huddled
    together.
<sup>8</sup> Irresponsible, of no account,
  they were driven out of the land.
<sup>9</sup> Yet now they sing of me in mockery;
  I have become a byword among
    them.<sup>l</sup>
<sup>10</sup> They abhor me, they stand aloof,
  they do not hesitate to spit in my
    face!
<sup>11</sup> <sup>‡</sup>Because he has loosened my bowstring
    and afflicted me,
  they have thrown off restraint in my
    presence.
<sup>12</sup> On my right the young rabble rise up;
  they trip my feet,
  they build their approaches for my
    ruin.
<sup>13</sup> They tear up my path,
  they promote my ruin,
  no helper is there against them.
<sup>14</sup> As through a wide breach they advance;
  amid the uproar they come on in
    waves;
<sup>15</sup>     terrors roll over me.
  My dignity is driven off like the wind,
  and my well-being vanishes like a
    cloud.
<sup>16</sup> And now my life ebbs away from me,
  days of affliction have taken hold
    of me.
<sup>17</sup> <sup>§</sup>At night he pierces my bones,
  my sinews have no rest.
<sup>18</sup> With great difficulty I change my clothes,
  the collar of my tunic fits around
    my waist.
<sup>19</sup> He has cast me into the mire;
  I have become like dust and ashes.
<sup>20</sup> I cry to you, but you do not answer me;<sup>m</sup>
  I stand, but you take no notice.
<sup>21</sup> You have turned into my tormentor,
  and with your strong hand you
    attack me.

---

<sup>†</sup>[30:4] **Saltwort:** found in salt marshes and very sour to
the taste; eaten by the extremely poor as a cooked vegetable.
**Broom plant:** the juniper or brushwood; cf. Ps 120:4; a figure
of bitterness and poverty, because of its bitter-tasting roots
which are practically inedible.
<sup>‡</sup>[30:11] God is the subject of the verbs. **Loosened my
bowstring:** i.e., disarmed and disabled me.
<sup>§</sup>[30:17–23] Job here refers to God's harsh treatment of
him. Cf. 16:9–17; 19:6–12.

---

*[29:18] **Phoenix:** a legendary bird which, after several
centuries of life, consumed itself in fire, then rose from its
ashes in youthful freshness.

---

j. [30:1] Jb 12:4; 19:18.   k. [30:3–8] Jb 24:5–6.

l. [30:9] Jb 17:6.   m. [30:20] Jb 19:7.

²² You raise me up and drive me before the
wind;
I am tossed about by the tempest.
²³ Indeed I know that you will return me to
death
to the house destined for everyone
alive.ⁿ
²⁴ Yet should not a hand be held out
to help a wretched person in
distress?
²⁵ Did I not weep for the hardships of
others;
was not my soul grieved for the
poor?ᵒ
²⁶ Yet when I looked for good, evil came;
when I expected light, darkness
came.
²⁷ My inward parts seethe and will not be
stilled;
days of affliction have overtaken me.
²⁸ I go about in gloom, without the sun;
I rise in the assembly and cry for
help.
²⁹ I have become a brother to jackals,
a companion to ostriches.
³⁰ My blackened skin falls away from me;
my very frame is scorched by the
heat.
³¹ My lyre is tuned to mourning,
and my reed pipe to sounds of
weeping.

## CHAPTER 31

¹ I made a covenant with my eyes
not to gaze upon a virgin.
² What portion comes from God above,
what heritage from the Almighty
on high?
³ Is it not calamity for the unrighteous,
and woe for evildoers?
⁴ Does he not see my ways,
and number all my steps?ᵖ
⁵ If I have walked in falsehood*
and my foot has hastened to deceit,
⁶ Let God weigh me in the scales of justice;
thus will he know my innocence!�q
⁷ If my steps have turned out of the way,
and my heart has followed my eyes,
or any stain clings to my hands,
⁸ Then may I sow, but another eat,
and may my produce be rooted up!
⁹ If my heart has been enticed toward a
woman,
and I have lain in wait at my
neighbor's door;
¹⁰ Then may my wife grind for another,
and may others kneel over her!

¹¹ For that would be heinous,
a crime to be condemned,ʳ
¹² A fire that would consume down to
Abaddon†
till it uprooted all my crops.ˢ
¹³ Had I refused justice to my manservant
or to my maidservant, when they
had a complaint against me,
¹⁴ What then should I do when God rises
up?
What could I answer when he
demands an account?
¹⁵ Did not he who made me in the belly
make him?
Did not the same One fashion us in
the womb?
¹⁶ If I have denied anything that the poor
desired,ᵗ
or allowed the eyes of the widow to
languish
¹⁷ While I ate my portion alone,
with no share in it for the fatherless,
¹⁸ Though like a father he‡ has reared me
from my youth,
guiding me even from my mother's
womb—
¹⁹ If I have seen a wanderer without
clothing,
or a poor man without covering,
²⁰ Whose limbs have not blessed me
when warmed with the fleece of my
sheep;
²¹ If I have raised my hand against the
innocent
because I saw that I had supporters
at the gate—§
²² Then may my arm fall from the shoulder,
my forearm be broken at the elbow!
²³ For I dread calamity from God,
and his majesty will overpower me.
²⁴ Had I put my trust in gold
or called fine gold my security;
²⁵ Or had I rejoiced that my wealth was
great,
or that my hand had acquired
abundance—
²⁶ Had I looked upon the lightⁿ as it shone,ᵘ
or the moon in the splendor of its
progress,
²⁷ And had my heart been secretly enticed
to blow them a kiss with my hand,
²⁸ This too would be a crime for
condemnation,
for I should have denied God above.ᵛ

---

†[31:12] **Abaddon**: see note on 26:6.
‡[31:18] **He**: presumably God.
§[31:21] **Gate**: cf. notes on 5:4; Ru 4:1.
¶[31:26–28] **Light**: of the sun. Job never sinned by worshiping the sun or the moon. **Blow them a kiss**: an act of idolatrous worship.

---

*[31:5–34] In a series of purificatory oaths, Job protests
his innocence.

n. [30:23] Heb 9:27.   o. [30:25] Jb 29:12–16.   p. [31:4] Jb 14:16;
34:21; Ps 139:3; Prv 5:21.   q. [31:6] Jb 23:10.

r. [31:11] Ex 20:14; Lv 20:10; Dt 22:22.   s. [31:12] Sir 9:8–9.
t. [31:16–23] Jb 29:12–16.   u. [31:26–27] Dt 4:19.   v. [31:28] Dt
17:2–7.

²⁹ Had I rejoiced at the destruction of my
        enemy
      or exulted when evil came upon
        him,ʷ
³⁰ Even though I had not allowed my mouth
        to sin
      by invoking a curse against his life—
³¹ Had not the men of my tent exclaimed,
      "Who has not been filled with his
        meat!"*
³² No stranger lodged in the street,
      for I opened my door to wayfarers—
³³ †Had I, all too human, hidden my sins
      and buried my guilt in my bosom
³⁴ Because I feared the great multitude
      and the scorn of the clans terrified
        me—
    then I should have remained silent,
      and not come out of doors!
³⁵ ‡Oh, that I had one to hear my case:
      here is my signature:§ let the
        Almighty answer me!
    Let my accuser write out his indictment!ˣ
³⁶ Surely, I should wear it on my shoulder¶
      or put it on me like a diadem;
³⁷ Of all my steps I should give him an
        account;
      like a prince** I should present myself
        before him.
³⁸ If my land has cried out against me
      till its furrows wept together;
³⁹ If I have eaten its strength without
        payment
      and grieved the hearts of its tenants;
⁴⁰ Then let the thorns grow instead of wheat
      and stinkweed instead of barley!

    The words of Job are ended.

## VII. ELIHU'S SPEECHES

### CHAPTER 32

¹Then the three men ceased to answer Job,
because in his own eyes he was in the right.ʸ ²ᵃBut
the anger of Elihu,†† son of Barachel the Buzite,

of the clan of Ram, was kindled. He was angry
with Job for considering himself rather than
God to be in the right. ³ᵃHe was angry also with
the three friends because they had not found a
good answer and had not condemned Job. ⁴But
since these men were older than he, Elihu bided
his time before addressing Job. ⁵When, however,
Elihu saw that there was no reply in the mouths of
the three men, his wrath was inflamed. ⁶So Elihu,
son of Barachel the Buzite, answered and said:

    I am young and you are very old;
      therefore I held back and was afraid
        to declare to you my knowledge.
⁷ I thought, days should speak,
      and many years teach wisdom!ᵇ
⁸ But there is a spirit in human beings,ᶜ
      the breath of the Almighty, that
        gives them understanding.
⁹ It is not those of many days who are wise,
      nor the aged who understand the
        right.
¹⁰ Therefore I say, listen to me;
      I also will declare my knowledge!
¹¹ Behold, I have waited for your words,
      have given ear to your arguments,
        as you searched out what to say.
¹² Yes, I followed you attentively:
      And look, none of you has convicted
        Job,
        not one could refute his statements.
¹³ So do not say, "We have met wisdom;‡‡
      God can vanquish him but no
        mortal!"
¹⁴ For had he addressed his words to me,
      I would not then have answered him
        with your words.
¹⁵ They are dismayed, they make no more
        reply;
      words fail them.
¹⁶ Must I wait? Now that they speak no
        more,
      and have ceased to make reply,
¹⁷ I too will speak my part;
      I also will declare my knowledge!
¹⁸ For I am full of words;
      the spirit within me compels me.
¹⁹ My belly is like unopened wine,
      like wineskins ready to burst.
²⁰ Let me speak and obtain relief;
      let me open my lips, and reply.

---

*[31:31] The members of his extended family will testify
to his hospitality.

†[31:33–34] Job's present protest is made, not in spite of
hidden sins which he had been unwilling to disclose, but out
of genuine innocence. **All too human**: can also be translated
"like Adam."

‡[31:35–37] This concluding bravado fits better after v.
40a.

§[31:35] **My signature**: lit., "*tau*," the last letter of the
Hebrew alphabet, shaped like a cross. Job issues a subpoena
to God, and challenges him to follow proper legal procedure
as well.

¶[31:36] **On my shoulder**: i.e., boldly, proudly.

**[31:37] **Like a prince**: not as a frightened criminal.

††[32:2] **Elihu** means "My God is he." This speaker was from
Buz, which, according to Jer 25:23, was near Tema and Dedan.
A young man, he impetuously and impatiently upbraids Job

for his boldness toward God, and the three friends for not
successfully answering Job. He undertakes to defend God's
absolute justice and to explain more clearly why there is suffering. While fundamentally his position is the same as that of
the three friends, he locates the place of suffering in the divine
plan. Because Elihu's four speeches (32:6–33:33; 34:2–37;
35:2–16; 36:2–37:24) repeat the substance of the earlier arguments of the three friends and also anticipate the content of
the divine speeches (chaps. 39–41), many scholars consider
them a later addition to the book.

‡‡[32:13] **Met wisdom**: in Job's arguments.

---

w. [31:29] Prv 24:17.   x. [31:35] Jb 19:23; 23:3–7.   y. [32:1] Jb
33:9.   z. [32:2] Jb 13:18; 27:6; 34:5; 35:2.

a. [32:3] Jb 22:5.   b. [32:7] Jb 12:12.   c. [32:8] Jb 33:4.

²¹ I would not be partial to anyone,
  nor give flattering titles to any.
²² For I know nothing of flattery;
  if I did, my Maker would soon take
    me away.

### CHAPTER 33

¹ Therefore, O Job, hear my discourse;
  listen to all my words.
² Behold, now I open my mouth;
  my tongue and voice form words.
³ I will state directly what is in my mind,
  my lips shall speak knowledge
    clearly;
⁴ For the spirit of God made me,
  the breath of the Almighty keeps
    me alive.ᵈ
⁵ If you are able, refute me;
  draw up your arguments and take
    your stand.
⁶ Look, I am like you before God,
  I too was pinched from clay.*ᵉ
⁷ Therefore fear of me should not dismay
    you,
  nor should I weigh heavily upon
    you.
⁸ But you have said in my hearing,
  as I listened to the sound of your
    words:
⁹ "I am clean, without transgression;
  I am innocent, there is no guilt in
    me.ᶠ
¹⁰ Yet he invents pretexts against me
  and counts me as an enemy.†ᵍ
¹¹ He puts my feet in the stocks,
  watches all my paths!"ʰ
¹² In this you are not just, let me tell you;
  for God is greater than mortals.
¹³ Why, then, do you make complaint
    against him
  that he gives no reply to their
    words?ⁱ
¹⁴ For God does speak, once,
  even twice, though you do not see it:‡
¹⁵ In a dream, in a vision of the night,
  when deep sleep falls upon mortals
  as they slumber in their beds.
¹⁶ It is then he opens their ears
  and with a warning, terrifies them,
¹⁷ By turning mortals from acting
  and keeping pride away from a man,
¹⁸ He holds his soul from the pit,
  his life from passing to the grave.

¹⁹ Or he is chastened on a bed of pain,
  suffering continually in his bones,
²⁰ So that to his appetite food is repulsive,
  his throat rejects the choicest
    nourishment.ʲ
²¹ His flesh is wasted, it cannot be seen;
  bones, once invisible, appear;
²² His soul draws near to the pit,
  his life to the place of the dead.
²³ If then there be a divine messenger,§
  a mediator, one out of a thousand,
  to show him what is right,
²⁴ He will take pity on him and say,
  "Deliver him from going down to
    the pit;
  I have found him a ransom."
²⁵ Then his flesh shall become soft as a boy's;
  he shall be again as in the days of
    his youth.
²⁶ He shall pray and God will favor him;
  he shall see God's face with
    rejoicing;ᵏ
  for he restores a person's
    righteousness.
²⁷ He shall sing before all and say,
  "I sinned and did wrong,
  yet I was not punished accordingly.
²⁸ He delivered me from passing to the pit,
  and my life sees light."
²⁹ See, all these things God does,
  two, even three times, for a man,
³⁰ Bringing back his soul from the pit
  to the light, in the light of the living.
³¹ Be attentive, Job, listen to me!
  Be silent and I will speak.
³² If you have anything to say, then answer
    me.
  Speak out! I should like to see you
    justified.
³³ If not, then you listen to me;
  be silent, and I will teach you
    wisdom.

### CHAPTER 34

¹ Then Elihu answered and said:¶

² Hear my discourse, you that are wise;
  you that have knowledge, listen to
    me!
³ For the ear tests words,
  as the palate tastes food.ˡ
⁴ Let us choose what is right;
  let us determine among ourselves
    what is good.

---

*[33:6] **Pinched from clay:** a reference to the tradition that human beings were made from clay; cf. Gn 2:7; Jb 10:9; Is 64:7.
†[33:10] **Enemy:** see note on 1:1; cf. 13:24.
‡[33:14] Elihu asserts that God speaks through warning in dream and also through pain. However, his presupposition is that the restored person admits sinfulness (v. 27). This of course is not relevant to Job's situation.

d. [33:4] Jb 32:8.  e. [33:6] Jb 31:15.  f. [33:9] Jb 10:7; 13:18; 27:5–6; 29:14; 32:1; 34:5.  g. [33:10] Jb 13:24; 19:11.  h. [33:11] Jb 13:27; 31:4.  i. [33:13] Jb 31:35.

§[33:23] **Divine messenger:** or "angel," one of the thousands who serve as mediators.
¶[34:1] Elihu replies, although no one else has spoken. This connective phrase (see also 35:1 and 36:1) may indicate that these speeches of Elihu are a secondary addition to the book (see note on 32:2).

j. [33:20] Jb 6:7.  k. [33:26] Jb 22:26–29.  l. [34:3] Jb 12:11.

5 For Job has said, "I am innocent,
    but God has taken away what is my
        right."[m]
6 I declare the judgment on me to be a lie;
    my arrow-wound is incurable,
        sinless though I am."[n]
7 What man is like Job?
    He drinks in blasphemies like water,
8 Keeps company with evildoers
    and goes along with the wicked,
9 When he says, "There is no profit
    in pleasing God."[o]
10 Therefore, you that have understanding,
        hear me:
    far be it from God to do wickedness;
    far from the Almighty to do wrong![p]
11 Rather, he requites mortals for their
        conduct,
    and brings home to them their way
        of life.[q]
12 Surely, God cannot act wickedly,
    the Almighty cannot pervert justice.[r]
13 Who gave him charge over the earth,
    or who set all the world in its place?[s]
14 If he were to set his mind to it,
    gather to himself his spirit and
        breath,
15 All flesh would perish together,
    and mortals return to dust.[t]
16 Now you[*]—understand, hear this!
    Listen to the words I speak!
17 Can an enemy of justice be in control,
    will you condemn the supreme Just
        One,
18 Who says to a king, "You are worthless!"
    and to nobles, "You are wicked!"
19 Who neither favors the person of princes,
    nor respects the rich more than the
        poor?
    For they are all the work of his hands;[u]
20     in a moment they die, even at
        midnight.[v]
    People are shaken, and pass away,
        the powerful are removed without
            lifting a hand;
21 For his eyes are upon our ways,
    and all our steps he sees.
22 There is no darkness so dense
    that evildoers can hide in it.
23 For no one has God set a time
    to come before him in judgment.
24 Without inquiry he shatters the mighty,[w]
    and appoints others in their place,
25 Thus he discerns their works;
    overnight they are crushed.

26 †Where the wicked are, he strikes them,
    in a place where all can see,
27 Because they turned away from him
    and did not understand his ways
        at all:
28 And made the cry of the poor reach him,
    so that he heard the cry of the
        afflicted.
29 If he is silent, who then can condemn?
    If he hides his face, who then can
        behold him,
    whether nation or individual?
30 Let an impious man not rule,
    nor those who ensnare their people.
31 Should anyone say to God,
    "I accept my punishment; I will
        offend no more;
32 What I cannot see, teach me:
    if I have done wrong, I will do so no
        more,"
33 Would you then say that God must
        punish,
    when you are disdainful?
    It is you who must choose, not I;
    speak, therefore, what you know.
34 Those who understand will say to me,
    all the wise who hear my views:
35 "Job speaks without knowledge,
    his words make no sense.[x]
36 Let Job be tested to the limit,
    since his answers are those of the
        impious;
37 For he is adding rebellion to his sin
    by brushing off our arguments
    and addressing many words to God."

## CHAPTER 35

1[‡]Then Elihu answered and said:

2 Do you think it right to say,
    "I am in the right, not God"?[y]
3 When you ask what it profits you,
    "What advantage do I have from not
        sinning?"[z]
4 I have words for a reply to you[§]
    and your friends as well.
5 Look up to the skies and see;
    behold the heavens high above you.
6 If you sin, what do you do to God?
    Even if your offenses are many, how
        do you affect him?
7 If you are righteous, what do you give him,
    or what does he receive from your
        hand?[a]

---

*[34:16] **Now you**: Elihu turns to Job and addresses him
directly.

m. [34:5] Jb 33:9–10.   n. [34:6] Jb 9:20.   o. [34:9] Jb 9:22–23,
30–31; 21:15; 35:3.   p. [34:10] Jb 36:23.   q. [34:11] Ps 62:13; Prv
24:12; Mt 16:27; Rom 2:6; 2 Cor 5:10; Rev 22:12.   r. [34:12] Jb
8:3.   s. [34:13] Jb 38:4–7.   t. [34:15] Jb 10:9.   u. [34:19] Dt 10:17;
2 Chr 19:7; Wis 6:7; Acts 10:34; Rom 2:11; Eph 6:9; Col 3:25; 1 Pt
1:17.   v. [34:20] Jb 21:13.   w. [34:24] Ps 2:9.

†[34:26, 29–30] The extant Hebrew text of these verses is
obscure.
‡[35:1] See note on 34:1.
§[35:4] **A reply to you**: Elihu refers to Job's statement that
the innocent suffer as much as the wicked, and especially to
Eliphaz's words in 22:2–3.

x. [34:35] Jb 35:16; 38:2; 42:3.   y. [35:2] Jb 32:2.   z. [35:3] Jb
34:9.   a. [35:7] Jb 22:3; 41:2; Lk 17:10; Rom 11:35.

8 Your wickedness affects only someone
     like yourself,
   and your justice, only a fellow
     human being.
9 In great oppression people cry out;
   they call for help because of the
     power of the great,
10 No one says, "Where is God, my Maker,
   who gives songs in the night,
11 Teaches us more than the beasts of the
     earth,
   and makes us wiser than the birds of
     the heavens?"
12 Though thus they cry out, he does not
     answer
   because of the pride of the wicked.
13 But it is idle to say God does not hear
   or that the Almighty does not take
     notice.
14 Even though you say, "You take no notice
     of it,"*
   the case is before him; with
     trembling wait upon him.
15 But now that you have done otherwise,
     God's anger punishes,
   nor does he show much concern
    `over a life.
16 Yet Job to no purpose opens his mouth,
   multiplying words without
     knowledge.[b]

## CHAPTER 36

1 Elihu continued and said:

2 Wait a little and I will instruct you,
   `for there are still words to be said
     for God.
3 I will assemble arguments from afar,
   and for my maker I will establish
     what is right.
4 For indeed, my words are not a lie;
   one perfect in knowledge is before
    `you.
5 Look, God is great, not disdainful;
   his strength of purpose is great.
   He does not preserve the life of the
     wicked.
6 He establishes the right of the poor;[c]
   he does not divert his eyes from
     the just
7 But he seats them upon thrones
   with kings, exalted forever.[d]
8 If they are bound with fetters,
   held fast by bonds of affliction,
9 He lets them know what they have done,
   and how arrogant are their sins.

10 He opens their ears to correction
   and tells them to turn back from evil.
11 If they listen and serve him,
   they spend their days in prosperity,
     their years in happiness.
12 But if they do not listen, they pass to the
     grave,
   they perish for lack of knowledge.
13 The impious in heart lay up anger;
   they do not cry for help when he
     binds them;
14 They will die young—
   their life[†] among the reprobate.
15 But he saves the afflicted through their
     affliction,
   and opens their ears through
     oppression.
16 [‡]He entices you from distress,
   to a broad place without constraint;
   what rests on your table is rich food.
17 Though you are full of the judgment of
     the wicked,
   judgment and justice will be
     maintained.
18 Let not anger at abundance entice you,
   nor great bribery lead you astray.
19 Will your wealth equip you against
     distress,
   or all your exertions of strength?
20 Do not long for the night,
   when peoples vanish in their place.
21 Be careful; do not turn to evil;
   for this you have preferred to
     affliction.
22 [§]Look, God is exalted in his power.
   What teacher is there like him?
23 Who prescribes for him his way?
   Who says, "You have done wrong"?[e]
24 Remember, you should extol his work,
   which people have praised in song.
25 All humankind beholds it;
   everyone views it from afar.
26 See, God is great beyond our knowledge,
   the number of his years past
     searching out.
27 He holds in check the waterdrops
   that filter in rain from his flood,
28 Till the clouds flow with them
   and they rain down on all humankind.
29 [¶]Can anyone understand the spreading
     clouds,
   the thunderings from his tent?

---

† [36:14] **Life:** a miserable life before death or a shadowy existence in Sheol. **Reprobate:** cf. Dt 23:18–19.

‡ [36:16–20] The Hebrew text here is obscure. Although each verse makes some sense, they do not constitute a logical sequence.

§ [36:22–25] These verses serve as an introduction to the hymn about the divine marvels, 36:26–37:24, which in some respects anticipates the tone and content of the Lord's speeches in chaps. 38–41.

¶ [36:29–31] The translation of these verses is uncertain.

e. [36:23] Jb 34:10; Is 40:13.

---

*[35:14–15] The text here is uncertain. It seems to indicate that Job should have realized God's indifference is only apparent, and that, because he has not done so, God will punish him.

b. [35:16] Jb 34:35; 38:2; 42:3.   c. [36:6] Ps 72:4, 12–13.   d. [36:7] Ps 113:7–8.

30 Look, he spreads his light over it,
   it covers the roots of the sea.
31 For by these he judges the nations,
   and gives food in abundance.
32 In his hands he holds the lightning,
   and he commands it to strike the
   mark.
33 His thunder announces him
   and incites the fury of the storm.

### CHAPTER 37

1 At this my heart trembles
   and leaps out of its place.
2 Listen to his angry voice*
   and the rumble that comes forth
   from his mouth!
3 Everywhere under the heavens he sends it,
   with his light, to the ends of the
   earth.
4 Again his voice roars,
   his majestic voice thunders;
   he does not restrain them when his
   voice is heard.
5 God thunders forth marvels with his
   voice;
   he does great things beyond our
   knowing.
6 He says to the snow, "Fall to the earth";
   likewise to his heavy, drenching rain.
7 He shuts up all humankind indoors,
   so that all people may know his
   work.
8 The wild beasts take to cover
   and remain quiet in their dens.
9 Out of its chamber the tempest comes
   forth;
   from the north winds, the cold.
10 With his breath God brings the frost,
    and the broad waters congeal.f
11 The clouds too are laden with moisture,
    the storm-cloud scatters its light.
12 †He it is who changes their rounds,
    according to his plans,
    to do all that he commands them
    across the inhabited world.
13 Whether for punishment or mercy,
    he makes it happen.
14 Listen to this, Job!
    Stand and consider the marvels of
    God!
15 Do you know how God lays his command
    upon them,
    and makes the light shine forth from
    his clouds?
16 Do you know how the clouds are banked,
    the marvels of him who is perfect in
    knowledge?

17 You, who swelter in your clothes
   when calm lies over the land from
   the south,
18 Can you with him spread out the
   firmament of the skies,
   hard as a molten mirror?‡
19 Teach us then what we shall say to him;
   we cannot, for the darkness, make
   our plea.
20 Will he be told about it when I speak?
   Can anyone talk when he is being
   destroyed?
21 Rather, it is as the light that cannot be
   seen
   while it is obscured by the clouds,
   till the wind comes by and sweeps
   them away.§
22 From Zaphon¶ the golden splendor
   comes,
   surrounding God's awesome
   majesty!
23 The Almighty! We cannot find him,
   preeminent in power and judgment,
   abundant in justice, who never
   oppresses.
24 Therefore people fear him;
   none can see him, however wise
   their hearts.**

### VIII. THE LORD AND JOB MEET

### CHAPTER 38

1 Then the LORD†† answered Job out of the storm
and said:

2 Who is this who darkens counsel
   with words of ignorance?
3 Gird up your loins‡‡ now, like a man;
   I will question you, and you tell me
   the answers!g
4 Where were you when I founded the
   earth?
   Tell me, if you have understanding.

---

* [37:2] **Voice:** the thunder.
† [37:12–13] The translation of these verses is uncertain.

‡ [37:18] **The firmament . . . mirror:** the ancients thought of the sky as a ceiling above which were the "upper waters" (cf. Gn 1:6–7; 7:11); when this ceiling became as hard as metal, the usual rain failed to fall on the earth (cf. Lv 26:19; Dt 28:23).
§ [37:21] Elihu argues that even though God seems not to know our circumstances, he does know them, just as surely as the sun shines behind the clouds.
¶ [37:22] **Zaphon:** the mythical mountain of the gods; cf. note on 26:7.
** [37:24] The concluding remark of Elihu is ironic in view of the appearance of the Lord in the next chapter and Job's claim in 42:5.
†† [38:1] Now the Lord enters the debate and addresses two discourses (chaps. 38–39 and 40–41) to Job, speaking of divine wisdom and power. Such things are altogether beyond the capacity of Job. **Out of the storm:** frequently the background of the appearances of the Lord in the Old Testament; cf. Ps 18; 50; Na 1:3; Hb 3:2–15.
‡‡ [38:3] **Gird up your loins:** prepare for combat—figuratively, be ready to defend yourself in debate.

---

f. [37:10] Ps 147:17.                g. [38:3] Jb 40:2.

⁵ Who determined its size? Surely you
      know?
      Who stretched out the measuring
         line for it?
⁶ Into what were its pedestals sunk,
      and who laid its cornerstone,
⁷ While the morning stars sang together
      and all the sons of God* shouted
         for joy?
⁸ Who shut within doors the sea,
      when it burst forth from the womb,ʰ
⁹ When I made the clouds its garment
      and thick darkness its swaddling
         bands?
¹⁰ When I set limits for it
      and fastened the bar of its door,
¹¹ And said: Thus far shall you come but no
         farther,
      and here shall your proud waves
         stop?
¹² Have you ever in your lifetime
         commanded the morning
      and shown the dawn its place
¹³ For taking hold of the ends of the earth,
      till the wicked are shaken from it?
¹⁴ The earth is changed as clay by the seal,
      and dyed like a garment;
¹⁵ But from the wicked their light is
         withheld,
      and the arm of pride is shattered.
¹⁶ Have you entered into the sources of the
         sea,
      or walked about on the bottom of
         the deep?
¹⁷ Have the gates of death been shown to
         you,
      or have you seen the gates of
         darkness?
¹⁸ Have you comprehended the breadth of
         the earth?
      Tell me, if you know it all.
¹⁹ What is the way to the dwelling of light,
      and darkness—where is its place?
²⁰ That you may take it to its territory
      and know the paths to its home?
²¹ You know, because you were born then,
      and the number of your days is
         great!†
²² Have you entered the storehouses of the
         snow,
      and seen the storehouses of the hail
²³ Which I have reserved for times of
         distress,
      for a day of war and battle?ⁱ
²⁴ What is the way to the parting of the
         winds,
      where the east wind spreads over
         the earth?

²⁵ Who has laid out a channel for the
         downpour
      and a path for the thunderstorm
²⁶ To bring rain to uninhabited land,
      the unpeopled wilderness;
²⁷ To drench the desolate wasteland
      till the desert blooms with verdure?
²⁸ Has the rain a father?
      Who has begotten the drops of dew?
²⁹ Out of whose womb comes the ice,
      and who gives the hoarfrost its birth
         in the skies,
³⁰ When the waters lie covered as though
         with stone
      that holds captive the surface of the
         deep?
³¹ Have you tied cords to the Pleiades,‡
      or loosened the bonds of Orion?
³² Can you bring forth the Mazzaroth in
         their season,
      or guide the Bear with her children?
³³ Do you know the ordinances of the
         heavens;
      can you put into effect their plan on
         the earth?
³⁴ Can you raise your voice to the clouds,
      for them to cover you with a deluge
         of waters?
³⁵ Can you send forth the lightnings on their
         way,
      so that they say to you, "Here we
         are"?
³⁶ Who gives wisdom to the ibis,
      and gives the rooster§
         understanding?
³⁷ Who counts the clouds with wisdom?
      Who tilts the water jars of heaven
³⁸ So that the dust of earth is fused into a
         mass
      and its clods stick together?
³⁹ Do you hunt the prey for the lion
      or appease the hunger of young lions?
⁴⁰ While they crouch in their dens,
      or lie in ambush in the thicket?
⁴¹ Who provides nourishment for the
         raven
      when its young cry out to God,ʲ
      wandering about without food?

## CHAPTER 39

¹ Do you know when mountain goats are
         born,
      or watch for the birth pangs of deer,
² Number the months that they must
         fulfill,
      or know when they give birth,

---

*[38:7] **Sons of God**: see note on 1:6.
†[38:21] Ironic, but not a harsh rebuke.

h. [38:8] Gn 1:9.   i. [38:23] Jos 10:11; Sir 46:5.

---

‡[38:31–32] **Pleiades . . . Orion . . . Bear**: cf. 9:9. **Mazzaroth**: it is uncertain what astronomical group is meant by
this Hebrew word; perhaps a southern constellation.
§[38:36] **Ibis . . . rooster**: the translation is uncertain.

j. [38:41] Ps 147:9.

3 When they crouch down and drop their
　　young,
　　when they deliver their progeny?
4 Their offspring thrive and grow in the
　　open,
　　they leave and do not return.
5 Who has given the wild donkey his
　　freedom,
　　and who has loosed the wild ass
　　　from bonds?
6 I have made the wilderness his home
　　and the salt flats his dwelling.
7 He scoffs at the uproar of the city,
　　hears no shouts of a driver.
8 He ranges the mountains for pasture,
　　and seeks out every patch of green.
9 Will the wild ox consent to serve you,
　　or pass the nights at your manger?
10 Will you bind the wild ox with a rope in
　　the furrow,
　　and will he plow the valleys after you?
11 Will you depend on him for his great
　　strength
　　and leave to him the fruits of your
　　　toil?
12 Can you rely on him to bring in your
　　grain
　　and gather in the yield of your
　　　threshing floor?
13 The wings of the ostrich* flap away;
　　her plumage is lacking in feathers.
14 When she abandons her eggs on the
　　ground†
　　and lets them warm in the sand,
15 She forgets that a foot may crush them,
　　that the wild beasts may trample
　　　them;
16 She cruelly disowns her young
　　and her labor is useless; she has no
　　　fear.
17 For God has withheld wisdom from her
　　and given her no share in
　　　understanding.
18 Yet when she spreads her wings high,
　　she laughs at a horse and rider.
19 Do you give the horse his strength,‡
　　and clothe his neck with a mane?
20 Do you make him quiver like a locust,
　　while his thunderous snorting
　　　spreads terror?
21 He paws the valley, he rejoices in his
　　strength,
　　and charges into battle.
22 He laughs at fear and cannot be terrified;
　　he does not retreat from the sword.
23 Around him rattles the quiver,
　　flashes the spear and the javelin.

24 Frenzied and trembling he devours the
　　ground;
　　he does not hold back at the sound
　　　of the trumpet;
25 at the trumpet's call he cries, "Aha!"
　　Even from afar he scents the battle,
　　the roar of the officers and the
　　　shouting.
26 Is it by your understanding that the hawk
　　soars,
　　that he spreads his wings toward the
　　　south?
27 Does the eagle fly up at your command
　　to build his nest up high?
28 On a cliff he dwells and spends the night,
　　on the spur of cliff or fortress.
29 From there he watches for his food;
　　his eyes behold it afar off.
30 His young ones greedily drink blood;
　　where the slain are, there is he.[k]

## CHAPTER 40

1 The Lord then answered Job and said:

2 Will one who argues with the Almighty
　　be corrected?
　　Let him who would instruct God
　　　give answer![l]

3 Then Job answered the Lord and said:

4 §Look, I am of little account; what can I
　　answer you?
　　I put my hand over my mouth.
5 I have spoken once, I will not reply;
　　twice, but I will do so no more.

6 Then the Lord answered Job out of the
storm and said:

7 Gird up your loins now, like a man.
　　I will question you, and you tell me
　　　the answers!
8 ¶Would you refuse to acknowledge my
　　right?
　　Would you condemn me that you
　　　may be justified?
9 Have you an arm like that of God,
　　or can you thunder with a voice
　　　like his?
10 Adorn yourself with grandeur and
　　majesty,
　　and clothe yourself with glory and
　　　splendor.

---

*[39:13] The wings of the ostrich cannot raise her from the ground, but they help her to run swiftly.

†[39:14–16] People thought that, because the ostrich laid her eggs on the sand, she was thereby cruelly abandoning them; cf. Lam 4:3.

‡[39:19–25] A classic description of a war horse.

§[40:4–5] Job's first reaction is humble, but also seemingly cautious.

¶[40:8–14] The issue is joined in these verses, and the Lord seems to challenge Job to play God and to bring down the proud and wicked.

k. [39:30] Mt 24:28; Lk 17:37.　l. [40:2] Jb 38:3.

¹¹ Let loose the fury of your wrath;
  look at everyone who is proud and
    bring them down.
¹² Look at everyone who is proud, and
    humble them.
    Tear down the wicked in their place,
¹³    bury them in the dust together;
    in the hidden world imprison them.
¹⁴ Then will I too praise you,
  for your own right hand can save
    you.
¹⁵ Look at Behemoth,* whom I made along
    with you,
  who feeds on grass like an ox.
¹⁶ See the strength in his loins,
  the power in the sinews of his belly.
¹⁷ He carries his tail like a cedar;
  the sinews of his thighs are like
    cables.
¹⁸ His bones are like tubes of bronze;
  his limbs are like iron rods.
¹⁹ He is the first of God's ways,
  only his maker can approach him
    with a sword.
²⁰ For the mountains bring him produce,
  and all wild animals make sport
    there.
²¹ Under lotus trees he lies,
  in coverts of the reedy swamp.
²² The lotus trees cover him with their
    shade;
  all about him are the poplars in the
    wadi.
²³ If the river grows violent, he is not
    disturbed;
  he is tranquil though the Jordan
    surges about his mouth.
²⁴ Who can capture him by his eyes,
  or pierce his nose† with a trap?
²⁵ Can you lead Leviathan‡ about with a
    hook,
  or tie down his tongue with a rope?
²⁶ Can you put a ring into his nose,
  or pierce through his cheek with a
    gaff?
²⁷ Will he then plead with you, time after
    time,
  or address you with tender words?
²⁸ Will he make a covenant with you
  that you may have him as a slave
    forever?
²⁹ Can you play with him, as with a bird?
  Can you tie him up for your little
    girls?

³⁰ Will the traders bargain for him?
  Will the merchants§ divide him up?
³¹ Can you fill his hide with barbs,
  or his head with fish spears?
³² Once you but lay a hand upon him,
  no need to recall any other conflict!

## CHAPTER 41

¹ Whoever might vainly hope to do so
  need only see him to be overthrown.
² No one is fierce enough to arouse him;
  who then dares stand before me?
³ Whoever has assailed me, I will pay back—
  Everything under the heavens is
    mine.
⁴ I need hardly mention his limbs,
  his strength, and the fitness of his
    equipment.
⁵ Who can strip off his outer garment,
  or penetrate his double armor?
⁶ Who can force open the doors of his face,
  close to his terrible teeth?
⁷ Rows of scales are on his back,
  tightly sealed together;
⁸ They are fitted so close to each other
  that no air can come between them;
⁹ So joined to one another
  that they hold fast and cannot be
    parted.
¹⁰ When he sneezes, light flashes forth;
  his eyes are like the eyelids of the
    dawn.
¹¹ Out of his mouth go forth torches;
  sparks of fire leap forth.
¹² From his nostrils comes smoke
  as from a seething pot or bowl.
¹³ His breath sets coals afire;
  a flame comes from his mouth.
¹⁴ Strength abides in his neck,
  and power leaps before him.
¹⁵ The folds of his flesh stick together,
  it is cast over him and immovable.
¹⁶ His heart is cast as hard as stone;
  cast as the lower millstone.
¹⁷ When he rises up, the gods are afraid;
  when he crashes down, they fall back.
¹⁸ Should a sword reach him, it will not
    avail;
  nor will spear, dart, or javelin.
¹⁹ He regards iron as chaff,
  and bronze as rotten wood.
²⁰ No arrow will put him to flight;
  slingstones used against him are but
    straw.
²¹ Clubs he regards as straw;
  he laughs at the crash of the spear.
²² Under him are sharp pottery fragments,
  spreading a threshing sledge upon
    the mire.

---

*[40:15] **Behemoth**: a primeval monster of chaos; identified by some scholars as the hippopotamus, on which the description of Behemoth is partially based. The point of the Behemoth-Leviathan passages is that only the Lord, not Job, can control the cosmic evil which these forces symbolize.

†[40:24] **Eyes . . . nose**: the only exposed parts of the submerged beast.

‡[40:25] **Leviathan**: although identified by some scholars as the crocodile, it is more likely another chaos monster; see note on 3:8.

§[40:30] **Merchants**: lit., "Canaanites," whose reputation for trading was so widespread that their name came to be used for merchants; cf. Prv 31:24.

23 He makes the depths boil like a pot;
      he makes the sea like a perfume
          bottle.
24 Behind him he leaves a shining path;
      you would think the deep had white
          hair.
25 Upon the earth there is none like him,
      he was made fearless.
26 He looks over all who are haughty,
      he is king over all proud beasts.

## CHAPTER 42

¹Then Job answered the LORD and said:

2   I know that you can do all things,*
        and that no purpose of yours can be
            hindered.
3   "Who is this who obscures counsel with
            ignorance?"
    I have spoken but did not understand;
        things too marvelous for me, which
            I did not know."ᵐ
4   "Listen, and I will speak;
    I will question you, and you tell me the
        answers."
5   By hearsay I had heard of you,
        but now my eye has seen you.†
6   Therefore I disown what I have said,
        and repent in dust and ashes.‡

## IX. EPILOGUE

**Job's Restoration.** ⁷And after the LORD had spoken these words to Job, the LORD said to Eliphaz
the Temanite, "My anger blazes against you
and your two friends!§ You have not spoken
rightly concerning me, as has my servant Job.
⁸So now take seven bulls and seven rams, and
go to my servant Job, and sacrifice a burnt offering for yourselves, and let my servant Job pray
for you.¶ To him I will show favor, and not punish your folly, for you have not spoken rightly
concerning me, as has my servant Job." ⁹Then
Eliphaz the Temanite, and Bildad the Shuhite,
and Zophar the Naamathite, went and did as the
LORD had commanded them. The LORD showed
favor to Job.

¹⁰The LORD also restored the prosperity
of Job, after he had prayed for his friends; the
LORD even gave to Job twice** as much as he had
before. ¹¹Then all his brothers and sisters came
to him, and all his former acquaintances, and
they dined with him in his house. They consoled
and comforted him for all the evil the LORD had
brought upon him, and each one gave him a
piece of money†† and a gold ring.

¹²ⁿThus the LORD blessed the later days of Job
more than his earlier ones. Now he had fourteen
thousand sheep, six thousand camels, a thousand yoke of oxen, and a thousand she-donkeys.
¹³He also had seven sons and three daughters:
¹⁴the first daughter he called Jemimah, the second Keziah, and the third Keren-happuch.‡‡ ¹⁵In
all the land no other women were as beautiful as
the daughters of Job; and their father gave them
an inheritance§§ among their brothers.

¹⁶After this, Job lived a hundred and forty
years; and he saw his children, his grandchildren, and even his great-grandchildren.ᵒ ¹⁷Then
Job died, old and full of years.

---

*[42:2–4] In his final speech, Job quotes God's own words
(see 38:2–3; 40:7).

†[42:5] In 19:25–27 Job had affirmed a hope to "see" (three
times) his vindicator. Now he has seen the Lord about whom
he had heard so much.

‡[42:6] A difficult verse. Some doubt, in view of God's
commendation in v. 7, that Job does in fact express repentance, and alternative translations are often given. Along with
v. 5, it describes a change in Job, which the encounter with
the Lord has brought about. **Dust and ashes:** an ambiguous
phrase. It can refer to the human condition (cf. Gn 18:27; Jb
30:19) or to Job's ash heap (2:8).

§[42:7] The three friends of Job (Elihu is ignored in the
epilogue) are criticized by the Lord because they had "not
spoken rightly" (vv. 7–8).

¶[42:8] An ironic touch: Job becomes the intercessor for
his friends.

**[42:10] **Twice:** this is the fine for damage inflicted upon
another; cf. Ex 22:3. The Lord pays up!

††[42:11] **A piece of money:** lit., *qesitah*, value unknown;
also used in Gn 33:19; Jos 24:32. **Gold ring:** for the nose or ear.

‡‡[42:14] Job's daughters had names symbolic of their
charms: **Jemimah,** dove; **Keziah,** precious perfume (cf. Ps
45:9); **Keren-happuch,** cosmetic jar—more precisely, a container for a black powder used like modern mascara.

§§[42:15] Ordinarily daughters did not inherit property
unless there were no sons; cf. Nm 27:1–11.

---

m. [42:3] Jb 34:35; 35:16; 38:2; Ps 131:1; Prv 30:18.

n. [42:12] Jb 1:3.   o. [42:16] Jb 5:25–26.

# THE BOOK OF
# PSALMS

The Hebrew Psalter numbers 150 songs. The corresponding number in the Septuagint differs because of a different division of certain Psalms. Hence the numbering in the Greek Psalter (which was followed by the Latin Vulgate) is usually one digit behind the Hebrew. In the New American Bible the numbering of the verses follows the Hebrew numbering; many of the traditional English translations are often a verse number behind the Hebrew because they do not count the superscriptions as a verse.

The superscriptions derive from pre-Christian Jewish tradition, and they contain technical terms, many of them apparently liturgical, which are no longer known to us. Seventy-three Psalms are attributed to David, but there is no sure way of dating any Psalm. Some are preexilic (before 587), and others are postexilic (after 539), but not as late as the Maccabean period (ca. 165). The Psalms are the product of many individual collections (e.g., Songs of Ascents, Ps 120–134), which were eventually combined into the present work in which one can detect five "books," because of the doxologies which occur at 41:14; 72:18–19; 89:53; 106:48.

Two important features of the Psalms deserve special notice. First, the majority were composed originally precisely for liturgical worship. This is shown by the frequent indication of liturgical leaders interacting with the community (e.g., Ps 118:1–4). Secondly, they follow certain distinct patterns or literary forms. Thus, the hymn is a song of praise, in which a community is urged joyfully to sing out the praise of God. Various reasons are given for this praise (often introduced by "for" or "because"): the divine work of creation and sustenance (Ps 135:1–12; 136). Some of the hymns have received a more specific classification, based on content. The "Songs of Zion" are so called because they exalt Zion, the city in which God dwells among the people (Ps 47; 96–99). Characteristic of the songs of praise is the joyful summons to get involved in the activity; Ps 104 is an exception to this, although it remains universal in its thrust.

Another type of Psalm is similar to the hymn: the thanksgiving Psalm. This too is a song of praise acknowledging the Lord as the rescuer of the psalmist from a desperate situation. Very often the psalmist will give a flashback, recounting the past distress, and the plea that was uttered (Ps 30; 116). The setting for such prayers seems to have been the offering of a *todah* (a "praise" sacrifice) with friends in the Temple.

There are more Psalms of lament than of any other type. They may be individual (e.g., Ps 3–7; 22) or communal (e.g., Ps 44). Although they usually begin with a cry for help, they develop in various ways. The description of the distress is couched in the broad imagery typical of the Bible (one is in Sheol, the Pit, or is afflicted by enemies or wild beasts, etc.)—in such a way that one cannot pinpoint the exact nature of the psalmist's plight. However, Ps 51 (cf. also Ps 130) seems to refer clearly to deliverance from sin. Several laments end on a note of certainty that the Lord has heard the prayer (cf. Ps 7, but contrast Ps 88), and the Psalter has been characterized as a movement from lament to praise. If this is somewhat of an exaggeration, it serves at least to emphasize the frequent expressions of trust which characterize the lament. In some cases it would seem as if the theme of trust has been lifted out to form a literary type all its own; cf. Ps 23, 62, 91. Among the communal laments can be counted Ps 74 and 79. They complain to the Lord about some national disaster, and try to motivate God to intervene in favor of the suffering people.

Other Psalms are clearly classified on account of content, and they may be in themselves laments or Psalms of thanksgiving. Among the "royal" Psalms that deal directly with the currently reigning king, are Ps 20, 21, and 72. Many of the royal Psalms were given a messianic interpretation by Christians. In Jewish tradition they were preserved, even after kingship had disappeared, because they were read in the light of the Davidic covenant reported in 2 Sm 7. Certain Psalms are called wisdom Psalms because they seem to betray the influence of the concerns of the ages (cf. Ps 37; 49), but there is no general agreement as to the number of these prayers. Somewhat related to the wisdom Psalms are the "torah" Psalms, in which the torah (instruction or law) of the Lord is glorified (Ps 1; 19:8–14; 119). Ps 78, 105, 106 can be considered as "historical" Psalms. Although the majority of the Psalms have a liturgical setting, there are certain prayers that may be termed "liturgies," so clearly does their structure reflect a liturgical incident (e.g., Ps 15; 24).

It is obvious that not all of the Psalms can be pigeon-holed into neat classifications, but even a brief sketch of these types help us to catch the structure and spirit of the Psalms we read. It has been rightly said that the Psalms are "a school of prayer." They not only provide us with models to follow, but inspire us to voice our own deepest feelings and aspirations.

## First Book—Psalms 1–41

### PSALM 1*
### True Happiness in God's Law

I

1 Blessed is the man who does not walk
    in the counsel of the wicked,
  Nor stand in the way† of sinners,
    nor sit in company with scoffers.ª
2 Rather, the law of the LORD‡ is his joy;
    and on his law he meditates day and
      night.ᵇ
3 He is like a treeᶜ
    planted near streams of water,
    that yields its fruit in season;
  Its leaves never wither;
    whatever he does prospers.

II

4 But not so are the wicked,§ not so!
  They are like chaff driven by the
      wind.ᵈ
5 Therefore the wicked will not arise at the
      judgment,
    nor will sinners in the assembly of
      the just.
6 Because the LORD knows the way of the
      just,ᵉ
    but the way of the wicked leads to
      ruin.

### PSALM 2¶
### A Psalm for a Royal Coronation

1 Why do the nations protest
    and the peoples conspire in vain?ᶠ
2 Kings on earth rise up
    and princes plot together
    against the LORD and against his
      anointed one:**ᵍ
3 "Let us break their shackles
    and cast off their chains from us!"ʰ
4 The one enthroned in heaven laughs;
    the Lord derides them,ⁱ
5 Then he speaks to them in his anger,
    in his wrath he terrifies them:
6 "I myself have installed my king
    on Zion, my holy mountain."
7 I will proclaim the decree of the LORD,
    he said to me, "You are my son;
    today I have begotten you.ʲ
8 Ask it of me,
    and I will give you the nations as
      your inheritance,
    and, as your possession, the ends of
      the earth.
9 With an iron rod you will shepherd them,
    like a potter's vessel you will shatter
      them."ᵏ
10 And now, kings, give heed;
    take warning, judges on earth.
11 Serve the LORD with fear;
    exult with trembling,
  Accept correction
    lest he become angry and you perish

---

*[Psalm 1] A preface to the whole Book of Psalms, contrasting with striking similes the destiny of the good and the wicked. The Psalm views life as activity, as choosing either the good or the bad. Each "way" brings its inevitable consequences. The wise through their good actions will experience rootedness and life, and the wicked, rootlessness and death.

†[1:1] The way: a common biblical term for manner of living or moral conduct (Ps 32:8; 101:2, 6; Prv 2:20; 1 Kgs 8:36).

‡[1:2] The law of the LORD: either the Torah, the first five books of the Bible, or, more probably, divine teaching or instruction.

§[1:4] The wicked: those who by their actions distance themselves from God's life-giving presence.

¶[Psalm 2] A royal Psalm. To rebellious kings (Ps 2:1–3) God responds vigorously (Ps 2:4–6). A speaker proclaims the divine decree (in the legal adoption language of the day), making the Israelite king the earthly representative of God (Ps 2:7–9) and warning kings to obey (Ps 2;10–11). The Psalm has a messianic meaning for the Church; the New Testament understands it of Christ (Acts 4:25–27; 13:33; Heb 1:5).

**[2:2] Anointed: in Hebrew mashiah, "anointed"; in Greek christos, whence English Messiah and Christ. In Israel kings (Jgs 9:8; 1 Sm 9:16; 16:12–13) and high priests (Lv 8:12; Nm 3:3) received the power of their office through anointing.

---

a. [1:1] Ps 26:4–5; 40:5.   b. [1:2] Jos 1:8; Ps 119; Sir 39:1.   c. [1:3] Ps 52:10; 92:13–15; Jer 17:8.   d. [1:4] Ps 35:5; 83:14–16; Jb 21:18.   e. [1:6] Ps 37:18.

f. [2:1] Rev 11:18.   g. [2:2] Ps 83:6.   h. [2:3] Ps 149:8.   i. [2:4] Ps 37:13; 59:9; Wis 4:18.   j. [2:7] Ps 89:27; 110:2–3; Is 49:1.   k. [2:9] Rev 2:27; 12:5; 19:15.

along the way
when his anger suddenly blazes up.*
Blessed are all who take refuge in him!

## PSALM 3*
### Threatened but Trusting

¹A psalm of David, when he fled from his son
Absalom.†ᵐ

I
² How many are my foes, LORD!
How many rise against me!
³ ‡How many say of me,
"There is no salvation for him in
God."ⁿ
*Selah*
⁴ But you, LORD, are a shield around me;
my glory, you keep my head high.ᵒ
II
⁵ With my own voice I will call out to the
LORD,
and he will answer me from his holy
mountain.
*Selah*
⁶ I lie down and I fall asleep,
[and] I will wake up, for the LORD
sustains me.ᵖ
⁷ I do not fear, then, thousands of people
arrayed against me on every side.
III
⁸ Arise, LORD! Save me, my God!
For you strike the cheekbone of all
my foes;
you break the teeth of the wicked.�q
⁹ Salvation is from the LORD!
May your blessing be upon your
people!ʳ
*Selah*

## PSALM 4§
### Trust in God

¹For the leader;⁵ with stringed instruments. A
psalm of David.

I
² Answer me when I call, my saving God.
When troubles hem me in, set me free;
take pity on me, hear my prayer.⁵
II
³ How long, O people, will you be hard of
heart?
Why do you love what is worthless,
chase after lies?"†
*Selah*
⁴ Know that the LORD works wonders for
his faithful one;
the LORD hears when I call out to him.
⁵ Tremble†† and sin no more;
weep bitterly†† within your hearts,
wail upon your beds.ᵘ
⁶ Offer fitting sacrifices
and trust in the LORD.ᵛ
⁷ Many say, "May we see better times!
LORD, show us the light of your face!"ʷ
*Selah*
⁸ But you have given my heart more joy
than they have when grain and wine
abound.
⁹ ˣ‡‡In peace I will lie down and fall asleep,
for you alone, LORD, make me secure.

## PSALM 5§§
### Prayer for Divine Help

¹For the leader; with wind instruments. A psalm
of David.

I
² Give ear to my words, O LORD;
understand my sighing.ʸ
³ Attend to the sound of my cry,
my king and my God!
For to you I will pray, LORD;
⁴ in the morning you will hear my voice;
in the morning I will plead before
you and wait.ᶻ

---

that such Psalms once stood together in a collection of "the
choirmaster," cf. 1 Chr 15:21.
**[4:3] **Love what is worthless . . . lies**: these expressions
probably refer to false gods worshiped by those the psalmist
is addressing.
††[4:5] **Tremble**: be moved deeply with fear for failing to
worship the true God. The Greek translation understood the
emotion to be anger, and it is so cited in Eph 4:26. **Weep bitterly . . . wail**: weeping within one's heart and wailing upon one's
bed denote sincere repentance because these actions are not
done in public or with the community but in the privacy of one's
heart and one's home. The same idiom is found in Hos 7:14.
‡‡[4:9] **In peace I will . . . fall asleep**: the last verse repeats
two themes in the Psalm. One is the security of one who
trusts in the true God; the other is the interior peace of those
who sincerely repent ("on [their] beds"), whose sleep is not
disturbed by a guilty conscience.
§§[Psalm 5] A lament contrasting the security of the house of
God (Ps 5:8–9, 12–13) with the danger of the company of evildoers (Ps 5:5–7, 10–11). The psalmist therefore prays that God will
hear (Ps 5:2–4) and grant the protection and joy of the Temple.

---

*[Psalm 3] An individual lament complaining of enemies
who deny that God will come to the rescue (Ps 3:2–3). Despite
such taunts the psalmist hopes for God's protection even in
sleep (Ps 3:4–7). The Psalm prays for an end to the enemies'
power to speak maliciously (Ps 3:8) and closes peacefully with
an expression of trust (Ps 3:9).
†[3:1] The superscription, added later, relates the Psalm to
an incident in the life of David.
‡[3:3, 3:5, 3:9] **Selah**: the term is generally considered a
direction to the cantor or musicians but its exact meaning is
not known. It occurs 71 times in 39 Psalms.
§[Psalm 4] An individual lament emphasizing trust in
God. The petition is based upon the psalmist's vivid experience of God as savior (Ps 4:2). That experience of God is the
basis for the warning to the wicked: revere God who intervenes on the side of the faithful (Ps 4:3–6). The faithful psalmist exemplifies the blessings given to the just (Ps 4:7–8).
¶[4:1] **For the leader**: many Psalm headings contain
this rubric. Its exact meaning is unknown but may signify

l. [2:11] Ps 34:9; 146:5; Prv 16:20.   m. [3:1] 2 Sm 15:13ff.   n. [3:3]
Ps 71:11.   o. [3:4] Ps 7:11; 18:3; 62:7–8; Dt 33:29; Is 60:19.   p. [3:6]
Ps 4:9; Prv 3:24.   q. [3:8] Ps 58:7.   r. [3:9] Ps 28:9; Jon 2:10.

s. [4:2] Ps 118:5.   t. [4:3] Ps 62:4.   u. [4:5] Prv 4:26.   v. [4:6] Ps
51:19.   w. [4:7] Ps 31:17; 44:4; 67:1; 80:4; Jb 13:24; Nm 6:25; Dn
9:17.   x. [4:9] Ps 3:6.   y. [5:2] Ps 86:6; 130:1–2.   z. [5:4] Wis 16:28.

**II**

⁵ You are not a god who delights in evil;
    no wicked person finds refuge with
        you;
⁶    the arrogant cannot stand before
        your eyes.
You hate all who do evil;
⁷    you destroy those who speak falsely.ᵃ
A bloody and fraudulent man
    the LORD abhors.

**III**

⁸ But I, through the abundance of your mercy,*
    will enter into your house.
I will bow down toward your holy
        sanctuary
    out of fear of you.ᵇ
⁹ LORD, guide me in your justice because of
        my foes;
    make straight your way before me.ᶜ

**IV**

¹⁰ For there is no sincerity in their mouth;
    their heart is corrupt.
Their throat† is an open grave;ᵈ
    on their tongue are subtle lies.
¹¹ Declare them guilty, God;
    make them fall by their own devices.ᵉ
Drive them out for their many sins;
    for they have rebelled against you.

**V**

¹² Then all who trust in you will be glad
    and forever shout for joy.ᶠ
You will protect them and those will
        rejoice in you
    who love your name.
¹³ For you, LORD, bless the just one;
    you surround him with favor like a
        shield.

## PSALM 6‡
### Prayer in Distress

¹For the leader; with stringed instruments,
"upon the eighth."§

A psalm of David.

**I**

² Do not reprove me in your anger, LORD,
    nor punish me in your wrath.ᵍ
³ Have pity on me, LORD, for I am weak;
    heal me, LORD, for my bones are
        shuddering.ʰ
⁴ My soul too is shuddering greatly—
    and you, LORD, how long . . . ?¶ⁱ
⁵ Turn back, LORD, rescue my soul;
    save me because of your mercy.
⁶ For in death there is no remembrance of
        you.
    Who praises you in Sheol?**ʲ

**II**

⁷ I am wearied with sighing;
    all night long I drench my bed with
        tears;
    I soak my couch with weeping.
⁸ My eyes are dimmed with sorrow,
    worn out because of all my foes.ᵏ

**III**

⁹ Away from me, all who do evil!ˡ
    The LORD has heard the sound of
        my weeping.
¹⁰ The LORD has heard my plea;
    the LORD will receive my prayer.
¹¹ My foes will all be disgraced and will
        shudder greatly;
    they will turn back in sudden
        disgrace.ᵐ

## PSALM 7††
### God the Vindicator

¹A plaintive song of David, which he sang to the
LORD concerning Cush, the Benjaminite.

**I**

² LORD my God, in you I trusted;
    save me; rescue me from all who
        pursue me,ⁿ
³ Lest someone maul me like a lion,
    tear my soul apart with no one to
        deliver.

---

*[5:8] **Mercy**: used to translate the Hebrew word, *hesed*. This term speaks to a relationship between persons. It is manifested in concrete actions to persons with some need or desire. The one who offers *hesed* has the ability to respond to that need of the other person. Other possible ways to translate *hesed* include "steadfast love" and "loving kindness."

†[5:10] **Their throat**: their speech brings harm to their hearers (cf. Jer 5:16). The verse mentions four parts of the body, each a source of evil to the innocent.

‡[Psalm 6] The first of the seven Penitential Psalms (Ps 6, 32, 38, 51, 102, 130, 143), a designation dating from the seventh century A.D. for Psalms suitable to express repentance. The psalmist does not, as in many laments, claim to be innocent but appeals to God's mercy (Ps 6:5). Sin here, as often in the Bible, is both the sinful act and its injurious consequences; here it is physical sickness (Ps 6:3–4, 7–8) and the attacks of enemies (Ps 6:8, 9, 11). The psalmist prays that the effects of personal and social sin be taken away.

§[6:1] **Upon the eighth**: apparently a musical notation, now lost.

¶[6:4] **How long?**: elliptical for "How long will it be before you answer my prayer?" cf. Ps 13:2–3.

**[6:6] A motive for God to preserve the psalmist from death: in the shadowy world of the dead no one offers you praise. Sheol is the biblical term for the underworld where the insubstantial souls of dead human beings dwelt. It was similar to the Hades of Greek and Latin literature. In the second century B.C., biblical books begin to speak positively of life with God after death (Dn 12:1–3; Wis 3).

††[Psalm 7] An individual lament. The psalmist flees to God's presence in the sanctuary for justice and protection (Ps 7:2–3) and takes an oath that only the innocent can swear (Ps 7:4–6). The innocent psalmist can thus hope for the just God's protection (Ps 7:7–14) and be confident that the actions of the wicked will come back upon their own heads (Ps 7:15–17). The justice of God leads the psalmist to praise (Ps 7:18).

a. [5:7] Ps 101:7; Wis 14:9; Heb 1:13.   b. [5:8] Ps 138:2; Jon 2:5.
c. [5:9] Ps 23:3; Prv 4:11; Is 26:7.   d. [5:10] Rom 3:13.   e. [5:11] Ps 141:10.   f. [5:12] Ps 64:11.

g. [6:2] Ps 38:2.   h. [6:3] Jer 17:14–15.   i. [6:4] Ps 13:2–3; 74:10; 89:47.   j. [6:6] Ps 30:10; 88:11; 115:17; Is 38:18.   k. [6:8] Ps 31:10; 38:11; 40:13.   l. [6:9] Ps 119:115; Mt 7:23; Lk 13:27.   m. [6:11] Ps 35:4, 26; 40:15; 71:13.   n. [7:2] Ps 6:5; 22:21.

## II

4 Lᴏʀᴅ my God, if I have done this,*
     if there is guilt on my hands,
5 If I have maltreated someone treating me
          equitably—
     or even despoiled my oppressor
          without cause—
6 Then let my enemy pursue and overtake
          my soul,
     trample my life to the ground,
     and lay my honor in the dust.*

                                        Selah

## III

7 Rise up, Lᴏʀᴅ, in your anger;
     be aroused against the outrages of
          my oppressors.*
     Stir up the justice, my God, you have
          commanded.
8 Have the assembly of the peoples gather
          about you;
     and return on high above them,
9      the Lᴏʀᴅ will pass judgment on the
          peoples.
   Judge me, Lᴏʀᴅ, according to my
          righteousness,
     and my integrity.
10 Let the malice of the wicked end.
     Uphold the just one,
     O just God,*
     who tries hearts and minds.

## IV

11 God is a shield above me
     saving the upright of heart.*
12 God is a just judge, powerful and patient,†
     not exercising anger every day.
13 If one does not repent,
     God sharpens his sword,
     strings and readies the bow,*
14 Prepares his deadly shafts,
     makes arrows blazing thunderbolts.*

## V

15 Consider how one conceives iniquity;
     is pregnant with mischief,
     and gives birth to deception.*
16 He digs a hole and bores it deep,
     but he falls into the pit he has made.*
17 His malice turns back upon his head;
     his violence falls on his own skull.

## VI

18 I will thank the Lᴏʀᴅ in accordance with
          his justice,
     I will sing the name of the Lᴏʀᴅ
          Most High.*

## PSALM 8‡
### Divine Majesty and Human Dignity

1 For the leader; "upon the *gittith*."§ A psalm of
   David.

2 O Lᴏʀᴅ, our Lord,
     how awesome is your name through
          all the earth!
   I will sing of your majesty above the heavens
3      with the mouths of babes* and
          infants.¶
   You have established a bulwark¶ against
          your foes,
     to silence enemy and avenger.¶

4 When I see your heavens, the work of
          your fingers,
     the moon and stars that you set in
          place—
5 "What is man that you are mindful of him,*
     and a son of man that you care for
          him?*
6 Yet you have made him little less than a
          god,††
     crowned him with glory and honor.
7 You have given him rule over the works of
          your hands,*
     put all things at his feet:
8 All sheep and oxen,
     even the beasts of the field,
9 The birds of the air, the fish of the sea,
     and whatever swims the paths of
          the seas.

10 O Lᴏʀᴅ, our Lord,
     how awesome is your name through
          all the earth!

‡[Psalm 8] While marvelling at the limitless grandeur of God
(Ps 8:2–3), the psalmist is struck first by the smallness of human
beings in creation (Ps 8:4–5), and then by the royal dignity and
power that God has graciously bestowed upon them (Ps 8:6–9).
§[8:1] **Upon the gittith:** probably the title of the melody
to which the Psalm was to be sung or a musical instrument.
¶[8:3] **With the mouths of babes and infants:** the psalmist realizes that his attempts to praise such an awesome God
are hopelessly inadequate and amount to little more than the
sounds made by infants. **Established a bulwark:** an allusion
to lost myth telling how God built a fortress for himself in the
heavens in primordial times in his battle with the powers of
chaos. This "bulwark" is the firmament. **Enemy and avenger:**
probably cosmic enemies. The primeval powers of watery
chaos are often personified in poetic texts (Ps 74:13–14; 89:11;
Jb 9:13; 26:12–13; Is 51:9).
**[8:5] **Man . . . a son of man:** the emphasis is on the fragility and mortality of human beings to whom God has given
great dignity.
††[8:6] **Little less than a god:** Hebrew *'elohim*, the ordinary
word for "God" or "the gods" or members of the heavenly
court. The Greek version translated *'elohim* by "angel, messenger"; several ancient and modern versions so translate. The
meaning seems to be that God created human beings almost
at the level of the beings in the heavenly world. Heb 2:9, translating "for a little while," finds the eminent fulfillment of this
verse in Jesus Christ, who was humbled before being glorified,
cf. also 1 Cor 15:27 where St. Paul applies to Christ the closing
words of Ps 8:7.

---

*[7:4] **Have done this:** in the accusation the enemies have
made against the psalmist.
†[7:12] **Powerful and patient:** the inclusion of these words
is drawn from the Septuagint tradition concerning this verse.

o. [7:6] Ps 143:3.   p. [7:7] Ps 9:4; 19:20.   q. [7:10] Ps 17:3; 26:2;
35:24; 43:1; 139:23; Jer 17:10; 20:12.   r. [7:11] Ps 3:4.   s. [7:13] Ps
11:2.   t. [7:14] Is 50:11.   u. [7:15] Jb 15:35; Is 59:4.   v. [7:16] Ps
9:16; 35:8; 57:7; Prv 26:27; Eccl 10:8; Sir 27:26.   w. [7:18] Ps 18:50;
30:5; 135:3; 146:2.

x. [8:3] Mt 21:16; Wis 10:21.   y. [8:5] Ps 144:3; Jb 7:17.   z. [8:5]
Heb 2:6ff.   a. [8:7ff] Gn 1:26, 28; Wis 9:2; 1 Cor 15:27.

## PSALM 9*
### Thanksgiving for Victory
### and Prayer for Justice

¹For the leader; according to *Muth Labben*.† A psalm of David.

### I

² I will praise you, LORD, with all my heart;
   I will declare all your wondrous
      deeds.
³ I will delight and rejoice in you;
   I will sing hymns to your name,
      Most High.
⁴ When my enemies turn back,
   they stumble and perish before you.

### II

⁵ For you upheld my right and my cause,
   seated on your throne, judging
      justly.
⁶ You rebuked the nations, you destroyed
      the wicked;
   their name you blotted out for all
      time.*b*
⁷ The enemies have been ruined forever;
   you destroyed their cities;
   their memory has perished.

### III

⁸ The LORD rules forever,
   has set up his throne for judgment.
⁹ It is he who judges the world with
      justice,*c*
   who judges the peoples with
      fairness.
¹⁰ The LORD is a stronghold for the
      oppressed,
   a stronghold in times of trouble.*d*
¹¹ Those who know your name trust in you;
   you never forsake those who seek
      you, LORD.

### IV

¹² Sing hymns to the LORD enthroned on
      Zion;
   proclaim his deeds among the
      nations!
¹³ For the avenger of bloodshed remembers,
   does not forget the cry of the
      afflicted.*e*

### V

¹⁴ Be gracious to me, LORD;
   see how my foes afflict me!

You alone can raise me from the
      gates of death.*f*
¹⁵ Then I will declare all your praises,
   sing joyously of your salvation
   in the gates of daughter Zion.‡

### VI

¹⁶ The nations fall into the pit they dig;
   in the snare they hide, their own
      foot is caught.
¹⁷ §The LORD is revealed in making
      judgments:
   by the deeds they do the wicked are
      trapped.*g*

                           *Higgaion. Selah*§

### VII

¹⁸ To Sheol the wicked will depart,
   all the nations that forget God.
¹⁹ For the needy will never be forgotten,
   nor will the hope of the afflicted ever
      fade.*h*
²⁰ Arise, LORD, let no mortal prevail;
   let the nations be judged in your
      presence.
²¹ Strike them with terror, LORD;
   show the nations they are only
      human.

                                    *Selah*

## PSALM 10

### I

¹ Why, LORD, do you stand afar
   and pay no heed in times of trouble?
² Arrogant scoundrels pursue the poor;
   they trap them by their cunning
      schemes.*i*

### II

³ The wicked even boast of their greed;
   these robbers curse and scorn the
      LORD.*j*
⁴ In their insolence the wicked boast:
   "God does not care; there is no God."*k*
⁵ Yet their affairs always succeed;
   they ignore your judgment on high;
   they sneer at all who oppose them.
⁶ They say in their hearts, "We will never
      fall;
   never will we see misfortune."
⁷ Their mouths are full of oaths, violence,
      and lies;
   discord and evil are under their
      tongues.*l*

---

*[Psalms 9–10] Ps 9 and Ps 10 in the Hebrew text have been transmitted as separate poems but they actually form a single acrostic poem and are so transmitted in the Greek and Latin tradition. Each verse of the two Psalms begins with a successive letter of the Hebrew alphabet (though several letters have no corresponding stanza). The Psalm states loosely connected themes: the rescue of the helpless poor from their enemies, God's worldwide judgment and rule over the nations, the psalmist's own concern for rescue (Ps 9:14–15).

†[9:1] **Muth Labben**: probably the melodic accompaniment of the Psalm, now lost.

b. [9:6] Jb 18:17.   c. [9:9] Ps 96:10; 98:9.   d. [9:10] Ps 37:39; Is 25:4.
e. [9:13] Jb 16:18.

---

‡[9:15] **Daughter Zion**: an ancient Near Eastern city could sometimes be personified as a woman or a queen, the spouse of the god of the city.

§[9:17] **The LORD is revealed in making judgments**: God has so made the universe that the wicked are punished by the very actions they perform. **Selah**: see note on Ps 3:3.

f. [9:14] Wis 16:13.   g. [9:17] Ps 35:8; Sir 27:26.   h. [9:19] Prv 23:18.   i. [10:2] Is 32:7.   j. [10:3] Ps 36:2.   k. [10:4] Ps 14:1; Jb 22:13; Is 29:15; Jer 5:12; Zep 1:12.   l. [10:7] Is 32:7; Rom 3:14.

8 They wait in ambush near towns;
  their eyes watch for the helpless
  to murder the innocent in secret.*m*
9 They lurk in ambush like lions in a
    thicket,
  hide there to trap the poor,
  snare them and close the net.*n*
10 The helpless are crushed, laid low;
  they fall into the power of the
    wicked,
11 Who say in their hearts, "God has
    forgotten,
  shows no concern, never bothers to
    look."*o*

III

12 Rise up, LORD! God, lift up your hand!
  Do not forget the poor!
13 Why should the wicked scorn God,
  say in their hearts, "God does not
    care"?
14 But you do see;
  you take note of misery and sorrow;*p*
  you take the matter in hand.
  To you the helpless can entrust their
    cause;
  you are the defender of orphans.*q*
15 Break the arm of the wicked and
    depraved;
  make them account for their crimes;
  let none of them survive.

IV

16 The LORD is king forever;*r*
  the nations have vanished from his
    land.
17 You listen, LORD, to the needs of the poor;
  you strengthen their heart and
    incline your ear.
18 You win justice for the orphaned and
    oppressed;*s*
  no one on earth will cause terror
    again.

### PSALM 11*
### Confidence in the Presence of God

1 For the leader. Of David.

I

  In the LORD I take refuge;
  how can you say to me,
  "Flee like a bird to the mountains!*t*
2 See how the wicked string their bows,
  fit their arrows to the string
  to shoot from the shadows at the
    upright of heart.*u*

3 †If foundations are destroyed,
  what can the just one do?"

II

4 The LORD is in his holy temple;
  the LORD's throne is in heaven.*v*
  God's eyes keep careful watch;
  they test the children of Adam.
5 The LORD tests the righteous and the
    wicked,
  hates those who love violence,
6 And rains upon the wicked
  fiery coals and brimstone,
  a scorching wind their allotted cup.‡w
7 The LORD is just and loves just deeds;
  the upright will see his face.

### PSALM 12§
### Prayer Against Evil Tongues

1 For the leader; "upon the eighth." A psalm of
David.

I

2 Help, LORD, for no one loyal remains;
  the faithful have vanished from the
    children of men.*x*
3 They tell lies to one another,
  speak with deceiving lips and a
    double heart.*y*

II

4 May the LORD cut off all deceiving lips,
  and every boastful tongue,
5 Those who say, "By our tongues we
    prevail;
  when our lips speak, who can lord it
    over us?"*z*

III

6 "Because they rob the weak, and the
    needy groan,
  I will now arise," says the LORD;
  "I will grant safety to whoever longs
    for it."*a*

IV

7 The promises of the LORD are sure,
  silver refined in a crucible,¶
  silver purified seven times.*b*

---

†[11:3] **Foundations**: usually understood of public order, cf. Ps 82:5.

‡[11:6] **Their allotted cup**: the cup that God gives people to drink is a common figure for their destiny, cf. Ps 16:5; 75:9; Mt 20:22; 26:39; Rev 14:10.

§[Psalm 12] A lament. The psalmist, thrown into a world where lying and violent people persecute the just (Ps 12:2–3), prays that the wicked be punished (Ps 12:4–5). The prayer is not simply for vengeance but arises from a desire to see God's justice appear on earth. Ps 12:6 preserves the word of assurance spoken by the priest to the lamenter; it is not usually transmitted in such Psalms. In Ps 12:7–8 the psalmist affirms the intention to live by the word of assurance.

¶[12:7] **A crucible**: lit., "in a crucible in the ground." The crucible was placed in the ground for support.

---

*[Psalm 11] A song of trust. Though friends counsel flight to the mountain country (a traditional hideout) to escape trouble (Ps 11:1–3), the innocent psalmist reaffirms confidence in God, who protects those who seek asylum in the Temple (Ps 11:4–7).

m. [10:8] Ps 11:2; Jb 24:14.   n. [10:9] Ps 17:12; Prv 1:11; Jer 5:26.   o. [10:11] Ps 44:25; 64:6; 73:11; 94:7; Ez 9:9.   p. [10:14] Ps 31:8; 56:9; 2 Kgs 20:5; Is 25:8; Rev 7:17.   q. [10:14] Ex 22:21–22.   r. [10:16] Ps 145:13; Jer 10:10.   s. [10:18] Dt 10:18.   t. [11:1] Ps 55:7; 91:4.   u. [11:2] Ps 7:13; 37:14; 57:5; 64:4.

v. [11:4] Ps 14:2; 102:20; Hab 2:20; Dt 26:15; Is 66:1; Mt 5:34.   w. [11:6] Ps 120:4; 140:11; Prv 16:27; Ez 38:22; Rev 8:5; 20:10.   x. [12:2] Ps 14:3; 116:11; Is 59:15; Mi 7:2.   y. [12:3] Ps 28:3; 55:22; Is 59:3–4; Jer 9:7.   z. [12:5] Sir 5:3.   a. [12:6] Is 33:10.   b. [12:7] Ps 18:31; 19:8; Prv 30:5.

⁸  You, O LORD, protect us always;
        preserve us from this generation.
⁹  On every side the wicked roam;
        the shameless are extolled by the
            children of men.

## PSALM 13*
### Prayer for Help

¹For the leader. A psalm of David.
                    I
²  How long, LORD? Will you utterly forget
        me?
        How long will you hide your face
            from me?ᶜ
³  How long must I carry sorrow in my soul,
        grief in my heart day after day?
        How long will my enemy triumph
            over me?
                    II
⁴  Look upon me, answer me, LORD, my
        God!
        Give light to my eyes lest I sleep in
            death,
⁵  Lest my enemy say, "I have prevailed,"
        lest my foes rejoice at my downfall.ᵈ
                    III
⁶  But I trust in your mercy.
        Grant my heart joy in your
            salvation,
    I will sing to the LORD,
        for he has dealt bountifully with
            me!ᵉ

## PSALM 14†
### A Lament over Widespread Corruption

¹For the leader. Of David.
                    I
    The fool says in his heart,
        "There is no God."
    Their deeds are loathsome and corrupt;
        not one does what is good.ᶠ
²  The LORD looks down from heaven
        upon the children of men,ᵍ
    To see if even one is wise,
        if even one seeks God.ʰ
³  All have gone astray;
        all alike are perverse.
    Not one does what is good,
        not even one.ⁱ

II
⁴  Will these evildoers never learn?
        They devour my people as they
            devour bread;ʲ
        they do not call upon the LORD.ᵏ
⁵  They have good reason, then, to fear;
        God is with the company of the
            just.
⁶  They would crush the hopes of the poor,
        but the poor have the LORD as their
            refuge.
                    III
⁷  ¹Oh, that from Zion might come
        the salvation of Israel!
    Jacob would rejoice, and Israel be glad
        when the LORD restores his people!‡

## PSALM 15§
### The Righteous Israelite

¹ᵐA psalm of David.
                    I
    LORD, who may abide in your tent?¶
        Who may dwell on your holy
            mountain?¶
                    II
²  Whoever walks without blame,ⁿ
        doing what is right,
        speaking truth from the heart;
³  Who does not slander with his tongue,
        does no harm to a friend,
        never defames a neighbor;
⁴  Who disdains the wicked,
        but honors those who fear the LORD;
    Who keeps an oath despite the cost,
⁵      lends no money at interest,**
        accepts no bribe against the
            innocent.ᵒ
                    III
    Whoever acts like this
        shall never be shaken.

---

the wicked, Ps 14:1–3) and "the company of the just" (Ps 14:4–6; also called "my people," and "the poor"). The wicked persecute the just, but the Psalm expresses the hope that God will punish the wicked and reward the good.

‡[14:7] **Jacob . . . Israel . . . his people**: the righteous poor are identified with God's people.

§[Psalm 15] The Psalm records a liturgical scrutiny at the entrance to the Temple court (cf. Ps 24:3–6; Is 33:14b–16). The Israelite wishing to be admitted had to ask the Temple official what conduct was appropriate to God's precincts. Note the emphasis on virtues relating to one's neighbor.

¶[15:1] **Your tent**: the Temple could be referred to as "tent" (Ps 61:5; Is 33:20), a reference to the tent of the wilderness period and the tent of David (2 Sm 6:17; 7:2), predecessors of the Temple. **Holy mountain**: a venerable designation of the divine abode (Ps 2:6; 3:5; 43:3; 48:2, etc.).

**[15:5] **Lends no money at interest**: lending money in the Old Testament was often seen as assistance to the poor in their distress, not as an investment; making money off the poor by charging interest was thus forbidden (Ex 22:24; Lv 25:36–37; Dt 23:20).

---

*[Psalm 13] A typical lament, in which the psalmist feels forgotten by God (Ps 13:2–3)—note the force of the repetition of "How long." The references to enemies may suggest some have wished evil on the psalmist. The heartfelt prayer (Ps 13:4–5) passes on a statement of trust (Ps 13:6a), intended to reinforce the prayer, and a vow to thank God when deliverance has come (Ps 13:6b).

†[Psalm 14] The lament (duplicated in Ps 53) depicts the world as consisting of two types of people: "the fool" (equals

---

c. [13:2] Ps 6:4; 44:25; 77:8; 79:5; 89:47; 94:3; Lam 5:20.
d. [13:5] Ps 38:17.    e. [13:6] Ps 116:7.    f. [14:1] Ps 10:4; 36:2; Is 32:6;
Jer 5:12.    g. [14:2–3] Rom 3:11–12.    h. [14:2] Ps 11:4; 102:20.
i. [14:3] Ps 12:1.

---

j. [14:4] Ps 27:2; Is 9:11.    k. [14:4] Ps 79:6.    l. [14:7] Ps 85:2.
m. [15:1] Is 56:7.    n. [15:2] Ps 119:1.    o. [15:5] Ex 22:24; 23:8.

## PSALM 16*
### God the Supreme Good

¹ᵖA *miktam*† of David.

#### I

Keep me safe, O God;
    in you I take refuge.
² I say to the Lord,
    you are my Lord,
    you are my only good.
³ As for the holy ones who are in the land,
    they are noble,
    in whom is all my delight.
⁴ ‡They multiply their sorrows
    who court other gods.
Blood libations to them I will not pour
    out,
    nor will I take their names upon
    my lips.
⁵ Lord, my allotted portion and my cup,
    you have made my destiny secure.�q
⁶ §Pleasant places were measured out for
    me;
    fair to me indeed is my
    inheritance.

#### II

⁷ I bless the Lord who counsels me;
    even at night my heart exhorts me.
⁸ I keep the Lord always before me;
    with him at my right hand, I shall
    never be shaken.ʳ
⁹ Therefore my heart is glad, my soul
    rejoices;
    my body also dwells secure,
¹⁰ For you will not abandon my soul to
    Sheol,
    nor let your devout one see the pit.§ˢ
¹¹ You will show me the path to life,
    abounding joy in your presence,
    the delights at your right hand
    forever.

## PSALM 17**
### Prayer for Rescue from Persecutors

¹A prayer of David.

#### I

Hear, Lord, my plea for justice;
    pay heed to my cry;
Listen to my prayer
    from lips without guile.
² From you let my vindication come;
    your eyes see what is right.
³ You have tested my heart,
    searched it in the night.ᵗ
You have tried me by fire,
    but find no malice in me.
My mouth has not transgressed
⁴     as others often do.
As your lips have instructed me,
    I have kept from the way of the
    lawless.
⁵ My steps have kept to your paths;
    my feet have not faltered.ᵘ

#### II

⁶ I call upon you; answer me, O God.
    Turn your ear to me; hear my
    speech.
⁷ Show your wonderful mercy,
    you who deliver with your right
    arm
    those who seek refuge from their
    foes.
⁸ ††Keep me as the apple of your eye;
    hide me in the shadow of your wings
⁹     from the wicked who despoil me.ᵛ

#### III

My ravenous enemies press upon me;ʷ
¹⁰     ‡‡they close their hearts,
    they fill their mouths with proud
    roaring.
¹¹ Their steps even now encircle me;
    they watch closely, keeping low to
    the ground,
¹² Like lions eager for prey,
    like a young lion lurking in
    ambush.
¹³ Rise, O Lord, confront and cast them
    down;
    rescue my soul from the wicked.
¹⁴ Slay them with your sword;
    with your hand, Lord, slay them;

---

*[Psalm 16] In the first section, the psalmist rejects the futile worship of false gods (Ps 16:2–5), preferring Israel's God (Ps 16:1), the giver of the land (Ps 16:6). The second section reflects on the wise and life-giving presence of God (Ps 16:7–11).

†[16:1] **Miktam**: a term occurring six times in Psalm superscriptions, always with "David." Its meaning is unknown.

‡[16:4] **Take their names**: to use the gods' names in oaths and hence to affirm them as one's own gods.

§[16:6] **Pleasant places were measured out for me**: the psalmist is pleased with the plot of land measured out to the family, which was to be passed on to succeeding generations ("my inheritance").

¶[16:10] **Nor let your devout one see the pit**: Hebrew *shahath* means here the pit, a synonym for Sheol, the underworld. The Greek translation derives the word here and elsewhere from the verb *shahath*, "to be corrupt." On the basis of the Greek, Acts 2:25–32; 13:35–37 apply the verse to Christ's resurrection, "Nor will you suffer your holy one to see corruption."

**[Psalm 17] A lament of an individual unjustly attacked. Confident of being found innocent, the psalmist cries out for God's just judgment (Ps 17:1–5) and requests divine help against enemies (Ps 17:6–9a). Those ravenous lions (Ps 17:9b–12) should be punished (Ps 17:13–14). The Psalm ends with a serene statement of praise (Ps 17:15). The Hebrew text of Ps 17:3–4, 14 is uncertain.

††[17:8] **Apple of your eye . . . shadow of your wings**: images of God's special care, cf. Dt 32:10; Prv 7:2; Is 49:2.

‡‡[17:10–12, 14] An extended metaphor: the enemies are lions.

p. [16:1] Ps 25:20.   q. [16:5] Ps 23:5; 73:26; Nm 18:20; Lam 3:24.
r. [16:8] Ps 73:23; 121:5, 8–12; Acts 2:25–28.  s. [16:10] Ps 28:1; 30:4; 49:16; 86:13; Jon 2:7; Acts 13:35.

t. [17:3] Ps 26:2; 139:23.  u. [17:5] Ps 18:36; Jb 23:11–12.  v. [17:9–12] Ps 10:9; 22:14, 22; 35:17; 58:7; Jb 4:10–11.  w. [17:9] Ps 36:8; 57:2; 61:5; 63:8; 91:4; Dt 32:10; Ru 2:12; Zec 2:12; Mt 23:37.

snatch them from the world in their
    prime.
Their bellies are being filled with your
    friends;
    their children are satisfied too,
    for they share what is left with their
    young.
15 I am just—let me see your face;
    when I awake, let me be filled with
    your presence.[x]

## PSALM 18[*]
### A King's Thanksgiving for Victory

¹For the leader. Of David, the servant of the
LORD, who sang to the LORD the words of this
song after the LORD had rescued him from the
clutches of all his enemies and from the hand of
Saul. ²He said:[y]

### I

I love you, LORD, my strength,
3    LORD, my rock, my fortress, my
    deliverer,
My God, my rock of refuge,
    my shield, my saving horn,[†] my
    stronghold![z]
4 Praised be the LORD, I exclaim!
    I have been delivered from my
    enemies.

### II

5 The cords of death encompassed me;
    the torrents of destruction terrified
    me.
6 The cords[‡] of Sheol encircled me;
    the snares of death lay in wait for me.[a]
7 In my distress I called out: LORD!
    I cried out to my God.[b]
From his temple he heard my voice;
    my cry to him reached his ears.
8 §The earth rocked and shook;
    the foundations of the mountains
    trembled;

they shook as his wrath flared up.[c]
9 Smoke rose from his nostrils,
    a devouring fire from his mouth;
    it kindled coals into flame.
10 He parted the heavens and came down,
    a dark cloud under his feet.[d]
11 Mounted on a cherub[¶] he flew,
    borne along on the wings of the
    wind.
12 He made darkness his cloak around him;
    his canopy, water-darkened
    stormclouds.
13 From the gleam before him, his clouds
    passed,
    hail and coals of fire.[e]
14 The LORD thundered from heaven;
    the Most High made his voice
    resound.[f]
15 He let fly his arrows[**] and scattered them;
    shot his lightning bolts and
    dispersed them.[g]
16 Then the bed of the sea appeared;
    the world's foundations lay bare,[h]
At your rebuke, O LORD,
    at the storming breath of your
    nostrils.
17 He reached down from on high and
    seized me;
    drew me out of the deep waters.[i]
18 He rescued me from my mighty enemy,
    from foes too powerful for me.
19 They attacked me on my day of distress,
    but the LORD was my support.
20 He set me free in the open;
    he rescued me because he loves me.

### III

21 The LORD acknowledged my
    righteousness,
    rewarded my clean hands.[j]
22 For I kept the ways of the LORD;
    I was not disloyal to my God.
23 For his laws were all before me,
    his decrees I did not cast aside.
24 I was honest toward him;
    I was on guard against sin.
25 So the LORD rewarded my righteousness,
    the cleanness of my hands in his
    sight.
26 Toward the faithful you are faithful;
    to the honest man you are honest;[k]
27 Toward the pure, you are pure;
    but to the perverse you are devious.

---

*[Psalm 18] A royal thanksgiving for a military victory,
duplicated in 2 Sm 22. Thanksgiving Psalms are in essence
reports of divine rescue. The Psalm has two parallel reports of
rescue, the first told from a heavenly perspective (Ps 18:5–20),
and the second from an earthly perspective (Ps 18:36–46).
The first report adapts old mythic language of a cosmic battle
between sea and rainstorm in order to depict God's rescue of
the Israelite king from his enemies. Each report has a short
hymnic introduction (Ps 18:2–4, 32–36) and conclusion (Ps
18:21–31, 47–50).

†[18:3] My saving horn: my strong savior. The horn
referred to is the weapon of a bull and the symbol of fertility,
cf. 1 Sm 2:10; Ps 132:17; Lk 1:69.

‡[18:6] Cords: hunting imagery, the cords of a snare.

§[18:8–16] God appears in the storm, which in Palestine
comes from the west. The introduction to the theophany (Ps
18:8–9) is probably a description of a violent, hot, and dry
east-wind storm. In the fall transition period from the rainless summer to the rainy winter such storms regularly precede
the rains, cf. Ex 14:21–22.

¶[18:11] Cherub: a winged creature, derived from myth,
in the service of the deity (Gn 3:24; Ex 25:18–20; 37:6–9).
Cherubim were the throne bearers of the deity (Ps 80:2; 99:1;
1 Kgs 6:23–28; 8:6–8).

**[18:15] Arrows: lightning.

---

x. [17:15] Ps 4:7; 31:17; 67:2; 80:4; Nm 6:25; Dn 9:17. y. [18:2–
51] 2 Sm 22:2–51. z. [18:3] Ps 3:4; 31:3–4; 42:10; Gn 49:24; Dt
32:4. a. [18:6] Ps 88:8; 93:3–4; 116:3–4. b. [18:7] Jon 2:3.

c. [18:8] Ps 97:3–4; 99:1; Jgs 5:4–5; Is 64:1; Heb 3:9–11. d. [18:10]
Ps 104:3; 144:5; Is 63:19. e. [18:13] Ex 13:21; 19:16. f. [18:14]
Ps 29; 77:19; Ex 19:19; Jb 37:3–4. g. [18:15] Ps 144:6; Wis
5:21. h. [18:16] Ps 77:17; Zec 9:14. i. [18:17] Ps 144:7. j. [18:21]
Ps 26; 1 Sm 26:23. k. [18:26] Ps 125:4.

28 For humble people you save;
    haughty eyes you bring low.[l]
29 For you, LORD, give light to my lamp;
    my God brightens my
    darkness.[m]
30 With you I can rush an armed band,
    with my God to help I can leap a
    wall.
31 God's way is unerring;
    the LORD's promise is refined;
    he is a shield for all who take refuge
    in him.[n]

IV

32 Truly, who is God except the LORD?
    Who but our God is the rock?[o]
33 This God who girded me with might,
    kept my way unerring,
34 Who made my feet like a deer's,
    and set me on the heights,[p]
35 Who trained my hands for war,
    my arms to string a bow of
    bronze.*[q]

V

36 You have given me your saving shield;
    your right hand has upheld me;
    your favor made me great.
37 You made room for my steps beneath
    me;
    my ankles never twisted.[r]
38 I pursued my enemies and overtook
    them;
    I did not turn back till I destroyed
    them.
39 I decimated them; they could not rise;
    they fell at my feet.
40 You girded me with valor for war,
    subjugated my opponents beneath
    me.
41 You made my foes expose their necks to
    me;
    those who hated me I silenced.
42 They cried for help, but no one saved
    them;
    cried to the LORD but received no
    answer.
43 I ground them to dust before the wind;
    I left them like mud in the streets.
44 You rescued me from the strife of
    peoples;
    you made me head over nations.
    A people I had not known served me;
45      as soon as they heard of me they
        obeyed.
    Foreigners submitted before me;
46      foreigners cringed;

they came cowering from their
    dungeons.[s]

VI

47 The LORD lives! Blessed be my rock![t]
    Exalted be God, my savior!
48 O God who granted me vengeance,
    made peoples subject to me,[u]
49      and saved me from my enemies,
    Truly you have elevated me above my
        opponents,
    from a man of lawlessness you have
        rescued me.
50 Thus I will praise you, LORD, among the
    nations;
    I will sing praises to your name.[v]
51 You have given great victories to your
    king,
    and shown mercy to his anointed,
    to David and his posterity forever.[w]

## PSALM 19[†]
### God's Glory in the Heavens and in the Law

1 For the leader. A psalm of David.

I

2   The heavens declare the glory of God;
        the firmament proclaims the works
        of his hands.[x]
3   Day unto day pours forth speech;
        night unto night whispers
        knowledge.
4   ‡There is no speech, no words;
        their voice is not heard;
5   A report goes forth through all the earth,
        their messages, to the ends of the
        world.
    He has pitched in them a tent for the
        sun;[§]
6       it comes forth like a bridegroom
            from his canopy,
        and like a hero joyfully runs its
            course.
7   From one end of the heavens it comes
        forth;
        its course runs through to the
            other;
        nothing escapes its heat.

---

†[Psalm 19] The heavenly elements of the world, now beautifully arranged, bespeak the power and wisdom of their creator (Ps 19:2–7). The creator's wisdom is available to human beings in the law (Ps 19:8–11), toward which the psalmist prays to be open (Ps 19:12–14). The themes of light and speech unify the poem.

‡[19:4] **No speech, no words**: the regular functioning of the heavens and the alternation of day and night inform human beings without words of the creator's power and wisdom.

§[19:5] **The sun**: in other religious literature the sun is a judge and lawgiver since it sees all in its daily course; Ps 19:5b–7 form a transition to the law in Ps 19:8–11. The six synonyms for God's revelation (Ps 19:8–11) are applied to the sun in comparable literature.

---

*[18:35] **Bow of bronze**: hyperbole for a bow difficult to bend and therefore capable of propelling an arrow with great force.

l. [18:28] Jb 22:29; Prv 3:34.   m. [18:29] Ps 27:1; 36:10; 43:3;
119:105; Jb 29:3; Mi 7:8.   n. [18:31] Ps 12:6; 77:13; Prv 30:5.
o. [18:32] Is 44:8; 45:21.   p. [18:34] Heb 3:19.   q. [18:35] Ps 144:1.
r. [18:37] Ps 17:5.

s. [18:46] Mi 7:17.   t. [18:47] Ps 144:1.   u. [18:48] Ps 144:2.   v.
[18:50] Ps 7:18; 30:5; 57:9; 135:3; 146:2; Rom 15:9.   w. [18:51] Ps
89:28–37; 144:10; 1 Sm 2:10.   x. [19:2] Ps 8:1; 50:6; 97:6.

II

8 The law of the LORD is perfect,
  refreshing the soul.
  The decree of the LORD is trustworthy,
  giving wisdom to the simple.^y
9 The precepts of the LORD are right,
  rejoicing the heart.
  The command of the LORD is clear,
  enlightening the eye.
10 The fear of the LORD is pure,
   enduring forever.
   The statutes of the LORD are true,
   all of them just;
11 More desirable than gold,
   than a hoard of purest gold,
   Sweeter also than honey
   or drippings from the comb.^z
12 By them your servant is warned;*
   obeying them brings much reward.

III

13 Who can detect trespasses?
   Cleanse me from my inadvertent sins.
14 Also from arrogant ones restrain your
   servant;
   let them never control me.
   Then shall I be blameless,
   innocent of grave sin.
15 Let the words of my mouth be acceptable,
   the thoughts of my heart before you,
   LORD, my rock and my redeemer.

## PSALM 20†
### Prayer for the King in Time of War

1 For the leader. A psalm of David.

I

2 The LORD answer you in time of distress;
  the name of the God of Jacob defend
  you!
3 May he send you help from the sanctuary,
  from Zion be your support.^a
4 May he remember‡ your every offering,
  graciously accept your burnt offering,
                                    Selah
5 Grant what is in your heart,
  fulfill your every plan.
6 May we shout for joy at your victory,§
  raise the banners in the name of our
  God.
  The LORD grant your every petition!

II

7 Now I know the LORD gives victory
  to his anointed.^b
  He will answer him from the holy heavens
  with a strong arm that brings victory.
8 Some rely on chariots, others on horses,
  but we on the name of the LORD our
  God.^c
9 They collapse and fall,
  but we stand strong and firm.^d
10 LORD, grant victory to the king;
   answer when we call upon you.

## PSALM 21¶
### Thanksgiving and Assurances for the King

1 For the leader. A psalm of David.

I

2 LORD, the king finds joy in your power;^e
  in your victory how greatly he
  rejoices!
3 You have granted him his heart's desire;
  you did not refuse the request of
  his lips.
                                    Selah
4 For you welcomed him with goodly
  blessings;
  you placed on his head a crown of
  pure gold.
5 He asked life of you;
  you gave it to him,
  length of days forever.^f
6 Great is his glory in your victory;
  majesty and splendor you confer
  upon him.
7 You make him the pattern of blessings
  forever,
  you gladden him with the joy of
  your face.
8 For the king trusts in the LORD,
  stands firm through the mercy of
  the Most High.

II

9 Your hand will find all your enemies;
  your right hand will find your foes!
10 At the time of your coming
   you will make them a fiery furnace.
   Then the LORD in his anger will consume
   them,
   devour them with fire.
11 Even their descendants you will wipe out
   from the earth,
   their offspring from the human race.

---

*[19:12] **Warned**: the Hebrew verb means both to shine
and to warn, cf. Dn 12:3.

†[Psalm 20] The people pray for the king before battle. The
people ask for divine help (Ps 20:2–6) and express confidence
that such help will be given (Ps 20:7–10). A solemn assurance
of divine help may well have been given between the two sections in the liturgy, something like the promises of Ps 12:6;
21:9–13. The final verse (Ps 20:10) echoes the opening verse.

‡[20:4] **Remember**: God's remembering implies readiness
to act, cf. Gn 8:1; Ex 2:24.

§[20:6] **Victory**: the Hebrew root is often translated "salvation," "to save," but in military contexts it can have the specific
meaning of "victory."

¶[Psalm 21] The first part of this royal Psalm is a thanksgiving (Ps 21:2–8), and the second is a promise that the king will
triumph over his enemies (Ps 21:9–13). The king's confident
prayer (Ps 21:3–5) and trust in God (Ps 21:8) enable him to
receive the divine gifts of vitality, peace, and military success.
Ps 21:14 reprises Ps 21:2. When kings ceased in Israel after the
sixth century B.C., the Psalm was sung of a future Davidic king.

b. [20:7] Ps 18:51; 144:10; 1 Sm 2:10.   c. [20:8] Ps 147:10–11; 2 Chr
14:10; Prv 21:31; 1 Sm 17:45; Is 31:1; 36:9.   d. [20:9] Is 40:30.
e. [21:2] Ps 63:12.   f. [21:5] 1 Kgs 3:14.

y. [19:8] Ps 12:7; 119.   z. [19:11] Sir 24:19.   a. [20:3] Ps 128:5; 134:3.

¹² Though they intend evil against you,
    devising plots, they will not succeed,
¹³ For you will put them to flight;
    you will aim at their faces with your
      bow.

### III

¹⁴ Arise, Lord, in your power!ᵍ
    We will sing and chant the praise of
      your might.

## PSALM 22*
### The Prayer of an Innocent Person

¹For the leader; according to "The deer of the
dawn."† A psalm of David.

### I

² My God, my God, why have you
    abandoned me?
    Why so far from my call for help,
    from my cries of anguish?ʰ
³ My God, I call by day, but you do not
    answer;
    by night, but I have no relief.ⁱ
⁴ Yet you are enthroned as the Holy One;
    you are the glory of Israel.ʲ
⁵ In you our fathers trusted;
    they trusted and you rescued them.
⁶ To you they cried out and they escaped;
    in you they trusted and were not
      disappointed.ᵏ
⁷ ‡But I am a worm, not a man,
    scorned by men, despised by the
      people.ˡ
⁸ All who see me mock me;
    they curl their lips and jeer;
    they shake their heads at me:ᵐ
⁹ "He relied on the Lord—let him deliver
    him;
    if he loves him, let him rescue him."ⁿ
¹⁰ For you drew me forth from the womb,
    made me safe at my mother's
      breasts.
¹¹ Upon you I was thrust from the womb;
    since my mother bore me you are
      my God.ᵒ

¹² Do not stay far from me,
    for trouble is near,
    and there is no one to help.ᵖ

### II

¹³ Many bulls§ surround me;
    fierce bulls of Bashan§ encircle
      me.
¹⁴ They open their mouths against me,
    lions that rend and roar.�q
¹⁵ Like water my life drains away;
    all my bones are disjointed.
    My heart has become like wax,
    it melts away within me.
¹⁶ As dry as a potsherd is my throat;
    my tongue cleaves to my palate;
    you lay me in the dust of death.§
¹⁷ Dogs surround me;
    a pack of evildoers closes in on me.
    They have pierced my hands and my feet
¹⁸ I can count all my bones.ʳ
    They stare at me and gloat;
¹⁹ they divide my garments among
    them;
    for my clothing they cast lots.ˢ
²⁰ But you, Lord, do not stay far off;
    my strength, come quickly to help
      me.
²¹ Deliver my soul from the sword,
    my life from the grip of the dog.
²² Save me from the lion's mouth,
    my poor life from the horns of wild
      bulls.ᵗ

### III

²³ Then I will proclaim your name to my
    brethren;
    in the assembly I will praise you:**ᵘ
²⁴ "You who fear the Lord, give praise!
    All descendants of Jacob, give
      honor;
    show reverence, all descendants of
      Israel!
²⁵ For he has not spurned or disdained
    the misery of this poor wretch,
    Did not turn away†† from me,
    but heard me when I cried out.

---

*[Psalm 22] A lament unusual in structure and in intensity of feeling. The psalmist's present distress is contrasted with God's past mercy in Ps 22:2–12. In Ps 22:13–22 enemies surround the psalmist. The last third is an invitation to praise God (Ps 22:23–27), becoming a universal chorus of praise (Ps 22:28–31). The Psalm is important in the New Testament. Its opening words occur on the lips of the crucified Jesus (Mk 15:34; Mt 27:46), and several other verses are quoted, or at least alluded to, in the accounts of Jesus' passion (Mt 27:35, 43; Jn 19:24).

†[22:1] **The deer of the dawn**: apparently the title of the melody.

‡[22:7] **I am a worm, not a man**: the psalmist's sense of isolation and dehumanization, an important motif of Ps 22, is vividly portrayed here.

§[22:13–14] **Bulls**: the enemies of the psalmist are also portrayed in less-than-human form, as wild animals (cf. Ps 22:17, 21–22). **Bashan**: a grazing land northeast of the Sea of Galilee, famed for its cattle, cf. Dt 32:14; Ez 39:18; Am 4:1.

¶[22:16] **The dust of death**: the netherworld, the domain of the dead.

**[22:23] **In the assembly I will praise you**: the person who offered a thanksgiving sacrifice in the Temple recounted to the other worshipers the favor received from God and invited them to share in the sacrificial banquet. The final section (Ps 22:24–32) may be a summary or a citation of the psalmist's poem of praise.

††[22:25] **Turn away**: lit., "hides his face from me," an important metaphor for God withdrawing from someone, e.g., Mi 3:4; Is 8:17; Ps 27:9; 69:18; 88:15.

g. [21:14] Nm 10:35. h. [22:2] Is 49:14; 54:7; Mt 27:46; Mk 15:34. i. [22:3] Sir 2:10. j. [22:4] Is 6:3. k. [22:6] Ps 25:3; Is 49:23; Dn 3:40. l. [22:7] Is 53:3. m. [22:8] Ps 109:25; Mt 27:39; Mk 15:29; Lk 23:35. n. [22:9] Ps 71:11; Wis 2:18–20; Mt 27:43. o. [22:11] Ps 71:6; Is 44:2; 46:3.

p. [22:12] Ps 35:22; 38:22; 71:12. q. [22:14] Ps 17:12; Jb 4:10; 1 Pt 5:8. r. [22:18] Ps 109:24. s. [22:19] Mt 27:35; Mk 15:24; Lk 23:34; Jn 19:24. t. [22:22] Ps 7:2–3; 17:12; 35:17; 57:5; 58:7; 2 Tm 4:17. u. [22:23] Ps 26:12; 35:18; 40:10; 109:30; 149:1; 2 Sm 22:50; Heb 2:12.

²⁶ I will offer praise in the great assembly;
    my vows I will fulfill before those
        who fear him.
²⁷ The poor* will eat their fill;
    those who seek the LORD will offer
        praise.
    May your hearts enjoy life forever!"ᵛ

**IV**

²⁸ All the ends of the earth
    will remember and turn to the
        LORD;
    All the families of nations
        will bow low before him.ʷ
²⁹ For kingship belongs to the LORD,
    the ruler over the nations.ˣ
³⁰ †All who sleep in the earth
    will bow low before God;
    All who have gone down into the dust
        will kneel in homage.
³¹ And I will live for the LORD;
    my descendants will serve you.
³² The generation to come will be told of the
    Lord,
    that they may proclaim to a people
        yet unborn
    the deliverance you have brought.ʸ

## PSALM 23‡
### The Lord, Shepherd and Host

¹A psalm of David.

**I**

    The LORD is my shepherd;§
        there is nothing I lack.ᶻ
² In green pastures he makes me lie down;
    to still waters he leads me;
³ ᵃhe restores my soul.
    He guides me along right paths¶
        for the sake of his name.
⁴ Even though I walk through the valley of
        the shadow of death,ᵇ
    I will fear no evil, for you are with
        me;

    your rod and your staff comfort me.

**II**

⁵ "You set a table before me
    in front of my enemies;**
    You anoint my head with oil;**ᶜ
    my cup overflows.ᵈ
⁶ Indeed, goodness and mercy†† will pursue
        me
    all the days of my life;
    I will dwell in the house of the LORDᵉ
        for endless days.

## PSALM 24‡‡
### The Glory of God in Procession to Zion

¹A psalm of David.

**I**

    The earth is the LORD's and all it holds,ᶠ
        the world and those who dwell in
        it.
² For he founded it on the seas,
    established it over the rivers.ᵍ

**II**

³ Who may go up the mountain of the
        LORD?ʰ
    Who can stand in his holy place?
⁴ §§"The clean of hand and pure of heart,
    who has not given his soul to useless
        things,
    what is vain.
⁵ He will receive blessings from the LORD,
    and justice from his saving God.
⁶ Such is the generation that seeks him,
    that seeks the face of the God of
        Jacob."

                        *Selah*

**III**

⁷ Lift up your heads, O gates;¶¶

---

\* [22:27] **The poor**: originally the poor, who were dependent on God; the term (*'anawim*) came to include the religious sense of "humble, pious, devout."

† [22:30] Hebrew unclear. The translation assumes that all on earth (Ps 22:27–28) and under the earth (Ps 22:29) will worship God.

‡ [Psalm 23] God's loving care for the psalmist is portrayed under the figures of a shepherd for the flock (Ps 23:1–4) and a host's generosity toward a guest (Ps 23:5–6). The imagery of both sections is drawn from traditions of the exodus (Is 40:11; 49:10; Jer 31:10).

§ [23:1] **My shepherd**: God as good shepherd is common in both the Old Testament and the New Testament (Ez 34:11–16; Jn 10:11–18).

¶ [23:3] **Right paths**: connotes "right way" and "way of righteousness."

** [23:5] **You set a table before me**: this expression occurs in an exodus context in Ps 78:19. **In front of my enemies**: my enemies see that I am God's friend and guest. **Oil**: a perfumed ointment made from olive oil, used especially at banquets (Ps 104:15; Mt 26:7; Lk 7:37, 46; Jn 12:2).

†† [23:6] **Goodness and mercy**: the blessings of God's covenant with Israel.

‡‡ [Psalm 24] The Psalm apparently accompanied a ceremony of the entry of God (invisibly enthroned upon the ark), followed by the people, into the Temple. The Temple commemorated the creation of the world (Ps 24:1–2). The people had to affirm their fidelity before being admitted into the sanctuary (Ps 24:3–6; cf. Ps 15). A choir identifies the approaching God and invites the very Temple gates to bow down in obeisance (Ps 24:7–10).

§§ [24:4–5] Lit., "the one whose hands are clean." The singular is used for the entire class of worshipers.

¶¶ [24:7, 9] **Lift up your heads, O gates . . . you ancient portals**: the literal meaning would involve disassembly of the gates, since the portcullis (a gate that moves up and down) was unknown in the ancient world. Extra-biblical parallels might also suggest a full personification of the circle of gate towers: they are like a council of elders, bowed down and anxious, awaiting the return of the army and the great warrior gone to battle.

---

v. [22:27] Ps 23:5; 69:33.  w. [22:28] Ps 86:9; Tb 13:11; Is 45:22; 52:10; Zec 14:16.  x. [22:29] Ps 103:19; Ob 21; Zec 14:9.  y. [22:32] Ps 48:14–15; 71:18; 78:6; 102:19; Is 53:10.  z. [23:1] Ps 80:2; 95:7; 100:3; Dt 2:7.  a. [23:3] Prv 4:11.  b. [23:4] Jb 10:21–22; Is 50:10.

c. [23:5] Ps 92:11.  d. [23:5] Ps 16:5.  e. [23:6] Ps 27:4.  f. [24:1] Ps 50:12; 89:12; Dt 10:14; 1 Cor 10:26.  g. [24:2] Ps 136:6; Is 42:5.  h. [24:3] Ps 15:1.

be lifted, you ancient portals,
    that the king of glory may enter.[i]
8 Who is this king of glory?
    The LORD, strong and mighty,
    the LORD, mighty in war.
9 Lift up your heads, O gates;
    rise up, you ancient portals,
    that the king of glory may enter.
10 Who is this king of glory?
    The LORD of hosts, he is the king of
    glory.

                                    *Selah*

## PSALM 25*
### Confident Prayer for
### Forgiveness and Guidance

1 Of David.

                    I

To you, O LORD, I lift up my soul,
2     [j]my God, in you I trust;
    do not let me be disgraced;[k]
    do not let my enemies gloat over
    me.
3 No one is disgraced who waits for you,[l]
    but only those who are treacherous
    without cause.
4 Make known to me your ways, LORD;
    teach me your paths.[m]
5 Guide me by your fidelity and teach me,
    for you are God my savior,
    for you I wait all the day long.
6 Remember your compassion and your
    mercy, O LORD,
    for they are ages old.[n]
7 Remember no more the sins of my
    youth;[o]
    remember me according to your
    mercy,
    because of your goodness, LORD.

                    II

8 Good and upright is the LORD,
    therefore he shows sinners the way,
9 He guides the humble in righteousness,
    and teaches the humble his way.
10 All the paths of the LORD are mercy and
    truth
    toward those who honor his
    covenant and decrees.
11 For the sake of your name, LORD,
    pardon my guilt, though it is great.
12 Who is the one who fears the LORD?
    God shows him the way he should
    choose.[p]

13 He will abide in prosperity,
    and his descendants will inherit the
    land.[q]
14 The counsel of the LORD belongs to those
    who fear him;
    and his covenant instructs them.
15 My eyes are ever upon the LORD,
    who frees my feet from the snare.[r]

                    III

16 Look upon me, have pity on me,
    for I am alone and afflicted.[s]
17 Relieve the troubles of my heart;
    bring me out of my distress.
18 Look upon my affliction and suffering;
    take away all my sins.
19 See how many are my enemies,
    see how fiercely they hate me.
20 Preserve my soul and rescue me;
    do not let me be disgraced; for in
    you I seek refuge.
21 Let integrity and uprightness preserve
    me;
    I wait for you, O LORD.
22 †Redeem Israel, O God,
    from all its distress!

## PSALM 26‡
### Prayer of Innocence

1 Of David.

                    I

Judge me, LORD!
    For I have walked in my integrity.[t]
In the LORD I trust;
    I do not falter.
2 Examine me, Lord, and test me;
    search my heart and mind.[u]
3 Your mercy is before my eyes;
    I walk guided by your faithfulness.[v]

                    II

4 I do not sit with worthless men,
    nor with hypocrites do I mingle.
5 I hate an evil assembly;
    with the wicked I do not sit.
6 I will wash my hands§ in innocence[w]
    so that I may process around your
    altar, Lord,

---

†[25:22] A final verse beginning with the Hebrew letter *pe* is added to the normal 22-letter alphabet. Thus the letters *aleph*, *lamed*, and *pe* open the first, middle (Ps 25:11), and last lines of the Psalm. Together, they spell *aleph*, the first letter of the alphabet, from a Hebrew root that means "to learn."

‡[Psalm 26] Like a priest washing before approaching the altar (Ex 30:17–21), the psalmist seeks God's protection upon entering the Temple. Ps 26:1–3, matched by Ps 26:11–12, remind God of past integrity while asking for purification; Ps 26:4–5, matched by Ps 26:9–10, pray for inclusion among the just; Ps 26:6–8, the center of the poem, express the joy in God at the heart of all ritual.

§[26:6] I will wash my hands: the washing of hands was a liturgical act (Ex 30:19, 21; 40:31–32), symbolic of inner as well as outer cleanness, cf. Is 1:16.

---

*[Psalm 25] A lament. Each verse begins with a successive letter of the Hebrew alphabet. Such acrostic Psalms are often a series of statements only loosely connected. The psalmist mixes ardent pleas (Ps 25:1–2, 16–22) with expressions of confidence in God who forgives and guides.

---

i. [24:7] Ps 118:19–20.   j. [25:2] Ps 86:4; 143:8.   k. [25:2] Ps 71:1.
l. [25:3] Ps 22:6; Is 49:23; Dn 3:40.   m. [25:4] Ps 27:11; 86:11;
119:12, 35; 143:8, 10.   n. [25:6] Sir 51:8.   o. [25:7] Jb 13:26; Is
64:8.   p. [25:12] Prv 19:23.

q. [25:13] Ps 37:9, 29.   r. [25:15] Ps 123:1, 2; 141:8.   s. [25:16] Ps
86:16; 119:132.   t. [26:1] Ps 7:9.   u. [26:2] Ps 17:3; 139:23.   v. [26:3]
Ps 86:11.   w. [26:6] Ps 73:13.

7 To hear the sound of thanksgiving,
  and recount all your wondrous
  deeds.
8 Lord, I love the refuge of your house,
  the site of the dwelling-place of your
  glory.[x]

### III

9 Do not take me away with sinners,
  nor my life with the men of blood,[y]
10 In whose hands there is a plot,
  their right hands full of bribery.
11 But I walk in my integrity;[z]
  redeem me, be gracious to me![a]
12 My foot stands on level ground;[*]
  in assemblies I will bless the LORD.[b]

## PSALM 27[†]
### Trust in God

1 Of David.

### A
### I

The LORD is my light and my salvation;
  whom should I fear?
The LORD is my life's refuge;
  of whom should I be afraid?
2 When evildoers come at me
  to devour my flesh,[‡d]
These my enemies and foes
  themselves stumble and fall.
3 Though an army encamp against me,
  my heart does not fear;
Though war be waged against me,
  even then do I trust.

### II

4 One thing I ask of the LORD;
  this I seek:
To dwell in the LORD's house
  all the days of my life,
To gaze on the LORD's beauty,
  to visit his temple.[e]
5 For God will hide me in his shelter
  in time of trouble;[f]
He will conceal me in the cover of his
  tent;
  and set me high upon a rock.

6 Even now my head is held high
  above my enemies on every side!
I will offer in his tent
  sacrifices with shouts of joy;
I will sing and chant praise to the
  LORD.

### B
### I

7 Hear my voice, LORD, when I call;
  have mercy on me and answer me.
8 "Come," says my heart, "seek his face";[§]
  your face, LORD, do I seek![g]
9 Do not hide your face from me;
  do not repel your servant in anger.
You are my salvation; do not cast me off;
  do not forsake me, God my savior!
10 Even if my father and mother forsake me,
  the LORD will take me in.[h]

### II

11 LORD, show me your way;
  lead me on a level path
  because of my enemies.[i]
12 Do not abandon me to the desire of my
  foes;
  malicious and lying witnesses have
  risen against me.
13 I believe I shall see the LORD's goodness
  in the land of the living.[¶j]
14 Wait for the LORD, take courage;
  be stouthearted, wait for the LORD!

## PSALM 28[**]
### Petition and Thanksgiving

1 Of David.

### I

To you, LORD, I call;
  my Rock, do not be deaf to me,[k]
Do not be silent toward me,
  so that I join those who go down to
  the pit.[l]
2 Hear the sound of my pleading when I cry
  to you for help
when I lift up my hands toward your
  holy place.[††m]
3 Do not drag me off with the wicked,
  with those who do wrong,[n]
Who speak peace to their neighbors

---

*[26:12] **On level ground**: in safety, where there is no danger of tripping and falling. **In assemblies**: at the Temple. Having walked around the altar, the symbol of God's presence, the psalmist blesses God.

†[Psalm 27] Tradition has handed down the two sections of the Psalm (Ps 27:1–6; 7–14) as one Psalm, though each part could be understood as complete in itself. Asserting boundless hope that God will bring rescue (Ps 27:1–3), the psalmist longs for the presence of God in the Temple, protection from all enemies (Ps 27:4–6). In part B there is a clear shift in tone (Ps 27:7–12); the climax of the poem comes with "I believe" (Ps 27:13), echoing "I trust" (Ps 27:3).

‡[27:2] **To devour my flesh**: the psalmist's enemies are rapacious beasts (Ps 7:3; 17:12; 22:14, 17).

§[27:8] **Seek his face**: to commune with God in the Temple. The idiom is derived from the practice of journeying to sacred places, cf. Hos 5:15; 2 Sm 21:1; Ps 24:6.

¶[27:13] **In the land of the living**: or "in the land of life," an epithet of the Jerusalem Temple (Ps 52:7; 116:9; Is 38:11), where the faithful had access to the life-giving presence of God.

**[Psalm 28] A lament asking that the psalmist, who has taken refuge in the Temple (Ps 28:2), not be punished with the wicked, who are headed inevitably toward destruction (Ps 28:1, 3–5). The statement of praise is exceptionally lengthy and vigorous (Ps 28:6–7). The Psalm ends with a prayer (Ps 28:8–9).

††[28:2] **Your holy place**: the innermost part of the Temple, the holy of holies, containing the ark, cf. 1 Kgs 6:16, 19–23; 8:6–8.

---

x. [26:8] Ps 29:9; 63:3; Ex 24:16; 25:8.    y. [26:9] Ps 28:3.    z. [26:11] Ps 101:6.    a. [26:11] Ps 25:16.    b. [26:12] Ps 22:23; 35:18; 149:1.    c. [27:1] Ps 18:29; 36:10; 43:3; Is 10:17; Mi 7:8.    d. [27:2] Ps 14:4.    e. [27:4] Ps 23:6; 61:5.    f. [27:5] Ps 31:21.

g. [27:8] Ps 24:6; Hos 5:15.    h. [27:10] Is 49:15.    i. [27:11] Ps 25:4; 86:11.    j. [27:13] Ps 116:9; Is 38:11.    k. [28:1] Ps 18:2.    l. [28:1] Ps 30:4; 88:5; 143:7; Prv 1:12.    m. [28:2] Ps 134:2.    n. [28:3] Ps 26:9.

though evil is in their hearts.⁰

4 Repay them for their deeds,
    for the evil that they do.
For the work of their hands repay them;
    give them what they deserve.ᵖ
5 Because they do not understand the
    Lord's works,
    the work of his hands,�q
He will tear them down,
    never to rebuild them.

### II

6 'Blessed be the Lord,
    who has heard the sound of my
    pleading.
7 The Lord is my strength and my shield,
    in whom my heart trusts.
I am helped, so my heart rejoices;
    with my song I praise him.

### III

8 †Lord, you are a strength for your people,
    the saving refuge of your anointed.
9 Save your people, bless your inheritance;
    pasture and carry them forever!

## PSALM 29‡
### The Lord of Majesty Acclaimed
### as King of the World

¹A psalm of David.

### I

Give to the Lord, you sons of God,§
    give to the Lord glory and might;
2 Give to the Lord the glory due his name.
    Bow down before the Lord's holy
    splendor!ʳ

### II

3 The voice of the Lordᵗ is over the waters;
    the God of glory thunders,
    the Lord, over the mighty waters.
4 The voice of the Lord is power;
    the voice of the Lord is splendor.ˢ
5 The voice of the Lord cracks the cedars;

the Lord splinters the cedars of
    Lebanon,
6 Makes Lebanon leap like a calf,
    and Sirion** like a young bull.
7 The voice of the Lord strikes with fiery
    flame;
8     the voice of the Lord shakes the
    desert;
    the Lord shakes the desert of
    Kadesh.
9 ††The voice of the Lord makes the deer
    dance
    and strips the forests bare.
    All in his Temple say, "Glory!"

### III

10 The Lord sits enthroned above the
    flood!‡‡
    The Lord reigns as king forever!
11 May the Lord give might to his people;§§
    may the Lord bless his people with
    peace!ᵘ

## PSALM 30¶¶
### Thanksgiving for Deliverance

¹A psalm. A song for the dedication of the Temple.*** Of David.

### I

2 I praise you, Lord, for you raised me up
    and did not let my enemies rejoice
    over me.
3 O Lord, my God,
    I cried out to you for help and you
    healed††† me.
4 Lord, you brought my soul up from
    Sheol;
    you let me live, from going down to
    the pit.‡‡‡ᵛ

### II

5 Sing praise to the Lord, you faithful;
    give thanks to his holy memory.
6 For his anger lasts but a moment;
    his favor a lifetime.

---

*[28:6] The psalmist shifts to fervent thanksgiving, prob-
ably responding to a priestly or prophetic oracle in Ps 28:5cd
(not usually transmitted) assuring the worshiper that the
prayer has been heard.

†[28:8] **Your people . . . your anointed**: salvation is more
than individual, affecting all the people and their God-given
leader.

‡[Psalm 29] The hymn invites the members of the heavenly court to acknowledge God's supremacy by ascribing
glory and might to God alone (Ps 29:1–2a, 9b). Divine glory
and might are dramatically visible in the storm (Ps 29:3–9a).
The storm apparently comes from the Mediterranean onto the
coast of Syria-Palestine and then moves inland. In Ps 29:10
the divine beings acclaim God's eternal kingship. The Psalm
concludes with a prayer that God will impart the power just
displayed to the Israelite king and through the king to Israel.

§[29:1] **Sons of God**: members of the heavenly court who
served Israel's God in a variety of capacities.

¶[29:3] **The voice of the Lord**: the sevenfold repetition of
the phrase imitates the sound of crashing thunder and may
allude to God's primordial slaying of Leviathan, the seven-
headed sea monster of Canaanite mythology.

o. [28:3] Ps 12:2; 55:22; 62:5; Prv 26:24–28.    p. [28:4] 2 Sm
3:39.    q. [28:5] Is 5:12.    r. [29:2] Ps 68:35; 96:7–9.    s. [29:4] Ps
46:7; 77:18–19; Jb 37:4; Is 30:30.

**[29:6] **Sirion**: the Phoenician name for Mount Hermon,
cf. Dt 3:9.

††[29:9b–10] Having witnessed God's supreme power (Ps
29:3–9a), the gods acknowledge the glory that befits the king
of the divine and human world.

‡‡[29:10] **The flood**: God defeated the primordial waters
and made them part of the universe, cf. Ps 89:10–13; 93:3–4.

§§[29:11] **His people**: God's people, Israel.

¶¶[Psalm 30] An individual thanksgiving in four parts:
praise and thanks for deliverance and restoration (Ps 30:2–4);
an invitation to others to join in (Ps 30:5–6); a flashback to the
time before deliverance (Ps 30:7–11); a return to praise and
thanks (Ps 30:12). Two sets of images recur: 1) going down,
death, silence; 2) coming up, life, praising. God has delivered
the psalmist from one state to the other.

***[30:1] **For the dedication of the Temple**: a later adapta-
tion of the Psalm to celebrate the purification of the Temple in
164 B.C. during the Maccabean Revolt.

†††[30:3] **Healed**: for God as healer, see also Ps 103:3;
107:20; Hos 6:1; 7:1; 11:3; 14:5.

‡‡‡[30:4] **Sheol . . . pit**: the shadowy underworld residence
of the spirits of the dead, here a metaphor for near-death.

t. [29:10] Bar 3:3.    u. [29:11] Ps 68:36.    v. [30:4] Ps 28:1; Jon 2:7.

At dusk weeping comes for the night;
    but at dawn there is rejoicing.

### III

7 Complacent,* I once said,
    "I shall never be shaken."
8 LORD, you showed me favor,
    established for me mountains of
      virtue.
But when you hid your face
    I was struck with terror.^w
9 To you, LORD, I cried out;
    with the Lord I pleaded for mercy:
10 †"What gain is there from my lifeblood,
    from my going down to the grave?
Does dust give you thanks
    or declare your faithfulness?
11 Hear, O LORD, have mercy on me;
    LORD, be my helper."

### IV

12 You changed my mourning into dancing;
    you took off my sackcloth
    and clothed me with gladness.^x
13 So that my glory may praise you
    and not be silent.
O LORD, my God,
    forever will I give you thanks.

## PSALM 31‡
### Prayer in Distress and
### Thanksgiving for Escape

1 For the leader. A psalm of David.

### I

2 In you, LORD, I take refuge;^y
    let me never be put to shame.
In your righteousness deliver me;
3     incline your ear to me;
    make haste to rescue me!
Be my rock of refuge,
    a stronghold to save me.
4 For you are my rock and my fortress;^z
    for your name's sake lead me and
      guide me.
5 Free me from the net they have set for me,
    for you are my refuge.
6 §Into your hands I commend my spirit;^a

you will redeem me, LORD, God of
    truth.
7 You hate those who serve worthless idols,
    but I trust in the LORD.
8 I will rejoice and be glad in your mercy,
    once you have seen my misery,
    [and] gotten to know the distress of
      my soul.^b
9 You will not abandon me into enemy
      hands,
    but will set my feet in a free and
      open space.

### II

10 Be gracious to me, LORD, for I am in
      distress;
    affliction is wearing down my eyes,
    my throat and my insides.
11 My life is worn out by sorrow,
    and my years by sighing.
My strength fails in my affliction;
    my bones are wearing down.^c
12 To all my foes I am a thing of scorn,
    and especially to my neighbors
    a horror to my friends.
When they see me in public,
    they quickly shy away.^d
13 I am forgotten, out of mind like the dead;
    I am like a worn-out tool.¶
14 I hear the whispers of the crowd;
    terrors are all around me.**
They conspire together against me;
    they plot to take my life.
15 But I trust in you, LORD;
    I say, "You are my God."^e
16 My destiny is in your hands;
    rescue me from my enemies,
    from the hands of my pursuers.
17 Let your face shine on your servant;^f
    save me in your mercy.
18 Do not let me be put to shame,
    for I have called to you, LORD.
Put the wicked to shame;
    reduce them to silence in Sheol.
19 Strike dumb their lying lips,
    which speak arrogantly against the
      righteous
    in contempt and scorn.^g

### III

20 How great is your goodness, Lord,
    stored up for those who fear you.
You display it for those who trust you,
    in the sight of the children of Adam.
21 You hide them in the shelter of your
      presence,
    safe from scheming enemies.

---

*[30:7] **Complacent**: untroubled existence is often seen as a source of temptation to forget God, cf. Dt 8:10–18; Hos 13:6; Prv 30:9.

†[30:10] In the stillness of Sheol no one gives you praise; let me live and be among your worshipers, cf. Ps 6:6; 88:11–13; 115:17; Is 38:18.

‡[Psalm 31] A lament (Ps 31:2–19) with a strong emphasis on trust (Ps 31:4, 6, 15–16), ending with an anticipatory thanksgiving (Ps 31:20–24). As is usual in laments, the affliction is couched in general terms. The psalmist feels overwhelmed by evil people but trusts in the "God of truth" (Ps 31:6).

§[31:6] **Into your hands I commend my spirit**: in Lk 23:46 Jesus breathes his last with this Psalm verse. Stephen in Acts 7:59 alludes to these words as he is attacked by enemies. The verse is used as an antiphon in the Divine Office at Compline, the last prayer of the day.

¶[31:13] **Like a worn-out tool**: a common comparison for something ruined and useless, cf. Is 30:14; Jer 19:11; 22:28.

**[31:14] **Terrors are all around me**: a cry used in inescapable danger, cf. Jer 6:25; 20:10; 46:5; 49:29.

---

w. [30:8] Ps 104:29.   x. [30:12] Is 61:3; Jer 31:13.   y. [31:2–4] Ps 71:1–3.   z. [31:4] Ps 18:2.   a. [31:6] Lk 23:46; Acts 7:59.

b. [31:8] Ps 10:14.   c. [31:11] Ps 32:3; 38:10–11.   d. [31:12] Jb 19:13–19.   e. [31:15] Ps 140:7; Is 25:1.   f. [31:17] Ps 67:1; Nm 6:24.   g. [31:19] Ps 12:4.

You conceal them in your tent,
away from the strife of tongues.[h]
22 Blessed be the LORD,
marvelously he showed to me
his mercy in a fortified city.
23 Though I had said in my alarm,
"I am cut off from your eyes."[i]
Yet you heard my voice, my cry for mercy,
when I pleaded with you for help.
24 Love the LORD, all you who are faithful to
him.
The LORD protects the loyal,
but repays the arrogant in full.
25 Be strong and take heart,
all who hope in the LORD.

## PSALM 32[*]
### Remission of Sin

1/Of David. A *maskil.*

I

Blessed is the one whose fault is removed,
whose sin is forgiven.
2 Blessed is the man to whom the LORD
imputes no guilt,
in whose spirit is no deceit.

II

3 Because I kept silent,[†] my bones wasted
away;
I groaned all day long.[k]
4 For day and night your hand was heavy
upon me;
my strength withered as in dry
summer heat.
*Selah*
5 Then I declared my sin to you;
my guilt I did not hide.[l]
I said, "I confess my transgression to the
LORD,"
and you took away the guilt of my sin.
*Selah*
6 Therefore every loyal person should pray
to you
in time of distress.
Though flood waters[‡] threaten,
they will never reach him.[m]
7 You are my shelter; you guard me from
distress;

with joyful shouts of deliverance you
surround me.
*Selah*

III

8 I will instruct you and show you the way
you should walk,
give you counsel with my eye upon
you.
9 Do not be like a horse or mule, without
understanding;
with bit and bridle their temper is
curbed,
else they will not come to you.

IV

10 Many are the sorrows of the wicked one,
but mercy surrounds the one who
trusts in the LORD.
11 Be glad in the LORD and rejoice, you
righteous;
exult, all you upright of heart.[n]

## PSALM 33[§]
### Praise of God's Power and Providence

I

1 Rejoice, you righteous, in the LORD;
praise from the upright is fitting.[o]
2 Give thanks to the LORD on the harp;
on the ten-stringed lyre offer praise.[p]
3 Sing to him a new song;
skillfully play with joyful chant.
4 For the LORD's word is upright;
all his works are trustworthy.
5 He loves justice and right.
The earth is full of the mercy of the
LORD.[q]

II

6 By the LORD's word the heavens were
made;
by the breath of his mouth all their
host.[¶r]
7 "He gathered the waters of the sea as a
mound;
he sets the deep into storage vaults.[s]

III

8 Let all the earth fear the LORD;
let all who dwell in the world show
him reverence.

---

*[Psalm 32] An individual thanksgiving and the second
of the seven Penitential Psalms (cf. Ps 6). The opening declaration—the forgiven are blessed (Ps 32:1–2)—arises from
the psalmist's own experience. At one time the psalmist was
stubborn and closed, a victim of sin's power (Ps 32:3–4), and
then became open to the forgiving God (Ps 32:5–7). Sin here,
as often in the Bible, is not only the personal act of rebellion
against God but also the consequences of that act—frustration and waning of vitality. Having been rescued, the psalmist can teach others the joys of justice and the folly of sin (Ps
32:8–11).

†[32:3] **I kept silent**: did not confess the sin before God.

‡[32:6] **Flood waters**: the untamed waters surrounding
the earth, a metaphor for danger.

h. [31:21] Ps 27:5.    i. [31:23] Jon 2:5.    j. [32:1] Is 1:18; Ps 65:3; Rom
4:7–8.    k. [32:3] Ps 31:11.    l. [32:5] Ps 38:19; 51:5.    m. [32:6] Ps
18:5.

§[Psalm 33] A hymn in which the just are invited (Ps 33:1–
3) to praise God, who by a mere word (Ps 33:4–5) created the
three-tiered universe of the heavens, the cosmic waters, and
the earth (Ps 33:6–9). Human words, in contrast, effect nothing (Ps 33:10–11). The greatness of human beings consists in
God's choosing them as a special people and their faithful
response (Ps 33:12–22).

¶[33:6] **All their host**: the stars of the sky are commonly
viewed as a vast army, e.g., Neh 9:6; Is 40:26; 45:12; Jer 33:22.

**[33:7] **The waters . . . as a mound**: ancients sometimes
attributed the power keeping the seas from overwhelming
land to a primordial victory of the storm-god over personified Sea.

n. [32:11] Ps 33:1.    o. [33:1] Ps 32:11; 147:1.    p. [33:2] Ps 92:4;
144:9.    q. [33:5] Ps 119:64.    r. [33:6] Gn 2:1.    s. [33:7] Ps 78:13;
Gn 1:9–10; Ex 15:8; Jos 3:16.

⁹ For he spoke, and it came to be,
    commanded, and it stood in place.ᵗ
¹⁰ The LORD foils the plan of nations,
    frustrates the designs of peoples.
¹¹ But the plan of the LORD stands forever,
    the designs of his heart through all
    generations.ᵘ
¹² Blessed is the nation whose God is the
    LORD,
    the people chosen as his
    inheritance.ᵛ

### IV

¹³ From heaven the LORD looks down
    and observes the children of Adam,ʷ
¹⁴ From his dwelling place he surveys
    all who dwell on earth.
¹⁵ The One who fashioned together their
    hearts
    is the One who knows all their
    works.

### V

¹⁶ A king is not saved by a great army,
    nor a warrior delivered by great
    strength.
¹⁷ Useless is the horse for safety;
    despite its great strength, it cannot
    be saved.
¹⁸ Behold, the eye of the LORD is upon those
    who fear him,
    upon those who count on his mercy,
¹⁹ To deliver their soul from death,
    and to keep them alive through
    famine.

### VI

²⁰ Our soul waits for the LORD,
    he is our help and shield.ˣ
²¹ For in him our hearts rejoice;
    in his holy name we trust.
²² May your mercy, LORD, be upon us;
    as we put our hope in you.

## PSALM 34*
### Thanksgiving to God Who Delivers the Just

¹Of David, when he feigned madness before
Abimelech,† who drove him out and he went
away.

### I

² I will bless the LORD at all times;
    his praise shall be always in my
    mouth.ʸ

³ My soul will glory in the LORD;
    let the poor hear and be glad.
⁴ Magnify the LORD with me;
    and let us exalt his name together.

### II

⁵ I sought the LORD, and he answered me,
    delivered me from all my fears.
⁶ Look to him and be radiant,
    and your faces may not blush for
    shame.
⁷ This poor one cried out and the LORD
    heard,
    and from all his distress he saved him.
⁸ The angel of the LORD encamps
    around those who fear him, and he
    saves them.ᶻ
⁹ Taste and see that the LORD is good;
    blessed is the stalwart one who takes
    refuge in him.ᵃ
¹⁰ Fear the LORD, you his holy ones;
    nothing is lacking to those who fear
    him.ᵇ
¹¹ The rich grow poor and go hungry,
    but those who seek the LORD lack
    no good thing.

### III

¹² Come, children,‡ listen to me;ᶜ
    I will teach you fear of the LORD.
¹³ Who is the man who delights in life,ᵈ
    who loves to see the good days?
¹⁴ Keep your tongue from evil,
    your lips from speaking lies.
¹⁵ Turn from evil and do good;ᵉ
    seek peace and pursue it.
¹⁶ The eyes of the LORD are directed toward
    the righteousᶠ
    and his ears toward their cry.
¹⁷ The LORD's face is against evildoers
    to wipe out their memory from the
    earth.
¹⁸ The righteous cry out, the LORD hears
    and he rescues them from all their
    afflictions.
¹⁹ The LORD is close to the brokenhearted,
    saves those whose spirit is crushed.
²⁰ Many are the troubles of the righteous,
    but the LORD delivers him from
    them all.
²¹ He watches over all his bones;
    not one of them shall be broken.ᵍ
²² Evil will slay the wicked;
    those who hate the righteous are
    condemned.
²³ The LORD is the redeemer of the souls of
    his servants;
    and none are condemned who take
    refuge in him.

---

*[Psalm 34] A thanksgiving in acrostic form, each line
beginning with a successive letter of the Hebrew alphabet. In
this Psalm one letter is missing and two are in reverse order.
The psalmist, fresh from the experience of being rescued (Ps
34:5, 7), can teach the "poor," those who are defenseless, to
trust in God alone (Ps 34:4, 12). God will make them powerful
(Ps 34:5–11) and give them protection (Ps 34:12–22).
    †[34:1] **Abimelech**: a scribal error for Achish. In 1 Sm 21:13–
16, David feigned madness before Achish, not Abimelech.

‡[34:12] **Children**: the customary term for students in
wisdom literature.

---

t. [33:9] Ps 148:5; Gn 1:3f; Jdt 16:14.   u. [33:11] Prv 19:21; Is
40:8.   v. [33:12] Ps 144:15; Ex 19:6; Dt 7:6.   w. [33:13] Jb 34:21;
Sir 15:19; Jer 16:17; 32:19.   x. [33:20] Ps 115:9.   y. [34:2] Ps 145:2.

z. [34:8] Ex 14:19.   a. [34:9] Ps 2:12.   b. [34:10] Prv 3:7.   c. [34:12]
Prv 1:8; 4:1.   d. [34:13–17] 1 Pt 3:10–12.   e. [34:15] Ps 37:27.
f. [34:16] Ps 33:18.   g. [34:21] Jn 19:36.

## PSALM 35*
### Prayer for Help Against Unjust Enemies

¹Of David.

**I**

†Oppose, O Lord, those who oppose me;
    war upon those who make war upon
    me.
² Take up the shield and buckler;
    rise up in my defense.
³ Brandish lance and battle-ax
    against my pursuers.
Say to my soul,
    "I am your salvation."
⁴ Let those who seek my life
    be put to shame and disgrace.
Let those who plot evil against me[h]
    be turned back and confounded.
⁵ Make them like chaff before the wind,[i]
    with the angel of the Lord driving
    them on.
⁶ Make their way slippery and dark,
    with the angel of the Lord pursuing
    them.

**II**

⁷ Without cause they set their snare for me;
    without cause they dug a pit for me.
⁸ Let ruin overtake them unawares;
    let the snare they have set catch them;
    let them fall into the pit they have
    dug.[j]
⁹ Then I will rejoice in the Lord,
    exult in God's salvation.
¹⁰ My very bones shall say,
    "O Lord, who is like you,[k]
Who rescue the afflicted from the powerful,
    the afflicted and needy from the
    despoiler?"

**III**

¹¹ Malicious witnesses rise up,
    accuse me of things I do not know.
¹² They repay me evil for good;
    my soul is desolate.[l]
¹³ ‡Yet I, when they were ill, put on
    sackcloth,
    afflicted myself with fasting,
    sobbed my prayers upon my bosom.

¹⁴ I went about in grief as for my brother,
    bent in mourning as for my mother.
¹⁵ Yet when I stumbled they gathered with
    glee,
    gathered against me and I did not
    know it.
They slandered me without ceasing;
¹⁶     without respect they mocked me,
    gnashed their teeth against me.

**IV**

¹⁷ O Lord, how long will you look on?
    Restore my soul from their
    destruction,
    my very life from lions![m]
¹⁸ Then I will thank you in the great
    assembly;
    I will praise you before the mighty
    throng.[n]
¹⁹ Do not let lying foes rejoice over me,
    my undeserved enemies wink
    knowingly.[o]
²⁰ They speak no words of peace,
    but against the quiet in the land
    they fashion deceitful speech.[p]
²¹ They open wide their mouths against me.
    They say, "Aha! Good!
    Our eyes have seen it!"[q]
²² You see this, Lord; do not be silent;[r]
    Lord, do not withdraw from me.
²³ Awake, be vigilant in my defense,
    in my cause, my God and my Lord.
²⁴ Defend me because you are just, Lord;
    my God, do not let them rejoice
    over me.
²⁵ Do not let them say in their hearts,
    "Aha! Our soul!"[§]
Do not let them say,
    "We have devoured that one!"
²⁶ Put to shame and confound
    all who relish my misfortune.
Clothe with shame and disgrace
    those who lord it over me.
²⁷ But let those who favor my just cause
    shout for joy and be glad.
May they ever say, "Exalted be the Lord
    who delights in the peace of his loyal
    servant."
²⁸ Then my tongue shall recount your justice,
    declare your praise, all the day long.[s]

## PSALM 36*
### Human Wickedness and Divine Providence

¹For the leader. Of David, the servant of the
Lord.

---

*[Psalm 35] A lament of a person betrayed by friends. The psalmist prays that the evildoers be publicly exposed as unjust (Ps 35:1–8), and gives thanks in anticipation of vindication (Ps 35:9–10). Old friends are the enemies (Ps 35:11–16). May their punishment come quickly (Ps 35:17–21)! The last part (Ps 35:22–26) echoes the opening in praying for the destruction of the psalmist's persecutors. The Psalm may appear vindictive, but one must keep in mind that the psalmist is praying for public redress now of a public injustice. There is at this time no belief in an afterlife in which justice will be redressed.

†[35:1–6] The mixture of judicial, martial, and hunting images shows that the language is figurative. The actual injustice is false accusation of serious crimes (Ps 35:11, 15, 20–21). The psalmist seeks lost honor through a trial before God.

‡[35:13, 15–17] The Hebrew is obscure.

§[35:25] **Aha! Our soul!:** an ancient idiomatic expression meaning that we have attained what we wanted.

¶[Psalm 36] A Psalm with elements of wisdom (Ps 36:2–5), the hymn (Ps 36:6–10), and the lament (Ps 36:11–13). The

h. [35:4] Ps 40:15; 71:13.  i. [35:5] Ps 1:4; 83:14; Jb 21:18.  j. [35:8] Ps 7:16; 9:16; 57:7; Prv 26:27; Eccl 10:8; Sir 27:26.  k. [35:10] Ps 86:8; 89:7, 9; Ex 15:11.  l. [35:12] Ps 27:12; 38:20–21; 109:5; Jer 18:20.

m. [35:17] Ps 17:12; 22:22; 58:7.  n. [35:18] Ps 22:23; 26:12; 35:18; 40:10; 149:1.  o. [35:19] Ps 38:17.  p. [35:20] Ps 120:6–7.  q. [35:21] Ps 40:16; Lam 2:16.  r. [35:22] Ps 22:12; 38:21; 109:1.  s. [35:28] Ps 71:15–16.

### I

2 Sin directs the heart of the wicked man;
   his eyes are closed to the fear of
      God.[t]
3 For he lives with the delusion:
   his guilt will not be known and
      hated.[*]
4 Empty and false are the words of his
      mouth;
   he has ceased to be wise and do
      good.
5 On his bed he hatches plots;
   he sets out on a wicked way;
   he does not reject evil.[u]

### II

6 [†]Lord, your mercy reaches to heaven;
   your fidelity, to the clouds.[v]
7 Your justice is like the highest mountains;
   your judgments, like the mighty
      deep;
   human being and beast you sustain,
      Lord.
8 How precious is your mercy, O God!
   The children of Adam take refuge in
      the shadow of your wings.[‡w]
9 They feast on the rich food of your house;
   from your delightful stream[x] you
      give them drink.
10 For with you is the fountain of life,[y]
    and in your light we see light.[z]
11 Show mercy on those who know you,
    your just defense to the upright of
       heart.
12 Do not let the foot of the proud overtake
       me,
    nor the hand of the wicked disturb
       me.
13 There make the evildoers fall;
    thrust them down, unable to rise.

### PSALM 37[§]
### The Fate of Sinners and
### the Reward of the Just

¹Of David.

### ALEPH
Do not be provoked by evildoers;
   do not envy those who do wrong.[a]
2 Like grass they wither quickly;
   like green plants they wilt away.[b]
### BETH
3 Trust in the Lord and do good
   that you may dwell in the land[c] and
      live secure.[c]
4 Find your delight in the Lord
   who will give you your heart's
      desire.[d]
### GIMEL
5 Commit your way to the Lord;
   trust in him and he will act[e]
6 And make your righteousness shine like
      the dawn,
   your justice like noonday.[f]
### DALETH
7 Be still before the Lord;
   wait for him.
Do not be provoked by the prosperous,
   nor by malicious schemers.
### HE
8 Refrain from anger; abandon wrath;
   do not be provoked; it brings only
      harm.
9 Those who do evil will be cut off,
   but those who wait for the Lord will
      inherit the earth.[g]
### WAW
10 Wait a little, and the wicked will be no
       more;
    look for them and they will not be
       there.
11 But the poor will inherit the earth,[h]
    will delight in great prosperity.
### ZAYIN
12 The wicked plot against the righteous
    and gnash their teeth at them;
13 But my Lord laughs at them,[i]
    because he sees that their day is
       coming.
### HETH
14 The wicked unsheath their swords;
    they string their bows
To fell the poor and oppressed,

---

rule of sin over the wicked (Ps 36:2–5) is contrasted with the rule of divine love and mercy over God's friends (Ps 36:6–10). The Psalm ends with a prayer that God's guidance never cease (Ps 36:11–12).
  *[36:3] **Hated**: punished by God.
  †[36:6–7] God actively controls the entire world.
  ‡[36:8] **The shadow of your wings**: metaphor for divine protection. It probably refers to the winged cherubim in the holy of holies in the Temple, cf. 1 Kgs 6:23–28, 32; 2 Chr 3:10–13; Ez 1:4–9.
  §[Psalm 37] The Psalm responds to the problem of evil, which the Old Testament often expresses as a question: why do the wicked prosper and the good suffer? The Psalm answers that the situation is only temporary. God will reverse things, rewarding the good and punishing the wicked here

on earth. The perspective is concrete and earthbound: people's very actions place them among the ranks of the good or wicked. Each group or "way" has its own inherent dynamism—eventual frustration for the wicked, eventual reward for the just. The Psalm is an acrostic, i.e., each section begins with a successive letter of the Hebrew alphabet. Each section has its own imagery and logic.
  ¶[37:3] **The land**: the promised land, Israel, which became for later interpreters a type or figure of heaven, cf. Heb 11:9–10, 13–16. The New Testament Beatitudes (Mt 5:3–12; Lk 6:20–26) have been influenced by the Psalm, especially their total reversal of the present and their interpretation of the happy future as possession of the land.

---

t. [36:2] Rom 3:18.   u. [36:5] Mi 2:1.   v. [36:6] Ps 57:11; 71:19.
w. [36:8] Ps 17:8.   x. [36:9] Gn 2:8, 10.   y. [36:10] Jn 4:14.
z. [36:10] Ps 80:4, 8, 20.

a. [37:1] Prv 3:31; 23:17; 24:1, 19.   b. [37:2] Ps 90:5–6; 102:12; 103:15–16; Jb 14:2; Is 40:7.   c. [37:3] Ps 128:2.   d. [37:4] Prv 10:24.   e. [37:5] Ps 55:23; Prv 3:5; 16:3.   f. [37:6] Wis 5:6; Is 58:10.   g. [37:9] Prv 25:13; Prv 2:21; Is 57:13.   h. [37:11] Mt 5:4.   i. [37:13] Ps 2:4; 59:9; Wis 4:18.

to slaughter those whose way is
upright.[j]

15 Their swords will pierce their own hearts;
their bows will be broken.

### TETH

16 Better the meagerness of the righteous one
than the plenty of the wicked.[k]

17 The arms of the wicked will be broken,
while the LORD will sustain the
righteous.

### YODH

18 The LORD knows the days of the
blameless;
their heritage lasts forever.

19 They will not be ashamed when times are
bad;
in days of famine they will be
satisfied.

### KAPH

20 The wicked perish,
enemies of the LORD;
They shall be consumed like fattened
lambs;
like smoke they disappear.[l]

### LAMEDH

21 The wicked one borrows but does not
repay;
the righteous one is generous and
gives.

22 For those blessed by the Lord will inherit
the earth,
but those accursed will be cut off.

### MEM

23 The valiant one whose steps are guided by
the LORD,
who will delight in his way,[m]

24 May stumble, but he will never fall,
for the LORD holds his hand.

### NUN

25 Neither in my youth, nor now in old age
have I seen the righteous one
abandoned[n]
or his offspring begging for bread.

26 All day long he is gracious and lends,
and his offspring become a blessing.

### SAMEKH

27 Turn from evil and do good,
that you may be settled forever.[o]

28 For the LORD loves justice
and does not abandon the faithful.

### AYIN

When the unjust are destroyed,
and the offspring of the wicked cut off,

29 The righteous will inherit the earth
and dwell in it forever.[p]

### PE

30 The mouth of the righteous utters
wisdom;[q]
his tongue speaks what is right.

31 God's teaching is in his heart;[r]
his steps do not falter.

### SADHE

32 The wicked spies on the righteous
and seeks to kill him.

33 But the LORD does not abandon him in
his power,
nor let him be condemned when
tried.

### QOPH

34 Wait eagerly for the LORD,
and keep his way;[s]
He will raise you up to inherit the earth;
you will see when the wicked are
cut off.

### RESH

35 I have seen a ruthless scoundrel,
spreading out like a green cedar.[t]

36 When I passed by again, he was gone;
though I searched, he could not be
found.

### SHIN

37 Observe the person of integrity and mark
the upright;
Because there is a future for a man
of peace.[u]

38 Sinners will be destroyed together;
the future of the wicked will be cut
off.

### TAW

39 The salvation of the righteous is from the
LORD,
their refuge in a time of distress.[v]

40 The LORD helps and rescues them,
rescues and saves them from the
wicked,
because they take refuge in him.

## PSALM 38*
### Prayer of an Afflicted Sinner

1 A psalm of David. For remembrance.

### I

2 LORD, do not punish me in your anger;
in your wrath do not chastise me![w]

3 Your arrows have sunk deep in me;[x]
your hand has come down upon me.

4 There is no wholesomeness in my flesh
because of your anger;
there is no health in my bones
because of my sin.[y]

5 My iniquities overwhelm me,
a burden too heavy for me.[z]

---

*[Psalm 38] In this lament, one of the Penitential Psalms
(cf. Ps 6), the psalmist acknowledges the sin that has brought
physical and mental sickness and social ostracism. There is
no one to turn to for help; only God can undo the past and
restore the psalmist.

r. [37:31] Ps 40:9; Dt 6:6; Is 51:7; Jer 31:33.  s. [37:34] Ps 31:24.
t. [37:35] Ps 92:8–9; Is 2:13; Ez 31:10–11.  u. [37:37] Prv 23:18;
24:14.  v. [37:39] Ps 9:10; Is 25:4.  w. [38:2] Ps 6:2.  x. [38:3] Jb 6:4;
Lam 3:12; Ps 31:11; 64:7.  y. [38:4] Is 1:5–6.  z. [38:5] Ps 40:13;
Ezr 9:6.

j. [37:14] Ps 11:2; 57:5; 64:4.  k. [37:16] Prv 15:16; 16:8.  l. [37:20]
Wis 5:14.  m. [37:23] Prv 20:24.  n. [37:25] Jb 4:7; Sir 2:10.
o. [37:27] Ps 34:14–15; Am 5:14.  p. [37:29] Ps 25:13; Prv 2:21; Is
57:13.  q. [37:30] Prv 10:31.

### II

6 Foul and festering are my sores
        because of my folly.
7 I am stooped and deeply bowed;[a]
        every day I go about mourning.
8 My loins burn with fever;
        there is no wholesomeness in my
            flesh.
9 I am numb and utterly crushed;
        I wail with anguish of heart.[b]
10 My Lord, my deepest yearning is before
            you;
        my groaning is not hidden from you.
11 My heart shudders, my strength forsakes
            me;
        the very light of my eyes has failed.[c]
12 Friends and companions shun my disease;
        my neighbors stand far off.
13 Those who seek my life lay snares for me;
        they seek my misfortune, they speak
            of ruin;
        they plot treachery every day.

### III

14 But I am like the deaf, hearing nothing,
        like the mute, I do not open my
            mouth,
15 I am even like someone who does not
            hear,
        who has no answer ready.
16 LORD, it is for you that I wait;
        O Lord, my God, you respond.[d]
17 For I have said that they would gloat over
            me,
        exult over me if I stumble.

### IV

18 I am very near to falling;
        my wounds are with me always.
19 I acknowledge my guilt
        and grieve over my sin.[e]
20 My enemies live and grow strong,
        those who hate me grow numerous
            fraudulently,
21 Repaying me evil for good,
        accusing me for pursuing good.[f]
22 Do not forsake me, O LORD;
        my God, be not far from me![g]
23 Come quickly to help me,[h]
        my Lord and my salvation!

## PSALM 39[*]
### The Vanity of Life

1 For the leader, for Jeduthun.[i] A psalm of David.

### I

2 I said, "I will watch my ways,
        lest I sin with my tongue;
        I will keep a muzzle on my mouth."
3 Mute and silent before the wicked,
        I refrain from good things.
    But my sorrow increases,
4        my heart smolders within me.[j]
    In my sighing a fire blazes up,
        and I break into speech:

### II

5 LORD, let me know my end, the number
            of my days,
        that I may learn how frail I am.
6 To be sure, you establish the expanse of
            my days;
        indeed, my life is as nothing before
            you.
    Every man is but a breath.[k]
                                        Selah

### III

7 Man goes about as a mere phantom;
        they hurry about, although in vain;
    he heaps up stores without knowing
            for whom.
8 And now, LORD, for what do I wait?
        You are my only hope.
9 From all my sins deliver me;
        let me not be the taunt of fools.

10 I am silent and do not open my mouth
        because you are the one who did this.
11 Take your plague away from me;
        I am ravaged by the touch of your
            hand.
12 You chastise man with rebukes for sin;
        like a moth you consume his
            treasures.
    Every man is but a breath.
                                        Selah
13 Listen to my prayer, LORD, hear my cry;
        do not be deaf to my weeping!
    For I am with you like a foreigner,
        a refugee, like my ancestors.[l]
14 Turn your gaze from me, that I may smile
        before I depart to be no more.

## PSALM 40[†]
### Gratitude and Prayer for Help

1 For the leader. A psalm of David.

---

*[Psalm 39] The lament of a mortally ill person who at first had resolved to remain silently submissive (Ps 39:2–4). But the grief was too much and now the psalmist laments the brevity and vanity of life (Ps 39:5–7), yet remaining hopeful (Ps 39:8–10). The psalmist continues to express both acceptance of the illness and hope for healing in Ps 39:11–13.

†[Psalm 40] A thanksgiving (Ps 40:2–13) has been combined with a lament (Ps 40:14–17) that appears also in Ps 70. The psalmist describes the rescue in spatial terms—being raised up from the swampy underworld to firm earth where one can praise God (Ps 40:2–4). All who trust God will experience like protection (Ps 40:5–6)! The Psalm stipulates the precise mode of thanksgiving: not animal sacrifice but open and enthusiastic proclamation of the salvation just experienced (Ps 40:7–11). A prayer for protection concludes (Ps 40:12–17).

a. [38:7] Ps 35:14.   b. [38:9] Ps 102:4–6.   c. [38:11] Ps 6:8; 31:10.
d. [38:16] Ps 13:4.   e. [38:19] Ps 32:5; 51:5.   f. [38:21] Ps 109:5.
g. [38:22] Ps 22:2, 12, 20; 35:22.   h. [38:23] Ps 40:14.   i. [39:1]
1 Chr 16:41; Ps 62:1; 77:1.

j. [39:4] Jer 20:9.   k. [39:6] Ps 62:10; 90:9–10; 144:4; Jb 7:6, 16; 14:1,
5; Eccl 6:12; Wis 2:5.   l. [39:13] Ps 119:19; Gn 23:4; Heb 11:13; 1 Pt
2:11.

A

2 Surely, I wait for the LORD;
　　who bends down to me and hears
　　　my cry;[m]
3 Draws me up from the pit of destruction,
　　out of the muddy clay,[n]
　Sets my feet upon rock,
　　steadies my steps,
4 And puts a new song* in my mouth,[o]
　　a hymn to our God.
　Many shall look on in fear
　　and they shall trust in the LORD.
5 Blessed the man who sets
　　his security in the LORD,
　who turns not to the arrogant
　　or to those who stray after falsehood.[p]
6 You, yes you, O LORD, my God,
　　have done many wondrous deeds!
　And in your plans for us
　　there is none to equal you.[q]
　Should I wish to declare or tell them,
　　too many are they to recount.[r]
7 †Sacrifice and offering you do not want;[s]
　　you opened my ears.
　Holocaust and sin-offering you do not
　　request;
8 　so I said, "See; I come
　　with an inscribed scroll written
　　　upon me.
9 I delight to do your will, my God;
　　your law is in my inner being!"[t]
10 When I sing of your righteousness
　　in a great assembly,
　See, I do not restrain my lips;
　　as you, LORD, know.[u]
11 I do not conceal your righteousness
　　within my heart;
　I speak of your loyalty and your salvation.
　　I do not hide your mercy or
　　　faithfulness from a great
　　　assembly.
12 LORD, may you not withhold
　　your compassion from me;
　May your mercy and your faithfulness
　　continually protect me.[v]

B

13 But evils surround me
　　until they cannot be counted.
　My sins overtake me,
　　so that I can no longer see.
　They are more numerous than the hairs of
　　my head;

　　my courage fails me.[w]
14 LORD, graciously rescue me![x]
　　Come quickly to help me, LORD!
15 May those who seek to destroy my life
　　be shamed and confounded.
　Turn back in disgrace
　　those who desire my ruin.[y]
16 Let those who say to me "Aha!"[z]
　　Be made desolate on account of
　　　their shame.
17 While those who seek you
　　rejoice and be glad in you.
　May those who long for your salvation
　　always say, "The LORD is great."[a]
18 Though I am afflicted and poor,
　　my Lord keeps me in mind.
　You are my help and deliverer;
　　my God, do not delay!

## PSALM 41‡
### Thanksgiving After Sickness

1 For the leader. A psalm of David.

I

2 Blessed the one concerned for the poor;[§]
　　on a day of misfortune, the LORD
　　　delivers him.[b]
3 The LORD keeps and preserves him,
　　makes him blessed in the land,
　　and does not betray him to his
　　　enemies.
4 The LORD sustains him on his sickbed,
　　you turn down his bedding
　　　whenever he is ill.[¶]

II

5 Even I have said, "LORD, take note of me;
　　heal me, although I have sinned
　　　against you.
6 My enemies say bad things against me:
　　'When will he die and his name be
　　　forgotten?'
7 When someone comes to visit me, he
　　speaks without sincerity.
　His heart stores up malice;
　　when he leaves, he gossips.[c]
8 All those who hate me whisper together
　　against me;
　　they imagine the worst about me:

---

‡[Psalm 41] A thanksgiving for rescue from illness (Ps 41:4, 5, 9). Many people, even friends, have interpreted the illness as a divine punishment for sin and have ostracized the psalmist (Ps 41:5–11). The healing shows the return of God's favor and rebukes the psalmist's detractors (Ps 41:12–13).

§[41:2] Blessed the one concerned for the poor: cf. Ps 32:1–2; 34:9; 40:5; 65:5. The psalmist's statement about God's love of the poor is based on the experience of being rescued (Ps 41:1–3).

¶[41:4] You turn down his bedding whenever he is ill: the Hebrew is obscure. It suggests ongoing attentive care of the one who is sick.

---

*[40:4] A new song: a song in response to the new action of God (cf. Ps 33:3; 96:1; 144:9; 149:1; Is 42:10). Giving thanks is not purely a human response but is itself a divine gift.

†[40:7–9] Obedience is better than sacrifice (cf. 1 Sm 15:22; Is 1:10–20; Hos 6:6; Am 5:22–25; Mi 6:6–8; Acts 7:42–43 [quoting Am 5:25–26]). Heb 10:5–9 quotes the somewhat different Greek version and interprets it as Christ's self-oblation.

---

m. [40:2] Lam 3:25.　n. [40:3] Ps 28:1; 30:4; 69:3, 15–16; 88:5; Prv 1:12; Jon 2:7.　o. [40:4] Ps 33:3.　p. [40:5] Ps 1:1; Prv 16:20; Jer 17:7.　q. [40:6] Ps 35:10.　r. [40:6] Ps 71:15; 139:17–18.　s. [40:7–9] Heb 10:5–7; Ps 51:18–19; Am 5:22; Hos 6:6; Is 1:11–15.　t. [40:9] Ps 37:31.　u. [40:10] Ps 22:23; 26:12; 35:18; 149:1.　v. [40:12] Ps 89:34.

w. [40:13] Ps 38:5, 11; Ezr 9:6.　x. [40:14–18] Ps 70:2–6; 71:12.　y. [40:15] Ps 35:4, 26.　z. [40:16] Ps 35:21, 25.　a. [40:17] Ps 35:27.　b. [41:2] Tb 4:7–11.　c. [41:7] Ps 31:12; 38:12–13; 88:8; Jb 19:13–19; Jer 20:10.

⁹ 'He has had ruin poured over him;
    that one lying down will never rise
      again.'
¹⁰ 'Even my trusted friend,
    who ate my bread,
    has raised his heel against me.ᵈ

### III

¹¹ "But you, LORD, take note of me to raise
    me up
    that I may repay them."†

¹² By this I will know you are pleased with
    me,
    that my enemy no longer shouts in
      triumph over me.
¹³ In my integrity may you support me
    and let me stand in your presence
      forever.
¹⁴ ‡Blessed be the LORD, the God of Israel,
    from all eternity and forever.
    Amen. Amen.ᵉ

### Second Book—Psalms 42–72

### PSALM 42§
### Longing for God's Presence in the Temple

¹For the leader. A *maskil* of the Korahites.¶

### I

² As the deer longs for streams of water,ᶠ
    so my soul longs for you, O God.
³ My soul thirsts for God, the living God.
    When can I enter and see the face
      of God?**ᵍ
⁴ My tears have been my bread day and
    night,ʰ
    as they ask me every day, "Where is
      your God?"ⁱ
⁵ Those times I recall
    as I pour out my soul,ʲ

When I would cross over to the shrine of
    the Mighty One,††
    to the house of God,
Amid loud cries of thanksgiving,
    with the multitude keeping festival.ᵏ
⁶ Why are you downcast, my soul;
    why do you groan within me?
Wait for God, for I shall again praise him,
    my savior and my God.

### II

⁷ My soul is downcast within me;
    therefore I remember you
From the land of the Jordan‡‡ and
    Hermon,
    from Mount Mizar,ˡ
⁸ §§Deep calls to deep
    in the roar of your torrents,
    and all your waves and breakers
      sweep over me.ᵐ
⁹ By day may the LORD send his mercy,
    and by night may his righteousness
      be with me!
    I will pray¶¶ to the God of my life,
¹⁰ I will say to God, my rock:
    "Why do you forget me?"ⁿ
Why must I go about mourning
    with the enemy oppressing me?"
¹¹ It shatters my bones, when my adversaries
    reproach me,
    when they say to me every day:
      "Where is your God?"
¹² Why are you downcast, my soul,
    why do you groan within me?
Wait for God, for I shall again praise him,
    my savior and my God.

### PSALM 43

¹ Grant me justice, O God;
    defend me from a faithless people;
    from the deceitful and unjust rescue
      me.ᵒ
² You, O God, are my strength.
    Why then do you spurn me?
Why must I go about mourning,
    with the enemy oppressing me?
³ ᵖSend your light and your fidelity,***
    that they may be my guide;�q

---

*[41:10] **Even my trusted friend . . . has raised his heel against me:** Jn 13:18 cites this verse to characterize Judas as a false friend. **Raised his heel against me:** an interpretation of the unclear Hebrew, "made great the heel against me."

†[41:11] **That I may repay them:** the healing itself is an act of judgment through which God decides for the psalmist and against the false friends. The prayer is not necessarily for strength to punish enemies.

‡[41:14] The doxology, not part of the Psalm, marks the end of the first of the five books of the Psalter, cf. Ps 72:18–20; 89:53; 106:48.

§[Psalms 42–43] Ps 42–43 form a single lament of three sections, each section ending in an identical refrain (Ps 42:6, 12; 43:5). The psalmist is far from Jerusalem, and longs for the divine presence that Israel experienced in the Temple liturgy. Despite sadness, the psalmist hopes once again to join the worshiping crowds.

¶[42:1] **The Korahites:** a major guild of Temple singers (2 Chr 20:19) whose name appears in the superscriptions of Ps 42; 44–49; 84–85; 87–88.

**[42:3] **See the face of God:** "face" designates a personal presence (Gn 33:10; Ex 10:28–29; 2 Sm 17:11). The expressions "see God/God's face" occur elsewhere (Ps 11:7; 17:15; cf. Ex 24:10; 33:7–11; Jb 33:26) for the presence of God in the Temple.

††[42:5] **The shrine of the Mighty One:** this reading follows the tradition of the Septuagint and the Vulgate.

‡‡[42:7] **From the land of the Jordan:** the sources of the Jordan in the foothills of Mount Hermon in present-day southern Lebanon. Mount Mizar is presumed to be a mountain in the same range.

§§[42:8] **Deep calls to deep:** to the psalmist, the waters arising in the north are overwhelming and far from God's presence, like the waters of chaos (Ps 18:5; 69:2–3, 15; Jon 2:3–6).

¶¶[42:9–10] **I will pray . . . I will say:** in the midst of his depression the psalmist turns to prayer. Despite his situation he trusts the Lord to deliver him from his sorrow so that he may enter the Temple precincts and praise him once again (Ps 43:3–4, 5b).

***[43:3] **Your light and your fidelity:** a pair of divine attributes personified as guides for the pilgrimage. As in Ps 42:9

---

d. [41:10] Ps 55:14–15; Jn 13:18.   e. [41:14] Neh 9:5.   f. [42:2–3] Ps 63:2; 84:3; 143:6; Is 26:9.   g. [42:3] Ps 27:4.   h. [42:4] Ps 80:6; 102:10.   i. [42:4] Ps 79:10; Jl 2:17.   j. [42:5] Lam 3:20.

k. [42:5] Ps 122:5.   l. [42:7] Ps 43:3.   m. [42:8] Ps 18:5; 32:6; 69:2; 88:8; Jon 2:4.   n. [42:10] Ps 18:2; 31:3–4.   o. [43:1] Ps 119:154.   p. [43:3] Ps 18:29; 27:1; 36:10; Mi 7:8.   q. [43:3] Ps 122:1.

Let them bring me to your holy
  mountain,
    to the place of your dwelling,
⁴ That I may come to the altar of God,
    to God, my joy, my delight.
  Then I will praise you with the harp,
    O God, my God.
⁵ Why are you downcast, my soul?
    Why do you groan within me?
  Wait for God, for I shall again praise him,
    my savior and my God.

## PSALM 44*
### God's Past Favor and Israel's Present Need

¹For the leader. A *maskil* of the Korahites.

I

² O God, we have heard with our own ears;
    our ancestors have told us*r*
  The deeds you did in their days,
    with your own hand in days of old:
³ You rooted out nations to plant them,*s*
    crushed peoples and expelled them.
⁴ Not with their own swords did they
      conquer the land,*t*
    nor did their own arms bring victory;
  It was your right hand, your own arm,
    the light of your face for you favored
      them.*u*
⁵ You are my king and my God,*v*
    who bestows victories on Jacob.
⁶ Through you we batter our foes;
    through your name we trample our
      adversaries.
⁷ Not in my bow do I trust,
    nor does my sword bring me victory.
⁸ You have brought us victory over our
      enemies,
    shamed those who hate us.
⁹ In God we have boasted all the day long;
    your name we will praise forever.
                                    *Selah*

II

¹⁰ *w*But now you have rejected and disgraced
      us;
    you do not march out with our
      armies.*x*
¹¹ You make us retreat† before the foe;

those who hate us plunder us at
      will.*y*
¹² You hand us over like sheep to be
      slaughtered,
    scatter us among the nations.*z*
¹³ You sell your people for nothing;
    you make no profit from their sale.*a*
¹⁴ You make us the reproach of our
      neighbors,*b*
    the mockery and scorn of those
      around us.
¹⁵ You make us a byword among the nations;
    the peoples shake their heads at us.
¹⁶ All day long my disgrace is before me;
    shame has covered my face
¹⁷ At the sound of those who taunt and
      revile,
    at the sight of the enemy and
      avenger.

III

¹⁸ All this has come upon us,
    though we have not forgotten you,
    nor been disloyal to your covenant.
¹⁹ ‡Our hearts have not turned back,
    nor have our steps strayed from
      your path.
²⁰ Yet you have left us crushed,
    desolate in a place of jackals;§*c*
    you have covered us with a shadow
      of death.
²¹ If we had forgotten the name of our God,
    stretched out our hands to another
      god,
²² Would not God have discovered this,
    God who knows the secrets of the
      heart?
²³ For you we are slain all the day long,
    considered only as sheep to be
      slaughtered.*d*

IV

²⁴ Awake! Why do you sleep, O Lord?
    Rise up! Do not reject us forever!*e*
²⁵ Why do you hide your face;*f*
    why forget our pain and misery?
²⁶ For our soul has been humiliated in the
      dust;*g*
    our belly is pressed to the earth.
²⁷ Rise up, help us!
    Redeem us in your mercy.

---

the psalmist prays that these divine attributes lead him back
to Jerusalem and ultimately to God's presence in the Temple.
   *[Psalm 44] In this lament the community reminds God
of past favors which it has always acknowledged (Ps 44:2–9).
But now God has abandoned Israel to defeat and humiliation
(Ps 44:10–17), though the people are not conscious of any sin
against the covenant (Ps 44:18–23). They struggle with being
God's special people amid divine silence; yet they continue to
pray (Ps 44:24–26).
   †[44:11] **You make us retreat**: the corollary of Ps 44:3.
Defeat, like victory, is God's doing; neither Israel nor its enemies can claim credit (Ps 44:23).

‡[44:19] **Our hearts have not turned back**: Israel's defeat
was not caused by its lack of fidelity.
   §[44:20] **A place of jackals**: following Israel's defeat and
exile (Ps 44:11–12), the land lies desolate, inhabited only by
jackals, cf. Is 13:22; Jer 9:10; 10:22. Others take *tannim* as "sea
monster" (cf. Ez 29:3; 32:2) and render: "you crushed us as
you did the sea monster."

---

r. [44:2] Ps 78:3.   s. [44:3] Ps 78:55; 80:9f.   t. [44:4] Dt 8:17f;
Jos 24:12.   u. [44:4] Ps 4:7; 31:17; 67:2; 80:4; Nm 6:25; Dn
9:17.   v. [44:5] Ps 145:1.   w. [44:10–27] Ps 89:39–52.   x. [44:10]
Ps 60:12.

y. [44:11] Lv 26:17; Dt 28:25.   z. [44:12] Lv 26:33; Dt 28:64.
a. [44:13] Dt 32:30; Is 52:3.   b. [44:14–17] Ps 79:4; 80:7; 123:3–4;
Jb 12:4; Dn 9:16.   c. [44:20] Jer 9:10.   d. [44:23] Rom 8:36.
e. [44:24] Ps 10:1; 74:1; 77:8; 79:5; 83:2.   f. [44:25] Ps 10:11; 89:47;
Jb 13:24.   g. [44:26] Ps 119:25.

## PSALM 45[*]
### Song for a Royal Wedding

[1] For the leader; according to "Lilies." A *maskil* of the Korahites. A love song.

I

[2] My heart is stirred by a noble theme,
     as I sing my ode to the king.
     My tongue is the pen of a nimble
       scribe.

II

[3] You are the most handsome of men;
     fair speech has graced your lips,
     for God has blessed you forever.[h]
[4] Gird your sword upon your hip, mighty
       warrior!
     In splendor and majesty ride on
       triumphant![i]
[5] In the cause of truth, meekness, and
       justice
     may your right hand show your
       wondrous deeds.
[6] Your arrows are sharp;
     peoples will cower at your feet;
     the king's enemies will lose heart.
[7] Your throne, O God,[†] stands forever;[j]
     your royal scepter is a scepter for
       justice.
[8] You love justice and hate wrongdoing;
     therefore God, your God, has
       anointed you
     with the oil of gladness above your
       fellow kings.
[9] With myrrh, aloes, and cassia
     your robes are fragrant.
     From ivory-paneled palaces[‡]
     stringed instruments bring you joy.
[10] Daughters of kings are your lovely wives;
     a princess arrayed in Ophir's gold[§]
     comes to stand at your right hand.

III

[11] Listen, my daughter, and understand;
     pay me careful heed.
     Forget your people and your father's house,[¶]

[12] that the king might desire your
       beauty.
     He is your lord;
[13]   [k]honor him, daughter of Tyre.
     Then the richest of the people
     will seek your favor with gifts.
[14] All glorious is the king's daughter as she
       enters,[l]
     her raiment threaded with gold;
[15] In embroidered apparel she is led to the
       king.
     The maids of her train are presented
       to the king.
[16] They are led in with glad and joyous
       acclaim;
     they enter the palace of the king.

IV

[17] The throne of your fathers your sons will
       have;
     you shall make them princes
       through all the land.[m]
[18] I will make your name renowned through
       all generations;
     thus nations shall praise you
       forever.[n]

## PSALM 46[**]
### God, the Protector of Zion

[1] For the leader. A song of the Korahites. According to *alamoth*.[††]

I

[2] God is our refuge and our strength,
     an ever-present help in distress.[o]
[3] [‡‡]Thus we do not fear, though earth be
       shaken
     and mountains quake to the depths
       of the sea,
[4] Though its waters rage and foam
     and mountains totter at its surging.[p]
                 *Selah*

II

[5] [§§]Streams of the river gladden the city of
       God,
     the holy dwelling of the Most High.[q]
[6] God is in its midst; it shall not be shaken;
     God will help it at break of day.[r]

---

*[Psalm 45] A song for the Davidic king's marriage to a foreign princess from Tyre in Phoenicia. The court poet sings (Ps 45:2, 18) of God's choice of the king (Ps 45:3, 8), of his role in establishing divine rule (Ps 45:4–8), and of his splendor as he waits for his bride (Ps 45:9–10). The woman is to forget her own house when she becomes wife to the king (Ps 45:11–13). Her majestic beauty today is a sign of the future prosperity of the royal house (Ps 45:14–17). The Psalm was retained in the collection when there was no reigning king, and came to be applied to the king who was to come, the messiah.

†[45:7] O God: the king, in courtly language, is called "god," i.e., more than human, representing God to the people. Heb 1:8–9 applies Ps 45:7–8 to Christ.

‡[45:9] Ivory-paneled palaces: lit., "palaces of ivory." Ivory paneling and furniture decoration have been found in Samaria and other ancient Near Eastern cities, cf. Am 3:15.

§[45:10] Ophir's gold: uncertain location, possibly a region on the coast of southern Arabia or eastern Africa, famous for its gold, cf. 1 Kgs 9:28; 10:11; Jb 22:24.

¶[45:11] Forget your people and your father's house: the bride should no longer consider herself a daughter of her father's house, but the wife of the king—the queen.

**[Psalm 46] A song of confidence in God's protection of Zion with close parallels to Ps 48. The dominant note in Ps 46 is sounded by the refrain, The LORD of hosts is with us (Ps 46:8, 12). The first strophe (Ps 46:2–4) sings of the security of God's presence even in utter chaos; the second (Ps 46:5–8), of divine protection of the city from its enemies; the third (Ps 46:9–11), of God's imposition of imperial peace.

††[46:1] Alamoth: the melody of the Psalm, now lost.

‡‡[46:3–4] Figurative ancient Near Eastern language to describe social and political upheavals.

§§[46:5] Jerusalem is not situated on a river. This description derives from mythological descriptions of the divine abode and symbolizes the divine presence as the source of all life (cf. Is 33:21; Ez 47:1–12; Jl 4:18; Zec 14:8; Rev 22:1–2).

h. [45:3] Sg 5:10–16.   i. [45:4] Ps 21:5.   j. [45:7–8] Heb 1:8–9.

k. [45:13] Ps 72:10–11; Is 60:5f.   l. [45:14–16] Ez 16:10–13. m. [45:17] Gn 17:6.   n. [45:18] Is 60:15.   o. [46:2] Ps 48:4; Is 33:2.   p. [46:4] Ps 93:3–4; Jb 9:5–6; Is 24:18–20; 54:10.   q. [46:5] Ps 48:2–3; 76:3.   r. [46:6] Is 7:14.

7 Though nations rage and kingdoms totter,
    he utters his voice and the earth melts.[s]
8 The LORD of hosts is with us;
    our stronghold is the God of Jacob.

Selah

### III

9 Come and see the works of the LORD,
    who has done fearsome deeds on
    earth;[t]
10 Who stops wars to the ends of the earth,
    breaks the bow, splinters the spear,
    and burns the shields with fire;[u]
11 v"Be still and know that I am God!
    I am exalted among the nations,
    exalted on the earth."
12 The LORD of hosts is with us;
    our stronghold is the God of Jacob.

Selah

## PSALM 47[†]
### The Ruler of All the Nations

1 For the leader. A psalm of the Korahites.

### I

2 All you peoples, clap your hands;
    shout to God with joyful cries.[w]
3 For the LORD, the Most High, is to be
    feared,
    the great king over all the earth,[x]
4 Who made people subject to us,
    nations under our feet,[y]
5 ‡Who chose our heritage for us,
    the glory of Jacob, whom he loves.[z]

Selah

### II

6 §God has gone up with a shout;
    the LORD, amid trumpet blasts.[a]
7 Sing praise to God, sing praise;
    sing praise to our king, sing praise.

### III

8 For God is king over all the earth;[b]
    sing hymns of praise.
9 God rules over the nations;
    God sits upon his holy throne.
10 The princes of the peoples assemble
    with the people of the God of
    Abraham.
    For the shields of the earth belong to God,
    highly exalted.[c]

## PSALM 48[¶]
### The Splendor of the Invincible City

1 A psalm of the Korahites.[**] A song.

### I

2 Great is the LORD and highly praised
    in the city of our God:[d]
    His holy mountain,
3     fairest of heights,
    the joy of all the earth,[e]
    Mount Zion, the heights of Zaphon,[††f]
    the city of the great king.

### II

4 God is in its citadel,
    renowned as a stronghold.
5 See! The kings assembled,
    together they advanced.
6 ‡‡When they looked they were astounded;
    terrified, they were put to flight![g]
7 Trembling seized them there,
    anguish, like a woman's labor,[h]
8 As when the east wind wrecks
    the ships of Tarshish![§§]

### III

9 §§What we had heard we have now seen
    in the city of the LORD of hosts,
    In the city of our God,
    which God establishes forever.

Selah

10 We ponder, O God, your mercy
    within your temple
11 Like your name, O God,
    so is your praise to the ends of the
    earth.[i]
    Your right hand is fully victorious.
12       Mount Zion is glad!
    The daughters of Judah rejoice
    because of your judgments![j]

---

¶[Psalm 48] A Zion hymn, praising the holy city as the invincible dwelling place of God. Unconquerable, it is an apt symbol of God who has defeated all enemies. After seven epithets describing the city (Ps 48:2–3), the Psalm describes the victory by the Divine Warrior over hostile kings (Ps 48:4–8). The second half proclaims the dominion of the God of Zion over all the earth (Ps 48:9–12) and invites pilgrims to announce that God is eternally invincible like Zion itself (Ps 48:13–14).

**[48:1] **Korahites:** see note on Ps 42:1.

††[48:3] **The heights of Zaphon:** the mountain abode of the Canaanite storm-god Baal in comparable texts. To speak of Zion as if it were Zaphon was to claim for Israel's God what Canaanites claimed for Baal. Though topographically speaking Zion is only a hill, viewed religiously it towers over other mountains as the home of the supreme God (cf. Ps 68:16–17).

‡‡[48:6] **When they looked:** the kings are stunned by the sight of Zion, touched by divine splendor. The language is that of holy war, in which the enemy panics and flees at the sight of divine glory.

§§[48:8] **The ships of Tarshish:** large ships, named after the distant land or port of Tarshish, probably ancient Tartessus in southern Spain, although other identifications have been proposed, cf. Is 2:16; 60:9; Jon 1:3.

§§[48:9] **What we had heard we have now seen:** the glorious things that new pilgrims had heard about the holy city—its beauty and awesomeness—they now see with their own eyes. The seeing here contrasts with the seeing of the hostile kings in Ps 48:6.

---

*[46:8] The first line of the refrain is similar in structure and meaning to Isaiah's name for the royal child, Emmanuel, With us is God (Is 7:14; 8:8, 10).

†[Psalm 47] A hymn calling on the nations to acknowledge the universal rule of Israel's God (Ps 47:2–5) who is enthroned as king over Israel and the nations (Ps 47:6–9).

‡[47:5] **Our heritage . . . the glory:** the land of Israel (cf. Is 58:14), which God has given Israel in an act of sovereignty.

§[47:6] **God has gone up:** Christian liturgical tradition has applied the verse to the Ascension of Christ.

---

s. [46:7] Ps 2:1–5; 48:5–8; 76:7–9; Is 17:12–14.   t. [46:9] Ps 48:9–10.
u. [46:10] Ps 76:4.   v. [46:11] Ps 48:11.   w. [47:2] Ps 89:16; Zep
3:14.   x. [47:3] Ps 95:3; Ex 15:18; Is 24:23; 52:7.   y. [47:4] Ps 2:8.
z. [47:5] Is 58:14.   a. [47:6] Ps 24:8, 10; 68:18–19; 98:6.   b. [47:8–9]
Ps 72:11; 93:1; 96:10; 97:1; 99:1; Jer 10:7.   c. [47:10] Ps 89:19; Ex 3:6;
Is 2:2–4.

d. [48:2] Ps 96:4; 145:3.   e. [48:3] Ps 50:2; Lam 2:15.   f. [48:3] Is
14:13.   g. [48:6] Jgs 5:19.   h. [48:7] Ex 15:14; Jer 4:31.   i. [48:11]
Mal 1:11.   j. [48:12] Ps 97:8.

## IV

13 Go about Zion, walk all around it,
     note the number of its towers.
14 Consider the ramparts, examine its
     citadels,
     that you may tell future generations:[k]
15 That this is God,
     our God for ever and ever.[*]
     He will lead us until death.

## PSALM 49[†]
### Confidence in God Rather than in Riches

1 For the leader. A psalm of the Korahites.[‡]
2 Hear this, all you peoples!
     Give ear, all who inhabit the world,
3 You of lowly birth or high estate,
     rich and poor together.
4 My mouth shall speak words of wisdom,
     my heart shall offer insights.[l]
5 I will turn my ear to a riddle,[§]
     expound my question on a lyre.

## I

6 Why should I fear in evil days,
     with the iniquity of my assailants
     surrounding me,
7 Of those who trust in their wealth
     and boast of their abundant riches?[m]
8 ¶No man can ransom even a brother,
     or pay to God his own ransom.[n]
9 The redemption of his soul is costly;
     and he will pass away forever.
10 Will he live on forever, then,
     and never see the Pit of Corruption?
11 Indeed, he will see that the wise die,
     and the fool will perish together
     with the senseless,[o]
     and they leave their wealth to
     others.[p]
12 Their tombs are their homes forever,
     their dwellings through all
     generations,

"They named countries after
     themselves"
13 —but man does not abide in
     splendor.
     He is like the beasts—they perish.[q]

## II

14 This is the way of those who trust in
     themselves,
     and the end of those who take
     pleasure in their own mouth.
                                              *Selah*
15 Like a herd of sheep they will be put into
     Sheol,
     and Death will shepherd them.
     Straight to the grave they descend,
     where their form will waste away,
     Sheol will be their palace.
16 But God will redeem my life,
     will take me[**] from the hand of
     Sheol.[r]
                                              *Selah*
17 Do not fear when a man becomes rich,
     when the wealth of his house grows
     great.
18 At his death he will not take along
     anything,
     his glory will not go down after
     him.[s]
19 During his life his soul uttered blessings;
     "They will praise you, for you do
     well for yourself."
20 But he will join the company of his
     fathers,
     never again to see the light.[t]
21 In his prime, man does not understand.
     He is like the beasts—they perish.

## PSALM 50[††]
### The Acceptable Sacrifice

1 A psalm of Asaph.

## I

The God of gods, the LORD,
     has spoken and summoned the
     earth
     from the rising of the sun to its
     setting.[u]
2 From Zion, the perfection of beauty,
     God shines forth.[v]

---

*[48:15] **Our God for ever and ever:** Israel's God is like Zion in being eternal and invincible. The holy city is therefore a kind of "sacrament" of God.

†[Psalm 49] The Psalm affirms confidence in God (cf. Ps 23; 27:1–6; 62) in the face of the apparent good fortune of the unjust rich, cf. Ps 37; 73. Reliance on wealth is misplaced (Ps 49:8–10) for it is of no avail in the face of death (Ps 49:18–20). After inviting all to listen to this axiom of faith (Ps 49:2–5), the psalmist depicts the self-delusion of the ungodly (Ps 49:6–13), whose destiny is to die like ignorant beasts (Ps 49:13, 18; cf. Prv 7:21–23). Their wealth should occasion no alarm, for they will come to nought, whereas God will save the just (Ps 49:14–20).

‡[49:1] **Korahites:** see note on Ps 42:1.

§[49:5] **Riddle:** the psalmist's personal solution to the perennial biblical problem of the prosperity of the wicked. **Question:** parallel in meaning to problem; in wisdom literature it means the mysterious way of how the world works.

¶[49:8] **No man can ransom even a brother:** an axiom. For the practice of redemption, cf. Jb 6:21–23. A play on the first Hebrew word of Ps 49:8, 16 relates the two verses.

**[49:16] **Will take me:** the same Hebrew verb is used of God "taking up" a favored servant: Enoch in Gn 5:24; Elijah in 2 Kgs 2:11–12; the righteous person in Ps 73:24. The verse apparently states the hope that God will rescue the faithful psalmist in the same manner.

††[Psalm 50] A covenant lawsuit stating that the sacrifice God really wants is the sacrifice of praise accompanied by genuine obedience (cf. Mi 6:1–8). It begins with a theophany and the summoning of the court (Ps 50:1–6). Then in direct address God explains what is required of the faithful (Ps 50:7–15), rebukes the hypocritical worshiper (Ps 50:16–21), and concludes with a threat and a promise (Ps 50:22–23; cf. Is 1:19–20).

---

k. [48:14]  Ps 22:31–32; 71:18.  l. [49:4]  Ps 78:2; Mt 13:35.
m. [49:7] Jb 31:24.  n. [49:8] Prv 10:15; 11:4; Ez 7:19; Mt 16:26.
o. [49:11] Eccl 2:16.  p. [49:11] Ps 39:7; Sir 11:18–19.

q. [49:13] Eccl 3:18–21.  r. [49:16]  Ps 16:10; 86:13; 103:4; 116:8.
s. [49:18] Sir 11:18–19; Eccl 5:15; 1 Tm 6:7.  t. [49:20] Jb 10:21–22.  u. [50:1] Dt 10:17; Jos 22:22.  v. [50:2] Ps 48:2.

³ Our God comes and will not be silent!
 Devouring fire precedes him,
 it rages strongly around him.ʷ
⁴ He calls to the heavens above
 and to the earth to judge his people:
⁵ "Gather my loyal ones to me,
 those who made a covenant with me
 by sacrifice."
⁶ The heavens proclaim his righteousness,
 for God himself is the judge.ˣ

*Selah*

II

⁷ "Listen, my people, I will speak;
 Israel, I will testify against you;
 God, your God, am I.
⁸ Not for your sacrifices do I rebuke you,
 your burnt offerings are always
 before me.
⁹ I will not take a bullock from your house,
 or he-goats from your folds.ʸ
¹⁰ For every animal of the forest is mine,
 beasts by the thousands on my
 mountains.
¹¹ I know every bird in the heights;
 whatever moves in the wild is mine.
¹² Were I hungry, I would not tell you,
 for mine is the world and all that
 fills it.ᶻ
¹³ Do I eat the flesh of bulls
 or drink the blood of he-goats?
¹⁴ Offer praise as your sacrifice to God;ᵃ
 fulfill your vows to the Most High.
¹⁵ Then call on me on the day of distress;ᵇ
 I will rescue you, and you shall
 honor me."

III

¹⁶ But to the wicked God says:
 "Why do you recite my
 commandments
 and profess my covenant with your
 mouth?
¹⁷ You hate discipline;
 you cast my words behind you!
¹⁸ If you see a thief, you run with him;
 with adulterers you throw in your
 lot.
¹⁹ You give your mouth free rein for evil;
 you yoke your tongue to deceit.
²⁰ You sit and speak against your brother,
 slandering your mother's son.
²¹ When you do these things should I be
 silent?
 Do you think that I am like you?
 I accuse you, I lay out the matter
 before your eyes.

IV

²² "Now understand this, you who forget
 God,
 lest I start ripping apart and there be
 no rescuer.

²³ Those who offer praise as a sacrifice
 honor me;
 I will let him whose way is steadfast
 look upon the salvation of God."ᶜ

## PSALM 51*
### The Miserere: Prayer of Repentance

¹For the leader. A psalm of David, ²when Nathan
the prophet came to him after he had gone in to
Bathsheba.ᵈ

I

³ Have mercy on me, God, in accord with
 your merciful love;
 in your abundant compassion blot
 out my transgressions.
⁴ Thoroughly wash away my guilt;
 and from my sin cleanse me.
⁵ For I know my transgressions;
 my sin is always before me.ᵉ
⁶ Against you, you alone have I sinned;
 I have done what is evil in your eyes
 So that you are just in your word,
 and without reproach in your
 judgment.ᶠ
⁷ Behold, I was born in guilt,
 in sin my mother conceived me.†ᵍ
⁸ Behold, you desire true sincerity;
 and secretly you teach me wisdom.
⁹ Cleanse me with hyssop,‡ that I may be
 pure;
 wash me, and I will be whiter than
 snow.ʰ
¹⁰ You will let me hear gladness and joy;
 the bones you have crushed will
 rejoice.

*[Psalm 51] A lament, the most famous of the seven Peni-
tential Psalms, prays for the removal of the personal and social
disorders that sin has brought. The poem has two parts of
approximately equal length: Ps 51:3–10 and Ps 51:11–19, and
a conclusion in Ps 51:20–21. The two parts interlock by repetition of "blot out" in the first verse of each section (Ps 51:3, 11),
of "wash (away)" just after the first verse of each section (Ps
51:4) and just before the last verse (Ps 51:9) of the first section,
and of "heart," "God," and "spirit" in Ps 51:12, 19. The first part
(Ps 51:3–10) asks deliverance from sin, not just a past act but its
emotional, physical, and social consequences. The second part
(Ps 51:11–19) seeks something more profound than wiping
the slate clean: nearness to God, living by the spirit of God (Ps
51:12–13), like the relation between God and people described
in Jer 31:33–34. Nearness to God brings joy and the authority
to teach sinners (Ps 51:15–16). Such proclamation is better than
offering sacrifice (Ps 51:17–19). The last two verses express the
hope that God's good will toward those who are cleansed and
contrite will prompt him to look favorably on the acts of worship offered in the Jerusalem Temple (Ps 51:19 [20–21]).

†[51:7] In sin my mother conceived me: lit., "In iniquity
was I conceived," an instance of hyperbole: at no time was the
psalmist ever without sin, cf. Ps 88:15, "I am mortally afflicted
since youth," i.e., I have always been afflicted. The verse does
not imply that the sexual act of conception is sinful.

‡[51:9] Hyssop: a small bush whose many woody twigs
make a natural sprinkler. It was prescribed in the Mosaic law
as an instrument for sprinkling sacrificial blood or lustral
water for cleansing, cf. Ex 12:22; Lv 14:4; Nm 19:18.

w. [50:3] Ps 97:3; Dn 7:10.   x. [50:6] Ps 19:2; 97:6.   y. [50:9] Ps
69:32; Am 5:21–22.   z. [50:12] Ps 24:1; 89:12; Dt 10:14; 1 Cor
10:26.   a. [50:14] Heb 13:15.   b. [50:15] Ps 77:3.

c. [50:23] Ps 91:16.   d. [51:2] 2 Sm 12.   e. [51:5] Ps 32:5; 38:19; Is
59:12.   f. [51:6] Rom 3:4.   g. [51:7] Jb 14:4.   h. [51:9] Jb 9:30; Is
1:18; Ez 36:25.

II

¹¹ Turn away your face from my sins;
   blot out all my iniquities.
¹² A clean heart create for me, God;
   renew within me a steadfast spirit.ⁱ
¹³ Do not drive me from before your face,
   nor take from me your holy spirit.ʲ
¹⁴ Restore to me the gladness of your
   salvation;
   uphold me with a willing spirit.
¹⁵ I will teach the wicked your ways,
   that sinners may return to you.
¹⁶ Rescue me from violent bloodshed, God,
   my saving God,
   and my tongue will sing joyfully of
   your justice.ᵏ
¹⁷ Lord, you will open my lips;
   and my mouth will proclaim your
   praise.
¹⁸ For you do not desire sacrifice* or I would
   give it;
   a burnt offering you would not accept.ˡ
¹⁹ My sacrifice, O God, is a contrite spirit;
   a contrite, humbled heart, O God,
   you will not scorn.

III

²⁰ †Treat Zion kindly according to your good
   will;
   build up the walls of Jerusalem.ᵐ
²¹ Then you will desire the sacrifices of the
   just,
   burnt offering and whole offerings;
   then they will offer up young bulls
   on your altar.

## PSALM 52‡
### The Deceitful Tongue

¹For the leader. A *maskil* of David, ²when Doeg
the Edomite entered and reported to Saul, saying to him: "David has entered the house of
Ahimelech."ⁿ

I

³ Why do you glory in what is evil, you who
   are mighty by the mercy of
   God?
   All day long
⁴ you are thinking up intrigues;

your tongue is like a sharpened
   razor,
   you worker of deceit.ᵒ
⁵ You love evil more than good,
   lying rather than saying what is
   right.ᵖ
                                    Selah
⁶ You love all the words that create
   confusion,
   you deceitful tongue.�q

II

⁷ God too will strike you down forever,
   he will lay hold of you and pluck you
   from your tent,
   uproot you from the land of the
   living.ʳ
                                    Selah
⁸ The righteous will see and they will fear;
   but they will laugh at him:ˢ
⁹ "Behold the man! He did not take God as
   his refuge,
   but he trusted in the abundance of
   his wealth,
   and grew powerful through his
   wickedness."ᵗ

III

¹⁰ But I, like an olive tree§ flourishing in the
   house of God,ᵘ
   I trust in God's mercy forever and
   ever.
¹¹ I will thank you forever
   for what you have done.
   I will put my hope in your name—for it
   is good,ᵛ
   —in the presence of those devoted
   to you.

## PSALM 53¶
### A Lament over Widespread Corruption

¹For the leader; according to *Mahalath*. A *maskil*
of David.

I

² The fool says in his heart,ʷ
   "There is no God."ˣ
   They act corruptly and practice injustice;
   there is none that does good.
³ God looks out from the heavens
   upon the children of Adam,ʸ
   To see if there is a discerning personᶻ
   who is seeking God.

---

*[51:18] **For you do not desire sacrifice**: the mere offering of the ritual sacrifice apart from good dispositions is not
acceptable to God, cf. Ps 50.

†[51:20–21] Most scholars think that these verses were
added to the Psalm some time after the destruction of the
Temple in 587 B.C. The verses assume that the rebuilt Temple
will be an ideal site for national reconciliation.

‡[Psalm 52] A condemnation of the powerful and arrogant (Ps 52:3–6), who bring down upon themselves God's
judgment (Ps 52:7). The just, those who trust in God alone,
are gladdened and strengthened by the downfall of their traditional enemies (Ps 52:8–9).

i. [51:12] Ez 11:19.   j. [51:13] Wis 1:5; 9:17; Is 63:11; Hg 2:5;
Rom 8:9.   k. [51:16] Ps 30:10.   l. [51:18] Ps 40:7; 50:8; Am
5:21–22; Hos 6:6; Is 1:11–15; Heb 10:5–7.   m. [51:20] Jer 31:4; Ez
36:33.   n. [52:2] 1 Sm 21:8; 22:6ff.

§[52:10] **Like an olive tree**: the righteous will flourish in
the house of God like a well-watered olive tree, cf. Ps 92:14;
128:3.

¶[Psalm 53] A lament of an individual, duplicated in Ps
14, except that "God" is used for "the LORD," and Ps 53:6 is
different, cf. Ps 14.

o. [52:4] Ps 12:3; 59:8; 120:2–3; Sir 51:3.   p. [52:5] Jer 4:22; Jn
3:19–20.   q. [52:6] Jer 9:4.   r. [52:7] Ps 27:13; 28:5; 56:14; Jb 18:14;
Prv 2:22; Is 38:11.   s. [52:8] Ps 44:14; 64:9.   t. [52:9] Jb 31:24; Prv
11:28.   u. [52:10] Ps 1:3; 92:12–14; Jer 11:16; 17:8.   v. [52:11] Ps
22:23; 26:12; 35:18; 149:1.   w. [53:2–6a] Ps 14:1–5a.   x. [53:2] Ps
10:4; 36:2; Is 32:6; Jer 5:12.   y. [53:2b–3] Rom 3:11–12.   z. [53:3]
Ps 11:4; 102:20.

4 All have gone astray;
>> each one is altogether perverse.
>> There is not one who does what is
>>> good, not even one.[a]

**II**

5 [b]Do they not know better, those who do
>> evil,
>> who feed upon my people as they
>>> feed upon bread?[c]
>> Have they not called upon God?
6 They are going to fear his name with great
>>> fear,
>> though they had not feared it before.
>> For God will scatter the bones
>> of those encamped against you.
>> They will surely be put to shame,
>> for God has rejected them.

**III**

7 Who will bring forth from Zion
>> the salvation of Israel?
>> When God reverses the captivity of his
>>> people
>> Jacob will rejoice and Israel will be
>>> glad.[d]

## PSALM 54*
### Confident Prayer in Great Peril

1 For the leader. On stringed instruments. A
*maskil* of David, 2 when the Ziphites came and
said to Saul, "David is hiding among us."[e]

**I**

3 O God, by your name[†] save me.
>> By your strength defend my cause.
4 O God, hear my prayer.
>> Listen to the words of my mouth.
5 Strangers have risen against me;
>> the ruthless seek my life;
>> they do not keep God before them.[f]
>>>>>> *Selah*

**II**

6 God is present as my helper;[g]
>> the Lord sustains my life.
7 Turn back the evil upon my foes;
>> in your faithfulness, destroy them.[h]
8 Then I will offer you generous sacrifice
>> and give thanks to your name,
>> LORD, for it is good.
9 Because it has rescued me from every
>>> trouble,
>> and my eyes look down on my foes.[i]

## PSALM 55[‡]
### A Lament over Betrayal

1 For the leader. On stringed instruments. A
*maskil* of David.

**I**

2 Listen, God, to my prayer;[j]
>> do not hide from my pleading;
3 hear me and give answer.
>> I rock with grief; I groan
4 at the uproar of the enemy,
>> the clamor of the wicked.
>> They heap trouble upon me,
>> savagely accuse me.
5 My heart pounds within me;
>> death's terrors fall upon me.
6 Fear and trembling overwhelm me;
>> shuddering sweeps over me.
7 I say, "If only I had wings like a dove
>> that I might fly away and find rest.[k]
8 Far away I would flee;
>> I would stay in the desert.[l]
>>>>>> *Selah*
9 "I would soon find a shelter from
>>> the raging wind and storm."

**II**

10 Lord, check and confuse their tongues.
>> For I see violence and strife in the
>>> city
11 making rounds on its walls day and
>>> night.
>> Within are mischief and trouble;
12 treachery is in its midst;
>> oppression and fraud never leave its
>>> streets.[m]
13 For it is not an enemy that reviled me—
>> that I could bear—
>> Not a foe who viewed me with contempt,
>> from that I could hide.
14 But it was you, my other self,
>> my comrade and friend,[n]
15 You, whose company I enjoyed,
>> at whose side I walked
>> in the house of God.

**III**

16 Let death take them;
>> let them go down alive to Sheol,[o]
>> for evil is in their homes and bellies.

---

*[Psalm 54] A lament in which the person under attack
calls directly upon God for help (Ps 54:3–5). Refusing to
despair, the psalmist hopes in God, who is active in history
and just (Ps 54:6–7). The Psalm ends with a serene promise to
return thanks (Ps 54:8–9).

†[54:3] **By your name**: one is present in one's name, hence
God as revealed to human beings.

‡[Psalm 55] The psalmist, betrayed by intimate friends (Ps
55:14–15, 20–21), prays that God punish those oath breakers
and thus be acknowledged as the protector of the wronged.
The sufferings of the psalmist include both ostracism (Ps 55:4)
and mental turmoil (Ps 55:5–6), culminating in the wish to
flee society (Ps 55:7–9). The wish for a sudden death for one's
enemies (Ps 55:16) occurs elsewhere in the Psalms; an example
of such a death is the earth opening under the wicked Dathan
and Abiram (Nm 16:31–32). The psalmist, confident of vindication, exhorts others to a like trust in the God of justice (Ps
55:23). The Psalm is not so much for personal vengeance as for
a public vindication of God's righteousness now. There was no
belief in an afterlife where such vindication could take place.

---

a. [53:4] Ps 12:2.   b. [53:5] Ps 79:6.   c. [53:5] Ps 27:2; Is 9:11.
d. [53:7] Ps 85:2.   e. [54:2] 1 Sm 23:19; 26:1.   f. [54:5] Ps 86:14.
g. [54:6] Ps 118:7.   h. [54:7] Ps 143:12.   i. [54:9] Ps 59:11; 91:8;
92:12.

j. [55:2–3] Ps 5:2–3; 86:6; 130:1–2; Lam 3:56; Jon 2:3.   k. [55:7]
Ps 11:1.   l. [55:8] Jer 9:1; Rev 12:6.   m. [55:12] Jer 5:1; 6:6; Ez
22:2; Heb 1:3; Zep 3:1.   n. [55:14] Ps 41:10; Jer 9:3; Mt 26:21–24
par.   o. [55:16] Ps 49:15; Nm 16:33; Prv 1:2; Is 5:14.

<sup>17</sup> But I will call upon God,
     and the LORD will save me.
<sup>18</sup> At dusk, dawn, and noon
     I will grieve and complain,
     and my prayer will be heard.<sup>p</sup>
<sup>19</sup> He will redeem my soul in peace
     from those who war against me,
     though there are many who oppose
     me.
<sup>20</sup> God, who sits enthroned forever,<sup>q</sup>
     will hear me and afflict them.

                            *Selah*

     For they will not mend their ways;
     they have no fear of God.
<sup>21</sup> He stretched out his hand at his friends
     and broke his covenant.
<sup>22</sup> Softer than butter is his speech,
     but war is in his heart.
     Smoother than oil are his words,
     but they are unsheathed swords.<sup>r</sup>
<sup>23</sup> Cast your care upon the LORD,
     who will give you support.
     He will never allow
     the righteous to stumble.<sup>s</sup>
<sup>24</sup> But you, God, will bring them down
     to the pit of destruction.<sup>t</sup>
     These bloodthirsty liars
     will not live half their days,
     but I put my trust in you.<sup>u</sup>

## PSALM 56<sup>*</sup>
### Trust in God

<sup>1</sup>For the director. According to *Yonath elem rehoqim.*<sup>†</sup> A *miktam* of David, when the Philistines seized him at Gath.<sup>v</sup>

                 I

<sup>2</sup> Have mercy on me, God,
     for I am treated harshly;
     attackers press me all the day.
<sup>3</sup> My foes treat me harshly all the day;
     yes, many are my attackers.
     O Most High, <sup>4</sup>when I am afraid,
     in you I place my trust.
<sup>5</sup> I praise the word of God;
     I trust in God, I do not fear.<sup>w</sup>
     What can mere flesh do to me?<sup>x</sup>

                 II

<sup>6</sup> All the day they foil my plans;
     their every thought is of evil against
     me.

<sup>7</sup> They hide together in ambush;
     they watch my every step;
     they lie in wait for my life.<sup>y</sup>
<sup>8</sup> They are evil; watch them, God!
     Cast the nations down in your anger!
<sup>9</sup> My wanderings you have noted;
     are my tears not stored in your flask,<sup>‡</sup>
     recorded in your book?<sup>z</sup>
<sup>10</sup> My foes turn back when I call on you.
     This I know: God is on my side.
<sup>11</sup> I praise the word of God,
     I praise the word of the LORD.
<sup>12</sup> In God I trust, I do not fear.
     What can man do to me?

                 III

<sup>13</sup> I have made vows to you, God;
     with offerings I will fulfill them,<sup>a</sup>
<sup>14</sup> For you have snatched me from death,
     kept my feet from stumbling,
     That I may walk before God
     in the light of the living.

## PSALM 57<sup>§</sup>
### Confident Prayer for Deliverance

<sup>1</sup>For the director. Do not destroy.<sup>¶</sup> A *miktam* of David, when he fled from Saul into a cave.<sup>b</sup>

                 I

<sup>2</sup> Have mercy on me, God,
     have mercy on me.
     In you I seek refuge.
     In the shadow of your wings<sup>**</sup> I seek refuge
     till harm pass by.<sup>c</sup>
<sup>3</sup> I call to God Most High,
     to God who provides for me.
<sup>4</sup> May God send help from heaven to save me,
     shame those who trample upon me.
     May God send fidelity and mercy.

                            *Selah*

<sup>5</sup> I must lie down in the midst of lions
     hungry for human prey.<sup>d</sup>
     Their teeth are spears and arrows;
     their tongue, a sharpened sword.<sup>e</sup>
<sup>6</sup> Be exalted over the heavens, God;
     may your glory appear above all the
     earth.<sup>f</sup>

---

‡[56:9] **Are my tears not stored in your flask:** a unique saying in the Old Testament. The context suggests that the tears are saved because they are precious; God puts a high value on each of the psalmist's troubles.

§[Psalm 57] Each of the two equal strophes contains a prayer for rescue from enemies, accompanied by joyful trust in God (Ps 57:2–5, 7–11). The refrain prays that God be manifested as saving (Ps 57:6, 12). Ps 108 is nearly identical to part of this Psalm (cf. Ps 57:8–11, Ps 108:2–6).

¶[57:1] **Do not destroy:** probably the title of the melody to which the Psalm was to be sung.

\*\*[57:2] **The shadow of your wings:** probably refers to the wings of the cherubim (powerful winged animals) whose wings spread over the ark in the inner chamber of the Temple (1 Kgs 6:23–28).

---

*[Psalm 56] Beset physically (Ps 56:2–3) and psychologically (Ps 56:6–7), the psalmist maintains a firm confidence in God (Ps 56:5, 9–10). Nothing will prevent the psalmist from keeping the vow to give thanks for God's gift of life (Ps 56:13). A refrain (Ps 56:5, 11–12) divides the Psalm in two equal parts.

†[56:1] **Yonath elem rehoqim:** Hebrew words probably designating the melody to which the Psalm was to be sung.

---

p. [55:18] Dn 6:11.   q. [55:20] Ps 29:10; 93:2; Bar 3:3.   r. [55:22] Ps 12:3; 28:3; 57:5; 62:5; 64:4; Prv 26:24–28; Jer 9:7.   s. [55:23] Ps 37:5; Prv 3:5; 16:3; 1 Pt 5:7.   t. [55:24] Ps 28:1; 30:4; 40:3; 88:5; 143:7; Prv 1:12; Jon 2:7.   u. [55:24] Ps 25:2; 56:4; 130:5.   v. [56:1] 1 Sm 21:10.   w. [56:5] Ps 130:5.   x. [56:5] Ps 118:6; Heb 13:6.

y. [56:7] Ps 140:5–6.   z. [56:9] Ps 10:14; 2 Kgs 20:5; Is 25:8; Rev 7:17.   a. [56:13] Nm 30:3.   b. [57:1] 1 Sm 22:1.   c. [57:2] Ps 17:8; 36:8.   d. [57:5] Ps 17:11–12; 22:22; 58:7.   e. [57:5] Ps 11:2; 64:4.   f. [57:6] Ps 72:19; Nm 14:21.

II

7  They have set a trap for my feet;
      my soul is bowed down;
   They have dug a pit before me.
      May they fall into it themselves!*g*

                                    *Selah*

8  My heart is steadfast, God,
      my heart is steadfast.
   I will sing and chant praise.*h*
9  Awake, my soul;
      awake, lyre and harp!
   I will wake the dawn.*i*
10 I will praise you among the peoples, Lord;
      I will chant your praise among the
         nations.*j*
11 For your mercy towers to the heavens;
      your faithfulness reaches to the
         skies.*k*
12 Exalt yourself over the heavens, God;
      may your glory appear above all the
         earth.

## PSALM 58†
### The Dethroning of Unjust Rulers

¹For the leader. Do not destroy.‡ A *miktam* of
David.

I

2  Do you indeed pronounce justice, O gods;§
      do you judge fairly you children of
         Adam?*l*
3  No, you freely engage in crime;
      your hands dispense violence to the
         earth.

II

4  The wicked have been corrupt since birth;
      liars from the womb, they have gone
         astray.
5  'Their venom is like the venom of a snake,
      like that of a serpent stopping its
         ears,*m*

---

6  So as not to hear the voice of the charmer
      or the enchanter with cunning
         spells.

III

7  O God, smash the teeth in their mouths;
      break the fangs of these lions,
         LORD!*n*
8  Make them vanish like water flowing
         away;*o*
      trodden down, let them wither like
         grass.*p*
9  Let them dissolve like a snail that oozes
         away,**
      like an untimely birth that never
         sees the sun.*q*
10 Suddenly, like brambles or thistles,
      have the whirlwind snatch them
         away.*r*
11 Then the just shall rejoice to see the
         vengeance
      and bathe their feet in the blood of
         the wicked.*s*
12 Then people will say:
      "Truly there is a reward for the just;
      there is a God who is judge on
         earth!"

## PSALM 59††
### Complaint Against Bloodthirsty Enemies

¹For the director. Do not destroy.‡‡ A *miktam* of
David, when Saul sent people to watch his house
and kill him.*t*

I

2  Rescue me from my enemies, my God;
      lift me out of reach of my foes.
3  Deliver me from evildoers;
      from the bloodthirsty save me.
4  They have set an ambush for my life;
      the powerful conspire against me.
   For no offense or misdeed of mine, LORD,
5     for no fault they hurry to take up
         arms.
   Come near and see my plight!
6     You, LORD God of hosts, are the
         God of Israel!
   Awake! Punish all the nations.
      Have no mercy on these worthless
         traitors.

                                    *Selah*

---

*[57:9] **I will wake the dawn**: by a bold figure the psalmist
imagines the sound of music and singing will waken a new
day.

†[Psalm 58] A lament expressing trust in God's power to
dethrone all powers obstructing divine rule of the world. First
condemned are "the gods," the powers that were popularly
imagined to control human destinies (Ps 58:2–3), then "the
wicked," the human instruments of these forces (Ps 58:4–6).
The psalmist prays God to prevent them from harming the
just (Ps 58:7–10). The manifestation of justice will gladden the
just; they will see that their God is with them (Ps 58:11). The
Psalm is less concerned with personal vengeance than with
public vindication of God's justice now.

‡[58:1] **Do not destroy**: probably the title of the melody to
which the Psalm was to be sung.

§[58:2] **Gods**: the Bible sometimes understands pagan
gods to be lesser divine beings who are assigned by Israel's
God to rule the foreign nations. Here they are accused of
injustice, permitting the human judges under their patronage
to abuse the righteous, cf. Ps 82.

¶[58:5–6] The image is that of a poisonous snake that is
controlled by the voice or piping of its trainer.

**[58:9] **A snail that oozes away**: empty shells suggested
to ancients that snails melted away as they left a slimy trail.

††[Psalm 59] A lament in two parts (Ps 59:2–9, 11b–17),
each ending in a refrain (Ps 59:10, 18). Both parts alternate
prayer for vindication (Ps 59:2–3, 4b–5, 11b–14) with vivid
depictions of the psalmist's enemies (Ps 59:4–5a, 7–8, 15–16).
The near curse in Ps 59:12–13 is not a crude desire for revenge
but a wish that God's just rule over human affairs be recognized now.

‡‡[59:1] **Do not destroy**: probably the title of the melody to
which the Psalm was to be sung.

---

g. [57:7] Ps 7:15; 9:16–17; 140:5–6.   h. [57:8] Ps 108:2.   i. [57:9] Jb
38:12.   j. [57:10] Ps 9:12; 18:50.   k. [57:11] Ps 36:6; 71:19.   l. [58:2]
Ps 82:2; Dt 16:19.   m. [58:5] Ps 64:4; 140:3; Rom 3:13.

n. [58:7] Ps 3:7.   o. [58:8] Wis 16:29.   p. [58:8] Ps 37:2.   q. [58:9]
Jb 3:16.   r. [58:10] Jb 21:18; Hos 13:3; Na 1:10.   s. [58:11] Ps 68:24;
Is 63:1–6.   t. [59:1] 1 Sm 19:11.

⁷ Each evening they return,
       growling like dogs, prowling the city.ᵘ
⁸ Their mouths pour out insult;
       sharp words are on their lips.
   They say: "Who is there to hear?"*
⁹ But you, LORD, laugh at them;
       you deride all the nations.ᵛ
¹⁰ My strength, for you I watch;
       you, God, are my fortress,
¹¹   my loving God.

                   II

   May God go before me,
       and show me my fallen foes.
¹² Slay them, God,
       lest they deceive my people.
   Shake them by your power;
       Lord, our shield, bring them down.
¹³ For the sinful words of their mouths and
           lips
       let them be caught in their pride.
   For the lies they have told under oathʷ
¹⁴   destroy them in anger,
       destroy till they are no more.
   Then people will know God rules over
           Jacob,
       yes, even to the ends of the earth.ˣ
                                    Selah

¹⁵ Each evening they return,
       growling like dogs, prowling the city.
¹⁶ They roam about as scavengers;
       if they are not filled, they howl.

                   III

¹⁷ But I shall sing of your strength,
       extol your mercy at dawn,
   For you are my fortress,
       my refuge in time of trouble.
¹⁸ My strength, your praise I will sing;
       you, God, are my fortress, my loving
           God.

## PSALM 60†
### Lament After Defeat in Battle

¹For the leader; according to "The Lily of. . . ."
A *miktam* of David (for teaching), ²when he
fought against Aram-Naharaim and Aram-
Zobah; and Joab, coming back, killed twelve
thousand Edomites in the Valley of Salt.ʸ

                   I

³ O God, you rejected us, broke our defenses;
       you were angry but now revive us.

⁴ You rocked the earth, split it open;ᶻ
       repair the cracks for it totters.
⁵ You made your people go through
           hardship,
       made us stagger from the wine you
           gave us.ᵃ
⁶ Raise up a banner for those who revere
           you,
       a refuge for them out of bow shot.
                                    Selah

⁷ ‡Help with your right hand and answer
           us
       that your loved ones may escape.

                   II

⁸ §In the sanctuary God promised:
       "I will exult, will apportion
           Shechem;
       the valley of Succoth§ I will measure
           out.
⁹ Gilead is mine, mine is Manasseh;
       Ephraim is the helmet for my head,
       Judah, my own scepter.¶
¹⁰ "Moab is my washbowl;
       upon Edom I cast my sandal."*ᵇ
   I will triumph over Philistia."

                   III

¹¹ Who will bring me to the fortified
           city?††
       Who will lead me into Edom?
¹² Was it not you who rejected us, God?
       Do you no longer march with our
           armies?ᶜ
¹³ Give us aid against the foe;
       worthless is human help.
¹⁴ We will triumph with the help of God,
       who will trample down our foes.

## PSALM 61‡‡
### Prayer of the King in Time of Danger

¹For the leader; with stringed instruments. Of
David.

                   I

² Hear my cry, O God,
       listen to my prayer!

---

*[59:8] **Who is there to hear?**: a sample of the enemies' godless reflection. The answer is that God hears their blasphemies.

†[Psalm 60] The community complains that God has let
the enemy win the battle (Ps 60:3–5) and asks for an assurance
of victory (Ps 60:6–7). In the oracle God affirms ownership of
the land; the invasion of other nations is not permanent and
will be reversed ultimately (Ps 60:8–10). With renewed confidence, the community resolves to fight again (Ps 60:11). The
opening lament is picked up again (Ps 60:12), but this time
with new awareness of God's power and human limitation.

---

‡[60:7–12] These verses occur again as the second half of
Ps 108.

§[60:8] **I will . . . apportion . . . measure out**: God lays
claim to these places. **The valley of Succoth**: probably the
lower stretch of the Jabbok valley.

¶[60:9] **Judah, my own scepter**: an allusion to the Testament of Jacob, Gn 49:10.

**[60:10] **Moab is my washbowl**: Moab borders the Dead
Sea, hence a metaphor for the country. **Upon Edom I cast my
sandal**: an ancient legal gesture of taking possession of land.

††[60:11] **The fortified city**: perhaps Bozrah, the fortified
capital of Edom, cf. Is 34:6; 63:1; Am 1:12.

‡‡[Psalm 61] A lament of the king who feels himself at the
brink of death (Ps 61:3) and cries out for the strong and saving presence of God (Ps 61:3b–5). The king cites the prayer
being made for him (Ps 61:7–8), and promises to give thanks
to God.

---

u. [59:7] Ps 55:11.   v. [59:9] Ps 2:4; 37:13; Wis 4:18.   w. [59:13] Prv
12:13; 18:7.   x. [59:14] Ps 83:18–19; Ez 5:13.   y. [60:2] 2 Sm 8:2, 3,
13; 1 Chr 18:2, 3, 12.

z. [60:4] Ps 75:4; Is 24:19.   a. [60:5] Ps 75:9; Is 51:17, 21–22; Jer
25:15.   b. [60:10] Ru 4:7–8.   c. [60:12] Ps 44:10.

<sup>3</sup> From the ends of the earth[*] I call;
    my heart grows faint.
Raise me up, set me on a rock,
<sup>4</sup>     for you are my refuge,
    a tower of strength against the foe.[d]
<sup>5</sup> Let me dwell in your tent forever,
    take refuge in the shelter of your
      wings.[e]

Selah

### II

<sup>6</sup> For you, O God, have heard my
    vows,
    you have granted me the heritage of
      those who revere your name.
<sup>7</sup> Add days to the life of the king;
    may his years be as from generation
      to generation;[f]
<sup>8</sup>  [g]May he reign before God forever;
    send your love and fidelity[†] to
      preserve him—[h]
<sup>9</sup> I will duly sing to your name forever,
    fulfill my vows day after day.

## PSALM 62[‡]
### Trust in God Alone

<sup>1</sup> For the leader; 'al Jeduthun.[§] A psalm of David.

### I

<sup>2</sup> My soul rests in God alone,[i]
    from whom comes my salvation.
<sup>3</sup> God alone is my rock and salvation,
    my fortress; I shall never fall.
<sup>4</sup> How long will you set yourself against a
    man?
    You shall all be destroyed,
Like a sagging wall
    or a tumbled down fence!
<sup>5</sup> Even highly placed people
    plot to overthrow him.
They delight in lies;
    they bless with their mouths,
    but inwardly they curse.[j]

Selah

### II

<sup>6</sup> My soul, be at rest in God alone,
    from whom comes my hope.
<sup>7</sup> God alone is my rock and my salvation,
    my fortress; I shall not fall.

<sup>8</sup> My deliverance and honor are with God,[k]
    my strong rock;
    my refuge is with God.
<sup>9</sup> Trust God at all times, my people!
    Pour out your hearts to God our
      refuge!

Selah

### III

<sup>10</sup> Mortals are a mere breath,
    the sons of man but an illusion;[l]
On a balance they rise;[¶]
    together they weigh nothing.
<sup>11</sup> Do not trust in extortion;
    in plunder put no empty hope.
On wealth that increases,
    do not set your heart.[m]
<sup>12</sup> "One thing God has said;
    two things I have heard:[n]
Strength belongs to God;
<sup>13</sup>     so too, my Lord, does mercy,
For you repay each man
    according to his deeds.[o]

## PSALM 63[††]
### Ardent Longing for God

<sup>1</sup> A psalm of David, when he was in the wilderness of Judah.[p]

### I

<sup>2</sup> O God, you are my God—
    it is you I seek!
For you my body yearns;
    for you my soul thirsts,
In a land parched, lifeless,
    and without water.[q]
<sup>3</sup> I look to you in the sanctuary
    to see your power and glory.
<sup>4</sup> For your love is better than life;[‡‡]
    my lips shall ever praise you!

### II

<sup>5</sup> I will bless you as long as I live;
    I will lift up my hands, calling on
      your name.
<sup>6</sup> My soul shall be sated as with choice food,

---

¶[62:10] **On a balance they rise**: precious objects were weighed by balancing two pans suspended from a beam. The lighter pan rises.

**[62:12] **One thing . . . two things**: parallelism of numbers for the sake of variation, a common device in Semitic poetry. One should not literally add up the numbers, cf. Am 1:3; Prv 6:16–19; 30:15, 18, 21.

††[Psalm 63] A Psalm expressing the intimate relationship between God and the worshiper. Separated from God (Ps 63:2), the psalmist longs for the divine life given in the Temple (Ps 63:3–6), which is based on a close relationship with God (Ps 63:7–9). May all my enemies be destroyed and God's true worshipers continue in giving praise (Ps 63:10–11)!

‡‡[63:4] **For your love is better than life**: only here in the Old Testament is anything prized above life—in this case God's love.

---

*[61:3] **Ends of the earth**: "earth" being taken in its occasional meaning "the underworld," cf. Jon 2:3.

†[61:8] **Send your love and fidelity**: as in Ps 43:3 the psalmist asks God to send these two divine attributes like angels to protect the king.

‡[Psalm 62] A song of trust displaying serenity from experiencing God's power (the refrains of Ps 62:2–3 and Ps 62:6–7) and anger toward unjust enemies (Ps 62:4–5). From the experience of being rescued, the psalmist can teach others to trust in God (Ps 62:9–12).

§[62:1] **'Al Jeduthun**: apparently the Hebrew name for the melody.

---

d. [61:4] Ps 46:2.   e. [61:5] Ps 17:8; 36:8; 57:2.   f. [61:7] Ps 21:5. g. [61:8] Ps 72:5; 89:5, 30, 37.   h. [61:8] Ps 85:11; 89:15, 25; Prv 20:28.   i. [62:2–3, 6–7] Ps 18:3; 31:3–4; 42:10; 118:8; 146:3.   j. [62:5] Ps 12:3; 28:3; 55:22; Prv 26:24–25.

k. [62:8] Ps 3:3; Is 26:4; 60:19.   l. [62:10] Ps 39:6–7; 144:4; Jb 7:16; Wis 2:5.   m. [62:11] Jb 31:25; Eccl 5:9; Jer 17:11; Mt 6:19–21, 24.   n. [62:12] Jb 40:5.   o. [62:13] Ps 28:4; 31:24; 2 Sm 3:39; Jb 34:11; Jer 17:10; Mt 16:27; Rom 2:6; 2 Tm 4:14.   p. [63:1] 1 Sm 24.   q. [63:2] Ps 42:2; 143:6; Is 26:9.

with joyous lips my mouth shall
      praise you!
7  I think of you upon my bed,
      I remember you through the
         watches of the night
8  You indeed are my savior,
      and in the shadow of your wings I
         shout for joy.[r]
9  My soul clings fast to you;
      your right hand upholds me.

### III

10  But those who seek my life will come to
      ruin;
      they shall go down to the depths of
         the netherworld!
11  Those who would hand over my life
      to the sword shall
      become the prey of jackals!
12  But the king shall rejoice in God;
      all who swear by the Lord[*] shall exult,
      but the mouths of liars will be shut![s]

### PSALM 64[†]
### Treacherous Conspirators Punished by God

1For the leader. A psalm of David.

### I

2  O God, hear my anguished voice;
      from a dreadful foe protect my life.
3  Hide me from the malicious crowd,
      the mob of evildoers.
4  They sharpen their tongues like swords,
      bend their bows of poison words.[t]
5  They shoot at the innocent from ambush,
      they shoot him in a moment and do
         not fear.
6  They resolve on their wicked plan;
      they conspire to set snares;
      they say: "Who will see us?"
7  They devise wicked schemes,
      conceal the schemes they devise;
      the designs of their hearts are hidden.[u]

### II

8  God shoots an arrow at them;
      in a moment they are struck down.[v]
9  They are brought down by their own
      tongues;
      all who see them flee.[w]
10  Every person fears and proclaims God's
      actions,
      they ponder his deeds.

11  The righteous rejoices and takes refuge in
      the Lord;
      all the upright give praise.[x]

### PSALM 65[‡]
### Thanksgiving for God's Blessings

1For the leader. A psalm of David. A song.

### I

2  To you we owe our hymn of praise,
      O God on Zion;
   To you our vows[§] must be fulfilled,
3      'you who hear our prayers.
   To you all flesh must come[y]
4      with its burden of wicked deeds.
   We are overcome by our sins;
      only you can pardon them.[z]
5  Blessed the one whom you will choose
         and bring
      to dwell in your courts.
   May we be filled with the good things of
         your house,
      your holy temple!

### II

6  You answer us with awesome deeds[**] of
      justice,
      O God our savior,
   The hope of all the ends of the earth
      and of those far off across the sea.[a]
7  You are robed in power,
      you set up the mountains by your
         might.
8  You still the roaring of the seas,[b]
      the roaring of their waves,
      the tumult of the peoples.[c]
9  Distant peoples stand in awe of your
         marvels;
      the places of morning and evening
         you make resound with joy.
10  ††You visit the earth and water it,
      make it abundantly fertile.[d]
   God's stream‡‡ is filled with water;
      you supply their grain.
   Thus do you prepare it:
11      you drench its plowed furrows,
      and level its ridges.

‡[Psalm 65] The community, aware of its unworthiness
(Ps 65:3–4), gives thanks for divine bounty (Ps 65:5), a bounty
resulting from God's creation victory (Ps 65:6–9). At God's touch
the earth comes alive with vegetation and flocks (Ps 65:10–13).

§[65:2] Vows: the Israelites were accustomed to promising
sacrifices in the Temple if their prayers were heard.

¶[65:3] To you all flesh must come: all must have recourse
to God's mercy.

**[65:6] Awesome deeds: the acts of creating—installing
mountains, taming seas, restraining nations (Ps 65:7–8)—that
are visible worldwide (Ps 65:6, 9).

††[65:10–14] Apparently a description of the agricultural
year, beginning with the first fall rains that soften the hard
sun-baked soil (Ps 65:9–10).

‡‡[65:10] God's stream: the fertile waters of the earth
derive from God's fertile waters in the heavenly realm.

*[63:12] All who swear by the Lord: to swear by a particu-
lar god meant that one was a worshiper of that god (Is 45:23;
48:1; Zep 1:5).

†[Psalm 64] A lament of a person overwhelmed by the
malice of the wicked who are depicted in the Psalms as the
enemies of the righteous (Ps 64:2–7). When people see God
bringing upon the wicked the evil they intended against others, they will know who is the true ruler of the world (Ps 64:8–
10). The final verse is a vow of praise (Ps 64:11).

r. [63:8] Ps 17:8; 36:8.   s. [63:12] Ps 107:42.   t. [64:4] Ps 11:2;
37:14; 55:22; 57:5.   u. [64:7] Ps 140:3; Prv 6:14.   v. [64:8] Ps 7:13–
14; 38:3; Dt 32:42.   w. [64:9] Ps 5:11; 44:14; 52:6.

x. [64:11] Ps 36:8; 57:2.   y. [65:3] Is 66:23.   z. [65:4] Ps 32:1–2; 78:38;
Is 1:18.   a. [65:6] Is 66:19.   b. [65:8] Ps 89:10; 107:29; Jb 38:11; Mt
8:26.   c. [65:8] Is 17:12.   d. [65:10] Lv 26:4; Is 30:23, 25; Jl 2:22–23.

With showers you keep it soft,
　　blessing its young sprouts.
12 You adorn the year with your bounty;
　　your paths* drip with fruitful rain.
13 The meadows of the wilderness also drip;
　　the hills are robed with joy.
14 The pastures are clothed with flocks,
　　the valleys blanketed with grain;
　　they cheer and sing for joy.ᵉ

## PSALM 66†
### Praise of God, Israel's Deliverer

¹For the leader. A song; a psalm.

### I

2 Shout joyfully to God, all the earth;
　　sing of his glorious name;
　　give him glorious praise.ᶠ
3 Say to God: "How awesome your deeds!
　　Before your great strength your
　　　enemies cringe.
4 All the earth falls in worship before you;ᵍ
　　they sing of you, sing of your name!"
　　　　　　　　　　　　　　　　Selah

### II

5 ‡Come and see the works of God,
　　awesome in deeds before the
　　　children of Adam.
6 He changed the sea to dry land;
　　through the river they passed on
　　　foot.ʰ
There we rejoiced in him,
7 　　who rules by his might forever,
His eyes are fixed upon the nations.
　　Let no rebel rise to challenge!
　　　　　　　　　　　　　　　　Selah

8 Bless our God, you peoples;
　　loudly sound his praise,
9 Who has kept us alive
　　and not allowed our feet to slip.ⁱ
10 You tested us, O God,
　　tried us as silver tried by fire.ʲ
11 You led us into a snare;
　　you bound us at the waist as
　　　captives.
12 §You let captors set foot on our neck;

we went through fire and water;
　　then you led us out to freedom.ᵏ

### III

13 I will bring burnt offerings¶ to your house;
　　to you I will fulfill my vows,
14 Which my lips pronounced
　　and my mouth spoke in my distress.
15 Burnt offerings of fatlings I will offer you
　　and sacrificial smoke of rams;
　　I will sacrifice oxen and goats.
　　　　　　　　　　　　　　　　Selah
16 Come and hear, all you who fear God,
　　while I recount what has been done
　　　for me.
17 I called to him with my mouth;
　　praise was upon my tongue.
18 Had I cherished evil in my heart,
　　the Lord would not have heard.
19 But God did hear
　　and listened to my voice in prayer.
20 Blessed be God, who did not reject my
　　　prayer
　　and refuse his mercy.

## PSALM 67**
### Harvest Thanks and Petition

¹For the leader; with stringed instruments. A
psalm; a song.

### I

2 May God be gracious to us†† and bless us;
　　may his face shine upon us.ˡ
　　　　　　　　　　　　　　　　Selah
3 So shall your way be known upon the earth,
　　your victory among all the nations.ᵐ
4 May the peoples praise you, God;
　　may all the peoples praise you!

### II

5 May the nations be glad and rejoice;
　　for you judge the peoples with
　　　fairness,
　　you guide the nations upon the earth.ⁿ
　　　　　　　　　　　　　　　　Selah
6 May the peoples praise you, God;
　　may all the peoples praise you!

### III

7 The earth has yielded its harvest;
　　God, our God, blesses us.ᵒ

---

*[65:12] **Paths**: probably the tracks of God's storm chariot dropping rain upon earth.

†[Psalm 66] In the first part (Ps 66:1–12), the community praises God for powerful acts for Israel, both in the past (the exodus from Egypt and the entry into the land [Ps 66:6]) and in the present (deliverance from a recent but unspecified calamity [Ps 66:8–12]). In the second part (Ps 66:13–20), an individual from the rescued community fulfills a vow to offer a sacrifice of thanksgiving. As often in thanksgivings, the rescued person steps forward to teach the community what God has done (Ps 66:16–20).

‡[66:5–6] cf. the events described in Ex 14:1–15, 21; Jos 3:11–4:24 and Ps 114.

§[66:12] **You let captors set foot on our neck**: lit., "you let men mount our heads." Conquerors placed their feet on

the neck of their enemies as a sign of complete defeat, cf. Jos 10:24. A ceremonial footstool of the Egyptian king Tutankhamen portrays bound and prostrate bodies of enemies ready for the king's feet on their heads, and one of Tutankhamen's ceremonial chariots depicts the king as a sphinx standing with paw atop the neck of an enemy.

¶[66:13] **Burnt offerings**: cf. Lv 1:3–13; 6:1–4; 22:17–20.

**[Psalm 67] A petition for a bountiful harvest (Ps 67:7), made in the awareness that Israel's prosperity will persuade the nations to worship its God.

††[67:2] **May God be gracious to us**: the people's petition echoes the blessing pronounced upon them by the priests, cf. Nm 6:22–27.

---

e. [65:14] Is 44:23.　f. [66:2] Ps 65:14; Is 44:23.　g. [66:3–4] Ps 18:45; Mi 7:17.　h. [66:6] Ps 74:15; 114:3; Ex 14:21f; Jos 3:14ff; Is 44:27; 50:2.　i. [66:9] Ps 91:12; 121:3; 1 Sm 2:9; Prv 3:23.　j. [66:10] Is 48:10.

k. [66:12] Is 43:2.　l. [67:2] Ps 4:7; 31:17; 44:4; 80:4; Dn 9:17.　m. [67:3] Jer 33:9.　n. [67:5] Ps 98:9.　o. [67:7] Ps 85:13; Lv 26:4; Ez 34:27; Hos 2:23–24.

8 May God bless us still;
   that the ends of the earth may revere
     him.

## PSALM 68*
### The Exodus and Conquest,
### Pledge of Future Help

¹For the leader. A psalm of David; a song.

### I

2 †May God arise;
   may his enemies be scattered;
   may those who hate him flee before
     him.ᵖ
3 As the smoke is dispersed, disperse them;
   as wax is melted by fire,
   so may the wicked perish before God.�q
4 Then the just will be glad;
   they will rejoice before God;
   they will celebrate with great joy.

### II

5 Sing to God, praise his name;
   exalt the rider of the clouds.‡
Rejoice before him
   whose name is the LORD.ʳ
6 Father of the fatherless, defender of
     widows—
   God in his holy abode,
7 God gives a home to the forsaken,
   who leads prisoners out to
     prosperity,
   while rebels live in the desert.§

### III

8 God, when you went forth before your
     people,ᵗ
   when you marched through the
     desert,
                   *Selah*
9 The earth quaked, the heavens poured,
   before God, the One of Sinai,
   before God, the God of Israel.
10 You poured abundant rains, God,
   your inheritance was weak and you
     repaired it.
11 Your creatures dwelt in it;
   you will establish it in your
     goodness for the poor, O God.

### IV

12 The Lord announced:
   "Those bringing news are a great
     Army.
13    The kings of the armies are in
     desperate flight.ᵘ
Every household will share the spoil,
14    though you lie down among the
     sheepfolds,ᵛ
   you shall be covered with silver as
     the wings of a dove,
   her feathers bright as fine gold."
15 When the Almighty routs the kings there,
   it will be as when snow fell on
     Zalmon.¶

### V

16 You mountain of God, mountain of
     Bashan,
   you rugged mountain, mountain of
     Bashan,
17 You rugged mountains, why look with
     envy
   at the mountain** where God has
     chosen to dwell,
   where the LORD resides forever?ʷ
18 God's chariots were myriad, thousands
     upon thousands;
   from Sinai the Lord entered the holy
     place.
19 You went up to its lofty height;
   you took captives, received slaves as
     tribute,ˣ
   even rebels, for the LORD God to
     dwell.

### VI

20 Blessed be the Lord day by day,
   God, our salvation, who carries us.ʸ
                    *Selah*

---

*[Psalm 68] The Psalm is extremely difficult because the Hebrew text is badly preserved and the ceremony that it describes is uncertain. The translation assumes the Psalm accompanied the early autumn Feast of Tabernacles (Sukkoth), which included a procession of the tribes (Ps 68:25–28). Israel was being oppressed by a foreign power, perhaps Egypt (Ps 68:31–32)—unless Egypt stands for any oppressor. The Psalm may have been composed from segments of ancient poems, which would explain why the transitions are implied rather than explicitly stated. At any rate, Ps 68:2 is based on Nm 10:35–36, and Ps 68:8–9 are derived from Jgs 5:4–5. The argument develops in nine stanzas (each of three to five poetic lines): 1. confidence that God will destroy Israel's enemies (Ps 68:2–4); 2. call to praise God as savior (Ps 68:5–7); 3. God's initial rescue of Israel from Egypt (Ps 68:8), the Sinai encounter (Ps 68:9), and the settlement in Canaan (Ps 68:10–11); 4. the defeat of the Canaanite kings (Ps 68:12–15); 5. the taking of Jerusalem, where Israel's God will rule the world (Ps 68:16–19); 6. praise for God's past help and for the future interventions that will be modeled on the ancient exodus-conquest (Ps 68:20–24); 7. procession at the Feast of Tabernacles (Ps 68:25–28); 8. prayer that the defeated enemies bring tribute to the Temple (Ps 68:29–32); 9. invitation for all kingdoms to praise Israel's God (Ps 68:33–35).

†[68:2] The opening line alluding to Nm 10:35 makes clear that God's assistance in the period of the exodus and conquest is the model and assurance of all future divine help.

‡[68:5] **Exalt the rider of the clouds**: God's intervention is in the imagery of Canaanite myth in which the storm-god mounted the storm clouds to ride to battle. Such theophanies occur throughout the Psalm: Ps 68:2–3, 8–10, 12–15, 18–19, 22–24, 29–32, 34–35. See Dt 33:26; Ps 18:8–16; Is 19:1.

§[68:7] **While rebels live in the desert**: rebels must live in the arid desert, whereas God's people will live in the well-watered land (Ps 68:8–11).

¶[68:15] **Zalmon**: generally taken as the name of a mountain where snow is visible in winter, perhaps to be located in the Golan Heights or in the mountains of Bashan or Hauran east of the Sea of Galilee.

**[68:17] **The mountain**: Mount Zion, the site of the Temple.

---

p. [68:2] Nm 10:35.   q. [68:3] Ps 97:5; Jdt 16:15; Wis 5:14; Mi 1:4.   r. [68:5] Ps 18:10; 104:3; Dt 33:26; Is 19:1.   s. [68:6–7] Ps 103:6; 146:7, 9; Ex 22:20–22; Bar 6:37.   t. [68:8–9] Ps 44:10; 114:4, 7; Jgs 5:4–5; Heb 12:26.   u. [68:13] Jgs 5:19, 22.   v. [68:14] Jgs 5:16.   w. [68:17] Ps 132:13–14; Ez 43:7.   x. [68:19] Ps 47:8; Eph 4:8–10.   y. [68:20] Ps 34:2; 145:2; Is 46:3–4; 63:9.

<sup>21</sup> Our God is a God who saves;
  escape from death is the LORD
    God's.
<sup>22</sup> God will crush the heads of his enemies,
  the hairy scalp of the one who walks
    in sin.<sup>z</sup>
<sup>23</sup> The Lord has said:
  "Even from Bashan I will fetch
    them,
  fetch them even from the depths of
    the sea.*
<sup>24</sup> You will wash your feet in your enemy's
    blood;
  the tongues of your dogs will lap
    it up."<sup>a</sup>

### VII

<sup>25</sup> †Your procession comes into view, O God,
  your procession into the holy place,
    my God and king.
<sup>26</sup> The singers go first, the harpists follow;
  in their midst girls sound the
    timbrels.<sup>b</sup>
<sup>27</sup> In your choirs, bless God;
  LORD, Israel's fountain.
<sup>28</sup> In the lead is Benjamin, few in number;
  there the princes of Judah, a large
    throng,
  the princes of Zebulun, the princes
    of Naphtali, too.<sup>c</sup>

### VIII

<sup>29</sup> Summon again, O God, your power,
  the divine power you once showed
    for us,
<sup>30</sup> From your temple on behalf of Jerusalem,
  that kings may bring you tribute.
<sup>31</sup> Roar at the wild beast of the reeds,<sup>‡</sup>
  the herd of mighty bulls, the calves
    of the peoples;
  trampling those who lust after silver
  scatter the peoples that delight in
    war.
<sup>32</sup> Let bronze be brought from Egypt,<sup>d</sup>
  Ethiopia hurry its hands to God.<sup>e</sup>

### IX

<sup>33</sup> You kingdoms of the earth, sing to God;<sup>f</sup>
  chant the praises of the Lord,

                                              *Selah*
<sup>34</sup> Who rides the heights of the ancient
    heavens,
  Who sends forth his voice as a
    mighty voice?

<sup>35</sup> Confess the power of God,
  whose majesty protects Israel,
  whose power is in the sky.
<sup>36</sup> Awesome is God in his holy place,
  the God of Israel,
  who gives power and strength to his
    people.<sup>g</sup>
Blessed be God!

## PSALM 69<sup>§</sup>
### A Cry of Anguish in Great Distress

<sup>1</sup>For the leader; according to "Lilies."<sup>¶</sup> Of David.

### I

<sup>2</sup> Save me, God,
  for the waters** have reached my
    neck.<sup>h</sup>
<sup>3</sup> I have sunk into the mire of the deep,
  where there is no foothold.
I have gone down to the watery depths;
  the flood overwhelms me.<sup>i</sup>
<sup>4</sup> I am weary with crying out;
  my throat is parched.
My eyes fail,
  from looking for my God.<sup>j</sup>
<sup>5</sup> More numerous than the hairs of my head
  are those who hate me without
    cause.<sup>k</sup>
Those who would destroy me are mighty,
  my enemies without reason.
Must I now restore
  what I did not steal?<sup>††</sup>

### II

<sup>6</sup> God, you know my folly;
  my faults are not hidden from you.
<sup>7</sup> Let those who wait in hope for you, LORD
    of hosts,
  not be shamed because of me.
Let those who seek you, God of Israel,<sup>l</sup>
  not be disgraced because of me.
<sup>8</sup> For it is on your account I bear insult,
  that disgrace covers my face.<sup>m</sup>

---

§[Psalm 69] A lament complaining of suffering in language both metaphorical (Ps 69:2–3, 15–16, the waters of chaos) and literal (Ps 69:4, 5, 9, 11–13, exhaustion, alienation from family and community, false accusation). In the second part the psalmist prays with special emphasis that the enemies be punished for all to see (Ps 69:23–29). Despite the pain, the psalmist does not lose hope that all be set right, and promises public praise (Ps 69:30–36). The Psalm, which depicts the suffering of the innocent just person vividly, is cited often by the New Testament especially in the passion accounts, e.g., Ps 69:5 in Jn 15:25; Ps 69:22 in Mk 15:23, 36 and parallels and in Jn 19:29. The Psalm prays not so much for personal vengeance as for public vindication of God's justice. There was, at this time, no belief in an afterlife where such vindication could take place. Redress had to take place now, in the sight of all.

¶[69:1] "Lilies": apparently the name of the melody.

**[69:2] Waters: the waters of chaos from which God created the world are a common metaphor for extreme distress, cf. Ps 18:5; 42:8; 88:8; Jon 2:3–6.

††[69:5] What I did not steal: the psalmist, falsely accused of theft, is being forced to make restitution.

---

*[68:23] Even from Bashan . . . from the depths of the sea: the heights and the depths, the farthest places where enemies might flee.

†[68:25–28] Your procession: the procession renews God's original taking up of residence on Zion, described in Ps 68:16–19.

‡[68:31] The wild beast of the reeds: probably the Nile crocodile, a symbol for Egypt; see Ps 68:32 and Ez 29:2–5.

z. [68:22] Dt 32:42.   a. [68:24] Ps 58:11; 1 Kgs 21:19; 22:38; Is 63:1–6.   b. [68:26] Ps 81:2–3; 87:7; 149:3; 150:3–5; 2 Sm 6:5.   c. [68:28] Is 8:23.   d. [68:32] Ez 29:2ff.   e. [68:32] Is 18:7; 45:14.   f. [68:33] Ps 138:4.

g. [68:36] Ps 28:8; 29:11.   h. [69:2] Ps 18:5; 93:3–4; Jb 22:11.   i. [69:3] Ps 40:2; 124:4–5.   j. [69:4] Ps 25:15; 119:82; 123:2; 141:8; Is 38:14.   k. [69:5] Ps 40:13; Lam 3:52; Jn 15:25.   l. [69:7] Ps 40:17.   m. [69:8] Jer 15:15.

9 I have become an outcast to my kindred,
   a stranger to my mother's children.[n]
10 Because zeal for your house has
    consumed me,[*]
   I am scorned by those who scorn
    you.[o]
11 When I humbled my spirit with fasting,[p]
   this led only to scorn.
12 When I clothed myself in sackcloth;
   I became a byword for them.
13 Those who sit in the gate gossip about
    me;
   drunkards make me the butt of
    songs.

### III

14 But I will pray to you, LORD,
   at a favorable time.
   God, in your abundant kindness, answer
    me
   with your sure deliverance.[q]
15 Rescue me from the mire,[r]
   and do not let me sink.
   Rescue me from those who hate me
   and from the watery depths.
16 Do not let the flood waters overwhelm
    me,
   nor the deep swallow me,
   nor the pit close its mouth over me.
17 Answer me, LORD, in your generous love;
   in your great mercy turn to me.
18 Do not hide your face from your servant;
   hasten to answer me, for I am in
    distress.[s]
19 Come and redeem my life;
   because of my enemies ransom me.
20 You know my reproach, my shame, my
    disgrace;
   before you stand all my foes.
21 Insult has broken my heart, and I
    despair;
   I looked for compassion, but there
    was none,[t]
   for comforters, but found none.
22 Instead they gave me poison for my food;
   and for my thirst they gave me
    vinegar.[u]

### IV

23 May their own table be a snare for them,
   and their communion offerings a
    trap.[v]
24 Make their eyes so dim they cannot see;
   keep their backs ever feeble.
25 Pour out your wrath upon them;

let the fury of your anger overtake
   them.
26 Make their camp desolate,
   with none to dwell in their tents.[w]
27 For they pursued the one you struck,
   added to the pain of the one you
    wounded.
28 Heap punishment upon their
    punishment;
   let them gain from you no
    vindication.
29 May they be blotted from the book of life;
   not registered among the just![x]

### V

30 But here I am miserable and in pain;
   let your saving help protect me,
    God,
31 [†]That I may praise God's name in song
   and glorify it with thanksgiving.
32 That will please the LORD more than oxen,
   more than bulls with horns and
    hooves;[y]
33 "See, you lowly ones, and be glad;
   you who seek God, take heart![z]
34 For the LORD hears the poor,
   and does not spurn those in
    bondage.
35 Let the heaven and the earth praise him,
   the seas and whatever moves in
    them!"

### VI

36 For God will rescue Zion,
   and rebuild the cities of Judah.[a]
   They will dwell there and possess it;
37 the descendants of God's servants will
    inherit it;
   those who love God's name will
    dwell in it.[b]

## PSALM 70[‡]
### Prayer for Divine Help

1 For the leader; of David. For remembrance.
2 Graciously rescue me, God![c]
   Come quickly to help me, LORD![d]
3 Let those who seek my life
   be confused and put to shame.[e]
   Let those who desire my ruin
   turn back in disgrace.
4 Let those who say "Aha!"[f]
   turn back in their shame.

---

*[69:10] **Zeal for your house has consumed me:** the psalmist's commitment to God's cause brings only opposition, cf. Jn 2:17. **I am scorned by those who scorn you:** Rom 15:3 uses the verse as an example of Jesus' unselfishness.

†[69:31] **That I may praise God's name in song:** the actual song is cited in Ps 69:33–35, the word "praise" in Ps 69:35 referring back to "praise" in Ps 69:31.

‡[Psalm 70] A lament of a poor and afflicted person (Ps 70:6) who has no resource except God, and who cries out to be saved from the enemy. The Psalm is almost identical to Ps 40:14–17.

n. [69:9] Jb 19:13–15.    o. [69:10] Ps 119:139; Jn 2:17; Rom 15:3.
p. [69:11–13] Ps 109:24–25; Jb 30:9; Lam 3:14.    q. [69:14] Is 49:8.
r. [69:15–16] Ps 28:1; 30:4; 32:6; 40:3; 88:5; Prv 1:12.    s. [69:18] Ps 102:3; 143:7.    t. [69:21] Lam 1:2.    u. [69:22] Lam 3:15; Mt 27:34, 48; Mk 15:23.    v. [69:23] Rom 11:9–10.

w. [69:26] Acts 1:20.    x. [69:29] Ps 139:16; Ex 32:32; Is 4:3; Dn 12:1; Mal 3:16; Rev 3:5.    y. [69:32] Ps 40:7; 50:8–9, 14; 51:18; Is 1:11–15; Hos 6:6; Am 5:21–22; Heb 10:5–8.    z. [69:33] Ps 22:27; 35:27; 70:5.    a. [69:36] Is 44:26; Ez 36:10.    b. [69:37] Ps 102:29; Is 65:9.    c. [70:2–6] Ps 40:14–18.    d. [70:2] Ps 71:12.    e. [70:3] Ps 35:4, 26.    f. [70:4] Ps 35:21, 25.

5 But may all who seek you
        rejoice and be glad in you,
    Those who long for your help
        always say, "God be glorified!"[g]
6 I am miserable and poor.
        God, come to me quickly!
    You are my help and deliverer.
    LORD, do not delay!

## PSALM 71[*]
### Prayer in Time of Old Age

### I

1 In you, LORD, I take refuge;[h]
        let me never be put to shame.[i]
2 In your justice rescue and deliver me;
        listen to me and save me!
3 Be my rock of refuge,
        my stronghold to give me safety;
        for you are my rock and fortress.[j]
4 My God, rescue me from the hand of the
        wicked,
        from the clutches of the evil and
        violent.[k]
5 You are my hope, Lord;
        my trust, GOD, from my youth.
6 On you I have depended since birth;
        from my mother's womb you are my
        strength;[l]
        my hope in you never wavers.
7 [†]I have become a portent to many,
        but you are my strong refuge!
8 My mouth shall be filled with your praise,
        shall sing your glory every day.

### II

9 Do not cast me aside in my old age;
        as my strength fails, do not forsake
        me.
10 For my enemies speak against me;
        they watch and plot against me.[m]
11 They say, "God has abandoned him.
        Pursue, and seize him!
        No one will come to the rescue!"
12 God, be not far from me;
        my God, hasten to help me.[n]
13 Bring to a shameful end
        those who attack me;
    Cover with contempt and scorn
        those who seek my ruin.[o]
14 I will always hope in you
        and add to all your praise.

15 My mouth shall proclaim your just deeds,
        day after day your acts of
        deliverance,
        though I cannot number them all.[p]
16 I will speak of the mighty works of the
        Lord;
        O GOD, I will tell of your singular
        justice.

### III

17 God, you have taught me from my youth;
        to this day I proclaim your
        wondrous deeds.
18 Now that I am old and gray,[q]
        do not forsake me, God,
    That I may proclaim your might
        to all generations yet to come,[r]
    Your power [19]and justice, God,
        to the highest heaven.
    You have done great things;[s]
        O God, who is your equal?[t]
20 Whatever bitter afflictions you sent me,
        you would turn and revive me.
    From the watery depths of the earth
        once more raise me up.
21 Restore my honor;
        turn and comfort me,
22 That I may praise you with the lyre
        for your faithfulness, my God,
    And sing to you with the harp,
        O Holy One of Israel!
23 My lips will shout for joy as I sing your
        praise;
        my soul, too, which you have
        redeemed.
24 Yes, my tongue shall recount
        your justice day by day.
    For those who sought my ruin
        have been shamed and disgraced.

## PSALM 72[‡]
### A Prayer for the King

1 Of Solomon.

### I

2 O God, give your judgment to the king;
        your justice to the king's son;[§u]
    That he may govern your people with
        justice,
        your oppressed with right judgment,[v]
3 That the mountains may yield their
        bounty for the people,
        and the hills great abundance,[w]

---

*[Psalm 71] A lament of an old person (Ps 71:9, 18) whose afflictions are interpreted by enemies as a divine judgment (Ps 71:11). The first part of the Psalm pleads for help (Ps 71:1–4) on the basis of a hope learned from a lifetime's experience of God; the second part describes the menace (Ps 71:9–13) yet remains buoyant (Ps 71:14–16); the third develops the theme of hope and praise.

†[71:7] **A portent to many**: the afflictions of the sufferer are taken as a manifestation of God's anger, cf. Dt 28:46; Ps 31:12.

‡[Psalm 72] A royal Psalm in which the Israelite king, as the representative of God, is the instrument of divine justice (Ps 72:1–4, 12–14) and blessing (Ps 72:5–7, 15–17) for the whole world. The king is human, giving only what he has received from God. Hence intercession must be made for him. The extravagant language is typical of oriental royal courts.

§[72:2] **The king … the king's son**: the crown prince is the king's son; the prayer envisages the dynasty.

g. [70:5] Ps 35:28.   h. [71:1–3] Ps 31:2–4.   i. [71:1] Ps 25:2.   j. [71:3] Ps 18:3.   k. [71:4] Ps 140:2.   l. [71:6] Ps 22:11.   m. [71:10] Ps 3:2; 22:8.   n. [71:12] Ps 22:20.   o. [71:13] Ps 35:4; 40:15; 70:3.   p. [71:15] Ps 35:28.   q. [71:18] Is 46:3–4.   r. [71:18] Ps 22:31–32; 48:14–15; 145:4.   s. [71:19] Ps 72:18.   t. [71:19] Ps 86:8.   u. [72:2] Ps 99:4; Jer 23:5.   v. [72:2] Prv 31:8–9.   w. [72:3] Is 52:7; 55:12.

4 That he may defend the oppressed among
    the people,
    save the children of the poor and
    crush the oppressor.

II

5 May they fear you with the sun,
    and before the moon, through all
    generations.ˣ
6 May he be like rain coming down upon
    the fields,
    like showers watering the earth,ʸ
7 That abundance may flourish in his days,
    great bounty, till the moon be no
    more.

III

8 *May he rule from sea to sea,
    from the river to the ends of the
    earth.ᶻ
9 May his foes kneel before him,
    his enemies lick the dust.ᵃ
10 May the kings of Tarshish and the islands†
    bring tribute,
    the kings of Sheba and Seba offer
    gifts.ᵇ
11 May all kings bow before him,
    all nations serve him.ᶜ
12 For he rescues the poor when they cry out,
    the oppressed who have no one to
    help.
13 He shows pity to the needy and the poorᵈ
    and saves the lives of the poor.
14 From extortion and violence he redeems
    them,
    for precious is their blood‡ in his
    sight.

IV

15 Long may he live, receiving gold from
    Sheba,
    prayed for without cease, blessed
    day by day.
16 §May wheat abound in the land,
    flourish even on the mountain
    heights.
    May his fruit be like that of Lebanon,
    and flourish in the city like the
    grasses of the land.ᵉ
17 May his name be forever;
    as long as the sun, may his name
    endure.ᶠ

May the tribes of the earth give blessings
    with his name;ᵍ
    may all the nations regard him as
    favored.ᵍ
18 **Blessed be the Lᴏʀᴅ God, the God of
    Israel,
    who alone does wonderful deeds.ʰ
19 Blessed be his glorious name forever;
    may he fill all the earth with his glory.ⁱ
    Amen and amen.

²⁰The end of the psalms of David, son of
Jesse.

## Third Book—Psalms 73–89

## PSALM 73††
### The Trial of the Just

¹A psalm of Asaph.

How good God is to the upright,
    to those who are pure of heart!

I

2 But, as for me, my feet had almost stumbled;
    my steps had nearly slipped,
3 Because I was envious of the arrogant
    when I saw the prosperity of the
    wicked.ʲ
4 For they suffer no pain;
    their bodies are healthy and sleek.
5 They are free of the burdens of life;
    they are not afflicted like others.
6 Thus pride adorns them as a necklace;
    violence clothes them as a robe.
7 Out of such blindness comes sin;
    evil thoughts flood their hearts.ᵏ
8 They scoff and spout their malice;
    from on high they utter threats.ˡ
9 ‡‡They set their mouths against the
    heavens,
    their tongues roam the earth.

---

¶[72:17] **May the tribes of the earth give blessings with his name:** an echo of the promise to the ancestors (Gn 12:3; 26:4; 28:14), suggesting that the monarchy in Israel fulfilled the promise to Abraham, Isaac, and Jacob.

**[72:18–19] A doxology marking the end of Book II of the Psalter.

††[Psalm 73] The opening verse of this probing poem (cf. Ps 37; 49) is actually the psalmist's hard-won conclusion from personal experience: God is just and good! The psalmist describes near loss of faith (Ps 73:2–3), occasioned by observing the wicked who blasphemed God with seeming impunity (Ps 73:4–12). Feeling abandoned despite personal righteousness, the psalmist could not bear the injustice until an experience of God's nearness in the Temple made clear how deluded the wicked were. Their sudden destruction shows their impermanence (Ps 73:13–20). The just can thus be confident, for, as the psalmist now knows, their security is from God (Ps 73:1, 23–28).

‡‡[73:9] **They set their mouths against the heavens:** in an image probably derived from mythic stories of half-divine giants, the monstrous speech of the wicked is likened to enormous jaws gaping wide, devouring everything in sight.

---

*[72:8] **From sea to sea . . . the ends of the earth:** the boundaries of the civilized world known at the time: from the Mediterranean Sea (the western sea) to the Persian Gulf (eastern sea), and from the Euphrates (the river) to the islands and lands of southwestern Europe, "the ends of the earth." The words may also have a mythic nuance—the earth surrounded by cosmic waters, hence everywhere.

†[72:10] **Tarshish and the islands:** the far west (Ps 48:6); Arabia and Seba: the far south (1 Kgs 10:1).

‡[72:14] **Their blood:** cf. Ps 116:15.

§[72:16] The translation of the difficult Hebrew is tentative.

x. [72:5] Ps 89:37–38; Jer 31:35.  y. [72:6] Dt 32:2; Is 45:8; Hos 6:3.  z. [72:8] Dt 11:24; Zec 9:10.  a. [72:9] Is 49:23; Mi 7:17.  b. [72:10] Ps 68:30; Is 60:5–6; 1 Kgs 10:1ff.  c. [72:11] Ps 47:8.  d. [72:13] Prv 31:9.  e. [72:16] Is 27:6; Hos 14:6–8; Am 9:13.  f. [72:17] Ps 21:7.

g. [72:17] Gn 12:3; 22:18; 26:4; Zec 8:13.  h. [72:18] Ps 41:14; 89:53; 106:48; 136:4.  i. [72:19] Ps 57:5; Nm 14:21.  j. [73:3] Ps 37:1; Jb 21:13.  k. [73:7] Jb 15:27.  l. [73:8] Ps 17:10.

<sup>10</sup> 'So my people turn to them
      and drink deeply of their words.
<sup>11</sup> They say, "Does God really know?"
      "Does the Most High have any
         knowledge?"<sup>m</sup>
<sup>12</sup> Such, then, are the wicked,
      always carefree, increasing their
         wealth.

                    II
<sup>13</sup> Is it in vain that I have kept my heart pure,
      washed my hands in innocence?<sup>n</sup>
<sup>14</sup> For I am afflicted day after day,
      chastised every morning.
<sup>15</sup> Had I thought, "I will speak as they do,"
      I would have betrayed this
         generation of your children.
<sup>16</sup> Though I tried to understand all this,
      it was too difficult for me,
<sup>17</sup> Till I entered the sanctuary of God
      and came to understand their end.<sup>†</sup>

                    III
<sup>18</sup> You set them, indeed, on a slippery road;
      you hurl them down to ruin.
<sup>19</sup> How suddenly they are devastated;
      utterly undone by disaster!
<sup>20</sup> They are like a dream after waking, Lord,
      dismissed like shadows when you
         arise.<sup>o</sup>

                    IV
<sup>21</sup> Since my heart was embittered
      and my soul deeply wounded,
<sup>22</sup> I was stupid and could not understand;
      I was like a brute beast in your
         presence.
<sup>23</sup> Yet I am always with you;
      you take hold of my right hand.<sup>p</sup>
<sup>24</sup> With your counsel you guide me,
      and at the end receive me with
         honor.<sup>‡</sup>
<sup>25</sup> Whom else have I in the heavens?
      None beside you delights me on
         earth.
<sup>26</sup> Though my flesh and my heart fail,
      God is the rock of my heart, my
         portion forever.
<sup>27</sup> But those who are far from you perish;
      you destroy those unfaithful to you.
<sup>28</sup> As for me, to be near God is my good,
      to make the Lord GOD my refuge.

I shall declare all your works
      in the gates of daughter Zion.<sup>§</sup>

## PSALM 74<sup>¶</sup>
### Prayer at the Destruction of the Temple

<sup>1</sup>A *maskil* of Asaph.
                    I
Why, God, have you cast us off forever?<sup>*q</sup>
      Why does your anger burn against
         the sheep of your pasture?<sup>r</sup>
<sup>2</sup> Remember your people, whom you
         acquired of old,
      the tribe you redeemed as your own
         heritage,
      Mount Zion where you dwell.<sup>s</sup>
<sup>3</sup> Direct your steps toward the utter
         destruction,
      everything the enemy laid waste in
         the sanctuary.
<sup>4</sup> Your foes roared triumphantly in the
         place of your assembly;
      they set up their own tokens of
         victory.
<sup>5</sup> They hacked away like a forester gathering
         boughs,
      swinging his ax in a thicket of trees.
<sup>6</sup> They smashed all its engraved work,
      struck it with ax and pick.
<sup>7</sup> They set your sanctuary on fire,
      profaned your name's abode by
         razing it to the ground.<sup>t</sup>
<sup>8</sup> They said in their hearts, "We will destroy
         them all!
      Burn all the assembly-places of God
         in the land!"
<sup>9</sup> <sup>††</sup>Even so we have seen no signs for us,
      there is no prophet any more,<sup>u</sup>
      no one among us who knows for
         how long.
<sup>10</sup> How long, O God, will the enemy jeer?<sup>v</sup>
      Will the enemy revile your name
         forever?

---

§[73:28] **In the gates of daughter Zion**: this reading follows the tradition of the Septuagint and Vulgate.

¶[Psalm 74] A communal lament sung when the enemy invaded the Temple; it would be especially appropriate at the destruction of Jerusalem in 587 B.C. Israel's God is urged to look upon the ruined sanctuary and remember the congregation who worshiped there (Ps 74:1–11). People and sanctuary are bound together; an attack on Zion is an attack on Israel. In the second half of the poem, the community brings before God the story of their origins—their creation (Ps 74:12–17)—in order to move God to reenact that deed of creation now. Will God allow a lesser power to destroy the divine project (Ps 74:18–23)?

**[74:1] **Forever**: the word implies that the disaster is already of long duration, cf. Ps 74:9 and note.

††[74:9] **Even so we have seen no signs . . .** : ancients often asked prophets to say for how long a divine punishment was to last, cf. 2 Sm 24:13. Here no prophet has arisen to indicate the duration.

---

*[73:10] The Hebrew is obscure.

†[73:17] **And came to understand their end**: the psalmist receives a double revelation in the Temple: 1) the end of the wicked comes unexpectedly (Ps 73:18–20); 2) God is with me.

‡[73:24] **And at the end receive me with honor**: a perhaps deliberately enigmatic verse. It is understood by some commentators as reception into heavenly glory, hence the traditional translation, "receive me into glory." The Hebrew verb can indeed refer to mysterious divine elevation of a righteous person into God's domain: Enoch in Gn 5:24; Elijah in 2 Kgs 2:11–12; the righteous psalmist in Ps 49:16. Personal resurrection in the Old Testament, however, is clearly attested only in the second century B.C. The verse is perhaps best left unspecified as a reference to God's nearness and protection.

m. [73:11] Ps 10:11; Jb 22:13.  n. [73:13] Ps 26:6; Mal 3:14.
o. [73:20] Jb 20:8.  p. [73:23] Ps 121:5.

q. [74:1] Ps 10:1; 44:24; 77:8.  r. [74:1] Ps 80:5.  s. [74:2] Ps 68:17; 132:13; Ex 15:17; Jer 10:16; 51:19.  t. [74:7] Ps 79:1; Is 64:10.  u. [74:9] Lam 2:9.  v. [74:10] Ps 89:47.

11 Why draw back your hand,
        why hold back your right hand
            within your bosom?*

        II

12 †Yet you, God, are my king from of old,
        winning victories throughout the
            earth.
13 You stirred up the sea by your might;ʷ
        you smashed the heads of the
            dragons on the waters.ˣ
14 You crushed the heads of Leviathan,ʸ
        gave him as food to the sharks.
15 You opened up springs and torrents,
        brought dry land out of the primeval
            waters.‡
16 Yours the day and yours the night too;
        you set the moon and sun in place.
17 You fixed all the limits of the earth;
        summer and winter you made.ᶻ
18 Remember how the enemy has jeered,
            LORD,
        how a foolish people has reviled
            your name.
19 Do not surrender to wild animals those
            who praise you;
        do not forget forever the life of your
            afflicted.
20 Look to your covenant,
        for the recesses of the land
        are full of the haunts of violence.
21 Let not the oppressed turn back in shame;
        may the poor and needy praise your
            name.
22 Arise, God, defend your cause;
        remember the constant jeering of
            the fools.
23 Do not forget the clamor of your foes,
        the unceasing uproar of your
            enemies.

## PSALM 75§
### God the Judge of the World

1 For the leader. Do not destroy! A psalm of
Asaph; a song.

        I

2 We thank you, God, we give thanks;
        we call upon your name,
        we declare your wonderful deeds.
[You said:]¶
3 "I will choose the time;
        I will judge fairly.
4 Though the earth and all its inhabitants
            quake,
        I make steady its pillars."ᵃ

                                        Selah

        II

5 So I say to the boastful: "Do not boast!"ᵇ
        to the wicked: "Do not raise your
            horns!"*
6 Do not raise your horns against heaven!
        Do not speak with a stiff neck!"ᶜ
7 For judgment comes not from east or
            from west,
        not from the wilderness or the
            mountains,ᵈ
8 But from God who decides,
        who brings some low and raises
            others high.ᵉ
9 Yes, a cup†† is in the LORD's hand,
        foaming wine, fully spiced.††
    When God pours it out,
        they will drain it even to the dregs;
        all the wicked of the earth will
            drink.ᶠ
10 But I will rejoice forever;
        I will sing praise to the God of
            Jacob,
11 ᵍ[Who has said:]
    "I will cut off all the horns of the wicked,
        but the horns of the righteous will
            be exalted."

## PSALM 76‡‡
### God Defends Zion

1 For the leader; a psalm with stringed instruments. A song of Asaph.

        I

2 Renowned in Judah is God,ʰ

---

*[74:11] **Why hold back . . . within your bosom**: i.e., idle
beneath your cloak.

†[74:12–17] Comparable Canaanite literature describes
the storm-god's victory over all-encompassing Sea and its
allies (dragons and Leviathan) and the subsequent peaceful
arrangement of the universe, sometimes through the placement of paired cosmic elements (day and night, sun and
moon), cf. Ps 89:12–13. The Psalm apparently equates the
enemies attacking the Temple with the destructive cosmic
forces already tamed by God. Why then are those forces now
raging untamed against your own people?

‡[74:15] **Waters**: lit., "rivers" (cf. Ps 24:7; Isa 50:2) upon
which, or from which, in primordial times the earth is created.

§[Psalm 75] The psalmist gives thanks and rejoices (Ps
75:2, 10) for the direct intervention of God, which is promised
in two oracles (Ps 75:3–4, 11). Expecting that divine intervention, the psalmist warns evildoers to repent (Ps 75:5–9).

¶[75:2] **You said**: supplied for clarity here and in Ps 75:11.
The translation assumes in both places that the psalmist is citing an oracle of God.

**[75:5] **Do not raise your horns!**: the horn is the symbol
of strength; to raise one's horn is to exalt one's own power as
Ps 75:5 explains.

††[75:9] **A cup**: "the cup of God's wrath" is the punishment
inflicted on the wicked, cf. Is 51:17; Jer 25:15–29; 49:12; Eze
23:31–33. **Spiced**: lit., "a mixed drink"; spices or drugs were
added to wine, cf. Prv 9:2, 5.

‡‡[Psalm 76] A song glorifying Zion, the mountain of Jerusalem where God destroyed Israel's enemies. Zion is thus the
appropriate site to celebrate the victory (Ps 76:3–4), a victory
described in parallel scenes (Ps 76:5–7, 8–11). Israel is invited
to worship its powerful patron deity (Ps 76:12).

---

w. [74:13] Ps 89:10.  x. [74:13] Is 51:9–10.  y. [74:14] Jb 3:8; 40:25;
Is 27:1.  z. [74:16–17] Gn 1.

a. [75:4] Ps 46:3; 60:4; 93:1; 96:10; 104:5; 1 Sm 2:8; Is 24:19.  b.
[75:5] 1 Sm 2:3; Zec 2:1–4.  c. [75:6] Jb 15:25.  d. [75:7] Mt 24:23–
27.  e. [75:8] Jb 5:11; 1 Sm 2:7.  f. [75:9] Ps 60:5; Jb 21:20; Is
51:17, 21–22; Jer 25:15ff; Hab 2:16.  g. [75:11] Ps 92:11.

whose name is great in Israel.
3 On Salem* is God's tent, his shelter on
    Zion.
4     There the flashing arrows were
        shattered,
    shield, sword, and weapons of war.*

                              *Selah*

**II**

5 Terrible and awesome are you,
    stronger than the ancient
        mountains.†
6 Despoiled are the stouthearted;
    they sank into sleep;
    the hands of all the men of valor
        have failed.*
7 At your roar, O God of Jacob,
    chariot and steed lay still.
8 You, terrible are you;
    who can stand before you and your
        great anger?*
9 From the heavens you pronounced
    sentence;
    the earth was terrified and reduced
        to silence,
10 When you arose, O God, for judgment
    to save the afflicted of the land.

                              *Selah*

11 Surely the wrath of man will give you
    thanks;
    the remnant of your furor will keep
        your feast.

**III**

12 Make and keep vows to the LORD your
    God.*
    May all around him bring gifts to
        the one to be feared,
13 Who checks the spirit of princes,
    who is fearful to the kings of earth.

**PSALM 77**‡
**Confidence in God During National Distress**

1 For the leader; According to *Jeduthun*. A psalm
of Asaph.

**I**

2 I cry aloud to God,
    I cry to God to hear me.
3 On the day of my distress I seek the
    Lord;

by night my hands are stretched out
    unceasingly;*
    I refuse to be consoled.
4 When I think of God, I groan;
    as I meditate, my spirit grows faint.*

                              *Selah*

5 You have kept me from closing my eyes in
    sleep;
    I am troubled and cannot speak.
6 I consider the days of old;
    the years long past 7 I remember.*
At night I ponder in my heart;
    and as I meditate, my spirit probes:
8 "Will the Lord reject us forever,*
    never again show favor?
9 Has God's mercy ceased forever?
    The promise to go unfulfilled for
        future ages?
10 Has God forgotten how to show mercy,
    in anger withheld his compassion?"

                              *Selah*

11 §I conclude: "My sorrow is this,
    the right hand of the Most High has
        abandoned us."*

**II**

12 ¶I will recall the deeds of the LORD;
    yes, recall your wonders of old.*
13 I will ponder all your works;
    on your exploits I will meditate.
14 Your way, God, is holy;
    what god is as great as our God?*
15 You are the God who does wonders;
    among the peoples you have
        revealed your might.*
16 With your mighty arm you redeemed
    your people,
    the children of Jacob and Joseph.*

                              *Selah*

17 The waters saw you, God;
    the waters saw you and lashed
        about,
    even the deeps of the sea** trembled.*
18 The clouds poured down their rains;
    the thunderheads rumbled;
    your arrows flashed back and forth.*
19 The thunder of your chariot wheels
    resounded;

---

*[76:3] **Salem**: an ancient name for Jerusalem, used here
perhaps on account of its allusion to the Hebrew word for
peace, *shalom*, cf. Gn 14:18; Heb 7:1–3.

†[76:5] **Ancient mountains**: conjectural translation of a
difficult Hebrew phrase on the basis of Gn 49:26. The mountains are part of the structure of the universe (Ps 89:12–13).

‡[Psalm 77] A community lament in which the speaker
("I") describes the anguish of Israel at God's silence when its
very existence is at stake (Ps 77:2–11). In response the speaker
recites the story of how God brought the people into existence
(Ps 77:12–20). The question is thus posed to God: Will you
allow the people you created to be destroyed?

§[77:11] **I conclude**: lit., "I said." The psalmist, after pondering the present distress and God's promises to Israel, has
decided that God has forgotten the people.

¶[77:12] **I will recall**: the verb sometimes means to make
present the great deeds of Israel's past by reciting them, cf. Ps
78:42; 105:5; 106:7.

**[77:17] **The deeps of the sea**: Heb. *tehom*; the same word
is used in Gn 1:2, where it alludes to the primeval seas which
in ancient Semitic cosmography are tamed by God in creation, cf. Ps 74:12–17; 89:12–13 and notes.

---

h. [76:2] Heb 3:2.  i. [76:4] Ps 46:10; 122:6–9.  j. [76:6] 2 Kgs
19:35; Jer 51:39; Na 3:18.  k. [76:8] Dt 7:21; 1 Sm 6:20; Na 1:6; Mal
3:2.  l. [76:12] Nm 30:3.

m. [77:3] Ps 50:15; 88:2.  n. [77:4] Jon 2:8.  o. [77:7] Ps 143:5;
Dt 32:7.  p. [77:8–10] Ps 13:2; 44:24; 74:1; 80:5; 89:47; Lam 3:31.
q. [77:11] Ps 17:7; 18:36; Ex 15:6, 12.  r. [77:12] Ps 143:5.  s. [77:14]
Ps 18:31; Ex 15:11.  t. [77:15] Ps 86:10; 89:6.  u. [77:16] Gn
46:26–27; Neh 1:10.  v. [77:17] Ps 18:16; 114:3; Na 1:4.  w. [77:18]
Ps 18:14–15; 29; 144:6; Jb 37:3–4; Wis 5:21; Hab 3:10–11; Zec 9:14.

your lightning lit up the world;
   the earth trembled and quaked.[x]

20 Through the sea was your way;
   your path, through the mighty waters,
      though your footsteps were unseen.[y]

21 You led your people like a flock
   by the hand of Moses and Aaron.[z]

## PSALM 78[*]
### A New Beginning in Zion and David

[1] A *maskil* of Asaph.

### I

Attend, my people, to my teaching;
   listen to the words of my mouth.

2 I will open my mouth in a parable,[†]
   unfold the puzzling events of the
      past.[a]

3 What we have heard and know;
   things our ancestors have recounted
      to us.[b]

4 We do not keep them from our children;
   we recount them to the next
      generation,
The praiseworthy deeds of the LORD and
   his strength,
      the wonders that he performed.[c]

5 God made a decree in Jacob,
   established a law in Israel:[d]
Which he commanded our ancestors,
   they were to teach their children;

6 That the next generation might come to
   know,
   children yet to be born.[e]
In turn they were to recount them to their
   children,

7        that they too might put their
            confidence in God,

And not forget God's deeds,
   but keep his commandments.

8 They were not to be like their ancestors,
   a rebellious and defiant generation,[f]
A generation whose heart was not
      constant,[g]
   and whose spirit was not faithful
      to God.

9 The ranks of Ephraimite archers,[‡]
   retreated on the day of battle.

10 They did not keep God's covenant;
   they refused to walk according to
      his law.

11 They forgot his deeds,
   the wonders that he had shown
      them.

### II
### A

12 In the sight of their ancestors God did
   wonders,
   in the land of Egypt, the plain of
      Zoan.[§h]

13 He split the sea and led them across,[i]
   making the waters stand like walls.[j]

14 He led them with a cloud by day,
   all night with the light of fire.[k]

15 He split rocks in the desert,
   gave water to drink, abundant as the
      deeps of the sea.[l]

16 He made streams flow from crags,
   caused rivers of water to flow down.

### B

17 But they went on sinning against him,
   rebelling against the Most High in
      the desert.[m]

18 They tested God in their hearts,
   demanding the food they craved.[n]

19 They spoke against God, and said,
   "Can God spread a table in the
      wilderness?[o]

20 True, when he struck the rock,
   water gushed forth,
   the wadies flooded.
But can he also give bread,
   or provide meat to his people?"

### C

21 The LORD heard and grew angry;[p]
   fire blazed up against Jacob;
   anger flared up against Israel.

22 For they did not believe in God,
   did not trust in his saving power.

---

*[Psalm 78] A recital of history to show that past generations did not respond to God's gracious deeds and were punished by God making the gift into a punishment. Will Israel fail to appreciate God's act—the choosing of Zion and of David? The tripartite introduction invites Israel to learn the lessons hidden in its traditions (Ps 78:1–4, 5–7, 8–11); each section ends with the mention of God's acts. There are two distinct narratives of approximately equal length: the wilderness events (Ps 78:12–39) and the movement from Egypt to Canaan (Ps 78:40–72). The structure of both is parallel: gracious act (Ps 78:12–16, 40–55), rebellion (Ps 78:17–20, 56–58), divine punishment (Ps 78:21–31, 59–64), God's readiness to forgive and begin anew (Ps 78:32–39, 65–72). While the Psalm has been thought to reflect the reunification program of either King Hezekiah (late eighth century) or King Josiah (late seventh century) in that the Northern Kingdom (Ephraim, Joseph) is especially invited to accept Zion and the Davidic king, a postexilic setting is also possible. Notable is the inclusion of the David-Zion tradition into the history of Israel recounted in the sources of the Pentateuch.

†[78:2] **Parable:** Hebrew *mashal* literally refers to some sort of relationship of comparison and can signify a story whose didactic potential becomes clear in the telling, as here in the retrospective examination of the history of Israel. Mt 13:35 cites the verse to explain Jesus' use of parables.

---

‡[78:9] **Ephraimite archers:** Ephraim was the most important tribe of the Northern Kingdom. Its military defeat (here unspecified) demonstrates its infidelity to God, who otherwise would have protected it.

§[78:12, 43] **Zoan:** a city on the arm of the Nile, a former capital of Egypt.

---

x. [77:19] Ps 18:8; 97:4; 99:1; Ex 19:16; Jgs 5:4–5.   y. [77:20] Neh 9:11; Wis 14:3; Is 51:10; Hab 3:15.   z. [77:21] Ps 78:52; Is 63:11–14; Hos 12:14; Mi 6:4.   a. [78:2] Ps 49:5; Mt 13:35.   b. [78:3] Ps 44:2.   c. [78:4] Ex 10:2; Dt 4:9; Jb 8:8.   d. [78:5] Ps 147:19; Dt 33:4.   e. [78:6] Ps 22:31–32; Dt 4:9; 6:7.

f. [78:8] Dt 31:27; 32:5.   g. [78:8] Ps 95:10.   h. [78:12] Ps 106:7.   i. [78:13–14] Ps 136:13; Ex 14–15.   j. [78:13] Ex 14:22; 15:8.   k. [78:14] Ps 105:39; Ex 13:21; Wis 18:3.   l. [78:15] Ps 105:41; 114:8; Ex 17:1–7; Nm 20:2–13; Dt 8:15; Wis 11:4; Is 48:21.   m. [78:17] Dt 9:7; Ez 20:13.   n. [78:18] Ps 106:14; Ex 16:2–36.   o. [78:19] Ps 23:5.   p. [78:21f] Nm 11; Dt 32:22.

²³ ˮSo he commanded the clouds above;
    and opened the doors of heaven.
²⁴ God rained manna upon them for food;
    grain from heaven he gave them.�q
²⁵ Man ate the bread of the angels;†
    food he sent in abundance.
²⁶ He stirred up the east wind in the skies;
    by his might God brought on the
      south wind.
²⁷ He rained meat upon them like dust,
    winged fowl like the sands of the
      sea,
²⁸ They fell down in the midst of their camp,
    all round their dwellings.
²⁹ They ate and were well filled;
    he gave them what they had craved.
³⁰ But while they still wanted more,
    and the food was still in their
      mouths,
³¹ God's anger flared up against them,
    and he made a slaughter of their
      strongest,
    laying low the youth of Israel.ʳ
³² In spite of all this they went on sinning,
    they did not believe in his wonders.

          D
³³ God ended their days abruptly,
    their years in sudden death.
³⁴ When he slew them, they began to seek
      him;
    they again looked for God.ˢ
³⁵ They remembered‡ that God was their
      rock,
    God Most High, their redeemer.
³⁶ But they deceived him with their mouths,
    lied to him with their tongues.
³⁷ Their hearts were not constant toward
      him;
    they were not faithful to his
      covenant.ᵗ
³⁸ §But God being compassionate forgave
      their sin;
    he did not utterly destroy them.
    Time and again he turned back his anger,
      unwilling to unleash all his rage.ᵘ
³⁹ He remembered that they were flesh,
    a breath that passes on and does not
      return.

          III
          A
⁴⁰ How often they rebelled against God in
      the wilderness,
    grieved him in the wasteland.
⁴¹ Again and again they tested God,
    provoked the Holy One of Israel.
⁴² They did not remember his power,
    the day he redeemed them from
      the foe,ᵛ
⁴³ ˮWhen he performed his signs in Egypt,
    his wonders in the plain of Zoan.ʷ
⁴⁴ God turned their rivers to blood;
    their streams they could not drink.
⁴⁵ He sent swarms of insects that devoured
      them,ˣ
    frogs that destroyed them.
⁴⁶ He gave their harvest to the caterpillar,
    the fruits of their labor to the locust.
⁴⁷ He killed their vines with hail,ʸ
    their sycamores with frost.
⁴⁸ He exposed their cattle to plague,
    their flocks to pestilence.ᶻ
⁴⁹ He let loose against them the heat of his
      anger,
    wrath, fury, and distress,
    a band of deadly messengers.
⁵⁰ He cleared a path for his anger;
    he did not spare them from death,
    but delivered their animals to the
      plague.
⁵¹ He struck all the firstborn of Egypt,ᵃ
    the first fruits of their vigor in the
      tents of Ham.
⁵² Then God led forth his people like sheep,
    guided them like a flock through the
      wilderness.ᵇ
⁵³ He led them on secure and unafraid,
    while the sea enveloped their
      enemies.ᶜ
⁵⁴ And he brought them to his holy
      mountain,
    the hill his right hand had won.ᵈ
⁵⁵ He drove out the nations before them,
    allotted them as their inherited
      portion,
    and settled in their tents the tribes
      of Israel.

          B
⁵⁶ But they tested and rebelled against God
      Most High,
    his decrees they did not observe.
⁵⁷ They turned disloyal, faithless like their
      ancestors;
    they proved false like a slack bow.

---

*[78:23–31] On the manna and the quail, see Ex 16 and
Nm 11. Unlike Ex 16, here both manna and quail are instruments of punishment, showing that a divine gift can become
deadly because of Israel's apostasy.

†[78:25] **Bread of the angels:** the translation "angels" com-
ports with the supernatural origin of the manna, though the
Hebrew *lechem 'abbirim* is more literally translated as "bread
of the strong ones" or "bread of the mighty." In the context of
the manna event, this phrase cannot possibly mean the Israelites or any human being.

‡[78:35] **Remembered:** invoked God publicly in worship.
Their words were insincere (Ps 78:36).

§[78:38] God is always ready to forgive and begin anew, as
in choosing Zion and David (Ps 78:65–72).

¶[78:43–55] Ex 7–12 records ten plagues. Here there are
six divine attacks upon Egypt; the seventh climactic act is
God's bringing Israel to the holy land.

q. [78:24] Ps 105:40; Ex 16:4, 14; Dt 8:3; Wis 16:20; Jn 6:31.    r. [78:31]
Nm 14:29.    s. [78:34] Dt 32:15, 18; Is 26:16.    t. [78:37] Ps 95:10; Is
29:13.    u. [78:38] Ps 85:4; Ex 32:14; Is 48:9; Ez 20:22.

v. [78:42] Ps 106:21.    w. [78:43f] Ps 105:27–36; 135:9; Ex 7:14–
11:10; 12:29–36; Wis 16–18.    x. [78:45] Ex 8:17.    y. [78:47]
Wis 16:16.    z. [78:48] Ex 9:3.    a. [78:51] Ps 105:36; 136:10; Ex
12:29.    b. [78:52] Ps 77:21.    c. [78:53] Ex 14:26–28.    d. [78:54]
Ex 15:17.

58 They enraged him with their high places,
    and with their idols provoked him*
       to jealous anger.*

C

59 God heard and grew angry;
    he rejected Israel completely.
60 He forsook the shrine at Shiloh,†ᶠ
    the tent he set up among human
       beings.
61 He gave up his might into captivity,
    his glorious ark into the hands of
       the foe.ᵍ
62 God delivered his people to the sword;
    he was enraged against his heritage.
63 Fire consumed their young men;
    their young women heard no
       wedding songs.ʰ
64 Their priests fell by the sword;
    their widows made no lamentation.

D

65 Then the Lord awoke as from sleep,
    like a warrior shouting from the
       effects of wine.
66 He put his foes to flight;
    everlasting shame he dealt them.
67 He rejected the tent of Joseph,
    chose not the tribe of Ephraim.
68 ‡God chose the tribe of Judah,
    Mount Zion which he loved.ⁱ
69 He built his shrine like the heavens,
    like the earth which he founded
       forever.
70 He chose David his servant,
    took him from the sheepfolds.ʲ
71 From tending ewes God brought him,
    to shepherd Jacob, his people,
    Israel, his heritage.ᵏ
72 He shepherded them with a pure heart;
    with skilled hands he guided them.

## PSALM 79§
### A Prayer for Jerusalem

¹A psalm of Asaph.

---

*[78:58] **Provoked him**: lit., "made him jealous."

†[78:60] **Shiloh**: an important shrine in the north prior to Jerusalem. Despite its holy status, it was destroyed (Ps 78:60–64; cf. Jer 7:12, 14).

‡[78:68, 70] God's ultimate offer of mercy to the sinful, helpless people is Zion and the Davidic king.

§[Psalm 79] A communal lament complaining that the nations have defiled the Temple and murdered the holy people, leaving their corpses unburied (Ps 79:1–4). The occasion is probably the destruction of Jerusalem by the Babylonian army in 587 B.C. The people ask how long the withdrawal of divine favor will last (Ps 79:5), pray for action now (Ps 79:6–7), and admit that their own sins have brought about the catastrophe (Ps 79:8–9). They seek to persuade God to act for reasons of honor: the nations who do not call upon the Name are running amok (Ps 79:6); the divine honor is compromised (Ps 79:1, 10, 12); God's own servants suffer (Ps 79:2–4, 11).

---

e. [78:58] Dt 32:16, 21.  f. [78:60] Jos 18:1; 1 Sm 1:3; Jer 7:12; 26:6.  g. [78:61] 1 Sm 4:11, 22. h. [78:63] Dt 32:25; Jer 7:34.  i. [78:68] Ps 48:2; 50:2; Lam 2:15.  j. [78:70] Ps 89:21; Ez 34:23; 37:24; 2 Chr 6:6.  k. [78:71] 1 Sm 16:11–13; 2 Sm 7:8.

I

O God, the nations have invaded your
    inheritance;
    they have defiled your holy temple;
    they have laid Jerusalem in ruins.ˡ
2 They have left the corpses of your servants
    as food for the birds of the sky,
    the flesh of those devoted to you for
       the beasts of the earth.ᵐ
3 They have poured out their blood like
    water
    all around Jerusalem,
    and no one is left to do the burying.ⁿ
4 We have become the reproach of our
    neighbors,
    the scorn and derision of those
       around us.ᵒ

II

5 How long, LORD? Will you be angry
    forever?
    Will your jealous anger keep
       burning like fire?ᵖ
6 Pour out your wrath on nations that do
    not recognize you,
    on kingdoms that do not call on
       your name,�q
7 For they have devoured Jacob,
    laid waste his dwelling place.
8 Do not remember against us the iniquities
    of our forefathers;
    let your compassion move quickly
       ahead of us,
    for we have been brought very low.ʳ

III

9 Help us, God our savior,
    on account of the glory of your name.
    Deliver us, pardon our sins
    for your name's sake.ˢ
10 Why should the nations say,
    "Where is their God?"ᵗ
    Before our eyes make known to the
       nations
    that you avenge the blood of your
       servants which has been
       poured out.ᵘ

IV

11 Let the groaning of the imprisoned come
    in before you;
    in accord with the greatness of your
       arm
    preserve those doomed to die.ᵛ
12 Turn back sevenfold into the bosom of
    our neighbors
    the insult with which they insulted
       you, Lord.ʷ
13 Then we, your people, the sheep of your
    pasture,

---

l. [79:1] 2 Kgs 25:9–10; Lam 1:10.  m. [79:2] Jer 7:33.  n. [79:3] 1 Mc 7:17; Jer 14:16.  o. [79:4] Ps 44:14; 80:7; 123:3–4; Jb 12:4; Dn 9:16; Zep 2:8.  p. [79:5] Ps 13:2; 44:24; 89:47; Dt 4:24.  q. [79:6] Ps 14:4; Jer 10:25.  r. [79:8] Ps 142:7.  s. [79:9] Ez 20:44; 36:22.  t. [79:10] Ps 42:4; 115:2; Jl 2:17.  u. [79:10] Jl 4:21.  v. [79:11] Ps 102:21.  w. [79:12] Ps 89:51–52.

will give thanks to you forever;
from generation to generation
we will recount your praise.

## PSALM 80[*]
### Prayer to Restore God's Vineyard

[1] For the leader; according to "Lilies." *Eduth.*[†] A psalm of Asaph.

### I

[2] O Shepherd of Israel, lend an ear,
you who guide Joseph like a flock!
Seated upon the cherubim, shine forth[x]
[3] upon Ephraim, Benjamin, and
Manasseh.
Stir up your power, and come to save us.
[4] ʾO God, restore us;
light up your face and we shall be
saved.

### II

[5] LORD of hosts,
how long will you smolder in anger
while your people pray?[z]
[6] You have fed them the bread of tears,
made them drink tears in great
measure.[‡a]
[7] You have left us to be fought over by our
neighbors;
our enemies deride us.[b]
[8] O God of hosts, restore us;
light up your face and we shall be
saved.

### III

[9] You brought a vine[§] out of Egypt;
you drove out nations and planted
it.
[10] You cleared out what was before it;
it took deep root and filled the land.
[11] The mountains were covered by its
shadow,
the cedars of God by its branches.
[12] It sent out its boughs as far as the sea,[¶]
its shoots as far as the river.[¶]

[13] Why have you broken down its walls,
so that all who pass along the way
pluck its fruit?[c]
[14] The boar from the forest strips the vine;
the beast of the field feeds upon it.[d]
[15] Turn back again, God of hosts;
look down from heaven and see;
Visit this vine,
[16] the stock your right hand has
planted,
and the son[**] whom you made strong
for yourself.
[17] Those who would burn or cut it down—
may they perish at your rebuke.
[18] May your hand be with the man on your
right,[††]
with the son of man whom you
made strong for yourself.
[19] Then we will not withdraw from you;
revive us, and we will call on your
name.
[20] LORD God of hosts, restore us;
light up your face and we shall be
saved.

## PSALM 81[‡‡]
### An Admonition to Fidelity

[1] For the leader; "upon the *gittith*."[§§] Of Asaph.

### I

[2] Sing joyfully to God our strength;[e]
raise loud shouts to the God of
Jacob!
[3] Take up a melody, sound the timbrel,
the pleasant lyre with a harp.
[4] "Blow the shofar at the new moon,
at the full moon, on our solemn
feast.[f]
[5] For this is a law for Israel,
an edict of the God of Jacob,[g]
[6] He made it a decree for Joseph
when he came out of the land of
Egypt.

---

*[Psalm 80] A community lament in time of military defeat. Using the familiar image of Israel as a vineyard, the people complain that God has broken down the wall protecting the once splendid vine brought from Egypt (Ps 80:9–14). They pray that God will again turn to them and use the Davidic king to lead them to victory (Ps 80:15–19).

†[80:1] **Lilies. . . . Eduth:** the first term is probably the title of the melody to which the Psalm was to be sung; the second is unexplained.

‡[80:6] Both the Septuagint and the Vulgate translate this verse in the first person, i.e., "You have fed us the bread of tears."

§[80:9] **A vine:** a frequent metaphor for Israel, cf. Is 5:1–7; 27:2–5; Jer 2:21; Hos 10:1; Mt 21:33.

¶[80:12] **The sea:** the Mediterranean. **The river:** the Euphrates, cf. Gn 15:18; 1 Kgs 5:1. The terms may also have a mythic nuance—the seas that surround the earth; sea and river are sometimes paralleled in poetry.

**[80:16] The Vulgate and Septuagint use "son of man."

††[80:18] **The man on your right:** the Davidic king who will lead the army in battle.

‡‡[Psalm 81] At a pilgrimage feast, probably harvest in the fall, the people assemble in the Temple in accord with the Sinai ordinances (Ps 81:2–6). They hear a divine word (mediated by a Temple speaker) telling how God rescued them from slavery in Egypt (Ps 81:7–9), gave them the fundamental commandment of fidelity (Ps 81:9–11), which would bring punishment if they refused to obey (Ps 81:12–13). But if Israel repents, God will be with them once again, bestowing protection and fertility (Ps 81:14–16).

§§[81:1] **Upon the gittith:** probably the title of the melody to which the Psalm was to be sung or a musical instrument.

¶¶[81:4] **New moon . . . full moon:** the pilgrimage feast of harvest began with a great assembly (Lv 23:24; Nm 29:1), used the new moon as a sign (Nm 29:6), and included trumpets (Lv 23:24)..

---

x. [80:2] Ps 23:1–3; 95:7; 100:3; Gn 48:15; Ex 25:22; 1 Sm 4:4; 2 Sm 6:2; Mi 7:14.   y. [80:4, 8, 20] Ps 4:7; 31:17; 67:2; 85:5; Nm 6:25; Dn 9:17.   z. [80:5] Ps 13:2; 44:24; 74:1; 79:5; 89:47; Dt 4:24.   a. [80:6] Ps 42:4; 102:10.   b. [80:7] Ps 44:14; 79:4; 123:3–4; Jb 12:4; Dn 9:16; Zep 2:8.

c. [80:13] Ps 89:41.   d. [80:14] Hos 2:14.   e. [81:2] Ps 43:4; 68:26; 149:3; 150:3–4; Jdt 16:1.   f. [81:4] Lv 23:24; Nm 29:1.   g. [81:5] Ex 23:14ff.

## II

7 'I heard a tongue I did not know:
  "I removed his shoulder from the
    burden;[†]
  his hands moved away from the
    basket.[†h]

8 In distress you called and I rescued you;
  I answered you in secret with thunder;
  At the waters of Meribah[‡] I tested you;[i]

9 'Listen, my people, I will testify against you
                                    *Selah*
  If only you will listen to me, Israel![j]

10 There shall be no foreign god among you;[§k]
  you shall not bow down to an alien
    god.

11 'I am the LORD your God,
  who brought you up from the land
    of Egypt.
  Open wide your mouth that I may
    fill it.'

12 But my people did not listen to my words;
  Israel would not submit to me.

13 So I thrust them away to the hardness of
    their heart;
  'Let them walk in their own
    machinations.'[l]

14 O that my people would listen to me,
  that Israel would walk in my ways,[m]

15 In a moment I would humble their foes,
  and turn back my hand against their
    oppressors.[n]

16 Those who hate the LORD will try
    flattering him,
  but their fate is fixed forever.

17 But Israel I will feed with the finest wheat,
  I will satisfy them with honey from
    the rock."[o]

## PSALM 82[¶]
### The Downfall of Unjust Gods

1 A psalm of Asaph.

## I

God takes a stand in the divine council,
  gives judgment in the midst of the
    gods.[p]

2 "How long will you judge unjustly
  and favor the cause of the wicked?[q]
                                    *Selah*

3 "Defend the lowly and fatherless;
  render justice to the afflicted and
    needy.

4 Rescue the lowly and poor;
  deliver them from the hand of the
    wicked."[r]

## II

5 "The gods neither know nor understand,
  wandering about in darkness,
  and all the world's foundations
    shake.

6 I declare: "Gods though you be,[††s]
  offspring of the Most High all of
    you,

7 Yet like any mortal you shall die;
  like any prince you shall fall."

8 Arise, O God, judge the earth,[‡‡]
  for yours are all the nations.

## PSALM 83[§§]
### Prayer Against a Hostile Alliance

1 A song; a psalm of Asaph.

## I

2 God, do not be silent;
  God, do not be deaf or remain
    unmoved![t]

3 See how your enemies rage;
  your foes proudly raise their heads.

4 They conspire against your people,
  plot against those you protect.[u]

5 They say, "Come, let us wipe them out as a
    nation;
  let Israel's name be remembered no
    more!"

6 They scheme with one mind,
  they have entered into a covenant
    against you:[v]

---

*[81:7] **I heard a tongue I did not know:** a Temple official speaks the word of God (Ps 81:5b–16), which is authoritative and unlike merely human words (cf. Ps 81:4, 16).

†[81:7] **I removed his shoulder from the burden:** A reference to the liberation of Israel from slavery in Egypt. The **basket:** for carrying clay to make bricks, cf. Ex 1:14.

‡[81:8] **Meribah:** place of rebellion in the wilderness; cf. Ex 17:7; Nm 20:13.

§[81:10] **There shall be no foreign god among you:** as in Ps 50 and 95, Israel is challenged to obey the first commandment of fidelity to God after the proclamation of the exodus.

¶[Psalm 82] As in Ps 58, the pagan gods are seen as subordinate divine beings to whom Israel's God had delegated oversight of the foreign countries in the beginning (Dt 32:8–9). Now God arises in the heavenly assembly (Ps 82:1) to rebuke the unjust "gods" (Ps 82:2–4), who are stripped of divine status and reduced in rank to mortals (Ps 82:5–7). They are accused of misruling the earth by not upholding the poor. A short prayer for universal justice concludes the Psalm (Ps 82:8).

**[82:5] The gods are blind and unable to declare what is right. Their misrule shakes earth's foundations (cf. Ps 11:3; 75:4), which God made firm in creation (Ps 96:10).

††[82:6] **I declare: "Gods though you be":** in Jn 10:34 Jesus uses the verse to prove that those to whom the word of God is addressed can fittingly be called "gods."

‡‡[82:8] **Judge the earth:** according to Dt 32:8–9, Israel's God had originally assigned jurisdiction over the foreign nations to the subordinate deities, keeping Israel as a personal possession. Now God will directly take over the rulership of the whole world.

§§[Psalm 83] The community lament complains to God of the nations' attempts to wipe out the name of Israel (Ps 83:1–8). The psalmist sees all Israel's enemies throughout its history united in a conspiracy (Ps 83:2–8). May God destroy the current crop of enemies as the enemies of old were destroyed (Ps 83:9–12), and may they be pursued until they acknowledge the name of Israel's God (Ps 83:13–18).

---

h. [81:7] Ex 1:14; 6:6.   i. [81:8] Ps 95:8; Ex 2:23ff; 17:7; 19:16; Nm 20:13; 27:14.   j. [81:9] Ex 1:14; 6:6.   k. [81:10–11] Ex 20:2–6; Dt 5:6–10.   l. [81:13] Jer 3:17; 7:24.   m. [81:14] Is 48:18.   n. [81:15] Lv 26:7–8.   o. [81:17] Ps 147:14; Dt 32:13–14.

p. [82:1] Is 3:13–14.   q. [82:2] Ps 58:2.   r. [82:4] Dt 1:17.   s. [82:6] 2 Pt 1:4.   t. [83:2] Ps 10:1; 44:24; 109:1.   u. [83:4] Jer 11:9.   v. [83:6] Ps 2:5.

7 The tents of Edom and the Ishmaelites,
   of Moab and the Hagrites,[w]
8 Gebal, Ammon, and Amalek,[x]
   Philistia and the inhabitants of
      Tyre.[y]
9 Assyria, too, in league with them,
   backs the descendants of Lot.

                                          *Selah*

                         II

10 Deal with them as with Midian;
   as with Sisera and Jabin at the wadi
      Kishon,[z]
11 Those destroyed at Endor,
   who became dung for the ground.[a]
12 Make their nobles like Oreb and Zeeb,
   all their princes like Zebah and
      Zalmunna,
13 Who made a plan together,
   "Let us take for ourselves the
      pastures of God."
14 My God, make them like tumbleweed,
   into chaff flying before the wind.[b]
15 As a fire raging through a forest,
   a flame setting mountains ablaze,[c]
16 Pursue them with your tempest;
   terrify them with your storm-wind.
17 Cover their faces with shame,
   till they seek your name,[+] LORD.
18 Let them be ashamed and terrified forever;
   let them perish in disgrace.
19 Let them know that your name is LORD,
   you alone are the Most High over all
      the earth.[d]

## PSALM 84[§]
### Prayer of a Pilgrim to Jerusalem

1 For the leader; "upon the *gittith*." A psalm of the
Korahites.

                         I

2  How lovely your dwelling,
   O LORD of hosts![e]

3 My soul yearns and pines
   for the courts of the LORD.[f]
My heart and flesh cry out
   for the living God.
4 As the sparrow finds a home
   and the swallow a nest to settle her
      young,
My home is by your altars,
   LORD of hosts, my king and my God![g]
5 Blessed are those who dwell in your house!
   They never cease to praise you.

                                          *Selah*

                         II

6 Blessed the man who finds refuge in you,
   in their hearts are pilgrim roads.
7 As they pass through the Baca valley,[**]
   they find spring water to drink.
The early rain covers it with blessings.
8 They will go from strength to strength[††]
   and see the God of gods on Zion.

                         III

9 LORD God of hosts, hear my prayer;
   listen, God of Jacob.

                                          *Selah*

10 ‡‡O God, watch over our shield;
   look upon the face of your anointed.[h]

                         IV

11 Better one day in your courts
   than a thousand elsewhere.
Better the threshold of the house of my
      God
   than a home in the tents of the
      wicked.
12 For a sun and shield is the LORD God,
   bestowing all grace and glory.
The LORD withholds no good thing
   from those who walk without
      reproach.
13 O LORD of hosts,
   blessed the man who trusts in you!

## PSALM 85[§§]
### Prayer for Divine Favor

1 For the leader. A psalm of the Korahites.

---

*[83:7–9] Apart from the Assyrians, all the nations listed here were neighbors of Israel. The Hagrites are a tribe of the desert regions east of Ammon and Moab (1 Chr 5:10, 19–22). Gebal is the Phoenician city of Byblos or perhaps a mountain region south of the Dead Sea. The descendants of Lot are Moab and Edom (Gn 19:36–38 and Dt 2:9). These nations were never united against Israel in the same period; the Psalm has lumped them all together.

†[83:10–13] For the historical events, see Jgs 4–8.

‡[83:17] **Seek your name:** a variant of the more typical phrase "to seek the face of God" (Ps 24:6; 27:8; 105:4). Seeking the face of God refers to the worshiper having recourse to a temple or sanctuary where in non-Jewish contexts a statue embodies the physical presence of the Deity. In Israel's aniconic tradition no visible image or statue can represent God. This understanding is conveyed here concretely by use of the term "your name" rather than the more typical "your face."

§[Psalm 84] Israelites celebrated three pilgrimage feasts in Jerusalem annually. The Psalm expresses the sentiments of the pilgrims eager to enjoy the divine presence.

¶[84:4] The desire of a restless bird for a secure home is an image of the desire of a pilgrim for the secure house of God, cf. Ps 42:2–3, where the image for the desire of the pilgrim is the thirst of the deer for water.

**[84:7] Baca valley: Hebrew obscure; probably a valley on the way to Jerusalem.

††[84:8] **Strength to strength:** pass through outer and inner wall.

‡‡[84:10] **Our shield . . . your anointed:** the king had a role in the liturgical celebration. For the king as shield, cf. Ps 89:19.

§§[Psalm 85] A national lament reminding God of past favors and forgiveness (Ps 85:2–4) and begging for forgiveness and grace now (Ps 85:5–8). A speaker represents the people who wait humbly with open hearts (Ps 85:9–10): God will be active on their behalf (Ps 85:11–13). The situation suggests the conditions of Judea during the early postexilic period, the fifth century B.C.; the thoughts are similar to those of postexilic prophets (Hg 1:5–11; 2:6–9).

---

w. [83:7] Nm 20:23; 1 Chr 5:10, 19.  x. [83:8] Ex 17:8.  y. [83:8] Jos 13:2.  z. [83:10] Ex 2:15; Is 9:3; 10:26.  a. [83:11] Jer 8:2.  b. [83:14] Ps 1:4; 35:5; 58:10; Is 5:24; 10:17; 17:13; 29:5; Ez 21:3.  c. [83:15] Ps 50:3.  d. [83:19] Ps 97:9; Dt 4:39; Dn 3:45.  e. [84:2] Ps 43:3–4; 122:1.

f. [84:3] Ps 42:2–3; 63:2–3; 143:6; Is 26:9.  g. [84:4] Ps 5:3. h. [84:10] Ps 89:19.

I

2 You once favored, LORD, your land,
    restored the captives of Jacob.[i]
3 You forgave the guilt of your people,
    pardoned all their sins.

                                              *Selah*

4 You withdrew all your wrath,
    turned back from your burning
        anger.[j]

II

5 Restore us, God of our salvation;
    let go of your displeasure with us.[k]
6 Will you be angry with us forever,
    prolong your anger for all
        generations?[l]
7 Certainly you will again restore our life,
    that your people may rejoice in you.
8 Show us, LORD, your mercy;
    grant us your salvation.

III

9 †I will listen for what God, the LORD, has
        to say;
    surely he will speak of peace
  To his people and to his faithful.
    May they not turn to foolishness!
10 Near indeed is his salvation for those who
        fear him;
    glory will dwell in our land.
11 †Love and truth will meet;
    justice and peace will kiss.[m]
12 Truth will spring from the earth;
    justice will look down from heaven.[n]
13 Yes, the LORD will grant his bounty;
    our land will yield its produce.[o]
14 Justice will march before him,
    and make a way for his footsteps.

## PSALM 86[‡]
### Prayer in Time of Distress

1 A prayer of David.

I

  Incline your ear, LORD, and answer me,
    for I am poor and oppressed.
2 Preserve my life, for I am devoted;
    save your servant who trusts in you.
  You are my God; 3be gracious to me, Lord;
    to you I call all the day.
4 Gladden the soul of your servant;
    to you, Lord, I lift up my soul.[p]
5 Lord, you are good and forgiving,

most merciful to all who call on
        you.[q]
6 LORD, hear my prayer;
    listen to my cry for help.[r]
7 On the day of my distress I call to you,
    for you will answer me.

II

8 None among the gods can equal you,
        O Lord;
    nor can their deeds compare to
        yours.[s]
9 All the nations you have made shall come
        to bow before you, Lord,
    and give honor to your name.[t]
10 For you are great and do wondrous deeds;
    and you alone are God.

III

11 Teach me, LORD, your way
    that I may walk in your truth,[u]
    single-hearted and revering your
        name.
12 I will praise you with all my heart,
    glorify your name forever, Lord my
        God.
13 Your mercy to me is great;
    you have rescued me from the
        depths of Sheol.[v]
14 O God, the arrogant have risen against
        me;
    a ruthless band has sought my life;
    to you they pay no heed.
15 But you, Lord, are a compassionate and
        gracious God,
    slow to anger, abounding in mercy
        and truth.[w]
16 Turn to me, be gracious to me;
    give your strength to your servant;
    save the son of your handmaid.[x]
17 Give me a sign of your favor:
    make my enemies see, to their
        confusion,
    that you, LORD, help and comfort me.

## PSALM 87[§]
### Zion the True Birthplace

1 A psalm of the Korahites. A song.

I

  His foundation is on holy
        mountains,
2 The LORD loves the gates[¶] of Zion
    more than any dwelling in Jacob.
3 Glorious things are said of you,
    O city of God!

                                              *Selah*

---

*[85:9] The prophet listens to God's revelation, cf. Heb 2:1.
†[85:11–13] Divine activity is personified as pairs of virtues.
‡[Psalm 86] An individual lament. The psalmist, "poor and oppressed" (Ps 86:1), "devoted" (Ps 86:2), "your servant" (Ps 86:2, 4, 16), "rescued . . . from the depths of Sheol" (Ps 86:13), attacked by the ruthless (Ps 86:14), desires only God's protection (Ps 86:1–7, 11–17).

i. [85:2] Ps 14:7; 126:4.  j. [85:4] Ps 78:38; Ex 32:14; Is 48:9.
k. [85:5] Ps 80:4.  l. [85:6] Ps 79:5; 89:47.  m. [85:11] Ps 89:15; 97:2.  n. [85:12] Is 45:8.  o. [85:13] Ps 67:7; Lv 26:4; Ez 34:27; Hos 2:23–24; Zec 8:12.  p. [86:4] Ps 25:1; 143:8.

§[Psalm 87] A song of Zion, like Ps 46; 48; 76; 132.
¶[87:2] **The gates**: the city itself, a common Hebrew idiom.

q. [86:5] Jl 2:13.  r. [86:6] Ps 5:2; 130:1–2.  s. [86:8] Ps 35:10; 89:9; Ex 15:11; Dt 3:24; Jer 10:6.  t. [86:9] Ps 22:28; Zec 14:16; Rev 15:4.  u. [86:11] Ps 25:4; 26:3; 27:11; 119:12, 35; 143:8, 10.  v. [86:13] Ps 30:4; 40:3; Jon 2:7.  w. [86:15] Ps 103:8; 130:7; 145:8; Ex 34:6.  x. [86:16] Ps 25:16; 116:16; Wis 9:5.  y. [87:1–2] Ps 76:2–3; 78:68–69.

II

4 Rahab and Babylon I count
        among those who know me.
See, Philistia and Tyre, with Ethiopia,
        "This one was born there."
5 *And of Zion it will be said:
        "Each one was born in it."[z]
The Most High will establish it;[a]
6        the LORD notes in the register of the
                peoples:
        "This one was born there."[b]

                                        Selah

7 So singers and dancers:
        "All my springs are in you."[c]

## PSALM 88[†]
### A Despairing Lament

[1]A song; a psalm of the Korahites. For the leader;
according to *Mahalath*. For singing; a *maskil* of
Heman the Ezrahite.

                    I

2 LORD, the God of my salvation, I call out
        by day;
        at night I cry aloud in your presence.[d]
3 Let my prayer come before you;
        incline your ear to my cry.[e]
4 ‡For my soul is filled with troubles;[f]
        my life draws near to Sheol.
5 I am reckoned with those who go down to
        the pit;
        I am like a warrior without strength.
6 My couch is among the dead,
        like the slain who lie in the grave.
You remember them no more;
        they are cut off from your influence.
7 You plunge me into the bottom of the pit,
        into the darkness of the abyss.
8 Your wrath lies heavy upon me;
        all your waves crash over me.[g]

                                        Selah

                    II

9 Because of you my acquaintances shun
        me;
        you make me loathsome to them;[h]
Caged in, I cannot escape;
10        my eyes grow dim from trouble.

All day I call on you, LORD;
        I stretch out my hands to you.

11 ⁵Do you work wonders for the dead?
        Do the shades arise and praise you?[i]

                                        Selah

                    III

12 Is your mercy proclaimed in the grave,
        your faithfulness among those who
                have perished?⁵
13 Are your marvels declared in the darkness,
        your righteous deeds in the land of
                oblivion?

                    IV

14 But I cry out to you, LORD;
        in the morning my prayer comes
                before you.
15 Why do you reject my soul, LORD,
        and hide your face from me?
16 I have been mortally afflicted since youth;
        I have borne your terrors and I am
                made numb.
17 Your wrath has swept over me;
        your terrors have destroyed me.[j]
18 All day they surge round like a flood;
        from every side they encircle me.
19 Because of you friend and neighbor shun
        me;[k]
        my only friend is darkness.

## PSALM 89[**]
### A Lament over God's Promise to David

[1]A *maskil* of Ethan the Ezrahite.

                    A
                    I

2 I will sing of your mercy forever, LORD[l]
        proclaim your faithfulness through
                all ages.
3 ††For I said, "My mercy is established
                forever;
        my faithfulness will stand as long as
                the heavens.
4 I have made a covenant with my chosen one;
        I have sworn to David my servant:
5 I will make your dynasty stand forever
        and establish your throne through
                all ages."[m]

                                        Selah

§[88:11–13] The psalmist seeks to persuade God to act out
of concern for divine honor: the shades give you no worship,
so keep me alive to offer you praise.

¶[88:12] **Perished:** lit., "Abaddon," the deepest part of Sheol.

**[Psalm 89] The community laments the defeat of the
Davidic king, to whom God promised kingship as enduring as
the heavens (Ps 89:2–5). The Psalm narrates how God became
king of the divine beings (Ps 89:6–9) and how the Davidic
king became king of earthly kings (Ps 89:20–38). Since the
defeat of the king calls into question God's promise, the community ardently prays God to be faithful to the original promise to David (Ps 89:39–52).

††[89:3–5] David's dynasty is to be as long-lasting as the
heavens, a statement reinforced by using the same verbs
(establish, stand) both of the divine love and loyalty and of the
Davidic dynasty and throne, cf. Ps 89:29–30.

*[87:5–6] The bond between the exile and the holy city was
so strong as to override the exile's citizenship of lesser cities.

†[Psalm 88] A lament in which the psalmist prays for
rescue from the alienation of approaching death. Each of the
three stanzas begins with a call to God (Ps 88:2, 10, 14) and
complains of the death that separates one from God. The tone
is persistently grim.

‡[88:4–8] In imagination the psalmist already experiences
the alienation of Sheol.

z. [87:5] Gal 4:26.   a. [87:5] Ps 48:9.   b. [87:6] Is 4:3.   c. [87:7] Ps
68:26; 149:3.   d. [88:2] Ps 77:3.   e. [88:3] Ps 119:170.   f. [88:4–7]
Ps 28:1; 30:4; 40:3; 86:13; 143:7; Nm 16:33; Jb 17:1; Jon 2:7.   g. [88:8]
Ps 18:5; 32:6; 42:8; 69:2; Jon 2:4.   h. [88:9] Ps 38:12; 79:4; 80:7;
123:3–4; 142:8; Jb 12:4; 19:13; Lam 3:7; Dn 9:16.

i. [88:11] Ps 6:6; 30:10; 38:18; 115:17.   j. [88:17] Jb 6:4; 20:25.
k. [88:19] Jb 19:13.   l. [89:2] Is 63:7.   m. [89:5] Ps 61:7–8; 132:11;
2 Sm 7:8–16.

## II

6 The heavens praise your marvels, LORD,
    your loyalty in the assembly of the
    holy ones.ⁿ

7 Who in the skies ranks with the LORD?
    Who is like the LORD among the
    sons of the gods?ᵒ

8 A God dreaded in the council of the holy
    ones,
    greater and more awesome than all
    those around him!

9 LORD, God of hosts, who is like you?
    Mighty LORD, your faithfulness
    surrounds you.

10 You rule the raging sea;ᵖ
    you still its swelling waves.

11 You crush Rahab† with a mortal blow;
    with your strong arm you scatter
    your foes.

12 Yours are the heavens, yours the earth;
    you founded the world and
    everything in it.�q

13 ‡Zaphon and Amanus you created;
    Tabor and Hermon rejoice in your
    name.

14 You have a mighty arm.
    Your hand is strong; your right hand
    is ever exalted.

15 Justice and judgment are the foundation
    of your throne;
    mercy and faithfulness march before
    you.ʳ

16 Blessed the people who know the war cry,
    who walk in the radiance of your
    face, LORD.

17 In your name they sing joyfully all the
    day;
    they rejoice in your righteousness.ˢ

18 You are their majestic strength;
    by your favor our hornˢ is exalted.ᵗ

19 Truly the LORD is our shield,
    the Holy One of Israel, our king!ᵘ

## III

20 Then you spoke in vision;ᵛ
    to your faithful ones you said:

"I have set a leader over the warriors;
    I have raised up a chosen one from
    the people.

21 I have chosen David, my servant;
    with my holy oil I have anointed
    him.

22 My hand will be with him;ʷ
    my arm will make him strong.

23 No enemy shall outwit him,
    nor shall the wicked defeat him.

24 I will crush his foes before him,
    strike down those who hate him.

25 My faithfulness and mercy will be with
    him;
    through my name his horn will be
    exalted.

26 ¶I will set his hand upon the sea,
    his right hand upon the rivers.

27 He shall cry to me, 'You are my father,ˣ
    my God, the Rock of my salvation!'

28 I myself make him the firstborn,
    Most High** over the kings of the
    earth.

29 Forever I will maintain my mercy for
    him;ʸ
    my covenant with him stands firm.

30 I will establish his dynasty forever,
    his throne as the days of the
    heavens.

31 If his descendants forsake my teaching,ᶻ
    do not follow my decrees,

32 If they fail to observe my statutes,
    do not keep my commandments,

33 I will punish their crime with a rod
    and their guilt with blows.

34 But I will not take my mercy from him,
    nor will I betray my bond of
    faithfulness.ᵃ

35 I will not violate my covenant;
    the promise of my lips I will not
    alter.ᵇ

36 By my holiness I swore once for all:ᶜ
    I will never be false to David.

37 ††His dynasty will continue forever,ᵈ
    his throne, like the sun before me.

38 Like the moon it will stand eternal,
    forever firm like the sky!"

*Selah*

---

*[89:7] **The sons of the gods**: "the holy ones" and "courtiers" of Ps 89:6, 8. These heavenly spirits are members of God's court.

†[89:11] **Rahab**: a mythological sea monster whose name is used in the Bible mainly as a personification of primeval chaos, cf. Jb 9:13; 26:12; Ps 74:13–14; Is 51:9.

‡[89:13] **Zaphon and Amanus**: two sacred mountains in northern Syria which came to designate the directions of north and south. **Tabor**: a high hill in the valley of Jezreel in northern Israel. **Hermon**: a mountain in Lebanon, forming the southern spur of the Anti-Lebanon range.

§[89:18, 25] **Horn**: a concrete noun for an abstract quality; horn is a symbol of strength.

n. [89:6] Ps 29:1; 82:1; Jb 1:6; 5:1.  o. [89:7–9] Ps 35:10; 86:8; 113:5; Ex 15:11; Jer 10:6.  p. [89:10–11] Ps 65:8; 74:13–15; 107:29; Jb 7:12; Is 51:9–10.  q. [89:12] Ps 24:1–2; 50:12; Dt 10:14; 1 Cor 10:26.  r. [89:15] Ps 85:11–12; 97:2.  s. [89:17] Ps 47:2; Zep 3:14.  t. [89:18] Ps 112:9; 148:14.  u. [89:19] Ps 47:9; 96:10; 97:1; 99:1; Is 6:3.  v. [89:20–21] Ps 78:70; 132:11–13; 2 Sm 7:4, 8–16; 1 Chr 17:3, 7–14; Is 42:1; Acts 13:22.

¶[89:26] **The sea . . . the rivers**: geographically the limits of the Davidic empire (the Mediterranean and the Euphrates); mythologically, the traditional forces of chaos. See note on Ps 89:11.

**[89:28] **Most High**: a divine title, which is here extended to David as God's own king, cf. Ps 2:7–9; Is 9:5. As God rules over the members of the heavenly council (Ps 89:6–9), so David, God's surrogate, rules over earthly kings.

††[89:37–38] **Like the sun before me . . . like the sky**: as enduring as the heavenly lights, cf. Ps 89:2–5 and Ps 72:5, 17.

w. [89:22–25] 1 Sm 2:9–10.  x. [89:27–28] Ps 2:7; 110:2–3; 2 Sm 7:9, 14; Col 1:15, 18; Rev 1:5.  y. [89:29–30] Ps 18:51; 61:8; 144:10; 2 Sm 7:11; Is 55:3.  z. [89:31–33] Lv 26:14–33.  a. [89:34] Ps 40:12; Sir 47:22.  b. [89:35] Jer 33:20–21.  c. [89:36] Am 4:2.  d. [89:37–38] Ps 61:8; 72:5; Sir 43:6.

## B
### IV

39 But now you have rejected and spurned,[e]
  been enraged at your anointed.
40 You renounced the covenant with your
    servant,
  defiled his crown in the dust.
41 You broke down all city walls,[f]
  left his strongholds in ruins.
42 All who pass through seize plunder;
  his neighbors deride him.
43 You have exalted the right hand of his foes,
  have gladdened all his enemies.[g]
44 You turned back his sharp sword,
  did not support him in battle.
45 You brought to an end his splendor,
  hurled his throne to the ground.
46 You cut short the days of his youth,
  covered him with shame.
                            *Selah*

### V

47 How long, LORD? Will you hide forever?
  Must your wrath smolder like fire?[h]
48 Remember how brief life is,
  how frail the sons of man you have
    created![i]
49 What is man, that he should live and not
    see death?
  Who can deliver his soul from the
    power of Sheol?[j]
                            *Selah*

### VI

50 Where are your former mercies, Lord,
  that you swore to David in your
    faithfulness?
51 Remember, Lord, the insults to your
    servants,
  how I have borne in my bosom the
    slander of the nations.[k]
52 Your enemies, LORD, insult;
  they insult each step of your anointed.
53 ˙Blessed be the LORD forever! Amen and
  amen![l]

## Fourth Book—Psalms 90–106

### PSALM 90[†]
### God's Eternity and Human Frailty

1 A prayer of Moses, the man of God.

### I
Lord, you have been our refuge
  through all generations.
2 Before the mountains were born,
  the earth and the world brought
    forth,
  from eternity to eternity you are
    God.[m]
3 You turn humanity back into dust,[‡]
  saying, "Return, you children of
    Adam!"[n]
4 A thousand years in your eyes
  are merely a day gone by,[o]
Before a watch passes in the night,
5   ⁵you wash them away;[p]
They sleep,
  and in the morning they sprout
    again like an herb.
6 In the morning it blooms only to pass
    away;
  in the evening it is wilted and
    withered.⁵[q]

### II
7 Truly we are consumed by your anger,
  filled with terror by your wrath.
8 You have kept our faults before you,
  our hidden sins in the light of your
    face.[r]
9 Our life ebbs away under your wrath;[s]
  our years end like a sigh.
10 Seventy is the sum of our years,
  or eighty, if we are strong;
Most of them are toil and sorrow;
  they pass quickly, and we are gone.
11 Who comprehends the strength of your
    anger?
  Your wrath matches the fear it
    inspires.
12 Teach us to count our days aright,
  that we may gain wisdom of heart.

### III
13 Relent, O LORD! How long?
  Have pity on your servants!
14 Fill us at daybreak with your mercy,[t]
  that all our days we may sing for joy.
15 Make us glad as many days as you
    humbled us,
  for as many years as we have seen
    trouble.[u]

---

*[89:53] The doxology at the end of the third book of the Psalms; it is not part of Ps 89.

†[Psalm 90] A communal lament that describes only in general terms the cause of the community's distress. After confidently invoking God (Ps 90:1), the Psalm turns to a complaint contrasting God's eternity with the brevity of human life (Ps 90:2–6) and sees in human suffering the punishment for sin (Ps 90:7–12). The Psalm concludes with a plea for God's intervention (Ps 90:13–17).

‡[90:3] **Dust:** one word of God is enough to return mortals to the dust from which they were created. Human beings were created from earth in Gn 2:7; 3:19.

§[90:5] **You wash them away:** the Hebrew of Ps 90:4–5 is unclear.

¶[90:6] **It is wilted and withered:** the transitory nature of the grass under the scorching sun was proverbial, cf. Ps 129:6; Is 40:6–8.

e. [89:39–47] Ps 44:10–25. f. [89:41–42] Ps 80:13–14. g. [89:43] Lam 1:5. h. [89:47] Ps 13:2; 44:25; 74:10; 79:5; Dt 4:24. i. [89:48] Ps 39:5–6; 62:10; 90:9–10; 144:4; Jb 7:6, 16; 14:1, 5; Eccl 6:12; Wis 2:5. j. [89:49] Ps 90:3. k. [89:51] Ps 79:12. l. [89:53] Ps 41:14; 72:18; 106:48.

m. [90:2] Ps 48:15; 55:20; 93:2; 102:13; Heb 1:12. n. [90:3] Ps 103:14; 104:29; 146:4; Gn 3:19; 1 Mc 2:63; Jb 34:14–15; Eccl 3:20; 12:7; Sir 40:11. o. [90:4] 2 Pt 3:8. p. [90:5] Ps 89:48. q. [90:6] Ps 37:2; 102:11; 103:15–16; Jb 14:1–2; Is 40:6–8. r. [90:8] Ps 109:14–15; Hos 7:2. s. [90:9–10] Ps 39:5–7; 62:10; 102:24–25; 144:4; Gn 6:3; Jb 7:6, 16; 14:5; Prv 10:27; Eccl 6:12; Wis 2:5; Sir 18:8; Is 65:20. t. [90:14] Ps 17:15. u. [90:15] Nm 14:34; Jer 31:13.

16 Show your deeds to your servants,
       your glory to their children.
17 May the favor of the Lord our God be
       ours.[v]
   Prosper the work of our hands!
   Prosper the work of our hands!

## PSALM 91[*]
### Security Under God's Protection

### I

1 You who dwell in the shelter of the Most
       High,[†]
   who abide in the shade of the
       Almighty,[†]
2 Say to the LORD, "My refuge and fortress,
       my God in whom I trust."[w]
3 He will rescue you from the fowler's
       snare,
   from the destroying plague,
4 He will shelter you with his pinions,
   and under his wings you may take
       refuge;[x]
   his faithfulness is a protecting
       shield.
5 You shall not fear the terror of the night
   nor the arrow that flies by day,[y]
6 Nor the pestilence that roams in
       darkness,
   nor the plague that ravages at
       noon.[z]
7 Though a thousand fall at your side,
   ten thousand at your right hand,
   near you it shall not come.
8 You need simply watch;
   the punishment of the wicked you
       will see.[a]
9 Because you have the LORD for your
       refuge
   and have made the Most High your
       stronghold,
10 No evil shall befall you,
   no affliction come near your tent.[b]
11 ‡For he commands his angels with regard
       to you,[c]

to guard you wherever you go.[d]
12 With their hands they shall support you,
   lest you strike your foot against a
       stone.[e]
13 You can tread upon the asp and the viper,
   trample the lion and the dragon.[f]

### II

14 Because he clings to me I will deliver him;
   because he knows my name I will set
       him on high.[g]
15 He will call upon me and I will answer;[h]
   I will be with him in distress;[i]
   I will deliver him and give him honor.
16 With length of days I will satisfy him,
   and fill him with my saving power.[j]

## PSALM 92[§]
### A Hymn of Thanksgiving for God's Fidelity

1 A psalm. A sabbath song.

### I

2 It is good to give thanks to the LORD,
   to sing praise to your name, Most
       High,[k]
3 To proclaim your love at daybreak,
   your faithfulness in the night,
4 With the ten-stringed harp,
   with melody upon the lyre.[l]
5 For you make me jubilant, LORD, by your
       deeds;
   at the works of your hands I shout
       for joy.

### II

6 How great are your works, LORD![m]
   How profound your designs!
7 A senseless person cannot know this;
   a fool cannot comprehend.
8 Though the wicked flourish like grass[n]
   and all sinners thrive,
   They are destined for eternal destruction;
9 but you, LORD, are forever on high.
10 Indeed your enemies, LORD,
   indeed your enemies shall perish;
   all sinners shall be scattered.[o]

### III

11 You have given me the strength of a wild
       ox;[p]
   you have poured rich oil upon me.[q]
12 My eyes look with glee on my wicked
       enemies;
   my ears shall hear what happens to
       my wicked foes.[r]

---

*[Psalm 91] A prayer of someone who has taken refuge in the Lord, possibly within the Temple (Ps 91:1–2). The psalmist is confident that God's presence will protect the people in every dangerous situation (Ps 91:3–13). The final verses are an oracle of salvation promising salvation to those who trust in God (Ps 91:14–16).

†[91:1] **The shelter of the Most High:** basically "hiding place" but in the Psalms a designation for the protected Temple precincts, cf. Ps 27:5; 31:21; 61:5. **The shade of the Almighty:** lit., "the shadow of the wings of the Almighty," cf. Ps 17:8; 36:8; 57:2; 63:8. Ps 91:4 makes clear that the shadow is an image of the safety afforded by the outstretched wings of the cherubim in the holy of holies.

‡[91:11–12] The words are cited in Lk 4:10–11; Mt 4:6, as Satan tempts Jesus in the desert.

§[Psalm 92] A hymn of praise and thanks for God's faithful deeds (Ps 92:2–5). The wicked, deluded by their prosperity (Ps 92:6–9), are punished (Ps 92:10), whereas the psalmist has already experienced God's protection (Ps 92:11–15).

---

v. [90:17] Ps 33:22.  w. [91:2] Ps 18:3; 31:3–4; 42:10; 142:6; 2 Sm 22:3.  x. [91:4] Ps 17:8; 36:8; 57:2; 63:8; Dt 32:11; Ru 2:12; Mt 23:37.  y. [91:5] Prv 3:25; Sg 3:8.  z. [91:6] Dt 32:24.  a. [91:8] Ps 92:12.  b. [91:10] Prv 12:21; Dt 7:15.  c. [91:11–12] Mt 4:6; Lk 4:10f.

d. [91:11] Heb 1:14.  e. [91:12] Ps 121:3; Prv 3:23.  f. [91:13] Is 11:8; Lk 10:19.  g. [91:14] Ps 9:11; 119:132.  h. [91:15] Jer 33:3; Zec 13:9.  i. [91:15] Is 43:2.  j. [91:16] Prv 3:2.  k. [92:2] Ps 33:1; 147:1.  l. [92:4] Ps 33:2; 144:9.  m. [92:6–7] Ps 131:1; 139:6, 17; Wis 13:1; 17:1.  n. [92:8] Ps 37:35.  o. [92:10] Ps 68:1–2; 125:5.  p. [92:11] Ps 75:11; Dt 33:17.  q. [92:11] Ps 23:5.  r. [92:12] Ps 91:8.

¹³ The just shall flourish like the palm tree,
    shall grow like a cedar of Lebanon.*
¹⁴ 'Planted in the house of the LORD,
    they shall flourish in the courts of
    our God.
¹⁵ They shall bear fruit even in old age,
    they will stay fresh and green,
¹⁶ To proclaim: "The LORD is just;
    my rock, in whom there is no wrong."ᵗ

## PSALM 93†
## God Is a Mighty King

¹ The LORD is king,‡ robed with majesty;
    the LORD is robed, girded with might.ᵘ
The world will surely stand in place,
    never to be moved.ᵛ
² Your throne stands firm from of old;
    you are from everlasting.ʷ
³ §The flood has raised up, LORD;
    the flood has raised up its roar;
    the flood has raised its pounding
    waves.
⁴ More powerful than the roar of many
    waters,
    more powerful than the breakers of
    the sea,
    powerful in the heavens is the LORD.
⁵ Your decrees are firmly established;
    holiness befits your house, LORD,
    for all the length of days.

## PSALM 94§
## A Prayer for Deliverance from the Wicked

I
¹ LORD, avenging God,
    avenging God, shine forth!ˣ

---

*[92:14] **Planted**: the just are likened to trees growing in the sacred precincts of the Temple, which is often seen as the source of life and fertility because of God's presence, cf. Ps 36:9, 10; Ez 47:1–12.

†[Psalm 93] A hymn celebrating the kingship of God, who created the world (Ps 93:1–2) by defeating the sea (Ps 93:3–4). In the ancient myth that is alluded to here, Sea completely covered the land, making it impossible for the human community to live. Sea, or Flood, roars in anger against God, who is personified in the storm. God's utterances or decrees are given authority by the victory over Sea (Ps 93:5).

‡[93:1] **The LORD is king**: lit., "the LORD reigns." This Psalm, and Ps 47; 96–99, are sometimes called enthronement Psalms. They may have been used in a special liturgy during which God's ascent to the throne was ritually reenacted. They have also been interpreted eschatologically, pointing to the coming of God as king at the end-time.

§[93:3] **The flood**: the primordial sea was tamed by God in the act of creation. It is a figure of chaos and rebellion, cf. Ps 46:4.

¶[Psalm 94] A lament of an individual who is threatened by wicked people. The danger affects the whole community. Calling upon God as judge (Ps 94:1–2), the Psalm complains about oppression of the holy community by people within (Ps 94:3–7). Bold declarations of faith follow: denunciation of evildoers (Ps 94:8–11) and assurance to the just (Ps 94:12–15). The Psalm continues with further lament (Ps 94:16–19) and ends with strong confidence in God's response (Ps 94:20–23).

s. [92:13] Ps 1:3; 52:10; Jer 17:8.    t. [92:16] Dt 32:4.    u. [93:1] Ps 47:8; 96:10; 97:1; 99:1.    v. [93:1] Ps 75:2–3; 104:5.    w. [93:2] Ps 55:20; 90:2; 102:13; Heb 1:12.    x. [94:1] Na 1:2.

---

² Rise up, O judge of the earth;
    give the proud what they deserve!ʸ
II
³ How long, LORD, shall the wicked,
    how long shall the wicked glory?ᶻ
⁴ How long will they mouth haughty
    speeches,
    go on boasting, all these evildoers?ᵃ
⁵ They crush your people, LORD,
    torment your very own.
⁶ They kill the widow and alien;
    the orphan they murder.ᵇ
⁷ They say, "The LORD does not see;
    the God of Jacob takes no notice."ᶜ
III
⁸ Understand, you stupid people!
    You fools, when will you be wise?ᵈ
⁹ Does the one who shaped the ear not
    hear?
    The one who formed the eye not see?ᵉ
¹⁰ Does the one who guides nations not
    rebuke?
    The one who teaches man not have
    knowledge?
¹¹ The LORD knows the plans of man;
    they are like a fleeting breath.ᶠ
IV
¹² Blessed the one whom you guide, LORD,ᵍ
    whom you teach by your
    instruction,
¹³ To give rest from evil days,
    while a pit is being dug for the
    wicked.
¹⁴ For the LORD will not forsake his people,
    nor abandon his inheritance.ʰ
¹⁵ Judgment shall again be just,
    and all the upright of heart will
    follow it.
V
¹⁶ Who will rise up for me against the
    wicked?
    Who will stand up for me against
    evildoers?
¹⁷ If the LORD were not my help,
    I would long have been silent in the
    grave.ⁱ
¹⁸ When I say, "My foot is slipping,"
    your mercy, LORD, holds me up.ʲ
¹⁹ When cares increase within me,
    your comfort gives me joy.
VI
²⁰ Can unjust judges be your allies,
    those who create burdens by decree,
²¹ Those who conspire against the just
    and condemn the innocent to death?
²² No, the LORD is my secure height,
    my God, my rock of refuge,

---

y. [94:2] Jer 51:56; Lam 3:64.    z. [94:3] Ps. 13:2; 75:5; Jer 12:1.
a. [94:4] Ps 73; Mal 2:17; 3:14.    b. [94:6] Ex 22:21–22; Dt 24:17–22.
c. [94:7] Ps 10:11; 64:6; 73:11; Jb 22:13–14; Ez 9:9.    d. [94:8] Prv 1:22; 8:5.    e. [94:9] Ex 4:11; Prv 20:12.    f. [94:11] Ps 33:15; 1 Cor 3:20.    g. [94:12] Ps 119:71; Jb 5:17.    h. [94:14] 1 Sm 12:22; Sir 47:22.    i. [94:17] Ps 6:6; 115:17.    j. [94:18] Ps 145:14.

23 [k]Who will turn back their evil upon them[l]
         and destroy them for their
            wickedness.
      Surely the LORD our God will
         destroy them!

## PSALM 95[*]
### A Call to Praise and Obedience

I

1 Come, let us sing joyfully to the LORD;
      cry out to the rock of our salvation.[m]
2 Let us come before him with a song of
      praise,
         joyfully sing out our psalms.
3 For the LORD is the great God,
      the great king over all gods,[n]
4 Whose hand holds the depths of the
      earth;
         who owns the tops of the
            mountains.
5 The sea and dry land belong to God,
      who made them, formed them by
         hand.[o]

II

6 Enter, let us bow down in worship;
      let us kneel before the LORD who
         made us.
7 For he is our God,
      we are the people he shepherds,
         the sheep in his hands.[p]

III

Oh, that today you would hear his voice:[q]
8      Do not harden your hearts as at
            Meribah,
         as on the day of Massah in the
            desert.[†]
9 There your ancestors tested me;
      they tried me though they had seen
         my works.[r]
10 Forty years I loathed that generation;
      I said: "This people's heart goes
         astray;
            they do not know my ways."[s]
11 Therefore I swore in my anger:
      "They shall never enter my rest."[‡]

---

*[Psalm 95] Twice the Psalm calls the people to praise and worship God (Ps 95:1–2, 6), the king of all creatures (Ps 95:3–5) and shepherd of the flock (Ps 95:7a, 7b). The last strophe warns the people to be more faithful than were their ancestors in the journey to the promised land (Ps 95:7c–11). This invitation to praise God regularly opens the Church's official prayer, the Liturgy of the Hours.

†[95:8] **Meribah:** lit., "contention"; the place where the Israelites quarreled with God. **Massah:** "testing," the place where they put God to the trial, cf. Ex 17:7; Nm 20:13.

‡[95:11] **My rest:** the promised land as in Dt 12:9. Heb 4 applies the verse to the eternal rest of heaven.

k. [94:23] Ps 7:16; 9:16; 35:8; 57:7; Prv 26:27; Eccl 10:8; Sir 27:26. l. [94:23] Ps 107:42. m. [95:1] Dt 32:15. n. [95:3] Ps 47:2; 135:5. o. [95:5] Ps 24:1–2. p. [95:7–11] Ps 81:8; 106:32; Heb 3:7–11, 15; 4:3, 5, 7. q. [95:7] Ps 23:1–3; 100:3; Mi 7:14. r. [95:9] Nm 14:22; 20:2–13; Dt 6:16; 33:8. s. [95:10] Ps 78:8; Nm 14:34; Dt 32:5.

## PSALM 96[§]
### God of the Universe

I

1 Sing to the LORD a new song;[t]
      sing to the LORD, all the earth.
2 Sing to the LORD, bless his name;
      proclaim his salvation day after day.
3 Tell his glory among the nations;
      among all peoples, his marvelous
         deeds.[u]

II

4 'For great is the LORD and highly to be
      praised,
         to be feared above all gods.[v]
5 For the gods of the nations are idols,
      but the LORD made the heavens.[w]
6 Splendor and power go before him;
      power and grandeur are in his holy
         place.

III

7 Give to the LORD, you families of nations,
      give to the LORD glory and might;
8      give to the LORD the glory due his
         name![x]
Bring gifts and enter his courts;
9      bow down to the LORD, splendid in
         holiness.
Tremble before him, all the earth;
10      [y]declare among the nations: The
         LORD is king.
The world will surely stand fast, never to
   be shaken.
      He rules the peoples with fairness.

IV

11 Let the heavens be glad and the earth rejoice;
      let the sea and what fills it resound;[z]
12      let the plains be joyful and all that is
         in them.
Then let all the trees of the forest rejoice
13      before the LORD who comes,
         who comes to govern the earth,[a]
To govern the world with justice
   and the peoples with faithfulness.

## PSALM 97[**]
### The Divine Ruler of All

I

1 The LORD is king; let the earth rejoice;
      let the many islands be glad.[b]

---

§[Psalm 96] A hymn inviting all humanity to praise the glories of Israel's God (Ps 96:1–3), who is the sole God (Ps 96:4–6). To the just ruler of all belongs worship (Ps 96:7–10); even inanimate creation is to offer praise (Ps 96:11–13). This Psalm has numerous verbal and thematic contacts with Is 40–55, as does Ps 98. Another version of the Psalm is 1 Chr 16:23–33.

¶[96:4] For references to other gods, see comments on Ps 58 and 82.

**[Psalm 97] The hymn begins with God appearing in a storm, a traditional picture of some ancient Near Eastern

t. [96:1] Ps 98:1; Is 42:10. u. [96:3] Ps 98:4; 105:1. v. [96:4] Ps 48:2; 95:3; 145:3. w. [96:5] Ps 97:7; 115:4–8; Is 40:17; 1 Cor 8:4. x. [96:8] Ps 29:2. y. [96:10] Ps 75:4; 93:1. z. [96:11] Ps 98:7. a. [96:13] Ps 98:9. b. [97:1] Ps 75:4; 93:1; 96:10.

2 Cloud and darkness surround him;
    justice and right are the foundation
      of his throne.[c]
3 Fire goes before him,
    consuming his foes on every side.
4 His lightening illumines the world;
    the earth sees and trembles.[d]
5 The mountains melt like wax before the
    Lord,
    before the Lord of all the earth.[e]
6 The heavens proclaim his justice;
    all peoples see his glory.[f]

II

7 All who serve idols are put to shame,
    who glory in worthless things;
    all gods' bow down before him.[g]
8 Zion hears and is glad,
    and the daughters of Judah rejoice
    because of your judgments,
    O Lord.[h]
9 For you, Lord, are the Most High over all
    the earth,[i]
    exalted far above all gods.
10 You who love the Lord, hate evil,
    he protects the souls of the faithful,[j]
    rescues them from the hand of the
      wicked.
11 Light dawns for the just,
    and gladness for the honest of
      heart.[k]
12 Rejoice in the Lord, you just,
    and give thanks at the remembrance
      of his holiness.[l]

## PSALM 98[†]
### The Coming of God

1 A psalm.

I

Sing a new song to the Lord,
    for he has done marvelous deeds.[m]
His right hand and holy arm
    have won the victory.[‡n]

2 The Lord has made his victory known;
    has revealed his triumph in the sight
      of the nations,
3 He has remembered his mercy and
      faithfulness
    toward the house of Israel.
All the ends of the earth have seen
    the victory of our God.

II

4 Shout with joy to the Lord, all the earth;
    break into song; sing praise.
5 Sing praise to the Lord with the lyre,
    with the lyre and melodious song.
6 With trumpets and the sound of the horn
    shout with joy to the King, the Lord.[o]

III

7 Let the sea and what fills it resound,[p]
    the world and those who dwell
      there.
8 Let the rivers clap their hands,
    the mountains shout with them for
      joy,[q]
9 'Before the Lord who comes,
    who comes to govern the earth,[s]
To govern the world with justice
    and the peoples with fairness.

## PSALM 99[§]
### The Holy King

I

1 The Lord is king, the peoples tremble;
    he is enthroned on the cherubim,[¶]
      the earth quakes.[t]
2 Great is the Lord in Zion,
    exalted above all the peoples.
3 Let them praise your great and awesome
      name:
    Holy is he![u]

II

4 O mighty king, lover of justice,
    you have established fairness;
    you have created just rule in Jacob.[v]
5 Exalt the Lord, our God;
    bow down before his footstool;[**w]
    holy is he!

---

gods (Ps 97:1–6); cf. Is 18:8–16; Mi 1:3–4; Heb 3:3–15. Israel rejoices in the overthrowing of idol worshipers and their gods (Ps 97:7–9) and the rewarding of the faithful righteous (Ps 97:10–12).

*[97:7] **All gods**: divine beings thoroughly subordinate to Israel's God. The Greek translates "angels," an interpretation adopted by Heb 1:6.

†[Psalm 98] A hymn, similar to Ps 96, extolling God for Israel's victory (Ps 98:1–3). All nations (Ps 98:4–6) and even inanimate nature (Ps 98:7–8) are summoned to welcome God's coming to rule over the world (Ps 98:9).

‡[98:1] **Marvelous deeds . . . victory**: the conquest of all threats to the peaceful existence of Israel, depicted in the Psalms variously as a cosmic force such as sea, or nations bent on Israel's destruction, or evildoers seemingly triumphant. **His right hand and holy arm**: God is pictured as a powerful warrior.

c. [97:2] Ps 85:11; 89:15; Ex 19:6; Dt 4:11; 5:22; 1 Kgs 8:12. d. [97:4] Ps 18:8; 50:3; 77:18; 99:1; Jgs 5:4–5.  e. [97:5] Jdt 16:15; Mi 1:4.  f. [97:6] Ps 50:6.  g. [97:7] Ps 96:5.  h. [97:8] Ps 48:12. i. [97:9] Ps83:19.  j. [97:10] Ps121:7.  k. [97:11] Ps112:4.  l. [97:12] Ps 30:5.  m. [98:1] Ps 96:1; Is 42:10.  n. [98:1] Is 59:16; 63:5.

§[Psalm 99] A hymn to God as the king whose grandeur is most clearly seen on Mount Zion (Ps 99:2) and in the laws given to Israel (Ps 99:4). Israel is special because of God's word of justice, which was mediated by the revered speakers, Moses, Aaron, and Samuel (Ps 99:6–8). The poem is structured by the threefold statement that God is holy (Ps 99:3, 5, 9) and by the twice-repeated command to praise (Ps 99:5, 9).

¶[99:1] **Enthroned on the cherubim**: cherubim were composite beings with animal and human features, common in ancient Near Eastern art. Two cherubim were placed on the ark (or box) of the covenant in the holy of holies. Upon them God was believed to dwell invisibly, cf. Ex 25:20–22; 1 Sm 4:4; 2 Sm 6:2; Ps 80:2.

**[99:5] **Footstool**: a reference to the ark, cf. 1 Chr 28:2; Ps 132:7.

o. [98:6] Ps 47:6–7.  p. [98:7] Ps 96:11.  q. [98:8] Is 44:23; 55:12.  r. [98:9] Ps 96:13.  s. [98:9] Ps 67:5.  t. [99:1] Ps 18:8–11; 80:2; 93:1; Ex 25:22; 1 Sm 4:4; 2 Sm 6:2.  u. [99:3] Is 6:3.  v. [99:4] Ps 72:1; Jer 23:5.  w. [99:5] Ps 132:7.

III

6 Moses and Aaron were among his priests,
    Samuel among those who called on
        his name;
  they called on the LORD, and he
        answered them.ˣ
7 From the pillar of cloud he spoke to them;
    they kept his decrees, the law he had
        given them.ʸ
8 O LORD, our God, you answered them;
    you were a forgiving God to them,
        though you punished their offenses.ᶻ
9 Exalt the LORD, our God;
    bow down before his holy mountain;
        holy is the LORD, our God.

## PSALM 100*
### Processional Hymn

¹A psalm of thanksgiving.

Shout joyfully to the LORD, all you lands;
2    serve the LORD with gladness;
    come before him with joyful song.
3 †Know that the LORD is God,
    he made us, we belong to him,
    we are his people, the flock he
        shepherds.ᵃ
4 Enter his gates with thanksgiving,
    his courts with praise.
  Give thanks to him, bless his name;ᵇ
5        good indeed is the LORD,
  His mercy endures forever,
        his faithfulness lasts through every
            generation.

## PSALM 101‡
### Norm of Life for Rulers

¹A psalm of David.

I

I sing of mercy and justice;
    to you, LORD, I sing praise.
2 I study the way of integrity;ᶜ
    when will you come to me?
  I act with integrity of heart
    within my household.§ᵈ
3 I do not allow into my presence anything
    base.

I hate wrongdoing;
    I will have no part of it.ᵉ
4 May the devious heart keep far from me;
    the wicked I will not acknowledge.
5 Whoever slanders a neighbor in secret
    I will reduce to silence.ᶠ
  Haughty eyes and arrogant heartsᵍ
    I cannot endure.

II

6 I look to the faithful of the land▪
    to sit at my side.
  Whoever follows the way of integrityʰ
    is the one to enter my service.
7 No one who practices deceit
    can remain within my house.
  No one who speaks falsely
    can last in my presence.ⁱ
8 ¨Morning after morning I clear all the
        wicked from the land,
    to rid the city of the LORD of all
        doers of evil.

## PSALM 102††
### Prayer in Time of Distress

¹The prayer of one afflicted and wasting away
whose anguish is poured out before the LORD.

I

2 LORD, hear my prayer;
    let my cry come to you.
3 Do not hide your face from me
    in the day of my distress.ʲ
  Turn your ear to me;
    when I call, answer me quickly.
4 For my days vanish like smoke;ᵏ
    my bones burn away as in a furnace.
5 My heart is withered, dried up like grass,
    too wasted to eat my food.
6 From my loud groaning
    I become just skin and bones.
7 I am like a desert owl,
    like an owl among the ruins.
8 I lie awake and moan,
    like a lone sparrow on the roof.
9 All day long my enemies taunt me;

---

*[Psalm 100] A hymn inviting the people to enter the Temple courts with thank offerings for the God who created them.
    †[100:3] Although the people call on all the nations of the world to join in their hymn, they are conscious of being the chosen people of God.
    ‡[Psalm 101] The king, grateful at being God's chosen (Ps 101:1), promises to be a ruler after God's own heart (Ps 101:2–3), allowing into the royal service only the God-fearing (Ps 101:3–8).
    §[101:2] **Within my household**: the king promises to make his own household, i.e., the royal court, a model for Israel, banning all officials who abuse their power.

¶[101:6] **I look to the faithful of the land**: the king seeks companions only among those faithful to God.
    **[101:8] **Morning after morning**: the morning is the normal time for the administration of justice (2 Sm 15:2; Jer 21:12) and for the arrival of divine aid (Ps 59:17; 143:8; Is 33:2). **I clear all the wicked from the land**: the king, as God's servant, is responsible for seeing that divine justice is carried out.
    ††[Psalm 102] A lament, one of the Penitential Psalms. The psalmist, experiencing psychological and bodily disintegration (Ps 102:4–12), cries out to God (Ps 102:1–3). In the Temple precincts where God has promised to be present, the psalmist recalls God's venerable promises to save the poor (Ps 102:13–23). The final part (Ps 102:24–28) restates the original complaint and prayer, and emphasizes God's eternity.

---

x. [99:6] Jer 15:1.    y. [99:7] Ex 33:9; Nm 12:5.    z. [99:8] Ex 32:11; Nm 20:12.    a. [100:3] Ps 23:1; 95:7; Mi 7:14; Is 64:7.    b. [100:4–5] Ps 106:1; 107:1; 118:1; 136:1; 138:8; Jer 33:11.    c. [101:2] Ps 26:11; Is 33:15.    d. [101:2] 1 Kgs 9:4.

e. [101:3] Prv 11:20.    f. [101:5] Prv 17:20; 30:10.    g. [101:5] Prv 21:4.    h. [101:6] Ps 26:11; Prv 20:7.    i. [101:7] Ps 5:5; Prv 25:5.    j. [102:3] Ps 69:18; 143:7.    k. [102:4–6] Ps 38:7–9.

in their rage, they make my name
    a curse.*

10 I eat ashes like bread,
    mingle my drink with tears.¹

11 Because of your furious wrath,
    you lifted me up just to cast me
    down.

12 ᵐMy days are like a lengthening shadow;ⁿ
    I wither like the grass.

### II

13 But you, LORD, are enthroned forever;
    your renown is for all generations.ᵒ

14 You will again show mercy to Zion;
    now is the time for pity;
    the appointed time has come.

15 Its stones are dear to your servants;
    its dust moves them to pity.

16 The nations shall fear your name, LORD,
    all the kings of the earth, your
    glory,ᵖ

17 Once the LORD has rebuilt Zion
    and appeared in glory,

18 Heeding the plea of the lowly,
    not scorning their prayer.

19 Let this be written for the next generation,
    for a people not yet born,
    that they may praise the LORD:�q

20 †"The LORD looked down from the holy
    heights,
    viewed the earth from heaven,ʳ

21 To attend to the groaning of the prisoners,
    to release those doomed to die."ˢ

22 Then the LORD's name will be declared on
    Zion,
    his praise in Jerusalem,

23 When peoples and kingdoms gather
    to serve the LORD.ᵗ

### III

24 He has shattered my strength in
    mid-course,
    has cut short my days.

25 I plead, O my God,
    do not take me in the midst of my
    days.ᵗᵘ
    Your years last through all
    generations.

26 Of old you laid the earth's foundations;ᵛ
    the heavens are the work of your
    hands.

27 They perish, but you remain;
    they all wear out like a garment;

Like clothing you change them and they
    are changed,

28 but you are the same, your years
    have no end.

29 May the children of your servants live on;
    may their descendants live in your
    presence.ʷ

## PSALM 103§
### Praise of Divine Goodness

¹Of David.

### I

Bless the LORD, my soul;
    all my being, bless his holy name!

2 Bless the LORD, my soul;
    and do not forget all his gifts,

3 Who pardons all your sins,
    and heals all your ills,

4 Who redeems your life from the pit,ˣ
    and crowns you with mercy and
    compassion,

5 Who fills your days with good things,
    so your youth is renewed like the
    eagle's.¶

### II

6 The LORD does righteous deeds,
    brings justice to all the oppressed.ʸ

7 He made known his ways to Moses,
    to the Israelites his deeds.

8 Merciful and gracious is the LORD,
    slow to anger, abounding in mercy.ᶻ

9 He will not always accuse,
    and nurses no lasting anger;

10 He has not dealt with us as our sins merit,
    nor requited us as our wrongs
    deserve.

### III

11 For as the heavens tower over the earth,
    so his mercy towers over those who
    fear him.ᵃ

12 As far as the east is from the west,
    so far has he removed our sins from
    us.

13 As a father has compassion on his
    children,
    so the LORD has compassion on
    those who fear him.

14 For he knows how we are formed,
    remembers that we are dust.ᵇ

---

*[102:9] **They make my name a curse:** enemies use the psalmist's name in phrases such as, "May you be as wretched as this person!"

†[102:20–23] Both Ps 102:20–21 and Ps 102:22–23 depend on Ps 102:19.

‡[102:25] **In the midst of my days:** when the normal span of life is but half completed, cf. Is 38:10; Jer 17:11.

l. [102:10] Ps 42:4; 80:6.  m. [102:12] Ps 109:23; 144:4; Jb 8:9; 14:2; Eccl 6:12; Wis 2:5.  n. [102:12] Ps 90:5–6.  o. [102:13] Ps 55:20; 90:2; 93:2; 135:13; 145:13; Lam 5:19; Heb 1:12.  p. [102:16] Is 59:19; 66:18.  q. [102:19] Ps 22:31–32.  r. [102:20] Ps 11:4; 14:2.  s. [102:21] Ps 79:11.  t. [102:23] Is 60:3–4; Zec 2:15; 8:22.  u. [102:25] Ps 39:5; 90:10; Jb 14:5.  v. [102:26–28] Heb 1:10–12.

§[Psalm 103] The speaker in this hymn begins by praising God for personal benefits (Ps 103:1–5), then moves on to God's mercy toward all the people (Ps 103:6–18). Even sin cannot destroy that mercy (Ps 103:11–13), for the eternal God is well aware of the people's human fragility (Ps 103:14–18). The psalmist invites the heavenly beings to join in praise (Ps 103:19–22).

¶[103:5] **Your youth is renewed like the eagle's:** because of the eagle's long life it was a symbol of perennial youth and vigor, cf. Is 40:31.

w. [102:29] Ps 69:36–37.  x. [103:4] Ps 28:1; 30:4; 40:3; 69:16; 88:5; 143:7; Prv 1:12; Jon 2:7.  y. [103:6] Ps 146:6–7.  z. [103:8] Ps 86:15; 145:8; Ex 34:6–7; Nm 14:18; Jer 3:12; Jl 2:13; Jon 4:2.  a. [103:11] Is 55:9.  b. [103:14] Ps 90:3.

<sup>15</sup> As for man, his days are like the grass;
 he blossoms like a flower in the
  field.<sup>c</sup>
<sup>16</sup> A wind sweeps over it and it is gone;
 its place knows it no more.
<sup>17</sup> But the LORD's mercy is from age to age,
 toward those who fear him.
 His salvation is for the children's children
<sup>18</sup>  of those who keep his covenant,
  and remember to carry out his
  precepts.

### IV

<sup>19</sup> The LORD has set his throne in heaven;
 his dominion extends over all.
<sup>20</sup> Bless the LORD, all you his angels,<sup>d</sup>
 mighty in strength, acting at his
  behest,
 obedient to his command.
<sup>21</sup> Bless the LORD, all you his hosts,
 his ministers who carry out his will.
<sup>22</sup> Bless the LORD, all his creatures,
 everywhere in his domain.
 Bless the LORD, my soul!

## PSALM 104*
### Praise of God the Creator

### I

<sup>1</sup> Bless the LORD, my soul!
 LORD, my God, you are great
  indeed!
 You are clothed with majesty and
  splendor,
<sup>2</sup>  robed in light as with a cloak.
 You spread out the heavens like a tent;<sup>e</sup>
<sup>3</sup>  setting the beams of your chambers
  upon the waters.<sup>†</sup>
 You make the clouds your chariot;
 traveling on the wings of the wind.
<sup>4</sup> You make the winds your messengers;<sup>f</sup>
 flaming fire, your ministers.<sup>f</sup>

### II

<sup>5</sup> <sup>‡</sup>You fixed the earth on its foundation,
 so it can never be shaken.
<sup>6</sup> The deeps covered it like a garment;

above the mountains stood the
 waters.
<sup>7</sup> At your rebuke they took flight;
 at the sound of your thunder they
  fled.<sup>g</sup>
<sup>8</sup> They rushed up the mountains, down the
  valleys
 to the place you had fixed for them.
<sup>9</sup> You set a limit they cannot pass;
 never again will they cover the
  earth.<sup>h</sup>

### III

<sup>10</sup> You made springs flow in wadies
 that wind among the mountains.
<sup>11</sup> They give drink to every beast of the field;<sup>i</sup>
 here wild asses quench their thirst.
<sup>12</sup> Beside them the birds of heaven nest;
 among the branches they sing.
<sup>13</sup> You water the mountains from your
  chambers;
 from the fruit of your labor the
  earth abounds.
<sup>14</sup> You make the grass grow for the cattle
 and plants for people's work
 to bring forth food from the earth,
<sup>15</sup> wine to gladden their hearts,
 oil to make their faces shine,
 and bread to sustain the human
  heart.
<sup>16</sup> <sup>§</sup>The trees of the LORD drink their fill,
 the cedars of Lebanon, which you
  planted.
<sup>17</sup> There the birds build their nests;
 the stork in the junipers, its home.<sup>j</sup>
<sup>18</sup> The high mountains are for wild goats;
 the rocky cliffs, a refuge for badgers.

### IV

<sup>19</sup> You made the moon to mark the seasons,<sup>k</sup>
 the sun that knows the hour of its
  setting.
<sup>20</sup> You bring darkness and night falls,
 then all the animals of the forest
  wander about.
<sup>21</sup> Young lions roar for prey;
 they seek their food from God.<sup>l</sup>
<sup>22</sup> When the sun rises, they steal away
 and settle down in their dens.
<sup>23</sup> People go out to their work,
 to their labor till evening falls.

### V

<sup>24</sup> How varied are your works, LORD!
 In wisdom you have made them all;
 the earth is full of your creatures.<sup>m</sup>
<sup>25</sup> There is the sea, great and wide!
 It teems with countless beings,
 living things both large and small.<sup>n</sup>

---

*[Psalm 104] A hymn praising God who easily and skillfully made rampaging waters and primordial night into a world vibrant with life. The psalmist describes God's splendor in the heavens (Ps 104:1–4), how the chaotic waters were tamed to fertilize and feed the world (Ps 104:5–18), and how primordial night was made into a gentle time of refreshment (Ps 104:19–23). The picture is like Gn 1:1–2: a dark and watery chaos is made dry and lighted so that creatures might live. The psalmist reacts to the beauty of creation with awe (Ps 104:24–34). May sin not deface God's work (Ps 104:35)!

†[104:3] **Your chambers upon the waters**: God's heavenly dwelling above the upper waters of the sky, cf. Gn 1:6–7; Ps 29:10.

‡[104:5–9] God places the gigantic disk of the earth securely on its foundation and then, as a warrior, chases away the enveloping waters and confines them under, above, and around the earth.

c. [103:15] Ps 37:2; 90:5–6; Is 40:7. d. [103:20] Ps 148:2; Dn 3:58. e. [104:2] Prv 8:27–28; Jb 9:8; Is 40:22; Gn 1:6–7; Am 9:6. f. [104:4] Heb 1:7.

---

§[104:16–18] Even the exotic flora and fauna of the high mountains of the Lebanon range receive adequate water.

g. [104:7] Ps 29:3. h. [104:9] Jer 5:22; Gn 9:11–15. i. [104:11–14] Ps 147:8–9. j. [104:17] Ez 31:6. k. [104:19] Sir 43:6. l. [104:21] Jb 38:39. m. [104:24] Ps 92:6; Sir 39:16. n. [104:25] Sir 43:26.

<sup>26</sup> There ships ply their course
> and Leviathan,<sup>*</sup> whom you formed
> to play with.<sup>o</sup>

### VI

<sup>27</sup> All of these look to you
> to give them food in due time.<sup>p</sup>
<sup>28</sup> When you give it to them, they gather;
> when you open your hand, they are
> well filled.
<sup>29</sup> <sup>†</sup>When you hide your face, they panic.
> Take away their breath, they perish
> and return to the dust.<sup>q</sup>
<sup>30</sup> Send forth your spirit, they are created
> and you renew the face of the earth.

### VII

<sup>31</sup> May the glory of the Lord endure forever;
> may the Lord be glad in his works!
<sup>32</sup> Who looks at the earth and it trembles,
> touches the mountains and they
> smoke!<sup>r</sup>
<sup>33</sup> I will sing to the Lord all my life;
> I will sing praise to my God while
> I live.<sup>s</sup>
<sup>34</sup> May my meditation be pleasing to him;
> I will rejoice in the Lord.
<sup>35</sup> May sinners vanish from the earth,
> and the wicked be no more.
> Bless the Lord, my soul! Hallelujah!<sup>‡</sup>

## PSALM 105<sup>§</sup>
### God's Fidelity to the Promise

### I

<sup>1</sup> Give thanks to the Lord, invoke his
> name;<sup>t</sup>
> make known among the peoples his
> deeds!<sup>u</sup>
<sup>2</sup> Sing praise to him, play music;
> proclaim all his wondrous deeds!
<sup>3</sup> Glory in his holy name;
> let hearts that seek the Lord rejoice!
<sup>4</sup> Seek out the Lord and his might;
> constantly seek his face.<sup>v</sup>

<sup>5</sup> Recall the wondrous deeds he has done,
> his wonders and words of judgment,
<sup>6</sup> You descendants of Abraham his servant,
> offspring of Jacob the chosen one!

### II

<sup>7</sup> He the Lord, is our God
> whose judgments reach through all
> the earth.
<sup>8</sup> He remembers forever his covenant,
> the word he commanded for a
> thousand generations,
<sup>9</sup> Which he made with Abraham,
> and swore to Isaac,<sup>w</sup>
<sup>10</sup> And ratified in a statute for Jacob,
> an everlasting covenant for Israel:
<sup>11</sup> "To you I give the land of Canaan,
> your own allotted inheritance."<sup>x</sup>

### III

<sup>12</sup> When they were few in number,<sup>y</sup>
> a handful, and strangers there,
<sup>13</sup> Wandering from nation to nation,
> from one kingdom to another people,
<sup>14</sup> He let no one oppress them;
> for their sake he rebuked kings:<sup>¶</sup>
<sup>15</sup> "Do not touch my anointed ones,
> to my prophets do no harm."

### IV

<sup>16</sup> Then he called down a famine on the
> land,
> destroyed the grain that sustained
> them.<sup>††z</sup>
<sup>17</sup> He had sent a man ahead of them,
> Joseph, sold as a slave.<sup>a</sup>
<sup>18</sup> They shackled his feet with chains;
> collared his neck in iron,<sup>b</sup>
<sup>19</sup> Till his prediction came to pass,
> and the word of the Lord proved
> him true.<sup>c</sup>
<sup>20</sup> The king sent and released him;
> the ruler of peoples set him free.<sup>d</sup>
<sup>21</sup> He made him lord over his household,
> ruler over all his possessions,<sup>e</sup>
<sup>22</sup> To instruct his princes as he desired,
> to teach his elders wisdom.

### V

<sup>23</sup> Then Israel entered Egypt;<sup>f</sup>
> Jacob sojourned in the land of Ham.<sup>‡‡</sup>
<sup>24</sup> God greatly increased his people,
> made them more numerous than
> their foes.<sup>g</sup>

---

*[104:26] **Leviathan**: a sea monster symbolizing primeval chaos, cf. Ps 74:14; Is 27:1; Jb 40:25. God does not destroy chaos but makes it part of the created order.

†[104:29–30] On one level, the spirit (or wind) of God is the fall and winter rains that provide food for all creatures. On another, it is the breath (or spirit) of God that makes beings live.

‡[104:35] **Hallelujah**: a frequent word in the last third of the Psalter. The word combines the plural imperative of praise (*hallelu*) with an abbreviated form of the divine name Yah(weh).

§[Psalm 105] A hymn to God who promised the land of Canaan to the holy people, cf. Ps 78; 106; 136. Israel is invited to praise and seek the presence of God (Ps 105:1–6), who is faithful to the promise of land to the ancestors (Ps 105:7–11). In every phase of the national story—the ancestors in the land of Canaan (Ps 105:12–15), Joseph in Egypt (Ps 105:16–22), Israel in Egypt (Ps 105:23–38), Israel in the desert on the way to Canaan (Ps 105:39–45)—God remained faithful, reiterating the promise of the land to successive servants.

¶[105:14] **Kings**: Pharaoh and Abimelech of Gerar, cf. Gn 12:17; 20:6–7.

**[105:15] **My anointed ones . . . my prophets**: the patriarchs Abraham, Isaac, and Jacob, who were "anointed" in the sense of being consecrated and recipients of God's revelation.

††[105:16] **The grain that sustained them**: lit., every "staff of bread."

‡‡[105:23, 27] **The land of Ham**: a synonym for Egypt, cf. Gn 10:6.

o. [104:26] Jb 3:8; 40:25, 29.   p. [104:27] Ps 136:25; 145:15–16.
q. [104:29] Ps 90:3; Jb 34:14–15; Eccl 3:20.   r. [104:32] Ps 144:5.
s. [104:33] Ps 146:2.   t. [105:1–15] 1 Chr 16:8–22.   u. [105:1] Ps 18:50; 96:3; 145:5; Is 12:4–5.   v. [105:4] Ps 24:6; 27:8.

w. [105:9] Gn 15:1ff; 26:3.   x. [105:11] Gn 12:7; 15:18.   y. [105:12–13] Dt 4:27; 26:5.   z. [105:16] Gn 41:54, 57.   a. [105:17] Gn 37:28, 36; 45:5.   b. [105:18] Gn 39:20.   c. [105:19] Gn 40–41.
d. [105:20] Gn 41:14.   e. [105:21] Gn 41:41–44.   f. [105:23] Gn 46:1–47:12; Acts 7:15.   g. [105:24] Ex 1:7; Acts 7:17.

25 He turned their hearts to hate his people,
      to treat his servants deceitfully.[h]
26 He sent his servant Moses,
      and Aaron whom he had chosen.[i]
27 They worked his signs in Egypt[j]
      and wonders in the land of Ham.
28 He sent darkness and it grew dark,
      but they rebelled against his word.
29 He turned their waters into blood
      and killed their fish.
30 Their land swarmed with frogs,
      even the chambers of their kings.
31 He spoke and there came swarms of flies,
      gnats through all their country.
32 For rain he gave them hail,
      flashes of lightning throughout their
         land.
33 He struck down their vines and fig trees,
      shattered the trees of their country.
34 He spoke and the locusts came,
      grasshoppers without number.[k]
35 They devoured every plant in the land;
      they devoured the crops of their
         fields.
36 He struck down every firstborn in the
         land,
      the first fruits of all their vigor.
37 He brought his people out,
      laden with silver and gold;[l]
      no one among the tribes stumbled.
38 Egypt rejoiced when they left,
      for fear had seized them.

                          VI
39 He spread a cloud out as a cover,
      and made a fire to light up the
         night.[m]
40 They asked and he brought them quail;
      with bread from heaven he filled
         them.[n]
41 He split the rock and water gushed forth;
      it flowed through the desert like a
         river.[o]
42 For he remembered his sacred promise
      to Abraham his servant.
43 He brought his people out with joy,
      his chosen ones with shouts of
         triumph.
44 He gave them the lands of the nations,
      they took possession of the wealth of
         the peoples,[p]
45 That they might keep his statutes
      and observe his teachings.[q]
   Hallelujah!

## PSALM 106[†]
### Israel's Confession of Sin

1 Hallelujah!

                          A
   Give thanks to the LORD, who is good,
      whose mercy endures forever.[r]
2 Who can recount the mighty deeds of the
         LORD,
      proclaim in full God's praise?
3 Blessed those who do what is right,
      whose deeds are always just.[s]
4 Remember me, LORD, as you favor your
         people;
      come to me with your saving help,[t]
5 That I may see the prosperity of your
         chosen ones,
      rejoice in the joy of your people,
      and glory with your heritage.

                          B
6 We have sinned like our ancestors;[u]
      we have done wrong and are guilty.

                          I
7 Our ancestors in Egypt
      did not attend to your wonders.
   They did not remember your manifold
         mercy;
      they defied the Most High at the
         Red Sea.
8 Yet he saved them for his name's sake
      to make his power known.[v]
9 He roared at the Red Sea and it dried up.
   He led them through the deep as
         through a desert.[w]
10 He rescued them from hostile hands,
      freed them from the power of the
         enemy.
11 The waters covered their oppressors;
      not one of them survived.
12 Then they believed his words
      and sang his praise.[x]

---

*[105:27–38] This Psalm and Ps 78:43–51 have an account of the plagues differing in number or in order from Ex 7:14–12:30. Several versions of the exodus story were current.

h. [105:25] Ex 1:8–14.   i. [105:26] Ex 3:10; 4:27.   j. [105:27–36] Ps 78:43–51; Ex 7–12.   k. [105:34] Jl 1:4.   l. [105:37] Ex 12:33–36.   m. [105:39] Ps 78:14; Ex 13:21–22; Wis 18:3.   n. [105:40] Ps 78:24–28; Ex 16:13–15; Nm 11:31ff; Wis 16:20.   o. [105:41] Ps 78:15–16; Ex 17:1–7; Nm 20:11.   p. [105:44] Dt 4:37–40.   q. [105:45] Dt 6:20–25; 7:8–11.

†[Psalm 106] Israel is invited to praise the God whose mercy has always tempered judgment of Israel (Ps 106:1–3). The speaker, on behalf of all, seeks solidarity with the people, who can always count on God's fidelity despite their sin (Ps 106:4–5). Confident of God's mercy, the speaker invites national repentance (Ps 106:6) by reciting from Israel's history eight instances of sin, judgment, and forgiveness. The sins are the rebellion at the Red Sea (Ps 106:6–12; see Ex 14–15), the craving for meat in the desert (Ps 106:13–15; see Nm 11), the challenge to Moses' authority (Ps 106:16–18; see Nm 16), the golden calf episode (Ps 106:19–23; see Ex 32–34), the refusal to take Canaan by the southern route (Ps 106:24–27; see Nm 13–14 and Dt 1–2), the rebellion at Baal-Peor (Ps 106:28–31; see Nm 25:1–10), the anger of Moses (Ps 106:32–33; see Nm 20:1–13), and mingling with the nations (Ps 106:34–47). The last, as suggested by its length and generalized language, may be the sin that invites the repentance of the present generation. The text gives the site of each sin: Egypt (Ps 106:7), the desert (Ps 106:14), the camp (Ps 106:16), Horeb (Ps 106:19), in their tents (Ps 106:25), Baal-Peor (Ps 106:28), the waters of Meribah (Ps 106:32), Canaan (Ps 106:38).

r. [106:1] Ps 100:5; 107:1; 1 Chr 16:34; Jer 33:11; Dn 3:89.   s. [106:3] Is 56:1–2.   t. [106:4] Ps 25:7; Neh 5:19.   u. [106:6–7] Ps 78:11–17; Ex 14:11; Lv 26:40; 1 Kgs 8:47; Bar 2:12; Dn 9:5.   v. [106:8] Ez 36:20–22.   w. [106:9] Ex 14:21–31; Is 50:2; 63:11–14; Na 1:4.   x. [106:12] Ex 15:1–21.

## II

13 But they soon forgot all he had done;
  they had no patience for his plan.
14 In the desert they gave in to their
    cravings,
  tempted God in the wasteland.[y]
15 So he gave them what they asked
  and sent a wasting disease against
    them.[z]

## III

16 In the camp they challenged Moses[a]
  and Aaron, the holy one of the Lord.
17 The earth opened and swallowed Dathan,
  it closed on the followers of Abiram.
18 Against their company the fire blazed;
  flames consumed the wicked.

## IV

19 At Horeb they fashioned a calf,[b]
  · worshiped a metal statue.
20 They exchanged their glory[*]
  for the image of a grass-eating bull.
21 They forgot the God who had saved them,
  who had done great deeds in Egypt,[c]
22 Amazing deeds in the land of Ham,
  fearsome deeds at the Red Sea.
23 He would have decreed their destruction,
    had not Moses, his chosen one,
  Withstood him in the breach[†]
  to turn back his destroying anger.[d]

## V

24 Next they despised the beautiful land;[e]
  they did not believe the promise.
25 In their tents they complained;
  they did not heed the voice of the
    Lord.
26 So with raised hand he swore
  he would destroy them in the desert,
27 And scatter their descendants among the
    nations,
  disperse them in foreign lands.

## VI

28 They joined in the rites of Baal of Peor,[f]
  · ate food sacrificed to the dead.
29 They provoked him by their actions,
  and a plague broke out among them.
30 Then Phinehas rose to intervene,
  and the plague was brought to a halt.
31 This was counted for him as a righteous
    deed
  for all generations to come.

## VII

32 At the waters of Meribah they angered
    God,[g]

and Moses suffered because of them.[‡]
33 They so embittered his spirit
  that rash words crossed his lips.

## VIII

34 They did not destroy the peoples
  as the Lord had commanded them,[h]
35 But mingled with the nations
  and imitated their ways.[i]
36 They served their idols
  and were ensnared by them.[j]
37 They sacrificed to demons[§]
  their own sons and daughters,
38 Shedding innocent blood,
    the blood of their own sons and
      daughters,
  Whom they sacrificed to the idols of
    Canaan,
  desecrating the land with bloodshed.
39 They defiled themselves by their actions,
  became adulterers by their conduct.
40 So the Lord grew angry with his people,
  abhorred his own heritage.
41 He handed them over to the nations,
  and their adversaries ruled over
    them.[k]
42 Their enemies oppressed them,
  kept them under subjection.
43 Many times did he rescue them,
    but they kept rebelling and
      scheming
  and were brought low by their own
    guilt.[l]
44 Still God had regard for their affliction
  when he heard their wailing.
45 For their sake he remembered his
    covenant
  and relented in his abundant mercy,[m]
46 Winning for them compassion
  from all who held them captive.

## C

47 Save us, Lord, our God;
    gather us from among the nations
  That we may give thanks to your holy
    name
  and glory in praising you.[n]
48 ¶Blessed be the Lord, the God of Israel,
    from everlasting to everlasting!
  Let all the people say, Amen![o]
Hallelujah!

---

‡[106:32] **Moses suffered because of them**: Moses was not allowed to enter the promised land because of his rash words (Nm 20:12). According to Dt 1:37, Moses was not allowed to cross because of the people's sin, not his own.
§[106:37] **Demons**: Hebrew *shedim* occurs in parallelism with "gods" in an important inscription from Transjordan and hence can also be translated "the gods."
¶[106:48] A doxology ending Book IV of the Psalter. It is not part of the Psalm.

---

*[106:20] **Their glory**: meant as a reference to God.
†[106:23] **Withstood him in the breach**: the image is that of Moses standing in a narrow break made in the wall to keep anyone from entering.

---

y. [106:14] Ps 78:18; Ex 15:24; 16:3; Nm 11:1–6. z. [106:15] Ps 78:26–31; Nm 11:33. a. [106:16–18] Nm 16; Dt 11:6; Is 26:11. b. [106:19–20] Ex 32; Dt 9:8–21; Jer 2:11; Acts 7:41; Rom 1:23. c. [106:21] Ps 78:42–58; Dt 32:18; Jer 2:32. d. [106:23] Ex 32:11; Dt 9:25; Ez 22:30. e. [106:24–27] Lv 26:33; Nm 14; Dt 1:25–36; Ez 20:15, 23. f. [106:28–31] Nm 25; Dt 26:14; Sir 45:23–24.

g. [106:32–33] Ps 95:8–9; Ex 17:1–7; Nm 20:2–13; Dt 6:16; 33:8. h. [106:34] Dt 7:1; Jgs 2:1–5. i. [106:35] Lv 18:3; Jgs 1:27–35; 3:5. j. [106:36–38] Lv 18:21; Nm 35:33; Dt 32:17; Jgs 2:11–13, 17, 19; 2 Kgs 16:3; Bar 4:7; 1 Cor 10:20. k. [106:41] Jgs 2:14–23. l. [106:43] Is 63:7–9. m. [106:45] Lv 26:42. n. [106:47] 1 Chr 16:35. o. [106:48] Ps 41:14; 72:18; 89:53; 1 Chr 16:36; Neh 9:5.

## Fifth Book—Psalms 107–150

### PSALM 107*
#### God the Savior of Those in Distress

1 "Give thanks to the LORD for he is good,
   his mercy endures forever!"[p]
2 Let that be the prayer of the LORD's
      redeemed,
   those redeemed from the hand of
      the foe,[q]
3 Those gathered from foreign lands,
   from east and west, from north and
      south.[r]

#### I

4 Some had lost their way in a barren
      desert;
   found no path toward a city to live in.
5 They were hungry and thirsty;
   their life was ebbing away.[s]
6 In their distress they cried to the LORD,
   who rescued them in their peril,
7 'Guided them by a direct path
   so they reached a city to live in.[u]
8 Let them thank the LORD for his mercy,
   such wondrous deeds for the
      children of Adam.
9 For he satisfied the thirsty,
   filled the hungry with good things.[v]

#### II

10 Some lived in darkness and gloom,
   imprisoned in misery and chains.
11 Because they rebelled against God's word,
   and scorned the counsel of the Most
      High,[w]
12 He humbled their hearts through
      hardship;
   they stumbled with no one to help.[x]
13 In their distress they cried to the LORD,
   who saved them in their peril;
14 He brought them forth from darkness and
      the shadow of death
   and broke their chains asunder.[y]
15 Let them thank the LORD for his mercy,
   such wondrous deeds for the
      children of Adam.
16 For he broke down the gates of bronze
   and snapped the bars of iron.

#### III

17 Some fell sick from their wicked ways,
   afflicted because of their sins.
18 They loathed all manner of food;[z]
   they were at the gates of death.
19 In their distress they cried to the LORD,
   who saved them in their peril,
20 Sent forth his word to heal them,[a]
   and snatched them from the grave.
21 Let them thank the LORD for his mercy,
   such wondrous deeds for the
      children of Adam.
22 Let them offer a sacrifice in thanks,
   recount his works with shouts of joy.

#### IV

23 Some went off to sea in ships,
   plied their trade on the deep waters.[b]
24 They saw the works of the LORD,
   the wonders of God in the deep. .
25 He commanded and roused a storm wind;
   it tossed the waves on high.[c]
26 They rose up to the heavens, sank to the
      depths;
   their hearts trembled at the danger.
27 They reeled, staggered like drunkards;
   their skill was of no avail.[d]
28 In their distress they cried to the LORD,
   who brought them out of their peril;
29 He hushed the storm to silence,
   the waves of the sea were stilled.[e]
30 They rejoiced that the sea grew calm,
   that God brought them to the
      harbor they longed for.
31 Let them thank the LORD for his mercy,
   such wondrous deeds for the
      children of Adam.
32 Let them extol him in the assembly of the
      people,
   and praise him in the council of the
      elders.

#### V

33 'God changed rivers into desert,
   springs of water into thirsty ground,[f]
34 Fruitful land into a salty waste,
   because of the wickedness of its
      people.[g]
35 He changed the desert into pools of water,
   arid land into springs of water,[h]
36 And settled the hungry there;
   they built a city to live in.[i]
37 They sowed fields and planted vineyards,
   brought in an abundant harvest.[j]

---

*[Psalm 107] A hymn inviting those who have been res-
cued by God to give praise (Ps 107:1–3). Four archetypal
divine rescues are described, each ending in thanksgiving:
from the sterile desert (Ps 107:4–9), from imprisonment in
gloom (Ps 107:10–16), from mortal illness (Ps 107:17–22),
and from the angry sea (Ps 107:23–32). The number four connotes totality, all the possible varieties of rescue. The same saving activity of God is shown in Israel's history (Ps 107:33–41);
whenever the people were endangered God rescued them.
The last verses invite people to ponder the persistent saving
acts of God (Ps 107:42–43).

†[107:33–41] God destroyed Sodom and Gomorrah in
Gn 18–19, which the Psalm sees as the destruction of the
wicked inhabitants of Canaan to prepare the way for Israel
(Ps 107:33–34). God then led Israel through the desert to give
them a fertile land (Ps 107:35–38) and protected them from
every danger (Ps 107:39–41).

p. [107:1] Ps 100:4–5; 106:1; Jer 33:11.  q. [107:2] Is 63:12.
r. [107:3] Is 43:5–6; 49:12; Zec 8:7.  s. [107:5] Dt 8:15; 32:10;
Is 49:10.  t. [107:7] Is 35:8; 40:3; 43:19.  u. [107:7] Dt 6:10.
v. [107:9] Lk 1:53.  w. [107:11] Is 42:7, 22; Jb 36:8–9; Prv 1:25.
x. [107:12] Ps 106:43.  y. [107:14] Is 42:7; 49:9; 51:14.

z. [107:18] Jb 6:6–7; 33:20.  a. [107:20] Ps 147:15; Wis 16:12;
Is 55:11;  Mt 8:8.  b. [107:23] Sir 43:25.  c. [107:25] Jon
1:4.  d. [107:27] Is 29:9.  e. [107:29] Ps 65:8; 89:10; Mt 8:26
par.  f. [107:33] Is 35:7; 42:15; 50:2.  g. [107:34] Gn 19:23–28;
Dt 29:22; Sir 39:23.  h. [107:35] Ps 114:8; Is 41:8.  i. [107:36] Ez
36:35.  j. [107:37] Is 65:21; Jer 31:5.

³⁸ ᵏGod blessed them, and they increased
        greatly,
    and their livestock did not decrease.ˡ
³⁹ But he poured out contempt on princes,
    made them wander trackless wastes,
⁴⁰ Where they were diminished and brought
        low
    through misery and cruel
        oppression.
⁴¹ While he released the poor man from
        affliction,
    and increased their families like
        flocks.ᵐ
⁴² The upright saw this and rejoiced;ⁿ
    all wickedness shut its mouth.
⁴³ Whoever is wise will take note of these
        things,ᵒ
    and ponder the merciful deeds of
        the LORD.

## PSALM 108*
### Prayer for Victory

¹A song; a psalm of David.
                I
² My heart is steadfast, God;ᵖ
    my heart is steadfast.
    Let me sing and chant praise.
³ Awake, lyre and harp!
    I will wake the dawn.�q
⁴ I will praise you among the peoples,
        LORD;
    I will chant your praise among the
        nations.ʳ
⁵ For your mercy is greater than the
        heavens;
    your faithfulness, to the skies.ˢ
                II
⁶ Appear on high over the heavens, God;
    your glory above all the earth.
⁷ Help with your right hand and answer us
    that your loved ones may escape.

⁸ God speaks in his holiness:ᵗ
    "I will exult, I will apportion
        Shechem;
    the valley of Succoth I will measure
        out.
⁹ Gilead is mine, mine is Manasseh;
    Ephraim is the helmet for my head,
        Judah, my scepter.

¹⁰ Moab is my washbowl;
    upon Edom I cast my sandal;ᵘ
    I will shout in triumph over
        Philistia."
¹¹ Who will bring me to the fortified city?
    Who will lead me into Edom?
¹² Was it not you who rejected us, God?
    Do you no longer march with our
        armies?ᵛ
¹³ Give us aid against the foe;
    worthless is human help.
¹⁴ We will triumph with the help of God,
    who will trample down our foes.

## PSALM 109‡
### Prayer of a Person Falsely Accused

¹For the leader. A psalm of David.
                I
² O God, whom I praise, do not be silent,ʷ
    for wicked and treacherous mouths
        attack me.
They speak against me with lying tongues;
³       with hateful words they surround
        me,
    attacking me without cause.
⁴ In return for my love they slander me,
    even though I prayed for them.
⁵ They repay me evil for good,
    hatred for my love.ˣ
                II
⁶ Appoint an evil one over him,
    an accuser§ to stand at his right
        hand,
⁷ That he may be judged and found guilty,
    that his plea may be in vain.
⁸ May his days be few;
    may another take his office.ʸ
⁹ May his children be fatherless,
    his wife, a widow.ᶻ
¹⁰ May his children wander and beg,
    driven from their hovels.
¹¹ May the usurer snare all he owns,
    strangers plunder all he earns.
¹² May no one treat him with mercy
    or pity his fatherless children.

---

*[Psalm 108] A prayer compiled from two other Psalms: Ps 108:2–6 are virtually the same as Ps 57:8–12; Ps 108:7–14 are the same as Ps 60:7–14. An old promise of salvation (Ps 108:8–10) is combined with a confident assurance (Ps 108:2–6, 13) and petition (Ps 108:7, 12–13).

†[108:8] **Holiness:** may also be translated as "sanctuary" or as referring to God's heavenly abode.

‡[Psalm 109] A lament notable for the length and vehemence of its prayer against evildoers (Ps 109:6–20); the cry to God (Ps 109:1) and the complaint (Ps 109:22–25) are brief in comparison. The psalmist is apparently the victim of a slander campaign, potentially devastating in a society where reputation and honor are paramount. In the emotional perspective of the Psalm, there are only two types of people: the wicked and their poor victims. The psalmist is a poor victim (Ps 109:22, 31) and by that fact a friend of God and enemy of the wicked. The psalmist seeks vindication not on the basis of personal virtue but because of God's promise to protect the poor.

§[109:6] **An accuser:** Hebrew *satan*, a word occurring in Job 1–2 and Zec 3:1–2. In the latter passage Satan stands at the right hand of the high priest to bring false accusations against him before God. Here the accuser is human.

---

k. [107:38] Jb 12:23–25.   l. [107:38] Dt 7:13–14.   m. [107:41] Ps 113:7.   n. [107:42] Ps 58:11; 63:12.   o. [107:43] Hos 14:10.   p. [108:2–6] Ps 57:8–12.   q. [108:3] Jb 38:12.   r. [108:4] Ps 9:12; 18:50; 148:13.   s. [108:5] Ps 36:6; 71:19.   t. [108:8–14] Ps 60:8–14.

u. [108:10] Ru 4:7–8.   v. [108:12] Ps 44:10.   w. [109:2] Ps 35:22; 83:1.   x. [109:5] Ps 35:12; 38:21; Prv 17:13; Jer 18:20.   y. [109:8] Acts 1:20.   z. [109:9] Ex 22:23; Jer 18:21.

13 May his posterity be destroyed,[a]
    their name rooted out in the next
        generation.
14 May his fathers' guilt be mentioned to the
        LORD;
    his mother's sin not rooted out.[b]
15 May their guilt be always before the
        LORD,[c]
    till their memory is banished from
        the earth,[d]
16 For he did not remember to show mercy,
    but hounded the wretched poor
    and brought death to the
        brokenhearted.
17 He loved cursing; may it come upon him;
    he hated blessing; may none come
        to him.
18 May cursing clothe him like a robe;
    may it enter his belly like water,
    his bones like oil.
19 May it be near as the clothes he wears,
    as the belt always around him.

20 'May this be the reward for my accusers
        from the LORD,
    for those speaking evil against me.

### III

21 But you, LORD, are my Lord,
    deal kindly with me for your name's
        sake;
    in your great mercy rescue me.
22 For I am poor and needy;
    my heart is pierced within me.
23 Like a lengthening shadow I am gone,
    I am shaken off like the locust.
24 My knees totter from fasting;[e]
    my flesh has wasted away.
25 I have become a mockery to them;
    when they see me, they shake their
        heads.
26 Help me, LORD, my God;
    save me in your mercy.
27 Make them know this is your hand,
    that you, LORD, have done this.
28 Though they curse, may you bless;
    arise, shame them, that your servant
        may rejoice.
29 Clothe my accusers with disgrace;
    make them wear their shame like a
        mantle.
30 I will give fervent thanks to the LORD;
    before a crowd I will praise him.[f]
31 For he stands at the right hand of the
        poor
    to save him from those who pass
        judgment on him.

## PSALM 110[†]
### God Appoints the King Both King and Priest

1 A psalm of David.

The LORD says to my lord:[‡]
    "Sit at my right hand,
    while I make your enemies your
        footstool."[*g]
2 The scepter of your might:
    the LORD extends your strong
        scepter from Zion.
    Have dominion over your enemies!
3 Yours is princely power from the day of
        your birth.
    In holy splendor before the daystar,
    like dew I begot you.[h]
4 The LORD has sworn and will not waver:
    "You are a priest forever in the
        manner of Melchizedek."[§i]
5 At your right hand is the Lord,
    who crushes kings on the day of his
        wrath,[j]
6 Who judges nations, heaps up corpses,
    crushes heads across the wide earth,
7 'Who drinks from the brook by the
        wayside
    and thus holds high his head.[k]

## PSALM 111[**]
### Praise of God for Goodness to Israel

1 Hallelujah!

I will praise the LORD with all my heart[l]

† [Psalm 110] A royal Psalm in which a court singer recites three oracles in which God assures the king that his enemies are conquered (Ps 110:1–2), makes the king "son" in traditional adoption language (Ps 110:3), gives priestly status to the king and promises to be with him in future military ventures (Ps 110:4–7).
‡ [110:1] The LORD says to my lord: a polite form of address of an inferior to a superior, cf. 1 Sm 25:25; 2 Sm 1:10. The court singer refers to the king. Jesus in the synoptic gospels (Mt 22:41–46 and parallels) takes the psalmist to be David and hence "my lord" refers to the messiah, who must be someone greater than David. Your footstool: in ancient times victorious kings put their feet on the prostrate bodies of their enemies.
§ [110:4] Melchizedek: Melchizedek was the ancient king of Salem (Jerusalem) who blessed Abraham (Gn 14:18–20); like other kings of the time he performed priestly functions. Heb 7 sees in Melchizedek a type of Christ.
¶ [110:7] Who drinks from the brook by the wayside: the meaning is uncertain. Some see an allusion to a rite of royal consecration at the Gihon spring (cf. 1 Kgs 1:33, 38). Others find here an image of the divine warrior (or king) pursuing enemies so relentlessly that he does not stop long enough to eat and drink.
** [Psalm 111] A Temple singer (Ps 111:1) tells how God is revealed in Israel's history (Ps 111:2–10). The deeds reveal God's very self, powerful, merciful, faithful. The poem is an acrostic, each verse beginning with a successive letter of the Hebrew alphabet.

* [109:20] May this be the reward . . . from the LORD: the psalmist prays that God ratify the curses of Ps 109:6–19 and bring them upon the wicked.

a. [109:13] Ps 21:11; Prv 10:7.  b. [109:14] Ex 20:5.  c. [109:15] Ps 90:8.  d. [109:15] Ps 34:16.  e. [109:24–25] Ps 69:11–13.  f. [109:30] Ps 111:1.

g. [110:1] Mt 22:44; Acts 2:34–35; 1 Cor 15:25; Heb 1:13; 8:1; 10:12–13; 1 Pt 3:22.  h. [110:3] Ps 2:7; 89:27; Is 49:1.  i. [110:4] Ps 89:35; 132:11; Gn 14:18; Heb 5:6; 7:21.  j. [110:5] Ps 2:9; Rev 2:27; 12:5; 19:15.  k. [110:7] Ps 3:4.  l. [111:1] Ps 138:1.

in the assembled congregation of the
upright.*

2 Great are the works of the LORD,
studied by all who delight in them.

3 Majestic and glorious is his work,
his righteousness endures forever.

4 He won renown for his wondrous deeds;
gracious and merciful is the LORD.*m*

5 He gives food to those who fear him,†
he remembers his covenant forever.

6 He showed his powerful deeds to his
people,
giving them the inheritance of the
nations.

7 The works of his hands are true and just,
reliable all his decrees,

8 Established forever and ever,
to be observed with truth and
equity.

9 He sent release to his people,
decreed his covenant forever;
holy and fearsome is his name.

10 ‡The fear of the LORD is the beginning of
wisdom;*n*
prudent are all who practice it.
His praise endures forever.

## PSALM 112§
### The Blessings of the Just

1Hallelujah!

Blessed the man who fears the LORD,
who greatly delights in his
commands.*o*

2 His descendants shall be mighty in the
land,
a generation of the upright will be
blessed.

3 Wealth and riches shall be in his house;
his righteousness¶ shall endure
forever.

4 Light shines through the darkness for the
upright;*p*
gracious, compassionate, and
righteous.

5 It is good for the man gracious in lending,
who conducts his affairs with justice.

6 For he shall never be shaken;
the righteous shall be remembered
forever.*q*

7 He shall not fear an ill report;
his heart is steadfast, trusting the
LORD.

8 His heart is tranquil, without fear,
till at last he looks down on his foes.

9 Lavishly he gives to the poor;
his righteousness shall endure
forever;*r*
his horn** shall be exalted in honor.

10 The wicked sees and is angry;
gnashes his teeth and wastes away;
the desire of the wicked come to
nothing.

## PSALM 113††
### Praise of God's Care for the Poor

1Hallelujah!

I

Praise, you servants of the LORD,
praise the name of the LORD.*s*

2 Blessed be the name of the LORD
both now and forever.

3 From the rising of the sun to its setting*t*
let the name of the LORD be praised.

II

4 High above all nations is the LORD;
above the heavens his glory.*u*

5 Who is like the LORD our God,
enthroned on high,

6 ⱽlooking down on heaven and earth?

7 He raises the needy from the dust,
lifts the poor from the ash heap,*w*

8 Seats them with princes,
the princes of the people,

9 Gives the childless wife a home,
the joyful mother of children.*x*
Hallelujah!

## PSALM 114‡‡
### The Lord's Wonders at the Exodus

1 When Israel came forth from Egypt,
the house of Jacob from an alien
people,

---

*[111:1] **In the assembled congregation of the upright**:
in the Temple, cf. Ps 149:1.

†[111:5] **Food to those who fear him**: probably a reference
to the manna in the desert, which elsewhere is seen as a type
of the Eucharist, cf. Jn 6:31–33, 49–51.

‡[111:10] **The fear of the LORD**: reverence for God.

§[Psalm 112] An acrostic poem detailing the blessings
received by those who remain close to God by obedience to
the commandments. Among their blessings are children (Ps
112:2), wealth that enables them to be magnanimous (Ps 112:3,
5, 9), and virtue by which they encourage others (Ps 112:4).
The just person is an affront to the wicked, whose hopes
remain unfulfilled (Ps 112:10). The logic resembles Ps 1; 111.

¶[112:3] **Righteousness**: in the Second Temple period the
word acquired the nuance of liberality and almsgiving, cf. Sir
3:30; 7:10; Mt 6:1–4.

**[112:9] **His horn**: the symbol for vitality and honor.

††[Psalm 113] A hymn exhorting the congregation to praise
God's name, i.e., the way in which God is present in the world;
the name is mentioned three times in Ps 113:1–3. The divine
name is especially honored in the Temple (Ps 113:1) but its
recognition is not limited by time (Ps 113:2) and space (Ps
113:3), for God is everywhere active (Ps 113:4–5) especially in
rescuing the lowly faithful (Ps 113:7–9).

‡‡[Psalm 114] A hymn celebrating Israel's escape from
Egypt, journey through the wilderness, and entry into the

---

m. [111:4] Ps 103:8; 112:4.   n. [111:10] Prv 1:7; 9:10; Sir 1:16.
o. [112:1] Ps 1:1–2; 119:1–2; 128:1.   p. [112:4] Ps 37:6; 97:11; Prv
13:9; Is 58:10.

q. [112:6] Prv 10:7; Wis 8:13.   r. [112:9] Prv 22:9; 2 Cor 9:9.
s. [113:1] Ps 135:1.   t. [113:3] Mal 1:11.   u. [113:4] Ps 148:13.
v. [113:6] Ps 89:7–9.   w. [113:7] Ps 107:41; 1 Sm 2:7–8.   x. [113:9]
1 Sm 2:5; Is 54:1.

2 Judah became God's sanctuary,
   Israel, God's domain.[y]
3 'The sea saw and fled;
   the Jordan turned back.[z]
4 The mountains skipped like rams;
   the hills, like lambs.[a]
5 Why was it, sea, that you fled?
   Jordan, that you turned back?
6 Mountains, that you skipped like rams?
   You hills, like lambs?
7 Tremble, earth, before the Lord,[b]
   before the God of Jacob,
8 'Who turned the rock into pools of water,
   flint into a flowing spring.[c]

## PSALM 115[‡]
### The Greatness of the True God

I

1 Not to us, Lord, not to us
   but to your name give glory
   because of your mercy and
     faithfulness.[d]
2 Why should the nations say,
   "Where is their God?"[§e]
3 Our God is in heaven
   and does whatever he wills.[f]

II

4 Their idols are silver and gold,[g]
   the work of human hands.[h]
5 They have mouths but do not speak,
   eyes but do not see.
6 They have ears but do not hear,
   noses but do not smell.
7 They have hands but do not feel,
   feet but do not walk;

they produce no sound from their
   throats.
8 Their makers will be like them,
   and anyone who trusts in them.

III

9 'The house of Israel trusts in the Lord,[i]
   who is their help and shield.[j]
10 The house of Aaron trusts in the Lord,
   who is their help and shield.
11 Those who fear the Lord trust in the
     Lord,
   who is their help and shield.
12 The Lord remembers us and will bless us,
   will bless the house of Israel,
   will bless the house of Aaron,
13 Will bless those who fear the Lord,
   small and great alike.
14 May the Lord increase your number,
   yours and your descendants.
15 May you be blessed by the Lord,
   maker of heaven and earth.
16 '''The heavens belong to the Lord,
   but he has given the earth to the
     children of Adam.[k]
17 ††The dead do not praise the Lord,
   not all those go down into silence.[l]
18 It is we who bless the Lord,
   both now and forever.
Hallelujah!

## PSALM 116[‡‡]
### Thanksgiving to God Who Saves from Death

I

1 I love the Lord, who listened
   to my voice in supplication,
2 Who turned an ear to me
   on the day I called.
3 I was caught by the cords of death;[§§m]
   the snares of Sheol had seized me;
   I felt agony and dread.
4 Then I called on the name of the Lord,
   "O Lord, save my life!"

---

promised land, and the miracles of nature that bore witness to God's presence in their midst. In the perspective of the Psalm, the people proceed directly from Egypt into the promised land (Ps 114:1–2). Sea and Jordan, which stood like soldiers barring the people from their land, flee before the mighty God as the earth recoils from the battle (Ps 114:3–4). The poet taunts the natural elements as one taunts defeated enemies (Ps 114:5–6).

*[114:3–4] Pairs of cosmic elements such as sea and rivers, mountains and hills, are sometimes mentioned in creation accounts. Personified here as warriors, the pairs tremble in fear before the Divine Warrior. The quaking also recalls the divine appearance in the storm at Sinai (Ex 19:16–19) and elsewhere (Jgs 5:4–5; Ps 18:7–15).

†[114:8] The miracles of giving drink to the people in the arid desert, cf. Ex 17:1–7; Is 41:17–18.

‡[114:8] A response to the enemy taunt, "Where is your God?" This hymn to the glory of Israel's God (Ps 115:1–3) ridicules the lifeless idols of the nations (Ps 115:4–8), expresses in a litany the trust of the various classes of the people in God (Ps 115:9–11), invokes God's blessing on them as they invoke the divine name (Ps 115:12–15), and concludes as it began with praise of God. Ps 135:15–18 similarly mocks the Gentile gods and has a similar litany and hymn (Ps 135:19–21).

§[115:2] Where is their God?: implies that God cannot help them.

¶[115:9–11] The house of Israel . . . the house of Aaron . . . those who fear the Lord: the laity of Israelite birth, the priests, and the converts to Judaism, cf. Ps 118:2–4; 135:19–21. In the New Testament likewise "those who fear the Lord" means converts to Judaism (cf. Acts 10:2, 22, 35; 13:16, 26).

**[115:16] The heavens: the Septuagint reads here "the heaven of heavens" or "the highest heavens," i.e., above the firmament. See note on Ps 148:4.

††[115:17] See note on Ps 6:5.

‡‡[Psalm 116] A thanksgiving in which the psalmist responds to God's rescue from mortal danger (Ps 116:3–4) and from near despair (Ps 116:10–11) with vows and Temple sacrifices (Ps 116:13–14, 17–19). The Greek and Latin versions divide the Psalm into two parts: Ps 116:1–9 and Ps 116:10–19, corresponding to its two major divisions.

§§[116:3] The cords of death: death is personified here; it attempts to capture the psalmist with snares and nets, cf. Ps 18:6.

y. [114:2]  Ex 19:6.   z. [114:3]  Ps 66:6; 74:15; Ex 14:21f; Jos 3:14ff.   a. [114:4]  Ps 29:6; Wis 19:9.   b. [114:7]  Ps 68:9.   c. [114:8]  Ex 17:6; Nm 20:11.   d. [115:1]  Ez 36:22–23.   e. [115:2]  Ps 79:10.   f. [115:3]  Ps 135:6.   g. [115:4–10]  Ps 135:15–19; Wis 15:15–16; Is 44:9f; Jer 10:1–5.   h. [115:4]  Is 40:19.

i. [115:9]  Ps 118:2–4.   j. [115:9]  Ps 33:20.   k. [115:16]  Gn 1:28.   l. [115:17]  Ps 6:6; 88:11ff; Sir 17:22f; Is 38:18.   m. [116:3]  Ps 18:5; Jon 2:3.

II

5 Gracious is the Lord and righteous;
  yes, our God is merciful.[n]
6 The Lord protects the simple;
  I was helpless, but he saved me.
7 Return, my soul, to your rest;
  the Lord has been very good to
  you.[o]
8 For my soul has been freed from death,
  my eyes from tears, my feet from
  stumbling.[p]
9 I shall walk before the Lord
  in the land of the living.*[q]

III

10 †I kept faith, even when I said,
   "I am greatly afflicted!"[r]
11 I said in my alarm,
   "All men are liars!"[s]
12 How can I repay the Lord
   for all the great good done for me?
13 I will raise the cup of salvation‡
   and call on the name of the Lord.
14 I will pay my vows to the Lord
   in the presence of all his people.
15 §Dear in the eyes of the Lord
   is the death of his devoted.[t]
16 Lord, I am your servant,
   your servant, the child of your
   maidservant;[u]
   you have loosed my bonds.
17 I will offer a sacrifice of praise
   and call on the name of the Lord.[v]
18 I will pay my vows to the Lord[w]
   in the presence of all his people,
19 In the courts of the house of the Lord,
   in your midst, O Jerusalem.
   Hallelujah!

## PSALM 117§
### The Nations Called to Praise

1 Praise the Lord, all you nations!
  Extol him, all you peoples![x]

---

*[116:9] **The land of the living**: the phrase elsewhere is an epithet of the Jerusalem Temple (cf. Ps 27:13; 52:5; Is 38:11). Hence the psalmist probably refers to being present to God in the Temple.

†[116:10] **I kept faith, even when I said**: even in the days of despair, the psalmist did not lose all hope.

‡[116:13] **The cup of salvation**: probably the libation of wine poured out in gratitude for rescue, cf. Ex 25:29; Nm 15:5, 7, 10.

§[116:15] **Dear in the eyes of the Lord**: the meaning is that the death of God's faithful is grievous to God, not that God is pleased with the death, cf. Ps 72:14. In Wis 3:5–6, God accepts the death of the righteous as a sacrificial burnt offering.

§[Psalm 117] This shortest of hymns calls on the nations to acknowledge God's supremacy. The supremacy of Israel's God has been demonstrated to them by the people's secure existence, which is owed entirely to God's gracious fidelity.

---

n. [116:5] Ex 34:6.  o. [116:7] Ps 13:6.  p. [116:8] Ps 56:14; Is 25:8; Rev 21:4.  q. [116:9] Ps 27:13; 56:14; Is 38:11.  r. [116:10] 2 Cor 4:13.  s. [116:11] Ps 12:2.  t. [116:15] Ps 72:14; Is 43:4.  u. [116:16] Ps 86:16; 143:12; Wis 9:5.  v. [116:17] Lv 7:12ff.  w. [116:18] Jon 2:10.  x. [117:1] Rom 15:11.

---

2 His mercy for us is strong;
  the faithfulness of the Lord is
  forever.
Hallelujah!

## PSALM 118**
### Hymn of Thanksgiving

I

1 Give thanks to the Lord, for he is good,[y]
  his mercy endures forever.
2 Let Israel say:
  his mercy endures forever.
3 Let the house of Aaron say,
  his mercy endures forever.
4 Let those who fear the Lord say,[z]
  his mercy endures forever.

II

5 In danger I called on the Lord;
  the Lord answered me and set me
  free.
6 The Lord is with me; I am not afraid;
  what can mortals do against me?[a]
7 The Lord is with me as my helper;
  I shall look in triumph on my foes.
8 Better to take refuge in the Lord[b]
  than to put one's trust in mortals.
9 Better to take refuge in the Lord
  than to put one's trust in princes.

III

10 All the nations surrounded me;
   in the Lord's name I cut them off.
11 They surrounded me on every side;
   in the Lord's name I cut them off.
12 They surrounded me like bees;[c]
   they burned up like fire among
   thorns;
   in the Lord's name I cut them off.
13 I was hard pressed and falling,
   but the Lord came to my help.[d]
14 The Lord, my strength and might,
   has become my savior.[e]

IV

15 The joyful shout of deliverance
   is heard in the tents of the righteous:
   "The Lord's right hand works valiantly;
16   the Lord's right hand is raised;
   the Lord's right hand works
   valiantly."

---

**[Psalm 118] A thanksgiving liturgy accompanying a procession of the king and the people into the Temple precincts. After an invocation in the form of a litany (Ps 118:1–4), the psalmist (very likely speaking in the name of the community) describes how the people confidently implored God's help (Ps 118:5–9) when hostile peoples threatened its life (Ps 118:10–16); vividly God's rescue is recounted (Ps 118:15–18). Then follows a possible dialogue at the Temple gates between the priests and the psalmist as the latter enters to offer the thanksgiving sacrifice (Ps 118:19–25). Finally, the priests impart their blessing (Ps 118:26–27), and the psalmist sings in gratitude (Ps 118:28–29).

---

y. [118:1] Ps 100:5; 136:1f.  z. [118:4] Ps 115:9–11.  a. [118:6] Ps 27:1; Heb 13:6.  b. [118:8f] Ps 146:3.  c. [118:12] Dt 1:44.  d. [118:13] Ps 129:1–2.  e. [118:14] Ex 15:2; Is 12:2.

¹⁷ I shall not die but live
    and declare the deeds of the LORD.
¹⁸ The LORD chastised me harshly,
    but did not hand me over to death.
                          V
¹⁹ Open the gates of righteousness;
    I will enter and thank the LORD.ᶠ
²⁰ This is the LORD's own gate,
    through it the righteous enter.
²¹ I thank you for you answered me;
    you have been my savior.
²² The stone the builders rejected
    has become the cornerstone.ᵍ
²³ By the LORD has this been done;
    it is wonderful in our eyes.
²⁴ This is the day the LORD has made;
    let us rejoice in it and be glad.
²⁵ LORD, grant salvation!†
    LORD, grant good fortune!
                          VI
²⁶ Blessed is he
    who comes in the name of the LORD.ʰ
    We bless you from the house of the LORD.
²⁷    The LORD is God and has
      enlightened us.
    Join in procession with leafy branches
    up to the horns of the altar.
                          VII
²⁸ You are my God, I give you thanks;
    my God, I offer you praise.
²⁹ Give thanks to the LORD, for he is good,
    his mercy endures forever.


## PSALM 119‡
### A Prayer to God, the Lawgiver

                        ALEPH
¹ Blessed those whose way is blameless,
    who walk by the law of the LORD.ⁱ

²  Blessed those who keep his testimonies,
    who seek him with all their heart.ʲ
³  They do no wrong;
    they walk in his ways.
⁴  You have given them the command
    to observe your precepts with care.
⁵  May my ways be firm
    in the observance of your statutes!
⁶  Then I will not be ashamed
    to ponder all your commandments.
⁷  I will praise you with sincere heart
    as I study your righteous judgments.
⁸  I will observe your statutes;
    do not leave me all alone.
                        BETH
⁹  How can the young keep his way without
      fault?
    Only by observing your words.
¹⁰ With all my heart I seek you;
    do not let me stray from your
      commandments.
¹¹ In my heart I treasure your promise,
    that I may not sin against you.
¹² Blessed are you, O LORD;
    teach me your statutes.ᵏ
¹³ With my lips I recite
    all the judgments you have spoken.
¹⁴ I find joy in the way of your testimonies
    more than in all riches.
¹⁵ I will ponder your precepts
    and consider your paths.
¹⁶ In your statutes I take delight;
    I will never forget your word.
                        GIMEL
¹⁷ Be kind to your servant that I may live,
    that I may keep your word.
¹⁸ Open my eyes to see clearly
    the wonders of your law.
¹⁹ I am a sojourner in the land;§ˡ
    do not hide your commandments
      from me.
²⁰ At all times my soul is stirred
    with longing for your judgments.
²¹ With a curse you rebuke the proud
    who stray from your commandments.
²² Free me from disgrace and contempt,
    for I keep your testimonies.
²³ Though princes meet and talk against me,
    your servant meditates on your
      statutes.

---

*[118:22] **The stone the builders rejected**: a proverb: what is insignificant to human beings has become great through divine election. The "stone" may originally have meant the foundation stone or capstone of the Temple. The New Testament interpreted the verse as referring to the death and resurrection of Christ (Mt 21:42; Acts 4:11; cf. Is 28:16 and Rom 9:33; 1 Pt 2:7).

†[118:25] **Grant salvation**: the Hebrew for this cry has come into English as "Hosanna." This cry and the words in Ps 118:26 were used in the gospels to welcome Jesus entering the Temple on Palm Sunday (Mk 11:9–10).

‡[Psalm 119] This Psalm, the longest by far in the Psalter, praises God for giving such splendid laws and instruction for people to live by. The author glorifies and thanks God for the Torah, prays for protection from sinners enraged by others' fidelity to the law, laments the cost of obedience, delights in the law's consolations, begs for wisdom to understand the precepts, and asks for the rewards of keeping them. Several expected elements do not appear in the Psalm: Mount Sinai with its story of God's revelation and gift to Israel of instruction and commandments, the Temple and other institutions related to revelation and laws (frequent in other Psalms). The Psalm is fascinated with God's word directing and guiding human life. The poem is an acrostic; its twenty-two stanzas (of eight verses each) are in the order of the Hebrew alphabet.

Each of the eight verses within a stanza begins with the same letter. Each verse contains one word for "instruction." The translation here given attempts to translate each Hebrew word for "instruction" with the same English word. There are, however, nine words for "instruction," not eight, so the principle of a different word for "instruction" in each verse cannot be maintained with perfect consistency. The nine words for "instruction" in the translation are: law, statute, commandment, precept, testimony, word, judgment, way, and promise.

§[119:19] **A sojourner in the land**: like someone without the legal protection of a native inhabitant, the psalmist has a special need for the guidance of God's teaching.

---

f. [118:19] Is 26:2.   g. [118:22] Mt 21:42; Lk 20:17; Acts 4:11; Rom 9:33; 1 Pt 2:7.   h. [118:26] Mt 21:9; 23:39.   i. [119:1] Ps 1:1–2; 15:2; 112:1.

j. [119:2] Dt 4:29.   k. [119:12] Ps 25:4; 27:11; 86:11; 143:8, 10.   l. [119:19] Ps 39:13.

²⁴ Your testimonies are my delight;
    they are my counselors.
          DALETH
²⁵ My soul clings to the dust;ᵐ
    give me life in accord with your
        word.
²⁶ I disclosed my ways and you answered
        me;
    teach me your statutes.
²⁷ Make me understand the way of your
        precepts;
    I will ponder your wondrous deeds.
²⁸ My soul is depressed;
    lift me up acccording to your word.
²⁹ Lead me from the way of deceit;
    favor me with your law.
³⁰ The way of loyalty I have chosen;
    I have kept your judgments.
³¹ I cling to your testimonies, LORD;
    do not let me come to shame.
³² I will run the way of your
        commandments,
    for you will broaden my heart.
          HE
³³ LORD, teach me the way of your statutes;
    I shall keep them with care.ⁿ
³⁴ Give me understanding to keep your law,
    to observe it with all my heart.
³⁵ Lead me in the path of your
        commandments,ᵒ
    for that is my delight.
³⁶ Direct my heart toward your testimonies
    and away from gain.
³⁷ Avert my eyes from what is worthless;
    by your way give me life.
³⁸ For your servant, fulfill your promise
    made to those who fear you.
³⁹ Turn away from me the taunts I dread,
    for your judgments are good.
⁴⁰ See how I long for your precepts;
    in your righteousness give me life.
          WAW
⁴¹ Let your mercy come to me, LORD,
    salvation in accord with your
        promise.
⁴² Let me answer my taunters with a word,
    for I trust in your word.
⁴³ Do not take the word of truth from my
        mouth,
    for in your judgments is my hope.
⁴⁴ I will keep your law always,
    for all time and forever.
⁴⁵ I will walk freely in an open space
    because I cherish your precepts.
⁴⁶ I will speak openly of your testimonies
    without fear even before kings.
⁴⁷ I delight in your commandments,
    which I dearly love.

⁴⁸ ʼI lift up my hands to your
        commandments;
    I study your statutes, which I love.
          ZAYIN
⁴⁹ Remember your word to your servant
    by which you give me hope.
⁵⁰ This is my comfort in affliction,
    your promise that gives me life.
⁵¹ Though the arrogant utterly scorn me,
    I do not turn from your law.
⁵² When I recite your judgments of old
    I am comforted, LORD.
⁵³ Rage seizes me because of the wicked;
    they forsake your law.
⁵⁴ Your statutes become my songs
    wherever I make my home.
⁵⁵ Even at night I remember your name
    in observance of your law, LORD.
⁵⁶ This is my good fortune,
    for I have kept your precepts.
          HETH
⁵⁷ My portion is the LORD;
    I promise to observe your words.
⁵⁸ I entreat you with all my heart:
    have mercy on me in accord with
        your promise.
⁵⁹ I have examined my ways
    and turned my steps to your
        testimonies.
⁶⁰ I am prompt, I do not hesitate
    in observing your commandments.
⁶¹ Though the snares of the wicked surround
        me,
    your law I do not forget.
⁶² At midnight I rise to praise you
    because of your righteous
        judgments.
⁶³ I am the friend of all who fear you,
    of all who observe your precepts.
⁶⁴ The earth, LORD, is filled with your
        mercy;ᵖ
    teach me your statutes.
          TETH
⁶⁵ You have treated your servant well,
    according to your word, O LORD.
⁶⁶ Teach me wisdom and knowledge,
    for in your commandments I trust.
⁶⁷ Before I was afflicted I went astray,
    but now I hold to your promise.
⁶⁸ You are good and do what is good;
    teach me your statutes.
⁶⁹ The arrogant smear me with lies,
    but I keep your precepts with all my
        heart.
⁷⁰ Their hearts are gross and fat;�q
    as for me, your law is my delight.
⁷¹ It was good for me to be afflicted,
    in order to learn your statutes.

---

*[119:48] **I lift up my hands to your commandments**: to
lift up the hands was an ancient gesture of reverence to God.
Here the picture is applied to God's law.

---

m. [119:25] Ps 44:26.  n. [119:33] Ps 19:12.  o. [119:35] Ps 25:4;
27:11; 86:11; 143:8, 10.

p. [119:64] Ps 33:5.  q. [119:70] Ps 17:10; 73:7; Jb 15:27.

72 The law of your mouth is more precious
   to me
    than heaps of silver and gold.

### YODH

73 Your hands made me and fashioned me;
    give me understanding to learn your
    commandments.

74 Those who fear you rejoice to see me,
    because I hope in your word.

75 I know, Lord, that your judgments are
    righteous;
    though you afflict me, you are
    faithful.

76 May your mercy comfort me
    in accord with your promise to your
    servant.

77 Show me compassion that I may live,
    for your law is my delight.

78 Shame the proud for leading me astray
    with falsehood,
    that I may study your testimonies.

79 Let those who fear you turn to me,
    those who acknowledge your
    testimonies.

80 May I be wholehearted toward your
    statutes,
    that I may not be put to shame.

### KAPH

81 My soul longs for your salvation;
    I put my hope in your word.[r]

82 My eyes long to see your promise.[s]
    When will you comfort me?

83 I am like a wineskin shriveled by smoke,[t]
    but I have not forgotten your
    statutes.

84 How long can your servant survive?
    When will your judgment doom
    my foes?

85 The arrogant have dug pits for me;
    defying your law.

86 All your commandments are steadfast.
    Help me! I am pursued without
    cause.

87 They have almost put an end to me on
    earth,
    but I do not forsake your precepts.

88 In your mercy give me life,
    to observe the testimonies of your
    mouth.

### LAMEDH

89 *Your word, Lord, stands forever;[u]
    it is firm as the heavens.

90 Through all generations your truth
    endures;
    fixed to stand firm like the earth.

91 By your judgments they stand firm to this
    day,
    for all things are your servants.

92 Had your law not been my delight,
    I would have perished in my
    affliction.

93 I will never forget your precepts;
    through them you give me life.

94 I am yours; save me,
    for I cherish your precepts.

95 The wicked hope to destroy me,
    but I seek to understand your
    testimonies.

96 I have seen the limits of all perfection,
    but your commandment is without
    bounds.

### MEM

97 How I love your law, Lord![†]
    I study it all day long.

98 Your commandment makes me wiser
    than my foes,
    as it is forever with me.

99 I have more insight than all my teachers,
    because I ponder your testimonies.

100 I have more understanding than my
    elders,
    because I keep your precepts.[v]

101 I keep my steps from every evil path,
    that I may observe your word.

102 From your judgments I do not turn,
    for you have instructed me.

103 How sweet to my tongue is your promise,
    sweeter than honey to my mouth![w]

104 Through your precepts I gain
    understanding;
    therefore I hate all false ways.

### NUN

105 Your word is a lamp for my feet,
    a light for my path.[x]

106 I make a solemn vow
    to observe your righteous
    judgments.

107 I am very much afflicted, Lord;
    give me life in accord with your
    word.

108 Accept my freely offered praise;[y]
    Lord, teach me your judgments.

109 My life is always at risk,
    but I do not forget your law.

110 The wicked have set snares for me,
    but from your precepts I do not
    stray.

111 Your testimonies are my heritage forever;
    they are the joy of my heart.

112 My heart is set on fulfilling your statutes;
    they are my reward forever.

### SAMEKH

113 I hate every hypocrite;
    your law I love.

114 You are my refuge and shield;
    in your word I hope.

---

*[119:89–91] God's word creates the world, which manifests that word by its permanence and reliability.

†[119:97] **Lord**: the inclusion of "Lord" follows the tradition of the Septuagint and the Vulgate.

r. [119:81] Ps 130:6.   s. [119:82] Ps 25:15; 123:1–2; 141:8.
t. [119:83] Jb 30:30.   u. [119:89] Is 40:8.

v. [119:100] Jb 32:6; Wis 4:8–9.   w. [119:103] Ps 19:11.   x. [119:105]
Ps 18:29; Prv 6:23.   y. [119:108] Ps 50:14, 23; Heb 13:15.

<sup>115</sup> Depart from me, you wicked,<sup>z</sup>
    that I may keep the commandments
      of my God.
<sup>116</sup> Sustain me by your promise that I may live;
    do not disappoint me in my hope.
<sup>117</sup> Strengthen me that I may be safe,
    ever to contemplate your statutes.
<sup>118</sup> You reject all who stray from your
      statutes,
    for vain is their deceit.
<sup>119</sup> Like dross you regard all the wicked on
      earth;
    therefore I love your testimonies.
<sup>120</sup> My flesh shudders with dread of you;
    I fear your judgments.

AYIN

<sup>121</sup> I have fulfilled your righteous judgment;
    do not abandon me to my
      oppressors.
<sup>122</sup> Guarantee your servant's welfare;
    do not let the arrogant oppress me.
<sup>123</sup> My eyes long to see your salvation
    and the promise of your
      righteousness.
<sup>124</sup> Act with mercy toward your servant;
    teach me your statutes.
<sup>125</sup> I am your servant; give me discernment
    that I may know your testimonies.
<sup>126</sup> It is time for the LORD to act;
    they have disobeyed your law.
<sup>127</sup> Truly I love your commandments
    more than gold, more than the finest
      gold.
<sup>128</sup> Thus, I follow all your precepts;
    every wrong way I hate.

PE

<sup>129</sup> Wonderful are your testimonies;
    therefore I keep them.
<sup>130</sup> The revelation of your words sheds light,
    gives understanding to the simple.
<sup>131</sup> I sigh with open mouth,
    yearning for your commandments.
<sup>132</sup> Turn to me and be gracious,<sup>a</sup>
    according to your judgment for
      those who love your name.
<sup>133</sup> Steady my feet in accord with your
      promise;
    do not let iniquity lead me.
<sup>134</sup> Free me from human oppression,
    that I may observe your precepts.
<sup>135</sup> Let your face shine upon your servant;
    teach me your statutes.
<sup>136</sup> My eyes shed streams of tears
    because your law is not observed.

SADHE

<sup>137</sup> You are righteous, LORD,
    and just are your judgments.<sup>b</sup>
<sup>138</sup> You have given your testimonies in
      righteousness
    and in surpassing faithfulness.

<sup>139</sup> I am consumed with rage,
    because my foes forget your words.
<sup>140</sup> Your servant loves your promise;
    it has been proved by fire.
<sup>141</sup> Though belittled and despised,
    I do not forget your precepts.
<sup>142</sup> Your justice is forever right,
    your law true.
<sup>143</sup> Though distress and anguish come upon
      me,
    your commandments are my
      delight.
<sup>144</sup> Your testimonies are forever righteous;
    give me understanding that I may
      live.

QOPH

<sup>145</sup> I call with all my heart, O LORD;
    answer me that I may keep your
      statutes.
<sup>146</sup> I call to you to save me
    that I may observe your testimonies.
<sup>147</sup> I rise before dawn and cry out;
    I put my hope in your words.
<sup>148</sup> My eyes greet the night watches
    as I meditate on your promise.<sup>c</sup>
<sup>149</sup> Hear my voice in your mercy, O LORD;
    by your judgment give me life.
<sup>150</sup> Malicious persecutors draw near me;
    they are far from your law.
<sup>151</sup> You are near, O LORD;
    reliable are all your commandments.
<sup>152</sup> Long have I known from your testimonies
    that you have established them
      forever.

RESH

<sup>153</sup> Look at my affliction and rescue me,
    for I have not forgotten your law.
<sup>154</sup> Take up my cause and redeem me;<sup>d</sup>
    for the sake of your promise give
      me life.
<sup>155</sup> Salvation is far from sinners
    because they do not cherish your
      statutes.
<sup>156</sup> Your compassion is great, O LORD;
    in accord with your judgments, give
      me life.
<sup>157</sup> Though my persecutors and foes are
      many,
    I do not turn from your testimonies.
<sup>158</sup> I view the faithless with loathing<sup>e</sup>
    because they do not heed your
      promise.
<sup>159</sup> See how I love your precepts, LORD;
    in your mercy give me life.
<sup>160</sup> Your every word is enduring;
    all your righteous judgments are
      forever.

SHIN

<sup>161</sup> Princes persecute me without reason,
    but my heart reveres only your
      word.

---

z. [119:115] Ps 6:9; 139:19; Jb 21:14.    a. [119:132] Ps 25:16; 86:16.
b. [119:137] Tb 3:2.

c. [119:148] Ps 63:7; 77:7.    d. [119:154] Ps 43:1.    e. [119:158] Ps
139:22.

162 I rejoice at your promise,
　　as one who has found rich spoil.
163 Falsehood I hate and abhor;
　　your law I love.
164 Seven times a day I praise you
　　because your judgments are
　　　righteous.
165 Lovers of your law have much peace;[f]
　　for them there is no stumbling
　　　block.
166 I look for your salvation, Lord,
　　and I fulfill your commandments.
167 I observe your testimonies;
　　I love them very much.
168 I observe your precepts and testimonies;
　　all my ways are before you.

TAW

169 Let my cry come before you, Lord;[g]
　　in keeping with your word, give me
　　　understanding.
170 Let my prayer come before you;
　　rescue me according to your
　　　promise.
171 May my lips pour forth your praise,
　　because you teach me your statutes.
172 May my tongue sing of your promise,
　　for all your commandments are
　　　righteous.
173 Keep your hand ready to help me,
　　for I have chosen your precepts.
174 I long for your salvation, Lord;
　　your law is my delight.
175 Let my soul live to praise you;
　　may your judgments give me help.
176 I have wandered like a lost sheep;
　　seek out your servant,
　　for I do not forget your
　　　commandments.[h]

## PSALM 120[*]
### Prayer of a Returned Exile

1 A song of ascents.[†]

The Lord answered me
　　when I called in my distress:[i]

2 Lord, deliver my soul from lying lips,
　　from a treacherous tongue.[j]

3 What will he inflict on you,
　　O treacherous tongue,
　　and what more besides?[‡]
4 A warrior's arrows
　　sharpened with coals of brush
　　　wood![§k]

5 'Alas, I am a foreigner in Meshech,
　　I live among the tents of Kedar!
6 Too long do I live
　　among those who hate peace.
7 When I speak of peace,
　　they are for war.[l]

## PSALM 121[**]
### The Lord My Guardian

1 A song of ascents.

I raise my eyes toward the mountains.[††]
　　From whence shall come my help?[m]
2 My help comes from the Lord,
　　the maker of heaven and earth.[n]

3 He will not allow your foot to slip;[o]
　　or your guardian to sleep.
4 Behold, the guardian of Israel
　　never slumbers nor sleeps.
5 [‡‡]The Lord is your guardian;
　　the Lord is your shade
　　at your right hand.[p]
6 By day the sun will not strike you,
　　nor the moon by night.[q]
7 The Lord will guard you from all evil;
　　he will guard your soul.[r]

---

‡[120:3] **More besides:** a common curse formula in Hebrew was "May the Lord do such and such evils to you [the evils being specified], and add still more to them," cf. 1 Sm 3:17; 14:44; 25:22. Here the psalmist is at a loss for a suitable malediction.

§[120:4] **Coals of brush wood:** coals made from the stalk of the broom plant burn with intense heat. The psalmist thinks of lighted coals cast at his enemies.

¶[120:5] Meshech was in the far north (Gn 10:2) and Kedar was a tribe of the north Arabian desert (Gn 25:13). The psalmist may be thinking generally of all aliens living among inhospitable peoples.

**[Psalm 121] A blessing given to someone embarking on a dangerous journey whether a soldier going on a campaign or a pilgrim returning home from the Temple. People look anxiously at the wooded hills. Will God protect them on their journey (Ps 121:1)? The speaker declares that God is not confined to a place or a time (Ps 121:2), that every step is guarded (Ps 121:3–4); night and day (Ps 121:5–6) God watches over their every movement (Ps 121:7–8).

††[121:1] **The mountains:** possibly Mount Zion, the site of the Temple and hence of safety, but more probably mountains as a place of dangers, causing anxiety to the psalmist.

‡‡[121:5–6] The image of shade, a symbol of protection, is apt: God as shade protects from the harmful effects that ancients believed were caused by the sun and moon.

---

*[Psalm 120] A thanksgiving, reporting divine rescue (Ps 120:1) yet with fervent prayer for further protection against lying attackers (Ps 120:2–4). The psalmist is acutely conscious of living away from God's own land where divine peace prevails (Ps 120:5–7).

†[120:1] **A song of ascents:** Ps 120–134 all begin with this superscription. Most probably these fifteen Psalms once formed a collection of Psalms sung when pilgrims went to Jerusalem, since one "ascended" to Jerusalem (1 Kgs 12:28; Ps 24:3; 122:4; Lk 2:42) or to the house of God or to an altar (1 Kgs 12:33; 2 Kgs 23:2; Ps 24:3). Less probable is the explanation that these Psalms were sung by the exiles when they "ascended" to Jerusalem from Babylonia (cf. Ezr 7:9). The idea, found in the Mishnah, that the fifteen steps on which the Levites sang corresponded to these fifteen Psalms (Middot 2:5) must underlie the Vulgate translation *canticum graduum,* "song of the steps" or "gradual song."

---

f. [119:165] Ps 72:7.　g. [119:169] Ps 88:3.　h. [119:176] Is 53:6; Jer 50:6; Lk 15:1–7.　i. [120:1] Jon 2:3.

j. [120:2] Ps 12:3–5; Sir 51:3.　k. [120:4] Ps 11:6; 140:11; Prv 16:27. l. [120:7] Ps 35:20; 140:3–4.　m. [121:1] Jer 3:23.　n. [121:2] Ps 124:8; 146:6.　o. [121:3] Ps 66:9; 91:12; 1 Sm 2:9; Prv 3:23.　p. [121:5] Ps 16:8; 73:23.　q. [121:6] Wis 18:3; Is 25:4; 49:10.　r. [121:7] Ps 97:10.

8 The LORD will guard your coming and
going
both now and forever.[s]

## PSALM 122[*]
### A Pilgrim's Prayer for Jerusalem

1 A song of ascents. Of David.

I

I rejoiced when they said to me,
"Let us go to the house of the
LORD."[t]

2 And now our feet are standing
within your gates, Jerusalem.

3 Jerusalem, built as a city,
walled round about.[t,u]

4 There the tribes go up,
the tribes of the LORD,
As it was decreed for Israel,
to give thanks to the name of the
LORD.[v]

5 There are the thrones of justice,
the thrones of the house of David.

II

6 For the peace of Jerusalem pray:
"May those who love you prosper!

7 May peace be within your ramparts,
prosperity within your towers."[w]

8 For the sake of my brothers and friends I
say,
"Peace be with you."[x]

9 For the sake of the house of the LORD, our
God,
I pray for your good.

## PSALM 123[‡]
### Reliance on the Lord

1 A song of ascents.

To you I raise my eyes,
to you enthroned in heaven.[y]

2 Yes, like the eyes of servants
on the hand of their masters,
Like the eyes of a maid
on the hand of her mistress,

So our eyes are on the LORD our God,
till we are shown favor.

3 Show us favor, LORD, show us favor,
for we have our fill of contempt.[z]

4 Our souls are more than sated
with mockery from the insolent,
with contempt from the
arrogant.

## PSALM 124[§]
### God, the Rescuer of the People

1 A song of ascents. Of David.

Had not the LORD been with us,
let Israel say,[a]

2 Had not the LORD been with us,
when people rose against us,

3 Then they would have swallowed us alive,[b]
for their fury blazed against us.

4 Then the waters would have engulfed us,
the torrent overwhelmed us;[c]

5 then seething water would have
drowned us.

6 Blessed is the LORD, who did not leave us
to be torn by their teeth.

7 We escaped with our lives like a bird
from the fowler's snare;
the snare was broken,
and we escaped.

8 ¶Our help is in the name of the LORD,
the maker of heaven and earth.[d]

## PSALM 125[**]
### Israel's Protector

1 A song of ascents.

Those trusting in the LORD are like Mount
Zion,
unshakable, forever enduring.[e]

2 As mountains surround Jerusalem,
the LORD surrounds his people
both now and forever.[f]

---

*[Psalm 122] A song of Zion, sung by pilgrims obeying the law to visit Jerusalem three times on a journey. The singer anticipates joining the procession into the city (Ps 122:1–3). Jerusalem is a place of encounter, where the people praise God (Ps 122:4) and hear the divine justice mediated by the king (Ps 122:5). The very buildings bespeak God's power (cf. Ps 48:13–15). May the grace of this place transform the people's lives (Ps 122:6–9)!

†[122:3] **Walled round about**: lit., "which is joined to it," probably referring both to the density of the buildings and to the dense population.

‡[Psalm 123] A lament that begins as a prayer of an individual (Ps 123:1), who expresses by a touching comparison exemplary confidence in God (Ps 123:2). The Psalm ends in prayer that God relieve the people's humiliation at the hands of the arrogant (Ps 123:3–4).

§[Psalm 124] A thanksgiving which teaches that Israel's very existence is owed to God who rescues them. In the first part Israel's enemies are compared to the mythic sea dragon (Ps 124:2b–3a; cf. Jer 51:34) and Flood (Ps 124:3b–5; cf. Is 51:9–10). The Psalm heightens the malice of human enemies by linking them to the primordial enemies of God's creation. Israel is a bird freed from the trapper's snare (Ps 124:6–8)— freed originally from Pharaoh and now from the current danger.

¶[124:8] **Our help is in the name**: for the idiom, see Ex 18:4.

**[Psalm 125] In response to exilic anxieties about the ancient promises of restoration, the Psalm expresses confidence that God will surround the people as the mountains surround Zion (Ps 125:1–2). The just will not be contaminated by the wicked (Ps 125:3). May God judge between the two groups (Ps 125:4–5).

---

s. [121:8] Dt 28:6.  t. [122:1] Ps 43:3–4; 84:2–5.  u. [122:3] Ps 48:13–14.  v. [122:4] Dt 16:16.  w. [122:7] Ps 128:5.  x. [122:8] Jn 20:19ff.  y. [123:1] Ps 25:15; 119:82; 141:8.

z. [123:3] Ps 44:13–14; Jb 12:4.  a. [124:1] Ps 129:1.  b. [124:3] Prv 1:12.  c. [124:4] Ps 18:5; 69:2.  d. [124:8] Ps 121:2; 146:6.  e. [125:1] Prv 10:25.  f. [125:2] Dt 32:11.

³ The scepter of the wicked will not prevail
   in the land allotted to the just,*
Lest the just themselves
   turn their hands to evil.

⁴ Do good, LORD, to the good,
   to those who are upright of heart.ᵍ
⁵ But those who turn aside to crooked ways
   may the LORD send down with the
     evildoers.ʰ
Peace upon Israel!ⁱ

## PSALM 126†
### The Reversal of Zion's Fortunes

¹A song of ascents.

### I

When the LORD restored the captives of
   Zion,ʲ
   we thought we were dreaming.
² Then our mouths were filled with
     laughter;
   our tongues sang for joy.ᵏ
Then it was said among the nations,
   "The LORD had done great things
     for them."
³ The LORD has done great things for us;
   Oh, how happy we were!
⁴ Restore our captives, LORD,
   like the dry stream beds of the Negeb.‡

### II

⁵ Those who sow in tears
   will reap with cries of joy.ˡ
⁶ Those who go forth weeping,
   carrying sacks of seed,
Will return with cries of joy,
   carrying their bundled sheaves.

## PSALM 127§
### The Need of God's Blessing

¹A song of ascents. Of Solomon.

### I

Unless the LORD build the house,
   they labor in vain who build.

Unless the LORD guard the city,
   in vain does the guard keep watch.
² It is vain for you to rise early
   and put off your rest at night,
To eat bread earned by hard toil—
   all this God gives to his beloved in
     sleep.ᵐ

### II

³ Certainly sons are a gift from the LORD,
   the fruit of the womb, a reward.ⁿ
⁴ Like arrows in the hand of a warrior
   are the sons born in one's youth.
⁵ Blessed is the man who has filled his
     quiver with them.
He will never be shamed
   for he will destroy his foes at the
     gate.¶

## PSALM 128**
### The Blessed Home of the Just

¹A song of ascents.

### I

Blessed are all who fear the LORD,
   and who walk in his ways.ᵒ
² What your hands provide you will enjoy;
   you will be blessed and prosper:ᵖ
³ Your wife will be like a fruitful vine
   within your home,
Your children like young olive plants
   around your table.�q
⁴ Just so will the man be blessed
   who fears the LORD.

### II

⁵ May the LORD bless you from Zion;
   may you see Jerusalem's prosperity
   all the days of your life,ʳ
⁶    and live to see your children's
     children.ˢ
Peace upon Israel!ᵗ

## PSALM 129††
### Against Israel's Enemies

¹A song of ascents.

---

*[125:3] **The land allotted to the just:** lit., "the lot of the righteous." The promised land was divided among the tribes of Israel by lot (Nm 26:55; Jos 18). The righteous are the members of the people who are obedient to God. If the domination of the wicked were to continue in the land, even the just would be infected by their evil attitudes.

†[Psalm 126] A lament probably sung shortly after Israel's return from exile. The people rejoice that they are in Zion (Ps 126:1–3) but mere presence in the holy city is not enough; they must pray for the prosperity and the fertility of the land (Ps 126:4). The last verses are probably an oracle of promise: the painful work of sowing will be crowned with life (Ps 126:5–6).

‡[126:4] **Like the dry stream beds of the Negeb:** the psalmist prays for rain in such abundance that the dry riverbeds will run.

§[Psalm 127] The Psalm puts together two proverbs (Ps 127:1–2, 3–5) on God establishing "houses" or families. The prosperity of human groups is not the work of human beings but the gift of God.

¶[127:5] **At the gate:** the reference is not to enemies besieging the walls of a city but to adversaries in litigation. Law courts functioned in the open area near the main city gate. The more adult sons a man had, the more forceful he would appear in disputes, cf. Prv 31:23.

**[Psalm 128] A statement that the ever-reliable God will bless the reverent (Ps 128:1). God's blessing is concrete: satisfaction and prosperity, a fertile spouse and abundant children (Ps 128:2–4). The perspective is that of the adult male, ordinarily the ruler and representative of the household to the community. The last verses extend the blessing to all the people for generations to come (Ps 128:5–6).

††[Psalm 129] A Psalm giving thanks for God's many rescues of Israel over the long course of their history (Ps 129:1–4); the people pray that their oppressors never know the joy of harvest (Ps 129:5–8).

m. [127:2] Eccl 2:24.   n. [127:3] Ps 115:14; 128:3; Dt 28:11; Prv 17:6.   o. [128:1] Ps 112:1.   p. [128:2] Ps 112:3.   q. [128:3] Ps 144:12; Jb 29:5.   r. [128:5] Ps 20:3; 134:3.   s. [128:6] Jb 42:16; Prv 17:6.   t. [128:6] Ps 125:5.

g. [125:4] Ps 18:25ff.   h. [125:5] Prv 3:32.   i. [125:5] Ps 128:6. j. [126:1] Ps 14:7.   k. [126:2] Jb 8:21.   l. [126:5] Bar 4:23; Is 65:19.

I

Viciously have they attacked me from my
youth,
let Israel say now.ᵘ
2 Viciously have they attacked me from my
youth,ᵛ
yet they have not prevailed against
me.
3 Upon my back the plowers plowed,
as they traced their long furrows.ʷ
4 But the just LORD cut me free
from the ropes of the wicked.ˣ

II

5 May they recoil in disgrace,
all who hate Zion.
6 May they be like grass on the rooftops†
withered in early growth,ˣ
7 Never to fill the reaper's hands,
nor the arms of the binders of sheaves,
8 And with none passing by to call out:
"The blessing of the LORD be upon
you!‡
We bless you in the name of the
LORD!"ʸ

## PSALM 130§
### Prayer for Pardon and Mercy

¹A song of ascents.

I

Out of the depths¶ I call to you, LORD;
2 Lord, hear my cry!
May your ears be attentive
to my cry for mercy.ᶻ
3 If you, LORD, keep account of sins,
Lord, who can stand?ᵃ
4 But with you is forgiveness
and so you are revered.**

II

5 I wait for the LORD,
my soul waits
and I hope for his word.ᵇ

6 My soul looks for the Lord
more than sentinels for daybreak.ᶜ
More than sentinels for daybreak,
7 let Israel hope in the LORD,
For with the LORD is mercy,
with him is plenteous redemption,ᵈ
8 And he will redeem Israel
from all its sins.ᵉ

## PSALM 131††
### Humble Trust in God

¹A song of ascents. Of David.

LORD, my heart is not proud;
nor are my eyes haughty.
I do not busy myself with great matters,
with things too sublime for me.ᶠ
2 Rather, I have stilled my soul,
Like a weaned child to its mother,
weaned is my soul.ᵍ
3 Israel, hope in the LORD,
now and forever.

## PSALM 132‡‡
### The Covenant Between David and God

¹A song of ascents.

I

Remember, O LORD, for David
all his hardships;
2 How he swore an oath to the LORD,
vowed to the Mighty One of Jacob:§§
3 "I will not enter the house where I live,ʰ
nor lie on the couch where I sleep;
4 I will give my eyes no sleep,
my eyelids no rest,
5 Till I find a place for the LORD,
a dwelling for the Mighty One of
Jacob."
6 "We have heard of it in Ephrathah;¶¶
we have found it in the fields of
Jaar.¶¶

---

*[129:4] **The ropes of the wicked**: usually understood as
the rope for yoking animals to the plow. If it is severed, the
plowing (cf. Ps 129:3) comes to a halt.

†[129:6] **Like grass on the rooftops**: after the spring rains,
grass would sprout from the coat of mud with which the flat
roofs of simple houses were covered, but when the dry summer began there was no moisture in the thin roof-covering to
sustain the grass.

‡[129:8] **The blessing of the LORD be upon you**: harvesters greeted one another with such blessings, cf. Ru 2:4.

§[Psalm 130] This lament, a Penitential Psalm, is the *De
profundis* used in liturgical prayers for the faithful departed.
In deep sorrow the psalmist cries to God (Ps 130:1–2), asking for mercy (Ps 130:3–4). The psalmist's trust (Ps 130:5–6)
becomes a model for the people (Ps 130:7–8).

¶[130:1] **The depths**: Sheol here is a metaphor of total
misery. Deep anguish makes the psalmist feel "like those
descending to the pit" (Ps 143:7).

**[130:4] **And so you are revered**: the experience of God's
mercy leads one to a greater sense of God.

††[Psalm 131] A song of trust, in which the psalmist gives
up self-sufficiency (Ps 131:1), like a babe enjoying the comfort of its mother's lap (Ps 131:2), thus providing a model for
Israel's faith (Ps 131:3).

‡‡[Psalm 132] A song for a liturgical ceremony in which the
ark, the throne of Israel's God, was carried in procession to the
Temple. The singer asks that David's care for the proper hous-
ing of the ark be regarded with favor (Ps 132:1–5), and tells
how it was brought to Jerusalem (Ps 132:6–10). There follows
God's promise of favor to the Davidic dynasty (Ps 132:11–12)
and to Zion (Ps 132:13–17). The transfer of the ark to the tent
in Jerusalem is described in 2 Sm 6.

§§[132:2, 132:5] **Mighty One of Jacob**: one of the titles of
Israel's God, cf. Gn 49:24; Is 49:26; 60:16.

¶¶[132:6] **Ephrathah**: the homeland of David, cf. Ru 4:11.
**The fields of Jaar**: poetic for Kiriath-jearim, a town west of
Jerusalem, where the ark remained for several generations, cf.
1 Sm 7:1–2; 2 Sm 6:2; 1 Chr 13:5–6.

---

u. [129:1] Ps 124:1.  v. [129:2] Ps 118:13.  w. [129:3] Is 51:23.
x. [129:6] Is 37:27.  y. [129:8] Ps 118:26.  z. [130:2] Ps 5:2–3;
55:2–3; 86:6; Lam 3:55–56; Jon 2:3.  a. [130:3] Na 1:6.  b. [130:5]
Ps 119:81.

c. [130:6] Is 21:11; 26:9.  d. [130:7] Ps 86:15; 100:5; 103:8.
e. [130:8] Ps 25:22; Mt 1:21.  f. [131:1] Ps 139:6.  g. [131:2] Is
66:12–13.  h. [132:3] 2 Sm 7; 1 Chr 28:2.

7 Let us enter his dwelling;
   let us worship at his footstool."*i*
8 "Arise, LORD, come to your resting place,*j*
   you and your mighty ark.
9 Your priests will be clothed with justice;
   your devout will shout for joy."
10 For the sake of David your servant,
   do not reject your anointed.

**II**

11 The LORD swore an oath to David in
   truth,
   he will never turn back from it:*k*
   "Your own offspring*l* I will set upon your
   throne.
12 If your sons observe my covenant,
   and my decrees I shall teach them,
   Their sons, in turn,
   shall sit forever on your throne."
13 Yes, the LORD has chosen Zion,
   desired it for a dwelling:
14 "This is my resting place forever;
   here I will dwell, for I desire it.
15 I will bless Zion with provisions;
   its poor I will fill with bread.
16 I will clothe its priests with salvation;
   its devout shall shout for joy.*m*
17 There I will make a horn sprout for
   David;*n*
   I will set a lamp for my anointed.
18 His foes I will clothe with shame,
   but on him his crown shall shine."

### PSALM 133†
### A Vision of a Blessed Community

1 A song of ascents. Of David.

How good and how pleasant it is,
   when brothers‡ dwell together as one!
2 Like fine oil on the head,§*o*
   running down upon the beard,

Upon the beard of Aaron,
   upon the collar of his robe.
3 Like dew* of Hermon* coming down
   upon the mountains of Zion.*p*
There the LORD has decreed a blessing,
   life for evermore!*q*

### PSALM 134**
### Exhortation to the Night Watch to Bless God

1 A song of ascents.

O come, bless the LORD,
   all you servants of the LORD††
You who stand in the house of the LORD
   throughout the nights.*r*
2 Lift up your hands toward the sanctuary,*s*
   and bless the LORD.
3 May the LORD bless you from Zion,
   the Maker of heaven and earth.*t*

### PSALM 135‡‡
### Praise of God, the Ruler
### and Benefactor of Israel

1 Hallelujah!

**I**

Praise the name of the LORD!
   Praise, you servants of the LORD,*u*
2 Who stand in the house of the LORD,
   in the courts of the house of our
   God!*v*
3 Praise the LORD, for the LORD is good!
   Sing to his name, for it brings joy!
4 §§For the LORD has chosen Jacob for
   himself,
   Israel as his treasured possession.*w*

**II**

5 For I know that the LORD is great,
   that our Lord is greater than all
   gods.*x*

---

*[132:17] **A horn sprout for David**: the image of the horn, a symbol of strength, is combined with that of a "sprout," a term used for the Davidic descendant (cf. Jer 23:5; 33:15; Zec 3:8; 6:12). Early Christians referred the latter designation to Christ as son of David (Lk 1:69).

†[Psalm 133] A benediction over a peaceful community, most probably the people Israel, but appropriate too for Israelite families (Ps 133:1). The history of Israel, whether of its ancestors in the Book of Genesis or of later periods, was a history of distinct groups struggling to live in unity. Here that unity is declared blessed, like the holy oils upon the priest Aaron or the dew of the rainless summer that waters the crops (Ps 133:2–3).

‡[133:1] **Brothers**: in biblical Hebrew this word includes both the male and female members of a group united by blood relationships or by shared experiences and values. In this Psalm, the term could be applied most appropriately to the people of Israel, those privileged by God to be his chosen children.

§[133:2] **Oil on the head**: oil was used at the consecration of the high priest (Ex 30:22–33).

¶[133:3] **Dew**: dew was an important source of moisture in the dry climate (Gn 27:28; Hos 14:6). **Hermon**: the majestic snow-capped mountain visible in the north of Palestine.

**[Psalm 134] A brief liturgy exhorting all those who serve in the Jerusalem Temple during the night (cf. Is 30:29) to praise God with words and gestures. Although he is the Creator of the whole universe, God's blessings emanate in a unique way from Zion, the city of Jerusalem.

††[134:1] **Servants of the LORD**: priests and Levites, cf. Dt 10:8; Ps 113:1; 135:1; Dn 3:85.

‡‡[Psalm 135] The hymn begins and ends with an invitation to praise God (Ps 135:1–3, 19–20) for the great act of choosing Israel (Ps 135:4). The story of Israel's emergence as a people is told in Ps 135:5–14; God created and redeemed the people, easily conquering all opposition. God's defeat of hostile powers means that the powers themselves and their images are useless (Ps 135:15–18). The last three verses appear also in Ps 115:4–8.

§§[135:4] Though all nations are God's, Israel has a special status as God's "treasured" people: Ex 19:5; Dt 7:6; 14:2; 26:18; Mal 3:17.

---

i. [132:7] Ps 99:5.   j. [132:8–10] Ps 2:2; 89:21; 95:11; Nm 10:35; 2 Chr 6:41–42; Sir 24:7.   k. [132:11–14] Ps 68:17; 1 Kgs 8:13; Sir 24:7.   l. [132:11] Ps 110:4; 2 Sm 7:12.   m. [132:16] 2 Chr 6:41; Is 61:10.   n. [132:17] Is 11:1; Jer 33:15; Ez 29:21; Zec 3:8; Lk 1:69.   o. [133:2] Ex 30:25, 30.

p. [133:3] Hos 14:6.   q. [133:3] Dt 28:8; 30:20.   r. [134:1] Ps 135:1–2; 1 Chr 9:33.   s. [134:2] Ps 28:2; 141:2.   t. [134:3] Ps 20:3; 128:5; Nm 6:24.   u. [135:1] Ps 113:1.   v. [135:2] Ps 134:1.   w. [135:4] Ps 33:12; 144:15; Ex 19:6; Dt 7:6.   x. [135:5] Ps 95:3; Ex 18:11.

<sup>6</sup> Whatever the LORD desires
  he does in heaven and on earth,
  in the seas and all the depths.<sup>y</sup>
<sup>7</sup> It is he who raises storm clouds from the
   end of the earth,
  makes lightning for the rain,
  and brings forth wind from his
   storehouse.<sup>z</sup>
      III
<sup>8</sup> He struck down Egypt's firstborn,<sup>a</sup>
  of human being and beast alike,
<sup>9</sup> And sent signs and wonders against you,
   Egypt,
  against Pharaoh and all his servants.
<sup>10</sup> It is he who struck down many nations,<sup>b</sup>
  and slew mighty kings—
<sup>11</sup> Sihon, king of the Amorites,
  and Og, king of Bashan,
  all the kings of Canaan—
<sup>12</sup> And made their land a heritage,
  a heritage for Israel his people.
<sup>13</sup> O LORD, your name is forever,
  your renown, from generation to
   generation!<sup>c</sup>
<sup>14</sup> For the LORD defends his people,
  shows mercy to his servants.<sup>d</sup>
      IV
<sup>15</sup> The idols of the nations are silver and
   gold,<sup>e</sup>
  the work of human hands.
<sup>16</sup> They have mouths but do not speak;
  they have eyes but do not see;
<sup>17</sup> They have ears but do not hear;
  nor is there breath in their mouths.
<sup>18</sup> Their makers will become like them,
  and anyone who trusts in them.
      V
<sup>19</sup> House of Israel, bless the LORD!<sup>f</sup>
  House of Aaron, bless the LORD!
<sup>20</sup> House of Levi, bless the LORD!
  You who fear the LORD, bless the
   LORD!
<sup>21</sup> Blessed be the LORD from Zion,
  who dwells in Jerusalem!
  Hallelujah!

## PSALM 136*
### Hymn of Thanksgiving for
### God's Everlasting Mercy

      I
<sup>1</sup> Praise the LORD, for he is good;<sup>g</sup>
  for his mercy endures forever;

<sup>2</sup> Praise the God of gods;
  for his mercy endures forever;
<sup>3</sup> Praise the Lord of lords;
  for his mercy endures forever;
      II
<sup>4</sup> Who alone has done great wonders,<sup>h</sup>
  for his mercy endures forever;
<sup>5</sup> Who skillfully made the heavens,<sup>i</sup>
  for his mercy endures forever;
<sup>6</sup> Who spread the earth upon the waters,<sup>j</sup>
  for his mercy endures forever;
<sup>7</sup> Who made the great lights,
  for his mercy endures forever;
<sup>8</sup> The sun to rule the day,
  for his mercy endures forever;
<sup>9</sup> The moon and stars to rule the night,<sup>k</sup>
  for his mercy endures forever;
      III
<sup>10</sup> Who struck down the firstborn of Egypt,<sup>l</sup>
  for his mercy endures forever;
<sup>11</sup> And led Israel from their midst,
  for his mercy endures forever;
<sup>12</sup> With mighty hand and outstretched arm,<sup>m</sup>
  for his mercy endures forever;
<sup>13</sup> Who split in two the Red Sea,
  for his mercy endures forever;
<sup>14</sup> And led Israel through its midst,
  for his mercy endures forever;
<sup>15</sup> But swept Pharaoh and his army into the
   Red Sea,<sup>n</sup>
  for his mercy endures forever;
<sup>16</sup> Who led the people through the desert,<sup>o</sup>
  for his mercy endures forever;
      IV
<sup>17</sup> Who struck down great kings,<sup>p</sup>
  for his mercy endures forever;
<sup>18</sup> Slew powerful kings,
  for his mercy endures forever;
<sup>19</sup> Sihon, king of the Amorites,
  for his mercy endures forever;
<sup>20</sup> Og, king of Bashan,
  for his mercy endures forever;
<sup>21</sup> And made their lands a heritage,
  for his mercy endures forever;
<sup>22</sup> †A heritage for Israel, his servant,
  for his mercy endures forever.
      V
<sup>23</sup> The Lord remembered us in our low
   estate,
  for his mercy endures forever;
<sup>24</sup> Freed us from our foes,
  for his mercy endures forever;

---

*[Psalm 136] The hymn praises Israel's God ("the God of gods," Ps 136:2), who has created the world in which Israel lives. The refrain occurring after every line suggests that a speaker and chorus sang the Psalm in antiphonal fashion. A single act of God is described in Ps 136:4–25. God arranges

the heavens and the earth as the environment for human community, and then creates the community by freeing them and giving them land. In the final section (Ps 136:23–25) God, who created the people and gave them land, continues to protect and nurture them.

†[136:22] **A heritage for Israel:** the land was given to Israel by God to be handed on to future generations.

y. [135:6] Ps 115:3.   z. [135:7] Ps 148:8; Jer 10:13; 51:16; Jb 37:9.   a. [135:8–9] Ps 78:51; 105:27, 36; 136:10; Ex 12:29.   b. [135:10–12] Ps 136:17–22; Nm 21:21–35; Dt 2:24–3:17.   c. [135:13] Ps 102:13; Ex 3:15.   d. [135:14] Dt 32:36.   e. [135:15–18] Ps 115:4–6, 8.   f. [135:19–20] Ps 118:2–4.   g. [136:1] Ps 100:5; 118:1.

h. [136:4] Ps 72:18.   i. [136:5] Gn 1:9–19.   j. [136:6] Ps 24:2.   k. [136:9] Jer 31:35.   l. [136:10] Ex 12:29, 51; 14:22, 27; 15:22; Ps 78:51–52; 135:8.   m. [136:12] Dt 4:34.   n. [136:15] Ex 14:21f.   o. [136:16] Dt 8:2, 15.   p. [136:17–22] Ps 135:10–12.

²⁵ And gives bread to all flesh,
　　　for his mercy endures forever.
　　　　　　　VI
²⁶ Praise the God of heaven,
　　　for his mercy endures forever.

## PSALM 137*
### Sorrow and Hope in Exile

　　　　　　　I
¹ By the rivers of Babylon
　　　there we sat weeping
　　　　when we remembered Zion.�q
² On the poplars in its midst
　　　we hung up our harps.ʳ
³ For there our captors asked us
　　　for the words of a song;
　Our tormentors, for joy:
　　　"Sing for us a song of Zion!"
⁴ But how could we sing a song of the Lord
　　　in a foreign land?
　　　　　　　II
⁵ If I forget you, Jerusalem,
　　　may my right hand forget.ˢ
⁶ May my tongue stick to my palate
　　　if I do not remember you,
　If I do not exalt Jerusalem
　　　beyond all my delights.
　　　　　　　III
⁷ Remember, Lord, against Edom
　　　that day at Jerusalem.
　They said: "Level it, level it
　　　down to its foundations!"ᵗ
⁸ Desolate Daughter Babylon, you shall be
　　　destroyed,
　　　blessed the one who pays you back
　　　　what you have done us!ᵘ
⁹ †Blessed the one who seizes your children
　　　and smashes them against the rock.ᵛ

## PSALM 138‡
### Hymn of a Grateful Heart

¹Of David.

---

*[Psalm 137] A singer refuses to sing the people's sacred songs in an alien land despite demands from Babylonian captors (Ps 137:1–4). The singer swears an oath by what is most dear to a musician—hands and tongue—to exalt Jerusalem always (Ps 137:5–6). The Psalm ends with a prayer that the old enemies of Jerusalem, Edom and Babylon, be destroyed (Ps 137:7–9).

†[137:9] **Blessed the one who seizes your children and smashes them against the rock**: the children represent the future generations, and so must be destroyed if the enemy is truly to be eradicated.

‡[Psalm 138] A thanksgiving to God, who came to the rescue of the psalmist. Divine rescue was not the result of the psalmist's virtues but of God's loving fidelity (Ps 138:1–3). The act is not a private transaction but a public act that stirs the surrounding nations to praise God's greatness and care for the people (Ps 138:4–6). The psalmist, having experienced salvation, trusts that God will always be there in moments of danger (Ps 138:7–8).

q. [137:1] Ez 3:15; Lam 3:48.　r. [137:2] Is 24:8; Lam 5:14.　s. [137:5] Jer 51:50.　t. [137:7] Jer 49:7; Lam 4:21–22; Ez 25:12–14.　u. [137:8] Is 47:1–3; Jer 50–51.　v. [137:9] Hos 14:1.

　　　　　　　I
I thank you, Lord, with all my heart;ʷ
　　　in the presence of the angels§ to you
　　　　I sing.
² I bow low toward your holy temple;
　　　I praise your name for your mercy
　　　　and faithfulness.
　For you have exalted over all
　　　your name and your promise.
³ On the day I cried out, you answered;
　　　you strengthened my spirit.
　　　　　　　II
⁴ All the kings of earth will praise you,
　　　Lord,
　　　when they hear the words of your
　　　　mouth.
⁵ They will sing of the ways of the Lord:
　　　"How great is the glory of the
　　　　Lord!"
⁶ The Lord is on high, but cares for the
　　　lowlyˣ
　　　and knows the proud from afar.
⁷ Though I walk in the midst of dangers,
　　　you guard my life when my enemies
　　　　rage.
　You stretch out your hand;
　　　your right hand saves me.
⁸ The Lord is with me to the end.
　　　Lord, your mercy endures forever.
　　　Never forsake the work of your
　　　　hands!

## PSALM 139¶
### The All-knowing and Ever-present God

¹For the leader. A psalm of David.
　　　　　　　I
　Lord, you have probed me, you know me:
²　　　you know when I sit and stand;**ʸ
　　　you understand my thoughts from
　　　　afar.
³ You sift through my travels and my rest;
　　　with all my ways you are familiar.
⁴ Even before a word is on my tongue,
　　　Lord, you know it all.
⁵ Behind and before you encircle me
　　　and rest your hand upon me.
⁶ Such knowledge is too wonderful for me,
　　　far too lofty for me to reach.ᶻ

---

§[138:1] **In the presence of the angels**: heavenly beings who were completely subordinate to Israel's God. The earthly Temple represents the heavenly palace of God.

¶[Psalm 139] A hymnic meditation on God's omnipresence and omniscience. The psalmist is keenly aware of God's all-knowing gaze (Ps 139:1–6), of God's presence in every part of the universe (Ps 139:7–12), and of God's control over the psalmist's very self (Ps 139:13–16). Summing up Ps 139:1–16, 17–18 express wonder. There is only one place hostile to God's rule—wicked people. The psalmist prays to be removed from their company (Ps 139:19–24).

**[139:2] **When I sit and stand**: in all my physical movement.

w. [138:1] Ps 9:1.　x. [138:6] Lk 1:51–52.　y. [139:2] 2 Kgs 19:27; Jb 12:3.　z. [139:6] Ps 131:1.

7 Where can I go from your spirit?
     From your presence, where can I
        flee?
8 If I ascend to the heavens, you are there;
     if I lie down in Sheol, there you are.[a]
9 If I take the wings of dawn*
     and dwell beyond the sea,*
10 Even there your hand guides me,
     your right hand holds me fast.
11 If I say, "Surely darkness shall hide me,
     and night shall be my light"[†]—
12 Darkness is not dark for you,
     and night shines as the day.
     Darkness and light are but one.[b]

                        II
13 You formed my inmost being;
     you knit me in my mother's womb.[c]
14 I praise you, because I am wonderfully
        made;
     wonderful are your works!
     My very self you know.
15 My bones are not hidden from you,
     When I was being made in secret,
     fashioned in the depths of the earth.[‡]
16 Your eyes saw me unformed;
     in your book all are written down;[d]
     my days were shaped, before one
        came to be.

                        III
17 How precious to me are your designs,
        O God;
     how vast the sum of them!
18 Were I to count them, they would
        outnumber the sands;
     when I complete them, still you are
        with me.[e]
19 When you would destroy the wicked,
        O God,
     the bloodthirsty depart from me![f]
20 Your foes who conspire a plot against
        you
     are exalted in vain.

                        IV
21 Do I not hate, LORD, those who hate you?
     Those who rise against you, do I not
        loathe?[g]
22 With fierce hatred I hate them,
     enemies I count as my own.

23 Probe me, God, know my heart;
     try me, know my thoughts.[h]

24 See if there is a wicked path in me;
     lead me along an ancient path.[§]

## PSALM 140[¶]
### Prayer for Deliverance from the Wicked

1 For the leader. A psalm of David.

                        I
2 Deliver me, LORD, from the wicked;
     preserve me from the violent,[i]
3 From those who plan evil in their hearts,
     who stir up conflicts every day,
4 **Who sharpen their tongue like a serpent,
     venom of asps upon their lips.[j]
                                        Selah

                        II
5 Keep me, LORD, from the clutches of the
        wicked;
     preserve me from the violent,
     who plot to trip me up.[k]
6 ††The arrogant have set a trap for me;
     they have spread out ropes for a net,
     laid snares for me by the wayside.
                                        Selah
7 I say to the LORD: You are my God;[l]
     listen, LORD, to the words of my pleas.
8 LORD, my master, my strong deliverer,
     you cover my head on the day of
        armed conflict.
9 LORD, do not grant the desires of the
        wicked one;
     do not let his plot succeed.
                                        Selah

                        III
10 Those who surround me raise their heads;
     may the mischief they threaten
        overwhelm them.
11 Drop burning coals upon them;[m]
     cast them into the watery pit never
        more to rise.

12 Slanderers will not survive on earth;
     evil will hunt down the man of
        violence to overthrow him.
13 For I know the LORD will take up the
        cause of the needy,
     justice for the poor.

---

§[139:24] **Lead me along an ancient path**: the manner of living of our ancestors, who were faithful to God's will, cf. Jer 6:16.

¶[Psalm 140] A lament seeking rescue from violent and treacherous foes (Ps 140:2–6). The psalmist remains trusting (Ps 140:7–8), vigorously praying that the plans of the wicked recoil upon themselves (Ps 140:9–12). A serene statement of praise ends the Psalm (Ps 140:13). The psalmist is content to be known as one of "the needy," "the poor," "the just," "the upright" (Ps 140:13), a class of people expecting divine protection.

**[140:4] Similar metaphors for a wicked tongue are used in Ps 52:2; 55:20; 58:3.

††[140:6] **Have set a trap . . . have spread out ropes for a net**: the same figure, of hunters setting traps, occurs in Ps 9:16; 31:5; 35:7; 64:6, cf. Mt 22:15; Lk 11:54.

---

*[139:9] **Take the wings of dawn**: go to the extremities of the east. **Beyond the sea**: uttermost bounds of the west; the sea is the Mediterranean.

†[139:11] **Night shall be my light**: night to me is what day is to others.

‡[139:15] **The depths of the earth**: figurative language for the womb, stressing the hidden and mysterious operations that occur there.

---

a. [139:8] Jb 23:8–9; Jer 23:23–24.   b. [139:12] Jb 12:22.   c. [139:13] Wis 7:1; Eccl 11:5; Jb 1:21.   d. [139:16] Mal 3:16.   e. [139:18] Jb 11:7.   f. [139:19] Jb 21:14.   g. [139:21] Ps 119:158.   h. [139:23] Ps 17:3; 26:2.

i. [140:2] Ps 71:4.   j. [140:4] Ps 64:4; Rom 3:13.   k. [140:5] Jer 18:22; Ps 56:7; 57:7.   l. [140:7] Ps 31:15.   m. [140:11] Ps 11:6; 120:4; Gn 19:24.

¹⁴ Then the righteous will give thanks to
          your name;
     the upright will dwell in your
          presence.ⁿ

## PSALM 141*
### Prayer for Deliverance from the Wicked

¹A psalm of David.

     LORD, I call to you; hasten to me;
          listen to my plea when I call.
²    Let my prayer be incense† before you;
          my uplifted hands† an evening
               offering.ᵒ
³    Set a guard, LORD, before my mouth,
          keep watch over the door of my
               lips.ᵖ
⁴    Do not let my heart incline to evil,
          to perform deeds in
               wickedness.
     On the delicacies of evildoers
          let me not feast.
⁵    ‡Let a righteous person strike me; it is
          mercy if he reproves me.
     Do not withhold oil from my
          head�q
     while my prayer opposes their evil
          deeds.
⁶    May their leaders be cast over the cliff,
          so that they hear that my speeches
               are pleasing.
⁷    Like the plowing and breaking up of the
          earth,
     our bones are strewn at the mouth
          of Sheol.
⁸    For my eyes are upon you, O LORD, my
          Lord;ʳ
     in you I take refuge; do not take
          away my soul.
⁹    Guard me from the trap they have set for
          me,
     from the snares of evildoers.ˢ
¹⁰   Let the wicked fall into their own nets,
          while only I pass over them
               safely.

## PSALM 142§
### A Prayer in Time of Trouble

¹A *maskil* of David, when he was in the cave.¶
A prayer.

²    With my own voice I cry to the LORD;
          with my own voice I beseech the LORD.
³    Before him I pour out my complaint,
          tell of my distress in front of him.
⁴    When my spirit is faint within me,ᵗ
          you know my path.ᵘ
     As I go along this path,
          they have hidden a trap for me.ᵛ
⁵    I look to my right hand to seeʷ
          that there is no one willing to
               acknowledge me.
     My escape has perished;
          no one cares for me.
⁶    I cry out to you, LORD,
          I say, You are my refuge,ˣ
     my portion in the land of the living.ʸ
⁷    Listen to my cry for help,
          for I am brought very low.ᶻ
     Rescue me from my pursuers,
          for they are too strong for me.
⁸    Lead my soul from prison,
          that I may give thanks to your name.
     Then the righteous shall gather around me**
          because you have been good to me.

## PSALM 143††
### A Prayer in Distress

¹A psalm of David.

     LORD, hear my prayer;
          in your faithfulness listen to my
               pleading;
          answer me in your righteousness.
²    Do not enter into judgment with your
          servant;
     before you no one can be just.ᵃ
³    The enemy has pursued my soul;

---

§[Psalm 142] In this lament imploring God for help (Ps 142:2–4), the psalmist tells how enemies have set a trap (Ps 142:4–5), and prays for rescue (Ps 142:6–8). The speaker feels utterly alone (Ps 142:5), exhausted (Ps 142:7), and may even be imprisoned (Ps 142:7). Prison is possibly a metaphor for general distress. The last two verses are the vow of praise, made after receiving an assurance of divine help (Ps 142:7).
¶[142:1] **In the cave**: cf. 1 Sm 22:1; 24:1–3; Ps 57:1.
**[142:8] **Then the righteous shall gather around me**: in the Temple, when the psalmist offers a thanksgiving sacrifice.
††[Psalm 143] One of the Church's seven Penitential Psalms, this lament is a prayer to be freed from death-dealing enemies. The psalmist addresses God, aware that there is no equality between God and human beings; salvation is a gift (Ps 143:1–2). Victimized by evil people (Ps 143:3–4), the psalmist recites ("remembers") God's past actions on behalf of the innocent (Ps 143:5–6). The Psalm continues with fervent prayer (Ps 143:7–9) and a strong desire for guidance and protection (Ps 143:10–12).

---

*[Psalm 141] A lament of an individual (Ps 141:1–2) who is keenly aware that only the righteous can worship God properly and who therefore prays to be protected from the doomed wicked (Ps 141:3–10).
†[141:2] **Incense**: lit., "smoke," i.e., the fragrant fumes arising from the altar at the burning of sacrificial animals or of aromatic spices; also used in Rev 5:8 as a symbol of prayer. **My uplifted hands**: the gesture of supplication, cf. Ps 28:2; 63:5; 88:10; 119:48; 134:2; 143:6.
‡[141:5–7] The Hebrew text is obscure.

---

n. [140:14]  Ps 11:7; 16:11; 17:15.  o. [141:2]  Ps 134:2; Ex 30:8.  p. [141:3]  Sir 22:27.  q. [141:5]  Prv 9:8; 25:12.  r. [141:8]  Ps 25:15; 123:1–2.  s. [141:9]  Ps 142:4.

t. [142:4]  Ps 143:4.  u. [142:4]  Ps 139:24.  v. [142:4]  Ps 141:9.  w. [142:5]  Ps 16:8; 73:23; 121:5.  x. [142:6]  Ps 91:2, 9.  y. [142:6]  Ps 16:5; 27:13; 116:9; Is 38:11.  z. [142:7]  Ps 79:8.  a. [143:2]  Eccl 7:20; Jb 4:17; Rom 3:20.

he has crushed my life to the ground.*[b]*
He has made me dwell in darkness
  like those long dead.*[c]*
4 My spirit is faint within me;
  my heart despairs.*[d]*
5 I remember the days of old;
  I ponder all your deeds;
  the works of your hands I recall.*[e]*
6 I stretch out my hands toward you,
  my soul to you like a parched land.*[f]*

                              Selah

7 Hasten to answer me, LORD;
  for my spirit fails me.
Do not hide your face from me,
  lest I become like those descending
    to the pit.*[g]*
8 In the morning let me hear of your mercy,
  for in you I trust.
Show me the path I should walk,
  for I entrust my life to you.*[h]*
9 Rescue me, LORD, from my foes,
  for I seek refuge in you.
10 Teach me to do your will,
  for you are my God.
May your kind spirit guide me
  on ground that is level.
11 For your name's sake, LORD, give me life;
  in your righteousness lead my soul
    out of distress.
12 In your mercy put an end to my foes;
  all those who are oppressing my soul,
  for I am your servant.*[i]*

## PSALM 144*
### A Prayer for Victory and Prosperity

¹Of David.

### I

†Blessed be the LORD, my rock,
  who trains my hands for battle,
  my fingers for war;
2 My safeguard and my fortress,
  my stronghold, my deliverer,
My shield, in whom I take refuge,
  who subdues peoples under me.

### II

3 ‡LORD, what is man that you take notice of
    him;
  the son of man, that you think of him?*[j]*
4 §Man is but a breath,
  his days are like a passing shadow.*[k]*
5 ¶LORD, incline your heavens and come down;
  touch the mountains and make
    them smoke.*[l]*
6 Flash forth lightning and scatter my foes;
  shoot your arrows and rout them.
7 Reach out your hand from on high;
  deliver me from the many waters;
  rescue me from the hands of foreign
    foes.
8 Their mouths speak untruth;
  their right hands are raised in lying
    oaths.**
9 O God, a new song I will sing to you;
  on a ten-stringed lyre I will play for
    you.*[m]*
10 You give victory to kings;
  you delivered David your servant.*[n]*
From the menacing sword ¹¹deliver me;
  rescue me from the hands of foreign
    foes.
Their mouths speak untruth;
  their right hands are raised in lying
    oaths.

### III

12 May our sons be like plants*[o]*
  well nurtured from their youth,
Our daughters, like carved columns,
  shapely as those of the temple.
13 May our barns be full
  with every kind of store.
May our sheep increase by thousands,
  by tens of thousands in our fields;
  may our oxen be well fattened.
14 May there be no breach in the walls,
  no exile, no outcry in our streets.*[p]*
15 Blessed the people so fortunate;
  blessed the people whose God is the
    LORD.*[q]*

## PSALM 145††
### The Greatness and Goodness of God

¹Praise. Of David.

---

*[Psalm 144] The Psalm may reflect a ceremony in which the king, as leader of the army, asked God's help (Ps 144:1–8). In Ps 144:9 the poem shifts abruptly from pleading to thanksgiving, and (except for Ps 144:11) shifts again to prayer for the people. The first section (Ps 144:1–2) is a prayer of thanks for victory; the second (Ps 144:3–7a), a humble acknowledgment of human nothingness and a supplication that God show forth saving power; the third (Ps 144:9–11), a promise of future thanksgiving; the fourth (Ps 144:12–15), a wish for prosperity and peace. A prayer for deliverance from treacherous foes serves as a refrain after the second and third sections (Ps 144:7b–8, 11). Except for its final section, the Psalm is made up almost entirely of verses from other Psalms.
†[144:1–2] Composed of phrases from Ps 18:3, 35, 47–48.

‡[144:3] Similar to Ps 8:4.
§[144:4] Composed of phrases from Ps 39:6; 102:12.
¶[144:5–7] Adapted in large part from Ps 18:10, 15, 17; 104:32.
**[144:8b, 11b] **Their right hands are raised in lying oaths:** the psalmist's enemies give false testimony.
††[Psalm 145] A hymn in acrostic form; every verse begins with a successive letter of the Hebrew alphabet. Acrostic poems usually do not develop ideas but consist rather of loosely connected statements. The singer invites all to praise God (Ps 145:1–3, 21). The "works of God" make God present and invite human praise (Ps 145:4–7); they climax in a confession (Ps 145:8–9). God's mighty acts show forth divine kingship (Ps 145:10–20), a major theme in the literature of early Judaism and in Christianity.

b. [143:3] Ps 7:6.  c. [143:3] Lam 3:6.  d. [143:4] Ps 142:4; Jb 17:1.  e. [143:5] Ps 77:6, 12.  f. [143:6] Ps 42:2; 63:2.  g. [143:7] Ps 28:1; 30:4; 88:5; Prv 1:12.  h. [143:8] Ps 25:4; 27:11; 86:11; 119:12, 35.  i. [143:12] Ps 116:16.

j. [144:3] Jb 7:17.  k. [144:4] Ps 62:10; 90:9–10; Jb 7:16; Eccl 6:12; Wis 2:5.  l. [144:5] Is 63:19.  m. [144:9] Ps 33:2–3.  n. [144:10] Ps 18:51.  o. [144:12] Ps 128:3.  p. [144:14] Is 65:19.  q. [144:15] Ps 33:12.

I will extol you, my God and king;
  I will bless your name forever and
    ever.
2 Every day I will bless you;
  I will praise your name forever and
    ever.[r]
3 Great is the LORD and worthy of much
    praise,[s]
  whose grandeur is beyond
    understanding.
4 One generation praises your deeds to the
    next
  and proclaims your mighty works.[t]
5 They speak of the splendor of your
    majestic glory,
  tell of your wonderful deeds.[u]
6 They speak of the power of your awesome
    acts
  and recount your great deeds.[v]
7 They celebrate your abounding goodness
  and joyfully sing of your justice.
8 The LORD is gracious and merciful,
  slow to anger and abounding in
    mercy.[w]
9 The LORD is good to all,
  compassionate toward all your
    works.[x]
10 All your works give you thanks, LORD
  and your faithful bless you.[y]
11 They speak of the glory of your reign
  and tell of your mighty works,
12 Making known to the sons of men your
    mighty acts,
  the majestic glory of your rule.
13 Your reign is a reign for all ages,
  your dominion for all generations.[z]
  The LORD is trustworthy in all his words,
  and loving in all his works.
14 The LORD supports all who are falling
  and raises up all who are bowed
    down.[a]
15 The eyes of all look hopefully to you;
  you give them their food in due
    season.[b]
16 You open wide your hand
  and satisfy the desire of every living
    thing.
17 The LORD is just in all his ways,
  merciful in all his works.[c]
18 The LORD is near to all who call upon
    him,
  to all who call upon him in truth.[d]
19 He fulfills the desire of those who fear
    him;
  he hears their cry and saves them.[e]

20 The LORD watches over all who love him,
  but all the wicked he destroys.[f]
21 My mouth will speak the praises of the LORD;
  all flesh will bless his holy name
    forever and ever.

## PSALM 146[*]
### Trust in God the Creator and Redeemer

1 Hallelujah!
2 Praise the LORD, my soul;
  I will praise the LORD all my life,
  sing praise to my God while I live.[g]

I

3 Put no trust in princes,
  in children of Adam powerless to
    save.[h]
4 Who breathing his last, returns to
    the earth;
  that day all his planning comes to
    nothing.[i]

II

5 Blessed the one whose help is the God of
    Jacob,
  whose hope is in the LORD, his God,
6 The maker of heaven and earth,
  the seas and all that is in them,[j]
  Who keeps faith forever,
7   secures justice for the oppressed,[k]
  who gives bread to the hungry.
  The LORD sets prisoners free;[l]
8   the LORD gives sight to the blind.
  The LORD raises up those who are bowed
    down;[m]
  the LORD loves the righteous.
9 The LORD protects the resident alien,
  comes to the aid of the orphan and
    the widow,[n]
  but thwarts the way of the wicked.
10 The LORD shall reign forever,
  your God, Zion, through all
    generations![o]
  Hallelujah!

## PSALM 147[†]
### God's Word Restores Jerusalem

1 Hallelujah!

---

*[Psalm 146] A hymn of someone who has learned there
is no other source of strength except the merciful God. Only
God, not mortal human beings (Ps 146:3–4), can help vulnerable and oppressed people (Ps 146:5–9). The first of the five
hymns that conclude the Psalter.

†[Psalm 147] The hymn is divided into three sections by
the calls to praise in Ps 147:1, 7, 12. The first section praises the
powerful creator who restores exiled Judah (Ps 147:1–6); the
second section, the creator who provides food to animals and
human beings; the third and climactic section exhorts the holy
city to recognize it has been re-created and made the place of
disclosure for God's word, a word as life-giving as water.

---

r. [145:2] Ps 34:2.   s. [145:3] Ps 48:2; 95:3; 96:4; Jb 36:26.   t. [145:4]
Ps 22:31–32; 48:14–15; 71:18; 78:4; Ex 10:2; Dt 4:9.   u. [145:5] Ps
96:3; 105:2.   v. [145:6] Ps 66:3.   w. [145:8] Ps 86:5, 15; 103:8; Ex
34:6; Sir 2:11.   x. [145:9] Ps 103:13; Wis 11:24.   y. [145:10] Dn
3:57.   z. [145:13] Ps 10:16; 102:13; 146:10; Lam 5:19; Dn 3:33;
Rev 11:15.   a. [145:14] Ps 94:18; 146:8.   b. [145:15] Ps 136:25;
104:27–28; Mt 6:25–26.   c. [145:17] Dt 32:4.   d. [145:18] Dt 4:7;
Is 55:6; 58:9.

e. [145:19] Ps 34:18.   f. [145:20] Jgs 5:31.   g. [146:2] Ps 103:1;
104:33.   h. [146:3] Ps 118:8–9.   i. [146:4] Ps 90:3; 104:29; 1 Mc 2:63;
Jb 34:14–15; Eccl 3:20; 12:7; Sir 40:11; Is 2:22.   j. [146:6] Ps 121:2;
124:8; Ex 20:11; Acts 14:15; Rev 14:7.   k. [146:7] Ps 103:6.   l. [146:7]
Ps 68:7; Is 49:9; 61:1.   m. [146:8] Ps 145:14.   n. [146:9] Ps 68:6; Dt
10:18.   o. [146:10] Ps 145:13; Lam 5:19.

I

How good to sing praise to our God;
　　how pleasant to give fitting praise.[p]
2 The LORD rebuilds Jerusalem,
　　and gathers the dispersed of Israel,[q]
3 Healing the brokenhearted,
　　and binding up their wounds.[r]
4 He numbers the stars,
　　and gives to all of them their names.[s]
5 Great is our Lord, vast in power,
　　with wisdom beyond measure.[t]
6 The LORD gives aid to the poor,
　　but casts the wicked to the ground.[u]

II

7 Sing to the LORD with thanksgiving;
　　with the lyre make music to our
　　　God,[v]
8 *Who covers the heavens with clouds,
　　provides rain for the earth,
　　makes grass sprout on the
　　　mountains,[w]
9 Who gives animals their food
　　and young ravens what they cry for.[x]
10 †He takes no delight in the strength of
　　　horses,
　　no pleasure in the runner's stride.[y]
11 Rather the LORD takes pleasure in those
　　　who fear him,
　　those who put their hope in his
　　　mercy.

III

12 Glorify the LORD, Jerusalem;
　　Zion, offer praise to your God,
13 For he has strengthened the bars of your
　　　gates,
　　blessed your children within you.[z]
14 He brings peace to your borders,
　　and satisfies you with finest wheat.[a]
15 ‡He sends his command to earth;
　　his word runs swiftly![b]
16 Thus he makes the snow like wool,
　　and spreads the frost like ash;[c]
17 He disperses hail like crumbs.
　　Who can withstand his cold?
18 Yet when again he issues his command, it
　　　melts them;
　　he raises his winds and the waters
　　　flow.

19 He proclaims his word to Jacob,
　　his statutes and laws to Israel.[d]
20 He has not done this for any other nation;
　　of such laws they know nothing.
Hallelujah!

### PSALM 148[§]
### All Creation Summoned to Praise

1 Hallelujah!

I

Praise the LORD from the heavens;
　　praise him in the heights.
2 Praise him, all you his angels;
　　give praise, all you his hosts.[e]
3 Praise him, sun and moon;
　　praise him, all shining stars.
4 Praise him, highest heavens,¶
　　you waters above the heavens.
5 Let them all praise the LORD's name;
　　for he commanded and they were
　　　created.[f]
6 Assigned them their station forever,
　　set an order that will never change.

II

7 Praise the LORD from the earth,
　　you sea monsters and all the deeps
　　　of the sea;[g]
8 Lightning and hail, snow and thick
　　　clouds,
　　storm wind that fulfills his
　　　command;
9 Mountains and all hills,
　　fruit trees and all cedars;[h]
10 Animals wild and tame,
　　creatures that crawl and birds that
　　　fly;[i]
11 Kings of the earth and all peoples,
　　princes and all who govern on earth;
12 Young men and women too,
　　old and young alike.
13 Let them all praise the LORD's name,
　　for his name alone is exalted,
　　His majesty above earth and heaven.[j]
14 **He has lifted high the horn of his people;
　　to the praise of all his faithful,
　　the Israelites, the people near to
　　　him.
Hallelujah!

---

*[147:8–9] God clothes the fields and feeds the birds, cf.
Mt 6:26, 30.

†[147:10–11] Acknowledging one's dependence upon God
rather than claiming self-sufficiency pleases God, cf. Ps 20:8;
33:16–19.

‡[147:15–19] God speaks through the thunder of nature
and the word of revealed law, cf. Is 55:10–11. The weather phenomena are well known in Jerusalem: a blizzard of snow and
hail followed by a thunderstorm that melts the ice.

§[Psalm 148] A hymn inviting the beings of heaven (Ps
148:1–6) and of earth (Ps 148:7–14) to praise God. The hymn
does not distinguish between inanimate and animate (and
rational) nature.

¶[148:4] **Highest heavens:** lit., "the heavens of the heavens,"
i.e., the space above the firmament, where the "upper waters"
are stored, cf. Gn 1:6–7; Dt 10:14; 1 Kgs 8:27; Ps 104:3, 13.

**[148:14] **Has lifted high the horn of his people:** the horn
symbolizes strength, the concrete noun for the abstract. Of all
peoples, God has chosen Israel to return praise and thanks in
a special way.

---

p. [147:1] Ps 33:1; 92:2.　q. [147:2] Is 11:12; 56:8; Jer 31:10.
r. [147:3] Jb 5:18; Is 30:26; 61:1; Jer 33:6.　s. [147:4] Is 40:26.
t. [147:5] Jdt 16:13; Jer 51:15.　u. [147:6] Ps 146:9; 1 Sm 2:7–
8.　v. [147:7] Ps 71:22.　w. [147:8] Ps 104:13f; Jb 5:10; Jer 14:22;
Jl 2:23.　x. [147:9] Jb 38:41; Mt 6:26.　y. [147:10] Ps 20:8; 33:16–
18.　z. [147:13] Ps 48:14.　a. [147:14] Ps 81:17.　b. [147:15] Ps
33:9.　c. [147:16] Jb 6:16; 37:10; 38:22.

d. [147:19] Ps 78:5; Bar 3:37; Dt 4:7–8.　e. [148:2] Ps 103:20f; Dn
3:58–63.　f. [148:5] Ps 33:9; Gn 1:3f; Jdt 16:14.　g. [148:7] Ps 135:6;
Gn 1:21.　h. [148:9] Is 44:23.　i. [148:10] Ps 30:5; Gn 1:21, 24f; Dt
4:7.　j. [148:13] Ps 30:5; Dt 4:7.

## PSALM 149*
### Praise God with Song and Sword

¹Hallelujah!

Sing to the LORD a new song,
    his praise in the assembly of the
        faithful.ᵏ
² Let Israel be glad in its maker,
    the people of Zion rejoice in their
        king.
³ Let them praise his name in dance,
    make music with tambourine and
        lyre.†ˡ
⁴ For the LORD takes delight in his people,
    honors the poor with victory.
⁵ Let the faithful rejoice in their glory,
    cry out for joy on their couches,‡
⁶ With the praise of God in their mouths,
    and a two-edged sword in their
        hands,ᵐ
⁷ To bring retribution on the nations,
    punishment on the peoples,ⁿ
⁸ To bind their kings in shackles,
    their nobles in chains of iron,
⁹ To execute the judgments decreed for
    them—

such is the gloryˢ of all God's
        faithful.
Hallelujah!

## PSALM 150*
### Final Doxology

¹Hallelujah!

Praise God in his holy sanctuary;**ᵒ
    give praise in the mighty dome of
        heaven.
² Give praise for his mighty deeds,ᵖ
    praise him for his great majesty.
³ Give praise with blasts upon the horn,�q
    praise him with harp and lyre.
⁴ Give praise with tambourines and dance,
    praise him with strings and pipes.ʳ
⁵ Give praise with crashing cymbals,
    praise him with sounding cymbals.
⁶ Let everything that has breath
    give praise to the LORD!ˢ
Hallelujah!

---

§[149:9] **The glory**: what brings honor to the people is their readiness to carry out the divine will, here conceived as punishing injustice done by the nations.

¶[Psalm 150] The Psalm is a closing doxology both for the fifth book of the Psalms (Ps 107–149) and for the Psalter as a whole. Temple musicians and dancers are called to lead all beings on earth and in heaven in praise of God. The Psalm proclaims to whom praise shall be given, and where (Ps 150:1); what praise shall be given, and why (Ps 150:2); how praise shall be given (Ps 150:3–5), and by whom (Ps 150:6).

**[150:1] **His holy sanctuary**: God's Temple on earth. **The mighty dome of heaven**: lit., "[God's] strong vault"; heaven is here imagined as a giant plate separating the inhabited world from the waters of the heavens.

---

*[Psalm 149] A hymn inviting the people of Israel to celebrate their God in song and festive dance (Ps 149:1–3, 5) because God has chosen them and given them victory (Ps 149:4). The exodus and conquest are the defining acts of Israel; the people must be ready to do again those acts in the future at the divine command (Ps 149:6–9).

†[149:3] **Make music with tambourine and lyre**: the verse recalls the great exodus hymn of Ex 15:20.

‡[149:5] **On their couches**: the people reclined to banquet.

---

k. [149:1]  Ps 22:23; 26:12; 35:18; 40:10; Jdt 16:1.  l. [149:3] Ps 68:26; 81:2–3; 87:7; 150:3–4.  m. [149:6] Neh 4:10–12; 2 Mc 15:27.  n. [149:7] Wis 3:8.

o. [150:1] Dn 3:53.  p. [150:2] Dt 3:24.  q. [150:3ff] Ps 81:3–4; 149:3; 2 Sm 6:5; 1 Chr 13:8; 16:5, 42; 2 Chr 5:12–13; 7:6.  r. [150:4] Ps 68:26; Ex 15:20.  s. [150:6] Rev 5:13.

# THE BOOK OF
# PROVERBS

❦

Proverbs is an anthology of collections of sayings and instructions. Many of the sayings and perhaps some instructions were composed in the monarchic period (late eleventh to the early sixth centuries). Editing of the whole book was done in the early postexilic period, in the view of most scholars; at that time chaps. 1–9 would have been added as the introduction. Whether the material originated among royal scribes (as 25:1 seems to suggest) imitating common literary genres, or whether it arose among tribal elders inculcating traditional ways, is disputed. The origin of the material, however, need not be imagined in an either/or scenario. Folk wisdom and observations could surely have been elaborated and re-expressed by learned scribes: "What oft was thought but ne'er so well expressed" (Alexander Pope). There can be no doubt, however, that Proverbs is sophisticated literature by talented writers, winning readers with its compelling portrait of wisdom and inviting them to see life afresh, "wisely," through its wit, originality, and shrewd observation.

The primary purpose of the book is to teach wisdom, not only to the young and inexperienced (1:2–4) but also to the advanced (1:5–6). Wisdom in the ancient Near East was not theoretical knowledge but practical expertise. Jewelers who cut precious stones were wise; kings who made their dominion peaceful and prosperous were wise. One could be wise in daily life, too, in knowing how to live successfully (having a prosperous household and living a long and healthy life) and without trouble in God's universe. Ultimately wisdom, or "sound guidance" (1:5), aims at the formation of character.

In the ancient Near East, people assumed that wisdom belonged to the gods, who were wise by reason of their divinity; human beings needed to have wisdom *granted* them by the gods. Creation accounts of neighboring cultures depict creation in two stages. In the first stage, human beings lived an animal-like existence, without clothes, writing, or kingship (proper governance). Over time, the gods came to realize that such a low grade of existence made the human race inadequate as their servants, so they endowed the race with "wisdom," which consisted of culture (e.g., kingship) and crafts (e.g., knowledge of farming, ability to weave). Such wisdom elevated the race to a "human" level and made them effective servants of the gods. Furthermore, divine wisdom was *mediated* to human beings through earthly institutions—the king, scribes (who produced wise writings), and heads of families (fathers, sometimes mothers). These traditional mediators appear in Proverbs: the book is credited to King Solomon, and kings are respectfully mentioned as pillars of society (e.g., 16:12–15); *writings* are a source of wisdom (1:1–7); the father instructing his son is the major paradigm of teaching. Proverbs differs, however, from other wisdom books in concentrating on wisdom itself, treating it as a virtually independent entity and personifying it as an attractive woman. Other books urge readers to perform wise acts, but Proverbs urges them to seek wisdom itself and portrays wisdom as a woman seeking human beings as disciples and companions.

Chapters 1–9 introduce the book, drawing attention to wisdom itself and its inherent value rather than exhorting to particular wise actions. The chapters personify wisdom as a woman and draw an extended analogy between finding a wife, or founding and maintaining a house(hold), and finding wisdom. The collections following chap. 9 consist largely of independent, two-line sayings, yielding their often indirect or paradoxical meaning only to readers willing to ponder them. To reflect on the sayings is perhaps what chaps. 1–9 mean by living with Wisdom and dwelling in her house.

The Book of Proverbs can make an important contribution to Christians and Jews today. First, it places the pursuit of wisdom over the performance of individual wise acts. To seek wisdom above all things is a fundamental option and a way of life. Second, it portrays the quest as filled with obstacles. There are men and women who offer a substitute for the real thing; discernment is required. Third, the book teaches that acquiring wisdom is both a human task and a divine gift. One can make oneself ready to receive by discipline, but one cannot take so divine a gift. Fourth, wisdom is in the world but it is not obvious to people entirely caught up with daily activities. The instructions and the aphorisms of the book can free the mind to see new things. Christians will see in personified Wisdom aspects of Jesus Christ, who they believe is divine wisdom sent to give human beings true and full life. Yet there is a universal dimension to Proverbs, for in its attention to human experience it creates a link to all people of good will.

The genres and themes of Proverbs continued on in Sirach, Wisdom of Solomon, and the later *Pirqe Abot* (The Sayings of the Fathers), a treatise in the Mishnah, which became the object of commentary in *Abot de Rabbi Nathan*. The New Testament saw Jesus as a wisdom teacher and employed the tradition of personified wisdom of chaps. 2 and 8 to express his incarnation. The Letter of James is an instruction resembling those in Proverbs. Wisdom traditions influenced the Gospels of Matthew and Luke through a common source (see, e.g., Mt 11:25–27 and Lk 10:21–22, which seem to derive their father-son language, at least in part, from the parental language of Proverbs). The Gospel of John regards Jesus as incarnate wisdom descended from on high to offer human beings life and truth and make disciples of them, a view largely reflected in Proverbs 1–9. In later Judaism, Hebrew ethical wills, in which parents hand on to their children their wisdom, borrowed from the genre of instruction.

The original audience of the instructions and sayings seems to have been male. The father addresses his son, marriage is finding a wife, success often is serving the king or farming effectively. The book itself, however, expands the traditional audience of youths (1:4) to include older, more experienced, people (1:5). It broadens the father-son language by mentioning the mother, and incorporates sayings on human experience generally. The father teaching his son becomes a model for anyone teaching a way of life to another person. The canonical process furthered such inclusiveness, for Proverbs was made part of the Bible that addresses *all* Israel.

The Book of Proverbs has nine sections:

    I.  Title and Introduction (1:1–7)
   II.  Instructions of Parents and of Woman Wisdom (1:8–9:18)
  III.  First Solomonic Collection of Sayings (10:1–22:16)
  IV.  Sayings of the Wise (22:17–24:22)
   V.  Further Sayings of the Wise (24:23–34)
  VI.  Second Solomonic Collection, Collected Under King Hezekiah (25:1–29:27)
 VII.  Sayings of Agur and Others (30:1–33)
VIII.  Sayings of King Lemuel (31:1–9)
  IX.  Poem on the Woman of Worth (31:10–31)

Part II is judged by many scholars to contain ten instructions (1:8–19; chap. 2; 3:1–12, 21–35; 4:1–9, 10–19, 20–27; chap. 5; 6:20–35; chap. 7), three wisdom poems (1:20–33; chap. 8; 9:1–6 + 11, 13–18), and two interludes (3:13–20; 6:1–19).

# I. TITLE AND INTRODUCTION

## CHAPTER 1

### Purpose of the Proverbs of Solomon*

1 The proverbs† of Solomon,*a* the son of
    David,
        king of Israel:
2 That people may know wisdom and
    discipline,‡
        may understand intelligent sayings;
3 May receive instruction in wise conduct,
        in what is right, just and fair;
4 That resourcefulness may be imparted to
    the naive,§
        knowledge and discretion to the
        young.
5 The wise by hearing them will advance in
    learning,
        the intelligent will gain sound
        guidance,
6 To comprehend proverb and byword,
        the words of the wise and their
        riddles.
7 Fear of the LORD¶ is the beginning of
    knowledge;*b*
        fools despise wisdom and discipline.

# II. INSTRUCTIONS OF PARENTS
# AND OF WOMAN WISDOM

### The Path of the Wicked: Greed and Violence**

8 Hear, my son, your father's instruction,
        and reject not your mother's teaching;
9 A graceful diadem will they be for your
    head;

a pendant for your neck.
10 My son, should sinners entice you,
11     do not go if they say, "Come along
        with us!
    Let us lie in wait for blood,
        unprovoked, let us trap the
        innocent;
12 Let us swallow them alive, like Sheol,
        whole, like those who go down to
        the pit!
13 All kinds of precious wealth shall we
    gain,
        we shall fill our houses with booty;
14 Cast in your lot with us,
        we shall all have one purse!"
15 My son, do not walk in the way with
    them,
        hold back your foot from their path!
16 [For their feet run to evil,
        they hasten to shed blood.*c*]
17 In vain a net is spread††
        right under the eyes of any bird—
18 They lie in wait for their own blood,
        they set a trap for their own lives.
19 This is the way of everyone greedy for
    loot:
        it takes away their lives.

### Wisdom in Person Gives a Warning‡‡

20 Wisdom cries aloud in the street,
        in the open squares she raises her
        voice;*d*
21 Down the crowded ways she calls out,
        at the city gates she utters her words:
22 §§"How long, you naive ones, will you

---

*[1:1-7] The prologue explains the purpose of the book.
The book has a sapiential, ethical, and religious dimension:
to bring the inexperienced to knowledge and right conduct,
to increase the facility of those already wise for interpreting
proverbs, parables and riddles, and to encourage the fulfillment of one's duties to God.

†[1:1] **Proverbs**: the Hebrew word *mashal* is broader than
English "proverb," embracing the instructions of chaps. 1–9 and
the sayings, observations, and comparisons of chaps. 10–31.

‡[1:2] **Discipline**: education or formation which dispels
ignorance and corrects vice. Note the reprise of v. 2a in v. 7b.

§[1:4] **Naive**: immature, inexperienced, sometimes the
young, hence easily influenced for good or evil.

¶[1:7] **Fear of the LORD**: primarily a disposition rather
than the emotion of fear; reverential awe and respect toward
God combined with obedience to God's will.

**[1:8–19] A parental warning to a young person leaving
home, for them to avoid the company of the greedy and violent. Two ways lie before the hearer, a way that leads to death
and a way that leads to life. The trap which the wicked set
for the innocent (v. 11) in the end takes away the lives of the
wicked themselves (v. 19). This theme will recur especially in
chaps. 1–9. A second theme introduced here is that of founding (or managing) a household and choosing a spouse. A third
theme is the human obstacles to attaining wisdom. Here (and
in 2:12–15 and 4:10–19), the obstacle is men (always in the
plural); in 2:16–19; 5:1–6; 6:20–35; chap. 7; 9:13–18, the obstacle to the quest is the "foreign" woman (always in the singular).

a. [1:1] Prv 10:1; 25:1; 1 Kgs 4:32.   b. [1:7] Prv 9:10; Jb 28:28; Ps
111:10; Sir 1:16.

††[1:17] A difficult verse. The most probable interpretation
is that no fowler lifts up the net so the bird can see it. The verse
might be paraphrased: God does not let those who walk on evil
paths see the net that will entrap them. The passive construction ("a net is spread") is sometimes used to express divine
activity. Verse 16 is a later attempt to add clarity. It is a quotation from Is 59:7 and is not in the best Greek manuscripts.

‡‡[1:20–33] Wisdom is personified as in chaps. 8 and 9:1–6.
With divine authority she proclaims the moral order, threatening to leave to their own devices those who disregard her
invitation. All three speeches of Woman Wisdom have common features: a setting in city streets; an audience of simple
or naive people; a competing appeal (chap. 7 is the competing
appeal for chap. 8); an invitation to a relationship that brings
long life, riches, repute.

The structure of the speeches is: A: setting (vv. 20–21); B:
Wisdom's withdrawal, rebuke and announcement (vv. 22–23);
reason and rejection I (vv. 24–27); reason and rejection II
(vv. 28–31); summary (v. 32); C: the effects of Wisdom's presence (v. 33). Wisdom's opening speech is an extended threat
ending with a brief invitation (v. 33). Her second speech is
an extended invitation ending with a brief threat (8:36). The
surprisingly abrupt and harsh tone of her speech is perhaps to
be explained as a response to the arrogant words of the men
in the previous scene (1:8–19).

§§[1:22–23] There is textual confusion. Verse 22bc (in the
third person) is an addition, interrupting vv. 22a and 23a (in
the second person). The addition has been put in brackets, to
separate it from the original poem. The original verses do not
ask for a change of heart but begin to detail the consequences
of disobedience to Wisdom.

c. [1:16] Is 59:7.   d. [1:20] Prv 8:1–3; 9:3.

love naivete,

23 How long will you turn away at my
reproof?
[The arrogant delight in their arrogance,
and fools hate knowledge.]
Lo! I will pour out to you my spirit,
I will acquaint you with my words:

24 'Because I called and you refused,
extended my hand and no one took
notice;*

25 Because you disdained all my counsel,
and my reproof you ignored—

26 I, in my turn, will laugh at your doom;
will mock when terror overtakes you;

27 When terror comes upon you like a storm,
and your doom approaches like a
whirlwind;
when distress and anguish befall you.'

28 Then they will call me, but I will not
answer;
they will seek me, but will not find me,

29 Because they hated knowledge,
and the fear of the LORD they did
not choose.

30 They ignored my counsel,
they spurned all my reproof;

31 Well, then, they shall eat the fruit* of their
own way,
and with their own devices be glutted.

32 For the straying of the naive kills them,
the smugness of fools destroys them.

33 But whoever obeys me dwells in security,
in peace, without fear of harm."*

## CHAPTER 2

### The Blessings of Wisdom†

1 My son, if you receive my words
and treasure my commands,

2 Turning your ear to wisdom,‡
inclining your heart to
understanding;

3 Yes, if you call for intelligence,
and to understanding raise your voice;

4 If you seek her like silver,
and like hidden treasures search
her out,

5 Then will you understand the fear of the
LORD;

the knowledge of God you will find;

6 For the LORD gives wisdom,
from his mouth come knowledge
and understanding;*

7 He has success in store for the upright,
is the shield of those who walk
honestly,

8 Guarding the paths of justice,
protecting the way of his faithful ones,

9 Then you will understand what is right
and just,
what is fair, every good path;

10 For wisdom will enter your heart,
knowledge will be at home in your
soul,

11 Discretion will watch over you,
understanding will guard you;

12 §Saving you from the way of the wicked,
from those whose speech is perverse.

13 From those who have left the straight
paths
to walk in the ways of darkness,

14 Who delight in doing evil
and celebrate perversity;

15 Whose ways are crooked,
whose paths are devious;

16 ¶Saving you from a stranger,
from a foreign woman with her
smooth words,*

17 One who forsakes the companion of her
youth
and forgets the covenant of her God;

18 For her path sinks down to death,
and her footsteps lead to the shades.**¡

19 None who enter there come back,
or gain the paths of life.

20 Thus you may walk in the way of the good,
and keep to the paths of the just.

21 ††For the upright will dwell in the land,ʲ
people of integrity will remain in it;

22 But the wicked will be cut off from the
land,
the faithless will be rooted out of it.

---

§[2:12–15] As in 1:8–19, there is an obstacle to the quest
for wisdom—deceitful and violent men. Cf. also 4:10–19.
They offer a way of life that is opposed to the way of wisdom.
¶[2:16–19] A second obstacle and counter-figure to Wisdom, personified as an attractive woman, is the "stranger," or
"foreigner," from outside the territory or kinship group, hence
inappropriate as a marriage partner. In Proverbs she comes to
be identified with Woman Folly, whose deceitful words promise life but lead to death. Woman Folly appears also in chap.
5, 6:20–35, chap. 7 and 9:13–18. **Covenant:** refers to the vow
uttered with divine sanction at the woman's previous marriage, as the parallel verse suggests. She is already married and
relations with her would be adulterous.
**[2:18] **Shades:** the inhabitants of Sheol.
††[2:21–22] Verses 21–22 echo the ending of Wisdom's
speech in 1:32–33, in which refusing Wisdom's invitation
meant death and obedience to her meant life. The same set of
ideas is found in Ps 37 (especially vv. 3, 9, 11, 22, 29, 34, and
38): to live on (or inherit) the land and to be uprooted from
the land are expressions of divine recompense.

*[1:31] **Eat the fruit:** sinners are punished by the consequences of their sins. Wisdom's voice echoes that of the parents in vv. 8–19. The parents mediate wisdom in vv. 8–19, but
here Wisdom herself speaks.
†[2:1–22] Chapter 2 is a single poem, an acrostic of twenty-
two lines, the number of consonants in the Hebrew alphabet.
In vv. 1–11, the letter *aleph,* the first letter of the alphabet, predominates, and in vv. 12–22, the letter *lamed,* the first letter of
the second half of the alphabet. A single structure runs through
the whole: if (*aleph*) you search . . . then (*aleph*) the Lord/
Wisdom will grant . . . saving (*lamed*) you from the wicked
man/woman . . . thus (*lamed*) you can walk in the safe way. . . .
‡[2:2–3] **Wisdom . . . understanding . . . intelligence:**
various names or aspects of the same gift.

e. [1:24] Is 65:2, 12; 66:4; Jer 7:13.   f. [1:33] Prv 8:33–34.

g. [2:6] Jb 32:8; Wis 7:25; Sir 1:1; Jas 1:5.   h. [2:16] Prv 5:3, 20; 6:24;
7:5; 22:14.   i. [2:18] Prv 5:5; 7:27.   j. [2:21] Prv 10:7, 30; Jb 18:17;
Ps 21:9–13; 37:22, 28.

## CHAPTER 3

### Confidence in God Leads to Prosperity[*]

1 My son, do not forget[†] my teaching,
   take to heart my commands;
2 For many days, and years of life,[k]
   and peace, will they bring you.
3 Do not let love and fidelity forsake you;
   bind them around your neck;
   write them on the tablet of your
   heart.
4 Then will you win favor and esteem
   before God and human beings.
5 Trust in the LORD with all your heart,
   on your own intelligence do not
   rely;
6 In all your ways be mindful of him,
   and he will make straight your
   paths.
7 Do not be wise in your own eyes,[l]
   fear the LORD and turn away from
   evil;
8 This will mean health for your flesh
   and vigor for your bones.
9 Honor the LORD with your wealth,
   with first fruits of all your produce;[m]
10 Then will your barns be filled with
   plenty,
   with new wine your vats will
   overflow.
11 The discipline of the LORD, my son, do
   not spurn;[n]
   do not disdain his reproof;
12 [‡]For whom the LORD loves he reproves,
   as a father, the son he favors.[o]

### The Benefits of Finding Wisdom[§]

13 Happy the one who finds wisdom,
   the one who gains understanding![p]
14 Her profit is better than profit in silver,
   and better than gold is her revenue;
15 She is more precious than corals,
   and no treasure of yours can
   compare with her.[q]
16 Long life is in her right hand,
   in her left are riches and honor;
17 Her ways are pleasant ways,
   and all her paths are peace;
18 She is a tree of life[s] to those who grasp her,
   and those who hold her fast are
   happy.[r]
19 The LORD by wisdom founded the earth,
   established the heavens by
   understanding;
20 By his knowledge the depths[**] are split,
   and the clouds drop down dew.

### Justice Toward One's Neighbor Brings Blessing[††]

21 My son, do not let these slip from your
   sight:
   hold to deliberation and planning;

---

[*][3:1–12] The instruction consists of a series of six four-line exhortations in which the second line of each exhortation mentions a reward or benefit. In the first five exhortations, the teacher promises a reward: long life, a good name, divine protection, health, abundant crops. The last exhortation, vv. 11–12, departs from the command-reward scheme, implying that being a disciple of the Lord does not guarantee unalloyed bliss: one must allow God freedom to "reprove" or educate. The process of education is like that described in chap. 2: the father first invites his son (or disciple) to memorize his teaching (v. 1), then to enter upon a relationship of trust with him (v. 3), and finally to place his trust in God, who takes up the parental task of education (v. 5). Education begun by the parent is brought to full completion by God.

[†][3:1] **Do not forget**: this word and several others in the section such as "teaching," "commands," "years of life," and the custom of affixing written teaching to one's body, occur also in Deuteronomy. This vocabulary suggests that Proverbs and Deuteronomy had a common origin in the scribal class of Jerusalem. This section (and vv. 21–34) subtly elaborates Dt 6:5–9, "You shall love the LORD with all your heart (v. 5) . . . Take to heart these words (v. 1) . . . Recite them when you are at home and when you are away (v. 23) . . . when you lie down (v. 24) . . . Bind them (v. 3) on your arm as a sign and let them be a pendant on your forehead" (v. 21).

[‡][3:12] One might be tempted to judge the quality of one's relationship to God by one's prosperity. It is an inadequate criterion, for God as a teacher might go counter to student expectations. The discipline of God can involve suffering.

[§][3:13–20] An encomium of Wisdom through the listing of her benefits to the human race and the depiction of her role in creation. Wisdom, or understanding, is more valuable than silver and gold. Its fruit is long life, riches, honor and happiness (vv. 13–18). Even the creation of the universe and its adornment (Gn 1) were not done without wisdom (vv. 19–20). The praise of Wisdom foreshadows the praise of a noble wife in the final poem (31:10–31), even to the singling out of the hands extended in a helpful way toward human beings.

[¶][3:18] **A tree of life**: in the Old Testament this phrase occurs only in Proverbs (11:30; 13:12; 15:4) and Genesis (2:9; 3:22, 24). The origins of the concept are obscure; there is no explicit mention of it in ancient Near Eastern literature, though on ancient seals trees are sometimes identified as trees of life. When the man and the woman were expelled from the garden, the tree of life was put off limits to them, lest they "eat of it and live forever" (Gn 3:22). The quest for wisdom gives access to the previously sequestered tree of life. The tree of life is mentioned also in the apocryphal work 1 Enoch 25:4–5. Rev 2 and 22 mention the tree of life as a source of eternal life.

[**][3:20] **Depths**: for the Hebrews, the depths enclosed the great subterranean waters; the rain and dew descended from the waters above the firmament; cf. Gn 1:6–10; Jb 26:8, 12; Ps 18:15; 24:2. The cosmogony provides the reason why Wisdom offers such benefits to human beings: the world was created in wisdom so that all who live in accord with wisdom live in tune with the universe.

[††][3:21–35] As in other instructions, the father in vv. 21–26 urges the son to seek wisdom, which in this case means practicing the virtues of "deliberation and planning," a specification of wisdom. Practicing these virtues brings protection from violence (vv. 22–26) and friendship with God (vv. 32–35). The language is like Ps 91.

Verses 27–35 are arranged according to a clear order. Serving God requires serving one's neighbor through kindness (vv. 27–28), maintaining peace with the good (vv. 29–31), having no envy of the wicked (v. 31), because the Lord's friendship and kindness are with the just, not with the wicked. Matching the six exhortations of vv. 1–12, vv. 27–34 contain six prohibitions. The righteous/wicked contrast is progressively developed: in contrast to the wicked, the righteous are in God's inner circle, their houses are blessed, they deal with a merciful God, and obtain honor.

---

k. [3:2] Prv 4:10; 9:11; 10:27.  l. [3:7] Rom 11:25; 12:16.  m. [3:9] Ex 34:26; Lv 27:30; Dt 26:2; Sir 7:31; 35:7.  n. [3:11] Heb 12:5–6.  o. [3:12] Jdt 8:27; Rev 3:19.

p. [3:13] Prv 8:34–35.  q. [3:15] Prv 8:11, 19; Wis 7:8–11.  r. [3:18] Prv 4:13; 8:35; 11:30; Gn 2:9; 3:22.

²² So will they be life to your soul,*
　　　　and an adornment for your neck.
²³ Then you may go your way securely;
　　　　your foot will never stumble;
²⁴ When you lie down, you will not be
　　　　afraid,
　　　　when you rest, your sleep will be
　　　　sweet.
²⁵ Do not be afraid of sudden terror,
　　　　of the ruin of the wicked when it
　　　　comes;
²⁶ For the LORD will be your confidence,
　　　　and will keep your foot from the
　　　　snare.
²⁷ Do not withhold any goods from the
　　　　owner
　　　　when it is in your power to act.
²⁸ Say not to your neighbor, "Go, come back
　　　　tomorrow,
　　　　and I will give it to you," when all
　　　　the while you have it.
²⁹ Do not plot evil against your neighbors,
　　　　when they live at peace with you.
³⁰ Do not contend with someone without
　　　　cause,
　　　　with one who has done you no harm.
³¹ Do not envy the violent
　　　　and choose none of their ways;ˢ
³² To the LORD the devious are an
　　　　abomination,
　　　　but the upright are close to him.
³³ The curse of the LORD is on the house of
　　　　the wicked,
　　　　but the dwelling of the just he
　　　　blesses;
³⁴ Those who scoff, he scoffs at,ᵗ
　　　　but the lowly he favors.
³⁵ The wise will possess glory,
　　　　but fools will bear shame.

## CHAPTER 4

### The Teacher as Model Disciple†

¹ Hear, O children, a father's instruction,
　　　　be attentive, that you may gain
　　　　understanding!

²　Yes, excellent advice I give you;
　　　　my teaching do not forsake.
³　When I was my father's child,
　　　　tender, the darling of my mother,
⁴　He taught me and said to me:
　　　　"Let your heart hold fast my words:ᵘ
　　　　keep my commands, and live!
⁵　Get wisdom,‡ get understanding!
　　　　Do not forget or turn aside from the
　　　　words of my mouth.
⁶　Do not forsake her, and she will preserve
　　　　you;
　　　　love her, and she will safeguard you;
⁷　The beginning of wisdom is: get wisdom;
　　　　whatever else you get, get
　　　　understanding.
⁸　Extol her, and she will exalt you;
　　　　she will bring you honors if you
　　　　embrace her;
⁹　She will put on your head a graceful
　　　　diadem;
　　　　a glorious crown will she bestow
　　　　on you."

### The Two Ways§

¹⁰ Hear, my son, and receive my words,
　　　　and the years of your life shall be
　　　　many.ᵛ
¹¹ On the way of wisdom I direct you,
　　　　I lead you on straight paths.
¹² When you walk, your step will not be
　　　　impeded,
　　　　and should you run, you will not
　　　　stumble.
¹³ Hold fast to instruction, never let it go;
　　　　keep it, for it is your life.
¹⁴ ¶The path of the wicked do not enter,
　　　　nor walk in the way of the evil;

---

*[3:22] **Your soul**: Heb. *nephesh* means "throat, esophagus;
life; soul." The meanings are connected. The throat area is the
moist, breathing center of the body, which stands for life and
for self. The figure of speech is called metonymy, in which one
word is substituted for another on the basis of a causal relation,
e.g., eye for sight, arm for power, or, as here, "throat area" for
life. Proverbs sometimes plays on this concrete meaning of life
(e.g., 21:23).

†[4:1–9] The teacher draws a parallel between his teaching the disciples now and his father's teaching him in his
youth (vv. 3–4): what my father taught me about wisdom is
what I am teaching you. The poem implies that the teacher
has acquired wisdom and has in fact been protected and honored as his father promised long ago. Thus the teacher has
the authority of someone who has been under wisdom's sway
since earliest youth.

There are two sections, a call for attention and introduction of the speaker (vv. 1–3) and the father's quoting of his own

father's teaching (vv. 4–9). Beginning with v. 5, the father's
words are no longer quoted, wisdom herself becoming the
active agent; she becomes the subject, not the object, of the
verbs. Three Hebrew verbs are repeated in the two parts, "to
forsake" in vv. 2 and 6, "to keep/guard" in vv. 4 and 6, and "to
give/bestow" in vv. 2 and 9. Each verb in its first appearance
has the father's words as its object; in its second appearance
each verb has wisdom as its subject or object. The teaching
process is like that in 2:1–22 and 3:1–12: heeding the words
of one's parent puts one in touch with wisdom, who completes
the process and bestows her gifts.

‡[4:5, 7] **Get wisdom**: the same Hebrew word "to get" can
mean to acquire merchandise and to acquire a wife (18:22;
31:10); both meanings are in keeping with Proverbs' metaphors of acquiring wisdom over gold and silver and of acquiring wisdom as a personified woman, a wife.

§[4:10–19] A central metaphor of the poem is "the way."
The way of wisdom leads directly to life (vv. 10–13); it is a light
that grows brighter (v. 18). The wise are bound to shun (vv.
14–17) the dark and violent path of the wicked (v. 19). Singleness of purpose and right conduct proceed from the heart of
the wise as from the source of life (vv. 23–26), saving them
from destruction on evil paths (4:27; 5:21–23). As in 1:8–19
and 2:12–15, the obstacles to the quest are men and their way.
Elsewhere in chaps. 1–9, the obstacle is the foreign woman
(2:16–19; chap. 5; 6:20–35; chap. 7; 9:13–18).

¶[4:14–15] One is always free to choose. The righteous
may choose to leave their path to walk on the wicked path and
the wicked may choose the righteous path.

---

s. [3:31] Prv 23:17; 24:1, 19; Ps 37:1.　　t. [3:34] Prv 1:26.

u. [4:4] Dt 6:1–6.　　v. [4:10] Prv 3:2.

<sup>15</sup> Shun it, do not cross it,
        turn aside from it, pass on.
<sup>16</sup> For they cannot rest unless they have
            done evil;
        if they do not trip anyone they lose
            sleep.
<sup>17</sup> For they eat the bread of wickedness
        and drink the wine of violence.
<sup>18</sup> But the path of the just is like shining
            light,
        that grows in brilliance till perfect
            day.*
<sup>19</sup> The way of the wicked is like darkness;
        they do not know on what they
            stumble.

### With Your Whole Being
### Heed My Words and Live†

<sup>20</sup> My son, to my words be attentive,
        to my sayings incline your ear;
<sup>21</sup> Let them not slip from your sight,
        keep them within your heart;
<sup>22</sup> For they are life to those who find them,ʷ
        bringing health to one's whole being.
<sup>23</sup> With all vigilance guard your heart,
        for in it are the sources of life.
<sup>24</sup> ‡Dishonest mouth put away from you,
        deceitful lips put far from you.
<sup>25</sup> Let your eyes look straight ahead
        and your gaze be focused forward.
<sup>26</sup> Survey the path for your feet,
        and all your ways will be sure.
<sup>27</sup> Turn neither to right nor to left,
        keep your foot far from evil.

## CHAPTER 5

### Warning Against Adultery§

<sup>1</sup> My son, to my wisdom be attentive,
        to understanding incline your ear,
<sup>2</sup> That you may act discreetly,

---

and your lips guard what you know.
<sup>3</sup> Indeed, the lips of the stranger drip
            honey,⁵
        and her mouth is smoother than oil;ˣ
<sup>4</sup> But in the end she is as bitter as
            wormwood,
        as sharp as a two-edged sword.
<sup>5</sup> Her feet go down to death,
        her steps reach Sheol;ʸ
<sup>6</sup> Her paths ramble, you know not where,
        lest you see before you the road to
            life.
<sup>7</sup> So now, children, listen to me,
        do not stray from the words of my
            mouth.
<sup>8</sup> Keep your way far from her,ᶻ
        do not go near the door of her
            house,
<sup>9</sup> Lest you give your honor** to others,ᵃ
        and your years to a merciless one;
<sup>10</sup> Lest outsiders take their fill of your
            wealth,
        and your hard-won earnings go to
            another's house;
<sup>11</sup> And you groan in the end,
        when your flesh and your body are
            consumed;
<sup>12</sup> And you say, "Oh, why did I hate
            instruction,
        and my heart spurn reproof!
<sup>13</sup> Why did I not listen to the voice of my
            teachers,
        incline my ear to my instructors!
<sup>14</sup> I am all but ruined,
        in the midst of the public assembly!"
<sup>15</sup> Drink water†† from your own cistern,
        running water from your own well.
<sup>16</sup> Should your water sources be dispersed
            abroad,
        streams of water in the streets?

---

astray and begets bitterness, bloodshed, and death (vv. 1–6). It destroys honor, wastes the years of life, despoils hard-earned wealth, and brings remorse in the end (vv. 7–14). Conjugal fidelity and love bring happiness and security (vv. 15–20). Cf. 6:20–7:27. The structure of the poem consists of a two-line introduction; part one consists of three stanzas of four lines each warning of the forbidden woman's effect on her lovers (vv. 3–14); part two consists of a stanza of twelve lines exhorting the disciple to marital fidelity (vv. 15–20); and a final stanza of six lines on the perils of the woman (vv. 21–23).

¶[5:3] A metaphorical level is established in the opening description of the forbidden woman: her lips drip honey and her feet lead to death. By her lies, she leads people away from the wisdom that gives life.

**[5:9] Honor: the words "life" and "wealth" have also been read in this place. A merciless one: the offended husband; cf. 6:34–35.

††[5:15–16] Water: water may have an erotic meaning as in Sg 4:15, "[You are] a garden fountain, a well of living water." Eating and drinking can be metaphors expressing the mutuality of love. The wife is the opposite of the adulterous woman; she is not an outsider, not unfeeling, not a destroyer of her husband's self and goods. The best defense against adultery is appreciating and loving one's spouse. The best defense against folly is to appreciate and love wisdom.

---

*[4:18] **Till perfect day**: lit., "till the day is established"; this may refer to full daylight or to noonday.

†[4:20–27] Acquiring wisdom brings life and health. The learning process involves two stages: (1) hearing the teacher's words and treasuring them in the heart; (2) speaking and acting in accord with the wisdom that one has stored in one's heart. Seven organs of the body are mentioned: ear, eyes, heart, mouth, lips, eyelids ("gaze," v. 25), feet. Each of the organs is to be strained to its limit as the disciple puts wisdom into practice. The physical organ stands for the faculty, e.g., the eye for sight, the foot for movement. The figure of speech is called metonymy; one word is substituted for another on the basis of a causal relation.

‡[4:24–27] In vv. 20–21 the faculties of hearing (ear) and seeing (eye) take in the teaching and the heart stores and ponders it, so in the second half of the poem, vv. 24–27, the faculties of speech, sight, and walking enable the disciple to put the teaching into practice.

§[5:1–23] This is the first of three poems on the forbidden woman, the "stranger" outside the social boundaries (cf. 2:16–19); the other two are 6:20–35 and chap. 7. Understanding and discretion are necessary to avoid adultery, which leads

w. [4:22] Prv 8:35.

---

x. [5:3] Prv 7:5.    y. [5:5] Prv 2:18; 7:27.    z. [5:8] Prv 7:25.    a. [5:9] Sir 9:6.

<sup>17</sup> Let them be yours alone,
 not shared with outsiders;
<sup>18</sup> Let your fountain be blessed and have joy
 of the wife of your youth,
<sup>19</sup>        your lovely hind, your graceful doe.<sup>*</sup>
 Of whose love you will ever have your fill,
 and by her ardor always be
 intoxicated.
<sup>20</sup> Why then, my son, should you be
 intoxicated with a stranger,
 and embrace another woman?
<sup>21</sup> Indeed, the ways of each person are plain
 to the Lord's sight;
 all their paths he surveys;<sup>b</sup>
<sup>22</sup> By their own iniquities the wicked will be
 caught,
 in the meshes of their own sin they
 will be held fast;
<sup>23</sup> They will die from lack of discipline,
 lost because of their great folly.

## CHAPTER 6

### Miscellaneous Proverbs<sup>†</sup>

*Against Going Surety for One's Neighbor*

<sup>1</sup> <sup>‡</sup>My son, if you have become surety to
 your neighbor,<sup>c</sup>
 given your hand in pledge to another,
<sup>2</sup> You have been snared by the utterance of
 your lips,
 caught by the words of your mouth;
<sup>3</sup> So do this, my son, to free yourself,
 since you have fallen into your
 neighbor's power:

Go, hurry, rouse your neighbor!
<sup>4</sup> Give no sleep to your eyes,
 nor slumber to your eyelids;
<sup>5</sup> Free yourself like a gazelle from the
 hunter,
 or like a bird from the hand of the
 fowler.

*The Ant and the Sluggard at Harvest*

<sup>6</sup> <sup>§</sup>Go to the ant,<sup>d</sup> O sluggard,
 study her ways and learn wisdom;
<sup>7</sup> For though she has no chief,
 no commander or ruler,
<sup>8</sup> She procures her food in the summer,
 stores up her provisions in the
 harvest.
<sup>9</sup> How long, O sluggard, will you lie there?
 when will you rise from your sleep?
<sup>10</sup> A little sleep, a little slumber,
 a little folding of the arms to rest—<sup>¶</sup>
<sup>11</sup> Then poverty will come upon you like a
 robber,
 and want like a brigand.

*The Scoundrel*

<sup>12</sup> <sup>**</sup>Scoundrels, villains, are they
 who deal in crooked talk.
<sup>13</sup> Shifty of eye,
 feet ever moving,
 pointing with fingers,
<sup>14</sup> They have perversity in their hearts,
 always plotting evil,
 sowing discord.
<sup>15</sup> Therefore their doom comes suddenly;
 in an instant they are crushed
 beyond cure.

*What the Lord Rejects*

<sup>16</sup> There are six things the Lord hates,
 yes, seven<sup>††</sup> are an abomination to him;

---

*[5:19] **Lovely hind . . . graceful doe**: ancient Near Eastern symbols of feminine beauty and charm; cf. Sg 2:7, 9, 17.

†[6:1–19] Four independent pieces akin to those in 30:1–5, 6–11, 12–15, and 16–19. Some judge the verses to be an ancient addition, but the fact that the pieces differ from the other material in chaps. 1–9 is not a strong argument against their originality. Ancient anthologies did not always have the symmetry of modern collections. An editor may have placed the four pieces in the midst of the three poems on the forbidden woman to shed light on some of their themes. Verses 1–5 warn against getting trapped by one's words to another person (the Hebrew word for "another" is the same used for the forbidden woman); vv. 6–11 proposes the ant as a model of forethought and diligence; vv. 12–15 describes the reprobate who bears some similarity to the seductive woman, especially as portrayed in chap. 7; vv. 16–19 depicts the typical enemy of God, underscoring the person's destructive words.

‡[6:1–5] Unlike other instructions that begin with "my son," this instruction does not urge the hearer to store up the father's words as a means to wisdom, but only to avoid one practice—going surety for one's neighbor. The warning is intensified by repetition of "neighbor" and "free yourself," the mention of bodily organs, and the imagery of hunting. **Given your hand in pledge**: lit., "struck your hands"; this was probably the legal method for closing a contract. To become surety meant intervening in favor of the insolvent debtor and assuming responsibility for the payment of the debt, either by obtaining it from the debtor or substituting oneself. Proverbs is strongly opposed to the practice (11:15; 17:18; 20:16; 22:26–27; 27:13) apparently because of the danger it poses to the freedom of the one providing surety.

§[6:6–11] The sluggard or lazybones is a type in Proverbs, like the righteous and the wicked. Sometimes the opposite type to the sluggard is the diligent person. Other extended passages on the sluggard are 24:30–34 and 26:13–16. The malice of the type is not low physical energy but the refusal to act. To describe human types, Proverbs often uses comparisons from the animal world, e.g., 27:8 (bird); 28:1, 15 (lion); 30:18–19 (eagle, snake); 30:24–28 (ant, badger, locust, lizard).

¶[6:10] This verse may be regarded as the sluggard's reply or as a continuation of the remonstrance.

**[6:12–15] Proverbs uses types to make the point that certain ways of acting have inherent consequences. The typifying intensifies the picture. All the physical organs—mouth, eyes, feet, fingers—are at the service of evil. Cf. Rom 6:12–13: "Therefore, sin must not reign over your mortal bodies so that you obey their desires. And do not present the parts of your bodies to sin as weapons for wickedness, but present yourselves to God as raised from the dead to life and the parts of your bodies to God as weapons of righteousness."

††[6:16] **Six . . . seven**: this literary pattern (n, n + 1) occurs frequently; cf., e.g., Am 1–2; Prv 30:18–19.

b. [5:21] Jb 14:16; 31:4; 34:21.   c. [6:1] Prv 11:15; 22:26; Sir 8:13; 29:19.

d. [6:6] Prv 30:25.

<sup>17</sup> ˚Haughty eyes, a lying tongue,
    hands that shed innocent blood,
<sup>18</sup> A heart that plots wicked schemes,
    feet that are quick to run to evil,
<sup>19</sup> The false witness who utters lies,
    and the one who sows discord
      among kindred.

### Warning Against Adultery[†]

<sup>20</sup> Observe, my son, your father's
    command,
    and do not reject your mother's
      teaching;
<sup>21</sup> Keep them fastened over your heart
    always,
    tie them around your neck.
<sup>22</sup> When you lie down they[‡] will watch over
    you,
    when you wake, they will share your
      concerns;
    wherever you turn, they will guide
      you.
<sup>23</sup> For the command is a lamp, and the
    teaching a light,
    and a way to life are the reproofs
      that discipline,
<sup>24</sup> Keeping you from another's wife,
    from the smooth tongue of the
      foreign woman.[e]
<sup>25</sup> Do not lust in your heart after her
    beauty,
    do not let her captivate you with her
      glance![f]
<sup>26</sup> For the price of a harlot
    may be scarcely a loaf of bread,
    But a married woman
      is a trap for your precious life.

<sup>27</sup> ⁵Can a man take embers into his bosom,
    and his garments not be burned?
<sup>28</sup> Or can a man walk on live coals,
    and his feet not be scorched?
<sup>29</sup> So with him who sleeps with another's
    wife—
    none who touches her shall go
      unpunished.[g]
<sup>30</sup> Thieves are not despised
    if out of hunger they steal to satisfy
      their appetite.
<sup>31</sup> Yet if caught they must pay back sevenfold,
    yield up all the wealth of their house.
<sup>32</sup> But those who commit adultery have no
    sense;
    those who do it destroy themselves.
<sup>33</sup> ˚They will be beaten and disgraced,
    and their shame will not be wiped
      away;
<sup>34</sup> For passion enrages the husband,
    he will have no pity on the day of
      vengeance;
<sup>35</sup> He will not consider any restitution,
    nor be satisfied by your many bribes.

## CHAPTER 7

### The Seduction[**]

<sup>1</sup> ††My son, keep my words,
    and treasure my commands.

---

§[6:27–29] There is a play on three words of similar sound, *'îsh*, "man," *'ishshâ*, "woman," and *ēsh*, "fire, embers." The question, "Can a man (*'îsh*) take embers (*ēsh*) into his bosom / and his garments not be burned?", has a double meaning. "Into his bosom" has an erotic meaning as in the phrase "wife of one's bosom" (Dt 13:6; 28:54; Sir 9:1). Hence one will destroy one's garments, which symbolize one's public position, by taking fire/another's wife into one's bosom.

¶[6:33–35] The nature of the husband's vengeance is disputed, some believing it is simply a physical beating whereas others hold it is public and involves the death penalty because Lv 20:20 and Dt 22:22 demand the death penalty.

**[7:1–27] The third and climactic instruction on adultery and seduction is an example story, of the same type as the example story in 24:30–34. By its negative portrayal of the deceitful woman, who speaks in the night to a lone youth, it serves as a foil to trustworthy Wisdom in chap. 8, who speaks in broad daylight to all who pass in the street.

As in 6:20–24, the father warns his son to keep his teaching to protect him from the dangerous forbidden woman. The father's language in 7:4 ("Say to Wisdom, 'You are my sister,' and call Understanding 'Friend'") sets this admonition apart, however; it is the language of courtship and love. If the son makes Woman Wisdom his companion and lover, she will protect him from the other woman. As in chap. 5, loving the right woman protects the man from the wrong woman.

As motivation, the father in vv. 6–23 tells his son of an incident he once observed while looking out his window— a young man went to the bed of an adulterous woman and wound up dead. As in chap. 5, the realistic details—the purposeful woman, the silent youth, the vow, the perfumed bed— have a metaphorical level. Ultimately the story is about two different kinds of love.

††[7:1–3] Verses 1–3 are artistically constructed. "Keep" in v. 1a recurs in v. 2a; "commands" in v. 1b recurs in v. 2a; the imperative verb "live" occurs in the very center of the three lines; v. 3, on preserving the teaching upon one's very person, matches vv. 1–2, on preserving the teaching internally by memorizing it.

---

*[6:17–19] The seven vices, symbolized for the most part by bodily organs, are pride, lying, murder, intrigue, readiness to do evil, false witness, and the stirring up of discord.

†[6:20–35] The second of three instructions on adultery (5:1–23; 6:20–35; and chap. 7). The instructions assume that wisdom will protect one from adultery and its consequences: loss of property and danger to one's person. In this poem, the father and the mother urge their son to keep their teaching constantly before his eyes. The teaching will light his way and make it a path to life (v. 23). The teaching will preserve him from the adulterous woman who is far more dangerous than a prostitute. Prostitutes may cost one money, but having an affair with someone else's wife puts one in grave danger. The poem bluntly urges self-interest as a motive to refrain from adultery.

The poem has three parts. I (vv. 20–24, ten lines), in which v. 23 repeats "command" and "teaching" of v. 20 and "keeping" in v. 24 completes the fixed pair initiated by "observe" in v. 20; II (vv. 25–29, ten lines) is a self-contained argument comparing the costs of a liaison with a prostitute and a married woman; III (vv. 30–35, twelve lines) draws conclusions from the comparison of adultery with theft: the latter involves property only but adultery destroys one's name and very self. The best protection against such a woman is heeding parental instruction, which is to be kept vividly before one's eyes like a written tablet.

‡[6:22] **They:** Heb. has "she." If this verse is not out of place, then the antecedent of "she" is command (v. 20), or perhaps wisdom.

---

e. [6:24] Prv 2:16; 7:5.   f. [6:25] Ex 20:17; Dt 5:21; Sir 9:8; 25:20; Mt 5:28.

g. [6:29] Sir 9:9.

2 Keep my commands and live,*
    and my teaching as the apple of
       your eye;
3 Bind them on your fingers,
    write them on the tablet of your
       heart.[h]
4 Say to Wisdom, "You are my sister!"†
    Call Understanding, "Friend!"
5 That they may keep you from a stranger,
    from the foreign woman with her
       smooth words.[i]
6 For at the window of my house,
    through my lattice I looked out‡
7 And I saw among the naive,
    I observed among the young men,
    a youth with no sense,
8 Crossing the street near the corner,
    then walking toward her house,
9 In the twilight, at dusk of day,
    in the very dark of night.
10 Then the woman comes to meet him,
    dressed like a harlot, with secret
       designs.
11 She is raucous and unruly,
    her feet cannot stay at home;
12 Now she is in the streets, now in the open
       squares,
    lurking in ambush at every corner.
13 Then she grabs him, kisses him,
    and with an impudent look says to
       him:
14 "I owed peace offerings,
    and today I have fulfilled my vows;
15 So I came out to meet you,
    to look for you, and I have found you!
16 With coverlets I have spread my couch,
    with brocaded cloths of Egyptian
       linen;
17 I have sprinkled my bed§ with myrrh,
    with aloes, and with cinnamon.
18 Come, let us drink our fill of love,
    until morning, let us feast on love!
19 For my husband is not at home,¶
    he has gone on a long journey;

20 A bag of money he took with him,
    he will not return home till the full
       moon."
21 She wins him over by repeated urging,
    with her smooth lips she leads him
       astray.**[j]
22 He follows her impulsively,
    like an ox that goes to slaughter;
    Like a stag that bounds toward the net,
23     till an arrow pierces its liver;
    Like a bird that rushes into a snare,
    unaware that his life is at stake.
24 So now, children, listen to me,††
    be attentive to the words of my
       mouth!
25 Do not let your heart turn to her ways,
    do not go astray in her paths;
26 For many are those she has struck down
       dead,
    numerous, those she has slain.
27 Her house is a highway to Sheol,
    leading down into the chambers of
       death.[k]

# CHAPTER 8

## The Discourse of Wisdom‡‡

1 Does not Wisdom call,
    and Understanding raise her voice?[l]

---

\*\*[7:21] The verbs "to win over" (lit., "to lead astray") and "to lead off" can be used of leading animals such as a donkey (Nm 22:23) or sheep (Jer 23:2 and 50:17). The animal imagery continues as the youth is compared to an ox, a fallow deer, and a bird in the moment they are slaughtered. None of the animals are aware of their impending death.

††[7:24–27] The father addresses "children," a larger audience than his own son; the story is typical, intended for others as an example. The story is a foil to the speech of the other woman in chap. 8.

‡‡[8:1–36] Chapter 8 is Wisdom's longest speech in the book. Wisdom is here personified as in 1:20–33. She exalts her grandeur and origin, and invites all (vv. 1–11) to be attentive to her salutary influence in human society (vv. 12–21), for she was privileged to be present at the creation of the world (vv. 22–31). Finally, she promises life and the favor of God to those who are devoted to her, death to those who reject her.

The poem has four sections, each (except the fourth) with two parts of five lines each:

| | | | |
|---|---|---|---|
| I. | A. vv. 1–5 | B. vv. 6–10 |
| II. | A. vv. 12–16 | B. vv. 17–21 |
| III. | A. vv. 22–26 | B. vv. 27–31 |
| IV. | vv. 32–36 | |

Within chaps. 1–9, chap. 8 is the companion piece to Wisdom's first speech in 1:20–33. There she spoke harshly, giving a promise only in the last line; here she speaks invitingly, giving a threat only in the last line.

Chapter 8 is the best-known chapter in Proverbs and has profoundly influenced Jewish and Christian thought. The most explicit and lengthy biblical comment is in Sir 24; it too has thirty-five lines in seven five-line stanzas and develops the theme of Wisdom's intimacy with God and desire to be with human beings. The Gospel of John portrays Jesus in the language of wisdom in Proverbs: Jesus, like Wisdom, calls out to people to listen to him, promises to tell them the truth, seeks disciples, invites them to a banquet, and gives them life. Writers in the patristic period used the language of pre-existent wisdom to express the idea of the pre-existent Word with God.

---

\*[7:2] **Live**: here as elsewhere (Gn 20:7; 42:18; 2 Kgs 18:32; Jer 27:12, 17; Ez 18:32), the imperative ("Live!") is uttered against the danger of death, e.g., "Do such and such and you will live (= survive the danger); why should you die?"

†[7:4] **You are my sister**: "sister" and "brother" are examples of love language in the ancient Near East, occurring in Egyptian love poetry and Mesopotamian marriage songs. In Sg 4:9, 10, 12; 5:1, the man calls the woman, "my sister, my bride." Intimate friendship with Woman Wisdom saves one from false and dangerous relationships.

‡[7:6–7] **I looked out . . . I saw** . . . : the perspective is unusual. The narrator looks through a window upon the drama in the street.

§[7:17] **Bed**: a bed can designate a place of burial in Is 57:2; Ez 32:25; 2 Chr 16:14. **Myrrh . . . aloes**: the spices could be used for funerals as for weddings (Jn 19:39). It is possible that the language is ambivalent, speaking of death as it seems to speak of life. As the woman offers the youth a nuptial feast, she is in reality describing his funerary feast.

¶[7:19–20] **For my husband is not at home**: the woman is calculating. She knows exactly how long her husband will be gone.

---

h. [7:3] Dt 6:8.   i. [7:5] Prv 2:16; 6:24.

j. [7:21] Prv 5:3; 6:24.   k. [7:27] Prv 2:18–19; 5:5.   l. [8:1] Prv 1:20–21; 9:3.

2 On the top of the heights along the road,
  at the crossroads she takes her stand;
3 By the gates at the approaches of the city,
  in the entryways she cries aloud:
4 "To you, O people, I call;
  my appeal is to you mortals.
5 You naive ones, gain prudence,
  you fools,* gain sense.
6 Listen! for noble things I speak;
  my lips proclaim honest words.
7 †Indeed, my mouth utters truth,
  and my lips abhor wickedness.
8 All the words of my mouth are sincere,
  none of them wily or crooked;
9 All of them are straightforward to the
    intelligent,
  and right to those who attain
    knowledge.
10 Take my instruction instead of silver,
   and knowledge rather than choice
     gold.
11 [For Wisdom is better than corals,
   and no treasures can compare with
     her.*]
12 I, Wisdom, dwell with prudence,
   and useful knowledge I have.
13 [The fear of the LORD is hatred of evil;]
   Pride, arrogance, the evil way,
   and the perverse mouth I hate.ⁿ
14 Mine are counsel and advice;
   Mine is strength; I am understanding.‡
15 By me kings reign,
   and rulers enact justice;
16 By me princes govern,
   and nobles, all the judges of the earth.
17 Those who love me I also love,
   and those who seek me find me.
18 With me are riches and honor,ᵒ
   wealth that endures, and
     righteousness.
19 My fruit is better than gold, even pure
     gold,
   and my yield than choice silver.ᵖ
20 On the way of righteousness I walk,
   along the paths of justice,
21 Granting wealth to those who love me,
   and filling their treasuries.

22 §"The LORD begot me, the beginning of
     his works,
   the forerunner of his deeds of long
     ago;�q

23 From of old I was formed,¶
   at the first, before the earth.ʳ
24 **When there were no deeps I was brought
     forth,
   when there were no fountains or
     springs of water;
25 Before the mountains were settled into
     place,
   before the hills, I was brought forth;
26 When the earth and the fields were not
     yet made,
   nor the first clods of the world.
27 When he established the heavens, there
     was I,ˢ
   when he marked out the vault over
     the face of the deep;
28 When he made firm the skies above,
   when he fixed fast the springs of the
     deep;
29 When he set for the sea its limit,
   so that the waters should not
     transgress his command;
   When he fixed the foundations of earth,
30   then was I beside him as artisan;††
   I was his delight day by day,
   playing before him all the while,
31 Playing over the whole of his earth,
   having my delight with human
     beings.
32 ‡‡Now, children, listen to me;
   happy are they who keep my ways.
33 Listen to instruction and grow wise,
   do not reject it!
34 Happy the one who listens to me,
   attending daily at my gates,
   keeping watch at my doorposts;
35 For whoever finds me finds life,ᵘ
   and wins favor from the LORD;

and created the universe, adorning it with beauty and variety,
and establishing its wonderful order (vv. 27–30). The purpose
of the two cosmogonies (vv. 22–26 and 27–31) is to ground
Wisdom's claims. The first cosmogony emphasizes that she
was born before all else (and so deserving of honor) and the
second underscores that she was with the Lord during the creation of the universe. The pre-existence of Woman Wisdom
with God is developed in Sir 24 and in New Testament hymns
to Christ, especially in Jn 1 and Col 1:15–20.
¶ [8:23] **Formed**: since the other verbs of the origin of Wisdom in these verses describe birth, it is likely that the somewhat
uncertain verb is to be understood of birth as in Ps 139:13.
**[8:24–26] Perhaps the formless mass from which God
created the heavens and the earth; cf. Gn 1:1–2; 2:4–6.
††[8:30] **Artisan**: the translation of the Hebrew word *āmôn*
has been controverted since antiquity. There have been three
main opinions: (1) artisan; (2) trustworthy (friend); (3) ward,
nursling. The most likely explanation is that *āmôn* is artisan,
related to Akkadian *ummānu*, legendary sages and heroes who
brought divine gifts and culture to the human race. **I was his
delight**: the chiastic or ABBA structure of vv. 30–31 unifies
the four lines and underscores the analogy between Woman
Wisdom's intimate relation to the Lord and her intimate relation to human beings, i.e., "delight" + "playing" parallels "playing" + "delight." She is God's friend and intimate and invites
human beings to a similar relationship to God through her.
‡‡[8:32–36] The final appeal of Woman Wisdom to her disciples is similar to the appeal of the father in 7:24–27.

* [8:5] **Naive ones . . . fools**: see note on 1:4.
† [8:7–8] The truth and sincerity of wisdom are absolute
because they are of divine origin. They can neither deceive nor
tolerate deception. The intelligent understand and accept this.
"Straight" and "crooked" in Hebrew and English are metaphors for true, trustworthy and false, deceitful.
‡ [8:14] What is here predicated of Wisdom is elsewhere
attributed to God (Jb 12:13–16).
§ [8:22–31] Wisdom is of divine origin. She is represented
as existing before all things (vv. 22–26), when God planned

m. [8:11] Prv 3:15; Wis 7:8.    n. [8:13] Prv 6:16–17; 16:5.    o. [8:18]
Prv 3:16.    p. [8:19] Prv 3:14.    q. [8:22] Wis 9:9; Sir 1:1; 24:9.

r. [8:23] Sir 1:4.    s. [8:27]  Prv 3:19; Sir 24:4–5.    t. [8:30] Wis
9:9.    u. [8:35] Prv 3:13–18; 4:22.

36 But those who pass me by do violence to
        themselves;
    all who hate me love death."

## CHAPTER 9

### The Two Women Invite
### Passersby to Their Banquets*

*Woman Wisdom Issues Her Invitation*

1 Wisdom has built her house,†
        she has set up her seven columns;
2 She has prepared her meat, mixed her
        wine,
        yes, she has spread her table.
3 She has sent out her maidservants; she
        calls‡
        from the heights out over the city:ᵛ
4 "Let whoever is naive turn in here;
        to any who lack sense I say,
5 Come, eat of my food,
        and drink of the wine I have mixed!
6 Forsake foolishness that you may live;§
        advance in the way of
        understanding."

*Miscellaneous Aphorisms*

7 Whoever corrects the arrogant earns
        insults;
        and whoever reproves the wicked
        incurs opprobrium.
8 Do not reprove the arrogant, lest they
        hate you;
        reprove the wise, and they will love
        you.ʷ
9 Instruct the wise, and they become still
        wiser;
        teach the just, and they advance in
        learning.
10 The beginning of wisdom is fear of the
        LORD,
        and knowledge of the Holy One is
        understanding.ˣ
11 For by me your days will be multiplied
        and the years of your life
        increased.ʸ
12 If you are wise, wisdom is to your
        advantage;
        if you are arrogant, you alone shall
        bear it.

*Woman Folly Issues Her Invitation*

13 ¶Woman Folly is raucous,ᶻ
        utterly foolish; she knows
        nothing.
14 She sits at the door of her house
        upon a seat on the city heights,
15 Calling to passersby
        as they go on their way straight
        ahead:
16 "Let those who are naive turn in here,
        to those who lack sense I say,
17 Stolen water is sweet,
        and bread taken secretly is
        pleasing!"**
18 Little do they know that the shades are
        there,
        that her guests are in the depths of
        Sheol!††

---

*[9:1–6, 13–18] Wisdom and folly are represented as women, each inviting people to her banquet. Wisdom's banquet symbolizes joy and closeness to God. Unstable and senseless Folly furnishes stolen bread and water of deceit and vice that bring death to her guests. The opposition between wisdom and folly was stated at the beginning of chaps. 1–9 (folly in 1:8–19 and wisdom in 1:20–33) and is maintained throughout, down to this last chapter.

In comparable literature, gods might celebrate their sovereign by building a palace and inviting the other gods to come to a banquet and celebrate with them. Presumably, Woman Wisdom is celebrating her grandeur (just described in chap. 8); her grand house is a symbol of her status as the Lord's friend. In order to enter the sacred building and take part in the banquet ("eat of my food"), guests must leave aside their old ways ("forsake foolishness").

Verses 7–12 are unrelated to the two invitations to the banquet. They appear to be based on chap. 1, especially on 1:1–7, 22. The Greek version has added a number of verses after v. 12 and v. 18. In the confusion, 9:11 seems to have been displaced from its original position after 9:6. It has been restored to its original place in the text.

†[9:1] **House**: house has a symbolic meaning. Woman Wisdom encourages marital fidelity (2:16–19; 5; 6:20–35; 7), which builds up a household (cf. chap. 5). Some scholars propose that an actual seven-pillared house is referred to, but so far none have been unearthed by archaeologists. Seven may simply connote completeness—a great house.

Some scholars see a connection between the woman's house here and the woman's house in the final poem (31:10–31). In chap. 9, she invites the young man to enter her house and feast, i.e., to marry her. Chapter 31 shows what happens to the man who marries her; he has a house and enjoys "life" understood as consisting of a suitable wife, children, wealth, and honor.

‡[9:3] **She calls**: i.e., invites; this is done indirectly through her maidservants, but the text could also mean that Wisdom herself publicly proclaims her invitation.

§[9:6] **That you may live**: life in Proverbs is this-worldly, consisting in fearing God or doing one's duty toward God, enjoying health and long life, possessing wealth, good reputation, and a family. Such a life cannot be attained without God's help. Hence Wisdom speaks not of life simply but of life with her; the guest is to live in Wisdom's house.

¶[9:13–18] Woman Folly is the mirror image of Woman Wisdom. Both make identical invitations but only one of the offers is trustworthy. Their hearers must discern which is the true offer. She is depicted with traits of the adulterous woman in 2:16–19; chap. 5; 6:20–35; chap. 7. Woman Folly is restless (cf. 7:11), her path leads to the underworld (2:18; 5:5; 7:27), and she is ignorant (5:6). In this final scene, she appears in single combat with her great nemesis, Woman Wisdom. Though the invitations of the two women appear at first hearing to be the same, they differ profoundly. Wisdom demands that her guests reject their ignorance, whereas Woman Folly trades on their ignorance.

**[9:17] "Stolen water" seems to refer to adultery, for "water" in 5:15–17 refers to the wife's sexuality; "stolen" refers to stealing the sexuality belonging to another's household. "Secret" evokes the furtive meeting of the wife and the youth in chap. 7.

††[9:18] The banquet chamber of Folly is a tomb from which no one who enters it is released; cf. 7:27. **Shades**: the Rephaim, the inhabitants of the underworld.

---

v. [9:3] Prv 8:1–2.

w. [9:8] Sir 10:27.  x. [9:10] Prv 1:7; Jb 28:28; Ps 111:10; Sir 1:16.  y. [9:11] Prv 3:2; 16:4, 10; 10:27.  z. [9:13–18] Prv 7:7–27.

## III. FIRST SOLOMONIC COLLECTION OF SAYINGS*

### CHAPTER 10

¹ The Proverbs of Solomon:
A wise son gives his father joy,
    but a foolish son is a grief to his
      mother.†ᵃ

² Ill-gotten treasures profit nothing,
    but justice saves from death.‡ᵇ

³ The Lord does not let the just go hungry,
    but the craving of the wicked he
      thwarts.§

⁴ The slack hand impoverishes,
    but the busy hand brings riches.ᶜ

⁵ A son who gathers in summer is a credit;
    a son who slumbers during harvest,
      a disgrace.

⁶ Blessings are for the head of the just;
    but the mouth of the wicked
      conceals violence.¶

⁷ The memory of the just serves as
    blessing,
    but the name of the wicked will rot.**

⁸ A wise heart accepts commands,
    but a babbling fool will be
      overthrown.††

⁹ Whoever walks honestly walks securely,
    but one whose ways are crooked will
      fare badly.

¹⁰ One who winks at a fault causes trouble,
    but one who frankly reproves
      promotes peace.

¹¹ The mouth of the just is a fountain of
    life,
    but the mouth of the wicked
      conceals violence.

¹² Hatred stirs up disputes,
    ᵈ but love covers all offenses.‡‡

¹³ On the lips of the intelligent is found
    wisdom,
    but a rod for the back of one without
      sense.§§

¹⁴ The wise store up knowledge,
    but the mouth of a fool is imminent
      ruin.

¹⁵ The wealth of the rich is their strong
    city;
    the ruin of the poor is their poverty.¶¶

¹⁶ The labor of the just leads to life,
    the gains of the wicked, to futility.***ᵉ

¹⁷ Whoever follows instruction is in the path
    to life,
    but whoever disregards reproof goes
      astray.ᶠ

¹⁸ Whoever conceals hatred has lying lips,
    and whoever spreads slander is a fool.

¹⁹ Where words are many, sin is not
    wanting;
    but those who restrain their lips do
      well.ᵍ

²⁰ Choice silver is the tongue of the just;
    the heart of the wicked is of little
      worth.

²¹ The lips of the just nourish many,
    but fools die for want of sense.†††

²² It is the Lord's blessing that brings
    wealth,ʰ

---

*[10:1–22:16] The Proverbs of Solomon are a collection of three hundred and seventy-five proverbs on a wide variety of subjects. No overall arrangement is discernible, but there are many clusters of sayings related by vocabulary and theme. One thread running through the whole is the relationship of the "son," the disciple, to the parents, and its effect upon the house(hold). In chaps. 10–14 almost all the proverbs are antithetical: "the righteous" and "the wicked" (ethical), "the wise" and "the foolish" (sapiential), and "the devout, the pious" and "the irreverent" (religious). Chapters 15–22 have fewer sharp antitheses. The sayings are generally witty, often indirect, and are rich in irony and paradox.

†[10:1] The opening saying ties the whole collection to the first section, for "son," "father," and "mother" evoke the opening line of the first instruction, "Hear, my son, your father's instruction, and reject not your mother's teaching." The son is the subject of parental exhortation throughout chaps. 1–9. This is the first of many sayings on domestic happiness or unhappiness, between parents and children (e.g., 15:20; 17:21) and between husband and wife (e.g., 12:4; 14:1). Founding or maintaining a household is an important metaphor in the book.

Adult children represented the family (headed by the oldest married male) to the outside world. Foolishness, i.e., malicious ignorance, brought dishonor to the parents and the family.

‡[10:2] **Death**: untimely, premature, or sorrowful. The word "death" can have other overtones (see Wis 1:15).

§[10:3] The last of the three introductory sayings in the collection, which emphasize, respectively, the sapiential (v. 1), ethical (v. 2), and religious (v. 3) dimensions of wisdom. In this saying, God will not allow the appetite of the righteous to go unfulfilled. The appetite of hunger is singled out; it stands for all the appetites.

¶[10:6] This saying, like several others in the chapter, plays on the different senses of the verb "to cover." As in English, "to cover" can mean to fill (as in Is 60:2) and to conceal (as in Jb 16:18). Colon B can be read either "violence *fills* the mouth (= head) of the wicked" or "the mouth of the wicked *conceals* violence." The ambiguity is intentional; the proverb is meant to be read both ways.

**[10:7] The name of the righteous continues to be used after their death in blessings such as "May you be as blessed as Abraham," but the wicked, being enemies of God, do not live on in anyone's memory. Their names rot with their bodies.

††[10:8] The wise take in instruction from their teachers but those who expel or pour out folly through their words will themselves be expelled.

‡‡[10:12] **Love covers all offenses**: a favorite maxim in the New Testament; cf. 1 Cor 13:7; Jas 5:20; 1 Pt 4:8. Cf. also Prv 17:9.

§§[10:13] An unusual juxtaposition of "lips" and "back." Those who have no wisdom on their lips (words) are fated to feel a punishing rod on their back.

¶¶[10:15] An observation rather than a moral evaluation of wealth and poverty; but cf. 18:10–11.

***[10:16] Wages are a metaphor for reward and punishment. The Hebrew word does not mean "sin" here but falling short, a meaning that is frequent in Proverbs. Cf. Rom 6:1: "But what profit did you get then from the things of which you are now ashamed? For the end of those things is death."

†††[10:21] The wise by their words maintain others in life whereas the foolish cannot keep themselves from sin that leads to premature death.

---

a. [10:1] Prv 1:1; 15:20; 17:25; 19:13; 25:1; 29:15.    b. [10:2] Prv 11:4, 6.    c. [10:4] Prv 6:11; 12:24; 13:4; 20:13; 28:19.

d. [10:12] 1 Cor 13:4–7; 1 Pt 4:8.    e. [10:16] Prv 11:18–19.    f. [10:17] Prv 15:10.    g. [10:19] Prv 17:27; Sir 20:17; Jas 1:19.    h. [10:22] Sir 11:22.

and no effort can substitute for it.*

23 Crime is the entertainment of the fool;
    but wisdom is for the person of
    understanding.

24 What the wicked fear will befall them,
    but the desire of the just will be
    granted.

25 When the tempest passes, the wicked are
    no more;
    but the just are established forever.

26 As vinegar to the teeth, and smoke to the
    eyes,
    are sluggards to those who send
    them.

27 Fear of the LORD prolongs life,
    but the years of the wicked are cut
    short.*i*

28 The hope of the just brings joy,
    but the expectation of the wicked
    perishes.†

29 The LORD is a stronghold to those who
    walk honestly,
    downfall for evildoers.

30 The just will never be disturbed,
    but the wicked will not abide in the
    land.

31 The mouth of the just yields wisdom,
    but the perverse tongue will be cut
    off.

32 The lips of the just know favor,
    but the mouth of the wicked,
    perversion.‡

## CHAPTER 11

1 False scales are an abomination to the
    LORD,
    but an honest weight, his delight.§j

2 When pride comes, disgrace comes;
    but with the humble is wisdom.¶

3 The honesty of the upright guides them;
    the faithless are ruined by their
    duplicity.

4 Wealth is useless on a day of wrath,**k
    but justice saves from death.

5 The justice of the honest makes their way
    straight,
    but by their wickedness the wicked
    fall.††l

6 The justice of the upright saves them,
    but the faithless are caught in their
    own intrigue.

7 When a person dies, hope is destroyed;m
    expectation pinned on wealth is
    destroyed.‡‡

8 The just are rescued from a tight spot,
    but the wicked fall into it instead.

9 By a word the impious ruin their neighbors,n
    but through their knowledge the just
    are rescued.§§

10 When the just prosper, the city rejoices;o
    when the wicked perish, there is
    jubilation.

11 Through the blessing of the upright the
    city is exalted,
    but through the mouth of the
    wicked it is overthrown.

12 Whoever reviles a neighbor lacks sense,
    but the intelligent keep silent.

13 One who slanders reveals secrets,p
    but a trustworthy person keeps a
    confidence.

14 For lack of guidance a people falls;
    security lies in many counselors.q

15 Harm will come to anyone going surety
    for another,r
    but whoever hates giving pledges is
    secure.¶¶

16 A gracious woman gains esteem,
    and ruthless men gain wealth.***

17 Kindly people benefit themselves,
    but the merciless harm themselves.

---

*[10:22] Human industry is futile without divine approval;
cf. Ps 127:1–2; Mt 6:25–34.

†[10:28] The thought is elliptical. Joy comes from fulfillment of one's plans, which the righteous can count on.
The opposite of joy thus is not sadness but unfulfillment
("perishes").

‡[10:32] The word used for "favor" is favor shown by an
authority (God or the king), not favor shown by a peer. A
righteous person's words create a climate of favor and acceptance, whereas crooked words will not gain acceptance. In
Hebrew as in English, straight and crooked are metaphors for
good and wicked.

§[11:1] The word pair "abomination" and "delight" (=
acceptable) to God is common in Proverbs. Originally the
language of ritual, the words came to be applied to whatever
pleases or displeases God (cf. also 11:20). False weights were a
constant problem even though weights were standardized. Cf.
20:23; Hos 12:8; Am 8:5.

¶[11:2] Disgrace is the very opposite of what the proud so
ardently want. Those who do not demand their due receive
wisdom.

**[11:4] Cf. note on 10:2. A day of wrath is an unforeseen
disaster (even death). Only one's relationship to God, which
makes one righteous, is of any help on such a day.

††[11:5] In Hebrew as in English, "way" means the course
of one's life; similarly, "straight" and "crooked" are metaphors
for morally straightforward and for bad, deviant, perverted.

‡‡[11:7] An ancient scribe added "wicked" to person in
colon A, for the statement that hope ends at death seemed to
deny life after death. The saying, however, is not concerned
with life after death but with the fact that in the face of death
all hopes based on one's own resources are vain. The aphorism
is the climax of the preceding six verses; human resources
cannot overcome mortality (cf. Ps 49:13).

§§[11:9] What the wicked express harms others; what the
righteous leave unsaid protects. Verses 9–14 are related in
theme: the effect of good and bad people, especially their words,
on their community.

¶¶[11:15] Proverbs is opposed to providing surety for
another's loan (see note on 6:1–5) and expresses this view
throughout the book.

***[11:16] Wealth and esteem are good things in Proverbs,
but the means for acquiring them are flawed. As precious gifts,
they must be granted, not taken. The esteem of others that
depends on beauty is as fleeting as beauty itself (cf. 31:30) and
the wealth acquired by aggressive behavior lasts only as long
as one has physical strength.

---

i. [10:27] Prv 3:2; 4:10; 9:11; 14:27.   j. [11:1] Prv 16:11; 20:10; Lv
19:35–36.

k. [11:4] Prv 10:2.   l. [11:5] Prv 28:18.   m. [11:7] Prv 10:28; Wis
3:18.   n. [11:9] Prv 29:5.   o. [11:10] Prv 28:12; 29:2.   p. [11:13]
Prv 20:19.   q. [11:14] Prv 15:22; 20:18; 24:6.   r. [11:15] Prv 6:1–2.

¹⁸ The wicked make empty profits,
    but those who sow justice have a
      sure reward.ˢ
¹⁹ Justice leads toward life,
    but pursuit of evil, toward death.
²⁰ The crooked in heart are an abomination
      to the LORD,
    but those who walk blamelessly are
      his delight.ᵃ
²¹ Be assured, the wicked shall not go
      unpunished,
    but the offspring of the just shall
      escape.
²² Like a golden ring in a swine's snout
    is a beautiful woman without
      judgment.†
²³ The desire of the just ends only in good;
    the expectation of the wicked is wrath.
²⁴ One person is lavish yet grows still richer;
    another is too sparing, yet is the
      poorer.‡
²⁵ Whoever confers benefits will be amply
      enriched,
    and whoever refreshes others will be
      refreshed.
²⁶ Whoever hoards grain, the people curse,
    but blessings are on the head of one
      who distributes it!
²⁷ Those who seek the good seek favor,
    but those who pursue evil will have
      evil come upon them.
²⁸ Those who trust in their riches will fall,
    but like green leaves the just will
      flourish.ᵗ
²⁹ Those who trouble their household
      inherit the wind,
    and fools become slaves to the wise
      of heart.
³⁰ The fruit of justice is a tree of life,
    and one who takes lives is a sage.¶
³¹ If the just are recompensed on the earth,
    how much more the wicked and the
      sinner!**ᵘ

# CHAPTER 12

¹ Whoever loves discipline loves
    knowledge,
    but whoever hates reproof is stupid.††ᵛ
² A good person wins favor from the LORD,
    but the schemer he condemns.‡‡
³ No one is made secure by wickedness,
    but the root of the just will never be
      disturbed.§§
⁴ A woman of worth is the crown of her
      husband,ʷ
    but a disgraceful one is like rot in his
      bones.¶¶
⁵ The plans of the just are right;
    the designs of the wicked are deceit.***
⁶ The words of the wicked are a deadly
      ambush,
    but the speech of the upright saves
      them.†††
⁷ Overthrow the wicked and they are no
      more,
    but the house of the just stands firm.
⁸ For their good sense people are praised,
    but the perverse of heart are
      despised.‡‡‡
⁹ Better to be slighted and have a servant
    than put on airs and lack bread.ˣ
¹⁰ The just take care of their livestock,
    but the compassion of the wicked
      is cruel.§§§
¹¹ Those who till their own land have food
      in plenty,
    but those who engage in idle
      pursuits lack sense.¶¶¶ʸ

---

*[11:20] The terminology of ritual (acceptable and unacceptable sacrifice, "abomination" and "delight") is applied to human conduct as in v. 1. The whole of human life is under divine scrutiny, not just ritual.

†[11:22] Ear and nose rings were common jewelry for women. A humorous saying on the priority of wisdom over beauty in choosing a wife.

‡[11:24] A paradox: spending leads to more wealth.

§[11:27] The saying is about seeking one thing and finding another. Striving for good leads to acceptance by God; seeking evil means only that trouble will come. The same Hebrew word means evil and trouble.

¶[11:30] Most translations emend Hebrew "wise person" in colon B on the basis of the Greek and Syriac translations to "violence" (similar in spelling), because the verb "to take a life" is a Hebrew idiom for "to kill" (as also in English). The emendation is unnecessary, however, for the saying deliberately plays on the odd meaning: the one who takes lives is not the violent but the wise person, for the wise have a profound influence upon life. There is a similar wordplay in 29:10.

**[11:31] The saying is not about life after death; "on the earth" means life in the present world. The meaning is that

divine judgment is exercised on all human action, even the best. The thought should strike terror into the hearts of habitual wrongdoers.

††[12:1] Discipline in Proverbs is both doctrine and training. The path to wisdom includes obedience to teachers and parents, acceptance of the community's traditions.

‡‡[12:2] The antithesis is between the good person who, by reason of that goodness, already has divine acceptance, and the wicked person who, despite great effort, gains only condemnation.

§§[12:3] Human beings are described as "made secure" in Jb 21:8; Ps 101:7; 102:29. "Root" in the context means enduring to succeeding generations, as in Mal 3:19 and Jb 8:17.

¶¶[12:4] In Proverbs a crown is the result and sign of wise conduct. A good wife is a public sign of the husband's shrewd judgment and divine blessing (crown), whereas a bad wife brings him inner pain (rot in the bones).

***[12:5] The opposite of "just" is not injustice but "deceit." The wicked will be deceived in their plans in the sense that their planning will not succeed.

†††[12:6] Words are a favorite theme of Proverbs. The words of the wicked effect harm to others whereas the words of the righteous protect themselves.

‡‡‡[12:8] The heart, the seat of intelligence, will eventually be revealed in the actions that people do, either for praise or for blame.

§§§[12:10] The righteous are sympathetically aware of the needs of their livestock and prosper from their herd's good health. The wicked will pay the price for their self-centeredness and cruelty.

¶¶¶[12:11] The second line clarifies the first: idleness will give one plenty of nothing. "Lacking sense" is a common phrase for fools.

---

s. [11:18] Prv 10:16.   t. [11:28] Ps 52:9–10.   u. [11:31] 1 Pt 4:18.

v. [12:1] Prv 15:5, 10; Sir 21:6.   w. [12:4] Prv 31:10; Sir 21:1, 16.
x. [12:9] Sir 10:26.   y. [12:11] Prv 28:19; Sir 20:27.

<sup>12</sup> A wicked person desires the catch of evil
　　　people,
　　but the root of the righteous will
　　　bear fruit.<sup>*</sup>
<sup>13</sup> By the sin of their lips the wicked are
　　　ensnared,
　　but the just escape from a tight spot.
<sup>14</sup> From the fruit of their mouths people
　　　have their fill of good,<sup>z</sup>
　　and the works of their hands come
　　　back upon them.<sup>†</sup>
<sup>15</sup> The way of fools is right in their own
　　　eyes,
　　but those who listen to advice are
　　　the wise.
<sup>16</sup> Fools immediately show their anger,
　　but the shrewd conceal contempt.
<sup>17</sup> Whoever speaks honestly testifies truly,
　　but the deceitful make lying
　　　witnesses.<sup>‡a</sup>
<sup>18</sup> The babble of some people is like sword
　　　thrusts,
　　but the tongue of the wise is healing.
<sup>19</sup> Truthful lips endure forever,
　　the lying tongue, for only a
　　　moment.<sup>§</sup>
<sup>20</sup> Deceit is in the heart of those who plot
　　　evil,
　　but those who counsel peace have
　　　joy.
<sup>21</sup> No harm befalls the just,
　　but the wicked are overwhelmed
　　　with misfortune.
<sup>22</sup> Lying lips are an abomination to the
　　　Lord,<sup>b</sup>
　　but those who are truthful, his
　　　delight.
<sup>23</sup> The shrewd conceal knowledge,
　　but the hearts of fools proclaim
　　　folly.<sup>5</sup>
<sup>24</sup> The diligent hand will govern,
　　but sloth makes for forced labor.<sup>c</sup>

<sup>25</sup> Worry weighs down the heart,
　　but a kind word gives it joy.<sup>d</sup>
<sup>26</sup> The just act as guides to their neighbors,
　　but the way of the wicked leads
　　　them astray.
<sup>27</sup> Sloth does not catch its prey,
　　but the wealth of the diligent is
　　　splendid.
<sup>28</sup> In the path of justice is life,
　　but the way of abomination leads
　　　to death.

## CHAPTER 13

<sup>1</sup> A wise son loves correction,
　　but the scoffer heeds no rebuke.<sup>**</sup>
<sup>2</sup> From the fruit of the mouth one enjoys
　　　good things,<sup>e</sup>
　　but from the throat of the
　　　treacherous comes violence.<sup>††</sup>
<sup>3</sup> Those who guard their mouths preserve
　　　themselves;<sup>‡‡</sup>
　　those who open wide their lips bring
　　　ruin.<sup>f</sup>
<sup>4</sup> The appetite of the sluggard craves but has
　　　nothing,
　　but the appetite of the diligent is
　　　amply satisfied.
<sup>5</sup> The just hate deceitful words,
　　but the wicked are odious and
　　　disgraceful.
<sup>6</sup> Justice guards one who walks
　　　honestly,
　　but sin leads the wicked astray.<sup>g</sup>
<sup>7</sup> One acts rich but has nothing;
　　another acts poor but has great
　　　wealth.<sup>§§</sup>
<sup>8</sup> People's riches serve as ransom for their
　　　lives,
　　but the poor do not even hear a
　　　threat.<sup>¶¶</sup>

---

*[12:12] A difficult, possibly corrupt saying, but there is no good alternative to the Hebrew text. The wicked desire what the malevolent have captured or killed, but their actions will go for naught because they invite punishment. The righteous, on the other hand, will bear fruit.

†[12:14] The saying contrasts words and deeds. "Fruit" here is not what one normally eats, as in 1:31; 8:19; 31:16, 31, but the consequences of one's actions. In the second line the things that issue from one's hands (one's deeds) come back to one in recompense or punishment. Prv 13:2a and 18:20 are variants. Cf. Mt 7:17; Gal 6:8.

‡[12:17] What is the rule of thumb for judging legal testimony? Look to the ordinary conduct and daily speech of a witness.

§[12:19] The saying has a double meaning: lies are quickly found out whereas truthful statements endure; truth-tellers, being favored by God, live long lives, whereas liars invite punishment.

¶[12:23] "Knowledge" here is "what one knows, has in one's heart," not knowledge in general. Fools reveal all they have stored in their heart and it naturally turns out to be folly. Revealing and concealing are constant themes in Proverbs.

**[13:1] Another in the series on the household, this one on the relation of parents and children. See under 10:1. The scoffer in Proverbs condemns discipline and thus can never become wise. Wise adult children advertise to the community what they received from their parents, for children become wise through a dialectical process involving the parents. A foolish adult child witnesses to foolish parents.

††[13:2] One's mouth normally eats food from outside, but in the moral life, things are reversed: one eats from the fruit of one's mouth, i.e., one experiences the consequences of one's own actions. Since the mouth of the treacherous is filled with violence, one must assume that they will some day endure violence.

‡‡[13:3] Preserve themselves: in Hebrew, literally to preserve the throat area, the moist breathing center of one's body, thus "life," "soul," or "self." There is wordplay: if you guard your mouth (= words) you guard your "soul." Fools, on the other hand, do not guard but open their lips and disaster strikes. A near duplicate is 21:23.

§§[13:7] Appearances can be deceiving; possessions do not always reveal the true state of a person.

¶¶[13:8] Related to v. 7. Possessions enable the wealthy to pay ransom but the poor are "protected" by lack of possessions: they never hear the threat of the pursuer. Cf. the use of the word "threat" in Is 30:17.

---

z. [12:14] Prv 13:2; 18:20.　a. [12:17] Prv 14:5.　b. [12:22] Prv 6:17.　c. [12:24] Prv 10:4; 13:4.

d. [12:25] Prv 15:13; 17:22.　e. [13:2] Prv 12:14; 18:20.　f. [13:3] Prv 18:7; 21:23.　g. [13:6] Prv 11:3, 5–6.

⁹ The light of the just gives joy,
  but the lamp* of the wicked goes out.ʰ
¹⁰ The stupid sow discord by their
    insolence,
  but wisdom is with those who take
    counsel.
¹¹ Wealth won quickly dwindles away,
  but gathered little by little, it grows.ⁱ
¹² Hope deferred makes the heart sick,
  but a wish fulfilled is a tree of life.†
¹³ Whoever despises the word must pay for
    it,‡
  but whoever reveres the command
    will be rewarded.
¹⁴ The teaching of the wise is a fountain of
    life,
  turning one from the snares of
    death.
¹⁵ Good sense brings favor,
  but the way of the faithless is their
    ruin.§
¹⁶ The shrewd always act prudently
  but the foolish parade folly.¶
¹⁷ A wicked messenger brings on disaster,
  but a trustworthy envoy is a healing
    remedy.
¹⁸ Poverty and shame befall those who let go
    of discipline,
  but those who hold on to reproof
    receive honor.**
¹⁹ Desire fulfilled delights the soul,
  but turning from evil is an
    abomination to fools.
²⁰ Walk with the wise and you become
    wise,
  but the companion of fools fares
    badly.ʲ
²¹ Misfortune pursues sinners,
  but the just shall be recompensed
    with good.
²² The good leave an inheritance to their
    children's children,
  but the wealth of the sinner is stored
    up for the just.

²³ The tillage of the poor yields abundant
    food,
  but possessions are swept away for
    lack of justice.††
²⁴ Whoever spares the rod hates the child,
  but whoever loves will apply
    discipline.ᵏ
²⁵ When the just eat, their hunger is
    appeased;
  but the belly of the wicked suffers
    want.

## CHAPTER 14

¹ Wisdom builds her house,
  but Folly tears hers down with her
    own hands.‡‡
² Those who walk uprightly fear the LORD,
  but those who are devious in their
    ways spurn him.
³ In the mouth of the fool is a rod for
    pride,
  but the lips of the wise preserve
    them.
⁴ Where there are no oxen, the crib is
    clean;
  but abundant crops come through
    the strength of the bull.§§
⁵ A trustworthy witness does not lie,
  but one who spouts lies makes a
    lying witness.¶¶ˡ
⁶ The scoffer seeks wisdom in vain,
  but knowledge is easy for the
    intelligent.
⁷ Go from the face of the fool;
  you get no knowledge from such
    lips.
⁸ The wisdom of the shrewd enlightens
    their way,
  but the folly of fools is deceit.***
⁹ The wicked scorn a guilt offering,
  but the upright find acceptance.
¹⁰ The heart knows its own bitterness,
  and its joy no stranger shares.†††

---

*[13:9] **Light . . . lamp**: symbols of life and prosperity; cf. 4:18–19.

†[13:12] "Tree of life" occurs in Gn 2–3, Prv 3:18; 11:30; 13:12; 15:4, and Rev 2:7; 22:2, 14, 19. It provides food and healing.

‡[13:13] **Must pay for it**: lit., "is pledge to it," i.e., just as one who has pledged or provided surety for another's loan is obligated to that pledge, so one is not free of a command until one performs it.

§[13:15] As the behavior of the wise wins them favor that increases their prosperity, like Abigail with David in 1 Sm 25, so the way (= conduct) of the faithless ruins their lives.

¶[13:16] Like 12:23 and 15:2, 3, the saying is about revealing and concealing. The wise reveal their wisdom in their actions whereas fools "parade," spread out their folly for all to see. The verb is used of vendors spreading their wares and of birds spreading their wings.

**[13:18] The saying plays on letting go and holding on. Wisdom consists in not rejecting discipline and being open to the comments of others, even if they are reproving comments.

††[13:23] An observation on the poor. The lands of the poor are as fertile as anyone's, for nature does not discriminate against them. Their problem is lack of justice, which puts their harvest at risk from unscrupulous human beings.

‡‡[14:1] The relationship between Wisdom, personified as a woman, and building a house is a constant theme. As elsewhere, the book here warns against the wrong woman and praises the right woman.

§§[14:4] If one has no animals, one does not have the burden of keeping the crib full, but without them one will have no crops to fill the barn. Colon B reverses the sense of colon A and also reverses the consonants of *bar* ("clean") to *rab* ("abundant").

¶¶[14:5] On discerning the truthfulness of witnesses; see 12:17.

***[14:8] Wisdom enables the shrewd to know their path is right but folly leads fools on the wrong path ("deceit"), which calls down retribution.

†††[14:10] The heart in Proverbs is where a person's sense impressions are stored and reflected upon. It is thus one's most personal and individual part. One's sorrows and joys (= the full

---

h. [13:9] Prv 24:20.   i. [13:11] Prv 28:20, 22.   j. [13:20] Sir 6:34; 8:8, 17.

k. [13:24] Prv 19:18; 22:15; 23:13–14; 29:15; Sir 30:1, 8–13.   l. [14:5] Prv 12:17.

¹¹ The house of the wicked will be
destroyed,
but the tent of the upright will
flourish.ᵐ
¹² Sometimes a way seems right,
but the end of it leads to death!ⁿ
¹³ Even in laughter the heart may be sad,
and the end of joy may be sorrow.
¹⁴ From their own ways turncoats are
sated,
from their own actions, the loyal.
¹⁵ The naïve believe everything,
but the shrewd watch their steps.†
¹⁶ The wise person is cautious and turns
from evil;
the fool is reckless and gets
embroiled.
¹⁷ The quick-tempered make fools of
themselves,
and schemers are hated.
¹⁸ The simple have folly as an adornment,
but the shrewd wear knowledge as
a crown.‡
¹⁹ The malicious bow down before the good,
and the wicked, at the gates of the
just.
²⁰ Even by their neighbors the poor are
despised,
but a rich person's friends are many.ᵒ
²¹ Whoever despises the hungry comes up
short,
but happy the one who is kind to
the poor!§
²² Do not those who plan evil go astray?
But those who plan good win
steadfast loyalty.
²³ In all labor there is profit,
but mere talk tends only to loss.
²⁴ The crown of the wise is wealth;
the diadem of fools is folly.
²⁵ The truthful witness saves lives,
but whoever utters lies is a betrayer.
²⁶ The fear of the LORD is a strong defense,
a refuge even for one's children.
²⁷ The fear of the LORD is a fountain of life,
turning one from the snares of death.
²⁸ A multitude of subjects is the glory of the
king;
but if his people are few, a prince is
ruined.

²⁹ Long-suffering results in great wisdom;
a short temper raises folly high.¶ᵖ
³⁰ A tranquil mind gives life to the body,
but jealousy rots the bones.
³¹ Those who oppress the poor revile their
Maker,
but those who are kind to the needy
honor him.�q
³² The wicked are overthrown by their
wickedness,
but the just find a refuge in their
integrity.
³³ Wisdom can remain silent in the
discerning heart,
but among fools she must make
herself known.**ʳ
³⁴ Justice exalts a nation,
but sin is a people's disgrace.††
³⁵ The king favors the skillful servant,
but the shameless one incurs his
wrath.

## CHAPTER 15

¹ ‡‡A mild answer turns back wrath,ˢ
but a harsh word stirs up anger.§§
² The tongue of the wise pours out
knowledge,
but the mouth of fools spews folly.
³ The eyes of the LORD are in every place,
keeping watch on the evil and the
good.
⁴ A soothing tongue is a tree of life,
but a perverse one breaks the spirit.
⁵ The fool spurns a father's instruction,
but whoever heeds reproof is
prudent.¶¶ᵗ
⁶ In the house of the just there are ample
resources,
but the harvest of the wicked is in peril.
⁷ The lips of the wise spread knowledge,
but the heart of fools is not steadfast.***
⁸ The sacrifice of the wicked is an
abomination to the LORD,ᵘ

---

¶[14:29] A series of puns on short and long; lit., "long
of nostrils (idiom for "patient"), large in wisdom, / short in
breath (idiom for "impatient"), makes folly tall."

**[14:33] Wisdom can remain silent in a wise person as a
welcome friend. But it must speak out among fools, for the
dissonance is so strong.

††[14:34] The rare noun "disgrace" occurs elsewhere only
in Lv 20:17. In measuring the greatness of a nation, one is
tempted to consider territory, wealth, history, but the most
important criterion is its relationship to God ("justice").

‡‡[15:1–7] These verses form a section beginning and ending with the topic of words.

§§[15:1] Paradoxically, where words are concerned soft is
powerful and hard is ineffective.

¶¶[15:5] One becomes wise by keeping and foolish by
rejecting. One must accept the tradition of the community.

***[15:7] "Lips" and "heart" are a fixed pair, in Proverbs sig-
nifying, respectively, expression and source. The wise dissemi-
nate what they have in their heart, and the wicked are unsound
even in the source of their words, their hearts.

---

range of emotions) cannot be shared fully with another. Verse
13 expresses the same individuality of the human person.

*[14:11] The traditional fixed pair "house" and "tent" is
used to express the paradox that a house can be less secure
than a tent if there is no justice.

†[14:15] The naive gullibly rely on others' words whereas
the shrewd watch their own steps.

‡[14:18] The inner quality of a person, simple or wise, will
eventually be revealed.

§[14:21] The paradox is that anyone who spurns the hungry will lack something, but anyone who shows mercy (presumably by giving to the poor) will gain prosperity.

---

m. [14:11] Prv 3:33; 12:7; 15:25. n. [14:12] Prv 16:25. o. [14:20]
Prv 19:4, 7; Sir 6:8, 12.

p. [14:29] Prv 16:32; 19:11; Jas 1:19. q. [14:31] Prv 17:5. r. [14:33]
Prv 1:22; 8:1. s. [15:1] Prv 25:15; Sir 6:5. t. [15:5] Prv 12:1;
13:18. u. [15:8] Prv 21:27; Eccl 4:17; Is 1:11–15.

but the prayer of the upright is his
delight.

9 The way of the wicked is an abomination
to the LORD,
but he loves one who pursues
justice.[v]

10 Discipline seems bad to those going
astray;
one who hates reproof will die.[*]

11 Sheol and Abaddon[†] lie open before the
LORD;
how much more the hearts of
mortals!

12 Scoffers do not love reproof;
to the wise they will not go.

13 A glad heart lights up the face,
but an anguished heart breaks the
spirit.[w]

14 The discerning heart seeks knowledge,
but the mouth of fools feeds on
folly.[‡]

15 All the days of the poor are evil,
but a good heart is a continual
feast.[§]

16 'Better a little with fear of the LORD
than a great fortune with anxiety.

17 Better a dish of herbs where love is
than a fatted ox and hatred with it.

18 The ill-tempered stir up strife,[x]
but the patient settle disputes.

19 The way of the sluggard is like a thorn
hedge,
but the path of the diligent is a
highway.

20 A wise son gives his father joy,
but a fool despises his mother.[y]

21 Folly is joy[**] to the senseless,
but the person of understanding
goes the straight way.

22 Plans fail where there is no counsel,
but they succeed when advisers are
many.[††z]

23 One has joy from an apt response;
a word in season, how good it is![‡‡a]

24 The path of life leads upward for the
prudent,
turning them from Sheol below.[§§]

25 The LORD pulls down the house of the
proud,
but preserves intact the widow's
landmark.

26 The schemes of the wicked are an
abomination to the LORD,[b]
but gracious words are pure.[¶¶]

27 The greedy tear down their own house,
but those who hate bribes will live.[***]

28 The heart of the just ponders a response,
but the mouth of the wicked spews
evil.

29 The LORD is far from the wicked,
but hears the prayer of the just.

30 A cheerful glance brings joy to the heart;
good news invigorates the bones.

31 The ear that listens to salutary reproof[c]
is at home among the wise.[†††]

32 Those who disregard discipline hate
themselves,
but those who heed reproof acquire
understanding.

33 The fear of the LORD is training for wisdom,
and humility goes before honors.[d]

## CHAPTER 16

1 Plans are made in human hearts,
but from the LORD comes the
tongue's response.[‡‡‡]

2 All one's ways are pure[§§§] in one's own eyes,
but the measurer of motives is the
LORD.[e]

3 Entrust your works to the LORD,
and your plans will succeed.

4 The LORD has made everything for a
purpose,
even the wicked for the evil day.[¶¶¶]

---

*[15:10] Discipline, always a good thing in Proverbs, seems bad to those deliberately wandering from justice.

†[15:11] **Sheol and Abaddon**: terms for the abode of the dead, signifying the profound obscurity which is open nevertheless to the sight and power of God; cf. 27:20.

‡[15:14] The contrasts include heart (organ of reflection) and mouth (organ of expression), and the wise and fools. One type feeds its mind with wisdom and the other feeds its face with folly.

§[15:15] Good heart does not refer to good intentions but to an instructed mind. Wisdom makes poverty not only bearable but even joyful like the joy of feast days.

¶[15:16] The sages favor wealth over poverty—but not at any price; cf. Ps 37:16.

**[15:21] The word "joy" occurs in the first line of vv. 20, 21, and 23. The state of folly is joy to a fool but the wise person is totally absorbed in keeping on the right or straight road.

††[15:22] Failure to consult makes it likely a plan will not succeed. The point is nicely made by contrasting the singular number in the first line ("no counsel") with the plural number in the second line ("many advisors").

‡‡[15:23] Conversation is the art of saying the right thing at the right time. It gives pleasure to speaker and hearer alike.

§§[15:24] Death is personified as Sheol, the underworld. "Up" and "down" in Hebrew as in English are metaphors for success and failure (see Dt 28:43). One who stays on the path of life need not fear the punishment that stalks sinners.

¶¶[15:26] "Pure" here means acceptable. The language of ritual (acceptable or pure) is applied to ordinary human actions. "Gracious words" are words that bring peace to the neighbor.

***[15:27] The same lesson as the opening scene of Proverbs (1:8–19): one cannot build a house by unjust gain. Injustice will come back upon a house so built.

†††[15:31] To become wise, one must hear and integrate perspectives contrary to one's own, which means accepting "reproof." Wisdom does not isolate one but places one in the company of the wise.

‡‡‡[16:1] Words, like actions, often produce results different from those which were planned, and this comes under the agency of God.

§§§[16:2] "Pure" in a moral sense for human action is found only in Job and Proverbs. As in v. 1, the contrast is between human intent and divine assessment.

¶¶¶[16:4] Even the wicked do not lie outside God's plan.

---

v. [15:9] Prv 11:20; 21:21.  w. [15:13] Prv 12:25; 17:22; Sir 30:22.
x. [15:18] Prv 6:21; 29:22; Sir 28:11.  y. [15:20] Prv 10:1; 29:3.
z. [15:22] Prv 11:14.

a. [15:23] Prv 25:11; Sir 20:6.  b. [15:26] Prv 6:18.  c. [15:31] Prv 25:12.  d. [15:33] Prv 1:7; 19:12; Sir 1:24.  e. [16:2] Prv 21:2.

5 Every proud heart* is an abomination to
      the LORD;ᶠ
      be assured that none will go
        unpunished.
6 By steadfast loyalty guilt is expiated,
      and by the fear of the LORD evil is
        avoided.†
7 When the LORD is pleased with someone's
      ways,
      he makes even enemies be at peace
        with them.
8 Better a little with justice,
      than a large income with injustice.
9 The human heart plans the way,
      but the LORD directs the steps.‡ᵍ
10 An oracle is upon the king's lips,
      no judgment of his mouth is false.§
11 Balance and scales belong to the LORD;
      every weight in the sack is his
        concern.ʰ
12 Wrongdoing is an abomination to kings,
      for by justice the throne endures.ⁱ
13 The king takes delight in honest lips,
      and whoever speaks what is right
        he loves.ʲ
14 The king's wrath is a messenger of death,ᵏ
      but a wise person can pacify it.
15 A king's smile means life,
      and his favor is like a rain cloud in
        spring.¶
16 How much better to get wisdom than
      gold!
      To get understanding is preferable
        to silver.**ˡ
17 The path of the upright leads away from
      misfortune;
      those who attend to their way guard
        their lives.††

18 Pride goes before disaster,
      and a haughty spirit before a fall.
19 It is better to be humble with the poor
      than to share plunder with the
        proud.ᵐ
20 Whoever ponders a matter will be
      successful;
      happy the one who trusts in the
        LORD!
21 The wise of heart is esteemed for
      discernment,
      and pleasing speech gains a
        reputation for learning.
22 Good sense is a fountain of life to those
      who have it,
      but folly is the training of fools.
23 The heart of the wise makes for eloquent
      speech,
      and increases the learning on their
        lips.
24 Pleasing words are a honeycomb,
      sweet to the taste and invigorating to
        the bones.
25 Sometimes a way seems right,
      but the end of it leads to death!ⁿ
26 The appetite of workers works for them,
      for their mouths urge them on.‡‡ᵒ
27 Scoundrels are a furnace of evil,
      and their lips are like a scorching fire.
28 Perverse speech sows discord,
      and talebearing separates bosom
        friends.ᵖ
29 The violent deceive their neighbors,
      and lead them into a way that is not
        good.
30 Whoever winks an eye plans perversity;
      whoever purses the lips does evil.§§
31 Gray hair is a crown of glory;�q
      it is gained by a life that is just.
32 The patient are better than warriors,
      and those who rule their temper,
      better than the conqueror of
        a city.ʳ
33 Into the bag the lot is cast,
      but from the LORD comes every
        decision.¶¶

## CHAPTER 17

1 Better a dry crust with quiet

---

*[16:5] **Proud heart:** lit., "high of heart." To forget one is a fallible human being is so basic an error that one cannot escape exposure and punishment.

†[16:6] As v. 5 used the language of worship to express what is acceptable or not to God, so this saying uses similar language to declare that lovingly loyal conduct undoes the effects of sin.

‡[16:9] As in vv. 1–3, the antithesis is between human plans and divine disposal. The saying uses the familiar metaphor of path for the course of life.

§[16:10] Six sayings on the king and his divine authority begin here, following the series of sayings about the Lord's governance in 15:33–16:9, in which "LORD" was mentioned nine times.

¶[16:15] The last of six sayings about the king. In the previous verse, royal wrath means death; in this verse royal favor means life. It is significant that royal favor is compared to something not under human control—the clouds preceding the spring rains.

**[16:16] The point of comparison is the superiority of the pursuit of wisdom and gold, not the relative merits of wealth and wisdom.

††[16:17] In the metaphor of the two ways, the way of the righteous is protected and the way of the wicked is unprotected. Since the path of the righteous leads therefore away from trouble, one's task is to stay on it, to "attend to" it.

‡‡[16:26] The adage puzzled ancient and modern commentators. The meaning seems to state the paradox that a person does not toil to feed the gullet but that the gullet itself "toils" in the sense that it forces the person to work. As often in Proverbs, the sense organ stands for the faculty by metonymy. Cf. Eccl 6:7.

§§[16:30] A restless or twitching eye or lip betrays the condition of the heart (cf. 6:13).

¶¶[16:33] Dice were given meanings of "yes" or "no" and then cast for their answer. What came out was the decision. Here the saying interprets the sequence of actions: a human being puts the dice in the bag but what emerges from the bag is the Lord's decision.

---

f. [16:5] Prv 6:16–17; 8:13.   g. [16:9] Prv 19:21; 20:24; Jer 10:23.   h. [16:11] Prv 11:1.   i. [16:12] Prv 25:5.   j. [16:13] Prv 14:35; 22:11.   k. [16:14] Prv 19:12; 20:2.   l. [16:16] Prv 8:10–11.
m. [16:19] Prv 11:2.   n. [16:25] Prv 14:12.   o. [16:26] Prv 10:4. p. [16:28] Prv 6:14, 19; 17:9; 26:22; Sir 28:15.   q. [16:31] Prv 20:29. r. [16:32] Prv 14:29.

than a house full of feasting with
strife.*
2 A wise servant will rule over an unworthy
son,
and will share the inheritance of the
children.†
3 The crucible for silver, and the furnace for
gold,
but the tester of hearts is the LORD.
4 The evildoer gives heed to wicked lips,
the liar, to a mischievous tongue.
5 Whoever mocks the poor reviles their
Maker;
whoever rejoices in their misfortune
will not go unpunished.ˢ
6 Children's children are the crown of the
elderly,
and the glory of children is their
parentage.
7 Fine words ill fit a fool;
how much more lying lips, a noble!
8 A bribe seems a charm to its user;
at every turn it brings success.‡
9 Whoever overlooks an offense fosters
friendship,
but whoever gossips about it
separates friends.§
10 A single reprimand does more for a
discerning person
than a hundred lashes for a fool.¶
11 The wicked pursue only rebellion,
and a merciless messenger is sent
against them.**
12 Face a bear robbed of her cubs,
but never fools in their folly!††
13 If you return evil for good,
evil will not depart from your house.‡‡ʹ
14 The start of strife is like the opening of a
dam;
check a quarrel before it bursts forth!
15 Whoever acquits the wicked,ᵘ whoever
condemns the just—
both are an abomination to the LORD.

16 Of what use is money in the hands of
fools
when they have no heart to acquire
wisdom?§§
17 A friend is a friend at all times,
and a brother is born for the time of
adversity.ᵛ
18 Those without sense give their hands in
pledge,
becoming surety for their neighbors.ʷ
19 Those who love an offense love a fight;ˣ
those who build their gate high¶¶
court disaster.
20 The perverse in heart come to no good,
and the double-tongued fall into
trouble.***
21 Whoever conceives a fool has grief;
the father of a numskull has no joy.
22 A joyful heart is the health of the body,
but a depressed spirit dries up the
bones.ʸ
23 A guilty person takes out a bribe from the
pocket,
thus perverting the course of
justice.†††
24 On the countenance of a discerning
person is wisdom,ᶻ
but the eyes of a fool are on the ends
of the earth.‡‡‡
25 A foolish son is vexation to his father,
and bitter sorrow to her who bore
him.ᵃ
26 It is wrong to fine an innocent person,
but beyond reason to scourge
nobles.
27 Those who spare their words are truly
knowledgeable,
and those who are discreet are
intelligent.ᵇ
28 Even fools, keeping silent, are considered
wise;
if they keep their lips closed,
intelligent.§§§

---

*[17:1] A "better than" saying, stating the circumstances
when a dry crust is better than a banquet. Peace and fellowship give joy to a meal, not the richness of the food. For a
similar thought, see 15:16 and 16:8.
†[17:2] Ability is esteemed more highly than ties of blood.
‡[17:8] An observation on the effect of the bribe upon the
bribe-giver: it gives an intoxicating feeling of power ("seems").
In v. 23 the evil effects of a bribe are noted.
§[17:9] A paradox. One finds (love, friend) by concealing
(an offense), one loses (a friend) by revealing (a secret). In
10:12 love also covers over a multitude of offenses.
¶[17:10] A wonderful comment on the openness and sensitivity of the wise and the foolish. One type learns from a single word and for the other one hundred blows are not enough.
**[17:11] The irony is that such people will meet up with
what they so energetically pursue—in the form of an unrelenting emissary sent to them.
††[17:12] Humorous hyperbole. An outraged dangerous
beast poses less danger than a fool.
‡‡[17:13] The paradox is that to pay out evil for good means
that the evil will never leave one's own house.

§§[17:16] The exhortation to acquire or purchase wisdom
is common in Proverbs. Fools misunderstand the metaphor,
assuming they can buy it with money. Their very misunderstanding shows they have no "heart" = mind, understanding. Money
in the hand is no good without such a "heart" to store it in.
¶¶[17:19] **Build their gate high**: a symbol of arrogance.
***[17:20] The saying employs the familiar metaphors of
walking = conducting oneself ("fall into trouble"), and of
straight and crooked = right and wrong ("perverse," "double-
tongued").
†††[17:23] A sharp look at the sly withdrawing of a bribe
from the pocket and a blunt judgment on its significance.
‡‡‡[17:24] Wisdom is visible on the countenance (i.e.,
mouth, lips, tongue) of the wise person; its ultimate source is
the heart. Fools have no such source of wisdom within them,
a point that is nicely made by referring to the eye of the fool,
roving over the landscape.
§§§[17:28] Related to v. 27. Words provide a glimpse into
the heart. In the unlikely event that fools, who usually pour
out words (15:2), were to say nothing, people would not be

---

s. [17:5] Prv 14:31.  t. [17:13] Mt 5:39; Rom 12:17; 1 Thes 5:15; 1 Pt
3:9.  u. [17:15] Prv 24:24; Is 5:23.

v. [17:17] Prv 18:24.  w. [17:18] Prv 6:1–2; 11:15.  x. [17:19] Prv
15:18.  y. [17:22] Prv 12:25; 15:13.  z. [17:24] Eccl 8:1.  a. [17:25]
Prv 10:1; 29:15.  b. [17:27] Prv 10:19; Sir 1:21; Jas 1:19.

## CHAPTER 18

¹ One who is alienated seeks a pretext,
    with all persistence picks a quarrel.
² Fools take no delight in understanding,
    but only in displaying what they
      think.*
³ With wickedness comes contempt,
    and with disgrace, scorn.
⁴ The words of one's mouth are deep waters,
    the spring of wisdom, a running
      brook.†ᶜ
⁵ It is not good to favor the guilty,
    nor to reject the claim of the just.ᵈ
⁶ The lips of fools walk into a fight,
    and their mouths are asking for a
      beating.‡
⁷ The mouths of fools are their ruin,
    their lips are a deadly snare.ᵉ
⁸ The words of a talebearer are like dainty
      morsels:
    they sink into one's inmost being.ᶠ
⁹ Those slack in their work
    are kin to the destroyer.
¹⁰ §The name of the LORD is a strong tower;
    the just run to it and are safe.
¹¹ The wealth of the rich is their strong
      city;ᵍ
    they fancy it a high wall.
¹² Before disaster the heart is haughty,ʰ
    but before honor is humility.
¹³ Whoever answers before listening,
    theirs is folly and shame.¶
¹⁴ One's spirit supports one when ill,
    but a broken spirit who can bear?**
¹⁵ The heart of the intelligent acquires
      knowledge,
    and the ear of the wise seeks
      knowledge.††
¹⁶ Gifts clear the way for people,
    winning access to the great.ʲ
¹⁷ Those who plead the case first seem to be
    in the right;

then the opponent comes and
      cross-examines them.‡‡
¹⁸ The lot puts an end to disputes,
    and decides a controversy between
      the mighty.§§
¹⁹ A brother offended is more unyielding
      than a stronghold;
    such strife is more daunting than
      castle gates.¶¶
²⁰ With the fruit of one's mouth one's belly is
      filled,
    with the produce of one's lips one is
      sated.***ᵏ
²¹ Death and life are in the power of the
      tongue;ˡ
    those who choose one shall eat its
      fruit.†††
²² To find a wife is to find happiness,
    a favor granted by the LORD.ᵐ
²³ The poor implore,
    but the rich answer harshly.
²⁴ There are friends who bring ruin,
    but there are true friends more loyal
      than a brother.ⁿ

## CHAPTER 19

¹ Better to be poor and walk in integrity
    than rich and crooked in one's ways.ᵒ
² Desire without knowledge is not good;
    and whoever acts hastily, blunders.‡‡‡
³ Their own folly leads people astray;
    in their hearts they rage against the
      LORD.§§§
⁴ Wealth adds many friends,
    but the poor are left friendless.ᵖ

---

‡‡[18:17] A persuasive speech in court can easily make one forget there is another side to the question. When the other party speaks, people realize they made a premature judgment. The experience at court is a lesson for daily life: there are two sides to every question.

§§[18:18] See note on 16:33.

¶¶[18:19] The Greek version, followed by several ancient versions, has the opposite meaning: "A brother helped by a brother is like a strong and lofty city; it is strong like a well-founded palace." The Greek is secondary as is shown by the need to supply the phrase "by a brother"; further, the parallelism is inadequate. The Hebrew is to be preferred.

***[18:20] Fruit from the earth is our ordinary sustenance, but "the fruit of one's lips," i.e., our words, also affect our well-being. If our words and our deeds are right, then we are blessed, our "belly is filled."

†††[18:21] This enigmatic saying has provoked many interpretations, e.g., judicious speech brings a reward; those who love the tongue in the sense of rattling on must face the consequences of their loquacity. This translation interprets the verb "love" in colon B in its occasional sense of "choose" (e.g., 12:1; 20:13; Dt 4:37) and interprets its pronominal object as referring to both death and life in colon A. Death and life are set before every person (cf. Dt 30:15–20) and we have the power to choose either one by the quality of our deeds. Words (= "the tongue") are regarded here as the defining actions of human beings.

‡‡‡[19:2] When not guided by wisdom, appetite—or desire—is not good. "Running feet" (so the Hebrew) miss the mark, i.e., do not reach their destination.

§§§[19:3] One's own folly destroys one's life. It is an indication of that folly that one blames God rather than oneself.

---

able to see their folly and would presume them intelligent. Alas, the saying is contrary to fact.

*[18:2] One grows in wisdom by listening to others, but fools take delight in expounding the contents of their minds.

†[18:4] Words express a person's thoughts ("deep waters"), which in turn become accessible to others. Cf. 20:5a.

‡[18:6] The bold personification of lips and mouth is similar to Ps 73:9, "They set their mouths against the heavens, their tongues roam the earth." Careless words can lead one into serious trouble.

§[18:10–11] Contrast this judgment with the observation in 10:15.

¶[18:13] To speak without first listening is characteristic of a fool; cf. 10:14; Sir 11:8.

**[18:14] The paradox is that something as slight as a column of air offers protection against the encroachment of death. If it is stilled, nothing, no matter how powerful, can substitute for it.

††[18:15] "Knowledge" here refers to what one knows, not knowledge in itself. The mind acquires and stores it, the ear strains toward it.

---

c. [18:4] Prv 20:5; Jn 7:38.    d. [18:5] Prv 24:23; 28:21.    e. [18:7] Prv 10:14; 12:13; 13:3; Eccl 10:12.    f. [18:8] Prv 26:22.    g. [18:11] Prv 10:15.    h. [18:12] Prv 11:2; 16:18; Sir 10:15.    i. [18:13] Sir 11:8.    j. [18:16] Prv 21:14.

k. [18:20] Prv 12:14; 13:2.    l. [18:21] Sir 37:18.    m. [18:22] Prv 12:4; 19:14; Sir 7:26.    n. [18:24] Prv 17:17.    o. [19:1] Prv 28:6.    p. [19:4] Prv 14:20; Sir 13:20–23.

⁵ The false witness will not go unpunished,
   and whoever utters lies will not
   escape.*�q
⁶ Many curry favor with a noble;
   everybody is a friend of a gift giver.
⁷ All the kin of the poor despise them;
   how much more do their friends
   shun them!†
⁸ Those who gain sense truly love
   themselves;
   those who preserve understanding
   will find success.‡
⁹ The false witness will not go unpunished,
   and whoever utters lies will perish.
¹⁰ Luxury is not befitting a fool;
   much less should a slave rule over
   princes.
¹¹ It is good sense to be slow to anger,
   and an honor to overlook an
   offense.§
¹² The king's wrath is like the roar of a lion,
   but his favor, like dew on the grass.ᶠʳ
¹³ The foolish son is ruin to his father,ˢ
   and a quarrelsome wife is water
   constantly dripping.**
¹⁴ Home and possessions are an inheritance
   from parents,
   but a prudent wife is from the LORD.ᵗ
¹⁵ Laziness brings on deep sleep,
   and the sluggard goes hungry.ᵘ
¹⁶ Those who keep commands keep their
   lives,
   but those who despise these ways
   will die.ᵛ
¹⁷ Whoever cares for the poor lends to the
   LORD,ʷ
   who will pay back the sum in full.
¹⁸ Discipline your son, for there is hope;
   but do not be intent on his death.††ˣ
¹⁹ A wrathful person bears the penalty;
   after one rescue, you will have it to
   do again.

²⁰ Listen to counsel and receive
   instruction,
   that you may eventually become
   wise.
²¹ Many are the plans of the human heart,
   but it is the decision of the LORD
   that endures.ʸ
²² What is desired of a person is fidelity;
   rather be poor than a liar.‡‡
²³ The fear of the LORD leads to life;
   one eats and sleeps free from any
   harm.
²⁴ The sluggard buries a hand in the dish;
   not even lifting it to the mouth.ᶻ
²⁵ Beat a scoffer and the naive learn a
   lesson;
   rebuke the intelligent and they gain
   knowledge.ᵃ
²⁶ Whoever mistreats a father or drives away
   a mother,
   is a shameless and disgraceful
   child.§§ᵇ
²⁷ My son, stop attending to correction;
   start straying from words of
   knowledge.¶¶
²⁸ An unprincipled witness scoffs at justice,
   and the mouth of the wicked pours
   out iniquity.
²⁹ Rods are prepared for scoffers,
   and blows for the backs of fools.ᶜ

## CHAPTER 20

¹ Wine is arrogant, strong drink is riotous;
   none who are intoxicated by them
   are wise.***ᵈ
² The terror of a king is like the roar of a
   lion;ᵉ
   those who incur his anger forfeit
   their lives.
³ A person gains honor by avoiding strife,
   while every fool starts a quarrel.†††
⁴ In seedtime sluggards do not plow;
   when they look for the harvest, it is
   not there.

---

*[19:5] The punishment fits the crime: those who abuse the legal system will be punished by the same system. They will not be acquitted.

†[19:7] Closely related to vv. 4 and 6. An observation, not without sympathy, on the social isolation of poor people.

‡[19:8] Wisdom benefits the one who practices it.

§[19:11] The paradox is that one obtains one thing by giving up another.

¶[19:12] An observation on the exercise of royal power. Both images suggest royal attitudes are beyond human control. Colon A is a variant of 20:2a and colon B of 16:15b.

**[19:13] One of many sayings about domestic happiness. The perspective is male; the two greatest pains to a father is a malicious son and an unsuitable wife. The immediately following saying is on the noble wife, perhaps to make a positive statement about women.

††[19:18] The pain of disciplining the young cannot be compared with the danger no discipline may bring. The chief reason for disciplining the young is their capacity to change; excluded thereby are revenge and punishment.

‡‡[19:22] The proverb has been read in two ways: (1) "Desire (greed) is a shame to a person," which assumes the rare Hebrew word for "shame" is being used; (2) "What is desired in a person is fidelity." The second interpretation is preferable. The context may be the court: better to forego money (a bribe) than perjure oneself.

§§[19:26] Children who disgrace the family equivalently plunder their father's wealth and expel their mother from the home.

¶¶[19:27] The meaning was disputed even in antiquity. The interpretation that most respects the syntax is to take it as ironic advice as in 22:6: to stop (listening) is to go (wandering).

***[20:1] The cause stands for its effect (wine, drunken behavior). In Proverbs wine is a sign of prosperity and a symbol of feasting (3:10; 4:17; 9:2, 5) but also a potential threat to wisdom as in 20:1; 21:17; 23:29–35.

†††[20:3] The honor that one might seek to gain from fighting comes of itself to the person who refrains from fighting.

---

q. [19:5] Dt 19:16–20; Dn 13:61.  r. [19:12] Prv 20:2.  s. [19:13] Prv 10:1; 17:25.  t. [19:14] Prv 18:22.  u. [19:15] Prv 6:9–10.  v. [19:16] Prv 13:13; 16:17.  w. [19:17] Prv 14:21; 22:9; 28:27.  x. [19:18] Prv 13:24; 23:13–14.

y. [19:21] Prv 16:9.  z. [19:24] Prv 26:15.  a. [19:25] Prv 17:10; 21:11.  b. [19:26] Sir 3:16.  c. [19:29] Prv 26:3.  d. [20:1] Prv 23:29–35.  e. [20:2] Prv 19:12.

5 The intention of the human heart is deep
     water,
    but the intelligent draw it forth.*f

6 Many say, "My loyal friend,"
    but who can find someone worthy
       of trust?

7 The just walk in integrity;
    happy are their children after them!

8 A king seated on the throne of judgment
    dispels all evil with his glance.†

9 Who can say, "I have made my heart
     clean,g
    I am cleansed of my sin"?‡

10 Varying weights, varying measures,
    are both an abomination to the
       LORD.h

11 In their actions even children can
       playact
    though their deeds be blameless and
       right.§

12 The ear that hears, the eye that sees—
    the LORD has made them both.¶

13 Do not love sleep lest you be reduced to
       poverty;
    keep your eyes open, have your fill
       of food.

14 "Bad, bad!" says the buyer,
    then goes away only to boast."

15 One can put on gold and abundant
       jewels,
    but wise lips are the most precious
       ornament.††

16 Take the garment of the one who became
       surety for a stranger;i
    if for foreigners, exact the pledge!‡‡

17 Bread earned by deceit is sweet,
    but afterward the mouth is filled
       with gravel.

18 Plans made with advice succeed;
    with wise direction wage your war.

19 A slanderer reveals secrets;
    so have nothing to do with a
       babbler!

20 Those who curse father or mother—
    their lamp will go out§§ in the dead
       of night.j

21 Possessions greedily guarded at the
       outset
    will not be blessed in the end.¶¶

22 Do not say, "I will repay evil!"
    Wait for the LORD, who will help
       you.***k

23 Varying weights are an abomination to
       the LORD,
    and false scales are not good.l

24 Our steps are from the LORD;m
    how, then, can mortals understand
       their way?†††

25 It is a trap to pledge rashly a sacred gift,
    and after a vow, then to reflect.‡‡‡

26 A wise king winnows the wicked,
    and threshes them under the
       cartwheel.§§§

27 A lamp from the LORD is human
       life-breath;
    it searches through the inmost
       being.¶¶¶

28 His steadfast loyalty safeguards the king,
    and he upholds his throne by
       justice.n

29 The glory of the young is their strength,
    and the dignity of the old is gray hair.o

30 Evil is cleansed away by bloody lashes,
    and a scourging to the inmost being.

## CHAPTER 21

1 A king's heart is channeled water in the
    hand of the LORD;

---

§§[20:20] **Their lamp will go out**: misfortune, even death, awaits them; cf. 13:9; Ex 21:17.

¶¶[20:21] By definition, an inheritance is not gained by one's own efforts but is received as a gift. If, when one first receives the inheritance, one drives everyone away, one treats it as if one acquired it by one's own efforts. In an agricultural society, an inheritance would often be a field that would require God's blessing to be fertile.

***[20:22] Appointing oneself an agent of divine retribution is dangerous. Better to wait for God to effect justice. Cf. 24:17–18.

†††[20:24] An indication of the Lord's inscrutable providence; cf. Jer 10:23; see Prv 21:2; cf. also 14:12.

‡‡‡[20:25] This verse cautions against making vows without proper reflection; cf. Dt 23:22–25; Eccl 5:4–5.

§§§[20:26] The king is responsible for effecting justice. Judgment is portrayed in agricultural imagery—exposing grain to a current of air so that the chaff is blown away, and passing a wheel over the cereal to break the husk. Winnowing as image for judgment is found throughout the Bible.

¶¶¶[20:27] A parallel is drawn between the life-breath that is God's gift (Jb 32:8; 33:2) coursing through the human body (Is 2:22) and the lamp of God, which can be a symbol of divine scrutiny. In Zep 1:12, God declares, "And in that day I will search through Jerusalem with lamps."

---

*[20:5] The heart is where human plans are made and stored; they remain "deep water" until words reveal them to others. The wise know how to draw up those waters, i.e., express them. Cf. 18:4.

†[20:8] The royal throne is established in justice and the king is the agent of that justice.

‡[20:9] A claim to sinlessness can be merely self-deception; see 16:2; cf. also 15:11.

§[20:11] The verb in colon A can mean either "to make oneself known" or "to play another person" (as in Gn 42:7 and 1 Kgs 14:5, 6). The second meaning makes a better parallel to colon B. The meaning is that if a child can playact, an adult can do so even more. Actions do not always reveal character.

¶[20:12] Human judgments are not ultimate; the Lord expects proper use of these faculties.

**[20:14] Bartering invites playacting and masking one's true intent. The truth of words depends on their context.

††[20:15] Wisdom is said to be preferable to gold in 3:14; 8:10, 19; 16:16. Colon B suggests that the gold and jewelry here are ornaments for the face (cf. Gn 24:53; Ex 3:22; Is 61:10). Wise lips are the most beautiful adornment, for they display the wisdom of the heart.

‡‡[20:16] The text is not clear. See 27:13. Caution in becoming surety is always advised (cf. 6:1–3), and it is especially advisable with strangers.

---

f. [20:5] Prv 18:4.   g. [20:9] 1 Kgs 8:46; 2 Chr 6:36; Eccl 7:20; 1 Jn 1:8.   h. [20:10] Prv 11:1; 20:23.   i. [20:16] Prv 27:13.

j. [20:20] Prv 30:11, 17; Ex 21:17; Lv 20:9; Mt 15:4.   k. [20:22] Prv 24:29; Sir 28:1; Mt 5:39; Rom 12:17, 19; 1 Thes 5:15; 1 Pt 3:9.   l. [20:23] Prv 11:1; 20:10.   m. [20:24] Prv 16:9.   n. [20:28] Prv 16:12.   o. [20:29] Prv 16:31.

God directs it where he pleases.*

2 All your ways may be straight in your
      own eyes,
   but it is the LORD who weighs
      hearts.ᵖ

3 To do what is right and justᵈ
   is more acceptable to the LORD than
      sacrifice.†

4 Haughty eyes and a proud heart—
   the lamp of the wicked will fail.‡

5 The plans of the diligent end in profit,
   but those of the hasty end in loss.§

6 Trying to get rich by lying
   is chasing a bubble over deadly
      snares.

7 The violence of the wicked will sweep
      them away,
   because they refuse to do what is
      right.

8 One's path may be winding and
      unfamiliar,
   but one's conduct is blameless and
      right.¶

9 It is better to dwell in a corner of the
      housetop
   than in a mansion with a
      quarrelsome woman.**ʳ

10 The soul of the wicked desires evil;
   their neighbor finds no pity in their
      eyes.

11 When scoffers are punished the naive
      become wise;
   when the wise succeed, they gain
      knowledge.ˢ

12 The Righteous One appraises the house of
      the wicked,
   bringing down the wicked to ruin.††

13 Those who shut their ears to the cry of the
      poor
   will themselves call out and not be
      answered.

14 A secret gift allays anger,
   and a present concealed, violent
      wrath.‡‡

15 When justice is done it is a joy for the
      just,
   downfall for evildoers.§§ᵗ

16 Whoever strays from the way of good
      sense
   will abide in the assembly of the
      shades.¶¶

17 The lover of pleasure will suffer want;
   the lover of wine and perfume will
      never be rich.

18 The wicked serve as ransom for the just,
   and the faithless for the upright.***ᵘ

19 It is better to dwell in a wilderness
   than with a quarrelsome wife and
      trouble.

20 Precious treasure and oil are in the house
      of the wise,
   but the fool consumes them.

21 Whoever pursues justice and kindness
   will find life and honor.†††

22 The wise person storms the city of the
      mighty,
   and overthrows the stronghold in
      which they trust.

23 Those who guard mouth and tongue
   guard themselves‡‡‡ from trouble.ᵛ

24 Proud, boastful—scoffer is the name:
   those who act with overbearing
      pride.

25 The desire of sluggards will slay them,
   for their hands refuse to work.§§§

---

*[21:1] "Channeled water" in Is 32:2 and Prv 5:16 is water that fertilizes arid land. It takes great skill to direct water, whether it be water to fertilize fields or cosmic floods harnessed at creation, for water is powerful and seems to have a mind of its own. It also requires great skill to direct the heart of a king, for it is inscrutable and beyond ordinary human control.

†[21:3] External rites or sacrifices do not please God unless accompanied by internal worship and right moral conduct; cf. 15:8; 21:27; Is 1:11–15; Am 5:22; Mal 1:12.

‡[21:4] Heart and eyes depict, respectively, the inner and the outer person. "Haughty eyes" peering out from a "proud heart" show a thoroughly arrogant person. How can such a person flourish! Their lamp, which signifies life, will go out.

§[21:5] The antitheses are diligent and impetuous. The metaphor characterizing each type is taken from the world of commerce. Planning is important; bustle leads to waste.

¶[21:8] One cannot always read others' hearts from their behavior. Unconventional conduct need not indicate evil motives.

**[21:9] In Proverbs, two great obstacles to a happy household are foolish children and quarrelsome spouses. The nagging wife is also mentioned in 19:13 and 27:15; 25:24 is a duplicate.

††[21:12] It is difficult to ascertain the subject of the saying. Some hold it is the Lord, the "Righteous One," who is normally the executor of justice in Proverbs. Others believe it is the just person who is the agent of divine justice. "Righteous One" is a title for God in Is 24:16. The best argument

for making God the subject of the verb is that elsewhere in Proverbs righteous human beings never do anything to the wicked; only God does.

‡‡[21:14] Proverbs offers several remedies for anger—a soft word (15:1), patience, and a bribe. The last remedy implies a certain disdain for the disordered passion of anger, for it can be so easily assuaged by a discreetly offered "gift."

§§[21:15] The second line is a duplicate of 10:29b.

¶¶[21:16] **Assembly of the shades**: those who dwell in Sheol.

***[21:18] In this bold paradox, the ransom that protects the righteous is the wicked person who attracts, like a lightning rod, the divine wrath that might have been directed at the righteous.

†††[21:21] The paradox is that one comes upon something other than what one pursued. The way to (long and healthy) life and honor is the vigorous pursuit of virtue.

‡‡‡[21:23] **Themselves**: see note on 13:3. To guard your "self" (lit., "throat," the moist and breathing center of the body, by metonymy, "life"), you must guard your tongue. Speech in Proverbs is the quintessential human activity and often has a meaning broader than speech alone; it can stand for all human activity. Acting rightly is the best way to protect yourself from evil.

§§§[21:25] Desire, or appetite, is the impulse toward food and drink (see Ps 42:3) which spurs animals and human beings into action. But sluggards cannot lift hand to mouth; they bury their hand in the dish (19:24), and so their appetite is thwarted.

---

p. [21:2] Prv 16:2.    q. [21:3] 1 Sm 15:22; Hos 6:6.    r. [21:9] Prv 21:19; 25:24; 27:15; Sir 25:23.    s. [21:11] Prv 19:25.

t. [21:15] Prv 10:29.    u. [21:18] Prv 11:8.    v. [21:23] Prv 13:3.

<sup>26</sup> Some are consumed with avarice all the
        day,
     but the just give unsparingly.
<sup>27</sup> The sacrifice of the wicked is an
        abomination,
     the more so when they offer it with
        bad intent.<sup>w</sup>
<sup>28</sup> The false witness will perish,<sup>x</sup>
     but one who listens will give lasting
        testimony.
<sup>29</sup> The face of the wicked hardens,
     but the upright maintains a straight
        course.<sup>*</sup>
<sup>30</sup> No wisdom, no understanding,
     no counsel prevail against the
        LORD.
<sup>31</sup> The horse is equipped for the day of
        battle,
     but victory is the LORD's.

### CHAPTER 22

<sup>1</sup> A good name is more desirable than great
        riches,
     and high esteem, than gold and
        silver.<sup>†y</sup>
<sup>2</sup> Rich and poor have a common bond:
     the LORD is the maker of them all.<sup>z</sup>
<sup>3</sup> The astute see an evil and hide,
     while the naive continue on and pay
        the penalty.<sup>‡a</sup>
<sup>4</sup> The result of humility and fear of the
        LORD
     is riches, honor and life.<sup>§</sup>
<sup>5</sup> Thorns and snares are on the path of the
        crooked;
     those who would safeguard their
        lives will avoid them.
<sup>6</sup> Train the young in the way they should
        go;
     even when old, they will not swerve
        from it.<sup>¶</sup>

<sup>7</sup> The rich rule over the poor,
     and the borrower is the slave of the
        lender.<sup>**</sup>
<sup>8</sup> Those who sow iniquity reap calamity,<sup>b</sup>
     and the rod used in anger will fail.<sup>††</sup>
<sup>9</sup> The generous will be blessed,
     for they share their food with the
        poor.
<sup>10</sup> Expel the arrogant and discord goes too;
     strife and insult cease.
<sup>11</sup> The LORD loves the pure of heart;<sup>c</sup>
     the person of winning speech has a
        king for a friend.
<sup>12</sup> The eyes of the LORD watch over the
        knowledgeable,
     but he defeats the projects of the
        faithless.
<sup>13</sup> The sluggard says, "A lion is outside;<sup>d</sup>
     I might be slain in the street."<sup>‡‡</sup>
<sup>14</sup> The mouth of the foreign woman is a deep
        pit;<sup>e</sup>
     whoever incurs the LORD's anger
        will fall into it.
<sup>15</sup> Folly is bound to the heart of a youth,
     but the rod of discipline will drive
        it out.<sup>§§</sup>
<sup>16</sup> Oppressing the poor for enrichment,
     giving to the rich: both are sheer
        loss.<sup>¶¶</sup>

### IV. SAYINGS OF THE WISE<sup>***</sup>

pronoun in the Hebrew phrase, lit., "his own way." The most
natural solution is to take the whole as ironic advice (like
19:27): yes, go ahead and let the young do exactly what they
want; they will become self-willed adults.

**[22:7] An observation on money and power. One who bor-
rows becomes poor in the sense of indebted, a slave to the lender.

††[22:8] Agricultural metaphors express the failure of malicious actions. In the first line, bad actions are seeds yielding
trouble. In the second line, "the rod" is a flail used to beat
grains as in Is 28:27.

‡‡[22:13] To avoid the effort required for action, the sluggard exaggerates the difficulties that must be overcome.

§§[22:15] Folly is attached to children as the husk is
attached to the grain. "Rod" here, as in v. 8, seems to be the
flail. Discipline is the process of winnowing away the folly.

¶¶[22:16] A difficult saying. One possibility is to take it as a
seemingly neutral observation on the plight of the poor: taking money from the poor is relatively easy for the powerful
but it is dangerous as the poor have the Lord as their defender
(24:22–23), who will punish their oppressors. Giving to the
rich, perhaps to win their favor by presents and bribes, is
equally a waste of money, for the rich will always do what they
please in any case.

***[22:17–24:22] This collection consists of an introduction
(22:17–21) urging openness and stating the purpose of the
Words and diverse admonitions, aphorisms, and counsels. It
is written with faith in the Lord, shrewdness, and a satirical
eye. The first part seems aimed at young people intent on a
career (22:22–23:11); the second is taken up with the concerns
of youth (23:12–35); the third part is interested in the ultimate
fate of the good and the wicked (24:1–22). The whole can be
described as a guidebook of professional ethics. The aim is to
inculcate trust in the Lord and to help readers avoid trouble
and advance their careers by living according to wisdom. Its
outlook is very practical: avoid bad companions because in
time you will take on some of their qualities; do not post bond
for others because you yourself will be encumbered; do not

*[21:29] The wicked cannot deter the righteous from
walking the straight path, i.e., from practicing virtue.

†[22:1] "Good name" (Heb. *shem*) and "high esteem"
(Heb. *chen*) are declared to be of more value than great riches.
Human beings belong to a community and without the acceptance of that community, which is built on esteem and trust,
human life is grievously damaged. Riches are less essential to
the human spirit.

‡[22:3] The wise see dangers before they are engulfed by
them whereas fools, through dullness or boldness, march
right on.

§[22:4] Humiliation can be an occasion for knowing one's
place in God's world. Such knowledge is part of fear (or revering) of the Lord. Revering the Lord brings the blessings of
wealth, honor, and long life. The saying is perhaps meant to
counter the view that humiliation is an unmixed evil; something good can come of it.

¶[22:6] One of the few exhortations in the collection (cf.
14:7; 16:3; 19:18, 20). "Way" in the first colon has been taken
in two different senses: (1) the morally right way, "according
to the way one ought to go"; (2) personal aptitude, i.e., the
manner of life for which one is destined, as "the way of Egypt"
(Is 10:24). Neither interpretation, however, accounts for the

w. [21:27] Prv 15:8; Sir 34:21–23.   x. [21:28] Prv 19:5, 9.   y. [22:1]
Eccl 7:1.   z. [22:2] Prv 29:13.   a. [22:3] Prv 27:12.

b. [22:8] Jb 4:8; Sir 7:3; Hos 8:7.   c. [22:11] Mt 5:8.   d. [22:13] Prv
26:13.   e. [22:14] Prv 23:27.

<sup>17</sup> The Words of the Wise:<sup>*</sup>
Incline your ear, and hear my words,<sup>f</sup>
and let your mind attend to my
teaching;
<sup>18</sup> For it will be well if you hold them within
you,
if they all are ready on your lips.
<sup>19</sup> That your trust may be in the LORD,
I make them known to you today—
yes, to you.
<sup>20</sup> Have I not written for you thirty sayings,
containing counsels and knowledge,
<sup>21</sup> To teach you truly
how to give a dependable report to
one who sends you?
<sup>22</sup> Do not rob the poor because they are poor,
nor crush the needy at the gate;<sup>†</sup>
<sup>23</sup> For the LORD will defend their cause,<sup>g</sup>
and will plunder those who plunder
them.
<sup>24</sup> Do not be friendly with hotheads,
nor associate with the wrathful,
<sup>25</sup> Lest you learn their ways,
and become ensnared.
<sup>26</sup> Do not be one of those who give their
hand in pledge,
those who become surety for debts;<sup>h</sup>

<sup>27</sup> For if you are unable to pay,
your bed will be taken from under
you.<sup>‡</sup>
<sup>28</sup> Do not remove the ancient landmark<sup>§</sup>
that your ancestors set up.<sup>i</sup>
<sup>29</sup> Do you see those skilled at their work?
They will stand in the presence of
kings,
but not in the presence of the obscure.

## CHAPTER 23

<sup>1</sup> ¶When you sit down to dine with a ruler,
mark well the one who is before you;
<sup>2</sup> Stick the knife in your gullet<sup>**</sup>
if you have a ravenous appetite.
<sup>3</sup> Do not desire his delicacies;
it is food that deceives.
<sup>4</sup> Do not wear yourself out to gain wealth,
cease to be worried about it;
<sup>5</sup> When your glance flits to it, it is gone!
For assuredly it grows wings,
like the eagle that flies toward
heaven.<sup>††</sup>
<sup>6</sup> ‡‡Do not take food with unwilling hosts,
and do not desire their delicacies;
<sup>7</sup> For like something stuck in the throat is
that food.
"Eat and drink," they say to you,
but their hearts are not with you;
<sup>8</sup> The little you have eaten you will vomit
up,

promote yourself too aggressively because such promotion is self-defeating; do not abuse sex or alcohol because they will harm you; do not emulate your peers if they are wicked (23:14; 24:1, 19) because such people have no future. Rather, trust the vocation of a sage (22:29–23:9).

The Egyptian *Instructions of Amenemope* (written ca. 1100 B.C.) was discovered in 1923. Scholars immediately recognized it as a source of Prv 22:17–23:11. The Egyptian work has thirty chapters (cf. Prv 22:20); its preface resembled Prv 22:17–21; its first two admonitions matched the first two in Proverbs (Prv 22:22–25). There are many other resemblances as well, some of which are pointed out in the notes. The instruction of a father to his son (or an administrator to his successor) was a well-known genre in Egypt; seventeen works are extant, spanning the period from 2500 B.C. to the first century A.D. The instructions aimed to help a young person live a happy and prosperous life and avoid mistakes that cause difficulties. They make concrete and pragmatic suggestions rather than hold up abstract ideals. Pragmatic though they were, the instructions were religious; they assumed that the gods implanted an order in the world (Egyptian *maat*), which is found both in nature and in the human world. *Amenemope* represents a stage in the development of the Egyptian genre, displaying a new inwardness and quest for serenity while still assuming that the practice of virtue brings worldly success. Proverbs borrows from the Egyptian work with great freedom: it does not, for example, import as such the Egyptian concept of order; it engages the reader with its characteristic wit, irony, and paradox (e.g., 22:26–27; 23:1–3).

\*[22:17–23:35] The maxims warn against: robbing the poor and defenseless (22:22–23), anger (22:24–25), giving surety for debts (22:26–27), advancing oneself by socializing with rulers (23:1–2), anxiety for riches (23:4–5), forcing oneself on a grudging host (23:6–8), intemperance in food and drink (23:19–21, 29–35), and adultery (23:26–28). They exhort to: careful workmanship (22:29), respect for the rights of orphans (23:10–11), correction of the young (23:13–14), filial piety (23:15–16, 22–25), and fear of the Lord (23:17–18).

†[22:22] **At the gate**: of the city, where justice was administered and public affairs discussed; cf. Ru 4:1. Cf. also Ps 69:13; 127:5; Prv 24:7; 31:23, 31. The Lord will personally avenge those who have no one to defend them.

f. [22:17] Prv 5:1.   g. [22:23] Prv 23:11.   h. [22:26] Prv 6:1–2; 11:15; 17:18.

‡[22:27] Providing surety for a debtor puts one in danger of having the very basics of one's life suddenly seized.

§[22:28] **Landmark**: marks the boundary of property. To remove it is the equivalent of stealing land. A similar warning is contained in 23:10.

¶[23:1–9] Four admonitions for someone aspiring to be a sage: be careful about advancing your career by socializing with the great (vv. 1–3); avoid greed (vv. 4–5); do not force yourself on an unwilling host (vv. 6–8); do not waste your wisdom on those who cannot profit from it (v. 9).

**[23:2] **Stick the knife in your gullet**: a metaphor for self-restraint. The usual translation, "Put a knife to your throat," is misleading, for in English it is a death threat. The exhortation is humorously exaggerated: stick the table-knife in your own gullet rather than take too much food. It assumes that the young courtier is unused to opulent banquets and will be tempted to overindulge.

††[23:5] The frustration of covetous intent and elusiveness of wealth are portrayed by the sudden flight of an eagle. *Amenemope*, chap. 7, has a similar statement: "Do not set your heart on wealth. There is no ignoring Fate and Destiny; / Do not let your heart go straying." Proverbs imagines covetous intent as a flight of the eyes, whereas *Amenemope* imagines it as a straying of the heart.

‡‡[23:6–8] Some humorous advice on not trading on the courtesy of unwilling hosts who, for convention's sake, use the language of welcome. *Amenemope*, chap. 11, gives similar advice: "Do not intrude on a man in his house, / Enter when you have been called; / He may say 'Welcome' with his mouth, / Yet deride you in his thoughts." "Unwilling," lit., "evil of eye," is usually translated "stingy," but the context suggests unwilling. In v. 8, the unwanted guest vomits up the food, thus destroying the desired good impression. Proverbs regards the uninvited banqueters as thieves who will suffer the consequences of their theft. *Amenemope*, chap. 11, is relevant: "Do not covet a poor man's goods, . . . A poor man's goods are a block in the throat, / It makes the gullet vomit."

i. [22:28] Prv 23:10; Dt 19:14; 27:17.

and you will have wasted your
    agreeable words.
9 Do not speak in the hearing of fools;
    they will despise the wisdom of your
    words.[j]
10 Do not remove the ancient landmark,[k]
    nor invade the fields of the
    fatherless;*
11 For their redeemer is strong;
    he will defend their cause against
    you.[l]
12 Apply your heart to instruction,
    and your ear to words of knowledge.
13 †Do not withhold discipline from youths;
    if you beat them with the rod, they
    will not die.[m]
14 Beat them with the rod,[n]
    and you will save them from Sheol.
15 My son, if your heart is wise,
    my heart also will rejoice;
16 And my inmost being will exult,
    when your lips speak what is right.
17 Do not let your heart envy sinners,[o]
    but only those who always fear the
    LORD;‡
18 For you will surely have a future,
    and your hope will not be cut off.[p]
19 Hear, my son, and be wise,
    and guide your heart in the right
    way.
20 Do not join with wine bibbers,
    nor with those who glut themselves
    on meat.
21 For drunkards and gluttons come to
    poverty,
    and lazing about clothes one in rags.
22 §Listen to your father who begot you,
    do not despise your mother when
    she is old.
23 Buy truth and do not sell:
    wisdom, instruction, understanding!
24 The father of a just person will exult
    greatly;
    whoever begets a wise son will
    rejoice in him.[q]

25 Let your father and mother rejoice;
    let her who bore you exult.
26 'My son, give me your heart,
    and let your eyes keep to my ways,
27 For the harlot is a deep pit,
    and the foreign woman a narrow
    well;
28 Yes, she lies in wait like a robber,[r]
    and increases the number of the
    faithless.
29 "Who scream? Who shout?
    Who have strife? Who have anxiety?
Who have wounds for nothing?
    Who have bleary eyes?
30 Whoever linger long over wine,
    whoever go around quaffing wine.[s]
31 Do not look on the wine when it is red,
    when it sparkles in the cup.
It goes down smoothly,
32     but in the end it bites like a serpent,
    and stings like an adder.
33 Your eyes behold strange sights,
    and your heart utters incoherent
    things;
34 You are like one sleeping on the high
    seas,
    sprawled at the top of the mast.
35 "They struck me, but it did not pain me;
    they beat me, but I did not feel it.
When can I get up,
    when can I go out and get more?"††

## CHAPTER 24

1 ‡‡Do not envy the wicked,
    nor desire to be with them;[t]
2 For their hearts plot violence,
    and their lips speak of foul play.
3 By wisdom a house is built,
    by understanding it is established;
4 And by knowledge its rooms are filled
    with every precious and pleasing
    possession.
5 The wise are more powerful than the
    strong,
    and the learned, than the mighty,[u]

---

*[23:10] In Israel ownership of property and other legal rights were vested mainly in the father as head of the family; thus the widow and fatherless child were vulnerable, left prey to those who would exploit them.

†[23:13–14] The young will not die from instructional blows but from their absence, for (premature) death results from uncorrected folly. The sardonic humor means the exhortation is not to be taken literally, as an argument for corporal punishment. The next verses (vv. 15–16) are exceedingly tender toward the young.

‡[23:17] Those whom one admires or associates with exercise enormous influence. Do not join the wicked, who are a doomed group. The warning is repeated in 24:1–2, 19–20.

§[23:22–23] Father and mother are associated with truth and wisdom. One should no more rid oneself of truth and wisdom than rid oneself of one's parents, who are their source.

¶[23:26–28] The exhortation is a condensed version of chap. 7 with its emotional appeal to "my son" to avoid the forbidden woman (7:1–5), her traps (7:21–23), and her intent to add the youth to her list of victims (7:24–27). As in 23:15, 19, 22, a trustful and affectionate relationship between student and teacher is the basis of teaching. The danger of the woman is expressed in imagery that has sexual overtones (cf. 22:14).

**[23:29–35] A vivid description of the evil effects, physical and psychological, of drunkenness. The emphasis is on the unwise behavior, the folly, caused by alcohol. Cf. 20:1.

††[23:35] Drunkards become insensible to bodily and moral harm. Their one desire is to indulge again.

‡‡[24:1–22] A new section (24:1–14)—on the fates of the wicked and foolish—begins with a warning not to take the foolish as role models. The same admonition is repeated in 23:17–18 and 24:19–20. In 24:1, the verb means "to be jealous, zealous; to emulate." The motive stated in the other passages—the wicked have no future—is indirectly stated here.

---

j. [23:9] Prv 9:7.  k. [23:10] Prv 22:28.  l. [23:11] Prv 23:23.
m. [23:13] Prv 13:24; 19:18; Sir 30:1.  n. [23:14] Prv 29:15, 17.
o. [23:17] Prv 3:31; 24:1, 19.  p. [23:18] Prv 24:14.  q. [23:24] Prv 10:1.

r. [23:28] Prv 7:10–27.  s. [23:30] Prv 20:1; Sir 19:2; Hos 4:11.
t. [24:1] Prv 3:31; 23:17; Ps 37:1.  u. [24:5] Prv 21:22.

6 For by strategy war is waged,
  and victory depends on many
  counselors.[v]
7 *Wise words are beyond fools' reach,[w]
  in the assembly they do not open
  their mouth;
8 As they calculate how to do evil,
  people brand them troublemakers.
9 The scheme of a fool gains no acceptance,
  the scoffer is an abomination to the
  community.
10 †Did you fail in a day of adversity,
   did your strength fall short?
11 Did you fail to rescue those who were
   being dragged off to death,‡
   those tottering, those near death,
12 because you said, "We didn't know
   about it"?
   Surely, the Searcher of hearts knows
   and will repay all according to their
   deeds.[x]
13 §If you eat honey, my son, because it is
   good,
   if pure honey is sweet to your taste,
14 Such, you must know, is wisdom to your
   soul.
   If you find it, you will have a future,
   and your hope will not be cut off.[y]
15 ¶Do not lie in wait at the abode of the just,
   do not ravage their dwelling places;
16 Though the just fall seven times, they rise
   again,
   but the wicked stumble from only
   one mishap.
17 **Do not rejoice when your enemies fall,
   and when they stumble, do not let
   your heart exult,
18 Lest the LORD see it, be displeased with
   you,
   and withdraw his wrath from your
   enemies.
19 Do not be provoked at evildoers,
   do not envy the wicked;

20 For the evil have no future,
   the lamp of the wicked will be put
   out.[z]
21 My son, fear the LORD and the king;
   have nothing to do with those who
   hate them;
22 For disaster will issue suddenly,
   and calamity from them both, who
   knows when?

## V. FURTHER SAYINGS OF THE WISE††

23 These also are Words of the Wise:
   To show partiality in judgment is not
   good.[a]
24 Whoever says to the guilty party, "You are
   innocent,"
   will be cursed by nations, scorned
   by peoples;
25 But those who render just verdicts will
   fare well,
   and on them will come the blessing
   of prosperity.
26 An honest reply—
   a kiss on the lips.‡‡
27 Complete your outdoor tasks,
   and arrange your work in the field;
   afterward you can build your house.§§
28 Do not testify falsely against your
   neighbor[b]
   and so deceive with your lips.
29 Do not say, "As they did to me, so will I
   do to them;[c]
   I will repay them according to their
   deeds."¶¶

---

††[24:23–34] A little collection between the thirty sayings of 22:17–24:22 and the Hezekiah collection in chaps. 25–29. Its title (v. 23) suggests that editors took it as an appendix. At this point, the Greek edition of Proverbs begins to arrange the later sections of the book in a different order than the Hebrew edition.

An editor has arranged originally separate sayings into two parallel groups.

|                     | I.                        | II.                    |
|---------------------|---------------------------|------------------------|
| Conduct in court:   | Judges (vv. 24–25)        | Witnesses (v. 28)      |
| Speaking, thinking: | Good speech (v. 26)       | Bad speech (v. 29)     |
| Wisdom in work:     | Positive (v. 27)          | Negative (vv. 30–34)   |

‡‡[24:26] The kiss is a gesture of respect and affection. The greatest sign of affection and respect for another is to tell that person the truth.

§§[24:27] **House**: can refer to both the building and the family (cf. 2 Sm 7). In the context established by the placement noted above under 24:23, the saying means that neglect of one's field is a sign that one is not building the house properly. In an agricultural society especially, the concept of household includes fields for animals and crops. On the metaphorical level, one must lay a careful preparation before embarking on a great project. This verse is sometimes interpreted as advocating careful and practical preparation for marriage.

¶¶[24:29] Retribution is a long and complex process that belongs to the Lord, not to individuals. Cf. vv. 12d, 17–18.

---

*[24:7–9] The verses are unclear; most scholars take them as two or even three single sayings, but, taken singly, the verses are banal. They are best taken as a single statement. Just as vv. 3–6 described the advantages of wisdom, so vv. 7–9 describe the disadvantages of its opposite, folly: it alienates one from the community (v. 7), for fools become notorious (v. 8), dooming their plans and ostracizing themselves.

†[24:10–12] Excuses for not coming to the aid of one's neighbor in serious trouble do not suffice before God, who sees through self-serving excuses.

‡[24:11] **Rescue . . . death**: perhaps refers to the legal rescue of those unjustly condemned to death.

§[24:13–14] God's word is sometimes said to be sweeter than honey, e.g., Ps 119:101–103. Cf. also Ps 19:11; Prv 16:24; Ez 3:3; Sir 24:19–22.

¶[24:15–16] The just will overcome every misfortune that oppresses them. *Seven times* is an indefinite number.

**[24:17–18] The admonition is linked to the previous by the words "fall" and "stumble." Premature public celebration of the downfall of enemies equivalently preempts the retribution that belongs to God.

---

v. [24:6] Prv 20:18.  w. [24:7] Sir 6:21.  x. [24:12] Ps 62:13; Sir 16:12; Mt 16:27; Rom 2:6.  y. [24:14] Prv 23:18.

z. [24:20] Prv 13:9.  a. [24:23] Prv 18:5; 28:21; Lv 19:15; Dt 1:17; 16:19.  b. [24:28] Prv 19:5; 25:18.  c. [24:29] Prv 20:22.

30 'I passed by the field of a sluggard,
  by the vineyard of one with no sense;
31 It was all overgrown with thistles;
  its surface was covered with nettles,
  and its stone wall broken down.
32 As I gazed at it, I reflected;
  I saw and learned a lesson:
33 A little sleep, a little slumber,[d]
  a little folding of the arms to rest—
34 Then poverty will come upon you like a
  robber,
  and want like a brigand.

## VI. SECOND SOLOMONIC COLLECTION, COLLECTED UNDER KING HEZEKIAH[†]

### CHAPTER 25

1 These also are proverbs of Solomon.[e] The servants of Hezekiah,[‡] king of Judah, transmitted them.

2 §It is the glory of God to conceal a matter,
  and the glory of kings to fathom a
  matter.¶
3 Like the heavens in height, and the earth
  in depth,
  the heart of kings is unfathomable.
4 "Remove the dross from silver,
  and it comes forth perfectly purified;
5 Remove the wicked from the presence of
  the king,
  and his throne is made firm through
  justice.
6 ††Claim no honor in the king's presence,
  nor occupy the place of superiors;

7 For it is better to be told, "Come up
  closer!"
  than to be humbled before the
  prince.[f]
8 What your eyes have seen
  do not bring forth too quickly
  against an opponent;
  For what will you do later on
  when your neighbor puts you to
  shame?
9 ‡‡Argue your own case with your
  neighbor,
  but the secrets of others do not
  disclose;
10 Lest, hearing it, they reproach you,
  and your ill repute never ceases.
11 Golden apples in silver settings
  are words spoken at the proper time.
12 A golden earring or a necklace of fine
  gold—
  one who gives wise reproof to a
  listening ear.
13 Like the coolness of snow in the heat of
  the harvest
  are faithful messengers for those
  who send them,
  lifting the spirits of their masters.
14 Clouds and wind but no rain—
  the one who boasts of a gift not
  given.
15 By patience is a ruler persuaded,[g]
  and a soft tongue can break a bone.
16 §§If you find honey, eat only what you
  need,
  lest you have your fill and vomit
  it up.
17 Let your foot be seldom in your
  neighbors' house,
  lest they have their fill of you—and
  hate you.
18 A club, sword, or sharp arrow—
  the one who bears false witness
  against a neighbor.[h]
19 A bad tooth or an unsteady foot—
  a trust betrayed in time of trouble.¶¶
20 Like the removal of clothes on a cold day,
  or vinegar on soda,
  is the one who sings to a troubled
  heart.

*[24:30–34] Neglect of one's fields through laziness ruins all plans to build a house (v. 27). This vignette is a teaching story, like those in 7:1–27; Ps 37:35–36.

†[25:1–29:27] Chaps. 25–29 make up the fifth collection in the book, and the third longest. King Hezekiah reigned in Judah in 715–687 B.C. According to 2 Kgs 18–20 and 2 Chr 29–32, he initiated political and religious reforms after the destruction of the Northern Kingdom in 722 B.C. Such reforms probably included copying and editing sacred literature such as Proverbs. Prv 25:1 is an important piece of evidence about the composition of the book, suggesting this collection was added to an already-existing collection also attributed to Solomon. The older collection is probably 10:1–22:16 (or part of it). By the end of the eighth century B.C., therefore, there existed in Israel two large collections of aphorisms.

Chap. 25 has two general themes: (1) social hierarchy, rank, or position; (2) social conflict and its resolution.

‡[25:1] The servants of Hezekiah: presumably scribes at the court of Hezekiah. Transmitted: lit., "to move, transfer from," hence "to collect," and perhaps also to arrange and compose.

§[25:2–7] The topic is the king—who he is (vv. 2–3) and how one is to behave in his presence (vv. 4–7).

¶[25:2] God and king were closely related in the ancient world and in the Bible. The king had a special responsibility for divine justice. Hence, God would give him special wisdom to search it out.

**[25:4–5] Wisdom involves virtue as well as knowledge. As in Ps 101 the king cannot tolerate any wickedness in the royal service.

††[25:6–7] An admonition with a practical motive for putting the teaching into practice. Pragmatic shrewdness suggests

that we not promote ourselves but let others do it for us. See Lk 14:7–11.

‡‡[25:9–10] Another admonition on the use of law courts to settle personal disputes. Speak privately with your opponent lest others' personal business become public and they resent you.

§§[25:16–17] The two admonitions are complementary, expressing nicely the need to restrain the inclination for delightful things, whether for honey or friendship.

¶¶[25:19] "A time of trouble" defeats all plans (cf. 10:2; 11:4). At such times human resources alone are like a tooth that falls out as one bites or a foot that goes suddenly lame.

d. [24:33] Prv 6:10–11.  e. [25:1] Prv 1:1.

f. [25:7] Lk 14:8–10.  g. [25:15] Prv 15:1, 4.  h. [25:18] Ex 20:16.

<sup>21</sup> *If your enemies are hungry, give them
        food to eat,
    if thirsty, give something to drink;<sup>i</sup>
<sup>22</sup> For live coals you will heap on their
        heads,
    and the LORD will vindicate you.
<sup>23</sup> The north wind brings rain,
    and a backbiting tongue, angry looks.
<sup>24</sup> It is better to dwell in a corner of the
        housetop
    than in a mansion with a
        quarrelsome wife.<sup>†j</sup>
<sup>25</sup> Cool water to one faint from thirst
    is good news from a far country.
<sup>26</sup> A trampled fountain or a polluted
        spring—<sup>‡</sup>
    a just person fallen before the wicked.
<sup>27</sup> To eat too much honey is not good;
    nor to seek honor after honor.<sup>§</sup>
<sup>28</sup> A city breached and left defenseless
    are those who do not control their
        temper.

### CHAPTER 26<sup>¶</sup>

<sup>1</sup> Like snow in summer, like rain in harvest,
    honor for a fool is out of place.<sup>**</sup>
<sup>2</sup> Like the sparrow in its flitting, like the
        swallow in its flight,
    a curse uncalled-for never lands.<sup>††</sup>
<sup>3</sup> The whip for the horse, the bridle for the
        ass,
    and the rod for the back of fools.<sup>k</sup>

<sup>4</sup> <sup>‡‡</sup>Do not answer fools according to their
        folly,
    lest you too become like them.
<sup>5</sup> Answer fools according to their folly,
    lest they become wise in their own
        eyes.
<sup>6</sup> Those who send messages by a fool
    cut off their feet; they drink down
        violence.
<sup>7</sup> <sup>§§</sup>A proverb in the mouth of a fool
    hangs limp, like crippled legs.
<sup>8</sup> Giving honor to a fool
    is like entangling a stone in the sling.
<sup>9</sup> A thorn stuck in the hand of a drunkard
    is a proverb in the mouth of fools.
<sup>10</sup> An archer wounding all who pass by
    is anyone who hires a drunken fool.
<sup>11</sup> As dogs return to their vomit,
    so fools repeat their folly.<sup>l</sup>
<sup>12</sup> You see those who are wise in their own
        eyes?
    There is more hope for fools than
        for them.
<sup>13</sup> <sup>¶¶</sup>The sluggard says, "There is a lion in the
        street,
    a lion in the middle of the square!"<sup>m</sup>
<sup>14</sup> The door turns on its hinges
    and sluggards, on their beds.
<sup>15</sup> The sluggard buries a hand in the dish,
    too weary to lift it to the mouth.<sup>n</sup>
<sup>16</sup> In their own eyes sluggards are wiser
    than seven who answer with good
        judgment.
<sup>17</sup> Whoever meddles in the quarrel of
        another
    is one who grabs a passing dog by
        the ears.
<sup>18</sup> Like a crazed archer
    scattering firebrands and deadly
        arrows,
<sup>19</sup> Such are those who deceive their
        neighbor,
    and then say, "I was only joking."
<sup>20</sup> ***Without wood the fire dies out;
    without a talebearer strife subsides.
<sup>21</sup> Charcoal for coals, wood for fire—

---

*[25:21–22] A memorable statement of humanity and
moderation; such sentiments could be occasionally found
even outside the Bible, e.g., "It is better to bless someone than
to do harm to one who has insulted you" (Egyptian *Papyrus
Insinger*). Cf. Ex 23:4 and Lv 19:17–18. Human beings should
not take it upon themselves to exact vengeance, leaving it
rather in God's hands. This saying has in view an enemy's vulnerability in time of need, in this case extreme hunger and
thirst; such a need should not be an occasion for revenge. The
motive for restraining oneself is to allow God's justice to take
its own course, as in 20:22 and 24:17–19. **Live coals**: either
remorse and embarrassment for the harm done, or increased
punishment for refusing reconciliation. Cf. Mt 5:44. Rom
12:20 cites the Greek version and interprets it, "Do not be
overcome by evil but overcome evil with good."

†[25:24] A humorous saying about domestic unhappiness: better to live alone outdoors than indoors with an angry
spouse. Prv 21:9 is identical and 21:19 is similar in thought.

‡[25:26] "Spring" is a common metaphor for source. The
righteous should be a source of life for others. When they fail,
it is as if a spring became foul and its water undrinkable. It is
not clear whether the righteous person yielded to a scoundrel
out of cowardice or was simply defeated by evil. The latter
seems more likely, for other proverbs say the just person will
never "fall" (lit., "be moved," 10:30; 12:3). The fall, even temporary, of a righteous person is a loss of life for others.

§[25:27] **Nor . . . honor**: the text is uncertain.

¶[26:1–28] Concrete images describe the vices of fools (vv.
1–12), of sluggards (vv. 13–16), of meddlers (vv. 17–19), of
talebearers (vv. 20–22), and of flatterers (vv. 23–28).

**[26:1] There is no fit ("out of place") between weather and
agricultural season.

††[26:2] The point is the similarity of actions: a hovering
bird that never lands, a groundless curse that never "lands." It
hangs in the air posing no threat to anyone.

‡‡[26:4–5] There is no contradiction between these two
proverbs. In their answers, the wise must protect their own
interests against fools. Or perhaps the juxtaposition of the two
proverbs suggests that no single proverb can resolve every
problem in life.

§§[26:7–9] Fools either abuse or are unable to use whatever
knowledge they have. **A thorn**: a proverb is "words spoken at the
proper time" (25:11). Fools have no sense of the right time; their
statements are like thorns that fasten on clothing randomly.

¶¶[26:13–16] Each verse mentions the sluggard, whom
Proverbs regards with derision. The criticism is not against
low energy but failure to act and take responsibility. Proverbs'
ideal is the active person who uses heart, lips, hands, feet to
keep to the good path. The verses are examples of the sardonic
humor of the book.

***[26:20–22] The three proverbs have a common theme—
the destructive power of slanderous words. Certain words are
repeated: wood and fire, talebearer.

---

i. [25:21] Rom 12:20.    j. [25:24] Prv 21:9.    k. [26:3] Prv 19:29; Sir
33:25.

l. [26:11] 2 Pt 2:22.    m. [26:13] Prv 22:13.    n. [26:15] Prv 19:24.

such are the quarrelsome,
    enkindling strife.°

22 The words of a talebearer are like dainty
    morsels:
    they sink into one's inmost being.*ᵖ

23 Like a glazed finish on earthenware
    are smooth lips and a wicked heart.†

24 With their lips enemies pretend,
    but inwardly they maintain deceit;

25 When they speak graciously, do not trust
    them,�q
    for seven abominations‡ are in their
    hearts.

26 Hatred can be concealed by pretense,
    but malice will be revealed in the
    assembly.§

27 Whoever digs a pit falls into it;
    and a stone comes back upon the
    one who rolls it.ʳ

28 The lying tongue is its owner's enemy,
    and the flattering mouth works ruin.

## CHAPTER 27

1 Do not boast about tomorrow,
    for you do not know what any day
    may bring forth.

2 Let another praise you, not your own
    mouth;
    a stranger, not your own lips.

3 Stone is heavy, and sand a burden,
    but a fool's provocation is heavier
    than both.ˢ

4 Anger is cruel, and wrath overwhelming,
    but before jealousy who can stand?¶

5 "Better is an open rebuke
    than a love that remains hidden.

6 Trustworthy are the blows of a friend,
    dangerous, the kisses of an enemy.††

7 One who is full spurns honey;
    but to the hungry, any bitter thing
    is sweet.

8 Like a bird far from the nest
    so is anyone far from home.‡‡

9 Perfume and incense bring joy to the heart,
    but by grief the soul is torn asunder.

10 Do not give up your own friend and your
    father's friend;
    do not resort to the house of your
    kindred when trouble strikes.
    Better a neighbor near than kin far away.§§

11 Be wise, my son, and bring joy to my heart,
    so that I can answer whoever taunts
    me.¶¶

12 The astute see an evil and hide;
    the naive continue on and pay the
    penalty.ᵗ

13 Take the garment of the one who became
    surety for a stranger;ᵘ
    if for a foreign woman, exact the
    pledge!***

14 Those who greet their neighbor with
    a loud voice††† in the early
    morning,
    a curse can be laid to their charge.

15 For a persistent leak on a rainy day
    the match is a quarrelsome wife;ᵛ

16 Whoever would hide her hides a
    stormwind
    and cannot tell north from south.

17 Iron is sharpened by iron;
    one person sharpens another.‡‡‡

18 Those who tend a fig tree eat its fruit;
    so those attentive to their master
    will be honored.

19 As face mirrors face in water,
    so the heart reflects the person.

20 Sheol and Abaddon can never be
    satisfied;ʷ
    so the eyes of mortals can never be
    satisfied.§§§

---

*[26:22] Malicious gossip is compared to delicious food that is swallowed and lodges in the deepest recesses of one's body. Negative comments are seldom forgotten. Prv 18:8 is a duplicate.

†[26:23] Heart = what is within, and lips (words) = what is expressed, are compared to an earthenware jar covered with glaze.

‡[26:25] **Seven abominations**: many evil intentions.

§[26:26] Hate may be concealed for a time, but it will eventually issue in a deed and become known in the public assembly. There is a play on words: the consonants of the word "hatred" (*śn*) are literally concealed in the word "pretense" (*mśn*).

¶[27:4] Anger generally subsides with time but jealousy coolly calculates and plots revenge.

**[27:5–6] Verses 5 and 6 are concerned with true friendship. "Better than" sayings often declare one thing superior to another in view of some value, e.g., 15:17, vegetables are better than meat in view of a milieu of love. In v. 5, a rebuke is better than an act of affection in view of discipline that imparts wisdom.

††[27:6] The present translation is conjectural. The meaning seems to be that a friend's rebuke can be life-giving and an enemy's kiss can be deadly (like the kiss of Judas in Mt 26:48).

---

o. [26:21] Prv 15:18; 29:22.  p. [26:22] Prv 18:8.  q. [26:25] Prv 12:10; 27:33.  r. [26:27] Eccl 10:8; Sir 27:25–26.  s. [27:3] Sir 22:14–15.

---

‡‡[27:8] The bird symbolizes vulnerability as it flees before danger as in Is 10:14; 16:2; and Ps 11:1. For the importance of place in human life, see Jb 20:8–9. People are defined by their place, but, tragically, war, poverty, or illness can force them from it.

§§[27:10] The adage is about the difference between friends and kin in a crisis. Two admonitions are grounded in one maxim (colon C). The same Hebrew word means both "one who is near" and "friend." The whole proverb urges the reader to cultivate old family friends and neighbors and not to rely exclusively on kin in times of trouble, for kin may not be there for us.

¶¶[27:11] A father's command to a son to be wise, another way of saying that sons or daughters bring joy or shame to their parents.

***[27:13] See note on 20:16.

†††[27:14] One interpretation takes the proverb as humorous and the other takes it as serious: (1) an overly loud and ill-timed greeting (lit., "blessing") invites the response of a curse rather than a "blessing" (greeting); (2) the loud voice suggests hypocrisy in the greeting.

‡‡‡[27:17] Iron sharpens the "face" (*panim* = surface, edge) of iron, and a human being sharpens the "face" (*panim* = face, words) of another. Human beings learn from each other and grow in wisdom by conversing.

§§§[27:20] Sheol, the underworld abode of the dead, is personified as a force that is never satisfied and always desires

---

t. [27:12] Prv 22:3.  u. [27:13] Prv 20:16.  v. [27:15] Prv 21:9; 25:24.  w. [27:20] Prv 30:16; Eccl 4:8.

21 The crucible for silver, the furnace for
      gold,
      so you must assay the praise you
        receive.
22 Though you pound fools with a pestle,
      their folly never leaves them.
23 Take good care of your flocks,
      give careful attention to your herds;
24 For wealth does not last forever,
      nor even a crown from age to age.
25 When the grass comes up and the new
      growth appears,
      and the mountain greens are
        gathered in,
26 The lambs will provide you with clothing,
      and the goats, the price of a field,
27 And there will be ample goat's milk for
      your food,
      food for your house, sustenance for
        your maidens.

## CHAPTER 28

1 The wicked flee though none pursue;
      but the just, like a lion, are
        confident.
2 If a land is rebellious, its princes will be
      many;
      but with an intelligent and wise
        ruler there is stability.†
3 One who is poor and extorts from the
      lowly
      is a devastating rain that leaves no
        food.‡
4 Those who abandon instruction§ praise
      the wicked,
      but those who keep instruction
        oppose them.
5 The evil understand nothing of justice,¶
      but those who seek the LORD
        understand everything.
6 Better to be poor and walk in integrity
      than rich and crooked in one's ways.ˣ

7 Whoever heeds instruction is a wise son,
      but whoever joins with wastrels
        disgraces his father.
8 Whoever amasses wealth by interest and
      overcharge**
      gathers it for the one who is kind to
        the poor.
9 Those who turn their ears from hearing
      instruction,ʸ
      even their prayer is an abomination.
10 Those who mislead the upright into an
      evil way
      will themselves fall into their own pit,
      but the blameless will attain
        prosperity.
11 The rich are wise in their own eyes,
      but the poor who are intelligent see
        through them.
12 When the just triumph, there is great
      glory;
      but when the wicked prevail, people
        hide.††
13 Those who conceal their sins do not
      prosper,
      but those who confess and forsake
        them obtain mercy.‡‡
14 Happy those who always fear;§§
      but those who harden their hearts
        fall into evil.
15 A roaring lion or a ravenous bear
      is a wicked ruler over a poor people.
16 The less prudent the rulers, the more
      oppressive their deeds.
      Those who hate ill-gotten gain
        prolong their days.
17 Though a person burdened with blood
      guilt is in flight even to the
        grave,
      let no one offer support.
18 Whoever walks blamelessly is safe,
      but one whose ways are crooked
        falls into a pit.
19 Those who cultivate their land will have
      plenty of food,
      but those who engage in idle pursuits
        will have plenty of want.ᶻ

---

more. Cf. Is 5:14 and Hos 13:14. The saying is applicable to
modern consumerism.
*[27:23–27] A little treatise on farming in the form of
admonitions. It proposes the advantages of field and flock
over other forms of wealth. Herds are the most productive
wealth, for their value does not diminish; they are a source of
money, clothing, and food. The thought is conservative and
traditional but the development is vivid and concrete.
†[28:2] The first line expresses the paradox that rebellion,
far from doing away with rulers, actually multiplies them. The
second line is corrupt.
‡[28:3] The reference may be to tax farmers who collected
taxes and took a commission. The collectors' lack of wealth
was the cause of their oppression of poor farmers. They are
like a rain too violent to allow crops to grow.
§[28:4] **Instruction**: *torah*; the word is used both for the
teaching of the wise and the law of Moses.
¶[28:5] **Understanding nothing of justice** plays on the
twofold sense of justice as righteousness and as punishment
that comes on the wicked. On the other hand, **those who seek
the LORD understand everything**, i.e., that the Lord punishes
the wicked and rewards the righteous (themselves).

**[28:8] Interest and overcharge were strictly forbidden in
the old law among Israelites because it was presumed that the
borrower was in distress; cf. Ex 22:25; Lv 25:35–37; Dt 23:20;
Ps 15:5; Ez 18:8. Divine providence will take the offender's
wealth; cf. Eccl 2:26.
††[28:12] People react in opposite ways to the triumph of
good and evil. To the triumph of good, they react by public display, public celebration, and to the triumph of evil, by hiding.
‡‡[28:13] Concealing the faults of another is a good thing in
Proverbs (17:9), but concealing one's own sins is not. Ps 32:1–5
expresses the anguish caused by concealing one's sins rather
than bringing them to light so they can be healed by God.
§§[28:14] **Fear** is a different verb than in the phrase "to fear
(or revere) the Lord." In its only other biblical occurrence (Is
51:13), the verb means to dread an oppressor. The saying states
a paradox: those who fear in the sense of being cautious are
declared happy, whereas those who are fearless will fall into
traps they did not "fear." In short, there is good fear and bad fear.

---

x. [28:6] Prv 19:1.

y. [28:9] Prv 15:8; 21:27.   z. [28:19] Prv 12:11.

20 The trustworthy will be richly blessed;
　　but whoever hastens to be rich will
　　　not go unpunished.*a*

21 To show partiality is never good:*b*
　　for even a morsel of bread one may
　　　do wrong.*

22 Misers hurry toward wealth,
　　not knowing that want is coming
　　　toward them.†

23 Whoever rebukes another wins more
　　favor
　　　than one who flatters with the
　　　　tongue.

24 Whoever defrauds father or mother and
　　says, "It is no sin,"*c*
　　　is a partner to a brigand.

25 The greedy person stirs up strife,
　　but the one who trusts in the LORD
　　　will prosper.

26 Those who trust in themselves are fools,
　　but those who walk in wisdom are
　　　safe.

27 Those who give to the poor have no lack,*d*
　　but those who avert their eyes, many
　　　curses.

28 When the wicked prevail, people
　　hide;
　　　but at their fall the just abound.*e*

## CHAPTER 29

1 Those stiff-necked in the face of reproof
　　in an instant will be shattered
　　　beyond cure.‡

2 When the just flourish, the people
　　rejoice;
　　　but when the wicked rule, the
　　　　people groan.§f

3 Whoever loves wisdom gives joy to his
　　father,
　　　but whoever consorts with harlots
　　　　squanders his wealth.

4 By justice a king builds up the land;
　　but one who raises taxes tears it
　　　down.¶

5 Those who speak flattery to their neighbor
　　cast a net at their feet.**

6 The sin of the wicked is a trap,
　　but the just run along joyfully.*g*

7 The just care for the cause of the poor;
　　the wicked do not understand such
　　　care.††

8 Scoffers enflame the city,
　　but the wise calm the fury.*h*

9 If a wise person disputes with a fool,
　　there is railing and ridicule but no
　　　resolution.

10 The bloodthirsty hate the blameless,
　　but the upright seek his life.‡‡

11 Fools give vent to all their anger;
　　but the wise, biding their time,
　　　control it.*i*

12 If rulers listen to lying words,
　　their servants all become
　　　wicked.

13 The poor and the oppressor meet:*j*
　　the LORD gives light to the eyes of
　　　both.

14 If a king is honestly for the rights of the
　　poor,
　　　his throne stands firm forever.*k*

15 The rod of correction gives wisdom,
　　but uncontrolled youths disgrace
　　　their mothers.*l*

16 When the wicked increase, crime
　　increases;
　　　but the just will behold their
　　　　downfall.§§

17 Discipline your children, and they will
　　bring you comfort,
　　　and give delight to your soul.

18 Without a vision the people lose
　　restraint;
　　　but happy is the one who follows
　　　　instruction.¶¶

19 Not by words alone can servants be
　　trained;*m*

---

*\*[28:21] Cf. 24:23. Verse 21b warns that even in a light matter one must remain impartial.*

*†[28:22] "Bad of eye" is the Hebrew idiom for miserly. Misers fail to see that poverty is hurrying toward them because of their wrong attitude toward wealth. Because misers are "bad of eye," they do not see the danger.*

*‡[29:1] The idiom "to stiffen one's neck" occurs in a context of not heeding a message in Dt 10:16 and 2 Kgs 17:14. To stiffen one's neck in this sense risks having it broken, as in 1 Sm 4:18.*

*§[29:2] Popular response to a just or unjust ruler is expressed in sound—shouts of joy or groans of anguish. "Rejoice" can mean to express one's joy, i.e., joyous shouts.*

*¶[29:4] In Hebrew as in English high and low are metaphors for prosperity and depression. A king who is just "causes the land to stand up," i.e., to be prosperous, and one who makes taxes high brings a country low.*

*\*\*[29:5] When one addresses deceptive words to someone's face, one equivalently throws a net at their feet to snare them.*

*††[29:7] As in 12:10 (on care for animals), the righteous care for those who are without a voice and often treated like animals. Colon B has a double meaning: the wicked have no such knowledge (care for the poor) and they have no knowledge (wisdom), for they are fools.*

*‡‡[29:10] An enigmatic saying in that "seek one's life" is a common idiom for killing. The saying probably plays on the idiom, interpreting "to seek the life of another" not as killing but as caring for another (as in 11:30).*

*§§[29:16] When the wicked grow numerous they sow the seeds of their own destruction, for there is a corresponding increase in offenses calling down divine retribution.*

*¶¶[29:18] This much-cited proverb has been interpreted in several different ways. "Vision" and "instruction" mean authoritative guidance for the community. People are demoralized without credible leadership, but any individual heeding traditional instruction can still find happiness. As in 15:15 wisdom enables an individual to surmount days of trouble.*

a. [28:20] Prv 13:11.　b. [28:21] Prv 24:23.　c. [28:24] Mk 7:11–13. d. [28:27] Prv 19:17; Sir 4:3–8.　e. [28:28] Prv 28:12.　f. [29:2] Prv 11:10; 28:12, 28.

g. [29:6] Prv 12:13.　h. [29:8] Prv 11:11.　i. [29:11] Prv 12:16; 25:28; Sir 21:26.　j. [29:13] Prv 22:2.　k. [29:14] Prv 16:12; 20:28; 25:5. l. [29:15] Prv 13:24; 22:15; 23:13–14; Sir 22:6; 30:1.　m. [29:19] Sir 33:25–30.

for they understand but do not
    respond.*
20 Do you see someone hasty in speech?[n]
    There is more hope for a fool!
21 If servants are pampered from
    childhood
    they will turn out to be stubborn.
22 The ill-tempered stir up strife,
    and the hotheaded cause many sins.[o]
23 Haughtiness brings humiliation,
    but the humble of spirit acquire
    honor.[†p]
24 Partners of a thief hate themselves;[‡]
    they hear the imprecation but do
    not testify.
25 Fear of others becomes a snare,
    but the one who trusts in the LORD
    is safe.
26 Many curry favor with a ruler,
    but it is from the LORD that one
    receives justice.
27 An abomination to the just, the evildoer;
    an abomination to the wicked, one
    whose way is straight.

## VII. SAYINGS OF AGUR AND OTHERS

## CHAPTER 30

1§The words of Agur, son of Jakeh the Massaite:

The pronouncement of mortal man: "I am
    weary, O God;
    I am weary, O God, and I am
    exhausted.
2 I am more brute than human being,
    without even human intelligence;
3 ¶Neither have I learned wisdom,

    nor have I the knowledge of the
    Holy One.
4 Who has gone up to heaven and come
    down again—
    who has cupped the wind in the
    hollow of the hand?
Who has bound up the waters in a cloak—
    who has established all the ends of
    the earth?
What is that person's name, or the name
    of his son?"**

5 ††Every word of God is tested;[q]
    he is a shield to those who take
    refuge in him.
6 Add nothing to his words,[r]
    lest he reprimand you, and you be
    proved a liar.

7 ‡‡Two things I ask of you,
    do not deny them to me before I die:
8 Put falsehood and lying far from me,
    give me neither poverty nor riches;
    provide me only with the food I need;
9 Lest, being full, I deny you,
    saying, "Who is the LORD?"
Or, being in want, I steal,
    and profane the name of my God.
10 Do not criticize servants to their master,
    lest they curse you, and you have to
    pay the penalty.
11 §§There are some who curse their fathers,
    and do not bless their mothers.[s]
12 There are some pure in their own eyes,
    yet not cleansed of their filth.
13 There are some—how haughty their eyes!
    how overbearing their glance!
14 There are some—their teeth are swords,
    their teeth are knives,
Devouring the needy from the earth,
    and the poor from the human race.
15 ¶¶The leech has two daughters:

---

*[29:19] The give and take of reproving is not possible for servants or slaves. Ancient custom dictated silent acquiescence for them. There is no open and free dialogue, which is part of ancient discipline.

†[29:23] One's prideful height brings one down and one's lowly state brings glory.

‡[29:24] **Hate themselves**: because they not only incur guilt as accomplices but, by their silence, bring down on themselves the curse invoked on the unknown guilty partner. Such a case is envisioned in Lv 5:1. After a theft, a public proclamation was made, enforced by a curse. No one in a town or city could avoid hearing it. The curse hung over the accomplice. By doing nothing, neither directly stealing nor confessing, accomplices put themselves in serious danger.

§[30:1–6] Scholars are divided on the original literary unit. Is it vv. 1–3, 1–4, 1–5, or 1–6? The unit is probably vv. 1–6, for a single contrast dominates: human fragility (and ignorance) and divine power (and knowledge). A similar contrast is found in Jb 28; Ps 73; Is 49:1–4. The language of self-abasement is hyperbolic; cf. 2 Sm 9:8; Ps 73:21–22; Jb 25:4–6. **Agur**: an unknown person. **Massaite**: from Massa in northern Arabia, elsewhere referred to as an encampment of the Ishmaelites (Gn 25:14). But Heb. *massa* may not be intended as a place name; it might signify "an oracle," "a prophecy," as in Is 15:1; 17:1; etc.

¶[30:3–4] Agur denies he has secret heavenly knowledge. The purpose of the denial is to underline that God directly gives wisdom to those whose conduct pleases him.

**[30:4] The Hebrew text has the phrase "do you know?" at the end of v. 4, which is supported by the versions. The phrase, however, does not appear in the important Greek manuscripts Vaticanus and Sinaiticus and spoils the sense, for Agur, not God, is the questioner. The phrase seems to be an addition to the Hebrew text, borrowed from Job 38:5, where it also follows a cosmic question.

††[30:5–6] Verse 5, like the confession of the king in Ps 18:31 (and its parallel, 2 Sm 22:31), expresses total confidence in the one who rescues from death. Agur has refused a word from any other except God and makes an act of trust in God.

‡‡[30:7–9] A prayer against lying words and for sufficiency of goods, lest reaction to riches or destitution lead to offenses against God.

§§[30:11–14] Perverted people are here classified as unfilial (v. 11), self-righteous (v. 12), proud (v. 13) and rapacious (v. 14).

¶¶[30:15–16] Here begins a series of numerical sayings; the pattern is n, n + 1. The slight variation in number (two and three, three and four) is an example of parallelism applied to numbers. The poetic technique is attested even outside the Bible. **Two daughters: "Give," and "Give"**: the text is obscure; as the leech (a bloodsucking worm) is insatiable in its desire for blood (v. 15), so are the nether world for victims, the barren womb for offspring, the earth for water,

n. [29:20] Sir 9:18; Prv 26:12.  o. [29:22] Prv 15:18; 22:24.
p. [29:23] Prv 11:2; 16:18; 18:12.

q. [30:5] Ps 12:7; 18:31.  r. [30:6] Dt 4:2; 13:1.  s. [30:11] Prv 20:20.

"Give," and "Give."
Three things never get their fill,
    four never say, "Enough!"
16 Sheòl, a barren womb,[t]
    land that never gets its fill of water,
    and fire, which never says, "Enough!"
17 The eye that mocks a father,
    or scorns the homage due a mother,
Will be plucked out by brook ravens;
    devoured by a brood of vultures.
18 *Three things are too wonderful for me,
    yes, four I cannot understand:
19 The way of an eagle in the sky,
    the way of a serpent upon a rock,
The way of a ship on the high seas,
    and the way of a man with a woman.
20 This is the way of an adulterous woman:
    she eats, wipes her mouth,
    and says, "I have done no wrong."[†]
21 ‡Under three things the earth trembles,
    yes, under four it cannot bear up:
22 Under a slave who becomes king,
    and a fool who is glutted with food;[u]
23 Under an unloved woman who is wed,
    and a maidservant who displaces
        her mistress.
24 §Four things are among the smallest on
        the earth,
    and yet are exceedingly wise:
25 Ants—a species not strong,
    yet they store up their food in the
        summer;
26 Badgers—a species not mighty,
    yet they make their home in the
        crags;
27 Locusts—they have no king,
    yet they march forth in formation;
28 Lizards—you can catch them with your
        hands,
    yet they find their way into kings'
        palaces.

29 °Three things are stately in their stride,
    yes, four are stately in their carriage:
30 The lion, mightiest of beasts,
    retreats before nothing;
31 The strutting cock, and the he-goat,
    and the king at the head of his
        people.
32 "If you have foolishly been proud
    or presumptuous—put your hand
        on your mouth;
33 For as the churning of milk produces
        curds,
    and the pressing of the nose
        produces blood,
    the churning of anger produces
        strife.

## VIII. SAYINGS OF KING LEMUEL[††]

### CHAPTER 31

¹The words of Lemuel, king of Massa,[‡‡] the instruction his mother taught him:

2   What are you doing, my son![§§]
    what are you doing, son of my
        womb;
    what are you doing, son of my vows!
3   Do not give your vigor to women,
    or your strength[¶¶] to those who ruin
        kings.
4   It is not for kings, Lemuel,
    not for kings to drink wine;
    strong drink is not for princes,
5   Lest in drinking they forget what has been
        decreed,
    and violate the rights of any who are
        in need.
6   Give strong drink to anyone who is
        perishing,
    and wine to the embittered;

---

and fire for fuel (v. 16). **Sheol:** here not so much the place of the dead as a force (death) that eventually draws all the living into it; cf. 27:20; Is 5:14; Hb 2:5. **Land . . . fire:** land (especially the dry land of Palestine) always absorbs more water; fire always requires more fuel.

*[30:18–19] The soaring flight of the eagle, the mysterious movement upon a rock of the serpent which has no feet, the path of the ship through the trackless deep, and the marvelous attraction between the sexes; there is a mysterious way common to them all.

†[30:20] This verse portrays the indifference of an adulterous woman who casually dismisses her guilt because it cannot be traced.

‡[30:21–23] Shaking heavens are part of general cosmic upheaval in Is 14:16; Jl 2:10; Am 8:8; Jb 9:6. Disturbances in nature mirror the disturbance of unworthy people attaining what they do not deserve. **Glutted with food:** someone unworthy ends up with the fulfillment that befits a wise person. **Unloved woman:** an older woman who, contrary to expectation, finds a husband.

§[30:24–28] The creatures may be small, but they are wise in knowing how to govern themselves—the definition of wisdom. **Badgers:** the rock badger is able to live on rocky heights that provide security from its enemies. **Locusts:** though vulnerable individually their huge swarms are impossible to deflect.

¶[30:29–31] Four beings with an imperiousness visible in their walk. Only the lion is described in detail; the reader is expected to transpose its qualities to the others.

**[30:32–33] The same Hebrew verb, "to churn, shake," is applied to milk, the nose (sometimes a symbol of anger), and wrath. In each case something is eventually produced by the constant agitation. The wise make peace and avoid strife, for strife eventually harms those who provoke it.

††[31:1–9] Though mothers are sources of wisdom in Proverbs (1:8; 6:20), the mother of Lemuel is special in being queen mother, which was an important position in the palace. Queen mothers played an important role in ancient palace life because of their longevity, knowledge of palace politics, and loyalty to their sons; they were in a good position to offer him sound counsel. The language of the poem contains Aramaisms, a sign of its non-Israelite origin.

The first section, vv. 3–5, warns against abuse of sex and alcohol (wine, strong drink) lest the king *forget the poor.* The second section, vv. 6–9, urges the use of alcohol (strong drink, wine) so that the downtrodden *poor* can *forget* their poverty. The real subject of the poem is justice for the poor.

‡‡[31:1] **Massa:** see note on 30:1–6.

§§[31:2] **My son:** in the Septuagint, "my son, my firstborn."

¶¶[31:3] The Hebrew word here translated "strength" normally means "ways," but the context and a cognate language support "authority" or "strength" here.

---

t. [30:16] Prv 27:20.    u. [30:22] Prv 19:10; Eccl 10:6–7.

7 When they drink, they will forget their
    misery,
    and think no more of their troubles.
8 Open your mouth in behalf of the mute,
    and for the rights of the destitute;
9 Open your mouth, judge justly,
    defend the needy and the poor!

## IX. POEM ON THE WOMAN OF WORTH*

10 Who can find† a woman of worth?ᵛ
    Far beyond jewels is her value.
11 Her husband trusts her judgment;
    he does not lack income.
12 She brings him profit, not loss,‡
    all the days of her life.
13 She seeks out wool and flax
    and weaves with skillful hands.
14 Like a merchant fleet,§
    she secures her provisions from afar.
15 She rises while it is still night,
    and distributes food to her
    household,
    a portion to her maidservants.
16 She picks out a field and acquires it;
    from her earnings she plants a
    vineyard.
17 She girds herself with strength;

she exerts her arms with vigor.¶
18 She enjoys the profit from her dealings;
    her lamp is never extinguished at
    night.**
19 She puts her hands to the distaff,
    and her fingers ply the spindle.††
20 She reaches out her hands to the poor,
    and extends her arms to the needy.
21 She is not concerned for her household
    when it snows—
    all her charges are doubly clothed.
22 She makes her own coverlets;
    fine linen and purple are her clothing.
23 Her husband is prominent at the city gates
    as he sits with the elders of the land.‡‡
24 She makes garments and sells them,
    and stocks the merchants with belts.
25 She is clothed with strength and dignity,
    and laughs at the days to come.§§
26 She opens her mouth in wisdom;
    kindly instruction is on her tongue.
27 She watches over¶¶ the affairs of her
    household,
    and does not eat the bread of idleness.
28 Her children rise up and call her blessed;
    her husband, too, praises her:
29 "Many are the women of proven worth,
    but you have excelled them all."ᵂ
30 Charm is deceptive and beauty fleeting;
    the woman who fears the Lord is to
    be praised.***
31 Acclaim her for the work of her hands,
    and let her deeds praise her at the
    city gates.

---

*[31:10–31] An acrostic poem of twenty-two lines; each line begins with a successive letter of the Hebrew alphabet. As with many other acrostic poems in the Bible, the unity of the poem is largely extrinsic, coming not from the narrative logic but from the familiar sequence of letters. The topic is the ideal woman described through her activity as a wife. Some have suggested that the traditional hymn extolling the great deeds of a warrior has been transposed to extol a heroic wife; the focus is on her exploits. She runs a household distinguished by abundant food and clothing for all within, by its trade (import of raw materials and export of finished products), and by the renown of its head, her husband, in the community. At v. 28, the voice is no longer that of the narrator but of her children and husband as they praise her. The purpose of the poem has been interpreted variously: an encomium to offset the sometimes negative portrayal of women in the book, or, more symbolically (and more likely), a portrait of a household ruled by Woman Wisdom and a disciple of Woman Wisdom, i.e., he now has a worthy wife and children, a great household, renown in the community.

†[31:10] **Who can find . . . ?**: in 20:6 and Eccl 8:1 the question implies that finding such a person is well-nigh impossible.

‡[31:12] **Profit, not loss**: a commercial metaphor.

§[31:14] **Like a merchant fleet**: she has her eye on the far horizon, like the ship of a merchant ready to bring supplies into her larder. It is the only simile ("like") in the poem.

ᵛ. [31:10] Prv 12:4; Sir 26:1–4, 13–18.

¶[31:17] The metaphor of clothing oneself is used to show the woman's readiness. One can gird on weapons of war and might and splendor (Ps 69:7; Is 52:9).

**[31:18] **Her lamp is never extinguished at night**: indicates abundance of productive work and its accompanying prosperity; cf. 20:20; Jb 18:6.

††[31:19] The wife weaves linen cloth from flax and wool from fleece, which she cultivated according to v. 13. **Distaff**: staff for holding the flax, tow, or wool, which in spinning was drawn out and twisted into yarn or thread by the spindle or round stick.

‡‡[31:23] The husband is mentioned for the first time since vv. 10–12 but as "her husband." He will not be mentioned again until v. 28, where he praises her.

§§[31:25] **Laughs at the days to come**: anticipates the future with joy, free of anxiety.

¶¶[31:27] **Watches over**: Hebrew ṣopiyyâ, perhaps a pun on the Greek *sophia* (= wisdom). **Bread of idleness**: she does not eat from the table of others but from her own labors.

***[31:30] The true charm of this woman is her religious spirit, for she fears the Lord; cf. note on 1:7.

# THE BOOK OF
# ECCLESIASTES

⁓⁓⁓

The Hebrew name of this book and of its author, Qoheleth, is actually a title, and it perhaps means "assembler" (of students, listeners) or "collector" (of wisdom sayings). The book's more common name, Ecclesiastes, is an approximate translation into Greek of this Hebrew word. The book comprises an extended reflective essay employing autobiographical narrative, proverbs, parables, and allegories. An almost unrelenting skepticism characterizes the tone or outlook. The issues with which the author deals and the questions he raises are aimed at those who would claim any absolute values in this life, including possessions, fame, success, or pleasure. Wisdom itself is challenged, but folly is condemned.

The refrain which begins and ends the book, "Vanity of vanities" (1:1; 12:8), recurs at key points throughout. The Hebrew word, *hebel* ("vanity"), has the sense of "emptiness, futility, absurdity": "I have seen all things that are done under the sun, and behold, all is vanity and a chase after wind" (1:14; 2:11, 17, 26; etc.). Everything in human life is subject to change, to qualification, to loss: "What profit have we from all the toil which we toil at under the sun?" (1:3). The answer is in the negative: No absolute profit or gain is possible. Even if some temporary profit or gain is achieved, it will ultimately be cancelled out by death, the great leveller (2:14–15; 3:19–20). Wisdom has some advantage over foolishness, but even wisdom's advantage is only a temporary and qualified one.

Many would locate Ecclesiastes in the third century B.C., when Judea was under the oppressive domination of Hellenistic kings from Egypt. These kings were highly efficient in their ruthless exploitation of the land and people (4:1; 5:7). The average Jew would have felt a sense of powerlessness and inability to change things for the better. For Qoheleth, God seems remote and uncommunicative, and we cannot hope to understand, much less influence, God's activity in the world (3:11; 8:16–17).

The book's honest and blunt appraisal of the human condition provides a healthy corrective to the occasionally excessive self-assurance of other wisdom writers. Its radical skepticism is somewhat tempered by the resigned conclusions to rejoice in whatever gifts God may give (2:24; 3:12–13, 22; 5:17–18; 8:15; 9:7–9; 11:9).

The Book of Ecclesiastes is divided as follows:

I. Qoheleth's Investigation of Life (1:12–6:9)
II. Qoheleth's Conclusions (6:10–12:14)
   A. No One Can Find Out the Best Way of Acting (7:1–8:17)
   B. No One Knows the Future (9:1–12:14)

## CHAPTER 1

¹The words of David's son, Qoheleth, king in Jerusalem:*ᵃ

² Vanity of vanities,† says Qoheleth,
　　vanity of vanities! All things are
　　　　vanity!ᵇ

---

### Vanity of Human Toil

³ What profit have we from all the toil
　　which we toil at under the sun?‡ᶜ
⁴ One generation departs and another
　　　　generation comes,
　　but the world forever stays.
⁵ The sun rises and the sun sets;
　　then it presses on to the place where
　　　　it rises.
⁶ Shifting south, then north,

---

*[1:1] **David's son . . . king in Jerusalem**: the intent of the author is to identify himself with Solomon. This is a literary device, by which the author hopes to commend his work to the public under the name of Israel's most famous sage (see 1 Kgs 5:9–14).

†[1:2] **Vanity of vanities**: a Hebrew superlative expressing the supreme degree of futility and emptiness.

‡[1:3] **Under the sun**: used throughout this book to signify "on the earth."

a. [1:1] Eccl 1:12; 12:9–10.　b. [1:2] Eccl 12:8.

c. [1:3] Eccl 2:11, 22; 3:9; 5:15.

back and forth shifts the wind,
 constantly shifting its course.
7 All rivers flow to the sea,
 yet never does the sea become
  full.
To the place where they flow,
 the rivers continue to flow.
8 All things are wearisome,*
 too wearisome for words.
The eye is not satisfied by seeing
 nor has the ear enough of hearing.*d*

9What has been, that will be; what has been done, that will be done. Nothing is new under the sun!*e* 10Even the thing of which we say, "See, this is new!" has already existed in the ages that preceded us.*f* 11There is no remembrance of past generations;*g* nor will future generations be remembered by those who come after them.†

## I. QOHELETH'S INVESTIGATION OF LIFE

**Twofold Introduction.** 12I, Qoheleth, was king over Israel in Jerusalem, 13and I applied my mind to search and investigate in wisdom all things that are done under the sun.*h*

A bad business God has given
 to human beings to be busied with.

14I have seen all things that are done under the sun, and behold, all is vanity and a chase after wind.‡*i*

15  What is crooked cannot be made
  straight,
 and you cannot count what is not
  there.§

16Though I said to myself, "See, I have greatly increased my wisdom beyond all who were before me in Jerusalem, and my mind has broad experience of wisdom and knowledge," 17yet when I applied my mind to know wisdom and knowledge, madness and folly, I learned that this also is a chase after wind.*k*

18  For in much wisdom there is much
  sorrow;

whoever increases knowledge
 increases grief.¶

## CHAPTER 2

**Study of Pleasure-seeking.** 1I said in my heart,** "Come, now, let me try you with pleasure and the enjoyment of good things." See, this too was vanity. 2Of laughter I said: "Mad!" and of mirth: "What good does this do?" 3Guided by wisdom,†† I probed with my mind how to beguile my senses with wine and take up folly, until I should understand what is good for human beings to do under the heavens during the limited days of their lives.

4I undertook great works; I built myself houses and planted vineyards; 5I made gardens and parks, and in them set out fruit trees of all sorts. 6And I constructed for myself reservoirs to water a flourishing woodland. 7I acquired male and female slaves, and had slaves who were born in my house. I also owned vast herds of cattle and flocks of sheep, more than all who had been before me in Jerusalem. 8I amassed for myself silver and gold, and the treasures of kings and provinces. I provided for myself male and female singers and delights of men, many women.‡‡ 9I accumulated much more than all others before me in Jerusalem; my wisdom, too, stayed with me. 10Nothing that my eyes desired did I deny them, nor did I deprive myself of any joy; rather, my heart rejoiced in the fruit of all my toil. This was my share for all my toil. 11But when I turned to all the works that my hands had wrought, and to the fruit of the toil for which I had toiled so much, see! all was vanity and a chase after wind. There is no profit under the sun. 12What about one who succeeds a king? He can do only what has already been done.§§

---

¶ [1:18] **Sorrow . . . grief**: these terms refer not just to a store of knowledge or to psychological or emotional pain. Corporal punishment, sometimes quite harsh, was also employed frequently by parents and teachers.

** [2:1–11] The author here assumes the role of Solomon who, as king, would have had the wealth and resources at his disposal to acquire wisdom and engage in pleasurable pursuits. Verses 4–8 in particular, with their description of abundant wealth and physical gratifications, parallel the descriptions in 1 Kgs 4–11 of the extravagances of Solomon's reign.

†† [2:3] **Guided by wisdom**: using all the means money can buy, the author sets out on a deliberate search to discover if pleasure constitutes true happiness.

‡‡ [2:8] **Many women**: the final phrase of this verse is difficult to translate. One word, *shiddah*, which appears here in both singular and plural, is found nowhere else in the Hebrew Bible. A suggested meaning is "woman" or "concubine," as it is interpreted here: "many women." The rest of the section (2:1–12) seems to be a description of Solomon's kingdom, and the "many women" would represent his huge harem (1 Kgs 11:1–3). In rabbinic Hebrew the word comes to mean "chest" or "coffer."

§§ [2:12] **What . . . been done**: the verse is difficult and elliptical. The words "He can do only" have been added for clarity. The two halves of the verse have been reversed. The author argues that it is useless to repeat the royal experiment described in vv. 1–11. The results would only be the same.

---

* [1:8] **All things are wearisome**: or, "All speech is wearisome."
† [1:11] Movement in nature and human activity appears to result in change and progress. The author argues that this change and progress are an illusion: "Nothing is new under the sun."
‡ [1:14] **A chase after wind**: an image of futile activity, like an attempt to corral the winds; cf. Hos 12:2. The ancient versions understood "affliction, dissipation of the spirit." This phrase concludes sections of the text as far as 6:9.
§ [1:15] **You cannot count what is not there**: perhaps originally a commercial metaphor alluding to loss or deficit in the accounts ledger.

---

d. [1:8] Eccl 4:8; 5:9–11.   e. [1:9] Eccl 3:15; 6:10.   f. [1:10] Eccl 3:15.   g. [1:11] Eccl 2:16.   h. [1:13] Eccl 8:9.   i. [1:14] Eccl 2:11, 17.   j. [1:16] Eccl 2:9.   k. [1:17] Eccl 1:3; 8:16.

l. [2:11] Eccl 1:3, 17; Sir 44:9.

**Study of Wisdom and Folly.** I went on to the consideration of wisdom, madness and folly. [13]And I saw that wisdom has as much profit over folly as light has over darkness.

[14]  Wise people have eyes in their heads,
      but fools walk in darkness.

Yet I knew that the same lot befalls both.*[m] [15]So I said in my heart, if the fool's lot is to befall me also, why should I be wise? Where is the profit? And in my heart I decided that this too is vanity. [16][n]The wise person will have no more abiding remembrance than the fool; for in days to come both will have been forgotten. How is it that the wise person dies[†] like the fool! [17]Therefore I detested life, since for me the work that is done under the sun is bad; for all is vanity and a chase after wind.

### Study of the Fruits of Toil

**To Others the Profits.** [18]And I detested all the fruits of my toil under the sun, because I must leave them to the one who is to come after me. [19]And who knows whether that one will be wise or a fool? Yet that one will take control of all the fruits of my toil and wisdom under the sun. This also is vanity. [20]So my heart turned to despair over all the fruits of my toil under the sun. [21]For here is one who has toiled with wisdom and knowledge and skill, and that one's legacy must be left to another who has not toiled for it. This also is vanity and a great evil. [22][o]For what profit comes to mortals from all the toil and anxiety of heart with which they toil under the sun? [23]Every day sorrow and grief are their occupation; even at night their hearts are not at rest. This also is vanity.

[24][‡][p]There is nothing better for mortals than to eat and drink and provide themselves with good things from their toil. Even this, I saw, is from the hand of God. [25]For who can eat or drink apart from God? [26][§][q]For to the one who pleases God, he gives wisdom and knowledge and joy; but to the one who displeases, God gives the task of gathering possessions for the one who pleases God. This also is vanity and a chase after wind.

## CHAPTER 3

### No One Can Determine the Right Time to Act

[1]  [r]There is an appointed time for
      everything,
      and a time for every affair under the
      heavens.
[2]  A time to give birth, and a time to die;
      a time to plant, and a time to uproot
      the plant.
[3]  A time to kill, and a time to heal;
      a time to tear down, and a time to
      build.
[4]  A time to weep, and a time to laugh;
      a time to mourn, and a time to
      dance.
[5]  A time to scatter stones, and a time to
      gather them;
      a time to embrace, and a time to be
      far from embraces.
[6]  A time to seek, and a time to lose;
      a time to keep, and a time to cast
      away.
[7]  A time to rend, and a time to sew;
      a time to be silent, and a time to
      speak.
[8]  A time to love, and a time to hate;
      a time of war, and a time of peace.

[9][s]What profit have workers from their toil? [10]I have seen the business that God has given to mortals to be busied about. [11][s]God has made everything appropriate to its time, but has put the timeless** into their hearts so they cannot find out, from beginning to end, the work which God has done. [12][t]I recognized that there is nothing better than to rejoice and to do well during life. [13]Moreover, that all can eat and drink and enjoy the good of all their toil—this is a gift of God. [14]I recognized that whatever God does will endure forever; there is no adding to it, or taking from it. Thus has God done that he may be revered. [15][††][u]What now is has already been; what is to be, already is: God retrieves what has gone by.

---

*[2:14] **Yet I knew . . . befalls both:** the author quotes a traditional saying upholding the advantages of wisdom, but then qualifies it. Nothing, not even wisdom itself, can give someone absolute control over their destiny and therefore guarantee any advantage.

†[2:16] **The wise person dies:** death, until now only alluded to (vv. 14–15), takes center stage and will constantly appear in the author's reflections through the remainder of the book.

‡[2:24–26] The author is not advocating unrestrained indulgence. Rather he counsels acceptance of the good things God chooses to give. This is the first of seven similar conclusions that Qoheleth provides; see 3:12–13, 22; 5:17–18; 8:15; 9:7–9; 11:9.

§[2:26] According to 7:15 and 9:1–3, God does not make an objective, evidential, moral distinction between saint and sinner. God "gives" as God pleases.

¶[3:1–8] The fourteen pairs of opposites describe various human activities. The poem affirms that God has determined the appropriate moment or "time" for each. Human beings cannot know that moment; further, the wider course of events and purposes fixed by God are beyond them as well.

**[3:11] **The timeless:** others translate "eternity," "the world," or "darkness." The author credits God with keeping human beings ignorant about God's "work"—present and future.

††[3:15] The verse is difficult. Literally it reads "and God seeks out what was pursued." It appears to be a variation of the theme in 1:9, "There is nothing new under the sun."

---

m. [2:14] Eccl 9:2–3.  n. [2:16] Eccl 1:11; Wis 2:4.  o. [2:22] Eccl 1:3.  p. [2:24] Eccl 3:12–13, 22; 5:17–19; 8:15.  q. [2:26] Eccl 7:26; Prv 13:22.

r. [3:9] Eccl 1:3.  s. [3:11] Eccl 8:17; 11:5.  t. [3:12] Eccl 2:24.  u. [3:15] Eccl 1:9.

**The Problem of Retribution.** [16v]And still under the sun in the judgment place I saw wickedness, and wickedness also in the seat of justice. [17w]I said in my heart, both the just and the wicked God will judge, since a time is set for every affair and for every work.* [18]I said in my heart: As for human beings, it is God's way of testing them and of showing that they are in themselves like beasts. [19]For the lot of mortals and the lot of beasts is the same lot: The one dies as well as the other. Both have the same life breath. Human beings have no advantage over beasts, but all is vanity. [20x]Both go to the same place; both were made from the dust, and to the dust they both return. [21]Who knows† if the life breath of mortals goes upward and the life breath of beasts goes earthward? [22y]And I saw that there is nothing better for mortals than to rejoice in their work; for this is their lot. Who will let them see what is to come after them?z

## CHAPTER 4

**Vanity of Toil.** [1]Again I saw all the oppressions that take place under the sun: the tears of the victims with none to comfort‡ them! From the hand of their oppressors comes violence, and there is none to comfort them!a [2]And those now dead, I declared more fortunate in death than are the living to be still alive.b [3]And better off than both is the yet unborn, who has not seen the wicked work that is done under the sun. [4]Then I saw that all toil and skillful work is the rivalry of one person with another. This also is vanity and a chase after wind.

[5] "Fools fold their arms
    and consume their own flesh"—§
[6] Better is one handful with tranquility
    than two with toil and a chase after
    wind!

**Companions and Successors.** [7]Again I saw this vanity under the sun: [8]those all alone with no companion, with neither child nor sibling—with no end to all their toil, and no satisfaction from riches. For whom do I toil and deprive myself of good things? This also is vanity and a bad business. [9]Two are better than one: They get a good wage for their toil. [10]If the one falls, the other will help the fallen one. But woe to the solitary person! If that one should fall, there is no other to help. [11]So also, if two sleep together, they keep each other warm. How can one alone keep warm? [12]Where one alone may be overcome, two together can resist. A three-ply cord¶ is not easily broken.

[13]**Better is a poor but wise youth than an old but foolish king who no longer knows caution; [14]for from a prison house he came forth to reign; despite his kingship he was born poor. [15]I saw all the living, those who move about under the sun, with the second youth who will succeed him.†† [16]There is no end to all this people, to all who were before them; yet the later generations will not have joy in him. This also is vanity and a chase after wind.

**Vanity of Many Words.** [17c]Guard your step when you go to the house of God.‡‡ Draw near for obedience, rather than for the fools' offering of sacrifice; for they know not how to keep from doing evil.

## CHAPTER 5

[1§§]Be not hasty in your utterance and let not your heart be quick to utter a promise in God's presence. God is in heaven and you are on earth; therefore let your words be few.d

[2]    As dreams come along with many cares,
        so a fool's voice along with a
            multitude of words.

[3e]When you make a vow to God, delay not its fulfillment. For God has no pleasure in fools; fulfill what you have vowed. [4]It is better not to make a vow than make it and not fulfill it. [5]Let not your utterances make you guilty, and say not before his representative, "It was a mistake." Why should God be angered by your words and destroy the

---

*[3:17] **A time is set . . . work:** another possible reading would see this verse referring to a judgment in or after death: "a time for every affair and for every work *there*" (that is, in death or in Sheol).

†[3:21] **Who knows:** the author presumes a negative answer: "No one knows." In place of speculation on impossible questions, the author counsels enjoyment of what is possible (cf. v. 22; but see also 2:10–11).

‡[4:1] **Oppressions . . . victims . . . none to comfort:** the author obviously feels deeply about the plight of the oppressed, but he seems to feel powerless to do anything. The repetition of "none to comfort" is purposeful, and emphatic.

§[4:5] **Consume their own flesh:** an enigmatic statement. In the context of vv. 4 and 6 it seems to warn that those who refuse to work for the necessities of life will suffer hunger and impair their bodily health. But the verse could also be intended for the industrious: Even the lazy may manage to have "their own flesh," that is, have sufficient food to eat.

¶[4:12] **A three-ply cord:** an ancient proverb known centuries before biblical times. The progression ("two together . . . three-ply") seems to imply, "If two are good, three are even better."

**[4:13–16] This passage deals with kingship and succession, but is obscure.

††[4:15] The king is no sooner dead than the people transfer their allegiance to his successor.

‡‡[4:17] **The house of God:** the Temple in Jerusalem. **Obedience . . . sacrifice:** the Temple was the place not only for sacrifice but also for instruction in the Law. Sacrifice without obedience was unacceptable; cf. 1 Sm 15:22; Hos 6:6.

§§[5:1–6] Further counsels on prudence and circumspection in fulfilling one's religious obligations. It is not the multitude of words but one's sincerity that counts in the acknowledgment of God's sovereignty (v. 1), especially through obedience (4:17) and reverence (v. 6).

---

v. [3:16] Eccl 4:1.   w. [3:17] Eccl 8:6a; 11:9; 12:14.   x. [3:20] Eccl 12:7; Gn 3:19; Sir 17:2.   y. [3:22] Eccl 3:12–13; 5:17–18.   z. [3:22] Eccl 8:7; 10:14.   a. [4:1] Eccl 3:16; 5:7; 9:4–5.   b. [4:2] Eccl 6:3–5.

c. [4:17] 1 Sm 15:22; Ps 40:7–9; Prv 15:8; 21:3; Hos 6:6.   d. [5:1] Ps 115:3, 16; Mt 6:7; Jas 1:19.   e. [5:3] Nm 30:3; Dt 23:22–24; Prv 20:25; Sir 18:22–23.

works of your hands? [6]Despite many dreams, futilities, and a multitude of words, fear God!

**Gain and Loss of Goods.** [7]If you see oppression of the poor, and violation of rights and justice in the realm, do not be astonished by the fact, for the high official has another higher than he watching him and above these are others higher still—. [8]But profitable for a land in such circumstances is a king concerned about cultivation.*

[9h]The covetous are never satisfied with money, nor lovers of wealth with their gain; so this too is vanity. [10]Where there are great riches, there are also many to devour them. Of what use are they to the owner except as a feast for the eyes alone? [11]Sleep is sweet to the laborer, whether there is little or much to eat; but the abundance of the rich allows them no sleep.

[12]This is a grievous evil which I have seen under the sun: riches hoarded by their owners to their own hurt. [13]Should the riches be lost through some misfortune, they may have offspring when they have no means. [14i]As they came forth from their mother's womb, so again shall they return, naked as they came, having nothing from their toil to bring with them. [15]This too is a grievous evil, that they go just as they came. What then does it profit them to toil for the wind? [16]All their days they eat in gloom with great vexation, sickness and resentment.

[17j]Here is what I see as good: It is appropriate to eat and drink and prosper from all the toil one toils at under the sun during the limited days of life God gives us; for this is our lot. [18]Those to whom God gives riches and property, and grants power to partake of them, so that they receive their lot and find joy in the fruits of their toil: This is a gift from God. [19]For they will hardly dwell on the shortness of life, because God lets them busy themselves with the joy of their heart.†

### CHAPTER 6

**Limited Worth of Enjoyment.** [1]There is another evil I have seen under the sun, and it weighs heavily upon humankind: [2k]There is one to whom God gives riches and property and honor, and who lacks nothing the heart could desire; yet God does not grant the power to partake of them, but a stranger devours them. This is vanity and a dire plague. [3]Should one have a hundred children and live many years, no matter to what great age, still if one has not the full

benefit of those goods, I proclaim that the child born dead, even if left unburied, is more fortunate.‡ [4l]Though it came in vain and goes into darkness and its name is enveloped in darkness, [5]though it has not seen the sun or known anything, yet the dead child has more peace. [6]Should such a one live twice a thousand years and not enjoy those goods, do not both go to the same place?§

[7]All human toil is for the mouth,¶ yet the appetite is never satisfied. [8]What profit have the wise compared to fools, or what profit have the lowly in knowing how to conduct themselves in life? [9**]What the eyes see is better than what the desires wander after.*** This also is vanity and a chase after wind.

## II. QOHELETH'S CONCLUSIONS

[10]Whatever is, was long ago given its name, and human nature is known; mortals cannot contend in judgment with One who is stronger.†† [11]For the more words, the more vanity; what profit is there for anyone? [12m]For who knows what is good for mortals in life, the limited days of their vain life, spent like a shadow? Because who can tell them what will come afterward under the sun?ⁿ

*A. No One Can Find Out the Best Way of Acting*

### CHAPTER 7

**Critique of Sages on the Day of Adversity**

1   A good name is better than good
         ointment,‡‡
     and the day of death than the day
         of birth.°
2   It is better to go to the house of mourning
         than to the house of feasting,
     For that is the end of every mortal,
         and the living should take it to
         heart.ᵖ

---

*[5:8] **A king concerned about cultivation:** the Hebrew text is ambiguous and obscure. The author does not criticize the oppression he describes in v. 7. Now perhaps he expresses the hope that the king would use his power to upbuild agriculture in order to alleviate the hunger and suffering of the poor and oppressed.

†[5:19] The joys of life, though temporary and never assured, keep one from dwelling on the ills which afflict humanity.

‡[6:3] Even a large family and exceptionally long life cannot compensate for the absence of good things and the joy which they bring.

§[6:6] **Same place:** the grave; cf. 3:20; 12:7.

¶[6:7] **The mouth:** symbolic of human desires.

**[6:9] Compare the English proverb, "A bird in the hand is worth two in the bush." However, it could also mean, "The seeing of the eyes is better than the wandering of the desire," with the emphasis on the actions of seeing and desiring. Seeing is a way of possessing whereas desire, by definition, can remain frustrated and unfulfilled.

††[6:10–11] **One who is stronger** is, of course, God. **The more vanity:** contending with God is futile.

‡‡[7:1] **Ointment:** a good name can be affirmed only with death, when one is normally anointed. The author dialogues in this section (vv. 1–14) with traditional wisdom, alternately affirming or countering its assertions. The real value of traditional wisdom lies in its ability to provoke one to thought and reflection, and not to absolve one from such activity.

---

f. [5:6] Eccl 3:14.   g. [5:7] Eccl 3:16; 4:1.   h. [5:9] Eccl 4:8; Prv 28:22.
i. [5:14] Jb 1:21; 1 Tm 6:7.   j. [5:17] Eccl 2:24.   k. [6:2] Eccl 2:18–19.

l. [6:4] Eccl 4:2–3; Jb 3:11, 16.   m. [6:12] Jb 8:9; 14:2; Ps 102:12.
n. [6:12] Eccl 3:22; 8:7.   o. [7:1] Eccl 4:2; Prv 22:1.   p. [7:2] Eccl 12:1.

3 Sorrow is better than laughter;
　　when the face is sad, the heart grows
　　　wise.
4 The heart of the wise is in the house of
　　mourning,
　　but the heart of fools is in the house
　　　of merriment.
5 It is better to listen to the rebuke of the
　　wise
　　than to listen to the song of fools;
6 For as the crackling of thorns under a pot,
　　so is the fool's laughter.
This also is vanity.
7 Extortion can make a fool out of the
　　wise,
　　and a bribe corrupts the heart.
8 Better is the end of a thing than its
　　beginning;
　　better is a patient spirit than a lofty
　　　one.
9 Do not let anger upset your spirit,
　　for anger lodges in the bosom of a
　　　fool.

10Do not say: How is it that former times
were better than these? For it is not out of wisdom that you ask about this.

11 Wisdom is as good as an inheritance
　　and profitable to those who see the
　　　sun.

12*For the protection of wisdom is as the protection of money; and knowledge is profitable
because wisdom gives life to those who possess it.
13Consider the work of God. Who can make
straight what God has made crooked?q 14On a
good day enjoy good things, and on an evil day
consider: Both the one and the other God has
made, so that no one may find the least fault
with him.
**Critique of Sages on Justice and Wickedness.**
15†I have seen all manner of things in my vain
days: the just perishing in their justice, and the
wicked living long in their wickedness. 16"Be not
just to excess, and be not overwise. Why work
your own ruin? 17Be not wicked to excess, and
be not foolish. Why should you die before your
time?" 18It is good to hold to this rule, and not to
let that one go; but the one who fears God will
succeed with both.

19Wisdom is a better defense for the wise
than ten princes in the city, 20yet there is no one
on earth so just as to do good and never sin.
21Do not give your heart to every word that is
spoken; you may hear your servant cursing you,
22for your heart knows that you have many times
cursed others.
23All these things I probed in wisdom. I said,
"I will acquire wisdom"; but it was far beyond
me. 24What exists is far-reaching; it is deep, very
deep:‡ Who can find it out? 25§I turned my heart
toward knowledge; I sought and pursued wisdom and its design, and I recognized that wickedness is foolishness and folly is madness.
**Critique of Advice on Women.** 26ʄMore bitter
than death I find the womanʄ who is a hunter's
trap, whose heart is a snare, whose hands are
prison bonds. The one who pleases God will be
delivered from her, but the one who displeases
will be entrapped by her. 27See, this have I found,
says Qoheleth, adding one to one to find the
sum. 28What my soul still seeks and has yet to
find is this: "One man out of a thousand have
I found, but a woman among them all I have
not found." 29But this alone I have found: God
made humankind honest, but they have pursued
many designs.

## CHAPTER 8

### Critique of Advice to Heed Authority

1 "Who is like the wise person,
　　and who knows the explanation of
　　　things?
Wisdom illumines the face
　　and transforms a grim countenance.

2Observe the command of the king, in view
of your oath to God. 3Be not hasty to withdraw
from the king; do not persist in an unpleasant
situation, for he does whatever he pleases. 4His
word is sovereign, and who can say to him,
"What are you doing?"
5††u"Whoever observes a command knows
no harm, and the wise heart knows times and

---

*[7:12] St. Jerome's translation of v. 12b gives an edge to
wisdom over money: "But learning and wisdom excel in this,
that they bestow life on the one who possesses them."

†[7:15–24] The author continues both to affirm and to
counter traditional wisdom. He affirms a certain validity to
wisdom, but challenges complacency and mindless optimism.
His sense of life's uncertainty and insecurity finds expression,
for example, in the irony evident when v. 16 is read in the light
of vv. 20–24: How can one be "excessively" just or wise, when
justice and wisdom may be out of reach to begin with? The
only sure thing is to "fear God" (v. 18).

q. [7:13] Eccl 1:15.

‡[7:24] **Far-reaching . . . deep**: the spatial metaphor here
emphasizes wisdom's inaccessibility, a frequent theme in
wisdom literature; cf. Jb 28; Prv 30:1–4; Sir 24:28–29; Bar
3:14–23.

§[7:25–29] The emphasis is on the devious designs of
human beings in general, reflecting the viewpoint of Genesis.

ʄ[7:26] **More bitter than death . . . the woman**: warnings against the scheming, adulterous woman are common in
ancient wisdom (e.g., Prv 2:16–19, etc.).

**[8:1–4] The author continues to quote traditional wis-
dom but then to counter and qualify it. He concedes wisdom's
advantages (v. 1), but then describes the subservience and
sometimes demeaning demands required of the sage in the
court of the king (vv. 2–4).

††[8:5–9] The wise exhibit keen insight about human
nature and the course of events (vv. 5–6a). Yet their knowledge and wisdom confront certain limits, such as the mystery
of evil and the time and inevitability of death (vv. 6b–9).

r. [7:20] Jb 9:2; 1 Kgs 8:46; Rom 3:23.　s. [7:25] Eccl 1:17.　t. [7:26]
Prv 5:4.　u. [8:5] Prv 19:16.

judgments." [6v]Yes, there is a time and a judgment for everything. But it is a great evil for mortals [7w]that they are ignorant of what is to come; for who will make known to them how it will be? [8]No one is master of the breath of life so as to retain it, and none has mastery of the day of death. There is no exemption in wartime, nor does wickedness deliver those who practice it. [9]All these things I saw and I applied my heart to every work that is done under the sun, while one person tyrannizes over another for harm.

**The Problem of Retribution.** [10]Meanwhile I saw the wicked buried. They would come and go from the holy place. But those were forgotten in the city who had acted justly. This also is vanity.[*] [11]Because the sentence against an evil deed is not promptly executed, the human heart is filled with the desire to commit evil— [12†]because the sinner does evil a hundred times and survives. Though indeed I know that it shall be well with those who fear God, for their reverence toward him; [13]and that it shall not be well with the wicked, who shall not prolong their shadowy days, for their lack of reverence toward God.

[14]This is a vanity that occurs on earth: There are those who are just but are treated as though they had done evil, and those who are wicked but are treated as though they had done justly. This, too, I say is vanity. [15x]Therefore I praised joy, because there is nothing better for mortals under the sun than to eat and to drink and to be joyful; this will accompany them in their toil through the limited days of life God gives them under the sun.

[16]I applied my heart to know wisdom and to see the business that is done on earth, though neither by day nor by night do one's eyes see sleep, [17y]and I saw all the work of God: No mortal can find out the work that is done under the sun. However much mortals may toil in searching, no one finds it out; and even if the wise claim to know, they are unable to find it out.

*B. No One Knows the Future*

# CHAPTER 9

[1]All this I have kept in my heart and all this I examined: The just, the wise, and their deeds are in the hand of God. Love from hatred[‡] mortals cannot tell; both are before them. [2]Everything is the same for everybody: the same lot for the just and the wicked, for the good, for the clean and the unclean, for the one who offers sacrifice and the one who does not. As it is for the good, so it is for the sinner; as it is for the one who takes an oath, so it is for the one who fears an oath. [3]Among all the things that are done under the sun, this is the worst, that there is one lot for all. Hence the hearts of human beings are filled with evil, and madness is in their hearts during life; and afterward—to the dead!

[4]For whoever is chosen among all the living has hope: "A live dog[§] is better off than a dead lion." [5a]For the living know that they are to die, but the dead no longer know anything. There is no further recompense for them, because all memory of them is lost. [6]For them, love and hatred and rivalry have long since perished. Never again will they have part in anything that is done under the sun.

[7b]Go, eat your bread[¶] with joy and drink your wine with a merry heart, because it is now that God favors your works. [8]At all times let your garments be white, and spare not the perfume for your head. [9]Enjoy life with the wife you love, all the days of the vain life granted you under the sun. This is your lot in life, for the toil of your labors under the sun. [10]Anything you can turn your hand to, do with what power you have; for there will be no work, no planning, no knowledge, no wisdom in Sheol where you are going.

**The Time of Misfortune Is Not Known.** [11]Again I saw under the sun that the race is not won by the swift, nor the battle by the valiant, nor a livelihood by the wise, nor riches by the shrewd, nor favor by the experts; for a time of misfortune comes to all alike. [12]Human beings no more know their own time than fish taken in the fatal net or birds trapped in the snare; like these, mortals are caught when an evil time suddenly falls upon them.

**The Uncertain Future and the Sages.** [13]On the other hand I saw this wise deed under the sun, which I thought magnificent. [14]Against a small city with few inhabitants advanced a mighty

---

*[8:10] This difficult verse seems to contrast the wicked, who die enjoying a good reputation as pious individuals, and the just, who are quietly forgotten.

†[8:12–17] The author admits that traditional wisdom affirms the long life and success of the just and the short unhappy life of the wicked (vv. 12b–13). But he points out clear exceptions: the wicked who live long, and the just who suffer for no apparent reason (v. 14). His puzzlement and frustration prompt a twofold response: acceptance of whatever joy God chooses to give each day, and honest acknowledgment that no one can discover "the work of God" (cf. 3:11; 7:13; 11:5).

‡[9:1–3] **Love from hatred . . . everything is the same**: God seems to bestow divine favor or disfavor (love or hatred) indiscriminately on the just and wicked alike. More ominously, the arbitrariness and inevitability of death and adversity confront every human being, whether good or bad.

§[9:4–6] **A live dog . . . no further recompense**: human reason and experience persuaded Qoheleth that death with its finality and annihilating power cruelly negates the supreme value—life, and with it, all possibilities (cf. v. 10). Faith in eternal life has its foundation only in hope and trust in God's promise and in God's love.

¶[9:7–10] **Go, eat your bread . . . enjoy life**: the author confesses his inability to imprison God in a fixed and predictable way of acting. Thus he ponders a practical and pragmatic solution: Seize whatever opportunity one has to find joy, if God grants it.

---

v. [8:6] Eccl 3:17; 9:12.   w. [8:7] Eccl 3:22; 6:12; 10:14.   x. [8:15] Eccl 2:24; 3:22; 5:17–18; 9:7.   y. [8:17] Eccl 3:11.

z. [9:2] Eccl 2:14; 3:15.   a. [9:5] Eccl 1:11; 2:16.   b. [9:7] Eccl 2:24; 8:15; 11:9.

king, who surrounded it and threw up great siegeworks about it. [15]But in the city lived a man who, though poor, was wise, and he delivered it through his wisdom. Yet no one remembered this poor man. [16c]Though I had said, "Wisdom is better than force," yet the wisdom of the poor man is despised and his words go unheeded.

[17] The quiet words of the wise are better
  heeded
    than the shout of a ruler of fools.
[18] Wisdom is better than weapons of war,
    but one bungler destroys much
      good.

## CHAPTER 10

[1] Dead flies corrupt and spoil the
    perfumer's oil;
  more weighty than wisdom or
    wealth is a little folly![*]
[2] The wise heart turns to the right;
  the foolish heart to the left.[†]

[3]Even when walking in the street the fool, lacking understanding, calls everyone a fool.[‡]

[4]Should the anger of a ruler burst upon you, do not yield your place; for calmness[§] abates great offenses.

[5]I have seen under the sun another evil, like a mistake that proceeds from a tyrant: [6]a fool put in high position, while the great and the rich sit in lowly places. [7]I have seen slaves on horseback, while princes[¶] went on foot like slaves.

[8] Whoever digs a pit may fall into it,[d]
    and whoever breaks through a wall,
      a snake may bite.
[9] Whoever quarries stones may be hurt by
      them,
    and whoever chops wood[**] is in
      danger from it.

[10]If the ax becomes dull, and the blade is not sharpened, then effort must be increased. But the advantage of wisdom is success.

[11] If the snake bites before it is charmed,
    then there is no advantage in a
      charmer.[††]
[12] Words from the mouth of the wise win
      favor,
    but the lips of fools consume them.
[13] [e]The beginning of their words is folly,
    and the end of their talk is utter
      madness;
[14]     yet fools multiply words.
No one knows what is to come,
    for who can tell anyone what will
      be?[f]
[15] The toil of fools wearies them,
    so they do not know even the way
      to town.

## No One Knows What Evil Will Come

[16] Woe to you, O land, whose king is a
      youth,[‡‡]
    and whose princes feast in the
      morning!
[17] Happy are you, O land, whose king is of
      noble birth,
    and whose princes dine at the right
      time—
    for vigor[§§] and not in drinking bouts.
[18] Because of laziness, the rafters sag;
    when hands are slack, the house
      leaks.
[19] A feast is made for merriment
    and wine gives joy to the living,
    but money answers[¶¶] for everything.
[20] Even in your thoughts do not curse the
      king,
    nor in the privacy of your bedroom
      curse the rich;
For the birds of the air may carry your
      voice,
    a winged creature[***] may tell what
      you say.

---

*[10:1] **Dead flies . . . a little folly**: wisdom is vulnerable to even the smallest amount of folly. The collection of proverbs and sayings in chaps. 10 and 11 demonstrates the author's sharp insight and strengthens his credentials as a sage. It thus adds weight to his critique of the wisdom tradition's tendencies to self-assurance and naive optimism.

†[10:2] **Right . . . left**: the right hand is identified with power, moral goodness, favor; the left hand with ineptness and bad luck.

‡[10:3] **Calls everyone a fool**: or, "tells everyone that he (himself) is a fool."

§[10:4] **Calmness**: a frequent motif of wisdom; silence and reserve characterize the wise, while boisterousness and impetuosity identify the fool.

¶[10:6–7] **A fool . . . the rich . . . slaves . . . princes**: another wisdom motif: astonishment at the reversal of the usual order in the world and in human affairs.

**[10:8–9] **A pit . . . a wall . . . stones . . . wood**: popular sayings reflecting the need for caution and alertness against the unexpected. Snakes could find a home in the stone walls of ancient Palestine; cf. Am 5:19.

††[10:10–11] **Ax . . . success . . . snake . . . charmer**: possession of the proper skill (a form of "wisdom") can ensure success, as in the case of a sharpened ax; but one must use it before it is too late (v. 11). Cf. Sir 12:13.

‡‡[10:16] **A youth**: thus too young and inexperienced to govern effectively. **Feast in the morning**: either concluding a whole night of revelry or beginning a new round of merrymaking.

§§[10:17] **For vigor**: or, "with self-control, restraint."

¶¶[10:19] **Money answers**: a stark reminder that such a life requires money. It could also be an affirmation of the power of wealth: "Money conquers all."

***[10:20] **Birds of the air . . . winged creature**: a common motif in ancient literature, and a vivid reminder of the need for caution in dealing with the rich and powerful.

---

c. [9:16] Prv 24:5.  d. [10:8] Prv 26:27; Ps 7:16; Sir 27:29.

e. [10:13] Eccl 5:2; 6:11.  f. [10:14] Eccl 3:22; 6:12; 10:14.

## CHAPTER 11

1 *Send forth your bread upon the face of
the waters;
after a long time you may find it
again.
2 Make seven, or even eight portions;
you know not what misfortune may
come upon the earth.

### No One Knows What Good Will Come

3 †When the clouds are full,
they pour out rain upon the earth.
Whether a tree falls to the south or to the
north,
wherever it falls, there shall it lie.
4 One who pays heed to the wind will never
sow,
and one who watches the clouds will
never reap.
5 Just as you do not know how the life
breath
enters the human frame in the
mother's womb,
So you do not know the work of God,
who is working in everything.g
6 In the morning sow your seed,
and at evening do not let your hand
be idle:
For you do not know which of the two
will be successful,
or whether both alike will turn out
well.

**Poem on Youth and Old Age.** 7‡Light is sweet!
and it is pleasant for the eyes to see the sun.
8However many years mortals live, let
them, as they enjoy them all, remember that
the days of darkness will be many. All that is to
come is vanity.

9 Rejoice, O youth, while you are young
and let your heart be glad in the
days of your youth.
Follow the ways of your heart,
the vision of your eyes;

Yet understand regarding all this
that God will bring you to judgment.
10 Banish misery from your heart
and remove pain from your body,
for youth and black hair are fleeting.§

## CHAPTER 12

1 ¶Remember your Creator in the days of
your youth,
before the evil days come
And the years approach of which you
will say,
"I have no pleasure in them";
2 Before the sun is darkened,
and the light and the moon and the
stars
and the clouds return after the rain; .
3 **When the guardians of the house
tremble,
and the strong men are bent;
When the women who grind are idle
because they are few,
and those who look through the
windows grow blind;
4 When the doors to the street are shut,
and the sound of the mill is low;
When one rises at the call of a bird,
and all the daughters of song are quiet;
5 When one is afraid of heights,
and perils in the street;
When the almond tree blooms,
and the locust grows sluggish
and the caper berry is without effect,
Because mortals go to their lasting home,
and mourners go about the streets;
6 ††Before the silver cord is snapped
and the golden bowl is broken,
And the pitcher is shattered at the spring,
and the pulley is broken at the well,
7 And the dust returns to the earth as it
once was,
and the life breath returns to God
who gave it.‡‡h

---

§[11:10] **Fleeting**: lit., "vanity."

¶[12:1–7] The homage to life of 11:7–10 is deliberately balanced by the sombre yet shimmering radiance of this poem
on old age and death. The poem's enigmatic imagery has often
been interpreted allegorically, especially in vv. 3–5. Above all
it seeks to evoke an atmosphere as well as an attitude toward
death and old age.

**[12:3–5] An allegorical reading of these verses sees ref-
erences to the human body—"guardians": the arms; "strong
men": the legs; "women who grind": the teeth; "those who
look": the eyes; "the doors": the lips; "daughters of song": the
voice; "the almond tree blooms": resembling the white hair of
old age; "the locust . . . sluggish": the stiffness in movement of
the aged; "the caper berry": a stimulant for appetite.

††[12:6] The golden bowl suspended by the silver cord is
a symbol of life; the snapping of the cord and the breaking
of the bowl, a symbol of death. **The pitcher . . . the pulley:**
another pair of metaphors for life and its ending.

‡‡[12:7] Death is portrayed in terms of the description of
creation in Gn 2:7: the body corrupts in the grave, and the
life breath (lit., "spirit"), or gift of life, returns to God who had
breathed upon what he had formed.

---

*[11:1–2] These two sayings can be understood against a
commercial background. They acknowledge the uncertainty
and risk such activity involves. At the same time they encourage action and a spirit of adventure. The first (v. 1) speaks of
trade and overseas investment: Export your grain ("bread") to
foreign markets and you may be surprised at the substantial profits. The second (v. 2) encourages diversification of
investment (seven, or even eight shipments of grain) to insure
against heavy losses.

†[11:3–6] Verses 3, 4, and 6 expand on the theme of
uncertainty and human inability to assess accurately every
situation. Verse 4, however, comments on the disadvantages
of too much caution: Only those willing to risk will enjoy success. But only the Creator knows the mystery of the "work of
God" (v. 5).

‡[11:7–10] The concluding part of the book opens with a
final bittersweet homage to life and an enthusiastic encouragement to rejoice in its gifts while they are within grasp.

g. [11:5] Eccl 3:11; 7:13; 8:17.

h. [12:7] Eccl 3:20–21; Jb 34:14–15.

8  Vanity of vanities, says Qoheleth,
    all things are vanity!^i

**Epilogue.** ^9*Besides being wise, Qoheleth taught the people knowledge, and weighed, scrutinized and arranged many proverbs. ^10Qoheleth sought to find appropriate sayings, and to write down true sayings with precision. ^11The sayings of the wise are like goads; like fixed spikes are the collected sayings given by one shepherd.^† ^12jAs to more than these,^‡ my son, beware. Of the

making of many books there is no end, and in much study there is weariness for the flesh.

^13§kThe last word, when all is heard: Fear God and keep his commandments, for this concerns all humankind; ^14lbecause God will bring to judgment every work, with all its hidden qualities, whether good or bad.

---

*[12:9] A disciple briefly describes and praises the master's skill and reputation as a sage.

†[12:11] **One shepherd**: perhaps referring to the book's author, who gathers or "shepherds" together its contents. God could also be "the one shepherd," the ultimate depository and source of true wisdom.

‡[12:12] **As to more than these**: the words seem to refer to the writings of Ecclesiastes and other sages. They are adequate and sufficient; any more involves exhaustive labor.

---

i. [12:8] Eccl 1:2.   j. [12:12] Eccl 1:18.

---

§[12:13–14] These words reaffirm traditional wisdom doctrine such as fear of God and faithful obedience, perhaps lest some of the more extreme statements of the author be misunderstood. Although the epilogue has been interpreted as a criticism of the book's author, it is really a summary that betrays the unruffled spirit of later sages, who were not shocked by Qoheleth's statements. They honored him as a *hakam* or sage (v. 9), even as they preserved his statements about the futility of life (v. 8), and the mystery of divine judgment (8:17; 11:5).

---

k. [12:13] Eccl 5:6.   l. [12:14] Eccl 11:9.

# THE SONG OF
# SONGS

❧

The Song of Songs (or Canticle of Canticles) is an exquisite collection of love lyrics, arranged to tell a dramatic tale of mutual desire and courtship. It presents an inspired portrayal of ideal human love, a resounding affirmation of the goodness of human sexuality that is applicable to the sacredness and the depth of married union.

Although the poem is attributed to Solomon in the traditional title (1:1), the language and style of the work, among other considerations, suggest a time after the end of the Babylonian exile (538 B.C.) when an unknown poet collected extant love poems, perhaps composing new material, and arranged the whole into the masterpiece we have before us. Some scholars argue the possibility of female authorship for at least portions of the Song.

The structure of the Song is difficult to analyze; this translation regards it as a lyric dialogue, with dramatic movement and interest. In both form and content, sections of the Song bear great similarity to the secular love songs of ancient Egypt and the "Sacred Marriage" cult songs of Mesopotamia which celebrate the union between divine partners.

While the lovers in the Song are clearly human figures, both Jewish and Christian traditions across the centuries have adopted "allegorical" interpretations. The Song is seen as a beautiful picture of the ideal Israel, the chosen people whom the Lord leads by degrees to a greater understanding and closer union in the bond of perfect love. Such readings of the Song build on Israel's covenant tradition. Isaiah (Is 5:1–7; 54:4–8; 62:5), Jeremiah (Jer 2:2–3, 32), and Ezekiel (Ez 16; 23) all characterize the covenant between the Lord and Israel as a marriage. Hosea the prophet sees the idolatry of Israel in the adultery of Gomer (Hos 1–3). He also represents the Lord speaking to Israel's heart (Hos 2:16) and changing her into a new spiritual people, purified by the Babylonian captivity and betrothed anew to her divine Lover "in justice and uprightness, in love and mercy" (Hos 2:21). Similar imagery has also been used frequently in Jewish mystical texts. The Song offers a welcome corrective to negative applications of the theological metaphor of the marriage/covenant in some prophetic texts. It frequently proclaims a joyous reciprocity between the lovers and highlights the active role of the female partner, now a pure figure to be cherished rather than an adulterous woman to be punished and abused. See also Is 62:3–5.

Christian tradition has followed Israel's example in using marriage as an image for the relationship with God. This image is found extensively in the New Testament (Mt 9:15; 25:1–13; Jn 3:29; 2 Cor 11:2; Eph 5:23–32; Rev 19:7–9; 21:9–11). Thus the Song has been read as a sublime portrayal and praise of this mutual love of the Lord and his people. Christian writers have interpreted the Song in terms of the union between Christ and the Church and of the union between Christ and the individual soul, particularly in the writings of Origen and St. Bernard.

## CHAPTER 1

¹The Song of Songs,* which is Solomon's.

### The Woman Speaks of Her Lover

2  **W** †ªLet him kiss me with kisses of his
            mouth,
        for your love is better than wine,‡
3      better than the fragrance of your
            perfumes.§
    Your name is a flowing perfume—
        therefore young women love you.
4  ᵇDraw me after you! Let us run!¶
    The king has brought me to his bed
            chambers.
    Let us exult and rejoice in you;
        let us celebrate your love: it is
            beyond wine!
    Rightly do they love you!

### Love's Boast

5  **W** I am black and beautiful,
        Daughters of Jerusalem**—
    Like the tents of Qedar,
        like the curtains of Solomon.
6  Do not stare at me because I am so
            black,††
        because the sun has burned me.
    The sons of my mother were angry with
            me;

they charged me with the care of the
            vineyards:
    my own vineyard I did not take
            care of.

### Love's Inquiry

7  **W** Tell me, you whom my soul loves,
        where you shepherd,‡‡ where you
            give rest at midday.
    Why should I be like one wandering
        after the flocks of your companions?
8  **M** If you do not know,
        most beautiful among women,
    Follow the tracks of the flock
        and pasture your lambs§§
            near the shepherds' tents.

### Love's Vision

9  **M** To a mare among Pharaoh's chariotry¶¶
        I compare you, my friend:
10  Your cheeks lovely in pendants,
        your neck in jewels.
11  We will make pendants of gold for you,
        and ornaments of silver.

### How Near Is Love!

12  **W** While the king was upon his couch,
        my spikenard*** gave forth its
            fragrance.
13  My lover††† is to me a sachet of myrrh;
        between my breasts he lies.
14  My lover is to me a cluster of henna‡‡‡
        from the vineyards of En-gedi.
15  **M** ᶜHow beautiful you are, my friend,
        how beautiful! your eyes are doves!§§§
16  **W** How beautiful you are, my lover—
        handsome indeed!

---

*[1:1] **Song of Songs**: in Hebrew and Aramaic the idiom "the X of Xs" denotes the superlative (e.g., "king of kings" = "the highest king"; cf. Dt 10:17; Eccl 1:2; 12:8; Ezr 7:12; Dn 2:37). The ascription of authorship to Solomon is traditional. The heading may also mean "for Solomon" or "about Solomon."

†[1:2–8:14] This translation augments the canonical text of the Song with the letters *W*, *M*, and *D*, placed in the margin, to indicate which of the characters in the Song is speaking: the woman, the man, or the "Daughters of Jerusalem." This interpretive gloss follows an early Christian scribal practice, attested in some Septuagint manuscripts from the first half of the first millennium A.D.

‡[1:2–7] The woman and her female chorus address the man, here viewed as king and shepherd (both are familiar metaphors for God; cf. Ps 23:1; Is 40:11; Jn 10:1–16). There is a wordplay between "kiss" (Hebrew *nashaq*) and "drink" (*shaqah*), anticipating 8:1–2. The change from third person ("let him kiss . . .") to second person (". . . for your love . . .") is not uncommon in the Song and elsewhere (1:4; 2:4; etc.; Ps 23:1–3, 4–5, 6; etc.) and reflects the woman's move from interior monologue to direct address to her partner.

§[1:3] **Your perfumes**: *shemen* (perfume) is a play on *shem* (name).

¶[1:4] Another change, but from second to third person (cf. 1:2). The "king" metaphor recurs in 1:12; 3:5–11; 7:6. **Let us exult**: perhaps she is addressing young women, calling on them to join in the praise of her lover.

**[1:5] **Daughters of Jerusalem**: the woman contrasts herself with the elite city women, who act as her female "chorus" (5:9; 6:1). **Qedar**: a Syrian desert region whose name suggests darkness; tents were often made of black goat hair. **Curtains**: tent coverings, or tapestries. **Solomon**: it could also be read Salma, a region close to Qedar.

††[1:6] **So black**: tanned from working outdoors in her brothers' vineyards, unlike the city women she addresses. **My own vineyard**: perhaps the woman herself; see 8:8–10 for her relationship to her brothers.

‡‡[1:7] **Shepherd**: a common metaphor for kings. Here and elsewhere in the Song (3:1; 5:8; 6:1), the woman expresses her desire to be in the company of her lover. The search for the lover and her failure to find him create a degree of tension. Only at the end (8:5–14) do the lovers finally possess each other.

§§[1:8] **Pasture your lambs**: both the woman and the man act as shepherds in the Song.

¶¶[1:9–11] The man compares the woman's beauty to the rich adornment of the royal chariot of Pharaoh. **My friend**: a special feminine form of the word "friend," appearing only in the Song (1:15; 2:2, 10, 13; 4:1, 7; 5:2; 6:4) and used to express endearment and equality in love. Cf. Hos 3:1 for the use of the masculine form of the term in a context with sexual overtones.

***[1:12] **Spikenard**: a precious perfumed ointment from India; in 4:13–14, a metaphor for the woman herself.

†††[1:13] **My lover**: the woman's favorite term for her partner (used 27 times). **Myrrh**: an aromatic resin of balsam or roses used in cosmetics, incense, and medicines.

‡‡‡[1:14] **Henna**: a plant which bears white scented flowers, used in cosmetics and medicines. **En-gedi**: a Judean desert oasis overlooking the Dead Sea.

§§§[1:15] **Doves**: doves are pictured in the ancient world as messengers of love.

---

a. [1:2–3] Sg 4:10.   b. [1:4] Sg 4:10.

c. [1:15] Sg 4:1, 7.

Verdant indeed is our couch;[*]
<sup>17</sup>     the beams of our house are cedars,
         our rafters, cypresses.

## CHAPTER 2

<sup>1</sup>   **W** I am a flower of Sharon,[†]
       a lily of the valleys.
<sup>2</sup>   **M** Like a lily among thorns,
       so is my friend among women.
<sup>3</sup>   **W** Like an apple tree among the trees of
           the woods,
       so is my lover among men.
   In his shadow[‡] I delight to sit,
       and his fruit is sweet to my taste.
<sup>4</sup>   [d]He brought me to the banquet hall[§]
       and his glance at me signaled love.
<sup>5</sup>   [e]Strengthen me with raisin cakes,[¶]
       refresh me with apples,
       for I am sick with love.
<sup>6</sup>   [f]His left hand is under my head
       and his right arm embraces me.
<sup>7</sup>   [g]I adjure you, Daughters of Jerusalem,[**]
       by the gazelles and the does of the
           field,
   Do not awaken, or stir up love
       until it is ready.

### Her Lover's Visit Remembered

<sup>8</sup>   **W** The sound of my lover! here he comes[††]
       springing across the mountains,
       leaping across the hills.
<sup>9</sup>   My lover is like a gazelle[‡‡]
       or a young stag.
   See! He is standing behind our wall,
       gazing through the windows,
       peering through the lattices.
<sup>10</sup>  My lover speaks and says to me,

   **M** "Arise, my friend, my beautiful one,
       and come!
<sup>11</sup>  For see, the winter is past,
       the rains are over and gone.
<sup>12</sup>  The flowers appear on the earth,
       the time of pruning the vines has
           come,
   and the song of the turtledove is
       heard in our land.
<sup>13</sup>  The fig tree puts forth its figs,
       and the vines, in bloom, give forth
           fragrance.
   Arise, my friend, my beautiful one,
       and come!
<sup>14</sup>  My dove in the clefts of the rock,[§§]
       in the secret recesses of the cliff,
   Let me see your face,
       let me hear your voice,
   For your voice is sweet,
       and your face is lovely."
<sup>15</sup>  **W** Catch us the foxes,[¶¶] the little foxes
       that damage the vineyards; for our
           vineyards are in bloom!
<sup>16</sup>  [h]My lover belongs to me and I to him;
       he feeds among the lilies.
<sup>17</sup>  [i]Until the day grows cool[***] and the
           shadows flee,
   roam, my lover,
   Like a gazelle or a young stag
       upon the rugged mountains.

## CHAPTER 3

### Loss and Discovery

<sup>1</sup>   **W** [j]On my bed at night I sought him[†††]
       whom my soul loves—
   I sought him but I did not find him.
<sup>2</sup>   "Let me rise then and go about the city,[‡‡‡]
       through the streets and squares;
   Let me seek him whom my soul loves."
       I sought him but I did not find him.
<sup>3</sup>   The watchmen found me,
       as they made their rounds in the
           city:
   "Him whom my soul loves—have
       you seen him?"
<sup>4</sup>   [k]Hardly had I left them

---

*[1:16–17] Continuing the royal metaphor, the meeting place of the lovers, a shepherd's hut of green branches, becomes a palace with beams of cedar and rafters of cypress when adorned with their love.

†[2:1] **Flower of Sharon**: probably the narcissus, which grows in the fertile Plain of Sharon lying between Mount Carmel and Jaffa on the Mediterranean coast. **Lily**: the lotus plant.

‡[2:3] **Shadow**: suggestive of protection (cf. Jgs 9:15; Ez 17:23; Ps 17:8; 121:5) and, here, of the woman's joy in the presence of her lover.

§[2:4–6] **The banquet hall**: the sweet things of the table, the embrace of the woman and man, express the richness of their affection and the intimacy of their love.

¶[2:5] **Raisin cakes**: perhaps pastries used in the worship of the fertility goddess (cf. Hos 3:1; Jer 7:18; 44:19). **Apples**: this is the common translation of a fruit that cannot be identified (cf. 2:3; 8:5); it appears frequently in Sumerian love poetry associated with the worship of the goddess Inanna. **Sick**: lovesickness is a popular motif in ancient love poetry.

**[2:7] Cf. 3:5; 5:8; 8:4. **By the gazelles and the does**: perhaps a mitigated invocation of the divinity based on the assonance in Hebrew of the names of these animals with terms for God.

††[2:8–13] In this sudden change of scene, the woman describes a rendezvous and pictures her lover hastening toward her dwelling until his voice is heard calling her to him.

‡‡[2:9] **Gazelle**: a frequent motif in ancient poems from Mesopotamia.

§§[2:14] The woman is addressed as though she were a dove in a mountain cleft out of sight and reach.

¶¶[2:15] A snatch of song in answer to the request of 2:14; cf. 8:13–14. **Foxes**: they threaten to disturb the security of vineyards. The vineyards are women sought after by young lovers, i.e., foxes.

***[2:17] **Grows cool**: in the evening when the sun is going down. Cf. Gn 3:8. **Rugged**: Hebrew obscure; some interpret it as a geographical name; others, in the sense of spices (cf. 8:14); still others, of sacrifice (Gn 15:10); the image probably refers here to the woman herself.

†††[3:1–5] See the parallel in 5:2–8.

‡‡‡[3:2] The motif of seeking/finding here and elsewhere is used by later Christian and Jewish mystics to speak of the soul's search for the divine.

---

d. [2:4] Sg 1:4.   e. [2:5] Sg 5:8.   f. [2:6] Sg 8:3.   g. [2:7] Sg 3:5; 8:4.

h. [2:16] Sg 6:3; 7:10.   i. [2:17] Sg 4:6; 8:14.   j. [3:1–5] Sg 5:2–8.
k. [3:4] Sg 8:2.

when I found him whom my soul
loves.*
I held him and would not let him go
until I had brought him to my
mother's house,
to the chamber of her who
conceived me.
5 ᴵI adjure you, Daughters of Jerusalem,
by the gazelles and the does of the
field,
Do not awaken or stir up love
until it is ready.

### Solomon's Wedding Procession

6 D ᵐWho is this coming up from the
desert,†
like columns of smoke
Perfumed with myrrh and frankincense,
with all kinds of exotic powders?
7 See! it is the litter of Solomon;
sixty valiant men surround it,
of the valiant men of Israel:
8 All of them expert with the sword,
skilled in battle,
Each with his sword at his side
against the terrors‡ of the night.
9 King Solomon made himself an enclosed
litter
of wood from Lebanon.
10 He made its columns of silver,
its roof of gold,
Its seat of purple cloth,
its interior lovingly fitted.§
Daughters of Jerusalem, ¹¹go out
and look upon King Solomon
In the crown with which his mother has
crowned him
on the day of his marriage,
on the day of the joy of his heart.

### CHAPTER 4

### The Beauty of the Woman

1 M ⁿ, ᵒHow beautiful you are, my friend,
how beautiful you are!
Your eyes are doves
behind your veil.

Your hair is like a flock of goats
streaming down Mount Gilead.ᵉ
2 Your teeth** are like a flock of ewes to be
shorn,
that come up from the washing,
All of them big with twins,
none of them barren.
3 Like a scarlet strand, your lips,
and your mouth—lovely!
Like pomegranate†† halves, your cheeks
behind your veil.
4 ᵖLike a tower of David, your neck,
built in courses,
A thousand shields hanging upon it,
all the armor of warriors.‡‡
5 ᵍYour breasts are like two fawns,
twins of a gazelle
feeding among the lilies.
6 ʳUntil the day grows cool
and the shadows flee,
I shall go to the mountain of myrrh,
to the hill of frankincense.§§
7 You are beautiful in every way, my
friend,
there is no flaw in you!¶¶
8 With me from Lebanon, my bride!
With me from Lebanon, come!
Descend from the peak of Amana,
from the peak of Senir and
Hermon,***
From the lairs of lions,
from the leopards' heights.
9 ˢYou have ravished my heart, my sister,†††
my bride;
you have ravished my heart with one
glance of your eyes,
with one bead of your necklace.
10 ᵗHow beautiful is your love,
my sister, my bride,
How much better is your love than wine,
and the fragrance of your perfumes
than any spice!

¶[4:1] This section (vv. 1–7) begins a *wasf*, a traditional
poetic form describing the physical attributes of one's partner
in terms of the natural world (cf. 5:10–16; 6:5b–7; 7:1–7). **Veil:**
women of the region customarily veiled their faces for some
occasions (cf. 4:3; 6:7; Gn 24:65–67; 38:14–19).
**[4:2] Teeth:** praised for whiteness and evenness.
††[4:3] **Pomegranate:** a fruit with a firm skin and deep red
color. The woman's cheek (or perhaps her brow) is compared,
in roundness and tint, to a half-pomegranate.
‡‡[4:4] The ornaments about her neck are compared to the
trophies and armaments on the city walls. Cf. 1 Kgs 10:10;
14:26–28; Ez 27:10.
§§[4:6] **Mountain of myrrh . . . hill of frankincense:** spoken figuratively of the woman; cf. 8:14.
¶¶[4:7] Cf. the description of the church in Eph 5:27.
***[4:8] **Amana . . . Senir and Hermon:** these rugged heights
symbolize obstacles that would separate the lovers; cf. 2:14.
†††[4:9] **Sister:** a term of endearment; brother-sister language forms part of the conventional language of love used in
this canticle, the Book of Tobit, and elsewhere in poetry from
Egypt, Mesopotamia, and Syro-Palestine.

*[3:4] **Whom my soul loves:** the fourfold repetition of this
phrase in vv. 1–4 highlights the depth of the woman's emotion and desire. **Mother's house:** cf. 8:2; a place of safety and
intimacy, one which implicitly signifies approval of the lovers'
relationship.
†[3:6–11] This may be an independent poem. In context it
portrays the lover as King Solomon, escorted by sixty armed
men, coming in royal procession to meet a bride.
‡[3:8] **Terrors:** cf. Ps 91:5; perhaps bandits lying in wait,
unidentified dangers lurking in darkness.
§[3:10] **Lovingly fitted:** translation uncertain. The phrase
"Daughters of Jerusalem" is read here with the following verse.

l. [3:5] Sg 2:7; 8:4.   m. [3:6] Sg 6:10; 8:5.   n. [4:1–3] Sg 6:5–7.
o. [4:1] Sg 1:15.

p. [4:4] Sg 7:5.   q. [4:5] Sg 7:4.   r. [4:6] Sg 2:17.   s. [4:9] Sg 6:5.
t. [4:10] Sg 1:2–3.

<sup>11</sup> Your lips drip honey,<sup>*</sup> my bride,
   honey and milk are under your
      tongue;
And the fragrance of your garments
   is like the fragrance of Lebanon.

### The Lover's Garden

<sup>12</sup> **M** "A garden enclosed, my sister, my bride,
   a garden enclosed, a fountain
      sealed!<sup>†</sup>
<sup>13</sup> Your branches are a grove of
      pomegranates,
   with fruits of choicest yield:
Henna with spikenard,
<sup>14</sup> spikenard and saffron,
Sweet cane and cinnamon,
   with all kinds of frankincense;
Myrrh and aloes,
   with all the finest spices;<sup>‡</sup>
<sup>15</sup> A garden fountain, a well of living
      water,
   streams flowing from Lebanon.
<sup>16</sup> Awake,<sup>§</sup> north wind!
   Come, south wind!
Blow upon my garden
   that its perfumes may spread
      abroad.
**W** Let my lover come to his garden
   and eat its fruits of choicest yield.

### CHAPTER 5

<sup>1</sup> **M** 'I have come to my garden, my sister,
      my bride;
   I gather my myrrh with my spices,
I eat my honeycomb with my honey,
   I drink my wine with my milk.
**D?** Eat, friends; drink!
   Drink deeply, lovers!<sup>¶</sup>

### A Fruitless Search

<sup>2</sup> **W** "I was sleeping, but my heart was awake."
   The sound of my lover knocking!
"Open to me, my sister, my friend,
   my dove, my perfect one!
For my head is wet with dew,

my hair, with the moisture of the
      night."
<sup>3</sup> I have taken off my robe,<sup>††</sup>
   am I then to put it on?
I have bathed my feet,
   am I then to soil them?
<sup>4</sup> My lover put his hand in through the
      opening:
   my innermost being<sup>‡‡</sup> trembled
      because of him.
<sup>5</sup> I rose to open for my lover,
   my hands dripping myrrh:
My fingers, flowing myrrh
   upon the handles of the lock.
<sup>6</sup> I opened for my lover—
   but my lover had turned and gone!
   At his leaving, my soul sank.
I sought him, but I did not find him;
   I called out after him, but he did not
      answer me.<sup>§§</sup>
<sup>7</sup> The watchmen<sup>¶¶</sup> found me,
   as they made their rounds in the city;
They beat me, they wounded me,
   they tore off my mantle,
   the watchmen of the walls.
<sup>8</sup> <sup>x</sup>I adjure you, Daughters of Jerusalem,
   if you find my lover
What shall you tell him?
   that I am sick with love.

### The Lost Lover Described

<sup>9</sup> **D** How does your lover differ from any
      other lover,
   most beautiful among women?
How does your lover differ from any
      other,
   that you adjure us so?
<sup>10</sup> **W** My lover is radiant and ruddy;<sup>***</sup>
   outstanding among thousands.
<sup>11</sup> His head is gold, pure gold,
   his hair like palm fronds,
   as black as a raven.
<sup>12</sup> His eyes are like doves
   beside streams of water,
Bathing in milk,
   sitting<sup>†††</sup> by brimming pools.

---

*[4:11] **Honey**: sweet words (cf. Prv 5:3) or perhaps kisses (1:2–3). **Honey and milk**: familiar descriptions for the fertile promised land (Ex 3:8, 17; Lv 20:24; Nm 13:27; Dt 6:3).

†[4:12] **Garden enclosed . . . fountain sealed**: reserved for the lover alone. Cf. Prv 5:15–19 for similar images used to describe fruitful, committed relationship.

‡[4:14] These plants are all known for their sweet fragrance.

§[4:16] **Awake**: the same verb is used of love in 3:5. The woman may be the speaker of 16a, as it is she who issues the invitation of 16b. **His garden**: the woman herself.

¶[5:1] **Eat . . . lovers**: the translation and meaning are uncertain.

**[5:2–8] An experience of anticipation and loss similar to that in 3:1–5. The lover's abrupt appearance resembles that in 2:8–9.

††[5:3] **Robe**: knee-length undergarment worn by men and women. **Am I then . . . ?**: the woman's refusal is a form of gentle teasing; that she does not really reject her lover is shown by her actions in vv. 5–6. See 1:7–8; 2:14–15, for other teasing interchanges.

‡‡[5:4] **My innermost being**: lit., "innards." In Gn 25:23, Is 49:1; Ps 71:6, the word appears to carry the meaning of "womb."

§§[5:6] The motif of the locked-out lover is common in classical Greek and Latin poetry.

¶¶[5:7] **The watchmen**: they do not know the reason for the woman's appearance in the city streets; cf. 3:2–4.

***[5:10–11] In answer to the question of 5:9 the woman sings her lover's praises (vv. 10–16). **Ruddy**: also used of David (1 Sm 16:12; 17:42). **Gold**: indicates how precious the lover is. **Palm fronds**: his thick, luxuriant growth of hair.

†††[5:12] **Sitting . . .**: the translation of this line is uncertain; it may continue the metaphor of the lover's eyes, or refer to

---

u. [4:12] Sg 6:2, 11.   v. [5:1] Sg 6:2.   w. [5:2] Sg 3:1–2.

x. [5:8] Sg 2:7; 8:4.

<sup>13</sup> His cheeks are like beds of spices
    yielding aromatic scents;
his lips are lilies
    that drip flowing myrrh.
<sup>14</sup> His arms are rods of gold
    adorned with gems;
His loins, a work of ivory
    covered with sapphires.
<sup>15</sup> His legs, pillars of alabaster,
    resting on golden pedestals.
His appearance, like the Lebanon,
    imposing as the cedars.
<sup>16</sup> His mouth is sweetness itself;
    he is delightful in every way.
Such is my lover, and such my friend,
    Daughters of Jerusalem!

## CHAPTER 6

### The Lost Lover Found

<sup>1</sup> **D** Where has your lover gone,
    most beautiful among women?
Where has your lover withdrawn
    that we may seek him with you?*
<sup>2</sup> **W** *y*My lover has come down to his garden,†
    to the beds of spices,
To feed in the gardens
    and to gather lilies.
<sup>3</sup> *z*I belong to my lover, and my lover
    belongs to me;
he feeds among the lilies.

### The Beauty of the Woman

<sup>4</sup> **M** Beautiful as Tirzah are you, my friend;‡
    fair as Jerusalem,
    fearsome as celestial visions!
<sup>5</sup> *a*Turn your eyes away from me,
    for they stir me up.
Your hair is like a flock of goats
    streaming down from Gilead.
<sup>6</sup> *b*Your teeth are like a flock of ewes
    that come up from the washing,
All of them big with twins,
    none of them barren.

<sup>7</sup> Like pomegranate halves,
    your cheeks behind your veil.
<sup>8</sup> Sixty are the queens, eighty the
    concubines,
    and young women without
    number—
<sup>9</sup> One alone*s* is my dove, my perfect one,
    her mother's special one,
    favorite of the one who bore her.
Daughters see her and call her happy,
    queens and concubines, and they
    praise her:
<sup>10</sup> *c*"Who*¶* is this that comes forth like the
    dawn,
    beautiful as the white moon, pure as
    the blazing sun,
    fearsome as celestial visions?"

### Love's Meeting

<sup>11</sup> **W** *d*To the walnut grove** I went down,
    to see the young growth of the
    valley;
To see if the vines were in bloom,
    if the pomegranates had blossomed.
<sup>12</sup> Before I knew it, my desire had made me
    the blessed one of the prince's
    people.††

## CHAPTER 7

### The Beauty of the Beloved

<sup>1</sup> **D?** Turn, turn, O Shulammite!‡‡
    turn, turn that we may gaze upon
    you!
**W** How can you gaze upon the Shulammite
    as at the dance of the two camps?
<sup>2</sup> **M** How beautiful are your feet in sandals,*§§*
    O noble daughter!

---

§[6:9] **One alone:** the incomparability of the woman is a favorite motif in love poetry.
¶[6:10] **"Who . . . ":** the speakers may be the women of vv. 8–9. **Moon . . . sun:** lit., "the white" and "the hot," respectively (cf. Is 24:23; 30:26). **Fearsome:** see note on 6:4–9.
**[6:11] **Walnut grove:** also a site of activity in a wedding hymn of the Syrian moon goddess Nikkal (cf. the woman compared to the moon in v. 10).
††[6:12] The text is obscure in Hebrew and in the ancient versions. The Vulgate reads: "I did not know; my soul disturbed me because of the chariots of Aminadab." Based on a parallel in Jgs 5:24, "chariots" is here emended to "blessed one."
‡‡[7:1] **Shulammite:** the woman is so designated because she is considered to be from Shulam (or Shunem) in the plain of Esdraelon (cf. 1 Kgs 1:3), or because the name may mean "the peaceful one," and thus recall the name of Solomon. **Turn:** she is asked to face the speaker(s). **How . . . :** she refuses to be regarded as a spectacle ("the dance of the two camps" is unknown). Some interpret the episode as an invitation to her to dance.
§§[7:2–6] Another description of the woman's charms. **Sandals:** the woman's sandaled foot was apparently considered quite seductive (Jdt 16:9). **Noble:** a possible connection to the enigmatic "prince" of 6:12. **Curving . . . jewels:** the meaning of these Hebrew words is not certain. Wine and wheat suggest fertility.

---

another part of his anatomy (e.g., teeth) which has been omitted from the text.
*[6:1] The Daughters of Jerusalem are won by this description of the lover and offer their aid in seeking him (cf. 5:6, 9).
†[6:2–3] The woman implies here that she had never really lost her lover, for he has come down to his garden (cf. 2:16; 4:5). **Feed . . . lilies:** the imagery here evokes both a shepherd pasturing his flocks and erotic play between the lovers (2:16; 4:5, 12, 16).
‡[6:4–9] The man again celebrates the woman's beauty. **Tirzah:** probably meaning "pleasant"; it was the early capital of the Northern Kingdom of Israel (1 Kgs 16). **Celestial visions:** the meaning is uncertain. Military images may be implied here, i.e., the "heavenly hosts" who fight along with God on Israel's behalf (cf. Jgs 5:20), or perhaps a reference to the awesome goddesses of the region who combined aspects of both fertility and war.

y. [6:2] Sg 4:12; 5:1.  z. [6:3] Sg 2:16; 7:11.  a. [6:5] Sg 4:9.
b. [6:6–7] Sg 4:1–3.

c. [6:10] Sg 3:6; 8:5.  d. [6:11] Sg 4:12–5:1; 7:13.

Your curving thighs like jewels,
the product of skilled hands.
³ Your valley,* a round bowl
that should never lack mixed wine.
Your belly, a mound of wheat,
encircled with lilies.
⁴ ᵉYour breasts are like two fawns,
twins of a gazelle.
⁵ ᶠYour neck like a tower of ivory;
your eyes, pools in Heshbon
by the gate of Bath-rabbim.
Your nose like the tower of Lebanon
that looks toward Damascus.†
⁶ Your head rises upon you like Carmel;‡
your hair is like purple;
a king is caught in its locks.

### Love's Desires

⁷ How beautiful you are, how fair,
my love, daughter of delights!
⁸ Your very form resembles a date-palm,§
and your breasts, clusters.
⁹ I thought, "Let me climb the date-palm!
Let me take hold of its branches!
Let your breasts be like clusters of the
vine
and the fragrance of your breath like
apples,
¹⁰ And your mouth like the best wine—
W that flows down smoothly for my
lover,
gliding⁹ over my lips and teeth.
¹¹ ᵍI belong to my lover,**
his yearning is for me.
¹² Come, my lover! Let us go out to the
fields,
let us pass the night among the
henna.
¹³ ʰLet us go early to the vineyards, and see
if the vines are in bloom,
If the buds have opened,
if the pomegranates have
blossomed;

There will I give you my love.
¹⁴ The mandrakes†† give forth fragrance,
and over our doors are all choice
fruits;
Fruits both fresh and dried, my lover,
have I kept in store for you.

### CHAPTER 8

¹ Would that you were a brother to me,
nursed at my mother's breasts!
If I met you out of doors, I would kiss
you
and none would despise me.
² ⁱI would lead you, bring you to my
mother's house,
where you would teach me,
Where I would give you to drink
spiced wine, my pomegranate‡‡
juice.
³ ʲHis left hand is under my head,
and his right arm embraces me.
⁴ ᵏI adjure you, Daughters of Jerusalem,
do not awaken or stir up love
until it is ready!

### The Return from the Desert

⁵ D? ˡWho is this coming up from the desert,
leaning upon her lover?
W Beneath the apple tree I awakened
you;§§
there your mother conceived you;
there she who bore you conceived.

### True Love

⁶ Set me as a seal¶¶ upon your heart,
as a seal upon your arm;
For Love is strong as Death,
longing is fierce as Sheol.
Its arrows are arrows of fire,
flames of the divine.

---

*[7:3] **Valley:** lit., navel; a discreet allusion to her sex.

†[7:5] The comparison emphasizes the stateliness of her neck, and the clarity of her eyes. **Bath-rabbim:** a proper name which occurs only here; there was a city of Rabbah northeast of Heshbon in Transjordan. Cf. Jer 49:3.

‡[7:6] **Carmel:** a prominent set of cliffs overlooking the Mediterranean.

§[7:8–9] **Date-palm:** a figure of stateliness. The lover is eager to enjoy the possession of his beloved.

¶[7:10] **Gliding:** the beloved interrupts her partner's compliment by referring to the intoxication of their union. The translation rests on an emendation of the enigmatic "the lips of the sleepers."

**[7:11–14] The woman's answer assures him of her love, and invites him to return with her to the rural delights associated with their love (cf. also 6:11–12). **Yearning:** used only here and in Gn 3:16; 4:7. The dependency and subordination of woman to man presented as a consequence of sin in the Genesis story is here transcended in the mutuality of true love.

††[7:14] **Mandrakes:** herbs believed to have power to arouse love and promote fertility; cf. Gn 30:14–16.

‡‡[8:2] **Wine . . . pomegranate:** sexual connotations are implied, since the root "drink" (*shaqah*) is a wordplay on "kiss" (*nashaq*) in v. 1; cf. 1:2.

§§[8:5] **Awakened you:** the speakers in this verse are difficult to identify. Someone (the poet? Daughters?) hails the couple in v. 5a. According to the Masoretic vocalization, the woman is the speaker in v. 5b.

¶¶[8:6] **Seal:** this could be worn bound to the arm, as here, or suspended at the neck, or as a ring (Jer 22:24). It was used for identification and signatures. **Strong . . . fierce:** in human experience, Death and Sheol are inevitable, unrelenting; in the end they always triumph. Love, which is just as certain of its victory, matches its strength against the natural enemies of life; waters cannot extinguish it nor floods carry it away. It is more priceless than all riches. **Flames of the divine:** the Hebrew is difficult: the short form (-Yah) of the divine name Yhwh found here may associate love with the Lord, or it may be acting as a superlative—i.e., god-sized flames.

---

e. [7:4] Sg 4:5.   f. [7:5] Sg 4:4.   g. [7:11] Sg 2:16; 6:3.   h. [7:13] Sg 6:11.

i. [8:2] Sg 3:4.   j. [8:3] Sg 2:6.   k. [8:4] Sg 2:7; 3:5.   l. [8:5] Sg 3:6; 6:10.

7 ᵐDeep waters* cannot quench love,
   nor rivers sweep it away.
Were one to offer all the wealth of his
   house for love,
   he would be utterly despised.

### An Answer to the Brothers

8 **W** "We have a little sister;†
   she has no breasts as yet.
What shall we do for our sister
   on the day she is spoken for?
9 If she is a wall,
   we will build upon her a silver
   turret;
But if she is a door,
   we will board her up with cedar
   planks."
10 I am a wall,‡
   and my breasts are like towers.

---

*[8:7] **Deep waters**: often used to designate chaos (Ps 93:4; 144:7; Is 17:12–13; Hb 3:15). The fires of love cannot be extinguished, even by waters of chaos. **Wealth**: love cannot be bought.

†[8:8–9] The woman quotes the course of action her elder brothers had decided on. While she is yet immature, they will shelter her in view of eventual marriage. **Wall . . . door**: if she is virtuous, she will be honored; if she is not, she will be kept under strict vigilance. **Silver turret**: a precious ornament.

‡[8:10] In reply to the officious and meddling attitude of the brothers, she answers with their terms: she is mature ("wall," "towers"). **Brings peace**: or, "finds peace."

m. [8:7] Prv 6:31.

I became in his eyes
   as one who brings peace.

### A Boast

11 **M?** Solomon had a vineyard at
   Baal-hamon;§
   he gave over the vineyard to
   caretakers.
For its fruit one would have to pay
   a thousand silver pieces.
12 My vineyard is at my own disposal;
   the thousand pieces are for you,
   Solomon,
   and two hundred for the caretakers
   of its fruit.

### The Lovers' Yearnings

13 **M** You who dwell in the gardens,ⁿ
   my companions are listening for
   your voice—
   let me hear it!
14 **W** "Swiftly, my lover,
   be like a gazelle or a young stag
   upon the mountains of spices.

---

§[8:11–12] These enigmatic verses have been variously interpreted, depending on who is taken to be the speaker. In v. 11, if the woman, she boasts that she is a vineyard of great value. If the man, he boasts over his possession of her.

¶[8:13–14] As in 2:14, her lover asks for a word or a song and she replies in words similar to those found in 2:17.

n. [8:14] Sg 2:9, 17; 4:6.

# THE BOOK OF
# WISDOM

൶൞

The Book of Wisdom was written about fifty years before the coming of Christ. Its author, whose name is not known to us, was probably a member of the Jewish community at Alexandria, in Egypt. He wrote in Greek, in a style patterned on that of Hebrew verse. At times he speaks in the person of Solomon, placing his teachings on the lips of the wise king of Hebrew tradition in order to emphasize their value. His profound knowledge of the earlier Old Testament writings is reflected in almost every line of the book, and marks him, like Ben Sira, as an outstanding representative of religious devotion and learning among the sages of postexilic Judaism.

The primary purpose of the author was the edification of his co-religionists in a time when they had experienced suffering and oppression, in part at least at the hands of apostate fellow Jews. To convey his message he made use of the most popular religious themes of his time, namely the splendor and worth of divine wisdom (6:22–11:1), the glorious events of the exodus (11:2–16; 12:23–27; 15:18–19:22), God's mercy (11:17–12:22), the folly of idolatry (13:1–15:17), and the manner in which God's justice operates in rewarding or punishing the individual (1:1–6:21). The first ten chapters in particular provide background for the teaching of Jesus and for some New Testament theology about Jesus. Many passages from this section of the book, notably 3:1–8, are used by the church in the liturgy.

The principal divisions of the Book of Wisdom are:

I. The Reward of Righteousness (1:1–6:21).
II. Praise of Wisdom by Solomon (6:22–11:1).
III. Special Providence of God During the Exodus (11:2–16; 12:23–27; 15:18–19:22) with digressions on God's mercy (11:17–12:22) and on the folly and shame of idolatry (13:1–15:17).

## I. THE REWARD OF RIGHTEOUSNESS*

### CHAPTER 1

### Exhortation to Righteousness, the Key to Life

1 Love righteousness,† you who judge the
    earth;[a]
  think of the LORD in goodness,
  and seek him in integrity of heart;[b]

2 Because he is found by those who do not
    test him,
  and manifests himself to those who
    do not disbelieve him.[c]

3 For perverse counsels separate people
    from God,
  and his power, put to the proof,
    rebukes the foolhardy;[d]

4 ‡Because into a soul that plots evil wisdom
    does not enter,
  nor does she dwell in a body under
    debt of sin.[e]

5 For the holy spirit of discipline§ flees deceit
  and withdraws from senseless
    counsels
  and is rebuked when
    unrighteousness occurs.[f]

---

*[1:1–6:21] The reward is the gift of immortality, to the righteous (1:15; 3:1–3), but not to the wicked (5:1–13). Contrasts between these two groups dominate chaps. 1–5. The philosophy of the wicked and their persecution of the righteous are dramatically presented in 1:16–2:24. New light is shed on the suffering of the righteous (3:1–9), childlessness (3:13–15), and premature death (4:7–16)—in contrast to the fate of the wicked (3:10–12, 16–19; 4:3–6, 17–20).

†[1:1] Righteousness: not merely the cardinal virtue of justice (cf. 8:7), but the universal moral quality which is the application of wisdom to moral conduct. You who judge: "judges" and "kings" (cf. 6:1) are addressed in accordance with the literary customs of the times and with the putative Solomonic authorship, but the real audience is the Jewish community.

a. [1:1] 1 Chr 29:17; Ps 2:10; Is 26:9.  b. [1:1–2] Sir 1:25.

‡[1:4] In these verses personified Wisdom is identified with the spirit of the Lord; so also in 9:17.

§[1:5] Discipline: here and elsewhere, another name for Wisdom.

c. [1:2] 1 Chr 28:9.  d. [1:3] Is 59:2.  e. [1:4] Sir 15:7–8; Rom 7:14.
f. [1:5] Is 63:10.

⁶ For wisdom is a kindly spirit,
   yet she does not acquit blasphemous
      lips;
Because God is the witness of the inmost
      self[g]
   and the sure observer of the heart
   and the listener to the tongue.[h]
⁷ For the spirit of the LORD fills the world,[i]
   is all-embracing, and knows
      whatever is said.
⁸ Therefore those who utter wicked things
      will not go unnoticed,
   nor will chastising condemnation
      pass them by.[j]
⁹ For the devices of the wicked shall be
      scrutinized,
   and the sound of their words shall
      reach the LORD,
   for the chastisement of their
      transgressions;
¹⁰ Because a jealous ear hearkens to
      everything,[k]
   and discordant grumblings are not
      secret.
¹¹ Therefore guard against profitless
      grumbling,
   and from calumny* withhold your
      tongues;
For a stealthy utterance will not go
      unpunished,
   and a lying mouth destroys the soul.

¹² Do not court death† by your erring way of
      life,
   nor draw to yourselves destruction
      by the works of your hands.
¹³ Because God did not make death,[l]
   nor does he rejoice in the
      destruction of the living.
¹⁴ For he fashioned all things that they
      might have being,
   and the creatures of the world are
      wholesome;
There is not a destructive drug among them
   nor any domain of Hades‡ on earth,
¹⁵ For righteousness is undying.§[m]

### The Wicked Reject Immortality and Righteousness Alike

¹⁶ It was the wicked who with hands and
      words invited death,

considered it a friend, and pined
      for it,
   and made a covenant with it,
Because they deserve to be allied with it.[n]

## CHAPTER 2

¹ For, not thinking rightly, they said
      among themselves:¶
"Brief and troubled is our lifetime;[o]
   there is no remedy for our dying,
   nor is anyone known to have come
      back from Hades.
² For by mere chance were we born,
   and hereafter we shall be as though
      we had not been;
Because the breath in our nostrils is smoke,
   and reason a spark from the beating
      of our hearts,
³ And when this is quenched, our body will
      be ashes
   and our spirit will be poured abroad
      like empty air.[p]
⁴ Even our name will be forgotten in time,
   and no one will recall our deeds.
So our life will pass away like the traces of
      a cloud,
   and will be dispersed like a mist
Pursued by the sun's rays
   and overpowered by its heat.
⁵ For our lifetime is the passing of a shadow;
   and our dying cannot be deferred
      because it is fixed with a seal; and no
         one returns.[q]
⁶ Come, therefore, let us enjoy the good
      things that are here,
   and make use of creation with
      youthful zest.[r]
⁷ Let us have our fill of costly wine and
      perfumes,
   and let no springtime blossom pass
      us by;
⁸ let us crown ourselves with rosebuds
      before they wither.
⁹ Let no meadow be free from our
      wantonness;
   everywhere let us leave tokens of our
      merriment,
   for this is our portion, and this our
      lot.[s]
¹⁰ Let us oppress the righteous poor;
   let us neither spare the widow
   nor revere the aged for hair grown
      white with time.[t]
¹¹ But let our strength be our norm of
      righteousness;
   for weakness proves itself useless.

---

*[1:11] **Calumny:** speech against God and divine providence is meant.
†[1:12] **Death:** as will become clear, the author is not speaking of physical death but of spiritual death, the eternal separation from God.
‡[1:14] **Hades:** the Greek term for the Hebrew Sheol, the dwelling place of the dead.
§[1:15] **Undying:** immortality is not seen as an innate quality of the soul but as a gift of God to the righteous.

¶[2:1–20] In this speech the wicked deny survival after death and indeed invite death by their evil deeds.

g. [1:6] Jer 17:10.  h. [1:6–7] Jer 23:24–25.  i. [1:7] Wis 12:1.
j. [1:8] Prv 19:5.  k. [1:10–11] Nm 14:27–28.  l. [1:13–14] Ez
18:32; 33:11; 2 Pt 3:9.  m. [1:15] Is 51:6–8.

n. [1:16] Is 28:15.  o. [2:1] Jb 14:1; 7:9.  p. [2:3] Jb 7:9; Jas 4:14.
q. [2:5] Ps 144:4.  r. [2:6] Is 22:13; 1 Cor 15:32.  s. [2:9] Jer 13:25.
t. [2:10] Ex 22:21–23; Lv 19:32.

¹² `Let us lie in wait for the righteous one,
          because he is annoying to us;
      he opposes our actions,
      Reproaches us for transgressions of the
            law†
      and charges us with violations of our
            training."ᵘ
¹³ He professes to have knowledge of God
          and styles himself a child of the
          LORD.ᵛ
¹⁴ To us he is the censure of our thoughts;
          merely to see him is a hardship for
          us,ʷ
¹⁵ Because his life is not like that of others,
          and different are his ways.
¹⁶ He judges us debased;
      he holds aloof from our paths as
            from things impure.
      He calls blest the destiny of the righteous
      and boasts that God is his Father.ˣ

¹⁷ Let us see whether his words be true;
          let us find out what will happen to
          him in the end.ʸ
¹⁸ For if the righteous one is the son of God,
          God will help him
      and deliver him from the hand of
            his foes.ᶻ
¹⁹ With violence and torture let us put him
          to the test
      that we may have proof of his
            gentleness
      and try his patience.
²⁰ Let us condemn him to a shameful death;
          for according to his own words, God
          will take care of him."ᵃ

²¹ These were their thoughts, but they erred;
          for their wickedness blinded them,ᵇ
²² ‡And they did not know the hidden
            counsels of God;
      neither did they count on a
            recompense for holiness
      nor discern the innocent souls'
            reward.ᶜ
²³ For God formed us to be imperishable;
          the image of his own nature he
          made us.ᵈ

²⁴ But by the envy§ of the devil, death
            entered the world,
      and they who are allied with him
            experience it.ᵉ

## CHAPTER 3

### The Hidden Counsels of God¶

#### A. On Suffering**

¹ The souls of the righteous are in the hand
          of God,ᶠ
      and no torment shall touch them.
² They seemed, in the view of the foolish, to
          be dead;
      and their passing away was thought
            an affliction
³     and their going forth from us, utter
            destruction.
      But they are in peace.ᵍ
⁴ For if to others, indeed, they seem
          punished,
      yet is their hope full of immortality;
⁵ Chastised a little, they shall be greatly
          blessed,
      because God tried them
      and found them worthy of himself.ʰ
⁶ As gold in the furnace, he proved them,
      and as sacrificial offerings†† he took
            them to himself.ⁱ
⁷ In the time of their judgment‡‡ they shall
          shine
      and dart about as sparks through
            stubble;ʲ
⁸ They shall judge nations and rule over
          peoples,
      and the LORD shall be their King
            forever.ᵏ
⁹ Those who trust in him shall understand
          truth,
      and the faithful shall abide with him
            in love:

§[2:24] **Envy**: perhaps because Adam was in the image of
God or because Adam had control over all creation. **Devil**: the
first biblical text to equate the serpent of Gn 3 with the devil.
¶[3:1–4:19] The central section of chaps. 1–6. The author
begins by stating that immortality is the reward of the righteous, and then in the light of that belief comments on three
points of the traditional discussion of the problem of retribution (suffering, childlessness, early death) each of which was
often seen as a divine punishment.
**[3:1–12] The author affirms that, for the righteous, suf-
ferings are not punishments but purification and opportunities to show fidelity, whereas for the wicked suffering is truly
a punishment.
††[3:6] **Offerings**: the image is that of the burnt offering, in
which the victim is completely consumed by fire.
‡‡[3:7] **Judgment**: the Greek *episkopē* is God's loving judgment of those who have been faithful to him; the same word
is used in 14:11 for the punishment of the wicked at God's
judgment. Cf. also v. 13.

---

*[2:12–5:23] From 2:12 to 5:23 the author draws heavily
on Is 52–62, setting forth his teaching in a series of characters
or types taken from Isaiah and embellished with additional
details from other texts. The description of the "righteous
one" in 2:12–20 seems to undergird the New Testament passion narrative.
†[2:12] **Law**: the law of Moses; "training" has the same
meaning.
‡[2:22] This verse announces the subject of the next
section.

u. [2:12] Hos 8:1.   v. [2:13] Mt 27:43; Jn 8:55; 10:36–39.   w. [2:14]
Mt 9:4.   x. [2:16] Jer 6:30.   y. [2:17] Gn 37:20.   z. [2:18] Ps
22:9; Is 42:1; Mt 27:43; Jn 5:18.   a. [2:20] Jas 5:6.   b. [2:21] Rom
1:21.   c. [2:22] Ps 18:24–25; Prv 11:18; Mt 11:25.   d. [2:23] Gn
1:26–27; Is 54:16 LXX.

e. [2:24] Gn 3:1–24; Rom 5:12.   f. [3:1] Jb 12:10.   g. [3:3] Is
57:2.   h. [3:5] Tb 12:13; 2 Cor 4:17; 1 Pt 1:6–7.   i. [3:6] Ps 51:19;
Prv 17:3; Sir 2:5; Is 48:10.   j. [3:7] Dn 12:3; Ob 18; Mal 3:3; Mt
13:43.   k. [3:8] Wis 8:14; Prv 8:16; Dn 7:22; 1 Cor 6:2; Rev 20:4.

Because grace and mercy are with his holy
ones,[l]
and his care is with the elect.
[10] But the wicked shall receive a punishment
to match their thoughts,[*]
since they neglected righteousness
and forsook the Lord.
[11] For those who despise wisdom and
instruction are doomed.[m]
Vain is their hope, fruitless their labors,
and worthless their works.[n]
[12] Their wives are foolish and their children
wicked,
accursed their brood.[o]

### B. On Childlessness[†]

[13] Yes, blessed is she who, childless and
undefiled,
never knew transgression of the
marriage bed;
for she shall bear fruit at the
judgment of souls.[‡]
[14] So also the eunuch whose hand wrought
no misdeed,
who held no wicked thoughts
against the Lord—
For he shall be given fidelity's choice
reward[§]
and a more gratifying heritage in the
Lord's temple.[p]
[15] For the fruit of noble struggles is a
glorious one;
and unfailing is the root of
understanding.[¶q]
[16] But the children of adulterers[**] will remain
without issue,
and the progeny of an unlawful bed
will disappear.[r]
[17] For should they attain long life, they will
be held in no esteem,
and dishonored will their old age be
in the end;
[18] Should they die abruptly, they will have
no hope
nor comfort in the day of scrutiny;
[19]     for dire is the end of the wicked
generation.[s]

---

*[3:10] **To match their thoughts**: a fate as empty as that
which they describe in 2:1–5.
†[3:13–4:6] The true fruit of life is not children but virtue
which leads to immortality. The many children of the wicked
will be a disappointing fruit.
‡[3:13] See vv. 7–9.
§[3:14] **Fidelity's choice reward**: cf. Is 56:1–8. **More gratifying**: better than sons and daughters; cf. Is 56:5.
¶[3:15] **Root of understanding**: the root that is understanding (wisdom).
**[3:16] **Adulterers**: understood here as a type of sinners in
general; cf. Is 57:3–5.

---

l. [3:9] Wis 4:15; Jb 10:12; Jn 15:10.   m. [3:11] Prv 1:7.   n. [3:11–
12] Sir 41:8.   o. [3:12] Dt 28:18.   p. [3:14] Is 56:2–5.   q. [3:15] Sir
1:18.   r. [3:16] 2 Sm 12:14.   s. [3:19] Ps 34:22.

## CHAPTER 4

[1] Better is childlessness with virtue;
for immortal is the memory of
virtue,
acknowledged both by God and
human beings.[t]
[2] When it is present people imitate it,
and they long for it when it is gone;
Forever it marches crowned in triumph,
victorious in unsullied deeds of valor.
[3] But the numerous progeny of the wicked
shall be of no avail;
their spurious offshoots shall not
strike deep root
nor take firm hold.[u]
[4] For even though their branches flourish
for a time,
they are unsteady and shall be
rocked by the wind
and, by the violence of the winds,
uprooted;[v]
[5] Their twigs shall be broken off untimely,
their fruit useless, unripe for eating,
fit for nothing.
[6] For children born of lawless unions
give evidence of the wickedness of
their parents, when they are
examined.

### C. On Early Death[††]

[7] But the righteous one, though he die early,
shall be at rest.[w]
[8] For the age that is honorable comes not
with the passing of time,[x]
nor can it be measured in terms of
years.
[9] Rather, understanding passes for gray hair,
and an unsullied life is the
attainment of old age.
[10] [‡‡]The one who pleased God was loved,[y]
living among sinners, was
transported—
[11] Snatched away, lest wickedness pervert
his mind
or deceit beguile his soul;[z]
[12] For the witchery of paltry things obscures
what is right
and the whirl of desire transforms
the innocent mind.[a]
[13] Having become perfect in a short while,
he reached the fullness of a long
career;

---

††[4:7–19] Early death is not a punishment for the righteous because genuine old age is the attainment of perfection
and early death is a preservation from corruption. The old age
and death of the wicked, however, will not be honorable.
‡‡[4:10–11] There are allusions here to Enoch (Gn 5:21–
24), who was young by patriarchal standards, and to Lot (Gn
19:10–11; 2 Pt 2:7–8). Cf. also Is 57:1–2.

---

t. [4:1] Prv 3:3–4; Sir 16:1–3.   u. [4:3] Sir 23:25.   v. [4:4] Sir
40:15; Is 40:24.   w. [4:7] Wis 3:3.   x. [4:8] Jb 12:12; 32:9; Sir
25:4–6.   y. [4:10] Gn 5:24; Sir 44:16; Heb 11:5.   z. [4:11] Is 57:1–2.
a. [4:12] Wis 2:21; Dn 13:9.

<sup>14</sup> for his soul was pleasing to the
LORD,
therefore he sped him out of the
midst of wickedness.<sup>b</sup>
But the people saw and did not
understand,
nor did they take that consideration
into account.<sup>*</sup>

<sup>16</sup> Yes, the righteous one who has died will
condemn
the sinful who live;
And youth, swiftly completed, will
condemn
the many years of the unrighteous
who have grown old.<sup>c</sup>
<sup>17</sup> For they will see the death of the wise
one
and will not understand what the
LORD intended,
or why he kept him safe.
<sup>18</sup> They will see, and hold him in contempt;
but the LORD will laugh them to
scorn.<sup>d</sup>
<sup>19</sup> And they shall afterward become
dishonored corpses<sup>e</sup>
and an unceasing mockery among
the dead.
For he shall strike them down speechless
and prostrate<sup>f</sup>
and rock them to their foundations;
They shall be utterly laid waste
and shall be in grief
and their memory shall perish.

### The Judgment of the Wicked

<sup>20</sup> Fearful shall they come, at the counting
up of their sins,
and their lawless deeds shall convict
them to their face.

### CHAPTER 5
<sup>1</sup> <sup>†</sup>Then shall the righteous one with great
assurance confront<sup>g</sup>
his oppressors who set at nought his
labors.<sup>h</sup>
<sup>2</sup> Seeing this, the wicked shall be shaken
with dreadful fear,
and be amazed at the unexpected
salvation.
<sup>3</sup> They shall say among themselves, rueful
and groaning through anguish of
spirit:

"This is the one whom once we held as a
laughingstock
and as a type for mockery,
<sup>4</sup>     fools that we were!
His life we accounted madness,
and death dishonored.
<sup>5</sup> See how he is accounted among the
heavenly beings;<sup>‡</sup>
how his lot is with the holy ones!<sup>i</sup>
<sup>6</sup> We, then, have strayed from the way of
truth,<sup>j</sup>
and the light of righteousness did
not shine for us,
and the sun did not rise for us.<sup>k</sup>
<sup>7</sup> We were entangled in the thorns of
mischief and of ruin;
we journeyed through trackless
deserts,
but the way of the LORD we never
knew.
<sup>8</sup> What did our pride avail us?
What have wealth and its
boastfulness afforded us?<sup>l</sup>
<sup>9</sup> All of them passed like a shadow
and like a fleeting rumor;<sup>m</sup>
<sup>10</sup> Like a ship traversing the heaving water:
when it has passed, no trace can be
found,
no path of its keel in the waves.
<sup>11</sup> Or like a bird flying through the air;
no evidence of its course is to be
found—
But the fluid air, lashed by the beating of
pinions,
and cleft by the rushing force
Of speeding wings, is traversed;
and afterward no mark of passage
can be found in it.
<sup>12</sup> Or as, when an arrow has been shot at a
mark,
the parted air straightway flows
together again
so that none discerns the way it
went—
<sup>13</sup> Even so, once born, we abruptly came to
nought
and held no sign of virtue to display,
but were consumed in our
wickedness."<sup>n</sup>

<sup>14</sup> <sup>§</sup>Yes, the hope of the wicked is like chaff
borne by the wind,
and like fine, storm-driven snow;

---

*[4:14] Verse 15 is omitted because it repeats the last two
lines of 3:9.
†[5:1–13] In contrast to their speech in chap. 2 the wicked
now regret their assessment of life and righteousness.

‡[5:5] **Heavenly beings**: lit., "sons of God." These are the
holy ones, members of the heavenly court, among whom the
righteous are to be found. A bodily resurrection does not
seem to be envisioned.
§[5:14–23] A picture of the reward of the righteous which
develops into an apocalyptic description of the divine warrior's destruction of evil. The author utilizes Is 59–62.

---

b. [4:14] Gn 19:22, 29; 2 Pt 2:7.   c. [4:16] Mt 12:41–42.   d. [4:18]
Ps 37:13.   e. [4:19] Neh 1:10 LXX; Ps 18:8; Is 14:19; Jer 23:39–40.
f. [4:19] 2 Mc 3:29.   g. [5:1–2] 2 Thes 1:6–7.   h. [5:1] Col 2:15.

i. [5:5] Acts 26:18; Col 1:12.   j. [5:6] Prv 4:18–19; Jn 12:35.   k. [5:6–
7] Prv 22:5; Is 59:6–14.   l. [5:8] Ps 49:7; Prv 10:2.   m. [5:9–12]
1 Chr 20:15; Jb 9:25–26 LXX; Ps 144:4.   n. [5:13] Ez 33:10.

Like smoke scattered by the wind,
and like the passing memory of the
nomad camping for a single
day.[o]
¹⁵ But the righteous live forever,
and in the LORD is their
recompense,
and the thought of them is with the
Most High.[p]
¹⁶ Therefore shall they receive the splendid
crown,
the beautiful diadem, from the hand
of the LORD,
For he will shelter them with his right hand,
and protect them with his arm.[q]
¹⁷ He shall take his zeal for armor[r]
and arm creation to requite the
enemy,
¹⁸ Shall put on righteousness for a
breastplate,
wear sure judgment for a helmet,
¹⁹ Shall take invincible holiness for a shield,[s]
²⁰ and sharpen his sudden anger for a
sword.
The universe will war with him against
the foolhardy;
²¹ Well-aimed bolts of lightning will go forth
and from the clouds will leap to the
mark as from a well-drawn
bow;[t]
²² and as from a sling, wrathful
hailstones shall be hurled.
The waters of the sea will be enraged
and flooding rivers will overwhelm
them;[u]
²³ A mighty wind will confront them
and winnow them like a tempest;
Thus lawlessness will lay waste the whole
earth
and evildoing overturn the thrones
of the mighty.[v]

## CHAPTER 6

### Exhortation to Seek Wisdom[*]

¹ Hear, therefore, kings, and understand;[w]
learn, you magistrates[†] of the earth's
expanse!
² Give ear, you who have power over
multitudes
and lord it over throngs of peoples!

³ Because authority was given you by the
Lord
and sovereignty by the Most High,
who shall probe your works and
scrutinize your counsels![x]
⁴ Because, though you were ministers of his
kingdom, you did not judge
rightly,
and did not keep the law,[‡]
nor walk according to the will of God,
⁵ Terribly and swiftly he shall come against
you,
because severe judgment awaits the
exalted—
⁶ For the lowly may be pardoned out of
mercy[y]
but the mighty shall be mightily put
to the test.
⁷ For the Ruler of all shows no partiality,
nor does he fear greatness,[z]
Because he himself made the great as well
as the small,
and provides for all alike;
⁸ but for those in power a rigorous
scrutiny impends.

⁹ To you, therefore, O princes, are my
words addressed[a]
that you may learn wisdom and that
you may not fall away.
¹⁰ For those who keep the holy precepts
hallowed will be found holy,
and those learned in them will have
ready a response.[§]
¹¹ Desire therefore my words;
long for them and you will be
instructed.

¹² Resplendent and unfading is Wisdom,
and she is readily perceived by those
who love her,
and found by those who seek her.[b]
¹³ She hastens to make herself known to
those who desire her;[c]
¹⁴ one who watches for her at dawn
will not be disappointed,
for she will be found sitting at the gate.
¹⁵ For setting your heart on her is the
perfection of prudence,
and whoever keeps vigil for her is
quickly free from care;
¹⁶ Because she makes her rounds, seeking
those worthy of her,
and graciously appears to them on
the way,

---

*[6:1–21] The first part of the book closes with an exhortation comparable to 1:1–15, and it leads into "Solomon's" personal comments on wisdom in chaps. 7–9.
†[6:1] **Kings . . . magistrates**: note the inclusion with v. 21 ("kings"). The address to earthly powers is in accord with the opening (1:1), but the true audience remains the Jewish community.

---

‡[6:4] **Law**: that of Moses; cf. 2:12; 6:10.
§[6:10] **Response**: a suitable plea before the great Judge. Cf. Prv 22:21; Jb 31:14; Hb 2:1; Sir 8:9.

---

o. [5:14] Jb 21:18; Ps 1:4; 37:20; Is 17:13.   p. [5:15] Is 62:1; Ez 18:9.   q. [5:16] Ex 33:22; Is 62:3; 2 Tm 4:8; 1 Pt 5:4.   r. [5:17] Is 59:17.   s. [5:19–20] Dt 32:40–43.   t. [5:21] Hb 3:9–11.   u. [5:22] Dt 11:4.   v. [5:23] Wis 11:20; Sir 10:13–14.   w. [6:1–2] Wis 1:1; Ps 2:10; Sir 33:19; Mi 3:1, 9.

x. [6:3] 2 Chr 36:23; Prv 8:15–16; Jn 19:11; Rom 13:1.   y. [6:6–7] Lk 12:48.   z. [6:7] Dt 1:17; Prv 22:2.   a. [6:9–11] Dt 4:10; Ps 2:12; Sir 32:14; 1 Jn 3:7.   b. [6:12] Wis 7:10; Prv 8:17; Jer 29:13.   c. [6:13–16] Prv 8:3, 17, 34.

and goes to meet them with full
    attention.[d]

17 *For the first step toward Wisdom is an
    earnest desire for discipline;[e]
18 then, care for discipline is love of
    her;
    love means the keeping of her laws;
To observe her laws is the basis for
    incorruptibility;
19 and incorruptibility makes one close
    to God;
20 thus the desire for Wisdom leads to
    a kingdom.
21 If, then, you find pleasure in throne and
    scepter, you princes of peoples,
    honor Wisdom, that you may reign
    as kings forever.

## II. PRAISE OF WISDOM BY SOLOMON[†]

### Introduction

22 Now what wisdom is, and how she came
    to be I shall proclaim;
    and I shall conceal no secrets from
    you,
But from the very beginning I shall search
    out
    and bring to light knowledge of her;
    I shall not diverge from the truth.[f]
23 Neither shall I admit consuming jealousy
    to my company,
    because that can have no fellowship
    with Wisdom.[g]
24 A multitude of the wise is the safety of the
    world,
    and a prudent king, the stability of
    the people;[h]
25 so take instruction from my words,
    to your profit.

### CHAPTER 7

### Solomon Is Like All Others

1 I too am a mortal, the same as all the rest,[i]
    and a descendant of the first one
    formed of earth.[‡]

And in my mother's womb I was molded
    into flesh
2 in a ten-month period[§]—body and
    blood,
    from the seed of a man, and the
    pleasure that accompanies
    marriage.
3 And I too, when born, inhaled the
    common air,
    and fell upon the kindred earth;
    wailing, I uttered that first sound
    common to all.
4 In swaddling clothes and with constant
    care I was nurtured.
5 For no king has any different origin or birth;
6 one is the entry into life for all,
    and in one same way they leave it.[j]

### Solomon Prayed and Wisdom and Riches Came to Him

7 Therefore I prayed, and prudence was
    given me;
    I pleaded and the spirit of Wisdom
    came to me.[k]
8 I preferred her to scepter and throne,[l]
And deemed riches nothing in
    comparison with her,
9 nor did I liken any priceless gem to
    her;
Because all gold, in view of her, is a bit
    of sand,
    and before her, silver is to be
    accounted mire.
10 Beyond health and beauty I loved her,
And I chose to have her rather than the
    light,
    because her radiance never ceases.[m]
11 Yet all good things together came to me
    with her,[n]
    and countless riches at her hands;
12 I rejoiced in them all, because Wisdom is
    their leader,
    though I had not known that she is
    their mother.[¶o]

### Solomon Prays for Help to Speak Worthily of Wisdom

13 Sincerely I learned about her, and
    ungrudgingly do I share—
    her riches I do not hide away;[p]
14 For she is an unfailing treasure;
    those who gain this treasure win the
    friendship of God,

---

*[6:17–20] This type of reasoning approximates the rhetorical sorites, a series of statements in which the predicate of each becomes the subject of the next. Cf. Rom 5:3–5.

†[6:22–9:18] In these verses the author identifies with Solomon (without mentioning that name anywhere), and praises the beauty of Wisdom, describing how he sought her out. Thus the readers of the book can find a model in their search for Wisdom.

‡[7:1] **First one formed of earth:** Adam. The author omits throughout the book the proper names of the characters in sacred history of whom he speaks; see especially chap. 10.

d. [6:16] Prv 8:20–21; Sir 15:1–5.   e. [6:17–21] Ps 2:10–12; Prv 4:4–9; 7:1–4; 8:15–16; Dn 7:27; Jn 14:15, 21; 1 Jn 5:3.   f. [6:22] Tb 12:7, 11; Mt 13:11; Jn 15:15.   g. [6:23] Wis 7:13; Jas 3:14–15.   h. [6:24] Prv 11:14; 24:6; 29:4; Sir 10:1–5.   i. [7:1–2] Wis 10:1; Gn 2:7; Jb 10:9–12; 33:6; 1 Cor 15:47–49.

§[7:2] **In a ten-month period:** ten lunar months.

¶[7:12] **Mother:** lit., "she who begets." Although Wisdom herself is begotten of God (Prv 8:22–24), she is here the one who brings into being.

j. [7:6] Jb 1:21; Lk 2:12; 1 Tm 6:7–8.   k. [7:7] 1 Kgs 3:5–15; Prv 2:3–11.   l. [7:8–9] Wis 8:5; 1 Kgs 10:21; Jb 28:15–19; Prv 3:14–16; 8:10, 18–19.   m. [7:10] Prv 6:23.   n. [7:11] Prv 8:21.   o. [7:12] Prv 8:14–15.   p. [7:13] Wis 6:23.

being commended by the gifts that
come from her discipline.*

<sup>15</sup> Now God grant I speak suitably
and value these endowments at their
worth:
For he is the guide of Wisdom
and the director of the wise.

<sup>16</sup> For both we and our words are in his
hand,
as well as all prudence and
knowledge of crafts.<sup>q</sup>

<sup>17</sup> †For he gave me sound knowledge of what
exists,
that I might know the structure of
the universe and the force of
its elements,

<sup>18</sup> The beginning and the end and the
midpoint of times,
the changes in the sun's course and
the variations of the seasons,

<sup>19</sup> Cycles of years, positions of stars,

<sup>20</sup>       natures of living things, tempers of
beasts,
Powers of the winds and thoughts of
human beings,
uses of plants and virtues of roots—

<sup>21</sup> Whatever is hidden or plain I learned,

<sup>22</sup>       for Wisdom, the artisan of all,
taught me.<sup>r</sup>

## Nature and Incomparable Dignity of Wisdom

‡ For in her is a spirit
intelligent, holy, unique,
Manifold, subtle, agile,
clear, unstained, certain,
Never harmful, loving the good, keen,<sup>s</sup>

<sup>23</sup>       unhampered, beneficent, kindly,
Firm, secure, tranquil,
all-powerful, all-seeing,
And pervading all spirits,
though they be intelligent, pure and
very subtle.

<sup>24</sup> For Wisdom is mobile beyond all motion,
and she penetrates and pervades all
things by reason of her purity.<sup>t</sup>

<sup>25</sup> §For she is a breath of the might of God
and a pure emanation of the glory of
the Almighty;

therefore nothing defiled can enter
into her.

<sup>26</sup> For she is the reflection of eternal light,
the spotless mirror of the power of
God,
the image of his goodness.<sup>u</sup>

<sup>27</sup> Although she is one, she can do all things,
and she renews everything while
herself perduring;
Passing into holy souls from age to age,
she produces friends of God and
prophets.<sup>v</sup>

<sup>28</sup> For God loves nothing so much as the one
who dwells with Wisdom.

<sup>29</sup> For she is fairer than the sun<sup>w</sup>
and surpasses every constellation of
the stars.
Compared to light, she is found more
radiant;

<sup>30</sup>       though night supplants light,
wickedness does not prevail over
Wisdom.

## CHAPTER 8

<sup>1</sup> Indeed, she spans the world from end to
end mightily
and governs all things well.<sup>x</sup>

### Wisdom, the Source of Blessings

<sup>2</sup> Her I loved and sought after from my
youth;
I sought to take her for my bride<sup>5</sup>
and was enamored of her beauty.<sup>y</sup>

<sup>3</sup> She adds to nobility the splendor of
companionship with God;
even the Ruler of all loved her.

<sup>4</sup> For she leads into the understanding of
God,
and chooses his works.<sup>z</sup>

<sup>5</sup> If riches are desirable in life,
what is richer than Wisdom, who
produces all things?<sup>a</sup>

<sup>6</sup> And if prudence is at work,<sup>b</sup>
who in the world is a better artisan
than she?

<sup>7</sup> Or if one loves righteousness,
whose works are virtues,
She teaches moderation and prudence,
righteousness and fortitude,**
and nothing in life is more useful
than these.

---

*[7:14] **Discipline**: cf. note on 1:5.

†[7:17–22a] Wisdom teaches not only righteousness and
friendship with God but also sound knowledge of the world,
the universe, plants, animals and human beings. See also
1 Kgs 5:9–14; these specialties reflect Hellenistic culture.

‡[7:22b–23] The twenty-one (7 × 3) attributes of the spirit
in Wisdom reflect the influence of contemporary philosophy,
especially the Stoa, but the personification rests also on Prv
8:22–31 and Sir 24.

§[7:25–26] Five strong metaphors underline the origins
and closeness of Wisdom with God. See the use of this language in Heb 1:3; Col 1:15.

¶[8:2] **I loved . . . my bride**: the erotic quality in the pursuit
of and living with Woman Wisdom, who is the Lord's consort
(9:4) and loved by him, continues throughout this chapter (vv.
16, 18). It is reflected already in Prv 4:5–9; 7:4–5. See also Sir
15:2–5; 51:13–21.

**[8:7] **Moderation . . . fortitude**: known also as the cardinal virtues, and recognized in Greek philosophy (Plato).

q. [7:16] Wis 3:1.   r. [7:22] Wis 14:2; Prv 8:30.   s. [7:22–23] Heb
4:12–13; Jas 3:17.   t. [7:24] Wis 8:1.

u. [7:26] 2 Cor 4:4; Col 1:15; Heb 1:3.   v. [7:27] Ex 33:11; Jb
42:2; Ps 104:29; Jl 3:1.   w. [7:29–30] Sg 6:3, 9.   x. [8:1] Wis 7:24;
15:1.   y. [8:2] Prv 5:13–18; 8:17.   z. [8:4] Prv 8:27–31.   a. [8:5]
Prv 8:18–19.   b. [8:6–7] Prv 8:14–15.

8 Or again, if one yearns for wide
        experience,
     she knows the things of old, and
          infers the things to come.
  She understands the turns of phrases and
        the solutions of riddles;
     signs and wonders she knows in
          advance
     and the outcome of times and ages.[c]

### Wisdom as Solomon's Counselor and Comfort

9 So I determined to take her to live with me,
     knowing that she would be my
          counselor while all was well,
     and my comfort in care and grief.
10 Because of her I have glory among the
          multitudes,[d]
     and esteem from the elders, though
          I am but a youth.
11 I shall become keen in judgment,
     and shall be a marvel before rulers.
12 They will wait while I am silent and listen
          when I speak;
     and when I shall speak the more,
     they will put their hands upon their
          mouths.[*]
13 Because of her I shall have immortality
     and leave to those after me an
          everlasting memory.[e]
14 I shall govern peoples, and nations will be
          my subjects—[f]
15      tyrannical princes, hearing of me,
          will be afraid;
     in the assembly I shall appear noble,
          and in war courageous.
16 Entering my house, I shall take my repose
          beside her;
  For association with her involves no
          bitterness
     and living with her no grief,
     but rather joy and gladness.[g]

### Wisdom Is a Gift of God

17 Reflecting on these things,
     and considering in my heart
  That immortality lies in kinship with
          Wisdom,[h]
18      great delight in love of her,
     and unfailing riches in the works of
          her hands;
  And that in associating with her there is
          prudence,
     and fair renown in sharing her
          discourses,

  I went about seeking to take her for
          my own.
19 [†]Now, I was a well-favored child,
     and I came by a noble nature;
20      or rather, being noble, I attained an
          unblemished body.
21 And knowing that I could not otherwise
          possess her unless God gave it—
     and this, too, was prudence, to know
          whose gift she is—
  I went to the LORD and besought him,[i]
     and said with all my heart:

## CHAPTER 9

### Solomon's Prayer[‡]

1 [§]God of my ancestors, Lord of mercy,[j]
     you who have made all things by
          your word[k]
2 And in your wisdom have established
          humankind
     to rule the creatures produced by
          you,[l]
3 And to govern the world in holiness and
          righteousness,
     and to render judgment in integrity
          of heart:[m]
4 Give me Wisdom, the consort at your
          throne,
     and do not reject me from among
          your children;[n]
5 For I am your servant, the child of your
          maidservant,
     a man weak and short-lived
     and lacking in comprehension of
          judgment and of laws.[o]
6 Indeed, though one be perfect among
          mortals,
     if Wisdom, who comes from you, be
          lacking,
     that one will count for nothing.[p]

7 You have chosen me king over your people
     and magistrate over your sons and
          daughters.[q]

---

[*][8:12] **Hands upon their mouths**: a sign of respect for
unanswerable wisdom; cf. Jb 40:4.

[†][8:19–20] Here the author mentions first bodily, then
spiritual, excellence. To make it plain that the latter is the governing factor in the harmonious development of the human
person, he then reverses the order. The Platonic doctrine of
the pre-existence of the soul is often read into these lines, but
such an anthropology does not seem to be the intent of the
author (cf. 7:1–6). Verse 20 appears to rule out any misunderstanding of v. 19. Verse 21 emphasizes that he did not bring
talent to his "birth"; his wisdom is the gift of God.

[‡][9:1–18] The author presents his version of Solomon's
prayer (1 Kgs 3:6–9; 2 Chr 1:8–10).

[§][9:1–2] The author identifies Wisdom with the word of
God just as he again identifies Wisdom with the spirit of God
in v. 17. All three are alternate ways of expressing God's activity in relationship with the world and its inhabitants.

c. [8:8] Prv 1:6; Sir 39:1–3; 42:19–20; Dn 2:21.   d. [8:10–12]
1 Kgs 3:28; Jb 29:8–10, 21–22.   e. [8:13] Sir 15:6; 41:12–13; Is
56:5.   f. [8:14] Wis 3:8; Ps 18:48; 47:4.   g. [8:16] Prv 29:6; Sir 15:6;
Bar 3:38.   h. [8:17] Prv 3:18.

i. [8:21] 1 Kgs 3:9; 1 Kgs 5:9; Prv 2:6; Jas 1:5.   j. [9:1–2] Ps
86:15.   k. [9:1] Gn 1; Ps 33:6; Prv 3:19; Jer 10:12; Jn 1:3, 10.   l. [9:2]
Ps 8:7–9; Sir 17:3–4.   m. [9:3] 1 Kgs 3:6; 9:4–5; Ps 9:8–9.   n. [9:4]
2 Chr 1:10.   o. [9:5] 1 Kgs 3:7; Ps 116:16.   p. [9:6] Wis 3:17; 1 Kgs
11:4; 1 Cor 3:18–21.   q. [9:7] 1 Chr 28:5.

<sup>8</sup> You have bid me build a temple on your
　　　holy mountain
　　and an altar in the city that is your
　　　dwelling place,
　　a copy of the holy tabernacle which
　　　you had established from of
　　　old.<sup>r</sup>
<sup>9</sup> Now with you is Wisdom, who knows
　　　your works
　　and was present when you made the
　　　world;
　　Who understands what is pleasing in
　　　your eyes
　　and what is conformable with your
　　　commands.<sup>s</sup>
<sup>10</sup> Send her forth from your holy heavens
　　and from your glorious throne
　　　dispatch her
　　That she may be with me and work with
　　　me,
　　that I may know what is pleasing
　　　to you.<sup>t</sup>
<sup>11</sup> For she knows and understands all
　　　things,
　　and will guide me prudently in my
　　　affairs
　　and safeguard me by her glory;<sup>u</sup>
<sup>12</sup> Thus my deeds will be acceptable,
　　and I will judge your people justly
　　and be worthy of my father's throne.<sup>v</sup>

<sup>13</sup> For who knows God's counsel,
　　　or who can conceive what the Lord
　　　intends?<sup>w</sup>
<sup>14</sup> For the deliberations of mortals are timid,
　　and uncertain our plans.
<sup>15</sup> *For the corruptible body burdens the
　　　soul
　　and the earthly tent weighs down
　　　the mind with its many
　　　concerns.<sup>x</sup>
<sup>16</sup> Scarcely can we guess the things on earth,
　　and only with difficulty grasp what
　　　is at hand;
　　but things in heaven, who can
　　　search them out?<sup>y</sup>
<sup>17</sup> Or who can know your counsel, unless
　　　you give Wisdom
　　and send your holy spirit from on
　　　high?<sup>z</sup>
<sup>18</sup> †Thus were the paths of those on earth
　　　made straight,

and people learned what pleases you,
　　and were saved by Wisdom.<sup>a</sup>

## CHAPTER 10‡

### Wisdom Preserves Her Followers

<sup>1</sup> She preserved the first-formed father¶ of
　　　the world<sup>b</sup>
　　when he alone had been created;<sup>c</sup>
And she raised him up from his fall,
<sup>2</sup>　　and gave him power to rule all
　　　things.<sup>d</sup>
<sup>3</sup> But when an unrighteous man¶ withdrew
　　　from her in his anger,
　　he perished through his fratricidal
　　　wrath.<sup>e</sup>
<sup>4</sup> When on his account the earth was
　　　flooded, Wisdom again saved it,
　　piloting the righteous man** on
　　　frailest wood.<sup>f</sup>

<sup>5</sup> She, when the nations were sunk in
　　　universal wickedness,
　　knew the righteous man,†† kept him
　　　blameless before God,
　　and preserved him resolute against
　　　pity for his child.<sup>g</sup>

<sup>6</sup> She rescued a righteous man‡‡ from among
　　　the wicked who were being
　　　destroyed,<sup>h</sup>
　　when he fled as fire descended upon
　　　the Pentapolis—
<sup>7</sup> Where as a testimony to its wickedness,
　　　even yet there remain a smoking
　　　desert,
　　Plants bearing fruit that never ripens,
　　　and the tomb of a disbelieving soul,§§
　　　a standing pillar of salt.<sup>i</sup>
<sup>8</sup> For those who forsook Wisdom
　　　not only were deprived of
　　　knowledge of the good,
　　But also left the world a memorial of their
　　　folly,
　　so that they could not even be
　　　hidden in their fall.
<sup>9</sup> But Wisdom rescued from tribulations
　　　those who served her.<sup>j</sup>

---

‡[10:1–21] This chapter prepares for the following section (Wis 11:2–19:22) on the history of Israel in the exodus, by reviewing the dealings of Wisdom with the patriarchs. It has a parallel in Sir 44–50; cf. also Wis 18:9.
§[10:1–2] Adam.
¶[10:3] Cain.
**[10:4] Noah.
††[10:5] Abraham.
‡‡[10:6] Lot. **Pentapolis**: the five cities, including Sodom; cf. Gn 14:2.
§§[10:7] **Disbelieving soul**: Lot's wife; cf. Gn 19:26.

*[9:15–17] Although the expressions in v. 15 draw on the language of Plato concerning the human condition, the conclusion is very biblical: God remains a mystery (Jb 38–39; Eccl 8:17; Is 40:12–14; Rom 11:33–34). The plight of humankind is clearly one of ignorance, unless the "holy spirit" is sent from God.
†[9:18] An announcement of the next section.

r. [9:8] Ex 25:8–9; 2 Sm 7:13; 1 Chr 28:5; 2 Chr 6:1–2; 7:7; Tb 1:4; Ps 15:1; 48:2–3.  s. [9:9] Dt 6:17–18; Prv 8:22–31; Jn 1:1–3, 10.  t. [9:10] Wis 18:15; Mt 5:34; Jn 3:17; 20:21.  u. [9:11] Wis 8:8.  v. [9:12] 1 Kgs 3:6–9.  w. [9:13] Is 40:13; Bar 3:31.  x. [9:15] Jb 4:19.  y. [9:16] Sir 1:3; Jn 3:12.  z. [9:17] Jn 14:26.

a. [9:18] Wis 10:9; Prv 28:26.  b. [10:1–16] Heb 11:17–27.  c. [10:1] Wis 7:1.  d. [10:2] Gn 1:28.  e. [10:3] Gn 4:1–16.  f. [10:4] Wis 14:5–6; Gn 6:5–9.  g. [10:5] Gn 22:7–10.  h. [10:6] Gn 18:22–33; 19:15–25; 2 Pt 2:6–7.  i. [10:7] Gn 19:26; Lk 17:32.  j. [10:9] Wis 16:8.

<sup>10</sup> She, when a righteous man* fled from his
    brother's anger,<sup>k</sup>
    guided him in right ways,
Showed him the kingdom of God
    and gave him knowledge of holy
    things;
She prospered him in his labors
    and made abundant the fruit of his
    works,
<sup>11</sup> Stood by him against the greed of his
    defrauders,
    and enriched him;<sup>l</sup>
<sup>12</sup> She preserved him from foes,
    and secured him against ambush,
And she gave him the prize for his hard
    struggle
    that he might know that devotion to
    God<sup>†</sup> is mightier than all else.<sup>m</sup>

<sup>13</sup> She did not abandon a righteous man<sup>‡</sup>
    when he was sold,<sup>n</sup>
    but rescued him from sin.<sup>o</sup>
<sup>14</sup> She went down with him into the
    dungeon,
    and did not desert him in his bonds,
Until she brought him the scepter of
    royalty
    and authority over his oppressors,
Proved false those who had defamed him,
    and gave him eternal glory.

<sup>15</sup> The holy people and their blameless
    descendants—it was she
    who rescued them from the nation
    that oppressed them.<sup>p</sup>
<sup>16</sup> She entered the soul of the Lord's
    servant,<sup>§</sup>
    and withstood fearsome kings with
    signs and wonders;<sup>q</sup>
<sup>17</sup> she gave the holy ones the reward of
    their labors,<sup>r</sup>
Conducted them by a wondrous road,
    became a shelter for them by day
    a starry flame by night.
<sup>18</sup> She took them across the Red Sea
    and brought them through the deep
    waters.
<sup>19</sup> Their enemies she overwhelmed,
    and churned them up* from the
    bottom of the depths.

<sup>20</sup> Therefore the righteous despoiled the
    wicked;
    and they sang of your holy name,
    Lord,
    and praised in unison your
    conquering hand,<sup>s</sup>
<sup>21</sup> Because Wisdom opened the mouths of
    the mute,
    and gave ready speech to infants.<sup>t</sup>

## CHAPTER 11

<sup>1</sup> She prospered their affairs through the
    holy prophet.<sup>u</sup>

## III. SPECIAL PROVIDENCE OF GOD DURING THE EXODUS**

### Introduction

<sup>2</sup> They journeyed through the uninhabited
    desert,
    and in lonely places they pitched
    their tents;<sup>v</sup>
<sup>3</sup> they withstood enemies and warded
    off their foes.<sup>w</sup>
<sup>4</sup> When they thirsted, they called upon
    you,
    and water was given them from the
    sheer rock,
    a quenching of their thirst from the
    hard stone.
<sup>5</sup> For by the things through which their
    foes were punished
    they in their need were benefited.<sup>x</sup>

### First Example: Water Punishes the Egyptians and Benefits the Israelites

<sup>6</sup> Instead of a river's<sup>††</sup> perennial source,
    troubled with impure blood<sup>y</sup>
<sup>7</sup> as a rebuke to the decree for the
    slaying of infants,
You gave them abundant water beyond
    their hope,
<sup>8</sup> after you had shown by the thirst
    they experienced
    how you punished their adversaries.
<sup>9</sup> For when they had been tried, though
    only mildly chastised,<sup>z</sup>

---

*[10:10–12] Jacob.

†[10:12] **Devotion to God**: in the Greek this signifies "piety" or "religion," and is the equivalent of the Hebrew "fear of the Lord"; cf. Prv 1:7.

‡[10:13–14] Joseph.

§[10:16] Moses.

¶[10:19] **Churned them up**: casting their bodies on the shore.

**[11:2–19:22] Few verses in chaps. 11–19 can be fully understood without consulting the passages in the Pentateuch which are indicated in the cross-references. The theme of this part of the book is expressed in v. 5 and is illustrated in the following chapters by five examples drawn from Exodus events.

††[11:6–8] **River**: the Nile; the contrast is between the first plague of Egypt (Ex 7:17–24) and the water drawn from the rock in Horeb (Ex 17:5–7; Nm 20:8–11).

---

k. [10:10] Gn 27:43–45; 28:12–15.  l. [10:11] Gn 30:29–30; 31:5–12.  m. [10:12] Gn 32:24–29; 1 Tm 4:8.  n. [10:13–14] Gn 37–45.  o. [10:13] Gn 39:7–10.  p. [10:15] Ex 3:9; 14:30; 19:6.  q. [10:16] Wis 1:4; 7:27; Ex 4:10; Ps 76:13.  r. [10:17–19] Wis 14:3; 19:7; Ex 13:21–22; Ex 14–15; Ps 77:20–21; 78:13, 53; Is 4:5–6.

s. [10:20] Ex 12:35–36; 15:1–21.  t. [10:21] Ex 4:10–15; Ps 8:3; Mt 11:25.  u. [11:1] Dt 2:7; Hos 12:14.  v. [11:2–5] Ex 17:2–6; Nm 20:1–13; Ps 63:2; 107:4–7; Jer 2:6.  w. [11:3] Ex 17:8–16; Nm 21:1–3, 21–35; 31:1–12; Ps 118:10–12.  x. [11:5] Wis 16:1–2.  y. [11:6–8] Wis 18:5; Ex 1:22; 7:17–24.  z. [11:9–11] Wis 3:5; 16:3–4; Dt 8:2–5; 2 Mc 6:12–16; Ps 6:2; Prv 3:12.

they recognized how the wicked,
    condemned in anger, were
    being tormented.

10 You tested your own people, admonishing
    them as a father;
    but as a stern king you probed and
    condemned the wicked.

11 Those near and far were equally afflicted:[a]

12 for a twofold grief* took hold of
    them[b]
    and a groaning at the remembrance
    of the ones who had departed.

13 For when they heard that the cause of
    their own torments
    was a benefit to these others, they
    recognized the Lord.

14 For though they had mocked and rejected
    him who had been cast out and
    abandoned long ago,
    in the final outcome, they marveled
    at him,
    since their thirst proved unlike that
    of the righteous.[c]

### Second Example: Animals Punish the Egyptians and Benefit the Israelites

15 In return for their senseless, wicked
    thoughts,
    which misled them into worshiping
    dumb† serpents and worthless
    insects,
    You sent upon them swarms of dumb
    creatures for vengeance;[d]

16 that they might recognize that one
    is punished by the very things
    through which one sins.[e]

### Digression on God's Mercy

17 For not without means was your almighty
    hand,[f]
    that had fashioned the universe
    from formless matter,‡
    to send upon them many bears or
    fierce lions,

18 Or newly created, wrathful, unknown
    beasts
    breathing forth fiery breath,
    Or pouring out roaring smoke,
    or flashing terrible sparks from their
    eyes.

19 Not only could these attack and
    completely destroy them;

even their frightful appearance itself
    could slay.

20 Even without these, they could have been
    killed at a single blast,
    pursued by justice
    and winnowed by your mighty spirit.
    But you have disposed all things by
    measure and number and
    weight.[g]

21 For great strength is always present with
    you;
    who can resist the might of your arm?[h]

22 Indeed, before you the whole universe is
    like a grain from a balance,§
    or a drop of morning dew come
    down upon the earth.[i]

23 'But you have mercy on all, because you
    can do all things;
    and you overlook sins for the sake of
    repentance.[j]

24 For you love all things that are
    and loathe nothing that you have
    made;
    for you would not fashion what you
    hate.[k]

25 How could a thing remain, unless you
    willed it;
    or be preserved, had it not been
    called forth by you?[l]

26 But you spare all things, because they are
    yours,
    O Ruler and Lover of souls,[m]

12:1 for your imperishable spirit is in all
    things![n]

### CHAPTER 12

2 Therefore you rebuke offenders little by
    little,
    warn them, and remind them of the
    sins they are committing,
    that they may abandon their
    wickedness and believe in you,
    Lord!

3 For truly, the ancient inhabitants of your
    holy land,[o]

4 whom you hated for deeds most
    odious—
    works of sorcery and impious
    sacrifices;

---

*[11:12] **Twofold grief**: the double distress described in vv. 13–14.

†[11:15] **Dumb**: that is, irrational.

‡[11:17] **Formless matter**: a Greek philosophical concept is used to interpret the chaos of Gn 1:2.

§[11:22] **Grain from a balance**: a tiny particle used for weighing on sensitive scales.

¶[11:23] The combination of divine mercy and power is an unusual paradox, but cf. 12:15–18; Ps 62:12–13; Sir 2:18. The main emphasis is on a creating that is motivated by love; the divine "imperishable spirit" (either Wisdom as in 1:4, 7, or perhaps the breath of life as in Gn 2:7) is in everything (12:1).

---

a. [11:11] Ps 6:2.  b. [11:12–13] Wis 16:8; Ex 14:4, 18.  c. [11:14] Ex 2:3.  d. [11:15] Wis 12:23–24; 15:18–16:1; Ex 7:26–8:11.  e. [11:16] Wis 12:23, 27; Ex 10:16; Prv 1:31–32; 26:27.  f. [11:17–19] Wis 12:8–9; 16:1, 5; Gn 1:1–2; Dt 32:24; 2 Kgs 17:25–26; Hos 13:4–8.

g. [11:20] Jb 4:9.  h. [11:21] Wis 12:12; 2 Chr 20:6.  i. [11:22] Hos 13:3.  j. [11:23] Wis 12:10; Dt 9:27; Acts 17:30; Rom 2:4; 11:32; 2 Pt 3:9.  k. [11:24] Ps 145:9.  l. [11:25] Is 41:4.  m. [11:26] Wis 12:16; Is 63:9.  n. [12:1] Wis 1:7.  o. [12:3–6] Wis 14:23; Dt 18:9–12; Ps 5:6; 106:28, 34–39; Jer 19:4–5; Ez 16:3, 20–21, 36.

⁵ These merciless murderers of children,
    devourers of human flesh,*
    and initiates engaged in a blood ritual,
⁶ and parents who took with their
        own hands defenseless lives,ᵖ
You willed to destroy by the hands of our
        ancestors,
⁷ that the land that is dearest of all to
        you
    might receive a worthy colony of
        God's servants.�q
⁸ But even these you spared, since they
        were but mortals
    and sent wasps as forerunners of
        your army
    that they might exterminate them by
        degrees.ʳ

⁹ Not that you were without power to have
        the wicked vanquished in
        battle by the righteous,
    or wiped out at once by terrible
        beasts or by one decisive word;ˢ
¹⁰ But condemning them by degrees, you
        gave them space for repentance.
You were not unaware that their origins
        were wicked
    and their malice ingrained,ᵗ
And that their dispositions would never
        change;
¹¹    for they were a people accursed
        from the beginning.
Neither out of fear for anyone
    did you grant release from their sins.ᵘ
¹² For who can say to you, "What have you
        done?"
    or who can oppose your decree?
Or when peoples perish, who can
        challenge you, their maker;
    or who can come into your presence
        to vindicate the unrighteous?ᵛ
¹³ For neither is there any god besides you
        who have the care of all,
    that you need show you have not
        unjustly condemned;ʷ
¹⁴ Nor can any king or prince confront you
        on behalf of those you have
        punished.ˣ

¹⁵ But as you are righteous, you govern all
        things righteously;
    you regard it as unworthy of your
        power
    to punish one who has incurred no
        blame.ʸ

¹⁶ For your might is the source of
        righteousness;
    your mastery over all things makes
        you lenient to all.ᶻ
¹⁷ For you show your might when the
        perfection of your power is
        disbelieved;
    and in those who know you, you
        rebuke insolence.†ᵃ
¹⁸ But though you are master of might, you
        judge with clemency,
    and with much lenience you govern
        us;
    for power, whenever you will,
        attends you.

¹⁹ You taught your people, by these deeds,ᵇ
    that those who are righteous must
        be kind;
And you gave your children reason to hope
    that you would allow them to repent
        for their sins.
²⁰ For these were enemies of your servants,
        doomed to death;
    yet, while you punished them with
        such solicitude and indulgence,
    granting time and opportunity to
        abandon wickedness,
²¹ With what exactitude you judged your
        children,
    to whose ancestors you gave the
        sworn covenants of goodly
        promises!ᶜ
²² Therefore to give us a lesson you punish
        our enemies with measured
        deliberation
    so that we may think earnestly of
        your goodness when we judge,
    and, when being judged, we may
        look for mercy.

### Second Example Resumed

²³ Hence those unrighteous who lived a life
        of folly,
    you tormented through their own
        abominations.ᵈ
²⁴ For they went far astray in the paths of
        error,
    taking for gods the worthless and
        disgusting among beasts,
    being deceived like senseless infants.ᵉ
²⁵ Therefore as though upon unreasoning
        children,
    you sent your judgment on them as
        a mockery;ᶠ

---

*[12:5] The horrible crimes here attributed to the Canaan-
ites (cf. also 14:23) were not unheard of in the ancient world.

p. [12:6] Nm 33:52.   q. [12:7] Dt 11:12.   r. [12:8] Ex 23:28–30;
Dt 7:17–24.   s. [12:9] Wis 11:18; 18:15; Nm 16:21.   t. [12:10]
Wis 11:23; Ps 55:20; Sir 16:9.   u. [12:11] Gn 9:25.   v. [12:12]
2 Sm 16:10; Eccl 8:4; Sir 46:19; Is 45:9; Dn 4:32; Rom 9:19–
21.   w. [12:13] Wis 6:7; Dt 3:24; 32:39; Is 44:6, 8.   x. [12:14] Jer
49:19; 50:44.   y. [12:15] Gn 18:23–32; Dt 32:4.

---

†[12:17] The brunt of divine anger and justice is borne by
those who know God but defy divine authority and might. Cf.
1:2; 15:2, but also 12:27; 18:13.

z. [12:16] Wis 2:11; 11:26; Ps 103:19.   a. [12:17] Wis 15:2–3;
Ex 9:16.   b. [12:19–20] Wis 11:23; Sir 17:24.   c. [12:21] Wis
18:22; Gn 50:24; Dt 7:6–14; Ps 105:8–11.   d. [12:23] Wis 11:16;
16:1.   e. [12:24] Dt 11:28; Jer 5:28; Rom 1:23.   f. [12:25] Jer 4:22.

<sup>26</sup> But they who took no heed of a
        punishment which was but
        child's play
    were to experience a condemnation
        worthy of God.
<sup>27</sup> For by the things through which they
        suffered distress,
    being tortured by the very things
        they deemed gods,
    They saw and recognized the true God
        whom formerly they had
        refused to know;
    with this, their final condemnation*
        came upon them.*

## CHAPTER 13

### Digression on False Worship

#### A. Nature Worship†

<sup>1</sup> Foolish by nature were all who were in
        ignorance of God,
    and who from the good things seen
        did not succeed in knowing
        the one who is,‡
    and from studying the works did not
        discern the artisan;*
<sup>2</sup> Instead either fire, or wind, or the swift air,
        or the circuit of the stars, or the
        mighty water,
    or the luminaries of heaven, the
        governors§ of the world, they
        considered gods.*
<sup>3</sup> Now if out of joy in their beauty they
        thought them gods,
    let them know how far more
        excellent is the Lord than these;
    for the original source of beauty
        fashioned them.*
<sup>4</sup> Or if they were struck by their might and
        energy,
    let them realize from these things
        how much more powerful is
        the one who made them.*
<sup>5</sup> For from the greatness and the beauty of
        created things

        their original author, by analogy, is
        seen.
<sup>6</sup> But yet, for these the blame is less;¶
    For they have gone astray perhaps,
        though they seek God and wish to
        find him.
<sup>7</sup> For they search busily among his works,
        but are distracted by what they see,
        because the things seen are fair.
<sup>8</sup> But again, not even these are pardonable.
<sup>9</sup> For if they so far succeeded in knowledge
        that they could speculate about the
        world,
    how did they not more quickly find
        its Lord?

#### B. Idolatry**

<sup>10</sup> But wretched are they, and in dead things
        are their hopes,
    who termed gods things made by
        human hands:
    Gold and silver, the product of art, and
        images of beasts,
    or useless stone, the work of an
        ancient hand.*

### The Carpenter and Wooden Idols

<sup>11</sup> A carpenter may cut down a suitable tree*
        and skillfully scrape off all its bark,
    And deftly plying his art
        produce something fit for daily use,*
<sup>12</sup> And use the scraps from his handiwork
        in preparing his food, and have his fill;
<sup>13</sup> Then the good-for-nothing refuse from
        these remnants,
    crooked wood grown full of knots,
        he takes and carves to occupy his
        spare time.*
    This wood he models with mindless skill,
        and patterns it on the image of a
        human being
<sup>14</sup>     or makes it resemble some worthless
        beast.
    When he has daubed it with red and
        crimsoned its surface with red
        stain,
    and daubed over every blemish in it,*
<sup>15</sup> He makes a fitting shrine for it
        and puts it on the wall, fastening it
        with a nail.*
<sup>16</sup> Thus he provides for it lest it fall down,
        knowing that it cannot help itself;

---

*[12:27] **Condemnation**: the death of Egyptian firstborn
and the destruction of their army in the sea.
    †[13:1–9] The author holds a relatively benign view of
the efforts of the philosophers to come to know God from
various natural phenomena. This is not a question of proving the existence of God in scholastic style. The author thinks
that the beauty and might of the world should have pointed
by analogy (v. 5) to the Maker. Instead, those "in ignorance
of God" remained fixed on the elements (v. 2, three named,
along with the stars). His Greek counterparts are not totally
blameless; they should have gone further and acknowledged
the creator of nature's wonders (vv. 4–5). Cf. Rom 1:18–23;
Acts 17:27–28.
    ‡[13:1] **One who is**: this follows the Greek translation of
the sacred name for God in Hebrew; cf. Ex 3:14.
    §[13:2] **Governors**: the sun and moon (cf. Gn 1:16).

---

¶[13:6] **The blame is less**: the greater blame is incurred by
those mentioned in v. 10; 15:14–16.
    **[13:10–19] The second digression is an example of the
polemic against idolatry (cf. Is 44:9–20; Jer 10:3–9; Ps 135:15–
18). Whether the idols be of wood or clay, they were made by
human beings and have become the source of evil.

l. [13:10] Wis 3:11; 15:5, 17; Dt 4:25–28; 7:25; 27:15; Ps 115:4; Hos
14:4; Acts 17:29.   m. [13:11–19] Is 44:9–20.   n. [13:11] Wis 15:7;
Bar 6:58.   o. [13:13] Dt 4:16.   p. [13:14] Jer 10:9.   q. [13:15] Is
40:20; 41:7; 44:13.

---

g. [12:27] Wis 16:16; Ex 14:4, 28.   h. [13:1] Acts 14:17; Eph 4:17–19.
i. [13:2] Gn 1:14–19; Dt 4:19; Jb 31:26–28.   j. [13:3] Ps 8:4.   k. [13:4]
Jer 10:2; Bar 6:39.

for, truly, it is an image and needs
help.[r]

[17] But when he prays about his goods or
marriage or children,[s]
he is not ashamed to address the
thing without a soul.
For vigor he invokes the powerless;
[18] for life he entreats the dead;
For aid he beseeches the wholly
incompetent;
for travel, something that cannot
even walk;
[19] For profit in business and success with his
hands
he asks power of a thing with hands
utterly powerless.

## CHAPTER 14

[1] Again, one preparing for a voyage and
about to traverse the wild waves
cries out to wood more unsound
than the boat that bears him.[t]
[2] For the urge for profits devised this latter,
and Wisdom the artisan produced it.

[3] ˙But your providence, O Father! guides it,
for you have furnished even in the
sea a road,
and through the waves a steady
path,[u]
[4] Showing that you can save from any
danger,
so that even one without skill may
embark.[v]
[5] But you will that the products of your
Wisdom be not idle;
therefore people trust their lives
even to most frail wood,
and were safe crossing the waves on
a raft.[w]
[6] For of old, when the proud giants were
being destroyed,
the hope of the universe, who took
refuge on a raft,[†]
left to the world a future for the
human family, under the
guidance of your hand.

[7] For blest is the wood through which
righteousness comes about;
[8] but the handmade idol is accursed,
and its maker as well:
he for having produced it, and the

corruptible thing, because it
was termed a god.[x]
[9] Equally odious to God are the evildoer
and the evil deed;
[10] and the thing made will be punished
with its maker.
[11] Therefore upon even the idols of the
nations shall a judgment come,
since they became abominable
among God's works,
Snares for human souls
and a trap for the feet of the senseless.[y]

### The Origin and Evils of Idolatry

[12] For the source of wantonness is the
devising of idols;
and their invention, a corruption
of life.[z]
[13] For in the beginning they were not,
nor can they ever continue;[a]
[14] for from human emptiness they
came into the world,
and therefore a sudden end is
devised for them.

[15] ‡For a father, afflicted with untimely
mourning,
made an image of the child so
quickly taken from him,
And now honored as a god what once
was dead
and handed down to his household
mysteries and sacrifices.
[16] Then, in the course of time, the impious
practice gained strength and
was observed as law,
and graven things were worshiped
by royal decrees.[b]
[17] People who lived so far away that they could
not honor him in his presence
copied the appearance of the distant
king
And made a public image of him they
wished to honor,
out of zeal to flatter the absent one
as though present.
[18] And to promote this observance among
those to whom it was strange,
the artisan's ambition provided a
stimulus.
[19] For he, perhaps in his determination to
please the ruler,
labored over the likeness§ to the best
of his skill;[c]

---

*[14:3–6] The wooden ship mentioned in vv. 1–2 prompts
a short meditation on the providence of God, who in fact has
watched over boats in their dangerous courses. The wood as
described in v. 7 became a favorite patristic type for the wood
of the cross.
†[14:6] Noah.

‡[14:15–21] The author develops two examples of idolatry:
cult of the dead, and cult of the king.
§[14:19] Likeness: he made this more flattering than the
reality.

---

r. [13:16] 1 Sm 5:3–5; Bar 6:57.　s. [13:17–19] Wis 15:15.　t. [14:1]
Is 46:7.　u. [14:3] Ps 107:23–30; Is 43:16.　v. [14:4] Wis 16:8.
w. [14:5] Wis 10:4.

x. [14:8] Rom 1:23.　y. [14:11] Wis 3:7; Nm 33:4; Jos 23:13; Ps 115:4;
Jer 6:15; 10:15; 46:25; Hos 9:15.　z. [14:12] Rom 1:23–32.
a. [14:13] Is 2:18.　b. [14:16] 1 Mc 1:47–50; Dn 3:4–7.　c. [14:19]
Is 44:12–13 LXX.

²⁰ And the masses, drawn by the charm of
the workmanship,
>soon took as an object of worship
the one who shortly before was
honored as a human being.ᵈ
²¹ And this became a snare for the world,
that people enslaved to either grief
or tyranny
>conferred the incommunicable
Name on stones and wood.

²² Then it was not enough for them to err in
their knowledge of God;ᵉ
>but even though they live in a great
war resulting from ignorance,
they call such evils peace.ᶠ
²³ For while they practice either child
sacrifices or occult mysteries,
or frenzied carousing in exotic rites,ᵍ
²⁴ They no longer respect either lives or
purity of marriage;
>but they either waylay and kill each
other, or aggrieve each other
by adultery.
²⁵ And all is confusion—blood and murder,
theft and guile,ʰ
>corruption, faithlessness, turmoil,
perjury,
²⁶ Disturbance of good people, neglect of
gratitude,
>besmirching of souls, unnatural lust,
disorder in marriage, adultery and
shamelessness.
²⁷ For the worship of infamous idols
is the reason and source and
extreme of all evil.ⁱ

²⁸ For they either go mad with enjoyment,
or prophesy lies,
or live lawlessly or lightly perjure
themselves.ʲ
²⁹ For as their trust is in lifeless idols,
they expect no harm when they have
sworn falsely.
³⁰ But on both counts justice shall overtake
them:
>because they thought perversely of
God by devoting themselves
to idols,ᵏ
>and because they deliberately swore
false oaths, despising piety.*
³¹ For it is not the might of those by whom
they swear,
>but the just retribution of sinners,
that ever follows upon the
transgression of the wicked.†

*[14:30] **Piety**: the sanctity of oaths.
†[14:31] Perjury is a form of deceit which calls for punishment even though it be practiced in the name of a lifeless idol.

d. [14:20] Wis 15:4.   e. [14:22–31] Jer 2:20; 3:1–25; Hos 4:1–2, 9–19; Rom 1:26–31; Gal 5:19–21; 1 Tm 1:9–10.   f. [14:22] Jer 6:14; Ez 13:10.   g. [14:23] Wis 12:4–5; 14:15; Is 57:5.   h. [14:25–26] Jer 7:8–9; 22:17.   i. [14:27] Ex 23:13.   j. [14:28] Jer 5:31; 29:26.   k. [14:30] Wis 1:1, 8; 11:20; Jer 5:2, 7.

# CHAPTER 15

¹ ‡But you, our God, are good and true,
slow to anger, and governing all with
mercy.ˡ
² For even if we sin, we are yours, and know
your might;
>but we will not sin, knowing that we
belong to you.ᵐ
³ For to know you well is complete
righteousness,
>and to know your might is the root
of immortality.ⁿ
⁴ For the evil creation of human fancy did
not deceive us,
nor the fruitless labor of painters,ᵒ
A form smeared with varied colors,
⁵ the sight of which arouses yearning
in a fool,
>till he longs for the inanimate form
of a dead image.
⁶ Lovers of evil things, and worthy of such
hopes
>are they who make them and long
for them and worship them.ᵖ

## The Potter's Clay Idols

⁷ For the potter, laboriously working the
soft earth,
>molds for our service each single
article:
He fashions out of the same clay
both the vessels that serve for clean
purposes
and their opposites, all alike;
As to what shall be the use of each vessel
of either class
the worker in clay is the judge.�q
⁸ §With misspent toil he molds a
meaningless god from the
selfsame clay,
>though he himself shortly before
was made from the earth,
And is soon to go whence he was taken,
when the life that was lent him is
demanded back.ʳ
⁹ But his concern is not that he is to die
nor that his span of life is brief;
Rather, he vies with goldsmiths and
silversmiths
and emulates molders of bronze,

‡[15:1–3] As often before (11:26; 12:2; 14:3–6), the author addresses God directly, so that chaps. 11–19 can be conceived as a more or less continuous prayer (cf. 11:7 and 19:22). This is the living God who is in stark contrast to the deadness of the idols that have been discussed. The merciful God (cf. Ex 34:6) is the source of immortality (1:15) for the community.
§[15:8–9] The author matches the irony of his words about the carpenter in 13:15–19 with this description of the potter's vain work.

l. [15:1] Ex 34:6–7; Ps 86:5, 15; 145:8, 9, 14.   m. [15:2] Jb 10:14–15 LXX.   n. [15:3] Wis 3:15; Jn 17:3.   o. [15:4] Wis 13:14.   p. [15:6] Ps 115:8.   q. [15:7] Wis 13:11; Jer 18:3–4; Rom 9:21; 2 Tm 2:20–21.   r. [15:8] Gn 3:19; Eccl 12:7.

and takes pride in fashioning
counterfeits.[s]

10 Ashes his heart is!* more worthless than
earth is his hope,[t]
more ignoble than clay his life;

11 Because he knew not the one who
fashioned him,
and breathed into him a
quickening soul,
and infused a vital spirit.[u]

12 Instead, he esteemed our life a mere game,
and our span of life a holiday for gain;
"For one must," says he, "make a profit
in every way, be it even from
evil."[v]

13 For more than anyone else he knows that
he is sinning,
when out of earthen stuff he creates
fragile vessels and idols alike.

14 But most stupid of all and worse than
senseless in mind,
are the enemies of your people who
enslaved them.[w]

15 For they esteemed all the idols of the
nations as gods,
which cannot use their eyes to see,
nor nostrils to breathe the air,
Nor ears to hear,
nor fingers on their hands for feeling;
even their feet are useless to walk
with.[x]

16 For it was a mere human being who made
them;[y]
one living on borrowed breath who
fashioned them.
For no one is able to fashion a god like
himself;

17 he is mortal, and what he makes
with lawless hands is dead.
For he is better than the things he
worships;
he at least lives, but never his idols.

### Second Example Resumed

18 †Besides, they worship the most
loathsome beasts—[z]
as regards stupidity, these are worse
than the rest,[‡]

19 For beasts are neither good-looking nor
desirable;

they have escaped both the approval
of God and his blessing.[a]

## CHAPTER 16

1 Therefore they§ were fittingly punished by
similar creatures,
and were tormented by a swarm of
insects.[b]

2 Instead of this punishment, you benefited
your people
with a novel dish, the delight they
craved,
by providing quail for their food,[c]

3 So that those others, when they desired
food,
should lose their appetite even for
necessities,
since the creatures sent to plague
them were so loathsome,
While these, after a brief period of privation,
partook of a novel dish.[d]

4 For inexorable want had to come upon
those oppressors;
but these needed only to be shown
how their enemies were being
tormented.[e]

5 For when the dire venom of beasts came
upon them[f]
and they were dying from the bite of
crooked serpents,
your anger endured not to the end.

6 But as a warning, for a short time they
were terrorized,
though they had a sign¶ of salvation,
to remind them of the precept
of your law.

7 For the one who turned toward it was
saved,
not by what was seen,
but by you, the savior of all.

8 By this also you convinced our foes
that you are the one who delivers
from all evil.[g]

9 For the bites of locusts and of flies slew
them,
and no remedy was found to save
their lives
because they deserved to be
punished by such means;[h]

---

*[15:10] **Ashes his heart is!**: the words of this cry are taken from Is 44:20 (the Septuagint).

†[15:18–19] The author here returns (11:15; 12:23–27) to the main theme of chaps. 11–19, which was interrupted by the digression of 13:1–15:17.

‡[15:18] **Worse than the rest**: this may mean that the creatures worshiped by the Egyptians (e.g., crocodiles, serpents, scarabs, etc.) were less intelligent than the general run of beasts.

§[16:1] **They**: the Egyptian idolaters, who are punished according to the principle laid down in 11:5, 15–16.

¶[16:6] **Sign**: the brazen serpent, as related in Numbers 21, but the author deliberately avoids any misunderstanding by addressing the Lord as responsible for the healing, since he is "the savior of all" (v. 7; see also vv. 12 and 26 for the role of the "word" of God).

s. [15:9] Bar 6:46.   t. [15:10] Jb 13:12 LXX.   u. [15:11] Gn 2:7; Zec 12:1.   v. [15:12] Jas 4:13–14.   w. [15:14] Ex 1:13.   x. [15:15] Wis 14:11; Dt 4:28; Ps 115:4–7; 135:15–18.   y. [15:16–17] Wis 13:10.   z. [15:18] Wis 11:15; 12:24.

a. [15:19] Gn 1:25; 3:14.   b. [16:1] Wis 11:15–16; 12:23, 27; Ex 7:27; 8:12, 17.   c. [16:2] Wis 11:13; 19:11–12; Ex 16:13; Nm 11:31–32; Ps 105:40.   d. [16:3] Wis 11:15; Ex 8:10; 16:3.   e. [16:4] Wis 11:8–9.   f. [16:5–6] Nm 21:4–9; Dt 32:24; Jer 8:17 LXX.   g. [16:8] Gn 48:16; 2 Mc 1:24–25.   h. [16:9] Ex 8:16–18; 10:4–19; Ps 78:45–46; 105:31, 34; Rev 9:1–11.

¹⁰ But not even the fangs of poisonous
reptiles overcame your
children,
for your mercy came forth and
healed them.ⁱ
¹¹ For as a reminder of your injunctions,
they were stung,
and swiftly they were saved,
Lest they should fall into deep
forgetfulness
and become unresponsive to your
beneficence.ʲ
¹² For indeed, neither herb nor application
cured them,
but your all-healing word, O LORD!ᵏ
¹³ *For you have dominion over life and death;ˡ
you lead down to the gates of Hades
and lead back.
¹⁴ Human beings, however, may kill another
with malice,
but they cannot bring back the
departed spirit,
or release the soul that death has
confined.
¹⁵ Your hand no one can escape.

### Third Example: A Rain
### of Manna for Israel Instead
### of the Plague of Storms

¹⁶ For the wicked who refused to know you
were punished by the might of your
arm,
Were pursued by unusual rains and
hailstorms and unremitting
downpours,
and were consumed by fire.ᵐ
¹⁷ For against all expectation, in water which
quenches everything,
the fire grew more active;
For the universe fights on behalf of the
righteous.ⁿ
¹⁸ Then the flame was temperedᵒ
so that the beasts that were sent
upon the wicked might not be
burnt up,
but that these might see and know
that they were struck by the
judgment of God;
¹⁹ And again, even in the water, fire blazed
beyond its strength
so as to consume the produce of the
wicked land.

²⁰ Instead of this, you nourished your people
with food of angels†
and furnished them bread from
heaven, ready to hand,
untoiled-for,
endowed with all delights and
conforming to every taste.ᵖ
²¹ For this substance of yours revealed
your sweetness toward your
children,
and serving the desire of the one
who received it,
was changed to whatever flavor each
one wished.�q
²² Yet snow and ice‡ withstood fire and were
not melted,
so that they might know that their
enemies' fruits
Were consumed by a fire that blazed in
the hail
and flashed lightning in the rain.ʳ

²³ But this fire, again, in order that the
righteous might be nourished,
forgot even its proper strength;ˢ
²⁴ For your creation, serving you, its maker,
grows tense for punishment against
the wicked,
but is relaxed in benefit for those
who trust in you.ᵗ
²⁵ Therefore at that very time, transformed
in all sorts of ways,
it was serving your all-nourishing
bounty
according to what they needed and
desired;
²⁶ That your children whom you loved
might learn, O LORD,
that it is not the various kinds of
fruits that nourish,
but your word that preserves those
who believe you!ᵘ
²⁷ For what was not destroyed by fire,
melted when merely warmed by a
momentary sunbeam;ᵛ
²⁸ To make known that one must give you
thanks before sunrise,
and turn to you at daybreak.ʷ
²⁹ For the hope of the ungrateful melts like a
wintry frost
and runs off like useless water.ˣ

---

*[16:13–14] The author recognizes the power of the Lord
over life and death, as expressed in 1 Sm 2:6; Tb 13:2. The
traditional imagery of Sheol (gates and confinement) colors
the passage.

---

†[16:20] **Food of angels**: the famous phrase (cf. the hymn
"Panis Angelicus") is taken from Ps 78:24 as rendered by the
Septuagint. The "bread from heaven" (cf. Ex 16:4; Ps 105:40)
with its marvelous "sweetness" becomes a type of the "bread
come down from heaven" in Jn 6:32–51, and plays a large role
in later Christian devotion.

‡[16:22] **Snow and ice**: the manna; cf. v. 27; 19:21.

---

i. [16:10] Dt 32:33. j. [16:11] Ps 78:11. k. [16:12] Ex 15:26.
l. [16:13–15] Dt 32:39; 1 Sm 2:6; Tb 13:2; 2 Mc 6:26; 7:23; Ps
78:34, 39; Eccl 8:8; Dn 5:19. m. [16:16] Wis 11:21; 12:27; Ex 5:2;
9:29–34. n. [16:17] Wis 10:20; 19:20; Ex 9:23–28; 2 Mc 8:36;
14:34. o. [16:18–19] Wis 19:20–21.

p. [16:20] Ex 16:4; Nm 11:8; Ps 78:24–25; Jn 6:31. q. [16:21]
Ps 34:9. r. [16:22] Ex 9:25–31; 10:12; Ps 148:8. s. [16:23] Wis
19:21. t. [16:24] Wis 5:17, 20; 19:6; Sir 39:25–27. u. [16:26]
Dt 8:3; Mt 4:4. v. [16:27] Ex 16:21. w. [16:28] Ps 57:9–10;
92:3. x. [16:29] Wis 5:14; 2 Sm 14:14.

## CHAPTER 17

### Fourth Example: Darkness Afflicts the Egyptians, While the Israelites Have Light*

1 For great are your judgments, and hard to describe;
   therefore the unruly souls went astray.[y]
2 For when the lawless thought to enslave the holy nation,
   they themselves lay shackled with darkness, fettered by the long night,
   confined beneath their own roofs as exiles from the eternal providence.[z]
3 For they, who supposed their secret sins were hid[a]
   under the dark veil of oblivion,
   Were scattered in fearful trembling, terrified by apparitions.
4 For not even their inner chambers kept them unafraid,
   for crashing sounds on all sides terrified them,
   and mute phantoms with somber looks appeared.
5 No fire had force enough to give light,
   nor did the flaming brilliance of the stars
   succeed in lighting up that gloomy night.[b]
6 But only intermittent, fearful fires flashed through upon them;
   And in their terror they thought beholding these was worse
   than the times when that sight was no longer to be seen.[c]
7 And mockeries of their magic art[†] failed,
   and there was a humiliating refutation of their vaunted shrewdness.[d]
8 For they who undertook to banish fears and terrors from the sick soul
   themselves sickened with ridiculous fear.
9 For even though no monstrous thing frightened them,
   they shook at the passing of insects and the hissing of reptiles,[e]

10 And perished trembling,
   reluctant to face even the air that they could nowhere escape.
11 For wickedness, of its nature cowardly, testifies in its own condemnation,
   and because of a distressed conscience, always magnifies misfortunes.[f]
12 For fear is nought but the surrender of the helps that come from reason;
13 and the more one's expectation is of itself uncertain,
   the more one makes of not knowing the cause that brings on torment.
14 So they, during that night, powerless though it was,
   since it had come upon them from the recesses of a powerless[‡] Hades,
   while all sleeping the same sleep,
15 Were partly smitten by fearsome apparitions
   and partly stricken by their souls' surrender;
   for fear overwhelmed them, sudden and unexpected.[g]
16 Thus, then, whoever was there fell into that prison without bars and was kept confined.[h]
17 For whether one was a farmer, or a shepherd,
   or a worker at tasks in the wasteland,
   Taken unawares, each served out the inescapable sentence;
18 for all were bound by the one bond of darkness.[i]
   And were it only the whistling wind,
   or the melodious song of birds in the spreading branches,
   Or the steady sound of rushing water,
19 or the rude crash of overthrown rocks,
   Or the unseen gallop of bounding animals,
   or the roaring cry of the fiercest beasts,
   Or an echo resounding from the hollow of the hills—
   these sounds, inspiring terror, paralyzed them.
20 For the whole world shone with brilliant light[j]
   and continued its works without interruption;
21 But over them alone was spread oppressive night,
   an image of the darkness[§] that was about to come upon them.

---

*[17:1–18:4] The description of the darkness of the ninth plague is a very creative development of Ex 10:21–29. It betrays a wide knowledge of contemporary thought. For the first and only time in the Septuagint the Greek word for "conscience" occurs, in 17:11. There is no Hebrew word that is equivalent; the idea is expressed indirectly. The horrendous darkness is illumined by "fires" (v. 6), i.e., lightnings that only contributed to the terror.

†[17:7] Magic art: the Egyptian magicians who were successful at first (Ex 7:11, 22) and then failed (Ex 8:14; 9:11) are now powerless against the darkness and the phantoms and are totally discredited.

y. [17:1] Ex 6:6 LXX.    z. [17:2] Wis 18:4; Ex 1:13–14; 9:6; 10:21–23.    a. [17:3–4] Wis 1:7–8; 10:8; 18:17.    b. [17:5] Wis 10:17; Jer 23:24 LXX.    c. [17:6] Ex 9:23–24.    d. [17:7] Wis 12:25–26; Ex 7:11–12, 22; 8:3; 9:11; 10:2.    e. [17:9] Wis 16:1; Jer 26:22 LXX.

‡[17:14] Powerless: Hades (or Sheol), i.e., the nether world, is often portrayed in the Old Testament as a hostile power, since all must die (Ps 49:8–13), but it has no power against God.

§[17:21] Darkness: of Hades or Sheol; see note on 16:13–14.

f. [17:11] Wis 4:6; 10:7; Rom 2:15.    g. [17:15] Ex 11:9–10.    h. [17:16] Wis 18:4; Ex 10:23.    i. [17:18–19] Lv 26:36.    j. [17:20–21] Ex 10:23; Is 9:1; 60:1–3; 2 Pt 2:17.

Yet they were more a burden to
themselves than was the
darkness.

## CHAPTER 18

1 But your holy ones had very great light;
And those others, who heard their voices
but did not see their forms,
counted them blest for not having
suffered;

2 And because they who formerly had been
wronged did not harm them,
they thanked them,
and because of the difference
between them,* pleaded with
them.

3 Instead of this, you furnished the flaming
pillar,
a guide on the unknown way,
and the mild sun for an honorable
migration.$^k$

4 †For they deserved to be deprived of light
and imprisoned by darkness,
they had kept your children confined,
through whom the imperishable
light of the law was to be given
to the world.$^l$

### Fifth Example: Death of the Egyptian Firstborn; the Israelites Are Spared

5 When they determined to put to death
the infants of the holy ones,
and when a single boy‡ had been
cast forth and then saved,
As a reproof you carried off a multitude of
their children
and made them perish all at once in
the mighty water.$^m$

6 That night was known beforehand to our
ancestors,
so that, with sure knowledge of the
oaths in which they put their
faith, they might have courage.$^n$

7 The expectation of your people
was the salvation of the righteous and
the destruction of their foes.$^o$

8 For by the same means with which you
punished our adversaries,
you glorified us whom you had
summoned.$^p$

9 For in secret the holy children of the good
were offering sacrifice

and carried out with one mind the
divine institution,$^§$
So that your holy ones should share
alike the same blessings and
dangers,
once they had sung the ancestral
hymns of praise.$^q$

10 But the discordant cry of their enemies
echoed back,
and the piteous wail of mourning for
children was borne to them.$^r$

11 And the slave was smitten with the same
retribution as the master;
even the commoner suffered the
same as the king.$^s$

12 And all alike by one common form of death
had countless dead;
For the living were not even sufficient for
the burial,
since at a single instant their most
valued offspring had been
destroyed.$^t$

13 For though they disbelieved at every turn
on account of sorceries,
at the destruction of the firstborn
they acknowledged that this
people¶ was God's son.$^u$

14 **For when peaceful stillness encompassed
everything
and the night in its swift course was
half spent,

15 Your all-powerful word from heaven's
royal throne
leapt into the doomed land,$^v$

16     a fierce warrior bearing the sharp
sword of your inexorable decree,
And alighted, and filled every place with
death,
and touched heaven, while standing
upon the earth.$^w$

17 Then, at once, visions in horrible dreams
perturbed them$^x$
and unexpected fears assailed them;

18 And cast half-dead, one here, another there,
they revealed why they were dying.

19 For the dreams that disturbed them had
proclaimed this beforehand,
lest they perish unaware of why they
endured such evil.

20 The trial of death touched even the
righteous,

---

*[18:2] **The difference between them**: God's distinctive manner of treating the Israelites and the Egyptians according to their respective deeds. **Pleaded**: perhaps, for their departure.

†[18:4] The discussion of physical light climaxes with a reference to the "imperishable light" of the torah.

‡[18:5] **Single boy**: Moses.

§[18:9] **Divine institution**: the Passover. **Ancestral hymns of praise**: possibly the Hallel psalms, the psalms sung at the end of the Passover meal; cf. Mt 26:30; Mk 14:26.

¶[18:13] **People**: the Israelites (cf. Ex 4:22).

**[18:14–16] These verses attribute to the personified "word" the actions of the Lord mentioned in Ex 12:13–17 (note the role of the "destroyer" in Ex 12:23 and compare Wis 18:22, 25).

---

k. [18:3] Ex 13:21. l. [18:4] Wis 17:2; Ps 119:105; Is 2:3, 5. m. [18:5] Wis 11:7, 14; Ex 1:16, 22; 2:3, 6–10; 15:10; Neh 9:11. n. [18:6] Wis 12:21; Ex 6:8; 13:5. o. [18:7] Ex 14:13. p. [18:8] Wis 19:22; Ex 3:18; Is 43:3–4.

q. [18:9] Ex 12:21–28; Sir 44–50. r. [18:10] Ex 12:30; Jer 9:17, 19. s. [18:11] Ex 11:5; 12:29. t. [18:12] Nm 33:4. u. [18:13] Wis 17:7; Ex 4:22–23; 12:12, 29; 13:2, 13, 15. v. [18:15] Wis 9:10; Ex 15:3. w. [18:16] 1 Chr 21:16; Heb 4:12; Rev 1:16. x. [18:17–19] Wis 17:3–4.

and in the desert a plague struck the
    multitude;
Yet not for long did the anger last.*y*
21 For the blameless man* hastened to be
    their champion,
    bearing the weapon of his special
      office,
    prayer and the propitiation of
      incense;
He withstood the wrath and put a stop to
    the calamity,
    showing that he was your servant.
22 He overcame the bitterness
    not by bodily strength, not by force
      of arms;
But by word he overcame the smiter,†
    recalling the sworn covenants with
      their ancestors.*z*
23 For when corpses had already fallen one
    on another in heaps,
    he stood in the midst and checked
      the anger,
    and cut off its way to the living.*a*
24 For on his full-length robe was the whole
    world,
    and ancestral glories were carved on
      the four rows of stones,
    and your grandeur‡ was on the
      crown upon his head.*b*
25 To these the destroyer yielded, these he
    feared;
    for this sole trial of anger sufficed.*c*

### CHAPTER 19
1 But merciless wrath assailed the wicked
    until the end,
    for God knew beforehand what they
      were yet to do:*d*
2 That though they themselves had agreed
    to the departure
    and had anxiously sent them on
      their way,
    they would regret it and pursue
      them.*e*
3 For while they were still engaged in
    funeral rites
    and mourning at the burials of the
      dead,
They adopted another senseless plan:
    those whom they had driven out
      with entreaties
    they now pursued as fugitives.*f*

4 For a compulsion appropriate to this
    ending drew them on,
    and made them forget what had
      befallen them,
That they might complete the torments of
    their punishment,
5    and your people might experience a
    glorious§ journey
    while those others met an extraordi-
      nary death.

6 ¶For all creation, in its several kinds, was
    being made over anew,
    serving your commands, that your
      children might be preserved
      unharmed.*g*
7 The cloud overshadowed their camp;
    and out of what had been water, dry
      land was seen emerging:
Out of the Red Sea an unimpeded road,
    and a grassy plain out of the mighty
      flood.*h*
8 Over this crossed the whole nation
    sheltered by your hand,
    and they beheld stupendous wonders.
9 For they ranged about like horses,
    and leapt like lambs,
    praising you, LORD, their deliverer.*i*
10 For they were still mindful of what had
    happened in their sojourn:
    how instead of the young of animals
      the land brought forth gnats,
    and instead of fishes the river
      swarmed with countless frogs.*j*
11 And later they saw also a new kind of
    bird*k*
    when, prompted by desire, they
      asked for pleasant foods;
12 For to appease them quail came to them
    from the sea.
13 And the punishments came upon the
    sinners
    not without forewarnings from the
      violence of the thunderbolts.

For they justly suffered for their own
    misdeeds,
    since they treated their guests with
      the more grievous** hatred.*l*
14 For those others†† did not receive
    unfamiliar visitors,*m*

---

§[19:5] **Glorious:** more precisely, "wondrous," but the word reflects "glorified" in 18:8 and 19:22.

¶[19:6] The cooperation of creation in Israel's deliverance (vv. 7–12) under the direction of the Lord is a favorite theme; cf. 16:24–25.

**[19:13] **More grievous:** than that of the people of Sodom (Gn 19) with whom the Egyptians are compared.

††[19:14] **Others:** the people of Sodom refused to receive strangers. **Beneficent:** because of the services rendered by Joseph.

---

*[18:21] **Blameless man:** Aaron, acting according to his office of high priest and intercessor (cf. Nm 17:9–15; Ex 28:15–21, 31–38).

†[18:22] **Smiter:** the destroying angel; cf. v. 25.

‡[18:24] **Glories . . . grandeur:** the name of God and the names of the tribes were inscribed on the high priest's apparel.

---

y. [18:20] Wis 16:5; Nm 17:9–15.  z. [18:22] Wis 12:21; Ex 32:12–13; Ps 20:8.  a. [18:23] Nm 14:29–30.  b. [18:24] Ex 28:15–21, 31–38; Sir 45:8–12; 50:11.  c. [18:25] 1 Chr 21:15.  d. [19:1] Ex 14:4.  e. [19:2] Ex 12:33; 14:5, 8.  f. [19:3] Wis 18:10, 12; Ex 12:30–36.

g. [19:6] Wis 5:17; 16:24.  h. [19:7] Ex 14:21–29.  i. [19:9] Wis 10:20; 16:8; Sir 15:1–18; Ps 114:4–6.  j. [19:10] Ex 7:27–8:3; 8:12–15; Ps 105:30–31.  k. [19:11–12] Wis 16:2; Ps 78:18.  l. [19:13] 2 Mc 7:18, 32.  m. [19:14–15] Gn 15:13; Ex 2:22.

but these were enslaving beneficent guests.

15 And not that only; but what punishment was to be theirs*
since they received strangers unwillingly!

16 Yet these,† after welcoming them with festivities,
oppressed with awful toils
those who had shared with them the same rights.ⁿ

17 And they were struck with blindness,‡
as those others had been at the doors of the righteous man—
When, surrounded by yawning darkness,
each sought the entrance of his own door.º

18 For the elements, in ever-changing harmony,

like strings of the harp, produce new melody,
while the flow of music steadily persists.
And this can be perceived exactly from a review of what took place.

19 For land creatures were changed into water creatures,
and those that swam went over on land.

20 Fire in water maintained its own strength,ᵖ
and water forgot its quenching nature;

21 Flames, by contrast, neither consumed the flesh
of the perishable animals that went about in them,
nor melted the icelike, quick-melting kind of ambrosial food.

22 For every way, Lord! you magnified and glorified your people;
unfailing, you stood by them in every time and circumstance.�q

---

*[19:15] **Theirs**: the people of Sodom.
†[19:16] **These**: the Egyptians.
‡[19:17] **Blindness**: the plague of darkness. **Righteous man**: Lot (Gn 19:11).

n. [19:16] Gn 45:17–20; 47:4–6; Ex 1:11.   o. [19:17] Wis 17:2; Gn 19:11.

p. [19:20–21] Wis 16:17–19, 22–23, 27.   q. [19:22] Wis 18:8; Lv 26:44; Ps 126:3.

# THE WISDOM OF
# BEN SIRA
## (ECCLESIASTICUS)

The Wisdom of Ben Sira derives its title from the author, "Yeshua [Jesus], son of Eleazar, son of Sira" (50:27). This seems to be the earliest title of the book. The designation "Liber Ecclesiasticus," meaning "Church Book," appended to some Greek and Latin manuscripts, is perhaps due to the extensive use the church made of this book in presenting moral teaching to catechumens and to the faithful. The title "Sirach" comes from the Greek form of the author's name.

The author, a sage who lived in Jerusalem, was thoroughly imbued with love for the wisdom tradition, and also for the law, priesthood, Temple, and divine worship. As a wise and experienced observer of life he addressed himself to his contemporaries with the motive of helping them to maintain religious faith and integrity through study of the books sacred to the Jewish tradition.

The book contains numerous well-crafted maxims, grouped by affinity, and dealing with a variety of subjects such as the individual, the family, and the community in their relations with one another and with God. It treats of friendship, education, poverty and wealth, laws, religious worship, and many other matters that reflect the religious and social customs of the time.

Written in Hebrew in the early years of the second century B.C., the book was finished by ca. 175. The text was translated into Greek by the author's grandson after 117 B.C. He also wrote a foreword which contains valuable information about the book, its author, and himself as translator. Until the close of the nineteenth century the Wisdom of Ben Sira was known to Christians in translations, of which the Greek rendering was the most important. From it the Latin version was made. Between 1896 and 1900, again in 1931, and several times since 1956, incomplete manuscripts were discovered, so that more than two thirds of the book in Hebrew is available; these Hebrew texts agree substantially with the Greek. One such text, from Masada, is pre-Christian in date. The New American Bible provides a critical translation based on the evidence of all the ancient texts.

Though not included in the Jewish Bible after the first century A.D., nor, therefore, accepted by Protestants, the Wisdom of Ben Sira has been recognized by the Catholic Church as inspired and canonical. The Foreword, though not properly part of the book, is always included with it because of its antiquity and importance.

The contents of the Wisdom of Ben Sira are of a discursive nature, not easily divided into separate parts. Chapters 1–43 deal largely with moral instruction; 44:1–50:24 contain a eulogy of the heroes of Israel. There are two appendixes in which the author expresses his gratitude to God (51:1–12), and invites the unschooled to acquire true wisdom (51:13–30).

## FOREWORD*

Inasmuch as many and great truths have been given to us through the Law, the prophets, and the authors who followed them,* for which the instruction and wisdom of Israel merit praise, it is the duty of those who read the scriptures not only to become knowledgeable themselves but also to use their love of learning in speech and in writing to help others less familiar. So my grandfather Jesus, who had long devoted himself to the study of the law, the prophets, and the rest of the books of our ancestors, and had acquired great familiarity with them, was moved to write something himself regarding instruction and wisdom. He did this so that those who love learning might, by accepting what he had written, make even greater progress in living according to the Law.

---

*[Foreword] **The Law, the prophets, and the authors who followed them:** an indication of the eventual tripartite division of the Hebrew Scriptures: Law (*torah*), Prophets (*nebi'im*), and Writings (*ketubim*), shortened in the acronym Tanak. **Thirty-eighth . . . Euergetes:** 132 B.C. The reference is to Ptolemy VII, Physkon Euergetes II (170–163; 145–117 B.C.).

You are invited therefore to read it with good will and attention, with indulgence for any failure on our part, despite earnest efforts, in the interpretation of particular passages. For words spoken originally in Hebrew do not have the same effect when they are translated into another language. That is true not only of this book but of the Law itself, the prophecies, and the rest of the books, which differ no little when they are read in the original.

I arrived in Egypt in the thirty-eighth year of the reign of King Euergetes, and while there, I had access to no little learning. I therefore considered it my duty to devote some diligence and industry to the translation of this book. During this time I applied my skill for many sleepless hours to complete the book and publish it for those living abroad who wish to acquire learning and are disposed to live their lives according to the Law.

## THE WISDOM OF BEN SIRA

## CHAPTER 1

### God's Gift of Wisdom[*]

1  All wisdom[†] is from the Lord
    and remains with him forever.[a]
2  The sands of the sea, the drops of rain,
    the days of eternity—who can count
    them?
3  Heaven's height, earth's extent,
    the abyss and wisdom—who can
    explore them?
4  Before all other things wisdom was created;
    and prudent understanding, from
    eternity.[‡]

6  The root of wisdom—to whom has it been
    revealed?
    Her subtleties—who knows them?[§b]
8  There is but one, wise and truly awesome,
    seated upon his throne—the Lord.

9  It is he who created her,
    saw her and measured her,[c]
   Poured her forth upon all his works,
10    upon every living thing according to
      his bounty,
      lavished her upon those who love him.

### Fear of the Lord Is Wisdom[**]

11  The fear of the Lord[††] is glory and exultation,
    gladness and a festive crown.
12  The fear of the Lord rejoices the heart,
    giving gladness, joy, and long life.[‡‡]
13  Those who fear the Lord will be happy at
    the end,
    even on the day of death they will be
    blessed.

14  The beginning of wisdom is to fear the
    Lord;
    she is created with the faithful in the
    womb.[d]
15  With the godly she was created from of old,
    and with their descendants she will
    keep faith.

16  The fullness of wisdom is to fear the Lord;
    she inebriates them with her fruits.[e]
17  Their entire house she fills with choice
    foods,
    their granaries with her produce.

18  The crown of wisdom is the fear of the Lord,
    flowering with peace and perfect
    health.[§§]
19  Knowledge and full understanding she
    rains down;
    she heightens the glory of those who
    possess her.

20  The root of wisdom is to fear the Lord;
    her branches are long life.
21  The fear of the Lord drives away sins;
    where it abides it turns back all
    anger.

---

[*] [1:1–10] This brief poem serves as an introduction to the book. The Lord is the source and preserver of all wisdom, which he pours out upon all. See Jb 28:20–28; Prv 2:6; 8:22–31; Wis 7:25–27.

[†] [1:1] **Wisdom**: throughout the book Ben Sira describes in great detail just what wisdom is: sometimes divine (1:6, 8), sometimes a synonym for God's law (24:22–23). Ben Sira makes clear that all wisdom comes from God.

‡ [1:4] Other ancient texts read as v. 5:

The wellspring of wisdom is the word of God in the heights,
    and its runlets are the ageless commandments.

§ [1:6] Other ancient texts read as v. 7:

An understanding of wisdom—to whom has this been disclosed;
    her resourcefulness, who has known?

¶[1:8–10] In contrast to Jb 28, wisdom is not only with God, but given to all, especially Israel; see Bar 3:9; 4:4.

---

a. [1:1] 1 Kgs 3:9.   b. [1:6] Bar 3:15; Jb 28:10, 20.

---

[**] [1:11–30] This is one of several poems of 22 bicola, or poetic lines, corresponding to the number of letters in the Hebrew alphabet. Ben Sira uses the expression "fear of the Lord" twelve times and the noun "wisdom" seven times to emphasize the connection between the two ideas. He describes the blessings that come to those who fear the Lord, i.e., those who practice true religion by loving and serving God and keeping the Law (2:7–10, 15–17; 4:11–16; see Dt 6:1–5, 24). Such blessings recur throughout the book.

[††] [1:11] **Fear of the Lord**: Ben Sira identifies wisdom with the fear of the Lord (vv. 26–27).

‡‡ [1:12] Other ancient texts read as v. 12cd:

Fear of the Lord is the Lord's gift;
    also for love he makes firm paths.

§§ [1:18] Other ancient texts read as v. 18cd:

Both are gifts of God toward peace;
    splendor opens out for those who love him.

---

c. [1:9] Jb 28:27.   d. [1:14] Jb 28:28; Ps 111:10; Prv 1:7; 9:10.
e. [1:16] Eccl 12:13.

22 Unjust anger can never be justified;
   anger pulls a person to utter ruin.
23 *Until the right time, the patient remain
   calm,
   then cheerfulness comes back to them.
24 Until the right time they hold back their
   words;
   then the lips of many will tell of
   their good sense.

25 Among wisdom's treasures is the model
   for knowledge;
   but godliness is an abomination to
   the sinner.
26 If you desire wisdom, keep the
   commandments,
   and the Lord will bestow her upon
   you;
27 For the fear of the Lord is wisdom and
   discipline;
   faithfulness and humility are his
   delight.

28 Do not disobey the fear of the Lord,†
   do not approach it with duplicity of
   heart.ᶠ
29 Do not be a hypocrite before others;
   over your lips keep watch.
30 Do not exalt yourself lest you fall
   and bring dishonor upon yourself;

   For then the Lord will reveal your secrets
   and cast you down in the midst of
   the assembly.
   Because you did not approach the fear of
   the Lord,
   and your heart was full of deceit.

## CHAPTER 2

### Trust in God

1 My child, when you come to serve the Lord,‡
   prepare yourself for trials.ᵍ
2 Be sincere of heart and steadfast,
   and do not be impetuous in time of
   adversity.
3 Cling to him, do not leave him,
   that you may prosper in your last days.

4 Accept whatever happens to you;
   in periods of humiliation be patient.

5 For in fire gold is tested,
   and the chosen, in the crucible of
   humiliation.ʰ
6 Trust in God, and he will help you;
   make your ways straight and hope
   in him.

7 You that fear the Lord, wait for his mercy,
   do not stray lest you fall.
8 You that fear the Lord, trust in him,
   and your reward will not be lost.
9 You that fear the LORD, hope for good things,
   for lasting joy and mercy.

10 Consider the generations long past and see:
   has anyone trusted in the Lord and
   been disappointed?
   Has anyone persevered in his fear and
   been forsaken?
   has anyone called upon him and
   been ignored?ⁱ
11 For the Lord is compassionate and merciful;
   forgives sins and saves in time of
   trouble.

12 Woe to timid hearts and drooping hands,§
   to the sinner who walks a double path!
13 Woe to the faint of heart! For they do not
   trust,
   and therefore have no shelter!
14 Woe to you that have lost hope!
   what will you do at the Lord's
   visitation?

15 Those who fear the Lord do not disobey
   his words;
   those who love him keep his ways.ʲ
16 Those who fear the Lord seek to please him;
   those who love him are filled with
   his law.
17 Those who fear the Lord prepare their
   hearts
   and humble themselves before him.

18 Let us fall into the hands of the Lord
   and not into the hands of mortals,
   For equal to his majesty is his mercy;
   and equal to his name are his works.ᵏ

## CHAPTER 3

### Responsibilities to Parents¶

1 Children, listen to me, your father;
   act accordingly, that you may be safe.

---

*[1:23–24] Ben Sira pays close attention to *kairos*, the right time, occurring some sixty times in his book.
†[1:28–30] Attempting to serve the Lord with duplicity of heart is hypocrisy and self-exaltation, deserving of public disgrace.
‡[2:1–11] Serving the Lord is not without its trials (v. 1); but no matter what happens, the genuine believer will remain sincere, steadfast, and faithful (vv. 2–3). Misfortune and humiliation are means of purification to prove one's worth (vv. 4–5). Ben Sira believed that patience and unwavering trust in God are ultimately rewarded with the benefits of God's mercy and of lasting joy (vv. 6–11).

§[2:12–18] A stern warning to those who compromise their faith in time of affliction; they fail in courage and trust and therefore have no security (vv. 12–14). But those who fear the Lord through obedience, reverence, love, and humility find his "mercy equal to his majesty" (vv. 15–18).
¶[3:1–16] Besides the virtues that must characterize our conduct toward God, special duties are enjoined, such as honor

---

f. [1:28] Jas 1:8; 2:8.   g. [2:1] 2 Tm 3:10–12.

h. [2:5] Prv 17:3; Wis 3:6; Is 48:10; 1 Pt 1:7.   i. [2:10] Ps 31:2; 145:18–20.   j. [2:15] Jn 14:23.   k. [2:18] Sir 17:29.

<sup>2</sup> For the Lord sets a father in honor over
     his children
       and confirms a mother's authority
         over her sons.
<sup>3</sup> Those who honor their father atone for sins;
<sup>4</sup>      they store up riches who respect
       their mother.
<sup>5</sup> Those who honor their father will have
       joy in their own children,
       and when they pray they are heard.
<sup>6</sup> Those who respect their father will live a
       long life;
       those who obey the Lord honor
         their mother.

<sup>7</sup> Those who fear the Lord honor their father,
       and serve their parents as masters.
<sup>8</sup> In word and deed honor your father,
       that all blessings may come to you.<sup>l</sup>
<sup>9</sup> A father's blessing gives a person firm
       roots,
       but a mother's curse uproots the
         growing plant.<sup>m</sup>
<sup>10</sup> Do not glory in your father's disgrace,
       for that is no glory to you!
<sup>11</sup> A father's glory is glory also for oneself;
       they multiply sin who demean their
         mother.<sup>n</sup>

<sup>12</sup> My son, be steadfast in honoring your
       father;
       do not grieve him as long as he lives.<sup>o</sup>
<sup>13</sup> Even if his mind fails, be considerate of him;
       do not revile him because you are in
         your prime.
<sup>14</sup> Kindness to a father will not be forgotten;
       it will serve as a sin offering—it will
         take lasting root.
<sup>15</sup> In time of trouble it will be recalled to
       your advantage,
       like warmth upon frost it will melt
         away your sins.
<sup>16</sup> Those who neglect their father are like
       blasphemers;
       those who provoke their mother are
         accursed by their Creator.<sup>p</sup>

### Humility*

<sup>17</sup> My son, conduct your affairs with
       humility,

       and you will be loved more than a
       giver of gifts.
<sup>18</sup> Humble yourself the more, the greater
       you are,
       and you will find mercy in the sight
         of God.<sup>†q</sup>
<sup>20</sup> For great is the power of the Lord;
       by the humble he is glorified.
<sup>21</sup> What is too sublime for you, do not seek;
       do not reach into things that are
         hidden from you.<sup>r</sup>
<sup>22</sup> What is committed to you, pay heed to;
       what is hidden is not your concern.
<sup>23</sup> In matters that are beyond you do not
       meddle,
       when you have been shown more
         than you can understand.
<sup>24</sup> Indeed, many are the conceits of human
       beings;
       evil imaginations lead them astray.

### Docility‡

<sup>25</sup> Without the pupil of the eye, light is
       missing;
       without knowledge, wisdom is
         missing.
<sup>26</sup> A stubborn heart will fare badly in the end;
       those who love danger will perish
         in it.
<sup>27</sup> A stubborn heart will have many a hurt;
       adding sin to sin is madness.
<sup>28</sup> When the proud are afflicted, there is no
       cure;
       for they are offshoots of an evil plant.<sup>s</sup>
<sup>29</sup> The mind of the wise appreciates
       proverbs,
       and the ear that listens to wisdom
         rejoices.

### Alms for the Poor

<sup>30</sup> As water quenches a flaming fire,
       so almsgiving atones for sins.<sup>t</sup>
<sup>31</sup> The kindness people have done crosses
       their paths later on;
       should they stumble, they will find
         support.

### CHAPTER 4

<sup>1</sup> My child, do not mock the life of the
       poor;
       do not keep needy eyes§ waiting.<sup>u</sup>

---

and respect toward parents, with corresponding blessings (vv. 1–9). By showing such respect especially to old and infirm parents (vv. 10–13), the sins of children are pardoned (vv. 14–15). Failure to honor father and mother is blasphemy and merits a curse from God (v. 16). Cf. Ex 20:12; Eph 6:2–3.

*[3:17–24] Humility gives you a true estimate of yourself (vv. 17–20; cf. 10:28), so that you will do what should be done, and avoid what is beyond your understanding and strength (vv. 21–23). Intellectual pride, however, leads you astray (v. 24). Ben Sira is perhaps warning his students against the perils of Greek philosophy.

---

† [3:18] Other ancient texts read as v. 19:

Many are lofty and famous,
     but to the humble he reveals his plan.

‡[3:25–29] The antidote for stubbornness is to be found in the search for knowledge and wisdom.
§[4:1] **Needy eyes:** when the poor look for help; cf. 18:18.

---

l. [3:8] Ex 20:12; Dt 5:16; Mt 15:4; 19:19; Mk 7:10; 10:19; Lk 18:20; Eph 6:2–3.   m. [3:9] Gn 27:27–29; 49:2–27.   n. [3:11] Prv 17:6. o. [3:12] Prv 23:22.   p. [3:16] Prv 19:26; 30:11, 14, 17.

q. [3:18] Mt 23:12; Lk 1:52; 14:11; 18:14.   r. [3:21] Ps 131:1. s. [3:28] Dt 32:32; Wis 12:10.   t. [3:30] Sir 7:32–36; 29:8–13; Dt 15:7–11; Tb 12:9; Dn 4:24.   u. [4:1] Tb 4:7–11.

2 Do not grieve the hungry,
   nor anger the needy.
3 Do not aggravate a heart already angry,
   nor delay giving to the needy.
4 A beggar's request do not reject;
   do not turn your face away from
   the poor.
5 From the needy do not turn your eyes;
   do not give them reason to curse
   you.
6 If in their pain they cry out bitterly,
   their Rock will hear the sound of
   their cry.

## Social Conduct

7 Endear yourself to the assembly;
   before the city's ruler bow your head.
8 Give a hearing to the poor,
   and return their greeting with
   deference;
9 Deliver the oppressed from their
   oppressors;[v]
   right judgment should not be
   repugnant to you.
10 Be like a father to orphans,
   and take the place of a husband to
   widows.
   Then God will call you his child,
   and he will be merciful to you and
   deliver you from the pit.

## The Rewards of Wisdom*

11 Wisdom teaches her children
   and admonishes all who can
   understand her.
12 Those who love her love life;
   those who seek her out win the
   LORD's favor.
13 Those who hold her fast will attain glory,
   and they shall abide in the blessing
   of the LORD.
14 Those who serve her serve the Holy One;
   those who love her the Lord loves.[w]

15 "Whoever obeys me will judge nations;
   whoever listens to me will dwell in
   my inmost chambers.
16 If they remain faithful, they will possess me;
   their descendants too will inherit me.

17 "I will walk with them in disguise,
   and at first I will test them with
   trials.

Fear and dread I will bring upon them
and I will discipline them with my
constraints.
When their hearts are fully with me,
18   then I will set them again on the
     straight path
     and reveal my secrets to them.
19 But if they turn away from me, I will
   abandon them
   and deliver them over to robbers."

## Sincerity and Justice[†]

20 My son, watch for the right time; fear
   what is evil;
   do not bring shame upon yourself.
21 There is a shame heavy with guilt,
   and a shame that brings glory and
   respect.
22 Show no favoritism to your own discredit;
   let no one intimidate you to your
   own downfall.
23 Do not refrain from speaking at the
   proper time,
   and do not hide your wisdom;
24 For wisdom becomes known through
   speech,
   and knowledge through the tongue's
   response.

25 Never speak against the truth,
   but of your own ignorance be ashamed.
26 Do not be ashamed to acknowledge your
   sins,
   and do not struggle against a
   rushing stream.
27 Do not abase yourself before a fool;
   do not refuse to do so before rulers.
28 Even to the death, fight for what is right,
   and the LORD will do battle for you.

29 Do not be haughty in your speech,
   or lazy and slack in your deeds.
30 Do not be like a lion at home,
   or sly and suspicious with your
   servants.
31 Do not let your hand be open to receive,
   but clenched when it is time to give.

## CHAPTER 5

## Against Presumption[‡]

1 Do not rely on your wealth,
   or say, "I have the power."[x]

---

*[4:11–19] The Hebrew text in vv. 15–19 presents wisdom speaking in the first person, as in chap. 24. The precious fruits of wisdom—life, favor, glory, blessings, God's love—arouse desire for her (vv. 11–14). Her disciples are like ministers (v. 14) and judges (v. 15), whose descendants have her for their heritage (v. 16). They enjoy happiness and learn her secrets after surviving her tests (vv. 17–18). Those who fail her are abandoned to destruction (v. 19).

v. [4:9] Jb 29:12, 17.   w. [4:14] Wis 7:28.

†[4:20–31] The student of wisdom is warned about interior trials of discipline and external dangers to sincerity and justice, namely evil, human respect (vv. 20–22), compromise of liberty in speech and action (vv. 23–25), false shame (v. 26). The student must fight for the truth (vv. 25, 28), avoiding cynicism and laziness (v. 29), and inconsistency (v. 30).

‡[5:1–8] The vices of the rich are pride and independence (vv. 1–2), presumption (v. 3), false security (vv. 4–6), and impenitence (v. 7), which cannot escape the divine wrath (vv. 7–8). Cf. Prv 18:23; 19:1; 28:6.

x. [5:1] Sir 11:24; Prv 27:1; Lk 12:19; 1 Tm 6:17.

² Do not rely on your strength
   in following the desires of your heart.
³ Do not say, "Who can prevail against me?"
   for the LORD will exact punishment.
⁴ Do not say, "I have sinned, yet what has
   happened to me?"
   for the LORD is slow to anger!
⁵ Do not be so confident of forgiveness
   that you add sin upon sin.
⁶ Do not say, "His mercy is great;
   my many sins he will forgive."
   For mercy and anger alike are with him;
   his wrath comes to rest on the wicked.
⁷ Do not delay turning back to the LORD,
   do not put it off day after day.
   For suddenly his wrath will come forth;
   at the time of vengeance, you will
   perish.
⁸ Do not rely on deceitful wealth,
   for it will be no help on the day of
   wrath.ʸ

### Use and Abuse of the Tongue*

⁹ Do not winnow in every wind,
   nor walk in every path.†
¹⁰ Be steadfast regarding your knowledge,
   and let your speech be consistent.
¹¹ Be swift to hear,
   but slow to answer.ᶻ
¹² If you can, answer your neighbor;
   if not, place your hand over your
   mouth!
¹³ Honor and dishonor through speaking!
   The tongue can be your downfall.
¹⁴ Do not be called double-tongued;
   and with your tongue do not slander
   a neighbor.
   For shame has been created for the thief,
   and sore disgrace for the
   double-tongued.
¹⁵ In little or in much, do not act corruptly;

## CHAPTER 6

¹ Do not be a foe instead of a friend.
   A bad name, disgrace, and dishonor you
   will inherit.
   Thus the wicked, the
   double-tongued!‡

### Unruly Passions

² Do not fall into the grip of your passion,ᵃ
   lest like fire it consume your strength.

³ It will eat your leaves and destroy your
   fruits,
   and you will be left like a dry tree.
⁴ For fierce passion destroys its owner
   and makes him the sport of his
   enemies.

### True Friendship§

⁵ Pleasant speech multiplies friends,
   and gracious lips, friendly greetings.
⁶ Let those who are friendly to you be many,
   but one in a thousand your confidant.
⁷ When you gain friends, gain them
   through testing,ᵇ
   and do not be quick to trust them.
⁸ For there are friends when it suits them,
   but they will not be around in time
   of trouble.
⁹ Another is a friend who turns into an
   enemy,
   and tells of the quarrel to your
   disgrace.
¹⁰ Others are friends, table companions,
   but they cannot be found in time of
   affliction.
¹¹ When things go well, they are your other
   self,
   and lord it over your servants.
¹² If disaster comes upon you, they turn
   against you
   and hide themselves.
¹³ Stay away from your enemies,
   and be on guard with your friends.
¹⁴ Faithful friends are a sturdy shelter;
   whoever finds one finds a treasure.
¹⁵ Faithful friends are beyond price,
   no amount can balance their worth.
¹⁶ Faithful friends are life-saving medicine;
   those who fear God will find them.
¹⁷ Those who fear the Lord enjoy stable
   friendship,
   for as they are, so will their
   neighbors be.

### Blessings of Wisdom¶

¹⁸ My child, from your youth choose
   discipline;
   and when you have gray hair you
   will find wisdom.

---

*[5:9–6:1] Proper use of the tongue requires constancy in speech (v. 10), prudence (vv. 11–12), good judgment (v. 13), charity (5:15; 6:1); detraction, calumny (v. 14), and double-talk bring shame and disgrace (5:14; 6:1).

†[5:9] The metaphors indicate careless behavior.

‡[6:1] **Thus . . . double-tongued!**: people will say this against those disgraced by lying and double-talk.

y. [5:8] Prv 10:2; 11:4, 28; Ps 52:9.   z. [5:11] Prv 29:20; Eccl 5:1; Jas 1:19.   a. [6:2–3] Sir 9:8; 23:16; 25:21; 41:20, 22; Jb 31:12.

§[6:5–17] One of several poems Ben Sira wrote on friendship; see also 9:10–16; 12:8–18; 13:1–23; 19:13–17; 22:19–26; 27:16–21. True friends are discerned not by prosperity (v. 11), but through the trials of adversity: distress, quarrels (v. 9), sorrow (v. 10) and misfortune (v. 12). Such friends are rare, a gift from God (vv. 14–17).

¶[6:18–37] The various figures in each of the eight stanzas urge the search for wisdom through patience (vv. 18–19), persistence (vv. 20–22), docility and perseverance (vv. 23–28). Wisdom bestows rich rewards (vv. 29–31) on those who apply themselves and learn from the wise (vv. 32–36). Although one must strive for wisdom, it is God who grants it (v. 37). Cf. 4:11–19.

b. [6:7–9] Sir 12:8–9; 37:1–5; Prv 19:4.

¹⁹ As though plowing and sowing, draw
        close to her;
    then wait for her bountiful crops.
    For in cultivating her you will work but little,
        and soon you will eat her fruit.
²⁰ She is rough ground to the fool!
        The stupid cannot abide her.
²¹ She will be like a burdensome stone to them,
        and they will not delay in casting
        her aside.
²² For discipline* is like her name,
        she is not accessible to many.
²³ Listen, my child, and take my advice;
        do not refuse my counsel.
²⁴ Put your feet into her fetters,
        and your neck under her yoke.
²⁵ Bend your shoulders and carry her
        and do not be irked at her bonds.
²⁶ With all your soul draw close to her;
        and with all your strength keep her
        ways.
²⁷ Inquire and search, seek and find;
        when you get hold of her, do not let
        her go.
²⁸ Thus at last you will find rest in her,
        and she will become your joy.
²⁹ Her fetters will be a place of strength;
        her snare, a robe of spun gold.
³⁰ Her yoke will be a gold ornament;ᶜ
        her bonds, a purple cord.
³¹ You will wear her as a robe of glory,
        and bear her as a splendid crown.
³² If you wish, my son, you can be wise;
        if you apply yourself, you can be shrewd.
³³ If you are willing to listen, you can learn;
        if you pay attention, you can be
        instructed.
³⁴ Stand in the company of the elders;
        stay close to whoever is wise.
³⁵ Be eager to hear every discourse;
        let no insightful saying escape you.ᵈ
³⁶ If you see the intelligent, seek them out;
        let your feet wear away their doorsteps!
³⁷ Reflect on the law of the Most High,
        and let his commandments be your
        constant study.
    Then he will enlighten your mind,
        and make you wise as you desire.ᵉ

## CHAPTER 7

### Conduct Toward God and Neighbor†

¹ Do no evil, and evil will not overtake you;‡

² avoid wickedness, and it will turn
        away from you.
³ Do not sow in the furrows of injustice,
        lest you harvest it sevenfold.ᶠ
⁴ Do not seek from God authority
        or from the king a place of honor.
⁵ Do not parade your righteousness before
        the LORD,
        and before the king do not flaunt
        your wisdom.ᵍ
⁶ Do not seek to become a judge
        if you do not have the strength to
        root out crime,
    Lest you show fear in the presence of the
        prominent
        and mar your integrity.
⁷ Do not be guilty of any evil before the city
        court
        or disgrace yourself before the
        assembly.
⁸ Do not plot to repeat a sin;
        even for one, you will not go
        unpunished.
⁹ Do not say, "He will appreciate my many
        gifts;
        the Most High God will accept my
        offerings."ʰ
¹⁰ Do not be impatient in prayer
        or neglect almsgiving.
¹¹ Do not ridicule the embittered;
        Remember: there is One who exalts
        and humbles.§
¹² Do not plot mischief against your relative
        or against your friend and
        companion.
¹³ Refuse to tell lie after lie,
        for it never results in good.
¹⁴ Do not babble in the assembly of the
        elders
        or repeat the words of your prayer.¶ⁱ
¹⁵ Do not hate hard work;
        work was assigned by God.ʲ
¹⁶ Do not esteem yourself more than your
        compatriots;
        remember, his wrath will not delay.
¹⁷ More and more, humble your pride;
        what awaits mortals is worms.**ᵏ

---

and partiality (vv. 4, 6), public disorder (v. 7), presumption
and impatience toward God (vv. 9–10), ridicule (v. 11), mischief and deceit toward one's neighbor (vv. 8, 12–13). See the
several wisdom poems in Prv 1–9.

‡[7:1] There is a play on "evil" which means both moral
wrong and material calamity.

§[7:11] **One who exalts and humbles**: God; cf. 1 Sm 2:7;
Ps 75:8; Lk 1:52.

¶[7:14] **Repeat . . . prayer**: brevity of speech is a wisdom
ideal; toward superiors and God it is a sign of respect; cf. Eccl
5:1; Mt 6:7.

**[7:17] **Worms**: i.e., corruption; the Septuagint adds "fire."

---

*[6:22] **Discipline**: musar (in the sense of wisdom) is a
perfect homonym for musar, "removed, withdrawn"; thus the
path of discipline is not accessible to many.

†[7:1–17] In the conduct of social relations wisdom forbids evil and injustice (vv. 1–3), pride (vv. 5, 15–17), ambition

c. [6:30] Is 62:3.    d. [6:35] Sir 8:8–9.    e. [6:37] Ps 1:2.

f. [7:3] Jb 4:8; Prv 22:8; Hos 8:7.    g. [7:5] Jb 9:2; Ps 143:2; Prv 25:6;
1 Cor 4:4.    h. [7:9] Sir 34:21–24; 35:14–15.    i. [7:14] Sir 32:7–10;
Mt 6:7.    j. [7:15] Gn 2:15; 3:17.    k. [7:17] Sir 10:11; Jb 17:14; Is
66:24.

## Duties of Family Life, Religion and Charity[*]

18 Do not barter a friend for money,
  or a true brother for the gold of Ophir.[†]
19 Do not reject a sensible wife;
  a gracious wife is more precious
    than pearls.
20 Do not mistreat a servant who works
    faithfully,
  or laborers who devote themselves
    to their task.[l]
21 Love wise servants as yourself;
  do not refuse them freedom.[‡]

22 Do you have livestock? Look after them;
  if they are dependable, keep them.
23 Do you have sons? Correct them
  and cure their stubbornness[§] in their
    early youth.[m]
24 Do you have daughters? Keep them chaste,
  and do not be indulgent to them.[n]
25 Give your daughter in marriage, and a
    worry comes to an end;
  but give her to a sensible man.
26 Do you have a wife? Do not mistreat her,
  but do not trust the wife you hate.

27 With your whole heart honor your father;
  your mother's birth pangs do not
    forget.[o]
28 Remember, of these parents you were born;
  what can you give them for all they
    gave you?

29 With all your soul fear God
  and revere his priests.
30 With all your strength love your Maker
  and do not neglect his ministers.
31 Honor God and respect the priest;
  give him his portion as you have
    been commanded:[p]
  First fruits and contributions,
    his portion of victims and holy
      offerings.[s]

32 To the poor also extend your hand,
  that your blessing may be complete.
33 Give your gift to all the living,
  and do not withhold your kindness
    from the dead.[**]
34 Do not avoid those who weep,
  but mourn with those who mourn.[q]
35 Do not hesitate to visit the sick,
  because for such things you will be
    loved.[r]

36 In whatever you do, remember your last
    days,
  and you will never sin.[††]

## CHAPTER 8

### Prudence in Dealing with Others[‡‡]

1 Do not contend with the mighty,
  lest you fall into their power.
2 Do not quarrel with the rich,
  lest they pay out the price of your
    downfall.
  For gold has unsettled many,
    and wealth perverts the character of
      princes.[s]

3 Do not quarrel with loud-mouths,
  or heap wood upon their fire.[§§t]
4 Do not associate with the senseless,
  lest your ancestors be insulted.

5 Do not reproach one who turns away
    from sin;[u]
  remember, we all are guilty.[¶¶]
6 Do not insult one who is old,
  for some of us will also grow old.
7 Do not rejoice when someone dies;
  remember, we are all to be gathered in.

8 Do not neglect the discourse of the wise,[v]
  but busy yourself with their proverbs;
  For in this way you will acquire the
    training
    to stand in the presence of princes.
9 Do not reject the tradition of the elders
    which they have heard from their
      ancestors;
  For from it you will learn
    how to answer when the need arises.

---

*[7:18–36] Respect and appreciation, justice and kindness should characterize relations toward members of the household (vv. 18–28), God and the priests (vv. 29–31), the poor and afflicted, the living and the dead (vv. 32–35).

†[7:18] **Ophir:** the port, at present unidentified, to which the ships of Solomon sailed and from which they brought back gold and silver; cf. note on Ps 45:10.

‡[7:21] After six years of service a Hebrew slave was entitled to freedom; cf. Ex 21:2; Dt 15:12–15.

§[7:23] **Cure their stubbornness:** keep them from rebellious pride; so with the Greek. Cf. 30:1–13. The Hebrew text, probably not original here, reads: "Choose wives for them while they are young."

¶[7:31] **First fruits . . . holy offerings:** cf. Ex 29:27; Lv 7:31–34; Nm 18:8–20; Dt 18:1–5.

**[7:33] This seems to refer to the observances ordained toward the dead, that is, proper mourning and burial. Cf. 2 Sm 21:12–14; Tb 1:17–18; 12:12.

††[7:36] **Never sin:** because the last days of the sinner, it was presumed, would be troubled.

‡‡[8:1–19] The prudent will be circumspect, avoiding conflict with the powerful, the rich and insolent, the impious, the irascible, and judges (vv. 1–3, 10–12, 14, 16). They will not associate with the undisciplined (v. 4) or the ruthless (v. 15), with fools or strangers (vv. 17–19), but with the wise and the elders of the people (vv. 8–9). Caution is a recurring theme in Ben Sira.

§§[8:3] One should avoid increasing the ire of those who are hotheaded; cf. vv. 10, 16.

¶¶[8:5] **We all are guilty:** cf. 1 Kgs 8:46; 2 Chr 6:36; Jb 25:4; Eccl 7:20; Rom 3:9–10; 5:12; 1 Jn 1:8.

---

l. [7:20] Lv 19:13; Dt 24:14–15; Jas 5:4.   m. [7:23] Sir 30:1–13; Prv 13:24; 19:18; 23:13–14; 29:15, 17.   n. [7:24] Sir 42:9–12.   o. [7:27] Sir 3:1–16; Ex 20:12; Dt 5:16; Tb 4:3–4; Prv 23:22.   p. [7:31] Lv 7:31; Nm 18:18.

q. [7:34] Rom 12:15.   r. [7:35] Mt 25:36.   s. [8:2] Sir 31:5–6; Dt 16:19.   t. [8:3] Prv 26:20–21.   u. [8:5] 1 Kgs 8:46; 1 Jn 1:8.   v. [8:8–9] Sir 6:34–36.

¹⁰ Do not kindle the coals of sinners,
    lest you be burned in their flaming
        fire.
¹¹ Do not give ground before scoundrels;
    it will set them in ambush against
        you.*
¹² Do not lend to one more powerful than
    yourself;
    or if you lend, count it as lost.ʷ
¹³ Do not give collateral beyond your means;
    consider any collateral a debt you
        must pay.

¹⁴ Do not go to court against a judge,
    for the case will be settled in his
        favor.
¹⁵ Do not travel with the ruthless
    lest they weigh you down with
        calamity;
For they will only go their own way,
    and through their folly you will also
        perish.
¹⁶ Do not defy the quick-tempered,
    or ride with them through the
        desert.
For bloodshed is nothing to them;
    when there is no one to help, they
        will destroy you.

¹⁷ Do not take counsel with simpletons,
    for they cannot keep a confidence.
¹⁸ Before a stranger do nothing that should
    be kept secret,
    for you do not know what it will
        produce later on.†ˣ
¹⁹ Open your heart to no one,
    do not banish your happiness.

## CHAPTER 9

### Advice Concerning Women‡

¹ Do not be jealous of the wife of your
    bosom,
    lest you teach her to do evil against
        you.§
² Do not give a woman power over you
    to trample on your dignity.ʸ
³ Do not go near a strange woman,
    lest you fall into her snares.
⁴ Do not dally with a singer,
    lest you be captivated by her charms.
⁵ Do not entertain any thoughts about a
    virgin,

    lest you be enmeshed in damages
        for her.¶
⁶ Do not give yourself to a prostitute
    lest you lose your inheritance.ᶻ
⁷ Do not look around the streets of the city
    or wander through its squares.
⁸ Avert your eyes from a shapely woman;
    do not gaze upon beauty that is not
        yours;
Through woman's beauty many have been
    ruined,
    for love of it burns like fire.ᵃ
⁹ Never recline at table with a married
    woman,
    or drink intoxicants with her,
Lest your heart be drawn to her
    and you go down in blood** to the
        grave.

### Choice of Friends††

¹⁰ Do not abandon old friends;
    new ones cannot equal them.
A new friend is like new wine—
    when it has aged, you drink it with
        pleasure.
¹¹ Do not envy the wicked
    for you do not know when their day
        will come.
¹² Do not delight in the pleasures of the
    ungodly;
    remember, they will not die
        unpunished.

¹³ Keep away from those who have power to
    kill,
    and you will not be filled with the
        dread of death.
But if you come near them, do not offend
    them,
    lest they take away your life.
Know that you are stepping among snares
    and walking over a net.

¹⁴ As best you can, answer your neighbor,
    and associate with the wise.
¹⁵ With the learned exchange ideas;
    and let all your conversation be
        about the law of the Most
        High.
¹⁶ Take the righteous for your table
    companions;
    and let your glory be in the fear of
        God.

---

*[8:11] Giving in to the wicked only encourages them to
take advantage.
†[8:18] To keep a secret, or a confidence, is a major concern of Ben Sira; cf. 1:30; 22:22; 27:16–21; 37:10; 42:1.
‡[9:1–9] Ben Sira writes about women only from the
androcentric viewpoint of his culture. Cf. 25:13–26:27.
§[9:1] Jealousy may lead to suspicion and may prompt a
wife to those actions her husband fears.

¶[9:5] Cf. Ex 22:15–16; Dt 22:28–29; Jb 31:1. Cf. note on
Ex 22:16.
**[9:9] **In blood:** perhaps refers to blood revenge; cf. Lv
20:10.
††[9:10–16] The second of Ben Sira's poems on friendship; cf.
note on 6:5–17. In choosing friends, adherence to the law of the
Lord should serve as a guide (v. 15). Associate with true friends
(v. 10), with the righteous and the learned (vv. 14–16); avoid the
company of the mighty and of sinners (vv. 11–13). Cf. 8:1–19.

---

w. [8:12] Sir 29:4–7; Prv 17:18.   x. [8:18] Prv 25:9–10.   y. [9:2] Sir
25:21.

z. [9:6] Prv 5:1–14; 6:24; 29:3.   a. [9:8] Sir 25:20; 41:21; Prv 6:25–29.

## Concerning Rulers*

[17] Work by skilled hands will earn praise;
　　but the people's leader is proved wise
　　　by his words.
[18] Loud mouths are feared in their city,
　　and whoever is reckless in speech
　　　is hated.

## CHAPTER 10

[1] A wise magistrate gives stability to his
　　people,
　　and government by the intelligent is
　　　well ordered.[b]
[2] As the people's judge, so the officials;[c]
　　as the head of a city, so the
　　　inhabitants.
[3] A reckless king destroys his people,
　　but a city grows through the
　　　intelligence of its princes.[d]
[4] Sovereignty over the earth is in the hand
　　of God,
　　who appoints the right person for
　　　the right time.
[5] Sovereignty over everyone is in the hand
　　of God,
　　who imparts his majesty to the ruler.

## The Sin of Pride

[6] No matter what the wrong, never harm
　　your neighbor
　　or go the way of arrogance.[e]
[7] Odious to the Lord and to mortals is pride,
　　and for both oppression is a crime.
[8] Sovereignty is transferred from one
　　people to another
　　because of the lawlessness of the
　　　proud.
[9] Why are dust and ashes proud?[†]
　　Even during life the body decays.
[10] A slight illness—the doctor jests;
　　a king today—tomorrow he is dead.
[11] When a people die,
　　they inherit corruption and worms,
　　　gnats and maggots.[f]

[12] The beginning of pride is stubbornness
　　in withdrawing the heart from one's
　　　Maker.
[13] For sin is a reservoir of insolence,
　　a source which runs over with vice;
　　Because of it God sends unheard-of
　　　afflictions

and strikes people with utter ruin.[g]
[14] God overturns the thrones of the proud
　　and enthrones the lowly in their
　　　place.
[15] God plucks up the roots of the proud,
　　and plants the lowly in their place.
[16] The Lord lays waste the lands of the nations,
　　and destroys them to the very
　　　foundations of the earth.
[17] He removes them from the earth,
　　destroying them,
　　erasing their memory from the world.
[18] Insolence does not befit mortals,
　　nor impudent anger those born of
　　　women.

## True Glory[‡]

[19] Whose offspring can be honorable?
　　Human offspring.
　　Those who fear the LORD are
　　　honorable offspring.
　　Whose offspring can be disgraceful?
　　　Human offspring.
　　Those who transgress the
　　　commandment are disgraceful
　　　offspring.
[20] Among relatives their leader is honored;
　　but whoever fears God is honored
　　　among God's people.[§]
[22] Resident alien, stranger, foreigner,
　　pauper—
　　their glory is the fear of the LORD.
[23] It is not right to despise anyone wise but
　　poor,
　　nor proper to honor the lawless.[h]

[24] The prince, the ruler, the judge are in
　　honor;
　　but none is greater than the one who
　　　fears God.
[25] When the free serve a wise slave,
　　the wise will not complain.[i]
[26] Do not flaunt your wisdom in managing
　　your affairs,
　　or boast in your time of need.
[27] Better the worker who has goods in plenty
　　than the boaster who has no food.[j]

[28] My son, with humility have self-esteem;
　　and give yourself the esteem you
　　　deserve.
[29] Who will acquit those who condemn
　　themselves?

---

*[9:17–10:5] Public office as conducted justly or unjustly benefits or destroys the people, according to the axiom, "as the prince, so the people." God, however, has sovereignty over both.
†[10:9–10] The general implication is that a slight illness today may be followed by death tomorrow. The uncertainty of life leaves no room for pride.

b. [10:1] Prv 29:4; Wis 6:24.　c. [10:2–3] Ez 16:44; Prv 29:12.
d. [10:3] Prv 29:4–8.　e. [10:6] Lv 19:18.　f. [10:11] Sir 7:17; Jb 17:14; Is 66:24.

‡ [10:19–11:6] Genuine honor comes not from one's place in society but from fear of the Lord and a true estimate of one-self. The Lord exalts the lowly and oppressed; transgressors of the commandment merit dishonor and disgrace.
§ [10:20] Other ancient texts read as v. 21:

　The beginning of acceptance is the fear of the Lord;
　　the beginning of rejection, effrontery and pride.

g. [10:13] Prv 11:2; 16:18; 18:12.　h. [10:23] Jas 2:1–4.　i. [10:25] Prv 17:2.　j. [10:27] Prv 12:9.

Who will honor those who disgrace
    themselves?

30 The poor are honored for their wisdom;
    the rich are honored for their wealth.
31 Honored in poverty, how much more so
    in wealth!
    Disgraced in wealth, in poverty how
    much the more!

## CHAPTER 11

1 The wisdom of the poor lifts their head high
    and sets them among princes.
2 Do not praise anyone for good looks;
    or despise anyone because of
    appearance.

3 The bee is least among winged creatures,
    but it reaps the choicest of harvests.
4 Do not mock the one who wears only a
    loin-cloth,
    or scoff at a person's bitter day.
    For strange are the deeds of the LORD,
    hidden from mortals his work.*
5 Many are the oppressed who rise to the
    throne;
    some that none would consider wear
    a crown.†
6 Many are the exalted who fall into utter
    disgrace,
    many the honored who are given
    into the power of the few.

### Moderation and Patience‡

7 Before investigating, do not find fault;
    examine first, then criticize.
8 Before listening, do not say a word,
    interrupt no one in the midst of
    speaking.ᵏ
9 Do not dispute about what is not your
    concern;
    in the quarrels of the arrogant do
    not take part.

10 My son, why increase your anxiety,
    since whoever is greedy for wealth
    will not be blameless?
    Even if you chase after it, you will never
    overtake it;
    and by fleeing you will not escape.
11 One may work and struggle and drive,
    and fall short all the same.ˡ
12 Others go their way broken-down
    drifters,

with little strength and great misery—
    Yet the eye of the LORD looks favorably
    upon them,
    shaking them free of the stinking
    mire.
13 He lifts up their heads and exalts them
    to the amazement of the many.

14 §"Good and evil, life and death,ᵐ
    poverty and riches—all are from the
    LORD.§
17 The Lord's gift remains with the devout;
    his favor brings lasting success.
18 Some become rich through a miser's life,
    and this is their allotted reward:
19 When they say: "I have found rest,ⁿ
    now I will feast on my goods,"
    They do not know how long it will be
    till they die and leave them to others.**

20 My child, stand by your agreement and
    attend to it,
    grow old while doing your work.
21 Do not marvel at the works of a sinner,
    but trust in the LORD and wait for
    his light;
    For it is easy in the eyes of the LORD
    suddenly, in an instant, to make the
    poor rich.

22 God's blessing is the lot of the righteous,
    and in due time their hope bears fruit.
23 Do not say: "What do I need?
    What further benefits can be mine?"
24 Do not say: "I am self-sufficient.
    What harm can come to me now?"
25 The day of prosperity makes one forget
    adversity;
    the day of adversity makes one
    forget prosperity.ᵒ

26 For it is easy for the Lord on the day of
    death††
    to repay mortals according to their
    conduct.
27 A time of affliction brings forgetfulness of
    past delights;
    at the end of life one's deeds are
    revealed.
28 Call none happy before death,
    for how they end, they are known.

---

§[11:14] In mysterious ways God ultimately governs the
lives of men and women.
¶ [11:14] Other ancient texts read as vv. 15–16:
   15 Wisdom and understanding and knowledge of the Law,
    love and virtuous paths, are from the Lord.
   16 Error and darkness were formed with sinners from
    their birth,
    and evil grows old with those who exult in evil.

**[11:19] Cf. the parable of the rich man, Lk 12:16–21.
††[11:26–28] Ben Sira thought that divine retribution took
place only in the present life, and even at the end of life; cf.
9:12; 14:16–17.

m. [11:14] Jb 1:21; 2:10.  n. [11:19] Eccl 4:8; 6:2; Lk 12:19.
o. [11:25] Sir 18:24–25.

---

*[11:4] The implication is similar to Eccl 7:13; 8:17: the
mysterious work of God.
†[11:5] Cf. 1 Sm 2:8; Ps 75:8; 105:17–22; Lk 1:52.
‡[11:7–28] Discretion should regulate conduct toward others (vv. 7–9); as regards personal interests, one should avoid
solicitude for the passing external benefits of life and property
(vv. 10–14, 18–19, 21, 23–25) and cultivate the lasting inward
gifts of wisdom, virtue (vv. 20, 22), and patience (vv. 25–28).

k. [11:8] Prv 18:13.  l. [11:11] Ps 127:2; Eccl 4:8.

## Care in Choosing Friends

29 Not everyone should be brought into your
house,
　　for many are the snares of the crafty.
30 Like a decoy partridge in a cage, so is the
heart of the proud,
　　and like a spy they will pick out the
weak spots.
31 For they lie in wait to turn good into evil,
　　and to praiseworthy deeds they
attach blame.
32 One spark kindles many coals;
　　a sinner lies in wait for blood.
33 Beware of scoundrels, for they breed only
evil,
　　and they may give you a lasting stain.
34 Admit strangers into your home, and they
will stir up trouble
　　and make you a stranger to your
own family.

## CHAPTER 12

1 If you do good, know for whom you are
doing it,[*]
　　and your kindness will have its effect.
2 Do good to the righteous and reward will
be yours,
　　if not from them, from the LORD.[p]
3 No good comes to those who give
comfort to the wicked,
　　nor is it an act of mercy that they do.
4 Give to the good but refuse the sinner;
5 　　refresh the downtrodden but give
nothing to the proud.
No arms for combat should you give
them,
　　lest they use these against you;
Twofold evil you will obtain for every
good deed you do for them.
6 For God also hates sinners,
　　and takes vengeance on evildoers.[†]

8 In prosperity we cannot know our
friends;[‡]
　　in adversity an enemy will not
remain concealed.[q]
9 When one is successful even an enemy is
friendly;
　　but in adversity even a friend
disappears.[r]
10 Never trust your enemies,
　　for their wickedness is like corrosion
in bronze.
11 Even though they act deferentially and
peaceably toward you,

take care to be on your guard against
them.[s]
Treat them as those who reveal secrets,[§]
　　and be certain that in the end there
will still be envy.
12 Do not let them stand near you,
　　lest they push you aside and take
your place.
Do not let them sit at your right hand,
　　or they will demand your seat,
And in the end you will appreciate my
advice,
　　when you groan with regret, as I
warned.

13 Who pities a snake charmer when he is
bitten,[¶]
　　or anyone who goes near a wild
beast?
14 So it is with the companion of the proud,
　　who is involved in their sins:
15 While you stand firm, they make no move;
　　but if you slip, they cannot hold
back.
16 With their lips enemies speak sweetly,
　　but in their heart they scheme to
plunge you into the abyss.
Though enemies have tears in their eyes,
　　given the chance, they will never
have enough of your blood.[t]
17 If evil comes upon you, you will find them
at hand;
　　pretending to help, they will trip
you up,
18 Then they will shake their heads and clap
their hands
　　and hiss repeatedly, and show their
true faces.

## CHAPTER 13

## Caution Regarding Associates[**]

1 Touch pitch and you blacken your hand;
　　associate with scoundrels and you
learn their ways.
2 Do not lift a weight too heavy for you,
　　or associate with anyone wealthier
than you.
How can the clay pot go with the metal
cauldron?
　　When they knock together, the pot
will be smashed:
3 The rich do wrong and boast of it,

---

§[12:11] Ben Sira has harsh words for those who reveal
secrets; see also 8:18; 27:16–21; 42:1; Prv 11:13; 20:19.
¶[12:13] For v. 13a, see especially Eccl 10:11.
**[13:1–14:2] By means of various images, most of them
unfavorable to the rich, Ben Sira indicates the practical
impossibility of genuine and sincere companionship between
the poor and the rich. He lays down a principle of associating
with equals (13:6–19).

---

*[12:1] The import of this verse is brought out in vv. 4–5.
†[12:6] Verse 7 is a variant of verse 4 and is omitted.
‡[12:8–18] Adversity distinguishes friends from enemies;
to trust the latter or permit them intimacy is to invite disaster.
Cf. note on 6:5–17.

p. [12:2] Dt 14:29.　q. [12:8] Prv 17:17.　r. [12:9] Prv 19:4–7.

s. [12:11] Prv 26:24–26.　t. [12:16] Jer 9:7.

while the poor are wronged and beg
forgiveness.

4 As long as the rich can use you they will
enslave you,
but when you are down and out they
will abandon you.

5 As long as you have anything they will
live with you,
but they will drain you dry without
remorse.

6 When they need you they will deceive you
and smile at you and raise your hopes;
they will speak kindly to you and
say, "What do you need?"

7 They will embarrass you at their dinner
parties,
and finally laugh at you.
Afterwards, when they see you, they will
pass you by,
and shake their heads at you.

8 Be on guard: do not act too boldly;
do not be like those who lack sense.

9 When the influential draw near, keep your
distance;
then they will urge you all the more.

10 Do not draw too close, lest you be rebuffed,
but do not keep too far away lest you
be regarded as an enemy.

11 Do not venture to be free with them,
do not trust their many words;
For by prolonged talk they will test you,
and though smiling they will probe
you.

12 Mercilessly they will make you a
laughingstock,
and will not refrain from injury or
chains.

13 Be on your guard and take care
never to accompany lawless people.*

15 Every living thing loves its own kind,
and we all love someone like
ourselves.

16 Every living being keeps close to its own
kind;
and people associate with their own
kind.

17 Is a wolf ever allied with a lamb?
So the sinner with the righteous.ᵘ

18 Can there be peace between the hyena
and the dog?
Or peace between the rich and the
poor?†

19 Wild donkeys of the desert are lion's prey;
likewise the poor are feeding
grounds for the rich.

20 Humility is an abomination to the proud;
and the poor are an abomination to
the rich.

21 When the rich stumble they are
supported by friends;
when the poor trip they are pushed
down by friends.

22 When the rich speak they have many
supporters;
though what they say is repugnant,
it wins approval.
When the poor speak people say, "Come,
come, speak up!"
though they are talking sense, they
get no hearing.

23 When the rich speak all are silent,
their wisdom people extol to the
clouds.
When the poor speak people say: "Who
is that?"
If they stumble, people knock them
down.ᵛ

24 Wealth is good where there is no sin;‡
but poverty is evil by the standards
of the proud.

25 The heart changes one's face,
either for good or for evil.ʷ

26 The sign of a good heart is a radiant face;
withdrawn and perplexed is the
toiling schemer.

## CHAPTER 14

1 §Happy those whose mouth causes them
no grief,
those who are not stung by remorse
for sin.ˣ

2 Happy are those whose conscience does
not reproach them,
those who have not lost hope.

### The Use of Wealth

3 Wealth is not appropriate for the
mean-spirited;¶
to misers, what use is gold?

---

* [13:13] Other ancient texts read as v. 14:

If you hear these things in your sleep, wake up!
With your whole life, love the Lord
and call on him for your salvation.

† [13:18] The hostility between the dogs which guard the
flocks (Jb 30:1) and the rapacious hyenas (Jer 12:9) is proverbial in Palestine.

‡ [13:24] Ben Sira allows that the rich can be virtuous—but
with difficulty; cf. 31:1–11.

§ [14:1–2] A clear conscience, the result of honoring personal commitments and responsibilities, brings contentment
and peace.

¶ [14:3–10] Ben Sira offers a case study about the miserable
life of the "small-hearted" (Heb. *leb qatan*) to verify vv. 1–2.
They are evil because they do not use their wealth properly
to benefit themselves or others. While they are never satisfied that they have enough, they ignore their own needs and
hospitality itself, feeding on the generosity of others, in order
to protect their own resources. Ironically, after their death,
strangers, with no obligation to keep their memory alive,
enjoy their wealth.

u. [13:17] 2 Cor 6:14–17.

v. [13:21–23] Prv 14:20; 19:4, 7.   w. [13:25] Prv 15:13.   x. [14:1]
Sir 5:13–14; 19:16; 25:8; Jas 1:26; 3:2.

⁴ What they deny themselves they collect
    for someone else,
    and strangers will live sumptuously
      on their possessions.ʸ

⁵ To whom will they be generous that are
    stingy with themselves
    and do not enjoy what is their own?

⁶ None are worse than those who are stingy
    with themselves;
    they punish their own avarice.

⁷ If ever they do good, it is by mistake;
    in the end they reveal their meanness.

⁸ Misers are evil people,
    they turn away and disregard others.

⁹ The greedy see their share as not enough;
    greedy injustice dries up the soul.

¹⁰ The eye of the miserly is rapacious for
    food,
    but there is none of it on their own
      table.

¹¹ *My son, if you have the means, treat
    yourself well,
    and enjoy life as best you can.ᶻ

¹² Remember that death does not delay,
    and you have not been told the
      grave's appointed time.

¹³ Before you die, be good to your friends;
    give them a share in what you
      possess.ᵃ

¹⁴ Do not deprive yourself of good things
    now
    or let a choice portion escape you.

¹⁵ Will you not leave your riches to others,
    and your earnings to be divided
      by lot?

¹⁶ Give and take, treat yourself well,
    for in Sheol there are no joys to seek.

¹⁷ All flesh grows old like a garment;
    the age-old law is: everyone must
      die.ᵇ

¹⁸ As with the leaves growing on a luxuriant
    tree—
    one falls off and another sprouts—
So with the generations of flesh and
    blood:
    one dies and another flourishes.ᶜ

¹⁹ All human deeds surely perish;
    the works they do follow after them.

### The Search for Wisdom and Her Blessings†

²⁰ Happy those who meditate on Wisdom,
    and fix their gaze on knowledge;ᵈ

²¹ Who ponder her ways in their heart,
    and understand her paths;

²² Who pursue her like a scout,
    and watch at her entry way;

²³ Who peep through her windows,
    and listen at her doors;

²⁴ Who encamp near her house
    and fasten their tent pegs next to
      her walls;

²⁵ Who pitch their tent beside her,
    and dwell in a good place;‡

²⁶ §Who build their nest in her leaves,
    and lodge in her branches;

²⁷ Who take refuge from the heat in her
    shade
    and dwell in her home.

## CHAPTER 15

¹ Whoever fears the Lᴏʀᴅ will do this;
    whoever is practiced in the Law will
      come to Wisdom.

² She will meet him like a mother;
    like a young bride she will receive
      him,

³ ¶She will feed him with the bread of
    learning,
    and give him the water of
      understanding to drink.ᵉ

⁴ He will lean upon her and not fall;
    he will trust in her and not be put
      to shame.

⁵ She will exalt him above his neighbors,
    and in the assembly she will make
      him eloquent.

⁶ Joy and gladness he will find,
    and an everlasting name he will
      inherit.ᶠ

⁷ The worthless will not attain her,
    and the haughty will not behold her.

⁸ She is far from the impious;
    liars never think of her.

⁹ **Praise is unseemly on the lips of sinners,
    for it has not been allotted to them
      by God.

¹⁰ But praise is uttered by the mouth of the
    wise,
    and its rightful owner teaches it.

---

*[14:11–19] Three realities govern Ben Sira's attitude toward a proper use of wealth: the inevitability and uncertainty of death, the ephemeral nature of human accomplishments, the lack of reward or punishment after death. He advises generous enjoyment of God's gift of wealth before death.

†[14:20–15:10] This poem charts the growing intimacy between those seeking Wisdom and Wisdom herself. They move from static reflection to playful pursuit, from camping outside the walls of her house to nesting inside her leafy shade. Ben Sira portrays Wisdom as both mother and bride, a feminine figure who is the fullness of womanhood according to his androcentric society.

‡[14:25] **In a good place**: i.e., where Wisdom dwells.

§[14:26–27] The shift in imagery creates a more intimate relationship. Those seeking Wisdom dwell within her as a bird nests within a leafy tree.

¶[15:3–6] In this role reversal Woman Wisdom teaches, nourishes, supports, and protects the vulnerable man. For similar imagery cf. Prv 8:4–21, 34–35; 9:1–5; 31:10–31.

**[15:9–10] There is an intimate association between wisdom and praise of the Lord.

---

y. [14:4] Eccl 2:18–19; 6:2.  z. [14:11–12] Eccl 5:17–19.  a. [14:13] Prv 3:27–28; Tb 4:7.  b. [14:17] Ps 103:14–16; Jb 14:1–2; Is 40:6; Jas 1:10; 1 Pt 1:24.  c. [14:18] Eccl 1:4.  d. [14:20] Ps 1:2.

e. [15:3] Jn 4:10; 6:31–33.  f. [15:6] Sir 6:28–33.

## Free Will[*]

11 Do not say: "It was God's doing that I fell
   away,"
   for what he hates he does not do.
12 Do not say: "He himself has led me astray,"
   for he has no need of the wicked.[g]
13 Abominable wickedness the LORD hates
   and he does not let it happen to
   those who fear him.

14 God in the beginning created human beings
   and made them subject to their own
   free choice.[h]
15 If you choose, you can keep the
   commandments;
   loyalty is doing the will of God.
16 Set before you are fire and water;
   to whatever you choose, stretch out
   your hand.
17 Before everyone are life and death,
   whichever they choose will be given
   them.[i]

18 Immense is the wisdom of the LORD;
   mighty in power, he sees all things.
19 The eyes of God behold his works,
   and he understands every human
   deed.[j]
20 He never commands anyone to sin,
   nor shows leniency toward
   deceivers.[†]

## CHAPTER 16

### God's Punishment of Sinners[‡]

1 Do not yearn for worthless children,
   or rejoice in wicked offspring.
2 Even if they be many, do not rejoice in
   them
   if they do not have fear of the LORD.
3 Do not count on long life for them,[k]
   or have any hope for their future.
   For one can be better than a thousand;
   rather die childless than have
   impious children!
4 Through one wise person a city can be
   peopled;
   but through a clan of rebels it
   becomes desolate.

5 Many such things my eye has seen,
   and even more than these my ear
   has heard.
6 Against a sinful band fire is kindled,[l]
   upon a godless people wrath blazes.[§]
7 He did not forgive the princes of old[¶]
   who rebelled long ago in their might.[m]
8 He did not spare the neighbors of Lot,[**][n]
   abominable in their pride.
9 He did not spare the doomed people,[††]
   dispossessed because of their sin;
10 Nor the six hundred thousand foot
   soldiers,[‡‡][o]
   sent to their graves for the arrogance
   of their hearts.
11 Had there been but one stiff-necked[§§]
   person,
   it would be a wonder had he gone
   unpunished.
   For mercy and anger alike are with him;
   he remits and forgives, but also
   pours out wrath.
12 Great as his mercy is his punishment;
   he judges people, each according to
   their deeds.
13 Criminals do not escape with their
   plunder;
   the hope of the righteous, God never
   leaves unfulfilled.
14 Whoever does good has a reward;
   each receives according to their
   deeds.[¶¶]

17 Do not say: "I am hidden from God;
   and on high who remembers me?
   Among so many people I am unknown;
   what am I in the world of spirits?
18 Look, the heavens and the highest heavens,

---

§[16:6] For Korah and his band (v. 6a), see 45:18–19; Nm 16:1–35; Ps 106:18; for the disgruntled Israelites (v. 6b), Ps 78:21–22.

¶[16:7] **The princes of old**: e.g., the mighty destroyed in the flood (Gn 6:1–4; Wis 14:6; Bar 3:26–28), as well as the king of Babylon (Is 14:4–21) and Nebuchadnezzar (Dn 4:7–30).

**[16:8] **Neighbors of Lot**: the people of Sodom and Gomorrah, condemned elsewhere for their sexual violence (Gn 19:24–25) and failure at hospitality (Ez 16:49–50).

††[16:9] **Doomed people**: the Canaanite tribes whose aberrant religious practices, at least in Israelite opinion, caused their downfall: Ex 23:23–24, 27–33; 33:2; 34:11–16; Dt 7:1–2; Wis 12:3–7.

‡‡[16:10] **Six hundred thousand foot soldiers**: the number given for those rescued by Moses, who murmured against the Lord in the wilderness and died there: 46:1, 7–8; Nm 11:20; 14:1–12, 22–24, 29, 36–38; 26:65; Dt 1:35–38.

§§[16:11] **Stiff-necked**: sinful Israelites; cf. Ex 32:9; 33:3, 5. Not even one Israelite would have gone unpunished for insolence or pride.

¶¶ [16:14] Other ancient texts read as vv. 15–16:

> 15 The LORD hardened the heart of Pharaoh so that he did
> not recognize him
> whose acts were manifest under the heavens;
> 16 His mercy was seen by all his creatures,
> and his light and his darkness he apportioned to
> humankind.

---

*[15:11–20] Here Ben Sira links freedom of the will with human responsibility. God, who sees everything, is neither the cause nor the occasion of sin. We have the power to choose our behavior and we are responsible for both the good and the evil we do (vv. 15–17).

†[15:20] **Deceivers**: those who hold the Lord responsible for their sins.

‡[16:1–23] One child who does God's will is a greater blessing than many sinful offspring (vv. 1–4), for history and experience show that God punishes sin (vv. 5–10). God judges everyone according to their deeds (vv. 11–14); no one can hide from God or escape retribution at his hand (vv. 17–23).

---

g. [15:12] Jas 1:13.  h. [15:14] Gn 1:27.  i. [15:17] Dt 30:15–20.  j. [15:19] Ps 33:18; 34:16; Heb 4:13.  k. [16:3–4] Wis 4:1–2.

l. [16:6] Sir 21:9.  m. [16:7] Gn 6:4; Wis 14:6; Bar 3:26–28.  n. [16:8] Gn 19:24–25.  o. [16:10] Nm 14:29.

the abyss and the earth tremble at
his visitation.
19 The roots of the mountains and the earth's
foundations—
at his mere glance they quiver and
quake.
20 Of me, therefore, he will take no notice;
with my ways who will be
concerned?
21 If I sin, no eye will see me;
if all in secret I act deceitfully, who
is to know?ᵖ
22 Who tells him about just deeds?
What can I expect for doing my
duty?"
23 Such the thoughts of the senseless;
only the foolish entertain them.

### Divine Wisdom Seen in Creation*

24 Listen to me, my son, and take my advice,
and apply your mind to my words,
25 While I pour out my spirit by measure
and impart knowledge with care.
26 When at the first God created his works
and, as he made them, assigned
their tasks,�q
27 He arranged for all time what they were
to do,
their domains from generation to
generation.
They were not to go hungry or grow
weary,
or ever cease from their tasks.
28 Never does a single one crowd its
neighbor,
or do any ever disobey his word.
29 Then the Lord looked upon the earth,
and filled it with his blessings.ʳ
30 Its surface he covered with every kind of
living creature
which must return into it again.

### CHAPTER 17

### Creation of Human Beings

1 The Lord created human beings from the
earth,
and makes them return to earth
again.ˢ
2 A limited number of days he gave them,ᵗ
but granted them authority over
everything on earth.

3 He endowed them with strength like his
own,
and made them in his image.
4 He put fear of them in all flesh,
and gave them dominion over beasts
and birds.†
6 Discernment, tongues, and eyes,
ears, and a mind for thinking he
gave them.
7 With knowledge and understanding he
filled them;
good and evil he showed them.
8 He put fear of him into their hearts
to show them the grandeur of his
works,
9 That they might describe the wonders of
his deeds
10 and praise his holy name.
11 He set before them knowledge,
and allotted to them the law of life.
12 An everlasting covenant he made with
them,
and his commandments‡ he revealed
to them.
13 His majesty glory their eyes beheld,
his glorious voice their ears heard.
14 He said to them, "Avoid all evil";
to each of them he gave precepts
about their neighbor.
15 Their ways are ever known to him,
they cannot be hidden from his eyes.§
17 Over every nation he appointed a ruler,¶
but Israel is the Lord's own portion."**ᵘ
19 All their works are clear as the sun to him,
and his eyes are ever upon their ways.
20 Their iniquities cannot be hidden from him;
all their sins are before the Lord.††

---

† [17:4] Other ancient texts read as v. 5:

They received the use of the Lord's five faculties;
of mind, the sixth, he granted them a share,
as also of speech, the seventh, the interpreter of
his actions.

‡[17:12] **An everlasting covenant . . . his commandments**: God made several covenants, e.g., Gn 9:8–17; 15:17–
21; 17:1–22, entered into with humankind, especially on
Mount Sinai, where the people saw God's glory and heard his
voice (v. 13; cf. Ex 19:16–24:18).

§ [17:15] Other ancient texts read as v. 16:

Their ways are directed toward evils from their youth,
and they are unable to make their hearts flesh
rather than stone.

¶[17:17] **Ruler**: this may refer to civil officials or to heavenly beings placed over nations as guardians; see note on Dt
32:8, and the cross-references.
** [17:17] Other ancient texts read as v. 18:

Israel, as his firstborn, he cares for with chastisement;
the light of his love he shares with him without
neglect.

†† [17:20] Other ancient texts read as v. 21:

But the Lord, being good and knowing how they are
formed,
neither neglected them nor ceased to spare them.

---

*[16:24–17:23] In harmony with Gn 1–2, the author
describes God's wisdom in creating the universe and everything in it (vv. 24–30), endowing human beings with a moral
nature, with wisdom, knowledge, and freedom of will (cf.
15:14) according to his own image (17:1–3, 7). Now they can
govern the earth (vv. 3–4), praise God's name (vv. 9–10), obey
his law (vv. 11–14), and render to him an account of their
deeds (v. 23). Cf. Ps 19; 104.

---

p. [16:21] Sir 23:18–20.   q. [16:26] Gn 1:3–30.   r. [16:29] Gn
1:11–31.   s. [17:1] Gn 2:7; 3:19.   t. [17:2–4] Gn 1:26–28; Ps 8:4–9.

u. [17:17] Ex 19:5; Dt 4:19–20; 32:8–9; Dn 10:13–21; 12:1.

²² Human goodness is like a signet ring with
        God,
        and virtue he keeps like the apple of
            his eye.
²³ Later he will rise up and repay them,
        requiting each one as they deserve.ᵛ

### Appeal for a Return to God*

²⁴ But to the penitent he provides a way back
        and encourages those who are losing
            hope!
²⁵ Turn back to the Lord and give up your
            sins,
        pray before him and make your
            offenses few.
²⁶ Turn again to the Most High and away
            from iniquity,
        and hate intensely what he loathes.
²⁷ †Who in Sheol can glorify the Most Highʷ
        in place of the living who offer their
            praise?
²⁸ The dead can no more give praise than
            those who have never lived;
        they who are alive and well glorify
            the Lord.
²⁹ How great is the mercy of the Lord,
        and his forgiveness for those who
            return to him!
³⁰ For not everything is within human reach,
        since human beings are not
            immortal.
³¹ Is anything brighter than the sun? Yet it
            can be eclipsed.
        How worthless‡ then the thoughts of
            flesh and blood!
³² God holds accountable the hosts of
            highest heaven,
        while all mortals are dust and ashes.

### CHAPTER 18

### The Divine Power and Mercy§

¹ He who lives forever created the whole
        universe;

² the LORD alone is just.¶
⁴ To whom has he given power to describe
        his works,
        and who can search out his mighty
            deeds?
⁵ Who can measure his majestic power,
        or fully recount his mercies?
⁶ No one can lessen, increase,
        or fathom the wonders of the Lord.
⁷ When mortals finish, they are only
            beginning,
        and when they stop they are still
            bewildered.
⁸ What are mortals? What are they worth?
        What is good in them, and what is
            evil?
⁹ The number of their days seems great
        if it reaches a hundred years.ˣ
¹⁰ Like a drop of water from the sea and a
            grain of sand,
        so are these few years among the
            days of eternity.
¹¹ That is why the Lord is patient with them
        and pours out his mercy on them.
¹² He sees and understands that their death
            is wretched,
        and so he forgives them all the more.
¹³ Their compassion is for their neighbor,
        but the Lord's compassion reaches
            all flesh,
    Reproving, admonishing, teaching,
        and turning them back, as a
            shepherd his flock.ʸ
¹⁴ He has compassion on those who accept
            his discipline,
        who are eager for his precepts.

### The Need for Prudence

¹⁵ My child, add no reproach to your
            charity,**
        or spoil any gift by harsh words.
¹⁶ Does not the dew give relief from the
            scorching heat?
        So a word can be better than a gift.
¹⁷ Indeed does not a word count more than
            a good gift?
        But both are offered by a kind person.
¹⁸ The fool is ungracious and abusive,
        and a grudging gift makes the eyes
            smart.ᶻ

---

*[17:24–32] Ben Sira opens this poem with a prophetic
summons to repent, urging sinners to give up their sins and
to pray for forgiveness (vv. 24–26, 29). Ben Sira reflects the
belief of his day that there was no life after death (vv. 27–28,
30; see note on 11:26–28). Cf. Ez 18:23, 30–32; 33:11–16. See
note on Ps 6:6.

†[17:27–28] True life consists in praise of God; this is not
possible in Sheol.

‡[17:31] **Worthless:** cf. Gn 6:5. Though moral fault is not
excluded, the thought here is the inability to understand the
designs of God. Cf. Wis 9:14–18.

§[18:1–14] Not only are God's justice and power beyond
human understanding (vv. 1–7), his mercy also is boundless
and surpasses all human compassion (vv. 8–14); he pities
human frailty and mortality.

¶ [18:2] Other ancient texts read as v. 3:

    He controls the world within the span of his hand,
        and everything obeys his will;
    For he in his might is the King of all,
        separating what is holy among them from what
            is profane.

**[18:15–27] The practice of charity, especially almsgiving, is
an art which avoids every offense to another (vv. 15–18). Prudence directs the changing circumstances of daily life in view of
the time of scrutiny (i.e., the day of reckoning, or death, v. 24).

---

v. [17:23] Ps 7:17; Jl 4:4, 7; Jer 23:19; Ez 22:31.   w. [17:27–28] Ps 6:6;
88:4–7; 115:17; Is 38:18.

x. [18:9] Ps 90:10.   y. [18:13] Ps 23:1–4; Is 40:11; 49:9–10; Jn 10:11–
16; Heb 13:20–21; Rev 7:17.   z. [18:18] Sir 20:14–15.

<sup>19</sup> Before you speak, learn;
 before you get sick, prepare the cure.
<sup>20</sup> Before you are judged, examine yourself,
 and at the time of scrutiny you will
 have forgiveness.
<sup>21</sup> Before you fall ill, humble yourself;
 and when you have sinned, show
 repentance.*
Do not delay forsaking your sins;
 do not neglect to do so until you are
 in distress.

<sup>22</sup> Let nothing prevent the prompt payment
 of your vows;
 do not wait until death to fulfill
 them.*a*
<sup>23</sup> Before making a vow prepare yourself;
 do not be like one who puts the
 Lord to the test.
<sup>24</sup> Think of wrath on the day of death,
 the time of vengeance when he will
 hide his face.*b*
<sup>25</sup> Think of the time of hunger in the time of
 plenty,
 poverty and need in the day of
 wealth.*c*
<sup>26</sup> Between morning and evening there is a
 change of time;
 before the Lord all things are
 fleeting.

<sup>27</sup> The wise are discreet in all things;
 where sin is rife they keep
 themselves from wrongdoing.
<sup>28</sup> Every wise person teaches wisdom,†
 and those who know her declare her
 praise;
<sup>29</sup> Those skilled in words become wise
 themselves,
 and pour forth apt proverbs.

### Self-Control‡

<sup>30</sup> Do not let your passions be your guide,*d*
 but keep your desires in check.
<sup>31</sup> If you allow yourself to satisfy your
 passions,
 they will make you the
 laughingstock of your enemies.
<sup>32</sup> Take no pleasure in too much luxury
 which brings on poverty redoubled.
<sup>33</sup> Do not become a glutton and a drunkard
 with nothing in your purse.

## CHAPTER 19

<sup>1</sup> Whoever does this grows no richer;
 those who waste the little they have
 will be stripped bare.
<sup>2</sup> Wine and women make the heart lustful,
 and the companion of prostitutes
 becomes reckless.*e*
<sup>3</sup> Rottenness and worms will possess him,
 and the reckless will be snatched
 away.*f*
<sup>4</sup> Whoever trusts others too quickly has a
 shallow mind,
 and those who sin wrong
 themselves.

### The Proper Use of Speech§

<sup>5</sup> Whoever gloats over evil will be
 destroyed,
<sup>6</sup> and whoever repeats gossip has no
 sense.
<sup>7</sup> Never repeat gossip,
 and no one will reproach you.*g*
<sup>8</sup> Tell nothing to friend or foe;
 and unless it be a sin for you, do not
 reveal a thing.*h*
<sup>9</sup> For someone may have heard you and
 watched you,
 and in time come to hate you.
<sup>10</sup> Let anything you hear die with you;
 never fear, it will not make you
 burst!
<sup>11</sup> Having heard something, the fool goes
 into labor,
 like a woman giving birth to a child.
<sup>12</sup> Like an arrow stuck in a fool's thigh,
 so is gossip in the belly of a fool.
<sup>13</sup> Admonish your friend—he may not have
 done it;
 and if he did, that he may not do it
 again.*i*
<sup>14</sup> Admonish your neighbor—he may not
 have said it;
 and if he did, that he may not say it
 again.
<sup>15</sup> Admonish your friend—often it may be
 slander;
 do not believe every story.
<sup>16</sup> Then, too, a person can slip and not mean
 it;
 who has not sinned with his
 tongue?*j*

---

*[18:21] Sickness was often viewed as a punishment for sin; hence, the need for repentance. Cf. 38:9–10; Jb 15:20–24.
†[18:28–29] A general statement on the teaching of wisdom, serving either as a conclusion to the preceding section or as an introduction to the following one.
‡[18:30–19:4] Inordinate gratification of the senses makes people unreasonable, slaves of passion, the laughingstock of their enemies, and it leads to an untimely death.

§[19:5–17] An excellent commentary on bearing false witness (Ex 20:16; Dt 5:20). Ben Sira speaks harshly about calumny, rash judgment, and detraction (vv. 5–7), and urges discreet silence (vv. 8–12). Justice requires that an accused neighbor be given a hearing, and charity urges fraternal correction; both together fulfill the law of the Most High (vv. 13–17); cf. Mt 7:1–2; 18:15–16.

---

a. [18:22] Nm 30:3; Dt 23:22; Ps 50:14; Prv 20:25; Eccl 5:4.
b. [18:24] Sir 7:16.   c. [18:25] Sir 11:25–27.   d. [18:30] Rom 6:12; 13:14; 2 Tm 2:22; Jas 1:14–15.

e. [19:2] Prv 20:1; 23:20–28.   f. [19:3] Gal 6:8.   g. [19:7] Prv 25:10.   h. [19:8] Sir 8:18–19.   i. [19:13] Lv 19:17; Mt 18:15; Lk 17:3.   j. [19:16] Sir 14:1; Jas 3:2.

<sup>17</sup> Admonish your neighbor before you
   break with him;
   and give due place to the Law of the
      Most High.<sup>*k</sup>

### How to Recognize True Wisdom[†]

<sup>20</sup> All wisdom is fear of the Lord;
   and in all wisdom, the observance of
      the Law.<sup>†l</sup>
<sup>22</sup> The knowledge of wickedness is not
      wisdom,
   nor is there prudence in the counsel
      of sinners.
<sup>23</sup> There is a shrewdness that is detestable,
   while the fool may be free from sin.
<sup>24</sup> Better are the God-fearing who have little
      understanding
   than those of great intelligence who
      violate the Law.

<sup>25</sup> There is a shrewdness keen but dishonest,
   and there are those who are
      duplicitous to win a judgment.
<sup>26</sup> There is the villain bowed in grief,
   but full of deceit within.
<sup>27</sup> He hides his face and pretends not to hear,
   but when not observed, he will take
      advantage of you:
<sup>28</sup> Even if his lack of strength keeps him
      from sinning,
   when he finds the right time he will
      do harm.
<sup>29</sup> People are known by their appearance;
   the sensible are recognized as such
      when first met.
<sup>30</sup> One's attire, hearty laughter, and gait
   proclaim him for what he is.

## CHAPTER 20

### Conduct of the Wise and the Foolish

<sup>1</sup> There is an admonition that is untimely,<sup>§</sup>
   but the silent person is the wise one.

<sup>2</sup> It is much better to admonish than to lose
      one's temper;
<sup>3</sup>    one who admits a fault will be kept
      from disgrace.
<sup>4</sup> Like a eunuch lusting to violate a young
      woman
   is the one who does right under
      compulsion.<sup>¶</sup>
<sup>5</sup> One is silent and is thought wise;
   another, for being talkative, is
      disliked.
<sup>6</sup> One is silent, having nothing to say;
   another is silent, biding his time.<sup>m</sup>
<sup>7</sup> The wise remain silent till the right time
      comes,
   but a boasting fool misses the
      proper time.
<sup>8</sup> Whoever talks too much is detested;
   whoever pretends to authority is
      hated.

<sup>9</sup> There is the misfortune that brings success;<sup>**</sup>
   and there is the gain that turns into
      loss.
<sup>10</sup> There is the gift that profits you nothing,
   and there is the gift that must be
      paid back double.
<sup>11</sup> There is the loss for the sake of glory,
   and there is the one who rises above
      humble circumstances.
<sup>12</sup> There is one who buys much for little,
   but pays for it seven times over.
<sup>13</sup> The wise make themselves beloved by a
      few words,
   but the courtesies of fools are wasted.
<sup>14</sup> A gift from a fool will do you no good,
   for in his eyes this one gift is equal
      to many.
<sup>15</sup> He gives little, criticizes often,
   and opens his mouth like a town
      crier.
He lends today and asks for it tomorrow;
   such a person is hateful.
<sup>16</sup> A fool says, "I have no friends
   nor thanks for my generosity."
Those who eat his bread have a mocking
      tongue.
<sup>17</sup> How many will ridicule him, and how
      often!

<sup>18</sup> A slip on the floor is better than a slip of
      the tongue;<sup>††</sup>
   in like manner the downfall of the
      wicked comes quickly.

---

* [19:17] Other ancient texts read as vv. 18–19:

<sup>18</sup> Fear of the Lord is the beginning of acceptance;
   and wisdom from him obtains love.
<sup>19</sup> Knowledge of the Lord's commandments is life-giving
      instruction;
   those who do what pleases him will harvest the
      fruit of the tree of immortality.

†[19:20–30] True wisdom is contrasted with a dishonest
shrewdness.
   ‡ [19:20] Other ancient texts read as v. 21:

The slave who says to his master, "What pleases you I will
      not do"—
   even if he does it later, provokes the one who
      feeds him.

§[20:1–8] The wise know the proper times for speech and
silence, that is, the occasions when the most benefit can be gained
from them. On the ambiguity of silences, see Prv 17:27–28.

k. [19:17] Lv 19:17.   l. [19:20] Sir 1:1, 12, 14; Jb 28:28; Ps 111:10;
Prv 1:7; 9:10.

¶[20:4] Force can prevent an external act of sin or compel a
good deed, but it does not eliminate the internal sin or desire
of wrongdoing.
**[20:9–17] In a series of paradoxes the author indicates
how much true and lasting values differ from apparent ones.
††[20:18–26] The ill-timed speech brings disaster (vv.
18–20); human respect may lead to rash promises and enmity
(vv. 22–23); lies bring dishonor and lasting disgrace (vv. 24–26).

m. [20:5–6] Prv 17:27–28.

<sup>19</sup> A coarse person, an untimely story;
    the ignorant are always ready to
        offer it.
<sup>20</sup> A proverb spoken by a fool is unwelcome,
    for he does not tell it at the proper
        time.

<sup>21</sup> There is a person whose poverty prevents
    him from sinning,
    but when he takes his rest he has no
        regrets.
<sup>22</sup> There is a person who is destroyed
    through shame,
    and ruined by foolish posturing.
<sup>23</sup> There is one who promises a friend out of
    shame,
    and so makes an enemy needlessly.

<sup>24</sup> A lie is a foul blot in a person,
    yet it is always on the lips of the
        ignorant.
<sup>25</sup> A thief is better than an inveterate liar,
    yet both will suffer ruin.
<sup>26</sup> A liar's way leads to dishonor,
    and his shame remains ever with him.

<sup>27</sup> The wise gain promotion with few words,*
    the prudent please the great.
<sup>28</sup> Those who work the land have abundant
    crops,
    and those who please the great are
        pardoned their faults.
<sup>29</sup> Favors and gifts blind the eyes;
    like a muzzle over the mouth they
        silence reproofs.ⁿ
<sup>30</sup> Hidden wisdom and unseen treasure—
    what value has either?
<sup>31</sup> Better are those who hide their folly
    than those who hide their wisdom.†

## CHAPTER 21

### Dangers from Sin‡

<sup>1</sup> My child, if you have sinned, do so no more,
    and for your past sins pray to be
        forgiven.
<sup>2</sup> Flee from sin as from a serpent
    that will bite you if you go near it;
    Its teeth, lion's teeth,
        destroying human lives.

<sup>3</sup> All lawlessness is like a two-edged sword;
    when it cuts, there is no healing.ᵒ
<sup>4</sup> Panic and pride wipe out wealth;
    so too the house of the proud is
        uprooted.
<sup>5</sup> Prayer from the lips of the poor is heard
    at once,
    and justice is quickly granted them.
<sup>6</sup> Whoever hates correction walks the
    sinner's path,ᵖ
    but whoever fears the Lord repents
        in his heart.
<sup>7</sup> Glib speakers are widely known,
    but when they slip the sensible
        perceive it.
<sup>8</sup> Those who build their houses with
    someone else's money
    are like those who collect stones for
        their funeral mounds.
<sup>9</sup> A band of criminals is like a bundle of tow;
    they will end in a flaming fire.�q
<sup>10</sup> The path of sinners is smooth stones,
    but its end is the pit of Sheol.§

### The Wise and Foolish: A Contrast¶

<sup>11</sup> Those who keep the Law control their
    thoughts;
    perfect fear of the Lord is wisdom.
<sup>12</sup> One who is not clever can never be taught,
    but there is a cleverness filled with
        bitterness.

<sup>13</sup> The knowledge of the wise wells up like a
    flood,
    and their counsel like a living spring.ʳ
<sup>14</sup> A fool's mind is like a broken jar:
    it cannot hold any knowledge at all.

<sup>15</sup> When the intelligent hear a wise saying,
    they praise it and add to it.
    The wanton hear it with distaste
    and cast it behind their back.

<sup>16</sup> A fool's chatter is like a load on a journey,
    but delight is to be found on the lips
        of the intelligent.
<sup>17</sup> The views of the prudent are sought in an
    assembly,
    and their words are taken to heart.

---

*[20:27–31] Through prudent speech the wise gain honor and esteem among the great (vv. 27–28). They must beware, however, of accepting bribes, lest they share in evil through silence when they should reprove (vv. 29–31).

† [20:31] Other ancient texts read as v. 32:

It is better to await the inevitable while serving the Lord
    than to be the ungoverned helmsman for the
        careening of one's life.

‡[21:1–10] Under various figures, the consequences of sin are described as destructive of wealth, and even of life, deserving of death (vv. 2–4, 6a, 8–10). Fear of the Lord motivates repentance (vv. 5, 6b).

n. [20:29] Ex 23:8; Dt 16:19.

§[21:10] **The path of sinners . . . Sheol**: Ben Sira refers to the death that awaits unrepentant sinners; see notes on 11:26–28; 17:24–32.

¶[21:11–28] The mind of the wise is a fountain of knowledge (vv. 13, 15); their will is trained to keep the Law (v. 11); their words are gracious, valued, carefully weighed, sincere (vv. 16–17, 25–26); their conduct is respectful, cultured and restrained (vv. 20, 22–24). The mind of the foolish is devoid of knowledge and impenetrable to it (vv. 12, 14, 18–19); their will rejects it (v. 15); their talk is burdensome (v. 16), their laughter unrestrained (v. 20), their conversation shallow and meddlesome (vv. 25–26); their conduct is bold and rude (vv. 22–24); their abuse of others redounds on themselves (vv. 27–28).

o. [21:3] Prv 5:4.   p. [21:6] Prv 12:1.   q. [21:9] Sir 16:6; Ps 21:10.
r. [21:13] Prv 13:14; 16:22; 18:4.

18 Like a house in ruins is wisdom to a fool;
    to the stupid, knowledge is
        incomprehensible chatter.
19 To the senseless, education is fetters on
        the feet,
    like manacles on the right hand.
20 Fools raise their voice in laughter,
    but the prudent at most smile quietly.[s]
21 Like a gold ornament is education to the
        wise,
    like a bracelet on the right arm.

22 A fool steps boldly into a house,
    while the well-bred are slow to make
        an entrance.[t]
23 A boor peeps through the doorway of a
        house,
    but the educated stay outside.
24 It is rude for one to listen at a door;
    the discreet person would be
        overwhelmed by the disgrace.

25 The lips of the arrogant talk of what is not
        their concern,
    but the discreet carefully weigh their
        words.
26 The mind of fools is in their mouths,
    but the mouth of the wise is in their
        mind.[*]
27 When the godless curse their adversary,[†]
    they really curse themselves.
28 Slanderers sully themselves,
    and are hated by their neighbors.

## CHAPTER 22

### On Laziness and Foolishness

1 ‡The sluggard is like a filthy stone;[§]
    everyone hisses at his disgrace.
2 The sluggard is like a lump of dung;
    whoever touches it shakes it off the
        hands.

3 An undisciplined child is a disgrace to its
        father;
    if it be a daughter, she brings him to
        poverty.[u]
4 A thoughtful daughter obtains a husband
        of her own,
    a shameless one is her father's grief.
5 A hussy shames her father and her husband;
    she is despised by both.

6 Like music at the time of mourning is
        ill-timed talk,[¶]
    but lashes and discipline are at all
        times wisdom.[**]
9 Teaching a fool is like gluing a broken pot,[v]
    or rousing another from deep sleep.
10 Whoever talks with a fool talks to
        someone asleep;
    when it is over, he says, "What was
        that?"

11 Weep over the dead, for their light has
        gone out;
    weep over the fool, for sense has
        left him.
Weep but less bitterly over the dead, for
        they are at rest;
    worse than death is the life of a fool.
12 Mourning for the dead, seven days—[w]
    but for the wicked fool, a whole
        lifetime.

13 Do not talk much with the stupid,
    or visit the unintelligent.
Beware of them lest you have trouble
    and be spattered when they shake
        themselves off.
Avoid them and you will find rest
    and not be wearied by their lack of
        sense.
14 What is heavier than lead?
    What is its name but "Fool"?
15 Sand, salt, and an iron weight
    are easier to bear than the stupid
        person.[x]

16 A wooden beam firmly bonded into a
        building[††]
    is not loosened by an earthquake;
So the mind firmly resolved after careful
        deliberation
    will not be afraid at any time.
17 The mind solidly backed by intelligent
        thought
    is like a stucco decoration on a
        smooth wall.
18 Small stones lying on an open height
    will not remain when the wind blows;
So a timid mind based on foolish plans
    cannot stand up to fear of any kind.

---

* [21:26] A clever play on words.
† [21:27] **Curse their adversary**: the curse of the godless
often recoils on their own head; cf. Gn 27:29; Nm 24:9.
‡ [22:1–15] To Ben Sira, a lazy person and an unruly child are
a cause of shame and disgrace; everyone wishes to be rid of them
(vv. 1–5). Speaking with a wicked fool is as senseless as talking
with someone who is asleep or dead (v. 10). The fool is an intolerable burden that merits a lifetime of mourning (v. 12). Seven
days was the usual mourning period. Cf. Gn 50:10; Jdt 16:24.
§ [22:1] **Stone**: used then and even today for wiping oneself
after a bowel movement.

¶ [22:6] As a joyful song is out of place among mourners
so a rebuke may be insufficient when corporal punishment
is called for.
** [22:6] Other ancient texts read as vv. 7–8:

7 Children whose upbringing leads to a wholesome life
    veil over the lowly origins of their parents.
8 Children whose pride is in scornful misconduct
    besmirch the nobility of their own family.

†† [22:16–18] A prudent mind firmly resolved is undisturbed by violent and conflicting thoughts, whereas a foolish
person is tossed about by the winds of fear, like small stones
whipped about by high winds.

---

s. [21:20] Eccl 7:6.    t. [21:22] Prv 25:17.    u. [22:3] Prv 10:1; 17:21,
25; 19:13.

v. [22:9–12] Prv 23:9.    w. [22:12] Gn 50:10; Jdt 16:24.    x. [22:15]
Prv 27:3.

## The Preservation of Friendship[*]

19 Whoever jabs the eye brings tears;
  whoever pierces the heart bares its
    feelings.
20 Whoever throws a stone at birds drives
      them away;
  whoever insults a friend breaks up
    the friendship.
21 Should you draw a sword against a friend,
  do not despair, for it can be undone.
22 Should you open your mouth against a
    friend,
  do not worry, for you can be
    reconciled.
But a contemptuous insult, a confidence
    broken,
  or a treacherous attack will drive any
    friend away.

23 Win your neighbor's trust while he is poor,
  so that you may rejoice with him in
    his prosperity.
In time of trouble remain true to him,
  so that you may share in his
    inheritance when it comes.
24 The billowing smoke of a furnace
    precedes the fire,
  so insults precede bloodshed.
25 I am not ashamed to shelter a friend,
  and I will not hide from him.
26 But if harm should come to me because of
    him,
  all who hear of it will beware of him.

### Prayer[†]

27 Who will set a guard over my mouth,
  an effective seal on my lips,
That I may not fail through them,
  and my tongue may not destroy me?[y]

## CHAPTER 23

1 Lord, Father and Master of my life,[‡]
  do not abandon me to their designs,
  do not let me fall because of them!

2 Who will apply the lash to my thoughts,
  and to my mind the rod of
    discipline,

That my failings may not be spared
  or the sins of my heart overlooked?
3 Otherwise my failings may increase,
  and my sins be multiplied;
And I fall before my adversaries,
  and my enemy rejoice over me?
4 Lord, Father and God of my life,
  do not give me haughty eyes;
5   remove evil desire from my heart.
6 Let neither gluttony nor lust overcome me;
  do not give me up to shameless
    desires.[z]

### Proper Use of the Tongue[§]

7 Listen, my children, to instruction
    concerning the mouth,
  for whoever keeps it will not be
    ensnared.
8 Through the lips the sinner is caught;
  by them the reviler and the arrogant
    are tripped up.
9 Do not accustom your mouth to oaths,
  or habitually utter the Holy Name.[a]
10 Just as a servant constantly under scrutiny
    will not be without bruises,
So one who swears continually by the
    Holy Name
  will never remain free from sin.
11 Those who swear many oaths heap up
    offenses;
  and the scourge will never be far
    from their houses.
If they swear in error, guilt is incurred;
  if they neglect their obligation, the
    sin is doubly great.[b]
If they swear without reason they cannot
    be declared innocent,
  for their households will be filled
    with calamities.

12 There are words comparable to death;
  may they never be heard in the
    inheritance of Jacob.
To the devout all such words are foreign;
  they do not wallow in sin.
13 Do not accustom your mouth to coarse
    talk,
  for it involves sinful speech.
14 Keep your father and mother in mind
    when you sit among the mighty,[c]
Lest you forget yourself in their presence
  and disgrace your upbringing.
Then you will wish you had never been
    born
  and will curse the day of your birth.

---

*[22:19–26] Disputes and violence weaken friendship,
and disloyalty and abuse of confidence destroy it utterly (vv.
19–22, 24, 26); but kindness to a poor person in time of poverty and adversity builds up friendship and merits a share in
his prosperity and inheritance (vv. 23, 25).

†[22:27–23:6] Ben Sira implores the divine assistance to
preserve him through stern discipline from sins of the tongue
(22:27; 23:1), from ignorance of mind and weakness of will
(vv. 2–3), and from inclinations of the senses and the flesh,
lest he fall into the hands of his enemies or become a prey of
shameful desires (vv. 4–6).

‡[23:1–6] **Lord, Father and Master of my life:** these words
express the tender personal relationship Ben Sira experiences
with God, and introduce his prayer for divine assistance and
providence in avoiding sins of pride and lust.

y. [22:27] Ps 141:3.

§[23:7–15] A warning against sins of the tongue through
misuse of the sacred Name, against thoughtless swearing (vv.
7–11), blasphemy (v. 12), coarse talk (vv. 13–14), and abusive
language (v. 15).

z. [23:6] Rom 13:13.   a. [23:9] Ex 20:7; Lv 19:12; 24:16; Dt 5:11;
Mt 5:33–37; Jas 5:12.   b. [23:11] Lv 5:4–10.   c. [23:14] Sir 7:27; Ex
20:12; Dt 5:16.

¹⁵ Those accustomed to using abusive
language
   will never acquire discipline as long
   as they live.

### Sins of the Flesh*

¹⁶ Two types of people multiply sins,
   and a third† draws down wrath:
Burning passion is like a blazing fire,
   not to be quenched till it burns itself
   out;
One unchaste with his kindred
   never stops until fire breaks forth.
¹⁷ To the unchaste all bread is sweet;
   he is never through till he dies.ᵈ

¹⁸ The man who dishonors his marriage bed
   says to himself, "Who can see me?
Darkness surrounds me, walls hide me,
   no one sees me. Who can stop me
   from sinning?"ᵉ
He is not mindful of the Most High,
¹⁹      fearing only human eyes.
He does not realize that the eyes of the
   Lord,
   ten thousand times brighter than
   the sun,
Observe every step taken
   and peer into hidden corners.
²⁰ The one who knows all things before they
   exist
   still knows them all after they are
   made.
²¹ Such a man will be denounced in the
   streets of the city;ᶠ
   and where he least suspects it, he
   will be apprehended.

²² So it is with the woman unfaithful to her
   husband,
   who offers him an heir by another
   man.
²³ First of all, she has disobeyed the law of
   the Most High;
   second, she has wronged her
   husband;
Third, through her wanton adultery
   she has brought forth children by
   another man.
²⁴ Such a woman will be dragged before the
   assembly,‡

and her punishment will extend to
   her children.
²⁵ Her children will not take root;
   her branches will not bring forth fruit.
²⁶ She will leave behind an accursed memory;
   her disgrace will never be blotted out.

²⁷ Thus all who dwell on the earth shall know,
   all who remain in the world shall
   understand,
That nothing is better than the fear of the
   Lord,
   nothing sweeter than obeying the
   commandments of the Lord.ᵍ§

## CHAPTER 24

### Praise of Wisdom

¹ Wisdom sings her own praises,¶
   among her own people she
   proclaims her glory.
² In the assembly of the Most High she
   opens her mouth,
   in the presence of his host she tells
   of her glory:

³ "From the mouth of the Most High I
   came forth,ʰ
   and covered the earth like a mist.
⁴ In the heights of heaven I dwelt,
   and my throne was in a pillar of
   cloud.
⁵ The vault of heaven I compassed alone,
   and walked through the deep abyss.
⁶ Over waves of the sea, over all the land,
   over every people and nation I held
   sway.
⁷ Among all these I sought a resting place.
   In whose inheritance should I abide?

⁸ "Then the Creator of all gave me his
   command,
   and my Creator chose the spot for
   my tent.
He said, 'In Jacob make your dwelling,
   in Israel your inheritance.'
⁹ Before all ages, from the beginning, he
   created me,
   and through all ages I shall not cease
   to be.

---

excluded them from the "community of the Lord" (Dt 23:3).
Cf. Wis 3:16–19; 4:3–6.

§ [23:27] Other ancient texts read as v. 28:

It is a great glory to follow after God,
   and for you to be received by him is length of days.

¶[24:1–29] Wisdom speaks in the first person, describing
her origin, her dwelling place in Israel, and the reward she
gives her followers. As in Proverbs 8, Wisdom is personified
as coming from God, yet distinct from him. This description
is reflected in the Johannine *logos*, or Word (Jn 1:1–14). It is
used extensively in the Roman liturgy.

---

*[23:16–27] Ben Sira treats sexual sins and their conse-
quences. Lust destroys its victims (vv. 16–17, 22–26). A false
sense of security aggravates the adulterer's inevitable fate (vv.
18–21).
   †[23:16] **Two types . . . a third**: a numerical proverb, as in
25:1–2, 7–11; 26:5–6, 28; 50:25–26; Prv 6:16–19; 30:15b–16,
18–19, 21–23, 29–31. Ben Sira condemns three kinds of sexual
sin: incest (v. 16), fornication (v. 17), and adultery (vv. 18–26).
   ‡[23:24–25] The judgment of the assembly determined
the illegitimacy of children born of adultery or incest and

d. [23:17] Prv 9:17.   e. [23:18–19] Jb 24:15; Prv 15:3, 11; 17:3;
24:12; Is 29:15; Ez 8:12.   f. [23:21–22] Lv 18:20; 20:10; Dt 22:21–22.

g. [23:27] Sir 1:11–30; Prv 3:1–2.   h. [24:3–6] Sir 1:1–4; Prv 2:6;
8:22–36; Wis 7:24–25.

<sup>10</sup> In the holy tent I ministered before him,
and so I was established in Zion.
<sup>11</sup> In the city he loves as he loves me, he gave
me rest;
in Jerusalem, my domain.
<sup>12</sup> I struck root among the glorious people,
in the portion of the Lord, his
heritage.

<sup>13</sup> "Like a cedar in Lebanon I grew tall,
like a cypress on Mount Hermon;
<sup>14</sup> I grew tall like a palm tree in Engedi,
like rosebushes in Jericho;
Like a fair olive tree in the field,
like a plane tree beside water I grew
tall.
<sup>15</sup> Like cinnamon and fragrant cane,
like precious myrrh I gave forth
perfume;
Like galbanum and onycha and mastic,<sup>i</sup>
like the odor of incense in the holy
tent.<sup>*</sup>

<sup>16</sup> "I spread out my branches like a terebinth,
my branches so glorious and so
graceful.
<sup>17</sup> I bud forth delights like a vine;
my blossoms are glorious and rich
fruit.<sup>†</sup>
<sup>19</sup> Come to me, all who desire me,
and be filled with my fruits.<sup>‡</sup>
<sup>20</sup> You will remember me as sweeter than
honey,
better to have than the honeycomb.
<sup>21</sup> Those who eat of me will hunger still,<sup>§</sup>
those who drink of me will thirst
for more.<sup>j</sup>
<sup>22</sup> Whoever obeys me will not be put to
shame,
and those who serve me will never
go astray."

<sup>23</sup> All this is the book of the covenant of the
Most High God,<sup>k</sup>
the Law which Moses commanded us<sup>¶</sup>
as a heritage for the community of
Jacob.<sup>**</sup>

<sup>25</sup> It overflows, like the Pishon, with wisdom,<sup>l</sup>
and like the Tigris at the time of first
fruits.
<sup>26</sup> It runs over, like the Euphrates, with
understanding,
and like the Jordan at harvest time.
<sup>27</sup> It floods like the Nile with instruction,
like the Gihon<sup>††</sup> at vintage time.
<sup>28</sup> The first human being never finished
comprehending wisdom,
nor will the last succeed in
fathoming her.
<sup>29</sup> For deeper than the sea are her thoughts,
and her counsels, than the great abyss.

<sup>30</sup> Now I, like a stream from a river,<sup>‡‡</sup>
and like water channeling into a
garden—
<sup>31</sup> I said, "I will water my plants,
I will drench my flower beds."
Then suddenly this stream of mine
became a river,
and this river of mine became a sea.
<sup>32</sup> Again I will make my teachings shine
forth like the dawn;
I will spread their brightness afar off.
<sup>33</sup> Again I will pour out instruction like
prophecy
and bestow it on generations yet to
come.

## CHAPTER 25

### Those Who Are Worthy of Praise

<sup>1</sup> <sup>§§</sup>With three things I am delighted,
for they are pleasing to the Lord and
to human beings:
Harmony among relatives, friendship
among neighbors,
and a wife and a husband living
happily together.
<sup>2</sup> Three kinds of people I hate,
and I loathe their manner of life:
A proud pauper, a rich liar,
and a lecherous old fool.

<sup>3</sup> In your youth you did not gather.
How will you find anything in your
old age?
<sup>4</sup> How appropriate is sound judgment in
the gray-haired,
and good counsel in the elderly!

---

<sup>*</sup>[24:15] These substances, associated with worship, are
mentioned in Ex 30:23–28, 34–35 as the ingredients of the
anointing oil and the sacred incense. Israel was a priestly
nation (Ex 19:6; Is 61:6).

† [24:17] Other ancient texts read as v. 18:

I am the mother of fair love, of reverence,
of knowledge, and of holy hope;
To all my children I give
to be everlasting: to those named by Him.

‡[24:19] Mt 11:28–30 contains a similar invitation.
§[24:21] The paradox of wisdom is that, far from being
satiated, those who partake of her will always desire more.
¶[24:23] Ben Sira now identifies Wisdom and the law of
Moses; see also Bar 4:1.
** [24:23] Other ancient texts read as v. 24:

Do not grow weary of striving with the Lord's help,
but cling to him that he may reinforce you.

i. [24:15] Ex 30:23–28, 34–35.    j. [24:21] Is 55:1; Jn 4:10–14; 6:35.
k. [24:23] Ex 24:7.

---

The Lord Almighty alone is God,
and apart from him there is no savior.

††[24:27] **Gihon**: understood by some to have been a name
for the Nile; cf. Gn 2:13.
‡‡[24:30–33] Ben Sira again speaks about himself. He had at
first drawn a small portion of the water of wisdom for his own
private benefit, but finding it so useful, he soon began to let others share in this boon by teaching them the lessons of wisdom.
Like the words of the prophets, Ben Sira's instruction is valuable
for all generations (v. 33). The comparison to prophecy is bold
and unique.
§§[25:1–2] A numerical saying in threes.

l. [24:23–27] Gn 2:11–14.

⁵ How appropriate is wisdom in the aged,
   understanding and counsel in the
   venerable!
⁶ The crown of the elderly, wide experience;
   their glory, the fear of the Lord.

⁷ There are nine who come to mind as
   blessed,
   a tenth whom my tongue proclaims:*
The man who finds joy in his children,
   and the one who lives to see the
   downfall of his enemies.
⁸ Happy the man who lives with a sensible
   woman,
   and the one who does not plow with
   an ox and a donkey combined.†
Happy the one who does not sin with the
   tongue,
   who does not serve an inferior.
⁹ Happy the one who finds a friend,
   who speaks to attentive ears.
¹⁰ How great is the one who finds wisdom,
   but none is greater than the one who
   fears the Lord.
¹¹ Fear of the Lord surpasses all else.
   To whom can we compare the one
   who has it?‡

### Wicked and Virtuous Women§

¹³ Any wound, but not a wound of the heart!
   Any wickedness, but not the
   wickedness of a woman!
¹⁴ Any suffering, but not suffering from
   one's foes!
   Any vengeance, but not the
   vengeance of one's enemies!
¹⁵ There is no poison worse than that of a
   serpent,
   no venom greater than that of a
   woman.
¹⁶ I would rather live with a dragon or a lion
   than live with a wicked woman.ᵐ
¹⁷ A woman's wicked disposition changes
   her appearance,
   and makes her face as dark as a bear.
¹⁸ When her husband sits among his
   neighbors,
   a bitter sigh escapes him unawares.

¹⁹ There is hardly an evil like that in a woman;
   may she fall to the lot of the sinner!

²⁰ Like a sandy hill to aged feet
   is a garrulous wife to a quiet husband.
²¹ Do not be enticed by a woman's beauty,
   or be greedy for her wealth.
²² Harsh is the slavery and great the shame
   when a wife supports her husband.

²³ Depressed mind, gloomy face,
   and a wounded heart—a wicked
   woman.
Drooping hands and quaking knees,
   any wife who does not make her
   husband happy.
²⁴ With a woman sin had a beginning,
   and because of her we all die.⁵
²⁵ Allow water no outlet,
   and no boldness of speech to a
   wicked woman.
²⁶ If she does not go along as you direct,
   cut her away from you.

### CHAPTER 26

¹ Happy the husband of a good wife;**
   the number of his days will be
   doubled.ⁿ
² A loyal wife brings joy to her husband,
   and he will finish his years in peace.
³ A good wife is a generous gift
   bestowed upon him who fears the
   Lord.ᵒ
⁴ Whether rich or poor, his heart is content,
   a smile ever on his face.

⁵ There are three things I dread,
   and a fourth which terrifies me:
Public slander, the gathering of a mob,
   and false accusation—all harder to
   bear than death.
⁶ A wife jealous of another wife is heartache
   and mourning;††
   everyone feels the lash of her tongue.

⁷ A wicked wife is a chafing yoke;
   taking hold of her is like grasping a
   scorpion.
⁸ A drunken wife arouses great anger,
   for she does not hide her shame.
⁹ By her haughty stare and her eyelids
   an unchaste wife can be recognized.

¹⁰ Keep a strict watch over an unruly wife,
   lest, finding an opportunity, she
   use it;ᵖ

---

*[25:7–11] A numerical proverb (9 + 1), in which the tenth
element, "the one who fears the Lord," is the most important.
   †[25:8] **An ox and a donkey combined**: the reference is to
a man married to two incompatible women (cf. 37:11a); the
imagery derives from Dt 22:10.
   ‡ [25:11] Other ancient texts read as v. 12:
   Fear of the Lord is the beginning of loving him,
      and fidelity is the beginning of clinging to him.
   §[25:13–26] The harsh statements Ben Sira makes about
women reflect the kind of instruction young Jewish males
were exposed to in the early second century B.C. His patriarchal perspective is as unfair as it is one-sided.

m. [25:16] Prv 21:9, 19; 25:24; 27:15.

¶[25:24] Ben Sira refers to the story of the first sin in Gn
3:1–6. Cf. 2 Cor 11:3 and 1 Tm 2:14. St. Paul, however, singles
out Adam; cf. Rom 5:12–19; 1 Cor 15:22.
   **[26:1–4, 13–18] A good wife is as a gift from God, bring-
ing joy and peace, happiness and contentment to her husband
(vv. 1–4) through her thoughtfulness, reserve, modesty and
chastity, beauty, grace, and virtue (vv. 13–18).
   ††[26:6–12] A repetition of the thought expressed in 25:13–26.

n. [26:1] Sir 25:8; Prv 18:22.   o. [26:3] Sir 36:27–29.   p. [26:10]
Sir 42:11.

11 Watch out for her impudent eye,
   and do not be surprised if she
      betrays you:
12 As a thirsty traveler opens his mouth
   and drinks from any water nearby,
So she sits down before every tent peg
   and opens her quiver for every arrow.

13 A gracious wife delights her husband;
   her thoughtfulness puts flesh on his
      bones.
14 A silent wife is a gift from the Lord;
   nothing is worth more than her
      self-discipline.
15 A modest wife is a supreme blessing;
   no scales can weigh the worth of her
      chastity.
16 The sun rising in the Lord's heavens—
   the beauty of a good wife in her
      well-ordered home.
17 The light which shines above the holy
      lampstand—*
   a beautiful face on a stately figure.
18 Golden columns on silver bases—
   so her shapely legs and steady feet.†

### Dangers to Integrity and Friendship

28 ‡Two things bring grief to my heart,
   and a third arouses my anger:
The wealthy reduced to want,
   the intelligent held in contempt,

---

*[26:17–18] The lampstand and the columns were located
in the holy place of the ancient tabernacle (Ex 25:31–40; 26:32).
† [26:18] Other ancient texts read as vv. 19–27:

19 My child, keep intact the bloom of your youth,
   and do not give your strength to strangers.
20 Seek out a fertile field from all the land,
   and sow it with your own seed, confident in your
      fine stock.
21 So shall your offspring prosper,
   and grow great, confident in their good descent.
22 A woman for hire is regarded as spittle,
   but a married woman is a deadly snare for her lovers.
23 A godless wife will be given to the lawless man as his
      portion,
   but a godly wife will be given to the man who
      fears the Lord.
24 A shameless woman wears out reproach,
   but a virtuous daughter will be modest even
      before her husband.
25 A headstrong wife is regarded as a bitch,
   but the one with a sense of shame fears the Lord.
26 The wife who honors her husband will seem wise to
      everyone,
   but if she dishonors him in her pride, she will be
      known to everyone as ungodly.
Happy is the husband of a good wife,
   for the number of his years will be doubled.
27 A loud-mouthed and garrulous wife will be regarded
   as a trumpet sounding the charge,
And every person who lives like this
   will spend his life in the anarchy of war.

‡[26:28–27:15] From proper conduct in family life, Ben
Sira proceeds to social morality, warning especially against
injustice in business (26:29–27:3), and perversity of speech in
daily life (27:4–7). The pursuit of justice in these matters is
all the more meritorious as it is difficult (27:8–10). The discourses of the godly are marked with wisdom, but the conversations of the wicked with offense, swearing, cursing, quarrels,
and even bloodshed (27:11–15).

---

And those who pass from righteousness
      to sin—
   the Lord prepares them for the sword.q

29 A merchant can hardly keep from
      wrongdoing,
   nor can a shopkeeper stay free from
      sin;

## CHAPTER 27

1 For the sake of profit many sin,
   and the struggle for wealth blinds
      the eyes.r
2 A stake will be driven between fitted
      stones—
   sin will be wedged in between
      buying and selling.
3 Unless one holds fast to the fear of the Lord,
   with sudden swiftness will one's
      house be thrown down.

4 When a sieve is shaken, the husks appear;
   so do people's faults when they
      speak.§
5 The furnace tests the potter's vessels;
   the test of a person is in
      conversation.s
6 The fruit of a tree shows the care it has
      had;
   so speech discloses the bent of a
      person's heart.t
7 Praise no one before he speaks,
   for it is then that people are tested.

8 If you strive after justice, you will attain it,
   and wear it like a splendid robe.
9 Birds nest with their own kind,
   and honesty comes to those who
      work at it.
10 A lion lies in wait for prey,
   so does sin for evildoers.

11 The conversation of the godly is always
      wisdom,
   but the fool changes like the moon.
12 Limit the time you spend among the
      stupid,
   but frequent the company of the
      thoughtful.
13 The conversation of fools is offensive,
   and their laughter is wanton sin.
14 Their oath-filled talk makes the hair stand
      on end,
   and their brawls make one stop the
      ears.
15 The wrangling of the proud ends in
      bloodshed,
   and their cursing is painful to hear.u

---

§[27:4–7, 11–15] The importance of effective speech is a
favorite wisdom topic; e.g., cf. 20:1–8, 18–20; 22:27–23:15.

q. [26:28] Ez 18:24–29.   r. [27:1] Sir 7:18; 31:5–6; Prv 30:7–
9.   s. [27:5] 1 Pt 1:7.   t. [27:6] Mt 7:20.   u. [27:15] Sir 23:8–15.

<sup>16</sup> Whoever betrays a secret destroys
confidence,[*]
and will never find a congenial
friend.[v]
<sup>17</sup> Cherish your friend, keep faith with him;
but if you betray his secrets, do not
go after him;
<sup>18</sup> For as one might kill another,
you have killed your neighbor's
friendship.
<sup>19</sup> Like a bird released from your hand,
you have let your friend go and
cannot recapture him.
<sup>20</sup> Do not go after him, for he is far away,
and has escaped like a gazelle from
a snare.
<sup>21</sup> For a wound can be bandaged, and an
insult forgiven,
but whoever betrays secrets does
hopeless damage.[w]

### Malice, Anger and Vengeance

<sup>22</sup> Whoever has shifty eyes plots mischief
and those who know him will keep
their distance;
<sup>23</sup> In your presence he uses honeyed talk,
and admires your words,
But later he changes his tone
and twists the words to your ruin.[x]
<sup>24</sup> I have hated many things but not as much
as him,
and the Lord hates him as well.[y]
<sup>25</sup> A stone falls back on the head of the one
who throws it high,[z]
and a treacherous blow causes many
wounds.
<sup>26</sup> Whoever digs a pit falls into it,
and whoever lays a snare is caught
in it.[†]
<sup>27</sup> The evil anyone does will recoil on him
without knowing how it came upon
him.

<sup>28</sup> Mockery and abuse will befall the arrogant,
and vengeance lies in wait for them
like a lion.
<sup>29</sup> Those who rejoice in the downfall of the
godly will be caught in a snare,

and pain will consume them before
they die.
<sup>30</sup> Wrath and anger, these also are
abominations,
yet a sinner holds on to them.

## CHAPTER 28

<sup>1</sup> The vengeful will face the Lord's vengeance;
indeed he remembers their sins in
detail.[a]

<sup>2</sup> Forgive your neighbor the wrong done to
you;
then when you pray, your own sins
will be forgiven.[b]
<sup>3</sup> Does anyone nourish anger against another
and expect healing from the LORD?[c]
<sup>4</sup> Can one refuse mercy to a sinner like
oneself,
yet seek pardon for one's own sins?
<sup>5</sup> If a mere mortal cherishes wrath,
who will forgive his sins?
<sup>6</sup> Remember your last days and set enmity
aside;
remember death and decay, and
cease from sin![d]
<sup>7</sup> Remember the commandments and
do not be angry with your
neighbor;
remember the covenant of the Most
High, and overlook faults.

<sup>8</sup> Avoid strife and your sins will be fewer,
for the hot-tempered kindle strife;
<sup>9</sup> The sinner disrupts friendships
and sows discord among those who
are at peace.[e]
<sup>10</sup> The more the wood, the greater the fire,[f]
the more the cruelty, the fiercer the
strife;
The greater the strength, the sterner the
anger,
the greater the wealth, the greater
the wrath.
<sup>11</sup> Pitch and resin make fire flare up,
and a hasty quarrel provokes
bloodshed.

### The Evil Tongue[‡]

<sup>12</sup> If you blow on a spark, it turns into flame,
if you spit on it, it dies out;
yet both you do with your mouth!

---

*[27:16–28:11] Betrayal of confidence through indiscretion destroys friendship and does irreparable harm (27:16–21); cf. 22:22. False friendship based on hypocrisy and deceit is hateful to Ben Sira and, he adds, to God as well (27:22–24); it soon becomes a victim of its own treachery (27:25–27). The same fate awaits the malicious and vengeful (27:28–28:1). They can obtain mercy and forgiveness only by first forgiving their neighbor, being mindful of death and of the commandments of the Most High (28:2–7). And they must avoid quarrels and strife (28:8–11).

†[27:26] This expresses a popular idea of act and consequence; an evil (or good) deed is repaid by an evil (or good) result. The frequent metaphor is the digging of a hole for another to fall into; cf. Prv 26:27; Ps 7:14; 9:16; Eccl 10:8.

v. [27:16] Prv 11:13; 20:19.   w. [27:21] Sir 22:20.   x. [27:23] Prv 26:24–28.   y. [27:24] Prv 6:16–19.   z. [27:25–27] Ps 7:16–17; Prv 26:27; Eccl 10:8.

‡[28:12–26] Further treatment of sins of the tongue and the havoc that results; cf. 5:9–6:1; 19:5–17; 20:18–26; 23:7–15. Gossips and the double-tongued destroy domestic peace (vv. 12–16). The whip, the sword, chains, even Sheol, are not so cruel as the suffering inflicted by an evil tongue (vv. 17–21). Not the godly but those who forsake the Lord are victims of their evil tongues (vv. 22–23). Therefore, guard your mouth and tongue as you would guard treasure against an enemy (vv. 24–26).

a. [28:1] Dt 32:35; Rom 12:19.   b. [28:2] Mt 6:14.   c. [28:3] Mt 18:23–35.   d. [28:6] Sir 7:36; 38:20.   e. [28:9] Prv 15:18.   f. [28:10–11] Prv 26:20–21.

¹³ Cursed be gossips and the
        double-tongued,
    for they destroy the peace of many.ᵍ
¹⁴ A meddlesome tongue subverts many,
        and makes them refugees among
        peoples.
    It destroys strong cities,
        and overthrows the houses of the
        great.
¹⁵ A meddlesome tongue drives virtuous
        women from their homes,
    and robs them of the fruit of their
        toil.
¹⁶ Whoever heed it will find no rest,
        nor will they dwell in peace.

¹⁷ A blow from a whip raises a welt,
        but a blow from the tongue will
        break bones.
¹⁸ Many have fallen by the edge of the sword,
        but not as many as by the tongue.ʰ
¹⁹ Happy the one who is sheltered from it,
        and has not endured its wrath;
    Who has not borne its yoke
        nor been bound with its chains.
²⁰ For its yoke is a yoke of iron,
        and its chains are chains of bronze;
²¹ The death it inflicts is an evil death,
        even Sheol is preferable to it.
²² It will have no power over the godly,
        nor will they be burned in its flame.
²³ But those who forsake the Lord will fall
        victim to it,
        as it burns among them
        unquenchably;
    It will hurl itself against them like a lion,
        and like a leopard, it will tear them
        to pieces.
²⁴ As you fence in your property with thorns,
        so make a door and a bolt for your
        mouth.ⁱ
²⁵ As you lock up your silver and gold,
        so make balances and scales for your
        words.
²⁶ Take care not to slip by your tongue
        and fall victim to one lying in ambush.

## CHAPTER 29

### Loans, Alms and Surety*

¹ The merciful lend to their neighbor,
    by holding out a helping hand, they
        keep the commandments.ʲ

² Lend to your neighbor in his time of need,
        and pay back your neighbor in time.ᵏ
³ Keep your promise and be honest with him,
        and at all times you will find what
        you need.
⁴ Many borrowers ask for a loan
        and cause trouble for those who
        help them.
⁵ Till he gets a loan, he kisses the lender's
        hand
        and speaks softly of his creditor's
        money,
    But at time of payment, delays,
        makes excuses, and finds fault with
        the timing.
⁶ If he can pay, the lender will recover
        barely half,
        and will consider that a windfall.
    If he cannot pay, the lender is cheated of
        his money
        and acquires an enemy at no extra
        charge;
    With curses and insults the borrower will
        repay,
        and instead of honor will repay with
        abuse.
⁷ Many refuse to lend, not out of meanness,
        but from fear of being cheated
        needlessly.

⁸ But with those in humble circumstances
        be patient;
        do not keep them waiting for your
        alms.
⁹ Because of the commandment, help the
        poor,
        and in their need, do not send them
        away empty-handed.ˡ
¹⁰ Lose your money for relative or friend;
        do not hide it under a stone to rot.
¹¹ Dispose of your treasure according to the
        commandments of the Most
        High,
        and that will profit you more than
        the gold.ᵐ
¹² †Store up almsgiving in your treasury,
        and it will save you from every evil.
¹³ Better than a mighty shield and a sturdy
        spear
        it will fight for you against the enemy.

¹⁴ ‡A good person will be surety for a neighbor,
        but whoever has lost a sense of
        shame will fail him.ⁿ
¹⁵ Do not forget the kindness of your backer,
        for he has given his very life for you.

---

*[29:1–20] Some practical maxims concerning the use of wealth. Give to the poor (vv. 8–9), lend to a needy neighbor, but repay when a loan falls due lest the lender's burden be increased (vv. 1–5) and his kindness abused (vv. 6–7); through charity build up defense against evil (vv. 10–13). Help your neighbor according to your means, but take care not to fall (v. 20), for the shameless play false and bring their protectors and themselves to misfortune and ruin (vv. 14–19).

g. [28:13] Sir 5:13–6:1.  h. [28:18] Jas 3:5–12.  i. [28:24] Sir 22:27; Ps 141:3.  j. [29:1] Dt 15:8; Ps 112:5; Prv 19:17.

†[29:12–13] In Ben Sira's day, almsgiving and righteousness were practically identified.
‡[29:14–17] Ben Sira is more lenient on going surety than earlier sages; cf. Prv 6:1–5.

k. [29:2] Ex 22:24–26; Lv 25:36; Mt 5:42.  l. [29:9] Sir 4:1–6; Lv 19:9–10; 23:22.  m. [29:11] Sir 17:22–23; Tb 4:7–11.  n. [29:14] Sir 8:13.

16  A sinner will turn the favor of a pledge
        into misfortune,
17      and the ungrateful will abandon his
            rescuer.
18  Going surety has ruined many who were
        prosperous
        and tossed them about like waves of
            the sea;[o]
    It has exiled the prominent
        and sent them wandering through
            foreign lands.
19  The sinner will come to grief through
        surety,
        and whoever undertakes too much
            will fall into lawsuits.
20  Help your neighbor according to your
        means,
        but take care lest you fall yourself.

### Frugality and Its Rewards[*]

21  Life's prime needs are water, bread, and
        clothing,
        and also a house for decent privacy.[p]
22  Better is the life of the poor under the
        shadow of their own roof
        than sumptuous banquets among
            strangers.[q]
23  Whether little or much, be content with
        what you have:
        then you will hear no reproach as a
            parasite.
24  It is a miserable life to go from house to
        house,
        for where you are a guest you dare
            not open your mouth.
25  You will entertain and provide drink
        without being thanked;
        besides, you will hear these bitter
            words:
26  "Come here, you parasite, set the table,
        let me eat the food you have there!
27  Go away, you parasite, for one more
        worthy;
        for my relative's visit I need the room!"
28  Painful things to a sensitive person
        are rebuke as a parasite and insults
            from creditors.

## CHAPTER 30

### The Training of Children[†]

1   Whoever loves a son will chastise him often,

        that he may be his joy when he
            grows up.[r]
2   Whoever disciplines a son will benefit
        from him,
        and boast of him among
            acquaintances.
3   Whoever educates a son will make his
        enemy jealous,
        and rejoice in him among his friends.
4   At the father's death, he will seem not
        dead,
        for he leaves after him one like
            himself,
5   Whom he looked upon through life with
        joy,
        and in death, without regret.
6   Against his enemies he has left an avenger,
        and one to repay his friends with
            kindness.

7   Whoever spoils a son will have wounds to
        bandage,
        and will suffer heartache at every cry.
8   An untamed horse turns out stubborn;
        and a son left to himself grows up
            unruly.
9   Pamper a child and he will be a terror for
        you,
        indulge him, and he will bring you
            grief.
10  Do not laugh with him lest you share
        sorrow with him,
        and in the end you will gnash your
            teeth.
11  Do not give him his own way in his youth,
        and do not ignore his follies.
12  Bow down his head in his youth,
        beat his sides while he is still young,
    Lest he become stubborn and disobey
        you,
        and leave you disconsolate.[s]
13  Discipline your son and make heavy his
        yoke,
        lest you be offended by his
            shamelessness.

### Health and Cheerfulness[‡]

14  Better the poor in vigorous health
        than the rich with bodily ills.

---

*[29:21–28] Those who provide their own basic needs of
food, clothing and dwelling, and are content with what they
have, preserve their freedom and self-respect (vv. 21–23). But
if they live as guests, even among the rich, they expose themselves to insult and rebuke (vv. 24–28).

†[30:1–13] Sound discipline (which would include physical
beating) and careful education of children correct self-indulgence and stubbornness, prevent remorse and humiliation,

and bring to parents lasting joy and delight, prestige among
friends, jealousy of enemies, perpetuation and vindication of
themselves through their offspring (vv. 1–6). Lack of discipline
and overindulgence of children bring sorrow and disappointment, terror and grief (vv. 7–13).

‡[30:14–25] Health of mind and body and joy of heart
Ben Sira judges to be more precious than wealth (vv. 14–16),
whereas bitterness, constant illness, and affliction are more
difficult to bear than death (vv. 17–20). Sadness, resentment,
anxiety, envy, and anger shorten days; they should be dis-
pelled by cheerfulness and gladness of heart, which help to
prolong one's days (vv. 21–25).

---

o. [29:18] Prv 6:1–2; 11:15.    p. [29:21] Sir 39:26.    q. [29:22] Sir
40:29.

r. [30:1] Prv 13:24; 19:18; 22:15; 23:13; 29:15; Heb 12:7.    s. [30:12]
Sir 7:23; Prv 23:14.

<sup>15</sup> I would rather have bodily health than
           any gold,
    and contentment of spirit than
           pearls.
<sup>16</sup> No riches are greater than a healthy body;
    and no happiness than a joyful heart.
<sup>17</sup> Better is death than a wretched life,<sup>t</sup>
    everlasting sleep than constant
           illness.
<sup>18</sup> Good things set before one who cannot
           eat
    are like food offerings placed before
           a tomb.<sup>*u</sup>
<sup>19</sup> What good is an offering to an idol
    that can neither eat nor smell?
    So it is with the one being punished by
           the Lord,
<sup>20</sup>     who groans at what his eyes behold.

<sup>21</sup> Do not give in to sadness,
    or torment yourself deliberately.<sup>v</sup>
<sup>22</sup> Gladness of heart is the very life of a
           person,
    and cheerfulness prolongs his days.
<sup>23</sup> Distract yourself and renew your courage,
    drive resentment far away from you;
    For grief has killed many,<sup>w</sup>
    and nothing is to be gained from
           resentment.
<sup>24</sup> Envy and anger shorten one's days,
    and anxiety brings on premature
           old age.
<sup>25</sup> Those who are cheerful and merry at table
    benefit from their food.<sup>†x</sup>

## CHAPTER 31

### The Proper Attitude Toward Riches<sup>‡</sup>

<sup>1</sup> Wakefulness over wealth wastes away the
           flesh,
    and anxiety over it drives away sleep.
<sup>2</sup> Wakeful anxiety banishes slumber;
    more than a serious illness it   .
           disturbs repose.
<sup>3</sup> The rich labor to pile up wealth,
    and if they rest, it is to enjoy
           pleasure;
<sup>4</sup> The poor labor for a meager living,
    and if they ever rest, they become
           needy.
<sup>5</sup> The lover of gold will not be free from sin;

whoever pursues money will be led
           astray by it.
<sup>6</sup> Many have come to ruin for the sake of
           gold,
    yet destruction lay before their very
           eyes;<sup>y</sup>
<sup>7</sup> It is a stumbling block for fools;
    any simpleton will be ensnared by it.

<sup>8</sup> Happy the rich person found without fault,
    who does not turn aside after wealth.<sup>z</sup>
<sup>9</sup> Who is he, that we may praise him?
    For he has done wonders among his
           people.
<sup>10</sup> Who has been tested by gold and been
           found perfect?
    Let it be for him his glory;
    Who could have sinned but did not,
    and could have done evil but did not?
<sup>11</sup> So his good fortune is secure,
    and the assembly will recount his
           praises.<sup>a</sup>

### Table Etiquette<sup>§</sup>

<sup>12</sup> Are you seated at the table of the great?
    Bring to it no greedy gullet,
    Nor say, "How much food there is here!"
<sup>13</sup>     Remember that the greedy eye is
           evil.
    What has been created more greedy than
           the eye?
    Therefore, it weeps for any cause.<sup>b</sup>
<sup>15</sup> Recognize that your neighbor feels as you
           do,
    and keep in mind everything you
           dislike.
<sup>14</sup> Toward what he looks at, do not put out a
           hand;
    nor reach for the same dish when
           he does.
<sup>16</sup> Eat, like anyone else, what is set before you,
    but do not eat greedily, lest you be
           despised.
<sup>17</sup> Be the first to stop, as befits good
           manners;
    and do not gorge yourself, lest you
           give offense.<sup>c</sup>
<sup>18</sup> If there are many with you at table,
    do not be the first to stretch out
           your hand.
<sup>19</sup> Does not a little suffice for a well-bred
           person?

---

*[30:18] The saying ridicules the practice of putting food
and drink on the tombs of the dead.

†[30:25(27)] Because of the dislocation of the Greek text,
the numbering of this verse follows Ziegler's edition. There
are no verses 25–26.

‡[31:1–11] Solicitude for acquiring wealth and anxiety over
preserving it disturb repose and easily lead to sin and ruin (vv.
1–7). Cf. Mt 6:25–34. The rich who have not sinned or been
seduced by wealth are worthy of highest praise (vv. 8–11).

§[31:12–32:13] Whoever observes etiquette at table avoids
greed and selfishness (31:12–13), is considerate of a neighbor's
likes and dislikes and is generous toward him (31:15, 14, 23,
24), observes proper manners (31:16–18), is moderate in eating and drinking (31:19–20, 25–30). A good host is solicitous
for the guests (32:1–2), provides conversation and diversion
(32:3–6), is modest in speech (32:7, 8, 10), is respectful of
elders (32:9), polite in comportment and grateful to God for
his favors (32:11–13).

---

t. [30:17] Sir 41:2.   u. [30:18] Tb 4:17.   v. [30:21] Prv 12:25; 15:13;
17:22.   w. [30:23] Sir 38:18–19.   x. [30:25] Prv 15:15.

y. [31:6] Sir 8:2.   z. [31:8] Sir 5:1, 8.   a. [31:11] Prv 29:14.
b. [31:13] Prv 23:1–2.   c. [31:17] Sir 37:27–31.

When he lies down, he does not
wheeze.*d*

20 Moderate eating ensures sound slumber
and a clear mind on rising the next
day.
The distress of sleeplessness and of nausea
and colic are with the glutton!

21 Should you have eaten too much,
get up to vomit* and you will have
relief.

22 Listen to me, my child, and do not scorn
me;
later you will find my advice good.
In whatever you do, be moderate,
and no sickness will befall you.

23 People bless one who is generous with
food,
and this testimony to his goodness
is lasting.*e*

24 The city complains about one who is
stingy with food,
and this testimony to his stinginess
is lasting.

25 Let not wine be the proof of your
strength,
for wine has been the ruin of many.

26 As the furnace tests the work of the smith,
so does wine the hearts of the
insolent.

27 Wine is very life to anyone,
if taken in moderation.
Does anyone really live who lacks the
wine
which from the beginning was
created for joy?*f*

28 Joy of heart, good cheer, and delight
is wine enough, drunk at the proper
time.

29 Headache, bitterness, and disgrace
is wine drunk amid anger and strife.

30 Wine in excess is a snare for the fool;
it lessens strength and multiplies
wounds.

31 Do not wrangle with your neighbor when
wine is served,
nor despise him while he is having a
good time;
Say no harsh words to him
nor distress him by making
demands.

## CHAPTER 32

1 If you are chosen to preside at a dinner,
do not be puffed up,
but with the guests be as one of
them;

2 Take care of them first and then sit down;
see to their needs, and then take
your place,
To share in their joy
and receive a wreath for a job well
done.

3 You who are older, it is your right to speak,
but temper your knowledge and do
not interrupt the singing.

4 Where there is entertainment, do not
pour out discourse,
and do not display your wisdom at
the wrong time.

5 Like a seal of carnelian in a setting of
gold:
a concert of music at a banquet of
wine.

6 A seal of emerald in a work of gold:
the melody of music with delicious
wine.

7 Speak, young man, only when necessary;*g*
when they have asked you more
than once.

8 Be brief, say much in few words;
be knowledgeable and yet quiet.

9 When among elders do not be forward,
and with officials do not be too
insistent.

10 The lightning that flashes before a
hailstorm:
the esteem that shines on modesty.

11 Leave in good time and do not be the last;
go home quickly without delay.

12 There enjoy doing as you wish,
but do not sin through words of
pride.

13 Above all, bless your Maker,
who showers his favors upon you.

## The Providence of God

14 Whoever seeks God must accept
discipline;*†*
and whoever resorts to him obtains
an answer.*h*

15 Whoever seeks the law will master it,
but the hypocrite will be ensnared
by it.*i*

16 Whoever fears the LORD will understand
what is right,
and out of obscurity he will draw
forth a course of action.*j*

17 The lawless turn aside warnings
and distort the law to suit their
purpose.*k*

---

*†[32:14–33:4]* God is shown to reveal himself through the
discipline of his law, a clear and safe plan of life for the pious.
Direction and deliberation are aids in following it (32:14–16,
18–24; 33:1, 3–4). Sinners and hypocrites, hating the law or
distorting it, fail in wisdom and are devoid of security (32:15b,
17, 18b; 33:2).

---

*\*[31:21]* **Get up to vomit**: the practice of induced vomit-
ing, well-known among Romans, and less well-known among
the Jews, seems to be referred to here.

---

d. [31:19] Eccl 5:11.   e. [31:23] Prv 22:9.   f. [31:27] Ps 104:15;
1 Tm 5:23.

g. [32:7–10] Sir 7:14.   h. [32:14] Sir 4:13.   i. [32:15] Sir 2:16.
j. [32:16] Ps 37:6.   k. [32:17] Sir 21:6; Prv 12:1.

<sup>18</sup> The sensible will not neglect direction;
 the proud and insolent are deterred
  by no fear.
<sup>19</sup> Do nothing without deliberation;
 then once you have acted, have no
  regrets.<sup>l</sup>
<sup>20</sup> Do not go on a way set with snares,
 and do not stumble on the same
  thing twice.
<sup>21</sup> Do not trust the road, because of bandits;
<sup>22</sup> be careful on your paths.
<sup>23</sup> Whatever you do, be on your guard,
 for whoever does so keeps the
  commandments.
<sup>24</sup> Whoever keeps the law preserves himself;
 and whoever trusts in the LORD
  shall not be put to shame.

## CHAPTER 33

<sup>1</sup> No evil can harm the one who fears the
 LORD;
 through trials, again and again he is
  rescued.<sup>m</sup>
<sup>2</sup> Whoever hates the law is without wisdom,
 and is tossed about like a boat in a
  storm.
<sup>3</sup> The prudent trust in the word of the LORD,
 and the law is dependable for them
  as a divine oracle.<sup>*</sup>
<sup>4</sup> Prepare your words and then you will be
 listened to;
 draw upon your training, and give
  your answer.

<sup>5</sup> Like the wheel of a cart is the mind of a
 fool,
 and his thoughts like a turning axle.
<sup>6</sup> A mocking friend is like a stallion
 that neighs, no matter who the rider
  may be.

<sup>7</sup> <sup>†</sup>Why is one day more important than
 another,
 when the same sun lights up every
  day of the year?
<sup>8</sup> By the LORD's knowledge they are kept
 distinct;
 and he designates the seasons and
  feasts.<sup>n</sup>
<sup>9</sup> Some he exalts and sanctifies,
 and others he lists as ordinary days.<sup>o</sup>

<sup>10</sup> Likewise, all people are of clay,
 and from earth humankind was
  formed;<sup>p</sup>
<sup>11</sup> In the fullness of his knowledge the Lord
 distinguished them,
 and he designated their different ways.
<sup>12</sup> Some he blessed and exalted,
 and some he sanctified and drew to
  himself.
Others he cursed and brought low,
 and expelled them from their place.
<sup>13</sup> Like clay in the hands of a potter,
 to be molded according to his
  pleasure,
So are people in the hands of their Maker,
 to be dealt with as he decides.<sup>q</sup>
<sup>14</sup> As evil contrasts with good, and death
 with life,
 so are sinners in contrast with the
  godly.<sup>r</sup>
<sup>15</sup> See now all the works of the Most High:
 they come in pairs, one the opposite
  of the other.

<sup>16</sup> Now I am the last to keep vigil,<sup>‡</sup>
 like a gleaner following the
  grape-pickers;
<sup>17</sup> Since by the Lord's blessing I have made
 progress
 till like a grape-picker I have filled
  my wine press,
<sup>18</sup> Consider that not for myself only have I
 labored,
 but for all who seek instruction.

### Property and Servants<sup>§</sup>

<sup>19</sup> Listen to me, leaders of the people;
 rulers of the congregation, pay heed!<sup>s</sup>
<sup>20a</sup> Let neither son nor wife, neither brother
 nor friend,
 have power over you as long as you
  live.
<sup>21</sup> While breath of life is still in you,
 let no one take your place.
<sup>20b</sup> Do not give your wealth to another,
 lest you must plead for support
  yourself.
<sup>22</sup> Far better that your children plead with
 you
 than that you should look for a
  handout from them.

---

*[33:3] **Oracle**: as the answer given through the Urim and
Thummim to the high priest is true, so the law proves itself
true to those who obey it. Cf. Ex 28:30; Nm 27:21.

†[33:7–15] An important doctrine of Ben Sira is his view of
the polarities in creation and history; cf. v. 15; 42:24. Contrasts
observable in the physical universe as well as in the moral order
serve the purposes of divine wisdom (vv. 5–9). All creatures are
like clay in the hands of their Maker—the fool and the wise, the
sinner and the just (vv. 10–15). This does not imply that some
are created to be sinners: God is not the author of wickedness.
Divine determinism and human freedom are a mysterious mix.

‡[33:16–18] Ben Sira refers to himself as the most recent
of the biblical writers who have endeavored to present true
wisdom to their readers.

§[33:19–33] Public officials should reject every influence
that would restrict their freedom in the management of their
affairs. They must make their own household subservient to
them rather than be subservient to it (vv. 19–24). Slaves are to
be given food and work and correction but never to be treated
unjustly (vv. 25–30). Great care should be taken of good slaves
(vv. 31–33).

---

l. [32:19] Sir 37:16; Tb 4:18. m. [33:1] Ps 91:10–13; Mt 4:6; Lk
4:10–11. n. [33:8] Gn 1:14. o. [33:9] Ex 20:11; Dt 5:13–14.

p. [33:10] Gn 2:7. q. [33:13] Wis 15:7; Jer 18:1–6; Rom 9:20–
21. r. [33:14] Sir 42:25. s. [33:19] Wis 6:1–2.

23 Keep control over all your affairs;
　　bring no stain on your honor.
24 When your few days reach their limit,
　　at the time of death distribute your
　　　inheritance.

25 Fodder and whip and loads for a donkey;
　　food, correction and work for a slave.
26 Make a slave work, and he will look for rest;
　　let his hands be idle and he will seek
　　　to be free.[t]
27 The yoke and harness will bow the neck;
　　and for a wicked slave, punishment
　　　in the stocks.
28 Force him to work that he be not idle,
29 　for idleness teaches much mischief.
30 Put him to work, as is fitting for him;
　　and if he does not obey, load him
　　　with chains.
　But never lord it over any human being,
　　and do nothing unjust.
31 If you have but one slave, treat him like
　　yourself,
　　for you have acquired him with your
　　　life's blood;
　If you have but one slave, deal with him as
　　a brother,
　　for you need him as you need your
　　　life.[u]
32 If you mistreat him and he runs away,
33 　in what direction will you look for
　　　him?

## CHAPTER 34

### Trust in the Lord and Not in Dreams[*]

1 Empty and false are the hopes of the
　　senseless,
　　and dreams give wings to fools.
2 Like one grasping at shadows or chasing
　　the wind,
　　so anyone who believes in dreams.
3 What is seen in dreams is a reflection,
　　the likeness of a face looking at
　　　itself.
4 How can the unclean produce what is
　　clean?
　　How can the false produce what is
　　　true?[v]
5 Divination, omens, and dreams are
　　unreal;
　　what you already expect, the mind
　　　fantasizes.
6 Unless they are specially sent by the Most
　　High,
　　do not fix your heart on them.

7 For dreams have led many astray,
　　and those who put their hope in
　　　them have perished.
8 Without such deceptions the Law will be
　　fulfilled,
　　and in the mouth of the faithful is
　　　complete wisdom.

9 A much-traveled person knows many
　　things;
　　and one with much experience
　　　speaks sense.
10 An inexperienced person knows little,
11 　whereas with travel one adds to
　　　resourcefulness.
12 I have seen much in my travels,
　　and learned more than I could ever
　　　say.
13 Often I was in danger of death,
　　but by these experiences I was saved.

14 Living is the spirit of those who fear the
　　Lord,
15 　for their hope is in their savior.
16 Whoever fear the Lord are afraid of nothing
　　and are never discouraged, for he is
　　　their hope.[w]
17 Happy the soul that fears the Lord!
18 　In whom does he trust, and who is
　　　his support?
19 The eyes of the Lord are upon those who
　　love him;
　　he is their mighty shield and strong
　　　support,
　A shelter from the heat, a shade from the
　　noonday sun,
　　a guard against stumbling, a help
　　　against falling.[x]
20 He lifts up spirits, brings a sparkle to the
　　eyes,
　　gives health and life and blessing.

### True Worship of God[†]

21 Ill-gotten goods offered in sacrifice are
　　tainted.
22 　Presents from the lawless do not win
　　　God's favor.[y]
23 The Most High is not pleased with the
　　gifts of the godless,
　　nor for their many sacrifices does he
　　　forgive their sins.
24 One who slays a son in his father's
　　presence—
　　whoever offers sacrifice from the
　　　holdings of the poor.

---

*[34:1–20] Confidence placed in dreams, divinations, and omens is false because these are devoid of reality (vv. 1–8). True confidence is founded on knowledge and experience (vv. 9–13), and above all on the fear of the Lord, with its accompanying blessings of divine assistance and protection (vv. 14–20).

†[34:21–31] To be acts of true religion, sacrifice and penance must be accompanied by the proper moral dispositions. To offer to God goods taken from the poor (vv. 21–27), or to practice penance without interior reform, is a mockery, worthless in the sight of God (vv. 28–31). Cf. Mt 15:4–7; Mk 7:9–13.

t. [33:26] Prv 29:19.　u. [33:31] Sir 7:20–21.　v. [34:4] Jb 14:4.

w. [34:16] Ps 23:4; 112:7–8; Prv 3:23–24; 28:1.　x. [34:19] Ps 33:18–19; 34:16.　y. [34:22] Sir 35:14–15; Prv 21:27.

<sup>25</sup> The bread of charity is life itself for the
needy;<sup>z</sup>
  whoever withholds it is a murderer.
<sup>26</sup> To take away a neighbor's living is to
  commit murder;
<sup>27</sup>  to deny a laborer wages is to shed
  blood.

<sup>28</sup> If one builds up and another tears down,
  what do they gain but trouble?
<sup>29</sup> If one prays and another curses,
  whose voice will God hear?
<sup>30</sup> If one again touches a corpse after bathing,
  what does he gain by the
  purification?<sup>a</sup>
<sup>31</sup> So one who fasts for sins,
  but goes and commits them again:
Who will hear his prayer,
  what is gained by mortification?

## CHAPTER 35<sup>*</sup>

<sup>1</sup> To keep the law is to make many
  offerings;<sup>b</sup>
<sup>2</sup>  whoever observes the
  commandments sacrifices a
  peace offering.
<sup>3</sup> By works of charity one offers fine flour,<sup>†</sup>
<sup>4</sup>  and one who gives alms presents a
  sacrifice of praise.
<sup>5</sup> To refrain from evil pleases the Lord,
  and to avoid injustice is atonement.

<sup>6</sup> Do not appear before the Lord
  empty-handed,
<sup>7</sup>  for all that you offer is in fulfillment
  of the precepts.<sup>c</sup>
<sup>8</sup> The offering of the just enriches the altar:
  a sweet odor before the Most High.
<sup>9</sup> The sacrifice of the just is accepted,
  never to be forgotten.
<sup>10</sup> With a generous spirit pay homage to the
  Lord,
  and do not spare your freewill gifts.<sup>d</sup>
<sup>11</sup> With each contribution show a cheerful
  countenance,
  and pay your tithes in a spirit of joy.<sup>e</sup>
<sup>12</sup> Give to the Most High as he has given to
  you,
  generously, according to your
  means.

<sup>13</sup> For he is a God who always repays
  and will give back to you sevenfold.<sup>f</sup>

<sup>14</sup> But offer no bribes; these he does not
  accept!
<sup>15</sup>  Do not trust in sacrifice of the fruits
  of extortion,<sup>g</sup>
For he is a God of justice,
  who shows no partiality.<sup>h</sup>
<sup>16</sup> He shows no partiality to the weak
  but hears the grievance of the
  oppressed.<sup>‡</sup>
<sup>17</sup> He does not forsake the cry of the
  orphan,<sup>i</sup>
  nor the widow when she pours out
  her complaint.
<sup>18</sup> Do not the tears that stream down her
  cheek
<sup>19</sup>  cry out against the one that causes
  them to fall?
<sup>20</sup> Those who serve God to please him are
  accepted;
  their petition reaches the clouds.
<sup>21</sup> The prayer of the lowly pierces the clouds;
  it does not rest till it reaches its goal;
Nor will it withdraw till the Most High
  responds,
<sup>22</sup>  judges justly and affirms the right.<sup>j</sup>

God indeed will not delay,
  and like a warrior, will not be still<sup>k</sup>
Till he breaks the backs of the merciless
<sup>23</sup>  and wreaks vengeance upon the
  nations;
Till he destroys the scepter of the proud,
  and cuts off the staff of the wicked;
<sup>24</sup> Till he requites everyone according to
  their deeds,
  and repays them according to their
  thoughts;
<sup>25</sup> Till he defends the cause of his people,
  and makes them glad by his
  salvation.
<sup>26</sup> Welcome is his mercy in time of distress
  as rain clouds in time of drought.

## CHAPTER 36

### A Prayer for God's People<sup>§</sup>

<sup>1</sup> Come to our aid, O God of the universe,
<sup>2</sup>  and put all the nations in dread of
  you!
<sup>3</sup> Raise your hand against the foreign people,

---

*[35:1–26] Keeping the commandments of the law and
avoiding injustice constitute sacrifice pleasing and acceptable to God (vv. 1–5). Offerings also should be made to him,
cheerfully and generously; these he repays sevenfold (vv.
6–13). Extortion from widows and orphans is injustice, and
God will hear their cries (vv. 14–22a). Punishing the proud
and the merciless and coming to the aid of the distressed, he
requites everyone according to their deeds (vv. 22b–26).
†[35:3] **Fine flour**, together with oil and frankincense, was
a prescribed offering to God; cf. Lv 2:1–3.

‡[35:16] Cf. Lv 19:15; Dt 1:17. The divine impartiality is
paradoxical, for it is tilted toward the poor.
§[36:1–22] A prayer that God hasten the day for the gathering of the tribes of Israel, and Zion once more be filled with
the divine glory. All the earth will then know that the Lord is
the eternal God.

---

z. [34:25–27] Lv 19:13; Dt 24:14–15; Tb 4:14.   a. [34:30] Nm
19:11–12; Prv 26:11; 2 Pt 2:22.   b. [35:1–5] 1 Sm 15:22; Ps 51:18–
19; Is 1:11–18; Hos 6:6; Am 5:21–24.   c. [35:7] Ex 23:15; 34:20; Dt
16:16.   d. [35:10] Sir 7:31.   e. [35:11] Dt 14:22; 2 Cor 9:7.

f. [35:13] Prv 19:17; Mt 25:34–40.   g. [35:15] Sir 34:21–23;
Prv 15:8; 21:27.   h. [35:15] Dt 10:17; 2 Chr 19:7; Jb 34:19; Wis
6:7; Acts 10:34; Rom 2:11; Gal 2:6; 1 Pt 1:17.   i. [35:17–19] Ex
22:22.   j. [35:22] Lk 18:7.   k. [35:22] Is 42:13–16; 2 Pt 3:9.

that they may see your mighty deeds.
⁴ As you have used us to show them your
holiness,*
so now use them to show us your
glory.
⁵ Thus they will know, as we know,
that there is no God but you.

⁶ Give new signs and work new wonders;
⁷ show forth the splendor of your
right hand and arm.
⁸ Rouse your anger, pour out wrath;
⁹ humble the enemy, scatter the foe.ˡ
¹⁰ Hasten the ending, appoint the time,
and let people proclaim your mighty
deeds.
¹¹ Let raging fire consume the fugitive,
and your people's oppressors meet
destruction.
¹² Crush the heads of the hostile rulers
who say, "There is no one besides
me."

¹³ Gather all the tribes of Jacob,†
¹⁶ that they may inherit the land as in
days of old.
¹⁷ Show mercy to the people called by your
name:
Israel, whom you named your
firstborn.ᵐ
¹⁸ Take pity on your holy city:
Jerusalem, your dwelling place.ⁿ
¹⁹ Fill Zion with your majesty,
your temple with your glory.

²⁰ Give evidence of your deeds of old;
fulfill the prophecies spoken in your
name.
²¹ Reward those who have hoped in you,
and let your prophets be proved true.
²² Hear the prayer of your servants,
according to your good will toward
your people.
Thus all the ends of the earth will know
that you are the eternal God.

### Choice of Associates‡

²³ The throat can swallow any food,
yet some foods are more agreeable
than others.

²⁴ The palate tests delicacies put forward as
gifts,
so does a keen mind test deceitful
tidbits.
²⁵ One with a tortuous heart brings about
grief,
but an experienced person can turn
the tables on him.

²⁶ A woman will accept any man as
husband,
but one woman will be preferable to
another.
²⁷ A woman's beauty makes her husband's
face light up,
for it surpasses all else that delights
the eye.ᵒ
²⁸ And if, besides, her speech is soothing,
her husband's lot is beyond that of
mortal men.
²⁹ A wife is her husband's richest treasure,
a help like himself and a staunch
support.ᵖ
³⁰ A vineyard with no hedge will be overrun;
and a man with no wife becomes a
homeless wanderer.
³¹ Who will trust an armed band
that shifts from city to city?
Or a man who has no nest,
who lodges wherever night
overtakes him?�q

### CHAPTER 37
¹ Every friend declares friendship,
but there are friends who are friends
in name only.ʳ
² Is it not a sorrow unto death
when your other self becomes your
enemy?
³ "Alas, my companion! Why were you
created
to fill the earth with deceit?"
⁴ A harmful friend will look to your table,
but in time of trouble he stands
aloof.
⁵ A good friend will fight with you against
the foe,
and against your enemies he will
hold up your shield.
⁶ Do not forget your comrade during the
battle,
and do not neglect him when you
distribute your spoils.

---

*[36:4] **Show . . . holiness**: this cultic language is used to indicate God's liberation of his people; cf. Ez 20:41; 28:25.

†[36:13] This verse marks the end of a major dislocation in the Greek text of Sirach (which is followed here) at the head of chap. 33. The verse numbers 1–13 come from the placement of these verses in Greek. Verse 13 here is the first half of a bicolon, the matching half of which is numbered in the Greek 36:16b. Thus although the numbering for vv. 14–15 is not used, none of the text is missing.

‡[36:23–37:15] In the choice of wife, friend, or associate, experience is a discerner of character (36:23–26). Beauty and soothing speech make a woman desirable as wife (36:27–28).

l. [36:9] Ps 79:6; Jer 10:25.   m. [36:17] Ex 4:22.   n. [36:18] 2 Chr 6:41; Ps 132:8, 14; Is 2:1–3; Mi 4:1–3.

---

The good wife becomes her husband's richest treasure, his help in establishing his household (36:29–31). Good friends fight for comrades and share the spoils with them (37:5–6); false friends deceive and abandon in time of need (37:1–4). A true counselor and associate should be sought among those who keep the commandments, not among those who break them and seek their own advantage (37:7–12). In all things one should pray to God for light and follow conscience (37:13–15).

---

o. [36:26–28] Sir 26:13–18; Prv 12:4; 18:22; 19:14.   p. [36:29] Gn 2:18.   q. [36:31] Prv 27:8.   r. [37:1] Sir 6:7–17.

<sup>7</sup> Every counselor points out a way,
    but some counsel ways of their own.
<sup>8</sup> Watch out when one offers advice;
    find out first of all what he wants.
  For he also may be thinking of himself—
    Why should the opportunity fall to
      him?
<sup>9</sup> He may tell you how good your way will
      be,
    and then stand by to see you
      impoverished.
<sup>10</sup> Seek no advice from your father-in-law,
    and from one who is envious of you,
      keep your intentions hidden.
<sup>11</sup> Seek no advice from a woman about her
      rival,
    from a coward about war,
    from a merchant about business,
    from a buyer about value,
    from a miser about generosity,
    from a cruel person about
      well-being,
    from a worthless worker about his
      work,
    from a seasonal laborer about the
      harvest,
    from an idle slave about a great
      task—
    pay no attention to any advice they
      give.

<sup>12</sup> Instead, associate with a religious person,
    who you know keeps the
      commandments;
  Who is like-minded with yourself
    and will grieve for you if you fall.
<sup>13</sup> Then, too, heed your own heart's counsel;
    for there is nothing you can depend
      on more.
<sup>14</sup> The heart can reveal your situation
    better than seven sentinels on a
      tower.
<sup>15</sup> Then with all this, pray to God
    to make your steps firm in the true
      path.

#### Wisdom and Temperance

<sup>16</sup> A word is the source of every deed;*
    a thought, of every act.ˢ
<sup>17</sup> The root of all conduct is the heart;
<sup>18</sup>    four branches it shoots forth:
  Good and evil, death and life,
    and their absolute mistress is the
      tongue.ᵗ
<sup>19</sup> One may be wise and benefit many,
    yet appear foolish to himself.

<sup>20</sup> One may be wise, but if his words are
      rejected,
    he will be deprived of all enjoyment.†
<sup>22</sup> When one is wise to his own advantage,
    the fruits of knowledge are seen in
      his own person.
<sup>23</sup> When one is wise to the advantage of
      people,
    the fruits of knowledge are lasting.ᵘ
<sup>24</sup> One wise for himself has full enjoyment,
    and all who see him praise him.
<sup>25</sup> The days of one's life are numbered,
    but the life of Israel, days without
      number.
<sup>26</sup> One wise among the people wins a
      heritage of glory,
    and his name lives on and on.ᵛ

<sup>27</sup> My son, while you are well, govern your
      appetite,‡
    and see that you do not allow it what
      is bad for you.
<sup>28</sup> For not everything is good for everyone,
    nor is everything suited to every
      taste.ʷ
<sup>29</sup> Do not go to excess with any enjoyment,ˣ
    neither become a glutton for choice
      foods;
<sup>30</sup> For sickness comes with overeating,
    and gluttony brings on nausea.
<sup>31</sup> Through lack of self-control many have
      died,
    but the abstemious one prolongs life.

### CHAPTER 38

#### Sickness and Death

<sup>1</sup> Make friends with the doctor, for he is
      essential to you;§
    God has also established him in his
      profession.
<sup>2</sup> From God the doctor has wisdom,
    and from the king he receives
      sustenance.
<sup>3</sup> Knowledge makes the doctor distinguished,
    and gives access to those in authority.
<sup>4</sup> God makes the earth yield healing herbs
    which the prudent should not
      neglect;

---

*[37:16–26] Thoughts determine action. Wisdom is the source of good and life; folly, of evil and death (vv. 16–18). If the fruits of a person's wisdom benefit himself, he may be praised in his own lifetime; if they benefit others, the praise endures after him, in their lives (vv. 19–26).

s. [37:16] Sir 32:19.    t. [37:18] Prv 18:21.

†[37:20] Verse 21 appears only in Greek, but not in the Hebrew, which is the basis for the translation here.
‡[37:27–31] Temperance and self-control should govern appetite for food, which is intended not to destroy but to preserve life.
§[38:1–15] The profession of medicine comes from God, who makes the earth yield healing herbs and gives the physician knowledge of their power (vv. 1–8). In illness the sick should cleanse their soul from sin and petition God for help through an offering of sacrifice; the physician, too, does well to invoke God that he may understand the illness and apply the proper remedy (vv. 9–14). The sinner, in contrast, defies both his Maker and the doctor (v. 15).

u. [37:23] Sir 39:10–11.    v. [37:26] Sir 39:9; 44:13–16.    w. [37:28] 1 Cor 6:12; 10:23.    x. [37:29–31] Sir 31:13, 16–21.

⁵ Was not the water sweetened by a twig,
    so that all might learn his power?ʸ
⁶ He endows people with knowledge,
    to glory in his mighty works,
⁷ Through which the doctor eases pain,
⁸     and the druggist prepares his
        medicines.
    Thus God's work continues without cease
        in its efficacy on the surface of the
        earth.

⁹ My son, when you are ill, do not delay,
    but pray to God, for it is he who heals.ᶻ
¹⁰ Flee wickedness and purify your hands;
    cleanse your heart of every sin.
¹¹ Offer your sweet-smelling oblation and
       memorial,
    a generous offering according to
       your means.ᵃ
¹² Then give the doctor his place
    lest he leave; you need him too,
¹³ For there are times when recovery is in
    his hands.
¹⁴     He too prays to God
    That his diagnosis may be correct
       and his treatment bring about a cure.
¹⁵ Whoever is a sinner before his Maker
    will be defiant toward the doctor.

¹⁶ My son, shed tears for one who is dead*
    with wailing and bitter lament;
    As is only proper, prepare the body,
       and do not absent yourself from the
       burial.
¹⁷ Weeping bitterly, mourning fully,
    pay your tribute of sorrow, as
       deserved:
    A day or two, to prevent gossip;
       then compose yourself after your grief.
¹⁸ For grief can bring on death,
    and heartache can sap one's strength.ᵇ
¹⁹ When a person is carried away, sorrow is
    over;
    and the life of the poor one is
       grievous to the heart.
²⁰ Do not turn your thoughts to him again;
    cease to recall him; think rather of
       the end.ᶜ
²¹ Do not recall him, for there is no hope of
    his return;
    you do him no good, and you harm
       yourself.ᵈ
²² Remember that his fate will also be yours;
    for him it was yesterday, for you
       today.ᵉ

²³ With the dead at rest, let memory cease;
    be consoled, once the spirit has gone.

## Vocations of the Skilled Worker
## and the Scribe†

²⁴ The scribe's wisdom increases wisdom;
    whoever is free from toil can
       become wise.
²⁵ How can one become learned who guides
    the plow,
    and thrills in wielding the goad like
       a lance,
    Who guides the ox and urges on the
       bullock,
    and whose every concern is for cattle?
²⁶ His concern is to plow furrows,
    and he is careful to fatten the
       livestock.

²⁷ So with every engraver and designer
    who, laboring night and day,
    Fashions carved seals,
    and whose concern is to vary the
       pattern.
    His determination is to produce a lifelike
       impression,
    and he is careful to finish the work.

²⁸ So too the smith sitting by the anvil,
    intent on the iron he forges.
    The flame from the fire sears his flesh,
       yet he toils away in the furnace heat.
    The clang of the hammer deafens his ears;
       his eyes are on the object he is
       shaping.
    His determination is to finish the work,
       and he is careful to perfect it in detail.

²⁹ So also the potter sitting at his labor,
    revolving the wheel with his feet.
    He is always concerned for his products,
       and turns them out in quantity.
³⁰ With his hands he molds the clay,
    and with his feet softens it.
    His determination is to complete the
       glazing,
    and he is careful to fire the kiln.

³¹ All these are skilled with their hands,
    each one an expert at his own work;
³² Without them no city could be lived in,
    and wherever they stay, they do not
       go hungry.

---

*[38:16–23] A period of mourning for the deceased and care for their burial are proper (vv. 16–17). But grief should not be excessive, for it cannot help the dead, who will not return, and may do harm to the living. The mourner should be realistic (vv. 18–23).

†[38:24–39:11] Ben Sira has a balanced view of the various vocations of skilled laborers—the farmer, engraver, smith and potter—but the profession of scribe is more excellent (38:24–34). He studies and meditates on the law of the Most High, seeks him in prayer of thanksgiving, petition and repentance for sin (39:1, 5, 7), explores the wisdom of the past and present, travels abroad to observe the conduct of many peoples, and attends rulers and great men. Through the spirit of understanding granted by God, he will show forth his wisdom to the glory of God's law, gaining renown for generations to come (39:2–4, 6–11).

y. [38:5] Ex 15:25. z. [38:9] Is 38:1–3. a. [38:11] Lv 2:1–3. b. [38:18] Prv 12:25; 15:13; 17:22. c. [38:20] Sir 7:36; 18:24; 30:21. d. [38:21] 2 Sm 12:23; Wis 2:1. e. [38:22] Jas 4:13–15.

But they are not sought out for the
	council of the people,
<sup>33</sup>	nor are they prominent in the
		assembly.
They do not sit on the judge's bench,
	nor can they understand law and
		justice.
They cannot expound discipline or
		judgment,
	nor are they found among the rulers.
<sup>34</sup> Yet they maintain the fabric of the world,
	and their concern is for exercise of
		their skill.

## CHAPTER 39

How different the person who devotes
		himself
	to the study of the law of the Most
		High!
<sup>1</sup> He explores the wisdom of all the ancients
	and is occupied with the prophecies;
<sup>2</sup> He preserves the discourses of the famous,
	and goes to the heart of involved
		sayings;
<sup>3</sup> He seeks out the hidden meaning of
		proverbs,
	and is busied with the enigmas
		found in parables.

<sup>4</sup> He is in attendance on the great,
	and appears before rulers.
He travels among the peoples of foreign
		lands
	to test what is good and evil among
		people.
<sup>5</sup> His care is to rise early
	to seek the Lord his Maker,
	to petition the Most High,
To open his mouth in prayer,
	to ask pardon for his sins.

<sup>6</sup> If it pleases the Lord Almighty,
	he will be filled with the spirit of
		understanding;
He will pour forth his words of wisdom
	and in prayer give praise to the Lord.
<sup>7</sup> He will direct his knowledge and his
		counsel,
	as he meditates upon God's mysteries.
<sup>8</sup> He will show the wisdom of what he has
		learned
	and glory in the Law of the Lord's
		covenant.

<sup>9</sup> Many will praise his understanding;
	his name can never be blotted out;
Unfading will be his memory,
	through all generations his name
		will live;<sup>f</sup>
<sup>10</sup> Peoples will speak of his wisdom,
	and the assembly will declare his
		praise.

<sup>11</sup> While he lives he is one out of a thousand,
	and when he dies he leaves a good
		name.

### Praise of God the Creator*

<sup>12</sup> Once more I will set forth my theme
	to shine like the moon in its fullness!
<sup>13</sup> Listen to me, my faithful children: open
		up your petals,
	like roses planted near running
		waters;
<sup>14</sup> Send up the sweet odor of incense,
	break forth in blossoms like the lily.
Raise your voices in a chorus of praise;
	bless the Lord for all his works!
<sup>15</sup> Proclaim the greatness of his name,
	loudly sing his praises,
With music on the harp and all stringed
		instruments;
	sing out with joy as you proclaim:

<sup>16</sup> The works of God are all of them good;
	he supplies for every need in its own
		time.<sup>g</sup>
<sup>17</sup> At his word the waters become still as in a
		flask;
	he had but to speak and the
		reservoirs were made.<sup>h</sup>
<sup>18</sup> He has but to command and his will is
		done;
	nothing can limit his saving action.
<sup>19</sup> The works of all humankind are present
		to him;
	nothing is hidden from his eyes.<sup>i</sup>
<sup>20</sup> His gaze spans all the ages:
	is there any limit to his saving action?
To him, nothing is small or insignificant,
	and nothing too wonderful or hard
		for him.
<sup>21</sup> No cause then to say: "What is the
		purpose of this?"
	Everything is chosen to satisfy a
		need.

<sup>22</sup> His blessing overflows like the Nile;
	like the Euphrates it enriches the
		surface of the earth.
<sup>23</sup> Even so, his wrath dispossesses the nations
	and turns fertile land into a salt
		marsh.<sup>j</sup>

---

*[39:12–35] Ben Sira invites his disciples to join him in joyfully proclaiming his favorite theme: The works of God are all good; God supplies for every need in its own time (vv. 12–16, 32–35). The sage describes God's omniscience, supreme power and wisdom, whereby all created things, good in themselves, are ever present to him, obey him, and fulfill their intended purpose (vv. 17–21), bringing blessing to the virtuous, but evil and punishment to the wicked who misuse them (vv. 22–31). Cf. similar hymns of praise, 36:1–22; 42:15–43:33.

g. [39:16] Sir 39:33; Gn 1:29–31; Eccl 3:11. h. [39:17] Gn 1:6–10; Ex 14:21–22; Jos 3:15–16. i. [39:19] Sir 15:18–19; 42:18–20. j. [39:23] Gn 13:10; 19:24–28; Dt 29:22; Jos 1:2–6; Ps 107:34; Wis 10:7.

f. [39:9] Sir 37:26; 44:14.

24 For the virtuous his paths are level,
  to the haughty they are clogged with
    stones.
25 Good things for the good he provided
    from the beginning,
  but for the wicked good things and
    bad.
26 Chief of all needs for human life
    are water and fire, iron and salt,
  The heart of the wheat, milk and honey,
    the blood of the grape, and oil, and
    clothing.^k
27 For the good all these are good,
  but for the wicked they turn out evil.

28 There are stormwinds created to punish;
  in their fury they can dislodge
    mountains.
  In a time of destruction they hurl their
    force
  and calm the anger of their Maker.
29 Fire and hail, famine and disease:
  these too were created for
    punishment.
30 Ravenous beasts, scorpions, vipers,
  and the avenging sword to
    exterminate the wicked:
  All these were created to meet a need,
  and are kept in his storehouse for
    the proper time.
31 When he commands them, they rejoice,
  in their assigned tasks they do not
    disobey his command.

32 That is why from the first I took my stand,
  and wrote down as my theme:
33 The works of God are all of them good;
  he supplies for every need in its own
    time.^l
34 There is no cause then to say: "This is not
    as good as that";
  for each shows its worth at the
    proper time.
35 So now with full heart and voice proclaim
  and bless his name!

## CHAPTER 40

### Joys and Miseries of Life

1 A great anxiety has God allotted,*
  and a heavy yoke, to the children of
    Adam,^m
  From the day they leave their mother's
    womb

until the day they return to the
    mother of all the living.†
2 Troubled thoughts and fear of heart are
    theirs
  and anxious foreboding until death.
3 Whether one sits on a lofty throne
  or grovels in dust and ashes,
4 Whether one wears a splendid crown
  or is clothed in the coarsest of
    garments—
5 There is wrath and envy, trouble and
    dread,
  terror of death, fury and strife.
  Even when one lies on his bed to rest,
  his cares disturb his sleep at night.
6 So short is his rest it seems like none,
  till in his dreams he struggles as he
    did by day,
  Troubled by the visions of his mind,
  like a fugitive fleeing from the
    pursuer.
7 As he reaches safety, he wakes up,
  astonished that there was nothing
    to fear.
8 To all flesh, human being and beast,
  but for sinners seven times more,
9 Come plague and bloodshed, fiery heat
    and drought,
  plunder and ruin, famine and death.^n
10 For the wicked evil was created,
  and because of them destruction
    hastens.

11 All that is of earth returns to earth,
  and what is from above returns
    above.‡
12 All that comes from bribes or injustice
    will be wiped out,
  but loyalty remains forever.
13 Wealth from injustice is like a flooding
    wadi,
  like a mighty stream with lightning
    and thunder,
14 Which, in its rising, rolls along the stones,
  but suddenly, once and for all,
    comes to an end.^o
15 The offshoot of violence will not flourish,
  for the root of the godless is on
    sheer rock.
16 They are like reeds on riverbanks,
  withered before all other plants;
17 But goodness, like eternity, will never be
    cut off,
  and righteousness endures forever.

---

*[40:1–17] The former idyllic description of the universe is contrasted with the picture of the evils afflicting humanity. Every person, high or low, is burdened from birth to death with fears, anxieties, and troubles, by day and often by night, the time appointed for rest (vv. 1–7). For sinners, the suffering is much greater (vv. 8–10). What they gained by violence and injustice is quickly destroyed; but righteousness will prevail (vv. 14–17).

k. [39:26] Sir 29:21.  l. [39:33] Sir 39:16; Gn 1:29–31; Eccl 3:11.
m. [40:1] Gn 3:17–19; Jb 7:1; 14:1–2; Eccl 2:23.

†[40:1] **Mother of all the living**: the earth from which human beings were taken. Cf. Gn 2:7; 3:19–20; Jb 1:21; Ps 139:15.
  ‡[40:11] **All that is of earth . . . returns above**: a reference to bodily mortality and to the divine origin of life. Cf. 41:10; Gn 2:7; 3:19; Jb 34:14–15; Ps 104:29–30; 146:4; Eccl 12:7. The Greek and the Latin render the second half of the verse: "all waters shall return to the sea."

n. [40:9] Sir 39:28–31.  o. [40:14] Sir 23:25–26; Wis 4:3–6.

<sup>18</sup> Wealth or wages can make life sweet,*
  but better than either, finding a
    treasure.
<sup>19</sup> A child or a city will preserve one's name,
  but better than either, finding
    wisdom.
Cattle and orchards make a person
    flourish;
  but better than either, a devoted
    wife.<sup>p</sup>
<sup>20</sup> Wine and strong drink delight the soul,
  but better than either, love of
    friends.<sup>q</sup>
<sup>21</sup> Flute and harp offer sweet melody,
  but better than either, a pure tongue.
<sup>22</sup> Grace and beauty delight the eye,
  but better than either, the produce
    of the field.
<sup>23</sup> A friend and a neighbor are timely guides,
  but better than either, a sensible
    wife.
<sup>24</sup> Relatives and helpers for times of stress;
  but better than either, charity that
    rescues.
<sup>25</sup> Gold and silver make one's way secure,
  but better than either, sound
    judgment.
<sup>26</sup> Wealth and vigor make the heart exult,
  but better than either, fear of God.
In the fear of the Lord there is no want;
  whoever has it need seek no other
    support.
<sup>27</sup> The fear of God is a paradise of blessings;
  its canopy is over all that is glorious.<sup>r</sup>

<sup>28</sup> My son, do not live the life of a beggar;<sup>†</sup>
  better to die than to beg.
<sup>29</sup> When one has to look to a stranger's table,
  life is not worth living.
The delicacies offered bring revulsion of
    spirit,
  and to the intelligent, inward
    torture.<sup>s</sup>
<sup>30</sup> In the mouth of the shameless begging is
    sweet,
  but within him it burns like fire.

## CHAPTER 41

<sup>1</sup> O death! How bitter is the thought of you<sup>‡</sup>
  for the one at peace in his home,

For the one who is serene and always
    successful,
  who can still enjoy life's pleasures.
<sup>2</sup> O death! How welcome is your sentence
  to the weak, failing in strength,
Stumbling and tripping on everything,
  with sight gone and hope lost.<sup>t</sup>
<sup>3</sup> Do not fear death's decree for you;
  remember, it embraces those before
    you and those to come.<sup>u</sup>
<sup>4</sup> This decree for all flesh is from God;
  why then should you reject a law of
    the Most High?
Whether one has lived a thousand years, a
    hundred, or ten,
  in Sheol there are no arguments
    about life.

<sup>5</sup> The children of sinners are a reprobate line,<sup>v</sup>
  and witless offspring are in the
    homes of the wicked.
<sup>6</sup> The inheritance of children of sinners will
    perish,
  and on their offspring will be
    perpetual disgrace.
<sup>7</sup> Children curse their wicked father,
  for they suffer disgrace because of
    him.
<sup>8</sup> Woe to you, O wicked people,
  who forsake the Law of the Most
    High.
<sup>9</sup> If you have children, calamity will be theirs;
  and if you beget them, it will be only
    for groaning.
When you stumble, there is lasting joy;
  and when you die, you become a
    curse.
<sup>10</sup> All that is nought returns to nought,
  so too the godless—from void to void.<sup>w</sup>

<sup>11</sup> The human body is a fleeting thing,
  but a virtuous name will never be
    annihilated.<sup>x</sup>
<sup>12</sup> Have respect for your name, for it will
    stand by you
  more than thousands of precious
    treasures.<sup>y</sup>
<sup>13</sup> The good things of life last a number of
    days,
  but a good name, for days without
    number.

### True and False Shame<sup>§</sup>

<sup>14b</sup> Hidden wisdom and concealed treasure,
  of what value is either?

---

*[40:18–27] Of the many treasures making life sweet, such
as children, friends, music, vigor, the best are called true married love, wisdom, and above all, fear of God; cf. 25:6–11.

†[40:28–30] Among the Jews, begging was considered
degrading to human dignity; it was agreeable only to the
shameless, who had lost their sense of honor. Cf. 29:22–23.

‡[41:1–13] Whether death seems bitter to one who enjoys
peace, success, and pleasure, or welcome to one who is weak
and in despair, it comes to all and must be accepted as the will
of God (vv. 1–4). The human body passes away (v. 11). Sinners
as well as their offspring pass away as if they had never been (vv.
5–10). Only the good name of the virtuous endures (vv. 11–13).

§[41:14–42:8] Ben Sira illustrates the subject of true and
false shame with numerous and detailed examples of wrongdoing (41:14–22) and virtue (42:1–8), following the norm of
the commandments.

---

p. [40:19] Prv 18:22; 19:14.   q. [40:20] Ps 104:15.   r. [40:27] Is
4:5–6.   s. [40:29] Sir 29:24.

t. [41:2] Sir 30:17.   u. [41:3] Sir 38:20–22.   v. [41:5–10] Sir 3:9–11;
Wis 3:16–19.   w. [41:10] Sir 40:11; Wis 4:19.   x. [41:11] Prv
10:7.   y. [41:12] Prv 22:1; Eccl 7:1.

15 Better is the person who hides his folly
     than the one who hides his wisdom.
14a My children, listen to instruction about
     shame;
16a     judge of disgrace according to my
     rules,
16b Not every kind of shame is shameful,
     nor is every kind of disgrace to be
     recognized.
17 Before father and mother be ashamed of
     immorality,
     before prince and ruler, of
     falsehood;
18 Before master and mistress, of deceit;
     before the public assembly, of crime;
Before associate and friend, of disloyalty,
19     and in the place where you settle, of
     theft.
Be ashamed of breaking an oath or a
     covenant,
     and of stretching your elbow at
     dinner;
Of refusing to give when asked,
21     of rebuffing your own relatives;
Of defrauding another of his appointed
     share,
20a    of failing to return a greeting;
21c Of gazing at a man's wife,
20b    of entertaining thoughts about
     another woman;z
22 Of trifling with a servant girl you have,
     of violating her bed;
Of using harsh words with friends,
     of following up your gifts with
     insults;a

## CHAPTER 42

1 Of repeating what you hear,
     of betraying any secret.b
Be ashamed of the right things,
     and you will find favor in the sight
     of all.

But of these things do not be ashamed,
     lest you sin to save face:c
2 Of the Law of the Most High and his
     precepts,
     or of justice that acquits the
     ungodly;
3 Of sharing the expenses of a business or a
     journey,
     of dividing an inheritance or
     property;
4 Of accuracy of scales and balances,
     of tested measures and weights;d
Of acquiring much or little,
5     of bargaining in dealing with a
     merchant;

Of constant training of children,
     of beating the sides of a wicked
     servant;e
6 Of a seal to keep a foolish wife at home,
     of a key where there are many hands;
7 Of numbering every deposit,
     of recording all that is taken in and
     given out;
8 Of chastisement for the silly and the
     foolish,
     for the aged and infirm answering
     for wanton conduct.
Thus you will be truly refined
     and recognized by all as discreet.

## A Father's Care for His Daughter*

9 A daughter is a treasure that keeps her
     father wakeful,
     and worry over her drives away
     sleep;f
Lest in her youth she remain unmarried,
     or when she is married, lest she be
     childless;
10 While unmarried, lest she be defiled,
     or in her husband's house, lest she
     prove unfaithful;
Lest she become pregnant in her father's
     house,
     or be sterile in that of her husband.
11 My son, keep a close watch on your
     daughter,
     lest she make you a laughingstock
     for your enemies,
A byword in the city and the assembly of
     the people,
     an object of derision in public
     gatherings.g
See that there is no lattice in her room,
     or spot that overlooks the
     approaches to the house.
12 Do not let her reveal her beauty to any
     male,h
     or spend her time with married
     women;
13 For just as moths come from garments,
     so a woman's wickedness comes
     from a woman.
14 Better a man's harshness than a woman's
     indulgence,
     a frightened daughter than any
     disgrace.

---

*[42:9–14] Ben Sira considers a daughter to be a source of anxiety to her father, lest she fail to marry, or be defiled, or lest, marrying, she be childless, prove unfaithful, or find herself sterile (vv. 9–10). He is advised to keep a close watch on her and on her companions, lest he suffer on her account among the people (vv. 11–12). The exhortations, which take into account only a father's concern, are quite unflattering to young women. The concluding statements (vv. 13–14) show the limitations of Ben Sira's perspective in the male-oriented society of his day.

---

z. [41:20] Sir 9:8; Mt 5:28.  a. [41:22] Sir 18:15; 20:14.  b. [42:1] Sir 27:16.  c. [42:1] Prv 24:23; Jas 2:1.  d. [42:4] Lv 19:35; Prv 11:1; 16:11; 20:10.

e. [42:5] Sir 30:1–13; 33:25–33.  f. [42:9] Sir 7:24–25.  g. [42:11] Dt 22:20–21.  h. [42:12–13] Sir 9:1–9.

### The Works of God in Nature*

<sup>15</sup> Now will I recall God's works;
　　what I have seen, I will describe.
By the Lord's word his works were
　　　brought into being;
　　he accepts the one who does his
　　　will.*ⁱ*

<sup>16</sup> As the shining sun is clear to all,
　　so the glory of the Lord fills all his
　　　works;

<sup>17</sup> Yet even God's holy ones must fail
　　in recounting the wonders of the
　　　Lord,
Though God has given his hosts the
　　　strength
　　to stand firm before his glory.

<sup>18</sup> He searches out the abyss and penetrates
　　　the heart;
　　their secrets he understands.
For the Most High possesses all
　　　knowledge,
　　and sees from of old the things that
　　　are to come.

<sup>19</sup> He makes known the past and the future,
　　and reveals the deepest secrets.

<sup>20</sup> He lacks no understanding;
　　no single thing escapes him.*ʲ*

<sup>21</sup> He regulates the mighty deeds of his
　　　wisdom;
　　he is from all eternity one and the
　　　same,
With nothing added, nothing taken away;
　　no need of a counselor for him!*ᵏ*

<sup>22</sup> How beautiful are all his works,
　　delightful to gaze upon and a joy to
　　　behold!

<sup>23</sup> Everything lives and abides forever;
　　and to meet each need all things are
　　　preserved.

<sup>24</sup> All of them differ, one from another,
　　yet none of them has he made in
　　　vain;

<sup>25</sup> For each in turn, as it comes, is good;
　　can one ever see enough of their
　　　splendor?*ˡ*

## CHAPTER 43

<sup>1</sup> The beauty of the celestial height and the
　　　pure firmament,*ᵐ*
　　heaven itself manifests its glory.

<sup>2</sup> The sun at its rising shines at its fullest,
　　a wonderful instrument, the work of
　　the Most High!

<sup>3</sup> At noon it scorches the earth,
　　and who can bear its fiery heat?

<sup>4</sup> Like a blazing furnace of solid metal,
　　the sun's rays set the mountains
　　　aflame;
Its fiery tongue consumes the world;
　　the eyes are burned by its fire.

<sup>5</sup> Great indeed is the Lord who made it,
　　at whose orders it urges on its
　　　steeds.

<sup>6</sup> It is the moon that marks the changing
　　　seasons,
　　governing the times, their lasting
　　　sign.*ⁿ*

<sup>7</sup> By it we know the sacred seasons and
　　　pilgrimage feasts,
　　a light which wanes in its course:

<sup>8</sup> The new moon like its name† renews
　　　itself;
　　how wondrous it is when it changes:
A military signal for the waterskins on
　　　high,
　　it paves the firmament with its
　　　brilliance,

<sup>9</sup> The beauty of the heavens and the glory of
　　　the stars,
　　a shining ornament in the heights
　　　of God.*ᵒ*

<sup>10</sup> By the Lord's command the moon keeps
　　　its appointed place,
　　and does not fade as the stars keep
　　　watch.

<sup>11</sup> Behold the rainbow! Then bless its Maker,
　　for majestic indeed is its splendor;*ᵖ*

<sup>12</sup> It spans the heavens with its glory,
　　the hand of God has stretched it out
　　　in power.

<sup>13</sup> His rebuke marks out the path for the hail,
　　and makes the flashes of his
　　　judgment shine forth.

<sup>14</sup> For his own purposes he opens the
　　　storehouse
　　and makes the rain clouds fly like
　　　vultures.

<sup>15</sup> His might gives the clouds their strength,
　　and breaks off the hailstones.

<sup>16</sup> The thunder of his voice makes the earth
　　　writhe;
　　by his power he shakes the
　　　mountains.

<sup>17</sup> A word from him drives on the south wind,
　　whirlwind, hurricane, and
　　　stormwind.
He makes the snow fly like birds;
　　it settles down like swarms of
　　　locusts.

---

*[42:15–43:33] These verses comprise another hymn; cf. 16:24–18:14. In them Ben Sira contemplates God's power, beauty, and goodness as manifested in the mighty work of creating and preserving the universe (42:15–17, 22–25; 43:1–26), his omniscience (42:18–20), perfect wisdom and eternity (42:21). The conclusion is a fervent hymn of praise (43:27–31).

i. [42:15] Ps 77:12–13.　j. [42:20] Sir 39:19; Wis 1:6–9.　k. [42:21] Wis 9:13; Is 40:13; Rom 11:34; 1 Cor 2:11.　l. [42:25] Sir 33:15.　m. [43:1–12] Ps 19:2–5.

†[43:8] **Like its name:** there is a play in the Hebrew text on the words for moon and renewal. **Waterskins:** clouds as source of rain.

n. [43:6] Lv 23:5; Nm 28:11–14; Ps 81:4–6.　o. [43:9] Ps 8:4.　p. [43:11] Gn 9:13.

<sup>18</sup> Its shining whiteness blinds the eyes,
    the mind marvels at its steady fall.
<sup>19</sup> He scatters frost like salt;
    it shines like blossoms on the
        thornbush.
<sup>20</sup> He sends cold northern blasts
    that harden the ponds like solid
        ground,
Spreads a crust over every body of water,
    and clothes each pool with a coat of
        armor.
<sup>21</sup> When mountain growth is scorched by
        heat,
    and flowering plains as by fire,
<sup>22</sup> The dripping clouds restore them all,
    and the scattered dew enriches the
        parched land.
<sup>23</sup> His is the plan that calms the deep,
    and plants the islands in the sea.
<sup>24</sup> Those who go down to the sea recount its
        extent,
    and when we hear them we are
        thunderstruck;<sup>q</sup>
<sup>25</sup> In it are his creatures, stupendous, amazing,
    all kinds of life, and the monsters of
        the deep.
<sup>26</sup> For him each messenger succeeds,
    and at his bidding accomplishes his
        will.<sup>r</sup>

<sup>27</sup> More than this we need not add;
    let the last word be, he is the all!<sup>*</sup>
<sup>28</sup> Let us praise him the more, since we
        cannot fathom him,
    for greater is he than all his works;
<sup>29</sup> Awesome indeed is the Lord,
    and wonderful his power.
<sup>30</sup> Lift up your voices to glorify the Lord
    as much as you can, for there is still
        more.
Extol him with renewed strength,
    do not grow weary, for you cannot
        fathom him.
<sup>31</sup> For who has seen him and can describe
        him?
Who can praise him as he is?<sup>s</sup>
<sup>32</sup> Beyond these, many things lie hidden;
    only a few of his works have I seen.
<sup>33</sup> It is the Lord who has made all things;
    to those who fear him he gives
        wisdom.<sup>t</sup>

## CHAPTER 44

### Praise of Israel's Great Ancestors<sup>†</sup>

<sup>1</sup> I will now praise the godly,
    our ancestors, in their own time,<sup>‡</sup>
<sup>2</sup> The abounding glory of the Most High's
        portion,
    his own part, since the days of old.<sup>u</sup>
<sup>3</sup> Subduers of the land in kingly fashion,
    renowned for their might,
Counselors in their prudence,
    seers of all things in prophecy,<sup>v</sup>
<sup>4</sup> Resolute princes of the flock,
    lawgivers and their rules,
Sages skilled in composition,
    authors of sharp proverbs,
<sup>5</sup> Composers of melodious psalms,
    writers of lyric poems;
<sup>6</sup> Stalwart, solidly established,
    at peace in their own estates—
<sup>7</sup> All these were glorious in their time,
    illustrious in their day.
<sup>8</sup> Some of them left behind a name
    so that people recount their praises.
<sup>9</sup> Of others no memory remains,
    for when they perished, they
        perished,
As if they had never lived,
    they and their children after them.
<sup>10</sup> Yet these also were godly;
    their virtues have not been
        forgotten.
<sup>11</sup> Their wealth remains in their families,
    their heritage with their
        descendants.
<sup>12</sup> Through God's covenant their family
        endures,
    and their offspring for their sake.
<sup>13</sup> And for all time their progeny will
        endure,
    their glory will never be blotted out;
<sup>14</sup> Their bodies are buried in peace,
    but their name lives on and on.<sup>w</sup>
<sup>15</sup> At gatherings their wisdom is retold,
    and the assembly proclaims their
        praises.

### The Early Ancestors

<sup>16</sup> [Enoch<sup>§</sup> walked with the Lord and was
    taken,<sup>x</sup>

---

through the history of God's people as seen in the lives of their ancestors, prophets, priests, and rulers. The example of these great people, whose virtues are recalled here, constitutes a high point of Ben Sira's teaching.

‡[44:1–15] The reader is here introduced to those people of Israel, later mentioned by name, who through various achievements and beneficial social activities have acquired great renown (vv. 1–8, 14–15); and also to those who, though forgotten, endure through the fruit of their virtues and through their families because of God's covenant with them (vv. 9–15).

§[44:16] **Enoch**: because of his friendship with God and his unusual disappearance from the earth, this prophet's renown was great among the chosen people, particularly in the two centuries just before the coming of Christ; cf. Gn 5:21–24; Heb 11:5. The present verse is an expansion of the original text; cf. 49:14.

---

*[43:27] **The all**: the perfections reflected in creation are found in a transcendent way in God, who alone is their source.
†[44:1–50:24] As in the previous section God's glory shone forth in the works of nature, so in these chapters it is revealed

q. [43:24–25] Ps 104:25–26.    r. [43:26] Ps 33:6.    s. [43:31] Ps 106:2.
t. [43:33] Sir 1:10.

u. [44:2] Dt 32:8–9.    v. [44:3] Sir 39:1.    w. [44:14] Wis 3:2–3.
x. [44:16] Sir 49:14; Gn 5:18–24; Heb 11:5.

that succeeding generations might
      learn by his example.]

[17] NOAH, found just and perfect,
      renewed the race in the time of
            devastation.[y]
Because of his worth there were survivors,
      and with a sign to him the deluge
            ended.

[18] A lasting covenant was made with him,
      that never again would all flesh be
            destroyed.

[19] ABRAHAM, father of many peoples,
      kept his glory without stain:[z]

[20] He observed the Most High's command,
      and entered into a covenant with
            him;
In his own flesh he incised the ordinance,[*]
      and when tested was found loyal.[a]

[21] For this reason, God promised him with
      an oath
      to bless the nations through his
            descendants,
To make him numerous as grains of dust,
      and to exalt his posterity like the
            stars,
Giving them an inheritance from sea to
      sea,
      and from the River[†] to the ends of
            the earth.

[22] For ISAAC, too, he renewed the same
      promise
      because of Abraham, his father.
The covenant with all his forebears was
      confirmed,
[23]      and the blessing rested upon the
            head of ISRAEL.[b]
God acknowledged him as the firstborn,
      and gave him his inheritance.
He fixed the boundaries for his tribes
      and their division into twelve.


## CHAPTER 45

### Praise of Moses, Aaron, and Phinehas

[1] From him came the man[‡]
      who would win the favor of all the
            living:[c]
Dear to God and human beings,
      MOSES, whose memory is a blessing.

[2] God made him like the angels in honor,
      and strengthened him with fearful
            powers.[d]

[3] At his words God performed signs
      and sustained him in the king's
            presence.
He gave him the commandments for his
      people,
      and revealed to him his glory.[e]

[4] Because of his trustworthiness and
      meekness
      God selected him from all flesh;[f]

[5] He let him hear his voice,
      and led him into the cloud,
Where he handed over the
      commandments,
      the law of life and understanding,[§]
That he might teach his precepts to Jacob,
      his judgments and decrees to Israel.

[6] He also raised up, like Moses in holiness,[¶]
      his brother AARON, of the tribe of Levi.[g]

[7] He made his office perpetual
      and bestowed on him priesthood for
            his people;
He established him in honor
      and crowned him with lofty majesty.

[8] He clothed him in splendid garments,
      and adorned him with glorious
            vestments:
Breeches, tunic, and robe
[9]      with pomegranates at the hem
And a rustle of bells round about,
      whose pleasing sound at each step
Would make him heard within the
            sanctuary,
      a reminder for the people;

[10] The sacred vestments of gold, violet,
      and crimson, worked with
            embroidery;
The breastpiece for decision, the ephod
      and cincture
[11]      with scarlet yarn, the work of the
            weaver;
Precious stones with seal engravings
      in golden settings, the work of the
            jeweler,
To commemorate in incised letters
      each of the tribes of Israel;

---

*[44:20] **In his own flesh . . . ordinance**: the covenant of circumcision; cf. Gn 17:10–14. **And when tested . . . loyal**: Abraham's willingness to sacrifice his son Isaac at the Lord's command; cf. Gn 22:1–12.

†[44:21] **The River**: the Euphrates; cf. Gn 2:14.

‡[44:23(end)]–45:5] Moses manifested God's power through marvels (vv. 1–3), God's authority through the commandments and the Law (v. 5), and God's mercy through the intimacy granted him by the Lord for his own faithfulness and meekness (v. 4).

§[45:5] On God's intimacy with Moses, see Ex 33:11; Nm 12:8; Dt 34:10.

¶[45:6–25] Ben Sira here expresses his reverence and esteem for the priesthood of the old covenant. He recalls God's choice of Aaron and his sons for this sublime office (vv. 6–7), and describes in detail the beauty of the high priest's vestments (vv. 8–13). He relates the ordination of Aaron at the hands of Moses (v. 15), and describes the priestly functions, namely, offering sacrifice to God (v. 16), and blessing (v. 15), teaching, governing, and judging the people (v. 17); the inheritance of the high priest (vv. 20–22); the punishment of those who were jealous of Aaron (vv. 18–19); and the confirmation of the covenant of the priesthood with Aaron's descendants through Phinehas (vv. 23–25).

---

y. [44:17] Gn 6:8–9:29; Heb 11:7.   z. [44:19] Gn 12:1–25:10; Rom 4:3; Gal 3:6; Heb 11:8–19; Jas 2:23.   a. [44:20] Gn 17:10–14; 22:1–12.   b. [44:22–23] Gn 26:3–5, 24; 27:28–29; 28:13–15.   c. [45:1] Ex 2:2; 11:3; 33:11; Nm 12:7.

d. [45:2–5] Ex 7–Dt 34.   e. [45:3] Ex 7:1–7; 20:2–17; Dt 5:6–21.   f. [45:4] Nm 12:3, 7.   g. [45:6–22] Ex 28–29; Wis 18:24.

12  On his turban a diadem of gold,
        its plate engraved with the sacred
            inscription—
    Majestic, glorious, renowned for splendor,
        a delight to the eyes, supremely
            beautiful.
13  Before him, no one had been adorned
        with these,
        nor may they ever be worn by any
            other
    Except his sons and them alone,
        generation after generation, for all
            time.
14  His grain offering is wholly burnt
        as an established offering twice each
            day;
15  For Moses ordained him
        and anointed him with the holy oil,
    In a lasting covenant with him and his
        family,
        as permanent as the heavens,
    That he should serve God in the priesthood
        and bless the people in his name.
16  He chose him from all the living
        to sacrifice burnt offerings and
            choice portions,
    To burn incense, sweet odor as a
        memorial,
        and to atone for the people of Israel.
17  He gave to him the laws,
        and authority to prescribe and to
            judge:
    To teach precepts to the people,
        and judgments to the Israelites.
18  Strangers rose in anger against him,
        grew jealous of him in the desert—
    The followers of Dathan and Abiram,
        and the band of Korah in their
            defiance.[h]
19  When the LORD saw this he became angry,
        and destroyed them in his burning
            wrath.
    He brought against them a marvel,
        and consumed them in flaming fire.
20  Then he increased the glory of Aaron[i]
        and bestowed upon him his
            inheritance:
    The sacred offerings he allotted to him,
        with the showbread[*] as his portion;
21  The oblations of the LORD are his food,
        a gift to him and his descendants.
22  But he holds no land among the people
        nor shares with them their heritage;
    For the LORD himself is his portion and
        inheritance
            among the Israelites.
23  PHINEHAS too, the son of Eleazar,
        was the courageous third of his line

When, zealous for the God of all,
    he met the crisis of his people[j]
And, at the prompting of his noble heart,
    atoned for the children of Israel.
24  Therefore, on him also God conferred the
        right,
        in a covenant of friendship, to
            provide for the sanctuary,
    So that he and his descendants
        should possess the high priesthood
            forever.
25  For even his covenant with David,
        the son of Jesse of the tribe of Judah,
    Was an individual heritage through one
        son alone;[k]
        but the heritage of Aaron is for all
            his descendants.

So now bless[†] the LORD
    who has crowned you with glory!
26  May he grant you wisdom of heart
        to govern his people in justice,
    Lest the benefits you confer should be
        forgotten,
        or your authority, throughout all
            time.

## CHAPTER 46

### Joshua, Caleb, the Judges, and Samuel

1  Valiant warrior was JOSHUA,[‡] son of Nun,
        aide to Moses in the prophetic office,
    Formed to be, as his name implies,
        the great savior of God's chosen ones,
    To punish the enemy
        and to give to Israel their heritage.[l]
2  What glory was his when he raised his
        hand,
        to brandish his sword against the
            city![m]
3  Who could withstand him
        when he fought the battles of the
            LORD?[§]
4  Was it not by that same hand the sun
        stopped,
        so that one day became two?[n]
5  He called upon the Most High God
        when his enemies beset him on all
            sides,
    And God Most High answered him
        with hailstones of tremendous
            power,

---

†[45:25–26] **So now bless**: Ben Sira addresses the whole
line of high priests, especially Simon II; cf. 50:1.
‡[46:1–6] **Joshua**: whose name means "the Lord is savior"
(v. 1), was the instrument through which God delivered his
people in marvelous ways (vv. 2–6) by destroying their enemies, whose land he gave to the Israelites as a heritage (v. 1).
§[46:3] **The battles of the Lord**: cf. Jos 6–11.

---

*[45:20] **Showbread**: cf. note on Ex 25:29–30.

h. [45:18] Nm 16:1–35.   i. [45:20–21] Nm 18:11–24; Dt 10:9.

j. [45:23] Nm 25:7–13; 1 Mc 2:26, 54; Ps 106:30–31.   k. [45:25]
2 Sm 7:12–16.   l. [46:1] Ex 17:9; Nm 27:18–23; Dt 34:9; Jos 1:1–9.
m. [46:2] Jos 8:18–19.   n. [46:4] Jos 10:12–13.

6 That rained down upon the hostile army
    till on the slope he destroyed the foe;
  That all the doomed nations might know
    the Lord was watching over his
    people's battles.
  He was indeed a devoted follower of God
7   and showed himself loyal in Moses'
    lifetime.
  He and Caleb,* son of Jephunneh,
    when they opposed the rebel
    assembly,
  Averted God's anger from the people
    and suppressed the wicked
    complaint.°
8 Because of this, these two alone were
    spared
    from the six hundred thousand
    infantry,
  To lead the people into their heritage,
    the land flowing with milk and
    honey.°
9 The strength God gave to Caleb
    remained with him even in old age
  Till he won his way onto the summits of
    the land;
    his family too received a heritage,°
10 That all the offspring of Jacob might know
    how good it is to be a devoted
    follower of the Lord.

11 The Judges,† each one of them,
    whose hearts were not deceived,
  Who did not abandon God—
    may their memory be ever blessed!°
12 May their bones flourish with new life
    where they lie,
  and their names receive fresh luster
    in their children!
13 Beloved of his people, dear to his Maker,
    pledged in a vow from his mother's
    womb,
  As one consecrated to the Lord in the
    prophetic office,
    was Samuel, the judge who offered
    sacrifice.
  At God's word he established the kingdom
    and anointed princes to rule the
    people.°
14 By the law of the Lord he judged the
    congregation,

and visited the encampments of
    Jacob.
15 As a trustworthy prophet he was sought
    out
    and his words proved him to be a
    true seer.
16 He, too, called upon the mighty Lord
    when his enemies pressed him on
    every side,
    and offered up a suckling lamb.°
17 Then the Lord thundered from heaven,
    and the tremendous roar of his voice
    was heard.°
18 He brought low the rulers of the enemy
    and destroyed all the lords of the
    Philistines.
19 When Samuel neared the end of life,
    he testified before the Lord and his
    anointed prince,
  "No bribe or secret gift have I taken from
    anyone!"
    and no one could accuse him.°
20 Even after death his guidance was sought;
    he made known to the king his fate.
  From the grave he spoke in prophecy
    to put an end to wickedness.°

## CHAPTER 47

### Nathan, David, and Solomon

1 After him came Nathan‡
    who served in David's presence.°
2 Like the choice fat of sacred offerings,
    so was David in Israel.°
3 He played with lions as though they were
    young goats,
    and with bears, like lambs of the
    flock.°
4 As a youth he struck down the giant
    and wiped out the people's disgrace;
  His hand let fly the slingstone
    that shattered the pride of Goliath.°
5 For he had called upon the Most High God,
    who gave strength to his right arm
  To defeat the skilled warrior
    and establish the might of his
    people.
6 Therefore the women sang his praises
    and honored him for "the tens of
    thousands."
  When he received the royal crown, he
    battled°
7   and subdued the enemy on every
    side.
  He campaigned against the hostile
    Philistines

---

*[46:7–10] **Caleb:** with Joshua he advised Moses to enter Canaan, despite the counsel of their companion scouts and the rebellion of the people. He led the next generation of Israelites into the promised land. He received a portion of land which he himself had conquered; cf. Jos 15:13–14.

†[46:11–20] Of the judges praised and blessed for their fidelity to God in opposing idolatry, Samuel was the greatest (vv. 11–13, 19). He was judge, prophet, and priest. Through his sacrificial offering he obtained victory over the Philistines. He established the kingdom, anointed kings (vv. 13–18), and even after his death foretold the king's fate (v. 20).

‡[47:1–11] An idealized portrait of David; cf. 1 Chronicles.

o. [46:7] Nm 13:30; 14:1–3.    p. [46:8] Nm 14:22–38.    q. [46:9] Jos 14:6–13; 15:13.    r. [46:11] Jgs 1:1–16:31.    s. [46:13] 1 Sm 1:10–20; 8:4–10:1; 16:12–13.

t. [46:16] 1 Sm 7:9.    u. [46:17] 1 Sm 7:10–13.    v. [46:19] 1 Sm 12:3.    w. [46:20] 1 Sm 28:14–19.    x. [47:1] 2 Sm 7:2–17.    y. [47:2] 1 Sm 16:1–13.    z. [47:3] 1 Sm 17:34–36.    a. [47:4] 1 Sm 17:49.    b. [47:6] 1 Sm 18:7.

and shattered their power till our
own day.[c]

8 With his every deed he offered thanks
to God Most High, in words of
praise.
With his whole heart he loved his Maker

9 and daily had his praises sung;

10 He added beauty to the feasts
and solemnized the seasons of each
year

9b With string music before the altar,
providing sweet melody for the
psalms[d]

10b So that when the Holy Name was praised,
before daybreak the sanctuary
would resound.

11 The LORD forgave him his sins
and exalted his strength forever;
He conferred on him the rights of royalty
and established his throne in Israel.[e]

12 Because of his merits he had as successor*
a wise son, who lived in security;[f]

13 SOLOMON reigned during an era of peace,
for God brought rest to all his
borders.
He built a house to the name of God,
and established a lasting sanctuary.[g]

14 How wise you were when you were young,
overflowing with instruction, like
the Nile in flood![h]

15 Your understanding covered the whole
earth,
and, like a sea, filled it with
knowledge.

16 Your fame reached distant coasts,
and you were beloved for your
peaceful reign.

17 With song and proverb and riddle,
and with your answers, you
astounded the nations.

18 You were called by that glorious name
which was conferred upon Israel.[†]
Gold you gathered like so much iron;
you heaped up silver as though it
were lead.

19 But you abandoned yourself to women
and gave them dominion over your
body.[i]

20 You brought a stain upon your glory,
shame upon your marriage bed,
Wrath upon your descendants,
and groaning upon your deathbed.

21 Thus two governments came into being,
when in Ephraim kingship was
usurped.[j]

22 But God does not withdraw his mercy,
nor permit even one of his promises
to fail.
He does not uproot the posterity of the
chosen,
nor destroy the offspring of his
friends.
So he gave to Jacob a remnant,
to David a root from his own family.[k]

### Rehoboam and Jeroboam

23 Solomon finally slept with his ancestors,
and left behind him one of his sons,
Broad[‡] in folly, narrow in sense,
whose policy made the people rebel.
Then arose the one who should not be
remembered,
the sinner who led Israel into sin,[l]
Who brought ruin to Ephraim

24 and caused them to be exiled from
their land.

### Elijah and Elisha

25 Their sinfulness grew more and more,
and they gave themselves to every
evil[§]

### CHAPTER 48

1 Until like fire a prophet appeared,
his words a flaming furnace.[m]

2 The staff of life, their bread, he shattered,
and in his zeal he made them few in
number.

3 By God's word he shut up the heavens
and three times brought down fire.[n]

4 How awesome are you, ELIJAH!
Whose glory is equal to yours?

5 You brought a dead body back to life
from Sheol, by the will of the LORD.[o]

6 You sent kings down to destruction,
and nobles, from their beds of
sickness.[p]

7 You heard threats at Sinai,
at Horeb avenging judgments.[q]

---

*[47:12–24] The standard view of Solomon is echoed by
Ben Sira, but he affirms the divine promise (v. 22) to David's
line.

†[47:18] Cf. 2 Sm 12:25, where Solomon is called Jedidiah,
"beloved of the Lord." A similar term is used of Israel in Jer
11:15.

‡[47:23] **Broad:** the name Rehoboam means "the people is
broad, or expansive," that is, widespread. **The sinner:** Jeroboam;
cf. 1 Kgs 12:1, 20, 26–32.

§[47:25–48:11] The prophetic ministry of Elijah amid
widespread idolatry is here described as a judgment by fire
(48:1). Through his preaching, marvels, and acts of vengeance
against God's enemies, he succeeded for a time in restoring
faith in and worship of the Lord (vv. 2–8). His mysterious
departure from this life gave rise to the belief that he did
not die but would return before the day of the Lord. Cf. Mal
3:23–24; Mt 17:9–13.

---

c. [47:7] 2 Sm 5:6–25.   d. [47:9] 1 Chr 16:4–37; 23:5; 25:1–7.
e. [47:11] 2 Sm 12:13; 7:12–16.   f. [47:12] 1 Kgs 2:12.   g. [47:13]
1 Kgs 5:1, 5; 6:2–38.   h. [47:14–18] 1 Kgs 5:9–14; 10:14–29.
i. [47:19] 1 Kgs 11:1–10.

j. [47:21] 1 Kgs 12:1–25.   k. [47:22] 2 Sm 7:15; Ps 89:34–38.
l. [47:23] 1 Kgs 11:43; 12:13, 21; 13:34; 2 Kgs 17:6–22.   m. [48:1]
1 Kgs 17:1.   n. [48:3] 2 Kgs 1:9–14.   o. [48:5] 1 Kgs 17:17–23.
p. [48:6] 1 Kgs 21:19; 2 Kgs 1:17.   q. [48:7] 1 Kgs 19:8–15.

8 You anointed the agent of these
        punishments,
        the prophet to succeed in your place.[r]
9 You were taken aloft in a whirlwind,
        in a chariot with fiery horses.[s]
10 You are destined, it is written, in time to
        come
        to put an end to wrath before the
            day of the LORD,
    To turn back the hearts of parents toward
        their children,
        and to re-establish the tribes of Israel.[t]
11 Blessed is the one who shall have seen you
        before he dies!*

12      When Elijah was enveloped in the
            whirlwind,
    ELISHA was filled with his spirit;[†]
    He worked twice as many marvels,[u]
        and every utterance of his mouth
            was wonderful.
    During his lifetime he feared no one,
        nor was anyone able to intimidate
            his will.
13 Nothing was beyond his power;[v]
        and from where he lay buried, his
            body prophesied.[‡]
14 In life he performed wonders,
        and after death, marvelous deeds.
15 Despite all this the people did not repent,
        nor did they give up their sins,
    Until they were uprooted from their land
        and scattered all over the earth.

### Judah

    But Judah remained, a tiny people,
        with its ruler from the house of
            David.[w]
16 Some of them did what was right,
        but others were extremely sinful.

### Hezekiah and Isaiah[§]

17 HEZEKIAH fortified his city
        and had water brought into it;[x]

    With bronze tools he cut through the
        rocks
        and dammed up a mountain site for
            water.[¶]
18 During his reign Sennacherib led an
        invasion
        and sent his adjutant;
    He shook his fist at Zion
        and blasphemed God in his pride.[y]
19 The people's hearts melted within them,
        and they were in anguish like that of
            childbirth.
20 But they called upon the Most High God
        and lifted up their hands to him;
    He heard the prayer they uttered,
        and saved them through ISAIAH.[z]
21 God struck the camp of the Assyrians
        and routed them with a plague.[a]
22 For Hezekiah did what was right
        and held fast to the paths of David,
    As ordered by the illustrious prophet
        Isaiah, who saw truth in visions.
23 In his lifetime he turned back the sun
        and prolonged the life of the king.[b]
24 By his powerful spirit he looked into the
        future[c]
        and consoled the mourners of Zion;
25 He foretold what would happen till the
        end of time,
        hidden things yet to be fulfilled.

## CHAPTER 49

### Josiah and the Prophets**

1      The name JOSIAH is like blended incense,
            made lasting by a skilled perfumer.[d]
    Precious is his memory, like honey to the
        taste,
        like music at a banquet.
2 For he grieved over our betrayals,
        and destroyed the abominable idols.
3 He kept his heart fixed on God,
        and in times of lawlessness practiced
            virtue.
4 Except for David, Hezekiah, and Josiah,
        they all were wicked;
    They abandoned the Law of the Most
        High,
        these kings of Judah, right to the
            very end.
5 So he gave over their power to others,
        their glory to a foreign nation

---

*[48:11] Verse 11b is not extant in the Hebrew; it is represented in the Greek tradition by "for we too shall certainly live." But this can hardly be the original reading.

†[48:12–16] Elisha continued Elijah's work (vv. 12–14), but the obstinacy of the people eventually brought on the destruction of the kingdom of Israel and the dispersion of its subjects. Judah, however, survived under the rule of Davidic kings, both good and bad (vv. 15–16).

‡[48:13] The reference in v. 13b seems to be to 2 Kgs 13:21 where it is related that a dead man, thrown into Elisha's grave, came back to life.

§[48:17–25] The fidelity of King Hezekiah (vv. 17, 22), the zeal of the prophet Isaiah, and the prayer of the people (v. 20) were effective. The Assyrian oppressors under Sennacherib withdrew (vv. 18–19, 21). The king's life was prolonged. The people were consoled by Isaiah's words about the future (vv. 23–25); the "consolations" refer to Is 40–66.

¶[48:17] The reference is to the famous Siloam tunnel in present-day Jerusalem.

**[49:1–10] Ben Sira's praise of King Josiah (vv. 1–3) and of the prophets Jeremiah and Ezekiel and the minor prophets (vv. 7–10) derives from their spirit of fidelity to the Lord and his Law (vv. 4–6, 10).

---

r. [48:8] 1 Kgs 19:16–17.   s. [48:9] 2 Kgs 2:11.   t. [48:10] Mal 3:23–24; Mt 17:10.   u. [48:12] 2 Kgs 2:9–12.   v. [48:13–14] 2 Kgs 13:21.   w. [48:15] 2 Kgs 15:29; 18:11–12.   x. [48:17] 2 Kgs 20:20; 2 Chr 32:30.

y. [48:18] 2 Kgs 18:13–37; Is 36:1–22.   z. [48:20] 2 Kgs 19:20.   a. [48:21] 2 Kgs 19:35; Is 37:36.   b. [48:23] 2 Kgs 20:11; Is 38:8.   c. [48:24–25] 2 Kgs 20:17; Is 40:1–11; 42:9; 46:10; 48:6; 61:2–3.   d. [49:1–2] 2 Kgs 22:1–2, 10–13, 19; 23:4–15, 19–20, 24; 2 Chr 34:1–7.

⁶ Who burned the holy city
  and left its streets desolate,
⁷ As foretold by JEREMIAH.ᵉ They
    mistreated him
  who even in the womb had been
    made a prophet,
  To root out, pull down, and destroy,
    and then to build and to plant.ᶠ
⁸ EZEKIEL beheld a vision
  and described the different creatures
    of the chariot;ᵍ
⁹ He also referred to JOB,
  who always persevered in the right
    path.ʰ
¹⁰ Then, too, the TWELVE PROPHETS—
  may their bones flourish with new
    life where they lie!—
  They gave new strength to Jacob
  and saved him with steadfast hope.

### The Heroes After the Exile

¹¹ How to extol ZERUBBABEL?*
  He was like a signet ring on the right
    hand,ⁱ
¹² And JESHUA, Jozadak's son?
  In their time they rebuilt the altar
  And erected the holy temple,
    destined for everlasting glory.
¹³ Exalted be the memory of NEHEMIAH!
  He rebuilt our ruined walls,
  Restored our shattered defenses,
    and set up gates and bars.ʲ

### The Earliest Patriarchs

¹⁴ Few on earth have been created like
    ENOCH;†
  he also was taken up bodily.ᵏ
¹⁵ Was ever a man born like JOSEPH?
  Even his dead body was provided
    for.ˡ
¹⁶ Glorious, too, were SHEM and SETH and
    ENOSH;
  but beyond that of any living being
    was the splendor of ADAM.ᵐ

## CHAPTER 50

### Simeon, Son of Jochanan

¹ Greatest of his family, the glory of his
    people,

was SIMEON the priest, son of
    Jochanan,‡
  In whose time the house of God was
    renovated,
  in whose days the temple was
    reinforced.
² In his time also the retaining wall was built
  with powerful turrets for the temple
    precincts.
³ In his time the reservoir was dug,
  a pool as vast as the sea.
⁴ He protected the people against brigands
  and strengthened the city against the
    enemy.
⁵ How splendid he was as he looked out
    from the tent,
  as he came from behind the veil!
⁶ Like a star shining among the clouds,
  like the full moon at the festal
    season;
⁷ Like sun shining upon the temple of the
    King,
  like a rainbow appearing in the
    cloudy sky;
⁸ Like blossoms on the branches in
    springtime,
  like a lily by running waters;
  Like a green shoot on Lebanon in
    summer,
⁹   like the fire of incense at sacrifice;
  Like a vessel of hammered gold,
    studded with all kinds of precious
      stones;
¹⁰ Like a luxuriant olive tree heavy with fruit,
  a plant with branches abounding
    in oil;
¹¹ Wearing his glorious robes,
  and vested in sublime magnificence,ⁿ
  As he ascended the glorious altar
  and lent majesty to the court of the
    sanctuary.
¹² When he received the portions from the
    priests
  while he stood before the sacrificial
    wood,
  His sons stood round him like a garland,
    like young cedars on Lebanon;
  And like poplars by the brook they
    surrounded him,
¹³   all the sons of Aaron in their glory,
  With the offerings to the LORD in their
    hands,
    in the presence of the whole
      assembly of Israel.
¹⁴ Once he had completed the service at the
    altar

---

*[49:11–13] The rebuilding of the Temple and the repair of the walls of the Holy City led to a restoration of religious worship and civil authority.
†[49:14–16] The patriarchs here mentioned were glorious because of their spirit of religion, i.e., their profound reverence for God and obedience to him. **The splendor of Adam**: suggests his direct origin from God (Gn 1:26–27; 2:7).

e. [49:7] 2 Kgs 25:9; 2 Chr 36:19.  f. [49:7] Jer 1:5, 10.  g. [49:8] Ez 1:4–21.  h. [49:9] Ez 14:14, 20.  i. [49:11–12] Ezr 3:2; Hg 1:12; Zec 3:1.  j. [49:13] Neh 1:1–3:32.  k. [49:14] Sir 44:16; Gn 5:18–24.  l. [49:15] Gn 37; 39–50; Ex 13:19; Jos 24:32.  m. [49:16] Gn 1:26–30; 2:7; 4:25–26.

‡[50:1–21] **Son of Jochanan**: Simeon II, in whose time as high priest (219–196 B.C.) great works were accomplished for the benefit of public worship and welfare (vv. 1–4). Ben Sira, a contemporary, describes detailed liturgical action, perhaps pertaining to the Day of Atonement (Yom Kippur, cf. Lv 16).

n. [50:11] Sir 45:8–13; Ex 28:2–43; 39:1–31.

and arranged the sacrificial hearth
　　for the Most High,

¹⁵ And had stretched forth his hand for the
　　　cup,
　　to offer blood of the grape,
And poured it out at the foot of the altar,
　　a sweet-smelling odor to God the
　　　Most High,ᵒ

¹⁶ Then the sons of Aaron would sound a blast,
　　the priests, on their trumpets of
　　　beaten metal;
A blast to resound mightily
　　as a reminder before the Most High.ᵖ

¹⁷ All the people with one accord
　　would fall with face to the ground
In adoration before the Most High,
　　before the Holy One of Israel.

¹⁸ Then hymns would re-echo,
　　and over the throng sweet strains of
　　　praise resound.

¹⁹ All the people of the land would shout for
　　　joy,
　　praying to the Merciful One,
As the high priest completed the service
　　at the altar
　　by presenting to God the fitting
　　　sacrifice.

²⁰ Then coming down he would raise his
　　　hands
　　over all the congregation of Israel;
The blessing of the LORD would be upon
　　his lips,
　　the name of the LORD would be his
　　　glory.�q

²¹ The people would again fall down
　　to receive the blessing of the Most
　　　High.

²² And now, bless the God of all,*
　　who has done wonders on earth;
Who fosters growth from the womb,
　　fashioning it according to his will!

²³ May he grant you a wise heart
　　and abide with you in peace;

²⁴ May his goodness toward Simeon last
　　forever;
　　may he fulfill for him the covenant
　　　with Phinehas
So that it may not be abrogated for him
　　or his descendants while the heavens
　　　last.

### Epilogue

²⁵ My whole being loathes two nations,
　　the third is not even a people:†

---

²⁶ The inhabitants of Seir‡ and Philistia,
　　and the foolish people who dwell in
　　　Shechem.ʳ

²⁷ Wise instruction, appropriate proverbs,§
　　I have written in this book—
I, Yeshua Ben Eleazar Ben Sira—
　　as they poured forth from my heart's
　　　understanding.

²⁸ Happy those who meditate upon these
　　　things;
　　wise those who take them to heart!

²⁹ If they put them into practice, they can
　　cope with anything,
　　for the fear of the LORD is their
　　　lamp.

## CHAPTER 51

### A Prayer of Thanksgiving

¹ I give you thanks, LORD and King,¶
　　I praise you, God my savior!
I declare your name, refuge of my life,ˢ

²　　　because you have ransomed my life
　　　　from death;
You held back my body from the pit,
　　and delivered my foot from the
　　　power of Sheol.ᵗ

You have preserved me from the scourge
　　of the slanderous tongue,
　　and from the lips of those who went
　　　over to falsehood.
You were with me against those who rise
　　up against me;

³　　　You have rescued me according to
　　　　your abundant mercyᵘ
From the snare of those who look for my
　　downfall,
　　and from the power of those who
　　　seek my life.

From many dangers you have saved me,

⁴　　　from flames that beset me on every
　　　　side,ᵛ
From the midst of fire till there was not a
　　whiff of it,**

⁵　　　from the deep belly of Sheol,
From deceiving lips and painters of lies,

⁶　　　from the arrows of a treacherous
　　　　tongue.

---

‡[50:26] **Seir**: Mount Seir in the territory of the Edomites.
**Shechem**: a city in Samaria.

§[50:27] This colophon may have been the original ending of the book. It is unusual for a biblical writer to append
his name.

¶[51:1–30] This chapter contains two appendixes: a prayer
(vv. 1–12) and an autobiographical poem praising wisdom
(vv. 13–30).

**[51:4] So complete is the deliverance from fire that even
the smell of smoke cannot be detected. Cf. Dn 3:27.

---

*[50:22–24] Ben Sira urges the reader to praise and bless
God for his wondrous works and then invokes a blessing on
all that they may enjoy peace and gladness of heart and the
abiding goodness of the Most High.

†[50:25] **Not even a people**: the Samaritans.

---

o. [50:15] Nm 15:5; 28:7.    p. [50:16] Nm 10:10.    q. [50:20] Nm
6:23–27.

r. [50:26] 2 Kgs 17:24; Jn 4:9.    s. [51:1] Ps 138:1.    t. [51:2] Ps
91:3.    u. [51:3] Ps 56:10–12; 124:2.    v. [51:4] Ps 66:12.

I was at the point of death,
  my life was nearing the depths of
    Sheol;[w]
7 I turned every way, but there was no one
    to help;
  I looked for support but there was
    none.[x]
8 Then I remembered the mercies of the
    LORD,
  his acts of kindness through ages
    past;
For he saves those who take refuge in him,
  and rescues them from every evil.

9 So I raised my voice from the grave;
  from the gates of Sheol I cried for
    help.
10 I called out: LORD, you are my Father,
  my champion, my savior!
Do not abandon me in time of trouble,
  in the midst of storms and dangers.[y]
11 I will always praise your name
  and remember you in prayer!

Then the LORD heard my voice,
  and listened to my appeal.
12 He saved me from every evil
  and preserved me in time of trouble.
For this reason I thank and praise him;
  I bless the name of the LORD.[*]

---

*[51:12] After this verse the Hebrew text gives the litany of praise contained below. It is similar to Ps 136. Though not found in any versions, and therefore of doubtful authenticity, the litany seems from internal evidence to go back to the time of Ben Sira.

> Give praise to the LORD, for he is good, for God's love
>   endures forever;
> Give praise to the God of glory, for God's love endures
>   forever;
> Give praise to the Guardian of Israel, for God's love
>   endures forever;
> Give praise to the creator of all things, for God's love
>   endures forever;
> Give praise to the redeemer of Israel, for God's love
>   endures forever;
> Give praise to God who gathers the dispersed of Israel, for
>   God's love endures forever;
> Give praise to God who builds the city and sanctuary, for
>   God's love endures forever;
> Give praise to God who makes a horn sprout forth for
>   the house of David, for God's love endures
>   forever;
> Give praise to God who has chosen the sons of Zadok as
>   priests, for God's love endures forever;
> Give praise to the Shield of Abraham, for God's love
>   endures forever;
> Give praise to the Rock of Isaac, for God's love endures
>   forever;
> Give praise to the Mighty One of Jacob, for God's love
>   endures forever;
> Give praise to God who has chosen Zion, for God's love
>   endures forever;
> Give praise to the King, the king of kings, for God's love
>   endures forever.
> He has lifted up the horn of his people! Let this be his
>   praise from all the faithful,
> From Israel, the people near to him. Hallelujah! (Cf. Ps
>   148:14.)

---

## Ben Sira's Pursuit of Wisdom

13 [†]When I was young and innocent,
  I sought wisdom.[z]
14 She came to me in her beauty,
  and until the end I will cultivate her.

15 As the blossoms yielded to ripening grapes,
    the heart's joy,
My feet kept to the level path
  because from earliest youth I was
    familiar with her.

16 In the short time I paid heed,
  I met with great instruction.
17 Since in this way I have profited,
  I will give my Teacher grateful praise.

18 I resolved to tread her paths;
  I have been jealous for the good and
    will not turn back.
19 I burned with desire for her,
    never relenting.
I became preoccupied with her,
  never weary of extolling her.

I spread out my hands to the heavens
  and I came to know her secrets.
20 For her I purified my hands;
  in cleanness I attained to her.

At first acquaintance with her, I gained
    understanding
  such that I will never forsake her.[a]
21 My whole being was stirred to seek her;
  therefore I have made her my prize
    possession.
22 The LORD has rewarded me with lips,
  with a tongue for praising him.

23 Come aside to me, you untutored,
  and take up lodging in the house of
    instruction;[‡b]
24 How long will you deprive yourself of
    wisdom's food,
  how long endure such bitter thirst?
25 I open my mouth and speak of her:
  gain wisdom for yourselves at no cost.[c]

26 Take her yoke upon your neck;
  that your mind may receive her
    teaching.

---

†[51:13–30] A Hebrew manuscript from Qumran demonstrates the acrostic style of vv. 13–20. This is an elegant twenty-three-line alphabetic acrostic hymn that describes Ben Sira's relationship to wisdom: (a) his approach to wisdom through prayer, persistent study, and instruction (vv. 13–17); (b) his purification from sin, his enlightenment, and ardent desire to possess wisdom (vv. 18–22). Ben Sira concludes with an urgent invitation to his students to receive instruction in wisdom from him, and to live by it, because wisdom gives herself to those who seek her (vv. 23–26); and for their labor, God will reward them in his own time (vv. 27–30). Cf. Mt 11:28; Eccl 12:14.
‡[51:23] House of instruction: this may be a metaphor for Ben Sira's teaching.

---

w. [51:6] Ps 88:4; 94:17.   x. [51:7] Ps 22:12; 142:5.   y. [51:10] Ps 89:27; 95:1.

z. [51:13] Sir 34:9–13; Prv 8:17.   a. [51:20] Prv 4:6.   b. [51:23] Prv 8:5.   c. [51:25] Sir 6:19; Is 55:1–3.

For she is close to those who seek her,
    and the one who is in earnest finds
    her.*d*

27 See for yourselves! I have labored only a
    little,
    but have found much.
28 Acquire but a little instruction,

and you will win silver and gold
    through her.

29 May your soul rejoice in God's mercy;
    do not be ashamed to give him praise.
30 Work at your tasks in due season,
    and in his own time God will give
    you your reward.*e*

d. [51:26] Sir 6:26–28.

e. [51:30] Sir 2:8; Jb 34:11; Jn 9:4.

# THE
# PROPHETIC BOOKS

❦

The prophetic books bear the names of the four major and twelve minor prophets, in addition to Lamentations and Baruch. The terms "major" and "minor" refer to the length of the respective compositions and not to their relative importance. Jonah is a story about a prophet rather than a collection of prophetic pronouncements. In the Hebrew Bible, Lamentations and Daniel are listed among the Writings (Hagiographa), not among the prophetic books. The former contains a series of laments over the destruction of Jerusalem by the Babylonians. The latter is considered to be a prophetic book, though it consists of a collection of six edifying diaspora tales (chaps. 1-6) and four apocalyptic visions about the end time (chaps. 7-12). Baruch is not included in the Hebrew canon, but is in the Septuagint or Old Greek version of the Bible, and the Church has from the beginning acknowledged its sacred and inspired character.

The prophetic books contain a deposit of prophetic preaching, and several of them in addition are filled out with narrative about prophets (e.g., Is 7; 36-39; Jer 26-29; 36-45; Am 7:10-17). In ancient Israel a prophet was understood to be an intermediary between God and the community, someone called to proclaim the word of God. Prophets received such communications through various means, including visions and dreams, often in a state of transformed consciousness, and transmitted them to the people as God's messengers through oracular utterances, sermons, writings, and symbolic actions.

It would be misleading to think of these works as books in our sense of the term. While some prophecies originated as written material, prophetic activity more commonly took the form of public speaking. Prophetic discourse addressed to different audiences in different situations would, typically, be committed first to memory, then to writing, often by the prophet's followers, sometimes by the prophet himself (e.g., Is 8:1-4, 16; Jer 36:1-2; Hb 2:2). Small compilations of such pronouncements and discourses would be put together, arranged according to subject matter (e.g., pronouncements against foreign nations), audience (e.g., Jeremiah to King Zedekiah, Jer 21:1-24:10), chronological sequence (e.g., in Ezekiel generally), or by verbal association (e.g., catchwords). These units would be circulated, edited, expanded and interpreted as the need arose to bring out the contemporary relevance of older prophecies, and eventually integrated into larger collections. The titles would have been added at a later date, in some instances centuries after the time of the prophet in question.

The office of the prophet came about as the result of a direct call from God. Unlike that of the priest, the prophetic function was not hereditary and did not correspond to a fixed office. In Israel as elsewhere in the ancient Near East and Levant, there were, however, prophets (*nĕbî'îm* in Hebrew) who were employed in temples and at royal courts, and some of the canonical prophets may have started out as "professionals" of this kind. Prophecy also differed from priesthood in ancient Israel in that there were both male and female prophets. Though none of the prophetic books is named for a female prophet, Miriam (Ex 15:20) and Deborah (Jgs 4:4) played important roles at the beginning of Israel's history and Huldah (2 Kgs 22:14) toward the end. The Bible gives great importance to the call or commissioning of the prophet, which was often accompanied by visionary or other extraordinary experiences (e.g., Jer 23:21-22; Ez 1-2). In these accounts the prophetic intermediary can be represented as a messenger commissioned by the Lord as king (e.g., Micaiah in 1 Kgs 22:19-23, and Isaiah in Is 6:1-13), and therefore prophetic speech is often introduced with the form used in the delivery of a message: "thus says the Lord" or some similar formula. Sometimes the prophetic calling could be expected to involve struggle, persecution, and suffering.

While prophetic messages sometimes bore on the future, their primary concern was with contemporary events in the public sphere of social life and politics, national and international. They focus on public morality, the treatment of the poor and disadvantaged, and the abuse of power, especially of the judicial system. They pass judgment in the strongest terms on the moral conduct of rulers and the ruling class, in the belief that a society that does not practice justice and righteousness will not survive. With equal rigor, they also condemn a religious formalism that would legitimate such a society (e.g., Is 1:10–17; Jer 7:1–15; Am 5:21–24). They view international affairs, the rise and fall of the great empires, in the light of their own passionate belief in the God of Israel and the destiny of Israel. The prophets never take political and military power as absolutes. They do not preach a new morality. They are radicals only in the sense of a radical commitment to and interpretation of the religious, legal, and moral traditions inherited from Israel's past.

Prophetic speech is not, however, confined to judgment and condemnation. The prophets also exhort, cajole, encourage; they announce salvation and a good prognosis for the future. Sometimes present realities and situations shade off into, or are taken up into, a panorama of a more distant future. In many instances, too, prophetic pronouncements are developed by a cumulative and incremental editorial process into a more inclusive and total vision of a final salvation and a final judgment, with or without the presence of a messianic figure. This process is particularly evident throughout the Book of Isaiah, and played an important part in the self-understanding of early Christian churches and their interpretation of the person and mission of Jesus. For early Christianity, therefore, prophetic texts were used to describe the new reality of Christ and the church (e.g., Mt 1:23; Acts 2:14–21; Gal 4:27).

# THE BOOK OF
# ISAIAH

Isaiah, one of the greatest of the prophets, appeared at a critical moment in Israel's history. The Northern Kingdom collapsed, under the hammerlike blows of Assyria, in 722/721 B.C., and in 701 Jerusalem itself saw the army of Sennacherib drawn up before its walls. In the year that Uzziah, king of Judah, died (742), Isaiah received his call to the prophetic office in the Temple of Jerusalem. Close attention should be given to chap. 6, where this divine summons to be the ambassador of the Most High is circumstantially described.

The vision of the Lord enthroned in glory stamps an indelible character on Isaiah's ministry and provides a key to the understanding of his message. The majesty, holiness and glory of the Lord took possession of his spirit and, at the same time, he gained a new awareness of human pettiness and sinfulness. The enormous abyss between God's sovereign holiness and human sinfulness overwhelmed the prophet. Only the purifying coal of the seraphim could cleanse his lips and prepare him for acceptance of the call: "Here I am, send me!"

The ministry of Isaiah extended from the death of Uzziah in 742 B.C. to Sennacherib's siege of Jerusalem in 701 B.C., and it may have continued even longer, until after the death of Hezekiah in 687 B.C. Later legend (the Martyrdom and Ascension of Isaiah) claims that Hezekiah's son, Manasseh, executed Isaiah by having him sawed in two; cf. Heb 11:37. During this long ministry, the prophet returned again and again to the same themes, and there are indications that he may have sometimes re-edited his older prophecies to fit new occasions. There is no evidence that the present arrangement of the oracles in the book reflects a chronological order. Indeed, it appears that there were originally separate smaller collections of oracles (note especially chaps. 6–12), each with its own logic for ordering, that were preserved fairly intact as blocks when the material was finally put together as a single literary work.

Isaiah's oracles cluster around several key historical events of the late eighth century: the Syro-Ephraimite War (735–732 B.C.), the accession of Hezekiah (715 B.C.), the revolt of Ashdod (714–711 B.C.), the death of Sargon (705 B.C.), and the revolt against Sennacherib (705–701 B.C.). In 738 B.C., with the Assyrian defeat of Calno/Calneh (Is 10:9; Am 6:2), the anti-Assyrian league, of which Judah may have been the ringleader, collapsed, and both Israel and the Arameans of Damascus paid tribute to Assyria. By 735 B.C., however, Rezin of Damascus had created a new anti-Assyrian league, and when Ahaz refused to join, the league attempted to remove Ahaz from the throne of Judah. The resulting Syro-Ephraimite War was the original occasion for many of Isaiah's oracles (cf. chaps. 7–8), in which he tried to reassure Ahaz of God's protection and dissuade him from seeking protection by an alliance with Assyria. Ahaz refused Isaiah's message, however.

When Hezekiah came to the throne in 715 B.C., Isaiah appears to have put great hopes in this new scion of David, and he undoubtedly supported the religious reform that Hezekiah undertook. But the old intrigues began again, and the king was sorely tempted to join with neighboring states in an alliance sponsored by Egypt against Assyria. Isaiah succeeded in keeping Hezekiah out of Ashdod's abortive revolt against Assyria, but when Sargon died in 705 B.C., with both Egypt and Babylon encouraging revolt, Hezekiah was won over to the pro-Egyptian party. Isaiah denounced this "covenant with death" (28:15, 18), and again summoned Judah to faith in the Lord as the only hope. But it was too late; the revolt had already begun. Assyria acted quickly and its army, after ravaging Judah, laid siege to Jerusalem (701). "I shut up Hezekiah like a bird in his cage," boasts the famous inscription of Sennacherib. The city was spared but at the cost of paying a huge indemnity to Assyria. Isaiah may have lived and prophesied for another dozen years after 701. There is material in the book that may plausibly be associated with Sennacherib's campaign against Babylon and its Arabian allies in 694–689 B.C.

For Isaiah, the vision of God's majesty was so overwhelming that military and political power faded into insignificance. He constantly called his people back to a reliance on God's promises and away from vain attempts to find security in human plans and intrigues. This vision also led him to insist on the ethical behavior that was required of human beings who wished to live in the presence of such a holy God. Isaiah couched this message in oracles of singular poetic beauty and power, oracles in which surprising shifts in syntax, audacious puns, and double- or triple-entendre are a constant feature.

The complete Book of Isaiah is an anthology of poems composed chiefly by the great prophet, but also by disciples, some of whom came many years after Isaiah. In 1–39 most of the oracles come from Isaiah and reflect the situation in eighth-century Judah. Sections such as the Apocalypse of Isaiah (24–27), the oracles against Babylon (13–14), and probably the poems of 34–35 were written by followers deeply influenced by the prophet, in some cases reusing earlier Isaianic material; cf., e.g., 27:2–8 with 5:1–7.

Chapters 40–55 (Second Isaiah, or Deutero-Isaiah) are generally attributed to an anonymous poet who prophesied toward the end of the Babylonian exile. From this section come the great oracles known as the Servant Songs, which are reflected in the New Testament understanding of the passion and glorification of Christ. Chapters 56–66 (Third Isaiah, or Trito-Isaiah) contain oracles from the postexilic period and were composed by writers imbued with the spirit of Isaiah who continued his work.

The principal divisions of the Book of Isaiah are the following:

I. Isaiah 1–39
    A. Indictment of Israel and Judah (1:1–5:30)
    B. The Book of Emmanuel (6:1–12:6)
    C. Oracles Against the Foreign Nations (13:1–23:18)
    D. Apocalypse of Isaiah (24:1–27:13)
    E. The Lord Alone, Israel's and Judah's Salvation (28:1–33:24)
    F. The Lord, Zion's Avenger (34:1–35:10)
    G. Historical Appendix (36:1–39:8)
II. Isaiah 40–55
    A. The Lord's Glory in Israel's Liberation (40:1–48:22)
    B. Expiation of Sin, Spiritual Liberation of Israel (49:1–55:13)
III. Isaiah 56–66

## I. ISAIAH 1–39

*A. Indictment of Israel and Judah*

### CHAPTER 1

¹The vision which Isaiah, son of Amoz, saw concerning Judah and Jerusalem in the days of Uzziah, Jotham, Ahaz and Hezekiah, kings of Judah.

#### Accusation and Appeal

² †Hear, O heavens, and listen, O earth,
    for the LORD speaks:

Sons have I raised and reared,
    but they have rebelled against me!ᵃ
³ An ox knows its owner,
    and an ass,‡ its master's manger;
But Israel does not know,
    my people has not understood.ᵇ
⁴ Ah!§ Sinful nation, people laden with wickedness,
    evil offspring, corrupt children!

---

*[1:1] The title, or inscription, of the book is an editorial addition to identify the prophet and the circumstances of his ministry. **Isaiah**: meaning "the salvation of the Lord," or "the Lord is salvation." **Amoz**: not Amos the prophet. **Judah**: the Southern Kingdom of the tribes of Judah and Benjamin. **Uzziah**: also called Azariah; cf. 2 Kgs 15:1; 2 Chr 26:1.
†[1:2–31] This chapter is widely considered to be a collection of oracles from various periods in Isaiah's ministry,

chosen by the editor as a compendium of his most characteristic teachings.
‡[1:3] **Ox . . . ass**: Isaiah uses animals proverbial for their stupidity and stubbornness to underline Israel's failure to respond to God. **Israel**: a term Isaiah (and other prophets) frequently applies to Judah, especially after the fall of the Northern Kingdom (which Isaiah normally calls Ephraim, as in 7:2, 9, 17; 9:8), but sometimes applies to the entire chosen people, as in 8:14.
§[1:4] **Ah**: see note on 5:8–24. **Holy One of Israel**: a title used frequently in the Book of Isaiah, rarely elsewhere in the Old Testament (see 5:19, 24; 10:20; 12:6; 17:7; 29:19; 30:11, 12, 15; 31:1; 37:23; 41:14, 16, 20; 43:3, 14; 45:11; 47:4; 48:17; 49:7; 54:5; 55:5; 60:9, 14).

a. [1:2] Dt 32:1, 5–6, 18.    b. [1:3] Jer 8:7; Lk 2:12.

They have forsaken the LORD,
    spurned the Holy One of Israel,
    apostatized,[c]
5 Why* would you yet be struck,
    that you continue to rebel?
The whole head is sick,
    the whole heart faint.
6 From the sole of the foot to the head
    there is no sound spot in it;
Just bruise and welt and oozing wound,
    not drained, or bandaged,
    or eased with salve.
7 Your country is waste,
    your cities burnt with fire;
Your land—before your eyes
    strangers devour it,
    a waste, like the devastation of
        Sodom.[†d]
8 And daughter Zion[‡] is left
    like a hut in a vineyard,
Like a shed in a melon patch,
    like a city blockaded.
9 If the LORD of hosts[§] had not
    left us a small remnant,
We would have become as Sodom,
    would have resembled Gomorrah.[e]

10 'Hear the word of the LORD,
    princes of Sodom!
Listen to the instruction of our God,
    people of Gomorrah!
11 What do I care for the multitude of your
        sacrifices?
    says the LORD.
I have had enough of whole-burnt rams
    and fat of fatlings;
In the blood of calves, lambs, and goats
    I find no pleasure.[f]
12 When you come to appear before me,
    who asks these things of you?
13 Trample my courts no more!
    To bring offerings is useless;

incense is an abomination to me.
New moon and sabbath, calling
        assemblies—
    festive convocations with
        wickedness—
    these I cannot bear.[g]
14 Your new moons and festivals I detest;[h]
    they weigh me down, I tire of the load.
15 When you spread out your hands,
    I will close my eyes to you;
Though you pray the more,
    I will not listen.
Your hands are full of blood!"*[i]
16     Wash yourselves clean!
Put away your misdeeds from before my
        eyes;
    cease doing evil;
17     learn to do good.
Make justice your aim: redress the wronged,
    hear the orphan's plea, defend the
        widow.[j]

18 Come now, let us set things right,[††]
    says the LORD:
Though your sins be like scarlet,
    they may become white as snow;
Though they be red like crimson,
    they may become white as wool.[k]
19 If you are willing, and obey,
    you shall eat the good things of the
        land;
20 But if you refuse and resist,
    you shall be eaten by the sword:
    for the mouth of the LORD has spoken!

### The Purification of Jerusalem

21 How she has become a prostitute,
    the faithful city,[‡‡] so upright!
Justice used to lodge within her,
    but now, murderers.[l]
22 Your silver is turned to dross,
    your wine is mixed with water.
23 Your princes are rebels
    and comrades of thieves;

---

*[1:5–6] The Hebrew expression translated "Why?" may also be translated "Where?" The ambiguity is probably intentional: "Why, O Israel, would you still be beaten, and where on your bruised body do you want the next blow?" The bruised body is a metaphor for the historical disaster that has overtaken Israel (see v. 7) because of its sins.

†[1:7] **Sodom**: Sodom and Gomorrah (see vv. 9–10; cf. Gn 19) were proverbial as wicked cities completely overthrown and destroyed by God. Judah, more fortunate, survives at least as a remnant. The devastation of the land and the isolation of Jerusalem suggest the time of Sennacherib's invasion of 701.

‡[1:8] **Daughter Zion**: Jerusalem, as isolated as a little hut erected in a field for the shelter of watchmen and laborers.

§[1:9] **LORD of hosts**: God, who is the Creator and Ruler of the armies of Israel, the angels, stars, etc.

¶[1:10–17] A powerful indictment of the religious hypocrisy of rulers and others who neglect just judgment and oppress the weaker members, yet believe they can please God with sacrifices and other external forms of worship. The long list of observances suggests the Lord's tedium with such attempts. **Sodom . . . Gomorrah**: the names are picked up from v. 9, but now to emphasize their wickedness rather than the good fortune of escaping total destruction.

**[1:15–16] **Hands . . . blood**: oppression of the poor is likened to violence that bloodies the hands, which explains why the hands spread out in prayer (v. 15) are not regarded by the Lord. This climax of the accusations is followed by positive admonitions for reversing the evil situation.

††[1:18] **Let us set things right**: the Hebrew word refers to the arbitration of legal disputes (Jb 23:7). God offers to settle his case with Israel on the basis of the change of behavior demanded above. For Israel it is a life or death choice; life in conformity with God's will or death for continued disobedience.

‡‡[1:21–28] **Faithful city**: the phrase, found in v. 21 and v. 28, forms an *inclusio* which marks off the passage and also suggests three chronological periods: the city's former ideal state, its present wicked condition (described in vv. 21b–23), and the future ideal conditions intended by God. This will be brought about by a purging judgment directed primarily against the leaders ("judges . . . counselors").

g. [1:13] Prv 15:8; Jer 6:20.   h. [1:14] Am 5:21–24.   i. [1:15] Prv 1:28; Sir 34:25–31.   j. [1:17] Ex 23:6; Dt 24:17; Sir 4:9–10; Jer 22:3; Ez 22:7; Am 5:14–15; Zec 7:9–10.   k. [1:18] Ps 51:9.   l. [1:21] Jer 3:8; Hos 2:7.

c. [1:4] Is 5:24; Dt 32:15.   d. [1:7] Is 13:19; Dt 29:22; Jer 49:18; 50:40; Am 4:11.   e. [1:9] Rom 9:29.   f. [1:11] Ps 50:8–13; Sir 34:23; Mi 6:7.

Each one of them loves a bribe
　　and looks for gifts.
The fatherless they do not defend,
　　the widow's plea does not reach
　　　them.*m*

24 Now, therefore, says the Lord,
　　the LORD of hosts, the Mighty One
　　　of Israel:
Ah! I will take vengeance on my foes
　　and fully repay my enemies!*n*

25 I will turn my hand against you,
　　and refine your dross in the furnace,
　　removing all your alloy.

26 I will restore your judges* as at first,
　　and your counselors as in the
　　　beginning;
After that you shall be called
　　city of justice, faithful city.*o*

27 †Zion shall be redeemed by justice,
　　and her repentant ones by
　　　righteousness.

28 Rebels and sinners together shall be
　　　crushed,
　　those who desert the LORD shall be
　　　consumed.

### Judgment on the Sacred Groves

29 ‡You shall be ashamed of the terebinths
　　　which you desired,
　　and blush on account of the gardens
　　　which you chose.

30 You shall become like a terebinth whose
　　　leaves wither,
　　like a garden that has no water.

31 The strong tree shall turn to tinder,
　　and the one who tends it shall
　　　become a spark;
Both of them shall burn together,
　　and there shall be none to quench
　　　them.

---

*[1:26] **Judges**: the reference must be to royal judges
appointed by David and his successors, not to the tribal judges
of the Book of Judges, since the "beginning" of Jerusalem as
an Israelite city dates only to the time of David. The Davidic
era is idealized here; obtaining justice in the historical Jerusalem of David's time was more problematic (see 2 Sm 15:1–6).

†[1:27–28] These verses expand the oracle that originally
ended at v. 26. The expansion correctly interprets the preceding text as proclaiming a purifying judgment on Zion in
which the righteous are saved while the wicked perish. The
meaning of "by justice" and "by righteousness" is ambiguous.
Do these terms refer to God's judgment or to the justice and
righteousness of Zion's surviving inhabitants? Is 33:14–16
suggests the latter interpretation.

‡[1:29–31] These verses were secondarily inserted here on
the catchword principle; like v. 28 they pronounce judgment
on certain parties "together" (v. 31). The terebinths and gardens refer to the sacred groves or asherahs that functioned as
idolatrous cultic symbols at the popular shrines or high places
(1 Kgs 14:23; 2 Kgs 17:10). Hezekiah cut down these groves
during his reform (2 Kgs 18:4); they were a religious issue
during Isaiah's ministry (cf. Is 17:7–11). Isaiah threatens those
who cultivate these symbols with the same fate that befalls
trees when deprived of water.

---

m. [1:23] Ex 23:8; Dt 16:19.　n. [1:24] Dt 32:41.　o. [1:26] Jer
33:7–11; Zec 8:8.

## CHAPTER 2

¹§This is what Isaiah, son of Amoz, saw concerning Judah and Jerusalem.

### Zion, the Royal City of God

2 ¶In days to come,
The mountain of the LORD's house
　　shall be established as the highest
　　　mountain
　　and raised above the hills.
All nations shall stream toward it.*p*

3 Many peoples shall come and say:
"Come, let us go up to the LORD's
　　　mountain,
　　to the house of the God of Jacob,
That he may instruct us in his ways,
　　and we may walk in his paths."*q*
For from Zion shall go forth instruction,
　　and the word of the LORD from
　　　Jerusalem.

4 **He shall judge between the nations,
　　and set terms for many peoples.
They shall beat their swords into
　　　plowshares
　　and their spears into pruning
　　　hooks;*r*
One nation shall not raise the sword
　　　against another,
　　nor shall they train for war again.*s*

5 ††House of Jacob, come,
　　let us walk in the light of the LORD!

### The Lord's Day of Judgment on Pride

6 You have abandoned your people,
　　the house of Jacob!

---

§[2:1] This editorial heading probably introduced the collection of chaps. 2–12, to which chap. 1 with its introduction
was added later (see note on 1:2–31).

¶[2:2–22] These verses contain two very important oracles,
one on the pilgrimage of nations to Mount Zion (vv. 2–4—
completed with an invitation to the "house of Jacob," v. 5), the
other on the day of the Lord (see note on Am 5:18), which was
probably composed from at least two earlier pieces. Whereas
vv. 6–8 indict Judah for trust in superstitious practices and
human resources rather than in the Lord, the following verses
are directed against humankind in general and emphasize the
effect of the "day of the Lord," the humbling of human pride.
This may be taken as a precondition for the glorious vision
of vv. 2–4. This vision of Zion's glorious future, which is also
found in a slightly variant form in Mi 4:1–4, is rooted in the
early Zion tradition, cultivated in the royal cult in Jerusalem.
It celebrated God's choice of Jerusalem as the divine dwelling place, along with God's choice of the Davidic dynasty
(Ps 68:16–17; 78:67–72; 132:13–18). **Highest mountain**: the
Zion tradition followed earlier mythological conceptions that
associate the abode of deities with very high mountains (Ps
48:2–3). The lifting of Mount Zion is a metaphor for universal
recognition of the Lord's authority.

**[2:4] Once the nations acknowledge God as sovereign,
they go up to Jerusalem to settle their disputes, rather than
having recourse to war.

††[2:5] This verse is added as a conclusion to vv. 2–4; cf. Mi
4:4–5, where a quite different conclusion is provided for the
parallel version of this oracle.

---

p. [2:2–4] Mi 4:1–4.　q. [2:3] Is 56:7; 2 Kgs 17:26–28; Jer 31:6–14;
Zec 8:20–23.　r. [2:4] Jl 4:10.　s. [2:4] Is 9:7; 11:4; Ps 46:10; Zec
9:10.

Because they are filled with diviners,
and soothsayers, like the Philistines;
with foreigners they clasp hands.[t]

7 Their land is full of silver and gold,
there is no end to their treasures;
Their land is full of horses,
there is no end to their chariots.

8 Their land is full of idols;
they bow down to the works of their
hands,
what their fingers have made.[u]

9 So all shall be abased,
each one brought low.[*]
Do not pardon them!

10 Get behind the rocks,
hide in the dust,
From the terror of the LORD
and the splendor of his majesty!

11 The eyes of human pride shall be lowered,
the arrogance of mortals shall be
abased,
and the LORD alone will be exalted,
on that day.[†]

12 For the LORD of hosts will have his day
against all that is proud and
arrogant,
against all that is high, and it will be
brought low;

13 Yes, against all the cedars of Lebanon[‡]
and against all the oaks of Bashan,

14 Against all the lofty mountains
and all the high hills,

15 Against every lofty tower
and every fortified wall,

16 Against all the ships of Tarshish
and all stately vessels.

17 Then human pride shall be abased,
the arrogance of mortals brought
low,
And the LORD alone will be exalted on
that day.

18 The idols will vanish completely.

19 People will go into caves in the rocks
and into holes in the earth,
At the terror of the LORD
and the splendor of his majesty,
as he rises to overawe the earth.

20 On that day people shall throw to moles
and bats
their idols of silver and their idols
of gold
which they made for themselves to
worship.

21 And they shall go into caverns in the rocks
and into crevices in the cliffs,

At the terror of the LORD
and the splendor of his majesty,
as he rises to overawe the earth.

22 [§]As for you, stop worrying about mortals,
in whose nostrils is but a breath;
for of what worth are they?

## CHAPTER 3

### Judgment on Jerusalem and Judah

1 [¶]The Lord, the LORD of hosts,
will take away from Jerusalem and
from Judah
Support and staff—
all support of bread,
all support of water:[v]

2 Hero and warrior,
judge and prophet, diviner and elder,

3 The captain of fifty and the nobleman,
counselor, skilled magician, and
expert charmer.

4 I will place boys as their princes;
the fickle will govern them,[w]

5 And the people will oppress one another,
yes, each one the neighbor.
The child will be insolent toward the
elder,
and the base toward the honorable.[x]

6 When anyone seizes a brother
in their father's house, saying,
"You have clothes! Be our ruler,
and take in hand this ruin!"—

7 He will cry out in that day:
"I cannot be a healer,[y]
when there is neither bread nor
clothing in my own house!
You will not make me a ruler of the
people!"

8 Jerusalem has stumbled, Judah has fallen;
for their speech and deeds affront
the LORD,
a provocation in the sight of his
majesty.

9 Their very look bears witness against
them;[z]
they boast of their sin like Sodom,[a]

---

§[2:22] The meaning of this verse, certainly a later addition, is not clear. It is not addressed to God but to a plural subject.

¶[3:1–12] These verses suggest deportation, with resulting social upheaval, and thus may date to sometime after Ahaz submitted as vassal to Assyria. The deportation practiced by Assyria, as later by Babylon, exiled the leading elements of society, such as those named in vv. 2–3; cf. 2 Kgs 24:12, 14–16 for a similar list of those exiled by the Babylonians. Denuding society of its leaders opens the way to near anarchy and a situation in which leadership is seized by or thrust upon those unqualified for it (vv. 5–7). The situation has been provoked by sinfully inept leadership (vv. 4, 8–9, 12). Some suggest that vv. 4 and 12 refer to Ahaz, who may have come to the throne at an early age. Verses 10–11 form a wisdom couplet that was inserted later.

---

*[2:9] Bowing down to idols will not bring deliverance to Israel, but rather total abasement. **Do not pardon them**: this line is so abrupt that it is almost certainly an intrusion in the text.
†[2:11] **That day**: i.e., the day of the Lord; cf. note on Am 5:18.
‡[2:13] **Lebanon**: Mount Lebanon in Syria, famed for its cedars. **Bashan**: the fertile uplands east of the Sea of Galilee.

t. [2:6] Is 10:32.  u. [2:8] Is 17:7–8; 31:1–3.

v. [3:1] Lv 26:26; Ez 4:16.  w. [3:4] Eccl 10:16.  x. [3:5] Mi 7:5–6.
y. [3:7] Is 1:6.  z. [3:9] Jer 3:3.  a. [3:9] Is 1:10.

They do not hide it.
>> Woe to them!
>> They deal out evil to themselves.
10 Happy the just, for it will go well with
>> them,
>> the fruit of their works they will eat.
11 Woe to the wicked! It will go ill with them,
>> with the work of their hands they
>> will be repaid.
12 My people—infants oppress them,
>> women rule over them!
My people, your leaders deceive you,[b]
>> they confuse the paths you should
>> follow.

13 The LORD rises to accuse,
>> stands to try his people.
14 The LORD enters into judgment
>> with the people's elders and princes:
You, you who have devoured the
>> vineyard;
>> the loot wrested from the poor is in
>> your houses.
15 What do you mean by crushing my
>> people,
>> and grinding down the faces of the
>> poor?
>> says the Lord, the GOD of hosts.

### The Haughty Women of Zion[†]

16 The LORD said:[c]
>> Because the daughters of Zion are
>> haughty,
>> and walk with necks outstretched,
Ogling and mincing as they go,
>> their anklets tinkling with every
>> step,
17 The Lord shall cover the scalps of Zion's
>> daughters with scabs,
>> and the LORD shall lay bare their
>> heads.[‡d]

18§On that day the Lord will do away with the finery of the anklets, sunbursts, and crescents; 19the
pendants, bracelets, and veils; 20the headdresses,
bangles, cinctures, perfume boxes, and amulets;
21the signet rings, and the nose rings; 22the court
dresses, wraps, cloaks, and purses; 23the lace
gowns, linen tunics, turbans, and shawls.

24 Instead of perfume there will be stench,
>> instead of a girdle, a rope,
And instead of elaborate coiffure,
>> baldness;
>> instead of a rich gown, a sackcloth
>> skirt.
Then, instead of beauty, shame.
25 Your men will fall by the sword,
>> and your champions,[¶] in war;[e]
26 Her gates will lament and mourn,
>> as the city sits desolate on the
>> ground.[f]

## CHAPTER 4

1 Seven women will take hold of one man[**]
>> on that day, saying:
"We will eat our own food
>> and wear our own clothing;
Only let your name be given us,
>> put an end to our disgrace!"

### Jerusalem Purified

2 ††On that day,
The branch‡‡ of the LORD will be beauty
>> and glory,
>> and the fruit of the land will be
>> honor and splendor
>> for the survivors of Israel.
3 Everyone who remains in Zion,
>> everyone left in Jerusalem
Will be called holy:
>> everyone inscribed for life§§ in
>> Jerusalem.[g]
4 When the Lord washes away
>> the filth of the daughters of Zion,
And purges Jerusalem's blood from her
>> midst
>> with a blast of judgment, a searing
>> blast,[h]
5 Then will the LORD create,
>> over the whole site of Mount Zion
>> and over her place of assembly,
A smoking cloud by day
>> and a light of flaming fire by night.[i]

---

¶ [3:25] **Your men . . . your champions**: the second person
feminine singular pronoun here shows that the prophet has
shifted his attention from the women of Zion to the personified city of Zion.
** [4:1] **Seven women . . . one man**: deportation (cf. note
on 3:1–12) would result in a disproportion of the sexes and
leave the female population without enough male partners.
The women are willing to marry, not for support, but to avoid
disgrace.
†† [4:2–6] Usually judged a later addition to the oracles of
Isaiah. It relieves the threatening tone of the surrounding
chaps. 3 and 5.
‡‡ [4:2] **Branch**: the term (Heb. *semah*) that is sometimes
used of the ideal Davidic king of the future (cf. Jer 23:5; 33:15;
Zec 3:8; 6:12). However, the parallel "fruit of the land" does
not favor that usage here.
§§ [4:3] **Inscribed for life**: in God's list of the elect; cf. Ex
32:32.

---

*[3:13–15] The princes and the elders, here accused of
despoiling the poor, are the very ones who should be their
defenders. **Loot**: by the Hebrew term (*gazela*) Isaiah conveys
the idea of violent seizure, though 10:1–4 suggests the poor
could be plundered by legal means.
†[3:16–4:1] Here and again in 32:9–14 Isaiah condemns
the women of the ruling class for their part in Jerusalem's
plight.
‡[3:17] A shaven head is a mark of social disgrace; cf. Nm
5:18.
§[3:18–23] The long list of women's apparel in these verses
suggests luxury and vanity; it contains a number of rare words,
and the precise meaning of many of the terms is uncertain.

---

b. [3:12] Mi 3:5.   c. [3:16] Is 32:9–14; Ez 16:50; Am 4:1–3.
d. [3:17] Jer 13:26; Ez 16:37.

e. [3:25] Hos 14:1.   f. [3:26] Is 47:1; Lam 2:10.   g. [4:3] Is 6:13; Ob
17; Mal 3:16.   h. [4:4] Is 1:21–28.   i. [4:5] Ex 13:21.

6 For over all, his glory will be shelter and
       protection:
     shade from the parching heat of day,
     refuge and cover from storm and rain.[j]

## CHAPTER 5

### The Song of the Vineyard[*]

1 Now let me sing of my friend,
     my beloved's song about his vineyard.
   My friend had a vineyard
     on a fertile hillside;
2 He spaded it, cleared it of stones,
     and planted the choicest vines;
   Within it he built a watchtower,
     and hewed out a wine press.
   Then he waited for the crop of grapes,
     but it yielded rotten grapes.[k]
3 Now, inhabitants of Jerusalem, people of
       Judah,
     judge between me and my vineyard:
4 What more could be done for my
       vineyard
     that I did not do?[l]
   Why, when I waited for the crop of grapes,
     did it yield rotten grapes?
5 Now, I will let you know
     what I am going to do to my
       vineyard:
   Take away its hedge, give it to grazing,
     break through its wall, let it be
       trampled![†]
6 Yes, I will make it a ruin:
     it shall not be pruned or hoed,
     but will be overgrown with thorns
       and briers;
   I will command the clouds
     not to rain upon it.
7 The vineyard of the LORD of hosts is the
       house of Israel,
     the people of Judah, his cherished
       plant;
   He waited for judgment, but see,
       bloodshed!
     for justice, but hark, the outcry![‡]

### Oracles of Reproach[§]

8 [§]Ah! Those who join house to house,
     who connect field with field,
   Until no space remains, and you alone dwell
     in the midst of the land![m]
9 In my hearing the LORD of hosts has sworn:[n]
     Many houses shall be in ruins,
     houses large and fine, with nobody
       living there.[o]
10 Ten acres of vineyard
     shall yield but one bath,[**]
   And a homer of seed
     shall yield but an ephah.
11 [††]Ah! Those who rise early in the morning
       in pursuit of strong drink,
     lingering late
       inflamed by wine,
12 Banqueting on wine with harp and lyre,
       timbrel and flute,[p]
   But the deed of the LORD they do not
       regard,
     the work of his hands they do not see![q]
13 Therefore my people go into exile
     for lack of understanding,[r]
   Its nobles starving,
     its masses parched with thirst.
14 Therefore Sheol enlarges its throat
     and opens its mouth beyond measure;[s]
   Down into it go nobility and masses,
     tumult and revelry.
15 All shall be abased, each one brought low,
     and the eyes of the haughty lowered,[t]
16 But the LORD of hosts shall be exalted by
       judgment,
     by justice the Holy God shown holy.[u]
17 Lambs shall graze as at pasture,
     young goats shall eat in the ruins of
       the rich.
18 Ah! Those who tug at guilt with cords of
       perversity,
     and at sin as if with cart ropes!
19 [‡‡]Who say, "Let him make haste,
     let him speed his work, that we may
       see it;

---

§[5:8–24] These verses contain a series of short oracles
introduced by the Hebrew particle *hoy* ("Ah!"), an emphatic
exclamation, sometimes translated "Woe!"

¶[5:8–10] An oracle against land-grabbers (v. 8); they will
be impoverished instead of enriched (vv. 9–10).

**[5:10] Ten acres: a field with ten times the surface area
a yoke of oxen could plow in one day. Bath: a liquid measure
equal to about twelve gallons. Homer: a dry measure equal to
what a donkey can carry, calculated to be about ten bushels.
Ephah: a dry measure of about one bushel. So small a harvest
is the fruit of the land-grabbers' greed.

††[5:11–13] An oracle against debauchery and indifference.
Strong drink: the Hebrew word *shekar* means either beer or a
type of wine, perhaps date wine, not distilled liquor.

‡‡[5:19] An indication that some, presumably of the ruling
class, scoff at Isaiah's teaching on the Lord's "plan" and "work"
(cf. v. 12; 14:26–27; 28:9–14; 30:10–11).

---

*[5:1–7] Vineyard: although the term is sometimes used
in an erotic context (Sg 1:6; 8:12), "vineyard" or "vine" is
used more frequently as a metaphor for God's people (27:2;
Ps 80:9, 14, 15; Jer 2:21; 12:10; Ez 17:7; Hos 10:1; Na 2:2). The
terms translated "friend" (*yadid*) and "beloved" (*dod*) suggest
the Lord's favor (Dt 33:12; 2 Sm 12:25; Ps 127:2) and familial background rather than introducing the piece as a "love
song," as is sometimes suggested. The prophet disguises the
real theme (the people's infidelity) so that the hearers will participate in the unfavorable judgment called for (vv. 3–4). Cf.
the reversal of this parable in 27:2–6.

†[5:5–6] Trampled . . . thorns and briers: this judgment
is echoed in the description of the devastated land in 7:23–25.

‡[5:7] Judgment . . . bloodshed . . . justice . . . outcry: in
Hebrew there is an impressive play on words: *mishpat* parallels *mispah*, *sedaqah* parallels *se'aqah*. See also the threefold
"waited for" in vv. 2, 4, 7.

---

j. [4:6] Is 32:1–2.   k. [5:2] Dt 32:32.   l. [5:4] Mi 6:3–5.

m. [5:8] Mi 2:1–3.   n. [5:9] Is 22:14.   o. [5:9] Is 6:12.   p. [5:12] Is
5:22; Am 6:1–7.   q. [5:12] Is 5:19; 10:12; 14:24–27; 19:12, 17; 23:9;
28:21; 30:1.   r. [5:13] Hos 4:6.   s. [5:14] Hb 2:5.   t. [5:15] Is 2:9,
11, 17.   u. [5:16] Is 1:27.

On with the plan of the Holy One of Israel!
 let it come to pass, that we may
  know it!"[v]
[20] Ah! Those who call evil good, and good evil,
 who change darkness to light, and
  light into darkness,
 who change bitter to sweet, and
  sweet into bitter![w]
[21] Ah! Those who are wise in their own eyes,
 prudent in their own view![x]
[22] Ah! Those who are champions at drinking
  wine,
 masters at mixing drink!
[23] Those who acquit the guilty for bribes,
 and deprive the innocent of justice![y]
[24] Therefore, as the tongue of fire licks up
  stubble,
 as dry grass shrivels in the flame,
Their root shall rot
 and their blossom scatter like dust;
For they have rejected the instruction of
  the LORD of hosts,
 and scorned the word of the Holy
  One of Israel.

[25] *Therefore the wrath of the LORD blazes
  against his people,
 he stretches out his hand to strike them;
The mountains quake,[z]
 their corpses shall be like refuse in
  the streets.
For all this, his wrath is not turned back,
 his hand is still outstretched.

### Invasion[†]

[26] He will raise a signal to a far-off nation,
 and whistle for it from the ends of
  the earth.[a]
 Then speedily and promptly they
  will come.
[27] None among them is weary, none stumbles,
 none will slumber, none will sleep.
None with waist belt loose,
 none with sandal thong broken.
[28] Their arrows are sharp,
 and all their bows are bent,
The hooves of their horses like flint,
 and their chariot wheels like the
  whirlwind.

[29] They roar like the lion,
 like young lions, they roar;
They growl and seize the prey,
 they carry it off and none can rescue.
[30] They will growl over it, on that day,
 like the growling of the sea,
Look to the land—
 darkness closing in,
 the light dark with clouds![b]

*B. The Book of Emmanuel*

## CHAPTER 6

**The Sending of Isaiah.** [1]In the year King Uzziah died,[‡] I saw the Lord seated on a high and lofty throne,[c] with the train of his garment filling the temple. [2]Seraphim[§] were stationed above; each of them had six wings: with two they covered their faces, with two they covered their feet, and with two they hovered.[d] [3]One cried out to the other:

"Holy, holy, holy[¶] is the LORD of hosts!
 All the earth is filled with his glory!"

[4]At the sound of that cry, the frame of the door shook and the house was filled with smoke.**[\*\*][e] [5]Then I said, "Woe is me, I am doomed![††] For I am a man of unclean lips, living among a people of unclean lips,[f] and my eyes have seen the King, the LORD of hosts!" [6]Then one of the seraphim flew to me, holding an ember which he had taken with tongs from the altar.

[7]He touched my mouth with it. "See," he said, "now that this has touched your lips,[‡‡] your wickedness is removed, your sin purged."[g]

‡[6:1] **In the year King Uzziah died**: probably 742 B.C., although the chronology of this period is disputed. **A high and lofty throne**: within the holy of holies of the Jerusalem Temple stood two cherubim, or winged sphinxes, whose outstretched wings served as the divine throne (1 Kgs 6:23–28; Ez 1:4–28; 10:1, 20). The ark of the covenant was God's footstool (Ps 132:7–8; 1 Chr 28:2), placed under the cherubim (1 Kgs 8:6–7). **Temple**: the holy place, just in front of the holy of holies.

§[6:2] **Seraphim**: the plural of *saraph* ("to burn"), a term used to designate the "fiery" serpents of the wilderness (Nm 21:8; Dt 8:15), and to refer to "winged" serpents (Is 14:29; 30:6). Here, however, it is used adjectivally of the cherubim, who are not serpent-like, as seen in the fact that they have faces and sexual parts ("feet"). See the adaptation of these figures by Ezekiel (Ez 1:10–12; 10:4–15).

¶[6:3] **Holy, holy, holy**: these words have been used in Christian liturgy from the earliest times.

\*\*[6:4] **Smoke**: reminiscent of the clouds which indicated God's presence at Mount Sinai (Ex 19:16–19; Dt 4:11) and which filled the tabernacle (Ex 40:34–38) and the Temple (1 Kgs 8:10–11) at their dedication.

††[6:5] **Doomed**: there are two roots from which the verb here could be derived; one means "to perish, be doomed," the other "to become silent," and given Isaiah's delight in puns and double entendre, he probably intended to sound both notes. "I am doomed!" is suggested by the popular belief that to see God would lead to one's death; cf. Gn 32:31; Ex 33:20; Jgs 13:22. "I am struck silent!" is suggested by the emphasis on the lips in vv. 5–6, and such silence is attested elsewhere as the appropriate response to the vision of the Lord in the Temple (Hb 2:20).

‡‡[6:7] **Touched your lips**: Isaiah is thus symbolically purified of sin in preparation for his mission as God's prophet.

---

*[5:25–30] These verses do not suit their present context. Apparently v. 25 was originally the conclusion of the poem of 9:7–20 directed against the Northern Kingdom; cf. the refrain that occurs here and in 9:11, 16, and 20. Verses 26–30 look to an invasion by Assyria and might originally have come immediately after the poem of 9:1–20 plus 5:25. The insertion of chaps. 6–8 may have occasioned the dislocation, as well as that of 10:1–4a, which may have originally belonged with the "reproach" oracles of 5:8–23.

†[5:26–30] This oracle threatens a future judgment, an invasion of the Assyrian army, God's instrument for punishing Judah (10:5, 15).

v. [5:19] Jer 17:15; 2 Pt 3:3–4. w. [5:20] Is 32:4–5. x. [5:21] Prv 3:7; 26:12; Rom 11:25; 12:16. y. [5:23] Ex 23:8; Prv 17:15. z. [5:25] Am 1:1; Zec 14:5; cf. Is 9:18a. a. [5:26] Is 7:18; 11:12; Jer 4:6; 50:2.

b. [5:30] Is 8:22. c. [6:1] 1 Kgs 22:19–23; Jn 12:41. d. [6:2] Rev 4:8.
e. [6:4] Rev 15:8. f. [6:5] Is 29:13; Mt 15:1–11; Mk 7:1–13; Col 2:20–23. g. [6:7] Jer 1:9; Dn 10:16.

⁸Then I heard the voice of the Lord saying, "Whom shall I send? Who will go for us?" "Here I am," I said; "send me!" ⁹And he replied: Go and say to this people:

> Listen carefully, but do not understand!
> Look intently, but do not perceive!ʰ
> 10  Make the heart of this people sluggish,
>         dull their ears and close their eyes;
>     Lest they see with their eyes, and hear
>             with their ears,
>         and their heart understand,
>         and they turn and be healed.ⁱ

¹¹"How long, O Lord?" I asked. And he replied:

> † Until the cities are desolate,
>         without inhabitants,
>     Houses, without people,
>         and the land is a desolate waste.
> 12  Until the LORD sends the people far away,
>         and great is the desolation in the
>             midst of the land.
> 13  If there remain a tenth part in it,
>         then this in turn shall be laid waste;
>     As with a terebinth or an oak
>         whose trunk remains when its leaves
>             have fallen.ᵗʲ
>     Holy offspring is the trunk.

## CHAPTER 7

### The Syro-Ephraimite Warᵇ

**Crisis in Judah.** ¹In the days of Ahaz,ᵗ king of Judah, son of Jotham, son of Uzziah, Rezin, king of Aram, and Pekah, king of Israel, son of Remaliah, went up to attack Jerusalem, but they were not able to conquer it.ᵏ ²When word came to the house of David that Aram had allied itself with Ephraim, the heart of the king and heart of the people trembled, as the trees of the forest tremble in the wind.

³Then the LORD said to Isaiah: Go out to meet Ahaz, you and your son Shear-jashub,** at the end of the conduit of the upper pool, on the highway to the fuller's field, ⁴and say to him: Take care you remain calm and do not fear; do not let your courage fail before these two stumps of smoldering brands,ⁱ the blazing anger of Rezin and the Arameans and of the son of Remaliah— ⁵because Aram, with Ephraim and the son of Remaliah, has planned†† evil against you. They say, ⁶"Let us go up against Judah, tear it apart, make it our own by force, and appoint the son of Tabeel‡‡ king there."

> 7   Thus says the Lord GOD:
>         It shall not stand, it shall not be!ᵐ
> 8   §§The head of Aram is Damascus,
>         and the head of Damascus is Rezin;
> 9   The head of Ephraim is Samaria,
>         and the head of Samaria is the son of
>             Remaliah.
>     Within sixty-five years,
>         Ephraim shall be crushed, no longer
>             a nation.
>     Unless your faith is firm,
>         you shall not be firm!ⁿ

**Emmanuel.** ¹⁰Again the LORD spoke to Ahaz: ¹¹Ask for a sign from the LORD, your God; let it be deep as Sheol, or high as the sky!¶¶ ¹²But Ahaz answered, "I will not ask! I will not tempt the LORD!"*** ¹³Then he said: Listen, house of David! Is it not enough that you weary human beings? Must you also weary my God? ¹⁴Therefore the Lord himself will give you a sign;††† the young

---

*[6:9–10] Isaiah's words give evidence that he attempted in every way, through admonition, threat, and promise, to bring the people to conversion (cf. 1:18–20), so it is unlikely that this charge to "harden" is to be understood as Isaiah's task; more probably it reflects the refusal of the people, more particularly the leaders, who were supposed to "see," "hear," and "understand," a refusal which would then lead to a disastrous outcome (vv. 11–12).

†[6:11–12] The desolation described would be the result of the sort of deportation practiced by the Assyrians and later by the Babylonians. Isaiah seems to expect this as an eventual consequence of Judah's submission as vassal to the Assyrians; cf. 3:1–3; 5:13.

‡[6:13] **When its leaves have fallen:** the meaning of the Hebrew is uncertain, and the text may be corrupt. **Holy offspring:** part of the phrase is missing from the Septuagint and may be a later addition; it provides a basis for hope for the future.

§[7:1–8:18] These verses (often termed Isaiah's "Memoirs") contain a series of oracles and narratives (some in first person), all closely related to the Syro-Ephraimite war of 735–732 B.C. Several passages feature three children whose symbolic names refer to the Lord's purposes: Shear-jashub (7:3), Emmanuel (7:10–17; 8:8–10), and Maher-shalal-hash-baz (8:1–4). Judah and its Davidic dynasty should trust God's promises and not fear the combined armies of Israel and Syria; within a very short time these two enemy states will be destroyed, and David's dynasty will continue.

¶[7:1] **Days of Ahaz:** who ruled from 735 to 715 B.C. This attack against Jerusalem by the kings of Aram (Syria) and Israel in 735 B.C. was occasioned by the refusal of Ahaz to enter with them into an anti-Assyrian alliance; cf. 2 Kgs 16.

**[7:3] **Shear-jashub:** this name means "a remnant will return" (cf. 10:20–22).

††[7:5] **Planned:** the plans of those who plot against Ahaz shall not be accomplished (v. 7). What the Lord plans will unfailingly come to pass, whereas human plans contrary to those of the Lord are doomed to frustration; cf. 8:10; 14:24–27; 19:11–14; 29:15; 30:1. See further the note on 14:24–27.

‡‡[7:6] **Son of Tabeel:** a puppet of Jerusalem's enemies. His appointment would interrupt the lawful succession from David.

§§[7:8–9] God had chosen and made a commitment to David's dynasty and his capital city Jerusalem, not to Rezin and his capital Damascus, nor to the son of Remaliah and his capital Samaria (2 Sm 7:12–16; Ps 2:6; 78:68–72; 132:11–18). **Within sixty-five years . . . nation:** this text occurs at the end of v. 8 in the Hebrew. Ahaz would not have been reassured by so distant a promise; the phrase is probably a later addition.

¶¶[7:11] **Deep . . . sky:** an extraordinary or miraculous sign that would prove God's firm will to save the royal house of David from its oppressors.

***[7:12] **Tempt the LORD:** Ahaz prefers to depend upon the might of Assyria rather than the might of God.

†††[7:14] Isaiah's sign seeks to reassure Ahaz that he need not fear the invading armies of Syria and Israel in the light of God's promise to David (2 Sm 7:12–16). The oracle follows

---

h. [6:9] Mt 13:10–17; Mk 4:10–12; Lk 8:9–10; Acts 28:25–28.  i. [6:10] Jer 5:21; Jn 12:40.  j. [6:13] Is 10:22.

k. [7:1] 2 Kgs 16:5; 2 Chr 28:5–15.  l. [7:4] Is 8:12; 30:15.  m. [7:7] Is 8:10; Ps 33:10.  n. [7:9] 2 Chr 20:20.

woman, pregnant and about to bear a son, shall name him Emmanuel. ¹⁵Curds and honey* he will eat so that he may learn to reject evil and choose good; ¹⁶for before the child learns to reject evil and choose good, the land of those two kings whom you dread shall be deserted.

¹⁷The LORD shall bring upon you and your people and your father's house such days as have not come since Ephraim seceded† from Judah (the king of Assyria). ¹⁸On that day

The LORD shall whistle
    for the fly in the farthest streams of
      Egypt,
    and for the bee in the land of
      Assyria.°
¹⁹ All of them shall come and settle
    in the steep ravines and in the rocky
      clefts,
    on all thornbushes and in all
      pastures.

²⁰‡On that day the Lord shall shave with the razor hired from across the River (the king of Assyria) the head, and the hair of the feet; it shall also shave off the beard.ᵖ ²¹On that day a man shall keep alive a young cow or a couple of sheep, ²²and from their abundant yield of milk he shall eat curds; curds and honey shall be the food of all who are left in the land. ²³ᵈOn that day every place where there were a thousand vines worth a thousand pieces of silver shall become briers and thorns. ²⁴One shall have to go there with bow and arrows, for all the country shall be briers and thorns.ᵍ ²⁵But as for all the hills which were hoed with a mattock, for fear of briers and thorns you will not go there; they shall become a place for cattle to roam and sheep to trample.ʳ

---

a traditional announcement formula by which the birth and sometimes naming of a child is promised to particular individuals (Gn 16:11; Jgs 13:3). **The young woman**: Hebrew *'almah* designates a young woman of marriageable age without specific reference to virginity. The Septuagint translated the Hebrew term as *parthenos*, which normally does mean virgin, and this translation underlies Mt 1:23. **Emmanuel**: the name means "with us is God." Since for the Christian the incarnation is the ultimate expression of God's willingness to "be with us," it is understandable that this text was interpreted to refer to the birth of Christ.

\*[7:15–16] **Curds and honey**: the only diet available to those who are left after the devastation of the land; cf. vv. 21–25.

†[7:17] **Such days as have not come since Ephraim seceded**: the days of the kingdom prior to the secession of Ephraim and the other northern tribes (1 Kgs 12). **The king of Assyria**: the final comment appears to be a later editorial gloss indicating days worse than any since the secession.

‡[7:20] God will use the Assyrians from across the River (the Euphrates) as his instrument ("razor") to inflict disgrace and suffering upon his people. Ahaz paid tribute to the Assyrian king Tiglath-pileser III, who decimated Syria and Israel in his campaigns of 734–732 B.C. (cf. 2 Kgs 16:7–9). **The feet**: euphemism for sexual parts; cf. Is 6:2.

§[7:23–25] Cf. note on 5:5–6.

---

o. [7:18] Is 5:26.   p. [7:20] Is 3:24; 2 Sm 10:4–6; Ez 5:1.   q. [7:24] Is 32:13.   r. [7:25] Is 5:5; 32:14.

# CHAPTER 8

**A Son of Isaiah.** ¹The LORD said to me: Take a large tablet, and inscribe on it with an ordinary stylus,¶ "belonging to Maher-shalal-hash-baz,"ˢ ²and call reliable witnesses" for me, Uriah the priest, and Zechariah, son of Jeberechiah.

³Then I went to the prophetess and she conceived and bore a son. The LORD said to me: Name him Maher-shalal-hash-baz, ⁴for before the child learns to say, "My father, my mother," the wealth of Damascus and the spoils of Samaria shall be carried off by the king of Assyria.

**The Choice: The Lord or Assyria.** ⁵Again the LORD spoke to me:

⁶ Because this people†† has rejected
    the waters of Shiloah that flow
      gently,
    And melts with fear at the display of
      Rezin and Remaliah's son,
⁷ Therefore the Lord is bringing up against
      them
    the waters of the River, great and
      mighty,
    the king of Assyria and all his glory.
It shall rise above all its channels,
    and overflow all its banks.
⁸ It shall roll on into Judah,
    it shall rage and pass on—
    up to the neck it shall reach.ᵗ
But his outspread wings will fill
    the width of your land, Emmanuel!
⁹ Band together, O peoples, but be
      shattered!
    Give ear, all you distant lands!
    Arm yourselves, but be shattered!
    Arm yourselves, but be
      shattered!
¹⁰ Form a plan, it shall be thwarted;
    make a resolve, it shall not be
      carried out,
    for "With us is God!"‡‡ᵘ

---

¶[8:1] **Ordinary stylus**: lit., "stylus of men." **Maher-shalal-hash-baz**: a symbolic name to be given to another son of Isaiah (v. 3); it means "quick spoils; speedy plunder," and describes what the Assyrians will do to Syria and Israel.

\*\*[8:2] **Reliable witnesses**: who would testify that Isaiah had indeed prophesied the future destruction. **Uriah the priest**: cf. 2 Kgs 16:10.

††[8:6–8] **This people**: Judah. **Waters of Shiloah**: the stream that flows from the Gihon spring into the pool of Shiloah in Jerusalem and provides a sure supply in time of siege; here it symbolizes the divine protection which Judah has rejected by seeking Assyrian support, symbolized by "the River" (i.e., the Euphrates). Ultimately Assyrian power will devastate Judah. **His outspread wings**: the Lord's wings, a recurring symbol for divine protection (Ps 17:8; 36:8; 57:2; 61:5; 91:4; Ru 2:12). Some understand the image to refer to the sides of the flooding river, but this use of the Hebrew word for "wings" is unparalleled elsewhere in classical Hebrew.

‡‡[8:10] The plan of Israel's enemies will be thwarted because, as the name "Emmanuel" signifies, "with us is God."

---

s. [8:1] Is 10:6.   t. [8:8] Is 30:28.   u. [8:10] Is 7:7; 17:12–14.

**Disciples of Isaiah.** [11]For thus said the LORD—his hand strong upon me—warning me not to walk in the way of this people:

[12] 'Do not call conspiracy what this people
        calls conspiracy,
    nor fear what they fear, nor feel dread.
[13] But conspire with the LORD of hosts;
        he shall be your fear, he shall be
        your dread.[v]
[14] He shall be a snare,
        a stone for injury,
    A rock for stumbling
        to both the houses of Israel,
    A trap and a snare
        to those who dwell in Jerusalem;[w]
[15] And many among them shall stumble;
        fallen and broken;
    snared and captured.[x]

[16]Bind up my testimony, seal the instruction with my disciples.[†] [17]I will trust in the LORD, who is hiding his face from the house of Jacob; yes, I will wait for him. [18]Here am I and the children whom the LORD has given me: we are signs[‡] and portents in Israel from the LORD of hosts, who dwells on Mount Zion.[y]

[19]And when they say to you, "Inquire of ghosts and soothsayers who chirp and mutter;[§z] should not a people inquire of their gods, consulting the dead on behalf of the living, [20]for instruction and testimony?" Surely, those who speak like this are the ones for whom there is no dawn.[¶]

[21] He will pass through it hard-pressed and
        hungry,
    and when hungry, shall become
        enraged,
    and curse king and gods.
    He will look upward,
[22]    and will gaze at the earth,
    But will see only distress and darkness,
        oppressive gloom,
    murky, without light.[**]

**The Promise of Salvation Under a New Davidic King.**[††] [23]There is no gloom where there had been distress. Where once he degraded the land of Zebulun and the land of Naphtali, now he has glorified the way of the Sea, the land across the Jordan, Galilee of the Nations.[‡‡]

## CHAPTER 9

[1] The people who walked in darkness
        have seen a great light;
    Upon those who lived in a land of gloom
        a light has shone.[a]
[2] You have brought them abundant joy
        and great rejoicing;
    They rejoice before you as people rejoice
        at harvest,
        as they exult when dividing the
        spoils.
[3] For the yoke that burdened them,
        the pole on their shoulder,
    The rod of their taskmaster,
        you have smashed, as on the day of
        Midian.[§§b]
[4] For every boot that tramped in battle,
        every cloak rolled in blood,
        will be burned as fuel for fire.[c]
[5] For a child[¶¶] is born to us, a son is given to
        us;
        upon his shoulder dominion rests.
    They name him Wonder-Counselor,
        God-Hero,[d]
        Father-Forever, Prince of Peace.
[6] His dominion is vast
        and forever peaceful,

---

††[8:23–9:6] The meaning of 8:23 is somewhat uncertain, for example, whether the expressions translated "once" and "now" refer to times or to individuals, and also whether the verbs speak of degrading and glorifying the territories. If this traditional translation is correct, the passage would seem to promise the former Northern Kingdom of Israel deliverance from the Assyrians and might relate to Hezekiah's program of trying to reincorporate the northern territories into the kingdom of Judah and thus restore the boundaries of the country as it was under David.

‡‡[8:23] The territories mentioned in this verse are those which the Assyrian king Tiglath-pileser III took from Israel and incorporated into the Assyrian provincial system as a result of the Syro-Ephraimite War of 735–732 B.C. (2 Kgs 15:29). **Zebulun . . . Naphtali**: regions of the former Northern Kingdom of Israel. **The way of the Sea**: the area along the Mediterranean coast south of Mount Carmel which became the Assyrian province of Dor. **Land across the Jordan**: the province of Gilead east of the Jordan. **Galilee of the Nations**: the territory north of Mount Carmel which was incorporated in the Assyrian province of Megiddo. Galilee apparently had a large non-Israelite population. Mt 4:15–16 cites this verse in the context of the beginning of Jesus' public mission in Galilee.

§§[9:3] **Day of Midian**: when God used the judge Gideon to deliver these northern territories from Midianite oppression (Jgs 6–7).

¶¶[9:5] **A child**: perhaps to be identified with the Emmanuel of 7:14 and 8:8; cf. 11:1–2, 9. This verse may reflect a coronation rather than a birth. **Upon his shoulder**: the reference may be to a particular act in the ritual in which a symbol of the king's authority was placed on his shoulder (cf. 2 Kgs 11:12; Is 22:22).

---

*[8:12–14] Because Isaiah and his followers resisted the official policy of seeking help from Assyria they were labeled "conspirators"; Isaiah uses the term to express what is really the case, cooperating with the Lord.

†[8:16] **Bind . . . seal . . . with my disciples**: because the prophet's message was not well received at the time, he wanted to preserve it until the future had vindicated him as God's true prophet (cf. 30:8–9).

‡[8:18] **Signs**: in the meantime, while awaiting the vindication of his message, Isaiah and his children with their symbolic names stood as a reminder of God's message to Israel.

§[8:19] **Chirp and mutter**: a mocking reference to necromancers.

¶[8:20] **Surely . . . no dawn**: reliance on necromancy brings futility.

**[8:22] **Oppressive gloom . . . without light**: the meaning of the Hebrew here is quite uncertain.

---

v. [8:13] Is 29:23; 1 Pt 3:14–15.   w. [8:14] Lk 2:34; Rom 9:32–33; 1 Pt 2:7–8.   x. [8:15] Mt 21:44.   y. [8:18] Is 2:2–5; 4:5; 11:9; 14:32; 28:16; 31:9; 33:5.   z. [8:19] Is 29:4.

a. [9:1] Mt 4:15–16.   b. [9:3] Is 10:26; Jgs 7:22–25.   c. [9:4] Ps 46:10.   d. [9:5] Is 10:21.

Upon David's throne, and over his kingdom,
which he confirms and sustains
By judgment and justice,
both now and forever.[e]
The zeal of the LORD of hosts will do this!

### Judgment on the Northern Kingdom[*]

7 The Lord has sent a word against Jacob,
and it falls upon Israel;

8 And all the people know it—
Ephraim and those who dwell in
Samaria—
those who say in arrogance and
pride of heart,

9 "Bricks have fallen,
but we will rebuild with cut stone;
Sycamores have been felled,
but we will replace them with cedars."[f]

10 So the LORD raises up their foes against
them
and stirs up their enemies to action—

11 Aram[†] from the east and the Philistines
from the west—
they devour Israel with open mouth.
For all this, his wrath is not turned back,
and his hand is still outstretched!

12 The people do not turn back to the one
who struck them,
nor do they seek the LORD of hosts.

13 So the LORD cuts off from Israel head and
tail,
palm branch and reed in one day.[g]

14 (The elder and the noble are the head,
the prophet who teaches falsehood
is the tail.)[h]

15 Those who lead this people lead them
astray,
and those who are led are swallowed
up.[i]

16 That is why the Lord does not spare their
young men,
and their orphans and widows he
does not pity;
For they are totally impious and wicked,
and every mouth speaks folly.
For all this, his wrath is not turned back,
his hand is still outstretched!

17 For wickedness burns like fire,
devouring brier and thorn;
It kindles the forest thickets,
which go up in columns of smoke.[j]

18 At the wrath of the LORD of hosts the land
quakes,
and the people are like fuel for fire;
no one spares his brother.[k]

19 They hack on the right, but remain hungry;
they devour on the left, but are not
filled.
Each devours the flesh of the
neighbor;

20 Manasseh devours Ephraim,[‡] and
Ephraim Manasseh,
together they turn on Judah.
For all this, his wrath is not turned back,
his hand is still outstretched!

## CHAPTER 10

### Perversion of Justice

1 [§]Ah! Those who enact unjust statutes,
who write oppressive decrees,[l]

2 Depriving the needy of judgment,
robbing my people's poor of justice,
Making widows their plunder,
and orphans their prey![m]

3 What will you do on the day of punishment,
when the storm comes from afar?
To whom will you flee for help?
Where will you leave your wealth,

4 Lest it sink beneath the captive
or fall beneath the slain?
For all this, his wrath is not turned back,
his hand is still outstretched![¶]

### Judgment on Assyria

5 [**]Ah! Assyria, the rod of my wrath,
the staff I wield in anger.[n]

6 Against an impious nation[††] I send him,
and against a people under my
wrath I order him
To seize plunder, carry off loot,

---

‡[9:20] **Manasseh . . . Ephraim**: two of the leading tribes of the Northern Kingdom. The reference is to the civil wars that marked the final decades of the Northern Kingdom (2 Kgs 15:10, 14–16, 25; cf. Hos 7:3–7).

§[10:1–4] This is another *hoy*-oracle; cf. note on 5:8–24. It may originally have been part of the collection at 5:8–24.

¶[10:4] **For all this . . . outstretched!**: this refrain appears to be out of place here; cf. 9:11, 16, 20.

**[10:5–34] These verses contain a series of oracles directed against Assyria. Verses 5–15 portray Assyria as simply the rod God uses to punish Israel, though Assyria does not realize this. The original conclusion to this unit may be the judgment found in vv. 24–27a, which continues the imagery and motifs found in vv. 5–15. Verses 16–23, because of the quite different imagery and motifs, may originally have been an insertion directed against Aram and Israel at the time of the Syro-Ephraimite War.

††[10:6] **Impious nation**: Judah. It was God's intention to use Assyria merely to punish, not to destroy, the nation.

---

*[9:7–20 + 5:25–30] These verses describe a series of judgments God sent against the Northern Kingdom of Israel because of its sins. Despite the judgments, however, Israel continued to rebel, and God's anger remained unabated, as the recurring refrain emphasizes (9:11, 16, 20). The refrain ties Is 9:7–20 together as a unit, but 9:20 is far too abrupt to be the original conclusion to the oracle. With its series of past judgments and repeated refrain, the oracle resembles Am 4:6–12; by analogy with that model one expects a conclusion in which the prophet turns from the narration of past judgments to the announcement of a future judgment. Is 5:25–30 fits the pattern found in 9:7–20 and provides a suitable and possibly original conclusion for the whole oracle.

†[9:11] **Aram**: the Syrian kingdom, with its capital at Damascus.

---

e. [9:6] Jer 23:5; Lk 1:32–33.   f. [9:9] Mal 1:4.   g. [9:13] Is 19:15; Dt 28:13, 44.   h. [9:14] Is 28:7.   i. [9:15] Is 3:12.

j. [9:17] Is 5:24; 33:11–12.   k. [9:18] Is 3:5.   l. [10:1] Jer 8:8.   m. [10:2] Is 1:23; 3:14–15.   n. [10:5] Jer 51:20–23.

and to trample them like the mud of
the street.
7 But this is not what he intends,
nor does he have this in mind;
Rather, it is in his heart to destroy,
to make an end of not a few nations.
8 For he says, "Are not my commanders all
kings?"
9 "'Is not Calno like Carchemish,
Or Hamath like Arpad,
or Samaria like Damascus?
10 Just as my hand reached out to idolatrous
kingdoms
that had more images than
Jerusalem and Samaria—
11 Just as I treated Samaria and her idols,
shall I not do to Jerusalem and her
graven images?"

12But when the LORD has brought to an end
all his work on Mount Zion and in Jerusalem,

I will punish the utterance
of the king of Assyria's proud heart,
and the boastfulness of his haughty
eyes.
13 For he says:
"By my own power I have done it,
and by my wisdom, for I am shrewd.
I have moved the boundaries of peoples,
their treasures I have pillaged,
and, like a mighty one, I have
brought down the enthroned.
14 My hand has seized, like a nest,
the wealth of nations.
As one takes eggs left alone,
so I took in all the earth;
No one fluttered a wing,
or opened a mouth, or chirped!"
15 Will the ax boast against the one who
hews with it?
Will the saw exalt itself above the
one who wields it?
As if a rod could sway the one who lifts it,
or a staff could lift the one who is
not wood!
16 Therefore the Lord, the LORD of hosts,
will send leanness among his fat ones,†
And under his glory there will be a
kindling
like the kindling of fire.º
17 The Light of Israel will become a fire,
the Holy One, a flame,
That burns and consumes its briers
and its thorns in a single day.ᵖ

18 And the glory of its forests and orchards
will be consumed, soul and body,
and it will be like a sick man who
wastes away.
19 And the remnant of the trees in his forest
will be so few,
that any child can record them.
20     On that day
The remnant of Israel,
the survivors of the house of Jacob,
will no more lean upon the one who
struck them;
But they will lean upon the LORD,
the Holy One of Israel, in truth.
21 A remnant will return,‡ the remnant of
Jacob,
to the mighty God.
22 Though your people, O Israel,
were like the sand of the sea,�q
Only a remnant of them will return;
their destruction is decreed,
as overflowing justice demands.ʳ

23For the Lord, the GOD of hosts, is about to
carry out the destruction decreed in the midst
of the whole land.ˢ
24,25Therefore thus says the Lord, the GOD of
hosts: My people, who dwell in Zion, do not fear
the Assyrian, though he strikes you with a rod,
and raises his staff against you as did the Egyptians. 25For just a brief moment more, and my
wrath shall be over, and my anger shall be set for
their destruction. 26Then the LORD of hosts will
raise against them a scourge such as struck Midian at the rock of Oreb;ᵗ and he will raise his staff
over the sea as he did in Egypt." 27On that day,

His burden shall be taken from your
shoulder,
and his yoke shattered from your
neck.ᵛ

### The March of an Enemy Armyˢ

He has come up from Rimmon,

---

‡[10:21] **A remnant will return**: in Hebrew, *shear-jashub*,
an allusion to the name of Isaiah's son, Shear-jashub; cf. 7:3.

§[10:24] This verse with its reference to Assyria's rod may
introduce the original conclusion to vv. 5–15.

¶[10:27b–32] A poetic description of the march of an
enemy army from the north, advancing south to the very
gates of Jerusalem, where the enemy waves his hand in a gesture of derision against the city. Though Sennacherib's troops
took a different route, advancing down the coast and then
approaching Jerusalem from the southeast, the arrogant attitude toward God's chosen city was the same. **Aiath**: the Ai of
Jos 7:22–8:29. **Migron**: modern Makrun north of Michmash.
**The ravine**: the deep valley between Michmash and Geba
(cf. 1 Sm 14:1–5). **Ramah . . . Gibeah . . . Bath-Gallim . . .
Laishah . . . Anathoth . . . Madmenah . . . Gebim**: cities north
of Jerusalem threatened by the sudden appearance of this
enemy army. **Nob**: probably to be identified with the present
Mount Scopus from where one has a clear view of Jerusalem.

---

*[10:9–10] The cities mentioned were all cities captured,
some more than once, by the Assyrians in the eighth century
B.C. Verse 9 suggests a certain historical order in the fall of
these cities, and v. 10 suggests that all of them had fallen before
Samaria (cf. Am 6:2). That implies that one should think primarily of events during the reign of Tiglath-pileser III (745–727).

†[10:16] **His fat ones**: the strong men of the enemy army.

o. [10:16] Is 17:4.   p. [10:17] Is 9:17–18; 30:27–33; 31:9; 33:14.

q. [10:22] Hos 2:1; Rom 9:27–28.   r. [10:22] Is 28:16–18.   s. [10:23]
Is 28:22.   t. [10:26] Is 9:3; Jgs 7:25.   u. [10:26] Ex 14:16.   v. [10:27]
Is 9:3.

28 he has reached Aiath, passed
  through Migron,
 at Michmash he has stored his
  supplies.
29 He has crossed the ravine,
 at Geba he has camped for the night.
Ramah trembles,
 Gibeah of Saul has fled.
30 Cry and shriek, Bath-Gallim!
 Hearken, Laishah! Answer her,
  Anathoth!
31 Madmenah is in flight,
 the inhabitants of Gebim seek
  refuge.
32 Even today he will halt at Nob,
 he will shake his fist at the mount of
  daughter Zion,
 the hill of Jerusalem!
33 ˊNow the Lord, the LORD of hosts,
 is about to lop off the boughs with
  terrible violence;
The tall of stature shall be felled,
 and the lofty ones shall be brought
  low;
34 He shall hack down the forest thickets
  with an ax,
 and Lebanon in its splendor shall
  fall.

## CHAPTER 11†

### The Ideal Davidic King‡

1 But a shoot shall sprout from the stump§
  of Jesse,
 and from his roots a bud shall
  blossom.ʷ
2 ˁThe spirit of the LORD shall rest upon
  him:ˣ
 a spirit of wisdom and of
  understanding,
A spirit of counsel and of strength,
 a spirit of knowledge and of fear of
  the LORD,

3  and his delight shall be the fear of
  the LORD.
Not by appearance shall he judge,
 nor by hearsay shall he decide,
4 But he shall judge the poor with justice,
 and decide fairly for the land's
  afflicted.ʸ
He shall strike the ruthless with the rod of
  his mouth,
 and with the breath of his lips he
  shall slay the wicked.ᶻ
5 Justice shall be the band around his waist,
 and faithfulness a belt upon his
  hips.ᵃ
6 ˀˀThen the wolf shall be a guest of the
  lamb,
 and the leopard shall lie down with
  the young goat;
The calf and the young lion shall browse
  together,
 with a little child to guide them.ᵇ
7 The cow and the bear shall graze,
 together their young shall lie down;
 the lion shall eat hay like the ox.ᶜ
8 The baby shall play by the viper's den,
 and the child lay his hand on the
  adder's lair.
9 They shall not harm or destroy on all my
  holy mountain;
 for the earth shall be filled with
  knowledge of the LORD,
  as water covers the sea.

### Restoration††

10  On that day,
The root of Jesse,
 set up as a signal for the peoples—
Him the nations will seek out;
 his dwelling shall be glorious.ᵈ
11  On that day,
The Lord shall again take it in hand
 to reclaim the remnant of his people
 that is left from Assyria and Egypt,
Pathros, Ethiopia, and Elam,
 Shinar, Hamath, and the isles of the
  sea.ᵉ

---

*[10:33–34] Just when the enemy is about to capture Jerusalem, God intervenes and destroys the hostile army. Cf. 29:1–8; 31:4–9.

†[11:1–16] Isaiah 11 contains a prophecy of the rise of a new Davidic king who will embody the ancient ideal of Davidic kingship (vv. 1–9), an elaboration of that prophecy in a further description of that king's rule (v. 10), and a prophecy of God's deliverance of the chosen people from exile and cessation of enmities (vv. 11–16).

‡[11:1–9 (10)] Here Isaiah looks forward to a new Davidide who will realize the ancient ideals (see Ps 72). The oracle does not seem to have a particular historical person in mind.

§[11:1] Shoot . . . stump: the imagery suggests the bankruptcy of the monarchy as embodied in the historical kings, along with the need for a new beginning, to spring from the very origin from which David and his dynasty arose. Jesse: David's father (cf. 1 Sm 16:1–13).

¶[11:2–3] The source of the traditional names of the gifts of the Holy Spirit. The Septuagint and the Vulgate read "piety" for "fear of the Lord" in its first occurrence, thus listing seven gifts.

**[11:6–9] This picture of the idyllic harmony of paradise is a dramatic symbol of universal peace and justice under the rule of the new Davidic king. The peace and harmony even among carnivores and their natural prey in this description suggest a paradisiac aspect of the reign of the new king.

††[11:10–16] This passage, with its reference to God's people in widely scattered lands, is probably from a much later period. God will restore them to their own land. The reconciliation of Ephraim (i.e., the Northern Kingdom) and Judah reverses what Isaiah saw as a disastrous event of the past (cf. 7:17). God's action is likened to a new exodus, analogous to the time God first acquired Israel in bringing them out of the land of Egypt. Pathros: upper Egypt. Elam: east of Babylonia. Shinar: Babylonia. Hamath: on the Orontes River in Syria. Isles: or coastlands, in the Mediterranean.

---

w. [11:1] Is 4:2; 53:2; Jer 23:5–6; 33:14–16; Zec 3:8; 6:12; Rev 22:16. x. [11:2] Is 42:1; 1 Sm 16:13; Mt 3:16; Mk 1:10; Jn 1:32.

y. [11:4] Ps 72:2, 4; 98:9. z. [11:4] 2 Thes 2:8; Rev 2:16. a. [11:5] Eph 6:14. b. [11:6] Hos 2:20. c. [11:7] Is 65:25. d. [11:10] Is 2:2–4; Rom 15:12. e. [11:11] Ex 3:20; Jer 23:7–8; 31:1–22; Zec 10:10.

12 He shall raise a signal to the nations[f]
   and gather the outcasts of Israel;
The dispersed of Judah he shall assemble
   from the four corners of the earth.
13 The envy of Ephraim shall pass away,
   and those hostile to Judah shall be
   cut off;
Ephraim shall not envy Judah,
   and Judah shall not be hostile to
   Ephraim;
14 But they shall swoop down on the
   foothills
   of the Philistines to the west,
together they shall plunder the
   people of the east;*
Edom and Moab shall be their
   possessions,
   and the Ammonites their subjects.
15 The LORD shall dry up the tongue[†] of the
   Sea of Egypt,
   and wave his hand over the
   Euphrates with his fierce wind,
And divide it into seven streamlets,
   so that it can be crossed in sandals.[g]
16 There shall be a highway for the remnant
   of his people
   that is left from Assyria,
As there was for Israel
   when it came up from the land of
   Egypt.[h]

## CHAPTER 12

### Song of Thanksgiving[‡]

1     On that day, you will say:
I give you thanks, O LORD;
   though you have been angry with
   me,
   your anger has abated, and you have
   consoled me.
2 God indeed is my salvation;
   I am confident and unafraid.
For the LORD is my strength and my
   might,
   and he has been my salvation.[i]
3 With joy you will draw water
   from the fountains of salvation.[j]
4 And you will say on that day:
   give thanks to the LORD, acclaim his
   name;
Among the nations make known his
   deeds,
   proclaim how exalted is his name.[k]

5 Sing praise to the LORD for he has done
   glorious things;
   let this be known throughout all the
   earth.[l]
6 Shout with exultation, City of Zion,
   for great in your midst
   is the Holy One of Israel![m]

*C. Oracles Against the Foreign Nations[§]*

## CHAPTER 13

**Babylon.[5]** [1]An oracle** concerning Babylon; a
vision of Isaiah, son of Amoz.

2     Upon the bare mountains set up a signal;
   cry out to them,[††]
Beckon for them to enter
   the gates of the nobles.[n]
3 I have commanded my consecrated ones,[‡‡]
   I have summoned my warriors,
   eager and bold to carry out my anger.[o]
4 Listen! the rumble on the mountains:
   that of an immense throng!
Listen! the noise of kingdoms, nations
   assembled!
The LORD of hosts is mustering
   an army for battle.[p]
5 They come from a far-off country,
   and from the end of the heavens,
The LORD and the instruments of his wrath,
   to destroy all the land.
6 Howl, for the day of the LORD[§§] is near;
   as destruction from the Almighty it
   comes.[q]
7 Therefore all hands fall helpless,[r]

§[13:1–23:18] These chapters, which probably existed at
one time as an independent collection, consist primarily of
oracles from various sources against foreign nations. While
some of the material is Isaianic, in many cases it has been
reworked by later editors or writers.

¶[13:1–22] Although attributed to Isaiah (v. 1), this oracle
does not reflect conditions of Isaiah's time. Babylon did not
achieve imperial status until a century later, after its victory
over Assyria in 609 B.C. The mention of the Medes (v. 17)
rather than Persia suggests a date prior to 550 B.C., when the
Median empire of Astyages fell to Cyrus the Persian. Tension
is created in that the attackers are not named until v. 17 and
the foe to be attacked until v. 19.

**[13:1] Oracle: Heb. *massa'*; used eight more times in this
collection.

††[13:2] To them: the Medes (v. 17), who are being summoned to destroy Babylon. Gates of the nobles: the reference
is apparently to the gates of Babylon and involves a wordplay
on the city name (Babylon = *bab ilani*, "gate of the gods").

‡‡[13:3] Consecrated ones: in the sense that they will wage
a "holy war" and carry out God's plan.

§§[13:6–8] Day of the LORD: described often in prophetic
writings, it generally signified the coming of the Lord in
power and majesty to destroy his enemies. The figures used
convey the idea of horror and destruction (Am 5:18–20). The
Almighty: Heb. *shaddai*; there is a play on words between
destruction (*shod*) and Shaddai, a title for God traditionally
rendered as "the Almighty" (cf. Gn 17:1; Ex 6:3).

*[11:14] People of the east: tribes in the Arabian Desert
(cf. Jgs 6:3, 33; 7:12).

†[11:15] Tongue: perhaps to be identified with the Gulf
of Suez.

‡[12:1–6] Israel's thanksgiving to the Lord, expressed in
language like that of the Psalms.

f. [11:12] Is 18:3.   g. [11:15] Zec 10:11; Rev 16:12.   h. [11:16] Is
51:10; Ex 14:29.   i. [12:2] Ex 15:2; Ps 118:14.   j. [12:3] Jgs 5:11; Jer
2:13; Jn 4:10, 14.   k. [12:4] Ps 105:1; 148:13.

l. [12:5] Is 11:9; Ex 15:1.   m. [12:6] Is 52:8–9; 54:1; Zep 3:14–15.
n. [13:2] Is 5:26; Jer 50:2.   o. [13:3] Jl 4:9.   p. [13:4] Jer 50:9.
q. [13:6] Is 2:12–21; Jer 46:10; Am 5:18–20; Jl 1:15; Zep 1:7; Rev
6:17.   r. [13:7] Jer 6:24; Ez 7:17.

8 every human heart melts,
  and they are terrified,
Pangs and sorrows take hold of them,
  like a woman in labor they writhe;
They look aghast at each other,
  their faces aflame.[s]

9 Indeed, the day of the LORD comes,
  cruel, with wrath and burning anger;
To lay waste the land
  and destroy the sinners within it![t]

10 The stars of the heavens and their
  constellations
  will send forth no light;
The sun will be dark at its rising,
  and the moon will not give its light.[u]

11 Thus I will punish the world for its evil
  and the wicked for their guilt.
I will put an end to the pride of the
  arrogant,
  the insolence of tyrants I will
  humble.[v]

12 I will make mortals more rare than pure
  gold,
  human beings, than the gold of
  Ophir.[*w]

13 For this I will make the heavens tremble
  and the earth shall be shaken from
  its place,
At the wrath of the LORD of hosts
  on the day of his burning anger.[x]

14 Like a hunted gazelle,
  or a flock that no one gathers,
They shall turn each to their own people
  and flee each to their own land.[y]

15 Everyone who is taken shall be run
  through;
  and everyone who is caught shall fall
  by the sword.

16 Their infants shall be dashed to pieces in
  their sight;
  their houses shall be plundered
  and their wives ravished.[z]

17 I am stirring up against them the Medes,
  who think nothing of silver
  and take no delight in gold.[a]

18 With their bows they shall shatter the
  young men,
And the fruit of the womb they shall not
  spare,
  nor shall their eye take pity on
  children.

19 And Babylon, the jewel of kingdoms,
  the glory and pride of the Chaldeans,
Shall become like Sodom and Gomorrah,
  overthrown by God.[b]

20 It shall never be inhabited,
  nor dwelt in, from age to age;
Arabians shall not pitch their tents there,
  nor shepherds rest their flocks
  there.[c]

21 But desert demons shall rest there
  and owls shall fill the houses;
There ostriches shall dwell,
  and satyrs[†] shall dance.[d]

22 Wild dogs shall dwell in its castles,
  and jackals in its luxurious palaces.
Its time is near at hand
  and its days shall not be prolonged.[e]

## CHAPTER 14

**Restoration of Israel.** [1]But the LORD will take pity on Jacob and again choose Israel, and will settle them on their own land; foreigners will join them and attach themselves to the house of Jacob.[f] [2]The nations will take them and bring them to their place, and the house of Israel will possess them[‡] as male and female slaves on the Lord's land; they will take captive their captors and rule over their oppressors.[g]

**Downfall of the King of Babylon.** [3]On the day when the LORD gives you rest from your sorrow and turmoil, from the hard service with which you served,[h] [4]you will take up this taunt-song[§] against the king of Babylon:[i]

How the oppressor has come to an end!
  how the turmoil has ended!
5 The LORD has broken the rod of the
  wicked,
  the staff of the tyrants[j]
6 That struck the peoples in wrath
  with relentless blows;
That ruled the nations in anger,
  with boundless persecution.[k]
7 The whole earth rests peacefully,
  song breaks forth;
8 The very cypresses rejoice over you,
  the cedars of Lebanon:
"Now that you are laid to rest,
  no one comes to cut us down."[l]

---

*[13:12] **Ophir:** cf. note on Ps 45:10.

†[13:21] **Satyrs:** in the popular mind, demons of goatlike form dwelling in ruins, symbols of immorality; cf. Lv 17:7; Is 34:14.

‡[14:2] **Possess them:** Israel will make slaves of the nations who escort it back to its land.

§[14:4–21] This taunt-song, a satirical funeral lament, is a beautiful example of classical Hebrew poetry. According to the prose introduction and the prosaic conclusion (vv. 22–23), it is directed against the king of Babylon, though Babylon is mentioned nowhere in the song itself. If the reference to Babylon is accurate, the piece was composed long after the time of Isaiah, for Babylon was not a threat to Judah in the eighth century. Some have argued that Isaiah wrote it at the death of an Assyrian king and the references to Babylon were made by a later editor, but this is far from certain.

s. [13:8] Is 21:3; Ps 48:7; Mi 4:9.  t. [13:9] Jer 4:7; 18:16; Mal 3:19.  u. [13:10] Is 24:23; Jer 4:23; Zep 1:15; Mt 24:29.  v. [13:11] Is 2:17; Jer 50:32.  w. [13:12] 1 Kgs 9:28; Jb 22:24.  x. [13:13] Hg 2:6; Lam 1:12.  y. [13:14] 1 Kgs 22:17; Jer 50:16; 51:9.  z. [13:16] 2 Kgs 8:12; Ps 137:9; Na 3:10.  a. [13:17] Is 21:2; Jer 51:11, 28.  b. [13:19] Dt 29:22; Is 1:7; Jer 49:18; 50:40; Am 4:11.

c. [13:20] Jer 51:62.  d. [13:21] Is 34:13–14; 35:7.  e. [13:22] Ez 32:23.  f. [14:1] Is 56:3; 60:4; Ps 102:14; Jer 24:6; Zec 1:17.  g. [14:2] Is 49:22–23; 60:14; 66:20.  h. [14:3] Ex 33:14; Jos 1:13; Jer 30:10.  i. [14:4] Hb 2:6.  j. [14:5] Is 10:24–27.  k. [14:6] Is 10:5–7.  l. [14:8] Is 37:24; 44:23; 55:12; Ez 31:16.

⁹ Below, Sheol is all astir
    preparing for your coming;
Awakening the shades to greet you,
    all the leaders of the earth;
Making all the kings of the nations
    rise from their thrones.
¹⁰ All of them speak out
    and say to you,
"You too have become weak like us,
    you are just like us!
¹¹ Down to Sheol your pomp is brought,
    the sound of your harps.
Maggots are the couch beneath you,
    worms your blanket."ᵐ
¹² How you have fallen from the heavens,
    O Morning Star,* son of the dawn!
How you have been cut down to the earth,
    you who conquered nations!ⁿ
¹³ In your heart you said:
    "I will scale the heavens;
Above the stars of God†
    I will set up my throne;
I will take my seat on the Mount of
    Assembly,
    on the heights of Zaphon.º
¹⁴ I will ascend above the tops of the clouds;
    I will be like the Most High!"ᵖ
¹⁵ No! Down to Sheol you will be brought
    to the depths of the pit!�q
¹⁶ When they see you they will stare,
    pondering over you:
"Is this the man who made the earth
    tremble,
    who shook kingdoms?
¹⁷ Who made the world a wilderness,
    razed its cities,
    and gave captives no release?"
¹⁸ All the kings of the nations lie in glory,
    each in his own tomb;ʳ
¹⁹ But you are cast forth without burial,
    like loathsome carrion,
Covered with the slain, with those struck
    by the sword,
    a trampled corpse,
Going down to the very stones of the pit.ˢ

²⁰ You will never be together with
    them in the grave,
For you have ruined your land,
    you have slain your people!
Let him never be named,
    that offshoot of evil!
²¹ Make ready to slaughter his sons
    for the guilt of their fathers;ᵗ
Lest they rise and possess the earth,
    and fill the breadth of the world with
    cities.‡

²²I will rise up against them, says the Lord of hosts, and cut off from Babylon name and remnant, progeny and offspring, says the Lord.ᵘ ²³I will make it a haunt of hoot owls and a marshland; I will sweep it with the broom of destruction, oracle of the Lord of hosts.

### God's Plan for Assyria§

²⁴ The Lord of hosts has sworn:
    As I have resolved,
        so shall it be;
    As I have planned,
        so shall it stand.
²⁵ To break the Assyrian in my land
        and trample him on my mountains;
    Then his yoke shall be removed from them,
        and his burden from their shoulder.ᵛ
²⁶ This is the plan proposed for the whole
        earth,
    and this the hand outstretched over
        all the nations.⁵
²⁷ The Lord of hosts has planned;
        who can thwart him?
    His hand is stretched out;
        who can turn it back?ʷ

**Philistia.**** ²⁸In the year that King Ahaz died,†† there came this oracle:

²⁹ ‡‡Do not rejoice, Philistia, not one of you,

---

*[14:12] **Morning Star**: term addressed to the king of Babylon. The Vulgate translates as "Lucifer," a name applied by the church Fathers to Satan. **Son of the dawn**: Heb., *ben shahar*, may reflect the name of a pagan deity.

†[14:13–15] **God**: not Elohim, the common word for God, but El, the name of the head of the pantheon in Canaanite mythology, a god who was early identified with the Lord in Israelite thought. **Mount of Assembly**: mountain where the council of the gods met, according to Canaanite mythology. **Zaphon**: the sacred mountain of Baal, originally the Jebel el-Aqra north of Ugarit, but other mountains have been identified with it, including Mount Zion in Jerusalem (Ps 48:3). The attempt to usurp the place of God (v. 14), coupled with the dramatic reversal ("above the stars of God" to "the depths of the pit") occasioned the interpretation that saw here the rebellion and fall of Satan.

‡[14:21] **Cities**: if the text is correct, it presumably refers to cities as expressions of human pride, authority, and oppression (cf. Gn 11:1–9; Na 3:1–4).

§[14:24–27] The motif of God's plan or work is a recurring thread running through Isaiah's oracles. The plans of Judah's enemies will not come to pass (7:5–7; 8:9–10; 10:7), but God's plan for his work of disciplining his own people (5:12, 19; 28:21), and then for punishing the foreign agents God used to administer that discipline (10:12) will come to pass.

¶[14:26] **Hand outstretched over all the nations**: as it was once outstretched over Israel (9:11, 16, 20; 5:25).

**[14:28–31] This oracle seems to reflect the political situation soon after the death of Ahaz in 715 B.C., when Ashdod and the other Philistine cities were trying to create a united front to rebel against Assyria. Ahaz had refused to join the rebels in 735 B.C. and remained loyal to Assyria during the rest of his reign, but the Philistines may have had higher hopes for his son Hezekiah. Judah, however, did not join in Ashdod's disastrous revolt in 713–711 B.C. (cf. 20:1).

††[14:28] **The year that King Ahaz died**: 715 B.C.

‡‡[14:29] The occasion for this oracle is usually taken to be the death of an Assyrian king; the Philistines were vassals of

---

m. [14:11] Sir 10:11.    n. [14:12] Jb 14:10.    o. [14:13] Jer 51:53; Am 9:2.    p. [14:14] Ez 28:2; Zep 2:15; 2 Thes 2:4.    q. [14:15] Ez 28:8–9; 32:23; Mt 11:23; Acts 12:23.    r. [14:18] Jb 3:14–15.    s. [14:19] Is 66:24.

t. [14:21] Ex 20:5; Mt 23:35.    u. [14:22] Jer 51:62; Jb 18:19.    v. [14:25] Is 9:3; 10:27a.    w. [14:27] Is 23:8–9; Jb 40:8; Jer 4:28.

that the rod which struck you is
broken;
For out of the serpent's root shall come
an adder,
its offspring shall be a flying saraph.
30 In my pastures the poor shall graze,
and the needy lie down in safety;
But I will kill your root with famine
that shall slay even your remnant.
31 Howl, O gate; cry out, O city!
Philistia, all of you melts away!
For there comes a smoke from the north,*
without a straggler in its ranks.
32 What will one answer the messengers of
the nations?†
"The LORD has established Zion,
and in her the afflicted of his people
find refuge."

## CHAPTER 15

### Moab‡

1
Oracle on Moab:
Laid waste in a night,
Ar of Moab is destroyed;
Laid waste in a night,
Kir of Moab is destroyed.
2 Daughter Dibon has gone up
to the high places to weep;
Over Nebo and over Medeba
Moab is wailing.
Every head is shaved,
every beard sheared off.§x
3 In the streets they wear sackcloth,
and on the rooftops;
In the squares
everyone wails, streaming with
tears.y
4 Heshbon and Elealeh cry out,
they are heard as far as Jahaz.
At this the loins of Moab tremble,
his soul quivers within him;z
5 My heart cries out for Moab,
his fugitives reach Zoar,
Eglath-shelishiyah:

The ascent of Luhith
they ascend weeping;
On the way to Horonaim
they utter rending cries;a
6 The waters of Nimrim
have become a waste,
The grass is withered,
new growth is gone,
nothing is green.
7 So now whatever they have acquired or
stored away
they carry across the Wadi of the
Poplars.
8 The cry has gone round
the territory of Moab;
As far as Eglaim his wailing,
even at Beer-elim his wailing.
9 ¶The waters of Dimon are filled with blood,
but I will bring still more upon
Dimon:
Lions for those who are fleeing from Moab
and for those who remain in the land!

## CHAPTER 16

1 Send them forth,** hugging the earth like
reptiles,
from Sela across the desert,
to the mount of daughter Zion.
2 Like flushed birds,
like scattered nestlings,
Are the daughters of Moab
at the fords of the Arnon.††b
3 ‡‡Offer counsel, take their part;
at high noon make your shade like
the night;
Hide the outcasts,
do not betray the fugitives.
4 Let the outcasts of Moab live with you,
be their shelter from the destroyer.
When there is an end to the oppressor,
when destruction has ceased,
and the marauders have vanished
from the land,
5 A throne shall be set up in mercy,
and on it shall sit in fidelity,
in David's tent,
A judge upholding right,
prompt to do justice.c
6 We have heard of the pride of Moab,
how very proud he is,

---

Assyria, whereas no victories of Ahaz over the Philistines are
recorded. The chronological notice (*in the year that King Ahaz
died*) may be incorrect, for no Assyrian king died around 715,
the date usually assigned for the death of Ahaz. **Flying saraph**:
a winged cobra, often portrayed in Egyptian art and on Israelite seals. The Hebrew *saraph* means "to burn" and perhaps
is applied to the cobra because of the burning sensation of
its bite.
*[14:31] **Smoke from the north**: the dust raised from the
approach of the Assyrian army.
†[14:32] **Messengers of the nations**: envoys from Philistia,
and from Egypt and Ethiopia, the real powers behind the Philistine revolt (cf. 18:1–2).
‡[15:1–16:14] Both the historical situation reflected in this
oracle against Moab and the date of composition are uncertain. Variants of the same poem are found in Jer 48, and there
are connections with Nm 21:27–30 as well.
§[15:2] **Shaved . . . sheared off**: traditional signs of grief.

x. [15:2] Jer 48:37; Ez 7:18; Am 8:10.   y. [15:3] Is 22:12; Jer
48:38.   z. [15:4] Jer 48:34.

¶[15:9] There is a play on words between "Dimon" and
*dam*, the Hebrew word for blood.
**[16:1] **Send them forth**: the Hebrew text is disturbed; it
could also be understood to refer to tribute (a lamb) sent from
Moab to Zion, presumably to encourage the king to receive
the Moabite refugees.
††[16:2] **The Arnon**: principal river of Moab.
‡‡[16:3–5] Directed to Jerusalem, which should receive the
suffering Moabites with mercy, as befits the city of David's
family, who were partly descended from Ruth the Moabite;
and cf. 1 Sm 22:3–4. This would be a gracious act on Judah's
part, since its relations with Moab were strained at best.

a. [15:5] Jer 48:5, 34.   b. [16:2] Nm 21:13.   c. [16:5] Is 9:6; 11:3–4;
32:1; Jer 23:5; Ps 89:14; Prv 20:28.

Of his haughtiness, pride, and arrogance
    that his empty words do not match.*d*

7 'Therefore let Moab wail,
    let everyone wail for Moab;
For the raisin cakes† of Kir-hareseth
    let them sigh, stricken with grief.

8 The terraced slopes of Heshbon languish,
    the vines of Sibmah,
Whose clusters once overpowered
    the lords of nations,
Reaching as far as Jazer
    winding through the wilderness,‡
Whose branches spread forth,
    crossing over the sea.

9 Therefore I weep with Jazer
    for the vines of Sibmah;
I drench you with my tears,
    Heshbon and Elealeh;
For on your summer fruits and harvests
    the battle cry§ has fallen.*e*

10 From the orchards are taken away
    joy and gladness,
In the vineyards there is no singing,
    no shout of joy;
In the wine presses no one treads grapes,
    the vintage shout is stilled.*f*

11 Therefore for Moab
    my heart moans like a lyre,
    my inmost being for Kir-hareseth.*g*

12 'When Moab wears himself out on the
    high places,
    and enters his sanctuary to pray,
    it shall avail him nothing.*h*

13'''That is the word the Lord spoke against Moab in times past. 14But now the Lord speaks: In three years, like the years of a hired laborer, the glory of Moab shall be empty despite all its great multitude; and the remnant shall be very small and weak.*i*

## CHAPTER 17

### Damascus

1     Oracle on Damascus:††

See, Damascus shall cease to be a city
    and become a pile of ruins;*j*

2 Her cities shall be forever abandoned,
    for flocks to lie in undisturbed.

3 The fortress shall vanish from Ephraim††
    and dominion from Damascus;
The remnant of Aram shall become like
        the glory
    of the Israelites—
    oracle of the Lord of hosts.

4     On that day
The glory of Jacob shall fade,
    and his full body shall grow thin.*k*

5 Like the reaper's mere armful of stalks,
    when he gathers the standing grain;
Or as when one gleans the ears
    in the Valley of Rephaim.§§

6 "Only gleanings shall be left in it,
    as when an olive tree has been
        beaten—
Two or three olives at the very top,
    four or five on its most fruitful
        branches—
    oracle of the Lord, the God of
        Israel.*l*

7 On that day people shall turn to their
        maker,
    their eyes shall look to the Holy One
        of Israel.*m*

8 They shall not turn to the altars, the work
        of their hands,
    nor shall they look to what their
        fingers have made:
    the asherahs*** or the incense stands.

9 On that day his strong cities shall be
    like those abandoned by the Hivites
        and Amorites
When faced with the Israelites;
    and there shall be desolation.*n*

10 Truly, you have forgotten the God who
    saves you,
    the Rock, your refuge, you have not
        remembered.*o*
Therefore, though you plant plants for the
    Pleasant One,†††

---

*[16:7–14] Moab had been prosperous; now it has become a desert.

†[16:7] **Raisin cakes**: masses of dried compressed grapes used as food (cf. 2 Sm 6:19; 1 Chr 16:3; Sg 2:5), and also in the worship of other gods (Hos 3:1).

‡[16:8] **Wilderness**: i.e., eastward. **Sea**: i.e., westward.

§[16:9–10] **Battle cry . . . shout of joy**: the same Hebrew word (*hedad*), which normally refers to the joyful shout of those treading the grapes (cf. Jer 25:30), here is used both for the triumphant shout of the enemy (v. 9) and for the vintagers' shout, which has ceased.

¶[16:12] In vain do the Moabites appeal to their god Chemosh.

**[16:13–14] A prose application of the preceding poetic oracle against Moab (15:1–16:12); cf. Jer 4:8. **Like the years of a hired laborer**: the fixed period of time for which the hired laborer contracted his services; cf. Is 21:16.

††[17:1] **Damascus**: capital of Aram or Syria, conquered by Tiglath-pileser III at the end of the Syro-Ephraimite War in 732 B.C.

‡‡[17:3] **Ephraim**: Israel, leagued with Aram against Judah in the Syro-Ephraimite War. Assyria ravaged and captured most of Israelite territory in 734–733 B.C. **Like the glory of the Israelites**: the remnant of Aram will be no more impressive than the pitiful remnant of the Northern Kingdom.

§§[17:5] **Valley of Rephaim**: a fertile plain just to the southwest of Jerusalem (cf. Jos 15:8; 2 Sm 5:18). Since it was near a large population center, the fields there would be thoroughly gleaned by the poor after the harvest, leaving very few ears of grain.

¶¶[17:6] Olives not easily picked by hand were knocked from the tree by means of a long stick; cf. 24:13.

***[17:8] **Asherahs**: see note on Ex 34:13. **Incense stands**: small altars on which incense was burned; cf. Is 27:9; Lv 26:30.

†††[17:10] **The Pleasant One**: an epithet for a foreign god of fertility, probably Adonis, in whose honor saplings were planted.

---

d. [16:6] Jer 48:29–30.  e. [16:9] Is 15:5; Jer 48:32.  f. [16:10] Is 24:8.
g. [16:11] Is 15:5; Jer 48:36.  h. [16:12] Jer 48:13.  i. [16:14] Dt 15:18.

j. [17:1] 2 Kgs 16:9; Jer 49:23; Am 1:3; Zec 9:1.  k. [17:4] Is 10:16.
l. [17:6] Is 24:13.  m. [17:7] Is 5:12.  n. [17:9] Is 27:10.  o. [17:10] Ps 106:13, 21; Jer 2:32; Hos 8:14.

and set out cuttings for a foreign
one,<sup>p</sup>
11 Though you make them grow the day you
plant them
and make them blossom the
morning you set them out,
The harvest shall disappear on a day of
sickness
and incurable pain.
12 Ah! the roaring of many peoples—*
a roar like the roar of the seas!
The thundering of nations—
thunder like the thundering of
mighty waters!<sup>q</sup>
13 †But God shall rebuke them,
and they shall flee far away,
Driven like chaff on the mountains before
a wind,
like tumbleweed before a storm.<sup>r</sup>
14 At evening, there is terror,
but before morning, they are gone!
Such is the portion of those who despoil
us,
the lot of those who plunder us.<sup>s</sup>

## CHAPTER 18

### Ethiopia

1 Ah! Land of buzzing insects,‡
beyond the rivers of Ethiopia,<sup>t</sup>
2 Sending ambassadors by sea,
in papyrus boats on the waters!
Go, swift messengers,
to a nation tall and bronzed,
To a people dreaded near and far,
a nation strong and conquering,
whose land is washed by rivers.<sup>u</sup>
3 §All you who inhabit the world,
who dwell on earth,
When the signal is raised on the
mountain, look!
When the trumpet blows, listen!
4 For thus says the LORD to me:

I will be quiet, looking on from
where I dwell,<sup>v</sup>
Like the shimmering heat in sunshine,
like a cloud of dew at harvest time.
5 Before the vintage, when the flowering
has ended,
and the blooms are succeeded by
ripening grapes,
Then comes the cutting of branches with
pruning hooks,
and the discarding of the lopped-off
shoots.
6 They shall all be left to the mountain
vultures
and to the beasts of the earth;
The vultures shall summer on them,
all the beasts of the earth shall
winter on them.

7Then will gifts be brought to the LORD of
hosts—to the place of the name of the LORD
of hosts, Mount Zion—from a people tall and
bronzed, from a people dreaded near and far,
a nation strong and conquering, whose land is
washed by rivers.<sup>w</sup>

## CHAPTER 19

### Egypt

1 Oracle on Egypt:
See, the LORD is riding on a swift cloud
on his way to Egypt;
The idols of Egypt tremble before him,
the hearts of the Egyptians melt
within them.<sup>x</sup>
2 I will stir up Egypt against Egypt:
brother will war against brother,
Neighbor against neighbor,
city against city, kingdom against
kingdom.
3 The courage of the Egyptians shall ebb
away within them,
and I will bring their counsel to
nought;
They shall consult idols and charmers,
ghosts and clairvoyants.<sup>y</sup>
4 I will deliver Egypt
into the power of a cruel master,
A harsh king¶ who shall rule over them—
oracle of the Lord, the LORD of hosts.<sup>z</sup>
5 The waters shall be drained from the sea,
the river shall parch and dry up;<sup>a</sup>
6 Its streams shall become foul,
and the canals of Egypt shall
dwindle and parch.<sup>b</sup>

---

*[17:12] **Many peoples**: the hordes that accompanied the
invading Assyrians, whom God repels just as he vanquished
the primeval waters of chaos; see notes on Jb 3:8; 7:12; Ps
89:11.

†[17:13–14] The passage seems to evoke the motif of
invincibility, part of the early Zion tradition that Jerusalem
could not be conquered because God protected it (Ps 48:1–8).

‡[18:1–2] **Land of buzzing insects**: the region of the
Upper Nile where these multiplied with great rapidity. **Ethiopia**: in Hebrew, *Kush*. The center of this ancient kingdom corresponds geographically to the modern Sudan, Roman Nubia.
**Papyrus boats**: light and serviceable vessels made of bundles
of papyrus stalks and sealed with pitch. Egypt, ruled by a
dynasty from Ethiopia, had invited Judah to join a coalition
against Assyria, but Isaiah told the ambassadors to return to
their own people.

§[18:3–6] A more general address but probably relating to
the same topic. The Lord will not act at once, but later there
will be a "harvest" of terrible destruction, probably directed
against Assyria (cf. 14:24–27).

¶[19:4] **Cruel master . . . harsh king**: possibly the Nubian
(Ethiopian) Shabaka who gained control of all of Egypt
around 712 B.C.

v. [18:4] Is 8:18; 18:7; 2 Chr 6:30; Ps 33:14.   w. [18:7] Is 45:14; Ps
68:30; Zep 3:10; Mal 1:11.   x. [19:1] Is 13:7.   y. [19:3] Is 8:19;
44:25; Lv 19:31.   z. [19:4] Ez 29:19; 30:10.   a. [19:5] Jer 51:36; Ez
30:12; 32:2.   b. [19:6] 2 Kgs 19:24.

p. [17:10] Is 1:29–31.   q. [17:12] Ps 46:3–7; 93:3–4.   r. [17:13] Ps
76:7; 83:14.   s. [17:14] Is 29:8.   t. [18:1] Zep 3:10.   u. [18:2] Is 18:7.

Reeds and rushes shall wither away,
    7    and bulrushes on the bank of the
            Nile;<sup>c</sup>

All the sown land along the Nile
    shall dry up and blow away, and be
    no more.
    8    The fishermen shall mourn and lament,
            all who cast hook in the Nile;
Those who spread their nets in the water
    shall pine away.
    9    The linen-workers shall be disappointed,
            the combers and weavers shall turn
            pale;<sup>d</sup>
    10    The spinners shall be crushed,
            all the hired laborers shall be
            despondent.
    11    Utter fools are the princes of Zoan!*
            the wisest of Pharaoh's advisers give
            stupid counsel.
How can you say to Pharaoh,
    "I am a descendant of wise men, of
    ancient kings"?
    12    Where then are your wise men?
            Let them tell you and make known
What the Lord of hosts has planned
    against Egypt.<sup>e</sup>
    13    The princes of Zoan have become fools,
            the princes of Memphis have been
            deceived.
The chiefs of its tribes
    have led Egypt astray.<sup>f</sup>
    14    The Lord has prepared among them
            a spirit of dizziness,
And they have made Egypt stagger in
    whatever she does,
    as a drunkard staggers in his vomit.<sup>g</sup>
    15    Egypt shall accomplish nothing—
            neither head nor tail, palm branch
            nor reed,† shall accomplish
            anything.

¹⁶On that day the Egyptians shall be like women, trembling with fear, because of the Lord of hosts shaking his fist at them.<sup>h</sup> ¹⁷And the land of Judah shall be a terror to the Egyptians. Every time they think of Judah, they shall stand in dread because of the plan the Lord of hosts has in mind for them.

¹⁸On that day there shall be five cities‡ in the land of Egypt that speak the language of Canaan and swear by the Lord of hosts; one shall be called "City of the Sun."

¹⁹On that day there shall be an altar to the Lord at the center of Egypt, and a sacred pillar to the Lord near its boundary. ²⁰This will be a sign and witness to the Lord of hosts in the land of Egypt, so that when they cry out to the Lord because of their oppressors, he will send them a savior to defend and deliver them.<sup>i</sup> ²¹The Lord shall make himself known to Egypt, and the Egyptians shall know the Lord in that day; they shall offer sacrifices and oblations, make vows to the Lord and fulfill them.<sup>j</sup> ²²Although the Lord shall smite Egypt severely, he shall heal them; they shall turn to the Lord and he shall be moved by their entreaty and heal them.<sup>k</sup>

²³On that day there shall be a highway from Egypt to Assyria; the Assyrians shall enter Egypt, and the Egyptians enter Assyria, and the Egyptians shall worship with the Assyrians. ²⁴On that day Israel shall be a third party with Egypt and Assyria, a blessing in the midst of the earth,<sup>l</sup> ²⁵when the Lord of hosts gives this blessing: "Blessed be my people Egypt, and the work of my hands Assyria, and my heritage, Israel."

## CHAPTER 20

**Isaiah's Warning Against Trust in Egypt and Ethiopia.** ¹In the year the general sent by Sargon, king of Assyria, came to Ashdod,§ fought against it, and captured it— ²*at that time the Lord had spoken through Isaiah, the son of Amoz: Go and take off the sackcloth from your waist, and remove the sandals from your feet. This he did, walking naked and barefoot.<sup>m</sup> ³Then the Lord said: Just as my servant Isaiah has gone naked and barefoot for three years as a sign and portent against Egypt and Ethiopia,<sup>n</sup> ⁴so shall the king of Assyria lead away captives from Egypt, and exiles from Ethiopia, young and old, naked and barefoot, with buttocks uncovered, the shame of Egypt.<sup>o</sup> ⁵They shall be dismayed and ashamed because of Ethiopia, their hope, and because of Egypt, their boast.<sup>p</sup> ⁶The inhabitants of this coastland shall say on that day, "See what has happened to those we hoped in, to whom we fled for help and deliverance from the king of Assyria! What escape is there for us now?"<sup>q</sup>

---

*[19:11, 13] **Zoan**, later known as Tanis, and **Memphis** (Hebrew *Noph*) were key cities in the Nile Delta.

†[19:15] **Head . . . reed**: the leaders and the people; cf. 9:13–14.

‡[19:18] **Five cities**: colonies of Jews living together and speaking their native language; cf. Jer 43. **City of the Sun**: the meaning is uncertain, but the reference seems to be to the city known later as Heliopolis.

---

§[20:1] **Ashdod**: a city of Philistia. In 713 B.C., Azuri, the king of Ashdod was deposed by Sargon for plotting rebellion, but the citizens of Ashdod rejected the ruler installed by the Assyrian king and followed a certain Yamani, who in 712 B.C., with the protection of Egypt, attempted to draw Edom, Moab, and Judah into a coalition against Assyria. In 711 B.C., Sargon's general marched against Ashdod, and Yamani fled to Ethiopia. Ashdod was captured, and a short time later Ethiopia handed Yamani over to the Assyrians for punishment.

¶[20:2–6] Isaiah's nakedness is a symbolic act to convey the message that Assyria would lead the Egyptians and Ethiopians away as captives. The Judeans and their allies would then realize the folly of having trusted in them. The purpose of the oracle was to dissuade Hezekiah, the Judean king, from being drawn into Ashdod's anti-Assyrian coalition (14:28–32).

---

i. [19:20] Ex 2:23; Jgs 2:18.   j. [19:21] Zec 14:16, 18.   k. [19:22] Hos 6:1.   l. [19:24] Gn 12:2; Zec 8:13.   m. [20:2] 1 Sm 19:24. n. [20:3] Is 8:18.   o. [20:4] 2 Sm 10:4.   p. [20:5] Is 30:3, 5.   q. [20:6] Is 31:3; 36:6.

c. [19:7] Jb 8:11.   d. [19:9] Ez 27:7.   e. [19:12] Is 14:26; 41:22–23. f. [19:13] Jer 2:16; Hos 9:6.   g. [19:14] Is 28:7; Jer 48:26.   h. [19:16] Na 3:13.

## CHAPTER 21

### Fall of Babylon[*]

1   Oracle on the wastelands by the sea:[†]
Like whirlwinds sweeping through the
        Negeb,
    it comes from the desert,
    from the fearful land.[r]

2   A harsh vision has been announced to
        me:
    "The traitor betrays,
    the despoiler spoils.[s]
Go up, O Elam; besiege, O Media;[‡]
    put an end to all its groaning!"[t]

3   Therefore my loins are filled with anguish,
    pangs have seized me like those of a
        woman in labor;
I am too bewildered to hear,
    too dismayed to look.[u]

4   My mind reels,
    shuddering assails me;
The twilight I yearned for
    he has turned into dread.[v]

5   They set the table,
    spread out the rugs;
    they eat, they drink.[§][w]
Rise up, O princes,
    oil the shield!

6   For thus my Lord said to me:
    Go, station a watchman,
    let him tell what he sees.

7   If he sees a chariot,
    a pair of horses,
Someone riding a donkey,
    someone riding a camel,
Then let him pay heed,
    very close heed.

8   Then the watchman cried,
    "On the watchtower, my Lord,
    I stand constantly by day;
And I stay at my post
    through all the watches of the night.[x]

9   Here he comes—
    a single chariot,
    a pair of horses—
He calls out and says,
    'Fallen, fallen is Babylon!
All the images of her gods
    are smashed to the ground!'"[y]

10  To you, who have been threshed,
    beaten on my threshing floor,
What I have heard
    from the LORD of hosts,
The God of Israel,
    I have announced to you.[z]

### Dumah

11  Oracle on Dumah:[¶]
They call to me from Seir,
    "Watchman, how much longer the
        night?
    Watchman, how much longer the
        night?"

12  The watchman replies,
    "Morning has come, and again night.
    If you will ask, ask; come back
        again."

### In the Steppe

13  Oracle: in the steppe:[**]
In the thicket in the steppe you will spend
        the night,
    caravans of Dedanites.

14  Meet the thirsty, bring them water,
    inhabitants of the land of Tema,
    greet the fugitives with bread.[a]

15  For they have fled from the sword,
    from the drawn sword;
From the taut bow,
    from the thick of battle.

16For thus the Lord has said to me: In another
year, like the years of a hired laborer,[††] all the
glory of Kedar shall come to an end. 17Few of
Kedar's stalwart archers shall remain, for the
LORD, the God of Israel, has spoken.

## CHAPTER 22

### The Valley of Vision

1   Oracle on the Valley of Vision:[‡‡][b]

¶[21:11–12] **Dumah:** an oasis in north Arabia (cf. Gn
25:14 and 1 Chr 1:30), may be identified with the north Arabian Adummatu mentioned in Assyrian records of Sennacherib's campaign against north Arabia. **Seir:** a site in Edom. The
Edomites ask the prophet how much longer they must suffer
("the night" of suffering); he answers ambiguously: "Liberation ("morning") and further suffering ("night")," but perhaps
they will later receive a more encouraging answer ("ask; come
back again").

**[21:13–14] **In the steppe:** the north Arabian steppe
where the oases referred to were located. **Dedanites:** a north
Arabian tribe associated with the oasis of Tema; cf. Gn 10:7;
25:3; Jer 25:23.

††[21:16] **Year . . . of a hired laborer:** see note on 16:13–14.
**Kedar:** a nomadic tribe in Arabia; cf. 42:11; 60:7; Ps 120:5.

‡‡[22:1–14] The title "oracle on the valley of vision," like
the other oracle headings in chaps. 13–23, was supplied by an
editor and is taken from v. 5. In all probability it relates to the
events of 701, the lifting of Sennacherib's siege of Jerusalem.
The death of the Assyrian king Sargon II in 705 occasioned

---

*[21:1–10] This oracle against Babylon is probably to be
dated to the period just before the fall of Babylon to the Persians in 539 B.C. (v. 9).

†[21:1] **Wastelands by the sea:** Babylonia. **Negeb:** the wilderness south of Judah.

‡[21:2] **Elam . . . Media:** nations which, under the leadership of Cyrus, captured Babylon in 539 B.C. **End to all its
groaning:** those who were captive in Babylon will be freed.

§[21:5] Babylon is destroyed while its leaders are feasting;
cf. Dn 5. **Oil the shield:** shields were oiled and greased so as
to divert blows more easily; cf. 2 Sm 1:21.

---

r. [21:1] Is 30:6; Dt 1:19; Jer 2:6.    s. [21:2] Is 24:16; 33:1.    t. [21:2]
Is 13:17; Jer 49:34.    u. [21:3] Is 16:11; Ps 38:8.    v. [21:4] Dt
28:67.    w. [21:5] Dn 5:5.    x. [21:8] Hb 2:1.    y. [21:9] Is 46:1; Jer
50:2; 51:8; Rev 14:8; 18:2.

z. [21:10] Is 51:23; Jer 51:33; Mi 4:13; Hb 3:12.    a. [21:14] Jb
6:19.    b. [22:1] Is 21:2.

What is the matter with you now, that you
    have gone up,
    all of you, to the housetops,
2 ˈYou who were full of noise,
    tumultuous city,
    exultant town?ᶜ
Your slain are not slain with the sword,
    nor killed in battle.
3 All your leaders fled away together,
    they were captured without use of
    bow;
All who were found were captured
    together,
    though they had fled afar off.
4 That is why I say: Turn away from me,
    let me weep bitterly;
Do not try to comfort me
    for the ruin of the daughter of my
    people.ᵈ
5 It is a day of panic, rout and confusion,
    from the Lord, the GOD of hosts, in
    the Valley of Vision†
Walls crash;
    a cry for help to the mountains.
6 Elam takes up the quiver,
    Aram mounts the horses
    and Kir‡ uncovers the shields.
7 Your choice valleys are filled with
    chariots,
    horses are posted at the gates—
8     and shelter over Judah is removed.§

On that day you looked to the weapons in the
House of the Forest; 9ᵃyou saw that the breaches

in the City of David were many; you collected
the water of the lower pool. 10You numbered
the houses of Jerusalem, tearing some down
to strengthen the wall; 11you made a reservoir
between the two walls for the water of the old
pool. But you did not look to the city's Maker,
nor consider the one who fashioned it long ago.

12 On that day the Lord,
    the GOD of hosts, called
For weeping and mourning,
    for shaving the head and wearing
    sackcloth.
13 But look! instead, there was celebration
    and joy,
    slaughtering cattle and butchering
    sheep,
Eating meat and drinking wine:
    "Eat and drink, for tomorrow we
    die!"ᵉ

14This message was revealed in my hearing from
the LORD of hosts:

    This iniquity will not be forgiven
    you until you die,
    says the Lord, the GOD of hosts.

### Shebna and Eliakim

15 Thus says the Lord, the GOD of hosts:
    Up, go to that official,
    Shebna,** master of the palace,
16 ††"What have you here? Whom have you
    here,
    that you have hewn for yourself a
    tomb here,
Hewing a tomb on high,
    carving a resting place in the rock?"
17 The LORD shall hurl you down headlong,
    mortal man!
He shall grip you firmly,
18 And roll you up and toss you like a ball
    into a broad land.
There you will die, there with the chariots
    you glory in,
    you disgrace to your master's house!
19 I will thrust you from your office
    and pull you down from your
    station.
20 On that day I will summon my servant
    Eliakim,‡‡ son of Hilkiah;ᶠ

the revolt of many of the vassal nations subject to Assyria, a
revolt in which Hezekiah joined, over Isaiah's bitter opposition. The biblical and other data concerning the outcome of
this adventure are conflicting and confusing. While 2 Kgs
19 (Is 37) tells of a miraculous deliverance of the city after
the siege had been renewed, Assyrian documents and 2 Kgs
18:13–16 report that Sennacherib, Sargon II's successor, devastated Judah (the destruction of 46 cities is mentioned in
Assyrian records); Hezekiah had to surrender and paid Sennacherib a heavy indemnity, taken from the Temple treasury
and adornments. The inhabitants of Jerusalem apparently
took the lifting of the siege as occasion for great rejoicing, a
response that Isaiah condemns. They should be mourning the
dead and learning that their confidence in allies rather than in
the Lord leads to disaster.
    *[22:2–3] The retreat of Judah's soldiers is a further reason
that rejoicing is not in order.
    †[22:5] **Valley of Vision:** frequently identified as the Hin-
nom Valley, west of Jerusalem.
    ‡[22:6] **Elam . . . Kir:** the Assyrian forces presumably
included auxiliary troops from various places.
    §[22:8] **Shelter over Judah is removed:** the reference is
obscure; it has been suggested that Judah's protection was
Jerusalem itself, and with the fall of the city the country was
exposed. **House of the Forest:** an armory built by Solomon;
its columns of wood suggested the trees of a forest; cf. 1 Kgs
7:2; 10:17.
    ¶[22:9–11] Frenetic efforts to fortify the city before
the impending siege; cf. 2 Kgs 20:20; 2 Chr 32:3–4, 30. Some
suggest that the description of these preparations comes from
the time of Nebuchadnezzar's assault on Jerusalem in 588.
**You did not look to the city's Maker:** Isaiah here makes the
crucial point. Jerusalem's safety lay not in military forces nor
in alliances with other nations nor in playing power politics

but in the Lord, here presented as the creator and founder of
the city. Isaiah may be alluding to the belief that the city was
inviolable.
    **[22:15] **Shebna:** by the time of the siege of Jerusalem in
36:3, Shebna, the scribe, no longer held the office of master
of the palace.
    ††[22:16] What is probably Shebna's inscribed tomb has
been discovered in the village of Silwan on the eastern slope
of Jerusalem.
    ‡‡[22:20] **Eliakim:** by the time of the events described in
36:3, Eliakim had replaced Shebna as master of the palace.

c. [22:2] Is 32:13.  d. [22:4] Jer 6:26; 9:1; 14:17.

e. [22:13] Is 56:12; Wis 2:6; 1 Cor 15:32.   f. [22:20] 2 Kgs 18:18, 37.

<sup>21</sup> I will clothe him with your robe,
    gird him with your sash,
    confer on him your authority.
He shall be a father to the inhabitants of
    Jerusalem,
    and to the house of Judah.<sup>g</sup>
<sup>22</sup> I will place the key* of the House of David
    on his shoulder;
    what he opens, no one will shut,
    what he shuts, no one will open.<sup>h</sup>
<sup>23</sup> I will fix him as a peg in a firm place,
    a seat of honor for his ancestral
      house;
<sup>24</sup> On him shall hang all the glory of his
    ancestral house:<sup>†</sup>
    descendants and offspring,
    all the little dishes, from bowls to
      jugs.

<sup>25</sup>On that day, says the LORD of hosts, the peg fixed in a firm place shall give way, break off and fall, and the weight that hung on it shall be done away with; for the LORD has spoken.

## CHAPTER 23

### Tyre and Sidon

<sup>1</sup>     <sup>‡</sup>Oracle on Tyre:
Wail, ships of Tarshish,
    for your port is destroyed;
From the land of the Kittim<sup>§</sup>
    the news reaches them.<sup>i</sup>
<sup>2</sup> Silence! you who dwell on the coast,
    you merchants of Sidon,
Whose messengers crossed the sea
    over the deep waters,
<sup>3</sup> Whose revenue was the grain of Shihor,<sup>¶</sup>
    the harvest of the Nile,
    you who were the merchant among
      the nations.<sup>j</sup>
<sup>4</sup> Be ashamed, Sidon, fortress on the sea,
    for the sea** has spoken,
"I have not been in labor, nor given birth,
    nor raised young men,
    nor reared young women."

<sup>5</sup> When the report reaches Egypt
    they shall be in anguish at the report
      about Tyre.
<sup>6</sup> Pass over to Tarshish,<sup>††</sup>
    wail, you who dwell on the coast!
<sup>7</sup> Is this your exultant city,
    whose origin is from old,
Whose feet have taken her
    to dwell in distant lands?
<sup>8</sup> Who has planned such a thing
    against Tyre, the bestower of crowns,
Whose merchants are princes,
    whose traders are the earth's
      honored men?
<sup>9</sup> The LORD of hosts has planned it,
    to disgrace the height of all beauty,
    to degrade all the honored of the
      earth.<sup>k</sup>
<sup>10</sup> Cross to your own land,
    ship of Tarshish;
    the harbor is no more.
<sup>11</sup> His hand he stretches out over the sea,
    he shakes kingdoms;
The LORD commanded the destruction
    of Canaan's strongholds:<sup>‡‡l</sup>
<sup>12</sup> Crushed, you shall exult no more,
    virgin daughter Sidon.
Arise, pass over to the Kittim,
    even there you shall find no rest.<sup>m</sup>
<sup>13</sup> <sup>§§</sup>Look at the land of the Chaldeans,
    the people that has ceased to be.
Assyria founded it for ships,
    raised its towers,
Only to tear down its palaces,
    and turn it into a ruin.<sup>n</sup>
<sup>14</sup> Lament, ships of Tarshish,
    for your stronghold is destroyed.

<sup>15</sup>On that day, Tyre shall be forgotten for seventy years,<sup>¶¶</sup> the lifetime of one king. At the end of seventy years, the song about the prostitute will be Tyre's song:

<sup>16</sup> Take a harp, go about the city,
    forgotten prostitute;
Pluck the strings skillfully, sing many
      songs,
    that you may be remembered.

---

*[22:22] **Key**: symbol of authority; cf. Mt 16:19; Rev 3:7.

†[22:24–25] Apparently Eliakim proved to be a disappointment, so an oracle of judgment was added to the originally positive oracle to Eliakim.

‡[23:1–17] This oracle, a satire directed against the Phoenician cities of Tyre and Sidon, is perhaps to be situated at the time of Sennacherib's campaign against the Phoenician cities in 701 B.C, following his subjugation of their Babylonian allies in 703 B.C.

§[23:1] **Kittim**: Cyprus. The Hebrew word is derived from the term for the well-known city of Cyprus, Kition. In later centuries the term Kittim is used for the Greeks, the Romans, and other distant peoples.

¶[23:3] **Shihor**: a synonym for the Nile.

**[23:4] **The sea**: here personified, it brings to distant coasts the news that Sidon must disown her children; her people are dispersed.

---

††[23:6–7] **Tarshish**: perhaps Tartessus in Spain. **Distant lands**: the reference is to the far-flung colonies established by the Phoenicians throughout the Mediterranean, including North Africa, Spain, and Sardinia. Oceangoing vessels were therefore called Tarshish ships.

‡‡[23:11] **Canaan's strongholds**: the fortresses of Phoenicia.

§§[23:13] The reference here seems to be to Assyria's subjugation of Babylon in 703 B.C., which left the coastal cities of Phoenicia as well as Judah open to Sennacherib's invasion in 701 B.C. **Founded it . . . its palaces . . . turn it**: the city of Babylon.

¶¶[23:15] **Seventy years**: a conventional expression for a long period of time; cf. Jer 25:11 and 29:10.

---

g. [22:21] Jb 29:16.  h. [22:22] Rev 3:7.  i. [23:1] Jer 25:22; Ez 26; Am 1:9; Zec 9:2, 4.  j. [23:3] Ez 27:3.

k. [23:9] Is 14:24–27; 22:11; Ez 28:7.  l. [23:11] Is 14:27; Ps 65:8.  m. [23:12] Ez 28:21–22.  n. [23:13] Is 13:21; 34:14; Jer 50:39.

<sup>17</sup>At the end of the seventy years the LORD shall visit Tyre. She shall return to her hire and serve as prostitute* with all the world's kingdoms on the face of the earth.<sup>o</sup> <sup>18</sup>But her merchandise and her hire shall be sacred to the LORD. It shall not be stored up or laid away; instead, her merchandise shall belong to those who dwell before the LORD, to eat their fill and clothe themselves in choice attire.

*D. Apocalypse of Isaiah*†

## CHAPTER 24

### Judgment upon the World and the Lord's Enthronement on Mount Zion‡

<sup>1</sup> See! The LORD is about to empty the earth
     and lay it waste;
  he will twist its surface,
     and scatter its inhabitants:<sup>p</sup>
<sup>2</sup> People and priest shall fare alike:
     servant and master,
  Maid and mistress,
     buyer and seller,
  Lender and borrower,
     creditor and debtor.<sup>q</sup>
<sup>3</sup> The earth shall be utterly laid waste,
     utterly stripped,
  for the LORD has decreed this word.
<sup>4</sup> The earth mourns and fades,
     the world languishes and fades,
     both heaven and earth languish.<sup>r</sup>
<sup>5</sup> The earth is polluted because of its
       inhabitants,
  for they have transgressed laws,
     violated statutes,
     broken the ancient covenant.<sup>§s</sup>
<sup>6</sup> Therefore a curse devours the earth,
     and its inhabitants pay for their
       guilt;

  Therefore they who dwell on earth have
       dwindled,
     and only a few are left.<sup>t</sup>
<sup>7</sup> The new wine mourns, the vine languishes,
     all the merry-hearted groan.<sup>u</sup>
<sup>8</sup> Stilled are the cheerful timbrels,
     ended the shouts of the jubilant,
     stilled the cheerful harp.<sup>v</sup>
<sup>9</sup> They no longer drink wine and sing;
     strong brew is bitter to those who
       drink it.<sup>w</sup>
<sup>10</sup> Broken down is the city of chaos,¶
     every house is shut against entry.<sup>x</sup>
<sup>11</sup> In the streets they cry out for lack of wine;
     all joy has grown dim,
     cheer is exiled from the land.<sup>y</sup>
<sup>12</sup> In the city nothing remains but
       desolation,
     gates battered into ruins.
<sup>13</sup> For thus it shall be in the midst of the earth,
       among the peoples,
  As when an olive tree has been beaten,
     as with a gleaning when the vintage
       is done.<sup>z</sup>
<sup>14</sup> These** shall lift up their voice,
     they shall sing for joy in the majesty
       of the LORD,
     they shall shout from the western sea:
<sup>15</sup> "Therefore, in the east
     give glory to the LORD!
  In the coastlands of the sea,
     to the name of the LORD, the God of
       Israel!"<sup>a</sup>
<sup>16</sup> From the end of the earth we hear songs:
     "Splendor to the Just One!"
  But I said, "I am wasted, wasted away.
     Woe is me! The traitors betray;
     with treachery have the traitors
       betrayed!<sup>b</sup>
<sup>17</sup> Terror, pit, and trap
     for you, inhabitant of the earth!<sup>c</sup>
<sup>18</sup> One who flees at the sound of terror
     will fall into the pit;
  One who climbs out of the pit
     will be caught in the trap.
  For the windows on high are open
     and the foundations of the earth
       shake.<sup>d</sup>
<sup>19</sup> The earth will burst asunder,
     the earth will be shaken apart,
     the earth will be convulsed.
<sup>20</sup> The earth will reel like a drunkard,
     sway like a hut;
  Its rebellion will weigh it down;
     it will fall, never to rise again."<sup>e</sup>

---

*[23:17–18] **Her hire . . . prostitute**: the international trade engaged in by Tyre will become a source of wealth to God's people (cf. 45:14; 60:4–14; Zec 14:14).

†[24:1–27:13] Although it has become traditional to call these chapters "Apocalypse of Isaiah," and although they do contain some apocalyptic traits, many others are lacking, so that the title is imprecise as a designation. These chapters are not a unified composition and their growth into their present form was a long, complicated process. They echo many themes from chaps. 13–23, "Oracles Against the Foreign Nations," as well as from earlier parts of Isaiah (e.g., the reversal of the "vineyard song," 5:1–7, in 27:2–5). Of particular interest is an unnamed city (24:10–13; 25:2; 26:5–6; 27:10–11), a wicked city, doomed to destruction; to the extent that it is identifiable, it may be Babylon, but more generally it symbolizes all forces hostile to God. And it stands in contrast to another city, also unnamed but no doubt to be identified with Jerusalem (26:1–2).

‡[24:1–23] The world is about to be shaken by a devastating judgment that will overthrow both the human and divine enemies of the Lord, who will then reign in glory over his people on Mount Zion.

§[24:5] **Ancient covenant**: God's commandments to all humankind (cf. Gn 9:4–6).

¶[24:10] **City of chaos**: a godless city which appears several times in chaps. 24–27; see note on 24:1–27:13.

**[24:14] **These**: the saved.

---

o. [23:17] Rev 17:5; 18:3, 11, 13.   p. [24:1] Is 13:9; Na 2:3, 11.   q. [24:2] Hos 4:9.   r. [24:4] Is 33:9.   s. [24:5] Nm 35:33; Hos 4:2–3.

t. [24:6] Lv 26:15–16.   u. [24:7] Jl 1:10–12.   v. [24:8] Jer 7:34; Hos 2:13.   w. [24:9] Am 6:5–7.   x. [24:10] Is 25:2.   y. [24:11] Jer 48:33; Lam 5:14–15.   z. [24:13] Is 17:6; Mi 7:1.   a. [24:15] Is 42:10, 12; Zep 2:11.   b. [24:16] Is 21:2; 33:1.   c. [24:17] Jer 48:43.   d. [24:18] Gn 7:11; Am 5:19.   e. [24:20] Am 5:2.

<sup>21</sup> On that day the LORD will punish
   the host of the heavens<sup>*</sup> in the
      heavens,
   and the kings of the earth on the
      earth.
<sup>22</sup> They will be gathered together
   like prisoners into a pit;
They will be shut up in a dungeon,
   and after many days they will be
      punished.<sup>f</sup>
<sup>23</sup> Then the moon will blush
   and the sun be ashamed,<sup>g</sup>
For the LORD of hosts will reign
   on Mount Zion and in Jerusalem,
   glorious in the sight of the elders.<sup>†h</sup>

## CHAPTER 25

### Praise for God's Deliverance and the Celebration in Zion<sup>‡</sup>

<sup>1</sup> O LORD, you are my God,
   I extol you, I praise your name;
For you have carried out your wonderful
      plans of old,
   faithful and true.<sup>i</sup>
<sup>2</sup> For you have made the city a heap,
   the fortified city a ruin,
The castle of the insolent, a city no more,
   not ever to be rebuilt.<sup>j</sup>
<sup>3</sup> Therefore a strong people will honor you,
   ruthless nations will fear you.
<sup>4</sup> For you have been a refuge to the poor,
   a refuge to the needy in their
      distress;
Shelter from the rain,
   shade from the heat.<sup>k</sup>
When the blast of the ruthless was like a
      winter rain,
<sup>5</sup>    the roar of strangers like heat in the
      desert,
You subdued the heat with the shade of
      a cloud,
   the rain of the tyrants was
      vanquished.
<sup>6</sup> On this mountain<sup>§</sup> the LORD of hosts
   will provide for all peoples
A feast of rich food and choice wines,
   juicy, rich food and pure, choice
      wines.

<sup>7</sup> On this mountain he will destroy
   the veil that veils all peoples,
The web that is woven over all nations.
<sup>8</sup> He will destroy death forever.
The Lord GOD will wipe away
   the tears from all faces;
The reproach of his people he will remove
   from the whole earth; for the LORD
      has spoken.<sup>l</sup>
<sup>9</sup> On that day it will be said:
"Indeed, this is our God; we looked to
      him, and he saved us!
This is the LORD to whom we looked;
   let us rejoice and be glad that he has
      saved us!"<sup>m</sup>

### Judgment on Moab<sup>¶</sup>

<sup>10</sup> For the hand of the LORD will rest on this
      mountain,
   but Moab will be trodden down
   as straw is trodden down in the
      mire.<sup>n</sup>
<sup>11</sup> He will spread out his hands in its midst,
   as a swimmer spreads out his hands
      to swim;
His pride will be brought low
   despite his strokes.<sup>o</sup>
<sup>12</sup> The high-walled fortress he will raze,
   bringing it low, leveling it to the
      ground, to the very dust.<sup>p</sup>

## CHAPTER 26
### Judah's Praise and Prayer for Deliverance.<sup>**</sup>
<sup>1</sup>On that day this song shall be sung in the land
of Judah:

"A strong city<sup>††</sup> have we;
   he sets up victory as our walls and
      ramparts.<sup>q</sup>
<sup>2</sup> Open up the gates
   that a righteous nation may enter,
   one that keeps faith.<sup>r</sup>
<sup>3</sup> With firm purpose you maintain peace;
   in peace, because of our trust in you."<sup>s</sup>
<sup>4</sup> Trust in the LORD forever!
   For the LORD is an eternal Rock.<sup>t</sup>
<sup>5</sup> He humbles those who dwell on high,
   the lofty city he brings down,
Brings it down to the ground,
   levels it to the dust.<sup>u</sup>

---

*[24:21] **Host of the heavens**: the stars, which were often regarded as gods; cf. Dt 4:19; Jer 8:2.

†[24:23] **The elders**: the tradition in Ex 24:9–11 suggests that this refers to the people of God who are to share in the banquet on Mount Zion (Is 25:6–8).

‡[25:1–9] These verses praise God for carrying out his plan to destroy the enemy and to save the poor of his people in Zion (14:32), and they announce the victory banquet to be celebrated in the Lord's city.

§[25:6] **This mountain**: i.e., Jerusalem's mountain, Zion.

¶[25:10–12] **Moab**: one of Israel's bitterest enemies.

**[26:1–19] This text is a mixture of praise for the salvation that will take place, a confession of Judah's inability to achieve deliverance on its own, and earnest prayer that God may quickly bring about the longed-for salvation.

††[26:1] **Strong city**: Jerusalem, the antithesis of the "city of chaos" (24:10); see note on 24:1–27:13.

f. [24:22] 2 Pt 2:4; Jude 6.   g. [24:23] Is 13:10; Jl 3:3–4; 4:15. h. [24:23] Is 4:5; 60:1–3; Ex 24:9–11; Mi 4:7; Rev 19:4–6.   i. [25:1] Is 12:1, 4; 22:11; 28:29; 37:26.   j. [25:2] Is 17:1; Jer 51:37.   k. [25:4] Is 14:32; 32:2; Na 1:7.

l. [25:8] Is 60:1, 3; 1 Cor 15:53–55; Rev 7:17; 21:4.   m. [25:9] Is 30:18–19.   n. [25:10] Zep 2:9–10.   o. [25:11] Is 16:6–7, 14. p. [25:12] Is 26:5.   q. [26:1] Is 60:18.   r. [26:2] Ps 118:19–20. s. [26:3] Is 32:17–18; Ps 112:7.   t. [26:4] Is 17:10; 30:29; Ps 62:8.   u. [26:5] Is 25:11–12; 32:19.

6 The feet of the needy trample on it—
    the feet of the poor.
7 The way of the just is smooth;
    the path of the just you make level.[v]
8 The course of your judgments, LORD, we
        await;
    your name and your memory are
        the desire of our souls.
9 My soul yearns for you at night,
    yes, my spirit within me seeks you
        at dawn;
When your judgment comes upon the
        earth,
    the world's inhabitants learn justice.[w]
10 The wicked, when spared, do not learn
        justice;
    in an upright land they act perversely,
    and do not see the majesty of the
        LORD.[x]
11 LORD, your hand is raised high,
    but they do not perceive it;
Let them be put to shame when they see
        your zeal for your people:
    let the fire prepared for your
        enemies consume them.[y]
12 LORD, you will decree peace for us,
    for you have accomplished all we
        have done.[z]
13 LORD, our God, lords other than you have
        ruled us;
    only because of you can we call
        upon your name.
14 Dead they are, they cannot live,
    shades that cannot rise;
Indeed, you have punished and destroyed
        them,
    and wiped out all memory of them.
15 You have increased the nation, LORD,
    you have increased the nation, have
        added to your glory,
    you have extended far all the
        boundaries of the land.[a]
16 LORD, oppressed by your punishment,
    we cried out in anguish under your
        discipline.[b]
17 As a woman about to give birth
    writhes and cries out in pain,
    so were we before you, LORD.[c]
18 We conceived and writhed in pain,
    giving birth only to wind;
Salvation we have not achieved for the
        earth,
    no inhabitants for the world were
        born.[d]
19 *But your dead shall live, their corpses
        shall rise!

Awake and sing, you who lie in the
        dust!
For your dew is a dew of light,
    and you cause the land of shades to
        give birth.[e]

### The Lord's Response[†]

20 Go, my people, enter your chambers,
    and close the doors behind you;
Hide yourselves for a brief moment,
    until the wrath is past.[f]
21 See, the LORD goes forth from his place,
    to punish the wickedness of the
        earth's inhabitants;
The earth will reveal the blood shed upon it,
    and no longer conceal the slain.[g]

## CHAPTER 27

### The Judgment and Deliverance of Israel

1            On that day,
The LORD will punish with his sword
    that is cruel, great, and strong,
Leviathan the fleeing serpent,
    Leviathan the coiled serpent;
he will slay the dragon[‡] in the sea.[h]

2            §On that day—
The pleasant vineyard, sing about it![i]
3     I, the LORD, am its keeper,
    I water it every moment;
Lest anyone harm it,
    night and day I guard it.[j]
4 I am not angry.
    But if I were to find briers and thorns,
In battle I would march against it;
    I would burn it all.[k]
5 But if it holds fast to my refuge,
    it shall have peace with me;[l]
    it shall have peace with me.

6 In days to come Jacob shall take root,
    Israel shall sprout and blossom,
    covering all the world with fruit.[m]

---

of Judah was radically reduced by the slaughter and deportations that the historical disasters of the late eighth and seventh
centuries B.C. brought upon the country. In this context, a
major concern for the future was for an increase in the population, a rebirth of the nation's life.

†[26:20–21] The time of wrath for Judah would soon be
over, and the just punishment of its enemies would begin (cf.
Hb 2:1–3).

‡[27:1] **Leviathan . . . dragon**: the description of Leviathan is almost identical to a passage from a much earlier Ugaritic text. The sea dragon became a symbol of the forces of evil
which God vanquishes even as he overcame primeval chaos;
cf. notes on 30:7; 51:9–10; Jb 3:8; 7:12; no power can challenge
God. Leviathan is even spoken of playfully in Ps 104:26.

§[27:2–5] This passage mitigates the harsh words on Israel
as the Lord's vineyard in 5:1–7; here is given the rain there withheld, though Israel's welfare is still made dependent on fidelity.

---

*[26:19] This verse refers not to resurrection of the dead,
but to the restoration of the people; cf. Ez 37. The population

---

v. [26:7] Ps 23:3–4; Prv 11:3, 5.    w. [26:9] Ps 63:2.    x. [26:10] Is
5:12; Eccl 8:11.    y. [26:11] Is 9:6; 30:27; 37:32.    z. [26:12] Jer 29:11;
Phil 2:13.    a. [26:15] Is 54:2–3.    b. [26:16] Hos 5:15.    c. [26:17]
Mi 4:10.    d. [26:18] Is 37:3.

e. [26:19] Ez 37:5–14;  Dn 12:2;  Hos 6:2.    f. [26:20]  Is 10:25.
g. [26:21] Gn 4:10; Jb 16:18; Ps 106:38; Mi 1:3.    h. [27:1] Jb 40:25–32;
Ps 74:12–14; Ez 32:2.    i. [27:2] Is 5:1; Am 5:11.    j. [27:3] Is 5:2–7.
k. [27:4] Is 10:17.    l. [27:5] Jb 22:21.    m. [27:6] Is 37:31–32; Hos
14:5–6.

7 'Was he smitten as his smiter was smitten?
   Was he slain as his slayer was slain?
8 Driving out and expelling, he struggled
         against it,
         carrying it off with his cruel wind on
            a day of storm.*

9 This, then, shall be the expiation of Jacob's
         guilt,
      this the result of removing his sin:
   He shall pulverize all the stones of the altars
         like pieces of chalk;
         no asherahs or incense altars shall
            stand.
10 For the fortified city shall be desolate,
         an abandoned pasture, a forsaken
            wilderness;
   There calves shall graze, there they shall
         lie down,
         and consume its branches.
11 When its boughs wither, they shall be
         broken off;
         and women shall come to kindle
            fires with them.
   For this is not an understanding people;
         therefore their maker shall not spare
            them;
         their creator shall not be gracious
            to them.*

12 On that day,
   The LORD shall beat out grain
         from the channel of the Euphrates to
            the Wadi of Egypt,*
         and you shall be gleaned* one by
            one, children of Israel.
13 On that day,*
   A great trumpet shall blow,
      and the lost in the land of Assyria
      and the outcasts in the land of Egypt
   Shall come and worship the LORD
      on the holy mountain, in Jerusalem.*

*E. The Lord Alone, Israel's and Judah's Salvation*

### CHAPTER 28

#### The Fate of Samaria*

1 Ah! majestic garland

of the drunkards of Ephraim,*
   Fading blooms of his glorious beauty,
         at the head of the fertile valley,
         upon those stupefied with wine.*
2 See, the LORD has a strong one, a mighty
         one,**
         who, like an onslaught of hail, a
            destructive storm,
   Like a flood of water, great and overflowing,
         levels to the ground with violence;*
3 With feet that will trample
         the majestic garland of the
            drunkards of Ephraim.
4 The fading blooms of his glorious beauty
         at the head of the fertile valley
   Will be like an early fig before summer:
         whoever sees it,
         swallows it as soon as it is in hand.*
5 On that day the LORD of hosts
         will be a glorious crown
   And a brilliant diadem
         for the remnant of his people,
6 A spirit of judgment
         for the one who sits in judgment,
   And strength for those
         who turn back the battle at the gate.

#### Against Judah

7 But these also stagger from wine
         and stumble from strong drink:
   Priest and prophet stagger from strong
            drink,
         overpowered by wine;
   They are confused by strong drink,
         they stagger in their visions,
         they totter when giving judgment.*
8 Yes, all the tables
         are covered with vomit,
         with filth, and no place left clean.
9 ††"To whom would he impart knowledge?
   To whom would he convey the message?
   To those just weaned from milk,
         those weaned from the breast?
10 For he says,
   'Command on command, command on
            command,

---

*[27:7–9] Israel was not treated as sternly as were its ene-
mies whom God used to punish it. God did, however, drive
Israel from its land, and if it wants to make peace with God,
it must change its former cultic practices, destroying its altars
and sacred groves (cf. 17:7–11).

†[27:12] **Gleaned**: God will harvest his people who have
been scattered from Assyria to Egypt. Note the same language
of gleaning to describe the remnant of the Northern Kingdom
in 17:5–6.

‡[27:13] The remnant of Israel will return to Jerusalem for
worship; cf. 11:10–16.

§[28:1–6] These verses once constituted an independent
oracle against the Northern Kingdom, probably originally
spoken during the time between its overthrow by Assyria in

732 and its destruction in 722/721. Isaiah has reused them
as an introduction to his oracle against Judah (vv. 7–22),
because the leaders of Judah were guilty of the same excesses
that had once marked Ephraim's leadership.

¶[28:1] **Ephraim**: the Northern Kingdom. Its capital,
Samaria, was built upon a hill, suggestive of a majestic garland
adorning a human head. The characterization of the leadership of Ephraim as drunken underscores its inattention to
justice and good government (cf. 5:11–13; Am 6:1–6).

**[28:2] **A strong one, a mighty one**: Assyria (cf. 8:7–8).

††[28:9–10] The words of those who ridicule Isaiah. The
Hebrew of v. 10, by its very sound, conveys the idea of mocking imitation of what the prophet says, as though he spoke like
a stammering child: "sau lasau, sau lasau, kau lakau, kau lakau,
ze'er sham, ze'er sham." But in v. 13 God repeats these words
in deadly earnest, putting them in the mouth of the victorious
Assyrian army.

---

n. [27:8] Jer 18:17.   o. [27:11] Is 1:3; 5:13; Jer 4:22.   p. [27:13] Is
11:11–16.

q. [28:1] Hos 7:5; Am 6:1–6.   r. [28:2] Is 25:4–5; 28:17–18;
30:30.   s. [28:4] Is 17:6; Na 3:12.   t. [28:7] Is 5:11–12; Mi 2:11.

rule on rule, rule on rule,
  here a little, there a little!'"
[11] 'Yes, with stammering lips and in a
        strange language
  he will speak to this people,[u]
[12]   to whom he said:
"This is the resting place,
  give rest to the weary;
And this is the place of repose"—
  but they refused to hear.[v]
[13] So for them the word of the LORD shall
        be:
"Command on command,
        command on command,
Rule on rule, rule on rule,
  here a little, there a little!"
So that when they walk, they shall
        stumble backward,
  broken, ensnared, and captured.[w]
[14] Therefore, hear the word of the LORD, you
        scoffers,
  who rule[†] this people in Jerusalem:[x]
[15] You have declared, "We have made a
        covenant with death,
  with Sheol[‡] we have made a pact;
When the raging flood passes through,
  it will not reach us;
For we have made lies our refuge,
  and in falsehood we have found a
        hiding place,"—[y]
[16] Therefore, thus says the Lord GOD:
  See, I am laying a stone in Zion,[§]
  a stone that has been tested,
A precious cornerstone as a sure
        foundation;
  whoever puts faith in it will not
        waver.[z]
[17] I will make judgment a measuring line,
  and justice a level.—[¶]

Hail shall sweep away the refuge of lies,
  and waters shall flood the hiding
        place.
[18] Your covenant with death shall be
        canceled
  and your pact with Sheol shall not
        stand.
When the raging flood passes through,
  you shall be beaten down by it.[a]
[19] Whenever it passes, it shall seize you;
  morning after morning it shall pass,
  by day and by night.
Sheer terror
  to impart the message!
[20] For the bed shall be too short to stretch
        out in,
  and the cover too narrow to wrap in.
[21] For the LORD shall rise up as on Mount
        Perazim,
  bestir himself as in the Valley of
        Gibeon,[**]
To carry out his work—strange his work!
  to perform his deed—alien his deed!
[22] Now, cease scoffing,
  lest your bonds be tightened,
For I have heard a decree of destruction
  from the Lord, the GOD of hosts,
  for the whole land.[b]

### The Parable of the Farmer

[23] [††]Give ear and hear my voice,
  pay attention and hear my word:
[24] Is the plowman forever plowing in order
        to sow,
  always loosening and harrowing the
        field?
[25] When he has leveled the surface,
  does he not scatter caraway and sow
        cumin,[‡‡]
Put in wheat and barley,
  with spelt as its border?
[26] His God has taught him this rule,
  he has instructed him.
[27] For caraway is not threshed with a sledge,
  nor does a cartwheel roll over cumin.
But caraway is beaten out with a staff,
  and cumin with a rod.
[28] Grain is crushed for bread, but not
        forever;

---

*[28:11] God will answer the mockers and defend Isaiah.
**Strange language**: spoken by the invading army.

†[28:14] **Who rule**: there is a play on words; the same
expression could also mean, "Proverb makers," that is, scoffers
of this people.

‡[28:15, 18] **A covenant with death, with Sheol**: an alliance
with foreign powers, such as Egypt and Babylon. **Have made
lies . . . a hiding place**: this confidence in human aid will prove
to be false and deceitful, incapable of averting the dreaded
disaster. **Raging flood**: the Assyrian invasion; cf. 8:7–8.

§[28:16] **A stone in Zion**: the true and sure foundation
of salvation, i.e., the presence of God, who had chosen and
founded Zion as his city (Ps 78:68–69; Is 14:32) and had chosen the Davidic dynasty to rule over his people (Ps 78:70–72;
Is 9:1–6; 11:1–10). **Cornerstone**: the assurance of salvation,
rejected by the people of Judah in the prophet's time, is picked
up in Ps 118:22 and applied to Christ; cf. Mt 21:42; Lk
20:17; Acts 4:11; Rom 9:33; 1 Pt 2:7. Chapters 28–31 alternate between threats of the danger of rebelling against Assyria
(with implied trust in Egypt) with assurances of the power
and protection of the Lord.

¶[28:17] **Line . . . level**: instruments used in constructing a building, to keep it true. They are used metaphorically here to refer to the qualities that Zion, the city of God, must
manifest, judgment and justice, not bloodshed (Mi 3:10), nor

deceit and violence, which would result in a bulging unstable
wall doomed to destruction (Is 30:12–14). Cf. 1 Cor 3:10–17.

**[28:21] **Mount Perazim . . . Valley of Gibeon**: where
David defeated the Philistines; cf. 2 Sm 5:20, 25; 1 Chr 14:11,
16. God's new work will be strange, because instead of fighting
for Judah as the Lord did in David's time, God will now fight
against Jerusalem (see 29:1–4).

††[28:23–29] The practical variation of the farmer's work
reflects the way God deals with his people, wisely adapted
to circumstances; he does not altogether crush them in their
weakness.

‡‡[28:25] **Caraway . . . cumin**: herbs used in seasoning
food. **Spelt**: a variety of wheat.

---

u. [28:11] Jer 5:15; 1 Cor 14:21; Dt 28:49; Bar 4:15.    v. [28:12] Is
30:9.    w. [28:13] Is 8:15.    x. [28:14] Is 3:1–4; 5:18–21.    y. [28:15]
Wis 1:16; Jer 5:12.    z. [28:16] Ps 118:22; Mt 21:42; Acts 4:11; Rom
9:33; 1 Pt 2:6.

a. [28:18] Is 28:2–3.    b. [28:22] Is 5:18–19; 10:23.

though he thresh it thoroughly,
and drive his cartwheel and horses
over it,
he does not pulverize it.
29 This too comes from the LORD of hosts;
wonderful is his counsel and great
his wisdom.c

## CHAPTER 29

### Judgment and Deliverance of Jerusalem

1 Ah! Ariel, Ariel,*
city where David encamped!
Let year follow year,
and feast follow feast,d
2 But I will bring distress upon Ariel,
and there will be mourning and
moaning.
You shall be to me like Ariel:e
3 I will encamp like David against
you;
I will circle you with outposts
and set up siege works against you.f
4 You shall speak from beneath the earth,
and from the dust below, your words
shall come.
Your voice shall be that of a ghost from
the earth,
and your words shall whisper from
the dust.g
5 The horde of your arrogant shall be like
fine dust,
a horde of tyrants like flying chaff.h
Then suddenly, in an instant,
6 you shall be visited by the LORD of
hosts,
With thunder, earthquake, and great
noise,
whirlwind, storm, and the flame of
consuming fire.i
7 †Then like a dream,
a vision of the night,
Shall be the horde of all the nations
who make war against Ariel:
All the outposts, the siege works against
it,
all who distress it.
8 As when a hungry man dreams he is
eating

and awakens with an empty
stomach,
Or when a thirsty man dreams he is
drinking
and awakens faint, his throat
parched,
So shall the horde of all the nations be,
who make war against Mount Zion.

### Blindness and Perversity

9 ‡Stupefy yourselves and stay stupid;
blind yourselves and stay blind!
You who are drunk, but not from wine,
who stagger, but not from strong
drink!j
10 For the LORD has poured out on you
a spirit of deep sleep.
He has shut your eyes (the prophets)
and covered your heads (the seers).§k

11For you the vision of all this has become like the words of a sealed scroll. When it is handed to one who can read, with the request, "Read this," the reply is, "I cannot, because it is sealed." 12When the scroll is handed to one who cannot read, with the request, "Read this," the reply is, "I cannot read."

13        The Lord said:
Since this people draws near with words
only
and honors me with their lips alone,
though their hearts are far from me,
And fear of me has become
mere precept of human teaching,l
14 Therefore I will again deal with this people
in surprising and wondrous fashion:
The wisdom of the wise shall perish,
the prudence of the prudent shall
vanish.m
15 Ah! You who would hide a plan
too deep for the LORD!
Who work in the dark, saying,
"Who sees us, who knows us?"n
16 Your perversity is as though the potter
were taken to be the clay:
As though what is made should say of its
maker,
"He did not make me!"
Or the vessel should say of the potter,
"He does not understand."o

---

*[29:1–2] **Ariel**: a poetic name for Jerusalem. It has been variously interpreted to mean "lion of God," "altar hearth of God" (Ez 43:15–16), "city of God," or "foundation of God." In v. 2 the term refers to "altar hearth," i.e., a place of burning for its people (cf. 30:33; 31:9). God will attack Jerusalem, as David did long ago.

†[29:7–8] Just when the attackers think their capture of Jerusalem is certain, the Lord will snatch victory from their hands and save the city. The sudden shift from the Lord's attack on the city to its deliverance by him is surprising and unexplained; it may reflect the account related in 37:36.

c. [28:29] Rom 11:33.   d. [29:1] 2 Sm 5:6–9.   e. [29:2] Is 33:7.
f. [29:3] 2 Kgs 25:1; Ez 4:2.   g. [29:4] Is 8:19; 1 Sm 28:14.   h. [29:5]
Is 17:13; Ps 18:43; Jb 21:18.   i. [29:6] Is 30:27, 30.

‡[29:9–16] Despite their show of piety, Judah's leaders refused to accept the prophet's words of assurance. They rejected prophetic advice (cf. 30:10–11), did not consult the prophetic oracle in forming their political plans (30:1–2; 31:1), and tried to hide their plans even from God's prophet (v. 15), who, they thought, simply did not understand military and political reality.
§[29:10] **Prophets . . . seers**: interpretive glosses.

j. [29:9] Is 19:14; 28:7–8.   k. [29:10] Is 6:10; Rom 11:8.   l. [29:13]
Ez 33:31; Mt 15:8–9; Mk 7:6–7.   m. [29:14] Jer 49:7; 1 Cor
1:19.   n. [29:15] Is 30:1–2; 31:1; Ez 8:12; Jn 3:19–20.   o. [29:16] Is
45:9; Jer 18:6; Rom 9:20.

### Redemption*

17 Surely, in a very little while,
    Lebanon shall be changed into an
        orchard,
        and the orchard be considered a
            forest!*p*
18 On that day the deaf shall hear
    the words of a scroll;
And out of gloom and darkness,
    the eyes of the blind shall see.*q*
19 The lowly shall again find joy in the LORD,
    the poorest rejoice in the Holy One
        of Israel.*r*
20 For the tyrant shall be no more,
    the scoffer shall cease to be;
All who are ready for evil shall be cut off,*s*
21     those who condemn with a mere
            word,
Who ensnare the defender at the gate,
    and leave the just with an empty
        claim.*t*
22 Therefore thus says the LORD,
    the God of the house of Jacob,
    who redeemed Abraham:†
No longer shall Jacob be ashamed,
    no longer shall his face grow pale.*u*
23 For when his children see
    the work of my hands in his midst,
They shall sanctify my name;
    they shall sanctify the Holy One of
        Jacob,
    be in awe of the God of Israel.*v*
24 Those who err in spirit shall acquire
        understanding,
    those who find fault shall receive
        instruction.

## CHAPTER 30

### Oracle on the Futility of
### an Alliance with Egypt‡

1  Ah! Rebellious children,
    oracle of the LORD,
Who carry out a plan that is not mine,
    who make an alliance§ I did not
        inspire,

thus adding sin upon sin;*w*
2  They go down to Egypt,
    without asking my counsel,§
To seek strength in Pharaoh's protection
    and take refuge in Egypt's shadow.*x*
3  Pharaoh's protection shall become your
        shame,
    refuge in Egypt's shadow your
        disgrace.*y*
4  When his princes are at Zoan
    and his messengers reach Hanes,*z*
5  All shall be ashamed
    of a people that gain them nothing,
Neither help nor benefit,
    but only shame and reproach.*a*
6      Oracle on the Beasts of the Negeb.
Through the distressed and troubled land**
    of the lioness and roaring lion,
    of the viper and flying saraph,
They carry their riches on the backs of
        donkeys
    and their treasures on the humps of
        camels
To a people good for nothing,
7      to Egypt whose help is futile and vain.
Therefore I call her
    "Rahab†† Sit-still."
8  ‡‡Now come, write it on a tablet they can
        keep,
    inscribe it on a scroll;
That in time to come it may be
    an eternal witness.*b*
9  For this is a rebellious people,
    deceitful children,
Children who refuse
    to listen to the instruction of the
        LORD;*c*
10 Who say to the seers, "Do not see";
    to the prophets,§§ "Do not prophesy
        truth for us;

¶[30:2] **Without asking my counsel:** it was a practice to consult God through the prophets or through the priestly oracle before making a major political decision (1 Sm 23:1–12; 1 Kgs 22:5), but Judah's leadership, in its concern for security, was apparently trying to keep its plan for a treaty with Egypt secret even from the prophets, thus implicitly from God (29:15).

\*\*[30:6] **Distressed . . . land:** the wilderness between Judah and Egypt, through which Judahite messengers had to pass, carrying their tribute to Egypt to buy assistance in the struggle against Assyria. **Flying saraph:** see notes on 6:2; 14:29.

††[30:7] Here as elsewhere (cf. Ps 87:4) Egypt is compared to Rahab, the raging, destructive sea monster (cf. Is 51:9; Jb 26:12; Ps 89:11); yet Egypt, when asked for aid by Judah, becomes silent and "sits still."

‡‡[30:8] Isaiah will write down his condemnation of the foolish policy pursued so that the truth of his warning of its dire consequences (vv. 12–17) may afterward be recognized.

§§[30:10] **Seers . . . prophets:** the two terms are synonyms for prophetic figures such as Isaiah (1:1; 2:1; 6:1, 5). There is word-play between the nouns and their cognate verbs, both of which mean "to see." The authorities are depicted as forbidding prophets to contradict their secret political and military policies.

---

\*[29:17–24] The prophet presents the positive aspects of God's plan in terms of a series of reversals: an end to pride, ignorance, and injustice. Cf. 32:3–5.

†[29:22] **Who redeemed Abraham:** perhaps by revealing himself and delivering Abraham from idolatrous worship; cf. Gn 12:1–3; 17:1; Jos 24:2–3.

‡[30:1–17] Several independent oracles against making an alliance with Egypt have been strung together in this chapter: vv. 1–5, vv. 6–7, and vv. 8–17. That these were originally separate oracles is indicated by the fact that the oracle in vv. 6–7 is still introduced by its own heading: Oracle on the Beasts of the Negeb.

§[30:1] **Make an alliance:** lit., "pour out a libation," namely, as part of the ritual of treaty making.

---

p. [29:17] Is 32:15.  q. [29:18] Is 35:5; 42:6–7.  r. [29:19] Is 61:1–2.  s. [29:20] Is 28:22.  t. [29:21] Is 5:23; 10:1–2; Am 5:10, 12.  u. [29:22] Is 45:17.  v. [29:23] Is 8:12–13.

w. [30:1] Is 1:4; 5:21; 28:15; 29:15.  x. [30:2] Is 31:1; 36:6.  y. [30:3] Is 20:5; Jer 2:36–37.  z. [30:4] Is 19:11.  a. [30:5] Is 36:6.  b. [30:8] Is 8:1, 16; Jer 36:2; Hb 2:2.  c. [30:9] Is 1:4; 28:12; Jer 7:28.

speak smooth things to us, see
visions that deceive!*d*

11 Turn aside from the way! Get out of the
path!
Let us hear no more
of the Holy One of Israel!"*e*

12 Therefore, thus says the Holy One of
Israel:
Because you reject this word,
And put your trust in oppression and
deceit,
and depend on them,*f*

13 This iniquity of yours shall be
like a descending rift
Bulging out in a high wall
whose crash comes suddenly, in an
instant,*g*

14 Crashing like a potter's jar
smashed beyond rescue,
And among its fragments cannot be found
a sherd to scoop fire from the hearth
or dip water from the cistern.*h*

15 For thus said the Lord God,
the Holy One of Israel:
By waiting and by calm you shall be saved,
in quiet and in trust shall be your
strength.
But this you did not will.*i*

16 "No," you said,
"Upon horses we will flee."
Very well, you shall flee!
"Upon swift steeds we will ride."
Very well, swift shall be your
pursuers!*j*

17 A thousand shall tremble at the threat of
one—
if five threaten, you shall flee.
You will then be left like a flagstaff on a
mountaintop,
like a flag on a hill.*k*

### Zion's Future Deliverance

18 Truly, the Lord is waiting to be gracious
to you,
truly, he shall rise to show you
mercy;
For the Lord is a God of justice:
happy are all who wait for him!*l*

19 Yes, people of Zion, dwelling in
Jerusalem,
you shall no longer weep;
He will be most gracious to you when you
cry out;
as soon as he hears he will answer
you.*m*

20 The Lord will give you bread in adversity
and water in affliction.

No longer will your Teacher* hide himself,
but with your own eyes you shall see
your Teacher,*n*

21 And your ears shall hear a word behind
you:
"This is the way; walk in it,"
when you would turn to the right or
the left.

22 You shall defile your silver-plated idols
and your gold-covered images;
You shall throw them away like filthy rags,
you shall say, "Get out!"*o*

23 He will give rain for the seed
you sow in the ground,
And the bread that the soil produces
will be rich and abundant.
On that day your cattle will graze
in broad meadows;*p*

24 The oxen and the donkeys that till the
ground
will eat silage tossed to them
with shovel and pitchfork.

25 Upon every high mountain and lofty hill
there will be streams of running
water.
On the day of the great slaughter,
when the towers fall,

26 The light of the moon will be like the light
of the sun,
and the light of the sun will be seven
times greater,
like the light of seven days,
On the day the Lord binds up the
wounds of his people
and heals the bruises left by his
blows.*q*

### Divine Judgment on Assyria†

27 See, the name of the Lord is coming from
afar,
burning with anger, heavy with threat,
His lips filled with fury,
tongue like a consuming fire,*r*

28 Breath like an overflowing torrent
that reaches up to the neck!
He will winnow the nations with a
destructive winnowing
and bridle the jaws of the peoples to
send them astray.*s*

29 For you, there will be singing
as on a night when a feast is
observed,

---

*[30:20] **Teacher**: God, who in the past made the people
blind and deaf through the prophetic message (6:9–10) and
who in his anger hid his face from the house of Jacob (8:17),
shall in the future help them to understand his teaching
clearly (cf. Jer 31:34).

†[30:27–33] God's punishment of Assyria. **The name of
the Lord**: here, God himself; cf. Ps 20:2.

---

d. [30:10] Is 29:10; Jer 5:31; 11:21; Am 2:12.    e. [30:11] Jb 21:14–
15.    f. [30:12] Is 28:15; Ps 62:11.    g. [30:13] Is 28:17; Ez 13:14.
h. [30:14] Jer 19:11.    i. [30:15] Is 7:4; 8:6; 28:12.    j. [30:16] Is 31:3.
k. [30:17] Is 11:10; Dt 32:30.    l. [30:18] Ex 34:6; Ps 34:9; Jer
17:7.    m. [30:19] Is 25:8; 58:9; 65:24.

n. [30:20] Is 6:9–10; 8:17; 29:18.    o. [30:22] Is 2:20; 27:9; 31:7.
p. [30:23] Lv 26:3–5.    q. [30:26] Is 1:6; Jer 30:17; Hos 6:1.    r. [30:27]
Is 10:17; 29:6.    s. [30:28] Is 8:7–8; 37:29.

And joy of heart
    as when one marches along with a
        flute
Going to the mountain of the LORD,
    to the Rock of Israel.

30 The LORD will make his glorious voice
        heard,
    and reveal his arm coming down
In raging fury and flame of consuming
        fire,
    in tempest, and rainstorm, and hail.[t]

31 For at the voice of the LORD, Assyria will
        be shattered,
    as he strikes with the rod;

32 And every sweep of the rod of his
        punishment,
    which the LORD will bring down
        on him,
Will be accompanied by timbrels and
        lyres,
    while he wages war against him.[u]

33 For his tophet[*] has long been ready,
    truly it is prepared for the king;
His firepit made both deep and wide,
    with fire and firewood in
        abundance,
And the breath of the LORD, like a stream
        of sulfur,
    setting it afire.[v]

## CHAPTER 31

### Against the Egyptian Alliance

1 Ah! Those who go down to Egypt for
        help,
    who rely on horses;
Who put their trust in chariots because of
        their number,
    and in horsemen because of their
        combined power,
But look not to the Holy One of Israel
    nor seek the LORD![†w]

2 Yet he too is wise and will bring disaster;
    he will not turn from his threats.
He will rise up against the house of the
        wicked
    and against those who help
        evildoers.[x]

3 The Egyptians are human beings, not God,
    their horses flesh, not spirit;
When the LORD stretches forth his hand,
    the helper shall stumble, the one
        helped shall fall,
    and both of them shall perish
        together.[y]

4 For thus says the LORD to me:
As a lion or its young
    growling over the prey,
With a band of shepherds
    assembled against it,
Is neither dismayed by their shouts
    nor cowed by their noise,
So shall the LORD of hosts come down
    to wage war upon Mount Zion,
        upon its height.[z]

5 Like hovering birds, so the LORD of hosts
    shall shield Jerusalem,
To shield and deliver,
    to spare and rescue.[a]

6Return, O Israelites, to him whom you have
utterly deserted.[b] 7On that day each one of you
shall reject his idols of silver and gold, which
your hands have made.[c]

8 Assyria shall fall by a sword, not wielded
        by human being,
    no mortal sword shall devour him;
He shall flee before the sword,
    and his young men shall be
        impressed as laborers.[d]

9 He shall rush past his crag[‡] in panic,
    and his princes desert the standard
        in terror,
Says the LORD who has a fire in Zion
    and a furnace in Jerusalem.[e]

## CHAPTER 32

### The Kingdom of Justice

1 See, a king will reign justly
    and princes will rule rightly.[f]

2 Each of them will be like a shelter from
        the wind,
    a refuge from the rain.
They will be like streams of water in a dry
        country,
    like the shade of a great rock in a
        parched land.[g]

3 The eyes of those who see will not be
        closed;

---

*[30:33] **Tophet**: a site, near Jerusalem, where children
were sacrificed by fire to Molech (2 Kgs 23:10), and where,
probably, Ahaz sacrificed his son (2 Kgs 16:3). Here, Isaiah
speaks of "his tophet," the site prepared for burning up the
king of Assyria. **King**: there seems to be a play on words
between the Heb. word for king (*melek*) and the name Molech.
This defeat of Assyria becomes the occasion for Israel's festal
rejoicing (v. 32).

†[31:1] **Seek the LORD**: a technical expression for seeking
a prophetic or priestly oracle, similar to the expression "asking my counsel" in 30:2. The prophet complains that Judah
has decided on its policy of alliance with Egypt without first
consulting the Lord.

‡[31:9] **Crag**: the king as the rallying point of the princes.
**Panic**: terror is an element of Israel's holy war tradition, in
which defeat of the enemy is accomplished by the Lord rather
than by human means (cf. v. 8).

---

t. [30:30] Is 10:17; 28:2; 29:6.  u. [30:32] Is 10:24–26; 14:24–27.
v. [30:33] Gn 19:24; Ez 38:22.  w. [31:1] Is 5:12, 24; 18:2; 22:11;
29:15; 30:2; 36:6.  x. [31:2] Is 28:21.

y. [31:3] Ps 146:3–5.  z. [31:4] Hos 5:14; Am 1:2; 3:8, 12.  a. [31:5]
Is 37:35; Dt 32:11; Ps 91:4.  b. [31:6] Is 1:2–4; Jer 3:12.  c. [31:7]
Is 2:20; 30:22.  d. [31:8] Is 27:1; 34:5–6; 37:36.  e. [31:9] Is 30:17,
33.  f. [32:1] Is 9:6; 11:4; 16:5; Ps 72:1–4; Jer 23:5–6.  g. [32:2] Is
4:6; 16:4; 25:4.

the ears of those who hear will be
attentive.[h]
4 The hasty of heart shall take thought to
know,
and tongues of stutterers shall speak
readily and clearly.
5 No more will the fool be called noble,
nor the deceiver be considered
honorable.[i]
6 For the fool speaks folly,
his heart plans evil:
Godless actions,
perverse speech against the LORD,
Letting the hungry go empty
and the thirsty without drink.[j]
7 The deceits of the deceiver are evil,
he plans devious schemes:
To ruin the poor with lies,
and the needy when they plead their
case.[k]
8 But the noble plan noble deeds,
and in noble deeds they persist.

### The Women of Jerusalem

9 You women so complacent, rise up and
hear my voice,
daughters so confident, give heed to
my words.[l]
10 In a little more than a year
your confidence will be shaken;
For the vintage will fail,
no fruit harvest will come in.[m]
11 Tremble, you who are so complacent!
Shudder, you who are so confident!
Strip yourselves bare,
with only a loincloth for cover.[n]
12 Beat your breasts
for the pleasant fields,
for the fruitful vine;[o]
13 For the soil of my people,
overgrown with thorns and briers;
For all the joyful houses,
the exultant city.[p]
14 The castle* will be forsaken,
the noisy city deserted;
Citadel and tower will become wasteland
forever,
the joy of wild donkeys, the pasture
of flocks;[q]
15 †Until the spirit from on high
is poured out on us.

And the wilderness becomes a garden land
and the garden land seems as
common as forest.[r]
16 Then judgment will dwell in the
wilderness
and justice abide in the garden land.
17 The work of justice will be peace;
the effect of justice, calm and
security forever.[s]
18 My people will live in peaceful country,
in secure dwellings and quiet resting
places.[t]
19 And the forest will come down completely,
the city will be utterly laid low.‡[u]
20 Happy are you who sow beside every
stream,
and let the ox and the donkey go
freely![v]

## CHAPTER 33

### Overthrow of Assyria§

1 Ah! You destroyer never destroyed,
betrayer never betrayed!
When you have finished destroying, you
will be destroyed;
when you have stopped betraying,
you will be betrayed.[w]
2 LORD, be gracious to us; for you we wait.
Be our strength every morning,
our salvation in time of trouble![x]
3 At the roaring sound, peoples flee;
when you rise in your majesty,
nations are scattered.[y]
4 Spoil is gathered up as caterpillars gather,
an onrush like the rush of locusts.[z]
5 The LORD is exalted, enthroned on high;
he fills Zion with right and justice.[a]
6 That which makes her seasons certain,
her wealth, salvation, wisdom, and
knowledge,
is the fear of the LORD, her treasure.[b]
7 See, the men of Ariel cry out in the streets,
the messengers of Shalem¶ weep
bitterly.

---

‡[32:19] Probably from a different context, perhaps after
v. 14a.

§[33:1–24] After an introductory address to Assyria (v. 1),
there follows a prayer on behalf of Jerusalem which recalls
what God had done in the past (vv. 2–6) and a description
of the present situation (vv. 7–9). In response, the Lord
announces a judgment on Assyria (vv. 10–12) that will lead
to the purification of Jerusalem's inhabitants (vv. 13–16). The
text ends with an idealized portrait of the redeemed Jerusalem
of the future (vv. 17–24).

¶[33:7] **Ariel . . . Shalem**: Jerusalem; cf. 29:1; Gn 14:18;
Ps 76:3. There is a play on words between "Shalem," the city
name, and *shalom*, Heb. for "peace."

---

*[32:14] **The castle**: the fortified royal palace in Jerusalem.
**Citadel**: Ophel, the fortified hill, with its stronghold called
"the great projecting tower" (Neh 3:27).
†[32:15–18, 20] Extraordinary peace and prosperity will
come to Israel under just rulers.

h. [32:3] Is 6:10; 29:18; 35:5.   i. [32:5] Is 5:20.   j. [32:6] Prv 15:2.
k. [32:7] Is 29:20–21; Mi 2:1.   l. [32:9] Is 3:16–24; Am 6:1.
m. [32:10] Zep 1:13.   n. [32:11] Is 20:2; Jer 4:8; Mi 1:8.   o. [32:12]
Is 16:9.   p. [32:13] Is 5:6; 7:23–25; 22:2; 34:13.   q. [32:14] Is 7:25;
24:10–11.

r. [32:15] Is 44:3; Ps 104:30; Ez 37:9–10; Jl 3:1–2.   s. [32:17] Is
9:6; 30:15; 33:15–16; Ps 72:2–3, 7; Jas 3:18.   t. [32:18] Jer 23:6;
Mi 4:4.   u. [32:19] Is 10:33–34; 26:5.   v. [32:20] Is 7:25; 30:18,
23.   w. [33:1] Is 10:12; 16:4; 21:2; 24:16.   x. [33:2] Is 25:9;
30:18–19.   y. [33:3] Is 17:13; Nm 10:35; Ps 68:2.   z. [33:4] Is 9:2;
33:23.   a. [33:5] Is 1:26–27; 2:11, 17; 32:1; 33:16.   b. [33:6] Is 11:2;
13:22; 60:22.

8 The highways are desolate,
   travelers have quit the paths,
  Covenants are broken, witnesses spurned;
   yet no one gives it a thought.[c]
9 The country languishes in mourning,
   Lebanon withers with shame;
  Sharon* is like the Arabah,
   Bashan and Carmel are stripped
    bare.[d]
10 Now I will rise up, says the LORD,
    now exalt myself,
    now lift myself up.[e]
11 You conceive dry grass, bring forth stubble;
    my spirit shall consume you like fire.
12 The peoples shall be burned to lime,
    thorns cut down to burn in fire.[f]
13 Hear, you who are far off, what I have
     done;
    you who are near, acknowledge my
     might.
14 In Zion sinners are in dread,
    trembling grips the impious:
   "Who of us can live with consuming fire?
    who of us can live with everlasting
     flames?"[g]
15 Whoever walks righteously and speaks
     honestly,
    who spurns what is gained by
     oppression,
   Who waves off contact with a bribe,
    who stops his ears so as not to hear
     of bloodshed,
    who closes his eyes so as not to look
     on evil—[h]
16 That one shall dwell on the heights,
    with fortresses of rock for
     stronghold,
    food and drink in steady supply.
17 Your eyes will see a king[†] in his splendor,
    they will look upon a vast land.[i]
18 Your mind will dwell on the terror:
   "Where is the one who counted,
    where the one who weighed?
   Where the one who counted the
     towers?"[j]
19 You shall no longer see a defiant people,
    a people of speech too obscure to
     comprehend,
    stammering in a tongue not
     understood.[k]
20 Look to Zion, the city of our festivals;
    your eyes shall see Jerusalem
    as a quiet abode, a tent not to be
     struck,
   Whose pegs will never be pulled up,
    nor any of its ropes severed.[l]

21 Indeed the LORD in majesty will be there
     for us
    a place of rivers and wide streams
    on which no galley may go,
    where no majestic ship[‡] may pass.[m]
22 For the LORD is our judge,
    the LORD is our lawgiver,
    the LORD is our king;
    he it is who will save us.
23 The rigging hangs slack;
    it cannot hold the mast in place,
    nor keep the sail spread out.
   Then the blind will divide great spoils
    and the lame will carry off the loot.[n]
24 No one who dwells there will say, "I am
     sick";
    the people who live there will be
     forgiven their guilt.[o]

F. The Lord, Zion's Avenger[§]

## CHAPTER 34

### Judgment upon Edom

1 Come near, nations, and listen;
   be attentive, you peoples!
  Let the earth and what fills it listen,
   the world and all it produces.[p]
2 The LORD is angry with all the nations,
   enraged against all their host;
  He has placed them under the ban,
   given them up to slaughter.[q]
3 Their slain shall be cast out,
   their corpses shall send up a stench;
   the mountains shall run with their
    blood,[r]
4 All the host of heaven shall rot;
   the heavens shall be rolled up like
    a scroll.
  All their host shall wither away,
   as the leaf wilts on the vine,
   or as the fig withers on the tree.[s]
5 When my sword has drunk its fill in the
    heavens,
   it shall come down upon Edom for
    judgment,
   upon a people under my ban.[t]

‡[33:21–23] **Galley . . . majestic ship**: of a foreign oppressor. Though the broad streams of the future Jerusalem will make it accessible by boat, no foreign invader will succeed in a naval attack on the city, for the Lord will protect it, the enemy fleet will be disabled, and even the weakest inhabitants will gather much plunder from the defeated enemy.
§[34:1–35:10] These two chapters form a small collection which looks forward to the vindication of Zion, first by defeat of its enemies (chap. 34), then by its restoration (chap. 35). They are generally judged to be later than the time of Isaiah (eighth century), perhaps during the Babylonian exile or thereafter; they are strongly influenced by Deutero-Isaiah (sixth century). In places they reflect themes from other parts of the Isaian collection.

*[33:9] **Sharon**: the fertile plain near the Mediterranean.
†[33:17] **King**: either the ideal Davidic king or God; cf. v. 22.

c. [33:8] Is 24:5; Jgs 5:6.   d. [33:9] Na 1:4.   e. [33:10] Ps 12:6; Zep 3:8.   f. [33:12] Is 10:17.   g. [33:14] Is 30:27, 30, 32; 31:9.   h. [33:15] Ps 15:2–6; 24:4–5.   i. [33:17] Is 26:15.   j. [33:18] Ps 48:13–14.   k. [33:19] Is 28:11.   l. [33:20] Is 32:18; Ps 46:5; 122:1–4.

m. [33:21] Ez 47:1–12; Ps 46:5; 48:7.   n. [33:23] 2 Sm 8:6–7.   o. [33:24] Mi 7:18–19.   p. [34:1] Mi 1:2.   q. [34:2] Is 24:21.   r. [34:3] Ez 32:4, 6.   s. [34:4] Is 13:10; 24:23; Ez 32:7; Jl 3:3–4; Mt 24:29; 2 Pt 3:10; Rev 6:12–14.   t. [34:5] Jer 46:10.

6 The LORD has a sword sated with blood,
   greasy with fat,
With the blood of lambs and goats,
   with the fat of rams' kidneys;
For the LORD has a sacrifice in Bozrah,
   a great slaughter in the land of
      Edom.ᵘ
7 Wild oxen shall be struck down with
      fatlings,
   and bullocks with bulls;
Their land shall be soaked with blood,
   and their soil greasy with fat.
8 ˙For the LORD has a day of vengeance,
   a year of requital for the cause of
      Zion.ᵛ
9 Edom's streams shall be changed into
      pitch,
   its soil into sulfur,
   and its land shall become burning
      pitch;
10 Night and day it shall not be quenched,
   its smoke shall rise forever.
From generation to generation it shall lie
      waste,
   never again shall anyone pass
      through it.ʷ
11 But the desert owl and hoot owl shall
      possess it,
   the screech owl and raven shall
      dwell in it.
The LORD will stretch over it the
      measuring line of chaos,
   the plumb line of confusion.†ˣ
12 Its nobles shall be no more,
   nor shall kings be proclaimed there;
   all its princes are gone.ʸ
13 Its castles shall be overgrown with thorns,
   its fortresses with thistles and briers.
It shall become an abode for jackals,
   a haunt for ostriches.ᶻ
14 Wildcats shall meet with desert beasts,
   satyrs‡ shall call to one another;
There shall the lilith repose,
   and find for herself a place to rest.
15 There the hoot owl shall nest and lay eggs,
   hatch them out and gather them in
      her shadow;
There shall the kites assemble,
   each with its mate.

16 Search through the book of the LORD§ and
      read:
   not one of these shall be lacking,
For the mouth of the LORD has ordered it,
   and his spirit gathers them there.
17 It is he who casts the lot for them;
   his hand measures off¶ their portions;
They shall possess it forever,
   and dwell in it from generation to
      generation.ᵃ

## CHAPTER 35

### Israel's Deliverance**

1 The wilderness and the parched land will
      exult;
   the Arabah will rejoice and bloom;ᵇ
2 Like the crocus it shall bloom abundantly,
   and rejoice with joyful song.
The glory of Lebanon will be given to it,
   the splendor of Carmel and Sharon;
They will see the glory of the LORD,
   the splendor of our God.ᶜ
3 Strengthen hands that are feeble,
   make firm knees that are weak,ᵈ
4 Say to the fearful of heart:
   Be strong, do not fear!
Here is your God,
   he comes with vindication;
With divine recompense
   he comes to save you.ᵉ
5 Then the eyes of the blind shall see,
   and the ears of the deaf be opened;ᶠ
6 Then the lame shall leap like a stag,
   and the mute tongue sing for joy.
For waters will burst forth in the
      wilderness,
   and streams in the Arabah.ᵍ
7 The burning sands will become pools,
   and the thirsty ground, springs of
      water;
The abode where jackals crouch
   will be a marsh for the reed and
      papyrus.
8 A highway will be there,
   called the holy way;

§[34:16] **Book of the LORD:** a list of God's creatures; cf. Ex 32:32–33; Ps 69:29, "the book of the living"; Ps 139:16, "your book."

¶[34:17] **Casts the lot . . . measures off:** an ironic reference to how land might be distributed to new possessors (cf. Jos 14–21; Mi 2:5).

**[35:1–10] This chapter contains a number of themes similar to those in Deutero-Isaiah (chaps. 40–55), for example, the blossoming of the wilderness (vv. 1–2; cf. 41:18–19), which is now well-irrigated (v. 7; cf. 43:19–20); sight to the blind (vv. 5–6; cf. 42:7, 16); a highway in the wilderness (v. 8; cf. 41:3); and the return of the redeemed/ransomed to Zion (vv. 9–10; cf. 51:11). Nevertheless, it forms a unit with chap. 34 (see note on 34:1–35:10) and reflects, along with that chapter, themes found in chaps. 1–33.

---

*[34:8–17] The extreme hostility against Edom in this passage is reflected in a number of other prophetic texts from the seventh and sixth centuries B.C. (cf. e.g., 63:1–6; Jer 49:7–22; Ez 25:12–14). The animus was probably prompted by Edomite infiltration of the southern territories of Judah, especially after the Babylonian conquest of Judah.

†[34:11] **Chaos . . . confusion:** *tohu . . . bohu* in Hebrew, the terms used to describe the primeval chaos in Gn 1:2.

‡[34:14] **Satyrs:** see note on 13:21. **The lilith:** a female demon thought to roam about the desert.

---

u. [34:6] Is 63:1; Lv 3:4; 2 Sm 1:22; Jer 49:12–13; Zep 1:7.   v. [34:8] Is 13:9; 63:4.   w. [34:10] Mal 1:4; Rev 14:11; 18:18.   x. [34:11] Is 14:23; 28:17; 2 Kgs 21:13; Zep 2:14.   y. [34:12] Ob 18.   z. [34:13] Is 13:21; Hos 9:6.

a. [34:17] Jos 18:10; Ps 78:55.   b. [35:1] Is 41:18–19; 55:12–13.   c. [35:2] Is 40:5; 60:13.   d. [35:3] Is 40:29–30; Jb 4:3–4; Heb 12:12.   e. [35:4] Is 41:10; Zec 8:13.   f. [35:5] Is 29:18; 32:3.   g. [35:6] Is 32:3–4; 41:18; 43:19–20; 44:3; Mt 11:5.

No one unclean may pass over it,
    but it will be for his people;
      no traveler, not even fools, shall go
        astray on it.[h]
9 No lion shall be there,
    nor any beast of prey approach,
      nor be found.
    But there the redeemed shall walk,[i]
10 And the ransomed of the LORD shall
      return,
    and enter Zion singing,
      crowned with everlasting joy;
They meet with joy and gladness,
    sorrow and mourning flee away.[j]

*G. Historical Appendix*[*]

## CHAPTER 36

**Invasion of Sennacherib.** [1]In the fourteenth year of King Hezekiah, Sennacherib, king of Assyria, went up against all the fortified cities of Judah and captured them.[†k] [2]From Lachish the king of Assyria sent his commander with a great army to King Hezekiah in Jerusalem. When he stopped at the conduit of the upper pool, on the highway of the fuller's field, [3]there came out to him the master of the palace, Eliakim, son of Hilkiah, and Shebna the scribe, and the chancellor, Joah, son of Asaph. [4]The commander said to them, "Tell Hezekiah: Thus says the great king, the king of Assyria: On what do you base this trust of yours? [5]Do you think mere words substitute for strategy and might in war? In whom, then, do you place your trust, that you rebel against me? [6]Do you trust in Egypt, that broken reed of a staff which pierces the hand of anyone who leans on it? That is what Pharaoh, king of Egypt, is to all who trust in him.[l] [7]Or do you say to me: It is in the LORD, our God, we trust? Is it not he whose high places and altars Hezekiah has removed,[‡] commanding Judah and Jerusalem, 'Worship before this altar'?[m]

[8]"Now, make a wager with my lord, the king of Assyria: I will give you two thousand horses, if you are able to put riders on them. [9]How then can you turn back even a captain, one of the least servants of my lord, trusting, as you do, in Egypt for chariots and horses? [10]Did I come up to destroy this land without the LORD? The LORD himself said to me, Go up and destroy that land!"[n]

[11]Then Eliakim and Shebna and Joah said to the commander, "Please speak to your servants in Aramaic; we understand it. Do not speak to us in the language of Judah within earshot of the people who are on the wall."[§]

[12]But the commander replied, "Was it to your lord and to you that my lord sent me to speak these words? Was it not rather to those sitting on the wall, who, with you, will have to eat their own excrement and drink their own urine?" [13]Then the commander stepped forward and cried out in a loud voice in the language of Judah, "Listen to the words of the great king, the king of Assyria. [14]Thus says the king: Do not let Hezekiah deceive you, for he cannot rescue you. [15]And do not let Hezekiah induce you to trust in the LORD, saying, 'The LORD will surely rescue us, and this city will not be handed over to the king of Assyria.' [16]Do not listen to Hezekiah, for thus says the king of Assyria:

Make peace with me
    and surrender to me!
Eat, each of you, from your vine,
    each from your own fig tree.
Drink water, each from your own well,[o]
17    until I arrive and take you
    to a land like your own,
A land of grain and wine,
    a land of bread and vineyards.

[18]Do not let Hezekiah seduce you by saying, 'The LORD will rescue us.' Has any of the gods of the nations rescued his land from the power of the king of Assyria?[p] [19]Where are the gods of Hamath and Arpad? Where are the gods of Sepharvaim? Where are the gods of Samaria? Have they saved Samaria from my power?[q] [20]Who among all the gods of these lands ever rescued their land from my power, that the LORD should save Jerusalem from my power?" [21]But they remained silent and did not answer at all, for the king's command was, "Do not answer him."

[22]Then the master of the palace, Eliakim, son of Hilkiah, Shebna the scribe, and the chancellor Joah, son of Asaph, came to Hezekiah with their garments torn, and reported to him the words of the commander.

---

[*][36:1–39:8] Except for 38:9–20 (Hezekiah's prayer of thanksgiving), this historical appendix describing the siege, etc., is paralleled in 2 Kgs 18:13–20:19, which, however, has certain details proper to itself. The events are also reflected in the cuneiform inscriptions of Sennacherib.

[†][36:1] The occasion for this Assyrian attack was Hezekiah's attempt to reject Judah's status as vassal to Assyria, relying on help from Egypt, a course of action condemned by Isaiah (see notes on 28:15, 18; 28:16; 29:7–8; 30:1–17; etc.). 2 Kgs 19:14–16 reports that Hezekiah surrendered to the Assyrians and paid the tribute imposed on him—a report omitted in the Isaiah text.

[‡][36:7] The Assyrians assert that Hezekiah's removal of the high places and altars (unofficial sanctuaries) was taken by the Lord as an insult. They declare to Jerusalem's emissaries that the city therefore no longer has a right to the Lord's protection and that they are the ones who truly carry out his will (cf. v. 10).

[§][36:11] The emissaries of King Hezekiah ask that the conversation be carried on in Aramaic, not in Hebrew, for they fear the effect of the Assyrian claims upon the morale of the people.

---

h. [35:8] Is 11:16; 43:19; 49:11.   i. [35:9] Is 62:10; Lv 26:6.   j. [35:10] Is 51:11.   k. [36:1] 2 Kgs 18:13; 2 Chr 32:1.   l. [36:6] Is 30:2–3, 7.   m. [36:7] 2 Kgs 18:4.

n. [36:10] Is 10:5–6.   o. [36:16] 1 Kgs 5:5; Zec 3:10.   p. [36:18] Is 37:11.   q. [36:19] Is 10:9; 37:13.

## CHAPTER 37

[1]*When King Hezekiah heard this, he tore his garments, covered himself with sackcloth, and went into the house of the LORD. [2]He sent Eliakim, the master of the palace, and Shebna the scribe, and the elders of the priests, covered with sackcloth, to tell the prophet Isaiah, son of Amoz,

[3] "Thus says Hezekiah:
A day of distress and rebuke,
    a day of disgrace is this day!
Children are due to come forth,
    but the strength to give birth is
        lacking.[†r]

[4]Perhaps the LORD, your God, will hear the words of the commander, whom his lord, the king of Assyria, sent to taunt the living God, and will rebuke him for the words which the LORD, your God, has heard. So lift up a prayer for the remnant that is here."

[5]When the servants of King Hezekiah had come to Isaiah, [6]he said to them: "Tell this to your lord: Thus says the LORD: Do not be frightened by the words you have heard, by which the deputies of the king of Assyria have blasphemed me.[s]

[7] I am putting in him such a spirit
    that when he hears a report
    he will return to his land.
I will make him fall by the sword in
    his land."

[8]When the commander, on his return, heard that the king of Assyria had withdrawn from Lachish, he found him besieging Libnah. [9]The king of Assyria heard a report: "Tirhakah,[‡] king of Ethiopia, has come out to fight against you." Again he sent messengers to Hezekiah to say: [10]"Thus shall you say to Hezekiah, king of Judah: Do not let your God in whom you trust deceive you by saying, 'Jerusalem will not be handed over to the king of Assyria.'[t] [11]You, certainly, have heard what the kings of Assyria have done to all the lands: they put them under the ban! And are you to be delivered? [12]Did the gods of the nations whom my fathers destroyed deliver them—Gozan, Haran, Rezeph, and the Edenites

in Telassar? [13]Where are the king of Hamath, the king of Arpad, or a king of the cities Sepharvaim, Hena or Ivvah?"

[14]Hezekiah took the letter from the hand of the messengers and read it; then he went up to the house of the LORD, and spreading it out before the LORD, [15]Hezekiah prayed to the LORD:

[16] "LORD of hosts, God of Israel,
    enthroned on the cherubim!
You alone are God
    over all the kingdoms of the earth.
It is you who made
    the heavens and the earth.[§]
[17] Incline your ear, LORD, and listen!
    open your eyes, LORD, and see!
Hear all the words Sennacherib has sent
    to taunt the living God.
[18] Truly, O LORD,
    the kings of Assyria have laid waste
    the nations and their lands.
[19] They gave their gods to the fire
    —they were not gods at all,
    but the work of human hands—
Wood and stone, they destroyed them.[u]
[20] Therefore, LORD, our God,
    save us from this man's power,
That all the kingdoms of the earth may
        know
    that you alone, LORD, are God."

[21]¶Then Isaiah, son of Amoz, sent this message to Hezekiah: "Thus says the LORD, the God of Israel, to whom you have prayed concerning Sennacherib, king of Assyria: I have listened! [22]This is the word the LORD has spoken concerning him:[v]

She despises you, laughs you to scorn,
    the virgin daughter Zion;
Behind you she wags her head,
    daughter Jerusalem.
[23] Whom have you insulted and
        blasphemed,
    at whom have you raised your voice
And lifted up your eyes on high?
    At the Holy One of Israel!"[w]
[24] Through the mouths of your messengers
    you have insulted the Lord when
        you said:
'With my many chariots I went up
    to the tops of the peaks,
    to the recesses of Lebanon,

---

*[37:1–35] There appear to be parallel accounts of Hezekiah's appeal and the response received (vv. 1–7 and vv. 14–35): in each, Hezekiah goes to the Temple, refers to the Assyrian boasts (found in 36:15–20; 37:10–14), and receives a favorable response from Isaiah.

†[37:3] A proverbial expression. In the Bible the pangs of childbirth often typify extreme anguish; cf. 13:8; Jer 6:24; Mi 4:9–10. In this instance there is reference to the desperate situation of Hezekiah from which he would scarcely be able to free himself.

‡[37:9] **Tirhakah:** may have been general of the Egyptian army in 701 B.C.; later he became pharaoh, one of the Ethiopian dynasty of Egyptian kings (ca. 690–664 B.C.). Many consider that this account in Isaiah combines features of two originally distinct sieges of Jerusalem by Sennacherib.

§[37:16] In contrast to the empty boasting of the Assyrians, Hezekiah proclaims the Lord as "God over all the kingdoms of the earth."

¶[37:21–37] The reversal of Isaiah's attitude toward Hezekiah's revolt (see note on 36:1) and a wonderful deliverance after Hezekiah had already submitted and paid tribute raise questions difficult to answer. See note on 22:1–14. Some have postulated that chaps. 36–37 combine accounts of two different Assyrian invasions.

r. [37:3] Is 26:18.   s. [37:6] Is 7:4; 10:24.   t. [37:10] Is 36:14.   u. [37:19] Jer 16:20.   v. [37:22] 2 Kgs 19:21.   w. [37:23] Is 10:12.

To cut down its lofty cedars,
    its choice cypresses;
I reached the farthest shelter,
    the forest ranges.
25 I myself dug wells
    and drank foreign water;
Drying up all the rivers of Egypt
    beneath the soles of my feet.'
26 Have you not heard?
    A long time ago I prepared it,
    from days of old I planned it,
Now I have brought it about:
    You are here to reduce
    fortified cities to heaps of ruins,ˣ
27 Their people powerless,
    dismayed and distraught,
They are plants of the field,
    green growth,
    thatch on the rooftops,
Grain scorched by the east wind.
28 I know when you stand or sit,
    when you come or go,
    and how you rage against me.
29 Because you rage against me
    and your smugness has reached my
      ears,
I will put my hook in your nose
    and my bit in your mouth,
And make you leave by the way you came.ʸ
30 This shall be a sign* for you:
This year you shall eat the aftergrowth,
    next year, what grows of itself;
But in the third year, sow and reap,
    plant vineyards and eat their fruit!
31 The remaining survivors of the house of
    Judah
    shall again strike root below
    and bear fruit above.ᶻ
32 For out of Jerusalem shall come a
    remnant,
    and from Mount Zion, survivors.
The zeal of the Lord of hosts shall do this.ᵃ

33 Therefore, thus says the Lord about the
king of Assyria:

He shall not come as far as this city,
    nor shoot there an arrow,
    nor confront it with a shield,
Nor cast up a siege-work against it.
34 By the way he came he shall leave,
    never coming as far as this city,
    oracle of the Lord.
35 I will shield and save this city

for my own sake and the sake of
    David my servant."ᵇ

36 Then the angel of the Lord went forth and struck down one hundred and eighty-five thousand in the Assyrian camp. Early the next morning, there they were, all those corpses, dead!†ᶜ 37 So Sennacherib, the king of Assyria, broke camp, departed, returned home, and stayed in Nineveh. 38 When he was worshiping in the temple of his god Nisroch, his sons Adrammelech and Sharezer struck him down with the sword and fled into the land of Ararat.‡ His son Esarhaddon reigned in his place.

## CHAPTER 38
**Sickness and Recovery of Hezekiah.** §¶In those days,¶ when Hezekiah was mortally ill, the prophet Isaiah, son of Amoz, came and said to him: "Thus says the Lord: Put your house in order, for you are about to die; you shall not recover."ᵈ 2 Hezekiah turned his face to the wall and prayed to the Lord:

3 "Ah, Lord, remember how faithfully and wholeheartedly I conducted myself in your presence, doing what was good in your sight!" And Hezekiah wept bitterly.ᵉ

4 Then the word of the Lord came to Isaiah: 5 Go, tell Hezekiah:** Thus says the Lord, the God of your father David: I have heard your prayer; I have seen your tears. Now I will add fifteen years to your life. 6 I will rescue you and this city from the hand of the king of Assyria; I will be a shield to this city.ᶠ

7 This will be the sign for you from the Lord that the Lord will carry out the word he has spoken: 8 See, I will make the shadow cast by the sun on the stairway to the terrace of Ahaz†† go back the ten steps it has advanced. So the sun came back the ten steps it had advanced.ᵍ

† [37:36] The destruction of Sennacherib's army is also recorded by Herodotus, a Greek historian of the fifth century B.C. It was possibly owing to a plague, which the author interprets as God's activity.

‡ [37:38] The violent death of Sennacherib (681 B.C.) is also mentioned in non-biblical sources. It occurred twenty years after his invasion of Judah. **Ararat:** the land of Urartu in the mountains north of Assyria.

§ [38:1–39:8] The events of this section—sickness and recovery of Hezekiah, embassy of Merodach-baladan—anticipate the rise of Babylon (chaps. 40–66). They occurred prior to the events of 36:1–37:38, which point back to Assyria (1:1–35:10).

¶ [38:1] **In those days:** before the siege of Jerusalem in 701 B.C.

** [38:5] Since Hezekiah died in 687 B.C., his sickness may have occurred in 702 B.C., that is, fifteen years before.

†† [38:8] **Stairway to the terrace of Ahaz:** this interpretation is based on a reading of the Hebrew text revised according to the Dead Sea Scroll of Isaiah; cf. 2 Kgs 23:12. Many translate the phrase as "steps of Ahaz" and understand this as referring to a sundial.

* [37:30] **A sign:** sets a time limit. After two years the normal conditions of life will be resumed. See the similar use of time limits as signs in 7:15–16; 8:4; 16:14; and 21:16. **You:** Hezekiah.

x. [37:26] Is 10:6, 15.   y. [37:29] Is 30:28.   z. [37:31] Is 27:6.
a. [37:32] Is 9:6.

b. [37:35] Is 31:5; 1 Kgs 15:4.   c. [37:36] Is 10:12; 17:14.   d. [38:1] 2 Kgs 20:1.   e. [38:3] 2 Kgs 18:5–6.   f. [38:6] Is 37:35.   g. [38:8] 2 Kgs 20:9–11.

**Hezekiah's Hymn of Thanksgiving.** ⁹The song of Hezekiah, king of Judah, after he had been sick and had recovered from his illness:

¹⁰ In the noontime of life* I said,
  I must depart!
To the gates of Sheol I have been
    consigned
  for the rest of my years.ʰ
¹¹ I said, I shall see the Lord† no more
    in the land of the living.
Nor look on any mortals
    among those who dwell in the
    world.
¹² My dwelling, like a shepherd's tent,
    is struck down and borne away from
    me;
You have folded up my life, like a weaver
    who severs me from the last thread.‡ⁱ
From morning to night you make an end
    of me;
¹³    I cry out even until the dawn.
Like a lion he breaks all my bones;
    from morning to night you make an
    end of me.ʲ
¹⁴ Like a swallow I chirp;
  I moan like a dove.
My eyes grow weary looking heavenward:
    Lord, I am overwhelmed; go
    security for me!
¹⁵ §What am I to say or tell him?
  He is the one who has done it!
All my sleep has fled,
    because of the bitterness of my soul.
¹⁶ Those live whom the Lord protects;
    yours is the life of my spirit.
You have given me health and restored
    my life!
¹⁷    Peace in place of bitterness!
You have preserved my life
    from the pit of destruction;
Behind your back
  you cast all my sins.¶
¹⁸ **"For it is not Sheol that gives you thanks,
    nor death that praises you;
Neither do those who go down into the
    pit
  await your kindness.ᵏ
¹⁹ The living, the living give you thanks,
    as I do today.

Parents declare to their children,
  O God, your faithfulness.
²⁰ The Lord is there to save us.
  We shall play our music
In the house of the Lord
    all the days of our life.

²¹††Then Isaiah said, "Bring a poultice of figs and apply it to the boil for his recovery." ²²Hezekiah asked, "What is the sign that I shall go up to the house of the Lord?"

## CHAPTER 39

**Embassy from Merodach-baladan.** ¹At that time Merodach-baladan,‡‡ son of Baladan, king of Babylon, sent letters and gifts to Hezekiah, when he heard that he had been sick and had recovered.ˡ ²Hezekiah was pleased at their coming, and then showed the messengers his treasury, the silver and gold, the spices and perfumed oil, his whole armory, and everything in his storerooms; there was nothing in his house or in all his realm that Hezekiah did not show them.ᵐ

³Then Isaiah the prophet came to King Hezekiah and asked him, "What did these men say to you? Where did they come from?" Hezekiah replied, "They came to me from a distant land, from Babylon." ⁴He asked, "What did they see in your house?" Hezekiah answered, "They saw everything in my house. There is nothing in my storerooms that I did not show them." ⁵Then Isaiah said to Hezekiah, "Hear the word of the Lord of hosts: ⁶The time is coming when all that is in your house, everything that your ancestors have stored up until this day, shall be carried off to Babylon;§§ nothing shall be left, says the Lord.ⁿ ⁷Some of your own descendants, your progeny, shall be taken and made attendants in the palace of the king of Babylon."ᵒ ⁸Hezekiah replied to Isaiah, "The word of the Lord which you have spoken is good."¶¶ For he thought, "There will be peace and stability in my lifetime."

---

††[38:21–22] These verses are clearly out of place. Logically they should come after v. 6, as they do in the parallel account in 2 Kgs 20, but the two accounts are not identical, and it appears that the version in Isaiah is abbreviated from that in Kings. If that is so, Is 38:21–22 would be a secondary addition from Kings, inserted by a later reader who thought the account incomplete.

‡‡[39:1] **Merodach-baladan**: twice king of Babylon, probably from 721 to 710 B.C., and again for nine months, in 704–703. This visit of his messengers, certainly before 701, was in reality a political one. Babylon hoped to lead an anti-Assyrian confederation composed of neighboring states and wanted Judah to join.

§§[39:6] Because Judah preferred to follow a pro-Babylonian policy, instead of trusting in the Lord, it would later be exiled to Babylon.

¶¶[39:8] Hezekiah was relieved that the disaster would not occur in his lifetime.

---

*[38:10] **In the noontime of life**: long before the end of a full span of life; cf. Ps 55:24; 102:25.
†[38:11] **See the Lord**: go to the Temple and take part in its service.
‡[38:12] These two metaphors emphasize the suddenness and finality of death.
§[38:15–16] The Hebrew text is very problematic and its meaning uncertain.
¶[38:17] **Behind your back you cast all my sins**: figurative language to express the divine forgiveness of sins, as if God no longer saw or cared about them.
**[38:18–19] See note on Ps 6:6.

---

h. [38:10] Jb 17:11–13; Ps 102:25.   i. [38:12] Jb 7:6.   j. [38:13] Jb 23:14.   k. [38:18] Ps 6:6; 88:11–13.

l. [39:1] 2 Kgs 20:12.   m. [39:2] 2 Chr 32:25–31.   n. [39:6] 2 Kgs 24:13; 25:13–17.   o. [39:7] Dn 1:3–19.

## II. ISAIAH 40–55*

*A. The Lord's Glory in Israel's Liberation*

### CHAPTER 40

#### Promise of Salvation

¹ †Comfort, give comfort to my people,
      says your God.
² Speak to the heart of Jerusalem, and
         proclaim to her
      that her service‡ has ended,
      that her guilt is expiated,
   That she has received from the hand of
         the LORD
      double for all her sins.ᵖ

³    A voice proclaims:§
   In the wilderness prepare the way of the
      LORD!
      Make straight in the wasteland a
         highway for our God!�q
⁴ Every valley shall be lifted up,
      every mountain and hill made low;
   The rugged land shall be a plain,
      the rough country, a broad valley.
⁵ Then the glory of the LORD shall be
         revealed,
      and all flesh shall see it together;
   for the mouth of the LORD has
         spoken.

⁶ A voice says, "Proclaim!"
      I answer, "What shall I proclaim?"
   "All flesh is grass,
      and all their loyalty like the flower of
         the field.ʳ
⁷ The grass withers, the flower wilts,
      when the breath of the LORD blows
         upon it."
   "Yes, the people is grass!
⁸    The grass withers, the flower wilts,
      but the word of our God stands
         forever."

⁹ Go up onto a high mountain,
      Zion, herald of good news!¶
   Cry out at the top of your voice,
      Jerusalem, herald of good news!
   Cry out, do not fear!
      Say to the cities of Judah:
      Here is your God!
¹⁰ Here comes with power
      the Lord GOD,
      who rules by his strong arm;
   Here is his reward with him,
      his recompense before him.
¹¹ Like a shepherd he feeds his flock;
      in his arms he gathers the lambs,
   Carrying them in his bosom,
      leading the ewes with care.ˢ

#### Power of God and the Vanity of Idols

¹² Who has measured with his palm the
         waters,
      marked off the heavens with a span,
      held in his fingers the dust of the
         earth,
      weighed the mountains in scales
      and the hills in a balance?˙˙
¹³ Who has directed the spirit of the LORD,
      or instructed him as his counselor?ᵗ
¹⁴ Whom did he consult to gain knowledge?
      Who taught him the path of judgment,
      or showed him the way of
         understanding?

¹⁵ See, the nations count as a drop in the
         bucket,
      as a wisp of cloud on the scales;
      the coastlands weigh no more than
         a speck.††

---

*[40:1–55:13] Chapters 40–55 are usually designated Second Isaiah (or Deutero-Isaiah) and are believed to have been written by an anonymous prophet toward the end of the Babylonian exile. Isaiah, who is named frequently in chaps. 1–39, does not appear here; the Assyrians, the great threat during the eighth century, hardly appear; the Judeans are in Babylon, having been taken there by the victorious Babylonians; Cyrus, the Persian king, is named; he will defeat Babylon and release the captives. Second Isaiah, who sees this not as a happy circumstance but as part of God's age-old plan, exhorts the Judeans to resist the temptations of Babylonian religion and stirs up hopes of an imminent return to Judah, where the Lord will again be acknowledged as King (52:7). Because the prophet proclaimed the triumph of Persia over Babylon, his message would have been considered seditious, and it is very likely for this reason that the collection would have circulated anonymously. At some point it was appended to Is 1–39 and consequently was long considered the work of Isaiah of Jerusalem of the eighth century. But the fact that it is addressed to Judean exiles in Babylon indicates a sixth-century date. Nevertheless, this eloquent prophet in many ways works within the tradition of Isaiah and develops themes found in the earlier chapters, such as the holiness of the Lord (cf. note on 1:4) and his lordship of history. Second Isaiah also develops other Old Testament themes, such as the Lord as Israel's redeemer or deliverer (cf. Ex 3:8; 6:6; 15:13; 18:8).

†[40:1] The "voices" of vv. 3, 6 are members of the heavenly court addressing the prophet; then v. 1 can be understood as the Lord addressing them. It is also possible to translate, with the Vulgate, "Comfort, give comfort, O my people" (i.e., the exiles are called to comfort Jerusalem). The juxtaposition of "my people" and "your God" recalls the covenant formulary.

‡[40:2] Service: servitude (cf. Jb 7:1) and exile.

§[40:3–5] A description of the return of the exiles from Babylon to Jerusalem (Zion). The language used here figuratively describes the way the exiles will take. The Lord leads them, so their way lies straight across the wilderness rather than along the well-watered routes usually followed from Mesopotamia to Israel. Mt 3:3 and gospel parallels adapt these verses to the witness of John the Baptizer to Jesus.

---

¶[40:9] Herald of good news: i.e., of the imminent restoration of the people to their land. This theme of the proclamation of the good news occurs elsewhere in Second Isaiah; cf. also 41:27; 52:7.

**[40:12] The implicit answer is "the hand of the LORD" (v. 2). Waters . . . heavens . . . earth: together form the universe; cf. Gn 1:1–2. Span: the distance between the extended little finger and the thumb. Fingers: lit., "three fingers" (i.e., thumb, index, and middle).

††[40:15] Drop . . . wisp of cloud . . . a speck: the smallest constituent parts of the cosmic waters, heavens, and earth mentioned in v. 12.

---

p. [40:2] Is 50:21.    q. [40:3] Mt 3:3; Mk 1:3; Lk 2:27; Jn 1:23.

r. [40:6] Jb 8:12; 14:2; Ps 37:2; Sir 14:18; Jas 1:10; 1 Pt 1:24.    s. [40:11] Is 49:9–10; 63:11; Ez 34:23; 37:24; Jn 10:11.    t. [40:13] Wis 9:13; Rom 11:34; 1 Cor 2:16; Jb 38:1–11.

<sup>16</sup> Lebanon would not suffice for fuel,<sup>*</sup>
　　nor its animals be enough for burnt
　　　　offerings.
<sup>17</sup> Before him all the nations are as nought,
　　as nothing and void he counts them.

<sup>18</sup> To whom can you liken God?<sup>u</sup>
　　With what likeness can you confront
　　　　him?
<sup>19</sup> An idol? An artisan casts it,
　　the smith plates it with gold,
　　fits it with silver chains.<sup>†v</sup>
<sup>20</sup> Is mulberry wood the offering?
　　A skilled artisan picks out
　　a wood that will not rot,
　　Seeks to set up for himself
　　an idol that will not totter.<sup>w</sup>

<sup>21</sup> Do you not know? Have you not heard?
　　Was it not told you from the
　　　　beginning?
　　Have you not understood from the
　　　　founding of the earth?
<sup>22</sup> The one who is enthroned above the vault
　　　　of the earth,
　　its inhabitants like grasshoppers,
　　Who stretches out the heavens like a veil
　　and spreads them out like a tent to
　　　　dwell in,<sup>x</sup>
<sup>23</sup> Who brings princes to nought
　　and makes the rulers of the earth as
　　　　nothing.
<sup>24</sup> Scarcely are they planted, scarcely sown,
　　scarcely their stem rooted in the earth,
　　When he breathes upon them and they
　　　　wither,
　　and the stormwind carries them
　　　　away like straw.

<sup>25</sup> To whom can you liken me as an equal?
　　says the Holy One.
<sup>26</sup> Lift up your eyes on high
　　and see who created<sup>‡</sup> these:
　　He leads out their army and numbers them,
　　　　calling them all by name.
　　By his great might and the strength of his
　　　　power
　　not one of them is missing!<sup>y</sup>
<sup>27</sup> Why, O Jacob, do you say,<sup>§</sup>
　　and declare, O Israel,
　　"My way is hidden from the LORD,
　　and my right is disregarded by my
　　　　God"?

<sup>28</sup> Do you not know?
　　Have you not heard?
　　The LORD is God from of old,
　　creator of the ends of the earth.
　　He does not faint or grow weary,
　　　　and his knowledge is beyond scrutiny.
<sup>29</sup> He gives power to the faint,
　　abundant strength to the weak.
<sup>30</sup> Though young men faint and grow weary,
　　and youths stagger and fall,
<sup>31</sup> They that hope in the LORD will renew
　　　　their strength,
　　they will soar on eagles' wings;
　　They will run and not grow weary,
　　walk and not grow faint.

## CHAPTER 41

### The Liberator of Israel

<sup>1</sup> Keep silence before me, O coastlands;<sup>¶</sup>
　　let the nations renew their strength.
　　Let them draw near and speak;
　　let us come together for judgment.
<sup>2</sup> Who has stirred up from the East the
　　　　champion of justice,
　　and summoned him to be his
　　　　attendant?
　　To him he delivers nations
　　　　and subdues kings;
　　With his sword he reduces them to dust,
　　　　with his bow, to driven straw.
<sup>3</sup> He pursues them, passing on without loss,
　　by a path his feet scarcely touch.
<sup>4</sup> Who has performed these deeds?
　　Who has called forth the
　　　　generations from the
　　　　beginning?<sup>z</sup>
　　I, the LORD, am the first,
　　and at the last<sup>**</sup> I am he.
<sup>5</sup> The coastlands see, and fear;
　　the ends of the earth tremble:
　　they approach, they come on.

<sup>6</sup> Each one helps his neighbor,
　　one says to the other, "Courage!"
<sup>7</sup> The woodworker encourages the goldsmith,
　　the one who beats with the hammer,
　　　　him who strikes on the anvil,

---

¶[41:1–4] Earlier prophets had spoken of the Assyrians and Babylonians as the Lord's instruments for the punishment of Israel's sins; here the Lord is described as raising up and giving victory to a foreign ruler in order to deliver Israel from the Babylonian exile. The ruler is Cyrus (44:28; 45:1), king of Anshan in Persia, a vassal of the Babylonians. He rebelled against the Babylonian overlords in 556 B.C., and after a series of victories, entered Babylon as victor in 539; the following year he issued a decree which allowed the Jewish captives to return to their homeland (2 Chr 36:22–23; Ezr 1:1–4). For Second Isaiah, the meteoric success of Cyrus was the work of the Lord to accomplish the deliverance promised by earlier prophets.

**[41:4] **The first . . . the last**: God as the beginning and end encompasses all reality. The same designation is used in 44:6 and 48:12.

---

*[40:16] **Lebanon . . . fuel**: the famed cedars would not be enough to keep the fires of sacrifice burning.
†[40:19] **Chains**: needed to hold the idol steady when carried in processions; cf. v. 20; Jer 10:4.
‡[40:26] **Created**: see note on Gn 1:1–2:3. **By name**: for he is their Creator.
§[40:27–28] The exiles, here called Jacob-Israel (Gn 32:29), must not give way to discouragement: their Lord is the eternal God.

---

u. [40:18–19] Acts 17:29.　v. [40:19] Ps 115:4–7; Jer 10:4.　w. [40:20] Is 44:13.　x. [40:22] Ps 104:2.　y. [40:26] Ps 147:4–5.

z. [41:4] Is 44:7; 46:10.

Saying of the soldering, "It is good!"
    then fastening it with nails so it will
        not totter.

8 But you, Israel, my servant,[a]
    Jacob, whom I have chosen,
    offspring of Abraham my friend—
9 You whom I have taken from the ends of
        the earth
    and summoned from its far-off
        places,
To whom I have said, You are my servant;
    I chose you, I have not rejected you—
10 Do not fear: I am with you;
    do not be anxious: I am your God.
I will strengthen you, I will help you,
    I will uphold you with my victorious
        right hand.

11 Yes, all shall be put to shame and disgrace
    who vent their anger against you;
Those shall be as nothing and perish
    who offer resistance.
12 You shall seek but not find
    those who strive against you;
They shall be as nothing at all
    who do battle with you.

13 For I am the LORD, your God,
    who grasp your right hand;
It is I who say to you, Do not fear,
    I will help you.
14 Do not fear, you worm Jacob,
    you maggot Israel;
I will help you—oracle of the LORD;
    the Holy One of Israel is your
        redeemer.*
15 I will make of you a threshing sledge,
    sharp, new, full of teeth,
To thresh the mountains and crush them,
    to make the hills like chaff.
16 When you winnow them, the wind shall
        carry them off,
    the storm shall scatter them.
But you shall rejoice in the LORD;
    in the Holy One of Israel you shall
        glory.

17 The afflicted and the needy seek water in
        vain,
    their tongues are parched with thirst.
I, the LORD, will answer them;
    I, the God of Israel, will not forsake
        them.
18 I will open up rivers on the bare heights,
    and fountains in the broad valleys;
I will turn the wilderness into a marshland,
    and the dry ground into springs of
        water.

19 In the wilderness I will plant the cedar,
    acacia, myrtle, and olive;
In the wasteland I will set the cypress,
    together with the plane tree and the
        pine,
20 That all may see and know,
    observe and understand,
That the hand of the LORD has done this,
    the Holy One of Israel has created it.

21 Present your case, says the LORD;†
    bring forward your arguments, says
        the King of Jacob.
22 Let them draw near and foretell to us
    what it is that shall happen!
What are the things of long ago?
    Tell us, that we may reflect on them
    and know their outcome;
Or declare to us the things to come,‡
23     tell what is to be in the future,
    that we may know that you are gods!
Do something, good or evil,
    that will put us in awe and in fear.
24 Why, you are nothing
    and your work is nought;
    to choose you is an abomination!

25 I have stirred up one from the north, and
        he comes;
    from the east I summon him§ by
        name;
He shall trample the rulers down like mud,
    like a potter treading clay.
26 Who announced this from the beginning,
    that we might know;
    beforehand, that we might say,
        "True"?
Not one of you foretold it, not one spoke;
    not one heard you say,
27 "The first news for Zion: here they come,"
    or, "I will give Jerusalem a herald of
        good news."
28 When I look, there is not one,
    not one of them to give counsel,
    to make an answer when I question
        them.
29 Ah, all of them are nothing,
    their works are nought,
    their idols, empty wind!

---

† [41:21–29] This indictment of Babylonian gods is patterned on a legal trial, in which they are challenged to prove power over events of history and so justify their status as gods (vv. 21–24). Israel's God, on the other hand, has foretold and now brings to pass Israel's deliverance (vv. 25–27). The accused are unable to respond (vv. 28–29). By such polemics (see also 43:12) the prophet declares that all gods other than the Lord are nonexistent; this implicit claim of monotheism later becomes explicit (see 43:10–11; 45:5–7, 14, 18, 21–22; 46:9; and note on 44:6).

‡ [41:22] **Things of long ago . . . things to come**: there are no predictions attributed to idols that have since been fulfilled. Second Isaiah makes frequent reference to "things of long ago," sometimes in conjunction with "things to come" or "new things" in connection with the Lord's activity (cf. 42:9; 43:9, 18; 46:9–10; 48:3–8); both the old things (e.g., creation, exodus) and the new things (release from exile) God brings to pass (cf. 51:9–11), which is why he can declare them beforehand.

§ [41:25] **I summon him**: Cyrus.

---

* [41:14] **Redeemer**: in Hebrew, *goel*, one who frees others from slavery and avenges their sufferings; cf. Lv 25:48; Dt 19:6, 12. Cf. note on Ru 2:20.

a. [41:8–9] Is 44:1–2, 21; 45:4.

## CHAPTER 42

### The Servant of the Lord

1 Here is my servant* whom I uphold,
    my chosen one with whom I am
      pleased.
  Upon him I have put my spirit;
    he shall bring forth justice to the
      nations.b
2 He will not cry out, nor shout,
    nor make his voice heard in the street.
3 A bruised reed† he will not break,
    and a dimly burning wick he will
      not quench.
  He will faithfully bring forth justice.
4 He will not grow dim or be bruised
    until he establishes justice on the
      earth;
    the coastlands‡ will wait for his
      teaching.

5 Thus says God, the LORD,
    who created the heavens and
      stretched them out,
    who spread out the earth and its
      produce,
  Who gives breath to its people
    and spirit to those who walk on it:
6 I, the LORD, have called you for justice,
    I have grasped you by the hand;
  I formed you, and set you
    as a covenant for the people,
    a light for the nations,c
7 To open the eyes of the blind,
    to bring out prisoners from
      confinement,
    and from the dungeon, those who
      live in darkness.
8 I am the LORD, LORD is my name;
    my glory I give to no other,
    nor my praise to idols.
9 See, the earlier things have come to pass,
    new ones I now declare;
  Before they spring forth
    I announce them to you.

### The Lord's Purpose for Israel

10 Sing to the LORD a new song,
    his praise from the ends of the earth:
  Let the sea and what fills it resound,
    the coastlands, and those who dwell
      in them.

11 Let the wilderness and its cities cry out,
    the villages where Kedar§ dwells;
  Let the inhabitants of Sela exult,
    and shout from the top of the
      mountains.
12 Let them give glory to the LORD,
    and utter his praise in the coastlands.

13 The LORD goes forth like a warrior,
    like a man of war he stirs up his
      fury;
  He shouts out his battle cry,
    against his enemies he shows his
      might:d
14 For a long time I have kept silent,
    I have said nothing, holding myself
      back;
  Now I cry out like a woman in labor,
    gasping and panting.
15 'I will lay waste mountains and hills,
    all their undergrowth I will dry up;
  I will turn the rivers into marshes,
    and the marshes I will dry up.e
16 I will lead the blind on a way they do not
      know;
    by paths they do not know I will
      guide them.
  I will turn darkness into light before them,
    and make crooked ways straight.
  These are my promises:
    I made them, I will not forsake
      them.f

17 They shall be turned back in utter shame
    who trust in idols;
  Who say to molten images,
    "You are our gods."
18 You deaf ones, listen,**
    you blind ones, look and see!
19 Who is blind but my servant,
    or deaf like the messenger I send?
  Who is blind like the one I restore,
    blind like the servant of the LORD?
20 You see many things but do not observe;
    ears open, but do not hear.
21 It was the LORD's will for the sake of his
      justice
    to make his teaching great and
      glorious.

22 This is a people†† plundered and despoiled,
    all of them trapped in holes,
    hidden away in prisons.

---

*[42:1–4] **Servant**: three other passages have been popularly called "servant of the Lord" poems: 49:1–7; 50:4–11; 52:13–53:12. Whether the servant is an individual or a collectivity is not clear (e.g., contrast 49:3 with 49:5). More important is the description of the mission of the servant. In the early Church and throughout Christian tradition, these poems have been applied to Christ; cf. Mt 12:18–21.

†[42:3] **Bruised reed . . .**: images to express the gentle manner of the servant's mission.

‡[42:4] **Coastlands**: for Israel, the world to the west: the islands and coastal nations of the Mediterranean.

b. [42:1] Is 45:6; 49:6.   c. [42:6] Is 45:13.

§[42:11] **Kedar**: cf. note on 21:16. **Sela**: Petra, the capital of Edom.

¶[42:15–16] Active once more, God will remove the obstacles that hinder the exiles' return, and will lead them by new roads to Jerusalem; cf. 40:3–4.

**[42:18–20] The LORD rebukes his people for their failures, but their role and their mission endure: they remain his servant, his messenger to the nations.

††[42:22] **A people**: Israel in exile.

d. [42:13] Ex 14:3.   e. [42:15] Ex 9:25; 10:15; 14:21; Ps 105:33–35.
f. [42:16] Ex 13:21.

They are taken as plunder, with no one to
        rescue them,
    as spoil, with no one to say, "Give
        back!"
²³ Who among you will give ear to this,
    listen and pay attention from now on?
²⁴ Who was it that gave Jacob to be
        despoiled,
    Israel to the plunderers?*
Was it not the LORD, against whom we
        have sinned?
    In his ways they refused to walk,
    his teaching they would not heed.
²⁵ So he poured out wrath upon them,
    his anger, and the fury of battle;
It blazed all around them, yet they did not
        realize,
    it burned them, but they did not
        take it to heart.


## CHAPTER 43

### Promises of Redemption and Restoration

¹ But now, thus says the LORD,
    who created you, Jacob, and formed
        you, Israel:
Do not fear, for I have redeemed you;
    I have called you by name: you are
        mine.
² When you pass through waters, I will be
        with you;
    through rivers, you shall not be
        swept away.
When you walk through fire, you shall
        not be burned,
    nor will flames consume you.
³ For I, the LORD, am your God,
    the Holy One of Israel, your savior.
I give Egypt as ransom for you,
    Ethiopia and Seba† in exchange for
        you.
⁴ Because you are precious in my eyes
    and honored, and I love you,
I give people in return for you
    and nations in exchange for your
        life.⁸
⁵ Fear not, for I am with you;
    from the east I will bring back your
        offspring,
    from the west I will gather you.
⁶ I will say to the north: Give them up!
    and to the south: Do not hold them!
Bring back my sons from afar,
    and my daughters from the ends of
        the earth:ʰ

⁷ All who are called by my name
    I created for my glory;
    I formed them, made them.
⁸ Lead out the people, blind though they
        have eyes,
    deaf though they have ears.

⁹ Let all the nations gather together,
    let the peoples assemble!
Who among them could have declared
        this,
    or announced to us the earlier things?‡
Let them produce witnesses to prove
        themselves right,
    that one may hear and say, "It is
        true!"
¹⁰ You are my witnesses§—oracle of the
        LORD—
    my servant whom I have chosen
To know and believe in me
    and understand that I am he.
Before me no god was formed,
    and after me there shall be none.
¹¹ I, I am the LORD;
    there is no savior but me.
¹² It is I who declared, who saved,
    who announced, not some strange
        god among you;
You are my witnesses—oracle of the LORD.
    I am God,
¹³    yes, from eternity I am he;
There is none who can deliver from my
        hand:
    I act and who can cancel it?ⁱ

¹⁴ Thus says the LORD, your redeemer,¶
    the Holy One of Israel:
For your sake I send to Babylon;
    I will bring down all her defenses,
    and the Chaldeans shall cry out in
        lamentation.
¹⁵ I am the LORD, your Holy One,
    the creator of Israel, your King.
¹⁶ Thus says the LORD,
    who opens a way in the sea,
    a path in the mighty waters,ʲ

---

‡[43:9] **Who among them . . . ?**: God, and only God, can
foretell the future because it is he who brings it to pass. The
argument from prediction is an important theme in Second
Isaiah and occurs also in 41:22; 43:10; 44:7–8, 26.

§[43:10] **You are my witnesses**: Israel's role as chosen
people now takes a new turn as they are given the active role
of bearing witness before humankind to the Lord's role in history by proclaiming events beforehand and bringing them to
pass; see also 44:8. The false gods, on the other hand, cannot
produce such witnesses (v. 9; cf. 44:9). **I am he**: this formula
of self-identification, repeated in vv. 13 and 25, is used here to
support the assertion that the Lord alone is God; see also 41:4;
46:4; 48:12; 51:12; 52:6. This expression in part may be behind
the self-identification formula used by Jesus in John's gospel
(cf. Jn 8:58). **Before . . . after**: another example of the same
assertion, that the Lord alone is God; see also note on 44:6.

¶[43:14–17] The destruction of Babylon is described in
language that recalls the drowning of the Egyptian army in
the Red Sea (Ex 14–15).

---

*[42:24] **Plunderers**: the Assyrians and Babylonians. **We
. . . they**: the switch from first- to third-person speech, though
puzzling, does not obscure the fact that "the people" is meant.

†[43:3–4] **Egypt . . . Ethiopia and Seba**: countries which
God permitted the Persians to conquer in return for having
given Israel its freedom.

---

g. [43:4] Dt 4:37; Hos 11:1.   h. [43:6] Is 49:22; Ez 16:20.

i. [43:13] Is 41:4.   j. [43:16] Is 51:10–11; Ex 14:21.

<sup>17</sup> Who leads out chariots and horsemen,
     a powerful army,
   Till they lie prostrate together, never to rise,
     snuffed out, quenched like a wick.<sup>k</sup>
<sup>18</sup> Remember not<sup>*</sup> the events of the past,
   the things of long ago consider not;
<sup>19</sup> See, I am doing something new!
     Now it springs forth, do you not
       perceive it?
   In the wilderness I make a way,
     in the wasteland, rivers.
<sup>20</sup> Wild beasts honor me,
     jackals and ostriches,
   For I put water in the wilderness
     and rivers in the wasteland
     for my chosen people to drink,
<sup>21</sup> The people whom I formed for myself,
     that they might recount my praise.

<sup>22</sup> Yet you did not call upon me, Jacob,<sup>†</sup>
     for you grew weary of me, Israel.
<sup>23</sup> You did not bring me sheep for your
       burnt offerings,
     nor honor me with your sacrifices.
   I did not exact from you the service of
       offerings,
     nor weary you for frankincense.<sup>l</sup>
<sup>24</sup> You did not buy me sweet cane,<sup>‡</sup>
     nor did you fill me with the fat of
       your sacrifices;
   Instead, you burdened me with your sins,
     wearied me with your crimes.
<sup>25</sup> It is I, I, who wipe out,
     for my own sake, your offenses;
     your sins I remember no more.
<sup>26</sup> Would you have me remember, have us
       come to trial?
     Speak up, prove your innocence!
<sup>27</sup> Your first father<sup>§</sup> sinned;
     your spokesmen rebelled against me
<sup>28</sup> Till I repudiated the holy princes,
     put Jacob under the ban,
     exposed Israel to scorn.

### CHAPTER 44
<sup>1</sup> Hear then, Jacob, my servant,
   Israel, whom I have chosen.
<sup>2</sup> Thus says the LORD who made you,
   your help, who formed you from the
       womb:

Do not fear, Jacob, my servant,
   Jeshurun,<sup>¶</sup> whom I have chosen.
<sup>3</sup> I will pour out water upon the thirsty
       ground,
     streams upon the dry land;
   I will pour out my spirit upon your
       offspring,
     my blessing upon your descendants.
<sup>4</sup> They shall spring forth amid grass
     like poplars beside flowing waters.<sup>m</sup>
<sup>5</sup> One shall say, "I am the LORD's,"
     another shall be named after Jacob,
   And this one shall write on his hand,<sup>**</sup>
       "The LORD's,"
     and receive the name Israel.<sup>n</sup>

### The True God and False Gods

<sup>6</sup> <sup>††</sup>Thus says the LORD, Israel's king,
     its redeemer, the LORD of hosts:
   I am the first, I am the last;
     there is no God but me.<sup>‡‡o</sup>
<sup>7</sup> Who is like me? Let him stand up and
       declare,
     make it evident, and confront me
       with it.
   Who of old announced future events?
     Let them foretell to us the things to
       come.
<sup>8</sup> Do not fear or be troubled.
   Did I not announce it to you long ago?
     I declared it, and you are my
       witnesses.
   Is there any God but me?
     There is no other Rock,<sup>§§</sup> I know of
       none!<sup>p</sup>

<sup>9</sup> ¶¶Those who fashion idols are all nothing;
     their precious works are of no avail.
   They are their witnesses:***
     they see nothing, know nothing,
     and so they are put to shame.<sup>q</sup>
<sup>10</sup> Who would fashion a god or cast an idol,
     that is of no use?
<sup>11</sup> Look, all its company will be shamed;
     they are artisans, mere human
       beings!

¶[44:2] **Jeshurun**: see note on Dt 32:15; cf. also Dt 33:5, 26.
**[44:5] **Write on his hand**: an allusion to the Babylonian custom of tattooing the owner's name on the hand of his slave.
††[44:6–8] Prediction and fulfillment are here seen as the hallmarks of true divinity. See note on 43:9.
‡‡[44:6] **No god but me**: with Second Isaiah, Israel's faith is declared to be explicitly monotheistic. However implicit it may have been, earlier formulas did not exclude the existence of other gods, not even that of the first commandment: "You shall not have other gods besides me" (Ex 20:3). Cf. also note on 41:21–29.
§§[44:8] **Rock**: place of refuge, a title here used of God; cf., e.g., Dt 32:4, 18; 1 Sm 2:2; Ps 18:3.
¶¶[44:9–20] A satire on the makers and worshipers of idols.
***[44:9] **Their witnesses**: Israel has been called to bear witness to the awesome power of God (cf. 43:10, 12; 44:8), but idol makers cannot testify in support of their creations, for idols cannot act (Dt 4:28; Ps 135:15–18).

*[43:18] **Remember not**: God's new act of delivering Israel from the Babylonian captivity is presented as so great a marvel as to eclipse even the memory of the exodus from Egypt. This comparison of the return from Babylon to the exodus from Egypt recurs throughout Second Isaiah (cf. 41:17–20; 43:18–21; 48:20–21; 49:8–13; 51:9–11).
†[43:22–28] The reason for the liberation of the Israelites is not their constancy but rather God's faithfulness to his promise (cf. 40:6–8).
‡[43:24] **Sweet cane**: a fragrant substance used in making incense and the sacred anointing oil; cf. Ex 30:23; Jer 6:20.
§[43:27] **First father**: Jacob. **Spokesmen**: leaders, priests, prophets.

k. [43:17] Ex 15:4.  l. [43:23] Jer 6:20.

m. [44:4] Is 54:1–3.  n. [44:5] Is 43:7; 45:14.  o. [44:6] Is 41:4; 43:15; 45:21; 48:3, 12; 51:15; 54:5.  p. [44:8] Is 43:10, 12; Dt 32:4.  q. [44:9] Is 48:5, 7.

They all assemble and stand there,
 only to cower in shame.
<sup>12</sup> The ironsmith fashions a likeness,
 he works it over the coals,
Shaping it with hammers,
 working it with his strong arm.
With hunger his strength wanes,
 without water, he grows faint.<sup>r</sup>
<sup>13</sup> The woodworker stretches a line,
 and marks out a shape with a stylus.
He shapes it with scraping tools,
 with a compass measures it off,
Making it the copy of a man,<sup>*</sup>
 human display, enthroned in a
  shrine.
<sup>14</sup> He goes out to cut down cedars,
 takes a holm tree or an oak.
He picks out for himself trees of the forest,
 plants a fir, and the rain makes it
  grow.
<sup>15</sup> It is used for fuel:
 with some of the wood he warms
  himself,
 makes a fire and bakes bread.
Yet he makes a god and worships it,
 turns it into an idol and adores it!
<sup>16</sup> Half of it he burns in the fire,
 on its embers he roasts meat;
 he eats the roast and is full.
He warms himself and says, "Ah!
 I am warm! I see the flames!"
<sup>17</sup> The rest of it he makes into a god,
 an image to worship and adore.
He prays to it and says,
 "Help me! You are my god!"
<sup>18</sup> They do not know, do not understand;
 their eyes are too clouded to see,
 their minds, to perceive.
<sup>19</sup> He does not think clearly;
 he lacks the wit and knowledge to
  say,
"Half the wood I burned in the fire,
 on its embers I baked bread,
 I roasted meat and ate.
Shall I turn the rest into an abomination?
 Shall I worship a block of wood?"
<sup>20</sup> He is chasing ashes!<sup>†</sup>
A deluded mind has led him astray;
 He cannot save himself,
 does not say, "This thing in my right
  hand—is it not a fraud?"

<sup>21</sup> Remember these things, Jacob,
 Israel, for you are my servant!
I formed you, a servant to me;
 Israel, you shall never be forgotten
  by me:

<sup>22</sup> I have brushed away your offenses like a
  cloud,
 your sins like a mist;
 return to me, for I have redeemed you.

<sup>23</sup> Raise a glad cry, you heavens—the Lord
  has acted!
 Shout, you depths of the earth.
Break forth, mountains, into song,
 forest, with all your trees.
For the Lord has redeemed Jacob,
 shows his glory through Israel.

## Cyrus, Anointed of the Lord, Agent of Israel's Liberation

<sup>24</sup> Thus says the Lord, your redeemer,
 who formed you from the womb:
I am the Lord, who made all things,
 who alone stretched out the heavens,
 I spread out the earth by myself.<sup>s</sup>
<sup>25</sup> I bring to nought the omens of babblers,
 make fools of diviners,
Turn back the wise
 and make their knowledge foolish.
<sup>26</sup> I confirm the words of my servant,
 carry out the plan my messengers
  announce.
I say to Jerusalem, Be inhabited!
 To the cities of Judah, Be rebuilt!
 I will raise up their ruins.
<sup>27</sup> I say to the deep, Be dry!
 I will dry up your rivers.<sup>t</sup>
<sup>28</sup> I say of Cyrus,<sup>‡</sup> My shepherd!
 He carries out my every wish,
Saying of Jerusalem, "Let it be rebuilt,"
 and of the temple, "Lay its
  foundations."<sup>u</sup>

## CHAPTER 45

<sup>1</sup> Thus says the Lord to his anointed,<sup>§</sup> Cyrus,
 whose right hand I grasp,
Subduing nations before him,
 stripping kings of their strength,
Opening doors before him,
 leaving the gates unbarred:
<sup>2</sup> I will go before you
 and level the mountains;
Bronze doors<sup>¶</sup> I will shatter,
 iron bars I will snap.<sup>v</sup>
<sup>3</sup> I will give you treasures of darkness,
 riches hidden away,

---

*[44:13] **Copy of a man**: in the biblical view human beings are made in the image of God; here gods are made in the image of human beings.

†[44:20] **Chasing ashes**: an exercise in futility.

‡[44:28] **Cyrus**: king of Persia (559–529 B.C.); cf. note on 41:1–4.

§[45:1] **Anointed**: in Hebrew, *mashiah*, from which the word "Messiah" is derived; from its Greek translation, *Christos*, we have the title "Christ." Applied to kings, "anointed" originally referred only to those of Israel, but it is here given to Cyrus because he is the agent of the Lord.

¶[45:2] **Bronze doors**: those defending the city gates of Babylon.

---

r. [44:12] Wis 13:11–16.

s. [44:24] Is 40:22; Jb 9:8. t. [44:27] Is 42:15; 51:10. u. [44:28] Jer 3:15; Ez 34:23. v. [45:2] Ps 107:16.

That you may know I am the LORD,
  the God of Israel, who calls you by
    name.

4  For the sake of Jacob, my servant,
     of Israel my chosen one,
   I have called you by name,
     giving you a title, though you do not
       know me.ʷ
5  I am the LORD, there is no other,
     there is no God besides me.
   It is I who arm you, though you do not
       know me,
6      so that all may know, from the rising
         of the sun
     to its setting, that there is none
       besides me.*
   I am the LORD, there is no other.
7      I form the light, and create the
         darkness,
   I make weal and create woe;†
     I, the LORD, do all these things.
8  Let justice descend, you heavens, like dew
       from above,
     like gentle rain let the clouds drop
       it down.
   Let the earth open and salvation bud forth;
     let righteousness spring up with
       them!‡
     I, the LORD, have created this.ˣ
9  Woe to anyone who contends with their
       Maker;ʸ
     a potsherd among potsherds of the
       earth!§
   Shall the clay say to the potter, "What are
       you doing?"
     or, "What you are making has no
       handles"?
10 Woe to anyone who asks a father, "What
       are you begetting?"
     or a woman, "What are you giving
       birth to?"
11 Thus says the LORD,
     the Holy One of Israel, his maker:
   Do you question me about my children,
     tell me how to treat the work of my
       hands?
12 It was I who made the earth
     and created the people upon it;
   It was my hands that stretched out the
       heavens;
     I gave the order to all their host.

13 It was I who stirred himˢ up for justice;
     all his ways I make level.
   He shall rebuild my city
     and let my exiles go free
   Without price or payment,
     says the LORD of hosts.

14     Thus says the LORD:
   The earnings of Egypt, the gain of
       Ethiopia,
     and the Sabeans,** tall of stature,
   Shall come over to you and belong to you;
     they shall follow you, coming in
       chains.
   Before you they shall bow down,
     saying in prayer:
   "With you alone is God; and there is none
       other,
     no other god!ᶻ
15 Truly with you God is hidden,††
     the God of Israel, the savior!ᵃ
16 They are put to shame and disgrace, all of
       them;
     they go in disgrace who carve
       images.
17 Israel has been saved by the LORD,
     saved forever!
   You shall never be put to shame or
       disgrace
     in any future age."

18     For thus says the LORD,
   The creator of the heavens,
     who is God,
   The designer and maker of the earth
     who established it,
   Not as an empty waste‡‡ did he create it,
     but designing it to be lived in:
   I am the LORD, and there is no other.
19     I have not spoken in secret
     from some place in the land of
       darkness,
   I have not said to the descendants of
       Jacob,
     "Look for me in an empty waste."

¶ [45:13] **Him:** Cyrus, called by God for the deliverance and restoration of Israel. **Justice:** the Hebrew word (*sedeq*) has multiple connotations; here it relates to the saving victory that the Lord will give to Cyrus for the deliverance of his people Israel. This word and others from the same root frequently have this connotation in Second Isaiah, occurring as a parallel term with "deliverance," "salvation," etc. Cf. its use in 41:10 (rendered "victorious") and 51:5 (rendered "victory").

** [45:14] **Egypt . . . Ethiopia . . . Sabeans:** the Egyptians and their allies who, when conquered by Cyrus, are seen as acknowledging the God of Israel; cf. 43:3.

†† [45:15] **God is hidden:** i.e., the one known only to Israel, who cannot be represented by wooden or molten images. The concept of the "Deus absconditus," "the hidden God," becomes an important theme in later theology.

‡‡ [45:18] **Empty waste:** an allusion to Gn 1:2, where the earth is waste and void; the same Hebrew word, *tohu*, is used in both passages. Here it points to devastated Judah and Jerusalem, where God wishes to resettle the returning exiles.

* [45:6] The nations will come to know that Israel's God is the only God; cf. also vv. 20–25.

† [45:7] **Create woe:** God created and controls all aspects of creation (light and darkness, order and chaos).

‡ [45:8] The Vulgate rendering gave a messianic sense to this verse, using "just one" and "savior" in place of "justice" and "salvation," phraseology taken over in the Advent liturgy, e.g., the "Rorate coeli."

§ [45:9] No one may challenge God's freedom of action, exemplified here by the selection of Cyrus as his anointed.

w. [45:4] Is 40:26; 44:5.   x. [45:8] Ps 72:6; 85:11.   y. [45:9] Jer 18:6;
Rom 9:20.

z. [45:14] Is 43:3.   a. [45:15] Is 55:8; Prv 25:2.

I, the LORD, promise justice,
    I declare what is right.

20 Come and assemble, gather together,
    you fugitives from among the
        nations!
They are without knowledge who bear
    wooden idols*
    and pray to gods that cannot save.
21 Come close and declare;
    let them take counsel together:
Who announced this from the beginning,
    declared it from of old?
Was it not I, the LORD,
    besides whom there is no other
        God?
    There is no just and saving God but
        me.

22 Turn to me and be safe,
    all you ends of the earth,
    for I am God; there is no other!
23 By myself I swear,
    uttering my just decree,
    a word that will not return:
To me every knee shall bend;
    by me every tongue shall swear,[b]
24 Saying, "Only in the LORD
    are just deeds and power.
Before him in shame shall come
    all who vent their anger against him.
25 In the LORD all the descendants of Israel
    shall have vindication and glory."

## CHAPTER 46

### The Gods of Babylon

1 Bel bows down, Nebo† stoops,
    their idols set upon beasts and cattle;
They must be borne upon shoulders,
    a load for weary animals.
2 They stoop and bow down together;
    unable to deliver those who bear
        them,
    they too go into captivity.

3 Hear me, O house of Jacob,
    all the remnant of the house of
        Israel,
My burden from the womb,
    whom I have carried since birth.[c]
4 Even to your old age I am he,
    even when your hair is gray I will
        carry you;

I have done this, and I will lift you up,
    I will carry you to safety.

5 To whom would you liken me as an equal,
    compare me, as though we were
        alike?
6 There are those who pour out gold from a
        purse
    and weigh out silver on the scales;
They hire a goldsmith to make it into a god
    before which they bow down in
        worship.
7 They lift it to their shoulders to carry;
    when they set it down, it stays,
    and does not move from the place.
They cry out to it, but it cannot answer;
    it delivers no one from distress.

8 Remember this and be firm,
    take it to heart, you rebels;
9     remember the former things, those
        long ago:
I am God, there is no other;
    I am God, there is none like me.
10 At the beginning I declare the outcome;
    from of old, things not yet done.
I say that my plan shall stand,
    I accomplish my every desire.

11 I summon from the east a bird of prey,‡
    from a distant land, one to carry out
        my plan.
Yes, I have spoken, I will accomplish it;
    I have planned it, and I will do it.
12 Listen to me, you fainthearted,
    far from the victory of justice:
13 I am bringing on that victory, it is not far
        off,
    my salvation shall not tarry;
I will put salvation within Zion,
    give to Israel my glory.

## CHAPTER 47

### The Fall of Babylon§

1 Come down, sit in the dust,
    virgin daughter Babylon;
Sit on the ground, dethroned,
    daughter of the Chaldeans.
No longer shall you be called
    dainty and delicate.[d]
2 Take the millstone and grind flour,
    remove your veil;
Strip off your skirt, bare your legs,
    cross through the streams.
3 Your nakedness shall be uncovered,
    and your shame be seen;

---

*[45:20] **Who bear wooden idols**: in their religious processions. Such gods have feet but cannot walk; cf. Ps 115:7; Bar 6:25.

†[46:1–4] **Bel . . . Nebo**: gods of Babylon; their complete helplessness is here contrasted with God's omnipotence; whereas they must be carried about, the Lord carries Israel as a parent does a child.

‡[46:11] **From the east a bird of prey**: Cyrus; cf. 41:2–4.
§[47:1–15] A taunt-song, mocking Babylon, once queen of the nations, now a mere slave.

b. [45:23] Rom 14:11; Phil 2:10.    c. [46:3] Is 44:2.

d. [47:1] Dt 28:56.

I will take vengeance,
    I will yield to no entreaty,
      says <sup>d</sup>our redeemer,
Whose name is the LORD of hosts,
    the Holy One of Israel.

<sup>5</sup> Go into darkness and sit in silence,
    daughter of the Chaldeans,
No longer shall you be called
    sovereign mistress of kingdoms.
<sup>6</sup> Angry at my people,
    I profaned my heritage
And gave them into your power;
    but you showed them no mercy;
Upon the aged
    you laid a very heavy yoke.
<sup>7</sup> You said, "I shall remain always,
    a sovereign mistress forever!"
You did not take these things to heart,
    but disregarded their outcome.<sup>e</sup>
<sup>8</sup> Now hear this, voluptuous one,
    enthroned securely,
Saying in your heart,
    "I, and no one else!"<sup>*</sup>
I shall never be a widow,
    bereft of my children"—<sup>f</sup>
<sup>9</sup> Both these things shall come to you
    suddenly, in a single day:
Complete bereavement and widowhood
    shall come upon you
Despite your many sorceries
    and the full power of your spells;<sup>†</sup>
<sup>10</sup> Secure in your wickedness,
    you said, "No one sees me."
Your wisdom and your knowledge
    led you astray,
And you said in your heart,
    "I, and no one else!"
<sup>11</sup> But upon you shall come an evil
    you will not be able to charm away;
Upon you shall fall a disaster
    you cannot ward off.
Upon you shall suddenly come
    a ruin you cannot imagine.

<sup>12</sup> Keep on with your spells
    and your many sorceries,
    at which you toiled from your youth.
Perhaps you can prevail,
    perhaps you can strike terror!
<sup>13</sup> You wore yourself out with so many
    consultations.
    Let the astrologers stand forth to
    save you,
The stargazers who forecast at each new
    moon

    what would happen to you.
<sup>14</sup> See, they are like stubble,
    fire consumes them;
They cannot deliver themselves
    from the spreading flames.
This is no warming ember,
    no fire to sit before!
<sup>15</sup> Thus do your wizards serve you
    with whom you have toiled from
    your youth;
They wander their separate ways,
    with none to save you.

## CHAPTER 48

### Exhortations to the Exiles

<sup>1</sup> Hear this, house of Jacob
    called by the name Israel,
    sprung from the stock of Judah,
You who swear by the name of the LORD
    and invoke the God of Israel
    without sincerity, without justice,
<sup>2</sup> Though you are named after the holy city
    and rely on the God of Israel,
    whose name is the LORD of hosts.
<sup>3</sup> Things of the past I declared long ago,
    they went forth from my mouth, I
    announced them;
    then suddenly I took action and
    they came to be.
<sup>4</sup> Because I know that you are stubborn
    and that your neck is an iron sinew
    and your forehead bronze,
<sup>5</sup> I declared them to you of old;
    before they took place I informed
    you,
That you might not say, "My idol did them,
    my statue, my molten image
    commanded them."
<sup>6</sup> Now that you have heard, look at all this;
    must you not admit it?<sup>g</sup>
From now on I announce new things to
    you,
    hidden events you never knew.
<sup>7</sup> Now, not from of old, they are created,
    before today you did not hear of
    them,
    so that you cannot claim, "I have
    known them."
<sup>8</sup> You never heard, you never knew,
    they never reached your ears
    beforehand.
Yes, I know you are utterly treacherous,
    a rebel you were named from the
    womb.<sup>h</sup>
<sup>9</sup> For the sake of my name I restrain my
    anger,
    for the sake of my renown I hold it
    back from you,
    lest I destroy you.

---

*[47:8, 10] **I, and no one else**: Babylon is mockingly presented as making the same claim as the Lord (cf. 45:6, 14, 22; 46:9), a claim that events will soon prove to be false and foolish (v. 11).

†[47:9–13, 15] Babylon was known for its sorcery and astrology.

e. [47:7] Is 14:13–14.   f. [47:8] Zep 2:15; Rev 18:7.

g. [48:6] Is 42:9.   h. [48:8] Is 43:22–24.

<sup>10</sup> See, I refined you, but not like silver;
　　I tested you in the furnace of
　　　affliction.<sup>i</sup>
<sup>11</sup> For my sake, for my own sake, I do this;
　　why should my name be profaned?
　　My glory I will not give to another.

<sup>12</sup> Listen to me, Jacob,
　　Israel, whom I called!
I, it is I who am the first,
　　and am I the last.<sup>j</sup>
<sup>13</sup> Yes, my hand laid the foundations of the
　　　earth;
　　my right hand spread out the heavens.
When I summon them,
　　they stand forth at once.<sup>k</sup>

<sup>14</sup> All of you assemble and listen:
　　Who among you declared these
　　　things?
The one the LORD loves<sup>*</sup> shall do his will
　　against Babylon and the offspring of
　　　Chaldea.
<sup>15</sup> I myself have spoken, I have summoned
　　　him,
　　I have brought him, and his way
　　　succeeds!
<sup>16</sup> Come near to me and hear this!
　　From the beginning I did not speak
　　　in secret;
At the time it happens, I am there:
　　"Now the Lord GOD has sent me,
　　　and his spirit."<sup>†</sup>

<sup>17</sup> Thus says the LORD, your redeemer,
　　the Holy One of Israel:
I am the LORD, your God,
　　teaching you how to prevail,
　　leading you on the way you should go.
<sup>18</sup> If only you would attend to my
　　　commandments,
　　your peace would be like a river,
　　your vindication like the waves of
　　　the sea,
<sup>19</sup> Your descendants like the sand,
　　the offspring of your loins like its
　　　grains,
Their name never cut off
　　or blotted out from my presence.
<sup>20</sup> Go forth from Babylon, flee from
　　　Chaldea!
　　With shouts of joy declare this,
　　　announce it;
Make it known to the ends of the earth,
　　Say: "The LORD has redeemed his
　　　servant Jacob.

<sup>21</sup> They did not thirst
　　when he led them through dry lands;
Water from the rock he set flowing for
　　　them;
　　he cleft the rock, and waters welled
　　　forth."<sup>l</sup>

<sup>22</sup> There is no peace<sup>‡</sup> for the wicked,
　　says the LORD.

*B. Expiation of Sin, Spiritual Liberation of Israel*

## CHAPTER 49

### The Servant of the Lord<sup>§</sup>

<sup>1</sup> Hear me, coastlands,
　　listen, distant peoples.<sup>m</sup>
Before birth the LORD called me,
　　from my mother's womb he gave me
　　　my name.<sup>¶</sup>
<sup>2</sup> He made my mouth like a sharp-edged
　　　sword,
　　concealed me, shielded by his hand.
He made me a sharpened arrow,
　　in his quiver he hid me.
<sup>3</sup> He said to me, You are my servant,
　　in you, Israel,<sup>**</sup> I show my glory.

<sup>4</sup> Though I thought I had toiled in vain,
　　for nothing and for naught spent my
　　　strength,
Yet my right is with the LORD,
　　my recompense is with my God.<sup>n</sup>
<sup>5</sup> For now the LORD has spoken
　　who formed me as his servant from
　　　the womb,
That Jacob may be brought back to him
　　and Israel gathered to him;
I am honored in the sight of the LORD,
　　and my God is now my strength!
<sup>6</sup> It is too little, he says, for you to be my
　　　servant,
　　to raise up the tribes of Jacob,
　　and restore the survivors of Israel;<sup>o</sup>
I will make you a light to the nations,
　　that my salvation may reach to the
　　　ends of the earth.<sup>††</sup>

---

‡[48:22] **No peace**: while the good news proclaimed by the prophet is directed to the people as a whole, "peace," which can represent the fullness of God's blessings and which would here include deliverance from exile, is not extended to all regardless of disposition.

§[49:1–7] The second of the four "servant of the Lord" oracles (cf. note on 42:1–4).

¶[49:1] **Gave me my name**: designated me for a special task or mission (cf. Jer 1:5).

**[49:3] **Israel**: the servant is identified with the people of Israel as their ideal representative; however, vv. 5–6 seem to distinguish the servant from Israel.

††[49:6] The servant's vocation extends beyond the restoration of Israel in order to bring the knowledge of Israel's God to the rest of the earth; cf. Lk 2:32.

---

*[48:14] **The one the LORD loves**: the reference is no doubt to Cyrus, who does the Lord's will by overcoming Babylon and releasing Israel from captivity.
†[48:16] **"Now the Lord . . . spirit"**: said by Cyrus; cf. v. 14.

i. [48:10] Is 1:25; Jer 6:29–30; Zec 13:9; Mal 3:2.　j. [48:12] Is 41:4; 44:6; 48:12; Rev 1:8, 17.　k. [48:13] Is 40:22, 26; 45:12, 18.

l. [48:21] Ex 17:6; Nm 20:11.　m. [49:1] Is 41:9; 43:1; 44:2, 24; 46:3.　n. [49:4] Is 40:27.　o. [49:6] Is 42:1–6; 44:5; 45:14; Lk 2:32; Acts 13:46–47.

⁷ Thus says the LORD,
   the redeemer, the Holy One of
      Israel,
To the one despised, abhorred by the
      nations,
   the slave of rulers:
When kings see you, they shall stand up,
   and princes shall bow down
Because of the LORD who is faithful,
   the Holy One of Israel who has
      chosen you.ᵖ

### The Liberation and Restoration of Zion

⁸ Thus says the LORD:
In a time of favor I answer you,*
   on the day of salvation I help you;
I form you and set you
   as a covenant for the people,
To restore the land
   and allot the devastated heritages,�q
⁹ To say to the prisoners: Come out!
   To those in darkness: Show
      yourselves!
Along the roadways they shall find
      pasture,
   on every barren height shall their
      pastures be.ʳ
¹⁰ They shall not hunger or thirst;
   nor shall scorching wind or sun
      strike them;
For he who pities them leads them
   and guides them beside springs of
      water.ˢ
¹¹ I will turn all my mountains into roadway,
   and make my highways level.ᵗ
¹² See, these shall come from afar:
   some from the north and the west,
   others from the land of Syene.†

¹³ Sing out, heavens, and rejoice, earth,
   break forth into song, you
      mountains,
For the LORD comforts his people
   and shows mercy to his afflicted.

¹⁴ But Zion said, "The LORD has forsaken
      me;
   my Lord has forgotten me."ᵘ
¹⁵ Can a mother forget her infant,
   be without tenderness for the child
      of her womb?
Even should she forget,
   I will never forget you.ᵛ

¹⁶ See, upon the palms of my hands I have
      engraved you;‡
   your walls are ever before me.
¹⁷ Your children hasten—
   your levelers, your destroyers
      go forth from you;
¹⁸ Look about and see,
   they are all gathering and coming
      to you.
As I live—oracle of the LORD—
   you shall don them as jewels,
   bedeck yourself like a bride.

¹⁹ Though you were waste and desolate,
   a land of ruins,
Now you shall be too narrow for your
      inhabitants,
   while those who swallowed you up
      will be far away.
²⁰ The children of whom you were bereft
   shall yet say in your hearing,
"This place is too narrow for me,
   make room for me to live in."
²¹ You shall ask yourself:
   "Who has borne me these,
   when I was bereft and barren?
Exiled and repudiated,
   who has reared them?
I was left all alone;
   where then do these come from?"ʷ
²² Thus says the Lord GOD:
See, I will lift up my hand to the nations,
   and to the peoples raise my signal;
They shall bring your sons in their arms,
   your daughters shall be carried on
      their shoulders.ˣ
²³ Kings shall be your guardians,
   their princesses your nursemaids;
Face to the ground, they shall bow down
      before you
   and lick the dust at your feet.
Then you shall know that I am the LORD,
   none who hope in me shall be
      ashamed.
²⁴ Can plunder be taken from a warrior,
   or captives rescued from a tyrant?
²⁵ Thus says the LORD:
Yes, captives can be taken from a warrior,
   and plunder rescued from a tyrant;
Those who oppose you I will oppose,
   and your sons I will save.
²⁶ I will make your oppressors eat their own
      flesh,
   and they shall be drunk with their
      own blood
   as though with new wine.
All flesh shall know
   that I, the LORD, am your savior,

---

*[49:8] **You:** the individual is not named; perhaps Cyrus
or the prophet.
†[49:12] **Syene:** now called Aswan, at the first cataract of
the Nile in southern Egypt.

p. [49:7] Is 49:23; 55:5.   q. [49:8] 2 Cor 6:2.   r. [49:9] Is 42:7, 18–20.
s. [49:10] Is 51:14; Rev 7:16.   t. [49:11] Is 40:3–4.   u. [49:14] Is
40:27.   v. [49:15] Is 43:4; 44:21; 46:3–4.

---

‡[49:16] **Upon the palms . . . you:** for continual remembrance; cf. Ex 13:9, 16; Dt 6:6–9.

w. [49:21] Is 54:1–3.   x. [49:22] Is 5:26; 13:2.

your redeemer, the Mighty One of
Jacob.[y]

## CHAPTER 50

### Salvation Through the Lord's Servant

1 Thus says the LORD:
Where is the bill of divorce
with which I dismissed your
mother?[*]
Or to which of my creditors
have I sold you?
It was for your sins you were sold,
for your rebellions your mother was
dismissed.[z]

2 Why was no one there when I came?
Why did no one answer when I
called?[†]
Is my hand too short to ransom?
Have I not the strength to deliver?
See, with my rebuke I dry up the sea,
I turn rivers into wilderness;
Their fish rot for lack of water,
and die of thirst.[a]
3 I clothe the heavens in black,
and make sackcloth their covering.

4 [‡]The Lord GOD has given me
a well-trained tongue,
That I might know how to answer the
weary
a word that will waken them.
Morning after morning
he wakens my ear to hear as
disciples do;
5 The Lord GOD opened my ear;
I did not refuse,
did not turn away.[§]
6 I gave my back to those who beat me,[*]
my cheeks to those who tore out my
beard;[¶]
My face I did not hide
from insults and spitting.[b]

7 The Lord GOD is my help,
therefore I am not disgraced;

Therefore I have set my face like flint,
knowing that I shall not be put to
shame.[c]
8 He who declares my innocence is near.
Who will oppose me?
Let us appear together.
Who will dispute my right?
Let them confront me.
9 See, the Lord GOD is my help;
who will declare me guilty?
See, they will all wear out like a garment,
consumed by moths.[d]
10 Who among you fears the LORD,[**]
heeds his servant's voice?
Whoever walk in darkness,
without any light,
Yet trust in the name of the LORD
and rely upon their God![e]
11 All you who kindle flames
and set flares alight,
Walk by the light of your own fire
and by the flares you have burnt!
This is your fate from my hand:
you shall lie down in a place of
torment.

## CHAPTER 51

### Exhortation to Trust in the Lord

1 Listen to me, you who pursue justice,
who seek the LORD;
Look to the rock from which you were
hewn,
to the quarry[††] from which you were
taken;[f]
2 Look to Abraham, your father,
and to Sarah, who gave you birth;
Though he was but one when I called
him,
I blessed him and made him many.[g]
3 Yes, the LORD shall comfort Zion,
shall comfort all her ruins;
Her wilderness he shall make like Eden,
her wasteland like the garden of the
LORD;
Joy and gladness shall be found in her,
thanksgiving and the sound of song.

4 Be attentive to me, my people;[‡‡]
my nation, give ear to me.
For teaching shall go forth from me,
and my judgment, as light to the
peoples.[h]
5 I will make my victory come swiftly;

---

*[50:1] Responding to the people's complaint of utter
abandonment by God, the prophet asserts that their sins were
responsible for their banishment. Since there was no bill of
divorce, the bond between the Lord and his people still exists
and he has the power to deliver them (v. 2).

†[50:2] Israel's faith in God is weak; the people do not
answer God's call, nor believe promises of deliverance.

‡[50:4–11] The third of the four "servant of the Lord"
oracles (cf. note on 42:1–4); in vv. 4–9 the servant speaks; in
vv. 10–11 God addresses the people directly.

§[50:5] The servant, like a well-trained disciple, does not
refuse the divine vocation.

¶[50:6] He willingly submits to insults and beatings. **Tore
out my beard**: a grave and painful insult.

**[50:10–11] The Lord offers a choice to those who walk in
darkness: either trust in the true light (v. 10), or walk in their
false light and suffer the consequences.

††[51:1] **Rock . . . quarry**: your glorious ancestry.

‡‡[51:4–5] The conversion of the nations.

---

y. [49:26] Is 19:2; Ez 38:21; Zec 14:13.    z. [50:1] Is 54:6–8; Dt 24:1–
4; Mt 19:3; Mk 10:2–4.    a. [50:2] Ex 7:18; Ps 105:29.    b. [50:6]
2 Sm 10:4–6; Mt 26:67; 27:30.

c. [50:7] Ez 3:9.    d. [50:9] Is 51:6–8; Ps 102:27.    e. [50:10] Is 43:1–
2; 44:1–2.    f. [51:1] Rom 9:30–31.    g. [51:2] Ez 33:24; Gn 12:2–4;
22:17.    h. [51:4] Is 2:3.

my salvation shall go forth
and my arm shall judge the nations;
In me the coastlands shall hope,
and my arm they shall await.

6 Raise your eyes to the heavens,
look at the earth below;
Though the heavens vanish like smoke,
the earth wear out like a garment
and its inhabitants die like flies,
My salvation shall remain forever
and my victory shall always be firm.*

7 Hear me, you who know justice,
you people who have my teaching
at heart:
Do not fear the reproach of others;
remain firm at their revilings.

8 They shall be like a garment eaten by
moths,
like wool consumed by grubs;
But my victory shall remain forever,
my salvation, for all generations.[i]

9 Awake, awake, put on strength,
arm of the LORD!
Awake as in the days of old,
in ages long ago!
Was it not you who crushed Rahab,†
you who pierced the dragon?[j]

10 Was it not you who dried up the sea,
the waters of the great deep,‡
You who made the depths of the sea into
a way
for the redeemed to pass through?

11 Those whom the LORD has ransomed will
return
and enter Zion singing,
crowned with everlasting joy;
They will meet with joy and gladness,
sorrow and mourning will flee.

12 I, it is I who comfort you.
Can you then fear mortals who die,
human beings who are just grass,

13 And forget the LORD, your maker,
who stretched out the heavens
and laid the foundations of earth?
All the day you are in constant dread
of the fury of the oppressor
When he prepares himself to destroy;
but where is the oppressor's fury?

14 The captives shall soon be released;
they shall not die and go down into
the pit,

nor shall they want for bread.

15 For I am the LORD, your God,
who stirs up the sea so that its waves
roar;
the LORD of hosts by name.[k]

16 I have put my words into your mouth,
I covered you, shielded by my hand,
Stretching out the heavens,
laying the foundations of the earth,
saying to Zion: You are my people.

### The Cup of the Lord

17 Wake up, wake up!
Arise, Jerusalem,
You who drank at the LORD's hand
the cup of his wrath;
Who drained to the dregs
the bowl of staggering![l]

18 She has no one to guide her
of all the children she bore;
She has no one to take her by the hand,
of all the children she reared!—

19 Your misfortunes are double;
who is there to grieve with you?
Desolation and destruction, famine and
sword!
Who is there to comfort you?

20 Your children lie helpless
at every street corner
like antelopes in a net.
They are filled with the wrath of the LORD,
the rebuke of your God.

21 But now, hear this, afflicted one,
drunk, but not with wine,[m]

22 Thus says the LORD, your Master,
your God, who defends his people:
See, I am taking from your hand
the cup of staggering;
The bowl of my wrath
you shall no longer drink.

23 I will put it into the hands of your
tormentors,
those who said to you,
"Bow down, that we may walk over
you."
So you offered your back like the ground,
like the street for them to walk on.

### CHAPTER 52

### Let Zion Rejoice

1 Awake, awake!
Put on your strength, Zion;
Put on your glorious garments,
Jerusalem, holy city.
Never again shall the uncircumcised
or the unclean enter you.

---

*[51:6] While the heavens and the earth appear eternal and changeless, they are not so firm and lasting as God's saving will for Israel.

†[51:9] **Rahab**: see note on 30:7. **The dragon**: see notes on 27:1; Ps 74:12–17.

‡[51:10] **Great deep**: a reference to the primeval chaos (cf. Gn 1:2; 7:11; 49:25; Jb 28:14; Ps 36:7; Jon 2:4).

i. [51:8] Is 50:9.   j. [51:9] Ex 15:16; Jb 9:13; 26:12; Ps 74:13; 89:11.

k. [51:15] Jer 31:35.   l. [51:17] Jer 25:15–17; Ez 23:32–34.   m. [51:21] Is 29:9.

2 Arise, shake off the dust,
    sit enthroned, Jerusalem;
Loose the bonds from your neck,
    captive daughter Zion!
3     For thus says the LORD:
For nothing you were sold,
    without money you shall be
      redeemed.

4     For thus says the Lord GOD:
To Egypt long ago my people went down,
    to sojourn there;
Assyria, too, oppressed them for
      nought.
5 But now, what am I to do here?
    —oracle of the LORD.
My people have been taken away for
      nothing;
    their rulers mock, oracle of the LORD;
constantly, every day, my name is
      reviled.
6 Therefore my people shall know my name
    on that day, that it is I who speaks:
    Here I am!
7 How beautiful upon the mountains*
    are the feet of the one bringing good
      news,
Announcing peace, bearing good news,
    announcing salvation, saying to
      Zion,
    "Your God is King!"ⁿ

8 Listen! Your sentinels raise a cry,
    together they shout for joy,
For they see directly, before their eyes,
    the LORD's return to Zion.º
9 Break out together in song,
    O ruins of Jerusalem!
For the LORD has comforted his people,
    has redeemed Jerusalem.
10 The LORD has bared his holy arm
    in the sight of all the nations;
All the ends of the earth can see
    the salvation of our God.

11 Depart, depart, go out from there,
    touch nothing unclean!
Out from there!† Purify yourselves,
    you who carry the vessels of the
      LORD.
12 But not in hurried flight will you go out,
    nor leave in headlong haste,
For the LORD goes before you,
    and your rear guard is the God of
      Israel.ᵖ

---

### Suffering and Triumph of the Servant of the Lord‡

13 See, my servant shall prosper,
    he shall be raised high and greatly
      exalted.
14 Even as many were amazed at him—
    so marred were his features,
    beyond that of mortals
    his appearance, beyond that of
      human beings—�q
15 So shall he startle many nations,
    kings shall stand speechless;
For those who have not been told shall see,
    those who have not heard shall
      ponder it.ʳ

## CHAPTER 53

1 Who would believe what we have heard?§
    To whom has the arm of the LORD
      been revealed?ˢ
2 He grew up like a sapling before him,ᵗ
    like a shoot from the parched earth;
He had no majestic bearing to catch our
      eye,
    no beauty to draw us to him.
3 He was spurned and avoided by men,
    a man of suffering, knowing pain,
Like one from whom you turn your face,
    spurned, and we held him in no
      esteem.ᵘ

4 Yet it was our pain that he bore,
    our sufferings he endured.
We thought of him as stricken,
    struck down by Godᵛ and afflicted,ᵛ

---

‡[52:13–53:12] The last of the "servant of the Lord" oracles (see note on 42:1–4). Taken together, these oracles depict a figure of one called by God for a vocation to Israel and the nations (42:4; 49:5–6); the servant's exaltation both opens and closes the passage (52:13; 53:12). The servant responded in fidelity but has suffered opposition (50:4–6). In this fourth oracle the servant is characterized as "a man of suffering" (53:3) and appears to be unjustly put to death (53:8–9). Those who have witnessed his career somehow recognize that he is innocent, has undergone suffering for their sins (53:4–6), and his death is referred to as a reparation offering (see note on 53:10–11). The servant is described in ways that identify him with Israel (which is frequently referred to as "servant" in the context of Second Isaiah—e.g., 41:8, 9; 44:2, 21; 43:4) and is designated as "Israel" in 49:3; yet Israel outside the "servant of the Lord" oracles is not presented as sinless, but rather in exile because of sin (40:2; 42:21–25) and even as servant as deaf and blind (42:18–19). The servant is thus both identified with Israel and distinguished from it. As with the previous servant poems, this chapter helped the followers of Jesus to interpret his suffering, death, and resurrection; see especially the passion narratives.

§[53:1–10] **What we have heard**: this fourth servant oracle is introduced by words of the Lord (52:13–15) but is now continued by speakers who are not identified, perhaps those referred to in 52:15, perhaps Israel (cf. "struck for the sins of his people"—v. 8). The Lord is again the speaker in vv. 11–13.

¶[53:4] **Struck down by God**: the Bible often sees suffering as a punishment for sin (e.g., Ps 6:2; 32:1–5), yet sin

---

*[52:7–10] God leads the people back from Babylon to Zion, from whose ruined walls sentinels greet the returning exiles.

†[52:11] **From there**: from Babylon. **Vessels of the LORD:** taken to Babylon by Nebuchadnezzar, now carried back by the exiles returning in procession to Zion; cf. Ezr 1:7.

n. [52:7] Is 40:9; Rom 10:15.   o. [52:8] Is 62:6.   p. [52:12] Ex 12:11.

q. [52:14] Ps 69:8.   r. [52:15] Mi 7:16.   s. [53:1] Is 52:10; Jn 12:38; Rom 10:16.   t. [53:2] Is 11:1.   u. [53:3] Jb 19:18; Ps 31:11–13; Mk 9:11.   v. [53:4] Jer 10:19; Mt 8:17.

5 But he was pierced for our sins,
  crushed for our iniquity.
He bore the punishment that makes us
  whole,
  by his wounds we were healed.[w]
6 We had all gone astray like sheep,
  all following our own way;
But the LORD laid upon him[*]
  the guilt of us all.[x]

7 Though harshly treated, he submitted
  and did not open his mouth;
Like a lamb led to slaughter
  or a sheep silent before shearers,
  he did not open his mouth.[y]
8 Seized and condemned, he was taken
  away.
  Who would have thought any more
    of his destiny?
For he was cut off from the land of the
  living,
  struck for the sins of his people.
9 He was given a grave among the wicked,
  a burial place with evildoers,
Though he had done no wrong,
  nor was deceit found in his mouth.[z]
10 But it was the LORD's will to crush him
  with pain.
By making his life as a reparation
  offering,[†]
  he shall see his offspring, shall
    lengthen his days,
  and the LORD's will shall be
    accomplished through him.
11 Because of his anguish he shall see the
  light;
  because of his knowledge he shall be
    content;
My servant, the just one, shall justify the
  many,
  their iniquity he shall bear.
12 Therefore I will give him his portion
  among the many,
  and he shall divide the spoils with
    the mighty,

Because he surrendered himself to death,
  was counted among the
    transgressors,
Bore the sins of many,
  and interceded for the
    transgressors.[a]

## CHAPTER 54

### The New Zion

1 Raise a glad cry, you barren one[‡] who
  never bore a child,
  break forth in jubilant song, you
    who have never been in labor,
For more numerous are the children of
  the deserted wife
  than the children of her who has a
    husband,
  says the LORD.[b]
2 Enlarge the space for your tent,
  spread out your tent cloths
    unsparingly;
  lengthen your ropes and make firm
    your pegs.[c]
3 For you shall spread abroad to the right
  and left;
  your descendants shall dispossess
    the nations
  and shall people the deserted cities.[§]

4 'Do not fear, you shall not be put to
  shame;
  do not be discouraged, you shall not
    be disgraced.
For the shame of your youth you shall
  forget,
  the reproach of your widowhood no
    longer remember.
5 For your husband is your Maker;
  the LORD of hosts is his name,
Your redeemer,[**] the Holy One of Israel,
  called God of all the earth.

6 The LORD calls you back,
  like a wife forsaken and grieved in
    spirit,

---

sometimes appears to go unpunished and the innocent often
suffer (cf. Ps 73; the Book of Job). In the case of the servant,
the onlookers initially judge him guilty because of his suffering but, in some way not explained, they come to understand
that his sufferings are for the sins of others. One notes the
element of surprise, for such vicarious suffering, in the form
described here, is without parallel in the Old Testament.

*[53:6] **The LORD laid upon him**: the servant's suffering is
no accidental or casual matter, but part of God's plan; see also
v. 10. The bystanders' speculation of v. 4 is verified, but not in
the sense intended by them.

†[53:10–11] **Reparation offering**: the Hebrew term *'asham*
is used of a particular kind of sacrifice, one that is intended as
compensation for that which is due because of guilt. See Lv
5:14–26 and note. **Justify**: the verb means "to be acquitted,"
"declared innocent," but since the servant bears "their iniquity," an effective rather than simply legal action is suggested.

‡[54:1] Jerusalem, pictured as a wife who had been barren
and deserted, now suddenly finds herself with innumerable
children (the returning exiles); cf. Gal 4:27 for an application
to a new context.

§[54:3] Those who had taken advantage of the exile to
encroach on Jerusalem's territory will be driven out, and the
returning exiles will repopulate the cities of Judah.

¶[54:4–8] As with some other Old Testament themes,
Second Isaiah uses that of Israel as the Lord's bride in a new
manner. Whereas Hosea and Jeremiah had depicted Israel as
the Lord's spouse to emphasize both Israel's infidelity and the
Lord's continued love (Hos 1–3; Jer 2:2; 3:1–15) and Ezekiel
to accuse Israel unsparingly (Ez 16; 23), Second Isaiah speaks
only of the love with which the Lord restores the people,
speaking tender words with no hint of reproach.

**[54:5] **Redeemer**: cf. note on 41:14.

---

w. [53:5] 1 Cor 15:3; 1 Pt 2:24.   x. [53:6] Lv 16:21–22.   y. [53:7] Mt
26:63; Acts 8:32.   z. [53:9] 1 Pt 2:22–23; 1 Jn 3:5.

a. [53:12] Mk 15:28; Lk 22:37.   b. [54:1] Gal 4:27.   c. [54:2] Is
49:20.

A wife married in youth and then cast off,
    says your God.[d]
7 For a brief moment I abandoned you,
    but with great tenderness I will take
        you back.
8 In an outburst of wrath, for a moment
    I hid my face from you;
But with enduring love I take pity on you,
    says the LORD, your redeemer.

9 This is for me like the days of Noah:
As I swore then that the waters of Noah
    should never again flood the earth,
So I have sworn now not to be angry with
    you,
    or to rebuke you.[e]
10 Though the mountains fall away
    and the hills be shaken,
My love shall never fall away from you
    nor my covenant of peace* be shaken,
    says the LORD, who has mercy on you.[f]

11 O afflicted one,† storm-battered and
        unconsoled,
    I lay your pavements in carnelians,
    your foundations in sapphires;[g]
12 I will make your battlements of rubies,
    your gates of jewels,
    and all your walls of precious stones.
13 All your children shall be taught by the
        LORD;
    great shall be the peace of your
        children.
14 In justice shall you be established,
    far from oppression, you shall not
        fear,
    from destruction, it cannot come
        near.
15 If there be an attack, it is not my doing;
    whoever attacks shall fall before you.

16 See, I have created the smith
    who blows on the burning coals
    and forges weapons as his work;
It is I also who have created
    the destroyer to work havoc.
17 Every weapon fashioned against you shall
        fail;
    every tongue that brings you to trial
    you shall prove false.

This is the lot of the servants of the LORD,
    their vindication from me—oracle
    of the LORD.

## CHAPTER 55

### An Invitation to Grace

1 All you who are thirsty,‡
    come to the water!
You who have no money,
    come, buy grain and eat;
Come, buy grain without money,
    wine and milk without cost![h]
2 Why spend your money for what is not
        bread;
    your wages for what does not satisfy?
Only listen to me, and you shall eat well,
    you shall delight in rich fare.
3 Pay attention and come to me;
    listen, that you may have life.
I will make with you an everlasting
        covenant,
    the steadfast loyalty promised to
        David.[i]
4 As I made him a witness to peoples,
    a leader and commander of peoples,
5 So shall you summon a nation you knew
        not,
    and a nation§ that knew you not
        shall run to you,
Because of the LORD, your God,
    the Holy One of Israel, who has
        glorified you.[j]

6 ¶Seek the LORD while he may be found,
    call upon him while he is near.
7 Let the wicked forsake their way,
    and sinners their thoughts;
Let them turn to the LORD to find mercy;
    to our God, who is generous in
        forgiving.
8 For my thoughts are not your thoughts,
    nor are your ways my ways—oracle
        of the LORD.
9 For as the heavens are higher than the
        earth,
    so are my ways higher than your
        ways,
    my thoughts higher than your
        thoughts.

10 **Yet just as from the heavens
    the rain and snow come down
And do not return there
    till they have watered the earth,
    making it fertile and fruitful,

---

*[54:10] **Covenant of peace**: this whole section, vv. 9–17, is given to various assurances of God's love for Israel and of safety from various possible threats; the phrase sums up both the positive aspects of *shalom*, which implies a fullness of blessing, and protection from all that might harm. Cf. also 55:3; Nm 25:12; Ez 34:25; 37:26; Mal 2:5.

†[54:11] **Afflicted one**: Jerusalem.

‡[55:1–3] The prophet invites all to return, under the figure of a banquet; cf. the covenant banquet in Ex 24:9–11 and wisdom's banquet in Prv 9:1–6. The Lord's covenant with David (2 Sm 7) is now to be extended beyond his dynasty.

§[55:5] The "nation" is Persia under Cyrus, but the perspective is worldwide.

¶[55:6–9] The invitation to seek the Lord is motivated by the mercy of a God whose "ways" are completely mysterious.

**[55:10–11] The efficacy of the word of God recalls 40:5, 8.

---

d. [54:6] Mal 2:14–15.  e. [54:9] Gn 9:15.  f. [54:10] Ps 46:3; 76:5.  g. [54:11] Rev 21:18–21.

h. [55:1] Jn 4:10–15; 6:35; 7:37–39; Rev 21:6; 22:17.  i. [55:3] 2 Sm 7:12–16.  j. [55:5] Acts 13:34.

Giving seed to the one who sows
    and bread to the one who eats,
11 So shall my word be
    that goes forth from my mouth;
It shall not return to me empty,
    but shall do what pleases me,
      achieving the end for which
        I sent it.

12 Yes, in joy you shall go forth,
    in peace you shall be brought home;
Mountains and hills shall break out in
      song before you,
    all trees of the field shall clap their
      hands.
13 In place of the thornbush, the cypress
      shall grow,
    instead of nettles,* the myrtle.
This shall be to the Lord's renown,
    as an everlasting sign that shall not
      fail.

### III. ISAIAH 56–66

### CHAPTER 56

**Salvation for the Just**[†]

1    ‡Thus says the Lord:
Observe what is right, do what is just,
    for my salvation is about to come,
    my justice, about to be revealed.[k]
2 Happy is the one who does this,
    whoever holds fast to it:

Keeping the sabbath without profaning it,
    keeping one's hand from doing any
      evil.[l]

### Obligations and Promises to Share in the Covenant

3    §The foreigner joined to the Lord should
      not say,
    "The Lord will surely exclude me
      from his people";
Nor should the eunuch say,
    "See, I am a dry tree."[m]
4      For thus says the Lord:
To the eunuchs who keep my sabbaths,
    who choose what pleases me,
    and who hold fast to my
      covenant,[n]
5 I will give them, in my house
    and within my walls, a monument
      and a name¶
Better than sons and daughters;
    an eternal name, which shall not be
      cut off, will I give them.
6 And foreigners who join themselves to
      the Lord,
    to minister to him,
To love the name of the Lord,
    to become his servants—
All who keep the sabbath without
      profaning it
    and hold fast to my covenant,
7    **Them I will bring to my holy mountain
    and make them joyful in my house
      of prayer;
Their burnt offerings and their sacrifices
    will be acceptable on my altar,
For my house shall be called
    a house of prayer for all peoples.[o]
8    ††Oracle of the Lord God,
    who gathers the dispersed of
      Israel—
Others will I gather to them
    besides those already
      gathered.[p]

---

*[55:13] **Thornbush . . . nettles:** suggestive of the desert and therefore symbolic of suffering and hardship; **cypress . . . myrtle:** suggestive of fertile land and therefore symbolic of joy and strength. **To the Lord's renown:** lit., "to the name of the Lord."

†[56:1–8] This poem inaugurates the final section of the Book of Isaiah, often referred to as Third or Trito-Isaiah. While Second or Deutero-Isaiah (Is 40–55) gave numerous references to the hopes of the community of Israel during the Babylonian exile (ca. 587–538 B.C.), Third Isaiah witnesses to the struggles and hoped-for blessings of the postexilic community now back in the homeland of Israel. In this opening poem, the references to "keeping the sabbath" (vv. 2, 4, 6), "holding fast to the covenant" (vv. 4, 6) and "God's holy mountain" as a house of prayer (v. 7) all tell of the postexilic community that was establishing itself again in the land according to the pattern of God's word given through the prophet. The poem can be classified as a "prophetic exhortation" in which the prophet gives instruction for those who wish to live according to God's word and covenant. What is important to note are the conditions placed upon the people of God; while Is 40–55 show an unconditional promise of redemption, these final chapters delineate clear expectations for receiving God's salvific promises. Both the expectations and the great promises of God will unfold in the succeeding chapters of Third Isaiah.

‡[56:1] This opening verse echoes themes that are well known throughout the Book of Isaiah: justice and right judgment (1:27; 5:7, 16; 9:6; 16:5; 26:9; 28:17; 32:1, 16; 33:5; 42:1, 4, 6; 45:8, 13, 19), salvation and deliverance (12:3; 26:18; 33:2; 45:8, 21; 46:13; 51:5, 6, 8). These themes will be developed also throughout Third Isaiah.

§[56:3] Eunuchs had originally been excluded from the community of the Lord; cf. Dt 23:2; Neh 13:1–3; Wis 3:14.

¶[56:5] **A monument and a name:** literally in Hebrew, "a hand and a name"; a memorial inscription to prevent oblivion for one who had no children; cf. 2 Sm 18:18; Neh 7:5; 13:14.

**[56:7] This verse continues the theme of universalism found in Is 49:6. As Israel was to be "a light to the nations" so that God's "salvation may reach to the ends of the earth," so now does that come to pass as foreigners, faithful to the divine commands, are brought to the Temple by God and joined to the covenant community of Israel.

††[56:8] For the gathering of the dispersed people of Israel, cf. Jer 23:3; 31:8–9; Ez 11:17. Here the Lord not only gathers the displaced of Israel, but also unites other peoples to them. Cf. Is 60:3–10; 66:18–21.

---

l. [56:2] Is 1:13; 58:13–14; Ex 23:12.   m. [56:3] Dt 23:3–5; Neh 13:1–3.   n. [56:4] Wis 3:14.   o. [56:7] 1 Kgs 8:29–30, 41; Mt 21:13.

k. [56:1] Is 59:9, 14, 19–20.   p. [56:8] Ps 147:2.

## Unworthy Shepherds[*]

9 All you beasts of the field,[†]
    come to devour,
    all you beasts in the forest![q]
10 [‡]All the sentinels of Israel are blind,
    they are without knowledge;
They are all mute dogs,
    unable to bark;
Dreaming, reclining,
    loving their sleep.
11 Yes, the dogs have a ravenous appetite;
    they never know satiety,
Shepherds who have no understanding;
    all have turned their own way,
    each one covetous for gain:
12 "Come, let me bring wine;
    let us fill ourselves with strong
        drink,
And tomorrow will be like today,
    or even greater."[r]

## CHAPTER 57

1 The just have perished,
    but no one takes it to heart;
The steadfast are swept away,
    while no one understands.
Yet the just are taken away from the
        presence of evil,
2     [§]and enter into peace;
They rest upon their couches,
    the sincere, who walk in integrity.[s]

## An Idolatrous People[¶]

3 But you, draw near,
    you children of a sorceress,
    offspring of an adulterer and a
        prostitute![**]

4 Against whom do you make sport,
    against whom do you open wide
        your mouth,
    and stick out your tongue?
Are you not rebellious children,
    deceitful offspring—
5 You who burn with lust among the oaks,
    under every green tree;
You who immolate children in the wadies,
    among the clefts of the rocks?[†††]
6 Among the smooth stones[‡‡] of the wadi is
        your portion,
    they, they are your allotment;
Indeed, you poured out a drink offering
        to them,
    and brought up grain offerings.
With these things, should I be
        appeased?
7 Upon a towering and lofty mountain
    you set up your bed,
    and there you went up to offer
        sacrifice.[u]
8 Behind the door and the doorpost
    you set up your symbol.
Yes, deserting me, you carried up your
        bedding;
    and spread it wide.
You entered an agreement with them,
    you loved their couch, you gazed
        upon nakedness.[§§]
9 You approached the king[¶¶] with oil,
    and multiplied your perfumes;
You sent your ambassadors far away,
    down even to deepest Sheol.
10 Though worn out with the length of your
        journey,
    you never said, "It is hopeless";
You found your strength revived,
    and so you did not weaken.
11 Whom did you dread and fear,
    that you told lies,
And me you did not remember
    nor take to heart?
Am I to keep silent and conceal,
    while you show no fear of me?

---

[*][56:9–57:21] This section is made up of two pronouncements of judgment (56:9–57:2; 57:3–13) and an oracle of salvation (57:14–21), each of which ends with a reversal of imagery and language. While there are harsh indictments against the corrupt leaders of Israel (56:9–12), a promise of peace is offered to those who are just (57:1–2). Then the judgment and its subsequent punishment for idolaters (57:3–13a) change to an announcement of reward for those who place their trust in God (57:13c). And the promises of salvation (57:14–19) then shift to a word of warning to the wicked (57:20–21).

[†][56:9] Beasts of the field: foreign nations, which are invited to come and ravage Israel.

[‡][56:10–11] These shepherds of Israel are without "knowledge," a theme developed earlier in the Isaian corpus; cf. 1:3; 6:9–10. Ezekiel 34 has similar condemnatory words against the unfaithful shepherds of Israel.

[§][57:2] Despite their sad fate, the just will ultimately attain peace (most likely in this world); cf. v. 13.

[¶][57:3–13] In this courtroom imagery, the idolaters are summoned before the judge (v. 3), their crimes are graphically described (vv. 4–11), their guilt is established, and condemnation is carried out (vv. 12–13b). In contrast to this, v. 13c describes the inheritance of God's land and holy mountain given to those who place their confidence in God instead of in idols.

[**][57:3] Language of sexual infidelity is often used in a figurative way to describe idolatry. Cf. Ez 16:15–22; Hos 2:4–7; Col 3:5.

[††][57:5] Child sacrifice is also attested in 2 Kgs 23:10; Jer 7:31; Ez 16:20; 20:28, 31; 23:37–39.

[‡‡][57:6] Smooth stones: the Hebrew word for this expression has the same consonants as the word for "portion"; instead of making the Lord their portion (cf. Ps 16:5), the people adored slabs of stone which they took from the streambeds in valleys and set up as idols; cf. Jer 3:9. Therefore, it is implied, they will be swept away as by a sudden torrent of waters carrying them down the rocky-bottomed gorge to destruction and death without burial.

[§§][57:8] Nakedness: literally in Hebrew, "hand." In this context, it may euphemistically refer to a phallus.

[¶¶][57:9] The king: in Hebrew, the word for king is melek, similar in sound to the Canaanite god Molech, to whom children were offered as a sacrifice in pagan ritual. The expression "your ambassadors" could be a figurative expression for the children whose death served as an offering to this deity.

---

q. [56:9] Jer 12:9–10; Ez 34:5.    r. [56:12] Is 22:13; 28:7; Wis 2:7.
s. [57:2] Wis 3:1–3.

t. [57:5] Dt 12:2; 2 Kgs 17:10; Jer 7:31; 19:5; Ez 20:28, 31.    u. [57:7] Jer 2:20; Ez 6:13; Hos 4:13.

12 I will proclaim your justice*
    and your works;
    but they shall not help you.
13 †When you cry out,
    let your collection of idols save you.
All these the wind shall carry off,
    a mere breath shall bear them away;
But whoever takes refuge in me shall
      inherit the land,
    and possess my holy mountain.

### The Way to Peace for God's People

14 And I say:
Build up, build up, prepare the way,
    remove every obstacle from my
      people's way.‡ᵛ
15 ⁵For thus says the high and lofty One,
    the One who dwells forever, whose
      name is holy:
I dwell in a high and holy place,
    but also with the contrite and lowly
      of spirit,
To revive the spirit of the lowly,
    to revive the heart of the crushed.
16 For I will not accuse forever,
    nor always be angry;
For without me their spirit fails,
    the life breath that I have given.ʷ
17 Because of their wicked avarice I grew
      angry;
    I struck them, hiding myself from
      them in wrath.
But they turned back, following the way
    of their own heart.ˣ
18 I saw their ways,
    but I will heal them.
I will lead them and restore full comfort
      to them
    and to those who mourn for them,ʸ

19     creating words of comfort.⁵
Peace! Peace to those who are far and
      near,
    says the LORD; and I will heal them.
20 But the wicked are like the tossing sea
    which cannot be still,
Its waters cast up mire and mud.ᶻ
21     There is no peace for the wicked!
    says my God.ᵃ

### CHAPTER 58

### Reasons for Judgment**

1 Cry out full-throated and unsparingly,
    lift up your voice like a trumpet
      blast;
Proclaim to my people their
      transgression,
    to the house of Jacob their sins.ᵇ
2 They seek me day after day,
    and desire to know my ways,
Like a nation that has done what is just
    and not abandoned the judgment of
      their God;
They ask of me just judgments,
    they desire to draw near to God.
3 "Why do we fast, but you do not see it?
    afflict ourselves, but you take no
      note?"
See, on your fast day you carry out your
      own pursuits,
    and drive all your laborers.ᶜ
4 See, you fast only to quarrel and fight
    and to strike with a wicked fist!
Do not fast as you do today
    to make your voice heard on high!
5 Is this the manner of fasting I would
      choose,
    a day to afflict oneself?
To bow one's head like a reed,
    and lie upon sackcloth and ashes?
Is this what you call a fast,
    a day acceptable to the LORD?ᵈ

### Authentic Fasting That Leads to Blessing††

6 Is this not, rather, the fast that I choose:
    releasing those bound unjustly,
    untying the thongs of the yoke;
Setting free the oppressed,
    breaking off every yoke?ᵉ
7 Is it not sharing your bread with the
      hungry,

---

*[57:12] **Justice**: here used sarcastically. The activity described in these verses is far from the justice which God demands of those who are aligned with the covenant (cf. 56:1, 4, 6). In the larger context of Third Isaiah and the whole of the Isaian tradition, justice is a key theological motif. The justice to which God calls Israel will eventually come to its fulfillment in an act of divine intervention (cf. 60:21; 61:3c). Until then, the people of God must strive to live in the ways of justice and right judgment (56:1).

†[57:13] In v. 6, the smooth stones of the valley are the portion which the unfaithful will receive as their due reward (cf. note on v. 6); while in v. 13c, an inheritance of the land and possession of God's holy mountain will be the portion of the upright.

‡[57:14] **The way . . . my people's way**: the language and imagery are reminiscent of 40:1–2, but in this context, when the people have already returned, the physical road through the desert is replaced by the spiritual way that leads to redemption.

§[57:15] The God of Israel is presented in both a transcendent and an immanent manner. God's holiness is the transcendent quality; the immanence is shown in the choice of dwelling among the downtrodden and humble.

⁵[57:19] **Creating words of comfort**: lit., "fruit of the lips," perhaps referring to praise and thanksgiving for the divine healing; cf. Hos 14:3.

**[58:1–5] The prophet is commanded to condemn the formalism of the people, specifically their hypocritical fasting.

††[58:6–12] Fasting is not genuine without reforming one's way of life. A true social morality will ensure prosperity.

---

v. [57:14] Is 40:3–4. w. [57:16] Gn 2:7. x. [57:17] Is 56:11. y. [57:18] Is 61:2.

z. [57:20] Jon 2:3–7. a. [57:21] Is 48:22. b. [58:1] Lv 25:9. c. [58:3] 1 Sm 7:6; 1 Kgs 21:12; 1 Mc 3:47; Jl 1:1–2:17. d. [58:5] Zec 7:5. e. [58:6] Is 35:5–6.

bringing the afflicted and the
homeless into your house;
Clothing the naked when you see them,
and not turning your back on your
own flesh?[f]

8 Then your light shall break forth like the
dawn,
and your wound shall quickly be
healed;
Your vindication shall go before you,
and the glory of the LORD shall be
your rear guard.

9 Then you shall call, and the LORD will
answer,
you shall cry for help, and he will
say: "Here I am!"
If you remove the yoke from among you,
the accusing finger, and malicious
speech;[g]

10 If you lavish your food on the hungry
and satisfy the afflicted;
Then your light shall rise in the darkness,
and your gloom shall become like
midday;

11 Then the LORD will guide you always
and satisfy your thirst in parched
places,
will give strength to your bones
And you shall be like a watered garden,
like a flowing spring whose waters
never fail.[h]

12 Your people shall rebuild the ancient
ruins;
the foundations from ages past you
shall raise up;
"Repairer of the breach," they shall call
you,
"Restorer of ruined dwellings."[i]

### Authentic Sabbath Observance
### That Leads to Blessing[*]

13 If you refrain from trampling the sabbath,
from following your own pursuits
on my holy day;
If you call the sabbath a delight,
the LORD's holy day glorious;
If you glorify it by not following your
ways,
seeking your own interests, or
pursuing your own affairs—

14 Then you shall delight in the LORD,
and I will make you ride upon the
heights of the earth;
I will nourish you with the heritage of
Jacob, your father,
for the mouth of the LORD has
spoken.[j]

## CHAPTER 59

### Salvation Delayed

1 [†]No, the hand of the LORD is not too short
to save,
nor his ear too dull to hear.[k]

2 Rather, it is your crimes
that separate you from your God,
It is your sins that make him hide his face
so that he does not hear you.

3 For your hands are defiled with blood,
and your fingers with crime;
Your lips speak falsehood,
and your tongue utters deceit.[l]

4 No one brings suit justly,
no one pleads truthfully;
They trust an empty plea and tell lies;
they conceive mischief and bring
forth malice.

5 [‡]They hatch adders' eggs,
and weave spiders' webs:
Whoever eats the eggs will die,
if one of them is crushed, it will
hatch a viper;[m]

6 Their webs cannot serve as clothing,
nor can they cover themselves with
their works.
Their works are evil works,
and deeds of violence are in their
hands.

7 Their feet run to evil,
and they hasten to shed innocent
blood;
Their thoughts are thoughts of
wickedness,
violence and destruction are on
their highways.[n]

8 The way of peace they know not,
and there is no justice on their paths;
Their roads they have made crooked,
no one who walks in them knows
peace.

### Acknowledgment of Transgressions

9 [§]That is why judgment is far from us
and justice does not reach us.

---

[†][59:1–20] This poem brings together a lament of the postexilic community and a harsh word of judgment from the prophet. After the opening rhetorical question, each of the stanzas begins with a reference to the justice and right judgment which are lacking among the people (vv. 4, 9, 14). Toward the end of the poem, God is depicted as a Divine Warrior (vv. 16–20) who is the only one who can intervene in order to bring redemption. This same Divine Warrior imagery is repeated in a similar fashion in 63:1–6.

[‡][59:5–6] The eggs signify evil works, doing positive harm; the webs are devices that serve no useful purpose.

[§][59:9–15] The turning point in the poem comes when the people acknowledge their transgressions and describe the horror of their present state. Light is a metaphor for salvation (cf. 9:1; 42:16; 60:1–3, 19–20) and darkness represents sin and disaster.

---

[*][58:13–14] Sabbath observance becomes a cornerstone of postexilic piety; cf. 56:2, 4, 6.

f. [58:7] Ez 18:7, 16; Mt 25:35.   g. [58:9] Am 5:7.   h. [58:11] Is 51:3; Ps 24.   i. [58:12] Is 61:4.   j. [58:14] Hb 3:19.

k. [59:1] Is 50:2; Nm 11:23.   l. [59:3] Is 1:15.   m. [59:5] Jb 20:12–16.   n. [59:7] Prv 1:15, 19; 2:8–9, 12–13, 15, 18–19; Rom 3:15.

We look for light, but there is darkness;
   for brightness, and we walk in gloom!°
¹⁰ Like those who are blind we grope along
     the wall,
   like people without eyes we feel our
     way.
We stumble at midday as if at twilight,
   among the vigorous, we are like the
     dead.
¹¹ Like bears we all growl,
   like doves we moan without ceasing.
We cry out for justice, but it is not there;
   for salvation, but it is far from us.ᵖ
¹² For our transgressions before you are
     many,
   our sins bear witness against us.
Our transgressions are present to us,
   and our crimes we acknowledge:
¹³ Transgressing, and denying the LORD,
   turning back from following our God,
Planning fraud and treachery,
   uttering lying words conceived in
     the heart.
¹⁴ Judgment is turned away,
   and justice stands far off;
For truth stumbles in the public square,
   and uprightness cannot enter. q
¹⁵ Fidelity is lacking,
   and whoever turns from evil is
     despoiled.

### Divine Intervention

The LORD saw this, and was aggrieved
   that there was no justice.
¹⁶ He saw that there was no one,
   was appalled that there was none to
     intervene;
Then his own arm brought about the
     victory,
   and his justice sustained him.
¹⁷ He put on justice as his breastplate,
   victory as a helmet on his head;
He clothed himself with garments of
     vengeance,
   wrapped himself in a mantle of zeal.ʳ
¹⁸ According to their deeds he repays his
     enemies
   and requites his foes with wrath;
to the coastlands he renders
     recompense.
¹⁹ Those in the west shall fear the name of
     the LORD,
   and those in the east, his glory,
Coming like a pent-up stream
   driven on by the breath of the LORD.
²⁰ Then for Zion shall come a redeemer,
   to those in Jacob who turn from
     transgression—oracle of the
     LORD.ˢ

²¹ *This is my covenant with them,
   which I myself have made, says the
     LORD:
My spirit which is upon you
   and my words that I have put in
     your mouth
Shall not depart from your mouth,
   nor from the mouths of your children
Nor the mouths of your children's
     children
   from this time forth and forever,
     says the LORD.ᵗ

## CHAPTER 60

### The Dawning of Divine Glory for Zion

¹ †Arise! Shine, for your light has come,
   the glory of the LORD has dawned
     upon you.ᵘ
² Though darkness covers the earth,
   and thick clouds, the peoples,
Upon you the LORD will dawn,
   and over you his glory will be seen.
³ Nations shall walk by your light,
   kings by the radiance of your
     dawning.ᵛ

### The Nations Come to Zion

⁴ Raise your eyes and look about;
   they all gather and come to you—
Your sons from afar,
   your daughters in the arms of their
     nurses.ʷ
⁵ Then you shall see and be radiant,
   your heart shall throb and overflow.
For the riches of the sea shall be poured
     out before you,
   the wealth of nations shall come to
     you.
⁶ Caravans of camels shall cover you,
   dromedaries of Midian and Ephah;
All from Sheba shall come
   bearing gold and frankincense,
   and heralding the praises of the
     LORD.
⁷ All the flocks of Kedar shall be gathered
     for you,
   the rams of Nebaioth shall serve
     your needs;
They will be acceptable offerings on my
     altar,
   and I will glorify my glorious house.

---

*[59:21] This verse makes the transition from chaps. 56–59 to chaps. 60–62. Oracles of judgment yield to oracles about God's redemptive action.

†[60:1–9] The light the prophet proclaims to Zion symbolizes the blessing to come to her: the glory of the Lord, the return of her children, the wealth of nations who themselves will walk by her light. The passage is famous from its use in the Latin liturgy for the feast of Epiphany.

---

o. [59:9] Am 5:18–19.  p. [59:11] Is 38:14.  q. [59:14] Jb 28:28.
r. [59:17] Wis 5:17–20; Eph 6:14–16; 1 Thes 5:8.  s. [59:20] Is 35:4;
Rom 11:26–27.

t. [59:21] Is 1:27.  u. [60:1] Is 40:5; 49:14–26; 51:17–23.  v. [60:3]
Is 42:6; 45:14; 49:6.  w. [60:4] Is 49:18.

8 Who are these that fly along like a cloud,
     like doves to their cotes?
9 The vessels of the coastlands are
        gathering,
        with the ships of Tarshish in the lead,
   To bring your children from afar,
        their silver and gold with them—
   For the name of the LORD, your God,
        for the Holy One of Israel who has
           glorified you.

### Honor and Service for Zion[*]

10 Foreigners shall rebuild your walls,
      their kings shall minister to you;
   Though in my wrath I struck you,
      yet in my good will I have shown
         you mercy.[x]
11 Your gates shall stand open constantly;
      day and night they shall not be
         closed
   So that they may bring you the wealth of
         nations,
      with their kings in the vanguard.[y]
12 For the nation or kingdom that will not
         serve you shall perish;
      such nations shall be utterly
         destroyed![z]
13 The glory of Lebanon shall come to you—
      the juniper, the fir, and the cypress
         all together—
   To bring beauty to my sanctuary,
      and glory to the place where I
         stand.[a]
14 The children of your oppressors shall
         come,
      bowing before you;
   All those who despised you,
      shall bow low at your feet.
   They shall call you "City of the LORD,"
      "Zion of the Holy One of Israel."
15 No longer forsaken and hated,
      with no one passing through,
   Now I will make you the pride of the ages,
      a joy from generation to generation.
16 You shall suck the milk of nations,
      and be nursed at royal breasts;
   And you shall know that I, the LORD, am
         your savior,
      your redeemer, the Mighty One of
         Jacob.
17 Instead of bronze I will bring gold,
      instead of iron I will bring silver;
   Instead of wood, bronze;
      instead of stones, iron.
   I will appoint peace your governor,
      and justice your ruler.[b]

18 No longer shall violence be heard of in
         your land,
      or plunder and ruin within your
         borders.
   You shall call your walls "Salvation"
      and your gates "Praise."

### Eternal Light for Zion

19 [†]No longer shall the sun
      be your light by day,
   Nor shall the brightness of the moon
      give you light by night;
   Rather, the LORD will be your light
         forever,
      your God will be your glory.[c]
20 No longer will your sun set,
      or your moon wane;
   For the LORD will be your light forever,
      and the days of your grieving will
         be over.
21 Your people will all be just;
      for all time they will possess the
         land;
   They are the shoot that I planted,
      the work of my hands, that I might
         be glorified.[d]
22 The least one shall become a clan,
      the smallest, a mighty nation;
   I, the LORD, will swiftly accomplish
      these things when the time comes.[e]

## CHAPTER 61

### The Anointed Bearer of Glad Tidings

1 [‡]The spirit of the Lord GOD is upon me,
      because the LORD has anointed me;
   He has sent me to bring good news to the
         afflicted,
      to bind up the brokenhearted,
   To proclaim liberty to the captives,
      release to the prisoners,[f]
2 To announce a year of favor from the
         LORD
      and a day of vindication by our God;
   To comfort all who mourn;[g]
3    to place on those who mourn in
         Zion
      a diadem instead of ashes,
   To give them oil of gladness instead of
         mourning,
      a glorious mantle instead of a faint
         spirit.

---

†[60:19–20] The theme of light is taken up again, but in an apocalyptic vein: the Lord's radiant presence replaces physical light.

‡[61:1–2] The prophet proclaims that he has been anointed by the Lord to bring good news (cf. 40:9) to the afflicted and to comfort Zion. The background to the "year of favor" is the jubilee year of release from debts (Lv 25:10–11; Is 49:8).

---

*[60:10–18] The glorious promises for the future continue: the wealth of the nations (vv. 5, 10), tribute from kings, glorification of the Temple, peace and justice (cf. Ps 85:11).

---

x. [60:10] Is 54:11–12.  y. [60:11] Rev 21:25.  z. [60:12] Is 61:2.
a. [60:13] Is 35:2; 66:1.  b. [60:17] Ps 85:11.

c. [60:19] Is 2:5; Rev 21:23; 22:5.  d. [60:21] Is 57:13c.  e. [60:22] Gn 12:2; 17:6.  f. [61:1] Is 40:9; 42:1; 48:16; 52:7; 58:7; Lk 4:18–19.  g. [61:2] Mt 5:4.

## Restoration and Blessing

They will be called oaks of justice,
　　the planting of the LORD to show
　　　his glory.
4 They shall rebuild the ancient ruins,
　　the former wastes they shall raise up
And restore the desolate cities,
　　devastations of generation upon
　　　generation.[h]
5 Strangers shall stand ready to pasture
　　your flocks,
　　foreigners shall be your farmers and
　　　vinedressers.
6 *You yourselves shall be called "Priests of
　　the LORD,"
　　"Ministers of our God" you shall be
　　　called.
You shall eat the wealth of the nations
　　and in their riches you will boast.[i]
7 Because their shame was twofold†
　　and disgrace was proclaimed their
　　　portion,
They will possess twofold in their own
　　land;
　　everlasting joy shall be theirs.[j]

## God's Word of Promise

8 For I, the LORD, love justice,
　　I hate robbery and wrongdoing;
I will faithfully give them their
　　recompense,
　　an everlasting covenant I will make
　　　with them.[k]
9 Their offspring shall be renowned among
　　the nations,
　　and their descendants in the midst
　　　of the peoples;
All who see them shall acknowledge them:
　　"They are offspring the LORD has
　　　blessed."

## Thanksgiving for God's Deliverance

10 ‡I will rejoice heartily in the LORD,
　　my being exults in my God;
For he has clothed me with garments of
　　salvation,
　　and wrapped me in a robe of justice,
Like a bridegroom adorned with a
　　diadem,
　　as a bride adorns herself with her
　　　jewels.[l]

11 As the earth brings forth its shoots,
　　and a garden makes its seeds spring
　　　up,
So will the Lord GOD make justice spring
　　up,
　　and praise before all the nations.

## CHAPTER 62

### A New Name for Zion

1 §For Zion's sake I will not be silent,
　　for Jerusalem's sake I will not keep
　　　still,
Until her vindication shines forth like the
　　dawn
　　and her salvation like a burning
　　　torch.[m]
2 Nations shall behold your vindication,
　　and all kings your glory;
You shall be called by a new name
　　bestowed by the mouth of the LORD.[n]
3 You shall be a glorious crown in the hand
　　of the LORD,
　　a royal diadem in the hand of your
　　　God.
4 No more shall you be called "Forsaken,"
　　nor your land called "Desolate,"
But you shall be called "My Delight is in
　　her,"
　　and your land "Espoused."
For the LORD delights in you,
　　and your land shall be espoused.[o]
5 For as a young man marries a virgin,
　　your Builder shall marry you;
And as a bridegroom rejoices in his bride
　　so shall your God rejoice in you.
6 Upon your walls, Jerusalem,
　　I have stationed sentinels;
By day and by night,
　　they shall never be silent.
You who are to remind the LORD,
　　take no rest,
7 And give him no rest,
　　until he re-establishes Jerusalem
And makes it the praise of the earth.

### The Blessings of Salvation for God's People

8 ¶The LORD has sworn by his right hand
　　and by his mighty arm:
No more will I give your grain
　　as food to your enemies;
Nor shall foreigners drink the wine,
　　for which you toiled.[p]

---

*[61:6] The bestowal of a new name suggests a new identity and mission. The whole people will be priests (cf. Ex 19:6), even ministering to nations who will serve God's people.

†[61:7] **Twofold**: Israel was punished double for infidelity (40:2); the blessings of its restoration will also be double.

‡[61:10–11] The new life of the restored Zion is expressed in nuptial (cf. also 62:5) and agricultural (cf. v. 3; 60:21) imagery.

§[62:1–12] As in chap. 60, the prophet addresses Zion, announcing the reversal of her fortune. Several motifs reappear: light and glory (60:1–3, 19–20), tribute of nations (60:11), and especially the marriage (61:10; cf. also 54:5–8).

¶[62:8–9] Peace and prosperity are indicated by the absence of invaders who would live off the land.

---

h. [61:4] Is 58:12.　i. [61:6] Ex 19:6; 1 Pt 2:9.　j. [61:7] Is 40:2.　k. [61:8] Is 55:3; 54:9–10; 59:21.　l. [61:10] 1 Sm 2:1; Ps 138:1–2.

m. [62:1] Is 42:14; 64:11.　n. [62:2] Rev 2:17; 3:12.　o. [62:4] Is 49:15–16; 54:7–8.　p. [62:8] Is 52:10.

<sup>9</sup> But those who harvest shall eat,
  and praise the LORD;
 Those who gather shall drink
  in my holy courts.<sup>q</sup>
<sup>10</sup> \*Pass through, pass through the gates,
  prepare a way for the people;<sup>r</sup>
 Build up, build up the highway, clear it of
   stones,
  raise up a standard over the nations.
<sup>11</sup> The LORD has proclaimed
  to the ends of the earth:
 Say to daughter Zion,
  "See, your savior comes!
 See, his reward is with him,
  his recompense before him."<sup>s</sup>
<sup>12</sup> They shall be called "The Holy People,"
  "The Redeemed of the LORD."
 And you shall be called "Cared For,"
  "A City Not Forsaken."<sup>t</sup>

## CHAPTER 63

### The Divine Warrior<sup>†</sup>

<sup>1</sup> Who is this that comes from Edom,
  in crimsoned garments, from
   Bozrah?
 Who is this, glorious in his apparel,
  striding in the greatness of his
   strength?
 "It is I, I who announce vindication,
  mighty to save."<sup>u</sup>
<sup>2</sup> Why is your apparel red,
  and your garments like one who
   treads the wine press?<sup>v</sup>
<sup>3</sup> "The wine press I have trodden alone,
  and from the peoples no one was
   with me.
 I trod them in my anger,
  and trampled them down in my
   wrath;
 Their blood spurted on my garments,
  all my apparel I stained.
<sup>4</sup> For a day of vindication was in my heart,
  my year for redeeming had come.<sup>w</sup>
<sup>5</sup> I looked about, but there was no one to
   help,
  I was appalled that there was no one
   to lend support;
 So my own arm brought me victory
  and my own wrath lent me support.<sup>x</sup>
<sup>6</sup> I trampled down the peoples in my anger,
  I made them drunk in my wrath,

 and I poured out their blood upon
  the ground."

### Prayer for the Return of God's Favor

<sup>7</sup> ‡The loving deeds of the LORD I will recall,
  the glorious acts of the LORD,
 Because of all the LORD has done for us,
  the immense goodness to the house
   of Israel,
 Which he has granted according to his
   mercy
  and his many loving deeds.<sup>y</sup>
<sup>8</sup> He said: "They are indeed my people,
  children who are not disloyal."
 So he became their savior
<sup>9</sup>   in their every affliction.
 It was not an envoy or a messenger,
  but his presence that saved them.
 Because of his love and pity
  the LORD redeemed them,
 Lifting them up and carrying them
  all the days of old.<sup>z</sup>
<sup>10</sup> But they rebelled
  and grieved his holy spirit;
 So he turned to become their enemy,
  and warred against them.<sup>a</sup>

<sup>11</sup>Then they remembered the days of old, of
Moses, his servant:

 Where is the one who brought up out of
  the sea
  the shepherd of his flock?
 Where is the one who placed in their midst
  his holy spirit,<sup>b</sup>
<sup>12</sup> Who guided Moses by the hand,
  with his glorious arm?
 Where is the one who divided the waters
  before them—
  winning for himself an everlasting
   renown—
<sup>13</sup> Who guided them through the depths,
  like horses in open country?
<sup>14</sup> As cattle going down into the valley,
  they did not stumble.
 The spirit of the LORD guided them.
 Thus you led your people,
  to make for yourself a glorious
   name.
<sup>15</sup> Look down from heaven and regard us
  from your holy and glorious palace!
 Where is your zealous care and your
   might,
  your surge of pity?<sup>c</sup>

---

\*[62:10–11] The gates of Babylon are to be opened for the exiles to return, led by the Lord, as in 40:3–5, 10.

†[63:1–6] Two questions are raised at the approach of a majestic figure coming from Edom. It is the Lord, his garments red with the blood from the judgment battle. Edom (its capital Bozrah) plundered Judah after the fall of Jerusalem; cf. 34:5–17. **Wine press**: here a symbol of a bloody judgment; cf. Lam 1:15; Jl 4:13.

‡[63:7–64:11] This lament of the exilic community recalls God's protection, and especially the memories of the exodus (vv. 7–14), before begging the Lord to come once more to their aid (63:15–64:3), as they confess their sins (64:4–11). The prayer is marked by God's "holy spirit" (63:10–11, 14) and fatherhood (63:8, 9, 16; 64:7).

---

q. [62:9] Dt 12:17–18; 14:23. r. [62:10] Is 58:14. s. [62:11] Is 40:10. t. [62:12] Is 62:4. u. [63:1] Is 34:6; 49:19. v. [63:2] Rev 19:13. w. [63:4] Is 34:8; 61:2. x. [63:5] Is 59:16.

y. [63:7] Is 26:15. z. [63:9] Dt 4:37–40. a. [63:10] Dt 32:15; Ps 51:12. b. [63:11] Heb 13:20. c. [63:15] Dt 26:15; Bar 2:16.

Your mercy hold not back!
16       For you are our father.
Were Abraham not to know us,
      nor Israel to acknowledge us,
You, LORD, are our father,
      our redeemer you are named from
            of old.
17  Why do you make us wander, LORD, from
            your ways,
      and harden our hearts so that we do
            not fear you?*
Return for the sake of your servants,
      the tribes of your heritage.
18  Why have the wicked invaded your holy
            place,
      why have our enemies trampled
            your sanctuary?
19  †Too long have we been like those you do
            not rule,
      on whom your name is not invoked.
Oh, that you would rend the heavens and
            come down,
      with the mountains quaking before
            you,*d*

## CHAPTER 64

1  As when brushwood is set ablaze,
      or fire makes the water boil!
Then your name would be made known
            to your enemies
      and the nations would tremble
            before you,
2  While you worked awesome deeds we
            could not hope for,‡
3      such as had not been heard of from
            of old.
No ear has ever heard, no eye ever seen,
      any God but you
      working such deeds for those who
            wait for him.*e*
4  Would that you might meet us doing
            right,
      that we might be mindful of you in
            our ways!
Indeed, you are angry; we have sinned,
      we have acted wickedly.
5  We have all become like something
            unclean,
      all our just deeds are like polluted
            rags;
We have all withered like leaves,
      and our crimes carry us away like
            the wind.*f*

6  There are none who call upon your name,
      none who rouse themselves to take
            hold of you;
For you have hidden your face from us
      and have delivered us up to our
            crimes.

### A Final Plea

7  §Yet, LORD, you are our father;
      we are the clay and you our potter:
      we are all the work of your hand.
8  Do not be so very angry, LORD,
      do not remember our crimes forever;
      look upon us, who are all your people!
9  Your holy cities have become a
            wilderness;
      Zion has become wilderness,
            Jerusalem desolation!*g*
10  Our holy and glorious house
      in which our ancestors praised you
Has been burned with fire;
      all that was dear to us is laid waste.
11  Can you hold back, LORD, after all this?
      Can you remain silent, and afflict us
            so severely?

## CHAPTER 65

1  ¶I was ready to respond to those who did
            not ask,
      to be found by those who did not
            seek me.
I said: Here I am! Here I am!
      To a nation that did not invoke my
            name.*h*
2  I have stretched out my hands all day
      to a rebellious people,
Who walk in a way that is not good,
      following their own designs;*i*
3  A people who provoke me
      continually to my face,
Offering sacrifices in gardens
      and burning incense on bricks,
4  Sitting in tombs
      and spending the night in caves,
Eating the flesh of pigs,
      with broth of unclean meat in their
            dishes;
5  Crying out, "Hold back,
      do not come near me, lest I render
            you holy!"**

---

*[63:17] The hardening of the heart (Ex 4:21; 7:3) serves to explain Israel's sins—a motif to induce the Lord to relent.

†[63:19–64:3] A new theophany, like Sinai of old, is invoked so that Israel's enemies will be humbled by God's intervention.

‡[64:2] The translation here omits some words repeated in the Hebrew from 63:19 ("would that you would come down, with the mountains trembling before you").

§[64:7–11] The motifs of father (63:16) and creator (clay and potter, 29:16; 45:9) are adduced to move the Lord to action in view of the damage done to his "holy cities" and "glorious house."

¶[65:1–7] These verses serve as a response to the preceding questions about God's inaction (64:6, 11). It is not God who has been absent, but the people who have walked away from God by idolatrous acts and rituals (vv. 3–4). That is the reason for their punishment (vv. 6–7).

**[65:5] **Render you holy:** unclean food is what these people claim has made them sacred! The prophet ridicules them.

---

d. [63:19] Ps 144:5; Mk 1:10.   e. [64:3] 1 Cor 2:9.   f. [64:5] Is 1:30; 34:4.

g. [64:9] Ps 79:1; Lam 1.   h. [65:1] Rom 10:20.   i. [65:2] Rom 10:21.

These things are smoke in my nostrils,
  a fire that burns all the day.
⁶ See, it stands written before me;
    I will not remain quiet until I have
      repaid in full
⁷ Your crimes and the crimes of your
      ancestors as well,
    says the LORD.
  Since they burned incense on the
      mountains,
    and insulted me on the hills,
  I will at once pour out in full measure
    their recompense into their laps.

### Fate of the Just and Unjust in Israel

⁸     *Thus says the LORD:
  As when the juice is pressed from a
      cluster,
    and someone says, "Do not destroy it,
      for there is still good in it,"
  So will I do for the sake of my servants:
    I will not destroy them all.
⁹ From Jacob I will bring forth offspring,
    from Judah, those who are to
      possess my mountains;
  My chosen ones shall possess the land,
    my servants shall dwell there.
¹⁰ Sharon shall become a pasture for the
      flocks,
    the Valley of Achor a resting place
      for the cattle,
  for my people who have sought me.ʲ
¹¹ But you who forsake the LORD,
    who forget my holy mountain,
  Who spread a table for Fortune
    and fill cups of mixed wine for
      Destiny,†
¹² You I will destine for the sword;
    you shall all bow down for slaughter;
  Because I called and you did not answer,
    I spoke and you did not listen,
  But did what is evil in my sight
    and things I do not delight in, you
      chose,ᵏ
¹³     therefore thus says the Lord GOD:
  My servants shall eat,
    but you shall go hungry;
  My servants shall drink,
    but you shall be thirsty;
  My servants shall rejoice,
    but you shall be put to shame;
¹⁴ My servants shall shout
    for joy of heart,
  But you shall cry out for grief of heart,
    and howl for anguish of spirit.

¹⁵ You will leave your name for a curse to
      my chosen ones
    when the Lord GOD slays you,
    and calls his servants by another
      name.
¹⁶ Whoever invokes a blessing in the land
    shall bless by the God of truth;‡
  Whoever takes an oath in the land
    shall swear by the God of truth;
  For the hardships of the past shall be
      forgotten
    and hidden from my eyes.

### A World Renewed

¹⁷ §See, I am creating new heavens
    and a new earth;
  The former things shall not be
      remembered
    nor come to mind.ˡ
¹⁸ Instead, shout for joy and be glad forever
    in what I am creating.
  Indeed, I am creating Jerusalem to be
      a joy
    and its people to be a delight;
¹⁹ I will rejoice in Jerusalem
    and exult in my people.
  No longer shall the sound of weeping be
      heard there,
    or the sound of crying;
²⁰ No longer shall there be in it
    an infant who lives but a few days,
    nor anyone who does not live a full
      lifetime;
  One who dies at a hundred years shall be
      considered a youth,
    and one who falls short of a hundred
      shall be thought accursed.ᵐ
²¹ They shall build houses and live in them,
    they shall plant vineyards and eat
      their fruit;
²² They shall not build and others live there;
    they shall not plant and others eat.
  As the years of a tree, so the years of my
      people;
    and my chosen ones shall long enjoy
      the work of their hands.
²³ They shall not toil in vain,
    nor beget children for sudden
      destruction;
  For they shall be a people blessed by the
      LORD
    and their descendants with them.
²⁴ Before they call, I will answer;
    while they are yet speaking, I will
      hear.

---

Sacredness was understood as something communicable (cf.
Ex 19:9–15).
  *[65:8] This verse reflects the remnant theology found
elsewhere in the Book of Isaiah: 1:8–9; 4:3; 6:11–13; etc.
  †[65:11–12] **Destiny**: the play on words is found in the
Hebrew, in which "destiny" and "destine" are *meni* and *manithi*.

  ‡[65:16] **God of truth**: lit., "God of Amen," i.e., the one
who keeps his word.
  §[65:17–18] The new creation (cf. 66:22) is described with
apocalyptic exuberance: long life, material prosperity, and so
forth. As the former events in 43:18 are to be forgotten, so
also the new creation wipes out memory of the first creation.

j. [65:10] Hos 2:17.   k. [65:12] Is 66:4; Prv 1:24; Jer 7:13.

l. [65:17] Is 66:22; Rev 21:1.   m. [65:20] Dt 4:40.

25 *The wolf and the lamb shall pasture
together,
and the lion shall eat hay like the
ox—
but the serpent's food shall be dust."
None shall harm or destroy
on all my holy mountain, says the
LORD.

## CHAPTER 66

### True and False Worship

1        †Thus says the LORD:
The heavens are my throne,
the earth, my footstool.
What house can you build for me?
Where is the place of my rest?°
2   My hand made all these things
when all of them came to be—oracle
of the LORD.
This is the one whom I approve:
the afflicted one, crushed in spirit,
who trembles at my word.ᵖ
3   ‡The one slaughtering an ox, striking a
man,
sacrificing a lamb, breaking a dog's
neck,
Making an offering of pig's blood,
burning incense, honoring an idol—
These have chosen their own ways,
and taken pleasure in their own
abominations.�q
4   I in turn will choose affliction for them
and bring upon them what they fear.
Because when I called, no one answered,
when I spoke, no one listened.
Because they did what was evil in my sight,
and things I do not delight in they
chose,ʳ
5   Hear the word of the LORD,
you who tremble at his word!
Your kin who hate you
and cast you out because of my
name say,
"May the LORD show his glory,
that we may see your joy";
but they shall be put to shame.
6   A voice roaring from the city,
a voice from the temple;

The voice of the LORD
rendering recompense to his
enemies!ˢ

### Blessings of Prosperity and Consolation

7   §Before she is in labor,
she gives birth;ᵗ
Before her pangs come upon her,
she delivers a male child.
8   Who ever heard of such a thing,
or who ever saw the like?
Can a land be brought forth in one day,
or a nation be born in a single
moment?
Yet Zion was scarcely in labor
when she bore her children.
9   Shall I bring a mother to the point of birth,
and yet not let her child be born?
says the LORD.
Or shall I who bring to birth
yet close her womb? says your God.
10   ¶Rejoice with Jerusalem and be glad
because of her,
all you who love her;
Rejoice with her in her joy,
all you who mourn over her—ᵘ
11   So that you may nurse and be satisfied
from her consoling breast;
That you may drink with delight
at her abundant breasts!
12        For thus says the LORD:
I will spread prosperity over her like a
river,
like an overflowing torrent,
the wealth of nations.
You shall nurse, carried in her arms,
cradled upon her knees;
13   As a mother comforts her child,
so I will comfort you;
in Jerusalem you shall find your
comfort.ᵛ
14   You will see and your heart shall exult,
and your bodies shall flourish like
the grass;
The LORD's power shall be revealed to his
servants,
but to his enemies, his wrath.
15   For see, the LORD will come in fire,
his chariots like the stormwind;
To wreak his anger in burning rage
and his rebuke in fiery flames.
16   For with fire the LORD shall enter into
judgment,

---

*[65:25] The imagery reflects the ideal era described in 11:6–9; see note there.

†[66:1–2] The Lord rejects the abuses associated with Temple worship in order to emphasize his concern for the sincere worshiper.

‡[66:3–6] The sacrificial abuses listed will only merit punishment. The true worshipers, the downtrodden, are those who "tremble" (vv. 2, 5) at God's word. Although they are ridiculed by those who reject them (v. 5), the latter will be afflicted with divine punishment; their "choice" will be met by the Lord's choice (v. 4).

§[66:7–9] The renewal of Zion is pictured in terms of a miraculous, instantaneous birth, facilitated by God's intervention.

¶[66:10–16] The poet addresses the children born of Jerusalem, their mother. In v. 13 the metaphor switches to the Lord as mother (cf. 49:15), comforting her charges but destroying the enemies.

n. [65:25] Is 11:6–9.   o. [66:1] 2 Sm 7:4–7; 1 Kgs 8:27; Acts 7:49; 17:24.   p. [66:2] Ps 24:1–2.   q. [66:3] Lv 11:7.   r. [66:4] Is 65:12; Prv 1:24; Jer 7:13.

s. [66:6] Jl 4:16; Am 1:2.   t. [66:7–9] Is 49:18–21; 54:1.   u. [66:10] Tb 13:14.   v. [66:13] Is 40:1; 49:13.

and, with his sword, against all flesh;
Those slain by the LORD shall be
    many.ʷ

¹⁷*Those who sanctify and purify themselves
to go into the gardens, following one who stands
within, eating pig's flesh, abominable things,
and mice, shall all together come to an end, with
their deeds and purposes—oracle of the LORD.
**God Gathers the Nations.** ¹⁸†I am coming to
gather all nations and tongues; they shall come
and see my glory.ˣ ¹⁹I will place a sign among
them; from them I will send survivors to the
nations: to Tarshish, Put and Lud, Mosoch,
Tubal and Javan, to the distant coastlands which
have never heard of my fame, or seen my glory;
and they shall proclaim my glory among the
nations. ²⁰They shall bring all your kin from
all the nations as an offering to the LORD, on
horses and in chariots, in carts, upon mules and
dromedaries, to Jerusalem, my holy mountain,

says the LORD, just as the Israelites bring their
grain offering in a clean vessel to the house of
the LORD. ²¹Some of these I will take as priests
and Levites, says the LORD.

²² Just as the new heavens and the new earth
        which I am making
    Shall endure before me—oracle of the
        LORD—
            so shall your descendants and your
                name endure.ʸ
²³ From new moon to new moon,
        and from sabbath to sabbath,
    All flesh shall come to worship
        before me, says the LORD.ᶻ
²⁴ ‡They shall go out and see the corpsesᵃ
        of the people who rebelled against
            me;
    For their worm shall not die,
        their fire shall not be extinguished;
        and they shall be an abhorrence to
            all flesh.

---

*[66:17] This verse seems to have some connection with
65:2–3.

†[66:18–21] God summons the neighboring nations to
Zion and from among them will send some to far distant
lands to proclaim the divine glory. **All your kin**: Jews in exile.
The "gathering of the people and the nations" is an eschatological motif common in the prophetic tradition; cf. 56:8.

w. [66:16] Lv 11:29.   x. [66:18] Is 56:1, 8; 59:20.

---

‡[66:24] God's enemies lie dead outside the walls of the
New Jerusalem; just as in the past, corpses, filth and refuse
lay in the Valley of Hinnom (Gehenna) outside the city; cf.
34:1–4; 2 Kgs 23:10.

y. [66:22] Is 65:17; Rev 21:1.   z. [66:23] Is 1:13.   a. [66:24] Is 1:27–28;
Mk 9:45.

# THE BOOK OF
# JEREMIAH

*೧ഏ೧*

The Book of Jeremiah combines history, biography, and prophecy. It portrays a nation in crisis and introduces the reader to an extraordinary person whom the Lord called to prophesy under the trying circumstances of the final days of the kingdom of Judah. Jeremiah was born, perhaps about 650 B.C., of a priestly family from the village of Anathoth, two and a half miles northeast of Jerusalem. He was called to his task in the thirteenth year of King Josiah (Jer 1:2). Josiah's reform, begun with enthusiasm and hope, ended with his death on the battlefield of Megiddo (609 B.C.) as he attempted to stop the northward march of the Egyptian Pharaoh Neco, who was going to provide assistance to the Assyrians who were in retreat before the Babylonians.

Nineveh, the capital of Assyria, fell in 612 B.C., preparing the way for the new colossus, Babylon, which was soon to put an end to the independence of Judah.

The prophet supported the reform of King Josiah (2 Kgs 22–23), but after the death of Josiah the old idolatry returned. Jeremiah opposed this as well as royal policy toward Babylon. Arrest, imprisonment, and public disgrace were his lot. In the nation's apostasy Jeremiah saw the sealing of its doom. Nebuchadnezzar captured Jerusalem (598 B.C.) and carried King Jehoiachin into exile (Jer 22:24).

During the years 598–587, Jeremiah counseled Zedekiah in the face of bitter opposition. The false prophet Hananiah proclaimed that the yoke of Babylon was broken and a strong pro-Egyptian party in Jerusalem induced Zedekiah to revolt. Nebuchadnezzar took swift vengeance; Jerusalem was destroyed in 587 and its leading citizens sent into exile.

The prophet remained in Jerusalem, but was later forced into Egyptian exile. We do not know the details of his death. The influence of Jeremiah was greater after his death than before. The exiled community read and meditated on the lessons of the prophet; his influence is evident in Ezekiel, some of the psalms, Is 40–66, and Daniel. In the postexilic period, the Book of Jeremiah circulated in various editions.*

The book may be divided as follows:

    I. Oracles in the Days of Josiah (1:1–6:30)
   II. Oracles Primarily from the Days of Jehoiakim (7:1–20:18)
  III. Oracles in the Last Years of Jerusalem (21:1–25:38)
  IV. The Temple Sermon (26:1–24; cf. 7:1–15)
   V. Controversies with the False Prophets (27:1–29:32)
  VI. Oracles of the Restoration of Israel and Judah (30:1–35:19)
 VII. Jeremiah and the Fall of Jerusalem (36:1–45:5)
VIII. Oracles Against the Nations (46:1–51:64)
  IX. Historical Appendix (52:1–34)

## I. ORACLES IN THE DAYS OF JOSIAH

### CHAPTER 1

¹The words of Jeremiah, son of Hilkiah, one of the priests from Anathoth,* in the land of Benjamin. ²The word of the LORD came to him in the days of Josiah, son of Amon, king of Judah, in the thirteenth year of his reign,ᵃ ³and again in the days of Jehoiakim, son of Josiah, king of Judah, until the end of the eleventh year of Zedekiah, son of Josiah, king of Judah—down to the exile of Jerusalem, in the fifth month.ᵇ

---

*[1:1] **Anathoth**: a village about three miles northeast of Jerusalem, to which Solomon had exiled Abiathar the priest (1 Kgs 2:26–27); it is likely that Jeremiah belonged to that priestly family.

a. [1:2] Jer 25:3.  b. [1:3] Jer 25:1.

## Call of Jeremiah

⁴ The word of the LORD came to me:
⁵ Before I formed you in the womb I knew
        you,
            before you were born I dedicated
                you,
                a prophet to the nations I appointed
                    you.*ᶜ
⁶ "Ah, Lord GOD!" I said,
        "I do not know how to speak. I am
            too young!"†
⁷ But the LORD answered me,
    Do not say, "I am too young."
        To whomever I send you, you shall
            go;
            whatever I command you, you shall
                speak.
⁸ Do not be afraid of them,
        for I am with you to deliver you—
            oracle of the LORD.

⁹Then the LORD extended his hand and
touched my mouth, saying to me,

    See, I place my words in your mouth!ᵈ
¹⁰        Today I appoint you
            over nations and over kingdoms,
    To uproot and to tear down,
        to destroy and to demolish,
        to build and to plant.

¹¹The word of the LORD came to me: What
do you see, Jeremiah? "I see a branch of the
almond tree,"‡ I replied. ¹²Then the LORD said to
me: You have seen well, for I am watching over
my word to carry it out. ¹³ᵉA second time the
word of the LORD came to me: What do you see?
I replied, "I see a boiling kettle whose mouth is
tipped away from the north."§
¹⁴The LORD said to me, And from the north
evil will pour out over all who dwell in the land.ᶠ

¹⁵    Look, I am summoning
        all the kingdoms of the north—
            oracle of the LORD—

Each king shall come and set up his
        throne
            in the gateways of Jerusalem,
    Against all its surrounding walls
        and against all the cities of Judah.ᵍ
¹⁶ I will pronounce my sentence against
        them
            for all their wickedness in
                forsaking me,
    In burning incense to other gods,
        in bowing down to the works of
            their hands.ʰ
¹⁷ But you, prepare yourself;
        stand up and tell them
            all that I command you.
    Do not be terrified on account of them,
        or I will terrify you before them;
¹⁸ For I am the one who today
        makes you a fortified city,
    A pillar of iron, a wall of bronze,
        against the whole land:
    Against Judah's kings and princes,
        its priests and the people of the
            land.ⁱ
¹⁹ They will fight against you, but not prevail
        over you,
            for I am with you to deliver you—
                oracle of the LORD.

## CHAPTER 2

**Infidelity of Israel.**¶ ¹The word of the LORD
came to me: ²Go, cry out this message for Jerusalem to hear!

    I remember the devotion** of your youth,
        how you loved me as a bride,
    Following me in the wilderness,
        in a land unsown.ʲ
³    Israel was dedicated to the LORD,
        the first fruits†† of his harvest;
    All who ate of it were held guilty,
        evil befell them—oracle of the
            LORD.ᵏ
⁴    Listen to the word of the LORD, house of
        Jacob!
        All you clans of the house of Israel,
⁵            thus says the LORD:
    What fault did your ancestors find in me
        that they withdrew from me,

---

*[1:5] Jeremiah was destined to become a prophet before
his birth; cf. Is 49:1, 5; Lk 1:15; Gal 1:15–16. **I knew you:** I
loved you and chose you. **I dedicated you:** I set you apart to
be a prophet. **The nations:** the neighbors of Judah, along with
Assyria, Babylonia, and Egypt.

†[1:6] **I am too young:** like Moses (Ex 3:11, 13; 4:10),
Jeremiah at first resists God's call. This narrative is perhaps
patterned after the story of Moses' call in order to identify Jeremiah as the prophet "like me" in Dt 18:15.

‡[1:11] There is wordplay between the Hebrew noun
*shaqed*, "almond tree," and the Hebrew verb *shoqed*, "watcher/
watching." Because the almond tree begins to bloom in late
winter in Palestine, it is called "the watcher" for the coming
of spring. God is also "watcher," observing the fulfillment of
the prophetic word.

§[1:13] **Kettle . . . the north:** symbol of an invasion from
the north; cf. vv. 14–15.

---

c. [1:5] Jer 49:1; Gal 1:15–16.   d. [1:9] Dt 18:18; Is 6:7.   e. [1:13] Ez
11:3, 7; 24:3.   f. [1:14] Jer 4:6; 6:1.

¶[2:1–3:5] These chapters may contain some of Jeremiah's
early preaching. He portrays Israel as the wife of the Lord,
faithful only in the beginning, when she walked behind him
(2:2–3, 5; 3:1). Consistent with the marriage metaphor, he
describes her present unfaithfulness as adultery (2:20; 3:2–3);
now she walks behind the Baals.

**[2:2] **Devotion:** Heb. *hesed*; Israel's gratitude, fidelity, and
love for God.

††[2:3] **First fruits:** the first yield of a harvest offered as a
sign of dependence and gratitude toward the Lord of the
land, thus divine property. Israel, then, is a gift made to God,
set apart for his use; cf. Ex 23:19.

---

g. [1:15] Jer 6:22.   h. [1:16] Is 2:8.   i. [1:18] Jer 6:27; 15:20; Ez
3:8.   j. [2:2] Dt 2:7; 32:9–12; Mi 6:4.   k. [2:3] Jer 12:14; Ex 4:22;
Dt 7:6; 14:2.

Went after emptiness,
    and became empty themselves?[l]

6 They did not ask, "Where is the LORD
    who brought us up from the land of
        Egypt,
Who led us through the wilderness,
    through a land of wastes and
        ravines,
A land of drought and darkness,
    a land which no one crosses,
    where no one dwells?"[m]

7 I brought you into the garden land
    to eat its fine fruits,
But you entered and defiled my land,
    you turned my heritage into an
        abomination.[n]

8 The priests did not ask,
    "Where is the LORD?"
The experts in the law* did not know me:
    the shepherds rebelled against me.
The prophets prophesied by Baal,
    and went after useless idols.[o]

9 Therefore I will again accuse you—oracle
        of the LORD—
    even your children's children I will
        accuse.[p]

10 Cross to the coast of Cyprus and see,
    send to Kedar† and carefully inquire:
    Where has anything like this been
        done?

11 Does any other nation change its gods?—
    even though they are not gods at all!
But my people have changed their glory
    for useless things.[q]

12 Be horrified at this, heavens;
    shudder, be appalled—oracle of the
        LORD.

13 Two evils my people have done:
    they have forsaken me, the source of
        living waters;
They have dug themselves cisterns,
    broken cisterns that cannot hold
        water.[r]

14 Is Israel a slave, a house-born servant?‡
    Why then has he become plunder?

15 Against him lions roar,
    they raise their voices.
They have turned his land into a waste,
    his cities are charred ruins, without
        an inhabitant.[s]

16 Yes, the people of Memphis§ and
        Tahpanhes
    shave the crown of your head.

17 Has not forsaking the LORD, your God,
    done this to you?[t]

18 And now, why go to Egypt,¶
    to drink the waters of the Nile?
Why go to Assyria,
    to drink the waters of the River?

19 Your own wickedness chastises you,
    your own infidelities punish you.
Know then, and see, how evil and bitter
    is your forsaking the LORD, your
        God,
And your showing no fear of me,
    oracle of the Lord, the GOD of hosts.[u]

20 Long ago you broke your yoke,[v]
    you tore off your bonds.
.You said, "I will not serve."
On every high hill, under every green
        tree,
    you sprawled and served as a
        prostitute.**

21 But I had planted you as a choice vine,
    all pedigreed stock;
How could you turn out so obnoxious
        to me,
    a spurious vine?[w]

22 Even if you scour it with lye,
    and use much soap,
The stain of your guilt is still before me,
    oracle of the Lord GOD.[x]

23 How can you say, "I am not defiled,
    I have not pursued the Baals"?
Consider your conduct in the Valley,††
    recall what you have done:
A skittish young camel,
    running back and forth,

24     a wild donkey bred in the
        wilderness,
Sniffing the wind in her desire—
    who can restrain her lust?
None seeking her need tire themselves;
    in her time they will find her.

25 Stop wearing out your feet
    and parching your throat!

---

§[2:16] **Memphis**: the capital of Lower Egypt. **Tahpanhes**: a frontier city of Egypt, east of the Delta. **Shave the crown of your head**: an image for Egypt plundering Judah; perhaps a reference to the capture of King Jehoahaz in 609 B.C. (2 Kgs 23:34).

¶[2:18] Egypt and Assyria were the competing foreign powers favored by rival parties within Judah. The desire for such foreign alliances is a further desertion of the Lord, the source of living waters (v. 13), in favor of the above-named powers, symbolized by the waters of the Nile and the Euphrates rivers.

**[2:20] **Served as a prostitute**: idolatry (because Israel is the "bride" of God); cf. vv. 2–3.

††[2:23] **The Valley**: probably Ben-hinnom, south of Jerusalem, site of the sanctuary of Topheth, where children were sacrificed to Molech; cf. 7:31.

---

*[2:8] **Experts in the law**: the priests. **The shepherds**: the kings and nobles.

†[2:10] **Kedar**: a nomadic tribe in north Arabia. Cyprus and Kedar represent west and east.

‡[2:14] **House-born servant**: one born in the master's house, in contrast to a slave acquired by purchase or as a captive; cf. Lv 22:11.

---

l. [2:5] 2 Kgs 17:15; Is 5:4; Mi 6:3.  m. [2:6] Ex 20:2–3; Dt 8:14; Is 63:11–14.  n. [2:7] Lv 18:24–25; Dt 8:7–10; 32:13–14.  o. [2:8] Jer 8:8–9; 23:1, 13.  p. [2:9] Ex 20:5.  q. [2:11] Jer 16:20; Ps 106:20.  r. [2:13] Jer 17:13; Ps 36:9; Is 1:4.  s. [2:15] Jer 9:11.

t. [2:17] Jer 4:18; 30:15.  u. [2:19] Prv 5:22; Hos 5:5.  v. [2:20] Jer 3:6, 13; Jgs 10:6.  w. [2:21] Ex 15:17; Ps 80:9; Is 5:4.  x. [2:22] Jb 9:30.

But you say, "No use! No!
How I love these strangers,
after them I must go."[y]

26 As the thief is shamed when caught,
so shall the house of Israel be
shamed:
They, their kings, their princes,
their priests and their prophets;[z]

27 They say to a piece of wood, "You are my
father,"
and to a stone, "You gave me birth."
They turn their backs to me, not their
faces;
yet in their time of trouble they cry
out,
"Rise up and save us!"

28 Where are the gods you made for
yourselves?
Let them rise up!
Will they save you in your time of
trouble?
For as numerous as your cities
are your gods, O Judah!
And as many as the streets of Jerusalem
are the altars you have set up for
Baal.[a]

29 Why are you arguing with me?
You have all rebelled against me—
oracle of the LORD.

30 In vain I struck your children;
correction they did not take.
Your sword devoured your prophets
like a ravening lion.[b]

31 You people of this generation,
consider the word of the Lord:
Have I become a wilderness to Israel,
a land of gloom?
Why then do my people say, "We have
moved on,
we will not come to you any more"?

32 Does a young woman forget her jewelry,
a bride her sash?
Yet my people have forgotten me
days without number.[c]

33 How well you pick your way
when seeking love!
In your wickedness,
you have gone by ways unclean!

34 On your clothing is
the life-blood of the innocent,
you did not find them committing
burglary;

35 Nonetheless you say, "I am innocent;
at least, his anger is turned away
from me."
Listen! I will judge you
on that word of yours, "I have not
sinned."

36 How frivolous you have become
in changing your course!

By Egypt you will be shamed,
just as you were shamed by Assyria.[d]

37 From there too you will go out,
your hands upon your head;
For the LORD has rejected those in whom
you trust,
with them you will have no success.[e]

## CHAPTER 3

1 If a man divorces his wife[f]
and she leaves him
and then becomes the wife of
another,
Can she return to the first?*
Would not this land be wholly
defiled?
But you have played the prostitute with
many lovers,
and yet you would return to me!—
oracle of the LORD.

2 Raise your eyes to the heights, and look,
where have men not lain with you?
Along the roadways you waited for them
like an Arabian† in the wilderness.
You defiled the land
by your wicked prostitution.[g]

3 Therefore the showers were withheld,
the spring rain did not fall.
But because you have a prostitute's brow,
you refused to be ashamed.[h]

4 Even now do you not call me, "My father,
you are the bridegroom of my
youth?

5 Will he keep his wrath forever,
will he hold his grudge to the end?"
This is what you say; yet you do
all the evil you can.

**Judah and Israel.** [6]The LORD said to me in the days of King Josiah: Do you see what rebellious Israel has done? She has gone up every high mountain, and under every green tree she has played the prostitute.[i] [7]And I thought: After she has done all this, she will return to me. But she did not return. Then, even though that traitor her sister Judah, saw [8]that, in response to all the adulteries rebel Israel had committed, I sent her away and gave her a bill of divorce, nevertheless Judah, the traitor, her sister, was not frightened; she too went off and played the prostitute.[j] [9]With her casual prostitution, she polluted the land, committing adultery with stone and wood.[k]

---

*[3:1] **Can she return to the first?**: i.e., her first husband. Here the Hebrew is emended in light of the Septuagint and Dt 24:1–4, which forbids a man to take back a woman once he has divorced her. The prophet uses this analogy to illustrate the presumption of Judah, the unfaithful wife, who assumes she can easily return to the Lord after worshiping other gods.

†[3:2] **An Arabian**: here depicted as a marauder lying in wait for caravans.

---

y. [2:25] Jer 18:12.   z. [2:26] Jer 48:27; Rom 6:21.   a. [2:28] Jer 11:13; Dt 32:38; Jgs 10:14.   b. [2:30] Jer 5:3; Neh 9:26.   c. [2:32] Jer 13:25; Dt 32:18.

d. [2:36] 2 Chr 28:16–21.   e. [2:37] 2 Sm 13:19.   f. [3:1] Dt 24:1–4.   g. [3:2] Ex 16:24–25.   h. [3:3] Jer 6:15; 8:12.   i. [3:6] Jer 2:20; Dt 12:2.   j. [3:8] 2 Kgs 17:6, 18–23; Ez 23:11.   k. [3:9] Jer 2:27.

¹⁰In spite of all this, Judah, the traitor, her sister, did not return to me wholeheartedly, but insincerely—oracle of the LORD.

**Restoration of Israel.** ¹¹Then the LORD said to me: Rebel Israel is more just than traitor Judah.*ˡ* ¹²Go, proclaim these words toward the north, and say:

> Return, rebel Israel—oracle of the LORD—
>     I will not remain angry with you;
> For I am merciful, oracle of the LORD,
>     I will not keep my anger forever.*ᵐ*

¹³ Only admit your guilt:
>     how you have rebelled against the
>         LORD, your God,
> How you ran here and there to strangers
>     under every green tree
>     and would not listen to my voice—
>         oracle of the LORD.*ⁿ*

¹⁴ Return, rebellious children—oracle of the
>         LORD—*
>     for I am your master;
> I will take you, one from a city, two from
>     a clan,
>     and bring you to Zion.*ᵒ*

¹⁵ I will appoint for you shepherds after my
>         own heart,
>     who will shepherd you wisely and
>         prudently.*ᵖ*

¹⁶ When you increase in number and are
>         fruitful in the land—
>     oracle of the LORD—
> They will in those days no longer say,
>     "The ark of the covenant of the
>         LORD!"
> They will no longer think of it, or
>     remember it,
>     or miss it, or make another one.

¹⁷At that time they will call Jerusalem "the LORD's throne." All nations will gather together there to honor the name of the LORD at Jerusalem, and they will no longer stubbornly follow their wicked heart.*q* ¹⁸In those days the house of Judah will walk alongside the house of Israel; together they will come from the land of the north to the land which I gave your ancestors as a heritage.*r*

### Conditions for Forgiveness

¹⁹ I thought:
>     How I would like to make you my
>         children!
> So I gave you a pleasant land,

the most beautiful heritage among
>     the nations!
> You would call me, "My Father," I
>     thought,
>     and you would never turn away
>         from me.*s*

²⁰ But like a woman faithless to her lover,
>     thus have you been faithless to me,
>     house of Israel—oracle of the LORD.*t*

²¹ A cry is heard on the heights!
>     the plaintive weeping of Israel's
>         children,
> Because they have perverted their way,
>     they have forgotten the LORD, their
>         God.

²² Return, rebellious children!
>     I will heal your rebellions.
> "Here we are! We belong to you,
>     for you are the LORD, our God.*u*

²³ Deceptive indeed are the hills,
>     the mountains, clamorous;
> Only in the LORD our God
>     is Israel's salvation.*v*

²⁴ The shameful thing† has devoured
>     our ancestors' worth from our
>         youth,
> Their sheep and cattle,
>     their sons and daughters.

²⁵ Let us lie down in our shame,
>     let our disgrace cover us,
>     for we have sinned against the LORD,
>         our God,
> We and our ancestors, from our youth to
>     this day;
>     we did not listen to the voice of the
>         LORD, our God."*w*

## CHAPTER 4

¹ If you return, Israel—oracle of the
>         LORD—
>     return to me.
> If you put your detestable things out of
>     my sight,
>     and do not stray,*x*

² And swear, "As the LORD lives,"‡
>     in truth, in judgment, and in justice,
> Then the nations shall bless themselves
>     in him
>     and in him glory.*y*

³For to the people of Judah and Jerusalem, thus says the LORD:

---

*[3:14–18] A remnant of Israel (v. 14) will reunite with Judah (v. 18). The former Israelite community, represented by the ark of the covenant, will be replaced by a universal alliance, symbolized by Jerusalem, the Lord's throne, to which all nations will be gathered (v. 17).

---

†[3:24] **The shameful thing:** Heb. *bosheth* ("shame"), a term often substituted for the name of Baal, a Canaanite god worshiped at local shrines.

‡[4:2] **As the LORD lives:** this oath, made sincerely, implies Israel's return and loyal adherence to God. Thus the ancient promises are fulfilled; cf. Gn 12:3; 18:18; 22:18; 26:4; Ps 72:17.

---

l. [3:11] Ez 16:51; 23:11.   m. [3:12] Dt 4:29–31.   n. [3:13] Jer 2:20, 25; Lv 26:40.   o. [3:14] Jer 23:3; Is 10:21–22.   p. [3:15] Ez 34:23; Jn 21:15.   q. [3:17] Is 2:2.   r. [3:18] Jer 30:3; 31:8.

s. [3:19] Jer 31:9, 20; Is 63:16.   t. [3:20] Jer 5:11.   u. [3:22] Hos 3:5.   v. [3:23] Jer 14:8.   w. [3:25] Jer 16:11–12; 22:21.   x. [4:1] Jer 25:5.   y. [4:2] Jer 12:16; Dt 10:20; Is 65:16.

Till your untilled ground,
and do not sow among thorns.[z]

4 Be circumcised for the LORD,[*]
remove the foreskins of your hearts,
people of Judah and inhabitants of
Jerusalem;
Or else my anger will break out like fire,
and burn so that no one can quench it,
because of your evil deeds.[a]

### The Invasion from the North

5 Proclaim it in Judah,
in Jerusalem announce it;
Blow the trumpet throughout the land,
call out, "Fill the ranks!"
Say, "Assemble, let us march
to the fortified cities."
6 Raise the signal—to Zion!
Seek refuge! Don't stand there!
Disaster I bring from the north,
and great destruction.
7 Up comes the lion from its lair,
the destroyer of nations has set out,
has left its place,
To turn your land into a desolation,
your cities into an uninhabited
waste.[b]
8 So put on sackcloth,
mourn and wail:
"The blazing anger of the LORD
has not turned away from us."[c]
9 In that day—oracle of the LORD—
The king will lose heart, and the princes;
the priests will be horrified,
and the prophets stunned.
10 "Ah! Lord GOD," they will say,
"You really did deceive[†] us
When you said: You shall have peace,
while the sword was at our very
throats."[d]
11 At that time it will be said
to this people and to Jerusalem,
A scorching wind from the bare heights
comes
through the wilderness toward my
daughter, the people.[‡]
Not to winnow, not to cleanse,
12         a strong wind from there comes at
my bidding.

Now I too pronounce
sentence upon them.[e]
13 See! like storm clouds he advances,
like a whirlwind, his chariots;
Swifter than eagles, his horses:
"Woe to us! we are ruined."
14 Cleanse your heart of evil, Jerusalem,
that you may be saved.
How long will you entertain
wicked schemes?
15 A voice proclaims it from Dan,
announces wickedness from Mount
Ephraim:
16 "Make this known to the nations,
announce it against Jerusalem:
Besiegers are coming from the distant
land,
shouting their war cry against the
cities of Judah."[f]
17 Like watchers in the fields they surround
her,
for she has rebelled against me—
oracle of the LORD.[g]
18 Your conduct, your deeds, have done this
to you;
how bitter is this evil of yours,
how it reaches to your very heart![h]
19 My body! my body! how I writhe![§]
The walls of my heart!
My heart beats wildly,
I cannot be still;
For I myself have heard the blast of the
horn,
the battle cry.
20 Ruin upon ruin is reported;
the whole land is laid waste.
In an instant my tents are ravaged;
in a flash, my shelters.[i]
21 How long must I see the signal,
hear the blast of the horn!
22 My people are fools,
they do not know me;
They are senseless children,
without understanding;
They are wise at evil,
but they do not know how to do
good.[j]
23 I looked at the earth—it was waste and
void;
at the heavens—their light had gone
out![k]
24 I looked at the mountains—they were
quaking!
All the hills were crumbling!
25 I looked—there was no one;
even the birds of the air had flown
away!

---

*[4:4] The external rite of circumcision accomplishes
nothing unless it is accompanied by the removal of blindness
and obstinacy of heart. Jeremiah's view is reflected in Rom
2:25, 29; 1 Cor 7:19; Gal 5:6; 6:13, 15.

†[4:10] **You really did deceive**: Jeremiah complains that
the Lord misled the people by fostering their complacency,
leaving them unprepared and unrepentant as judgment
approaches.

‡[4:11] **My daughter, the people**: the covenant people
personified as a young woman. Ezekiel 16 presents Israel and
Judah as female infants whom the Lord adopts and then abandons and punishes because they desire other lords.

§[4:19–21] Probably the prophet's own anguish at the
coming destruction of Judah.

---

z. [4:3] Hos 10:12; Mt 13:7, 22.   a. [4:4] Jer 9:24.   b. [4:7] Jer 2:15;
5:6.   c. [4:8] Jer 6:26; Is 5:25.   d. [4:10] Jer 6:14.

e. [4:12] Jer 1:16.   f. [4:16] Jer 5:15.   g. [4:17] Jer 6:3.   h. [4:18]
Jer 2:17, 19.   i. [4:20] Jer 10:20.   j. [4:22] Dt 32:5–6, 28.   k. [4:23]
Is 24:1, 3.

<sup>26</sup> I looked—the garden land was a
        wilderness,
    with all its cities destroyed
    before the LORD, before his blazing
        anger.<sup>l</sup>
<sup>27</sup>    For thus says the LORD:
    The whole earth shall be waste,
        but I will not wholly destroy it.<sup>m</sup>
<sup>28</sup> Because of this the earth shall mourn,
        the heavens above shall darken;
    I have spoken, I will not change my mind,
        I have decided, I will not turn back.<sup>n</sup>
<sup>29</sup> At the shout of rider and archer
        each city takes to flight;
    They shrink into the thickets,
        they scale the rocks:
    All the cities are abandoned,
        no one lives in them.
<sup>30</sup> You now who are doomed, what are you
        doing
        dressing in purple,
        bedecking yourself with gold,
    Enlarging your eyes with kohl?
        You beautify yourself in vain!
    Your lovers reject you,
        they seek your life.
<sup>31</sup> Yes, I hear the cry, like that of a woman in
        labor,
        like the anguish of a mother bearing
            her first child—
    The cry of daughter Zion gasping,
        as she stretches out her hands:
    "Ah, woe is me! I sink exhausted
        before my killers!"<sup>o</sup>

## CHAPTER 5

### Universal Corruption

<sup>1</sup>    Roam the streets of Jerusalem,
        look about and observe,
    Search through her squares,
        to find even one
    Who acts justly
        and seeks honesty,
        and I will pardon her!
<sup>2</sup>    They say, "As the LORD lives,"
        but in fact they swear falsely.
<sup>3</sup>        LORD, do your eyes not search for
            honesty?
    You struck them, but they did not flinch;
        you laid them low, but they refused
            correction;
    They set their faces harder than stone,
        and refused to return.<sup>p</sup>
<sup>4</sup>    I thought: These are only the lowly,
        they behave foolishly;
    For they do not know the way of the
        LORD,
        the justice of their God.<sup>q</sup>

<sup>5</sup>    Let me go to the leaders
        and speak with them;
    For they must know the way of the LORD,
        the justice of their God.
    But, one and all, they have broken the
        yoke,
        torn off the harness.<sup>r</sup>
<sup>6</sup>    Therefore, lions from the forest slay them,
        wolves of the desert ravage them,
    Leopards keep watch round their cities:
        all who come out are torn to pieces,
    For their crimes are many,
        their rebellions numerous.
<sup>7</sup>    Why should I pardon you?
        Your children have forsaken me,
        they swear by gods that are no gods.
    I fed them, but they commit adultery;
        to the prostitute's house they throng.
<sup>8</sup>    They are lustful stallions,
        each neighs after the other's wife.<sup>s</sup>
<sup>9</sup>    Should I not punish them for this?—
            oracle of the
            LORD;
        on a nation like this should I not
            take vengeance?
<sup>10</sup> Climb her terraces, and ravage them,
        destroy them completely.
    Tear away her tendrils,
        they do not belong to the LORD.<sup>t</sup>
<sup>11</sup> For they have openly rebelled against me,
        both the house of Israel and the
            house of Judah—
        oracle of the LORD.<sup>u</sup>
<sup>12</sup> They denied the LORD,<sup>*</sup>
        saying, "He is nothing,
    No evil shall come to us,
        neither sword nor famine shall we
            see.<sup>v</sup>
<sup>13</sup> The prophets are wind,
        and the word is not with them.
    Let it be done to them!"
<sup>14</sup> Therefore, thus says the LORD, the God of
        hosts,
        because you have said this—
    See! I make my words
        a fire in your mouth,
    And this people the wood
        that it shall devour!—
<sup>15</sup> Beware! I will bring against you
        a nation from far away,
        O House of Israel—oracle of the
            LORD;
    A long-lived nation, an ancient nation,
        a people whose language you do not
            know,
        whose speech you cannot
            understand.<sup>w</sup>
<sup>16</sup> Their quivers are like open graves;
        all of them are warriors.

---

*[5:12] **They denied the LORD**: the people act as though
God does not matter and will not interfere.

---

l. [4:26] Lv 26:31.   m. [4:27] Jer 5:18.   n. [4:28] Is 24:4.   o. [4:31]
Jer 6:24.   p. [5:3] Jer 2:30.   q. [5:4] Jer 8:7.

r. [5:5] Jer 6:13.   s. [5:8] Jer 13:27.   t. [5:10] Jer 2:21.   u. [5:11] Jer
3:20.   v. [5:12] Jer 14:13; Is 28:15.   w. [5:15] Dt 28:49.

17 They will devour your harvest and your
    bread,
    devour your sons and your
        daughters,
Devour your sheep and cattle,
    devour your vines and fig trees;
With their swords they will beat down
    the fortified cities in which you
        trust.[x]

18 Yet even in those days—oracle of the
LORD—I will not completely destroy you.[y] 19 And
when they ask, "Why has the LORD our God
done all these things to us?" say to them, "As
you have abandoned me to serve foreign gods in
your own land, so shall you serve foreigners in a
land not your own."

20 Announce this to the house of Jacob,
    proclaim it in Judah:
21 Pay attention to this,
    you foolish and senseless people,
Who have eyes and do not see,
    who have ears and do not hear.[z]
22 Should you not fear me—oracle of the
    LORD—
    should you not tremble before me?
I made the sandy shore the sea's limit,
    which by eternal decree it may not
        overstep.
Toss though it may, it is to no avail;
    though its billows roar, they cannot
        overstep.[a]
23 But this people's heart is stubborn and
    rebellious;
    they turn and go away,
24 And do not say in their hearts,
    "Let us fear the LORD, our God,
Who gives us rain
    early and late,* in its time;
Who watches for us
    over the appointed weeks of
        harvest."[b]
25 Your crimes have prevented these things,
    your sins have turned these
        blessings away from you.[c]
26 For criminals lurk among my people;
    like fowlers they set traps,
    but it is human beings they catch.[d]
27 Their houses are as full of treachery
    as a bird-cage is of birds;
Therefore they grow powerful and rich,
28     fat and sleek.
They pass over wicked deeds;
    justice they do not defend

By advancing the claim of the orphan
    or judging the cause of the poor.[e]
29 Shall I not punish these things?—oracle of
    the LORD;
    on a nation such as this shall I not
        take vengeance?
30 Something shocking and horrible
    has happened in the land:
31 The prophets prophesy falsely,
    and the priests teach on their own
        authority;
Yet my people like it this way;
    what will you do when the end
        comes?[f]

# CHAPTER 6

## The Enemy at the Gates

1 Seek refuge, Benjaminites,
    from the midst of Jerusalem!
Blow the trumpet in Tekoa,
    raise a signal over Beth-haccherem;
For disaster threatens from the north,
    and mighty destruction.[g]
2 Lovely and delicate
    daughter Zion, you are ruined!
3 Against her, shepherds come with their
    flocks;[†]
    all around, they pitch their tents
        against her;
    each one grazes his portion.[h]
4 "Prepare for war against her,
    Up! let us rush upon her at midday!"
"Woe to us! the day is waning,
    evening shadows lengthen!"
5 "Up! let us rush upon her by night,
    destroy her palaces!"[i]
6     For thus says the LORD of hosts:
Hew down her trees,
    throw up a siege mound against
        Jerusalem.
Woe to the city marked for punishment;
    there is nothing but oppression
        within her![j]
7 As a well keeps its waters fresh,
    so she keeps fresh her wickedness.
Violence and destruction resound in her;
    ever before me are wounds and
        blows.[k]
8 Be warned, Jerusalem,
    or I will be estranged from you,
And I will turn you into a wilderness,
    a land where no one dwells.
9     Thus says the LORD of hosts:
Glean, glean like a vine
    the remnant of Israel;

---

*[5:24] **Rain early and late**: autumn and spring rains
respectively. **Appointed weeks of harvest**: the seven weeks
between the Passover (Dt 16:9–10) and the feast of Weeks
(Pentecost), when it did not ordinarily rain.

x. [5:17] Dt 28:31.  y. [5:18] Jer 4:27.  z. [5:21] Is 6:9.  a. [5:22]
Jb 38:10–11.  b. [5:24] Gn 8:22; Dt 11:14.  c. [5:25] Jer 2:17,
19.  d. [5:26] Prv 1:11.

---

†[6:3] **Shepherds come with their flocks**: foreign invaders
with their armies.

e. [5:28] Jer 12:1; Is 1:23.  f. [5:31] Jer 14:14; Mi 2:11.  g. [6:1] Jer
1:14–15.  h. [6:3] Jer 4:17.  i. [6:5] 2 Chr 36:19.  j. [6:6] Jer 32:24;
Zep 3:1–4.  k. [6:7] Is 57:20.

Pass your hand, like a vintager,
  repeatedly over the tendrils.
10 To whom shall I speak?
  whom shall I warn, and be heard?
See! their ears are uncircumcised,
  they cannot pay attention;
See, the word of the LORD has become
    for them
  an object of scorn, for which they
    have no taste.*l*
11 But the wrath of the LORD brims up
    within me,
  I am weary of holding it in.
I will pour it out upon the child in the
    street,
  upon the young men gathered
    together.
Yes, husband and wife will be taken,
  elder with ancient.*m*
12 Their houses will fall to others,
  their fields and their wives as well;
For I will stretch forth my hand
  against those who dwell in the
    land—oracle of the LORD.*n*
13 Small and great alike, all are greedy for
    gain;
  prophet and priest, all practice
    fraud.*o*
14 They have treated lightly
  the injury to my people:
"Peace, peace!" they say,
  though there is no peace.*p*
15 They have acted shamefully, committing
    abominations,
  yet they are not at all ashamed,
  they do not know how to blush.
Therefore they will fall among the fallen;
  in the time of their punishment they
    shall stumble,
  says the LORD.*q*
16 Thus says the LORD:
Stand by the earliest roads,
  ask the pathways of old,*
"Which is the way to good?" and walk it;
  thus you will find rest for yourselves.
  But they said, "We will not walk it."*r*
17 I raised up watchmen† for them:
  "Pay attention to the sound of the
    trumpet!"
  But they said, "We will not pay
    attention!"
18 Therefore hear, O nations,
  and know, O earth,
  what I will do with them:
19 See, I bring evil upon this people,

the fruit of their own schemes,
Because they did not pay attention to my
    words,
  because they rejected my law.*s*
20 Of what use to me is incense that comes
    from Sheba,
  or sweet cane from far-off lands?
Your burnt offerings find no favor with
    me,
  your sacrifices do not please me.*t*
21 Therefore, thus says the LORD:
See, I will place before this people
  obstacles to trip them up;
Parents and children alike,
  neighbors and friends shall perish.*u*
22 Thus says the LORD:
See, a people comes from the land of the
    north,
  a great nation, rising from the very
    ends of the earth.*v*
23 Bow and javelin they wield;
  cruel and pitiless are they.
They sound like the roaring sea
  as they ride forth on horses,
Each in his place for battle
  against you, daughter Zion.
24 We hear news of them;
  our hands hang helpless,
Anguish takes hold of us,
  pangs like a woman in childbirth.*w*
25 Do not go out into the field,
  do not step into the street,
For the enemy has a sword;
  terror on every side!
26 Daughter of my people, dress in
    sackcloth,
  roll in the ashes.
Mourn as for an only child
  with bitter wailing:
"How suddenly the destroyer
  comes upon us!"*x*
27 ‡A tester for my people I have appointed
    you,
  to search and test their way.*y*
28 Arch-rebels are they all,
  dealers in slander,
bronze and iron, all of them,
  destroyers they are.
29 The bellows are scorched,
  the lead is consumed by the fire;
In vain has the refiner refined,
  the wicked are not drawn off.
30 "Silver rejected" they shall be called,
  for the LORD has rejected them.

---

* [6:16] **Pathways of old**: history and the lessons to be
learned from it.
† [6:17] **Watchmen**: the prophets who, like Jeremiah, had
upheld God's moral law.

‡ [6:27–30] God appoints Jeremiah to be a "tester" of his
people. The passage uses the metaphor of the refining of silver: the silver was extracted from lead ore, but the process in
ancient times was inexact, so that sometimes all that was left
was a scummy mess, to be thrown out.

---

l. [6:10] Jer 7:26; 20:8.  m. [6:11] Ez 9:6.  n. [6:12] Jer 8:10; Dt
28:30–32.  o. [6:13] Jer 8:10; 23:11.  p. [6:14] Jer 8:11.  q. [6:15]
Jer 3:3; 8:12.  r. [6:16] Jer 7:23–24; 18:15.

s. [6:19] Prv 1:31.  t. [6:20] Is 1:11; 43:24.  u. [6:21] Is 8:14–15.
v. [6:22] Jer 1:15; 5:15.  w. [6:24] Jer 4:31.  x. [6:26] Jer 25:34; Am
8:10.  y. [6:27] Jer 1:18.

## II. ORACLES PRIMARILY FROM THE DAYS OF JEHOIAKIM

### CHAPTER 7

**The Temple Sermon.**[*] [1]The word came to Jeremiah from the LORD: [2]Stand at the gate of the house of the LORD and proclaim this message there: Hear the word of the LORD, all you of Judah who enter these gates to worship the LORD! [3]Thus says the LORD of hosts, the God of Israel: Reform your ways and your deeds so that I may dwell with you in this place.[z] [4]Do not put your trust in these deceptive words: "The temple of the LORD! The temple of the LORD! The temple of the LORD!"[a] [5]Only if you thoroughly reform your ways and your deeds; if each of you deals justly with your neighbor; [6]if you no longer oppress the alien,[†] the orphan, and the widow; if you no longer shed innocent blood in this place or follow after other gods to your own harm,[b] [7]only then will I let you continue to dwell in this place, in the land I gave your ancestors long ago and forever.[c]

[8]But look at you! You put your trust in deceptive words to your own loss! [9]Do you think you can steal and murder, commit adultery and perjury, sacrifice to Baal, follow other gods that you do not know,[d] [10]and then come and stand in my presence in this house, which bears my name, and say: "We are safe! We can commit all these abominations again!"?[e] [11]Has this house which bears my name become in your eyes a den of thieves? I have seen it for myself!—oracle of the LORD.[f] [12]Go to my place at Shiloh,[‡] where I made my name dwell in the beginning. See what I did to it because of the wickedness of my people Israel.[g] [13]And now, because you have committed all these deeds—oracle of the LORD—because you did not listen, though I spoke to you untiringly, and because you did not answer, though I called you, [14]I will do to this house, which bears my name, in which you trust, and to the place which I gave you and your ancestors, exactly what I did to Shiloh.[h] [15]I will cast you out of my sight, as I cast away all your kindred, all the offspring of Ephraim.[i]

**Abuses in Worship.** [16]You, now, must not intercede for this people! Do not raise a cry or prayer in their behalf![j] Do not press me, for I will not listen to you! [17]Do you not see what they are doing in the cities of Judah, in the streets of Jerusalem? [18]The children gather wood, their fathers light the fire, and the women knead dough to make cakes for the Queen of Heaven,[§] while libations are poured out to other gods—all to offend me![k] [19]Are they really offending me—oracle of the LORD—or rather themselves, to their own disgrace?[l] [20]Therefore, thus says the Lord GOD: my anger and my wrath will pour out upon this place, upon human being and beast, upon the trees of the field and the fruits of the earth; it will burn and not be quenched.[m]

[21]Thus says the LORD of hosts, the God of Israel: Heap your burnt offerings upon your sacrifices; eat up the meat! [22]In speaking to your ancestors on the day I brought them out of the land of Egypt, I gave them no command[¶] concerning burnt offering or sacrifice. [23]This rather is what I commanded them: Listen to my voice; then I will be your God and you shall be my people. Walk exactly in the way I command you, so that you may prosper.[n]

[24]But they did not listen to me, nor did they pay attention. They walked in the stubbornness of their evil hearts and turned their backs, not their faces, to me.[o] [25]From the day that your ancestors left the land of Egypt even to this day, I kept on sending all my servants the prophets to you.[p] [26]Yet they have not listened to me nor have they paid attention; they have stiffened their necks and done worse than their ancestors.[q] [27]When you speak all these words to them, they will not listen to you either. When you call to them, they will not answer you. [28]Say to them: This is the nation which does not listen to the voice of the LORD, its God, or take correction. Faithfulness has disappeared; the word itself is banished from their speech.

[29]     Cut off your hair[**] and throw it away!
         on the heights raise a lament;
     The LORD has indeed rejected and cast off
         the generation that draws down his
             wrath.

[30]The people of Judah have done what is evil in my eyes—oracle of the LORD. They have set

---

[*][7:1–15] The Temple of the Lord will not guarantee safety against enemy invasion or any other misfortune.

[†][7:6] **The alien:** specially protected within Israelite society; cf. Ex 22:20; Nm 9:14; 15:14; Dt 5:14; 28:43.

[‡][7:12] **Shiloh:** an important sanctuary where the ark of the covenant was kept, according to the Books of Joshua, Judges, and 1 Samuel. In response to the corrupt behavior of the priests serving there, God allows the Philistines to destroy Shiloh and take the ark of the covenant. Cf. 1 Sm 1:9; 4:3–4; Ps 78:60, 68–69.

[§][7:18] **Queen of Heaven:** probably Astarte, goddess of fertility (cf. 1 Sm 31:10; 1 Kgs 11:5), worshiped particularly by women (cf. Jer 44:15–19). Such worship was evidently reinforced during the reign of King Manasseh (2 Kgs 21:3–7) and was revived after Josiah's death.

[¶][7:22] **I gave them no command:** right conduct rather than formal ritual was God's will concerning his people (v. 23).

[**][7:29] **Hair:** the unshorn hair of the nazirite, regarded as sacred because of a vow, temporary or permanent, to abstain from cutting or shaving the hair; nazirites also avoided contact with a corpse and with all products of the vine; cf. Nm 6:4–8. The cutting of this hair was a sign of extreme mourning.

---

z. [7:3] Jer 18:11; 26:13.   a. [7:4] Mi 3:11.   b. [7:6] Ex 22:21–24.   c. [7:7] Dt 4:40.   d. [7:9] Jer 44:17.   e. [7:10] Jer 32:34.   f. [7:11] Mt 21:13.   g. [7:12] Jos 18:1.   h. [7:14] Jer 26:9.   i. [7:15] 1 Kgs 9:7; 2 Kgs 17:23.   j. [7:16] Jer 11:14; 14:11.

k. [7:18] Jer 44:17, 19.   l. [7:19] Jb 35:6.   m. [7:20] Jer 36:29; 2 Kgs 22:17.   n. [7:23] Jer 11:4; Lv 26:3, 12.   o. [7:24] Jer 17:23.   p. [7:25] 2 Chr 36:15–16; Bar 1:19.   q. [7:26] Jer 19:15; 2 Chr 30:8.   r. [7:29] Jer 9:17–21.

up their detestable things in the house which bears my name, thereby defiling it.[s] [31]In the Valley of Ben-hinnom[*] they go on building the high places of Topheth to sacrifice their sons and daughters by fire, something I never commanded or considered. [32]Be assured! Days are coming—oracle of the Lord—when they will no longer say "Topheth" or "Valley of Ben-hinnom" but "Valley of Slaughter." For want of space, Topheth will become burial ground.[t] [33]The corpses of this people will be food for the birds of the sky and beasts of the earth, which no one will drive away.[u] [34]I will silence the cry of joy, the cry of gladness, the voice of the bridegroom and the voice of the bride, in the cities of Judah and in the streets of Jerusalem; for the land will be turned to rubble.[v]

## CHAPTER 8

[1]At that time—oracle of the Lord—the bones of the kings and princes of Judah, the bones of the priests and the prophets, and the bones of the inhabitants of Jerusalem will be brought out of their graves[w] [2]and spread out before the sun, the moon, and the whole host of heaven,[†] which they loved and served, which they followed, consulted, and worshiped. They will not be gathered up for burial, but will lie like dung upon the ground.[x] [3]Death will be preferred to life by all the survivors of this wicked people who remain in any of the places to which I banish them—oracle of the Lord of hosts.

### Israel's Conduct Incomprehensible

[4]       Tell them: Thus says the Lord:
    When someone falls, do they not rise
        again?
        if they turn away, do they not turn
            back?
[5]   Why then do these people resist
        with persistent rebellion?
    Why do they cling to deception,
        refuse to turn back?[y]
[6]   I have listened closely:
        they speak what is not true;
    No one regrets wickedness,
        saying, "What have I done?"
    Everyone keeps on running their course,
        like a horse dashing into battle.[z]
[7]   Even the stork in the sky
        knows its seasons;
    Turtledove, swift, and thrush
        observe the time of their return,

But my people do not know
    the order of the Lord.[a]
[8]   How can you say, "We are wise,[b]
        we have the law of the Lord"?
    See, that has been changed into falsehood
        by the lying pen of the scribes![‡]
[9]   The wise are put to shame,
        terrified, and trapped;
    Since they have rejected the word of the
        Lord,
        what sort of wisdom do they have?[c]

### Shameless in Their Crimes

[10]  Therefore, I will give their wives to other
        men,
        their fields to new owners.
    Small and great alike, all are greedy for
        gain,
        prophet and priest, all practice fraud.[d]
[11]  They have treated lightly
        the injury to the daughter of my
            people:[§]
    "Peace, peace!" they say,
        though there is no peace.[e]
[12]  They have acted shamefully; they have
        done abominable things,
        yet they are not at all ashamed,
        they do not know how to blush.
    Hence they shall be among those who fall;
        in their time of punishment they
            shall stumble,
        says the Lord.[f]

### Threats of Punishment

[13]  I will gather them all in—oracle of the
        Lord:
        no grapes on the vine,
    No figs on the fig trees,
        foliage withered!
    Whatever I have given them is gone.
[14]  Why do we remain here?
        Let us assemble and flee to the
            fortified cities,
        where we will meet our doom;
    For the Lord our God has doomed us,
        he has given us poisoned water to
            drink,
        because we have sinned against the
            Lord.[g]
[15]  We wait for peace to no avail;
        for a time of healing, but terror
            comes instead.[h]
[16]  From Dan is heard
        the snorting of horses;

---

*[7:31] **Valley of Ben-hinnom**: this valley was probably south of Jerusalem. **Topheth**: perhaps, "fire pit."

†[8:2] **Host of heaven**: the stars, worshiped by other nations and even by the inhabitants of Jerusalem, particularly during the reigns of Manasseh and Amon.

‡[8:8] **Lying pen of the scribes**: because the teachings and interpretations of the scribes ran counter to the word of the Lord.

§[8:11] **Daughter of my people**: see note on 4:11.

---

s. [7:30] Jer 32:34.   t. [7:32] Jer 19:6; 32:35.   u. [7:33] Jer 16:4; 34:20.   v. [7:34] Jer 16:9.   w. [8:1] Bar 2:24.   x. [8:2] Dt 4:19. y. [8:5] Jer 5:3; 7:24, 26.   z. [8:6] Jb 34:31–32.

a. [8:7] Is 1:3.   b. [8:8] Mal 2:8; Rom 2:17–23.   c. [8:9] 1 Cor 3:20.   d. [8:10] Jer 6:13; Dt 28:30.   e. [8:11] Jer 6:14.   f. [8:12] Jer 6:15.   g. [8:14] Jer 9:14; 23:15.   h. [8:15] Jer 14:19.

The neighing of stallions
shakes the whole land.
They come to devour the land and
everything in it,
the city and its inhabitants.
[17] Yes, I will send against you
poisonous snakes.
Against them no charm will work
when they bite you—oracle of the
LORD.[i]

### The Prophet's Grief
### over the People's Suffering

[18] My joy is gone,
grief is upon me,
my heart is sick.
[19] Listen! the cry of the daughter of my
people,
far and wide in the land!
"Is the LORD no longer in Zion,
is her King no longer in her midst?"
Why do they provoke me with their idols,
with their foreign nonentities?[j]
[20] "The harvest is over, the summer ended,
but we have not yet been saved!"
[21] I am broken by the injury of the daughter
of my people.
I am in mourning; horror has seized
me.[k]
[22] Is there no balm in Gilead,[*]
no healer there?
Why does new flesh not grow
over the wound of the daughter of
my people?[l]
[23] Oh, that my head were a spring of water,
my eyes a fountain of tears,
That I might weep day and night
over the slain from the daughter of
my people!

### CHAPTER 9

### The Corruption of the People

[1] Oh, that I had in the wilderness
a travelers' lodging!
That I might leave my people
and depart from them.
They are all adulterers,
a band of traitors.
[2] They ready their tongues like a drawn
bow;
with lying, and not with truth,
they are powerful in the land.
They go from evil to evil,
and me they do not know—oracle of
the LORD.

[3] Be on your guard, everyone against his
neighbor;
put no trust in any brother.
Every brother imitates Jacob, the
supplanter,[†]
every neighbor is guilty of slander.
[4] Each one deceives the other,
no one speaks the truth.
They have accustomed their tongues to
lying,
they are perverse and cannot
repent.[m]
[5] Violence upon violence,
deceit upon deceit:
They refuse to know me—
oracle of the LORD.
[6] Therefore, thus says the LORD of hosts:
I will refine them and test them;
how else should I deal with the
daughter of my people?
[7] A murderous arrow is their tongue,
their mouths utter deceit;
They speak peaceably with their
neighbors,
but in their hearts they lay an
ambush![n]
[8] Should I not punish them for these
deeds—oracle of the LORD;
on a nation such as this should I not
take vengeance?[o]

### Dirge over the Ravaged Land

[9] Over the mountains I shall break out in
cries of lamentation,
over the pastures in the wilderness,
in a dirge:
They are scorched, and no one crosses
them,
no sound of lowing cattle;
Birds of the air as well as beasts,
all have fled and are gone.[p]
[10] I will turn Jerusalem into a heap of ruins,
a haunt of jackals;
The cities of Judah I will make a waste,
where no one dwells.[q]

[11]Who is wise enough to understand this? To
whom has the mouth of the LORD spoken? Let
him declare it!

Why is the land ravaged,
scorched like a wilderness no one
crosses?[r]

---

*[8:22] **Gilead**: a region southeast of the Sea of Galilee noted for its healing balm.

†[9:3] **Jacob, the supplanter**: in Hebrew, a play on words. In the popular etymology given in Gn 25:26, the name Jacob means "he supplants," for he deprived his brother Esau of his birthright (cf. Gn 25:33).

---

i. [8:17] Dt 32:24.   j. [8:19] Dt 32:21; Mi 4:9.   k. [8:21] Jer 14:17.
l. [8:22] Jer 46:11.

m. [9:4] Jer 12:6.   n. [9:7] Ps 28:3; 62:4.   o. [9:8] Jer 5:9, 29.
p. [9:9] Jer 4:25; 12:4.   q. [9:10] Is 13:22.   r. [9:11] Ps 107:43; Hos 14:10.

¹²The LORD said: Because they have abandoned my law, which I set before them, and did not listen to me or follow it, ¹³but followed instead their stubborn hearts and the Baals, as their ancestors had taught them,ˢ ¹⁴therefore, thus says the LORD of hosts, the God of Israel: See now, I will give this people wormwood to eat and poisoned water to drink.ᵗ ¹⁵I will scatter them among nations whom neither they nor their ancestors have known; I will send the sword to pursue them until I have completely destroyed them.ᵘ

¹⁶         Thus says the LORD of hosts:
Inquire, and call the wailing women to
                 come;
         summon the most skilled of them.
¹⁷ Let them come quickly
         and raise for us a dirge,
That our eyes may run with tears,
         our pupils flow with water.ᵛ
¹⁸ The sound of the dirge is heard from
                 Zion:
         We are ruined and greatly ashamed;
We have left the land,
         given up our dwellings!
¹⁹ Hear, you women, the word of the LORD,
         let your ears receive the word of his
                 mouth.
Teach your daughters a dirge,
         and each other a lament:
²⁰ Death has come up through our windows,
         has entered our citadels,
To cut down children in the street,
         young people in the squares.ʷ
²¹ Corpses shall fall
         like dung in the open field,
Like sheaves behind the harvester,
         with no one to gather them.

### True Glory

²²         Thus says the LORD:
Let not the wise boast of his wisdom,
         nor the strong boast of his strength,
         nor the rich man boast of his riches;
²³ But rather, let those who boast, boast of
                 this,
         that in their prudence they know
                 me,ˣ
Know that I, the LORD, act with fidelity,
         justice, and integrity on earth.
How I take delight in these—oracle of the
         LORD.

**False Circumcision.** ²⁴See, days are coming—oracle of the LORD—when I will demand an account of all those circumcised in the foreskin:ʸ ²⁵Egypt and Judah, Edom and the Ammonites, Moab, and those who live in the wilderness and shave their temples.* For all the nations are uncircumcised, even the whole house of Israel is uncircumcised at heart.

## CHAPTER 10

**The Folly of Idolatry.** ¹Hear the word the LORD speaks to you, house of Israel. ²Thus says the LORD:

Do not learn the ways of the nations,
         and have no fear of the signs in the
                 heavens,†
         even though the nations fear them.ᶻ
³ For the carvings of the nations are
                 nonentities,
         wood cut from the forest,
Fashioned by artisans with the adze,ᵃ
⁴         adorned with silver and gold.
With nails and hammers they are
                 fastened,
         so they do not fall.ᵇ
⁵ Like a scarecrow in a cucumber field are
                 they,
         they cannot speak;
They must be carried about,
         for they cannot walk.
Do not fear them, they can do no harm,
         neither can they do good.ᶜ
⁶ No one is like you, LORD,
         you are great,
         great and mighty is your name.ᵈ
⁷ Who would not fear you,
         King of the nations,
         for it is your due!
Among all the wisest of the nations,
         and in all their domains,
         there is none like you.ᵉ
⁸ One and all they are stupid and senseless,
         the instruction from nonentities—
                 only wood!
⁹ Silver plates brought from Tarshish,
         and gold from Ophir,
The work of the artisan
         and the handiwork of the smelter,
Clothed with violet and purple—
         all of them the work of skilled
                 workers.
¹⁰ The LORD is truly God,
         he is the living God, the eternal
                 King,
Before whose anger the earth quakes,
         whose wrath the nations cannot
                 endure.ᶠ

---

*[9:25] **Shave their temples:** some Arabian tribes practiced this custom. None of the nations who practice circumcision understand the meaning of their action, not even Israel; no one conforms to life under the covenant.

†[10:2] **Signs in the heavens:** phenomena in the sky, such as eclipses or comets, used to predict disasters.

---

s. [9:13] Jer 7:24; 19:4–5.   t. [9:14] Jer 23:15.   u. [9:15] Lv 26:33; Dt 28:36, 64.   v. [9:17] Jer 14:17.   w. [9:20] Jer 14:16.   x. [9:23] Prv 21:30.   y. [9:24] Jer 4:4.

z. [10:2] Bar 6:6.   a. [10:3] Wis 13:1; Is 44:9.   b. [10:4] Is 40:19; 41:7.   c. [10:5] Ps 115:4–8; Bar 6:15.   d. [10:6] Ps 86:8–10.   e. [10:7] Jer 5:22; Ps 47:2, 8.   f. [10:10] Ps 10:16.

¹¹Thus shall you say of them: The gods that did not make heaven and earth—let these perish from earth and from beneath heaven!'*

¹² The one who made the earth by his power,
    established the world by his wisdom,
        and by his skill stretched out the heavens.ʰ
¹³ When he thunders, the waters in the heavens roar,
    and he brings up clouds from the end of the earth,
Makes lightning flash in the rain,
    and brings forth the wind from his storehouses.
¹⁴ Everyone is too stupid to know;
    every artisan is put to shame by his idol:
He has molded a fraud,
    without breath of life.ⁱ
¹⁵ They are nothing, objects of ridicule;
    they will perish in their time of punishment.
¹⁶ Jacob's portion is nothing like them:
    for he is the maker of everything!
Israel is his very own tribe,
    LORD of hosts is his name.ʲ

### Abandonment of Judah

¹⁷ Gather up your bundle from the land,
    City living under siege!
¹⁸    For thus says the LORD:
Now, at this time
    I will sling away the inhabitants of the land;
I will hem them in,
    that they may be taken.
¹⁹ Woe is me! I am undone,
    my wound is beyond healing.
Yet I had thought:
    if I make light of my sickness, I can bear it.
²⁰ My tent is ruined,
    all its cords are severed.
My children have left me, they are no more:
    no one to pitch my tent,
    no one to raise its curtains.ᵏ
²¹ How stupid are the shepherds!
    The LORD they have not sought;
For this reason they have failed,
    and all their flocks scattered.ˡ
²² Listen! a rumor! here it comes,
    a great commotion from the land of the north:
To make the cities of Judah a desolation,
    the haunt of jackals.

---

*[10:11] This verse is in Aramaic.

g. [10:11] Ps 96:5.  h. [10:12] Ps 104:5.  i. [10:14] Rom 1:22–23.  j. [10:16] Ps 33:12; Jer 31:35.  k. [10:20] Jer 4:20.  l. [10:21] Jer 23:1; Ez 34:5–6.

### Prayer of Jeremiah

²³ I know, LORD,
    that no one chooses their way,
Nor determines their course
    nor directs their own step.
²⁴ Correct me, LORD, but with equity,
    not in anger, lest you diminish me.
²⁵ Pour out your wrath on the nations that
        do not know you,
    on the tribes that do not call your name;
For they have utterly devoured Jacob,
    and laid waste his home.ᵐ

## CHAPTER 11

**Plea for Fidelity to the Covenant.** ¹The word that came to Jeremiah from the LORD: ²Speak to the people of Judah and the inhabitants of Jerusalem, ³and say to them: Thus says the LORD, the God of Israel: Cursed be anyone who does not observe the words of this covenant,ⁿ ⁴which I commanded your ancestors the day I brought them up out of the land of Egypt, that iron furnace, saying: Listen to my voice and do all that I command you. Then you shall be my people, and I will be your God.° ⁵Thus I will fulfill the oath I swore to your ancestors, to give them a land flowing with milk and honey, the one you have today. "Amen, LORD," I answered.

⁶Then the LORD said to me: Proclaim all these words in the cities of Judah and in the streets of Jerusalem: Hear the words of this covenant and obey them. ⁷I warned your ancestors unceasingly from the day I brought them up out of the land of Egypt even to this day: obey my voice. ⁸But they did not listen or obey. They each walked in the stubbornness of their evil hearts, till I brought upon them all the threats of this covenant which they had failed to observe as I commanded them.ᵖ

⁹A conspiracy has been found, the LORD said to me, among the people of Judah and the inhabitants of Jerusalem: ¹⁰They have returned to the crimes of their ancestors who refused to obey my words. They also have followed and served other gods; the house of Israel and the house of Judah have broken the covenant I made with their ancestors.�q ¹¹Therefore, thus says the LORD: See, I am bringing upon them a disaster they cannot escape. Though they cry out to me, I will not listen to them.ʳ ¹²Then the cities of Judah and the inhabitants of Jerusalem will go and cry out to the gods to whom they have been offering incense. But these gods will give them no help whatever in the time of their disaster.ˢ

¹³ For as many as your cities
    are your gods, O Judah!

---

m. [10:25] Ps 79:6–7.  n. [11:3] Dt 27:26.  o. [11:4] Dt 4:20; 1 Kgs 8:51.  p. [11:8] 2 Kgs 17:14.  q. [11:10] Dt 31:16; Ez 20:21–30.  r. [11:11] Jer 14:12; Mi 3:4.  s. [11:12] Dt 32:37–38.

As many as the streets of Jerusalem
    are the altars for sacrifice to Baal.*

<sup>14</sup>Now, you must not intercede for this people;
do not raise on their behalf a cry or prayer! I
will not listen when they call to me in the time
of their disaster.*

### Sacrifices of No Avail

<sup>15</sup> What right has my beloved in my house,
    while she devises her plots?
Can vows and sacred meat turn away
    your disaster from you?
Will you still be jubilant
<sup>16</sup>     when you hear the great tumult?
The LORD has named you
    "a spreading olive tree, a pleasure to
        behold";
Now he sets fire to it,
    its branches burn.

<sup>17</sup>The LORD of hosts who planted you has
decreed disaster for you because of the evil done
by the house of Israel and by the house of Judah,
who provoked me by sacrificing to Baal.*
**The Plot Against Jeremiah.** <sup>18</sup>I knew it because
the LORD informed me: at that time you showed
me their doings.
    <sup>19</sup>Yet I was like a trusting lamb led to slaugh-
ter, not knowing that they were hatching plots
against me: "Let us destroy the tree in its vigor;
let us cut him off from the land of the living, so
that his name will no longer be remembered."*

<sup>20</sup> But, you, LORD of hosts, just Judge,
    searcher of mind and heart,
Let me witness the vengeance you take
      on them,
    for to you I have entrusted my
      cause!*

    <sup>21</sup>Therefore, thus says the LORD concerning
the men of Anathoth who seek your life and say,
"Do not prophesy in the name of the LORD; otherwise you shall die by our hand."* <sup>22</sup>Therefore,
thus says the LORD of hosts: I am going to punish them. The young men shall die by the sword;
their sons and daughters shall die by famine.*
<sup>23</sup>None shall be spared among them, for I will
bring disaster upon the men of Anathoth, the
year of their punishment.*

### CHAPTER 12

<sup>1</sup> You would be in the right, O LORD,
    if I should dispute with you;
    even so, I must lay out the case
      against you.

Why does the way of the wicked prosper,
    why do all the treacherous live in
      contentment?*
<sup>2</sup> You planted them; they have taken root,
    they flourish and bear fruit as well.
You are upon their lips,
    but far from their thoughts.*
<sup>3</sup> LORD, you know me, you see me,
    you have found that my heart is with
      you.*
Pick them out like sheep for the butcher,
    set them apart for the day of
      slaughter.*
<sup>4</sup> How long must the land mourn,
    the grass of the whole countryside
      wither?
Because of the wickedness of those who
      dwell in it
beasts and birds disappear,
    for they say, "God does not care
      about our future."

<sup>5</sup> If running against men has wearied you,
    how will you race against horses?
And if you are safe only on a level stretch,
    what will you do in the jungle of the
      Jordan?

<sup>6</sup>Your kindred and your father's house, even they
betray you; they have recruited a force against
you. Do not believe them, even when they speak
fair words to you.*

### The Lord's Complaint

<sup>7</sup> I have abandoned my house,
    cast off my heritage;
The beloved of my soul I have delivered
    into the hand of her foes.*
<sup>8</sup> My heritage has become for me
    like a lion in the thicket;
She has raised her voice against me,
    therefore she has incurred my
      hatred.*
<sup>9</sup> My heritage is a prey for hyenas,
    is surrounded by vultures;
Come, gather together, all you wild
      animals,
    come and eat!*
<sup>10</sup> Many shepherds have ravaged my
      vineyard,
    have trampled down my heritage;
My delightful portion they have turned
    into a desert waste.*

---

*[12:3] Jeremiah calls the Lord to account for allowing the
wicked to flourish while he himself is persecuted for his fidelity to the Lord's mission; cf. 20:12. See Jesus' judgment, Mk
9:42. The metaphors indicate that Jeremiah has even greater
trials ahead of him.

---

t. [11:13] Jer 2:28; Hos 10:1.  u. [11:14] Jer 7:16; 14:11.  v. [11:17]
Is 5:2.  w. [11:19] Jer 18:18; 20:10; Wis 2:20.  x. [11:20] Jer
15:15.  y. [11:21] Am 7:13, 16.  z. [11:22] Jer 18:21–22.  a. [11:23]
Jer 23:12.

b. [12:1] Jb 21:7; Mal 3:15.  c. [12:2] Is 29:13.  d. [12:3] Jer
17:18; Jb 23:10.  e. [12:6] Jer 9:4.  f. [12:7] Ps 78:62; Lam 2:1–2.
g. [12:8] Ps 106:40.  h. [12:9] 2 Kgs 24:2; Is 56:9.  i. [12:10] Jer 6:3;
Is 63:18.

<sup>11</sup> They have made it a mournful waste,
    desolate before me,
Desolate, the whole land,
    because no one takes it to heart.
<sup>12</sup> Upon every height in the wilderness
    marauders have appeared.
The Lord has a sword that consumes
    the land from end to end:
    no peace for any living thing.<sup>j</sup>
<sup>13</sup> They have sown wheat and reaped thorns,
    they have tired themselves out for
      no purpose;
They are shamed by their harvest,
    the burning anger of the Lord.

**Judah's Neighbors.** <sup>14</sup>Thus says the Lord, against all my evil neighbors* who plunder the heritage I gave my people Israel as their own: See, I will uproot them from their land; the house of Judah I will uproot in their midst.<sup>k</sup>

<sup>15</sup>But after uprooting them, I will have compassion on them again and bring them back, each to their heritage, each to their land.<sup>l</sup> <sup>16</sup>And if they truly learn my people's custom of swearing by my name, "As the Lord lives," just as they taught my people to swear by Baal, then they shall be built up in the midst of my people.<sup>m</sup> <sup>17</sup>But if they do not obey, I will uproot and destroy that nation entirely—oracle of the Lord.<sup>n</sup>

## CHAPTER 13

**Judah's Corruption.**<sup>†</sup> <sup>1</sup>The Lord said to me: Go buy yourself a linen loincloth; wear it on your loins, but do not put it in water. <sup>2</sup>I bought the loincloth, as the Lord commanded, and put it on. <sup>3</sup>A second time the word of the Lord came to me thus: <sup>4</sup>Take the loincloth which you bought and are wearing, and go at once to the Perath; hide it there in a cleft of the rock. <sup>5</sup>Obedient to the Lord's command, I went to the Perath and buried the loincloth. <sup>6</sup>After a long time, the Lord said to me: Go now to the Perath and fetch the loincloth which I told you to hide there. <sup>7</sup>So I went to the Perath, looked for the loincloth and took it from the place I had hidden it. But it was rotted, good for nothing! <sup>8</sup>Then the word came to me from the Lord: <sup>9</sup>Thus says the Lord: So also I will allow the pride of Judah to rot, the great pride of Jerusalem.<sup>o</sup> <sup>10</sup>This wicked people who refuse to obey my words, who walk in the stubbornness of their hearts and follow other gods, serving and worshiping them, will be like this loincloth, good for nothing.<sup>p</sup> <sup>11</sup>For, as the loincloth clings to a man's loins, so I made the whole house of Israel and the whole house of Judah cling to me—oracle of the Lord—to be my people, my fame, my praise, my glory. But they did not listen.<sup>q</sup>

**The Broken Wineflask.** <sup>12</sup>Now speak to them this word: Thus says the Lord, the God of Israel: Every wineflask should be filled with wine. If they reply, "Do we not know that every wineflask should be filled with wine?" <sup>13</sup>say to them: Thus says the Lord: Beware! I am making all the inhabitants of this land drunk, the kings who sit on David's throne, the priests and prophets, and all the inhabitants of Jerusalem.<sup>r</sup> <sup>14</sup>I will smash them against each other, parents and children together—oracle of the Lord—showing no compassion, I will neither spare nor pity, but I will destroy them.<sup>s</sup>

### A Last Warning

<sup>15</sup> Listen and give ear, do not be arrogant,
    for the Lord speaks.
<sup>16</sup> Give glory to the Lord, your God,
    before he brings darkness;
Before your feet stumble
    on mountains at twilight;
Before the light you look for turns to
      darkness,
    changes into black clouds.<sup>t</sup>
<sup>17</sup> If you do not listen to this in your pride,
    I will weep many tears in secret;
My eyes will run with tears
    for the Lord's flock, led away to
      exile.<sup>u</sup>

### Exile

<sup>18</sup> Say to the king and to the queen mother:
    come down from your throne;
From your heads
    your splendid crowns will fall.<sup>v</sup>
<sup>19</sup> The cities of the Negeb are besieged,
    with no one to relieve them;
Judah is taken into exile—all of it—
    in total exile.

### Jerusalem's Disgrace

<sup>20</sup> Lift up your eyes and see
    those coming in from the north.
Where is the flock entrusted to you,
    your splendid sheep?<sup>w</sup>
<sup>21</sup> What will you say when rulers are
      appointed over you,
    those you taught to be allies?
Will not pains seize you
    like those of a woman giving birth?<sup>x</sup>

---

* [12:14] **My evil neighbors:** nations surrounding Israel, the land belonging to the Lord; cf. Is 8:8.

† [13:1–11] In this symbolic action, Jeremiah probably went to the village and spring of Parah, two and a half miles northeast of Anathoth, whose name closely resembled the Hebrew name of the river Euphrates (*Perath*), in order to dramatize the religious corruption of Judah at the hands of the Babylonians.

---

j. [12:12] Is 42:25; 57:21.   k. [12:14] 2 Kgs 24:2.   l. [12:15] Am 9:14.   m. [12:16] Dt 6:13.   n. [12:17] Is 60:12.   o. [13:9] Prv 16:18.

p. [13:10] Jer 2:20; 7:24; 16:11.   q. [13:11] Ex 19:5; Dt 26:18–19.   r. [13:13] Jer 25:15–18; Is 51:17.   s. [13:14] Jer 19:10–11.   t. [13:16] Prv 4:18–19; Is 5:30; Am 8:9.   u. [13:17] Jer 14:17; Ps 119:136.   v. [13:18] Jer 22:26; 2 Kgs 24:12, 15.   w. [13:20] Jer 6:22–23.   x. [13:21] 2 Kgs 16:7.

<sup>22</sup> If you say to yourself:
  "Why have these things happened
        to me?"
  For your great guilt your skirts are
        stripped away
  and you are violated.<sup>y</sup>
<sup>23</sup> Can Ethiopians change their skin,
        leopards their spots?
  As easily would you be able to do good,
        accustomed to evil as you are.<sup>z</sup>
<sup>24</sup> I will scatter them like chaff that flies
        on the desert wind.<sup>a</sup>
<sup>25</sup> This is your lot, the portion I have
        measured out to you—
        oracle of the LORD.
  Because you have forgotten me,
        and trusted in deception,<sup>*b</sup>
<sup>26</sup> I now will strip away your skirts,
        so that your shame is visible.<sup>c</sup>
<sup>27</sup> Your adulteries, your neighings,
        your shameless prostitutions:
  On the hills, in the fields
        I see your detestable crimes.
  Woe to you, Jerusalem! How long will
        it be
  before you are clean?<sup>d</sup>

## CHAPTER 14

**The Great Drought.** <sup>1</sup>The word of the LORD that
came to Jeremiah concerning the drought:<sup>e</sup>

<sup>2</sup> Judah mourns,
        her gates are lifeless;
  They are bowed to the ground,
        and the outcry of Jerusalem goes up.<sup>f</sup>
<sup>3</sup> The nobles send their servants for water,
        but when they come to the cisterns
  They find no water
        and return with empty jars.<sup>g</sup>
  Confounded, despairing, they cover their
        heads
<sup>4</sup>       because of the ruined soil;
  Because there is no rain in the land
        the farmers are confounded, they
        cover their heads.<sup>h</sup>
<sup>5</sup> Even the doe in the field deserts her
        young
        because there is no grass.
<sup>6</sup> The wild donkeys stand on the bare
        heights,
        gasping for breath like jackals;
  Their eyes grow dim;
        there is no grass.
<sup>7</sup> Even though our crimes bear witness
        against us,
        act, LORD, for your name's sake—

  Even though our rebellions are many,
        and we have sinned against you.<sup>i</sup>
<sup>8</sup> Hope of Israel, LORD,
        our savior in time of need!
  Why should you be a stranger in the land,
        like a traveler stopping only for a
        night?
<sup>9</sup> Why are you like someone bewildered,
        a champion who cannot save?
  You are in our midst, LORD,
        your name we bear:
        do not forsake us!<sup>j</sup>
<sup>10</sup> Thus says the LORD about this
        people:
  They so love to wander
        that they cannot restrain their feet.
  The LORD takes no pleasure in them;
        now he remembers their guilt,
        and will punish their sins.<sup>k</sup>

<sup>11</sup>Then the LORD said to me: Do not inter-
cede for the well-being of this people.<sup>l</sup> <sup>12</sup>If they
fast, I will not listen to their supplication. If they
sacrifice burnt offerings or grain offerings, I will
take no pleasure in them. Rather, I will destroy
them with the sword, famine, and plague.<sup>m</sup>
<sup>13</sup>"Ah! Lord GOD," I replied, "it is the proph-
ets who say to them, 'You shall not see the
sword; famine shall not befall you. Indeed, I will
give you lasting peace in this place.'"<sup>n</sup>
<sup>14</sup>These prophets utter lies in my name, the
LORD said to me: I did not send them; I gave
them no command, nor did I speak to them.
They prophesy to you lying visions, foolish divination, deceptions from their own imagination.<sup>o</sup>
<sup>15</sup>Therefore, thus says the LORD: Concerning the
prophets who prophesy in my name, though I
did not send them, and who say, "Sword and
famine shall not befall this land": by sword and
famine shall these prophets meet their end.<sup>p</sup>
<sup>16</sup>The people to whom they prophesy shall be
thrown out into the streets of Jerusalem because
of famine and the sword. No one shall bury
them, their wives, their sons, or their daughters, for I will pour out upon them their own
wickedness.<sup>q</sup> <sup>17</sup>Speak to them this word:

  Let my eyes stream with tears
        night and day, without rest,
  Over the great destruction which
        overwhelms
        the virgin daughter of my people,
        over her incurable wound.<sup>r</sup>
<sup>18</sup> If I walk out into the field,
        look! those slain by the sword;
  If I enter the city,
        look! victims of famine.
  Both prophet and priest ply their trade
        in a land they do not know.

---

*[13:25] Heb. *sheqer*: lit., "deception," often used to designate an idol.

---

y. [13:22] Is 47:2–3.   z. [13:23] Ps 55:20.   a. [13:24] Ps 1:4; 83:14.
b. [13:25] Jb 20:29.   c. [13:26] Ez 16:32.   d. [13:27] Jer 2:20.
e. [14:1] Lv 26:19–20.   f. [14:2] Is 3:26.   g. [14:3] Am 4:8.
h. [14:4] Dt 28:23.
i. [14:7] Dn 9:4–14.   j. [14:9] Is 59:1–2; 63:19.   k. [14:10] Jer
2:25.   l. [14:11] Jer 11:14; Ex 32:10.   m. [14:12] Jer 6:20; Is 1:11,
13.   n. [14:13] Jer 4:10; 5:12.   o. [14:14] Jer 5:31; 23:16.   p. [14:15]
Jer 5:12–13.   q. [14:16] Jer 7:33; 19:7.   r. [14:17] Jer 9:17.

<sup>19</sup> Have you really cast Judah off?
    Is Zion loathsome to you?
Why have you struck us a blow
    that cannot be healed?
We wait for peace, to no avail;
    for a time of healing, but terror
      comes instead.<sup>s</sup>

<sup>20</sup> We recognize our wickedness, LORD,
    the guilt of our ancestors:
    we have sinned against you.<sup>t</sup>

<sup>21</sup> Do not reject us, for your name's sake,
    do not disgrace your glorious
      throne.
    Remember! Do not break your
      covenant with us.<sup>u</sup>

<sup>22</sup> Among the idols of the nations are there
    any that give rain?
    Or can the mere heavens send
      showers?
Is it not you, LORD,
    our God, to whom we look?
    You alone do all these things.<sup>v</sup>

## CHAPTER 15

<sup>1</sup>The LORD said to me: Even if Moses and Samuel stood before me, my heart would not turn toward this people. Send them away from me and let them go.<sup>w</sup> <sup>2</sup>If they ask you, "Where should we go?" tell them, Thus says the LORD: Whoever is marked for death, to death; whoever is marked for the sword, to the sword; whoever is marked for famine, to famine; whoever is marked for captivity, to captivity.<sup>x</sup> <sup>3</sup>Four kinds of scourge I have decreed against them—oracle of the LORD—the sword to kill them; dogs to drag them off; the birds of the sky and the beasts of the earth to devour and destroy them.<sup>y</sup> <sup>4</sup>And I will make them an object of horror to all the kingdoms of the earth because of what Manasseh, son of Hezekiah, king of Judah, did in Jerusalem.<sup>z</sup>

### Scene of Tragedy

<sup>5</sup> Who will pity you, Jerusalem,
    who will grieve for you?
Who will stop to ask
    about your welfare?<sup>a</sup>

<sup>6</sup> It is you who have disowned me—oracle
    of the LORD—
    turned your back upon me;
I stretched out my hand to destroy you,
    because I was weary of relenting.<sup>b</sup>

<sup>7</sup> I winnowed them with a winnowing fork
    at the gates of the land;
I have bereaved, destroyed my people;
    they have not turned from their evil
      ways.<sup>c</sup>

<sup>8</sup> Their widows were more numerous before
    me
    than the sands of the sea.
I brought against the mother of youths
    the destroyer at midday;
Suddenly I struck her
    with anguish and terror.

<sup>9</sup> The mother of seven faints away,
    breathing out her life;
Her sun sets in full day,
    she is ashamed, abashed.
Their survivors I will give to the sword
    in the presence of their enemies—
      oracle of the LORD.<sup>d</sup>

### Jeremiah's Complaint

<sup>10</sup> Woe to me, my mother, that you gave me
    birth!
    a man of strife and contention to all
      the land!
I neither borrow nor lend,
    yet everyone curses me.<sup>e</sup>

<sup>11</sup> Tell me, LORD, have I not served you for
    their good?
    Have I not interceded with you
    in time of misfortune and anguish?<sup>f</sup>

<sup>12</sup> Can one break iron,
    iron from the north, and bronze?

<sup>13</sup> *Your wealth and your treasures
    I give as plunder, demanding no
      payment,
    because of all your sins, throughout
      all your territory.

<sup>14</sup> And I shall enslave you to your enemies
    in a land you do not know,
For fire has broken out from my anger,
    it is kindled against you.

<sup>15</sup>     You know, LORD;
Remember me and take care of me,
    avenge me on my persecutors.
Because you are slow to anger, do not
    banish me;
    know that for you I have borne insult.<sup>g</sup>

<sup>16</sup> When I found your words, I devoured
    them;
    your words were my joy, the
      happiness of my heart,
Because I bear your name,
    LORD, God of hosts.

<sup>17</sup> I did not sit celebrating
    in the circle of merrymakers;
Under the weight of your hand I sat alone
    because you filled me with rage.<sup>h</sup>

---

*[15:13–14] Though the wording of these verses is close to that in 17:3–4, the present passage is evidently God's word to Jeremiah, whereas 17:3–4 is evidently a word of judgment on Judah. It is noteworthy that the references to "you" in the present passage are singular, until a shift to plural in "against you" in the last line; this "you" is then doubtless a reference to both the prophet and his enemies.

s. [14:19] Jer 8:15; 2 Chr 36:16.   t. [14:20] Ps 106:6; Dn 9:5, 8.   u. [14:21] Jer 14:7; Lv 26:44; Ps 25:11.   v. [14:22] Jer 5:24; Zec 10:1.   w. [15:1] Ps 99:6; Ez 14:14, 16.   x. [15:2] Jer 14:12; Ez 5:12.   y. [15:3] Ez 14:21.   z. [15:4] Jer 24:9; 2 Kgs 21:11–16; 23:26; 24:3–4.   a. [15:5] Is 51:19.   b. [15:6] Am 7:8.   c. [15:7] Is 41:16.

d. [15:9] 1 Sm 2:5.   e. [15:10] Jer 20:14.   f. [15:11] Jer 39:11–14.   g. [15:15] Jer 11:20; 12:3; Ps 69:8.   h. [15:17] Ps 25:4.

18 Why is my pain continuous,
    my wound incurable, refusing to be
      healed?
To me you are like a deceptive brook,
    waters that cannot be relied on!^i
19 Thus the LORD answered me:
If you come back and I take you back,
    in my presence you shall stand;
If you utter what is precious and not what
      is worthless,
    you shall be my mouth.
Then they will be the ones who turn to you,
    not you who turn to them.
20 And I will make you toward this people
    a fortified wall of bronze.
Though they fight against you,
    they shall not prevail,
For I am with you,
    to save and rescue you—oracle of
      the LORD.^j
21 I will rescue you from the hand of the
      wicked,
    and ransom you from the power of
      the violent.

## CHAPTER 16

**Jeremiah's Life a Warning.** ¹This word came to
me from the LORD: ²Do not take a wife and do
not have sons and daughters in this place, ³for
thus says the LORD concerning the sons and
daughters born in this place, the mothers who
give them birth, the fathers who beget them in
this land: ⁴Of deadly disease they shall die. Unla-
mented and unburied they will lie like dung on
the ground. Sword and famine will make an end
of them, and their corpses will become food for
the birds of the sky and the beasts of the earth.^k

⁵Thus says the LORD: Do not go into a house
of mourning; do not go there to lament or grieve
for them. For I have withdrawn my peace from
this people—oracle of the LORD—my love and
my compassion.^l ⁶They shall die, the great and
the lowly, in this land, unburied and unlament-
ed.* No one will gash themselves or shave their
heads for them.^m ⁷They will not break bread with
the bereaved to offer consolation for the dead;
they will not give them the cup of consolation to
drink over the death of father or mother.^n

⁸Do not enter a house of feasting to sit eating
and drinking with them. ⁹For thus says the LORD
of hosts, the God of Israel: Before your eyes and
in your lifetime, I will silence in this place the
song of joy and the song of gladness, the song of
the bridegroom and the song of the bride.^o

¹⁰When you proclaim all these words to this
people and they ask you: "Why has the LORD

pronounced all this great disaster against us?
What is our crime? What sin have we committed against the LORD, our God?"—^p ¹¹qyou
shall answer them: It is because your ancestors
have forsaken me—oracle of the LORD—and
followed other gods that they served and worshiped; but me they have forsaken, and my law
they did not keep. ¹²And you have done worse
than your ancestors. Here you are, every one of
you, walking in the stubbornness of your evil
heart instead of listening to me.^r ¹³I will throw
you out of this land into a land that neither you
nor your ancestors have known; there you can
serve other gods day and night because I will
not show you mercy.

**Return from Exile.** ¹⁴Therefore, days are coming—oracle of the LORD—when it will no longer be said, "As the LORD lives, who brought
the Israelites out of Egypt";^s ¹⁵but rather, "As the
LORD lives, who brought the Israelites out of the
land of the north and out of all the countries to
which he had banished them." I will bring them
back to the land I gave their ancestors.^t

**Double Punishment.** ¹⁶Look!—oracle of the
LORD—I will send many fishermen to catch
them. After that, I will send many hunters to
hunt them out from every mountain and hill
and rocky crevice.^u ¹⁷For my eyes are upon all
their ways; they are not hidden from me, nor
does their guilt escape my sight.^v ¹⁸I will at once
repay them double for their crime and their sin
because they profaned my land with the corpses
of their detestable idols, and filled my heritage
with their abominations.^w

### Conversion of the Nations

19 LORD, my strength, my fortress,
    my refuge in the day of distress!
To you nations will come
    from the ends of the earth, and say,
"Our ancestors inherited mere frauds,
    empty, worthless."^x
20 Can human beings make for themselves
      gods?
    But these are not gods at all!^y
21 Therefore, I will indeed give them
      knowledge;
    this time I will make them
      acknowledge
My strength and my power:
    they shall know that my name is LORD.^z

## CHAPTER 17

### The Sin of Judah and Its Punishment

1 The sin of Judah is written
    with an iron stylus,

---

*[16:6–7] These verses refer to popular mourning prac-
tices in the land; cf. Dt 14:1–2.

---

i. [15:18] Jer 14:19; 30:15.   j. [15:20] Jer 1:18; 6:27.   k. [16:4]
Jer 7:33; 22:18.   l. [16:5] Ez 24:16–17.   m. [16:6] Lv 19:28; Dt
14:1.   n. [16:7] Ez 24:17.   o. [16:9] Jer 7:34; 25:10.

p. [16:10] Jer 2:35; 5:19; 13:22.   q. [16:11] Jer 22:9; Dt 29:25.
r. [16:12] Jer 7:24–26.   s. [16:14] Jer 23:7–8.   t. [16:15] Jer 24:6.
u. [16:16] 2 Kgs 24:2; Lam 4:19.   v. [16:17] Jer 32:19; Jb 34:21.
w. [16:18] Is 40:2.   x. [16:19] Jer 2:11; Is 2:2–3.   y. [16:20] Jer 2:11;
Gal 4:8.   z. [16:21] Am 5:8.

Engraved with a diamond point
    upon the tablets of their hearts,[a]

And the horns of their altars, [2]when their children remember their altars and their asherahs,
beside the green trees, on the high hills, [3]the
peaks in the country.

Your wealth and all your treasures
    I give as plunder,
As payment for all your sins
    throughout your territory,
[4] You will relinquish your hold on your
    heritage
    which I have given you.
I will enslave you to your enemies
    in a land you do not know:
For a fire has broken out from my anger,
    burning forever.[b]

### True Wisdom

[5]     Thus says the LORD:
Cursed is the man who trusts in human
    beings,
    who makes flesh his strength,
    whose heart turns away from the
    LORD.[c]
[6] He is like a barren bush in the wasteland
    that enjoys no change of season,
But stands in lava beds in the wilderness,
    a land, salty and uninhabited.
[7] Blessed are those who trust in the LORD;
    the LORD will be their trust.[d]
[8] They are like a tree planted beside the
    waters
    that stretches out its roots to the
    stream:
It does not fear heat when it comes,
    its leaves stay green;
In the year of drought it shows no distress,
    but still produces fruit.[e]
[9] More tortuous than anything is the
    human heart,
    beyond remedy; who can
    understand it?
[10] I, the LORD, explore the mind
    and test the heart,
Giving to all according to their ways,
    according to the fruit of their deeds.[f]
[11] A partridge that broods but does not hatch
    are those who acquire wealth unjustly:
In midlife it will desert them;
    in the end they are only fools.[g]

### The Source of Life

[12] A throne of glory, exalted from the
    beginning,
    such is our holy place.[h]

[13] O Hope of Israel, LORD!
    all who forsake you shall be put to
    shame;
The rebels shall be enrolled in the
    netherworld;
    they have forsaken the LORD, source
    of living waters.[i]

### Prayer for Vengeance

[14] Heal me, LORD, that I may be healed;
    save me, that I may be saved,
    for you are my praise.
[15] See how they say to me,
    "Where is the word of the LORD?
    Let it come to pass!"[j]
[16] Yet I did not press you to send disaster;
    the day without remedy I have not
    desired.
You know what passed my lips;
    it is present before you.
[17] Do not become a terror to me,
    you are my refuge in the day of
    disaster.[k]
[18] Let my persecutors be confounded—not
    me!
    let them be terrified—not me!
Bring upon them the day of disaster,
    crush them with double destruction.[l]

**Observance of the Sabbath.** [19]Thus said the
LORD to me: Go, stand at the Gate of Benjamin,*
where the kings of Judah enter and leave, and
at the other gates of Jerusalem.[m] [20]There say to
them: Hear the word of the LORD, you kings of
Judah, and all Judah, and all you inhabitants of
Jerusalem who enter these gates! [21]Thus says the
LORD: As you love your lives, take care not to
carry burdens on the sabbath, to bring them
in through the gates of Jerusalem.[n] [22]Bring no
burden from your homes on the sabbath. Do no
work whatever, but keep holy the sabbath day, as
I commanded your ancestors,[o] [23]though they did
not listen or give ear, but stiffened their necks
so they could not hear or take correction.[p] [24]If
you truly obey me—oracle of the LORD—and
carry no burden through the gates of this city on
the sabbath, keeping the sabbath day holy and
abstaining from all work on it,[q] [25]then, through
the gates of this city, kings who sit upon the
throne of David will continue to enter, riding in
their chariots or upon their horses, along with
their princes, and the people of Judah, and the
inhabitants of Jerusalem. This city will remain
inhabited forever.[r] [26]To it people will come from
the cities of Judah and the neighborhood of

---

*[17:19] **The Gate of Benjamin**: this gate, probably part of
the Temple area, is otherwise unknown.

---

i. [17:13] Jer 2:13.  j. [17:15] Is 5:19; 2 Pt 3:4.  k. [17:17] Jer
16:19.  l. [17:18] Jer 15:15; 18:20–23; Ps 35:5–6.  m. [17:19] Jer
7:2.  n. [17:21] Neh 13:15–19.  o. [17:22] Ex 20:8; 23:12.  p. [17:23]
Jer 5:3; 7:24.  q. [17:24] Is 58:14.  r. [17:25] Jer 22:4.

---

a. [17:1] Jb 19:24.  b. [17:4] Jer 5:19; Dt 32:22.  c. [17:5] Ps 146:2–3.
d. [17:7] Ps 1:3.  e. [17:8] Is 58:11.  f. [17:10] Jer 32:19; 1 Sm 16:7;
Eccl 12:14.  g. [17:11] Prv 13:11; Lk 12:20.  h. [17:12] Jer 14:21.

Jerusalem, from the land of Benjamin and from the Shephelah, from the hill country and the Negeb, to bring burnt offerings and sacrifices, grain offerings, incense, and thank offerings to the house of the Lord.⁵ ²⁷But if you do not obey me and keep holy the sabbath day, if you carry burdens and come through the gates of Jerusalem on the sabbath, I will set fire to its gates—a fire never to be extinguished—and it will consume the palaces of Jerusalem.ᵗ

## CHAPTER 18

**The Potter's Vessel.**˙ ¹This word came to Jeremiah from the Lord: ²Arise and go down to the potter's house; there you will hear my word. ³I went down to the potter's house and there he was, working at the wheel. ⁴Whenever the vessel of clay he was making turned out badly in his hand, he tried again, making another vessel of whatever sort he pleased.ᵘ ⁵Then the word of the Lord came to me: ⁶Can I not do to you, house of Israel, as this potter has done?—oracle of the Lord. Indeed, like clay in the hand of the potter, so are you in my hand, house of Israel.ᵛ ⁷ᵂAt one moment I may decree concerning a nation or kingdom that I will uproot and tear down and destroy it; ⁸but if that nation against whom I have decreed turns from its evil, then I will have a change of heart regarding the evil which I have decreed.ˣ ⁹At another moment, I may decree concerning a nation or kingdom that I will build up and plant it; ¹⁰but if that nation does what is evil in my eyes, refusing to obey my voice, then I will have a change of heart regarding the good with which I planned to bless it.ʸ

¹¹And now, tell this to the people of Judah and the inhabitants of Jerusalem: Thus says the Lord: Look, I am fashioning evil against you and making a plan. Return, all of you, from your evil way; reform your ways and your deeds.ᶻ ¹²But they will say, "No use! We will follow our own devices; each one of us will behave according to the stubbornness of our evil hearts!"ᵃ

### Unnatural Apostasy

¹³     Therefore thus says the Lord:
Ask among the nations—
who has ever heard the like?
Truly horrible things
virgin Israel has done!ᵇ
¹⁴ Does the snow of Lebanon†
desert the rocky heights?

Do the gushing waters dry up
that flow fresh down the mountains?
¹⁵ Yet my people have forgotten me:
they offer incense in vain.
They stumble off their paths,
the ways of old,
Traveling on bypaths,
not the beaten track.ᶜ
¹⁶ Their land shall be made a waste,
an object of endless hissing;‡
All passersby will be horrified,
shaking their heads.ᵈ
¹⁷ Like the east wind, I will scatter them
before their enemies;
I will show them my back, not my face,
in their day of disaster.ᵉ

**Another Prayer for Vengeance.** ¹⁸"Come," they said, "let us devise a plot against Jeremiah, for instruction will not perish from the priests, nor counsel from the wise, nor the word from the prophets. Come, let us destroy him by his own tongue. Let us pay careful attention to his every word."ᶠ

¹⁹ Pay attention to me, O Lord,
and listen to what my adversaries say.
²⁰ Must good be repaid with evil
that they should dig a pit to take my life?
Remember that I stood before you
to speak on their behalf,
to turn your wrath away from them.ᵍ
²¹ So now, give their children§ to famine,ʰ
deliver them to the power of the sword.
Let their wives be childless and widows;
let their husbands die of pestilence,
their youths be struck down by the sword in battle.
²² May cries be heard from their homes,
when suddenly you send plunderers against them.
For they have dug a pit to capture me,
they have hidden snares for my feet;
²³ But you, Lord, know
all their planning for my death.
Do not forgive their crime,
and their sin do not blot out from your sight!

---

*[18:1–12] The lesson of the potter is that God has the power to destroy or restore, changing his plans accordingly as these nations disobey him or fulfill his will. Cf. Jon 3:10.

†[18:14] **Lebanon**: here apparently including Mount Hermon, whose snow-capped peak can be seen from parts of Palestine all year round. The prophet contrasts the certainties of

nature with Israel's unnatural desertion of the Lord for idols (v. 15).

‡[18:16] **Hissing**: in some ancient Near Eastern cultures hissing was not only a sign of derision but a magical means of keeping demons away; people hissed in order to ward off danger, like whistling in a cemetery.

§[18:21] **Give their children**: often an extended family is meant, to be rewarded or punished as a unit.

---

s. [17:26] Jer 32:44.   t. [17:27] Ez 22:8.   u. [18:4] Rom 9:20–21.
v. [18:6] Wis 15:7; Is 45:9.   w. [18:7] Jer 1:10.   x. [18:8] Jer 26:3; Is 55:7; Ez 18:21, 27; Jon 3:10.   y. [18:10] Nm 14:22–23.   z. [18:11] Jer 7:3; 25:5; 35:15.   a. [18:12] Jer 2:25; 7:24.   b. [18:13] Jer 2:10–11; 5:30.

c. [18:15] Jer 2:13, 32.   d. [18:16] Jer 19:8; Lv 26:32; 1 Kgs 9:8.
e. [18:17] Prv 1:24–31.   f. [18:18] Jer 11:19; Ps 35:15–16.   g. [18:20] Ps 35:12.   h. [18:21] Ps 109:9–10.

Let them stumble before you,
in the time of your anger act against
them.[i]

## CHAPTER 19

**Symbol of the Potter's Flask.** [1]Thus said the
LORD: Go, buy a potter's earthenware flask.
Take along some of the elders of the people and
some of the priests, [2]and go out toward the Valley of Ben-hinnom, at the entrance of the Potsherd Gate;* there proclaim the words which I
will speak to you: [3]You shall say, Listen to the
word of the LORD, kings of Judah and inhabitants of Jerusalem: Thus says the LORD of hosts,
the God of Israel: I am going to bring such evil
upon this place that the ears of all who hear of
it will ring. [4]All because they have forsaken me
and profaned this place by burning incense to
other gods which neither they nor their ancestors knew; and because the kings of Judah have
filled this place with innocent blood,[j] [5]build-
ing high places for Baal to burn their children
in fire as offerings to Baal—something I never
considered or said or commanded.[k] [6]†Therefore,
days are coming—oracle of the LORD—when
this place will no longer be called Topheth, or
the Valley of Ben-hinnom, but rather, the Valley
of Slaughter.[l] [7]In this place I will foil the plan of
Judah and Jerusalem; I will make them fall by
the sword before their enemies, at the hand of
those who seek their lives. Their corpses I will
give as food to the birds of the sky and the beasts
of the earth.[m] [8]I will make this city a waste and
an object of hissing. Because of all its wounds,
every passerby will be horrified and hiss. [9]I will
have them eat the flesh of their sons and daughters; they shall eat one another's flesh during
the harsh siege under which their enemies and
those who seek their lives will confine them.[n]

[10]And you shall break the flask in the sight of
the men who went with you, [11]and say to them:
Thus says the LORD of hosts: Thus will I smash
this people and this city, as one smashes a clay
pot so that it cannot be repaired. And Topheth
shall be its burial place, for there will be no other
place for burial.[o] [12]Thus I will do to this place
and to its inhabitants—oracle of the LORD; I will
make this city like Topheth.[p] [13]And the houses of
Jerusalem and the houses of the kings of Judah
shall be defiled like the place of Topheth, all the
houses upon whose roofs they burnt incense to
the whole host of heaven and poured out libations to other gods.[q]

[14]When Jeremiah returned from Topheth,
where the LORD had sent him to prophesy, he
stood in the court of the house of the LORD and
said to all the people:[r] [15]Thus says the LORD of
hosts, the God of Israel: I will bring upon this
city all the evil I have spoken against it, because
they have become stubborn and have not
obeyed my words.[s]

## CHAPTER 20

[1]Now the priest Pashhur,[t] son of Immer, chief
officer in the house of the LORD,[‡] heard Jeremiah
prophesying these things. [2]So he struck the
prophet and put him in the stocks at the upper
Gate of Benjamin in the house of the LORD.[u]
[3]The next morning, after Pashhur had released
Jeremiah from the stocks, the prophet said to
him:[v] "Instead of Pashhur, the LORD names you
'Terror on every side.'[§] [4]For thus says the LORD:
Indeed, I will hand you over to terror, you and all
your friends. Your own eyes shall see them fall
by the sword of their enemies. All Judah I will
hand over to the power of the king of Babylon,[¶]
who shall take them captive to Babylon or strike
them down with the sword. [5]All the wealth of
this city, all its resources and its valuables, all the
treasures of the kings of Judah, I will hand over
to their enemies, who shall plunder it and carry
it away to Babylon.[w] [6]You, Pashhur, and all the
members of your household shall go into exile.
To Babylon you shall go; there you shall die and
be buried, you and all your friends, because you
have prophesied lies to them."[x]

### Jeremiah's Interior Crisis

[7]  You seduced me,** LORD, and I let myself
        be seduced;
    you were too strong for me, and you
        prevailed.
    All day long I am an object of laughter;
        everyone mocks me.
[8]  Whenever I speak, I must cry out,
        violence and outrage I proclaim;
    The word of the LORD has brought me
        reproach and derision all day long.
[9]  I say I will not mention him,
        I will no longer speak in his name.

---

‡[20:1] **Chief officer in the house of the LORD**: head
of the Temple police; cf. 29:26. By entering the Temple
court (19:14), Jeremiah had put himself under Pashhur's
jurisdiction.

§[20:3] **Terror on every side**: the name indicates the siege
that will beset Jerusalem.

¶[20:4] **Babylon**: mentioned here for the first time in
Jeremiah as the land of exile. The prophecy dates from after
605 B.C., when Nebuchadnezzar defeated Egypt and made
the Babylonian (Chaldean) empire dominant in Syria and
Palestine.

**[20:7] **You seduced me**: Jeremiah accuses the Lord of
having deceived him; cf. 15:18.

---

*[19:2] **Potsherd Gate**: perhaps in the south wall of Jerusalem, through which potsherds and other refuse were thrown
into the Valley of Ben-hinnom.

†[19:6] Cf. note on 7:31.

---

i. [18:23] Neh 4:5; Ps 35:4; 37:32–33.  j. [19:4] Jer 1:16; 2 Kgs 21:16;
24:4.  k. [19:5] Jer 7:31–32; 32:35.  l. [19:6] Jer 7:32.  m. [19:7]
Jer 7:33.  n. [19:9] Lv 26:29.  o. [19:11] Jer 7:32.  p. [19:12] 2 Kgs
23:10.  q. [19:13] Jer 32:29.

r. [19:14] Jer 26:2.  s. [19:15] Jer 7:26; Prv 29:1.  t. [20:1] Jer
21:1.  u. [20:2] Jer 29:26.  v. [20:3] Jer 6:25.  w. [20:5] 2 Kgs
20:17; 24:12–16.  x. [20:6] Jer 14:13–14; 28:15.

But then it is as if fire is burning in my
    heart,
    imprisoned in my bones;
I grow weary holding back,
    I cannot!*y*

10 Yes, I hear the whisperings of many:
    "Terror on every side!
    Denounce! let us denounce him!"
All those who were my friends
    are on the watch for any misstep of
      mine.
"Perhaps he can be tricked; then we will
      prevail,
    and take our revenge on him."*z*

11 But the LORD is with me, like a mighty
      champion:
    my persecutors will stumble, they
      will not prevail.
In their failure they will be put to utter
      shame,
    to lasting, unforgettable confusion.*a*

12 LORD of hosts, you test the just,
    you see mind and heart,
Let me see the vengeance you take on
      them,
    for to you I have entrusted my
      cause.*b*

13 Sing to the LORD,
    praise the LORD,
For he has rescued the life of the poor
    from the power of the evildoers!*c*

14 Cursed be the day*
    on which I was born!
May the day my mother gave me birth
    never be blessed!*d*

15 Cursed be the one who brought the news
    to my father,
"A child, a son, has been born to you!"
    filling him with great joy.

16 Let that man be like the cities
    which the LORD relentlessly
      overthrew;
Let him hear war cries in the morning,
    battle alarms at noonday,*e*

17 because he did not kill me in the
      womb!
Then my mother would have been my
      grave,
    her womb confining me forever.*f*

18 Why did I come forth from the womb,
    to see sorrow and pain,
    to end my days in shame?*g*

---

*\*[20:14–18] Deception, sorrow and terror have brought
the prophet to the point of despair; nevertheless he maintains
confidence in God (vv. 11–13); cf. Jb 3:3–12.*

*y. [20:9] Jer 6:11; Jb 32:18.  z. [20:10] Jb 19:19; Ps 31:13; Lk
20:20.  a. [20:11] Jer 1:8; 15:20.  b. [20:12] Jer 11:20.  c. [20:13]
Ps 35:9–10; 109:30–31.  d. [20:14] Jer 15:10; Jb 3:1–10;
10:18.  e. [20:16] Gn 19:25; Is 13:19.  f. [20:17] Jb 3:10–11;
10:19.  g. [20:18] Jb 14:1.*

---

## III. ORACLES IN THE LAST YEARS OF JERUSALEM

### CHAPTER 21

**Fate of Zedekiah and Jerusalem.** ¹The word
which came to Jeremiah from the LORD when
King Zedekiah† sent Pashhur, son of Malchiah,
and the priest Zephaniah, son of Maaseiah, to
him with this request: ²Inquire for us of the
LORD, because Nebuchadnezzar, king of Babylon, is attacking us. Perhaps the LORD will act
for us in accord with his wonderful works by
making him withdraw from us. ³But Jeremiah
answered them: This is what you shall report
to Zedekiah: ⁴Thus says the LORD, the God of
Israel: I will turn against you the weapons with
which you are fighting the king of Babylon and
the Chaldeans who besiege you outside the
walls. These weapons I will pile up in the midst
of this city,*h* ⁵and I myself will fight against you
with outstretched hand and mighty arm, in
anger, wrath, and great rage!*i* ⁶I will strike down
the inhabitants of this city, human being and
beast; they shall die in a great pestilence.*j* ⁷After
that—oracle of the LORD—I will hand over
Zedekiah, king of Judah, and his ministers and
the people in this city who survive pestilence,
sword, and famine, to Nebuchadnezzar, king of
Babylon, to their enemies and those who seek
their lives. He shall strike them down with the
edge of the sword, without quarter, without
mercy or compassion.*k* ⁸And to this people you
shall say: Thus says the LORD: See, I am giving
you a choice between the way to life and the way
to death.*l* ⁹Whoever remains in this city shall
die by the sword or famine or pestilence. But
whoever leaves and surrenders to the Chaldeans
who are besieging you shall live and escape with
his life. ¹⁰I have set my face against this city,
for evil and not for good—oracle of the LORD.
It shall be given into the power of the king of
Babylon who shall set it on fire.‡

### Oracles Regarding the Kings§

11 To the royal house of Judah:
    Hear the word of the LORD,
12     house of David!

---

*†[21:1] **Zedekiah:** brother of Jehoiakim, appointed king by
Nebuchadnezzar after he had carried Jehoiachin away to captivity (2 Kgs 24:17). **Pashhur:** different from the one in 20:1–3
but also one of Jeremiah's enemies; cf. 38:1, 4.*

*‡[21:10] Jeremiah consistently pointed out the uselessness
of resistance to Babylon, since the Lord had delivered Judah
to Nebuchadnezzar (27:6). Because of this the prophet was
denounced and imprisoned as a traitor (37:13–14).*

*§[21:11–23:8] This section contains an editor's collec-
tion of Jeremiah's oracles against the kings of Judah. They
are placed in the chronological order of the kings, and are
prefaced by oracles against the kings of Judah in general
(21:11–22:9).*

*h. [21:4] Jer 37:8–10.  i. [21:5] Is 63:10; Lam 2:4–5.  j. [21:6] Jer
16:4.  k. [21:7] Jer 24:8–10; Dt 28:49–50.  l. [21:8] Jer 21:9; Dt
30:15, 19.*

Thus says the Lord:
Each morning dispense justice,
   rescue the oppressed from the hand
     of the oppressor,
Or my fury will break out like fire
   and burn with no one to quench it
     because of your evil deeds.[m]

13 Beware! I am against you, Ruler of the
    Valley,
   Rock of the Plain*—oracle of the
    Lord.
You say, "Who will attack us,
   who can storm our defenses?"
14 I will punish you—oracle of the Lord—
   as your deeds deserve!
I will kindle a fire in its forest[†]
   that shall devour all its
    surroundings.[n]

## CHAPTER 22

¹Thus says the Lord: Go down to the palace of the king of Judah and there deliver this word: ²You shall say: Listen to the word of the Lord, king of Judah, who sit on the throne of David, you, your ministers, and your people who enter by these gates![o] ³Thus says the Lord: Do what is right and just. Rescue the victims from the hand of their oppressors. Do not wrong or oppress the resident alien, the orphan, or the widow, and do not shed innocent blood in this place.[p] ⁴If you carry out these commands, kings who succeed to the throne of David will continue to enter the gates of this house, riding in chariots or mounted on horses, with their ministers, and their people. ⁵But if you do not obey these commands, I swear by myself—oracle of the Lord: this house shall become rubble. ⁶For thus says the Lord concerning the house of the king of Judah:

Though you be to me like Gilead,
   like the peak of Lebanon,
I swear I shall turn you into a waste,
   with cities uninhabited.
7 Against you I will send destroyers,
   each with their tools;
They shall cut down your choice cedars,
   and cast them into the fire.[q]

⁸Many nations will pass by this city and ask one another: "Why has the Lord done this to so great a city?"[r] ⁹And they will be told: "Because

they have deserted their covenant with the Lord, their God, by worshiping and serving other gods."[s]

### Jehoahaz

10 Do not weep for him who is dead,[‡]
   nor mourn for him!
Weep rather for him who is going away;
   never again to see
   the land of his birth.[t]

¹¹Thus says the Lord concerning Shallum,[§] son of Josiah, king of Judah, his father's successor, who left this place: He shall never return, ¹²but in the place where they exiled him, there he shall die; he shall never see this land again.

### Jehoiakim

13 Woe to him who builds his house on
    wrongdoing,
   his roof-chambers on injustice;
Who works his neighbors without pay,[¶]
   and gives them no wages.[u]
14 Who says, "I will build myself a spacious
    house,
   with airy rooms,"
Who cuts out windows for it,
   panels it with cedar,
   and paints it with vermilion.
15 Must you prove your rank among kings[**]
   by competing with them in cedar?
Did not your father eat and drink,
   And act justly and righteously?
   Then he prospered.[v]
16 Because he dispensed justice to the weak
    and the poor,
   he prospered.
Is this not to know me?—
   oracle of the Lord.[w]
17 But your eyes and heart are set on nothing
    except your own gain,
On shedding innocent blood
   and practicing oppression and
    extortion.[x]

---

‡[22:10] **Him who is dead**: Josiah. His successor, Jehoahaz, was deported by Pharaoh Neco to Egypt, where he died (2 Kgs 23:33–34).

§[22:11] **Shallum**: i.e., Jehoahaz; cf. 1 Chr 3:15. This may have been his name at birth, in which case Jehoahaz would have been his throne name.

¶[22:13] **Without pay**: either by forced labor in public works, or by defrauding the workers. Despite the impoverishment caused in Judah by the payment of foreign tribute, Jehoiakim embarked on a building program in Jerusalem (v. 14); cedar was an expensive building material which had to be imported. Social injustice is the cause of much of the prophetic condemnation of the kings (v. 17).

**[22:15–16] The rule of Josiah, Jehoiakim's father, shows that authentic kingship is rooted in knowledge of the Lord and creates a society in which the most disadvantaged can expect and receive justice.

---

*[21:13] **Ruler of the Valley, Rock of the Plain**: Mount Zion, surrounded by valleys, was regarded by the royal house as impregnable. Despite this natural fortification, God derides it as no more than a rock rising from the plain, useless against the attack of his fury.

†[21:14] **Its forest**: probably the royal palace, built of cedar wood; cf. 22:14; in 1 Kgs 7:2 the palace is called "the house of the forest of Lebanon."

---

m. [21:12] Jer 4:4; 22:3; Zec 7:9.  n. [21:14] 2 Kgs 25:9; 2 Chr 36:19.  o. [22:2] Jer 17:20.  p. [22:3] Jer 21:12; Ex 22:21–24; Dt 24:17.  q. [22:7] Jer 21:14.  r. [22:8] Dt 29:24–27.

s. [22:9] Jer 19:4; 40:2–3.  t. [22:10] 2 Chr 35:23–25.  u. [22:13] Lv 19:13; Dt 24:14; Hb 2:9, 12.  v. [22:15] 2 Sm 5:11; 7:2; 2 Kgs 23:25.  w. [22:16] Prv 31:9.  x. [22:17] Ez 22:13, 27.

¹⁸Therefore, thus says the LORD concerning Jehoiakim, son of Josiah, king of Judah:

They shall not lament him,
"Alas! my brother"; "Alas! sister.'"
They shall not lament him,
"Alas, Lord! alas, Majesty!"ʸ
¹⁹ The burial of a donkey† he shall be given,
dragged forth and cast out
beyond the gates of Jerusalem.ᶻ

### Jeconiah

²⁰ Climb Lebanon and cry out,‡
in Bashan lift up your voice;
Cry out from Abarim,
for all your lovers are crushed.ᵃ
²¹ I spoke to you when you were secure,
but you answered, "I will not listen."
This has been your way from your youth,
not to listen to my voice.
²² The wind shall shepherd all your
shepherds,
your lovers shall go into exile.
Surely then you shall be ashamed and
confounded
because of all your wickedness.
²³ You who dwell on Lebanon,
who nest in the cedars,
How you shall groan when pains come
upon you,
like the pangs of a woman in
childbirth!

²⁴As I live—oracle of the LORD—even if you, Coniah,§ son of Jehoiakim, king of Judah, were a signet ringᵇ on my right hand, I would snatch you off. ²⁵I will hand you over to those who seek your life, to those you dread: Nebuchadnezzar, king of Babylon, and the Chaldeans.ᶜ ²⁶I will cast

you out, you and the mother who bore you,ᵉ into a land different from the land of your birth; and there you will die;ᵈ ²⁷Neither shall return to the land for which they yearn.ᵉ

²⁸ Is this man Coniah a thing despised, to be
broken,
a vessel that no one wants?
Why are he and his offspring cast out?
why thrown into a land they do not
know?
²⁹ O land, land, land,
hear the word of the LORD—
³⁰ Thus says the LORD:
ᶠ Write this man down as childless,**
a man who will never prosper in
his life!
Nor shall any of his descendants prosper,
to sit upon the throne of David,
to rule again over Judah.

## CHAPTER 23

**A Just Shepherd.**†† ¹Woe to the shepherds who destroy and scatter the flock of my pasture— oracle of the LORD. ²Therefore, thus says the LORD, the God of Israel, against the shepherds who shepherd my people: You have scattered my sheep and driven them away. You have not cared for them, but I will take care to punish your evil deeds.ʰ ³I myself will gather the remnant of my flock from all the lands to which I have banished them and bring them back to their folds; there they shall be fruitful and multiply.ⁱ ⁴I will raise up shepherds for them who will shepherd them so that they need no longer fear or be terrified; none shall be missing—oracle of the LORD.ʲ

⁵ See, days are coming—oracle of the LORD—
when I will raise up a righteous
branch for David;

---

*[22:18] **"Alas! my brother"; "Alas! sister"**: customary cries of mourning.

†[22:19] **The burial of a donkey**: no burial at all, except to be cast outside the city as refuse. This prophecy describes the popular feeling toward Jehoiakim rather than the actual circumstances of his burial. According to 2 Kgs 24:5 he was buried with his ancestors in Jerusalem.

‡[22:20–23] The prophet first bids Jerusalem to scale Lebanon, Bashan, and Abarim, i.e., the highest surrounding mountains to the north, northeast, and southeast, and gaze on the ruin of its lovers, i.e., the false leaders of Judah, called its shepherds (v. 22); cf. 2:8. Jerusalem still stands (v. 23), apparently as secure as the heights of Lebanon, but destruction is to follow (cf. v. 6).

§[22:24] **Coniah**: a shortened form of Jeconiah, the name Jeremiah gives King Jehoiachin (cf. 24:1). **A signet ring**: the seal used by kings and other powerful figures—a symbol of their power and status—mounted in a ring worn constantly on the hand. The Lord says that even were Jehoiachin such a precious possession, he would reject him. Hg 2:23 uses the same imagery to signal the restoration of Zerubbabel. The words in Jer 22:24–30 date from the short three-month reign of Jehoiachin, before he was deported by Nebuchadnezzar.

¶[22:26] **You and the mother who bore you**: the queen mother held a special position in the monarchy of Judah, and in the Books of Kings she is invariably mentioned by name along with the king (1 Kgs 15:2; 2 Kgs 18:2). Jehoiachin did indeed die in Babylon.

**[22:30] **Childless**: Jehoiachin is considered childless because none of his seven sons became king. His grandson Zerubbabel presided for a time over the Judahite community after the return from exile, but not as king. According to Ezekiel, whose oracles are dated by Jehoiachin's fictitious regnal years, the people expected Jehoiachin to return. Jeremiah's prophecy dispels this hope, despite the words of Hananiah (28:4).

††[23:1–8] With the false rulers (shepherds) who have governed his people the Lord contrasts himself, the true shepherd, who will in the times of restoration appoint worthy rulers (vv. 1–4). He will provide a new king from David's line who will rule justly, fulfilling royal ideals (vv. 5, 6). "The Lord our justice" is an ironic wordplay on the name of the weak King Zedekiah ("The Lord is justice"). Unlike Zedekiah, the future king will be true to the name he bears. Verses 7–8 may have been added during the exile.

---

y. [22:18] Jer 16:4–7; 1 Kgs 13:30.   z. [22:19] Jer 36:30.   a. [22:20] Jer 30:14–15; Dt 32:49.   b. [22:24] Hg 2:23.   c. [22:25] Jer 21:7; 34:20.

d. [22:26] 2 Kgs 24:15.   e. [22:27] Jer 44:14.   f. [22:30] Jer 36:30; 1 Chr 3:16–17; Mt 1:12.   g. [23:1] Jer 22:22.   h. [23:2] Ez 34:4–10; Zec 11:16–17.   i. [23:3] Jer 29:14; 32:37.   j. [23:4] Jer 3:15; Ez 34:11–12.

As king he shall reign and govern wisely,
    he shall do what is just and right in
      the land.[k]
6  In his days Judah shall be saved,
    Israel shall dwell in security.
    This is the name to be given him:
      "The LORD our justice."[l]

[7m]Therefore, the days are coming—oracle of
the LORD—when they shall no longer say, "As
the LORD lives, who brought the Israelites out
of the land of Egypt"; [8]but rather, "As the LORD
lives, who brought the descendants of the house
of Israel up from the land of the north"—and
from all the lands to which I banished them;
they shall again live on their own soil.

### The False Prophets[*]

9  Concerning the prophets:
My heart is broken within me,
    all my bones tremble;
I am like a drunk,
    like one overcome by wine,
Because of the LORD,
    because of his holy words.
10  The land is filled with adulterers;
    because of the curse the land
      mourns,
    the pastures of the wilderness are
      withered.[n]
Theirs is an evil course,
    theirs is unjust power.
11  Both prophet and priest are godless!
    In my very house I find their
      wickedness—
    oracle of the LORD.[o]
12  Hence their way shall become for them
      slippery ground.
Into the darkness they shall be driven,
    and fall headlong;
For I will bring disaster upon them,
    the year of their punishment—
      oracle of the LORD.[p]
13  Among Samaria's prophets
    I saw something unseemly:
They prophesied by Baal
    and led my people Israel astray.[q]
14  But among Jerusalem's prophets
    I saw something more shocking:
Adultery, walking in deception,[†]
    strengthening the power of the
      wicked,
    so that no one turns from evil;

To me they are all like Sodom,
    its inhabitants like Gomorrah.[r]

15Therefore, thus says the LORD of hosts
against the prophets:

Look, I will give them wormwood to eat,
    and poisoned water to drink;
For from Jerusalem's prophets
    ungodliness has gone forth into the
      whole land.[s]
16  Thus says the LORD of hosts:
Do not listen to the words of your
      prophets,
    who fill you with emptiness;
They speak visions from their own fancy,
    not from the mouth of the LORD.[t]
17  They say to those who despise the word of
      the LORD,[‡]
    "Peace shall be yours";
And to everyone who walks in hardness
      of heart,
    "No evil shall overtake you."[u]
18  Now, who has stood in the council of the
      LORD,
    to see him and to hear his word?
    Who has heeded his word so as to
      announce it?[v]
19  See, the storm of the LORD!
    His wrath breaks forth
In a whirling storm
    that bursts upon the heads of the
      wicked.[w]
20  The anger of the LORD shall not abate
    until he has carried out completely
      the decisions of his heart.
In days to come
    you will understand fully.
21  I did not send these prophets,
    yet they ran;
I did not speak to them,
    yet they prophesied.[x]
22  Had they stood in my council,
    they would have proclaimed my
      words to my people,
They would have brought them back from
      their evil ways
    and from their wicked deeds.
23  Am I a God near at hand only—oracle of
      the LORD—[y]
    and not a God far off?[s]

---

‡[23:17–20] Not only are the false prophets personally
immoral, but they encourage immorality by prophesying
good for evildoers. The true prophet, on the other hand, sees
the inevitable consequences of evil behavior.

§[23:23–24] **Near at hand only . . . far off:** a divine claim
that no one can hide from God and that God is aware of all
that happens.

---

*[23:9–40] After the collection of oracles against the kings,
the editor of the book placed this collection of oracles against
the false prophets. With them are associated the priests, for
both have betrayed their trust as instructors in the ways of the
Lord; cf. 2:8; 4:9; 6:13–14.

†[23:14] Cf. note on 13:25.

---

k. [23:5] Jer 33:14–16; Is 4:2; 9:5–6; 11:1–5.  l. [23:6] Dn 9:24.
m. [23:7–8] Jer 16:14–15.  n. [23:10] Jer 4:22; 5:7–8; 9:2, 10.
o. [23:11] Jer 6:13.  p. [23:12] Ps 35:6.  q. [23:13] 1 Kgs 18:19.

r. [23:14] Jer 29:21–23; Is 1:9–10.  s. [23:15] Jer 8:14; 9:14.
t. [23:16] Jer 14:14.  u. [23:17] Jer 5:12; Ez 13:10; Mi 3:11; Zec
10:2.  v. [23:18] Jb 15:8; Is 40:13; 1 Cor 2:16.  w. [23:19] Jer 30:23.
x. [23:21] Jer 29:9.  y. [23:23] Jer 16:17; Ps 139:8.

24 Can anyone hide in secret
                without my seeing them?—oracle of
                the LORD.
    Do I not fill
                heaven and earth?—oracle of the
                LORD.

25I have heard the prophets who prophesy lies in my name say, "I had a dream! I had a dream!" 26How long? Will the hearts of the prophets who prophesy lies and their own deceitful fancies ever turn back? 27By the dreams they tell each other, they plan to make my people forget my name, just as their ancestors forgot my name for Baal.z 28Let the prophets who have dreams tell their dreams; let those who have my word speak my word truthfully!

    What has straw to do with wheat?*
                —oracle of the LORD.a
29  Is not my word like fire—oracle of the
                LORD—
                like a hammer shattering rock?

30Therefore I am against the prophets—oracle of the LORD—those who steal my words from each other.b 31Yes, I am against the prophets—oracle of the LORD—those who compose their own speeches and call them oracles. 32Yes, I am against the prophets who tell lying dreams—oracle of the LORD—those who lead my people astray by recounting their reckless lies. It was not I who sent them or commanded them; they do this people no good at all—oracle of the LORD.c

33†And when this people or a prophet or a priest asks you, "What is the burden of the LORD?" you shall answer, "You are the burden, and I cast you off"—oracle of the LORD. 34If a prophet or a priest or anyone else mentions "the burden of the LORD," I will punish that man and his household. 35Thus you shall ask, when speaking to one another, "What answer did the LORD give?" or "What did the LORD say?" 36But "the burden of the LORD" you shall mention no more. For each of you, your own word becomes the burden so that you pervert the words of the living God, the LORD of hosts, our God. 37Thus shall you ask the prophet, "What answer did the LORD give?" or "What did the LORD say?" 38But if you ask about "the burden of the LORD," then thus says the LORD: Because you use this phrase, "the burden of the LORD," though I forbade you

to use it, 39therefore I will lift you on high and cast you from my presence, you and the city which I gave to you and your ancestors. 40And I will bring upon you eternal reproach, eternal shame, never to be forgotten.d

## CHAPTER 24
**The Two Baskets of Figs.**‡ 1The LORD showed me two baskets of figs placed before the temple of the LORD.e This was after Nebuchadnezzar, king of Babylon, had exiled from Jerusalem Jeconiah,§ son of Jehoiakim, king of Judah, and the princes of Judah, the artisans and smiths, and brought them to Babylon. 2One basket contained excellent figs, those that ripen early. But the other basket contained very bad figs, so bad they could not be eaten. 3Then the LORD said to me: What do you see, Jeremiah?f "Figs," I replied; "the good ones are very good, but the bad ones very bad, so bad they cannot be eaten." 4Thereupon this word of the LORD came to me: 5Thus says the LORD, the God of Israel: Like these good figs, I will also regard with favor Judah's exiles whom I sent away from this place into the land of the Chaldeans.g 6I will look after them for good and bring them back to this land, to build them up, not tear them down; to plant them, not uproot them.h 7I will give them a heart to know me, that I am the LORD. They shall be my people and I will be their God, for they shall return to me with their whole heart.i 8But like the figs that are bad, so bad they cannot be eaten—yes, thus says the LORD—even so will I treat Zedekiah, king of Judah, and his princes, the remnant of Jerusalem remaining in this land and those who have settled in the land of Egypt.j 9I will make them an object of horror to all the kingdoms of the earth, a reproach and a byword, a taunt and a curse, in all the places to which I will drive them.k 10I will send upon them sword, famine, and pestilence, until they have disappeared from the land which I gave them and their ancestors.l

## CHAPTER 25
**Seventy Years of Exile.** 1The word that came to Jeremiah concerning all the people of Judah, in the fourth year of Jehoiakim,¶ son of Josiah, king

---

‡[24:1–10] For Jeremiah, as for Ezekiel, no good could be expected from the people who had been left in Judah under Zedekiah or who had fled into Egypt; a future might be expected only for those who would pass through the purifying experience of the exile to form the new Israel.

§[24:1] **Jeconiah:** alternative form of Jehoiachin (cf. note on 22:24).

¶[25:1–14] **The fourth year of Jehoiakim:** 605 B.C. Officially, the first year of Nebuchadnezzar began the following year; but as early as his victory over Egypt at Carchemish in 605, Nebuchadnezzar wielded dominant power in the Near East. Jeremiah saw in him the fulfillment of his prophecy of

---

*[23:28–29] **Straw . . . wheat:** a contrast between false and true prophecy. True prophecy is also like fire (cf. 5:14; 20:9), producing violent results (v. 29); Jeremiah's own life is a testimony of this.

†[23:33–40] A wordplay on *massa',* which means both "oracle" (usually of woe) and "burden." In vv. 34–40 the word *massa'* itself is forbidden to the people under the meaning of a divine oracle.

---

z. [23:27]  Jgs 3:7; 8:33.  a. [23:28]  Nm 12:6.  b. [23:30]  Dt 18:20.  c. [23:32]  Jer 28:15–17.

d. [23:40] Jer 20:11.  e. [24:1] Am 8:1–2.  f. [24:3] Jer 1:11.  g. [24:5] Jer 29:11; Lv 26:44–45.  h. [24:6] Jer 12:15; Am 9:15.  i. [24:7] Jer 30:22; 31:1; 32:37; Bar 2:31.  j. [24:8] Jer 29:18.  k. [24:9] Jer 15:4; Dt 28:37.  l. [24:10] Jer 14:12.

of Judah (the first year of Nebuchadnezzar, king of Babylon).<sup>m</sup> <sup>2</sup>This word the prophet Jeremiah spoke to all the people of Judah and all the inhabitants of Jerusalem: <sup>3</sup>Since the thirteenth year of Josiah, son of Amon, king of Judah, to this day—that is, twenty-three years—the word of the LORD has come to me and I spoke to you untiringly, but you would not listen.<sup>n</sup> <sup>4</sup>The LORD kept sending you all his servants the prophets,<sup>o</sup> but you refused to listen or pay attention <sup>5</sup>to this message: Turn back, each of you, from your evil way and from your evil deeds; then you shall remain in the land which the LORD gave you and your ancestors, from of old and forever. <sup>6</sup>Do not follow other gods to serve and bow down to them; do not provoke me with the works of your hands, or I will bring evil upon you.<sup>p</sup> <sup>7</sup>But you would not listen to me—oracle of the LORD— and so you provoked me with the works of your hands to your own harm.<sup>q</sup> <sup>8</sup>Hence, thus says the LORD of hosts: Since you would not listen to my words, <sup>9</sup>I am about to send for and fetch all the tribes from the north—oracle of the LORD—and I will send for Nebuchadnezzar, king of Babylon, my servant; I will bring them against this land, its inhabitants, and all these neighboring nations. I will doom them, making them an object of horror, of hissing, of everlasting reproach.<sup>r</sup> <sup>10</sup>Among them I will put to an end the song of joy and the song of gladness, the voice of the bridegroom and the voice of the bride, the sound of the millstone and the light of the lamp. <sup>11</sup>This whole land shall be a ruin and a waste. Seventy years these nations shall serve the king of Babylon;<sup>s</sup> <sup>12</sup>but when the seventy years have elapsed, I will punish the king of Babylon and that nation and the land of the Chaldeans for their guilt—oracle of the LORD. Their land I will turn into everlasting waste.<sup>t</sup> <sup>13</sup>Against that land I will fulfill all the words I have spoken against it, all that is written in this book, which Jeremiah prophesied against all the nations. <sup>14</sup>They also shall serve many nations and great kings, and thus I will repay them according to their own deeds and according to the works of their hands.<sup>u</sup>

**The Cup of Judgment on the Nations.** <sup>15*</sup>For thus said the LORD, the God of Israel, to me: Take this cup of the wine of wrath<sup>†</sup> from my hand and have all the nations to whom I will send you drink it.<sup>v</sup> <sup>16</sup>They shall drink, and retch, and go mad, because of the sword I will send among them.<sup>w</sup> <sup>17</sup>I took the cup from the hand of the LORD and gave it as drink to all the nations to whom the LORD sent me: <sup>18</sup>to Jerusalem, the cities of Judah, its kings and princes, to make them a ruin and a waste, an object of hissing and cursing, as they are today; <sup>19</sup>to Pharaoh, king of Egypt, and his servants, princes, all his people <sup>20</sup>and those of mixed ancestry; all the kings of the land of Uz;<sup>‡</sup> all the kings of the land of the Philistines: Ashkelon, Gaza, Ekron, and the remnant of Ashdod; <sup>21</sup>Edom, Moab, and the Ammonites; <sup>22</sup>all the kings of Tyre, of Sidon, and of the shores beyond the sea;<sup>§</sup> <sup>23</sup>Dedan and Tema and Buz,<sup>¶</sup> all the desert dwellers who shave their temples; <sup>24</sup>all the kings of Arabia; <sup>25</sup>all the kings of Zimri, of Elam, of the Medes; <sup>26</sup>all the kings of the north, near and far, one after the other; all the kingdoms upon the face of the earth and after them the king of Sheshach<sup>**</sup> shall drink.

<sup>27</sup>Tell them: Thus says the LORD of hosts, the God of Israel: Drink! Get drunk and vomit! Fall, never to rise, before the sword that I will send among you!<sup>x</sup> <sup>28</sup>If they refuse to take the cup from your hand and drink, say to them: Thus says the LORD of hosts: You must drink!<sup>y</sup> <sup>29</sup>Now that I am inflicting evil on this city, called by my name, how can you possibly escape? You shall not escape! I am calling down the sword upon all the inhabitants of the earth—oracle of the LORD of hosts. <sup>30</sup>As for you, prophesy against them all these words and say to them:

> The LORD roars from on high,
>> from his holy dwelling he raises his voice;
> Mightily he roars over his sheepfold,
>> a shout like that of vintagers echoes<sup>z</sup>
>> over all the inhabitants of the earth.
> <sup>31</sup> The uproar spreads
>> to the end of the earth;
> For the LORD has an indictment against the nations,
>> he enters into judgment against all flesh:
> The wicked shall be given to the sword—
>> oracle of the LORD.
> <sup>32</sup> Thus says the LORD of hosts:
> Look! disaster stalks
>> nation after nation;
> A violent storm surges
>> from the recesses of the earth.

---

the enemy to come from the north (cf. 1:13; 6:22–24). In vv. 11–12 the prophecy of the seventy years' exile occurs for the first time; cf. 29:10. This number signifies that the present generation must die out; cf. forty in the exodus tradition (Nm 14:20–23).

\*[25:15–17] Jeremiah is a prophet to the nations (cf. 1:5) as well as to his own people. All the nations mentioned here appear again in the more extensive collection of Jeremiah's oracles against the nations in chaps. 46–51.

†[25:15] **Cup . . . wrath:** a metaphor for destruction that occurs often in the Old Testament (cf. Ps 11:6; 75:9; Hb 2:15–16; Ez 23:31–33, etc.).

‡[25:20] **Uz:** the homeland of legendary Job, in Edomite or Arabian territory.

§[25:22] **The shores beyond the sea:** Phoenician commercial colonies located throughout the Mediterranean world.

¶[25:23] **Dedan and Tema and Buz:** North Arabian tribes.

\*\*[25:26] **Sheshach:** a contrived word from the Hebrew letters of Babylon.

m. [25:1] Jer 36:1.    n. [25:3] Jer 1:2.    o. [25:4] 2 Chr 36:15.    p. [25:6] Jer 7:6–7.    q. [25:7] Jer 7:17–19.    r. [25:9] Jer 1:15; 43:10.    s. [25:11] Lv 26:32–35.    t. [25:12] Is 13:20–22.    u. [25:14] Jer 27:7; 50:9, 41–42; 51:6, 24.

v. [25:15] Rev 14:10.    w. [25:16] Jer 51:7.    x. [25:27] Ob 16. y. [25:28] Jer 49:12.    z. [25:30] Jer 51:14.

³³On that day, those whom the Lord has slain will be strewn from one end of the earth to the other. They will not be mourned, they will not be gathered, they will not be buried; they shall lie like dung upon the ground.ᵃ

³⁴ Howl, you shepherds, and wail!
    roll on the ground, leaders of the
       flock!
The time for your slaughter has come;
    like choice rams you shall fall.
³⁵ There is no flight for the shepherds,
    no escape for the leaders of the
       flock.ᵇ
³⁶ Listen! Wailing from the shepherds,
    howling from the leaders of the
       flock!
For the Lord lays waste their grazing
    place;
³⁷    desolate are the peaceful pastures,
    from the burning wrath of the Lord.
³⁸ Like a lion he leaves his lair,
    and their land is made desolate
By the sweeping sword,
    and the burning wrath of the Lord.ᶜ

### IV. THE TEMPLE SERMON

## CHAPTER 26

**Jeremiah Threatened with Death.** ¹In the beginning of the reign* of Jehoiakim, son of Josiah, king of Judah, this word came from the Lord: ²Thus says the Lord: Stand in the court of the house of the Lord and speak to the inhabitants of all the cities of Judah who come to worship in the house of the Lord; whatever I command you, tell them, and hold nothing back.ᵈ ³Perhaps they will listen and turn, all of them from their evil way, so that I may repent of the evil I plan to inflict upon them for their evil deeds.ᵉ ⁴Say to them: Thus says the Lord: If you do not obey me, by walking according to the law I set before you ⁵and listening to the words of my servants the prophets, whom I kept sending you, even though you do not listen to them,ᶠ ⁶I will treat this house like Shiloh, and make this city a curse for all the nations of the earth.ᵍ

⁷Now the priests, the prophets, and all the people heard Jeremiah speaking these words in the house of the Lord. ⁸When Jeremiah finished speaking all that the Lord commanded him to speak to all the people, then the priests, the prophets, and all the people laid hold of him, crying, "You must die! ⁹Why do you prophesy in

the name of the Lord: 'This house shall become like Shiloh,' and 'This city shall be desolate, without inhabitant'?" And all the people crowded around Jeremiah in the house of the Lord.

¹⁰When the princes of Judah heard about these things, they came up from the house of the king to the house of the Lord and convened at the New Gate of the house of the Lord. ¹¹The priests and prophets said to the princes and to all the people, "Sentence this man to death! He has prophesied against this city! You heard it with your own ears."ʰ ¹²Jeremiah said to the princes and all the people: "It was the Lord who sent me to prophesy against this house and city everything you have heard. ¹³Now, therefore, reform your ways and your deeds; listen to the voice of the Lord your God, so that the Lord will have a change of heart regarding the evil he has spoken against you.ⁱ ¹⁴As for me, I am in your hands; do with me what is good and right in your eyes. ¹⁵But you should certainly know that by putting me to death, you bring innocent blood on yourselves, on this city and its inhabitants. For in truth it was the Lord who sent me to you, to speak all these words for you to hear."

¹⁶Then the princes and all the people said to the priests and the prophets, "This man does not deserve a death sentence; it is in the name of the Lord, our God, that he speaks to us." ¹⁷At this, some of the elders of the land arose and said to the whole assembly of the people, ¹⁸"Micah of Moresheth† used to prophesy in the days of Hezekiah, king of Judah, and he said to all the people of Judah: Thus says the Lord of hosts:

Zion shall be plowed as a field,
    Jerusalem, a heap of ruins,
    and the temple mount,
    a forest ridge.ʲ

¹⁹Did Hezekiah, king of Judah, and all Judah condemn him to death? Did he not fear the Lord and entreat the favor of the Lord, so that the Lord had a change of heart regarding the evil he had spoken against them? We, however, are about to do great evil against ourselves."ᵏ **The Fate of Uriah.** ²⁰There was another man who used to prophesy in the name of the Lord, Uriah, son of Shemaiah, from Kiriath-jearim; he prophesied against this city and this land the same message as Jeremiah. ²¹When King Jehoiakim and all his officers and princes heard his words, the king sought to have him killed. But Uriah heard of it and fled in fear to Egypt. ²²Then King Jehoiakim sent Elnathan, son of Achbor, and others with him into Egypt, ²³and they brought Uriah out of Egypt and took him to Jehoiakim the king, who struck him down

---

*[26:1] **The beginning of the reign**: a technical expression for the time between a king's accession to the throne and the beginning of his first official (calendar) year as king. Jehoiakim's first regnal year was 608 B.C.

a. [25:33] Jer 8:2; 16:4, 6.  b. [25:35] Jer 32:4.  c. [25:38] Jer 4:7.
d. [26:2] Jer 7:2.  e. [26:3] Jer 18:3.  f. [26:5] Jer 25:4.  g. [26:6] Jer 7:12, 14.

†[26:18] **Micah of Moresheth**: the prophet Micah, who appears among the canonical minor prophets (cf. Mi 1:1).

h. [26:11] Jer 38:4.  i. [26:13] Jer 7:3.  j. [26:18] Mi 1:1; 3:12.
k. [26:19] 2 Chr 32:26.

with the sword and threw his corpse into the common burial ground. [24]But the hand of Ahikam, son of Shaphan,* protected Jeremiah, so they did not hand him over to the people to be put to death.

## V. CONTROVERSIES WITH THE FALSE PROPHETS[†]

### CHAPTER 27

**Serve Babylon or Perish.** [1]In the beginning of the reign of Zedekiah,[‡] son of Josiah, king of Judah, this word came to Jeremiah from the LORD: [2]The LORD said to me: Make for yourself thongs and yoke bars and put them on your shoulders. [3]Send them to the kings of Edom, Moab, the Ammonites, Tyre, and Sidon, through the ambassadors who have come to Jerusalem to Zedekiah, king of Judah,[§] [4]and command them to tell their lords: Thus says the LORD of hosts, the God of Israel, Thus shall you say to your lords: [5]It was I who made the earth, human being and beast on the face of the earth, by my great power, with my outstretched arm; and I can give them to whomever I think fit.[l] [6]Now I have given all these lands into the hand of Nebuchadnezzar, king of Babylon, my servant; even the wild animals I have given him to serve him.[m] [7]All nations shall serve him and his son and his grandson, until the time comes for him and his land; then many nations and great kings will enslave him.[n] [8]Meanwhile, the nation or the kingdom that will not serve him, Nebuchadnezzar, king of Babylon, or bend its neck under the yoke of the king of Babylon, I will punish that nation with sword, famine, and pestilence—oracle of the LORD—until I finish them by his hand.[o]

[9]You, however, must not listen to your prophets,[¶] to your diviners and dreamers, to your soothsayers and sorcerers, who say to you, "Do not serve the king of Babylon."[p] [10]For they prophesy lies to you, so as to drive you far from your land, making me banish you so that you

perish.[q] [11]The people that bends the neck to the yoke of the king of Babylon to serve him, I will leave in peace on its own land—oracle of the LORD—to cultivate it and dwell on it.[r]

[12]To Zedekiah, king of Judah, I spoke the same words: Bend your necks to the yoke of the king of Babylon; serve him and his people, so that you may live.[s] [13]Why should you and your people die by sword, famine, and pestilence, in accordance with the word the LORD has spoken to the nation that will not serve the king of Babylon?[t] [14]Do not listen to the words of the prophets who say to you, "Do not serve the king of Babylon." They prophesy lies to you![u] [15]I did not send them—oracle of the LORD—but they prophesy falsely in my name. As a result I must banish you, and you will perish, you and the prophets who are prophesying to you.[v]

[16w]To the priests and to all the people I said: Thus says the LORD: Do not listen to the words of your prophets who prophesy to you: "The vessels of the house of the LORD will soon be brought back from Babylon," for they prophesy lies to you. [17]Do not listen to them! Serve the king of Babylon that you may live. Why should this city become rubble? [18]If they were prophets, if the word of the LORD were with them, then they would intercede with the LORD of hosts, that the vessels remaining in the house of the LORD and in the house of the king of Judah and in Jerusalem should not also go to Babylon. [19]For thus says the LORD of hosts concerning the pillars, the sea, the stands, and the rest of the vessels remaining in this city; [20]which Nebuchadnezzar, king of Babylon, did not take when he exiled Jeconiah, son of Jehoiakim, king of Judah, from Jerusalem to Babylon, along with all the nobles of Judah and Jerusalem— [21]thus says the LORD of hosts, the God of Israel, concerning the vessels remaining in the house of the LORD, in the house of the king of Judah, and in Jerusalem:[x] [22]To Babylon they shall go, and there they shall remain, until the day I look for them—oracle of the LORD; then I will bring them back and restore them to this place.

### CHAPTER 28

**The Two Yokes.** [1]That same year, in the beginning of the reign of Zedekiah, king of Judah, in the fifth month of the fourth year, Hananiah the prophet, son of Azzur, from Gibeon, said to me in the house of the LORD in the sight of the priests and all the people: [2]"Thus says the LORD of hosts, the God of Israel: I have broken the yoke of the king of Babylon. [3]Within two years I will restore to this place all the vessels of the house of the LORD which Nebuchadnezzar, king of Babylon, took from this place and carried

---

*[26:24] **Ahikam, son of Shaphan**: one of Josiah's officials (2 Kgs 22:12) and Jeremiah's friend. He was the father of Gedaliah, who was governor of Judah after Zedekiah's deportation (cf. Jer 39:14; 40:5–7).

†[27:1–29:32] A special collection of Jeremiah's prophecies dealing with false prophets. Stylistic peculiarities evident in the Hebrew suggest that these three chapters once existed as an independent work.

‡[27:1] **Zedekiah**: The Hebrew text actually has "Jehoiakim," but the content of the chapter indicates that Zedekiah is intended.

§[27:3] The time is the fourth year of Zedekiah, 594 B.C., the occasion of a delegation from the neighboring states, doubtless for the purpose of laying plans against Nebuchadnezzar.

¶[27:9] **Your prophets**: seers and diviners served non-Israelite kings just as the professional prophets served the kings of Judah.

---

l. [27:5] Jer 32:17.  m. [27:6] Jer 25:9; 43:10; Ez 30:21, 25.  n. [27:7] Jer 25:11; 2 Chr 36:20.  o. [27:8] Jer 25:9; Bar 2:22.  p. [27:9] Jer 29:8.

q. [27:10] Jer 14:13–16.  r. [27:11] Bar 2:21.  s. [27:12] Jer 38:17.  t. [27:13] Jer 24:8–10.  u. [27:14] Jer 14:14; 23:21.  v. [27:15] Jer 2:6.  w. [27:16] Jer 28:3; 2 Chr 36:7, 10, 18.  x. [27:21–22] 2 Kgs 25:13–17; 2 Chr 36:18, 22.

away to Babylon. ⁴And Jeconiah, son of Jehoiakim, king of Judah, and all the exiles of Judah who went to Babylon, I will bring back to this place—oracle of the LORD—for I will break the yoke of the king of Babylon."

⁵Jeremiah the prophet answered the prophet Hananiah in the sight of the priests and all the people standing in the house of the LORD, ⁶and said: Amen! thus may the LORD do! May the LORD fulfill your words that you have prophesied, by bringing back the vessels of the house of the LORD and all the exiles from Babylon to this place! ⁷But now, listen to the word I am about to speak in your hearing and the hearing of all the people. ⁸In the past, the prophets who came before you and me prophesied war, disaster, and pestilence against many lands and mighty kingdoms. ⁹But the prophet who prophesies peace is recognized as the prophet whom the LORD has truly sent only when his word comes to pass.ʸ

¹⁰Thereupon Hananiah the prophet took the yoke bar from the neck of Jeremiah the prophet and broke it. ¹¹He said in the sight of all the people: "Thus says the LORD: Like this, within two years I will break the yoke of Nebuchadnezzar, king of Babylon, from the neck of all the nations." At that, the prophet Jeremiah went on his way.

¹²After Hananiah the prophet had broken the yoke bar off the neck of the prophet Jeremiah, the word of the LORD came to Jeremiah: ¹³Go tell Hananiah this: Thus says the LORD: By breaking a wooden yoke bar, you make an iron yoke! ¹⁴For thus says the LORD of hosts, the God of Israel: A yoke of iron I have placed on the necks of all these nations serving Nebuchadnezzar, king of Babylon, and they shall serve him; even the wild animals I have given him.ᶻ ¹⁵And Jeremiah the prophet said to Hananiah the prophet: Listen to this, Hananiah! The LORD has not sent you, and you have led this people to rely on deception. ¹⁶For this, says the LORD, I am sending you from the face of the earth; this very year you shall die, because you have preached rebellion against the LORD.ᵃ ¹⁷Hananiah the prophet died in that year, in the seventh month.

## CHAPTER 29

**Letter to the Exiles in Babylon.** ¹These are the words of the scroll which Jeremiah the prophet sent from Jerusalem to the remaining elders among the exiles, to the priests, the prophets, and all the people whom Nebuchadnezzar exiled from Jerusalem to Babylon. ²This was after King Jeconiah and the queen mother, the court officials, the princes of Judah and Jerusalem, the artisans and smiths had left Jerusalem.ᵇ

³Delivered in Babylon by Elasah,⁎ son of Shaphan, and by Gemariah, son of Hilkiah, whom Zedekiah, king of Judah, sent to the king of Babylon, the letter read:

⁴Thus says the LORD of hosts, the God of Israel, to all the exiles whom I exiled from Jerusalem to Babylon: ⁵Build houses and live in them; plant gardens and eat their fruits. ⁶Take wives and have sons and daughters; find wives for your sons and give your daughters to husbands, so that they may bear sons and daughters. Increase there; do not decrease. ⁷Seek the welfare of the city to which I have exiled you; pray for it to the LORD, for upon its welfare your own depends.ᶜ ⁸For thus says the LORD of hosts, the God of Israel: Do not be deceived by the prophets and diviners who are among you; do not listen to those among you who dream dreams,ᵈ ⁹for they prophesy lies to you in my name; I did not send them—oracle of the LORD.ᵉ

¹⁰For thus says the LORD: Only after seventy years have elapsed for Babylon will I deal with you and fulfill for you my promise to bring you back to this place.ᶠ ¹¹For I know well the plans I have in mind for you—oracle of the LORD—plans for your welfare and not for woe, so as to give you a future of hope. ¹²When you call me, and come and pray to me, I will listen to you.ᵍ ¹³When you look for me, you will find me. Yes, when you seek me with all your heart, ¹⁴I will let you find me—oracle of the LORD—and I will change your lot; I will gather you together from all the nations and all the places to which I have banished you—oracle of the LORD—and bring you back to the place from which I have exiled you.ʰ ¹⁵As for your saying, "The LORD has raised up for us prophets here in Babylon"—

¹⁶Thus says the LORD concerning the king sitting on David's throne and all the people living in this city, your kinsmen who did not go with you into exile; ¹⁷thus says the LORD of hosts: I am sending against them sword, famine, and pestilence. I will make them like rotten figs, so spoiled that they cannot be eaten. ¹⁸I will pursue them with sword, famine, and pestilence, and make them an object of horror to all the kingdoms of the earth, a curse, a desolation, a hissing, and a reproach to all the nations among which I have banished them,ⁱ ¹⁹because they did not listen to my words—oracle of the LORD—even though I kept sending them my servants the prophets, but they would not listen to them—oracle of the LORD.ʲ

---

⁎[29:3] **Elasah:** probably the brother of Ahikam (cf. 26:24). **Gemariah:** probably the son of the high priest Hilkiah; cf. 2 Kgs 22:4. Zedekiah had dispatched these men to Nebuchadnezzar for some other purpose, possibly the payment of tribute, but Jeremiah took advantage of their mission to send his letter with them.

y. [28:9] Dt 18:22.   z. [28:14] Jer 27:6–7; Dt 28:48.   a. [28:16] Dt 13:6.   b. [29:2] 2 Kgs 24:15.

c. [29:7] 1 Tm 2:1–2.   d. [29:8] Jer 27:9, 14.   e. [29:9] Jer 5:31. f. [29:10] Jer 25:11; 2 Chr 36:21–22; Ezr 1:1; Dn 9:2; Zec 1:12; 7:5.   g. [29:12] Jer 33:3.   h. [29:14] Jer 23:3, 8.   i. [29:18] Jer 15:4; 24:9; 34:17–18.   j. [29:19] Jer 25:4.

²⁰As for you, listen to the word of the LORD, all you exiles whom I sent away from Jerusalem to Babylon. ²¹This is what the LORD of hosts, the God of Israel, says about Ahab, son of Kolaiah, and Zedekiah, son of Maaseiah, who prophesy lies to you in my name: I am handing them over to Nebuchadnezzar, king of Babylon, who will kill them before your eyes.ᵏ ²²And because of them this curse will be used by all the exiles of Judah in Babylon: "May the LORD make you like Zedekiah and Ahab, whom the king of Babylon roasted in fire," ²³because they have committed an outrage in Israel, committing adultery with their neighbors' wives, and alleging in my name things I did not command. I know, I am witness —oracle of the LORD.ˡ

**The False Prophet Shemaiah.** ²⁴To Shemaiah, the Nehelamite, say: ²⁵Thus says the LORD of hosts, the God of Israel: Because you sent documents in your own name to all the people in Jerusalem, to Zephaniah, the priest, son of Maaseiah, and to all the priests saying: ²⁶"It is the LORD who has appointed you priest in place of the priest Jehoiada, to provide officers for the house of the LORD, that you may confine in stocks or pillory any madman who poses as a prophet. ²⁷Why, then, have you not rebuked Jeremiah of Anathoth who poses as a prophet among you? ²⁸For he sent this message to us in Babylon: It will be a long time; build houses to live in; plant gardens and eat their fruit. . . ."

²⁹When the priest Zephaniah read this letter to Jeremiah the prophet, ³⁰the word of the LORD came to Jeremiah: ³¹Send to all the exiles: Thus says the LORD concerning Shemaiah, the Nehelamite: Because Shemaiah prophesies to you, although I did not send him, and has led you to rely on a lie, ³²therefore thus says the LORD, I will punish Shemaiah, the Nehelamite, and his descendants. None of them shall dwell among this people to see the good I will do for this people—oracle of the LORD—because he preached rebellion against the LORD.

## VI. ORACLES OF THE RESTORATION OF ISRAEL AND JUDAH

### CHAPTER 30

**The Restoration.**† ¹This word came to Jeremiah from the LORD: ²Thus says the LORD, the God of Israel: Write down on a scroll all the words I have spoken to you.ᵐ ³For indeed, the days are coming—oracle of the LORD—when I will restore the fortunes of my people Israel and Judah—oracle of the LORD. I will bring them back to the land which I gave to their ancestors, and they shall take possession of it.ⁿ

⁴These are the words the LORD spoke to Israel and to Judah: ⁵Thus says the LORD:

We hear a cry of fear:
    terror, not peace.
⁶ Inquire and see:
    does a male give birth?
Why, then, do I see all these men,
    their hands on their loins
Like women in labor,
    all their faces drained of color?ᵒ
⁷ Ah! How mighty is that day—
    there is none like it!
A time of distress for Jacob,
    though he shall be saved from it.ᵖ

⁸On that day—oracle of the LORD of hosts— I will break his yoke off your neck and snap your bonds. Strangers shall no longer enslave them;�q ⁹instead, they shall serve the LORD, their God, and David, their king,‡ whom I will raise up for them.ʳ

¹⁰ But you, my servant Jacob, do not fear!—
    oracle of the LORD—
    do not be dismayed, Israel!
For I will soon deliver you from places
    far away,
    your offspring from the land of their
    exile;
Jacob shall again find rest,
    secure, with none to frighten him,ˢ
¹¹     for I am with you—oracle of the
    LORD—to save you.
I will bring to an end all the nations
    among whom I have scattered you;
    but you I will not bring to an end.
I will chastise you as you deserve,
    I will not let you go unpunished.ᵗ
¹²     For thus says the LORD:
Incurable is your wound,
    grievous your injury;ᵘ

---

*[29:26–29] Jeremiah's message to Shemaiah is not completely preserved in the current Hebrew text, hence the incomplete sentence in vv. 25–28.

†[30:1–31:40] These two chapters contain salvation oracles that originally expressed the double expectation that the Lord would return the exiled survivors of the Northern Kingdom of Israel and reunite Israel and Judah as one kingdom under a just Davidic king. They were probably composed early in Josiah's reign (the reference of v. 9), when he took advantage of Assyria's internal disintegration and asserted control over northern Israel (cf. 2 Kgs 23:15–17). With the destruction of Jerusalem, the oracles were re-worked to include Judah and their fulfillment along with the renewal of the Davidic dynasty became associated with the eschatological "day of the Lord."

‡[30:9] **David, their king**: a descendant of David ("his leader" in v. 21) who, like his ancestor, would rule a unified kingdom and "walk in the ways of the Lord," as the Deuteronomistic historians claimed David did. Other prophets also refer to this idealized ruler as "David"; cf. Ez 34:23–24; 37:24–25; Hos 3:5.

k. [29:21] Jer 14:14.  l. [29:23] Jer 23:14.

m. [30:2] Jer 36:2; Hb 2:2; Rev 1:11.  n. [30:3] Jer 29:14; 31:8, 10, 23; 32:37, 44; Ez 39:25; Am 9:14.  o. [30:6] Jer 6:24; 50:43.  p. [30:7] Am 5:18; Zep 1:14–15.  q. [30:8] Is 14:5–6; Ez 34:27.  r. [30:9] Ez 34:23; 37:24; Hos 3:5; Lk 1:69.  s. [30:10] Jer 46:27; Is 43:5.  t. [30:11] Jer 46:28; Ez 11:16–17; Am 9:8–9.  u. [30:12] Jer 10:19; 14:17; 15:18.

<sup>13</sup> There is none to plead your case,
  no remedy for your running sore,
  no healing for you.
<sup>14</sup> All your lovers have forgotten you,
  they do not seek you out.
I struck you as an enemy would strike,
  punishing you cruelly.<sup>v</sup>
<sup>15</sup> Why cry out over your wound?
  There is no relief for your pain.
Because of your great guilt,
  your numerous sins,
  I have done this to you.<sup>w</sup>
<sup>16</sup> Yet all who devour you shall be devoured,
  all your enemies shall go into exile.
All who plunder you shall become
  plunder,
  all who pillage you I will hand over
  to be pillaged.<sup>x</sup>
<sup>17</sup> For I will restore your health;
  I will heal your injuries—oracle of
  the LORD.
"The outcast" they have called you,
  "whom no one looks for."<sup>y</sup>
<sup>18</sup> Thus says the LORD:
See! I will restore the fortunes of Jacob's
  tents,
  on his dwellings I will have
  compassion;
A city shall be rebuilt upon its own ruins,
  a citadel restored where it should be.<sup>z</sup>
<sup>19</sup> From them will come praise,
  the sound of people rejoicing.
I will increase them, they will not
  decrease,
I will glorify them, they will not be
  insignificant.<sup>a</sup>
<sup>20</sup> His children shall be as of old,
  his assembly shall stand firm in my
  presence,
  I will punish all his oppressors.<sup>b</sup>
<sup>21</sup> His leader<sup>*</sup> shall be one of his own,
  and his ruler shall emerge from his
  ranks.
He shall approach me when I summon
  him;
  Why else would he dare
  approach me?—oracle of the LORD.
<sup>22</sup> You shall be my people,
  and I will be your God.<sup>c</sup>
<sup>23</sup> Look! The storm of the LORD!
  His wrath breaks out
In a whirling storm
  that bursts upon the heads of the
  wicked.<sup>d</sup>

<sup>24</sup> The anger of the LORD will not abate
  until he has carried out completely
  the decisions of his heart.
In days to come
  you will fully understand it.<sup>e</sup>

## CHAPTER 31

### Good News of the Return

<sup>1</sup> At that time—oracle of the LORD—
  I will be the God of all the families
  of Israel,
  and they shall be my people.<sup>f</sup>
<sup>2</sup>  <sup>†</sup>Thus says the LORD:
The people who escaped the sword
  find favor in the wilderness.
As Israel comes forward to receive rest,
<sup>3</sup>  from afar the LORD appears:
With age-old love I have loved you;
  so I have kept my mercy toward
  you.<sup>g</sup>
<sup>4</sup> Again I will build you, and you shall stay
  built,
  virgin Israel;
Carrying your festive tambourines,
  you shall go forth dancing with
  merrymakers.
<sup>5</sup> You shall again plant vineyards
  on the mountains of Samaria;
  those who plant them shall enjoy
  their fruits.<sup>h</sup>
<sup>6</sup> Yes, a day will come when the watchmen
  call out on Mount Ephraim:
"Come, let us go up to Zion,
  to the LORD, our God."<sup>i</sup>

### The Road of Return

<sup>7</sup>  For thus says the LORD:
Shout with joy for Jacob,
  exult at the head of the nations;
  proclaim your praise and say:
The LORD has saved his people,
  the remnant of Israel.<sup>j</sup>
<sup>8</sup> Look! I will bring them back
  from the land of the north;
I will gather them from the ends of the
  earth,
  the blind and the lame in their
  midst,
Pregnant women, together with those in
  labor—

---

*[30:21] **His leader**: cf. v. 9. **Approach me**: i.e., in the
sanctuary of the Temple for worship. This new David is given
a priestly function to perform on behalf of the assembly. To
approach God on one's own brings death; cf. Lv 16:1–2.

†[31:2–3] Jeremiah describes the exiles of the Northern
Kingdom on their way home from the nations where the
Assyrians had resettled them (722/721 B.C.). The favor they
discover in the wilderness is the appearance of the Lord (v. 3)
coming to guide them to Jerusalem. Implicit in these verses is
the presentation of the people's return from captivity as a second exodus, a unifying theme in Second Isaiah (chaps. 40–55).

v. [30:14] Jer 22:22; Lam 1:19.  w. [30:15] Jer 15:18.  x. [30:16]
Jer 2:3.  y. [30:17] Jer 33:6.  z. [30:18] Jer 33:7, 11; Ezr 6:3–15; Ez
36:10.  a. [30:19] Is 35:10; 51:11.  b. [30:20] Is 49:26.  c. [30:22]
Jer 24:7; 31:1, 33; 32:38; Lv 26:12; Ez 11:20; 36:28.  d. [30:23] Jer
23:19.

e. [30:24] Jer 23:20.  f. [31:1] Jer 30:22.  g. [31:3] Dt 7:8; 10:15;
Is 43:4; 63:9; Hos 11:1, 4.  h. [31:5] Dt 28:30; Is 65:21; Am
9:14.  i. [31:6] Is 2:3; 27:13; Mi 4:2.  j. [31:7] Is 12:6.

an immense throng—they shall
    return.[k]
9 With weeping they shall come,
    but with compassion I will guide
      them;
I will lead them to streams of water,
    on a level road, without stumbling.
For I am a father to Israel,
    Ephraim is my firstborn.[l]
10 Hear the word of the LORD, you nations,
    proclaim it on distant coasts, and
      say:
The One who scattered Israel, now
      gathers them;
he guards them as a shepherd his
      flock.
11 The LORD shall ransom Jacob,
    he shall redeem him from a hand
      too strong for him.[m]
12 Shouting, they shall mount the heights of
      Zion,
    they shall come streaming to the
      LORD's blessings:
The grain, the wine, and the oil,
    flocks of sheep and cattle;
They themselves shall be like watered
      gardens,
    never again neglected.[n]
13 Then young women shall make merry and
      dance,
    young men and old as well.
I will turn their mourning into joy,
    I will show them compassion and
      have them rejoice after their
      sorrows.
14 I will lavish choice portions on the priests,
    and my people shall be filled with
      my blessings—
      oracle of the LORD.

### End of Rachel's Mourning

15     Thus says the LORD:
In Ramah[*] is heard the sound of sobbing,
    bitter weeping!
Rachel mourns for her children,
    she refuses to be consoled
    for her children—they are no more![o]
16     Thus says the LORD:
Cease your cries of weeping,
    hold back your tears!
There is compensation for your labor—
    oracle of the LORD—

they shall return from the enemy's
    land.
17 There is hope for your future—oracle of
      the LORD—
    your children shall return to their
      own territory.[p]
18 Indeed, I heard Ephraim rocking in grief:
    You chastised me, and I was
      chastised;
    I was like an untamed calf.
Bring me back, let me come back,
    for you are the LORD, my God.[q]
19 For after I turned away, I repented;
    after I came to myself, I struck my
      thigh;[†]
I was ashamed, even humiliated,
    because I bore the disgrace of my
      youth.[r]
20 Is Ephraim not my favored son,
    the child in whom I delight?
Even though I threaten him,
    I must still remember him!
My heart stirs for him,
    I must show him compassion!—
      oracle of the LORD.[s]

### Summons to Return Home

21 Set up road markers,
    put up signposts;
Turn your attention to the highway,
    the road you walked.
Turn back, virgin Israel,
    turn back to these your cities.
22 How long will you continue to hesitate,
    rebellious daughter?
The LORD has created a new thing upon
    the earth:
    woman encompasses man.[‡]

23 Thus says the LORD of hosts, the God of
Israel: When I restore their fortunes in the land
of Judah and in its cities, they shall again use this
greeting: "May the LORD bless you, Tent of Justice, Holy Mountain!"[t] 24 Judah and all its cities,
the farmers and those who lead the flock shall
dwell there together. 25 For I will slake the thirst
of the faint; the appetite of all the weary I will
satisfy. 26 At this I awoke and opened my eyes; my
sleep was satisfying.[§]

†[31:19] **Struck my thigh**: a gesture signifying grief and
dread (cf. Ez 21:17).

‡[31:22] No satisfactory explanation has been given for
this text. Jerome, for example, saw the image as a reference
to the infant Jesus enclosed in Mary's womb. Since Jeremiah
often uses marital imagery in his description of a restored
Israel, the phrase may refer to a wedding custom, perhaps
women circling the groom in a dance. It may also be a metaphor describing the security of a new Israel, a security so complete that it defies the imagination and must be expressed as
hyperbolic role reversal: any danger will be so insignificant
that women can protect their men.

§[31:26] **I awoke . . . satisfying**: an intrusive comment.

---

*[31:15] **Ramah**: a village about five miles north of Jerusalem, where one tradition locates Rachel's tomb (1 Sm 10:2).
The wife of Jacob/Israel, Rachel is the matriarchal ancestor of
Ephraim, chief among the northern tribes. She personified
Israel as a mother whose grief for her lost children is especially poignant because she had to wait a long time to bear
them. Mt 2:18 applies this verse to Herod's slaughter of the
innocents.

k. [31:8] Jer 3:18; 23:3, 8; Is 35:5–6.  l. [31:9] Ex 4:22.  m. [31:11]
Is 44:23; 48:20.  n. [31:12] Is 58:11.  o. [31:15] Mt 2:18.

p. [31:17] Jer 29:10–14.  q. [31:18] Lv 26:40–42.  r. [31:19] Dt
30:1–3.  s. [31:20] Hos 11:8.  t. [31:23] Jer 30:3; Ps 122:8.

²⁷See, days are coming—oracle of the LORD—
when I will sow the house of Israel and the house
of Judah with the seed of human beings and
the seed of animals. ²⁸As I once watched over
them to uproot and tear down, to demolish, to
destroy, and to harm, so I will watch over them
to build and to plant—oracle of the LORD.ᵘ ²⁹In
those days they shall no longer say,

"The parents ate unripe grapes,ᵛ
       and the children's teeth are set on
       edge,"

³⁰but all shall die because of their own iniquity:
the teeth of anyone who eats unripe grapes shall
be set on edge.

**The New Covenant.**† ³¹See, days are coming—
oracle of the LORD—when I will make a new
covenant with the house of Israel and the house
of Judah.ʷ ³²It will not be like the covenant I
made with their ancestors the day I took them
by the hand to lead them out of the land of
Egypt. They broke my covenant, though I was
their master—oracle of the LORD.ˣ ³³But this is
the covenant I will make with the house of Israel
after those days—oracle of the LORD. I will place
my law within them, and write it upon their
hearts; I will be their God, and they shall be my
people.ʸ ³⁴They will no longer teach their friends
and relatives, "Know the LORD!" Everyone, from
least to greatest, shall know me—oracle of the
LORD—for I will forgive their iniquity and no
longer remember their sin.ᶻ

### Certainty of God's Promise

³⁵       Thus says the LORD,
Who gives the sun to light the day,
       moon and stars to light the night;
Who stirs up the sea so that its waves roar,
       whose name is LORD of hosts:ᵃ
³⁶ If ever this fixed order gives way
       before me—oracle of the LORD—
Then would the offspring of Israel cease
       as a people before me forever.ᵇ

³⁷       Thus says the LORD:
If the heavens on high could be measured,
       or the foundations below the earth
              be explored,
Then would I reject all the offspring of
              Israel
       because of all they have done—
              oracle of the LORD.

**Jerusalem Rebuilt.**‡ ³⁸See, days are coming—
oracle of the LORD—when the city shall be
rebuilt as the LORD's,ᶜ from the Tower of Hananel to the Corner Gate. ³⁹A measuring line
shall be stretched from there straight to the hill
Gareb and then turn to Goah. ⁴⁰The whole valley of corpses and ashes, all the terraced slopes
toward the Wadi Kidron, as far as the corner of
the Horse Gate at the east, shall be holy to the
LORD. Never again shall the city be uprooted or
demolished.

## CHAPTER 32

**Pledge of Restoration.**§ ¹The word came to
Jeremiah from the LORD in the tenth year of
Zedekiah,¶ king of Judah, the eighteenth year
of Nebuchadnezzar. ²At that time the army of
the king of Babylon was besieging Jerusalem,
while Jeremiah the prophet was confined to the
court of the guard, in the house of the king of
Judah.ᵈ ³Zedekiah, king of Judah, had confined
him there, saying: "How dare you prophesy:
Thus says the LORD: I am handing this city over
to the king of Babylon that he may capture it.ᵉ
⁴Zedekiah, king of Judah, shall not escape the
hands of the Chaldeans: he shall indeed be
handed over to the king of Babylon. He shall
speak with him face to face and see him eye to
eye.ᶠ ⁵He shall take Zedekiah to Babylon. There
he shall remain, until I attend to him—oracle
of the LORD. If you fight against the Chaldeans,
you cannot win!"ᵍ

---

‡[31:38–40] The landmarks in these verses outline the
borders of Jerusalem during the time of Nehemiah: the Tower
of Hananel (Neh 3:1; 12:39) in the northeast and the Corner
Gate (2 Kgs 14:13) in the northwest; Goah in the southeast
and Gareb Hill in the southwest; the Valley of Ben-hinnom
("the Valley of corpses and ashes"), which met the Wadi
Kidron in the southeast, and the Horse Gate in the eastern
wall at the southeast corner of the Temple area.

§[32:1–44] This chapter recounts a prophecy "in action."
At the Lord's command, Jeremiah fulfills his family duty to
purchase the land of his cousin, carrying out all the legal
details, even putting the deed away for safekeeping against the
day he will have to produce it to verify his ownership of the
land. The Lord defines the meaning of this symbolic action:
In the future, Judah will be restored and daily life will return
to normal.

¶[32:1] **The tenth year of Zedekiah:** 588 B.C. **The eighteenth year of Nebuchadnezzar:** dating his reign from his
victory at Carchemish; see note on 25:1–14.

---

\*[31:29] **"The parents . . . on edge":** Jeremiah's opponents
use this proverb to complain that they are being punished for
sins of their ancestors. Jeremiah, however, insists that the Lord
knows the depth of their wickedness and holds them accountable for their actions.

†[31:31–34] The new covenant is an occasional prophetic
theme, beginning with Hosea. According to Jeremiah, (a) it
lasts forever; (b) its law (*torah*) is written in human hearts; (c)
it gives everyone true knowledge of God, making additional
instruction (*torah*) unnecessary. The Dead Sea Scroll community claimed they were partners in a "new covenant." The
New Testament presents the death and resurrection of Jesus of
Nazareth as inaugurating a new covenant open to anyone who
professes faith in Jesus the Christ. Cf. Lk 22:20; 1 Cor 11:25;
Heb 8:8–12. **Know the LORD:** cf. note on 22:15–16.

---

u. [31:28] Jer 1:10; 18:7.   v. [31:29] Dt 24:16; Ez 18:2.   w. [31:31]
Jer 32:40; Heb 9:15.   x. [31:32] Ex 24:7–8; Dt 5:2.   y. [31:33] Jer
32:40; Ez 37:26; Heb 10:16.   z. [31:34] Is 54:13.   a. [31:35] Gn
1:14–18.   b. [31:36] Jer 33:20–21.

c. [31:38] Neh 12:38; Zec 14:10–11.   d. [32:2] Jer 33:1; 37:20; 38:6;
39:14.   e. [32:3] Jer 26:9; 34:2; 37:6–10.   f. [32:4] Jer 34:3; 38:18,
23; 39:4–7.   g. [32:5] Jer 39:7; 52:11.

⁶*Jeremiah said, This word came to me from the LORD: ⁷Hanamel, son of your uncle Shallum, will come to you with the offer:ʰ "Purchase my field in Anathoth, since you, as nearest relative, have the first right of purchase."† ⁸And, just as the LORD had said, my cousin Hanamel came to me in the court of the guard and said, "Please purchase my field in Anathoth, in the territory of Benjamin; as nearest relative, you have the first right of possession—purchase it for yourself." Then I knew this was the word of the LORD. ⁹So I bought the field in Anathoth from my cousin Hanamel, weighing out for him the silver, seventeen shekels of silver.

¹⁰When I had written and sealed the deed, called witnesses and weighed out the silver on the scales, ¹¹I accepted the deed of purchase, both the sealed copy, containing title and conditions, and the open copy.‡ ¹²I gave this deed of purchase to Baruch, son of Neriah, son of Mahseiah, in the presence of my cousin Hanamel and the witnesses who had signed the deed of purchase and before all the Judahites sitting around in the court of the guard.ⁱ

¹³In their presence I gave Baruch this charge: ¹⁴Thus says the LORD of hosts, the God of Israel: Take these deeds of purchase, both the sealed and the open deeds, and put them in an earthenware jar,§ so they can last a long time. ¹⁵For thus says the LORD of hosts, the God of Israel: They shall again purchase houses and fields and vineyards in this land.

¹⁶After I had given the deed of purchase to Baruch, son of Neriah, I prayed to the LORD: ¹⁷Ah, my Lord GOD! You made the heavens and the earth with your great power and your outstretched arm; nothing is too difficult for you.ʲ ¹⁸You continue your kindness through a thousand generations; but you repay the ancestors' guilt upon their children who follow them. Great and mighty God, whose name is LORD of hosts,ᵏ ¹⁹great in counsel, mighty in deed, whose eyes are fixed on all the ways of mortals, giving to all according to their ways, according to the fruit of their deeds:ˡ ²⁰you performed signs and wonders in the land of Egypt and to this day, in Israel and among all peoples, you have made a name for yourself as on this day.ᵐ ²¹You brought your people Israel out of the land of Egypt with signs and wonders, with a strong hand and an outstretched arm, and great terror. ²²And you gave them this land, as you had sworn to their ancestors to give them, a land flowing with milk and honey.ⁿ ²³They went in and took possession of it, but they did not listen to your voice. They did not live by your law; they did not do anything you commanded them to do. Then you made all this evil fall upon them.º ²⁴See, the siegeworks have arrived at this city to capture it; the city is handed over to the Chaldeans who are attacking it, with sword, starvation, and disease. What you threatened has happened—you can see it for yourself.ᵖ ²⁵Yet you told me, my Lord GOD: Purchase the field with silver and summon witnesses, when the city has already been handed over to the Chaldeans!

²⁶Then this word of the LORD came to Jeremiah: ²⁷I am the LORD, the God of all the living! Is anything too difficult for me? ²⁸Therefore the LORD says: I am handing over this city to the Chaldeans and to Nebuchadnezzar, king of Babylon, and he shall capture it. ²⁹The Chaldeans who are attacking this city shall go in and set the city on fire, burning it and the houses, on whose roofs incense was burned to Baal and libations were poured out to other gods in order to provoke me.�q ³⁰From their youth the Israelites and the Judahites have been doing only what is evil in my eyes; the Israelites have been provoking me with the works of their hands—oracle of the LORD.ʳ ³¹This city has so stirred my anger and wrath, from the day it was built to this day, that I must put it out of my sight, ³²for all the evil the Israelites and Judahites have done to provoke me—they, their kings, their princes, their priests, and their prophets, the people of Judah and the inhabitants of Jerusalem.ˢ ³³They turned their backs to me, not their faces; though I taught them persistently, they would not listen or accept correction.ᵗ ³⁴Instead they set up their abominations in the house which bears my name in order to defile it.ᵘ ³⁵They built high places to Baal in the Valley of Ben-hinnom to sacrifice their sons and daughters to Molech;¶ I never commanded them to do this, nor did it even enter my mind that they would practice this abomination, so as to bring sin upon Judah.ᵛ

³⁶Now, therefore, thus says the LORD, the God of Israel, concerning this city, which you say is being handed over to the king of Babylon by means of the sword, starvation, and disease:

---

*[32:6–9] Jeremiah's imprisonment by the weak-willed Zedekiah was a technical custody that did not deprive him of all freedom of action.

†[32:7] The first right of purchase: the obligation of the closest relative to redeem the property of a family member in economic distress so that the ancestral land remains within the family (Lv 25:25–28); see note on Ru 2:20.

‡[32:11] The sealed copy . . . and the open copy: the legal deed of sale was written on a scroll, which was then rolled up and sealed; a second scroll containing a copy of the legal deed was then rolled around it and left unsealed so the contents of the legal deed would be accessible without destroying the original seal.

§[32:14] In an earthenware jar: to protect the scroll from drying out and disintegrating. Some of the Dead Sea Scrolls were found in such jars.

¶[32:35] Molech: a god to whom human sacrifice was offered in the Valley of Ben-hinnom. Here, as in 19:5, he is called "Baal"; see note on Lv 18:21.

---

h. [32:7] Lv 25:24–34; Ru 4:4.   i. [32:12] Jer 36:4.   j. [32:17] 2 Kgs 19:15; Jb 42:2.   k. [32:18] Ex 20:5–6; 34:6; Dt 5:9.   l. [32:19] Jb 34:21; Ps 33:13–15.

m. [32:20] Ex 6:6; Ps 135:9.   n. [32:22] Jer 11:5; Gn 15:18; 17:8; 26:3.   o. [32:23] Jer 7:24–26; Dn 9:10–14.   p. [32:24] Jer 21:5; 33:4.   q. [32:29] Jer 21:10; 37:8–10.   r. [32:30] Jer 3:25; 44:8.   s. [32:32] Jer 2:26; Is 3:8.   t. [32:33] Jer 7:24.   u. [32:34] Jer 7:30; 2 Kgs 21:4–5.   v. [32:35] Jer 7:31; 19:5; Ps 106:37–38.

³⁷See, I am gathering them from all the lands to which I drove them in my rising fury and great anger; I will bring them back to this place and settle them here in safety.ʷ ³⁸They shall be my people, and I will be their God.ˣ ³⁹I will give them one heart and one way, that they may fear me always, for their own good and the good of their children after them. ⁴⁰With them I will make an everlasting covenant, never to cease doing good to them; I will put fear of me in their hearts so that they never turn away from me.ʸ ⁴¹I will take delight in doing good to them: I will plant them firmly in this land, with all my heart and soul.ᶻ

⁴²For thus says the LORD: Just as I have brought upon this people all this great evil, so I will bring upon them all the good I have promised them.ᵃ ⁴³Fields shall be purchased in this land, about which you say, "It is a wasteland, without human beings or animals, handed over to the Chaldeans."ᵇ ⁴⁴They will purchase fields with silver, write up deeds, seal them, and have them witnessed in the land of Benjamin, in the neighborhood of Jerusalem, in the cities of Judah and of the hill country, in the cities of the Shephelah and the Negeb, when I restore their fortunes—oracle of the LORD.ᶜ

## CHAPTER 33

**Restoration of Jerusalem.** ¹The word of the LORD came to Jeremiah a second time while he was still confined in the court of the guard: ²Thus says the LORD who made the earth, giving it shape and stability, LORD is his name: ³Call to me, and I will answer you; I will tell you great things beyond the reach of your knowledge.ᵈ ⁴Thus says the LORD, the God of Israel, concerning the houses of this city and the houses of the kings of Judah, which are being torn down because of the siegeworks and the sword:ᵉ ⁵men come to battle the Chaldeans, and to fill these houses with the corpses of those whom I have struck down in my raging anger, when I hid my face from this city because of all their wickedness.ᶠ

⁶Look! I am bringing the city recovery and healing; I will heal them and reveal to them an abundance of lasting peace.ᵍ ⁷I will restore the fortunes of Judah and Israel, and rebuild them as they were in the beginning.ʰ ⁸I will purify them of all the guilt they incurred by sinning against me; I will forgive all their offenses by which they sinned and rebelled against me.ⁱ ⁹Then this city shall become joy for me, a name of praise and pride, before all the nations of the earth, as they hear of all the good I am doing for them. They shall fear and tremble because of all the prosperity I give it.

¹⁰Thus says the LORD: In this place, about which you say: "It is a waste without people or animals!" and in the cities of Judah, in the streets of Jerusalem now deserted, without people, without inhabitant, without animal, there shall yet be heardʲ ¹¹the song of joy, the song of gladness, the song of the bridegroom, the song of the bride, the song of those bringing thank offerings to the house of the LORD: "Give thanks to the LORD of hosts, for the LORD is good; God's love endures forever." For I will restore the fortunes of this land as they were in the beginning, says the LORD.ᵏ

¹²Thus says the LORD of hosts: In this place, now a waste, without people or animals, and in all its cities there shall again be sheepfolds for the shepherds to rest their flocks. ¹³In the cities of the hill country, of the Shephelah and the Negeb, in the land of Benjamin and the neighborhood of Jerusalem, and in the cities of Judah, flocks will again pass under the hands of the one who counts them, says the LORD.

¹⁴The days are coming—oracle of the LORD—when I will fulfill the promise I made to the house of Israel and the house of Judah. ¹⁵In those days, at that time, I will make a just shoot spring up for David; he shall do what is right and just in the land.ˡ ¹⁶In those days Judah shall be saved and Jerusalem shall dwell safely; this is the name they shall call her: "The LORD our justice." ¹⁷For thus says the LORD: David shall never lack a successor on the throne of the house of Israel,ᵐ ¹⁸nor shall the priests of Levi ever be lacking before me, to sacrifice burnt offerings, to burn cereal offerings, and to make sacrifices.ⁿ

¹⁹This word of the LORD also came to Jeremiah: ²⁰Thus says the LORD: If you can break my covenant with dayᵒ and my covenant with night so that day and night no longer appear in their proper time, ²¹only then can my covenant with my servant David be broken, so that he will not have a descendant to act as king upon his throne, and my covenant with the priests of Levi who minister to me. ²²Just as the host of heaven cannot be numbered and the sands of the sea cannot be counted, so I will multiply the descendants of David my servant and the Levites who minister to me.

²³This word of the LORD came to Jeremiah: ²⁴Have you not noticed what these people are saying: "The LORD has rejected the two tribes he had chosen"? They hold my people

---

\*[33:14–26] This is the longest continuous passage in the Hebrew text of Jeremiah that is missing from the Greek text of Jeremiah. It is probably the work of a postexilic writer who applied parts of Jeremiah's prophecies to new situations. The hope for an eternal Davidic dynasty (vv. 14–17; cf. 2 Sm 7:11–16) and for a perpetual priesthood and sacrificial system (v. 18) was not realized after the exile. On the canonical authority of the Septuagint, see note on Dn 13:1–14:42.

---

w. [32:37] Jer 23:3; 29:14; Is 11:12; Ez 11:17.   x. [32:38] Jer 24:7; 31:33.   y. [32:40] Jer 31:31–33.   z. [32:41] Dt 30:9.   a. [32:42] Jer 33:10–14; Zec 8:13.   b. [32:43] Jer 33:10.   c. [32:44] Jer 17:26; 33:7.   d. [33:3] Is 48:6.   e. [33:4] Jer 32:24.   f. [33:5] Jer 21:4–6.   g. [33:6] Is 57:18.   h. [33:7] Jer 30:3; 32:44.   i. [33:8] Ez 36:25.

j. [33:10] Jer 32:43.   k. [33:11] 1 Chr 16:34; Ezr 3:11; Ps 136:1.   l. [33:15] Jer 23:5; Ps 72:1–4, 12–14; Is 11:1.   m. [33:17] 2 Sm 7:16; 1 Kgs 2:4; Ps 89:4–5, 29, 36–37.   n. [33:18] Ez 44:15–16.   o. [33:20–21] Jer 31:36–37; Ps 89:37–38.

in contempt as if it were no longer a nation in their eyes.[p] [25q]Thus says the LORD: If I have no covenant with day and night, if I did not establish statutes for heaven and earth, [26]then I will also reject the descendants of Jacob and of David my servant, no longer selecting from his descendants rulers for the offspring of Abraham, Isaac, and Jacob. Yes, I will restore their fortunes and show them mercy.

## CHAPTER 34

**Fate of Zedekiah.** [1]The word which came to Jeremiah from the LORD while Nebuchadnezzar, king of Babylon, and all his army and all the earth's kingdoms under his rule, and all the peoples were attacking Jerusalem and all her cities:[r] [2]Thus says the LORD, the God of Israel: Go to Zedekiah, king of Judah, and tell him: Thus says the LORD: I am handing this city over to the king of Babylon; he will burn it with fire.[s] [3]You yourself shall not escape his hand; rather you will be captured and fall into his hand. You shall see the king of Babylon eye to eye and speak to him face to face. Then you shall go to Babylon.[t]

[4]Just hear the word of the LORD, Zedekiah, king of Judah! Then, says the LORD concerning you, you shall not die by the sword. [5]You shall die in peace, and they will burn spices for you as they did for your ancestors, the earlier kings who preceded you, and they shall make lament over you, "Alas, Lord." I myself make this promise—oracle of the LORD.

[6]Jeremiah the prophet told all these things to Zedekiah, king of Judah, in Jerusalem, [7]while the army of the king of Babylon was attacking Jerusalem and the remaining cities of Judah, Lachish, and Azekah.[*] Only these fortified cities were left standing out of all the cities of Judah!

**The Pact Broken.**[†] [8]This is the word that came to Jeremiah from the LORD after King Zedekiah had made a covenant with all the people in Jerusalem to proclaim freedom: [9]Everyone must free their Hebrew slaves, male and female, so that no one should hold another Judahite in servitude.[u] [10]All the princes and the people who entered this covenant agreed to set free their

slaves, their male and female servants, so that they should no longer be in servitude. But even though they agreed and freed them, [11]afterward they took back their male and female servants whom they had set free and again forced them into servitude.

[12]Then this word of the LORD came to Jeremiah: [13]Thus says the LORD, the God of Israel: I myself made a covenant with your ancestors the day I brought them out of the land of Egypt, out of the house of slavery: [14]Every seventh year each of you must set free all Hebrews who have sold themselves to you; six years they shall serve you, but then you shall let them go free. Your ancestors, however, did not listen to me or obey me. [15]As for you, today you repented and did what is right in my eyes by proclaiming freedom for your neighbor and making a covenant before me in the house which bears my name. [16]But then you again profaned my name by taking back your male and female slaves whom you had just set free for life; you forced them to become your slaves again.[v] [17]Therefore, thus says the LORD: You for your part did not obey me by proclaiming freedom for your families and neighbors. So I now proclaim freedom for you—oracle of the LORD—for the sword, starvation, and disease. I will make you an object of horror to all the kingdoms of the earth. [18‡]Those who violated my covenant and did not observe the terms of the covenant they made in my presence—I will make them like the calf which they cut in two so they could pass between its parts— [19]the princes of Judah and of Jerusalem, the court officials, the priests, and all the people of the land, who passed between the parts of the calf. [20]These I will hand over to their enemies, to those who seek their lives: their corpses shall become food for the birds of the air and the beasts of the field.[w]

[21]Zedekiah, king of Judah, and his princes, I will hand also over to their enemies, to those who seek their lives, to the army of the king of Babylon which is now withdrawing from you.[x] [22]I am giving the command—oracle of the LORD—to bring them back to this city. They shall attack and capture it, and burn it with fire; the cities of Judah I will turn into a waste, where no one dwells.[y]

## CHAPTER 35

**The Faithful Rechabites.** [1]The word that came to Jeremiah from the LORD in the days of

---

*[34:7] **Lachish, and Azekah:** fortress towns southwest of Jerusalem which Nebuchadnezzar besieged to prevent any help coming to Jerusalem from Egypt. At Lachish, archaeologists found several letters written on ostraca (pottery fragments) dated to 598 or 588 B.C., which mention both Lachish and Azekah.

†[34:8–22] During the siege of Jerusalem, its citizens made a covenant at Zedekiah's instigation to free Judahites they held in servitude, thus providing additional defenders for the city, leaving slave owners with fewer mouths to feed, and making reparation for past violations of the law, which dictated that Hebrew slaves should serve no longer than six years (Dt 15:12–15). But when the siege was temporarily lifted, when the assistance promised by Pharaoh Hophra arrived (cf. Jer 37:5), the inhabitants of Jerusalem broke the covenant and once more pressed their fellow citizens into slavery (v. 11).

‡[34:18–19] Both the Old Testament (Gn 15:10–17) and the eighth century B.C. Sefire inscription indicate that sometimes contracting parties ratified an agreement by walking between dismembered animals, invoking upon themselves the animals' fate if they failed to keep their word. **The covenant:** that mentioned in vv. 10, 15.

p. [33:24] Rom 11:1–2.   q. [33:25–26] Jer 31:36–37; 32:44.   r. [34:1] Jer 52:4; 2 Kgs 25:1.   s. [34:2] Jer 21:10; 32:3, 28.   t. [34:3] Jer 32:4; 52:11.   u. [34:9] Ex 21:2–4; Lv 25:39, 46; Dt 15:12–15.

v. [34:16] Lv 19:12.   w. [34:20] Jer 7:33; 16:4; 19:7.   x. [34:21] Jer 37:5, 11.   y. [34:22] Jer 37:8; 52:7–13; 2 Chr 36:17, 19.

Jehoiakim,* son of Josiah, king of Judah: ²Go to the house† of the Rechabites, speak to them, and bring them to the house of the Lord, to one of the rooms there, and give them wine to drink. ³So I took Jaazaniah, son of Jeremiah, son of Habazziniah, his brothers and all his sons—the whole house of the Rechabites— ⁴and I brought them to the house of the Lord, to the room of the sons of Hanan,‡ son of Igdaliah, the man of God, next to the room of the princes above the room of Maaseiah, son of Shallum, the guard at the entrance. ⁵I set before the Rechabites bowls full of wine, and cups, and said to them, "Drink some wine."

⁶"We do not drink wine," they said to me; "Jonadab,§ Rechab's son, our father, commanded us, 'Neither you nor your children shall ever drink wine.ᶻ ⁷Build no house and sow no seed; do not plant vineyards or own any. You must dwell in tents all your lives, so that you may live long on the land where you live as resident aliens.' ⁸We have obeyed Jonadab, Rechab's son, our father, in everything that he commanded us: not drinking wine as long as we live—neither we nor our wives nor our sons nor our daughters; ⁹not building houses to live in; not owning vineyards or fields or crops. ¹⁰We live in tents, doing everything our father Jonadab commanded us. ¹¹But when Nebuchadnezzar, king of Babylon, invaded this land, we said, 'Come, let us go into Jerusalem to escape the army of the Chaldeans and the army of the Arameans.'¶ That is why we are now living in Jerusalem."ᵃ

¹²Then the word of the Lord came to Jeremiah: ¹³Thus says the Lord of hosts, the God of Israel: Go, say to the people of Judah and to the inhabitants of Jerusalem: Will you not take correction and obey my words?—oracle of the Lord.ᵇ ¹⁴The words of Jonadab, Rechab's son, by which he commanded his children not to drink

wine, have been upheld: to this day they have not drunk wine; they obeyed their ancestor's command. I, however, have spoken to you time and again. But you did not obey me!ᶜ ¹⁵Time and again I sent you all my servants the prophets, saying: Turn away, each of you, from your evil way and reform your actions! Do not follow other gods to serve them that you may remain in the land which I gave you and your ancestors. But you did not pay attention. You did not obey me.ᵈ ¹⁶Yes, the children of Jonadab, Rechab's son, upheld the command which their father laid on them. But this people has not obeyed me! ¹⁷Now, therefore, says the Lord God of hosts, the God of Israel: I will soon bring upon Judah and all the inhabitants of Jerusalem every evil with which I threatened them because I spoke but they did not obey, I called but they did not answer.ᵉ

¹⁸But to the house of the Rechabites Jeremiah said: Thus says the Lord of hosts, the God of Israel: Since you have obeyed the command of Jonadab, your father, kept all his commands and done everything he commanded you, ¹⁹therefore, thus says the Lord of hosts, the God of Israel: Never shall there fail to be a descendant of Jonadab, Rechab's son, standing in my presence.

## VII. JEREMIAH AND THE FALL
## OF JERUSALEM

### CHAPTER 36

**Baruch, the Scribe of Jeremiah.** ¹In the fourth year of Jehoiakim, son of Josiah, king of Judah, this word came to Jeremiah from the Lord: ²Take a scroll and write on it all the words I have spoken to you about Israel, Judah, and all the nations, from the day I first spoke to you, from the days of Josiah, until today. ³Perhaps, if the house of Judah hears all the evil I have in mind to do to them, so that all of them turn from their evil way, then I can forgive their wickedness and their sin.ᶠ ⁴So Jeremiah called Baruch, son of Neriah, and he wrote down on a scroll what Jeremiah said, all the words which the Lord had spoken to him. ⁵Then Jeremiah commanded Baruch: "I cannot enter the house of the Lord; I am barred** from it. ⁶So you yourself must go. On a fast day in the hearing of the people in the Lord's house, read the words of the Lord from the scroll you wrote at my dictation; read them also to all the people of Judah who come up from their cities. ⁷Perhaps they will present their supplication before the Lord and will all turn back from their evil way;

---

*[35:1] **In the days of Jehoiakim**: probably in 599 or 598 B.C. (cf. 2 Kgs 24:1–2).

†[35:2] **House**: both members of the family of Rechab (cf. v. 3) and the place where they live; cf. note on v. 11. The **Rechabites**: traditionalists who rejected the settled agricultural and urban cultures to which other Israelites had assimilated, maintaining their loyalty to the Lord by perpetuating the semi-nomadic life of their distant ancestors (cf. 2 Kgs 10:15–17). Jeremiah contrasts their adherence to their vows with the Judahites' disregard for divine commands.

‡[35:4] **The sons of Hanan**: probably disciples of Hanan. **Man of God**: occurring only here in Jeremiah, the title frequently is applied to prophets: e.g., Samuel (1 Sm 9:6–10), Elijah (2 Kgs 1:9–13), Elisha (2 Kgs 4–13). Whatever the function of the sons of Hanan, they encourage Jeremiah by lending him their room. **Maaseiah**: perhaps the father of the priest Zephaniah (29:25; 37:3). **Guard at the entrance**: an important priestly responsibility (cf. 52:24).

§[35:6] **Jonadab**: another spelling of Jehonadab, a contemporary of King Jehu; cf. 2 Kgs 10:15–17.

¶[35:11] **The army of the Arameans**: Nebuchadnezzar enlisted the help of Judah's neighbors in his assault on Jerusalem. **Living in Jerusalem**: the current military threat and the prospect of being killed or captured as plunder drove the Rechabites into the city and away from their tents.

---

**[36:5] **I am barred**: Jeremiah could have been forbidden to enter the Temple for any number of reasons: e.g., his inflammatory preaching (the Temple sermon, 7:1–15; the broken pot); the hostility of Temple guards; the restrictions of arrest.

---

z. [35:6] Jgs 4:17, 24; 1 Sm 15:6; 2 Kgs 10:15–17.   a. [35:11] 2 Kgs 24:1–2.   b. [35:13] Jer 32:33.

c. [35:14] Jer 7:13; 25:3; 2 Chr 36:15–16.   d. [35:15] Jer 25:4–5, 7.
e. [35:17] Jer 11:8–9.   f. [36:3] Jer 26:3; Is 55:6–7.

for great is the anger and wrath with which the Lord has threatened this people."[g]

[8]Baruch, son of Neriah, did everything Jeremiah the prophet commanded; from the scroll he read the Lord's words in the Lord's house. [9]In the ninth month, in the fifth year of Jehoiakim, son of Josiah, king of Judah, all the people of Jerusalem and all those who came from Judah's cities to Jerusalem proclaimed a fast before the Lord. [10]So Baruch read the words of Jeremiah from the scroll in the room of Gemariah,[*] son of the scribe Shaphan, in the upper court of the Lord's house, at the entrance of the New Temple Gate, in the hearing of all the people.

[11]Now Micaiah, son of Gemariah, son of Shaphan, heard all the words of the Lord read from the scroll. [12]So he went down to the house of the king, into the scribe's chamber,[†] where the princes were meeting in session: Elishama, the scribe; Delaiah, son of Shemaiah; Elnathan, son of Achbor; Gemariah, son of Shaphan; Zedekiah, son of Hananiah; and the other princes. [13]Micaiah reported to them all that he had heard Baruch read from his scroll in the hearing of the people. [14]The princes immediately sent Jehudi, son of Nethaniah, son of Shelemiah, son of Cushi, to Baruch with the order: "The scroll you read in the hearing of the people—bring it with you and come." Scroll in hand, Baruch, son of Neriah, went to them. [15]"Sit down," they said to him, "and read it in our hearing." Baruch read it in their hearing, [16]and when they had heard all its words, they turned to each other in alarm and said to Baruch, "We have to tell the king all these things." [17]Then they asked Baruch: "Tell us, please, how did you come to write down all these words? Was it at his dictation?" [18]"Yes, he would dictate all these words to me," Baruch answered them, "while I wrote them down with ink in the scroll." [19]The princes said to Baruch, "Go into hiding, you and Jeremiah; do not let anyone know where you are."

[20]They went in to the king, into the courtyard; they had deposited the scroll in the room of Elishama the scribe. When they told the king everything that had happened, [21]the king sent Jehudi to get the scroll. Jehudi brought it from the room of Elishama the scribe, and read it to the king and to all the princes who were attending the king. [22]Now the king was sitting in his winter house, since it was the ninth month, and a fire was burning in the brazier before him. [23]Each time Jehudi finished reading three or four columns, he would cut off the piece with

a scribe's knife[‡] and throw it into the fire in the brazier, until the entire scroll was consumed in the fire in the brazier. [24]As they were listening to all these words the king and all his officials did not become alarmed, nor did they tear their garments. [25]And though Elnathan, Delaiah, and Gemariah urged the king not to burn the scroll, he would not listen to them. [26]He commanded Jerahmeel, a royal prince, and Seraiah, son of Azriel, and Shelemiah, son of Abdeel, to arrest Baruch, the scribe, and Jeremiah the prophet. But the Lord had hidden them away.

[27]The word of the Lord came to Jeremiah, after the king burned the scroll and the words Jeremiah had dictated to Baruch: [28]Take another scroll, and write on it all the words in the first scroll, which Jehoiakim, king of Judah, burned. [29]And against Jehoiakim, king of Judah, say this: Thus says the Lord: You are the one who burned that scroll, saying, "Why did you write on it: Babylon's king shall surely come and ravage this land, emptying it of every living thing"? [30]The Lord now says of Jehoiakim, king of Judah:[h] No descendant of his shall sit on David's throne; his corpse shall be thrown out, exposed to heat by day, frost by night.[§] [31]I will punish him and his descendants and his officials for their wickedness; upon them, the inhabitants of Jerusalem, and the people of Judah I will bring all the evil threats to which they did not listen.

[32]Then Jeremiah took another scroll and gave it to his scribe, Baruch, son of Neriah, who wrote on it at Jeremiah's dictation all the words contained in the scroll which Jehoiakim, king of Judah, had burned in the fire, adding many words like them.

## CHAPTER 37

**Jeremiah in the Dungeon.** [1]Zedekiah, son of Josiah, became king, succeeding Coniah, son of Jehoiakim; Nebuchadnezzar, king of Babylon, appointed him king over the land of Judah.[i] [2]Neither he, nor his officials, nor the people of the land would listen to the words which the Lord spoke through Jeremiah the prophet. [3]Yet King Zedekiah sent Jehucal, son of Shelemiah, and Zephaniah, son of Maaseiah the priest, to Jeremiah the prophet with this request: "Please appeal to the Lord, our God, for us."[j] [4]At this time Jeremiah still came and went freely among the people; he had not yet been put into prison.[¶] [5]Meanwhile, Pharaoh's army[**] had set out

---

‡[36:23] **A scribe's knife**: used to sharpen reed pens.

§[36:30] Jehoiakim's son Jehoiachin was named king, but reigned only three months; he was better known for his long exile in Babylon. **His corpse shall be thrown out**: just as Jehoiakim had thrown pieces of the scroll into the fire (cf. 22:19).

¶[37:4] **Put into prison**: as described in 32:1–3. Chronologically, the present episode follows 34:1–7.

**[37:5] **Pharaoh's army**: the force sent by Pharaoh Hophra; when they arrived, the Chaldeans temporarily lifted the siege against Jerusalem (cf. 34:21).

---

*[36:10] **Gemariah**: member of a family friendly to Jeremiah with rights to a room in the gateway fortress overlooking the court of the Temple. His father Shaphan had been Josiah's secretary of state (2 Kgs 22:3). From a window in this room Baruch read Jeremiah's scroll to the people.

†[36:12] **The scribe's chamber**: the office of the royal secretary.

---

g. [36:7] 2 Kgs 22:13.

h. [36:30] Jer 22:19.  i. [37:1] Jer 52:1; 2 Kgs 24:17; 2 Chr 36:10.  j. [37:3] Jer 21:1.

from Egypt, and when the Chaldeans who were besieging Jerusalem heard this report, they withdrew from the city.[k]

[6]Then the word of the LORD came to Jeremiah the prophet: [7]Thus says the LORD, the God of Israel: Thus you must say to the king of Judah who sent you to consult me: Listen! Pharaoh's army, which has set out to help you, will return to Egypt, its own land.[l] [8]The Chaldeans shall return and attack this city; they shall capture it and destroy it by fire.[m]

[9]Thus says the LORD: Do not deceive yourselves, saying: "The Chaldeans are surely leaving us forever." They are not! [10]Even if you could defeat the whole Chaldean army that is now attacking you, and only the wounded remained, each in his tent, these would rise up and destroy the city with fire.[n]

[11]Now when the Chaldean army withdrew from Jerusalem because of the army of Pharaoh,[o] [12]Jeremiah set out from Jerusalem to go to the territory of Benjamin, to receive his share of property among the people. [13]But at the Gate of Benjamin, the captain of the guard, by the name of Irijah, son of Shelemiah, son of Hananiah, arrested Jeremiah the prophet, saying, "You are deserting to the Chaldeans!" [14]"That is a lie!" Jeremiah answered, "I am not deserting to the Chaldeans." Without listening to him, Irijah kept Jeremiah in custody and brought him to the princes.

[15]The princes were enraged at Jeremiah and had Jeremiah beaten and imprisoned in the house of Jonathan the scribe, for they were using it as a jail.[p] [16]And so Jeremiah went into a room in the dungeon, where he remained many days.

[17]Then King Zedekiah had him brought to his palace, and he asked him secretly, "Is there any word from the LORD?" "There is!" Jeremiah answered: "You shall be handed over to the king of Babylon."[q] [18]Jeremiah then asked King Zedekiah: "How have I wronged you or your officials or this people, that you should put me in prison?[r] [19]Where are your own prophets who prophesied for you, saying: 'The King of Babylon will not attack you or this land'? [20]Please hear me, my lord king! Grant my petition: do not send me back into the house of Jonathan the scribe, or I shall die there."

[21]So King Zedekiah ordered that Jeremiah be confined in the court of the guard and given a ration of bread every day from the bakers' street until all the bread in the city was eaten up. Thus Jeremiah remained in the court of the guard.[s]

## CHAPTER 38
**Jeremiah in the Muddy Cistern.** [1]Shephatiah, son of Mattan, Gedaliah, son of Pashhur, Jucal,

son of Shelemiah, and Pashhur, son of Malchiah, heard the words Jeremiah was speaking to all the people:[*] [2]Thus says the LORD: Those who remain in this city shall die by means of the sword, starvation, and disease; but those who go out to the Chaldeans shall live. Their lives shall be spared them as spoils of war that they may live.[t] [3]Thus says the LORD: This city shall certainly be handed over to the army of the king of Babylon; he shall capture it.

[4]Then the princes said to the king, "This man ought to be put to death. He is weakening the resolve[†] of the soldiers left in this city and of all the people, by saying such things to them; he is not seeking the welfare of our people, but their ruin."[u] [5]King Zedekiah answered: "He is in your hands," for the king could do nothing with them. [6]And so they took Jeremiah and threw him into the cistern of Prince Malchiah, in the court of the guard, letting him down by rope. There was no water in the cistern, only mud, and Jeremiah sank down into the mud.[v]

[7]Now Ebed-melech, an Ethiopian, a court official in the king's house, heard that they had put Jeremiah in the cistern. The king happened to be sitting at the Gate of Benjamin, [8]and Ebed-melech went there from the house of the king and said to him, [9]"My lord king, these men have done wrong in all their treatment of Jeremiah the prophet, throwing him into the cistern. He will starve to death on the spot, for there is no more bread in the city."[w] [10]Then the king ordered Ebed-melech the Ethiopian: "Take three men with you, and get Jeremiah the prophet out of the cistern before he dies." [11]Ebed-melech took the men with him, and went first to the linen closet in the house of the king. He took some old, tattered rags and lowered them by rope to Jeremiah in the cistern. [12]Then he said to Jeremiah, "Put these old, tattered rags between your armpits and the ropes." Jeremiah did so, [13]and they pulled him up by rope out of the cistern. But Jeremiah remained in the court of the guard.

[14]King Zedekiah summoned Jeremiah the prophet to meet him at the third entrance of the house of the LORD. "I have a question to ask you," the king said to Jeremiah. "Do not hide anything from me."[x] [15]Jeremiah answered Zedekiah: "If I tell you anything, will you not have me put to death? If I counsel you, you will not listen to me!"[y] [16]But King Zedekiah swore to Jeremiah secretly: "As the LORD lives who gave

---

*[38:1] Jeremiah enjoyed sufficient liberty in the court of the guard (37:21) to speak to the people; cf. 32:6–9. **Gedaliah, son of Pashhur**: the latter is possibly the Pashhur of 20:1. **Pashhur, son of Malchiah**: mentioned in 21:1.

†[38:4] **He is weakening the resolve**: lit., "he weakens the hands." One of the Lachish ostraca (cf. note on 34:7) makes the same claim against the princes in Jerusalem.

k. [37:5] Ez 17:15; 29:6–7.  l. [37:7] Ez 17:17.  m. [37:8] Jer 34:22.
n. [37:10] Jer 21:4.  o. [37:11] Zec 14:10.  p. [37:15] Jer 38:6–13.  q. [37:17] Jer 21:7; 32:3; 34:21.  r. [37:18] Jer 26:19.
s. [37:21] Jer 32:2; 38:28.

t. [38:2] Jer 21:9–10; 39:18; 45:5.  u. [38:4] Jer 26:11.  v. [38:6] Jer 37:14–15.  w. [38:9] Jer 52:6.  x. [38:14] Jer 37:16.  y. [38:15] Lk 22:67–68.

us our lives, I will not kill you, nor will I hand you over to those men who seek your life."

[17]Jeremiah then said to Zedekiah: "Thus says the LORD God of hosts, the God of Israel: If you will only surrender to the princes of Babylon's king, you shall save your life; this city shall not be destroyed by fire, and you and your household shall live.[z] [18]But if you do not surrender to the princes of Babylon's king, this city shall fall into the hand of the Chaldeans, who shall destroy it by fire, and you shall not escape their hand."[a]

[19]King Zedekiah said to Jeremiah, "I am afraid of the Judahites who have deserted to the Chaldeans; I could be handed over to them, and they will mistreat me."[b] [20]"You will not be handed over to them," Jeremiah answered. "I beg you! Please listen to the voice of the LORD regarding what I tell you so that it may go well with you and your life be spared.[c] [21]But if you refuse to surrender, this is what the LORD has shown: [22]I see all the women who remain in the house of Judah's king being brought out to the princes of Babylon's king, and they are crying:

'They betrayed you, outdid you,
    your good friends!
Now that your feet are sunk in mud,
    they slink away.'[d]

[23]All your wives and children shall be brought out to the Chaldeans, and you shall not escape their hands; you shall be handed over to the king of Babylon, and this city shall be destroyed by fire."[e]

[24]Then Zedekiah said to Jeremiah, "Let no one know about this conversation, or you shall die. [25]If the princes should hear I spoke with you and if they should come and ask you, 'Tell us what you said to the king; do not hide it from us, or we will kill you,' or, 'What did the king say to you?' [26]then give them this answer: 'I petitioned the king not to send me back to Jonathan's house lest I die there.'" [27]When all the princes came to Jeremiah and questioned him, he answered them with the very words the king had commanded. They said no more to him, for nothing had been overheard of the conversation. [28]Thus Jeremiah stayed in the court of the guard until the day Jerusalem was taken.[f]

## CHAPTER 39

**The Capture of Jerusalem.** When Jerusalem was taken, [1]in the ninth year of Zedekiah,[g] king of Judah, in the tenth month,* Nebuchadnezzar, king of Babylon, and all his army marched

against Jerusalem and placed it under siege. [2]In the eleventh year of Zedekiah, on the ninth day of the fourth month,† the city wall was breached. [3]All the princes of the king of Babylon came and took their seats at the middle gate: Nergal-sharezer of Simmagir, a chief officer; Nebushazban, a high dignitary; and all the rest of the princes of the king of Babylon.‡ [4]When Zedekiah, king of Judah, and all his warriors saw this, they fled, leaving the city at night by way of the king's garden,§ through a gate between the two walls. He went in the direction of the Arabah,¶ [5]but the Chaldean army pursued them; they caught up with Zedekiah in the wilderness near Jericho and took him prisoner. They brought him to Nebuchadnezzar, king of Babylon, in Riblah,¶ in the land of Hamath, and he pronounced sentence upon him.[i] [6]The king of Babylon executed the sons of Zedekiah at Riblah before his very eyes; the king of Babylon also executed all the nobles of Judah.[j] [7]He then blinded Zedekiah and bound him in chains to bring him to Babylon.[k]

[8]The Chaldeans set fire to the king's house and the houses of the people and tore down the walls of Jerusalem.[l] [9]Nebuzaradan, captain of the bodyguard, deported to Babylon the rest of the people left in the city, those who had deserted to him, and the rest of the workers.[m] [10]But Nebuzaradan, captain of the bodyguard, left in the land of Judah some of the poor who had nothing and at the same time gave them vineyards and farms.[n]

**Jeremiah Released to Gedaliah's Custody.** [11]Concerning Jeremiah, Nebuchadnezzar, king of Babylon, gave these orders through Nebuzaradan, captain of the bodyguard: [12]"Take him and look after him; do not let anything happen to him. Whatever he may ask, you must do for him."[o] [13]Thereupon Nebuzaradan, captain of the bodyguard, and Nebushazban, a high dignitary, and Nergal-sharezer, a chief officer, and all the nobles of the king of Babylon, [14]had Jeremiah taken out of the courtyard of the guard and entrusted to Gedaliah, son of Ahikam,

589/588 B.C., according to the Babylonian calendar, whose New Year began in March/April.

†[39:2] **In the eleventh year . . . the ninth day of the fourth month:** in July, 587 B.C.

‡[39:3] The Babylonian officers act as a military tribunal or government, headed by Nergal-sharezer, Nebuchadnezzar's son and successor.

§[39:4] **By way of the king's garden:** along the southeast side of the city; the royal garden was in the Kidron Valley. **A gate between the two walls:** the southernmost city gate, at the end of the Tyropoeon Valley. **The Arabah:** the southern Jordan Valley. Zedekiah was perhaps trying to escape across the Jordan when he was captured near Jericho.

¶[39:5] **Riblah:** Nebuchadnezzar's headquarters north of Damascus; Pharaoh Neco had once used the town as a military post (2 Kgs 23:33).

*[39:1] **In the ninth year . . . in the tenth month:** the month Tebet (mid-December to mid-January) of the year

z. [38:17] Jer 27:12–13; 2 Kgs 24:12.  a. [38:18] Jer 32:4.  b. [38:19] 1 Sm 31:4.  c. [38:20] 2 Chr 20:20.  d. [38:22] Jb 6:15; 19:13–14, 19.  e. [38:23] Jer 41:10.  f. [38:28] Jer 39:14.  g. [39:1–2] Jer 52:4–16; 2 Kgs 25:1–12; Ez 24:1.

h. [39:4] Jer 52:7.  i. [39:5] Jer 32:4–5; 38:18.  j. [39:6] Jer 34:21.  k. [39:7] Jer 32:4–5; Ez 12:13.  l. [39:8] Jer 21:10; 34:2; 52:13.  m. [39:9] 2 Kgs 25:11.  n. [39:10] 2 Kgs 25:12, 22.  o. [39:12] Jer 40:4.

son of Shaphan, to bring him home. And so he remained among the people.[p]

**A Word of Comfort for Ebed-melech.** [15]While Jeremiah was still imprisoned in the court of the guard, the word of the LORD came to him: [16]Go, tell this to Ebed-melech the Ethiopian: Thus says the LORD of hosts, the God of Israel: See, I am now carrying out my words against this city, for evil and not for good; this will happen in your presence on that day.[q] [17]But on that day I will deliver you—oracle of the LORD; you shall not be handed over to the men you dread. [18]I will make certain that you escape and do not fall by the sword. Your life will be your spoils of war because you trusted in me—oracle of the LORD.[r]

## CHAPTER 40

**Jeremiah Still in Judah.** [1]The word* which came to Jeremiah from the LORD, after Nebuzaradan, captain of the bodyguard, had released him in Ramah, where he found him a prisoner in chains among the captives of Jerusalem and Judah being exiled to Babylon.[s] [2]The captain of the bodyguard took charge of Jeremiah and said to him, "The LORD, your God, decreed ruin for this place. [3]Now he has made it happen, accomplishing what he decreed; because you sinned against the LORD and did not listen to his voice, this decree has been realized against you. [4]Now, I release you today from the chains upon your hands; if you want to come with me to Babylon, then come: I will look out for you. But if you do not want to come to Babylon, very well. See, the whole land lies before you; go wherever you think good and proper.[t] [5]Or go to Gedaliah, son of Ahikam, son of Shaphan, whom the king of Babylon has set over the cities of Judah. Stay with him among the people. Or go wherever you want!" The captain of the bodyguard gave him food and gifts and let him go.[u] [6]So Jeremiah went to Gedaliah, son of Ahikam, in Mizpah,[†] and dwelt with him among the people left in the land.[v]

[7]When the military leaders still in the field with their soldiers heard that the king of Babylon had set Gedaliah, son of Ahikam, over the land and had put him in charge of men, women, and children, from the poor of the land who had not been deported to Babylon, [8]they and their soldiers came to Gedaliah in Mizpah: Ishmael, son of Nethaniah; Johanan, son of Kareah; Seraiah, son of Tanhumeth; the sons of Ephai of Netophah; and Jezaniah of Beth-maacah.

[9]Gedaliah, son of Ahikam, son of Shaphan, swore an oath to them and their men: "Do not be afraid to serve the Chaldeans. Stay in the land and serve the king of Babylon, so that everything may go well with you.[w] [10]As for me, I will remain in Mizpah, as your representative before the Chaldeans when they come to us. You, for your part, harvest the wine, the fruit, and the oil, store them in jars, and remain in the cities you occupied." [11]Then all the Judahites in Moab, in Ammon, in Edom, and those in all other lands heard that the king of Babylon had left a remnant in Judah and had set over them Gedaliah, son of Ahikam, son of Shaphan. [12]They all returned to the land of Judah from the places to which they had scattered. They went to Gedaliah at Mizpah and had a rich harvest of wine and fruit.

**Assassination of Gedaliah.** [13]Now Johanan, son of Kareah, and all the military leaders in the field came to Gedaliah in Mizpah [14]and said to him, "Surely you are aware that Baalis, the Ammonite king,[‡] has sent Ishmael, son of Nethaniah, to assassinate you?"[x] But Gedaliah, son of Ahikam, would not believe them. [15]Then Johanan, son of Kareah, said secretly to Gedaliah in Mizpah: "Please let me go and kill Ishmael, son of Nethaniah; no one will know it. What if he assassinates you? All the Judahites who have now rallied behind you would scatter and the remnant of Judah would perish." [16]Gedaliah, son of Ahikam, answered Johanan, son of Kareah, "You must not do that. What you are saying about Ishmael is a lie!"

## CHAPTER 41

[1]In the seventh month, Ishmael, son of Nethaniah, son of Elishama, of royal descent, one of the king's nobles, came with ten men to Gedaliah, son of Ahikam, at Mizpah.[y] While they were together at table in Mizpah, [2]Ishmael, son of Nethaniah, and the ten with him, stood up and struck down Gedaliah, son of Ahikam, son of Shaphan, with swords. They killed him, since the king of Babylon had set him over the land; [3]Ishmael also killed all the Judahites of military age who were with Gedaliah and the Chaldean soldiers stationed there.

[4]The day after the murder of Gedaliah, before anyone learned about it, [5]eighty men, in ragged clothes, with beards shaved off and gashes on their bodies, came from Shechem, Shiloh, and Samaria, bringing grain offerings and incense for the house of the LORD. [6]Weeping as he went, Ishmael son of Nethaniah, set out from Mizpah to meet them. "Come to Gedaliah,

---

*[40:1] **The word**: this "word" does not actually appear until 42:7.

†[40:6] While Jerusalem had suffered a great deal of damage, the Babylonian leaders' selection of Mizpah as their local headquarters was probably as much a symbolic statement as it was a utilitarian one: Jerusalem and its political and religious worldview had given way to disorder and no longer existed as a symbol of order.

‡[40:14] In an attempt, perhaps, to weaken Babylon's hold on the area and to add Judah to the Ammonite kingdom, Baalis supported Ishmael's claim to the throne of David (cf. 41:1 for Ishmael's genealogy).

---

p. [39:14] Jer 26:24; 38:28.   q. [39:16] Jer 21:10; Dn 9:12.   r. [39:18] Jer 45:5; Ps 25:3; 37:40.   s. [40:1] Jer 39:14.   t. [40:4] Jer 39:12.   u. [40:5] Jer 39:14; 2 Kgs 25:22.   v. [40:6] Jer 39:14.

w. [40:9] Jer 27:12–13; 2 Kgs 25:24.   x. [40:14] Jer 41:1–3, 10.   y. [41:1] Jer 40:14–16; 2 Kgs 25:25.

son of Ahikam," he said as he met them. ⁷Once they were inside the city, Ishmael, son of Nethaniah, and his men slaughtered them and threw them into the cistern. ⁸Ten of them said to Ishmael: "Do not kill us! We have stores of wheat and barley, oil and honey hidden in the field." So he spared them and did not kill them as he had killed their companions. ⁹The cistern into which Ishmael threw all the bodies of the men he had killed was the large one King Asa made to defend himself against Baasha, king of Israel; Ishmael, son of Nethaniah, filled this cistern with the slain.ᶻ

¹⁰Ishmael led away the rest of the people left in Mizpah, including the princesses,* whom Nebuzaradan, captain of the bodyguard, had consigned to Gedaliah, son of Ahikam. With these captives, Ishmael, son of Nethaniah, set out to cross over to the Ammonites.

**Flight to Egypt.** ¹¹But when Johanan, son of Kareah, and the other army leaders with him heard about the crimes Ishmael, son of Nethaniah, had committed, ¹²they took all their men and set out to attack Ishmael, son of Nethaniah. They overtook him at the great pool in Gibeon.† ¹³At the sight of Johanan, son of Kareah, and the other army leaders, the people with Ishmael rejoiced; ¹⁴all of those whom Ishmael had taken captive from Mizpah went back to Johanan, son of Kareah. ¹⁵But Ishmael, son of Nethaniah, escaped from Johanan with eight men and fled to the Ammonites. ¹⁶Then Johanan, son of Kareah, and all the military leaders took charge of all the rest of the people whom Ishmael, son of Nethaniah, had taken away from Mizpah after he killed Gedaliah, son of Ahikam—the soldiers, the women with children, and court officials, whom he brought back from Gibeon. ¹⁷They set out and stopped at Geruth Chimham near Bethlehem, intending to go into Egypt. ¹⁸They were afraid of the Chaldeans, because Ishmael, son of Nethaniah, had slain Gedaliah, son of Ahikam, whom the king of Babylon had set over the land.

## CHAPTER 42

¹Then all the military leaders, including Johanan, son of Kareah, Azariah, son of Hoshaiah, and all the people, from the least to the greatest, ²approached Jeremiah the prophet and said, "Please grant our petition; pray for us to the LORD, your God, for all this remnant. As you see, only a few of us remain, but once we were many. ³May the LORD, your God, show us the way we should take and what we should do." ⁴"Very well!" Jeremiah the prophet answered

them: "I will pray to the LORD, your God, as you desire; whatever the LORD answers, I will tell you; I will withhold nothing from you."ᵃ ⁵And they said to Jeremiah, "May the LORD be a true and faithful witness against us if we do not follow all the instructions the LORD, your God, sends us through you.ᵇ ⁶Whether we like it or not, we will obey the command of the LORD, our God, to whom we are sending you, so that it may go well with us for obeying the command of the LORD, our God."ᶜ

⁷Ten days passed before the word of the LORD came to Jeremiah. ⁸Then he called Johanan, son of Kareah, his army leaders, and all the people, from the least to the greatest, ⁹and said to them: Thus says the LORD, the God of Israel, to whom you sent me to offer your petition: ¹⁰If indeed you will remain in this land, I will build you up, and not tear you down; I will plant you, not uproot you; for I repent of the evil I have done you.ᵈ ¹¹Do not fear the king of Babylon, as you do now. Do not fear him—oracle of the LORD—for I am with you to save you, to rescue you from his power.ᵉ ¹²I will take pity on you, so that he will have pity on you and let you return to your land.ᶠ ¹³But if you keep saying, "We will not stay in this land," thus disobeying the voice of the LORD, your God, ¹⁴and saying, "No, we will go to the land of Egypt, where we will not see war, nor hear the trumpet alarm, nor hunger for bread. There we will live!"ᵍ ¹⁵then listen to the word of the LORD, remnant of Judah: Thus says the LORD of hosts, the God of Israel: If you are set on going to Egypt and settling down there once you arrive, ¹⁶the sword you fear shall overtake you in the land of Egypt; the hunger you dread shall pursue you to Egypt and there you shall die.ʰ ¹⁷All those determined to go to Egypt to live shall die by the sword, famine, and disease: not one shall survive or escape the evil that I am bringing upon them.ⁱ ¹⁸For thus says the LORD of hosts, the God of Israel: Just as my furious wrath was poured out upon the inhabitants of Jerusalem, so shall my anger be poured out on you when you reach Egypt. You shall become a malediction and a horror, a curse and a reproach, and you shall never see this place again.ʲ

¹⁹The LORD has spoken to you, remnant of Judah. Do not go to Egypt! Mark well that I am warning you this day. ²⁰At the cost of your lives you have been deceitful, for you yourselves sent me to the LORD, your God, saying, "Pray for us to the LORD, our God; whatever the LORD, our God, shall say, tell us and we will do it." ²¹Today I have told you, but you have not listened to the voice of the LORD your God, in anything that he has sent me to tell you.ᵏ ²²Have no doubt about

---

*[41:10] **The princesses**: the women of Judah's royal house.

†[41:12] **Gibeon**: modern El-Jib; northwest of Jerusalem. A huge pit carved into limestone provided water in time of siege, here called the great pool, lit., "many waters"; cf. 2 Sm 2:12–14.

z. [41:9] 1 Kgs 15:16; 2 Chr 16:6.

a. [42:4] 1 Sm 3:18.  b. [42:5] Jgs 11:10.  c. [42:6] Jer 7:23; Dt 5:33; 6:3.  d. [42:10] Jer 31:28; 32:41.  e. [42:11] Jer 30:10–11.  f. [42:12] Ps 106:45–46; Prv 16:7.  g. [42:14] Dt 28:68.  h. [42:16] Jer 44:13–14, 27.  i. [42:17] Jer 29:17–18; 44:14, 28.  j. [42:18] Jer 44:12.  k. [42:21] Zec 7:11–12.

this: you shall die by the sword, famine, and disease in the place where you want to go and live.[l]

## CHAPTER 43

[1]When Jeremiah finished telling the people all the words the LORD, their God, sent to them, [2]Azariah, son of Hoshaiah, Johanan, son of Kareah, and all the others had the insolence to say to Jeremiah: "You lie; the LORD, our God, did not send you to tell us, 'Do not to go to Egypt to live there.' [3]Baruch, son of Neriah, is inciting you against us, to hand us over to the Chaldeans to be killed or exiled to Babylon."[m]

[4]So Johanan, son of Kareah, and the rest of the leaders and the people did not listen to the voice of the LORD to stay in the land of Judah.[n] [5]Instead, Johanan, son of Kareah, and the military leaders took along all the remnant of Judah who had been dispersed among the nations and then had returned to dwell in the land of Judah: [6]men, women, and children, the princesses and everyone whom Nebuzaradan, captain of the bodyguard, had consigned to Gedaliah, son of Ahikam, son of Shaphan; also Jeremiah, the prophet, and Baruch, son of Neriah.[o] [7]They went to Egypt—they did not listen to the voice of the LORD—and came to Tahpanhes.[p]

**Jeremiah in Egypt.** [8]The word of the LORD came to Jeremiah in Tahpanhes: [9]Take some large stones in your hand and set them in mortar in the terrace at the entrance to the house of Pharaoh in Tahpanhes, while the Judahites watch. [10]Then say to them: Thus says the LORD of hosts, the God of Israel: I will send for my servant Nebuchadnezzar, king of Babylon. He will place his throne upon these stones which I, Jeremiah, have set up, and stretch his canopy above them.[q] [11]He shall come and strike the land of Egypt: with death, those marked for death; with exile, those marked for exile; with the sword, those marked for the sword.[r] [12]He shall set fire to the temples of Egypt's gods, burn the gods and carry them off. He shall pick the land of Egypt clean, as a shepherd picks lice off his cloak, and then depart victorious.[s] [13]He shall smash the obelisks at the Temple of the Sun in the land of Egypt and destroy with fire the temples of the Egyptian gods.

## CHAPTER 44

[1]The word that came to Jeremiah for all the Judahites who were living in Egypt, those living in Migdol, Tahpanhes, and Memphis, and in Upper Egypt: [2]Thus says the LORD of hosts,

the God of Israel: You yourselves have seen all the evil I brought upon Jerusalem and the other cities of Judah. Today they lie in ruins uninhabited,[t] [3]because of the evil they did to provoke me, going after other gods, offering incense and serving other gods they did not know, neither they, nor you, nor your ancestors.[u] [4]Though I repeatedly sent you all my servants the prophets, saying: "You must not commit this abominable deed I hate," [5]they did not listen or incline their ears in order to turn from their evil, no longer offering incense to other gods.[v] [6]Therefore the fury of my anger poured forth and kindled fire in the cities of Judah and the streets of Jerusalem, to turn them into the ruined wasteland they are today.

[7]Now thus says the LORD God of hosts, the God of Israel: Why inflict so great an evil upon yourselves, cutting off from Judah man and woman, child and infant, not leaving yourselves even a remnant? [8]Why do you provoke me with the works of your hands, offering sacrifice to other gods here in the land of Egypt where you have come to live? Will you cut yourselves off and become a curse, a reproach among all the nations of the earth?[w] [9]Have you forgotten the evil of your ancestors, the evil of the kings of Judah, the evil of their wives, and your own evil and the evil of your wives—all that they did in the land of Judah and in the streets of Jerusalem?[x] [10]To this day they have not been crushed down, nor have they shown fear. They have not followed my law and my statutes that I set before you and your ancestors.[y]

[11]Therefore, thus says the LORD of hosts, the God of Israel: I have set my face against you for evil, to cut off all Judah. [12]I will take away the remnant of Judah who insisted on going to the land of Egypt to live there; in the land of Egypt they shall meet their end. They shall fall by the sword or be consumed by hunger. From the least to the greatest, they shall die by sword or hunger; they shall become a malediction, a horror, a curse, a reproach.[z] [13]Thus I will punish those who live in Egypt, just as I punished Jerusalem, with sword, hunger, and disease, [14]so that none of the remnant of Judah who came to live in the land of Egypt shall escape or survive.[a] No one shall return to the land of Judah. Even though they long to return and live there, they shall not return except as refugees.

[15]They answered Jeremiah—all the men who knew that their wives were offering sacrifices to other gods, all the women standing there in the immense crowd, and all the people who lived in Lower and Upper Egypt: [16]"Regarding the word you have spoken to us in the name of the LORD, we are not listening to you.[b] [17]Rather we will go on doing what we proposed; we will

* [44:2–30] Chronologically, these are the last of Jeremiah's words to his people. As the narrative ends, Jeremiah meets with rejection. According to tradition, recorded in a much later work, he was murdered in Egypt by fellow Judahites.

l. [42:22] Jer 44:12; Hos 9:6.   m. [43:3] Jer 38:4.   n. [43:4] Jer 41:16.   o. [43:6] Jer 41:10.   p. [43:7] Jer 42:13–14; 44:1.   q. [43:10] Jer 27:6; Ez 29:19.   r. [43:11] Jer 46:13; Ez 30:10.   s. [43:12] Jer 46:25; Ez 30:13–14.

t. [44:2] Jer 34:22; Lv 26:32–33.   u. [44:3] Jer 11:17; Dt 32:17.   v. [44:5] Jer 7:24, 26; 19:4.   w. [44:8] Jer 25:6–7.   x. [44:9] 1 Kgs 11:1, 8; Ezr 9:7, 14.   y. [44:10] Jer 7:24.   z. [44:12] Jer 42:15, 18, 22.   a. [44:14] Jer 43:11.   b. [44:16] Jer 6:16–17.

offer incense to the Queen of Heaven and pour out libations to her, just as we have done, along with our ancestors, our kings and princes, in the cities of Judah and in the streets of Jerusalem. Then we had plenty to eat, we prospered, and we suffered no misfortune.[c] [18]But ever since we stopped offering sacrifices to the Queen of Heaven and pouring out libations to her, we lack everything and are being destroyed by sword and hunger." [19]And the women said, "When we offered sacrifices to the Queen of Heaven and poured out libations to her, did we bake cakes in her image and pour out libations to her without our husbands' consent?"[d]

[20]To all the people, men and women, who gave him this answer, Jeremiah said: [21]As for the sacrifices you offered in the cities of Judah and in the streets of Jerusalem—you, your ancestors, your kings and princes, and the people of the land—did not the LORD remember them? Did it not enter his mind?[e] [22]The LORD could no longer bear the evil of your deeds, the abominations you were doing; then your land became a waste, a horror, a curse, without even one inhabitant, as it is today.[f] [23]Because you offered sacrifice and sinned against the LORD, not listening to the voice of the LORD, not following his law, his statutes, and his decrees, therefore this evil has overtaken you, as it is today.[g]

[24]Jeremiah said to all the people and to all the women: Hear the word of the LORD, all you Judahites in the land of Egypt: [25]Thus says the LORD of hosts, the God of Israel: You and your wives have carried out with your hands what your mouths have spoken: "We will go on fulfilling the vows we have made to offer sacrifice to the Queen of Heaven and to pour out libations to her." Very well! keep your vows, fulfill your vows! [26]And then listen to the word of the LORD, all you Judahites living in Egypt; I swear by my own great name, says the LORD: in the whole land of Egypt, my name shall no longer be pronounced by the lips of any Judahite, saying, "As the Lord GOD lives." [27]I am watching over them for evil, not for good. All the Judahites in Egypt shall come to an end by sword or famine until they are completely destroyed.[h] [28]Those who escape the sword to return from the land of Egypt to the land of Judah shall be few in number. The whole remnant of Judah who came to Egypt to live shall know whose word stands, mine or theirs.[i]

[29]And this shall be a sign to you—oracle of the LORD—I will punish you in this place so that you will know that my words stand solidly against you for evil. [30]Thus says the LORD: See! I will hand over Pharaoh Hophra,* king of Egypt,

to his enemies, to those seeking his life, just as I handed over Zedekiah, king of Judah, to his enemy Nebuchadrezzar, king of Babylon, to the one seeking his life.[j]

## CHAPTER 45

**A Message to Baruch.**[†] [1]The word that Jeremiah the prophet spoke to Baruch, son of Neriah, when he wrote on a scroll words from Jeremiah's own mouth in the fourth year of Jehoiakim, son of Josiah, king of Judah:[k] [2]Thus says the LORD, God of Israel, to you, Baruch. [3]You said, "Woe is me! the LORD has added grief to my pain.[l] I have worn myself out with groaning; rest eludes me." [4]You must say this to him. Thus says the LORD: What I have built, I am tearing down; what I have planted, I am uprooting: all this land.[m] [5]And you, do you seek great things for yourself? Do not seek them! I am bringing evil on all flesh—oracle of the LORD—but I will grant you your life as spoils of war, wherever you may go.[n]

## VIII. ORACLES AGAINST THE NATIONS[‡]

## CHAPTER 46

[1]The word of the LORD that came to Jeremiah the prophet concerning the nations.
**Against Egypt.** [2]Concerning Egypt. Against the army of Pharaoh Neco, king of Egypt, defeated at Carchemish on the Euphrates[§] by Nebuchadrezzar, king of Babylon, in the fourth year of Jehoiakim, son of Josiah, king of Judah:

[3]   Prepare buckler and shield!
           move forward to battle!
[4]   Harness the horses,
           charioteers, mount up!
     Fall in, with helmets on;
           polish your spears, put on your
                          armor.
[5]   What do I see?
           Are they panicking, falling apart?
           Their warriors are hammered back,
     They flee headlong
           never making a stand.

---

†[45:1–5] At the conclusion of his narrative, Baruch appends a message Jeremiah had given him when he first wrote down Jeremiah's words (cf. 36:4). The future revealed by the prophet overwhelmed Baruch; now he learns his own safety is assured, even though the Lord will destroy Judah.

‡[46:1–51:64] A collection of oracles against foreign nations constitutes the final section of the Hebrew text of Jeremiah; in the Greek text they follow 25:13. The oracles here appear to be arranged in loose chronological order: 46:2 mentions the fourth year of Jehoiakim; the oracles in 50:1–51:64 are evidently from the end of Jeremiah's life.

§[46:2] **Carchemish on the Euphrates**: the western terminus of the Mesopotamian trade route, where Nebuchadnezzar defeated Pharaoh Neco in 605 B.C., thus gaining undisputed control of Syria and Palestine.

---

*[44:30] **Hophra**: killed by his own people. Hophra's successor, Amasis, ruled Egypt when Nebuchadnezzar took control of the country.

---

c. [44:17] Jer 5:3; 7:18.   d. [44:19] Jer 7:18.   e. [44:21] Jer 11:13.   f. [44:22] Jer 15:6.   g. [44:23] 2 Kgs 17:15; Dn 9:11–12.   h. [44:27] Ezr 7:3–7.   i. [44:28] Dt 28:62; Is 10:22.

j. [44:30] Jer 39:5–7; 46:25–26; Ez 29:3–4; 30:21.   k. [45:1] Jer 36:4, 18, 32.   l. [45:3] Lam 1:3; 5:5.   m. [45:4] Jer 18:7; Is 5:5–6.   n. [45:5] Jer 25:26–29.

Terror on every side—
  oracle of the LORD!°
6  The swift cannot flee,
  nor the warrior escape:
There up north, on the banks of the
  Euphrates
  they stumble and fall.
7  Who is this? Like the Nile, it rears up;
  like rivers, its waters surge.
8  Egypt rears up like the Nile,
  like rivers, its waters surge.
"I will rear up," it says, "and cover the earth,
  destroying the city and its people.ᵖ
9  Forward, horses!
  charge, chariots!
March forth, warriors,
  Cush and Put, bearing shields,
  Archers of Lud, stretching bows!"
10  Today belongs to the Lord GOD of hosts,
  a day of vengeance, vengeance on
  his foes!
The sword devours and is sated, drunk
  with their blood:
  for the Lord GOD of hosts holds a
  sacrifice
  in the land of the north, on the River
  Euphrates.�q
11  Go up to Gilead, procure balm,
  Virgin daughter Egypt!
No use to multiply remedies;
  for you there is no healing.ʳ
12  The nations hear your cries,
  your screaming fills the earth.
Warrior stumbles against warrior,
  both collapse together.ˢ

13ʳThe word that the LORD spoke to Jeremiah
the prophet when Nebuchadrezzar, king of Babylon, came to attack the land of Egypt:ᵗ

14  Proclaim in Egypt, announce in Migdol,
  announce in Memphis and
  Tahpanhes!
Say: Fall in, get ready,
  the sword has devoured your
  neighbors.ᵘ
15  Why has Apisᵗ fled?
  Your champion did not stand,
Because the LORD thrust him down;
16  he stumbled repeatedly then
  collapsed.
They said to each other,
  "Get up! We must return to our own
  people,

To the land of our birth,
  away from the destroying sword."ᵛ
17  Give Pharaoh, king of Egypt, the name
  "Braggart-missed-his-chance."‡
18  As I live, says the King
  whose name is LORD of hosts,
Like Tabor above mountains,
  like Carmel§ above the sea, he comes.
19  Pack your bags for exile,
  enthroned daughter Egypt;
Memphis shall become a wasteland,
  an empty ruin.
20  Egypt is a beautiful heifer,
  a horsefly from the north keeps
  coming.
21  Even the mercenaries in her ranks
  are like fattened calves;
They too turn and flee together—
  they do not stand their ground,
For their day of ruin comes upon them,
  their time of punishment.
22  Her voice is like a snake!
  Yes, they come in force;
They attack her with axes,
  like those who fell trees.
23  They cut down her forest—oracle of the
  LORD—
  impenetrable though it be;
More numerous than locusts,
  they cannot be counted.
24  Shamed is daughter Egypt,
  handed over to a people from the
  north.

25The LORD of hosts, the God of Israel, has
said: See! I will punish Amon⁵ of Thebes and
Egypt, gods, kings, Pharaoh, and those who trust
in him.ʷ  26I will hand them over to those who
seek their lives, to Nebuchadrezzar, king of Babylon, and to his officers. But later, Egypt shall be
inhabited again, as in days of old—oracle of the
LORD.ˣ

27  But you, my servant Jacob, do not fear;
  do not be dismayed, Israel!
Listen! I will deliver you from far-off
  lands;
  your offspring, from the land of
  their exile.
Jacob shall again find rest,
  secure, with none to frighten him.ʸ
28  You, Jacob my servant, must not fear—
  oracle of the LORD—

---

*[46:13] In 601 B.C. Nebuchadnezzar advanced into Egypt
itself, but finally had to withdraw to Syria.
†[46:15]  **Apis**: the chief god of Memphis; the black bull
honored as an incarnation of the god Ptah and, later, of the
god Osiris.

o. [46:5] Jer 6:25; 49:29.  p. [46:8] Ez 29:3; 32:2.  q. [46:10] Dt
32:42; Is 13:9; Ez 39:17–20.  r. [46:11] Jer 8:22; 51:8; Ez 30:21–22.
s. [46:12] Ez 32:9–12.  t. [46:13] Jer 43:10–11; 44:30; Is 19:1.
u. [46:14] Jer 44:1.

‡[46:17]  **"Braggart-missed-his-chance"**: the Hebrew
phrase may contain a pun on the Pharaoh's name or royal title.
§[46:18]  **Tabor . . . Carmel**: mountains in Palestine that
seem to tower over their surroundings as Nebuchadnezzar towers over the nations in his path as he makes his way
toward Egypt.
¶[46:25]  **Amon**: the sun-god worshiped at Thebes in
Upper Egypt.

v. [46:16] Lv 26:37.  w. [46:25] Ez 30:15–16.  x. [46:26] Jer 44:30;
Ez 30:4; 32:11–12.  y. [46:27] Jer 30:10; 43:5.

for I am with you;
    I will make an end of all the nations
        to which I have driven you,
    But of you I will not make an end:
    I will chastise you as you deserve,
        I cannot let you go unpunished.[z]

## CHAPTER 47

**Against the Philistines.** [1]The word of the LORD
that came to Jeremiah the prophet concerning
the Philistines, before Pharaoh attacked Gaza:[a]

[2] Thus says the LORD:
    [*] See: waters are rising from the north,
        to become a torrent in flood;
    They shall flood the land and all it
            contains,
        the cities and their inhabitants.
    People will howl and wail,
        every inhabitant of the land.
[3] At the noise of the pounding hooves of
            his steeds,
    the clanking chariots, the rumbling
            wheels,
    Parents do not turn back for their
            children;
        their hands hang helpless,
[4] Because of the day that is coming
        to destroy all the Philistines
    And cut off from Tyre and Sidon[†]
        the last of their allies.
    Yes, the LORD is destroying the
            Philistines,
        the remnant from the coasts of
            Caphtor.[b]
[5] Baldness is visited upon Gaza,[c]
        Ashkelon is reduced to silence;
    Ashdod, remnant of their strength,
        how long will you gash yourself?[‡]
[6] Ah! Sword of the LORD!
        When will you find rest?
    Return to your scabbard;
        stop, be still!
[7] How can it find rest
        when the LORD has commanded it?
    Against Ashkelon and the seacoast,
        there he has appointed it.[d]

---

*[47:2–7] Nebuchadnezzar's military campaign against
Ashkelon in 604 B.C. may provide some historical background for this poem.

†[47:4] **Tyre and Sidon:** Phoenician seaports allied commercially with the Philistines and often rebelling against
Nebuchadnezzar; cf. 27:1–4. After the capture of Jerusalem,
Nebuchadnezzar carried out a partially successful thirteen-
year siege of Tyre. **Caphtor:** Crete and other Aegean islands,
points of origin for the Philistines and other sea peoples; cf.
Am 9:7.

‡[47:5] **Baldness . . . gash yourself:** close-cropped hair,
silence, and ritual slashing of the body express mourning and
grief and here represent the mourner's awareness that chaos
has overcome order (cf. 41:5).

---

z. [46:28] Jer 30:11.   a. [47:1] Ez 25:15–16; Zep 2:4.   b. [47:4] Jer
25:22; Ez 25:16–17; Am 1:8; 9:7.   c. [47:5] Am 1:7.   d. [47:7] Zep
2:5–6.

## CHAPTER 48

**Against Moab.**[§] [1]Concerning Moab. Thus says
the LORD of hosts, the God of Israel:

    Ah, Nebo! it is ravaged;
        Kiriathaim is disgraced, captured;
    Disgraced and overthrown is the
            stronghold:
[2]        Moab's glory is no more.
    In Heshbon they plot evil against her:
        "Come! We will put an end to her as
            a nation."
    You, too, Madmen,[¶] shall be silenced;
        you the sword stalks!
[3] Listen! an outcry from Horonaim,[e]
        "Ruin and great destruction!"
[4] "Moab is crushed!"
        their outcry is heard in Zoar.
[5] Up the ascent of Luhith
        they go weeping;
    At the descent to Horonaim
        they hear cries of anguish:
[6] "Flee, save your lives!
        Be like a wild donkey in the
            wilderness!"
[7] Because you trusted in your works and
            your treasures,
        you also shall be captured.
    Chemosh[**] shall go into exile,
        his priests and princes with him.[f]
[8] The destroyer comes upon every city,
        not a city escapes;
    Ruined is the valley,
        wasted the plateau—oracle of the
            LORD.
[9] Set up a tombstone for Moab;
        it will soon become a complete
            wasteland,
    Its cities turned into ruins
        where no one dwells.
[10] Cursed are they who do the LORD's work
            carelessly,
        cursed those who keep their sword
            from shedding blood.
[11] [††]Moab has been resting from its youth,
        suspended above its dregs,
    Never poured from flask to flask,
        never driven into exile.
    Thus it retained its flavor,
        its bouquet is not lost.[g]

---

§[48:1–47] Moab, located east of the Dead Sea, was one of
Israel's bitter enemies (cf., e.g., Is 15–16; Am 2:1–3). According to Flavius Josephus, Nebuchadnezzar conquered Moab
and Ammon in his twenty-third year (582 B.C.), five years
after the destruction of Jerusalem. This chapter is full of local
place names in Moab.

¶[48:2] **Madmen:** a place name, not mentioned elsewhere
in the Old Testament.

**[48:7] **Chemosh:** chief god of Moab (cf. Nm 21:29).

††[48:11–12] Moabite wine was known for its high quality.
Here the wine is a metaphor for Moab's complacency.

---

e. [48:3–5] Is 15:5.   f. [48:7] Nm 21:29.   g. [48:11] Zep 1:12.

¹²Be assured! The days are coming—oracle of the LORD—when I will send him wine-makers to decant the wine; they shall empty its flasks and smash its jars. ¹³Chemosh shall disappoint Moab, just as the house of Israel was disappointed by Bethel, in which they trusted.ʰ

¹⁴ How can you say, "We are heroes,
    mighty warriors"?
¹⁵ The one who ravages Moab and its cities
    comes up,
    the best of its youth go down to
        slaughter—
    oracle of the King, whose name is
        LORD of hosts.
¹⁶ Moab's ruin is near at hand,
    its disaster approaches swiftly.
¹⁷ Mourn, all you neighbors,
    all you who know its name!
  Say: How the mighty scepter is broken,
    the glorious staff!
¹⁸ Come down from glory, sit on the
        parched ground,
    enthroned daughter Dibon;*
  Moab's destroyer has fallen upon you,
    has shattered your strongholds.ⁱ
¹⁹ Stand along the road, keep watch,
    enthroned Aroer;
  Ask the fleeing man, the escaping woman:
    ask them what has happened.ʲ
²⁰ "Moab is put to shame, destroyed."
    Wail and cry out,
  Proclaim it at the Arnon:
    "Moab is destroyed!"ᵏ

²¹Judgment has come upon the plateau: on Holon, Jahzah, and Mephaath,ˡ ²²on Dibon, Nebo, and Beth-diblathaim, ²³on Kiriathaim, Beth-gamul, and Beth-meon, ²⁴on Kerioth and on Bozrah: on all the cities of the land of Moab, far and near.

²⁵ The horn of Moab is cut off,
    its arm is broken—oracle of the LORD.

²⁶Make him drunk because he set himself over against the LORD; let Moab swim in his vomit and become a laughingstock. ²⁷Has Israel not been a laughingstock to you? Was he caught among thieves that you wag your heads whenever you speak of him?ᵐ

²⁸ Abandon the cities, take shelter in the
    crags,
    inhabitants of Moab.
  Be like the dove that nests
    in the walls of a gorge.

²⁹ We have heard of the pride of Moab,ⁿ
    pride beyond bounds:
  His loftiness, his pride, his scorn,
    his insolent heart.
³⁰ I myself know his arrogance—oracle of
    the LORD—
    liar in word, liar in deed.
³¹ And so I wail over Moab,
    over all Moab I cry,
    over the people of Kir-heres I moan.º
³² More than for Jazer I weep for you,
    vine of Sibmah.
  Your tendrils trailed down to the sea,
    as far as Jazer they stretched.
  Upon your summer harvest and your
        vintage,
    the destroyer has fallen.ᵖ
³³ Joy and gladness are taken away
    from the garden land, the land of
        Moab.
  I dry up the wine from the wine vats,
    the treader treads no more,
    the vintage shout is stilled.

³⁴The cry of Heshbon and Elealeh is heard as far as Jahaz; they call from Zoar to Horonaim and to Eglath-shelishiyah; even the waters of Nimrim turn into a wasteland.�q ³⁵I will leave no one in Moab—oracle of the LORD—to offer burnt offerings on the high place or to make sacrifices to their gods. ³⁶Hence my heart wails like a flute for Moab; my heart wails like a flute for the people of Kir-heres: the wealth they accumulated has perished.ʳ ³⁷Every head has been shaved bald, every beard cut off; every hand gashed, and all their loins are draped in sackcloth.ˢ ³⁸On all the rooftops of Moab and in all its squares there is mourning. I have shattered Moab like a pot that no one wants—oracle of the LORD. ³⁹How terrified they are, how they wail! How Moab turns its back in shame! Moab has become a laughingstock and a horror to all its neighbors!

⁴⁰ For thus says the LORD:
  Look there! Like an eagle he swoops,
    spreading his wings over Moab.ᵗ
⁴¹ Cities are captured,
    strongholds seized:
  On that day the hearts of Moab's warriors
    become like the heart of a woman
        in labor.ᵘ
⁴² Moab shall be wiped out, a people no
    more,
    because it set itself over against the
        LORD.ᵛ
⁴³ Terror, pit, and trap be upon you,
    enthroned Moab—oracle of the
        LORD.ʷ

---

*[48:18] Dibon, the capital of Moab at that time, is situated on a height. The prophet here offers a personification of the city, pictured as a confident ruler.

h. [48:13] Is 16:12.  i. [48:18] Nm 21:30.  j. [48:19] Dt 2:36. k. [48:20] Is 16:7.  l. [48:21] Is 15:4.  m. [48:27] Zep 2:8–10.

n. [48:29–30] Is 16:6.  o. [48:31] Is 16:7.  p. [48:32] Is 16:8–9. q. [48:34] Is 15:4–5.  r. [48:36] Is 16:11.  s. [48:37] Jer 47:5; Is 15:2–3; Ez 7:18.  t. [48:40] Jer 49:22.  u. [48:41] Jer 6:24; 30:6. v. [48:42] Zep 2:9–10.  w. [48:43] Is 24:17–18.

⁴⁴ Those fleeing the terror
        fall into the pit;
    Those climbing out of the pit
        are caught in the trap;
    Ah, yes! I will bring these things upon
            Moab
        in the year of their punishment—
            oracle of the LORD.
⁴⁵ In Heshbon's shadow the fugitives
        stop short, exhausted;
    For fire blazes up from Heshbon,
        and flames up from the house of
            Sihon:
    It consumes the forehead of Moab,
        the scalp of the noisemakers.ˣ
⁴⁶ Woe to you, Moab!
        You are finished, people of
            Chemosh!
    Your sons are taken into exile,
        your daughters into captivity.
⁴⁷ Yet I will restore the fortunes of Moab
        in the days to come—oracle of the
            LORD.ʸ
Thus far the judgment on Moab.

### CHAPTER 49

**Against the Ammonites.** ¹Concerning the
Ammonites. Thus says the LORD:

    Has Israel no sons?
        none to inherit?
    Why has Milcom* disinherited Gad,
        why are his people living in its
            cities?
² Therefore the days are coming—oracle of
            the LORD—
        when I will sound the battle alarm
            against Rabbah of the Ammonites;
    It shall become a mound of ruins,
        and its villages destroyed by fire.
    Israel shall then inherit those who
            disinherited it—
        oracle of the LORD.ᶻ
³ Wail, Heshbon, "The ruin is destroyed!"
        shriek, villages of Rabbah!
    Put on sackcloth and lament!
        Run back and forth in the
            sheepfolds.
    For Milcom is going into exile,
        taking priest and prince with him.ᵃ
⁴ Why boast in your strength,
        your ebbing strength, rebellious
            daughter?
    Why trust in your treasures, saying,
        "Who would dare attack me?"
⁵ See, I am bringing terror upon you—

        oracle of the Lord GOD of hosts—
            from all around you;
    You shall be scattered, each in headlong
            flight,
        with no one to gather the fugitives.ᵇ
⁶ But afterward I will restore the fortunes
        of the Ammonites—oracle of the
            LORD.

**Against Edom.**† ⁷Concerning Edom. Thus says
the LORD of hosts:

    Is there no more wisdom in Teman,‡
        has counsel perished from the
            prudent,
        is their wisdom gone?
⁸ Flee, retreat, hide deep for lodging,
        inhabitants of Dedan:
    For I bring disaster upon Esau§
        when I come to punish them.ᶜ
⁹ If vintagers came upon you,
        they would leave no gleanings;
    If thieves by night,
        they would destroy as they pleased.ᵈ
¹⁰ So I myself will strip Esau;
        I will uncover his lairs so he cannot
            hide.
    Offspring and family are destroyed,
        neighbors, too; he is no more.ᵉ
¹¹ Leave your orphans behind, I will keep
            them alive;
        your widows, let them trust in me.ᶠ

¹²For thus says the LORD: Look, even those
not sentenced to drink the cup must drink it!
Shall you then go unpunished? You shall not!
You shall drink every bit of it!ᵍ ¹³By myself I
have sworn—oracle of the LORD—Bozrah¶ shall
become an object of horror, a disgrace, a desolation, and a curse. Bozrah and all its cities shall
become ruins forever.ʰ

¹⁴ I have heard a report from the LORD,
        a herald has been sent among the
            nations:
    "Gather together, move against it,
        get ready for battle!"
¹⁵ I will make you the least among the
            nations,
        despised by all people!ⁱ

---

*[49:1] **Milcom**: chief god of the Ammonites (cf. 1 Kgs
11:5). The Ammonites shared a border with Gad, an Israelite
tribe in Transjordan (Jos 13:8–10); the Ammonites occupied
its territory after the collapse of the Northern Kingdom.

†[49:7–22] **Edom**: southeast of the Dead Sea, a traditional
enemy who profited from Judah's downfall; cf. Ps 137:7; Lam
4:21–22; Ob 11–12.

‡[49:7] Teman, a district of Edom (cf. Jb 2:11), represents
the whole country, which was famous for the wisdom of its
sages.

§[49:8] **Esau**: Jacob's brother, the traditional ancestor of
the Edomites; cf. Gn 36:1.

¶[49:13] **Bozrah**: capital of Edom.

x. [48:45] Nm 21:28–29.  y. [48:47] Jer 49:39.  z. [49:2] Am 1:14.
a. [49:3] Is 15:2–5.

b. [49:5] Jer 48:47.  c. [49:8] Ez 25:13.  d. [49:9] Ob 5.  e. [49:10]
Mal 1:3.  f. [49:11] Dt 10:18; Ps 68:6.  g. [49:12] Jer 25:15, 28; Lam
4:21–22.  h. [49:13] Is 34:6; Ez 35:3–9; Ob 16.  i. [49:15] Ob 2.

<sup>16</sup> The terror you spread,
    the pride of your heart, beguiled
      you.
You denizens of rocks and crevices,
    occupying towering peaks:
Though you build your nest high as the
      eagle,
    from there I will bring you down—
      oracle of the Lord.<sup>j</sup>

<sup>17</sup>Edom shall become an object of horror. Passersby recoil in terror, hissing at all its wounds. <sup>18</sup>As when Sodom, Gomorrah, and their neighbors were overthrown—oracle of the Lord—no one shall live in it, nor anyone settle there.<sup>k</sup>

<sup>19</sup> As when a lion comes up from a thicket of
      the Jordan
    to a permanent pasture,
So in an instant, I will chase them off;
    I will establish there whomever I
      choose.
For who is like me? Who holds me
      accountable?
    What shepherd can stand against
      me?<sup>l</sup>
<sup>20</sup> Therefore, listen to the strategy
    the Lord devised for Edom;
The plans he has drawn up
    against the inhabitants of Teman:
They shall be dragged away, even the
      smallest of the flock;
    their pasture shall be aghast because
      of them.
<sup>21</sup> With the din of their collapse the earth
      quakes,
    to the Red Sea the outcry is heard!
<sup>22</sup> Look! like an eagle he soars aloft,
    and spreads his wings over Bozrah;
On that day the hearts of Edom's warriors
      become
    like the heart of a woman in labor.<sup>m</sup>

**Against Damascus.** <sup>23</sup>Concerning Damascus.

Hamath and Arpad<sup>*</sup> are shamed,
    for they have heard bad news;
Anxious, they surge like the sea
    which cannot calm down.<sup>n</sup>
<sup>24</sup> Damascus loses heart, turns to flee;
    panic has seized it.
Distress and pangs take hold,
    like the pain of a woman in labor.
<sup>25</sup> How can the glorious city be abandoned,
    the town of joy!

<sup>26</sup> But now its young men shall fall in its
      squares,
    all the warriors destroyed on that
      day—
    oracle of the Lord of hosts.
<sup>27</sup> I will set fire to the wall of Damascus;
    it shall devour the palaces of
      Ben-hadad.<sup>†</sup>

**Against Arabia.** <sup>28</sup>About Kedar and the kingdoms of Hazor, which Nebuchadnezzar, king of Babylon, defeated.

Thus says the Lord:
Rise up, attack Kedar,
    destroy the people from the east.<sup>o</sup>
<sup>29</sup> Their tents and flocks shall be taken away,
    their tent curtains and all their
      goods;
    Their camels they carry off,
    they shout over them, "Terror on
      every side!"<sup>p</sup>
<sup>30</sup> Flee! wander about, hide deep for lodging,
    inhabitants of Hazor—oracle of the
      Lord;
For Nebuchadnezzar, king of Babylon, has
      devised a strategy against you,
    drawn up a plan against you,
<sup>31</sup> Get up! set out against a tranquil nation,
    living in security—oracle of the
      Lord—
Without gates or bars,
    dwelling alone.
<sup>32</sup> Their camels shall become spoils,
    their hordes of cattle, plunder;
I will scatter to the winds those who shave
      their temples;
    from every side I will bring their
      ruin—
    oracle of the Lord.<sup>q</sup>
<sup>33</sup> Hazor shall become a haunt for jackals,
    a wasteland forever,
Where no one lives,
    no mortal stays.

**Against Elam.** <sup>34</sup>The word of the Lord that came to Jeremiah the prophet concerning Elam<sup>‡</sup> at the beginning of the reign of Zedekiah, king of Judah:

<sup>35</sup> Thus says the Lord of hosts:
Look! I will break the bow of Elam,
    the mainstay of their might.
<sup>36</sup> I will bring upon Elam the four winds
    from the four ends of the heavens:
I will scatter them to all these winds, until
    there is no nation

---

<sup>*</sup>[49:23] **Hamath and Arpad**: independent Aramean states north of Damascus, the direction from which the invasion is coming. Cf. Is 10:9–10.

---

j. [49:16] Jer 48:29–30.   k. [49:18] Jer 50:40; Dt 29:23.   l. [49:19] Jer 12:5; 25:9; 50:44–45.   m. [49:22] Jer 4:13.   n. [49:23] Is 36:19; 37:13.

<sup>†</sup>[49:27] **Ben-hadad**: a dynastic name for some of the kings who ruled in Damascus; cf. 1 Kgs 15:18, 20.
<sup>‡</sup>[49:34] **Elam**: an ancient kingdom east of Babylonia.

---

o. [49:28] Is 21:16.   p. [49:29] Jer 4:20.   q. [49:32] Jer 9:25.

to which the outcasts of Elam have
    not gone.
[37] I will terrify Elam before their foes,
    those seeking their life;
I will bring evil upon them,
    my burning wrath—oracle of the
        LORD.
I will send sword after them
    until I have finished them off;
[38] I will set up my throne in Elam
    and destroy from there king and
        princes—
    oracle of the LORD.
[39] But at the end of days I will restore
    the fortunes of Elam—oracle of the
        LORD.

## CHAPTER 50

**The First Oracle Against Babylon.** [1]The word
the LORD spoke against Babylon,* against the
land of the Chaldeans, through Jeremiah the
prophet:[r]

[2] Proclaim this among the nations,
        announce it!
    Announce it, do not hide it, but say:
    Babylon is captured, Bel[†] put to shame,
        Marduk terrified;
    its images are put to shame, its idols
        shattered.
[3] A nation from the north advances against
        it,
    making the land desolate
    So that no one can live there;
        human beings and animals have fled.[s]
[4] In those days and at that time—oracle of
        the LORD—
    Israelite and Judahite shall come
        together,
    Weeping as they come, to seek the LORD,
        their God;[t]
[5] They shall ask for Zion,
        seeking out the way.
    "Come, let us join ourselves to the LORD
        in an everlasting covenant, never to
            be forgotten."[u]
[6] Lost sheep were my people,
        their shepherds misled them,
        leading them astray on the
            mountains;
    From mountain to hill they wandered,
        forgetting their fold.[v]
[7] Whoever happened upon them devoured
        them;

their enemies said, "We are not guilty,
Because they sinned against the LORD,
    the abode of justice, the hope of
        their ancestors."[w]
[8] Flee from the midst of Babylon,
    leave the land of the Chaldeans,
    be like rams at the head of the flock.[x]
[9] See, I am stirring up against Babylon
    a band of great nations from the
        land of the north;
They are arrayed against her,
    from there she shall be taken.
Their arrows are like the arrows of a
    skilled warrior
    who never returns empty-handed.[y]
[10] Chaldea shall become plunder;
    all its plunderers shall be enriched—
        oracle of the LORD.
[11] Yes, rejoice and exult,
    you that plunder my heritage;
Frisk like calves on the grass,
    neigh like stallions!
[12] Your mother will indeed be put to shame,
    she that bore you shall be abashed;
See, the last of the nations,
    a wilderness, a dry wasteland.[z]
[13] Because of the LORD's wrath it shall be
        uninhabited,
    become an utter wasteland;
Everyone who passes by Babylon will be
        appalled
    and hiss at all its wounds.[a]
[14] Take your posts encircling Babylon,
    you who bend the bow;
Shoot at it, do not spare your arrows,[b]
[15]    raise the war cry against it on every
        side.
It surrenders, its bastions fall,
    its walls are torn down:[‡]
This is retribution from the LORD! Take
        retribution on her,
    as she has done, do to her;
    for she sinned against the LORD.[c]
[16] Cut off the sower from Babylon
    and those who wield sickles at
        harvest time!
Before the destroying sword,
    all of them turn back to their own
        people,
    all flee to their own land.[d]
[17] Israel was a stray sheep
    that lions pursued;
The king of Assyria once devoured him;
    now Nebuchadnezzar of Babylon
        gnaws his bones.[e]

---

*[50:1–51:58] A collection of miscellaneous oracles
against Babylon introducing the story in 51:59–64.

†[50:2] **Bel:** originally the title of the god of Nippur in
Mesopotamia, later associated with *Merodach* (Marduk), chief
god of Babylon (cf. Is 46:1).

---

‡[50:15] **Its walls are torn down:** the prophet describes
the downfall of Babylon in conventional language. Babylon
surrendered peacefully to the Persians in 539 B.C.

---

r. [50:1] Jer 51:1; Is 13:1–14; 21:1–10.    s. [50:3] Jer 51:48; Is 13:17.
t. [50:4] Jer 3:18; Ps 126:6.    u. [50:5] Jer 31:31; 32:40.    v. [50:6]
Is 53:6; 1 Pt 2:25.

w. [50:7] Jer 31:23.    x. [50:8] Jer 51:6, 45; Is 48:20.    y. [50:9] Jer
51:27.    z. [50:12] Jer 51:43; Is 13:20–22.    a. [50:13] Jer 25:12.
b. [50:14] Jer 51:11; Is 21:2.    c. [50:15] Jer 51:11, 44, 58; Ps 137:8.
d. [50:16] Is 13:14.    e. [50:17] 2 Kgs 17:24; 18:14.

<sup>18</sup> Therefore, thus says the LORD of hosts,
 the God of Israel:
I will punish the king of Babylon and his
 land,
  as I once punished the king of
  Assyria;<sup>f</sup>
<sup>19</sup> But I will bring Israel back to its pasture,
 to feed on Carmel and Bashan,
And on Mount Ephraim and Gilead,
 until they have their fill.<sup>g</sup>

<sup>20</sup>In those days, at that time—oracle of the
LORD:

The guilt of Israel may be sought, but it no
 longer exists,
 the sin of Judah, but it can no longer
  be found;
 for I will forgive the remnant I
  preserve.<sup>h</sup>
<sup>21</sup> Attack the land of Merathaim,
 and those who live in Pekod;<sup>*</sup>
Slaughter and put them under the ban—
 oracle of the LORD—
 do all I have commanded you.
<sup>22</sup> Battle alarm in the land,
 great destruction!
<sup>23</sup> How the hammer of the whole earth
 has been cut off and broken!
What an object of horror
 Babylon has become among the
  nations!<sup>i</sup>
<sup>24</sup> You ensnared yourself and were caught,
 Babylon, before you knew it!
You were discovered and seized,
 because you challenged the LORD.<sup>j</sup>
<sup>25</sup> The LORD opens his armory,
 brings out the weapons of his wrath;
The Lord GOD of hosts has work to do
 in the land of the Chaldeans.<sup>k</sup>
<sup>26</sup> Come upon them from every side,
 open their granaries,
Pile them up in heaps and put them under
 the ban;
 do not leave a remnant.
<sup>27</sup> Slay all the oxen,
 take them down to slaughter;
Woe to them! their day has come,
 the time of their punishment.
<sup>28</sup> Listen! the fugitives, the refugees
 from the land of Babylon:
They announce in Zion
 the retribution of the LORD, our
  God.<sup>l</sup>

<sup>29</sup> Call archers out against Babylon,
 all who bend the bow;
Encamp around them;
 let no one escape.
Repay them for their deeds;
 what they have done, do to them,
For they insulted the LORD,
 the Holy One of Israel.<sup>m</sup>
<sup>30</sup> Therefore their young men shall fall in the
 squares,
 all their warriors shall be stilled on
  that day—
 oracle of the LORD.<sup>n</sup>
<sup>31</sup> I am against you, O Insolence—
 oracle of the Lord GOD of hosts;
For your day has come,
 the time for me to punish you.
<sup>32</sup> Insolence stumbles and falls,
 there is no one to raise him up.
I will kindle a fire in his cities
 to devour everything around him.
<sup>33</sup> Thus says the LORD of hosts:
Oppressed are the people of Israel,
 together with the people of Judah;
All their captors hold them fast
 and refuse to let them go.
<sup>34</sup> Strong is their Redeemer,
 whose name is LORD of hosts,
The sure defender of their cause,
 who gives rest to their land,
 but unrest to those who live in
  Babylon.<sup>o</sup>
<sup>35</sup> A sword upon the Chaldeans—oracle of
 the LORD—
 upon the inhabitants of Babylon, her
  princes and sages!
<sup>36</sup> A sword upon the soothsayers,
 and they become fools!
A sword upon the warriors,
 and they tremble!
<sup>37</sup> A sword upon their motley throng,
 and they become women!
A sword upon their treasures,
 and they are plundered;<sup>p</sup>
<sup>38</sup> A drought upon the waters,
 and they dry up!
For it is a land of idols,
 soon made frantic by phantoms.<sup>q</sup>
<sup>39</sup> Hence, wildcats shall dwell there with
 hyenas,
 and ostriches occupy it;
Never again shall it be inhabited or settled,
 from age to age.<sup>r</sup>
<sup>40</sup> As happened when God overturned
 Sodom
 and Gomorrah and their
  neighbors—oracle of the
  LORD—
No one shall dwell there,
 no mortal shall settle there.<sup>s</sup>

---

*[50:21] **Merathaim . . . Pekod:** "twice bitter," "punishment," symbolic terms for Babylon that recall the names of regions in the country.

---

f. [50:18] Is 10:12; 14:24–25. g. [50:19] Jer 23:3; Ez 34:13–14.
h. [50:20] Jer 31:34; Is 43:25; Mi 7:19. i. [50:23] Jer 51:20; Is 14:6. j. [50:24] Jer 51:57. k. [50:25] Jer 51:11–12; Is 13:5.
l. [50:28] Jer 51:10–11.

m. [50:29] Jer 51:56. n. [50:30] Jer 49:26; 51:4. o. [50:34] Jer 51:36. p. [50:37] Jer 51:30; Na 3:13. q. [50:38] Jer 51:32, 36.
r. [50:39] Jer 51:37; Is 13:21–22. s. [50:40] Jer 51:43.

41 See, a people comes from the north,
    a great nation, and mighty kings
        rising from the ends of the earth.[t]
42 Bow and javelin they wield,
    cruel and pitiless are they;
They sound like the roaring sea,
    as they ride forth on horses,
Each in place for battle
    against you, daughter Babylon.
43 The king of Babylon hears news of them,
    and his hands hang helpless;
Anguish takes hold of him,
    like the pangs of a woman giving
        birth.[u]
44 As happens when a lion comes up from a
        thicket of the Jordan
    to permanent pasture,
So I, in an instant, will chase them off,
    and establish there whomever I
        choose!
For who is like me? Who can call me to
        account?
    What shepherd can stand against
        me?[v]
45 Therefore, hear the strategy of the LORD,
    which he has devised against
        Babylon;
Hear the plans drawn up
    against the land of the Chaldeans:
They shall be dragged away, even the
        smallest sheep;
    their own pasture aghast because of
        them.[w]
46 At the cry "Babylon is captured!" the
        earth quakes;
    the outcry is heard among the
        nations.[x]

## CHAPTER 51

### The Second Oracle Against Babylon

1     Thus says the LORD:
See! I rouse against Babylon,
    and the inhabitants of Chaldea,
    a destroyer wind.[*]
2 To Babylon I will send winnowers
    to winnow and lay waste the land;
They shall besiege it on every side
    on the day of affliction.[y]
3 How can the archers draw back their
        bows,
    lift their armor?
Do not spare her young men,
    put the entire army under the ban.[z]
4 The slain shall fall in the land of Chaldea,
    the wounded, in its streets;[a]

5 For Israel and Judah are not left widowed
    by their God, the LORD of hosts,
Even though the land is full of guilt
    against the Holy One of Israel.
6 Flee from Babylon;
    each of you save your own life,
    do not perish because of her guilt;
This is a time of retribution from the
    LORD,
7     who pays out her due.[b]
Babylon was a golden cup in the hand of
    the LORD
    making the whole earth drunk;
The nations drank its wine,
    thus they have gone mad.[c]
8 Babylon suddenly falls and is broken:
    wail over her!
Bring balm for her wounds,
    in case she can be healed.[d]
9 "We have tried to heal Babylon,
    but she cannot be healed.
    Leave her, each of us must go to our
        own land."
The judgment against her reaches the
        heavens,
    it touches the clouds.[e]
10 The LORD has brought forth our
        vindication;
    come, let us tell in Zion
    what the LORD, our God, has done.[f]
11 Sharpen the arrows,
    fill the quivers;
The LORD has stirred up the spirit of the
        kings of the Medes,[†]
    for his resolve is Babylon's
        destruction.
Yes, it is retribution from the LORD,
    retribution for his temple.[g]
12 Over the walls of Babylon raise a signal,
    reinforce the watch;
Post sentries,
    arrange ambushes!
For the LORD has both planned and
        carried out
    what he spoke against the
        inhabitants of Babylon.
13 You who dwell by mighty waters,
    rich in treasure,
Your end has come,
    the time at which you shall be cut
        off![h]
14 The LORD of hosts has sworn by himself:
    I will fill you with people as
        numerous as locusts,
    who shall raise over you a joyous
        shout!

---

*[51:1] The destroyer wind is the fierce dry wind from the east (cf. 4:11).

†[51:11] **Kings of the Medes**: the Medes and the Persians lived in the area known today as Iran.

---

t. [50:41] Jer 51:27–28.  u. [50:43] Is 13:7.  v. [50:44] Jer 49:19. w. [50:45] Jer 51:12, 29.  x. [50:46] Jer 51:29.  y. [51:2] Jer 15:7; Is 41:16.  z. [51:3] Jer 50:14, 29.  a. [51:4] Jer 50:30.

b. [51:7] Jer 50:8, 15, 29; Is 48:20.  c. [51:7] Rev 14:8; 17:4.  d. [51:8] Rev 18:9–18.  e. [51:9] Is 13:14; Rev 18:5.  f. [51:10] Jer 50:28. g. [51:11] 2 Kgs 17:6; Is 13:17.  h. [51:13] Na 2:1.

15 He made the earth by his power,
   established the world by wisdom,
   and by his skill stretched out the
      heavens.*i*

16 When he thunders, the waters in the
      heavens roar,
   he summons clouds from the ends
      of the earth,
   Makes lightning flash in the rain,
      and brings out winds from their
      storehouses.

17 Every man is stupid, ignorant;
      every artisan is put to shame by his
      idol:
   He molds a fraud,
      without life-breath.

18 They are nothing, a ridiculous work,
      that will perish at the time of
      punishment.

19 Jacob's portion is nothing like them:
      he is the creator of all things.
   Israel is his very own tribe;
      LORD of hosts is his name.

20 You are my hammer,
      a weapon for war;
   With you I shatter nations,
      with you I destroy kingdoms.

21 With you I shatter horse and rider,
      with you I shatter chariot and
      driver.*j*

22 With you I shatter man and woman,
      with you I shatter old and young,
      with you I shatter the young man
      and young woman.*k*

23 With you I shatter shepherd and flock,
      with you I shatter farmer and team,
      with you I shatter governors and
      officers.

24 Thus I will repay Babylon,
      all the inhabitants of Chaldea,
   For all the evil they committed against
      Zion,
      before your very eyes—oracle of the
      LORD.*l*

25 Beware! I am against you,
      destroying mountain—oracle of the
      LORD—
      destroyer of the entire earth,
   I will stretch forth my hand against you,
      roll you down over the cliffs,
      and make you a burnt mountain:*m*

26 They will not take from you a
      cornerstone,
      or a foundation stone;
   You shall remain ruins forever—
      oracle of the LORD.*n*

27 Raise a signal in the land,
      sound the trumpet among the
      nations;

Dedicate nations for war against her,
      summon against her the kingdoms:
   Ararat, Minni, and Ashkenaz;.*
Appoint a recruiting officer against her,
      dispatch horses like bristling
      locusts.*o*

28 Dedicate nations for war against her:
      the king of the Medes,
   Its governors and all its officers,
      every land in its domain.

29 The earth quakes and writhes,
      the LORD's plan against Babylon is
      carried out,
   Turning the land of Babylon
      into a wasteland without
      inhabitants.

30 Babylon's warriors have ceased to fight,
      they remain in their strongholds;
   Dried up is their strength,
      they have become women.
   Burned down are their homes,
      broken their gates.

31 One runner meets another,
      herald meets herald,
   Telling the king of Babylon
      that his entire city has been taken.*p*

32 The fords have been seized,
      marshes set on fire,
      warriors panic.

33For thus says the LORD of hosts, the God
of Israel:

Daughter Babylon is like a threshing floor
      at the time of treading;
   Yet a little while,
      and the harvest time will come for
      her.*q*

34 "He consumed me, defeated me,
      Nebuchadnezzar, king of Babylon;
      he left me like an empty vessel,
   Swallowed me like a sea monster,
      filled his belly with my delicacies
      and cast me out.

35 Let my torn flesh be visited upon Babylon,"
      says enthroned Zion;
   "My blood upon the inhabitants of
      Chaldea,"
      says Jerusalem.

36 But now, thus says the LORD:
   I will certainly defend your cause,
      I will certainly avenge you;
   I will dry up her sea,
      and drain her fountain.

37 Babylon shall become a heap of ruins,
      a haunt of jackals;
   A place of horror and hissing,
      without inhabitants.*r*

---

*[51:27] **Ararat, Minni, and Ashkenaz**: regions in eastern
Asia Minor under the control of the Medes.

---

i. [51:15] Jer 10:12.   j. [51:21] Dn 7:7, 19, 23.   k. [51:22] Is 13:16,
18.   l. [51:24] Jer 25:14; 50:29; Ps 137:8.   m. [51:25] Rev 8:7; 18:8–9.
n. [51:26] Jer 25:12; Ps 118:22.

o. [51:27] Na 3:17.   p. [51:31] 2 Chr 36:6; Jb 1:14–18.   q. [51:33]
Rev 14:15.   r. [51:37] Is 25:2.

38 They roar like lions,
    growl like lion cubs.*
39 When they are parched, I will set drink
        before them
    to make them drunk, that they may
        be overcome
    with everlasting sleep, never to
        awaken—
    oracle of the LORD.
40 I will bring them down like lambs to
        slaughter,
    like rams and goats.
41 How she has been seized, taken captive,
    the glory of the whole world!
    What a horror Babylon has become
        among the nations:*
42      against Babylon the sea rises,
    she is overwhelmed by roaring
        waves!
43 Her cities have become wasteland,
    a parched and arid land
    Where no one lives,
        no one passes through.
44 I will punish Bel in Babylon,
    and make him vomit up what he
        swallowed;
    nations shall no longer stream to
        him.
    Even the wall of Babylon falls!
45      Leave her, my people; each of you
        save your own life
    from the burning wrath of the LORD.

46 Do not be discouraged when rumors
spread through the land; this year one rumor
comes, next year another: "Violence in the
land!" or "Ruler against ruler!"* 47Realize that
the days are coming when I will punish the
idols of Babylon; the whole land shall be put to
shame, all her slain shall fall in her midst. 48Then
heaven and earth and everything in them shall
shout over Babylon with joy, when the destroyers come against her from the north—oracle of
the LORD.* 49Babylon, too, must fall, you slain of
Israel, because by the hand of Babylon the slain
of all the earth have fallen.

50 You who have escaped the sword,
    go, do not stand idle;
    Remember the LORD from far away,
    let Jerusalem come to mind.
51 We are ashamed because we have heard
        taunts,
    disgrace covers our faces;
    strangers have entered sanctuaries in
        the LORD's house.*
52 Therefore see, the days are coming—
    oracle of the LORD—
    when I will punish her idols,

    and throughout the land the
        wounded will groan.
53 Though Babylon scale the heavens,
    and make her strong heights
        inaccessible,
    my destroyers shall reach her—
        oracle of the LORD.*
54 A sound of crying from Babylon,
    great destruction from the land of
        the Chaldeans;
55 For the LORD lays Babylon waste,
    silences her loud cry,
    Waves roaring like mighty waters,
        a clamor resounding.
56 For the destroyer comes upon her, upon
        Babylon;
    warriors are captured, their bows
        broken;
    The LORD is a God of recompense,
    he will surely repay.*

57 I will make her princes and sages drunk,
with her governors, officers, and warriors, so that
they sleep an everlasting sleep, never to awaken—
oracle of the King, whose name is LORD of hosts.

58      Thus says the LORD of hosts:
    The walls of spacious Babylon shall be
        leveled to the ground,
    its lofty gates destroyed by fire.
    The toil of the peoples is for nothing;
    the nations weary themselves for
        what the flames consume.*

**The Prophecy Sent to Babylon.** 59The mission
Jeremiah the prophet gave to Seraiah,* son of
Neriah, son of Mahseiah, when he went to Babylon with King Zedekiah, king of Judah, in the
fourth year of his reign; Seraiah was chief quar-
termaster. 60Jeremiah wrote down on one scroll
the disaster that would befall Babylon;† all these
words were written against Babylon. 61And Jeremiah said to Seraiah: "When you reach Babylon,
see that you read all these words aloud,* 62and
then say: LORD, you yourself spoke against this
place in order to cut it down so that nothing,
human being or beast, could live in it, because
it is to remain a wasteland forever. 63When you
have finished reading this scroll, tie a stone to it
and throw it into the Euphrates,* 64and say: Thus
Babylon shall sink. It will never rise, because of
the disaster I am bringing upon it." Thus far the
words of Jeremiah.

---

*[51:59] **Seraiah:** the brother of Baruch; cf. 32:12. He may
have gone to Babylon to explain away the presence of foreign
ambassadors in Jerusalem that same year; cf. 27:3.

†[51:60] Jeremiah prophesied against Babylon, even as he
foretold Judah's release from Babylon's power (3:14–18; 32:15;
33:6–9, 12–13); but his scroll against Babylon was thrown in
the Euphrates (v. 63). Some of the preceding oracles may have
been composed by later writers; see note on 50:1–51:58.

---

s. [51:38] Na 2:11–12.   t. [51:41] Is 13:19.   u. [51:46] Mt 24:6–7.
v. [51:48] Rev 18:20.   w. [51:51] Ps 44:16–17; 78:1–4.

x. [51:53] Is 14:13.   y. [51:56] Na 1:2.   z. [51:58] Hb 2:13.   a. [51:61]
Jer 50:1–51.   b. [51:63] Rev 18:21.

## IX. HISTORICAL APPENDIX*

### CHAPTER 52

**Capture of Jerusalem.** ¹Zedekiah was twenty-one years old when he became king; he reigned eleven years in Jerusalem.ᶜ His mother's name was Hamutal, daughter of Jeremiah from Libnah. ²He did what was evil in the sight of the LORD, just as Jehoiakim had done. ³Indeed, the things done in Jerusalem and in Judah so angered the LORD that he cast them out from his presence. Thus Zedekiah rebelled against the king of Babylon. ⁴ᵈIn the tenth month of the ninth year of his reign, on the tenth day of the month,† Nebuchadnezzar, king of Babylon, and his entire army advanced against Jerusalem, encamped around it, and built siege walls on every side. ⁵The siege of the city continued until the eleventh year of King Zedekiah.

⁶On the ninth day of the fourth month, when famine had gripped the city and the people had no more bread, ⁷the city walls were breached. All the soldiers fled and left the city by night through the gate between the two walls which was near the king's garden. With the Chaldeans surrounding the city, they went in the direction of the Arabah. ⁸But the Chaldean army pursued the king and overtook Zedekiah in the wilderness near Jericho; his whole army fled from him.

⁹The king, therefore, was arrested and brought to Riblah, in the land of Hamath, to the king of Babylon, who pronounced judgment on him. ¹⁰As Zedekiah looked on, the king of Babylon slaughtered his sons before his eyes! All the nobles of Judah were slaughtered at Riblah. ¹¹And the eyes of Zedekiah he then blinded, bound him with chains, and the King of Babylon brought him to Babylon and kept him in prison until the day he died.

**Destruction of Jerusalem.** ¹²On the tenth day of the fifth month, this was in the nineteenth year‡ of Nebuchadnezzar, king of Babylon, Nebuzaradan, captain of the bodyguard, came to Jerusalem as the representative of the king of Babylon. ¹³He burned the house of the LORD, the palace of the king, and all the houses of Jerusalem; every large building he destroyed with fire. ¹⁴Then the Chaldean troops with the captain of the guard tore down all the walls that surrounded Jerusalem.

¹⁵Nebuzaradan, captain of the guard, led into exile the remnant of people left in the city, those who had deserted to the king of Babylon, and the rest of the artisans. ¹⁶But Nebuzaradan, captain of the guard, left behind some of the country's poor as vinedressers and farmers.

¹⁷The bronze pillars that belonged to the house of the LORD, and the wheeled carts and the bronze sea in the house of the LORD, the Chaldeans broke into pieces; they carried away all the bronze to Babylon. ¹⁸They also took the pots, shovels, snuffers, bowls, pans, and all the bronze vessels used for service; ¹⁹the basins, fire holders, bowls, pots, lampstands, pans, the sacrificial bowls made of gold or silver. Along with these furnishings the captain of the guard carried off ²⁰the two pillars, the one sea and its base of twelve oxen cast in bronze, and the wheeled carts King Solomon had commissioned for the house of the LORD. The bronze from all these furnishings was impossible to weigh.

²¹As for the pillars, each of them was eighteen cubits high and twelve cubits in diameter; each was four fingers thick and hollow inside. ²²A bronze capital five cubits high crowned the one pillar, and a network with pomegranates encircled the capital, all of bronze; and so for the other pillar, with pomegranates. ²³There were ninety-six pomegranates on the sides, a hundred pomegranates surrounding the network.

²⁴The captain of the guard also took Seraiah the high priest, Zephaniah the second priest, and the three keepers of the entrance. ²⁵From the city he took one courtier, a commander of soldiers, and seven men in the personal service of the king still in the city, the scribe of the army commander who mustered the people of the land, and sixty of the common people remaining in the city. ²⁶The captain of the guard, Nebuzaradan, arrested them and brought them to the king of Babylon at Riblah, ²⁷who had them struck down and executed in Riblah, in the land of Hamath.

Thus Judah was exiled from the land. ²⁸§This is the number of people Nebuchadnezzar led away captive: in his seventh year, three thousand twenty-three people of Judah; ²⁹in the eighteenth year of Nebuchadnezzar, eight hundred thirty-two persons from Jerusalem; ³⁰in the twenty-third year of Nebuchadnezzar, Nebuzaradan, captain of the guard, deported seven hundred forty-five Judahites: four thousand six hundred persons in all.

**Favor Shown to Jehoiachin.**¶ ³¹ᵉIn the thirty-seventh year of the exile of Jehoiachin, king of Judah, on the twenty-fifth day of the twelfth

---

*[52:1–34] One of the editors of the Book of Jeremiah took most of this supplement from 2 Kgs 24:18–25:30 and placed it here to show the fulfillment of Jeremiah's prophecies. The supplement repeats part of the history given in Jeremiah 39–41, but omits the history of Gedaliah in 2 Kgs 25:22–26.

†[52:4] **In the tenth month of the ninth year of his reign, on the tenth day of the month:** January 15, 588 B.C. Cf. 39:1.

‡[52:12] **On the tenth day of the fifth month . . . nineteenth year:** the tenth of Ab—July/August in 587/586 B.C.

§[52:28–30] These verses, missing in the Greek text, do not come from 2 Kgs 25 but from a source using a different chronology. Besides the deportations of 598 and 587 B.C., this passage mentions a final deportation in 582/581, possibly a response to the murder of Gedaliah; cf. Jer 41:2.

¶[52:31–34] In the year 561/560 B.C., Nebuchadnezzar's successor Awel-Marduk (Evil-merodach), who reigned only two years, released Jehoiachin. Babylonian records confirm that Jehoiachin and his family were supported at public expense.

c. [52:1–27] 2 Kgs 24:18–25:21.   d. [52:4–16] Jer 39:1–10.          e. [52:31–34] 2 Kgs 25:27–30.

month, Evil-merodach, king of Babylon, in the inaugural year of his reign, raised up Jehoiachin, king of Judah, and released him from prison. [32]He spoke kindly to him and gave him a throne higher than the thrones of the other kings* who were with him in Babylon. [33]Jehoiachin took off his prison garb and ate at the king's table as long as he lived. [34]The allowance given him by the king of Babylon was a perpetual allowance, in fixed daily amounts, all the days of his life until the day of his death.

*[52:32] **The other kings**: heads of state brought as captives to Babylon.

# THE BOOK OF
# LAMENTATIONS

The Book of Lamentations is a collection of five poems that serve as an anguished response to the destruction of Jerusalem in 587 B.C., after a long siege by the invading Babylonian army. (See 2 Kgs 25 for a prose account of the fall of Jerusalem.) Although the poems are traditionally ascribed to the prophet Jeremiah, this is unlikely. The Hebrew text of the book does not mention Jeremiah at all, and it is difficult to square some of the content of the poetry with what one finds in the Book of Jeremiah itself (cf. Lam 1:10; 2:9; 4:17, 20). While there are connections in theme and vocabulary among all five chapters (and especially between chaps. 1 and 2), the poems may have been composed separately and grouped together later. In any case, they are anonymous compositions probably used by survivors of the catastrophe of 587 B.C. in a communal expression of grief and mourning.

Jewish liturgical tradition considers the book one of the "scrolls" (*megillot*); it is read once a year on the ninth of Av (August–September), a fast day commemorating the destruction of both the first Temple in 587 B.C. and the second Temple in A.D. 70. While passages from chap. 3 are often incorporated into Christian services for Holy Thursday or Good Friday, the Church has otherwise tended to neglect the book. It is not hard to see why; a more anguished piece of writing is scarcely imaginable: from its portrayal of Jerusalem in chaps. 1 and 2 as an abandoned widow exposed to endless dangers, to the broken man of chap. 3, to the bleak description in chap. 4 of the inhabitants of the devastated city, to the final unanswered communal lament of chap. 5, the reader is not so much engaged by the Book of Lamentations as assaulted by it. But with its unsparing focus on destruction, pain, and suffering the book serves an invaluable function as part of Scripture, witnessing to a biblical faith determined to express honestly the harsh realities of a violent world and providing contemporary readers the language to do the same.

As a literary work, the Book of Lamentations combines elements of communal and individual laments (in which the speakers attempt to persuade God to intervene in the face of an acute crisis), funeral dirges (in which a death is mourned), and ancient Near Eastern city-laments (in which the destruction of a city is mourned). The meter is called *Qinah* (lament), that is, each verse normally has three beats followed by two. The poems are acrostics: in chaps. 1–4, the separate stanzas begin with successive letters of the Hebrew alphabet from the first to the last. The last chapter, while not strictly an acrostic, nevertheless partially conforms to the pattern in its use of 22 lines, the number of letters in the Hebrew alphabet. Far from destroying the spontaneous pathos of the songs, this feature conveys the expression of a profound grief that might otherwise seem to be without limit (cf. 2:13).

The book may be divided as follows:

I. The Desolation of Jerusalem (1:1–22)
II. The Lord's Wrath and Zion's Ruin (2:1–22)
III. The Voice of a Suffering Individual (3:1–66)
IV. Miseries of the Besieged City (4:1–22)
V. The Community's Lament to the Lord (5:1–22)

## CHAPTER 1

### The Desolation of Jerusalem[*]

1 How solitary sits the city,
　　once filled with people.
She who was great among the nations
　　is now like a widow.
Once a princess among the provinces,
　　now a toiling slave.

2 She weeps incessantly in the night,
　　her cheeks damp with tears.
She has no one to comfort her
　　from all her lovers;[†]
Her friends have all betrayed her,
　　and become her enemies.[a]

3 Judah has gone into exile,
　　after oppression and harsh labor;
She dwells among the nations,
　　yet finds no rest:[b]
All her pursuers overtake her
　　in the narrow straits.

4 The roads to Zion mourn,
　　empty of pilgrims to her feasts.
All her gateways are desolate,
　　her priests groan,
Her young women grieve;
　　her lot is bitter.[c]

5 Her foes have come out on top,
　　her enemies are secure;
Because the LORD has afflicted her
　　for her many rebellions.
Her children have gone away,
　　captive before the foe.

6 From daughter Zion has gone
　　all her glory:
Her princes have become like rams
　　that find no pasture.
They have gone off exhausted
　　before their pursuers.

7 Jerusalem remembers
　　in days of wretched homelessness,
All the precious things she once had
　　in days gone by.
But when her people fell into the hands
　　of the foe,
　　and she had no help,

Her foes looked on and laughed
　　at her collapse.

8 Jerusalem has sinned grievously,
　　therefore she has become a
　　　　mockery;
Those who honored her now demean her,
　　for they saw her nakedness;
She herself groans out loud,
　　and turns away.[d]

9 Her uncleanness is on her skirt;
　　she has no thought of her future.
Her downfall is astonishing,
　　with no one to comfort her.
"Look, O LORD, at my misery;
　　how the enemy triumphs!"[‡]

10 The foe stretched out his hands
　　to all her precious things;
She has seen the nations
　　enter her sanctuary,
Those you forbade to come
　　into your assembly.[e]

11 All her people groan,
　　searching for bread;
They give their precious things for food,
　　to retain the breath of life.
"Look, O LORD, and pay attention
　　to how I have been demeaned!

12 Come, all who pass by the way,
　　pay attention and see:
Is there any pain like my pain,
　　which has been ruthlessly inflicted
　　　　upon me,
With which the LORD has tormented me
　　on the day of his blazing wrath?

13 From on high he hurled fire down
　　into my very bones;
He spread out a net for my feet,
　　and turned me back.
He has left me desolate,
　　in misery all day long.[f]

14 The yoke of my rebellions is bound together,
　　fastened by his hand.
His yoke is upon my neck;
　　he has made my strength fail.
The Lord has delivered me into the grip
　　of those I cannot resist.

15 All my valiant warriors
　　my Lord has cast away;
He proclaimed a feast against me
　　to crush my young men;

---

*[1:1–22] In this poem the poet first takes on the persona of
an observer describing Jerusalem's abject state after the destruction wrought by the Babylonian army (vv. 1–11a); but the
detached tone gives way to a more impassioned appeal when
the city itself—personified as the grieving widow and mother
Zion—abruptly intrudes upon this description (vv. 9c, 11c–16,
18–22) to demand that God look squarely at her misery.

†[1:2] **Lovers**: language of love was typically used to
describe the relationship between treaty partners, thus here it
connotes Judah's allies (see v. 19).

‡[1:9] Zion breaks in on the poet's description in v. 9c,
albeit briefly, to demand that the Lord face squarely her misery.
She takes up the lament in a more sustained fashion in v. 11c.

a. [1:2] Jer 30:14; Ez 16:37.　b. [1:3] Dt 28:65; Jer 45:3.　c. [1:4] Is
33:8–9; Jer 14:2.

d. [1:8] Is 47:2–3; Jer 13:22, 26; Na 3:5.　e. [1:10] Dt 23:3–6; Ps
74:4–8; Is 56:6; 66:20–21; Jer 51:51.　f. [1:13] Ez 12:13.

My Lord has trodden in the wine press
    virgin daughter Judah.

16 For these things I weep—My eyes! My eyes!
    They stream with tears!
How far from me is anyone to comfort,
    anyone to restore my life.
My children are desolate;
    the enemy has prevailed."[g]

17 Zion stretches out her hands,
    with no one to comfort her;
The LORD has ordered against Jacob
    his foes all around;
Jerusalem has become in their midst
    a thing unclean.

18 "The LORD is in the right;
    I had defied his command.
Listen, all you peoples,
    and see my pain:
My young women and young men
    have gone into captivity.[h]

19 I cried out to my lovers,
    but they failed me.[i]
My priests and my elders
    perished in the city;
How desperately they searched for food,
    to save their lives!

20 Look, O LORD, at the anguish I suffer!
    My stomach churns,
And my heart recoils within me:
    How bitter I am!
Outside the sword bereaves—
    indoors, there is death.[j]

21 Hear how I am groaning;
    there is no one to comfort me.
All my enemies hear of my misery and
    rejoice
    over what you have done.
Bring on the day you proclaimed,
    and let them become like me!

22 Let all their evil come before you
    and deal with them
As you have so ruthlessly dealt with me
    for all my rebellions.
My groans are many,
    my heart is sick."[k]

## CHAPTER 2

### The Lord's Wrath and Zion's Ruin*

1 How the Lord in his wrath
    has abhorred daughter Zion,

Casting down from heaven to earth
    the glory of Israel,[†]
Not remembering his footstool
    on the day of his wrath!

2 The Lord has devoured without pity
    all of Jacob's dwellings;
In his fury he has razed
    daughter Judah's defenses,
Has brought to the ground in dishonor
    a kingdom and its princes.

3 In blazing wrath, he cut down entirely
    the horn[‡] of Israel;
He withdrew the support of his right hand
    when the enemy approached;
He burned against Jacob like a blazing fire
    that consumes everything in its path.

4 He bent his bow like an enemy;
    the arrow in his right hand
Like a foe, he killed
    all those held precious;
On the tent of daughter Zion
    he poured out his wrath like fire.

5 The Lord has become the enemy,
    he has devoured Israel:
Devoured all its strongholds,
    destroyed its defenses,
Multiplied moaning and groaning
    throughout daughter Judah.

6 He laid waste his booth like a garden,
    destroyed his shrine;[§]
The LORD has blotted out in Zion
    feast day and sabbath,
Has scorned in fierce wrath
    king and priest.[l]

7 The Lord has rejected his altar,
    spurned his sanctuary;
He has handed over to the enemy
    the walls of its strongholds.
They shout in the house of the LORD
    as on a feast day.[m]

8 The LORD was bent on destroying
    the wall of daughter Zion:
He stretched out the measuring line;[¶]

20–22). The persona of the poet, first portrayed in chap. 1 as a detached observer recounting both the desolation as well as the sins of the city, becomes in this chapter an advocate for Zion in her appeal to the Lord and never once mentions her sins.

†[2:1] **The glory of Israel**: the Temple. **His footstool**: the ark of the covenant (1 Chr 28:2; Ps 99:5; 132:7); or again, the Temple (Ez 43:7).

‡[2:3] **Horn**: a symbol of power and strength; cf. v. 17; 1 Sm 2:1, 10; Ps 89:18, 25; 92:11; 112:9.

§[2:6] **Booth . . . shrine**: synonyms for the Temple; cf. Ps 27:5; 74:4, 8. The term for "shrine" in Hebrew (*mo'ed*) figures prominently in the pentateuchal expression "tent of meeting" ('ohel mo'ed).

¶[2:8] **The measuring line**: normally used for building, here employed ironically as an instrument of destruction; cf. Is 34:11; 2 Kgs 21:13.

*[2:1–22] This chapter continues to move between the voice of the poet (vv. 1–20) and that of personified Zion (vv.

g. [1:16] Ps 69:21; Eccl 4:1; Jer 13:17; 14:17; Na 3:7.    h. [1:18] Dt 28:41.    i. [1:19] Jer 30:14.    j. [1:20] Lam 2:11.    k. [1:22] Lam 3:64.

l. [2:6] Is 1:13; 5:5.    m. [2:7] Ez 24:21.

did not hesitate to devour,
Brought grief on rampart and wall
    till both succumbed.[n]

9 Her gates sank into the ground;
    he smashed her bars to bits.
Her king and her princes are among the
        nations;
    instruction is wanting,
Even her prophets do not obtain
    any vision from the Lord.[o]

10 The elders of daughter Zion
    sit silently on the ground;
They cast dust[*] on their heads
    and dress in sackcloth;
The young women of Jerusalem
    bow their heads to the ground.[p]

11 My eyes are spent with tears,
    my stomach churns;[†]
My bile is poured out on the ground
    at the brokenness of the daughter of
        my people,
As children and infants collapse
    in the streets of the town.[q]

12 They cry out to their mothers,
    "Where is bread and wine?"
As they faint away like the wounded
    in the streets of the city,
As their life is poured out
    in their mothers' arms.

13 To what can I compare you[‡]—to what can
    I liken you—
    O daughter Jerusalem?
What example can I give in order to
        comfort you,
    virgin daughter Zion?
For your breach is vast as the sea;
    who could heal you?[r]

14 Your prophets provided you visions
    of whitewashed illusion;
They did not lay bare your guilt,
    in order to restore your fortunes;
They saw for you only oracles
    of empty deceit.[s]

15 All who pass by on the road,
    clap their hands at you;
They hiss and wag their heads
    over daughter Jerusalem:
"Is this the city they used to call
    perfect in beauty and joy of all the
        earth?"[t]

16 They open their mouths against you,
    all your enemies;
They hiss and gnash their teeth,
    saying, "We have devoured her!
How we have waited for this day—
    we have lived to see it!"[u]

17 The Lord has done what he planned.
    He has fulfilled the threat
Decreed from days of old,
    destroying without pity!
He let the enemy gloat over you
    and exalted the horn of your foes.[v]

18 Cry out to the Lord from your heart,
    wall of daughter Zion!
Let your tears flow like a torrent
    day and night;
Give yourself no rest,
    no relief for your eyes.

19 Rise up! Wail in the night,
    at the start of every watch;
Pour out your heart like water
    before the Lord;
Lift up your hands to him
    for the lives of your children,
Who collapse from hunger
    at the corner of every street.[§]

20 "Look, O Lord, and pay attention:
    to whom have you been so ruthless?
Must women eat their own offspring,[¶]
    the very children they have borne?
Are priest and prophet to be slain
    in the sanctuary of the Lord?[w]

21 They lie on the ground in the streets,
    young and old alike;
Both my young women and young men
    are cut down by the sword;

---

*[2:10] **They cast dust**: as a sign of mourning; cf. Jos 7:6; Jb 2:12; Ez 27:30.

†[2:11] **My eyes are spent with tears, my stomach churns**: the poet appropriates the emotional language used by Zion in 1:16 and 1:20 to express a progressively stronger commitment to her cause. After describing the systematic dismantling of the city in vv. 5–9, the poet turns to the plight of the inhabitants in vv. 10–12. It is the description of children dying in the streets that finally brings about the poet's emotional breakdown, even as it did for Zion in 1:16.

‡[2:13] **To what can I compare you . . . ?**: the author calls attention to the poetic task: to find language that speaks adequately of the atrocities and incomparable suffering experienced by Zion, and thus to attempt to offer comfort.

§[2:19] The poet urges Zion to appeal to the Lord once more on behalf of her dying children. The image of Zion's children effectively condenses the metaphorical sense of all residents of the city (young and old alike) into the more poignant picture of actual children at the point of death. It was precisely this image, no doubt well known to survivors of besieged cities, that led to the emotional breakdown of both Zion (1:16) and the poet (2:11). The hope is that the Lord will be similarly affected by such a poignant image and respond with mercy.

¶[2:20] **Must women eat their own offspring**: extreme famine in a besieged city sometimes led to cannibalism; this becomes a stereotypical way of expressing the nearly unthinkable horrors of war; cf. Lam 4:10; Dt 28:53; 2 Kgs 6:28–29; Bar 2:3; Ez 5:10.

---

n. [2:8] Jer 52:12–14.   o. [2:9] Dt 28:36.   p. [2:10] Is 3:26.   q. [2:11] Lam 1:16, 20; 3:48; Jer 8:18.   r. [2:13] Lam 1:12; Jer 8:21.   s. [2:14] Is 58:1; Jer 2:8; 23:16; Ez 13:9; 22:28.

t. [2:15] Ps 48:3; 50:12; Jer 18:16.   u. [2:16] Lam 3:46.   v. [2:17] Dt 28:15.   w. [2:20] Lam 4:10.

You killed them on the day of your wrath,
    slaughtered without pity.ˣ

²² You summoned as to a feast day
    terrors on every side;
On the day of the LORD's wrath,
    none survived or escaped.
Those I have borne and nurtured,
    my enemy has utterly destroyed."ʸ

## CHAPTER 3

### The Voice of a Suffering Individual*

¹ I am one who has known affliction
    under the rod of God's anger,ᶻ
² One whom he has driven and forced to
    walk
    in darkness, not in light;
³ Against me alone he turns his hand—
    again and again all day long.

⁴ He has worn away my flesh and my skin,
    he has broken my bones;ᵃ
⁵ He has besieged me all around
    with poverty and hardship;
⁶ He has left me to dwell in dark places
    like those long dead.ᵇ

⁷ He has hemmed me in with no escape,
    weighed me down with chains;
⁸ Even when I cry for help,
    he stops my prayer;ᶜ
⁹ He has hemmed in my ways with fitted
    stones,
    and made my paths crooked.

¹⁰ He has been a bear lying in wait for me,
    a lion in hiding!ᵈ
¹¹ He turned me aside and tore me apart,
    leaving me ravaged.ᵉ
¹² He bent his bow, and set me up
    as a target for his arrow.ᶠ

¹³ He pierced my kidneys
    with shafts from his quiver.ᵍ
¹⁴ I have become a laughingstock to all my
    people,
    their taunt all day long;ʰ
¹⁵ He has sated me with bitterness,
    filled me with wormwood.ⁱ

¹⁶ He has made me eat gravel,
    trampled me into the dust;
¹⁷ My life is deprived of peace,
    I have forgotten what happiness is;
¹⁸ My enduring hope, I said,
    has perished before the LORD.

¹⁹ The thought of my wretched homelessness
    is wormwood and poison;
²⁰ Remembering it over and over,
    my soul is downcast.
²¹ But this I will call to mind;†
    therefore I will hope:

²² The LORD's acts of mercy are not
    exhausted,
    his compassion is not spent;ʲ
²³ They are renewed each morning—
    great is your faithfulness!
²⁴ The LORD is my portion, I tell myself,
    therefore I will hope in him.ᵏ

²⁵ The LORD is good to those who trust in
    him,
    to the one that seeks him;ˡ
²⁶ It is good to hope in silence
    for the LORD's deliverance.
²⁷ It is good for a person, when young,
    to bear the yoke,

²⁸ To sit alone and in silence,
    when its weight lies heavy,
²⁹ To put one's mouth in the dust—‡
    there may yet be hope—
³⁰ To offer one's cheek to be struck,
    to be filled with disgrace.ᵐ

³¹ For the Lord does not
    reject forever;ⁿ
³² Though he brings grief, he takes pity,
    according to the abundance of his
    mercy;ᵒ
³³ He does not willingly afflict
    or bring grief to human beings.ᵖ

³⁴ That someone tramples underfoot
    all the prisoners in the land,
³⁵ Or denies justice to anyone
    in the very sight of the Most High,
³⁶ Or subverts a person's lawsuit—
    does the Lord not see?

³⁷ Who speaks so that it comes to pass,
    unless the Lord commands it?

---

*[3:1–66] This chapter is focused less on the destruction of Jerusalem than are chaps. 1 and 2 and more on the suffering of an individual. The identity of the individual is never given, and one probably should not search for a specific identification of the speaker. The figure of the representative sufferer makes concrete the pain of the people in a way similar to the personification of Zion as a woman in chaps. 1 and 2. Indeed, in vv. 40–48 the individual voice gives way to a communal voice, returning in vv. 49–66 to the individual sufferer.

x. [2:21] Lam 3:43; 2 Chr 36:17; Jer 6:11.   y. [2:22] Jer 42:17.
z. [3:1] Jer 20:18.   a. [3:4] Jb 30:30; Is 38:13.   b. [3:6] Ps 143:3.
c. [3:8] Ps 18:41; 22:2; 88:14–15.   d. [3:10] Jb 10:16; Hos 13:8.
e. [3:11] Lam 1:13.   f. [3:12] Lam 2:4; Jb 16:12.   g. [3:13] Jb 6:4; Ps 38:3.   h. [3:14] Jb 30:9; Ps 69:13.   i. [3:15] Jer 9:14; 23:15.

†[3:21–24] In the midst of a description of suffering, the speaker offers this brief but compelling statement of hope in God's ultimate mercy. It is a hard-won and precarious hope, nearly submerged by the volume and intensity of the surrounding lament, but it is hope nonetheless.

‡[3:29] **To put one's mouth in the dust**: a sign of humiliation and submission; cf. v. 16; Ps 72:9.

j. [3:22] 1 Sm 20:15; Neh 9:31.   k. [3:24] Ps 16:5; 73:26.   l. [3:25] Ps 130:6; Is 30:18.   m. [3:30] Is 50:6; Mt 5:39.   n. [3:31] Ps 85:6; 103:9.   o. [3:32] 1 Sm 2:6–7; Tb 13:2; Is 54:8.   p. [3:33] Ex 34:6–7.

³⁸ ˙ Is it not at the word of the Most High
that both good and bad take place?�q
³⁹ What should the living complain about?
about their sins!

⁴⁰ *Let us search and examine our ways,
and return to the LORD!ʳ
⁴¹ Let us lift up our hearts as well as our
hands
toward God in heaven!
⁴² We have rebelled and been obstinate;
you have not forgiven us.

⁴³ You wrapped yourself in wrath and
pursued us,
killing without pity;ˢ
⁴⁴ You wrapped yourself in a cloud,
which no prayer could pierce.
⁴⁵ You have made us filth and rubbish
among the peoples.ᵗ

⁴⁶ They have opened their mouths against us,
all our enemies;
⁴⁷ Panic and the pit have been our lot,
desolation and destruction;ᵘ
⁴⁸ †My eyes stream with tears over the
destruction
of the daughter of my people.ᵛ

⁴⁹ My eyes will flow without ceasing,
without rest,
⁵⁰ Until the LORD from heaven
looks down and sees.
⁵¹ I am tormented by the sight
of all the daughters of my city.

⁵² Without cause, my enemies snared me
as though I were a bird;
⁵³ They tried to end my life in the pit,
pelting me with stones.
⁵⁴ The waters flowed over my head:
and I said, "I am lost!"ʷ

⁵⁵ I have called upon your name, O LORD,ˣ
from the bottom of the pit;
⁵⁶ You heard me call, "Do not let your ear be
deaf
to my cry for help."
⁵⁷ You drew near on the day I called you;
you said, "Do not fear!"

⁵⁸ You pleaded my case, Lord,
you redeemed my life.

⁵⁹ You see, LORD, how I am wronged;
do me justice!ʸ
⁶⁰ You see all their vindictiveness,
all their plots against me.

⁶¹ You hear their reproach, LORD,
all their plots against me,
⁶² The whispered murmurings of my
adversaries,
against me all day long;
⁶³ Look! Whether they sit or stand,
I am the butt of their taunt.

⁶⁴ Give them what they deserve, LORD,
according to their deeds;
⁶⁵ Give them hardness of heart;
your curse be upon them;ᶻ
⁶⁶ Pursue them in wrath and destroy them
from under the LORD's heaven!

# CHAPTER 4

### Miseries of the Besieged City‡

¹ How the gold has lost its luster,
the noble metal changed;
Jewels§ lie scattered
at the corner of every street.

² And Zion's precious children,
worth their weight in gold—
How they are treated like clay jugs,
the work of any potter!ᵃ

³ Even jackals offer their breasts
to nurse their young;
But the daughter of my people is as cruel
as the ostrich¶ in the wilderness.ᵇ

⁴ The tongue of the infant cleaves
to the roof of its mouth in thirst;
Children beg for bread,
but no one gives them a piece.

⁵ Those who feasted on delicacies
are abandoned in the streets;
Those who reclined on crimson**
now embrace dung heaps.ᶜ

---

‡[4:1–22] This chapter returns to the focus of chaps. 1 and
2, namely the horrors of a siege. Unlike chaps. 1 and 2, however,
the character of personified Zion never interrupts the voice of
the poet to protest her abject state. As a result, the emotion of
the poem is less intense, while at the same time seeming more
grim on account of its lack of petition to the Lord.

§[4:1–2] Jewels: lit., "holy stones." These precious things
designate the children who are abandoned, starving, and
killed in the siege of Jerusalem (cf. Zec 9:16). Another explanation is that these are the stones of the destroyed Temple.

¶[4:3] Cruel as the ostrich: see note on Jb 39:14–16. Jerusalem, in her distress, has abandoned her children.

**[4:5] Crimson: a sign of luxury. Tyrian purple, a red-
purple or blue-purple dye produced from shellfish, was very
expensive and the only colorfast dye in the ancient Near East.
Thus purple or crimson cloth was available only to the wealthy.

---

*[3:40–66] The plural voice in this lament suggests that a
communal lament begins here; it then continues in the singular voice in vv. 55–66.

†[3:48–51] These verses are more appropriate on the lips
of the poet, who speaks of "my city" (v. 51). Daughters of my
city: here as elsewhere "daughter" may refer to villages dependent on a larger city.

---

q. [3:38] Is 45:7.   r. [3:40] Jl 2:12–13.   s. [3:43] Lam 2:21.   t. [3:45]
1 Cor 4:13.   u. [3:47] Is 24:17–18; Jer 48:43–44.   v. [3:48] Lam 1:16;
2:11; Jer 8:23; 9:17.   w. [3:54] Ps 69:2–3; 88:8; Jon 2:4.   x. [3:55–56]
Ps 130:1–2.

y. [3:58–59] Ps 35:23–24; 43:1; 119:154.   z. [3:65] Jer 11:20; 2 Tm
4:14.   a. [4:2] Jer 19:11.   b. [4:3] Jb 39:16.   c. [4:5] Dt 28:56.

⁶ The punishment of the daughter of my
     people
          surpassed the penalty of Sodom,
Which was overthrown in an instant
     with no hand laid on it.ᵈ

⁷ Her princes were brighter than snow,
     whiter than milk,
Their bodies more ruddy than coral,
     their beauty like the sapphire.

⁸ Now their appearance is blacker than
     soot,
          they go unrecognized in the streets;
Their skin has shrunk on their bones,
     and become dry as wood.ᵉ

⁹ Better for those pierced by the sword
     than for those pierced by hunger,
Better for those who bleed from wounds
     than for those who lack food.

¹⁰ The hands of compassionate women
     have boiled their own children!
They became their food
     when the daughter of my people was
          shattered.ᶠ

¹¹ The LORD has exhausted his anger,
     poured out his blazing wrath;
He has kindled a fire in Zion
     that has consumed her foundations.ᵍ

¹² The kings of the earth did not believe,
     nor any of the world's inhabitants,
That foe or enemy could enter
     the gates of Jerusalem.

¹³ Except for the sins of her prophets
     and the crimes of her priests,
Who poured out in her midst
     the blood of the just.ʰ

¹⁴ They staggered blindly in the streets,
     defiled with blood,
So that people could not touch
     even their garments:ⁱ

¹⁵ "Go away! Unclean!" they cried to them,
     "Away, away, do not touch!"
If they went away and wandered,
     it would be said among the nations,
          "They can no longer live here!

¹⁶ The presence of the LORD was their portion,
     but he no longer looks upon them.
The priests are shown no regard,
     the elders, no mercy.

¹⁷ Even now our eyes are worn out,
     searching in vain for help;

From our watchtower we have watched
     for a nation* unable to save.

¹⁸ They dogged our every step,
     we could not walk in our squares;
Our end drew near, our time was up;
     yes, our end had come.

¹⁹ Our pursuers were swifter
     than eagles in the sky,
In the mountains they were hot on our
     trail,
          they ambushed us in the wilderness.ʲ

²⁰ The LORD's anointed—our very
     lifebreath!—†
          was caught in their snares,
He in whose shade we thought
     to live among the nations.ᵏ

²¹ Rejoice and gloat, daughter Edom,
     dwelling in the land of Uz,‡
The cup will pass to you as well;
     you shall become drunk and strip
          yourself naked!ˡ

²² Your punishment is completed, daughter
     Zion,
          the Lord will not prolong your exile;
The Lord will punish your iniquity,
     daughter Edom,
          will lay bare your sins.ᵐ

## CHAPTER 5

### The Community's Lament to the Lord

¹ Remember, LORD, what has happened to
     us,
          pay attention, and see our disgrace:
² Our heritage is turned over to strangers,
     our homes, to foreigners.ⁿ
³ We have become orphans, without
     fathers;
          our mothers are like widows.
⁴ We pay money to drink our own water,
     our own wood comes at a price.
⁵ With a yoke on our necks, we are driven;
     we are worn out, but allowed no
          rest.

---

*[4:17] **A nation:** probably Egypt, which failed to give effective aid against Babylon.

†[4:20] **Our very lifebreath:** lit., "the breath of our nostrils," that is, the king. This expression occurs in Egyptian texts of the late second millennium B.C., and may have survived as a royal epithet in the Jerusalem court. After the disaster of 598 B.C. (2 Kgs 24:1–17), Jerusalem could have hoped to live in peace amidst her neighbors; but they (vv. 21–22) as well as Babylon turned against her to ensure her total devastation in 587 B.C.

‡[4:21] **Rejoice:** the address is sarcastic, since Edom (where Uz may have been located) ravaged the land after the fall of Jerusalem (cf. Ps 137).

---

d. [4:6] Gn 19:23–29; 2 Pt 2:6; Jude 7.   e. [4:8] Lam 3:4.   f. [4:10] Lam 2:20; Dt 28:56–57; 2 Kgs 6:29.   g. [4:11] Jer 7:20; Ez 5:13.   h. [4:13] Jer 6:13.   i. [4:14] Dt 28:29; Is 59:10.

j. [4:19] Jer 4:13; Hb 1:8.   k. [4:20] Lam 2:9; Ez 19:4, 8.   l. [4:21] Lam 1:21; Jer 25:15.   m. [4:22] Is 40:2.   n. [5:2] Ps 79:1.

⁶ We extended a hand to Egypt and Assyria,
    to satisfy our need of bread.*
⁷ Our ancestors, who sinned, are no more;
    but now we bear their guilt.
⁸ Servants† rule over us,
    with no one to tear us from their
        hands.
⁹ We risk our lives just to get bread,
    exposed to the desert heat;°
¹⁰ Our skin heats up like an oven,
    from the searing blasts of famine.ᵖ

¹¹ Women are raped in Zion,
    young women in the cities of Judah;�q
¹² Princes have been hanged by them,
    elders shown no respect.ʳ
¹³ Young men carry millstones,
    boys stagger under loads of wood;
¹⁴ The elders have abandoned the gate,‡
    the young men their music.

¹⁵ The joy of our hearts has ceased,
    dancing has turned into mourning;ˢ
¹⁶ The crown has fallen from our head:
    woe to us that we sinned!
¹⁷ Because of this our hearts grow sick,
    at this our eyes grow dim:
¹⁸ Because of Mount Zion, lying desolate,
    and the jackals roaming there!

¹⁹ But you, LORD, are enthroned forever;
    your throne stands from age to age.ᵗ
²⁰ §Why have you utterly forgotten us,
    forsaken us for so long?ᵘ
²¹ Bring us back to you, LORD, that we may
       return:
    renew our days as of old.ᵛ
²² For now you have indeed rejected us
    and utterly turned your wrath
       against us.ʷ

---

*[5:6] **Extended a hand**: that is, made an alliance. In its
state of abjection, Judah was forced to depend on the major
powers to the west and the east for subsistence.

†[5:8] **Servants**: the Hebrew word for "servant" is also
the word used for an official of relatively high status (servant
of the ruler; cf. 2 Kgs 25:24, where the term is used to refer
to Babylonian rulers over occupied Jerusalem); the author
doubtless intends the double meaning here.

‡[5:14] **The gate**: a place of assembly, where city decisions
were made and judgment given by the elders and other community leaders; see note on Ru 4:1.

---

§[5:20–22] Unlike most of the laments found in the
Book of Psalms, the Book of Lamentations never moves
from lament to thanksgiving. It ends with this question still
unanswered by God: "Why have you utterly forgotten us?"

---

o. [5:9] Lam 1:11.   p. [5:10] Lam 4:8.   q. [5:11] Zec 14:2.   r. [5:12]
Lam 4:16.

s. [5:15] Jer 16:9; 25:10; Am 8:10.   t. [5:19] Ps 9:8; 45:7; 102:13, 27.
u. [5:20] Ps 13:2; 42:10; Is 49:14.   v. [5:21] Ps 80:19–20.   w. [5:22]
Jer 14:19.

# THE BOOK OF
# BARUCH

The opening verses ascribe the book to the well-known assistant to Jeremiah (Jer 32:12; 36:4, 32; 45:1). It is a collection of four very different compositions, ending with a work entitled "The Letter of Jeremiah," which circulated separately in major manuscripts of the Greek tradition. The original language may have been Hebrew, but only the Greek and other versions have been preserved. The fictional setting is Babylon, where Baruch reads his scroll to King Jechoniah (Jehoiachin) and the exiles; they react by sending gifts and the scroll to Jerusalem (1:1–14), presumably by the hand of Baruch (1:7). No certain date can be given for the book, but it may have been edited in final form during the last two centuries B.C. The work attempts to explain the trauma of the exile in terms of a Deuteronomic cycle: sin (of Israel), punishment, repentance, and return (cf. Jgs 2; also Dt 28–33).

The prayer of the exiles (2:11–3:8) is a confession of sin and a request for mercy, and has remarkable similarities to Dn 9 and to parts of Jeremiah. The poem on personified Wisdom is concerned with three themes: the importance of Wisdom, the elusive character of Wisdom (cf. Jb 28), and the identification of Wisdom with Torah (cf. Sir 24:23). Baruch's Poem of Consolation resembles parts of Is 40–66, and it offers encouragement to the exiles in view of their eventual return; there are two addresses by personified Zion. The Letter of Jeremiah, unlike the letter in Jer 29, is a polemic against idolatry, a well-known theme (cf. Jer 10:2–11; Ps 115:4–8; 135:15–18; Is 44:9–20; Wis 13:10–15:17). It contains ten warnings that end in a kind of refrain that the idols are not gods and are not to be feared (vv. 14, 22, 28, 39, 44, 51, 56, 64, 68).

The book can be divided thus:

I. Letter to Jerusalem (1:1–3:8)
    A. Historical Setting (1:1–9)
    B. Confession of Guilt (1:10–2:10)
    C. Prayer for Deliverance (2:11–3:8)
II. Praise of Wisdom (3:9–4:4)
    A. Importance of Wisdom (3:9–23)
    B. Inaccessibility of Wisdom (3:24–36)
    C. Wisdom Contained in the Law (3:37–4:4)
III. Baruch's Poem of Consolation (4:5–5:9)
    A. Baruch Addresses Diaspora (4:5–9a)
    B. Jerusalem Addresses Neighbors (4:9b–16)
    C. Jerusalem Addresses Diaspora (4:17–29)
    D. Baruch Addresses Jerusalem (4:30–5:9)
IV. Letter of Jeremiah (6:1–72)

## I. LETTER TO JERUSALEM

### CHAPTER 1

#### A. Historical Setting

¹Now these are the words of the scroll which Baruch, son of Neriah, son of Mahseiah, son of Zedekiah, son of Hasadiah, son of Hilkiah, wrote in Babylon,ᵃ ²in the fifth year, on the seventh day of the month,* at the time the Chaldeans took Jerusalem and destroyed it with fire.ᵇ ³Baruch read the words of this scroll in the hearing of Jeconiah, son of Jehoiakim, king

---

*[1:2] **In the fifth year, on the seventh day of the month:** Jerusalem fell on the seventh day of the fifth month in 587

a. [1:1] Jer 32:12; 36:4; 45:1–5.　b. [1:2] 2 Kgs 25:8–10.　c. [1:3–4] 2 Kgs 23:1–2.

of Judah, and all the people who came to the reading:[d] [4]the nobles, kings' sons, elders, and all the people, small and great—all who lived in Babylon by the river Sud.[*]

[5]They wept, fasted, and prayed before the Lord, [6]and collected such funds as each could afford.[e] [7]These they sent to Jerusalem, to Jehoiakim the priest, son of Hilkiah, son of Shallum, and to the priests and the whole people who were with him in Jerusalem. [8](At the same time he[†] received the vessels of the house of the LORD that had been removed from the temple, to restore them to the land of Judah, on the tenth of Sivan. These silver vessels Zedekiah, son of Josiah, king of Judah, had had made [9/]after Nebuchadnezzar, king of Babylon, carried off as captives Jeconiah and the princes, the skilled workers, the nobles, and the people of the land from Jerusalem, and brought them to Babylon.)

### B. Confession of Guilt

[10]The message was: "We send you funds, with which you are to procure burnt offerings, sin offerings, and frankincense, and to prepare grain offerings; offer these[‡] on the altar of the LORD our God,[g] [11]and pray for the life of Nebuchadnezzar, king of Babylon, and of Belshazzar, his son,[§] that their lifetimes may be as the days of the heavens above the earth.[h] [12]Pray that the LORD may give us strength, and light to our eyes, that we may live under the protective shadow of Nebuchadnezzar, king of Babylon, and of Belshazzar, his son, to serve them many days, and find favor in their sight. [13]Pray for us to the LORD, our God, for we have sinned against the LORD, our God. Even to this day the wrath of the LORD and his anger have not turned away from us. [14]On the feast day and during the days

of assembly, read aloud in the house of the LORD this scroll that we send you:[i]

[15]"To the Lord our God belongs justice; to us, people of Judah and inhabitants of Jerusalem, to be shamefaced, as on this day—[j] [16]to us, our kings, rulers, priests, and prophets, and our ancestors. [17]We have sinned in the LORD's sight [18]and disobeyed him. We have not listened to the voice of the LORD, our God, so as to follow the precepts the LORD set before us. [19]From the day the LORD led our ancestors out of the land of Egypt until the present day, we have been disobedient to the LORD, our God, and neglected to listen to his voice. [20]Even today evils cling to us, the curse the LORD pronounced to Moses, his servant, at the time he led our ancestors out of the land of Egypt to give us a land flowing with milk and honey.[k] [21]For we did not listen to the voice of the LORD, our God, in all the words of the prophets he sent us, [22]but each of us has followed the inclinations of our wicked hearts, served other gods, and done evil in the sight of the LORD, our God.

## CHAPTER 2

[1]"So the LORD carried out the warning he had uttered against us: against our judges, who governed Israel, against our kings and princes, and against the people of Israel and Judah. [2]Nowhere under heaven has anything been done like what he did in Jerusalem, as was written in the law of Moses:[*][/] [3]that we would each eat[††] the flesh of our sons, each the flesh of our daughters. [4]He has made us subject to all the kingdoms around us, an object of reproach and horror among all the peoples around us, where the LORD has scattered us.[m] [5]We are brought low, not raised high,[n] because we sinned against the LORD, our God, not listening to his voice.

[6]"To the LORD, our God, belongs justice; to us and to our ancestors, to be shamefaced, as on this day.[o] [7]All the evils of which the LORD had warned us have come upon us. [8]We did not entreat the favor of the LORD by turning, each one, from the designs of our evil hearts. [9]The LORD kept watch over the evils, and brought them home to us; for the LORD is just in all the works he commanded us to do,[p] [10]but we did not listen to his voice, or follow the precepts of the LORD which he had set before us.

---

B.C.; cf. 2 Kgs 25:8; Jer 52:12. Either the text read originally "the fifth month," or it refers to the observance of an anniversary of the fall of Jerusalem.

[*][1:4] **The river Sud:** probably one of the Babylonian canals, not otherwise identified; or possibly a misreading of Ahava; cf. Ezr 8:21, 31.

[†][1:8–9] **He:** apparently Baruch; less likely Jehoiakim the priest (v. 7). The silver vessels here described are distinct from the vessels referred to in 2 Kgs 25:14 and Ezr 1:7–9. The author of this note may have thought of the fifth year (v. 1) of Zedekiah, in view of Jer 28:1; 29:1–3. A "fifth year," again with no month mentioned, is given in Ez 1:2 for the inaugural vision of Ezekiel's prophetic career.

[‡][1:10] **Offer these:** since 2:26 suggests that the Temple is destroyed, the mention of sacrifices here may be an anachronism. Nevertheless, Jer 41:5 indicates that some people continued to worship at the Temple site after Nebuchadnezzar's destruction of the Temple.

[§][1:11] **Nebuchadnezzar . . . Belshazzar, his son:** Belshazzar was the son of Nabonidus, the last king of Babylon, not of Nebuchadnezzar, the destroyer of Jerusalem. Belshazzar was co-regent for a few years while his father was away in Arabia. Later Jewish tradition seems to have simplified the end of the Babylonian empire (cf. Dn 5:1–2), for three kings came between Nebuchadnezzar and Nabonidus.

d. [1:3] 2 Kgs 24:8–17; Jer 22:24–30; 27:20; 51:59–64.    e. [1:6] Dt 16:17.    f. [1:9] Jer 24:1.    g. [1:10] Jer 17:26; 41:5.    h. [1:11] Dt 11:21; Ps 89:30; Jer 29:7; Dn 5:1–2; 1 Tm 2:1–2.

[¶][1:15–2:10] This confession of sin is similar to Dn 9:7–14, and echoes ideas from Deuteronomy and Jeremiah; cf. also Neh 9.

[**][2:2] **Law of Moses:** cf. Dt 28:53–57.

[††][2:3] **We would each eat:** such dreadful events were the result of the prolonged siege of Jerusalem; cf. Lam 2:20.

---

i. [1:14] Ex 23:14–17; Lv 23:35–36; Sir 50:6; Hos 9:5.    j. [1:15] Bar 2:6; 3:8; Ezr 9:6–15; Neh 9:6–37; Dn 9:4–19.    k. [1:20] Lv 26:14–39; Dt 28:15–68.    l. [2:2–3] Dt 28:52–57; 2 Kgs 6:28–29; Jer 19:9; Lam 2:20; 4:10; Ez 5:10; Dn 9:12.    m. [2:4] Jer 29:18; Dn 9:16.    n. [2:5] Dt 28:13, 43–44.    o. [2:6] Bar 1:15; Dn 9:7.    p. [2:9] Jer 1:12; 31:28; 44:27; Dn 9:14.

## C. Prayer for Deliverance

¹¹*"And now, LORD, God of Israel, who led your people out of the land of Egypt with a strong hand, with signs and wonders and great might, and with an upraised arm, so that you have made for yourself a name to the present day:�q ¹²we have sinned, we have committed sacrilege, we have violated all your statutes, LORD, our God.ʳ ¹³Withdraw your anger from us, for we are left few in number among the nations where you have scattered us. ¹⁴Hear, LORD, our prayer of supplication, and deliver us for your own sake: grant us favor in the sight of those who brought us into exile, ¹⁵that the whole earth may know that you are the LORD, our God, and that Israel† and his descendants bear your name.ˢ ¹⁶LORD, look down from your holy dwelling and take thought of us; LORD, incline your ear to hear us.ᵗ ¹⁷Open your eyes and see: it is not the dead in Hades,‡ whose breath has been taken from within them, who will declare the glory and vindication to the LORD.ᵘ ¹⁸The person who is deeply grieved, who walks bowed and feeble, with failing eyes and famished soul, will declare your glory and justice, LORD!ᵛ

¹⁹"Not on the just deeds of our ancestors and our kings do we base our plea for mercy in your sight, LORD, our God. ²⁰You have sent your wrath and anger upon us, as you had warned us through your servants the prophets: ²¹Thus says the LORD: Bend your necks and serve the king of Babylon, that you may continue in the land I gave your ancestors;ʷ ²²for if you do not listen to the LORD's voice so as to serve the king of Babylon, ²³I will silence from the cities of Judah and from the streets of Jerusalem the cry of joy and the cry of gladness, the voice of the bridegroom and the voice of the bride; and all the land shall be deserted, without inhabitants.ˣ ²⁴But we did not listen to your voice, or serve the king of Babylon, and you carried out the threats you had made through your servants the prophets, that the bones of our kings and the bones of our ancestors would be brought out from their burial places.ʸ ²⁵And indeed, they lie exposed◗ to the heat of day and the frost of night. They died in great suffering, by famine and sword and plague.ᶻ ²⁶And you reduced the house which

bears your name** to what it is today, because of the wickedness of the house of Israel and the house of Judah.ᵃ

**God's Promises Recalled.** ²⁷"But with us, Lord, our God, you have dealt in all your clemency and in all your great mercy. ²⁸††Thus you spoke through your servant Moses, the day you ordered him to write down your law in the presence of the Israelites: ²⁹°If you do not listen to my voice, surely this great and numerous throng will dwindle away among the nations to which I will scatter them.ᵇ ³⁰For I know they will not listen to me, because they are a stiff-necked people. But in the land of their exile they shall have a change of heart;ᶜ ³¹they shall know that I, the LORD, am their God. I will give them a heart and ears that listen;ᵈ ³²and they shall praise me in the land of their exile, and shall remember my name.ᵉ ³³Then they shall turn back from their stiff-necked stubbornness, and from their evil deeds, because they shall remember the ways of their ancestors, who sinned against the LORD.ᶠ ³⁴And I will bring them back to the land I promised on oath to their ancestors, to Abraham, Isaac, and Jacob; and they shall rule it. I will make them increase; they shall not be few. ³⁵And I will establish for them an eternal covenant: I will be their God, and they shall be my people; and I will never again remove my people Israel from the land I gave them.'ᵍ

# CHAPTER 3

¹"LORD Almighty, God of Israel, the anguished soul, the dismayed spirit cries out to you. ²Hear, LORD, and have mercy, for you are a merciful God; have mercy on us, who have sinned against you: ³for you are enthroned forever, while we are perishing forever.ʰ ⁴LORD Almighty, God of Israel, hear the prayer of the dead of Israel, children who sinned against you; they did not listen to the voice of the LORD, their God, and their evils cling to us.ⁱ ⁵Do not remember the wicked deeds of our ancestors, but remember at this time your power and your name, ⁶for you are the LORD our God; and you, LORD, we will praise! ⁷This is why you put into our hearts the fear of you: that we may call upon your name, and praise you in our exile, when we have removed from our hearts all the wickedness of our ancestors who sinned against you.ʲ ⁸See, today we are in exile, where you have scattered us, an object

---

*[2:11–35] An earnest appeal for divine mercy, along with confession of sin; cf. Dn 9:15–19.

†[2:15] **Israel**: the Israelites claimed descent from the patriarch Jacob, who had received the name Israel in a mysterious encounter with God (Gn 32:29). Thus the Deity was sometimes referred to as "the God of Israel" (Gn 33:20; Ex 5:1).

‡[2:17] **Hades**: this is the Greek translation of Hebrew *sheol*, the nether world.

§[2:22–24] These words are very similar to Jer 7:34; 27:9, 12.

◗[2:25] **They lie exposed**: Jeremiah's words threatened Jehoiakim with being left unburied (Jer 22:19; 36:30).

**[2:26] **The house which bears your name**: the Temple of Jerusalem; cf. Dt 12:11; Jer 7:11. **What it is today**: during the exile it lay in ruins.

††[2:28–35] These words do not actually quote anything Moses is recorded as having said, but they present the substance of a passage such as Dt 30:1–10, which envisions exile, repentance, and restoration.

---

q. [2:11] Dt 6:21–22.    r. [2:12] Ps 106:6.    s. [2:15] Gn 33:20; Sir 36:11; Jer 14:9; 35:17.    t. [2:16] Dt 26:15.    u. [2:17] Ps 6:6; Is 38:18.    v. [2:18] Zep 2:3.    w. [2:21] Jer 27:12.    x. [2:23] Jer 7:34.    y. [2:24] Jer 8:1–2.    z. [2:25] Jer 7:34; 14:12; 31:30.

a. [2:26] Jer 7:10–15; 11:17.    b. [2:29] Lv 26:39.    c. [2:30] Dt 30:1–2; 31:27.    d. [2:31] Ps 40:7; Jer 24:7; Ez 36:26.    e. [2:32] Tb 13:6.    f. [2:33–35] Lv 26:42–45; Dt 30:1–10.    g. [2:35] Jer 31:31; Lam 4:22.    h. [3:3] Ps 29:10; 102:12–13.    i. [3:4] Jer 31:29.    j. [3:7] Jer 31:33.

of reproach and cursing and punishment for all the wicked deeds of our ancestors, who withdrew from the LORD, our God."

## II. PRAISE OF WISDOM*

### A. Importance of Wisdom

9 Hear, Israel, the commandments of life:
  listen, and know prudence!ᵏ
10 How is it, Israel,
    that you are in the land of your foes,
    grown old in a foreign land,
11 Defiled with the dead,
    counted among those destined for
      Hades?ˡ
12 You have forsaken the fountain of
      wisdom!ᵐ
13 Had you walked in the way of God,
    you would have dwelt in enduring
      peace.ⁿ

14 Learn where prudence is,
    where strength, where
      understanding;
  That you may know also
    where are length of days, and life,
    where light of the eyes, and peace.ᵒ
15 Who has found the place of wisdom?ᵖ
    Who has entered into her treasuries?
16 Where are the rulers of the nations,
    who lorded it over the wild beasts of
      the earth,�q
17   made sport of the birds in the heavens,
  Who heaped up the silver,
    the gold in which people trust,
    whose possessions were unlimited,
18 Who schemed anxiously for money,
    their doings beyond discovery?
19 They have vanished, gone down to Hades,
    and others have risen up in their
      stead.
20 Later generations have seen the light of day,
    have dwelt on the earth,
  But the way to understanding they have
    not known,
21   they have not perceived her paths or
      reached her;
    their children remain far from the
      way to her.
22 She has not been heard of in Canaan,†
    nor seen in Teman.ʳ

23 The descendants of Hagar who seek
      knowledge on earth,
    the merchants of Medan and Tema,ˢ
  the storytellers and those seeking
      knowledge—
These have not known the way to wisdom,
    nor have they kept her paths in mind.

### B. Inaccessibility of Wisdom

24 O Israel, how vast is the dwelling of God,‡
    how broad the scope of his dominion:
25 Vast and endless,
    high and immeasurable!
26 In it were born the giants,§
    renowned at the first,
    huge in stature, skilled in war.ᵗ
27 These God did not choose,
    nor did he give them the way of
      understanding;ᵘ
28 They perished for lack of prudence,
    perished through their own folly.ᵛ

29 Who has gone up to the heavens and
      taken her,
    bringing her down from the clouds?ʷ
30 Who has crossed the sea and found her,
    bearing her away rather than choice
      gold?
31 None knows the way to her,
    nor has at heart her path.
32 But the one who knows all things knows
      her;
    he has probed her by his
      knowledge—
  The one who established the earth for all
      time,
    and filled it with four-footed
      animals,
33 Who sends out the lightning, and it goes,
    calls it, and trembling it obeys him;
34 Before whom the stars at their posts
      shine and rejoice.
35 When he calls them, they answer, "Here
      we are!"
    shining with joy for their Maker.ˣ
36 Such is our God;
    no other is to be compared to him:

### C. Wisdom Contained in the Law

37 ¶He has uncovered the whole way of
      understanding,

---

*[3:9–4:4] This poem in praise of personified Wisdom utilizes the theme of Jb 28 (where is wisdom to be found?) and it identifies wisdom and law, as in Sir 24:22–23.

†[3:22–23] Despite the renown for wisdom of the peoples of Canaan and Phoenicia (Ez 28:3–4), of Teman (Jer 49:7), of the descendants of Hagar or the Arabians of Medan and Tema, they did not possess true wisdom, which is found only in the law of God (Bar 4:1).

‡[3:24] The dwelling of God: here, the whole universe; cf. Is 66:1.

§[3:26] The giants: Gn 6:1–4 reflects a tradition about giants who existed before the flood; this was developed in the non-canonical Book of Enoch.

¶[3:37–38] As in Sir 24:8, Wisdom is given to Israel but also is said to live with all human beings (Prv 8:31).

---

k. [3:9] Dt 6:4–5; Prv 4:20–22.  l. [3:11] Ps 88:5.  m. [3:12] Jer 2:13; Jn 4:10, 14.  n. [3:13] Is 48:18.  o. [3:14] Prv 3:2; 8:14.  p. [3:15–37] Jb 28:1–28.  q. [3:16] Jer 27:6; 1 Cor 1:20.  r. [3:22] Jb 2:11; Jer 49:7; Ez 28:4–5; Zec 9:2.

s. [3:23] Gn 25:2, 15; Jb 6:19; Jer 25:23.  t. [3:26] Gn 6:4; Wis 14:6; Sir 16:7.  u. [3:27] 1 Sm 16:7–10.  v. [3:28] Sir 10:8.  w. [3:29] Dt 30:12–13; Sir 24:4; Rom 10:6–7.  x. [3:35] Jb 38:7; Ps 147:4; Is 40:26.

and has given her to Jacob, his servant,
to Israel, his beloved.<sup>y</sup>

<sup>38</sup> Thus she has appeared on earth,
is at home with mortals.<sup>z</sup>

## CHAPTER 4

<sup>1</sup> *She is the book of the precepts of God,
the law that endures forever;
All who cling to her will live,
but those will die who forsake her.<sup>a</sup>
<sup>2</sup> Turn, O Jacob, and receive her:
walk by her light toward splendor.<sup>b</sup>
<sup>3</sup> Do not give your glory to another,
your privileges to an alien nation.
<sup>4</sup> Blessed are we, O Israel;
for what pleases God is known to us!<sup>c</sup>

### III. BARUCH'S POEM OF CONSOLATION<sup>†</sup>

*A. Baruch Addresses Diaspora*

<sup>5</sup> Take courage, my people!
Remember, O Israel,
<sup>6</sup> You were sold to the nations
not for destruction;
It was because you angered God
that you were handed over to your
foes.<sup>d</sup>
<sup>7</sup> For you provoked your Maker<sup>e</sup>
with sacrifices to demons and not
to God;
<sup>8</sup> You forgot the eternal God who
nourished you,
and you grieved Jerusalem who
nurtured you.
<sup>9</sup> She indeed saw coming upon you
the wrath of God; and she said:

*B. Jerusalem Addresses Neighbors*

"Hear, you neighbors of Zion!
God has brought great mourning
upon me,
<sup>10</sup> For I have seen the captivity
that the Eternal One has brought
upon my sons and daughters.
<sup>11</sup> With joy I nurtured them;
but with mourning and lament I
sent them away.

<sup>12</sup> Let no one gloat over me,
a widow, bereft of many;
For the sins of my children I am left
desolate,
because they turned from the law
of God,<sup>f</sup>
<sup>13</sup> and did not acknowledge his
statutes;
In the ways of God's commandments they
did not walk,
nor did they tread the disciplined
paths of his justice.

<sup>14</sup> "Let Zion's neighbors come—
Remember the captivity of my sons
and daughters,
brought upon them by the Eternal
One.
<sup>15</sup> He has brought against them a nation
from afar,
a nation ruthless and of alien speech,
That has neither reverence for old age
nor pity for the child;<sup>g</sup>
<sup>16</sup> They have led away this widow's beloved
sons,
have left me solitary, without
daughters.

*C. Jerusalem Addresses Diaspora*

<sup>17</sup> What can I do to help you?
<sup>18</sup> The one who has brought this evil
upon you
must himself deliver you from your
enemies' hands.<sup>h</sup>
<sup>19</sup> Farewell, my children, farewell;
I am left desolate.
<sup>20</sup> I have taken off the garment of peace,
have put on sackcloth for my prayer
of supplication;
while I live I will cry out to the
Eternal One.<sup>i</sup>

<sup>21</sup> "Take courage, my children; call upon
God;
he will deliver you from oppression,
from enemy hands.<sup>j</sup>
<sup>22</sup> I have put my hope for your deliverance
in the Eternal One,
and joy has come to me from the
Holy One
Because of the mercy that will swiftly
reach you
from your eternal Savior.
<sup>23</sup> With mourning and lament I sent you
away,
but God will give you back to me
with gladness and joy forever.<sup>k</sup>
<sup>24</sup> As Zion's neighbors lately saw you taken
captive,

---

*[4:1–4] The poem ends with the identification of Wisdom and Torah, as in Sir 24:22–23; cf. also Dt 4:5–8.
†[4:5–5:9] The poet addresses the exiles (vv. 5–9a), and then Zion personified is introduced, speaking to the nations and mourning the loss of her children (vv. 9b–16). She then addresses the exiles (vv. 17–29). Finally (4:30–5:9) the poet issues three calls to Jerusalem (4:30, 36; 5:5): she will see her children returning (4:22, 36–37; 5:5).

y. [3:37] Ps 147:19; Sir 24:8–12.   z. [3:38] Wis 9:18; Jn 1:14.   a. [4:1] Dt 4:6–8; Prv 8:35–36; Sir 24:22.   b. [4:2] Prv 4:13, 19.   c. [4:4] Dt 4:32–37; 33:29.   d. [4:6] Jgs 2:14; Is 50:1; 52:3.   e. [4:7–8] Dt 32:13–18; 1 Cor 10:20.

f. [4:12] Lam 1:1, 2, 7.   g. [4:15] Dt 28:49–50; Jer 5:15; 6:22–23.   h. [4:18] Jer 32:42.   i. [4:20] Jdt 9:1; Est 4:16.   j. [4:21] Jer 51:5.   k. [4:23] Jer 31:12–13.

so shall they soon see God's
　　salvation come to you,
with great glory and the splendor of
　　the Eternal One.[l]

25 "My children, bear patiently the wrath[m]
　　　that has come upon you from God;
Your enemies have persecuted you,
　　　but you will soon see their
　　　　destruction
　　and trample upon their necks.*

26 My pampered children have trodden
　　　rough roads,
　　carried off by their enemies like
　　　sheep in a raid.[n]

27 Take courage, my children; call out to
　　　God!
　　The one who brought this upon you
　　　will remember you.[o]

28 As your hearts have been disposed to
　　　stray from God,
　　so turn now ten times the more to
　　　seek him;

29 For the one who has brought disaster
　　　upon you
　　will, in saving you, bring you eternal
　　　joy."[p]

*D. Baruch Addresses Jerusalem*

30 Take courage, Jerusalem!
　　The one who gave you your name
　　　will console you.[q]

31 Wretched shall be those who harmed you,
　　who rejoiced at your downfall;

32 Wretched shall be the cities where your
　　　children were enslaved,
　　wretched the city that received your
　　　children.[r]

33 As that city rejoiced at your collapse,[s]
　　and made merry at your downfall,
　　so shall she grieve over her own
　　　desolation.

34 I will take from her the rejoicing crowds,
　　and her exultation shall be turned to
　　　mourning:

35 For fire shall come upon her[t]
　　from the Eternal One, for many a
　　　day,
　　to be inhabited by demons for a long
　　　time.†

36 Look to the east, Jerusalem;
　　see the joy that comes to you from
　　　God![u]

---

*[4:25] **Trample upon their necks**: a sign of victory over
the enemy (cf. Ps 44:6; Is 14:25). The Israelites considered
their enemies to be God's enemies as well.

†[4:35] Deserts and desolate places were looked upon as
the habitation of demons; cf. Tb 8:3; Lk 11:24.

l. [4:24] Is 60:1–7.   m. [4:25] Is 51:23.   n. [4:26] Lam 2:22.
o. [4:27] Is 40:1.   p. [4:29] Is 35:10.   q. [4:30] Ps 46:5; Is 60:14.
r. [4:32] Jer 51:43.   s. [4:33–34] Is 13:20–22; 47:1–11; Jer 50:13.
t. [4:35] Is 34:9–14.   u. [4:36] Is 60:4–5.

37 Here come your children whom you sent
　　　away,
　　gathered in from east to west
By the word of the Holy One,
　　rejoicing in the glory of God.

## CHAPTER 5

1 Jerusalem, take off your robe of mourning
　　　and misery;
　　put on forever the splendor of glory
　　　from God:[v]

2 Wrapped in the mantle of justice from
　　　God,
　　place on your head the diadem
　　　of the glory of the Eternal One.[w]

3 For God will show your splendor to all
　　　under the heavens;

4 　　you will be named by God forever:
　　the peace of justice, the glory of
　　　God's worship.[x]

5 Rise up, Jerusalem! stand upon the
　　　heights;
　　look to the east and see your children
Gathered from east to west
　　at the word of the Holy One,
　　rejoicing that they are remembered
　　　by God.

6 Led away on foot by their enemies they
　　　left you:
　　but God will bring them back to you
　　carried high in glory as on royal
　　　thrones.[y]

7 For God has commanded
　　that every lofty mountain
　　and the age-old hills be made low,
That the valleys be filled to make level
　　　ground,
　　that Israel may advance securely in
　　　the glory of God.[z]

8 The forests and every kind of fragrant tree
　　have overshadowed Israel at God's
　　　command;[a]

9 For God is leading Israel in joy
　　by the light of his glory,
　　with the mercy and justice that are his.

### IV. LETTER OF JEREMIAH

## CHAPTER 6

¹A copy of the letter which Jeremiah sent to
those led captive to Babylon by the king of the
Babylonians, to tell them what God had commanded him:[b]

　For the sins you committed before God, you
are being led captive to Babylon by Nebuchadnezzar, king of the Babylonians. ²When you
reach Babylon you will be there many years, a

v. [5:1] Is 52:1.   w. [5:2] Ex 39:30; Wis 18:24; Is 61:10; 62:3.
x. [5:4] Is 1:26; 32:17; Jer 33:16.   y. [5:6] Is 49:22.   z. [5:7] Is 40:3–4.
a. [5:8] Is 41:19.   b. [6:1] Jer 29:1.

long time—seven generations;* after that I will bring you back from there in peace. ³And now in Babylon you will see gods of silver and gold and wood, carried shoulder high, to cast fear upon the nations.ᶜ ⁴ᵃTake care that you yourselves do not become like these foreigners and let not such fear possess you. ⁵When you see the crowd before them and behind worshiping them, say in your hearts, "You, Lord, are the one to be worshiped!"ᵈ ⁶For my angel‡ is with you, and he will keep watch on you.ᵉ

⁷Their tongues are smoothed by woodworkers; they are covered with gold and silver—but they are frauds, and cannot speak.ᶠ ⁸People bring gold, as though for a girl fond of dressing up, ⁹and prepare crowns for the heads of their gods. Then sometimes the priests filch the gold and silver from their gods and spend it on themselves, ¹⁰or give part of it to harlots§ in the brothel. They dress them up in clothes like human beings, these gods of silver and gold and wood. ¹¹Though they are wrapped in purple clothing, they are not safe from rust and corrosion. ¹²Their faces are wiped clean of the cloud of dust which is thick upon them. ¹³Each has a scepter, like the human ruler of a district, but none can do away with those that offend against it. ¹⁴Each has in its right hand an ax or dagger, but it cannot save itself from war or pillage. Thus it is known they are not gods; do not fear them.

¹⁵As useless as a broken potᵍ ¹⁶are their gods, set up in their temples, their eyes full of dust from the feet of those who enter. ¹⁷Their courtyards are walled in like those of someone brought to execution for a crime against the king; the priests reinforce their temples with gates and bars and bolts, so they will not be carried off by robbers. ¹⁸They light more lamps for them than for themselves, yet not one of these can they see. ¹⁹They are like any timber in the temple; their hearts, it is said, are eaten away. Though crawling creatures from the ground

consume them and their garments, they do not feel it. ²⁰Their faces become sooty from the smoke in the temple. ²¹Bats and swallows alight on their bodies and heads—any bird, and cats as well. ²²Know, therefore, that they are not gods; do not fear them.

²³Gold adorns them, but unless someone wipes away the corrosion, they do not shine; they felt nothing when they were molded. ²⁴They are bought at whatever price, but there is no spirit in them. ²⁵Since they have no feet, they are carried shoulder high, displaying to all how worthless they are; even those who worship them are put to shameʰ ²⁶because, if they fall to the ground, the worshipers must pick them up. They neither move of themselves if one sets them upright, nor come upright if they are tipped over; offerings are set out for them as for the dead.ⁱ ²⁷ᵃTheir priests sell their sacrifices for their own advantage. Likewise their wives cure some of the meat, but they do not share it with the poor and the weak;ʲ ²⁸women ritually unclean or at childbirth handle their sacrifices. From such things, know that they are not gods; do not fear them.

²⁹How can they be called gods? Women set out the offerings for these gods of silver and gold and wood, ³⁰and in their temples the priests squat with torn tunic and with shaven hair and beard, and with their heads uncovered.ᵏ ³¹They shout and wail before their gods as others do at a funeral banquet. ³²The priests take some of the clothing from their gods and put it on their wives and children. ³³ᵃWhether these gods are treated well or badly by anyone, they cannot repay it. They can neither set up nor remove a king.ˡ ³⁴They cannot give anyone riches or pennies; if one fails to fulfill a vow to them, they will not exact it. ³⁵They neither save anyone from death, nor deliver the weak from the strong,ᵐ ³⁶nor do they restore sight to the blind, or rescue anyone in distress. ³⁷The widow they do not pity, the orphan they do not help. ³⁸These gilded and silvered wooden statues are no better than stones from the mountains; their worshipers will be put to shame. ³⁹How then can it be thought or claimed that they are gods?

⁴⁰Even the Chaldeans themselves have no respect for them; for when they see a deaf mute, unable to speak, they bring forward Bel†† and expect him to make a sound, as though he could hear. ⁴¹They themselves are unable to reflect and

---

*[6:2] **Seven generations**: this number may be symbolic. If it is not, it may indicate the date of this composition by an author writing for his contemporaries for whom the conditions of the exile were still realities. He has multiplied the seventy years of Jer 29:10 by three or four.

†[6:4–72] This whole chapter is a sustained argument against the temptation to worship Babylonian gods. A pattern is repeated throughout the chapter: various reasons are set forth to prove that the idols in the Babylonian temples are not gods (e.g., they are weak, helpless, attended by unworthy ministers); each section is followed by an exhortation not to be deceived, not to worship them. Note the refrain at vv. 14, 22, 28, 39, 44, 51, 56, 64. Israelite religion was aniconic, i.e., it prohibited images; as elsewhere in the Old Testament (e.g., Is 42:17; 44:9–20), the polemic against idols here oversimplifies by identifying the god worshiped with the image that represents it.

‡[6:6] **My angel**: the prophet assures the people that God's watchful care is with them, just as he was with their ancestors during their journey to the promised land (Ex 23:20).

§[6:10] **Harlots**: cult prostitutes, common in some religions of the ancient Near East.

¶[6:27–31] From the viewpoint of Jewish ritual law, the practices named here were grotesque and depraved; cf. Lv 12:2–8; 15:19–23.

**[6:33–39] All that the Babylonian gods cannot do, the true God does; they have neither power nor inclination to save those in need, unlike the God of Israel, who champions the cause of the weak over the strong, and who defends the widow and the orphan. Cf. 1 Sm 2:7; Ps 68:6; 146:7–9; Is 35:4–5.

††[6:40] **Bel**: cf. note on Jer 50:2.

c. [6:3] Is 46:7; Jer 10:1–16.  d. [6:5] Dt 6:13; 10:20; Mt 4:10; Lk 4:8.  e. [6:6] Ex 23:20.  f. [6:7] Ps 135:16.  g. [6:15] Jer 22:28.  h. [6:25] Wis 13:16.  i. [6:26] Sir 30:18–19.  j. [6:27] Lv 12:4; 15:19–20; Dt 14:28–29.  k. [6:30] Lv 10:6; 21:5, 10.  l. [6:33] Dn 2:21.  m. [6:35] Ps 68:6; 146:7–9.

abandon these gods, for they have no sense. <sup>42*</sup>And the women, with cords around them, sit by the roads, burning chaff for incense;<sup>n</sup> <sup>43</sup>and whenever one of them is taken aside by some passerby who lies with her, she mocks her neighbor who has not been thought thus worthy, and has not had her cord broken. <sup>44</sup>All that is done for these gods is a fraud; how then can it be thought or claimed that they are gods?

<sup>45</sup>They are produced by woodworkers and goldsmiths; they are nothing other than what these artisans wish them to be. <sup>46</sup>Even those who produce them are not long-lived; <sup>47</sup>how then can the things they have produced be gods? They have left frauds and disgrace to their successors. <sup>48</sup>For when war or disaster comes upon them, the priests deliberate among themselves where they can hide with them. <sup>49</sup>How then can one not understand that these are not gods, who save themselves neither from war nor from disaster? <sup>50</sup>Beings that are wooden, gilded and silvered, they will later be known for frauds. To all nations and kings it will be clear that they are not gods, but human handiwork; and that God's work is not in them. <sup>51</sup>Is it not obvious that they are not gods?

<sup>52†</sup>They set no king over the land, nor do they give rain. <sup>53</sup>They neither vindicate their own rights, nor do they rescue anyone wronged, for they are powerless. <sup>54</sup>They are like crows in midair. For when fire breaks out in the temple of these wooden or gilded or silvered gods, though the priests flee and are safe, they themselves are burned up in the fire like timbers. <sup>55</sup>They cannot resist a king or enemy forces. <sup>56</sup>How then can it be admitted or thought that they are gods?

They are safe from neither thieves nor bandits, these wooden and silvered and gilded gods.

<sup>57</sup>Anyone who can will strip off the gold and the silver, and go away with the clothing that was on them; they cannot help themselves. <sup>58</sup>How much better to be a king displaying his valor, or a handy tool in a house, the joy of its owner, than these false gods; better the door of a house, protecting whatever is within, than these false gods; better a wooden post in a palace, than these false gods!<sup>o</sup> <sup>59‡</sup>The sun and moon and stars are bright, obedient in the task for which they are sent. <sup>60</sup>Likewise the lightning, when it flashes, is a great sight; and the one wind blows over every land. <sup>61</sup>The clouds, too, when commanded by God to proceed across the whole world, fulfill the command; <sup>62</sup>and fire, sent from on high to burn up the mountains and the forests, carries out its command. But these false gods are not their equal, whether in appearance or in power. <sup>63</sup>So it is unthinkable, and cannot be claimed that they are gods. They can neither execute judgment, nor benefit anyone. <sup>64</sup>Know, therefore, that they are not gods; do not fear them.

<sup>65</sup>Kings they can neither curse nor bless. <sup>66</sup>They show the nations no signs in the heavens, nor do they shine like the sun, nor give light like the moon. <sup>67</sup>The beasts are better than they— beasts can help themselves by fleeing to shelter. <sup>68</sup>Thus is it in no way apparent to us that they are gods; so do not fear them.

<sup>69</sup>For like a scarecrow in a cucumber patch,<sup>p</sup> providing no protection, are their wooden, gilded, silvered gods. <sup>70</sup>Just like a thornbush in a garden on which perches every kind of bird, or like a corpse hurled into darkness, are their wooden, gilded, silvered gods. <sup>71</sup>From the rotting of the purple and the linen upon them, you can know that they are not gods; they themselves will in the end be consumed, and be a disgrace in the land. <sup>72</sup>Better the just who has no idols; such shall be far from disgrace!

---

*[6:42–43] Perhaps a reference to the Babylonian practice of cultic prostitution mentioned by Herodotus, the fifth-century Greek historian. The unbroken cord was a sign that this service had not yet been rendered.
†[6:52–53] Unlike the God of Israel, the Babylonian gods are unable to set up and depose kings, or to provide life-giving rain.

n. [6:42–43] Jer 3:2.

‡[6:59–62] The elements of nature, obedient to God's orders and accomplishing the divine purpose, are better than the Babylonian gods.

o. [6:58] Wis 13:10–15; 15:7–17.   p. [6:69] Jer 10:5.

# THE BOOK OF
# EZEKIEL

〜◆〜

In response to the rebellion of Jehoiakim of Judah in 601 B.C., Nebuchadnezzar, the Babylonian ruler, besieged Jerusalem. When Jehoiakim's successor, Jehoiachin, surrendered in 597, Nebuchadnezzar appointed Zedekiah king and deported to Babylon Jehoiachin and the royal family, along with members of the upper class, including Ezekiel the priest. Five years later, as Zedekiah planned his own revolt against Babylon, Ezekiel became the first prophet to be commissioned outside Judah or Israel (chaps. 1–3). Before Jerusalem is destroyed (587 B.C.), Ezekiel is concerned to convince his audience that they are responsible for the punishment of exile and to justify the Lord's decision to destroy their city and Temple. Later, Ezekiel argues that the Judahites who embrace his preaching are the people whom the Lord has chosen as a new Israel, enlivened by a new heart, imbued with new breath (chaps. 36–37), and restored to a re-created land, Temple, and covenant relationship (chaps. 40–48). Ezekiel is clear on one point: the Lord punishes and restores for one reason—for the sake of his name, in order to demonstrate once and for all that he is Lord.

Ezekiel's symbolic actions or performances foreshadow the inevitable destruction of Jerusalem (4:1–5:4; 12:1–20; 24:15–24). The closely related judgment oracles are directed against increasingly larger groups: the inhabitants of Jerusalem (5:5–17); refugees who have fled into the mountains (6:1–14); Judah's total population, "the four corners of the land" (7:1–27). Particularly chilling is Ez 8–11, the prophet's vision of the violent injustice and idolatrous worship that fills Jerusalem. When Ezekiel protests the Lord's order to slaughter Jerusalem's wicked inhabitants, the Lord refuses to relent; the Lord's glory leaves the Temple, affirming his judgment on Jerusalem (11:22–25), whom Ezekiel portrays as a promiscuous woman, rebel from the beginning, more violent and sinful than Sodom (chap. 16). Appeals for a speedy end to the exile on the basis of a past relationship with the Lord or of Jerusalem's privileged status are futile gestures.

Ezekiel uses stereotypic oracles against the nations (chaps. 25–32) to claim universal sovereignty for Israel's God, to exemplify the consequences of arrogant national pride, and to set the stage for Israel's restoration. In order to demonstrate to all the nations that "I am the Lord," God becomes Israel's just shepherd (34:15) under whose rule a restored people (37:1–14) enjoy prosperity in a restored land. God again acts "for the sake of my name" when the mysterious forces of Gog attack Israel (chaps. 38–39). Their defeat is prelude to Ezekiel's vision of a new Israel whose source of life and prosperity is a well-ordered cult in a new Temple, where the divine glory again dwells (chaps. 40–48).

The Book of Ezekiel has the following divisions:

  I. Call of the Prophet (1:1–3:27)
 II. Before the Siege of Jerusalem (4:1–24:27)
III. Prophecies Against Foreign Nations (25:1–32:32)
 IV. Hope for the Future (33:1–39:29)
  V. The New Israel (40:1–48:35)

## I. CALL OF THE PROPHET

### CHAPTER 1

**The Vision: God on the Cherubim.** ¹In the thirtieth year,* on the fifth day of the fourth month, while I was among the exiles by the river Chebar, the heavens opened, and I saw divine visions.ᵃ— ²On the fifth day of the month—this was the fifth year† of King Jehoiachin's exileᵇ— ³the word of the LORD came to the priest Ezekiel, the son of Buzi, in the land of the Chaldeans by the river Chebar. There the hand of the LORD came upon him.ᶜ

⁴As I watched, a great stormwind came from the North,‡ a large cloud with flashing fire, a bright glow all around it, and something like polished metal gleamed at the center of the fire.ᵈ ⁵From within it figures in the likeness of four living creatures§ appeared. This is what they looked like:ᵉ ⁶They were in human form, but each had four faces and four wings,ᶠ ⁷and their legs were straight, the soles of their feet like the hooves of a bull, gleaming like polished brass.ᵍ ⁸Human hands were under their wings, and the wings of one touched those of another.ʰ ⁹Their faces and their wings looked out on all their four sides; they did not turn when they moved, but each went straight ahead.ⁱ

¹⁰¶Their faces were like this:ʲ each of the four had a human face, and on the right the face of a lion, and on the left, the face of an ox, and each had the face of an eagle. ¹¹Such were their faces. Their wings were spread out above. On each one, two wings touched one another, and the other two wings covered the body.ᵏ ¹²Each went straight ahead. Wherever the spirit would go, they went; they did not change direction when they moved.ˡ ¹³**And the appearance of the living creatures seemed like burning coals of fire. Something indeed like torches moved back and forth among the living creatures. The fire gleamed intensely, and from it lightning flashed. ¹⁴The creatures darting back and forth flashed like lightning.

¹⁵††As I looked at the living creatures, I saw wheels on the ground, one alongside each of the four living creatures.ᵐ ¹⁶The wheels and their construction sparkled like yellow topaz, and all four of them looked the same: their construction seemed as though one wheel was inside the other. ¹⁷When they moved, they went in any of the four directions without veering as they moved. ¹⁸ⁿThe four of them had rims, high and fearsome—eyes filled the four rims all around. ¹⁹When the living creatures moved, the wheels moved with them; and when the living creatures were raised from the ground, the wheels also were raised. ²⁰Wherever the spirit would go, they went. And they were raised up together with the living creatures, for the spirit of the living creatures was in the wheels. ²¹Wherever the living creatures moved, the wheels moved; when they stood still, the wheels stood still. When they were lifted up from the earth, the wheels were lifted up with them.ᵒ For the spirit of the living creatures was in the wheels.

²²‡‡Above the heads of the living creatures was a likeness of the firmament; it was awesome, stretching upwards like shining crystal over their heads.ᵖ ²³Beneath the firmament their wings stretched out toward one another; each had two wings covering the body. ²⁴Then I heard the sound of their wings, like the roaring of mighty waters, like the voice of the Almighty. When they moved, the sound of the tumult was like the din of an army. And when they stood still, they lowered their wings.�q ²⁵While they stood with their wings lowered, a voice came from above the firmament over their heads.

²⁶Above the firmament over their heads was the likeness of a throne that looked like sapphire; and upon this likeness of a throne was seated, up above, a figure that looked like a human being.§§ʳ ²⁷And I saw something like polished metal, like the appearance of fire enclosed on all sides, from what looked like the waist up; and from what

---

*[1:1] **The thirtieth year,** which corresponds to the fifth year of exile (v. 2), has never been satisfactorily explained; possibly it refers to the prophet's age, or the anniversary of the finding of the book of the law in the Temple during Josiah's reform of 622 (2 Kgs 22:1–13). **The river Chebar:** probably a canal near Nippur, southeast of Babylon, one of the sites on which the Jewish exiles were settled.

†[1:2] **The fifth day . . . the fifth year:** the end of July, 593 B.C.; cf. v. 1.

‡[1:4] **The North:** Zaphon, the traditional abode of the gods; see notes on Jb 37:22; Ps 48:3; Is 14:13–15.

§[1:5] **Four living creatures:** identified as cherubim in 10:1–2, 20. Known from Assyrian religion as minor guardian deities of palaces and temples, the cherubim were usually portrayed in gigantic sculpture with the bodies of bulls or lions, wings like an eagle and a human head. In the Jerusalem Temple, the Lord was enthroned above in the holy of holies (Is 6:1–2).

¶[1:10] The four faces together represent animate creation: wild animals, domesticated livestock, birds, and human beings. Christian tradition associates them with the four evangelists: the lion with Mark, the ox with Luke, the eagle with John, and the man with Matthew.

**[1:13–14] The coals and flashing lightning moving among the four creatures and yet coming from them identify this vision as a theophany. See note on 10:2–13.

††[1:15–21] The repetitions and inconsistencies in the description of the wheels and the direction of their movements evoke the vision's mysterious quality and emphasize the difficulty of describing the divine world in human language.

‡‡[1:22–23, 26] This symbolic description of God's throne is similar to that in Ex 24:9–10.

§§[1:26] **Looked like a human being:** the God who transcends the powers of the human imagination is pictured here in the likeness of an enthroned human king.

---

a. [1:1] Ez 10:20; 11:24–25; 43:3; Ps 137:1. b. [1:2] 2 Kgs 24:15. c. [1:3] Ez 3:14, 22; 8:1; 33:22; 37:1; 40:1; 2 Kgs 3:15; Is 8:11. d. [1:4] Ez 8:2; Jb 38:1. e. [1:5] Is 6:2. f. [1:6] Ez 10:14. g. [1:7] Rev 1:15. h. [1:8] Ez 10:8. i. [1:9] Ez 10:22. j. [1:10] Ez 10:14; Rev 4:6–7. k. [1:11] Is 6:2.

l. [1:12] Ez 10:16–19. m. [1:15] Ez 10:2. n. [1:18] Ez 10:12; Rev 4:6, 8. o. [1:21] Ez 10:9–12. p. [1:22] Ez 10:1; Gn 1:6. q. [1:24] Ez 3:13; 10:5; 43:2; Rev 1:15. r. [1:26] Rev 1:13.

looked like the waist down, I saw something like the appearance of fire and brilliant light surrounding him.ˢ ²⁸Just like the appearance of the rainbow in the clouds on a rainy day so was the appearance of brilliance that surrounded him. Such was the appearance of the likeness of the glory of the LORD. And when I saw it, I fell on my face and heard a voice speak.ᵗ

## CHAPTER 2

**Eating of the Scroll.** ¹The voice said to me: Son of man,* stand up! I wish to speak to you. ²As he spoke to me, the spirit† entered into me and set me on my feet, and I heard the one who was speakingᵘ ³say to me: Son of man, I am sending you to the Israelites, a nation of rebels who have rebelled against me; they and their ancestors have been in revolt against me to this very day.ᵛ ⁴Their children are bold of face and stubborn of heart—to them I am sending you. You shall say to them: Thus says the Lord GOD.ʷ ⁵And whether they hear or resist—they are a rebellious house—they shall know that a prophet has been among them.ˣ ⁶But as for you, son of man, do not fear them or their words. Do not fear, even though there are briers or thorns and you sit among scorpions.‡ Do not be afraid of their words or be terrified by their looks for they are a rebellious house.ʸ ⁷You must speak my words to them, whether they hear or resist, because they are rebellious.ᶻ ⁸But you, son of man, hear me when I speak to you and do not rebel like this rebellious house. Open your mouth and eat what I am giving you.ᵃ

⁹ᵇIt was then I saw a hand stretched out to me; in it was a written scroll. ¹⁰He unrolled it before me; it was covered with writing front and back. Written on it was: Lamentation, wailing, woe!ᶜ

## CHAPTER 3

¹He said to me: Son of man, eat what you find here: eat this scroll, then go, speak to the house of Israel. ²So I opened my mouth, and he gave me the scroll to eat. ³ᵈSon of man, he said to me, feed your stomach and fill your belly with this scroll I am giving you. I ate it, and it was as sweet as honey§ in my mouth. ⁴Then he said to me, Son of man, go now to the house of Israel, and speak my words to them.

⁵Not to a people with obscure speech and difficult language am I sending you, but to the house of Israel.ᵉ ⁶Nor to many nations of obscure speech and difficult language whose words you cannot understand. For if I were to send you to these, they would listen to you.ᶠ ⁷But the house of Israel will refuse to listen to you, since they refuse to listen to me. For the whole house of Israel is stubborn of brow and hard of heart.ᵍ ⁸Look! I make your face as hard as theirs, and your brow as stubborn as theirs.ʰ ⁹Like diamond, harder than flint, I make your brow. Do not be afraid of them, or be terrified by their looks, for they are a rebellious house.ⁱ

¹⁰Then he said to me, Son of man, take into your heart all my words that I speak to you; hear them well. ¹¹Now go to the exiles, to your own people, and speak to them. Say to them, whether they hear or refuse to hear: Thus says the LORD God!

¹²Then the spirit lifted me up, and I heard behind me a loud rumbling noise as the glory of the LORD** rose from its place:ʲ ¹³the noise of the wings of the living creatures beating against one another, and the noise of the wheels alongside them, a loud rumbling.ᵏ ¹⁴And the spirit lifted me up and took me away, and I went off, my spirit angry and bitter, for the hand of the LORD pressed hard on me. ¹⁵Thus I came to the exiles who lived at Tel-abib†† by the river Chebar; and there where they dwelt, I stayed among them distraught for seven days. ¹⁶ᴵAt the end of the seven days, the word of the LORD came to me: **The Prophet as Sentinel.**‡‡ ¹⁷Son of man, I have appointed you a sentinel for the house of Israel.ᵐ When you hear a word from my mouth, you shall warn them for me.

¹⁸If I say to the wicked, You shall surely die—and you do not warn them or speak out to dissuade the wicked from their evil conduct in order to save their lives—then they shall die for their sin, but I will hold you responsible for their blood. ¹⁹If, however, you warn the wicked and they still do not turn from their wickedness and

---

*[2:1] **Son of man**: in Hebrew, "son/daughter of . . ." is a common idiom expressing affiliation in a group; in this case, "a human being." The title is God's habitual way of addressing the prophet throughout this book, probably used to emphasize the separation of the divine and the human.

†[2:2] **The spirit**: lit., wind, breath; a vital power, coming from God, which enables the prophet to hear the divine word; cf. 8:3; 11:1, 24.

‡[2:6] **And you sit among scorpions**: the prophet must be prepared for bitter opposition.

s. [1:27] Ez 8:2.   t. [1:28] Rev 4:2–3.   u. [2:2] Ez 3:24; Dn 8:18.
v. [2:3] Ez 20:8, 13.   w. [2:4] Ex 32:9.   x. [2:5] Ez 3:11, 27; 33:33.
y. [2:6] Dt 31:6.   z. [2:7] Ez 3:10–11; Jer 7:27.   a. [2:8] Jer 15:16.   b. [2:9] Ez 8:3; Rev 10:2.   c. [2:10] Zec 5:3; Rev 5:1.
d. [3:3] Jer 15:16; Rev 10:9–10.

§[3:3] **As sweet as honey**: though the prophet must foretell terrible things, the word of God is sweet to the one who receives it.

¶[3:8] Cf. Jer 1:18. The prophet must face fierce opposition with the determination and resistance shown by his opponents.

**[3:12] **The glory of the LORD**: the divine presence, manifested here in audible form. Cf. Ex 40:34; Lk 2:9.

††[3:15] **Tel-abib**: one of the sites where the exiles were settled, probably near Nippur.

‡‡[3:17–21] This passage refers to the prophet's role as sentinel, placed here and in chap. 33 as introductions to sections containing judgment oracles and salvation oracles respectively; cf. Hb 2:1.

e. [3:5] Is 28:11.   f. [3:6] cf. Mt 11:21.   g. [3:7] Jer 7:27.   h. [3:8] Jer 1:18.   i. [3:9] Is 48:4.   j. [3:12] Ez 8:3; 43:5.   k. [3:13] Ez 10:16–17.   l. [3:16] Ez 33:7–9; cf. 18:5–18.   m. [3:17] Is 52:8; Jer 1:17; Hb 2:1.

evil conduct, they shall die for their sin, but you shall save your life.

²⁰But if the just turn away from their right conduct and do evil when I place a stumbling block before them, then they shall die. Even if you warned them about their sin, they shall still die, and the just deeds that they performed will not be remembered on their behalf. I will, however, hold you responsible for their blood.ⁿ ²¹If, on the other hand, you warn the just to avoid sin, and they do not sin, they will surely live because of the warning, and you in turn shall save your own life.

**Ezekiel Mute.** ²²The hand of the LORD came upon me there and he said to me: Get up and go out into the plain, where I will speak with you.ᵒ ²³ᵖSo I got up and went out into the plain. There it was! The glory of the LORD was standing there like the glory I had seen by the river Chebar. Then I fell on my face, ²⁴but the spirit entered into me, set me on my feet; he spoke to me, and said: Go, shut yourself in your house. ²⁵As for you, son of man, know that they will put ropes on you and bind you with them, so that you cannot go out among them.�q ²⁶And I will make your tongue stick to the roof of your mouth so that you will be mute,* no longer one who rebukes them for being a rebellious house.ʳ ²⁷Only when I speak to you and open your mouth, shall you say to them: Thus says the LORD God: Let those who hear, hear! Let those who resist, resist! They are truly a rebellious house.

## II. BEFORE THE SIEGE OF JERUSALEM

### CHAPTER 4

**Acts Symbolic of Siege and Exile.** ¹†You, son of man, take a clay tablet; place it in front of you, and draw on it a city, Jerusalem. ²Lay siege to it: build up siege works, raise a ramp against it, pitch camps and set up battering rams all around it. ³Then take an iron pan and set it up as an iron wall between you and the city. Set your face toward it and put it under siege. So you must lay siege to it as a sign for the house of Israel.ˢ ⁴Then lie down on your left side, while I place the guilt of the house of Israel upon you. As many days as you lie like this, you shall bear their guilt. ⁵I allot you three hundred and ninety days‡ during which you must bear the guilt of

the house of Israel, the same number of years they sinned. ⁶When you have completed this, you shall lie down a second time, on your right side to bear the guilt of the house of Judah forty days; I allot you one day for each year.ᵗ ⁷Turning your face toward the siege of Jerusalem, with bared arm§ you shall prophesy against it. ⁸See, I bind you with ropes so that you cannot turn from one side to the other until you have completed the days of your siege.ᵘ

⁹¶Then take wheat and barley, beans and lentils, millet and spelt; put them into a single pot and make them into bread. Eat it for as many days as you lie upon your side, three hundred and ninety days. ¹⁰The food you eat shall be twenty shekels a day by weight; each day you shall eat it. ¹¹And the water you drink shall be the sixth of a hin** by measure; each day you shall drink it. ¹²And the barley cake you eat you must bake on human excrement in the sight of all. ¹³The LORD said: Thus the Israelites shall eat their food, unclean, among the nations where I drive them.ᵛ ¹⁴"Oh no, Lord GOD," I protested. "Never have I defiled myself nor have I eaten carrion flesh or flesh torn by wild beasts, nor from my youth till now has any unclean meat entered my mouth."ʷ ¹⁵Very well, he replied, I will let you use cow manure in place of human dung. You can bake your bread on that. ¹⁶Then he said to me: Son of man, I am about to break the staff of bread†† in Jerusalem so they shall eat bread which they have weighed out anxiously and drink water which they have measured out fearfully.ˣ ¹⁷Because they lack bread and water they shall be devastated; each and every one will waste away because of their guilt.ʸ

### CHAPTER 5

¹Now you, son of man, take a sharp sword and use it like a barber's razor, to shave your head and your beard. Then take a balance scale for weighing and divide the hair.ᶻ ²Set a third on fire within the city,‡‡ when the days of your siege are completed; place another third around the city and strike it with the sword; the final third scatter to the wind and then unsheathe the sword after it.ᵃ ³But take a few of the hairs and tie them in the hem of your garment. ⁴Take some of these and throw them into the fire and burn them in

---

translated "the days of your siege" (v. 8) is three hundred and ninety. Forty years conventionally represents one generation.

§[4:7] **Bared arm**: a symbol of unrestrained power.

¶[4:9–13] This action represents the scarcity of food during the siege of Jerusalem, and the consequent need to eat whatever is at hand. **Twenty shekels**: about nine ounces. **The sixth of a hin**: about one quart.

**[4:11] **Hin**: see note on 45:24.

††[4:16] **Break the staff of bread**: reducing the supply of bread that supports life as the walking staff supports a traveler; cf. 5:16; 14:13; Lv 26:26; Ps 105:16; Is 3:1.

‡‡[5:2] **The city**: the one drawn on the tablet (4:1).

---

\*[3:26–27] **Mute**: here the prophet's inability to speak to the people in exile while Jerusalem was being besieged is seen as a consequence of God's direct intervention (cf. 24:27).

†[4:1–5:4] The symbolic actions in this section prepare for the series of oracles that follow in 5:5–7:27.

‡[4:5–6] **Three hundred and ninety days . . . forty days**: a symbol to represent the respective lengths of exile for the Northern Kingdom of Israel and the Southern Kingdom of Judah. Israel had already fallen to Assyria in 722/721 B.C. The numerical value of the Hebrew consonants in the phrase

---

n. [3:20] Is 8:14.   o. [3:22] Ez 1:3; 8:4.   p. [3:23] Ez 10:15; 40:3.   q. [3:25] Ez 4:8.   r. [3:26] Ps 22:15.   s. [4:3] Is 8:18.

t. [4:6] Dn 9:24–25; 12:11–12.   u. [4:8] Ez 3:25.   v. [4:13] Hos 9:4.   w. [4:14] Dn 1:8.   x. [4:16] Ez 5:16; Lv 26:26.   y. [4:17] Lv 26:39.   z. [5:1] Is 7:20.   a. [5:2] Jer 13:24.

the fire. Because of this, fire will flash out against the whole house of Israel.

[5]Thus says the Lord God: This is Jerusalem! I placed it in the midst of the nations, surrounded by foreign lands. [6]But it rebelled against my ordinances more wickedly than the nations, and against my statutes more than the foreign lands around it; they rejected my ordinances and did not walk in my statutes.[b] [7]Therefore, thus says the Lord God: Because you have caused more uproar than the nations surrounding you, not living by my statutes nor carrying out my judgments, nor even living by the ordinances of the surrounding nations; [8]therefore, thus says the Lord God: See, I am coming against you![*] I will carry out judgments among you while the nations look on.[c] [9]Because of all your abominations I will do to you what I have never done before, the like of which I will never do again. [10]Therefore, parents will eat their children in your midst, and children will eat their parents.[†] I will inflict punishments upon you and scatter all who remain to the winds.[d]

[11]Therefore, as I live, says the Lord God, because you have defiled my sanctuary with all your atrocities and all your abominations, I will surely withdraw and not look upon you with pity nor spare you.[e] [12]A third of your people shall die of disease or starve to death within you; another third shall fall by the sword all around you; a third I will scatter to the winds and pursue them with the sword.[j]

[13]Thus my anger will spend itself; I will vent my wrath against them until I am satisfied. Then they will know that I the Lord spoke in my passion when I spend my wrath upon them.[g] [14]I will make you a desolation and a reproach among the nations around you, in the sight of every passerby.[h] [15]And you will be a reproach and a taunt, a warning and a horror to the nations around you when I execute judgments against you in angry wrath, with furious chastisements. I, the Lord, have spoken! [16]When I loose against you the deadly arrows of starvation that I am sending to destroy you, I will increase starvation and will break your staff of bread.[i] [17]I will send against you starvation and wild beasts who will leave you childless, while disease and bloodshed sweep through you. I will bring the sword against you. I, the Lord, have spoken.[j]

## CHAPTER 6
**Against the Mountains of Israel.** [1]The word of the Lord came to me: [2]Son of man, set your face toward the mountains of Israel and prophesy against them:[k] [3]You shall say: Mountains of Israel, hear the word of the Lord God. Thus says the Lord God to the mountains and hills, to the ravines and valleys:[l] Pay attention! I am bringing a sword against you, and I will destroy your high places.[‡] [4]Your altars shall be laid waste, your incense stands smashed, and I will throw your slain down in front of your idols. [5]Yes, I will lay the corpses of the Israelites in front of their idols, and scatter your bones around your altars.[§m] [6]Wherever you live, cities shall be ruined and high places laid waste, in order that your altars be laid waste and devastated, your idols broken and smashed, your incense altars hacked to pieces, and whatever you have made wiped out.[n] [7]The slain shall fall in your midst, and you shall know that I am the Lord.[¶o] [8]But I will spare some of you from the sword to live as refugees among the nations when you are scattered to foreign lands. [9]Then your refugees will remember me among the nations to which they have been exiled, after I have broken their lusting hearts that turned away from me and their eyes that lusted after idols. They will loathe themselves for all the evil they have done, for all their abominations.[p] [10]Then they shall know that I the Lord did not threaten in vain to inflict this evil on them.

[11]Thus says the Lord God: Clap your hands, stamp your feet,[**] and cry "Alas!" for all the evil abominations of the house of Israel! They shall fall by the sword, starvation, and disease.[q] [12]Those far off shall die of disease, those nearby shall fall by the sword, and those who survive and are spared shall perish by starvation; thus will I spend my fury upon them. [13]They shall know that I am the Lord, when their slain lie among their idols, all around their altars, on every high hill and mountaintop, beneath every green tree and leafy oak[††]—any place they offer sweet-smelling oblations to all their idols.[r] [14]I will stretch out my hand against them; I will

---

‡[6:3] **High places**: raised platforms usually built on hills outside towns for making sacrifices to the Lord or to Canaanite deities. They became synonymous with places of idolatry after the centralization of worship in the Jerusalem Temple.

§[6:5] **Scatter your bones . . . altars**: the bones of the dead defiled a place; cf. 2 Kgs 23:14.

¶[6:7] **You shall know that I am the Lord**: this formula is repeated after most of Ezekiel's oracles from this point on. Whatever happens to Israel happens at the Lord's command; because the Lord uses the nations to punish or reward Israel for its behavior, Israel will learn that its God has sole rule over the nations and the universe, and will acknowledge that rule in obedience.

**[6:11] **Clap your hands, stamp your feet**: these gestures may express grief, even horror, at Israel's infidelities; in 25:6, they are signs of gloating.

††[6:13] **Every green tree and leafy oak**: trees often identified with fertility deities and the "tree of life"; sacred groves had a long history in Palestine and throughout the Mediterranean basin as places of worship; cf. Dt 12:2.

---

*[5:8] **I am coming against you**: an expression borrowed from the language of warfare in which an enemy attacked another with the sword. "You" in vv. 8–17 is Jerusalem.

†[5:10] **Parents will eat their children . . . parents**: the prophet describes the consequences of the prolonged Babylonian siege of Jerusalem in 587/586 B.C. See note on Lam 2:20.

---

b. [5:6] Ez 16:47–51.   c. [5:8] Jer 21:5.   d. [5:10] Lv 26:29, 33; Dt 28:53; Jer 19:9.   e. [5:11] Ez 7:4, 9; 8:18.   f. [5:12] Ez 6:11–12; Rev 6:8.   g. [5:13] Ez 16:42.   h. [5:14] Lv 26:32.   i. [5:16] Ez 4:16; 14:13; Lv 26:26.   j. [5:17] Lv 26:25.

k. [6:2] Ez 36:1.   l. [6:3] Lv 26:34; Lv 26:30.   m. [6:5] Lv 26:30; Jer 8:12.   n. [6:6] Lv 26:30.   o. [6:7] Ez 11:10–12.   p. [6:9] Ez 20:7, 24; Ps 137:1.   q. [6:11] Ez 21:14–17.   r. [6:13] Ez 20:28; Lv 26:30.

make the land a desolate waste, from the wilderness to Riblah,* wherever they live. Thus they shall know that I am the LORD.*

## CHAPTER 7

**The End Has Come.** ¹The word of the LORD came to me: ²Son of man, now say: Thus says the Lord GOD to the land of Israel: An end! The end comes upon the four corners of the land!' ³Now the end is upon you; I will unleash my anger against you, judge you according to your ways, and hold against you all your abominations. ⁴My eye will not spare you, nor will I have pity; but I will hold your conduct against you, since your abominations remain within you; then shall you know that I am the LORD."

⁵Thus says the Lord GOD: Evil upon evil! See it coming! ⁶An end is coming, the end is coming; it is ripe for you! See it coming! ⁷The crisis has come for you who dwell in the land! The time has come, near is the day: panic, no rejoicing on the mountains.ʸ ⁸Soon now I will pour out my fury upon you and spend my anger against you; I will judge you according to your ways and hold against you all your abominations.ʷ ⁹My eye will not spare, nor will I take pity; I will hold your conduct against you since your abominations remain within you, then you shall know that it is I, the LORD, who strikes.ˣ

¹⁰The day is here! Look! it is coming! The crisis has come! Lawlessness is blooming, insolence budding; ¹¹the violent have risen up to wield a scepter of wickedness. But none of them shall remain; none of their crowd, none of their wealth, for none of them are innocent. ¹²†The time has come, the day dawns. The buyer must not rejoice, nor the seller mourn, for wrath is coming upon all the throng.ʸ ¹³Assuredly, the seller shall not regain what was sold, as long as they all live; for the vision is for the whole crowd: it shall not be revoked! Yes, because of their guilt, they shall not hold on to life. ¹⁴They will sound the trumpet and get everything ready, but no one will go out to battle, for my wrath weighs upon all the crowd.

¹⁵The sword is outside; disease and hunger are within. Whoever is in the fields will die by the sword; whoever is in the city disease and hunger will devour.ᶻ ¹⁶If their survivors flee, they will die on the mountains, moaning like doves of the valley on account of their guilt. ¹⁷All their hands will hang limp, and all their knees‡ turn to water.ᵃ ¹⁸ᵇThey put on sackcloth, horror clothes

them; shame is on all their faces, all their heads are shaved bald.§ ¹⁹They fling their silver into the streets, and their gold is considered unclean.ᶜ Their silver and gold cannot save them on the day of the LORD's wrath. They cannot satisfy their hunger or fill their bellies, for it has been the occasion of their sin. ²⁰In their beautiful ornaments they took pride; out of them they made their abominable images, their detestable things. For this reason I will make them unclean.ᵈ ²¹I will hand them over as spoils to foreigners, as plunder to the wicked of the earth, so that they may defile them. ²²I will turn my face away from them. My treasure will be defiled; the violent will enter and defile it.ᵉ ²³They will wreak slaughter, for the land is filled with bloodshed and the city with violence.ᶠ ²⁴I will bring in the worst of the nations to take possession of their houses. I will put an end to their proud strength,** and their sanctuaries will be defiled.ᵍ ²⁵When anguish comes, they will seek peace, but there is none.ʰ ²⁶Disaster after disaster, rumor upon rumor. They keep seeking a vision from the prophet; instruction from the priest is missing, and counsel from the elders.ⁱ ²⁷The king mourns, the prince is terror-stricken, the hands of the common people tremble. I will deal with them according to their ways, and according to their judgments I will judge them. They shall know that I am the LORD.

## CHAPTER 8

¹In the sixth year, on the fifth day of the sixth month,†† as I was sitting in my house, with the elders of Judah sitting before me, the hand of the Lord GOD fell upon me there.ʲ ²I looked up and there was a figure that looked like a man.‡‡ Downward from what looked like his waist, there was fire; from his waist upward, like the brilliance of polished bronze.ᵏ

**Vision of Abominations in the Temple.** ³He stretched out the form of a hand and seized me by the hair of my head. The spirit lifted me up§§

§[7:18] **Shaved bald:** shaving the head was a sign of mourning.

¶[7:20] Assyrian wall paintings show that statues of deities were often cast in precious metals and then decorated with jewelry. Cf. Is 40:19–20; 41:6–7; 44:9–20.

**[7:24] **Proud strength:** misplaced trust in the might and power of their kings and army. Cf. v. 22; 33:28 and related ideas in Is 2:12; 10:12; 13:11; Jer 48:29; Ez 24:21; 30:18.

††[8:1] **In the sixth year, on the fifth day of the sixth month:** September, 592 B.C.

‡‡[8:2] **Looked like a man:** the divine presence which accompanies Ezekiel in these visions. Cf. 40:3–4.

§§[8:3] **The spirit lifted me up:** the prophet is transported in vision from Babylon to Jerusalem. Ezekiel may be drawing on his memory of the Temple from before his exile in 598 B.C. **The statue of jealousy:** the statue which provokes the Lord's outrage against the insults of his own people; perhaps the statue of the goddess Asherah set up by Manasseh, king of Judah (cf. 2 Kgs 21:7; 2 Chr 33:7, 15). Although his successor,

---

*[6:14] **From the wilderness to Riblah:** the whole land, from the far south to the far north.

†[7:12–13] Normal affairs will cease to have any meaning in view of the disaster that is to come.

‡[7:17] **Hands . . . knees:** image of profound terror; loss of control of body movement and functions.

s. [6:14] Jer 48:22.    t. [7:2] Rev 7:1; 20:8.    u. [7:4] Ez 5:11; Jer 13:14.
v. [7:7] Ez 12:23; 30:3; Am 5:18–19; Zep 1:14.    w. [7:8] Ez 20:8, 13, 21.
x. [7:9] Ez 22:31; Jer 21:7.    y. [7:12] Is 24:2; cf. Mt 24:17–18.    z. [7:15]
Dt 32:25.    a. [7:17] Jer 47:3.    b. [7:18] Is 15:2–3; Jer 4:8; 48:3.

c. [7:19] Zep 1:7, 18; 2:2.    d. [7:20] Jer 10:3–4.    e. [7:22] Ps 74:7–8.
f. [7:23] Ez 22:9; 24:6.    g. [7:24] Lam 2:7.    h. [7:25] Jer 6:1.    i. [7:26]
Jer 18:18; Mi 3:6–7.    j. [8:1] Ez 14:1; 33:31.    k. [8:2] Ez 1:4, 26–27.

between earth and heaven and brought me in divine vision to Jerusalem[l] to the entrance of the inner gate facing north where the statue of jealousy that provokes jealousy stood. [4]There I saw the glory of the God of Israel, like the vision I had seen in the plain.[m] [5]He said to me: Son of man, lift your eyes to the north! I looked to the north and there in the entry north of the altar gate was this statue of jealousy.[n] [6]He asked, Son of man, do you see what they are doing? Do you see the great abominations that the house of Israel is practicing here, so that I must depart from my sanctuary? You shall see even greater abominations![o]

[7]Then he brought me to the entrance of the courtyard, and there I saw a hole in the wall. [8]Son of man, he ordered, dig through the wall. I dug through the wall—there was a doorway. [9]Go in, he said to me, and see the evil abominations they are doing here. [10]I went in and looked—figures of all kinds of creeping things and loathsome beasts,[*] all the idols of the house of Israel,[p] pictured around the wall. [11]Before them stood seventy of the elders of the house of Israel. Among them stood Jaazaniah, son of Shaphan, each with censer in hand; a cloud of incense drifted upward.[q] [12]Then he said to me: Do you see, son of man, what the elders of the house of Israel are doing in the dark, each in his idol chamber? They think: "The LORD cannot see us; the LORD has forsaken the land."[r] [13]He said: You will see them practicing even greater abominations.

[14]Then he brought me to the entrance of the north gate of the house of the LORD. There women sat and wept for Tammuz.[†s] [15]He said to me: Do you see this, son of man? You will see other abominations, greater than these!

[16]Then he brought me into the inner court of the house of the LORD. There at the door of the LORD's temple, between the porch and the altar, were about twenty-five men with their backs to the LORD's temple and their faces toward the east; they were bowing eastward[‡] to the sun.[t] [17]He said: Do you see, son of man? Are the

abominable things the house of Judah has done here so slight that they should also fill the land with violence, provoking me again and again? Now they are putting the branch to my nose![§] [18]Therefore I in turn will act furiously: my eye will not spare, nor will I take pity. Even if they cry out in a loud voice for me to hear, I shall not listen to them.

## CHAPTER 9

**Slaughter of the Idolaters.** [1]Then he cried aloud for me to hear: Come, you scourges of the city! [2]And there were six men coming from the direction of the upper gate which faces north, each with a weapon of destruction in his hand. In their midst was a man dressed in linen, with a scribe's case at his waist. They entered and stood beside the bronze altar.[u] [3]Then the glory of the God of Israel moved off the cherub and went up to the threshold of the temple. He called to the man dressed in linen with the scribe's case at his waist,[v] [4"]and the LORD said to him:[¶] Pass through the city, through the midst of Jerusalem, and mark an X on the foreheads of those who grieve and lament over all the abominations practiced within it. [5]To the others he said in my hearing: Pass through the city after him and strike! Do not let your eyes spare; do not take pity. [6]Old and young, male and female, women and children—wipe them out! But do not touch anyone marked with the X. Begin at my sanctuary. So they began with the elders who were in front of the temple.[x] [7]Defile the temple, he said to them, fill its courts with the slain. Then go out and strike in the city.

[8]As they were striking, I was left alone. I fell on my face, crying out, "Alas, Lord GOD! Will you destroy all that is left of Israel when you pour out your fury on Jerusalem?" [9]He answered me: The guilt of the house of Israel and the house of Judah is too great to measure; the land is filled with bloodshed, the city with lawlessness. They think that the LORD has abandoned the land, that he does not see them. [10]My eye, however, will not spare, nor shall I take pity, but I will bring their conduct down upon their heads.

[11]Just then the man dressed in linen with the scribe's case at his waist made his report: "I have done as you commanded!"

---

Josiah, had removed it (2 Kgs 23:6), the statue may have been set up again after his death.

[*] [8:10] **Creeping things and loathsome beasts**: perhaps images of Egyptian deities, often represented in animal form. During the last days of Jerusalem Zedekiah, king of Judah, was allied with Egypt, hoping for protection against the Babylonians.

[†] [8:14] **Wept for Tammuz**: the withering of trees and plants that began in late spring was attributed to the descent of Tammuz, the Mesopotamian god of fertility, to the world of the dead beneath the earth. During the fourth month of the year, female worshipers of Tammuz would wail and mourn the god's disappearance.

[‡] [8:16] **Bowing eastward**: sun worship was perhaps introduced as a condition of alliance with other nations. While Josiah removed some elements of this worship (2 Kgs 23:11), Manasseh, for example, built altars to all the "hosts of heaven" in two Temple courtyards (2 Kgs 21:5).

[§] [8:17] **Putting the branch to my nose**: the meaning is uncertain. It may be connected with the social injustice mentioned in v. 17b and in 9:9, e.g., "with their violence they tweak my nose," i.e., "goad my fury." The Masoretic text reads "their noses" as a euphemism for "my nose," thus avoiding the impropriety of these idolaters coming into contact with God even figuratively.

[¶] [9:4] Ezekiel emphasizes personal accountability; the innocent inhabitants of Jerusalem are spared while the idolatrous are punished. **An X**: lit., the Hebrew letter *taw*.

---

l. [8:3] Ez 2:9; 3:12; Dn 14:6.   m. [8:4] Ez 3:22.   n. [8:5] Ps 78:58.
o. [8:6] Ps 78:60.   p. [8:10] Ez 23:14.   q. [8:11] Nm 11:16.   r. [8:12]
Is 29:15.   s. [8:14] cf. Dn 11:37.   t. [8:16] Jb 31:26–28.

u. [9:2] Ez 10:2; Dn 10:5; 12:6; Rev 8:2; 15:6.   v. [9:3] Ez 11:22.
w. [9:4] Ex 12:7; Rev 7:2–4; 13:16.   x. [9:6] Gn 4:15; Ex 12:7.

## CHAPTER 10

[1]Then I looked and there above the firmament over the heads of the cherubim was something like a sapphire, something that looked like a throne.[y] [2]*And he said to the man dressed in linen: Go within the wheelwork under the cherubim; fill both your hands with burning coals from the place among the cherubim, then scatter them over the city. As I watched, he entered.[z] [3]Now the cherubim were standing to the south of the temple when the man went in and a cloud filled the inner court. [4]The glory of the LORD had moved off the cherubim to the threshold of the temple; the temple was filled with the cloud, the whole court brilliant with the glory of LORD. [5]The sound of the wings of the cherubim could be heard as far as the outer court; it was like the voice of God Almighty speaking.[a] [6]He commanded the man dressed in linen: Take fire from within the wheelwork among the cherubim. The man entered and stood by one of the wheels. [7]Thereupon a cherub stretched out a hand from among the cherubim toward the fire in the midst of the cherubim, took some, and put it in the hands of the one dressed in linen. He took it and came out. [8]Something like a human hand was visible under the wings of the cherubim. [9]I also saw four wheels beside the cherubim, one wheel beside each cherub, and the wheels appeared to have the sparkle of yellow topaz. [10]And the appearance of the four all seemed alike, as though one wheel were inside the other. [11]When they moved, they went in any of the four directions without veering as they moved; in whatever direction the first cherub faced, the others followed without veering as they went. [12]Their entire bodies—backs, hands, and wings—and wheels were covered with eyes all around like the four wheels.[b] [13]I heard the wheels called "wheelwork." [14]Each living creature had four faces: the first a cherub, the second a human being, the third a lion, the fourth an eagle.[c] [15]*When the cherubim rose up, they were indeed the living creatures I had seen by the river Chebar.[d] [16]When the cherubim moved, the wheels went beside them; when the cherubim lifted up their wings to rise from the earth, even then the wheels did not leave their sides. [17]When they stood still, the wheels stood still; when they rose up, the wheels rose up with them, for the spirit of the living creatures was in them. [18]Then the glory of the LORD left the threshold of the temple and took its place upon the cherubim. [19]The cherubim lifted their wings and rose up from the earth before my eyes as they departed with the wheels beside them. They stopped at the entrance of the eastern gate of the LORD's house, and the glory of the God of Israel was up above them.[e] [20]‡These were the living creatures I had seen beneath the God of Israel by the river Chebar. Now I knew they were cherubim.[f] [21]Each of them had four faces and four wings, and something like human hands under their wings. [22]Their faces looked just like the faces I had seen by the river Chebar; and each one went straight ahead.

## CHAPTER 11

**Death for the Remnant in Jerusalem.** [1]The spirit lifted me up and brought me to the east gate of the house of the LORD facing east. There at the entrance of the gate were twenty-five men; among them I saw the public officials Jaazaniah, son of Azzur, and Pelatiah, son of Benaiah. [2]The LORD said to me: Son of man, these are the men who are planning evil and giving wicked counsel in this city. [3]They are saying, "No need to build houses! The city is the pot, and we are the meat."[§g] [4]Therefore prophesy against them, son of man, prophesy! [5]Then the spirit of the LORD fell upon me and told me to say: Thus says the LORD: This is how you talk, house of Israel. I know the things that come into your mind! [6]You have slain many in this city, filled its streets with the slain. [7]Therefore thus says the Lord GOD: The slain whom you piled up in it, that is the meat, the pot is the city. But you I will bring out of it.[h] [8]You fear the sword—that sword I will bring upon you—oracle of the Lord GOD.[i] [9]I will bring you out of the city, hand you over to foreigners, and execute judgments against you. [10]By the sword you shall fall. At the borders of Israel I will judge you so that you will know that I am the LORD. [11]The city shall not be a pot for you, nor shall you be meat within it. At the borders of Israel I will judge you,[j] [12]so you shall know that I am the LORD, whose statutes you did not follow, whose ordinances you did not keep. Instead, you acted according to the ordinances of the nations around you.

---

\*[10:2–13] The burning coals, a sign of the divine presence (cf. 28:14; Ps 18:9), represent the judgment of destruction that God is visiting upon the city; they may also represent the judgment of purification that prepares the land to become the Lord's sanctuary (cf. Is 6:6–7).

†[10:15–19] The throne represents God's presence as ruler and protector of the land. In chap. 1, God is revealed as the lord of the world who can appear even in a far-off land; here God is about to abandon the Temple, that is, hand the city over to its enemies. God and the throne return again in 43:1–3.

‡[10:20–22] The repetition of description from the preceding verses is a device intended to suggest the rapid, constantly changing motion of the vision and the difficulty of describing the divine in human language.

§[11:3] **No need to build houses . . . meat:** this advice is based on the conviction that invincible Jerusalem will protect its citizens from further danger just as a pot shields the meat inside from the fire. The poorer citizens of Jerusalem and the refugees from nearby villages can now appropriate the property abandoned by the city's wealthier upper class when they were deported (v. 15). The metaphor of the pot and its contents reappears in chap. 24.

y. [10:1] Ex 24:10; Rev 4:2.  z. [10:2] Rev 8:2.  a. [10:5] Jb 40:9.  
b. [10:12] Ez 1:15–20; Rev 4:6–8.  c. [10:14] cf. Gn 3:24.  d. [10:15] Ps 137:1.

e. [10:19] Ez 43:4.  f. [10:20] Ez 1:1.  g. [11:3] Ez 24:3; Jer 1:13.  
h. [11:7] Mi 3:2–3.  i. [11:8] Lv 26:25.  j. [11:11] 2 Kgs 25:20–21.

¹³While I was prophesying, Pelatiah, the son of Benaiah, dropped dead. I fell down on my face and cried out in a loud voice: "Alas, Lord God! You are finishing off what remains of Israel!"[k]

**Restoration for the Exiles.** ¹⁴The word of the Lord came to me: ¹⁵†Son of man, the inhabitants of Jerusalem are saying about all your relatives, the other exiles, and all the house of Israel, "They are far away from the Lord. The land is given to us as a possession."[l] ¹⁶Therefore say: Thus says the Lord God: I have indeed sent them far away among the nations, scattered them over the lands, and have been but little sanctuary for them in the lands to which they have gone. ¹⁷Therefore, thus says the Lord God, I will gather you from the nations and collect you from the lands through which you were scattered, so I can give you the land of Israel.[m] ¹⁸They will enter it and remove all its atrocities and abominations. ¹⁹ⁿAnd I will give them another heart and a new spirit I will put within them. From their bodies I will remove the hearts of stone, and give them hearts of flesh, ²⁰so that they walk according to my statutes, taking care to keep my ordinances. Thus they will be my people, and I will be their God.[o] ²¹But as for those whose hearts are devoted to their atrocities and abominations, I will bring their conduct down upon their heads—oracle of the Lord God.

²²Then the cherubim lifted their wings and the wheels alongside them, with the glory of the God of Israel above them.[p] ²³‡The glory of the Lord rose up from the middle of the city and came to rest on the mountain east of the city.[q] ²⁴In a vision, the spirit lifted me up and brought me back to the exiles in Chaldea, by the spirit of God. The vision I had seen left me,[r] ²⁵and I told the exiles everything the Lord had shown me.[s]

## CHAPTER 12

**Acts Symbolic of the Exile.** ¹The word of the Lord came to me: ²Son of man, you live in the midst of a rebellious house; they have eyes to see, but do not see, and ears to hear but do not hear. They are such a rebellious house![r] ³Now,

son of man, during the day while they watch, pack a bag for exile,[§] and again while they watch, go into exile from your place to another place; perhaps they will see that they are a rebellious house. ⁴During the day, while they watch, bring out your bag, an exile's bag. In the evening, again while they watch, go out as if into exile.[u] ⁵While they watch, dig a hole through the wall[¶] and go out through it. ⁶While they watch, shoulder your load and go out in darkness. Cover your face so you cannot see the land, for I am making you a sign for the house of Israel![v]

⁷I did just as I was commanded. During the day I brought out my bag, an exile's bag. In the evening while they watched, I dug a hole through the wall with my hands and set out in darkness, shouldering my load.

⁸In the morning, the word of the Lord came to me: ⁹Son of man, did not the house of Israel, that house of rebels, say, "What are you doing?"[w] ¹⁰Tell them: Thus says the Lord God: This load is the prince in Jerusalem and the whole house of Israel within it. ¹¹Say, I am a sign for you: just as I have done, so it shall be done to them; into exile, as captives they shall go.[x] ¹²The prince among them shall shoulder his load in darkness and go out through the hole they dug in the wall to bring him out. His face shall be covered so that he cannot even see the ground.[y] ¹³*I will spread my net over him and he shall be caught in my snare. I will bring him into Babylon, to the land of the Chaldeans, though he shall not see it,** and there he shall die. ¹⁴All his retinue, his aides and all his troops, I will scatter to the winds and pursue them with the sword.[a] ¹⁵Then they shall know that I am the Lord, when I disperse them among the nations and scatter them throughout the lands.[b] ¹⁶But I will let a few of them escape the sword, starvation, and plague, so that they may recount all their abominations among the nations to which they go. Thus they may know that I am the Lord.[††]

¹⁷The word of the Lord came to me: ¹⁸Son of man, eat your bread trembling and drink your water shaking with fear.[c] ¹⁹And say to the

---

*[11:13] In Ezekiel's vision Pelatiah represents the people left in Jerusalem, "the remnant of Israel." His sudden death in the vision, but not in reality, is a figure for the judgment described in vv. 8–10 and prompts Ezekiel's anguished question about the survival of the people left in the land after the deportations in 597.

†[11:15–21] Ezekiel insists that those who remained in Judah are doomed; the exiles, under a new covenant, will constitute a new Israel. Cf. chap. 36; Jer 24:7; 29.

‡[11:23] The glory of the Lord departs toward the east, to the exiles in Babylon; it will return once the Temple is rebuilt (43:1–3).

§[12:3–10] An exile's bag contains bare necessities, probably no more than a bowl, a mat, and a waterskin. The prophet's action foreshadows the fate of ruler and people (vv. 11–14).

¶[12:5] **Through the wall**: mud-brick outer wall of a private home. In this symbolic action, Ezekiel represents the enemy forces, and the house wall, the city wall of Jerusalem breached by the Babylonian army.

**[12:13] **Though he shall not see it**: according to a Targum, an allusion to Nebuchadnezzar having Zedekiah blinded before deporting him to Babylonia (cf. 2 Kgs 25:7); according to the Septuagint, the king is ashamed of his flight from the city and disguises himself so others will not recognize him.

††[12:16] Both exiles and nations shall know that the exile is divine punishment for Israel's betrayal of the Lord and the covenant, not evidence that the Lord is too weak to fight off the Babylonian deity.

k. [11:13] Ez 9:8.  l. [11:15] Ez 33:24.  m. [11:17] Ez 34:13; 36:28.  n. [11:19] Ez 18:31; 36:26; 2 Cor 3:3.  o. [11:20] Ex 6:7; Jer 31:33; 32:38.  p. [11:22] Ez 24:16.  q. [11:23] Zec 14:4.  r. [11:24] Ez 37:1.  s. [11:25] Ez 3:4, 11.  t. [12:2] Is 6:9–10; Jer 5:21; cf. Mt 13:15; Mk 4:12; 8:18.

u. [12:4] 2 Kgs 25:4.  v. [12:6] Is 8:18.  w. [12:9] Ez 20:49; 24:19.  x. [12:11] 2 Kgs 25:7; Jer 52:15.  y. [12:12] Jer 23:33; 52:7.  z. [12:13] Ez 17:20; 19:8; 32:3.  a. [12:14] 2 Kgs 25:5; Jer 21:7.  b. [12:15] Lv 26:33.  c. [12:18] Lam 5:9.

people of the land:* Thus says the Lord God about the inhabitants of Jerusalem in the land of Israel: they shall eat their bread in fear and drink their water in horror, because the land will be emptied of what fills it—the lawlessness of all its inhabitants. ²⁰Inhabited cities shall be in ruins, the land a desolate place. Then you shall know that I am the Lord.

**Prophecy Ridiculed.** ²¹The word of the Lord came to me: ²²Son of man, what is this proverb you have in the land of Israel: "The days drag on, and every vision fails"?*†*ᵈ ²³Say to them therefore: Thus says the Lord God: I will put an end to that proverb; they shall never use it again in Israel. Say to them instead: "The days are at hand and every vision fulfilled."ᵉ ²⁴No longer shall there be any false visions or deceitful divinations within the house of Israel,ᶠ ²⁵for whatever word I speak shall happen without delay. In your days, rebellious house, whatever I speak I will bring about—oracle of the Lord God.ᵍ

²⁶The word of the Lord came to me: ²⁷Son of man, listen! The house of Israel is saying, "The vision he sees is a long time off; he prophesies for distant times!"ʰ ²⁸Say to them therefore: Thus says the Lord God: None of my words shall be delayed any longer. Whatever I say is final; it shall be done—oracle of the Lord God.

## CHAPTER 13

**Against the Prophets of Peace.** ¹The word of the Lord came to me: ²Son of man, prophesy against the prophets of Israel, prophesy! Say to those who prophesy their own thoughts: Hear the word of the Lord!ⁱ ³Thus says the Lord God: Woe to those prophets, the fools who follow their own spirit and see nothing.ʲ ⁴Like foxes among ruins are your prophets, Israel! ⁵You did not step into the breach, nor repair the wall around the house of Israel so it would stand firm against attack on the day of the Lord. ⁶False visions! Lying divinations! They say, "The oracle of the Lord," even though the Lord did not send them. Then they expect their word to be confirmed!ᵏ ⁷Was not the vision you saw false? Did you not report a lying divination when you said, "Oracle of the Lord," even though I never spoke? ⁸Therefore thus says the Lord God: Because you have spoken falsehood and seen lying visions, therefore, for certain I am coming at you—oracle of the Lord God. ⁹My hand is against the prophets who see false visions and who make lying divinations. They shall not belong to the community of my people. They

shall not be written in the register of the house of Israel, nor shall they enter the land of Israel. Thus you shall know that I am the Lord.ˡ

¹⁰Because they led my people astray, saying, "Peace!" when there is no peace, and when a wall is built, they cover it with whitewash,‡ ¹¹say then to the whitewashers: I will bring down a flooding rain; hailstones shall fall, and a stormwind shall break forth.ᵐ ¹²When the wall has fallen, will you not be asked: "Where is the whitewash you spread on it?"

¹³Therefore thus says the Lord God: In my fury I will let loose stormwinds; because of my anger there will be flooding rain, and hailstones will fall with destructive wrath.ⁿ ¹⁴I will tear down the wall you whitewashed and level it to the ground, laying bare its foundations. When it falls, you shall be crushed beneath it. Thus you shall know that I am the Lord. ¹⁵When I have poured out my fury on the wall and its white-washers, it will fall. Then I will say to you: No wall! No whitewashers— ¹⁶the prophets of Israel who prophesy to Jerusalem and see visions of peace for it when there is no peace—oracle of the Lord God.ᵒ

**Against Witches.** ¹⁷As for you, son of man, now set your face against the daughters of your people who play the prophet from their own thoughts, and prophesy against them.ᵖ ¹⁸You shall say, Thus says the Lord God: Woe to those who sew amulets for the wrists of every arm and make veils§ for every head size to snare lives! You ensnare the lives of my people, even as you preserve your own lives! ¹⁹You have profaned me among my people for handfuls of barley and crumbs of bread,¶ slaying those who should not be slain, and keeping alive those who should not live, lying to my people, who listen to lies. ²⁰Therefore thus says the Lord God: See! I am coming after your amulets by which you ensnare lives like prey. I will tear them from your arms and set free the lives of those you have ensnared like prey.�q ²¹I will tear off your veils and deliver my people from your power, so that they shall never again be ensnared by your hands. Thus you shall know that I am the Lord. ²²Because you discourage the righteous with lies when I did not want them to be distressed, and encourage the wicked so they do not turn from their evil ways and save their lives,ʳ ²³therefore you

---

\*[12:19] **The people of the land**: the exiles in Babylon who, ironically, are now outside the land.

†[12:22–28] This proverb conveys the skepticism the people of Jerusalem have; cf. Jer 20:7–9.

‡[13:10] The false prophets contributed to popular illusions of security by predictions of peace, like those who whitewash a wall to conceal its defects.

§[13:18] **Sew amulets . . . make veils**: used by sorcerers to mark individuals for life or for death. For a small price (v. 19), these women promised protection for the wicked, who, in the Lord's estimation, "should not live" (v. 19), and death for the righteous, "who should not be slain" (v. 19). Both decisions belong to the Lord.

¶[13:19] **Handfuls of barley and crumbs of bread**: payment for the amulets and scarves.

d. [12:22] Ps 49:4.   e. [12:23] Ez 7:7.   f. [12:24] Ez 13:23; Jer 14:14; Zec 13:2–4.   g. [12:25] Hb 2:3.   h. [12:27] cf. Mt 24:48; 2 Pt 3:4.   i. [13:2] Jer 23:16, 21–22; 28:15.   j. [13:3] Ez 14:9; Nm 16:28; Is 32:6; Jer 23:1, 16, 25–40; Mi 2:11.   k. [13:6] cf. Is 30:10.

l. [13:9] Ex 32:32.   m. [13:11] cf. Ps 18:7–15; 77:17–18.   n. [13:13] Rev 11:19; 16:21.   o. [13:16] Jer 6:14.   p. [13:17] Rev 2:20.   q. [13:20] Ps 124:7.   r. [13:22] Ez 18:21; 33:14–16.

shall no longer see false visions or practice divination again. I will deliver my people from your hand. Thus you shall know that I am the LORD.

## CHAPTER 14

**Idolatry and Unfaithfulness.** [1]Some elders of Israel came and sat down before me.[s] [2]Then the word of the LORD came to me: [3]Son of man, these men keep the memory of their idols alive in their hearts, setting the stumbling block of their sin before them. Should I allow myself to be consulted by them? [4]Therefore say to them: Thus says the Lord GOD: If any of the house of Israel who keep the memory of their idols in their hearts, setting the stumbling block of their sin before them, come to a prophet, the LORD will answer in person because of their many idols, [5]in order to catch the hearts of the house of Israel, estranged from me because of all their idols.

[6]Therefore say to the house of Israel: Thus says the Lord GOD: Return, turn away from your idols; from all your abominations, turn your faces.[t] [7]For if anyone of the house of Israel or any alien residing in Israel who are estranged from me and who keep their idols in their hearts, setting the stumbling block of their sin before them, come to ask a prophet to consult me on their behalf, I the LORD will answer them in person. [8]I will set my face against them and make them a sign and a byword, and cut them off from the midst of my people. Thus you shall know that I am the LORD.

[9]"As for the prophet, if he speaks a deceiving word, I the LORD am the one who deceives that prophet.[*] I will stretch out my hand against him and destroy him from the midst of my people Israel. [10]They will be punished for their own sins, the inquirer and the prophet alike, [11]so that the house of Israel may no longer stray from me, no longer defile themselves by all their sins. Then they shall be my people, and I shall be their God—oracle of the Lord GOD.

**Just Cause.**[†] [12]The word of the LORD came to me: [13]"Son of man, if a land sins against me by breaking faith, and I stretch out my hand against it, breaking its staff of bread and setting famine loose upon it, cutting off from it human being and beast alike— [14]even if these three were in it, Noah, Daniel, and Job,[‡] they could only save

themselves by their righteousness—oracle of the Lord GOD.[w] [15]If I summoned wild beasts to prowl the land, depopulating it so that it became a wasteland which no one would cross because of the wild beasts,[x] [16]and these three were in it, as I live—oracle of the Lord GOD—I swear they could save neither sons nor daughters; they alone would be saved, but the land would become a wasteland.[y] [17]Or if I bring the sword upon this land, commanding the sword to pass through the land cutting off from it human being and beast alike,[z] [18]and these three were in it, as I live—oracle of the Lord GOD—they could save neither sons nor daughters; they alone would be saved. [19]Or if I send plague into this land, pouring out upon it my bloody wrath, cutting off from it human being and beast alike, [20]even if Noah, Daniel, and Job were in it, as I live—oracle of the Lord GOD—they could save neither son nor daughter; they would save only themselves by their righteousness.

[21]Thus says the Lord GOD: Even though I send against Jerusalem my four evil punishments—sword, famine, wild beasts, and plague—to cut off from it human being and beast alike,[a] [22]there will still be some survivors in it who will bring out sons and daughters. When they come out to you and you see their ways and their deeds, you shall be consoled regarding the evil I brought on Jerusalem, everything I brought upon it. [23]They shall console you when you see their ways and their deeds, and you shall know that not without reason did I do to it everything I did—oracle of the Lord GOD.[b]

## CHAPTER 15

**Parable of the Vine.** [1]The word of the LORD came to me:

[2]   Son of man,
         what makes the wood of the vine
      Better than the wood of branches
         found on the trees in the forest?[c]
[3]   Can wood be taken from it
         to make something useful?
      Can someone make even a peg out of it
         on which to hang a vessel?
[4]   Of course not! If it is fed to the fire for
         fuel,
         and the fire devours both ends of it,
      Leaving the middle charred,
         is it useful for anything then?
[5]   Even when it is whole
         it cannot be used for anything;
      So when fire has devoured and charred it,
         how useful can it be?

---

*[14:9] The ancient Israelites thought that God could use deception as a means of promoting divine justice; cf. 2 Sm 24:1–3; 1 Kgs 22:19–23.

†[14:12–23] According to Ezekiel, the people in Jerusalem deserve destruction because they are corrupt. Yet he admits an exception to the principle of individual responsibility when he affirms that some of those deserving death will survive and be reunited with family in exile. The depravity of Jerusalem testifies that the punishment of Jerusalem was just and necessary.

‡[14:14] **Noah, Daniel, and Job**: righteous folk heroes whom Israel shared with other ancient Near Eastern cultures. Daniel was the just judge celebrated in Ugaritic literature, perhaps the model for the hero of Dn 13.

§[15:1–8] Verses 2–5 point out that the wood of the vine-stock may be burned for fuel, fit only for destruction. In vv. 6–8 Ezekiel asserts that Jerusalem has the same destiny.

---

s. [14:1] Ez 8:1; 20:1.   t. [14:6] Is 2:20; cf. Ez 18:30; 33:11.   u. [14:9] cf. 1 Kgs 22:23; 2 Chr 18:22.   v. [14:13] Lv 26:26.

w. [14:14] Ez 28:3; Dn 1:6; cf. Gn 6:9; Jb 1:1.   x. [14:15] cf. Lv 26:22.   y. [14:16] cf. Ez 18:20.   z. [14:17] Lv 26:25.   a. [14:21] cf. Rev 6:8.   b. [14:23] Jer 22:8–9.   c. [15:2] cf. Ps 80; Is 5:1–7.

⁶  Therefore, thus says the Lord GOD:
    Like vine wood among forest trees,
        which I have given as fuel for fire,
    So I will give the inhabitants of Jerusalem.
⁷  I will set my face against them:
    Although they have escaped the fire,
        the fire will still devour them;
    You shall know that I am the LORD,
        when I set my face against them.*d*
⁸  Yes, I will make the land desolate,
        because they are so unfaithful—
        oracle of the Lord GOD.

## CHAPTER 16

**A Parable of Infidelity.** ¹The word of the LORD
came to me: ²Son of man, make known to Jerusalem her abominations.*e* ³You shall say, Thus
says the Lord GOD to Jerusalem: By origin and
birth you belong to the land of the Canaanites; your father was an Amorite, your mother
a Hittite.*⁄* ⁴*As for your birth, on the day you
were born your navel cord was not cut; you were
not washed with water or anointed; you were
not rubbed with salt or wrapped in swaddling
clothes.*g* ⁵No eye looked on you with pity or
compassion to do any of these things for you.
Rather, on the day you were born you were left
out in the field, rejected.

⁶Then I passed by and saw you struggling
in your blood, and I said to you in your blood,
"Live!" ⁷I helped you grow up like a field plant,
so that you grew, maturing into a woman with
breasts developed and hair grown; but still you
were stark naked. ⁸I passed by you again and
saw that you were now old enough for love. So
I spread the corner of my cloak‡ over you to
cover your nakedness; I swore an oath to you
and entered into covenant with you—oracle of
the Lord GOD—and you became mine.*h* ⁹Then I
bathed you with water, washed away your blood,
and anointed you with oil.*i* ¹⁰I clothed you with
an embroidered gown, put leather sandals on
your feet; I gave you a fine linen sash and silk

robes to wear.*⁄* ¹¹I adorned you with jewelry, putting bracelets on your arms, a necklace about
your neck,*k* ¹²a ring in your nose, earrings in
your ears, and a beautiful crown on your head.
¹³Thus you were adorned with gold and silver;
your garments made of fine linen, silk, and
embroidered cloth. Fine flour, honey, and olive
oil were your food. You were very, very beautiful,
fit for royalty.*l* ¹⁴You were renowned among the
nations for your beauty, perfected by the splendor I showered on you—oracle of the Lord GOD.

¹⁵But you trusted in your own beauty and
used your renown to serve as a prostitute. You
poured out your prostitution on every passerby—let it be his.*m* ¹⁶You took some of your
garments and made for yourself gaudy high
places, where you served as a prostitute. It
has never happened before, nor will it happen
again!*n* ¹⁷You took the splendid gold and silver
ornaments that I had given you and made for
yourself male images and served as a prostitute
with them. ¹⁸You took your embroidered garments to cover them; my oil and my incense you
set before them; ¹⁹the food I had given you, the
fine flour, the oil, and the honey with which I fed
you, you set before them as a pleasant odor, says
the Lord GOD.*o* ²⁰*⁄*The sons and daughters you
bore for me you took and offered as sacrifices
for them to devour! Was it not enough that you
had become a prostitute? ²¹*q*You slaughtered and
immolated my children to them, making them
pass through fire. ²²In all your abominations and
prostitutions you did not remember the days of
your youth when you were stark naked, struggling in your blood.*r*

²³Then after all your evildoing—woe, woe to
you! oracle of the Lord GOD— ²⁴you built yourself a platform and raised up a dais** in every
public place.*s* ²⁵*At every intersection you built
yourself a dais so that you could degrade your
beauty by spreading your legs for every passerby,
multiplying your prostitutions. ²⁶You served as
a prostitute with the Egyptians, your big-mem-
bered neighbors, and multiplied your prostitutions to provoke me. ²⁷Therefore I stretched
out my hand against you and reduced your
allotment, and delivered you over to the whim

---

*[16:3–4] **By origin and birth . . . Hittite:** Jerusalem's pre-
Israelite origins are the breeding ground for its inability to
respond faithfully to the Lord's generosity.

†[16:4–5] In this chapter, Ezekiel represents Jerusalem
and Samaria as unwanted, abandoned sisters whom the Lord
rescues and cares for. Here the prophet depicts Jerusalem as
a newborn female, abandoned and left to die, an accepted
practice in antiquity for females, who were considered financial liabilities by their families. That the infant has no one, not
even her mother, to tie off her umbilical cord, wash her clean,
and wrap her in swaddling clothes emphasizes Jerusalem's
death-like isolation and accentuates the Lord's gracious action
in her behalf. The practice of rubbing the skin of newborns
with salt is an attested Palestinian custom that survived into
the twentieth century.

‡[16:8] **I spread the corner of my cloak:** one way to
acquire a woman for marriage; cf. Ru 3:9. In Dt 23:1 a son's
illicit sexual relations with his father's wife is described as
"uncovering the edge of the father's garment."

§[16:16] In the allegory of this chapter the viewpoint often
shifts from the figure (prostitution) to the reality (idolatry).
A symbol of the woman's depravity supersedes her parents'
cruel abandonment when she was an infant. It overrides the
loyalty she owes her covenant partner and the care she owes
their children.

¶[16:20–21] Also a reference to the practice of child sacrifice introduced under Judah's impious kings; cf. 2 Kgs 16:3;
17:17; Jer 7:31; 19:5; 32:35.

**[16:24] **A platform . . . a dais:** associated with rituals borrowed from the Canaanites.

---

d. [15:7] Is 24:18; Am 9:1–4.   e. [16:2] cf Ez 8:17.   f. [16:3] cf Dt
26:5; Gn 23:10; 48:22.   g. [16:4] cf Lk 2:2.   h. [16:8] cf Ez 16:59;
Ru 3:9.   i. [16:9] cf Ru 3:3.

j. [16:10] cf Ps 45:14.   k. [16:11] cf Ez 23:40–42.   l. [16:13] Dt
32:13–14; Hos 2:8.   m. [16:15] Is 57:7–8.   n. [16:16] cf 2 Kgs
23:7.   o. [16:19] Hos 2:13.   p. [16:20] Jer 7:31; cf Lv 18:21; Dt
18:10; 2 Kgs 21:6; 23:10.   q. [16:21] cf 2 Kgs 16:3; 17:17.   r. [16:22]
Jer 2:2; Hos 2:15; 11:1.   s. [16:24] Is 57:7.   t. [16:25] Jer 2:20; 3:2;
5:7; Hos 2:4.

of your enemies, the Philistines,* who were revolted by your depraved conduct.ᵘ ²⁸You also served as a prostitute for the Assyrians, because you were not satisfied. Even after serving as a prostitute for them, you were still not satisfied.ᵛ ²⁹You increased your prostitutions again, now going to Chaldea, the land of traders; but despite this, you were still not satisfied.ʷ

³⁰How wild your lust!—oracle of the Lord God—that you did all these works of a shameless prostitute, ³¹when you built your platform at every intersection and set up your high place in every public square. But unlike a prostitute, you disdained payment. ³²Adulterous wife, taking strangers in place of her husband! ³³Prostitutes usually receive gifts. But you bestowed gifts on all your lovers, bribing them to come to you for prostitution from every side.ˣ ³⁴Thus in your prostitution you were different from any other woman. No one solicited you for prostitution. Instead, you yourself offered payment; what a reversal!

³⁵Therefore, prostitute, hear the word of the Lord! ³⁶Thus says the Lord God: Because you poured out your lust and exposed your nakedness in your prostitution with your lovers and your abominable idols, because you gave the life-blood of your children to them, ³⁷ʸtherefore, I will now gather together all your lovers with whom you found pleasure, both those you loved and those you hated; I will gather them against you from all sides and expose you naked for them to see. ³⁸†I will inflict on you the sentence of adultery and murder; I will bring on you bloody wrath and jealous anger.ᶻ ³⁹I will hand you over to them to tear down your platform and demolish your high place, to strip you of your garments and take away your splendid ornaments, leaving you stark naked.ᵃ ⁴⁰They shall lead an assembly against you to stone you and hack you to pieces with their swords.ᵇ ⁴¹ᶜThey shall set fire to your homes and inflict punishments on you while many women watch. Thus I will put an end to your prostitution, and you shall never again offer payment. ⁴²When I have spent my fury upon you I will stop being jealous about you, and calm down, no longer angry. ⁴³Because you did not remember the days of your youth but enraged me with all these things, see, I am bringing down your ways upon your head—oracle of the Lord God. Have you not added depravity to your other abominations?

⁴⁴See, everyone who makes proverbs will make this proverb about you, "Like mother, like daughter." ⁴⁵Yes, you are truly the daughter of your mother‡ who rejected her husband and children: you are truly a sister to your sisters who rejected their husbands and children—your mother was a Hittite and your father an Amorite.ᵈ ⁴⁶§Your elder sister was Samaria with her daughters to the north of you; and your younger sister was Sodom and her daughters, south of you.ᵉ ⁴⁷Not only did you walk in their ways and act as abominably as they did, but in a very short time you became more corrupt in all your ways than they were.ᶠ ⁴⁸As I live—oracle of the Lord God—I swear that your sister Sodom with her daughters have not done the things you and your daughters have done!ᵍ ⁴⁹ʰNow look at the guilt of your sister Sodom: she and her daughters were proud, sated with food, complacent in prosperity. They did not give any help to the poor and needy. ⁵⁰Instead, they became arrogant and committed abominations before me; then, as you have seen, I removed them.ⁱ ⁵¹Samaria did not commit half the sins you did. You have done more abominable things than they did. You even made your sisters look righteous, with all the abominations you have done. ⁵²You, then, must bear your disgrace, for you have made a case for your sisters! Because your sins are more abominable than theirs, they seem righteous compared to you. Blush for shame, and bear the disgrace of having made your sisters appear righteous.

⁵³I will restore their fortunes, the fortunes of Sodom and her daughters, the fortunes of Samaria and her daughters—and your fortunes along with them. ⁵⁴Thus you must bear your disgrace and be ashamed of all you have done to bring them comfort. ⁵⁵Yes, your sisters, Sodom and her daughters, Samaria and her daughters, shall return to the way they were,ʲ and you and your daughters shall return to the way you were. ⁵⁶Did you not hold your sister Sodom in bad repute while you felt proud of yourself, ⁵⁷before your evil was exposed? Now you are like her, reproached by the Arameans and all their neighbors, despised on all sides by the Philistines.ᵏ ⁵⁸The penalty of your depravity and your abominations—you must bear it all—oracle of the Lord.

---

*[16:27] **Philistines**: lit., "daughters of the Philistines," a common expression when referring to the various towns that make up a territory.

†[16:38] As a jealous husband, Yhwh severely punishes Jerusalem for her adultery: i.e., her worship of idols. Adultery was considered a capital crime in ancient Israel; cf. Lv 20:10–14; Nm 5:11–28; Dt 22:22.

‡[16:45] **Truly the daughter of your mother**: Jerusalem's depraved behavior follows from the bad behavior of its non-Israelite forebears; cf. v. 3.

§[16:46–47] Jerusalem is so much more corrupt than Samaria, the elder sister in size, and the smaller Sodom that both now appear just and righteous. Ezekiel's reference to Sodom indicates that the city's identification with wickedness and evil was already an established tradition in fifth century B.C. Judah.

---

u. [16:27] cf. 2 Chr 28:18.   v. [16:28] 2 Kgs 16:7.   w. [16:29] cf. Ez 23:14–17.   x. [16:33] Hos 8:9–10.   y. [16:37] cf. Ez 23:10, 22; Is 47:3; Rev 17:16.   z. [16:38] Lv 20:10; Dt 22:22.   a. [16:39] cf. 2 Kgs 18:11.   b. [16:40] cf. Ez 23:47; Jn 8:5, 7.   c. [16:41] 2 Kgs 25:9; cf. Jgs 12:1; 15:6.

d. [16:45] cf. Ez 23:2.   e. [16:46] Jer 3:8–11; Rev 11:8.   f. [16:47] cf. Dt 29:23; 32:32; Is 1:9–10.   g. [16:48] cf. Gn 19:25; Mt 10:15; 11:23–24.   h. [16:49] cf. Is 1:10; cf. Gn 49:24.   i. [16:50] cf. Gn 18:20–21.   j. [16:55] cf. Ez 36:11.   k. [16:57] cf. Ez 25:12–14; 35:1–15; 2 Kgs 16:6.

⁵⁹For thus says the Lord GOD: I will deal with you for what you did; you despised an oath by breaking a covenant.[l] ⁶⁰But I will remember the covenant I made with you when you were young; I will set up an everlasting covenant* with you.[m] ⁶¹Then you shall remember your ways and be ashamed when you receive your sisters, those older and younger than you; I give them to you as daughters, but not by reason of your covenant. ⁶²For I will re-establish my covenant with you, that you may know that I am the LORD,[n] ⁶³that you may remember and be ashamed, and never again open your mouth because of your disgrace, when I pardon you for all you have done—oracle of the Lord GOD.[o]

## CHAPTER 17

**The Eagles and the Vine.** ¹The word of the LORD came to me: ²Son of man, propose a riddle, and tell this proverb to the house of Israel: ³Thus says the Lord GOD:

The great eagle, with wide wingspan
  and long feathers, with thick
    plumage,
      many-hued, came to Lebanon.
He plucked the crest of the cedar,[p]
⁴    broke off its topmost branch,
And brought it to a land of merchants,
    set it in a city of traders.
⁵  Then he took some native seed
    and planted it in fertile soil;
A shoot beside plentiful waters,
    like a willow he planted it,[q]
⁶  That it might sprout and become a vine,
    dense and low-lying,
With its branches turned toward him,
    its roots beneath it.
Thus it became a vine, produced
    branches,
      and put forth shoots.
⁷  Then another great eagle appeared,
    with wide wingspan, rich in
      plumage,
And see! This vine bent its roots to him,
    sent out branches for him to water.
From the bed where it was planted,[r]
⁸    it was transplanted to a fertile field
By abundant waters, to produce branches,
    to bear fruit, to become a majestic
      vine.
⁹  Say: Thus says the Lord GOD: Can it
    thrive?

Will he not tear up its roots
    and strip its fruit?
Then all its green leaves will wither—
    neither strong arm nor mighty
      nation
        is needed to uproot it.
¹⁰  True, it is planted; but will it thrive?
    Will it not wither up
When the east wind strikes it,
    wither in the very bed where it
      sprouted?[s]

¹¹†The word of the LORD came to me:

¹²  Now say to the rebellious house:
    Do you not understand this? Tell
      them!
The king of Babylon came to Jerusalem
    and took away its king and officials
    and brought them to him in
      Babylon.[t]
¹³  After removing the nobles from the land,
    he then took one of the royal line
And made a covenant with him,
    binding him under oath,[u]
¹⁴  To be a humble kingdom,
    without high aspirations,
    to keep his covenant and so survive.
¹⁵  But this one rebelled against him
    by sending envoys to Egypt
To obtain horses and a mighty army.
    Can he thrive?
Can he escape if he does this?
    Can he break a covenant and go
      free?[v]
¹⁶  As I live—oracle of the Lord GOD—
    in the house of the king who set him
      up to rule,
Whose oath he ignored and whose
    covenant he broke,
      there in Babylon I swear he shall
        die![w]
¹⁷  Pharaoh shall not help him on the day of
    battle,
    with a great force and mighty horde,
When ramps are thrown up and siege
    works built
      for the cutting down of many lives.
¹⁸  He ignored his oath, breaking his
    covenant;
    even though he gave his hand, he
      did all these things—
        he shall not escape![x]

---

*[16:60] **Everlasting covenant:** Ezekiel foresees God renewing the covenant of Sinai in a new and spirit-empowered way that will not be fatally broken as in the present exile or force God to abandon Israel again; cf. 11:19–21; 36:25–27; 37:26–28.

l. [16:59] cf. Ez 17:19.    m. [16:60] cf. Ez 37:26; Is 55:3; Jer 32:40.
n. [16:62] Dt 29:14.    o. [16:63] Dn 9:7–8.    p. [17:3] Dt 28:49; Jer 49:22; Dn 7:4.    q. [17:5] cf. 2 Kgs 24:17.    r. [17:7] cf. Ez 31:4–5; Jer 37:5; 44:30.

---

, †[17:11–21] These verses explain the allegory in vv. 3–10. In 597 B.C., Nebuchadnezzar removed Jehoiachin from the throne and took him into exile; in his place he set Zedekiah, Jehoiachin's uncle, on the throne and received from him the oath of loyalty. But Zedekiah was persuaded to rebel by Pharaoh Hophra of Egypt and thus deserved punishment; cf. 2 Kgs 24:10–25:7.

---

s. [17:10] cf. Ez 19:12.    t. [17:12] 2 Kgs 24:15.    u. [17:13] 2 Chr 36:13.    v. [17:15] Jer 52:3.    w. [17:16] 2 Kgs 24:17; 25:7; Jer 52:11.    x. [17:18] cf. 2 Kgs 10:15.

<sup>19</sup> Therefore, thus says the Lord God:
> As I live, my oath which he spurned,
> And my covenant which he broke,
> I will bring down on his head.

<sup>20</sup> I will spread my net over him,
> and he will be caught in my snare.
> I will bring him to Babylon
> to judge him there
> because he broke faith with me.<sup>y</sup>

<sup>21</sup> Any among his forces who escape
> will fall by the sword,
> And whoever might survive
> will be scattered to the winds.<sup>z</sup>
> Thus you will know that I the Lord have
> spoken.

<sup>22</sup> Thus says the Lord God:
> I, too, will pluck from the crest of the
> cedar
> the highest branch.
> From the top a tender shoot
> I will break off and transplant<sup>*</sup>
> on a high, lofty mountain.

<sup>23</sup> On the mountain height of Israel
> I will plant it.
> It shall put forth branches and bear fruit,
> and become a majestic cedar.
> Every small bird will nest under it,
> all kinds of winged birds will dwell
> in the shade of its branches.<sup>a</sup>

<sup>24</sup> Every tree of the field will know
> that I am the Lord.
> I bring low the high tree,
> lift high the lowly tree,
> Wither up the green tree,
> and make the dry tree bloom.<sup>b</sup>
> As I, the Lord, have spoken, so will I do!

## CHAPTER 18

**Personal Responsibility.** <sup>1</sup>The word of the Lord came to me: Son of man, <sup>2</sup>what is the meaning of this proverb you recite in the land of Israel:

> "Parents eat sour grapes,<sup>c</sup>
> but the children's teeth are set on
> edge"?<sup>†</sup>

<sup>3</sup>As I live—oracle of the Lord God: I swear that none of you will ever repeat this proverb in Israel. <sup>4</sup>For all life is mine: the life of the parent is like the life of the child, both are mine. Only the one who sins shall die!

<sup>5</sup>If a man is just—if he does what is right, <sup>6</sup>if he does not eat on the mountains,<sup>‡</sup> or raise his eyes to the idols of the house of Israel; if he does not defile a neighbor's wife, or have relations with a woman during her period;<sup>d</sup> <sup>7e</sup>if he oppresses no one, gives back the pledge received for a debt, commits no robbery; gives food to the hungry and clothes the naked; <sup>8</sup>if he does not lend at interest or exact usury; if he refrains from evildoing and makes a fair judgment between two opponents;<sup>f</sup> <sup>9</sup>if he walks by my statutes and is careful to observe my ordinances, that man is just—he shall surely live—oracle of the Lord God.<sup>g</sup>

<sup>10</sup>But if he begets a son who is violent and commits murder, or does any of these things,<sup>h</sup> <sup>11</sup>even though the father does none of them—a son who eats on the mountains, defiles the wife of his neighbor, <sup>12</sup>oppresses the poor and needy, commits robbery, does not give back a pledge, raises his eyes to idols, does abominable things, <sup>13</sup>lends at interest and exacts usury—this son certainly shall not live. Because he practiced all these abominations, he shall surely be put to death; his own blood shall be on him.<sup>i</sup>

<sup>14</sup>But, in turn, if he begets a son who sees all the sins his father commits, yet fears and does not imitate him— <sup>15</sup>a son who does not eat on the mountains, or raise his eyes to the idols of the house of Israel, or defile a neighbor's wife; <sup>16</sup>who does not oppress anyone, or exact a pledge, or commit robbery; who gives his food to the hungry and clothes the naked;<sup>j</sup> <sup>17</sup>who refrains from evildoing, accepts no interest or usury, but keeps my ordinances and walks in my statutes—this one shall not die for the sins of his father. He shall surely live! <sup>18</sup>Only the father, since he committed extortion and robbed his brother, and did what was not good among his people—he will die because of his sin! <sup>19</sup>You ask: "Why is not the son charged with the guilt of his father?" Because the son has done what is just and right and has been careful to observe all my statutes—he shall surely live! <sup>20k</sup>Only the one who sins shall die. The son shall not be charged with the guilt of his father, nor shall the father be charged with the guilt of his son. Justice belongs to the just, and wickedness to the wicked.

<sup>21</sup>But if the wicked man turns away from all the sins he has committed, if he keeps all my statutes and does what is just and right, he shall surely live. He shall not die! <sup>22</sup>None of the crimes he has committed shall be remembered against him; he shall live because of the justice he has shown. <sup>23</sup>l Do I find pleasure in the death

---

*[17:22–23] The Lord will undo the actions of the Babylonian king by rebuilding the Davidic dynasty so the nations realize that only Israel's God can restore a people's destiny.

†[18:2] **Parents . . . on edge:** a proverb the people quoted to complain that they were being punished for their ancestors' sins; cf. Jer 31:29.

‡[18:6] **Eat on the mountains:** take part in meals after sacrifice at the high places.

---

y. [17:20] cf. Ez 12:13; 32:3.    z. [17:21] Jer 26:33; 2 Kgs 25:5.
a. [17:23] Dn 4:12; Hos 14:5–7.    b. [17:24] Dn 5:21.    c. [18:2] Jer
31:29; cf. Ez 21:19.

d. [18:6] Lv 15:19–24; cf. Hos 4:13.    e. [18:7] Ex 22:26; Is 58:7; Mt
25:35.    f. [18:8] Ex 22:25; Lv 25:35–37; Dt 23:19–20.    g. [18:9] Lv
18:5.    h. [18:10] cf. Ez 22:6–9.    i. [18:13] Ex 22:25; Lv 20:9–11.
j. [18:16] cf. Ez 16:49; Is 58:7–10.    k. [18:20] Dt 24:16; 2 Kgs 14:6;
cf. Mt 16:27; Jn 9:2.    l. [18:23] cf. Ez 33:11; 2 Pt 3:9.

of the wicked—oracle of the Lord GOD? Do I not rejoice when they turn from their evil way and live?

[24]And if the just turn from justice and do evil, like all the abominations the wicked do, can they do this evil and still live? None of the justice they did shall be remembered, because they acted treacherously and committed these sins; because of this, they shall die.[m] [25n]You say, "The LORD's way is not fair!"[p] Hear now, house of Israel: Is it my way that is unfair? Are not your ways unfair? [26]When the just turn away from justice to do evil and die, on account of the evil they did they must die. [27]But if the wicked turn from the wickedness they did and do what is right and just, they save their lives; [28]since they turned away from all the sins they committed, they shall live; they shall not die. [29]But the house of Israel says, "The Lord's way is not fair!" Is it my way that is not fair, house of Israel? Is it not your ways that are not fair?

[30o]Therefore I will judge you, house of Israel, all of you according to your ways—oracle of the Lord GOD. Turn, turn back from all your crimes, that they may not be a cause of sin for you ever again. [31]Cast away from you all the crimes you have committed, and make for yourselves a new heart and a new spirit. Why should you die, house of Israel?[p] [32q]For I find no pleasure in the death of anyone who dies—oracle of the Lord GOD. Turn back and live!

## CHAPTER 19

### Allegory of the Lions[†]

[1]As for you, raise a lamentation over the princes of Israel, [2]and say:

> What a lioness was your mother,
>     a lion among lions!
> She made her lair among young lions,
>     to raise her cubs;
> [3] One cub she raised up,
>     a young lion he became;
> He learned to tear apart prey,
>     he devoured people.[r]
> [4] Nations heard about him;
>     in their pit he was caught;
> They took him away with hooks
>     to the land of Egypt.[‡s]

[5] When she realized she had waited in vain,
>     she lost hope.
> She took another of her cubs,
>     and made him a young lion.
> [6] He prowled among the lions,
>     became a young lion;
> He learned to tear apart prey,
>     he devoured people.[t]
> [7] He ravaged their strongholds,
>     laid waste their cities.
> The earth and everything in it were terrified
>     at the sound of his roar.
> [8] Nations laid out against him
>     snares all around;
> They spread their net for him,
>     in their pit he was caught.[u]
> [9] They put him in fetters and took him away
>     to the king of Babylon,
> So his roar would no longer be heard
>     on the mountains of Israel.

### Allegory of the Vine Branch

> [10] Your mother was like a leafy vine[§]
>     planted by water,
> Fruitful and full of branches
>     because of abundant water.
> [11] One strong branch grew
>     into a royal scepter.
> So tall it towered among the clouds,
>     conspicuous in height,
>     with dense foliage.[v]
> [12] But she was torn out in fury
>     and flung to the ground;
> The east wind withered her up,
>     her fruit was plucked away;
> Her strongest branch dried up,
>     fire devoured it.[w]
> [13] Now she is planted in a wilderness,
>     in a dry, parched land.[x]
> [14] Fire flashed from her branch,
>     and devoured her shoots;
> Now she does not have a strong branch,
>     a royal scepter!

This is a lamentation and serves as a lamentation.

## CHAPTER 20

**Israel's History of Infidelity.** [1]In the seventh year, on the tenth day of the fifth month,[¶] some

---

*[18:25] **The LORD's way is not fair:** this chapter rejects the idea that punishment is transferred from one generation to the next and emphasizes individual responsibility and accountability.

†[19:1–9] Some commentators identify Jehoahaz and Zedekiah, sons of the same mother, as the "two young lions"; they were deported to Egypt and Babylon respectively. Cf. 2 Kgs 23:31–34; 24:18–20.

‡[19:4] A common fate for royal prisoners: e.g., Assurbanipal claims he put a ring in the jaw of a captive king and a

dog collar around his neck (cf. v. 9). A wall relief shows Esarhaddon holding two royal captives with ropes tied to rings in their lips.

§[19:10–14] **Vine:** Judah. **One strong branch:** the Davidic king. This allegory describes the deportation of the Davidic dynasty to Babylon and laments the destruction of the house of David. From Ezekiel's perspective, the arrogance of Judah's kings leads to this tragedy (vv. 12–14).

¶[20:1] **The seventh year . . . the fifth month:** August 14, 591 B.C.

---

m. [18:24] cf. 2 Pt 2:20–22.   n. [18:25] cf. Ez 33:20.   o. [18:30] Jer 35:15; cf. Mt 3:2; Lk 3:3.   p. [18:31] cf. Ez 11:19; 36:26.   q. [18:32] cf. Ez 18:23; 33:11.   r. [19:3] 2 Kgs 23:31–34.   s. [19:4] 2 Chr 36:4.

t. [19:6] 2 Kgs 24:9.   u. [19:8] 2 Kgs 24:2–15.   v. [19:11] Dn 4:11.   w. [19:12] Hos 13:15.   x. [19:13] cf. Ez 20:35.

of the elders of Israel came to consult the LORD and sat down before me.[y] [2]Then the word of the LORD came to me: [3]Son of man, speak to the elders of Israel and say to them: Thus says the Lord GOD: Have you come to consult me? As I live, I will not allow myself to be consulted by you!—oracle of the Lord GOD.

[4]Will you judge them? Will you judge, son of man? Tell them about the abominations of their ancestors,[z] [5]and say to them: Thus says the Lord GOD: The day I chose Israel, I swore to the descendants of the house of Jacob; I revealed myself to them in the land of Egypt and swore to them, saying: I am the LORD, your God. [6]That day I swore to bring them out of the land of Egypt to the land I had searched out for them, a land flowing with milk and honey, a jewel among all lands.[a] [7]Then I said to them: Throw away, each of you, the detestable things[*] that held your eyes; do not defile yourselves with the idols of Egypt: I am the LORD, your God.[b]

[8]But they rebelled and refused to listen to me; none of them threw away the detestable things that held their eyes, nor did they abandon the idols of Egypt. Then I considered pouring out my fury and spending my anger against them there in the land of Egypt.[c] [9]I acted for the sake of my name, that it should not be desecrated in the eyes of the nations among whom they were: in the eyes of the nations I had made myself known to them, to bring them out of the land of Egypt.[d] [10]Therefore I led them out of the land of Egypt and brought them into the wilderness. [11e]Then I gave them my statutes and made known to them my ordinances, so that everyone who keeps them has life through them. [12f]I also gave them my sabbaths to be a sign between me and them, to show that it is I, the LORD, who makes them holy.

[13]But the house of Israel rebelled against me in the wilderness. They did not observe my statutes, and they rejected my ordinances that bring life to those who keep them. My sabbaths, too, they desecrated grievously. Then I considered pouring out my fury on them in the wilderness to put an end to them,[g] [14]but I acted for the sake of my name, so it would not be desecrated in the eyes of the nations in whose sight I had brought them out.[h] [15]Nevertheless in the wilderness I swore to them that I would not bring them into the land I had given them—a land flowing

with milk and honey, a jewel among all the lands. [16]Their hearts followed after their idols so closely that they did not live by my statutes, but rejected my ordinances and desecrated my sabbaths. [17]But I looked on them with pity, not wanting to destroy them, so I did not put an end to them in the wilderness.

[18]Then I said to their children in the wilderness: Do not follow the statutes of your parents. Do not keep their ordinances. Do not defile yourselves with their idols. [19]I am the LORD, your God: follow my statutes and be careful to observe my ordinances; [20]keep holy my sabbaths as a sign between me and you so that you may know that I am the LORD, your God.[i] [21]But their children rebelled against me: they did not follow my statutes or keep my ordinances that bring life to those who observe them; my sabbaths they desecrated. Then I considered pouring out my fury on them, spending my anger against them in the wilderness; [22]but I stayed my hand, acting for the sake of my name, lest it be desecrated in the eyes of the nations, in whose sight I had brought them out. [23]Nevertheless I swore to them in the wilderness that I would disperse them among the nations and scatter them in other lands, [24]because they did not carry out my ordinances, but rejected my statutes and desecrated my sabbaths, having eyes only for the idols of their ancestors. [25]Therefore I gave them statutes that were not good,[†] and ordinances through which they could not have life.[j] [26]I let them become defiled by their offerings, by having them make a fiery offering of every womb's firstborn, in order to ruin them so they might know that I am the LORD.[k]

[27]Therefore speak to the house of Israel, son of man, and tell them: Thus says the Lord GOD: In this way also your ancestors blasphemed me, breaking faith with me. [28]When I brought them to the land I had sworn to give them, and they saw all its high hills and leafy trees, there they offered sacrifices, there they made offerings to provoke me, there they sent up sweet-smelling oblations, there they poured out their libations.[l] [29]So I said to them, "What is this high place[‡] to

---

[*][20:7] **Detestable things**: in the Book of Ezekiel, Israel's continued worship of idols in Egypt and in the wilderness, despite the Lord's powerful deeds on their behalf, is the reason God punishes them so severely; they must learn and acknowledge that he is their only Lord. Cf., e.g., Exodus (5:1–6:9; 14:10–30; 16:1–36) and Numbers (11:1–15; 14:1–12; 20:1–9), where the people's failure to trust Moses and the Lord brings punishment.

[†][20:25–26] **I gave them statutes that were not good**: because Israel rejected the Lord's life-giving laws, he "gave" laws (e.g., the sacrifice of every firstborn) that would lead only to death and destruction. Dt 12:29–31; Jer 7:31; 19:4–5 may address a popular assumption that the Lord accepted and perhaps required child sacrifice, especially as evidence of great trust during national emergencies (2 Kgs 3:27; Mi 6:7). By combining language from Ex 22:28 with the vocabulary of child sacrifice, Ezekiel suggests that firstborn sons were regularly sacrificed in Israel.

[‡][20:29] **High place**: a cultic site, originally a hilltop, but often a raised platform in a sacred area. Until Deuteronomy's insistence that official and legitimate worship of the Lord take place only in Jerusalem, these local shrines were popular places for worship (e.g., 1 Sm 9–10) or for consulting the Lord (1 Kgs 3:4–5). In order to unite the Kingdom of Judah politically and religiously, Dt 12:2 demands destruction of the

---

y. [20:1] cf. Ez 8:1.  z. [20:4] cf. Ez 16:2; Mt 23:32.  a. [20:6] Ex 3:8; 6:8; Dt 8:7–10.  b. [20:7] Ex 20:2–4.  c. [20:8] cf. Ez 16:26; Ex 32:7.  d. [20:9] cf. Ez 36:22.  e. [20:11] Lv 18:5; Dt 4:7–8; Rom 10:5.  f. [20:12] Ex 20:8, 10; 31:13; Dt 5:12; Neh 13:17–18.  g. [20:13] Jer 11:7–8; 17:21–23.  h. [20:14] Is 48:11.

i. [20:20] Ex 31:13.  j. [20:25] cf. Rom 1:28.  k. [20:26] Lv 18:21.  l. [20:28] Ps 78:57–58.

which you go?" Thus its name became "high place" even to this day.*[m] [30]Therefore say to the house of Israel: Thus says the Lord GOD: Will you defile yourselves in the way your ancestors did? Will you lust after their detestable idols? [31]By offering your gifts, by making your children pass through the fire, you defile yourselves with all your idols even to this day. Shall I let myself be consulted by you, house of Israel? As I live— oracle of the Lord GOD—I swear I will not let myself be consulted by you!*[n]

[32]What has entered your mind shall never happen: You are thinking, "We shall be like the nations, like the peoples of foreign lands, serving wood and stone." [33]As I live—oracle of the Lord GOD—with mighty hand and outstretched arm, with wrath poured out, I swear I will be king over you!*[o] [34]With mighty hand and outstretched arm, with wrath poured out, I will bring you out from the nations and gather you from the countries over which you are scattered;*[p] [35]I will lead you to the wilderness of the peoples and enter into judgment with you face to face. [36]Just as I entered into judgment with your ancestors in the wilderness of the land of Egypt, so will I enter into judgment with you—oracle of the Lord GOD. [37]Thus I will make you pass under the staff†[q] and will impose on you the terms of the covenant.*[q] [38]I will sort out from you those who defied me and rebelled against me; from the land where they resided as aliens I will bring them out, but they shall not return to the land of Israel. Thus you shall know that I am the LORD.

[39]As for you, house of Israel, thus says the Lord GOD: Go! each of you, and worship your idols. Listen to me! You shall never again desecrate my holy name with your offerings and your idols!*[r] [40]For on my holy mountain,‡ on the highest mountain in Israel—oracle of the Lord GOD—there the whole house of Israel shall worship me; there in the land I will accept them all, there I will claim your tributes, the best of your offerings, from all your holy things.*[s] [41]As a sweet-smelling oblation I will accept you, when I bring you from among the nations and gather

you out of the lands over which you were scattered; and through you I will manifest my holiness in the sight of the nations.*[t] [42]Thus you shall know that I am the LORD, when I bring you back to the soil of Israel, the land I swore to give your ancestors. [43]There you shall remember your ways, all the deeds by which you defiled yourselves; and you shall loathe yourselves because of all the evil you did.*[u] [44]And you shall know that I am the LORD when I deal with you thus, for the sake of my name, not according to your evil ways and wanton deeds, house of Israel— oracle of the Lord GOD.*[v]

## CHAPTER 21

**The Sword of the Lord.** [1]The word of the LORD came to me: [2]Son of man, turn your face to the south: preach against the south, prophesy against the forest land in the south. [3]Say to the forest in the south: Hear the word of the LORD! Thus says the Lord GOD: See! I am kindling a fire in you that shall devour every green tree as well as every dry tree. The blazing flame shall not be quenched so that from south to north every face shall be scorched by it. [4]All flesh shall see that I, the LORD, have kindled it; it shall not be quenched.*[w]

[5]But I said, "Ah! Lord GOD, they are saying about me, 'Is not this the one who is forever spinning parables?'" [6]Then the word of the LORD came to me: [7]Son of man, turn your face toward Jerusalem: preach against its sanctuary, prophesy against the land of Israel.*[x] [8]Say to the land of Israel: Thus says the LORD: See! I am coming against you; I will draw my sword from its scabbard and cut off from you the righteous and the wicked.*[¶] [9]Thus my sword shall come out from its scabbard against all flesh from south to north [10]and all flesh shall know that I, the LORD, have drawn my sword from its scabbard. It cannot return again.*[y]

**Act Symbolic of the City's Fall.** [11]As for you, son of man, groan! with shattered loins and bitter grief, groan in their sight. [12]When they ask you, "Why are you groaning?" you shall say: Because of what I heard!*[**] When it comes every heart shall melt, every hand fall helpless; every spirit will grow faint, and every knee run with water. See, it is coming, it is here!—oracle of the Lord GOD.

**Song of the Sword.** [13]The word of the LORD came to me:*[z] [14]Son of man, prophesy! say: Thus says the LORD:

high places. Ezekiel, like other prophets, condemns Israelite worship at these places and identifies this illegitimate worship as one reason for the punishment of exile.

*[20:35–38] Exile among other lands occasions a new exodus and a new wilderness journey back to Israel. The Lord will eliminate the rebellious, as he did on the first journey, and use the surviving remnant to reveal his power to the nations.

†[20:37] **Pass under the staff**: in Lv 27:32–33, a method of counting off animals to select those to be dedicated for the tithe. In Ezekiel, on the other hand, those who survive the selection process are marked for destruction for violating the covenant.

‡[20:40] **Holy mountain**: the Temple mount and Jerusalem in contrast to "every high hill" in v. 28 (cf. the royal Zion theology in Ps 48:2). Acceptable worship takes place here among a restored people, a theme taken up in chaps. 40–48 (cf. 40:2).

§[21:2–4] In Babylon Ezekiel looks toward Judah, pictured as a forest about to be destroyed by fire.

¶[21:8] **Cut off from you the righteous and the wicked**: a more complete devastation of Jerusalem than that described in 9:6.

**[21:12] **What I heard**: the news of the fall of Jerusalem; cf. 33:21–22.

m. [20:29] cf. Ez 16:16.   n. [20:31] Ps 106:37–39.   o. [20:33] Dt 4:34; 5:1.   p. [20:34] Ps 106:47.   q. [20:37] Lv 27:3; Jer 33:13.   r. [20:39] Ex 20:7.   s. [20:40] cf. Ps 2:6; Is 11:9; 56:7.

t. [20:41] cf. 2 Cor 2:14.   u. [20:43] Lv 26:41.   v. [20:44] cf. Ez 36:22.   w. [21:4] Lv 26:25.   x. [21:7] Lv 26:36.   y. [21:10] Is 34:5–6.   z. [21:13] Gn 49:10.

A sword, a sword has been sharpened,
    a sword, a sword has been
        burnished:[a]
[15] Sharpened to make a slaughter,
    burnished to flash lightning!
Why should I stop now?
    You have rejected the rod and every
        judgment!
[16] I have given it over to the burnisher
    that he might hold it in his hand,
A sword sharpened and burnished
    to be put in the hands of an
        executioner.
[17] Cry out and howl, son of man,
    for it is destined for my people,
For all the princes of Israel,
    victims of the sword with my
        people.
Therefore, slap your thigh,[*]
[18]     for it is tested, and why not?
Since you rejected my staff,
    should it not happen?—
        oracle of the Lord GOD.
[19] As for you, son of man, prophesy,
    and clap your hands!
Let the sword strike twice, a third time.
    It is a sword of slaughter,
A sword for slaughtering,
    whirling around them all,
[20] That every heart may tremble;
    for many will be made to stumble.
At all their gates
    I have stationed the sword for
        slaughter,
Made it flash lightning,
    drawn for slaughter.
[21] Slash to the right!
    turn to the left,
    Wherever your edge is directed![b]
[22] Then I, too, shall clap my hands,[†]
    and spend my fury.
I, the LORD, have spoken.

**Nebuchadnezzar at the Crossroads.** [23]The word of the LORD came to me: [24]Son of man, make for yourself two roads over which the sword of the king of Babylon can come. Both roads shall start out from the same land. Then put a signpost at the head of each road [25]so the sword can come to Rabbah of the Ammonites or to Judah and its fortress, Jerusalem. [26]For the king of Babylon is standing at the fork of the two roads to read the omens:[‡] he shakes out the arrows, inquires of the teraphim, inspects the liver.[c] [27]Into his right hand has fallen the lot marked "Jerusalem";[§] to order the slaughter, to raise the battle cry, to set the battering rams against the gates, to throw up a ramp, to build siege works. [28]In the eyes of those bound by oath this seems like a false omen; yet the lot taken in hand exposes the wickedness for which they, still bound by oath, will be taken in hand.

[29]Therefore thus says the Lord GOD: Because your guilt has been exposed, your crimes laid bare, your sinfulness revealed in all your deeds—because you have been exposed, you shall be taken in hand.[d] [30]And as for you, depraved and wicked prince of Israel, a day is coming to end your life of crime.[e] [31]Thus says the Lord GOD: Off with the turban and away with the crown! Nothing shall be as it was! Exalt the lowly and bring the exalted low! [32]A ruin, a ruin, a ruin, I shall make it! Nothing will be the same until the one comes to whom I have given it for judgment.[f]

**To the Ammonites.**[¶] [33]As for you, son of man, prophesy: Thus says the Lord GOD to the Ammonites and their insults:

O sword, sword drawn for slaughter,
    burnished to consume, to flash
        lightning!
[34] Your false visions and lying omens,
    Set you over the necks of the slain,
    the wicked whose day had come—
        an end to their life of crime.
[35] Return to your scabbard!
    In the place you were created,
In the land of your origin,
    I will judge you.
[36] I will pour out my anger upon you,
    breathing my fiery wrath against
        you;
I will hand you over to ravagers,
    artisans of destruction!
[37] You shall be fuel for the fire,
    your blood shall flow throughout
        the land;
You shall not be remembered,
    for I, the LORD, have spoken.

## CHAPTER 22

**Crimes of Jerusalem.** [1]The word of the LORD came to me: [2]You,[**] son of man, will you judge?

---

of the configurations of the livers of newly slaughtered animals, a common form of divination in Mesopotamia.

§[21:27–28] A lot marked "Jerusalem" falls out, which marks the guilt of the city's inhabitants.

¶[21:33–37] In vv. 23–32 Ezekiel imagines Nebuchadnezzar deciding whether to attack Jerusalem or Rabbath-Ammon. As it happened, the Babylonians decided to attack Jerusalem first. Here (vv. 33–37) Ezekiel prophesies to the Ammonites that a nation which serves as an instrument of the Lord's judgment will itself be judged.

**[22:2–16] This first oracle focuses on Jerusalem as a "city of bloodshed" (cf. Na 3:1). Here transgressions involving

*[21:17] **Slap your thigh**: a gesture signifying grief and dread; cf. Jer 31:19.

†[21:22] **Clap my hands**: the Lord declares himself no longer responsible for Judah; cf. 22:13; Nm 24:10; Jb 27:23; Lam 2:15.

‡[21:26] Three forms of divination are mentioned: arrow divination, consisting in the use of differently marked arrows extracted or shaken from a case at random; the consultation of the teraphim or household idols; and liver divination, scrutiny

a. [21:14] cf. 2 Kgs 13:18–19.  b. [21:21] Prv 16:33; Zec 10:2.

c. [21:26]Is28:5;Ps75:8.  d. [21:29]Jer8:11–12;27:9–10.  e. [21:30] cf. Ez 16:3.  f. [21:32] Mal 3:19.

will you judge the city of bloodshed? Then make known all its abominations, ³and say: Thus says the Lord GOD: O city that sheds blood within itself so that its time has come, that has made idols for its own defilement: ⁴By the blood you shed you have become guilty, and by the idols you made you have become defiled. You have brought on your day, you have come to the end of your years. Therefore I make you an object of scorn for the nations and a laughingstock for all lands.ᵍ ⁵Those near and those far off will mock you: "Defiled of Name! Queen of Tumult!" ⁶See! the princes of Israel within you use their power to shed blood. ⁷Within you, father and mother are dishonored; they extort the resident alien in your midst; within you, they oppress orphans and widows.ʰ ⁸What I consider holy you have rejected, and my sabbaths you have desecrated. ⁹In you are those who slander to cause bloodshed; within you are those who feast on the mountains; in your midst are those whose actions are depraved.ⁱ ¹⁰In you are those who uncover the nakedness of their fathers; in you those who coerce women to intercourse during their period.ʲ ¹¹ᵏThere are those in you who do abominable things with their neighbors' wives, men who defile their daughters-in-law by incest, men who coerce their sisters to intercourse, the daughters of their own fathers. ¹²There are those in you who take bribes to shed blood. You exact interest and usury; you extort profit from your neighbor by violence. But me you have forgotten—oracle of the Lord GOD.ˡ

¹³See, I am clapping my hands because of the profits you extorted and the blood shed in your midst. ¹⁴Will your heart remain firm, will your hands be strong, in the days when I deal with you? I am the LORD; I have spoken, and I will act! ¹⁵I will disperse you among the nations and scatter you over other lands, so that I may purge your filth. ¹⁶In you I will allow myself to be desecrated in the eyes of the nations; thus you shall know that I am the LORD.

¹⁷The word of the LORD came to me: ¹⁸‡Son of man, the house of Israel has become dross to me. All of them are copper, tin, iron, and lead within a furnace; they have become the dross from silver.ᵐ ¹⁹Therefore thus says the Lord GOD: Because all of you have become dross, See! I

am gathering you within Jerusalem. ²⁰Just as silver, copper, iron, lead, and tin are gathered within a furnace to be blasted with fire to smelt it, so I will gather you together in my furious wrath, put you in, and smelt you." ²¹When I have assembled you, I will blast you with the fire of my anger and smelt you with it. ²²Just as silver is smelted in a furnace, so you shall be smelted in it. Thus you shall know that I, the LORD, have poured out my fury on you.

²³The word of the LORD came to me: ²⁴‡Son of man, say to her: You are an unclean land receiving no rain at the time of my fury. ²⁵A conspiracy of its princes is like a roaring lion tearing prey; they devour people, seizing their wealth and precious things, making many widows within her.ᵒ ²⁶Her priests violate my law and desecrate what I consider holy; they do not distinguish between holy and common, nor teach the difference between unclean and clean; they pay no attention to my sabbaths, so that I have been desecrated in their midst.ᵖ ²⁷‡Within her, her officials are like wolves tearing prey, shedding blood and destroying lives to extort profit. ²⁸ʳAnd her prophets cover them with whitewash, seeing false visions and performing lying divinations, saying, "Thus says the Lord GOD," although the LORD has not spoken. ²⁹The people of the land practice extortion and commit robbery; they wrong the poor and the needy, and oppress the resident alien without justice. ³⁰Thus I have searched among them for someone who would build a wall or stand in the breach before me to keep me from destroying the land; but I found no one. ³¹Therefore I have poured out my fury upon them; with my fiery wrath I have consumed them, bringing down their ways upon their heads—oracle of the Lord GOD.

## CHAPTER 23

**The Two Sisters.** ¹The word of the LORD came to me: ²Son of man, there were two women, daughters of the same mother.ᵗ ³Even as young girls, they were prostitutes, serving as prostitutes in Egypt. There the Egyptians fondled their breasts and caressed their virgin nipples.ᵘ ⁴Oholah was the name of the elder, and the name of her sister was Oholibah.⁵ They became mine and gave birth to sons and daughters.ᵛ As for their names: Samaria was Oholah and Jerusalem, Oholibah. ⁵ʷOholah became a prostitute while married to me and lusted after her lovers, the Assyrians: warriors ⁶dressed in purple, governors and

---

blood, the oppression of the poor, and improper cultic practices are seen as interrelated, for blood as the carrier of life is fundamental to both the cultic and social spheres of life.

\*[22:6] **To shed blood**: a very serious charge in light of the solemn command of God to Noah in Gn 9:6 against human bloodshed.

†[22:9–11] The charges against Jerusalem echo the commandments of Lv 20:10–18.

‡[22:18–22] The image of smelting metals for purifying the people by the attacks of their enemies is common among the prophets; cf. Is 1:22, 25; Jer 6:27–30.

g. [22:4] Ps 44:13–14.  h. [22:7] Ex 22:21–22; 23:9; Dt 5:16.  i. [22:9] cf. Ez 18:11.  j. [22:10] Lv 18:7–8, 19.  k. [22:11] Lv 18:7–20; 20:10–21; Dt 23:1–30; Jer 5:8.  l. [22:12] Ez 18:8; Dt 27:25; Am 5:12.  m. [22:18] Is 1:21–26; 48:10; Jer 6:27–30.

§[22:24–31] For a similar oracle, cf. Zep 3:1–8.

¶[23:4] **Oholah . . . Oholibah**: symbolic names for Samaria, "her own tent," and Jerusalem, "my tent is in her." Cf. Ps 15:1 where "tent" is a synonym for "holy mountain." The names refer to the temple set up in the Northern Kingdom of Samaria (1 Kgs 12:28–29) and the Jerusalem Temple.

n. [22:20] Hos 8:10; Mal 3:2.  o. [22:25] Jer 15:8.  p. [22:26] Lv 20:25; Hg 2:11–14.  q. [22:27] Mi 3:11; Zep 3:3.  r. [22:28–29] cf. Ez 13:2–10.  s. [23:1] cf. Ez 16.  t. [23:2] Jer 3:7.  u. [23:3] Is 1:21.  v. [23:4] Jer 3:6–12.  w. [23:5] Hos 5:3; 8:9.

officers, all of them handsome young soldiers, mounted on horses. ⁷She gave herself as a prostitute to them, to all the Assyrian elite; with all those for whom she lusted, she also defiled herself with their idols. ⁸She did not abandon the prostitution she had begun with the Egyptians, who had lain with her when she was young, fondling her virgin breasts and pouring out their lust upon her.ˣ ⁹Therefore I handed her over to her lovers, to the Assyrians for whom she lusted. ¹⁰ʸThey exposed her nakedness; her sons and daughters they took away, and her they killed with the sword. She became a byword for women because of the sentence carried out against her.

¹¹Although her sister Oholibah saw all this, her lust was more depraved than her sister's; she outdid her in prostitution.ᶻ ¹²She too lusted after the Assyrians, governors and officers, warriors impeccably clothed, mounted on horses, all of them handsome young soldiers.ᵃ ¹³I saw that she had defiled herself—now both had gone down the same path. ¹⁴She went further in her prostitution: She saw male figures drawn on the wall, images of Chaldeans drawn with vermilion, ¹⁵with sashes tied about their waists, flowing turbans on their heads, all looking like chariot warriors, images of Babylonians, natives of Chaldea. ¹⁶As soon as she set eyes on them she lusted for them, and she sent messengers to them in Chaldea.ᵇ ¹⁷The Babylonians came to her, to her love couch; they defiled her with their impurities. But as soon as they had defiled her, she recoiled from them. ¹⁸When her prostitution was discovered and her shame revealed, I recoiled from her as I had recoiled from her sister. ¹⁹But she increased her prostitution, recalling the days of her youth when she had served as a prostitute in the land of Egypt. ²⁰She lusted for the lechers of Egypt, whose members are like those of donkeys, whose thrusts are like those of stallions.

²¹You reverted to the depravity of your youth, when Egyptians fondled your breasts, caressing your young nipples. ²²Therefore, Oholibah, thus says the Lord GOD: I will now stir up your lovers against you, those from whom you recoiled, and I will bring them against you from every side: ²³the men of Babylon and all of Chaldea, Pekod, Shoa and Koa,* along with all the Assyrians, handsome young soldiers, all of them governors and officers, charioteers and warriors, all of them horsemen. ²⁴They shall invade you with armor, chariots and wagons, a horde of peoples; they will array against you on every side bucklers and shields and helmets. I will give them the right of judgment, and they will judge you according to their standards.ᶜ ²⁵I will direct

my jealousy against you, so that they deal with you in fury, cutting off your nose and ears; what is left of you shall fall by the sword. They shall take away your sons and daughters, and what is left of you shall be devoured by fire. ²⁶They shall strip off your clothes and seize your splendid jewelry. ²⁷I will put an end to your depravity and to your prostitution from the land of Egypt; you shall no longer look to them, nor even remember Egypt again.

²⁸For thus says the Lord GOD: I am now handing you over to those whom you hate, to those from whom you recoil. ²⁹They shall treat you with hatred, seizing all that you worked for and leaving you stark naked, so that your indecent nakedness is exposed.ᵈ Your depravity and prostitution ³⁰brought these things upon you because you served as a prostitute to the nations, defiling yourself with their idols.ᵉ

³¹Because you followed your sister's path, I will put her cup into your hand.†ᶠ

³²  Thus says the Lord GOD:ᵍ
    The cup of your sister you shall drink,
        deep and wide;
    It brings ridicule and mockery,
        it holds so much;
³³  You will be filled with drunkenness and
            grief—
        A cup of horror and devastation,
        the cup of your sister Samaria;
³⁴  You shall drink it dry,
        its very sherds you will gnaw;
    And you shall tear out your breasts;
        for I have spoken—oracle of the
        Lord GOD.

³⁵Therefore thus says the Lord GOD: You have forgotten me and cast me behind your back; now suffer for your depravity and prostitution.

³⁶‡Then the LORD said to me: Son of man, would you judge Oholah and Oholibah? Then make known to them their abominations.ʰ ³⁷For they committed adultery, and blood covers their hands. They committed adultery with their idols; even the children they bore for me they burnt as food for them. ³⁸And they also did this to me: on that day, they defiled my sanctuary and desecrated my sabbaths. ³⁹On the very day they slaughtered their children for their idols, they entered my sanctuary to desecrate it. Thus

---

*[23:23] **Pekod, Shoa and Koa**: nations along the Tigris River, part of "greater Babylonia."

x. [23:8] cf. Ez 20:5–8.   y. [23:10] cf. Ez 16:37.   z. [23:11] Jer 3:8–11.
a. [23:12] 2 Kgs 16:7–15; 2 Chr 28:16.   b. [23:16] Is 57:8–9.
c. [23:24] Jer 30:5–6.

†[23:31] The cup is a metaphor for divine punishment, the lot of all who rebel against the Lord (cf. Ps 75:9; Jer 25:15–16; 51:7; Is 51:21–23; Lam 4:21; Hb 2:15–16).

‡[23:36–49] Unlike vv. 1–35, this short poem juxtaposes the careers of the two sisters and looks to a future punishment. The male lovers of the first poem become the sisters' executioners, and the guests at the love feast a lynch mob. So corrupt and depraved are the two sisters that their executioners win the esteemed title "righteous," for they have acted appropriately as agents of the Lord's judgment.

d. [23:29] Jer 13:27; Mi 1:11.   e. [23:30] Ps 106:37–38.   f. [23:31] Ps 75:8; Ob 16; Mt 20:22; Rev 14:10.   g. [23:32–33] Jer 25:15–16.   h. [23:36] Is 58:1; Mi 3:8.

they acted within my house!ʲ ⁴⁰Moreover, they sent for men who had to come from afar; when a messenger was sent to them, they came. On their account you bathed, painted your eyes, and put on jewelry.ʲ ⁴¹You sat on a magnificent couch, set before it a table, on which to lay my incense and oil. ⁴²The cries of a mob! The shouts of men coming in from the wilderness! They put bracelets on the women's arms and splendid crowns on their heads. ⁴³I said: "That worn-out one still has adulteries in her! Now they engage her as a prostitute and she . . . ⁴⁴And indeed they did come in to her as men come in to a prostitute. Thus they came to Oholah and Oholibah, the depraved women. ⁴⁵The righteous shall certainly punish them with sentences given to adulterers and murderers, for they committed adultery, and blood is on their hands.ᵏ

⁴⁶Indeed, thus says the Lord GOD: Raise up an army against them and hand them over to terror and plunder. ⁴⁷The army will stone them and hack them to pieces with their swords. They will kill their sons and daughters and set fire to their houses. ⁴⁸Thus I will put an end to depravity in the land, and all women will be warned not to imitate your depravity. ⁴⁹They shall inflict on you the penalty of your depravity, and you shall pay for your sins of idolatry. Then you shall know that I am the Lord GOD.ˡ

## CHAPTER 24

**Allegory of the Pot.** * ¹On the tenth day of the tenth month, in the ninth year,† the word of the LORD came to me:ᵐ ²Son of man, write down today's date this very day, for on this very day the king of Babylon lays siege to Jerusalem. ³ⁿPropose this parable to the rebellious house and say to them: Thus says the Lord GOD:

Put the pot on, put it on!
　　Pour in some water;
⁴　Add to it pieces of meat,
　　all choice pieces;
With thigh and shoulder,
　　with choice cuts fill it.
⁵　Choose the pick of the flock,
　　then pile logs beneath it;
Bring it to a boil,
　　cook all the pieces in it.ᵒ

⁶　Therefore thus says the Lord GOD:
　　Woe to the city full of blood!ᵖ
A pot containing filth,
　　whose filth cannot be removed!
Take out its pieces one by one,
　　for no lot has fallen on their behalf.
⁷　For her blood is still in her midst;
　　on a bare rock she left it;
She did not pour it on the ground
　　to be covered with dirt.‡
⁸　To arouse wrath, to exact vengeance,
　　I have left her blood on bare rock
　　not to be covered.
⁹　Therefore, thus says the Lord GOD:
Woe to the city full of blood!
　　I will make the pyre great!
¹⁰　Pile on the wood, kindle the fire.
Cook the meat, stir the spicy mixture,
　　char the bones!
¹¹　Then set it empty on the coals,
　　to heat up until its copper glows,
So its impurities melt,
　　its filth disappears.
¹²　§The toil is exhausting,
　　but the great filth will not come
　　　　out—
Filth, even with fire.
¹³　Even in defiling yourself with depravity
　　I would still have cleansed you,
　　but you would not have your
　　　　impurity cleansed.
You will not be cleansed now
　　until I wreak my fury on you.�q
¹⁴　I, the LORD, have spoken;
　　it will happen!
I will do it and not hold back!
　　I will not have pity or relent.
By your conduct and deeds you shall be
　　　　judged—
　　oracle of the Lord GOD.

**Ezekiel as a Sign for the Exiles.** ¹⁵The word of the LORD came to me: ¹⁶Son of man, with a sudden blow I am taking away from you the delight of your eyes, but do not mourn or weep or shed any tears.ʳ ¹⁷Groan, moan for the dead, but make no public lament; bind on your turban, put your sandals on your feet, but do not cover your beard or eat the bread of mourners.¶ ¹⁸I spoke to the people in the morning. In the evening my wife died. The next morning I did as I had

---

*[24:1–14] As the Babylonian siege of Jerusalem begins (588 B.C.), Ezekiel uses allegory to depict Jerusalem and its over-confident inhabitants as a pot of meat set on the fire for boiling (vv. 3–5; cf. 11:3) and left there until only burnt bones remain (v. 10). In vv. 6–8, the innocent blood shed by Jerusalem's inhabitants is the rust that, despite efforts to remove it, coats the interior of the pot filled with meat. Once emptied (v. 8), the rust-encrusted pot is set on hot coals (v. 11), but the rust remains (v. 12). Only the brunt of the Lord's fury can cleanse Jerusalem of its guilt (vv. 13–14).

†[24:1] **The tenth day . . . the ninth year**: January 15, 588 B.C. The same wording appears in 2 Kgs 25:1 (Jer 52:4).

‡[24:7] **Blood . . . to be covered with dirt**: since blood was sacred to God, it had to be covered with earth (Gn 37:26; Lv 17:13); the blood of innocent victims left uncovered cried out for vengeance; cf. Gn 4:10; Jb 16:18; Is 26:21.

§[24:12] A cryptic line in Hebrew.

¶[24:17] **The bread of mourners**: a post-burial meal that mourners shared to comfort one another; cf. 2 Sm 3:35; Jer 16:7. The other gestures mentioned here were also popular mourning customs. Because Ezekiel does not observe any of the mourning customs mentioned, the people are puzzled and ask him to explain.

i. [23:39] 2 Kgs 21:4. j. [23:40] Jer 27:3. k. [23:45] Lv 20:10. l. [23:49] cf. Ez 24:13. m. [24:1] cf. Ez 8:1. n. [24:3–6] cf. Ez 11:3–12. o. [24:5] Jer 52:24–27.

p. [24:6] Na 3:1; Hb 2:12. q. [24:13] Is 22:14; Jer 6:28–30. r. [24:16] Jer 16:5–7.

been commanded.[s] [19]Then the people asked me, "Will you not tell us what all these things you are doing mean for us?" [20]I said to them, The word of the LORD came to me: [21]Say to the house of Israel: Thus says the Lord GOD: I will now desecrate my sanctuary, the pride of your strength, the delight of your eyes, the concern of your soul. The sons and daughters you left behind shall fall by the sword.[t] [22]Then you shall do as I have done, not covering your beards nor eating the bread of mourning. [23]Your turbans shall remain on your heads, your sandals on your feet. You shall not mourn or weep, but you shall waste away because of your sins and groan to one another. [24]Ezekiel shall be a sign for you: everything he did, you shall do. When it happens, you shall know that I am the Lord GOD.

**End of Ezekiel's Muteness.** [25]As for you, son of man, truly, on the very day I take away from them their strength, their glorious joy, the delight of their eyes, the desire of their soul, the pride of their hearts, their sons and daughters, [26]on that day a survivor will come to you so that you may hear it with your own ears.[w] [27]On that day, with the survivor, your mouth shall be opened; you shall speak and be mute[u] no longer. You shall be a sign to them, and they shall know that I am the LORD.

## III. PROPHECIES AGAINST FOREIGN NATIONS[‡]

### CHAPTER 25[§]

**Against Ammon.** [1]The word of the LORD came to me: [2]Son of man, turn toward the Ammonites and prophesy against them.[x] [3]Say to the Ammonites: Hear the word of the LORD! Thus says the Lord GOD: Because you jeered at my sanctuary when it was desecrated, at the land of Israel when it was destroyed, and at the house of Judah when they went into exile, [4]therefore I am giving you to people from the east[v] as a possession. They shall set up their encampments among you and pitch their tents in your midst; they shall eat your produce and drink your milk.[y] [5]And I will

turn Rabbah into a pasture for camels and all of Ammon into a grazing place for flocks. Then you shall know that I am the LORD.

[6]For thus says the Lord GOD: Because you rejoiced over the land of Israel with scorn in your heart, clapping your hands and stamping your feet, [7]therefore, see, I am stretching out my hand against you and giving you up as plunder to the nations. I will cut you off from the peoples and wipe you out of the lands. I will destroy you, and you shall know that I am the LORD.[z]

**Against Moab.** [8]Thus says the Lord GOD: Because Moab said, "See! the house of Judah is like all the other nations," [9]therefore, I am exposing the whole flank of Moab** with its cities, the jewels of its land: Beth-jesimoth, Baalmeon, and Kiriathaim. [10]I will hand it over, along with the Ammonites, to the people from the east that it may not be remembered among the nations. [11]I will execute judgment upon Moab that they may know that I am the LORD.[b]

**Against Edom.** [12]Thus says the Lord GOD: Because Edom took vengeance on the house of Judah and incurred terrible guilt by taking vengeance on them, [13]therefore thus says the Lord GOD: I will stretch out my hand against Edom and cut off from it human being and beast alike. I will turn it into ruins from Teman to Dedan; they shall fall by the sword.[d] [14]I will put my vengeance against Edom into the hands of my people Israel; they will deal with Edom in accord with my furious anger. Thus they shall know my vengeance!—oracle of the Lord GOD.[e]

**Against the Philistines.** [15]Thus says the Lord GOD: Because the Philistines acted vengefully and exacted vengeance with intentional malice, destroying with undying hostility,[f] [16]therefore thus says the Lord GOD: See! I am stretching out my hand against the Philistines, and I will cut off the Cherethites[††] and wipe out the remnant on the seacoast. [17]Thus I will execute great acts of vengeance on them, punishing them furiously. Then they shall know that I am the LORD, when I wreak my vengeance on them.

### CHAPTER 26

**Against the City of Tyre.** [1][‡‡]On the first day of the eleventh month of the eleventh year, the word of the LORD came to me:

---

*[24:22–24] The fall of the city will be so sudden and final that the exiles will have no time to go into mourning.

†[24:27] **Mute**: unable to preach anything but the Lord's judgment against Judah and Jerusalem; cf. 3:27 and note on 33:21–22.

‡[25:1–32:32] These chapters form a body of oracles directed against foreign nations. They follow the prophet's condemnation of Judah and oracles announcing its destruction. The unit precedes the announcement of Judah's salvation in chaps. 33–48.

§[25:1–17] Ezekiel condemns four nations for their reactions to Judah's destruction and exile: Ammon to the east (vv. 2–7); Moab to the southeast (vv. 8–11); Edom to the south (vv. 12–14); Philistia to the west (vv. 15–17). Their hostility was not unprovoked; at one time or another, each one either lost territory to Israel or had been under Israelite control.

¶[25:4] **People from the east**: nomadic tribes from the desert east of Ammon and Moab (cf. Is 11:14; Jer 49:28), often a threat to outlying towns and villages.

**[25:9] **The whole flank of Moab**: the eastern edge of the Moabite plateau, perhaps lightly fortified because the vast desert to the east provided a natural barrier to invasion.

††[25:16] **Cherethites**: people from the island of Crete in the Aegean, the Philistines' point of origin. In Zep 2:5, the terms "Philistines," "Cherethites," and "seacoast people" describe the same group of people.

‡‡[26:1] The Hebrew text does not give a number with the month. This translation assumes a scribal error, the omission of the second occurrence of the number eleven.

s. [24:18] cf. Ez 12:9.   t. [24:21] Lv 26:31.   u. [24:23–24] Is 20:2–3.   v. [24:25] cf. Ez 3:22–27.   w. [24:26] cf. Ez 33:22.   x. [25:2] Jer 49:1–6; Am 1:13–15; Zep 2:8–11.   y. [25:4] Dt 28:33, 51.

z. [25:7] Am 1:14–15.   a. [25:8] Sir 50:26; Is 15–16; Jer 48; Am 2:1–3.   b. [25:11] Am 2:1–3.   c. [25:12] 2 Sm 8:13–14; 2 Chr 28:17; Ob 11–14.   d. [25:13] cf. Ez 35; Is 34:5–17; 63:1–6; Jer 49:7–11.   e. [25:14] cf. Ez 35:11.   f. [25:15] Is 14:29–31; Jer 47:1–7; Am 1:6–8; Zep 2:4–7.

2  'Son of man, because Tyre said of
           Jerusalem:
   "Aha! The gateway of the peoples is
           smashed!
       It has been turned over to me;
       I will be enriched by its ruin!"g
3      therefore thus says the Lord GOD:
   See! I am coming against you, Tyre;
       I will churn up against you many
           nations,
       just as the sea churns up its waves.
4  They will destroy the walls of Tyre
       and tear down its towers;
   I will scrape off its debris
       and leave it a bare rock.†
5  It will become a place for drying nets
       in the midst of the sea.
   For I have spoken—oracle of the Lord GOD:
       she will become plunder for the
           nations.
6  Her daughter cities‡ on the mainland
       will be slaughtered by the sword;
       then they shall know that I am the
           LORD.
7  Indeed thus says the Lord GOD:
   I am bringing up against Tyre
       from the north, Nebuchadnezzar,
   King of Babylon, king of kings,
       with horses and chariots, with
           cavalry,
       and a mighty horde of troops.h
8  Your daughter cities on the mainland
       he shall slay with the sword.
   He shall build a siege wall around you,
       throw up a ramp against you,
       and raise his shields about you.
9  He shall pound your walls with
           battering-rams
       and break down your towers with
           his axes.
10 From the surging of his horses
       he will cover you with dust;
       from the noise of warhorses,
           wheels and chariots.
   Your walls will shake
       when he enters your gates,
       even as one enters a city that is
           breached.
11 With the hooves of his horses
       he will trample all your streets;
   Your people he will slay by the sword;
       your mighty pillars will collapse.i

12 They shall plunder your wealth
       and pillage your goods;
   They will tear down your walls
       and demolish your splendid houses.
   Your stones, timbers, and debris
       they will cast into the sea.
13 I will bring an end to the noise of your
           songs;
       the music of your lyres will be heard
           no more.
14 I will turn you into bare rock,
       you will become a place for drying
           nets.
   You shall never be rebuilt,
       for I the LORD have spoken—
       oracle of the Lord GOD.
15 Thus says the Lord GOD to Tyre:
   At the sound of your downfall,
       at the groaning of the wounded,
   When victims are slain within you,
       will the islands not quake?
16 All the princes of the sea§
       will step down from their thrones,
   Lay aside their robes,
       and strip off their embroidered
           garments.
   Clothed in mourning,
       they will sit on the ground
   And tremble, horror-struck
       and appalled at you.j
17 They will raise lament¶ over you
       and say to you:
   How you have perished,
       gone from the seas,
       Renowned City!
   Once she was mighty on the sea,
       she and her inhabitants,
   Those who spread their terror
       to all who dwelt nearby.k
18 On this, the day of your fall,
       the islands quake!
   The islands in the sea
       are terrified at your passing.
19 Indeed thus says the Lord GOD:
   When I make you a ruined city
       like cities no longer inhabited,
   When I churn up the deep
       and its mighty waters cover you,
20 Then I will thrust you down
       with those who go down to the pit,**
       to those of the bygone age;
   I will make you dwell in the netherworld,
       in the everlasting ruins,

---

*[26:2] Tyre is pictured rejoicing over Jerusalem's fall to
Babylon because now the wealth from caravans and other
trade will go to Tyrian merchants.

†[26:4–5] A bare rock: the Tyre of Ezekiel's time was situated on a rocky island just off the Phoenician coast. During
the time of Alexander the Great a causeway was built to connect it to the mainland.

‡[26:6] Daughter cities: tributary towns and villages on
the mainland.

---

§[26:16] The princes of the sea: the rulers of the islands
and coastal cities leagued commercially with Tyre.

¶[26:17] Lament: the princes sing a funeral dirge at the
burial of the personified Tyre; cf. the similar lamentation over
Egypt in 32:3–8.

**[26:20] Those who go down to the pit: the dead, pictured
as dwelling in Sheol, a place or cave of darkness. Cf. 32:17–32;
Is 14:4–21 for other examples.

---

g. [26:2] Is 23:1–18; Jl 3:4–5; Am 1:9–10; Zec 9:2–4.   h. [26:7] Jer
27:6; Na 2:3–4.   i. [26:11] Na 3:11.

j. [26:16] cf. Ez 32:10.   k. [26:17] cf. Ez 19:1.

with those who have gone down to
    the pit,
So you will never return
    or have a place in the land of the
       living.[*l*]
²¹ I will make you a horror,
    and you shall be no more;
You shall be sought for,
    but never found again—
       oracle of the Lord God.

## CHAPTER 27

**The Ship Tyre.** ¹The word of the Lord came to
me: ²You, son of man, raise a lament over Tyre,
³and say to Tyre, who sits at the entrance to the
sea, trader to peoples on many coastlands, Thus
says the Lord God:

Tyre, you said, "I am a ship,
    perfect in beauty;[*m*]
⁴ In the heart of the sea was your territory;
    your builders perfected your beauty.[*n*]
⁵ With juniper wood from Senir[*]
    they built all your decks;
A cedar from Lebanon they took
    to make you a mast.
⁶ With oaks of Bashan[†]
    they fashioned your oars,
Your bridge, of ivory-inlaid cypress wood
    from the coasts of Kittim.
⁷ Fine embroidered linen from Egypt
    became your sail;
Your awnings were made of purple and
    scarlet
    from the coasts of Elishah.[‡o]
⁸ Inhabitants of Sidon[§] and Arvad
    were your oarsmen;
Your own sages, Tyre, were on board,
    serving as your sailors.[*p*]
⁹ The elders and sages of Gebal
    were with you to caulk your seams.
Every ship and sailor on the sea
    came to you to carry on trade.[*q*]
¹⁰ Persia and Lud and Put
    were warriors in your army;
Shield and helmet they hung on you
    to enhance your splendor.
¹¹ The men of Arvad and Helech[¶]
    were on your walls all around
And Gamadites on your towers;

they hung their shields around your
    walls,
    they made your beauty perfect.
¹² Tarshish traded with you,
    so great was your wealth,
Exchanging for your wares
    silver, iron, tin, and lead.
¹³ Javan, Tubal, and Meshech
    also traded with you,
Exchanging slaves and bronze vessels
    for your merchandise.[*r*]
¹⁴ Horses, steeds, and mules from
    Beth-togarmah
    were exchanged for your wares.
¹⁵ Men of Rhodes trafficked with you;
    many coastlands were your agents;
Ivory tusks and ebony wood
    they brought back as your payment.
¹⁶ Edom traded with you for your many
    wares:
    garnets, purple dye, embroidered
      cloth,
Fine linen, coral, and rubies
    they gave you as merchandise.
¹⁷ Judah and the land of Israel
    trafficked with you:
Minnith wheat, grain,[**] honey, oil, and
    balm[*s*]
    they gave you as merchandise.
¹⁸ Damascus traded with you for your many
    wares,
    so great was your wealth,
    exchanging Helbon wine and Zahar
      wool.
¹⁹ Javan exchanged wrought iron, cassia, and
    aromatic cane
    from Uzal for your wares.
²⁰ Dedan traded with you for riding gear.[*t*]
²¹ Arabia and the sheikhs of Kedar were
    your agents,
    dealing in lambs, rams, and goats.[*u*]
²² The merchants of Sheba and Raamah also
    traded with you,
    exchanging for your wares the very
      best spices,
    all kinds of precious stones, and
      gold.
²³ Haran, Canneh, and Eden,
    the merchants of Sheba, Asshur, and
      Chilmad,
²⁴ Traded with you, marketing rich
    garments,
    purple cloth, embroidered fabric,
    varicolored carpets, and braided
      cords.
²⁵ The ships of Tarshish sailed for you with
    your goods;

---

*[27:5] **Senir:** another name for Mount Hermon; cf. Dt
3:9.
†[27:6] **Bashan:** an area in northern Transjordan, noted
for its lush growth and great forests (cf. Is 2:13). **Kittim:** here,
probably Cyprus.
‡[27:7] **Elishah:** perhaps another term for Cyprus.
§[27:8–9] **Sidon . . . Gebal:** Phoenician cities in Tyre's orbit
of influence; Gebal is classical Byblos.
¶[27:11] **Helech:** perhaps in Asia Minor; otherwise
unknown.

---

l. [26:20]cf. Ez31:14;32:18,24,30.   m. [27:3]Is23:9.   n. [27:4]cf. Ez
28:1.   o. [27:7] Is 19:9–10.   p. [27:8] cf. Ez 28:20–23.   q. [27:9]
Ps 104:26.

---

**[27:17] **Grain:** most commentators have read "figs," but
Hebrew *panag* more properly describes milled grains or prepared meal.

---

r. [27:13] cf. Ez 38:2; 39:1.   s. [27:17] 1 Kgs 5:9.   t. [27:20] Is 21:13.
u. [27:21] Is 21:17; Jer 49:28.

You were full and heavily laden
    in the heart of the sea.
26 Out into deep waters
    your oarsmen brought you;
The east wind shattered you
    in the heart of the sea.<sup>v</sup>
27 Your wealth, your goods, your wares,
    your sailors, your crew,
The caulkers of your seams,
    those who traded for your goods,
All the warriors with you,
    the whole crowd with you
Sank into the heart of the sea
    on the day of your downfall.<sup>w</sup>
28 At the sound of your sailors' shouts
    the waves shudder,<sup>x</sup>
29 Down from their ships
    come all who ply the oars;
Sailors, all the seafaring crew,
    stand on the shore.
30 They raise their voices over you
    and shout their bitter cries;
They pour dust on their heads
    and cover themselves with ashes.
31 For you they shave their heads bald
    and put on sackcloth;
For you they weep bitterly,
    in anguished lament.<sup>y</sup>
32 They raise a lament for you;
    they wail over you:
"Who was ever destroyed like Tyre
    in the midst of the sea?"<sup>z</sup>
33 By exporting your goods by sea
    you satisfied many peoples,
With your great wealth and merchandise
    you enriched the kings of the earth.<sup>a</sup>
34 Now you are wrecked in the sea,
    in the watery depths;
Your wares and all your crew
    have fallen down with you.
35 All who dwell on the coastlands
    are aghast over you;
Their kings are terrified,
    their faces distorted.
36 The traders among the peoples
    now hiss at you;
You have become a horror,
    you shall be no more.

## CHAPTER 28

**The Prince of Tyre.** <sup>1</sup>The word of the LORD came to me: <sup>2</sup>Son of man, say to the prince of Tyre: Thus says the Lord GOD:

Because you are haughty of heart,
    you say, "I am a god!
I sit on a god's throne
    in the heart of the sea!"
But you are a man, not a god;
    yet you pretend
    you are a god at heart!
3 Oh yes, you are wiser than Daniel,<sup>†</sup>
    nothing secret is too obscure for
      you!<sup>b</sup>
4 By your wisdom and intelligence
    you made yourself rich,
    filling your treasuries with gold and
      silver.
5 Through your great wisdom in trading
    you heaped up riches for yourself—
    your heart is haughty because of
      your riches.
6     Therefore thus says the Lord GOD:
Because you pretend you are a god at
      heart,
7 Therefore, I will bring against you
    strangers, the most bloodthirsty of
      nations.
They shall draw their swords
    against your splendid wisdom,
    and violate your radiance.<sup>c</sup>
8 They shall thrust you down into the pit:
    you shall die a violent death
    in the heart of the sea.
9 Then, face to face with your killers,
    will you still say, "I am a god"?
No, you are a man, not a god,
    handed over to those who slay you.
10 You shall die the death of the
      uncircumcised
    handed over to strangers,
for I have spoken—oracle of the
      Lord GOD.<sup>d</sup>

<sup>11</sup>The word of the LORD came to me: <sup>12</sup>Son of man, raise a lament over the king of Tyre, and say to him: Thus says the Lord GOD:

<sup>‡</sup> You were a seal of perfection,
    full of wisdom, perfect in beauty.<sup>e</sup>
13 In Eden, the garden of God, you lived;
    precious stones of every kind were
      your covering:
Carnelian, topaz, and beryl,
    chrysolite, onyx, and jasper,
    sapphire, garnet, and emerald.
Their mounts and settings
    were wrought in gold,
    fashioned for you the day you were
      created.<sup>f</sup>

---

* [28:1–10] Ezekiel mocks the arrogance of Tyre's leader, who mistakes the city's commercial success for evidence of his divinity. At the hands of a foreign army, commissioned by the only God worthy of the name, this leader dies a humiliating, unceremonious death.

† [28:3] **Wiser than Daniel:** see note on 14:14.
‡ [28:12–19] Ezekiel describes the leader of Tyre in language that recalls the imagery of Gn 2–3.

---

v. [27:26] Ps 48:7; Jer 18:17.   w. [27:27] cf. Ez 28:8.   x. [27:28] Jer 49:21.   y. [27:31] Is 15:2; Jer 48:37.   z. [27:32] Is 23:1–6.   a. [27:33] cf. Ez 28:4–5.

b. [28:3] cf. Ez 14:14; Dn 1:20; 2:20–23.   c. [28:7] cf. Ez 30:11; 31:12; 32:12.   d. [28:10] cf. Ez 32:19, 24.   e. [28:12] Is 14:12–15.   f. [28:13] cf. Ez 31:8–9; Gn 2:8, 15.

14 With a cherub I placed you;
  I put you on the holy mountain of
    God,*
  where you walked among fiery
    stones.
15 Blameless were you in your ways
    from the day you were created,
  Until evil was found in you.
16   Your commerce was full of
    lawlessness, and you sinned.
  Therefore I banished you from the
    mountain of God;
  the cherub drove you out
    from among the fiery stones.g
17 Your heart had grown haughty
    because of your beauty;
  You corrupted your wisdom
    because of your splendor.
  I cast you to the ground,
  I made you a spectacle
    in the sight of kings.h
18 Because of the enormity of your guilt,
    and the perversity of your trade,
    you defiled your sanctuary.
  I brought fire out of you;
    it devoured you;
  I made you ashes on the ground
    in the eyes of all who see you.i
19 All the nations who knew you
    are appalled on account of you;
  You have become a horror,
    never to be again.j

**Against Sidon.** 20The word of the LORD came to
me: 21Son of man, turn your face toward Sidon
and prophesy against it. 22Thus says the Lord
GOD:

  Watch out! I am against you, Sidon;
    I will win glory for myself in your
      midst.
  They shall know that I am the LORD,
    when I deliver judgment upon it
    and manifest my holiness in it.
23 I will send disease into it;
    blood will fill its streets,
  Within it shall fall
    those slain by the sword
    raised against it on every side.
  Then they shall know that I am the LORD.
24 No longer will there be a thorn that tears
    or a brier that scratches for the
      house of Israel
  From the surrounding neighbors
    who despise them;
  thus they shall know that I am the
    LORD.k

25Thus says the Lord GOD: When I gather the
house of Israel from the peoples among whom
they are scattered, and I manifest my holiness
through them in the sight of the nations, then
they shall live on the land I gave my servant
Jacob.l 26They shall dwell on it securely, building
houses and planting vineyards. They shall dwell
securely while I execute judgment on all their
neighbors who treated them with contempt; then
they shall know that I, the LORD, am their God.m

## CHAPTER 29

**Egypt the Crocodile.** 1In the tenth year, on the
twelfth day of the tenth month,† the word of the
LORD came to me: 2Son of man, turn your face
toward Pharaoh, king of Egypt, and prophesy
against him and against all Egypt.‡n 3Say to him:
Thus says the Lord GOD:

  Pay attention! I am against you,
    Pharaoh, king of Egypt,
  Great dragon§ crouching
    in the midst of the Nile,
  Who says, "The Nile belongs to me;
    I made it myself!"o
4 ❛I will put hooks in your jaws
    and make all the fish of your Nile
  Cling to your scales;
    I will drag you up from your Nile,
  With all the fish of your Nile
    clinging to your scales.p
5 I will hurl you into the wilderness,
    you and all the fish of your Nile.
  You will fall into an open field,
    you will not be picked up or
      gathered together.
  To the beasts of the earth
    and the birds of the sky
    I give you as food.q
6 ❛Then all the inhabitants of Egypt
    will know that I am the LORD.
  Because you were a staff of reeds**
    for the house of Israel:
7 When they took hold of you, you would
    splinter,

---

†[29:1] The date is calculated to be January 7, 587 B.C. The
siege of Jerusalem had begun a year earlier; cf. 24:1.
‡[29:2] Egypt was allied with Judah against the Babylonians.
§[29:3] **Dragon:** Hebrew reads *tannim*, usually translated
"jackals," here a byform of *tannin*, the mythical dragon, or
sea monster, representing chaos (cf. Is 27:1; 51:9; Jer 51:34;
Ps 91:13; Jb 7:12), and the crocodile native to the Nile. **Nile:**
the many rivulets of the Nile that branch out into the Delta.
¶[29:4–5] Ezekiel's repetition of detail creates a vivid picture
of Egypt's destruction: God hauls the crocodile (Pharaoh) and
the fish clinging to it for protection (the Egyptian populace)
out of the Nile and lands them in an open field, where their
corpses are torn apart by wildlife rather than being properly
buried (cf. Dt 28:26; 2 Kgs 9:36–37; Jer 34:20; Ez 39:17–20).
**[29:6] **Staff of reeds:** Pharaoh is like a reed that looks
sturdy but breaks under pressure. For a similar image, cf.
2 Kgs 18:21 (Is 36:6).

---

*[28:14] **The holy mountain of God:** the residence of gods
in Israelite and non-Israelite myth; cf. Is 14:13. **Fiery stones:**
associated with the divine presence; cf. Ez 1:13; Ps 18:13.

g. [28:16] Gn 3:24.   h. [28:17] Is 10:12.   i. [28:18] Ob 18.   j. [28:19]
Lv 26:12.   k. [28:24] Nm 33:55.

l. [28:25] cf. Ez 20:41.   m. [28:26] Lv 25:18–19; Jer 23:6.   n. [29:2]
Is 19:1–17; Jer 25:19.   o. [29:3] cf. Ez 32:2.   p. [29:4] Is 19:5.
q. [29:5] Jer 7:33.   r. [29:6–7] 2 Kgs 18:21; Is 36:6.

throwing shoulders out of joint.
When they leaned on you, you would
	break,
	pitching them down headlong.
8 Therefore thus says the Lord GOD:
	Look! I am bringing the sword against
		you
	to cut off from you people and
		animals.
9 The land of Egypt shall become a desolate
		waste;
	then they shall know that I am the
		LORD.
	Because you said, "The Nile belongs to me;
		I made it!"
10 Beware! I am against you
		and against your Nile.
	I will turn the land of Egypt into ruins,
		into a dry, desolate waste,
	From Migdol to Syene,*
		up to the border of Ethiopia.ˢ
11 No foot shall pass through it,
	no human being or beast cross it;
	it will remain uninhabited for forty
		years.
12 I will make the land of Egypt the most
		desolate
		among desolate lands;
	Its cities, the most deserted
		among deserted cities for forty years;
	I will scatter the Egyptians among the
		nations
		and disperse them throughout other
		lands.ᵗ
13 But thus says the Lord GOD:
	At the end of forty years
	I will gather the Egyptians
		from among the peoples
		where they are scattered;
14 I will restore Egypt's fortunes,
		bringing them back to the land of
		Pathros,†
		the land of their origin.
	But there it will be a lowly kingdom,
15		lower than any other kingdom,
	no longer able to set itself above the
		nations.
	I will make them few in number,
		so they cannot rule other nations.
16 No longer shall they be security
		for the house of Israel,
	But a reminder of its iniquity
		in turning away to follow them.

Then they shall know that I am the Lord
	GOD.ᵘ

**Wages for Nebuchadnezzar.** ¹⁷In the twenty-seventh year on the first day of the first month,‡ the word of the LORD came to me: ¹⁸Son of man, Nebuchadnezzar, the king of Babylon, has made his army wage a hard campaign against Tyre;§ their heads grew bald, their shoulders rubbed raw, yet neither he nor his army received compensation from Tyre for all the effort they expended against it.ᵛ ¹⁹Therefore thus says the Lord GOD:ʷ See! I am giving to Nebuchadnezzar, king of Babylon, the land of Egypt! He will carry off its wealth, plundering and pillaging whatever he can find to provide pay for his army. ²⁰As payment for his toil I give him the land of Egypt— oracle of the Lord GOD.

²¹On that day I will make a hornˢ sprout for the house of Israel, and I will let you again open your mouth in their midst; then they shall know that I am the LORD.ˣ

# CHAPTER 30

**The Day of the Lord Against Egypt.** ¹The word of the LORD came to me: ²Son of man, prophesy and say: Thus says the Lord GOD:

	Wail: "Alas the day!"
3	Yes, a day approaches,
		a day of the Lord approaches:
	A day of dark cloud,
		a time appointed for the nations.ʸ
4	A sword will come against Egypt,
		there will be anguish in Ethiopia,
	When the slain fall in Egypt
		when its hordes are seized,
		its foundations razed.ᶻ
5	Ethiopia, Put, and Lud,
		all the mixed rabble** and Kub,
	and the people of allied lands
		shall fall by the sword with them.
6	Thus says the LORD:
	The pillars of Egypt shall fall,
		and its proud strength sink;

---

*[29:10] **From Migdol to Syene**: from the northeastern to the southern limits of Egypt. Syene is the modern Aswan, at the first cataract of the Nile; Ethiopia (Heb. *kush*) is the territory south of Aswan.

†[29:14] **Pathros**: an Egyptian word for upper, i.e., southern, Egypt, above Memphis/Thebes. As silt filled the Delta region and richer land became available there, the population spread north, creating the tradition of a migration from the south (Is 11:11; Jer 44:1, 15).

‡[29:17] **In the twenty-seventh year on the first day of the first month**: April 26, 571 B.C. This is the latest date attached to any of Ezekiel's prophecies.

§[29:18–19] Nebuchadnezzar's thirteen-year siege (587–574 B.C.) ended with Tyre's surrender on the condition that the Babylonian army would not loot and pillage (*pace* 26:3–14). According to Ezekiel, Nebuchadnezzar and his army should collect their wages for serving as God's instrument in Tyre's punishment, by plundering and controlling Egypt.

¶[29:21] **A horn**: God will give Israel renewed strength. For horn as a symbol of strength, cf. Dt 33:17; Ps 92:11; 132:17. Ezekiel suggests that the Babylonian conquest of Egypt precedes Israel's restoration, an event he expects to witness and acknowledge when God removes his muteness.

**[30:5] **Mixed rabble**: mercenaries.

---

s. [29:10] cf. Ez 30:4, 6.    t. [29:12] Jer 46:19.

u. [29:16] Ps 40:5; Is 20:5.    v. [29:18] Is 26:7–14.    w. [29:19] Is 19:4. x. [29:21] Ps 132:17; Lk 1:69.    y. [30:3] cf. Ez 7:7; Is 13:6.    z. [30:4] Jer 25:19–20.

From Migdol to Syene,
  its people will fall by the sword—
  oracle of the Lord GOD.[a]
7 It shall be the most desolate
  among desolate lands,
Its cities the most ruined
  among ruined cities.
8 They shall know that I am the LORD,
  when I set fire to Egypt,
  and all its allies are shattered.[b]
9 On that day, messengers from me
  will go forth in ships
  to terrorize confident Ethiopia.
Anguish will be among them
  on Egypt's day—it is certainly
  coming!*
10 Thus says the Lord GOD:
I will put an end to Egypt's hordes
  by the hand of Nebuchadnezzar,
  king of Babylon:
11 He and his army with him,
  the most ruthless of nations,
  will be brought in to devastate the
  land.
They will draw their swords against Egypt
  and fill the land with the slain.
12 Then I will dry up the streams of the Nile,
  and sell the land into evil hands;
By the hand of foreigners I will devastate
  the land and everything in it.
  I, the LORD, have spoken.[c]
13 †Thus says the Lord GOD:
I will destroy idols,
  and put an end to images in
  Memphis.
There will never again be a prince
  over the land of Egypt.
Instead, I will spread fear
  throughout the land of Egypt.[d]
14 I will devastate Pathros,
  set fire to Zoan,
  and execute judgment against
  Thebes.[e]
15 I will pour out my wrath on Pelusium,
  the fortress of Egypt,
  and cut off the troops of Thebes.
16 I will set fire to Egypt;
  Pelusium will writhe in anguish,
Thebes will be breached,
  and Memphis besieged in daylight.
17 The warriors of On and Pi-beseth
  will fall by the sword,
  the cities taken captive.

18 In Tahpanhes, the day will turn dark
  when I break the scepter of Egypt
  there
  and put an end to its proud strength.
Dark clouds will cover it,
  and its women will go into captivity.[f]
19 I will execute judgment against Egypt
  that they may know that I am the
  LORD.

**Pharaoh's Broken Arm.** [20]On the seventh day of the first month in the eleventh year,[‡] the word of the LORD came to me: [21§]Son of man, I have broken the arm of Pharaoh, king of Egypt. See! It has not been immobilized for healing, nor set with a splint to make it strong enough to grasp a sword.[g] [22]Therefore thus says the Lord GOD: See! I am coming against Pharaoh, king of Egypt. I will break both his arms, the strong one and the broken one, making the sword fall from his hand. [23]I will scatter the Egyptians among the nations and disperse them throughout other lands. [24]I will, however, strengthen the arms of the king of Babylon and put my sword in his hand so he can bring it against Egypt for plunder and pillage.[h] [25]When I strengthen the arms of the king of Babylon, and the arms of Pharaoh collapse, they shall know that I am the LORD, because I put my sword into the hand of the king of Babylon to wield against the land of Egypt. [26]When I scatter the Egyptians among the nations and disperse them throughout other lands, they shall know that I am the LORD.

## CHAPTER 31

**Allegory of the Cedar.** [1]On the first day of the third month in the eleventh year,[¶] the word of the LORD came to me: [2]Son of man, say to Pharaoh, the king of Egypt, and to his hordes: In your greatness, whom do you resemble?

3 Assyria! It is Assyria!**
    A cedar of Lebanon—
  Beautiful branches,
    thick shade,
  Towering heights,
    its crown in the clouds![i]

---

*[30:9] God spreads panic throughout Ethiopia, ancient Cush, by sending messengers with news of Egypt's fall. Rivers at its borders insulated Ethiopia and made it inaccessible except by boat.

†[30:13–19] The prophet enumerates a list of major Egyptian cities that shall each bear the judgment proclaimed in the previous oracle, vv. 1–12.

‡[30:20] **The seventh day of the first month in the eleventh year**: April 29, 587 B.C.

§[30:21–26] This oracle was delivered more than a year into the siege of Jerusalem (24:1). When Pharaoh Hophra came to help Jerusalem, the Babylonians temporarily lifted the siege; cf. Jer 34:21; 37:6–7. In Ezekiel's eyes, Hophra was interfering with the punishment God intended the Babylonians to inflict on Judah. The Babylonians routed the Egyptians, who could not offer Jerusalem any more help; cf. chap. 31.

¶[31:1] **The first day of the third month in the eleventh year**: June 21, 587 B.C.

**[31:3] **Assyria**: this translates te'ashshur, which some interpret as "cypress tree." The oracle, however, compares the fate of Pharaoh to the terrible demise of Assyria because of its arrogant pride (cf. Na 1–3). Ezekiel may have drawn on an ancient myth of a cosmic tree of life to emphasize the greatness of Egypt's fall.

a. [30:6] cf. Ez 29:10.   b. [30:8] Jer 49:27.   c. [30:12] Is 19:6.
d. [30:13] Is 19:13.   e. [30:14] Is 19:11, 13; Jer 46:25.

f. [30:18] Jer 43:4–7.   g. [30:21] Jer 37:10; 44:30; 48:25.   h. [30:24] cf. Ez 21:14.   i. [31:3] Ps 92:12; Jer 50:18.

⁴ The waters made it grow,
  the deep made it tall,
Letting its currents flow
  around the place it was planted,
Then sending its channels
  to all the other trees of the field.ʲ
⁵ Thereupon it towered in height
  above all the trees in the field;
Its branches were numerous
  and its boughs long,
Because of the many waters
  sent to its shoots.
⁶ In its branches nested
  all the birds of the sky;
Under its boughs all the wild animals
  gave birth,
And in its shade* dwelt
  all the mighty nations.ᵏ
⁷ It was magnificent in size
  and in the length of its branches,
For its roots reached down
  to the many waters.
⁸ In the garden of God,
  no cedars could rival it,
No juniper could equal its branches,
  no plane tree match its boughs.
No tree in the garden of God
  could match its beauty.ˡ
⁹ I made it beautiful
  with abundant foliage,
So that all the trees in Eden
  were envious of it.†
¹⁰ Therefore, thus says the Lord God:
Because it was arrogant about its height,
  lifting its crown among the clouds
  and exalting itself because of its size,ᵐ
¹¹ I handed it over to a ruler of nations
  to deal with it according to its evil.
I have cast it off,
¹²  and foreigners have cut it down,
The most ruthless nations,
  have hurled it on the mountains.
Its boughs fell into every valley
  and its branches lay broken
  in every ravine in the land.
All the peoples of the earth
  departed from its shade
  when it was hurled down.ⁿ
¹³ On its fallen trunk
  sit all the birds of the sky;
Beside its fallen branches,
  are found all the beasts of the field.
¹⁴ This has happened so no well-watered
  tree
  will gain such lofty height,
  or lift its crown to the clouds.

Not one of those fed by water
  will tower in height over the rest.
For all of them are destined for death,
  for the underworld, among mere
   mortals,
  with those who go down to the pit.
¹⁵ Thus says the Lord God:
On the day it went down to Sheol,
  I made the deep close up
  in mourning for it.
I restrained the currents of the deep,
  and held back the many waters.
I darkened Lebanon because of it,
  and all the trees of the field
  languished because of it.
¹⁶ At the sound of its fall,
  I made nations shudder,
When I cast it down to Sheol
  with those who go down to the pit.
In the underworld
  all the trees of Eden took comfort:
Lebanon's choicest and best,
  all that were fed by the waters.ᵒ
¹⁷ They too will go down to Sheol,
  to those slain by the sword,
Its allies‡ who dwelt
  in its shade among the nations.
¹⁸ To whom among the trees of Eden
  do you compare in glory and
   greatness?
You will be brought down
  with the trees of Eden to the
   underworld,
And lie among the uncircumcised,
  with those slain by the sword.
Such is Pharaoh and all his hordes—
  oracle of the Lord God.

## CHAPTER 32

**Lament over Pharaoh.** ¹On the first day of the twelfth month in the twelfth year,§ the word of the Lord came to me: ²Son of man, utter a lament over Pharaoh, the king of Egypt, and say to him:

You liken yourself to a lion among nations,
  but you are like the monster in the
   sea!
Thrashing about in your streams,
  churning the water with your feet,
  polluting the streams.ᵖ
³ Thus says the Lord God:
I will cast my net over you
  by assembling many armies,
  and I will hoist you up in my mesh.
⁴ I will hurl you onto the land,
  cast you into an open field.

---

*[31:6] **Shade**: a metaphor for protection (cf. Lam 4:20).
 †[31:9] Here Israel's God is responsible for Assyria's splendor, whereas in Is 10:13 Assyria claims to have created its own might.

j. [31:4] Dn 4:10. k. [31:6] Dn 4:12; cf. Mt 13:32. l. [31:8] Ps 80:14. m. [31:10] Is 2:11. n. [31:12] Dn 4:14.

---

‡[31:17] **Allies**: lit., "arm."
 §[32:1] **The first day of the twelfth month in the twelfth year**: March 3, 585 B.C.

o. [31:16] Is 14:8, 15. p. [32:2] cf. Ez 19:1; 20:3.

I will make all the birds of the sky
    roost upon you,
The beasts of the whole earth
    gorge themselves on you.
5 I will strew your flesh on the mountains,
    and fill the valleys with your corpse.^q
6 I will drench the land,
    pouring out your blood on the
        mountain;
    filling up the ravines with you.
7 When I extinguish you,
    I will cover the heavens
    and darken all its stars.
The sun I will cover with clouds;
    the moon will not give light.^r
8 All the shining lights in the heavens
    I will darken over you;
I will spread darkness over your land—
    oracle of the Lord God.
9 I will trouble the hearts
    of many peoples,
When I bring you captive
    among the nations,
    to lands you do not know.
10 I will fill many nations with horror;
    their kings will shudder at you,
    when I brandish my sword in their
        faces.
They will tremble violently
    fearing for their lives on the day of
        your fall.^s
11 For thus says the Lord God:
The sword of the king of Babylon
    will come against you.
12 I will cut down your hordes
    with the swords of warriors,
    all of them, ruthless nations;
They will lay waste the glory of Egypt,
    and all its hordes will be destroyed.^t
13 I will wipe out all the livestock
    from the banks of its many waters;
No human foot will disturb them again,
    no animal hoof stir them up.
14 Then I will make their waters clear
    and their streams flow like oil—
    oracle of the Lord God.
15 When I make Egypt a wasteland
    and the land destitute of everything,
When I strike down all its inhabitants
    they shall know that I am the Lord.
16 This is the lamentation
    women of all nations will chant;
They will raise it over Egypt;
    over all its hordes they will chant
        it—
    oracle of the Lord God.

**Another Lament over Egypt.** 17*On the fifteenth day of that month in the twelfth year, the word of the Lord came to me:

18 Son of man, wail over the hordes of
    Egypt—
    you and the women of mighty
        nations—
Send them down to the underworld,
    with those who go down into the pit.
19 Whom do you excel in beauty? Go down!
    Be laid to rest with the
        uncircumcised!
20 Among those slain by the sword they will
    fall,
    for the sword has been appointed!
Seize Egypt and all its hordes.^u
21 Out of Sheol the mighty warriors
    will speak to him and his allies:
Let them descend and lie down among
        the uncircumcised,
    those slain by the sword!^v
22 There is Assyria and all its company,
    around it are its graves,
    all of them slain, fallen by the sword.
23 The graves are set
    in the recesses of the pit;
Its company is assembled
    around its grave,
All of them slain, fallen by the sword,
    those who spread terror in the land
        of the living.^w
24 There is Elam and all its horde
    around its grave,
All of them slain, fallen by the sword;
    they descended uncircumcised
        into the underworld,
Those who spread their terror
    in the land of the living.
They bear their disgrace
    with those who go down into the pit.
25 Among the slain is set its bed,
    with all its horde around its grave;
All of them uncircumcised,
    slain by the sword
Because of the terror they spread
    in the land of the living.
They bear their disgrace
    with those who go down into the pit.
    Among the slain it is set!
26 There is Meshech and Tubal† and all the
    hordes
    surrounding it with their graves.
All of them uncircumcised,
    slain by the sword

---

*[32:17–32] The description of Pharaoh in Sheol shifts rapidly between the single individual and the collective body, between corpses speaking and corpses lying inert, between singular (his, hers, its) and plural (them, theirs) pronouns to emphasize that all the enemies of Israel come to the same end.
†[32:26] **Meshech and Tubal:** see note on 38:2.

q. [32:5] Is 34:3.  r. [32:7] Is 3:10.  s. [32:10] Rev 18:9–10. t. [32:12] Cf. Ez 31:11–12.

u. [32:20] cf. Ez 31:17–18.  v. [32:21] Is 14:9.  w. [32:23] Is 14:15.

Because they spread their terror
    in the land of the living.[x]
27 They do not rest with the warriors
    who fell in ancient times,
    who went down to Sheol fully
      armed.
Their swords were placed under their
    heads
    and their shields laid over their
      bones;
For there was terror of these warriors
    in the land of the living.
28 But as for you, among the uncircumcised
    you will be broken and laid to rest
    with those slain by the sword.
29 There is Edom, all its kings and princes,
    who, despite their might,
    are put with those slain by the
      sword.
They lie among the uncircumcised,
    with those who go down into the
      pit.[y]
30 There are the generals of the north
    and all the Sidonians
Who have gone down with the slain,
    because of the terror their might
      inspired.
They lie uncircumcised
    with those slain by the sword,
And bear their shame with those
    who have gone down into the pit.[z]
31 When Pharaoh sees them,
    he will be consoled on behalf of all
      his hordes,
    slain by the sword—
Pharaoh and all his army—
    oracle of the Lord GOD.
32 I spread terror of him
    in the land of the living;
Now he is laid among the uncircumcised,
    with those slain by the sword—
Pharaoh and all his horde—
    oracle of the Lord GOD.

## IV. HOPE FOR THE FUTURE

### CHAPTER 33

**The Prophet as Sentinel.** [1]The word of the LORD came to me: [2]Son of man, speak to your people and tell them: When I bring the sword against a land, if the people of that land select one of their number as a sentinel[*] for them,[a] [3]and the sentinel sees the sword coming against the land, he should blow the trumpet to warn the people.[b] [4]If they hear the trumpet but do not take the warning and a sword attacks and kills them, their blood will be on their own heads.[c] [5]They heard the trumpet blast but ignored the warning; their blood is on them. If they had heeded the warning, they could have escaped with their lives. [6]If, however, the sentinel sees the sword coming and does not blow the trumpet, so that the sword attacks and takes someone's life, his life will be taken for his own sin, but I will hold the sentinel responsible for his blood.

[7d]You, son of man—I have appointed you as a sentinel for the house of Israel; when you hear a word from my mouth, you must warn them for me. [8]When I say to the wicked, "You wicked, you must die," and you do not speak up to warn the wicked about their ways, they shall die in their sins, but I will hold you responsible for their blood. [9]If, however, you warn the wicked to turn from their ways, but they do not, then they shall die in their sins, but you shall save your life. **Individual Retribution.** [10]As for you, son of man, speak to the house of Israel: You people say, "Our crimes and our sins weigh us down; we are rotting away because of them. How can we survive?"[e] [11f]Answer them: As I live—oracle of the Lord GOD—I swear I take no pleasure in the death of the wicked, but rather that they turn from their ways and live. Turn, turn from your evil ways! Why should you die, house of Israel?

[12]As for you, son of man, say to your people: The justice of the just will not save them on the day they sin; the wickedness of the wicked will not bring about their downfall on the day they turn from their wickedness. No, the just cannot save their lives on the day they sin.[g] [13]Even though I say to the just that they shall surely live, if they, relying on their justice, do wrong, none of their just deeds shall be remembered; because of the wrong they have done, they shall die.[h] [14]And though I say to the wicked that they shall die, if they turn away from sin and do what is just and right— [15]returning pledges, restoring stolen goods, walking by statutes that bring life, doing nothing wrong—they shall surely live; they shall not die.[i] [16]None of the sins they committed shall be remembered against them. If they do what is right and just, they shall surely live.

[17]Your people say, "The way of the LORD is not fair!" But it is their way that is not fair. [18]When the just turn away from justice and do wrong, they shall die for it.[j] [19]When the wicked turn away from wickedness and do what is right and just, because of this they shall live. [20]But still you say, "The way of the LORD is not fair!" I will judge each of you according to your ways, house of Israel.

**The Survivor from Jerusalem.** [21]On the fifth day of the tenth month,[†] in the twelfth year of

---

*[33:2] **Sentinel**: the theme of the sentinel's duty initiates a new commission to announce salvation (chaps. 33–48), just as the same command (3:17–21) opened Ezekiel's ministry to announce judgment (chaps. 3–24).

†[33:21–22] **The fifth day of the tenth month**: January 8, 585 B.C. According to Jeremiah (39:2), Jerusalem was taken

x. [32:26] cf. Ez 27:13.  y. [32:29] Is 34:5–15.  z. [32:30] Jer 25:26.  a. [33:2] Lv 26:25.  b. [33:3] Hos 5:8; 8:1.

c. [33:4] Lv 20:9; Jer 6:17.  d. [33:7] Jer 1:17.  e. [33:10] Lv 26:16, 39.  f. [33:11] Jer 44:7–8; cf. Ez 18:23.  g. [33:12] cf. Ez 3:20.  h. [33:13] Heb 10:38.  i. [33:15] Ex 22:1–4, 26.  j. [33:18] Jer 18:7–10.

our exile, the survivor came to me from Jerusalem and said, "The city is taken!"[k] [22]The hand of the LORD had come upon me the evening before the survivor arrived and opened my mouth when he reached me in the morning. My mouth was opened, and I was mute no longer.[l]

**Those Left in Judah.**[*] [23]The word of the LORD came to me: [24]Son of man, these who live among the ruins in the land of Israel are saying: "Abraham was only one person, yet he was given possession of the land. Since we are many, the land must be given to us as our possession."[m] [25]Therefore say to them: Thus says the Lord GOD: You eat on the mountains, you raise your eyes to your idols, you shed blood—yet you would keep possession of the land?[n] [26]You rely on your swords, you commit abominations, each defiles his neighbor's wife—yet you would keep possession of the land? [27]Say this to them: Thus says the Lord GOD: As I live, those among the ruins shall fall by the sword; those in the open field I have made food for the wild beasts; and those in rocky hideouts and caves shall die by the plague. [28]I will make the land a desolate waste, so that its proud strength will come to an end, and the mountains of Israel shall be so desolate that no one will cross them. [29]Thus they shall know that I am the LORD, when I make the land a desolate waste because of all the abominations they committed.

**Popular Misunderstanding.** [30]As for you, son of man, your people are talking about you beside the walls and in the doorways of houses. They say to one another, "Let's go hear the latest word that comes from the LORD." [31]My people come to you, gathering as a crowd and sitting in front of you to hear your words, but they will not act on them. Love songs are on their lips, but in their hearts they pursue dishonest gain.[o] [32]For them you are only a singer[†] of love songs, with a pleasant voice and a clever touch. They listen to your words, but they do not obey them. [33]But when it comes—and it is surely coming!—they shall know that there was a prophet among them.

## CHAPTER 34

**Parable of the Shepherds.** [1]The word of the LORD came to me: [2]Son of man, prophesy against the shepherds[‡] of Israel. Prophesy and say to them: To the shepherds, thus says the Lord GOD: Woe to the shepherds of Israel who have been pasturing themselves![p] Should not shepherds pasture the flock? [3]You consumed milk, wore wool, and slaughtered fatlings, but the flock you did not pasture.[q] [4]You did not strengthen the weak nor heal the sick nor bind up the injured. You did not bring back the stray or seek the lost but ruled them harshly and brutally.[r] [5]So they were scattered for lack of a shepherd, and became food for all the wild beasts. They were scattered[s] [6]and wandered over all the mountains and high hills; over the entire surface of the earth my sheep were scattered. No one looked after them or searched for them.

[7]Therefore, shepherds, hear the word of the LORD: [8]As I live—oracle of the Lord GOD—because my sheep became plunder, because my sheep became food for wild beasts, for lack of a shepherd, because my shepherds did not look after my sheep, but pastured themselves and did not pasture my sheep,[t] [9]therefore, shepherds, hear the word of the LORD: [10]Thus says the Lord GOD: Look! I am coming against these shepherds. I will take my sheep out of their hand and put a stop to their shepherding my flock, so that these shepherds will no longer pasture them. I will deliver my flock from their mouths so it will not become their food.[u]

[11]For thus says the Lord GOD: Look! I myself will search for my sheep and examine them. [12]As a shepherd examines his flock while he himself is among his scattered sheep, so will I examine my sheep. I will deliver them from every place where they were scattered on the day of dark clouds.[v] [13]I will lead them out from among the peoples and gather them from the lands; I will bring them back to their own country and pasture them upon the mountains of Israel, in the ravines and every inhabited place in the land.[w] [14]In good pastures I will pasture them; on the mountain heights of Israel will be their grazing land. There they will lie down on good grazing ground; in rich pastures they will be pastured on the mountains of Israel.[x] [15]I myself will pasture my sheep; I myself will give them rest—oracle of the Lord GOD. [16]The lost I will search out, the strays I will bring back, the injured I will bind up, and the sick I will heal; but the sleek and the strong I will destroy. I will shepherd them in judgment.

---

in July, 587. Some manuscripts read "eleventh" for "twelfth" year (January, 586); even so, there was ample time between the fall of Jerusalem and the arrival of the survivor from that city to journey to Babylon. However, this is the survivor sent to fulfill the promise of Ez 24:25–27, the eyewitness whose arrival would release Ezekiel from his muteness; cf. 3:26–27.

[*][33:23–29] News brought by the survivor furnished the occasion for this prophecy. Like Jeremiah, Ezekiel rejects the idea that those left in Judah have any claim to the land. The new Israel is to be formed from the exiles.

[†][33:32] **Singer:** perhaps the term indicates an entertainer whom one enjoys and then forgets.

---

[‡][34:2] **Shepherds:** the leaders of the people. A frequent title for kings and deities in the ancient Near East; the ideal ruler took care of his subjects and anticipated their needs. Ezekiel's oracle broadens the reference to include the whole class of Jerusalem's leaders (v. 17). The prophet assures his audience, the exiles in Babylon, that God holds these leaders responsible for what has happened to Jerusalem and will give Israel a new shepherd worthy of the title.

---

k. [33:21] 2 Kgs 25:4, 10; Is 39:1–2. l. [33:22] cf. Ez 3:26–27. m. [33:24] Is 51:2. n. [33:25] Gn 9:4; Jer 7:9–10. o. [33:31] cf. Ez 8:1; Mt 13:22.

p. [34:2] Ps 78:70–72; Jn 10:11. q. [34:3] Is 56:11. r. [34:4] Ex 1:13; Zec 11:15–17; Mt 18:12–14. s. [34:5] cf. Mk 6:34. t. [34:8] Jude 12. u. [34:10] Ps 72:14. v. [34:12] Is 40:11; Lk 19:10. w. [34:13] cf. Ez 36:24, 29–30. x. [34:14] Ps 23:2; Is 40:11.

**Separation of the Sheep.** [17]As for you, my flock, thus says the Lord God: I will judge between one sheep and another, between rams and goats.[y] [18]Was it not enough for you to graze on the best pasture, that you had to trample the rest of your pastures with your hooves? Or to drink the clearest water, that you had to pollute the rest with your hooves? [19]Thus my flock had to graze on what your hooves had trampled and drink what your hooves had polluted. [20]Therefore thus says the Lord God: Now I will judge between the fat and the lean. [21]Because you push with flank and shoulder, and butt all the weak sheep with your horns until you drive them off, [22]I will save my flock so they can no longer be plundered; I will judge between one sheep and another. [23]I will appoint one shepherd[*] over them to pasture them, my servant David; he shall pasture them and be their shepherd. [24]I, the Lord, will be their God, and my servant David will be prince in their midst. I, the Lord, have spoken.[a]

[25]I will make a covenant of peace with them and rid the country of wild beasts so they will dwell securely in the wilderness and sleep in the forests.[b] [26]I will settle them around my hill and send rain in its season, the blessing of abundant rain. [27]The trees of the field shall bear their fruits, and the land its crops, and they shall dwell securely on their own soil. They shall know that I am the Lord when I break the bars of their yoke and deliver them from the power of those who enslaved them.[c] [28]They shall no longer be plundered by the nations nor will wild beasts devour them, but they shall dwell securely, with no one to frighten them.[d] [29]I will prepare for them peaceful fields for planting so they are never again swept away by famine in the land or bear taunts from the nations. [30]Thus they shall know that I, the Lord, their God, am with them, and that they are my people, the house of Israel—oracle of the Lord God.[e] [31]Yes, you are my flock: you people are the flock of my pasture, and I am your God—oracle of the Lord God.[f]

## CHAPTER 35

**Against Edom.**[†] [1]The word of the Lord came to me: [2]Son of man, set your face against Mount Seir and prophesy against it. [3]Say to it: Thus says the Lord God: Watch out! I am against you, Mount Seir. I will stretch out my hand against you and turn you into a desolate waste.[g] [4]Your cities I will turn into ruins, and you shall be a desolation; then you shall know that I am the Lord.[h]

[5]Because you nursed a long-standing hatred and handed the Israelites over to the sword at the time of their collapse, at the time of their final punishment,[‡i] [6]therefore, as I live—oracle of the Lord God—you are guilty of blood, and blood, I swear, shall pursue you. [7]I will make Mount Seir a desolate waste and cut off from it anyone who travels across it and back.[j] [8]I will fill its mountains with the slain; those slain by the sword shall fall on your hills, into your valleys and all your ravines.

[9]  I will make you a desolation forever,
      your cities will not be inhabited,
      and you shall know that I am the
            Lord.[k]

[10]Because you said: The two nations and the two lands[§] belong to me; let us take possession of them—although the Lord was there—[11]therefore, as I live—oracle of the Lord God—I will deal with you according to the anger and envy you dealt out to them in your hatred, and I will make myself known to them when I execute judgment on you,[l] [12]then you shall know that I am the Lord.

I have heard all the insults you spoke against the mountains of Israel, saying: They are desolate; they have been given to us to devour. [13]You boasted against me with your mouths and used insolent words against me. I heard everything! [14]Thus says the Lord God: Because you rejoiced that the whole land was desolate, so I will do to you. [15]As you rejoiced over the devastation of the heritage of the house of Israel, the same I will do to you: you will become a ruin, Mount Seir, and the whole of Edom, all of it! Then they shall know that I am the Lord.[m]

## CHAPTER 36

**Regeneration of the Land.** [1]As for you, son of man, prophesy to the mountains of Israel and say: Mountains of Israel, hear the word of the Lord! [2]Thus says the Lord God: Because the

---

*[34:23] **One shepherd:** a future king to rule over a unified, restored Israel, in the image of the idealized David present in the Book of Kings (cf., e.g., 1 Kgs 3:3; 11:38; 2 Kgs 14:3; 22:2). **My servant David:** a common characterization of David; e.g., 1 Kgs 11:34, 36, 38; 2 Kgs 8:19; Ps 36:1; 78:70. See Ez 37:25.

†[35:1–15] After the fall of Jerusalem, Edom assisted the Babylonians in devastating the land and subduing the population in order to occupy part of Judah's former territory. For this reason these oracles against Edom are found in the context of the city's fall.

‡[35:5] **Final punishment:** throughout this oracle the prophet echoes the threat against the mountains of Israel found in chaps. 6–7.

§[35:10] **The two nations and the two lands:** by presenting Edom's excursion into the southern territory of Judah as its claim to both kingdoms, Ezekiel exaggerates Edom's greed and arrogance. **Lord was there:** Edom's betrayal of Judah becomes an attack on Judah's God, the land's sovereign. In 11:15 and 33:24, Ezekiel condemns Judahites who annex land that does not belong to them. Now the exiles in Babylon learn that even though God had left Jerusalem (chap. 11), he witnesses Edom's insolence and pronounces judgment against it. Cf. 48:35, "The Lord is there!"

---

y. [34:17] Mt 25:32–33.  z. [34:23] Ps 89:4, 20; Jer 23:5–6.  a. [34:24] cf. Ez 36:28; Ps 89:49; Jn 10:16.  b. [34:25] Is 11:6–9.  c. [34:27] Lv 26:13; Ps 72:16; Jer 28:10–13.  d. [34:28] Jer 30:10.  e. [34:30] Ex 6:7.  f. [34:31] Ps 28:9.

g. [35:3] cf. Ez 25:12–14.  h. [35:4] Ob 13.  i. [35:5] Ob 11–15.  j. [35:7] Jer 46:19.  k. [35:9] Is 34:5–6; Ob 10.  l. [35:11] Ob 15.  m. [35:15] Is 34:11; Ob 12.

enemy said about you, "Ha! the ancient heights have become our possession," [3]therefore prophesy and say: Thus says the Lord GOD: because you have been ridiculed and hounded on all sides for becoming a possession for the remaining nations and have become a byword and a popular jeer,[n] [4]therefore, mountains of Israel, hear the word of the Lord GOD: Thus says the Lord GOD to the mountains and hills, to the ravines and valleys, to the desolate ruins and abandoned cities, plundered and mocked by the nations remaining around you:[o] [5]therefore thus says the Lord GOD: Truly, with burning jealousy I speak against the remaining nations and against Edom; they all took possession of my land for plunder with wholehearted joy and utter contempt. [6]Therefore, prophesy concerning the land of Israel and say to the mountains and hills, to the ravines and valleys: Thus says the Lord GOD: See! in my jealous fury I speak, because you endured the reproach of the nations. [7]Therefore, thus says the Lord GOD: I raise my hand and swear: the nations around you shall bear their own reproach.

[8]But you, mountains of Israel, you will sprout branches and bear fruit for my people Israel, for they are coming soon.[p] [9]Look! I am for you! I will turn my face toward you; you will be plowed and planted.[q] [10]Upon you I will multiply the whole house of Israel; cities shall be resettled and ruins rebuilt.[r] [11]Upon you I will multiply people and animals so they can multiply and be fruitful. I will resettle you as in the past, and make you more prosperous than at your beginning; then you shall know that I am the LORD.[s]

[12]Upon you I will have them walk, my people Israel. They shall possess you, and you shall be their heritage. Never again shall you rob them of their children.

[13]Thus says the Lord GOD: Because they say of you, "You devour your own people,[*] you rob your nation of its children,"[t] [14]therefore, you shall never again devour your people or rob your nation of its children—oracle of the Lord GOD. [15]I will no longer make you listen to the reproach of nations. You will never again endure insults from the peoples. Never again shall you rob your nation of its children—oracle of the Lord GOD.

**Regeneration of the People.** [16]The word of the LORD came to me: [17]Son of man, when the house of Israel lived in its land, they defiled it with their behavior and their deeds. In my sight their behavior was like the impurity of a woman in menstruation.[u] [18]So I poured out my fury

upon them for the blood they poured out on the ground and for the idols with which they defiled it. [19]I scattered them among the nations, and they were dispersed through other lands; according to their behavior and their deeds I carried out judgment against them.[v] [20†]But when they came to the nations, where they went, they desecrated my holy name, for people said of them: "These are the people of the LORD, yet they had to leave their land." [21]So I relented because of my holy name which the house of Israel desecrated among the nations to which they came. [22]Therefore say to the house of Israel: Thus says the Lord GOD: Not for your sake do I act, house of Israel, but for the sake of my holy name, which you desecrated among the nations to which you came.[w] [23]But I will show the holiness of my great name, desecrated among the nations, in whose midst you desecrated it. Then the nations shall know that I am the LORD—oracle of the Lord GOD—when through you I show my holiness before their very eyes.[x] [24]I will take you away from among the nations, gather you from all the lands, and bring you back to your own soil. [25‡]I will sprinkle clean water over you to make you clean; from all your impurities and from all your idols I will cleanse you. [26]I will give you a new heart, and a new spirit I will put within you. I will remove the heart of stone from your flesh and give you a heart of flesh.[a] [27]I will put my spirit within you so that you walk in my statutes, observe my ordinances, and keep them.[b] [28]You will live in the land I gave to your ancestors; you will be my people, and I will be your God.[c] [29]I will deliver you from all your impurities. I will summon the grain and make it plentiful; I will not send famine against you. [30]I will increase the fruit on your trees and the crops in your fields so that you no longer endure reproach from the nations because of famine.[d] [31]Then you will remember your evil behavior and your deeds that were not good; you will loathe yourselves for your sins and your abominations. [32]Not for your sake do I act—oracle of the Lord GOD. Let this be known to you! Be ashamed and humbled because of your behavior, house of Israel.

---

†[36:20–24] These verses make clear that Israel's restoration is God's initiative, independent of the people's shame and repentance (v. 31). By their wickedness, Israel provoked the exile; its presence among the nations gave the impression that God could not protect his people. God's gracious return of Israel to its land will restore his honor among these same nations.

‡[36:25–26] God's initiative to cleanse Israel (cf. 24:13–14) is the first act in the creation of a new people, no longer disposed to repeating Israel's wicked past (chap. 20). To make this restoration permanent, God replaces Israel's rebellious and obdurate interiority ("heart of stone") with an interiority ("heart of flesh") susceptible to and animated by God's intentions ("my spirit," v. 27).

---

*[36:13] **You devour your own people**: i.e., the land destroys its own population; this phrase also occurs in Nm 13:32, where Israelite spies describe Canaan as "a land that devours its inhabitants."

---

n. [36:3] Ob 13.   o. [36:4] cf. Ez 6:3.   p. [36:8] Lv 26:3–5.   q. [36:9] Lv 26:9.   r. [36:10] Is 49:8, 17–23.   s. [36:11] cf. Gn 1:22, 28.   t. [36:13] Nm 13:32.   u. [36:17] Ps 106:37–38.

v. [36:19] Lv 18:24–28.   w. [36:22] cf. Ez 20:44; Dt 9:4–6; Is 37:35.   x. [36:23] cf. Ez 20:41; Is 37:23.   y. [36:25] Ezr 6:21; Ps 51:2–7.   z. [36:26–27] Jer 31:33–34.   a. [36:26] cf. Rom 8:5–8.   b. [36:27] Ps 51:7–11.   c. [36:28] Jer 30:22; 31:33.   d. [36:30] Lv 26:4–5.

<sup>33</sup>Thus says the Lord GOD: When I cleanse you of all your guilt, I will resettle the cities and the ruins will be rebuilt.<sup>e 34</sup>The desolate land will be tilled—once a wasteland in the eyes of every passerby. <sup>35</sup>They will say, "This once-desolate land has become like the garden of Eden. The cities once ruined, laid waste and destroyed, are now resettled and fortified."<sup>f 36</sup>Then the surrounding nations that remain shall know that I, the LORD, have rebuilt what was destroyed and replanted what was desolate. I, the LORD, have spoken: I will do it. <sup>37</sup>Thus says the Lord GOD: This also I will be persuaded to do for the house of Israel: to multiply them like sheep. <sup>38</sup>Like sheep for sacrifice, like the sheep of Jerusalem on its feast days, the ruined cities shall be filled with flocks of people; then they shall know that I am the LORD.<sup>g</sup>

## CHAPTER 37

**Vision of the Dry Bones.**<sup>*</sup> <sup>1</sup>The hand of the LORD came upon me, and he led me out in the spirit of the LORD and set me in the center of the broad valley. It was filled with bones. <sup>2</sup>He made me walk among them in every direction. So many lay on the surface of the valley! How dry they were! <sup>3</sup>He asked me: Son of man, can these bones come back to life? "Lord GOD," I answered, "you alone know that."<sup>h 4</sup>Then he said to me: Prophesy over these bones, and say to them: Dry bones, hear the word of the LORD! <sup>5</sup>Thus says the Lord GOD to these bones: Listen! I will make breath enter you so you may come to life. <sup>6</sup>I will put sinews on you, make flesh grow over you, cover you with skin, and put breath into you so you may come to life. Then you shall know that I am the LORD. <sup>7</sup>I prophesied as I had been commanded. A sound started up, as I was prophesying, rattling like thunder. The bones came together, bone joining to bone. <sup>8</sup>As I watched, sinews appeared on them, flesh grew over them, skin covered them on top, but there was no breath in them. <sup>9</sup>Then he said to me: Prophesy to the breath, prophesy, son of man! Say to the breath: Thus says the Lord GOD: From the four winds come, O breath, and breathe into these slain that they may come to life.<sup>†i 10</sup>I prophesied as he commanded me, and

the breath entered them; they came to life and stood on their feet, a vast army.<sup>j 11</sup>He said to me: Son of man, these bones are the whole house of Israel! They are saying, "Our bones are dried up, our hope is lost, and we are cut off." <sup>12</sup>Therefore, prophesy and say to them: Thus says the Lord GOD: Look! I am going to open your graves; I will make you come up out of your graves, my people, and bring you back to the land of Israel.<sup>k 13</sup>You shall know that I am the LORD, when I open your graves and make you come up out of them, my people! <sup>14</sup>I will put my spirit in you that you may come to life, and I will settle you in your land. Then you shall know that I am the LORD. I have spoken; I will do it—oracle of the LORD.<sup>l</sup>

**The Two Sticks.** <sup>15*</sup>Thus the word of the LORD came to me: <sup>16</sup>As for you, son of man, take one stick and write on it, "Judah and those Israelites associated with it." Then take another stick and write on it: "Joseph, Ephraim's stick, and the whole house of Israel associated with it." <sup>17</sup>Join the two sticks together so they become one stick in your hand. <sup>18</sup>When your people ask you, "Will you not tell us what you mean by all this?" <sup>19</sup>answer them: Thus says the Lord GOD: I will take the stick of Joseph, now in Ephraim's hand, and the tribes of Israel associated with it, and join to it the stick of Judah, making them one stick; they shall become one in my hand.<sup>m</sup> <sup>20</sup>The sticks on which you write, you must hold in your hand in their sight. <sup>21</sup>Say to them: Thus says the Lord GOD: I will soon take the Israelites from among the nations to which they have gone and gather them from all around to bring them back to their land. <sup>22</sup>I will make them one nation in the land, upon the mountains of Israel, and there shall be one king for them all. They shall never again be two nations, never again be divided into two kingdoms.<sup>n</sup>

<sup>23</sup>No longer shall they defile themselves with their idols, their abominations, and all their transgressions. I will deliver them from all their apostasy through which they sinned. I will cleanse them so that they will be my people, and I will be their God.<sup>o 24p</sup>David my servant shall be king over them; they shall all have one shepherd. They shall walk in my ordinances, observe my statutes, and keep them. <sup>25</sup>They shall live on the land I gave to Jacob my servant, the land where their ancestors lived; they shall live on it always, they, their children, and their children's

---

<sup>*</sup>[37:1–14] This account is a figurative description of God's creation of a new Israel. Even though that creation begins with the remains of the old Israel, the exiles under the image of dry bones, depicting a totally hopeless situation, the new Israel is radically different: it is an ideal people, shaped by God's spirit to live the covenant faithfully, something the old Israel, exiles included, were unable to do. While this passage in its present context is not about the doctrine of individual or communal resurrection, many Jewish and Christian commentators suggest that the doctrine is foreshadowed here.

<sup>†</sup>[37:9] The Hebrew word *rûah* has multiple related meanings expressed by different English words: wind, spirit, breath. In this translation, *rûah* is rendered "spirit," a powerful force that creates vision and insight (v. 1); "breath," physical energy

that quickens and enlivens (vv. 5–6); "wind," invisible physical energy, sometimes destructive, sometimes invigorating (e.g., the rain-bearing winter winds), also a metaphor for restoration and new life (vv. 9–10); "my spirit," a share in God's power so the people observe the law that assures them life in the land (v. 14).

<sup>‡</sup>[37:15–22] The symbolic action of joining two sticks into one continues Ezekiel's description of God's future saving action: the unification of Judah and Israel under an ideal ruler.

j. [37:10] cf. Rev 11:11.   k. [37:12] Is 26:19; Jer 19:14.   l. [37:14] cf. Ez 36:27–28; Jer 43:2; Jl 3:1–2.   m. [37:19] Zec 10:6.   n. [37:22] cf. Ez 17:22; 34:13–14.   o. [37:23] cf. Ez 11:18; 36:28; Na 2:2.   p. [37:24] Ps 78:70–71; Is 55:4.

e. [36:33] Lv 26:31.   f. [36:35] cf. Ez 28:13; 31:9.   g. [36:38] 1 Kgs 8:63.   h. [37:3] Is 26:19.   i. [37:9] Ps 104:30; Is 32:15; Dn 7:2.

children, with David my servant as their prince forever. [26q]I will make a covenant of peace with them; it shall be an everlasting covenant with them. I will multiply them and put my sanctuary among them forever. [27]My dwelling shall be with them; I will be their God, and they will be my people.[r] [28]Then the nations shall know that I, the LORD, make Israel holy, by putting my sanctuary among them forever.

## CHAPTER 38

**First Prophecy Against Gog.** [1]The word of the LORD came to me: [2]Son of man, turn your face against Gog[†] of the land of Magog, the chief prince of Meshech and Tubal, and prophesy against him.[s] [3]Say: Thus says the Lord GOD: See! I am coming against you, Gog, chief prince of Meshech and Tubal. [4]I will turn you around and put hooks in your jaws to lead you out with all your army, horses and riders, all well armed, a great company, all of them with bucklers and shields, carrying swords: [5]Persia, Cush, and Put with them, all with shields and helmets; [6]Gomer and all its troops, Beth-togarmah from the recesses of Zaphon and all its troops—many nations will accompany you. [7]Prepare and get ready, you and the company mobilized for you, but in my service. [8]After many days you will be called to battle; in the last years you will invade a land that has survived the sword—a people gathered from many nations back to the long-deserted mountains of Israel, brought forth from the nations to dwell securely.[u] [9]You shall come up like a sudden storm, covering the land like a cloud, you and all your troops and the many nations with you.[v]

[10]Thus says the Lord GOD: On that day thoughts shall cross your mind, and you shall devise an evil plan. [11]You will say, "I will invade a land of open villages and attack a peaceful people who live in security—all of them living without city walls, bars, or gates"—[w] [12]in order to plunder and pillage, turning your hand against resettled ruins, against a people gathered from the nations, a people whose concern is cattle and goods, dwelling at the center[‡] of the earth.

[13]Sheba and Dedan, the merchants of Tarshish and all its "young lions" shall ask you: "Have you come here to plunder? Have you summoned your army for pillage, to carry off silver and gold, to take away cattle and goods, to seize much plunder?"[x]

**Second Prophecy Against Gog.** [14]Therefore, prophesy, son of man, and say to Gog: Thus says the Lord GOD: On that day, when my people Israel dwell securely, will you not take action, [15]leaving your base in the recesses of Zaphon,[§] you and many nations with you, all mounted on horses, a great company, a mighty army?[y] [16]You shall rise up over my people Israel like a cloud covering the land. In those last days, I will let you invade my land so that the nations acknowledge me, when in their sight I show my holiness through you, Gog.

[17]Thus says the Lord GOD: About you I spoke in earlier times through my servants, the prophets of Israel, who prophesied at that time that I would let you invade them. [18]But on that day, the day Gog invades the land of Israel—oracle of the Lord GOD—my fury will flare up in my anger, [19]and in my jealousy, with fiery wrath, I swear on that day there will be a great earthquake in the land of Israel.[z] [20]Before me will tremble the fish of the sea and the birds of the air, the beasts of the field and everything that crawls on the ground, and everyone on the face of the earth. Mountains will be overturned, terraces will collapse, and every wall will fall to the ground.[a] [21]Against him I will summon every terror—oracle of the Lord GOD; every man's sword will be raised against his brother.[b] [22]I will execute judgment on him: disease and bloodshed; flooding rain and hailstones, fire and brimstone, I will rain down on him, on his troops and on the many nations with him.[c] [23]And so I will show my greatness and holiness and make myself known in the sight of many nations. Then they shall know that I am the LORD.[d]

## CHAPTER 39

**Third Prophecy Against Gog.** [1]You, son of man, prophesy against Gog, saying: Thus says the Lord GOD: Here I am, Gog, coming at you, chief prince of Meshech and Tubal. [2]I will turn you around, even though I urged you on and brought you up from the recesses of Zaphon and let you attack the mountains of Israel.[e] [3]Then I will strike the bow from your left hand and make the arrows drop from your right. [4]Upon the mountains of Israel you shall fall, you and all your troops and the peoples with you. I will give you as food to birds of prey of every kind

---

*[38:1–39:20] These three oracles against Gog (38:2–13; 14–23; 39:1–20) describe a mythic attack of God against a final enemy of his people sometime in the future. Like the oracles against the nations, their purpose is to strengthen Israel's hope in God, since they end with God's triumph on behalf of the people.

†[38:2] **Gog:** the name is symbolic, probably derived from Gyges, king of Lydia. The gloss Magog may be an Akkadian expression, *mat-Gog*, "the land of Gog." Meshech and Tubal, as well as Gomer and Beth-togarmah (v. 6), were countries around the Black Sea, the northernmost countries known to the Israelites. The north was the traditional direction from which invasion was expected; cf. Jer 1:13–15.

‡[38:12] **Center:** lit., "navel." Many ancient peoples spoke of their own homelands as "the navel," that is, the center of the earth.

§[38:15] **Zaphon:** cf. note on Jb 37:22.

---

q. [37:26] Gn 9:16; Nm 25:12; Heb 13:20.   r. [37:27] Lv 26:11.
s. [38:2] cf. Gn 10:2; Ez 27:13.   t. [38:5–6] Gn 10:2–3, 6.   u. [38:8]
Is 24:22.   v. [38:9] Is 25:4; Jer 4:13; Rev 20:8.   w. [38:11] Zec 2:4–5.

x. [38:13] Gn 10:4, 7.   y. [38:15] cf. Ez 39:2.   z. [38:19] Is 24:18; Rev
6:12.   a. [38:20] Is 42:15.   b. [38:21] Is 34:5–6; 66:16.   c. [38:22]
cf. Rev 9:17; 16:21.   d. [38:23] Rev 20:8.   e. [39:2] cf. Ez 32:30;
38:6, 15.

and to wild beasts to be eaten. [5]In the open field you shall fall, for I have spoken—oracle of the Lord God.[f]

[6]I will send fire against Magog and against those who live securely on the seacoast, and they will know that I am the Lord.[g] [7]I will reveal my holy name among my people Israel, and I will never again allow my holy name to be defiled. Then the nations shall know that I am the Lord, the Holy One of Israel.[h] [8]Yes, it is coming! It shall happen—oracle of the Lord God. This is the day I decreed.

[9]Everyone living in the cities of Israel shall go out and set fire to the weapons, buckler and shield, bows and arrows, clubs and spears; for seven years they shall make fires with them.[i] [10]They will not need to bring in wood from the fields or cut down trees in the forests, for they will make fires with the weapons, plundering those who plundered them, pillaging those who pillaged them—oracle of the Lord God.

[11]On that day I will give Gog a place for his tomb in Israel, the Valley of Abarim,[*] east of the sea. It will block the way of travelers. There Gog shall be buried with all his horde; it shall be called "Valley of Hamon-Gog."[j] [12]For seven months the house of Israel shall bury them in order to cleanse the land. [13]All the people of the land shall take part in the burials, making a name for themselves on the day I am glorified—oracle of the Lord God. [14]Men shall be permanently assigned to pass through the land, burying those who lie unburied in order to cleanse the land. For seven months they shall keep searching. [15]When these pass through the land and see a human bone, they must set up a marker beside it, until the gravediggers bury it in the Valley of Hamon-Gog. [16]Also the name of the city is Hamonah. Thus the land will be cleansed.

[17]As for you, son of man, thus says the Lord God: Say to birds of every kind and to every wild beast: "Assemble! Come from all sides for the sacrifice I am making for you, a great slaughter on the mountains of Israel. You shall eat flesh and drink blood! [18]You shall eat the flesh of warriors and drink the blood of the princes of the earth: rams, lambs, and goats, bulls and fatlings from Bashan, all of them.[k] [19]From the sacrifice I slaughtered for you, you shall eat fat until you are sated and drink blood until you are drunk. [20]At my table you shall be sated with horse and rider, with warrior and soldier of every kind—oracle of the Lord God.

**Israel's Return.** [21]Then I will display my glory among the nations, and all the nations will see

the judgment I executed, the hand I laid upon them. [22]From that day forward the house of Israel shall know that I am the Lord, their God. [23]The nations shall know that the house of Israel went into exile because of its sins. Because they betrayed me, I hid my face from them, handing them over to their foes, so they all fell by the sword.[l] [24]According to their defilement and their crimes I dealt with them, hiding my face from them.[m]

[25]Therefore, thus says the Lord God: Now I will restore the fortunes of Jacob and take pity on the whole house of Israel; I am zealous for my holy name.[n] [26]They will forget their shame and all the infidelities they committed against me when they live securely on their own land with no one to frighten them. [27]When I bring them back from the nations and gather them from the lands of their enemies, I will show my holiness through them in the sight of many nations.[o] [28]Thus they shall know that I, the Lord, am their God, since I who exiled them among the nations will gather them back to their land, not leaving any of them behind. [29]I will no longer hide my face from them once I pour out my spirit upon the house of Israel—oracle of the Lord God.[p]

# V. THE NEW ISRAEL[†]

## The New Temple

## CHAPTER 40

**The Man with a Measure.** [1]In the twenty-fifth year of our exile, at the beginning of the year, on the tenth day of the month, fourteen years after the city had been captured, on that very day the hand of the Lord came upon me and brought me back there.[q] [2]In a divine vision he brought me to the land of Israel, where he set me down on a very high mountain. In front of me, there was something like a city built on it.[r] [3]He brought me there, and there standing in the gateway was a man whose appearance was like bronze! He held in his hand a linen cord and a measuring rod.[s] [4]The man said to me, "Son of man, look carefully and listen intently. Pay strict attention to everything I show you, for you have been brought here so that I might show it

---

†[40:1–48:35] This lengthy vision of a new Temple and a restored Israel is dated in v. 1 to April 28, 573 B.C. The literary form of the vision is sometimes compared to a mandala, a sacred model through which one can move symbolically to reach the world of the divine. Ezekiel describes the Temple through its boundaries, entrances, and exits in chaps. 40–43; by its sacred and profane use and space in 44–46; and by its central place within the land itself in 47–48. The prophet could not have expected a literal fulfillment of much of what he described. The passage doubtless went through several editorial stages, both from the prophet and from later writers.

---

*[39:11] **The Valley of Abarim**: in the Abarim mountains, east of the Jordan. "Abarim" plays on the word *oberim*, "travelers." Hamon-Gog: "the horde of Gog."

f. [39:5] cf. Ez 32:4.   g. [39:6] Rev 20:9.   h. [39:7] Is 12:6.   i. [39:9] Ps 46:9; 76:3.   j. [39:11] cf. Ez 38:2.   k. [39:18] Jer 51:40; Rev 19:17–21.

l. [39:23] Ps 30:7; Is 54:8.   m. [39:24] 2 Kgs 17:23.   n. [39:25] Is 27:13.   o. [39:27] cf. Ez 20:41.   p. [39:29] cf. Ez 37:9; Is 11:2.   q. [40:1] 2 Kgs 25:7; Jer 39:1–10; 52:4–11.   r. [40:2] Is 2:2; Mi 4:1; Zec 14:10; cf. Rev 21:10.   s. [40:3] Zec 2:1–2; Rev 1:15; 11:1; 21:15.

to you. Then you must tell the house of Israel everything you see." ⁵There an outer wall completely surrounded the temple. The measuring rod in the man's hand was six cubits long, each cubit being a cubit plus a handbreadth;* he measured the width of the structure, one rod, and its height, one rod.

**The East Gate.†** ⁶Going to the gate facing east, he climbed its steps and measured the threshold of the outer gateway as one rod wide.ᵗ ⁷Each cell was one rod long and one rod wide, and there were five cubits between the cells; the threshold of the inner gateway adjoining the vestibule of the gate facing the temple was one rod wide. ⁸He also measured the vestibule of the inner gate, ⁹eight cubits, and its posts, two cubits each. The vestibule faced the inside. ¹⁰On each side of the east gatehouse were three cells, all the same size; their posts were all the same size. ¹¹He measured the width of the gate's entryway, ten cubits, and the length of the gate itself, thirteen cubits. ¹²The borders in front of the cells on both sides were one cubit, while the cells themselves measured six cubits by six cubits from one opening to the next. ¹³Next he measured the gatehouse from the back wall of one cell to the back wall of the cell on the opposite side through the openings facing each other, a width of twenty-five cubits. ¹⁴All around the courtyard of the gatehouse were posts six cubits high. ¹⁵From the front of the gatehouse at its outer entry to the gateway of the porch facing inward, the length was fifty cubits. ¹⁶There were recessed windows in the cells on all sides and in the posts on the inner side of the gate. Posts and windows were all around the inside, with palm trees decorating the posts.ᵘ

**The Outer Court.** ¹⁷Then he brought me to the outer court,‡ where there were chambers and pavement laid all around the courtyard: thirty chambers facing the pavement.ᵛ ¹⁸The pavement lay alongside the gatehouses, the same length as the gates; this was the lower pavement. ¹⁹He measured the length of the pavement from the front of the lower gate to the outside of the inner gate, one hundred cubits. He then moved from the east to the north side.

**The North Gate.** ²⁰He measured the length and width of the north gate of the outer courtyard. ²¹Its cells, three on each side, its posts, and its vestibule had the same measurements as those

of the first gate, fifty cubits long and twenty-five cubits wide. ²²Its windows, its vestibule, and its palm decorations had the same proportions as those of the gate facing east. Seven steps led up to it, and its vestibule faced the inside. ²³The inner court had a gate opposite the north gate, just as at the east gate; he measured one hundred cubits from one gate to the other.

**The South Gate.** ²⁴Then he led me to the south. There, too, facing south, was a gate! He measured its posts and vestibule; they were the same size as the others. ²⁵The gate and its vestibule had windows on both sides, like the other windows, fifty cubits long and twenty-five cubits wide. ²⁶Seven steps led up to it, its vestibule faced inside; and palms decorated each of the posts opposite one another. ²⁷The inner court also had a gate facing south. He measured it from gate to gate, facing south, one hundred cubits.

**Gates of the Inner Court.§** ²⁸Then he brought me to the inner courtyard by the south gate, where he measured the south gateway; its measurements were the same as the others. ²⁹Its cells, posts, and vestibule were the same size as the others, fifty cubits long and twenty-five cubits wide. ³⁰¶The vestibules all around were twenty-five cubits long and five cubits wide. ³¹Its vestibule faced the outer court; palms decorated its posts, and its stairway had eight steps. ³²Then he brought me to the inner courtyard on the east and measured the gate there; its dimensions were the same as the others. ³³Its cells, posts, and vestibule were the same size as the others. The gate and its vestibule had windows on both sides, fifty cubits long and twenty-five cubits wide. ³⁴Its vestibule faced the outer court, palms decorated the posts opposite each other, and it had a stairway of eight steps. ³⁵Then he brought me to the north gate,ʷ where he measured the dimensions ³⁶of its cells, posts, and vestibule; they were the same. The gate and its vestibule had windows on both sides, fifty cubits long and twenty-five cubits wide. ³⁷Its vestibule faced the outer court; palm trees decorated its posts opposite each other, and it had a stairway of eight steps.

**Side Rooms.** ³⁸There was a chamber opening off the vestibule of the gate where burnt offerings were washed.ˣ ³⁹In the vestibule of the gate there were two tables on either side for slaughtering the burnt offerings, purification offerings, and reparation offerings.ʸ ⁴⁰Two more tables stood along the wall of the vestibule by the entrance of the north gate, and two tables on the other

---

*[40:5] **A cubit plus a handbreadth**: a great cubit. The ordinary cubit consisted of six handbreadths; the great cubit, of seven. In measuring the Temple, a rod six great cubits long was used. The ordinary cubit was about one and a half feet, or, more exactly, 17.5 inches; the large cubit, 20.4 inches.

†[40:6–16] The gate facing east, leading into the outer court of the Temple, is described more fully than the north and south gates, which, however, have the same dimensions. On the west side of the outer court there is a large building instead of a gate (cf. 41:12).

‡[40:17] **The outer court**: the court outside the Temple area proper, which had its own inner court (vv. 28–37).

§[40:28–37] The gates leading into the inner court of the Temple area correspond to the gates leading into the outer court, with the exception that their vestibules are on the outer rather than the inner side.

¶[40:30] The reference to vestibules all around is uncertain, and the verse may have arisen as a partial repetition of v. 29.

---

t. [40:6] cf. Ez 8:16.   u. [40:16] 1 Kgs 6:29, 32, 35.   v. [40:17] cf. Ez 41:6; 42:1.

w. [40:35] cf. Ez 44:4; 47:2.   x. [40:38] 2 Chr 4:6.   y. [40:39] cf. Ez 46:2.

side of the vestibule of the gate. [41]There were thus four tables on one side of the gate and four tables on the other side, eight tables in all, for slaughtering. [42]The four tables for burnt offerings were made of cut stone, one and a half cubits long, one and a half cubits wide, and one cubit high; the instruments used for slaughtering burnt offerings and other sacrifices were kept [43]on shelves the width of one hand, fixed all around the room; but on the tables themselves was the meat for the sacrifices. [44]Outside the inner gatehouse there were two rooms on the inner courtyard, one beside the north gate, facing south, and the other beside the south gate, facing north. [45]He said to me, "This chamber facing south is reserved for the priests who have charge of the temple area, [46]while this chamber facing north is reserved for the priests who have charge of the altar; they are the sons of Zadok,* the only Levites who may come near to minister to the LORD." [47]He measured the courtyard, a square one hundred cubits long and a hundred cubits wide, with the altar standing in front of the temple.[z]

**The Temple Building.**[†] [48a]Then he brought me into the vestibule of the temple and measured the posts, five cubits on each side. The gateway was fourteen cubits wide, its side walls three cubits. [49]The vestibule was twenty cubits long and twelve cubits wide; ten steps led up to it, and there were columns by the posts, one on each side.

# CHAPTER 41

[1]Then he brought me to the nave and measured the posts; each was six cubits wide.[b] [2]The width of the entrance was ten cubits, and the walls on either side measured five cubits. He measured the nave, forty cubits long and twenty cubits wide.

[3]Then he went inside and measured the posts at the other entrance, two cubits wide. The entrance was six cubits wide, with walls seven cubits long on each side. [4]Next he measured the length and width of the room beyond the nave, twenty cubits long and twenty cubits wide. He said to me, "This is the holy of holies."[‡c]

[5]Then he measured the wall of the temple, six cubits wide, and the width of the side chambers stretching all around the temple, four cubits each. [6§]There were thirty side chambers,

chamber upon chamber in three stories; terraces on the outside wall of the temple enclosing the side chambers provided support, but there were no supports for the temple wall itself. [7]A broad passageway led up the side chambers, for the house was enclosed all the way up and all the way around. Thus the temple was widened by the ascent that went from the lowest story through the middle one to the highest story.[d] [8]I saw a raised platform all around the temple, the foundation for all the side chambers; the width of this terrace was a full rod, six cubits. [9]The width of the outside wall enclosing the side chambers was five cubits. There was an open space between the side chambers of the temple [10]and the other chambers that measured twenty cubits around the temple on all sides. [11]The side chambers had entrances to the open space, one entrance on the north and the other on the south. The width of the wall surrounding the open space was five cubits. [12]The building¶ opposite the restricted area on the west side was seventy cubits long and ninety cubits wide, with walls five cubits thick all around it. [13]Thus he measured the temple, one hundred cubits long. The restricted area, its building and walls, measured a hundred cubits in length. [14]The temple facade, along with the restricted area to the east, was also one hundred cubits wide. [15]He measured the building opposite the restricted area which was behind it, together with its terraces on both sides, one hundred cubits.

**Interior of the Temple.** The inner nave and the outer vestibule [16]were paneled; the windows had recesses and precious wood trim around all three sides except the sill. Paneling covered the walls from the floor up to the windows and even the window sections.[e] [17]Even above the doorway and in the inner part of the temple and outside as well, around all the walls inside and out, [18]were figures of cherubim and palm trees: a palm tree between each pair of cherubim. Each cherub had two faces:[f] [19]the face of a human being looked toward one palm tree and the face of a lion looked toward the other palm tree. Thus the figures covered all the walls around the temple. [20]From the floor to the lintel of the door, cherubim and palm trees decorated the walls. [21]The nave had a square door frame, and inside facing the holy place was something that looked like [22]a wooden altar,** three cubits high, two cubits long, and two cubits wide. It had corners and a wooden base and sides. He said to me, "This is the table that stands before the LORD."[g]

---

*[40:46] **Sons of Zadok**: descendants of the priestly line of Zadok; cf. 2 Sm 15:24–29; 1 Kgs 1:32–34; 2:35.

†[40:48–41:15] The description of Ezekiel's visionary Temple closely follows the description of the Temple of Solomon (1 Kgs 6), along with some crucial differences.

‡[40:49–41:4] **Vestibule . . . nave . . . holy of holies**: the three divisions of the Temple building in progressing order of sanctity. The last is called "the inner sanctuary" in 1 Kgs 6.

§[41:6] The description of the three stories of rooms surrounding the Temple building can be compared with

Solomon's Temple in 1 Kgs 6:6; there a step-like or terraced retaining wall supported the Temple building so no beams or nails from these chambers would enter the Temple wall itself.

¶[41:12] **The building**: the function of this structure behind the Temple is never specified.

**[41:22] **A wooden altar**: the altar of incense, standing in the nave at the entrance to the holy of holies.

---

z. [40:47] cf. Ez 41:13–14; 43:14–17.   a. [40:48] 1 Kgs 6:2.   b. [41:1] 1 Kgs 6:3–5.   c. [41:4] 1 Kgs 6:20; cf. Ex 26:33; Heb 9:3–8.

d. [41:7] 1 Kgs 6:8.   e. [41:16] 1 Kgs 6:4, 15.   f. [41:18] 1 Kgs 6:18, 29; 7:36.   g. [41:22] Ex 25:23; Lv 24:5–9.

[23]The nave had a double door,[h] and the holy place [24]also had a double door; each door had two sections that could move; two sections on one door, and two on the other.[i] [25]Cherubim and palm trees decorated the doors of the nave like the decoration on the walls. Outside a wooden lattice faced the vestibule. [26]There were recessed windows and palm trees on the side walls of the vestibule. The side chambers of the temple also had latticework.

## CHAPTER 42

**Other Structures.** [1]Then he led me north to the outer court, bringing me to some chambers on the north side opposite the restricted area and the north building.[j] [2]They were a hundred cubits long on the north side and fifty cubits wide. [3]Built in rows at three different levels, they stood between the twenty cubits of the inner court and the pavement of the outer court. [4]In front of the chambers was a walkway ten cubits wide on the inside of a wall one cubit wide. The doorways faced north. [5]The upper chambers were shorter because they lost space to the lower and middle tiers of the building. [6]Because they were in three tiers, they did not have foundations like the court, but were set back from the lower and middle levels from the ground up. [7]The outside walls ran parallel to the chambers along the outer court, a length of fifty cubits. [8]The chambers facing the outer court were fifty cubits long; thus the wall along the nave was a hundred cubits. [9]At the base of these chambers, there was an entryway from the east so that one could enter from the outer court [10]where the wall of the court began.

To the south along the side of the restricted area and the building there were also chambers [11]with a walkway in front of them. They looked like the chambers on the north side in length and width, in their exits, their design, and their doorways. [12]At the base of the chambers on the south side there was an entry at the end of a walkway in front of the protective wall by which one could enter from the east. [13]He said to me, "The north and south chambers facing the restricted area are the chambers of the holy place where the priests who approach the LORD shall eat the most holy meals. Here they shall place the most holy offerings: the grain offerings, the purification offerings, and the reparation offerings; for the place is holy.[†k] [14]When the priests have entered, they must not go out again from the holy place into the outer court without leaving the garments in which they ministered because

they are holy. They shall put on other garments before approaching the area for the people."[l]

**Measuring the Outer Court.** [15]When he finished measuring the interior of the temple area, he brought me out by way of the gate facing east and measured all around it. [16]He measured the east side, five hundred cubits by his measuring rod. Then he turned [17]and measured the north side: five hundred cubits by his measuring rod. He turned [18]and measured the south side, five hundred cubits by his measuring rod. He turned and measured the west side, also five hundred cubits by his measuring rod. [20]Thus he measured it on the four sides. It was surrounded by a wall five hundred cubits long and five hundred cubits wide, to separate the sacred from the profane.

*Restoration of the Temple*

## CHAPTER 43

**The Glory of the Lord Returns.** [1]Then he led me to the gate facing east,[m] [2]and there was the glory of the God of Israel coming from the east! His voice was like the roar of many waters, and the earth shone with his glory. [3]The vision I saw was like the vision I had seen when he came to destroy the city and like the vision I had seen by the river Chebar—I fell on my face. [4]The glory of the LORD entered the temple by way of the gate facing east.[n] [5]Then the spirit lifted me up and brought me to the inner court. And there the glory of the LORD filled the temple![o] [6]I heard someone speaking to me from the temple, but the man was standing beside me. [7]The voice said to me: Son of man, do you see the place for my throne, and the place for the soles of my feet? Here I will dwell among the Israelites forever. The house of Israel, neither they nor their kings, will never again defile my holy name, with their prostitutions and the corpses of their kings at their death.[p] [8]When they placed their threshold against my threshold[‡] and their doorpost next to mine, with only a wall between me and them, they defiled my holy name by the abominations they committed, and I devoured them in my wrath.[q] [9]From now on, let them put their prostitution and the corpses of their kings far from me, and I will dwell in their midst forever.[r]

**The Law of the Temple.** [10]As for you, son of man, describe the temple to the house of Israel so they are ashamed for their sins. Let them measure its layout. [11]If they are ashamed for all

---

‡[43:8] **They placed their threshold against my threshold**: in preexilic Jerusalem, the Temple and the palace belonged to the same complex of buildings; kings like Ahaz and Manasseh treated it as their private chapel for the religious practices Ezekiel condemns. In the new Israel the Temple is free, even spatially, from civil jurisdiction; cf. 45:7–8. This is an instance of Ezekiel's broader program to separate the sacred from the secular.

---

*[42:5–6] The three rows of identical chambers, on different ground levels, necessarily had roofs on correspondingly different levels.

†[42:13] The function of these chambers is explained again in 46:19–20.

---

h. [41:23] 1 Kgs 6:32.  i. [41:24] 1 Kgs 6:34.  j. [42:1] Ex 27:9.  k. [42:13] Lv 10:12–13, 17.

l. [42:14] Ex 29:9; Lv 8:7–9.  m. [43:1] 1 Chr 9:18.  n. [43:4] cf. Ez 10:19.  o. [43:5] cf. Ez 11:24.  p. [43:7] 1 Chr 28:2; Ps 132:7; Is 6:1; Jer 3:17.  q. [43:8] 1 Kgs 7:1–12.  r. [43:9] cf. Ez 37:26–28.

they have done, tell them about the layout and design of the temple, its exits and entrances, with all its regulations and instructions; write it down for them to see, that they may carefully observe all its laws and statutes. [12]This is the law for the temple: the entire area on top of the mountain all around will be a most holy place. This is the law for the temple.

**The Altar.** [13]These were the dimensions of the altar* in cubits, a cubit being one cubit plus a handbreadth. The channel was one cubit deep by one cubit wide, and its rim had a lip one span wide all around it.[s] The height of the altar itself was as follows: [14]from the channel at floor level up to the lower ledge was two cubits, with the ledge one cubit wide; from the lower ledge to the upper ledge, four cubits, with the ledge one cubit wide. [15]The altar hearth was four cubits high, and extending up from the top of the hearth were four horns. [16]The hearth was twelve cubits long and twelve cubits wide, a square with four equal sides. [17]The upper ledge was fourteen cubits long and fourteen cubits wide on all four sides. The rim around it was half a cubit, with a channel one cubit all around. The steps faced east.[t]

[18]Then he said to me: Son of man, thus says the Lord GOD: These are the statutes for the altar when it is set up for sacrificing burnt offerings and splashing blood on it.[u] [19]A young bull must be brought as a purification offering to the priests, the Levites descended from Zadok, who come near to serve me—oracle of the Lord GOD.[v] [20]You shall take some of its blood and smear it on the four horns of the altar, and on the four corners of the ledge, and all around its rim. Thus you shall purify and purge it.[w] [21]Then take the bull as purification offering and burn it in the appointed place outside the sanctuary.[x] [22]On the second day present an unblemished male goat as a purification offering, to purify the altar as you did with the bull. [23]When you have completed the purification,[y] you must bring an unblemished young bull and an unblemished ram from the flock [24]and present them before the LORD. The priests shall throw salt on them and sacrifice them as burnt offerings to the LORD. [25]Daily for seven days you shall give a male goat as a purification offering; and a young bull and a ram from the flock, all unblemished,[z] shall be offered [26]for seven days. Thus they shall purge the altar, in order to cleanse and dedicate it. [27]And when these days are over, from the eighth day on, the priests shall sacrifice

your burnt offerings and communion offerings on the altar. Then I will be pleased with you— oracle of the Lord GOD.

## CHAPTER 44

**The Closed Gate.** [1]Then he brought me back to the outer gate of the sanctuary facing east, but it was closed. [2]The LORD said to me: This gate must remain closed; it must not be opened, and no one should come through it. Because the LORD, the God of Israel, came through it, it must remain closed. [3]Only the prince may sit in it to eat a meal in the presence of the LORD; he must enter through the vestibule of the gate and leave the same way.[†a]

*The New Law*

**Admission to the Temple.** [4]Then he brought me by way of the north gate to the facade of the temple. I looked—and the glory of the LORD filled the LORD's house! I fell on my face.[b] [5]The LORD said to me: Son of man, pay close attention, look carefully, and listen intently to everything I tell you about all the statutes and laws of the LORD's house. Pay close attention to the entrance into the temple and all the exits of the sanctuary. [6]Say to that rebellious house, the house of Israel: Thus says the Lord GOD: Enough of all your abominations, house of Israel! [7]You have admitted foreigners, uncircumcised in heart and flesh, into my sanctuary to profane it when you offered me food, the fat and blood.[‡] Thus you have broken my covenant by all your abominations.[c] [8]Instead of caring for the service of my sanctuary, you appointed these foreigners to care for the service of my sanctuary. [9]Thus says the Lord GOD: No foreigners, uncircumcised in heart and flesh, shall ever enter my sanctuary: not even any of the foreigners who live among the Israelites.[d]

**Levites.** [10]As for the Levites who went far away from me when Israel strayed from me after their idols, they will bear the consequences of their sin. [11]They will serve in my sanctuary only as gatekeepers and temple servants; they will slaughter burnt offerings and sacrifices for the people. They will stand before the people to serve them.[e] [12]Because they used to serve them before their idols, thus becoming a stumbling

---

\*[43:13–17] **The altar**: like altars from Assyria and other parts of the ancient Near East, this altar has three parts: a base, a pedestal, and an upper block with a channel cut into the surface on all sides. The rim around the upper block (v. 17) stopped blood and other sacrificial material from falling to the ground.

s. [43:13] cf. Ex 20:24.  t. [43:17] Ex 20:26.  u. [43:18] Ex 29:16; Lv 4:6; 5:9.  v. [43:19] Lv 4:3.  w. [43:20] Lv 4:7.  x. [43:21] Ex 29:14; Lv 4:12; 8:17; cf. Heb 13:11–13.  y. [43:23] Ex 29:1.  z. [43:25] Ex 29:37; Lv 8:33.

†[44:3] Ezekiel imagines a scene like this: The prince stands at the eastern gate of the inner court while his sacrifice is being offered (46:2); he then goes to the vestibule of the outer court to eat the sacrificial meal. The closed outer gate on the eastern side signifies that the Lord has entered the Temple permanently, not to depart again.

‡[44:7–14] According to Ezekiel, the Levites' priestly role is reduced to the performance of menial tasks as punishment for their misdeeds (cf. vv. 10–14). This demotion was enforced during the restoration of Temple worship under Ezra and Nehemiah; this may explain the small number of Levites willing to return to Jerusalem after the exile.

a. [44:3] Ex 24:9–11; 2 Chr 26:16–20.  b. [44:4] Is 6:4; Rev 15:8.  c. [44:7] Lv 26:41.  d. [44:9] Jl 4:17; Neh 13:8.  e. [44:11] Nm 3:5–37; 1 Chr 26:12–19.

block to the house of Israel, therefore I have sworn an oath against them, says the Lord God, and they will bear the consequences of their sin. [13]They shall no longer come near to serve as my priests, nor shall they touch any of my sacred things or my most sacred offerings, for they must bear their shame, the abominations they committed. [14]Instead I will make them responsible for the service of the temple and all its work, for everything that must be done in it.[f]

**Priests.** [15]As for the levitical priests, sons of Zadok, who took charge of my sanctuary when the Israelites strayed from me, they may approach me to serve me and stand before me to offer the fat and the blood—oracle of the Lord God.[g] [16]They may enter my sanctuary; they may approach my table to serve me and carry out my service.[h] [17]Whenever they enter the gates of the inner court, they shall wear linen garments; they shall not put on anything woolen when they serve at the gates of the inner court or within the temple. [18]They shall have linen turbans on their heads and linen undergarments on their loins; they shall not gird themselves with anything that causes sweat. [19][j]And when they go out to the people in the outer court, they shall take off the garments in which they served and leave them in the rooms of the sanctuary, and put on other garments so they do not transmit holiness to the people[*] by their garments.

[20][k]They shall not shave their heads nor let their hair hang loose, but they shall keep their hair carefully trimmed. [21]No priest shall drink wine before he enters the inner court. [22][l]They shall not take as wives either widows or divorced women, but only unmarried women from the line of Israel; however, they may take as wives widows who are widows of priests. [23][m]They shall teach my people to distinguish between sacred and profane and make known to them the difference between clean and unclean. [24][n]In legal cases they shall stand as judges, judging according to my ordinances. They shall observe all my laws and statutes regarding all my appointed feasts, and they shall keep my sabbaths holy.

[25][o]They shall not make themselves unclean by going near a dead body; only for their father, mother, son, daughter, brother, or unmarried sister may they make themselves unclean. [26]After he is again clean, he must wait an additional seven days; [27]on the day he enters the inner court to serve in the sanctuary, he shall present a purification offering for himself—oracle of the

Lord God. [28][p]I will be their heritage: I am their heritage! You shall not give them any property in Israel, for I am their property! [29][q]They shall eat grain offerings, purification offerings, and reparation offerings; anything under the ban[†] in Israel belongs to them; [30][r]all the choicest first fruits of every kind and all the best of your offerings of every kind shall belong to the priests; the best of your dough you shall also give to the priests to bring a blessing upon your house. [31][s]The priests shall not eat anything, whether bird or animal, that died naturally or was killed by wild beasts.

## CHAPTER 45

**The Holy Portion.** [1]When you apportion the land heritage by heritage, you shall set apart a holy portion for the Lord, holier than the rest of the land—twenty-five thousand cubits long and twenty thousand cubits wide; the entire area shall be holy. [2]Of this land a square plot, five hundred by five hundred cubits, shall be assigned to the sanctuary, with fifty cubits of free space around it. [3]From this tract also measure off a length of twenty-five thousand cubits and a width of ten thousand cubits; on it the sanctuary, the holy of holies, shall stand. [4]This shall be the sacred part of the land belonging to the priests, the ministers of the sanctuary, who draw near to minister to the Lord; it shall be a place for their homes and an area set apart for the sanctuary. [5]There shall also be a strip twenty-five thousand cubits long and ten thousand wide for the Levites, the ministers of the temple, so they have cities to live in. [6]You shall assign a strip five thousand cubits wide and twenty-five thousand long as the property of the city parallel to the sacred tract; this shall belong to the whole house of Israel. [7]A section shall belong to the prince, bordering both sides of the sacred tract and city combined, extending westward on the west side and eastward on the east side, corresponding in length to one of the tribal portions from the west boundary to the east boundary [8]of the land. This shall be his property in Israel so that my princes will no longer oppress my people, but will leave the land to the house of Israel according to its tribes. [9]Thus says the Lord God: Enough, you princes of Israel! Put away violence and oppression, and do what is just and right! Stop evicting my people!—oracle of the Lord God.

**Weights and Measures.**[‡] [10][t]You shall have honest scales, an honest ephah, and an honest bath.

---

*[44:19] **Transmit holiness to the people**: holiness was considered to have a physical quality that could be communicated from person to person. It is a danger to those who have not prepared themselves to be in God's presence. The priests remove their ceremonial garments out of concern for the people.

f. [44:14] 1 Chr 23:28–32.   g. [44:15] 1 Chr 6:50–53.   h. [44:16] Lv 3:16–17.   i. [44:18] Ex 28:39, 42.   j. [44:19] Ex 39:27–29; Lv 6:10–11.   k. [44:20] Lv 21:5.   l. [44:22] Lv 21:7.   m. [44:23] Hg 2:10–13.   n. [44:24] Dt 17:8–9.   o. [44:25] Lv 21:1–4.

†[44:29] **Under the ban**: dedicated to the Lord.
‡[45:10–12] Besides the land monopoly fostered by royal greed and collusion with the wealthy (Mi 2:2; Is 3:12–15; 5:8–10), one grave social evil of preexilic Israel was dishonesty in business; cf. Hos 12:8; Am 8:5. **Ephah, bath**: see note on Is 5:10.

p. [44:28] Nm 18:23–24; Dt 18:1–2.   q. [44:29] Lv 6:16; 27:28.   r. [44:30] Nm 15:18–21; 18:12–13.   s. [44:31] Lv 11:39.   t. [45:10] Lv 19:35–36; Dt 25:13–16; Mi 6:10–12.

¹¹The ephah and the bath shall be the same size: the bath equal to one tenth of a homer, and the ephah equal to one tenth of a homer; their capacity is based on the homer. ¹²The shekel shall be twenty gerahs. Twenty shekels plus twenty-five shekels plus fifteen shekels make up a mina* for you.

**Offerings.** ¹³This is the offering you must make: one sixth of an ephah from each homer of wheat and one sixth of an ephah from each homer of barley. ¹⁴This is the regulation for oil: for every bath of oil, one tenth of a bath, computed by the kor,† made up of ten baths, that is, a homer, for ten baths make a homer. ¹⁵Also, one sheep from the flock for every two hundred from the pasture land of Israel, for the grain offering, the burnt offering, and communion offerings, to make atonement on their behalf—oracle of the Lord GOD.ᵘ ¹⁶All the people of the land shall be responsible for these offerings to the prince in Israel. ¹⁷It shall be the duty of the prince to provide burnt offerings, grain offerings, and libations on feast days, new moons, and sabbaths, on all the festivals of the house of Israel. He shall provide the purification offering, grain offering, burnt offering, and communion offerings, to make atonement on behalf of the house of Israel.ᵛ

**The Passover.** ¹⁸Thus says the Lord GOD: On the first day of the first month you shall take an unblemished young bull to purify the sanctuary.ʷ ¹⁹The priest shall take some of the blood from the purification offering and smear it on the doorposts of the house, on the four corners of the ledge of the altar, and on the doorposts of the gates of the inner courtyard.ˣ ²⁰You shall repeat this on the seventh day of the month for those who have sinned inadvertently or out of ignorance; thus you shall purge the temple.ʸ ²¹On the fourteenth day of the first month you shall observe the feast of Passover; for seven days unleavened bread must be eaten. ²²On that day the prince shall sacrifice, on his own behalf and on behalf of all the people of the land, a bull as a purification offering. ²³On each of the seven days of the feast he shall sacrifice, as a burnt offering to the LORD, seven bulls and seven rams without blemish, and as a purification offering he shall sacrifice one male goat each day.ᶻ ²⁴As a grain offering he shall offer one ephah for each bull and one ephah for each ram and one hin‡ of oil for each ephah.ᵃ

**The Feast of Booths.** ²⁵In the seventh month, on the fifteenth day of the seventh month, on the feast day and for the next seven days, he shall make the same offerings: the same purification offerings, burnt offerings, grain offerings, and offerings of oil.ᵇ

## CHAPTER 46

**Sabbaths.** ¹Thus says the Lord GOD: The gate of the inner court facing east shall remain closed throughout the six working days, but on the sabbath and on the day of the new moon it shall be open. ²ᵃThen the prince shall enter from outside by way of the vestibule of the gate and remain standing at the doorpost of the gateway while the priests sacrifice his burnt offerings and communion offerings; then he shall bow down in worship at the opening of the gate and leave. But the gate shall not be closed until evening. ³The people of the land also shall bow down in worship before the LORD at the opening of this gate on the sabbaths and new moons. ⁴The burnt offerings which the prince sacrifices to the LORD on the sabbath shall consist of six unblemished lambs and an unblemished ram, ⁵together with a grain offering of one ephah for the ram and whatever he pleases for the lambs, and a hin of oil for each ephah. ⁶ᶜOn the day of the new moon, he shall provide an unblemished young bull, six lambs, and a ram without blemish, ⁷with a grain offering of one ephah for the bull and an ephah for the ram, and for the lambs whatever he can, and for each ephah a hin of oil.ᵈ

**Ritual Laws.** ⁸When the prince enters, he shall always enter and depart by the vestibule of the gate. ⁹When the people of the land come before the LORD to bow down on the festivals, if they enter by the north gate they shall leave by the south gate, and if they enter by the south gate they shall leave by the north gate. They shall not go back by the gate through which they entered; everyone shall leave by the opposite gate. ¹⁰When they come in, the prince shall be with them; he shall also leave with them. ¹¹On feasts and festivals, the grain offering shall be an ephah for a bull, an ephah for a ram, but for the lambs whatever they please, and a hin of oil with each ephah. ¹²When the prince makes a freewill offering to the LORD, whether a burnt offering or communion offering, the gate facing east shall be opened for him, and he shall bring his burnt offering or peace offering as he does on the sabbath. Then he shall leave, and the gate

---

*[45:12] **Mina**: before the exile, a mina was worth fifty shekels; later, in imitation of Babylonian practice, its value increased to sixty shekels. A shekel weighed slightly less than half an ounce. A shekel's monetary value depended on whether it was gold or silver.

†[45:14] **Kor**: a liquid and a dry measure, equal to a homer.

‡[45:24] **Hin**: one sixth of the liquid measure known as a bath.

§[46:2–12] The prophet describes the inner eastern gateway opening on the inner court of the priests in front of the Temple itself where the altar of sacrifice stands. The people may watch the priests making offerings on sabbaths and feast days only by looking through the open gate; the prince, however, may stand inside the gate, in the vestibule on the edge of the inner court, to observe the offerings. Only priests could stand in the court itself.

---

u. [45:15] Lv 1:4; 6:23.   v. [45:17] cf. Ez 46:4–12.   w. [45:18] Lv 16:33.   x. [45:19] Lv 16:18–19.   y. [45:20] Lv 4:27.   z. [45:23] Nm 22:40; 28:16–25.   a. [45:24] Nm 28:12–13.

b. [45:25] Ex 23:16; 34:22; Lv 23:34–43; Nm 29:12–38.   c. [46:6] Lv 22:20.   d. [46:7] cf. Nm 28:12.

shall be closed after his departure. [13]*Every day you shall bring as a burnt offering to the LORD an unblemished year-old lamb; you shall offer it every morning, [14]and with it every morning a grain offering of one sixth of an ephah, with a third of a hin of oil to moisten the fine flour. This grain offering for the LORD is a perpetual statute. [15]*The lamb, the grain offering, and the oil you must bring every morning as a perpetual burnt offering.

**The Prince and the Land.** [16]Thus says the Lord GOD: If the prince makes a gift of part of his heritage to any of his sons, it belongs to his sons; that property is their heritage. [17]But if he makes a gift of part of his heritage to one of his servants, it belongs to him until the year of release;* then it reverts to the prince. Only the heritage given to his sons belongs to him.[g] [18]The prince shall not seize any part of the heritage of the people by forcing them off their property. From his own property he shall provide heritage for his sons, so that none of my people will be driven off their property.

**The Temple Kitchens.** [19]Then he brought me through the entrance at the side of the gateway to the chambers reserved for the priests, which faced north. There I saw a place at the far west end, [20]about which he said to me, "This is the place where the priests cook the reparation offerings and the purification offerings and bake the grain offerings, so they do not have to bring them into the outer court and so transmit holiness to the people."[†h] [21]Then he led me into the outer court and had me cross to the four corners of the court, and there, in each corner, was another court! [22]In all four corners of the courtyard there were courts set off, each forty cubits long by thirty cubits wide, all four of them the same size. [23]A stone wall surrounded them on four sides, and ovens were built along the bottom of the walls all the way around. [24]He said to me, "These are the kitchens where the temple ministers cook the sacrifices of the people."

## CHAPTER 47

**The Wonderful Stream.**[‡] [1]Then he brought me back to the entrance of the temple, and there! I saw water flowing out from under the threshold of the temple toward the east, for the front of the temple faced east. The water flowed out toward the right side of the temple to the south of the altar.[i] [2]He brought me by way of the north gate

and around the outside to the outer gate facing east; there I saw water trickling from the southern side. [3]When he continued eastward with a measuring cord in his hand, he measured off a thousand cubits and had me wade through the water; it was ankle-deep. [4]He measured off another thousand cubits and once more had me wade through the water; it was up to the knees. He measured another thousand cubits and had me wade through the water; it was up to my waist. [5]Once more he measured off a thousand cubits. Now it was a river I could not wade across. The water had risen so high, I would have to swim—a river that was impassable. [6]Then he asked me, "Do you see this, son of man?" He brought me to the bank of the river and had me sit down. [7]As I was returning, I saw along the bank of the river a great many trees on each side.[j] [8]He said to me, "This water flows out into the eastern district, runs down into the Arabah and empties into the polluted waters of the sea§ to freshen them.[k] [9]Wherever it flows, the river teems with every kind of living creature; fish will abound. Where these waters flow they refresh; everything lives where the river goes. [10]Fishermen will stand along its shore from En-gedi to En-eglaim;¶ it will become a place for drying nets, and it will abound with as many kinds of fish as the Great Sea.[l] [11]Its marshes and swamps shall not be made fresh, but will be left for salt. [12]Along each bank of the river every kind of fruit tree will grow; their leaves will not wither, nor will their fruit fail. Every month they will bear fresh fruit because the waters of the river flow out from the sanctuary. Their fruit is used for food, and their leaves for healing."[m]

### The New Israel

**Boundaries of the Land.**** [13]Thus says the Lord GOD: These are the boundaries of the land which you shall apportion among the twelve tribes of Israel, with Joseph having two portions.[n] [14]You shall apportion it equally because I swore to give it to your ancestors as a heritage; this land, then, is your heritage.[o] [15]*These are the borders of the land: on the northern side, from the Great Sea in the direction of Hethlon, Lebo-hamath to Zedad, [16]Berothah, and Sibraim, along the frontiers of Damascus and Hamath, to Hazar-enon,

---

*[46:17] **The year of release**: the jubilee year; cf. Lv 25:23–55.
†[46:20] Cf. note on 44:19.
‡[47:1–12] The life and refreshment produced wherever the Temple stream flows evoke the order and abundance of paradise (cf. Gn 1:20–22; 2:10–14; Ps 46:5) and represent the coming transformation Ezekiel envisions for the exiles and their land. Water signifies great blessings and evidence of the Lord's presence (cf. Jl 2:14).

§[47:8] **The sea**: the Dead Sea, in which nothing can live. This vision of the Temple stream which transforms places of death into places of life is similar in purpose to the oracle of dry bones in 37:1–14: it offers the exiles hope for the future.
¶[47:10] **From En-gedi to En-eglaim**: En-gedi is about halfway down the western shore of the Dead Sea; En-eglaim may have been at its northern end.
**[47:13–20] These boundaries for a restored Israel correspond to the boundaries of the Davidic kingdom at its fullest extent; they are the "ideal boundaries" of the promised land; cf. Nm 34:3–12.

e. [46:13] Ex 29:38; Nm 28:3–8.  f. [46:15] Ex 29:42; Nm 28:5–6.  g. [46:17] Lv 25:8–17.  h. [46:20] Lv 6:20.  i. [47:1] cf. Gn 2:10; Ps 46:4; Rev 22:1.

j. [47:7] Rev 22:2.  k. [47:8] Zec 14:8.  l. [47:10] Ps 104:25.  m. [47:12] Ps 1:3; Jer 17:8.  n. [47:13] Gn 48:16; Nm 34:2–12.  o. [47:14] Gn 12:7; 15:9–21.  p. [47:15] Nm 34:1–12.

on the border of Hauran.*q* *17*Thus the border extends from the sea to Hazar-enon, north of the border of Damascus, the frontier of Hamath to the north. This is the northern boundary. *18*The eastern border shall be between Damascus and Hauran, while the Jordan will form the border between Gilead and the land of Israel down to the eastern sea as far as Tamar. This is the eastern boundary. *19*The southern border shall go southward from Tamar to the waters of Meribath-kadesh, on to the Wadi of Egypt, and into the Great Sea. This is the southern boundary.*r* *20*The western border shall have the Great Sea as a boundary as far as a point opposite Lebohamath. This is the western boundary.

**The Northern Portions.** *21*You shall divide this land according to the tribes of Israel. *22*You shall allot it as heritage for yourselves and for the resident aliens in your midst who have fathered children among you. You shall treat them like native Israelites; along with you they shall receive a heritage among the tribes of Israel. *23*In whatever tribe the resident alien lives, there you shall assign his heritage—oracle of the Lord GOD.

## CHAPTER 48

*1*These are the names* of the tribes:

At the northern end, along the side of the way to Hethlon, Lebo-hamath, and Hazar-enon, the border of Damascus, and northward up to the frontier with Hamath, from the eastern border to the western: Dan, one portion. *2*Along the territory of Dan from the eastern border to the western border: Asher, one portion.*t* *3*Along the territory of Asher from the eastern border to the western border: Naphtali, one portion.*u* *4*Along the territory of Naphtali from the eastern border to the western border: Manasseh, one portion.*v* *5*Along the territory of Manasseh from the eastern border to the western border: Ephraim, one portion.*w* *6*Along the territory of Ephraim from the eastern border to the western border: Reuben, one portion.*x* *7*Along the territory of Reuben from the eastern border to the western border: Judah, one portion.*y*

**The Sacred Tract.** *8*Along the territory of Judah from the eastern border to the western border is the tract you shall set apart, twenty-five thousand cubits wide and as long as one of the portions from the eastern border to the western border. The sanctuary shall stand in the center of the tract. *9*The tract you set apart for the LORD shall be twenty-five thousand cubits long by twenty thousand wide. *10*The sacred tract

will be given to the following: the priests shall have twenty-five thousand cubits on the north, ten thousand on the west, ten thousand on the east, and twenty-five thousand on the south. The sanctuary of the LORD shall be in its center. *11*The consecrated priests, the Zadokites, who fulfilled my service and did not stray with the Israelites as the Levites did, *12*shall have their own tract set apart, next to the territory of the Levites, separate from the most holy tract. *13*The Levites shall have territory corresponding to that of the priests, twenty-five thousand cubits long and ten thousand cubits wide. The whole tract shall be twenty-five thousand cubits long and twenty thousand wide. *14*They may not sell or exchange or transfer any of it, the best part of the land, for it is sacred to the LORD. *15*The remaining section, five thousand cubits long and twenty-five thousand cubits wide, is profane land, assigned to the city for dwellings and pasture. The city is at its center. *16*These are the dimensions of the city: the north side, forty-five hundred cubits; the south side, forty-five hundred cubits; the east side, forty-five hundred cubits; and the west side, forty-five hundred cubits.*z* *17*The pasture land for the city extends north two hundred fifty cubits, south two hundred fifty cubits, east two hundred fifty cubits, and west two hundred fifty cubits. *18*The remaining section runs eastward along the sacred tract for ten thousand cubits and westward ten thousand cubits. Its produce shall provide food for the workers of the city. *19*The workers of the city, from all the tribes of Israel, shall cultivate it. *20*The entire sacred tract measures twenty-five thousand by twenty-five thousand cubits; as a square you shall set apart the sacred tract together with the city property.

*21*The remaining land on both sides of the sacred tract and the property of the city shall belong to the prince, extending eastward twenty-five thousand cubits up to the eastern boundary, and westward twenty-five thousand cubits to the western boundary. This portion belongs to the prince and corresponds to the tribal portions. The sacred tract and the sanctuary of the temple shall be in the middle. *22*Except for the Levites' property and the city's property, which are in the middle of the prince's property, the territory between the portion of Judah and the portion of Benjamin shall belong to the prince.

**The Southern Portions.** *23*These are the remaining tribes:

From the eastern border to the western border: Benjamin, one portion.*a* *24*Along the territory of Benjamin from the eastern border to the western border: Simeon, one portion.*b* *25*Along the territory of Simeon from the eastern border to the western border: Issachar, one portion.*c* *26*Along the territory of Issachar from the eastern border to the western border: Zebulun, one

---

*[48:1–29] This distribution of the land among the tribes does not correspond to the geographical realities of Palestine. It is another idealizing element in Ezekiel's representation of a restored and transformed Israel.

q. [47:16] 2 Sm 8:8. r. [47:19] Nm 34:4; Dt 32:51. s. [47:22] Lv 24:22; Nm 15:29; 26:55–56; Is 56:6–7. t. [48:2] Jos 19:24–31. u. [48:3] Jos 19:32–39. v. [48:4] Jos 17:1–11. w. [48:5] Jos 16:5–9. x. [48:6] Jos 13:15–21. y. [48:7] Jos 15:1–63.

z. [48:16] Rev 21:16. a. [48:23] Jos 18:11–28. b. [48:24] Jos 19:1–9. c. [48:25] Jos 19:17–23.

portion.[d] [27]Along the territory of Zebulun from the eastern border to the western border: Gad, one portion.[e] [28]Along the territory of Gad shall be the southern border. This boundary shall extend from Tamar to the waters of Meribath-kadesh, and along the Wadi of Egypt to the Great Sea. [29]This is the land you shall apportion as a heritage among the tribes of Israel, and these are their portions—oracle of the Lord God.

**The Gates of the City.** [30]These are the exits from the city: On the north side, measuring forty-five hundred cubits— [31]the gates are named after the tribes of Israel—on the north, three gates: the

gate of Reuben, one; the gate of Judah, one; and the gate of Levi, one. [32]On the east side, measuring forty-five hundred cubits, three gates: the gate of Joseph, one; the gate of Benjamin, one; and the gate of Dan, one. [33]On the south side, measuring forty-five hundred cubits, three gates: the gate of Simeon, one; the gate of Issachar, one; and the gate of Zebulun, one. [34]On the west side, measuring forty-five hundred cubits, three gates: the gate of Gad, one; the gate of Asher, one; and the gate of Naphtali, one.[f] [35]The circuit of the city shall be eighteen thousand cubits. From now on the name of the city is "The Lord is there."[g]

---

d. [48:26] Jos 19:10–16.    e. [48:27] Jos 13:24–28.

f. [48:34] Rev 21:12–13.    g. [48:35] Is 2:6; Rev 3:12; 21:3.

# THE BOOK OF
# DANIEL

This book takes its name not from the author, who is actually unknown, but from its hero, who was allegedly among the first Jews deported to Babylon, where he lived at least until 538 B.C. Strictly speaking, the book does not belong to the prophetic writings but rather to a distinctive type of literature known as "apocalyptic," of which it is an early specimen. Apocalyptic writing first appears about 200 B.C. and flourished among Jews and Christians down to the Middle Ages, especially in times of persecution. Apocalyptic literature has its roots in the older teaching of the prophets, who often pointed ahead to the day of the Lord, the consummation of history. For both prophet and apocalyptist there was one Lord of history, who would ultimately vindicate the chosen people. Apocalyptic also has roots in the wisdom tradition. Daniel has the gift of discernment from God. Greek wisdom (represented by the Babylonian "magicians and enchanters") is ridiculed (see especially chaps. 2 and 5), whereas God reveals hidden things to faithful servants.

This work was composed during the bitter persecution carried on by Antiochus IV Epiphanes (167–164 B.C.) and was written to strengthen and comfort the Jewish people in their ordeal. The persecution was occasioned by Antiochus's efforts to unify his kingdom, in face of the rising power of Rome, by continuing the hellenization begun by Alexander the Great; Antiochus tried to force Jews to adopt Greek ways, including religious practices. Severe penalties, including death, were exacted against those who refused (cf., e.g., 1 Mc 1:41–63).

The book contains traditional stories (chaps. 1–6), which tell of the trials and triumphs of the wise Daniel and his three companions. The moral is that people of faith can resist temptation and conquer adversity. The stories bristle with historical problems and have the character of historical novels rather than factual records. What is more important than the question of historicity, and closer to the intention of the author, is the fact that persecuted Jews of the second century B.C. would quickly see the application of these stories to their own plight.

There follows in chaps. 7–12 a series of visions promising deliverance and glory to the Jews in the days to come. The great nations of the ancient world have risen in vain against the Lord; his kingdom shall overthrow existing powers and last forever; in the end the dead will be raised for reward or punishment. Under this apocalyptic imagery some of the best elements of prophetic and sapiential teaching are synthesized: the insistence on right conduct, the divine control over events, the certainty that the kingdom of God will ultimately triumph and humanity attain the goal intended for it at the beginning of creation. The arrival of the kingdom is a central theme of the gospels, where Jesus is identified as the human figure (or "Son of Man") who appears in Daniel's vision in chap. 7. The message in both parts of the first twelve chapters (i.e., chaps. 1–6 and chaps. 7–12) is that history unrolls under the watchful eye of God, who does not abandon those who trust in him and will finally deliver and re-establish them. Moreover, it can be pointed out that chaps. 2 and 7 present the same teaching in different symbolism; 2:31 even describes the king's dream as a "vision."

The added episodes of Susanna, Bel, and the Dragon, found only in the Greek version, are edifying short stories with a didactic purpose (chaps. 13–14). The Greek version also adds a long prayer, numbered in the NAB and the Greek, 3:24–90, between 3:23–24 in the Hebrew text.

These three sections constitute the divisions of the Book of Daniel:

I. Daniel and the Kings of Babylon (1:1–6:29)
II. Daniel's Visions (7:1–12:13)
III. Appendix: Susanna, Bel, and the Dragon (13:1–14:42)

## I. DANIEL AND THE KINGS OF BABYLON

### CHAPTER 1

**The Food Test.** [1]In the third year of the reign of Jehoiakim,* king of Judah, King Nebuchadnezzar of Babylon came and laid siege to Jerusalem.[a] [2b]The Lord handed over to him Jehoiakim, king of Judah, and some of the vessels of the temple of God, which he carried off to the land of Shinar[†] and placed in the temple treasury of his god.

[3]The king told Ashpenaz,[‡] his chief chamberlain, to bring in some of the Israelites, some of the royal line and of the nobility. [4]They should be young men without any defect, handsome, proficient in wisdom, well informed, and insightful, such as could take their place in the king's palace; he was to teach them the language and literature of the Chaldeans. [5]The king allotted them a daily portion of food and wine from the royal table. After three years' training they were to enter the king's service. [6]Among these were Judeans, Daniel, Hananiah, Mishael, and Azariah. [7§]The chief chamberlain changed their names: Daniel to Belteshazzar, Hananiah to Shadrach, Mishael to Meshach, and Azariah to Abednego.

[8]But Daniel was resolved not to defile himself with the king's food or wine; so he begged the chief chamberlain to spare him this defilement.[¶] [9]Though God had given Daniel the favor and sympathy of the chief chamberlain, [10]he said to Daniel, "I am afraid of my lord the king, who allotted your food and drink. If he sees that you look thinner in comparison to the other young men of your age, you will endanger my life with the king." [11]Then Daniel said to the guardian whom the chief chamberlain had put in charge of Daniel, Hananiah, Mishael, and Azariah, [12]"Please test your servants for ten days. Let us be given vegetables to eat and water to drink. [13]Then see how we look in comparison with the other young men who eat from the royal table, and treat your servants according to what you see." [14]He agreed to this request, and tested them for ten days; [15]after ten days they looked healthier and better fed than any of the young men who ate from the royal table. [16]So the steward continued to take away the food and wine they were to receive, and gave them vegetables.

[17]To these four young men God gave knowledge and proficiency in all literature and wisdom, and to Daniel the understanding of all visions and dreams. [18]At the end of the time the king had specified for their preparation, the chief chamberlain brought them before Nebuchadnezzar. [19]When the king had spoken with all of them, none was found equal to Daniel, Hananiah, Mishael, and Azariah; and so they entered the king's service. [20]In any question of wisdom or understanding which the king put to them, he found them ten times better than any of the magicians and enchanters in his kingdom. [21c]Daniel remained there until the first year of King Cyrus.**

### CHAPTER 2

**Nebuchadnezzar's Dream.**[†† ] [1]In the second year of his reign, King Nebuchadnezzar had a dream which left his spirit no rest and robbed him of his sleep. [2]So he ordered that the magicians, enchanters, sorcerers, and Chaldeans[‡‡] be summoned to interpret the dream for him. When they came and presented themselves to the king, [3]he said to them, "I had a dream which will allow my spirit no rest until I know what it means." [4]The Chaldeans answered the king in Aramaic:[§§] "O king, live forever! Tell your servants the dream and we will give its meaning." [5]The king answered the Chaldeans, "This is what I have decided: unless you tell me the dream and its meaning, you shall be cut to pieces and your houses made into a refuse heap. [6]But if you tell me the dream and its meaning, you shall receive from me gifts and presents and great honors. Therefore tell me the dream and its meaning."

[7]Again they answered, "Let the king tell his servants the dream and we will give its meaning." [8]But the king replied: "I know for certain that you are bargaining for time, since you know what I have decided. [9]If you do not tell me the dream, there can be but one decree for you. You have conspired to present a false and deceitful interpretation to me until the crisis is past. Tell me the dream, therefore, that I may be sure that you can also give its correct interpretation."

---

*[1:1] According to 2 Kgs 24, the siege of Jerusalem took place after the death of Jehoiakim, but 2 Chr 36:5–8 says that Jehoiakim was taken to Babylon.

†[1:2] **Shinar**: ancient name for Babylonia, a deliberate archaism in this text; cf. Gn 10:10; 11:2.

‡[1:3] The proper name Ashpenaz is sometimes taken as a title, major-domo.

§[1:7] Other prominent Jews with Babylonian names include Sheshbazzar and Zerubbabel, who were leaders of the postexilic community.

¶[1:8] **This defilement**: the bread, meat, and wine of the Gentiles were unclean (Hos 9:3; Tb 1:12; Jdt 10:5; 12:1–2) because they might have been offered to idols; and the meat may not have been drained of blood, as Jewish dietary law requires. This test relates to the attempt of Antiochus to force Jews to eat forbidden foods in contempt of their religion (1 Mc 1:62–63; 2 Mc 6:18; 7:1).

**[1:21] **The first year of King Cyrus**: the year of this Persian king's conquest of Babylon, 539/538 B.C.

††[2:1–49] The chronology of v. 1 is in conflict with that of 1:5, 18, and in 2:25 Daniel appears to be introduced to the king for the first time. It seems that the story of this chapter was originally entirely independent of chap. 1 and later retouched slightly to fit its present setting. The Septuagint (Papyrus 967) reads the twelfth year instead of the second.

‡‡[2:2] **Chaldeans**: because the Babylonians gave serious study to the stars and planets, "Chaldeans" were identified with astrologers throughout the Hellenistic world.

§§[2:4] **Aramaic**: a gloss to indicate that at this point the text switches from Hebrew to Aramaic, which continues through the end of chap. 7; at 8:1, the text switches back to Hebrew.

a. [1:1] 2 Kgs 24:1; 2 Chr 36:6; Jer 25:1.  b. [1:2] Dn 5:2; 2 Chr 36:7; Gn 10:10.

c. [1:21] Dn 6:29.

¹⁰The Chaldeans answered the king: "There is not a man on earth who can do what you ask, O king; never has any king, however great and mighty, asked such a thing of any magician, enchanter, or Chaldean. ¹¹What you demand, O king, is too difficult; there is no one who can tell it to the king except the gods, who do not dwell among people of flesh." ¹²At this the king became violently angry and ordered all the wise men* of Babylon to be put to death. ¹³When the decree was issued that the wise men should be slain, Daniel and his companions were also sought out.

¹⁴Then Daniel prudently took counsel with Arioch, the chief of the king's guard, who had set out to kill the wise men of Babylon. ¹⁵He asked Arioch, the officer of the king, "What is the reason for this harsh order from the king?" When Arioch told him, ¹⁶Daniel went and asked for time from the king, that he might give him the interpretation.

¹⁷Daniel went home and informed his companions Hananiah, Mishael, and Azariah, ¹⁸that they might implore the mercy of the God of heaven in regard to this mystery, so that Daniel and his companions might not perish with the rest of the wise men of Babylon. ¹⁹During the night the mystery was revealed to Daniel in a vision, and he blessed the God of heaven:

²⁰ "Blessed be the name of God forever and ever,
    for wisdom and power are his.
²¹ He causes the changes of the times and seasons,
    establishes kings and deposes them.
   He gives wisdom to the wise
    and knowledge to those who understand.
²² He reveals deep and hidden things
    and knows what is in the darkness,
    for the light dwells with him.ᵈ
²³ To you, God of my ancestors,
    I give thanks and praise,
   because you have given me wisdom and power.
   Now you have shown me what we asked of you,
    you have made known to us the king's dream."

²⁴So Daniel went to Arioch, whom the king had appointed to destroy the wise men of Babylon, and said to him, "Do not put the wise men of Babylon to death. Bring me before the king, and I will tell him the interpretation of the

dream." Arioch quickly brought Daniel to the king and said, ²⁵"I have found a man among the Judean exiles who can give the interpretation to the king." ²⁶The king asked Daniel, whose name was Belteshazzar, "Can you tell me the dream that I had and its meaning?" ²⁷In the king's presence Daniel made this reply:

"The mystery about which the king has inquired, the wise men, enchanters, magicians, and diviners could not explain to the king. ²⁸But there is a God in heaven who reveals mysteries, and he has shown King Nebuchadnezzar what is to happen in the last days; this was your dream, the visions† you saw as you lay in bed. ²⁹To you in your bed there came thoughts about what should happen in the future, and he who reveals mysteries showed you what is to be. ³⁰To me also this mystery has been revealed; not that I am wiser than any other living person, but in order that its meaning may be made known to the king, that you may understand the thoughts of your own mind.

³¹"In your vision, O king, you saw a statue, very large and exceedingly bright, terrifying in appearance as it stood before you. ³²Its head was pure gold, its chest and arms were silver, its belly and thighs bronze, ³³its legs iron, its feet partly iron and partly clay.‡ ³⁴While you watched, a stone was hewn from a mountain without a hand being put to it, and it struck its iron and clay feet, breaking them in pieces. ³⁵The iron, clay, bronze, silver, and gold all crumbled at once, fine as the chaff on the threshing floor in summer, and the wind blew them away without leaving a trace. But the stone that struck the statue became a great mountain and filled the whole earth.

³⁶§"This was the dream; the interpretation we shall also give in the king's presence. ³⁷You, O king, are the king of kings; to you the God of heaven has given dominion and strength, power and glory; ³⁸human beings, wild beasts, and birds of the air, wherever they may dwell, he has handed over to you, making you ruler over them

---

*[2:12] **Wise men**: the satire, although directed against the Babylonian diviners in the text, refers to the Hellenistic Greeks, who made special claims to wisdom; the assertion here is that true wisdom comes from God and resides with the Jews. Cf. also chap. 5.

d. [2:22] Jn 1:9; 8:12; 1 Cor 4:5; 1 Jn 1:6.

†[2:28] **The visions**: lit., "the visions of your head," a phrasing which distinguishes visionary experiences that are personal from those that are observable by others (see 4:2, 7, 10). That Daniel, unlike the Chaldeans, has access to these visions testifies to his God-given wisdom. Actually, this "dream" is more properly an apocalyptic vision; cf. the very similar message in Daniel's vision of chap. 7.

‡[2:33] **Clay**: it has been suggested that the motif of iron mixed with clay implies a hollow metal statue packed with clay to stabilize it. In the interpretation of the dream, however, the mixture is taken as a sign of weakness.

§[2:36–45] The four successive kingdoms in this apocalyptic perspective are the Babylonian (gold), the Median (silver), the Persian (bronze), and the Hellenistic (iron). The last, after Alexander's death, was divided among his generals (vv. 41–42). Of the kingdoms which emerged from this partitioning, the two that most affected the Jews were the dynasties of the Ptolemies in Egypt and the Seleucids in Syria. They tried in vain, by war and through intermarriage, to restore the unity of Alexander's empire (v. 43). The stone hewn from the mountain is the kingdom of God awaited by the Jews (vv. 44–45). Compare the image of the stone applied to Jesus in Luke 20:17–18.

all; you are the head of gold. ³⁹Another kingdom shall take your place, inferior to yours, then a third kingdom, of bronze, which shall rule over the whole earth. ⁴⁰There shall be a fourth kingdom, strong as iron; it shall break in pieces and subdue all these others, just as iron breaks in pieces and crushes everything else. ⁴¹The feet and toes you saw, partly of clay and partly of iron, mean that it shall be a divided kingdom, but yet have some of the hardness of iron. As you saw the iron mixed with clay tile, ⁴²and the toes partly iron and partly clay, the kingdom shall be partly strong and partly fragile. ⁴³The iron mixed with clay means that they shall seal their alliances by intermarriage, but they shall not stay united, any more than iron mixes with clay. ⁴⁴In the lifetime of those kings the God of heaven will set up a kingdom that shall never be destroyed or delivered up to another people; rather, it shall break in pieces all these kingdoms and put an end to them, and it shall stand forever. ⁴⁵ᵉThat is the meaning of the stone you saw hewn from the mountain without a hand being put to it, which broke in pieces the iron, bronze, clay, silver, and gold. The great God has revealed to the king what shall be in the future; this is exactly what you dreamed, and its meaning is sure."

⁴⁶Then King Nebuchadnezzar fell down and worshiped Daniel and ordered sacrifice and incense offered to him. ⁴⁷To Daniel the king said, "Truly your God is the God of gods and Lord of kings and a revealer of mysteries; that is why you were able to reveal this mystery." ⁴⁸He advanced Daniel to a high post, gave him many generous presents, made him ruler of the whole province of Babylon and chief prefect over all the wise men of Babylon. ⁴⁹At Daniel's request the king made Shadrach, Meshach, and Abednego administrators of the province of Babylon, while Daniel himself remained at the king's court.

## CHAPTER 3

**The Fiery Furnace.** ¹King Nebuchadnezzar had a golden statue made, sixty cubits high and six cubits wide, which he set up in the plain of Dura* in the province of Babylon. ²He then ordered the satraps,† prefects, and governors, the counselors, treasurers, judges, magistrates and all the officials of the provinces to be summoned to the dedication of the statue which he had set up. ³The satraps, prefects, and governors, the counselors, treasurers, judges, magistrates and all the officials of the provinces came together for the dedication and stood before the statue which King Nebuchadnezzar had set up. ⁴A herald

cried out: "Nations and peoples of every language, ⁵‡when you hear the sound of the horn, pipe, zither, dulcimer, harp, double-flute, and all the other musical instruments, you must fall down and worship the golden statue which King Nebuchadnezzar has set up. ⁶Whoever does not fall down and worship shall be instantly cast into a white-hot furnace." ⁷Therefore, as soon as they heard the sound of the horn, pipe, zither, dulcimer, harp, double-flute, and all the other musical instruments, the nations and peoples of every language all fell down and worshiped the golden statue which King Nebuchadnezzar had set up.

⁸At that point, some of the Chaldeans came and accused the Jews ⁹to King Nebuchadnezzar: "O king, live forever! ¹⁰O king, you issued a decree that everyone who heard the sound of the horn, pipe, zither, dulcimer, harp, and double-flute, and all the other musical instruments should fall down and worship the golden statue; ¹¹whoever did not was to be cast into a white-hot furnace. ¹²There are certain Jews whom you have made administrators of the province of Babylon: Shadrach, Meshach, and Abednego; these men, O king, have paid no attention to you; they will not serve your god or worship the golden statue which you set up."

¹³Nebuchadnezzar flew into a rage and sent for Shadrach, Meshach, and Abednego, who were promptly brought before the king. ¹⁴King Nebuchadnezzar questioned them: "Is it true, Shadrach, Meshach, and Abednego, that you will not serve my god, or worship the golden statue that I set up? ¹⁵Now, if you are ready to fall down and worship the statue I made, whenever you hear the sound of the horn, pipe, zither, dulcimer, harp, double-flute, and all the other musical instruments, then all will be well;§ if not, you shall be instantly cast into the white-hot furnace; and who is the God who can deliver you out of my hands?" ¹⁶Shadrach, Meshach, and Abednego answered King Nebuchadnezzar, "There is no need for us to defend ourselves before you in this matter. ¹⁷If our God, whom we serve, can save us¶ from the white-hot furnace and from your hands, O king, may he save us! ¹⁸But even if he will not, you should know, O king, that we will not serve your god or worship the golden statue which you set up."

¹⁹Nebuchadnezzar's face became livid with utter rage against Shadrach, Meshach, and Abednego. He ordered the furnace to be heated seven times more than usual ²⁰and had some of the strongest men in his army bind Shadrach, Meshach, and Abednego and cast them into the

---

*[3:1] **Dura**: several places in Babylonia bore this name. Probably the present reference is to one located close to Babylon. Giant statues of the type mentioned here were not uncommon in antiquity; a cubit was about a foot and a half. The unrealistic proportions of this statue suggest a comic effect.

†[3:2] **Satraps**: Persian provincial governors.

e. [2:45] Mt 21:44; Lk 20:18.

‡[3:5] The precise identification of the instruments is disputed. Several of the names are Greek.

§[3:15] **Then all will be well**: lacking in Aramaic; this phrase is supplied from the context.

¶[3:17] **If our God . . . can save us**: the youths do not question the efficacy of the divine power, but whether it will be exercised (v. 18).

white-hot furnace. ²¹They were bound and cast into the white-hot furnace with their trousers, shirts, hats and other garments, ²²for the king's order was urgent. So huge a fire was kindled in the furnace that the flames devoured the men who threw Shadrach, Meshach, and Abednego into it. ²³But these three fell, bound, into the midst of the white-hot furnace.

**Prayer of Azariah.** ²⁴They walked about in the flames, singing to God and blessing the Lord. ²⁵Azariah† stood up in the midst of the fire and prayed aloud:

²⁶ "Blessed are you, and praiseworthy,
　　O Lord, the God of our ancestors,
　　and glorious forever is your name.
²⁷ For you are just in all you have done;
　　all your deeds are faultless, all your
　　　ways right,
　　and all your judgments proper.
²⁸ You have executed proper judgments
　　in all that you have brought upon us
　　and upon Jerusalem, the holy city of
　　　our ancestors.
　　By a proper judgment you have done all
　　　this
　　because of our sins;
²⁹ For we have sinned and transgressed
　　by departing from you,
　　and we have done every kind of evil.
³⁰ Your commandments we have not heeded
　　or observed,
　　nor have we done as you ordered us
　　　for our good.
³¹ Therefore all you have brought upon us,
　　all you have done to us,
　　you have done by a proper
　　　judgment.
³² You have handed us over to our enemies,
　　lawless and hateful rebels;
　　to an unjust king, the worst in all
　　　the world.
³³ Now we cannot open our mouths;
　　shame and reproach have come
　　　upon us,
　　your servants, who revere you.
³⁴ For your name's sake, do not deliver us up
　　forever,
　　or make void your covenant.
³⁵ Do not take away your mercy from us,
　　for the sake of Abraham, your
　　　beloved,
　　Isaac your servant, and Israel your
　　　holy one,
³⁶ To whom you promised to multiply their
　　offspring

like the stars of heaven,
　　or the sand on the shore of the sea.
³⁷ For we are reduced, O Lord, beyond any
　　other nation,
　　brought low everywhere in the
　　　world this day
　　because of our sins.
³⁸ We have in our day no prince, prophet, or
　　leader,
　　no burnt offering, sacrifice, oblation,
　　　or incense,
　　no place to offer first fruits, to find
　　　favor with you.
³⁹ But with contrite heart and humble spirit
　　let us be received;
　　As though it were burnt offerings of rams
　　　and bulls,
　　or tens of thousands of fat lambs,
⁴⁰ So let our sacrifice be in your presence
　　today
　　and find favor before you;
　　for those who trust in you cannot be
　　　put to shame.
⁴¹ And now we follow you with our whole
　　heart,
　　we fear you and we seek your face.
　　Do not put us to shame,
⁴² but deal with us in your kindness
　　　and great mercy.
⁴³ Deliver us in accord with your wonders,
　　and bring glory to your name,
　　　O Lord:
⁴⁴ Let all those be put to shame
　　who inflict evils on your servants;
　　Let them be shamed and powerless,
　　　and their strength broken;
⁴⁵ Let them know that you alone are the
　　　Lord God,
　　glorious over the whole world."

⁴⁶Now the king's servants who had thrown them in continued to stoke the furnace with naphtha, pitch, tow, and brush. ⁴⁷The flames rose forty-nine cubits above the furnace, ⁴⁸and spread out, burning the Chaldeans that it caught around the furnace. ⁴⁹But the angel of the Lord went down into the furnace with Azariah and his companions, drove the fiery flames out of the furnace, ⁵⁰and made the inside of the furnace as though a dew-laden breeze were blowing through it. The fire in no way touched them or caused them pain or harm. ⁵¹Then these three in the furnace with one voice sang, glorifying and blessing God:

⁵² "Blessed are you, O Lord, the God of our
　　　ancestors,
　　praiseworthy and exalted above all
　　　forever;
　　And blessed is your holy and glorious
　　　name,
　　praiseworthy and exalted above all
　　　for all ages.

---

*[3:24–90] These verses are additions to the Aramaic text of Daniel, translated from the Greek form of the book. They were probably first composed in Hebrew or Aramaic, but are no longer extant in the original language. The Roman Catholic Church has always regarded them as part of the canonical Scriptures.

†[3:25] **Azariah:** i.e., Abednego; cf. Dn 1:7.

53 Blessed are you in the temple of your holy
glory,
   praiseworthy and glorious above all
   forever.
54 Blessed are you on the throne of your
kingdom,
   praiseworthy and exalted above all
   forever.
55 Blessed are you who look into the depths
from your throne upon the
cherubim,
   praiseworthy and exalted above all
   forever.
56 Blessed are you in the firmament of
heaven,
   praiseworthy and glorious forever.
57 Bless the Lord, all you works of the Lord,
   praise and exalt him above all forever.
58 Angels of the Lord, bless the Lord,
   praise and exalt him above all
   forever.
59 You heavens, bless the Lord,
   praise and exalt him above all
   forever.f
60 All you waters above the heavens, bless
the Lord,
   praise and exalt him above all forever.
61 All you powers, bless the Lord;
   praise and exalt him above all forever.
62 Sun and moon, bless the Lord;
   praise and exalt him above all forever.
63 Stars of heaven, bless the Lord;
   praise and exalt him above all forever.
64 Every shower and dew, bless the Lord;
   praise and exalt him above all forever.
65 All you winds, bless the Lord;
   praise and exalt him above all forever.
66 Fire and heat, bless the Lord;
   praise and exalt him above all forever.
67 Cold and chill, bless the Lord;
   praise and exalt him above all forever.
68 Dew and rain, bless the Lord;
   praise and exalt him above all forever.
69 Frost and chill, bless the Lord;
   praise and exalt him above all forever.
70 Hoarfrost and snow, bless the Lord;
   praise and exalt him above all forever.
71 Nights and days, bless the Lord;
   praise and exalt him above all forever.
72 Light and darkness, bless the Lord;
   praise and exalt him above all forever.
73 Lightnings and clouds, bless the Lord;
   praise and exalt him above all forever.
74 Let the earth bless the Lord,
   praise and exalt him above all forever.
75 Mountains and hills, bless the Lord;
   praise and exalt him above all forever.
76 Everything growing on earth, bless the
Lord;
   praise and exalt him above all forever.

77 You springs, bless the Lord;
   praise and exalt him above all forever.
78 Seas and rivers, bless the Lord;
   praise and exalt him above all forever.
79 You sea monsters and all water creatures,
bless the Lord;
   praise and exalt him above all forever.
80 All you birds of the air, bless the Lord;
   praise and exalt him above all forever.
81 All you beasts, wild and tame, bless the
Lord;
   praise and exalt him above all forever.
82 All you mortals, bless the Lord;
   praise and exalt him above all forever.
83 O Israel, bless the Lord;
   praise and exalt him above all forever.
84 Priests of the Lord, bless the Lord;
   praise and exalt him above all forever.
85 Servants of the Lord, bless the Lord;
   praise and exalt him above all forever.
86 Spirits and souls of the just, bless the
Lord;
   praise and exalt him above all forever.
87 Holy and humble of heart, bless the Lord;
   praise and exalt him above all forever.
88 Hananiah, Azariah, Mishael, bless the
Lord;
   praise and exalt him above all forever.
For he has delivered us from Sheol,
   and saved us from the power of
   death;
He has freed us from the raging flame
   and delivered us from the fire.
89 Give thanks to the Lord, who is good,
   whose mercy endures forever.
90 Bless the God of gods, all you who fear
the Lord;
   praise and give thanks,
   for his mercy endures forever."

**Deliverance from the Furnace.** 91Then King
Nebuchadnezzar was startled and rose in
haste, asking his counselors, "Did we not cast
three men bound into the fire?" "Certainly, O
king," they answered. 92"But," he replied, "I see
four men unbound and unhurt, walking in the
fire, and the fourth looks like a son of God."
93Then Nebuchadnezzar came to the opening
of the white-hot furnace and called: "Shadrach,
Meshach, and Abednego, servants of the Most
High God, come out." Thereupon Shadrach,
Meshach, and Abednego came out of the fire.
94When the satraps, prefects, governors, and
counselors of the king came together, they saw
that the fire had had no power over the bodies
of these men; not a hair of their heads had been
singed, nor were their garments altered; there
was not even a smell of fire about them. 95Nebu-
chadnezzar exclaimed, "Blessed be the God of
Shadrach, Meshach, and Abednego, who sent
his angel to deliver the servants that trusted in
him; they disobeyed the royal command and

---

f. [3:59] Ps 148:4.

yielded their bodies rather than serve or worship any god except their own God. ⁹⁶Therefore I decree for nations and peoples of every language that whoever blasphemes the God of Shadrach, Meshach, and Abednego shall be cut to pieces and his house made into a refuse heap. For there is no other God who can rescue like this." ⁹⁷Then the king promoted Shadrach, Meshach, and Abednego in the province of Babylon.

⁹⁸*King Nebuchadnezzar to the nations and peoples of every language, wherever they dwell on earth: May your peace abound! ⁹⁹It has seemed good to me to publish the signs and wonders which the Most High God has accomplished in my regard.

¹⁰⁰ How great are his signs, how mighty his
        wonders;
    his kingship is an everlasting
        kingship,
    and his dominion endures through
        all generations.ᵍ

## CHAPTER 4

**Nebuchadnezzar's Madness.** ¹I, Nebuchadnezzar, was at home in my palace, content and prosperous. ²I had a terrifying dream as I lay in bed, and the images and my visions frightened me. ³So I issued a decree that all the wise men of Babylon should be brought before me to give the interpretation of the dream. ⁴When the magicians, enchanters, Chaldeans, and diviners had come in, I related the dream before them; but none of them could tell me its meaning. ⁵Finally there came before me Daniel, whose name is Belteshazzar after the name of my god,† and in whom is a spirit of the holy gods.ʰ I repeated the dream to him: ⁶"Belteshazzar, chief of the magicians, I know that a spirit of the holy gods is in you and no mystery is too difficult for you; this is the dream that I saw, tell me its meaning.

⁷"These were the visions I saw while in bed: I saw a tree of great height at the center of the earth. ⁸It was large and strong, with its top touching the heavens, and it could be seen to the ends of the earth. ⁹Its leaves were beautiful, its fruit abundant, providing food for all. Under it the wild beasts found shade, in its branches the birds of the air nested; all flesh ate of it. ¹⁰In the vision I saw while in bed, a holy watcher‡

---

*[3:98–4:34] This section has the form of a letter written by Nebuchadnezzar to his subjects.

†[4:5] **After the name of my god:** Belteshazzar, the Babylonian name given to Daniel at the king's orders (1:7), is *Balāṭ-šu-uṣur,* "protect his life." This passage implies a name connected with Bel, a Babylonian god. **A spirit of the holy gods:** or a holy divine spirit; or spirit of a holy God. See also vv. 6, 15; 5:11–12, 14; 6:4.

‡[4:10] **A holy watcher:** lit., "a watcher and a holy one." Two terms for angels. The term watcher is found in the Bible only in this chapter of Daniel, but it is common in extracanonical Jewish literature. In 1 Enoch, the fallen angels are called watchers.

g. [3:100] Dn 4:31; 7:14.    h. [4:5] Gn 41:38.

---

came down from heaven ¹¹and cried aloud in these words:

'Cut down the tree and lop off its
        branches,
    strip off its leaves and scatter its
        fruit;
Let the beasts flee from beneath it, and
        the birds from its branches,
¹²    but leave its stump in the earth.
Bound with iron and bronze,
    let him be fed with the grass of the
        field
    and bathed with the dew of heaven;
    let his lot be with the beasts in the
        grass of the earth.
¹³ Let his mind be changed from a human
        one;
    let the mind of a beast be given him,
        till seven years pass over him.
¹⁴ By decree of the watchers is this
        proclamation,
    by order of the holy ones, this
        sentence;
That all who live may know
    that the Most High is sovereign over
        human kingship,
Giving it to whom he wills,
    and setting it over the lowliest of
        mortals.'ⁱ

¹⁵"This is the dream that I, King Nebuchadnezzar, had. Now, Belteshazzar, tell me its meaning. None of the wise men in my kingdom can tell me the meaning, but you can, because the spirit of the holy gods is in you."

¹⁶Then Daniel, whose name was Belteshazzar, was appalled for a time, dismayed by his thoughts. "Belteshazzar," the king said to him, "do not let the dream or its meaning dismay you." "My lord," Belteshazzar replied, "may this dream be for your enemies, and its meaning for your foes. ¹⁷The tree that you saw, large and strong, its top touching the heavens, that could be seen by the whole earth, ¹⁸its leaves beautiful, its fruit abundant, providing food for all, under which the wild beasts lived, and in whose branches the birds of the air dwelt— ¹⁹you are that tree, O king, large and strong! Your majesty has become so great as to touch the heavens, and your rule reaches to the ends of the earth. ²⁰As for the king's vision of a holy watcher, who came down from heaven and proclaimed: 'Cut down the tree and destroy it, but leave its stump in the earth. Bound with iron and bronze, let him be fed with the grass of the field, and bathed with the dew of heaven; let his lot be with wild beasts till seven years pass over him'— ²¹here is its meaning, O king, here is the sentence that the Most High has passed upon my lord king: ²²You shall be cast out from human society

i. [4:14] 1 Sm 2:8.    j. [4:22] Dn 5:21.

and dwell with wild beasts; you shall be given grass to eat like an ox and be bathed with the dew of heaven; seven years shall pass over you, until you know that the Most High is sovereign over human kingship and gives it to whom he will. ²³The command that the stump of the tree is to be left means that your kingdom shall be preserved for you, once you have learned that heaven is sovereign. ²⁴Therefore, O king, may my advice be acceptable to you; atone for your sins by good deeds,* and for your misdeeds by kindness to the poor; then your contentment will be long lasting."

²⁵All this happened to King Nebuchadnezzar. ²⁶Twelve months later, as he was walking on the roof of the royal palace in Babylon, ²⁷the king said, "Babylon the great! Was it not I, with my great strength, who built it as a royal residence for my splendor and majesty?" ²⁸While these words were still on the king's lips, a voice spoke from heaven, "It has been decreed for you, King Nebuchadnezzar, that your kingship is taken from you! ²⁹You shall be cast out from human society, and shall dwell with wild beasts; you shall be given grass to eat like an ox, and seven years shall pass over you, until you learn that the Most High is sovereign over human kingship and gives it to whom he will." ³⁰†At once this was fulfilled. Nebuchadnezzar was cast out from human society, he ate grass like an ox, and his body was bathed with the dew of heaven, until his hair grew like the feathers of an eagle, and his nails like the claws of a bird.

³¹When this period was over, I, Nebuchadnezzar, raised my eyes to heaven; my reason was restored to me, and I blessed the Most High, I praised and glorified the One who lives forever,

Whose dominion is an everlasting dominion,
and whose kingdom endures
through all generations.ᵏ
³² All who live on the earth are counted as nothing;
he does as he wills with the powers of heaven
and with those who live on the earth.
There is no one who can stay his hand
or say to him, "What have you done?"

³³At the same time my reason returned to me, and for the glory of my kingdom, my majesty and my splendor returned to me. My counselors and nobles sought me out; I was restored to my kingdom and became much greater than before. ³⁴Now, I, Nebuchadnezzar, praise and exalt and glorify the King of heaven, all of whose works are right and ways just; and who is able to humble those who walk in pride.

## CHAPTER 5

**The Writing on the Wall.** ¹King Belshazzar gave a great banquet for a thousand of his nobles, with whom he drank. ²Under the influence of the wine, he ordered the gold and silver vessels which Nebuchadnezzar, his father,‡ had taken from the temple in Jerusalem, to be brought in so that the king, his nobles, his consorts, and his concubines might drink from them. ³When the gold vessels taken from the temple, the house of God in Jerusalem, had been brought in, and while the king, his nobles, his consorts, and his concubines were drinking ⁴wine from them, they praised their gods of gold and silver, bronze and iron, wood and stone.

⁵Suddenly, opposite the lampstand, the fingers of a human hand appeared, writing on the plaster of the wall in the king's palace. When the king saw the hand that wrote, ⁶his face became pale; his thoughts terrified him, his hip joints shook, and his knees knocked. ⁷The king shouted for the enchanters, Chaldeans, and diviners to be brought in. "Whoever reads this writing and tells me what it means," he said to the wise men of Babylon, "shall be clothed in purple, wear a chain of gold around his neck, and be third in governing the kingdom." ⁸But though all the king's wise men came in, none of them could either read the writing or tell the king what it meant. ⁹Then King Belshazzar was greatly terrified; his face became pale, and his nobles were thrown into confusion.

¹⁰When the queen heard of the discussion between the king and his nobles, she entered the banquet hall and said, "O king, live forever! Do not let your thoughts terrify you, or your face become so pale! ¹¹There is a man in your kingdom in whom is a spirit of the holy gods; during the lifetime of your father he showed brilliant insight and god-like wisdom. King Nebuchadnezzar, your father, made him chief of the magicians, enchanters, Chaldeans, and diviners. ¹²Because this Daniel, whom the king named Belteshazzar, has shown an extraordinary spirit, knowledge, and insight in interpreting dreams, explaining riddles and solving problems, let him now be summoned to tell you what this means."

*[4:24] **Good deeds**: the Aramaic word ṣidqâ has the root meaning of "righteousness," but in a late text such as this could mean "almsgiving."

†[4:30–32] There is no historical record that these events happened to Nebuchadnezzar. Scholars have long suspected that the story originally involved Nabonidus, the father of Belshazzar, who was absent from Babylon and lived at Teima in the Arabian desert for a number of years. This suggestion is now strengthened by the Prayer of Nabonidus, found at Qumran, which is closely related to chap. 4. The biblical author's chief interest was not in the historicity of this popular tale, but in the object lesson it contained for the proud "divine" kings of the Seleucid dynasty.

k. [4:31] Dn 3:33; 7:14.

‡[5:2] **Nebuchadnezzar, his father**: between Nebuchadnezzar and Belshazzar several kings ruled in Babylon. Belshazzar was the son of Nabonidus, and he acted as regent in Babylon during his father's absence.

¹³Then Daniel was brought into the presence of the king. The king asked him, "Are you the Daniel, one of the Jewish exiles, whom my father, the king, brought from Judah? ¹⁴I have heard that the spirit of the gods is in you, that you have shown brilliant insight and extraordinary wisdom. ¹⁵The wise men and enchanters were brought in to me to read this writing and tell me its meaning, but they could not say what the words meant. ¹⁶But I have heard that you can give interpretations and solve problems; now, if you are able to read the writing and tell me what it means, you shall be clothed in purple, wear a chain of gold around your neck, and be third in governing the kingdom."

¹⁷Daniel answered the king: "You may keep your gifts, or give your presents to someone else; but the writing I will read for the king, and tell what it means. ¹⁸The Most High God gave your father Nebuchadnezzar kingship, greatness, splendor, and majesty. ¹⁹Because he made him so great, the nations and peoples of every language dreaded and feared him. Whomever he willed, he would kill or let live; whomever he willed, he would exalt or humble. ²⁰But when his heart became proud and his spirit hardened by insolence, he was put down from his royal throne and deprived of his glory; ²¹he was cast out from human society and his heart was made like that of a beast; he lived with wild asses, and ate grass like an ox; his body was bathed with the dew of heaven, until he learned that the Most High God is sovereign over human kingship and sets over it whom he will. ²²You, his son, Belshazzar, have not humbled your heart, though you knew all this; ²³you have rebelled against the Lord of heaven. You had the vessels of his temple brought before you, so that you and your nobles, your consorts and your concubines, might drink wine from them; and you praised the gods of silver and gold, bronze and iron, wood and stone, that neither see nor hear nor have intelligence. But the God in whose hand is your very breath and the whole course of your life, you did not glorify. ²⁴By him was the hand sent, and the writing set down.

²⁵"This is the writing that was inscribed: MENE, TEKEL, and PERES.* These words mean: ²⁶†MENE, God has numbered your kingdom and put an end to it; ²⁷TEKEL, you have been weighed on the scales and found wanting; ²⁸PERES, your kingdom has been divided and given to the Medes and Persians."

²⁹Then by order of Belshazzar they clothed Daniel in purple, with a chain of gold around his neck, and proclaimed him third in governing the kingdom. ³⁰That very night Belshazzar, the Chaldean king, was slain:

## CHAPTER 6

¹And Darius the Mede‡ succeeded to the kingdom at the age of sixty-two.

**The Lions' Den.** ²Darius decided to appoint over his entire kingdom one hundred and twenty satraps. ³These were accountable to three ministers, one of whom was Daniel; the satraps reported to them, so that the king should suffer no loss. ⁴Daniel outshone all the ministers and satraps because an extraordinary spirit was in him, and the king considered setting him over the entire kingdom. ⁵Then the ministers and satraps tried to find grounds for accusation against Daniel regarding the kingdom. But they could not accuse him of any corruption. Because he was trustworthy, no fault or corruption was to be found in him. ⁶Then these men said to themselves, "We shall find no grounds for accusation against this Daniel except in connection with the law of his God." ⁷So these ministers and satraps stormed in to the king and said to him, "King Darius, live forever! ⁸ᵐAll the ministers of the kingdom, the prefects, satraps, counselors, and governors agree that the following prohibition ought to be put in force by royal decree: for thirty days, whoever makes a petition to anyone, divine or human, except to you, O king, shall be thrown into a den of lions. ⁹Now, O king, let the prohibition be issued over your signature, immutable and irrevocable¶ according to the law of the Medes and Persians." ¹⁰So King Darius signed the prohibition into law.

¹¹Even after Daniel heard that this law had been signed, he continued his custom of going home to kneel in prayer and give thanks to his God in the upper chamber three times a day, with the windows open toward Jerusalem. ¹²So these men stormed in and found Daniel

---

‡[6:1] **Darius the Mede**: unknown outside of the Book of Daniel. The Median kingdom did not exist at this time because it had already been conquered by Cyrus the Persian. Apparently the author of Daniel is following an apocalyptic view of history, linked to prophecy (cf. Is 13:17–19; Jer 51:11, 28–30), according to which the Medes formed the second of four world kingdoms preceding the messianic times; see note on Dn 2:36–45. The character of Darius the Mede has probably been modeled on that of the Persian king Darius the Great (522–486 B.C.), the second successor of Cyrus. The Persian Darius did appoint satraps over his empire.

§[6:8–11] The Jews of the second century B.C. could relate the king's attempt to force upon them, under pain of death, the worship of a foreign deity to the decrees of Antiochus IV; cf. 1 Mc 1:41–50.

¶[6:9] **Immutable and irrevocable**: Est 1:19 and 8:8 also refer to the immutability of Medo-Persian laws. The same idea is found in the historian Diodorus Siculus with reference to the time of Darius III (335–331 B.C.), the last of the Persian kings. Cf. Dn 6:13, 16.

---

*[5:25] **MENE, TEKEL, and PERES**: these seem to be the Aramaic names of weights and monetary values: the mina, the shekel (the sixtieth part of a mina), and the parsu (a half-mina).

†[5:26–28] Daniel interprets these three terms by a play on the words: *MENE*, connected with the verb meaning to number; *TEKEL*, with the verb meaning to weigh; *PERES*, with the verb meaning to divide. There is also a play on the last term with the word for Persians.

l. [5:21] Dn 4:22.

m. [6:8] Est 1:19.

praying and pleading before his God. ¹³Then they went to remind the king about the prohibition: "Did you not sign a decree, O king, that for thirty days, whoever makes a petition to anyone, divine or human, except to you, O king, shall be cast into a den of lions?" The king answered them, "The decree is absolute, irrevocable under the law of the Medes and Persians." ¹⁴To this they replied, "Daniel, one of the Jewish exiles, has paid no attention to you, O king, or to the prohibition you signed; three times a day he offers his prayer." ¹⁵The king was deeply grieved at this news and he made up his mind to save Daniel; he worked till sunset to rescue him. ¹⁶But these men pressed the king. "Keep in mind, O king," they said, "that under the law of the Medes and Persians every royal prohibition or decree is irrevocable." ¹⁷So the king ordered Daniel to be brought and cast into the lions' den.* To Daniel he said, "Your God, whom you serve so constantly, must save you." ¹⁸To forestall any tampering, the king sealed with his own ring and the rings of the lords the stone that had been brought to block the opening of the den.

¹⁹Then the king returned to his palace for the night; he refused to eat and he dismissed the entertainers. Since sleep was impossible for him, ²⁰the king rose very early the next morning and hastened to the lions' den. ²¹As he drew near, he cried out to Daniel sorrowfully, "Daniel, servant of the living God, has your God whom you serve so constantly been able to save you from the lions?" ²²Daniel answered the king: "O king, live forever! ²³My God sent his angel and closed the lions' mouths so that they have not hurt me.ⁿ For I have been found innocent before him; neither have I done you any harm, O king!" ²⁴This gave the king great joy. At his order Daniel was brought up from the den; he was found to be unharmed because he trusted in his God. ²⁵The king then ordered the men who had accused Daniel, along with their children and their wives, to be cast into the lions' den. Before they reached the bottom of the den, the lions overpowered them and crushed all their bones.

²⁶Then King Darius wrote to the nations and peoples of every language, wherever they dwell on the earth: "May your peace abound! ²⁷I decree that throughout my royal domain the God of Daniel is to be reverenced and feared:

"For he is the living God, enduring forever,
   whose kingdom shall not be
      destroyed,
   whose dominion shall be without end,
²⁸ A savior and deliverer,
   working signs and wonders in
      heaven and on earth,

who saved Daniel from the lions'
   power."

²⁹So Daniel fared well during the reign of Darius and the reign of Cyrus the Persian.ᵒ

## II. DANIEL'S VISIONS

### CHAPTER 7

**The Beasts and the Judgment.**† ¹In the first year of King Belshazzar of Babylon, as Daniel lay in bed he had a dream, visions in his head. Then he wrote down the dream; the account began: ²In the vision I saw during the night, suddenly the four winds of heaven stirred up the great sea,‡ ³from which emerged four immense beasts,ᵖ each different from the others. ⁴The first was like a lion, but with eagle's wings.§ While I watched, the wings were plucked; it was raised from the ground to stand on two feet like a human being, and given a human mind. ⁵The second beast was like a bear;¶ it was raised up on one side, and among the teeth in its mouth were three tusks. It was given the order, "Arise, devour much flesh." ⁶After this I looked and saw another beast, like a leopard;** on its back were four wings like those of a bird, and it had four heads. To this beast dominion was given. ⁷††After this, in the visions of the night I saw a fourth beast, terrifying, horrible, and of extraordinary strength; it had great iron teeth with which it devoured and crushed, and it trampled with its feet what was left. It differed from the beasts that preceded it. It had ten horns. ⁸I was considering the ten horns it had,

---

*[6:17] **The lions' den**: a pit too deep to be easily scaled; its opening was blocked with a stone (v. 18).

---

†[7:1–27] This vision continues the motif of the four kingdoms from chap. 2; see note on 2:36–45. To the four succeeding world kingdoms, Babylonian, Median, Persian, and Greek, is opposed the heavenly kingdom of God and the kingdom of God's people on earth. The beast imagery of this chapter has been used extensively in the Book of Revelation, where it is applied to the Roman empire, the persecutor of the Church.

‡[7:2] **The great sea**: the primordial ocean beneath the earth, according to ancient Near Eastern cosmology (Gn 7:11; 49:25). It was thought to contain various monsters (Is 27:1; Jb 7:12), and in particular mythological monsters symbolizing the chaos which God had vanquished in primordial times (Jb 9:13; 26:12; Is 51:9–10; etc.).

§[7:4] In ancient times the Babylonian empire was commonly represented as a winged lion, in the rampant position (raised up on one side). The two wings that were plucked may represent Nebuchadnezzar and Belshazzar. **On two feet like a human being . . . a human mind**: contrasts with what is said in 4:13, 30.

¶[7:5] **A bear**: represents the Median empire, its three tusks symbolizing its destructive nature; hence, the command: "Arise, devour much flesh."

**[7:6] **A leopard**: used to symbolize the swiftness with which Cyrus the Persian established his kingdom. **Four heads**: corresponding to the four Persian kings of 11:2.

††[7:7–8] Alexander's empire was different from all the others in that it was Western rather than Eastern in inspiration, and far exceeded the others in power. The ten horns represent the kings of the Seleucid dynasty, the only part of the Hellenistic empire that concerned the author. The little horn is Antiochus IV Epiphanes (175–164 B.C.), who usurped the throne and persecuted the Jews.

---

n. [6:23] 1 Mc 2:60.

o. [6:29] Dn 1:21.   p. [7:3] Rev 13:1.

when suddenly another, a little horn, sprang out of their midst, and three of the previous horns were torn away to make room for it. This horn had eyes like human eyes, and a mouth that spoke arrogantly. [9*]As I watched,

> Thrones were set up
> and the Ancient of Days took his
> throne.
> His clothing was white as snow,
> the hair on his head like pure wool;
> His throne was flames of fire,
> with wheels of burning fire.
> [10] A river of fire surged forth,
> flowing from where he sat;
> Thousands upon thousands were
> ministering to him,
> and myriads upon myriads stood
> before him.[q]

The court was convened, and the books were opened. [11]I watched, then, from the first of the arrogant words which the horn spoke, until the beast was slain and its body destroyed and thrown into the burning fire. [12]As for the other beasts, their dominion was taken away, but they were granted a prolongation of life for a time and a season. [13]As the visions during the night continued, I saw coming with the clouds of heaven[r]

> One like a son of man.[†]
> When he reached the Ancient of Days
> and was presented before him,
> [14] He received dominion, splendor, and
> kingship;
> all nations, peoples and tongues will
> serve him.
> His dominion is an everlasting dominion
> that shall not pass away,
> his kingship, one that shall not be
> destroyed.[s]

[15]Because of this, my spirit was anguished and I, Daniel, was terrified by my visions. [16]I approached one of those present and asked him the truth of all this; in answer, he made known to me its meaning: [17]"These four great beasts stand for four kings which shall arise on the earth. [18]But the holy ones[‡] of the Most High shall receive the kingship, to possess it forever and ever."

[19]Then I wished to make certain about the fourth beast, so very terrible and different from the others, devouring and crushing with its iron teeth and bronze claws, and trampling with its feet what was left; [20]and about the ten horns on its head, and the other one that sprang up, before which three horns fell; and about the horn with the eyes and the mouth that spoke arrogantly, which appeared greater than its fellows. [21]For, as I watched, that horn made war against the holy ones and was victorious [22]until the Ancient of Days came, and judgment was pronounced in favor of the holy ones of the Most High, and the time arrived for the holy ones to possess the kingship. [23]He answered me thus:

> "The fourth beast shall be a fourth
> kingdom on earth,
> different from all the others;
> The whole earth it shall devour,
> trample down and crush.
> [24] The ten horns shall be ten kings
> rising out of that kingdom;
> another shall rise up after them,
> Different from those before him,
> who shall lay low three kings.
> [25] He shall speak against the Most High
> and wear down the holy ones of the
> Most High,
> intending to change the feast days
> and the law.[§]
> They shall be handed over to him
> for a time, two times, and half a
> time.
> [26] But when the court is convened,
> and his dominion is taken away
> to be abolished and completely
> destroyed,
> [27] Then the kingship and dominion and
> majesty
> of all the kingdoms under the heavens
> shall be given to the people of God
> the holy ones of the Most High,
> Whose kingship shall be an everlasting
> kingship,
> whom all dominions shall serve and
> obey."

---

*[7:9–10] A vision of the heavenly throne of God (the Ancient of Days), who sits in judgment over the nations. Some of the details of the vision, depicting the divine majesty and omnipotence, are to be found in Ezekiel 1. Others are paralleled in 1 Enoch, a contemporary Jewish apocalypse.

†[7:13–14] **One like a son of man**: In contrast to the worldly kingdoms opposed to God, which are represented as grotesque beasts, the coming Kingdom of God is represented by a human figure. Scholars disagree as to whether this figure should be taken as a collective symbol for the people of God (cf. 7:27) or identified as a particular individual, e.g., the archangel Michael (cf. 12:1) or the messiah. The phrase "Son of Man" becomes a title for Jesus in the gospels, especially in passages dealing with the Second Coming (Mk 13 and parallels).

‡[7:18] "Holy ones" in Hebrew and Aramaic literature are nearly always members of the heavenly court or angels (cf. 4:10, 14, 20; 8:13), though here the term is commonly taken to refer to Israel.

§[7:25] The reference is to the persecution of Antiochus IV and specifically to the disruption of the Temple cult (1 Mc 1:41–64). **A time, two times, and half a time**: an indefinite, evil period of time. Probably here, three and a half years, which becomes the standard period of tribulation in apocalyptic literature (Rev 11:2; 13:5 [in months]; 11:3 [in days]; and cf. 12:14). As seven is the Jewish "perfect" number, half of it signifies great imperfection. Actually, the Temple was desecrated for three years (1 Mc 4:52–54). The duration of the persecution was a little longer, since it was already under way before the Temple was desecrated.

q. [7:10] Rev 5:11.    r. [7:13] Mk 13:26; 14:62.    s. [7:14] Dn 3:33; 4:31.

²⁸This is the end of the report. I, Daniel, was greatly terrified by my thoughts, and my face became pale, but I kept the matter to myself.*

## CHAPTER 8

**The Ram and the He-goat.**† ¹After this first vision, I, Daniel, had another, in the third year of the reign of King Belshazzar. ²In my vision I saw myself in the fortress of Susa‡ in the province of Elam; I was beside the river Ulai. ³I looked up and saw standing by the river a ram with two great horns, the one larger and newer than the other. ⁴I saw the ram butting toward the west, north, and south. No beast could withstand it or be rescued from its power; it did what it pleased and grew powerful.

⁵As I was reflecting, a he-goat with a prominent horn on its forehead suddenly came from the west across the whole earth without touching the ground. ⁶It came to the two-horned ram I had seen standing by the river, and rushed toward it with savage force. ⁷I saw it reach the ram; enraged, the he-goat attacked and shattered both its horns. The ram did not have the strength to withstand it; the he-goat threw the ram to the ground and trampled upon it. No one could rescue the ram from its power.

⁸The he-goat grew very powerful, but at the height of its strength the great horn was shattered, and in its place came up four others, facing the four winds of heaven. ⁹Out of one of them came a little horn§ which grew and grew toward the south, the east, and the glorious land. ¹⁰It grew even to the host of heaven,¶ so that it cast down to earth some of the host and some of the stars and trampled on them. ¹¹It grew even to the Prince of the host, from whom the daily sacrifice was removed, and whose sanctuary was cast down. ¹²The host was given over together with the daily sacrifice in the course of transgression. It cast truth to the ground, and was succeeding in its undertaking.

¹³I heard a holy one speaking, and another said to whichever one it was that spoke, "How long shall the events of this vision last concerning the daily sacrifice, the desolating sin,** the giving over of the sanctuary and the host for trampling?" ¹⁴He answered him, "For two thousand three hundred evenings and mornings; then the sanctuary shall be set right."

¹⁵While I, Daniel, sought the meaning of the vision I had seen, one who looked like a man stood before me, ¹⁶and on the Ulai I heard a human voice that cried out, "Gabriel,†† explain the vision to this man." ¹⁷When he came near where I was standing, I fell prostrate in terror. But he said to me, "Understand, O son of man, that the vision refers to the end time."‡‡ ¹⁸As he spoke to me, I fell forward unconscious; he touched me and made me stand up. ¹⁹"I will show you," he said, "what is to happen in the last days of wrath; for it is for the appointed time of the end.

²⁰"The two-horned ram you saw represents the kings of the Medes and Persians.§§ ²¹The he-goat is the king of the Greeks, and the great horn on its forehead is the first king. ²²The four that rose in its place when it was shattered are four kingdoms that will issue from his nation, but without his strength.

²³ "At the end of their reign,
    when sinners have reached their
        measure,
There shall arise a king,
    impudent, and skilled in intrigue.
²⁴ He shall be strong and powerful,
    bring about fearful ruin,
    and succeed in his undertaking.
He shall destroy powerful peoples;
²⁵    his cunning shall be against the holy
        ones,
    his treacherous conduct shall
        succeed.
He shall be proud of heart
    and destroy many by stealth.
But when he rises against the Prince of
        princes,
    he shall be broken without a hand
        being raised.
²⁶ As for the vision of the evenings and the
        mornings,
    what was spoken is true.
But you, keep this vision secret:
    it is for the distant future."

*[7:28] This verse ends the Aramaic part of the Book of Daniel.

†[8:1–27] This vision continues images of the preceding one, and develops it in more detail. As explained in vv. 20–22 the two-horned ram represents the combined kingdom of the Medes and Persians, destroyed by Alexander's Hellenistic empire originating in the west. Once again the author is interested only in the Seleucid dynasty, which emerged from the dissolution of Alexander's empire after his death in 323 B.C.

‡[8:2] The fortress of Susa: the royal palace of the Persian kings in the ancient territory of Elam, east of Babylonia. The river Ulai: a canal along the northern side of Susa. Some scholars argue that the Hebrew word understood as "river" here should instead be translated "gate."

§[8:9] A little horn: as in chap. 7, Antiochus IV. The glorious land: Israel.

¶[8:10–12] The host of heaven: the angelic host, symbolized by the stars. The Prince of the host: the Most High God, whose worship Antiochus suppressed (1 Mc 1:45).

**[8:13] The desolating sin: the Hebrew contains a wordplay (shomem) on the name Baal Shamem ("lord of the heavens," identified by some as the Greek Zeus Olympios). The reference is to some object with which Antiochus profaned the Temple of Jerusalem (2 Mc 6:2), most probably a pagan altar.

††[8:16] The angel Gabriel is mentioned here for the first time in the Bible. There is wordplay in the preceding verse on geber, "manlike figure."

‡‡[8:17] The end time: the time when God sits in judgment on the wicked (v. 19).

§§[8:20] The Medes and Persians: the Medes had been allies of the Babylonians in destroying the Assyrian empire (late seventh century B.C.), and Cyrus the Persian defeated the Medes en route to conquering the Babylonians. The Book of Daniel, however, treats the Medes and Persians as a dual kingdom; cf. also 5:28; 6:9; and note on 6:1.

²⁷I, Daniel, was weak and ill for some days; then I arose and took care of the king's affairs. But the vision left me desolate, without understanding.

## CHAPTER 9

**The Seventy Weeks of Years.** ¹It was the first year that Darius,* son of Ahasuerus, of the race of the Medes, reigned over the kingdom of the Chaldeans; ²in the first year of his reign, I, Daniel, perceived in the books the number of years the LORD had decreed to the prophet Jeremiah: Jerusalem was to lie in ruins for seventy years.†

³I turned to the Lord God, to seek help, in prayer and petition, with fasting, sackcloth, and ashes. ⁴ᵘI prayed to the LORD, my God, and confessed, "Ah, Lord, great and awesome God, you who keep your covenant and show mercy toward those who love you and keep your commandments and your precepts! ⁵We have sinned, been wicked and done evil; we have rebelled and turned from your commandments and your laws. ⁶We have not obeyed your servants the prophets, who spoke in your name to our kings, our princes, our ancestors, and all the people of the land. ⁷Justice, O Lord, is on your side; we are shamefaced even to this day: the men of Judah, the residents of Jerusalem, and all Israel, near and far, in all the lands to which you have scattered them because of their treachery toward you. ⁸O LORD, we are ashamed, like our kings, our princes, and our ancestors, for having sinned against you. ⁹But to the Lord, our God, belong compassion and forgiveness, though we rebelled against him ¹⁰and did not hear the voice of the LORD, our God, by walking in his laws given through his servants the prophets. ¹¹ᵛThe curse and the oath written in the law of Moses, the servant of God, were poured out over us for our sins, because all Israel transgressed your law and turned aside, refusing to hear your voice. ¹²He fulfilled the words he spoke against us and against those who ruled us, by bringing upon us an evil—no evil so great has happened under heaven as happened in Jerusalem. ¹³As it is written‡ in the law of Moses, this evil has come upon us. We did not appease the LORD, our God, by turning back from our wickedness and acting

according to your truth, ¹⁴so the LORD kept watch over the evil and brought it upon us. The LORD, our God, is just in all that he has done: we did not listen to his voice.

¹⁵"Now, Lord, our God, who led your people out of the land of Egypt with a strong hand, and made a name for yourself even to this day, we have sinned, we are guilty. ¹⁶Lord, in keeping with all your just deeds, let your anger and your wrath be turned away from your city Jerusalem, your holy mountain. On account of our sins and the crimes of our ancestors, Jerusalem and your people have become the reproach of all our neighbors. ¹⁷Now, our God, hear the prayer and petition of your servant; and for your own sake, Lord, let your face shine upon your desolate sanctuary. ¹⁸Give ear, my God, and listen; open your eyes and look upon our desolate city upon which your name is invoked. When we present our petition before you, we rely not on our just deeds, but on your great mercy. ¹⁹Lord, hear! Lord, pardon! Lord, be attentive and act without delay, for your own sake, my God, because your name is invoked upon your city and your people!"

²⁰I was still praying to the LORD, my God, confessing my sin and the sin of my people Israel, presenting my petition concerning the holy mountain of my God— ²¹I was still praying, when the man, Gabriel, whom I had seen in vision before, came to me in flight at the time of the evening offering.§ ²²He instructed me in these words: "Daniel, I have now come to give you understanding. ²³When you began your petition, an answer was given which I have come to announce, because you are beloved. Therefore, mark the answer and understand the vision.

²⁴    "Seventy weeks¶ are decreed
            for your people and for your holy
                    city:
        Then transgression will stop and sin will
                    end,
            guilt will be expiated,
        Everlasting justice will be introduced,
            vision and prophecy ratified,
            and a holy of holies will be anointed.
²⁵        Know and understand:
        From the utterance of the word
            that Jerusalem was to be rebuilt**

---

*[9:1] **Darius**: see note on 6:1.

†[9:2] **Seventy years**: Jeremiah was understood to prophesy a Babylonian captivity of seventy years, a round number signifying the complete passing away of the existing generation (Jer 25:11; 29:10). On this view Jeremiah's prophecy was seen to be fulfilled in the capture of Babylon by Cyrus and the subsequent return of the Jews to Palestine. However, the author of Daniel, living during the persecution of Antiochus, extends Jeremiah's number to seventy weeks of years (Dn 9:24), i.e., seven times seventy years, to encompass the period of Seleucid persecution.

‡[9:13] **As it is written**: the first time that this formula of Scriptural citation is used in the Bible. The reference (v. 11) is to the sanctions of Lv 26:14–16; Dt 28:15–17.

t. [9:2] Jer 25:11; 29:10.    u. [9:4] Ezr 9:6–14; Neh 9:6–37.    v. [9:11] Dt 27:15.

§[9:21] **At the time of the evening offering**: between three and four in the afternoon.

¶[9:24] **Seventy weeks**: i.e., of years. Just as Jeremiah's seventy years was an approximation (see note on v. 2), the four hundred and ninety years here is not to be taken literally. Similarly, the distribution of the "weeks" in the following verses indicates only relative proportions of the total figure. **A holy of holies**: or "most holy"; could be understood as a place (e.g., the Jerusalem Temple) or a person (cf. 1 Chr 23:13).

**[9:25] **From the utterance . . . to be rebuilt**: from the time of Jeremiah's prophecy. **Anointed ruler**: either Cyrus, who was called the anointed of the Lord to end the exile (Is 45:1), or the high priest Jeshua who presided over the rebuilding of the altar of sacrifice after the exile (Ezr 3:2). **Seven weeks**: forty-nine years, an approximation of the time of the exile. **In the course of sixty-two weeks . . . rebuilt**: a period

Until there is an anointed ruler,
    there shall be seven weeks.
In the course of sixty-two weeks
    it shall be rebuilt,
With squares and trenches,
    in time of affliction.
26 After the sixty-two weeks
    an anointed one* shall be cut down
    with no one to help him.
And the people of a leader who will come
    shall destroy the city and the
    sanctuary.
His end shall come in a flood;
    until the end of the war, which is
    decreed,
    there will be desolation.
27 For one week† he shall make
    a firm covenant with the many;
Half the week
    he shall abolish sacrifice and
    offering;
In their place shall be the desolating
    abomination
    until the ruin that is decreed
    is poured out upon the desolator."w

## CHAPTER 10

**An Angelic Vision.**‡ 1In the third year of Cyrus, king of Persia, a revelation was given to Daniel, who had been named Belteshazzar. The revelation was certain: a great war;§ he understood this from the vision. 2In those days, I, Daniel, mourned three full weeks. 3I ate no savory food, took no meat or wine, and did not anoint myself at all until the end of the three weeks.

4On the twenty-fourth day of the first month¶ I was on the bank of the great river, the Tigris. 5As I looked up, I saw a man** dressed in linen with a belt of fine gold around his waist.x 6His body was like chrysolite, his face shone like lightning, his eyes were like fiery torches, his

arms and feet looked like burnished bronze, and the sound of his voice was like the roar of a multitude. 7I alone, Daniel, saw the vision; but great fear seized those who were with me; they fled and hid themselves, although they did not see the vision. 8So I was left alone to see this great vision. No strength remained in me; I turned the color of death and was powerless. 9When I heard the sound of his voice, I fell face forward unconscious.

10But then a hand touched me, raising me to my hands and knees. 11"Daniel, beloved," he said to me, "understand the words which I am speaking to you; stand up, for my mission now is to you." When he said this to me, I stood up trembling. 12"Do not fear, Daniel," he continued; "from the first day you made up your mind to acquire understanding and humble yourself before God, your prayer was heard. Because of it I started out, 13but the prince of the kingdom of Persia†† stood in my way for twenty-one days, until finally Michael, one of the chief princes, came to help me. I left him there with the prince of the kingdom of Persia, 14and came to make you understand what shall happen to your people in the last days; for there is yet a vision concerning those days."

15While he was speaking thus to me, I fell forward and kept silent. 16Then something like a hand touched my lips; I opened my mouth and said to the one standing before me, "My lord, I was seized with pangs at the vision and I was powerless. 17How can my lord's servant speak with you, my lord? For now no strength or even breath is left in me." 18The one who looked like a man touched me again and strengthened me, saying, 19"Do not fear, beloved. Peace! Take courage and be strong." When he spoke to me, I grew strong and said, "Speak, my lord, for you have strengthened me." 20"Do you know," he asked, "why I have come to you? Soon I must fight the prince of Persia again. When I leave, the prince of Greece will come; 21but I shall tell you what is written in the book of truth.‡‡ No one supports me against these except Michael,y your prince, 11:1and in the first year of Darius the Mede I stood to strengthen him and be his refuge.

## CHAPTER 11

**The Hellenistic Age.** 2"Now I shall tell you the truth.

"Three kings of Persia§§ are yet to appear; and a fourth shall acquire the greatest riches of all.

of four hundred thirty-four years, roughly approximating the interval between the rebuilding of Jerusalem after the exile and the beginning of the Seleucid persecution.

*[9:26] **An anointed one**: the high priest Onias III, murdered in 171 B.C., from which the author dates the beginning of the persecution. Onias was in exile when he was killed. **A leader**: Antiochus IV.

†[9:27] **One week**: the final phase of the period in view, the time of Antiochus' persecution. **He**: Antiochus himself. **The many**: the faithless Jews who allied themselves with the Seleucids; cf. 1 Mc 1:11–13. **Half the week**: three and a half years; the Temple was desecrated by Antiochus from 167 to 164 B.C. **The desolating abomination**: see note on 8:13; probably a pagan altar. Jesus refers to this passage in his prediction of the destruction of Jerusalem in Mt 24:15.

‡[10:1–12:13] This final vision is concerned with history from the time of Cyrus to the death of Antiochus Epiphanes.

§[10:1] **A great war**: or "the service was great," or "a mighty host." The Hebrew is ambiguous.

¶[10:4] **The first month**: the month Nisan (mid-March to mid-April).

**[10:5–6] The heavenly person of the vision is probably the angel Gabriel, as in 9:21. **Chrysolite**: or topaz, a yellowish precious stone. Cf. the visions in Ez 1 and 8.

††[10:13] **The prince of the kingdom of Persia**: the angelic guardian of Persia. Where other texts speak of the gods of various countries (Dt 32:8), Daniel speaks of "princes." **Michael**: the patron angel of Israel (v. 21).

‡‡[10:21] **The book of truth**: a heavenly book in which future events are already recorded; cf. 7:10; 12:1.

§§[11:2] **Three kings of Persia**: it is unclear which kings are intended because there were more than three Persian kings between Cyrus and the dissolution of the kingdom.

w. [9:27] Mt 24:15; 1 Mc 1:54.   x. [10:5] Ez 10:2.

y. [10:21] Rev 12:7.

Strengthened by his riches, he shall stir up all kingdoms, even that of Greece. ³But a powerful king* shall appear and rule with great might, doing as he wills. ⁴No sooner shall he appear than his kingdom shall be broken and divided in four directions under heaven; but not among his descendants or in keeping with his mighty rule, for his kingdom shall be torn to pieces and belong to others.

⁵†"The king of the south shall grow strong, but one of his princes shall grow stronger still and govern a domain greater than his. ⁶†After some years they shall become allies: the daughter of the king of the south shall come to the king of the north to carry out the alliance. But she shall not retain power: and his offspring shall not survive, and she shall be given up, together with those who brought her, her son, and her supporter in due time. ⁷A descendant of her line shall succeed to his place, and shall come against the army, enter the stronghold of the king of the north, attack and conquer them. ⁸Even their gods, with their molten images and their precious vessels of silver and gold, he shall carry away as spoils of war into Egypt. For years he shall have nothing to do with the king of the north. ⁹Then the latter shall invade the land of the king of the south, and return to his own country.

¹⁰"But his sons shall be aroused and assemble a great armed host, which shall pass through like a flood and again surge around the stronghold. ¹¹§The king of the south, enraged, shall go out to fight against the king of the north, who shall field a great host, but the host shall be given into his hand. ¹²When the host is carried off, in the pride of his heart he shall bring down tens of thousands, but he shall not triumph. ¹³¶For the king of the north shall raise another army, greater than before; after some years he shall attack with this large army and great resources. ¹⁴In those times many shall resist the king of the south, and violent ones among your people shall rise up in fulfillment of vision, but they shall stumble. ¹⁵**When the king of the north comes, he shall set up siegeworks and take the fortified city by storm. The forces of the south shall not withstand him, and not even his picked troops shall have the strength to withstand.

¹⁶The invader shall do as he wills, with no one to withstand him. He shall stop in the glorious land, and it shall all be in his power. ¹⁷††He shall resolve to come with the entire strength of his kingdom. He shall make an alliance with him and give him a daughter in marriage in order to destroy him, but this shall not stand. ¹⁸‡‡He shall turn to the coastland and take many prisoners, but a commander shall put an end to his shameful conduct, so that he cannot retaliate. ¹⁹He shall turn to the strongholds of his own land, but shall stumble and fall, to be found no more. ²⁰§§In his stead one shall arise who will send a collector of tribute through the glorious kingdom, but he shall soon be destroyed, though not in conflict or in battle.

²¹¶¶"There shall arise in his place a despicable person, to whom the royal insignia shall not be given. He shall enter by stealth and seize the kingdom by fraud. ²²Armed forces shall be completely overwhelmed by him and crushed, even the prince of the covenant.*** ²³After making alliances, he shall treacherously rise to power with only a few supporters. ²⁴By stealth he shall enter prosperous provinces and do that which his fathers or grandfathers never did; he shall distribute spoil, plunder, and riches among them and devise plots against their strongholds. ²⁵He shall rouse his strength and courage to meet the king of the south with a great army; the king of the south shall go into battle with a very large and strong army, but he shall not stand because of the plots devised against him. ²⁶Even his table companions shall seek to destroy him, his army shall be overwhelmed, and many shall be struck down. ²⁷The two kings, resolved on evil, shall sit at table together and exchange lies, but they shall have no success, because the appointed end is not yet.

²⁸"He††† shall turn back toward his land with great riches, his mind set against the holy covenant; he shall take action and return to his land. ²⁹At the time appointed he shall come again to the south, but this time it shall not be as before. ³⁰When ships of the Kittim‡‡‡ confront him, he shall lose heart and retreat. Then he shall rage against the holy covenant and take action; he shall again favor those who forsake the holy covenant. ³¹Armed forces shall rise at his command and defile the sanctuary stronghold, abolishing

The fourth is Xerxes I (486–465 B.C.), the great campaigner against Greece.

*[11:3] **A powerful king:** Alexander the Great, who broke Persian dominance by his victory at Issus in 333 B.C.

†[11:5–45] These verses describe the dynastic histories of the Ptolemies in Egypt (the king of the south) and the Seleucids in Syria (the king of the north), the two divisions of the Hellenistic empire that were of interest to the author (v. 6). Verses 10–20 describe the struggle between the two kingdoms for the control of Palestine; the Seleucids were eventually victorious.

‡[11:6] The marriage of Antiochus II Theos and Berenice of Egypt about 250 B.C., which ended in tragedy.

§[11:11] The battle of Raphia (217 B.C.), in which Egypt defeated Syria.

¶[11:13] Syria defeated Egypt at the battle of Paneas in 200 B.C. Judea then passed under Syrian rule.

**[11:15] The siege of Sidon after the battle of Paneas.

††[11:17] Antiochus III, the Great, betrothed his daughter to Ptolemy Epiphanes in 197 B.C.

‡‡[11:18] The Roman general Scipio defeated Antiochus at Magnesia in 190 B.C.

§§[11:20] Seleucus IV, who sent Heliodorus to Jerusalem (cf. 2 Mc 3).

¶¶[11:21] Here begins the career of Antiochus IV Epiphanes.

***[11:22] **The prince of the covenant:** the high priest Onias III, who was murdered.

†††[11:28] **He:** the king of the north, probably Antiochus IV.

‡‡‡[11:30] **Kittim:** originally this word meant Cypriots or other westerners. It is sometimes used for the Greeks (1 Mc 1:1). Here it refers to the Romans, who forced Antiochus to withdraw from Egypt during his second campaign there.

the daily sacrifice and setting up the desolating abomination. ³²By his deceit he shall make some who were disloyal forsake the covenant; but those who remain loyal to their God shall take strong action. ³³Those with insight among the people shall instruct the many; though for a time the sword, flames, exile, and plunder will cause them to stumble. ³⁴When they stumble, they will be helped,* but only a little; many shall join them, but out of treachery. ³⁵Some of those with insight shall stumble so that they may be tested, refined, and purified, until the end time which is still appointed to come.

³⁶"The king shall do as he wills, exalting himself and making himself greater than any god; he shall utter dreadful blasphemies against the God of gods. He shall prosper only till the wrath is finished, for what is determined must take place. ³⁷He shall have no regard for the gods of his ancestors or for the one in whom women delight;† for no god shall he have regard, because he shall make himself greater than all. ³⁸Instead, he shall give glory to the god of strongholds;‡ a god unknown to his ancestors he shall glorify with gold, silver, precious stones, and other treasures. ³⁹He shall act for those who fortify strongholds, a people of a foreign god, whom he has recognized. He shall greatly honor them; he shall make them rule over the many and distribute the land as a reward.

⁴⁰§"At the end time the king of the south shall engage him in battle but the king of the north shall overwhelm him with chariots and horsemen and a great fleet, passing through the lands like a flood. ⁴¹He shall enter the glorious land and many shall fall, except Edom, Moab, and the chief part of Ammon, which shall escape his power. ⁴²He shall extend his power over the land, and not even Egypt shall escape. ⁴³He shall control the riches of gold and silver and all the treasures of Egypt; Libya and Ethiopia shall be in his entourage. ⁴⁴When reports from the east and the north disturb him, he shall set out with great fury to destroy many, putting them under the ban. ⁴⁵He shall pitch the tents of his royal pavilion between the sea and the glorious holy mountain, but he shall come to his end with none to help him.

---

# CHAPTER 12

## The Resurrection

¹ "At that time there shall arise Michael,ᶻ
the great prince,
guardian of your people;
It shall be a time unsurpassed in distress
since the nation began until that time.
At that time your people shall escape,
everyone who is found written in
the book.¶
² Many of those who sleep**
in the dust of the earth shall awake;
Some to everlasting life,
others to reproach and everlasting
disgrace.ᵃ
³ But those with insight shall shine brightly
like the splendor of the firmament,
And those who lead the many to justice
shall be like the stars†† forever.ᵇ

⁴"As for you, Daniel, keep secret the message and seal the book until the end time; many shall wander aimlessly and evil shall increase."

⁵I, Daniel, looked and saw two others, one standing on either bank of the river. ⁶One of them said to the man clothed in linen, who was upstream, "How long shall it be to the end of these appalling things?" ⁷The man clothed in linen,ᶜ who was upstream, lifted his hands to heaven; and I heard him swear by him who lives forever that it should be for a time, two times, and half a time;‡‡ and that, when the power of the destroyer of the holy people was brought to an end, all these things should end. ⁸I heard, but I did not understand; so I asked, "My lord, what follows this?" ⁹"Go, Daniel," he said, "because the words are to be kept secret and sealed until the end time. ¹⁰Many shall be refined, purified, and tested, but the wicked shall prove wicked; the wicked shall have no understanding, but those with insight shall. ¹¹§§From the time that the daily sacrifice is abolished and the desolating abomination is set up, there shall be one thousand two hundred and ninety days. ¹²Blessed are they who

---

*[11:34] **Helped**: this may be a reference to the Maccabean revolt. The apocalyptic author expects deliverance from God and has little regard for human efforts. In fact, the Maccabees routed the Syrian troops, recaptured Jerusalem, purified and rededicated the Temple, and brought to an end the Syrian persecution.

†[11:37] **The one in whom women delight**: Tammuz. Antiochus favored the cult of Zeus. Daniel takes this to imply the neglect of all other gods, although this does not appear to have been the case.

‡[11:38] **The god of strongholds**: the god worshiped in the fortress Akra, which Antiochus established in Jerusalem.

§[11:40–45] In these concluding verses, the events described no longer correspond to the history of the Maccabean period. Daniel imagines the death of Antiochus on the model of Gog in Ez 38–39. Antiochus actually died in Persia.

¶[12:1] **Written in the book**: cf. 10:21.

**[12:2] **Many of those who sleep**: Daniel does not envisage the universal resurrection as later developed. Two groups are distinguished, one that rises to eternal life, the other to reproach and disgrace. Then "those with insight" (11:33–35) are singled out for special honor.

††[12:3] **Like the stars**: like the heavenly host, or angels. Cf. Mt 22:30.

‡‡[12:7] **A time, two times, and half a time**: see note on 7:25.

§§[12:11] The specific numbers of days given in vv. 11–12 represent attempts to calculate the precise duration of the three and a half years. Most probably, when the first date (1,290 days) passed, the author attempted another calculation. Another, earlier calculation is preserved in 8:14. It is noteworthy, however, that the contradictory numbers were allowed to stand in the text; this is a reminder that it is not possible to calculate a precise date for God's judgment; cf. Mk 13:32.

z. [12:1] Rev 12:7.    a. [12:2] Is 66:24; Mt 25:46; Jn 5:29.    b. [12:3] Wis 3:7.    c. [12:7] Rev 10:5–6.

have patience and persevere for the one thousand three hundred and thirty-five days. ¹³Go, take your rest, you shall rise for your reward at the end of days."

## III. APPENDIX: SUSANNA, BEL, AND THE DRAGON*

### CHAPTER 13

**Susanna.** ¹In Babylon there lived a man named Joakim, ²who married a very beautiful and God-fearing woman, Susanna, the daughter of Hilkiah; ³her parents were righteous and had trained their daughter according to the law of Moses. ⁴Joakim was very rich and he had a garden near his house. The Jews had recourse to him often because he was the most respected of them all.

⁵That year, two elders of the people were appointed judges, of whom the Lord said, "Lawlessness has come out of Babylon, that is, from the elders who were to govern the people as judges." ⁶These men, to whom all brought their cases, frequented the house of Joakim. ⁷When the people left at noon, Susanna used to enter her husband's garden for a walk. ⁸When the elders saw her enter every day for her walk, they began to lust for her. ⁹They perverted their thinking; they would not allow their eyes to look to heaven, and did not keep in mind just judgments. ¹⁰Though both were enamored of her, they did not tell each other their trouble, ¹¹for they were ashamed to reveal their lustful desire to have her. ¹²Day by day they watched eagerly for her. ¹³One day they said to each other, "Let us be off for home, it is time for the noon meal." So they went their separate ways. ¹⁴But both turned back and arrived at the same spot. When they asked each other the reason, they admitted their lust, and then they agreed to look for an occasion when they could find her alone.

¹⁵One day, while they were waiting for the right moment, she entered as usual, with two maids only, wanting to bathe in the garden, for the weather was warm. ¹⁶Nobody else was there except the two elders, who had hidden themselves and were watching her. ¹⁷"Bring me oil and soap," she said to the maids, "and shut the garden gates while I bathe." ¹⁸They did as she said; they shut the garden gates and left by the side gate to fetch what she had ordered, unaware that the elders were hidden inside.

¹⁹As soon as the maids had left, the two old men got up and ran to her. ²⁰"Look," they said,

"the garden doors are shut, no one can see us, and we want you. So give in to our desire, and lie with us. ²¹If you refuse, we will testify against you that a young man was here with you and that is why you sent your maids away."

²²"I am completely trapped," Susanna groaned. "If I yield, it will be my death; if I refuse, I cannot escape your power. ²³Yet it is better for me not to do it and to fall into your power than to sin before the Lord." ²⁴Then Susanna screamed, and the two old men also shouted at her, ²⁵as one of them ran to open the garden gates. ²⁶When the people in the house heard the cries from the garden, they rushed in by the side gate to see what had happened to her. ²⁷At the accusations of the old men, the servants felt very much ashamed, for never had any such thing been said about Susanna.

²⁸When the people came to her husband Joakim the next day, the two wicked old men also came, full of lawless intent to put Susanna to death. ²⁹Before the people they ordered: "Send for Susanna, the daughter of Hilkiah, the wife of Joakim." When she was sent for, ³⁰she came with her parents, children and all her relatives. ³¹Susanna, very delicate and beautiful, ³²was veiled; but those transgressors of the law ordered that she be exposed so as to sate themselves with her beauty. ³³All her companions and the onlookers were weeping.

³⁴In the midst of the people the two old men rose up and laid their hands on her head. ³⁵As she wept she looked up to heaven, for she trusted in the Lord wholeheartedly. ³⁶The old men said, "As we were walking in the garden alone, this woman entered with two servant girls, shut the garden gates and sent the servant girls away. ³⁷A young man, who was hidden there, came and lay with her. ³⁸When we, in a corner of the garden, saw this lawlessness, we ran toward them. ³⁹We saw them lying together, but the man we could not hold, because he was stronger than we; he opened the gates and ran off. ⁴⁰Then we seized this one and asked who the young man was, ⁴¹but she refused to tell us. We testify to this." The assembly believed them, since they were elders and judges of the people, and they condemned her to death.

⁴²But Susanna cried aloud: "Eternal God, you know what is hidden and are aware of all things before they come to be: ⁴³you know that they have testified falsely against me. Here I am about to die, though I have done none of the things for which these men have condemned me."

⁴⁴The Lord heard her prayer. ⁴⁵As she was being led to execution, God stirred up the holy spirit of a young boy named Daniel, ⁴⁶and he cried aloud: "I am innocent of this woman's blood." ⁴⁷All the people turned and asked him, "What are you saying?" ⁴⁸He stood in their midst and said, "Are you such fools, you Israelites, to condemn a daughter of Israel without investigation

---

*[13:1–14:42] The short stories in these two chapters exist now only in Greek and other translations, but probably were first composed in Hebrew or Aramaic. They were never part of the Hebrew-Aramaic Book of Daniel, or of the Hebrew Bible. They are excluded from the Protestant canon of Scripture, but the Catholic Church has always included them among the inspired writings; they existed in the Septuagint, which was used as its Bible by the early church.

and without clear evidence? [49]Return to court, for they have testified falsely against her."

[50]Then all the people returned in haste. To Daniel the elders said, "Come, sit with us and inform us, since God has given you the prestige of old age." [51]But he replied, "Separate these two far from one another, and I will examine them."

[52]After they were separated from each other, he called one of them and said: "How you have grown evil with age! Now have your past sins come to term: [53]passing unjust sentences, condemning the innocent, and freeing the guilty,[d] although the Lord says, 'The innocent and the just you shall not put to death.' [54]Now, then, if you were a witness, tell me under what tree you saw them together." [55]"Under a mastic tree," he answered. "Your fine lie has cost you your head," said Daniel; "for the angel of God has already received the sentence from God and shall split you in two." [56]Putting him to one side, he ordered the other one to be brought. "Offspring of Canaan, not of Judah," Daniel said to him, "beauty has seduced you, lust has perverted your heart. [57]This is how you acted with the daughters of Israel, and in their fear they yielded to you; but a daughter of Judah did not tolerate your lawlessness. [58]Now, then, tell me under what tree you surprised them together." [59]"Under an oak," he said. "Your fine lie has cost you also your head," said Daniel; "for the angel of God waits with a sword to cut you in two so as to destroy you both."

[60]The whole assembly cried aloud, blessing God who saves those who hope in him. [61]They rose up against the two old men, for by their own words Daniel had convicted them of bearing false witness.[e] They condemned them to the fate they had planned for their neighbor: [62]in accordance with the law of Moses they put them to death. Thus was innocent blood spared that day.

[63]Hilkiah and his wife praised God for their daughter Susanna, with Joakim her husband and all her relatives, because she was found innocent of any shameful deed. [64]And from that day onward Daniel was greatly esteemed by the people.

## CHAPTER 14

### Bel and the Dragon.[†] [1]After King Astyages[‡] was gathered to his ancestors, Cyrus the Per-

sian succeeded to his kingdom. [2]Daniel was a companion of the king and was held in higher honor than any of the Friends of the King. [3]The Babylonians had an idol called Bel,[§] and every day they provided for it six bushels of fine flour, forty sheep, and six measures of wine. [4]The king revered it and went every day to worship it; but Daniel worshiped only his God. [5]When the king asked him, "Why do you not worship Bel?" Daniel replied, "Because I do not revere idols made with hands, but only the living God who made heaven and earth and has dominion over all flesh." [6]Then the king continued, "You do not think Bel is a living god? Do you not see how much he eats and drinks every day?" [7]Daniel began to laugh. "Do not be deceived, O king," he said; "it is only clay inside and bronze outside; it has never eaten or drunk anything." [8]Enraged, the king called his priests and said to them, "Unless you tell me who it is that consumes these provisions, you shall die. But if you can show that Bel consumes them, Daniel shall die for blaspheming Bel." [9]Daniel said to the king, "Let it be as you say!"

There were seventy priests of Bel, besides their wives and children. [10¶]When the king went with Daniel into the temple of Bel, [11]the priests of Bel said, "See, we are going to leave. You, O king, set out the food and prepare the wine; then shut the door and seal it with your ring. [12]*If you do not find that Bel has eaten it all when you return in the morning, we are to die; otherwise Daniel shall die for his lies against us." [13]They were not perturbed, because under the table they had made a secret entrance through which they always came in to consume the food. [14]After they departed the king set the food before Bel, while Daniel ordered his servants to bring some ashes, which they scattered through the whole temple; the king alone was present. Then they went outside, sealed the closed door

---

*[13:55–59] The contrast between the mastic tree, which is small, and the majestic oak emphasizes the contradiction between the statements of the two elders. In the Greek there is a play on words between the names of these two trees and the mortal punishment decreed by Daniel for the elders. The mastic tree (*schinon*) sounds like the verb "to split" (*schisai*). The oak tree (*prinon*) suggests a play on *poisai* (to saw).

†[14:1–22] In chap. 14, readings in the Septuagint differ markedly from those in Theodotion, which is followed here. See individual notes on 1–3a, 10–11, 12–14, 15–17 and 21–22; the translation is that of Collins, *Daniel*, pp. 405ff, with brackets indicating additions to the Septuagint according to Collins.

‡[14:1–3a] These verses in the Septuagint Greek text read: "From the prophecy of Habakkuk, son of Joshua, of the tribe of Levi. [2] There was a certain man, a priest, whose name was Daniel, son of Abal, a companion of the king of Babylon. [3] There was an idol, Bel, which the Babylonians revered, . . . " This may represent an earlier form of the story, before it was attached to the Book of Daniel. **King Astyages:** the last of the Median kings, defeated by Cyrus in 550 B.C. This story preserves the fiction of a successive Median and Persian rule of Babylon.

§[14:3] **Bel:** see note on 4:5.

¶[14:10–11] These verses in the Septuagint Greek text read: "(Now, there were seventy priests of Bel, apart from women and children.) They led the king to the idol shrine. [11] The food was set out in the presence of the king and of Daniel, and mixed wine was brought in and set before Bel. Daniel said, 'You yourself see that these things are laid out, O king. You, therefore, seal the door of temple when it is closed.' [The word pleased the king.]"

**[14:12–14] Theodotion's vv. 12–13 and 14's "After they departed the king set the food before Bel" are lacking in the Septuagint Greek text, which continues vv. 15–17 from v. 11 as follows: "Then Daniel commanded his attendants to make everyone go out from the temple and sprinkle the whole temple with ashes, unknown to anyone outside. Then he ordered them to apply the seal with the king's ring [and the seals of certain illustrious priests, and so it was done]."

---

d. [13:53] Ex 23:7.   e. [13:61] Dt 19:18–19.

with the king's ring, and departed. [15]*The priests entered that night as usual, with their wives and children, and they ate and drank everything.

[16]Early the next morning, the king came with Daniel. [17]"Are the seals unbroken, Daniel?" he asked. And Daniel answered, "They are unbroken, O king." [18]As soon as he had opened the door, the king looked at the table and cried aloud, "You are great, O Bel; there is no deceit in you." [19]†But Daniel laughed and kept the king from entering. He said, "Look at the floor and consider whose footprints these are." [20]"I see the footprints of men, women, and children!" said the king. [21]‡In his wrath the king arrested the priests, their wives, and their children. They showed him the secret door by which they used to enter to consume what was on the table. [22]The king put them to death, and handed Bel over to Daniel, who destroyed it and its temple.

[23]There was a great dragon§ which the Babylonians revered. [24]The king said to Daniel, "You cannot deny that this is a living god, so worship it." [25]But Daniel answered, "I worship the Lord, my God, for he is the living God. [26]Give me permission, O king, and I will kill this dragon without sword or club." "I give you permission," the king said. [27]Then Daniel took some pitch, fat, and hair; these he boiled together and made into cakes. He put them into the mouth of the dragon, and when the dragon ate them, he burst. "This," he said, "is what you revered."

[28]When the Babylonians heard this, they were angry and turned against the king. "The king has become a Jew," they said; "he has destroyed Bel, killed the dragon, and put the priests to death." [29]They went to the king and demanded: "Hand Daniel over to us, or we will kill you and your family." [30]When he saw himself threatened with violence, the king was forced to hand Daniel over to them. [31]They threw Daniel into a lions' den,¶ where he remained six days. [32]In the den were seven lions. Two carcasses and two sheep had been given to them daily, but now they were given nothing, so that they would devour Daniel.

[33]The prophet Habakkuk was in Judea. He mixed some bread in a bowl with the stew he had boiled, and was going to bring it to the reapers in the field, [34]when an angel of the Lord told him, "Take the meal you have to Daniel in the lions' den at Babylon." [35]But Habakkuk answered, "Sir, I have never seen Babylon, and I do not know the den!" [36]The angel of the Lord seized him by the crown of his head and carried him by the hair;f with the speed of the wind, he set him down in Babylon above the den. [37]"Daniel, Daniel," cried Habakkuk, "take the meal God has sent you." [38]"You have remembered me, O God," said Daniel; "you have not forsaken those who love you." [39]So Daniel ate, but the angel of God at once brought Habakkuk back to his own place.

[40]On the seventh day the king came to mourn for Daniel. As he came to the den and looked in, there was Daniel, sitting there. [41]The king cried aloud, "You are great, O Lord, the God of Daniel, and there is no other besides you!" [42]He brought Daniel out, but those who had tried to destroy him he threw into the den, and they were devoured in a moment before his eyes.

---

*[14:15–17] These verses in the Septuagint Greek text read: "[15]On the next day they came to the place. But the priests of Bel had entered through false doors and had eaten all that was set forth for Bel and drunk the wine. Daniel said, 'See whether your seals remain, O priests, and you, O king, see that nothing has happened that seems improper to you.' They found the seal as it had been, and they removed the seal."

†[14:19] Note that here the king seems unaware of Daniel's ruse.

‡[14:21–22] These verses in the Septuagint Greek text read: "[21]And he went to the house where the priests had come, and he found Bel's food and the wine, and Daniel showed the king the false doors through which the priests entered and consumed what had been set before Bel. [22]The king led them out of the temple of Bel and gave them over to Daniel. He gave Daniel what was expended on him and destroyed Bel."

§[14:23] Dragon: or "serpent," and see v. 27. Sacred snakes are well attested in the ancient world (e.g., in the temple of the god of healing Asclepius at Epidaurus), though evidence for their veneration in Babylon is doubtful.

¶[14:31] A lions' den: this story provides a different account from chap. 6 as to why Daniel was associated with the lions' den.

f. [14:36] Ez 8:3.

# THE BOOK OF
# HOSEA

❧

Hosea, a prophet from the Northern Kingdom, preached in his homeland, which he addresses as Israel, Jacob or, frequently, Ephraim. Hosea began his mission in a period of prosperity, the last years of Jeroboam II (783–743 B.C.). This was followed by a period of internal instability, with intrigues at the royal court leading to the assassination of several kings. Hosea witnessed the revival of Assyria, the Syro-Ephraimite war, and the numerous treaties the Israelite kings made with Egypt and Assyria to survive. Hosea's long ministry (ca. 750–725) seems to have ended before the capture of Samaria in 722/721.

The only information the text provides us about the life of Hosea concerns his marriage. Even if we cannot reconstruct what happened exactly, the text as it now stands speaks of three moments in the relationship: first love, separation, reunion. This marriage is a symbol of the covenant between the Lord and Israel. Hosea speaks about the first love, the short period of Israel's loyalty in the desert, which was then followed by a long history of unfaithfulness lasting until his day. Hosea accuses Israel of three crimes in particular. Instead of putting their trust in the Lord alone, the people break the covenant: (1) by counting on their own military strength, (2) by making treaties with foreign powers (Assyria and Egypt), and (3) by running after the Baals, the gods of fertility. Israel thus forgets that the Lord is its strength, its covenant partner, and giver of fertility. This unfaithful behavior will lead to Israel's destruction by Assyria, but God's love will have the last word. The back and forth movement from doom to salvation is typical of the Book of Hosea.

Hosea began the Old Testament tradition of describing the relation between the Lord and Israel in terms of marriage (e.g., Jer 3:1; Ez 16:23; Is 50:1). The New Testament uses the marriage imagery to describe the union between Christ and the Church (e.g., Mk 2:19–20; Eph 5:25).

The Hebrew of the Book of Hosea is challenging to translate, possibly because the text is corrupt or because it is written in a nonstandard dialect of Hebrew. As a result, the English translations of the book sometimes offer very different readings of the same passage.

The book, which opens with a superscription (1:1) and ends with a final challenge (14:10), is divided into two major parts:

I. The Prophet's Marriage and Its Symbolism (1:2–3:5)
II. Israel's Guilt, Punishment, and Restoration (4:1–14:9)

---

### CHAPTER 1

¹The word of the Lord that came to Hosea son of Beeri, in the days of Uzziah, Jotham, Ahaz, Hezekiah, kings of Judah, and in the days of Jeroboam, son of Joash, king of Israel.†

---

*[1:1–3] This section begins with Hosea's marriage to Gomer, which symbolizes Israel's relationship to God. Hence the symbolic names of Hosea's children and their later renaming (1:2–9; 2:1–3). The prophet foresees God's punishment for the unfaithful covenant partner, but knows that God's last word is always hope (2:4–25).

†[1:1] This superscription is from a Judean editor, who lists the kings of Judah in the south first, even though Hosea preached in the Northern Kingdom of Israel.

## I. THE PROPHET'S MARRIAGE AND ITS SYMBOLISM

**Marriage of Hosea and Gomer.** ²When the Lord began to speak with Hosea, the Lord said to Hosea: Go, get for yourself a woman of prostitution‡ and children of prostitution, for the land prostitutes itself,ᵃ turning away from the Lord.

---

‡[1:2] **A woman of prostitution**: this does not necessarily mean that Gomer was a prostitute when Hosea married her; the verse describes the event in its final consequences.

a. [1:2] Jer 2:20, 23; Ez 23:3.

³So he went and took Gomer, daughter of Diblaim; and she conceived and bore him a son. ⁴Then the LORD said to him: Give him the name "Jezreel,"* for in a little while I will punish the house of Jehu for the bloodshed at Jezreel and bring to an end the kingdom of the house of Israel; ⁵on that day I will break the bow of Israel in the valley of Jezreel.

⁶She conceived again and bore a daughter. The LORD said to him: Give her the name "Not-Pitied,"† for I will no longer feel pity for the house of Israel: rather, I will utterly abhor them. ⁷‡Yet for the house of Judah I will feel pity; I will save them by the LORD, their God; but I will not save them by bow or sword, by warfare, by horses or horsemen.ᵇ

⁸After she weaned Not-Pitied, she conceived and bore a son. ⁹Then the LORD said: Give him the name "Not-My-People,"§ for you are not my people, and I am not "I am" for you.

## CHAPTER 2

¹ ¶The number of the Israelites
　　will be like the sand of the sea,
　　which can be neither measured nor
　　　counted.ᶜ
Instead of being told,
　　"You are Not-My-People,"
They will be called,
　　"Children of the living God."ᵈ
² Then the people of Judah and of Israel
　　will gather together;
They will appoint for themselves one head
　　and rise up from the land;
　　great indeed shall be the day of Jezreel!
³ Say to your brothers, "My People,"
　　and to your sisters, "Pitied."

Prostitution here may refer to Gomer's participation in the worship of other gods.
　*[1:4] **Give him the name "Jezreel"**: the names of the three children are symbolic, and predict God's punishment in a crescendo. These names are frequently repeated in chaps. 1–2. **Jezreel**: (lit., "God will sow") the strategic valley in northern Israel where Jehu brought the dynasty of Omri to an end through bloodshed (2 Kgs 9–10). Jeroboam II was the next to the last king of the house of Jehu. The prophecy in this verse of the end of the house of Jehu was fulfilled by the murder of Zechariah, son of Jeroboam II (2 Kgs 15:8–10).
　†[1:6] **"Not-Pitied"**: in Hebrew *lo-ruhama*.
　‡[1:7] Probably written by a later editor when the prophecies of Hosea circulated in the south, after the dissolution of the Northern Kingdom had occurred. The second part of the verse emphasizes the power of the Lord, who needs no human agents to fulfill the divine will. It may refer to the deliverance of Jerusalem from the siege of Sennacherib in 701 (2 Kgs 19:35–37).
　§[1:9] **"Not-My-People"**: in Hebrew *lo-ammi*. **I am not "I am" for you**: a reference to the divine name revealed to Moses, "I am" (Ex 3:14). This reversal of the relationship marks the end of the covenant (Ex 6:7).
　¶[2:1–3] These verses abruptly reverse the tone of the judgments of 1:2–9 with words of hope for the covenant people: the name Jezreel is given a favorable interpretation in contrast to its negative meaning in 1:4; the child named "Not-Pitied" in 1:6 is renamed "Pitied" in 2:3; the child named "Not-My-People" is renamed "My People." The reversal of these names occurs again in 2:25.

b. [1:7] Zec 4:6.　　c. [2:1] Gn 15:5; 22:17; 32:13.　　d. [2:1] Rom 9:26–27.

## The Lord and Israel His Spouse**

⁴ Accuse your mother, accuse!
　　for she is not my wife,
　　and I am not her husband.††
Let her remove her prostitution from her
　　face.
　　her adultery from between her
　　　breasts,

⁵ Or I will strip her naked,‡‡
　　leaving her as on the day of her
　　　birth;
I will make her like the wilderness,
　　make her like an arid land,
　　and let her die of thirst.
⁶ I will have no pity on her children,
　　for they are children of prostitution.
⁷ Yes, their mother has prostituted herself;
　　she who conceived them has acted
　　　shamefully.
For she said, "I will go after my lovers,§§
　　who give me my bread and my
　　　water,
　　my wool and my flax, my oil and my
　　　drink."ᵉ
⁸ ***Therefore, I will hedge in her way with
　　　thorns
　　and erect a wall against her,
　　so that she cannot find her paths.
⁹ If she runs after her lovers, she will not
　　　overtake them;
　　if she seeks them she will not find
　　　them.
Then she will say,
　　"I will go back to my first husband,
　　for I was better off then than now."ᶠ

¹⁰ She did not know
　　that it was I who gave her
　　the grain, the wine, and the oil,
I who lavished upon her silver,
　　and gold, which they used for Baal,***
¹¹ Therefore I will take back my grain in its
　　　time,
　　and my wine in its season;

　**[2:4–25] The section contains three oracles of doom (vv. 4–6, 7–9, 10–15), a transition (vv. 16–17), and three oracles of salvation (vv. 18–19, 20–22, 23–25).
　††[2:4] The Lord speaks of Israel, still using the example of Hosea's wife.
　‡‡[2:5] **I will strip her naked**: it was the husband's responsibility to provide food and clothing for his wife (Ex 21:10) and now, because of her adultery, he takes back his support.
　§§[2:7] **My lovers**: even though Israel had experienced the Lord as the God of the desert, covenant and conquest, the people were inclined to turn to the local fertility deities, the Baals, who were believed to be responsible for agricultural success. They easily forgot that the Lord provides them with everything (v. 10; cf. Dt 7:13), and thus prostituted themselves by worshiping other gods.
　¶¶[2:8] The crop failures sent by the Lord are meant to make Israel see the folly of its ways.
　***[2:10] **For Baal**: as an offering to Baal or to make statues of Baal.

e. [2:7] Jer 2:25.　　f. [2:9] Lk 15:17–18.

I will snatch away my wool and my flax,
    which were to cover her nakedness.
12 Now I will lay bare her shame
    in full view of her lovers,<sup>g</sup>
    and no one can deliver her out of
        my hand.<sup>h</sup>
13 I will put an end to all her joy,
    her festivals, her new moons, her
        sabbaths—
    all her seasonal feasts.
14 I will lay waste her vines and fig trees,
    of which she said, "These are the fees
        my lovers have given me";
    I will turn them into rank growth
    and wild animals shall devour them.
15 I will punish her for the days of the Baals,<sup>*</sup>
    for whom she burnt incense,
    When she decked herself out with her
        rings and her jewelry,
    and went after her lovers—
    but me she forgot—oracle of the
        Lord.<sup>i</sup>
16 Therefore,<sup>†</sup> I will allure her now;
    I will lead her into the wilderness<sup>j</sup>
    and speak persuasively to her.
17 Then I will give her the vineyards she had,
    and the valley of Achor<sup>‡</sup> as a door
        of hope.<sup>k</sup>
    There she will respond as in the days of
        her youth,
    as on the day when she came up
        from the land of Egypt.

18 On that day—oracle of the Lord—
    You shall call me "My husband,"
    and you shall never again call me
        "My baal."<sup>§</sup>
19 I will remove from her mouth the names
    of the Baals;
    they shall no longer be mentioned
        by their name.

20 I will make a covenant for them on that day,<sup>l</sup>
    with the wild animals,
    With the birds of the air,
    and with the things that crawl on
        the ground.

Bow and sword and warfare
    I will destroy from the land,
    and I will give them rest in safety.

21 I will betroth you to me forever:
    I will betroth you to me with<sup>¶</sup> justice
        and with judgment,
    with loyalty and with compassion;
22 I will betroth you to me with fidelity,
    and you shall know the Lord.
23 On that day I will respond—oracle of the
        Lord—
    I will respond to the heavens,
    and they will respond to the earth;
24 The earth will respond to the grain, and
        wine, and oil,
    and these will respond to Jezreel.
25 I will sow her for myself in the land,
    and I will have pity on Not-Pitied.
    I will say to Not-My-People, "You are my
        people,"<sup>m</sup>
    and he will say, "My God!"

## CHAPTER 3

**Hosea and His Wife Reunited**<sup>**</sup> <sup>1</sup>Again the
Lord said to me:

Go, love a woman
    who is loved by her spouse but
        commits adultery;
Just as the Lord loves the Israelites,
    though they turn to other gods
    and love raisin cakes.<sup>††</sup>

<sup>2‡‡</sup>So I acquired her for myself for fifteen
pieces of silver and a homer and a lethech of
barley. <sup>3</sup>Then I said to her:

"You will wait for me for many days;
    you will not prostitute yourself
Or belong to any man;
    I in turn will wait for you."

---

*[2:15] **The days of the Baals**: feast days of the Baal cult (v. 13), or the whole period of Israel's apostasy.

†[2:16] **Therefore**: this word in Hebrew normally introduces an oracle of doom; here, surprisingly, it leads to hope. **Allure**: as though seducing a virgin (Ex 22:15–16). Ordinarily this word connotes deception (Jgs 14:15; 16:5; 1 Kgs 22:20–22).

‡[2:17] **Valley of Achor**: lit., valley of trouble (Jos 7:26). Here this valley becomes a valley of hope, a new entry into the promised land.

§[2:18–19] **Baal**: the word means "lord, master." It was commonly used by women of their husbands, but it is to be shunned as a title for the Lord because of its association with the fertility gods, the Baals. Many Israelites saw little if any difference between the worship of the Lord and the worship of the Baals, thereby dishonoring the true source of the land's fertility.

g. [2:12] Ez 16:37.  h. [2:12] Jn 10:29.  i. [2:15] Jer 2:32.  j. [2:16] Jer 2:2–7.  k. [2:17] Jos 7:24–26.  l. [2:20] Gn 9:8–11; Ez 34:25; Jb 5:23.

---

¶[2:21–22] **Betroth . . . with**: the betrothal was the legal moment before cohabitation when the dowry was paid to the father of the bride. In this remarriage the Lord gives the bride price to Israel herself "forever." **Justice . . . judgment**: refer to equity and fairness of conduct. The next two terms, "loyalty" (*hesed*), the steadfast love between the covenant partners, and "compassion," maternal love (cf. 1:6; 2:3, 25) are characteristic of Hosea. **You shall know**: not an abstract but a practical knowledge which means acknowledgment of God's will and obedience to his law (4:1; 5:4; 6:3, 6).

**[3:1–5] Just as the Lord is ready to take Israel back, Hosea takes his wife back. She must undergo a period of purification, just as Israel must experience purification before the restoration of the covenant relationship.

††[3:1] **Raisin cakes**: offerings to the fertility goddess Asherah, the female counterpart of Baal, cf. Jer 7:18; 44:19; Dn 14:5–8.

‡‡[3:2] Just as the Lord offered a new bride price to Israel (2:21–22), so Hosea offers a new bride price to his wife. He returns to her what he has taken away from her (2:5): "fifteen (shekels) of silver"; "a homer of barley," a unit of dry measurement, which according to the etymology means "a mule load"; and "a lethech of barley," which is a half-homer.

---

m. [2:25] Rom 9:25–26; 1 Pt 2:10.

4 'For the Israelites will remain many days
    without king or prince,
Without sacrifice or sacred pillar,
    without ephod or household gods.
5 Afterward the Israelites will turn back
    and seek the LORD, their God,
    and David, their king;'ⁿ
They will come trembling to the LORD
    and to his bounty, in the last days.

## II. ISRAEL'S GUILT, PUNISHMENT, AND RESTORATION

### CHAPTER 4

#### Indictment of Israel‡

1 Hear the word of the LORD, Israelites,
    for the LORD has a dispute
    with the inhabitants of the land:ᵒ
There is no fidelity, no loyalty,
    no knowledge of God in the land.
2 Swearing, lying, murder,
    stealing and adultery break out;§
    bloodshed follows bloodshed.ᵖ
3 Therefore the land dries up,
    and everything that dwells in it
      languishes:
The beasts of the field,
    the birds of the air,
    and even the fish of the sea perish.�q

#### Guilt of Priest and of People

4 But let no one accuse, let no one rebuke;
    with you is my dispute, priest!¶
5 You will stumble in the day,
    and the prophet will stumble with
      you at night;
    I will make an end of your mother.**

6 My people are ruined for lack of
      knowledge!
Since you have rejected knowledge,
    I will reject you from serving as my
      priest;
Since you have forgotten the law of your
      God,
    I will also forget your children.

7 The more they multiplied, the more they
      sinned against me,
    I will change their glory†† into shame.ʳ
8 They feed on the sin of my people,
    and are greedy for their iniquity.‡‡
9 Like people, like priest:ˢ
    I will punish them for their ways,
    and repay them for their deeds.
10 They will eat but not be satisfied,ᵗ
    they will promote prostitution§§ but
      not increase,
Because they have abandoned the LORD,
    devoting themselves
11     to prostitution.
Aged wine and new wine
    take away understanding.ᵘ
12 My people consult their piece of wood,¶¶
    and their wand makes
      pronouncements for them,
For the spirit of prostitution has led them
      astray;
    they prostitute themselves, forsaking
      their God.
13 On the mountaintops they offer sacrifice
    and on the hills they burn incense,
Beneath oak and poplar and terebinth,
    because of their pleasant shade.***
Therefore your daughters prostitute
      themselves,
    and your daughters-in-law commit
      adultery.
14 I will not punish your daughters for their
      prostitution,
    nor your daughters-in-law for their
      adultery,
Because the men themselves consort with
      prostitutes,

---

\*[3:4] Israel will lose its political and cultic institutions. **Sacred pillar**: originally perhaps a phallic symbol, representing Baal. These were also used in Israelite worship (cf. notes on Gn 28:18; Ex 34:13). **Ephod**: an instrument used in consulting the deity (1 Sm 23:6–12; 30:7; cf. notes on Ex 28:6, 15–30). **Household gods**: in Hebrew, *teraphim*; images regarded as the tutelary deities of the household (Gn 31:19; Jgs 17:5; 18:14, 17–18).

†[3:5] **David, their king**: the king belonging to the line of David who will restore the Israelite nation (Jer 23:5; Ez 34:23, 24). **The last days**: a future time of transformation.

‡[4:1–3] The introduction to the oracles (chaps. 4–11) which begin with "Hear the word of the Lord" (4:1) and end with "oracle of the Lord" (11:11).

§[4:2] Similar to the decalogue (Ex 20:1–17; cf. Jer 7:9).

¶[4:4–6] Hosea is particularly severe with the priests in the Northern Kingdom who had led the way in the general apostasy from God's law. The prophets here associated with the priests (v. 5) were doubtless cult prophets; cf. Jer 2:8; 4:9–10; 6:13–14; 23:9–40.

\*\*[4:5] **Your mother**: the one who gave life to the priest, understood here as an extension of the punishment to his whole family (Am 7:17), or "mother" taken as a metaphor for the community of Israel, of which the priest is a member (Hos 2:4).

††[4:7] **Their glory**: possibly connoting "their children." See 9:11; Is 22:24. Or "Glory" may refer to the Lord in contrast to Ba'al. The Hebrew word for shame, *bosheth*, is often substituted for Ba'al in biblical names. See Ishbaal (Heb. *Ishbosheth*, 2 Sm 2:8, 10, 12, 15) and Meribaal (Heb. *Mephibosheth*, 2 Sm 9:6, 10–13).

‡‡[4:8] The priest receives part of the sacrifice (Lv 6:19; 7:7).

§§[4:10–11] **Prostitution**: often a synonym for idolatry. The covenant bond was symbolized as the relationship between husband and wife (see chaps. 1–2). Thus, abandoning the Lord for a foreign god was called prostitution or adultery.

¶¶[4:12] **Piece of wood**: a derogatory term for an idol. **Wand**: a sacred wooden object, perhaps some kind of staff, used for divination.

\*\*\*[4:13] The shrines on the "high places" typically had an altar, a grove of trees, and a stone pillar representing a god (Dt 12:2; Jer 2:20).

---

n. [3:5] Jer 30:9; Ez 34:23.    o. [4:1] Is 3:10–15; Mi 6:1–5.    p. [4:2] Ex 20:13–17.    q. [4:3] Is 24:4–7; Zep 1:2–3.

r. [4:7] Jer 2:11; Ps 106:20.    s. [4:9] Is 24:2.    t. [4:10] Mi 6:14. u. [4:11] Is 28:7.

and with temple women* they offer
     sacrifice!
Thus a people without understanding
     comes to ruin.

15 Though you prostitute yourself, Israel,
     do not let Judah become guilty!
   Do not come to Gilgal,†
     do not go up to Beth-aven,ᵛ
     do not swear, "As the Lord lives!"ʷ
16 For like a stubborn cow,
     Israel is stubborn;
   Will the LORD now pasture them,
     like lambs in a broad meadow?
17 Ephraim‡ is bound to idols,
     let him alone!
18 §When their drinking is over,
     they give themselves to prostitution;ˣ
   they love shame more than their
     honor.
19 A wind¶ has bound them up in its wings;ʸ
     they shall be ashamed because of
     their altars.ᶻ

## CHAPTER 5

### Guilt of the Religious and Political Leaders

1 Hear this, priests,
     Pay attention, house of Israel,
   Household of the king, give ear!ᵃ
     For you are responsible for
     judgment.**
   But you have been a snare at Mizpah,††
     a net spread upon Tabor,
2 a pit dug deep in Shittim.
   Now I will discipline them all.

3 I know Ephraim,
     and Israel is not hidden from me:
   Now, Ephraim, you have practiced
     prostitution,
   Israel is defiled.
4 Their deeds do not allow them
     to return to their God;ᵇ
   For the spirit of prostitution is in them,
     and they do not know the LORD.

5 The arrogance of Israel bears witness
     against him;
   Israel and Ephraim stumble because
     of their iniquity,
     and Judah stumbles with them.
6 With their flocks and herds they will go
     to seek the LORD, but will not find
     him;ᶜ
   he has withdrawn from them.
7 They have betrayed the LORD,
     for they have borne illegitimate
     children;
   Now the new moon‡‡ will devour them
     together with their fields.

### Political Upheavals§§

8 Blow the ram's horn in Gibeah,
     the trumpet in Ramah!
   Sound the alarm in Beth-aven:ᵈ
     "Look behind you, Benjamin!"¶¶
9 Ephraim shall become a wasteland
     on the day of punishment:
   Among the tribes of Israel
     I announce what is sure to be.
10 The princes of Judah have become
     like those who move a boundary
     line;***ᵉ
   Upon them I will pour out
     my wrath like water.
11 Ephraim is oppressed, crushed by
     judgment,
   for he has willingly gone after filth!†††
12 I am like a moth for Ephraim,ᶠ
     like rot for the house of Judah.
13 When Ephraim saw his infirmity,
     and Judah his sore,

---

*[4:14] **Temple women**: plural of Heb. *qedesha*; the exact import of the term is disputed. See notes on Gn 38:21 and Dt 23:18–19.

†[4:15] **Gilgal**: close to Jericho (Jos 4:19–20; 5:2–9). **Beth-aven**: (lit., "house of iniquity") Hosea's derogatory term for the sanctuary of Bethel (lit., "house of God"), the major shrine of the Northern Kingdom (10:5, 8; cf. Am 5:5). **As the Lord lives**: a legitimate oath formula (1 Sm 26:10, 16), but unacceptable here because Israel is guilty of religious syncretism and the idolatrous worship of other gods.

‡[4:17] **Ephraim**: the name of one of the sons of Joseph, son of Jacob (Gn 41:52), also used to designate one of the tribes living in the heartland of the Northern Kingdom. Hosea often uses the name Ephraim to refer to the whole Northern Kingdom of Israel. During the latter part of his ministry, after the Assyrians occupied Galilee, Ephraim was all that remained of Israel.

§[4:18] Cf. v. 11.

¶[4:19] **A wind**: (Heb. *ruah*), a metaphor for Israel's addiction to the Baal cult, which is nothing but wind, a "spirit (*ruah*) of prostitution" (v. 12).

**[5:1] **For you . . . judgment**: possibly "for you are called to judgment."

††[5:1–2] **Mizpah**: several places bear this name; the best known is in Benjamin (1 Sm 7:6, 16; 10:17). Perhaps this is a wordplay on *mishpat*, "justice," "judgment." **Tabor**: the mountain that dominates the valley of Jezreel. **Shittim**: in Transjordan, where Israel committed its first act of idolatry with the Baal of Peor (9:10; cf. Nm 25). At these three places the leaders had misled the people by an idolatrous cult or by an abuse of justice.

‡‡[5:7] **New moon**: normally a feast day of joy (2:13), but, because of infidelity, it will be a day of destruction.

§§[5:8–14] This passage describes political and military conflict between Judah and Israel. Perhaps some allusion is made to the Syro-Ephraimite war of 735–734 B.C., when a coalition of Arameans and Israelites attempted to dethrone the king of Judah (2 Kgs 16:5; Is 7:1–9). Judah repulsed the attempt with the aid of Assyria, and the latter devastated both Aram and Israel.

¶¶[5:8] A vision of invasion, from Gibeah and Ramah in northern Judah, into Israel.

***[5:10] **Move a boundary line**: invasion by Judah (v. 8) is compared to a case of social injustice (Dt 19:14; 27:17; Prv 23:10–11).

†††[5:11] **Filth**: Ephraim's reliance on foreign nations and their gods.

---

v. [4:15] Am 4:4.   w. [4:15] Am 8:14.   x. [4:18] Am 2:8.   y. [4:19] Jer 4:11–12.   z. [4:19] Is 1:29.   a. [5:1] Mi 3:1.

b. [5:4] Jer 13:23.   c. [5:6] Is 55:6; Jer 29:13; Am 5:4–6; 8:12; Jn 7:34.   d. [5:8] Jer 4:5; Jl 2:1.   e. [5:10] Dt 19:14; 27:17.   f. [5:12] Is 50:9.

Ephraim went to Assyria,
  and sent to the great king.*g
But he cannot heal you,
  nor take away your sore.
14 For I am like a lion to Ephraim,
  like a young lion to the house of
    Judah;h
It is I who tear the prey and depart,
  I carry it away and no one can save
    it.i

### Insincere Conversion

15 I will go back to my place
  until they make reparation
  and seek my presence.
In their affliction, they shall look for me.j

### CHAPTER 6

1 "Come, let us return to the LORD,k
For it is he who has torn, but he will heal
    us;
  he has struck down, but he will bind
    our wounds.
2 He will revive us after two days;
  on the third day† he will raise us up,l
  to live in his presence.
3 Let us know, let us strive to know the
    LORD;
  as certain as the dawn is his coming.
He will come to us like the rain,
  like spring rain that waters the
    earth."m

4 What can I do with you, Ephraim?
  What can I do with you, Judah?
Your loyalty is like morning mist,
  like the dew that disappears early.
5 For this reason I struck them down
    through the prophets,
  I killed them by the words of my
    mouth;‡n
  my judgment shines forth like the
    light.
6 For it is loyalty that I desire, not sacrifice,
  and knowledge of God rather than
    burnt offerings.o

### Further Crimes of Israel

7 But they, at Adam,§ violated the covenant;
  there they betrayed me.

8 Gilead¶ is a city of evildoers,
  tracked with blood.
9 Like brigands lying in wait
  is the band of priests.
They murder on the road to Shechem,**
  indeed they commit a monstrous
    crime.
10 In the house of Israel I have seen a
    horrible thing:
  there is found Ephraim's
    prostitution,
  Israel is defiled.
11 For you also, Judah,
  a harvest†† has been appointed!

### CHAPTER 7

When I would have restored the fortunes
  of my people,
1   when I would have healed Israel,
The guilt of Ephraim was revealed,
  the wickedness of Samaria:
  They practiced falsehood.
Thieves break in,
  bandits roam outside.
2 Yet they do not call to mind
  that I remember all their
    wickedness.p
Now their crimes surround them,
  present to my sight.q

### Israel's Domestic Politics‡‡

3 With their wickedness they make the king
    rejoice,
  the princes too, with their
    treacherous deeds.
4 They are all adulterers,§§
  like a blazing oven,
Which the baker quits stoking,
  after the dough's kneading until its
    rising.

---

*[5:13] **Ephraim went . . . king**: in 738 the Israelite king Menahem had to pay tribute to the Assyrian king Tiglath-pileser III, whose vassal he became (2 Kgs 15:19–20). Under the threat of the Syro-Ephraimite invasion King Ahaz of Judah also submitted to Tiglath-pileser (2 Kgs 16:7–9). **Great king**: Heb. *melek-yarev*, may be a proper name: King Yarev, but unknown; or "the defender king": irony about the great king of Assyria (see note on 10:6).
†[6:2] **After two days; on the third day**: presumptuous Israel expects that soon God will renew them (cf. Ez 37).
‡[6:5] The word of God proclaimed by the prophets is effective, it accomplished what it promised: punishment.

§[6:7] **At Adam**: the violation of the covenant at Adam is mentioned nowhere else in the Bible. The place Adam, the location of which is unknown, may be referred to in Jos 3:16.
¶[6:8] **Gilead**: city in Transjordan (Gn 31:46–48; 2 Kgs 15:25).
**[6:9] **Shechem**: an important ancient religious and political center (Jos 24).
††[6:11] **Harvest**: God's judgment, when Judah will reap what it has sown.
‡‡[7:3–7] This passage perhaps refers to a conspiracy at the royal court. Between the death of Jeroboam II (743 B.C.) and the fall of Samaria (722/721), nearly all the kings were murdered (2 Kgs 15:10, 14, 25, 30).
§§[7:4] **Adulterers**: the unfaithful nobles who kill the king. Their passion is compared to the fire of the oven. The point of the metaphor is that, like this oven whose fire is always ready to blaze up again, the conspirators are always ready for rebellion.

---

g. [5:13] 2 Kgs 15:19–20; 16:7–9.  h. [5:14] Is 5:29; Am 1:2; 3:12.  i. [5:14] Dt 32:39.  j. [5:15] Jer 29:13; Ps 78:34.  k. [6:1] Lam 3:40.  l. [6:2] Lk 24:7, 46; 1 Cor 15:4.  m. [6:3] Dt 11:14; Ps 72:6.  n. [6:5] Is 11:4; 49:2; Jer 5:14; Heb 4:12–13.  o. [6:6] 1 Sm 15:22; Am 5:22–24; Mi 6:6–8; Eccl 4:17; Mt 9:13; 12:7.

p. [7:2] Ps 10:11.  q. [7:2] Prv 5:21–22.

5 On the day of our king,
    they made the princes sick with
      poisoned wine;
    he extended his hand to the scoffers.
6 For they draw near in ambush
    with their hearts like an oven.
All the night their anger sleeps;
    in the morning it flares like a blazing
      fire.
7 They are all heated like ovens,
    and consume their rulers.
All their kings have fallen;
    none of them calls upon me.

### Israel's Foreign Politics

8 Ephraim is mixed with the nations,*
    Ephraim is an unturned cake.
9 Strangers have consumed his strength,
    but he does not know it;*r*
Gray hairs are strewn on his head,
    but he takes no notice of it.
10 The arrogance of Israel bears witness
    against him;
    yet they do not return to the LORD,
      their God,
    nor seek him, despite all this.*s*
11 Ephraim is like a dove,
    silly and senseless;
They call upon Egypt,
    they go to Assyria.
12 When they go I will spread my net around
    them,
    like birds in the air I will bring them
      down.*t*
I will chastise them when I hear of
    their assembly.
13 Woe to them, for they have strayed from
    me!
    Ruin to them, for they have rebelled
      against me!
Though I wished to redeem them,
    they spoke lies against me.
14 They have not cried to me from their hearts
    when they wailed upon their beds;
For wheat and wine they lacerated
    themselves;*t*
    they rebelled against me.
15 Though I trained and strengthened their
    arms,
    yet they devised evil against me.
16 They have again become useless,
    they have been like a treacherous
      bow.*u*

Their princes shall fall by the sword
    because of the insolence of their
      tongues;
    thus they shall be mocked in the
      land of Egypt.

## CHAPTER 8

### Corruption of Cult, Domestic and Foreign Politics

1 Put the trumpet to your lips!*v*
    One like an eagle‡ is over the house
      of the LORD!
Because they have violated my covenant,
    and rebelled against my law,
2 They cry out to me,
    "My God! We know you!"
3 But Israel has rejected what is good;
    the enemy§ shall pursue him.

4 ¶They made kings, but not by my authority;
    they established princes, but without
      my knowledge.
With their silver and gold
    they made idols for themselves,
    to their own destruction.
5 He has rejected your calf,** Samaria!*w*
    My wrath is kindled against them;
How long will they be incapable of
      innocence
    in Israel?
6 An artisan made it,
    it is no god at all.*x*
The calf of Samaria
    will be dashed to pieces.

7 When they sow the wind,
    they will reap the whirlwind;*y*
The stalk of grain that forms no head
    can yield no flour;
Even if it could,
    strangers would swallow it.
8 Israel is swallowed up;
    now they are among the nations,
    like a useless vessel.
9 For they went up to Assyria—††
    a wild ass off on its own—
    Ephraim bargained for lovers.*z*

---

‡[8:1] **Eagle**: perhaps an image for Tiglath-pileser III of Assyria, who overran the land of Israel in 733 B.C. (Jer 48:40; 49:22; Ez 17:3).

§[8:3] **Enemy**: Assyria.

¶[8:4] Hosea is not against the monarchy, but against the conspiracies at the royal court (see note on 7:3–7). The king should be chosen by God (1 Kgs 19:15–16).

**[8:5] **Calf**: a cultic object introduced by Jeroboam I after the separation of the Northern Kingdom from the Southern Kingdom (1 Kgs 12:26–30; cf. Ex 32).

††[8:9] **They went up to Assyria**: a reference to the politics of appealing to Assyria (cf. 5:13; 7:11). There is a play on the Hebrew word for "wild ass" (*pere*) and "Ephraim."

---

*[7:8] **Is mixed with the nations**: the people reject exclusive allegiance to the Lord, and they now try to find their salvation in alliances with foreign nations. **An unturned cake**: burnt on one side, but not baked at all on the other, and thus worthless.

†[7:14] **Lacerated themselves**: a ritual to obtain a good harvest from Baal (2:7–10; 1 Kgs 18:28; Jer 16:6; 41:5). This practice was forbidden (Lv 19:28; Dt 14:1).

r. [7:9] Jer 5:3; Rev 3:17.   s. [7:10] Is 9:12; Am 4:6.   t. [7:12] Ez 12:13; 32:3.   u. [7:16] Ps 78:57.

v. [8:1] Jl 2:1.   w. [8:5] 1 Kgs 12:28.   x. [8:6] Ex 20:4; 34:17; Is 40:19–20; 44:9–20; Jer 10:1–16.   y. [8:7] Jb 4:8; Prv 22:8; 2 Cor 9:6; Gal 6:7–8.   z. [8:9] Ez 16:32–34.

10 Even though they bargain with the
          nations,
   I will now gather them* together;
   They will soon succumb
          under the burden of king and
          princes.

11 †When Ephraim made many altars to
          expiate sin,
   they became altars for sinning.
12 Though I write for him my many
          instructions,
   they are considered like a stranger's.
13 They love sacrifice,
   they sacrifice meat and eat it,
          but the LORD is not pleased with
          them.*a*
   Now he will remember their guilt
          and punish their sins;*b*
   they shall return to Egypt.‡*c*
14 Israel has forgotten his maker*d*
          and has built palaces.
   Judah, too, has fortified many cities,
          but I will send fire upon his cities,
   to devour their strongholds.*e*

## CHAPTER 9

### From Days of Celebration
### to Days of Punishment

1  Do not rejoice, Israel,
          do not exult like the nations!
   For you have prostituted yourself,
          abandoning your God,
          loving a prostitute's fee
          upon every threshing floor.§
2  Threshing floor and wine press will not
          nourish them,
          the new wine will fail them.

3  They will not dwell in the LORD's land;
          Ephraim will return to Egypt,
          and in Assyria they will eat unclean
          food.
4  They will not pour libations of wine to the
          LORD,
          and their sacrifices will not please
          him.
   Their bread will be like mourners' bread,¶*f*

that makes unclean all who eat of it;
   Their food will be for their own appetites;
          it cannot enter the house of the
          LORD.

5  What will you do on the festival day,
          the day of the LORD's feast?**
6  ††When they flee from the devastation,
          Egypt will gather them, Memphis
          will bury them.
   Weeds will overgrow their silver treasures,
          and thorns, their tents.

7  They have come, the days of punishment!
          they have come, the days of
          recompense!
   Let Israel know it!
          "The prophet is a fool,*g*
          the man of the spirit is mad!"
   Because your iniquity is great,
          great, too, is your hostility.
8  ‡‡The watchman of Ephraim, the people of
          my God, is the prophet;*h*
          yet a fowler's snare is on all his ways,
          hostility in the house of his God.
9  They have sunk to the depths of
          corruption,
          as in the days of Gibeah;§§*i*
   God will remember their iniquity
          and punish their sins.

### From Former Glory
### to a History of Corruption

10 Like grapes in the desert,
          I found Israel;
   Like the first fruits of the fig tree, its first
          to ripen,*j*
          I looked on your ancestors.
   But when they came to Baal-peor¶¶*k*
          and consecrated themselves to the
          Shameful One,
          they became as abhorrent as the
          thing they loved.
11 Ephraim is like a bird:
          their glory flies away—

---

*[8:10] **I will now gather them**: for judgment and for
deportation.
†[8:11] The altars had become places of self-serving worship (cf. v. 13).
‡[8:13] **Return to Egypt**: to punish their violation of the
covenant they will experience a reversal of the exodus.
§[9:1] **Threshing floor**: an allusion to harvest festivals in
honor of Baal, to whom the Israelites had attributed the fertility of the land; cf. 2:7.
¶[9:4] **Mourners' bread**: bread eaten at funeral rites (Dt
26:14). The presence of a corpse also made all food prepared
in that house unclean (Jer 16:5–7).

**[9:5] **The LORD's feast**: probably the important autumn
feast of Booths, the most important of the Israelite public celebrations (Lv 23:34).
††[9:6] Instead of gathering for celebration (v. 5), they will
be gathered for death. **Memphis**: known for the monumental pyramid tombs. **Silver treasures**: the silver statues of Baal
(8:4).
‡‡[9:8] Prophets, like Hosea himself, are called to be sentinels for Israel, warning Israel of God's coming wrath (see Ez
3:17; 33:7), but often meet rejection.
§§[9:9] **The days of Gibeah**: the precise allusion is not clear.
Perhaps it is a reference to the outrage committed at Gibeah in
the days of the judges (Jgs 19–21), or to questions surrounding Saul's kingship at Gibeah (1 Sm 10:26; 14:2; 22:6).
¶¶[9:10] **Baal-peor**: where the Israelites consecrated themselves for the first time to Baal (Nm 25; see note on Hos 5:1–
2). Baal is here called the Shameful One.

a. [8:13] Am 5:22.  b. [8:13] Jer 14:10.  c. [8:13] Dt 28:68.
d. [8:14] Dt 32:15, 18; Is 51:13.   e. [8:14] Am 1:7, 10, 12, 14; 2:2, 5.
f. [9:4] Dt 26:14.

g. [9:7] 2 Kgs 9:11; Jn 10:20.   h. [9:8] Jer 6:17; Ez 3:17; 33:2, 6,
7.   i. [9:9] Jgs 19–21.   j. [9:10] Is 28:4; Jer 2:2.   k. [9:10] Nm 25.

no birth, no pregnancy, no
  conception.[l]
12 Even though they bring up their children,
    I will make them childless, until no
      one is left.
Indeed, woe to them
    when I turn away from them!
13 Ephraim, as I saw, was a tree
    planted in a meadow;
But now Ephraim will bring out
    his children to the slaughterer!
14 Give them, Lord!
    give them what?
Give them a miscarrying womb,
    and dry breasts![m]
15 All their misfortune began in Gilgal;[*]
    yes, there I rejected them.
Because of their wicked deeds
    I will drive them out of my house.
I will love them no longer;
    all their princes are rebels.
16 [†]Ephraim is stricken,
    their root is dried up;[n]
    they will bear no fruit.[o]
Were they to bear children,
    I would slay the beloved of their
      womb.
17 My God will disown them
    because they have not listened to him;
    they will be wanderers among the
      nations.[p]

## CHAPTER 10

### Destruction of Idolatrous Cultic Objects

1 [q]Israel is a luxuriant vine
    whose fruit matches its growth.
The more abundant his fruit,
    the more altars he built;
The more productive his land,
    the more sacred pillars[‡] he set up.
2 Their heart is false!
    Now they will pay for their guilt:
God will break down their altars
    and destroy their sacred pillars.
3 For now they will say,
    "We have no king![§]
Since we do not fear the Lord,
    the king—what could he do for us?"

4 They make promises,
    swear false oaths, and make
      covenants,
While lawsuits sprout
    like poisonous weeds[¶] in the furrows
      of a field!

5 The inhabitants of Samaria are afraid
    for the calf of Beth-aven;[**]
Its people mourn for it
    and its idolatrous priests wail over it,
    —over its glory which has departed
      from it.[r]
6 It too will be carried to Assyria,
    as an offering to the great king.[††s]
Ephraim will be put to shame,
    Israel will be shamed by his
      schemes.

7 Samaria and her king will disappear,
    like a twig upon the waters.
8 The high places of Aven[‡‡] will be
      destroyed,
    the sin of Israel;
    thorns and thistles will overgrow
      their altars.
Then they will cry out to the mountains,
    "Cover us!"
    and to the hills, "Fall upon us!"[t]

### War Because of Israel's Wickedness

9 Since the days of Gibeah[u]
    you have sinned, Israel.
There they took their stand;
    will war not reach them in Gibeah?
Against a perverse people
10   I came and I chastised them;
Peoples will be gathered against them
    when I bind them to their two
      crimes.[§§]
11 Ephraim was a trained heifer,
    that loved to thresh;
I myself laid a yoke
    upon her beautiful neck;
I will make Ephraim break ground, Judah
      must plow,
Jacob must harrow for himself:
12 "Sow for yourselves justice,
    reap the reward of loyalty;
Break up for yourselves a new field,[v]

---

*[9:15] **Gilgal**: possibly a reference to Saul's disobedience to Samuel (1 Sm 13:7–14; 15), or to the idolatry practiced in that place (see note on Hos 4:15).

†[9:16] Wordplay on the Hebrew word for "fruit" (*peri*) and Ephraim (see note on 8:9). The whole passage (vv. 10–17) presents a reversal of Ephraim's name (Gn 41:52). He will have no fruit, a condition which will result in extinction.

‡[10:1] **Sacred pillars**: see note on 3:4.

§[10:3] **No king**: the instability of the monarchy (7:3–7) and its vassalage to foreign kings (7:8–16) render the monarchy ineffective. The kings do the opposite of what they are supposed to do (10:4).

¶[10:4] **Lawsuits . . . like poisonous weeds**: the administration of justice, which should have been the mainstay of the people, has in corrupt hands become another instrument of oppression; cf. Am 6:12.

**[10:5] **The calf of Beth-aven**: see note on 4:15.

††[10:6] **The great king**: a title used by the Assyrian kings. See also note on 5:13.

‡‡[10:8] **Aven**: wickedness, first of all at Bethel (v. 5), but also at all the high places.

§§[10:10] **Two crimes**: the allusion is not clear; a possible reference is the outrage described in Jgs 19.

---

l. [9:11] Dt 28:18.   m. [9:14] Jb 3:11–12; Lk 23:29.   n. [9:16] Am 2:9.   o. [9:16] Mt 21:19.   p. [9:17] Gn 4:12, 14; Dt 28:64–65.   q. [10:1] Is 5:1–7.

r. [10:5] 1 Sm 4:21–22.   s. [10:6] Am 5:27.   t. [10:8] Is 2:10, 19; Lk 23:30; Rev 6:16.   u. [10:9] Jgs 19–21.   v. [10:12] Jer 4:3.

for it is time to seek the LORD,
    till he comes and rains justice upon
        you."[w]
13 But you have plowed wickedness,
    reaped perversity,
    and eaten the fruit of falsehood.
Because you have trusted in your own
        power,
    and in your many warriors,[x]
14 The clamor of war shall break out among
        your people
    and all your fortresses shall be
        ravaged
As Salman ravaged Beth-arbel* on the day
        of war,
    smashing mothers along with their
        children.[y]
15 So it will be done to you, Bethel,
    because of your utter wickedness:
At dawn† the king of Israel
    will utterly disappear.

## CHAPTER 11

### The Disappointment of a Parent

1 ‡When Israel was a child I loved him,[z]
    out of Egypt§ I called my son.[a]
2 The more I called them,
    the farther they went from me,
Sacrificing to the Baals
    and burning incense to idols.
3 Yet it was I who taught Ephraim to walk,
    who took them in my arms;[b]
    but they did not know that I cared
        for them.
4 I drew them with human cords,
    with bands of love;¶
I fostered them like those
    who raise an infant to their cheeks;
    I bent down to feed them.[c]

5 He shall return to the land of Egypt,[d]
    Assyria shall be his king,
    because they have refused to repent.
6 The sword shall rage in his cities:
    it shall destroy his diviners,

and devour them because of their
    schemings.
7 My people have their mind set on
        apostasy;
    though they call on God in unison,
    he shall not raise them up.

### But Love Is Stronger and Restores

8 How could I give you up, Ephraim,
    or deliver you up, Israel?
How could I treat you as Admah,
    or make you like Zeboiim?**[e]
My heart is overwhelmed,
    my pity is stirred.
9 I will not give vent to my blazing anger,
    I will not destroy Ephraim again;
For I am God and not a man,[f]
    the Holy One present among you;
    I will not come in wrath.
10 They shall follow the LORD,
    who roars like a lion;[g]
When he roars,
    his children shall come frightened
        from the west,
11 Out of Egypt they shall come trembling,
    like birds,
    like doves, from the land of Assyria;
And I will resettle them in their homes,
    oracle of the LORD.

## CHAPTER 12

### Infidelity of Israel††

1 Ephraim has surrounded me with lies,
    the house of Israel, with deceit;
Judah still wanders about with gods,
    and is faithful to holy ones.‡‡
2 §§Ephraim shepherds the wind,
    and pursues the east wind all day
        long.
He multiplies lies and violence:
    They make a covenant with Assyria,
    and oil is carried to Egypt.

3 The LORD has a dispute with Judah,
    and will punish Jacob¶¶ for his
        conduct,
    and repay him for his deeds.
4 In the womb he supplanted his brother,[h]

---

*[10:14] **As Salman ravaged Beth-arbel**: perhaps Sala-
manu, king of Moab, mentioned in an inscription of Tiglath-
pileser III, after an invasion in Gilead (Transjordan), where
there was a Beth-arbel, close to present Irbid.

†[10:15] **At dawn**: normally the moment of God's victory
over Israel's enemies, and thus his salvation (Is 17:14; Ps 46:6).
Here it is a reversal of this expectation.

‡[11:1–3] After the image of husband-wife (chaps. 1–3),
Hosea uses the image of parent-child (Ex 4:22; Is 1:2; Jer 3:19).

§[11:1] **Out of Egypt**: Hosea dates the real beginning of
Israel from the time of the exodus. Mt 2:15 applies this text to
the return of Jesus from Egypt.

¶[11:4] **I drew them . . . with bands of love**: perhaps a
reversal of the yoke imagery of the previous chapter, i.e.,
not forcing them like draft animals, but drawing them with
kindness and affection.

**[11:8] **Admah . . . Zeboiim**: cities in the vicinity of
Sodom and Gomorrah (Gn 14:2, 8) and destroyed with them
(Gn 19:24–25; Dt 29:22).

††[12:1–15] This chapter draws a parallel between the history of Israel and events in the life of Jacob-Israel, the ancestor.

‡‡[12:1] An attack on the idolatry of both kingdoms, Israel
and Judah. **Holy ones**: subordinate gods, members of the
divine council.

§§[12:2] Hosea frequently condemns the alliances with
Assyria and Egypt, the two world powers (7:8–16).

¶¶[12:3] **Jacob**: whose name was changed to Israel (Gn
35:10).

---

w. [10:12] Is 45:8; Jl 2:23.  x. [10:13] Is 31:1.  y. [10:14] Ps 137:9;
Am 1:13.  z. [11:1] Dt 7:8; 10:15; Jer 2:1–9.  a. [11:1] Ex 4:22; Mt
2:15.  b. [11:3] Dt 1:31; 8:5.  c. [11:4] Dt 8:16.  d. [11:5] Dt 17:16.

e. [11:8] Dt 29:22.  f. [11:9] Nm 23:19; Is 31:3; Ez 28:2.  g. [11:10]
Jl 4:16; Am 1:2; Jer 25:30.  h. [12:4] Gn 25:26; 27:35–36.

and in his vigor he contended with a
    divine being;
5 He contended with an angel and prevailed,[i]
    he wept and entreated him.
At Bethel he met with him,
    and there he spoke with him.[j]
6 The Lord is the God of hosts,
    the Lord is his name![k]
7 You must return to your God.
    Maintain loyalty and justice
    and always hope in your God.

8 A merchant who holds a false balance,
    he loves to extort!
9 Ephraim has said,
    "How rich I have become;
    I have made a fortune!"[l]
All his gain will not suffice
    for the guilt of his sin.
10 I the Lord have been your God,
    since the land of Egypt;[m]
I will again have you live in tents,
    as on feast days.
11 I spoke to the prophets,
    I granted many visions,[n]
    and through the prophets I told
      parables.
12 In Gilead is falsehood, they have come to
    nothing;
    in Gilgal they sacrifice bulls,
But their altars are like heaps of stones[o]
    in the furrows of the field.

13 Jacob fled to the land of Aram,
    and Israel served for a wife;
    for a wife he tended sheep.[p]
14 But by a prophet[*] the Lord brought Israel
    out of Egypt,
    and by a prophet Israel was tended.[q]
15 Ephraim has aroused bitter anger,
    so his Lord shall cast his bloodguilt
      upon him
    and repay him for his scorn.

## CHAPTER 13

### The Death of Ephraim

1 When Ephraim spoke there was terror;
    he was exalted in Israel;[†]
    but he became guilty through Baal
      and died.

2 Now they continue to sin,
    making for themselves molten
      images,

Silver idols according to their skill,[r]
    all of them the work of artisans.
"To these, offer sacrifice," they say.
    People kiss calves![‡s]
3 Therefore, they will be like a morning
    cloud
    or like the dew that vanishes with
      the dawn,
Like chaff storm-driven from the
      threshing floor[t]
    or like smoke out of the window.

4 I, the Lord, am your God,
    since the land of Egypt;[§u]
Gods apart from me you do not know;
    there is no savior but me.[v]
5 I fed you in the wilderness,
    in the parched land.
6 When I fed them, they were satisfied;
    when satisfied, they became proud,
    therefore they forgot me.
7 So, I will be like a lion to them,
    like a leopard by the road I will keep
      watch.
8 [w]I will attack them like a bear robbed of
      its young,
    and tear their hearts from their
      breasts;
I will devour them on the spot like a lion,
    as a wild animal would rip them
      open.

9 [¶]I destroy you, Israel!
    who is there to help you?
10 Where now is your king,
    that he may rescue you?
And all your princes,
    that they may defend you?
Of whom you said,
    "Give me a king and princes"?[x]
11 I give you a king in my anger,
    and I take him away in my wrath.[**]

12 The guilt of Ephraim is wrapped up,
    his sin is stored away.
13 [††]The birth pangs will come for him,[y]
    but this is an unwise child,

---

‡ [13:2] **Kiss calves**: apparently a reference to a ritual gesture associated with the worship of Baal represented as a calf (1 Kgs 19:18).

§ [13:4] **I, the Lord . . . land of Egypt**: according to 1 Kgs 12:28, Jeroboam introduced the calves used in the worship at the sanctuaries in Bethel and Dan with the words: "Here are your gods, O Israel, who brought you up from the land of Egypt."

¶ [13:9–10] Only God can save Israel, not the king, whom Israel had requested from the Lord (1 Sm 8:1–9).

** [13:11] **I give you a king . . . in my wrath**: the Lord punished the people of the Northern Kingdom by giving them kings who were soon deposed (see notes on 7:3–7 and 8:4).

†† [13:13] Ephraim will die along with its stored-up sin, just as a mother dies along with a child that she cannot deliver.

---

\* [12:14] **A prophet**: Moses.

† [13:1] **Exalted in Israel**: Ephraim enjoyed a privileged position in Israel (Gn 48:14–19).

---

i. [12:5] Gn 32:25–30.  j. [12:5] Gn 28:12–19; 35:15.  k. [12:6] Ex 3:15; Am 4:13.  l. [12:9] Rev 3:17.  m. [12:10] Ex 20:2.  n. [12:11] Ps 74:9.  o. [12:12] Gn 31:45–54; Jos 4–5.  p. [12:13] Gn 28:5; 29:15–30; 30:31.  q. [12:14] Ex 3:7–10; Dt 18:18.

r. [13:2] Is 40:19–20; 44:9–20.  s. [13:2] 1 Kgs 19:18.  t. [13:3] Is 17:13; Zep 2:2; Ps 1:4.  u. [13:4] Ex 20:2.  v. [13:4] Is 43:11.  w. [13:8] 2 Sm 17:8.  x. [13:10] 1 Sm 8:5.  y. [13:13] Is 26:17–18; Jer 6:24; 22:23.

Who, when it is time, does not present
    himself
    at the mouth of the womb.*

14 *Shall I deliver them from the power of
    Sheol?
    shall I redeem them from death?
Where are your plagues, O death!
    where is your sting, Sheol!*ª*
    Compassion is hidden from my
      eyes.

15 Though Ephraim† may flourish among his
    brothers,
    an east wind*b* will come, a wind
      from the LORD,
    rising from the wilderness,
That will dry up his spring,
    and leave his fountain dry.
It will loot his treasury
    of every precious thing.

## CHAPTER 14

1 Samaria‡ has become guilty,
    for she has rebelled against her God.
They shall fall by the sword,
    their infants shall be dashed to
      pieces,*c*
    their pregnant women shall be
      ripped open.*d*

### Sincere Conversion and New Life

2 Return, Israel, to the LORD, your God;
    you have stumbled because of your
      iniquity.
3 Take with you words,
    and return to the LORD;
Say to him, "Forgive all iniquity,
    and take what is good.
Let us offer the fruit of our lips.*e*

4 §Assyria will not save us,
    nor will we mount horses;*f*
We will never again say, 'Our god,'
    to the work of our hands;
    for in you the orphan finds
      compassion."*g*

5 I will heal their apostasy,
    I will love them freely;
    for my anger is turned away from
      them.

6 I will be like the dew for Israel:*h*
    he will blossom like the lily;
He will strike root like the Lebanon cedar,
7     and his shoots will go forth.*i*
His splendor will be like the olive tree
    and his fragrance like Lebanon
      cedar.*j*

8 Again they will live in his shade;
    they will raise grain,
They will blossom like the vine,
    and his renown will be like the wine
      of Lebanon.

9 Ephraim! What more have I to do with
    idols?*k*
    I have humbled him, but I will take
      note of him.
I am like a verdant cypress tree.¶
    From me fruit will be found for you!

### Epilogue

10 **Who is wise enough to understand these
    things?*l*
    Who is intelligent enough to know
      them?
Straight are the paths of the LORD,*m*
    the just walk in them,*n*
    but sinners stumble in them.

---

\*[13:14] God calls upon "death" and "Sheol" to send their auxiliaries, "plagues" and "sting," to punish Israel (Hb 3:5; Ps 91:6). Paul uses this text in a different way to speak about the victory over death (1 Cor 15:54–55).

†[13:15] Although "Ephraim" is not explicitly mentioned in the text (the Hebrew text has the word "he"), the wordplay with the Hebrew word for "flourish" (*yaphrî*) suggests the use of "Ephraim" in the translation. **Wind**: possibly Assyria.

‡[14:1] **Samaria**: the capital of the Northern Kingdom will fall; this is the punishment predicted for Ephraim, the Northern Kingdom.

§[14:4] These good intentions promise a reversal of Israel's sins: no more reliance on "Assyria," i.e., on foreign alliances (see notes on 8:9 and 12:2), on "horses," i.e., on human power (10:13), and on idolatry (8:4–6; 13:2). Israel will trust in the Lord alone.

¶[14:9] **Verdant cypress tree**: the symbol of lasting life, the opposite of the sacred trees of the Baal cult (4:13). The Lord provides the "fruit" (*peri*) to Israel (2:7, 10), another instance of the wordplay on Ephraim (see notes on 9:16 and 13:15).

**[14:10] A challenge to the reader in the style of the wisdom literature.

z. [13:13] Is 37:3.   a. [13:14] 1 Cor 15:55.   b. [13:15] Ez 19:12.
c. [14:1] Ps 137:9.   d. [14:1] Am 1:13.   e. [14:3] Heb 13:15.

f. [14:4] Is 31:1.   g. [14:4] Lam 5:3.   h. [14:6] Is 26:19.   i. [14:7] Is 27:6.   j. [14:7] Sg 4:11.   k. [14:9] 2 Cor 6:16.   l. [14:10] Ps 107:43; Jer 9:11; Eccl 8:1.   m. [14:10] Dt 32:4.   n. [14:10] Dt 8:6; 11:22; Mi 6:8.

# THE BOOK OF
# JOEL

*❦*

In the two speeches that make up this book, Joel uses an agricultural crisis to measure his audience's knowledge of its God, warn them of a worse disaster if they ignore his preaching, and express his conviction that all faithful Judahites would someday enjoy a secure future. Although the superscription, or title (1:1), does not place Joel's preaching or the book's composition in a specific historical context, internal evidence favors a postexilic date for its composition, probably 450–400 B.C. This evidence includes: Joel's reliance on an established, possibly written, prophetic tradition; the existence of an organized temple liturgy; the dominance of priests and the absence of a king; and vocabulary characteristic of later material like Chronicles and Zechariah.

Inadequate winter rains and a spring locust infestation have devastated Judah's grain fields, vineyards, and orchards. Because the people carry on with business as usual, unaware that this crisis is the work of the Lord in their midst, Joel fears that the Lord may soon deliver a death blow by withholding the rains that normally fall in the late autumn. However, Joel's efforts to avert this crisis are successful. The first speech ends with Joel's assurance that at the end of the next agricultural year the people will enjoy a superabundant harvest.

The second speech begins with a summary description (chap. 3) of the prophet's hope that Judah's God will one day destroy its enemies and make Jerusalem secure once and for all. This divine intervention will create a more inclusive community, cutting across boundaries of gender, class, and age. In Peter's first public speech at Pentecost (Acts 2:16–21), the author uses Jl 3:1–5 to announce the formation of such a community among Christians in Jerusalem and the proximity of the day of the Lord. The rest of Joel's second speech (chap. 4) uses the imagery of drought and locusts from the first speech and introduces the metaphor of a grape harvest and wine making to describe the attack of the Lord's heavenly army on Judah's enemies. In the renewal of Judah's hillsides by the winter rains, the prophet sees the revitalization of the people because the Lord dwells with them.

The Book of Joel may be divided as follows:

I. Announcement of Unprecedented Disaster (1:2–20)
II. The Day of the Lord (2:1–27)
III. The Lord's Final Judgment (3:1–4:21)

## CHAPTER 1

¹The word of the LORD which came to Joel, the son of Pethuel.

### I. ANNOUNCEMENT OF
### UNPRECEDENTED DISASTER

² Listen to this, you elders!
  Pay attention, all who dwell in the
    land!
  Has anything like this ever happened in
    your lifetime,
    or in the lifetime of your ancestors?
³ Report it to your children.
  Have your children report it to their
    children,

and their children to the next
    generation.
⁴ What the cutter left,
    the swarming locust has devoured;
  What the swarming locust left,
    the hopper has devoured;
  What the hopper left,
    the consuming locust* has devoured.
⁵ Wake up, you drunkards,† and weep;

---

*[1:4] **Cutter . . . swarming locust . . . hopper . . . consuming locust**: these names may refer to various species of locusts, or to some phases in the insect's life cycle, or to successive waves of locusts ravaging the countryside.

†[1:5] **Drunkards**: this metaphor expresses both the urgency behind Joel's preaching and his ironic assessment of his audience. There are no grapes to process into new wine,

wail, all you wine drinkers,
Over the new wine,
    taken away from your mouths.
6 For a nation* invaded my land,
    powerful and past counting,
With teeth like a lion's,
    fangs like those of a lioness.
7 It has stripped bare my vines,
    splintered my fig tree,
Shearing off its bark and throwing it away,
    until its branches turn white.
8 Wail like a young woman† dressed in
    sackcloth
    for the husband of her youth.
9 Grain offering and libation are cut off
    from the house of the LORD;
In mourning are the priests,
    the ministers of the LORD.
10 The field is devastated;
    the farmland mourns,‡
Because the grain is devastated,
    the wine has dried up,
    the oil has failed.
11 Be appalled, you farmers!
    wail, you vinedressers,
Over the wheat and the barley,
    because the harvest in the field is
    ruined.
12 The vine has dried up,
    the fig tree has withered;
The pomegranate, even the date palm and
    the apple—
    every tree in the field has dried up.
Joy itself has dried up
    among the people.

### Cry Out to the Lord

13 §Gird yourselves and lament, you priests!
    wail, ministers of the altar!
Come, spend the night in sackcloth,
    ministers of my God!
For the grain offering and the libation
    are withheld from the house of your
    God.ª
14 Proclaim a holy fast!
    Call an assembly!
Gather the elders,
    all who dwell in the land,

To the house of the LORD, your God,
    and cry out to the LORD!ᵇ
15 O! The day!¶
    For near is the day of the LORD,
    like destruction from the Almighty
    it is coming!ᶜ
16 Before our very eyes**
    has not food been cut off?
And from the house of our God,
    joy and gladness?
17 The seed lies shriveled beneath clods of
    dirt;††
    the storehouses are emptied.
The granaries are broken down,
    for the grain is dried up.
18 ‡‡How the animals groan!
    The herds of cattle are bewildered!
Because they have no pasture,
    even the flocks of sheep are starving.
19 To you, LORD, I cry!
    for fire has devoured the wilderness
    pastures,
    flame has scorched all the trees in
    the field.
20 Even the animals in the wild
    cry out to you;
For the streams of water have run dry,
    and fire has devoured the wilderness
    pastures.ᵈ

## II. THE DAY OF THE LORD

### CHAPTER 2

### The Day Approaches

1 ¶¶Blow the horn in Zion,
    sound the alarm on my holy
    mountain!

¶[1:15] As in Am 5:18–20, the day of the Lord in Joel's first speech brings punishment, not victory, for Judah. In his second speech, this event means victory for those faithful to the Lord and death for the nations who are the Lord's enemies. **Almighty**: Hebrew *shaddai*. There is wordplay between *shod* ("destruction") and *shaddai*.

**[1:16] Before our very eyes**: Joel's audience should have discerned the significance of the winter drought and the locust invasion they witnessed. **Joy and gladness**: the loss of field crops has reduced Joel's audience to subsistence living, with no means for liturgical or personal celebration, as in v. 12.

††[1:17] The seed . . . clods of dirt: the meaning of the Hebrew is uncertain. Most commentators use the translation given here, since it fits the prophet's description of an agricultural year plagued by winter drought and a spring locust infestation.

‡‡[1:18–19] In figurative language, Joel describes how the insufficient winter rain, the locust invasions, and summer's heat on pasture lands and water sources drive domestic and wild animals to cry out for rain.

§§[2:1–11] Joel warns the people about the destruction he sees galloping toward Jerusalem. He combines the imagery of the locust invasion (chap. 1) with language from the holy war tradition in order to describe the Lord leading a heavenly army against the enemy, in this case, Jerusalem.

---

yet people view their situation as just another agricultural crisis. Joel argues that the problems they now face are lessons the Lord is using to provide the knowledge they lack.

*[1:6] **A nation**: the locusts are compared to an invading army, whose numbers are overwhelming. The ravaged landscape resembles the wasteland left behind by marauding troops; the order and peace associated with agricultural productivity (1 Kgs 5:5; Mi 4:4) has been destroyed.

†[1:8] **Like a young woman**: this simile personifies Jerusalem as a youthful widow, left unprotected and without resources by her husband's sudden death.

‡[1:10] **The farmland mourns**: or "the farmland is dried up."

§[1:13] Judah's situation is so grave and the day of the Lord so imminent that priests must lament day and night if they hope to reverse the divine punishment.

---

a. [1:13] Jer 4:8.

b. [1:14] Jl 2:15.   c. [1:15] Is 13:6; Ez 30:2–3; Ob 15; Zep 1:7.
d. [1:20] Ps 42:2.

Let all the inhabitants of the land tremble,
for the day of the LORD is coming!^e
Yes, it approaches,

2     a day of darkness and gloom,
a day of thick clouds!
Like dawn* spreading over the mountains,
a vast and mighty army!
Nothing like it has ever happened in ages
past,
nor will the future hold anything
like it,
even to the most distant
generations.^f

3 Before it,† fire devours,
behind it flame scorches.
The land before it is like the garden of
Eden,
and behind it, a desolate wilderness;
from it nothing escapes.^g

4 Their appearance is that of horses;
like war horses they run.

5 Like the rumble of chariots
they hurtle across mountaintops;
Like the crackling of fiery flames
devouring stubble;
Like a massive army
in battle formation.^h

6 Before them peoples tremble,
every face turns pale.^i

7 Like warriors they run,
like soldiers they scale walls,
Each advancing in line,
without swerving from the course.

8 No one crowds the other;
each advances in its own track;
They plunge through the weapons;
they are not checked.

9 They charge the city,
they run upon the wall,
they climb into the houses;
Through the windows
they enter like thieves.

10 Before them the earth trembles;
the heavens shake;
Sun and moon are darkened,
and the stars withhold their
brightness.^j

11 The LORD raises his voice
at the head of his army;
How immense is his host!
How numerous those who carry out
his command!

How great is the day of the LORD!
Utterly terrifying! Who can survive it?^k

## Return to the Lord

12 Yet even now—oracle of the LORD—
return to me with your whole heart,
with fasting, weeping, and
mourning.

13 Rend your hearts, not your garments,
and return to the LORD, your God,
For he is gracious and merciful,
slow to anger, abounding in
steadfast love,
and relenting in punishment.^l

14 Perhaps he will again relent
and leave behind a blessing,‡
Grain offering and libation
for the LORD, your God.^m

15 Blow the horn in Zion!
Proclaim a fast,
call an assembly!^n

16 Gather the people,
sanctify the congregation;
Assemble the elderly;
gather the children,
even infants nursing at the breast;
Let the bridegroom leave his room,
and the bride^§ her bridal tent.

17 Between the porch and the altar¶
let the priests weep,
let the ministers of the LORD weep
and say:
"Spare your people, LORD!
do not let your heritage become a
disgrace,
a byword among the nations!
Why should they say among the peoples,
'Where is their God?'"^o

**The Lord Relents.** ^18Then the LORD grew jealous** for his land and took pity on his people. ^19In response the LORD said to his people:

I am sending you
grain, new wine, and oil,
and you will be satisfied by them;

---

‡[2:14] **Blessing**: the rain that makes possible the grapes and grain (v. 19) that workers will process into Temple offerings.

§[2:16] **Elderly . . . infants . . . bridegroom . . . bride**: Jerusalem is in such great danger that even those normally excused from fasting or working are called upon to participate in activities to ward off the imminent catastrophe.

¶[2:17] **Between the porch and the altar**: the priests stood in the open space between the outdoor altar for burnt offerings and the Temple building.

**[2:18] **Jealous**: the Hebrew word describes the passionate empathetic bond the Lord has with Israel. The people's wholehearted participation in Joel's call for fasting and prayer sparks the Lord's longing to protect and love his people Israel. This desire moves him to withhold punishment and to send the blessing of v. 14 instead.

---

*[2:2] **Like dawn**: from the east comes dark destruction rather than a new day's light.

†[2:3] **Before it**: fire precedes and follows the army's advance. Even the ravaged landscape of chap. 1 looks like a lush garden compared to the devastation this army leaves behind.

e. [2:1] Is 13:9; Jer 4:5; 6:1; 51:27; Hos 5:8; Zep 1:16.   f. [2:2] Is 13:14; Zep 1:4–15.   g. [2:3] Is 13:9; 51:3; Ez 36:35.   h. [2:5] Jer 6:23.   i. [2:6] Na 2:11.   j. [2:10] Jl 4:15; Is 13:10, 13; Ez 32:7–8; Mt 24:29; Mk 13:24; Lk 21:25–26.

k. [2:11] Jer 30:7; Am 5:18; Zep 1:15.   l. [2:13] Ex 34:6; Ps 86:5; Jon 4:2.   m. [2:14] Jon 3:9.   n. [2:15] Jl 1:14.   o. [2:17] Ps 42:4, 11; 79:10; 115:2.

Never again will I make you
　　a disgrace among the nations.
20 The northerner* I will remove far from
　　　　you,
　　driving them out into a dry and
　　　　desolate land,
Their vanguard to the eastern sea,
　　their rearguard to the western sea,
And their stench will rise,
　　their stink will ascend,
What great deeds the Lord has done!
21 Do not fear, O land!
　　delight and rejoice,
　　for the Lord has done great things!ᵖ
22 Do not fear, you animals in the wild,
　　for the wilderness pastures sprout
　　　　green grass.
The trees bear fruit,
　　the fig tree and the vine produce
　　　　their harvest.
23 Children of Zion, delight
　　and rejoice in the Lord, your God!
For he has faithfully given you the early
　　　　rain,†
　　sending rain down on you,
　　the early and the late rains as
　　　　before.�q
24 The threshing floors will be full of grain,
　　the vats spilling over with new wine
　　　　and oil.
25 I will repay you double
　　what the swarming locust has eaten,
The hopper, the consuming locust, and
　　　　the cutter,
　　my great army I sent against you.ʳ
26 You will eat until you are fully satisfied,
　　then you will praise the name of the
　　　　Lord, your God,
Who acts so wondrously on your behalf!
　　My people will never again be put
　　　　to shame.
27 Then you will know that I am in the midst
　　　　of Israel:
　　I, the Lord, am your God, and there
　　　　is no other;
　　my people will never again be put to
　　　　shame.ˢ

## III. THE LORD'S FINAL JUDGMENT

## CHAPTER 3

### The Day of the Lordᵗ

1 ‡It shall come to pass
　　I will pour out my spirit upon all
　　　　flesh.
Your sons and daughters will prophesy,
　　your old men will dream dreams,
　　your young men will see visions.
2 Even upon your male and female
　　　　servants,
　　in those days, I will pour out my
　　　　spirit.
3 I will set signs in the heavens and on the
　　　　earth,
　　blood, fire, and columns of smoke;
4 The sun will darken,
　　the moon turn blood-red,
Before the day of the Lord arrives,
　　that great and terrible day.ᵘ
5 Then everyone who calls upon the name
　　　　of the Lord
　　will escape harm.
For on Mount Zion there will be a
　　　　remnant,
　　as the Lord has said,
And in Jerusalem survivors
　　whom the Lord will summon.ᵛ

## CHAPTER 4

### The Lord's Case Against the Nations

1 For see, in those days and at that time,ʷ
　　when I restore the fortunes
　　of Judah and Jerusalem,
2 I will gather all the nations
　　and bring them down to the Valley
　　　　of Jehoshaphat.§
There I will enter into judgment with
　　　　them
　　on behalf of my people, my heritage,
　　　　Israel;

---

*[2:20] **The northerner**: the locusts, pictured as an invading army, which traditionally came from the north (Jer
1:14–15; Ez 26:7; 38:6, 15). Locusts are not usually an annual
threat in Palestine, nor are they often associated with the
north. However, to demonstrate the extent of the Lord's care
for Judah and control over what happens within its borders,
Joel assures his audience that the Lord will quickly drive the
locusts out of Judah the coming spring, should they reappear.
Dead locusts will litter the shores of the "eastern" (the Dead
Sea) and the "western" (the Mediterranean) seas.

†[2:23] This autumn rain teaches the people to recognize
God's compassionate presence in nature and history. There is a
play on the double meaning of the Hebrew word *moreh*: "early
rain" and "teacher." In the Dead Sea Scrolls, the word is used
in the phrase "teacher (= *moreh*) of righteousness."

‡[3:1–5] In many places in the Old Testament, Hebrew
*ruah* is God's power, or spirit, bestowed on chosen individuals. The word can also mean "breath" or "wind." In this summary introduction to his second speech, Joel anticipates that
the Lord will someday renew faithful Judahites with the divine
spirit. In Acts 2:17–21 the author has Peter cite Joel's words
to suggest that the newly constituted Christian community,
filled with divine life and power, inaugurates the Lord's Day,
understood as salvation for all who believe that Jesus of Nazareth is the Christ.

§[4:2] **Valley of Jehoshaphat**: one of the symbolic names
of the place of punishment for Judah's enemies; the other is
"Valley of Decision" (v. 14). The name Jehoshaphat means "the
Lord judges." If the popular identification of this place as the
Kidron Valley is accurate, Joel may imagine the Lord seated
above the valley on Mount Zion directing his troops in the
destruction of nations in the valley below.

---

p. [2:21] Ps 126:3.　q. [2:23] Hos 10:12.　r. [2:25] Jer 5:17.　s. [2:27]
Is 45:5–6, 18; 46:9.

t. [3:1] Is 44:3; Ez 39:28–29; Acts 2:17–21.　u. [3:4] Jl 2:10; Mal
3:23.　v. [3:5] Ob 17–18; Rom 10:13.　w. [4:1] Jer 33:15; 50:4, 20.

Because they scattered them among the
       nations,
   they divided up my land.$^x$
$^3$ For my people they cast lots,
       trading a young boy for the price of
          a prostitute,
       exchanging a young girl for the wine
          they drank.$^y$

$^4$*Moreover, what are you doing to me, Tyre
and Sidon, and all the regions of Philistia? Are
you paying me back for something? If you are,
I will very quickly turn your deeds back upon
your own head.$^z$ $^5$You took my silver and my
gold and brought my priceless treasures into
your temples! $^6$You sold the people of Judah and
Jerusalem to the Greeks, taking them far from
their own country! $^7$Look! I am rousing them
from the place to which you sold them, and I
will turn your deeds back upon your own head.
$^8$I will sell your sons and daughters to the Judahites who will sell them to the Sabeans,$^†$ a distant
nation. The LORD has spoken!

### The Nations Destroyed

$^9$ Announce this to the nations:
       Proclaim a holy war!
       Alert the warriors!
   Let all the soldiers
       report and march!$^a$
$^{10}$ ‡Beat your plowshares into swords,
       and your pruning knives into spears;
       let the weakling boast, "I am a
          warrior!"$^b$

$^{11}$ Hurry and come, all you neighboring
          peoples,
       assemble there!
   Bring down, LORD, your warriors!
$^{12}$ Let the nations rouse themselves and
          come up
       to the Valley of Jehoshaphat;
   For there I will sit in judgment
       upon all the neighboring nations.

$^{13}$ Wield the sickle,$^c$
       for the harvest is ripe;
   Come and tread,
       for the wine press is full;

The vats overflow,
       for their crimes are numerous.$^§$
$^{14}$ Crowds upon crowds
       in the Valley of Decision;
   For near is the day of the LORD
       in the Valley of Decision.$^d$
$^{15}$ Sun and moon are darkened,
       and the stars withhold their
          brightness,$^e$
$^{16}$ The LORD roars from Zion,
       and from Jerusalem raises his voice,$^f$
   The heavens and the earth quake,
       but the LORD will be a shelter for his
          people,
       a fortress for the people of Israel.

### A Secure Future for Judah

$^{17}$ Then you will know$^§$ that I the LORD am
          your God,$^g$
       dwelling on Zion, my holy
          mountain;
   Jerusalem will be holy,
       and strangers will never again travel
          through her.
$^{18}$ **On that day
       the mountains will drip new wine,
       and the hills flow with milk,
   All the streams of Judah
       will flow with water.
   A spring will rise from the house of the
          LORD,
       watering the Valley of Shittim.$^h$
$^{19}$ Egypt will be a waste,
       Edom a desolate wilderness,
   Because of violence done to the Judahites,
       because they shed innocent blood in
          their land.$^i$
$^{20}$ But Judah will be inhabited forever,
       and Jerusalem for all generations.
$^{21}$ I will avenge their blood,
       and I will not acquit the guilt.
   The LORD dwells in Zion.

§[4:13] **Their crimes are numerous**: the nations are ripe
for punishment. Joel uses the vocabulary of the autumn grape
harvest to describe the assault of the Lord's army against these
nations. In Is 63:1–6, grape harvest imagery also controls the
description of the Lord's return from Edom with blood-spat-
tered clothing after having trod his enemies into the ground
as if they were grapes (cf. Jer 25:30).
   ¶[4:17] **Then you will know**: this verse further develops
the motif of knowledge introduced in 2:27. The Judahites will
learn that the Lord is present in their economic prosperity and
political autonomy, even though they did not associate God's
presence with their crop failure.
   **[4:18] Images of agricultural abundance illustrate the
harmony and order Joel expects the Lord to establish in Judah;
like 2:18–27, this section reverses the deprivation and drought
of chap. 1. **A spring . . . house of the LORD**: streams of water
flowing from the Temple of an ideal Jerusalem also appear in
Ez 47:1. **The Valley of Shittim**: or "the ravine of the acacia
trees"; while there is a Shittim east of the Jordan, the reference
here is probably to that rocky part of the Kidron Valley southeast of Jerusalem, an arid region where acacia trees flourished.

*[4:4–8] This prose material may be a later addition to the
book. It illustrates a common biblical theme (cf. Ps 7:16; 9:16;
35:8; 37:14–15; 57:7), having one's evil deed (selling Judahites
into slavery) turned into one's own punishment (being sold
into slavery by the Judahites).
   †[4:8] **Sabeans**: traders from the southwestern tip of the
Arabian peninsula, present-day Yemen (cf. 1 Kgs 10:1–2; Ps
72:10; Jer 6:20).
   ‡[4:10] The Lord directs the troops to forge military
weapons out of the agricultural tools necessary for life during
peacetime. In Is 2:4 and Mi 4:3, both in contexts presuming
the defeat of Israel's enemies, this imagery is reversed.

x. [4:2] Is 66:18; Zec 14:2.   y. [4:3] Ob 11, 16.   z. [4:4] Ob 15.
a. [4:9] Jer 6:4.   b. [4:10] Is 2:4; Mi 4:3.   c. [4:13] Is 63:1–6; Rev
14:15.

d. [4:14] Ob 15.   e. [4:15] Jl 2:10; 3:4.   f. [4:16] Jer 25:30; Am
1:2.   g. [4:17] Ob 17; Na 2:1.   h. [4:18] Ez 47:1–12; Am 9:13; Zec
14:8.   i. [4:19] Ob 10.

# THE BOOK OF
# AMOS

᜵ᔇᔒ

Amos was a sheepbreeder of Tekoa in Judah, who delivered his oracles in the Northern Kingdom during the prosperous reign of Jeroboam II (786–746 B.C.). He prophesied in Israel at the great cult center of Bethel, from which he was finally expelled by the priest in charge of this royal sanctuary (7:10–17). The poetry of Amos, who denounces the hollow prosperity of the Northern Kingdom, is filled with imagery and language taken from his own pastoral background. The book is an anthology of his oracles and was compiled either by the prophet or by some of his disciples.

The prophecy begins with a sweeping indictment of Damascus, Philistia, Tyre, and Edom; but the forthright herdsman saves his climactic denunciation for Israel, whose injustice and idolatry are sins against the light granted to her. Israel could indeed expect the day of the Lord, but it would be a day of darkness and not light (5:18). When Amos prophesied the overthrow of the sanctuary, the fall of the royal house, and the captivity of the people, it was more than Israelite officialdom could bear. The priest of Bethel drove Amos from the shrine—but not before hearing a terrible sentence pronounced upon himself.

Amos is a prophet of divine judgment, and the sovereignty of the Lord in nature and history dominates his thought. But he was no innovator; his conservatism was in keeping with the whole prophetic tradition calling the people back to the high moral and religious demands of the Lord's revelation.

Amos's message stands as one of the most powerful voices ever to challenge hypocrisy and injustice. He boldly indicts kings, priests, and leaders (6:1; 7:9, 16–17). He stresses the importance and the divine origin of the prophetic word (3:3–8); one must either heed that word in its entirety or suffer its disappearance (8:11–12). Religion without justice is an affront to the God of Israel and, far from appeasing God, can only provoke divine wrath (5:21–27; 8:4–10). The Lord is not some petty national god but the sovereign creator of the cosmos (4:13; 5:8; 9:5–6). Amos alludes to historical forces at work through which God would exercise judgment on Israel (6:14). Several times he mentions deportation as the fate that awaits the people and their corrupt leaders (4:3; 5:5, 27; 7:17), a standard tactic of Assyrian foreign policy during this period. Through the prophetic word and various natural disasters (4:6–12) the Lord has tried to bring Israel to repentance, but to no avail. Israel's rebelliousness has exhausted the divine patience and the destruction of Israel as a nation and as God's people is inevitable (2:4, 13–16; 7:8–9). As it is presented in this book, Amos's message is one of almost unrelieved gloom (but see 5:14–15). A later appendix (9:11–15), however, ends the book on a hopeful note, looking beyond the judgment that had already taken place in fulfillment of Amos's word.

The Book of Amos may be divided as follows:

   I. Editorial Introduction (1:1–2)
  II. Oracles Against the Nations (1:3–2:16)
 III. Threefold Summons to Hear the Word of the Lord (3:1–5:9)
 IV. Three Woes (5:7–6:14)
  V. Symbolic Visions (7:1–9:10)
 VI. Epilogue: Restoration Under a Davidic King (9:11–15)

# I. EDITORIAL INTRODUCTION

## CHAPTER 1

¹The words of Amos, who was one of the sheep-breeders from Tekoa,*a* which he received in a vision concerning Israel in the days of Uzziah, king of Judah, and in the days of Jeroboam, son of Joash, king of Israel, two years before the earthquake.* ²He said:

The LORD roars from Zion,†
 and raises his voice from Jerusalem;
The pastures of the shepherds languish,
 and the summit of Carmel withers.*b*

## II. ORACLES AGAINST THE NATIONS‡

### Aram

³Thus says the LORD:

For three crimes of Damascus, and now
 four—§
I will not take it back—
Because they threshed Gilead
 with sledges of iron,
⁴ I will send fire upon the house of Hazael,
 and it will devour the strongholds of
 Ben-hadad.¶*c*
⁵ I will break the barred gate of Damascus;
 From the Valley of Aven** I will cut
 off the one enthroned,
And the sceptered ruler from Beth-eden;
 the people of Aram shall be exiled to
 Kir,*d* says the LORD.

### Philistia

⁶Thus says the LORD:

For three crimes of Gaza, and now four—
 I will not take it back—
Because they exiled an entire population,
 handing them over to Edom,
⁷ I will send fire upon the wall of Gaza,
 and it will devour its strongholds;
⁸ From Ashdod I will cut off the one
 enthroned
 and the sceptered ruler from
 Ashkelon;
I will turn my hand against Ekron,
 and the last of the Philistines shall
 perish,
 says the Lord GOD.

### Tyre

⁹Thus says the LORD:

For three crimes of Tyre, and now four—
 I will not take it back—
Because they handed over an entire
 population to Edom,
 and did not remember their
 covenant of brotherhood,††
¹⁰ I will send fire upon the wall of Tyre,
 and it will devour its strongholds.

### Edom

¹¹Thus says the LORD:

For three crimes of Edom, and now four—
 I will not take it back—
Because he pursued his brother‡‡ with the
 sword,
 suppressing all pity,
Persisting in his anger,
 his wrath raging without end,
¹² I will send fire upon Teman,
 and it will devour the strongholds of
 Bozrah.§§

### Ammon

¹³Thus says the LORD:

For three crimes of the Ammonites, and
 now four—
 I will not take it back—
Because they ripped open pregnant
 women in Gilead,*e*

---

*[1:1] **The earthquake**: a major earthquake during the reign of Uzziah (ca. 783–742 B.C.), so devastating that it was remembered long afterwards (cf. Zec 14:5). See the description of an earthquake in Amos's final vision (9:1).

†[1:2] Significantly, the roar comes to the Northern Kingdom from Jerusalem. This verse, perhaps an editorial remark, sets the tone of Amos's message.

‡[1:3–2:16] All the nations mentioned here may have been part of the ideal empire of David-Solomon (cf. 1 Kgs 5:1; 2 Kgs 14:25). Certain standards of conduct were expected not only in their relations with Israel but also with one another.

§[1:3] **For three crimes . . . and now four**: this formula (n, n + 1) is frequent in poetry (e.g., Prv 6:16–19; 30:18–19). The progression "three" followed by "four" here suggests a climax. The fourth crime is one too many and exhausts the Lord's forbearance.

¶[1:4] **Hazael . . . Ben-hadad**: kings of the Arameans whose capital was Damascus (v. 5); they fought against Israel (2 Kgs 13:3) and had long occupied the region of Gilead (v. 3) in Transjordan.

**[1:5] **Valley of Aven**: lit., "valley of wickedness," perhaps a distortion of a place name in Aramean territory, identity unknown. **Beth-eden**: an Aramean city-state on the Euphrates, about two hundred miles northeast of Damascus, called *Bit-adini* in Assyro-Babylonian texts. **Kir**: cf. 9:7; probably to be identified with the city of Emar on the Euphrates, a major Aramean center in the Late Bronze Age. One text from this site calls the king of Emar "the king of the people of the land of Kir."

††[1:9] **Did not remember their covenant of brotherhood**: standard diplomatic language of this period, meaning "violated the treaty." The violation may not have been against Israel itself but against a fellow "subject" nation of the ideal Davidic-Solomonic empire (cf. 2:1).

‡‡[1:11] **Pursued his brother**: "brother" here may denote a fellow vassal or subject of Israel.

§§[1:12] **Teman . . . Bozrah**: two of the chief cities of Edom; cf. Jer 49:20.

---

a. [1:1] Zec 14:5.  b. [1:2] Jer 25:30; Jl 4:16.  c. [1:4] 2 Kgs 13:3–7; Hos 8:14.  d. [1:5] 2 Kgs 16:9.

e. [1:13] 2 Kgs 8:12; 15:16.

in order to extend their territory,
14 I will kindle a fire upon the wall of
        Rabbah,*
    and it will devour its strongholds
Amid war cries on the day of battle,
    amid stormwind on the day of
        tempest.
15 Their king shall go into exile,
    he and his princes with him, says
        the Lord.

## CHAPTER 2

### Moab

¹Thus says the Lord:

For three crimes of Moab, and now four—
    I will not take it back—
Because he burned to ashes†
    the bones of Edom's king,
2 I will send fire upon Moab,
    and it will devour the strongholds of
        Kerioth;
Moab shall meet death amid uproar,
    battle cries and blasts of the ram's
        horn.
3 I will cut off the ruler from its midst,
    and all the princes I will slay with
        him, says the Lord.

### Judah

4‡Thus says the Lord:

For three crimes of Judah, and now four—
    I will not take it back—
Because they spurned the instruction of
        the Lord,ᶠ
    and did not keep his statutes;
Because the lies§ which their ancestors
        followed
    have led them astray,
5 I will send fire upon Judah,
    and it will devour the strongholds of
        Jerusalem.

### Israel

⁶Thus says the Lord:

For three crimes of Israel,¶ and now
        four—
    I will not take it back—
Because they hand over the just for silver,
    and the poor for a pair of sandals;ᵍ
7 They trample the heads of the destitute
        into the dust of the earth,
    and force the lowly out of the way.
Son and father sleep with the same girl,**
    profaning my holy name.
8 Upon garments taken in pledge
    they recline beside any altar.††ʰ
Wine at treasury expense
    they drink in their temples.
9 Yet it was I who destroyed the Amorites
        before them,
    who were as tall as cedars,
    and as strong as oak trees.
I destroyed their fruit above
    and their roots beneath.ⁱ
10 It was I who brought you up from the
        land of Egypt,
    and who led you through the desert
        for forty years,
    to occupy the land of the Amorites;
11 I who raised up prophets among your
        children,
    and nazirites‡‡ among your young
        men.
Is this not so, Israelites?—
    oracle of the Lord.
12 But you made the nazirites drink wine,
    and commanded the prophets, "Do
        not prophesy!"ʲ
13 Look, I am groaning beneath you,
    as a wagon groans when laden with
        sheaves.
14 Flight shall elude the swift,
    and the strong shall not retain
        strength;ᵏ

---

¶[2:6] **Israel**: Amos's audience would applaud his condemnation of foreign kingdoms in the foregoing seven oracles, especially of Judah. But now he adds an eighth, unexpected oracle—against Israel itself. This is the real "punch line" of this whole section, to which the preceding oracles serve mainly as introduction.

**[2:7] **Son and father sleep with the same girl**: the crime condemned here may be the misuse of power by the rich who take unfair advantage of young women from the ranks of the poor and force themselves on them, thus adding oppression to the sin of impurity.

††[2:8] **Upon garments . . . any altar**: creditors kept the garments taken as pledges from the poor instead of returning them to their owners before nightfall as the law commanded (Ex 22:25; cf. Dt 24:12). **Wine . . . in their temples**: lavish feasts for the rich, serving the finest wines in great abundance (see 6:4–7) and funded by the treasuries of local temples (e.g., at Dan and Bethel). The Hebrew in this verse is difficult. Another possible translation would be: "And the wine of those who have been fined / they drink in the house of their god."

‡‡[2:11] **Nazirites**: see note on Nm 6:2–21. **Oracle of the Lord**: a phrase used extensively in prophetic books to indicate divine speech.

---

*[1:14] **Rabbah**: now called Amman, the modern capital of Jordan.

†[2:1] **He burned to ashes**: to the peoples of the Near East, burning the bones of the dead was a particularly heinous crime, as it was believed to cause the spirits of these dead to wander without any hope of interment in their graves, where they could rest in peace.

‡[2:4–8, 12] Unlike the crimes of the nations detailed in this section, which are wrongs against other nations, those of Judah and Israel named here are violations of the Lord's demands.

§[2:4] **The lies**: false gods worshiped by the Judahites.

f. [2:4] Is 5:24.

g. [2:6] Am 8:6; Sir 46:19.   h. [2:8] Dt 24:12–13.   i. [2:9] Nm 21:21–32; Dt 2:24–37; Jb 18:16; Hos 9:16.   j. [2:12] Am 7:13; Nm 6:1–4; Is 30:10; Jer 11:21.   k. [2:14] Ps 33:16.

The warrior shall not save his life,
<sup>15</sup>     nor shall the archer stand his ground;
The swift of foot shall not escape,
     nor shall the horseman save his life.
<sup>16</sup> And the most stouthearted of warriors
     shall flee naked on that day—
     oracle of the LORD.

## III. THREEFOLD SUMMONS TO HEAR THE WORD OF THE LORD

### CHAPTER 3

#### First Summons

<sup>1</sup> Hear this word, Israelites, that the LORD
     speaks concerning you,
     concerning the whole family I
     brought up from the land of
     Egypt:
<sup>2</sup> You alone I have known,*
     among all the families of the earth;<sup>l</sup>
Therefore I will punish you
     for all your iniquities.

<sup>3</sup> †Do two journey together
     unless they have agreed?
<sup>4</sup> Does a lion roar in the forest
     when it has no prey?
Does a young lion cry out from its den
     unless it has seized something?
<sup>5</sup> Does a bird swoop down on a trap on the
     ground
     when there is no lure for it?
Does a snare spring up from the ground
     without catching anything?
<sup>6</sup> Does the ram's horn sound in a city
     without the people becoming
     frightened?
Does disaster befall a city
     unless the LORD has caused it?<sup>m</sup>

<sup>7</sup>(Indeed, the Lord GOD does nothing without
revealing his plan to his servants the prophets.)

<sup>8</sup> The lion has roared,
     who would not fear?<sup>n</sup>
The Lord GOD has spoken,
     who would not prophesy?

<sup>9</sup> Proclaim this in the strongholds of
     Assyria,<sup>‡</sup>

in the strongholds of the land of
     Egypt:
"Gather on the mount of Samaria,
     and see the great disorders within it,
     the oppressions within its midst."<sup>§</sup>
<sup>10</sup> They do not know how to do what is
     right—
     oracle of the LORD—
Storing up in their strongholds
     violence and destruction.
<sup>11</sup> Therefore thus says the Lord GOD:
An enemy shall surround the land,
     tear down your fortresses,
     and pillage your strongholds.
<sup>12</sup> Thus says the LORD:
As the shepherd rescues from the mouth
     of the lion
     a pair of sheep's legs or the tip of
     an ear,
So shall the Israelites escape,
     those who dwell in Samaria,
With the corner of a couch
     or a piece of a cot.<sup>¶</sup>

<sup>13</sup> Hear and bear witness against the house
     of Jacob—
     an oracle of the Lord GOD, the God
     of hosts:
<sup>14</sup> On the day when I punish Israel for its
     crimes,
     I will also punish the altars of Bethel;
The horns of the altar shall be broken off
     and fall to the ground."<sup>o</sup>
<sup>15</sup> I will strike the winter house
     and the summer house;
The houses of ivory shall lie in ruin,
     and their many rooms shall be no
     more—
     oracle of the LORD.

### CHAPTER 4

#### Second Summons

<sup>1</sup> Hear this word, you cows of Bashan,<sup>††</sup>
     who live on the mount of Samaria:
Who oppress the destitute
     and abuse the needy;
Who say to your husbands,
     "Bring us a drink!"

---

*[3:2] **You alone I have known**: precisely because Israel enjoyed a special status among the nations of the world in the eyes of the Lord (but see 9:7) it was called to a high degree of fidelity to God. Because Israel has failed in this expectation, it must experience God's punishment.

†[3:3–8] The metaphors in these sayings illustrate the principle of cause and effect, and lead up to the conclusion in v. 8.

‡[3:9] **Assyria**: following the Greek version, the Hebrew text has "Ashod." It is supposed that this was a copyist's error:

---

"Assyria" seems intended, in order to parallel "Egypt" in the next line.

§[3:9] With a keen sense of irony, Amos invites the most powerful oppressors in Israel's memory, past and present—Egypt and Assyria—to see and marvel at the great oppression and injustice being wrought within Samaria by the people of Israel.

¶[3:12] The "escape" is clearly a disaster, not a deliverance.

**[3:14] On Bethel, see also 4:4; 5:5–6; and 7:13. The prophet is condemning the religiosity and formalism of the worship by Israel's leaders.

††[4:1] **Cows of Bashan**: the pampered women of Samaria; Bashan was a region east of the Sea of Galilee, famous for its rich pasture and fattened herds.

---

l. [3:2] Gn 18:19; Dt 7:6.   m. [3:6] Jl 2:1.   n. [3:8] Am 1:2.

o. [3:14] Am 9:1; 1 Kgs 13:1–5.

2 The Lord God has sworn by his holiness:
  Truly days are coming upon you
        when they shall drag you away with
            ropes,
        your children with fishhooks;
3 You shall go out through the breached walls
        one in front of the other,
  And you shall be exiled to Harmon—*
        oracle of the Lord.

4 Come to Bethel† and sin,
        to Gilgal and sin all the more!
  Each morning bring your sacrifices,
        every third day your tithes;
5 Burn leavened bread as a thanksgiving
            sacrifice,
        proclaim publicly your voluntary
            offerings,
  For so you love to do, Israelites—
        oracle of the Lord God.

6 Though I made your teeth
        clean of food in all your cities,
        and made bread scarce in all your
            dwellings,
  Yet you did not return to me—
        oracle of the Lord.ᵖ
7 �q And I withheld the rain from you
        when the harvest was still three
            months away;
  I sent rain upon one city
        but not upon another;
  One field was watered by rain,
        but the one I did not water dried up;
8 Two or three cities staggered to another to
            drink water
        but were not satisfied;
  Yet you did not return to me—
        oracle of the Lord.
9 I struck you with blight and mildew;
        locusts devoured your gardens and
            vineyards,
        the caterpillar consumed your fig
            trees and olive trees;
  Yet you did not return to me—
        oracle of the Lord.ʳ
10 I sent upon you pestilence like that of
            Egypt;ˢ
        with the sword I killed your young
            men and your captured horses,
        and to your nostrils I brought the
            stench of your camps;
  Yet you did not return to me—
        oracle of the Lord.

11 I overthrew you
        as when God overthrew Sodom and
            Gomorrah;
        you were like a brand plucked from
            the fire,ᵗ
  Yet you did not return to me—
        oracle of the Lord.
12 Therefore thus I will do to you,‡ Israel:
        and since I will deal thus with you,
        prepare to meet your God, O Israel!
13 The one who forms mountains and
            creates winds,
        and declares to mortals their
            thoughts;
  Who makes dawn into darkness
        and strides upon the heights of the
            earth,
        the Lord, the God of hosts, is his
            name!

## CHAPTER 5

### Third Summons§

1 Hear this word which I utter concerning
            you,
        this dirge, house of Israel:
2 She is fallen, to rise no more,
        virgin Israel;
  She lies abandoned on her land,
        with no one to raise her up.ᵘ
3 For thus says the Lord God
        to the house of Israel:
  The city that marched out with a thousand
        shall be left with a hundred,
  Another that marched out with a hundred
        shall be left with ten.
4 For thus says the Lordᐟ
        to the house of Israel:
  Seek me, that you may live,ᵛ
5      but do not seek Bethel;
  Do not come to Gilgal,
        and do not cross over to Beer-sheba;
  For Gilgal shall be led into exile
        and Bethel shall be no more.
6 ** Seek the Lord, that you may live,

---

‡[4:12] **Therefore thus I will do to you**: this climax of vv. 6–12, announcing the sentence the Lord intends to pass on Israel, is open-ended.

§[5:1–17] These verses form a chiastic section beginning and ending with a lament over Israel (vv. 2, 16–17) and containing a double appeal to "seek" the Lord (vv. 4, 14). This editorial arrangement gives the whole section a negative cast, in effect nullifying the only hopeful verse in Amos (v. 15). Israel is as good as dead.

¶[5:4–5] **For thus says the Lord . . . Bethel shall be no more**: these two verses continue the sarcasm of 4:4–5, verses in which Amos invites the people to come and "sin" at Bethel and Gilgal. The cult cities of Samaria should have been places where God could be "sought" but, because of the sins of the Northern Kingdom, these cities would cease to exist.

**[5:6] These verses have been rearranged to achieve the proper sequence according to the best possible manuscript tradition. Cf. the Textual Notes accompanying the translation.

---

*[4:3] **Harmon**: or perhaps "Mount Mon"; an unidentified site, probably far to the north of Israel, under the control of Assyria.

†[4:4] **Come to Bethel**: Amos's invitation to the people to come and "sin" at two of the major religious centers in Samaria is sarcastic. His point is that sacrifice and worship without justice is an abomination to the God of Israel; cf. 5:21–24.

---

p. [4:6] Wis 12:2, 10.   q. [4:7] Jer 14:1–6.   r. [4:9] Dt 28:22; Jl 1:4; 2:25; Hg 2:17.   s. [4:10] Dt 7:15; 28:27.

t. [4:11] Gn 19:24–25; Zec 3:2.   u. [5:2] Am 8:13.   v. [5:4] Hos 5:6; 10:12.

lest he flare up against the house of
Joseph* like a fire
that shall consume the house of
Israel, with no one to quench it.

8 The one who made the Pleiades and Orion,
who turns darkness into dawn,
and darkens day into night;
Who summons the waters of the sea,
and pours them out on the surface
of the earth;ʷ
9 Who makes destruction fall suddenly
upon the stronghold
and brings ruin upon the fortress,
the Lord is his name.

## IV. THREE WOES

### First Woe

7 Woe to those who turn justice into
wormwood
and cast righteousness to the
ground,
10 They hate those who reprove at the gate
and abhor those who speak with
integrity;
11 Therefore, because you tax the destitute
and exact from them levies of grain,
Though you have built houses of hewn
stone,
you shall not live in them;
Though you have planted choice
vineyards,
you shall not drink their wine.ˣ
12 Yes, I know how many are your crimes,
how grievous your sins:
Oppressing the just, accepting bribes,
turning away the needy at the gate.
13 (Therefore at this time the wise are struck
dumb
for it is an evil time.)

14 Seek good and not evil,
that you may live;
Then truly the Lord, the God of hosts,
will be with you as you claim.
15 Hate evil and love good,
and let justice prevail at the gate;
Then it may be that the Lord, the God
of hosts,
will have pity on the remnant of
Joseph.ʸ

16 Therefore, thus says the Lord,
the God of hosts, the Lord:

In every square there shall be lamentation,
and in every street they shall cry,
"Oh, no!"
They shall summon the farmers to wail
and the professional mourners to
lament.
17 And in every vineyard there shall be
lamentation
when I pass through your midst,
says the Lord.

### Second Woe

18 Woe to those who yearn
for the day of the Lord!†
What will the day of the Lord mean for
you?
It will be darkness, not light!ᶻ
19 As if someone fled from a lion
and a bear met him;
Or as if on entering the house
he rested his hand against the wall,
and a snake bit it.
20 Truly, the day of the Lord will be
darkness, not light,
gloom without any brightness!

21 ‡ᵃI hate, I despise your feasts,
I take no pleasure in your
solemnities.
22 Even though you bring me your burnt
offerings and grain offerings
I will not accept them;
Your stall-fed communion offerings,
I will not look upon them.
23 Take away from me
your noisy songs;
The melodies of your harps,
I will not listen to them.
24 Rather let justice surge like waters,
and righteousness like an unfailing
stream.
25 ᵇDid you bring me sacrifices and grain
offerings
for forty years in the desert, O house
of Israel?ᶜ

---

†[5:18] **The day of the Lord:** first mentioned in Amos,
this refers to a specific time in the future, known to the Lord
alone, when God's enemies would be decisively defeated. The
common assumption among Israelites was that the Lord's foes
and Israel's foes were one and the same. But Amos makes it
clear that because the people have become God's enemies by
refusing to heed the prophetic word, they too would experience the divine wrath on that fateful day. However, during the
exile this expression comes to mean a time when God would
avenge Israel against its oppressors and bring about its restoration (Jer 50:27; Ez 30:3–5).
‡[5:21–27] The prophet does not condemn cultic activity
as such but rather the people's attempt to offer worship with
hands unclean from oppression of their fellow Israelites (cf. Ps
15:2–5; 24:3–4). But worship from those who disregard justice
and righteousness (v. 24) is never acceptable to the God of
Israel. Through the Sinai covenant the love of God and the
love of neighbor are inextricably bound together.

---

*[5:6] **House of Joseph:** the kingdom of Israel or Northern Kingdom, the chief tribes of which were descended from
Ephraim and Manasseh, the sons of Joseph; cf. 5:15; 6:6.

---

w. [5:8] Am 9:6; Jb 9:9; 38:31.   x. [5:11] Am 9:14; Dt 28:30; Zep
1:13.   y. [5:15] Jl 2:14; Rom 12:9.

z. [5:18] Jer 14:16; Jl 2:1–2, 11; Zep 1:14–18.   a. [5:21–24] Is 1:10–
17; Jer 6:20.   b. [5:25–26] Acts 7:42–43.   c. [5:25] Jer 7:21–26.

26 Yet you will carry away Sukuth,* your king,
    and Kaiwan, your star-image,
    your gods that you have made for
       yourselves,[d]
27 As I exile you beyond Damascus,
    says the Lord,
    whose name is the God of hosts.

## CHAPTER 6

### Third Woe

1 Woe to those who are complacent in
       Zion,
    secure on the mount of Samaria,
  Leaders of the first among nations,
    to whom the people of Israel turn.
2 Pass over to Calneh and see,
    go from there to Hamath the great,
    and down to Gath[†] of the Philistines.
  Are you better than these kingdoms,
    or is your territory greater than
      theirs?
3 You who would put off the day of disaster,
    yet hasten the time of violence!
4 Those who lie on beds of ivory,
    and lounge upon their couches;
  Eating lambs taken from the flock,
    and calves from the stall;
5 Who improvise to the music of the harp,
    composing on musical instruments
      like David,
6 Who drink wine from bowls,
    and anoint themselves with the best
      oils,
  but are not made ill by the collapse
      of Joseph;
7 Therefore, now they shall be the first to go
    into exile,
  and the carousing of those who
      lounged shall cease.

8 The Lord God has sworn by his very
      self—
  an oracle of the Lord, the God of
      hosts:
  I abhor the pride of Jacob,
    I hate his strongholds,
    and I will hand over the city with
      everything in it;[e]

9 Should there remain ten people
    in a single house, these shall die.
10 When a relative or one who prepares the
      body picks up the remains
    to carry them out of the house,
  If he says to someone in the recesses of
      the house,
    "Is anyone with you?" and the
      answer is, "No one,"
  Then he shall say, "Silence!"
    for no one must mention the name
      of the Lord.[‡][f]
11 Indeed, the Lord has given the command
    to shatter the great house to bits,
    and reduce the small house to
      rubble.
12 Can horses run over rock,
    or can one plow the sea with oxen?
  Yet you have turned justice into gall,
    and the fruit of righteousness into
      wormwood,[g]
13 You who rejoice in Lodebar,
    and say, "Have we not, by our own
      strength,
    seized Karnaim[§] for ourselves?"
14 Look, I am raising up against you, house
      of Israel—
    oracle of the Lord, the God of
      hosts—
  A nation[¶] that shall oppress you
    from Lebo-hamath even to the Wadi
      Arabah.

## V. SYMBOLIC VISIONS

## CHAPTER 7

### First Vision: The Locust Swarm

1 This is what the Lord God showed me: He was forming a locust swarm when the late growth began to come up (the late growth after the king's mowing**). 2 When they had finished eating the grass in the land, I said:

  Forgive, O Lord God!
    Who will raise up Jacob?
    He is so small!

---

*[5:26] **Sukuth:** probably a hebraized form of Assyro-Babylonian *Shukudu* ("the Arrow"), a name of Sirius, the brightest star in the night sky. It was associated with the god Ninurta, who was widely worshiped in Mesopotamia. According to 2 Kgs 17:30 the cult of Sirius was introduced into Samaria by deportees from Babylonia. **Kaiwan:** a hebraized form of an Akkadian name for the planet Saturn, also worshiped as a deity in Mesopotamia.

†[6:2] **Calneh . . . Hamath . . . Gath:** city-states overcome by the Assyrians in the eighth century B.C., whose fate should be a lesson to the Israelites. The prophet castigates the leaders for being more intent on pursuing a luxurious lifestyle (vv. 1, 4–6) than reading the signs of the times.

‡[6:10] In this desperate situation there seems to be a profound fear of the Lord, who is the cause of the deaths (cf. 3:6).

§[6:13] **Lodebar . . . Karnaim:** two towns recaptured from Judah by Israelite forces during the reign of Jeroboam II (see 2 Kgs 14:25). Some mockery of at least the first of these victories is probably intended by the prophet here, as Lodebar can be translated "nothing."

¶[6:14] **A nation:** Assyria. **Lebo-hamath . . . Wadi Arabah:** the territorial limits of Solomon's kingdom, north and south respectively, as re-established by Jeroboam II (see 2 Kgs 14:25).

**[7:1] **The king's mowing:** the first harvesting of the crops apparently belonged to the king as a kind of tax.

---

d. [5:26] 2 Kgs 17:30; Jer 2:28.   e. [6:8] Is 28:1–4; Jer 51:14.

f. [6:10] Zep 1:7.   g. [6:12] Am 5:7.

³The LORD relented concerning this. "This shall not be," said the Lord GOD.

## Second Vision: The Rain of Fire

⁴This is what the Lord GOD showed me: He was summoning a rain of fire. It had devoured the great abyss and was consuming the fields. ⁵Then I said:

Cease, O Lord GOD!
Who will raise up Jacob?
He is so small!

⁶The LORD relented concerning this. "This also shall not be," said the Lord GOD.

## Third Vision: The Plummet

⁷ᵏThis is what the Lord GOD showed me: He was standing, plummet in hand, by a wall built with a plummet.* ⁸The Lord GOD asked me, "What do you see, Amos?" And I answered, "A plummet." Then the LORD said:

See, I am laying the plummet
    in the midst of my people Israel;
    I will forgive them no longer.
⁹    The high places of Isaac shall be laid
        waste,
        and the sanctuaries of Israel made
            desolate;
        and I will attack the house of
            Jeroboam with the sword.

## Biographical Interlude: Amos and Amaziah

¹⁰Amaziah, the priest of Bethel, sent word to Jeroboam, king of Israel: "Amos has conspired against you within the house of Israel; the country cannot endure all his words. ¹¹For this is what Amos says:

'Jeroboam shall die by the sword,
    and Israel shall surely be exiled from
        its land.'"

¹²To Amos, Amaziah said: "Off with you, seer, flee to the land of Judah and there earn your bread by prophesying! ¹³But never again prophesy in Bethel;ⁱ for it is the king's sanctuary and a royal temple." ¹⁴Amos answered Amaziah, "I am not a prophet,† nor do I belong to a company of prophets. I am a herdsman and a dresser of sycamores,ʲ ¹⁵but the LORD took me from following the flock, and the LORD said to me, 'Go, prophesy to my people Israel.'ᵏ ¹⁶Now hear the word of the LORD:

You say: 'Do not prophesy against Israel,
    do not preach against the house of
        Isaac.'
¹⁷ Therefore thus says the LORD:
Your wife shall become a prostitute in
    the city,
    and your sons and daughters shall
        fall by the sword.
Your land shall be parcelled out by
    measuring line,
    and you yourself shall die in an
        unclean land;
    and Israel shall be exiled from its
        land."

# CHAPTER 8

## Fourth Vision: The Summer Fruit

¹This is what the Lord GOD showed me: a basket of end-of-summer fruit.‡ ²He asked, "What do you see, Amos?" And I answered, "A basket of end-of-summer fruit." And the LORD said to me:

The end has come for my people Israel;
    I will forgive them no longer.
³ The temple singers will wail on that day—
    oracle of the Lord GOD.
Many shall be the corpses,
    strewn everywhere—Silence!ˡ

⁴ Hear this, you who trample upon the needy
    and destroy the poor of the land:
⁵ "When will the new moon be over," you
    ask,
    "that we may sell our grain,
And the sabbath,
    that we may open the grain-bins?
We will diminish the ephah,§
    add to the shekel,
    and fix our scales for cheating!ᵐ
⁶ We will buy the destitute for silver,
    and the poor for a pair of sandals;ⁿ
    even the worthless grain we will
        sell!"

---

*[7:7] **A plummet**: with this vision, the pleas of the prophet (vv. 1–6) disappear, and disaster is announced. One use of the plummet in ancient times was to see how far out of line a wall or building had become, to determine whether it could be repaired or would have to be torn down. Like a structure that had become architecturally unsound, Israel was unsalvageable and would have to be demolished (cf. 2 Kgs 21:13; Is 34:11; Lam 2:8).

†[7:14] **I am not a prophet**: Amos reacts strongly to Amaziah's attempt to classify him as a "prophet-for-hire" who "earns [his] bread" by giving oracles in exchange for payment (cf. 1 Sm 9:3–10; Mi 3:5). To disassociate himself from this kind of "professional" prophet, Amos rejects outright the title of *nabi'* ("prophet"). By profession he is a herdsman/sheep-breeder and a dresser of sycamore trees, but God's call was commissioned him to prophesy to Israel.

‡[8:1–2] **End-of-summer fruit . . . the end has come**: the English translation attempts to capture the wordplay of the Hebrew. The Hebrew word for "fruit picked late in the season" is *qayis*, while the word for "end" is *qes*.

§[8:5] **Ephah**: see note on Is 5:10.

h. [7:7–8] Jer 1:11–14.   i. [7:13] Am 2:12.

j. [7:14] Am 1:1; 2 Sm 7:8.   k. [7:15] Am 3:8.   l. [8:3] Am 6:10.
m. [8:5] Dt 25:13; Hos 12:8.   n. [8:6] Am 2:6.

7 The LORD has sworn by the pride of
    Jacob:
        Never will I forget a thing they have
            done!
8 Shall not the land tremble because of this,
        and all who dwell in it mourn?
    It will all rise up and toss like the Nile,
        and subside like the river of Egypt.°
9 On that day—oracle of the Lord GOD—
        I will make the sun set at midday
        and in broad daylight cover the land
            with darkness.
10 I will turn your feasts into mourning
        and all your songs into dirges.
    I will cover the loins of all with sackcloth
        and make every head bald.
    I will make it like the time of mourning
        for an only child,
        and its outcome like a day of bitter
            weeping.ᵖ

11 See, days are coming—oracle of the Lord
        GOD—
        when I will send a famine upon the
            land:
    Not a hunger for bread, or a thirst for
        water,
        but for hearing the word of the
            LORD.
12 They shall stagger from sea to sea
        and wander from north to east
    In search of the word of the LORD,
        but they shall not find it.q

13 On that day, beautiful young women and
        young men
        shall faint from thirst,
14 Those who swear by Ashima of Samaria,*ʳ
        and who say, "By the life of your
        god, O Dan,"
    "By the life of the Power of Beer-sheba!"
        They shall fall, never to rise again.

## CHAPTER 9

### Fifth Vision: The Destruction
### of the Sanctuary

¹I saw the Lord standing beside the altar. And
he said:

    Strike the capitals
        so that the threshold shakes!

    Break them off on the heads of them
        all!
    Those who are left I will slay with the
        sword.
    Not one shall get away,
        no survivor shall escape.†ˢ
2 Though they dig down to Sheol,
        even from there my hand shall take
        them;
    Though they climb to the heavens,
        even from there I shall bring them
        down.ᵗ
3 Though they hide on the summit of
        Carmel,
        there too I will hunt them down and
        take them;
    Though they hide from my gaze at the
        bottom of the sea,
        there I will command the serpent‡ to
        bite them.ᵘ
4 Though they go into captivity before their
        enemies,
        there I will command the sword to
        slay them.
    I will fix my gaze upon them
        for evil and not for good.

5 The Lord GOD of hosts,
    Who melts the earth with his touch,
        so that all who dwell on it mourn,
    So that it will all rise up like the Nile,
        and subside like the river of Egypt;ᵛ
6 Who has built his upper chamber in
        heaven,
        and established his vault over the
        earth;
    Who summons the waters of the sea
        and pours them upon the surface of
        the earth—
        the LORD is his name.ʷ

7 Are you not like the Ethiopians to me,
        O Israelites?—oracle of the LORD—
    Did I not bring the Israelites from the
        land of Egypt
        as I brought the Philistines from
        Caphtor
        and the Arameans§ from Kir?

*[8:14] **Ashima of Samaria**: a high-ranking goddess
worshiped in Hamath, whose cult was transplanted by the
people of that city when they were deported to Samaria by
the Assyrians (2 Kgs 17:30). **The Power of Beer-sheba**: possibly an epithet of a deity worshiped in Beer-sheba, either a
syncretistic form of the worship of Israel's God or of another
god. **Dan . . . Beer-sheba**: the traditional designation for the
northern and southern limits of Israel to which the Israelites
made pilgrimages.

†[9:1] This vision may describe the destruction of the
temple at Bethel and the fulfillment of the oracle in 3:14, linking God's judgment upon Israel with the "punishment" of the
altars of Bethel. This dramatic event (perhaps to be identified
with the earthquake mentioned in 1:1) symbolizes the end of
the Northern Kingdom as the Lord's people, the consequence
of their steadfast refusal to heed the prophetic word and
return to the God of Israel.

‡[9:3] **The serpent**: a name for the primeval chaos monster, vanquished by God at the time of creation but not annihilated. He was a personification of the sea, another primary
archetype of chaos in the ancient Near East.

§[9:7] **The Ethiopians . . . the Philistines . . . the Arameans**: although Israel's relationship to the Lord was special,
even unique in some respects (3:2), Israel was not the only

o. [8:8] Am 1:1; 9:1, 5.    p. [8:10] Tb 2:6; Zec 12:10.    q. [8:12] Hos
5:6.    r. [8:14] 2 Kgs 17:30.

s. [9:1] Am 2:13–16.    t. [9:2] Ps 139:7–12; Jb 20:6.    u. [9:3] Jb 7:12;
Is 27:1.    v. [9:5] Am 8:8.    w. [9:6] Am 5:8.

8 See, the eyes of the Lord GOD are on this
    sinful kingdom,
    and I will destroy it from the face of
      the earth—
But I will not destroy the house of Jacob
    completely—
    oracle of the LORD.
9 For see, I have given the command
    to sift the house of Israel among all
      the nations,
As one sifts with a sieve,
    letting no pebble fall to the ground.
10 All sinners among my people shall die by
    the sword,
    those who say, "Disaster will not
      reach or overtake us."[x]

## VI. EPILOGUE: RESTORATION UNDER A DAVIDIC KING

11 *On that day I will raise up
    the fallen hut of David;
I will wall up its breaches,
    raise up its ruins,

    and rebuild it as in the days of old,[y]
12 That they may possess the remnant of
    Edom,
    and all nations claimed in my
      name—
    oracle of the LORD, the one who
      does this.
13 Yes, days are coming—
    oracle of the LORD—
When the one who plows shall overtake
    the one who reaps
    and the vintager, the sower of the
      seed;
The mountains shall drip with the juice
    of grapes,
    and all the hills shall run with it.[z]
14 I will restore my people Israel,
    they shall rebuild and inhabit their
      ruined cities,
Plant vineyards and drink[†] the wine,
    set out gardens and eat the fruits.[a]
15 I will plant them upon their own ground;
    never again shall they be plucked
From the land I have given them—
    the LORD, your God, has spoken.

---

people on earth that God cared for. Striking here is the reference to divine intervention in the history of the Philistines and Arameans, not unlike the Lord's saving intervention to bring Israel out of Egypt. **Caphtor**: the island of Crete.

*[9:11–15] These verses are most likely an editorial supplement to Amos, added to bring the book into harmony with the positive thrust of the prophetic books in general, especially those written after the exile, when the final edition of Amos was probably completed. The editors would have seen the destruction of Samaria in 722/721 B.C. as the fulfillment of Amos's prophecies, but in this epilogue they express the

view that destruction was not the Lord's final word for Israel. In Acts 15:15–17, James interprets this passage in a messianic sense. **The fallen hut of David**: the Davidic kingdom, which included what later became the divided Northern and Southern Kingdoms. **All nations claimed in my name**: lit., "all nations over whom my name has been pronounced." This idiom denotes ownership.

†[9:14] **Rebuild . . . inhabit . . . plant . . . drink**: in this era of restoration, the Lord nullifies the curse of 5:11, which uses these same four verbs, and turns it into a blessing for Israel.

---

x. [9:10] Jer 5:12; 23:17.

y. [9:11] Acts 15:16–17.   z. [9:13] Jl 4:18.   a. [9:14] Is 65:21–22.

# THE BOOK OF
# OBADIAH

This book, the shortest among the twelve minor prophets, is a single twenty-one-verse oracle against Edom. Nothing is known of the author, although his prophecy against Edom, a neighbor and rival of Israel, indicates a date of composition sometime after the Babylonian destruction of Jerusalem in 587 B.C., when the Edomites apparently took advantage of the helpless people of Judah and Jerusalem (v. 11; Ps 137:7). The relations and rivalries between Israel and Edom are reflected in oracles against Edom (Is 34; Ez 35) and in the stories of their ancestors, the brothers Jacob and Esau (Gn 25–33).

The prophecy is a bitter cry for vengeance against Edom for its pride and its crimes. Mount Esau in Edom will be occupied and ravaged by the enemy, while Mount Zion will be restored to its former sanctity and security. The triumphant refrain of Israelite eschatology will be heard once more: "The kingdom is the Lord's!" The opening verses of this prophecy (vv. 1–5) are very similar to part of an oracle against Edom in Jer 49 (vv. 9, 14–16), suggesting that Israel's prophets drew upon traditional language and idioms in the composition of prophetic speech.

The book may be divided as follows:

I. Edom's Fall Decreed (1–7)
II. Edom's Betrayal of Judah (8–14)
III. Edom's Fall and Judah's Restoration (15–21)

## Edom's Fall Decreed

1 The vision of Obadiah.
Thus says the Lord GOD concerning
Edom:
We have heard a message from the LORD,
and a herald has been sent among
the nations:
"Rise up, so we may go to war
against it!"[a] •
2 Now I make you least among the nations;
you are utterly contemptible.
3 The pride of your heart has deceived
you—
you who dwell in mountain crevices,
in your lofty home,*
Who say in your heart,
"Who will bring me down to earth?"
4 Though you soar like the eagle,
and your nest is set among the stars,
From there I will bring you down—
oracle of the LORD.
5 If thieves came to you, robbers by night
—how you have been destroyed!—
would they not steal merely till they
had enough?

If grape pickers came to you,
would they not leave some
gleanings?[†b]
6 ‡How Esau has been searched out,
his treasures hunted down!
7 To the border they have driven you—
all your allies;
Your partners have deceived you,
they have overpowered you;
Those who eat your bread§
will replace you with foreigners,
who have no understanding.

## Edom's Betrayal of Judah

8 On that day—oracle of the LORD—will I
not
make the wise disappear from Edom,
and understanding from Mount
Esau?[c]

---

†[5] Something of value may escape the thief, and the grape picker always leaves something for the gleaners, but God's devastation of Edom will be complete.

‡[6] With the past tense in vv. 5–7, the prophet presents a future event as if it had already happened.

§[7] **Those who eat your bread**: alliances were often established by covenant meals (cf. Gn 31:44–46). When Edom is destroyed, foreigners will replace the Edomites, who were known for wisdom (cf. v. 8; Jer 49:7; Jb 2:11).

---

*[3] Edom occupied the mountains southeast of Israel and the Dead Sea.

---

a. [1:1–4] Jer 49:14–16.

b. [1:5] Jer 49:9.  c. [1:8] Is 29:14; 1 Cor 1:19.

9 Teman,* your warriors will be
    terror-stricken,
    so that everyone on Mount Esau will
        be cut down.
10 Because of violence to your brother† Jacob,
    disgrace will cover you,
    you will be done away with forever!*d*
11 On the day you stood by,
    the day strangers carried off his
        possessions,
    And foreigners entered his gates
        and cast lots for Jerusalem,
    you too were like one of them.‡e

12 §Do not gloat over the day of your brother,
    the day of his disaster;
    Do not exult over the people of Judah
        on the day of their ruin;
    Do not speak haughtily
        on the day of distress!
13 Do not enter the gate of my people
        on the day of their calamity;
    Do not gloat—especially you—over his
        misfortune
        on the day of his calamity;
    Do not lay hands upon his possessions
        on the day of his calamity!
14 Do not stand at the crossroads
        to cut down his survivors;
    Do not hand over his fugitives
        on the day of distress!

### Edom's Fall and Judah's Restoration

15 Near is the day of the LORD*f*
    against all the nations!

As you have done, so will it be done to
    you,
    your conduct will come back upon
        your own head;
16 As you drank¶ upon my holy mountain,
    so will all the nations drink
        continually.
    Yes, they will drink and swallow,
        and will become as though they had
            not been.
17 But on Mount Zion there will be some
    who escape;**
    the mountain will be holy,
    And the house of Jacob will take
        possession
        of those who dispossessed them.*g*
18 The house of Jacob will be a fire,
    the house of Joseph a flame,
    and the house of Esau stubble.
    They will set it ablaze and devour it;
    none will survive of the house of
        Esau,
    for the LORD has spoken.

19They will take possession of the Negeb,†† Mount
Esau, the Shephelah, and Philistia, possess the
countryside of Ephraim, the countryside of
Samaria, Benjamin, and Gilead.*h* 20The exiles
of this Israelite army will possess the Canaanite land as far as Zarephath,‡‡ and the exiles of
Jerusalem who are in Sepharad will possess the
cities of the Negeb. 21And deliverers§§ will ascend
Mount Zion to rule Mount Esau, and the kingship shall be the LORD's.

---

*[9] **Teman**: a synonym for Edom; perhaps the name of a
region or a city, the part representing the whole. **Mount Esau**:
whatever its geographic reference, the phrase is an effective
representation of Edom's arrogance.

†[10] **Your brother**: used with a double meaning referring
to the common lineage of Israel and Edom, in which their
ancestors were brothers, Jacob and Esau (Gn 25:19–26), and
referring also to their political alliance, in which allies were
called brothers (cf. Am 1:9, 11).

‡[11] In 587 B.C., Edomites joined the invading Babylonian forces (v. 13) and captured escaping Judahites. The
destruction of Jerusalem strengthened and expanded Edom's
hold on Judah's southern territory.

§[12–14] The commands in vv. 12–14 are not to be understood as future prohibitions but as descriptions of crimes
Edom in fact already committed on the day of Jerusalem's fall
described in v. 11.

---

d. [1:10] Gn 27:41–45; Ez 25:12–14.   e. [1:11] Ps 137:7.   f. [1:15] Jl
4:11–12, 14.

¶[16] **As you drank**: i.e., Judah has suffered the punishment of divine wrath in 587 B.C. The oracle promises a similar
fate for the nations, especially Edom (v. 18). The metaphor
"drinking the cup of God's wrath" occurs often in the Bible; cf.
Jb 21:20; Is 51:17–23; Jer 25:15–16; Rev 14:10.

**[17–19] The Israelites will be restored and will occupy the
lands of those who oppressed them. The survivors of Judah
will be rejoined by the returned exiles from northern Israel.

††[19] **Negeb**: the area south of Judah and west of Edom.
**Gilead**: east of the Jordan River.

‡‡[20] **Zarephath**: a town in Phoenicia, north of Tyre; cf.
1 Kgs 17:10. **Sepharad**: perhaps Sardis in western Asia Minor.
The later rabbis thought it was Spain.

§§[21] **Deliverers**: the victorious Israelites who will rule
over their enemies, as the ancient judges did; cf. Jgs 3:9, 15,
31; 10:1.

---

g. [1:17] Jer 49:2.   h. [1:19] Jer 50:19.

# THE BOOK OF
# JONAH

✥

The story of Jonah has great theological import. It concerns a disobedient prophet who rejected his divine commission, was cast overboard in a storm and swallowed by a great fish, rescued in a marvelous manner, and returned to his starting point. Now he obeys and goes to Nineveh, the capital of Israel's ancient enemy. The Ninevites listen to his message of doom and repent immediately. All, from king to lowliest subject, humble themselves in sackcloth and ashes. Seeing their repentance, God does not carry out the punishment planned for them. At this, Jonah complains, angry because the Lord spares them. This fascinating story caricatures a narrow mentality which would see God's interest extending only to Israel, whereas God is presented as concerned with and merciful to even the inhabitants of Nineveh (4:11), the capital of the Assyrian empire which brought the Northern Kingdom of Israel to an end and devastated Jerusalem in 701 B.C.. The Lord is free to "repent" and change his mind. Jonah seems to realize this possibility and wants no part in it (4:2; cf. Ex 34:6). But the story also conveys something of the ineluctable character of the prophetic calling.

The book is replete with irony, wherein much of its humor lies. The name "Jonah" means "dove" in Hebrew, but Jonah's character is anything but dove-like. Jonah is commanded to go east to Nineveh but flees toward the westernmost possible point (1:2–3), only to be swallowed by a great fish and dumped back at this starting point (2:1, 11). The sailors pray to their gods, but Jonah is asleep in the hold (1:5–6). The prophet's preaching is a minimum message of destruction, while it is the king of Nineveh who calls for repentance and conversion (3:4–10); the instant conversion of the Ninevites is greeted by Jonah with anger and sulking (4:1). He reproaches the Lord in words that echo Israel's traditional praise of his mercy (4:2; cf. Ex 34:6–7). Jonah is concerned about the loss of the gourd but not about the possible destruction of 120,000 Ninevites (4:10–11).

Unlike other prophetic books, this is not a collection of oracles but the story of a disobedient, narrow-minded prophet who is angry at the outcome of the sole message he delivers (3:4). It is difficult to date but almost certainly is postexilic and may reflect the somewhat narrow, nationalistic reforms of Ezra and Nehemiah. As to genre, it has been classified in various ways, such as parable or satire. The "sign" of Jonah is interpreted in two ways in the New Testament: His experience of three days and nights in the fish is a "type" of the experience of the Son of Man (Mt 12:39–40), and the Ninevites' reaction to the preaching of Jonah is contrasted with the failure of Jesus' generation to obey the preaching of one who is "greater than Jonah" (Mt 12:41–42; Lk 11:29–32).

The Book of Jonah may be divided as follows:

I. Jonah's Disobedience and Flight (1:1–16)
II. Jonah's Prayer (2:1–11)
III. Jonah's Obedience and the Ninevites' Repentance (3:1–10)
IV. Jonah's Anger and God's Reproof (4:1–11)

## CHAPTER 1
**Jonah's Disobedience and Flight.** ¹The word of the Lord came to Jonah,ᵃ son of Amittai:* ²Set out for the great city† of Nineveh, and preach against it; for their wickedness has come before me.ᵇ ³But Jonah made ready to flee to Tarshish,‡ away from the Lord. He went down to Joppa,

---

*[1:1] **Jonah, son of Amittai:** a prophet of this name lived at the time of Jeroboam II (786–746 B.C.).

†[1:2] **Great city:** exaggeration is characteristic of this book; the word "great" (Heb. *gadol*) occurs fourteen times.

‡[1:3] **Tarshish:** identified by many with Tartessus, an ancient Phoenician colony in southwest Spain; precise identification with any particular Phoenician center in the western Mediterranean is uncertain. To the Israelites it stood for the far west.

a. [1:1] 2 Kgs 14:25.

b. [1:2] Jon 3:3; 4:11.

found a ship going to Tarshish, paid the fare, and went down in it to go with them to Tarshish, away from the LORD.

4The LORD, however, hurled a great wind upon the sea, and the storm was so great that the ship was about to break up. 5Then the sailors were afraid and each one cried to his god. To lighten the ship for themselves, they threw its cargo into the sea. Meanwhile, Jonah had gone down into the hold of the ship, and lay there fast asleep. 6The captain approached him and said, "What are you doing asleep? Get up, call on your god! Perhaps this god will be mindful of us so that we will not perish."

7Then they said to one another, "Come, let us cast lots to discover on whose account this evil has come to us." So they cast lots, and the lot fell on Jonah.d 8They said to him, "Tell us why this evil has come to us! What is your business? Where do you come from? What is your country, and to what people do you belong?" 9"I am a Hebrew," he replied; "I fear the LORD, the God of heaven, who made the sea and the dry land."

10Now the men were seized with great fear and said to him, "How could you do such a thing!"—They knew that he was fleeing from the LORD, because he had told them. 11They asked, "What shall we do with you, that the sea may calm down for us?" For the sea was growing more and more stormy. 12Jonah responded, "Pick me up and hurl me into the sea and then the sea will calm down for you. For I know that this great storm has come upon you because of me."

13Still the men rowed hard to return to dry land, but they could not, for the sea grew more and more stormy. 14Then they cried to the LORD: "Please, O LORD, do not let us perish for taking this man's life; do not charge us with shedding innocent blood, for you, LORD, have accomplished what you desired."* 15Then they picked up Jonah and hurled him into the sea, and the sea stopped raging. 16Seized with great fear of the LORD, the men offered sacrifice to the LORD and made vows.

## CHAPTER 2

**Jonah's Prayer.** 1But the LORD sent a great fish to swallow Jonah, and he remained in the belly of the fish three days and three nights.e 2Jonah prayed to the LORD, his God, from the belly of the fish:

3 †Out of my distress I called to the LORD,
　　and he answered me;
　From the womb of Sheol‡ I cried for help,
　　and you heard my voice.f
4 You cast me into the deep, into the heart
　　of the sea,
　　and the flood enveloped me;
　All your breakers and your billows
　　passed over me.g
5 Then I said, "I am banished from your
　　sight!
　How will I again look upon your
　　holy temple?"h
6 The waters surged around me up to my
　　neck;
　　the deep enveloped me;
　seaweed wrapped around my head.i
7 I went down to the roots of the
　　mountains;
　　to the land whose bars closed
　　behind me forever,
　But you brought my life up from the pit,
　　O LORD, my God.j

8 When I became faint,
　　I remembered the LORD;
　My prayer came to you
　　in your holy temple.k
9 Those who worship worthless idols
　　abandon their hope for mercy.l
10 But I, with thankful voice,
　　will sacrifice to you;
　What I have vowed I will pay:
　　deliverance is from the LORD.m

11Then the LORD commanded the fish to vomit Jonah upon dry land.

## CHAPTER 3

**Jonah's Obedience and the Ninevites' Repentance.** 1The word of the LORD came to Jonah a second time: 2Set out for the great city of Nineveh, and announce to it the message that I will tell you. 3So Jonah set out for Nineveh, in accord with the word of the LORD. Now Nineveh was an awesomely great city; it took three days to walk through it. 4Jonah began his journey through the city, and when he had gone only a single day's walk announcing, "Forty days more and Nineveh shall be overthrown," 5the people of Nineveh believed God; they proclaimed a fast and all of them, great and small,§ put on sackcloth.n

6When the news reached the king of Nineveh, he rose from his throne, laid aside his robe, covered himself with sackcloth, and sat in

---

*[1:14] Aware that this disaster is a divine punishment on Jonah, the sailors ask that in ridding themselves of him they not be charged with the crime of murder.

†[2:3–10] These verses, which may have originally been an independent composition, are a typical example of a song of thanksgiving, a common psalm genre (e.g., Ps 116; Is 38:9–20). Such a song is relevant here, since Jonah has not drowned, and the imagery of vv. 4, 6 is appropriate.

‡[2:3] **Sheol**: cf. note on Ps 6:6.

§[3:5] **Great and small**: the contrast can refer to distinctions of social class (prominent citizens and the poor).

c. [1:4–6] Mk 4:37–38.   d. [1:7] Jos 7:16–18; 1 Sm 14:40–42.
e. [2:1] Mt 12:40; 16:4; Lk 11:30; 1 Cor 15:4.

f. [2:3] Ps 18:7; 120:1.   g. [2:4] Ps 42:8.   h. [2:5] Ps 31:23; Is 38:11.
i. [2:6] Ps 18:5; 69:2.   j. [2:7] Ps 16:10; 30:4.   k. [2:8] Ps 5:8; 18:7; 88:3.
l. [2:9] Ps 31:7.   m. [2:10] Ps 50:14.   n. [3:5] Mt 12:41; Lk 11:32.

ashes. ⁷Then he had this proclaimed throughout Nineveh:* "By decree of the king and his nobles, no man or beast, no cattle or sheep, shall taste anything; they shall not eat, nor shall they drink water. ⁸Man and beast alike must be covered with sackcloth and call loudly to God; they all must turn from their evil way and from the violence of their hands. ⁹†Who knows? God may again repent and turn from his blazing wrath, so that we will not perish." ˢ ¹⁰When God saw by their actions how they turned from their evil way, he repented of the evil he had threatened to do to them; he did not carry it out.

## CHAPTER 4

**Jonah's Anger and God's Reproof.** ¹But this greatly displeased Jonah, and he became angry.‡ ²He prayed to the Lord, "O Lord, is this not what I said while I was still in my own country? This is why I fled at first toward Tarshish. I knew that you are a gracious and merciful God, slow to anger, abounding in kindness, repenting of punishment.ᵖ ³So now, Lord, please take my life from me; for it is better for me to die than to live."�q ⁴But the Lord asked, "Are you right to be angry?"¶

⁵Jonah then left the city for a place to the east of it, where he built himself a hut and waited** under it in the shade, to see what would happen to the city. ⁶Then the Lord God provided a gourd plant.†† And when it grew up over Jonah's head, giving shade that relieved him of any discomfort, Jonah was greatly delighted with the plant. ⁷But the next morning at dawn God provided a worm that attacked the plant, so that it withered. ⁸And when the sun arose, God provided a scorching east wind; and the sun beat upon Jonah's head till he became faint. Then he wished for death, saying, "It is better for me to die than to live."

⁹But God said to Jonah, "Do you have a right to be angry over the gourd plant?" Jonah answered, "I have a right to be angry—angry enough to die." ¹⁰Then the Lord said, "You are concerned‡‡ over the gourd plant which cost you no effort and which you did not grow; it came up in one night and in one night it perished. ¹¹And should I not be concerned over the great city of Nineveh, in which there are more than a hundred and twenty thousand persons who cannot know their right hand from their left, not to mention all the animals?"§§

---

*[3:7–8] Fasting and wearing sackcloth are signs of human repentance; here they are legislated even for the animals—a humorous touch, perhaps anticipating 4:11.

†[3:9–10] Scripture frequently presents the Lord as repenting (or, changing his mind) of the evil that he threatens; e.g., Gn 6:6–7; Jer 18:8.

‡[4:1] **He became angry**: because of his narrow vindictiveness, Jonah did not wish the Lord to forgive the Ninevites.

§[4:2] **Punishment**: lit., "evil"; see 1:2, 7, 8; 3:8, 10; 4:1.

¶[4:4] The Lord's question is as unexpected as it is pithy. It is also a mysterious reply to Jonah's wish to die; perhaps it serves to invite Jonah to think over his situation. However, it goes unanswered, and the request and reply will be repeated in vv. 8–9.

**[4:5] **Waited**: Jonah still hopes his threat of doom will be fulfilled.

††[4:6] **Gourd plant**: the Hebrew word, qiqayon, means here a wide-leafed plant of the cucumber or castor-bean variety.

‡‡[4:10] **Concerned**: the meaning of the Hebrew verb suggests "pity, care for," and this appears in the Lord's attitude to Nineveh in v. 11. Jonah has shown only a selfish concern over the plant in contrast to the Lord's true "concern" for his creatures.

§§[4:11] A selfish Jonah bemoans his personal loss of a gourd plant for shade without any concern over the threat of loss of life to the Ninevites through the destruction of their city. If a solicitous God provided the plant for a prophet without the latter's effort or merit, how much more is God disposed to show love and mercy toward all people, Jew and Gentile, when they repent of their sins and implore divine pardon. God's care goes beyond human beings to all creation, as in Job 38.

---

o. [3:9] Jl 2:14.   p. [4:2] Ex 34:6–7; Ps 86:5; Jl 2:13.   q. [4:3] 1 Kgs 19:4.

# THE BOOK OF
# MICAH

This book consists of a collection of speeches, proclamations of punishment and of salvation, attributed to the prophet Micah. Following its superscription (1:1), the book has two major sections, each with two parts. The organization of the material is thematic, moving from judgment to salvation in both major sections. In the first section (Mi 1–5), chaps. 1–3 consist almost entirely of prophecies of punishment, and chaps. 4–5 of prophecies of salvation. The second section (chaps. 6–7) also moves from prophecies of punishment (6:1–7:6) to confidence in God's salvation (7:7–20).

Micah was a contemporary of the prophet Isaiah. The book's superscription (1:1) places his prophetic activity during the reigns of three kings of Judah: Jotham, Ahaz, and Hezekiah. It identifies him as a resident of Moresheth, a village in the Judean foothills. The solitary reference to Micah outside the book (Jer 26:17–18) places him in the reign of Hezekiah and reports that he went from his small town to proclaim the word of the Lord in the capital, and asserts that his announcements of judgment against Jerusalem moved the king and the people to repentance. Unlike Isaiah, who was a native of the holy city, Micah was an outsider from the countryside and must have been a controversial figure. He would have been unpopular with the leaders whom he condemned (3:1–4) and the wealthy whom he criticized (2:1–5). He was quick to separate himself from priests and other prophets, whom he considered to be corrupt (3:5–8).

Just how much of the Book of Micah can be traced to the eighth-century prophet is uncertain. Tradition considers all of the words to be the recorded speeches of Micah, and some contemporary commentators agree. On the other hand, some modern scholars have thought of Micah as exclusively a prophet of doom, and therefore attributed as few as three of the seven chapters to him. The style, content, theological viewpoint, and historical perspective of some of the material reflect not the period of the Assyrian threat to Judah in the eighth century but the Babylonian exile in the sixth century B.C. and later. This is particularly evident in chap. 7, but also at other points in the book. The composition of this book, like most other prophetic texts, involved a complex editorial process. This is apparent from the fact that the stirring prophecy of peace and justice in 4:1–5 is virtually identical to Is 2:2–5.

Like Is 1–39, the Book of Micah is focused on Jerusalem, Zion, and the Judean leadership. The Micah who speaks in this prophetic book knows the tradition that Zion is the Lord's chosen place, but he is critical of the popular view that this election ensures the city's security (2:6–13; 3:9–12). Through the prophetic voice, the Lord announces the impending punishment of God's people by means of military defeat and exile because of their failure to establish justice. After that punishment God will bring the people back to their land and establish perpetual peace. The will of God for human beings is that they do justice, love goodness, and walk humbly with God (6:6–8).

The Book of Micah is divided as follows:

 I. Oracles of Punishment (1:2–3:12)
 II. Oracles of Salvation (4:1–5:14)
 III. Announcement of Judgment (6:1–7:6)
 IV. Confidence in God's Future (7:7–20)

## CHAPTER 1

¹The word of the LORD which came to Micah of Moresheth in the days of Jotham, Ahaz, and Hezekiah, kings of Judah, which he saw concerning Samaria and Jerusalem.

### I. ORACLES OF PUNISHMENT

²  Hear, O peoples, all of you,
        give heed, O earth, and all that is
            in it!*
    Let the Lord GOD be witness against you,
        the Lord from his holy temple!*
³  For see, the LORD goes out from his place*
        and descending, treads upon the
            heights of the earth.†
⁴  The mountains melt under him
        and the valleys split open,
    Like wax before the fire,
        like water poured down a slope.
⁵  All this is for the crime of Jacob,
        for the sins of the house of Israel.‡
    What is the crime of Jacob? Is it not
            Samaria?
    And what is the sin of the house of Judah?
        Is it not Jerusalem?
⁶  So I will make Samaria a ruin in the field,
        a place to plant vineyards;
    I will throw its stones into the valley,
        and lay bare its foundations.§
⁷  All its carved figures shall be broken to
            pieces,ᶜ
        all its wages shall be burned in the
            fire,
        and all its idols I will destroy.
    As the wages of a prostitute⁵ it gathered
            them,
        and to the wages of a prostitute they
            shall return.

⁸  "For this I will lament and wail,
        go barefoot and naked;
    I will utter lamentation like the jackals,
        mourning like the ostriches,ᵈ
⁹  For her wound is incurable;
        it has come even to Judah.
    It has reached to the gate of my people,
        even to Jerusalem.

¹⁰  ††Do not announce it in Gath,*
        do not weep at all;
    In Beth-leaphrah
        roll in the dust.ᵉ
¹¹  Pass by,
        you who dwell in Shaphir!
    The inhabitants of Zaanan
        do not come forth from their city.
    There is lamentation in Beth-ezel.
        It will withdraw its support from
            you.
¹²  The inhabitants of Maroth
        hope for good,
    But evil has come down from the LORD
        to the gate of Jerusalem.
¹³  Harness steeds to the chariots,
        inhabitants of Lachish;
    You are the beginning of sin
        for daughter Zion,
    For in you were found
        the crimes of Israel.
¹⁴  Therefore you must give back the dowry
        to Moresheth-gath;
    The houses of Achzib‡‡ are a dry stream
            bed
        to the kings of Israel.
¹⁵  Again I will bring the conqueror to you,
        inhabitants of Mareshah;
    The glory of Israel shall come
        even to Adullam.
¹⁶  Make yourself bald, cut off your hair,
        for the children whom you
            cherish;
    Make yourself bald as a vulture,
        for they are taken from you into
            exile.§§

---

*[1:2] The prophet summons all the peoples to hear the divine accusations against them. What follows in 1:2–3:12 is a series of prophecies of punishment addressed to the capital cities of both the Northern and Southern Kingdoms, Samaria and Jerusalem. The prophecies indict the leaders and main officials, including prophets. Because of the corruption and selfishness of their leaders, Samaria and Jerusalem will fall to their enemies.

†[1:3] The Lord comes in a theophany which has devastating effects on the natural world (1:4).

‡[1:5] Although the summons (1:2) had been addressed to all people, the Lord speaks against Israel and Judah, identifying their crimes with the respective capital cities of Samaria and Jerusalem. Only Samaria, however, is scheduled for destruction in the announcement of punishment (vv. 6–7).

§[1:6] The punishment of Samaria will be a military disaster such as the one that actually came at the hands of the Assyrian army in 722/721 B.C.

¶[1:7] **The wages of a prostitute**: as often in the prophets, prostitution is a metaphor for idolatry (Hos 1–3; 4:14). **They shall return**: i.e., Samaria's idols shall come to nothing just as the wages of a prostitute are counted as nothing.

a. [1:2] Dt 32:1; Is 1:2.   b. [1:3–4] Is 26:21; Na 1:5; Hb 3:10.   c. [1:7] Hos 9:1.

**[1:8–16] The prophet laments and wails, singing a funeral song or dirge over the city of Jerusalem. Finally (1:16) he calls upon the people of Jerusalem to join in the mourning.

††[1:10–15] Not all of the cities and villages in this long list can be located with certainty. However, those which can be identified, including the prophet's hometown, lie southwest of Jerusalem. In the Hebrew, wordplays on the names of these cities abound. The territory involved corresponds to that decimated by the Assyrian king Sennacherib in 701 B.C., during the reign of Hezekiah. **Do not weep at all**: some commentators and translators understand the Hebrew differently. They argue that the translation "in (unknown place name) weep!" fits the context better.

‡‡[1:14] **The houses of Achzib**: there is a wordplay here. In the Hebrew, the word translated here as "dry stream bed" is 'achzab; this word is sometimes translated as "deception" or "disappointment."

§§[1:16] Shaving the head was a sign of mourning; cf. Is 3:24; Am 8:10.

d. [1:8] Jb 30:29.   e. [1:10] 2 Sm 1:20.

# CHAPTER 2

1 ˙ Ah! you plotters of iniquity,
  who work out evil on your beds!
In the morning light you carry it out
  for it lies within your power.
2 † You covet fields, and seize them;
  houses, and take them;
You cheat owners of their houses,
  people of their inheritance.

3   Therefore thus says the LORD:
  Look, I am planning against this family
    an evil
  from which you cannot free your
    necks;
  Nor shall you walk with head held high,
    for it will be an evil time.
4 On that day you shall be mocked,
    and there will be bitter lament:
  "Our ruin is complete,
    our fields are divided among our
      captors,
  The fields of my people are measured out,
    and no one can get them back!"‡
5 Thus you shall have no one
    in the assembly of the LORD
    to allot to you a share of land.

6 §"Do not preach," they preach,
    "no one should preach of these
      things!
    Shame will not overtake us."
7 How can it be said, house of Jacob,
    "Is the LORD short of patience;
    are these the Lord's deeds?"
  Do not my words promise good
    to the one who walks in justice?
8 But you rise up against my people as an
    enemy:

you have stripped off the garment
  from the peaceful,
From those who go their way in confidence,
  as though it were spoils of war.
9 The women of my people you drive out
  from their pleasant houses;
From their children you take away
  forever the honor I gave them.

10 ¶"Get up! Leave,
    this is no place to rest";
  Because of uncleanness that destroys
    with terrible destruction.
11 If one possessed of a lying spiritᶠ
    speaks deceitfully, saying,
  "I will preach to you wine and strong
    drink,"
    that one would be the preacher for
      this people.

12 **"I will gather you, Jacob, each and every
    one,
  I will assemble all the remnant of
    Israel;
I will group them like a flock in the fold,
  like a herd in its pasture;
  the noise of the people will resound.

13 The one who makes a breach goes up
    before them;
  they make a breach and pass
    through the gate;
Their king shall go through before them,
  the LORD at their head.

# CHAPTER 3

1   ††And I said:
  Hear, you leaders of Jacob,
    rulers of the house of Israel!
  Is it not your duty to know what is right,
2     you who hate what is good, and love
      evil?
  You who tear their skin from them,
    and their flesh from their bones;ᵍ
3 Who eat the flesh of my people,
    flay their skin from them,
    and break their bones;

---

*[2:1–5] The cry "Ah" (*hoy*) begins a typical prophetic speech that is usually continued, as here (vv. 1–2), by a description of the addressees in terms of their unrighteous activities. This description is an indictment which gives the reasons for punishment announced to a particular group of people (vv. 3–5). The prophet spells out the crimes; the Lord announces the punishment, which corresponds to the crime: those who take the land of others will have their own land taken.

Those who plot iniquity and have the power to do it are wealthy landowners. The evil which they do consists in coveting the fields and houses of others and taking them.

†[2:2] To covet the "house" and other property of the neighbor was a violation of the Decalogue (Ex 20:17; 34:24; Dt 5:21).

The Lord, as owner of the earth, allotted the land by tribes and families to the people of Israel (Jos 13–19). Losing one's inheritance diminished one's place in the community and threatened the family's economic viability and existence. According to Micah, those who used their power to expand their estates at the expense of weaker Israelites took more than land from them: they were tampering with the divine order.

‡[2:4] Those who take land from the less powerful will in turn have their land taken away by invaders.

§[2:6–11] This unit is a disputation, an argument in which the prophet is debating with his opponents. The words of the opponents are given to us only as the prophet quotes them. The opponents accuse Micah of being a false prophet, and he reacts by accusing them of injustice and of preferring prophets and preachers who speak lies (v. 11).

¶[2:10] The meaning of the Hebrew is uncertain.

**[2:12–13] This announcement of salvation to the "remnant of Israel" stands out dramatically in the context, and is probably a later addition to the words of Micah, coming from the time of the Babylonian exile. The content of the promise and the images are similar to those found in Second Isaiah, the great poet of Israel's salvation and restoration (see Is 40:11; 43:5).

††[3:1–4] This prophecy of punishment has an introductory call to hear (v. 1a–b) and two major parts, the indictment or reasons for punishment (vv. 1c–3) and the announcement of judgment (v. 4). The prophet accuses the leaders and rulers of Israel of treating the people so badly that their actions are comparable to cannibalism. Those who, above all, should know and maintain justice are the most corrupt of all. In the time of trouble the Lord will withdraw (v. 4); that is, God will abandon the leaders to their fate and refuse to answer their prayers.

---

f. [2:11] 1 Kgs 22:22–23.   g. [3:2] Am 2:7.

Who chop them in pieces like flesh in a
        kettle,
    like meat in a pot.
[4] When they cry to the LORD,
        he will not answer them;
    He will hide his face from them at that
        time,
        because of the evil they have done.

[5] *Thus says the LORD regarding the
        prophets:
    O you who lead my people astray,
    When your teeth have something to bite
        you announce peace,
    But proclaim war against the one
        who fails to put something in your
        mouth.[h]
[6] Therefore you shall have night, not vision,
        darkness, not divination;
    The sun shall go down upon the prophets,
        and the day shall be dark for them.[i]
[7] Then the seers shall be put to shame,
        and the diviners confounded;
    They shall all cover their lips,
        because there is no answer from
        God.
[8] But as for me, I am filled with power,
        with the spirit of the LORD,
        with justice and with might;
    To declare to Jacob his crimes
        and to Israel his sins.

[9] †Hear this, you leaders of the house of
        Jacob,
        you rulers of the house of Israel!
    You who abhor justice,
        and pervert all that is right;
[10] Who build up Zion with bloodshed,
        and Jerusalem with wickedness!
[11] Its leaders render judgment for a bribe,
        the priests teach for pay,
        the prophets divine for money,
    While they rely on the LORD, saying,
        "Is not the LORD in the midst of us?
        No evil can come upon us!"[j]
[12] Therefore, because of you,
        Zion shall be plowed like a field,

    and Jerusalem reduced to rubble,
    And the mount of the temple
        to a forest ridge.[k]

## II. ORACLES OF SALVATION

### CHAPTER 4

[1] ‡In days to come
        the mount of the LORD's house
    Shall be established as the highest
        mountain;
        it shall be raised above the hills,
    And peoples shall stream to it:[l]
[2]     Many nations shall come, and say,
    "Come, let us climb the LORD's mountain,
        to the house of the God of Jacob,
    That he may instruct us in his ways,
        that we may walk in his paths."
    For from Zion shall go forth instruction,
        and the word of the LORD from
        Jerusalem.
[3] He shall judge between many peoples
        and set terms for strong and distant
        nations;
    They shall beat their swords into
        plowshares,
        and their spears into pruning hooks;
    One nation shall not raise the sword
        against another,
        nor shall they train for war again.
[4] They shall all sit under their own vines,
        under their own fig trees,
        undisturbed;
        for the LORD of hosts has spoken.[m]
[5] Though all the peoples walk,
        each in the name of its god,
    We will walk in the name of the LORD,
        our God, forever and ever.

[6] §On that day—oracle of the LORD—
        I will gather the lame,
    And I will assemble the outcasts,
        and those whom I have afflicted.
[7] I will make of the lame a remnant,
        and of the weak a strong nation;

---

*[3:5–8] This prophecy of punishment concerns and is addressed to false prophets. The prophets in Jerusalem who mislead the people are corrupt because their word can be bought (v. 5). Therefore such prophets, seers, and diviners shall be disgraced, put to shame, left in the dark without vision or answer (vv. 6–7). But Micah is convinced that he is filled with power and the spirit of the Lord, which corresponds to justice and might (v. 8).

†[3:9–12] This is the most comprehensive of Micah's prophecies of punishment concerning the leaders in Jerusalem. The indictment (vv. 9–11) includes all political and religious leaders. They combine corruption and greed with a false confidence that the Lord is on their side. But the announcement of judgment (v. 12) is not limited to the punishment of the leaders but includes Mount Zion where the Temple stands and the entire city, thus encompassing the entire population.

‡[4:1–4] This magnificent prophecy of salvation is almost identical to Is 2:2–5, with the exception of its last verse. See also Jl 4:9–10, which transforms the promise into a call to war. It is not known if Micah or an editor of the book picked up the announcement from his contemporary Isaiah or if Isaiah borrowed it from Micah. Perhaps both Isaiah and Micah depended upon another, more ancient tradition. The ground of the prophetic hope voiced here is the justice and grace of the God who has chosen Israel. The basis for peace shall be a just order where all are obedient to the divine will. While the vision is a universal one, including all peoples and nations (vv. 3–4), its center and wellspring is the Temple of the Lord of Israel on Mount Zion in Jerusalem.

§[4:6–8] An announcement of salvation proclaiming that the Lord will restore the lame and afflicted people of God as a nation on Mount Zion. **Oracle of the LORD**: a phrase used extensively in prophetic books to indicate divine speech.

h. [3:5] Ez 13:10.   i. [3:6] Jer 15:9; Am 8:9; Zec 13:3.   j. [3:11] Ez 22:27; Zep 3:3.

k. [3:12] Jer 26:18.   l. [4:1–3] Is 2:2–4.   m. [4:4] Hos 14:8; Am 9:14.

The LORD shall be king over them on
  Mount Zion,
    from now on and forever."

8 And you, O tower of the flock,*
    hill of daughter Zion!
  To you it shall come:
    the former dominion shall be
      restored,
    the reign of daughter Jerusalem.

9 Now why do you cry out so?
    Are you without a king?
    Or has your adviser perished,
  That you are seized with pains
    like a woman in labor?
10 †Writhe, go into labor,
    O daughter Zion,
    like a woman giving birth;
  For now you shall leave the city
    and camp in the fields;
  To Babylon you shall go,
    there you shall be rescued.
  There the LORD shall redeem you
    from the hand of your enemies.

11 ‡And now many nations are gathered
      against you!
    They say, "Let her be profaned,
    let our eyes see Zion's downfall!"
12 But they do not know the thoughts of the
      LORD,
    nor understand his plan:
  He has gathered them
    like sheaves to the threshing floor.
13 Arise and thresh, O daughter Zion;
    your horn I will make iron
  And your hoofs I will make bronze,
    that you may crush many peoples;
  You shall devote their spoils to the LORD,§
    their riches to the Lord of the whole
      earth.°

14 Now grieve, O grieving daughter!¶
    "They have laid siege against us!"
  With the rod they strike on the cheek
    the ruler of Israel.

## CHAPTER 5

1 **But you, Bethlehem-Ephrathahᵖ
    least among the clans of Judah,
  From you shall come forth for me
    one who is to be ruler in Israel;
  Whose origin is from of old,
    from ancient times.
2 Therefore the Lord will give them up,
    until the time
    when she who is to give birth has
      borne,††
  Then the rest of his kindred shall return
    to the children of Israel.�q
3 He shall take his place as shepherd
    by the strength of the LORD,
    by the majestic name of the LORD,
      his God;
  And they shall dwell securely, for now his
      greatness
    shall reach to the ends of the earth:
4   he shall be peace.‡‡
  If Assyria invades our country
    and treads upon our land,
  We shall raise against it seven shepherds,
    eight of royal standing;
5 They shall tend the land of Assyria with
      the sword,
    and the land of Nimrod§§ with the
      drawn sword;
  They will deliver us from Assyria,
    when it invades our land,
    when it treads upon our borders.

6 The remnant of Jacob shall be
    in the midst of many peoples,
  Like dew coming from the LORD,
    like showers on the grass,
  Which wait for no one,
    delay for no human being.
7 And the remnant of Jacob shall be among
      the nations,
    in the midst of many peoples,
  Like a lion among beasts of the forest,
    like a young lion among flocks of
      sheep;
  When it passes through it tramples;
    it tears and no one can rescue.
8 Your hand shall be lifted above your foes,
    and all your enemies shall be cut
      down.

---

*[4:8] **Tower of the flock**: in Hebrew *migdal-eder*, a place name in Gn 35:21.

†[4:10] Frequently the prophets personify the city of Jerusalem as a woman, and here as a woman in labor.

‡[4:11–13] The nations who have ridiculed Zion (v. 11) will be threshed like grain (v. 13).

§[4:13] **Devote their spoils to the LORD**: the fulfillment of the ancient ordinance of the holy war in which all plunder taken in the war was "put under the ban," i.e., belonged to the Lord.

¶[4:14] **Grieve, O grieving daughter!**: the Hebrew actually reflects the ancient Near Eastern mourning practice of afflicting oneself with cuts and gashes, as evidence of grief. A literal rendering would be "gash yourself, O woman who gashes."

n. [4:7] Is 6:13; Dn 7:14; Zep 3:19; Lk 1:32.   o. [4:13] Is 41:15; Hos 10:11.

---

**[5:1–6] Salvation will come through a "messiah," an anointed ruler. The Book of Micah shares with Isaiah the expectation that God will deliver Israel through a king in the line of David. Bethlehem-Ephrathah is the home of the Davidic line.

††[5:2] These words are sometimes understood as a reference to Isaiah's Emmanuel oracle, given some thirty years earlier (Is 7:14). The Gospel of Matthew reports that the chief priests and scribes cite this passage as the ancient promise of a messiah in the line of David to be born in Bethlehem (Mt 2:5–6).

‡‡[5:4] **Peace**: he will not only symbolize but also bring about harmony and wholeness.

§§[5:5] **Nimrod**: the legendary ancestor of the Mesopotamians; cf. Gn 10:10–12.

p. [5:1] Ru 1:2; 1 Sm 17:12; Mt 2:6; Jn 7:42.   q. [5:2–3] Is 7:14; 11:1–2.

⁹    ˙On that day—oracle of the LORD—
    I will destroy the horses from your midst
        and ruin your chariots;
¹⁰   I will destroy the cities of your land
        and tear down all your fortresses.
¹¹   I will destroy the sorcery you practice,
        and there shall no longer be
            soothsayers among you.
¹²   I will destroy your carved figures
        and the sacred stones† from your
            midst;
    And you shall no longer worship
        the works of your hands.ʳ
¹³   I will tear out the asherahs from your
            midst,
        and destroy your cities.
¹⁴   I will wreak vengeance in anger and wrath
        upon the nations that have not
            listened.

## III. ANNOUNCEMENT OF JUDGMENT

### CHAPTER 6
¹    ‡Hear, then, what the LORD says:
    Arise, plead your case before the
        mountains,
        and let the hills hear your voice!ˢ
²    Hear, O mountains, the LORD's case,
        pay attention, O foundations of the
            earth!
    For the LORD has a case against his
        people;
        he enters into trial with Israel.
³    My people, what have I done to you?
        how have I wearied you? Answer
            me!ᵗ
⁴    I brought you up from the land of Egypt,
        from the place of slavery I ransomed
            you;
    And I sent before you Moses,
        Aaron, and Miriam.ᵘ
⁵    §My people, remember what Moab's King
        Balak planned,

and how Balaam, the son of Beor,
        answered him.
    Recall the passage from Shittim to Gilgal,
        that you may know the just deeds of
            the LORD.ᵛ
⁶    ¶With what shall I come before the LORD,
        and bow before God most high?
    Shall I come before him with burnt
        offerings,
        with calves a year old?ʷ
⁷    Will the LORD be pleased with thousands
            of rams,
        with myriad streams of oil?
**   Shall I give my firstborn for my crime,
        the fruit of my body for the sin of
            my soul?
⁸    ††You have been told, O mortal, what is
            good,
        and what the LORD requires of you:
    Only to do justice and to love goodness,
        and to walk humbly with your God.ˣ
⁹    ‡‡The LORD cries aloud to the city
        (It is prudent to fear your name!):
        Hear, O tribe and city assembly,
¹⁰   Am I to bear criminal hoarding
        and the accursed short ephah?§§
¹¹   Shall I acquit crooked scales,
        bags of false weights?
¹²   You whose wealthy are full of violence,
        whose inhabitants speak falsehood
        with deceitful tongues in their
            mouths!
¹³   I have begun to strike you
        with devastation because of your
            sins.
¹⁴   You shall eat, without being satisfied,
        food that will leave you empty;

---

¶[6:6–8] These verses continue the previous unit (6:1–5), the dialogue between the Lord and the people in the pattern of a trial. The Lord has initiated proceedings against them, and they ask how to re-establish the broken relationship with God (vv. 6–7), and are given an answer (v. 8). The form of the passage borrows from a priestly liturgical pattern. When worshipers came to the temple, they inquired of the priest concerning the appropriate offering or sacrifice, and the priest answered them (see Ps 15; 24; Is 1:10–17; Am 5:21–24).

**[6:7] The questions reach their climax with the possibility of child sacrifice, a practice known in antiquity (cf. 2 Kgs 16:3; 21:6).

††[6:8] To do justice refers to human behavior in relationship to others. To love goodness refers to the kind of love and concern which is at the heart of the covenant between the Lord and Israel; it is persistently faithful. To walk humbly with your God means to listen carefully to the revealed will of God.

‡‡[6:9–16] The language of the trial resumes as the Lord accuses the people of their sins (vv. 9–12, 16a) and announces their punishment (vv. 13–15, 16b). The city is Jerusalem, and those addressed are its inhabitants. Their wickedness includes cheating in business with false weights and measures, violence, lies, and following the practices of the Israelite kings Omri and Ahab (v. 16a), whose reigns came to symbolize a time of syncretistic worship. The punishment, which has already begun, will include a series of disasters. Finally, the Lord will destroy the city and see that its inhabitants are ridiculed (v. 16b).

§§[6:10] Ephah: see note on Is 5:10.

---

*[5:9–13] The Lord will destroy all those features of the nation's life that have stood between the people and their God. These false supports include horses, chariots, fortifications, and forbidden practices such as sorcery and idolatry.

†[5:12–13] Sacred stones . . . asherahs: the Hebrew *asherah* is a sacred pole. All forms of idolatry (standing stones and sacred poles were part of forbidden cult practices) were violations of Israel's covenant with the Lord.

‡[6:1–5] The Lord, through the prophet, initiates a legal case against the people. The initial calls (vv. 1–2) signal the beginning of a trial, and the proclamation that the Lord intends to enter into a legal dispute with Israel. One would expect accusations to follow such an introduction, but instead the Lord speaks in self-defense, reciting mighty acts done in behalf of Israel (vv. 3–5).

§[6:5] The Lord calls for the people to remember the saving events of the past, from the encounters with Balak and Balaam (Nm 22:23) during the wandering in the wilderness to the entrance into the promised land ("from Shittim to Gilgal," Jos 3–5).

---

r. [5:12] Hos 3:4; 10:1–2.  s. [6:1] Is 6:2; Ob 1.  t. [6:3] Jer 2:5.
u. [6:4] Ex 15:20.

v. [6:5] Nm 22:23; Jos 3–5.  w. [6:6–7] Hos 6:6; 8:13; Am 5:21.
x. [6:8] Dt 26:16; Zec 7:9; Mt 23:23.

What you acquire, you cannot save;
  what you do save, I will deliver up to
    the sword.*y*
<sup>15</sup> You shall sow, yet not reap,
  tread out the olive, yet pour no oil,
  crush the grapes, yet drink no wine.*z*
<sup>16</sup> You have kept the decrees of Omri,
  and all the works of the house of
    Ahab,
  and you have walked in their counsels;
Therefore I will deliver you up to ruin,
  and your citizens to derision;
  and you shall bear the reproach of
    the nations.

## CHAPTER 7

<sup>1</sup> Woe is me! I am like the one who gathers
    summer fruit,
  when the vines have been gleaned;
There is no cluster to eat,
  no early fig that I crave.
<sup>2</sup> The faithful have vanished from the earth,
  no mortal is just!
They all lie in wait to shed blood,
  each one ensnares the other.*a*
<sup>3</sup> Their hands succeed at evil;
  the prince makes demands,
The judge is bought for a price,
  the powerful speak as they please.*b*
<sup>4</sup> The best of them is like a brier,
  the most honest like a thorn hedge.
The day announced by your sentinels!
  Your punishment has come;
  now is the time of your confusion.
<sup>5</sup> Put no faith in a friend,
  do not trust a companion;
With her who lies in your embrace
  watch what you say.*c*
<sup>6</sup> For the son belittles his father,
  the daughter rises up against her
    mother,
The daughter-in-law against her
    mother-in-law,
  and your enemies are members of
    your household.*d*

## IV. CONFIDENCE IN GOD'S FUTURE

<sup>7</sup> But as for me, I will look to the LORD,
  I will wait for God my savior;
  my God will hear me!*e*
<sup>8</sup> *Do not rejoice over me, my enemy!†

though I have fallen, I will arise;
  though I sit in darkness, the LORD is
    my light.
<sup>9</sup> I will endure the wrath of the LORD
  because I have sinned against him,
Until he pleads my case,
  and establishes my right.
He will bring me forth to the light;
  I will see his righteousness.
<sup>10</sup> When my enemy sees this,
  shame shall cover her:
She who said to me,
  "Where is the LORD, your God?"
My eyes shall see her downfall;
  now she will be trampled‡
    underfoot,
  like mud in the streets.
<sup>11</sup> §It is the day for building your walls;
  on that day your boundaries shall be
    enlarged.
<sup>12</sup> It is the day when those from Assyria to
    Egypt
  shall come to you,
And from Tyre even to the River,
  from sea to sea, and from mountain
    to mountain;*f*
<sup>13</sup> And the earth shall be a waste
  because of its inhabitants,
  as a result of their deeds.

<sup>14</sup> ¶Shepherd your people with your staff,
  the flock of your heritage,
That lives apart*g* in a woodland,
  in the midst of an orchard.
Let them feed in Bashan and Gilead,
  as in the days of old;
<sup>15</sup> As in the days when you came from the
    land of Egypt,
  show us wonderful signs.
<sup>16</sup> The nations will see and will be put to
    shame,
  in spite of all their strength;
They will put their hands over their
    mouths;
  their ears will become deaf.
<sup>17</sup> They will lick the dust like a snake,
  like crawling things on the ground;
They will come quaking from their
    strongholds;
  they will tremble in fear of you, the
    LORD, our God.

---

‡[7:10] **She who said . . . she will be trampled**: in the Old Testament, cities are often personified as women. Here, the prophet is speaking of the enemies' cities.

§[7:11–13] An announcement of salvation to Zion. The walls of Jerusalem will be rebuilt, its inhabitants who are now scattered from Assyria to Egypt shall return, but the other peoples will suffer for their evil deeds.

¶[7:14–17] A prayer that God will care for the people as in ancient days (v. 14) is answered (vv. 15–17) when the Lord promises to do marvelous things. The nations shall be afraid and turn to the Lord.

---

*[7:8–20] The book concludes with a collection of confident prayers for deliverance, affirmations of faith, and announcements of salvation. Most of these verses bear the marks of use in worship, and probably arose in the exilic or postexilic periods.

†[7:8–10] An individual, possibly personified Jerusalem, expresses confidence that the Lord will deliver her from her enemy (cf. Ps 23).

---

y. [6:14] Dt 28:38; Am 5:11; Hg 1:6.   z. [6:15] Hos 4:10.   a. [7:2] Is 1:21; Hos 4:2.   b. [7:3] Is 1:23.   c. [7:5] Jer 9:3.   d. [7:6] Mt 10:35–36.   e. [7:7] Is 8:17.

f. [7:12] Zec 14:16.   g. [7:14] Nm 23:9.

18 *Who is a God like you, who removes
          guilt
      and pardons sin for the remnant of
          his inheritance;
      Who does not persist in anger forever,

---

*[7:18–20] The final lines of the book contain a hymn
of praise for the incomparable God, who pardons sin and
delights in mercy. Thus the remnant, those left after the exile,
is confident in God's compassion and in the ancient promises
sworn to the ancestors.

but instead delights in mercy,[h]
19   And will again have compassion on us,
          treading underfoot our iniquities?
      You will cast into the depths of the sea all
          our sins;
20   You will show faithfulness to Jacob,
          and loyalty to Abraham,
      As you have sworn to our ancestors
          from days of old.[i]

---

h. [7:18] Jer 10:6; Acts 10:43.   i. [7:20] Ps 105:6; Is 41:8; 63:16.

# THE BOOK OF
# NAHUM

～⁂～

Shortly before the fall of Nineveh, the capital of Assyria, in 612 B.C., Nahum uttered his prophecy against the hated city. To understand the prophet's exultant outburst of joy over the impending destruction it is necessary to recall the savage cruelty of Assyria, which had made it the scourge of the ancient Near East for almost three centuries. The royal inscriptions of Assyria afford the best commentary on Nahum's burning denunciation of "the bloody city." In the wake of their conquests, mounds of heads, impaled bodies, enslaved citizens, and avaricious looters testified to the ruthlessness of the Assyrians. Just such a conquest was suffered by Israel, when its capital Samaria fell to the Assyrians in 722/721 B.C., and by Judah, when its capital Jerusalem nearly fell to invading Assyrian armies twenty years later. Little wonder that in 3:19 Judah is shown as joining in the general outburst of joy over the destruction of Nineveh!

But Nahum is not a prophet of unrestrained revenge. He asserts God's moral government of the world. Nineveh's doom is evidence that God stands against oppression and the abuse of power. As an ancient Near Eastern superpower, Assyria had terrorized its smaller and weaker neighbors, exploiting their economies and subjugating their people for its own ends. Thus Nineveh's demise is viewed as an act of divine justice, and it is greeted by the small, oppressed countries as a time of deliverance, as a moment of renewal, and as a message of peace (2:1; 3:19).

The book is divided as follows:

I. God's Terrifying Appearance (1:2–8)
II. Nineveh's Judgment and Judah's Restoration (1:9–2:1)
III. The Attack on Nineveh (2:2–3:7)
IV. Nineveh's Inescapable Fate (3:8–19)

## CHAPTER 1

¹Oracle* concerning Nineveh. The book of the vision of Nahum of Elkosh.

### God's Terrifying Appearance

² †A jealous and avenging God‡ is the LORD,
  an avenger is the LORD, full of wrath;
The LORD takes vengeance on his
    adversaries,
  and rages against his enemies;
³ The LORD is slow to anger, yet great in
    power;
  the LORD will not leave the guilty
    unpunished.ᵃ

In stormwind§ and tempest he comes,
  and clouds are the dust at his feet;
⁴ He roars at the sea and leaves it dry,
  and all the rivers he dries up.
Laid low are Bashan and Carmel,
  and the bloom of Lebanon
    withers;¶
⁵ The mountains quake before him,
  and the hills dissolve;
The earth is laid waste before him,
  the world and all who dwell in it.
⁶ **Before his wrath, who can stand firm,
  and who can face his blazing anger?ᵇ
His fury is poured out like fire,
  and boulders break apart before
    him.

---

*[1:1] **Oracle**: (Heb. *Massa'*) a word used frequently to describe a prophetic statement against a foreign nation or occasionally Israel; it is used favorably for Israel in Zec 12:1 and Mal 1:1. **Nahum of Elkosh**: Nahum means "comfort." Elkosh is a clan or village of unknown location, perhaps in southern Judah.

†[1:2–8] A poem written in the style of the alphabetic psalms (cf. Ps 9; 25; 111; 119) in which each verse unit begins with a successive letter of the Hebrew alphabet. The second half of the alphabet is not represented here.

‡[1:2] **A jealous . . . God**: see note on Ex 20:5.

a. [1:3] Ex 34:6–7; Jl 2:13.

§[1:3–6] **In stormwind**: the power of God is often pictured by natural forces and cosmic disruption (Ex 19:9–25; Ps 18:8–16; 104:1–9).

¶[1:4] Bashan, Carmel, and Lebanon were famous for their mountainous terrain and lush forests.

**[1:6–7] When God comes in judgment those who oppose God will be destroyed, and those who trust in God will be saved.

b. [1:6] Is 30:27–28; Zep 1:15.

⁷ The LORD is good to those who wait for
        him,
    a refuge on the day of distress,
  Taking care of those who look to him for
        protection,
⁸      when the flood rages;
  He makes an end of his opponents,
    and pursues his enemies into
        darkness.

### Nineveh's Judgment and Judah's Restoration

⁹ What do you plot against the LORD,
    the one about to bring total
        destruction?
  No opponent rises a second time!
¹⁰ *Like a thorny thicket, they are tangled,
    and like drunkards, they are drunk;
  like dry stubble, they are utterly
        consumed.
¹¹ From you has come
    one plotting evil against the LORD,
    one giving sinister counsel.†
¹² Thus says the LORD:
    though fully intact and so numerous,
    they‡ shall be mown down and
        disappear.
  Though I have humbled you,
    I will humble you no more.
¹³ Now I will break his yoke off of you,
    and tear off your bonds.ᶜ

¹⁴ The LORD has commanded regarding
        you:§
  no descendant will again bear your
        name;
  From the house of your gods I will abolish
    the carved and the molten image;
  I will make your grave a dung heap.

### CHAPTER 2

¹ At this moment on the mountains
    the footsteps of one bearing good
        news,
  of one announcing peace!ᵈ
  Celebrate your feasts, Judah,
    fulfill your vows!
  For never again will destroyers invade
        you;¶
    they are completely cut off.

### The Attack on Nineveh

² One who scatters has come up against
        you;**
    guard the rampart,
  Watch the road, brace yourselves,
    marshal all your strength!
³ ††The LORD will restore the vine of Jacob,
    the honor of Israel,
  Because ravagers have ravaged them
    and ruined their branches.
⁴ The shields of his warriors are crimsoned,
    the soldiers clad in scarlet;
  Like fire are the trappings of the chariots
    on the day he prepares for war;
    the cavalry is agitated!
⁵ The chariots dash madly through the
        streets
    and wheel in the squares,
  Looking like torches,
    bolting like lightning.
⁶ His picked troops are called,
    ranks break at their charge;
  To the wall they rush,
    their screen‡‡ is set up.
⁷ The river gates§§ are opened,
    the palace is washed away.
⁸ The mistress is led forth captive,
    and her maidservants¶¶ led away,
  Moaning like doves,
    beating their breasts.
⁹ Nineveh is like a pool
    whose waters escape;
  "Stop! Stop!"
    but none turns back.ᵉ
¹⁰ "Plunder the silver, plunder the gold!"
    There is no end to the treasure,
    to wealth in every precious thing!

¹¹ Emptiness, desolation, waste;
    melting hearts and trembling knees,
  Churning in every stomach,
    every face turning pale!ᶠ

Romans. The prophets were convinced that Israel held a key
place in God's plan and looked for the people to survive all
catastrophes, always blessed by the Lord, though the manner
was not always as they expected; the "fallen hut of David" was
not rebuilt as Am 9:11 suggests, except in the coming of Jesus,
and in a way far different than the prophet expected. Often the
prophet speaks in hyperbole, as when Second Isaiah speaks
of the restored Jerusalem being built with precious stones (Is
54:12) as a way of indicating a glorious future.

**[2:2] One who scatters has come up against you: the
enemy is about to crush Nineveh, dispersing and deporting
its people (v. 8; 3:18).

††[2:3] This verse does not fit its context well; it may have
been the conclusion for the preceding section and have once
followed v. 1, or it may be a later scribal addition.

‡‡[2:6] Their screen: that is, a mantelet, a movable military
shelter protecting the besiegers.

§§[2:7] River gates: a network of canals brought water into
Nineveh from the Tigris and Khosr Rivers on which the city
was located.

¶¶[2:8] Mistress . . . and her maidservants: either the
queen of Nineveh with the ladies of her court, or the city of
Nineveh itself, pictured as a noblewoman (3:4).

*[1:10] Thorns (Is 34:13), drunkenness (Lam 4:21; Na
3:11), and burning stubble (Ob 18) are all images of the judgment of God's enemies.

†[1:11] From you . . . giving sinister counsel: addressed to
Nineveh, the capital city of Sennacherib, king of Assyria, who
besieged Jerusalem ca. 700 B.C.

‡[1:12–13] They: the enemies of Judah. You: Judah. His
yoke: the dominion of the Assyrian king over Judah.

§[1:14] You: the king of Assyria.

¶[2:1] For never again will destroyers invade you: prophets are not always absolutely accurate in the things they fore-
see. Nineveh was destroyed, as Nahum expected, but Judah
was later invaded by the Babylonians and (much later) by the

c. [1:13] Is 9:4; 10:27.    d. [2:1] Is 52:7; Rom 10:15.

e. [2:9] Is 8:7–8.    f. [2:11] Jl 2:6.

12 Where is the lionesses' den,
        the young lions' cave,
Where the lion* went in and out,
        and the cub, with no one to disturb
            them?*ᵍ
13 The lion tore apart enough for his cubs,
        and strangled for his lionesses;
He filled his lairs with prey,
        and his dens with torn flesh.
14 I now come against you—
        oracle of the Lᴏʀᴅ of hosts—
I will consume your chariots in smoke,
        and the sword will devour your
            young lions;
Your preying on the land I will bring to
        an end,
        the cry of your lionesses will be
            heard no more.

## CHAPTER 3

1 Ah! The bloody city,
        all lies,
Full of plunder,
        whose looting never stops!ʰ
2 The crack of the whip,
        the rumbling of wheels;
Horses galloping,
        chariots bounding,
3 Cavalry charging,
        the flash of the sword,
        the gleam of the spear;
A multitude of slain,
        a mass of corpses,
Endless bodies
        to stumble upon!
4 For the many debaucheries of the
            prostitute,
        a charming mistress of witchcraft,
Who enslaved nations with her
            prostitution,
        and peoples by her witchcraft:ⁱ
5 †I now come against you—
        oracle of the Lᴏʀᴅ of hosts—
        and I will lift your skirt above your
            face;
I will show your nakedness to the nations,
        to the kingdoms your shame!ʲ
6 I will cast filth upon you,
        disgrace you and make you a
            spectacle;
7 Until everyone who sees you
        runs from you saying,
"Nineveh is destroyed;
        who can pity her?
Where can I find
        any to console you?"

### Nineveh's Inescapable Fate

8 Are you better than No-amon‡ᵏ
        that was set among the Nile's canals,
Surrounded by waters,
        with the river for her rampart
        and water for her wall?
9 Ethiopia was her strength,
        and Egypt without end;
Put§ and the Libyans
        were her allies.
10 Yet even she became an exile,
        and went into captivity;
Even her little ones were dashed to pieces
        at the corner of every street;
For her nobles they cast lots,
        and all her great ones were put into
            chains.
11 You, too, will drink of this;
        you will be overcome;ˡ
You, too, will seek
        a refuge from the foe.
12 But all your fortresses are fig trees,
        bearing early figs;¶
When shaken, they fall
        into the devourer's mouth.
13 Indeed your troops
        are women in your midst;
To your foes are open wide
        the gates of your land,
        fire has consumed their bars.

14 Draw water for the siege,**
        strengthen your fortresses;
Go down into the mud
        and tread the clay,
        take hold of the brick mold!
15 There the fire will consume you,
        the sword will cut you down;
        it will consume you like the
            grasshoppers.

Multiply like the grasshoppers,
        multiply like the locusts!ᵐ
16 You have made your traders†† more
            numerous
        than the stars of the heavens;
        like grasshoppers that shed their
            skins and fly away.

---

‡[3:8] **No-amon:** "No" was the Egyptian name of the capital of Upper Egypt, called Thebes by the Greeks; its patron deity was Amon. This great city was destroyed by the Assyrians in 663 B.C.

§[3:9] **Put:** a North African people often associated with Egypt and Ethiopia (Jer 46:8–9).

¶[3:12] **Early figs:** the refugees from Nineveh who escape to presumably secure fortresses.

**[3:14] An ironic exhortation to prepare the city for a futile defense. **Go down . . . brick mold:** make bricks for the city walls.

††[3:16] **Traders:** agents of the economic exploitation that sustained and enriched the Assyrian empire.

---

*[2:12] **The lion:** the king of Assyria.
†[3:5–6] The punishment for adulterous women.

---

g. [2:12] Ez 19:2–7.   h. [3:1] Is 10:13–14; Hb 2:12.   i. [3:4] Mi 1:7;
Rev 17:1.   j. [3:5] Is 47:3; Jer 13:26.

k. [3:8] Jer 46:25.   l. [3:11] Jer 25:15–16; Ob 16.   m. [3:15] Jer 46:23.

<sup>17</sup> Your sentries are like locusts,
  and your scribes like locust swarms
Gathered on the rubble fences
  on a cold day!
Yet when the sun rises, they vanish,
  and no one knows where they have
   gone.

<sup>18</sup> Your shepherds slumber,
  O king of Assyria,

your nobles have gone to rest;
Your people are scattered upon the
  mountains,
  with none to gather them.
<sup>19</sup> There is no healing for your hurt,
  your wound is fatal.
All who hear this news of you
  clap their hands over you;
For who has not suffered
  under your endless malice?

# THE BOOK OF
# HABAKKUK

Habakkuk is the only prophet to devote his entire work to the question of the justice of God's government of the world. In the Bible as a whole, only Job delivers a more pointed challenge to divine rule. Habakkuk's challenge is set up as a dialogue between the prophet and God, in which Habakkuk's opening complaint about injustices in Judean society (1:2–4) is followed in 1:5–11 by God's promise that the perpetrators will be punished by invading Chaldeans, i.e., Babylonians. Habakkuk's second complaint about the violence of the Chaldeans themselves (1:12–2:1) is followed by a second divine response assuring the prophet of the reliability of God's rule and calling for human faithfulness (2:2–4).

This dialogue is followed by a series of observations on the disastrous nature of tyranny (2:5–20), and by a vivid description in chap. 3 of God's appearance to save the people. Chapter 3 may be the prophet's prayer that God fulfill the promises made earlier to Habakkuk, or a hymn praising God's power added to Habakkuk's speeches by editors. In either case, the description of the theophany draws heavily upon ancient traditions in which God establishes order by defeating chaos, symbolized by rebellious waters (see Jb 7:12; Ps 74:13–14; 77:17–21; 89:10–11; Is 51:9).

Two important events frame Habakkuk's prophecy: the great Babylonian (Chaldean) victory over the Egyptians at Carchemish (605 B.C.) and the second Babylonian invasion of Judah (587 B.C.), which ended with the destruction of Jerusalem. The desperate conditions in Judah during these years, arising from internal and external threats, provoked Habakkuk's struggle with difficult and important theological questions about divine justice.

The book may be divided as follows:

I. Habakkuk's First Complaint (1:2–4)
II. God's Response (1:5–11)
III. Habakkuk's Second Complaint (1:12–2:1)
IV. God's Response (2:2–4)
V. Sayings Against Tyrants (2:5–20)
VI. Hymn About God's Reign (3:1–19)

## CHAPTER 1

¹The oracle which Habakkuk the prophet received in a vision.

### Habakkuk's First Complaint

² How long, O Lord, must I cry for help*
    and you do not listen?ª
Or cry out to you, "Violence!"
    and you do not intervene?
³ Why do you let me see iniquity?
    why do you simply gaze at evil?
Destruction and violence are before me;ᵇ
    there is strife and discord.

⁴ This is why the law is numb†
    and justice never comes,
For the wicked surround the just;ᶜ
    this is why justice comes forth
        perverted.

### God's Response

⁵ ‡Look over the nations and see!

---

*[1:2–4] The prophet complains about God's apparent disregard for Judah's internal evils in language that echoes the preaching of prophets like Amos, Isaiah, and Jeremiah.

†[1:4] **The law is numb:** because the Lord has been silent, the Law, whether in the form of the scroll found in the Temple in the time of Josiah (2 Kgs 22) or in the form of divine instruction given by priests and prophets, has proved ineffective and so appeared to be cold, unreceptive, and powerless. For the Law to be credible, the Lord must see to it that the wicked are punished and the just rewarded.

‡[1:5–7] Habakkuk interprets the Babylonian defeat of Egypt at Carchemish (605 B.C.) as the answer to his complaint:

a. [1:2] Ps 13:2.  b. [1:3] Ez 45:9.

c. [1:4] Is 29:20–21.

Be utterly amazed!
For a work is being done in your days
　　that you would not believe, were it
　　told.[d]
6 For now I am raising up the Chaldeans,[e]
　　that bitter and impulsive people,
Who march the breadth of the land
　　to take dwellings not their own.
7 They are terrifying and dreadful;
　　their right and their exalted position
　　　are of their own making.
8 Swifter than leopards are their horses,
　　and faster than desert wolves.
Their horses spring forward;
　　they come from far away;
　　they fly like an eagle hastening to
　　　devour.
9 All of them come for violence,
　　their combined onslaught, a
　　　stormwind
　　to gather up captives like sand.
10 They scoff at kings,
　　ridicule princes;
They laugh at any fortress,
　　heap up an earthen ramp, and
　　　conquer it.
11 Then they sweep through like the wind
　　and vanish—
　　they make their own strength their
　　　god!'

### Habakkuk's Second Complaint

12 Are you not from of old, O LORD,
　　my holy God, immortal?[f]
LORD, you have appointed them for
　　judgment,[†]
O Rock,[‡] you have set them in place
　　to punish!
13 Your eyes are too pure to look upon
　　wickedness,
　　and the sight of evil you cannot
　　　endure.
Why, then, do you gaze on the faithless
　　in silence
　　while the wicked devour those more
　　　just than themselves?
14 You have made mortals like the fish in the
　　sea,
　　like creeping things without a leader.

15 He[§] brings them all up with a hook,
　　and hauls them away with his net;
He gathers them in his fishing net,
　　and then rejoices and exults.
16 Therefore he makes sacrifices to his net,[¶]
　　and burns incense to his fishing net;
For thanks to them his portion is rich,
　　and his meal lavish.
17 Shall they, then, keep on drawing his
　　sword
　　to slaughter nations without mercy?

## CHAPTER 2

1 I will stand at my guard post,
　　and station myself upon the rampart;[g]
I will keep watch to see what he will say
　　to me,
　　and what answer he will give to my
　　　complaint.

### God's Response

2 Then the LORD answered me and said:
　　Write down the vision;[**h]
Make it plain upon tablets,
　　so that the one who reads it may
　　　run.
3 For the vision is a witness for the
　　appointed time,
　　a testimony to the end; it will not
　　　disappoint.
If it delays, wait for it,
　　it will surely come, it will not be late.
4 See, the rash have no integrity;
　　but the just one who is righteous
　　　because of faith shall live.[††i]

### Sayings Against Tyrants

5 ‡‡Indeed wealth is treacherous;
　　a proud man does not succeed.
He who opens wide his throat like Sheol,
　　and is insatiable as death,
Who gathers to himself all the nations,
　　and collects for himself all the
　　　peoples—

---

§[1:15] **He**: the Babylonian king (cf. vv. 6, 13), who easily conquers other nations and treats them as objects for his entertainment and enrichment.

¶[1:16] **He makes sacrifices to his net**: the leader attributes victory to the military weapons he wields; he and his weapons have won victory, not any god.

**[2:2] **Write down the vision**: the vision is written down for two reasons: so that a herald may carry and proclaim its contents to the people, and so that the reception of the vision and its truth can be verified by its fulfillment (v. 3).

††[2:4] **The just one who is righteous because of faith shall live**: the faithful survive the impending doom because they trust in God's justice and wait patiently for God to carry it out. Several New Testament passages cite these words (Rom 1:17; Gal 3:11; cf. Heb 10:38) to confirm the teaching that people receive justification and supernatural life through faith in Christ.

‡‡[2:5] This verse describes any tyrant who, like the Babylonians, possesses insatiable greed.

---

the Lord will send the Chaldean empire against Judah as punishment for their sins.

*[1:11] The primary aim of military campaigns by ancient Near Eastern rulers was usually the gathering of spoils and the collection of tribute rather than the annexation of territory. However, in the eighth century B.C., the Assyrians began to administer many conquered territories as provinces.

†[1:12–2:1] **Appointed them for judgment**: this complaint is directed against the violent Babylonians, the very nation God chose to punish Judah.

‡[1:12] **Rock**: an ancient title celebrating the Lord's power and fidelity; cf. Dt 32:4; Is 26:4; 30:29; Ps 18:3, 32, 47; 95:1.

---

d. [1:5] Acts 13:41.　e. [1:6] Jer 32:28.　f. [1:12] Ps 90:2.

g. [2:1] Is 21:8.　h. [2:2] Is 30:8.　i. [2:4] Rom 1:17; Gal 3:11; Heb 10:38.

6 Shall not all these take up a taunt against
       him,ʲ
    and make a riddle about him,
       saying:

  Ah! you who store up what is not yours
    —how long can it last!—
    you who load yourself down with
       collateral.
7 Will your debtors* not rise suddenly?
    Will they not awake, those who
       make you tremble?
    You will become their spoil!
8 Because you plundered many nations,
       the remaining peoples shall plunder
       you;
    Because of the shedding of human blood,
       and violence done to the land,
    to the city and to all who live in it.

9 Ah! you who pursue evil gain for your
       household,
    setting your nest on high
    to escape the reach of misfortune!
10 You have devised shame for your
       household,
    cutting off many peoples, forfeiting
       your own life;
11 For the stone in the wall shall cry out,†
    and the beam in the frame shall
       answer it!

12 Ah! you who build a city by bloodshed,
    and who establish a town with
       injustice!ᵏ
13 Is this not from the LORD of hosts:
    peoples toil‡ for what the flames
       consume,
    and nations grow weary for nothing!
14 But the earth shall be filled
    with the knowledge of the LORD's
       glory,
    just as the water covers the sea.ˡ

15 Ah! you who give your neighbors
    the cup of your wrath to drink, and
       make them drunk,
    until their nakedness is seen!ᵐ
16 You are filled with shame instead of glory;
    drink, you too, and stagger!

The cup from the LORD's right hand shall
       come around to you,
    and utter shame shall cover your glory.
17 For the violence done to Lebanon§ shall
       cover you,ⁿ
    and the destruction of the animals
       shall terrify you;
    Because of the shedding of human blood,
       and violence done to the land,
    to the city and to all who live in it.

18 Of what use is the carved image,⁵
    that its maker should carve it?
    Or the molten image, the lying oracle,
       that its very maker should trust in it,
    and make mute idols?
19 Ah! you who say to wood, "Awake!"
    to silent stone, "Arise!"
    Can any such thing give oracles?ᵒ
    It is only overlaid with gold and silver,
       there is no breath in it at all.
20 But the LORD is in his holy temple;
    silence before him, all the earth!ᵖ

## CHAPTER 3

### Hymn About God's Reign

¹Prayer of Habakkuk, the prophet. According to
Shigyonot.**

2 O LORD, I have heard your renown,
    and am in awe, O LORD, of your work.
  In the course of years revive it,††
    in the course of years make yourself
       known;
    in your wrath remember compassion!

3 ‡‡God came from Teman,§§
    the Holy One from Mount Paran.�q
                                    *Selah*

---

§[2:17] **The violence done to Lebanon**: the destruction of
the cedar forests of Lebanon, used in lavish building projects
by the great conquerors; cf. Is 14:8; 37:24. **The destruction of
the animals**: the killing off of the wild animals through excessive hunting by the same conquerors; cf. Bar 3:16.

¶[2:18–20] Idolatrous worship is here shown to be folly by
contrasting idols with the majesty of the one true God. Verse
18 may originally have followed v. 19, since the term "Ah!"
begins each new saying in this section.

**[3:1] **Shigyonot**: a Hebrew technical term no longer
understood, but probably a musical notation regarding the
following hymn. This term, the references to the leader and
stringed instruments at the end of the hymn (v. 19), and the
use of the term *selah* in vv. 3, 9, and 13 are found elsewhere
in the Bible only in the Psalter, and they indicate that, like the
psalms, this poem was once used in worship.

††[3:2] **In the course of years revive it**: a plea for God to
renew the works of the past.

‡‡[3:3–15] Cf. the theophanies in Dt 33:2–3; Jgs 5:4–5; Ps
18:8–16; 68:8–9; 77:17–21; 97:1–5; Na 1:3–6, etc. Conventional language is employed to describe the appearance of the
Lord, as in Ex 19:16–19.

§§[3:3] **Teman**: a region in Edom. **Mount Paran**: in the territory of Edom, or the northern part of the Sinai peninsula.

---

*[2:7] **Debtors**: the Hebrew term can mean either debtors or creditors, and this double meaning is likely intended:
the debtor nations rise up against their creditor nation and
become its creditors in the reversal of affairs described here.

†[2:11–12] The palaces, built at the expense of gross injustice (vv. 6–10), call down vengeance on their builders. This
is typical prophetic language for the condemnation of social
crimes within Israel and Judah.

‡[2:13] **Peoples toil**: those oppressed by the Babylonians
do not benefit from their work. Verses 13–14 break the pattern of reversal in the oracles that precede and may have been
added by an editor.

---

j. [2:6] Is 14:4.   k. [2:12] Ez 24:6; Mi 3:10; Na 3:1.   l. [2:14] Is 11:9.
m. [2:15] Jer 51:7; Lam 4:21.

n. [2:17] Is 14:8.   o. [2:19] Is 44:18–19.   p. [2:20] Ps 11:4.   q. [3:3]
Dt 33:2.

His glory covered the heavens,
    and his praise filled the earth;
4  his splendor spread like the light.
He raised his horns high,<sup>r</sup>
    he rejoiced on the day of his
    strength.
5 Before him went pestilence,
    and plague* followed in his steps.
6 He stood and shook the earth;
    he looked and made the nations
    tremble.
Ancient mountains were shattered,
    the age-old hills bowed low,
    age-old orbits† collapsed.

7 The tents of Cushan trembled,
    the pavilions of the land of Midian.‡
8 Was your anger against the rivers,
    O LORD?
    your wrath against the rivers,
    your rage against the sea,§s
That you mounted your steeds,
    your victorious chariot?
9 You readied your bow,
    you filled your bowstring with
    arrows.

                              *Selah*

You split the earth with rivers;
10     at the sight of you the mountains
    writhed.
The clouds poured down water;
    the deep roared loudly.
The sun¹ forgot to rise,
11     the moon left its lofty station,<sup>t</sup>

At the light of your flying arrows,
    at the gleam of your flashing spear.

12 In wrath you marched on the earth,
    in fury you trampled the nations.
13 You came forth to save your people,
    to save your anointed one.**
You crushed the back of the wicked,
    you laid him bare, bottom to neck.
                            *Selah*
14 ††You pierced his head with your shafts;
    his princes you scattered with your
    stormwind,
    as food for the poor in unknown
    places.
15 You trampled the sea with your horses
    amid the churning of the deep
    waters.

16 I hear, and my body trembles;
    at the sound, my lips quiver.
Decay invades my bones,
    my legs tremble beneath me.
I await the day of distress
    that will come upon the people who
    attack us.

17 For though the fig tree does not blossom,
    and no fruit appears on the vine,
Though the yield of the olive fails
    and the terraces produce no
    nourishment,
Though the flocks disappear from the fold
    and there is no herd in the stalls,
18 Yet I will rejoice in the LORD
    and exult in my saving God.
19 GOD, my Lord, is my strength;
    he makes my feet swift as those of
    deer
    and enables me to tread upon the
    heights.‡‡u

For the leader; with stringed instruments.

---

*[3:5] **Pestilence . . . plague:** these may be figures who are part of the heavenly armies God leads into battle.

†[3:6] **Age-old orbits:** the regular paths through the skies of heavenly bodies are disrupted at the appearance of the divine warrior, as are the ancient mountains on earth. Such cosmic disruption is typical of divine appearances (Ps 18:8; Na 1:5).

‡[3:7] **Cushan . . . Midian:** the inhabitants of the area southeast of Judah where the divine march originates (Teman, Mount Paran), who are shaken, together with the cosmos, at God's appearance.

§[3:8] **Rivers . . . sea:** the forces of chaos personified as *yam* (Sea) and *nahar* (River) try to destroy the order God imposed at creation by sweeping past their boundaries and covering the earth. Their mention here and in v. 15 emphasizes that God is both creator and deliverer, subduing historical enemies and cosmic forces.

¶[3:10–11] **Sun . . . moon:** heavenly figures who, like pestilence and plague (v. 5), serve in God's army, or are startled at God's appearance, as are the ancient constellations (v. 6).

r. [3:4] Ps 18:3.   s. [3:8] Ps 74:13; 89:11; Is 51:9; Na 1:4.   t. [3:11] Jos 10:12–13.

**[3:13] **Your anointed one:** the theocratic king, the head of God's people. **The back of the wicked:** this may refer both to God's cosmic enemy, River/Sea, and to the leader of Israel's historical enemy.

††[3:14] The last two lines of this verse are obscure in Hebrew and difficult to translate.

‡‡[3:19] **The heights:** this term can also mean "backs" and may be an image of conquest over the poet's foes.

u. [3:19] Ps 18:32–34.

# THE BOOK OF
# ZEPHANIAH

❧

Zephaniah's prophecy of judgment on Judah and Jerusalem emphasizes, perhaps more than any other prophecy, the devastation and death that divine judgment will bring. Described as the day of the Lord, the day of judgment is pictured as a time of darkness, of anguish and distress, of destruction and plunder of cities, and of threat to all life, human and animal alike. The major sins motivating this judgment, in Zephaniah's view, are Judah's worship of other deities (1:4–9) and its unjust and abusive leadership (3:1–4).

The title of the prophecy informs us that the ministry of Zephaniah took place during the reign of Josiah (640–609 B.C.), not long before the fall of Jerusalem in 587 B.C. The protest against the worship of false gods and the condemnation of foreign practices (1:8–9) may indicate that Zephaniah spoke during the height of Assyrian influence in the early years of Josiah's reign, before Josiah launched the religious reforms praised by Israel's historians (2 Kgs 22:1–23:30). If so, the prophecy of Zephaniah would be contemporary with the early prophecy of Jeremiah, with which it shares both language and ideas.

Following are the book's four sections:

   I. The Day of the Lord: Judgment on Judah (1:2–2:3)
  II. Judgment on the Nations (2:4–15)
 III. Jerusalem Reproached (3:1–7)
 IV. The Nations Punished and Jerusalem Restored (3:8–20)

## CHAPTER 1

¹The word of the LORD which came to Zephaniah, the son of Cushi, the son of Gedaliah, the son of Amariah, the son of Hezekiah,[*] in the days of Josiah, the son of Amon, king of Judah.

### The Day of the Lord: Judgment on Judah

2 I will completely sweep away all things
    from the face of the land—oracle of
    the LORD.
3 I will sweep away human being and beast
    alike,
    I will sweep away the birds of the sky,
    and the fish of the sea.
I will make the wicked stumble;
    I will eliminate the people
    from the face of the land—oracle of
    the LORD.[a]
4 I will stretch out my hand against Judah,
    and against all the inhabitants of
    Jerusalem;

I will eliminate from this place
    the last vestige of Baal,
    the name of the idolatrous priests.
5 And those who bow down on the roofs
    to the host of heaven,[†]
And those who bow down to the LORD
    but swear by Milcom;[b]
6 And those who have turned away from
      the LORD,
    and those who have not sought the
      LORD,
    who have not inquired of him.

7 Silence in the presence of the Lord GOD!
    for near is the day of the LORD,
Yes, the LORD has prepared a sacrifice,
    he has consecrated his guests.[c]
8 On the day of the LORD's sacrifice
I will punish the officials and the king's
      sons,

---

[†][1:5] **The host of heaven**: the sun, moon, planets, and stars, the worship of which became widespread in Judah under Assyrian influence; cf. 1 Kgs 11:5, 7, 33; 2 Kgs 23:13. **Milcom**: the god of the Ammonites; cf. 1 Kgs 11:5, 7, 33; 2 Kgs 23:13.
[‡][1:7] **He has consecrated his guests**: God has consecrated the troops, presumably foreign, who have been invited to share in the spoil on the day of slaughter.

---

[*][1:1] **Hezekiah**: it is possible, but not certain, that Zephaniah's ancestor was King Hezekiah who reigned in Judah from 715 to 687 B.C. (2 Kgs 18–20).

a. [1:3] Hos 4:3.

b. [1:5] Jer 8:2; 2 Kgs 23:13.   c. [1:7] Is 34:6; Am 5:18.

and all who dress in foreign apparel.
9 I will punish, on that day,
   all who leap over the threshold,*
Who fill the house of their master
   with violence and deceit.
10    On that day—oracle of the LORD—
A cry will be heard from the Fish Gate,
   a wail from the Second Quarter,†
   loud crashing from the hills.
11 Wail, O inhabitants of Maktesh!
   for all the merchants are destroyed,
   all who weigh out silver, done away
      with.

12    At that time,
I will search Jerusalem with lamps,
   I will punish the people
   who settle like dregs in wine,‡
Who say in their hearts,
   "The Lord will not do good,
      nor will he do harm."
13 Their wealth shall be given to plunder
   and their houses to devastation;
They will build houses,
   but not dwell in them;
They will plant vineyards,
   but not drink their wine.d
14 Near is the great day of the LORD,
   near and very swiftly coming.
The sound of the day of the LORD!
            Piercing—
   there a warrior shrieks!
15 A day of wrath is that day,
   a day of distress and anguish,
   a day of ruin and desolation,
A day of darkness and gloom,
   a day of thick black clouds,e
16 A day of trumpet blasts and battle cries
   against fortified cities,
   against lofty battlements.f
17 I will hem the people in
   till they walk like the blind,
   because they have sinned against
      the LORD;
And their blood shall be poured out like
      dust,
   and their bowels like dung.
18 Neither their silver nor their gold
   will be able to save them.
On the day of the LORD's wrath,
   in the fire of his passion,
   all the earth will be consumed.

For he will make an end, yes, a sudden
            end,
   of all who live on the earth.g

## CHAPTER 2

1 §Gather, gather yourselves together,
   O nation without shame!
2 Before you are driven away,
   like chaff that disappears;
Before there comes upon you
   the blazing anger of the LORD;
Before there comes upon you
   the day of the LORD's anger.
3 Seek the LORD,
   all you humble of the land,
   who have observed his law;
Seek justice,
   seek humility;
Perhaps you will be sheltered
   on the day of the LORD's anger.h

### Judgment on the Nations

4 For Gaza shall be forsaken,
   and Ashkelon shall be a waste,
Ashdod they shall drive out at midday,
   and Ekron§ shall be uprooted.i
5 Ah! You who dwell by the seacoast,
   the nation of Cherethites,**
   the word of the LORD is against you!
O Canaan, land of the Philistines,
   I will leave you to perish without an
      inhabitant!
6 You shall become fields for shepherds,
   and folds for flocks.
7 The seacoast shall belong
   to the remnant of the house of
      Judah;
   by the sea they shall pasture.
In the houses of Ashkelon
   they shall lie down in the evening.
For the LORD their God will take care of
      them,
   and bring about their restoration.

8 I have heard the taunts uttered by Moab,
   and the insults of the Ammonites,††
When they taunted my people
   and made boasts against their
      territory.j

---

*[1:9] **Leap over the threshold**: the reference may be to a religious ritual like that practiced by the priests of the Philistine deity Dagon (1 Sm 5:5).
†[1:10–11] **The Second Quarter . . . Maktesh**: sections of Jerusalem (cf. 2 Kgs 22:14).
‡[1:12] **Settle like dregs in wine**: those who are overconfident because, like the sediment that settles to the bottom of a bottle of wine, they have remained at peace and undisturbed for a long time.

d. [1:13] Am 5:11.   e. [1:15] Is 13:9; Jl 2:1–2.   f. [1:16] Am 2:2.

§[2:1–3] This oracle is a classic description of the day of the Lord as an overwhelming disaster, concluding with a call for repentance and reform. **Nation without shame**: Judah.
§[2:4] **Gaza . . . Ashkelon . . . Ashdod . . . Ekron**: cities of the Philistine confederation.
**[2:5] **Cherethites**: a synonym for, or subgroup of, the Philistines, which may be associated with Crete, a part of the larger Aegean area from which the Philistines came.
††[2:8] **Moab . . . Ammonites**: Judah's neighbors to the East across the Jordan.

g. [1:18] Zep 3:8; Jer 4:26–27.   h. [2:3] Am 5:14–15.   i. [2:4] Jer 47:5; Am 1:6–8.   j. [2:8] Jer 48:1; 49:1.

⁹ Therefore, as I live—
  oracle of the LORD of hosts—
  the God of Israel,
Moab shall become like Sodom,
  the Ammonites like Gomorrah:
A field of weeds,
  a salt pit,
  a waste forever.
The remnant of my people shall plunder
    them,
  the survivors of my nation
    dispossess them.
¹⁰ This will be the recompense for their pride,
  because they taunted and boasted
    against
  the people of the LORD of hosts.
¹¹ The LORD shall inspire them with terror
  when he makes all the gods of earth
    waste away;
Then the distant shores of the nations,
  each from its own place,
  shall bow down to him.

¹² You too, O Cushites,*
  *shall be slain by the sword of the
    LORD.ᵏ
¹³ He will stretch out his hand against the
    north,
  to destroy Assyria;
He will make Nineveh a waste,
  dry as the desert.ˡ
¹⁴ In her midst flocks shall lie down,
  all the wild life of the hollows;
The screech owl and the desert owl
  shall roost in her columns;
The owl shall hoot from the window,
  the raven croak from the doorway.ᵐ
¹⁵ Is this the exultant city†
  that dwelt secure,
That told itself,
  "I and there is no one else"?
How it has become a waste,
  a lair for wild animals!
Those who pass by it
  hiss, and shake their fists!

## CHAPTER 3

### Jerusalem Reproached

¹ Ah! Rebellious and polluted,
  the tyrannical city!‡
² It listens to no voice,
  accepts no correction;
In the LORD it has not trusted,
  nor drawn near to its God.ⁿ

---

*[2:12] **Cushites**: the Ethiopians, who had ruled Egypt a
generation before Zephaniah's career.
†[2:15] **The exultant city**: Nineveh. **Hiss, and shake their
fists**: gestures of derision.
‡[3:1] **The tyrannical city**: Jerusalem.

k. [2:12] 2 Chr 14:7-14.   l. [2:13] Na 3:7.   m. [2:14] Is 34:11.
n. [3:2] Jer 2:30; 7:28.

---

³ Its officials within it
  are roaring lions;
Its judges are desert wolves
  that have no bones to gnaw by
    morning.ᵒ
⁴ Its prophets are reckless,
  treacherous people;
Its priests profane what is holy,
  and do violence to the law.ᵖ
⁵ But the LORD in its midst is just,
  doing no wrong;
Morning after morning rendering
    judgment
  unfailingly, at dawn;
  the wicked, however, know no
    shame.

⁶ I have cut down nations,
  their battlements are laid waste;
I have made their streets deserted,
  with no one passing through;
Their cities are devastated,
  with no one dwelling in them.�q
⁷ I said, "Surely now you will fear me,
  you will accept correction;
They cannot fail to see
  all I have brought upon them."
Yet the more eagerly they have done
  all their corrupt deeds.

### The Nations Punished and Jerusalem Restored

⁸ Therefore, wait for me—oracle of the
    LORD—
  until the day when I arise as accuser;
For it is my decision to gather nations,
  to assemble kingdoms,
In order to pour out upon them my
    wrath,
  all my blazing anger;
For in the fire of my passion
  all the earth will be consumed.ʳ

⁹ For then I will make pure
  the speech of the peoples,
That they all may call upon the name of
  the LORD,
  to serve him with one accord;
¹⁰ From beyond the rivers of Ethiopia
  and as far as the recesses of the
    North,
  they shall bring me offerings.

¹¹       On that day
You will not be ashamed
  of all your deeds,
  when you rebelled against me;
For then I will remove from your midst
  the proud braggarts,

---

o. [3:3] Ez 22:27; Mi 3:11.   p. [3:4] Ez 22:26; Hb 1:4.   q. [3:6] Jer
2:15.   r. [3:8] Zep 1:18; Jl 4:2.

And you shall no longer exalt yourself
    on my holy mountain.
12 But I will leave as a remnant in your midst
    a people humble and lowly,
Who shall take refuge in the name of the
    Lord—ˢ
13     the remnant of Israel.
They shall do no wrong
    and speak no lies;
Nor shall there be found in their mouths
    a deceitful tongue;
They shall pasture and lie down
    with none to disturb them.ᵗ
14 Shout for joy, daughter Zion!
    sing joyfully, Israel!
Be glad and exult with all your heart,
    daughter Jerusalem!ᵘ
15 The Lord has removed the judgment
    against you,
    he has turned away your enemies;
The King of Israel, the Lord, is in your
    midst,
    you have no further misfortune to
    fear.
16     On that day, it shall be said to
    Jerusalem:

Do not fear, Zion,
    do not be discouraged!
17 The Lord, your God, is in your midst,
    a mighty savior,
Who will rejoice over you with gladness,
    and renew you in his love,
Who will sing joyfully because of you,ᵛ
18     as on festival days.

I will remove disaster from among you,
    so that no one may recount your
    disgrace.
19 At that time I will deal
    with all who oppress you;
I will save the lame,
    and assemble the outcasts;
I will give them praise and renown
    in every land where they were
    shamed.ʷ
20 At that time I will bring you home,
    and at that time I will gather you;
For I will give you renown and praise,
    among all the peoples of the earth,
When I bring about your restoration
    before your very eyes, says the
    Lord.ˣ

s. [3:12] Is 57:13; Ob 17.    t. [3:13] Mi 4:4.    u. [3:14] Zec 9:9.

v. [3:17] Jl 2:27.    w. [3:19] Mi 4:6.    x. [3:20] Jl 4:1.

# THE BOOK OF
# HAGGAI

⁓⁓

Haggai's words concern conditions in the Persian province of Judah at the beginning of the postexilic period during the reign of the Persian king Darius I (522–486 B.C.). The community in Judah is struggling with its identity in light of the loss of its statehood through the demise of the monarchy and the destruction of the Temple. Haggai's oracles address both these problems. First, the provincial government, despite its subordination to Persian hegemony, is seen as the legitimate heir to the Davidic monarchy; the governor Zerubbabel, himself a descendant of the Davidic line, and the high priest Joshua together provide political, economic, and religious leadership for the survivors of the Babylonian destruction and the returnees from the Babylonian exile who live together in Judah. Still, the possibility for restoration of Davidic rule is not relinquished but rather is shifted to the eschatological future. Second, the Temple's ruined state is addressed by a rebuilding program. The prophet links the well-being of the community to the work of Temple restoration, and his exhortations to the leaders and the people to begin work on this project are apparently heeded. The brief period of Haggai's ministry (August to December 520 B.C.) marks the resumption of work on the Temple, the symbol of divine presence among the people.

Six date formulas (1:1, 15; 2:1, 10, 18, 20) are an important feature of the Book of Haggai. In their specificity and in their link to the reign of a foreign king (Darius), the dates underscore God's control over history, as do similar chronological references in Zechariah, a prophetic book connected in literary and thematic ways to Haggai.

The prophecies of Haggai can be divided into two major parts:

I. The Restoration of the Temple (1:1–15)
II. Oracles of Encouragement (2:1–23)

## CHAPTER 1
**Prophetic Call to Work on the Temple.** ¹On the first day of the sixth month in the second year* of Darius the king, the word of the LORD came through Haggai the prophet to the governor of Judah, Zerubbabel,ᵃ son of Shealtiel, and to the high priest Joshua, son of Jehozadak:ᵇ ²Thus says the LORD of hosts: This people has said: "Now is not the time to rebuild the house of the LORD."

³Then the word of the LORD came through Haggai the prophet: ⁴Is it time for you to dwell in your paneled houses while this house lies in ruins?†ᶜ

⁵ Now thus says the LORD of hosts:
  Reflect on your experience!‡
⁶ You have sown much, but have brought in little;
   you have eaten, but have not been satisfied;ᵈ
You have drunk, but have not become intoxicated;
   you have clothed yourselves, but have not been warmed;
And the hired worker labors for a bag full of holes.

⁷Thus says the LORD of hosts:

Reflect on your experience!

---

*[1:1] **First day of the sixth month in the second year**: August 29, 520 B.C. This is the first of six chronological indicators in Haggai. **Darius**: Darius I, emperor of Persia from 522 to 486 B.C. **Governor**: term used for local rulers of provinces in the Persian imperial structure. **Zerubbabel**: grandson of King Jehoiachin (cf. 2 Kgs 24:8–17).

†[1:4] **Your paneled houses . . . house lies in ruins**: the contrast here is between the unfinished Temple and the completed houses of the Judeans.

‡[1:5] **Reflect on your experience**: the prophet exhorts the people to consider the futility of their efforts as a result of their neglecting work on the Temple. The following verses call attention to harsh conditions in Judah after the return from exile and the preoccupation of the people with their personal concerns.

a. [1:1] Zec 4:6–10.   b. [1:1] Zec 3:1–10.   c. [1:4] 2 Sm 7:2.   d. [1:6] Lv 26:26; Hos 4:10.

8 Go up into the hill country;
    bring timber, and build the house
that I may be pleased with it,
    and that I may be glorified,* says the
        LORD.
9 You expected much, but it came to little;
    and what you brought home, I blew
        away.
Why is this?—oracle of the LORD† of
        hosts—
    Because my house is the one which
        lies in ruins,
    while each of you runs to your own
        house.
10 Therefore, the heavens withheld the dew,
    and the earth its yield.
11 And I have proclaimed a devastating heat‡
    upon the land and upon the
        mountains,
Upon the grain, the new wine, and the
        olive oil,
    upon all that the ground brings
        forth;
Upon human being and beast alike,
    and upon all they produce.

**Response of Leaders and People.** 12Then
Zerubbabel, son of Shealtiel, and the high priest
Joshua, son of Jehozadak, and all the remnant
of the people§ obeyed the LORD their God, and
the words of Haggai the prophet, since the LORD
their God had sent him; thus the people feared
the LORD. 13Then Haggai, the messenger of the
LORD, proclaimed to the people as the message
of the LORD: I am with you!—oracle of the LORD.

14And so the LORD stirred up the spirit of the
governor of Judah, Zerubbabel, son of Shealtiel,
and the spirit of the high priest Joshua, son of
Jehozadak, and the spirit of all the remnant of
the people,e so that they came to do the work in
the house of the LORD of hosts, their God, 15on
the twenty-fourth day of the sixth month in the
second year¶ of Darius the king.

**CHAPTER 2**

**Assurance of God's Presence.** 1On the twenty-
first day of the seventh month,** the word of the
LORD came through Haggai the prophet: 2Speak
to the governor of Judah, Zerubbabel, son of
Shealtiel, and to the high priest Joshua, son of
Jehozadak, and to the remnant of the people:

3 Who is left among you††
    who saw this house in its former
        glory?
And how do you see it now?
    Does it not seem like nothing in
        your eyes?f
4 Now be strong, Zerubbabel—oracle of the
        LORD—
    be strong, Joshua, son of Jehozadak,
        high priest,
Be strong, all you people of the land—
        oracle of the LORD—
    and work! For I am with you—
        oracle of the LORD of hosts.
5 This is the commitment I made to you
    when you came out of Egypt.
My spirit remains in your midst;
    do not fear!

6For thus says the LORD of hosts:‡‡

In just a little while,
    I will shake the heavens and the earth,g
    the sea and the dry land.
7 I will shake all the nations,
    so that the treasures of all the
        nations will come in.
And I will fill this house with glory—
    says the LORD of hosts.h

8Mine is the silver and mine the gold—oracle of
the LORD of hosts.

9 Greater will be the glory of this housei
    the latter more than the former—
        says the LORD of hosts;
And in this place I will give you peace—§§
    oracle of the LORD of hosts.

---

*[1:8] **That I may be glorified:** for the prophet, the
rebuilding of the Temple restores the glory God had lost in
the eyes of the nations by the Temple's destruction.

†[1:9] **Oracle of the LORD:** a phrase used extensively in
prophetic books to indicate divine speech.

‡[1:11] **Devastating heat:** this pronouncement of natural
disaster, which functions as a warning to the people for their
failure to rebuild the Temple, concludes the opening oracular
section of Haggai.

§[1:12] **The remnant of the people:** here the phrase
appears to refer to the prophet's audience, but the "remnant"
theme, though often in different Hebrew terminology, suggesting especially those whom the Lord will call back from
exile and re-establish as his people, is important in the prophets (cf. Is 4:3; 37:31–32; Jl 3:5; Mi 4:7; Ob 17) and in the New
Testament (cf. Rom 11:1–10).

¶[1:15] **Twenty-fourth day of the sixth month in the second year:** September 21, 520 B.C. The resumption of work on
the Temple occurred twenty-three days from the beginning of
Haggai's prophecy. This date formula repeats in reverse order
the formula of v. 1, thereby bringing to conclusion chap. 1; it
also initiates the next unit in 2:1.

e. [1:14] Ezr 1:5; 5:1–2.

---

**[2:1] **Twenty-first day of the seventh month:** October
17, 520 B.C.

††[2:3] **Who is left among you:** i.e., who is old enough to
have seen the first Temple prior to its destruction in 587 B.C.?
Compare the reaction of priests who were alive then (Ezr
3:12–13).

‡‡[2:6–9] These verses emphasize that the total fulfillment
of God's promises to Israel is on the horizon. Such an eschatological event, which will shake the nations (v. 6; cf. v. 21), finds
an echo not only in the political revolts in the Persian empire
in 521 but also in the formative events of Israel's history (Ex
19:18; Jgs 5:4; Ps 68:8–9) when God intervened on behalf of
the Israelites. The bringing of treasures of all the nations (v.
7) to Jerusalem recalls the visionary passages of Isaiah of the
pilgrimage of all nations to Jerusalem (Is 2:2–4; 60:6–9).

§§[2:9] **Peace:** after God's presence or glory has returned
to the Temple, Jerusalem will receive the treasures from the

f. [2:3] Ezr 3:10–13.  g. [2:6] Heb 12:26.  h. [2:7] Is 60:7–11.
i. [2:9] 1 Kgs 8:11.

**Priestly Ruling with Prophetic Interpretation.**\* <sup></sup>¹⁰On the twenty-fourth day of the ninth month in the second year† of Darius, the word of the LORD came to Haggai the prophet: ¹¹Thus says the LORD of hosts: Ask the priests for a ruling:‡ ¹²If someone carries sanctified meat in the fold of a garment and the fold touches bread, soup, wine, oil, or any other food, do they become sanctified? "No," the priests answered. ¹³Then Haggai asked: "If a person defiled from contact with a corpse touches any of these, do they become defiled?" The priests answered, "They become defiled."ʲ ¹⁴Then Haggai replied:

> So is this people,§ and so is this nation
> in my sight—oracle of the LORD—
> And so is all the work of their hands;
> what they offer there is defiled.

¹⁵Now reflect,¶ from this day forward—before you set stone to stone in the temple of the LORD, ¹⁶what was your experience?

> When one went to a heap of grain for
> twenty ephahs,
> there were only ten;
> When one went to a vat to draw fifty
> ephahs,\*\*
> there were only twenty.ᵏ
¹⁷ I struck you, and all the work of your
> hands,
> with searing wind, blight, and hail,

yet you did not return to me—oracle of the LORD.ˡ

¹⁸Reflect from this day forward, from the twenty-fourth day of the ninth month.†† From the day on which the temple of the LORD was founded, reflect!

¹⁹ Is there still seed in the storehouse?
> Have the vine, the fig, the
> pomegranate,
> and the olive tree still not borne
> fruit?
> From this day, I will bless you.‡‡

**Future Hope.**§§ ²⁰The word of the LORD came a second time to Haggai on the twenty-fourth day of the month:¶¶ ²¹Speak to Zerubbabel, the governor of Judah:

> I will shake the heavens and the earth;
²²    I will overthrow the thrones of
> kingdoms,
> and destroy the power of the
> kingdoms of the nations.
> I will overthrow the chariots and their
> riders,
> and the riders with their horses
> will fall by each other's swords.ᵐ

²³On that day—oracle of the LORD of hosts—I will take you, my servant, Zerubbabel, son of Shealtiel—oracle of the LORD—and I will make you like a signet ring,\*\*\* for I have chosen you—oracle of the LORD of hosts.ⁿ

---

the nations, making the Temple more glorious than ever; and from that place God will extend *shalom*, a peace which embraces prosperity, well-being, harmony.

\*[2:10–14] A request for a priestly ruling (Heb. *torah*) is made in the form of a dialogue between Haggai and the priests. Explicit examples where such priestly rulings are quoted are rare in prophetic books. The interchange illustrates an essential role of the priesthood: the interpretation of God's law (cf. Lv 10:9–11).

†[2:10] **Twenty-fourth day of the ninth month in the second year**: December 18, 520 B.C.

‡[2:11] **Ask the priests for a ruling**: i.e., a determination on whether defilement and sanctity can be physically transmitted. The priests are expected to make a legal decision. The answer is that sanctity cannot be transmitted (v. 12) but defilement can (v. 13). Priestly duties are enumerated in Lv 10:10–20.

§[2:14] **So is this people**: the prophet's interpretation is that the restored sacrifices were not acceptable because the people's behavior was tainted.

¶[2:15–19] This prophecy is retrospective and should be read with 1:5–11, a description of the conditions of economic deprivation before the rebuilding of the Temple.

\*\*[2:16] **Ephahs**: see note on Is 5:10.

††[2:18] **Twenty-fourth day of the ninth month**: December 18, 520 B.C., the date of the refounding of the Temple (vv. 10, 20), the central date in Haggai.

‡‡[2:19] **I will bless you**: from the day of the refounding of the Temple, agricultural plenty and fertility are assured. This link between temple and prosperity is part of the ancient Near Eastern temple ideology that underlies Haggai and Zec 1–8.

§§[2:20–23] This final oracle of hope is uttered on the day of the refounding of the Temple. Unlike the other oracles it is addressed to Zerubbabel alone, who, as a Davidic descendant, will have a servant role in God's future Israelite kingdom to be established when God intervenes to overthrow the nations.

¶¶[2:20] **Twenty-fourth day of the month**: December 18, 520 B.C. (as in v. 18).

\*\*\*[2:23] **Like a signet ring**: this promise to Zerubbabel reverses the punishment of his grandfather (Jer 22:23–25). A signet is a ring or other instrument used to mark documents or materials with the equivalent of an official signature. A lower official could thus be authorized to act on behalf of a higher official. Like a signet ring, Zerubbabel represents the Lord.

---

j. [2:13] Lv 22:4–7.   k. [2:16] Hos 4:3a.

l. [2:17] Am 4:9.   m. [2:22] Sir 49:11.   n. [2:23] Zec 6:12–13.

# THE BOOK OF
# ZECHARIAH

The Book of Zechariah, because of its great variation in style, content, and language, is widely believed to be a composite work. Made up of First Zechariah (chaps. 1–8) and Second Zechariah (chaps. 9–14), the book has been attributed to at least two different prophets. The prophecies of First Zechariah can be dated to the late sixth century B.C., contemporary with those of Haggai; the oracles of Second Zechariah are somewhat later.

The most striking feature of First Zechariah is a series of visions in which the prophet describes the centrality of Jerusalem, its Temple, and its leaders, who function both in the politics of the region and of the Persian empire and in God's universal rule. These visions clearly relate to the Temple restoration begun in 520 B.C.

The prophecies of First Zechariah can be divided into three literary units. A brief introductory unit (1:1–6) links the prophecies of chaps. 1–8 with those of Haggai. The visionary unit (1:7–6:15) consists of seven visionary images plus an associated vision dealing with the high priest Joshua. The third unit (7:1–8:23) consists of two parts: (1) an address (7:1–14) to a delegation sent from Bethel in anticipation of the end of the seventy years of exile; (2) a series of oracles (8:1–23): seven oracles dealing with the restoration of Judah and Zion (vv. 1–17), followed by three oracles of hope concerning Judah and the nations (vv. 18–23).

Coming nearly a century later, the prophecies of Second Zechariah are extraordinarily diverse. A complex assortment of literary genres appears in these six chapters, which consist of two distinct parts (chaps. 9–11 and chaps. 12–14), each introduced by an unusual Hebrew word for "oracle." Despite the diversity of materials, the structural links among the chapters along with verbal and thematic connections point to an overall integrity for Zec 9–14.

Second Zechariah draws heavily on the words and ideas of earlier biblical prophets. The prophet is acutely aware of the devastation that comes from disobedience to God's word, as had been spoken by God's prophetic emissaries. Yet, it was now clear in this century after the rebuilding of the Temple and the repatriation of many of the exiles, that Judah would not soon regain political autonomy and a Davidic king. So the various poems, narratives, oracles, and parables of Second Zechariah maintain the hope of previous prophets by depicting a glorious eschatological restoration. At that time all nations will recognize Jerusalem's centrality and acknowledge God's universal sovereignty.

## CHAPTER 1

**Call for Obedience.** ¹In the second year of Darius,* in the eighth month, the word of the LORD came to the prophet Zechariah, son of Berechiah, son of Iddo: ²The LORD was very angry with your ancestors.†ª ³Say to them: Thus says the LORD of hosts, Return to me—oracle of the LORD‡ of hosts—and I will return to you, says the LORD of hosts. ⁴Do not be like your ancestors to whom the earlier prophets§ proclaimed: Thus says the LORD of hosts: Turn from your evil ways and from your wicked deeds.ᵇ But they did not listen or pay attention to meᶜ—oracle of the LORD.— ⁵Your ancestors, where are they? And the prophets, can they live forever? ⁶But my words and my statutes, with which I charged my servants the prophets, did

---

*[1:1] **Darius:** Darius I, emperor of Persia from 522 to 486 B.C. **The second year . . . eighth month:** October/November 520 B.C., i.e., prior to the latest date in Haggai (Dec. 18, 520 B.C., Hg 2:10). Unlike other prophets, Haggai and Zechariah 1–8 contain specific chronological information, probably because they were sensitive to the imminent end of the expected seventy years of exile. See note on Zec 1:12.

†[1:2] **Your ancestors:** refers to the preexilic people of Judah, who were subjected to Babylonian destruction and exile.

‡[1:3] **Oracle of the LORD:** a phrase used extensively in prophetic books to indicate divine speech.

§[1:4] **Earlier prophets:** preexilic prophets of the Lord. There are many allusions to them in Zechariah, indicating their influence on the postexilic community (see 7:7, 12).

a. [1:2] Mi 3:7.

b. [1:4] Is 55:7.   c. [1:4] Lk 20:15.

these not overtake your ancestors?*d* Then they repented* and admitted: "Just as the LORD of hosts intended to treat us according to our ways and deeds, so the LORD has done."

**First Vision: Horses Patrolling the Earth.***e* 7In the second year of Darius, on the twenty-fourth day of Shebat, the eleventh month,† the word of the LORD came to the prophet Zechariah, son of Berechiah, son of Iddo:

8‡I looked out in the night,§ and there was a man mounted on a red horse standing in the shadows among myrtle trees; and behind him were red, sorrel, and white horses. 9I asked, "What are these, my lord?"¶ Then the angel who spoke with me answered, "I will show you what these are." 10Then the man who was standing among the myrtle trees spoke up and said, "These are the ones whom the LORD has sent to patrol the earth."*f* 11And they answered the angel of the LORD,** who was standing among the myrtle trees: "We have been patrolling the earth, and now the whole earth rests quietly." 12Then the angel of the LORD replied, "LORD of hosts, how long will you be without mercy for Jerusalem and the cities of Judah that have felt your anger these seventy years?"††g 13To the angel who spoke with me, the LORD replied favorably, with comforting words.

**Oracular Response.** 14The angel who spoke with me then said to me, Proclaim: Thus says the LORD of hosts:

I am jealous for Jerusalem
    and for Zion‡‡ intensely jealous.*h*
15 I am consumed with anger
    toward the complacent nations;§§

When I was only a little angry,
    they compounded the disaster.*i*
16 Therefore, thus says the LORD:
I return to Jerusalem in mercy;*j*
    my house¶¶ will be rebuilt there*k*—
        oracle of the LORD of hosts—
    and a measuring line will be
        stretched over Jerusalem.
17 Proclaim further: Thus says the LORD of
        hosts:
My cities will again overflow with
        prosperity;
    the LORD will again comfort Zion,
    and will again choose Jerusalem.*l*

## CHAPTER 2

**Second Vision: The Four Horns and the Four Smiths.** 1I raised my eyes and looked and there were four horns.*** 2Then I asked the angel who spoke with me, "What are those?" He answered, "Those are the horns that scattered††† Judah, Israel, and Jerusalem."*m* 3Then the LORD showed me four workmen.‡‡‡ 4And I said, "What are these coming to do?" And the LORD said, "Those are the horns that scattered Judah, so that none could raise their heads any more;*n* and these have come to terrify them—to cut down the horns of the nations that raised their horns to scatter the land of Judah."

**Third Vision: The Man with the Measuring Cord.** 5I raised my eyes and looked, and there was a man with a measuring cord§§§ in his hand.*o* 6I asked, "Where are you going?" And he said, "To measure Jerusalem—to see how great its width is and how great its length."

7Then the angel who spoke with me advanced as another angel came out to meet him 8and he said to the latter, "Run, speak to that official:¶¶¶ Jerusalem will be unwalled, because of the abundance of people and beasts in its midst.*p*

---

*[1:6] **Repented**: the Hebrew word *shub* literally means "turn back." This term is often used to speak of repentance as a return to the covenantal relationship between Israel and the Lord.

†[1:7] **The second year . . . eleventh month**: February 15, 519 B.C. The largest set of visions (1:7–6:15) is dated to a time just prior to the beginning of the new year in the spring.

‡[1:8–11] Four riders on horses of three different colors are sent by God to patrol the four corners of the earth. Compare the four chariots of the seventh vision, 6:1–8.

§[1:8] **In the night**: nighttime, or this night. This setting of darkness is meant only for the first vision.

¶[1:9] **My lord**: this expression in Hebrew (*'adoni*) is used as a polite form of address. **Angel who spoke with me**: angelic being (not identical to the angel of the Lord who is one of the four horsemen) who serves as an interpreter, bringing a message from God to the prophet, who himself is a messenger of God.

**[1:11] **Angel of the LORD**: chief angelic figure in God's heavenly court, and perhaps the "man" of 1:8.

††[1:12] **These seventy years**: allusion to the period of divine anger mentioned in Jer 25:11–12 and 29:10. Here the symbolic number seventy is understood to mark the period without a Temple in Jerusalem. Since these seventy years would have been almost over at this point, this symbolic number would have provided motivation for rebuilding the Temple as a sign of the end of the exile.

‡‡[1:14] **For Jerusalem and for Zion**: rather than the usual order, Zion and Jerusalem, elsewhere in the Bible. The reversal highlights the centrality of Jerusalem, which is mentioned in all three of the brief oracles of 1:14–17.

§§[1:15] **Complacent nations**: probably a reference to the Persian empire, which in its imperial extent included many

national groups that maintained separate identities. **Compounded the disaster**: the surrounding nations took advantage of the Lord's anger against Judah to further their own interests.

¶¶[1:16] **My house**: the Temple. See note on Hg 1:4. **Measuring line**: a builder's string, not for devastation, as in Is 34:11, but for reconstruction.

***[2:1] **Four horns**: symbols of the total political and military might of Judah's imperial adversaries, probably representing Assyria, Babylonia, and Persia. The number four represents universality rather than any specific number of foes.

†††[2:2] **Scattered**: sent part of the population into exile. This was standard imperial policy initiated in the ancient Near East by the Assyrians for dealing with a conquered state.

‡‡‡[2:3] **Four workmen**: four agents of God's power. The imagery follows that of four horns: the workers cut down, or make ineffectual, the horns, i.e., enemy.

§§§[2:5] **Measuring cord**: a string for measuring, as opposed to a builder's string, 1:16.

¶¶¶[2:8] **That official**: probably the man with the measuring cord of v. 5.

---

i. [1:15] Is 47:6.  j. [1:16] Is 54:6–10.  k. [1:16] Zec 2:5–9.
l. [1:17] Zec 2:15; 13:9.  m. [2:2] Dt 33:17; Dn 7:8.  n. [2:4] Jer 48:25.  o. [2:5] Jer 31:38–39; Ez 41:13; Rev 11:1; 21:15.  p. [2:8] Is 49:19–20; 54:2–3; Jer 31:27; Ez 38:11.

---

d. [1:6] Zec 7:7–14.  e. [1:7] Zec 6:1–7; Rev 5:6; 6:1–9.  f. [1:10] Zec 7:5; Jer 25:11–12; 29:10.  g. [1:12] Rev 6:10.  h. [1:14] Zec 8:2.

[9]I will be an encircling wall of fire* for it—oracle of the Lord—and I will be the glory in its midst."[q] **Expansion on the Themes of the First Three Visions.** [10]Up! Up! Flee from the land of the north[†]—oracle of the Lord;—For like the four winds of heaven I have dispersed you—oracle of the Lord.[r] [11]Up, Zion! Escape, you who dwell in daughter Babylon! [12]For thus says the Lord of hosts after the Lord's glory had sent me, concerning the nations that have plundered you: Whoever strikes you strikes me directly in the eye.[s] [13]Now I wave my hand over them, and they become plunder for their own servants.[t] Thus you shall know that the Lord of hosts has sent me. [14]Sing and rejoice, daughter Zion! Now, I am coming to dwell in your midst—oracle of the Lord. [15]Many nations will bind themselves to the Lord on that day.[u] They will be my people,[‡] and I will dwell in your midst. Then you shall know that the Lord of hosts has sent me to you. [16]The Lord will inherit Judah[v] as his portion of the holy land,[§] and the Lord will again choose Jerusalem. [17]Silence, all people, in the presence of the Lord, who stirs forth from his holy dwelling.[w]

## CHAPTER 3

**Prophetic Vision: Joshua the High Priest.** [1]Then he showed me Joshua the high priest standing before the angel of the Lord, while the adversary[¶] stood at his right side to accuse him.[x] [2]And the angel of the Lord said to the adversary, "May the Lord rebuke you, O adversary; may the Lord who has chosen Jerusalem rebuke you![y] Is this not a brand plucked from the fire?"[z]

[3]"Now Joshua was standing before the angel, clad in filthy garments. [4]Then the angel said to those standing before him, "Remove his filthy garments."[a] And to him he said, "Look, I have taken your guilt from you,[b] and I am clothing

you in stately robes." [5]Then he said, "Let them put a clean turban on his head." And they put a clean turban on his head and clothed him with the garments while the angel of the Lord was standing by. [6]Then the angel of the Lord charged Joshua: [7]"Thus says the Lord of hosts: If you walk in my ways and carry out my charge, you will administer my house and watch over my courts;[††] and I will give you access to those standing here."

**Supplementary Oracle.** [8]"Hear, O Joshua, high priest! You and your associates who sit before you! For they are signs of things to come![‡‡] I will surely bring my servant the Branch. [9]Look at the stone[d] that I have placed before Joshua. On this one stone with seven facets[§§] I will engrave its inscription—oracle of the Lord of hosts—and I will take away the guilt of that land in one day. [10]On that day—oracle of the Lord of hosts—you will invite one another under your vines and fig trees."[f]

## CHAPTER 4

**Fourth Vision: The Lampstand and the Two Olive Trees.** [1]Then the angel who spoke with me returned and aroused me, like one awakened from sleep. [2]He said to me, "What do you see?" I replied, "I see a lampstand[¶¶] all of gold,[g] with a bowl on top of it. There are seven lamps on it, with seven spouts on each of the lamps that are on top of it. [3]And beside it are two olive trees,[***] one on the right of the bowl and one to its left." [4]Then I said to the angel who spoke with me, "What are these things, my lord?" [5]And the

---

*[2:9] **Encircling wall of fire**: divine protection for an unwalled Jerusalem. Urban centers were generally walled, and Jerusalem's walls were eventually rebuilt in the late fifth century B.C. (Neh 2:17–20).

†[2:10] **Land of the north**: refers to Babylon (v. 11), in a geographic rather than a political sense, as the place from which exiles will return. The designation is "north" because imperial invaders historically entered Palestine from that direction (see Jer 3:18; 23:8).

‡[2:15] **Many nations . . . my people**: a way of expressing God's relationship to people in covenant language. The covenant between God and Israel (see Jer 31:33; 32:38) is here universalized to include all nations.

§[2:16] **The holy land**: the Lord's earthly territory, a designation found only rarely in the Old Testament.

¶[3:1] **Adversary**: Hebrew *satan*, here, the prosecuting attorney, a figure in the Lord's heavenly courtroom. Cf. Jb 1:6–2:7. Later tradition understands this figure to be Satan.

**[3:3–4] The filthy garments of Joshua symbolized the guilt of the Israelite people who have become unclean by going into exile. The angel of the Lord purifies the high priest by the removal of his garments.

††[3:7] **If you walk . . . watch over my courts**: four components of priestly activity: (1) following God's commandments and teaching them to the people, (2) carrying out cultic functions, (3) participating in the judicial system in certain difficult cases, and (4) administering the laborers and lands in the Temple's domain.

‡‡[3:8] **Signs of things to come**: the restoration of the priesthood is a sign of the expected restoration of the Davidic line. **The Branch**: a tree metaphor for the expected future ruler as a descendant of the Davidic dynasty. This imagery also appears in Is 11:1, 10; Jer 23:5; 33:15; and Zec 6:12.

§§[3:9] **Stone with seven facets**: represents both the precious stones that were part of the high priest's apparel and the building stone (see 4:7, 10) that initiated a major construction project. The seven facets (or "eyes") indicate the totality of its role as an instrument of God's vigilance and action. **Inscription**: can refer both to words engraved on the high priest's apparel (Ex 28:9, 11) and to words chiseled on a cornerstone.

¶¶[4:2] **Lampstand**: receptacle for lamps and one of the furnishings of the main room of the Temple. This visionary object does not correspond to the biblical descriptions of the menorah in either the tabernacle (Ex 25:31–40) or the Solomonic Temple (1 Kgs 7:49) but rather has properties of both. **Seven lamps . . . seven spouts**: seven lamps, each with seven pinched wick holes. Such objects were part of the repertoire of cultic vessels throughout the Old Testament period. Here they symbolize God's eyes, i.e., divine omniscience; see v. 10.

***[4:3] **Olive trees**: visionary image that picks up the botanical language describing the Israelite cultic lampstands, with the olive trees specifically connoting fertility, permanence, and righteousness.

---

q. [2:9] Rev 21:23; 22:3–5.   r. [2:10] Zec 6:5; Is 48:20; Jer 50:8; 51:6. s. [2:12] Dt 32:10; Ps 17:8.   t. [2:13] Is 14:2; Zep 3:15.   u. [2:15] Is 56:6; 66:18.   v. [2:16] Zec 1:17.   w. [2:17] Hb 2:20; Zep 1:7; Rev 8:1a.   x. [3:1] Jb 1:6–2:7; 1 Chr 21:1.   y. [3:2] Jude 9.   z. [3:2] Am 4:11.   a. [3:4] Lk 15:22; Rev 19:8.   b. [3:4] Is 6:7; Jer 31:34; Ez 36:33.

c. [3:8] Is 8:18.   d. [3:9] Zec 4:7, 10; Is 28:16.   e. [3:9] Rev 5:6. f. [3:10] 1 Kgs 5:5; Mi 4:4.   g. [4:2] Ex 25:31–40; 1 Kgs 7:49; Rev 11:4.

angel who spoke with me replied, "Do you not know what these things are?" I said, "No, my lord."

**An Oracle.** [6]Then he said to me: "This is the word of the LORD to Zerubbabel: Not by might, and not by power, but by my spirit,*[h] says the LORD of hosts. [7]Who are you, O great mountain?[†] Before Zerubbabel you become a plain. He will bring forth the first stone amid shouts of 'Favor, favor be upon it!'"

[8]Then the word of the LORD came to me: [9]The hands of Zerubbabel have laid the foundations of this house, and his hands will finish it. Thus you shall know that the LORD of hosts has sent me to you. [10]For whoever has scorned such a day of small things will rejoice to see the capstone[‡] in the hand of Zerubbabel. **Resumption of the Vision: Explanation of Lamps and Trees.** "These seven are the eyes of the LORD that range over the whole earth."[i] [11]I then asked him, "What are these two olive trees, on the right of the lampstand and on its left?" [12]A second time I asked, "What are the two streams from the olive trees that pour out golden oil through two taps of gold?" [13]He said to me, "Do you not know what these are?" I answered, "No, my lord." [14]Then he said, "These are the two anointed ones[§] who stand by the Lord of the whole earth."[j]

## CHAPTER 5

**Fifth Vision: The Flying Scroll.** [1]Then I raised my eyes again and saw a flying scroll. [2]He asked me, "What do you see?" I answered, "I see a flying scroll, twenty cubits long and ten cubits wide."[¶k] [3]Then he said to me: "This is the curse

which is to go forth over the whole land. According to it, every thief and every perjurer** will be expelled. [4]I will send it forth—oracle of the LORD of hosts—so that it will come to the house of the thief, and into the house of the one who swears falsely by my name.[l] It shall lodge within each house, consuming it, timber and stones." **Sixth Vision: The Basket of Wickedness.** [5]Then the angel who spoke with me came forward and said to me, "Raise your eyes and look. What is this that comes forth?" [6]I said, "What is it?" And he answered, "This is the basket[††] that is coming." And he said, "This is their guilt in all the land." [7]Then a leaden cover was lifted, and there was a woman sitting inside the basket.[‡‡] [8]He said, "This is Wickedness," and he thrust her inside the basket, pushing the leaden weight into the opening.

[9]Then I raised my eyes and saw two women coming forth with wind under their wings[§§]— they had wings like the wings of a stork—and they lifted the basket into the air. [10]I said to the angel who spoke with me, "Where are they taking the basket?" [11]He replied, "To build a temple for it in the land of Shinar.[¶¶] When the temple is constructed, they will set it there on its base."

## CHAPTER 6

**Seventh Vision: Four Chariots.**[m] [1]Again I raised my eyes and saw four chariots*** coming out from between two mountains; and the mountains were of bronze. [2]The first chariot had red horses, the second chariot black horses, [3]the third chariot white horses, and the fourth chariot dappled horses—all of them strong horses. [4]I asked the angel who spoke with me, "What are these, my lord?" [5]The angel answered me, "These are the four winds of the heavens,[†††] which are coming forth after presenting themselves before the LORD of all the earth.[n] [6]The one with the black horses is going toward the land of the north,

---

*[4:6] **Not by might . . . my spirit:** one of the most quoted verses from the Old Testament, particularly in Jewish tradition, which connects it with the theme of Hanukkah, sometimes called the Festival of Lights.

†[4:7] **Great mountain:** part of symbolic imagery for the Temple on Mount Zion, as embodiment of the cosmic mountain where heaven and earth connect. **Plain:** leveled ground serving as the foundation area for the construction of the Temple, and symbolizing the foundation of the cosmos. **First stone:** foundation stone of a major public building. Such stones were laid with great ceremony in foundation rituals when monumental buildings were newly built or rebuilt in the biblical world.

‡[4:10] **Capstone:** topmost stone of a structure, which finishes the construction. This translation is based on the context. Other translations read: "stone of distinction," "plummet," "tin-stone."

§[4:14] **Two anointed ones:** two leadership positions in the ideal restored nation. The concept of a state headed by both priestly and political leaders harks back to premonarchic traditions (Aaron and Moses) and finds an echo in the two messianic figures—a Davidic and a levitical messiah—in the Dead Sea Scrolls and in apocryphal literature. See also the two crowns of 6:11–14.

¶[5:2] **Twenty cubits long and ten cubits wide:** ca. thirty feet by fifteen feet. These dimensions may represent the ratio of height to width in the exposed portion of a scroll being opened for liturgical reading; at the same time it may symbolize the approach to God's presence since the entryway to the Temple has the same measurements (1 Kgs 6:3). The scroll

itself may represent God's covenant with the people, insofar as it contains curses against those who break the law.

**[5:3] **Thief . . . perjurer:** a pair of miscreants representing all those who disobey God's covenant (see note on v. 2) and who must therefore be punished according to covenant curses.

††[5:6] **Basket:** literally, ephah, a dry measure; see note on Is 5:10.

‡‡[5:7] **Woman sitting inside the basket:** figure representing wickedness or foreign idolatry being transported back to Babylonia (vv. 1–11). Returning exiles were apparently worshiping deities they had learned to accept in Babylonia, and that "wickedness" (v. 8) must be removed.

§§[5:9] **Two women . . . wings:** composite beings, part human and part animal, similar to the cherubim flanking the holy ark (Ex 25:18–22; 1 Kgs 6:23–28; Ez 10:18–22). Such creatures accompany foreign deities as here, or the biblical God.

¶¶[5:11] **Shinar:** land of Babylonia; this name for Babylonia is found also in Gn 1:10; 11:2; 14:1; Is 11:11; and Dn 1:2.

***[6:1] **Four chariots:** vehicles with horses of four different colors (vv. 2–3) represent God's presence throughout the world and correspond to the four horses of 1:7–11.

†††[6:5] **Four winds of the heavens:** four compass directions and therefore the whole world.

---

h. [4:6] Hos 1:7.  i. [4:10] Zec 1:11; 6:7; Rev 5:6.  j. [4:14] Jos 3:11; Mi 4:13; Rev 11:4.  k. [5:2] Ez 2:9–10; Rev 10:9–11.

l. [5:4] Ex 20:7, 16.  m. [6:1] Rev 6:2–8.  n. [6:5] Rev 7:1.

and the white horses go toward the west, and the dappled ones go toward the land of the south." ⁷These strong horses went out, eager to set about patrolling the earth, for he said, "Go, patrol the earth!" So they patrolled the earth. ⁸Then he cried out to me and said, "See, those who go forth to the land of the north provide rest for my spirit in the land of the north.'"

**The Crowning.** ⁹Then the word of the LORD came to me: ¹⁰Take from the exiles—Heldai, Tobijah, Jedaiah—and go the same day to the house of Josiah, son of Zephaniah. (These had come from Babylon.) ¹¹You will take silver and gold, and make crowns;ᵗ place one on the head of Joshua, son of Jehozadak, the high priest. ¹²And say to him: Thus says the LORD of hosts: There is a man whose name is Branch‡ᵒ—and from his place he will branch out and he will build the temple of the LORD. ¹³He will build the temple of the LORD, and taking up the royal insignia, he will sit as ruler upon his throne. The priest will be at his right hand, and between the two of them there will be peaceful understanding.§ᵖ ¹⁴The other crown will be in the temple of the LORD as a gracious reminder to Heldai, Tobijah, Jedaiah, and the son of Zephaniah. ¹⁵And they who are from afar will come and build the temple of the LORD, and you will know that the LORD of hosts has sent me to you. This will happen if you truly obey the LORD your God.�q

### CHAPTER 7

**A Question About Fasting.** ¹In the fourth year of Darius the king, the word of the LORD came to Zechariah, on the fourth day of the ninth month, Kislev.¶ ²Bethelsarezer sent Regemmelech and his men to implore the favor of the LORD ³and to ask the priests of the house of the LORD of hosts, and the prophets, "Must I weep and abstain in the fifth month" as I have been doing these many years?" ⁴Then the word of

the LORD of hosts came to me: ⁵Say to all the people of the land and to the priests: When you fasted and lamented in the fifth and in the seventh month†† these seventy years, was it really for me that you fasted?ʳ ⁶When you were eating and drinking, was it not for yourselves that you ate and for yourselves that you drank?

⁷Are these not the words which the LORD proclaimed through the earlier prophets,‡‡ when Jerusalem and its surrounding cities were inhabited and secure, when the Negeb and the Shephelah were inhabited? ⁸The word of the LORD came to Zechariah: ⁹Thus says the LORD of hosts: Judge with true justice, and show kindness and compassion toward each other.ˢ ¹⁰Do not oppress the widow or the orphan, the resident alien or the poor;§§ do not plot evil against one another in your hearts.ᵗ ¹¹But they refused to listen; they stubbornly turned their backs and stopped their ears so as not to hear.ᵘ ¹²And they made their hearts as hard as diamondᵛ so as not to hear the instruction and the words that the LORD of hosts had sent by his spirit through the earlier prophets. So great anger came from the LORD of hosts: ¹³Just as when I called out and they did not listen, so they will call out and I will not listen, says the LORD of hosts. ¹⁴And I will scatter them among all the nations that they do not know.ʷ So the land was left desolate behind them with no one moving about, and they made a pleasant land into a wasteland.

### CHAPTER 8

**Seven Oracles: Judah and Zion Restored.** ¹Then the word of the LORD of hosts came: ²Thus says the LORD of hosts:

I am intensely jealous for Zion,ˣ
    stirred to jealous wrath for her.

³Thus says the LORD:

I have returned to Zion,
    and I will dwell within Jerusalem;
Jerusalem will be called the faithful city,¶¶ʸ
    and the mountain of the LORD of
        hosts, the holy mountain.

---

*[6:8] **Land of the north**: the enemy (cf. 2:10). This emphasis on the land of the north refers to the fact that God will deal with Israel's foes and order will be re-established.

†[6:11] **Crowns**: two crowns made of precious metals and representing two high offices (compare the symbolism of the two olive trees in 4:14). One crown is for the high priest Joshua, who, with the governor Zerubbabel, was one of the recognized rulers of the Persian province of Judah. The other crown would have been for a royal ruler, a Davidic descendant. Zerubbabel was a Davidide but could not be king because the Persians would not allow such autonomy. The second crown was thus put in storage in the Temple (v. 14) for the crowning of a future king, or "branch" (see 3:8), from the house of David.

‡[6:12] **Branch**: future Davidic ruler. See note on 3:8.

§[6:13] **Peaceful understanding**: harmonious rule of both the high priest and the king.

¶[7:1] **The fourth year of Darius . . . the ninth month, Kislev**: December 7, 518 B.C., the last chronological heading in Zechariah.

**[7:3] **Weep . . . fifth month**: a mourning ritual commemorating the destruction of Jerusalem and the Temple on the seventh day of the fifth month in the nineteenth year of Nebuchadnezzar's reign (ca. 587/586 B.C.; see 2 Kgs 25:8).

††[7:5] **Seventh month**: the time of a fast in memory of the murder of Gedaliah, the governor installed by the Babylonians after they conquered Jerusalem (see 2 Kgs 25:25; Jer 41:1–3). **Seventy years**: see note on 1:12.

‡‡[7:7, 12] **Earlier prophets**: see note on 1:4.

§§[7:10] **Widow . . . orphan . . . resident alien . . . poor**: four categories of socially and economically marginalized persons. Concern for their well-being is commanded in both pentateuchal and prophetic literature.

¶¶[8:3] **Faithful city**: a unique biblical epithet for Jerusalem, signaling the importance of the holy city and its leaders for establishing justice in society (see also vv. 8, 16, 19). **Holy mountain**: Jerusalem and its Temple, the sacred center of the holy land (2:16) and of the whole world.

---

o. [6:12] Zec 3:8; Jer 23:5.   p. [6:13] Zec 4:14.   q. [6:15] Dt 28:1.

r. [7:5] Am 5:21.   s. [7:9] Is 1:17; 58:6.   t. [7:10] Ex 22:20–24; Dt 24:17; Jer 5:28; Mi 2:1.   u. [7:11] Ex 32:9; Is 48:4.   v. [7:12] Ez 11:19.   w. [7:14] Dt 4:27.   x. [8:2] Zec 1:14.   y. [8:3] Is 1:26.

⁴Thus says the LORD of hosts:

Old men and old women will again sit in the streets of Jerusalem, each with staff in hand because of old age.ᶻ ⁵The city will be filled with boys and girls playing in its streets.

⁶Thus says the LORD of hosts:

Even if this should seem impossible in the eyes of the remnant of this people in those days, should it seem impossible in my eyes also?ᵃ—oracle of the LORD of hosts.

⁷Thus says the LORD of hosts:

I am going to rescue my people from the land of the rising sun, and from the land of the setting sun. ⁸I will bring them back to dwell within Jerusalem. They will be my people, and I will be their God,ᵇ in faithfulness and justice.

⁹Thus says the LORD of hosts:

Let your hands be strong, you who now hear these words which were spoken by the prophets when the foundation of the house of the LORD of hosts was laid* for the building of the temple.ᶜ ¹⁰For before those days, there were no wages for people, nor hire for animals. Those who came and went were not safe from the enemy, for I set neighbor against neighbor. ¹¹But now I will not deal with the remnant of this people as in former days—oracle of the LORD of hosts.

¹² For there will be a sowing of peace:
　　the vine will yield its fruit,
　　the land will yield its crops,
　　and the heavens† will yield their dew.

I will give all these things to the remnant of this people to possess. ¹³Just as you became a curse among the nations, O house of Judah and house of Israel, so will I save you that you may be a blessing.ᵈ Do not fear; let your hands be strong.

¹⁴Thus says the LORD of hosts:

Just as I intended to harm you when your ancestors angered me—says the LORD of hosts—and I did not relent, ¹⁵so again in these days I intend to favor Jerusalem and the house of Judah; do not fear! ¹⁶These then are the things you must do: Speak the truth to one another;ᵉ judge with honesty and complete justice in your gates.†ᶠ ¹⁷Let none of you plot evil against another in your heart, nor love a false oath. For all these things I hate—oracle of the LORD.

**Three Oracles: Judah and the Nations.** ¹⁸The word of the LORD of hosts came to me:

¹⁹Thus says the LORD of hosts:

The fast days of the fourth, the fifth, the seventh, and the tenth months§ᵍ will become occasions of joy and gladness, and happy festivals for the house of Judah.ʰ So love faithfulness and peace!

²⁰Thus says the LORD of hosts:

There will yet come peoples and inhabitants of many cities;ⁱ ²¹and the inhabitants of one city will approach those of another, and say, "Come! let us go to implore the favor of the LORD and to seek the LORD of hosts. I too am going." ²²Many peoples and strong nations will come to seek the LORD of hosts in Jerusalem and to implore the favor of the LORD.

²³Thus says the LORD of hosts:

In those days ten people from nations of every language will take hold,ʲ yes, will take hold of the cloak of every Judahite and say, "Let us go with you, for we have heard that God is with you."

# CHAPTER 9

## Restoration of the Land of Israelˢ

1　An oracle:** the word of the LORD is
　　　　against the land of Hadrach,
　　and Damascus is its destination,
　　For the cities of Aram are the LORD's,
　　　　as are all the tribes of Israel.

2　Hamath also on its border,
　　　　Tyre too, and Sidon, no matter how
　　　　　　clever they be.

3　Tyre built itself a stronghold,
　　　　and heaped up silver like dust,
　　　　and gold like the mud of the streets.

4　But now the Lord will dispossess it,
　　　　and cast its wealth into the sea,
　　　　and it will be devoured by fire.

5　Ashkelon will see it and be afraid;
　　　　Gaza too will be in great anguish;
　　　　Ekron also, for its hope will wither.
　　The king will disappear from Gaza,
　　　　Ashkelon will not be inhabited,

---

*[8:9] **When the foundation . . . was laid**: December 18, 520 B.C., the date of the Temple refoundation ceremony, marking the beginning of the project to restore the Temple (see Hg 2:10, 18, 20).

†[8:12] **Vine . . . land . . . heavens**: future prosperity, reversing the hardships of Hg 1:10.

‡[8:16] **Gates**: important gathering places in ancient Near Eastern cities, where legal proceedings were often carried out.

§[8:19] **Fast days of the fourth, the fifth, the seventh, and the tenth months**: all these fast days were probably held in connection with Jerusalem's demise. The fasts of the fourth month (commemorating the departure of Judahite leadership from Jerusalem, 2 Kgs 25:3–7) and of the tenth month (marking the beginning of the siege of Jerusalem, 2 Kgs 25:1) were added to the fasts of the fifth and seventh months mentioned in Zec 7:3 and 5 (see notes).

¶[9:1–8] The opening verses of Second Zechariah delineate the ideal boundaries of a restored Israel. Echoing the ideas of Haggai and First Zechariah (chaps. 1–8), the prophet reiterates the notion that the rebuilt Temple will bring about peace. The areas to be returned to Israel include Syria (Aram), with the cities of Hadrach and Damascus; Phoenicia, with the cities of Tyre and Sidon; and Philistia, with the cities of Ashkelon, Gaza, Ekron, and Ashdod.

**[9:1] **An oracle**: this designation also introduces Zec 12:1 and Mal 1:1, suggesting a connection among the three units. The term functions as both a title to the larger literary unit (Zec 9–11) and a part of the message of the opening oracular statement.

---

z. [8:4] Dt 4:40.　a. [8:6] Jer 32:27.　b. [8:8] Zec 13:9; Jer 31:33.
c. [8:9] Hg 1:14.　d. [8:13] Gn 12:3; Ps 72:17.　e. [8:16] Eph 4:25.
f. [8:16] Zec 7:9; Dt 21:19; 22:24; Ru 4:1, 11.

g. [8:19] Zec 7:1–3; Mt 9:14–15.　h. [8:19] Is 35:10; Jer 31:13.
i. [8:20] 1 Kgs 8:43.　j. [8:23] 1 Sm 15:27; Tb 13:11.

6          and the illegitimate will rule in
                Ashdod.
       I will destroy the pride of the Philistines
7          and take from their mouths their
                bloody prey,
           their disgusting meat from between
                their teeth.
       They will become merely a remnant for
                our God,[k]
           and will be like a clan in Judah;
           Ekron will be like the Jebusites.[*]
8      I will encamp at my house,
           a garrison against invaders;
       No oppressor will overrun them again,
           for now I have seen their affliction.

### The King's Entry into Jerusalem[†]

9      Exult greatly, O daughter Zion!
           Shout for joy, O daughter Jerusalem!
       Behold: your king[‡] is coming to you,
           a just savior is he,
       Humble, and riding on a donkey,
           on a colt, the foal of a donkey.[l]
10     He shall banish the chariot from Ephraim,[m]
           and the horse from Jerusalem;
       The warrior's bow will be banished,
           and he will proclaim peace to the
                nations.[n]
       His dominion will be from sea to sea,
           and from the River[§] to the ends of
                the earth.[o]

### Restoration of the People

11     As for you, by the blood of your covenant,[¶][p]
           I have freed your prisoners from a
                waterless pit.
12     Return to a fortress,[**]
           O prisoners of hope;

This very day, I announce
           I am restoring double to you.
13     For I have bent Judah as my bow,
           I have set Ephraim as its arrow;
       I will arouse your sons, O Zion,
           against your sons, O Yavan,[††]
           and I will use you as a warrior's
                sword.
14     The LORD will appear over them,
           God's arrow will shoot forth as
                lightning;
       The Lord GOD will sound the ram's horn,
           and come in a storm from the
                south.[q]
15     The LORD of hosts will protect them;
           they will devour and conquer with
                sling stones,
           they will drink and become heated
                as with wine;
           they will be full like bowls—like the
                corners of the altar.[r]
16     And the LORD their God will save them:
           the people, like a flock on that day;[s]
       For like gemstones of a crown[‡‡]
           they will shine on the land.
17     Then how good and how lovely!
           Grain will make the young men
                flourish,
           and new wine the young women.[t]

## CHAPTER 10

### The Lord Strengthens Judah
### and Rescues Ephraim

1      Ask the LORD for rain in the spring
                season,[u]
           the LORD who brings storm clouds,
                and heavy rains,[v]
           who gives to everyone grain in the
                fields.
2      For the teraphim[§§] have spoken nonsense,[w]
           the diviners have seen false visions;
       Deceitful dreams they have told,
           empty comfort they have offered.
       This is why they wandered like sheep,
           wretched, for they have no
                shepherd.[x]
3      My wrath is kindled against the
                shepherds,[¶¶]

---

*[9:7] **The Jebusites**: the pre-Israelite inhabitants of Jerusalem, conquered by David and incorporated into Israel.

†[9:9–10] These two verses form the centerpiece of chap.
9. The restoration of a royal figure connects the first part of
the chapter (vv. 1–8), which depicts the restored land of Israel,
with the second part (vv. 11–17), which concerns the restoration of the people Israel.

‡[9:9] **Your king**: a just savior, a figure of humble
demeanor, but riding on a donkey like royalty in the ancient
Near East (Gn 49:11; Jgs 5:10; 10:4). The announcement of
the coming of such a king marks a departure from the view
of the royal figure as a conquering warrior. This depiction is
in keeping with the tone of First Zechariah (3:8; 4:6–10; 6:12)
but contrasts with Haggai (2:20–23). New Testament authors
apply this prophecy to Jesus' triumphant entry into Jerusalem
(Mt 21:4–5; Jn 12:14–15).

§[9:10] **The River**: probably the Euphrates; see note on Ps
72:8.

¶[9:11] **The blood of your covenant**: the covenant between
the Lord and Israel sealed with sacrificial blood (Ex 24:8).

**[9:12] **Fortress**: the Hebrew word for "fortress" (*bissaron*)
plays upon the Hebrew word for Zion (*siyyon*). Those who
return to Zion will be protected by the Lord. **O prisoners of
hope**: imagery of exile, conveying a sense that the future in
Israel will be better.

††[9:13] **Your sons, O Yavan**: the reference is to the Greeks
and their struggle with the Persians for control of Syria-Palestine and the eastern Mediterranean in the mid-fifth century
B.C.

‡‡[9:16] **Like gemstones of a crown**: imagery reminiscent
of First Zechariah (3:9; 4:7, 10; 6:11, 14) and evocative of the
Temple and the priestly headgear (cf. Ex 29:6 and Lv 8:9).

§§[10:2] **Teraphim**: household idols or cult objects (see Gn
31:19, 30–35; Jgs 17:5; 1 Sm 19:11–17), or ancestor statuettes
(see 2 Kgs 23:24; Hos 3:4).

¶¶[10:3] **Against the shepherds**: bad leaders or false
prophets.

---

k. [9:7] Is 4:3.   l. [9:9] Is 9:6; 62:11; Jer 23:5; Mt 21:5; Jn 12:15.
m. [9:10] Mi 5:9.   n. [9:10] Is 2:4; 11:6; Hos 2:20; Eph 2:17.
o. [9:10] Ps 72:8.   p. [9:11] Ex 24:4–8; Mt 26:28; Heb 13:20.

q. [9:14] Dt 33:2; Ps 18:14; Hb 3:4.   r. [9:15] Ex 27:3; 38:3; Nm
4:14.   s. [9:16] Ez34:11.   t. [9:17] Jer31:12–13.   u. [10:1] Dt11:14.
v. [10:1] Ps 135:7.   w. [10:2] 1 Sm 15:23.   x. [10:2] Ez 34:5; Mt 9:36.

and I will punish the leaders.
For the Lord of hosts attends to the flock,
    the house of Judah,
    'and will make them like a splendid
      horse in battle.

4 From them will come the tower,
    from them the tent peg,
    from them the bow of war,
    from them every officer.

5 Together they will be like warriors,
    trampling the mud of the streets in
      battle.
They will wage war because the Lord is
    with them,
    and will put the horsemen to shame.

6 I will strengthen the house of Judah,[y]
    the house of Joseph[*] I will save;
I will bring them back, because I have
    mercy on them;
    they will be as if I had never cast
      them off,
    for I am the Lord their God, and I
      will answer them.[z]

7 Then Ephraim will be like a hero,
    and their hearts will be cheered as
      by wine.[a]
Their children will see and rejoice—
    their hearts will exult in the Lord.

8 I will whistle for them and gather them in;
    for I will redeem them
    and they will be as numerous as
      before.[†]

9 I sowed them among the nations,
    yet in distant lands they will
      remember me;
    they will bear their children and
      return.[b]

10 I will bring them back from the land of
    Egypt,
    and gather them from Assyria.
To the land of Gilead and to Lebanon I
    will bring them,
    until no room is found for them.

11 I will cross over to Egypt
    and smite the waves of the sea,
    and all the depths of the Nile will
      dry up.
The pride of Assyria will be cast down,
    and the scepter of Egypt disappear.

12 I will strengthen them in the Lord,[c]
    in whose name they will walk—
      oracle of the Lord.

---

*[10:6] **The house of Joseph**: represents the Northern Kingdom (Israel), as does Ephraim in v. 7 below.

†[10:8] **Gather them in . . . be as numerous as before**: God's intention is to bring back the exiles and redeem them as at the time of the exodus. This image, resumed in vv. 10–11, anticipates an expanded population, echoes the ancestral promise (Gn 1:22, 28; 9:1, 7; 35:11), and also suggests an awareness of the acute demographic decline of Jews in Palestine in the Persian period.

y. [10:6] Zec 12:5.  z. [10:6] Is 41:17.  a. [10:7] Ps 104:15.
b. [10:9] Dt 30:1–3; Bar 2:30–32.  c. [10:12] Zec 12:5.

---

# CHAPTER 11

## The Cry of Trees, Shepherds, and Lions

1 Open your doors, Lebanon,
    that fire may devour your cedars!

2 Wail, cypress trees,
    for the cedars are fallen,
    the mighty are destroyed!
Wail, oaks of Bashan,
    for the dense forest is cut down!

3 Listen! the wailing of shepherds,
    their glory has been destroyed.
Listen! the roaring of young lions,
    the thickets of the Jordan are
      destroyed.

**The Shepherd Narrative.**[‡d] 4Thus says the Lord, my God: Shepherd the flock to be slaughtered.[e] 5For they who buy them slay them and are not held accountable; while those who sell them say, "Blessed be the Lord, I have become rich!" Even their own shepherds will not pity them. 6For I will no longer pity the inhabitants of the earth—oracle of the Lord.—Yes, I will deliver them into each other's power, or into the power of their kings; they will crush the earth, and I will not deliver it out of their power.

7So I shepherded the flock to be slaughtered for the merchants of the flock. I took two staffs: one I called Delight, and the other Union. Thus I shepherded the flock. 8In a single month, I did away with the three shepherds, for I wearied of them, and they disdained me. 9"I will not shepherd you," I said. "Whoever is to die shall die; whoever is to be done away with shall be done away with; and those who are left shall devour one another's flesh."

10Then I took my staff Delight and snapped it in two, breaking my covenant which I had made with all peoples. 11So it was broken on that day. The merchants of the flock, who were watching me, understood that this was the word of the Lord. 12Then I said to them, "If it seems good to you, give me my wages; but if not, withhold

---

‡[11:4–17] This narrative has features of an allegory, a parable, and a commissioning narrative. The use of a symbolic action (vv. 7, 10, 14), however, places this text squarely in the tradition of classical prophecy. For example, the staff "Delight" signifies the Mosaic covenant, and the staff "Union" signifies the union of Israel and Judah. Breaking the staffs signifies the breaking of the Mosaic covenant (resulting in the destruction of Jerusalem and the exile) and the historical schism between north and south. In this narrative the prophet is the "shepherd" of God's flock, which is to be slaughtered. The "three shepherds" of v. 8 represent either leaders responsible for the decay in Israelite society or false prophets (cf. vv. 15, 17 and 13:2–6). The service of the good shepherd is contemptuously valued at thirty pieces of silver, the legal indemnity for a gored slave (Ex 21:32). The prophet throws the money into the Temple treasury, showing how poorly God's love is requited (cf. Mt 26:14–16; 27:5). With great rhetorical irony, payment is rejected. The entire wage-payment scenario may be regarded as another symbolic action, embedded within the primary action.

d. [11:4] Ez 34:1.  e. [11:4] Jer 12:3.

them."ʲ And they counted out my wages,ᵍ thirty pieces of silver. ¹³Then the LORD said to me, Throw it in the treasury—the handsome price at which they valued me. So I took the thirty pieces of silver and threw them into the treasury in the house of the LORD. ¹⁴Then I snapped in two my second staff, Union, breaking the kinship between Judah and Israel.

¹⁵The LORD said to me: This time take the gear of a foolish shepherd.ʰ ¹⁶For I am raising up a shepherd in the land who will take no note of those that disappear, nor seek the strays, nor heal the injured,ⁱ nor feed the exhausted; but he will eat the flesh of the fat ones and tear off their hoofs!

### Oracle to the Worthless Shepherd

¹⁷ Ah! my worthless shepherd
    who forsakes the flock!ʲ
May the sword fall upon his arm
    and upon his right eye;
His arm will surely wither,
    and his right eye surely go blind!

## CHAPTER 12
### Oracles Concerning the Nations and Judah.*
¹An oracle:† The word of the LORD concerning Israel—oracle of the LORD, who spreads out the heavens, lays the foundations of the earth, and fashions the human spirit within:ᵏ ²See, I will make Jerusalem a cup of reeling‡ for all peoples round about.ʲ Judah will be besieged, even Jerusalem. ³On that day I will make Jerusalem a heavy stone for all peoples. All who attempt to lift it will injure themselves badly, though all the nations of the earth will gather against it. ⁴On that day—oracle of the LORD—I will strike every horse with fright, and its rider with madness. But over the house of Judah I will keep watch, while I strike blind all the horses of the peoples. ⁵Then the clans of Judah will say to themselves, "The inhabitants of Jerusalem have their strength in the LORD of hosts, their God."ᵐ ⁶On that day I will make the clans of Judah like a brazier of fire in the woodland and like a burning torch among

sheaves, and they will devour right and left all the surrounding peoples; but Jerusalem will again inhabit its own place.ⁿ

⁷The LORD will save the tents of Judah first, that the glory of the house of David and the glory of the inhabitants of Jerusalem may not be exalted over Judah. ⁸On that day the LORD will shield the inhabitants of Jerusalem, so that the weakest among them will be like David on that day; and the house of David will be like God, like the angel of the LORD before them.

⁹On that day I will seek the destruction of all nations that come against Jerusalem.ᵒ ¹⁰I will pour out on the house of David and on the inhabitants of Jerusalem a spirit of mercy and supplication, so that when they look on him whom they have thrust through,§ᵖ they will mourn for him as one mourns for an only child, and they will grieve for him as one grieves over a firstborn.�q

**Catalogue of Mourners.** ¹¹On that day the mourning in Jerusalem will be as great as the mourning for Hadadrimmon in the plain of Megiddo.§ ¹²And the land shall mourn, each family apart: the family of the house of David, and their women; the family of the house of Nathan, and their women; ¹³the family of the house of Levi, and their women; the family of Shimei, and their women; ¹⁴and all the rest of the families, each family apart, and the women apart.

## CHAPTER 13
### Oracles Concerning the End of False Prophecy.** ¹On that day a fountain will be opened for the house of David†† and the inhabitants of Jerusalem, to purify from sin and uncleanness.ʳ

²On that day—oracle of the LORD of hosts—I will destroy the names of the idols from the

---

§[12:10] **They look on him . . . thrust through:** another possible rendering is "they shall look to me concerning him . . . thrust through." In either case, the victim is an enigmatic figure, perhaps referring to a Davidic descendant, a priestly leader, or even a true prophet. Some historical event, unknown to us from any surviving source, may underlie this reference. The Gospel of John applies this text to the piercing of Christ's side after his death (19:37).

¶[12:11] The mourning for the pierced victim in Jerusalem is compared to the annual ritual mourning in the plain of Megiddo over the death of the Phoenician fertility god, Hadadrimmon. According to others, Hadadrimmon is the name of a place near Megiddo, and the reference would then be to the mourning over the death of King Josiah at the hands of Pharaoh Neco in 609 B.C.; cf. 2 Kgs 23:29–30; 2 Chr 35:22–25.

**[13:1–6] False prophecy is a major theme of Second Zechariah (chaps. 9–14) and figures in many other passages (10:1–2; 11; 12:10). Problems of idolatry and false prophecy occurred in postexilic Judah as they had in preexilic times. The understanding of the role of the prophet as an intermediary was challenged because (1) there was no king in Jerusalem, and (2) the texts of earlier prophets were beginning to be accorded the authority of prophetic tradition.

††[13:1] **For the house of David:** anticipation that a cleansed leadership will enable the re-established monarchy to be rid of the misdeeds of its past.

---

*[12:1–10] The oracles deal with (1) the status of Judah in relation to other political powers in the world that threaten its existence and (2) the reordering of Judah's internal structures so that its future can be realized. That future is linked to the fortunes of the house of David, which is mentioned five times between 12:7 and 13:1 (12:7, 8, 10, 12; 13:1).

†[12:1] **An oracle:** part two of Second Zechariah begins with the same heading as that of part one (9:1; also Mal 1:1), suggesting two distinct blocks of material. The unusual cluster of introductory terms that follow the heading greatly intensifies the claim of prophetic authority, apparently an issue in postexilic prophecy.

‡[12:2] **Cup of reeling:** like a cup filled with intoxicating drink, Jerusalem will cause the nations to stumble and fall (cf. Is 51:17, 22; Jer 25:15; 49:12; Lam 4:21).

---

f. [11:12] Mt 27:3–10.    g. [11:12] 2 Kgs 12:11; 22:4.    h. [11:15] Ez 34:1–10.    i. [11:16] Is 42:3; Mt 12:20.    j. [11:17] Jer 23:1; Jn 10:12–13.    k. [12:1] Gn 2:7; Is 42:5.    l. [12:2] Is 51:17.    m. [12:5] Zec 10:6, 12.

n. [12:6] Zec 14:10.    o. [12:9] Zec 14:3.    p. [12:10] Jn 19:37; Rev 1:7.    q. [12:10] Am 8:10.    r. [13:1] Ez 36:25; 47:1; Jn 7:38.

land, so that they will be mentioned no more; I will also remove the prophets and the spirit of uncleanness from the land. ³If any still prophesy, their father and mother who bore them will say, "You will not live, because you have spoken a lie in the name of the Lord." Their father and mother who bore them will thrust them through when they prophesy.ˢ

⁴On that day, all prophets will be ashamed of the visions they prophesy; and they will not put on the hairy mantle* to mislead,ᵗ ⁵but each will say, "I am not a prophet. I am a tiller of the soil, for I have owned land since my youth."ᵘ ⁶And if anyone asks, "What are these wounds on your chest?"† each will answer, "I received these wounds in the house of my friends."ᵛ

### The Song of the Sword

7  Awake, O sword, against my shepherd,
        against the one who is my associate
        —oracle of the Lord of hosts.
    Strike the shepherd
        that the sheep may be scattered;‡ʷ
    I will turn my hand against the little
        ones.
8  In all the land—oracle of the Lord—
        two thirds of them will be cut off
        and perish,
        and one third will be left.
9  I will bring the one third through the fire;
        I will refine them as one refines
        silver,ˣ
        and I will test them as one tests gold.
    They will call upon my name, and I will
        answer them;ʸ
    I will say, "They are my people,"ᶻ
        and they will say, "The Lord is my
        God."

### CHAPTER 14

**Devastation and Rescue of Jerusalem.** ¹§A day is coming for the Lord when the spoils taken

from you will be divided in your midst. ²And I will gather all the nations against Jerusalem for battle: The city will be taken, houses will be plundered, women raped; half the city will go into exile, but the rest of the people will not be removed from the city. ³Then the Lord will go forth and fight against those nations, fighting as on a day of battle.ᵃ ⁴On that day God's feet will stand‖ on the Mount of Olives, which is opposite Jerusalem to the east. The Mount of Olives will be split in two from east to west by a very deep valley,ᵇ and half of the mountain will move to the north and half of it to the south. ⁵You will flee by the valley between the mountains, for the valley between the mountains will reach to Azal. Thus you will flee as you fled because of the earthquake** in the days of Uzziah king of Judah.ᶜ Then the Lord, my God, will come, and all his holy ones with him.ᵈ

**Jerusalem Restored.** ⁶On that day there will no longer be cold or frost. ⁷There will be one continuous day—it is known to the Lord—not day and night, for in the evening there will be light. ⁸On that day, fresh water will flow from Jerusalem,ᵉ half to the eastern sea, and half to the western sea. This will be so in summer and in winter. ⁹The Lord will be king over the whole earth;ᶠ on that day the Lord will be the only one, and the Lord's name the only one. ¹⁰All the land will turn into a plain, from Geba to Rimmon, south of Jerusalem, which will stand exalted in its place—from the Gate of Benjamin to the place of the first gate, to the Corner Gate and from the Tower of Hananel to the king's wine presses. ¹¹The city will be inhabited; never again will it be doomed. Jerusalem will dwell securely.ᵍ

**The Fate of Jerusalem's Foes.** ¹²And this will be the plague with which the Lord will strike all the peoples that have fought against Jerusalem: their flesh will rot while they stand on their feet, and their eyes will rot in their sockets, and their tongues will rot in their mouths.ʰ ¹³On that day a great panic from the Lord will be upon them.ⁱ They will seize each other's hands, and their hands will be raised against each other. ¹⁴Even

---

*[13:4] **Hairy mantle**: worn by prophets as a sign of their calling, for example, Elijah (1 Kgs 19:13; 2 Kgs 1:8) and John the Baptist (Mt 3:4).

†[13:6] **Wounds on your chest**: lit., "wounds between your hands." The false prophets, like the prophets of Baal (1 Kgs 18:28), apparently inflicted wounds on themselves. Here it seems that persons accused of false prophecy deny having inflicted wounds on themselves and instead claim that they have received them at the houses of their friends.

‡[13:7] **Strike the shepherd . . . may be scattered**: in Matthew's Gospel (26:31) Jesus makes use of this text before his arrest in the Garden of Gethsemane and the flight of the disciples.

§[14:1–21] The marked eschatological thrust of Zec 9–14 culminates in this apocalyptic description, with its astonishing images of the day of the Lord. This last and longest chapter focuses on the restoration of Jerusalem and the return of the people of Zion so that the rest of the world will acknowledge

God's sovereignty. Four units constitute this chapter: vv. 1–5 concentrate on the destruction and rescue of Jerusalem and the escape of a remnant; vv. 6–11 describe the transformation of the climate and the topography of Jerusalem; vv. 12–15 depict the defeat of Jerusalem's enemies; and vv. 16–21 outline a vision for the end time, in which even foreign nations will make the pilgrimage to Jerusalem to acknowledge God's universal reign.

‖[14:4] **God's feet will stand**: a remarkable anthropomorphic image adds emphasis to the traditional Old Testament scene of God appearing on a mountain and causing extreme reactions such as quaking, melting, shattering (see Ex 19:18; Ps 97:5; Hb 3:6). The Mount of Olives is split, which opens a way for those fleeing from the Lord's appearance to escape from Jerusalem.

**[14:5] **Earthquake**: Amos 1:1 mentions an earthquake in the time of King Uzziah (cf. Is 6:4).

a. [14:3] Is 31:4.  b. [14:4] Mi 1:4.  c. [14:5] Am 1:1.  d. [14:5] Dt 33:2–3; Mt 16:27; 1 Thes 3:13.  e. [14:8] Zec 13:1; Ez 47:1–8; Jl 4:18.  f. [14:9] Ps 96:7–10; 97:1; 98:4–6; Rev 11:15.  g. [14:11] Dt 33:28; Jer 31:40; Rev 22:3.  h. [14:12] Is 66:24.  i. [14:13] 1 Sm 5:9, 11; 14:18–20; Is 22:5.

s. [13:3] Jn 19:34.  t. [13:4] 2 Kgs 1:8; Mt 3:4.  u. [13:5] Am 7:14.  v. [13:6] 1 Kgs 18:28.  w. [13:7] Ez 34:1–8; Mt 26:31.  x. [13:9] Is 1:25; 48:10.  y. [13:9] Ps 91:15; Is 65:24.  z. [13:9] Zec 8:8; Jer 31:31.

Judah will fight against Jerusalem. The riches of all the surrounding nations will be gathered together—gold, silver, and garments—in great abundance. [15]Like the plague on human beings will be the plague upon the horses, mules, camels, donkeys, and upon all the beasts that are in those camps.

**The Future: Jerusalem, Judah, and the Nations.** [16]Everyone who is left of all the nations that came against Jerusalem will go up year after year to bow down to the King, the LORD of hosts, and to celebrate the feast of Booths.*[j] [17]Should any of the families of the earth[k] not go up to Jerusalem to bow down to the King, the LORD of hosts, then there will be no rain for them. [18]And

---

*[14:16] **Feast of Booths**: fall harvest festival, also known as the "festival of Ingathering" (Ex 23:16; 34:22) or "Booths" (Lv 23:33–36; Dt 16:13–15; 31:9–13). The singling out of this festival indicates its special status in the sacred calendar; it is frequently referred to as "the feast" (1 Kgs 8:1–2; 2 Chr 5:3; Ez 45:25).

j. [14:16] Lv 23:33–36; Dt 16:13–15.    k. [14:17] Zec 8:20–23; Is 2:1–4; Mi 4:1–3.

if the family of Egypt does not go up or enter, upon them will fall the plague,[l] with which the LORD strikes the nations that do not go up to celebrate the feast of Booths. [19]This will be the punishment of Egypt and the punishment of all the nations that do not go up to celebrate the feast of Booths.

[20]On that day, "Holy to the LORD"[m] will be written on the horses' bells.† The pots in the house of the LORD will be as the basins before the altar. [21]Every pot‡ in Jerusalem and in Judah will be holy to the LORD of hosts. All who come to sacrifice will take them and cook in them. No longer will there be merchants in the house of the LORD of hosts on that day.

---

†[14:20] **Horses' bells**: even these bells, part of the trappings of animals used for war, will become holy in the end time, like the bells of the high priest's garb (cf. Ex 28:34).

‡[14:21] **Every pot**: vessels used for mundane food preparation will, in the end time, be as holy as Temple vessels.

l. [14:18] Ex 5:3; 9:15.    m. [14:20] Lv 23:20; 27:30, 32.

# THE BOOK OF
# MALACHI

This short book may have been written before Nehemiah's first return to Jerusalem in 445 B.C.; it is also possible that it was written while Nehemiah was there, or even later. What seems to be the author's name, *mal'ākî*, is found in 1:1 ("the word of the Lord to Israel through Malachi"), but many believe that this is a pseudonym based on *mal'ākî*, "my messenger," in 3:1 and that the author's real name is unknown. In any case, he shows us attitudes and behaviors characteristic of the Jewish community a few generations after the end of the Babylonian exile, and describes God's response.

God loves Israel (1:2–5), but the people return that love poorly. Taking advantage of the negligent attitude of the priests, they withhold tithes and sacrificial contributions (3:6–11) and cheat God by providing defective goods for sacrifice (1:6–14). People divorce their spouses and marry worshipers of other gods (2:10–16). Sorcerers, adulterers, perjurers, and people who take advantage of workers and the needy abound (3:5). Priests, who could strengthen discipline by their instruction, connive with the people, telling them what they want to hear (2:1–9). Underlying all this is a weary attitude, a cynical notion that nothing is to be gained by doing what God wants and that wrongdoers prosper (2:17; 3:14–15). God condemns the wrongdoing and the underlying attitude, issuing a challenge to immediate reform (3:10–12), but also announcing a general reckoning at a future moment (3:16–21).

The Book of Malachi may be divided as follows:

I. Israel Preferred to Edom (1:2–5)
II. Offense in Sacrifice and Priestly Duty (1:6–2:9)
III. Marriage and Divorce (2:10–16)
IV. Purification and Just Judgment (2:17)
V. The Messenger of the Covenant (3:1–5)
VI. Gifts for God, Blessings for the People (3:6–12)
VII. The Need to Serve God (3:13–21)
VIII. Moses and Elijah (3:22–24)

## CHAPTER 1

¹An oracle. The word of the LORD to Israel through Malachi.

### Israel Preferred to Edom

² ᵃI love you, says the LORD;
   but you say, "How do you love us?"
³ ᵗᵇWas not Esau Jacob's brother?—oracle of
      the LORD.
   I loved Jacob, but rejected Esau;
   I made his mountains a waste,
      his heritage a desert for jackals.

---

*[1:1] See note on Zec 9:1.
†[1:3–5] The thought passes from the person Esau to his descendants, Edom, and from the person Jacob to his descendants, Israel; cf. Gn 25:21–23. In the New Testament, Paul uses this passage as an example of God's freedom of choice in calling the Gentiles to faith (Rom 9:13).

a. [1:2] Dt 7:8; Ez 16; Hos 11:1; Am 1:11.   b. [1:3] Gn 25:23; Rom 9:13.

---

⁴ ᶜIf Edom says, "We have been crushed,
      but we will rebuild the ruins,"
   Thus says the LORD of hosts:
   They indeed may build, but I will
      tear down,
   And they shall be called "territory of
         wickedness,"
      the people with whom the LORD is
      angry forever.
⁵ ᵈYour own eyes will see it, and you will
      say,
      "Great is the LORD, even beyond the
      territory of Israel."

### Offense in Sacrifice and Priestly Duty

⁶ ᵉA son honors his father,
      and a servant fears his master;
   If, then, I am a father,

---

c. [1:4] Is 34:2–15; 63:1–6; Jer 49:7–22; Ob 21.   d. [1:5] Is 60.   e. [1:6] Prv 1:7; Is 29:13.

where is the honor due to me?
And if I am a master,
   where is the fear due to me?
So says the LORD of hosts to you, O priests,
   who disdain my name.
But you ask, "How have we disdained
   your name?"
7     By offering defiled food on my altar!
You ask, "How have we defiled it?"
   By saying that the table of the LORD
   may be disdained!
8  *When you offer a blind animal for
   sacrifice,
   is there no wrong in that?
When you offer a lame or sick animal,
   is there no wrong in that?
Present it to your governor!
   Will he be pleased with you—or
   show you favor?
   says the LORD of hosts.
9  So now implore God's favor, that he may
   have mercy on us!
You are the ones who have done this;
Will he show favor to any of you?
   says the LORD of hosts.
10  †Oh, that one of you would just shut the
   temple gates
   to keep you from kindling fire on
   my altar in vain!
I take no pleasure in you, says the LORD
   of hosts;
   and I will not accept any offering
   from your hands!
11  ᵍFrom the rising of the sun to its setting,
   my name is great among the nations;
Incense offerings are made to my name
   everywhere,
   and a pure offering;
For my name is great among the nations,
   says the LORD of hosts.
12  But you profane it by saying
   that the LORD's table is defiled,
   and its food may be disdained.
13  You say, "See what a burden this is!"
   and you exasperate me, says the
   LORD of hosts;

You bring in what is mutilated, or lame,
   or sick;
   you bring it as an offering!
Will I accept it from your hands?
   says the LORD.
14  Cursed is the cheat who has in his flock
   an intact male,
   and vows it, but sacrifices to the
   LORD a defective one instead;
For a great king am I, says the LORD of
   hosts,
   and my name is feared among the
   nations.

## CHAPTER 2

1  And now, priests, this commandment is
   for you:
   If you do not listen,
2  ʰAnd if you do not take to heart
   giving honor to my name, says the
   LORD of hosts,
I will send a curse upon you
   and your blessing I will curse.
In fact, I have already cursed it,
   because you do not take it to heart.
3  I will rebuke your offspring;
   I will spread dung on your faces,
Dung from your feasts,
   and will carry you to it.
4  You should know that I sent you this
   commandment
   so that my covenant with Levi might
   endure,
   says the LORD of hosts.
5  ⁱMy covenant with him was the life and
   peace which I gave him,
   and the fear he had for me,
   standing in awe of my name.
6  ʲReliable instruction was in his mouth,
   no perversity was found upon his
   lips;
He walked with me in integrity and
   uprightness,
   and turned many away from evil.
7  ᵏFor a priest's lips preserve knowledge,
   and instruction is to be sought from
   his mouth,
   because he is the messenger of the
   LORD of hosts.
8  But you have turned aside from the way,
   and have caused many to stumble by
   your instruction;
You have corrupted the covenant of Levi,‡
   says the LORD of hosts.
9  I, therefore, have made you contemptible
   and base before all the people,

---

*[1:8] The sacrificial offering of a lame, sick, or blind ani-
mal was forbidden in the law (Lv 22:17–25; Dt 17:1).

†[1:10–11] The imperfect sacrifices offered by the people
of Judah are displeasing to the Lord. **Kindling fire on my
altar**: kindle the altar fire for sacrifice. In contrast, the Lord
is pleased with the sacrifices offered by other peoples in
other places (**the rising of the sun**: the far east; **its setting**:
the far west). Since the people of other nations could not be
expected to know the Lord's name as did the people of Judah,
the rhetorical purpose of this statement is to shame the latter. **Incense offerings**: in the ancient world, the hallmark of
an offering made to a god was the smoke it produced on an
altar. In the Old Testament, this was true not only of animals
(Lv 8:20–21) but also of incense (Ex 30:7), suet (Lv 3:11), and
grain offerings (Lv 6:8). In a Christian interpretation of Mal
1:10–11, the "pure offering" of Mal 1:11 is seen as a reference to sacrifice in the Messianic Age. The Council of Trent
endorsed this interpretation (DS 1724).

f. [1:8] Lv 22:17–25; Dt 15:21; 17:1.   g. [1:11] Ps 113:3; Is 59:19.

‡[2:8] **The covenant of Levi**: not mentioned elsewhere in
the Bible. The covenant with Phinehas the grandson of Aaron
(Nm 25:11–13) and the Blessing of Levi (Dt 33:8–11) may lie
in the background.

h. [2:2] Lv 26:14–45; Dt 28:15.   i. [2:5] Ez 37:26.   j. [2:6] Dt 33:8–
11.   k. [2:7] Lv 10:10–11; Dt 17:9–10; Hg 2:11–13.

For you do not keep my ways,
  but show partiality in your
    instruction.

## Marriage and Divorce

10 *lHave we not all one father?
  Has not one God created us?
Why, then, do we break faith with each
    other,
  profaning the covenant of our
    ancestors?
11 mJudah has broken faith; an abominable
    thing
  has been done in Israel and in
    Jerusalem.
Judah has profaned the LORD's holy place,
  which he loves,
  and has married a daughter of a
    foreign god.†
12 May the LORD cut off from the man who
    does this
  both witness and advocate from the
    tents of Jacob,
  and anyone to bring an offering to
    the LORD of hosts!
13 This also you do: the altar of the LORD
    you cover
  with tears, weeping, and groaning,
Because the Lord no longer takes note of
    your offering
  or accepts it favorably from your
    hand.
14 nAnd you say, "Why?"—
  Because the LORD is witness
  between you and the wife of your
    youth
With whom you have broken faith,
  though she is your companion, your
    covenanted wife.‡
15 oDid he not make them one, with flesh
    and spirit?
  And what does the One require?
    Godly offspring!

You should be on guard, then, for your life,
  and do not break faith with the wife
    of your youth.
16 For I hate divorce,
  says the LORD, the God of Israel,
And the one who covers his garment with
    violence,
  says the LORD of hosts.
You should be on guard, then, for your life,
  and you must not break faith.

## Purification and Just Judgment

17 You have wearied the LORD with your
    words,
  yet you say, "How have we wearied
    him?"
By saying, "All evildoers
  are good in the sight of the LORD,
And he is pleased with them,"
  or "Where is the just God?"

## CHAPTER 3

### The Messenger of the Covenant

1 pNow I am sending my messenger—
  he will prepare the way before me;§
And the lord whom you seek will come
  suddenly to his temple;
The messenger of the covenant whom you
    desire—
  see, he is coming! says the LORD of
    hosts.
2 But who can endure the day of his coming?
  Who can stand firm when he
    appears?
For he will be like a refiner's fire,
  like fullers' lye.
3 qHe will sit refining and purifying silver,
  and he will purify the Levites,
Refining them like gold or silver,
  that they may bring offerings to the
    LORD in righteousness.
4 Then the offering of Judah and Jerusalem
  will please the LORD,
  as in ancient days, as in years gone
    by.
5 I will draw near to you for judgment,
  and I will be swift to bear witness
Against sorcerers, adulterers, and
    perjurers,
  those who deprive a laborer of
    wages,

---

*[2:10–16] Intermarriage of Israelites with foreigners was forbidden according to Dt 7:1–4. After the exile, attempts were made to enforce this law (Ezr 9–10). Foreign marriages are here portrayed as a covenantal violation (v. 10). They are all the more reprehensible when they were accompanied by the divorce of Israelite wives (vv. 14–16), and God finds their sacrifices unacceptable (vv. 13–14). In Mk 10:2–12, Jesus forbids divorce; in Mt 19:3–12, this ideal is maintained with the provision that unlawful marriage may be grounds for divorce (see 1 Cor 7:10–16). **You should be on guard, then, for your life**: a warning of punishment for failure to obey God (cf. Dt 4:9; Jos 23:11; Jer 17:21).

†[2:11] **Daughter of a foreign god**: this unusual phrase connotes a woman who does not share the same father/creator (v. 10), since she does not share the same covenant.

‡[2:14] **Companion . . . covenanted wife**: the Hebrew word *haberet* signifies an equal, a partner. This woman, in contrast to the daughter of a foreign god, shares with her husband the same covenant with the Lord.

l. [2:10] Dt 32:6; Jb 31:15; Mt 23:9; Eph 4:6.  m. [2:11] Ezr 9:2; Neh 13:25.  n. [2:14] Gn 31:49–50; Prv 5:18–19.  o. [2:15] Gn 2:7, 22–24.

---

§[3:1] **My messenger . . . before me**: Mt 11:10 applies these words to John the Baptist; Mt 11:14 further identifies John as Elijah (see Mal 3:23). Some take God's messenger in v. 1a to be a person distinct from "the lord" and "the messenger of the covenant" in v. 1b; others hold that they are one and the same person. Some consider "the lord" and "the messenger of the covenant" to be divine, while others hold that in the text's literal sense he is a messianic earthly ruler.

p. [3:1] Ex 23:20–22; Is 40:3; Mt 11:10; Mk 1:2; Lk 1:17; 7:27. q. [3:3] Is 1:25; Zec 13:9.

Oppress a widow or an orphan,
　　or turn aside a resident alien,
　　without fearing me, says the LORD
　　　of hosts.

## Gifts for God, Blessings for the People

6　For I, the LORD, do not change,*
　　and you, sons of Jacob, do not cease
　　　to be.
7　'Since the days of your ancestors you have
　　　turned aside
　　from my statutes and have not kept
　　　them.
　Return to me, that I may return to you,
　　says the LORD of hosts.
　But you say, "Why should we return?"
8　'Can anyone rob God? But you are
　　　robbing me!
　And you say, "How have we robbed you?"
　　Of tithes and contributions!
9　You are indeed accursed,
　　for you, the whole nation, rob me.
10　'Bring the whole tithe
　　into the storehouse,†
　That there may be food in my house.
　　Put me to the test, says the LORD of
　　　hosts,
　And see if I do not open the floodgates of
　　　heaven for you,
　　and pour down upon you blessing
　　　without measure!
11　I will rebuke the locust for you
　　so that it will not destroy your crops,
　And the vine in the field will not be barren,
　　says the LORD of hosts.
12　"All the nations will call you blessed,
　　for you will be a delightful land,
　　says the LORD of hosts.

## The Need to Serve God

13　Your words are too much for me, says the
　　　LORD.
　　You ask, "What have we spoken
　　　against you?"
14　'You have said, "It is useless to serve God;
　　what do we gain by observing God's
　　　requirements,
　And by going about as mourners‡
　　before the LORD of hosts?
15　But we call the arrogant blessed;
　　for evildoers not only prosper
　　but even test God and escape."

16　"Then those who fear the LORD spoke
　　　with one another,
　　and the LORD listened attentively;
　A record book§ was written before him
　　of those who fear the LORD and
　　　esteem his name.
17　*They shall be mine, says the LORD of
　　　hosts,
　　my own special possession, on the
　　　day when I take action.
　And I will have compassion on them,
　　as a man has compassion on his son
　　　who serves him.
18　Then you will again distinguish
　　between the just and the wicked,
　Between the person who serves God,
　　and the one who does not.
19　'For the day is coming, blazing like an
　　　oven,
　　when all the arrogant and all
　　　evildoers will be stubble,
　And the day that is coming will set them
　　　on fire,
　　leaving them neither root nor branch,
　　says the LORD of hosts.
20　'But for you who fear my name, the sun of
　　　justice
　　will arise with healing in its wings;¶
　And you will go out leaping like calves
　　　from the stall
21　　and tread down the wicked;
　They will become dust under the soles of
　　　your feet,
　　on the day when I take action, says
　　　the LORD of hosts.

## Moses and Elijah

22　'Remember the law of Moses my servant,
　　whom I charged at Horeb
　With statutes and ordinances
　　for all Israel.
23　'Now I am sending to you
　　Elijah** the prophet,
　Before the day of the LORD comes,
　　the great and terrible day;
24　He will turn the heart of fathers to their
　　　sons,
　　and the heart of sons to their fathers,
　Lest I come and strike
　　the land with utter destruction.

---

§[3:16] **Record book**: see note on Ex 32:32.
¶[3:20] **Wings**: a common symbol of the manifestation of
a god in the ancient Near East is the winged sun disk found,
for example, on premonarchic jar handles. Cf. Nm 6:25; Ps
4:7; 31:17; 34:6; 84:12.
**[3:23] **Elijah**: taken up in a whirlwind, according to 2 Kgs
2:11. Here his return seems to be foretold. A Jewish tradition
interpreted this literally; the gospels saw Elijah in the person
of John the Baptist (Mt 11:13–14; 17:10–13; Mk 9:9–13).

---

*[3:6–7] **Not change**: God remains faithful to the covenant
even when the human partners break it.
†[3:10] **Storehouse**: the temple treasury.
‡[3:14] **As mourners**: the adverb translated "as mourners"
means something like "with a long face."

---

r. [3:7] Zec 1:3–4; Acts 7:51.　　s. [3:8] Neh 13:10–14.　　t. [3:10] Dt
28:2, 12; 2 Chr 31:10–11; Neh 10:38; 13:12; Prv 3:9–10.　u. [3:12]
Dt 28:10; Is 61:9.　　v. [3:14] Jb 21:14–15; 22:17; Ps 73:11–12; Is 58:3;
Zec 7:2–7.

w. [3:16] Rev 20:12.　　x. [3:17] Ex 19:5; Dt 7:6; Ps 103:13; 135:4.
y. [3:19] Is 13:9; 34:8; Jl 3:3; Zep 1:18; 2 Pt 3:7.　z. [3:20] Lk 1:78–
79.　a. [3:22] Ex 20; Lv 26; Dt 4:1, 5–6.　b. [3:23] 2 Kgs 2:10–12; Sir
48:10; Mt 11:13–14; 17:10–13; Mk 9:9–13; Lk 1:17.

# THE
# NEW TESTAMENT

# NEW AMERICAN BIBLE

## FIRST EDITION OF THE NEW TESTAMENT

The New Testament translation has been approached with essentially the same fidelity to the thought and individual style of the biblical writers as was applied in the Old Testament. In some cases, however, the problem of marked literary peculiarities had to be met. What by any Western standard are the limited vocabularies and stylistic infelicities of the evangelists cannot be retained in the exact form in which they appear in the originals without displeasing the modern ear. A compromise is here attempted whereby some measure of the poverty of the evangelists' expression is kept and placed at the service of their message in its richness. Similarly, the syntactical shortcomings of Paul, his frequent lapses into anacoluthon, and the like, are rendered as they occur in his epistles rather than "smoothed out." Only thus, the translators suppose, will contemporary readers have some adequate idea of the kind of writing they have before them. When the prose of the original flows more smoothly, as in Luke, Acts, and Hebrews, it is reflected in the translation.

The Gospel according to John comprises a special case. Absolute fidelity to his technique of reiterated phrasing would result in an assault on the English ear, yet the softening of the vocal effect by substitution of other words and phrases would destroy the effectiveness of his poetry. Again, resort is had to compromise. This is not an easy matter when the very repetitiousness which the author deliberately employed is at the same time regarded by those who read and speak English to be a serious stylistic defect. Only those familiar with the Greek originals can know what a relentless tattoo Johannine poetry can produce. A similar observation could be made regarding other New Testament books as well. Matthew and Mark are given to identical phrasing twice and three times in the same sentence. As for the rhetorical overgrowth and mixed figures of speech in the letters of Peter, James, and Jude, the translator must resist a powerful compulsion to tidy them up if only to render these letters intelligibly.

Without seeking refuge in complaints against the inspired authors, however, the translators of *The New American Bible* here state that what they have attempted is a translation rather than a paraphrase. To be sure, all translation can be called paraphrase by definition. Any striving for complete fidelity will shortly end in infidelity. Nonetheless, it must be pointed out that the temptation to improve overladen sentences by the consolidation or elimination of multiplied adjectives, or the simplification of clumsy hendiadys, has been resisted here. For the most part, rhetorically ineffective words and phrases are retained in this translation in some form, even when it is clear that a Western contemporary writer would never have employed them.

The spelling of proper names in *The New American Bible* follows the customary forms found in most English Bibles since the Authorized Version.

Despite the arbitrary character of the divisions into numbered verses (a scheme which in its present form is only four centuries old), the translators have made a constant effort to keep within an English verse the whole verbal content of the Greek verse. At times the effort has not seemed worth the result since it often does violence to the original author's flow of expression, which preceded it by so many centuries. If this translation had been prepared for purposes of public reading only, the editors would have forgone the effort at an early stage. But since they never departed from the threefold objective of preparing a translation suitable for liturgical use, private reading, and the purposes of students, the last-named consideration prevailed. Those familiar with Greek should be able to discover how the translators of the New Testament have rendered any given original verse of scripture, if their exegetical or theological tasks require them to know this. At the same time, the fact should be set down here that the editors did not commit themselves in the synoptic gospels to rendering repeated words or phrases identically.

This leads to a final consideration: the Greek text used for the New Testament. Here, punctuation and verse division are at least as important as variant readings. In general, Nestle-Aland's *Novum Testamentum Graece* (25th edition, 1963) was followed. Additional help was derived from *The Greek New Testament* (Aland, Black, Metzger, Wikgren), produced for the use of translators by the United Bible Societies in 1966. However, the editors did not confine themselves strictly to these texts; at times, they inclined toward readings otherwise attested. The omission of alternative translations does not mean that the translators think them without merit, but only that in every case they had to make a choice.

Poorly attested readings do not occur in this translation. Doubtful readings of some merit appear within brackets; public readers may include such words or phrases, or omit them entirely without any damage to sense. Parentheses are used, as ordinarily in English, as a punctuation device. Material they enclose is in no sense textually doubtful. It is simply thought to be parenthetical in the intention of the biblical author, even though there is no such punctuation mark in Greek. The difficulty in dealing with quotation marks is well known. Since they do not appear in any form in the original text, wherever they occur here they constitute an editorial decision.

## PREFACE TO THE REVISED EDITION

The New Testament of *The New American Bible*, a fresh translation from the Greek text, was first published in complete form in 1970, together with the Old Testament translation that had been completed the previous year. Portions of the New Testament had appeared earlier, in somewhat different form, in the provisional Mass lectionary of 1964 and in the *Lectionary for Mass* of 1970.

Since 1970 many different printings of the New Testament have been issued by a number of publishers, both separately and in complete bibles, and the text has become widely known both in the United States and in other English-speaking countries. Most American Catholics have been influenced by it because of its widespread use in the liturgy, and it has received a generally favorable reception from many other Christians as well. It has taken its place among the standard contemporary translations of the New Testament, respected for its fidelity to the original and its attempt to render this into current American English.

Although the scriptures themselves are timeless, translations and explanations of them quickly become dated in an era marked by rapid cultural change to a degree never previously experienced. The explosion of biblical studies that has taken place in our century and the changing nature of our language itself require periodic adjustment both in translations and in the accompanying explanatory materials. The experience of actual use of the New Testament of The New American Bible, especially in oral proclamation, has provided a basis for further improvement. Accordingly, it was decided in 1978 to proceed with a thorough revision of the New Testament to reflect advances in scholarship and to satisfy needs identified through pastoral experience.

For this purpose a steering committee was formed to plan, organize, and direct the work of revision, to engage collaborators, and to serve as an editorial board to coordinate the work of the various revisers and to determine the final form of the text and the explanatory materials. Guidelines were drawn up and collaborators selected in 1978 and early 1979, and November of 1980 was established as the deadline for manuscripts. From December 1980 through September 1986 the editorial board met a total of fifty times and carefully reviewed and revised all the material in order to ensure accuracy and consistency of approach. The editors also worked together with the bishops' ad hoc committee that was appointed by the National Conference of Catholic Bishops in 1982 to oversee the revision.

The threefold purpose of the translation that was expressed in the preface to the first edition has been maintained in the revision: to provide a version suitable for liturgical proclamation, for private reading, and for purposes of study. Special attention has been given to the first of these purposes, since oral proclamation demands special qualities in a translation, and experience had provided insights and suggestions that could lead to improvement in this area. Efforts have also been made, however, to facilitate devotional reading by providing suitable notes and introductory materials, and to assist the student by achieving greater accuracy and consistency in the translation and supplying more abundant information in the introductions and notes.

The primary aim of the revision is to produce a version as accurate and faithful to the meaning of the Greek original as is possible for a translation. The editors have consequently moved in the direction of a formal-equivalence approach to translation, matching the vocabulary, structure, and even word order of the original as closely as possible in the receptor language. Some other contemporary biblical versions have adopted, in varying degrees, a dynamic-equivalence approach, which attempts to respect the individuality of each language by expressing the meaning of the original in a linguistic structure suited to English, even though this may be very different from the corresponding Greek structure. While this approach often results in fresh and brilliant renderings, it has the disadvantages of more or less radically abandoning traditional biblical and liturgical terminology and phraseology, of expanding the text to include what more properly belongs in notes, commentaries, or preaching, and of tending toward paraphrase. A more formal approach seems better suited to the specific purposes intended for this translation.

At the same time, the editors have wished to produce a version in English that reflects contemporary American usage and is readily understandable to ordinary educated people, but one that will be recognized as dignified speech, on the level of formal rather than colloquial usage. These aims are not in fact contradictory, for there are different levels of language in current use: the language of formal situations as not that of colloquial conversation, though people understand both and may pass from one to the other without adverting to the transition. The liturgy is a formal situation that requires a level of discourse more dignified, formal, and hieratic than the world of business, sport, or informal communication. People readily understand this more formal level even though they may not often use it; our passive vocabulary is much larger than our active vocabulary. Hence this revision, while avoiding archaisms, does not shrink from traditional biblical terms that are easily understood even though not in common use in everyday speech. The level of language consciously aimed at is one appropriate for liturgical proclamation; this may also permit the translation to serve the purposes of devotional reading and serious study.

A particular effort has been made to insure consistency of vocabulary. Always to translate a given Greek word by the same English equivalent would lead to ludicrous results and to infidelity to the meaning of the text. But in passages where a particular Greek term retains the same meaning, it has been rendered in the same way insofar as this has been feasible; this is particularly significant in the case of terms that have a specific theological meaning. The synoptic gospels have been carefully translated so as to reveal both the similarities and the differences of the Greek.

An especially sensitive problem today is the question of discrimination in language. In recent years there has been much discussion about allegations of anti-Jewish expressions in the New Testament and of language that discriminates against various minorities. Above all, however, the question of discrimination against women affects the largest number of people and arouses the greatest degree of interest and concern. At present there is little agreement about these problems or about the best way to deal with them. In all these areas the present translation attempts to display a sensitivity appropriate to the present state of the questions under discussion, which are not yet resolved and in regard to which it is impossible to please everyone, since intelligent and sincere participants in the debate hold mutually contradictory views.

The primary concern in this revision is fidelity to what the text says. When the meaning of the Greek is inclusive of both sexes, the translation seeks to reproduce such inclusivity insofar as this is possible in normal English usage, without resort to inelegant circumlocutions or neologisms that would offend against the dignity of the language. Although the generic sense of *man* is traditional in English, many today reject it; its use has therefore generally been avoided, though it is retained in cases where no fully satisfactory equivalent could be found. English does not possess a gender-inclusive third personal pronoun in the singular, and this translation continues to use the masculine resumptive pronoun after *everyone* or *anyone*, in the traditional way, where this cannot be avoided without infidelity to the meaning.

The translation of the Greek word *adelphos*, particularly in the plural form *adelphoi*, poses an especially delicate problem. While the term literally means brothers or other male blood relatives, even in profane Greek the plural can designate two persons, one of either sex, who were born of the same parents. It was adopted by the early Christians to designate, in a figurative sense, the members of the Christian community, who were conscious of a new familial relationship to one another by reason of their adoption as children of God. They are consequently addressed as *adelphoi*. This has traditionally been rendered into English by *brothers* or, more archaically, *brethren*. There has never been any doubt that this designation includes *all* the members of the Christian community, both male and female. Given the absence in English of a corresponding term that explicitly includes both sexes, this translation retains the usage of *brothers*, with the inclusive meaning that has been traditionally attached to it in this biblical context.

Since the New Testament is the product of a particular time and culture, the views expressed in it and the language in which they are expressed reflect a particular cultural conditioning, which sometimes makes them quite different from contemporary ideas and concerns. Discriminatory language should be eliminated insofar as possible whenever it is unfaithful to the meaning of the New Testament, but the text should not be altered in order to adjust it to contemporary concerns. This translation does not introduce any changes, expansions, additions to, or subtractions from the text of scripture. It further retains the traditional biblical ways of speaking about God and about Christ, including the use of masculine nouns and pronouns.

The Greek text followed in this translation is that of the third edition of *The Greek New Testament*, edited by Kurt Aland, Matthew Black, Carlo Martini, Bruce Metzger, and Allen Wikgren, and published by the United Bible Societies in 1975. The same text, with a different critical apparatus and variations in punctuation and typography, was published as the twenty-sixth edition of the Nestle-Aland *Novum Testamentum Graece* in 1979 by the Deutsche Bibelstiftung, Stuttgart. This edition has also been consulted. When variant readings occur, the translation, with few exceptions, follows the reading that was placed in the text of these Greek editions, though the occurrence of the principal variants is pointed out in the notes.

The editors of the Greek text placed square brackets around words or portions of words of which the authenticity is questionable because the evidence of textual witnesses is inconclusive. The same has been done in the translation insofar as it is possible to reproduce this convention in English. It should be possible to read the text either with or without the disputed words, but in English it is not always feasible to provide this alternative, and in some passages the bracketed words must be included to make sense. As in the first edition, parentheses do not indicate textual uncertainty, but are simply a punctuation device to indicate a passage that in the editors' judgment appears parenthetical to the thought of the author.

Citations from the Old Testament are placed within quotation marks; longer citations are set off as block quotations in a separate indented paragraph. The sources of such citations, as well as those of many more or less subtle allusions to the Old Testament, are identified in the biblical cross-reference section at the bottom of each page. Insofar as possible, the translation of such Old Testament citations agrees with that of *The New American Bible* Old Testament whenever the underlying Greek agrees with the Hebrew (or, in some cases, the Aramaic or Greek) text from which the Old Testament translation was made. But citations in the New Testament frequently follow the Septuagint or some other version, or were made from memory, hence, in many cases the translation in the New Testament passage will not agree with what appears in the Old Testament. Some of these cases are explained in the notes.

It is a further aim of the revised edition to supply explanatory materials more abundantly than in the first edition. In most cases the introductions and notes have been entirely rewritten and expanded, and the cross-references checked and revised. It is intended that these materials should reflect the present state of sound biblical scholarship and should be presented in such a form that they can be assimilated by the ordinary intelligent reader without specialized biblical training. While they have been written with the ordinary educated Christian in mind, not all technical vocabulary can be entirely dispensed with in approaching the Bible, any more than in any other field. It is the hope of the editors that these materials, even if they sometimes demand an effort, will help the reader to a fuller and more intelligent understanding of the New Testament and a fruitful appropriation of its meaning for personal spiritual growth.

*The New American Bible* is a Roman Catholic translation. This revision, however, like the first edition, has been accomplished with the collaboration of scholars from other Christian churches, both among the revisers and on the editorial board, in response to the encouragement of Vatican Council II (*Dei Verbum*, 22). The editorial board expresses gratitude to all who have collaborated in the revision: to all the revisers, consultants, and bishops who contributed to it, to reviewers of the first edition, and to those who voluntarily submitted suggestions. May this translation fulfill its threefold purpose, "so that the word of the Lord may speed forward and be glorified" (2 Thes 3:1).

The Feast of St. Jerome
September 30, 1986

# THE
# GOSPELS

The collection of writings that constitutes the New Testament begins with four gospels. Next comes the Acts of the Apostles, followed by twenty-one letters that are attributed to Paul, James, Peter, John, and Jude. Finally, at the end of the early church's scriptures stands the Revelation to John. Virtually all Christians agree that these twenty-seven books constitute the "canon," a term that means "rule" and designates the list of writings that are regarded as authoritative for Christian faith and life.

It is the purpose of this Introduction to describe those features that are common to the four gospels. A similar treatment of the letters of the New Testament is provided in the two Introductions that appear before the Letter to the Romans and before the Letter of James, respectively. The Acts of the Apostles, a work that is both historical and theological, and Revelation, an apocalyptic work, have no counterparts in the New Testament; the special Introductions prefixed to these books treat of the literary characteristics proper to each of them.

While the New Testament contains four writings called "gospels," there is in reality only one gospel running through all of the Christian scriptures, the gospel of and about Jesus Christ. Our English word "gospel" translates the Greek term *euangelion*, meaning "good news." This noun was used in the plural by the Greek translators of the Old Testament to render the Hebrew term for "good news" (2 Sm 4:10; possibly also 2 Sm 18:20, 25). But it is the corresponding verb *euangelizomai*, "to proclaim good news," that was especially significant in preparing for the New Testament idea of "gospel," since this term is used by Deutero-Isaiah of announcing the great victory of God that was to establish his universal kingship and inaugurate the new age (Is 40:9; 52:7; 61:1).

Paul used the word *euangelion* to designate the message that he and the other apostles proclaimed, the "gospel of God" (Rom 1:1; 15:16; 2 Cor 11:7; 1 Thes 2:2, 8–9). He often referred to it simply as "the gospel" (Rom 1:16; 10:16; 11:28; etc) or, because of its content and origin, as "the gospel of Christ" (Rom 15:19; 1 Cor 9:12; 1 Thes 3:2; etc). Because of its personal meaning for him and his own particular manner of telling the story about Jesus Christ and of explaining the significance of his cross and resurrection, Paul also referred to this message as "my gospel" (Rom 2:16; cf. Gal 1:11; 2:2) or "our gospel" (2 Cor 4:3; 1 Thes 1:5; 2 Thes 2:14).

It was Mark, as far as we know, who first applied the term "gospel" to a book telling the story of Jesus; see Mk 1:1 and the note there. This form of presenting Jesus' life, works, teachings, passion, and resurrection was developed further by the other evangelists; see the Introduction to each gospel. The first three of the canonical gospels, Matthew, Mark, and Luke, are so similar at many points when viewed together, particularly when arranged in parallel columns or lines, that they are called "synoptic" gospels, from the Greek word for such a general view. The fourth gospel, John, often differs significantly from the synoptics in outline and approach. This work never uses the word "gospel" or its corresponding verb; nevertheless, its message concerns the same Jesus, and the reader is urged to believe in him as the Messiah, "that through this belief you may have life in his name" (Jn 20:31).

From the second century onward, the practice arose of designating each of these four books as a "gospel," understood as a title, and of adding a phrase with a name that identified the traditional author, e.g., "The Gospel according to Matthew." The arrangement of the canon that was adopted, with the four gospels grouped together at the beginning followed by Acts, provides a massive focus upon Jesus and allows Acts to serve as a framework for the letters of the New Testament. This order, however, conceals the fact that Luke's two volumes, a gospel and Acts, were intended by their author to go together. It further obscures the point that Paul's letters were written before any of our gospels, though the sayings and deeds of Jesus stand behind all the New Testament writings.

# THE GOSPEL ACCORDING TO
# MATTHEW

The position of the Gospel according to Matthew as the first of the four gospels in the New Testament reflects both the view that it was the first to be written, a view that goes back to the late second century A.D., and the esteem in which it was held by the church; no other was so frequently quoted in the noncanonical literature of earliest Christianity. Although the majority of scholars now reject the opinion about the time of its composition, the high estimation of this work remains. The reason for that becomes clear upon study of the way in which Matthew presents his story of Jesus, the demands of Christian discipleship, and the breaking-in of the new and final age through the ministry but particularly through the death and resurrection of Jesus.

The gospel begins with a narrative prologue (Mt 1:1–2:23), the first part of which is a genealogy of Jesus starting with Abraham, the father of Israel (Mt 1:1–17). Yet at the beginning of that genealogy Jesus is designated as "the son of David, the son of Abraham" (Mt 1:1). The kingly ancestor who lived about a thousand years after Abraham is named first, for this is the genealogy of Jesus Christ, the Messiah, the royal anointed one (Mt 1:16). In the first of the episodes of the infancy narrative that follow the genealogy, the mystery of Jesus' person is declared. He is conceived of a virgin by the power of the Spirit of God (Mt 1:18–25). The first of the gospel's fulfillment citations, whose purpose it is to show that he was the one to whom the prophecies of Israel were pointing, occurs here (Mt 1:23): he shall be named Emmanuel, for in him God is with us.

The announcement of the birth of this newborn king of the Jews greatly troubles not only King Herod but all Jerusalem (Mt 2:1–3), yet the Gentile magi are overjoyed to find him and offer him their homage and their gifts (Mt 2:10–11). Thus his ultimate rejection by the mass of his own people and his acceptance by the Gentile nations is foreshadowed. He must be taken to Egypt to escape the murderous plan of Herod. By his sojourn there and his subsequent return after the king's death he relives the Exodus experience of Israel. The words of the Lord spoken through the prophet Hosea, "Out of Egypt I called my son," are fulfilled in him (Mt 2:15); if Israel was God's son, Jesus is so in a way far surpassing the dignity of that nation, as his marvelous birth and the unfolding of his story show (see Mt 3:17; 4:1–11; 11:27; 14:33; 16:16; 27:54). Back in the land of Israel, he must be taken to Nazareth in Galilee because of the danger to his life in Judea, where Herod's son Archelaus is now ruling (Mt 2:22–23). The sufferings of Jesus in the infancy narrative anticipate those of his passion, and if his life is spared in spite of the dangers, it is because his destiny is finally to give it on the cross as "a ransom for many" (Mt 20:28). Thus the word of the angel will be fulfilled, ". . . he will save his people from their sins" (Mt 1:21; cf. Mt 26:28).

In Mt 4:12 Matthew begins his account of the ministry of Jesus, introducing it by the preparatory preaching of John the Baptist (Mt 3:1–12), the baptism of Jesus that culminates in God's proclaiming him his "beloved Son" (Mt 3:13–17), and the temptation in which he proves his true sonship by his victory over the devil's attempt to deflect him from the way of obedience to the Father (Mt 4:1–11). The central message of Jesus' preaching is the coming of the kingdom of heaven and the need for repentance, a complete change of heart and conduct, on the part of those who are to receive this great gift of God (Mt 4:17). Galilee is the setting for most of his ministry; he leaves there for Judea only in Mt 19:1, and his ministry in Jerusalem, the goal of his journey, is limited to a few days (Mt 21:1–25:46).

In this extensive material there are five great discourses of Jesus, each concluding with the formula "When Jesus finished these words" or one closely similar (Mt 7:28; 11:1; 13:53; 19:1; 26:1). These are an important structure of the gospel. In every case the discourse is preceded by a narrative section, each narrative and discourse together constituting a "book" of the gospel. The discourses are, respectively, the "Sermon on the Mount" (Mt 5:3–7:27), the missionary discourse (Mt 10:5–42), the parable discourse (Mt 13:3–52), the "church order" discourse (Mt 18:3–35), and the eschatological discourse (Mt 24:4–25:46). In large measure the material of these discourses came to Matthew from his tradition, but his work in modifying and adding to what he had received is abundantly evident. No other evangelist gives the teaching of Jesus with such elegance and order as he.

In the "Sermon on the Mount" the theme of righteousness is prominent, and even at this early stage of the ministry the note of opposition is struck between Jesus and the Pharisees, who are designated as "the hypocrites" (Mt 6:2, 5, 16). The righteousness of his disciples must surpass that of the scribes and Pharisees; otherwise, in spite of their alleged following of Jesus, they will not enter into the kingdom of heaven (Mt 5:20). Righteousness means doing the will of the heavenly Father (Mt 7:21), and his will is proclaimed in a manner that is startling to all who have identified it with the law of Moses. The antitheses of the Sermon (Mt 5:21–48) both accept (Mt 5:21–30, 43–48) and reject (Mt 5:31–42) elements of that law, and in the former case the understanding of the law's demands is deepened and extended. The antitheses are the best commentary on the meaning of Jesus' claim that he has come not to abolish but to fulfill the law (Mt 5:17). What is meant by fulfillment of the law is not the demand to keep it exactly as it stood before the coming of Jesus, but rather his bringing the law to be a lasting expression of the will of God, and in that fulfillment there is much that will pass away. Should this appear contradictory to his saying that "until heaven and earth pass away" not even the smallest part of the law will pass (Mt 5:18), that time of fulfillment is not the dissolution of the universe but the coming of the new age, which will occur with Jesus' death and resurrection. While righteousness in the new age will continue to mean conduct that is in accordance with the law, it will be conduct in accordance with the law as expounded and interpreted by Jesus (cf. Mt 28:20, ". . . all that I have commanded you").

Though Jesus speaks harshly about the Pharisees in the Sermon, his judgment is not solely a condemnation of them. The Pharisees are portrayed as a negative example for his disciples, and his condemnation of those who claim to belong to him while disobeying his word is no less severe (Mt 7:21–23, 26–27).

In Mt 4:23 a summary statement of Jesus' activity speaks not only of his teaching and proclaiming the gospel but of his "curing every disease and illness among the people"; this is repeated almost verbatim in Mt 9:35. The narrative section that follows the Sermon on the Mount (Mt 8:1–9:38) is composed principally of accounts of those merciful deeds of Jesus, but it is far from being simply a collection of stories about miraculous cures. The nature of the community that Jesus will establish is shown; it will always be under the protection of him whose power can deal with all dangers (Mt 8:23–27), but it is only for those who are prepared to follow him at whatever cost (Mt 8:16–22), not only believing Israelites but Gentiles who have come to faith in him (Mt 8:10–12). The disciples begin to have some insight, however imperfect, into the mystery of Jesus' person. They wonder about him whom "the winds and the sea obey" (Mt 8:27), and they witness his bold declaration of the forgiveness of the paralytic's sins (Mt 9:2). That episode of the narrative moves on two levels. When the crowd sees the cure that testifies to the authority of Jesus, the Son of Man, to forgive sins (Mt 9:6), they glorify God "who had given such authority to human beings" (Mt 9:8). The forgiveness of sins is now not the prerogative of Jesus alone but of "human beings," that is, of the disciples who constitute the community of Jesus, the church. The ecclesial character of this narrative section could hardly be more plainly indicated.

The end of the section prepares for the discourse on the church's mission (Mt 10:5–42). Jesus is moved to pity at the sight of the crowds who are like sheep without a shepherd (Mt 9:36), and he sends out the twelve disciples to make the proclamation with which his own ministry began, "The kingdom of heaven is at hand" (Mt 10:7; cf. Mt 4:17), and to drive out demons and cure the sick as he has done (Mt 10:1). Their mission is limited to Israel (Mt 10:5–6) as Jesus' own was (Mt 15:24), yet in Mt 15:16 that perspective broadens and the discourse begins to speak of the mission that the disciples will have after the resurrection and of the severe persecution that will attend it (Mt 10:18). Again, the discourse moves on two levels: that of the time of Jesus and that of the time of the church.

The narrative section of the third book (Mt 11:2–12:50) deals with the growing opposition to Jesus. Hostility toward him has already been manifested (Mt 8:10; 9:3, 10–13, 34), but here it becomes more intense. The rejection of Jesus comes, as before, from Pharisees, who take "counsel against him to put him to death" (Mt 12:14) and repeat their earlier accusation that he drives out demons because he is in league with demonic power (Mt 12:22–24). But they are not alone in their rejection. Jesus complains of the lack of faith of "this generation" of Israelites (Mt 11:16–19) and reproaches the towns "where most of his mighty deeds had been done" for not heeding his call to repentance (Mt 11:20–24). This dark picture is relieved by Jesus' praise of the Father who has enabled "the childlike" to accept him (Mt 11:25–27), but on the whole the story is one of opposition to his word and blindness to the meaning of his deeds. The whole section ends with his declaring that not even the most intimate blood relationship with him counts for anything; his only true relatives are those who do the will of his heavenly Father (Mt 12:48–50).

The narrative of rejection leads up to the parable discourse (Mt 13:3–52). The reason given for Jesus' speaking to the crowds in parables is that they have hardened themselves against his clear teaching, unlike the disciples to whom knowledge of "the mysteries of the kingdom has been granted" (Mt 13:10–16). In Mt 13:36 he dismisses the crowds and continues the discourse to his disciples alone, who claim, at the end, to have understood all that he has said (Mt 13:51). But, lest the impression be given that the church of Jesus is made up only of true disciples, the explanation of the parable of the weeds among the wheat (Mt 13:37–43), as well as the parable of the net thrown into the sea "which collects fish of every kind" (Mt 13:47–49), shows that it is composed of both the righteous and the wicked, and that separation between the two will be made only at the time of the final judgment.

In the narrative that constitutes the first part of the fourth book of the gospel (Mt 13:54–17:27), Jesus is shown preparing for the establishment of his church with its teaching authority that will supplant the blind guidance of the Pharisees (Mt 15:13–14), whose teaching, curiously said to be that of the Sadducees also, is repudiated by Jesus as the norm for his disciples (Mt 16:6, 11–12). The church of Jesus will be built on Peter (Mt 16:18), who will be given authority to bind and loose on earth, an authority whose exercise will be confirmed in heaven (Mt 16:19). The metaphor of binding and loosing has a variety of meanings, among them that of giving authoritative teaching. This promise is made to Peter directly after he has confessed Jesus to be the Messiah, the Son of the living God (Mt 16:16), a confession that he has made as the result of revelation given to him by the heavenly Father (Mt 16:17); Matthew's ecclesiology is based on his high christology.

Directly after that confession Jesus begins to instruct his disciples about how he must go the way of suffering and death (Mt 16:21). Peter, who has been praised for his confession, protests against this and receives from Jesus the sharpest of rebukes for attempting to deflect Jesus from his God-appointed destiny. The future rock upon whom the church will be built is still a man of "little faith" (see Mt 14:31). Both he and the other disciples must know not only that Jesus will have to suffer and die but that they too will have to follow him on the way of the cross if they are truly to be his disciples (Mt 16:24–25).

The discourse following this narrative (Mt 18:1–35) is often called the "church order" discourse, although that title is perhaps misleading since the emphasis is not on the structure of the church but on the care that the disciples must have for one another in respect to guarding each other's faith in Jesus (Mt 18:6–7), to seeking out those who have wandered from the fold (Mt 18:10–14), and to repeated forgiving of their fellow disciples who have offended them (Mt 18:21–35). But there is also the obligation to correct the sinful fellow Christian and, should one refuse to be corrected, separation from the community is demanded (Mt 18:15–18).

The narrative of the fifth book (Mt 19:1–23:39) begins with the departure of Jesus and his disciples from Galilee for Jerusalem. In the course of their journey Jesus for the third time predicts the passion that awaits him at Jerusalem and also his resurrection (Mt 20:17–19). At his entrance into the city he is hailed as the Son of David by the crowds accompanying him (Mt 21:9). He cleanses the temple (Mt 21:12–17), and in the few days of his Jerusalem ministry he engages in a series of controversies with the Jewish religious leaders (Mt 21:23–27; 22:15–22, 23–33, 34–40, 41–46), meanwhile speaking parables against them (Mt 21:28–32, 33–46), against all those Israelites who have rejected God's invitation to the messianic banquet (Mt 22:1–10), and against all, Jew and Gentile, who have accepted but have shown themselves unworthy of it (Mt 22:11–14). Once again, the perspective of the evangelist includes not only the time of Jesus' ministry but that of the preaching of the gospel after his resurrection. The narrative culminates in Jesus' denunciation of the scribes and Pharisees, reflecting not only his own opposition to them but that of Matthew's church (Mt 23:1–36), and in Jesus' lament over Jerusalem (Mt 23:37–39).

In the discourse of the fifth book (Mt 24:1–25:46), the last of the great structural discourses of the gospel, Jesus predicts the destruction of the temple and his own final coming. The time of the latter is unknown (Mt 24:36, 44), and the disciples are exhorted in various parables to live in readiness for it, a readiness that entails faithful attention to the duties of the interim period (Mt 24:45–25:30). The coming of Jesus will bring with it the great judgment by which the everlasting destiny of all will be determined (Mt 25:31–46).

The story of Jesus' passion and resurrection (Mt 26:1–28:20), the climax of the gospel, throws light on all that has preceded. In Matthew "righteousness" means both the faithful response to the will of God demanded of all to whom that will is announced and also the saving activity of God for his people (see Mt 3:15; 5:6; 6:33). The passion supremely exemplifies both meanings of that central Matthean word. In Jesus' absolute faithfulness to the Father's will that he drink the cup of suffering (Mt 26:39), the incomparable model for Christian obedience is given; in his death "for the forgiveness of sins" (Mt 26:28), the saving power of God is manifested as never before.

Matthew's portrayal of Jesus in his passion combines both the majestic serenity of the obedient Son who goes his destined way in fulfillment of the scriptures (Mt 26:52–54), confident of his ultimate vindication by God, and the depths of fear and abandonment that he feels in face of death (Mt 26:38–39; 27:46). These two aspects are expressed by an Old Testament theme that occurs often in the narrative, i.e., the portrait of the suffering Righteous One who complains to God in his misery, but is certain of eventual deliverance from his terrible ordeal.

The passion-resurrection of God's Son means nothing less than the turn of the ages, a new stage of history, the coming of the Son of Man in his kingdom (Mt 28:18; cf. Mt 16:28). That is the sense of the apocalyptic signs that accompany Jesus' death (Mt 27:51–53) and resurrection (Mt 28:2). Although the old age continues, as it will until the manifestation of Jesus' triumph at his parousia, the final age has now begun. This is known only to those who have seen the Risen One and to those, both Jews and Gentiles, who have believed in their announcement of Jesus' triumph and have themselves become his disciples (cf. Mt 28:19). To them he is constantly, though invisibly, present (Mt 28:20), verifying the name Emmanuel, "God is with us" (cf. Mt 1:23).

The questions of authorship, sources, and the time of composition of this gospel have received many answers, none of which can claim more than a greater or lesser degree of probability. The one now favored by the majority of scholars is the following.

The ancient tradition that the author was the disciple and apostle of Jesus named Matthew (see Mt 10:3) is untenable because the gospel is based, in large part, on the Gospel according to Mark (almost all the verses of that gospel have been utilized in this), and it is hardly likely that a companion of Jesus would have followed so extensively an account that came from one who admittedly never had such an association rather than rely on his own memories. The attribution of the gospel to the disciple Matthew may have been due to his having been responsible for some of the traditions found in it, but that is far from certain.

The unknown author, whom we shall continue to call Matthew for the sake of convenience, drew not only upon the Gospel according to Mark but upon a large body of material (principally, sayings of Jesus) not found in Mark that corresponds, sometimes exactly, to material found also in the Gospel according to Luke. This material, called "Q" (probably from the first letter of the German word Quelle, meaning "source"), represents traditions, written and oral, used by both Matthew and Luke. Mark and Q are sources common to the two other synoptic gospels; hence the name the "Two-Source Theory" given to this explanation of the relation among the synoptics.

In addition to what Matthew drew from Mark and Q, his gospel contains material that is found only there. This is often designated "M," written or oral tradition that was available to the author. Since Mark was written shortly before or shortly after A.D. 70 (see Introduction to Mark), Matthew was composed certainly after that date, which marks the fall of Jerusalem to the Romans at the time of the First Jewish Revolt (A.D. 66–70), and probably at least a decade later since Matthew's use of

Mark presupposes a wide diffusion of that gospel. The post-A.D. 70 date is confirmed within the text by Mt 22:7, which refers to the destruction of Jerusalem.

As for the place where the gospel was composed, a plausible suggestion is that it was Antioch, the capital of the Roman province of Syria. That large and important city had a mixed population of Greek-speaking Gentiles and Jews. The tensions between Jewish and Gentile Christians there in the time of Paul (see Gal 2:1–14) in respect to Christian obligation to observe Mosaic law are partially similar to tensions that can be seen between the two groups in Matthew's gospel. The church of Matthew, originally strongly Jewish Christian, had become one in which Gentile Christians were predominant. His gospel answers the question how obedience to the will of God is to be expressed by those who live after the "turn of the ages," the death and resurrection of Jesus.

The principal divisions of the Gospel according to Matthew are the following:

   I. The Infancy Narrative (1:1–2:23)
  II. The Proclamation of the Kingdom (3:1–7:29)
 III. Ministry and Mission in Galilee (8:1–11:1)
  IV. Opposition from Israel (11:2–13:53)
   V. Jesus, the Kingdom, and the Church (13:54–18:35)
  VI. Ministry in Judea and Jerusalem (19:1–25:46)
 VII. The Passion and Resurrection (26:1–28:20)

## I. THE INFANCY NARRATIVE

### CHAPTER 1

**The Genealogy of Jesus.**[*] [1a]The book of the genealogy of Jesus Christ, the son of David, the son of Abraham.[†]

---

[*][1:1–2:23] The infancy narrative forms the prologue of the gospel. Consisting of a genealogy and five stories, it presents the coming of Jesus as the climax of Israel's history, and the events of his conception, birth, and early childhood as the fulfillment of Old Testament prophecy. The genealogy is probably traditional material that Matthew edited. In its first two sections (Mt 1:2–11) it was drawn from Ru 4:18–22; 1 Chr 1–3. Except for Jechoniah, Shealtiel, and Zerubbabel, none of the names in the third section (Mt 1:12–16) is found in any Old Testament genealogy. While the genealogy shows the continuity of God's providential plan from Abraham on, discontinuity is also present. The women Tamar (Mt 1:3), Rahab and Ruth (Mt 1:5), and the wife of Uriah, Bathsheba (Mt 1:6), bore their sons through unions that were in varying degrees strange and unexpected. These "irregularities" culminate in the supreme "irregularity" of the Messiah's birth of a virgin mother; the age of fulfillment is inaugurated by a creative act of God.

Drawing upon both biblical tradition and Jewish stories, Matthew portrays Jesus as reliving the Exodus experience of Israel and the persecutions of Moses. His rejection by his own people and his passion are foreshadowed by the troubled reaction of "all Jerusalem" to the question of the magi who are seeking the "newborn king of the Jews" (Mt 2:2–3), and by Herod's attempt to have him killed. The magi who do him homage prefigure the Gentiles who will accept the preaching of the gospel. The infancy narrative proclaims who Jesus is, the savior of his people from their sins (Mt 1:21), Emmanuel in whom "God is with us" (Mt 1:23), and the Son of God (Mt 2:15).

[†][1:1] **The Son of David, the son of Abraham**: two links of the genealogical chain are singled out. Although the later, David is placed first in order to emphasize that Jesus is the royal Messiah. The mention of Abraham may be due not only to his being the father of the nation Israel but to Matthew's interest in the universal scope of Jesus' mission; cf. Gn 22:18 ". . . in your descendants all the nations of the earth shall find blessing."

a. [1:1] Gn 5:1; 1 Chr 17:11; Gn 22:18.

[2b]Abraham became the father of Isaac, Isaac the father of Jacob, Jacob the father of Judah and his brothers.[c] [3]Judah became the father of Perez and Zerah, whose mother was Tamar.[d] Perez became the father of Hezron, Hezron the father of Ram, [4e]Ram the father of Amminadab. Amminadab became the father of Nahshon, Nahshon the father of Salmon, [5f]Salmon the father of Boaz, whose mother was Rahab. Boaz became the father of Obed, whose mother was Ruth. Obed became the father of Jesse, [6g]Jesse the father of David the king.

David became the father of Solomon, whose mother had been the wife of Uriah. [7‡h]Solomon became the father of Rehoboam, Rehoboam the father of Abijah, Abijah the father of Asaph. [8]Asaph became the father of Jehoshaphat, Jehoshaphat the father of Joram, Joram the father of Uzziah. [9]Uzziah became the father of Jotham, Jotham the father of Ahaz, Ahaz the father of Hezekiah. [10]Hezekiah became the father of Manasseh, Manasseh the father of Amos,[§] Amos the father of Josiah. [11]Josiah

---

[‡][1:7] The successor of Abijah was not Asaph but Asa (see 1 Chr 3:10). Some textual witnesses read the latter name; however, **Asaph** is better attested. Matthew may have deliberately introduced the psalmist Asaph into the genealogy (and in Mt 1:10 the prophet Amos) in order to show that Jesus is the fulfillment not only of the promises made to David (see 2 Sm 7) but of all the Old Testament.

[§][1:10] **Amos**: some textual witnesses read **Amon**, who was the actual successor of Manasseh (see 1 Chr 3:14).

b. [1:2–17] Lk 3:23–38.  c. [1:2] Gn 21:3; 25:26; 29:35; 1 Chr 2:1.  d. [1:3] Gn 38:29–30; Ru 4:18; 1 Chr 2:4–9.  e. [1:4] Ru 4:19–20; 1 Chr 2:10–11.  f. [1:5] Ru 4:21–22; 1 Chr 2:11–12.  g. [1:6] 2 Sm 12:24; 1 Chr 2:15; 3:5.  h. [1:7–11] 2 Kgs 25:1–21; 1 Chr 3:10–15.

became the father of Jechoniah and his brothers at the time of the Babylonian exile.

¹²ʲAfter the Babylonian exile, Jechoniah became the father of Shealtiel, Shealtiel the father of Zerubbabel, ¹³Zerubbabel the father of Abiud. Abiud became the father of Eliakim, Eliakim the father of Azor, ¹⁴Azor the father of Zadok. Zadok became the father of Achim, Achim the father of Eliud, ¹⁵Eliud the father of Eleazar. Eleazar became the father of Matthan, Matthan the father of Jacob, ¹⁶Jacob the father of Joseph, the husband of Mary. Of her was born Jesus who is called the Messiah.

¹⁷Thus the total number of generations from Abraham to David is fourteen generations; from David to the Babylonian exile, fourteen generations; from the Babylonian exile to the Messiah, fourteen generations.*

**The Birth of Jesus.**† ¹⁸Now this is how the birth of Jesus Christ came about. When his mother Mary was betrothed to Joseph,‡ but before they lived together, she was found with child through the holy Spirit. ¹⁹Joseph her husband, since he was a righteous man,§ yet unwilling to expose her to shame, decided to divorce her quietly. ²⁰Such was his intention when, behold, the angel of the Lord¶ appeared to him in a dream and said, "Joseph, son of David, do not be afraid to take Mary your wife into your home. For it is through the holy Spirit that this child has been conceived in her. ²¹She will bear a son and you are to name him Jesus,** because he will save his people from their sins." ²²All this took place to fulfill what the Lord had said through the prophet:

²³ ††ᵏ"Behold, the virgin shall be with child
      and bear a son,
   and they shall name him
      Emmanuel,"

which means "God is with us." ²⁴When Joseph awoke, he did as the angel of the Lord had commanded him and took his wife into his home. ²⁵He had no relations with her until she bore a son,‡‡ and he named him Jesus.ˡ

## CHAPTER 2

**The Visit of the Magi.**§§ ¹When Jesus was born in Bethlehem of Judea, in the days of King Herod,¶¶ behold, magi from the east arrived in Jerusalem, ²saying, "Where is the newborn king of the Jews? We saw his star*** at its rising and have come to do him homage."ᵐ ³When King Herod heard this, he was greatly troubled, and all Jerusalem with him. ⁴Assembling all the chief priests and the scribes of the people, he inquired of them where the Messiah was to be born.††† ⁵ⁿThey said

---

*[1:17] Matthew is concerned with fourteen generations, probably because fourteen is the numerical value of the Hebrew letters forming the name of David. In the second section of the genealogy (Mt 1:6b–11), three kings of Judah, Ahaziah, Joash, and Amaziah, have been omitted (see 1 Chr 3:11–12), so that there are fourteen generations in that section. Yet the third (Mt 1:12–16) apparently has only thirteen. Since Matthew here emphasizes that each section has fourteen, it is unlikely that the thirteen of the last was due to his oversight. Some scholars suggest that **Jesus who is called the Messiah** (Mt 1:16b) doubles the final member of the chain: **Jesus**, born within the family of David, opens up the new age as **Messiah**, so that in fact there are fourteen generations in the third section. This is perhaps too subtle, and the hypothesis of a slip not on the part of Matthew but of a later scribe seems likely. On **Messiah**, see note on Lk 2:11.

†[1:18–25] This first story of the infancy narrative spells out what is summarily indicated in Mt 1:16. The virginal conception of Jesus is the work of the Spirit of God. Joseph's decision to divorce Mary is overcome by the heavenly command that he take her into his home and accept the child as his own. The natural genealogical line is broken but the promises to David are fulfilled; through Joseph's adoption the child belongs to the family of David. Matthew sees the virginal conception as the fulfillment of Is 7:14.

‡[1:18] **Betrothed to Joseph**: betrothal was the first part of the marriage, constituting a man and woman as husband and wife. Subsequent infidelity was considered adultery. The betrothal was followed some months later by the husband's taking his wife into his home, at which time normal married life began.

§[1:19] **A righteous man**: as a devout observer of the Mosaic law, Joseph wished to break his union with someone whom he suspected of gross violation of the law. It is commonly said that the law required him to do so, but the texts usually given in support of that view, e.g., Dt 22:20–21 do not clearly pertain to Joseph's situation. **Unwilling to expose her to shame**: the penalty for proved adultery was death by stoning; cf. Dt 22:21–23.

¶[1:20] **The angel of the Lord**: in the Old Testament a common designation of God in communication with a human being. **In a dream**: set Mt 2:13, 19, 22. These dreams may be meant to recall the dreams of Joseph, son of Jacob

the patriarch (Gn 37:5–11, 19). A closer parallel is the dream of Amram, father of Moses, related by Josephus (*Antiquities* 2:212, 215–16).

**[1:21] **Jesus**: in first-century Judaism the Hebrew name Joshua (Greek *Iēsous*) meaning "Yahweh helps" was interpreted as "Yahweh saves."

††[1:23] **God is with us**: God's promise of deliverance to Judah in Isaiah's time is seen by Matthew as fulfilled in the birth of Jesus, in whom God is with his people. The name Emmanuel is alluded to at the end of the gospel where the risen Jesus assures his disciples of his continued presence, ". . . I am with you always, until the end of the age" (Mt 28:20).

‡‡[1:25] **Until she bore a son**: the evangelist is concerned to emphasize that Joseph was not responsible for the conception of Jesus. The Greek word translated "until" does not imply normal marital conduct after Jesus' birth, nor does it exclude it.

§§[2:1–12] The future rejection of Jesus by Israel and his acceptance by the Gentiles are retrojected into this scene of the narrative.

¶¶[2:1] **In the days of King Herod**: Herod reigned from 37 to 4 B.C. **Magi**: originally a designation of the Persian priestly caste, the word became used of those who were regarded as having more than human knowledge. Matthew's magi are astrologers.

***[2:2] **We saw his star**: it was a common ancient belief that a new star appeared at the time of a ruler's birth. Matthew also draws upon the Old Testament story of Balaam, who had prophesied that "A star shall advance from Jacob" (Nm 24:17), though there the star means not an astral phenomenon but the king himself.

†††[2:4] Herod's consultation with the chief priests and scribes has some similarity to a Jewish legend about the child Moses in which the "sacred scribes" warn Pharaoh about the imminent birth of one who will deliver Israel from Egypt and the king makes plans to destroy him.

---

k. [1:23] Is 7:14 LXX.   l. [1:25] Lk 2:7.   m. [2:2] Nm 24:17.   n. [2:5–6] Mi 5:1; 2 Sm 5:2.

---

i. [1:12–16] 1 Chr 3:16–19.   j. [1:20] 2:13, 19; Lk 1:35.

to him, "In Bethlehem of Judea, for thus it has been written through the prophet:

6 'And you, Bethlehem, land of Judah,
        are by no means least among the
            rulers of Judah;
    since from you shall come a ruler,
        who is to shepherd my people
            Israel.'"

[7]Then Herod called the magi secretly and ascertained from them the time of the star's appearance. [8]He sent them to Bethlehem and said, "Go and search diligently for the child. When you have found him, bring me word, that I too may go and do him homage." [9]After their audience with the king they set out. And behold, the star that they had seen at its rising preceded them, until it came and stopped over the place where the child was. [10]They were overjoyed at seeing the star, [11°]and on entering the house they saw the child with Mary his mother. They prostrated themselves and did him homage. Then they opened their treasures and offered him gifts of gold, frankincense, and myrrh. [12]And having been warned in a dream not to return to Herod, they departed for their country by another way.

**The Flight to Egypt.** [13†]When they had departed, behold, the angel of the Lord appeared to Joseph in a dream and said, "Rise, take the child and his mother, flee to Egypt,‡ and stay there until I tell you. Herod is going to search for the child to destroy him." [14]Joseph rose and took the child and his mother by night and departed for Egypt. [15§]He stayed there until the death of Herod, that what the Lord had said through the prophet[p] might be fulfilled, "Out of Egypt I called my son."

**The Massacre of the Infants.** [16]When Herod realized that he had been deceived by the magi, he became furious. He ordered the massacre of all the boys in Bethlehem and its vicinity two years old and under, in accordance with the time he had ascertained from the magi. [17]Then was fulfilled what had been said through Jeremiah the prophet:

18 [q]"A voice was heard in Ramah,
        sobbing and loud lamentation;
    Rachel weeping for her children,
        and she would not be consoled,
            since they were no more."

**The Return from Egypt.** [19]When Herod had died, behold, the angel of the Lord appeared in a dream to Joseph in Egypt [20]and said,[r] "Rise, take the child and his mother and go to the land of Israel, for those who sought the child's life are dead."[**] [21]He rose, took the child and his mother, and went to the land of Israel. [22]But when he heard that Archelaus was ruling over Judea in place of his father Herod,[††] he was afraid to go back there. And because he had been warned in a dream, he departed for the region of Galilee. [23‡‡s]He went and dwelt in a town called Nazareth, so that what had been spoken through the prophets might be fulfilled, "He shall be called a Nazorean."

## II. THE PROCLAMATION OF THE KINGDOM

### CHAPTER 3

**The Preaching of John the Baptist.**[§§t] [1]In those days John the Baptist appeared, preaching in the desert of Judea[¶¶] [2][and] saying, "Repent,[***] for

---

¶[2:18] Jer 31:15 portrays Rachel, wife of the patriarch Jacob, weeping for her children taken into exile at the time of the Assyrian invasion of the northern kingdom (722–21 B.C.). Bethlehem was traditionally identified with Ephrath, the place near which Rachel was buried (see Gn 35:19; 48:7), and the mourning of Rachel is here applied to her lost children of a later age. **Ramah**: about six miles north of Jerusalem. The lamentation of Rachel is so great as to be heard at a far distance.

**[2:20] For those who sought the child's life are dead**: Moses, who had fled from Egypt because the Pharaoh sought to kill him (see Ex 2:15), was told to return there, "for all the men who sought your life are dead" (Ex 4:19).

††[2:22] With the agreement of the emperor Augustus, Archelaus received half of his father's kingdom, including Judea, after Herod's death. He had the title "ethnarch" (i.e., "ruler of a nation") and reigned from 4 B.C. to A.D. 6.

‡‡[2:23] **Nazareth . . . he shall be called a Nazorean**: the tradition of Jesus' residence in Nazareth was firmly established, and Matthew sees it as being in accordance with the forean-nounced plan of God. The town of Nazareth is not mentioned in the Old Testament, and no such prophecy can be found there. The vague expression "through the prophets" may be due to Matthew's seeing a connection between Nazareth and certain texts in which there are words with a remote similarity to the name of that town. Some such Old Testament texts are Is 11:1 where the Davidic king of the future is called "a bud" (nēṣer) that shall blossom from the roots of Jesse, and Jgs 13:5, 7 where Samson, the future deliverer of Israel from the Philistines, is called one who shall be consecrated (a nāzîr) to God.

§§[3:1–12] Here Matthew takes up the order of Jesus' ministry found in the gospel of Mark, beginning with the preparatory preaching of John the Baptist.

¶¶[3:1] Unlike Luke, Matthew says nothing of the Baptist's origins and does not make him a relative of Jesus. **The desert of Judea**: the barren region west of the Dead Sea extending up the Jordan valley.

***[3:2] **Repent**: the Baptist calls for a change of heart and conduct, a turning of one's life from rebellion to obedience towards God. The **kingdom of heaven is at hand**: "heaven"

---

*[2:11] Cf. Ps 72:10, 15; Is 60:6. These Old Testament texts led to the interpretation of the magi as kings.

†[2:13–23] Biblical and nonbiblical traditions about Moses are here applied to the child Jesus, though the dominant Old Testament type is not Moses but Israel (Mt 2:15).

‡[2:13] **Flee to Egypt**: Egypt was a traditional place of refuge for those fleeing from danger in Palestine (see 1 Kgs 11:40; Jer 26:21), but the main reason why the child is to be taken to Egypt is that he may relive the Exodus experience of Israel.

§[2:15] The fulfillment citation is taken from Hos 11:1. Israel, God's son, was called out of Egypt at the time of the Exodus; Jesus, the Son of God, will similarly be called out of that land in a new exodus. The father-son relationship between God and the nation is set in a higher key. Here the son is not a group adopted as "son of God," but the child who, as conceived by the holy Spirit, stands in unique relation to God. He is son of David and of Abraham, of Mary and of Joseph, but, above all, of God.

---

o. [2:11] Ps 72:10–11, 15; Is 60:6.  p. [2:15] Hos 11:1.

q. [2:18] Jer 31:15.  r. [2:20] Ex 4:19.  s. [2:23] 13:54; Mk 1:9; Lk 2:39; 4:34; Jn 19:19.  t. [3:1–12] Mk 1:2–8; Lk 3:2–17.

the kingdom of heaven is at hand!"ᵘ ³ᵗIt was of him that the prophet Isaiahᵛ had spoken when he said:

"A voice of one crying out in the desert,
    'Prepare the way of the Lord,
        make straight his paths.'"

⁴ᵗʷJohn wore clothing made of camel's hair and had a leather belt around his waist. His food was locusts and wild honey. ⁵At that time Jerusalem, all Judea, and the whole region around the Jordan were going out to him ⁶and were being baptized by him in the Jordan River as they acknowledged their sins.‡

⁷When he saw many of the Pharisees and Sadducees§ coming to his baptism, he said to them, "You brood of vipers! Who warned you to flee from the coming wrath?ˣ ⁸Produce good fruit as evidence of your repentance. ⁹And do not presume to say to yourselves, 'We have Abraham as our father.' For I tell you, God can raise up children to Abraham from these stones.ʸ ¹⁰Even now the ax lies at the root of the trees. Therefore every tree that does not bear good fruit will be cut down and thrown into the fire. ¹¹ᶻI am baptizing you with water, for repentance, but the one who is coming after me is mightier than I. I am not worthy to carry his sandals. He will baptize you with the holy Spirit and fire.¶

¹²**ᵃHis winnowing fan is in his hand. He will clear his threshing floor and gather his wheat into his barn, but the chaff he will burn with unquenchable fire."

**The Baptism of Jesus.**†† ¹³ᵇThen Jesus came from Galilee to John at the Jordan to be baptized by him. ¹⁴‡‡John tried to prevent him, saying, "I need to be baptized by you, and yet you are coming to me?" ¹⁵Jesus said to him in reply, "Allow it now, for thus it is fitting for us to fulfill all righteousness." Then he allowed him. ¹⁶§§ᶜAfter Jesus was baptized, he came up from the water and behold, the heavens were opened [for him], and he saw the Spirit of God descending like a dove [and] coming upon him. ¹⁷And a voice came from the heavens, saying, "This is my beloved Son,¶¶ with whom I am well pleased."ᵈ

## CHAPTER 4

**The Temptation of Jesus.** ¹***ᵉThen Jesus was led by the Spirit into the desert to be tempted by the devil. ²ᶠHe fasted for forty days and forty nights,†††

---

(lit., "the heavens") is a substitute for the name "God" that was avoided by devout Jews of the time out of reverence. The expression "the kingdom of heaven" occurs only in the gospel of Matthew. It means the effective rule of God over his people. In its fullness it includes not only human obedience to God's word, but the triumph of God over physical evils, supremely over death. In the expectation found in Jewish apocalyptic, the kingdom was to be ushered in by a judgment in which sinners would be condemned and perish, an expectation shared by the Baptist. This was modified in Christian understanding where the kingdom was seen as being established in stages, culminating with the parousia of Jesus.

\* [3:3] See note on Jn 1:23.
† [3:4] The clothing of John recalls the austere dress of the prophet Elijah (2 Kgs 1:8). The expectation of the return of Elijah from heaven to prepare Israel for the final manifestation of God's kingdom was widespread, and according to Matthew this expectation was fulfilled in the Baptist's ministry (Mt 11:14; 17:11–13).
‡ [3:6] Ritual washing was practiced by various groups in Palestine between 150 B.C. and A.D. 250. John's baptism may have been related to the purificatory washings of the Essenes at Qumran.
§ [3:7] **Pharisees and Sadducees:** the former were marked by devotion to the law, written and oral, and the scribes, experts in the law, belonged predominantly to this group. The Sadducees were the priestly aristocratic party, centered in Jerusalem. They accepted as scripture only the first five books of the Old Testament, followed only the letter of the law, rejected the oral legal traditions, and were opposed to teachings not found in the Pentateuch, such as the resurrection of the dead. Matthew links both of these groups together as enemies of Jesus (Mt 16:1, 6, 11, 12; cf. Mk 8:11–13, 15). The threatening words that follow are addressed to them rather than to "the crowds" as in Lk 3:7. **The coming wrath:** the judgment that will bring about the destruction of unrepentant sinners.
¶ [3:11] **Baptize you with the holy Spirit and fire:** the water baptism of John will be followed by an "immersion" of the repentant in the cleansing power of the Spirit of God,

and of the unrepentant in the destroying power of God's judgment. However, some see **the holy Spirit and fire** as synonymous, and the effect of this "baptism" as either purification or destruction. See note on Lk 3:16.
\*\* [3:12] The discrimination between the good and the bad is compared to the procedure by which a farmer separates wheat and chaff. The **winnowing fan** was a forklike shovel with which the threshed wheat was thrown into the air. The kernels fell to the ground; the light chaff, blown off by the wind, was gathered and burned up.
†† [3:13–17] The baptism of Jesus is the occasion on which he is equipped for his ministry by the holy Spirit and proclaimed to be the Son of God.
‡‡ [3:14–15] This dialogue, peculiar to Matthew, reveals John's awareness of Jesus' superiority to him as the mightier one who is coming and who will baptize with the holy Spirit (Mt 3:11). His reluctance to admit Jesus among the sinners whom he is baptizing with water is overcome by Jesus' response. **To fulfill all righteousness:** in this gospel to **fulfill** usually refers to fulfillment of prophecy, and **righteousness** to moral conduct in conformity with God's will. Here, however, as in Mt 5:6; 6:33, **righteousness** seems to mean the saving activity of God. **To fulfill all righteousness** is to submit to the plan of God for the salvation of the human race. This involves Jesus' identification with sinners; hence the propriety of his accepting John's baptism.
§§ [3:16] **The Spirit . . . coming upon him:** cf. Is 42:1.
¶¶ [3:17] **This is my beloved Son:** the Marcan address to Jesus (Mk 1:11) is changed into a proclamation. The Father's voice speaks in terms that reflect Is 42:1; Ps 2:7; Gn 22:2.
\*\*\* [4:1–11] Jesus, proclaimed Son of God at his baptism, is subjected to a triple temptation. Obedience to the Father is a characteristic of true sonship, and Jesus is tempted by the devil to rebel against God, overtly in the third case, more subtly in the first two. Each refusal of Jesus is expressed in language taken from the Book of Deuteronomy (Dt 8:3; 6:13, 16). The testings of Jesus resemble those of Israel during the wandering in the desert and later in Canaan, and the victory of Jesus, the true Israel and the true Son, contrasts with the failure of the ancient and disobedient "son," the old Israel. In the temptation account Matthew is almost identical with Luke; both seem to have drawn upon the same source.
††† [4:2] **Forty days and forty nights:** the same time as that during which Moses remained on Sinai (Ex 24:18). The time reference, however, seems primarily intended to recall the

u. [3:2] 4:17; 10:7.    v. [3:3] Is 40:3.    w. [3:4] 11:7–8; 2 Kgs 1:8; Zec 13:4.    x. [3:7] 12:34; 23:33; Is 59:5.    y. [3:9] Jn 8:33, 39; Rom 9:7–8; Gal 4:21–31.    z. [3:11] Jn 1:26–27, 33; Acts 1:5.

a. [3:12] 13:30; Is 41:16; Jer 15:7.    b. [3:13–17] Mk 1:9–11; Lk 3:21–22; Jn 1:31–34.    c. [3:16] Is 42:1.    d. [3:17] 12:18; 17:5; Gn 22:2; Ps 2:7; Is 42:1.    e. [4:1–11] Mk 1:12–13; Lk 4:1–13.    f. [4:2] Ex 24:18; Dt 8:2.

and afterwards he was hungry. ³The tempter approached and said to him, "If you are the Son of God, command that these stones become loaves of bread." ⁴*He said in reply, "It is written:ᵍ

'One does not live by bread alone,
　　but by every word that comes forth
　　　　from the mouth of God.'"

⁵†Then the devil took him to the holy city, and made him stand on the parapet of the temple, ⁶and said to him, "If you are the Son of God, throw yourself down. For it is written:

'He will command his angels concerning
　　you'
and 'with their hands they will
　　support you,
lest you dash your foot against a stone.'"ʰ

⁷Jesus answered him, "Again it is written, 'You shall not put the Lord, your God, to the test.'"ⁱ ⁸Then the devil took him up to a very high mountain, and showed him all the kingdoms of the world in their magnificence, ⁹and he said to him, "All these I shall give to you, if you will prostrate yourself and worship me."‡ ¹⁰At this, Jesus said to him, "Get away, Satan! It is written:

'The Lord, your God, shall you worship
　　and him alone shall you serve.'"ʲ

¹¹Then the devil left him and, behold, angels came and ministered to him.

**The Beginning of the Galilean Ministry.**§ ¹²ᵏWhen he heard that John had been arrested, he withdrew to Galilee. ¹³He left Nazareth and went to live in Capernaum by the sea, in the region of Zebulun and Naphtali,ˡ ¹⁴that what had been said through Isaiah the prophet might be fulfilled:

¹⁵ "Land of Zebulun and land of Naphtali,ᵐ
　　the way to the sea, beyond the
　　　　Jordan,
　　　　Galilee of the Gentiles,
¹⁶ the people who sit in darkness
　　have seen a great light,
　　on those dwelling in a land overshadowed
　　　　by death
　　　　light has arisen."ⁿ

¹⁷¶From that time on, Jesus began to preach and say,ᵒ "Repent, for the kingdom of heaven is at hand."

**The Call of the First Disciples.**** ¹⁸ᵖAs he was walking by the Sea of Galilee, he saw two brothers, Simon who is called Peter, and his brother Andrew, casting a net into the sea; they were fishermen. ¹⁹He said to them, "Come after me, and I will make you fishers of men." ²⁰††At once they left their nets and followed him. ²¹He walked along from there and saw two other brothers, James, the son of Zebedee, and his brother John. They were in a boat, with their father Zebedee, mending their nets. He called them, ²²and immediately they left their boat and their father and followed him.

**Ministering to a Great Multitude.**‡‡ ²³He went around all of Galilee, teaching in their synagogues,§§ proclaiming the gospel of the kingdom, and curing every disease and illness among the people.�q ²⁴¶¶His fame spread to all of Syria, and they brought to him all who were sick with various diseases and racked with pain, those who were possessed, lunatics, and paralytics, and he cured them. ²⁵ʳAnd great crowds from Galilee, the Decapolis,*** Jerusalem, and Judea, and from beyond the Jordan followed him.

---

¶[4:17] At the beginning of his preaching Jesus takes up the words of John the Baptist (Mt 3:2) although with a different meaning; in his ministry the kingdom of heaven has already begun to be present (Mt 12:28).

**[4:18–22] The call of the first disciples promises them a share in Jesus' work and entails abandonment of family and former way of life. Three of the four, Simon, James, and John, are distinguished among the disciples by a closer relation with Jesus (Mt 17:1; 26:37).

††[4:20] Here and in Mt 4:22, as in Mark (Mk 1:16–20) and unlike the Lucan account (Lk 5:1–11), the disciples' response is motivated only by Jesus' invitation, an element that emphasizes his mysterious power.

‡‡[4:23–25] This summary of Jesus' ministry concludes the narrative part of the first book of Matthew's gospel (Mt 3–4). The activities of his ministry are teaching, proclaiming the gospel, and healing; cf. Mt 9:35.

§§[4:23] **Their synagogues**: Matthew usually designates the Jewish synagogues as **their synagogue(s)** (Mt 9:35; 10:17; 12:9; 13:54) or, in address to Jews, **your synagogues** (Mt 23:34), an indication that he wrote after the break between church and synagogue.

¶¶[4:24] **Syria**: the Roman province to which Palestine belonged.

***[4:25] **The Decapolis**: a federation of Greek cities in Palestine, originally ten in number, all but one east of the Jordan.

---

forty years during which Israel was tempted in the desert (Dt 8:2).

*[4:4] Cf. Dt 8:3. Jesus refuses to use his power for his own benefit and accepts whatever God wills.

†[4:5–7] The devil supports his proposal by an appeal to the scriptures, Ps 91:11a, 12. Unlike Israel (Dt 6:16), Jesus refuses to "test" God by demanding from him an extraordinary show of power.

‡[4:9] The worship of Satan to which Jesus is tempted is probably intended to recall Israel's worship of false gods. His refusal is expressed in the words of Dt 6:13.

§[4:12–17] Isaiah's prophecy of the light rising upon Zebulun and Naphtali (Is 8:22–9:1) is fulfilled in Jesus' residence at Capernaum. The territory of these two tribes was the first to be devastated (733–32 B.C.) at the time of the Assyrian invasion. In order to accommodate Jesus' move to Capernaum to the prophecy, Matthew speaks of that town as being "in the region of Zebulun and Naphtali" (Mt 4:13), whereas it was only in the territory of the latter, and he understands the sea of the prophecy, the Mediterranean, as the sea of Galilee.

---

g. [4:4] Dt 8:3.　h. [4:6] Ps 91:11–12.　i. [4:7] Dt 6:16.　j. [4:10] 16:23; Dt 6:13.　k. [4:12–13] Mk 1:14–15; Lk 4:14, 31.　l. [4:13] Jn 2:12.

m. [4:15–16] Is 8:23 LXX; 9:1.　n. [4:16] Lk 1:79.　o. [4:17] 3:2.　p. [4:18–22] Mk 1:16–20; Lk 5:1–11.　q. [4:23] 9:35; Mk 1:39; Lk 4:15, 44.　r. [4:25] Mk 3:7–8; Lk 6:17–19.

## CHAPTER 5

**The Sermon on the Mount.** [1]*When he saw the crowds,[†] he went up the mountain, and after he had sat down, his disciples came to him. ²He began to teach them, saying:

### The Beatitudes[‡]

³ "Blessed are the poor in spirit,[§]
   for theirs is the kingdom of heaven.[s]

⁴ 'Blessed are they who mourn,[t]
   for they will be comforted.

⁵ "Blessed are the meek,[u]
   for they will inherit the land.

⁶ Blessed are they who hunger and thirst
      for righteousness,[††]
   for they will be satisfied.

⁷ Blessed are the merciful,
   for they will be shown mercy.[v]

⁸ ‡‡Blessed are the clean of heart,[w]
   for they will see God.

⁹ Blessed are the peacemakers,
   for they will be called children of
      God.

¹⁰ Blessed are they who are persecuted for
      the sake of righteousness,[§§]
   for theirs is the kingdom of heaven.[x]

¹¹Blessed are you when they insult you and persecute you and utter every kind of evil against you [falsely] because of me.[y] ¹²¶¶Rejoice and be glad, for your reward will be great in heaven.[z] Thus they persecuted the prophets who were before you.

**The Similes of Salt and Light.**[***] ¹³ᵃ"You are the salt of the earth. But if salt loses its taste, with what can it be seasoned? It is no longer good for anything but to be thrown out and trampled underfoot.[†††] ¹⁴You are the light of the world. A city set on a mountain cannot be hidden.[b] ¹⁵Nor do they light a lamp and then put it under a bushel basket; it is set on a lampstand, where it gives light to all in the house.[c] ¹⁶Just so, your light must shine before others, that they may see your good deeds and glorify your heavenly Father.[d]

**Teaching About the Law.** ¹⁷‡‡‡"Do not think that I have come to abolish the law or the prophets. I have come not to abolish but to fulfill. ¹⁸Amen, I say to you, until heaven and earth pass away, not the smallest letter or the smallest part of a letter will pass from the law, until all things have taken place.[e] ¹⁹Therefore, whoever breaks one of the least of these commandments and teaches others to do so will be called least in the kingdom of heaven. But whoever obeys and teaches these commandments will be called greatest in

---

* [5:1–7:29] The first of the five discourses that are a central part of the structure of this gospel. It is the discourse section of the first book and contains sayings of Jesus derived from Q and from M. The Lucan parallel is in that gospel's "Sermon on the Plain" (Lk 6:20–49), although some of the sayings in Matthew's "Sermon on the Mount" have their parallels in other parts of Luke. The careful topical arrangement of the sermon is probably not due only to Matthew's editing; he seems to have had a structured discourse of Jesus as one of his sources. The form of that source may have been as follows: four beatitudes (Mt 5:3–4, 6, 11–12), a section on the new righteousness with illustrations (Mt 5:17, 20–24, 27–28, 33–48), a section on good works (Mt 6:1–6, 16–18), and three warnings (Mt 7:1–2, 15–21, 24–27).

† [5:1–2] Unlike Luke's sermon, this is addressed not only to the disciples but to the crowds (see Mt 7:28).

‡ [5:3–12] The form **Blessed are (is)** occurs frequently in the Old Testament in the Wisdom literature and in the psalms. Although modified by Matthew, the first, second, fourth, and ninth beatitudes have Lucan parallels (Mt 5:3 // Lk 6:20; Mt 5:4 // Lk 6:21b; Mt 5:6 // Lk 6:21a; Mt 5:11–12 // Lk 5:22–23). The others were added by the evangelist and are probably his own composition. A few manuscripts, Western and Alexandrian, and many versions and patristic quotations give the second and third beatitudes in inverted order.

§ [5:3] **The poor in spirit:** in the Old Testament, the poor (*'anāwîm*) are those who are without material possessions and whose confidence is in God (see Is 61:1; Zep 2:3; in the NAB the word is translated **lowly** and **humble**, respectively, in those texts). Matthew added **in spirit** in order either to indicate that only the devout poor were meant or to extend the beatitude to all, of whatever social rank, who recognized their complete dependence on God. The same phrase **poor in spirit** is found in the Qumran literature (1QM 14:7).

¶ [5:4] Cf. Is 61:2, "(The Lord has sent me) . . . to comfort all who mourn." **They will be comforted:** here the passive is a "theological passive" equivalent to the active "God will comfort them"; so also in Mt 5:6, 7.

** [5:5] Cf. Ps 37:11, ". . . the meek shall possess the land." In the psalm "the land" means the land of Palestine; here it means the kingdom.

†† [5:6] **For righteousness:** a Matthean addition. For the meaning of **righteousness** here, see note on Mt 3:14–15.

‡‡ [5:8] Cf. Ps 24:4. Only one "whose heart is clean" can take part in the temple worship. To be with God in the temple is described in Ps 42:3 as "beholding his face," but here the promise is that the **clean of heart** is that they will **see God** not in the temple but in the coming kingdom.

§§ [5:10] **Righteousness** here, as usually in Matthew, means conduct in conformity with God's will.

¶¶ [5:12] **The prophets who were before you:** the disciples of Jesus stand in the line of the persecuted prophets of Israel. Some would see the expression as indicating also that Matthew considered all Christian disciples as prophets.

*** [5:13–16] By their deeds the disciples are to influence the world for good. They can no more escape notice than **a city set on a mountain.** If they fail in good works, they are as useless as flavorless salt or as a lamp whose light is concealed.

††† [5:13] The unusual supposition of salt losing its flavor has led some to suppose that the saying refers to the salt of the Dead Sea that, because chemically impure, could lose its taste.

‡‡‡ [5:17–20] This statement of Jesus' position concerning the Mosaic law is composed of traditional material from Matthew's sermon documentation (see note on Mt 5:1–7:29), other Q material (cf. Mt 18; Lk 16:17), and the evangelist's own editorial touches. **To fulfill** the law appears at first to mean a literal enforcement of the law in the least detail: **until heaven and earth pass away** nothing of the law will pass (Mt 5:18). Yet the "passing away" of heaven and earth is not necessarily the end of the world understood, as in much apocalyptic literature, as the dissolution of the existing universe. The "turning of the ages" comes with the apocalyptic event of Jesus' death and resurrection, and those to whom this gospel is addressed are living in the new and final age, prophesied by Isaiah as the time of "new heavens and a new earth" (Is 65:17; 66:22). Meanwhile, during Jesus' ministry when the kingdom is already breaking in, his mission remains within the framework of the law, though with significant anticipation of the age to come, as the following antitheses (Mt 5:21–48) show.

x. [5:10] 1 Pt 2:20; 3:14; 4:14.   y. [5:11] 10:22; Acts 5:41.   z. [5:12] 2 Chr 36:16; Heb 11:32–38; Jas 5:10.   a. [5:13] Mk 9:50; Lk 14:34–35.   b. [5:14] Jn 8:12.   c. [5:15] Mk 4:21; Lk 8:16; 11:33.   d. [5:16] Jn 3:21.   e. [5:18] Lk 16:17.

s. [5:3–12] Lk 6:20–23.   t. [5:4] Is 61:2–3; Rev 21:4.   u. [5:5] Ps 37:11.   v. [5:7] 18:33; Jas 2:13.   w. [5:8] Ps 24:4–5; 73:1.

the kingdom of heaven.* 20I tell you, unless your righteousness surpasses that of the scribes and Pharisees, you will not enter into the kingdom of heaven.

**Teaching About Anger.**† 21"You have heard that it was said to your ancestors,f 'You shall not kill; and whoever kills will be liable to judgment.'‡ 22But I say to you, whoever is angry⸋ with his brother will be liable to judgment,g and whoever says to his brother, 'Raqa,' will be answerable to the Sanhedrin, and whoever says, 'You fool,' will be liable to fiery Gehenna. 23Therefore, if you bring your gift to the altar, and there recall that your brother has anything against you,h 24leave your gift there at the altar, go first and be reconciled with your brother, and then come and offer your gift. 25Settle with your opponent quickly while on the way to court with him.i Otherwise your opponent will hand you over to the judge, and the judge will hand you over to the guard, and you will be thrown into prison. 26Amen, I say to you, you will not be released until you have paid the last penny.

**Teaching About Adultery.** 27**"You have heard that it was said,j 'You shall not commit adultery.' 28But I say to you, everyone who looks at a woman with lust has already committed adultery with her in his heart. 29††If your right eye causes you to sin, tear it out and throw it away.k It is better for you to lose one of your members than to have your whole body thrown into Gehenna. 30And if your right hand causes you to sin, cut it off and throw it away. It is better for you to lose one of your members than to have your whole body go into Gehenna.

**Teaching About Divorce.** 31‡‡"It was also said, 'Whoever divorces his wife must give her a bill of divorce.'l 32But I say to you, whoever divorces his wife (unless the marriage is unlawful) causes her to commit adultery, and whoever marries a divorced woman commits adultery.m

**Teaching About Oaths.** 33§§n"Again you have heard that it was said to your ancestors, 'Do not take a false oath, but make good to the Lord all that you vow.' 34oBut I say to you, do not swear at all;⸋⸋ not by heaven, for it is God's throne; 35nor by the earth, for it is his footstool; nor by Jerusalem, for it is the city of the great King. 36Do not swear by your head, for you cannot make a single hair white or black. 37***Let your 'Yes' mean 'Yes,' and your 'No' mean 'No.' Anything more is from the evil one.

**Teaching About Retaliation.** 38†††"You have heard that it was said,p 'An eye for an eye and a tooth

---

*[5:19] Probably **these commandments** means those of the Mosaic law. But this is an interim ethic "until heaven and earth pass away."

†[5:21–48] Six examples of the conduct demanded of the Christian disciple. Each deals with a commandment of the law, introduced by **You have heard that it was said to your ancestors** or an equivalent formula, followed by Jesus' teaching in respect to that commandment, **But I say to you;** thus their designation as "antitheses." Three of them accept the Mosaic law but extend or deepen it (Mt 5:21–22; 27–28; 43–44); three reject it as a standard of conduct for the disciples (Mt 5:31–32; 33–37; 38–39).

‡[5:21] Cf. Ex 20:13; Dt 5:17. The second part of the verse is not an exact quotation from the Old Testament, but cf. Ex 21:12.

§[5:22–26] Reconciliation with an offended brother is urged in the admonition of Mt 5:23–24 and the parable of Mt 5:25–26 (// Lk 12:58–59). The severity of the judge in the parable is a warning of the fate of unrepentant sinners in the coming judgment by God.

⸋[5:22] Anger is the motive behind murder, as the insulting epithets are steps that may lead to it. They, as well as the deed, are all forbidden. **Raqa:** an Aramaic word rêqā' or rēqā probably meaning "imbecile," "blockhead," a term of abuse. The ascending order of punishment, **judgment** (by a local council?), trial before the **Sanhedrin**, condemnation to **Gehenna**, points to a higher degree of seriousness in each of the offenses. **Sanhedrin:** the highest judicial body of Judaism. **Gehenna:** in Hebrew gê-hinnōm, "Valley of Hinnom," or gê ben-hinnōm, "Valley of the son of Hinnom," southwest of Jerusalem, the center of an idolatrous cult during the monarchy in which children were offered in sacrifice (see 2 Kgs 23:10; Jer 7:31). In Jos 18:16 (Septuagint, Codex Vaticanus) the Hebrew is transliterated into Greek as gaienna, which appears in the New Testament as geenna. The concept of punishment of sinners by fire either after death or after the final judgment is found in Jewish apocalyptic literature (e.g., Enoch 90:26) but the name geenna is first given to the place of punishment in the New Testament.

**[5:27] See Ex 20:14; Dt 5:18.

††[5:29–30] No sacrifice is too great to avoid total destruction in **Gehenna.**

‡‡[5:31–32] See Dt 24:1–5. The Old Testament commandment that a bill of divorce be given to the woman assumes the legitimacy of divorce itself. It is this that Jesus denies. **(Unless the marriage is unlawful):** this "exceptive clause," as it is often called, occurs also in Mt 19:9, where the Greek is slightly different. There are other sayings of Jesus about divorce that prohibit it absolutely (see Mk 10:11–12; Lk 16:18; cf. 1 Cor 7:10, 11b), and most scholars agree that they represent the stand of Jesus. Matthew's "exceptive clauses" are understood by some as a modification of the absolute prohibition. It seems, however, that the unlawfulness that Matthew gives as a reason why a marriage must be broken refers to a situation peculiar to his community: the violation of Mosaic law forbidding marriage between persons of certain blood and/or legal relationship (Lv 18:6–18). Marriages of that sort were regarded as incest (porneia), but some rabbis allowed Gentile converts to Judaism who had contracted such marriages to remain in them. Matthew's "exceptive clause" is against such permissiveness for Gentile converts to Christianity; cf. the similar prohibition of porneia in Acts 15:20, 29. In this interpretation, the clause constitutes no exception to the absolute prohibition of divorce when the marriage is lawful.

§§[5:33] This is not an exact quotation of any Old Testament text, but see Ex 20:7; Dt 5:11; Lv 19:12. The purpose of an oath was to guarantee truthfulness by one's calling on God as witness.

⸋⸋[5:34–36] The use of these oath formularies that avoid the divine name is in fact equivalent to swearing by it, for all the things sworn by are related to God.

***[5:37] **Let your 'Yes' mean 'Yes,' and your 'No' mean 'No':** literally, "let your speech be 'Yes, yes,' 'No, no.'" Some have understood this as a milder form of oath, permitted by Jesus. In view of Mt 5:34, "Do not swear at all," that is unlikely. **From the evil one:** i.e., from the devil. Oath-taking presupposes a sinful weakness of the human race, namely, the tendency to lie. Jesus demands of his disciples a truthfulness that makes oaths unnecessary.

†††[5:38–42] See Lv 24:20. The Old Testament commandment was meant to moderate vengeance; the punishment

---

f. [5:21] Ex 20:13; Dt 5:17.　g. [5:22] Jas 1:19–20.　h. [5:23] Mk 11:25.　i. [5:25–26] 18:34–35; Lk 12:58–59.　j. [5:27] Ex 20:14; Dt 5:18.

k. [5:29–30] 18:8–9; Mk 9:43–47.　l. [5:31] 19:3–9; Dt 24:1.　m. [5:32] Lk 16:18; 1 Cor 7:10–11.　n. [5:33] Lv 19:12; Nm 30:3.　o. [5:34–37] Ps 48:3; Sir 23:9; Is 66:1; Jas 5:12.　p. [5:38] Ex 21:24; Lv 24:19–20.

for a tooth.' ³⁹�q But I say to you, offer no resistance to one who is evil. When someone strikes you on [your] right cheek, turn the other one to him as well. ⁴⁰If anyone wants to go to law with you over your tunic, hand him your cloak as well. ⁴¹Should anyone press you into service for one mile,* go with him for two miles.ʳ ⁴²Give to the one who asks of you, and do not turn your back on one who wants to borrow.ˢ

**Love of Enemies.**† ⁴³ᵗ"You have heard that it was said, 'You shall love your neighbor and hate your enemy.'ᵘ ⁴⁴But I say to you, love your enemies, and pray for those who persecute you, ⁴⁵that you may be children of your heavenly Father, for he makes his sun rise on the bad and the good, and causes rain to fall on the just and the unjust. ⁴⁶For if you love those who love you, what recompense will you have? Do not the tax collectors‡ do the same? ⁴⁷And if you greet your brothers only, what is unusual about that? Do not the pagans do the same?§ ⁴⁸So be perfect,¶ just as your heavenly Father is perfect.ᵛ

## CHAPTER 6

**Teaching About Almsgiving.**** ¹"[But] take care not to perform righteous deeds in order that people may see them;ʷ otherwise, you will have no recompense from your heavenly Father. ²When you give alms, do not blow a trumpet

before you, as the hypocrites†† do in the synagogues and in the streets to win the praise of others. Amen, I say to you, they have received their reward.ˣ ³But when you give alms, do not let your left hand know what your right is doing, ⁴so that your almsgiving may be secret. And your Father who sees in secret will repay you.

**Teaching About Prayer.** ⁵"When you pray, do not be like the hypocrites, who love to stand and pray in the synagogues and on street corners so that others may see them. Amen, I say to you, they have received their reward. ⁶But when you pray, go to your inner room, close the door, and pray to your Father in secret. And your Father who sees in secret will repay you. ⁷‡‡In praying, do not babble like the pagans, who think that they will be heard because of their many words.§§ ⁸Do not be like them. Your Father knows what you need before you ask him.

**The Lord's Prayer.** ⁹¶¶"This is how you are to pray:ʸ

> Our Father in heaven,***
>     hallowed be your name,
> 10     your kingdom come,†††
>     your will be done,
>        on earth as in heaven.ᶻ
> 11     ‡‡‡ᵃGive us today our daily bread;

---

should not exceed the injury done. Jesus forbids even this proportionate retaliation. Of the five examples that follow, only the first deals directly with retaliation for evil; the others speak of liberality.

* [5:41] Roman garrisons in Palestine had the right to requisition the property and services of the native population.

† [5:43–48] See Lv 19:18. There is no Old Testament commandment demanding hatred of one's enemy, but the "neighbor" of the love commandment was understood as one's fellow countryman. Both in the Old Testament (Ps 139:19–22) and at Qumran (1QS 9:21) hatred of evil persons is assumed to be right. Jesus extends the love commandment to the enemy and the persecutor. His disciples, as children of God, must imitate the example of their Father, who grants his gifts of sun and rain to both the good and the bad.

‡ [5:46] **Tax collectors:** Jews who were engaged in the collection of indirect taxes such as tolls and customs. See note on Mk 2:14.

§ [5:47] Jesus' disciples must not be content with merely usual standards of conduct; see Mt 5:20 where the verb "surpass" (Greek *perisseuō*) is cognate with the **unusual** (*perisson*) of this verse.

¶ [5:48] **Perfect:** in the gospels this word occurs only in Matthew, here and in Mt 19:21. The Lucan parallel (Lk 6:36) demands that the disciples be **merciful.**

** [6:1–18] The sermon continues with a warning against doing good in order to be seen and gives three examples, almsgiving (Mt 6:2–4), prayer (Mt 6:5–15), and fasting (Mt 6:16–18). In each, the conduct of the hypocrites (Mt 6:2) is contrasted with that demanded of the disciples. The sayings about reward found here and elsewhere (Mt 5:12, 46; 10:41–42) show that this is a genuine element of Christian moral exhortation. Possibly to underline the difference between the Christian idea of reward and that of the hypocrites, the evangelist uses two different Greek verbs to express the rewarding of the disciples and that of the hypocrites; in the latter case it is the verb *apechō*, a commercial term for giving a receipt for what has been paid in full (Mt 6:2, 5, 16).

†† [6:2] **The hypocrites:** the scribes and Pharisees, see Mt 23:13, 15, 23, 25, 27, 29. The designation reflects an attitude resulting not only from the controversies at the time of Jesus' ministry but from the opposition between Pharisaic Judaism and the church of Matthew. **They have received their reward:** they desire praise and have received what they were looking for.

‡‡ [6:7–15] Matthew inserts into his basic traditional material an expansion of the material on prayer that includes the model prayer, the "Our Father." That prayer is found in Lk 11:2–4 in a different context and in a different form.

§§ [6:7] The example of what Christian prayer should be like contrasts it now not with the prayer of the hypocrites but with that of **the pagans.** Their babbling probably means their reciting a long list of divine names, hoping that one of them will force a response from the deity.

¶¶ [6:9–13] Matthew's form of the "Our Father" follows the liturgical tradition of his church. Luke's less developed form also represents the liturgical tradition known to him, but it is probably closer than Matthew's to the original words of Jesus.

*** [6:9] **Our Father in heaven:** this invocation is found in many rabbinic prayers of the post-New Testament period. **Hallowed be your name:** though the "hallowing" of the divine name could be understood as reverence done to God by human praise and by obedience to his will, this is more probably a petition that God hallow his own name, i.e., that he manifest his glory by an act of power (cf. Ez 36:23), in this case, by the establishment of his kingdom in its fullness.

††† [6:10] **Your kingdom come:** this petition sets the tone of the prayer, and inclines the balance toward divine rather than human action in the petitions that immediately precede and follow it. **Your will be done, on earth as in heaven:** a petition that the divine purpose to establish the kingdom, a purpose present now **in heaven**, be executed **on earth.**

‡‡‡ [6:11] **Give us today our daily bread:** the rare Greek word *epiousios*, here **daily**, occurs in the New Testament only here and in Lk 11:3. A single occurrence of the word outside of these texts and of literature dependent on them has been claimed, but the claim is highly doubtful. The word may mean **daily** or "future" (other meanings have also been proposed). The latter would conform better to the eschatological tone of the whole prayer. So understood, the petition would be for a speedy coming of the kingdom (**today**), which is often

---

q. [5:39–42] Lk 6:29–30.   r. [5:41] Lam 3:30.   s. [5:42] Dt 15:7–8.   t. [5:43–48] Lk 6:27, 32–36.   u. [5:43] Lv 19:18.   v. [5:48] Lv 11:44; 19:2; Dt 18:13; Jas 1:4; 1 Pt 1:16; 1 Jn 3:3.   w. [6:1] 23:5.

x. [6:2] Jn 12:43.   y. [6:9–13] Lk 11:2–4.   z. [6:10] 26:42.   a. [6:11] Prv 30:8–9.

¹² and forgive us our debts,*
    as we forgive our debtors;[b]
¹³ and do not subject us to the final test,†
    but deliver us from the evil one.[c]

¹⁴*If you forgive others their transgressions, your heavenly Father will forgive you.[d] ¹⁵But if you do not forgive others, neither will your Father forgive your transgressions.[e]

**Teaching About Fasting.** ¹⁶"When you fast,§ do not look gloomy like the hypocrites. They neglect their appearance, so that they may appear to others to be fasting. Amen, I say to you, they have received their reward. ¹⁷But when you fast, anoint your head and wash your face, ¹⁸so that you may not appear to others to be fasting, except to your Father who is hidden. And your Father who sees what is hidden will repay you.

**Treasure in Heaven.** ¹⁹*"Do not store up for yourselves treasures on earth, where moth and decay destroy, and thieves break in and steal.[f] ²⁰But store up treasures in heaven, where neither moth nor decay destroys, nor thieves break in and steal. ²¹For where your treasure is, there also will your heart be.[g]

**The Light of the Body.**** ²²"The lamp of the body is the eye. If your eye is sound, your whole body will be filled with light; ²³but if your eye is bad, your whole body will be in darkness. And if the light in you is darkness, how great will the darkness be.[h]

**God and Money.** ²⁴††"No one can serve two masters.[i] He will either hate one and love the other, or be devoted to one and despise the other. You cannot serve God and mammon.

**Dependence on God.**‡ ²⁵*"Therefore I tell you, do not worry about your life, what you will eat

[or drink], or about your body, what you will wear. Is not life more than food and the body more than clothing? ²⁶Look at the birds in the sky; they do not sow or reap, they gather nothing into barns, yet your heavenly Father feeds them. Are not you more important than they?[k] ²⁷Can any of you by worrying add a single moment to your life-span?§§ ²⁸Why are you anxious about clothes? Learn from the way the wild flowers grow. They do not work or spin. ²⁹But I tell you that not even Solomon in all his splendor was clothed like one of them. ³⁰*If God so clothes the grass of the field, which grows today and is thrown into the oven tomorrow, will he not much more provide for you, O you of little faith? ³¹So do not worry and say, 'What are we to eat?' or 'What are we to drink?' or 'What are we to wear?' ³²All these things the pagans seek. Your heavenly Father knows that you need them all. ³³But seek first the kingdom [of God] and his righteousness,*** and all these things will be given you besides. ³⁴Do not worry about tomorrow; tomorrow will take care of itself. Sufficient for a day is its own evil.

## CHAPTER 7

**Judging Others.** ¹†††"Stop judging,‡‡‡ that you may not be judged.[m] ²For as you judge, so will you be judged, and the measure with which you measure will be measured out to you.[n] ³Why do you notice the splinter in your brother's eye, but do not perceive the wooden beam in your own eye? ⁴How can you say to your brother, 'Let me remove that splinter from your eye,' while the wooden beam is in your eye? ⁵You hypocrite,§§§ remove the wooden beam from your eye first; then you will see clearly to remove the splinter from your brother's eye.

**Pearls Before Swine.** ⁶"Do not give what is holy to dogs,*** or throw your pearls before swine, lest

portrayed in both the Old Testament and the New under the image of a feast (Is 25:6; Mt 8:11; 22:1–10; Lk 13:29; 14:15–24).

*[6:12] **Forgive us our debts:** the word **debts** is used metaphorically of sins, "debts" owed to God (see Lk 11:4). The request is probably for forgiveness at the final judgment.

†[6:13] Jewish apocalyptic writings speak of a period of severe trial before the end of the age, sometimes called the "messianic woes." This petition asks that the disciples be spared that **final test**.

‡[6:14–15] These verses reflect a set pattern called "Principles of Holy Law." Human action now will be met by a corresponding action of God at the final judgment.

§[6:16] The only fast prescribed in the Mosaic law was that of the Day of Atonement (Lv 16:31), but the practice of regular fasting was common in later Judaism; cf. *Didache* 9:1.

¶[6:19–34] The remaining material of this chapter is taken almost entirely from Q. It deals principally with worldly possessions, and the controlling thought is summed up in Mt 6:24: the disciple can serve only one master and must choose between God and wealth (**mammon**). See further the note on Lk 16:9.

**[6:22–23] In this context the parable probably points to the need for the disciple to be enlightened by Jesus' teaching on the transitory nature of earthly riches.

††[6:24] **Mammon:** an Aramaic word meaning wealth or property.

‡‡[6:25–34] Jesus does not deny the reality of human needs (Mt 6:32), but forbids making them the object of anxious care and, in effect, becoming their slave.

§§[6:27] **Life-span:** the Greek word can also mean "stature." If it is taken in that sense, the word here translated **moment** (literally, "cubit") must be translated literally as a unit not of time but of spatial measure. The cubit is about eighteen inches.

¶¶[6:30] **Of little faith:** except for the parallel in Lk 12:28, the word translated **of little faith** is found in the New Testament only in Matthew. It is used by him of those who are disciples of Jesus but whose faith in him is not as deep as it should be (see Mt 8:26; 14:31; 16:8 and the cognate noun in Mt 17:20).

***[6:33] **Righteousness:** see note on Mt 3:14–15.

†††[7:1–12] In Mt 7:1 Matthew returns to the basic traditional material of the sermon (Lk 6:37–38, 41–42). The governing thought is the correspondence between conduct toward one's fellows and God's conduct toward the one so acting.

‡‡‡[7:1] This is not a prohibition against recognizing the faults of others, which would be hardly compatible with Mt 7:5, 6 but against passing judgment in a spirit of arrogance, forgetful of one's own faults.

§§§[7:5] **Hypocrite:** the designation previously given to the scribes and Pharisees is here given to the Christian disciple who is concerned with the faults of another and ignores his own more serious offenses.

¶¶¶[7:6] **Dogs** and **swine** were Jewish terms of contempt for Gentiles. This saying may originally have derived from a Jewish Christian community opposed to preaching the gospel

b. [6:12] 18:21–22; Sir 28:2.   c. [6:13] Jn 17:15; 2 Thes 3:3.   d. [6:14] 18:35; Sir 28:1–5; Mk 11:25.   e. [6:15] Jas 2:13.   f. [6:19] Jas 5:2–3.   g. [6:20–21] Lk 12:33–34.   h. [6:22–23] Lk 11:34–36.   i. [6:24] Lk 16:13.   j. [6:25–33] Lk 12:22–31.

k. [6:26] Ps 145:15–16; 147:9.   l. [7:1–5] Lk 6:37–38, 41–42.   m. [7:1] Rom 2:1–2; 1 Cor 4:5.   n. [7:2] Wis 12:22; Mk 4:24.

they trample them underfoot, and turn and tear you to pieces.[o]

**The Answer to Prayers.** [7p]"Ask and it will be given to you; seek and you will find; knock and the door will be opened to you.[q] [8]For everyone who asks, receives; and the one who seeks, finds; and to the one who knocks, the door will be opened.[r] [9]Which one of you would hand his son a stone when he asks for a loaf of bread,[s] [10]or a snake when he asks for a fish? [11]If you then, who are wicked, know how to give good gifts to your children, how much more will your heavenly Father give good things to those who ask him.[s]

**The Golden Rule.** [12]"Do to others whatever you would have them do to you.[t] This is the law and the prophets.

**The Narrow Gate.** [13‡]"Enter through the narrow gate;[§] for the gate is wide and the road broad that leads to destruction, and those who enter through it are many.[u] [14]How narrow the gate and constricted the road that leads to life. And those who find it are few.

**False Prophets.**[¶] [15]"Beware of false prophets, who come to you in sheep's clothing, but underneath are ravenous wolves.[v] [16w]By their fruits you will know them. Do people pick grapes from thornbushes, or figs from thistles? [17]Just so, every good tree bears good fruit, and a rotten tree bears bad fruit. [18]A good tree cannot bear bad fruit, nor can a rotten tree bear good fruit. [19]Every tree that does not bear good fruit will be cut down and thrown into the fire. [20]So by their fruits you will know them.[x]

**The True Disciple.** [21]"Not everyone who says to me, 'Lord, Lord,' will enter the kingdom of heaven," but only the one who does the will of my Father in heaven.[y] [22]Many will say to me on that day,[z] 'Lord, Lord, did we not prophesy in your name? Did we not drive out demons in your name? Did we not do mighty deeds in your name?'[a] [23]Then I will declare to them solemnly, 'I never knew you.[††] Depart from me, you evildoers.'[b]

**The Two Foundations.** [24‡‡]"Everyone who listens to these words of mine and acts on them will be like a wise man who built his house on rock.[c] [25]The rain fell, the floods came, and the winds blew and buffeted the house.[d] But it did not collapse; it had been set solidly on rock. [26]And everyone who listens to these words of mine but does not act on them will be like a fool who built his house on sand. [27]The rain fell, the floods came, and the winds blew and buffeted the house. And it collapsed and was completely ruined."

[28§§]When Jesus finished these words, the crowds were astonished at his teaching, [29¶¶]for he taught them as one having authority, and not as their scribes.

## III. MINISTRY AND MISSION IN GALILEE[***]

## CHAPTER 8

**The Cleansing of a Leper.** [1]When Jesus came down from the mountain, great crowds followed

---

**[7:21–23]** The attack on the false prophets is continued, but is broadened to include those disciples who perform works of healing and exorcism in the name of Jesus (**Lord**) but live evil lives. Entrance into the kingdom is only for those who do the will of the Father. On the day of judgment (**on that day**) the morally corrupt prophets and miracle workers will be rejected by Jesus.

**††[7:23]** I never knew you: cf. Mt 10:33. **Depart from me, you evildoers**: cf. Ps 6:9.

**‡‡[7:24–27]** The conclusion of the discourse (cf. Lk 6:47–49). Here the relation is not between saying and doing as in Mt 7:15–23 but between hearing and doing, and the words of Jesus are applied to every Christian (**everyone who listens**).

**§§[7:28–29]** When Jesus finished these words: this or a similar formula is used by Matthew to conclude each of the five great discourses of Jesus (cf. Mt 11:1; 13:53; 19:1; 26:1).

**¶¶[7:29]** Not as their scribes: scribal instruction was a faithful handing down of the traditions of earlier teachers; Jesus' teaching is based on his own authority. **Their scribes**: for the implications of **their**, see note on Mt 4:23.

**\*\*\*[8:1–9:38]** This narrative section of the second book of the gospel is composed of nine miracle stories, most of which are found in Mark, although Matthew does not follow the Marcan order and abbreviates the stories radically. The stories are arranged in three groups of three, each group followed by a section composed principally of sayings of Jesus about discipleship. Mt 9:35 is an almost verbatim repetition of Mt 4:23. Each speaks of Jesus' teaching, preaching, and healing. The teaching and preaching form the content of Mt 5–7; the healing, that of Mt 8–9. Some scholars speak of a portrayal of Jesus as "Messiah of the Word" in Mt 5–7 and "Messiah of the Deed" in Mt 8–9. That is accurate so far as it goes, but there is also a strong emphasis on discipleship in Mt 8–9; these chapters have not only christological but ecclesiological import.

---

(what is holy, pearls) to Gentiles. In the light of Mt 28:19 that can hardly be Matthew's meaning. He may have taken the saying as applying to a Christian dealing with an obstinately impenitent fellow Christian (Mt 18:17).

*\*[7:9–10]* There is a resemblance between a stone and a round loaf of bread and between a serpent and the scaleless fish called *barbut*.

†[7:12] See Lk 6:31. This saying, known since the eighteenth century as the "Golden Rule," is found in both positive and negative form in pagan and Jewish sources, both earlier and later than the gospel. This is the law and the prophets is an addition probably due to the evangelist.

‡[7:13–28] The final section of the discourse is composed of a series of antitheses, contrasting two kinds of life within the Christian community, that of those who obey the words of Jesus and that of those who do not. Most of the sayings are from Q and are found also in Luke.

§[7:13–14] The metaphor of the "two ways" was common in pagan philosophy and in the Old Testament. In Christian literature it is found also in the *Didache* (1–6) and the *Epistle of Barnabas* (18–20).

¶[7:15–20] Christian disciples who claimed to speak in the name of God are called **prophets** (Mt 7:15) in Mt 10:41; Mt 23:34. They were presumably an important group within the church of Matthew. As in the case of the Old Testament prophets, there were both true and false ones, and for Matthew the difference could be recognized by the quality of their deeds, the **fruits** (Mt 7:16). The mention of **fruits** leads to the comparison with trees, some producing good fruit, others bad.

---

o. [7:6] Prv 23:9.    p. [7:7–11] Mk 11:24; Lk 11:9–13.    q. [7:7] 18:19.    r. [7:8] Lk 18:1–8; Jn 14:13.    s. [7:11] 1 Jn 5:14–15.    t. [7:12] Lk 6:31.    u. [7:13] Lk 13:24.    v. [7:15] 2 Pt 2:1.    w. [7:16–17] 12:33; Lk 6:43–44.    x. [7:20] 3:10.

y. [7:21] Is 29:13; Lk 6:46.    z. [7:22–23] Lk 13:26–27.    a. [7:22] 25:11–12.    b. [7:23] Ps 5:5; 6:9.    c. [7:24–27] Lk 6:47–49.    d. [7:25–26] Prv 10:25.    e. [7:29] Mk 1:22; Lk 4:32.    f. [8:1–4] Mk 1:40–44; Lk 5:12–14.

him. [2]And then a leper* approached, did him homage, and said, "Lord, if you wish, you can make me clean." [3]He stretched out his hand, touched him, and said, "I will do it. Be made clean." His leprosy was cleansed immediately. [4†]Then Jesus said to him, "See that you tell no one, but go show yourself to the priest, and offer the gift that Moses prescribed;[g] that will be proof for them."

**The Healing of a Centurion's Servant.**[‡] [5h]When he entered Capernaum,[§] a centurion approached him and appealed to him, [6]saying, "Lord, my servant is lying at home paralyzed, suffering dreadfully." [7]He said to him, "I will come and cure him." [8]The centurion said in reply,[¶] "Lord, I am not worthy to have you enter under my roof; only say the word and my servant will be healed. [9]For I too am a person subject to authority, with soldiers subject to me. And I say to one, 'Go,' and he goes; and to another, 'Come here,' and he comes; and to my slave, 'Do this,' and he does it." [10]When Jesus heard this, he was amazed and said to those following him, "Amen, I say to you, in no one in Israel** have I found such faith. [11]I say to you,[††] many will come from the east and the west, and will recline with Abraham, Isaac, and Jacob at the banquet in the kingdom of heaven, [12]but the children of the kingdom will be driven out into the outer darkness, where there will be wailing and grinding of teeth." [13]And Jesus said to the centurion, "You may go; as you have believed, let it be done for you." And at that very hour [his] servant was healed.

**The Cure of Peter's Mother-in-Law.**[‡‡] [14i]Jesus entered the house of Peter, and saw his mother-in-law lying in bed with a fever. [15]He touched her hand, the fever left her, and she rose and waited on him.[k]

**Other Healings.** [16]When it was evening, they brought him many who were possessed by demons, and he drove out the spirits by a word[§§] and cured all the sick, [17]to fulfill what had been said by Isaiah the prophet:[¶¶l]

> "He took away our infirmities
> and bore our diseases."

**The Would-be Followers of Jesus.**[***] [18m]When Jesus saw a crowd around him, he gave orders to cross to the other side.[†††] [19n]A scribe approached and said to him, "Teacher,[‡‡‡] I will follow you wherever you go." [20]Jesus answered him, "Foxes have dens and birds of the sky have nests, but the Son of Man[§§§] has nowhere to rest his head." [21]Another of [his] disciples said to him, "Lord, let me go first and bury my father." [22¶¶¶]But Jesus answered him, "Follow me, and let the dead bury their dead."

**The Calming of the Storm at Sea.** [23****o]He got into a boat and his disciples followed him. [24]Suddenly a violent storm[††††] came up on the sea, so that the boat was being swamped by waves;

---

*[8:2] **A leper:** see note on Mk 1:40.

†[8:4] Cf. Lv 14:2–9. **That will be proof for them:** the Greek can also mean "that will be proof against them." It is not clear whether **them** refers to the priests or the people.

‡[8:5–13] This story comes from Q (see Lk 7:1–10) and is also reflected in Jn 4:46–54. The similarity between the Q story and the Johannine is due to a common oral tradition, not to a common literary source. As in the later story of the daughter of the Canaanite woman (Mt 15:21–28) Jesus breaks with his usual procedure of ministering only to Israelites and anticipates the mission to the Gentiles.

§[8:5] **A centurion:** a military officer commanding a hundred men. He was probably in the service of Herod Antipas, tetrarch of Galilee; see note on Mt 14:1.

¶[8:8–9] Acquainted by his position with the force of a command, the centurion expresses faith in the power of Jesus' mere word.

**[8:10] **In no one in Israel:** there is good textual attestation (e.g., Codex Sinaiticus) for a reading identical with that of Lk 7:9, "not even in Israel." But that seems to be due to a harmonization of Matthew with Luke.

††[8:11–12] Matthew inserts into the story a Q saying (see Lk 13:28–29) about the entrance of Gentiles into the kingdom and the exclusion of those Israelites who, though descended from the patriarchs and members of the chosen nation (**the children of the kingdom**), refused to believe in Jesus. **There will be wailing and grinding of teeth:** the first occurrence of a phrase used frequently in this gospel to describe final condemnation (Mt 13:42, 50; 22:13; 24:51; 25:30). It is found elsewhere in the New Testament only in Lk 13:28.

‡‡[8:14–15] Cf. Mk 1:29–31. Unlike Mark, Matthew has no implied request by others for the woman's cure. Jesus acts on his own initiative, and the cured woman rises and waits not on "them" (Mk 1:31) but on **him.**

§§[8:16] **By a word:** a Matthean addition to Mk 1:34; cf. 8:8.

¶¶[8:17] This fulfillment citation from Is 53:4 follows the MT, not the LXX. The prophet speaks of the Servant of the Lord who suffers vicariously for the sins ("infirmities") of others; Matthew takes the **infirmities** as physical afflictions.

***[8:18–22] This passage between the first and second series of miracles about following Jesus is taken from Q (see Lk 9:57–62). The third of the three sayings found in the source is absent from Matthew.

†††[8:18] **The other side:** i.e., of the Sea of Galilee.

‡‡‡[8:19] **Teacher:** for Matthew, this designation of Jesus is true, for he has Jesus using it of himself (Mt 10:24, 25; 23:8; 26:18), yet when it is used of him by others they are either his opponents (Mt 9:11; 12:38; 17:24; 22:16, 24, 36) or, as here and in Mt 19:16, well-disposed persons who cannot see more deeply. Thus it reveals an inadequate recognition of who Jesus is.

§§§[8:20] **Son of Man:** see note on Mk 8:31. This is the first occurrence in Matthew of a term that appears in the New Testament only in sayings of Jesus, except for Acts 7:56 and possibly Mt 9:6 (// Mk 2:10; Lk 5:24). In Matthew it refers to Jesus in his ministry (seven times, as here), in his passion and resurrection (nine times, e.g., Mt 17:22), and in his glorious coming at the end of the age (thirteen times, e.g., Mt 24:30).

¶¶¶[8:22] **Let the dead bury their dead:** the demand of Jesus overrides what both the Jewish and the Hellenistic world regarded as a filial obligation of the highest importance. See note on Lk 9:60.

****[8:23] **His disciples followed him:** the first miracle in the second group (Mt 8:23–9:8) is introduced by a verse that links it with the preceding sayings by the catchword "follow." In Mark the initiative in entering the boat is taken by the disciples (Mk 4:35–41); here, Jesus enters first and the disciples follow.

††††[8:24] **Storm:** literally, "earthquake," a word commonly used in apocalyptic literature for the shaking of the old world when God brings in his kingdom. All the synoptics use it in depicting the events preceding the parousia of the Son of Man (Mt 24:7; Mk 13:8; Lk 21:11). Matthew has introduced it here and in his account of the death and resurrection of Jesus (Mt 27:51–54; 28:2).

---

g. [8:4] Lv 14:2–32; Lk 17:14.   h. [8:5–13] Lk 7:1–10; Jn 4:46–53.   i. [8:11–12] 13:42, 50; 22:13; 24:51; 25:30; Lk 13:28–29.   j. [8:14–16] Mk 1:29–34; Lk 4:38–41.

k. [8:15] 9:25.   l. [8:17] Is 53:4.   m. [8:18] Mk 4:35.   n. [8:19–22] Lk 9:57–60.   o. [8:23–27] Mk 4:35–40; Lk 8:22–25.

but he was asleep. 25ᵖThey came and woke him, saying, "Lord, save us! We are perishing!" 26He said to them, "Why are you terrified, O you of little faith?"† Then he got up, rebuked the winds and the sea, and there was great calm. 27The men were amazed and said, "What sort of man is this, whom even the winds and the sea obey?"

**The Healing of the Gadarene Demoniacs.** 28qWhen he came to the other side, to the territory of the Gadarenes,‡ two demoniacs who were coming from the tombs met him. They were so savage that no one could travel by that road. 29They cried out, "What have you to do with us,§ Son of God? Have you come here to torment us before the appointed time?" 30Some distance away a herd of many swine was feeding.ʳ 31The demons pleaded with him, "If you drive us out, send us into the herd of swine."ʳ 32And he said to them, "Go then!" They came out and entered the swine, and the whole herd rushed down the steep bank into the sea where they drowned. 33The swineherds ran away, and when they came to the town they reported everything, including what had happened to the demoniacs. 34Thereupon the whole town came out to meet Jesus, and when they saw him they begged him to leave their district.

## CHAPTER 9

**The Healing of a Paralytic.** 1"ˢHe entered a boat, made the crossing, and came into his own town. 2And there people brought to him a paralytic lying on a stretcher. When Jesus saw their faith, he said to the paralytic, "Courage, child, your sins are forgiven."ᵗ 3At that, some of the scribes††

said to themselves, "This man is blaspheming." 4Jesus knew what they were thinking, and said, "Why do you harbor evil thoughts? 5Which is easier, to say, 'Your sins are forgiven,' or to say, 'Rise and walk'? 6‡‡But that you may know that the Son of Man has authority on earth to forgive sins"—he then said to the paralytic, "Rise, pick up your stretcher, and go home."ᵘ 7He rose and went home. 8§§When the crowds saw this they were struck with awe and glorified God who had given such authority to human beings.

**The Call of Matthew.**¶¶ 9As Jesus passed on from there,ᵛ he saw a man named Matthew*** sitting at the customs post. He said to him, "Follow me." And he got up and followed him. 10While he was at table in his house,††† many tax collectors and sinners came and sat with Jesus and his disciples.ʷ 11The Pharisees saw this and said to his disciples, "Why does your teacher‡‡‡ eat with tax collectors and sinners?" 12He heard this and said, "Those who are well do not need a physician, but the sick do.§§§ 13Go and learn the meaning of the words,ˣ 'I desire mercy, not sacrifice.'¶¶¶ I did not come to call the righteous but sinners."

**The Question About Fasting.** 14ʸThen the disciples of John approached him and said, "Why do we and the Pharisees fast [much], but your disciples do not fast?" 15Jesus answered them, "Can the wedding guests mourn as long as the bridegroom is with them? The days will come when the bridegroom is taken away from them,

---

*[8:25] The reverent plea of the disciples contrasts sharply with their reproach of Jesus in Mk 4:38.

†[8:26] **You of little faith:** see note on Mt 6:30. **Great calm:** Jesus' calming the sea may be meant to recall the Old Testament theme of God's control over the chaotic waters (Ps 65:8; 89:10; 93:3–4; 107:29).

‡[8:28] **Gadarenes:** this is the reading of Codex Vaticanus, supported by other important textual witnesses. The original reading of Codex Sinaiticus was Gazarenes, later changed to Gergesenes, and a few versions have Gerasenes. Each of these readings points to a different territory connected, respectively, with the cities Gadara, Gergesa, and Gerasa (modern Jerash). There is the same confusion of readings in the parallel texts, Mk 5:1 and Lk 8:26; there the best reading seems to be "Gerasenes," whereas "Gadarenes" is probably the original reading in Matthew. The town of Gadara was about five miles southeast of the Sea of Galilee, and Josephus (*Life* 9:42) refers to it as possessing territory that lay on that sea. **Two demoniacs:** Mark (5:1–20) has one.

§[8:29] **What have you to do with us?** see note on Jn 2:4. **Before the appointed time:** the notion that evil spirits were allowed by God to afflict human beings until the time of the final judgment is found in Enoch 16:1 and Jubilees 10:7–10.

¶[8:30] The tending of pigs, animals considered unclean by Mosaic law (Lv 11:6–7), indicates that the population was Gentile.

**[9:1] **His own town:** Capernaum; see Mt 4:13.

††[9:3] **Scribes:** see note on Mk 2:6. Matthew omits the reason given in the Marcan story for the charge of blasphemy: "Who but God alone can forgive sins?" (Mk 2:7).

‡‡[9:6] It is not clear whether **But that you may know . . . to forgive sins** is intended to be a continuation of the words of Jesus or a parenthetical comment of the evangelist to those who would hear or read this gospel. In any case, Matthew here follows the Marcan text.

§§[9:8] **Who had given such authority to human beings:** a significant difference from Mk 2:12 ("They . . . glorified God, saying, 'We have never seen anything like this'"). Matthew's extension to **human beings** of the authority to forgive sins points to the belief that such authority was being claimed by Matthew's church.

¶¶[9:9–17] In this section the order is the same as that of Mk 2:13–22.

***[9:9] **A man named Matthew:** Mark names this tax collector Levi (Mk 2:14). No such name appears in the four lists of the twelve who were the closest companions of Jesus (Mt 10:2–4; Mk 3:16–19; Lk 6:14–16; Acts 1:13 [eleven, because of the defection of Judas Iscariot]), whereas all four list a Matthew, designated in Mt 10:3 as "the tax collector." The evangelist may have changed the "Levi" of his source to **Matthew** so that this man, whose call is given special notice, like that of the first four disciples (Mt 4:18–22), might be included among the twelve. Another reason for the change may be that the disciple Matthew was the source of traditions peculiar to the church for which the evangelist was writing.

†††[9:10] **His house:** it is not clear whether **his** refers to Jesus or Matthew. **Tax collectors:** see note on Mt 5:46. Table association with such persons would cause ritual impurity.

‡‡‡[9:11] **Teacher:** see note on Mt 8:19.

§§§[9:12] See note on Mk 2:17.

¶¶¶[9:13] **Go and learn . . . not sacrifice:** Matthew adds the prophetic statement of Hos 6:6 to the Marcan account (see also Mt 12:7). If mercy is superior to the temple sacrifices, how much more to the laws of ritual impurity.

---

p. [8:25–26] Ps 107:28–29.  q. [8:28–34] Mk 5:1–17; Lk 8:26–37.  r. [8:31] Lk 4:34, 41.  s. [9:1–8] Mk 2:3–12; Lk 5:18–26.  t. [9:2] Lk 7:48.

u. [9:6] Jn 5:27.  v. [9:9–13] Mk 2:14–17; Lk 5:27–32.  w. [9:10] 11:19; Lk 15:1–2.  x. [9:13] 12:7; Hos 6:6.  y. [9:14–17] Mk 2:18–22; Lk 5:33–39.

and then they will fast.* ¹⁶No one patches an old cloak with a piece of unshrunken cloth,† for its fullness pulls away from the cloak and the tear gets worse. ¹⁷People do not put new wine into old wineskins. Otherwise the skins burst, the wine spills out, and the skins are ruined. Rather, they pour new wine into fresh wineskins, and both are preserved."

**The Official's Daughter and the Woman with a Hemorrhage.** ¹⁸‡While he was saying these things to them,ᶻ an official§ came forward, knelt down before him, and said, "My daughter has just died. But come, lay your hand on her, and she will live." ¹⁹Jesus rose and followed him, and so did his disciples. ²⁰A woman suffering hemorrhages for twelve years came up behind him and touched the tasselᶜ on his cloak. ²¹She said to herself, "If only I can touch his cloak, I shall be cured."ᵃ ²²Jesus turned around and saw her, and said, "Courage, daughter! Your faith has saved you." And from that hour the woman was cured.

²³When Jesus arrived at the official's house and saw the flute players and the crowd who were making a commotion, ²⁴he said, "Go away! The girl is not dead but sleeping."** And they ridiculed him. ²⁵When the crowd was put out, he came and took her by the hand, and the little girl arose. ²⁶And news of this spread throughout all that land.

**The Healing of Two Blind Men.**†† ²⁷ᵇAnd as Jesus passed on from there, two blind men followed [him], crying out, "Son of David,‡‡ have pity on us!"ᶜ ²⁸When he entered the house, the blind men approached him and Jesus said to them, "Do you believe that I can do this?" "Yes, Lord," they said to him. ²⁹Then he touched their eyes and said, "Let it be done for you according to your faith." ³⁰And their eyes were opened. Jesus warned them sternly, "See that no one knows about this." ³¹But they went out and spread word of him through all that land.

**The Healing of a Mute Person.** ³²ᵈAs they were going out,§§ a demoniac who could not speak was brought to him, ³³and when the demon was driven out the mute person spoke. The crowds were amazed and said, "Nothing like this has ever been seen in Israel."ᵉ ³⁴¶¶But the Pharisees said,ᶠ "He drives out demons by the prince of demons."

**The Compassion of Jesus.** ³⁵***ᵍJesus went around to all the towns and villages, teaching in their synagogues, proclaiming the gospel of the kingdom, and curing every disease and illness. ³⁶ʰAt the sight of the crowds, his heart was moved with pity for them because they were troubled and abandoned,††† like sheep without a shepherd. ³⁷‡‡‡ⁱThen he said to his disciples, "The harvest is abundant but the laborers are few; ³⁸so ask the master of the harvest to send out laborers for his harvest."

## CHAPTER 10

**The Mission of the Twelve.** ¹§§§Then he summoned his twelve disciples¶¶¶ and gave them

---

*[9:15] Fasting is a sign of mourning and would be as inappropriate at this time of joy, when Jesus is proclaiming the kingdom, as it would be at a marriage feast. Yet the saying looks forward to the time when Jesus will no longer be with the disciples visibly, the time of Matthew's church. **Then they will fast**: see *Didache* 8:1.

†[9:16–17] Each of these parables speaks of the unsuitability of attempting to combine the old and the new. Jesus' teaching is not a patching up of Judaism, nor can the gospel be contained within the limits of Mosaic law.

‡[9:18–34] In this third group of miracles, the first (Mt 9:18–26) is clearly dependent on Mark (Mk 5:21–43). Though it tells of two miracles, the cure of the woman had already been included within the story of the raising of the official's daughter, so that the two were probably regarded as a single unit. The other miracles seem to have been derived from Mark and Q, respectively, though here Matthew's own editing is much more evident.

§[9:18] **Official**: literally, "ruler." Mark calls him "one of the synagogue officials" (Mk 5:22). **My daughter has just died**: Matthew heightens the Marcan "my daughter is at the point of death" (Mk 5:23).

¶[9:20] **Tassel**: possibly "fringe." The Mosaic law prescribed that tassels be worn on the corners of one's garment as a reminder to keep the commandments (see Nm 15:37–39; Dt 22:12).

**[9:24] **Sleeping**: sleep is a biblical metaphor for death (see Ps 87:6 LXX; Dn 12:2; 1 Thes 5:10). Jesus' statement is not a denial of the child's real death, but an assurance that she will be roused from her sleep of death.

††[9:27–31] This story was probably composed by Matthew out of Mark's story of the healing of a blind man named Bartimaeus (Mk 10:46–52). Mark places the event late in Jesus' ministry, just before his entrance into Jerusalem, and Matthew has followed his Marcan source at that point in his gospel also (see Mt 20:29–34). In each of the Matthean stories the single blind man of Mark becomes two. The reason why

Matthew would have given a double version of the Marcan story and placed the earlier one here may be that he wished to add a story of Jesus' curing the blind at this point in order to prepare for Jesus' answer to the emissaries of the Baptist (Mt 11:4–6) in which Jesus, recounting his works, begins with his giving sight to the blind.

‡‡[9:27] **Son of David**: this messianic title is connected once with the healing power of Jesus in Mark (Mk 10:47–48) and Luke (Lk 18:38–39) but more frequently in Matthew (see also Mt 12:23; 15:22; 20:30–31).

§§[9:32–34] The source of this story seems to be Q (see Lk 11:14–15). As in the preceding healing of the blind, Matthew has two versions of this healing, the later in Mt 12:22–24 and the earlier here.

¶¶[9:34] This spiteful accusation foreshadows the growing opposition to Jesus in Mt 11 and 12.

***[9:35] See notes on Mt 4:23–25; Mt 8:1–9:38.

†††[9:36] See Mk 6:34; Nm 27:17; 1 Kgs 22:17.

‡‡‡[9:37–38] This Q saying (see Lk 10:2) is only imperfectly related to this context. It presupposes that only God (**the master of the harvest**) can take the initiative in sending out preachers of the gospel, whereas in Matthew's setting it leads into Mt 10 where Jesus does so.

§§§[10:1–11:1] After an introductory narrative (Mt 10:1–4), the second of the discourses of the gospel. It deals with the mission now to be undertaken by the disciples (Mt 10:5–15), but the perspective broadens and includes the missionary activity of the church between the time of the resurrection and the parousia.

¶¶¶[10:1] **His twelve disciples**: although, unlike Mark (Mk 3:13–14) and Luke (Lk 6:12–16), Matthew has no story of Jesus' choosing the Twelve, he assumes that the group is known

c. [9:27] 15:22.   d. [9:32–34] 12:22–24; Lk 11:14–15.   e. [9:33] Mk 2:12; 7:37.   f. [9:34] 10:25; Mk 3:22.   g. [9:35] 4:23; Lk 8:1.
h. [9:36] Nm 27:17; 1 Kgs 22:17; Jer 50:6; Ez 34:5; Mk 6:34.   i. [9:37–38] Lk 10:2; Jn 4:35.

z. [9:18–26] Mk 5:22–43; Lk 8:41–56.   a. [9:21] 14:36; Nm 15:37.
b. [9:27–31] 20:29–34.

authority over unclean spirits to drive them out and to cure every disease and every illness.[j] [2]The names of the twelve apostles[*] are these: first, Simon called Peter, and his brother Andrew; James, the son of Zebedee, and his brother John; [3]Philip and Bartholomew, Thomas and Matthew the tax collector; James, the son of Alphaeus, and Thaddeus; [4]Simon the Cananean, and Judas Iscariot who betrayed him.

**The Commissioning of the Twelve.** [5k]Jesus sent out these twelve[†] after instructing them thus, "Do not go into pagan territory or enter a Samaritan town. [6]Go rather to the lost sheep of the house of Israel. [7]As you go, make this proclamation: 'The kingdom of heaven is at hand.'[m] [8‡]Cure the sick, raise the dead, cleanse lepers, drive out demons. Without cost you have received; without cost you are to give. [9n]Do not take gold or silver or copper for your belts; [10]no sack for the journey, or a second tunic, or sandals, or walking stick. The laborer deserves his keep. [11p]Whatever town or village you enter, look for a worthy person in it, and stay there until you leave. [12]As you enter a house, wish it peace. [13]If the house is worthy, let your peace come upon it; if not, let your peace return to you.[§] [14§q]Whoever will not receive you or listen

to your words—go outside that house or town and shake the dust from your feet. [15]Amen, I say to you, it will be more tolerable for the land of Sodom and Gomorrah on the day of judgment than for that town.[r]

**Coming Persecutions.** [16s]"Behold, I am sending you like sheep in the midst of wolves; so be shrewd as serpents and simple as doves. [17**]But beware of people,[t] for they will hand you over to courts and scourge you in their synagogues,[u] [18]and you will be led before governors and kings for my sake as a witness before them and the pagans. [19]When they hand you over, do not worry about how you are to speak or what you are to say. You will be given at that moment what you are to say.[v] [20]For it will not be you who speak but the Spirit of your Father speaking through you. [21††w]Brother will hand over brother to death, and the father his child; children will rise up against parents and have them put to death. [22]You will be hated by all because of my name, but whoever endures to the end[‡‡] will be saved. [23]When they persecute you in one town, flee to another. Amen, I say to you, you will not finish the towns of Israel before the Son of Man comes.[§§] [24x]No disciple is above his teacher, no slave above his master. [25]It is enough for the disciple that he become like his teacher, for the slave that he become like his master. If they have called the master of the house Beelzebul,[¶¶] how much more those of his household!

**Courage Under Persecution.** [26y]"Therefore do not be afraid of them. Nothing is concealed that will not be revealed, nor secret that will not be known.[***z] [27]What I say to you in the darkness, speak in the light; what you hear whispered,

---

to the reader. The earliest New Testament text to speak of it is 1 Cor 15:5. The number probably is meant to recall the twelve tribes of Israel and implies Jesus' authority to call all Israel into the kingdom. While Luke (Lk 6:13) and probably Mark (Mk 4:10, 34) distinguish between the Twelve and a larger group also termed disciples, Matthew tends to identify the disciples and the Twelve. **Authority . . . every illness:** activities the same as those of Jesus; see Mt 4:23; Mt 9:35; 10:8. The Twelve also share in his proclamation of the kingdom (Mt 10:7). But although he teaches (Mt 4:23; 7:28; 9:35), they do not. Their commission to teach comes only after Jesus' resurrection, after they have been fully instructed by him (Mt 28:20).

*[10:2–4] Here, for the only time in Matthew, the Twelve are designated **apostles**. The word "apostle" means "one who is sent," and therefore fits the situation here described. In the Pauline letters, the place where the term occurs most frequently in the New Testament, it means primarily one who has seen the risen Lord and has been commissioned to proclaim the resurrection. With slight variants in Luke and Acts, the names of those who belong to this group are the same in the four lists given in the New Testament (see note on Mt 9:9). **Cananean:** this represents an Aramaic word meaning "zealot." The meaning of that designation is unclear (see note on Lk 6:15).

†[10:5–6] Like Jesus (Mt 15:24), the Twelve are sent only to Israel. This saying may reflect an original Jewish Christian refusal of the mission to the Gentiles, but for Matthew it expresses rather the limitation that Jesus himself observed during his ministry.

‡[10:8–11] The Twelve have received their own call and mission through God's gift, and the benefits they confer are likewise to be given freely. They are not to take with them money, provisions, or unnecessary clothing; their lodging and food will be provided by those who receive them.

§[10:13] The greeting of peace is conceived of not merely as a salutation but as an effective word. If it finds no worthy recipient, it will return to the speaker.

¶[10:14] **Shake the dust from your feet:** this gesture indicates a complete disassociation from such unbelievers.

**[10:17] The persecutions attendant upon the post-resurrection mission now begin to be spoken of. Here Matthew brings into the discourse sayings found in Mk 13 which deals with events preceding the parousia.

††[10:21] See Mi 7:6 which is cited in Mt 10:35, 36.

‡‡[10:22] **To the end:** the original meaning was probably "until the parousia." But it is not likely that Matthew expected no missionary disciples to suffer death before then, since he envisages the martyrdom of other Christians (Mt 10:21). For him, **the end** is probably that of the individual's life (see Mt 10:28).

§§[10:23] **Before the Son of Man comes:** since the coming of the Son of Man at the end of the age had not taken place when this gospel was written, much less during the mission of the Twelve during Jesus' ministry, Matthew cannot have meant the coming to refer to the parousia. It is difficult to know what he understood it to be: perhaps the "proleptic parousia" of Mt 28:16–20, or the destruction of the temple in A.D. 70, viewed as a coming of Jesus in judgment on unbelieving Israel.

¶¶[10:25] **Beelzebul:** see Mt 9:34 for the charge linking Jesus with "the prince of demons," who is named **Beelzebul** in Mt 12:24. The meaning of the name is uncertain; possibly, "lord of the house."

***[10:26] The **concealed** and **secret** coming of the kingdom is to be proclaimed by them, and no fear must be allowed to deter them from that proclamation.

---

j. [10:1–4] Mk 3:14–19; Lk 6:13–16; Acts 1:13.   k. [10:5–15] Mk 6:7–13; Lk 9:1–6.   l. [10:6] 15:24.   m. [10:7] 3:2; 4:17.   n. [10:9–10] Mk 6:8–9; Lk 9:3; 10:4.   o. [10:10] Lk 10:7; 1 Cor 9:14; 1 Tm 5:18.   p. [10:11–15] Mk 6:10–11; Lk 9:4–5; 10:5–12.   q. [10:14] Acts 13:51; 18:6.

r. [10:15] 11:24; Gn 19:1–29; Jude 7.   s. [10:16] Lk 10:3.   t. [10:17–22] Mk 13:9–13; Lk 21:12–19.   u. [10:17] Acts 5:40.   v. [10:19] Ex 4:11–12; Jer 1:6–10; Lk 12:11–12.   w. [10:21–22] 24:9,13.   x. [10:24–25] Lk 6:40; Jn 13:16; 15:20.   y. [10:26–33] Lk 12:2–9.   z. [10:26] Mk 4:22; Lk 8:17; 1 Tm 5:25.

proclaim on the housetops. ²⁸And do not be afraid of those who kill the body but cannot kill the soul; rather, be afraid of the one who can destroy both soul and body in Gehenna.ᵃ ²⁹Are not two sparrows sold for a small coin? Yet not one of them falls to the ground without your Father's knowledge. ³⁰Even all the hairs of your head are counted. ³¹So do not be afraid; you are worth more than many sparrows. ³²*Everyone who acknowledges me before others I will acknowledge before my heavenly Father. ³³But whoever denies me before others, I will deny before my heavenly Father.ᵇ

**Jesus: A Cause of Division.** ³⁴ᶜ"Do not think that I have come to bring peace upon the earth. I have come to bring not peace but the sword. ³⁵For I have come to set

a man 'against his father,
　a daughter against her mother,
and a daughter-in-law against her
　　mother-in-law;
³⁶　and one's enemies will be those of
　　his household.'

**The Conditions of Discipleship.** ³⁷ᵈ"Whoever loves father or mother more than me is not worthy of me, and whoever loves son or daughter more than me is not worthy of me; ³⁸and whoever does not take up his cross† and follow after me is not worthy of me. ³⁹ᵗᵉWhoever finds his life will lose it, and whoever loses his life for my sake will find it.

**Rewards.** ⁴⁰"Whoever receives you receives me,§ and whoever receives me receives the one who sent me.ᶠ ⁴¹"Whoever receives a prophet because he is a prophet will receive a prophet's reward, and whoever receives a righteous man because he is righteous will receive a righteous man's reward. ⁴²And whoever gives only a cup

of cold water to one of these little ones to drink because he is a disciple—amen, I say to you, he will surely not lose his reward."ᵍ

# CHAPTER 11

¹When Jesus finished giving these commands to his twelve disciples," he went away from that place to teach and to preach in their towns.

## IV. OPPOSITION FROM ISRAEL

**The Messengers from John the Baptist.** ²ᵗᵗʰWhen John heard in prison‡‡ of the works of the Messiah, he sent his disciples to him ³§§with this question, "Are you the one who is to come, or should we look for another?" ⁴Jesus said to them in reply, "Go and tell John what you hear and see: ⁵§§the blind regain their sight, the lame walk, lepers are cleansed, the deaf hear, the dead are raised, and the poor have the good news proclaimed to them.ⁱ ⁶And blessed is the one who takes no offense at me."

**Jesus' Testimony to John.***** ⁷As they were going off, Jesus began to speak to the crowds about John, "What did you go out to the desert to see? A reed swayed by the wind?ʲ ⁸Then what did you go out to see? Someone dressed in fine clothing? Those who wear fine clothing are in royal palaces. ⁹Then why did you go out? To see a prophet?††† Yes, I tell you, and more than a prophet. ¹⁰This is the one about whom it is written:

'Behold, I am sending my messenger
　　ahead of you;
　he will prepare your way before you.'ᵏ

---

***[11:1] The closing formula of the discourse refers back to the original addressees, the Twelve.

††[11:2–12:50] The narrative section of the third book deals with the growing opposition to Jesus. It is largely devoted to disputes and attacks relating to faith and discipleship and thus contains much sayings-material, drawn in large part from Q.

‡‡[11:2] **In prison:** see Mt 4:12; 14:1–12. **The works of the Messiah:** the deeds of Mt 8–9.

§§[11:3] The question probably expresses a doubt of the Baptist that Jesus is **the one who is to come** (cf. Mal 3:1) because his mission has not been one of fiery judgment as John had expected (Mt 3:2).

¶¶[11:5–6] Jesus' response is taken from passages of Isaiah (Is 26:19; 29:18–19; 35:5–6; 61:1) that picture the time of salvation as marked by deeds such as those that Jesus is doing. The beatitude is a warning to the Baptist not to disbelieve because his expectations have not been met.

***[11:7–19] Jesus' rebuke of John is counterbalanced by a reminder of the greatness of the Baptist's function (Mt 11:7–15) that is followed by a complaint about those who have heeded neither John nor Jesus (Mt 11:16–19).

†††[11:9–10] In common Jewish belief there had been no prophecy in Israel since the last of the Old Testament prophets, Malachi. The coming of a new prophet was eagerly awaited, and Jesus agrees that John was such. Yet he was **more than a prophet,** for he was the precursor of the one who would bring in the new and final age. The Old Testament quotation is a combination of Mal 3:1; Ex 23:20 with the significant change that the **before me** of Malachi becomes **before you.** The messenger now precedes not God, as in the original, but Jesus.

---

*[10:32–33] In the Q parallel (Lk 12:8–9), the Son of Man will acknowledge those who have acknowledged Jesus, and those who deny him will be denied (by the Son of Man) before the angels of God at the judgment. Here Jesus and the Son of Man are identified, and the acknowledgment or denial will be before his heavenly Father.

†[10:38] The first mention of the cross in Matthew, explicitly that of the disciple, but implicitly that of Jesus (**and follow after me**). Crucifixion was a form of capital punishment used by the Romans for offenders who were not Roman citizens.

‡[10:39] One who denies Jesus in order to save one's earthly life will be condemned to everlasting destruction; loss of earthly life for Jesus' sake will be rewarded by everlasting life in the kingdom.

§[10:40–42] All who receive the disciples of Jesus receive him, and God who sent him, and will be rewarded accordingly.

¶[10:41] **A prophet:** one who speaks in the name of God; here, the Christian prophets who proclaim the gospel. **Righteous man:** since righteousness is demanded of all the disciples, it is difficult to take the **righteous man** of this verse and **one of these little ones** (Mt 10:42) as indicating different groups within the followers of Jesus. Probably all three designations are used here of Christian missionaries as such.

---

a. [10:28] Jas 4:12.　b. [10:33] Mk 8:38; Lk 9:26; 2 Tm 2:12; Rev 3:5.　c. [10:34–35] Lk 12:51–53.　d. [10:37–39] 16:24–25; Lk 14:26–27.　e. [10:39] Mk 8:35; Lk 9:24; Jn 12:25.　f. [10:40] Lk 10:16; Jn 12:44; 13:20.

g. [10:42] 25:40; Mk 9:41.　h. [11:2–11] Lk 7:18–28.　i. [11:5] Is 26:19; 29:18–19; 35:5–6; 61:1.　j. [11:7] 3:3, 5.　k. [11:10] Ex 23:20; Mal 3:1; Mk 1:2; Lk 1:76.

¹¹Amen, I say to you, among those born of women there has been none greater than John the Baptist; yet the least in the kingdom of heaven is greater than he.* ¹²From the days of John the Baptist until now, the kingdom of heaven suffers violence,† and the violent are taking it by force.ˡ ¹³All the prophets and the law‡ prophesied up to the time of John. ¹⁴And if you are willing to accept it, he is Elijah, the one who is to come.ᵐ ¹⁵Whoever has ears ought to hear.

¹⁶ⁿ"To what shall I compare this generation?§ It is like children who sit in marketplaces and call to one another, ¹⁷'We played the flute for you, but you did not dance, we sang a dirge but you did not mourn.' ¹⁸For John came neither eating nor drinking, and they said, 'He is possessed by a demon.'ᵒ ¹⁹The Son of Man came eating and drinking and they said, 'Look, he is a glutton and a drunkard, a friend of tax collectors and sinners.' But wisdom is vindicated by her works."ᵖ

**Reproaches to Unrepentant Towns.** ²⁰�q Then he began to reproach the towns where most of his mighty deeds had been done, since they had not repented. ²¹"Woe to you, Chorazin! Woe to you, Bethsaida! For if the mighty deeds done in your midst had been done in Tyre and Sidon,ᵉ they would long ago have repented in sackcloth and ashes.ʳ ²²But I tell you, it will be more tolerable for Tyre and Sidon on the day of judgment than for you. ²³"And as for you, Capernaum:

'Will you be exalted to heaven?ˢ
  You will go down to the
    netherworld.'

For if the mighty deeds done in your midst had been done in Sodom, it would have remained until this day. ²⁴But I tell you, it will be more tolerable for the land of Sodom on the day of judgment than for you."ᵗ

**The Praise of the Father.** ²⁵ᵘAt that time Jesus said in reply,†† "I give praise to you, Father, Lord of heaven and earth, for although you have hidden these things from the wise and the learned you have revealed them to the childlike. ²⁶Yes, Father, such has been your gracious will. ²⁷All things have been handed over to me by my Father. No one knows the Son except the Father, and no one knows the Father except the Son and anyone to whom the Son wishes to reveal him.ᵛ

**The Gentle Mastery of Christ.** ²⁸‡‡"Come to me, all you who labor and are burdened,§§ and I will give you rest. ²⁹¶¶"Take my yoke upon you and learn from me, for I am meek and humble of heart; and you will find rest for yourselves. ³⁰For my yoke is easy, and my burden light."

## CHAPTER 12

**Picking Grain on the Sabbath.** ¹***At that time Jesus was going through a field of grain on the sabbath.ˣ His disciples were hungry and began to pick the heads††† of grain and eat them.ʸ ²When the Pharisees saw this, they said to him, "See, your disciples are doing what is unlawful to do on the sabbath." ³He said to them,‡‡‡ "Have

---

*[11:11] John's preeminent greatness lies in his function of announcing the imminence of the kingdom (Mt 3:1). But to be in the kingdom is so great a privilege that the least who has it is greater than the Baptist.

†[11:12] The meaning of this difficult saying is probably that the opponents of Jesus are trying to prevent people from accepting the kingdom and to snatch it away from those who have received it.

‡[11:13] **All the prophets and the law**: Matthew inverts the usual order, "law and prophets," and says that both have **prophesied**. This emphasis on the prophetic character of the law points to its fulfillment in the teaching of Jesus and to the transitory nature of some of its commandments (see note on Mt 5:17–20).

§[11:16–19] See Lk 7:31–35. The meaning of the parable (Mt 11:16–17) and its explanation (Mt 11:18–19b) is much disputed. A plausible view is that the **children** of the parable are two groups, one of which proposes different entertainments to the other that will not agree with either proposal. The first represents John, Jesus, and their disciples; the second those who reject John for his asceticism and Jesus for his table association with those despised by the religiously observant. Mt 11:19c (**her works**) forms an inclusion with Mt 11:2 ("the works of the Messiah"). The original form of the saying is better preserved in Lk 7:35 ". . . wisdom is vindicated by all her children." There John and Jesus are the children of Wisdom; here the works of Jesus the Messiah are those of divine Wisdom, of which he is the embodiment. Some important textual witnesses, however, have essentially the same reading as in Luke.

¶[11:21] Tyre and Sidon were pagan cities denounced for their wickedness in the Old Testament; cf. Jl 4:4–7.

**[11:23] Capernaum's pride and punishment are described in language taken from the taunt song against the king of Babylon (Is 14:13–15).

††[11:25–27] This Q saying, identical with Lk 10:21–22 except for minor variations, introduces a joyous note into this section, so dominated by the theme of unbelief. **While the wise and the learned**, the scribes and Pharisees, have rejected Jesus' preaching and the significance of his mighty deeds, **the childlike** have accepted them. Acceptance depends upon the Father's revelation, but this is granted to those who are open to receive it and refused to the arrogant. Jesus can speak of all mysteries because he is **the Son** and there is perfect reciprocity of knowledge between him and the Father; what has been **handed over** to him is revealed only to those whom he wishes.

‡‡[11:28–29] These verses are peculiar to Matthew and are similar to Ben Sirach's invitation to learn wisdom and submit to her yoke (Sir 51:23, 26).

§§[11:28] **Who labor and are burdened**: burdened by the law as expounded by the scribes and Pharisees (Mt 23:4).

¶¶[11:29] In place of the yoke of the law, complicated by scribal interpretation, Jesus invites the burdened to take the yoke of obedience to his word, under which they **will find rest**; cf. Jer 6:16.

***[12:1–14] Matthew here returns to the Marcan order that he left in Mt 9:18. The two stories depend on Mk 2:23–28; 3:1–6, respectively, and are the only places in either gospel that deal explicitly with Jesus' attitude toward sabbath observance.

†††[12:1–2] The picking of the heads of grain is here equated with reaping, which was forbidden on the sabbath (Ex 34:21).

‡‡‡[12:3–4] See 1 Sm 21:2–7. In the Marcan parallel (Mk 2:25–26) the high priest is called Abiathar, although in 1 Samuel this action is attributed to Ahimelech. The Old Testament story is not about a violation of the sabbath rest; its pertinence

---

l. [11:12] Lk 16:16.   m. [11:14] 17:10–13; Mal 3:23; Lk 1:17.
n. [11:16–19] Lk 7:31–35.   o. [11:18] Lk 1:15.   p. [11:19] 9:10–11.
q. [11:20–24] Lk 10:12–15.   r. [11:21] Jl 4:4–7.

s. [11:23] Is 14:13–15.   t. [11:24] 10:15.   u. [11:25–27] Lk 10:21–22.
v. [11:27] Jn 3:35; 6:46; 7:28; 10:15.   w. [11:29] Sir 51:26; Jer 6:16.
x. [12:1–8] Mk 2:23–28; Lk 6:1–5.   y. [12:1] Dt 23:26.

you not read what David*z* did when he and his companions were hungry, *4*how he went into the house of God and ate the bread of offering,*a* which neither he nor his companions but only the priests could lawfully eat? *5*Or have you not read in the law that on the sabbath the priests serving in the temple violate the sabbath and are innocent?*b* *6*I say to you, something greater than the temple is here. *7†*If you knew what this meant, 'I desire mercy, not sacrifice,'*c* you would not have condemned these innocent men. *8‡d*For the Son of Man is Lord of the sabbath."

**The Man with a Withered Hand.** *9e*Moving on from there, he went into their synagogue. *10*And behold, there was a man there who had a withered hand. They questioned him, "Is it lawful to cure on the sabbath?"*§* so that they might accuse him. *11¶*He said to them, "Which one of you who has a sheep that falls into a pit on the sabbath will not take hold of it and lift it out? *12*How much more valuable a person is than a sheep. So it is lawful to do good on the sabbath." *13*Then he said to the man, "Stretch out your hand." He stretched it out, and it was restored as sound as the other. *14*But the Pharisees** went out and took counsel against him to put him to death.*f*

**The Chosen Servant.**†† *15*When Jesus realized this, he withdrew from that place. Many [people] followed him, and he cured them all,‡‡ *16*but he warned them not to make him known. *17*This was to fulfill what had been spoken through Isaiah the prophet:

*18* "Behold, my servant whom I have chosen,*g* my beloved in whom I delight; I shall place my spirit upon him, and he will proclaim justice to the Gentiles.
*19* He will not contend§§ or cry out, nor will anyone hear his voice in the streets.
*20* A bruised reed he will not break, a smoldering wick he will not quench, until he brings justice to victory.
*21* And in his name the Gentiles will hope."¶¶

**Jesus and Beelzebul.*** *22h*Then they brought to him a demoniac who was blind and mute. He cured the mute person so that he could speak and see. *23†††*All the crowd was astounded, and said, "Could this perhaps be the Son of David?" *24‡‡‡i*But when the Pharisees heard this, they said, "This man drives out demons only by the power of Beelzebul, the prince of demons." *25k*But he knew what they were thinking and said to them,§§§ "Every kingdom divided against itself will be laid waste, and no town or house divided against itself will stand. *26*And if Satan drives out Satan, he is divided against himself; how, then, will his kingdom stand? *27*And if I drive out demons by Beelzebul, by whom do your own people¶¶¶ drive them out? Therefore they will be your judges. *28****j*But if it is by the Spirit of God that I drive out demons, then the kingdom of God has come upon you. *29††††*How can anyone

---

to this dispute is that a violation of the law was permissible because of David's men being without food.

*\*[12:5–6] This and the following argument (Mt 12:7) are peculiar to Matthew. The temple service seems to be the changing of the showbread on the sabbath (Lv 24:8) and the doubling on the sabbath of the usual daily holocausts (Nm 28:9–10). The argument is that the law itself requires work that breaks the sabbath rest, because of the higher duty of temple service. If temple duties outweigh the sabbath law, how much more does the presence of Jesus, with his proclamation of the kingdom (**something greater than the temple**), justify the conduct of his disciples.*

*†[12:7] See note on Mt 9:13.*

*‡[12:8] The ultimate justification for the disciples' violation of the sabbath rest is that Jesus, the Son of Man, has supreme authority over the law.*

*§[12:10] Rabbinic tradition later than the gospels allowed relief to be given to a sufferer on the sabbath if life was in danger. This may also have been the view of Jesus' Pharisaic contemporaries. But the case here is not about one in danger of death.*

*¶[12:11] Matthew omits the question posed by Jesus in Mk 3:4 and substitutes one about rescuing a sheep on the sabbath, similar to that in Lk 14:5.*

*\*\*[12:14] See Mk 3:6. Here the plan to bring about Jesus' death is attributed to the Pharisees only. This is probably due to the situation of Matthew's church, when the sole opponents were the Pharisees.*

*††[12:15–21] Matthew follows Mk 3:7–12 but summarizes his source in two verses (Mt 12:15, 16) that pick up the withdrawal, the healings, and the command for silence. To this he adds a fulfillment citation from the first Servant Song (Is 42:1–4) that does not correspond exactly to either the Hebrew or the LXX of that passage. It is the longest Old Testament citation in this gospel, emphasizing the meekness of Jesus, the Servant of the Lord, and foretelling the extension of his mission to the Gentiles.*

*‡‡[12:15] Jesus' knowledge of the Pharisees' plot and his healing all are peculiar to Matthew.*

*§§[12:19] The servant's not contending is seen as fulfilled in Jesus' withdrawal from the disputes narrated in Mt 12:1–14.*

*¶¶[12:21] Except for a minor detail, Matthew here follows the LXX, although the meaning of the Hebrew ("the coastlands will wait for his teaching") is similar.*

*\*\*\*[12:22–32] For the exorcism, see note on Mt 9:32–34. The long discussion combines Marcan and Q material (Mk 3:22–30; Lk 11:19–20, 23; 12:10). Mk 3:20–21 is omitted, with a consequent lessening of the sharpness of Mt 12:48.*

*†††[12:23] See note on Mt 9:27.*

*‡‡‡[12:24] See note on Mt 10:25.*

*§§§[12:25–26] Jesus' first response to the Pharisees' charge is that if it were true, Satan would be destroying his own kingdom.*

*¶¶¶[12:27] Besides pointing out the absurdity of the charge, Jesus asks how the work of Jewish exorcists (**your own people**) is to be interpreted. Are they, too, to be charged with collusion with Beelzebul? For an example of Jewish exorcism see Josephus, Antiquities 8:42–49.*

*\*\*\*\*[12:28] The Q parallel (Lk 11:20) speaks of the "finger" rather than of the "spirit" of God. While the difference is probably due to Matthew's editing, he retains **the kingdom of God** rather than changing it to his usual "kingdom of heaven." **Has come upon you:** see Mt 4:17.*

*††††[12:29] A short parable illustrates what Jesus is doing. The **strong man** is Satan, whom Jesus has tied up and whose **house** he is plundering. Jewish expectation was that Satan*

---

z. [12:3–4] 1 Sm 21:2–7.  a. [12:4] Lv 24:5–9.  b. [12:5] Lv 24:8; Nm 28:9–10.  c. [12:7] Hos 6:6.  d. [12:8] Jn 5:16–17.  e. [12:9–15] Mk 3:1–6; Lk 6:6–11.  f. [12:14] Jn 5:18.

g. [12:18–21] Is 42:1–4.  h. [12:22–24] 9:32–34; Lk 11:14–15.  i. [12:23] 9:27.  j. [12:24] 10:25; Mk 3:22.  k. [12:25–29] Mk 3:23–27; Lk 11:17–22.  l. [12:28] Lk 11:20.

enter a strong man's house and steal his property, unless he first ties up the strong man? Then he can plunder his house. ³⁰*ᵐWhoever is not with me is against me, and whoever does not gather with me scatters. ³¹ⁿTherefore, I say to you, every sin and blasphemy will be forgiven people, but blasphemy against the Spirit† will not be forgiven. ³²And whoever speaks a word against the Son of Man will be forgiven; but whoever speaks against the holy Spirit will not be forgiven, either in this age or in the age to come.

**A Tree and Its Fruits.** ³³ᵒ"Either declare‡ the tree good and its fruit is good, or declare the tree rotten and its fruit is rotten, for a tree is known by its fruit. ³⁴ᵖYou brood of vipers, how can you say good things when you are evil? For from the fullness of the heart the mouth speaks. ³⁵A good person brings forth good out of a store of goodness, but an evil person brings forth evil out of a store of evil. ³⁶ᵠI tell you, on the day of judgment people will render an account for every careless word they speak. ³⁷By your words you will be acquitted, and by your words you will be condemned."

**The Demand for a Sign.**⁎ ³⁸Then some of the scribes and Pharisees said to him, "Teacher,†† we wish to see a sign from you."ʳ ³⁹He said to them in reply, "An evil and unfaithful‡‡ generation seeks a sign, but no sign will be given it except

the sign of Jonah the prophet. ⁴⁰Just as Jonah was in the belly of the whale three days and three nights,§§ so will the Son of Man be in the heart of the earth three days and three nights. ⁴¹⁎⁎At the judgment, the men of Nineveh will arise with this generation and condemn it, because they repented at the preaching of Jonah; and there is something greater than Jonah here. ⁴²At the judgment the queen of the south will arise with this generation and condemn it, because she came from the ends of the earth to hear the wisdom of Solomon; and there is something greater than Solomon here.ˢ

**The Return of the Unclean Spirit.**⁎⁎⁎ ⁴³"When an unclean spirit goes out of a person it roams through arid regions searching for rest but finds none. ⁴⁴Then it says, 'I will return to my home from which I came.' But upon returning, it finds it empty, swept clean, and put in order. ⁴⁵Then it goes and brings back with itself seven other spirits more evil than itself, and they move in and dwell there; and the last condition of that person is worse than the first. Thus it will be with this evil generation."

**The True Family of Jesus.**††† ⁴⁶ᵘWhile he was still speaking to the crowds, his mother and his brothers appeared outside, wishing to speak with him. ⁴⁷[Someone told him, "Your mother and your brothers are standing outside, asking to speak with you."]‡‡‡ ⁴⁸But he said in reply to the one who told him, "Who is my mother? Who are my brothers?" ⁴⁹And stretching out his hand toward his disciples, he said, "Here are my mother and my brothers. ⁵⁰For whoever does the will of my heavenly Father is my brother, and sister, and mother."

# CHAPTER 13

**The Parable of the Sower.** ¹§§§On that day, Jesus went out of the house and sat down by the sea.ᵛ

---

would be chained up in the last days (Rev 20:2); Jesus' exorcisms indicate that those days have begun.

*[12:30] This saying, already attached to the preceding verses in Q (see Lk 11:23), warns that there can be no neutrality where Jesus is concerned. Its pertinence in a context where Jesus is addressing not the neutral but the bitterly opposed is not clear. The accusation of scattering, however, does fit the situation. Jesus is the shepherd of God's people (Mt 2:6), his mission is to the lost sheep of Israel (Mt 15:24); the Pharisees, who oppose him, are guilty of scattering the sheep.

†[12:31] **Blasphemy against the Spirit**: the sin of attributing to Satan (Mt 12:24) what is the work of the Spirit of God (Mt 12:28).

‡[12:33] **Declare**: literally, "make." The meaning of this verse is obscure. Possibly it is a challenge to the Pharisees either to declare Jesus and his exorcisms good or both of them bad. A tree is known by its fruit; if the fruit is good, so must the tree be. If the driving out of demons is good, so must its source be.

§[12:34] The admission of Jesus' goodness cannot be made by the Pharisees, for they are evil, and the words that proceed from their evil hearts cannot be good.

¶[12:36–37] If on the day of judgment people will be held accountable for even their **careless** words, the vicious accusations of the Pharisees will surely lead to their condemnation.

**[12:38–42] This section is mainly from Q (see Lk 11:29–32). Mk 8:11–12, which Matthew has followed in Mt 16:1–4, has a similar demand for a sign. The scribes and Pharisees refuse to accept the exorcisms of Jesus as authentication of his claims and demand a sign that will end all possibility of doubt. Jesus' response is that no such sign will be given. Because his opponents are evil and see him as an agent of Satan, nothing will convince them.

††[12:38] **Teacher**: see note on Mt 8:19. In Mt 16:1 the request is for a sign "from heaven" (Mk 8:11).

‡‡[12:39] **Unfaithful**: literally, "adulterous." The covenant between God and Israel was portrayed as a marriage bond, and unfaithfulness to the covenant as adultery; cf. Hos 2:4–14; Jer 3:6–10.

§§[12:40] See Jon 2:1. While in Q the sign was simply Jonah's preaching to the Ninevites (Lk 11:30, 32), Matthew here adds Jonah's sojourn **in the belly of the whale** for **three days and three nights**, a prefigurement of Jesus' sojourn in the abode of the dead and, implicitly, of his resurrection.

¶¶[12:41–42] The Ninevites who **repented** (see Jon 3:1–10) and **the queen of the south** (i.e., of Sheba; see 1 Kgs 10:1–13) were pagans who responded to lesser opportunities than have been offered to Israel in the ministry of Jesus, **something greater than Jonah** or **Solomon**. At the final judgment they will condemn the faithless **generation** that has rejected him.

***[12:43–45] Another Q passage; cf. Mt 11:24–26. Jesus' ministry has broken Satan's hold over Israel, but the refusal of **this evil generation** to accept him will lead to a worse situation than what preceded his coming.

†††[12:46–50] See Mk 3:31–35. Matthew has omitted Mk 3:20–21 which is taken up in Mk 3:31 (see note on Mt 12:22–32), yet the point of the story is the same in both gospels: natural kinship with Jesus counts for nothing; only one who **does the will** of his **heavenly Father** belongs to his true family.

‡‡‡[12:47] This verse is omitted in some important textual witnesses, including Codex Sinaiticus (original reading) and Codex Vaticanus.

§§§[13:1–53] The discourse in parables is the third great discourse of Jesus in Matthew and constitutes the second part of

---

m. [12:30] Lk 11:23.  n. [12:31–32] Mk 3:28–30; Lk 12:10. o. [12:33–35] Lk 6:43–45.  p. [12:34] 3:7; 23:33; 15:11–12; Lk 3:7.  q. [12:36–37] Jas 3:1–2.  r. [12:38–42] 16:1–4; Jon 2:1; 3:1–10; Mk 8:11–12; Lk 11:29–32.

s. [12:42] 1 Kgs 10:1–10.  t. [12:43–45] Lk 11:24–26.  u. [12:46–50] Mk 3:31–35; Lk 8:19–21.  v. [13:1–15] Mk 4:1–12; Lk 8:4–10.

²Such large crowds gathered around him that he got into a boat and sat down, and the whole crowd stood along the shore. ³*And he spoke to them at length in parables,† saying: "A sower went out to sow. ⁴And as he sowed, some seed fell on the path, and birds came and ate it up. ⁵Some fell on rocky ground, where it had little soil. It sprang up at once because the soil was not deep, ⁶and when the sun rose it was scorched, and it withered for lack of roots. ⁷Some seed fell among thorns, and the thorns grew up and choked it. ⁸But some seed fell on rich soil, and produced fruit, a hundred or sixty or thirtyfold. ⁹Whoever has ears ought to hear."

**The Purpose of Parables.** ¹⁰The disciples approached him and said, "Why do you speak to them in parables?" ¹¹‡He said to them in reply, "Because knowledge of the mysteries of the kingdom of heaven has been granted to you, but to them it has not been granted. ¹²ʷTo anyone who has, more will be given§ and he will grow rich;

from anyone who has not, even what he has will be taken away. ¹³ˣThis is why I speak to them in parables, because 'they look but do not see and hear but do not listen or understand.' ¹⁴ʸIsaiah's prophecy is fulfilled in them, which says:

'You shall indeed hear but not understand,
　　you shall indeed look but never see.
¹⁵ Gross is the heart of this people,
　　they will hardly hear with their ears,
　　　they have closed their eyes,
　　　　lest they see with their eyes
　　and hear with their ears
and understand with their heart and be
　　converted,
　　and I heal them.'

**The Privilege of Discipleship.** ¹⁶ᶻ"But blessed are your eyes, because they see, and your ears, because they hear. ¹⁷Amen, I say to you, many prophets and righteous people longed to see what you see but did not see it, and to hear what you hear but did not hear it.

**The Explanation of the Parable of the Sower.**†† ¹⁸ᵃ"Hear then the parable of the sower. ¹⁹The seed sown on the path is the one who hears the word of the kingdom without understanding it, and the evil one comes and steals away what was sown in his heart. ²⁰The seed sown on rocky ground is the one who hears the word and receives it at once with joy. ²¹But he has no root and lasts only for a time. When some tribulation or persecution comes because of the word, he immediately falls away. ²²The seed sown among thorns is the one who hears the word, but then worldly anxiety and the lure of riches choke the

---

the third book of the gospel. Matthew follows the Marcan outline (Mk 4:1–35) but has only two of Mark's parables, the five others being from Q and M. In addition to the seven parables, the discourse gives the reason why Jesus uses this type of speech (Mt 13:10–15), declares the blessedness of those who understand his teaching (Mt 13:16–17), explains the parable of the sower (Mt 13:18–23) and of the weeds (Mt 13:36–43), and ends with a concluding statement to the disciples (Mt 13:51–52).

*[13:3] **In parables:** the word "parable" (Greek *parabolē*) is used in the LXX to translate the Hebrew *māshāl*, a designation covering a wide variety of literary forms such as axioms, proverbs, similitudes, and allegories. In the New Testament the same breadth of meaning of the word is found, but there it primarily designates stories that are illustrative comparisons between Christian truths and events of everyday life. Sometimes the event has a strange element that is quite different from usual experience (e.g., in Mt 13:33 the enormous amount of dough in the parable of the yeast); this is meant to sharpen the curiosity of the hearer. If each detail of such a story is given a figurative meaning, the story is an allegory. Those who maintain a sharp distinction between parable and allegory insist that a parable has only one point of comparison, and that while parables were characteristic of Jesus' teaching, to see allegorical details in them is to introduce meanings that go beyond their original intention and even falsify it. However, to exclude any allegorical elements from a parable is an excessively rigid mode of interpretation, now abandoned by many scholars.

†[13:3–8] Since in Palestine sowing often preceded plowing, much of the seed is scattered on ground that is unsuitable. Yet while much is wasted, the seed that falls on good ground bears fruit in extraordinarily large measure. The point of the parable is that, in spite of some failure because of opposition and indifference, the message of Jesus about the coming of the kingdom will have enormous success.

‡[13:11] Since a parable is figurative speech that demands reflection for understanding, only those who are prepared to explore its meaning can come to know it. To understand is a gift of God, granted to the disciples but not to the crowds. In Semitic fashion, both the disciples' understanding and the crowd's obtuseness are attributed to God. The question of human responsibility for the obtuseness is not dealt with, although it is asserted in Mt 13:13. **The mysteries:** as in Lk 8:10; Mk 4:11 has "the mystery." The word is used in Dn 2:18, 19, 27 and in the Qumran literature (1QpHab 7:8; 1QS 3:23; 1QM 3:9) to designate a divine plan or decree affecting the course of history that can be known only when revealed. **Knowledge of the mysteries of the kingdom of heaven** means recognition that the kingdom has become present in the ministry of Jesus.

§[13:12] In the New Testament use of this axiom of practical "wisdom" (see Mt 25:29; Mk 4:25; Lk 8:18; 19:26), the reference

transcends the original level. God gives further understanding to one who accepts the revealed mystery; from the one who does not, he will take it away (note the "theological passive," **more will be given, what he has will be taken away**).

¶[13:13] **Because 'they look . . . or understand':** Matthew softens his Marcan source, which states that Jesus speaks in parables so that the crowds may not understand (Mk 4:12), and makes such speaking a punishment given **because** they have not accepted his previous clear teaching. However, his citation of Is 6:9–10 in Mt 13:14 supports the harsher Marcan view.

**[13:16–17] Unlike the unbelieving crowds, the disciples have seen that which the **prophets** and the **righteous** of the Old Testament **longed to see** without having their longing fulfilled.

††[13:18–23] See Mk 4:14–20; Lk 8:11–15. In this explanation of the parable the emphasis is on the various types of soil on which the seed falls, i.e., on the dispositions with which the preaching of Jesus is received. The second and third types particularly are explained in such a way as to support the view held by many scholars that the explanation derives not from Jesus but from early Christian reflection upon apostasy from the faith that was the consequence of persecution and worldliness, respectively. Others, however, hold that the explanation may come basically from Jesus even though it was developed in the light of later Christian experience. The four types of persons envisaged are (1) those who never accept **the word of the kingdom** (Mt 13:19); (2) those who believe for a while but fall away because of **persecution** (Mt 13:20–21); (3) those who believe, but in whom **the word** is choked by **worldly anxiety** and the seduction of **riches** (Mt 13:22); (4) those who respond to **the word** and produce **fruit** abundantly (Mt 13:23).

---

x. [13:13] Jn 9:39.　y. [13:14–15] Is 6:9–10; Jn 12:40; Acts 28:26–27; Rom 11:8.　z. [13:16–17] Lk 10:23–24; 1 Pt 1:10–12.　a. [13:18–23] Mk 4:13–20; Lk 8:11–15.

w. [13:12] 25:29; Mk 4:25; Lk 8:18; 19:26.

word and it bears no fruit. [23]But the seed sown on rich soil is the one who hears the word and understands it, who indeed bears fruit and yields a hundred or sixty or thirtyfold."

**The Parable of the Weeds Among the Wheat.** [24]He proposed another parable to them.* "The kingdom of heaven may be likened to a man who sowed good seed in his field. [25]While everyone was asleep his enemy came and sowed weeds† all through the wheat, and then went off. [26]When the crop grew and bore fruit, the weeds appeared as well. [27]The slaves of the householder came to him and said, 'Master, did you not sow good seed in your field? Where have the weeds come from?' [28]He answered, 'An enemy has done this.' His slaves said to him, 'Do you want us to go and pull them up?' [29]He replied, 'No, if you pull up the weeds you might uproot the wheat along with them. [30]Let them grow together until harvest;‡ then at harvest time I will say to the harvesters, "First collect the weeds and tie them in bundles for burning; but gather the wheat into my barn."'"b

**The Parable of the Mustard Seed.**§ [31]cHe proposed another parable to them. "The kingdom of heaven is like a mustard seed that a person took and sowed in a field. [32]dIt is the smallest of all the seeds, yet when full-grown it is the largest of plants. It becomes a large bush, and the 'birds of the sky come and dwell in its branches.'"

**The Parable of the Yeast.** [33]He spoke to them another parable. "The kingdom of heaven is like yeast** that a woman took and mixed with three measures of wheat flour until the whole batch was leavened."e

**The Use of Parables.** [34]††fAll these things Jesus spoke to the crowds in parables. He spoke to them only in parables, [35]to fulfill what had been said through the prophet:‡‡

"I will open my mouth in parables,
    I will announce what has lain
        hidden from the foundation
            [of the world]."g

**The Explanation of the Parable of the Weeds.** [36]Then, dismissing the crowds,§§ he went into the house. His disciples approached him and said, "Explain to us the parable of the weeds in the field." [37]¶¶He said in reply, "He who sows good seed is the Son of Man, [38]the field is the world,*** the good seed the children of the kingdom. The weeds are the children of the evil one, [39]and the enemy who sows them is the devil. The harvest is the end of the age,††† and the harvesters are angels. [40]Just as weeds are collected and burned [up] with fire, so will it be at the end of the age. [41]The Son of Man will send his angels, and they will collect out of his kingdom‡‡‡ all who cause others to sin and all evildoers. [42]hThey will throw them into the fiery furnace, where there will be wailing and grinding of teeth. [43]§§§iThen the righteous will shine like the sun in the kingdom of their Father. Whoever has ears ought to hear.

**More Parables.**¶¶¶ [44]j"The kingdom of heaven is like a treasure buried in a field,**** which a person

---

* [13:24–30] This parable is peculiar to Matthew. The comparison in Mt 13:24 does not mean that **the kingdom of heaven may be likened** simply to the person in question but to the situation narrated in the whole story. The refusal of the **householder** to allow his **slaves** to separate **the wheat** from **the weeds** while they are still growing is a warning to the disciples not to attempt to anticipate the final judgment of God by a definitive exclusion of sinners from the kingdom. In its present stage it is composed of the good and the bad. The judgment of God alone will eliminate the sinful. Until then there must be patience and the preaching of repentance.

† [13:25] **Weeds:** darnel, a poisonous weed that in its first stage of growth resembles wheat.

‡ [13:30] **Harvest:** a common biblical metaphor for the time of God's judgment; cf. Jer 51:33; Jl 4:13; Hos 6:11.

§ [13:31–33] See Mk 4:30–32; Lk 13:18–21. The parables of the mustard seed and the yeast illustrate the same point: the amazing contrast between the small beginnings of the kingdom and its marvelous expansion.

¶ [13:32] See Dn 4:7–9, 17–19 where the birds nesting in the tree represent the people of Nebuchadnezzar's kingdom. See also Ez 17:23; 31:6.

** [13:33] Except in this Q parable and in Mt 16:12, **yeast** (or "leaven") is, in New Testament usage, a symbol of corruption (see Mt 16:6, 11–12; Mk 8:15; Lk 12:1; 1 Cor 5:6–8; Gal 5:9). **Three measures:** an enormous amount, enough to feed a hundred people. The exaggeration of this element of the parable points to the greatness of the kingdom's effect.

†† [13:34] **Only in parables:** see Mt 13:10–15.

‡‡ [13:35] **The prophet:** some textual witnesses read "Isaiah the prophet." The quotation is actually from Ps 78:2; the first line corresponds to the LXX text of the psalm. The psalm's title ascribes it to Asaph, the founder of one of the guilds of temple musicians. He is called "the prophet" (NAB "the seer") in 2 Chr 29:30, but it is doubtful that Matthew averted to that; for him, any Old Testament text that could be seen as fulfilled in Jesus was prophetic.

§§ [13:36] **Dismissing the crowds:** the return of Jesus to the house marks a break with the crowds, who represent unbelieving Israel. From now on his attention is directed more and more to his disciples and to their instruction. The rest of the discourse is addressed to them alone.

¶¶ [13:37–43] In the explanation of the parable of the weeds emphasis lies on the fearful end of the wicked, whereas the parable itself concentrates on patience with them until judgment time.

*** [13:38] **The field is the world:** this presupposes the resurrection of Jesus and the granting to him of "all power in heaven and on earth" (Mt 28:18).

††† [13:39] **The end of the age:** this phrase is found only in Matthew (13:40, 49; 24:3; 28:20).

‡‡‡ [13:41] **His kingdom:** the **kingdom** of the **Son of Man** is distinguished from that of the Father (Mt 13:43); see 1 Cor 15:24–25. The church is the place where Jesus' kingdom is manifested, but his royal authority embraces the entire world; see note on Mt 13:38.

§§§ [13:43] See Dn 12:3.

¶¶¶ [13:44–50] The first two of the last three parables of the discourse have the same point. The **person** who **finds** a buried **treasure** and the **merchant** who finds a **pearl of great price** sell **all** that they have to acquire these finds; similarly, the one who understands the supreme value of the kingdom gives up whatever he must to obtain it. The **joy** with which this is done is made explicit in the first parable, but it may be presumed in the second also. The concluding parable of the fishnet resembles the explanation of the parable of the weeds with its stress upon the final exclusion of evil persons from the kingdom.

**** [13:44] In the unsettled conditions of Palestine in Jesus' time, it was not unusual to guard valuables by burying them in the ground.

---

b. [13:30] 3:12.   c. [13:31–32] Mk 4:30–32; Lk 13:18–19.   d. [13:32] Ez 17:23; 31:6; Dn 4:7–9, 17–19.   e. [13:33] Lk 13:20–21.   f. [13:34–35] Mk 4:33–34.

g. [13:35] Ps 78:2.   h. [13:42] 8:12; Rev 21:8.   i. [13:43] Dn 12:3.   j. [13:44–45] Prv 2:4; 4:7.

finds and hides again, and out of joy goes and sells all that he has and buys that field. ⁴⁵Again, the kingdom of heaven is like a merchant searching for fine pearls. ⁴⁶When he finds a pearl of great price, he goes and sells all that he has and buys it. ⁴⁷Again, the kingdom of heaven is like a net thrown into the sea, which collects fish of every kind. ⁴⁸When it is full they haul it ashore and sit down to put what is good into buckets. What is bad they throw away. ⁴⁹Thus it will be at the end of the age. The angels will go out and separate the wicked from the righteous ⁵⁰and throw them into the fiery furnace, where there will be wailing and grinding of teeth.

**Treasures New and Old.** ⁵¹"Do you understand* all these things?" They answered, "Yes." ⁵²*And he replied, "Then every scribe who has been instructed in the kingdom of heaven is like the head of a household who brings from his storeroom both the new and the old." ⁵³When Jesus finished these parables, he went away from there.

## V. JESUS, THE KINGDOM, AND THE CHURCH

**The Rejection at Nazareth.** ⁵⁴‡He came to his native place and taught the people in their synagogue.ᵏ They were astonished§ and said, "Where did this man get such wisdom and mighty deeds?ˡ ⁵⁵Is he not the carpenter's son? Is not his mother named Mary and his brothers James, Joseph, Simon, and Judas?ᵐ ⁵⁶Are not his sisters all with us? Where did this man get all this?" ⁵⁷And they took offense at him. But Jesus said to them, "A prophet is not without honor except in his native place and in his own house."ⁿ

---

*[13:51] Matthew typically speaks of the understanding of the disciples.

†[13:52] Since Matthew tends to identify the disciples and the Twelve (see note on Mt 10:1), this saying about the Christian **scribe** cannot be taken as applicable to all who accept the message of Jesus. While the Twelve are in many ways representative of all who believe in him, they are also distinguished from them in certain respects. The church of Matthew has leaders among whom are a group designated as "scribes" (Mt 23:34). Like the scribes of Israel, they are teachers. It is the Twelve and these their later counterparts to whom this verse applies. **The scribe . . . instructed in the kingdom of heaven** knows both the teaching of Jesus (**the new**) and the law and prophets (**the old**) and provides in his own teaching **both the new and the old** as interpreted and fulfilled by **the new**. On the translation **head of a household** (for the same Greek word translated **householder** in Mt 13:27), see note on Mt 24:45–51.

‡[13:54–17:27] This section is the narrative part of the fourth book of the gospel.

§[13:54–58] After the Sermon on the Mount the crowds are in admiring astonishment at Jesus' teaching (Mt 7:28); here the astonishment is of those who take **offense at him**. Familiarity with his background and family leads them to regard him as pretentious. Matthew modifies his Marcan source (Mt 6:1–6). Jesus is not the carpenter but **the carpenter's son** (Mt 13:55), "and among his own kin" is omitted (Mt 13:57), **he did not work many mighty deeds** in face of such unbelief (Mt 13:58) rather than the Marcan ". . . he was not able to perform any mighty deed there" (Mt 6:5), and there is no mention of his amazement at his townspeople's lack of faith.

k. [13:54–58] Mk 6:1–6; Lk 4:16–30.   l. [13:54] 2:23; Jn 1:46; 7:15.   m. [13:55] 12:46; 27:56; Jn 6:42.   n. [13:57] Jn 4:44.

---

⁵⁸And he did not work many mighty deeds there because of their lack of faith.

## CHAPTER 14

**Herod's Opinion of Jesus.** ¹*°At that time Herod the tetrarch**ᵖ heard of the reputation of Jesus�q ²and said to his servants, "This man is John the Baptist. He has been raised from the dead; that is why mighty powers are at work in him."

**The Death of John the Baptist.** ³ʳNow Herod had arrested John, bound [him], and put him in prison on account of Herodias,†† the wife of his brother Philip, ⁴ˢfor John had said to him, "It is not lawful for you to have her." ⁵ᵗAlthough he wanted to kill him, he feared the people, for they regarded him as a prophet. ⁶But at a birthday celebration for Herod, the daughter of Herodias performed a dance before the guests and delighted Herod ⁷so much that he swore to give her whatever she might ask for. ⁸Prompted by her mother, she said, "Give me here on a platter the head of John the Baptist." ⁹The king was distressed, but because of his oaths and the guests who were present, he ordered that it be given, ¹⁰and he had John beheaded in the prison. ¹¹His head was brought in on a platter and given to the girl, who took it to her mother. ¹²His disciples came and took away the corpse and buried him; and they went and told Jesus.

**The Return of the Twelve and the Feeding of the Five Thousand.** ‡‡ ¹³ᵘWhen Jesus heard of it, he withdrew in a boat to a deserted place by himself. The crowds heard of this and followed him on foot from their towns. ¹⁴When he

---

¶[14:1–12] The murder of the Baptist by Herod Antipas prefigures the death of Jesus (see Mt 17:12). The Marcan source (Mk 6:14–29) is much reduced and in some points changed. In Mark Herod reveres John as a holy man and the desire to kill him is attributed to Herodias (Mk 6:19, 20), whereas here that desire is Herod's from the beginning (Mt 14:5).

**[14:1] **Herod the tetrarch**: Herod Antipas, son of Herod the Great. When the latter died, his territory was divided among three of his surviving sons, Archelaus who received half of it (Mt 2:23), Herod Antipas who became ruler of Galilee and Perea, and Philip who became ruler of northern Transjordan. Since he received a quarter of his father's domain, Antipas is accurately designated **tetrarch** ("ruler of a fourth [part]"), although in Mt 14:9 Matthew repeats the "king" of his Marcan source (Mk 6:26).

††[14:3] Herodias was not the wife of Herod's half-brother Philip but of another half-brother, Herod Boethus. The union was prohibited by Lv 18:16; 20:21. According to Josephus (*Antiquities* 18:116–19), Herod imprisoned and then executed John because he feared that the Baptist's influence over the people might enable him to lead a rebellion.

‡‡[14:13–21] The feeding of the five thousand is the only miracle of Jesus that is recounted in all four gospels. The principal reason for that may be that it was seen as anticipating the Eucharist and the final banquet in the kingdom (Mt 8:11; 26:29), but it looks not only forward but backward, to the feeding of Israel with manna in the desert at the time of the Exodus (Ex 16), a miracle that in some contemporary Jewish expectation would be repeated in the messianic age (2 Bar 29:8). It may also be meant to recall Elisha's feeding a hundred men with small provisions (2 Kgs 4:42–44).

---

o. [14:1–12] Mk 6:14–29.   p. [14:1–2] Lk 9:7–9.   q. [14:1] Lk 3:1.   r. [14:3–4] Lk 3:19–20.   s. [14:4] Lv 18:16; 20:21.   t. [14:5] 21:26.   u. [14:13–21] 15:32–38; Mk 6:32–44; Lk 9:10–17; Jn 6:1–13.

disembarked and saw the vast crowd, his heart was moved with pity for them, and he cured their sick. ¹⁵When it was evening, the disciples approached him and said, "This is a deserted place and it is already late; dismiss the crowds so that they can go to the villages and buy food for themselves." ¹⁶[Jesus] said to them, "There is no need for them to go away; give them some food yourselves." ¹⁷But they said to him, "Five loaves and two fish are all we have here." ¹⁸Then he said, "Bring them here to me," ¹⁹and he ordered the crowds to sit down on the grass. Taking* the five loaves and the two fish, and looking up to heaven, he said the blessing, broke the loaves, and gave them to the disciples, who in turn gave them to the crowds. ²⁰They all ate and were satisfied, and they picked up the fragments left over†—twelve wicker baskets full. ²¹Those who ate were about five thousand men, not counting women and children.

**The Walking on the Water.**‡ ²²ᵛThen he made the disciples get into the boat and precede him to the other side, while he dismissed the crowds. ²³ʷAfter doing so, he went up on the mountain by himself to pray. When it was evening he was there alone. ²⁴Meanwhile the boat, already a few miles offshore, was being tossed about by the waves, for the wind was against it. ²⁵During the fourth watch of the night,§ he came toward them, walking on the sea. ²⁶When the disciples saw him walking on the sea they were terrified. "It is a ghost," they said, and they cried out in fear. ²⁷At once [Jesus] spoke to them, "Take courage, it is I;¶ do not be afraid." ²⁸Peter said to him in reply, "Lord, if it is you, command me to come to you on the water." ²⁹He said, "Come." Peter got out of the boat and began to walk on the water toward Jesus. ³⁰ˣBut when he saw how [strong] the wind was he became frightened; and, beginning to sink, he cried out, "Lord, save me!" ³¹Immediately Jesus stretched out his hand and caught him, and said to him, "O you of little

faith," why did you doubt?" ³²After they got into the boat, the wind died down. ³³††ʸThose who were in the boat did him homage, saying, "Truly, you are the Son of God."

**The Healings at Gennesaret.** ³⁴ᶻAfter making the crossing, they came to land at Gennesaret. ³⁵When the men of that place recognized him, they sent word to all the surrounding country. People brought to him all those who were sick ³⁶ᵃand begged him that they might touch only the tassel on his cloak, and as many as touched it were healed.

# CHAPTER 15

**The Tradition of the Elders.**‡‡ ¹ᵇThen Pharisees and scribes came to Jesus from Jerusalem and said, ²ᶜ"Why do your disciples break the tradition of the elders?§§ They do not wash [their] hands when they eat a meal." ³He said to them in reply, "And why do you break the commandment of God¶¶ for the sake of your tradition? ⁴ᵈFor God said, 'Honor your father and your mother,' and 'Whoever curses father or mother shall die.' ⁵***But you say, 'Whoever says to father or mother, "Any support you might have had from me is dedicated to God," ⁶need not honor his father.' You have nullified the word of God for the sake of your tradition. ⁷Hypocrites, well did Isaiah prophesy about you when he said:

**\*\*[14:31] You of little faith:** see note on Mt 6:30. **Why did you doubt?:** the verb is peculiar to Matthew and occurs elsewhere only in Mt 28:17.

††[14:33] This confession is in striking contrast to the Marcan parallel (Mk 6:51) where the disciples are "completely astounded."

‡‡[15:1–20] This dispute begins with the question of the Pharisees and scribes why Jesus' disciples are breaking **the tradition of the elders** about washing one's hands before eating (Mt 15:2). Jesus' counterquestion accuses his opponents of breaking **the commandment of God for the sake of** their **tradition** (Mt 15:3) and illustrates this by their interpretation of the commandment of the Decalogue concerning parents (Mt 15:4–6). Denouncing them as hypocrites, he applies to them a derogatory prophecy of Isaiah (Mt 15:7–8). Then with a wider audience (**the crowd**, Mt 15:10) he goes beyond the violation of tradition with which the dispute has started. The parable (Mt 15:11) is an attack on the Mosaic law concerning clean and unclean foods, similar to those antitheses that abrogate the law (Mt 5:31–32, 33–34, 38–39). After a warning to his disciples not to follow the moral guidance of the Pharisees (Mt 15:13–14), he explains the **parable** (Mt 15:15) to them, saying that defilement comes not from what **enters the mouth** (Mt 15:17) but from the evil thoughts and deeds that rise from within, **from the heart** (Mt 15:18–20). The last verse returns to the starting point of the dispute (eating **with unwashed hands**). Because of Matthew's omission of Mk 7:19b, some scholars think that Matthew has weakened the Marcan repudiation of the Mosaic food laws. But that half verse is ambiguous in the Greek, which may be the reason for its omission here.

§§[15:2] **The tradition of the elders:** see note on Mk 7:5. The purpose of the handwashing was to remove defilement caused by contact with what was ritually unclean.

¶¶[15:3–4] For the commandment see Ex 20:12 (// Dt 5:16); 21:17. The honoring of one's parents had to do with supporting them in their needs.

\*\*\*[15:5] See note on Mk 7:11.

*[14:19] The **taking,** saying the blessing, breaking, and giving to the disciples correspond to the actions of Jesus over the bread at the Last Supper (Mt 26:26). Since they were usual at any Jewish meal, that correspondence does not necessarily indicate a eucharistic reference here. Matthew's silence about Jesus' dividing the fish among the people (Mk 6:41) is perhaps more significant in that regard.

†[14:20] The **fragments left over:** as in Elisha's miracle, food was **left over** after all had been fed. The word **fragments** (Greek klasmata) is used, in the singular, of the broken bread of the Eucharist in Didache 9:3–4.

‡[14:22–33] The disciples, laboring against the turbulent sea, are saved by Jesus. For his power over the waters, see note on Mt 8:26. Here that power is expressed also by his **walking on the sea** (Mt 14:25; cf. Ps 77:20; Jb 9:8). Matthew has inserted into the Marcan story (Mk 6:45–52) material that belongs to his special traditions on Peter (Mt 14:28–31).

§[14:25] **The fourth watch of the night:** between 3 a.m. and 6 a.m. The Romans divided the twelve hours between 6 p.m. and 6 a.m. into four equal parts called "watches."

¶[14:27] **It is I:** see note on Mk 6:50.

v. [14:22–33] Mk 6:45–52; Jn 6:16–21.  w. [14:23] Mk 1:35; Lk 5:16; 6:12.  x. [14:30–31] 8:25–26.

y. [14:33] 16:16.  z. [14:34–36] Mk 6:53–56.  a. [14:36] 9:20–22.  b. [15:1–20] Mk 7:1–23.  c. [15:2] Lk 11:38.  d. [15:4] Ex 20:12; 21:17; Lv 20:9; Dt 5:16; Prv 20:20.

<sup>8</sup> "'This people honors me with their lips,*
     but their hearts are far from me;
<sup>9</sup> /in vain do they worship me,
     teaching as doctrines human
       precepts.'"

<sup>10g</sup>He summoned the crowd and said to them, "Hear and understand. <sup>11</sup>It is not what enters one's mouth that defiles that person; but what comes out of the mouth is what defiles one." <sup>12</sup>Then his disciples approached and said to him, "Do you know that the Pharisees took offense when they heard what you said?" <sup>13</sup>He said in reply,<sup>†</sup> "Every plant that my heavenly Father has not planted will be uprooted. <sup>14h</sup>Let them alone; they are blind guides [of the blind]. If a blind person leads a blind person, both will fall into a pit." <sup>15</sup>Then Peter<sup>‡</sup> said to him in reply, "Explain [this] parable to us." <sup>16</sup>He said to them, "Are even you still without understanding? <sup>17</sup>Do you not realize that everything that enters the mouth passes into the stomach and is expelled into the latrine? <sup>18i</sup>But the things that come out of the mouth come from the heart, and they defile. <sup>19j</sup>For from the heart come evil thoughts, murder, adultery, unchastity, theft, false witness, blasphemy. <sup>20</sup>These are what defile a person, but to eat with unwashed hands does not defile."

**The Canaanite Woman's Faith.**<sup>ʲ</sup> <sup>21j</sup>Then Jesus went from that place and withdrew to the region of Tyre and Sidon. <sup>22</sup>And behold, a Canaanite woman of that district came and called out, "Have pity on me, Lord, Son of David! My daughter is tormented by a demon." <sup>23</sup>But he did not say a word in answer to her. His disciples came and asked him, "Send her away, for she keeps calling out after us." <sup>24</sup>He said in reply, "I was sent only to the lost sheep of the house of Israel." <sup>25k</sup>But the woman came and did him homage, saying, "Lord, help me." <sup>26</sup>He said in reply, "It is not right to take the food of the children<sup>††</sup> and throw it to the dogs." <sup>27</sup>She said, "Please, Lord, for even the dogs eat the scraps that fall from the table of their masters." <sup>28l</sup>Then

Jesus said to her in reply, "O woman, great is your faith!<sup>‡‡</sup> Let it be done for you as you wish." And her daughter was healed from that hour.

**The Healing of Many People.** <sup>29</sup>Moving on from there Jesus walked by the Sea of Galilee, went up on the mountain, and sat down there. <sup>30m</sup>Great crowds came to him, having with them the lame, the blind, the deformed, the mute, and many others. They placed them at his feet, and he cured them. <sup>31</sup>The crowds were amazed when they saw the mute speaking, the deformed made whole, the lame walking, and the blind able to see, and they glorified the God of Israel.

**The Feeding of the Four Thousand.**<sup>§§</sup> <sup>32n</sup>Jesus summoned his disciples and said, "My heart is moved with pity for the crowd, for they have been with me now for three days and have nothing to eat. I do not want to send them away hungry, for fear they may collapse on the way." <sup>33</sup>The disciples said to him, "Where could we ever get enough bread in this deserted place to satisfy such a crowd?" <sup>34</sup>Jesus said to them, "How many loaves do you have?" "Seven," they replied, "and a few fish." <sup>35</sup>He ordered the crowd to sit down on the ground. <sup>36</sup>Then he took the seven loaves and the fish, gave thanks,<sup>¶¶</sup> broke the loaves, and gave them to the disciples, who in turn gave them to the crowds. <sup>37o</sup>They all ate and were satisfied. They picked up the fragments left over—seven baskets full. <sup>38</sup>Those who ate were four thousand men, not counting women and children. <sup>39</sup>And when he had dismissed the crowds, he got into the boat and came to the district of Magadan.

## CHAPTER 16

**The Demand for a Sign.** <sup>1***p</sup>The Pharisees and Sadducees came and, to test him, asked him to show them a sign from heaven. <sup>2†††</sup>He said to them in reply, "[In the evening you say, 'Tomorrow will be fair, for the sky is red'; <sup>3q</sup>and, in the morning, 'Today will be stormy, for the sky is

---

*[15:8] The text of Is 29:13 is quoted approximately according to the Septuagint.

†[15:13–14] Jesus leads his disciples away from the teaching authority of the Pharisees.

‡[15:15] Matthew specifies **Peter** as the questioner, unlike Mk 7:17. Given his tendency to present the disciples as more understanding than in his Marcan source, it is noteworthy that here he retains the Marcan rebuke, although in a slightly milder form. This may be due to his wish to correct the Jewish Christians within his church who still held to the food laws and thus separated themselves from Gentile Christians who did not observe them.

§[15:19] The Marcan list of thirteen things that defile (Mk 7:21–22) is here reduced to seven that partially cover the content of the Decalogue.

¶[15:21–28] See note on Mt 8:5–13.

**[15:24] See note on Mt 10:5–6.

††[15:26] **The children:** the people of Israel. **Dogs:** see note on Mt 7:6.

‡‡[15:28] As in the case of the cure of the centurion's servant (Mt 8:10), Matthew ascribes Jesus' granting the request to the woman's **great faith**, a point not made equally explicit in the Marcan parallel (Mk 7:24–30).

§§[15:32–39] Most probably this story is a doublet of that of the feeding of the five thousand (Mt 14:13–21). It differs from it notably only in that Jesus takes the initiative, not the disciples (Mt 15:32), and in the numbers: the crowd has been with Jesus **three days** (Mt 15:32), **seven loaves** are multiplied (Mt 15:36), **seven baskets** of **fragments** remain after the feeding (Mt 15:37), and **four thousand** men are fed (Mt 15:38).

¶¶[15:36] **Gave thanks:** see Mt 14:19, "said the blessing." There is no difference in meaning. The thanksgiving was a blessing of God for his benefits.

***[16:1] **A sign from heaven:** see note on Mt 12:38–42.

†††[16:2–3] The answer of Jesus in these verses is omitted in many important textual witnesses, and it is very uncertain that it is an original part of this gospel. It resembles Lk 12:54–56 and may have been inserted from there. It rebukes the Pharisees and Sadducees who are able to read indications of coming weather but not the indications of the coming kingdom in the signs that Jesus does offer, his mighty deeds and teaching.

---

e. [15:8] Is 29:13 LXX.   f. [15:9] Col 2:23.   g. [15:10] Mk 7:14.
h. [15:14] 23:16, 19, 24; Lk 6:39; Jn 9:40.   i. [15:18] 12:34.
j. [15:21–28] Mk 7:24–30.   k. [15:25] 10:6.   l. [15:28] 8:10.

m. [15:30] Is 35:5–6.   n. [15:32–39] Mk 8:1–10.   o. [15:37] 16:10.
p. [16:1–10] Mk 8:11–21.   q. [16:3] Lk 12:54–56.

red and threatening.' You know how to judge the appearance of the sky, but you cannot judge the signs of the times.] [4*]An evil and unfaithful generation seeks a sign, but no sign will be given it except the sign of Jonah."* Then he left them and went away.

## The Leaven of the Pharisees and Sadducees.
[5†]In coming to the other side of the sea,† the disciples had forgotten to bring bread. [6*]Jesus said to them, "Look out, and beware of the leaven† of the Pharisees and Sadducees." [7*]They concluded among themselves, saying, "It is because we have brought no bread." [8*]When Jesus became aware of this he said, "You of little faith, why do you conclude among yourselves that it is because you have no bread? [9u]Do you not yet understand, and do you not remember the five loaves for the five thousand, and how many wicker baskets you took up? [10v]Or the seven loaves for the four thousand, and how many baskets you took up? [11]How do you not comprehend that I was not speaking to you about bread? Beware of the leaven of the Pharisees and Sadducees." [12]Then they understood* that he was not telling them to beware of the leaven of bread, but of the teaching of the Pharisees and Sadducees.

## Peter's Confession About Jesus.** [13w]When Jesus went into the region of Caesarea Philippi†† he

asked his disciples, "Who do people say that the Son of Man is?" [14x]They replied, "Some say John the Baptist,‡‡ others Elijah, still others Jeremiah or one of the prophets." [15]He said to them, "But who do you say that I am?" [16§§y]Simon Peter said in reply, "You are the Messiah, the Son of the living God." [17]Jesus said to him in reply, "Blessed are you, Simon son of Jonah. For flesh and blood¶¶ has not revealed this to you, but my heavenly Father. [18z]And so I say to you, you are Peter, and upon this rock I will build my church,*** and the gates of the netherworld shall not prevail against it. [19a]I will give you the keys to the kingdom of heaven.††† Whatever you bind

---

* [16:4] See notes on Mt 12:39, 40.

† [16:5–12] Jesus' warning his disciples against **the teaching of the Pharisees and Sadducees** comes immediately before his promise to confer on Peter the authority to bind and to loose on earth (Mt 16:19), an authority that will be confirmed in heaven. Such authority most probably has to do, at least in part, with teaching. The rejection of the teaching authority of the Pharisees (see also Mt 12:12–14) prepares for a new one derived from Jesus.

‡ [16:6] **Leaven:** see note on Mt 13:33. **Sadducees:** Matthew's Marcan source speaks rather of "the leaven of Herod" (Mk 8:15).

§ [16:7–11] The disciples, men **of little faith**, misunderstand Jesus' metaphorical use of **leaven**, forgetting that, as the feeding of the crowds shows, he is not at a loss to provide them with bread.

¶ [16:12] After his rebuke, the disciples understand that by **leaven** he meant the corrupting influence of **the teaching of the Pharisees and Sadducees.** The evangelist probably understands this **teaching** as common to both groups. Since at the time of Jesus' ministry the two differed widely on points of teaching, e.g., the resurrection of the dead, and at the time of the evangelist the Sadducee party was no longer a force in Judaism, the supposed common teaching fits neither period. The disciples' eventual understanding of Jesus' warning contrasts with their continuing obtuseness in the Marcan parallel (Mk 8:14–21).

** [16:13–20] The Marcan confession of Jesus as Messiah, made by Peter as spokesman for the other disciples (Mk 8:27–29; cf. also Lk 9:18–20), is modified significantly here. The confession is of Jesus both as **Messiah** and as **Son of the living God** (Mt 16:16). Jesus' response, drawn principally from material peculiar to Matthew, attributes the confession to a divine revelation granted to Peter alone (Mt 16:17) and makes him the **rock** on which Jesus **will build** his **church** (Mt 16:18) and the disciple whose authority in the church **on earth** will be confirmed in **heaven**, i.e., by God (Mt 16:19).

†† [16:13] **Caesarea Philippi:** situated about twenty miles north of the Sea of Galilee in the territory ruled by Philip, a son of Herod the Great, tetrarch from 4 B.C. until his death in

---

A.D. 34 (see note on Mt 14:1). He rebuilt the town of Paneas, naming it **Caesarea** in honor of the emperor, and **Philippi** ("of Philip") to distinguish it from the seaport in Samaria that was also called Caesarea. **Who do people say that the Son of Man is?:** although the question differs from the Marcan parallel (Mk 8:27: "Who . . . that I am?"), the meaning is the same, for Jesus here refers to himself as the **Son of Man** (cf. Mt 16:15).

‡‡ [16:14] **John the Baptist:** see Mt 14:2. **Elijah:** cf. Mal 3:23–24; Sir 48:10; and see note on Mt 3:4. **Jeremiah:** an addition of Matthew to the Marcan source.

§§ [16:16] **The Son of the living God:** see Mt 2:15; 3:17. The addition of this exalted title to the Marcan confession eliminates whatever ambiguity was attached to the title Messiah. This, among other things, supports the view proposed by many scholars that Matthew has here combined his source's confession with a post-resurrectional confession of faith in Jesus as Son of the living God that belonged to the appearance of the risen Jesus to Peter; cf. 1 Cor 15:5; Lk 24:34.

¶¶ [16:17] **Flesh and blood:** a Semitic expression for human beings, especially in their weakness. **Has not revealed this . . . but my heavenly Father:** that Peter's faith is spoken of as coming not through human means but through a revelation from God is similar to Paul's description of his recognition of who Jesus was; see Gal 1:15–16, ". . . when he [God] . . . was pleased to reveal his Son to me . . . ."

*** [16:18] **You are Peter, and upon this rock I will build my church:** the Aramaic word *kēpaʾ* meaning **rock** and transliterated into Greek as *Kēphas* is the name by which Peter is called in the Pauline letters (1 Cor 1:12; 3:22; 9:5; 15:4; Gal 1:18; 2:9, 11, 14) except in Gal 2:7–8 ("Peter"). It is translated as *Petros* ("Peter") in Jn 1:42. The presumed original Aramaic of Jesus' statement would have been, in English, "You are the Rock (*Kēpaʾ*) and upon this rock (*kēpaʾ*) I will build my church." The Greek text probably means the same, for the difference in gender between the masculine noun *petros*, the disciple's new name, and the feminine noun *petra* (rock) may be due simply to the unsuitability of using a feminine noun as the proper name of a male. Although the two words were generally used with slightly different nuances, they were also used interchangeably with the same meaning, "rock." **Church:** this word (Greek *ekklēsia*) occurs in the gospels only here and in Mt 18:17 (twice). There are several possibilities for an Aramaic original. Jesus' **church** means the community that he **will** gather and that, like a building, will have Peter as its solid foundation. That function of Peter consists in his being witness to Jesus as the **Messiah, the Son of the living God. The gates of the netherworld shall not prevail against it:** the netherworld (Greek *Hadēs*, the abode of the dead) is conceived of as a walled city whose **gates** will not close in upon the church of Jesus, i.e., it will not be overcome by the power of death.

††† [16:19] **The keys to the kingdom of heaven:** the image of the keys is probably drawn from Is 22:15–25 where Eliakim, who succeeds Shebna as master of the palace, is given "the key of the House of David," which he authoritatively "opens" and "shuts" (Is 22:22). **Whatever you bind . . . loosed in heaven:** there are many instances in rabbinic literature of the binding-loosing imagery. Of the several meanings given there to the metaphor, two are of special importance here: the giving of

---

r. [16:4] 12:39; Jon 2:1.    s. [16:5–12] Mk 8:14–21.    t. [16:6] Lk 12:1.    u. [16:9] 14:17–21; Jn 6:9.    v. [16:10] 15:34–38.    w. [16:13–16] Mk 8:27–29; Lk 9:18–20.

x. [16:14] 14:2.    y. [16:16] Jn 6:69.    z. [16:18] Jn 1:42.    a. [16:19] Is 22:22; Rev 3:7.

on earth shall be bound in heaven; and whatever you loose on earth shall be loosed in heaven." [20]*[b]Then he strictly ordered his disciples to tell no one that he was the Messiah.

**The First Prediction of the Passion.**[†] [21][c]From that time on, Jesus began to show his disciples that he[‡] must go to Jerusalem and suffer greatly from the elders, the chief priests, and the scribes, and be killed and on the third day be raised.[d] [22]§Then Peter took him aside and began to rebuke him, "God forbid, Lord! No such thing shall ever happen to you." [23][e]He turned and said to Peter, "Get behind me, Satan! You are an obstacle to me. You are thinking not as God does, but as human beings do."

**The Conditions of Discipleship.**¶ [24][f]Then Jesus said to his disciples, "Whoever wishes to come after me must deny himself," take up his cross,

and follow me. [25]gFor whoever wishes to save his life will lose it, but whoever loses his life for my sake will find it.[††] [26]What profit would there be for one to gain the whole world and forfeit his life? Or what can one give in exchange for his life? [27]‡‡[h]For the Son of Man will come with his angels in his Father's glory, and then he will repay everyone according to his conduct. [28]§§Amen, I say to you, there are some standing here who will not taste death until they see the Son of Man coming in his kingdom."

## CHAPTER 17

**The Transfiguration of Jesus.**¶¶ [1][i]After six days Jesus took Peter, James, and John his brother, and led them up a high mountain by themselves.*** [2]†††[j]And he was transfigured before them; his face shone like the sun and his clothes became white as light. [3]‡‡‡And behold, Moses and Elijah appeared to them, conversing with him. [4]Then Peter said to Jesus in reply, "Lord, it is good that we are here. If you wish, I will make three tents§§§ here, one for you, one for Moses, and one for Elijah." [5][k]While he was still speaking, behold, a bright cloud cast a shadow over

authoritative teaching, and the lifting or imposing of the ban of excommunication. It is disputed whether the image of **the keys** and that of binding and loosing are different metaphors meaning the same thing. In any case, the promise of the keys is given to Peter alone. In Mt 18:18 all the disciples are given the power of binding and loosing, but the context of that verse suggests that there the power of excommunication alone is intended. That **the keys** are those to the **kingdom of heaven** and that Peter's exercise of authority in the church **on earth** will be confirmed **in heaven** show an intimate connection between, but not an identification of, the church and **the kingdom of heaven**.

\* [16:20] Cf. Mk 8:30. Matthew makes explicit that the prohibition has to do with speaking of Jesus as **the Messiah**; see note on Mk 8:27–30.

† [16:21–23] This first prediction of the passion follows Mk 8:31–33 in the main and serves as a corrective to an understanding of Jesus' messiahship as solely one of glory and triumph. By his addition of **from that time on** (Mt 16:21) Matthew has emphasized that Jesus' revelation of his coming suffering and death marks a new phase of the gospel. Neither this nor the two later passion predictions (Mt 17:22–23; 20:17–19) can be taken as sayings that, as they stand, go back to Jesus himself. However, it is probable that he foresaw that his mission would entail suffering and perhaps death, but was confident that he would ultimately be vindicated by God (see Mt 26:29).

‡ [16:21] **He:** the Marcan parallel (Mk 8:31) has "the Son of Man." Since Matthew has already designated Jesus by that title (Mt 15:13), its omission here is not significant. The Matthean prediction is equally about the sufferings of the Son of Man. **Must:** this necessity is part of the tradition of all the synoptics; cf. Mk 8:31; Lk 9:21. **On the third day:** so also Lk 9:22, against the Marcan "after three days" (Mk 8:31). Matthew's formulation is, in the Greek, almost identical with the pre-Pauline fragment of the kerygma in 1 Cor 15:4 and also in Hos 6:2, which many take to be the Old Testament background to the confession that Jesus was raised **on the third day**. Josephus uses "after three days" and "on the third day" interchangeably (*Antiquities* 7:280–81; 8:214, 218) and there is probably no difference in meaning between the two phrases.

§ [16:22–23] Peter's refusal to accept Jesus' predicted suffering and death is seen as a satanic attempt to deflect Jesus from his God-appointed course, and the disciple is addressed in terms that recall Jesus' dismissal of the devil in the temptation account (Mt 4:10: "Get away, Satan!"). Peter's satanic purpose is emphasized by Matthew's addition to the Marcan source of the words **You are an obstacle to me**.

¶ [16:24–28] A readiness to follow Jesus even to giving up one's life for him is the condition for true discipleship; this will be repaid by him at the final judgment.

\*\* [16:24] **Deny himself:** to deny someone is to disown him (see Mt 10:33; 26:34–35) and to deny oneself is to disown oneself as the center of one's existence.

†† [16:25] See notes on Mk 10:38, 39.

‡‡ [16:27] The parousia and final judgment are described in Mt 25:31 in terms almost identical with these.

§§ [16:28] **Coming in his kingdom:** since the **kingdom of the Son of Man** has been described as "the world" and Jesus' sovereignty precedes his final coming in glory (Mt 13:38, 41), the coming in this verse is not the parousia as in the preceding but the manifestation of Jesus' rule after his resurrection; see notes on Mt 13:38, 41.

¶¶ [17:1–8] The account of the transfiguration confirms that Jesus is the **Son** of God (Mt 17:5) and points to fulfillment of the prediction that he will come **in his Father's glory** at the end of the age (Mt 16:27). It has been explained by some as a resurrection appearance retrojected into the time of Jesus' ministry, but that is not probable since the account lacks many of the usual elements of the resurrection-appearance narratives. It draws upon motifs from the Old Testament and noncanonical Jewish apocalyptic literature that express the presence of the heavenly and the divine, e.g., brilliant light, white garments, and the overshadowing cloud.

\*\*\* [17:1] These three disciples are also taken apart from the others by Jesus in Gethsemane (Mt 26:37). **A high mountain:** this has been identified with Tabor or Hermon, but probably no specific mountain was intended by the evangelist or by his Marcan source (Mk 9:2). Its meaning is theological rather than geographical, possibly recalling the revelation to Moses on Mount Sinai (Ex 24:12–18) and to Elijah at the same place (1 Kgs 19:8–18; Horeb = Sinai).

††† [17:2] **His face shone like the sun:** this is a Matthean addition; cf. Dn 10:6. **His clothes became white as light:** cf. Dn 7:9, where the clothing of God appears "snow bright." For the white garments of other heavenly beings, see Rev 4:4; 7:9; 19:14.

‡‡‡ [17:3] See note on Mk 9:5.

§§§ [17:4] **Three tents:** the booths in which the Israelites lived during the feast of Tabernacles (cf. Jn 7:2) were meant to recall their ancestors' dwelling in booths during the journey from Egypt to the promised land (Lv 23:39–42). The same Greek word, *skēnē*, here translated **tents**, is used in the LXX for the booths of that feast, and some scholars have suggested that there is an allusion here to that liturgical custom.

b. [16:20] Mk 8:30; Lk 9:21.   c. [16:21–28] Mk 8:31–9:1; Lk 9:22–27. d. [16:21] 17:22–23; 20:17–19.   e. [16:23] 4:10.   f. [16:24] Lk 14:27.

g. [16:25] Lk 17:33; Jn 12:25.   h. [16:27] 25:31–33; Jb 34:11; Ps 62:13; Jer 17:10; 2 Thes 1:7–8.   i. [17:1–8] Mk 9:2–8; Lk 9:28–36.   j. [17:2] 28:3; Dn 7:9; 10:6; Rev 4:4; 7:9; 19:14.   k. [17:5] 3:17; Dt 18:15; 2 Pt 1:17.

them,* then from the cloud came a voice that said, "This is my beloved Son, with whom I am well pleased; listen to him." [6†]When the disciples heard this, they fell prostrate and were very much afraid. [7]But Jesus came and touched them, saying, "Rise, and do not be afraid." [8]And when the disciples raised their eyes, they saw no one else but Jesus alone.

### The Coming of Elijah.[‡] [9l]As they were coming down from the mountain, Jesus charged them, "Do not tell the vision[§] to anyone until the Son of Man has been raised from the dead." [10¶m]Then the disciples asked him, "Why do the scribes say that Elijah must come first?" [11n]He said in reply, "Elijah will indeed come and restore all things; [12o]but I tell you that Elijah has already come, and they did not recognize him but did to him whatever they pleased. So also will the Son of Man suffer at their hands." [13††]Then the disciples understood that he was speaking to them of John the Baptist.

### The Healing of a Boy with a Demon.[‡‡] [14p]When they came to the crowd a man approached, knelt down before him, [15]and said, "Lord, have pity on my son, for he is a lunatic[§§] and suffers severely; often he falls into fire, and often into water. [16]I brought him to your disciples, but they could not cure him." [17q]Jesus said in reply, "O faithless and perverse[¶¶] generation, how long will I be with

you? How long will I endure you? Bring him here to me." [18]Jesus rebuked him and the demon came out of him,[***] and from that hour the boy was cured. [19]Then the disciples approached Jesus in private and said, "Why could we not drive it out?" [20†††r]He said to them, "Because of your little faith. Amen, I say to you, if you have faith the size of a mustard seed, you will say to this mountain, 'Move from here to there,' and it will move. Nothing will be impossible for you." [21†‡‡]

### The Second Prediction of the Passion.[§§§] [22s]As they were gathering in Galilee, Jesus said to them, "The Son of Man is to be handed over to men, [23]and they will kill him, and he will be raised on the third day." And they were overwhelmed with grief.

### Payment of the Temple Tax.[¶¶¶] [24t]When they came to Capernaum, the collectors of the temple tax[****] approached Peter and said, "Doesn't your

---

translated **perverse** is the same as that in Dt 32:5 LXX, where Moses speaks to his people. There is a problem in knowing to whom the reproach is addressed. Since the Matthean Jesus normally chides his disciples for their **little faith** (as in Mt 17:20), it would appear that the charge of lack of faith could not be made against them and that the reproach is addressed to unbelievers among the Jews. However in Mt 17:20b (**if you have faith the size of a mustard seed**), which is certainly addressed to the disciples, they appear to have not even the smallest faith; if they had, they would have been able to cure the boy. In the light of Mt 17:20b the reproach of Mt 17:17 could have applied to the disciples. There seems to be an inconsistency between the charge of **little faith** in Mt 17:20a and that of not even a little in Mt 17:20b.

[***][17:18] **The demon came out of him**: not until this verse does Matthew indicate that the boy's illness is a case of demoniacal possession.

[†††][17:20] The entire verse is an addition of Matthew who (according to the better attested text) omits the reason given for the disciples' inability in Mk 9:29. **Little faith**: see note on Mt 6:30. **Faith the size of a mustard seed . . . and it will move**: a combination of a Q saying (cf. Lk 17:6) with a Marcan saying (cf. Mk 11:23).

[‡‡‡][17:21] Some manuscripts add, "But this kind does not come out except by prayer and fasting"; this is a variant of the better reading of Mk 9:29.

[§§§][17:22–23] The second passion prediction (cf. Mt 16:21–23) is the least detailed of the three and may be the earliest. In the Marcan parallel the disciples do not understand (Mk 9:32); here they understand and are **overwhelmed with grief** at the prospect of Jesus' death (Mt 17:23).

[¶¶¶][17:24–27] Like Mt 14:28–31 and Mt 16:16b–19, this episode comes from Matthew's special material on Peter. Although the question of **the collectors** concerns Jesus' payment of **the temple tax**, it is put to **Peter**. It is he who receives instruction from Jesus about freedom from the obligation of payment and yet why it should be made. The means of doing so is provided miraculously. The pericope deals with a problem of Matthew's church, whether its members should pay the temple tax, and the answer is given through a word of Jesus conveyed to Peter. Some scholars see here an example of the teaching authority of Peter exercised in the name of Jesus (see Mt 16:19). The specific problem was a Jewish Christian one and may have arisen when the Matthean church was composed largely of that group.

[****][17:24] **The temple tax**: before the destruction of the Jerusalem temple in A.D. 70 every male Jew above nineteen years of age was obliged to make an annual contribution to its upkeep (cf. Ex 30:11–16; Neh 10:33). After the destruction the Romans imposed upon Jews the obligation of paying that tax for the temple of Jupiter Capitolinus. There is disagreement about which period the story deals with.

---

*[17:5] **Cloud cast a shadow over them**: see note on Mk 9:7. **This is my beloved Son . . . listen to him**: cf. Mt 3:17. The voice repeats the baptismal proclamation about Jesus, with the addition of the command **listen to him**. The latter is a reference to Dt 18:15 in which the Israelites are commanded to **listen to** the prophet like Moses whom God will raise up for them. The command to listen to Jesus is general, but in this context it probably applies particularly to the preceding predictions of his passion and resurrection (Mt 16:21) and of his coming (Mt 16:27, 28).

†[17:6–7] A Matthean addition; cf. Dn 10:9–10, 18–19.

‡[17:9–13] In response to the disciples' question about the expected return of Elijah, Jesus interprets the mission of the Baptist as the fulfillment of that expectation. But that was not suspected by those who opposed and finally killed him, and Jesus predicts a similar fate for himself.

§[17:9] **The vision**: Matthew alone uses this word to describe the transfiguration. **Until the Son of Man has been raised from the dead**: only in the light of Jesus' resurrection can the meaning of his life and mission be truly understood; until then no testimony to **the vision** will lead people to faith.

¶[17:10] See notes on Mt 3:4; 16:14.

**[17:11–12] The preceding question and this answer may reflect later controversy with Jews who objected to the Christian claims for Jesus if Elijah had not yet come.

††[17:13] See Mt 11:14.

‡‡[17:14–20] Matthew has greatly shortened the Marcan story (Mk 9:14–29). Leaving aside several details of the boy's illness, he concentrates on the need for faith, not so much on the part of the boy's father (as does Mark, for Matthew omits Mk 9:22b–24) but on that of his own disciples whose inability to drive out the demon is ascribed to their **little faith** (Mt 17:20).

§§[17:15] **A lunatic**: this description of the boy is peculiar to Matthew. The word occurs in the New Testament only here and in Mt 4:24 and means one affected or struck by the moon. The symptoms of the boy's illness point to epilepsy, and attacks of this were thought to be caused by phases of the moon.

¶¶[17:17] **Faithless and perverse**: so Matthew and Luke (Lk 9:41) against Mark's **faithless** (Mk 9:19). The Greek word here

---

l. [17:9–13] Mk 9:9–13.   m. [17:10] Mal 3:23–24.   n. [17:11] Lk 1:17.   o. [17:12–13] 11:14.   p. [17:14–21] Mk 9:14–29; Lk 9:37–43.
q. [17:17] Dt 32:5 LXX.

r. [17:20] 21:21; Lk 17:6; 1 Cor 13:2.   s. [17:22–23] 16:21; 20:18–19.   t. [17:24] Ex 30:11–16; Neh 10:33.

teacher pay the temple tax?" [25]"Yes," he said.[*] When he came into the house, before he had time to speak, Jesus asked him, "What is your opinion, Simon? From whom do the kings of the earth take tolls or census tax? From their subjects or from foreigners?" [26†]When he said, "From foreigners," Jesus said to him, "Then the subjects are exempt. [27]But that we may not offend them,[‡] go to the sea, drop in a hook, and take the first fish that comes up. Open its mouth and you will find a coin worth twice the temple tax. Give that to them for me and for you."

## CHAPTER 18[§]

**The Greatest in the Kingdom.** [1u]At that time the disciples[u] approached Jesus and said, "Who is the greatest in the kingdom of heaven?" [2]He called a child over, placed it in their midst, [3v]and said, "Amen, I say to you, unless you turn and become like children,[**] you will not enter the kingdom of heaven. [4w]Whoever humbles himself like this child is the greatest in the kingdom of heaven. [5††]And whoever receives one child such as this in my name receives me.

**Temptations to Sin.** [6x]"Whoever causes one of these little ones[‡‡] who believe in me to sin, it would be better for him to have a great millstone hung around his neck and to be drowned in the depths of the sea. [7§§]Woe to the world because of things that cause sin! Such things must come, but woe to the one through whom they come! [8y]If your hand or foot causes you to sin,[¶] cut it off and throw it away. It is better for you to enter into life maimed or crippled than with two hands or two feet to be thrown into eternal fire. [9]And if your eye causes you to sin, tear it out and throw it away. It is better for you to enter into life with one eye than with two eyes to be thrown into fiery Gehenna.

**The Parable of the Lost Sheep.**[***] [10z]"See that you do not despise one of these little ones,[†††] for I say to you that their angels in heaven always look upon the face of my heavenly Father. [[11]‡‡‡a]

---

*[17:25] **From their subjects or from foreigners?**: the Greek word here translated **subjects** literally means "sons."

†[17:26] **Then the subjects are exempt**: just as **subjects** are not bound by laws applying to **foreigners**, neither are Jesus and his disciples, who belong to the kingdom of heaven, bound by the duty of paying the temple tax imposed on those who are not of the kingdom. If the Greek is translated "sons," the freedom of Jesus, the Son of God, and of his disciples, children ("sons") of the kingdom (cf. Mt 13:38), is even more clear.

‡[17:27] **That we may not offend them**: though they are exempt (Mt 17:26), Jesus and his disciples are to avoid giving offense; therefore the tax is to be paid. **A coin worth twice the temple tax**: literally, "a stater," a Greek coin worth two double drachmas. Two double drachmas were equal to the Jewish shekel and the tax was a half-shekel. **For me and for you**: not only Jesus but Peter pays the tax, and this example serves as a standard for the conduct of all the disciples.

§[18:1–35] This discourse of the fourth book of the gospel is often called the "church order" discourse, but it lacks most of the considerations usually connected with church order, such as various offices in the church and the duties of each, and deals principally with the relations that must obtain among the members of the church. Beginning with the warning that greatness in the **kingdom of heaven** is measured not by rank or power but by childlikeness (Mt 18:1–5), it deals with the care that the disciples must take not to cause the **little ones to sin** or to neglect them if they stray from the community (Mt 18:6–14), the correction of members who sin (Mt 18:15–18), the efficacy of the prayer of the disciples because of the presence of Jesus (Mt 18:19–20), and the forgiveness that must be repeatedly extended to sinful members who repent (Mt 18:21–35).

¶[18:1] The initiative is taken not by Jesus as in the Marcan parallel (Mk 9:33–34) but by the disciples. **Kingdom of heaven**: this may mean **the kingdom** in its fullness, i.e., after the parousia and the final judgment. But what follows about causes of sin, church discipline, and forgiveness, all dealing with the present age, suggests that the question has to do with rank also in the church, where the kingdom is manifested here and now, although only partially and by anticipation; see notes on Mt 3:2; 4:17.

**[18:3] **Become like children**: the child is held up as a model for the disciples not because of any supposed innocence of children but because of their complete dependence on, and trust in, their parents. So must the disciples be, in respect to God.

††[18:5] Cf. Mt 10:40.

‡‡[18:6] **One of these little ones**: the thought passes from the child of Mt 18:2–4 to the disciples, **little ones** because of their becoming **like children**. It is difficult to know whether this is a designation of all who are disciples or of those who are insignificant in contrast to others, e.g., the leaders of the community. Since apart from this chapter the designation **little ones** occurs in Matthew only in Mt 10:42 where it means disciples as such, that is its more likely meaning here. **Who believe in me**: since discipleship is impossible without at least some degree of faith, this further specification seems superfluous. However, it serves to indicate that the warning against causing a **little one** to sin is principally directed against whatever would lead such a one to a weakening or loss of faith. The Greek verb *skandalizein*, here translated **causes . . . to sin**, means literally "causes to stumble"; what the stumbling is depends on the context. It is used of falling away from faith in Mt 13:21. According to the better reading of Mk 9:42, **in me** is a Matthean addition to the Marcan source. **It would be better . . . depths of the sea**: cf. Mk 9:42.

§§[18:7] This is a Q saying; cf. Lk 17:1. The inevitability of **things that cause sin** (literally, "scandals") does not take away the responsibility of **the one through whom they come.**

¶¶[18:8–9] These verses are a doublet of Mt 5:29–30. In that context they have to do with causes of sexual sin. As in the Marcan source from which they have been drawn (Mk 9:42–48), they differ from the first warning about scandal, which deals with causing another person to sin, for they concern what **causes** oneself **to sin** and they do not seem to be related to another's loss of faith, as the first warning is. It is difficult to know how Matthew understood the logical connection between these verses and Mt 18:6–7.

***[18:10–14] The first and last verses are peculiar to Matthew. The parable itself comes from Q; see Lk 15:3–7. In Luke it serves as justification for Jesus' table-companionship with sinners; here, it is an exhortation for the disciples to seek out fellow disciples who have gone **astray**. Not only must no one cause a fellow disciple to sin, but those who have strayed must be sought out and, if possible, brought back to the community. The joy of the shepherd on finding the sheep, though not absent in Mt 18:13 is more emphasized in Luke. By his addition of Mt 18:10, 14 Matthew has drawn out explicitly the application of the parable to the care of the **little ones.**

†††[18:10] **Their angels in heaven . . . my heavenly Father**: for the Jewish belief in angels as guardians of nations and individuals, see Dn 10:13, 20–21; Tb 5:4–7; 1QH 5:20–22; as intercessors who present the prayers of human beings to God, see Tb 13:12, 15. The high worth of the **little ones** is indicated by their being represented before God by these heavenly beings.

‡‡‡[18:11] Some manuscripts add, "For the Son of Man has come to save what was lost"; cf. Mt 9:13. This is practically identical with Lk 19:10 and is probably a copyist's addition from that source.

---

u. [18:1–5] Mk 9:36–37; Lk 9:46–48.   v. [18:3] 19:14; Mk 10:15; Lk 18:17.   w. [18:4] 23:12.

x. [18:6–7] Mk 9:42; Lk 17:1–2.   y. [18:8–9] 5:29–30; Mk 9:43–47.   z. [18:10–14] Ez 34:1–3, 16; Lk 15:3–7.   a. [18:11] Lk 19:10.

¹²What is your opinion? If a man has a hundred sheep and one of them goes astray, will he not leave the ninety-nine in the hills and go in search of the stray? ¹³And if he finds it, amen, I say to you, he rejoices more over it than over the ninety-nine that did not stray. ¹⁴In just the same way, it is not the will of your heavenly Father that one of these little ones be lost.

**A Brother Who Sins.**ᵇ ¹⁵ᵇ"If your brotherᵗ sins [against you], go and tell him his fault between you and him alone. If he listens to you, you have won over your brother. ¹⁶ᶜIf he does not listen, take one or two others along with you, so that 'every fact may be established on the testimony of two or three witnesses.' ¹⁷ᵈIf he refuses to listen to them, tell the church.§ If he refuses to listen even to the church, then treat him as you would a Gentile or a tax collector. ¹⁸ᵉAmen, I say to you, whatever you bind on earth shall be bound in heaven, and whatever you loose on earth shall be loosed in heaven. ¹⁹ᵃᵗᶠAgain, [amen,] I say to you, if two of you agree on earth about anything for which they are to pray, it shall be granted to them by my heavenly Father. ²⁰ᵗᵗᵍFor where two or three are gathered together in my name, there am I in the midst of them."

**The Parable of the Unforgiving Servant.**‡‡ ²¹ʰThen Peter approaching asked him, "Lord, if my brother sins against me, how often must I forgive him? As many as seven times?" ²²§§Jesus answered, "I say to you, not seven times but seventy-seven times. ²³ⁱThat is why the kingdom of heaven may be likened to a king who decided to settle accounts with his servants. ²⁴¶¶When he began the accounting, a debtor was brought before him who owed him a huge amount. ²⁵Since he had no way of paying it back, his master ordered him to be sold, along with his wife, his children, and all his property, in payment of the debt. ²⁶***At that, the servant fell down, did him homage, and said, 'Be patient with me, and I will pay you back in full.' ²⁷Moved with compassion the master of that servant let him go and forgave him the loan. ²⁸When that servant had left, he found one of his fellow servants who owed him a much smaller amount.††† He seized him and started to choke him, demanding, 'Pay back what you owe.' ²⁹Falling to his knees, his fellow servant begged him, 'Be patient with me, and I will pay you back.' ³⁰But he refused.

---

*[18:15–20] Passing from the duty of Christian disciples toward those who have strayed from their number, the discourse now turns to how they are to deal with one who sins and yet remains within the community. First there is to be private correction (Mt 18:15); if this is unsuccessful, further correction before **two or three witnesses** (Mt 18:16); if this fails, the matter is to be brought before the assembled community (the church), and if the sinner refuses to attend to the correction of **the church**, he is to be expelled (Mt 18:17). The church's judgment will be ratified **in heaven**, i.e., by God (Mt 18:18). This three-step process of correction corresponds, though not exactly, to the procedure of the Qumran community; see 1QS 5:25–6:1; 6:24–7:25; CD 9:2–8. The section ends with a saying about the favorable response of God to prayer, even to that of a very small number, for Jesus is in the midst of any gathering of his disciples, however small (Mt 18:19–20). Whether this prayer has anything to do with the preceding judgment is uncertain.

†[18:15] **Your brother:** a fellow disciple; see Mt 23:8. The bracketed words, **against you**, are widely attested but they are not in the important codices Sinaiticus and Vaticanus or in some other textual witnesses. Their omission broadens the type of sin in question. **Won over:** literally, "gained."

‡[18:16] Cf. Dt 19:15.

§[18:17] **The church:** the second of the only two instances of this word in the gospels; see note on Mt 16:18. Here it refers not to the entire **church** of Jesus, as in Mt 16:18, but to the local congregation. **Treat him . . . a Gentile or a tax collector:** just as the observant Jew avoided the company of Gentiles and tax collectors, so must the congregation of Christian disciples separate itself from the arrogantly sinful member who refuses to repent even when convicted of his sin by the whole **church**. Such a one is to be set outside the fellowship of the community. The harsh language about **Gentile** and **tax collector** probably reflects a stage of the Matthean **church** when it was principally composed of Jewish Christians. That time had long since passed, but the principle of exclusion for such a sinner remained. Paul makes a similar demand for excommunication in 1 Cor 5:1–13.

¶[18:18] Except for the plural of the verbs **bind** and **loose**, this verse is practically identical with Mt 16:19b and many scholars understand it as granting to all the disciples what was previously given to Peter alone. For a different view, based on the different contexts of the two verses, see note on Mt 16:19.

**[18:19–20] Some take these verses as applying to prayer on the occasion of the church's gathering to deal with the sinner of Mt 18:17. Unless an *a fortiori* argument is supposed, this seems unlikely. God's answer to the prayer of **two or three** envisages a different situation from one that involves the entire congregation. In addition, the object of this prayer is expressed in most general terms as **anything for which they are to pray**.

††[18:20] **For where two or three . . . midst of them:** the presence of Jesus guarantees the efficacy of the prayer. This saying is similar to one attributed to a rabbi executed in A.D. 135 at the time of the second Jewish revolt: ". . . When two sit and there are between them the words of the Torah, the divine presence (*Shekinah*) rests upon them" (*Pirqê 'Abôt* 3,3).

‡‡[18:21–35] The final section of the discourse deals with the forgiveness that the disciples are to give to their fellow disciples who sin against them. To the question of Peter how often forgiveness is to be granted (Mt 18:21), Jesus answers that it is to be given without limit (Mt 18:22) and illustrates this with the parable of the unmerciful servant (Mt 18:23–34), warning that his **heavenly Father** will give those who do not forgive the same treatment as that given to the unmerciful servant (Mt 18:35). Mt 18:21–22 correspond to Lk 17:4; the parable and the final warning are peculiar to Matthew. That the parable did not originally belong to this context is suggested by the fact that it really does not deal with repeated forgiveness, which is the point of Peter's question and Jesus' reply.

§§[18:22] **Seventy-seven times:** the Greek corresponds exactly to the LXX of Gn 4:24. There is probably an allusion, by contrast, to the limitless vengeance of Lamech in the Genesis text. In any case, what is demanded of the disciples is limitless forgiveness.

¶¶[18:24] **A huge amount:** literally, "ten thousand talents." The talent was a unit of coinage of high but varying value depending on its metal (gold, silver, copper) and its place of origin. It is mentioned in the New Testament only here and in Mt 25:14–30.

***[18:26] **Pay you back in full:** an empty promise, given the size of the debt.

†††[18:28] **A much smaller amount:** literally, "a hundred denarii." A denarius was the normal daily wage of a laborer. The difference between the two debts is enormous and brings out the absurdity of the conduct of the Christian who has received the great forgiveness of God and yet refuses to forgive the relatively minor offenses done to him.

---

b. [18:15] Lv 19:17; Sir 19:13; Gal 6:1.   c. [18:16] Dt 19:15; Jn 8:17; 1 Tm 5:19.   d. [18:17] 1 Cor 5:1–13.   e. [18:18] 16:19; Jn 20:23.   f. [18:19] 7:7–8; Jn 15:7.

g. [18:20] 1 Cor 5:4.   h. [18:21–22] 6:12; Lk 17:4.   i. [18:23] 25:19.

Instead, he had him put in prison until he paid back the debt. ³¹Now when his fellow servants saw what had happened, they were deeply disturbed, and went to their master and reported the whole affair. ³²His master summoned him and said to him, 'You wicked servant! I forgave you your entire debt because you begged me to. ³³Should you not have had pity on your fellow servant, as I had pity on you?' ³⁴Then in anger his master handed him over to the torturers until he should pay back the whole debt.* ³⁵†kSo will my heavenly Father do to you, unless each of you forgives his brother from his heart."

## VI. MINISTRY IN JUDEA AND JERUSALEM‡

### CHAPTER 19

**Marriage and Divorce.** ¹§When Jesus§ finished these words,¶ he left Galilee and went to the district of Judea across the Jordan. ²Great crowds followed him, and he cured them there. ³lSome Pharisees approached him, and tested him,** saying, "Is it lawful for a man to divorce his wife for any cause whatever?" ⁴††mHe said in reply, "Have you not read that from the beginning the Creator 'made them male and female' ⁵ⁿand said, 'For this reason a man shall leave his father and mother and be joined to his wife, and the two shall become one flesh'? ⁶So they are no longer two, but one flesh. Therefore, what God has joined together, no human being must separate." ⁷‡‡oThey said to him, "Then why did Moses command that the man give the woman a bill of divorce and dismiss [her]?" ⁸He said to them, "Because of the hardness of your hearts Moses allowed you to divorce your wives, but from the beginning it was not so. ⁹pI say to you,§§ whoever divorces his wife (unless the marriage is unlawful) and marries another commits adultery." ¹⁰[His] disciples said to him, "If that is the case of a man with his wife, it is better not to marry." ¹¹He answered, "Not all can accept [this] word,¶¶ but only those to whom that is granted. ¹²Some are incapable of marriage because they were born so; some, because they were made so by others; some, because they have renounced marriage*** for the sake of the kingdom of heaven. Whoever can accept this ought to accept it."

* [18:34] Since the debt is so great as to be unpayable, the punishment will be endless.

† [18:35] The Father's forgiveness, already given, will be withdrawn at the final judgment for those who have not imitated his forgiveness by their own.

‡ [19:1–23:39] The narrative section of the fifth book of the gospel. The first part (Mt 19:1–20:34) has for its setting the journey of Jesus from Galilee to Jerusalem; the second (Mt 21:1–23:39) deals with Jesus' ministry in Jerusalem up to the final great discourse of the gospel (Mt 24–25). Matthew follows the Marcan sequence of events, though adding material both special to this gospel and drawn from Q. The second part ends with the denunciation of the scribes and Pharisees (Mt 23:1–36) followed by Jesus' lament over Jerusalem (Mt 23:37–39). This long and important speech raises a problem for the view that Matthew is structured around five other discourses of Jesus (see Introduction) and that this one has no such function in the gospel. However, it is to be noted that this speech lacks the customary concluding formula that follows the five discourses (see note on Mt 7:28), and that those discourses are all addressed either exclusively (Mt 10; 18; 24; 25) or primarily (Mt 5–7; 13) to the disciples, whereas this is addressed primarily to the scribes and Pharisees (Mt 23:13–36). Consequently, it seems plausible to maintain that the evangelist did not intend to give it the structural importance of the five other discourses, and that, in spite of its being composed of sayings-material, it belongs to the narrative section of this book. In that regard, it is similar to the sayings-material of Mt 11:7–30. Some have proposed that Matthew wished to regard it as part of the final discourse of Mt 24–25, but the intervening material (Mt 24:1–4) and the change in matter and style of those chapters do not support that view.

§ [19:1] In giving Jesus' teaching on divorce (Mt 19:3–9), Matthew here follows his Marcan source (Mk 10:2–12) as he does Q in Mt 5:31–32 (cf. Lk 16:18). Mt 19:10–12 are peculiar to Matthew.

¶ [19:1] When Jesus finished these words: see note on Mt 7:28–29. The district of Judea across the Jordan: an inexact designation of the territory. Judea did not extend across the Jordan; the territory east of the river was Perea. The route to Jerusalem by way of Perea avoided passage through Samaria.

** [19:3] Tested him: the verb is used of attempts of Jesus' opponents to embarrass him by challenging him to do something they think impossible (Mt 16:1; Mk 8:11; Lk 11:16) or by having him say something that they can use against him

(Mt 22:18, 35; Mk 10:2; 12:15). **For any cause whatever**: this is peculiar to Matthew and has been interpreted by some as meaning that Jesus was being asked to take sides in the dispute between the schools of Hillel and Shammai on the reasons for divorce, the latter holding a stricter position than the former. It is unlikely, however, that to ask Jesus' opinion about the differing views of two Jewish schools, both highly respected, could be described as "testing" him, for the reason indicated above.

†† [19:4–6] Matthew recasts his Marcan source, omitting Jesus' question about Moses' command (Mk 10:3) and having him recall at once two Genesis texts that show the will and purpose of **the Creator** in making human beings **male and female** (Gn 1:27), namely, that **a man** may **be joined to his wife** in marriage in the intimacy of **one flesh** (Gn 2:24). **What God has** thus **joined** must not be separated by any human being. (The NAB translation of the Hebrew *bāsār* of Gn 2:24 as "body" rather than "flesh" obscures the reference of Matthew to that text.)

‡‡ [19:7] See Dt 24:1–4.

§§ [19:9] Moses' concession to human sinfulness (**the hardness of your hearts**, Mt 19:8) is repudiated by Jesus, and the original will of the Creator is reaffirmed against that concession. (**Unless the marriage is unlawful**): see note on Mt 5:31–32. There is some evidence suggesting that Jesus' absolute prohibition of divorce was paralleled in the Qumran community (see 11QTemple 57:17–19; CD 4:12b–5:14). Matthew removes Mark's setting of this verse as spoken to the disciples alone "in the house" (Mk 10:10) and also his extension of the divorce prohibition to the case of a woman's divorcing her husband (Mk 10:12), probably because in Palestine, unlike the places where Roman and Greek law prevailed, the woman was not allowed to initiate the divorce.

¶¶ [19:11] [This] **word**: probably the disciples' "**it is better not to marry**" (Mt 19:10). Jesus agrees but says that celibacy is not for all but only for those **to whom that is granted** by God.

*** [19:12] Incapable of marriage: literally, "eunuchs." Three classes are mentioned, eunuchs from birth, eunuchs by castration, and those who have voluntarily **renounced marriage** (literally, "have made themselves eunuchs") **for the sake of the kingdom**, i.e., to devote themselves entirely to its service. Some scholars take the last class to be those who have been divorced by their spouses and have refused to enter another marriage. But it is more likely that it is rather those who have chosen never to marry, since that suits better the optional nature of the decision: **whoever can . . . ought to accept it**.

m. [19:4] Gn 1:27.   n. [19:5] Gn 2:24; 1 Cor 6:16; Eph 5:31.   o. [19:7] Dt 24:1–4.   p. [19:9] 5:32; Lk 16:18; 1 Cor 7:10–11.

j. [18:33] Sir 28:4.   k. [18:35] 6:15; Jas 2:13.   l. [19:3–9] Mk 10:2–12.

**Blessing of the Children.** ¹³ᵖThen children were brought to him that he might lay his hands on them and pray. The disciples rebuked them, ¹⁴but Jesus said, "Let the children come to me, and do not prevent them; for the kingdom of heaven belongs to such as these." ¹⁵After he placed his hands on them, he went away.

**The Rich Young Man.**† ¹⁶ˢNow someone approached him and said, "Teacher, what good must I do to gain eternal life?"‡ ¹⁷He answered him, "Why do you ask me about the good? There is only One who is good.§ If you wish to enter into life, keep the commandments." ¹⁸ᵠHe asked him, "Which ones?" And Jesus replied, "'You shall not kill; you shall not commit adultery; you shall not steal; you shall not bear false witness; ¹⁹honor your father and your mother'; and 'you shall love your neighbor as yourself.'" ²⁰"The young man said to him, "All of these I have observed. What do I still lack?" ²¹ᵘJesus said to him, "If you wish to be perfect,†† go, sell what you have and give to [the] poor, and you will have treasure in heaven. Then come, follow me."

²²When the young man heard this statement, he went away sad, for he had many possessions. ²³‡‡Then Jesus said to his disciples, "Amen, I say to you, it will be hard for one who is rich to enter the kingdom of heaven. ²⁴ᵛAgain I say to you, it is easier for a camel to pass through the eye of a needle than for one who is rich to enter the kingdom of God." ²⁵§§When the disciples heard this, they were greatly astonished and said, "Who then can be saved?" ²⁶ʷJesus looked at them and said, "For human beings this is impossible, but for God all things are possible." ²⁷ˣThen Peter said to him in reply, "We have given up everything and followed you. What will there be for us?" ²⁸¶¶ʸJesus said to them, "Amen, I say to you that you who have followed me, in the new age, when the Son of Man is seated on his throne of glory, will yourselves sit on twelve thrones, judging the twelve tribes of Israel. ²⁹And everyone who has given up houses or brothers or sisters or father or mother or children or lands for the sake of my name will receive a hundred times more, and will inherit eternal life. ³⁰***ᶻBut many who are first will be last, and the last will be first.

**CHAPTER 20**

**The Workers in the Vineyard.**††† ¹"The kingdom of heaven is like a landowner who went out at dawn to hire laborers for his vineyard. ²After

---

*[19:13–15] This account is understood by some as intended to justify the practice of infant baptism. That interpretation is based principally on the command not to **prevent** the children from coming, since that word sometimes has a baptismal connotation in the New Testament; see Acts 8:36.

†[19:16–30] Cf. Mk 10:17–31. This story does not teach a "two-tier" morality, that of those who seek (only) **eternal life** (Mt 19:16) and that of those who **wish to be perfect** (Mt 19:21). It speaks rather of the obstacle that riches constitute for the following of Jesus and of the impossibility, humanly speaking, for one who has **many possessions** (Mt 19:22) **to enter the kingdom** (Mt 19:24). Actual renunciation of riches is not demanded of all; Matthew counts the rich Joseph of Arimathea as a disciple of Jesus (Mt 27:57). But only the poor in spirit (Mt 5:3) can **enter the kingdom** and, as here, such poverty may entail the sacrifice of one's **possessions**. The Twelve, who **have given up everything** (Mt 19:27) to follow Jesus, will have as their reward a share in Jesus' (the Son of Man's) **judging the twelve tribes of Israel** (Mt 19:28), and all who have similarly sacrificed family or property for his sake **will inherit eternal life** (Mt 19:29).

‡[19:16] **Gain eternal life:** this is equivalent to "entering into life" (Mt 19:17) and "being saved" (Mt 19:25); the **life** is that of the new age after the final judgment (see Mt 25:46). It probably is also equivalent here to "entering the kingdom of heaven" (Mt 19:23) or "the kingdom of God" (Mt 19:24), but see notes on Mt 3:2; 4:17; 18:1 for the wider reference of **the kingdom** in Matthew.

§[19:17] By Matthew's reformulation of the Marcan question and reply (Mk 10:17–18) Jesus' repudiation of the term "good" for himself has been softened. Yet the Marcan assertion that "no one is good but God alone" stands, with only unimportant verbal modification.

¶[19:18–19] The first five commandments cited are from the Decalogue (see Ex 20:12–16; Dt 5:16–20). Matthew omits Mark's "you shall not defraud" (Mk 10:19; see Dt 24:14) and adds Lv 19:18. This combination of commandments of the Decalogue with Lv 19:18 is partially the same as Paul's enumeration of the demands of Christian morality in Rom 13:9.

**[19:20] Young man:** in Matthew alone of the synoptics the questioner is said to be a **young man;** thus the Marcan "from my youth" (Mk 10:20) is omitted.

††[19:21] **If you wish to be perfect: to be perfect** is demanded of all Christians; see Mt 5:48. In the case of this man, it involves selling his possessions and giving to the poor; only so can he **follow** Jesus.

‡‡[19:23–24] Riches are an obstacle to entering **the kingdom** that cannot be overcome by human power. The comparison with the impossibility of a camel's passing **through the eye of a needle** should not be mitigated by such suppositions as that **the eye of a needle** means a low or narrow gate. The **kingdom of God:** as in Mt 12:28; 21:31, 43 instead of Matthew's usual **kingdom of heaven.**

§§[19:25–26] See note on Mk 10:23–27.

¶¶[19:28] This saying, directed to the Twelve, is from Q; see Lk 22:29–30. **The new age:** the Greek word here translated "new age" occurs in the New Testament only here and in Ti 3:5. Literally, it means "rebirth" or "regeneration," and is used in Titus of spiritual rebirth through baptism. Here it means the "rebirth" effected by the coming of the kingdom. Since that coming has various stages (see notes on Mt 3:2; 4:17), **the new age** could be taken as referring to the time after the resurrection when the Twelve will govern the true Israel, i.e., the church of Jesus. (For "judge" in the sense of "govern," cf. Jgs 12:8, 9, 11; 15:20; 16:31; Ps 2:10). But since it is connected here with the time when **the Son of Man** will be **seated on his throne of glory,** language that Matthew uses in Mt 25:31 for the time of final judgment, it is more likely that what the Twelve are promised is that they will be joined with Jesus then in judging the people of Israel.

***[19:30] Different interpretations have been given to this saying, which comes from Mk 10:31. In view of Matthew's associating it with the following parable (Mt 20:1–15) and substantially repeating it (in reverse order) at the end of that parable (Mt 20:16), it may be that its meaning is that all who respond to the call of Jesus, at whatever time (**first** or **last**), will be the same in respect to inheriting the benefits of the kingdom, which is the gift of God.

†††[20:1–16] This parable is peculiar to Matthew. It is difficult to know whether the evangelist composed it or received it as part of his traditional material and, if the latter is the case, what its original reference was. In its present context its close association with Mt 19:30 suggests that its teaching

---

q. [19:13–15] Mk 10:13–16; Lk 18:15–17.   r. [19:14] 18:3; Acts 8:36.   s. [19:16–30] Mk 10:17–31; Lk 18:18–30.   t. [19:18–19] Ex 20:12–16; Dt 5:16–20 / Lv 19:18; Rom 13:9.   u. [19:21] 5:48; 6:20.

v. [19:24] 7:14.   w. [19:26] Gn 18:14; Jb 42:2; Lk 1:37.   x. [19:27] 4:20, 22.   y. [19:28] 25:31; Dn 7:9, 22; Lk 22:30; Rev 3:21; 20:4.   z. [19:30] 20:16.

agreeing with them for the usual daily wage, he sent them into his vineyard. ³Going out about nine o'clock, he saw others standing idle in the marketplace, ⁴ᵃand he said to them, 'You too go into my vineyard, and I will give you what is just.' ⁵So they went off. [And] he went out again around noon, and around three o'clock, and did likewise. ⁶Going out about five o'clock, he found others standing around, and said to them, 'Why do you stand here idle all day?' ⁷They answered, 'Because no one has hired us.' He said to them, 'You too go into my vineyard.' ⁸ᵗᵃWhen it was evening the owner of the vineyard said to his foreman, 'Summon the laborers and give them their pay, beginning with the last and ending with the first.' ⁹When those who had started about five o'clock came, each received the usual daily wage. ¹⁰So when the first came, they thought that they would receive more, but each of them also got the usual wage. ¹¹And on receiving it they grumbled against the landowner, ¹²saying, 'These last ones worked only one hour, and you have made them equal to us, who bore the day's burden and the heat.' ¹³He said to one of them in reply, 'My friend, I am not cheating you.‡ Did you not agree with me for the usual daily wage? ¹⁴§Take what is yours and go. What if I wish to give this last one the same as you? ¹⁵[Or] am I not free to do as I wish with my own money? Are you envious because I am generous?' ¹⁶¶Thus, the last will be first, and the first will be last."

**The Third Prediction of the Passion.**** ¹⁷ᵇAs Jesus was going up to Jerusalem, he took the twelve [disciples] aside by themselves, and said to them on the way, ¹⁸"Behold, we are going up to Jerusalem, and the Son of Man will be handed over to the chief priests and the scribes, and they will condemn him to death, ¹⁹and hand him over to the Gentiles to be mocked and scourged and crucified, and he will be raised on the third day."

---

is the equality of all the disciples in the reward of inheriting eternal life.

*[20:4] **What is just**: although the wage is not stipulated as in the case of those first hired, it will be fair.

†[20:8] **Beginning with the last . . . the first**: this element of the parable has no other purpose than to show how **the first** knew what **the last** were given (Mt 20:12).

‡[20:13] **I am not cheating you**: literally, "I am not treating you unjustly."

§[20:14–15] The owner's conduct involves no violation of justice (Mt 20:4, 13), and that all the workers receive the same wage is due only to his generosity to the latest arrivals; the resentment of the first comes from envy.

¶[20:16] See note on Mt 19:30.

**[20:17–19] Cf. Mk 10:32–34. This is the third and the most detailed of the passion predictions (Mt 16:21–23; 17:22–23). It speaks of Jesus' being **handed over to the Gentiles** (Mt 27:2), his being **mocked** (Mt 27:27–30), **scourged** (Mt 27:26), and **crucified** (Mt 27:31, 35). In all but the last of these points Matthew agrees with his Marcan source, but whereas Mark speaks of Jesus' being killed (Mk 10:34), Matthew has the specific **to be . . . crucified.**

a. [20:8] Lv 19:13; Dt 24:15.   b. [20:17–19] 16:21; 17:22–23; Mk 10:32–34; Lk 18:31–33.

---

**The Request of James and John.**†† ²⁰ᶜThen the mother‡‡ of the sons of Zebedee approached him with her sons and did him homage, wishing to ask him for something. ²¹He said to her, "What do you wish?" She answered him, "Command that these two sons of mine sit, one at your right and the other at your left, in your kingdom." ²²Jesus said in reply, "You do not know what you are asking.§§ Can you drink the cup that I am going to drink?" They said to him, "We can." ²³He replied, "My cup you will indeed drink, but to sit at my right and at my left [, this] is not mine to give but is for those for whom it has been prepared by my Father." ²⁴ᵈWhen the ten heard this, they became indignant at the two brothers. ²⁵But Jesus summoned them and said, "You know that the rulers of the Gentiles lord it over them, and the great ones make their authority over them felt. ²⁶But it shall not be so among you. Rather, whoever wishes to be great among you shall be your servant; ²⁷ᵉwhoever wishes to be first among you shall be your slave. ²⁸ᶠJust so, the Son of Man did not come to be served but to serve and to give his life as a ransom¶¶ for many."

**The Healing of Two Blind Men.***** ²⁹ᵍAs they left Jericho, a great crowd followed him. ³⁰ʰTwo blind men were sitting by the roadside, and

---

††[20:20–28] Cf. Mk 10:35–45. The request of the sons of Zebedee, made through their mother, for the highest places of honor in the **kingdom**, and the indignation of **the** other **ten** disciples at this request, show that neither **the two brothers** nor the others have understood that what makes for greatness in the kingdom is not lordly power but humble service. Jesus gives the example, and his ministry of service will reach its highest point when he gives his life for the deliverance of the human race from sin.

‡‡[20:20–21] The reason for Matthew's making **the mother** the petitioner (cf. Mk 10:35) is not clear. Possibly he intends an allusion to Bathsheba's seeking the kingdom for Solomon; see 1 Kgs 1:11–21. **Your kingdom**: see note on Mt 16:28.

§§[20:22] **You do not know what you are asking**: the Greek verbs are plural and, with the rest of the verse, indicate that the answer is addressed not to the woman but to her sons. **Drink the cup**: see note on Mk 10:38–40. Matthew omits the Marcan "or be baptized with the baptism with which I am baptized" (Mk 10:38).

¶¶[20:28] **Ransom**: this noun, which occurs in the New Testament only here and in the Marcan parallel (Mk 10:45), does not necessarily express the idea of liberation by payment of some price. The cognate verb is used frequently in the LXX of God's liberating Israel from Egypt or from Babylonia after the Exile; see Ex 6:6; 15:13; Ps 77:16 (76 LXX); Is 43:1; 44:22. The liberation brought by Jesus' death will be **for many**; cf. Is 53:12. **Many** does not mean that some are excluded, but is a Semitism designating the collectivity who benefit from the service of the one, and is equivalent to "all." While there are few verbal contacts between this saying and the fourth Servant Song (Is 52:13–53:12), the ideas of that passage are reflected here.

***[20:29–34] The cure of the blind men is probably symbolic of what will happen to the disciples, now blind to the meaning of Jesus' passion and to the necessity of their sharing his suffering. As the men are given sight, so, after the resurrection, will the disciples come to see that to which they are now blind. Matthew has abbreviated his Marcan source (Mk 10:46–52) and has made Mark's one man two. Such doubling is characteristic of this gospel; see Mt 8:28–34 (// Mk 5:1–20) and the note on Mt 9:27–31.

c. [20:20–28] Mk 10:35–45.   d. [20:24–27] Lk 22:25–27.   e. [20:27] Mk 9:35.   f. [20:28] 26:28; Is 53:12; Rom 5:6; 1 Tm 2:6.   g. [20:29–34] Mk 10:46–52; Lk 18:35–43.   h. [20:30] 9:27.

when they heard that Jesus was passing by, they cried out, "[Lord,]* Son of David, have pity on us!" ³¹The crowd warned them to be silent, but they called out all the more, "Lord, Son of David, have pity on us!" ³²Jesus stopped and called them and said, "What do you want me to do for you?" ³³They answered him, "Lord, let our eyes be opened." ³⁴Moved with pity, Jesus touched their eyes. Immediately they received their sight, and followed him.

## CHAPTER 21

**The Entry into Jerusalem.**† ¹ᵃWhen they drew near Jerusalem and came to Bethphage‡ on the Mount of Olives, Jesus sent two disciples, ²saying to them, "Go into the village opposite you, and immediately you will find an ass tethered, and a colt with her.§ Untie them and bring them here to me. ³And if anyone should say anything to you, reply, 'The master has need of them.' Then he will send them at once." ⁴ᵇThis happened so that what had been spoken through the prophet might be fulfilled:

5    ʲ"Say to daughter Zion,
      'Behold, your king comes to you,
         meek and riding on an ass,
            and on a colt, the foal of a beast
               of burden.'"

⁶The disciples went and did as Jesus had ordered them. ⁷ᵏThey brought the ass and the colt and

laid their cloaks over them, and he sat upon them. ⁸†††ᵏThe very large crowd spread their cloaks on the road, while others cut branches from the trees and strewed them on the road. ⁹ᵖThe crowds preceding him and those following kept crying out and saying:

   "Hosanna‡‡ to the Son of David;
      blessed is he who comes in the name
         of the Lord;
   hosanna in the highest."

¹⁰And when he entered Jerusalem the whole city was shaken§§ and asked, "Who is this?" ¹¹And the crowds replied, "This is Jesus the prophet,¶¶ from Nazareth in Galilee."

**The Cleansing of the Temple.***** ¹²ᵐJesus entered the temple area and drove out all those engaged in selling and buying there. He overturned the tables of the money changers and the seats of those who were selling doves.†††ⁿ ¹³ᵒAnd he said to them, "It is written:

   'My house shall be a house of prayer,'‡‡‡
      but you are making it a den of thieves."

---

*[20:30] **[Lord,]**: some important textual witnesses omit this, but that may be because copyists assimilated this verse to Mt 9:27. **Son of David**: see note on Mt 9:27.

†[21:1–11] Jesus' coming to Jerusalem is in accordance with the divine will that he must go there (cf. Mt 16:21) to suffer, die, and be raised. He prepares for his entry into the city in such a way as to make it a fulfillment of the prophecy of Zec 9:9 (Mt 21:2) that emphasizes the humility of the **king** who **comes** (Mt 21:5). That prophecy, absent from the Marcan parallel account (Mk 11:1–11) although found also in the Johannine account of the entry (Jn 12:15), is the center of the Matthean story. During the procession from Bethphage to Jerusalem, Jesus is acclaimed as the Davidic messianic king by the crowds who accompany him (Mt 21:9). On his arrival **the whole city was shaken**, and to the inquiry of the amazed populace about Jesus' identity the crowds with him reply that he is **the prophet, from Nazareth in Galilee** (Mt 21:10, 11).

‡[21:1] **Bethphage**: a village that can no longer be certainly identified. Mark mentions it before Bethany (Mk 11:1), which suggests that it lay to the east of the latter. **The Mount of Olives**: the hill east of Jerusalem that is spoken of in Zec 14:4 as the place where the Lord will come to rescue Jerusalem from the enemy nations.

§[21:2] **An ass tethered, and a colt with her**: instead of the one animal of Mk 11:2, Matthew has two, as demanded by his understanding of Zec 9:9.

¶[21:4–5] **The prophet**: this fulfillment citation is actually composed of two distinct Old Testament texts, Is 62:11 (**Say to daughter Zion**) and Zec 9:9. The **ass** and the **colt** are the same animal in the prophecy, mentioned twice in different ways, the common Hebrew literary device of poetic parallelism. That Matthew takes them as two is one of the reasons why some scholars think that he was a Gentile rather than a Jewish Christian who would presumably not make that mistake (see Introduction).

**[21:7] **Upon them**: upon the two animals; an awkward picture resulting from Matthew's misunderstanding of the prophecy.

††[21:8] **Spread . . . on the road**: cf. 2 Kgs 9:13. There is a similarity between the cutting and strewing of the **branches** and the festivities of Tabernacles (Lv 23:39–40); see also 2 Mc 10:5–8 where the celebration of the rededication of the temple is compared to that of Tabernacles.

‡‡[21:9] **Hosanna**: the Hebrew means "(O Lord) grant salvation"; see Ps 118:25, but that invocation had become an acclamation of jubilation and welcome. **Blessed is he . . . in the name of the Lord**: see Ps 118:26 and the note on Jn 12:13. **In the highest**: probably only an intensification of the acclamation, although **Hosanna in the highest** could be taken as a prayer, "May God save (him)."

§§[21:10] **Was shaken**: in the gospels this verb is peculiar to Matthew where it is used also of the earthquake at the time of the crucifixion (Mt 27:51) and of the terror of the guards at Jesus' tomb at the appearance of the angel (Mt 28:4). For Matthew's use of the cognate noun, see note on Mt 8:24.

¶¶[21:11] **The prophet**: see Mt 16:14 ("one of the prophets") and 21:46.

***[21:12–17] Matthew changes the order of (Mk 11:11, 12, 15) and places the cleansing of the temple on the same day as the entry into Jerusalem, immediately after it. The activities going on in **the temple area** were, not secular but connected with the temple worship. Thus Jesus' attack on those so engaged and his charge that they were making God's **house of prayer a den of thieves** (Mt 21:12–13) constituted a claim to authority over the religious practices of Israel and were a challenge to the priestly authorities. Mt 21:14–17 are peculiar to Matthew. Jesus' healings and his countenancing the children's cries of praise rouse the indignation of **the chief priests and the scribes** (Mt 21:15). These two groups appear in the infancy narrative (Mt 2:4) and have been mentioned in the first and third passion predictions (Mt 16:21; 20:18). Now, as the passion approaches, they come on the scene again, exhibiting their hostility to Jesus.

†††[21:12] These activities were carried on in the court of the Gentiles, the outermost court of **the temple area**. Animals for sacrifice were sold; the **doves** were for those who could not afford a more expensive offering; see Lv 5:7. **Tables of the money changers**: only the coinage of Tyre could be used for the purchases; other money had to be exchanged for that.

‡‡‡[21:13] **'My house . . . prayer'**: cf. Is 56:7. Matthew omits the final words of the quotation, "for all peoples" ("all nations"), possibly because for him the worship of the God of Israel by all nations belongs to the time after the resurrection; see Mt 28:19. **A den of thieves**: the phrase is taken from Jer 7:11.

---

i. [21:1–11] Mk 11:1–11; Lk 19:28–38; Jn 12:12–15.    j. [21:5] Is 62:11; Zec 9:9.

k. [21:8] 2 Kgs 9:13.    l. [21:9] Ps 118:25–26.    m. [21:12–17] Mk 11:15–19; Lk 19:45–48; Jn 2:14–22.    n. [21:12] Lv 5:7.    o. [21:13] Is 56:7; Jer 7:11.

¹⁴ᵖThe blind and the lame* approached him in the temple area, and he cured them. ¹⁵When the chief priests and the scribes saw the wondrous things† he was doing, and the children crying out in the temple area, "Hosanna to the Son of David," they were indignant ¹⁶ᵠand said to him, "Do you hear what they are saying?" Jesus said to them, "Yes; and have you never read the text, 'Out of the mouths of infants and nurslings you have brought forth praise'?" ¹⁷And leaving them, he went out of the city to Bethany, and there he spent the night.

**The Cursing of the Fig Tree.**§ ¹⁸ʳWhen he was going back to the city in the morning, he was hungry. ¹⁹ˢSeeing a fig tree by the road, he went over to it, but found nothing on it except leaves. And he said to it, "May no fruit ever come from you again." And immediately the fig tree withered. ²⁰When the disciples saw this, they were amazed and said, "How was it that the fig tree withered immediately?" ²¹ᵗJesus said to them in reply, "Amen, I say to you, if you have faith and do not waver, not only will you do what has been done to the fig tree, but even if you say to this mountain, 'Be lifted up and thrown into the sea,' it will be done. ²²ᵘWhatever you ask for in prayer with faith, you will receive."

**The Authority of Jesus Questioned.**** ²³ᵛWhen he had come into the temple area, the chief priests and the elders of the people approached him as he was teaching and said, "By what authority are you doing these things?†† And who gave you this authority?"ʷ ²⁴Jesus said to them in reply, "I shall ask you one question,‡‡ and if you answer it for me, then I shall tell you by what authority I do these things. ²⁵Where was John's

baptism from? Was it of heavenly or of human origin?" They discussed this among themselves and said, "If we say 'Of heavenly origin,' he will say to us, 'Then why did you not believe him?' ²⁶§§But if we say, 'Of human origin,' we fear the crowd, for they all regard John as a prophet." ²⁷So they said to Jesus in reply, "We do not know." He himself said to them, "Neither shall I tell you by what authority I do these things.¶¶

**The Parable of the Two Sons.***** ²⁸"What is your opinion? A man had two sons. He came to the first and said, 'Son, go out and work in the vineyard today.' ²⁹He said in reply, 'I will not,' but afterwards he changed his mind and went. ³⁰The man came to the other son and gave the same order. He said in reply, 'Yes, sir,' but did not go. ³¹†††Which of the two did his father's will?" They answered, "The first." Jesus said to them, "Amen, I say to you, tax collectors and prostitutes are entering the kingdom of God before you. ³²‡‡‡When John came to you in the way of righteousness, you did not believe him; but tax collectors and prostitutes did. Yet even when you saw that, you did not later change your minds and believe him.

**The Parable of the Tenants.**§§§ ³³ᶻ"Hear another parable. There was a landowner who planted a

---

§§[21:26] **We fear . . . as a prophet:** cf. Mt 14:5.

¶¶[21:27] Since through embarrassment on the one hand and fear on the other the religious authorities claim ignorance of the origin of John's baptism, they show themselves incapable of speaking with authority; hence Jesus refuses to discuss with them the grounds of his authority.

***[21:28–32] The series of controversies is interrupted by three parables on the judgment of Israel (Mt 21:28–22:14) of which this, peculiar to Matthew, is the first. The second (Mt 21:33–46) comes from Mark (12:1–12), and the third (Mt 22:1–14) from Q; see Lk 14:15–24. This interruption of the controversies is similar to that in Mark, although Mark has only one parable between the first and second controversy. As regards Matthew's first parable, Mt 21:28–30 if taken by themselves could point simply to the difference between saying and doing, a theme of much importance in this gospel (cf. Mt 7:21; 12:50); that may have been the parable's original reference. However, it is given a more specific application by the addition of Mt 21:31–32. The two sons represent, respectively, the religious leaders and the religious outcasts who followed John's call to repentance. By the answer they give to Jesus' question (Mt 21:31) the leaders condemn themselves. There is much confusion in the textual tradition of the parable. Of the three different forms of the text given by important textual witnesses, one has the leaders answer that the son who agreed to go but did not was the one who did the father's will. Although some scholars accept that as the original reading, their arguments in favor of it seem unconvincing. The choice probably lies only between a reading that puts the son who agrees and then disobeys before the son who at first refuses and then obeys, and the reading followed in the present translation. The witnesses to the latter reading are slightly better than those that support the other.

†††[21:31] **Entering . . . before you:** this probably means "they enter; you do not."

‡‡‡[21:32] Cf. Lk 7:29–30. Although the thought is similar to that of the Lucan text, the formulation is so different that it is improbable that the saying comes from Q. **Came to you . . . way of righteousness:** several meanings are possible: that John himself was righteous, that he taught righteousness to others, or that he had an important place in God's plan of salvation. For the last, see note on Mt 3:14–15.

§§§[21:33–46] In this parable there is a close correspondence between most of the details of the story and the

---

*[21:14] **The blind and the lame:** according to 2 Sm 5:8 LXX **the blind and the lame** were forbidden to enter "the house of the Lord," the temple. These are the last of Jesus' healings in Matthew.

†[21:15] **The wondrous things:** the healings.

‡[21:16] **'Out of the mouths . . . praise':** cf. Ps 8:3 LXX.

§[21:18–22] In Mark the effect of Jesus' cursing the fig tree is not immediate; see Mk 11:14, 20. By making it so, Matthew has heightened the miracle. Jesus' act seems arbitrary and ill-tempered, but it is a prophetic action similar to those of Old Testament prophets that vividly symbolize some part of their preaching; see, e.g., Ez 12:1–20. It is a sign of the judgment that is to come upon the Israel that with all its apparent piety lacks the fruit of good deeds (Mt 3:10) and will soon bear the punishment of its fruitlessness (Mt 21:43). Some scholars propose that this story is the development in tradition of a parable of Jesus about the destiny of a fruitless tree, such as Lk 13:6–9. Jesus' answer to the question of the amazed disciples (Mt 21:20) makes the miracle an example of the power of prayer made with unwavering **faith** (Mt 21:21–22).

¶[21:21] See Mt 17:20.

**[21:23–27] Cf. Mk 11:27–33. This is the first of five controversies between Jesus and the religious authorities of Judaism in Mt 21:23–22:46, presented in the form of questions and answers.

††[21:23] **These things:** probably his entry into the city, his cleansing of the temple, and his healings there.

‡‡[21:24] To reply by counterquestion was common in rabbinical debate.

---

p. [21:14] 2 Sm 5:8 LXX.   q. [21:16] Ps 8:2 LXX; Wis 10:21.
r. [21:18–22] Mk 11:12–14, 20–24.   s. [21:19] Jer 8:13; Lk 13:6–9.
t. [21:21] 17:20; Lk 17:6.   u. [21:22] 7:7; 1 Jn 3:22.   v. [21:23–27] Mk 11:27–33; Lk 20:1–8.   w. [21:23] Jn 2:18.

x. [21:26] 14:5.   y. [21:32] Lk 7:29–30.   z. [21:33–46] Mk 12:1–12; Lk 20:9–19.

vineyard,* put a hedge around it, dug a wine press in it, and built a tower. Then he leased it to tenants and went on a journey.[a] ³⁴When vintage time drew near, he sent his servants† to the tenants to obtain his produce. ³⁵But the tenants seized the servants and one they beat, another they killed, and a third they stoned. ³⁶Again he sent other servants, more numerous than the first ones, but they treated them in the same way. ³⁷Finally, he sent his son to them, thinking, 'They will respect my son.' ³⁸‡But when the tenants saw the son, they said to one another, 'This is the heir. Come, let us kill him and acquire his inheritance.' ³⁹§They seized him, threw him out of the vineyard, and killed him. ⁴⁰What will the owner of the vineyard do to those tenants when he comes?" ⁴¹They answered¶ him, "He will put those wretched men to a wretched death and lease his vineyard to other tenants who will give him the produce at the proper times." ⁴²**ᶜJesus said to them, "Did you never read in the scriptures:

The stone that the builders rejected
      has become the cornerstone;
by the Lord has this been done,
      and it is wonderful in our eyes'?

⁴³††Therefore, I say to you, the kingdom of God will be taken away from you and given to a people that will produce its fruit. ⁴⁴[‡‡ The one who falls on this stone will be dashed to pieces; and it will crush anyone on whom it falls.]" ⁴⁵When the chief priests and the Pharisees§§ heard his parables, they knew that he was speaking about them. ⁴⁶And although they were attempting to arrest him, they feared the crowds, for they regarded him as a prophet.

## CHAPTER 22

**The Parable of the Wedding Feast.**¶¶ ¹ᵈJesus again in reply spoke to them in parables, saying, ²"The kingdom of heaven may be likened to a king who gave a wedding feast*** for his son. ³†††He dispatched his servants to summon the invited guests to the feast, but they refused to come. ⁴A second time he sent other servants, saying, 'Tell those invited: "Behold, I have prepared my banquet, my calves and fattened cattle are killed, and everything is ready; come to the feast."' ⁵Some ignored the invitation and went away, one to his farm, another to his business. ⁶"The rest laid hold of his servants, mistreated them, and killed them. ⁷‡‡‡The king was enraged and sent his troops, destroyed those murderers, and burned their city. ⁸Then he said to his servants, 'The feast is ready, but those who were invited were not worthy to come. ⁹Go out, therefore, into the main roads and invite to the feast whomever you find.' ¹⁰The servants went out into the streets and gathered all they found, bad and good alike,§§§ and the hall was filled with guests. ¹¹¶¶¶But

---

situation that it illustrates, the dealings of God with his people. Because of that heavy allegorizing, some scholars think that it does not in any way go back to Jesus, but represents the theology of the later church. That judgment applies to the Marcan parallel as well, although the allegorizing has gone farther in Matthew. There are others who believe that while many of the allegorical elements are due to church sources, they have been added to a basic parable spoken by Jesus. This view is now supported by the Gospel of Thomas 65, where a less allegorized and probably more primitive form of the parable is found.

*[21:33] **Planted a vineyard . . . a tower:** cf. Is 5:1–2. The **vineyard** is defined in Is 5:7 as "the house of Israel."

†[21:34–35] **His servants:** Matthew has two sendings of **servants** as against Mark's three sendings of a single servant (Mk 11:2–5a) followed by a statement about the sending of "many others" (Mk 11:2, 5b). That these servants stand for the prophets sent by God to Israel is clearly implied but not made explicit here, but see Mt 23:37. **His produce:** cf. Mk 12:2 "some of the produce." The **produce** is the good works demanded by God, and his claim to them is total.

‡[21:38] **Acquire his inheritance:** if a Jewish proselyte died without heir, the tenants of his land would have final claim on it.

§[21:39] **Threw him out . . . and killed him:** the change in the Marcan order where the son is killed and his corpse then thrown out (Mk 12:8) was probably made because of the tradition that Jesus died outside the city of Jerusalem; see Jn 19:17; Heb 13:12.

¶[21:41] **They answered:** in Mk 12:9 the question is answered by Jesus himself; here the leaders answer and so condemn themselves; cf. Mt 21:31. Matthew adds that the new **tenants** to whom the vineyard will be transferred **will give** the owner **the produce at the proper times.**

**[21:42] Cf. Ps 118:22–23. The psalm was used in the early church as a prophecy of Jesus' resurrection; see Acts 4:11; 1 Pt 2:7. If, as some think, the original parable ended at Mt 21:39 it was thought necessary to complete it by a reference to Jesus' vindication by God.

††[21:43] Peculiar to Matthew. **Kingdom of God:** see note on Mt 19:23–24. Its presence here instead of Matthew's usual "kingdom of heaven" may indicate that the saying came from Matthew's own traditional material. **A people that will produce its fruit:** believing Israelites and Gentiles, the church of Jesus.

‡‡[21:44] The majority of textual witnesses omit this verse. It is probably an early addition to Matthew from Lk 20:18 with which it is practically identical.

§§[21:45] **The Pharisees:** Matthew inserts into the group of Jewish leaders (Mt 21:23) those who represented the Judaism of his own time.

¶¶[22:1–14] This parable is from Q; see Lk 14:15–24. It has been given many allegorical traits by Matthew, e.g., the burning of the **city** of the guests who refused the invitation (Mt 22:7), which corresponds to the destruction of Jerusalem by the Romans in A.D. 70. It has similarities with the preceding parable of the tenants: the sending of two groups of ser-vants (Mt 22:3, 4), the murder of the **servants** (Mt 22:6), the punishment of the **murderers** (Mt 22:7), and the entrance of a new group into a privileged situation of which the others had proved themselves unworthy (Mt 22:8–10). The parable ends with a section that is peculiar to Matthew (Mt 22:11–14), which some take as a distinct parable. Matthew presents the **kingdom** in its double aspect, already present and something that can be entered here and now (Mt 22:1–10), and something that will be possessed only by those present members who can stand the scrutiny of the final judgment (Mt 22:11–14). The parable is not only a statement of God's judgment on Israel but a warning to Matthew's church.

***[22:2] **Wedding feast:** the Old Testament's portrayal of final salvation under the image of a banquet (Is 25:6) is taken up also in Mt 8:11; cf. Lk 13:15.

†††[22:3–4] **Servants . . . other servants:** probably Christian missionaries in both instances; cf. Mt 23:34.

‡‡‡[22:7] See note on Mt 22:1–14.

§§§[22:10] **Bad and good alike:** cf. Mt 13:47.

¶¶¶[22:11] **A wedding garment:** the repentance, change of heart and mind, that is the condition for entrance into the

---

a. [21:33] Is 5:1–2, 7.   b. [21:39] Heb 13:12.   c. [21:42] Ps 118:22–23; Is 28:16; Acts 4:11; 1 Pt 2:7.

d. [22:1–14] Lk 14:15–24.   e. [22:6] 21:35.

when the king came in to meet the guests he saw a man there not dressed in a wedding garment. [12]He said to him, 'My friend, how is it that you came in here without a wedding garment?' But he was reduced to silence. [13]*'Then the king said to his attendants, 'Bind his hands and feet, and cast him into the darkness outside, where there will be wailing and grinding of teeth.' [14]Many are invited, but few are chosen."

**Paying Taxes to the Emperor.**[†] [15]*Then the Pharisees[‡] went off and plotted how they might entrap him in speech. [16]They sent their disciples to him, with the Herodians,[§] saying, "Teacher, we know that you are a truthful man and that you teach the way of God in accordance with the truth. And you are not concerned with anyone's opinion, for you do not regard a person's status. [17]**Tell us, then, what is your opinion: Is it lawful to pay the census tax to Caesar or not?" [18]Knowing their malice, Jesus said, "Why are you testing me, you hypocrites? [19]**Show me the coin that pays the census tax." Then they handed him the Roman coin. [20]He said to them, "Whose image is this and whose inscription?" [21]*They replied, "Caesar's."[††] At that he said to them, "Then repay to Caesar what belongs to Caesar and to God what belongs to God." [22]When they heard this they *were amazed, and leaving him they went away.

**The Question About the Resurrection.**[‡‡] [23]*On that day Sadducees approached him, saying that

there is no resurrection.[§§] They put this question to him, [24]*saying, "Teacher, Moses said, 'If a man dies[¶¶] without children, his brother shall marry his wife and raise up descendants for his brother.' [25]Now there were seven brothers among us. The first married and died, and, having no descendants, left his wife to his brother. [26]The same happened with the second and the third, through all seven. [27]Finally the woman died. [28]Now at the resurrection, of the seven, whose wife will she be? For they all had been married to her." [29]***Jesus said to them in reply, "You are misled because you do not know the scriptures or the power of God. [30]At the resurrection they neither marry nor are given in marriage but are like the angels in heaven. [31]And concerning the resurrection of the dead, have you not read what was said to you[†††] by God, [32]**'I am the God of Abraham, the God of Isaac, and the God of Jacob'? He is not the God of the dead but of the living." [33]When the crowds heard this, they were astonished at his teaching.

**The Greatest Commandment.**[‡‡‡] [34]*When the Pharisees heard that he had silenced the Sadducees, they gathered together, [35]and one of them

on Mt 3:7. Denying the resurrection of the dead, a teaching of relatively late origin in Judaism (cf. Dn 12:2), they appeal to a law of the Pentateuch (Dt 25:5–10) and present a case based on it that would make resurrection from the dead ridiculous (Mt 22:24–28). Jesus chides them for knowing neither **the scriptures** nor **the power of God** (Mt 22:29). His argument in respect to God's power contradicts the notion, held even by many proponents as well as by opponents of the teaching, that the life of those raised from the dead would be essentially a continuation of the type of life they had had before death (Mt 22:30). His argument based on the scriptures (Mt 22:31–32) is of a sort that was accepted as valid among Jews of the time.

§§[22:23] **Saying that there is no resurrection**: in the Marcan parallel (Mk 22:12, 18) the Sadducees are correctly defined as those "who say there is no resurrection"; see also Lk 20:27. Matthew's rewording of Mark can mean that these particular Sadducees deny the resurrection, which would imply that he was not aware that the denial was characteristic of the party. For some scholars this is an indication of his being a Gentile Christian; see note on Mt 21:4–5.

¶¶[22:24] **'If a man dies . . . his brother'**: this is known as the "law of the levirate," from the Latin *levir*, "brother-in-law." Its purpose was to continue the family line of the deceased brother (Dt 25:6).

***[22:29] The sexual relationships of this world will be transcended; the risen body will be the work of the creative **power of God**.

†††[22:31–32] Cf. Ex 3:6. In the Pentateuch, which the Sadducees accepted as normative for Jewish belief and practice, God speaks even now (**to you**) of himself as the God of the patriarchs who died centuries ago. He identifies himself in relation to them, and because of their relation to him, the living God, they too are alive. This might appear no argument for the resurrection, but simply for life after death as conceived in Wis 3:1–3. But the general thought of early first-century Judaism was not influenced by that conception; for it human immortality was connected with the existence of the body.

‡‡‡[22:34–40] The Marcan parallel (Mk 12:28–34) is an exchange between Jesus and a scribe who is impressed by the way in which Jesus had conducted himself in the previous controversy (Mk 12:28), who compliments him for the answer he gives him (Mk 12:32), and who is said by Jesus to be "not far from the kingdom of God" (Mk 12:34). Matthew has sharpened that scene. The questioner, as the representative of other Pharisees, tests Jesus by his question (Mt 22:34–35), and both

kingdom (Mt 3:2; 4:17) must be continued in a life of good deeds (Mt 7:21–23).

*[22:13] **Wailing and grinding of teeth**: the Christian who lacks the wedding garment of good deeds will suffer the same fate as those Jews who have rejected Jesus; see note on Mt 8:11–12.

†[22:15–22] The series of controversies between Jesus and the representatives of Judaism (see note on Mt 21:23–27) is resumed. As in the first (Mt 21:23–27), here and in the following disputes Matthew follows his Marcan source with few modifications.

‡[22:15] **The Pharisees**: while Matthew retains the Marcan union of Pharisees and Herodians in this account, he clearly emphasizes the Pharisees' part. They alone are mentioned here, and the Herodians are joined with them only in a prepositional phrase of Mt 22:16. **Entrap him in speech**: the question that they will pose is intended to force Jesus to take either a position contrary to that held by the majority of the people or one that will bring him into conflict with the Roman authorities.

§[22:16] **Herodians**: see note on Mk 3:6. They would favor payment of the tax; the Pharisees did not.

¶[22:17] **Is it lawful**: the law to which they refer is the law of God.

**[22:19] **They handed him the Roman coin**: their readiness in producing the money implies their use of it and their acceptance of the financial advantages of the Roman administration in Palestine.

††[22:21] **Caesar's**: the emperor Tiberius (A.D. 14–37). **Repay to Caesar what belongs to Caesar**: those who willingly use the coin that is Caesar's should **repay** him in kind. The answer avoids taking sides in the question of the lawfulness of the tax. **To God what belongs to God**: Jesus raises the debate to a new level. Those who have hypocritically asked about tax in respect to its relation to the law of **God** should be concerned rather with repaying God with the good deeds that are his due; cf. Mt 21:41, 43.

‡‡[22:23–33] Here Jesus' opponents are the **Sadducees**, members of the powerful priestly party of his time; see note

f. [22:13] 8:12; 25:30.    g. [22:15–22] Mk 12:13–17; Lk 20:20–26.
h. [22:21] Rom 13:7.    i. [22:23–33] Mk 12:18–27; Lk 20:27–40.

j. [22:24] Gn 38:8; Dt 25:5–6.    k. [22:32] Ex 3:6.    l. [22:34–40] Mk 12:28–34; Lk 10:25–28.

[a scholar of the law]* tested him by asking, [36]"Teacher,[†] which commandment in the law is the greatest?" [37m]He said to him,[‡] "You shall love the Lord, your God, with all your heart, with all your soul, and with all your mind. [38]This is the greatest and the first commandment. [39n]The second is like it:[§] You shall love your neighbor as yourself. [40§o]The whole law and the prophets depend on these two commandments."

**The Question About David's Son.** [41p]While the Pharisees were gathered together, Jesus questioned them,[††] [42‡‡]saying, "What is your opinion about the Messiah? Whose son is he?" They replied, "David's." [43]He said to them, "How, then, does David, inspired by the Spirit, call him 'lord,' saying:

[44] [q]'The Lord said to my lord,
"Sit at my right hand
until I place your enemies under
your feet"'?

[45§§]If David calls him 'lord,' how can he be his son?" [46r]No one was able to answer him a word,

nor from that day on did anyone dare to ask him any more questions.

# CHAPTER 23[¶]

**Denunciation of the Scribes and Pharisees.** [1s]Then Jesus spoke to the crowds and to his disciples, [2***]saying, "The scribes and the Pharisees have taken their seat on the chair of Moses. [3]Therefore, do and observe all things whatsoever they tell you, but do not follow their example. For they preach but they do not practice. [4]They tie up heavy burdens[†††] [hard to carry] and lay them on people's shoulders, but they will not lift a finger to move them. [5‡‡‡u]All their works

---

his reaction to Jesus' reply and Jesus' commendation of him are lacking.

*[22:35] [A scholar of the law]: meaning "scribe." Although this reading is supported by the vast majority of textual witnesses, it is the only time that the Greek word so translated occurs in Matthew. It is relatively frequent in Luke, and there is reason to think that it may have been added here by a copyist since it occurs in the Lucan parallel (Lk 10:25–28). Tested: see note on Mt 19:3.

†[22:36] For the devout Jew all the commandments were to be kept with equal care, but there is evidence of preoccupation in Jewish sources with the question put to Jesus.

‡[22:37–38] Cf. Dt 6:5. Matthew omits the first part of Mark's fuller quotation (Mk 12:29; Dt 6:4–5), probably because he considered its monotheistic emphasis needless for his church. The love of God must engage the total person (**heart, soul, mind**).

§[22:39] Jesus goes beyond the extent of the question put to him and joins **to the greatest and the first commandment** a **second**, that of **love** of **neighbor**, Lv 19:18; see note on Mt 19:18–19. This combination of the two commandments may already have been made in Judaism.

¶[22:40] The double commandment is the source from which **the whole law and the prophets** are derived.

**[22:41–46] Having answered the questions of his opponents in the preceding three controversies, Jesus now puts a question to them about the sonship of the Messiah. Their easy response (Mt 22:43a) is countered by his quoting a verse of Ps 110 that raises a problem for their response (43b–45). They are unable to solve it and **from that day on** their questioning of him is ended.

††[22:41] **The Pharisees . . . questioned them**: Mark is not specific about who are questioned (Mk 12:35).

‡‡[22:42–44] **David's**: this view of the Pharisees was based on such Old Testament texts as Is 11:1–9; Jer 23:5; and Ez 34:23; see also the extrabiblical Psalms of Solomon 17:21. **How, then . . . saying**: Jesus cites Ps 110:1, accepting the Davidic authorship of the psalm, a common view of his time. The psalm was probably composed for the enthronement of a Davidic king of Judah. Matthew assumes that the Pharisees interpret it as referring to the Messiah, although there is no clear evidence that it was so interpreted in the Judaism of Jesus' time. It was widely used in the early church as referring to the exaltation of the risen Jesus. **My lord**: understood as the Messiah.

§§[22:45] Since Matthew presents Jesus both as Messiah (Mt 16:16) and as Son of David (Mt 1:1; see also note on Mt 9:27),

the question is not meant to imply Jesus' denial of Davidic sonship. It probably means that although he is the Son of David, he is someone greater, Son of Man and Son of God, and recognized as greater by David who calls him my '**lord**.'

¶¶[23:1–39] The final section of the narrative part of the fifth book of the gospel is a denunciation by Jesus of the scribes and the Pharisees (see note on Mt 3:7). It depends in part on Mark and Q (cf. Mk 12:38–39; Lk 11:37–52; 13:34–35), but in the main it is peculiar to Matthew. (For the reasons against considering this extensive body of sayings-material either as one of the structural discourses of this gospel or as part of the one that follows in Mt 24–25, see note on Mt 19:1–23:39.) While the tradition of a deep opposition between Jesus and the Pharisees is well founded, this speech reflects an opposition that goes beyond that of Jesus' ministry and must be seen as expressing the bitter conflict between Pharisaic Judaism and the church of Matthew at the time when the gospel was composed. The complaint often made that the speech ignores the positive qualities of Pharisaism and of its better representatives is true, but the complaint overlooks the circumstances that gave rise to the invective. Nor is the speech purely anti-Pharisaic. The evangelist discerns in his church many of the same faults that he finds in its opponents and warns his fellow Christians to look to their own conduct and attitudes.

***[23:2–3] **Have taken their seat . . . Moses**: it is uncertain whether this is simply a metaphor for Mosaic teaching authority or refers to an actual **chair** on which the teacher sat. It has been proved that there was a seat so designated in synagogues of a later period than that of this gospel. **Do and observe . . . they tell you**: since the Matthean Jesus abrogates Mosaic law (Mt 5:31–42), warns his disciples against the teaching of the Pharisees (Mt 14:1–12), and, in this speech, denounces the Pharisees as blind guides in respect to their teaching on oaths (Mt 23:16–22), this commandment **to observe all things whatsoever they** (the scribes and Pharisees) **tell you** cannot be taken as the evangelist's understanding of the proper standard of conduct for his church. The saying may reflect a period when the Matthean community was largely Jewish Christian and was still seeking to avoid a complete break with the synagogue. Matthew has incorporated this traditional material into the speech in accordance with his view of the course of salvation history, in which he portrays the time of Jesus' ministry as marked by the fidelity to the law, although with significant pointers to the new situation that would exist after his death and resurrection (see note on Mt 5:17–20). The crowds and the disciples (Mt 23:1) are exhorted not to **follow** the **example** of the Jewish leaders, whose deeds do not conform to their teaching (Mt 23:3).

†††[23:4] **Tie up heavy burdens**: see note on Mt 11:28.

‡‡‡[23:5] To the charge of preaching but not practicing (Mt 23:3), Jesus adds that of acting in order to earn praise. The disciples have already been warned against this same fault (see note on Mt 6:1–18). **Phylacteries**: the Mosaic law required that during prayer small boxes containing parchments on which verses of scripture were written be worn on the left forearm and the forehead (see Ex 13:9, 16; Dt 6:8; 11:18). **Tassels**: see note on Mt 9:20. The widening of **phylacteries** and the lengthening of **tassels** were for the purpose of making these evidences of piety more noticeable.

---

m. [22:37] Dt 6:5.   n. [22:39] Lv 19:18; Jas 2:8.   o. [22:40] Rom 13:8–10; Gal 5:14.   p. [22:41–46] Mk 12:35–37; Lk 20:41–44.   q. [22:44] Ps 110:1; Acts 2:35; Heb 1:13.   r. [22:46] Lk 20:40.

s. [23:1–39] Mk 12:38–39; Lk 11:37–52; 13:34–35.   t. [23:4] Lk 11:46.   u. [23:5] 6:1–6; Ex 13:9, 16; Nm 15:38–39; Dt 6:8; 11:18.

are performed to be seen. They widen their phylacteries and lengthen their tassels. [6*v]They love places of honor at banquets, seats of honor in synagogues, [7]greetings in marketplaces, and the salutation 'Rabbi.' [8†]As for you, do not be called 'Rabbi.' You have but one teacher, and you are all brothers. [9]Call no one on earth your father; you have but one Father in heaven. [10]Do not be called 'Master'; you have but one master, the Messiah. [11w]The greatest among you must be your servant. [12x]Whoever exalts himself will be humbled; but whoever humbles himself will be exalted.

[13‡y]"Woe to you, scribes and Pharisees, you hypocrites. You lock the kingdom of heaven§ before human beings. You do not enter yourselves, nor do you allow entrance to those trying to enter. [[14]]¶

[15**]"Woe to you, scribes and Pharisees, you hypocrites. You traverse sea and land to make one convert, and when that happens you make him a child of Gehenna twice as much as yourselves.

[16††z]"Woe to you, blind guides, who say, 'If one swears by the temple, it means nothing, but if one swears by the gold of the temple, one is obligated.' [17]Blind fools, which is greater, the gold, or the temple that made the gold sacred? [18]And you say, 'If one swears by the altar, it means nothing, but if one swears by the gift on the altar, one is obligated.' [19]You blind ones, which is greater, the gift, or the altar that makes the gift sacred? [20a]One who swears by the altar swears by it and all that is upon it; [21]one who swears by the temple swears by it and by him who dwells in it; [22]one who swears by heaven swears by the throne of God and by him who is seated on it.

[23b]"Woe to you, scribes and Pharisees, you hypocrites. You pay tithes‡‡ of mint and dill and cummin, and have neglected the weightier things of the law: judgment and mercy and fidelity. [But] these you should have done, without neglecting the others. [24§§c]Blind guides, who strain out the gnat and swallow the camel!

[25¶¶d]"Woe to you, scribes and Pharisees, you hypocrites. You cleanse the outside of cup and dish, but inside they are full of plunder and self-indulgence. [26]Blind Pharisee, cleanse first the inside of the cup, so that the outside also may be clean.

[27***]"Woe to you, scribes and Pharisees, you hypocrites. You are like whitewashed tombs, which appear beautiful on the outside, but inside are full of dead men's bones and every kind of filth. [28e]Even so, on the outside you appear righteous, but inside you are filled with hypocrisy and evildoing.

---

*[23:6–7] Cf. Mk 12:38–39. 'Rabbi': literally, "my great one," a title of respect for teachers and leaders.

†[23:8–12] These verses, warning against the use of various titles, are addressed to the disciples alone. While only the title **'Rabbi'** has been said to be used in addressing the scribes and Pharisees (Mt 23:7), the implication is that **Father** and **'Master'** also were. The prohibition of these titles to the disciples suggests that their use was present in Matthew's church. The Matthean Jesus forbids not only the titles but the spirit of superiority and pride that is shown by their acceptance. **Whoever exalts . . . will be exalted:** cf. Lk 14:11.

‡[23:13–36] This series of seven "woes," directed against the **scribes and Pharisees** and addressed to them, is the heart of the speech. The phrase **woe to** occurs often in the prophetic and apocalyptic literature, expressing horror of a sin and punishment for those who commit it. **Hypocrites:** see note on Mt 6:2. The hypocrisy of the **scribes and Pharisees** consists in the difference between their speech and action (Mt 23:3) and in demonstrations of piety that have no other purpose than to enhance their reputation as religious persons (Mt 23:5).

§[23:13] **You lock the kingdom of heaven:** cf. Mt 16:19 where Jesus tells Peter that he will give him the keys to **the kingdom of heaven.** The purpose of the authority expressed by that metaphor is to give entrance into the kingdom (the kingdom is closed only to those who reject the authority); here the charge is made that the authority of the **scribes and Pharisees** is exercised in such a way as to be an obstacle to entrance. Cf. Lk 11:52 where the accusation against the "scholars of the law" (Matthew's **scribes**) is that they "have taken away the key of knowledge."

¶[23:14] Some manuscripts add a verse here or after Mt 23:12, "Woe to you, scribes and Pharisees, you hypocrites. You devour the houses of widows and, as a pretext, recite lengthy prayers. Because of this, you will receive a very severe condemnation." Cf. Mk 12:40; Lk 20:47. This "woe" is almost identical with Mk 12:40 and seems to be an interpolation derived from that text.

**[23:15] In the first century A.D. until the First Jewish Revolt against Rome (A.D. 66–70); many Pharisees conducted a vigorous missionary campaign among Gentiles. **Convert:** literally, "proselyte," a Gentile who accepted Judaism fully by submitting to circumcision and all other requirements of Mosaic law. **Child of Gehenna:** worthy of everlasting punishment; for **Gehenna,** see note on Mt 5:22. **Twice as much as yourselves:** possibly this refers simply to the zeal of the **convert,** surpassing that of the one who converted him.

††[23:16–22] An attack on the casuistry that declared some oaths binding (**one is obligated**) and others not (**it means nothing**) and held the binding oath to be the one made by something of lesser value (**the gold; the gift on the altar**). Such teaching, which inverts the order of values, reveals the teachers to be **blind guides;** cf. Mt 15:14. Since the Matthean Jesus forbids all oaths to his disciples (Mt 5:33–37), this vow does not set up a standard for Christian moral conduct, but ridicules the Pharisees on their own terms.

‡‡[23:23] The Mosaic law ordered tithing of the produce of the land (Lv 27:30; Dt 14:22–23), and the scribal tradition is said here to have extended this law to even the smallest herbs. The practice is criticized not in itself but because it shows the Pharisees' preoccupation with matters of less importance while they neglect **the weightier things of the law.**

§§[23:24] Cf. Lv 11:41–45 that forbids the eating of any "swarming creature." The Pharisees' scrupulosity about minor matters and neglect of greater ones (Mt 23:23) is further brought out by this contrast between straining liquids that might contain a tiny "swarming creature" and yet swallowing **the camel.** The latter was one of the unclean animals forbidden by the law (Lv 11:4), but it is hardly possible that the scribes and Pharisees are being denounced as guilty of so gross a violation of the food laws. To **swallow the camel** is only a hyperbolic way of speaking of their neglect of what is important.

¶¶[23:25–26] The ritual washing of utensils for dining (cf. Mk 7:4) is turned into a metaphor illustrating a concern for appearances while inner purity is ignored. The **scribes and Pharisees** are compared to cups carefully washed on the outside but filthy within. **Self-indulgence:** the Greek word here translated means lack of self-control, whether in drinking or in sexual conduct.

***[23:27–28] The sixth **woe,** like the preceding one, deals with concern for externals and neglect of what is **inside.** Since contact with dead bodies, even when one was unaware of it, caused ritual impurity (Nm 19:11–22), tombs were whitewashed so that no one would contract such impurity inadvertently.

---

v. [23:6–7] Mk 12:38–39; Lk 11:43; 20:46.   w. [23:11] 20:26.   x. [23:12] Lk 14:11; 18:14.   y. [23:13] Lk 11:52.   z. [23:16] 15:14.

a. [23:20–22] 5:34–35.   b. [23:23] Lv 27:30; Dt 14:22; Lk 11:42.   c. [23:24] Lv 11:41–45.   d. [23:25–26] Mk 7:4; Lk 11:39.   e. [23:28] Lk 16:15; 18:9.

²⁹"'Woe to you, scribes and Pharisees,† you hypocrites. You build the tombs of the prophets and adorn the memorials of the righteous, ³⁰and you say, 'If we had lived in the days of our ancestors, we would not have joined them in shedding the prophets' blood.' ³¹ᵉThus you bear witness against yourselves that you are the children of those who murdered the prophets; ³²now fill up what your ancestors measured out! ³³ʰYou serpents, you brood of vipers, how can you flee from the judgment of Gehenna? ³⁴ᶠTherefore, behold, I send to you prophets and wise men and scribes; some of them you will kill and crucify, some of them you will scourge in your synagogues and pursue from town to town, ³⁵so that there may come upon you all the righteous blood shed upon earth, from the righteous blood of Abel to the blood of Zechariah, the son of Barachiah, whom you murdered between the sanctuary and the altar. ³⁶Amen, I say to you, all these things will come upon this generation.

**The Lament over Jerusalem.**§ ³⁷ʲ"Jerusalem, Jerusalem, you who kill the prophets and stone those sent to you, how many times I yearned to gather your children together, as a hen gathers her young under her wings, but you were unwilling!ᵏ ³⁸ˡBehold, your house will be abandoned, desolate. ³⁹ᵐI tell you, you will not see me again until you say, 'Blessed is he who comes in the name of the Lord.'"

**CHAPTER 24**

**The Destruction of the Temple Foretold.** ¹ⁿJesus left the temple area and was going away, when his disciples approached him to point out the temple buildings. ²"He said to them in reply, "You see all these things, do you not? Amen, I say to you, there will not be left here a stone upon another stone that will not be thrown down."

**The Beginning of Calamities.** ³As he was sitting on the Mount of Olives,†† the disciples approached him privately and said, "Tell us, when will this happen, and what sign will there be of your coming, and of the end of the age?" ⁴‡‡Jesus said to

§[24:1–25:46] The discourse of the fifth book, the last of the five around which the discourse is structured. It is called the "eschatological" discourse since it deals with the coming of the new age (the *eschaton*) in its fullness, with events that will precede it, and with how the disciples are to conduct themselves while awaiting an event that is as certain as its exact time is unknown to all but the Father (Mt 24:36). The discourse may be divided into two parts, Mt 24:1–44 and Mt 24:45–25:46. In the first, Matthew follows his Marcan source (Mk 13:1–37) closely. The second is drawn from Q and from the evangelist's own traditional material. Both parts show Matthew's editing of his sources by deletions, additions, and modifications. The vigilant waiting that is emphasized in the second part does not mean a cessation of ordinary activity and concentration only on what is to come, but a faithful accomplishment of duties at hand, with awareness that the end, for which the disciples must always be ready, will entail the great judgment by which the everlasting destiny of all will be determined.

**[24:2] As in Mark, Jesus predicts the destruction of the temple. By omitting the Marcan story of the widow's contribution (Mk 12:41–44) that immediately precedes the prediction in that gospel, Matthew has established a close connection between it and Mt 23:38, ". . . your house will be abandoned desolate."

††[24:3] The Mount of Olives: see note on Mt 21:1. The disciples: cf. Mk 13:3–4 where only Peter, James, John, and Andrew put the question that is answered by the discourse. In both gospels, however, the question is put privately: the ensuing discourse is only for those who are disciples of Jesus. When will this happen . . . end of the age?: Matthew distinguishes carefully between the destruction of the temple (this) and the coming of Jesus that will bring the end of the age. In Mark the two events are more closely connected, a fact that may be explained by Mark's believing that the one would immediately succeed the other. Coming: this translates the Greek word *parousia*, which is used in the gospels only here and in Mt 24:27, 37, 39. It designated the official visit of a ruler to a city or the manifestation of a saving deity, and it was used by Christians to refer to the final coming of Jesus in glory, a term first found in the New Testament with that meaning in 1 Thes 2:19. The end of the age: see note on Mt 13:39.

‡‡[24:4–14] This section of the discourse deals with calamities in the world (Mt 24:6–7) and in the church (Mt 24:9–12). The former must happen before the end comes (Mt 24:6), but they are only the beginning of the labor pains (Mt 24:8). (It may be noted that the Greek word translated the end in Mt 24:6 and in Mt 24:13–14 is not the same as the phrase "the end of the age" in Mt 24:3, although the meaning is the same.) The latter are sufferings of the church, both from within and without, that will last until the gospel is preached . . . to all

*[23:29–36] The final woe is the most serious indictment of all. It portrays the scribes and Pharisees as standing in the same line as their ancestors who murdered the prophets and the righteous.

†[23:29–32] In spite of honoring the slain dead by building their tombs and adorning their memorials, and claiming that they would not have joined in their ancestors' crimes if they had lived in their days, the scribes and Pharisees are true children of their ancestors and are defiantly ordered by Jesus to fill up what those ancestors measured out. This order reflects the Jewish notion that there was an allotted measure of suffering that had to be completed before God's final judgment would take place.

‡[23:34–36] There are important differences between the Matthean and the Lucan form of this Q material; cf. Lk 11:49–51. In Luke the one who sends the emissaries is the "wisdom of God." If, as many scholars think, that is the original wording of Q, Matthew, by making Jesus the sender, has presented him as the personified divine wisdom. In Luke, wisdom's emissaries are the Old Testament "prophets" and the Christian "apostles." Matthew's prophets and wise men and scribes are probably Christian disciples alone; cf. Mt 10:41 and see note on Mt 13:52. You will kill: see Mt 24:9. Scourge in your synagogues . . . town to town: see Mt 10:17, 23 and the note on Mt 10:17. All the righteous blood shed upon the earth: the slaying of the disciples is in continuity with all the shedding of righteous blood beginning with that of Abel. The persecution of Jesus' disciples by this generation involves the persecutors in the guilt of their murderous ancestors. The blood of Zechariah: see note on Lk 11:51. By identifying him as the son of Barachiah Matthew understands him to be Zechariah the Old Testament minor prophet; see Zec 1:1.

§[23:37–39] Cf. Lk 13:34–35. The denunciation of Pharisaic Judaism ends with this lament over Jerusalem, which has repeatedly rejected and murdered those whom God has sent to her. How many times: this may refer to various visits of Jesus to the city, an aspect of his ministry found in John but otherwise not in the synoptics. As a hen . . . under her wings: for imagery similar to this, see Ps 17:8; 91:4. Your house . . . desolate: probably an allusion to the destruction of the temple in A.D. 70. You will not see me . . . in the name of the Lord: Israel will not see Jesus again until he comes in glory for the final judgment. The acclamation has been interpreted in contrasting ways, as an indication that Israel will at last accept Jesus at that time, and as its troubled recognition of him as its dreaded judge who will pronounce its condemnation; in support of the latter view see Mt 24:30.

f. [23:30] Lk 11:47.    g. [23:31] Acts 7:52.    h. [23:33] 3:7; 12:34.    i. [23:34–36] 5:12; Gn 4:8; 2 Chr 24:20–22; Zec 1:1; Lk 11:49–51; Rev 18:24.    j. [23:37–39] Lk 13:34–35; 19:41–44.

k. [23:37] 21:35.    l. [23:38] Jer 12:7.    m. [23:39] Ps 118:26.    n. [24:1–44] Mk 13:1–37; Lk 21:5–36.

them in reply, "See that no one deceives you. [5]For many will come in my name, saying, 'I am the Messiah,' and they will deceive many. [6]*You will hear of wars* and reports of wars; see that you are not alarmed, for these things must happen, but it will not yet be the end. [7]*Nation will rise against nation, and kingdom against kingdom; there will be famines and earthquakes from place to place. [8]†All these are the beginning of the labor pains. [9]‡*Then they will hand you over to persecution, and they will kill you. You will be hated by all nations because of my name. [10]And then many will be led into sin; they will betray and hate one another. [11]Many false prophets will arise and deceive many; [12]and because of the increase of evildoing, the love of many will grow cold. [13]*But the one who perseveres to the end will be saved. [14]§And this gospel of the kingdom will be preached throughout the world as a witness to all nations,§ and then the end will come.

## The Great Tribulation.¶ [15]*"When you see the desolating abomination** spoken of through Daniel the prophet standing in the holy place (let the reader understand), [16]then those in Judea must flee†† to the mountains, [17]‡‡*a person on the housetop must not go down to get things out of his house, [18]a person in the field must not return to get his cloak. [19]Woe to pregnant women and nursing mothers in those days. [20]§§Pray that your flight not be in winter or on the sabbath, [21]¶¶*for at that time there will be great tribulation, such as has not been since the beginning of the world until now, nor ever will be. [22]And if those days had not been shortened, no one would be saved; but for the sake of the elect they will be shortened. [23]*If anyone says to you then, 'Look, here is the Messiah!' or, 'There he is!' do not believe it. [24]False messiahs and false prophets will arise, and they will perform signs and wonders so great as to deceive, if that were possible, even the elect. [25]Behold, I have told it to you beforehand. [26]So if they say to you, 'He is in the desert,' do not go out there; if they say, 'He is in the inner rooms,' do not believe it.*** [27]*For just as lightning comes from the east and is seen as far as the west, so will the coming of the Son of Man be. [28]Wherever the corpse is, there the vultures will gather.

## The Coming of the Son of Man. [29]†††*Immediately after the tribulation of those days,

---

nations. Then the end will come and those who have endured the sufferings with fidelity will be saved (Mt 24:13–14).

*[24:6–7] The disturbances mentioned here are a commonplace of apocalyptic language, as is the assurance that they must happen (see Dn 2:28 LXX), for that is the plan of God. Kingdom against kingdom: see Is 19:2.

†[24:8] The labor pains: the tribulations leading up to the end of the age are compared to the pains of a woman about to give birth. There is much attestation for rabbinic use of the phrase "the woes (or birth pains) of the Messiah" after the New Testament period, but in at least one instance it is attributed to a rabbi who lived in the late first century A.D. In this Jewish usage it meant the distress of the time preceding the coming of the Messiah; here, the labor pains precede the coming of the Son of Man in glory.

‡[24:9–12] Matthew has used Mk 13:9–12 in his missionary discourse (Mt 10:17–21) and omits it here. Besides the sufferings, including death, and the hatred of all nations that the disciples will have to endure, there will be worse affliction within the church itself. This is described in Mt 24:10–12, which are peculiar to Matthew. Will be led into sin: literally, "will be scandalized," probably meaning that they will become apostates; see Mt 13:21 where "fall away" translates the same Greek word as here. Betray: in the Greek this is the same word as the hand over of Mt 24:9. The handing over to persecution and hatred from outside will have their counterpart within the church. False prophets: these are Christians; see note on Mt 7:15–20. Evildoing: see Mt 7:23. Because of the apocalyptic nature of much of this discourse, the literal meaning of this description of the church should not be pressed too hard. However, there is reason to think that Matthew's addition of these verses reflects in some measure the condition of his community.

§[24:14] Except for the last part (and then the end will come), this verse substantially repeats Mk 13:10. The Matthean addition raises a problem since what follows in Mt 24:15–23 refers to the horrors of the First Jewish Revolt including the destruction of the temple, and Matthew, writing after that time, knew that the parousia of Jesus was still in the future. A solution may be that the evangelist saw the events of those verses as foreshadowing the cosmic disturbances that he associates with the parousia (Mt 24:29) so that the period in which the former took place could be understood as belonging to the end.

¶[24:15–28] Cf. Mk 13:14–23; Lk 17:23–24, 37. A further stage in the tribulations that will precede the coming of the Son of Man, and an answer to the question of Mt 24:3a, "when will this (the destruction of the temple) happen?"

**[24:15] The desolating abomination: in 167 B.C. the Syrian king Antiochus IV Epiphanes desecrated the temple by

setting up in it a statue of Zeus Olympios (see 1 Mc 1:54). That event is referred to in Dn 12:11 LXX as the "desolating abomination" (NAB "horrible abomination") and the same Greek term is used here; cf. also Dn 9:27; 11:31. Although the desecration had taken place before Daniel was written, it is presented there as a future event, and Matthew sees that "prophecy" fulfilled in the desecration of the temple by the Romans. In the holy place: the temple; more precise than Mark's where he should not (Mk 13:14). Let the reader understand: this parenthetical remark, taken from Mk 13:14 invites the reader to realize the meaning of Daniel's "prophecy."

††[24:16] The tradition that the Christians of Jerusalem fled from that city to Pella, a city of Transjordan, at the time of the First Jewish Revolt is found in Eusebius (Ecclesiastical History 3.5.3), who attributes the flight to "a certain oracle given by revelation before the war." The tradition is not improbable but the Matthean command, derived from its Marcan source, is vague in respect to the place of flight (to the mountains), although some scholars see it as applicable to the flight to Pella.

‡‡[24:17–19] Haste is essential, and the journey will be particularly difficult for women who are burdened with unborn or infant children.

§§[24:20] On the sabbath: this addition to in winter (cf. Mk 13:18) has been understood as an indication that Matthew was addressed to a church still observing the Mosaic law of sabbath rest and the scribal limitations upon the length of journeys that might lawfully be made on that day. That interpretation conflicts with Matthew's view on sabbath observance (cf. Mt 12:1–14). The meaning of the addition may be that those undertaking on the sabbath a journey such as the one here ordered would be offending the sensibilities of law-observant Jews and would incur their hostility.

¶¶[24:21] For the unparalleled distress of that time, see Dn 12:1.

***[24:26–28] Claims that the Messiah is to be found in some distant or secret place must be ignored. The coming of the Son of Man will be as clear as lightning to all and as the corpse of an animal is to vultures; cf. Lk 17:24, 37. Here there is clear identification of the Son of Man and the Messiah; cf. Mt 24:23.

†††[24:29] The answer to the question of Mt 24:3b, "What sign will there be of your coming?" Immediately after . . .

o. [24:6] Dn 2:28 LXX.    p. [24:7] Is 19:2.    q. [24:9] 10:17.    r. [24:13] 10:22.    s. [24:14] 28:19; Rom 10:18.    t. [24:15] Dn 9:27; 11:31; 12:11; Mk 13:14.

u. [24:17] Lk 17:31.    v. [24:21] Dn 12:1.    w. [24:23] Lk 17:23.    x. [24:27–28] Lk 17:24, 37.    y. [24:29] Is 13:10, 13; Ez 32:7; Am 8:9.

the sun will be darkened,
> and the moon will not give its light,
and the stars will fall from the sky,
> and the powers of the heavens will
> be shaken.

30gAnd then the sign of the Son of Man* will appear in heaven, and all the tribes of the earth will mourn, and they will see the Son of Man coming upon the clouds of heaven with power and great glory. 31aAnd he will send out his angels† with a trumpet blast, and they will gather his elect from the four winds, from one end of the heavens to the other.

**The Lesson of the Fig Tree.‡** 32"Learn a lesson from the fig tree. When its branch becomes tender and sprouts leaves, you know that summer is near. 33In the same way, when you see all these things, know that he is near, at the gates. 34Amen, I say to you, this generation§ will not pass away until all these things have taken place. 35bHeaven and earth will pass away, but my words will not pass away.

**The Unknown Day and Hour.¶** 36c"But of that day and hour no one knows, neither the angels of heaven, nor the Son,** but the Father alone. 37††dFor as it was in the days of Noah, so it will be at the coming of the Son of Man. 38In [those] days before the flood, they were eating and drinking, marrying and giving in marriage, up to the day that Noah entered the ark. 39They did not know until the flood came and carried them all away. So will it be [also] at the coming of the Son of Man. 40‡‡eTwo men will be out in the field; one will be taken, and one will be left. 41Two women will be grinding at the mill; one will be taken, and one will be left. 42§§fTherefore, stay awake! For you do not know on which day your Lord will come. 43gBe sure of this: if the master of the house had known the hour of night when the thief was coming, he would have stayed awake and not let his house be broken into. 44So too, you also must be prepared, for at an hour you do not expect, the Son of Man will come.

**The Faithful or the Unfaithful Servant.¶¶** 45h"Who, then, is the faithful and prudent servant, whom the master has put in charge of his household to distribute to them their food at the proper time?*** 46Blessed is that servant whom his master on his arrival finds doing so. 47Amen, I say to you, he will put him in charge of all his property. 48†††But if that wicked servant says to himself, 'My master is long delayed,' 49and begins to beat his fellow servants, and eat and drink with drunkards, 50the servant's master will come on an unexpected day and at an unknown hour 51iiand will punish him severely‡‡‡ and assign him a place with the hypocrites, where there will be wailing and grinding of teeth. .

## CHAPTER 25

**The Parable of the Ten Virgins.§§§** 1"Then¶¶¶ the kingdom of heaven will be like ten virgins

---

**those days**: the shortening of time between the preceding **tribulation** and the parousia has been explained as Matthew's use of a supposed device of Old Testament prophecy whereby certainty that a predicted event will occur is expressed by depicting it as imminent. While it is questionable that this is an acceptable understanding of the Old Testament predictions, it may be applicable here, for Matthew knew that the parousia had not come **immediately after** the fall of Jerusalem, and it is unlikely that he is attributing a mistaken calculation of time to Jesus. **The sun . . . be shaken**: cf. Is 13:10, 13.

*[24:30] **The sign of the Son of Man**: perhaps this means **the sign** that is the glorious appearance of **the Son of Man**; cf. Mt 12:39–40 where "the sign of Jonah" is Jonah's being in the "belly of the whale." **Tribes of the earth will mourn**: peculiar to Matthew; cf. Zec 12:12–14. **Coming upon the clouds . . . glory**: cf. Dn 7:13, although there the "one like a son of man" comes to God to receive kingship; here **the Son of Man** comes from heaven for judgment.

†[24:31] **Send out his angels**: cf. Mt 13:41 where they are sent out to collect the wicked for punishment. **Trumpet blast**: cf. Is 27:13; 1 Thes 4:16.

‡[24:32–35] Cf. Mk 13:28–31.

§[24:34] The difficulty raised by this verse cannot be satisfactorily removed by the supposition that **this generation** means the Jewish people throughout the course of their history, much less the entire human race. Perhaps for Matthew it means the **generation** to which he and his community belonged.

¶[24:36–44] The statement of Mt 24:34 is now counterbalanced by one that declares that the exact time of the parousia is known only to **the Father** (Mt 24:36), and the disciples are warned to be always ready for it. This section is drawn from Mark and Q (cf. Lk 17:26–27, 34–35; 12:39–40).

**[24:36] Many textual witnesses omit **nor the Son**, which follows Mk 13:32. Since its omission can be explained by reluctance to attribute this ignorance to **the Son**, the reading that includes it is probably original.

††[24:37–39] Cf. Lk 17:26–27. **In the days of Noah**: the Old Testament account of the flood lays no emphasis upon what is central for Matthew, i.e., the unexpected coming of the flood upon those who were unprepared for it.

‡‡[24:40–41] Cf. Lk 17:34–35. **Taken . . . left**: the former probably means **taken** into the kingdom; the latter, **left** for destruction. People in the same situation will be dealt with in opposite ways. In this context, the discrimination between them will be based on their readiness for the coming of the Son of Man.

§§[24:42–44] Cf. Lk 12:39–40. The theme of vigilance and readiness is continued with the bold comparison of the Son of Man to a thief who comes to break into a house.

¶¶[24:45–51] The second part of the discourse (see note on Mt 24:1–25:46) begins with this parable of **the faithful** or unfaithful **servant**; cf. Lk 12:41–46. It is addressed to the leaders of Matthew's church; **the servant has** been put in charge of his master's **household** (Mt 24:45) even though that household is composed of those who are his **fellow servants** (Mt 24:49).

***[24:45] **To distribute . . . proper time**: readiness for the master's return means a vigilance that is accompanied by faithful performance of the duty assigned.

†††[24:48] **My master . . . delayed**: the note of delay is found also in the other parables of this section; cf. Mt 25:5, 19.

‡‡‡[24:51] **Punish him severely**: the Greek verb, found in the New Testament only here and in the Lucan parallel (Lk 12:46), means, literally, "cut in two." **With the hypocrites**: see note on Mt 6:2. Matthew classes the unfaithful Christian leader with the unbelieving leaders of Judaism. **Wailing and grinding of teeth**: see note on Mt 8:11–12.

§§§[25:1–14] Peculiar to Matthew.

¶¶¶[25:1] **Then**: at the time of the parousia. **Kingdom . . . will be like**: see note on Mt 13:24–30.

---

z. [24:30] Dn 7:13; Dn 12:12–14; Rev 1:7.   a. [24:31] Is 27:13; 1 Cor 15:52; 1 Thes 4:16.   b. [24:35] Is 40:8.   c. [24:36] Acts 1:7.   d. [24:37–39] Gn 6:5–7:23; Lk 17:26–27; 2 Pt 3:6.

e. [24:40–41] Lk 17:34–35.   f. [24:42–44] 25:13; Lk 12:39–40.   g. [24:43] 1 Thes 5:2.   h. [24:45–51] Lk 12:41–46.   i. [24:51] 13:42; 25:30.

who took their lamps and went out to meet the bridegroom. [2]*Five of them were foolish and five were wise. [3]The foolish ones, when taking their lamps, brought no oil with them, [4]but the wise brought flasks of oil with their lamps. [5]Since the bridegroom was long delayed, they all became drowsy and fell asleep. [6]At midnight, there was a cry, 'Behold, the bridegroom! Come out to meet him!' [7]Then all those virgins got up and trimmed their lamps. [8]The foolish ones said to the wise, 'Give us some of your oil, for our lamps are going out.' [9]But the wise ones replied, 'No, for there may not be enough for us and you. Go instead to the merchants and buy some for yourselves.' [10]While they went off to buy it, the bridegroom came and those who were ready went into the wedding feast with him. Then the door was locked. [11]j/Afterwards the other virgins came and said, 'Lord, Lord, open the door for us!' [12]But he said in reply, 'Amen, I say to you, I do not know you.' [13]kTherefore, stay awake,‡ for you know neither the day nor the hour.

**The Parable of the Talents.**§ [14]l"It will be as when a man who was going on a journey⁋ called in his servants and entrusted his possessions to them. [15]To one he gave five talents;** to another, two; to a third, one—to each according to his ability. Then he went away. Immediately [16]the one who received five talents went and traded with them, and made another five. [17]Likewise, the one who received two talents made another two. [18]But the man who received one went off and dug a hole in the ground and buried his master's money. [19]After a long time the master of those servants came back and settled accounts with them. [20]The one who had received five talents came forward bringing the additional five.‡‡ He said, 'Master, you gave me five talents. See, I have made five more.' [21]mHis master said to him, 'Well done,

my good and faithful servant. Since you were faithful in small matters, I will give you great responsibilities. Come, share your master's joy.' [22][Then] the one who had received two talents also came forward and said, 'Master, you gave me two talents. See, I have made two more.' [23]His master said to him, 'Well done, my good and faithful servant. Since you were faithful in small matters, I will give you great responsibilities. Come, share your master's joy.' [24]Then the one who had received the one talent came forward and said, 'Master, I knew you were a demanding person, harvesting where you did not plant and gathering where you did not scatter; [25]so out of fear I went off and buried your talent in the ground. Here it is back.' [26]His master said to him in reply, 'You wicked, lazy servant!§§ So you knew that I harvest where I did not plant and gather where I did not scatter? [27]Should you not then have put my money in the bank so that I could have got it back with interest on my return? [28]Now then! Take the talent from him and give it to the one with ten. [29]⁋⁋nFor to everyone who has, more will be given and he will grow rich; but from the one who has not, even what he has will be taken away. [30]***And throw this useless servant into the darkness outside, where there will be wailing and grinding of teeth.'

**The Judgment of the Nations.**††† [31]o"When the Son of Man comes in his glory, and all the angels with him, he will sit upon his glorious throne, [32]pand all the nations‡‡‡ will be assembled

---

§§[25:26–28] **Wicked, lazy servant:** this man's inactivity is not negligible but seriously culpable. As punishment, he loses the gift he had received, that is now given to the first servant, whose possessions are already great.

⁋⁋[25:29] See note on Mt 13:12 where there is a similar application of this maxim.

***[25:30] See note on Mt 8:11–12.

†††[25:31–46] The conclusion of the discourse, which is peculiar to Matthew, portrays the final judgment that will accompany the parousia. Although often called a "parable," it is not really such, for the only parabolic elements are the depiction of **the Son of Man** as a **shepherd** and of **the righteous** and the wicked as **sheep** and **goats,** respectively (Mt 25:32–33). The criterion of judgment will be the deeds of mercy that have been done for the **least** of Jesus' **brothers** (Mt 25:40). A difficult and important question is the identification of these **least brothers.** Are they all people who have suffered hunger, thirst, etc. (Mt 25:35, 36) or a particular group of such sufferers? Scholars are divided in their response and arguments can be made for either side. But leaving aside the problem of what the traditional material that Matthew edited may have meant, it seems that a stronger case can be made for the view that in the evangelist's sense the sufferers are Christians, probably Christian missionaries whose sufferings were brought upon them by their preaching of the gospel. The criterion of judgment for **all the nations** is their treatment of those who have borne to the world the message of Jesus, and this means ultimately their acceptance or rejection of Jesus himself; cf. Mt 10:40, "Whoever receives you, receives me." See note on Mt 16:27.

‡‡‡[25:32] **All the nations:** before the end the gospel will have been preached throughout the world (Mt 24:14); thus the Gentiles will be judged on their response to it. But the phrase **all the nations** includes the Jews also, for at the judgment "the Son of Man . . . will repay everyone according to his conduct" (Mt 16:27).

---

*[25:2–4] **Foolish . . . wise:** cf. the contrasted "wise man" and "fool" of Mt 7:24, 26, where the two are distinguished by good deeds and lack of them, and such deeds may be signified by the **oil** of this parable.

†[25:11–12] **Lord, Lord:** cf. Mt 7:21. **I do not know you:** cf. Mt 7:23 where the Greek verb is different but synonymous.

‡[25:13] **Stay awake:** some scholars see this command as an addition to the original parable of Matthew's traditional material, since in Mt 25:5 all the virgins, wise and foolish, fall asleep. But the wise virgins are adequately equipped for their task, and stay awake may mean no more than to be prepared; cf. Mt 24:42, 44.

§[25:14–30] Cf. Lk 19:12–27.

⁋[25:14] **It will be as when . . . journey:** literally, "For just as a man who was going on a journey." Although the comparison is not completed, the sense is clear; the kingdom of heaven is like the situation here described. Faithful use of one's gifts will lead to participation in the fullness of the kingdom, lazy inactivity to exclusion from it.

**[25:15] **Talents:** see note on Mt 18:24.

††[25:18] **Buried his master's money:** see note on Mt 13:44.

‡‡[25:20–23] Although the first two servants have received and doubled large sums, their faithful trading is regarded by the master as fidelity **in small matters** only, compared with the **great responsibilities** now to be given to them. The latter are unspecified. **Share your master's joy:** probably the joy of the banquet of the kingdom; cf. Mt 8:11.

---

j. [25:11–12] 7:21, 23; Lk 13:25–27.    k. [25:13] 24:42; Mk 13:33.
l. [25:14–30] Lk 19:12–27.    m. [25:21] Lk 16:10.

n. [25:29] 13:12; Mk 4:25; Lk 8:18; 19:26.    o. [25:31] 16:27; Dt 33:2 LXX.    p. [25:32] Ez 34:17.

before him. And he will separate them one from another, as a shepherd separates the sheep from the goats. ³³He will place the sheep on his right and the goats on his left. ³⁴Then the king will say to those on his right, 'Come, you who are blessed by my Father. Inherit the kingdom prepared for you from the foundation of the world. ³⁵qFor I was hungry and you gave me food, I was thirsty and you gave me drink, a stranger and you welcomed me, ³⁶naked and you clothed me, ill and you cared for me, in prison and you visited me.' ³⁷Then the righteous* will answer him and say, 'Lord, when did we see you hungry and feed you, or thirsty and give you drink? ³⁸When did we see you a stranger and welcome you, or naked and clothe you? ³⁹When did we see you ill or in prison, and visit you?' ⁴⁰rAnd the king will say to them in reply, 'Amen, I say to you, whatever you did for one of these least brothers of mine, you did for me.' ⁴¹†sThen he will say to those on his left, 'Depart from me, you accursed, into the eternal fire prepared for the devil and his angels. ⁴²tFor I was hungry and you gave me no food, I was thirsty and you gave me no drink, ⁴³a stranger and you gave me no welcome, naked and you gave me no clothing, ill and in prison, and you did not care for me.' ⁴⁴‡Then they will answer and say, 'Lord, when did we see you hungry or thirsty or a stranger or naked or ill or in prison, and not minister to your needs?' ⁴⁵He will answer them, 'Amen, I say to you, what you did not do for one of these least ones, you did not do for me.' ⁴⁶uAnd these will go off to eternal punishment, but the righteous to eternal life."

## VII. THE PASSION AND RESURRECTION

### CHAPTER 26

**The Conspiracy Against Jesus.** ¹vWhen Jesus finished all these words,¶ he said to his disciples,

²v"You know that in two days' time it will be Passover, and the Son of Man will be handed over to be crucified." ³wThen the chief priests and the elders of the people assembled in the palace of the high priest, who was called Caiaphas,** ⁴wand they consulted together to arrest Jesus by treachery and put him to death. ⁵But they said, "Not during the festival,†† that there may not be a riot among the people."

**The Anointing at Bethany.**‡‡ ⁶xNow when Jesus was in Bethany in the house of Simon the leper, ⁷a woman came up to him with an alabaster jar of costly perfumed oil, and poured it on his head while he was reclining at table. ⁸When the disciples saw this, they were indignant and said, "Why this waste? ⁹It could have been sold for much, and the money given to the poor." ¹⁰Since Jesus knew this, he said to them, "Why do you make trouble for the woman? She has done a good thing for me. ¹¹yThe poor you will always have with you; but you will not always have me. ¹²§§In pouring this perfumed oil upon my body, she did it to prepare me for burial. ¹³Amen, I say to you, wherever this gospel is proclaimed in the whole world, what she has done will be spoken of, in memory of her."

**The Betrayal by Judas.** ¹⁴zThen one of the Twelve, who was called Judas Iscariot,¶¶ went to the chief priests ¹⁵***aand said, "What are you willing to give me if I hand him over to you?" They paid him thirty pieces of silver, ¹⁶and from that time on he looked for an opportunity to hand him over.

**Preparations for the Passover.** ¹⁷bOn the first day of the Feast of Unleavened Bread,††† the disciples approached Jesus and said, "Where do you

*[25:37–40] **The righteous** will be astonished that in caring for the needs of the sufferers they were ministering to the **Lord** himself. **One of these least brothers of mine:** cf. Mt 10:42.

†[25:41] **Fire prepared . . . his angels:** cf. 1 Enoch 10:13 where it is said of the evil angels and Semyaza, their leader, "In those days they will lead them into the bottom of the fire—and in torment—in the prison (where) they will be locked up forever."

‡[25:44–45] **The accursed** (Mt 25:41) will be likewise astonished that their neglect of the sufferers was neglect of the **Lord** and will receive from him a similar answer.

§[26:1–28:20] The five books with alternating narrative and discourse (Mt 3:1–25:46) that give this gospel its distinctive structure lead up to the climactic events that are the center of Christian belief and the origin of the Christian church, the passion and resurrection of Jesus. In his passion narrative (Mt 26 and 27) Matthew follows his Marcan source closely but with omissions (e.g., Mk 14:51–52) and additions (e.g., Mt 27:3–10, 19). Some of the additions indicate that he utilized traditions that he had received from elsewhere; others are due to his own theological insight (e.g., Mt 26:28, ". . . for the forgiveness of sins"; Mt 27:52). In his editing Matthew also altered Mark in some minor details. But there is no need to suppose that he knew any passion narrative other than Mark's.

¶[26:1–2] **When Jesus finished all these words:** see note on Mt 7:28–29. **"You know . . . crucified":** Matthew turns

q. [25:35–36] Is 58:7; Ez 18:7.  r. [25:40] 10:40, 42.  s. [25:41] 7:23; Lk 13:27.  t. [25:42–43] Jb 22:7; Jas 2:15–16.  u. [25:46] Dn 12:2.

Mark's statement of the time (Mk 14:1) into Jesus' final prediction of his passion. **Passover:** see note on Mk 14:1.

**[26:3] **Caiaphas** was high priest from A.D. 18 to 36.

††[26:5] **Not during the festival:** the plan to delay Jesus' arrest and execution until after **the festival** was not carried out, for according to the synoptics he was arrested on the night of Nisan 14 and put to death the following day. No reason is given why the plan was changed.

‡‡[26:6–13] See notes on Mk 14:3–9 and Jn 12:1–8.

§§[26:12] **To prepare me for burial:** cf. Mk 14:8. In accordance with the interpretation of this act as Jesus' **burial** anointing, Matthew, more consistent than Mark, changes the purpose of the visit of the women to Jesus' tomb; they do not go to anoint him (Mk 16:1) but "to see the tomb" (Mt 28:1).

¶¶[26:14] **Iscariot:** see note on Lk 6:16.

***[26:15] The motive of avarice is introduced by Judas's question about the price for betrayal, which is absent in the Marcan source (Mk 14:10–11). **Hand him over:** the same Greek verb is used to express the saving purpose of God by which Jesus is handed over to death (cf. Mt 17:22; 20:18; 26:2) and the human malice that hands him over. **Thirty pieces of silver:** the price of the betrayal is found only in Matthew. It is derived from Zec 11:12 where it is the wages paid to the rejected shepherd, a cheap price (Zec 11:13). That amount is also the compensation paid to one whose slave has been gored by an ox (Ex 21:32).

†††[26:17] **The first day of the Feast of Unleavened Bread:** see note on Mk 14:1. Matthew omits Mark's "when they sacrificed the Passover lamb."

v. [26:2–5] Mk 14:1–2; Lk 22:1–2.  w. [26:4] Jn 11:47–53.  x. [26:6–13] Mk 14:3–9; Jn 12:1–8.  y. [26:11] Dt 15:11.  z. [26:14–16] Mk 14:10–11; Lk 22:3–6.  a. [26:15] Zec 11:12.  b. [26:17–25] Mk 14:12–21; Lk 22:7–23.

want us to prepare for you to eat the Passover?"[c] [18*]He said, "Go into the city to a certain man and tell him, 'The teacher says, "My appointed time draws near; in your house I shall celebrate the Passover with my disciples."'" [19]The disciples then did as Jesus had ordered, and prepared the Passover.

**The Betrayer.** [20]When it was evening, he reclined at table with the Twelve. [21]And while they were eating, he said, "Amen, I say to you, one of you will betray me."[†] [22]Deeply distressed at this, they began to say to him one after another, "Surely it is not I, Lord?" [23]He said in reply, "He who has dipped his hand into the dish with me is the one who will betray me. [24‡d]The Son of Man indeed goes, as it is written of him, but woe to that man by whom the Son of Man is betrayed. It would be better for that man if he had never been born." [25§]Then Judas, his betrayer, said in reply, "Surely it is not I, Rabbi?" He answered, "You have said so."

**The Lord's Supper.** [26¶e]While they were eating, Jesus took bread, said the blessing, broke it, and giving it to his disciples said, "Take and eat; this is my body."[**f] [27]Then he took a cup, gave thanks,[††]

and gave it to them, saying, "Drink from it, all of you, [28g]for this is my blood of the covenant, which will be shed on behalf of many for the forgiveness of sins. [29‡‡]I tell you, from now on I shall not drink this fruit of the vine until the day when I drink it with you new in the kingdom of my Father." [30§§]Then, after singing a hymn, they went out to the Mount of Olives.

**Peter's Denial Foretold.** [31h]Then Jesus said to them, "This night all of you will have your faith in me shaken,[¶¶] for it is written:[i]

'I will strike the shepherd,
     and the sheep of the flock will be
          dispersed';

[32]but after I have been raised up, I shall go before you to Galilee." [33]Peter said to him in reply, "Though all may have their faith in you shaken, mine will never be." [34***j]Jesus said to him, "Amen, I say to you, this very night before the cock crows, you will deny me three times."[k] [35]Peter said to him, "Even though I should have to die with you, I will not deny you." And all the disciples spoke likewise.

**The Agony in the Garden.** [36†††l]Then Jesus came with them to a place called Gethsemane,[‡‡‡] and he said to his disciples, "Sit here while I go over there and pray."[m] [37n]He took along Peter and the

---

*[26:18] By omitting much of Mk 14:13–15, adding **My appointed time draws near**, and turning the question into a statement, **in your house I shall celebrate the Passover**, Matthew has given this passage a solemnity and majesty greater than that of his source.

†[26:21] Given Matthew's interest in the fulfillment of the Old Testament, it is curious that he omits the Marcan designation of Jesus' betrayer as "one who is eating with me" (Mk 14:18), since that is probably an allusion to Ps 41:10. However, the shocking fact that the betrayer is one who shares table fellowship with Jesus is emphasized in Mt 26:23.

‡[26:24] **It would be better . . . born**: the enormity of the deed is such that it would be better not to exist than to do it.

§[26:25] Peculiar to Matthew. **You have said so**: cf. Mt 26:64; 27:11. This is a half-affirmative. Emphasis is laid on the pronoun and the answer implies that the statement would not have been made if the question had not been asked.

¶[26:26–29] See note on Mk 14:22–24. The Marcan-Matthean is one of the two major New Testament traditions of the words of Jesus when instituting the Eucharist. The other (and earlier) is the Pauline-Lucan (1 Cor 11:23–25; Lk 22:19–20). Each shows the influence of Christian liturgical usage, but the Marcan-Matthean is more developed in that regard than the Pauline-Lucan. The words over the bread and cup succeed each other without the intervening meal mentioned in 1 Cor 11:25; Lk 22:20; and there is parallelism between the consecratory words (**this is my body . . . this is my blood**). Matthew follows Mark closely but with some changes.

**[26:26] See note on Mt 14:19. **Said the blessing**: a prayer blessing God. **Take and eat**: literally, **Take, eat**. **Eat** is an addition to Mark's "take it" (literally, "take"; Mk 14:22). **This is my body**: the bread is identified with Jesus himself.

††[26:27–28] **Gave thanks**: see note on Mt 15:36. **Give it to them . . . all of you**: cf. Mk 14:23–24. In the Marcan sequence the disciples drink and then Jesus says the interpretative words. Matthew has changed this into a command to **drink** followed by those words. **My blood**: see Lv 17:11 for the concept that the **blood** is "the seat of life" and that when placed on the altar it "makes atonement." **Which will be shed**: the present participle, "being shed" or "going to be shed," is future in relation to the Last Supper. **On behalf of**: Greek *peri*; see note on Mk 14:24. **Many**: see note on Mt 20:28. **For the forgiveness of sins**: a Matthean addition. The same phrase occurs in Mk 1:4 in connection with John's baptism but Matthew avoids it there (Mt 3:11). He places it here probably because he wishes

to emphasize that it is the sacrificial death of Jesus that brings **forgiveness of sins**.

‡‡[26:29] Although his death will interrupt the table fellowship he has had with the disciples, Jesus confidently predicts his vindication by God and a new table fellowship with them at the banquet of the kingdom.

§§[26:30] See note on Mt 14:26.

¶¶[26:31] **Will have . . . shaken**: literally, "will be scandalized in me"; see note on Mt 24:9–12. **I will strike . . . dispersed**: cf. Zec 13:7.

***[26:34] **Before the cock crows**: see note on Mt 14:25. The third watch of the night was called "cockcrow." **Deny me**: see note on Mt 16:24.

†††[26:36–56] Cf. Mk 14:32–52. The account of Jesus in Gethsemane is divided between that of his agony (Mt 26:36–46) and that of his betrayal and arrest (Mt 26:47–56). Jesus' **sorrow and distress** (Mt 26:37) in face of death is unrelieved by the presence of his three disciples who, though urged to **watch** with him (Mt 26:38, 41), fall asleep (Mt 26:40, 43). He prays that **if . . . possible** his death may be avoided (Mt 26:39) but that his Father's will be done (Mt 26:39, 42, 44). Knowing then that his death must take place, he announces to his companions that **the hour** for his being **handed over** has come (Mt 26:45). Judas arrives with an armed band provided by the Sanhedrin and greets Jesus with a kiss, the prearranged sign for his identification (Mt 26:47–49). After his arrest, he rebukes a disciple who has attacked the **high priest's servant** with a **sword** (Mt 26:51–54), and chides those who have come out to seize him with **swords and clubs** as if he were a **robber** (Mt 26:55–56). In both rebukes Jesus declares that the treatment he is now receiving is the fulfillment of the scriptures (Mt 26:55, 56). The subsequent flight of **all the disciples** is itself the fulfillment of his own prediction (cf. 31). In this episode, Matthew follows Mark with a few alterations.

‡‡‡[26:36] **Gethsemane**: the Hebrew name means "oil press" and designates an olive orchard on the western slope of the Mount of Olives; see note on Mt 21:1. The name appears only in Matthew and Mark. The place is called a "garden" in Jn 18:1.

---

g. [26:28] Ex 24:8; Is 53:12.  h. [26:31–35] Mk 14:7–31.  i. [26:31] Zec 13:7; Jn 16:32.  j. [26:34–35] Lk 22:33–34; Jn 13:37–38.  k. [26:34] Mk 26:69–75.  l. [26:36–46] Mk 14:32–42; Lk 22:39–46.  m. [26:36] Jn 18:1.  n. [26:37–39] Heb 5:7.

---

c. [26:17] Ex 12:14–20.  d. [26:24] Is 53:8–10.  e. [26:26–30] Mk 14:22–26; Lk 22:14–23; 1 Cor 11:23–25.  f. [26:26–27] 1 Cor 10:16.

two sons of Zebedee,* and began to feel sorrow and distress. 38ªThen he said to them, "My soul is sorrowful even to death.† Remain here and keep watch with me." 39ªHe advanced a little and fell prostrate in prayer, saying, "My Father,‡ if it is possible, let this cup pass from me; yet, not as I will, but as you will." 40When he returned to his disciples he found them asleep. He said to Peter, "So you could not keep watch with me for one hour? 41Watch and pray that you may not undergo the test.§ The spirit is willing, but the flesh is weak." 42ªᵈWithdrawing a second time, he prayed again, "My Father, if it is not possible that this cup pass without my drinking it, your will be done!" 43Then he returned once more and found them asleep, for they could not keep their eyes open. 44He left them and withdrew again and prayed a third time, saying the same thing again. 45ʳThen he returned to his disciples and said to them, "Are you still sleeping and taking your rest? Behold, the hour is at hand when the Son of Man is to be handed over to sinners. 46Get up, let us go. Look, my betrayer is at hand."

**The Betrayal and Arrest of Jesus.** 47ˢWhile he was still speaking, Judas, one of the Twelve, arrived, accompanied by a large crowd, with swords and clubs, who had come from the chief priests and the elders of the people. 48His betrayer had arranged a sign with them, saying, "The man I shall kiss is the one; arrest him." 49Immediately he went over to Jesus and said, "Hail, Rabbi!"** and he kissed him. 50Jesus answered him, "Friend, do what you have come for." Then stepping forward they laid hands on Jesus and arrested him. 51And behold, one of those who accompanied Jesus put his hand to his sword, drew it, and struck the high priest's servant, cutting off his ear. 52Then Jesus said to him, "Put your sword back into its sheath, for

all who take the sword will perish by the sword. 53Do you think that I cannot call upon my Father and he will not provide me at this moment with more than twelve legions of angels? 54But then how would the scriptures be fulfilled which say that it must come to pass in this way?" 55††At that hour Jesus said to the crowds, "Have you come out as against a robber, with swords and clubs to seize me? Day after day I sat teaching in the temple area, yet you did not arrest me. 56ªBut all this has come to pass that the writings of the prophets may be fulfilled." Then all the disciples left him and fled.

**Jesus Before the Sanhedrin.** ‡‡ 57ᵘThose who had arrested Jesus led him away to Caiaphas§§ the high priest, where the scribes and the elders were assembled. 58Peter was following him at a distance as far as the high priest's courtyard, and going inside he sat down with the servants to see the outcome. 59The chief priests and the entire Sanhedrin¶¶ kept trying to obtain false testimony against Jesus in order to put him to death, 60ᵛbut they found none, though many false witnesses came forward. Finally two*** came forward 61who stated, "This man said, 'I can destroy the temple

---

††[26:55] **Day after day . . . arrest me:** cf. Mk 14:49. This suggests that Jesus had taught for a relatively long period in Jerusalem, whereas Mt 21:1–11 puts his coming to the city for the first time only a few days before.

‡‡[26:57–68] Following Mk 14:53–65 Matthew presents the nighttime appearance of Jesus before the **Sanhedrin** as a real trial. After **many false witnesses** bring charges against him that do not suffice for the death sentence (Mt 26:60), **two came forward** who charge him with claiming to be able to **destroy the temple . . . and within three days** to **rebuild it** (Mt 26:60–61). Jesus makes no answer even when challenged to do so by **the high priest,** who then orders him to declare **under oath . . . whether** he is the **Messiah, the Son of God** (Mt 26:62–63). Matthew changes Mark's clear affirmative response (Mk 14:62) to the same one as that given to Judas (Mt 26:25), but follows Mark almost verbatim in Jesus' predicting that his judges will see him **(the Son of Man) seated at the right hand** of God **and coming on the clouds of heaven** (Mt 26:64). **The high priest** then charges him with blasphemy (Mt 26:65), a charge with which the other members of **the Sanhedrin** agree by declaring that **he deserves to die** (Mt 26:66). They then attack him (Mt 26:67) and mockingly demand that he **prophesy** (Mt 26:68). This account contains elements that are contrary to the judicial procedures prescribed in the Mishnah, the Jewish code of law that dates in written form from ca. A.D. 200, e.g., trial on a feast day, a night session of the court, pronouncement of a verdict of condemnation at the same session at which testimony was received. Consequently, some scholars regard the account entirely as a creation of the early Christians without historical value. However, it is disputable whether the norms found in the Mishnah were in force at the time of Jesus. More to the point is the question whether the Matthean-Marcan night trial derives from a combination of two separate incidents, a nighttime preliminary investigation (cf. Jn 18:13, 19–24) and a formal trial on the following morning (cf. Lk 22:66–71).

§§[26:57] **Caiaphas:** see note on Mt 26:3.

¶¶[26:59] **Sanhedrin:** see note on Lk 22:66.

***[26:60] **Two:** cf. Dt 19:15. **I can destroy . . . rebuild it:** there are significant differences from the Marcan parallel (Mk 14:58). Matthew omits "made with hands" and "not made with hands" and changes Mark's "will destroy" and "will build another" to **can destroy** and (can) **rebuild.** The charge is probably based on Jesus' prediction of the temple's destruction; see notes on Mt 23:37–39; 24:2; and Jn 2:19. A similar

---

*[26:37] **Peter and the two sons of Zebedee:** cf. Mt 17:1.

†[26:38] Cf. Ps 42:6, 12. In the Septuagint (Ps 41:5, 12) the same Greek word for **sorrowful** is used as here. **To death:** i.e., "enough to die"; cf. Jon 4:9.

‡[26:39] **My Father:** see note on Mk 14:36. Matthew omits the Aramaic *'abbā'* and adds the qualifier **my. This cup:** see note on Mk 10:38–40.

§[26:41] **Undergo the test:** see note on Mt 6:13. In that verse "the final test" translates the same Greek word as is here translated **the test,** and these are the only instances of the use of that word in Matthew. It is possible that the passion of Jesus is seen here as an anticipation of the great tribulation that will precede the parousia (see notes on Mt 24:8; 24:21) to which Mt 6:13 refers, and that just as Jesus prays to be delivered from death (Mt 26:39), so he exhorts the disciples to pray that they will not have to **undergo** the great **test** that his passion would be for them. Some scholars, however, understand **not undergo** (literally, "not enter") **the test** as meaning not that the disciples may be spared **the test** but that they may not yield to the temptation of falling away from Jesus because of his passion even though they will have to endure it.

¶[26:42] **Your will be done:** cf. Mt 6:10.

**[26:49] **Rabbi:** see note on Mt 23:6–7. Jesus is so addressed twice in Matthew (Mt 26:25), both times by Judas. For the significance of the closely related address "teacher" in Matthew, see note on Mt 8:19.

---

o. [26:38] Ps 42:6, 12; Jon 4:9.    p. [26:39] Jn 4:34; 6:38; Phil 2:8.
q. [26:42] 6:10; Heb 10:9.    r. [26:45] Jn 12:23; 13:1; 17:1.    s. [26:47–56] Mk 14:43–50; Lk 22:47–53; Jn 18:3–11.

t. [26:56] 26:31.    u. [26:57–68] Mk 14:53–65; Lk 22:54–55, 63–71; Jn 18:12–14, 19–24.    v. [26:60–61] Dt 19:15; Jn 2:19; Acts 6:14.

of God and within three days rebuild it.'" ⁶²The high priest rose and addressed him, "Have you no answer? What are these men testifying against you?" ⁶³ʷBut Jesus was silent.* Then the high priest said to him, "I order you to tell us under oath before the living God whether you are the Messiah, the Son of God." ⁶⁴ˣJesus said to him in reply, "You have said so.† But I tell you:

From now on you will see 'the Son of Man seated at the right hand of the Power' and 'coming on the clouds of heaven.'"

⁶⁵Then the high priest tore his robes and said, "He has blasphemed!‡ What further need have we of witnesses? You have now heard the blasphemy; ⁶⁶what is your opinion?" They said in reply, "He deserves to die!" ⁶⁷ʸThen they spat in his face and struck him, while some slapped him, ⁶⁸saying, "Prophesy for us, Messiah: who is it that struck you?"

**Peter's Denial of Jesus.** ⁶⁹ᶻNow Peter was sitting outside in the courtyard. One of the maids came over to him and said, "You too were with Jesus the Galilean." ⁷⁰But he denied it in front of everyone, saying, "I do not know what you are talking about!" ⁷¹As he went out to the gate, another girl saw him and said to those who were there, "This man was with Jesus the Nazorean." ⁷²Again he denied it with an oath, "I do not know the man!" ⁷³**A little later the bystanders came over and said to Peter, "Surely you too are one of them; even your speech gives you away." ⁷⁴At that he began to curse and to swear, "I do not know the man." And immediately a cock crowed. ⁷⁵ᵃThen Peter remembered the word

that Jesus had spoken: "Before the cock crows you will deny me three times." He went out and began to weep bitterly.

# CHAPTER 27

**Jesus Before Pilate.** ¹††When it was morning,ᵇ all the chief priests and the elders of the people took counsel‡‡ against Jesus to put him to death. ²They bound him, led him away, and handed him over to Pilate, the governor.

**The Death of Judas.** ³ᶜThen Judas, his betrayer, seeing that Jesus had been condemned, deeply regretted what he had done. He returned the thirty pieces of silver§§ to the chief priests and elders,ᵈ ⁴saying, "I have sinned in betraying innocent blood." They said, "What is that to us? Look to it yourself." ⁵¶¶Flinging the money into the temple, he departed and went off and hanged himself. ⁶The chief priests gathered up the money, but said, "It is not lawful to deposit this in the temple treasury, for it is the price of blood." ⁷After consultation, they used it to buy the potter's field as a burial place for foreigners. ⁸That is why that field even today is called the Field of Blood. ⁹Then was fulfilled what had been said through Jeremiah the prophet,*** "And they took the thirty pieces of silver, the value

---

prediction by Jeremiah was considered as deserving death; cf. Jer 7:1–15; 26:1–8.

*[26:63] **Silent:** possibly an allusion to Is 53:7. **I order you . . . living God:** peculiar to Matthew; cf. Mk 14:61.

†[26:64] **You have said so:** see note on Mt 26:25. **From now on . . . heaven:** the Son of Man who is to be crucified (cf. Mt 20:19) will be seen in glorious majesty (cf. Ps 110:1) and **coming on the clouds of heaven** (cf. Dn 7:13). **The Power:** see note on Mk 14:61–62.

‡[26:65] **Blasphemed:** the punishment for **blasphemy** was death by stoning (see Lv 24:10–16). According to the Mishnah, to be guilty of blasphemy one had to pronounce "the Name itself," i.e., Yahweh; cf. *Sanhedrin* 7:4, 5. Those who judge the legal accounts of Jesus' trial by the later Mishnah standards point out that Jesus uses the surrogate "the Power," and hence no Jewish court would have regarded him as guilty of blasphemy; others hold that the Mishnah's narrow understanding of blasphemy was a later development.

§[26:67–68] The physical abuse, apparently done to Jesus by the members of the Sanhedrin themselves, recalls the sufferings of the Isaian Servant of the Lord; cf. Is 50:6. The mocking challenge to **prophesy** is probably motivated by Jesus' prediction of his future glory (Mt 26:64).

¶[26:70] **Denied it in front of everyone:** see Mt 10:33. Peter's repentance (Mt 26:75) saves him from the fearful destiny of which Jesus speaks there.

**[26:73] **Your speech . . . away:** Matthew explicates Mark's "you too are a Galilean" (Mk 14:70).

††[27:1–31] Cf. Mk 15:1–20. Matthew's account of the Roman trial before **Pilate** is introduced by a consultation of the Sanhedrin after which Jesus is **handed over to . . . the governor** (Mt 27:1–2). Matthew follows his Marcan source closely but adds some material that is peculiar to him, the death of **Judas** (Mt 27:3–10), possibly the name **Jesus** as the name of **Barabbas** also (Mt 27:16–17), the intervention of Pilate's **wife** (Mt 27:19), Pilate's washing **his hands** in token of his disclaiming responsibility for Jesus' death (Mt 27:24), and the assuming of that responsibility by **the whole people** (Mt 27:25).

‡‡[27:1] There is scholarly disagreement about the meaning of the Sanhedrin's taking **counsel** (*symboulion elabon*; cf. Mt 12:14; 22:15; 27:7; 28:12); see note on Mk 15:1. Some understand it as a discussion about the strategy for putting their death sentence against **Jesus** into effect since they lacked the right to do so themselves. Others see it as the occasion for their passing that sentence, holding that Matthew, unlike Mark (Mk 14:64), does not consider that it had been passed in the night session (Mt 26:66). Even in the latter interpretation, their handing **him over to Pilate** is best explained on the hypothesis that they did not have competence to put their sentence into effect, as is stated in Jn 18:31.

§§[27:3] **The thirty pieces of silver:** see Mt 26:15.

¶¶[27:5–8] For another tradition about the death of Judas, cf. Acts 1:18–19. The two traditions agree only in the purchase of a field with **the money** paid to Judas for his betrayal of Jesus and the name given to the field, **the Field of Blood.** In Acts Judas himself buys the field and its name comes from his own blood shed in his fatal accident on it. **The potter's field:** this designation of the field is based on the fulfillment citation in Mt 27:10.

***[27:9–10] Cf. Mt 26:15. Matthew's attributing this text to Jeremiah is puzzling, for there is no such text in that book, and **the thirty pieces of silver** thrown by Judas "into the temple" (Mt 27:5) recall rather Zec 11:12–13. It is usually said that the attribution of the text to Jeremiah is due to Matthew's combining the Zechariah text with texts from Jeremiah that speak of a **potter** (Jer 18:2–3), the buying of a **field** (Jer 32:6–9), or the breaking of a potter's flask at Topheth in the valley of Ben-Hinnom with the prediction that it will become a burial place (Jer 19:1–13).

---

w. [26:63] Is 53:7.   x. [26:64] Ps 110:1; Dn 7:13.   y. [26:67] Wis 2:19; Is 50:6.   z. [26:69–75] Mk 14:66–72; Lk 22:56–62; Jn 18:17–18, 25–27.   a. [26:75] 26:34.

b. [27:1–2] Mk 15:1; Lk 23:1; Jn 18:28.   c. [27:3–10] Acts 1:18–19.   d. [27:3] 26:15.

of a man with a price on his head, a price set by some of the Israelites, <sup>10e</sup>and they paid it out for the potter's field just as the Lord had commanded me."

**Jesus Questioned by Pilate.** <sup>11f</sup>Now Jesus stood before the governor, and he questioned him, "Are you the king of the Jews?"* Jesus said, "You say so." <sup>12g</sup>And when he was accused by the chief priests and elders,† he made no answer. <sup>13</sup>Then Pilate said to him, "Do you not hear how many things they are testifying against you?" <sup>14</sup>But he did not answer him one word, so that the governor was greatly amazed.

**The Sentence of Death.** <sup>15‡h</sup>Now on the occasion of the feast the governor was accustomed to release to the crowd one prisoner whom they wished. <sup>16§</sup>And at that time they had a notorious prisoner called [Jesus] Barabbas. <sup>17</sup>So when they had assembled, Pilate said to them, "Which one do you want me to release to you, [Jesus] Barabbas, or Jesus called Messiah?" <sup>18¶</sup>For he knew that it was out of envy that they had handed him over. <sup>19**</sup>While he was still seated on the bench, his wife sent him a message, "Have nothing to do with that righteous man. I suffered much in a dream today because of him." <sup>20i</sup>The chief priests and the elders persuaded the crowds to ask for Barabbas but to destroy Jesus. <sup>21</sup>The governor said to them in reply, "Which of the two do you want me to release to you?" They answered, "Barabbas!" <sup>22††</sup>Pilate said to them, "Then what shall I do with Jesus called Messiah?" They all said, "Let him be crucified!" <sup>23</sup>But he said, "Why? What evil has he done?" They only shouted the louder, "Let him be crucified!" <sup>24‡‡j</sup>When Pilate saw that he was not succeeding at all, but that a riot was breaking out instead, he took water and washed his hands in the sight of the crowd, saying, "I am innocent of this man's blood. Look to it yourselves." <sup>25</sup>And the whole people said in reply, "His blood be upon us and upon our children." <sup>26</sup>Then he released Barabbas to them, but after he had Jesus scourged,<sup>§§</sup> he handed him over to be crucified.

**Mockery by the Soldiers.** <sup>27k</sup>Then the soldiers of the governor took Jesus inside the praetorium¶¶ and gathered the whole cohort around him. <sup>28</sup>They stripped off his clothes and threw a scarlet military cloak*** about him. <sup>29l</sup>Weaving a crown out of thorns,††† they placed it on his head, and a reed in his right hand. And kneeling before him, they mocked him, saying, "Hail, King of the Jews!" <sup>30m</sup>They spat upon him‡‡‡ and took the reed and kept striking him on the head. <sup>31</sup>And when they had mocked him, they stripped him of the cloak, dressed him in his own clothes, and led him off to crucify him.

---

*[27:11] **King of the Jews**: this title is used of Jesus only by pagans. The Matthean instances are, besides this verse, Mt 2:2; 27:29, 37. Matthew equates it with "Messiah"; cf. Mt 2:2, 4 and Mt 27:17, 22 where he has changed "the king of the Jews" of his Marcan source (Mk 15:9, 12) to "(Jesus) called Messiah." The normal political connotation of both titles would be of concern to the Roman **governor. You say so**: see note on Mt 26:25. An unqualified affirmative response is not made because Jesus' kingship is not what Pilate would understand it to be.

†[27:12–14] Cf. Mt 26:62–63. As in the trial before the Sanhedrin, Jesus' silence may be meant to recall Is 53:7. **Greatly amazed**: possibly an allusion to Is 52:14–15.

‡[27:15–26] The choice that Pilate offers **the crowd** between **Barabbas** and **Jesus** is said to be in accordance with a custom of releasing at the Passover feast **one prisoner** chosen by **the crowd** (Mt 27:15). This custom is mentioned also in Mk 15:6 and Jn 18:39 but not in Luke; see note on Lk 23:17. Outside of the gospels there is no direct attestation of it, and scholars are divided in their judgment of the historical reliability of the claim that there was such a practice.

§[27:16–17] **[Jesus] Barabbas**: it is possible that the double name is the original reading; **Jesus** was a common Jewish name; see note on Mt 1:21. This reading is found in only a few textual witnesses, although its absence in the majority can be explained as an omission of **Jesus** made for reverential reasons. That name is bracketed because of its uncertain textual attestation. The Aramaic name **Barabbas** means "son of the father"; the irony of the choice offered between him and Jesus, the true son of the Father, would be evident to those addressees of Matthew who knew that.

¶[27:18] Cf. Mk 14:10. This is an example of the tendency, found in varying degree in all the gospels, to present Pilate in a relatively favorable light and emphasize the hostility of the Jewish authorities and eventually of the people.

**[27:19] Jesus' innocence is declared by a Gentile woman. **In a dream**: in Matthew's infancy narrative, dreams are the means of divine communication; cf. Mt 1:20; 2:12, 13, 19, 22.

††[27:22] **Let him be crucified**: incited by the chief priests and elders (Mt 27:20), the crowds demand that Jesus be executed by crucifixion, a peculiarly horrible form of Roman capital punishment. The Marcan parallel, "Crucify him" (Mk 15:3), addressed to Pilate, is changed by Matthew to the passive, probably to emphasize the responsibility of the crowds.

‡‡[27:24–25] Peculiar to Matthew. **Took water . . . blood**: cf. Dt 21:1–8, the handwashing prescribed in the case of a murder when the killer is unknown. The elders of the city nearest to where the corpse is found must wash their hands, declaring, "Our hands did not shed this blood. **Look to it yourselves**: cf. Mt 27:4. **The whole people**: Matthew sees in those who speak these words **the** entire **people** (Greek *laos*) of Israel. **His blood . . . upon our children**: cf. Jer 26:15. The responsibility for Jesus' death is accepted by the nation that was God's special possession (Ex 19:5), his own **people** (Hos 2:25), and they thereby lose that high privilege; see Mt 21:43 and the note on that verse. The controversy between Matthew's church and Pharisaic Judaism about which was the true people of God is reflected here. As the Second Vatican Council has pointed out, guilt for Jesus' death is not attributable to all the Jews of his time or to any Jews of later times.

§§[27:26] **He had Jesus scourged**: the usual preliminary to crucifixion.

¶¶[27:27] **The praetorium**: the residence of the Roman governor. His usual place of residence was at Caesarea Maritima on the Mediterranean coast, but he went to Jerusalem during the great feasts, when the influx of pilgrims posed the danger of a nationalistic riot. It is disputed whether the **praetorium** in Jerusalem was the old palace of Herod in the west of the city or the fortress of Antonia northwest of the temple area. **The whole cohort**: normally six hundred soldiers.

***[27:28] **Scarlet military cloak**: so Matthew as against the royal purple of Mk 15:17 and Jn 19:2.

†††[27:29] **Crown out of thorns**: probably of long **thorns** that stood upright so that it resembled the "radiant" **crown**, a diadem with spikes worn by Hellenistic kings. The soldiers' purpose was mockery, not torture. **A reed**: peculiar to Matthew; a mock scepter.

‡‡‡[27:30] **Spat upon him**: cf. Mt 26:67 where there also is a possible allusion to Is 50:6.

---

e. [27:10] Zec 11:12–13.   f. [27:11–14] Mk 15:2–5; Lk 23:2–3; Jn 18:29–38.   g. [27:12] Is 53:7.   h. [27:15–26] Mk 15:6–15; Lk 23:17–25; Jn 18:39–19:16.   i. [27:20] Acts 3:14.

j. [27:24] Dt 21:1–8.   k. [27:27–31] Mk 15:16–20; Jn 19:2–3.   l. [27:29] 27:11.   m. [27:30] Is 50:6.

**The Way of the Cross.**[*] ³²ⁿAs they were going out, they met a Cyrenian named Simon; this man they pressed into service to carry his cross. **The Crucifixion.** ³³ᵒAnd when they came to a place called Golgotha (which means Place of the Skull), ³⁴ᵖthey gave Jesus wine to drink mixed with gall.[†] But when he had tasted it, he refused to drink. ³⁵�qAfter they had crucified him, they divided his garments[‡] by casting lots; ³⁶then they sat down and kept watch over him there. ³⁷And they placed over his head the written charge[§] against him: This is Jesus, the King of the Jews. ³⁸Two revolutionaries[‖] were crucified with him, one on his right and the other on his left. ³⁹ᵗʳThose passing by reviled him, shaking their heads ⁴⁰ˢand saying, "You who would destroy the temple and rebuild it in three days, save yourself, if you are the Son of God, [and] come down from the cross!" ⁴¹Likewise the chief priests with the scribes and elders mocked him and said, ⁴²"He saved others; he cannot save himself. So he is the king of Israel![††] Let him come down from the cross now, and we will believe in him. ⁴³ᵗ‡He trusted in God; let him deliver him now if he wants him. For he said, 'I am the Son of God.'" ⁴⁴The revolutionaries who were crucified with him also kept abusing him in the same way. **The Death of Jesus.** ⁴⁵§§ᵘFrom noon onward,[ᵛ] darkness came over the whole land until three

in the afternoon. ⁴⁶ʷAnd about three o'clock Jesus cried out in a loud voice, "*Eli, Eli, lema sabachthani?*"[¶] which means, "My God, my God, why have you forsaken me?" ⁴⁷***Some of the bystanders who heard it said, "This one is calling for Elijah." ⁴⁸ˣImmediately one of them ran to get a sponge; he soaked it in wine, and putting it on a reed, gave it to him to drink. ⁴⁹But the rest said, "Wait, let us see if Elijah comes to save him." ⁵⁰†††But Jesus cried out again in a loud voice, and gave up his spirit. ⁵¹ʸAnd behold, the veil of the sanctuary was torn in two from top to bottom.[‡‡‡] The earth quaked, rocks were split, ⁵²ᶻtombs were opened, and the bodies of many saints who had fallen asleep were raised. ⁵³And coming forth from their tombs after his resurrection, they entered the holy city and appeared to many. ⁵⁴§§§The centurion and the men with him who were keeping watch over Jesus feared greatly when they saw the earthquake and all that was happening, and they said, "Truly, this was the Son of God!" ⁵⁵There were many women

¶[27:46] *Eli, Eli, lema sabachthani?*: Jesus cries out in the words of Ps 22:2a, a psalm of lament that is the Old Testament passage most frequently drawn upon in this narrative. In Mark the verse is cited entirely in Aramaic, which Matthew partially retains but changes the invocation of God to the Hebrew *Eli*, possibly because that is more easily related to the statement of the following verse about Jesus' calling for Elijah.

***[27:47] **Elijah**: see note on Mt 3:4. This prophet, taken up into heaven (2 Kgs 2:11), was believed to come to the help of those in distress, but the evidences of that belief are all later than the gospels.

†††[27:50] **Gave up his spirit**: cf. the Marcan parallel (Mk 15:37), "breathed his last." Matthew's alteration expresses both Jesus' control over his destiny and his obedient giving up of his life to God.

‡‡‡[27:51–53] **Veil of the sanctuary ... bottom**: cf. Mk 15:38; Lk 23:45. Luke puts this event immediately before the death of Jesus. There were two veils in the Mosaic tabernacle on the model of which the temple was constructed, the outer one before the entrance of the Holy Place and the inner one before the Holy of Holies (see Ex 26:31–36). Only the high priest could pass through the latter and that only on the Day of Atonement (see Lv 16:1–18). Probably the torn veil of the gospels is the inner one. The meaning of the scene may be that now, because of Jesus' death, all people have access to the presence of God, or that the temple, its holiest part standing exposed, is now profaned and will soon be destroyed. **The earth quaked ... appeared to many**: peculiar to Matthew. The earthquake, the splitting of the **rocks**, and especially the resurrection of the dead **saints** indicate the coming of the final age. In the Old Testament the coming of God is frequently portrayed with the imagery of an earthquake (see Ps 68:9; 77:19), and Jesus speaks of the earthquakes that will accompany the "labor pains" that signify the beginning of the dissolution of the old world (Mt 24:7–8). For the expectation of the resurrection of the dead at the coming of the new and final age, see Dn 12:1–3. Matthew knows that the end of the old age has not yet come (Mt 28:20), but the new age has broken in with the death (and resurrection; cf. the earthquake in Mt 28:2) of Jesus; see note on Mt 16:28. **After his resurrection**: this qualification seems to be due to Matthew's wish to assert the primacy of Jesus' **resurrection** even though he has placed the resurrection of the dead **saints** immediately after Jesus' death.

§§§[27:54] Cf. Mk 15:39. The Christian confession of faith is made by Gentiles, not only **the centurion**, as in Mark, but the other soldiers **who were keeping watch over Jesus** (cf. Mt 27:36).

*[27:32] See note on Mk 15:21. **Cyrenian named Simon**: Cyrenaica was a Roman province on the north coast of Africa and Cyrene was its capital city. The city had a large population of Greek-speaking Jews. **Simon** may have been living in Palestine or have come there for the Passover as a pilgrim. **Pressed into service**: see note on Mt 5:41.

†[27:34] **Wine ... mixed with gall**: cf. Mk 15:23 where the drink is "wine drugged with myrrh," a narcotic. Matthew's text is probably an inexact allusion to Ps 69:22. That psalm belongs to the class called the individual lament, in which a persecuted just man prays for deliverance in the midst of great suffering and also expresses confidence that his prayer will be heard. That theme of the suffering Just One is frequently applied to the sufferings of Jesus in the passion narratives.

‡[27:35] The clothing of an executed criminal went to his executioner(s), but the description of that procedure in the case of Jesus, found in all the gospels, is plainly inspired by Ps 22:19. However, that psalm verse is quoted only in Jn 19:24.

§[27:37] The offense of a person condemned to death by crucifixion was written on a tablet that was displayed on his cross. The **charge** against Jesus was that he had claimed to be the **King of the Jews** (cf. Mt 27:11), i.e., the Messiah (cf. Mt 27:17, 22).

‖[27:38] **Revolutionaries**: see note on Jn 18:40 where the same Greek word as that found here is used for Barabbas.

**[27:39–40] **Reviled him ... heads**: cf. Ps 22:8. **You who would destroy ... three days**; cf. Mt 26:61. **If you are the Son of God**: the same words as those of the devil in the temptation of Jesus; cf. Mt 4:3, 6.

††[27:42] **King of Israel**: in their mocking of Jesus the members of the Sanhedrin call themselves and their people not "the Jews" but **Israel**.

‡‡[27:43] Peculiar to Matthew. **He trusted in God ... wants him**: cf. Ps 22:9. **He said ... of God**: probably an allusion to Wis 2:12–20 where the theme of the suffering Just One appears.

§§[27:45] Cf. Am 8:9 where on the day of the Lord "the sun will set at midday."

n. [27:32] Mk 15:21; Lk 23:26. o. [27:33–44] Mk 15:22–32; Lk 23:32–38; Jn 19:17–19, 23–24. p. [27:34] Ps 69:21. q. [27:35] Ps 22:19. r. [27:39] Ps 22:8. s. [27:40] 4:3; 26:61. t. [27:43] Ps 22:9; Wis 2:12–20. u. [27:45–46] Mk 15:33–41; Lk 23:44–49; Jn 19:28–30. v. [27:45] Am 8:9.

w. [27:46] Ps 22:2. x. [27:48] Ps 69:21. y. [27:51] Ex 26:31–36; Ps 68:9; 77:19. z. [27:52] Dn 12:1–3.

there, looking on from a distance,* who had followed Jesus from Galilee, ministering to him. [56a]Among them were Mary Magdalene and Mary the mother of James and Joseph, and the mother of the sons of Zebedee.

**The Burial of Jesus.**[†] [57b]When it was evening, there came a rich man from Arimathea named Joseph, who was himself a disciple of Jesus.[c] [58]He went to Pilate and asked for the body of Jesus; then Pilate ordered it to be handed over. [59]Taking the body, Joseph wrapped it [in] clean linen [60]and laid it in his new tomb that he had hewn in the rock. Then he rolled a huge stone across the entrance to the tomb and departed. [61]But Mary Magdalene and the other Mary remained sitting there, facing the tomb.

**The Guard at the Tomb.**[‡] [62]The next day, the one following the day of preparation,[§] the chief priests and the Pharisees gathered before Pilate [63a]and said, "Sir, we remember that this impostor while still alive said, 'After three days I will be raised up.' [64]Give orders, then, that the grave be secured until the third day, lest his disciples come and steal him and say to the people, 'He has been raised from the dead.' This last imposture would be worse than the first."[¶] [65]Pilate said to them, "The guard is yours;** go secure it as best you can." [66]So they went and secured the tomb by fixing a seal to the stone and setting the guard.

---

\*[27:55–56] **Looking on from a distance:** cf. Ps 38:12. **Mary Magdalene . . . Joseph:** these two women are mentioned again in Mt 27:61 and 28:1 and are important as witnesses of the reality of the empty tomb. A **James** and **Joseph** are referred to in Mt 13:55 as brothers of Jesus.

†[27:57–61] Cf. Mk 15:42–47. Matthew drops Mark's designation of **Joseph** of **Arimathea** as "a distinguished member of the council" (the Sanhedrin), and makes him a **rich man** and a **disciple of Jesus.** The former may be an allusion to Is 53:9 (the Hebrew reading of that text is disputed and the one followed in the NAB OT has nothing about the rich, but they are mentioned in the LXX version). That the tomb was the **new tomb** of a **rich man** and that it was seen by the women are indications of an apologetic intent of Matthew; there could be no question about the identity of Jesus' burial place. **The other Mary:** the mother of James and Joseph (Mt 27:56).

‡[27:62–66] Peculiar to Matthew. The story prepares for Mt 28:11–15 and the Jewish charge that the tomb was empty because the disciples had stolen the body of Jesus (Mt 28:13, 15).

§[27:62] **The next day . . . preparation:** the sabbath. According to the synoptic chronology, in that year **the day of preparation** (for the sabbath) was the Passover; cf. Mk 15:42. **The Pharisees:** the principal opponents of Jesus during his ministry and, in Matthew's time, of the Christian church, join with **the chief priests** to guarantee against a possible attempt of Jesus' **disciples** to steal his body.

¶[27:64] **This last imposture . . . the first:** the claim that Jesus **has been raised from the dead** is clearly the **last imposture;** the **first** may be either his claim that he would **be raised up** (Mt 27:63) or his claim that he was the one with whose ministry the kingdom of God had come (see Mt 12:28).

\*\*[27:65] **The guard is yours:** literally, "have a guard" or "you have a guard." Either the imperative or the indicative could mean that Pilate granted the petitioners some Roman soldiers as guards, which is the sense of the present translation. However, if the verb is taken as an indicative it could also mean that Pilate told them to use their own Jewish guards.

---

a. [27:56] 13:55.  b. [27:57–61] Mk 15:42–47; Lk 23:50–56; Jn 19:38–42.  c. [27:57] Is 53:9.  d. [27:63] 12:40; 16:21; 17:23; 20:19.

## CHAPTER 28[††]

**The Resurrection of Jesus.** [1e]After the sabbath, as the first day of the week was dawning,[‡‡] Mary Magdalene and the other Mary came to see the tomb. [2f]And behold, there was a great earthquake; for an angel of the Lord descended from heaven, approached, rolled back the stone, and sat upon it. [3g]His appearance was like lightning and his clothing was white as snow. [4]The guards were shaken with fear of him and became like dead men. [5]Then the angel said to the women in reply, "Do not be afraid! I know that you are seeking Jesus the crucified. [6]He is not here, for he has been raised just as he said. Come and see the place where he lay. [7h]Then go quickly and tell his disciples, 'He has been raised from the dead, and he is going before you to Galilee; there you

---

††[28:1–20] Except for Mt 28:1–8 based on Mk 16:1–8, the material of this final chapter is peculiar to Matthew. Even where he follows Mark, Matthew has altered his source so greatly that a very different impression is given from that of the Marcan account. The two points that are common to the resurrection testimony of all the gospels are that the tomb of Jesus had been found empty and that the risen Jesus had appeared to certain persons, or, in the original form of Mark, that such an appearance was promised as soon to take place (see Mk 16:7). On this central and all-important basis, Matthew has constructed an account that interprets the resurrection as the turning of the ages (Mt 28:2–4), shows the Jewish opposition to Jesus as continuing **to the present** in the claim that the resurrection is a deception perpetrated by the **disciples** who stole his body from the tomb (Mt 28:11–15), and marks a new stage in the mission of **the disciples** once limited to Israel (Mt 10:5–6); now they are to **make disciples of all nations.** In this work they will be strengthened by the presence of the exalted Son of Man, who will be with them **until** the kingdom comes in fullness at **the end of the age** (Mt 28:16–20).

‡‡[28:1] **After the sabbath . . . dawning:** since the sabbath ended at sunset, this could mean in the early evening, for **dawning** can refer to the appearance of the evening star; cf. Lk 23:54. However, it is probable that Matthew means the morning dawn of the day after the sabbath, as in the similar though slightly different text of Mark, "when the sun had risen" (Mk 16:2). **Mary Magdalene and the other Mary:** see notes on Mt 27:55–56; 57–61. **To see the tomb:** cf. Mk 16:1–2 where the purpose of the women's visit is to anoint Jesus' body.

§§[28:2–4] Peculiar to Matthew. **A great earthquake:** see note on Mt 27:51–53. **Descended from heaven:** this trait is peculiar to Matthew, although his interpretation of the "young man" of his Marcan source (Mk 16:5) as an **angel** is probably true to Mark's intention; cf. Lk 24:23 where the "two men" of Mt 24:4 are said to be "angels." **Rolled back the stone . . . upon it:** not to allow the risen Jesus to leave the tomb but to make evident that the tomb is empty (see Mt 24:6). Unlike the apocryphal Gospel of Peter (9:35—11:44), the New Testament does not describe the resurrection of Jesus, nor is there anyone who sees it. **His appearance was like lightning . . . snow:** see note on Mt 17:2.

¶¶[28:6–7] Cf. Mk 16:6–7. **Just as he said:** a Matthean addition referring to Jesus' predictions of his resurrection, e.g., Mt 16:21; 17:23; 20:19. **Tell his disciples:** like the angel of the Lord of the infancy narrative, the angel interprets a fact and gives a commandment about what is to be done; cf. Mt 1:20–21. Matthew omits Mark's "and Peter" (Mk 16:7); considering his interest in Peter, this omission is curious. Perhaps the reason is that the Marcan text may allude to a first appearance of Jesus to Peter alone (cf. 1 Cor 15:5; Lk 24:34) which Matthew has already incorporated into his account of Peter's confession at Caesarea Philippi; see note on Mt 16:16. **He is going . . . Galilee:** like Mk 16:7, a reference to Jesus' prediction at the Last Supper (Mt 26:32; Mk 14:28). Matthew changes Mark's "as he told you" to a declaration of the angel.

---

e. [28:1–10] Mk 16:1–8; Lk 24:1–12; Jn 20:1–10.  f. [28:2] 25:51.  g. [28:3] 17:2.  h. [28:7] 26:32.

will see him.' Behold, I have told you." [8]Then they went away quickly from the tomb, fearful yet overjoyed, and ran to announce* this to his disciples. [9]i And behold, Jesus met them on their way and greeted them. They approached, embraced his feet, and did him homage. [10]Then Jesus said to them, "Do not be afraid. Go tell my brothers to go to Galilee, and there they will see me."

**The Report of the Guard.**[‡] [11]While they were going, some of the guard went into the city and told the chief priests all that had happened. [12]They assembled with the elders and took counsel; then they gave a large sum of money to the soldiers, [13]telling them, "You are to say, 'His disciples came by night and stole him while we were asleep.' [14]And if this gets to the ears of the governor, we will satisfy [him] and keep you out of trouble." [15]The soldiers took the money and did as they were instructed. And this story has circulated among the Jews to the present [day].

**The Commissioning of the Disciples.**[§] [16]jThe eleven[¶] disciples went to Galilee, to the mountain to which Jesus had ordered them. [17]**When they saw him, they worshiped, but they doubted. [18]†† kThen Jesus approached and said to them, "All power in heaven and on earth has been given to me. [19]Go, therefore,‡‡ and make disciples of all nations, baptizing them in the name of the Father, and of the Son, and of the holy Spirit, [20]mteaching them to observe all that I have commanded you.§§ And behold, I am with you always, until the end of the age."

---

since the message to the **disciples** was simply that they were to go to Galilee (Mt 28:10), some think that **the mountain** comes from a tradition of the message known to Matthew and alluded to here. For the significance of **the mountain**, see note on Mt 17:1.

**[28:17] But they doubted:** the Greek can also be translated, "but some doubted." The verb occurs elsewhere in the New Testament only in Mt 14:31 where it is associated with Peter's being of "little faith." For the meaning of that designation, see note on Mt 6:30.

††[28:18] **All power . . . me:** the Greek word here translated **power** is the same as that found in the LXX translation of Dn 7:13–14 where one "like a son of man" is given **power** and an everlasting kingdom by God. The risen Jesus here claims universal power, i.e., **in heaven and on earth.**

‡‡[28:19] **Therefore:** since universal power belongs to the risen Jesus (Mt 28:18), he gives the eleven a mission that is universal. They are to **make disciples of all nations.** While **all nations** is understood by some scholars as referring only to all Gentiles, it is probable that it included the Jews as well. **Baptizing them:** baptism is the means of entrance into the community of the risen one, the Church. **In the name of the Father . . . holy Spirit:** this is perhaps the clearest expression in the New Testament of trinitarian belief. It may have been the baptismal formula of Matthew's church, but primarily it designates the effect of baptism, the union of the one baptized with the Father, Son, and holy Spirit.

§§[28:20] **All that I have commanded you:** the moral teaching found in this gospel, preeminently that of the Sermon on the Mount (Mt 5–7). The commandments of Jesus are the standard of Christian conduct, not the Mosaic law as such, even though some of the Mosaic commandments have now been invested with the authority of Jesus. **Behold, I am with you always:** the promise of Jesus' real though invisible presence echoes the name Emmanuel given to him in the infancy narrative; see note on Mt 1:23. **End of the age:** see notes on Mt 13:39 and Mt 24:3.

---

*[28:8] Contrast Mk 16:8 where the women in their fear "said nothing to anyone."

†[28:9–10] Although these verses are peculiar to Matthew, there are similarities between them and John's account of the appearance of Jesus to Mary Magdalene (Jn 20:17). In both there is a touching of Jesus' body, and a command of Jesus to bear a message to his disciples, designated as his **brothers**. Matthew may have drawn upon a tradition that appears in a different form in John. Jesus' words to the women are mainly a repetition of those of the angel (Mt 28:5a, 7b).

‡[28:11–15] This account indicates that the dispute between Christians and Jews about the empty tomb was not whether the tomb was empty but why.

§[28:16–20] This climactic scene has been called a "proleptic parousia," for it gives a foretaste of the final glorious coming of the Son of Man (Mt 26:64). Then his triumph will be manifest to all; now it is revealed only to **the disciples**, who are commissioned to announce it to **all nations** and bring them to belief in Jesus and obedience to his commandments.

¶[28:16] **The eleven:** the number recalls the tragic defection of Judas Iscariot. **To the mountain . . . ordered them:**

---

i. [28:9–10] Jn 20:17.    j. [28:16–20] Mk 16:14–16; Lk 24:36–49; Jn 20:19–23.

k. [28:18] Dn 7:14 LXX.    l. [28:19] Acts 1:8.    m. [28:20] 1:23; 13:39; 24:3.

# THE GOSPEL ACCORDING TO
# MARK

⸙

This shortest of all New Testament gospels is likely the first to have been written, yet it often tells of Jesus' ministry in more detail than either Matthew or Luke (for example, the miracle stories at Mk 5:1–20 or Mk 9:14–29). It recounts what Jesus did in a vivid style, where one incident follows directly upon another. In this almost breathless narrative, Mark stresses Jesus' message about the kingdom of God now breaking into human life as good news (Mk 1:14–15) and Jesus himself as the gospel of God (Mk 1:1; 8:35; 10:29). Jesus is the Son whom God has sent to rescue humanity by serving and by sacrificing his life (Mk 10:45).

The opening verse about good news in Mark (Mk 1:1) serves as a title for the entire book. The action begins with the appearance of John the Baptist, a messenger of God attested by scripture. But John points to a mightier one, Jesus, at whose baptism God speaks from heaven, declaring Jesus his Son. The Spirit descends upon Jesus, who eventually, it is promised, will baptize "with the holy Spirit." This presentation of who Jesus really is (Mk 1:1–13) is rounded out with a brief reference to the temptation of Jesus and how Satan's attack fails. Jesus as Son of God will be victorious, a point to be remembered as one reads of Jesus' death and the enigmatic ending to Mark's Gospel.

The key verses at Mk 1:14–15, which are programmatic, summarize what Jesus proclaims as gospel: fulfillment, the nearness of the kingdom, and therefore the need for repentance and for faith. After the call of the first four disciples, all fishermen (Mk 1:16–20), we see Jesus engaged in teaching (Mk 1:21, 22, 27), preaching (Mk 1:38, 39), and healing (Mk 1:29–31, 34, 40–45), and exorcising demons (Mk 1:22–27, 34–39). The content of Jesus' teaching is only rarely stated, and then chiefly in parables (Mk 4) about the kingdom. His cures, especially on the sabbath (Mk 3:1–5); his claim, like God, to forgive sins (Mk 2:3–12); his table fellowship with tax collectors and sinners (Mk 2:14–17); and the statement that his followers need not now fast but should rejoice while Jesus is present (Mk 2:18–22), all stir up opposition that will lead to Jesus' death (Mk 3:6).

In Mark, Jesus is portrayed as immensely popular with the people in Galilee during his ministry (Mk 2:2; 3:7; 4:1). He appoints twelve disciples to help preach and drive out demons, just as he does (Mk 3:13–19). He continues to work many miracles; the blocks Mk 4:35–6:44 and Mk 6:45–7:10 are cycles of stories about healings, miracles at the Sea of Galilee, and marvelous feedings of the crowds. Jesus' teaching in Mk 7 exalts the word of God over "the tradition of the elders" and sees defilement as a matter of the heart, not of unclean foods. Yet opposition mounts. Scribes charge that Jesus is possessed by Beelzebul (Mk 3:22). His relatives think him "out of his mind" (Mk 3:21). Jesus' kinship is with those who do the will of God, in a new eschatological family, not even with mother, brothers, or sisters by blood ties (Mk 3:31–35; cf. Mk 6:1–6). But all too often his own disciples do not understand Jesus (Mk 4:13, 40; 6:52; 8:17–21). The fate of John the Baptist (Mk 6:17–29) hints ominously at Jesus' own passion (Mk 9:13; cf. Mk 8:31).

A breakthrough seemingly comes with Peter's confession that Jesus is the Christ (Messiah; Mk 8:27–30). But Jesus himself emphasizes his passion (Mk 8:31; 9:31; 10:33–34), not glory in the kingdom (Mk 10:35–45). Momentarily he is glimpsed in his true identity when he is transfigured before three of the disciples (Mk 9:2–8), but by and large Jesus is depicted in Mark as moving obediently along the way to his cross in Jerusalem. Occasionally there are miracles (Mk 9:17–27; 10:46–52; 11:12–14, 20–21, the only such account in Jerusalem), sometimes teachings (Mk 10:2–11, 23–31), but the greatest concern is with discipleship (Mk 8:34–9:1; 9:33–50). For the disciples do not grasp the mystery being revealed (Mk 9:32; 10:32, 38). One of them will betray him, Judas (Mk 14:10–11, 43–45); one will deny him, Peter (Mk 14:27, 31, 54, 66–72); all eleven men will desert Jesus (Mk 14:27, 50).

The passion account, with its condemnation of Jesus by the Sanhedrin (Mk 14:53, 55–65; 15:1a) and sentencing by Pilate (Mk 15:1b–15), is prefaced with the entry into Jerusalem (Mk 11:1–11), ministry and controversies there (Mk 11:15–12:44), Jesus' Last Supper with the disciples (Mk 14:1–26), and his arrest at Gethsemane (Mk 14:32–52). A chapter of apocalyptic tone about the destruction of the temple (Mk 13:1–2, 14–23) and the coming of the Son of Man (Mk 13:24–27), a discourse filled with promises (Mk 13:11, 31) and admonitions to be watchful (Mk 13:2, 23, 37), is significant for Mark's Gospel, for it helps one see that God, in Jesus, will be victorious after the cross and at the end of history.

The Gospel of Mark ends in the most ancient manuscripts with an abrupt scene at Jesus' tomb, which the women find empty (Mk 16:1–8). His own prophecy of Mk 14:28 is reiterated, that Jesus goes before the disciples into Galilee; "there you will see him." These words may imply resurrection appearances there, or Jesus' parousia there, or the start of Christian mission, or a return to the roots depicted in Mk 1:9, 14–15 in Galilee. Other hands have attached additional endings after Mk 16:8; see note on Mk 16:9–20.

The framework of Mark's Gospel is partly geographical: Galilee (Mk 1:14–9:49), through the area "across the Jordan" (Mk 10:1) and through Jericho (Mk 10:46–52), to Jerusalem (Mk 11:1–16:8). Only rarely does Jesus go into Gentile territory (Mk 5:1–20; 7:24–37), but those who acknowledge him there and the centurion who confesses Jesus at the cross (Mk 15:39) presage the gospel's expansion into the world beyond Palestine.

Mark's Gospel is even more oriented to christology. Jesus is the Son of God (Mk 1:11; 9:7; 15:39; cf. Mk 1:1; 14:61). He is the Messiah, the anointed king of Davidic descent (Mk 12:35; 15:32), the Greek for which, *Christos*, has, by the time Mark wrote, become in effect a proper name (Mk 1:1; 9:41). Jesus is also seen as Son of Man, a term used in Mark not simply as a substitute for "I" or for humanity in general (cf. Mk 2:10, 27–28; 14:21) or with reference to a mighty figure who is to come (Mk 13:26; 14:62), but also in connection with Jesus' predestined, necessary path of suffering and vindication (Mk 8:31; 10:45).

The unfolding of Mark's story about Jesus is sometimes viewed by interpreters as centered around the term "mystery." The word is employed just once, at Mk 4:11, in the singular, and its content there is the kingdom, the open secret that God's reign is now breaking into human life with its reversal of human values. There is a related sense in which Jesus' real identity remained a secret during his lifetime, according to Mark, although demons and demoniacs knew it (Mk 1:24; 3:11; 5:7); Jesus warned against telling of his mighty deeds and revealing his identity (Mk 1:44; 3:12; 5:43; 7:36; 8:26, 30), an injunction sometimes broken (Mk 1:45; cf. Mk 5:19–20). Further, Jesus teaches by parables, according to Mark, in such a way that those "outside" the kingdom do not understand, but only those to whom the mystery has been granted by God.

Mark thus shares with Paul, as well as with other parts of the New Testament, an emphasis on election (Mk 13:20, 22) and upon the gospel as Christ and his cross (cf. 1 Cor 1:23). Yet in Mark the person of Jesus is also depicted with an unaffected naturalness. He reacts to events with authentic human emotion: pity (Mk 1:44), anger (Mk 3:5), triumph (Mk 4:40), sympathy (Mk 5:36; 6:34), surprise (Mk 6:9), admiration (Mk 7:29; 10:21), sadness (Mk 14:33–34), and indignation (Mk 14:48–49).

Although the book is anonymous, apart from the ancient heading "According to Mark" in manuscripts, it has traditionally been assigned to John Mark, in whose mother's house (at Jerusalem) Christians assembled (Acts 12:12). This Mark was a cousin of Barnabas (Col 4:10) and accompanied Barnabas and Paul on a missionary journey (Acts 12:25; 13:3; 15:36–39). He appears in Pauline letters (2 Tm 4:11; Phlm 24) and with Peter (1 Pt 5:13). Papias (ca. A.D. 135) described Mark as Peter's "interpreter," a view found in other patristic writers. Petrine influence should not, however, be exaggerated. The evangelist has put together various oral and possibly written sources—miracle stories, parables, sayings, stories of controversies, and the passion—so as to speak of the crucified Messiah for Mark's own day.

Traditionally, the gospel is said to have been written shortly before A.D. 70 in Rome, at a time of impending persecution and when destruction loomed over Jerusalem. Its audience seems to have been Gentile, unfamiliar with Jewish customs (hence Mk 7:3–4, 11). The book aimed to equip such

Christians to stand faithful in the face of persecution (Mk 13:9–13), while going on with the proclamation of the gospel begun in Galilee (Mk 13:10; 14:9). Modern research often proposes as the author an unknown Hellenistic Jewish Christian, possibly in Syria, and perhaps shortly after the year 70.

The principal divisions of the Gospel according to Mark are the following:

I. The Preparation for the Public Ministry of Jesus (1:1–13)
II. The Mystery of Jesus (1:14–8:26)
III. The Mystery Begins to Be Revealed (8:27–9:32)
IV. The Full Revelation of the Mystery (9:33–16:8)
      The Longer Ending (16:9–20)
      The Shorter Ending
      The Freer Logion (in the note on 16:9–20)

## I. THE PREPARATION FOR THE PUBLIC MINISTRY OF JESUS[*]

### CHAPTER 1

[1]The beginning of the gospel of Jesus Christ [the Son of God].[†]

**The Preaching of John the Baptist.** [2a]As it is written in Isaiah the prophet:[‡b]

"Behold, I am sending my messenger
    ahead of you;
he will prepare your way.
[3] 'A voice of one crying out in the desert:
    'Prepare the way of the Lord,
    make straight his paths.'"

[4]John [the] Baptist appeared in the desert proclaiming a baptism of repentance for the forgiveness of sins. [5]People of the whole Judean countryside and all the inhabitants of Jerusalem were going out to him and were being baptized by him in the Jordan River as they acknowledged their sins. [6]John was clothed in camel's hair, with a leather belt around his waist.[§] He

fed on locusts and wild honey. [7]And this is what he proclaimed: "One mightier than I is coming after me. I am not worthy to stoop and loosen the thongs of his sandals. [8]*d*I have baptized you with water; he will baptize you with the holy Spirit."

**The Baptism of Jesus.** [9]*e*It happened in those days that Jesus came from Nazareth of Galilee and was baptized in the Jordan by John. [10]On coming up out of the water he saw the heavens being torn open and the Spirit, like a dove, descending upon him." [11]*f*And a voice came from the heavens, "You are my beloved Son; with you I am well pleased."

**The Temptation of Jesus.**[††] [12]At once the Spirit drove him out into the desert,[g] [13]and he remained in the desert for forty days, tempted

---

*[1:1–13] The prologue of the Gospel according to Mark begins with the title (Mk 1:1) followed by three events preparatory to Jesus' preaching: (1) the appearance in the Judean wilderness of John, baptizer, preacher of repentance, and precursor of Jesus (Mk 1:2–8); (2) the baptism of Jesus, at which a voice from heaven acknowledges Jesus to be God's Son, and the holy Spirit descends on him (Mk 1:9–11); (3) the temptation of Jesus by Satan (Mk 1:12–13).

†[1:1] **The gospel of Jesus Christ [the Son of God]:** the "good news" of salvation in and through Jesus, crucified and risen, acknowledged by the Christian community as Messiah (Mk 8:29; 14:61–62) and Son of God (Mk 1:11; 9:7; 15:39), although some important manuscripts here omit **the Son of God**.

‡[1:2–3] Although Mark attributes the prophecy to Isaiah, the text is a combination of Mal 3:1; Is 40:3; Ex 23:20; cf. Mt 11:10; Lk 7:27. John's ministry is seen as God's prelude to the saving mission of his Son. **The way of the Lord:** this prophecy of Deutero-Isaiah concerning the end of the Babylonian exile is here applied to the coming of Jesus; John the Baptist is to prepare the way for him.

§[1:6] **Clothed in camel's hair . . . waist:** the Baptist's garb recalls that of Elijah in 2 Kgs 1:8. Jesus speaks of the Baptist

as Elijah who has already come (Mk 9:11–13; Mt 17:10–12; cf. Mal 3:23–24; Lk 1:17).

¶[1:8–9] Through the life-giving baptism with the holy Spirit (Mk 1:8), Jesus will create a new people of God. But first he identifies himself with the people of Israel in submitting to John's baptism of repentance and in bearing on their behalf the burden of God's decisive judgment (Mk 1:9; cf. Mk 1:4). As in the desert of Sinai, so here in the wilderness of Judea, Israel's sonship with God is to be renewed.

**[1:10–11] He saw the heavens . . . and the Spirit . . . upon him:** indicating divine intervention in fulfillment of promise. Here the descent of the Spirit on Jesus is meant, anointing him for his ministry; cf. Is 11:2; 42:1; 61:1; 63:9. **A voice . . . with you I am well pleased:** God's acknowledgment of Jesus as his unique Son, the object of his love. His approval of Jesus is the assurance that Jesus will fulfill his messianic mission of salvation.

††[1:12–13] The same Spirit who descended on Jesus in his baptism now drives him into the desert for forty days. The result is radical confrontation and temptation by Satan who attempts to frustrate the work of God. The presence of wild beasts may indicate the horror and danger of the desert regarded as the abode of demons or may reflect the paradise motif of harmony among all creatures; cf. Is 11:6–9. The presence of ministering angels to sustain Jesus recalls the angel who guided the Israelites in the desert in the first Exodus (Ex 14:19; 23:20) and the angel who supplied nourishment to Elijah in the wilderness (1 Kgs 19:5–7). The combined forces of good and evil were present to Jesus in the desert. His sustained obedience brings forth the new Israel of God there where Israel's rebellion had brought death and alienation.

---

d. [1:8] Jn 1:27; Acts 1:5; 11:16. e. [1:9–11] Mt 3:13–17; Lk 3:21–23; Jn 1:32–33. f. [1:11] Ps 2:7. g. [1:12–13] Mt 4:1–11; Lk 4:1–13.

a. [1:2–8] Mt 3:1–11; Lk 3:2–16. b. [1:2] Mal 3:1. c. [1:3] Is 40:3; Jn 1:23.

by Satan. He was among wild beasts, and the angels ministered to him.

## II. THE MYSTERY OF JESUS

**The Beginning of the Galilean Ministry.** ¹⁴ʰAfter John had been arrested,* Jesus came to Galilee proclaiming the gospel of God: ¹⁵ᐟ"This is the time of fulfillment. The kingdom of God is at hand. Repent, and believe in the gospel."

**The Call of the First Disciples.**† ¹⁶ʲAs he passed by the Sea of Galilee, he saw Simon and his brother Andrew casting their nets into the sea; they were fishermen. ¹⁷Jesus said to them, "Come after me, and I will make you fishers of men." ¹⁸Then they abandoned their nets and followed him. ¹⁹He walked along a little farther and saw James, the son of Zebedee, and his brother John. They too were in a boat mending their nets. ²⁰Then he called them. So they left their father Zebedee in the boat along with the hired men and followed him.

**The Cure of a Demoniac.** ²¹ᵏThen they came to Capernaum, and on the sabbath he entered the synagogue and taught. ²²ˡThe people were astonished at his teaching, for he taught them as one having authority and not as the scribes. ²³§In their synagogue was a man with an unclean spirit; ²⁴*he cried out, "What have you to do with us,** Jesus of Nazareth? Have you come to destroy us? I know who you are—the Holy One of God!" ²⁵Jesus rebuked him and said, "Quiet! Come out of him!" ²⁶The unclean spirit convulsed him and with a loud cry came out of him. ²⁷All were

amazed and asked one another, "What is this? A new teaching with authority. He commands even the unclean spirits and they obey him." ²⁸His fame spread everywhere throughout the whole region of Galilee.

**The Cure of Simon's Mother-in-Law.** ²⁹ᵐOn leaving the synagogue he entered the house of Simon and Andrew with James and John. ³⁰Simon's mother-in-law lay sick with a fever. They immediately told him about her. ³¹He approached, grasped her hand, and helped her up. Then the fever left her and she waited on them.

**Other Healings.** ³²When it was evening, after sunset, they brought to him all who were ill or possessed by demons. ³³The whole town was gathered at the door. ³⁴He cured many who were sick with various diseases, and he drove out many demons, not permitting them to speak because they knew him.

**Jesus Leaves Capernaum.** ³⁵ⁿRising very early before dawn, he left and went off to a deserted place, where he prayed. ³⁶Simon and those who were with him pursued him ³⁷and on finding him said, "Everyone is looking for you." ³⁸He told them, "Let us go on to the nearby villages that I may preach there also. For this purpose have I come." ³⁹So he went into their synagogues, preaching and driving out demons throughout the whole of Galilee.

**The Cleansing of a Leper.** ⁴⁰ᵒA leper†† came to him [and kneeling down] begged him and said, "If you wish, you can make me clean." ⁴¹Moved with pity, he stretched out his hand, touched him, and said to him, "I do will it. Be made clean."ᵖ ⁴²The leprosy left him immediately, and he was made clean.�q ⁴³Then, warning him sternly, he dismissed him at once. ⁴⁴Then he said to him, "See that you tell no one anything, but go, show yourself to the priest and offer for your cleansing what Moses prescribed; that will be proof for them."ʳ ⁴⁵The man went away and began to publicize the whole matter. He spread the report abroad so that it was impossible for Jesus to enter a town openly. He remained outside in deserted places, and people kept coming to him from everywhere.

## CHAPTER 2

**The Healing of a Paralytic.** ¹‡‡When Jesus returned to Capernaumˢ after some days, it

---

*[1:14–15] **After John had been arrested**: in the plan of God, Jesus was not to proclaim the good news of salvation prior to the termination of the Baptist's active mission. **Galilee**: in the Marcan account, scene of the major part of Jesus' public ministry before his arrest and condemnation. **The gospel of God**: not only the good news from God but about God at work in Jesus Christ. **This is the time of fulfillment**: i.e., of God's promises. **The kingdom of God . . . Repent**: see note on Mt 3:2.

†[1:16–20] These verses narrate the call of the first Disciples. See notes on Mt 4:18–22 and Mt 4:20.

‡[1:21–45] The account of a single day's ministry of Jesus on a sabbath in and outside the synagogue of Capernaum (Mk 1:21–31) combines teaching and miracles of exorcism and healing. Mention is not made of the content of the teaching but of the effect of astonishment and alarm on the people. Jesus' teaching with authority, making an absolute claim on the hearer, was in the best tradition of the ancient prophets, not of the scribes. The narrative continues with events that evening (Mk 1:32–34; see notes on Mt 8:14–17) and the next day (Mk 1:35–39). The cleansing in Mk 1:40–45 stands as an isolated story.

§[1:23] **An unclean spirit**: so called because of the spirit's resistance to the holiness of God. The spirit knows and fears the power of Jesus to destroy his influence; cf. Mk 1:32, 34; 3:11; 6:13.

¶[1:24–25] **The Holy One of God**: not a confession but an attempt to ward off Jesus' power, reflecting the notion that use of the precise name of an opposing spirit would guarantee mastery over him. Jesus silenced the cry of the unclean spirit and drove him out of the man.

**[1:24] **What have you to do with us?**: see note on Jn 2:4.

††[1:40] **A leper**: for the various forms of skin disease, see Lv 13:1–50 and the note on Lv 13:2–4. There are only two instances in the Old Testament in which God is shown to have cured a leper (Nm 12:10–15; 2 Kgs 5:1–14). The law of Moses provided for the ritual purification of a leper. In curing the leper, Jesus assumes that the priests will reinstate the cured man into the religious community. See also note on Lk 5:14.

‡‡[2:1–3:6] This section relates a series of conflicts between Jesus and the scribes and Pharisees in which the growing opposition of the latter leads to their plot to put Jesus to death (Mk 3:6).

---

h. [1:14–15] Mt 4:12–17; Lk 4:14–15.  i. [1:15] Mt 3:2.  j. [1:16–20] Mt 4:18–22; Lk 5:2–11.  k. [1:21–28] Lk 4:31–37.  l. [1:22] Mt 7:28–29.

m. [1:29–34] Mt 8:14–16; Lk 4:38–41.  n. [1:35–39] Lk 4:42–44.  o. [1:40–44] Mt 8:2–4; Lk 5:12–14.  p. [1:41] 5:30.  q. [1:42] Lk 17:14.  r. [1:44] Lv 14:2–32.  s. [2:1–12] Mt 9:2–8; Lk 5:18–26.

became known that he was at home.* ²Many gathered together so that there was no longer room for them, not even around the door, and he preached the word to them. ³They came bringing to him a paralytic carried by four men. ⁴Unable to get near Jesus because of the crowd, they opened up the roof above him. After they had broken through, they let down the mat on which the paralytic was lying. ⁵ᵗWhen Jesus saw their faith, he said to the paralytic, "Child, your sins are forgiven." ⁶ᵗNow some of the scribes were sitting there asking themselves, ⁷"Why does this man speak that way? He is blaspheming. Who but God alone can forgive sins?"ᵗ ⁸Jesus immediately knew in his mind what they were thinking to themselves, so he said, "Why are you thinking such things in your hearts? ⁹Which is easier, to say to the paralytic, 'Your sins are forgiven,' or to say, 'Rise, pick up your mat and walk'? ¹⁰ᵗBut that you may know that the Son of Man has authority to forgive sins on earth"— ¹¹he said to the paralytic, "I say to you, rise, pick up your mat, and go home." ¹²He rose, picked up his mat at once, and went away in the sight of everyone. They were all astounded and glorified God, saying, "We have never seen anything like this."

**The Call of Levi.** ¹³**°Once again he went out along the sea. All the crowd came to him and he taught them. ¹⁴ᵛAs he passed by,ᵗᵗ he saw Levi, son of Alphaeus, sitting at the customs post. He said to him, "Follow me." And he got up and followed

him. ¹⁵While he was at table in his house,‡‡ many tax collectors and sinners sat with Jesus and his disciples; for there were many who followed him. ¹⁶§§Some scribes who were Pharisees saw that he was eating with sinners and tax collectors and said to his disciples, "Why does he eat with tax collectors and sinners?" ¹⁷Jesus heard this and said to them [that], "Those who are well do not need a physician,¶¶ but the sick do. I did not come to call the righteous but sinners."

**The Question About Fasting.**\*\*\* ¹⁸The disciples of John and of the Pharisees were accustomed to fast.ʷ People came to him and objected, "Why do the disciples of John and the disciples of the Pharisees fast, but your disciples do not fast?" ¹⁹Jesus answered them, "Can the wedding guests fast†††while the bridegroom is with them? As long as they have the bridegroom with them they cannot fast. ²⁰But the days will come when the bridegroom is taken away from them, and then they will fast on that day. ²¹No one sews a piece of unshrunken cloth on an old cloak. If he does, its fullness pulls away, the new from the old, and the tear gets worse. ²²Likewise, no one pours new wine into old wineskins. Otherwise, the wine will burst the skins, and both the wine and the skins are ruined. Rather, new wine is poured into fresh wineskins."

**The Disciples and the Sabbath.**‡‡‡ ²³As he was passing through a field of grain on the sabbath, his disciples began to make a path while picking the heads of grain.ˣ ²⁴At this the Pharisees said to him, "Look, why are they doing what is unlawful on the sabbath?"ʸ ²⁵He said to them, "Have you never read what David did§§§when he was in need and he and his companions were hungry? ²⁶How

---

*[2:1–2] **He was at home**: to the crowds that gathered in and outside the house Jesus **preached the word**, i.e., the gospel concerning the nearness of the kingdom and the necessity of repentance and faith (Mk 1:14).

†[2:5] It was the faith of the paralytic and those who carried him that moved Jesus to heal the sick man. Accounts of other miracles of Jesus reveal more and more his emphasis on faith as the requisite for exercising his healing powers (Mk 5:34; 9:23–24; 10:52).

‡[2:6] **Scribes**: trained in oral interpretation of the written law; in Mark's gospel, adversaries of Jesus, with one exception (Mk 12:28, 34).

§[2:7] **He is blaspheming**: an accusation made here and repeated during the trial of Jesus (Mk 14:60–64).

¶[2:10] **But that you may know that the Son of Man . . . on earth**: although Mk 2:8–9 are addressed to the scribes, the sudden interruption of thought and structure in Mk 2:10 seems not addressed to them nor to the paralytic. Moreover, the early public use of the designation "Son of Man" to unbelieving scribes is most unlikely. The most probable explanation is that Mark's insertion of Mk 2:10 is a commentary addressed to Christians for whom he recalls this miracle and who already accept in faith that Jesus is Messiah and Son of God.

\*\*[2:13] **He taught them**: see note on Mk 1:21–45.

††[2:14] **As he passed by**: see note on Mk 1:16–20. **Levi, son of Alphaeus**: see note on Mt 9:9. **Customs post**: such tax collectors paid a fixed sum for the right to collect customs duties within their districts. Since whatever they could collect above this amount constituted their profit, the abuse of extortion was widespread among them. Hence, Jewish customs officials were regarded as sinners (Mk 2:16), outcasts of society, and disgraced along with their families. **He got up and followed him**: i.e., became a disciple of Jesus.

‡‡[2:15] **In his house**: cf. Mk 2:1; Mt 9:10. Lk 5:29 clearly calls it Levi's house.

§§[2:16–17] This and the following conflict stories reflect a similar pattern: a statement of fact, a question of protest, and a reply by Jesus.

¶¶[2:17] **Do not need a physician**: this maxim of Jesus with its implied irony was uttered to silence his adversaries who objected that he ate with **tax collectors and sinners** (Mk 2:16). Because the scribes and Pharisees were self-righteous, they were not capable of responding to Jesus' call to repentance and faith in the gospel.

\*\*\*[2:18–22] This conflict over the question of fasting has the same pattern as Mk 2:16–17; see notes on Mt 9:15; 9:16–17.

†††[2:19] **Can the wedding guests fast?**: the bridal metaphor expresses a new relationship of love between God and his people in the person and mission of Jesus to his disciples. It is the inauguration of the new and joyful messianic time of fulfillment and the passing of the old. Any attempt at assimilating the Pharisaic practice of fasting, or of extending the preparatory discipline of John's disciples beyond the arrival of the bridegroom, would be as futile as sewing **a piece of unshrunken cloth on an old cloak** or pouring **new wine into old wineskins** with the resulting destruction of both cloth and wine (Mk 2:21–22). Fasting is rendered superfluous during the earthly ministry of Jesus; cf. Mk 2:20.

‡‡‡[2:23–28] This conflict regarding the sabbath follows the same pattern as Mk 2:18–22.

§§§[2:25–26] **Have you never read what David did?**: Jesus defends the action of his disciples on the basis of 1 Sm 21:2–7 in which an exception is made to the regulation of Lv 24:9 because of the extreme hunger of David and his men. According to

---

t. [2:7] Is 43:25.   u. [2:13] 4:1.   v. [2:14–17] Mt 9:9–13; Lk 5:27–32.

w. [2:18–22] Mt 9:14–17; Lk 5:33–39.   x. [2:23–28] Mt 12:1–8; Lk 6:1–5.   y. [2:24] Dt 23:25.

he went into the house of God when Abiathar was high priest and ate the bread of offering that only the priests could lawfully eat, and shared it with his companions?"ᶻ ²⁷Then he said to them, "The sabbath was made for man,* not man for the sabbath.ᵃ ²⁸†That is why the Son of Man is lord even of the sabbath."

## CHAPTER 3

**A Man with a Withered Hand.** ¹‡Again he entered the synagogue.ᵇ There was a man there who had a withered hand. ²They watched him closely to see if he would cure him on the sabbath so that they might accuse him. ³He said to the man with the withered hand, "Come up here before us." ⁴Then he said to them, "Is it lawful to do good on the sabbath rather than to do evil, to save life rather than to destroy it?" But they remained silent. ⁵Looking around at them with anger and grieved at their hardness of heart, he said to the man, "Stretch out your hand." He stretched it out and his hand was restored.ᶜ ⁶§The Pharisees went out and immediately took counsel with the Herodians against him to put him to death.

**The Mercy of Jesus.** ⁷¶Jesus withdrew toward the sea with his disciples.ᵈ A large number of people [followed] from Galilee and from Judea. ⁸Hearing what he was doing, a large number of people came to him also from Jerusalem, from Idumea, from beyond the Jordan, and from the neighborhood of Tyre and Sidon. ⁹He told his disciples to have a boat ready for him because of the crowd, so that they would not crush him. ¹⁰He

had cured many and, as a result, those who had diseases were pressing upon him to touch him.ᵉ ¹¹"And whenever unclean spirits saw him they would fall down before him and shout, "You are the Son of God."ᶠ ¹²He warned them sternly not to make him known.

**The Mission of the Twelve.** ¹³ᵍHe went up the mountain†† and summoned those whom he wanted and they came to him. ¹⁴ʰHe appointed twelve [whom he also named apostles] that they might be with him‡‡ and he might send them forth to preach ¹⁵and to have authority to drive out demons: ¹⁶§§[he appointed the twelve:] Simon, whom he named Peter; ¹⁷James, son of Zebedee, and John the brother of James, whom he named Boanerges, that is, sons of thunder;ⁱ ¹⁸Andrew, Philip, Bartholomew, Matthew, Thomas, James the son of Alphaeus; Thaddeus, Simon the Cananean, ¹⁹and Judas Iscariot who betrayed him.

**Blasphemy of the Scribes.** ²⁰¶¶He came home.*** Again [the] crowd gathered, making it impossible for them even to eat.ʲ ²¹When his relatives heard of this they set out to seize him, for they said, "He is out of his mind."ᵏ ²²The scribes who had come from Jerusalem said, "He is possessed by Beelzebul,"††† and "By the prince of demons he drives out demons."ˡ

**Jesus and Beelzebul.** ²³Summoning them, he began to speak to them in parables, "How can Satan drive out Satan? ²⁴If a kingdom is divided against itself, that kingdom cannot stand. ²⁵And if a house is divided against itself, that house will not be able to stand. ²⁶And if Satan has risen up against himself and is divided, he cannot stand;

---

1 Samuel, the priest who gave the bread to David was Ahimelech, father of Abiathar.

*[2:27] **The sabbath was made for man**: a reaffirmation of the divine intent of the sabbath to benefit Israel as contrasted with the restrictive Pharisaic tradition added to the law.

†[2:28] **The Son of Man is lord even of the sabbath:** Mark's comment on the theological meaning of the incident is to benefit his Christian readers; see note on Mk 2:10.

‡[3:1–5] Here Jesus is again depicted in conflict with his adversaries over the question of sabbath-day observance. His opponents were already ill disposed toward him because they regarded Jesus as a violator of the sabbath. Jesus' question **Is it lawful to do good on the sabbath rather than to do evil?** places the matter in the broader theological context outside the casuistry of the scribes. The answer is obvious. Jesus heals the man with the withered hand in the sight of all and reduces his opponents to silence; cf. Lk 5:17–18.

§[3:6] In reporting the plot of the Pharisees and Herodians to put Jesus to death after this series of conflicts in Galilee, Mark uses a pattern that recurs in his account of later controversies in Jerusalem (Mk 11:17–18; 12:13–17). The help of the Herodians, supporters of Herod Antipas, tetrarch of Galilee and Perea, is needed to take action against Jesus. Both series of conflicts point to their gravity and to the impending passion of Jesus.

¶[3:7–19] This overview of the Galilean ministry manifests the power of Jesus to draw people to himself through his teaching and deeds of power. The crowds of Jews from many regions surround Jesus (Mk 3:7–12). This phenomenon prepares the way for creating a new people of Israel. The choice and mission of the Twelve is the prelude (Mk 3:13–19).

**[3:11–12] See note on Mk 1:24–25.

††[3:13] **He went up the mountain**: here and elsewhere the mountain is associated with solemn moments and acts in the mission and self-revelation of Jesus (Mk 6:46; 9:2–8; 13:3). Jesus acts with authority as he **summoned those whom he wanted and they came to him.**

‡‡[3:14–15] **He appointed twelve [whom he also named apostles] that they might be with him**: literally "he made," i.e., instituted them as apostles to extend his messianic mission through them (Mk 6:7–13). See notes on Mt 10:1 and 10:2–4.

§§[3:16] **Simon, whom he named Peter**: Mark indicates that Simon's name was changed on this occasion. Peter is first in all lists of the apostles (Mt 10:2; Lk 6:14; Acts 1:13; cf. 1 Cor 15:5–8).

¶¶[3:20–35] Within the narrative of the coming of Jesus' relatives (Mk 3:20–21) is inserted the account of the unbelieving scribes from Jerusalem who attributed Jesus' power over demons to Beelzebul (Mk 3:22–30); see note on Mk 3:21–43. There were those even among the relatives of Jesus who disbelieved and regarded Jesus as **out of his mind** (Mk 3:21). Against this background, Jesus is informed of the arrival of his mother and brothers [and sisters] (Mk 3:32). He responds by showing that not family ties but doing God's will (Mk 3:35) is decisive in the kingdom; cf. note on Mt 12:46–50.

***[3:20] **He came home**: cf. Mk 2:1–2 and see note on Mk 2:15.

†††[3:22] **By Beelzebul**: see note on Mt 10:25. Two accusations are leveled against Jesus: (1) that **he is possessed** by an unclean spirit and (2) **by the prince of demons he drives out demons**. Jesus answers the second charge by a parable (Mk 3:24–27) and responds to the first charge in Mk 3:28–29.

---

z. [2:26] 1 Sm 21:2–7; Lv 24:5–9.  a. [2:27] 2 Mc 5:19.  b. [3:1–6] Mt 12:9–14; Lk 6:6–11.  c. [3:5] Lk 14:4.  d. [3:7–12] Mt 4:23–25; 12:15; Lk 6:17–19.

e. [3:10] 5:30.  f. [3:11] 1:34; Lk 4:41.  g. [3:13–19] Mt 10:1–4; Lk 6:12–16.  h. [3:14] 6:7.  i. [3:17] Mt 16:18; Jn 1:42.  j. [3:20] 2:2.  k. [3:21] Jn 10:20.  l. [3:22–30] Mt 12:24–32; Lk 11:15–22; 12:10.

that is the end of him. ²⁷But no one can enter a strong man's house to plunder his property unless he first ties up the strong man. Then he can plunder his house. ²⁸Amen, I say to you, all sins and all blasphemies that people utter will be forgiven them.ᵐ ²⁹But whoever blasphemes against the holy Spirit* will never have forgiveness, but is guilty of an everlasting sin." ³⁰For they had said, "He has an unclean spirit."

**Jesus and His Family.** ³¹ⁿHis mother and his brothers arrived. Standing outside they sent word to him and called him. ³²A crowd seated around him told him, "Your mother and your brothers† [and your sisters] are outside asking for you." ³³But he said to them, "Who are my mother and [my] brothers?" ³⁴And looking around at those seated in the circle he said, "Here are my mother and my brothers. ³⁵[For] whoever does the will of God is my brother and sister and mother."

## CHAPTER 4

**The Parable of the Sower.** ¹‡On another occasion° he began to teach by the sea.§ A very large crowd gathered around him so that he got into a boat on the sea and sat down. And the whole crowd was beside the sea on land.ᵖ ²And he taught them at length in parables, and in the course of his instruction he said to them, ³¶"Hear this! A sower went out to sow. ⁴And as he sowed, some seed fell on the path, and the birds came and ate it up. ⁵Other seed fell on rocky ground where it had little soil. It sprang up at once because the soil was not deep. ⁶And when the sun rose, it was scorched and it withered for lack of roots. ⁷Some seed fell among thorns, and the thorns grew up and choked it and it produced no grain. ⁸And some seed fell on rich soil and produced fruit. It came up and grew and yielded thirty, sixty, and a hundredfold." ⁹He added, "Whoever has ears to hear ought to hear."

**The Purpose of the Parables.** ¹⁰And when he was alone, those present along with the Twelve questioned him about the parables. ¹¹**"He answered them, "The mystery of the kingdom of God has been granted to you. But to those outside everything comes in parables, ¹²so that

'they may look and see but not perceive,
and hear and listen but not
understand,
in order that they may not be converted
and be forgiven.'"�q

¹³††Jesus said to them, "Do you not understand this parable?ʳ Then how will you understand any of the parables? ¹⁴The sower sows the word. ¹⁵These are the ones on the path where the word is sown. As soon as they hear, Satan comes at once and takes away the word sown in them. ¹⁶And these are the ones sown on rocky ground who, when they hear the word, receive it at once with joy. ¹⁷But they have no root; they last only for a time. Then when tribulation or persecution comes because of the word, they quickly fall away. ¹⁸Those sown among thorns are another sort. They are the people who hear the word, ¹⁹but worldly anxiety, the lure of riches, and the craving for other things intrude and choke the word, and it bears no fruit. ²⁰But those sown on rich soil are the ones who hear the word and accept it and bear fruit thirty and sixty and a hundredfold."

**Parable of the Lamp.** ²¹He said to them, "Is a lamp brought in to be placed under a bushel basket or under a bed, and not to be placed on a lampstand?ᵗ ²²For there is nothing hidden except to be made visible; nothing is secret except to come to light.ᵘ ²³Anyone who has ears to hear ought to hear." ²⁴He also told them, "Take care what you hear. The measure with which you measure will be measured out to you, and still more will be given to you.ᵛ ²⁵To the one who has, more will be given; from the one who has not, even what he has will be taken away."ʷ

**Seed Grows of Itself.** ²⁶He said, "This is how it is with the kingdom of God;‡‡ it is as if a man

---

*[3:29] **Whoever blasphemes against the holy Spirit**: this sin is called **an everlasting sin** because it attributes to Satan, who is the power of evil, what is actually the work of the holy Spirit, namely, victory over the demons.

†[3:32] **Your brothers**: see note on Mk 6:3.

‡[4:1–34] **In parables** (Mk 4:2): see note on Mt 13:3. The use of parables is typical of Jesus' enigmatic method of teaching the crowds (Mk 4:2–9, 12) as compared with the interpretation of the parables he gives to his disciples (Mk 4:10–25, 33–34) to each group according to its capacity to understand (Mk 4:9–11). The key feature of the parable at hand is the sowing of the seed (Mk 4:3), representing the breakthrough of the kingdom of God into the world. The various types of soil refer to the diversity of response accorded the word of God (Mk 4:4–7). The climax of the parable is the harvest of thirty, sixty, and a hundredfold, indicating the consummation of the kingdom (Mk 4:8). Thus both the present and the future action of God, from the initiation to the fulfillment of the kingdom, is presented through this and other parables (Mk 4:26–29, 30–32).

§[4:1] **By the sea**: the shore of the Sea of Galilee or a boat near the shore (Mk 2:13; 3:7–8) is the place where Mark depicts Jesus teaching the crowds. By contrast the mountain is the scene of Jesus at prayer (Mk 6:46) or in the process of forming his disciples (Mk 3:13; 9:2).

¶[4:3–8] See note on Mt 13:3–8.

**[4:11–12] These verses are to be viewed against their background in Mk 3:6, 22 concerning the unbelief and opposition Jesus encountered in his ministry. It is against this background that the distinction in Jesus' method becomes clear of presenting the kingdom to the disbelieving crowd in one manner and to the disciples in another. To the former it is presented in parables and the truth remains hidden; for the latter the parable is interpreted and the mystery is partially revealed because of their faith; see notes on Mt 13:11 and Mt 13:13.

††[4:13–20] See note on Mt 13:18–23.

‡‡[4:26–29] Only Mark records the parable of the seed's growth. Sower and harvester are the same. The emphasis is on the power of the seed to grow of itself without human

m. [3:28] Lk 12:10.  n. [3:31–35] Mt 12:46–50; Lk 8:19–21.  o. [4:1–12] Mt 13:1–13; Lk 8:4–10.  p. [4:1] 2:13; Lk 5:1.

q. [4:12] Is 6:9; Jn 12:40; Acts 28:26; Rom 11:8.  r. [4:13–20] Mt 13:18–23; Lk 8:11–15.  s. [4:21–25] Lk 8:16–18.  t. [4:21] Mt 5:15; Lk 11:33.  u. [4:22] Mt 10:26; Lk 12:2.  v. [4:24] Mt 7:2; Lk 6:38.  w. [4:25] Mt 13:12; Lk 19:26.

were to scatter seed^x on the land ²⁷and would sleep and rise night and day and the seed would sprout and grow, he knows not how. ²⁸Of its own accord the land yields fruit, first the blade, then the ear, then the full grain in the ear. ²⁹And when the grain is ripe, he wields the sickle at once, for the harvest has come."

**The Mustard Seed.** ³⁰ʸHe said, "To what shall we compare the kingdom of God, or what parable can we use for it? ³¹It is like a mustard seed that, when it is sown in the ground, is the smallest of all the seeds on the earth. ³²*But once it is sown, it springs up and becomes the largest of plants and puts forth large branches, so that the birds of the sky can dwell in its shade." ³³With many such parables^z he spoke the word to them as they were able to understand it. ³⁴Without parables he did not speak to them, but to his own disciples he explained everything in private.

**The Calming of a Storm at Sea.** ³⁵†On that day, as evening drew on, he said to them, "Let us cross to the other side."^a ³⁶Leaving the crowd, they took him with them in the boat just as he was. And other boats were with him. ³⁷A violent squall came up and waves were breaking over the boat, so that it was already filling up. ³⁸Jesus was in the stern, asleep on a cushion. They woke him and said to him, "Teacher, do you not care that we are perishing?" ³⁹He woke up, rebuked the wind, and said to the sea, "Quiet! Be still!"‡ The wind ceased and there was great calm. ⁴⁰Then he asked them, "Why are you terrified? Do you not yet have faith?" ⁴¹ᵇThey were filled with great awe and said to one another, "Who then is this whom even wind and sea obey?"

## CHAPTER 5

**The Healing of the Gerasene Demoniac.** ¹ᶜThey came to the other side of the sea, to the territory of the Gerasenes. ²When he got out of the boat, at once a man** from the tombs who had an unclean spirit met him. ³The man had been dwelling among the tombs, and no one could restrain him any longer, even with a chain. ⁴In fact, he had frequently been bound with shackles and chains, but the chains had been pulled apart by him and the shackles smashed, and no one was strong enough to subdue him. ⁵Night and day among the tombs and on the hillsides he was always crying out and bruising himself with stones. ⁶Catching sight of Jesus from a distance, he ran up and prostrated himself before him, ⁷crying out in a loud voice, "What have you to do with me,†† Jesus, Son of the Most High God? I adjure you by God, do not torment me!" ⁸(He had been saying to him, "Unclean spirit, come out of the man!") ⁹‡‡He asked him, "What is your name?" He replied, "Legion is my name. There are many of us."^d ¹⁰And he pleaded earnestly with him not to drive them away from that territory.

¹¹Now a large herd of swine§§ was feeding there on the hillside. ¹²And they pleaded with him, "Send us into the swine. Let us enter them." ¹³And he let them, and the unclean spirits came out and entered the swine. The herd of about two thousand rushed down a steep bank into the sea, where they were drowned. ¹⁴The swineherds ran away and reported the incident in the town and throughout the countryside. And people came out to see what had happened. ¹⁵As they approached Jesus, they caught sight of the man who had been possessed by Legion, sitting there clothed and in his right mind. And they were seized with fear. ¹⁶Those who witnessed the incident explained to them what had happened to the possessed man and to the swine. ¹⁷Then they began to beg him to leave their district. ¹⁸As he was getting into the boat, the man who had been possessed pleaded to remain with him. ¹⁹But he would not permit him but told him instead, "Go home§§ to your family and announce to them all that the Lord in his pity has done for you." ²⁰Then the man went off and began to proclaim in the Decapolis what Jesus had done for him; and all were amazed.

**Jairus's Daughter and the Woman with a Hemorrhage.*** ²¹When Jesus had crossed again

---

intervention (Mk 4:27). Mysteriously it produces **blade and ear** and **full grain** (Mk 4:28). Thus the kingdom of God initiated by Jesus in proclaiming the word develops quietly yet powerfully until it is fully established by him at the final judgment (Mk 4:29); cf. Rev 14:15.

*[4:32] The universality of the kingdom of God is indicated here; cf. Ez 17:23; 31:6; Dn 4:17–19.

†[4:35–5:43] After the chapter on parables, Mark narrates four miracle stories: Mk 4:35–41; 5:1–20; and two joined together in Mk 5:21–43. See also notes on Mt 8:23–34 and 9:8–26.

‡[4:39] **Quiet! Be still!**: as in the case of silencing a demon (Mk 1:25), Jesus rebukes the wind and subdues the turbulence of the sea by a mere word; see note on Mt 8:26.

§[4:41] Jesus is here depicted as exercising power over wind and sea. In the Christian community this event was seen as a sign of Jesus' saving presence amid persecutions that threatened its existence.

¶[5:1] **The territory of the Gerasenes**: the reference is to pagan territory; cf. Is 65:1. Another reading is "Gadarenes"; see note on Mt 8:28.

**[5:2–6] The man was an outcast from society, dominated by unclean spirits (Mk 5:8, 13), living among the tombs. The prostration before Jesus (Mk 5:6) indicates Jesus' power over evil spirits.

††[5:7] **What have you to do with me?**: cf. Mk 1:24 and see note on Jn 2:4.

‡‡[5:9] **Legion is my name**: the demons were numerous and the condition of the possessed man was extremely serious; cf. Mt 12:45.

§§[5:11] **Herd of swine**: see note on Mt 8:30.

¶¶[5:19] **Go home**: Jesus did not accept the man's request to remain with him as a disciple (Mk 5:18), yet invited him to announce to his own people what the Lord had done for him, i.e., proclaim the gospel message to his pagan family; cf. Mk 1:14, 39; 3:14; 13:10.

***[5:21–43] The story of the raising to life of Jairus's daughter is divided into two parts: Mk 5:21–24; 5:35–43.

---

x. [4:26–29] Jas 5:7. y. [4:30–32] Mt 13:31–32; Lk 13:18–19. z. [4:33–34] Mt 13:34. a. [4:35–40] Mt 8:18, 23–37; Lk 8:22–25. b. [4:41] 1:27. c. [5:1–20] Mt 8:28–34; Lk 8:26–39.

d. [5:9] Mt 12:45; Lk 8:2; 11:26.

[in the boat] to the other side, a large crowd gathered around him, and he stayed close to the sea.ᵉ ²²One of the synagogue officials, named Jairus, came forward.ᶠ Seeing him he fell at his feet ²³and pleaded earnestly with him, saying, "My daughter is at the point of death. Please, come lay your hands on her* that she may get well and live." ²⁴He went off with him, and a large crowd followed him and pressed upon him.

²⁵There was a woman afflicted with hemorrhages for twelve years. ²⁶She had suffered greatly at the hands of many doctors and had spent all that she had. Yet she was not helped but only grew worse. ²⁷She had heard about Jesus and came up behind him in the crowd and touched his cloak. ²⁸ᵗShe said, "If I but touch his clothes, I shall be cured." ²⁹Immediately her flow of blood dried up. She felt in her body that she was healed of her affliction. ³⁰Jesus, aware at once that power had gone out from him, turned around in the crowd and asked, "Who has touched my clothes?" ³¹But his disciples said to him, "You see how the crowd is pressing upon you, and yet you ask, 'Who touched me?'" ³²And he looked around to see who had done it. ³³The woman, realizing what had happened to her, approached in fear and trembling. She fell down before Jesus and told him the whole truth. ³⁴He said to her, "Daughter, your faith has saved you. Go in peace and be cured of your affliction."ᵍ

³⁵ᵗWhile he was still speaking, people from the synagogue official's house arrived and said, "Your daughter has died; why trouble the teacher any longer?" ³⁶Disregarding the message that was reported, Jesus said to the synagogue official, "Do not be afraid; just have faith." ³⁷He did not allow anyone to accompany him inside except Peter, James, and John, the brother of James. ³⁸When they arrived at the house of the synagogue official, he caught sight of a commotion, people weeping and wailing loudly. ³⁹ᵍʰSo he went in and said to them, "Why this commotion and weeping? The child is not dead but asleep." ⁴⁰And they ridiculed him. Then he put

them all out. He took along the child's father and mother and those who were with him and entered the room where the child was. ⁴¹¶He took the child by the hand and said to her, "*Talitha koum*," which means, "Little girl, I say to you, arise!" ⁴²The girl, a child of twelve, arose immediately and walked around. [At that] they were utterly astounded. ⁴³He gave strict orders that no one should know this and said that she should be given something to eat.

## CHAPTER 6

**The Rejection at Nazareth.** ¹ⁱHe departed from there and came to his native place,** accompanied by his disciples. ²ᵗᵗWhen the sabbath came he began to teach in the synagogue, and many who heard him were astonished. They said, "Where did this man get all this? What kind of wisdom¹ has been given him? What mighty deeds are wrought by his hands! ³Is he not the carpenter,‡‡ the son of Mary, and the brother of James and Joses and Judas and Simon? And are not his sisters here with us?" And they took offense at him. ⁴§§ᵏJesus said to them, "A prophet is not without honor except in his native place and among his own kin and in his own house." ⁵So he was not able to perform any mighty deed there,¶¶ apart from curing a few sick people by

---

¶[5:41] **Arise**: the Greek verb *egeirein* is the verb generally used to express resurrection from death (Mk 6:14, 16; Mt 11:5; Lk 7:14) and Jesus' own resurrection (Mk 16:6; Mt 28:6; Lk 24:6).

**[6:1] **His native place**: the Greek word *patris* here refers to Nazareth (cf. Mk 1:9; Lk 4:16, 23–24) though it can also mean native land.

††[6:2–6] See note on Mt 13:54–58.

‡‡[6:3] **Is he not the carpenter?**: no other gospel calls Jesus a carpenter. Some witnesses have "the carpenter's son," as in Mt 13:55. **Son of Mary**: contrary to Jewish custom, which calls a man the son of his father, this expression may reflect Mark's own faith that God is the Father of Jesus (Mk 1:1, 11; 8:38; 13:32; 14:36). **The brother of James . . . Simon**: in Semitic usage, the terms "brother," "sister" are applied not only to children of the same parents, but to nephews, nieces, cousins, half-brothers, and half-sisters; cf. Gn 14:16; 29:15; Lv 10:4. While one cannot suppose that the meaning of a Greek word should be sought in the first place from Semitic usage, the Septuagint often translates the Hebrew *āh* by the Greek word *adelphos*, "brother," as in the cited passages, a fact that may argue for a similar breadth of meaning in some New Testament passages. For instance, there is no doubt that in v 17, "brother" is used of Philip, who was actually the half-brother of Herod Antipas. On the other hand, Mark may have understood the terms literally; see also Mk 3:31–32; Mt 12:46; 13:55–56; Lk 8:19; Jn 7:3, 5. The question of meaning here would not have arisen but for the faith of the church in Mary's perpetual virginity.

§§[6:4] **A prophet is not without honor except . . . in his own house**: a saying that finds parallels in other literatures, especially Jewish and Greek, but without reference to a prophet. Comparing himself to previous Hebrew prophets whom the people rejected, Jesus intimates his own eventual rejection by the nation especially in view of the dishonor his own relatives had shown him (Mk 3:21) and now his townspeople as well.

¶¶[6:5] **He was not able to perform any mighty deed there**: according to Mark, Jesus' power could not take effect because of a person's lack of faith.

---

Between these two separated parts the account of the cure of the hemorrhage victim (Mk 5:25–34) is interposed. This technique of intercalating or sandwiching one story within another occurs several times in Mk 3:19b–21; 3:22–30; 3:31–35; 6:6b–13; 6:14–29; 6:30; 11:12–14; 11:15–19; 11:20–25; 14:53; 14:54; 14:55–65; 14:66–73.

*[5:23] **Lay your hands on her**: this act for the purpose of healing is frequent in Mk 6:5; 7:32–35; 8:23–25; 16:18 and is also found in Mt 9:18; Lk 4:40; 13:13; Acts 9:17; 28:8.

†[5:28] Both in the case of Jairus and his daughter (Mk 5:23) and in the case of the hemorrhage victim, the inner conviction that physical contact (Mk 5:30) accompanied by faith in Jesus' saving power could effect a cure was rewarded.

‡[5:35] The faith of Jairus was put to a twofold test: (1) that his daughter might be cured and, now that she had died, (2) that she might be restored to life. His faith contrasts with the lack of faith of the crowd.

§[5:39] **Not dead but asleep**: the New Testament often refers to death as sleep (Mt 27:52; Jn 11:11; 1 Cor 15:6; 1 Thes 4:13–15); see note on Mt 9:24.

---

e. [5:21] 2:13.   f. [5:22–43] Mt 9:18–26; Lk 8:41–56.   g. [5:34] Lk 7:30.   h. [5:39–40] Acts 9:40.

i. [6:1–6] Mt 13:54–58; Lk 4:16–30.   j. [6:3] 15:40; Mt 12:46; Jn 6:42.   k. [6:4] Jn 4:44.

laying his hands on them. ⁶He was amazed at their lack of faith.

**The Mission of the Twelve.** He went around to the villages in the vicinity teaching. ⁷He summoned the Twelve* and began to send them out two by two and gave them authority over unclean spirits. ⁸†He instructed them to take nothing for the journey but a walking stick—no food, no sack, no money in their belts. ⁹They were, however, to wear sandals but not a second tunic. ¹⁰‡He said to them, "Wherever you enter a house, stay there until you leave from there. ¹¹Whatever place does not welcome you or listen to you, leave there and shake the dust off your feet in testimony against them." ¹²So they went off and preached repentance. ¹³§They drove out many demons, and they anointed with oil many who were sick^m and cured them.

**Herod's Opinion of Jesus.**¶ ¹⁴King Herod" heard about it, for his fame had become widespread, and people were saying,ⁿ "John the Baptist has been raised from the dead; that is why mighty powers are at work in him."ᵒ ¹⁵Others were saying, "He is Elijah"; still others, "He is a prophet like any of the prophets."ᵖ ¹⁶But when Herod learned of it, he said, "It is John whom I beheaded. He has been raised up."

**The Death of John the Baptist.**†† ¹⁷Herod was the one who had John arrested and bound in prison on account of Herodias, the wife of his brother

Philip, whom he had married.�q ¹⁸John had said to Herod, "It is not lawful for you to have your brother's wife."ʳ ¹⁹Herodias‡‡ harbored a grudge against him and wanted to kill him but was unable to do so. ²⁰Herod feared John, knowing him to be a righteous and holy man, and kept him in custody. When he heard him speak he was very much perplexed, yet he liked to listen to him. ²¹She had an opportunity one day when Herod, on his birthday, gave a banquet for his courtiers, his military officers, and the leading men of Galilee. ²²Herodias's own daughter came in and performed a dance that delighted Herod and his guests. The king said to the girl, "Ask of me whatever you wish and I will grant it to you." ²³He even swore [many things] to her, "I will grant you whatever you ask of me, even to half of my kingdom."ˢ ²⁴She went out and said to her mother, "What shall I ask for?" She replied, "The head of John the Baptist." ²⁵The girl hurried back to the king's presence and made her request, "I want you to give me at once on a platter the head of John the Baptist." ²⁶The king was deeply distressed, but because of his oaths and the guests he did not wish to break his word to her. ²⁷So he promptly dispatched an executioner with orders to bring back his head. He went off and beheaded him in the prison. ²⁸He brought in the head on a platter and gave it to the girl. The girl in turn gave it to her mother. ²⁹When his disciples heard about it, they came and took his body and laid it in a tomb.

**The Return of the Twelve.** ³⁰The apostles§§ gathered together with Jesus and reported all they had done and taught.ᵘ ³¹¶¶He said to them, "Come away by yourselves to a deserted place and rest a while." People were coming and going in great numbers, and they had no opportunity even to eat.ᵛ ³²So they went off in the boat by themselves to a deserted place.ʷ ³³People saw them leaving and many came to know about it. They hastened there on foot from all the towns and arrived at the place before them.

**The Feeding of the Five Thousand.** ³⁴When he disembarked and saw the vast crowd, his heart was moved with pity for them, for they were like sheep without a shepherd; and he began to teach them many things. ³⁵***By now it was already

---

*[6:7–13] The preparation for the mission of the Twelve is seen in the call (1) of the first disciples to be fishers of men (Mk 1:16–20), (2) then of the Twelve set apart to be with Jesus and to receive authority to preach and expel demons (Mk 3:13–19). Now they are given the specific mission to exercise that authority in word and power as representatives of Jesus during the time of their formation.

†[6:8–9] In Mark the use of a **walking stick** (Mk 6:8) and **sandals** (Mk 6:9) is permitted, but not in Mt 10:10 nor in Lk 10:4. Mark does not mention any prohibition to visit pagan territory and to enter Samaritan towns. These differences indicate a certain adaptation to conditions in and outside of Palestine and suggest in Mark's account a later activity in the church. For the rest, Jesus required of his apostles a total dependence on God for food and shelter; cf. Mk 6:35–44; 8:1–9.

‡[6:10–11] Remaining in the same house as a guest (Mk 6:10) rather than moving to another offering greater comfort avoided any impression of seeking advantage for oneself and prevented dishonor to one's host. Shaking the dust off one's feet served as testimony against those who rejected the call to repentance.

§[6:13] **Anointed with oil . . . cured them**: a common medicinal remedy, but seen here as a vehicle of divine power for healing.

¶[6:14–16] The various opinions about Jesus anticipate the theme of his identity that reaches its climax in Mk 8:27–30.

**[6:14] **King Herod**: see note on Mt 14:1.

††[6:17–29] Similarities are to be noted between Mark's account of the imprisonment and death of John the Baptist in this pericope, and that of the passion of Jesus (Mk 15:1–47). Herod and Pilate, each in turn, acknowledges the holiness of life of one over whom he unjustly exercises the power of condemnation and death (Mk 6:26–27; 15:9–10, 14–15). The hatred of Herodias toward John parallels that of the Jewish leaders toward Jesus. After the deaths of John and of Jesus, well-disposed persons request the bodies of the victims of Herod and of Pilate in turn to give them respectful burial (Mk 6:29; 15:45–46).

‡‡[6:19] **Herodias**: see note on Mt 14:3.

§§[6:30] **Apostles**: here, and in some manuscripts at Mk 3:14, Mark calls apostles (i.e., those sent forth) the Twelve whom Jesus sends as his emissaries, empowering them to preach, to expel demons, and to cure the sick (Mk 6:13). Only after Pentecost is the title used in the technical sense.

¶¶[6:31–34] The withdrawal of Jesus with his disciples to a desert place to rest attracts a great number of people to follow them. Toward this people of the new exodus Jesus is moved with pity; he satisfies their spiritual hunger by teaching them many things, thus gradually showing himself the faithful shepherd of a new Israel; cf. Nm 27:17; Ez 34:15.

***[6:35–44] See note on Mt 14:13–21. Compare this section with Mk 8:1–9. The various accounts of the multiplication

---

l. [6:7–11] Mt 10:1, 9–14; Lk 9:15; 10:4–11.   m. [6:13] Jas 5:14.   n. [6:14–29] Mt 14:1–12.   o. [6:14–16] Lk 9:7–8.   p. [6:15] Mt 16:14.

q. [6:17] Lk 3:19–20.   r. [6:18] Lv 18:16.   s. [6:23] Est 5:3.   t. [6:27–28] Lk 9:9.   u. [6:30] Lk 9:10.   v. [6:31] 3:20; Mt 14:13; Lk 9:10.   w. [6:32–44] Mt 14:13–21; Lk 9:10–17; Jn 6:1–13.

late and his disciples approached him and said, "This is a deserted place and it is already very late. ³⁶Dismiss them so that they can go to the surrounding farms and villages and buy themselves something to eat." ³⁷He said to them in reply, "Give them some food yourselves." But they said to him, "Are we to buy two hundred days' wages worth of food and give it to them to eat?" ³⁸He asked them, "How many loaves do you have? Go and see." And when they had found out they said, "Five loaves and two fish." ³⁹So he gave orders to have them sit down in groups on the green grass. ⁴⁰The people took their places in rows by hundreds and by fifties. ⁴¹Then, taking the five loaves and the two fish and looking up to heaven, he said the blessing, broke the loaves, and gave them to [his] disciples to set before the people; he also divided the two fish among them all.[†] ⁴²They all ate and were satisfied. ⁴³And they picked up twelve wicker baskets full of fragments and what was left of the fish. ⁴⁴Those who ate [of the loaves] were five thousand men.

**The Walking on the Water.**[‡] ⁴⁵Then he made his disciples get into the boat[x] and precede him to the other side toward Bethsaida,[§] while he dismissed the crowd. ⁴⁶¶And when he had taken leave of them, he went off to the mountain to pray. ⁴⁷When it was evening, the boat was far out on the sea and he was alone on shore. ⁴⁸Then he saw that they were tossed about while rowing, for the wind was against them. About the fourth watch of the night, he came toward them walking on the sea.[**] He meant to pass by them. ⁴⁹But when they saw him walking on the sea, they thought it was a ghost and cried out. ⁵⁰††They had all seen him and were terrified. But at once he spoke with them, "Take courage, it is I, do not be afraid!" ⁵¹He got into the boat with them and the wind died down. They were [completely]

astounded. ⁵²They had not understood the incident of the loaves.[‡‡] On the contrary, their hearts were hardened.[y]

**The Healings at Gennesaret.** ⁵³ᶻAfter making the crossing, they came to land at Gennesaret and tied up there. ⁵⁴As they were leaving the boat, people immediately recognized him. ⁵⁵They scurried about the surrounding country and began to bring in the sick on mats to wherever they heard he was. ⁵⁶Whatever villages or towns or countryside he entered, they laid the sick in the marketplaces and begged him that they might touch only the tassel on his cloak; and as many as touched it were healed.[a]

## CHAPTER 7

**The Tradition of the Elders.**[§§] ¹Now when the Pharisees with some scribes who had come from Jerusalem gathered around him,[b] ²they observed that some of his disciples ate their meals with unclean, that is, unwashed, hands. ³(For the Pharisees and, in fact, all Jews, do not eat without carefully washing their hands,[¶¶] keeping the tradition of the elders. ⁴And on coming from the marketplace they do not eat without purifying themselves. And there are many other things that they have traditionally observed, the purification of cups and jugs and kettles [and beds].) ⁵So the Pharisees and scribes questioned him, "Why do your disciples not follow the tradition of the elders*** but instead eat a meal with unclean hands?" ⁶He responded, "Well did Isaiah prophesy about you hypocrites, as it is written:[c]

'This people honors me with their lips,
    but their hearts are far from me;
⁷ In vain do they worship me,
    teaching as doctrines human
        precepts.'

---

of loaves and fishes, two each in Mark and in Matthew and one each in Luke and in John, indicate the wide interest of the early church in their eucharistic gatherings; see, e.g., Mk 6:41; 8:6; 14:22; and recall also the sign of bread in Ex 16; Dt 8:3–16; Ps 78:24–25; 105:40; Wis 16:20–21.

*[6:40] **The people . . . in rows by hundreds and by fifties**: reminiscent of the groupings of Israelites encamped in the desert (Ex 18:21–25) and of the wilderness tradition of the prophets depicting the transformation of the wasteland into pastures where the true shepherd feeds his flock (Ez 34:25–26) and makes his people beneficiaries of messianic grace.

†[6:41] On the language of this verse as eucharistic (cf. Mk 14:22), see notes on Mt 14:19, 20. Jesus observed the Jewish table ritual of blessing God before partaking of food.

‡[6:45–52] See note on Mt 14:22–33.

§[6:45] **To the other side toward Bethsaida**: a village at the northeastern shore of the Sea of Galilee.

¶[6:46] **He went off to the mountain to pray**: see Mk 1:35–38. In Jn 6:15 Jesus withdrew to evade any involvement in the false messianic hopes of the multitude.

**[6:48] **Walking on the sea**: see notes on Mt 14:22–33 and on Jn 6:19.

††[6:50] **It is I, do not be afraid!**: literally, "I am." This may reflect the divine revelatory formula of Ex 3:14; Is 41:4, 10, 14; 43:1–3, 10, 13. Mark implies the hidden identity of Jesus as Son of God.

‡‡[6:52] **They had not understood . . . the loaves**: the revelatory character of this sign and that of the walking on the sea completely escaped the disciples. **Their hearts were hardened**: in Mk 3:5–6 hardness of heart was attributed to those who did not accept Jesus and plotted his death. Here the same disposition prevents the disciples from comprehending Jesus' self-revelation through signs; cf. Mk 8:17.

§§[7:1–23] See note on Mt 15:1–20. Against the Pharisees' narrow, legalistic, and external practices of piety in matters of purification (Mk 7:2–5), external worship (Mk 7:6–7), and observance of commandments, Jesus sets in opposition the true moral intent of the divine law (Mk 7:8–13). But he goes beyond contrasting the law and Pharisaic interpretation of it. The parable of Mk 7:14–15 in effect sets aside the law itself in respect to clean and unclean food. He thereby opens the way for unity between Jew and Gentile in the kingdom of God, intimated by Jesus' departure for pagan territory beyond Galilee. For similar contrast see Mk 2:1–3:6; 3:20–35; 6:1–6.

¶¶[7:3] **Carefully washing their hands**: refers to ritual purification.

***[7:5] **Tradition of the elders**: the body of detailed, unwritten, human laws regarded by the scribes and Pharisees to have the same binding force as that of the Mosaic law; cf. Gal 1:14.

---

y. [6:52] 4:13.  z. [6:53–56] Mt 14:34–36.  a. [6:56] 5:27–28; Acts 5:15.  b. [7:1–23] Mt 15:1–20.  c. [7:6] Is 29:13.

x. [6:45–51] Mt 14:22–32; Jn 6:15–21.

⁸"You disregard God's commandment but cling to human tradition." ⁹He went on to say, "How well you have set aside the commandment of God in order to uphold your tradition! ¹⁰For Moses said, 'Honor your father and your mother,' and 'Whoever curses father or mother shall die.'*ᵈ ¹¹Yet you say, 'If a person says to father or mother, "Any support you might have had from me is *qorban*"'* (meaning, dedicated to God), ¹²you allow him to do nothing more for his father or mother. ¹³You nullify the word of God in favor of your tradition that you have handed on. And you do many such things." ¹⁴He summoned the crowd again and said to them, "Hear me, all of you, and understand. ¹⁵Nothing that enters one from outside can defile that person; but the things that come out from within are what defile."[¹⁶]†

¹⁷‡When he got home away from the crowd his disciples questioned him about the parable. ¹⁸He said to them, "Are even you likewise without understanding? Do you not realize that everything that goes into a person from outside cannot defile, ¹⁹§§since it enters not the heart but the stomach and passes out into the latrine?" (Thus he declared all foods clean.) ²⁰"But what comes out of a person, that is what defiles. ²¹ʰFrom within people, from their hearts, come evil thoughts, unchastity, theft, murder, ²²adultery, greed, malice, deceit, licentiousness, envy, blasphemy, arrogance, folly. ²³All these evils come from within and they defile."

**The Syrophoenician Woman's Faith.** ²⁴ⁱFrom that place he went off to the district of Tyre.⁵ He entered a house and wanted no one to know about it, but he could not escape notice. ²⁵Soon a woman whose daughter had an unclean spirit heard about him. She came and fell at his feet. ²⁶The woman was a Greek, a Syrophoenician by birth, and she begged him to drive the demon out of her daughter.ʲ ²⁷He said to her, "Let the

children be fed first." For it is not right to take the food of the children and throw it to the dogs." ²⁸She replied and said to him, "Lord, even the dogs under the table eat the children's scraps." ²⁹Then he said to her, "For saying this, you may go. The demon has gone out of your daughter." ³⁰When the woman went home, she found the child lying in bed and the demon gone.

**The Healing of a Deaf Man.** ³¹ᵏAgain he left the district of Tyre and went by way of Sidon to the Sea of Galilee, into the district of the Decapolis. ³²And people brought to him a deaf man who had a speech impediment and begged him to lay his hand on him. ³³He took him off by himself away from the crowd. He put his finger into the man's ears and, spitting, touched his tongue; ³⁴then he looked up to heaven and groaned, and said to him, "*Ephphatha!*" (that is, "Be opened!") ³⁵And [immediately] the man's ears were opened, his speech impediment was removed, and he spoke plainly. ³⁶††He ordered them not to tell anyone. But the more he ordered them not to, the more they proclaimed it. ³⁷They were exceedingly astonished and they said, "He has done all things well. He makes the deaf hear and [the] mute speak."ˡ

# CHAPTER 8

**The Feeding of the Four Thousand.**‡‡ ¹In those days when there again was a great crowd without anything to eat,ᵐ he summoned the disciples and said, ²"My heart is moved with pity for the crowd, because they have been with me now for three days and have nothing to eat. ³If I send them away hungry to their homes, they will collapse on the way, and some of them have come a great distance." ⁴His disciples answered him, "Where can anyone get enough bread to satisfy them here in this deserted place?" ⁵Still he asked them, "How many loaves do you have?" "Seven," they replied. ⁶§§He ordered the crowd to sit down on the ground. Then, taking the seven loaves

---

* [7:11] **Qorban:** a formula for a gift to God, dedicating the offering to the temple, so that the giver might continue to use it for himself but not give it to others, even needy parents.

† [7:16] Mk 7:16, "Anyone who has ears to hear ought to hear," is omitted because it is lacking in some of the best Greek manuscripts and was probably transferred here by scribes from Mk 4:9, 23.

‡ [7:17] **Away from the crowd . . . the parable:** in this context of privacy the term *parable* refers to something hidden, about to be revealed to the disciples; cf. Mk 4:10–11, 34. Jesus sets the Mosaic food laws in the context of the kingdom of God where they are abrogated, and he declares moral defilement the only cause of uncleanness.

§ [7:19] **(Thus he declared all foods clean):** if this bold declaration goes back to Jesus, its force was not realized among Jewish Christians in the early church; cf. Acts 10:1–11:18.

¶ [7:24–37] The withdrawal of Jesus to the district of Tyre may have been for a respite (Mk 7:24), but he soon moved onward to Sidon and, by way of the Sea of Galilee, to the Decapolis. These districts provided a Gentile setting for the extension of his ministry of healing because the people there acknowledged his power (Mk 7:29, 37). The actions attributed to Jesus (Mk 7:33–35) were also used by healers of the time.

** [7:27–28] The figure of a household in which children at table are fed first and then their leftover food is given to the dogs under the table is used effectively to acknowledge the prior claim of the Jews to the ministry of Jesus; however, Jesus accedes to the Gentile woman's plea for the cure of her afflicted daughter because of her faith.

†† [7:36] **The more they proclaimed it:** the same verb *proclaim* attributed here to the crowd in relation to the miracles of Jesus is elsewhere used in Mark for the preaching of the gospel on the part of Jesus, of his disciples, and of the Christian community (Mk 1:14; 13:10; 14:9). Implied in the action of the crowd is a recognition of the salvific mission of Jesus; see note on Mt 11:5–6.

‡‡ [8:1–10] The two accounts of the multiplication of loaves and fishes (Mk 8:1–10; 6:31–44) have eucharistic significance. Their similarity of structure and themes but dissimilarity of detail are considered by many to refer to a single event that, however, developed in two distinct traditions, one Jewish Christian and the other Gentile Christian, since Jesus in Mark's presentation (Mk 7:24–37) has extended his saving mission to the Gentiles.

§§ [8:6] See note on Mk 6:41.

---

d. [7:10] Ex 21:17; Lv 20:9; Dt 5:16; Eph 6:2.   e. [7:14–23] Mt 15:10–20.   f. [7:17] 4:10, 13.   g. [7:19] Acts 10:15.   h. [7:21] Jer 17:9.   i. [7:24–30] Mt 15:21–28.   j. [7:26] Mt 8:29.

k. [7:31–37] Mt 15:29–31.   l. [7:37] Mt 15:31.   m. [8:1–10] 6:34–44; Mt 15:32–39.

he gave thanks, broke them, and gave them to his disciples to distribute, and they distributed them to the crowd. [7]They also had a few fish. He said the blessing over them and ordered them distributed also. [8]They ate and were satisfied. They picked up the fragments left over—seven baskets. [9]There were about four thousand people.

He dismissed them [10]and got into the boat with his disciples and came to the region of Dalmanutha.

**The Demand for a Sign.** [11]*The Pharisees came forward and began to argue with him,*[n] seeking from him a sign from heaven to test him.[o] [12]He sighed from the depth of his spirit and said, "Why does this generation seek a sign? Amen, I say to you, no sign will be given to this generation." [13]Then he left them, got into the boat again, and went off to the other shore.

**The Leaven of the Pharisees.** [14]*p*They had forgotten to bring bread, and they had only one loaf with them in the boat. [15]*He enjoined them, "Watch out, guard against the leaven of the Pharisees and the leaven of Herod." [16]They concluded among themselves that it was because they had no bread. [17]When he became aware of this he said to them, "Why do you conclude that it is because you have no bread? Do you not yet understand or comprehend? Are your hearts hardened?[q] [18]Do you have eyes and not see, ears and not hear? And do you not remember,[r] [19]when I broke the five loaves for the five thousand, how many wicker baskets full of fragments you picked up?" They answered him, "Twelve." [20]"When I broke the seven loaves for the four thousand, how many full baskets of fragments did you pick up?" They answered [him], "Seven." [21]He said to them, "Do you still not understand?"

**The Blind Man of Bethsaida.**[‡] [22]When they arrived at Bethsaida, they brought to him a blind man and begged him to touch him. [23]He took the blind man by the hand and led him outside the village. Putting spittle on his eyes he laid his hands on him and asked, "Do you see anything?"[s] [24]Looking up he replied, "I see people looking like trees and walking." [25]Then he

laid hands on his eyes a second time and he saw clearly; his sight was restored and he could see everything distinctly. [26]Then he sent him home and said, "Do not even go into the village."

## III. THE MYSTERY BEGINS TO BE REVEALED

**Peter's Confession About Jesus.**[§] [27]Now Jesus and his disciples set out for the villages of Caesarea Philippi.[t] Along the way he asked his disciples, "Who do people say that I am?" [28]They said in reply, "John the Baptist, others Elijah, still others one of the prophets." [29]And he asked them, "But who do you say that I am?" Peter said to him in reply, "You are the Messiah." [30]Then he warned them not to tell anyone about him.

**The First Prediction of the Passion.** [31]*u*He began to teach them that the Son of Man[¶] must suffer greatly and be rejected by the elders, the chief priests, and the scribes, and be killed, and rise after three days. [32]He spoke this openly. Then Peter took him aside and began to rebuke him. [33]At this he turned around and, looking at his disciples, rebuked Peter and said, "Get behind me, Satan. You are thinking not as God does, but as human beings do."

**The Conditions of Discipleship.** [34]He summoned the crowd with his disciples and said[**] to them, "Whoever wishes to come after me must

§[8:27–30] This episode is the turning point in Mark's account of Jesus in his public ministry. Popular opinions concur in regarding him as a prophet. The disciples by contrast believe him to be the Messiah. Jesus acknowledges this identification but prohibits them from making his messianic office known to avoid confusing it with ambiguous contemporary ideas on the nature of that office. See further the notes on Mt 16:13–20.

¶[8:31] Son of Man: an enigmatic title. It is used in Dn 7:13–14 has a symbol of "the saints of the Most High," the faithful Israelites who receive the everlasting kingdom from the Ancient One (God). They are represented by a human figure that contrasts with the various beasts who represent the previous kingdoms of the earth. In the Jewish apocryphal books of 1 Enoch and 4 Ezra the "Son of Man" is not, as in Daniel, a group, but a unique figure of extraordinary spiritual endowments, who will be revealed as the one through whom the everlasting kingdom decreed by God will be established. It is possible though doubtful that this individualization of the Son of Man figure had been made in Jesus' time, and therefore his use of the title in that sense is questionable. Of itself, this expression means simply a human being, or, indefinitely, someone, and there are evidences of this use in pre-Christian times. Its use in the New Testament is probably due to Jesus' speaking of himself in that way, "a human being," and the later church's taking this in the sense of the Jewish apocrypha and applying it to him with that meaning. **Rejected by the elders, the chief priests, and the scribes:** the supreme council called the Sanhedrin was made up of seventy-one members of these three groups and presided over by the high priest. It exercised authority over the Jews in religious matters. See note on Mt 8:20.

**[8:34–35] This utterance of Jesus challenges all believers to authentic discipleship and total commitment to himself through self-renunciation and acceptance of the cross of suffering, even to the sacrifice of life itself. **Whoever wishes to save his life will lose it . . . will save it:** an expression of the ambivalence of life and its contrasting destiny. Life seen as mere self-centered earthly existence and lived in denial of Christ ends in destruction, but when lived in loyalty to Christ, despite earthly death, it arrives at fullness of life.

*[8:11–12] The objection of the Pharisees that Jesus' miracles are unsatisfactory for proving the arrival of God's kingdom is comparable to the request of the crowd for a sign in Jn 6:30–31. Jesus' response shows that a sign originating in human demand will not be provided; cf. Nm 14:11, 22.

†[8:15] The leaven of the Pharisees . . . of Herod: the corruptive action of leaven (1 Cor 5:6–8; Gal 5:9) was an apt symbol of the evil dispositions both of the Pharisees (Mk 8:11–13; 7:5–13) and of Herod (Mk 6:14–29) toward Jesus. The disciples of Jesus are warned against sharing such rebellious attitudes toward Jesus; cf. Mk 8:17, 21.

‡[8:22–26] Jesus' actions and the gradual cure of the blind man probably have the same purpose as in the case of the deaf man (Mk 7:31–37). Some commentators regard the cure as an intended symbol of the gradual enlightenment of the disciples concerning Jesus' messiahship.

n. [8:11–12] Mt 12:38–39; 16:1–4.    o. [8:11] Lk 11:16.    p. [8:14–21] Mt 16:5–12; Lk 12:1.    q. [8:17] 4:13.    r. [8:18] Jer 5:21; Ez 12:2.    s. [8:23] 7:33; Jn 9:6.

t. [8:27–30] Mt 16:13–20; Lk 9:18–21.    u. [8:31–38] Mt 16:21–27; Lk 9:22–26.

deny himself, take up his cross, and follow me.[v] [35]For whoever wishes to save his life will lose it, but whoever loses his life for my sake and that of the gospel[*] will save it.[w] [36]What profit is there for one to gain the whole world and forfeit his life? [37]What could one give in exchange for his life? [38]Whoever is ashamed of me and of my words in this faithless and sinful generation, the Son of Man will be ashamed of when he comes in his Father's glory with the holy angels."[x]

## CHAPTER 9

[1y]He also said to them, "Amen, I say to you, there are some standing here who will not taste death until they see that the kingdom of God has come in power."

**The Transfiguration of Jesus.**[‡] [2]After six days Jesus took Peter, James, and John and led them up a high mountain apart by themselves.[z] And he was transfigured before them, [3]and his clothes became dazzling white, such as no fuller on earth could bleach them. [4]Then Elijah appeared to them along with Moses, and they were conversing with Jesus. [5b]Then Peter said to Jesus in reply, "Rabbi, it is good that we are here! Let us make three tents: one for you, one for Moses, and one for Elijah." [6]He hardly knew what to say, they were so terrified. [7]Then a cloud came, casting a shadow over them;[¶] then from the cloud came a voice, "This is my beloved Son. Listen to him." [8]Suddenly, looking around, they no longer saw anyone but Jesus alone with them.

**The Coming of Elijah.**[**] [9]As they were coming down from the mountain, he charged them not to relate what they had seen to anyone, except when the Son of Man had risen from the dead.[a] [10]So they kept the matter to themselves, questioning what rising from the dead meant. [11b]Then they asked him, "Why do the scribes say that Elijah must come first?" [12]He told them, "Elijah will indeed come first and restore all things, yet how is it written regarding the Son of Man that he must suffer greatly and be treated with contempt? [13]But I tell you that Elijah has come and they did to him whatever they pleased, as it is written of him."[c]

**The Healing of a Boy with a Demon.**[††] [14]When they came to the disciples,[d] they saw a large crowd around them and scribes arguing with them. [15]Immediately on seeing him, the whole crowd was utterly amazed. They ran up to him and greeted him. [16]He asked them, "What are you arguing about with them?" [17]Someone from the crowd answered him, "Teacher, I have brought to you my son possessed by a mute spirit. [18]Wherever it seizes him, it throws him down; he foams at the mouth, grinds his teeth, and becomes rigid. I asked your disciples to drive it out, but they were unable to do so." [19]He said to them in reply, "O faithless generation, how long will I be with you? How long will I endure you? Bring him to me." [20]They brought the boy to him. And when he saw him, the spirit immediately threw the boy into convulsions. As he fell to the ground, he began to roll around and foam at the mouth. [21]Then he questioned his father, "How long has this been happening to him?" He replied, "Since childhood. [22]It has often thrown him into fire and into water to kill him. But if you can do anything, have compassion on us and help us." [23]Jesus said to him, "'If you can!' Everything is possible to one who has faith." [24]Then the boy's father cried out, "I do believe, help my unbelief!" [25]Jesus, on seeing a crowd rapidly gathering, rebuked the unclean spirit and said to it, "Mute and deaf spirit, I command you: come out of him and never enter him again!" [26]Shouting and throwing the boy into convulsions, it came out. He became like a corpse, which caused many to say, "He is dead!" [27]But Jesus took him by the hand, raised him, and he stood up. [28]When he entered the house, his disciples asked him in private, "Why could

---

*[8:35] **For my sake and that of the gospel**: Mark here, as at Mk 10:29 equates Jesus with the gospel.

†[9:1] **There are some standing . . . come in power**: understood by some to refer to the establishment by God's power of his kingdom on earth in and through the church; more likely, as understood by others, a reference to the imminent parousia.

‡[9:2–8] Mark and Mt 17:1 place the transfiguration of Jesus six days after the first prediction of his passion and death and his instruction to the disciples on the doctrine of the cross; Lk 9:28 has "about eight days." Thus the transfiguration counterbalances the prediction of the passion by affording certain of the disciples insight into the divine glory that Jesus possessed. His glory will overcome his death and that of his disciples; cf. 2 Cor 3:18; 2 Pt 1:16–19. The heavenly voice (Mk 9:7) prepares the disciples to understand that in the divine plan Jesus must die ignominiously before his messianic glory is made manifest; cf. Lk 24:25–27. See further the note on Mt 17:1–8.

§[9:5] Moses and Elijah represent, respectively, law and prophecy in the Old Testament and are linked to Mount Sinai; cf. Ex 19:16–20:17; 1 Kgs 19:2, 8–14. They now appear with Jesus as witnesses to the fulfillment of the law and the prophets taking place in the person of Jesus as he appears in glory.

¶[9:7] **A cloud came, casting a shadow over them**: even the disciples enter into the mystery of his glorification. In the Old Testament the cloud covered the meeting tent, indicating the Lord's presence in the midst of his people (Ex 40:34–35) and came to rest upon the temple in Jerusalem at the time of its dedication (1 Kgs 8:10).

**[9:9–13] At the transfiguration of Jesus his disciples had seen Elijah. They were perplexed because, according to the rabbinical interpretation of Mal 3:23–24, Elijah was to come

first. Jesus' response shows that Elijah has come, in the person of John the Baptist, to prepare for the day of the Lord. Jesus **must suffer greatly and be treated with contempt** (Mk 9:12) like the Baptist (Mk 9:13); cf. Mk 6:17–29.

††[9:14–29] The disciples' failure to effect a cure seems to reflect unfavorably on Jesus (Mk 9:14–18, 22). In response Jesus exposes their lack of trust in God (Mk 9:19) and scores their lack of prayer (Mk 9:29), i.e., of conscious reliance on God's power when acting in Jesus' name. For Matthew, see note on Mt 17:14–20. Lk 9:37–43 centers attention on Jesus' sovereign power.

---

v. [8:34] Mt 10:38–39; 16:24–27; Lk 14:26–27.  w. [8:35] Jn 12:25. x. [8:38] Mt 10:33; Lk 12:8.  y. [9:1] Mt 16:28; Lk 9:27.  z. [9:2–13] Mt 17:1–13; Lk 9:28–36.

a. [9:9] 8:31.  b. [9:11–12] Is 53:3; Mal 3:23.  c. [9:13] 1 Kgs 19:2–10.  d. [9:14–29] Mt 17:14–21; Lk 9:37–43.

we not drive it out?" ²⁹He said to them, "This kind can only come out through prayer."

**The Second Prediction of the Passion.** ³⁰ᵉThey left from there and began a journey through Galilee, but he did not wish anyone to know about it.ᶠ ³¹He was teaching his disciples and telling them, "The Son of Man is to be handed over to men and they will kill him, and three days after his death he will rise." ³²But they did not understand the saying, and they were afraid to question him.

## IV. THE FULL REVELATION OF THE MYSTERY

**The Greatest in the Kingdom.**† ³³They came to Capernaum and, once inside the house, he began to ask them, "What were you arguing about on the way?"ᵍ ³⁴But they remained silent. They had been discussing among themselves on the way who was the greatest. ³⁵Then he sat down, called the Twelve, and said to them, "If anyone wishes to be first, he shall be the last of all and the servant of all."ʰ ³⁶Taking a child he placed it in their midst, and putting his arms around it he said to them, ³⁷"Whoever receives one child such as this in my name, receives me; and whoever receives me, receives not me but the One who sent me."ⁱ

**Another Exorcist.**‡ ³⁸John said to him,ʲ "Teacher, we saw someone driving out demons in your name, and we tried to prevent him because he does not follow us." ³⁹Jesus replied, "Do not prevent him. There is no one who performs a mighty deed in my name who can at the same time speak ill of me. ⁴⁰For whoever is not against us is for us.ᵏ ⁴¹Anyone who gives you a cup of water to drink because you belong to Christ, amen, I say to you, will surely not lose his reward.ˡ

**Temptations to Sin.** ⁴²ᵐ"Whoever causes one of these little ones who believe [in me] to sin, it would be better for him if a great millstone were put around his neck and he were thrown into the sea. ⁴³If your hand causes you to sin, cut it off. It is better for you to enter into life maimed than with two hands to go into Gehenna,§ into

the unquenchable fire. [⁴⁴]⁶ ⁴⁵And if your foot causes you to sin, cut it off. It is better for you to enter into life crippled than with two feet to be thrown into Gehenna. [⁴⁶] ⁴⁷And if your eye causes you to sin, pluck it out. Better for you to enter into the kingdom of God with one eye than with two eyes to be thrown into Gehenna, ⁴⁸where 'their worm does not die, and the fire is not quenched.'ⁿ

**The Simile of Salt.** ⁴⁹**"Everyone will be salted with fire. ⁵⁰Salt is good, but if salt becomes insipid, with what will you restore its flavor? Keep salt in yourselves and you will have peace with one another."ᵒ

## CHAPTER 10

**Marriage and Divorce.** ¹He set out from there and went into the district of Judea [and] across the Jordan. Again crowds gathered around him and, as was his custom, he again taught them. ²††The Pharisees approached and asked, "Is it lawful for a husband to divorce his wife?" They were testing him.ᵖ ³He said to them in reply, "What did Moses command you?" ⁴They replied, "Moses permitted him to write a bill of divorce and dismiss her."�q ⁵But Jesus told them, "Because of the hardness of your hearts he wrote you this commandment. ⁶But from the beginning of creation, 'God made them male and female.'ʳ ⁷For this reason a man shall leave his father and mother [and be joined to his wife],ˢ ⁸and the two shall become one flesh.' So they are no longer two but one flesh. ⁹Therefore what God has joined together, no human being must separate." ¹⁰In the house the disciples again questioned him about this. ¹¹He said to them, "Whoever divorces his wife and marries another commits adultery against her; ¹²and if she divorces her husband and marries another, she commits adultery."

**Blessing of the Children.** ¹³"And people were bringing children to him that he might touch them, but the disciples rebuked them.ᵛ ¹⁴When Jesus saw this he became indignant and said

---

*[9:29] **This kind can only come out through prayer**: a variant reading adds "and through fasting."

†[9:33–37] Mark probably intends this incident and the sayings that follow as commentary on the disciples' lack of understanding (Mk 9:32). Their role in Jesus' work is one of service, especially to the poor and lowly. Children were the symbol Jesus used for the *anawim*, the poor in spirit, the lowly in the Christian community.

‡[9:38–41] Jesus warns against jealousy and intolerance toward others, such as exorcists who do **not follow us**. The saying in Mk 9:40 is a broad principle of the divine tolerance. Even the smallest courtesies shown to those who teach in Jesus' name do not go unrewarded.

§[9:43, 45, 47] **Gehenna**: see note on Mt 5:22.

¶[9:44, 46] These verses, lacking in some important early manuscripts, are here omitted as scribal additions. They simply repeat Mk 9:48 itself a modified citation of Is 66:24.

**[9:49] **Everyone will be salted with fire**: so the better manuscripts. Some add "every sacrifice will be salted with salt." The purifying and preservative use of salt in food (Lv 2:13) and the refinement effected through fire refer here to comparable effects in the spiritual life of the disciples of Jesus.

††[10:2–9] In the dialogue between Jesus and the Pharisees on the subject of divorce, Jesus declares that the law of Moses permitted divorce (Dt 24:1) only **because of the hardness of your hearts** (Mk 10:4–5). In citing Gn 1:27 and 2:24 Jesus proclaims permanence to be the divine intent from the beginning concerning human marriage (Mk 10:6–8). He reaffirms this with the declaration that **what God has joined together, no human being must separate** (Mk 10:9). See further the notes on Mt 5:31–32; 19:3–9.

---

e. [9:30–32] 8:31; Mt 17:22–23; Lk 9:43–45. f. [9:30] Jn 7:1. g. [9:33–37] Mt 18:1–5; Lk 9:46–48. h. [9:35] Mt 20:27. i. [9:37] Mt 10:40; 18:5; Jn 13:20. j. [9:38–41] Nm 11:28; Lk 9:49–50; 1 Cor 12:3. k. [9:40] Mt 12:30. l. [9:41] Mt 10:42; 1 Cor 3:23. m. [9:42–47] Mt 5:29–30; 18:6–9; Lk 17:1–2.

n. [9:48] Is 66:24. o. [9:50] Lv 2:13; Mt 5:13; Lk 14:34–35; Col 4:6. p. [10:2–12] Mt 19:3–9. q. [10:4] Dt 24:1–4. r. [10:6] Gn 1:27. s. [10:7–8] Gn 2:24; 1 Cor 6:16; Eph 5:31. t. [10:11–12] Mt 5:32; Lk 16:18; 1 Cor 7:10–11. u. [10:13–16] Mt 19:13–15; Lk 18:15–17. v. [10:13] Lk 9:47.

to them, "Let the children come to me; do not prevent them, for the kingdom of God belongs to such as these. [15]Amen, I say to you, whoever does not accept the kingdom of God like a child[*] will not enter it."[w] [16]Then he embraced them and blessed them, placing his hands on them.

**The Rich Man.** [17x]As he was setting out on a journey, a man ran up, knelt down before him, and asked him, "Good teacher, what must I do to inherit eternal life?" [18]Jesus answered him, "Why do you call me good?[†] No one is good but God alone. [19]You know the commandments: 'You shall not kill; you shall not commit adultery; you shall not steal; you shall not bear false witness; you shall not defraud; honor your father and your mother.'"[y] [20]He replied and said to him, "Teacher, all of these I have observed from my youth." [21]Jesus, looking at him, loved him and said to him, "You are lacking in one thing. Go, sell what you have, and give to [the] poor and you will have treasure in heaven; then come, follow me." [22]At that statement his face fell, and he went away sad, for he had many possessions.

[23‡]Jesus looked around and said to his disciples, "How hard it is for those who have wealth to enter the kingdom of God!"[z] [24]The disciples were amazed at his words. So Jesus again said to them in reply, "Children, how hard it is to enter the kingdom of God! [25]It is easier for a camel to pass through [the] eye of [a] needle than for one who is rich to enter the kingdom of God." [26]They were exceedingly astonished and said among themselves, "Then who can be saved?" [27]Jesus looked at them and said, "For human beings it is impossible, but not for God. All things are possible for God." [28]Peter began to say to him, "We have given up everything and followed you." [29]Jesus said, "Amen, I say to you, there is no one who has given up house or brothers or sisters or mother or father or children or lands for my sake and for the sake of the gospel [30]who will not receive a hundred times more now in this present age: houses and brothers and sisters and mothers and children and lands, with persecutions, and eternal life in the age to come. [31]But many that are first will be last, and [the] last will be first."[a]

**The Third Prediction of the Passion.** [32b]They were on the way, going up to Jerusalem, and Jesus went ahead of them. They were amazed, and those who followed were afraid. Taking the Twelve aside again, he began to tell them what was going to happen to him. [33]"Behold, we are going up to Jerusalem, and the Son of Man will be handed over to the chief priests and the scribes, and they will condemn him to death and hand him over to the Gentiles [34]who will mock him, spit upon him, scourge him, and put him to death, but after three days he will rise."

**Ambition of James and John.** [35c]Then James and John, the sons of Zebedee, came to him and said to him, "Teacher, we want you to do for us whatever we ask of you." [36]He replied, "What do you wish [me] to do for you?" [37]They answered him, "Grant that in your glory we may sit one at your right and the other at your left." [38§d]Jesus said to them, "You do not know what you are asking. Can you drink the cup that I drink or be baptized with the baptism with which I am baptized?" [39]They said to him, "We can." Jesus said to them, "The cup that I drink, you will drink, and with the baptism with which I am baptized, you will be baptized; [40]but to sit at my right or at my left is not mine to give but is for those for whom it has been prepared." [41]When the ten heard this, they became indignant at James and John. [42e]Jesus summoned them and said to them,[e] "You know that those who are recognized as rulers over the Gentiles lord it over them, and their great ones make their authority over them felt. [43]But it shall not be so among you. Rather, whoever wishes to be great among you will be your servant; [44]whoever wishes to be first among you will be the slave of all. [45]For the Son of Man did not come to be served but to serve and to give his life as a ransom for many."

**The Blind Bartimaeus.**[**] [46]They came to Jericho.[f] And as he was leaving Jericho with his disciples and a sizable crowd, Bartimaeus, a blind man, the son of Timaeus, sat by the roadside begging. [47]On hearing that it was Jesus of Nazareth, he

---

*[10:15] **Whoever does not accept the kingdom of God like a child:** i.e., in total dependence upon and obedience to the gospel; cf. Mt 18:3–4.

†[10:18] **Why do you call me good?** Jesus repudiates the term "good" for himself and directs it to God, the source of all goodness who alone can grant the gift of eternal life; cf. Mt 19:16–17.

‡[10:23–27] In the Old Testament wealth and material goods are considered a sign of God's favor (Jb 1:10; Ps 128:1–2; Is 3:10). The words of Jesus in Mk 10:23–25 provoke astonishment among the disciples because of their apparent contradiction of the Old Testament concept (Mk 10:24, 26). Since wealth, power, and merit generate false security, Jesus rejects them utterly as a claim to enter the kingdom. Achievement of salvation is beyond human capability and depends solely on the goodness of God who offers it as a gift (Mk 10:27).

§[10:38–40] **Can you drink the cup . . . I am baptized?:** the metaphor of drinking the cup is used in the Old Testament to refer to acceptance of the destiny assigned by God; see note on Psalm 11:6. In Jesus' case, this involves divine judgment on sin that Jesus the innocent one is to expiate on behalf of the guilty (Mk 14:24; Is 53:5). His baptism is to be his crucifixion and death for the salvation of the human race; cf. Lk 12:50. The request of James and John for a share in the glory (Mk 10:35–37) must of necessity involve a share in Jesus' sufferings, the endurance of tribulation and suffering for the gospel (Mk 10:39). The authority of assigning places of honor in the kingdom is reserved to God (Mk 10:40).

¶[10:42–45] Whatever authority is to be exercised by the disciples must, like that of Jesus, be rendered as service to others (Mk 10:45) rather than for personal aggrandizement (Mk 10:42–44). The service of Jesus is his passion and death for the sins of the human race (Mk 10:45); cf. Mk 14:24; Is 53:11–12; Mt 26:28; Lk 22:19–20.

**[10:46–52] See notes on Mt 9:27–31 and 20:29–34.

---

w. [10:15] Mt 18:3.  x. [10:17–31] Mt 19:16–30; Lk 18:18–30.
y. [10:19] Ex 20:12–16; Dt 5:16–21.  z. [10:23] Prv 11:28.
a. [10:31] Mt 19:30; Lk 13:30.

b. [10:32–34] 8:31; Mt 20:17–19; Lk 18:31–33.  c. [10:35–45] Mt 20:20–28.  d. [10:38] Lk 12:50.  e. [10:42–45] Lk 22:25–27.
f. [10:46–52] Mt 20:29–34; Lk 18:35–43.

began to cry out and say, "Jesus, son of David, have pity on me." [48]And many rebuked him, telling him to be silent. But he kept calling out all the more, "Son of David, have pity on me." [49]Jesus stopped and said, "Call him." So they called the blind man, saying to him, "Take courage; get up, he is calling you." [50]He threw aside his cloak, sprang up, and came to Jesus. [51]Jesus said to him in reply, "What do you want me to do for you?" The blind man replied to him, "Master, I want to see." [52]Jesus told him, "Go your way; your faith has saved you." Immediately he received his sight and followed him on the way.

## CHAPTER 11

**The Entry into Jerusalem.**[*] [1]When they drew near to Jerusalem,[g] to Bethphage and Bethany at the Mount of Olives, he sent two of his disciples [2]and said to them, "Go into the village opposite you, and immediately on entering it, you will find a colt tethered on which no one has ever sat. Untie it and bring it here. [3]If anyone should say to you, 'Why are you doing this?' reply, 'The Master has need of it and will send it back here at once.'" [4]So they went off and found a colt tethered at a gate outside on the street, and they untied it. [5]Some of the bystanders said to them, "What are you doing, untying the colt?" [6]They answered them just as Jesus had told them to, and they permitted them to do it. [7]So they brought the colt to Jesus and put their cloaks over it. And he sat on it. [8]Many people spread their cloaks on the road, and others spread leafy branches that they had cut from the fields. [9]Those preceding him as well as those following kept crying out:[h]

"Hosanna!
    Blessed is he who comes in the
        name of the Lord!
[10]    Blessed is the kingdom of our father
        David that is to come!
Hosanna in the highest!"

[11]He entered Jerusalem and went into the temple area. He looked around at everything and, since it was already late, went out to Bethany with the Twelve.[i]

**Jesus Curses a Fig Tree.**[†] [12]The next day as they were leaving Bethany he was hungry.[j] [13]Seeing

from a distance a fig tree in leaf, he went over to see if he could find anything on it. When he reached it he found nothing but leaves; it was not the time for figs. [14]And he said to it in reply, "May no one ever eat of your fruit again!" And his disciples heard it.

**Cleansing of the Temple.**[‡] [15]They came to Jerusalem,[k] and on entering the temple area he began to drive out those selling and buying there. He overturned the tables of the money changers and the seats of those who were selling doves. [16]He did not permit anyone to carry anything through the temple area. [17]Then he taught them saying, "Is it not written:

'My house shall be called a house of
        prayer for all peoples'?
But you have made it a den of
        thieves."[l]

[18]The chief priests and the scribes came to hear of it and were seeking a way to put him to death, yet they feared him because the whole crowd was astonished at his teaching. [19]When evening came, they went out of the city.

**The Withered Fig Tree.** [20n]Early in the morning, as they were walking along, they saw the fig tree withered to its roots. [21]Peter remembered and said to him, "Rabbi, look! The fig tree that you cursed has withered." [22]Jesus said to them in reply, "Have faith in God. [23]Amen, I say to you, whoever says to this mountain, 'Be lifted up and thrown into the sea,' and does not doubt in his heart but believes that what he says will happen, it shall be done for him.[o] [24]Therefore I tell you, all that you ask for in prayer, believe that you will receive it and it shall be yours.[p] [25]When you stand to pray, forgive anyone against whom you have a grievance, so that your heavenly Father may in turn forgive you your transgressions."[q] [[26]][§]

**The Authority of Jesus Questioned.**[¶] [27]They returned once more to Jerusalem.[r] As he was walking in the temple area, the chief priests, the scribes, and the elders approached him [28]and said to him, "By what authority are you doing

---

in action representing Jesus' judgment (Mk 11:20) on barren Israel and the fate of Jerusalem for failing to receive his teaching; cf. Is 34:4; Hos 2:14; Lk 13:6–9.

‡[11:15–19] See note on Mt 21:12–17.

§[11:26] This verse, which reads, "But if you do not forgive, neither will your heavenly Father forgive your transgressions," is omitted in the best manuscripts. It was probably added by copyists under the influence of Mt 6:15.

¶[11:27–33] The mounting hostility toward Jesus came from the chief priests, the scribes, and the elders (Mk 11:27); the Herodians and the Pharisees (Mk 12:13); and the Sadducees (Mk 12:18). By their rejection of God's messengers, John the Baptist and Jesus, they incurred the divine judgment implied in Mk 11:27–33 and confirmed in the parable of the vineyard tenants (Mk 12:1–12).

*[11:1–11] In Mark's account Jesus takes the initiative in ordering the preparation for his entry into Jerusalem (Mk 11:1–6) even as he later orders the preparation of his last Passover supper (Mk 14:12–16). In Mk 10:9–10 the greeting Jesus receives stops short of proclaiming him Messiah. He is greeted rather as the prophet of the coming messianic kingdom. Contrast Mt 21:9.

†[11:12–14] Jesus' search for fruit on the fig tree recalls the prophets' earlier use of this image to designate Israel; cf. Jer 8:13; 29:17; Jl 1:7; Hos 9:10, 16. Cursing the fig tree is a parable

g. [11:1–10] Mt 21:1–9; Lk 19:29–38; Jn 12:12–15.  h. [11:9–10] 2 Sm 7:16; Ps 118:26.  i. [11:11] Mt 21:10, 17.  j. [11:12–14] Mt 21:18–20; Lk 13:6–9.

k. [11:15–18] Mt 21:12–13; Lk 19:45–46; Jn 2:14–16.  l. [11:17] Is 56:7; Jer 7:11.  m. [11:19] Lk 21:37.  n. [11:20–24] Mt 21:20–22.  o. [11:23] Mt 17:20–21; Lk 17:6.  p. [11:24] Mt 7:7; Jn 11:22; 14:13.  q. [11:25] Mt 6:14; 18:35.  r. [11:27–33] Mt 21:23–27; Lk 20:1–8.

these things? Or who gave you this authority to do them?" [29]Jesus said to them, "I shall ask you one question. Answer me, and I will tell you by what authority I do these things. [30]Was John's baptism of heavenly or of human origin? Answer me." [31]They discussed this among themselves and said, "If we say, 'Of heavenly origin,' he will say, '[Then] why did you not believe him?' [32]But shall we say, 'Of human origin'?"— they feared the crowd, for they all thought John really was a prophet. [33]So they said to Jesus in reply, "We do not know." Then Jesus said to them, "Neither shall I tell you by what authority I do these things."

## CHAPTER 12

**Parable of the Tenants.**[*] [1]He began to speak to them in parables.[s] "A man planted a vineyard, put a hedge around it, dug a wine press, and built a tower. Then he leased it to tenant farmers and left on a journey.[t] [2]At the proper time he sent a servant to the tenants to obtain from them some of the produce of the vineyard. [3]But they seized him, beat him, and sent him away empty-handed. [4]Again he sent them another servant. And that one they beat over the head and treated shamefully. [5]He sent yet another whom they killed. So, too, many others; some they beat, others they killed. [6]He had one other to send, a beloved son. He sent him to them last of all, thinking, 'They will respect my son.' [7]But those tenants said to one another, 'This is the heir. Come, let us kill him, and the inheritance will be ours.' [8]So they seized him and killed him, and threw him out of the vineyard. [9]What [then] will the owner of the vineyard do? He will come, put the tenants to death, and give the vineyard to others. [10]Have you not read this scripture passage:[u]

'The stone that the builders rejected
　　has become the cornerstone;
[11]　by the Lord has this been done,
　　and it is wonderful in our eyes'?"

[12]They were seeking to arrest him, but they feared the crowd, for they realized that he had addressed the parable to them. So they left him and went away.

**Paying Taxes to the Emperor.** [13][†]They sent some Pharisees[v] and Herodians to him to ensnare

him[w] in his speech.[‡] [14]They came and said to him, "Teacher, we know that you are a truthful man and that you are not concerned with anyone's opinion. You do not regard a person's status but teach the way of God in accordance with the truth. Is it lawful to pay the census tax to Caesar or not? Should we pay or should we not pay?" [15]Knowing their hypocrisy he said to them, "Why are you testing me? Bring me a denarius to look at." [16]They brought one to him and he said to them, "Whose image and inscription is this?" They replied to him, "Caesar's." [17]So Jesus said to them, "Repay to Caesar what belongs to Caesar and to God what belongs to God." They were utterly amazed at him.[x]

**The Question About the Resurrection.**[§] [18]Some Sadducees, who say there is no resurrection, came to him and put this question to him, [19]saying, "Teacher, Moses wrote for us, 'If someone's brother dies, leaving a wife but no child, his brother must take the wife and raise up descendants for his brother.'[y] [20]Now there were seven brothers. The first married a woman and died, leaving no descendants. [21]So the second married her and died, leaving no descendants, and the third likewise. [22]And the seven left no descendants. Last of all the woman also died. [23]At the resurrection [when they arise] whose wife will she be? For all seven had been married to her." [24]Jesus said to them, "Are you not misled because you do not know the scriptures or the power of God? [25]When they rise from the dead, they neither marry nor are given in marriage, but they are like the angels in heaven. [26]As for the dead being raised, have you not read in the Book of Moses, in the passage about the bush, how God told him, 'I am the God of Abraham, [the] God of Isaac, and [the] God of Jacob'?[z] [27]He is not God of the dead but of the living. You are greatly misled."

**The Greatest Commandment.**[¶] [28]One of the scribes,[a] when he came forward and heard them disputing and saw how well he had answered them, asked him, "Which is the first of all the commandments?" [29]Jesus replied, "The first is this: 'Hear, O Israel! The Lord our God is Lord alone! [30]You shall love the Lord your God with all your heart, with all your soul, with all your mind, and with all your strength.'[b] [31]The second is this: 'You shall love your neighbor as yourself.' There is no other commandment greater than these."[c] [32]The scribe said to him, "Well said, teacher. You are right in saying, 'He is One and there is no other than he.' [33]And 'to love him with all your heart, with all your understanding, with all your strength, and to love your neighbor as

---

*[12:1–12] The vineyard denotes Israel (Is 5:1–7). The tenant farmers are the religious leaders of Israel. God is the owner of the vineyard. His servants are his messengers, the prophets. The beloved son is Jesus (Mk 1:11; 9:7; Mt 3:17; 17:5; Lk 3:22; 9:35). The punishment of the tenants refers to the religious leaders, and the transfer of the vineyard to others refers to the people of the new Israel.

†[12:13–34] In the ensuing conflicts (cf. also Mk 2:1–3:6) Jesus vanquishes his adversaries by his responses to their questions and reduces them to silence (Mk 12:34).

‡[12:13–17] See note on Mt 22:15–22.

§[12:18–27] See note on Mt 22:23–33.

¶[12:28–34] See note on Mt 22:34–40.

s. [12:1–12] Mt 21:33–46; Lk 20:9–19.   t. [12:1] Is 5:1–7; Jer 2:21.   u. [12:10–11] Ps 118:22–23; Is 28:16.   v. [12:13–27] Mt 22:15–33; Lk 20:20–39.

w. [12:13]3:6.   x. [12:17]Rom 13:7.   y. [12:19]Dt 25:5.   z. [12:26] Ex 3:6.   a. [12:28–34] Mt 22:34–40; Lk 10:25–28.   b. [12:30] Dt 6:4–5.   c. [12:31] Lv 18:18; Rom 13:9; Gal 5:14; Jas 2:8.

yourself' is worth more than all burnt offerings and sacrifices."^d ^34And when Jesus saw that [he] answered with understanding, he said to him, "You are not far from the kingdom of God." And no one dared to ask him any more questions.^e

**The Question About David's Son.**^* ^35As Jesus was teaching in the temple area he said,^f "How do the scribes claim that the Messiah is the son of David? ^36David himself, inspired by the holy Spirit, said:

> 'The Lord said to my lord,
> "Sit at my right hand
>    until I place your enemies under
>       your feet."'^g

^37David himself calls him 'lord'; so how is he his son?" [The] great crowd heard this with delight.

**Denunciation of the Scribes.**^† ^38In the course of his teaching he said,^h "Beware of the scribes, who like to go around in long robes and accept greetings in the marketplaces, ^39seats of honor in synagogues, and places of honor at banquets. ^40They devour the houses of widows and, as a pretext, recite lengthy prayers. They will receive a very severe condemnation."

**The Poor Widow's Contribution.**^‡ ^41He sat down opposite the treasury and observed how the crowd put money into the treasury.^i Many rich people put in large sums. ^42A poor widow also came and put in two small coins worth a few cents. ^43Calling his disciples to himself, he said to them, "Amen, I say to you, this poor widow put in more than all the other contributors to the treasury. ^44For they have all contributed from their surplus wealth, but she, from her poverty, has contributed all she had, her whole livelihood."

## CHAPTER 13

**The Destruction of the Temple Foretold.**^§ ^1As he was making his way out of the temple area one of his disciples said to him, "Look, teacher, what stones and what buildings!"^j ^2Jesus said to him, "Do you see these great buildings? There will not be one stone left upon another that will not be thrown down."

**The Signs of the End.** ^3As he was sitting on the Mount of Olives opposite the temple area, Peter, James, John, and Andrew asked him privately,^k ^4"Tell us, when will this happen, and what sign will there be when all these things are about to come to an end?" ^5Jesus began to say to them, "See that no one deceives you.^l ^6Many will come in my name saying, 'I am he,' and they will deceive many. ^7When you hear of wars and reports of wars do not be alarmed; such things must happen, but it will not yet be the end. ^8Nation will rise against nation and kingdom against kingdom. There will be earthquakes from place to place and there will be famines. These are the beginnings of the labor pains.

**The Coming Persecution.** ^9m"Watch out for yourselves. They will hand you over to the courts. You will be beaten in synagogues. You will be arraigned before governors and kings because of me, as a witness before them. ^10But the gospel must first be preached to all nations."^** ^11When they lead you away and hand you over, do not worry beforehand about what you are to say.^n But say whatever will be given to you at that hour. For it will not be you who are speaking but the holy Spirit. ^12Brother will hand over brother to death, and the father his child; children will rise up against parents and have them put to death. ^13You will be hated by all because of my name. But the one who perseveres to the end will be saved.

**The Great Tribulation.** ^14o"When you see the desolating abomination standing^†† where he should not (let the reader understand), then those in Judea must flee to the mountains,^p ^15[and] a person on a housetop must not go down or enter to get anything out of his house,^q ^16and a person in a field must not return to get his cloak. ^17Woe to pregnant women and nursing mothers in those days. ^18Pray that this does not happen in winter. ^19For those times will have tribulation such as has not been since the

---

§ [13:3–37] Jesus' prediction of the destruction of the temple (Mk 13:2) provoked questions that the four named disciples put to him in private regarding the time and the sign when all **these things are about to come to an end** (Mk 13:3–4). The response to their questions was Jesus' eschatological discourse prior to his imminent death. It contained instruction and consolation exhorting the disciples and the church to faith and obedience through the trials that would confront them (Mk 13:5–13). The sign is the presence of **the desolating abomination** (Mk 13:14; see Dn 9:27), i.e., of the Roman power profaning the temple. Flight from Jerusalem is urged rather than defense of the city through misguided messianic hope (Mk 13:14–23). Intervention will occur only after destruction (Mk 13:24–27), which will happen before the end of the first Christian generation (Mk 13:28–31). No one but the Father knows the precise time, or that of the parousia (Mk 13:32); hence the necessity of constant vigilance (Mk 13:33–37). Luke sets the parousia at a later date, after "the time of the Gentiles" (Lk 21:24). See also notes on Mt 24:1–25:46.

** [13:10] **The gospel . . . to all nations**: the period of the Christian mission.

†† [13:14] The participle **standing** is masculine, in contrast to the neuter at Mt 24:15.

---

\* [12:35–37] Jesus questions the claim of the scribes about the Davidic descent of the Messiah, not to deny it (Mt 1:1; Acts 2:20, 34; Rom 1:3; 2 Tm 2:8) but to imply that he is more than this. His superiority derives from his transcendent origin, to which David himself attested when he spoke of the Messiah with the name "Lord" (Ps 110:1). See also note on Mt 22:41–46.

† [12:38–40] See notes on Mk 7:1–23 and Mt 23:1–39.

‡ [12:41–44] See note on Lk 21:1–4.

§ [13:1–2] The reconstructed temple with its precincts, begun under Herod the Great ca. 20 B.C., was completed only some seven years before it was destroyed by fire in A.D. 70 at the hands of the Romans; cf. Jer 26:18; Mt 24:1–2. For the dating of the reconstruction of the temple, see further the note on Jn 2:20.

---

d. [12:33] Dt 6:4; Ps 40:7–9.  e. [12:34] Mt 22:46; Lk 20:40.  f. [12:35–37] Mt 22:41–45; Lk 20:41–44.  g. [12:36] Ps 110:1.  h. [12:38–40] Mt 23:1–7; Lk 11:43; 20:45–47.  i. [12:41–44] Lk 21:1–4.  j. [13:1–2] Mt 24:1–2; Lk 21:5–6.

k. [13:3–8] Mt 24:3–8; Lk 21:7–11.  l. [13:5] Eph 5:6; 2 Thes 2:3.  m. [13:9–13] Mt 24:9–14; Lk 21:12–19.  n. [13:11–12] Mt 10:19–22; Lk 12:11–12.  o. [13:14–23] Mt 24:15–22; Lk 21:20–24.  p. [13:14] Dn 9:27; Mt 24:15.  q. [13:15] Lk 17:31.

beginning of God's creation until now, nor ever will be.[r] [20]If the Lord had not shortened those days, no one would be saved; but for the sake of the elect whom he chose, he did shorten the days. [21]If anyone says to you then, 'Look, here is the Messiah! Look, there he is!' do not believe it. [22]False messiahs and false prophets will arise and will perform signs and wonders in order to mislead, if that were possible, the elect. [23]Be watchful! I have told it all to you beforehand.

**The Coming of the Son of Man.** [24s]"But in those days after that tribulation

the sun will be darkened,
and the moon will not give its light,[t]
[25] and the stars will be falling from the sky,
and the powers in the heavens will be shaken.

[26*u]And then they will see 'the Son of Man coming in the clouds' with great power and glory, [27]and then he will send out the angels and gather [his] elect from the four winds, from the end of the earth to the end of the sky.

**The Lesson of the Fig Tree.** [28v]"Learn a lesson from the fig tree. When its branch becomes tender and sprouts leaves, you know that summer is near. [29]In the same way, when you see these things happening, know that he is near, at the gates. [30]Amen, I say to you, this generation will not pass away until all these things have taken place. [31]Heaven and earth will pass away, but my words will not pass away.

**Need for Watchfulness.** [32]"But of that day or hour, no one knows, neither the angels in heaven, nor the Son, but only the Father. [33w]Be watchful! Be alert! You do not know when the time will come. [34]It is like a man traveling abroad. He leaves home and places his servants in charge, each with his work, and orders the gatekeeper to be on the watch.[x] [35]Watch, therefore; you do not know when the lord of the house is coming, whether in the evening, or at midnight, or at cockcrow, or in the morning. [36]May he not come suddenly and find you sleeping. [37]What I say to you, I say to all: 'Watch!'"

## CHAPTER 14

**The Conspiracy Against Jesus.** [1†]The Passover and the Feast of Unleavened Bread[‡] were to take

place in two days' time.[y] So the chief priests and the scribes were seeking a way to arrest him by treachery and put him to death. [2]They said, "Not during the festival, for fear that there may be a riot among the people."

**The Anointing at Bethany.**[§] [3]When he was in Bethany reclining at table in the house of Simon the leper,[z] a woman came with an alabaster jar of perfumed oil, costly genuine spikenard. She broke the alabaster jar and poured it on his head. [4]There were some who were indignant. "Why has there been this waste of perfumed oil? [5]It could have been sold for more than three hundred days' wages and the money given to the poor." They were infuriated with her. [6]Jesus said, "Let her alone. Why do you make trouble for her? She has done a good thing for me. [7]The poor you will always have with you, and whenever you wish you can do good to them, but you will not always have me. [8]She has done what she could. She has anticipated anointing my body for burial. [9]Amen, I say to you, wherever the gospel is proclaimed to the whole world, what she has done will be told in memory of her."

**The Betrayal by Judas.** [10a]Then Judas Iscariot, one of the Twelve, went off to the chief priests to hand him over to them. [11]When they heard him they were pleased and promised to pay him money. Then he looked for an opportunity to hand him over.

**Preparations for the Passover.** [12b]On the first day of the Feast of Unleavened Bread, when they sacrificed the Passover lamb,[¶] his disciples said to him, "Where do you want us to go and prepare for you to eat the Passover?" [13]He sent two of his disciples and said to them, "Go into the city and a man will meet you, carrying a jar

12:3–20; 34:18; Lv 23:4–8; Nm 9:2–14; 28:16–17; Dt 16:1–8. The Passover commemorated the redemption from slavery and the departure of the Israelites from Egypt by night. It began at sundown after the Passover lamb was sacrificed in the temple in the afternoon of the fourteenth day of the month of Nisan. With the Passover supper on the same evening was associated the eating of unleavened bread. The latter was continued through Nisan 21, a reminder of the affliction of the Israelites and of the haste surrounding their departure. Praise and thanks to God for his goodness in the past were combined at this dual festival with the hope of future salvation. **The chief priests . . . to death:** the intent to put Jesus to death was plotted for a long time but delayed for fear of the crowd (Mk 3:6; 11:18; 12:12).

§[14:3] At Bethany on the Mount of Olives, a few miles from Jerusalem, in **the house of Simon the leper,** Jesus defends a woman's loving action of anointing his head with perfumed oil in view of his impending death and burial as a criminal, in which case his body would not be anointed. See further the note on Jn 12:7. He assures the woman of the remembrance of her deed in the worldwide preaching of the good news.

¶[14:12] **The first day of the Feast of Unleavened Bread . . . the Passover lamb:** a less precise designation of the day for sacrificing the Passover lamb as evidenced by some rabbinical literature. For a more exact designation, see note on Mk 14:1. It was actually Nisan 14.

---

*[13:26] **Son of Man . . . with great power and glory:** Jesus cites this text from Dn 7:13 in his response to the high priest, **Are you the Messiah?** (Mk 14:61). In Ex 34:5; Lv 16:2; and Nm 11:25 the clouds indicate the presence of the divinity. Thus in his role of Son of Man, Jesus is a heavenly being who will come in power and glory.

†[14:1–16:8] In the movement of Mark's gospel the cross is depicted as Jesus' way to glory in accordance with the divine will. Thus the passion narrative is seen as the climax of Jesus' ministry.

‡[14:1] **The Passover and the Feast of Unleavened Bread:** the connection between the two festivals is reflected in Ex

r. [13:19] Dn 12:1.   s. [13:24–27] Mt 24:29–31; Lk 21:25–27.
t. [13:24] Is 13:10; Ez 32:7; Jl 2:10.   u. [13:26] 14:62; Dn 7:13–14.
v. [13:28–32] Mt 24:32–36; Lk 21:29–33.   w. [13:33–37] Mt 24:42;
25:13–15.   x. [13:34] Mt 25:14–30; Lk 19:12–27.

y. [14:1–2] Mt 26:2–5; Lk 22:1–2; Jn 11:45–53.   z. [14:3–9] Mt 26:6–13; Jn 12:1–8.   a. [14:10–11] Mt 26:14–16; Lk 22:3–6.
b. [14:12–16] Mt 26:17–19; Lk 22:7–13.

of water.* Follow him. ¹⁴Wherever he enters, say to the master of the house, 'The Teacher says, "Where is my guest room where I may eat the Passover with my disciples?"' ¹⁵Then he will show you a large upper room furnished and ready. Make the preparations for us there." ¹⁶The disciples then went off, entered the city, and found it just as he had told them; and they prepared the Passover.

**The Betrayer.** ¹⁷ᶜWhen it was evening, he came with the Twelve. ¹⁸†And as they reclined at table and were eating, Jesus said, "Amen, I say to you, one of you will betray me, one who is eating with me." ¹⁹They began to be distressed and to say to him, one by one, "Surely it is not I?" ²⁰He said to them, "One of the Twelve, the one who dips with me into the dish. ²¹For the Son of Man indeed goes, as it is written of him,‡ but woe to that man by whom the Son of Man is betrayed. It would be better for that man if he had never been born."

**The Lord's Supper.** ²²§While they were eating,ᵈ he took bread, said the blessing, broke it, and gave it to them, and said, "Take it; this is my body." ²³Then he took a cup, gave thanks, and gave it to them, and they all drank from it. ²⁴He said to them, "This is my blood of the covenant, which will be shedᶠ for many. ²⁵Amen, I say to you, I shall not drink again the fruit of the vine until the day when I drink it new in the kingdom of God." ²⁶Then, after singing a hymn,** they went out to the Mount of Olives.ᵉ

**Peter's Denial Foretold.**†† ²⁷Then Jesus said to them, "All of you will have your faith shaken, for it is written:

'I will strike the shepherd,
    and the sheep will be dispersed.'ᶠ

²⁸But after I have been raised up, I shall go before you to Galilee." ²⁹Peter said to him, "Even though all should have their faith shaken, mine will not be." ³⁰Then Jesus said to him, "Amen, I say to you, this very night before the cock crows twice you will deny me three times." ³¹But he vehemently replied, "Even though I should have to die with you, I will not deny you." And they all spoke similarly.

**The Agony in the Garden.** ³²‡‡Then they came to a place named Gethsemane,ᵍ and he said to his disciples, "Sit here while I pray."ʰ ³³He took with him Peter, James, and John, and began to be troubled and distressed. ³⁴Then he said to them, "My soul is sorrowful even to death. Remain here and keep watch." ³⁵He advanced a little and fell to the ground and prayed that if it were possible the hour might pass by him; ³⁶he said, "Abba, Father,§§ all things are possible to you. Take this cup away from me, but not what I will but what you will." ³⁷When he returned he found them asleep. He said to Peter, "Simon, are you asleep? Could you not keep watch for one hour? ³⁸¶¶Watch and pray that you may not undergo the test.ⁱ The spirit is willing but the flesh is weak." ³⁹Withdrawing again, he prayed, saying the same thing. ⁴⁰Then he returned once more and found them asleep, for they could not keep their eyes open and did not know what to answer him. ⁴¹He returned a third time and said to them, "Are you still sleeping and taking your rest? It is enough. The hour has come. Behold, the Son of Man is to be handed over to sinners. ⁴²Get up, let us go. See, my betrayer is at hand."

**The Betrayal and Arrest of Jesus.** ⁴³ʲThen, while he was still speaking, Judas, one of the Twelve, arrived, accompanied by a crowd with swords and clubs who had come from the chief priests, the scribes, and the elders. ⁴⁴His betrayer had arranged a signal with them, saying, "The man

---

\* [14:13] **A man . . . carrying a jar of water:** perhaps a prearranged signal, for only women ordinarily carried water in jars. The Greek word used here, however, implies simply a person and not necessarily a male.

† [14:18] **One of you will betray me, one who is eating with me:** contrasts the intimacy of table fellowship at the Passover meal with the treachery of the traitor; cf. Ps 41:10.

‡ [14:21] **The Son of Man indeed goes, as it is written of him:** a reference to Ps 41:10 cited by Jesus concerning Judas at the Last Supper; cf. Jn 13:18–19.

§ [14:22–24] The actions and words of Jesus express within the framework of the Passover meal and the transition to a new covenant the sacrifice of himself through the offering of his body and blood in anticipation of his passion and death. His **blood of the covenant** both alludes to the ancient rite of Ex 24:4–8 and indicates the new community that the sacrifice of Jesus will bring into being (Mt 26:26–28; Lk 22:19–20; 1 Cor 11:23–25).

¶ [14:24] **Which will be shed:** see note on Mt 26:27–28. **For many:** the Greek preposition *hyper* is a different one from that at Mt 26:28 but the same as that found at Lk 22:19, 20 and 1 Cor 11:24. The sense of both words is vicarious, and it is difficult in Hellenistic Greek to distinguish between them. For **many** in the sense of "all," see note on Mt 20:28.

\*\* [14:26] **After singing a hymn:** Ps 114–118, thanksgiving songs concluding the Passover meal.

†† [14:27–31] Jesus predicted that the Twelve would waver in their faith, even abandon him, despite their protestations to the contrary. Yet he reassured them that after his resurrection he would regather them in Galilee (Mk 16:7; cf. Mk 26:32;

28:7, 10, 16; Jn 21), where he first summoned them to be his followers as he began to preach the good news (Mk 1:14–20).

‡‡ [14:32–34] The disciples who had witnessed the raising to life of the daughter of Jairus (Mk 5:37) and the transfiguration of their Master (Mk 9:2) were now invited to witness his degradation and agony and to watch and pray with him.

§§ [14:36] **Abba, Father:** an Aramaic term, here also translated by Mark, Jesus' special way of addressing God with filial intimacy. The word *'abbā* seems not to have been used in earlier or contemporaneous Jewish sources to address God without some qualifier. Cf. Rom 8:15; Gal 4:6 for other occurrences of the Aramaic word in the Greek New Testament. **Not what I will but what you will:** note the complete obedient surrender of the human will of Jesus to the divine will of the Father; cf. Jn 4:34; 8:29; Rom 5:19; Phil 2:8; Heb 5:8.

¶¶ [14:38] **The spirit is willing but the flesh is weak:** the spirit is drawn to what is good yet found in conflict with the flesh, inclined to sin; cf. Ps 51:7, 12. Everyone is faced with this struggle, the full force of which Jesus accepted on our behalf and, through his bitter passion and death, achieved the victory.

---

c. [14:17–21] Mt 26:20–24; Lk 22:21–23; Jn 13:21–26.  d. [14:22–25] Mt 26:26–30; Lk 22:19–20; 1 Cor 11:23–25.  e. [14:26–31] Mt 26:30–35; Lk 22:34, 39; Jn 13:36–38.

f. [14:27] Zec 13:7; Jn 16:32.  g. [14:32–42] Mt 26:36–46; Lk 22:40–46.  h. [14:32] Jn 18:1.  i. [14:38] Rom 7:5.  j. [14:43–50] Mt 26:47–56; Lk 22:47–53; Jn 18:3–11.

I shall kiss is the one; arrest him and lead him away securely." ⁴⁵He came and immediately went over to him and said, "Rabbi." And he kissed him. ⁴⁶At this they laid hands on him and arrested him. ⁴⁷One of the bystanders drew his sword, struck the high priest's servant, and cut off his ear. ⁴⁸Jesus said to them in reply, "Have you come out as against a robber, with swords and clubs, to seize me? ⁴⁹Day after day I was with you teaching in the temple area, yet you did not arrest me; but that the scriptures may be fulfilled." ⁵⁰And they all left him and fled. ⁵¹Now a young man followed him wearing nothing but a linen cloth about his body. They seized him, ⁵²but he left the cloth behind and ran off naked.

**Jesus Before the Sanhedrin.** ⁵³*ᵏThey led Jesus away to the high priest, and all the chief priests and the elders and the scribes came together. ⁵⁴Peter followed him at a distance into the high priest's courtyard and was seated with the guards, warming himself at the fire. ⁵⁵The chief priests and the entire Sanhedrin kept trying to obtain testimony against Jesus in order to put him to death, but they found none. ⁵⁶Many gave false witness against him, but their testimony did not agree. ⁵⁷†Some took the stand and testified falsely against him, alleging, ⁵⁸"We heard him say, 'I will destroy this temple made with hands and within three days I will build another not made with hands.'" ⁵⁹Even so their testimony did not agree. ⁶⁰The high priest rose before the assembly and questioned Jesus, saying, "Have you no answer? What are these men testifying against you?" ⁶¹‡But he was silent and answered nothing. Again the high priest asked him and said to him, "Are you the Messiah, the son of the Blessed One?" ⁶²Then Jesus answered, "I am;

and 'you will see the Son of Man
seated at the right hand of the Power
and coming with the clouds of
heaven.'"ᵐ

⁶³At that the high priest tore his garments and said, "What further need have we of witnesses?

⁶⁴You have heard the blasphemy. What do you think?" They all condemned him as deserving to die. ⁶⁵Some began to spit on him. They blindfolded him and struck him and said to him, "Prophesy!" And the guards greeted him with blows.ⁿ

**Peter's Denial of Jesus.** ⁶⁶ᵒWhile Peter was below in the courtyard, one of the high priest's maids came along. ⁶⁷Seeing Peter warming himself, she looked intently at him and said, "You too were with the Nazarene, Jesus." ⁶⁸§But he denied it saying, "I neither know nor understand what you are talking about." So he went out into the outer court. [Then the cock crowed.] ⁶⁹The maid saw him and began again to say to the bystanders, "This man is one of them." ⁷⁰Once again he denied it. A little later the bystanders said to Peter once more, "Surely you are one of them; for you too are a Galilean." ⁷¹He began to curse and to swear, "I do not know this man about whom you are talking." ⁷²And immediately a cock crowed a second time. Then Peter remembered the word that Jesus had said to him, "Before the cock crows twice you will deny me three times." He broke down and wept.ᵖ

# CHAPTER 15

**Jesus Before Pilate.** ¹ᵃAs soon as morning came,ʳ the chief priests with the elders and the scribes, that is, the whole Sanhedrin, held a council.¶ They bound Jesus, led him away, and handed him over to Pilate. ²Pilate questioned him, "Are you the king of the Jews?"** He said to him in reply, "You say so." ³The chief priests accused him of many things. ⁴Again Pilate questioned him, "Have you no answer? See how many things they accuse you of." ⁵Jesus gave him no further answer, so that Pilate was amazed.

**The Sentence of Death.**†† ⁶Now on the occasion of the feast he used to release to them one prisoner whom they requested.ˢ ⁷A man called Barabbas‡‡ was then in prison along with the rebels who had committed murder in a rebellion.

---

*[14:53] **They led Jesus away . . . came together:** Mark presents a formal assembly of the whole Sanhedrin (chief priests, elders, and scribes) at night, leading to the condemnation of Jesus (Mk 14:64), in contrast to Lk 22:66, 71 where Jesus is condemned in a daytime meeting of the council; see also Jn 18:13, 19–24.

†[14:57–58] See notes on Mt 26:60–61 and Jn 2:19.

‡[14:61–62] **The Blessed One:** a surrogate for the divine name, which Jews did not pronounce. **I am:** indicates Jesus' acknowledgment that he is the Messiah and Son of God; cf. Mk 1:1. Contrast Mt 26:64 and Lk 22:67–70, in which Jesus leaves his interrogators to answer their own question. **You will see the Son of Man . . . with the clouds of heaven:** an allusion to Dn 7:13 and Ps 110:1 portending the enthronement of Jesus as judge in the transcendent glory of God's kingdom. **The Power:** another surrogate for the name of God.

§[14:68] [**Then the cock crowed**]: found in most manuscripts, perhaps in view of Mk 14:30, 72 but omitted in others.

¶[15:1] **Held a council:** the verb here, *poieō*, can mean either "convene a council" or "take counsel." This reading is preferred to a variant "reached a decision" (cf. Mk 3:6), which Mk 14:64 describes as having happened at the night trial; see note on Mt 27:1–2. **Handed him over to Pilate:** lacking authority to execute their sentence of condemnation (Mk 14:64), the Sanhedrin had recourse to Pilate to have Jesus tried and put to death (Mk 15:15); cf. Jn 18:31.

**[15:2] **The king of the Jews:** in the accounts of the evangelists a certain irony surrounds the use of this title as an accusation against Jesus (see note on Mk 15:26). While Pilate uses this term (Mk 15:2, 9, 12), he is aware of the evil motivation of the chief priests who handed Jesus over for trial and condemnation (Mk 15:10; Lk 23:14–16, 20; Mt 27:18, 24; Jn 18:38; 19:4, 6, 12).

††[15:6–15] See note on Mt 27:15–26.

‡‡[15:7] **Barabbas:** see note on Mt 27:16–17.

k. [14:53–65] Mt 26:57–68; Lk 22:54–55, 63–65, 67–71; Jn 18:12–13. l. [14:58] 15:29; 2 Cor 5:1. m. [14:62] 13:26; Ps 110:1; Dn 7:13; Mt 24:30.

n. [14:65] Lk 22:63–65.   o. [14:66–72] Mt 26:69–75; Lk 22:56–62; Jn 18:16–18, 25–27.   p. [14:72] Jn 13:38.   q. [15:1–5] Mt 27:1–2, 11–14; Lk 23:1–3.   r. [15:1] Jn 18:28.   s. [15:6–15] Mt 27:15–26; Lk 23:17–25; Jn 18:39–40.

⁸The crowd came forward and began to ask him to do for them as he was accustomed. ⁹Pilate answered, "Do you want me to release to you the king of the Jews?" ¹⁰For he knew that it was out of envy that the chief priests had handed him over. ¹¹But the chief priests stirred up the crowd to have him release Barabbas for them instead. ¹²Pilate again said to them in reply, "Then what [do you want] me to do with [the man you call] the king of the Jews?" ¹³*They shouted again, "Crucify him." ¹⁴Pilate said to them, "Why? What evil has he done?" They only shouted the louder, "Crucify him." ¹⁵†So Pilate, wishing to satisfy the crowd, released Barabbas to them and, after he had Jesus scourged, handed him over to be crucified.

**Mockery by the Soldiers.** ¹⁶‡*The soldiers led him away inside the palace, that is, the praetorium, and assembled the whole cohort. ¹⁷They clothed him in purple and, weaving a crown of thorns, placed it on him. ¹⁸They began to salute him with, "Hail, King of the Jews!" ¹⁹and kept striking his head with a reed and spitting upon him. They knelt before him in homage. ²⁰And when they had mocked him, they stripped him of the purple cloak, dressed him in his own clothes, and led him out to crucify him.

**The Way of the Cross.** ²¹ᵗThey pressed into service a passer-by, Simon, a Cyrenian,§ who was coming in from the country, the father of Alexander and Rufus, to carry his cross.ᵘ

**The Crucifixion.** ²²ᵛThey brought him to the place of Golgotha (which is translated Place of the Skull). ²³They gave him wine drugged with myrrh, but he did not take it. ²⁴¶ʷThen they crucified him and divided his garments by casting lots for them to see what each should take. ²⁵It was nine o'clock in the morning** when they crucified him. ²⁶††The inscription of the charge against him read, "The King of the Jews." ²⁷With him they crucified two revolutionaries, one

on his right and one on his left.ˣ [²⁸]‡‡ ²⁹§§Those passing by reviled him, shaking their heads and saying,ʸ "Aha! You who would destroy the temple and rebuild it in three days, ³⁰save yourself by coming down from the cross." ³¹Likewise the chief priests, with the scribes, mocked him among themselves and said, "He saved others; he cannot save himself. ³²Let the Messiah, the King of Israel, come down now from the cross that we may see and believe." Those who were crucified with him also kept abusing him.ᶻ

**The Death of Jesus.** ³³At noon darkness came over the whole land until three in the afternoon. ³⁴And at three o'clock Jesus cried out in a loud voice, "*Eloi, Eloi, lema sabachthani?*"¶¶ which is translated, "My God, my God, why have you forsaken me?"ᵃ ³⁵***Some of the bystanders who heard it said, "Look, he is calling Elijah." ³⁶One of them ran, soaked a sponge with wine, put it on a reed, and gave it to him to drink, saying, "Wait, let us see if Elijah comes to take him down." ³⁷Jesus gave a loud cry and breathed his last. ³⁸†††The veil of the sanctuary was torn in two from top to bottom. ³⁹‡‡‡ᵇWhen the centurion who stood facing him saw how he breathed his last he said, "Truly this man was the Son of God!" ⁴⁰§§§There were also women looking on from a distance.ᶜ Among them were Mary Magdalene, Mary the mother of the younger James and of Joses, and Salome. ⁴¹These women had followed him when he was in Galilee and ministered to him. There were also many other women who had come up with him to Jerusalem.

**The Burial of Jesus.** ⁴²ᵈWhen it was already evening, since it was the day of preparation, the day before the sabbath, ⁴³Joseph of Arimathea,¶¶¶ a distinguished member of the council, who was himself awaiting the kingdom of God, came and courageously went to Pilate and asked for the body of Jesus. ⁴⁴Pilate was amazed that he was already dead. He summoned the centurion and asked him if Jesus had already died. ⁴⁵And when he learned of it from the centurion, he gave the body to Joseph. ⁴⁶Having bought a linen cloth, he took him down, wrapped him in the linen

---

*[15:13] **Crucify him:** see note on Mt 27:22.

†[15:15] See note on Mt 27:26.

‡[15:16] **Praetorium:** see note on Mt 27:27.

§[15:21] **They pressed into service . . . Simon, a Cyrenian:** a condemned person was constrained to bear his own instrument of torture, at least the crossbeam. The precise naming of Simon and his sons is probably due to their being known among early Christian believers to whom Mark addressed his gospel. See also notes on Mt 27:32; Lk 23:26–32.

¶[15:24] See notes on Mt 27:35 and Jn 19:23–25a.

**[15:25] **It was nine o'clock in the morning:** literally, "the third hour," thus between 9 a.m. and 12 noon. Cf. Mk 15:33, 34, 42 for Mark's chronological sequence, which may reflect liturgical or catechetical considerations rather than the precise historical sequence of events; contrast the different chronologies in the other gospels, especially Jn 19:14.

††[15:26] **The inscription . . . the King of the Jews:** the political reason for the death penalty falsely charged by the enemies of Jesus. See further the notes on Mt 27:37 and Jn 19:19.

‡‡[15:28] This verse, "And the scripture was fulfilled that says, 'And he was counted among the wicked,'" is omitted in the earliest and best manuscripts. It contains a citation from Is 53:12 and was probably introduced from Lk 22:37.

§§[15:29] See note on Mt 27:39–40.

¶¶[15:34] An Aramaic rendering of Ps 22:2. See also note on Mt 27:46.

***[15:35] **Elijah:** a verbal link with Eloi (Mk 15:34). See note on Mk 9:9–13; cf. Mal 3:23–24. See also note on Mt 27:47.

†††[15:38] See note on Mt 27:51–53.

‡‡‡[15:39] The closing portion of Mark's gospel returns to the theme of its beginning in the Gentile centurion's climactic declaration of belief that Jesus **was the Son of God**. It indicates the fulfillment of the good news announced in the prologue (Mk 1:1) and may be regarded as the firstfruit of the passion and death of Jesus.

§§§[15:40–41] See note on Mt 27:55–56.

¶¶¶[15:43] **Joseph of Arimathea:** see note on Mt 27:57–61.

---

t. [15:16–20] Mt 27:27–31; Jn 19:2–3.   u. [15:21] Mt 27:32; Lk 23:26.
v. [15:22–38] Mt 27:33–51; Lk 23:32–46; Jn 19:17–30.   w. [15:24] Ps 22:18.

x. [15:27] Lk 23:33.   y. [15:29] Jn 2:19.   z. [15:32] Lk 23:39.   a. [15:34] Ps 22:2.   b. [15:39–41] Mt 27:54–56; Lk 23:47–49.   c. [15:40] 6:3; Lk 8:2–3.   d. [15:42–47] Mt 27:57–61; Lk 23:50–56; Jn 19:38–42.

cloth and laid him in a tomb that had been hewn out of the rock. Then he rolled a stone against the entrance to the tomb. [47]Mary Magdalene and Mary the mother of Joses watched where he was laid.

## CHAPTER 16

**The Resurrection of Jesus.**[*] [1]When the sabbath was over,[e] Mary Magdalene, Mary, the mother of James, and Salome bought spices so that they might go and anoint him.[f] [2]Very early when the sun had risen, on the first day of the week, they came to the tomb. [3]They were saying to one another, "Who will roll back the stone for us from the entrance to the tomb?" [4]When they looked up, they saw that the stone had been rolled back; it was very large. [5]On entering the tomb they saw a young man sitting on the right side, clothed in a white robe, and they were utterly amazed.[g] [6]He said to them, "Do not be amazed! You seek Jesus of Nazareth, the crucified. He has been raised; he is not here. Behold, the place where they laid him. [7]But go and tell his disciples and Peter, 'He is going before you to Galilee; there you will see him, as he told you.'"[h] [8]Then they went out and fled from the tomb, seized with trembling and bewilderment. They said nothing to anyone, for they were afraid.

### The Longer Ending[†]

**The Appearance to Mary Magdalene.** [[9]When he had risen, early on the first day of the week, he appeared first to Mary Magdalene, out of whom he had driven seven demons. [10]She went and told his companions who were mourning and weeping. [11]When they heard that he was alive and had been seen by her, they did not believe.
**The Appearance to Two Disciples.** [12]After this he appeared in another form to two of them walking along on their way to the country.

[13]They returned and told the others; but they did not believe them either.
**The Commissioning of the Eleven.** [14][But] later, as the eleven were at table, he appeared to them and rebuked them for their unbelief and hardness of heart because they had not believed those who saw him after he had been raised. [15]He said to them, "Go into the whole world and proclaim the gospel to every creature. [16]Whoever believes and is baptized will be saved; whoever does not believe will be condemned. [17]These signs will accompany those who believe: in my name they will drive out demons, they will speak new languages. [18]They will pick up serpents [with their hands], and if they drink any deadly thing, it will not harm them. They will lay hands on the sick, and they will recover."[n]
**The Ascension of Jesus.** [19]So then the Lord Jesus, after he spoke to them, was taken up into heaven and took his seat at the right hand of God.[o] [20]But they went forth and preached everywhere, while the Lord worked with them and confirmed the word through accompanying signs.][p]

### The Shorter Ending

[And they reported all the instructions briefly to Peter's companions. Afterwards Jesus himself, through them, sent forth from east to west the sacred and imperishable proclamation of eternal salvation. Amen.]

found in some less important manuscripts, has traditionally been accepted as a canonical part of the gospel and was defined as such by the Council of Trent. Early citations of it by the Fathers indicate that it was composed by the second century, although vocabulary and style indicate that it was written by someone other than Mark. It is a general resume of the material concerning the appearances of the risen Jesus, reflecting, in particular, traditions found in Lk 24 and Jn 20.

The Shorter Ending: Found after Mk 16:8 before the Longer Ending in four seventh-to-ninth-century Greek manuscripts as well as in one Old Latin version, where it appears alone without the Longer Ending.

The Freer Logion: Found after Mk 16:14 in a fourth-fifth century manuscript preserved in the Freer Gallery of Art, Washington, DC, this ending was known to Jerome in the fourth century. It reads: "And they excused themselves, saying, 'This age of lawlessness and unbelief is under Satan, who does not allow the truth and power of God to prevail over the unclean things dominated by the spirits [or, does not allow the unclean things dominated by the spirits to grasp the truth and power of God]. Therefore reveal your righteousness now.' They spoke to Christ. And Christ responded to them, 'The limit of the years of Satan's power is completed, but other terrible things draw near. And for those who sinned I was handed over to death, that they might return to the truth and no longer sin, in order that they might inherit the spiritual and incorruptible heavenly glory of righteousness. But . . . .'"

---

*[16:1–8] The purpose of this narrative is to show that the tomb is empty and that Jesus **has been raised** (Mk 16:6) and is **going before you to Galilee** (Mk 16:7) in fulfillment of Mk 14:28. The women find the tomb empty, and an angel stationed there announces to them what has happened. They are told to proclaim the news to Peter and the disciples in order to prepare them for a reunion with him. Mark's composition of the gospel ends at Mk 16:8 with the women telling no one, because they were afraid. This abrupt termination causes some to believe that the original ending of this gospel may have been lost. See the following note.

†[16:9–20] This passage, termed the Longer Ending to the Marcan gospel by comparison with a much briefer conclusion

e. [16:1–8] Mt 28:1–8; Lk 24:1–10; Jn 20:1–10.   f. [16:1–2] Mt 28:1; Lk23:56.   g. [16:5]Jn20:12.   h. [16:7]14:28.   i. [16:9–20]Mt28:1–10; Jn 20:11–18.   j. [16:10–11] Lk 24:10–11; Jn 20:18.   k. [16:12–14] Lk 24:13–35.

l. [16:14]  Lk  24:36–49;  1  Cor  15:5.   m. [16:15–16]  13:10; Mt 28:18–20; Lk 24:47; Jn 20:21.   n. [16:18] Mt 10:1; Lk 10:19; Acts 28:3–6.   o. [16:19] Lk 24:50–53.   p. [16:20] 1 Tm 3:16.

# THE GOSPEL ACCORDING TO
# LUKE

The Gospel according to Luke is the first part of a two-volume work that continues the biblical history of God's dealings with humanity found in the Old Testament, showing how God's promises to Israel have been fulfilled in Jesus and how the salvation promised to Israel and accomplished by Jesus has been extended to the Gentiles. The stated purpose of the two volumes is to provide Theophilus and others like him with certainty—assurance—about earlier instruction they have received (Lk 1:4). To accomplish his purpose, Luke shows that the preaching and teaching of the representatives of the early church are grounded in the preaching and teaching of Jesus, who during his historical ministry (Acts 1:21–22) prepared his specially chosen followers and commissioned them to be witnesses to his resurrection and to all else that he did (Acts 10:37–42). This continuity between the historical ministry of Jesus and the ministry of the apostles is Luke's way of guaranteeing the fidelity of the Church's teaching to the teaching of Jesus.

Luke's story of Jesus and the church is dominated by a historical perspective. This history is first of all salvation history. God's divine plan for human salvation was accomplished during the period of Jesus, who through the events of his life (Lk 22:22) fulfilled the Old Testament prophecies (Lk 4:21; 18:31; 22:37; 24:26–27, 44), and this salvation is now extended to all humanity in the period of the church (Acts 4:12). This salvation history, moreover, is a part of human history. Luke relates the story of Jesus and the church to events in contemporary Palestinian (Lk 1:5; 3:1–2; Acts 4:6) and Roman (Lk 2:1–2; 3:1; Acts 11:28; 18:2, 12) history for, as Paul says in Acts 26:26, "this was not done in a corner." Finally, Luke relates the story of Jesus and the church to contemporaneous church history. Luke is concerned with presenting Christianity as a legitimate form of worship in the Roman world, a religion that is capable of meeting the spiritual needs of a world empire like that of Rome. To this end, Luke depicts the Roman governor Pilate declaring Jesus innocent of any wrongdoing three times (Lk 23:4, 14, 22). At the same time Luke argues in Acts that Christianity is the logical development and proper fulfillment of Judaism and is therefore deserving of the same toleration and freedom traditionally accorded Judaism by Rome (Acts 13:16–41; 23:6–9; 24:10–21; 26:2–23).

The prominence given to the period of the church in the story has important consequences for Luke's interpretation of the teachings of Jesus. By presenting the time of the church as a distinct phase of salvation history, Luke accordingly shifts the early Christian emphasis away from the expectation of an imminent parousia to the day-to-day concerns of the Christian community in the world. He does this in the gospel by regularly emphasizing the words "each day" (Lk 9:23; cf. Mk 8:34; Lk 11:3; 16:19; 19:47) in the sayings of Jesus. Although Luke still believes the parousia to be a reality that will come unexpectedly (Lk 12:38, 45–46), he is more concerned with presenting the words and deeds of Jesus as guides for the conduct of Christian disciples in the interim period between the ascension and the parousia and with presenting Jesus himself as the model of Christian life and piety.

Throughout the gospel, Luke calls upon the Christian disciple to identify with the master Jesus, who is caring and tender toward the poor and lowly, the outcast, the sinner, and the afflicted, toward all those who recognize their dependence on God (Lk 4:18; 6:20–23; 7:36–50; 14:12–14; 15:1–32; 16:19–31; 18:9–14; 19:1–10; 21:1–4), but who is severe toward the proud and self-righteous, and particularly toward those who place their material wealth before the service of God and his people (Lk 6:24–26; 12:13–21; 16:13–15, 19–31; 18:9–14, 15–25; cf. Lk 1:50–53). No gospel writer is more concerned than Luke with the mercy and compassion of Jesus (Lk 7:41–43; 10:29–37; 13:6–9; 15:11–32). No gospel writer is more concerned with the role of the Spirit in the life of Jesus and the Christian disciple (Lk 1:35, 41; 2:25–27; 4:1, 14, 18; 10:21; 11:13; 24:49), with the importance of prayer (Lk 3:21; 5:16; 6:12; 9:28; 11:1–13; 18:1–8), or with Jesus' concern for women (Lk 7:11–17,

36–50; 8:2–3; 10:38–42). While Jesus calls all humanity to repent (Lk 5:32; 10:13; 11:32; 13:1–5; 15:7–10; 16:30; 17:3–4; 24:47), he is particularly demanding of those who would be his disciples. Of them he demands absolute and total detachment from family and material possessions (Lk 9:57–62; 12:32–34; 14:25–35). To all who respond in faith and repentance to the word Jesus preaches, he brings salvation (Lk 2:30–32; 3:6; 7:50; 8:48, 50; 17:19; 19:9) and peace (Lk 2:14; 7:50; 8:48; 19:38, 42) and life (Lk 10:25–28; 18:26–30).

Early Christian tradition, from the late second century on, identifies the author of this gospel and of the Acts of the Apostles as Luke, a Syrian from Antioch, who is mentioned in the New Testament in Col 4:14, Phlm 24 and 2 Tm 4:11. The prologue of the gospel makes it clear that Luke is not part of the first generation of Christian disciples but is himself dependent upon the traditions he received from those who were eyewitnesses and ministers of the word (Lk 1:2). His two-volume work marks him as someone who was highly literate both in the Old Testament traditions according to the Greek versions and in Hellenistic Greek writings.

Among the likely sources for the composition of this gospel (Lk 1:3) were the Gospel of Mark, a written collection of sayings of Jesus known also to the author of the Gospel of Matthew (Q; see Introduction to Matthew), and other special traditions that were used by Luke alone among the gospel writers. Some hold that Luke used Mark only as a complementary source for rounding out the material he took from other traditions. Because of its dependence on the Gospel of Mark and because details in Luke's Gospel (Lk 13:35a; 19:43–44; 21:20; 23:28–31) imply that the author was acquainted with the destruction of the city of Jerusalem by the Romans in A.D. 70, the Gospel of Luke is dated by most scholars after that date; many propose A.D. 80–90 as the time of composition.

Luke's consistent substitution of Greek names for the Aramaic or Hebrew names occurring in his sources (e.g., Lk 23:33; Mk 15:22; Lk 18:41; Mk 10:51), his omission from the gospel of specifically Jewish Christian concerns found in his sources (e.g., Mk 7:1–23), his interest in Gentile Christians (Lk 2:30–32; 3:6, 38; 4:16–30; 13:28–30; 14:15–24; 17:11–19; 24:47–48), and his incomplete knowledge of Palestinian geography, customs, and practices are among the characteristics of this gospel that suggest that Luke was a non-Palestinian writing to a non-Palestinian audience that was largely made up of Gentile Christians.

The principal divisions of the Gospel according to Luke are the following:

I. The Prologue (1:1–4)
II. The Infancy Narrative (1:5–2:52)
III. The Preparation for the Public Ministry (3:1–4:13)
IV. The Ministry in Galilee (4:14–9:50)
V. The Journey to Jerusalem: Luke's Travel Narrative (9:51–19:27)
VI. The Teaching Ministry in Jerusalem (19:28–21:38)
VII. The Passion Narrative (22:1–23:56)
VIII. The Resurrection Narrative (24:1–53)

## I. THE PROLOGUE*

### CHAPTER 1

¹Since many have undertaken to compile a narrative of the events that have been fulfilled among us,ᵃ ²just as those who were eyewitnesses from the beginning and ministers of the word have handed them down to us,ᵇ ³I too have decided, after investigating everything accurately anew, to write it down in an orderly sequence for you, most excellent Theophilus, ⁴so that you may realize the certainty of the teachings you have received.

---

*[1:1–4] The Gospel according to Luke is the only one of the synoptic gospels to begin with a literary prologue. Making use of a formal, literary construction and vocabulary, the author writes the prologue in imitation of Hellenistic Greek writers and, in so doing, relates his story about Jesus to contemporaneous Greek and Roman literature. Luke is not only interested in the words and deeds of Jesus, but also in the larger context of the birth, ministry, death, and resurrection of Jesus as the fulfillment of the promises of God in the Old Testament. As a second- or third-generation Christian, Luke acknowledges his debt to earlier **eyewitnesses** and **ministers of the word**, but claims that his contribution to this developing tradition is a complete and accurate account, told in an orderly manner, and intended to provide **Theophilus** ("friend of God," literally) and other readers with certainty about earlier teachings they have received.

a. [1:1–4] Acts 1:1; 1 Cor 15:3.

b. [1:2] 24:48; Jn 15:27; Acts 1:21–22.

## II. THE INFANCY NARRATIVE*

**Announcement of the Birth of John.** [5]In the days of Herod, King of Judea,[†] there was a priest named Zechariah of the priestly division of Abijah; his wife was from the daughters of Aaron, and her name was Elizabeth.[c] [6]Both were righteous in the eyes of God, observing all the commandments and ordinances of the Lord blamelessly. [7]But they had no child,[‡] because Elizabeth was barren and both were advanced in years.[d] [8]Once when he was serving as priest in his division's turn before God, [9]according to the practice of the priestly service, he was chosen by lot to enter the sanctuary of the Lord to burn incense.[e] [10]Then, when the whole assembly of the people was praying outside at the hour of the incense offering, [11]the angel of the Lord appeared to him, standing at the right of the altar of incense. [12]Zechariah was troubled by what he saw, and fear came upon him. [13]But the angel said to him, "Do not be afraid,[§] Zechariah, because your prayer has been heard. Your wife Elizabeth will bear you a son, and you shall name him John.[f] [14]And you will have joy and gladness, and many will rejoice at his birth, [15]for he will be great in the sight of [the] Lord. He will drink neither wine nor strong drink.[¶] He will be filled with the holy Spirit even from his mother's womb,[g] [16]and he will turn many of the children of Israel to the Lord their God. [17]He will go before him in the spirit and power of Elijah** to turn the hearts of fathers toward children and the disobedient to the understanding of the righteous, to prepare a people fit for the Lord."[h] [18]Then Zechariah said to the angel, "How shall I know this? For I am an old man, and my wife is advanced in years." [19]And the angel said to him in reply, "I am Gabriel,[††] who stand before God. I was sent to speak to you and to announce to you this good news.[i] [20]But now you will be speechless and unable to talk[‡‡] until the day these things take place, because you did not believe my words, which will be fulfilled at their proper time."[j]

[21]Meanwhile the people were waiting for Zechariah and were amazed that he stayed so long in the sanctuary. [22]But when he came out, he was unable to speak to them, and they realized that he had seen a vision in the sanctuary. He was gesturing to them but remained mute. [23]Then, when his days of ministry were completed, he went home. [24]After this time his wife Elizabeth conceived, and she went into seclusion for five months, saying, [25]"So has the Lord done for me at a time when he has seen fit to take away my disgrace before others."[k]

**Announcement of the Birth of Jesus.**[§§] [26]In the sixth month, the angel Gabriel was sent from

---

*[1:5–2:52] Like the Gospel according to Matthew, this gospel opens with an infancy narrative, a collection of stories about the birth and childhood of Jesus. The narrative uses early Christian traditions about the birth of John the Baptist, and canticles such as the Magnificat (Lk 1:46–55) and Benedictus (Lk 1:67–79), composed of phrases drawn from the Greek Old Testament. It is largely, however, the composition of Luke who writes in imitation of Old Testament birth stories, combining historical and legendary details, literary ornamentation and interpretation of scripture, to answer in advance the question, "Who is Jesus Christ?" The focus of the narrative, therefore, is primarily christological. In this section Luke announces many of the themes that will become prominent in the rest of the gospel: the centrality of Jerusalem and the temple, the journey motif, the universality of salvation, joy and peace, concern for the lowly, the importance of women, the presentation of Jesus as savior, Spirit-guided revelation and prophecy, and the fulfillment of Old Testament promises. The account presents parallel scenes (diptychs) of angelic announcements of the birth of John the Baptist and of Jesus, and of the birth, circumcision, and presentation of John and Jesus. In this parallelism, the ascendency of Jesus over John is stressed: John is prophet of the Most High (Lk 1:76); Jesus is Son of the Most High (Lk 1:32). John is great in the sight of the Lord (Lk 1:15); Jesus will be Great (a LXX attribute, used absolutely, of God) (Lk 1:32). John will go before the Lord (Lk 1:16–17); Jesus will be Lord (Lk 1:43; 2:11).

†[1:5] **In the days of Herod, King of Judea**: Luke relates the story of salvation history to events in contemporary world history. Here and in Lk 3:1–2 he connects his narrative with events in Palestinian history; in Lk 2:1–2 and Lk 3:1 he casts the Jesus story in the light of events of Roman history. Herod the Great, the son of the Idumean Antipater, was declared "King of Judea" by the Roman Senate in 40 B.C., but became the undisputed ruler of Palestine only in 37 B.C. He continued as king until his death in 4 B.C. **Priestly division of Abijah**: a reference to the eighth of the twenty-four divisions of priests who, for a week at a time, twice a year, served in the Jerusalem temple.

‡[1:7] **They had no child**: though childlessness was looked upon in contemporaneous Judaism as a curse or punishment for sin, it is intended here to present Elizabeth in a situation similar to that of some of the great mothers of important Old Testament figures: Sarah (Gn 15:3; 16:1); Rebekah (Gn 25:21); Rachel (Gn 29:31; 30:1); the mother of Samson and wife of Manoah (Jgs 13:2–3); Hannah (1 Sm 1:2).

§[1:13] **Do not be afraid**: a stereotyped Old Testament phrase spoken to reassure the recipient of a heavenly vision

(Gn 15:1; Jos 1:9; Dn 10:12, 19 and elsewhere in Lk 1:30; 2:10). **You shall name him John**: the name means "Yahweh has shown favor," an indication of John's role in salvation history.

¶[1:15] **He will drink neither wine nor strong drink**: like Samson (Jgs 13:4–5) and Samuel (1 Sm 1:11 LXX and 4QSamᵃ), John is to be consecrated by Nazirite vow and set apart for the Lord's service.

**[1:17] **He will go before him in the spirit and power of Elijah**: John is to be the messenger sent before Yahweh, as described in Mal 3:1–2. He is cast, moreover, in the role of the Old Testament fiery reformer, the prophet Elijah, who according to Mal 3:23 (4:5) is sent before "the great and terrible day of the Lord comes."

††[1:19] **I am Gabriel**: "the angel of the Lord" is identified as Gabriel, the angel who in Dn 9:20–25 announces the seventy weeks of years and the coming of an anointed one, a prince. By alluding to Old Testament themes in Lk 1:17, 19 such as the coming of the day of the Lord and the dawning of the messianic era, Luke is presenting his interpretation of the significance of the births of John and Jesus.

‡‡[1:20] **You will be speechless and unable to talk**: Zechariah's becoming mute is the sign given in response to his question in v 18. When Mary asks a similar question in Lk 1:34, unlike Zechariah who was punished for his doubt, she, in spite of her doubt, is praised and reassured (Lk 1:35–37).

§§[1:26–38] The announcement to Mary of the birth of Jesus is parallel to the announcement to Zechariah of the birth of John. In both the angel Gabriel appears to the parent who is troubled by the vision (Lk 1:11–12, 26–29) and then told by

---

f. [1:13] 1:57, 60, 63; Mt 1:20–21. g. [1:15] 7:33; Nm 6:1–21; Jgs 13:4; 1 Sm 1:11 LXX. h. [1:17] Sir 48:10; Mal 3:1; 3:23–24; Mt 11:14; 17:11–13. i. [1:19] Dn 8:16; 9:21. j. [1:20] 1:45. k. [1:25] Gn 30:23.

c. [1:5] 1 Chr 24:10. d. [1:7] Gn 18:11; Jgs 13:2–5; 1 Sm 1:5–6. e. [1:9] Ex 30:7.

God to a town of Galilee called Nazareth, ²⁷to a virgin betrothed to a man named Joseph, of the house of David, and the virgin's name was Mary.ˡ ²⁸And coming to her, he said, "Hail, favored one! The Lord is with you."ᵐ ²⁹But she was greatly troubled at what was said and pondered what sort of greeting this might be. ³⁰Then the angel said to her, "Do not be afraid, Mary, for you have found favor with God. ³¹ⁿBehold, you will conceive in your womb and bear a son, and you shall name him Jesus. ³²ᵒHe will be great and will be called Son of the Most High,* and the Lord God will give him the throne of David his father, ³³and he will rule over the house of Jacob forever, and of his kingdom there will be no end.ᵖ ³⁴But Mary said to the angel, "How can this be, since I have no relations with a man?"† ³⁵And the angel said to her in reply, "The holy Spirit will come upon you, and the power of the Most High will overshadow you. Therefore the child to be born will be called holy, the Son of God.�q ³⁶And behold, Elizabeth, your relative, has also conceived‡ a son in her old age, and this is the sixth month for her who was called barren; ³⁷for nothing will be impossible for God."ʳ ³⁸Mary said, "Behold, I am the handmaid of the Lord. May it be done to me according to your word." Then the angel departed from her.

**Mary Visits Elizabeth.** ³⁹During those days Mary set out and traveled to the hill country in haste to a town of Judah, ⁴⁰where she entered the house of Zechariah and greeted Elizabeth. ⁴¹When Elizabeth heard Mary's greeting, the infant leaped in her womb, and Elizabeth, filled with the holy Spirit,ˢ ⁴²cried out in a loud voice and said, "Most blessed are you among women, and blessed is the fruit of your womb.ᵗ ⁴³And how does this happen to me, that the mother of my Lord§ should come to me? ⁴⁴For at the

moment the sound of your greeting reached my ears, the infant in my womb leaped for joy. ⁴⁵Blessed are you who believed§ that what was spoken to you by the Lord would be fulfilled."ᵘ **The Canticle of Mary.** ⁴⁶ᵛAnd Mary said:**

"My soul proclaims the greatness of the
        Lord;ʷ
⁴⁷    my spirit rejoices in God my savior.ˣ
⁴⁸ For he has looked upon his handmaid's
        lowliness;
    behold, from now on will all ages
        call me blessed.ʸ
⁴⁹ The Mighty One has done great things for
        me,
    and holy is his name.ᶻ
⁵⁰ His mercy is from age to age
    to those who fear him.ᵃ
⁵¹ He has shown might with his arm,
    dispersed the arrogant of mind and
        heart.ᵇ
⁵² He has thrown down the rulers from their
        thrones
    but lifted up the lowly.ᶜ
⁵³ The hungry he has filled with good things;
    the rich he has sent away empty.ᵈ
⁵⁴ He has helped Israel his servant,
    remembering his mercy,ᵉ
⁵⁵ according to his promise to our fathers,
    to Abraham and to his descendants
        forever."ᶠ

⁵⁶Mary remained with her about three months and then returned to her home.
**The Birth of John.**†† ⁵⁷When the time arrived for Elizabeth to have her child she gave birth to a

---

the angel not to fear (Lk 1:13, 30). After the announcement is made (Lk 1:14–17, 31–33) the parent objects (Lk 1:18, 34) and a sign is given to confirm the announcement (Lk 1:20, 36). The particular focus of the announcement of the birth of Jesus is on his identity as Son of David (Lk 1:32–33) and Son of God (Lk 1:32, 35).

*[1:32] **Son of the Most High**: cf. Lk 1:76 where John is described as "prophet of the Most High." "Most High" is a title for God commonly used by Luke (Lk 1:35; 76; 6:35; 8:28; Acts 7:48; 16:17).

†[1:34] Mary's questioning response is a denial of sexual relations and is used by Luke to lead to the angel's declaration about the Spirit's role in the conception of this child (Lk 1:35). According to Luke, the virginal conception of Jesus takes place through the holy Spirit, the power of God, and therefore Jesus has a unique relationship to Yahweh: he is Son of God.

‡[1:36–37] The sign given to Mary in confirmation of the angel's announcement to her is the pregnancy of her aged relative Elizabeth. If a woman past the childbearing age could become pregnant, why, the angel implies, should there be doubt about Mary's pregnancy, for **nothing will be impossible for God**.

§[1:43] Even before his birth, Jesus is identified in Luke as the Lord.

¶[1:45] **Blessed are you who believed**: Luke portrays Mary as a believer whose faith stands in contrast to the disbelief of Zechariah (Lk 1:20). Mary's role as believer in the infancy narrative should be seen in connection with the explicit mention of her presence among "those who believed" after the resurrection at the beginning of the Acts of the Apostles (Acts 1:14).

**[1:46–55] Although Mary is praised for being the mother of the Lord and because of her belief, she reacts as the servant in a psalm of praise, the Magnificat. Because there is no specific connection of the canticle to the context of Mary's pregnancy and her visit to Elizabeth, the Magnificat (with the possible exception of v 48) may have been a Jewish Christian hymn that Luke found appropriate at this point in his story. Even if not composed by Luke, it fits in well with themes found elsewhere in Luke: joy and exultation in the Lord; the lowly being singled out for God's favor; the reversal of human fortunes; the fulfillment of Old Testament promises. The loose connection between the hymn and the context is further seen in the fact that a few Old Latin manuscripts identify the speaker of the hymn as Elizabeth, even though the overwhelming textual evidence makes Mary the speaker.

††[1:57–66] The birth and circumcision of John above all emphasize John's incorporation into the people of Israel by the

u. [1:45] 1:20.   v. [1:46–55] 1 Sm 2:1–10.   w. [1:46] Ps 35:9; Is 61:10; Heb 3:18.   x. [1:47] Ti 3:4; Jude 25.   y. [1:48] 11:27; 1 Sm 1:11; 2 Sm 16:12; 2 Kgs 14:26; Ps 113:7.   z. [1:49] Dt 10:21; Ps 71:19; 111:9; 126:2–3.   a. [1:50] Ps 89:2; 103:13, 17.   b. [1:51] Ps 89:10; 118:15; Jer 32:17 (39:17 LXX).   c. [1:52] 1 Sm 2:7; 2 Sm 22:28; Jb 5:11; 12:19; Ps 147:6; Sir 10:14; Jas 4:6; 1 Pt 5:5.   d. [1:53] 1 Sm 2:5; Ps 107:9.   e. [1:54] Ps 98:3; Is 41:8–9.   f. [1:55] Gn 13:15; 17:7; 18:18; 22:17–18; Mi 7:20.

---

l. [1:27] 2:5; Mt 1:16, 18.   m. [1:28] Jgs 6:12; Ru 2:4; Jdt 13:18.
n. [1:31] Gn 16:11; Jgs 13:3; Is 7:14; Mt 1:21–23.   o. [1:32–33]
2 Sm 7:12, 13, 16; Is 9:7.   p. [1:33] Dn 2:44; 7:14; Mi 4:7; Mt 28:18.
q. [1:35] Mt 1:20.   r. [1:37] Gn 18:14; Jer 32:27; Mt 19:26.   s. [1:41]
1:15; Gn 25:22 LXX.   t. [1:42] 11:27–28; Jgs 5:24; Jdt 13:18; Dt 28:4.

son. [58]Her neighbors and relatives heard that the Lord had shown his great mercy toward her, and they rejoiced with her.[g] [59]When they came on the eighth day to circumcise[h] the child, they were going to call him Zechariah after his father, [60]but his mother said in reply, "No. He will be called John."[i] [61]But they answered her, "There is no one among your relatives who has this name." [62]So they made signs, asking his father what he wished him to be called. [63]He asked for a tablet and wrote, "John is his name," and all were amazed. [64]Immediately his mouth was opened, his tongue freed, and he spoke blessing God.[j] [65]Then fear came upon all their neighbors, and all these matters were discussed throughout the hill country of Judea. [66]All who heard these things took them to heart, saying, "What, then, will this child be?" For surely the hand of the Lord was with him.

**The Canticle of Zechariah.** [67]Then Zechariah his father, filled with the holy Spirit, prophesied, saying:

[68] †"Blessed be the Lord, the God of Israel,
    for he has visited and brought
        redemption to his people.[k]
[69] ‡He has raised up a horn for our salvation
    within the house of David his
        servant,[l]
[70] even as he promised through the mouth
        of his holy prophets from of old:
[71]     salvation from our enemies and
        from the hand of all who hate
        us,[m]

[72] to show mercy to our fathers[n]
    and to be mindful of his holy
        covenant[o]
[73] and of the oath he swore to Abraham our
        father,[p]
    and to grant us that, [74]rescued from
        the hand of enemies,
without fear we might worship him [75]in
        holiness and righteousness
    before him all our days.[q]
[76] And you, child, will be called prophet of
        the Most High,
    for you will go before the Lord[s] to
        prepare his ways,[r]
[77] to give his people knowledge of salvation
        through the forgiveness of their sins,
[78] because of the tender mercy of our God[s]
    by which the daybreak from on
        high[s] will visit us[t]
[79] to shine on those who sit in darkness and
        death's shadow,
    to guide our feet into the path of
        peace."

[80]The child grew and became strong in spirit, and he was in the desert until the day of his manifestation to Israel.[u]

## CHAPTER 2

**The Birth of Jesus.** [1]*In those days a decree went out from Caesar Augustus†† that the whole

---

sign of the covenant (Gn 17:1–12). The narrative of John's circumcision also prepares the way for the subsequent description of the circumcision of Jesus in Lk 2:21. At the beginning of his two-volume work Luke shows those who play crucial roles in the inauguration of Christianity to be wholly a part of the people of Israel. At the end of the Acts of the Apostles (Acts 21:20; 22:3; 23:6–9; 24:14–16; 26:2–8, 22–23) he will argue that Christianity is the direct descendant of Pharisaic Judaism.

\*[1:59] The practice of Palestinian Judaism at this time was to name the child at birth; moreover, though naming a male child after the father is not completely unknown, the usual practice was to name the child after the grandfather (see Lk 1:61). The naming of the child John and Zechariah's recovery from his loss of speech should be understood as fulfilling the angel's announcement to Zechariah in Lk 1:13, 20.

†[1:68–79] Like the canticle of Mary (Lk 1:46–55) the canticle of Zechariah is only loosely connected with its context. Apart from Lk 1:76–77, the hymn in speaking of **a horn for our salvation** (Lk 1:69) and **the daybreak from on high** (Lk 1:78) applies more closely to Jesus and his work than to John. Again like Mary's canticle, it is largely composed of phrases taken from the Greek Old Testament and may have been a Jewish Christian hymn of praise that Luke adapted to fit the present context by inserting Lk 1:76–77 to give Zechariah's reply to the question asked in Lk 1:66.

‡[1:69] **A horn for our salvation**: the horn is a common Old Testament figure for strength (Ps 18:3; 75:5–6; 89:18; 112:9; 148:14). This description is applied to God in Ps 18:2 and is here transferred to Jesus. The connection of the phrase with **the house of David** gives the title messianic overtones and may indicate an allusion to a phrase in Hannah's song of praise (1 Sm 2:10), "the horn of his anointed."

§[1:76] **You will go before the Lord**: here **the Lord** is most likely a reference to Jesus (contrast Lk 1:15–17 where Yahweh is meant) and John is presented as the precursor of Jesus.

¶[1:78] **The daybreak from on high**: three times in the LXX (Jer 23:5; Zec 3:8; 6:12), the Greek word used here for **daybreak** translates the Hebrew word for "scion, branch," an Old Testament messianic title.

\*\*[2:1–2] Although universal registrations of Roman citizens are attested in 28 B.C., 8 B.C., and A.D. 14 and enrollments in individual provinces of those who are not Roman citizens are also attested, such a universal census of the Roman world under Caesar Augustus is unknown outside the New Testament. Moreover, there are notorious historical problems connected with Luke's dating the census **when Quirinius was governor of Syria**, and the various attempts to resolve the difficulties have proved unsuccessful. P. Sulpicius Quirinius became legate of the province of Syria in A.D. 6–7 when Judea was annexed to the province of Syria. At that time, a provincial census of Judea was taken up. If Quirinius had been legate of Syria previously, it would have to have been before 10 B.C. because the various legates of Syria from 10 B.C. to 4 B.C. (the death of Herod) are known, and such a dating for an earlier census under Quirinius would create additional problems for dating the beginning of Jesus' ministry (Lk 3:1, 23). A previous legateship after 4 B.C. (and before A.D. 6) would not fit with the dating of Jesus' birth in the days of Herod (Lk 1:5; Mt 2:1). Luke may simply be combining Jesus' birth in Bethlehem with his vague recollection of a census under Quirinius (see also Acts 5:37) to underline the significance of this birth for the whole Roman world: through this child born in Bethlehem peace and salvation come to the empire.

††[2:1] **Caesar Augustus**: the reign of the Roman emperor Caesar Augustus is usually dated from 27 B.C. to his death in A.D. 14. According to Greek inscriptions, Augustus was

---

g. [1:58] 1:14.   h. [1:59] 2:21; Gn 17:10, 12; Lv 12:3.   i. [1:60] 1:13.   j. [1:64] 1:20.   k. [1:68] 7:16; Ps 41:13; 72:18; 106:48; 111:9.   l. [1:69] Ps 18:3.   m. [1:71] Ps 106:10.

n. [1:72–73] Gn 17:7; Lv 26:42; Ps 105:8–9; Mi 7:20.   o. [1:72] Ps 106:45–46.   p. [1:73–74] Gn 22:16–17.   q. [1:75] Ti 2:12.   r. [1:76] Is 40:3; Mal 3:1; Mt 3:3; 11:10.   s. [1:78–79] Is 60:1–2.   t. [1:78] Mal 3:20.   u. [1:80] 2:40; Mt 3:1.

world should be enrolled. [2]This was the first enrollment, when Quirinius was governor of Syria. [3]So all went to be enrolled, each to his own town. [4]And Joseph too went up from Galilee from the town of Nazareth to Judea, to the city of David that is called Bethlehem, because he was of the house and family of David,[v] [5]to be enrolled with Mary, his betrothed, who was with child.[w] [6]While they were there, the time came for her to have her child, [7]and she gave birth to her firstborn son.[*] She wrapped him in swaddling clothes and laid him in a manger, because there was no room for them in the inn.[x]

[8][†]Now there were shepherds in that region living in the fields and keeping the night watch over their flock. [9]The angel of the Lord appeared to them and the glory of the Lord shone around them, and they were struck with great fear.[y] [10]The angel said to them, "Do not be afraid; for behold, I proclaim to you good news of great joy that will be for all the people. [11][‡]For today in the city of David a savior has been born for you who is Messiah and Lord. [12]And this will be a sign for you: you will find an infant wrapped in swaddling clothes and lying in a manger." [13]And suddenly there was a multitude of the heavenly host with the angel, praising God and saying:

[14] [§]"Glory to God in the highest[a]
    and on earth peace to those on
        whom his favor rests."

**The Visit of the Shepherds.** [15]When the angels went away from them to heaven, the shepherds said to one another, "Let us go, then, to Bethlehem to see this thing that has taken place, which the Lord has made known to us." [16]So they went in haste and found Mary and Joseph, and the infant lying in the manger. [17]When they saw this, they made known the message that had been told them about this child. [18]All who heard it were amazed by what had been told them by the shepherds. [19]And Mary kept all these things, reflecting on them in her heart. [20]Then the shepherds returned, glorifying and praising God for all they had heard and seen, just as it had been told to them.

**The Circumcision and Naming of Jesus.** [21]When eight days were completed for his circumcision,[¶] he was named Jesus, the name given him by the angel before he was conceived in the womb.[b]

**The Presentation in the Temple.** [22][**]When the days were completed for their purification[††]

regarded in the Roman Empire as "savior" and "god," and he was credited with establishing a time of peace, the *pax Augusta*, throughout the Roman world during his long reign. It is not by chance that Luke relates the birth of Jesus to the time of Caesar Augustus: the real savior (Lk 2:11) and peace-bearer (Lk 2:14; see also Lk 19:38) is the child born in Bethlehem. The great emperor is simply God's agent (like the Persian king Cyrus in Is 44:28–45:1) who provides the occasion for God's purposes to be accomplished. **The whole world:** that is, the whole Roman world: Rome, Italy, and the Roman provinces.

*[2:7] **Firstborn son:** the description of Jesus as **firstborn** son does not necessarily mean that Mary had other sons. It is a legal description indicating that Jesus possessed the rights and privileges of the firstborn son (Gn 27; Ex 13:2; Nm 3:12–13; 18:15–16; Dt 21:15–17). See notes on Mt 1:25; Mk 6:3. **Wrapped him in swaddling clothes:** there may be an allusion here to the birth of another descendant of David, his son Solomon, who though a great king was wrapped in swaddling clothes like any other infant (Wis 7:4–6). **Laid him in a manger:** a feeding trough for animals. A possible allusion to Is 1:3 LXX.

†[2:8–20] The announcement of Jesus' birth to the shepherds is in keeping with Luke's theme that the lowly and neglected are the recipients of God's favors and blessings (see also Lk 1:48, 52).

‡[2:11] The basic message of the infancy narrative is contained in the angel's announcement: this child is **savior, Messiah,** and **Lord.** Luke is the only synoptic gospel writer to use the title **savior** for Jesus (Lk 2:11; Acts 5:31; 13:23; see also Lk 1:69; 19:9; Acts 4:12). As savior, Jesus is looked upon by Luke as the one who rescues humanity from sin and delivers humanity from the condition of alienation from God. The title *christos,* "Christ," is the Greek equivalent of the Hebrew *māšîaḥ,* "Messiah," "anointed one." Among certain groups in first-century Palestinian Judaism, the title was applied to an expected royal leader from the line of David who would restore the kingdom to Israel (see Acts 1:6). The political overtones of the title are played down in Luke and instead the Messiah of the Lord (Lk 2:26) or the Lord's anointed is the one who now brings salvation to all humanity, Jew and Gentile (Lk 2:29–32). Lord is the most frequently used title for Jesus in Luke and Acts. In the New Testament it is also applied to Yahweh, as it is in the Old Testament. When used of Jesus it points to his transcendence and dominion over humanity.

§[2:14] **On earth peace to those on whom his favor rests:** the peace that results from the Christ event is for those whom God has favored with his grace. This reading is found in the oldest representatives of the Western and Alexandrian text traditions and is the preferred one; the Byzantine text tradition, on the other hand, reads: "on earth peace, good will toward men." The peace of which Luke's gospel speaks (Lk 2:14; 7:50; 8:48; 10:5–6; 19:38, 42; 24:36) is more than the absence of war of the *pax Augusta;* it also includes the security and well-being characteristic of peace in the Old Testament.

¶[2:21] Just as John before him had been incorporated into the people of Israel through his circumcision, so too this child (see note on Lk 1:57–66).

**[2:22–40] The presentation of Jesus in the temple depicts the parents of Jesus as devout Jews, faithful observers of the law of the Lord (Lk 2:23–24, 39), i.e., the law of Moses. In this respect, they are described in a fashion similar to the parents of John (Lk 1:6) and Simeon (Lk 2:25) and Anna (Lk 2:36–37).

††[2:22] **Their purification:** syntactically, **their** must refer to Mary and Joseph, even though the Mosaic law never mentions the purification of the husband. Recognizing the problem, some Western scribes have altered the text to read "his purification," understanding the presentation of Jesus in the temple as a form of purification; the Vulgate version has a Latin form that could be either "his" or "her." According to the Mosaic law (Lv 12:2–8), the woman who gives birth to a boy is unable for forty days to touch anything sacred or to enter the temple area by reason of her legal impurity. At the end of this period she is required to offer a year-old lamb as a burnt offering and a turtledove or young pigeon as an expiation of sin. The woman who could not afford a lamb offered instead two turtledoves or two young pigeons, as Mary does here. **They took him up to Jerusalem to present him to the Lord:** as the firstborn son (Lk 2:7) Jesus was consecrated to the Lord as the law required (Ex 13:2, 12), but there was no requirement that this be done at the temple. The concept of a presentation at the temple is probably derived from 1 Sm 1:24–28, where Hannah offers the child Samuel for sanctuary services. The law further stipulated (Nm 3:47–48) that the firstborn son

v. [2:4] Mi 5:2; Mt 2:6.   w. [2:5] 1:27; Mt 1:18.   x. [2:7] Mt 1:25.
y. [2:9] 1:11, 26.   z. [2:11] Mt 1:21; 16:16; Jn 4:42; Acts 2:36; 5:31; Phil 2:11.

a. [2:14] 19:38.   b. [2:21] 1:31; Gn 17:12; Mt 1:21.

according to the law of Moses, they took him up to Jerusalem to present him to the Lord,[c 23]just as it is written in the law of the Lord, "Every male that opens the womb shall be consecrated to the Lord,"[d 24]and to offer the sacrifice of "a pair of turtledoves or two young pigeons," in accordance with the dictate in the law of the Lord.

[25]Now there was a man in Jerusalem whose name was Simeon. This man was righteous and devout, awaiting the consolation of Israel,* and the holy Spirit was upon him. [26]It had been revealed to him by the holy Spirit that he should not see death before he had seen the Messiah of the Lord. [27]He came in the Spirit into the temple; and when the parents brought in the child Jesus to perform the custom of the law in regard to him, [28]he took him into his arms and blessed God, saying:

[29] "Now, Master, you may let your servant
        go
        in peace, according to your word,
[30] for my eyes have seen your salvation,[e]
[31]     which you prepared in sight of all
        the peoples,
[32] a light for revelation to the Gentiles,
        and glory for your people Israel."[f]

[33]The child's father and mother were amazed at what was said about him; [34]and Simeon blessed them and said to Mary his mother, "Behold, this child is destined for the fall and rise of many in Israel, and to be a sign that will be contradicted[g] [35](and you yourself a sword will pierce)[†] so that the thoughts of many hearts may be revealed." [36]There was also a prophetess, Anna, the daughter of Phanuel, of the tribe of Asher. She was advanced in years, having lived seven years with her husband after her marriage, [37]and then as a widow until she was eighty-four. She never left the temple, but worshiped night and day with fasting and prayer. [38]And coming forward at that very time, she gave thanks to God and spoke about the child to all who were awaiting the redemption of Jerusalem.[h]

**The Return to Nazareth.** [39]When they had fulfilled all the prescriptions of the law of the Lord, they returned to Galilee, to their own town of Nazareth.[i] [40]The child grew and became strong, filled with wisdom; and the favor of God was upon him.[j]

**The Boy Jesus in the Temple.**[‡] [41]Each year his parents went to Jerusalem for the feast of Passover,[k] [42]and when he was twelve years old, they went up according to festival custom. [43]After they had completed its days, as they were returning, the boy Jesus remained behind in Jerusalem, but his parents did not know it. [44]Thinking that he was in the caravan, they journeyed for a day and looked for him among their relatives and acquaintances, [45]but not finding him, they returned to Jerusalem to look for him. [46]After three days they found him in the temple, sitting in the midst of the teachers, listening to them and asking them questions, [47]and all who heard him were astounded at his understanding and his answers. [48]When his parents saw him, they were astonished, and his mother said to him, "Son, why have you done this to us? Your father and I have been looking for you with great anxiety." [49]And he said to them, "Why were you looking for me? Did you not know that I must be in my Father's house?"[§] [50]But they did not understand what he said to them. [51]He went down with them and came to Nazareth, and was obedient to them; and his mother kept all these things in her heart.[l] [52]And Jesus advanced [in] wisdom and age and favor before God and man.[m]

## III. THE PREPARATION FOR THE PUBLIC MINISTRY

### CHAPTER 3

**The Preaching of John the Baptist.**[¶] [1]In the

---

should be redeemed by the parents through their payment of five shekels to a member of a priestly family. About this legal requirement Luke is silent.

*[2:25] **Awaiting the consolation of Israel:** Simeon here and later Anna who speak about the child to all who were awaiting the redemption of Jerusalem represent the hopes and expectations of faithful and devout Jews who at this time were looking forward to the restoration of God's rule in Israel. The birth of Jesus brings these hopes to fulfillment.

†[2:35] **(And you yourself a sword will pierce):** Mary herself will not be untouched by the various reactions to the role of Jesus (Lk 2:34). Her blessedness as mother of the Lord will be challenged by her son who describes true blessedness as "hearing the word of God and observing it" (Lk 11:27–28 and Lk 8:20–21).

‡[2:41–52] This story's concern with an incident from Jesus' youth is unique in the canonical gospel tradition. It presents Jesus in the role of the faithful Jewish boy, raised in the traditions of Israel, and fulfilling all that the law requires. With this episode, the infancy narrative ends just as it began, in the setting of the Jerusalem temple.

§[2:49] **I must be in my Father's house:** this phrase can also be translated, "I must be about my Father's work." In either translation, Jesus refers to God as his Father. His divine sonship, and his obedience to his heavenly Father's will, take precedence over his ties to his family.

¶[3:1–20] Although Luke is indebted in this section to his sources, the Gospel of Mark and a collection of sayings of John the Baptist, he has clearly marked this introduction to the ministry of Jesus with his own individual style. Just as the gospel began with a long periodic sentence (Lk 1:1–4), so too this section (Lk 3:1–2). He casts the call of John the Baptist in the form of an Old Testament prophetic call (Lk 3:2) and extends the quotation from Isaiah found in Mk 1:3 (Is 40:3) by the addition of Is 40:4–5 in Lk 3:5–6. In doing so, he presents his theme of the universality of salvation, which he has announced earlier in the words of Simeon (Lk 2:30–32). Moreover, in describing the expectation of the people (Lk 3:15), Luke is characterizing the time of John's preaching in the same way as he had earlier described the situation of other

---

c. [2:22–24] Lv 12:2–8.   d. [2:23] Ex 13:2, 12.   e. [2:30–31] 3:6; Is 40:5 LXX; 52:10.   f. [2:32] Is 42:6; 46:13; 49:6; Acts 13:47; 26:23.   g. [2:34] 12:51; Is 8:14; Jn 9:39; Rom 9:33; 1 Cor 1:23; 1 Pt 2:7–8.   h. [2:38] Is 52:9.

i. [2:39] Mt 2:23.   j. [2:40] 1:80; 2:52.   k. [2:41] Ex 12:24–27; 23:15; Dt 16:1–8.   l. [2:51] 2:19.   m. [2:52] 1:80; 2:40; 1 Sm 2:26.

fifteenth year of the reign of Tiberius Caesar,* when Pontius Pilate was governor of Judea,ⁿ and Herod was tetrarch of Galilee, and his brother Philip tetrarch of the region of Ituraea and Trachonitis, and Lysanias was tetrarch of Abilene, ²during the high priesthood of Annas and Caiaphas,† the word of God came to John° the son of Zechariah in the desert. ³*He went throughout [the] whole region of the Jordan, proclaiming a baptism of repentance for the forgiveness of sins,ᵖ ⁴‡as it is written in the book of the words of the prophet Isaiah:�q

"A voice of one crying out in the desert:
'Prepare the way of the Lord,ʳ
     make straight his paths.
⁵   Every valley shall be filled
        and every mountain and hill shall be
        made low.
The winding roads shall be made straight,
     and the rough ways made smooth,
⁶   and all flesh shall see the salvation of God.'"ˢ

⁷He said to the crowds who came out to be baptized by him, "You brood of vipers! Who warned you to flee from the coming wrath?ᵗ ⁸Produce good fruits as evidence of your repentance; and do not begin to say to yourselves, 'We have Abraham as our father,' for I tell you, God can raise up children to Abraham from these stones.ᵘ ⁹Even now the ax lies at the root of the trees. Therefore every tree that does not produce good fruit will be cut down and thrown into the fire."ᵛ

¹⁰And the crowds asked him, "What then should we do?" ¹¹He said to them in reply, "Whoever has two tunics should share with the person who has none. And whoever has food should do likewise." ¹²Even tax collectors came to be baptized and they said to him, "Teacher, what should we do?"ʷ ¹³He answered them, "Stop collecting more than what is prescribed." ¹⁴Soldiers also asked him, "And what is it that we should do?" He told them, "Do not practice extortion, do not falsely accuse anyone, and be satisfied with your wages."

¹⁵ˣNow the people were filled with expectation, and all were asking in their hearts whether John might be the Messiah. ¹⁶¶John answered them all, saying,ʸ "I am baptizing you with water, but one mightier than I is coming. I am not worthy to loosen the thongs of his sandals. He will baptize you with the holy Spirit and fire. ¹⁷His winnowing fan** is in his hand to clear his threshing floor and to gather the wheat into his barn, but the chaff he will burn with unquenchable fire."ᶻ ¹⁸Exhorting them in many other ways, he preached good news to the people. ¹⁹††Now Herod the tetrarch,ᵃ who had been censured by him because of Herodias, his brother's wife, and because of all the evil deeds Herod had committed, ²⁰added still another to these by [also] putting John in prison.

**The Baptism of Jesus.**‡‡ ²¹ᵇAfter all the people had been baptized and Jesus also had been

---

devout Israelites in the infancy narrative (Lk 2:25–26, 37–38). In Lk 3:7–18 Luke presents the preaching of John the Baptist who urges the crowds to reform in view of **the coming wrath** (Lk 3:7, 9: eschatological preaching), and who offers the crowds certain standards for reforming social conduct (Lk 3:10–14: ethical preaching), and who announces to the crowds the coming of **one mightier than** he (Lk 3:15–18: messianic preaching).

*[3:1] **Tiberius Caesar**: Tiberius succeeded Augustus as emperor in A.D. 14 and reigned until A.D. 37. The fifteenth year of his reign, depending on the method of calculating his first regnal year, would have fallen between A.D. 27 and 29. **Pontius Pilate**: prefect of Judea from A.D. 26 to 36. The Jewish historian Josephus describes him as a greedy and ruthless prefect who had little regard for the local Jewish population and their religious practices (see Lk 13:1). **Herod**: i.e., Herod Antipas, the son of Herod the Great. He ruled over Galilee and Perea from 4 B.C. to A.D. 39. His official title **tetrarch** means literally, "ruler of a quarter," but came to designate any subordinate prince. **Philip**: also a son of Herod the Great, tetrarch of the territory to the north and east of the Sea of Galilee from 4 B.C. to A.D. 34. Only two small areas of this territory are mentioned by Luke. **Lysanias**: nothing is known about this Lysanias who is said here to have been tetrarch of Abilene, a territory northwest of Damascus.

†[3:2] **During the high priesthood of Annas and Caiaphas**: after situating the call of John the Baptist in terms of the civil rulers of the period, Luke now mentions the religious leadership of Palestine (see note on Lk 1:5). Annas had been high priest A.D. 6–15. After being deposed by the Romans in A.D. 15 he was succeeded by various members of his family and eventually by his son-in-law, Caiaphas, who was high priest A.D. 18–36. Luke refers to Annas as high priest at this time (but see Jn 18:13, 19), possibly because of the continuing influence of Annas or because the title continued to be used for the ex-high priest. **The word of God came to John**: Luke is alone among the New Testament writers in associating the preaching of John with a call from God. Luke is thereby identifying John with the prophets whose ministries began with similar calls. In Lk 7:26 John will be described as "more than a prophet"; he is also the precursor of Jesus (Lk 7:27), a transitional figure inaugurating the period of the fulfillment of prophecy and promise.

‡[3:3] See note on Mt 3:2.

§[3:4] The Essenes from Qumran used the same passage to explain why their community was in the desert studying and observing the law and the prophets (1QS 8:12–15).

¶[3:16] **He will baptize you with the holy Spirit and fire**: in contrast to John's baptism with water, Jesus is said to baptize with the holy Spirit and with fire. From the point of view of the early Christian community, the Spirit and fire must have been understood in the light of the fire symbolism of the pouring out of the Spirit at Pentecost (Acts 2:1–4); but as part of John's preaching, the Spirit and fire should be related to their purifying and refining characteristics (Ez 36:25–27; Mal 3:2–3). See note on Mt 3:11.

**[3:17] **Winnowing fan**: see note on Mt 3:12.

††[3:19–20] Luke separates the ministry of John the Baptist from that of Jesus by reporting the imprisonment of John before the baptism of Jesus (Lk 3:21–22). Luke uses this literary device to serve his understanding of the periods of salvation history. With John the Baptist, the time of promise, the period of Israel, comes to an end; with the baptism of Jesus and the descent of the Spirit upon him, the time of fulfillment, the period of Jesus, begins. In his second volume, the Acts of the Apostles, Luke will introduce the third epoch in salvation history, the period of the church.

‡‡[3:21–22] This episode in Luke focuses on the heavenly message identifying Jesus as Son and, through the allusion to

---

n. [3:1–20] Mt 3:1–12; Mk 1:1–8; Jn 1:19–28.   o. [3:2] 1:80.   p. [3:3] Acts 13:24; 19:4.   q. [3:4–6] Is 40:3–5.   r. [3:4] Jn 1:23.   s. [3:6] 2:30–31.

t. [3:7] Mt 12:34.   u. [3:8] Jn 8:39.   v. [3:9] Mt 7:19; 15:6.   w. [3:12] 7:29.   x. [3:15–16] Acts 13:25.   y. [3:16] 7:19–20; Jn 1:27; Acts 1:5; 11:16.   z. [3:17] Mt 3:12.   a. [3:19–20] Mt 14:3–4; Mk 6:17–18.   b. [3:21–22] Mt 3:13–17; Mk 1:9–11.

baptized and was praying,* heaven was opened ²²ᵗᶜand the holy Spirit descended upon him in bodily form like a dove. And a voice came from heaven, "You are my beloved Son; with you I am well pleased."

**The Genealogy of Jesus.**‡ ²³ᵈWhen Jesus began his ministry he was about thirty years of age. He was the son, as was thought, of Joseph, the son of Heli,ᵉ ²⁴the son of Matthat, the son of Levi, the son of Melchi, the son of Jannai, the son of Joseph, ²⁵the son of Mattathias, the son of Amos, the son of Nahum, the son of Esli, the son of Naggai, ²⁶the son of Maath, the son of Mattathias, the son of Semein, the son of Josech, the son of Joda, ²⁷the son of Joanan, the son of Rhesa, the son of Zerubbabel, the son of Shealtiel, the son of Neri,ᶠ ²⁸the son of Melchi, the son of Addi, the son of Cosam, the son of Elmadam, the son of Er, ²⁹the son of Joshua, the son of Eliezer, the son of Jorim, the son of Matthat, the son of Levi, ³⁰the son of Simeon, the son of Judah, the son of Joseph, the son of Jonam, the son of Eliakim, ³¹the son of Melea, the son of Menna, the son of Mattatha, the son of Nathan, the son of David,§ ³²the son of Jesse,ʰ the son of Obed, the son of Boaz, the son of Sala, the son of Nahshon, ³³the son of Amminadab, the son of Admin, the son of Arni, the son of Hezron, the son of Perez,ⁱ the son of Judah,ʲ ³⁴the son of Jacob, the son of Isaac, the son of Abraham,ᵏ the son of Terah, the son of Nahor, ³⁵the son of Serug, the son of Reu, the son of Peleg, the son of Eber, the son of Shelah, ³⁶the son of Cainan, the son of Arphaxad, the son of Shem,ˡ the son of Noah, the son of Lamech, ³⁷the son of Methuselah, the son of Enoch, the son of Jared, the son of Mahalaleel,

the son of Cainan, ³⁸the son of Enos, the son of Seth, the son of Adam,ᵐ the son of God.

## CHAPTER 4

**The Temptation of Jesus.**¶ ¹ⁿFilled with the holy Spirit,** Jesus returned from the Jordan and was led by the Spirit into the desert ²for forty days,†† to be tempted by the devil. He ate nothing during those days, and when they were over he was hungry.º ³The devil said to him, "If you are the Son of God, command this stone to become bread." ⁴Jesus answered him, "It is written, 'One does not live by bread alone.'"ᵖ ⁵Then he took him up and showed him all the kingdoms of the world in a single instant. ⁶The devil said to him, "I shall give to you all this power and their glory; for it has been handed over to me, and I may give it to whomever I wish.�q ⁷All this will be yours, if you worship me." ⁸Jesus said to him in reply, "It is written:

'You shall worship the Lord, your God, and him alone shall you serve.'"ʳ

⁹‡‡Then he led him to Jerusalem, made him stand on the parapet of the temple, and said to him, "If you are the Son of God, throw yourself down from here, ¹⁰for it is written:

'He will command his angels concerning you, to guard you,'ˢ

¹¹and:

'With their hands they will support you, lest you dash your foot against a stone.'"ᵗ

¹²Jesus said to him in reply, "It also says, 'You shall not put the Lord, your God, to the test.'"ᵘ ¹³§§When the devil had finished every temptation,ᵛ he departed from him for a time.

---

Is 42:1, as Servant of Yahweh. The relationship of Jesus to the Father has already been announced in the infancy narrative (Lk 1:32, 35; 2:49); it occurs here at the beginning of Jesus' Galilean ministry and will reappear in Lk 9:35 before another major section of Luke's gospel, the travel narrative (Lk 9:51–19:27). Elsewhere in Luke's writings (Lk 4:18; Acts 10:38), this incident will be interpreted as a type of anointing of Jesus.

*[3:21] **Was praying:** Luke regularly presents Jesus at prayer at important points in his ministry: here at his baptism; at the choice of the Twelve (Lk 6:12); before Peter's confession (Lk 9:18); at the transfiguration (Lk 9:28); when he teaches his disciples to pray (Lk 11:1); at the Last Supper (Lk 22:32); on the Mount of Olives (Lk 22:41); on the cross (Lk 23:46).

†[3:22] **You are my beloved Son; with you I am well pleased:** this is the best attested reading in the Greek manuscripts. The Western reading, "You are my Son, this day I have begotten you," is derived from Ps 2:7.

‡[3:23–38] Whereas Mt 1:2 begins the genealogy of Jesus with Abraham to emphasize Jesus' bonds with the people of Israel, Luke's universalism leads him to trace the descent of Jesus beyond Israel to Adam and beyond that to God (Lk 3:38) to stress again Jesus' divine sonship.

§[3:31] **The son of Nathan, the son of David:** in keeping with Jesus' prophetic role in Luke and Acts (e.g., Lk 7:16, 39; 9:8; 13:33; 24:19; Acts 3:22–23; 7:37) Luke traces Jesus' Davidic ancestry through the prophet Nathan (see 2 Sm 7:2) rather than through King Solomon, as Mt 1:6–7.

¶[4:1–13] See note on Mt 4:1–11.

**[4:1] **Filled with the holy Spirit:** as a result of the descent of the Spirit upon him at his baptism (Lk 3:21–22), Jesus is now equipped to overcome the devil. Just as the Spirit is prominent at this early stage of Jesus' ministry (Lk 4:1, 14, 18), so too it will be at the beginning of the period of the church in Acts (Acts 1:4; 2:4, 17).

††[4:2] **For forty days:** the mention of forty days recalls the forty years of the wilderness wanderings of the Israelites during the Exodus (Dt 8:2).

‡‡[4:9] **To Jerusalem:** the Lucan order of the temptations concludes on the parapet of the temple in Jerusalem, the city of destiny in Luke-Acts. It is in Jerusalem that Jesus will ultimately face his destiny (Lk 9:51; 13:33).

§§[4:13] **For a time:** the devil's opportune time will occur before the passion and death of Jesus (Lk 22:3, 31–32, 53).

---

c. [3:22] 9:35; Ps 2:7; Is 42:1; Mt 12:18; 17:5; Mk 9:7; Jn 1:32; 2 Pt 1:17.　d. [3:23–38] Mt 1:1–17.　e. [3:23] 4:22; Jn 6:42.　f. [3:27] 1 Chr 3:17; Ez 3:2.　g. [3:31] 2 Sm 5:14.　h. [3:31–32] 1 Sm 16:1, 18.　i. [3:31–33] Ru 4:17–22; 1 Chr 2:1–15.　j. [3:33] Gn 29:35; 38:29.　k. [3:34] Gn 21:3; 25:26; 1 Chr 1:34; 28:34.　l. [3:34–36] Gn 11:10–26; 1 Chr 1:24–27.

m. [3:36–38] Gn 4:25–5:32; 1 Chr 1:1–4.　n. [4:1–13] Mt 4:1–11; Mk 1:12–13.　o. [4:2] Heb 4:15.　p. [4:4] Dt 8:3.　q. [4:6] Jer 27:5; Mt 28:18.　r. [4:8] Dt 6:13.　s. [4:10] Ps 91:11.　t. [4:11] Ps 91:12.　u. [4:12] Dt 6:16; 1 Cor 10:9.　v. [4:13] 22:3; Jn 13:2, 27; Heb 4:15.

## IV. THE MINISTRY IN GALILEE

**The Beginning of the Galilean Ministry.**
¹⁴ʷJesus returned to Galilee in the power of the Spirit, and news of him spread* throughout the whole region.ˣ ¹⁵He taught in their synagogues and was praised by all.

**The Rejection at Nazareth.**†ʸ ¹⁶He came to Nazareth, where he had grown up, and went according to his custom‡ into the synagogue on the sabbath day. He stood up to read ¹⁷and was handed a scroll of the prophet Isaiah. He unrolled the scroll and found the passage where it was written:

¹⁸ "The Spirit of the Lord is upon me,§
   because he has anointed me
      to bring glad tidings to the poor.ᶻ
He has sent me to proclaim liberty to
      captives
   and recovery of sight to the blind,
      to let the oppressed go free,
¹⁹ and to proclaim a year acceptable to the
      Lord."

²⁰Rolling up the scroll, he handed it back to the attendant and sat down, and the eyes of all in the synagogue looked intently at him. ²¹He said to them, "Today this scripture passage is fulfilled in your hearing."¶ ²²And all spoke highly of him and were amazed at the gracious words that came from his mouth. They also asked, "Isn't this the son of Joseph?"ᵃ ²³He said to them, "Surely you will quote me this proverb, 'Physician, cure yourself,' and say, 'Do here in your native place the things that we heard were done in Capernaum.'"** ²⁴And he said, "Amen, I say to you, no prophet is accepted in his own native place. ²⁵††Indeed, I tell you, there were many widows in Israel in the days of Elijah when the sky was closed for three and a half years and a severe famine spread over the entire land.ᵇ ²⁶‡‡It was to none of these that Elijah was sent, but only to a widow in Zarephathᶜ in the land of Sidon. ²⁷Again, there were many lepers in Israel during the time of Elisha the prophet; yet not one of them was cleansed, but only Naaman the Syrian.ᵈ ²⁸When the people in the synagogue heard this, they were all filled with fury. ²⁹They rose up, drove him out of the town, and led him to the brow of the hill on which their town had been built, to hurl him down headlong. ³⁰But he passed through the midst of them and went away.

**The Cure of a Demoniac.** ³¹§§Jesus then went down to Capernaum,ᵉ a town of Galilee.ᶠ He taught them on the sabbath, ³²and they were astonished at his teaching because he spoke with authority.ᵍ ³³In the synagogue there was a man with the spirit of an unclean demon,ʰ and he cried out in a loud voice, ³⁴"Ha! What have you to do with us, Jesus of Nazareth? Have you come to destroy us?¶¶ I know who you are—the Holy One of God!"ⁱ ³⁵Jesus rebuked him and said, "Be quiet! Come out of him!" Then the demon threw the man down in front of them and came out of him without doing him any harm. ³⁶They were all amazed and said to one another, "What is there about his word? For with authority and power he commands the unclean spirits, and they come out." ³⁷And news of him spread everywhere in the surrounding region.

---

*[4:14] **News of him spread**: a Lucan theme; see Lk 4:37; 5:15; 7:17.

†[4:16–30] Luke has transposed to the beginning of Jesus' ministry an incident from his Marcan source, which situated it near the end of the Galilean ministry (Mk 6:1–6a). In doing so, Luke turns the initial admiration (Lk 4:22) and subsequent rejection of Jesus (Lk 4:28–29) into a foreshadowing of the whole future ministry of Jesus. Moreover, the rejection of Jesus in his own hometown hints at the greater rejection of him by Israel (Acts 13:46).

‡[4:16] **According to his custom**: Jesus' practice of regularly attending synagogue is carried on by the early Christians' practice of meeting in the temple (Acts 2:46; 3:1; 5:12).

§[4:18] **The Spirit of the Lord is upon me, because he has anointed me**: see note on Lk 3:21–22. As this incident develops, Jesus is portrayed as a prophet whose ministry is compared to that of the prophets Elijah and Elisha. Prophetic anointings are known in first-century Palestinian Judaism from the Qumran literature that speaks of prophets as God's anointed ones. **To bring glad tidings to the poor**: more than any other gospel writer Luke is concerned with Jesus' attitude toward the economically and socially poor (see Lk 6:20, 24; 12:16–21; 14:12–14; 16:19–26; 19:8). At times, the poor in Luke's gospel are associated with the downtrodden, the oppressed and afflicted, the forgotten and the neglected (Lk 4:18; 6:20–22; 7:22; 14:12–14), and it is they who accept Jesus' message of salvation.

¶[4:21] **Today this scripture passage is fulfilled in your hearing**: this sermon inaugurates the time of fulfillment of Old Testament prophecy. Luke presents the ministry of Jesus as fulfilling Old Testament hopes and expectations (Lk 7:22); for Luke, even Jesus' suffering, death, and resurrection are done in fulfillment of the scriptures (Lk 24:25–27, 44–46; Acts 3:18).

**[4:23] **The things that we heard were done in Capernaum**: Luke's source for this incident reveals an awareness of an earlier ministry of Jesus in Capernaum that Luke has not yet made use of because of his transposition of this Nazareth episode to the beginning of Jesus' Galilean ministry. It is possible that by use of the future tense **you will quote me . . . ,** Jesus is being portrayed as a prophet.

††[4:25–26] The references to Elijah and Elisha serve several purposes in this episode: they emphasize Luke's portrait of Jesus as a prophet like Elijah and Elisha; they help to explain why the initial admiration of the people turns to rejection; and they provide the scriptural justification for the future Christian mission to the Gentiles.

‡‡[4:26] **A widow in Zarephath in the land of Sidon**: like Naaman the Syrian in Lk 4:27, a non-Israelite becomes the object of the prophet's ministry.

§§[4:31–44] The next several incidents in Jesus' ministry take place in Capernaum and are based on Luke's source, Mk 1:21–39. To the previous portrait of Jesus as prophet (Lk 4:16–30) they now add a presentation of him as teacher (Lk 4:31–32), exorcist (Lk 4:32–37, 41), healer (Lk 4:38–40), and proclaimer of God's kingdom (Lk 4:43).

¶¶[4:34] **What have you to do with us?**: see note on Jn 2:4. **Have you come to destroy us?**: the question reflects the current belief that before the day of the Lord control over humanity would be wrested from the evil spirits, evil destroyed, and God's authority over humanity reestablished. The synoptic gospel tradition presents Jesus carrying out this task.

---

w. [4:14–15] Mt 4:12–17; Mk 1:14–15.   x. [4:14] 5:15; Mt 3:16.
y. [4:16–30] Mt 13:53–58; Mk 6:1–6.   z. [4:18–19] Is 61:1–2;
58:6.   a. [4:22] 3:23; Jn 6:42.

b. [4:25] 1 Kgs 17:1–7; 18:1; Jas 5:17.   c. [4:26] 1 Kgs 17:9.   d. [4:27]
2 Kgs 5:1–14.   e. [4:31–37] Mk 1:21–28.   f. [4:31] Mt 4:13; Jn
2:12.   g. [4:32] Mt 7:28–29.   h. [4:33–34] 8:28; Mt 8:29; Mk 1:23–
24; 5:7.   i. [4:34] 4:41; Jn 6:69.

**The Cure of Simon's Mother-in-Law.** [38j]After he left the synagogue, he entered the house of Simon.* Simon's mother-in-law was afflicted with a severe fever, and they interceded with him about her. [39]He stood over her, rebuked the fever, and it left her. She got up immediately and waited on them.

**Other Healings.**[k] [40]At sunset, all who had people sick with various diseases brought them to him. He laid his hands on each of them and cured them. [41]And demons also came out from many, shouting, "You are the Son of God."[l] But he rebuked them and did not allow them to speak because they knew that he was the Messiah.[†]

**Jesus Leaves Capernaum.**[m] [42‡]At daybreak, Jesus left and went to a deserted place. The crowds went looking for him, and when they came to him, they tried to prevent him from leaving them. [43]But he said to them, "To the other towns also I must proclaim the good news of the kingdom of God, because for this purpose I have been sent."[n] [44]And he was preaching in the synagogues of Judea.[§]

## CHAPTER 5

**The Call of Simon the Fisherman.**[o] [1p]While the crowd was pressing in on Jesus and listening to the word of God, he was standing by the Lake of Gennesaret. [2]He saw two boats there alongside the lake; the fishermen had disembarked and were washing their nets. [3]Getting into one of the boats, the one belonging to Simon, he asked him to put out a short distance from the shore. Then he sat down and taught the crowds from the boat. [4q]After he had finished speaking, he said to Simon, "Put out into deep water and lower your nets for a catch." [5]Simon said in reply, "Master, we have worked hard all night and have caught nothing, but at your command I will lower the nets." [6]When they had done this, they caught a great number of fish and their nets were tearing. [7]They signaled to their partners in the other boat to come to help them. They came and filled both boats so that they were in danger of sinking. [8]When Simon Peter saw this, he fell at the knees of Jesus and said, "Depart from me, Lord, for I am a sinful man." [9]For astonishment at the catch of fish they had made seized him and all those with him, [10]and likewise James and John, the sons of Zebedee, who were partners of Simon. Jesus said to Simon, "Do not be afraid; from now on you will be catching men."[r] [11]When they brought their boats to the shore, they left everything** and followed him.[s]

**The Cleansing of a Leper.**[t] [12]Now there was a man full of leprosy[††] in one of the towns where he was; and when he saw Jesus, he fell prostrate, pleaded with him, and said, "Lord, if you wish, you can make me clean." [13]Jesus stretched out his hand, touched him, and said, "I do will it. Be made clean." And the leprosy left him immediately. [14]Then he ordered him not to tell anyone, but "Go, show yourself to the priest and offer for your cleansing what Moses prescribed;[‡‡] that will be proof for them."[u] [15]The report about him spread all the more, and great crowds assembled to listen to him and to be cured of their ailments, [16]but he would withdraw to deserted places to pray.[v]

**The Healing of a Paralytic.**[w] [17§§]One day as Jesus was teaching, Pharisees[¶¶] and teachers of the law

---

* [4:38] **The house of Simon:** because of Luke's arrangement of material, the reader has not yet been introduced to Simon (cf. Mk 1:16–18, 29–31). Situated as it is before the call of Simon (Lk 5:1–11), it helps the reader to understand Simon's eagerness to do what Jesus says (Lk 5:5) and to follow him (Lk 5:11).

† [4:41] **They knew that he was the Messiah:** that is, the Christ (see note on Lk 2:11).

‡ [4:42] **They tried to prevent him from leaving them:** the reaction of these strangers in Capernaum is presented in contrast to the reactions of those in his hometown who rejected him (Lk 4:28–30).

§ [4:44] **In the synagogues of Judea:** instead of **Judea,** which is the best reading of the manuscript tradition, the Byzantine text tradition and other manuscripts read "Galilee," a reading that harmonizes Luke with Mt 4:23 and Mk 1:39. Up to this point Luke has spoken only of a ministry of Jesus in Galilee. Luke may be using **Judea** to refer to the land of Israel, the territory of the Jews, and not to a specific portion of it.

¶ [5:1–11] This incident has been transposed from his source, Mk 1:16–20, which places it immediately after Jesus makes his appearance in Galilee. By this transposition Luke uses this example of Simon's acceptance of Jesus to counter the earlier rejection of him by his hometown people, and since several incidents dealing with Jesus' power and authority have already been narrated, Luke creates a plausible context for the acceptance of Jesus by Simon and his partners. Many commentators have noted the similarity between the wondrous catch of fish reported here (Lk 4:4–9) and the post-resurrectional appearance of Jesus in Jn 21:1–11. There are traces in Luke's story that the post-resurrectional context is the original one: in Lk 4:8 Simon addresses Jesus as **Lord** (a post-resurrectional title for Jesus—see Lk 24:34; Acts 2:36—that has been read back into the historical ministry of Jesus) and recognizes himself as a sinner (an appropriate recognition for one who had denied knowing Jesus—Lk 22:54–62). As used by Luke, the incident looks forward to Peter's leadership in Luke-Acts (Lk 6:14; 9:20; 22:31–32; 24:34; Acts 1:15; 2:14–40; 10:11–18; 15:7–12) and symbolizes the future success of Peter as fisherman (Acts 2:41).

** [5:11] **They left everything:** in Mk 1:16–20 and Mt 4:18–22 the fishermen who follow Jesus leave their nets and their father; in Luke, they leave **everything** (see also Lk 5:28; 12:33; 14:33; 18:22), an indication of Luke's theme of complete detachment from material possessions.

†† [5:12] **Full of leprosy:** see note on Mk 1:40.

‡‡ [5:14] **Show yourself to the priest . . . what Moses prescribed:** this is a reference to Lv 14:2–9 that gives detailed instructions for one who had been a victim of leprosy and thereby excluded from contact with others (see Lv 13:45–46, 49; Nm 5:2–3). **That will be proof for them:** see note on Mt 8:4.

§§ [5:17–6:11] From his Marcan source, Luke now introduces a series of controversies with Pharisees: controversy over Jesus' power to forgive sins (Lk 5:17–26); controversy over his eating and drinking with tax collectors and sinners (Lk 5:27–32); controversy over not fasting (Lk 5:33–36); and finally two episodes narrating controversies over observance of the sabbath (Lk 5:1–11).

¶¶ [5:17] **Pharisees:** see note on Mt 3:7.

---

j. [4:38–39] Mt 8:14–15; Mk 1:29–31.    k. [4:40–41] Mt 8:16; Mk 1:32–34.    l. [4:41] 4:34; Mt 8:29; Mk 3:11–12.    m. [4:42–44] Mk 1:35–39.    n. [4:43] 8:1; Mk 1:14–15.    o. [5:1–11] Mt 4:18–22; Mk 1:16–20.    p. [5:1–3] Mt 13:1–2; Mk 2:13; 3:9–10; 4:1–2.

q. [5:4–9] Jn 21:1–11.    r. [5:10] Jer 16:16.    s. [5:11] Mt 19:27.    t. [5:12–16] Mt 8:2–4; Mk 1:40–45.    u. [5:14] 8:56; Lv 14:2–32; Mk 7:36.    v. [5:16] Mk 1:35.    w. [5:17–26] Mt 9:1–8; Mk 2:1–12.

were sitting there who had come from every village of Galilee and Judea and Jerusalem, and the power of the Lord was with him for healing. ¹⁸And some men brought on a stretcher a man who was paralyzed; they were trying to bring him in and set [him] in his presence. ¹⁹But not finding a way to bring him in because of the crowd, they went up on the roof and lowered him on the stretcher through the tiles* into the middle in front of Jesus. ²⁰When he saw their faith, he said, "As for you, your sins are forgiven."† ²¹Then the scribes‡ and Pharisees began to ask themselves, "Who is this who speaks blasphemies? Who but God alone can forgive sins?"ˣ ²²Jesus knew their thoughts and said to them in reply, "What are you thinking in your hearts?ʸ ²³Which is easier, to say, 'Your sins are forgiven,' or to say, 'Rise and walk'? ²⁴ᶻBut that you may know that the Son of Man has authority on earth to forgive sins"—he said to the man who was paralyzed, "I say to you, rise, pick up your stretcher, and go home." ²⁵He stood up immediately before them, picked up what he had been lying on, and went home, glorifying God. ²⁶Then astonishment seized them all and they glorified God, and, struck with awe, they said, "We have seen incredible things today."

**The Call of Levi.**ᵃ ²⁷After this he went out and saw a tax collector named Levi sitting at the customs post. He said to him, "Follow me." ²⁸And leaving everything behind,¶ he got up and followed him. ²⁹ᵇThen Levi gave a great banquet for him in his house, and a large crowd of tax collectors and others were at table with them. ³⁰The Pharisees and their scribes complained to his disciples, saying, "Why do you eat and drink with tax collectors and sinners?" ³¹Jesus said to them in reply, "Those who are healthy do not need a physician, but the sick do. ³²I have not come to call the righteous to repentance but sinners."

**The Question About Fasting.**ᶜ ³³And they said to him, "The disciples of John fast often and offer prayers, and the disciples of the Pharisees do the same; but yours eat and drink." ³⁴**Jesus answered them, "Can you make the wedding guests†† fast while the bridegroom is with them? ³⁵But the days will come, and when the bridegroom is taken away from them, then they will fast in those days." ³⁶‡‡And he also told them a parable. "No one tears a piece from a new cloak to patch an old one. Otherwise, he will tear the new and the piece from it will not match the old cloak. ³⁷Likewise, no one pours new wine into old wineskins. Otherwise, the new wine will burst the skins, and it will be spilled, and the skins will be ruined. ³⁸Rather, new wine must be poured into fresh wineskins. ³⁹[And] no one who has been drinking old wine desires new, for he says, 'The old is good.'"§§

## CHAPTER 6

**Debates About the Sabbath.**¶¶ ¹ᵈWhile he was going through a field of grain on a sabbath, his disciples were picking the heads of grain, rubbing them in their hands, and eating them.ᵉ ²Some Pharisees said, "Why are you doing what is unlawful on the sabbath?" ³ᶠJesus said to them in reply, "Have you not read what David did when he and those [who were] with him were hungry? ⁴[How] he went into the house of God, took the bread of offering,*** which only the priests could lawfully eat, ate of it, and shared it with his companions."ᵍ ⁵Then he said to them, "The Son of Man is lord of the sabbath."

⁶ʰOn another sabbath he went into the synagogue and taught, and there was a man there whose right hand was withered. ⁷The scribes and the Pharisees watched him closely to see if he would cure on the sabbath so that they might discover a reason to accuse him.ⁱ ⁸But he realized their intentions and said to the man with the withered hand, "Come up and stand before us." And he rose and stood there.ʲ ⁹Then Jesus said to them, "I ask you, is it lawful to do good on the sabbath rather than to do evil, to save life rather than to destroy it?" ¹⁰Looking around at them all, he then said to him, "Stretch out your hand." He did so and his hand was restored. ¹¹But they became enraged and discussed together what they might do to Jesus.

---

*[5:19] **Through the tiles:** Luke has adapted the story found in Mark to his non-Palestinian audience by changing "opened up the roof" (Mk 2:4, a reference to Palestinian straw and clay roofs) to **through the tiles,** a detail that reflects the Hellenistic Greco-Roman house with tiled roof.

†[5:20] **As for you, your sins are forgiven:** literally, "O man, your sins are forgiven you." The connection between the forgiveness of sins and the cure of the paralytic reflects the belief of first-century Palestine (based on the Old Testament: Ex 20:5; Dt 5:9) that sickness and infirmity are the result of sin, one's own or that of one's ancestors (see also Lk 13:2; Jn 5:14; 9:2).

‡[5:21] **The scribes:** see note on Mk 2:6.

§[5:24] See notes on Mt 9:6 and Mk 2:10.

¶[5:28] **Leaving everything behind:** see note on Lk 5:11.

**[5:34–35] See notes on Mt 9:15 and Mk 2:19.

††[5:34] **Wedding guests:** literally, "sons of the bridal chamber."

‡‡[5:36–39] See notes on Mt 9:16–17 and Mk 2:19.

§§[5:39] **The old is good:** this saying is meant to be ironic and offers an explanation for the rejection by some of the new wine that Jesus offers: satisfaction with old forms will prevent one from sampling the new.

¶¶[6:1–11] The two episodes recounted here deal with gathering grain and healing, both of which were forbidden on the sabbath. In his defense of his disciples' conduct and his own charitable deed, Jesus argues that satisfying human needs such as hunger and performing works of mercy take precedence even over the sacred sabbath rest. See also notes on Mt 12:1–14 and Mk 2:25–26.

***[6:4] **The bread of offering:** see note on Mt 12:5–6.

x. [5:21] 7:49; Is 43:25.   y. [5:22] 6:8; 9:47.   z. [5:24–25] Jn 5:8–9, 27.   a. [5:27–32] Mt 9:9–13; Mk 2:13–17.   b. [5:29–30] 15:1–2.   c. [5:33–39] Mt 9:14–17; Mk 2:18–22.

d. [6:1–5] Mt 12:1–8; Mk 2:23–28.   e. [6:1] Dt 23:26.   f. [6:3–4] 1 Sm 21:1–6.   g. [6:4] Lv 24:5–9.   h. [6:6–11] Mt 12:9–14; Mk 3:1–6.   i. [6:7] 14:1.   j. [6:8] 5:22; 9:47.

**The Mission of the Twelve.*** $^{12k}$In those days he departed to the mountain to pray, and he spent the night in prayer† to God. $^{13}$When day came, he called his disciples to himself, and from them he chose Twelve,‡ whom he also named apostles: $^{14l}$Simon, whom he named Peter,§ and his brother Andrew, James, John, Philip, Bartholomew, $^{15}$Matthew, Thomas, James the son of Alphaeus, Simon who was called a Zealot,¶ $^{16}$and Judas the son of James, and Judas Iscariot,** who became a traitor.

**Ministering to a Great Multitude.**$^m$ $^{17}$†And he came down with them and stood on a stretch of level ground. A great crowd of his disciples and a large number of the people from all Judea and Jerusalem and the coastal region of Tyre and Sidon $^{18}$came to hear him and to be healed of their diseases; and even those who were tormented by unclean spirits were cured. $^{19}$Everyone in the crowd sought to touch him because power came forth from him and healed them all.

**Sermon on the Plain.**$^n$ $^{20}$‡‡And raising his eyes toward his disciples he said:

"Blessed are you who are poor,§§
 for the kingdom of God is yours.
$^{21}$ Blessed are you who are now hungry,
 for you will be satisfied.
 Blessed are you who are now weeping,
 for you will laugh.$^o$
$^{22}$ Blessed are you when people hate you,
 and when they exclude and insult you,
 and denounce your name as evil
 on account of the Son of Man.$^p$

$^{23}$Rejoice and leap for joy on that day! Behold, your reward will be great in heaven. For their ancestors treated the prophets in the same way.$^q$

$^{24}$ But woe to you who are rich,
 for you have received your
 consolation.$^r$
$^{25}$ But woe to you who are filled now,
 for you will be hungry.
 Woe to you who laugh now,
 for you will grieve and weep.$^s$
$^{26}$ Woe to you when all speak well of you,
 for their ancestors treated the false
 prophets in this way.$^t$

**Love of Enemies.**¶¶ $^{27u}$"But to you who hear I say, love your enemies, do good to those who hate·you,$^v$ $^{28}$bless those who curse you, pray for those who mistreat you.$^w$ $^{29}$To the person who strikes you on one cheek, offer the other one as well, and from the person who takes your cloak, do not withhold even your tunic. $^{30}$Give to everyone who asks of you, and from the one who takes what is yours do·not demand it back. $^{31}$Do to others as you would have them do to you.$^x$ $^{32}$For if you love those who love you, what

---

*[6:12–16] See notes on Mt 10:1–11:1 and Mk 3:14–15.

†[6:12] **Spent the night in prayer:** see note on Lk 3:21.

‡[6:13] **He chose Twelve:** the identification of this group as the **Twelve** is a part of early Christian tradition (see 1 Cor 15:5), and in Matthew and Luke, the **Twelve** are associated with the twelve tribes of Israel (Lk 22:29–30; Mt 19:28). After the fall of Judas from his position among the Twelve, the need is felt on the part of the early community to reconstitute this group before the Christian mission begins at Pentecost (Acts 1:15–26). From Luke's perspective, they are an important group who because of their association with Jesus from the time of his baptism to his ascension (Acts 1:21–22) provide the continuity between the historical Jesus and the church of Luke's day and who as the original eyewitnesses guarantee the fidelity of the church's beliefs and practices to the teachings of Jesus (Lk 1:1–4). **Whom he also named apostles:** only Luke among the gospel writers attributes to Jesus the bestowal of the name **apostles** upon the Twelve. See note on Mt 10:2–4. "Apostle" becomes a technical term in early Christianity for a missionary sent out to preach the word of God. Although Luke seems to want to restrict the title to the Twelve (only in Acts 4:4, 14 are Paul and Barnabas termed apostles), other places in the New Testament show an awareness that the term was more widely applied (1 Cor 15:5–7; Gal 1:19; 1 Cor 1:1; 9:1; Rom 16:7).

§[6:14] **Simon, whom he named Peter:** see note on Mk 3:16.

¶[6:15] **Simon who was called a Zealot:** the Zealots were the instigators of the First Revolt of Palestinian Jews against Rome in A.D. 66–70. Because the existence of the Zealots as a distinct group during the lifetime of Jesus is the subject of debate, the meaning of the identification of Simon as a Zealot is unclear.

**[6:16] **Judas Iscariot:** the name **Iscariot** may mean "man from Kerioth."

††[6:17] **The coastal region of Tyre and Sidon:** not only Jews from Judea and Jerusalem, but even Gentiles from outside Palestine come to hear Jesus (see Lk 2:31–32; 3:6; 4:24–27).

‡‡[6:20–49] Luke's "Sermon on the Plain" is the counterpart to Matthew's "Sermon on the Mount" (Mt 5:1–7:27). It is addressed to the disciples of Jesus, and, like the sermon in Matthew, it begins with beatitudes (Lk 6:20–22) and ends with the parable of the two houses (Lk 6:46–49). Almost all the words of Jesus reported by Luke are found in Matthew's version, but because Matthew includes sayings that were related to specifically Jewish Christian concerns (e.g., Mt 5:17–20; 6:1–8, 16–18) that Luke did not find appropriate for his predominantly Gentile Christian audience, the "Sermon on the Mount" is considerably longer. Luke's sermon may be outlined

as follows: an introduction consisting of blessings and woes (Lk 6:20–26); the love of one's enemies (Lk 6:27–36); the demands of loving one's neighbor (Lk 6:37–42); good deeds as proof of one's goodness (Lk 6:43–45); a parable illustrating the result of listening to and acting on the words of Jesus (Lk 6:46–49). At the core of the sermon is Jesus' teaching on the love of one's enemies (Lk 6:27–36) that has as its source of motivation God's graciousness and compassion for all humanity (Lk 6:35–36) and Jesus' teaching on the love of one's neighbor (Lk 6:37–42) that is characterized by forgiveness and generosity.

§§[6:20–26] The introductory portion of the sermon consists of blessings and woes that address the real economic and social conditions of humanity (the poor—the rich; the hungry—the satisfied; those grieving—those laughing; the outcast—the socially acceptable). By contrast, Matthew emphasizes the religious and spiritual values of disciples in the kingdom inaugurated by Jesus ("poor in spirit," Mt 5:3; "hunger and thirst for righteousness," Mt 5:6). In the sermon, **blessed** extols the fortunate condition of persons who are favored with the blessings of God; the woes, addressed as they are to the disciples of Jesus, threaten God's profound displeasure on those so blinded by their present fortunate situation that they do not recognize and appreciate the real values of God's kingdom. In all the blessings and woes, the present condition of the persons addressed will be reversed in the future.

¶¶[6:27–36] See notes on Mt 5:43–48 and Mt 5:48.

---

o. [6:21] Ps 126:5–6; Is 61:3; Jer 31:25; Rev 7:16–17. p. [6:22] Jn 15:19; 16:2; 1 Pt 4:14. q. [6:23] 11:47–48; 2 Chr 36:16; Mt 23:30–31. r. [6:24] Jas 5:1. s. [6:25] Is 65:13–14. t. [6:26] Jas 4:4. u. [6:27–36] Mt 5:38–48. v. [6:27] Prv 25:21; Rom 12:20–21. w. [6:28] Rom 12:14; 1 Pt 3:9. x. [6:31] Mt 7:12.

k. [6:12–16] Mt 10:1–4; Mk 3:13–19. l. [6:14–16] Acts 1:13. m. [6:17–19] Mt 4:23–25; Mk 3:7–10. n. [6:20–26] Mt 5:1–12.

credit is that to you? Even sinners love those who love them. ³³And if you do good to those who do good to you, what credit is that to you? Even sinners do the same. ³⁴If you lend money to those from whom you expect repayment, what credit [is] that to you? Even sinners lend to sinners, and get back the same amount.ʸ ³⁵But rather, love your enemies and do good to them, and lend expecting nothing back; then your reward will be great and you will be children of the Most High, for he himself is kind to the ungrateful and the wicked.ᶻ ³⁶Be merciful, just as [also] your Father is merciful.

**Judging Others.**˙ ³⁷ᵃ"Stop judging and you will not be judged. Stop condemning and you will not be condemned. Forgive and you will be forgiven.ᵇ ³⁸Give and gifts will be given to you; a good measure, packed together, shaken down, and overflowing, will be poured into your lap. For the measure with which you measure will in return be measured out to you."ᶜ ³⁹And he told them a parable, "Can a blind person guide a blind person? Will not both fall into a pit?ᵈ ⁴⁰No disciple is superior to the teacher; but when fully trained, every disciple will be like his teacher.ᵉ ⁴¹Why do you notice the splinter in your brother's eye, but do not perceive the wooden beam in your own? ⁴²How can you say to your brother, 'Brother, let me remove that splinter in your eye,' when you do not even notice the wooden beam in your own eye? You hypocrite! Remove the wooden beam from your eye first; then you will see clearly to remove the splinter in your brother's eye.

**A Tree Known by Its Fruit.**ᶠ ⁴³†"A good tree does not bear rotten fruit, nor does a rotten tree bear good fruit. ⁴⁴For every tree is known by its own fruit. For people do not pick figs from thornbushes, nor do they gather grapes from brambles. ⁴⁵A good person out of the store of goodness in his heart produces good, but an evil person out of a store of evil produces evil; for from the fullness of the heart the mouth speaks.

**The Two Foundations.** ⁴⁶ᵍ"Why do you call me, 'Lord, Lord,' but not do what I command? ⁴⁷‡I will show you what someone is like who comes to me, listens to my words, and acts on them.ʰ ⁴⁸That one is like a person building a house, who dug deeply and laid the foundation on rock; when the flood came, the river burst against that house but could not shake it because it had been well built. ⁴⁹But the one who listens and does not act is like a person who built a house on the ground without a foundation. When the river

burst against it, it collapsed at once and was completely destroyed."

## CHAPTER 7

**The Healing of a Centurion's Slave.**ⁱ ¹When he had finished all his words to the people, he entered Capernaum.* ²A centurion** there had a slave who was ill and about to die, and he was valuable to him. ³When he heard about Jesus, he sent elders of the Jews to him, asking him to come and save the life of his slave. ⁴They approached Jesus and strongly urged him to come, saying, "He deserves to have you do this for him, ⁵for he loves our nation and he built the synagogue for us." ⁶And Jesus went with them, but when he was only a short distance from the house, the centurion sent friends to tell him, "Lord, do not trouble yourself, for I am not worthy to have you enter under my roof.†† ⁷Therefore, I did not consider myself worthy to come to you; but say the word and let my servant be healed. ⁸For I too am a person subject to authority, with soldiers subject to me. And I say to one, 'Go,' and he goes; and to another, 'Come here,' and he comes; and to my slave, 'Do this,' and he does it." ⁹When Jesus heard this he was amazed at him and, turning, said to the crowd following him, "I tell you, not even in Israel have I found such faith." ¹⁰When the messengers returned to the house, they found the slave in good health.

**Raising of the Widow's Son.**‡‡ ¹¹Soon afterward he journeyed to a city called Nain, and his disciples and a large crowd accompanied him. ¹²As he drew near to the gate of the city, a man who had died was being carried out, the only son of his mother, and she was a widow. A large crowd from the city was with her.ᵏ ¹³When the Lord

§[7:1–8:3] The episodes in this section present a series of reactions to the Galilean ministry of Jesus and reflect some of Luke's particular interests: the faith of a Gentile (Lk 7:1–10); the prophet Jesus' concern for a widowed mother (Lk 7:11–17); the ministry of Jesus directed to the afflicted and unfortunate of Is 61:1 (Lk 7:18–23); the relation between John and Jesus and their role in God's plan for salvation (Lk 7:24–35); a forgiven sinner's manifestation of love (Lk 7:36–50); the association of women with the ministry of Jesus (Lk 8:1–3).

¶[7:1–10] This story about the faith of the centurion, a Gentile who cherishes the Jewish nation (Lk 7:5), prepares for the story in Acts of the conversion by Peter of the Roman centurion Cornelius who is similarly described as one who is generous to the Jewish nation (Acts 10:2). See also Acts 10:34–35 in the speech of Peter: "God shows no partiality . . . whoever fears him and acts righteously is acceptable to him." See also notes on Mt 8:5–13 and Jn 4:43–54.

**[7:2] A centurion:** see note on Mt 8:5.

††[7:6] **I am not worthy to have you enter under my roof:** to enter the house of a Gentile was considered unclean for a Jew; cf. Acts 10:28.

‡‡[7:11–17] In the previous incident Jesus' power was displayed for a Gentile whose servant was dying; in this episode it is displayed toward a widowed mother whose only son has already died. Jesus' power over death prepares for his reply to John's disciples in Lk 7:22: "the dead are raised." This resuscitation in alluding to the prophet Elijah's resurrection of the only son of a widow of Zarephath (1 Kgs 7:8–24) leads to the reaction of the crowd: "A great prophet has arisen in our midst" (Lk 7:16).

---

*[6:37–42] See notes on Mt 7:1–12; 7:1; 7:5.
†[6:43–46] See notes on Mt 7:15–20 and 12:33.
‡[6:47–49] See note on Mt 7:24–27.

y. [6:34] Dt 15:7–8.  z. [6:35] Lv 25:35–36.  a. [6:37–42] Mt 7:1–5.
b. [6:37] Mt 6:14; Jas 2:13.  c. [6:38] Mk 4:24.  d. [6:39] Mt 15:14; 23:16–17, 24.  e. [6:40] Mt 10:24–25; Jn 13:16; 15:20.  f. [6:43–45] Mt 7:16–20; 12:33, 35.  g. [6:46] Mt 7:21; Rom 2:13; Jas 1:22.  h. [6:47–49] Mt 7:24–27.

i. [7:1–10] Mt 8:5–13; Jn 4:43–54.  j. [7:11–17] 4:25–26; 1 Kgs 17:8–24.  k. [7:12] 8:42; 1 Kgs 17:17.

saw her, he was moved with pity for her and said to her, "Do not weep." [14]He stepped forward and touched the coffin; at this the bearers halted, and he said, "Young man, I tell you, arise!" [15]The dead man sat up and began to speak, and Jesus gave him to his mother.[l] [16]Fear seized them all, and they glorified God, exclaiming, "A great prophet has arisen in our midst," and "God has visited his people."[m] [17]This report about him spread through the whole of Judea and in all the surrounding region.

**The Messengers from John the Baptist.**[*] [18n]The disciples of John told him about all these things. John summoned two of his disciples [19]and sent them to the Lord to ask, "Are you the one who is to come, or should we look for another?"[o] [20]When the men came to him, they said, "John the Baptist has sent us to you to ask, 'Are you the one who is to come, or should we look for another?'" [21]At that time he cured many of their diseases, sufferings, and evil spirits; he also granted sight to many who were blind. [22]And he said to them in reply, "Go and tell John what you have seen and heard: the blind regain their sight, the lame walk, lepers are cleansed, the deaf hear, the dead are raised, the poor have the good news proclaimed to them.[p] [23]And blessed is the one who takes no offense at me."[†]

**Jesus' Testimony to John.** [24‡]When the messengers of John had left, Jesus began to speak to the crowds about John.[q] "What did you go out to the desert to see—a reed swayed by the wind? [25]Then what did you go out to see? Someone dressed in fine garments? Those who dress luxuriously and live sumptuously are found in royal palaces. [26]Then what did you go out to see? A prophet? Yes, I tell you, and more than a prophet.[r] [27]This is the one about whom scripture says:

'Behold, I am sending my messenger
        ahead of you,
    he will prepare your way before
        you.'[s]

[28]I tell you, among those born of women, no one is greater than John; yet the least in the kingdom of God is greater than he." [29](All the people who listened, including the tax collectors, and who were baptized with the baptism of John, acknowledged the righteousness of God; [30]but the Pharisees and scholars of the law, who were not baptized by him, rejected the plan of God for themselves.)

[31]"Then to what shall I compare the people of this generation? What are they like?[u] [32]They are like children who sit in the marketplace and call to one another,

'We played the flute for you, but you did
        not dance.
    We sang a dirge, but you did not
        weep.'

[33]For John the Baptist came neither eating food nor drinking wine, and you said, 'He is possessed by a demon.' [34]The Son of Man came eating and drinking and you said, 'Look, he is a glutton and a drunkard, a friend of tax collectors and sinners.'[v] [35]But wisdom is vindicated by all her children."

**The Pardon of the Sinful Woman.**[¶] [36w]A Pharisee invited him to dine with him, and he entered the Pharisee's house and reclined at table.[**] [37]Now there was a sinful woman in the city who learned that he was at table in the house of the Pharisee.[x] Bringing an alabaster flask of ointment,[y] [38]she stood behind him at his feet weeping and began to bathe his feet with her tears. Then she wiped them with her hair, kissed them, and anointed them with the ointment. [39]When the Pharisee who had invited him saw this he said to himself, "If this man were a prophet, he would know who and what sort of woman this is who is touching him, that she is a sinner." [40]Jesus said to him in reply, "Simon, I have something to say to you." "Tell me, teacher," he said. [41]"Two people were in debt to a certain creditor; one owed five hundred days' wages[††] and the other owed fifty.

---

* [7:18–23] In answer to John's question, **Are you the one who is to come?**—a probable reference to the return of the fiery prophet of reform, Elijah, "before the day of the Lord comes, the great and terrible day" (Mal 3:23)—Jesus responds that his role is rather to bring the blessings spoken of in Is 61:1 to the oppressed and neglected of society (Lk 7:22; cf. Lk 4:18).

† [7:23] **Blessed is the one who takes no offense at me:** this beatitude is pronounced on the person who recognizes Jesus' true identity in spite of previous expectations of what "the one who is to come" would be like.

‡ [7:24–30] In his testimony to John, Jesus reveals his understanding of the relationship between them: John is the precursor of Jesus (Lk 7:27); John is the messenger spoken of in Mal 3:1 who in Mal 3:19 is identified as Elijah. Taken with the previous episode, it can be seen that Jesus identifies John as precisely the person John envisioned Jesus to be: the Elijah who prepares the way for the coming of the day of the Lord.

§ [7:31–35] See note on Mt 11:16–19.

¶ [7:36–50] In this story of the pardoning of the sinful woman Luke presents two different reactions to the ministry of Jesus. A Pharisee, suspecting Jesus to be a prophet, invites Jesus to a festive banquet in his house, but the Pharisee's self-righteousness leads to little forgiveness by God and consequently little love shown toward Jesus. The sinful woman, on the other hand, manifests a faith in God (Lk 7:50) that has led her to seek forgiveness for her sins, and because so much was forgiven, she now overwhelms Jesus with her display of love; cf. the similar contrast in attitudes in Lk 18:9–14. The whole episode is a powerful lesson on the relation between forgiveness and love.

** [7:36] **Reclined at table:** the normal posture of guests at a banquet. Other oriental banquet customs alluded to in this story include the reception by the host with a kiss (Lk 7:45), washing the feet of the guests (Lk 7:44), and the anointing of the guests' heads (Lk 7:46).

†† [7:41] **Days' wages:** one denarius is the normal daily wage of a laborer.

---

l. [7:15] 1 Kgs 17:23; 2 Kgs 4:36.    m. [7:16] 1:68; 19:44.    n. [7:18–23] Mt 11:2–6.    o. [7:19] Mal 3:1; Rev 1:4, 8; 4:8.    p. [7:22] 4:18; Is 35:5–6; 61:1.    q. [7:24–30] Mt 11:7–15.    r. [7:26] 1:76.    s. [7:27] Mal 3:1 / Is 40:3.

t. [7:29–30] 3:7, 12; Mt 21:32.    u. [7:31–35] Mt 11:16–19.    v. [7:34] 15:2.    w. [7:36] 11:37; 14:1.    x. [7:37] Mt 26:7; Mk 14:3.    y. [7:37–38] Jn 12:3.

[42]Since they were unable to repay the debt, he forgave it for both. Which of them will love him more?" [43]Simon said in reply, "The one, I suppose, whose larger debt was forgiven." He said to him, "You have judged rightly." [44]Then he turned to the woman and said to Simon, "Do you see this woman? When I entered your house, you did not give me water for my feet, but she has bathed them with her tears and wiped them with her hair. [45]You did not give me a kiss, but she has not ceased kissing my feet since the time I entered. [46]You did not anoint my head with oil, but she anointed my feet with ointment. [47]So I tell you, her many sins have been forgiven; hence, she has shown great love.* But the one to whom little is forgiven, loves little." [48]He said to her, "Your sins are forgiven."z [49]The others at table said to themselves, "Who is this who even forgives sins?"a [50]But he said to the woman, "Your faith has saved you; go in peace."

## CHAPTER 8

**Galilean Women Follow Jesus.**† [1]Afterward he journeyed from one town and village to another, preaching and proclaiming the good news of the kingdom of God.b Accompanying him were the Twelve [2]cand some women who had been cured of evil spirits and infirmities, Mary, called Magdalene, from whom seven demons had gone out, [3]Joanna, the wife of Herod's steward Chuza, Susanna, and many others who provided for them out of their resources.

**The Parable of the Sower.**d [4]‡When a large crowd gathered, with people from one town after another journeying to him, he spoke in a parable.§ [5]"A sower went out to sow his seed. And as he sowed, some seed fell on the path and was trampled, and the birds of the sky ate it up. [6]Some seed fell on rocky ground, and when it

grew, it withered for lack of moisture. [7]Some seed fell among thorns, and the thorns grew with it and choked it. [8]And some seed fell on good soil, and when it grew, it produced fruit a hundredfold." After saying this, he called out, "Whoever has ears to hear ought to hear."e

**The Purpose of the Parables.**f [9]Then his disciples asked him what the meaning of this parable might be. [10]He answered, "Knowledge of the mysteries of the kingdom of God has been granted to you; but to the rest, they are made known through parables so that 'they may look but not see, and hear but not understand.'g

**The Parable of the Sower Explained.**¶ [11]h"This is the meaning of the parable. The seed is the word of God.i [12]Those on the path are the ones who have heard, but the devil comes and takes away the word from their hearts that they may not believe and be saved. [13]Those on rocky ground are the ones who, when they hear, receive the word with joy, but they have no root; they believe only for a time and fall away in time of trial. [14]As for the seed that fell among thorns, they are the ones who have heard, but as they go along, they are choked by the anxieties and riches and pleasures of life, and they fail to produce mature fruit. [15]But as for the seed that fell on rich soil, they are the ones who, when they have heard the word, embrace it with a generous and good heart, and bear fruit through perseverance.

**The Parable of the Lamp.**** [16]"No one who lights a lamp conceals it with a vessel or sets it under a bed; rather, he places it on a lampstand so that those who enter may see the light.k [17]For there is nothing hidden that will not become visible, and nothing secret that will not be known and come to light.l [18]Take care, then, how you hear. To anyone who has, more will be given, and from the one who has not, even what he seems to have will be taken away."m

**Jesus and His Family.**n [19]Then his mother and his brothers†† came to him but were unable to join him because of the crowd. [20]He was told, "Your mother and your brothers are standing outside and they wish to see you." [21]He said to them in reply, "My mother and my brothers are those who hear the word of God and act on it."‡‡

---

*[7:47] **Her many sins have been forgiven; hence, she has shown great love**: literally, "her many sins have been forgiven, seeing that she has loved much." That the woman's sins have been forgiven is attested by the great love she shows toward Jesus. Her love is the consequence of her forgiveness. This is also the meaning demanded by the parable in Lk 7:41–43.

†[8:1–3] Luke presents Jesus as an itinerant preacher traveling in the company of the Twelve and of the Galilean women who are sustaining them out of their means. These Galilean women will later accompany Jesus on his journey to Jerusalem and become witnesses to his death (Lk 23:49) and resurrection (Lk 24:9–11, where Mary Magdalene and Joanna are specifically mentioned; cf. also Acts 1:14). The association of women with the ministry of Jesus is most unusual in the light of the attitude of first-century Palestinian Judaism toward women. The more common attitude is expressed in Jn 4:27, and early rabbinic documents caution against speaking with women in public.

‡[8:4–21] The focus in this section is on how one should hear the word of God and act on it. It includes the parable of the sower and its explanation (Lk 8:4–15), a collection of sayings on how one should act on the word that is heard (Lk 8:16–18), and the identification of the mother and brothers of Jesus as the ones who hear the word and act on it (Lk 8:19–21). See also notes on Mt 13:1–53 and Mk 4:1–34.

§[8:4–8] See note on Mt 13:3–8.

¶[8:11–15] On the interpretation of the parable of the sower, see note on Mt 13:18–23.

**[8:16–18] These sayings continue the theme of responding to the word of God. Those who hear the word must become a light to others (Lk 8:16); even the mysteries of the kingdom that have been made known to the disciples (Lk 8:9–10) must come to light (Lk 8:17); a generous and persevering response to the word of God leads to a still more perfect response to the word.

††[8:19] **His brothers**: see note on Mk 6:3.

‡‡[8:21] The family of Jesus is not constituted by physical relationship with him but by obedience to the word of God.

---

z. [7:48] 5:20; Mt 9:20; Mk 2:5.   a. [7:49] 5:21.   b. [8:1] 4:43.   c. [8:2–3] 23:49; 24:10; Mt 27:55–56; Mk 15:40–41; Jn 19:5.   d. [8:4–8] Mt 13:1–9; Mk 4:1–9.

e. [8:8] 14:35; Mt 11:15; 13:43; Mk 4:23.   f. [8:9–10] Mt 13:10–13; Mk 4:10–12.   g. [8:10] Is 6:9.   h. [8:11–15] Mt 13:18–23; Mk 4:13–20.   i. [8:11] 1 Pt 1:23.   j. [8:16–19] Mk 4:21–25.   k. [8:16] 11:33; Mt 5:15.   l. [8:17] 12:2; Mt 10:26.   m. [8:18] 19:26; Mt 13:12; 25:29.   n. [8:19–21] Mt 12:46–50; Mk 3:31–35.   o. [8:20–21] 11:27–28.

## The Calming of a Storm at Sea.ᵖ ²²One day

he got into a boat with his disciples and said to them, "Let us cross to the other side of the lake." So they set sail, ²³and while they were sailing he fell asleep. A squall blew over the lake, and they were taking in water and were in danger. ²⁴They came and woke him saying, "Master, master, we are perishing!" He awakened, rebuked the wind and the waves, and they subsided and there was a calm. ²⁵Then he asked them, "Where is your faith?" But they were filled with awe and amazed and said to one another, "Who then is this, who commands even the winds and the sea, and they obey him?"

## The Healing of the Gerasene Demoniac.�q

²⁶Then they sailed to the territory of the Gerasenes,† which is opposite Galilee. ²⁷When he came ashore a man from the town who was possessed by demons met him. For a long time he had not worn clothes; he did not live in a house, but lived among the tombs. ²⁸ʳWhen he saw Jesus, he cried out and fell down before him; in a loud voice he shouted, "What have you to do with me, Jesus, son of the Most High God? I beg you, do not torment me!" ²⁹For he had ordered the unclean spirit to come out of the man. (It had taken hold of him many times, and he used to be bound with chains and shackles as a restraint, but he would break his bonds and be driven by the demon into deserted places.) ³⁰Then Jesus asked him, "What is your name?"‡ He replied, "Legion," because many demons had entered him. ³¹And they pleaded with him not to order them to depart to the abyss.§

³²A herd of many swine was feeding there on the hillside, and they pleaded with him to allow them to enter those swine; and he let them. ³³The demons came out of the man and entered the swine, and the herd rushed down the steep bank into the lake and was drowned. ³⁴When the swineherds saw what had happened, they ran away and reported the incident in the town and throughout the countryside. ³⁵People came out to see what had happened and, when they approached Jesus, they discovered the man from whom the demons had come out sitting at his feet.⁵ He was clothed and in his right mind, and they were seized with fear. ³⁶Those who witnessed it told them how the possessed man had been saved. ³⁷The entire population of the region of the Gerasenes asked Jesus to leave them because they were seized with great fear. So he got into a boat and returned. ³⁸The man from whom the demons had come out begged to remain with him, but he sent him away, saying, ³⁹"Return home and recount what God has done for you." The man went off and proclaimed throughout the whole town what Jesus had done for him.

## Jairus's Daughter and the Woman with a Hemorrhage.** ⁴⁰ˢWhen Jesus returned, the crowd

welcomed him, for they were all waiting for him. ⁴¹And a man named Jairus, an official of the synagogue, came forward. He fell at the feet of Jesus and begged him to come to his house, ⁴²because he had an only daughter,†† about twelve years old, and she was dying. As he went, the crowds almost crushed him. ⁴³And a woman afflicted with hemorrhages for twelve years,‡‡ who [had spent her whole livelihood on doctors and] was unable to be cured by anyone, ⁴⁴came up behind him and touched the tassel on his cloak. Immediately her bleeding stopped. ⁴⁵Jesus then asked, "Who touched me?" While all were denying it, Peter said, "Master, the crowds are pushing and pressing in upon you." ⁴⁶But Jesus said, "Someone has touched me; for I know that power has gone out from me."ᵗ ⁴⁷When the woman realized that she had not escaped notice, she came forward trembling. Falling down before him, she explained in the presence of all the people why she had touched him and how she had been healed immediately. ⁴⁸He said to her, "Daughter, your faith has saved you; go in peace."ᵘ

⁴⁹While he was still speaking, someone from the synagogue official's house arrived and said, "Your daughter is dead; do not trouble the

---

In this, Luke agrees with the Marcan parallel (Mk 3:31–35), although by omitting Mk 3:33 and especially Mk 3:20–21 Luke has softened the Marcan picture of Jesus' natural family. Probably he did this because Mary has already been presented in Lk 1:38 as the obedient handmaid of the Lord who fulfills the requirement for belonging to the eschatological family of Jesus; cf. also Lk 11:27–28.

*[8:22–56] This section records four miracles of Jesus that manifest his power and authority: (1) the calming of a storm on the lake (Lk 8:22–25); (2) the exorcism of a demoniac (Lk 8:26–39); (3) the cure of a hemorrhaging woman (Lk 8:40–48); (4) the raising of Jairus's daughter to life (Lk 8:49–56). They parallel the same sequence of stories at Mk 4:35–5:43.

†[8:26] **Gerasenes**: other manuscripts read Gadarenes or Gergesenes. See also note on Mt 8:28. **Opposite Galilee**: probably Gentile territory (note the presence in the area of pigs—unclean animals to Jews) and an indication that the person who receives salvation (Lk 8:36) is a Gentile.

‡[8:30] **What is your name?**: the question reflects the popular belief that knowledge of the spirit's name brought control over the spirit. **Legion**: to Jesus' question the demon replies with a Latin word transliterated into Greek. The Roman legion at this period consisted of 5,000 to 6,000 foot soldiers; hence the name implies a very large number of demons.

§[8:31] **Abyss**: the place of the dead (Rom 10:7) or the prison of Satan (Rev 20:3) or the subterranean "watery deep" that symbolizes the chaos before the order imposed by creation (Gn 1:2).

¶[8:35] **Sitting at his feet**: the former demoniac takes the position of a disciple before the master (Lk 10:39; Acts 22:3).

**[8:40–56] Two interwoven miracle stories, one a healing and the other a resuscitation, present Jesus as master over sickness and death. In the Lucan account, faith in Jesus is responsible for the cure (Lk 8:48) and for the raising to life (Lk 8:50).

††[8:42] **An only daughter**: cf. the son of the widow of Nain whom Luke describes as an "only" son (Lk 7:12; see also Lk 9:38).

‡‡[8:43] **Afflicted with hemorrhages for twelve years**: according to the Mosaic law (Lv 15:25–30) this condition would render the woman unclean and unfit for contact with other people.

---

p. [8:22–25] Mt 8:18, 23–27; Mk 4:35–41.  q. [8:26–39] Mt 8:28–34; Mk 5:1–20.  r. [8:28–29] 4:33–35; Mt 8:29; Mk 1:23–24.

s. [8:40–56] Mt 9:18–26; Mk 5:21–43.  t. [8:46] 6:19.  u. [8:48] 7:50; 17:19; 18:42.

teacher any longer." ⁵⁰On hearing this, Jesus answered him, "Do not be afraid; just have faith and she will be saved." ⁵¹When he arrived at the house he allowed no one to enter with him except Peter and John and James, and the child's father and mother. ⁵²ᵛAll were weeping and mourning for her, when he said, "Do not weep any longer, for she is not dead, but sleeping." ⁵³And they ridiculed him, because they knew that she was dead. ⁵⁴But he took her by the hand and called to her, "Child, arise!" ⁵⁵Her breath returned and she immediately arose. He then directed that she should be given something to eat. ⁵⁶Her parents were astounded, and he instructed them to tell no one what had happened.

## CHAPTER 9

**The Mission of the Twelve.**† ¹ʷHe summoned the Twelve and gave them power and authority over all demons and to cure diseases, ²and he sent them to proclaim the kingdom of God and to heal [the sick]. ³He said to them, "Take nothing for the journey,‡ neither walking stick, nor sack, nor food, nor money, and let no one take a second tunic. ⁴Whatever house you enter, stay there and leave from there.ˣ ⁵And as for those who do not welcome you, when you leave that town, shake the dust from your feet§ in testimony against them."ʸ ⁶Then they set out and went from village to village proclaiming the good news and curing diseases everywhere.

**Herod's Opinion of Jesus.**ᶻ ⁷"Herod the tetrarch" heard about all that was happening, and he was greatly perplexed because some were saying, "John has been raised from the dead";ᵃ ⁸others were saying, "Elijah has appeared"; still others, "One of the ancient prophets has arisen." ⁹††ᵇBut

Herod said, "John I beheaded. Who then is this about whom I hear such things?" And he kept trying to see him.

**The Return of the Twelve and the Feeding of the Five Thousand.**ᶜ ¹⁰When the apostles returned, they explained to him what they had done. He took them and withdrew in private to a town called Bethsaida. ¹¹The crowds, meanwhile, learned of this and followed him. He received them and spoke to them about the kingdom of God, and he healed those who needed to be cured. ¹²As the day was drawing to a close, the Twelve approached him and said, "Dismiss the crowd so that they can go to the surrounding villages and farms and find lodging and provisions; for we are in a deserted place here." ¹³ᵈHe said to them, "Give them some food yourselves." They replied, "Five loaves and two fish are all we have, unless we ourselves go and buy food for all these people." ¹⁴Now the men there numbered about five thousand. Then he said to his disciples, "Have them sit down in groups of [about] fifty." ¹⁵They did so and made them all sit down. ¹⁶Then taking‡‡ the five loaves and the two fish, and looking up to heaven, he said the blessing over them, broke them, and gave them to the disciples to set before the crowd.ᵉ ¹⁷They all ate and were satisfied. And when the leftover fragments were picked up, they filled twelve wicker baskets.

**Peter's Confession About Jesus.**§§ ¹⁸Once when Jesus was praying in solitude,¶¶ and the disciples were with him, he asked them, "Who do the crowds say that I am?" ¹⁹They said in reply, "John the Baptist; others, Elijah; still others, 'One of the ancient prophets has arisen.'"ᵍ ²⁰Then he said to them, "But who do you say that I am?" Peter said in reply, "The Messiah of God."*** ²¹He rebuked them and directed them not to tell this to anyone.

**The First Prediction of the Passion.** ²²He said, "The Son of Man must suffer greatly and be rejected by the elders, the chief priests, and the scribes, and be killed and on the third day be raised."ʰ

---

* [8:52] **Sleeping**: her death is a temporary condition; cf. Jn 11:11–14.

† [9:1–6] Armed with the power and authority that Jesus himself has been displaying in the previous episodes, the Twelve are now sent out to continue the work that Jesus has been performing throughout his Galilean ministry: (1) proclaiming the kingdom (Lk 4:43; 8:1); (2) exorcising demons (Lk 4:33–37, 41; 8:26–39) and (3) healing the sick (Lk 4:38–40; 5:12–16, 17–26; 6:6–10; 7:1–10, 17, 22; 8:40–56).

‡ [9:3] **Take nothing for the journey**: the absolute detachment required of the disciple (Lk 14:33) leads to complete reliance on God (Lk 12:22–31).

§ [9:5] **Shake the dust from your feet**: see note on Mt 10:14.

¶ [9:7–56] This section in which Luke gathers together incidents that focus on the identity of Jesus is introduced by a question that Herod is made to ask in this gospel: "Who then is this about whom I hear such things?" (Lk 9:9) In subsequent episodes, Luke reveals to the reader various answers to Herod's question: Jesus is one in whom God's power is present and who provides for the needs of God's people (Lk 9:10–17); Peter declares Jesus to be "the Messiah of God" (Lk 9:18–21); Jesus says he is the suffering Son of Man (Lk 9:22, 43–45); Jesus is the Master to be followed, even to death (Lk 9:23–27); Jesus is God's son, his Chosen One (Lk 9:28–36).

** [9:7] **Herod the tetrarch**: see note on Lk 3:1.

†† [9:9] **And he kept trying to see him**: this indication of Herod's interest in Jesus prepares for Lk 13:31–33 and for Lk

23:8–12 where Herod's curiosity about Jesus' power to perform miracles remains unsatisfied.

‡‡ [9:16] **Then taking . . .**: the actions of Jesus recall the institution of the Eucharist in Lk 22:19; see also note on Mt 14:19.

§§ [9:18–22] This incident is based on Mk 8:27–33, but Luke has eliminated Peter's refusal to accept Jesus as suffering Son of Man (Mk 8:32) and the rebuke of Peter by Jesus (Mk 8:33). Elsewhere in the gospel, Luke softens the harsh portrait of Peter and the other apostles found in his Marcan source (cf. Lk 22:39–46, which similarly lacks a rebuke of Peter that occurs in the source, Mk 14:37–38).

¶¶ [9:18] **When Jesus was praying in solitude**: see note on Lk 3:21.

*** [9:20] **The Messiah of God**: on the meaning of this title in first-century Palestinian Judaism, see notes on Lk 2:11 and on Mt 16:13–20 and Mk 8:27–30.

c. [9:10–17] Mt 14:13–21; Mk 6:30–44; Jn 6:1–14.  d. [9:13–17] 2 Kgs 4:42–44.  e. [9:16] 22:19; 24:30–31; Acts 2:42; 20:11; 27:35.  f. [9:18–21] Mt 16:13–20; Mk 8:27–30.  g. [9:19] 9:7–8. h. [9:22] 24:7, 26; Mt 16:21; 20:18–19; Mk 8:31; 10:33–34.

v. [8:52] 7:13.  w. [9:1–6] Mt 10:1, 5–15; Mk 6:7–13.  x. [9:4] 10:5–7.  y. [9:5] 10:10–11; Acts 13:51.  z. [9:7–9] Mt 14:1–12; Mk 6:14–29.  a. [9:7–8] 9:19; Mt 16:14; Mk 8:28.  b. [9:9] 23:8.

**The Conditions of Discipleship.**[i] [23]Then he said to all, "If anyone wishes to come after me, he must deny himself and take up his cross daily* and follow me.[j] [24]For whoever wishes to save his life will lose it, but whoever loses his life for my sake will save it.[k] [25]What profit is there for one to gain the whole world yet lose or forfeit himself? [26]Whoever is ashamed of me and of my words, the Son of Man will be ashamed of when he comes in his glory and in the glory of the Father and of the holy angels.[l] [27]Truly I say to you, there are some standing here who will not taste death until they see the kingdom of God."

**The Transfiguration of Jesus.**[†] [28]About eight days after he said this, he took Peter, John, and James and went up the mountain to pray.[‡] [29]While he was praying his face changed in appearance and his clothing became dazzling white. [30]And behold, two men were conversing with him, Moses and Elijah,[§] [31]*who appeared in glory and spoke of his exodus that he was going to accomplish in Jerusalem. [32]Peter and his companions had been overcome by sleep, but becoming fully awake, they saw his glory** and the two men standing with him.[o] [33]As they were about to part from him, Peter said to Jesus, "Master, it is good that we are here; let us make three tents,[††] one for you, one for Moses, and one for Elijah." But he did not know what he was saying. [34]‡‡While he was still speaking, a cloud came and cast a shadow over them, and they became frightened when they entered the cloud. [35]§§*Then from the cloud came a voice that said, "This is my chosen Son; listen to him." [36]After the voice had spoken, Jesus was found alone. They fell silent and did not at that time** tell anyone what they had seen.

**The Healing of a Boy with a Demon.**[***] [37q]On the next day, when they came down from the mountain, a large crowd met him. [38]There was a man in the crowd who cried out, "Teacher, I beg you, look at my son; he is my only child. [39]For a spirit seizes him and he suddenly screams and it convulses him until he foams at the mouth; it releases him only with difficulty, wearing him out. [40]I begged your disciples to cast it out but they could not." [41]Jesus said in reply, "O faithless and perverse generation, how long will I be with you and endure you? Bring your son here." [42]As he was coming forward, the demon threw him to the ground in a convulsion; but Jesus rebuked the unclean spirit, healed the boy, and returned him to his father. [43]And all were astonished by the majesty of God.

**The Second Prediction of the Passion.**[r] While they were all amazed at his every deed, he said to his disciples, [44]"Pay attention to what I am telling you. The Son of Man is to be handed over to men." [45]But they did not understand this saying; its meaning was hidden from them so that they should not understand it, and they were afraid to ask him about this saying.

**The Greatest in the Kingdom.**[s] [46†††]An argument arose among the disciples about which of them was the greatest.[t] [47]Jesus realized the intention of their hearts and took a child and placed it by his side [48]and said to them, "Whoever receives this child in my name receives me, and whoever receives me receives the one who sent me. For the one who is least among all of you is the one who is the greatest."[u]

**Another Exorcist.**[v] [49]Then John said in reply, "Master, we saw someone casting out demons in your name and we tried to prevent him because he does not follow in our company." [50]Jesus said to him, "Do not prevent him, for whoever is not against you is for you."

---

*[9:23] **Daily:** this is a Lucan addition to a saying of Jesus, removing the saying from a context that envisioned the imminent suffering and death of the disciple of Jesus (as does the saying in Mk 8:34–35) to one that focuses on the demands of daily Christian existence.

†[9:28–36] Situated shortly after the first announcement of the passion, death, and resurrection, this scene of Jesus' transfiguration provides the heavenly confirmation to Jesus' declaration that his suffering will end in glory (Lk 9:32); see also notes on Mt 17:1–8 and Mk 9:2–8.

‡[9:28] **Up the mountain to pray:** the "mountain" is the regular place of prayer in Luke (see Lk 6:12; 22:39–41).

§[9:30] **Moses and Elijah:** the two figures represent the Old Testament law and the prophets. At the end of this episode, the heavenly voice will identify Jesus as the one to be listened to now (Lk 9:35). See also note on Mk 9:5.

¶[9:31] **His exodus that he was going to accomplish in Jerusalem:** Luke identifies the subject of the conversation as the **exodus** of Jesus, a reference to the death, resurrection, and ascension of Jesus that will take place in Jerusalem, the city of destiny (see Lk 9:51). The mention of exodus, however, also calls to mind the Israelite Exodus from Egypt to the promised land.

**[9:32] **They saw his glory:** the **glory** that is proper to God is here attributed to Jesus (see Lk 24:26).

††[9:33] **Let us make three tents:** in a possible allusion to the feast of Tabernacles, Peter may be likening his joy on the occasion of the transfiguration to the joyful celebration of this harvest festival.

‡‡[9:34] **Over them:** it is not clear whether **them** refers to Jesus, Moses, and Elijah, or to the disciples. For the cloud casting its shadow, see note on Mk 9:7.

§§[9:35] Like the heavenly voice that identified Jesus at his baptism prior to his undertaking the Galilean ministry (Lk 3:22), so too here before the journey to the city of destiny is begun (Lk 9:51) the heavenly voice again identifies Jesus as Son. **Listen to him:** the two representatives of Israel of old depart (Lk 9:33) and Jesus is left alone (Lk 9:36) as the teacher whose words must be heeded (see also Acts 3:22).

¶¶[9:36] **At that time:** i.e., before the resurrection.

***[9:37–43a] See note on Mk 9:14–29.

†††[9:46–50] These two incidents focus on attitudes that are opposed to Christian discipleship: rivalry and intolerance of outsiders.

i. [9:23–27] Mt 16:24–28; Mk 8:34–9:1.  j. [9:23] 14:27; Mt 10:38.  k. [9:24] 17:33; Mt 10:39; Jn 12:25.  l. [9:26] 12:9; Mt 10:33; 2 Tm 2:12.  m. [9:28–36] Mt 17:1–8; Mk 9:2–8.  n. [9:31] 9:22; 13:33.  o. [9:32] Jn 1:14; 2 Pt 1:16.

p. [9:35] 3:22; Dt 18:15; Ps 2:7; Is 42:1; Mt 3:17; 12:18; Mk 1:11; 2 Pt 1:17–18.  q. [9:37–43] Mt 17:14–18; Mk 9:14–27.  r. [9:43–45] 18:32–34; Mt 17:22–23; Mk 9:30–32.  s. [9:46–48] Mt 18:1–5; Mk 9:33–37.  t. [9:46] 22:24.  u. [9:48] 10:16; Mt 10:40; Jn 13:20.  v. [9:49–50] Mk 9:38–40.

# V. THE JOURNEY TO JERUSALEM: LUKE'S TRAVEL NARRATIVE*

**Departure for Jerusalem; Samaritan Inhospitality.** [51]When the days for his being taken up[‡] were fulfilled, he resolutely determined to journey to Jerusalem,[w] [52§]and he sent messengers ahead of him.[x] On the way they entered a Samaritan village to prepare for his reception there, [53]but they would not welcome him because the destination of his journey was Jerusalem. [54]When the disciples James and John saw this they asked, "Lord, do you want us to call down fire from heaven to consume them?"[y] [55]Jesus turned and rebuked them, [56]and they journeyed to another village.

**The Would-be Followers of Jesus.¶** [57z]As they were proceeding on their journey someone said to him, "I will follow you wherever you go." [58]Jesus answered him, "Foxes have dens and birds of the sky have nests, but the Son of Man has nowhere to rest his head." [59]And to another he said, "Follow me." But he replied, "[Lord,] let me go first and bury my father." [60]But he answered him, "Let the dead bury their dead.** But you, go and proclaim the kingdom of God."

[61a]And another said, "I will follow you, Lord, but first let me say farewell to my family at home." [62][To him] Jesus said, "No one who sets a hand to the plow and looks to what was left behind is fit for the kingdom of God."

# CHAPTER 10

**The Mission of the Seventy-two.††** [1]After this the Lord appointed seventy[-two][‡‡] others whom he sent ahead of him in pairs to every town and place he intended to visit.[b] [2]He said to them, "The harvest is abundant but the laborers are few; so ask the master of the harvest to send out laborers for his harvest.[c] [3]Go on your way; behold, I am sending you like lambs among wolves.[d] [4§§]Carry no money bag,[e] no sack, no sandals;[f] and greet no one along the way. [5]Into whatever house you enter, first say, 'Peace to this household.'¶¶ [6]If a peaceful person*** lives there, your peace will rest on him; but if not, it will return to you. [7]Stay in the same house and eat and drink what is offered to you, for the laborer deserves his payment. Do not move about from one house to another.[g] [8]Whatever town you enter and they welcome you, eat what is set before you,[h] [9]cure the sick in it and say to them, 'The kingdom of God is at hand for you.'[i] [10]Whatever town you enter and they do not receive you, go out into the streets and say,[j] [11]'The dust of your town that clings to our feet, even that we shake off against you.' Yet know this: the kingdom of God is at hand.[k] [12]I tell you, it will be more tolerable for Sodom on that day than for that town.[l]

**Reproaches to Unrepentant Towns.†††** [13m]"Woe to you, Chorazin! Woe to you, Bethsaida! For if

---

* [9:51–18:14] The Galilean ministry of Jesus finishes with the previous episode and a new section of Luke's gospel begins, the journey to Jerusalem. This journey is based on Mk 10:1–52 but Luke uses his Marcan source only in Lk 18:15–19:27. Before that point he has inserted into his gospel a distinctive collection of sayings of Jesus and stories about him that he has drawn from Q, a collection of sayings of Jesus used also by Matthew, and from his own special traditions. All of the material collected in this section is loosely organized within the framework of a journey of Jesus to Jerusalem, the city of destiny, where his exodus (suffering, death, resurrection, ascension) is to take place (Lk 9:31), where salvation is accomplished, and from where the proclamation of God's saving word is to go forth (Lk 24:47; Acts 1:8). Much of the material in the Lucan travel narrative is teaching for the disciples. During the course of this journey Jesus is preparing his chosen Galilean witnesses for the role they will play after his exodus (Lk 9:31): they are to be his witnesses to the people (Acts 10:39; 13:31) and thereby provide certainty to the readers of Luke's gospel that the teachings they have received are rooted in the teachings of Jesus (Lk 1:1–4).

† [9:51–56] Just as the Galilean ministry began with a rejection of Jesus in his hometown, so too the travel narrative begins with the rejection of him by Samaritans. In this episode Jesus disassociates himself from the attitude expressed by his disciples that those who reject him are to be punished severely. The story alludes to 2 Kgs 1:10, 12 where the prophet Elijah takes the course of action Jesus rejects, and Jesus thereby rejects the identification of himself with Elijah.

‡ [9:51] **Days for his being taken up:** like the reference to his exodus in Lk 9:31 this is probably a reference to all the events (suffering, death, resurrection, ascension) of his last days in Jerusalem. **He resolutely determined:** literally, "he set his face."

§ [9:52] **Samaritan:** Samaria was the territory between Judea and Galilee west of the Jordan river. For ethnic and religious reasons, the Samaritans and the Jews were bitterly opposed to one another (see Jn 4:9).

¶ [9:57–62] In these sayings Jesus speaks of the severity and the unconditional nature of Christian discipleship. Even family ties and filial obligations, such as burying one's parents, cannot distract one no matter how briefly from proclaiming the kingdom of God. The first two sayings are paralleled in Mt 8:19–22; see also notes there.

** [9:60] **Let the dead bury their dead:** i.e., let the spiritually dead (those who do not follow) bury their physically dead. See also note on Mt 8:22.

†† [10:1–12] Only the Gospel of Luke contains two episodes in which Jesus sends out his followers on a mission: the first (Lk 10:1–6) is based on the mission in Mk 6:6b–13 and recounts the sending out of the Twelve; here in Lk 10:1–12 a similar report based on Q describes the sending out of seventy-two in this gospel. The episode continues the theme of Jesus preparing witnesses to himself and his ministry. These witnesses include not only the Twelve but also the seventy-two who may represent the Christian mission in Luke's own day. Note that the instructions given to the Twelve and to the seventy-two are similar and that what is said to the seventy-two in Lk 10:4 is directed to the Twelve in Lk 22:35.

‡‡ [10:1] **Seventy[-two]:** important representatives of the Alexandrian and Caesarean text types read "seventy," while other important Alexandrian texts and Western readings have "seventy-two."

§§ [10:4] **Carry no money bag . . . greet no one along the way:** because of the urgency of the mission and the single-mindedness required of missionaries, attachment to material possessions should be avoided and even customary greetings should not distract from the fulfillment of the task.

¶¶ [10:5] **First say, 'Peace to this household':** see notes on Lk 2:14 and Mt 10:13.

*** [10:6] **A peaceful person:** literally, "a son of peace."

††† [10:13–16] The call to repentance that is a part of the proclamation of the kingdom brings with it a severe judgment for those who hear it and reject it.

---

a. [9:61–62] 1 Kgs 19:20.   b. [10:1] Mk 6:7.   c. [10:2] Mt 9:37–38; Jn 4:35.   d. [10:3] Mt 10:16.   e. [10:4–11] Mt 10:7–14.   f. [10:4] 9:3; 2 Kgs 4:29.   g. [10:7] 9:4; Mt 10:10; 1 Cor 9:6–14; 1 Tm 5:18.   h. [10:8] 1 Cor 10:27.   i. [10:9] Mt 3:2;4:17;Mk1:15.   j. [10:10–11] 9:5.   k. [10:11] Acts 13:51;18:6.   l. [10:12] Mt 10:15;11:24.   m. [10:13–15] Mt 11:20–24.   n. [10:13–14] Is 23; Ez 26–28; Jl 3:4–8; Am 1:1–10; Zec 9:2–4.

w. [9:51] 9:53; 13:22, 33; 17:11; 18:31; 19:28; 24:51; Acts 1:2, 9–11, 22.   x. [9:52] Mal 3:1.   y. [9:54] 2 Kgs 1:10, 12.   z. [9:57–60] Mt 8:19–22.

the mighty deeds done in your midst had been done in Tyre and Sidon, they would long ago have repented, sitting in sackcloth and ashes. [14]But it will be more tolerable for Tyre and Sidon at the judgment than for you. [15]*[o]And as for you, Capernaum, 'Will you be exalted to heaven? You will go down to the netherworld.'" [16]Whoever listens to you listens to me. Whoever rejects you rejects me. And whoever rejects me rejects the one who sent me."[p]

**Return of the Seventy-two.** [17]The seventy[-two] returned rejoicing, and said, "Lord, even the demons are subject to us because of your name." [18]Jesus said, "I have observed Satan fall like lightning[†] from the sky.[q] [19]Behold, I have given you the power 'to tread upon serpents' and scorpions and upon the full force of the enemy and nothing will harm you.[r] [20]Nevertheless, do not rejoice because the spirits are subject to you, but rejoice because your names are written in heaven."[s]

**Praise of the Father.**[t] [21]At that very moment he rejoiced [in] the holy Spirit and said, "I give you praise, Father, Lord of heaven and earth, for although you have hidden these things from the wise and the learned you have revealed them to the childlike.[‡] Yes, Father, such has been your gracious will.[u] [22]All things have been handed over to me by my Father. No one knows who the Son is except the Father, and who the Father is except the Son and anyone to whom the Son wishes to reveal him."[v]

**The Privileges of Discipleship.**[w] [23]Turning to the disciples in private he said, "Blessed are the eyes that see what you see. [24]For I say to you, many prophets and kings desired to see what you see, but did not see it, and to hear what you hear, but did not hear it."

**The Greatest Commandment.**[x] [25]§There was a scholar of the law[¶] who stood up to test him and said, "Teacher, what must I do to inherit eternal life?"[y] [26]Jesus said to him, "What is written in the law? How do you read it?" [27]He said in reply, "You shall love the Lord, your God, with all your heart, with all your being, with all your strength, and with all your mind, and your neighbor as yourself."[z] [28]He replied to him, "You have answered correctly; do this and you will live."[a]

**The Parable of the Good Samaritan.** [29]But because he wished to justify himself, he said to Jesus, "And who is my neighbor?" [30]Jesus replied, "A man fell victim to robbers as he went down from Jerusalem to Jericho. They stripped and beat him and went off leaving him half-dead. [31]"A priest happened to be going down that road, but when he saw him, he passed by on the opposite side. [32]Likewise a Levite came to the place, and when he saw him, he passed by on the opposite side. [33]But a Samaritan traveler who came upon him was moved with compassion at the sight. [34]He approached the victim, poured oil and wine over his wounds and bandaged them. Then he lifted him up on his own animal, took him to an inn and cared for him. [35]The next day he took out two silver coins and gave them to the innkeeper with the instruction, 'Take care of him. If you spend more than what I have given you, I shall repay you on my way back.' [36]Which of these three, in your opinion, was neighbor to the robbers' victim?" [37]He answered, "The one who treated him with mercy." Jesus said to him, "Go and do likewise."

**Martha and Mary.**[†† 38b]As they continued their journey he entered a village where a woman whose name was Martha welcomed him. [39]‡‡She had a sister named Mary [who] sat beside the Lord at his feet listening to him speak. [40]Martha, burdened with much serving, came to him and said, "Lord, do you not care that my sister has left me by myself to do the serving? Tell her to help me." [41]The Lord said to her in reply, "Martha, Martha, you are anxious and worried about many things. [42]§§There is need of only one thing. Mary has chosen the better part and it will not be taken from her."

---

*[10:15] **The netherworld**: the underworld, the place of the dead (Acts 2:27, 31) here contrasted with heaven; see also note on Mt 11:23.

†[10:18] **I have observed Satan fall like lightning**: the effect of the mission of the seventy-two is characterized by the Lucan Jesus as a symbolic fall of Satan. As the kingdom of God is gradually being established, evil in all its forms is being defeated; the dominion of Satan over humanity is at an end.

‡[10:21] **Revealed them to the childlike**: a restatement of the theme announced in Lk 8:10: the mysteries of the kingdom are revealed to the disciples. See also note on Mt 11:25–27.

§[10:25–37] In response to a question from a Jewish legal expert about inheriting eternal life, Jesus illustrates the superiority of love over legalism through the story of the good Samaritan. The law of love proclaimed in the "Sermon on the Plain" (Lk 6:27–36) is exemplified by one whom the legal expert would have considered ritually impure (see Jn 4:9). Moreover, the identity of the "neighbor" requested by the legal expert (Lk 10:29) turns out to be a Samaritan, the enemy of the Jew (see note on Lk 9:52).

¶[10:25] **Scholar of the law**: an expert in the Mosaic law, and probably a member of the group elsewhere identified as the scribes (Lk 5:21).

**[10:31–32] Priest . . . Levite**: those religious representatives of Judaism who would have been expected to be models of "neighbor" to the victim pass him by.

††[10:38–42] The story of Martha and Mary further illustrates the importance of hearing the words of the teacher and the concern with women in Luke.

‡‡[10:39] **Sat beside the Lord at his feet**: it is remarkable for first-century Palestinian Judaism that a woman would assume the posture of a disciple at the master's feet (see also Lk 8:35; Acts 22:3), and it reveals a characteristic attitude of Jesus toward women in this gospel (see Lk 8:2–3).

§§[10:42] **There is need of only one thing**: some ancient versions read, "there is need of few things"; another important, although probably inferior, reading found in some manuscripts is, "there is need of few things, or of one."

---

o. [10:15] Is 14:13–15.   p. [10:16] Mt 10:40; Jn 5:23; 13:20; 15:23.   q. [10:18] Is 14:12; Jn 12:31; Rev 12:7–12.   r. [10:19] Ps 91:13; Mk 16:18.   s. [10:20] Ex 32:32; Dn 12:1; Mt 7:22; Phil 4:3; Heb 12:23; Rev 3:5; 21:27.   t. [10:21–22] Mt 11:25–27.   u. [10:21] 1 Cor 1:26–28.   v. [10:22] Jn 3:35; 10:15.   w. [10:23–24] Mt 13:16–17.   x. [10:25–28] Mt 22:34–40; Mk 12:28–34.

y. [10:25] 18:18; Mt 19:16; Mk 10:17.   z. [10:27] Lv 19:18; Dt 6:5; 10:12; Jos 22:5; Mt 19:19; 22:37–39; Rom 13:9; Gal 5:14; Jas 2:8.   a. [10:28] Lv 18:5; Prv 19:16; Rom 10:5; Gal 3:12.   b. [10:38–39] Jn 11:1; 12:2–3.

## CHAPTER 11

**The Lord's Prayer.**[c] [1]He was praying in a certain place, and when he had finished, one of his disciples said to him, "Lord, teach us to pray just as John taught his disciples."[†] [2]He said to them, "When you pray, say:

Father, hallowed be your name,
　　your kingdom come.
[3]　　Give us each day our daily bread[§]
[4]　　and forgive us our sins
　　for we ourselves forgive everyone in
　　　　debt to us,
　　and do not subject us to the final
　　　　test."

**Further Teachings on Prayer.**[d] [5]And he said to them, "Suppose one of you has a friend to whom he goes at midnight and says, 'Friend, lend me three loaves of bread, [6]for a friend of mine has arrived at my house from a journey and I have nothing to offer him,' [7]and he says in reply from within, 'Do not bother me; the door has already been locked and my children and I are already in bed. I cannot get up to give you anything.' [8]I tell you, if he does not get up to give him the loaves because of their friendship, he will get up to give him whatever he needs because of his persistence.

**The Answer to Prayer.**[e] [9]"And I tell you, ask and you will receive; seek and you will find; knock and the door will be opened to you.[f] [10]For everyone who asks, receives; and the one who seeks, finds; and to the one who knocks, the door will be opened. [11]What father among you would hand his son a snake when he asks for a fish? [12]Or hand him a scorpion when he asks for an egg? [13]If you then, who are wicked, know how to give good gifts to your children, how much more will the Father in heaven give the holy Spirit[§] to those who ask him?"

**Jesus and Beelzebul.**[g] [14]He was driving out a demon [that was] mute, and when the demon had gone out, the mute person spoke and the crowds were amazed. [15]Some of them said, "By the power of Beelzebul, the prince of demons, he drives out demons."[h] [16]Others, to test him, asked him for a sign from heaven.[i] [17]But he knew their thoughts and said to them, "Every kingdom divided against itself will be laid waste and house will fall against house. [18]And if Satan is divided against himself, how will his kingdom stand? For you say that it is by Beelzebul that I drive out demons. [19]If I, then, drive out demons by Beelzebul, by whom do your own people[**] drive them out? Therefore they will be your judges. [20]But if it is by the finger of God that [I] drive out demons, then the kingdom of God has come upon you.[j] [21]When a strong man fully armed guards his palace, his possessions are safe. [22]But when one stronger[††] than he attacks and overcomes him, he takes away the armor on which he relied and distributes the spoils. [23]Whoever is not with me is against me, and whoever does not gather with me scatters.[k]

**The Return of the Unclean Spirit.**[l] [24]"When an unclean spirit goes out of someone, it roams through arid regions searching for rest but, finding none, it says, 'I shall return to my home from which I came.' [25]But upon returning, it finds it swept clean and put in order. [26]Then it goes and brings back seven other spirits more wicked than itself who move in and dwell there, and the last condition of that person is worse than the first."[m]

**True Blessedness.**[‡‡] [27]While he was speaking, a woman from the crowd called out and said to him, "Blessed is the womb that carried you and the breasts at which you nursed."[n] [28]He replied, "Rather, blessed are those who hear the word of God and observe it."

**The Demand for a Sign.**[§§] [29]While still more people gathered in the crowd, he said to them,[o] "This generation is an evil generation; it seeks a sign, but no sign will be given it, except the sign of Jonah.[p] [30]Just as Jonah became a sign to the Ninevites, so will the Son of Man be to this

---

\*[11:1–13] Luke presents three episodes concerned with prayer. The first (Lk 11:1–4) recounts Jesus teaching his disciples the Christian communal prayer, the "Our Father"; the second (Lk 11:5–8), the importance of persistence in prayer; the third (Lk 11:9–13), the effectiveness of prayer.

†[11:1–4] The Matthean form of the "Our Father" occurs in the "Sermon on the Mount" (Mt 6:9–15); the shorter Lucan version is presented while Jesus is at prayer (see note on Lk 3:21) and his disciples ask him to teach them to pray just as John taught his disciples to pray. In answer to their question, Jesus presents them with an example of a Christian communal prayer that stresses the fatherhood of God and acknowledges him as the one to whom the Christian disciple owes daily sustenance (Lk 11:3), forgiveness (Lk 11:4), and deliverance from the final trial (Lk 11:4). See also notes on Mt 6:9–13.

‡[11:2] **Your kingdom come**: in place of this petition, some early church Fathers record: "May your holy Spirit come upon us and cleanse us," a petition that may reflect the use of the "Our Father" in a baptismal liturgy.

§[11:3–4] **Daily bread**: see note on Mt 6:11. **The final test**: see note on Mt 6:13.

¶[11:13] **The holy Spirit**: this is a Lucan editorial alteration of a traditional saying of Jesus (see Mt 7:11). Luke presents

the gift of the holy Spirit as the response of the Father to the prayer of the Christian disciple.

\*\*[11:19] **Your own people**: the Greek reads "your sons." Other Jewish exorcists (see Acts 19:13–20), who recognize that the power of God is active in the exorcism, would themselves convict the accusers of Jesus. See also note on Mt 12:27.

††[11:22] **One stronger**: i.e., Jesus. Cf. Lk 3:16 where John the Baptist identifies Jesus as "mightier than I."

‡‡[11:27–28] The beatitude in Lk 11:28 should not be interpreted as a rebuke of the mother of Jesus; see note on Lk 8:21. Rather, it emphasizes (like Lk 2:35) that attentiveness to God's word is more important than biological relationship to Jesus.

§§[11:29–32] The "sign of Jonah" in Luke is the preaching of the need for repentance by a prophet who comes from afar. Cf. Mt 12:38–42 (and see notes there) where the "sign of Jonah" is interpreted by Jesus as his death and resurrection.

---

c. [11:1–4] Mt 6:9–15. d. [11:5–8] 18:1–5. e. [11:9–13] Mt 7:7–11. f. [11:9] Mt 21:22; Mk 11:24; Jn 14:13; 15:7; 1 Jn 5:14–15.

g. [11:14–23] Mt 12:22–30; Mk 3:20–27. h. [11:15] Mt 9:34. i. [11:16] Mt 12:38; 16:1; Mk 8:11; 1 Cor 1:22. j. [11:20] Ex 8:19. k. [11:23] 9:50; Mk 9:40. l. [11:24–26] Mt 12:43–45. m. [11:26] Jn 5:14. n. [11:27] 1:28, 42, 48. o. [11:29–32] Mt 12:38–42; Mk 8:12. p. [11:29] Mt 16:1, 4; Jn 6:30; 1 Cor 1:22.

generation. ³¹At the judgment the queen of the south will rise with the men of this generation and she will condemn them, because she came from the ends of the earth to hear the wisdom of Solomon, and there is something greater than Solomon here.*q* ³²At the judgment the men of Nineveh will arise with this generation and condemn it, because at the preaching of Jonah they repented, and there is something greater than Jonah here.*r*

**The Simile of Light.** *•* ³³"No one who lights a lamp hides it away or places it [under a bushel basket], but on a lampstand so that those who enter might see the light.*s* ³⁴The lamp of the body is your eye.*t* When your eye is sound, then your whole body is filled with light, but when it is bad, then your body is in darkness. ³⁵Take care, then, that the light in you not become darkness. ³⁶If your whole body is full of light, and no part of it is in darkness, then it will be as full of light as a lamp illuminating you with its brightness."

**Denunciation of the Pharisees and Scholars of the Law.** *•* ³⁷*u*After he had spoken, a Pharisee invited him to dine at his home. He entered and reclined at table to eat.*v* ³⁸The Pharisee was amazed to see that he did not observe the prescribed washing before the meal.*w* ³⁹The Lord said to him, "Oh you Pharisees! Although you cleanse the outside of the cup and the dish, inside you are filled with plunder and evil. ⁴⁰You fools! Did not the maker of the outside also make the inside? ⁴¹But as to what is within, give alms, and behold, everything will be clean for you. ⁴²Woe to you Pharisees! You pay tithes of mint and of rue and of every garden herb, but you pay no attention to judgment and to love for God. These you should have done, without overlooking the others.*y* ⁴³Woe to you Pharisees! You love the seat of honor in synagogues and greetings in marketplaces.*z* ⁴⁴Woe to you! You are like unseen graves† over which people unknowingly walk."*a*

⁴⁵Then one of the scholars of the law‡ said to him in reply, "Teacher, by saying this you are insulting us too."*b* ⁴⁶And he said, "Woe also to you scholars of the law! You impose on people burdens hard to carry, but you yourselves do not lift one finger to touch them. ⁴⁷*c*Woe to you! You build the memorials of the prophets whom your ancestors killed. ⁴⁸Consequently, you bear witness and give consent to the deeds of your ancestors, for they killed them and you do the building. ⁴⁹*d*Therefore, the wisdom of God said, 'I will send to them prophets and apostles;§ some of them they will kill and persecute' ⁵⁰in order that this generation might be charged with the blood of all the prophets shed since the foundation of the world, ⁵¹from the blood of Abel to the blood of Zechariah¶ who died between the altar and the temple building. Yes, I tell you, this generation will be charged with their blood! ⁵²Woe to you, scholars of the law! You have taken away the key of knowledge. You yourselves did not enter and you stopped those trying to enter."*f* ⁵³When he left, the scribes and Pharisees began to act with hostility toward him and to interrogate him about many things,*g* ⁵⁴for they were plotting to catch him at something he might say.*h*

# CHAPTER 12

**The Leaven of the Pharisees.** *•* ¹Meanwhile, so many people were crowding together that they were trampling one another underfoot.*i* He began to speak, first to his disciples, "Beware of the leaven—that is, the hypocrisy—of the Pharisees.

**Courage Under Persecution.** †† ²*j*"There is nothing concealed that will not be revealed, nor secret that will not be known.*k* ³Therefore whatever you have said in the darkness will be heard in the light, and what you have whispered behind closed doors will be proclaimed on the housetops. ⁴I tell you, my friends, do not be afraid of those who kill the body but after that can do no more. ⁵I shall show you whom to fear. Be afraid of the one who after killing has the power to cast into Gehenna;‡‡ yes, I tell you, be afraid of that one. ⁶Are not five sparrows sold for two small coins?§§ Yet not one of them has escaped the notice of God. ⁷Even the hairs of your head

---

§[11:49] **I will send to them prophets and apostles:** Jesus connects the mission of the church (apostles) with the mission of the Old Testament prophets who often suffered the rebuke of their contemporaries.

¶[11:51] **From the blood of Abel to the blood of Zechariah:** the murder of Abel is the first murder recounted in the Old Testament (Gn 4:8). The Zechariah mentioned here may be the Zechariah whose murder is recounted in 2 Chr 24:20–22, the last murder presented in the Hebrew canon of the Old Testament.

**[12:1] See notes on Mk 8:15 and Mt 16:5–12.

††[12:2–9] Luke presents a collection of sayings of Jesus exhorting his followers to acknowledge him and his mission fearlessly and assuring them of God's protection even in times of persecution. They are paralleled in Mt 10:26–33.

‡‡[12:5] **Gehenna:** see note on Mt 5:22.

§§[12:6] **Two small coins:** the Roman copper coin, the assarion (Latin *as*), was worth about one-sixteenth of a denarius (see note on Lk 7:41).

---

*[11:37–54] This denunciation of the Pharisees (Lk 11:39–44) and the scholars of the law (Lk 11:45–52) is set by Luke in the context of Jesus' dining at the home of a Pharisee. Controversies with or reprimands of Pharisees are regularly set by Luke within the context of Jesus' eating with Pharisees (see Lk 5:29–39; 7:36–50; 14:1–24). A different compilation of similar sayings is found in Mt 23 (see also notes there).

†[11:44] **Unseen graves:** contact with the dead or with human bones or graves (see Nm 19:16) brought ritual impurity. Jesus presents the Pharisees as those who insidiously lead others astray through their seeming attention to the law.

‡[11:45] **Scholars of the law:** see note on Lk 10:25.

---

q. [11:31]  1 Kgs 10:1–10; 2 Chr 9:1–12.   r. [11:32]  Jon 3:8, 10.   s. [11:33]  8:16; Mk 4:21.   t. [11:34–36]  Mt 6:22–23.   u. [11:37–54]  20:45–47; Mt 23:1–36; Mk 12:38–40.   v. [11:37]  7:36; 14:1.   w. [11:38]  Mt 15:2; Mk 7:2–5.   x. [11:39–41]  Mt 23:25–26.   y. [11:42]  Lv 27:30; Mt 23:23.   z. [11:43]  20:46; Mt 23:6; Mk 12:38–39.   a. [11:44]  Mt 23:27.   b. [11:45]  Mt 23:4.

c. [11:47–48]  Mt 23:29–32.   d. [11:49–51]  Mt 23:34–36.   e. [11:51]  Gn 4:8; 2 Chr 24:20–22.   f. [11:52]  Mt 23:13.   g. [11:53]  6:11; Mt 22:15–22.   h. [11:54]  20:20.   i. [12:1]  Mt 16:6; Mk 8:15.   j. [12:2–9]  Mt 10:26–33.   k. [12:2]  8:17; Mk 4:22.

have all been counted. Do not be afraid. You are worth more than many sparrows.[l] [8]I tell you, everyone who acknowledges me before others the Son of Man will acknowledge before the angels of God. [9]But whoever denies me before others will be denied before the angels of God.[m]

**Sayings About the Holy Spirit.** [10]"Everyone who speaks a word against the Son of Man will be forgiven, but the one who blasphemes against the holy Spirit will not be forgiven.[n] [11]When they take you before synagogues and before rulers and authorities,[o] do not worry about how or what your defense will be or about what you are to say. [12]For the holy Spirit will teach you at that moment what you should say."

**Saying Against Greed.** [13]†Someone in the crowd said to him, "Teacher, tell my brother to share the inheritance with me." [14]He replied to him, "Friend, who appointed me as your judge and arbitrator?"[p] [15]Then he said to the crowd, "Take care to guard against all greed, for though one may be rich, one's life does not consist of possessions."[q]

**Parable of the Rich Fool.** [16]Then he told them a parable. "There was a rich man whose land produced a bountiful harvest. [17]He asked himself, 'What shall I do, for I do not have space to store my harvest?' [18]And he said, 'This is what I shall do: I shall tear down my barns and build larger ones. There I shall store all my grain and other goods [19]and I shall say to myself, "Now as for you, you have so many good things stored up for many years, rest, eat, drink, be merry!"' [20]But God said to him, 'You fool, this night your life will be demanded of you; and the things you have prepared, to whom will they belong?' [21]Thus will it be for the one who stores up treasure for himself but is not rich in what matters to God."‡

**Dependence on God.** [22]†He said to [his] disciples, "Therefore I tell you, do not worry about your life and what you will eat, or about your body and what you will wear. [23]For life is more than food and the body more than clothing. [24]Notice the ravens: they do not sow or reap; they have neither storehouse nor barn, yet God feeds them. How much more important are you

than birds![u] [25]Can any of you by worrying add a moment to your life-span? [26]If even the smallest things are beyond your control, why are you anxious about the rest? [27]Notice how the flowers grow. They do not toil or spin. But I tell you, not even Solomon in all his splendor was dressed like one of them.[v] [28]If God so clothes the grass in the field that grows today and is thrown into the oven tomorrow, will he not much more provide for you, O you of little faith? [29]As for you, do not seek what you are to eat and what you are to drink, and do not worry anymore. [30]All the nations of the world seek for these things, and your Father knows that you need them. [31]Instead, seek his kingdom, and these other things will be given you besides. [32]Do not be afraid any longer, little flock, for your Father is pleased to give you the kingdom.[w] [33]Sell your belongings and give alms. Provide money bags for yourselves that do not wear out, an inexhaustible treasure in heaven that no thief can reach nor moth destroy.[x] [34]For where your treasure is, there also will your heart be.

**Vigilant and Faithful Servants.**§ [35]†"Gird your loins and light your lamps [36]and be like servants who await their master's return from a wedding, ready to open immediately when he comes and knocks.[z] [37]Blessed are those servants whom the master finds vigilant on his arrival. Amen, I say to you, he will gird himself, have them recline at table, and proceed to wait on them. [38]And should he come in the second or third watch and find them prepared in this way, blessed are those servants. [39]Be sure of this: if the master of the house had known the hour when the thief was coming, he would not have let his house be broken into. [40]You also must be prepared, for at an hour you do not expect, the Son of Man will come."

[41]Then Peter said, "Lord, is this parable meant for us or for everyone?" [42]And the Lord replied, "Who, then, is the faithful and prudent steward whom the master will put in charge of his servants to distribute [the] food allowance at the proper time? [43]Blessed is that servant whom his master on arrival finds doing so. [44]Truly, I say to you, he will put him in charge of all his property. [45]But if that servant says to himself, 'My master is delayed in coming,'¶ and begins to beat the menservants and the maidservants, to eat and drink and get drunk, [46]then that servant's master will come on an unexpected day and at

---

* [12:10–12] The sayings about the holy Spirit are set in the context of fearlessness in the face of persecution (Lk 12:2–9; cf. Mt 12:31–32). The holy Spirit will be presented in Luke's second volume, the Acts of the Apostles, as the power responsible for the guidance of the Christian mission and the source of courage in the face of persecution.

† [12:13–34] Luke has joined together sayings contrasting those whose focus and trust in life is on material possessions, symbolized here by the rich fool of the parable (Lk 12:16–21), with those who recognize their complete dependence on God (Lk 12:21), those whose radical detachment from material possessions symbolizes their heavenly treasure (Lk 12:33–34).

‡ [12:21] **Rich in what matters to God:** literally, "rich for God."

l. [12:7] 12:24; 21:18; Acts 27:34.   m. [12:9] 9:26; Mk 8:38; 2 Tm 2:12.   n. [12:10] Mt 12:31–32; Mk 3:28–29.   o. [12:11–12] 21:12–15; Mt 10:17–20; Mk 13:11.   p. [12:14] Ex 2:14; Acts 7:27.   q. [12:15] 1 Tm 6:9–10.   r. [12:19–21] 6:19–21; 1 Tm 6:17.   s. [12:19–20] Sir 11:19.   t. [12:22–32] Mt 6:25–34.

§ [12:35–48] This collection of sayings relates to Luke's understanding of the end time and the return of Jesus. Luke emphasizes for his readers the importance of being faithful to the instructions of Jesus in the period before the parousia.

¶ [12:45] **My master is delayed in coming:** this statement indicates that early Christian expectations for the imminent return of Jesus had undergone some modification. Luke cautions his readers against counting on such a delay and acting irresponsibly. Cf. the similar warning in Mt 24:48.

u. [12:24] 12:7.   v. [12:27] 1 Kgs 10:4–7; 2 Chr 9:3–6.   w. [12:32] 22:29; Rev 1:6.   x. [12:33] 18:22; Mt 6:20–21; Mk 10:21.   y. [12:35–46] Mt 24:45–51.   z. [12:36] Mt 25:1–13; Mk 13:35–37.   a. [12:39–40] Mt 24:43–44; 1 Thes 5:2.

an unknown hour and will punish him severely and assign him a place with the unfaithful. [47]That servant who knew his master's will but did not make preparations nor act in accord with his will shall be beaten severely;[b] [48]and the servant who was ignorant of his master's will but acted in a way deserving of a severe beating shall be beaten only lightly. Much will be required of the person entrusted with much, and still more will be demanded of the person entrusted with more.

**Jesus: A Cause of Division.[*]** [49]"I have come to set the earth on fire, and how I wish it were already blazing! [50†]There is a baptism with which I must be baptized, and how great is my anguish until it is accomplished![c] [51]Do you think that I have come to establish peace on the earth?[d] No, I tell you, but rather division.[e] [52]From now on a household of five will be divided, three against two and two against three; [53]a father will be divided against his son and a son against his father, a mother against her daughter and a daughter against her mother, a mother-in-law against her daughter-in-law and a daughter-in-law against her mother-in-law."[f]

**Signs of the Times.[g]** [54]He also said to the crowds, "When you see [a] cloud rising in the west you say immediately that it is going to rain—and so it does; [55]and when you notice that the wind is blowing from the south you say that it is going to be hot—and so it is. [56]You hypocrites! You know how to interpret the appearance of the earth and the sky; why do you not know how to interpret the present time?

**Settlement with an Opponent.[h]** [57]"Why do you not judge for yourselves what is right? [58]If you are to go with your opponent before a magistrate, make an effort to settle the matter on the way; otherwise your opponent will turn you over to the judge, and the judge hand you over to the constable, and the constable throw you into prison. [59]I say to you, you will not be released until you have paid the last penny."[‡]

## CHAPTER 13

**A Call to Repentance.[§]** [1]At that time some people who were present there told him about the Galileans whose blood Pilate[*] had mingled with the blood of their sacrifices. [2]He said to them in reply, "Do you think that because these Galileans suffered in this way they were greater sinners than all other Galileans?[i] [3]By no means! But I tell you, if you do not repent,[j] you will all perish as they did! [4]Or those eighteen people who were killed when the tower at Siloam fell on them[**]—do you think they were more guilty than everyone else who lived in Jerusalem? [5]By no means! But I tell you, if you do not repent, you will all perish as they did!"

**The Parable of the Barren Fig Tree.[††]** [6k]And he told them this parable: "There once was a person who had a fig tree planted in his orchard, and when he came in search of fruit on it but found none, [7]he said to the gardener, 'For three years now I have come in search of fruit on this fig tree but have found none. [So] cut it down. Why should it exhaust the soil?' [8]He said to him in reply, 'Sir, leave it for this year also, and I shall cultivate the ground around it and fertilize it; [9]it may bear fruit in the future. If not you can cut it down.'"

**Cure of a Crippled Woman on the Sabbath.[‡‡]** [10]He was teaching in a synagogue on the sabbath. [11]And a woman was there who for eighteen years had been crippled by a spirit; she was bent over, completely incapable of standing erect. [12]When Jesus saw her, he called to her and said, "Woman, you are set free of your infirmity." [13]He laid his hands on her, and she at once stood up straight and glorified God. [14]But the leader of the synagogue, indignant that Jesus had cured on the sabbath, said to the crowd in reply, "There are six days when work should be done. Come on those days to be cured, not on the

---

¶[13:1] The slaughter of the Galileans by Pilate is unknown outside Luke; but from what is known about Pilate from the Jewish historian Josephus, such a slaughter would be in keeping with the character of Pilate. Josephus reports that Pilate had disrupted a religious gathering of the Samaritans on Mount Gerizim with a slaughter of the participants (*Antiquities* 18:86–87), and that on another occasion Pilate had killed many Jews who had opposed him when he appropriated money from the temple treasury to build an aqueduct in Jerusalem (*Jewish Wars* 2:175–77; *Antiquities* 18:60–62).

**[13:4] Like the incident mentioned in Lk 13:1 nothing of this accident in Jerusalem is known outside Luke and the New Testament.

††[13:6–9] Following on the call to repentance in Lk 13:1–5, the parable of the barren fig tree presents a story about the continuing patience of God with those who have not yet given evidence of their repentance (see Lk 3:8). The parable may also be alluding to the delay of the end time, when punishment will be meted out, and the importance of preparing for the end of the age because the delay will not be permanent (Lk 13:8–9).

‡‡[13:10–17] The cure of the crippled woman on the sabbath and the controversy that results furnishes a parallel to an incident that will be reported by Luke in 14:1–6, the cure of the man with dropsy on the sabbath. A characteristic of Luke's style is the juxtaposition of an incident that reveals Jesus' concern for a man with an incident that reveals his concern for a woman; cf., e.g., Lk 7:11–17 and Lk 8:49–56.

---

*[12:49–53] Jesus' proclamation of the kingdom is a refining and purifying fire. His message that meets with acceptance or rejection will be a source of conflict and dissension even within families.

†[12:50] **Baptism:** i.e., his death.

‡[12:59] **The last penny:** Greek, **lepton**, a very small amount. Mt 5:26 has for "the last penny" the Greek word *kodrantēs* (Latin *quadrans*, "farthing").

§[13:1–5] The death of the Galileans at the hands of Pilate (Lk 13:1) and the accidental death of those on whom the tower fell (Lk 13:4) are presented by the Lucan Jesus as timely reminders of the need for all to repent, for the victims of these tragedies should not be considered outstanding sinners who were singled out for punishment.

---

b. [12:47] Jas 4:17.  c. [12:50] Mk 10:38–39.  d. [12:51–53] Mt 10:34–35.  e. [12:51] 2:14.  f. [12:53] Mi 7:6.  g. [12:54–56] Mt 16:2–3.  h. [12:57–59] Mt 5:25–26.

i. [13:2] Jn 9:2.  j. [13:3–5] Jn 8:24.  k. [13:6–9] Jer 8:13; Heb 3:17; Mt 21:19; Mk 11:13.  l. [13:14] 6:7; 14:3; Ex 20:8–11; Dt 5:12–15; Mt 12:10; Mk 3:2–4; Jn 5:16; 7:23; 9:14, 16.

sabbath day." [15]"The Lord said to him in reply, "Hypocrites! Does not each one of you on the sabbath untie his ox or his ass from the manger and lead it out for watering?[m 16†]This daughter of Abraham, whom Satan has bound for eighteen years now, ought she not to have been set free on the sabbath day from this bondage?"[n 17]When he said this, all his adversaries were humiliated; and the whole crowd rejoiced at all the splendid deeds done by him.

### The Parable of the Mustard Seed.[o] [18†]Then he said, "What is the kingdom of God like? To what can I compare it? [19]It is like a mustard seed that a person took and planted in the garden. When it was fully grown, it became a large bush and 'the birds of the sky dwelt in its branches.'"[p]

### The Parable of the Yeast.[q] [20]Again he said, "To what shall I compare the kingdom of God? [21]It is like yeast that a woman took and mixed [in] with three measures of wheat flour until the whole batch of dough was leavened."

### The Narrow Door; Salvation and Rejection.[§] [22]He passed through towns and villages, teaching as he went and making his way to Jerusalem. [23]Someone asked him, "Lord, will only a few people be saved?" He answered them, [24r]"Strive to enter through the narrow door, for many, I tell you, will attempt to enter but will not be strong enough.[s] [25]After the master of the house has arisen and locked the door, then will you stand outside knocking and saying, 'Lord, open the door for us.' He will say to you in reply, 'I do not know where you are from.'[t] [26]And you will say, 'We ate and drank in your company and you taught in our streets.' [27u]Then he will say to you, 'I do not know where [you] are from. Depart from me, all you evildoers!'[u] [28v]And there will be wailing and grinding of teeth when you see Abraham, Isaac, and Jacob and all the prophets in the kingdom of God and you yourselves cast out. [29]And people will come from the east and the west and from the north and the south and will recline at table in the kingdom of God.[w] [30]For behold, some are last who will be first, and some are first who will be last."[x]

### Herod's Desire to Kill Jesus. [31]At that time some Pharisees came to him and said, "Go away, leave this area because Herod wants to kill you." [32]He replied, "Go and tell that fox, 'Behold, I cast out demons and I perform healings today and tomorrow, and on the third day I accomplish my purpose.[¶] [33†]Yet I must continue on my way today,[y] tomorrow, and the following day, for it is impossible that a prophet should die outside of Jerusalem.'

### The Lament over Jerusalem.[z] [34]"Jerusalem, Jerusalem, you who kill the prophets and stone those sent to you, how many times I yearned to gather your children together as a hen gathers her brood under her wings, but you were unwilling! [35]Behold, your house will be abandoned. [But] I tell you, you will not see me until [the time comes when] you say, 'Blessed is he who comes in the name of the Lord.'"[a]

## CHAPTER 14

### Healing of the Man with Dropsy on the Sabbath.[†† 1b]On a sabbath he went to dine at the home of one of the leading Pharisees, and the people there were observing him carefully.[c] [2]In front of him there was a man suffering from dropsy.[‡‡] [3]Jesus spoke to the scholars of the law and Pharisees in reply, asking, "Is it lawful to cure on the sabbath or not?"[d] [4]But they kept silent; so he took the man and, after he had healed him, dismissed him. [5]Then he said to them, "Who among you, if your son or ox[§§] falls into a cistern, would not immediately pull him out on the sabbath day?"[e] [6]But they were unable to answer his question.[f]

### Conduct of Invited Guests and Hosts.[¶¶] [7g]He told a parable to those who had been invited,

---

*[13:15–16] If the law as interpreted by Jewish tradition allowed for the untying of bound animals on the sabbath, how much more should this woman who has been bound by Satan's power be freed on the sabbath from her affliction.

†[13:16] **Whom Satan has bound:** affliction and infirmity are taken as evidence of Satan's hold on humanity. The healing ministry of Jesus reveals the gradual wresting from Satan of control over humanity and the establishment of God's kingdom.

‡[13:18–21] Two parables are used to illustrate the future proportions of the kingdom of God that will result from its deceptively small beginning in the preaching and healing ministry of Jesus. They are paralleled in Mt 13:31–33 and Mk 4:30–32.

§[13:22–30] These sayings of Jesus follow in Luke upon the parables of the kingdom (Lk 13:18–21) and stress that great effort is required for entrance into the kingdom (Lk 13:24) and that there is an urgency to accept the present opportunity to enter because the narrow door will not remain open indefinitely (Lk 13:25). Lying behind the sayings is the rejection of Jesus and his message by his Jewish contemporaries (Lk 13:26) whose places at table in the kingdom will be taken by Gentiles from the four corners of the world (Lk 13:29). Those called last (the Gentiles) will precede those to whom the invitation to enter was first extended (the Jews). See also Lk 14:15–24.

¶[13:32] Nothing, not even Herod's desire to kill Jesus, stands in the way of Jesus' role in fulfilling God's will and in establishing the kingdom through his exorcisms and healings.

**[13:33] It is impossible that a prophet should die outside of Jerusalem:** Jerusalem is the city of destiny and the goal of the journey of the prophet Jesus. Only when he reaches the holy city will his work be accomplished.

††[14:1–6] See note on Lk 13:10–17.

‡‡[14:2] **Dropsy:** an abnormal swelling of the body because of the retention and accumulation of fluid.

§§[14:5] **Your son or ox:** this is the reading of many of the oldest and most important New Testament manuscripts. Because of the strange collocation of **son** and **ox**, some copyists have altered it to "your ass or ox," on the model of the saying in Lk 13:15.

¶¶[14:7–14] The banquet scene found only in Luke provides the opportunity for these teachings of Jesus on humility and presents a setting to display Luke's interest in Jesus' attitude

---

m. [13:15] 14:5; Dt 22:4; Mt 12:11.  n. [13:16] 19:9.  o. [13:18–19] Mt 13:31–32; Mk 4:30–32.  p. [13:19] Ez 17:23–24; 31:6.  q. [13:20–21] Mt 13:33.  r. [13:24–30] Mt 7:13–14, 21–23.  s. [13:24] Mk 10:25.  t. [13:25] Mt 25:10–12.  u. [13:27] Ps 6:9; Mt 7:23; 25:41.  v. [13:28–29] Mt 8:11–12.

w. [13:29] Ps 107:2–3.  x. [13:30] Mt 19:20; 20:16; Mk 10:31.  y. [13:33] 2:38; Jn 6:30; 8:20.  z. [13:34–35] 19:41–44; Mt 23:37–39.  a. [13:35] 19:38; 1 Kgs 9:7–8; Ps 118:26; Jer 7:4–7, 13–15; 12:7; 22:5.  b. [14:1–6] 6:6–11; 13:10–17.  c. [14:1] 11:37.  d. [14:3] 6:9; Mk 3:4.  e. [14:5] 13:15; Dt 22:4; Mt 12:11.  f. [14:6] Mt 22:46.  g. [14:7] 11:43; Mt 23:6; Mk 12:38–39.

noticing how they were choosing the places of honor at the table. [8h]"When you are invited by someone to a wedding banquet, do not recline at table in the place of honor. A more distinguished guest than you may have been invited by him, [9]and the host who invited both of you may approach you and say, 'Give your place to this man,' and then you would proceed with embarrassment to take the lowest place. [10]Rather, when you are invited, go and take the lowest place so that when the host comes to you he may say, 'My friend, move up to a higher position.' Then you will enjoy the esteem of your companions at the table. [11]For everyone who exalts himself will be humbled, but the one who humbles himself will be exalted."[i] [12]Then he said to the host who invited him, "When you hold a lunch or a dinner, do not invite your friends or your brothers or your relatives or your wealthy neighbors, in case they may invite you back and you have repayment.[j] [13]Rather, when you hold a banquet, invite the poor, the crippled, the lame, the blind; [14]blessed indeed will you be because of their inability to repay you. For you will be repaid at the resurrection of the righteous."[k]

**The Parable of the Great Feast.**[*] [15]One of his fellow guests on hearing this said to him, "Blessed is the one who will dine in the kingdom of God." [16l]He replied to him, "A man gave a great dinner to which he invited many. [17]When the time for the dinner came, he dispatched his servant to say to those invited, 'Come, everything is now ready.' [18]But one by one, they all began to excuse themselves. The first said to him, 'I have purchased a field and must go to examine it; I ask you, consider me excused.' [19]And another said, 'I have purchased five yoke of oxen and am on my way to evaluate them; I ask you, consider me excused.' [20]And another said, 'I have just married a woman, and therefore I cannot come.' [21]The servant went and reported this to his master. Then the master of the house in a rage commanded his servant, 'Go out quickly into the streets and alleys of the town and bring in here the poor and the crippled, the blind and the lame.' [22]The servant reported, 'Sir, your orders have been carried out and still there is room.' [23]The master then ordered the servant, 'Go out to the highways and hedgerows and make people come in that my home may be filled. [24]For, I tell you, none of those men who were invited will taste my dinner.'"

**Sayings on Discipleship.**[†] [25]Great crowds were traveling with him, and he turned and addressed them, [26m]"If anyone comes to me without hating his father[‡] and mother, wife and children, brothers and sisters, and even his own life, he cannot be my disciple.[n] [27]Whoever does not carry his own cross and come after me cannot be my disciple.[o] [28]Which of you wishing to construct a tower does not first sit down and calculate the cost to see if there is enough for its completion? [29]Otherwise, after laying the foundation and finding himself unable to finish the work the onlookers should laugh at him [30]and say, 'This one began to build but did not have the resources to finish.' [31]Or what king marching into battle would not first sit down and decide whether with ten thousand troops he can successfully oppose another king advancing upon him with twenty thousand troops? [32]But if not, while he is still far away, he will send a delegation to ask for peace terms. [33]In the same way, everyone of you who does not renounce all his possessions cannot be my disciple.[p]

**The Simile of Salt.**[§] [34]"Salt is good, but if salt itself loses its taste, with what can its flavor be restored?[q] [35]It is fit neither for the soil nor for the manure pile; it is thrown out. Whoever has ears to hear ought to hear."[r]

# CHAPTER 15

**The Parable of the Lost Sheep.**[¶] [1s]The tax collectors and sinners were all drawing near to listen to him, [2]but the Pharisees and scribes began to complain, saying, "This man welcomes sinners and eats with them."[t] [3]So to them he addressed this parable. [4u]"What man among you having a hundred sheep and losing one of them would not leave the ninety-nine in the desert and go after the lost one[v] until he finds it?[w] [5]And when

---

†[14:25–33] This collection of sayings, most of which are peculiar to Luke, focuses on the total dedication necessary for the disciple of Jesus. No attachment to family (Lk 14:26) or possessions (Lk 14:33) can stand in the way of the total commitment demanded of the disciple. Also, acceptance of the call to be a disciple demands readiness to accept persecution and suffering (Lk 14:27) and a realistic assessment of the hardships and costs (Lk 14:28–32).

‡[14:26] **Hating his father . . . :** cf. the similar saying in Mt 10:37. The disciple's family must take second place to the absolute dedication involved in following Jesus (see also Lk 9:59–62).

§[14:34–35] The simile of salt follows the sayings of Jesus that demanded of the disciple total dedication and detachment from family and possessions and illustrates the condition of one who does not display this total commitment. The halfhearted disciple is like salt that cannot serve its intended purpose. See the simile of salt in Mt 5:13 and the note there.

¶[15:1–32] To the parable of the lost sheep (Lk 15:1–7) that Luke shares with Matthew (Mt 18:12–14), Luke adds two parables (the lost coin, Lk 15:8–10; the prodigal son, Lk 15:11–32) from his own special tradition to illustrate Jesus' particular concern for the lost and God's love for the repentant sinner.

---

toward the rich and the poor (see notes on Lk 4:18; 6:20–26; 12:13–34).

*[14:15–24] The parable of the great dinner is a further illustration of the rejection by Israel, God's chosen people, of Jesus' invitation to share in the banquet in the kingdom and the extension of the invitation to other Jews whose identification as the poor, crippled, blind, and lame (Lk 14:21) classifies them among those who recognize their need for salvation, and to Gentiles (Lk 14:23). A similar parable is found in Mt 22:1–10.

---

h. [14:8–10] Prv 25:6–7.   i. [14:11] 18:14.   j. [14:12] 6:32–35.
k. [14:14] Jn 5:29.   l. [14:16–24] Mt 22:2–10.

m. [14:26–27] Mt 10:37–38.   n. [14:26] 9:57–62; 18:29; Jn 12:25.
o. [14:27] 9:23; Mt 16:24; Mk 8:34.   p. [14:33] 5:11.   q. [14:34] Mt 5:13; Mk 9:50.   r. [14:35] 8:8; Mt 11:15; 13:9; Mk 4:9, 23.   s. [15:1–7] Mt 9:10–13.   t. [15:2] 5:30; 19:7.   u. [15:4–7] Mt 18:12–14.   v. [15:4–6] 19:10.   w. [15:4] Ez 34:11–12, 16.

he does find it, he sets it on his shoulders with great joy ⁶and, upon his arrival home, he calls together his friends and neighbors and says to them, 'Rejoice with me because I have found my lost sheep.' ⁷I tell you, in just the same way there will be more joy in heaven over one sinner who repents than over ninety-nine righteous people who have no need of repentance.ˣ

**The Parable of the Lost Coin.** ⁸"Or what woman having ten coins* and losing one would not light a lamp and sweep the house, searching carefully until she finds it? ⁹And when she does find it, she calls together her friends and neighbors and says to them, 'Rejoice with me because I have found the coin that I lost.' ¹⁰In just the same way, I tell you, there will be rejoicing among the angels of God over one sinner who repents."

**The Parable of the Lost Son.** ¹¹Then he said, "A man had two sons, ¹²and the younger son said to his father, 'Father, give me the share of your estate that should come to me.' So the father divided the property between them. ¹³After a few days, the younger son collected all his belongings and set off to a distant country where he squandered his inheritance on a life of dissipation.ʸ ¹⁴When he had freely spent everything, a severe famine struck that country, and he found himself in dire need. ¹⁵So he hired himself out to one of the local citizens who sent him to his farm to tend the swine. ¹⁶And he longed to eat his fill of the pods on which the swine fed, but nobody gave him any. ¹⁷Coming to his senses he thought, 'How many of my father's hired workers have more than enough food to eat, but here am I, dying from hunger. ¹⁸I shall get up and go to my father and I shall say to him, "Father, I have sinned against heaven and against you. ¹⁹I no longer deserve to be called your son; treat me as you would treat one of your hired workers."' ²⁰So he got up and went back to his father. While he was still a long way off, his father caught sight of him, and was filled with compassion. He ran to his son, embraced him and kissed him. ²¹His son said to him, 'Father, I have sinned against heaven and against you; I no longer deserve to be called your son.' ²²But his father ordered his servants, 'Quickly bring the finest robe and put it on him; put a ring on his finger and sandals on his feet. ²³Take the fattened calf and slaughter it. Then let us celebrate with a feast, ²⁴because this son of mine was dead, and has come to life again; he was lost, and has been found.' Then the celebration began. ²⁵Now the older son had been out in the field and, on his way back, as he neared the house, he heard the sound of music and dancing. ²⁶He called one of the servants and asked what this might mean. ²⁷The servant said to him, 'Your brother has returned and your father has slaughtered the fattened calf

because he has him back safe and sound.' ²⁸He became angry, and when he refused to enter the house, his father came out and pleaded with him. ²⁹He said to his father in reply, 'Look, all these years I served you and not once did I disobey your orders; yet you never gave me even a young goat to feast on with my friends. ³⁰But when your son returns who swallowed up your property with prostitutes, for him you slaughter the fattened calf.' ³¹He said to him, 'My son, you are here with me always; everything I have is yours. ³²But now we must celebrate and rejoice, because your brother was dead and has come to life again; he was lost and has been found.'"

## CHAPTER 16

**The Parable of the Dishonest Steward.**† ¹Then he also said to his disciples, "A rich man had a steward who was reported to him for squandering his property. ²He summoned him and said, 'What is this I hear about you? Prepare a full account of your stewardship, because you can no longer be my steward.' ³The steward said to himself, 'What shall I do, now that my master is taking the position of steward away from me? I am not strong enough to dig and I am ashamed to beg. ⁴I know what I shall do so that, when I am removed from the stewardship, they may welcome me into their homes.' ⁵He called in his master's debtors one by one. To the first he said, 'How much do you owe my master?' ⁶He replied, 'One hundred measures of olive oil.' He said to him, 'Here is your promissory note. Sit down and quickly write one for fifty.' ⁷Then to another he said, 'And you, how much do you owe?' He replied, 'One hundred kors§ of wheat.' He said to him, 'Here is your promissory note; write one for eighty.' ⁸And the master commended that dishonest steward for acting prudently.

**Application of the Parable.**¶ "For the children of this world are more prudent in dealing with their own generation than are the children of light."** ⁹I tell you, make friends for yourselves

†[16:1–8a] The parable of the dishonest steward has to be understood in the light of the Palestinian custom of agents acting on behalf of their masters and the usurious practices common to such agents. The dishonesty of the steward consisted in the squandering of his master's property (Lk 16:1) and not in any subsequent graft. The master commends the dishonest steward who has forgone his own usurious commission on the business transaction by having the debtors write new notes that reflected only the real amount owed the master (i.e., minus the steward's profit). The dishonest steward acts in this way in order to ingratiate himself with the debtors because he knows he is being dismissed from his position (Lk 16:3). The parable, then, teaches the prudent use of one's material goods in light of an imminent crisis.

‡[16:6] **One hundred measures:** literally, "one hundred baths." A bath is a Hebrew unit of liquid measurement equivalent to eight or nine gallons.

§[16:7] **One hundred kors:** a **kor** is a Hebrew unit of dry measure for grain or wheat equivalent to ten or twelve bushels.

¶[16:8b–13] Several originally independent sayings of Jesus are gathered here by Luke to form the concluding application of the parable of the dishonest steward.

**[16:8b–9] The first conclusion recommends the prudent use of one's wealth (in the light of the coming of the end of

*[15:8] **Ten coins:** literally, "ten drachmas." A drachma was a Greek silver coin.

x. [15:7] Ez 18:23.   y. [15:13] Prv 29:3.

z. [16:8] Eph 5:8; 1 Thes 5:5.

with dishonest wealth,* so that when it fails, you will be welcomed into eternal dwellings.*[10†]The person who is trustworthy in very small matters is also trustworthy in great ones; and the person who is dishonest in very small matters is also dishonest in great ones.[b] [11]If, therefore, you are not trustworthy with dishonest wealth, who will trust you with true wealth? [12]If you are not trustworthy with what belongs to another, who will give you what is yours? [13]No servant can serve two masters.[‡] He will either hate one and love the other, or be devoted to one and despise the other. You cannot serve God and mammon."[c]

**A Saying Against the Pharisees.** [14§]The Pharisees, who loved money,[¶] heard all these things and sneered at him. [15]And he said to them, "You justify yourselves in the sight of others, but God knows your hearts; for what is of human esteem is an abomination in the sight of God.[d]

**Sayings About the Law.** [16]"The law and the prophets lasted until John;** but from then on the kingdom of God is proclaimed, and everyone who enters does so with violence.[e] [17]It is easier for heaven and earth to pass away than for the smallest part of a letter of the law to become invalid.[f]

**Sayings About Divorce.** [18]"Everyone who divorces his wife and marries another commits adultery, and the one who marries a woman divorced from her husband commits adultery.[g]

**The Parable of the Rich Man and Lazarus.**[††] [19]"There was a rich man[‡‡] who dressed in purple garments and fine linen and dined sumptuously each day. [20]And lying at his door was a poor man named Lazarus, covered with sores,[h] [21]who would gladly have eaten his fill of the scraps that fell from the rich man's table. Dogs even used to come and lick his sores. [22]When the poor man died, he was carried away by angels to the bosom of Abraham. The rich man also died and was buried, [23]and from the netherworld,[§§] where he was in torment, he raised his eyes and saw Abraham far off and Lazarus at his side. [24]And he cried out, 'Father Abraham, have pity on me. Send Lazarus to dip the tip of his finger in water and cool my tongue, for I am suffering torment in these flames.' [25]Abraham replied, 'My child, remember that you received what was good during your lifetime while Lazarus likewise received what was bad; but now he is comforted here, whereas you are tormented.[i] [26]Moreover, between us and you a great chasm is established to prevent anyone from crossing who might wish to go from our side to yours or from your side to ours.' [27]He said, 'Then I beg you, father, send him to my father's house, [28]for I have five brothers, so that he may warn them, lest they too come to this place of torment.' [29]But Abraham replied, 'They have Moses and the prophets. Let them listen to them.' [30]He said, 'Oh no, father Abraham, but if someone from the dead goes to them, they will repent.' [31]Then Abraham said, 'If they will not listen to Moses and the prophets, neither will they be persuaded if someone should rise from the dead.'"[j]

## CHAPTER 17

**Temptations to Sin.** [1k]He said to his disciples, "Things that cause sin will inevitably occur, but woe to the person through whom they occur. [2]It would be better for him if a millstone were put around his neck and he be thrown into the sea than for him to cause one of these little ones to sin. [3]Be on your guard!*** If your brother sins, rebuke him; and if he repents, forgive him.[l] [4]And if he wrongs you seven times in one day and returns to you seven times saying, 'I am sorry,' you should forgive him."[m]

**Saying of Faith.** [5]And the apostles said to the Lord, "Increase our faith." [6]The Lord replied, "If you have faith the size of a mustard seed, you

---

the age) after the manner of the children of this world, represented in the parable by the dishonest steward.

*[16:9] **Dishonest wealth:** literally, "mammon of iniquity." Mammon is the Greek transliteration of a Hebrew or Aramaic word that is usually explained as meaning "that in which one trusts." The characterization of this wealth as **dishonest** expresses a tendency of wealth to lead one to dishonesty. **Eternal dwellings:** or, "eternal tents," i.e., heaven.

†[16:10–12] The second conclusion recommends constant fidelity to those in positions of responsibility.

‡[16:13] The third conclusion is a general statement about the incompatibility of serving God and being a slave to riches. To be dependent upon wealth is opposed to the teachings of Jesus who counseled complete dependence on the Father as one of the characteristics of the Christian disciple (Lk 12:22–39). **God and mammon:** see note on Lk 16:9. Mammon is used here as if it were itself a god.

§[16:14–18] The two parables about the use of riches in chap. 16 are separated by several isolated sayings of Jesus on the hypocrisy of the Pharisees (Lk 16:14–15), on the law (Lk 16:16–17), and on divorce (Lk 16:18).

¶[16:14–15] The Pharisees are here presented as examples of those who are slaves to wealth (see Lk 16:13) and, consequently, they are unable to serve God.

**[16:16] John the Baptist is presented in Luke's gospel as a transitional figure between the period of Israel, the time of promise, and the period of Jesus, the time of fulfillment. With John, the fulfillment of the Old Testament promises has begun.

††[16:19–31] The parable of the rich man and Lazarus again illustrates Luke's concern with Jesus' attitude toward the rich and the poor. The reversal of the fates of the rich man and Lazarus (Lk 16:22–23) illustrates the teachings of Jesus in Luke's "Sermon on the Plain" (Lk 6:20–21, 24–25).

‡‡[16:19] The oldest Greek manuscript of Luke dating from ca. A.D. 175–225 records the name of the rich man as an abbreviated form of "Nineveh," but there is very little textual support in other manuscripts for this reading. "Dives" of popular tradition is the Latin Vulgate's translation for "rich man" (Lk 16:19–31).

§§[16:23] **The netherworld:** see note on Lk 10:15.

¶¶[16:30–31] A foreshadowing in Luke's gospel of the rejection of the call to repentance even after Jesus' resurrection.

***[17:3] **Be on your guard:** the translation takes Lk 17:3a as the conclusion to the saying on scandal in Lk 17:1–2. It is not impossible that it should be taken as the beginning of the saying on forgiveness in Lk 17:3b–4.

---

a. [16:9] 12:33.　b. [16:10] 19:17; Mt 25:20–23.　c. [16:13] Mt 6:24.　d. [16:15] 18:9–14.　e. [16:16] Mt 11:12–13.　f. [16:17] Mt 5:18.　g. [16:18] Mt 5:32; 19:9; Mk 10:11–12; 1 Cor 7:10–11.

h. [16:20] Mt 15:27; Mk 7:28.　i. [16:25] 6:24–25.　j. [16:31] Jn 5:46–47; 11:44–48.　k. [17:1–2] Mt 18:6–7.　l. [17:3] Mt 18:15.　m. [17:4] Mt 6:14; 18:21–22, 35; Mk 11:25.

would say to [this] mulberry tree, 'Be uprooted and planted in the sea,' and it would obey you."

**Attitude of a Servant.**⃰ ⁷"Who among you would say to your servant who has just come in from plowing or tending sheep in the field, 'Come here immediately and take your place at table'? ⁸Would he not rather say to him, 'Prepare something for me to eat. Put on your apron and wait on me while I eat and drink. You may eat and drink when I am finished'? ⁹Is he grateful to that servant because he did what was commanded? ¹⁰So should it be with you. When you have done all you have been commanded, say, 'We are unprofitable servants; we have done what we were obliged to do.'"

**The Cleansing of Ten Lepers.**† ¹¹As he continued his journey to Jerusalem,ᵒ he traveled through Samaria and Galilee.‡ ¹²As he was entering a village, ten lepers met [him]. They stood at a distance from him ¹³and raised their voice, saying, "Jesus, Master! Have pity on us!"ᵖ ¹⁴And when he saw them, he said, "Go show yourselves to the priests."§ As they were going they were cleansed.�q ¹⁵And one of them, realizing he had been healed, returned, glorifying God in a loud voice; ¹⁶and he fell at the feet of Jesus and thanked him. He was a Samaritan. ¹⁷Jesus said in reply, "Ten were cleansed, were they not? Where are the other nine? ¹⁸Has none but this foreigner returned to give thanks to God?" ¹⁹Then he said to him, "Stand up and go; your faith has saved you."ʳ

**The Coming of the Kingdom of God.** ²⁰¶Asked by the Pharisees when the kingdom of God would come, he said in reply, "The coming of the kingdom of God cannot be observed,ˢ ²¹⃰⃰and

no one will announce, 'Look, here it is,' or, 'There it is.'ᵗ For behold, the kingdom of God is among you."

**The Day of the Son of Man.** ²²Then he said to his disciples, "The days will come when you will long to see one of the days of the Son of Man, but you will not see it. ²³There will be those who will say to you, 'Look, there he is,' [or] 'Look, here he is.' Do not go off, do not run in pursuit.ᵘ ²⁴For just as lightning flashes and lights up the sky from one side to the other, so will the Son of Man be [in his day].ᵛ ²⁵But first he must suffer greatly and be rejected by this generation.ʷ ²⁶As it was in the days of Noah,ˣ so it will be in the days of the Son of Man; ²⁷they were eating and drinking, marrying and giving in marriage up to the day that Noah entered the ark, and the flood came and destroyed them all. ²⁸ʸSimilarly, as it was in the days of Lot: they were eating, drinking, buying, selling, planting, building; ²⁹on the day when Lot left Sodom, fire and brimstone rained from the sky to destroy them all. ³⁰So it will be on the day the Son of Man is revealed. ³¹ᶻOn that day, a person who is on the housetop and whose belongings are in the house must not go down to get them, and likewise a person in the field must not return to what was left behind.ᵃ ³²Remember the wife of Lot. ³³Whoever seeks to preserve his life will lose it, but whoever loses it will save it.ᵇ ³⁴I tell you, on that night there will be two people in one bed; one will be taken, the other left. ³⁵ᶜAnd there will be two women grinding meal together; one will be taken, the other left." ³⁶††  ³⁷They said to him in reply, "Where, Lord?" He said to them, "Where the body is, there also the vultures will gather."ᵈ

# CHAPTER 18

**The Parable of the Persistent Widow.** ¹‡‡Then he told them a parable about the necessity for them to pray always without becoming weary.ᵉ He said, ²"There was a judge in a certain town who

---

⃰[17:7–10] These sayings of Jesus, peculiar to Luke, which continue his response to the apostles' request to increase their faith (Lk 17:5–6), remind them that Christian disciples can make no claim on God's graciousness; in fulfilling the exacting demands of discipleship, they are only doing their duty.

†[17:11–19] This incident recounting the thankfulness of the cleansed Samaritan leper is narrated only in Luke's gospel and provides an instance of Jesus holding up a non-Jew (Lk 17:18) as an example to his Jewish contemporaries (cf. Lk 10:33 where a similar purpose is achieved in the story of the good Samaritan). Moreover, it is the faith in Jesus manifested by the foreigner that has brought him salvation (Lk 17:19; cf. the similar relationship between faith and salvation in Lk 7:50; 8:48, 50).

‡[17:11] **Through Samaria and Galilee:** or, "between Samaria and Galilee."

§[17:14] See note on Lk 5:14.

¶[17:20–37] To the question of the Pharisees about the time of the coming of God's kingdom, Jesus replies that the kingdom is **among you** (Lk 17:20–21). The emphasis has thus been shifted from an imminent observable coming of the kingdom to something that is already present in Jesus' preaching and healing ministry. Luke has also appended further traditional sayings of Jesus about the unpredictable suddenness of the day of the Son of Man, and assures his readers that in spite of the delay of that day (Lk 12:45), it will bring judgment unexpectedly on those who do not continue to be vigilant.

⃰⃰[17:21] **Among you:** the Greek preposition translated **as among** can also be translated as "within." In the light of other statements in Luke's gospel about the presence of the kingdom (see Lk 10:9, 11; 11:20) "among" is to be preferred.

††[17:36] The inclusion of Lk 17:36, "There will be two men in the field; one will be taken, the other left behind," in some Western manuscripts appears to be a scribal assimilation to Mt 24:40.

‡‡[18:1–14] The particularly Lucan material in the travel narrative concludes with two parables on prayer. The first (Lk 18:1–8) teaches the disciples the need of persistent prayer so that they not fall victims to apostasy (Lk 18:8). The second (Lk 18:9–14) condemns the self-righteous, critical attitude of the Pharisee and teaches that the fundamental attitude of the Christian disciple must be the recognition of sinfulness and complete dependence on God's graciousness. The second parable recalls the story of the pardoning of the sinful woman (Lk 7:36–50) where a similar contrast is presented between the critical attitude of the Pharisee Simon and the love shown by the pardoned sinner.

---

n. [17:6] Mt 17:20; 21:21; Mk 11:23.  o. [17:11] 9:51–53; 13:22, 33; 18:31; 19:28; Jn 4:4.  p. [17:13] 18:38; Mt 9:27; 15:22.  q. [17:14] 5:14; Lv 14:2–32; Mt 8:4; Mk 1:44.  r. [17:19] 7:50; 18:42.  s. [17:20] Jn 3:3.

t. [17:21] 17:23; Mt 24:23; Mk 13:21.  u. [17:23] 17:21; Mt 24:23, 26; Mk 13:21.  v. [17:24] Mt 24:27.  w. [17:25] 9:22; 18:32–33; Mt 16:21; 17:22–23; 20:18–19; Mk 8:31; 9:31; 10:33–34.  x. [17:26–27] Gn 6–8; Mt 24:37–39.  y. [17:28–29] Gn 18:20–21; 19:1–29.  z. [17:31–32] Gn 19:17,26.  a. [17:31] Mt 24:17–18; Mk 13:15–16.  b. [17:33] 9:24; Mt 10:39; 16:25; Mk 8:35; Jn 12:25.  c. [17:35] Mt 24:40–41.  d. [17:37] Jb 39:30; Mt 24:28.  e. [18:1] Rom 12:12; Col 4:2; 1 Thes 5:17.

neither feared God nor respected any human being. ³And a widow in that town used to come to him and say, 'Render a just decision for me against my adversary.' ⁴For a long time the judge was unwilling, but eventually he thought, 'While it is true that I neither fear God nor respect any human being, ⁵*because this widow keeps bothering me I shall deliver a just decision for her lest she finally come and strike me.'" ⁶The Lord said, "Pay attention to what the dishonest judge says. ⁷Will not God then secure the rights of his chosen ones who call out to him day and night? Will he be slow to answer them? ⁸I tell you, he will see to it that justice is done for them speedily. But when the Son of Man comes, will he find faith on earth?"

**The Parable of the Pharisee and the Tax Collector.** ⁹He then addressed this parable to those who were convinced of their own righteousness and despised everyone else.ᵍ ¹⁰"Two people went up to the temple area to pray; one was a Pharisee and the other was a tax collector. ¹¹The Pharisee took up his position and spoke this prayer to himself, 'O God, I thank you that I am not like the rest of humanity—greedy, dishonest, adulterous—or even like this tax collector. ¹²I fast twice a week, and I pay tithes on my whole income.'ʰ ¹³But the tax collector stood off at a distance and would not even raise his eyes to heaven but beat his breast and prayed, 'O God, be merciful to me a sinner.'ⁱ ¹⁴I tell you, the latter went home justified, not the former; for everyone who exalts himself will be humbled, and the one who humbles himself will be exalted."ʲ

**Saying on Children and the Kingdom.** ¹⁵†People were bringing even infants to him that he might touch them,ᵏ and when the disciples saw this, they rebuked them.ᵏ ¹⁶Jesus, however, called the children to himself and said, "Let the children come to me and do not prevent them; for the kingdom of God belongs to such as these. ¹⁷Amen, I say to you, whoever does not accept the kingdom of God like a child will not enter it."ˡ

**The Rich Official.** ¹⁸ᵐAn official asked him this question, "Good teacher, what must I do to inherit eternal life?"ⁿ ¹⁹Jesus answered him, "Why do you call me good? No one is good but God alone. ²⁰You know the commandments, 'You shall not commit adultery; you shall not kill; you shall not steal; you shall not bear false witness; honor your father and your mother.'"ᵒ ²¹And he replied, "All of these I have observed from my youth." ²²§ᵖWhen Jesus heard this he said to him, "There is still one thing left for you: sell all that you have and distribute it to the poor, and you will have a treasure in heaven. Then come, follow me." ²³But when he heard this he became quite sad, for he was very rich.

**On Riches and Renunciation.** ²⁴Jesus looked at him [now sad] and said, "How hard it is for those who have wealth to enter the kingdom of God! ²⁵For it is easier for a camel to pass through the eye of a needle than for a rich person to enter the kingdom of God." ²⁶Those who heard this said, "Then who can be saved?" ²⁷And he said, "What is impossible for human beings is possible for God."�q ²⁸Then Peter said, "We have given up our possessions and followed you." ²⁹He said to them, "Amen, I say to you, there is no one who has given up house or wife or brothers or parents or children for the sake of the kingdom of God ³⁰who will not receive [back] an overabundant return in this present age and eternal life in the age to come."

**The Third Prediction of the Passion.**ˢ ³¹¶Then he took the Twelve aside and said to them, "Behold, we are going up to Jerusalem and everything written by the prophets about the Son of Man will be fulfilled.** ³²He will be handed over to the Gentiles and he will be mocked and insulted and spat upon; ³³and after they have scourged him they will kill him, but on the third day he will rise." ³⁴But they understood nothing of this; the word remained hidden from them and they failed to comprehend what he said.ᵘ

**The Healing of the Blind Beggar.**ᵛ ³⁵Now as he approached Jericho a blind man was sitting by the roadside begging, ³⁶and hearing a crowd going by, he inquired what was happening.

---

*[18:5] **Strike me:** the Greek verb translated as strike means "to strike under the eye" and suggests the extreme situation to which the persistence of the widow might lead. It may, however, be used here in the much weaker sense of "to wear one out."

†[18:15–19:27] Luke here includes much of the material about the journey to Jerusalem found in his Marcan source (Lk 10:1–52) and adds to it the story of Zacchaeus (Lk 19:1–10) from his own particular tradition and the parable of the gold coins (minas) (Lk 19:11–27) from Q, the source common to Luke and Matthew.

‡[18:15–17] The sayings on children furnish a contrast to the attitude of the Pharisee in the preceding episode (Lk 18:9–14) and that of the wealthy official in the following one (Lk 18:18–23) who think that they can lay claim to God's favor by their own merit. The attitude of the disciple should be marked by the receptivity and trustful dependence characteristic of the child.

§[18:22] Detachment from material possessions results in the total dependence on God demanded of one who would inherit eternal life. **Sell all that you have:** the original saying (cf. Mk 10:21) has characteristically been made more demanding by Luke's addition of "all."

¶[18:31–33] The details included in this third announcement of Jesus' suffering and death suggest that the literary formulation of the announcement has been directed by the knowledge of the historical passion and death of Jesus.

**[18:31] **Everything written by the prophets . . . will be fulfilled:** this is a Lucan addition to the words of Jesus found in the Marcan source (Mk 10:32–34). Luke understands the events of Jesus' last days in Jerusalem to be the fulfillment of Old Testament prophecy, but, as is usually the case in Luke-Acts, the author does not specify which Old Testament prophets he has in mind; cf. Lk 24:25, 27, 44; Acts 3:8; 13:27; 26:22–23.

---

f. [18:5] 11:8.  g. [18:9] 16:5; Mt 23:25–28.  h. [18:12] Mt 23:23.
i. [18:13] Ps 51:3.  j. [18:14] 14:11; Mt 23:12.  k. [18:15–17] Mt 19:13–15; Mk 10:13–16.  l. [18:17] Mt 18:3.  m. [18:18–30] Mt 19:16–30; Mk 10:17–31.

n. [18:18] 10:25.  o. [18:20] Ex 20:12–16; Dt 5:16–20.  p. [18:22] 12:33; Sir 29:11; Mt 6:20.  q. [18:27] Mk 14:36.  r. [18:29–30] 14:26.  s. [18:31–34] 24:25–27, 44; Mt 20:17–19; Mk 10:32–34; Acts 3:18.  t. [18:32–33] 9:22, 44.  u. [18:34] Mk 9:32.  v. [18:35–43] Mt 20:29–34; Mk 10:46–52.

³⁷They told him, "Jesus of Nazareth is passing by." ³⁸ʷHe shouted, "Jesus, Son of David,* have pity on me!" ³⁹The people walking in front rebuked him, telling him to be silent, but he kept calling out all the more, "Son of David, have pity on me!" ⁴⁰Then Jesus stopped and ordered that he be brought to him; and when he came near, Jesus asked him, ⁴¹"What do you want me to do for you?" He replied, "Lord, please let me see."ˣ ⁴²Jesus told him, "Have sight; your faith has saved you."ʸ ⁴³He immediately received his sight and followed him, giving glory to God. When they saw this, all the people gave praise to God.

## CHAPTER 19

**Zacchaeus the Tax Collector.**† ¹He came to Jericho and intended to pass through the town. ²Now a man there named Zacchaeus, who was a chief tax collector and also a wealthy man, ³was seeking to see who Jesus was; but he could not see him because of the crowd, for he was short in stature. ⁴So he ran ahead and climbed a syca-more tree in order to see Jesus, who was about to pass that way. ⁵When he reached the place, Jesus looked up and said to him, "Zacchaeus, come down quickly, for today I must stay at your house." ⁶And he came down quickly and received him with joy. ⁷When they all saw this, they began to grumble, saying, "He has gone to stay at the house of a sinner."ᶻ ⁸But Zacchaeus stood there and said to the Lord, "Behold, half of my possessions, Lord, I shall give to the poor, and if I have extorted anything from anyone I shall repay it four times over."ᵃ ⁹ᵃAnd Jesus said to him, "Today salvationᵇ has come to this house because this man too is a descendant of Abra-ham. ¹⁰ᶜFor the Son of Man has come to seek and to save what was lost."

---

*[18:38] **Son of David:** the blind beggar identifies Jesus with a title that is related to Jesus' role as Messiah (see note on Lk 2:11). Through this Son of David, salvation comes to the blind man. Note the connection between salvation and house of David mentioned earlier in Zechariah's canticle (Lk 1:69). See also note on Mt 9:27.

†[19:1–10] The story of the tax collector Zacchaeus is unique to this gospel. While a rich man (Lk 19:2), Zacchaeus provides a contrast to the rich man of Lk 18:18–23 who can-not detach himself from his material possessions to become a follower of Jesus. Zacchaeus, according to Luke, exemplifies the proper attitude toward wealth: he promises to give half of his possessions to the poor (Lk 19:8) and consequently is the recipient of salvation (Lk 19:9–10).

‡[19:9] **A descendant of Abraham:** literally, "a son of Abraham." The tax collector Zacchaeus, whose repentance is attested by his determination to amend his former ways, shows himself to be a true descendant of Abraham, the true heir to the promises of God in the Old Testament. Underlying Luke's depiction of Zacchaeus as a descendant of Abraham, the father of the Jews (Lk 1:73; 16:22–31), is his recognition of the central place occupied by Israel in the plan of salvation.

§[19:10] This verse sums up for Luke his depiction of the role of Jesus as savior in this gospel.

**The Parable of the Ten Gold Coins.**§ ¹¹ᵈWhile they were listening to him speak, he proceeded to tell a parable because he was near Jerusalem and they thought that the kingdom of God would appear there immediately. ¹²So he said, "A nobleman went off to a distant country to obtain the kingship for himself and then to return.ᵉ ¹³He called ten of his servants and gave them ten gold coins** and told them, 'Engage in trade with these until I return.' ¹⁴His fellow citizens, however, despised him and sent a del-egation after him to announce, 'We do not want this man to be our king.' ¹⁵But when he returned after obtaining the kingship, he had the ser-vants called, to whom he had given the money, to learn what they had gained by trading. ¹⁶The first came forward and said, 'Sir, your gold coin has earned ten additional ones.' ¹⁷He replied, 'Well done, good servant! You have been faith-ful in this very small matter; take charge of ten cities.'ᶠ ¹⁸Then the second came and reported, 'Your gold coin, sir, has earned five more.' ¹⁹And to this servant too he said, 'You, take charge of five cities.' ²⁰Then the other servant came and said, 'Sir, here is your gold coin; I kept it stored away in a handkerchief, ²¹for I was afraid of you, because you are a demanding person; you take up what you did not lay down and you har-vest what you did not plant.' ²²He said to him, 'With your own words I shall condemn you, you wicked servant. You knew I was a demanding person, taking up what I did not lay down and harvesting what I did not plant; ²³why did you not put my money in a bank? Then on my return I would have collected it with interest.' ²⁴And to those standing by he said, 'Take the gold coin from him and give it to the servant who has ten.' ²⁵But they said to him, 'Sir, he has ten gold coins.' ²⁶'I tell you, to everyone who has, more will be given, but from the one who has not, even what he has will be taken away.ᵍ ²⁷Now as for those enemies of mine who did not want me as their king, bring them here and slay them before me.'"

¶[19:11–27] In this parable Luke has combined two origi-nally distinct parables: (1) a parable about the conduct of faithful and productive servants (Lk 19:13, 15b–26) and (2) a parable about a rejected king (Lk 19:12, 14–15a, 27). The story about the conduct of servants occurs in another form in Mt 25:14–20. The story about the rejected king may have originated with a contemporary historical event. After the death of Herod the Great, his son Archelaus traveled to Rome to receive the title of king. A delegation of Jews appeared in Rome before Caesar Augustus to oppose the request of Arche-laus. Although not given the title of king, Archelaus was made ruler over Judea and Samaria. As the story is used by Luke, however, it furnishes a correction to the expectation of the imminent end of the age and of the establishment of the king-dom in Jerusalem (Lk 19:11). Jesus is not on his way to Jerusa-lem to receive the kingly power; for that, he must go away and only after returning from the distant country (a reference to the parousia) will reward and judgment take place.

**[19:13] **Ten gold coins:** literally, "ten minas." A mina was a monetary unit that in ancient Greece was the equivalent of one hundred drachmas.

---

w. [18:38–39] 17:13; Mt 9:27; 15:22.   x. [18:41] Mk 10:36.   y. [18:42] 7:50; 17:19.   z. [19:7] 5:30; 15:2.   a. [19:8] Ex 21:37; Nm 5:6–7; 2 Sm 12:6.   b. [19:9] 13:16; Mt 21:31.   c. [19:10] 15:4–10; Ez 34:16.

d. [19:11–27] Mt 25:14–30.   e. [19:12] Mk 13:34.   f. [19:17] 16:10.   g. [19:26] 8:18; Mt 13:12; Mk 4:25.

## VI. THE TEACHING MINISTRY
## IN JERUSALEM[*]

**The Entry into Jerusalem.**[h] [28]After he had said this, he proceeded on his journey up to Jerusalem. [29]As he drew near to Bethphage and Bethany at the place called the Mount of Olives, he sent two of his disciples.[i] [30]He said, "Go into the village opposite you, and as you enter it you will find a colt tethered on which no one has ever sat. Untie it and bring it here.[j] [31]And if anyone should ask you, 'Why are you untying it?' you will answer, 'The Master has need of it.'" [32]So those who had been sent went off and found everything just as he had told them.[k] [33]And as they were untying the colt, its owners said to them, "Why are you untying this colt?" [34]They answered, "The Master has need of it." [35]So they brought it to Jesus, threw their cloaks over the colt, and helped Jesus to mount. [36]As he rode along, the people were spreading their cloaks on the road; [37]and now as he was approaching the slope of the Mount of Olives, the whole multitude of his disciples began to praise God aloud with joy for all the mighty deeds they had seen. [38]They proclaimed:

"Blessed is the king who comes
    in the name of the Lord.[†]
Peace in heaven
    and glory in the highest."[m]

[39]Some of the Pharisees in the crowd said to him, "Teacher, rebuke your disciples."[‡] [40]He said in reply, "I tell you, if they keep silent, the stones will cry out!"

**The Lament for Jerusalem.**[§] [41n]As he drew near, he saw the city and wept over it,[o] [42]saying, "If this day you only knew what makes for peace—but now it is hidden from your eyes.[p] [43]For the days are coming upon you when your enemies will raise a palisade against you; they will encircle you and hem you in on all sides.[q] [44]They will smash you to the ground and your children within you, and they will not leave one stone upon another within you because you did not recognize the time of your visitation."[r]

**The Cleansing of the Temple.** [45s]Then Jesus entered the temple area[**] and proceeded to drive out those who were selling things,[t] [46]saying to them, "It is written, 'My house shall be a house of prayer, but you have made it a den of thieves.'"[u] [47]And every day he was teaching in the temple area.[v] The chief priests, the scribes, and the leaders of the people, meanwhile, were seeking to put him to death,[w] [48]but they could find no way to accomplish their purpose because all the people were hanging on his words.

## CHAPTER 20[††]

**The Authority of Jesus Questioned.**[x] [1]One day as he was teaching the people in the temple area and proclaiming the good news, the chief priests and scribes, together with the elders, approached him [2]and said to him, "Tell us, by what authority are you doing these things? Or who is the one who gave you this authority?"[y] [3]He said to them in reply, "I shall ask you a question. Tell me, [4]was John's baptism of heavenly or of human origin?"[z] [5]They discussed this among themselves, and said, "If we say, 'Of heavenly origin,' he will say, 'Why did you not believe him?'[a] [6]But if we say, 'Of human origin,' then all the people will stone us, for they are convinced that John was a prophet." [7]So they answered that they did not know from where it came. [8]Then Jesus said to them, "Neither shall I tell you by what authority I do these things."

**The Parable of the Tenant Farmers.**[‡‡] [9b]Then he proceeded to tell the people this parable. "[A]

---

*[19:28–21:38] With the royal entry of Jesus into Jerusalem, a new section of Luke's gospel begins, the ministry of Jesus in Jerusalem before his death and resurrection. Luke suggests that this was a lengthy ministry in Jerusalem (Lk 19:47; 20:1; 21:37–38; 22:53) and it is characterized by Jesus' daily teaching in the temple (Lk 21:37–38). For the story of the entry of Jesus into Jerusalem, see also Mt 21:1–11; Mk 11:1–10; Jn 12:12–19 and the notes there.

†[19:38] **Blessed is the king who comes in the name of the Lord:** only in Luke is Jesus explicitly given the title **king** when he enters Jerusalem in triumph. Luke has inserted this title into the words of Ps 118:26 that heralded the arrival of the pilgrims coming to the holy city and to the temple. Jesus is thereby acclaimed as **king** (see Lk 1:32) and as the one who **comes** (see Mal 3:1; Lk 7:19). **Peace in heaven . . . :** the acclamation of the disciples of Jesus in Luke echoes the announcement of the angels at the birth of Jesus (Lk 2:14). The peace Jesus brings is associated with the salvation to be accomplished here in Jerusalem.

‡[19:39] **Rebuke your disciples:** this command, found only in Luke, was given so that the Roman authorities would not interpret the acclamation of Jesus as king as an uprising against them; cf. Lk 23:2–3.

§[19:41–44] The lament for Jerusalem is found only in Luke. By not accepting Jesus (the one who mediates peace), Jerusalem will not find peace but will become the victim of devastation.

¶[19:43–44] Luke may be describing the actual disaster that befell Jerusalem in A.D. 70 when it was destroyed by the Romans during the First Revolt.

**[19:45–46] Immediately upon entering the holy city, Jesus in a display of his authority enters the temple (see Mal 3:1–3) and lays claim to it after cleansing it that it might become a proper place for his teaching ministry in Jerusalem (Lk 19:47; 20:1; 21:37; 22:53). See Mt 21:12–17; Mk 11:15–19; Jn 2:13–17 and the notes there.

††[20:1–47] The Jerusalem religious leaders or their representatives, in an attempt to incriminate Jesus with the Romans and to discredit him with the people, pose a number of questions to him (about his authority, Lk 20:2; about payment of taxes, Lk 20:22; about the resurrection, Lk 20:28–33).

‡‡[20:9–19] This parable about an absentee landlord and a tenant farmers' revolt reflects the social and economic

---

h. [19:28–40] Mt 21:1–11; Mk 11:1–11; Jn 12:12–19.   i. [19:29] Zec 14:4.   j. [19:30] Nm 19:2; Dt 21:3; 1 Sm 6:7; Zec 9:9.   k. [19:32] 22:13.   l. [19:35–36] 2 Kgs 9:13.   m. [19:38] 2:14; Ps 118:26.   n. [19:41] 2 Kgs 8:11–12; Jer 14:17; 15:5.

p. [19:42] 8:10; Is 6:9–10; Mt 13:14; Mk 4:12; Acts 28:26–27; Rom 11:8, 10.   q. [19:43] Is 29:3.   r. [19:44] 1:68; 21:6; Ps 137:9; Mt 24:2; Mk 13:2.   s. [19:45–46] Mt 21:12–13; Mk 11:15–17; Jn 2:13–17.   t. [19:45] 3:1 / Hos 9:15.   u. [19:46] Is 56:7; Jer 7:11.   v. [19:47–48] 20:19; 22:2; Mt 21:46; Mk 11:18; 12:12; 14:1–2; Jn 5:18; 7:30.   w. [19:47] 21:37; 22:53; Jn 18:20.   x. [20:1–8] Mt 21:23–27; Mk 11:27–33.   y. [20:2] Acts 4:7.   z. [20:4] 3:3, 16.   a. [20:5] Mt 21:32.   b. [20:9–19] Mt 21:33–46; Mk 12:1–12.

man planted a vineyard, leased it to tenant farmers, and then went on a journey for a long time.<sup>c</sup> <sup>10</sup>At harvest time he sent a servant<sup>d</sup> to the tenant farmers to receive some of the produce of the vineyard. But they beat the servant and sent him away empty-handed. <sup>11</sup>So he proceeded to send another servant, but him also they beat and insulted and sent away empty-handed. <sup>12</sup>Then he proceeded to send a third, but this one too they wounded and threw out. <sup>13</sup>The owner of the vineyard said, 'What shall I do? I shall send my beloved son; maybe they will respect him.'<sup>e</sup> <sup>14</sup>But when the tenant farmers saw him they said to one another, 'This is the heir. Let us kill him that the inheritance may become ours.' <sup>15</sup>So they threw him out of the vineyard and killed him.<sup>*</sup> What will the owner of the vineyard do to them? <sup>16</sup>He will come and put those tenant farmers to death and turn over the vineyard to others." When the people heard this, they exclaimed, "Let it not be so!" <sup>17</sup>But he looked at them and asked, "What then does this scripture passage mean:

'The stone which the builders rejected
has become the cornerstone'?<sup>f</sup>

<sup>18</sup>Everyone who falls on that stone will be dashed to pieces; and it will crush anyone on whom it falls." <sup>19</sup>The scribes and chief priests sought to lay their hands on him at that very hour, but they feared the people, for they knew that he had addressed this parable to them.<sup>g</sup>

**Paying Taxes to the Emperor.**<sup>h</sup> <sup>20</sup>They watched him closely and sent agents pretending to be righteous who were to trap him in speech,<sup>i</sup> in order to hand him over to the authority and power of the governor. <sup>21</sup>They posed this question to him, "Teacher, we know that what you say and teach is correct, and you show no partiality, but teach the way of God in accordance with the truth.<sup>j</sup> <sup>22</sup>Is it lawful for us to pay tribute to Caesar or not?"<sup>‡</sup> <sup>23</sup>Recognizing their craftiness

he said to them, <sup>24</sup>"Show me a denarius;<sup>§</sup> whose image and name does it bear?" They replied, "Caesar's." <sup>25</sup>So he said to them, "Then repay to Caesar what belongs to Caesar and to God what belongs to God."<sup>k</sup> <sup>26</sup>They were unable to trap him by something he might say before the people, and so amazed were they at his reply that they fell silent.

**The Question About the Resurrection.**<sup>l</sup> <sup>27</sup>Some Sadducees,<sup>¶</sup> those who deny that there is a resurrection, came forward and put this question to him,<sup>m</sup> <sup>28</sup>saying, "Teacher, Moses wrote for us, 'If someone's brother dies leaving a wife but no child, his brother must take the wife and raise up descendants for his brother.'<sup>n</sup> <sup>29</sup>Now there were seven brothers; the first married a woman but died childless. <sup>30</sup>Then the second <sup>31</sup>and the third married her, and likewise all the seven died childless. <sup>32</sup>Finally the woman also died. <sup>33</sup>Now at the resurrection whose wife will that woman be? For all seven had been married to her." <sup>34</sup>Jesus said to them, "The children of this age marry and are given in marriage; <sup>35</sup>but those who are deemed worthy to attain to the coming age and to the resurrection of the dead neither marry nor are given in marriage. <sup>36</sup>They can no longer die, for they are like angels; and they are the children of God because they are the ones who will rise.<sup>††</sup> <sup>37</sup>That the dead will rise even Moses made known in the passage about the bush, when he called 'Lord' the God of Abraham, the God of Isaac, and the God of Jacob;<sup>o</sup> <sup>38</sup>and he is not God of the dead, but of the living, for to him all are alive."<sup>p</sup> <sup>39</sup>Some of the scribes said in reply, "Teacher, you have answered well." <sup>40</sup>And they no longer dared to ask him anything.<sup>q</sup>

**The Question About David's Son.**<sup>‡‡</sup> <sup>41</sup>Then he said to them, "How do they claim that the Messiah is the Son of David? <sup>42</sup>For David himself in the Book of Psalms says:<sup>s</sup>

'The Lord said to my lord,
"Sit at my right hand

---

conditions of rural Palestine in the first century. The synoptic gospel writers use the parable to describe how the rejection of the landlord's son becomes the occasion for the vineyard to be taken away from those to whom it was entrusted (the religious leadership of Judaism that rejects the teaching and preaching of Jesus; Lk 20:19).

\* [20:15] **They threw him out of the vineyard and killed him**: cf. Mk 12:8. Luke has altered his Marcan source and reports that the murder of the son takes place outside the vineyard to reflect the tradition of Jesus' death outside the walls of the city of Jerusalem (see Heb 13:12).

† [20:20] **The governor**: i.e., Pontius Pilate, the Roman administrator responsible for the collection of taxes and maintenance of order in Palestine.

‡ [20:22] Through their question the agents of the Jerusalem religious leadership hope to force Jesus to take sides on one of the sensitive political issues of first-century Palestine. The issue of nonpayment of taxes to Rome becomes one of the focal points of the First Jewish Revolt (A.D. 66–70) that resulted in the Roman destruction of Jerusalem and the temple. See also note on Mt 22:15–22.

§ [20:24] **Denarius**: a Roman silver coin (see note on Lk 7:41).

¶ [20:27] **Sadducees**: see note on Mt 3:7.

\*\* [20:28–33] The Sadducees' question, based on the law of levirate marriage recorded in Dt 25:5–10, ridicules the idea of the resurrection. Jesus rejects their naive understanding of the resurrection (Lk 20:35–36) and then argues on behalf of the resurrection of the dead on the basis of the written law (Lk 20:37–38) that the Sadducees accept. See also notes on Mt 22:23–33.

†† [20:36] **Because they are the ones who will rise**: literally, "being sons of the resurrection."

‡‡ [20:41–44] After successfully answering the three questions of his opponents, Jesus now asks them a question. Their inability to respond implies that they have forfeited their position and authority as the religious leaders of the people because they do not understand the scriptures. This series of controversies between the religious leadership of Jerusalem and Jesus reveals Jesus as the authoritative teacher whose words are to be listened to (see Lk 9:35). See also notes on Mt 22:41–46.

---

c. [20:9] Is 5:1–7.   d. [20:10–12] 2 Chr 36:15–16.   e. [20:13] 3:22.
f. [20:17] Ps 118:22; Is 28:16.   g. [20:19] 19:47–48; 22:2; Mt 21:46; Mk 11:18; 12:12; 14:1–2; Jn 5:18; 7:30.   h. [20:20–26] Mt 22:15–22; Mk 12:13–17.   i. [20:20] 11:54.   j. [20:21] Jn 3:2.

k. [20:25] Rom 13:6–7.   l. [20:27–40] Mt 22:23–33; Mk 12:18–27. m. [20:27] Acts 23:8.   n. [20:28] Gn 38:8; Dt 25:5.   o. [20:37] Ex 3:2, 6, 15–16.   p. [20:38] Rom 14:8–9.   q. [20:40] Mt 22:46; Mk 12:34. r. [20:41–44] Mt 22:41–45; Mk 12:35–37.   s. [20:42–43] Ps 110:1.

43 till I make your enemies your
footstool.'"

[44]Now if David calls him 'lord,' how can he be
his son?"

**Denunciation of the Scribes.**[t] [45]Then, within
the hearing of all the people, he said to [his] disciples, [46]"Be on guard against the scribes, who
like to go around in long robes and love greetings in marketplaces, seats of honor in synagogues, and places of honor at banquets.[u] [47]They
devour the houses of widows and, as a pretext,
recite lengthy prayers. They will receive a very
severe condemnation."

## CHAPTER 21

**The Poor Widow's Contribution.**[*] [1v]When he
looked up he saw some wealthy people putting
their offerings into the treasury [2]and he noticed
a poor widow putting in two small coins. [3]He
said, "I tell you truly, this poor widow put in
more than all the rest; [4]for those others have all
made offerings from their surplus wealth, but
she, from her poverty, has offered her whole
livelihood."

**The Destruction of the Temple Foretold.**[w]
[5†]While some people were speaking about how
the temple was adorned with costly stones
and votive offerings, he said, [6]"All that you see
here—the days will come when there will not be
left a stone upon another stone that will not be
thrown down."[x]

**The Signs of the End.** [7y]Then they asked him,
"Teacher, when will this happen? And what sign
will there be when all these things are about to
happen?" [8]He answered, "See that you not be
deceived, for many will come in my name, saying, 'I am he,' and 'The time has come.'[‡] Do not

follow them! [z] [9]When you hear of wars and insur-
rections, do not be terrified; for such things must
happen first, but it will not immediately be the
end." [10]Then he said to them, "Nation will rise
against nation, and kingdom against kingdom.[a]
[11]There will be powerful earthquakes, famines,
and plagues from place to place; and awesome
sights and mighty signs will come from the sky.
**The Coming Persecution.** [12b]"Before all this
happens,[§] however, they will seize and persecute
you, they will hand you over to the synagogues
and to prisons, and they will have you led before
kings and governors because of my name.[c] [13]It
will lead to your giving testimony. [14]Remember,
you are not to prepare your defense beforehand,
[15d]for I myself shall give you a wisdom in speaking[¶] that all your adversaries will be powerless to
resist or refute. [16e]You will even be handed over
by parents, brothers, relatives, and friends, and
they will put some of you to death.[f] [17]You will
be hated by all because of my name, [18]but not a
hair on your head will be destroyed.[g] [19]By your
perseverance you will secure your lives.[h]
**The Great Tribulation.**[*] [20i]"When you see Jerusalem surrounded by armies, know that its desolation is at hand.[j] [21]Then those in Judea must
flee to the mountains. Let those within the city
escape from it, and let those in the countryside
not enter the city,[k] [22]for these days are the time of
punishment when all the scriptures are fulfilled.
[23]Woe to pregnant women and nursing mothers
in those days, for a terrible calamity will come
upon the earth and a wrathful judgment upon
this people.[l] [24]They will fall by the edge of the
sword and be taken as captives to all the Gentiles; and Jerusalem will be trampled underfoot
by the Gentiles until the times of the Gentiles[††]
are fulfilled.[m]
**The Coming of the Son of Man.**[n] [25]"There will
be signs in the sun, the moon, and the stars, and
on earth nations will be in dismay, perplexed by
the roaring of the sea and the waves.[o] [26]People

* [21:1–4] The widow is another example of the poor ones
in this gospel whose detachment from material possessions
and dependence on God leads to their blessedness (Lk 6:20).
Her simple offering provides a striking contrast to the pride
and pretentiousness of the scribes denounced in the preceding
section (Lk 20:45–47). The story is taken from Mk 12:41–44.

† [21:5–36] Jesus' eschatological discourse in Luke is
inspired by Mk 13 but Luke has made some significant
alterations to the words of Jesus found there. Luke maintains,
though in a modified form, the belief in the early expectation
of the end of the age (see Lk 21:27, 28, 31, 32, 36), but, by
focusing attention throughout the gospel on the importance
of the day-to-day following of Jesus and by reinterpreting
the meaning of some of the signs of the end from Mk 13 he
has come to terms with what seemed to be the early Christian
community to be a delay of the parousia. Mark, for example,
described the desecration of the Jerusalem temple by the
Romans (Mk 13:14) as the apocalyptic symbol (see Dn 9:27;
12:11) accompanying the end of the age and the coming of
the Son of Man. Luke (Lk 21:20–24), however, removes the
apocalyptic setting and separates the historical destruction of
Jerusalem from the signs of the coming of the Son of Man by
a period that he refers to as "the times of the Gentiles" (Lk
21:24). See also notes on Mt 24:1–36 and Mk 13:1–37.

‡ [21:8] **The time has come:** in Luke, the proclamation of
the imminent end of the age has itself become a false teaching.

§ [21:12] **Before all this happens . . . :** to Luke and his
community, some of the signs of the end just described (Lk
21:10–11) still lie in the future. Now in dealing with the persecution of the disciples (Lk 21:12–19) and the destruction
of Jerusalem (Lk 21:20–24) Luke is pointing to eschatological
signs that have already been fulfilled.

¶ [21:15] **A wisdom in speaking:** literally, "a mouth and
wisdom."

** [21:20–24] The actual destruction of Jerusalem by Rome
in A.D. 70 upon which Luke and his community look back
provides the assurance that, just as Jesus' prediction of Jerusalem's destruction was fulfilled, so too will be his announcement of their final redemption (Lk 21:27–28).

†† [21:24] **The times of the Gentiles:** a period of indetermi-
nate length separating the destruction of Jerusalem from the
cosmic signs accompanying the coming of the Son of Man.

t. [20:45–47] 11:37–54; Mt 23:1–36; Mk 12:38–40.   u. [20:46] 14:7–
11.   v. [21:1–4] Mk 12:41–44.   w. [21:5–6] Mt 24:1–2; Mk 13:1–
2.   x. [21:6] 19:44.   y. [21:7–19] Mt 24:3–14; Mk 13:3–13.

z. [21:8] 17:23; Mk 13:5, 6, 21; 1 Jn 2:18.   a. [21:10] 2 Chr 15:6; Is
19:2.   b. [21:12–15] 12:11–12; Mt 10:17–20; Mk 13:9–11.   c. [21:12]
Jn 16:2; Acts 25:24.   d. [21:15] Acts 6:10.   e. [21:16–18] Mt 10:21–
22.   f. [21:16] 12:52–53.   g. [21:18] 12:7; 1 Sm 14:45; Mt 10:30;
Acts 27:34.   h. [21:19] 8:15.   i. [21:20–24] Mt 24:15–21; Mk 13:14–
19.   j. [21:20–22] 19:41–44.   k. [21:21] 17:31.   l. [21:23] 1 Cor
7:26.   m. [21:24] Tb 14:5; Ps 79:1; Is 63:18; Jer 21:7; Rom 11:25; Rev
11:2.   n. [21:25–28] Mt 24:29–31; Mk 13:24–27.   o. [21:25] Wis
5:22; Is 13:10; Ez 32:7; Jl 2:10; 3:3–4; 4:15; Rev 6:12–14.

will die of fright in anticipation of what is coming upon the world, for the powers of the heavens* will be shaken.*p* 27And then they will see the Son of Man coming in a cloud with power and great glory.*q* 28But when these signs begin to happen, stand erect and raise your heads because your redemption is at hand."*r*

**The Lesson of the Fig Tree.***s* 29He taught them a lesson. "Consider the fig tree and all the other trees. 30When their buds burst open, you see for yourselves and know that summer is now near; 31in the same way, when you see these things happening, know that the kingdom of God is near. 32Amen, I say to you, this generation will not pass away until all these things have taken place.*t* 33Heaven and earth will pass away, but my words will not pass away.*u*

**Exhortation to Be Vigilant.** 34"Beware that your hearts do not become drowsy from carousing and drunkenness and the anxieties of daily life, and that day catch you by surprise*v* 35like a trap. For that day will assault everyone who lives on the face of the earth. 36Be vigilant at all times and pray that you have the strength to escape the tribulations that are imminent and to stand before the Son of Man."*w*

**Ministry in Jerusalem.** 37During the day, Jesus was teaching in the temple area, but at night he would leave and stay at the place called the Mount of Olives.*x* 38And all the people would get up early each morning to listen to him in the temple area.

## VII. THE PASSION NARRATIVE†

### CHAPTER 22
**The Conspiracy Against Jesus.** 1yNow the feast of Unleavened Bread, called the Passover,‡ was

drawing near, 2and the chief priests and the scribes were seeking a way to put him to death, for they were afraid of the people.*z* 3aThen Satan entered into Judas,§ the one surnamed Iscariot, who was counted among the Twelve,*b* 4and he went to the chief priests and temple guards to discuss a plan for handing him over to them. 5They were pleased and agreed to pay him money. 6He accepted their offer and sought a favorable opportunity to hand him over to them in the absence of a crowd.

**Preparations for the Passover.***c* 7When the day of the feast of Unleavened Bread arrived, the day for sacrificing the Passover lamb,*d* 8he sent out Peter and John, instructing them, "Go and make preparations for us to eat the Passover." 9They asked him, "Where do you want us to make the preparations?" 10And he answered them, "When you go into the city, a man will meet you carrying a jar of water.¶ Follow him into the house that he enters 11and say to the master of the house, 'The teacher says to you, "Where is the guest room where I may eat the Passover with my disciples?"' 12He will show you a large upper room that is furnished. Make the preparations there." 13Then they went off and found everything exactly as he had told them, and there they prepared the Passover.*e*

**The Last Supper.***f* 14When the hour came, he took his place at table with the apostles. 15He said to them, "I have eagerly desired to eat this Passover** with you before I suffer, 16for, I tell you, I shall not eat it [again] until there is fulfillment in the kingdom of God."*g* 17Then he took a cup,†† gave thanks, and said, "Take this and share it among yourselves; 18for I tell you [that] from this time on I shall not drink of the fruit of the vine until the kingdom of God comes." 19‡‡hThen he took the bread, said the blessing, broke it, and

---

*[21:26] **The powers of the heavens**: the heavenly bodies mentioned in Lk 21:25 and thought of as cosmic armies.

†[22:1–23:56a] The passion narrative. Luke is still dependent upon Mark for the composition of the passion narrative but has incorporated much of his own special tradition into the narrative. Among the distinctive sections in Luke are: (1) the tradition of the institution of the Eucharist (Lk 22:15–20); (2) Jesus' farewell discourse (Lk 22:21–38); (3) the mistreatment and interrogation of Jesus (Lk 22:63–71); (4) Jesus before Herod and his second appearance before Pilate (Lk 23:6–16); (5) words addressed to the women followers on the way to the crucifixion (Lk 23:27–32); (6) words to the penitent thief (Lk 23:39–41); (7) the death of Jesus (Lk 23:46, 47b–49). Luke stresses the innocence of Jesus (Lk 23:4, 14–15, 22) who is the victim of the powers of evil (Lk 22:3, 31, 53) and who goes to his death in fulfillment of his Father's will (Lk 22:42, 46). Throughout the narrative Luke emphasizes the mercy, compassion, and healing power of Jesus (Lk 22:51; 23:43) who does not go to death lonely and deserted, but is accompanied by others who follow him on the way of the cross (Lk 23:26–31, 49).

‡[22:1] **Feast of Unleavened Bread, called the Passover**: see note on Mk 14:1.

§[22:3] **Satan entered into Judas**: see note on Lk 4:13.

¶[22:10] **A man will meet you carrying a jar of water**: see note on Mk 14:13.

**[22:15] **This Passover**: Luke clearly identifies this last supper of Jesus with the apostles as a Passover meal that commemorated the deliverance of the Israelites from slavery in Egypt. Jesus reinterprets the significance of the Passover by setting it in the context of the kingdom of God (Lk 22:16). The "deliverance" associated with the Passover finds its new meaning in the blood that will be shed (Lk 22:20).

††[22:17] Because of a textual problem in Lk 22:19–20 some commentators interpret this cup as the eucharistic cup.

‡‡[22:19c–20] **Which will be given . . . do this in memory of me**: these words are omitted in some important Western text manuscripts and a few Syriac manuscripts. Other ancient text types, including the oldest papyrus manuscript of Luke dating from the late second or early third century, contain the longer reading presented here. The Lucan account of the words of institution of the Eucharist bears a close resemblance to the words of institution in the Pauline tradition (see 1 Cor 11:23–26). See also notes on Mt 26:26–29; 26:27–28; and Mk 14:22–24.

---

p. [21:26] Hg 2:6, 21.  q. [21:27] Dn 7:13–14; Mt 26:64; Rev 1:7.  r. [21:28] 2:38.  s. [21:29–33] Mt 24:32–35; Mk 13:28–31.  t. [21:32] 9:27; Mt 16:28.  u. [21:33] 16:17.  v. [21:34] 12:45–46; Mt 24:48–50; 1 Thes 5:3, 6–7.  w. [21:36] Mk 13:33.  x. [21:37] 19:47; 22:39.  y. [22:1–2] Mt 26:1–5; Mk 14:1–2; Jn 11:47–53.

z. [22:2] 19:47–48; 20:19; Mt 21:46; Mk 12:12; Jn 5:18; 7:30.  a. [22:3–6] Mt 26:14–16; Mk 14:10–11; Jn 13:2, 27.  b. [22:3] Acts 1:17.  c. [22:7–13] Mt 26:17–19; Mk 14:12–16.  d. [22:7] Ex 12:6, 14–20.  e. [22:13] 19:32.  f. [22:14–20] Mt 26:20, 26–30; Mk 14:17, 22–26; 1 Cor 11:23–25.  g. [22:16] 13:29.  h. [22:19] 24:30; Acts 27:35.

gave it to them, saying, "This is my body, which will be given for you; do this in memory of me." [20]And likewise the cup after they had eaten, saying, "This cup is the new covenant in my blood, which will be shed for you.[i]

**The Betrayal Foretold.**[j] [21]"And yet behold, the hand of the one who is to betray me is with me on the table; [22]for the Son of Man indeed goes as it has been determined; but woe to that man by whom he is betrayed." [23]And they began to debate among themselves who among them would do such a deed.

**The Role of the Disciples.** [24]"Then an argument broke out among them[k] about which of them should be regarded as the greatest. [25†]He said to them, "The kings of the Gentiles lord it over them and those in authority over them are addressed as 'Benefactors'; [26]but among you it shall not be so. Rather, let the greatest among you be as the youngest, and the leader as the servant.[m] [27]For who is greater: the one seated at table or the one who serves? Is it not the one seated at table? I am among you as the one who serves. [28]It is you who have stood by me in my trials; [29]and I confer a kingdom on you, just as my Father has conferred one on me,[n] [30]that you may eat and drink at my table in my kingdom; and you will sit on thrones judging the twelve tribes of Israel.[o]

**Peter's Denial Foretold.**[p] [31†]"Simon, Simon, behold Satan has demanded to sift all of you[§] like wheat,[q] [32]but I have prayed that your own faith may not fail; and once you have turned back, you must strengthen your brothers." [33]He said to him, "Lord, I am prepared to go to prison and to die with you."[r] [34]But he replied, "I tell you, Peter, before the cock crows this day, you will deny three times that you know me."[s]

**Instructions for the Time of Crisis.** [35†]He said to them, "When I sent you forth without a money bag or a sack or sandals, were you in need of anything?" "No, nothing," they replied. [36u]He said to them,[¶] "But now one who has a money bag should take it, and likewise a sack, and one who does not have a sword should sell his cloak and buy one. [37]For I tell you that this scripture must be fulfilled in me, namely, 'He was counted among the wicked'; and indeed what is written about me is coming to fulfillment."[v] [38]Then they said, "Lord, look, there are two swords here." But he replied, "It is enough!"[*]

**The Agony in the Garden.**[w] [39]Then going out he went, as was his custom, to the Mount of Olives, and the disciples followed him. [40]When he arrived at the place he said to them, "Pray that you may not undergo the test."[x] [41]After withdrawing about a stone's throw from them and kneeling, he prayed,[y] [42]saying, "Father, if you are willing, take this cup away from me; still, not my will but yours be done."[z] [††43]And to strengthen him an angel from heaven appeared to him. [44]He was in such agony and he prayed so fervently that his sweat became like drops of blood falling on the ground.] [45]When he rose from prayer and returned to his disciples, he found them sleeping from grief. [46]He said to them, "Why are you sleeping? Get up and pray that you may not undergo the test."[a]

**The Betrayal and Arrest of Jesus.**[b] [47]While he was still speaking, a crowd approached and in front was one of the Twelve, a man named Judas. He went up to Jesus to kiss him. [48]Jesus said to him, "Judas, are you betraying the Son of Man with a kiss?" [49]His disciples realized what was about to happen, and they asked, "Lord, shall we strike with a sword?"[c] [50]And one of them struck the high priest's servant and cut off his right ear.[d] [51‡‡]But Jesus said in reply, "Stop, no more of this!" Then he touched the servant's ear and healed him. [52]And Jesus said to the chief priests and temple guards and elders who had come for him, "Have you come out as against a robber, with swords and clubs?[e] [53]Day after day I was with you in the temple area, and you did not seize me; but this is your hour, the time for the power of darkness."[f]

**Peter's Denial of Jesus.** [54g]After arresting him they led him away and took him into the house of the high priest; Peter was following at a

---

\*[22:24–38] The Gospel of Luke presents a brief farewell discourse of Jesus; compare the lengthy farewell discourses and prayer in Jn 13–17.

†[22:25] '**Benefactors**': this word occurs as a title of rulers in the Hellenistic world.

‡[22:31–32] Jesus' prayer for Simon's faith and the commission to strengthen his brothers anticipates the postresurrectional prominence of Peter in the first half of Acts, where he appears as the spokesman for the Christian community and the one who begins the mission to the Gentiles (Acts 10–11).

§[22:31] **All of you**: literally, "you." The translation reflects the meaning of the Greek text that uses a second person plural pronoun here.

¶[22:36] In contrast to the ministry of the Twelve and of the seventy-two during the period of Jesus (Lk 9:3; 10:4), in

the future period of the church the missionaries must be prepared for the opposition they will face in a world hostile to their preaching.

\*\*[22:38] **It is enough!**: the farewell discourse ends abruptly with these words of Jesus spoken to the disciples when they take literally what was intended as figurative language about being prepared to face the world's hostility.

††[22:43–44] These verses, though very ancient, were probably not part of the original text of Luke. They are absent from the oldest papyrus manuscripts of Luke and from manuscripts of wide geographical distribution.

‡‡[22:51] **And healed him**: only Luke recounts this healing of the injured servant.

---

i. [22:20] Ex 24:8; Jer 31:31; 32:40; Zec 9:11.  j. [22:21–23] Ps 41:10; Mt 26:21–25; Mk 14:18–21; Jn 13:21–30.  k. [22:24] 9:46; Mt 18:1; Mk 9:34.  l. [22:25–27] Mt 20:25–27; Mk 10:42–44; Jn 13:3–16.  m. [22:26] Mt 23:11; Mk 9:35.  n. [22:29] 12:32.  o. [22:30] Mt 19:28.  p. [22:31–34] Mt 26:33–35; Mk 14:29–31; Jn 13:37–38.  q. [22:31] Jb 1:6–12; Am 9:9.  r. [22:33] 22:54.  s. [22:34] 22:54–62.  t. [22:35] 9:3; 10:4; Mt 10:9–10; Mk 6:7–9.  u. [22:36] 22:49.

v. [22:37] Is 53:12.  w. [22:39–46] Mt 26:30, 36–46; Mk 14:26, 32–42; Jn 18:1–2.  x. [22:40] 22:46.  y. [22:41] Heb 5:7–8.  z. [22:42] Mt 6:10.  a. [22:46] 22:40.  b. [22:47–53] Mt 26:47–56; Mk 14:43–50; Jn 18:3–4.  c. [22:49] 22:36.  d. [22:50] Jn 18:26.  e. [22:52] 22:37.  f. [22:53] 19:47; 21:37; Jn 7:30; 8:20; Col 1:13.  g. [22:54–62] Mt 26:57–58, 69–75; Mk 14:53–54, 66–72; Jn 18:12–18, 25–27.

distance.[h] [55]They lit a fire in the middle of the courtyard and sat around it, and Peter sat down with them. [56]When a maid saw him seated in the light, she looked intently at him and said, "This man too was with him." [57]But he denied it saying, "Woman, I do not know him." [58]A short while later someone else saw him and said, "You too are one of them"; but Peter answered, "My friend, I am not." [59]About an hour later, still another insisted, "Assuredly, this man too was with him, for he also is a Galilean." [60]But Peter said, "My friend, I do not know what you are talking about." Just as he was saying this, the cock crowed, [61]and the Lord turned and looked at Peter;[*] and Peter remembered the word of the Lord, how he had said to him, "Before the cock crows today, you will deny me three times."[i] [62]He went out and began to weep bitterly. [63]The men who held Jesus in custody were ridiculing and beating him. [64]They blindfolded him and questioned him, saying, "Prophesy! Who is it that struck you?" [65]And they reviled him in saying many other things against him.

**Jesus Before the Sanhedrin.**[†] [66k]When day came the council of elders of the people met, both chief priests and scribes,[j] and they brought him before their Sanhedrin.[‡] [67]They said, "If you are the Messiah, tell us," but he replied to them, "If I tell you, you will not believe,[m] [68]and if I question, you will not respond. [69]But from this time on the Son of Man will be seated at the right hand of the power of God."[n] [70]They all asked, "Are you then the Son of God?" He replied to them, "You say that I am." [71]Then they said, "What further need have we for testimony? We have heard it from his own mouth."

### CHAPTER 23

**Jesus Before Pilate.**[o] [1]Then the whole assembly of them arose and brought him before Pilate.

[2]They brought charges against him, saying, "We found this man misleading our people; he opposes the payment of taxes to Caesar and maintains that he is the Messiah, a king."[p] [3]Pilate asked him, "Are you the king of the Jews?" He said to him in reply, "You say so."[q] [4]Pilate then addressed the chief priests and the crowds, "I find this man not guilty." [5]But they were adamant and said, "He is inciting the people with his teaching throughout all Judea, from Galilee where he began even to here."[r]

**Jesus Before Herod.** [6]On hearing this Pilate asked if the man was a Galilean; [7]and upon learning that he was under Herod's jurisdiction, he sent him to Herod who was in Jerusalem at that time.[s] [8]Herod was very glad to see Jesus; he had been wanting to see him for a long time, for he had heard about him and had been hoping to see him perform some sign.[t] [9]He questioned him at length, but he gave him no answer.[u] [10]The chief priests and scribes, meanwhile, stood by accusing him harshly.[v] [11][Even] Herod and his soldiers treated him contemptuously and mocked him, and after clothing him in resplendent garb, he sent him back to Pilate.[w] [12]Herod and Pilate became friends that very day, even though they had been enemies formerly. [13]Pilate then summoned the chief priests, the rulers, and the people [14]and said to them, "You brought this man to me and accused him of inciting the people to revolt. I have conducted my investigation in your presence and have not found this man guilty of the charges you have brought against him,[x] [15]nor did Herod, for he sent him back to us. So no capital crime has been committed by him. [16y]Therefore I shall have him flogged and then release him." [[17]]**

**The Sentence of Death.**[z] [18]But all together they shouted out, "Away with this man! Release Barabbas to us." [19](Now Barabbas had been imprisoned for a rebellion that had taken place in the city and for murder.) [20]Again Pilate addressed them, still wishing to release Jesus, [21]but they continued their shouting, "Crucify him! Crucify him!" [22]Pilate addressed them a third time, "What evil has this man done? I found him guilty of no

---

*[22:61] Only Luke recounts that **the Lord turned and looked at Peter**. This look of Jesus leads to Peter's weeping bitterly over his denial (Lk 22:62).

†[22:66–71] Luke recounts one daytime trial of Jesus (Lk 22:66–71) and hints at some type of preliminary nighttime investigation (Lk 22:54–65). Mark (and Matthew who follows Mark) has transferred incidents of this day into the nighttime interrogation with the result that there appear to be two Sanhedrin trials of Jesus in Mark (and Matthew); see note on Mk 14:53.

‡[22:66] **Sanhedrin**: the word is a Hebraized form of a Greek word meaning a "council," and refers to the elders, chief priests, and scribes who met under the high priest's leadership to decide religious and legal questions that did not pertain to Rome's interests. Jewish sources are not clear on the competence of the Sanhedrin to sentence and to execute during this period.

§[23:1–5, 13–25] Twice Jesus is brought before Pilate in Luke's account, and each time Pilate explicitly declares Jesus innocent of any wrongdoing (Lk 23:4, 14, 22). This stress on the innocence of Jesus before the Roman authorities is also characteristic of John's gospel (Jn 18:38; 19:4, 6). Luke presents the Jerusalem Jewish leaders as the ones who force the hand of the Roman authorities (Lk 23:1–2, 5, 10, 13, 18, 21, 23–25).

¶[23:6–12] The appearance of Jesus before Herod is found only in this gospel. Herod has been an important figure in Luke (Lk 9:7–9; 13:31–33) and has been presented as someone who has been curious about Jesus for a long time. His curiosity goes unrewarded. It is faith in Jesus, not curiosity, that is rewarded (Lk 7:50; 8:48, 50; 17:19).

**[23:17] This verse, "He was obliged to release one prisoner for them at the festival," is not part of the original text of Luke. It is an explanatory gloss from Mk 15:6 (also Mt 27:15) and is not found in many early and important Greek manuscripts. On its historical background, see notes on Mt 27:15–26.

---

h. [22:54] 22:33.  i. [22:61] 22:34.  j. [22:63–65] Mt 26:67–68; Mk 14:65.  k. [22:66–71] Mt 26:59–66; Mk 14:55–64.  l. [22:66] Mt 27:1; Mk 15:1.  m. [22:67] Jn 3:12; 8:45; 10:24.  n. [22:69] Ps 110:1; Dn 7:13–14; Acts 7:56.  o. [23:1–5] Mt 27:1–2, 11–14; Mk 15:1–5; Jn 18:28–38.

p. [23:2] 20:22–25; Acts 17:7; 24:5.  q. [23:3] 22:70; 1 Tm 6:13.  r. [23:5] 23:14, 22, 41; Mt 27:24; Jn 19:4, 6; Acts 13:28.  s. [23:7] 3:1; 9:7.  t. [23:8] 9:9; Acts 4:27–28.  u. [23:9] Mk 15:5.  v. [23:10] Mt 27:12; Mk 15:3.  w. [23:11] Mt 27:28–30; Mk 15:17–19; Jn 19:2–3.  x. [23:14] 23:4, 22, 41.  y. [23:16] 23:22; Jn 19:12–14.  z. [23:18–25] Mt 27:20–26; Mk 15:6–7, 11–15; Jn 18:38b–40; 19:14–16; Acts 3:13–14.

capital crime. Therefore I shall have him flogged and then release him." ²³With loud shouts, however, they persisted in calling for his crucifixion, and their voices prevailed. ²⁴The verdict of Pilate was that their demand should be granted. ²⁵So he released the man who had been imprisoned for rebellion and murder, for whom they asked, and he handed Jesus over to them to deal with as they wished.

**The Way of the Cross.** * ²⁶ᵃAs they led him away they took hold of a certain Simon, a Cyrenian, who was coming in from the country; and after laying the cross on him, they made him carry it behind Jesus. ²⁷A large crowd of people followed Jesus, including many women who mourned and lamented him. ²⁸ᵇJesus turned to them and said, "Daughters of Jerusalem, do not weep for me; weep instead for yourselves and for your children, ²⁹for indeed, the days are coming when people will say, 'Blessed are the barren, the wombs that never bore and the breasts that never nursed.' ³⁰At that time people will say to the mountains, 'Fall upon us!' and to the hills, 'Cover us!'ᶜ ³¹for if these things are done when the wood is green what will happen when it is dry?" ³²Now two others, both criminals, were led away with him to be executed.

**The Crucifixion.**ᵈ ³³When they came to the place called the Skull, they crucified him and the criminals there, one on his right, the other on his left.ᵉ ³⁴[Then Jesus said, "Father, forgive them, they know not what they do."]† They divided his garments by casting lots.ᶠ ³⁵The people stood by and watched; the rulers, meanwhile, sneered at him and said,ᵍ "He saved others, let him save himself if he is the chosen one, the Messiah of God."ʰ ³⁶Even the soldiers jeered at him. As they approached to offer him wineⁱ ³⁷they called out, "If you are King of the Jews, save yourself." ³⁸Above him there was an inscription that read, "This is the King of the Jews."

³⁹†Now one of the criminals hanging there reviled Jesus, saying, "Are you not the Messiah? Save yourself and us." ⁴⁰The other, however, rebuking him, said in reply, "Have you no fear

of God, for you are subject to the same condemnation? ⁴¹And indeed, we have been condemned justly, for the sentence we received corresponds to our crimes, but this man has done nothing criminal."ʲ ⁴²Then he said, "Jesus, remember me when you come into your kingdom."ᵏ ⁴³He replied to him, "Amen, I say to you, today you will be with me in Paradise."ˡ

**The Death of Jesus.**ᵐ ⁴⁴§It was now about noonⁿ and darkness came over the whole land until three in the afternoon ⁴⁵because of an eclipse of the sun. Then the veil of the temple was torn down the middle.ᵒ ⁴⁶Jesus cried out in a loud voice, "Father, into your hands I commend my spirit"; and when he had said this he breathed his last.ᵖ ⁴⁷The centurion who witnessed what had happened glorified God and said, "This man was innocent¶ beyond doubt." ⁴⁸When all the people who had gathered for this spectacle saw what had happened, they returned home beating their breasts;�q ⁴⁹but all his acquaintances stood at a distance, including the women who had followed him from Galilee and saw these events.ʳ

**The Burial of Jesus.**ˢ ⁵⁰Now there was a virtuous and righteous man named Joseph who, though he was a member of the council, ⁵¹had not consented to their plan of action. He came from the Jewish town of Arimathea and was awaiting the kingdom of God.ᵗ ⁵²He went to Pilate and asked for the body of Jesus. ⁵³After he had taken the body down, he wrapped it in a linen cloth and laid him in a rock-hewn tomb in which no one had yet been buried.ᵘ ⁵⁴It was the day of preparation, and the sabbath was about to begin. ⁵⁵The women who had come from Galilee with him followed behind, and when they had seen the tomb and the way in which his body was laid in it,ᵛ ⁵⁶they returned and prepared spices and perfumed oils. Then they rested on the sabbath according to the commandment.ʷ

# VIII. THE RESURRECTION NARRATIVE**

## CHAPTER 24

**The Resurrection of Jesus.** ¹ˣBut at daybreak on the first day of the week they took the spices they

---

*[23:26–32] An important Lucan theme throughout the gospel has been the need for the Christian disciple to follow in the footsteps of Jesus. Here this theme comes to the fore with the story of Simon of Cyrene who takes up the cross and follows Jesus (see Lk 9:23; 14:27) and with the large crowd who likewise follow Jesus on the way of the cross. See also note on Mk 15:21.

†[23:34] [**Then Jesus said, "Father, forgive them, they know not what they do."**]: this portion of Lk 23:34 does not occur in the oldest papyrus manuscript of Luke and in other early Greek manuscripts and ancient versions of wide geographical distribution.

‡[23:39–43] This episode is recounted only in this gospel. The penitent sinner receives salvation through the crucified Jesus. Jesus' words to the penitent thief reveal Luke's understanding that the destiny of the Christian is "to be with Jesus."

§[23:44] **Noon . . . three in the afternoon:** literally, the sixth and ninth hours. See note on Mk 15:25.

¶[23:47] **This man was innocent:** or, "This man was righteous."

**[24:1–53] The resurrection narrative in Luke consists of five sections: (1) the women at the empty tomb (Lk 23:56b–24:12); (2) the appearance to the two disciples on the way to Emmaus (Lk 24:13–35); (3) the appearance to the disciples in Jerusalem (Lk 24:36–43); (4) Jesus' final instructions (Lk 24:44–49); (5) the ascension (Lk 24:50–53). In Luke, all the

j. [23:41] 23:4, 14, 22.   k. [23:42] 9:27; 23:2, 3, 38.   l. [23:43] 2 Cor 12:3; Rev 2:7.   m. [23:44–49] Mt 27:45–56; Mk 15:33–41; Jn 19:25–30.   n. [23:44–45] Am 8:9.   o. [23:45] Ex 26:31–33; 36:35.   p. [23:46] Ps 31:6; Acts 7:59.   q. [23:48] 18:13; Zec 12:10.   r. [23:49] 8:1–3; 23:55–56; 24:10; Ps 38:12.   s. [23:50–56] Mt 27:57–61; Mk 15:42–47; Jn 19:38–42; Acts 13:29.   t. [23:51] 2:25, 38.   u. [23:53] 19:30; Acts 13:29.   v. [23:55] 8:2; 23:49; 24:10.   w. [23:56] Ex 12:16; 20:10; Dt 5:14.   x. [24:1–8] Mt 28:1–8; Mk 16:1–8; Jn 20:1–17.

a. [23:26–32] Mt 27:32, 38; Mk 15:21, 27; Jn 19:17.   b. [23:28–31] 19:41–44; 21:23–24.   c. [23:30] Hos 10:8; Rev 6:16.   d. [23:33–43] Mt 27:33–44; Mk 15:22–32; Jn 19:17–24.   e. [23:33] 22:37; Is 53:12.   f. [23:34] Nm 15:27–31; Ps 22:19; Mt 5:44; Acts 7:60.   g. [23:35–36] Ps 22:8–9.   h. [23:35] 4:23.   i. [23:36] Ps 69:22; Mt 27:48; Mk 15:36.

had prepared and went to the tomb. ²They found the stone rolled away from the tomb; ³but when they entered, they did not find the body of the Lord Jesus. ⁴While they were puzzling over this, behold, two men in dazzling garments appeared to them.ʸ ⁵They were terrified and bowed their faces to the ground. They said to them, "Why do you seek the living one among the dead?ᶻ ⁶He is not here, but he has been raised.* Remember what he said to you while he was still in Galilee, ⁷that the Son of Man must be handed over to sinners and be crucified, and rise on the third day."ᵃ ⁸And they remembered his words.ᵇ ⁹†ᶜThen they returned from the tomb and announced all these things to the eleven and to all the others. ¹⁰The women were Mary Magdalene, Joanna, and Mary the mother of James; the others who accompanied them also told this to the apostles,ᵈ ¹¹but their story seemed like nonsense and they did not believe them. ¹²‡ᵉBut Peter got up and ran to the tomb, bent down, and saw the burial cloths alone; then he went home amazed at what had happened.

**The Appearance on the Road to Emmaus.**§ ¹³Now that very day two of them were going to a village seven miles¶ from Jerusalem called Emmaus,ᶠ ¹⁴and they were conversing about all the things that had occurred. ¹⁵And it happened that while they were conversing and debating, Jesus himself drew near and walked with them, ¹⁶**ᵍbut their eyes were prevented from recognizing him.

¹⁷He asked them, "What are you discussing as you walk along?" They stopped, looking downcast. ¹⁸One of them, named Cleopas, said to him in reply, "Are you the only visitor to Jerusalem who does not know of the things that have taken place there in these days?" ¹⁹And he replied to them, "What sort of things?" They said to him, "The things that happened to Jesus the Nazarene, who was a prophet mighty in deed and word before God and all the people,ʰ ²⁰how our chief priests and rulers both handed him over to a sentence of death and crucified him. ²¹ⁱBut we were hoping that he would be the one to redeem Israel; and besides all this, it is now the third day since this took place. ²²ʲSome women from our group, however, have astounded us: they were at the tomb early in the morning ²³and did not find his body; they came back and reported that they had indeed seen a vision of angels who announced that he was alive. ²⁴ᵏThen some of those with us went to the tomb and found things just as the women had described, but him they did not see." ²⁵And he said to them, "Oh, how foolish you are! How slow of heart to believe all that the prophets spoke! ²⁶Was it not necessary that the Messiah should suffer†† these things and enter into his glory?" ²⁷Then beginning with Moses and all the prophets, he interpreted to them what referred to him in all the scriptures.ᵐ ²⁸As they approached the village to which they were going, he gave the impression that he was going on farther. ²⁹But they urged him, "Stay with us, for it is nearly evening and the day is almost over." So he went in to stay with them. ³⁰And it happened that, while he was with them at table, he took bread, said the blessing, broke it, and gave it to them. ³¹With that their eyes were opened and they recognized him, but he vanished from their sight. ³²Then they said to each other, "Were not our hearts burning [within us] while he spoke to us on the way and opened the scriptures to us?" ³³So they set out at once and returned to Jerusalem where they found gathered together the eleven and those with them ³⁴who were saying, "The Lord has truly been raised and has appeared to Simon!"ⁿ ³⁵Then the two recounted what had taken place on the way and how he was made known to them in the breaking of the bread.

resurrection appearances take place in and around Jerusalem; moreover, they are all recounted as having taken place on Easter Sunday. A consistent theme throughout the narrative is that the suffering, death, and resurrection of Jesus were accomplished in fulfillment of Old Testament promises and of Jewish hopes (Lk 24:19a, 21, 26–27, 44, 46). In his second volume, Acts, Luke will argue that Christianity is the fulfillment of the hopes of Pharisaic Judaism and its logical development (see Acts 24:10–21).

*[24:6] **He is not here, but he has been raised:** this part of the verse is omitted in important representatives of the Western text tradition, but its presence in other text types and the slight difference in wording from Mt 28:6 and Mk 16:6 argue for its retention.

†[24:9] The women in this gospel do not flee from the tomb and tell no one, as in Mk 16:8 but return and tell the disciples about their experience. The initial reaction to the testimony of the women is disbelief (Lk 24:11).

‡[24:12] This verse is missing from the Western textual tradition but is found in the best and oldest manuscripts of other text types.

§[24:13–35] This episode focuses on the interpretation of scripture by the risen Jesus and the recognition of him in the breaking of the bread. The references to the quotations of scripture and explanation of it (Lk 24:25–27), the kerygmatic proclamation (Lk 24:34), and the liturgical gesture (Lk 24:30) suggest that the episode is primarily catechetical and liturgical rather than apologetic.

¶[24:13] **Seven miles:** literally, "sixty stades." A stade was 607 feet. Some manuscripts read "160 stades" or more than eighteen miles. The exact location of Emmaus is disputed.

**[24:16] A consistent feature of the resurrection stories is that the risen Jesus was different and initially unrecognizable (Lk 24:37; Mk 16:12; Jn 20:14; 21:4).

††[24:26] **That the Messiah should suffer . . . :** Luke is the only New Testament writer to speak explicitly of a suffering Messiah (Lk 24:26, 46; Acts 3:18; 17:3; 26:23). The idea of a suffering Messiah is not found in the Old Testament or in other Jewish literature prior to the New Testament period, although the idea is hinted at in Mk 8:31–33. See notes on Mt 26:63 and 26:67–68.

y. [24:4] 2 Mc 3:26; Acts 1:10.   z. [24:5] Acts 2:9.   a. [24:7] 9:22, 44; 17:25; 18:32–33; Mt 16:21; 17:22–23; Mk 9:31; Acts 17:3.   b. [24:8] Jn 2:22.   c. [24:9–11] Mk 16:10–11; Jn 20:18.   d. [24:10] 8:2–3; Mk 16:9.   e. [24:12] Jn 20:3–7.   f. [24:13] Mk 16:12–13.   g. [24:16] Jn 20:14; 21:4.

h. [24:19] Mt 2:23; 21:11; Acts 2:22.   i. [24:21] 1:54, 68; 2:38.   j. [24:22–23] 24:1–11; Mt 28:1–8; Mk 16:1–8.   k. [24:24] Jn 20:3–10.   l. [24:25–26] 9:22; 18:31; 24:44; Acts 3:24; 17:3.   m. [24:27] 24:44; Dt 18:15; Ps 22:1–18; Is 53; 1 Pt 1:10–11.   n. [24:34] 1 Cor 15:4–5.

**The Appearance to the Disciples in Jerusalem.** [36]*While they were still speaking about this,[o] he stood in their midst and said to them, "Peace be with you."[p] [37]But they were startled and terrified and thought that they were seeing a ghost.[q] [38]Then he said to them, "Why are you troubled? And why do questions arise in your hearts? [39]†Look at my hands and my feet, that it is I myself. Touch me and see, because a ghost does not have flesh and bones as you can see I have." [40]rAnd as he said this, he showed them his hands and his feet. [41]While they were still incredulous for joy and were amazed, he asked them, "Have you anything here to eat?" [42]They gave him a piece of baked fish;[s] [43]he took it and ate it in front of them.

[44]He said to them, "These are my words that I spoke to you while I was still with you, that everything written about me in the law of Moses and in the prophets and psalms must be fulfilled."[t] [45]Then he opened their minds to understand the scriptures.[u] [46]‡And he said to them,[v] "Thus it is written that the Messiah would suffer and rise from the dead on the third day [47]and that repentance, for the forgiveness of sins, would be preached in his name to all the nations, beginning from Jerusalem.[w] [48]You are witnesses of these things.[x] [49]And [behold] I am sending the promise of my Father[$] upon you; but stay in the city until you are clothed with power from on high."[y]

**The Ascension.**¶ [50]zThen he led them [out] as far as Bethany, raised his hands, and blessed them. [51]As he blessed them he parted from them and was taken up to heaven. [52]They did him homage and then returned to Jerusalem with great joy,[a] [53]and they were continually in the temple praising God.**

---

*[24:36–43, 44–49] The Gospel of Luke, like each of the other gospels (Mt 28:16–20; Mk 16:14–15; Jn 20:19–23), focuses on an important appearance of Jesus to the Twelve in which they are commissioned for their future ministry. As in Lk 24:6, 12, so in Lk 24:36, 40 there are omissions in the Western text.

†[24:39–42] The apologetic purpose of this story is evident in the concern with the physical details and the report that Jesus ate food.

‡[24:46] See note on Lk 24:26.

§[24:49] **The promise of my Father**: i.e., the gift of the holy Spirit.

¶[24:50–53] Luke brings his story about the time of Jesus to a close with the report of the ascension. He will also begin the story of the time of the church with a recounting of the ascension. In the gospel, Luke recounts the ascension of Jesus on Easter Sunday night, thereby closely associating it with the resurrection. In Acts 1:3, 9–11; 13:31 he historicizes the ascension by speaking of a forty-day period between the resurrection and the ascension. The Western text omits some phrases in Lk 24:51, 52 perhaps to avoid any chronological conflict with Acts 1 about the time of the ascension.

**[24:53] The Gospel of Luke ends as it began (Lk 1:9), in the Jerusalem temple.

---

o. [24:36–53] Mk 16:14–19; Jn 20:19–20.   p. [24:36] 1 Cor 15:5.   q. [24:37] Mt 14:26.   r. [24:40–41] Jn 21:5, 9–10, 13.   s. [24:42] Acts 10:41.   t. [24:44] 18:31; 24:27; Mt 16:21; Jn 5:39, 46.   u. [24:45] Jn 20:9.

v. [24:46] 9:22; Is 53; Hos 6:2.   w. [24:47] Mt 3:2; 28:19–20; Mk 16:15–16; Acts 10:41.   x. [24:48] Acts 1:8.   y. [24:49] Jn 14:26; Acts 1:4; 2:3–4.   z. [24:50–51] Mk 16:19; Acts 1:9–11.   a. [24:52] Acts 1:12.

# THE GOSPEL ACCORDING TO
# JOHN

୧୦୧ଅ

The Gospel according to John is quite different in character from the three synoptic gospels. It is highly literary and symbolic. It does not follow the same order or reproduce the same stories as the synoptic gospels. To a much greater degree, it is the product of a developed theological reflection and grows out of a different circle and tradition. It was probably written in the 90s of the first century.

The Gospel of John begins with a magnificent prologue, which states many of the major themes and motifs of the gospel, much as an overture does for a musical work. The prologue proclaims Jesus as the preexistent and incarnate Word of God who has revealed the Father to us. The rest of the first chapter forms the introduction to the gospel proper and consists of the Baptist's testimony about Jesus (there is no baptism of Jesus in this gospel—John simply points him out as the Lamb of God), followed by stories of the call of the first disciples, in which various titles predicated of Jesus in the early church are presented.

The gospel narrative contains a series of "signs"—the gospel's word for the wondrous deeds of Jesus. The author is primarily interested in the significance of these deeds, and so interprets them for the reader by various reflections, narratives, and discourses. The first sign is the transformation of water into wine at Cana (Jn 2:1–11); this represents the replacement of the Jewish ceremonial washings and symbolizes the entire creative and transforming work of Jesus. The second sign, the cure of the royal official's son (Jn 4:46–54) simply by the word of Jesus at a distance, signifies the power of Jesus' life-giving word. The same theme is further developed by other signs, probably for a total of seven. The third sign, the cure of the paralytic at the pool with five porticoes in chap. 5, continues the theme of water offering newness of life. In the preceding chapter, to the woman at the well in Samaria Jesus had offered living water springing up to eternal life, a symbol of the revelation that Jesus brings; here Jesus' life-giving word replaces the water of the pool that failed to bring life. Jn 6 contains two signs, the multiplication of loaves and the walking on the waters of the Sea of Galilee. These signs are connected much as the manna and the crossing of the Red Sea are in the Passover narrative and symbolize a new exodus. The multiplication of the loaves is interpreted for the reader by the discourse that follows, where the bread of life is used first as a figure for the revelation of God in Jesus and then for the Eucharist. After a series of dialogues reflecting Jesus' debates with the Jewish authorities at the Feast of Tabernacles in Jn 7; 8, the sixth sign is presented in Jn 9, the sign of the young man born blind. This is a narrative illustration of the theme of conflict in the preceding two chapters; it proclaims the triumph of light over darkness, as Jesus is presented as the Light of the world. This is interpreted by a narrative of controversy between the Pharisees and the young man who had been given his sight by Jesus, ending with a discussion of spiritual blindness and spelling out the symbolic meaning of the cure. And finally, the seventh sign, the raising of Lazarus in chap. 11, is the climax of signs. Lazarus is presented as a token of the real life that Jesus, the Resurrection and the Life, who will now ironically be put to death because of his gift of life to Lazarus, will give to all who believe in him once he has been raised from the dead.

After the account of the seven signs, the "hour" of Jesus arrives, and the author passes from sign to reality, as he moves into the discourses in the upper room that interpret the meaning of the passion, death, and resurrection narratives that follow. The whole gospel of John is a progressive revelation of the glory of God's only Son, who comes to reveal the Father and then returns in glory to the Father. The author's purpose is clearly expressed in what must have been the original ending of the gospel at the end of Jn 20: "Now Jesus did many other signs in the presence of [his] disciples that are not written in this book. But these are written that you may [come to] believe that Jesus is the Messiah, the Son of God, and that through this belief you may have life in his name."

Critical analysis makes it difficult to accept the idea that the gospel as it now stands was written by one person. Jn 21 seems to have been added after the gospel was completed; it exhibits a Greek style somewhat different from that of the rest of the work. The prologue (Jn 1:1–18) apparently contains an independent hymn, subsequently adapted to serve as a preface to the gospel. Within the gospel itself there are also some inconsistencies, e.g., there are two endings of Jesus' discourse in the upper room (Jn 14:31; 18:1). To solve these problems, scholars have proposed various rearrangements that would produce a smoother order. However, most have come to the conclusion that the inconsistencies were probably produced by subsequent editing in which homogeneous materials were added to a shorter original.

Other difficulties for any theory of eyewitness authorship of the gospel in its present form are presented by its highly developed theology and by certain elements of its literary style. For instance, some of the wondrous deeds of Jesus have been worked into highly effective dramatic scenes (Jn 9); there has been a careful attempt to have these followed by discourses that explain them (Jn 5; 6); and the sayings of Jesus have been oven into long discourses of a quasi-poetic form resembling the speeches of personified Wisdom in the Old Testament.

The gospel contains many details about Jesus not found in the synoptic gospels, e.g., that Jesus engaged in a baptizing ministry (Jn 3:22) before he changed to one of preaching and signs; that Jesus' public ministry lasted for several years (see note on Jn 2:13); that he traveled to Jerusalem for various festivals and met serious opposition long before his death (Jn 2:14–25; 5; 7–8); and that he was put to death on the day before Passover (Jn 18:28). These events are not always in chronological order because of the development and editing that took place. However, the accuracy of much of the detail of the fourth gospel constitutes a strong argument that the Johannine tradition rests upon the testimony of an eyewitness. Although tradition identified this person as John, the son of Zebedee, most modern scholars find that the evidence does not support this.

The fourth gospel is not simply history; the narrative has been organized and adapted to serve the evangelist's theological purposes as well. Among them are the opposition to the synagogue of the day and to John the Baptist's followers, who tried to exalt their master at Jesus' expense, the desire to show that Jesus was the Messiah, and the desire to convince Christians that their religious belief and practice must be rooted in Jesus. Such theological purposes have impelled the evangelist to emphasize motifs that were not so clear in the synoptic account of Jesus' ministry, e.g., the explicit emphasis on his divinity.

The polemic between synagogue and church produced bitter and harsh invective, especially regarding the hostility toward Jesus of the authorities—Pharisees and Sadducees—who are combined and referred to frequently as "the Jews" (see note on Jn 1:19). These opponents are even described in Jn 8:44 as springing from their father the devil, whose conduct they imitate in opposing God by rejecting Jesus, whom God has sent. On the other hand, the author of this gospel seems to take pains to show that women are not inferior to men in the Christian community: the woman at the well in Samaria (Jn 4) is presented as a prototype of a missionary (Jn 4:4–42), and the first witness of the resurrection is a woman (Jn 20:11–18).

The final editing of the gospel and arrangement in its present form probably dates from between A.D. 90 and 100. Traditionally, Ephesus has been favored as the place of composition, though many support a location in Syria, perhaps the city of Antioch, while some have suggested other places, including Alexandria.

The principal divisions of the Gospel according to John are the following:

I. Prologue (1:1–18)
II. The Book of Signs (1:19–12:50)
III. The Book of Glory (13:1–20:31)
IV. Epilogue: The Resurrection Appearance in Galilee (21:1–25)

# I. PROLOGUE*

## CHAPTER 1

¹ In the beginning† was the Word,
　　and the Word was with God,
　　and the Word was God.ᵃ
² He was in the beginning with God.
³ ‡All things came to be through him,
　　and without him nothing came to be.ᵇ
　What came to be ⁴through him was life,
　　and this life was the light of the
　　　human race;ᶜ
⁵ ⁵the light shines in the darkness,ᵈ
　　and the darkness has not overcome it.

⁶‡A man named John was sent from God.ᵉ ⁷He
came for testimony,** to testify to the light, so
that all might believe through him.ᶠ ⁸He was not
the light, but came to testify to the light.ᵍ ⁹The
true light, which enlightens everyone, was coming into the world.ʰ

¹⁰ He was in the world,
　　and the world came to be through him,
　　but the world did not know him.
¹¹ He came to what was his own,
　　but his own people†† did not accept
　　　him.

¹²ᶦBut to those who did accept him he gave
power to become children of God, to those who
believe in his name, ¹³‡‡ᶦwho were born not by
natural generation nor by human choice nor by
a man's decision but of God.

¹⁴ And the Word became flesh⁵⁵
　　and made his dwelling among us,
　　and we saw his glory,
　　the glory as of the Father's only Son,
　　full of grace and truth.ᵏ

¹⁵⁵⁵John testified to him and cried out, saying,
"This was he of whom I said,ᶦ 'The one who is
coming after me ranks ahead of me because he
existed before me.'" ¹⁶From his fullness we have
all received, grace in place of grace,*** ¹⁷because
while the law was given through Moses, grace
and truth came through Jesus Christ.ᵐ ¹⁸No one
has ever seen God. The only Son, God,††† who is at
the Father's side, has revealed him.ⁿ

## II. THE BOOK OF SIGNS

**John the Baptist's Testimony to Himself.**
¹⁹‡‡‡And this is the testimony of John. When the

---

*[1:1–18] The prologue states the main themes of the gos-
pel: life, light, truth, the world, testimony, and the preexistence
of Jesus Christ, the incarnate *Logos*, who reveals God the Father.
In origin, it was probably an early Christian hymn. Its closest
parallel is in other christological hymns, Col 1:15–20 and Phil
2:6–11. Its core (Jn 1:1–5, 10–11, 14) is poetic in structure, with
short phrases linked by "staircase parallelism," in which the last
word of one phrase becomes the first word of the next. Prose
inserts (at least Jn 1:6–8, 15) deal with John the Baptist.

†[1:1] **In the beginning**: also the first words of the Old
Testament (Gn 1:1). **Was**: this verb is used three times with
different meanings in this verse: existence, relationship, and
predication. **The Word** (Greek *logos*): this term combines God's
dynamic, creative word (Genesis), personified preexistent Wisdom as the instrument of God's creative activity (Proverbs), and
the ultimate intelligibility of reality (Hellenistic philosophy).
**With God**: the Greek preposition here connotes communication with another. **Was God**: lack of a definite article with
"God" in Greek signifies predication rather than identification.

‡[1:3] **What came to be**: while the oldest manuscripts
have no punctuation here, the corrector of Bodmer Papyrus
P⁷⁵, some manuscripts, and the Ante-Nicene Fathers take this
phrase with what follows, as staircase parallelism. Connection
with Jn 1:3 reflects fourth-century anti-Arianism.

§[1:5] The ethical dualism of light and darkness is paralleled in intertestamental literature and in the Dead Sea Scrolls.
**Overcome**: "comprehend" is another possible translation, but
cf. Jn 12:35; Wis 7:29–30.

¶[1:6] John was **sent** just as Jesus was "sent" (Jn 4:34) in
divine mission. Other references to John the Baptist in this gospel
emphasize the differences between them and John's subordinate role.

**[1:7] **Testimony**: the testimony theme of John is introduced, which portrays Jesus as if on trial throughout his ministry. All testify to Jesus: John the Baptist, the Samaritan woman,
scripture, his works, the crowds, the Spirit, and his disciples.

††[1:11] **What was his own . . . his own people**: first a
neuter, literally, "his own property/possession" (probably =
Israel), then a masculine, "his own people" (the Israelites).

‡‡[1:13] Believers in Jesus become children of God not
through any of the three natural causes mentioned but
through God who is the immediate cause of the new spiritual life. **Were born**: the Greek verb can mean "begotten" (by
a male) or "born" (from a female or of parents). The variant
"he who was begotten," asserting Jesus' virginal conception, is
weakly attested in Old Latin and Syriac versions.

§§[1:14] **Flesh**: the whole person, used probably against
docetic tendencies (cf. 1 Jn 4:2; 2 Jn 7). **Made his dwelling**:
literally, "pitched his tent/tabernacle." Cf. the tabernacle or
tent of meeting that was the place of God's presence among
his people (Ex 25:8–9). The incarnate Word is the new mode
of God's presence among his people. The Greek verb has the
same consonants as the Aramaic word for God's presence
(Shekinah). **Glory**: God's visible manifestation of majesty in
power, which once filled the tabernacle (Ex 40:34) and the
temple (1 Kgs 8:10–11, 27), is now centered in Jesus. **Only
Son**: Greek, *monogenēs*, but see note on Jn 1:18. **Grace and
truth**: these words may represent two Old Testament terms
describing Yahweh in covenant relationship with Israel (cf. Ex
34:6), thus God's "love" and "fidelity." The Word shares Yahweh's covenant qualities.

¶¶[1:15] This verse, interrupting Jn 1:14, 16 seems drawn
from Jn 1:30.

***[1:16] **Grace in place of grace**: replacement of the Old
Covenant with the New (cf. Jn 1:17). Other possible translations are "grace upon grace" (accumulation) and "grace for
grace" (correspondence).

†††[1:18] **The only Son, God**: while the vast majority of
later textual witnesses have another reading, "the Son, the
only one" or "the only Son," the translation above follows
the best and earliest manuscripts, *monogenēs theos*, but takes
the first term to mean not just "Only One" but to include a
filial relationship with the Father, as at Lk 9:38 ("only child")
or Heb 11:17 ("only son") and as translated at Jn 1:14. The
Logos is thus "only Son" and God but not Father/God.

‡‡‡[1:19–51] The testimony of John the Baptist about the
Messiah and Jesus' self-revelation to the first disciples. This
section constitutes the introduction to the gospel proper and
is connected with the prose inserts in the prologue. It develops
the major theme of testimony in four scenes: John's negative
testimony about himself; his positive testimony about Jesus;

---

a. [1:1] 10:30; Gn 1:1–5; Jb 28:12–27; Prv 8:22–25; Wis 9:1–2; 1 Jn
1:1–2; Col 1:1, 15; Rev 3:14; 19:13.　b. [1:3] Ps 33:9; Wis 9:1; Sir
42:15; 1 Cor 8:6; Col 1:16; Heb 1:2; Rev 3:14.　c. [1:4] 5:26; 8:12;
1 Jn 1:2.　d. [1:5] 3:19; 8:12; 9:5; 12:35, 46; Wis 7:29–30; 1 Thes
5:4; 1 Jn 2:8.　e. [1:6] Mt 3:1; Mk 1:4; Lk 3:2–3.　f. [1:7] 1:19–34;
5:33.　g. [1:8] 5:35.　h. [1:9] 3:19; 8:12; 9:39; 12:46.

i. [1:12] 3:11–12; 5:43–44; 12:46–50; Gal 3:26; 4:6–7; Eph 1:5; 1 Jn
3:2.　j. [1:13] 3:5–6.　k. [1:14] Ex 16:10; 24:17; 25:8–9; 33:22; 34:6; Sir
24:4, 8; Is 60:1; Ez 43:7; Jl 4:17; Heb 2:14; 1 Jn 1:2; 4:2; 2 Jn 7.　l. [1:15]
1:30; 3:27–30.　m. [1:17] 7:19; Ex 31:18; 34:28.　n. [1:18] 5:37; 6:46;
Ex 33:20; Jgs 13:21–22; 1 Tm 6:16; 1 Jn 4:12.

Jews* from Jerusalem sent priests and Levites [to him] to ask him, "Who are you?" ²⁰ʰe admitted and did not deny it, but admitted,ᵒ "I am not the Messiah." ²¹So they asked him, "What are you then? Are you Elijah?"‡ And he said, "I am not." "Are you the Prophet?" He answered, "No."ᵖ ²²So they said to him, "Who are you, so we can give an answer to those who sent us? What do you have to say for yourself?" ²³He said:

"I am 'the voice of one crying out in the
desert,�q
"Make straight the way of the Lord,'"ˢ

as Isaiah the prophet said." ²⁴Some Pharisees¶ were also sent. ²⁵They asked him, "Why then do you baptize if you are not the Messiah or Elijah or the Prophet?"ʳ ²⁶John answered them, "I baptize with water;** but there is one among you whom you do not recognize,ˢ ²⁷the one who is coming after me, whose sandal strap I am not worthy to untie." ²⁸This happened in Bethany across the Jordan,†† where John was baptizing.
**John the Baptist's Testimony to Jesus.** ²⁹The next day he saw Jesus coming toward him and said, "Behold, the Lamb of God,‡‡ who takes away the sin of the world.ᵗ ³⁰§§He is the one of whom I said,ᵘ 'A man is coming after me who ranks

ahead of me because he existed before me.' ³¹I did not know him,¶¶ but the reason why I came baptizing with water was that he might be made known to Israel." ³²John testified further, saying, "I saw the Spirit come down like a dove*** from the sky and remain upon him. ³³I did not know him,ᵛ but the one who sent me to baptize with water told me, 'On whomever you see the Spirit come down and remain, he is the one who will baptize with the holy Spirit.'ʷ ³⁴††††ˣNow I have seen and testified that he is the Son of God."
**The First Disciples.**ʸ ³⁵The next day John was there again with two of his disciples, ³⁶and as he watched Jesus walk by, he said, "Behold, the Lamb of God."‡‡‡ ³⁷The two disciples§§§ heard what he said and followed Jesus. ³⁸Jesus turned and saw them following him and said to them, "What are you looking for?" They said to him, "Rabbi" (which translated means Teacher), "where are you staying?" ³⁹He said to them, "Come, and you will see." So they went and saw where he was staying, and they stayed with him that day. It was about four in the afternoon.¶¶¶ ⁴⁰Andrew, the brother of Simon Peter, was one of the two who heard John and followed Jesus. ⁴¹He first found his own brother Simon and told him, "We have found the Messiah"**** (which is translated Anointed).ᶻ ⁴²Then he brought him to Jesus. Jesus looked at him and said, "You are Simon the son of John;†††† you will be called Cephas" (which is translated Peter).ᵃ

the revelation of Jesus to Andrew and Peter; the revelation of Jesus to Philip and Nathanael.

*[1:19] **The Jews:** throughout most of the gospel, the "Jews" does not refer to the Jewish people as such but to the hostile authorities, both Pharisees and Sadducees, particularly in Jerusalem, who refuse to believe in Jesus. The usage reflects the atmosphere, at the end of the first century, of polemics between church and synagogue, or possibly it refers to Jews as representative of a hostile world (Jn 1:10–11).

†[1:20] **Messiah:** the anointed agent of Yahweh, usually considered to be of Davidic descent. See further the note on Jn 1:41.

‡[1:21] **Elijah:** the Baptist did not claim to be Elijah returned to earth (cf. Mal 3:19; Mt 11:14). **The Prophet:** probably the prophet like Moses (Dt 18:15; cf. Acts 3:22).

§[1:23] This is a repunctuation and reinterpretation (as in the synoptic gospels and Septuagint) of the Hebrew text of Is 40:3 which reads, "A voice cries out: In the desert prepare the way of the LORD."

¶[1:24] **Some Pharisees:** other translations, such as "Now they had been sent from the Pharisees," misunderstand the grammatical construction. This is a different group from that in Jn 1:19; the priests and Levites would have been Sadducees, not Pharisees.

**[1:26] **I baptize with water:** the synoptics add "but he will baptize you with the holy Spirit" (Mk 1:8) or ". . . holy Spirit and fire" (Mt 3:11; Lk 3:16). John's emphasis is on purification and preparation for a better baptism.

††[1:28] **Bethany across the Jordan:** site unknown. Another reading is "Bethabara."

‡‡[1:29] **The Lamb of God:** the background for this title may be the victorious apocalyptic lamb who would destroy evil in the world (Rev 5–7; 17:14); the paschal lamb, whose blood saved Israel (Ex 12); and/or the suffering servant led like a lamb to the slaughter as a sin-offering (Is 53:7, 10).

§§[1:30] **He existed before me:** possibly as Elijah (to come, Jn 1:27); for the evangelist and his audience, Jesus' preexistence would be implied (see note on Jn 1:1).

¶¶[1:31] **I did not know him:** this gospel shows no knowledge of the tradition (Lk 1) about the kinship of Jesus and John the Baptist. **The reason why I came baptizing with water:** in this gospel, John's baptism is not connected with forgiveness of sins; its purpose is revelatory, that Jesus may be made known to Israel.

***[1:32] **Like a dove:** a symbol of the new creation (Gn 8:8) or the community of Israel (Hos 11:11). **Remain:** the first use of a favorite verb in John, emphasizing the permanency of the relationship between Father and Son (as here) and between the Son and the Christian. Jesus is the permanent bearer of the Spirit.

†††[1:34] **The Son of God:** this reading is supported by good Greek manuscripts, including the Chester Beatty and Bodmer Papyri and the Vatican Codex, but is suspect because it harmonizes this passage with the synoptic version: "This is my beloved Son" (Mt 3:17; Mk 1:11; Lk 3:22). The poorly attested alternate reading, "God's chosen One," is probably a reference to the Servant of Yahweh (Is 42:1).

‡‡‡[1:36] John the Baptist's testimony makes his disciples' following of Jesus plausible.

§§§[1:37] **The two disciples:** Andrew (Jn 1:40) and, traditionally, John, son of Zebedee (see note on Jn 13:23).

¶¶¶[1:39] **Four in the afternoon:** literally, the tenth hour, from sunrise, in the Roman calculation of time. Some suggest that the next day, beginning at sunset, was the sabbath; they would have stayed with Jesus to avoid travel on it.

****[1:41] **Messiah:** the Hebrew word *māšîaḥ*, "anointed one" (see note on Lk 2:11), appears in Greek as the transliterated *messias* only here and in Jn 4:25. Elsewhere the Greek translation *christos* is used.

††††[1:42] **Simon, the son of John:** in Mt 16:17, Simon is called *Bariōna*, "son of Jonah," a different tradition for the name of Simon's father. **Cephas:** in Aramaic = the Rock; cf. Mt 16:18. Neither the Greek equivalent **Petros** nor, with one

o. [1:20] 3:28; Lk 3:15; Acts 13:25.   p. [1:21] Dt 18:15, 18; 2 Kgs 2:11; Sir 48:10; Mal 3:1, 23; Mt 11:14; 17:11–13; Mk 9:13; Acts 3:22.   q. [1:23] Is 40:3; Mt 3:3; Mk 1:2; Lk 3:4.   r. [1:25] Ez 36:25; Zec 13:1; Mt 16:14.   s. [1:26] Mt 3:11; Mk 1:7–8; Lk 3:16; Acts 13:25.   t. [1:29] 1:36; Ex 12; Is 53:7; Rev 5–7; 17:14.   u. [1:30] 1:15; Mt 3:11; Mk 1:7; Lk 3:16.

v. [1:33] Sg 5:2; Is 11:2; Hos 11:11; Mt 3:16; Mk 1:10; Lk 3:21–22.   w. [1:33] Is 42:1; Mt 3:11; Mk 1:8; Lk 3:16.   x. [1:34] Is 42:1; Mt 3:17; Mk 1:11; Lk 9:35.   y. [1:35–51] Mt 4:18–22; Mk 1:16–20; Lk 5:1–11.   z. [1:41] 4:25.   a. [1:42] Mt 16:18; Mk 3:16.

<sup>43</sup>The next day he<sup>*</sup> decided to go to Galilee, and he found Philip. And Jesus said to him, "Follow me." <sup>44</sup>Now Philip was from Bethsaida, the town of Andrew and Peter. <sup>45</sup>Philip found Nathanael and told him, "We have found the one about whom Moses wrote in the law, and also the prophets, Jesus son of Joseph, from Nazareth."<sup>b</sup> <sup>46</sup>But Nathanael said to him, "Can anything good come from Nazareth?" Philip said to him, "Come and see." <sup>47</sup>Jesus saw Nathanael coming toward him and said of him, "Here is a true Israelite.<sup>†</sup> There is no duplicity in him." <sup>48‡c</sup>Nathanael said to him, "How do you know me?" Jesus answered and said to him, "Before Philip called you, I saw you under the fig tree." <sup>49</sup>Nathanael answered him, "Rabbi, you are the Son of God;<sup>§</sup> you are the King of Israel."<sup>d</sup> <sup>50</sup>Jesus answered and said to him, "Do you believe because I told you that I saw you under the fig tree?<sup>¶</sup> You will see greater things than this." <sup>51</sup>And he said to him, "Amen, amen," I say to you, you will see the sky opened and the angels of God ascending and descending on the Son of Man."<sup>e</sup>

### CHAPTER 2

**The Wedding at Cana.** <sup>1††</sup>On the third day there was a wedding<sup>‡‡</sup> in Cana<sup>§§</sup> in Galilee, and the mother of Jesus was there.<sup>f</sup> <sup>2</sup>Jesus and his disciples were also invited to the wedding. <sup>3</sup>When the wine ran short, the mother of Jesus said to him, "They have no wine." <sup>4¶¶</sup>[And] Jesus said to her,

"Woman, how does your concern affect me? My hour has not yet come."<sup>g</sup> <sup>5</sup>His mother said to the servers, "Do whatever he tells you."<sup>h</sup> <sup>6***</sup>Now there were six stone water jars there for Jewish ceremonial washings,<sup>i</sup> each holding twenty to thirty gallons. <sup>7</sup>Jesus told them, "Fill the jars with water." So they filled them to the brim. <sup>8</sup>Then he told them, "Draw some out now and take it to the headwaiter."<sup>†††</sup> So they took it. <sup>9</sup>And when the headwaiter tasted the water that had become wine, without knowing where it came from (although the servers who had drawn the water knew), the headwaiter called the bridegroom <sup>10</sup>and said to him, "Everyone serves good wine first, and then when people have drunk freely, an inferior one; but you have kept the good wine until now." <sup>11</sup>Jesus did this as the beginning of his signs<sup>‡‡‡</sup> in Cana in Galilee and so revealed his glory, and his disciples began to believe in him.<sup>j</sup>

<sup>12§§§</sup>After this, he and his mother, [his] brothers, and his disciples went down to Capernaum and stayed there only a few days.<sup>¶¶¶</sup>

**Cleansing of the Temple.** <sup>13****</sup>Since the Passover<sup>††††</sup> of the Jews was near,<sup>k</sup> Jesus went up to Jerusalem. <sup>14‡‡‡‡</sup>He found in the temple area those who sold oxen, sheep, and doves,<sup>§§§§</sup> as well

---

isolated exception, **Cephas** is attested as a personal name before Christian times.

*[1:43] **He**: grammatically, could be Peter, but logically is probably Jesus.

†[1:47] **A true Israelite. There is no duplicity in him**: Jacob was the first to bear the name "Israel" (Gn 32:29), but Jacob was a man of duplicity (Gn 27:35–36).

‡[1:48] **Under the fig tree**: a symbol of messianic peace (cf. Mi 4:4; Zec 3:10).

§[1:48] **Son of God**: this title is used in the Old Testament, among other ways, as a title of adoption for the Davidic king (2 Sm 7:14; Ps 2:7; 89:27), and thus here, with **King of Israel**; in a messianic sense. For the evangelist, **Son of God** also points to Jesus' divinity (cf. Jn 20:28).

¶[1:50] Possibly a statement: "You [singular] believe because I saw you under the fig tree."

**[1:51] The double "Amen" is characteristic of John. **You** is plural in Greek. The allusion is to Jacob's ladder (Gn 28:12).

††[2:1–6:71] Signs revealing Jesus as the Messiah to all Israel. "Sign" (*sēmeion*) is John's symbolic term for Jesus' wondrous deeds (see Introduction). The Old Testament background lies in the Exodus story (cf. Dt 11:3; 29:2). John is interested primarily in what the *sēmeia* signify: God's intervention in human history in a new way through Jesus.

‡‡[2:1–11] The first sign. This story of replacement of Jewish ceremonial washings (Jn 2:6) presents the initial revelation about Jesus at the outset of his ministry. He manifests his glory; the disciples believe. There is no synoptic parallel.

§§[2:1] **Cana**: unknown from the Old Testament. **The mother of Jesus**: she is never named in John.

¶¶[2:4] This verse may seek to show that Jesus did not work miracles to help his family and friends, as in the apocryphal gospels. **Woman**: a normal, polite form of address, but

unattested in reference to one's mother. Cf. also Jn 19:26. **How does your concern affect me?**: literally, "What is this to me and to you?"—a Hebrew expression of either hostility (Jgs 11:12; 2 Chr 35:21; 1 Kgs 17:18) or denial of common interest (Hos 14:9; 2 Kgs 3:13). Cf. Mk 1:24; 5:7 used by demons to Jesus. **My hour has not yet come**: the translation as a question ("Has not my hour now come?"), while preferable grammatically and supported by Greek Fathers, seems unlikely from a comparison with Jn 7:6, 30. The "hour" is that of Jesus' passion, death, resurrection, and ascension (Jn 13:1).

***[2:6] **Twenty to thirty gallons**: literally, "two or three measures"; the Attic liquid measure contained 39.39 liters. The vast quantity recalls prophecies of abundance in the last days; cf. Am 9:13–14; Hos 14:7; Jer 31:12.

†††[2:8] **Headwaiter**: used of the official who managed a banquet, but there is no evidence of such a functionary in Palestine. Perhaps here a friend of the family acted as master of ceremonies; cf. Sir 32:1.

‡‡‡[2:11] **The beginning of his signs**: the first of seven (see Introduction).

§§§[2:12–3:21] The next three episodes take place in Jerusalem. Only the first is paralleled in the synoptic gospels.

¶¶¶[2:12] This transitional verse may be a harmonization with the synoptic tradition in Lk 4:31 and Mt 4:13. There are many textual variants. John depicts no extended ministry in Capernaum as do the synoptics.

****[2:13–22] This episode indicates the post-resurrectional replacement of the temple by the person of Jesus.

††††[2:13] **Passover**: this is the first Passover mentioned in John; a second is mentioned in Jn 6:4 a third in Jn 13:1. Taken literally, they point to a ministry of at least two years.

‡‡‡‡[2:14–22] The other gospels place the cleansing of the temple in the last days of Jesus' life (Matthew, on the day Jesus entered Jerusalem; Mark, on the next day). The order of events in the gospel narratives is often determined by theological motives rather than by chronological data.

§§§§[2:14] **Oxen, sheep, and doves**: intended for sacrifice. The doves were the offerings of the poor (Lv 5:7). **Money-changers**: for a temple tax paid by every male Jew more than nineteen years of age, with a half-shekel coin (Ex 30:11–16), in Syrian currency. See note on Mt 17:24.

---

b. [1:45] 21:2.    c. [1:48] Mi 4:4; Zec 3:10.    d. [1:49] 12:13; Ex 4:22; Dt 14:1; 2 Sm 7:14; Jb 1:6; 2:1; 38:7; Ps 2:7; 29:1; 89:27; Wis 2:18; Sir 4:10; Dn 3:92; Hos 11:1; Mt 14:33; 16:16; Mk 13:32.    e. [1:51] Gn 28:10–17; Dn 7:13.    f. [2:1] 4:46; Jgs 14:12; Tb 11:8.

g. [2:4] 7:30; 8:20; 12:23; 13:1; Jgs 11:12; 1 Kgs 17:18; 2 Kgs 3:13; 2 Chr 35:21; Hos 14:9; Mk 1:24; 5:7; 7:30; 8:20; 12:23; 13:1.    h. [2:5] Gn 41:55.    i. [2:6] 3:25, Lv 11:33; Am 9:13–14; Mt 15:2; 23:25–26; Mk 7:2–4; Lk 11:38.    j. [2:11] 4:54.    k. [2:13–22] Mt 21:12–13; Mk 11:15–17; Lk 19:45–46.

as the money changers seated there.[l] [15]He made a whip out of cords and drove them all out of the temple area, with the sheep and oxen, and spilled the coins of the money changers and overturned their tables, [16]and to those who sold doves he said, "Take these out of here, and stop making my Father's house a marketplace."[m] [17]His disciples recalled the words of scripture,[n] "Zeal for your house will consume me." [18]At this the Jews answered and said to him, "What sign can you show us for doing this?"[o] [19]Jesus answered and said to them,[†p] "Destroy this temple and in three days I will raise it up." [20]The Jews said, "This temple has been under construction for forty-six years,[‡] and you will raise it up in three days?" [21]But he was speaking about the temple of his body. [22]Therefore, when he was raised from the dead, his disciples remembered that he had said this, and they came to believe the scripture and the word Jesus had spoken.[q]

[23]While he was in Jerusalem for the feast of Passover, many began to believe in his name when they saw the signs he was doing.[r] [24]But Jesus would not trust himself to them because he knew them all, [25]and did not need anyone to testify about human nature. He himself understood it well.[s]

## CHAPTER 3

**Nicodemus.**[§] [1]Now there was a Pharisee named Nicodemus, a ruler of the Jews.[¶] [2]He came to Jesus at night and said to him, "Rabbi, we know that you are a teacher who has come from God, for no one can do these signs that you are doing unless God is with him."[u] [3]Jesus answered and said to him, "Amen, amen, I say to you, no one

can see the kingdom of God without being born** from above." [4]Nicodemus said to him, "How can a person once grown old be born again? Surely he cannot reenter his mother's womb and be born again, can he?"[v] [5]Jesus answered, "Amen, amen, I say to you, no one can enter the kingdom of God without being born of water and Spirit.[w] [6]What is born of flesh is flesh and what is born of spirit is spirit.[x] [7]Do not be amazed that I told you, 'You must be born from above.' [8]The wind[††] blows where it wills, and you can hear the sound it makes, but you do not know where it comes from or where it goes; so it is with everyone who is born of the Spirit.[y] [9]Nicodemus answered and said to him, "How can this happen?" [10]Jesus answered and said to him, "You are the teacher of Israel and you do not understand this? [11]Amen, amen, I say to you, we speak of what we know and we testify to what we have seen, but you people do not accept our testimony.[z] [12]If I tell you about earthly things and you do not believe, how will you believe if I tell you about heavenly things?[a] [13]No one has gone up to heaven except the one who has come down from heaven, the Son of Man.[b] [14]And just as Moses lifted up[‡‡] the serpent in the desert, so must the Son of Man be lifted up,[15§§] so that everyone who believes in him may have eternal life."

[16]For God so loved the world that he gave[¶¶] his only Son, so that everyone who believes in him might not perish but might have eternal life.[d] [17]For God did not send his Son into the world to condemn*** the world, but that the world might be saved through him.[e] [18]Whoever believes in him will not be condemned, but whoever does not believe has already been condemned, because he has not believed in the name of the only Son of God.[f] [19†††]And this is the verdict,[g] that the light came into the world,

---

\* [2:17] Ps 69:10, changed to future tense to apply to Jesus.

† [2:19] This saying about the destruction of the temple occurs in various forms (Mt 24:2; 27:40; Mk 13:2; 15:29; Lk 21:6; cf. Acts 6:14). Mt 26:61 has: "I can destroy the temple of God . . ."; see note there. In Mk 14:58, there is a metaphorical contrast with a new temple: "I will destroy this temple made with hands and within three days I will build another not made with hands." Here it is symbolic of Jesus' resurrection and the resulting community (see Jn 2:21 and Rev 21:2). In three days: an Old Testament expression for a short, indefinite period of time; cf. Hos 6:2.

‡ [2:20] Forty-six years: based on references in Josephus (Jewish Wars 1:401; Antiquities 15:380), possibly the spring of A.D. 28. Cf. note on Lk 3:1.

§ [3:1–21] Jesus instructs Nicodemus on the necessity of a new birth from above. This scene in Jerusalem at Passover exemplifies the faith engendered by signs (Jn 2:23). It continues the self-manifestation of Jesus in Jerusalem begun in Jn 2. This is the first of the Johannine discourses, shifting from dialogue to monologue (Jn 3:11–15) to reflection of the evangelist (Jn 3:16–21). The shift from singular through Jn 3:10 to plural in Jn 3:11 may reflect the early church's controversy with the Jews.

¶ [3:1] A ruler of the Jews: most likely a member of the Jewish council, the Sanhedrin; see note on Mk 8:31.

** [3:3] Born: see note on Jn 1:13. From above: the Greek adverb anōthen means both "from above" and "again." Jesus means "from above" (see Jn 3:31) but Nicodemus misunderstands it as "again." This misunderstanding serves as a springboard for further instruction.

†† [3:8] Wind: the Greek word pneuma (as well as the Hebrew rûah) means both "wind" and "spirit." In the play on the double meaning, "wind" is primary.

‡‡ [3:14] Lifted up: in Nm 21:9, Moses simply "mounted" a serpent upon a pole. John here substitutes a verb implying glorification. Jesus, exalted to glory at his cross and resurrection, represents healing for all.

§§ [3:15] Eternal life: used here for the first time in John, this term stresses quality of life rather than duration.

¶¶ [3:16] Gave: as a gift in the incarnation, and also "over to death" in the crucifixion; cf. Rom 8:32.

*** [3:17–19] Condemn: the Greek root means both judgment and condemnation. Jesus' purpose is to save, but his coming provokes judgment; some condemn themselves by turning from the light.

††† [3:19] Judgment is not only future but is partially realized here and now.

---

l. [2:14] Ex 30:11–16; Lv 5:7.　m. [2:16] Zec 14:21.　n. [2:17] Ps 69:9.　o. [2:18] 6:30.　p. [2:19] Mt 24:2; 26:61; 27:40; Mk 13:2; 14:58; 15:29; Lk 21:6; Acts 6:14.　q. [2:22] 5:39; 12:16; 14:26; 20:9; Mt 12:6; Lk 24:6–8; Rev 21:22.　r. [2:23] 4:45.　s. [2:25] 1 Kgs 8:39; Ps 33:15; 94:11; Sir 42:18; Jer 17:10; 20:12.　t. [3:1] 7:50–51; 19:39.　u. [3:2] 9:4, 16, 33; 10:21; 11:10; 13:30; Mt 22:16; Mk 12:14; Lk 20:21.

v. [3:4] 1:13.　w. [3:5] 1:32; 7:39; 19:30, 34–35; Is 32:15; 44:3; Ez 36:25–27; Jl 3:1–2.　x. [3:6] 6:63; 1 Cor 15:44–50.　y. [3:8] Eccl 11:4–5; Acts 2:2–4.　z. [3:11] 3:32, 34; 8:14; Mt 11:27.　a. [3:12] 6:62–65; Wis 9:16–17; 1 Cor 15:40; 2 Cor 5:1; Phil 2:10; 3:19–20.　b. [3:13] 1:18; 6:62; Dn 7:13; Rom 10:6; Eph 4:9.　c. [3:14] 8:28; 12:32, 34; Nm 21:4–9; Wis 16:5–7.　d. [3:16] 1 Jn 4:9.　e. [3:17] 5:22, 30; 8:15–18; 12:47.　f. [3:18] 5:24; Mk 16:16.　g. [3:19] 1:5, 9–11; 8:12; 9:5.

but people preferred darkness to light, because their works were evil. [20]For everyone who does wicked things hates the light and does not come toward the light, so that his works might not be exposed.[h] [21]But whoever lives the truth comes to the light, so that his works may be clearly seen as done in God.[i]

**Final Witness of the Baptist.** [22]*After this, Jesus and his disciples went into the region of Judea, where he spent some time with them baptizing.[j] [23]John was also baptizing in Aenon near Salim,[†] because there was an abundance of water there, and people came to be baptized,. [24]‡*[k]for John had not yet been imprisoned. [25]Now a dispute arose between the disciples of John and a Jew[§] about ceremonial washings. [26]So they came to John and said to him, "Rabbi, the one who was with you across the Jordan, to whom you testified, here he is baptizing and everyone is coming to him."[l] [27]John answered and said, "No one can receive anything except what has been given him from heaven.[m] [28]You yourselves can testify that I said [that] I am not the Messiah, but that I was sent before him.[n] [29]The one who has the bride is the bridegroom; the best man,[¶] who stands and listens to him, rejoices greatly at the bridegroom's voice. So this joy of mine has been made complete.[o] [30]He must increase; I must decrease."[p]

**The One from Heaven.**** [31]The one who comes from above is above all. The one who is of the earth is earthly and speaks of earthly things. But the one who comes from heaven [is above all].[q] [32]He testifies to what he has seen and heard, but no one accepts his testimony.[r] [33]Whoever does accept his testimony certifies that God is trustworthy.[s] [34]For the one whom God sent speaks the words of God. He does not ration his gift[††] of the Spirit. [35]The Father loves the Son and

has given everything over to him.[t] [36]Whoever believes in the Son has eternal life, but whoever disobeys the Son will not see life, but the wrath of God remains upon him.[u]

## CHAPTER 4

[1]‡‡Now when Jesus learned that the Pharisees had heard that Jesus was making and baptizing more disciples than John [2](although Jesus himself was not baptizing, just his disciples),[§§] [3]he left Judea and returned to Galilee.

**The Samaritan Woman.** [4]He had to[¶¶] pass through Samaria. [5]So he came to a town of Samaria called Sychar,*** near the plot of land that Jacob had given to his son Joseph.[v] [6]Jacob's well was there. Jesus, tired from his journey, sat down there at the well. It was about noon.

[7]A woman of Samaria came to draw water. Jesus said to her, "Give me a drink." [8]His disciples had gone into the town to buy food. [9]†††The Samaritan woman said to him, "How can you, a Jew, ask me, a Samaritan woman, for a drink?"[w] (For Jews use nothing in common with Samaritans.) [10]‡‡‡Jesus answered and said to her,[x] "If you knew the gift of God and who is saying to you, 'Give me a drink,' you would have asked him and he would have given you living water." [11][The woman] said to him, "Sir,[§§§] you do not even have a bucket and the well is deep; where then can you get this living water? [12]Are you greater than our father Jacob, who gave us this well and drank from it himself with his children and his flocks?"[y] [13]Jesus answered and said to her, "Everyone who drinks this water will be thirsty again; [14]but whoever drinks the water I shall give will never thirst; the water I shall give will become in him a spring of water welling up to eternal life."[z] [15]The woman said to him, "Sir,

---

*[3:22–26] Jesus' ministry in Judea is only loosely connected with Jn 2:13–3:21; cf. Jn 1:19–36. Perhaps John the Baptist's further testimony was transposed here to give meaning to "water" in Jn 3:5. Jesus is depicted as baptizing (Jn 3:22); contrast Jn 4:2.

†[3:23] **Aenon near Salim**: site uncertain, either in the upper Jordan valley or in Samaria.

‡[3:24] A remark probably intended to avoid objections based on a chronology like that of the synoptics (Mt 4:12; Mk 1:14).

§[3:25] **A Jew**: some think Jesus is meant. Many manuscripts read "Jews."

¶[3:29] **The best man**: literally, "the friend of the groom," the *shoshben* of Jewish tradition, who arranged the wedding. Competition between him and the groom would be unthinkable.

**[3:31–36] It is uncertain whether these are words by the Baptist, Jesus, or the evangelist. They are reflections on the two preceding scenes.

††[3:34] **His gift**: of God or to Jesus, perhaps both. This verse echoes Jn 3:5, 8.

‡‡[4:1–42] Jesus in Samaria. The self-revelation of Jesus continues with his second discourse, on his mission to "half-Jews." It continues the theme of replacement, here with regard to cult (Jn 4:21). Water (Jn 4:7–15) serves as a symbol (as at Cana and in the Nicodemus episode).

§§[4:2] An editorial refinement of Jn 3:22, perhaps directed against followers of John the Baptist who claimed that Jesus imitated him.

¶¶[4:4] **He had to**: a theological necessity; geographically, Jews often bypassed Samaria by taking a route across the Jordan.

***[4:5] **Sychar**: Jerome identifies this with Shechem, a reading found in Syriac manuscripts.

†††[4:9] Samaritan women were regarded by Jews as ritually impure, and therefore Jews were forbidden to drink from any vessel they had handled.

‡‡‡[4:10] **Living water**: the water of life, i.e., the revelation that Jesus brings; the woman thinks of "flowing water," so much more desirable than stagnant well water. On John's device of such misunderstanding, cf. note on Jn 3:3.

§§§[4:11] **Sir**: the Greek *kyrios* means "master" or "lord," as a respectful mode of address for a human being or a deity; cf. Jn 4:19. It is also the word used in the Septuagint for the Hebrew *'adonai*, substituted for the tetragrammaton YHWH.

---

h. [3:20] Jb 24:13–17.  i. [3:21] Gn 47:29 LXX; Jos 2:14 LXX; 2 Sm 2:6 LXX; 15:20 LXX; Tb 4:6 LXX; 13:6; Is 26:10 LXX; Mt 5:14–16.  j. [3:22–23] 4:1–2.  k. [3:24] Mt 4:12; 14:3; Mk 1:14; 6:17; Lk 3:20.  l. [3:26] 1:26, 32–34, 36.  m. [3:27] 19:11; 1 Cor 4:7; 2 Cor 3:5; Heb 5:4.  n. [3:28] 1:20–23; Lk 3:15.  o. [3:29] 15:11; 17:13; Mt 9:15.  p. [3:30] 2 Sm 3:1.  q. [3:31] 8:23.  r. [3:32] 3:11.  s. [3:33–34] 8:26; 12:44–50; 1 Jn 5:10.

t. [3:35] 13:3; Mt 11:27; 28:18; Lk 10:22.  u. [3:36] 3:16; 1 Jn 5:13.  v. [4:5] Gn 33:18–19; 48:22; Jos 24:32.  w. [4:9] Sir 50:25–26; Mt 10:5.  x. [4:10] Sir 24:20–21; Is 55:1; Jer 2:13.  y. [4:12] 8:53; Mt 12:41.  z. [4:14] 6:35, 58; 7:37–39; Is 44:3; 49:10; Jl 4:18; Rev 7:16; 21:6.

give me this water, so that I may not be thirsty or have to keep coming here to draw water." <sup>16</sup>Jesus said to her, "Go call your husband and come back." <sup>17</sup>The woman answered and said to him, "I do not have a husband." Jesus answered her, "You are right in saying, 'I do not have a husband.' <sup>18</sup>For you have had five husbands, and the one you have now is not your husband. What you have said is true."<sup>a</sup> <sup>19</sup>The woman said to him, "Sir, I can see that you are a prophet.<sup>b</sup> <sup>20</sup>Our ancestors worshiped on this mountain;* but you people say that the place to worship is in Jerusalem."<sup>c</sup> <sup>21</sup>Jesus said to her, "Believe me, woman, the hour is coming when you will worship the Father neither on this mountain nor in Jerusalem. <sup>22</sup>You people worship what you do not understand; we worship what we understand, because salvation is from the Jews.<sup>d</sup> <sup>23</sup>But the hour is coming, and is now here, when true worshipers will worship the Father in Spirit and truth;<sup>†</sup> and indeed the Father seeks such people to worship him. <sup>24</sup>God is Spirit, and those who worship him must worship in Spirit and truth."<sup>e</sup> <sup>25*</sup>The woman said to him, "I know that the Messiah is coming,<sup>f</sup> the one called the Anointed; when he comes, he will tell us everything." <sup>26</sup>Jesus said to her, "I am he,<sup>§</sup> the one who is speaking with you."<sup>g</sup>

<sup>27</sup>At that moment his disciples returned, and were amazed that he was talking with a woman,<sup>¶</sup> but still no one said, "What are you looking for?" or "Why are you talking with her?" <sup>28</sup>The woman left her water jar and went into the town and said to the people, <sup>29</sup>"Come see a man who told me everything I have done. Could he possibly be the Messiah?" <sup>30</sup>They went out of the town and came to him. <sup>31</sup>Meanwhile, the disciples urged him, "Rabbi, eat." <sup>32</sup>But he said to them, "I have food to eat of which you do not know." <sup>33</sup>So the disciples said to one another, "Could someone have brought him something to eat?" <sup>34</sup>Jesus said to them, "My food is to do the will of the one who sent me and to finish his work.<sup>h</sup> <sup>35</sup>Do you not say, 'In four months"

the harvest will be here'? I tell you, look up and see the fields ripe for the harvest.<sup>i</sup> <sup>36</sup>The reaper is already<sup>††</sup> receiving his payment and gathering crops for eternal life, so that the sower and reaper can rejoice together.<sup>j</sup> <sup>37</sup>For here the saying is verified that 'One sows and another reaps.'<sup>k</sup> <sup>38</sup>I sent you to reap what you have not worked for; others have done the work, and you are sharing the fruits of their work."

<sup>39</sup>Many of the Samaritans of that town began to believe in him because of the word of the woman<sup>‡‡</sup> who testified, "He told me everything I have done." <sup>40</sup>When the Samaritans came to him, they invited him to stay with them; and he stayed there two days. <sup>41</sup>Many more began to believe in him because of his word, <sup>42</sup>and they said to the woman, "We no longer believe because of your word; for we have heard for ourselves, and we know that this is truly the savior of the world."<sup>l</sup>

**Return to Galilee.** <sup>43§§</sup>After the two days, he left there for Galilee. <sup>44¶¶</sup>For Jesus himself testified that a prophet has no honor in his native place. <sup>45</sup>When he came into Galilee, the Galileans welcomed him, since they had seen all he had done in Jerusalem at the feast; for they themselves had gone to the feast.

**Second Sign at Cana.** *** <sup>46n</sup>Then he returned to Cana in Galilee, where he had made the water wine. Now there was a royal official whose son was ill in Capernaum. <sup>47</sup>When he heard that Jesus had arrived in Galilee from Judea, he went to him and asked him to come down and heal his son, who was near death. <sup>48</sup>Jesus said to him, "Unless you people see signs and wonders, you will not believe."<sup>o</sup> <sup>49</sup>The royal official said to him, "Sir, come down before my child dies." <sup>50</sup>Jesus said to him, "You may go; your son will live." The man believed what Jesus said to him and left.<sup>p</sup> <sup>51</sup>While he was on his way back, his slaves met him and told him that his boy would live. <sup>52</sup>He asked them when he began to recover. They told him, "The fever left him yesterday, about one in the afternoon." <sup>53</sup>The father realized that just at

---

*[4:20] **This mountain:** Gerizim, on which a temple was erected in the fourth century B.C. by Samaritans to rival Mount Zion in Jerusalem; cf. Dt 27:4 (Mount Ebal = the Jews' term for Gerizim).

†[4:23] **In Spirit and truth:** not a reference to an interior worship within one's own spirit. The Spirit is the spirit given by God that reveals truth and enables one to worship God appropriately (Jn 14:16–17). Cf. "born of water and Spirit" (Jn 3:5).

‡[4:25] The expectations of the Samaritans are expressed here in Jewish terminology. They did not expect a messianic king of the house of David but a prophet like Moses (Dt 18:15).

§[4:26] **I am he:** it could also be translated "I am," an Old Testament self-designation of Yahweh (Is 43:3, etc.); cf. Jn 6:20; 8:24, 28, 58; 13:19; 18:5–6, 8. See note on Mk 6:50.

¶[4:27] **Talking with a woman:** a religious and social restriction that Jesus is pictured treating as unimportant.

**[4:35] **'In four months . . .':** probably a proverb; cf. Mt 9:37–38.

††[4:36] **Already:** this word may go with the preceding verse rather than with Jn 4:36.

‡‡[4:39] The woman is presented as a missionary, described in virtually the same words as the disciples are in Jesus' prayer (Jn 17:20).

§§[4:43–54] Jesus' arrival in Cana in Galilee; the second sign. This section introduces another theme, that of the life-giving word of Jesus. It is explicitly linked to the first sign (Jn 2:11). The royal official believes (Jn 4:50). The natural life given his son is a sign of eternal life.

¶¶[4:44] Probably a reminiscence of a tradition as in Mk 6:4. Cf. Gospel of Thomas 31: "No prophet is acceptable in his village, no physician heals those who know him."

***[4:46–54] The story of the cure of the royal official's son may be a third version of the cure of the centurion's son (Mt 8:5–13) or servant (Lk 7:1–10). Cf. also Mt 15:21–28; Mk 7:24–30.

---

a. [4:18] 2 Kgs 17:24–34.  b. [4:19] 9:17; Hos 1:3.  c. [4:20] Dt 11:29; 27:4; Jos 8:33; Ps 122:1–5.  d. [4:22] 2 Kgs 17:27; Ps 76:2–3.  e. [4:24] 2 Cor 3:17.  f. [4:25] 1:41.  g. [4:26] 9:37.  h. [4:34] 5:30, 36; 6:38; 9:4; 17:4.

i. [4:35] Mt 9:37–38; Lk 10:2; Rev 14:15.  j. [4:36] Ps 126:5–6; Am 9:13–14.  k. [4:37] Dt 20:6; 28:30; Jb 31:8; Mi 6:15.  l. [4:42] 1 Jn 4:14.  m. [4:44] Mt 13:57; Mk 6:4; Lk 4:24.  n. [4:46–54] 2:1–11; Mt 8:5–13; 15:21–28; Mk 7:24–30; Lk 7:1–10.  o. [4:48] 2:18, 23; Wis 8:8; Mt 12:38; 1 Cor 1:22.  p. [4:50] 1 Kgs 17:23.

that time Jesus had said to him, "Your son will live," and he and his whole household came to believe. [54][Now] this was the second sign Jesus did when he came to Galilee from Judea.[q]

## CHAPTER 5*

**Cure on a Sabbath.** [1]After this, there was a feast[†] of the Jews, and Jesus went up to Jerusalem.[r] [2]Now there is in Jerusalem at the Sheep [Gate][‡] a pool called in Hebrew Bethesda, with five porticoes.[s] [3]In these lay a large number of ill, blind, lame, and crippled.[§] [4][¶] [5]One man was there who had been ill for thirty-eight years. [6]When Jesus saw him lying there and knew that he had been ill for a long time, he said to him, "Do you want to be well?" [7]The sick man answered him, "Sir, I have no one to put me into the pool when the water is stirred up; while I am on my way, someone else gets down there before me." [8]Jesus said to him, "Rise, take up your mat, and walk."[t] [9]Immediately the man became well, took up his mat, and walked.[u]

Now that day was a sabbath. [10]So the Jews said to the man who was cured, "It is the sabbath, and it is not lawful for you to carry your mat."[v] [11]He answered them, "The man who made me well told me, 'Take up your mat and walk.'" [12]They asked him, "Who is the man who told you, 'Take it up and walk'?" [13]The man who was healed did not know who it was, for Jesus had slipped away, since there was a crowd there.[w]

[14]After this Jesus found him in the temple area and said to him,[x] "Look, you are well; do not sin any more, so that nothing worse may happen to you." [15]The man went and told the Jews that Jesus was the one who had made him well. [16]Therefore, the Jews began to persecute Jesus because he did this on a sabbath.[y] [17†]But Jesus answered them,[z] "My Father is at work until now, so I am at work." [18]For this reason the Jews tried all the more to kill him, because he not only broke the sabbath but he also called God his own father, making himself equal to God.[a]

**The Work of the Son.** [19‡]Jesus answered and said to them, "Amen, amen, I say to you, a son cannot do anything on his own, but only what he sees his father doing;[b] for what he does, his son will do also. [20]For the Father loves his Son and shows him everything that he himself does, and he will show him greater works than these, so that you may be amazed.[c] [21]For just as the Father raises the dead and gives life,[§§] so also does the Son give life to whomever he wishes.[d] [22]Nor does the Father judge anyone, but he has given all judgment[¶¶] to his Son,[e] [23]so that all may honor the Son just as they honor the Father. Whoever does not honor the Son does not honor the Father who sent him. [24]Amen, amen, I say to you, whoever hears my word and believes in the one who sent me has eternal life and will not come to condemnation, but has passed from death to life.[f] [25]Amen, amen, I say to you, the hour is coming and is now here when the dead will hear the voice of the Son of God, and those who hear will live.[g] [26]For just as the Father has life in himself, so also he gave to his Son the possession of life in himself.[h] [27]And he gave him power to exercise judgment, because he is the Son of Man.[i]

---

*[5:1–47] The self-revelation of Jesus continues in Jerusalem at a feast (cf. Jn 2:11; 4:54) is performed, the cure of a paralytic by Jesus' life-giving word. The water of the pool fails to bring life; Jesus' word does.

†[5:1] The reference in Jn 5:45–46 to Moses suggests that the feast was Pentecost. The connection of that feast with the giving of the law to Moses on Sinai, attested in later Judaism, may already have been made in the first century. The feast could also be Passover (cf. Jn 6:4). John stresses that the day was a sabbath (Jn 5:9).

‡[5:2] There is no noun with **Sheep**. "Gate" is supplied on the grounds that there must have been a gate in the NE wall of the temple area where animals for sacrifice were brought in; cf. Neh 3:1, 32; 12:39. **Hebrew**: more precisely, Aramaic. **Bethesda**: preferred to variants "Be(th)zatha" and "Bethsaida"; *bêt-'ešdatayin* is given as the name of a double pool northeast of the temple area in the Qumran Copper Roll. **Five porticoes**: a pool excavated in Jerusalem actually has five porticoes.

§[5:3] The Caesarean and Western recensions, followed by the Vulgate, add "waiting for the movement of the water." Apparently an intermittent spring in the pool bubbled up occasionally (see Jn 5:7). This turbulence was believed to cure.

¶[5:4] Toward the end of the second century in the West and among the fourth-century Greek Fathers, an additional verse was known: "For [from time to time] an angel of the Lord used to come down into the pool; and the water was stirred up, so the first one to get in [after the stirring of the water] was healed of whatever disease afflicted him." The angel was a popular explanation of the turbulence and the healing powers attributed to it. This verse is missing from all early Greek manuscripts and the earliest versions, including the original Vulgate. Its vocabulary is markedly non-Johannine.

**[5:14] While the cure of the paralytic in Mk 2:1–12 is associated with the forgiveness of sins, Jesus never drew a one-to-one connection between sin and suffering (cf. Jn 9:3; Lk 12:1–5), as did Ez 18:20.

††[5:17] Sabbath observance (Jn 5:10) was based on God's resting on the seventh day (cf. Gn 2:2–3; Ex 20:11). Philo and some rabbis insisted that God's providence remains active on the sabbath, keeping all things in existence, giving life in birth and taking it away in death. Other rabbis taught that God rested from creating, but not from judging (= ruling, governing). Jesus here claims the same authority to work as the Father, and, in the discourse that follows, the same divine prerogatives: power over life and death (Jn 5:21, 24–26) and judgment (Jn 5:22, 27).

‡‡[5:19] This proverb or parable is taken from apprenticeship in a trade: the activity of a son is modeled on that of his father. Jesus' dependence on the Father is justification for doing what the Father does.

§§[5:21] **Gives life**: in the Old Testament, a divine prerogative (Dt 32:39; 1 Sm 2:6; 2 Kgs 5:7; Tb 13:2; Is 26:19; Dn 12:2).

¶¶[5:22] **Judgment**: another divine prerogative, often expressed as acquittal or condemnation (Dt 32:36; Ps 43:1).

q. [4:54] 2:11.   r. [5:1] 6:4.   s. [5:2] Neh 3:1, 32; 12:39.   t. [5:8] Mt 9:6; Mk 2:11; Lk 5:24; Acts 3:6.   u. [5:9] Mk 2:12; Lk 5:25; 9:14.   v. [5:10] Ex 20:8; Jer 17:21–27; Mk 3:2; Lk 13:10 / 14:1.   w. [5:13] Mt 8:18; 13:36; Mk 4:36; 7:17.

x. [5:14] 8:11; 9:2; Ez 18:20.   y. [5:16] 7:23; Mt 12:8.   z. [5:17] Ex 20:11.   a. [5:18] 7:1, 25; 8:37, 40; 10:33, 36; 14:28; Gn 3:5–6; Wis 2:16; Mt 26:4; 2 Thes 2:4.   b. [5:19] 3:34; 8:26; 12:49; 9:4; 10:30.   c. [5:20] 3:35.   d. [5:21] 11:25; Dt 32:39; 1 Sm 2:6; 2 Kgs 5:7; Tb 13:2; Wis 16:13; Is 26:19; Dn 7:10, 13; 12:2; Rom 4:17; 2 Cor 1:9.   e. [5:22] Acts 10:42; 17:31.   f. [5:24] 3:18; 8:51; 1 Jn 3:14.   g. [5:25] 5:28; 8:51; 11:25–26; Eph 2:1; 5:14; Rev 3:1.   h. [5:26] 1:4; 1 Jn 5:11.   i. [5:27] 5:22; Dn 7:13, 22; Mt 25:31; Lk 21:36.

²⁸*Do not be amazed at this, because the hour is coming in which all who are in the tombs will hear his voiceʲ ²⁹and will come out, those who have done good deeds to the resurrection of life, but those who have done wicked deeds to the resurrection of condemnation.ᵏ

³⁰"I cannot do anything on my own; I judge as I hear, and my judgment is just, because I do not seek my own will but the will of the one who sent me.ˡ

**Witnesses to Jesus.** ³¹ᵐ"If I testify on my own behalf, my testimony cannot be verified. ³²But there is anotherᵗ who testifies on my behalf, and I know that the testimony he gives on my behalf is true. ³³You sent emissaries to John, and he testified to the truth.ⁿ ³⁴I do not accept testimony from a human being, but I say this so that you may be saved.ᵒ ³⁵He was a burning and shining lamp,ᵗ and for a while you were content to rejoice in his light.ᵖ ³⁶But I have testimony greater than John's. The works that the Father gave me to accomplish, these works that I perform testify on my behalf that the Father has sent me.�q ³⁷Moreover, the Father who sent me has testified on my behalf. But you have never heard his voice nor seen his form,ʳ ³⁸and you do not have his word remaining in you, because you do not believe in the one whom he has sent.ˢ ³⁹You searchˢ the scriptures, because you think you have eternal life through them; even they testify on my behalf.ᵗ ⁴⁰But you do not want to come to me to have life.

**Unbelief of Jesus' Hearers.** ⁴¹"I do not accept human praise;⁵ ⁴²moreover, I know that you do not have the love of God in you.ᵘ ⁴³I came in the name of my Father, but you do not accept me; yet if another comes in his own name, you will accept him.ᵛ ⁴⁴How can you believe, when you accept praise from one another and do not seek the praise that comes from the only God?ʷ ⁴⁵Do not think that I will accuse you before the Father: the one who will accuse you is Moses, in whom you have placed your hope.ˣ ⁴⁶For if you had believed Moses, you would have believed

me, because he wrote about me.ʸ ⁴⁷But if you do not believe his writings, how will you believe my words?"

## CHAPTER 6

**Multiplication of the Loaves.**** ¹ᶻAfter this, Jesus went across the Sea of Galilee [of Tiberias].†† ²A large crowd followed him, because they saw the signs he was performing on the sick. ³Jesus went up on the mountain, and there he sat down with his disciples. ⁴The Jewish feast of Passover was near.ᵃ ⁵‡‡When Jesus raised his eyes and saw that a large crowd was coming to him, he said to Philip,ᵇ "Where can we buy enough food for them to eat?" ⁶§§He said this to test him, because he himself knew what he was going to do. ⁷Philip answered him, "Two hundred days' wages¶¶ worth of food would not be enough for each of them to have a little [bit]."ᶜ ⁸One of his disciples, Andrew, the brother of Simon Peter, said to him, ⁹"There is a boy here who has five barley loaves*** and two fish; but what good are these for so many?"ᵈ ¹⁰Jesus said, "Have the people recline." Now there was a great deal of grass††† in that place. So the men reclined, about five thousand in number.ᵉ ¹¹Then Jesus took the loaves, gave thanks, and distributed them to those who were reclining, and also as much of the fish as they wanted.ᶠ ¹²When they had had their fill, he said to his disciples, "Gather the fragments left over, so that nothing will be wasted." ¹³So they collected them, and filled twelve wicker baskets‡‡‡ with fragments from the five barley loaves that had been more than they could eat. ¹⁴When the people saw the sign he had done, they said, "This is truly the Prophet,§§§

---

*[5:28–29] While Jn 5:19–27 present realized eschatology, Jn 5:28–29 are future eschatology; cf. Dn 12:2.

†[5:32] **Another:** likely the Father, who in four different ways gives testimony to Jesus, as indicated in the verse groupings Jn 5:33–34, 36, 37–38, 39–40.

‡[5:35] **Lamp:** cf. Ps 132:17—"I will place a lamp for my anointed (= David)," and possibly the description of Elijah in Sir 48:1. But only **for a while,** indicating the temporary and subordinate nature of John's mission.

§[5:39] **You search:** this may be an imperative: "Search the scriptures, because you think that you have eternal life through them."

¶[5:41] **Praise:** the same Greek word means "praise" or "honor" (from others) and "glory" (from God). There is a play on this in Jn 5:44.

**[6:1–15] This story of the multiplication of the loaves is the fourth sign (cf. note on Jn 5:1–47). It is the only miracle story found in all four gospels (occurring twice in Mark and Matthew). See notes on Mt 14:13–21; 15:32–39. John differs on the roles of Philip and Andrew, the proximity of Passover (Jn 6:4), and the allusion to Elisha (see Jn 6:9). The story here symbolizes the food that is readily available through Jesus. It connotes a new exodus and has eucharistic overtones.

††[6:1] **[Of Tiberias]:** the awkward apposition represents a later name of the Sea of Galilee. It was probably originally a marginal gloss.

‡‡[6:5] Jesus takes the initiative (in the synoptics, the disciples do), possibly pictured as (cf. Jn 6:14) the new Moses (cf. Nm 11:13).

§§[6:6] Probably the evangelist's comment; in this gospel Jesus is never portrayed as ignorant of anything.

¶¶[6:7] **Days' wages:** literally, "denarii"; a Roman denarius is a day's wage in Mt 20:2.

***[6:9] **Barley loaves:** the food of the poor. There seems an allusion to the story of Elisha multiplying the barley bread in 2 Kgs 4:42–44.

†††[6:10] **Grass:** implies springtime, and therefore Passover. **Five thousand:** so Mk 6:39, 44 and parallels.

‡‡‡[6:13] **Baskets:** the word describes the typically Palestinian wicker basket, as in Mk 6:43 and parallels.

§§§[6:14] **The Prophet:** probably the prophet like Moses (see note on Jn 1:21). **The one who is to come into the world:** probably Elijah; cf. Mal 3:1, 23.

---

j. [5:28] 11:43.  k. [5:29] Dn 12:2; Mt 16:27; 25:46; Acts 24:15; 2 Cor 5:10.  l. [5:30] 6:38.  m. [5:31–32] 8:13–14, 18.  n. [5:33] 1:19–27; Mt 11:10–11.  o. [5:34] 1 Jn 5:9.  p. [5:35] 1:8; Ps 132:17; Sir 48:1.  q. [5:36] 10:25.  r. [5:37] 8:18; Dt 4:12, 15; 1 Jn 5:9.  s. [5:38] 1 Jn 2:14.  t. [5:39] 12:16; 19:28; 20:9; Lk 24:27, 44; 1 Pt 1:10.  u. [5:42] 1 Jn 2:15.  v. [5:43] Mt 24:5, 24.  w. [5:44] 12:43.  x. [5:45] Dt 31:26.

y. [5:46] 5:39; Dt 18:15; Lk 16:31; 24:44.  z. [6:1–13] Mt 14:13–21; Mk 6:32–44; Lk 9:10–17.  a. [6:4] 2:13; 11:55.  b. [6:5] Nm 11:13.  c. [6:7] Mt 20:2.  d. [6:9] 2 Kgs 4:42–44.  e. [6:10] Mt 14:21; Mk 6:44.  f. [6:11] 21:13.

the one who is to come into the world."[g] [15]Since Jesus knew that they were going to come and carry him off to make him king, he withdrew again to the mountain alone.[h]

**Walking on the Water.*** [16t]When it was evening, his disciples went down to the sea, [17]embarked in a boat, and went across the sea to Capernaum. It had already grown dark, and Jesus had not yet come to them. [18]The sea was stirred up because a strong wind was blowing. [19]When they had rowed about three or four miles, they saw Jesus walking on the sea[†] and coming near the boat, and they began to be afraid.[j] [20]But he said to them, "It is I.[‡] Do not be afraid." [21]They wanted to take him into the boat, but the boat immediately arrived at the shore to which they were heading.

**The Bread of Life Discourse.** [22§]The next day, the crowd that remained across the sea saw that there had been only one boat there, and that Jesus had not gone along with his disciples in the boat, but only his disciples had left. [23¶]Other boats came from Tiberias near the place where they had eaten the bread when the Lord gave thanks. [24]When the crowd saw that neither Jesus nor his disciples were there, they themselves got into boats and came to Capernaum looking for Jesus. [25]And when they found him across the sea they said to him, "Rabbi, when did you get here?" [26]Jesus answered them and said, "Amen, amen, I say to you, you are looking for me not because you saw signs but because you ate the loaves and were filled. [27]Do not work for food that perishes but for the food that endures for eternal life,** which the Son of Man will give you. For on him the Father, God, has set his seal."[k] [28]So they said to him, "What can we do to accomplish the works of God?" [29]Jesus answered and said to them, "This is the work of God, that you believe in the one he sent." [30]So they said to him, "What sign can you do, that we may see and believe in you? What can you do?[l] [31††]Our ancestors ate manna in the desert, as it is written:[m]

'He gave them bread from heaven to eat.'"

[32]So Jesus said to them, "Amen, amen, I say to you, it was not Moses who gave the bread from heaven; my Father gives you the true bread from heaven.[n] [33]For the bread of God is that which comes down from heaven and gives life to the world." [34]So they said to him, "Sir, give us this bread always." [35‡‡]Jesus said to them, "I am the bread of life; whoever comes to me will never hunger, and whoever believes in me will never thirst.[p] [36]But I told you that although you have seen [me], you do not believe.[q] [37]Everything that the Father gives me will come to me, and I will not reject anyone who comes to me, [38]because I came down from heaven not to do my own will but the will of the one who sent me.[r] [39]And this is the will of the one who sent me, that I should not lose anything of what he gave me, but that I should raise it [on] the last day.[s] [40]For this is the will of my Father, that everyone who sees the Son and believes in him may have eternal life, and I shall raise him [on] the last day."[t]

[41]The Jews murmured about him because he said, "I am the bread that came down from heaven," [42]and they said, "Is this not Jesus, the son of Joseph? Do we not know his father and mother? Then how can he say, 'I have come down from heaven'?"[u] [43]Jesus answered and said to them, "Stop murmuring[§§] among yourselves.[v] [44]No one can come to me unless the Father who sent me draw him, and I will raise him on the last day. [45]It is written in the prophets:

'They shall all be taught by God.'

Everyone who listens to my Father and learns from him comes to me.[w] [46]Not that anyone has seen the Father except the one who is from God; he has seen the Father.[x] [47]Amen, amen, I say to you, whoever believes has eternal life. [48]I am the bread of life. [49]Your ancestors ate the manna in the desert, but they died;[y] [50]this is the bread that comes down from heaven so that one may eat it and not die. [51]I am the living bread that came down from heaven; whoever eats this bread will live forever; and the bread that I will give is my flesh for the life of the world."[z]

[52]The Jews quarreled among themselves, saying, "How can this man give us [his] flesh

*[6:16–21] The fifth sign is a nature miracle, portraying Jesus sharing Yahweh's power. Cf. the parallel stories following the multiplication of the loaves in Mk 6:45–52 and Mt 14:22–33.

†[6:19] **Walking on the sea:** although the Greek (cf. Jn 6:16) could mean "on the seashore" or "by the sea" (cf. Jn 21:1), the parallels, especially Mt 14:25, make clear that Jesus walked upon the water. John may allude to Jb 9:8: God "treads upon the crests of the sea."

‡[6:20] **It is I:** literally, "I am." See also notes on Jn 4:26 and Mk 6:50.

§[6:22–71] Discourse on the bread of life; replacement of the manna. Jn 6:22–34 serve as an introduction, Jn 6:35–59 constitute the discourse proper, Jn 6:60–71 portray the reaction of the disciples and Peter's confession.

¶[6:23] Possibly a later interpolation, to explain how the crowd got to Capernaum.

**[6:27] **The food that endures for eternal life:** cf. Jn 4:14, on water "springing up to eternal life."

††[6:31] **Bread from heaven:** cf. Ex 16:4, 15, 32–34 and the notes there; Ps 78:24. The manna, thought to have been

hidden by Jeremiah (2 Mc 2:5–8), was expected to reappear miraculously at Passover, in the last days.

‡‡[6:35–59] Up to Jn 6:50 "bread of life" is a figure for God's revelation in Jesus; in Jn 6:51–58, the eucharistic theme comes to the fore. There may thus be a break between Jn 6:50–51.

§§[6:43] **Murmuring:** the word may reflect the Greek of Ex 16:2, 7–8.

n. [6:32] Mt 6:11.  o. [6:34] 4:15.  p. [6:35] Is 55:1–3; Am 8:11–13.  q. [6:36] 20:29.  r. [6:38] 4:34; Mt 26:39; Heb 10:9.  s. [6:39] 10:28–29; 17:12; 18:9.  t. [6:40] 1 Jn 2:25.  u. [6:42] Mt 13:54–57; Mk 6:1–4; Lk 4:22.  v. [6:43] Ex 16:2, 7, 8; Lk 4:22.  w. [6:45] Is 54:13; Jer 31:33–34.  x. [6:46] 1:18; 7:29; Ex 33:20.  y. [6:49] 1 Cor 10:3, 5.  z. [6:51] Mt 26:26–27; Lk 22:19.

g. [6:14] Dt 18:15, 18; Mal 3:1, 23; Acts 3:22.  h. [6:15] 18:36.  i. [6:16–21] Mt 14:22–27; Mk 6:45–52.  j. [6:19] Jb 9:8; Ps 29:3–4; 77:20; Is 43:16.  k. [6:27] 6:50, 51, 54, 58.  l. [6:30] Mt 16:1–4; Lk 11:29–30.  m. [6:31] Ex 16:4–5; Nm 11:7–9; Ps 78:24.

to eat?" ⁵³Jesus said to them, "Amen, amen, I say to you, unless you eat the flesh of the Son of Man and drink his blood, you do not have life within you. ⁵⁴Whoever eats* my flesh and drinks my blood has eternal life, and I will raise him on the last day. ⁵⁵For my flesh is true food, and my blood is true drink. ⁵⁶Whoever eats my flesh and drinks my blood remains in me and I in him. ⁵⁷Just as the living Father sent me and I have life because of the Father, so also the one who feeds on me will have life because of me.ᵃ ⁵⁸This is the bread that came down from heaven. Unlike your ancestors who ate and still died, whoever eats this bread will live forever." ⁵⁹These things he said while teaching in the synagogue in Capernaum.

**The Words of Eternal Life.**† ⁶⁰Then many of his disciples who were listening said, "This saying is hard; who can accept it?" ⁶¹Since Jesus knew that his disciples were murmuring about this, he said to them, "Does this shock you? ⁶²What if you were to see the Son of Man ascending to where he was before?‡ ⁶³It is the spirit that gives life, while the flesh§ is of no avail. The words I have spoken to you are spirit and life. ⁶⁴But there are some of you who do not believe." Jesus knew from the beginning the ones who would not believe and the one who would betray him.ᵇ ⁶⁵And he said, "For this reason I have told you that no one can come to me unless it is granted him by my Father."

⁶⁶As a result of this, many [of] his disciples returned to their former way of life and no longer accompanied him. ⁶⁷Jesus then said to the Twelve, "Do you also want to leave?" ⁶⁸Simon Peter answered him, "Master, to whom shall we go? You have the words of eternal life. ⁶⁹We have come to believe and are convinced that you are the Holy One of God."ᶜ ⁷⁰Jesus answered them, "Did I not choose you twelve? Yet is not one of you a devil?" ⁷¹He was referring to Judas, son of Simon the Iscariot; it was he who would betray him, one of the Twelve.ᵈ

---

*[6:54–58] **Eats:** the verb used in these verses is not the classical Greek verb used of human eating, but that of animal eating: "munch," "gnaw." This may be part of John's emphasis on the reality of the flesh and blood of Jesus (cf. Jn 6:55), but the same verb eventually became the ordinary verb in Greek meaning "eat."

†[6:60–71] These verses refer more to themes of Jn 6:35–50 than to those of Jn 6:51–58 and seem to be addressed to members of the Johannine community who found it difficult to accept the high christology reflected in the bread of life discourse.

‡[6:62] This unfinished conditional sentence is obscure. Probably there is a reference to Jn 6:49–51. Jesus claims to be **the bread that comes down from heaven** (Jn 6:50); this claim provokes incredulity (Jn 6:60); and so Jesus is pictured as asking what his disciples will say when he goes up to heaven.

§[6:63] **Spirit . . . flesh:** probably not a reference to the eucharistic body of Jesus but to the supernatural and the natural, as in Jn 3:6. **Spirit and life:** all Jesus said about the bread of life is the revelation of the Spirit.

a. [6:57] 5:26.   b. [6:64] 13:11.   c. [6:69] 11:27; Mt 16:16; Mk 1:24; Lk 4:34.   d. [6:71] 12:4; 13:2, 27.

## CHAPTER 7

**The Feast of Tabernacles.** ¶ᵃAfter this, Jesus moved about within Galilee; but he did not wish to travel in Judea, because the Jews were trying to kill him.ᵉ ²But the Jewish feast of Tabernacles was near.ᶠ ³So his brothers** said to him, "Leave here and go to Judea, so that your disciples also may see the works you are doing. ⁴No one works in secret if he wants to be known publicly. If you do these things, manifest yourself to the world."ᵍ ⁵For his brothers did not believe in him. ⁶††So Jesus said to them, "My time is not yet here, but the time is always right for you. ⁷The world cannot hate you, but it hates me, because I testify to it that its works are evil.ʰ ⁸You go up to the feast. I am not going up‡‡ to this feast, because my time has not yet been fulfilled." ⁹After he had said this, he stayed on in Galilee.

¹⁰But when his brothers had gone up to the feast, he himself also went up, not openly but [as it were] in secret. ¹¹The Jews were looking for him at the feast and saying, "Where is he?" ¹²And there was considerable murmuring about him in the crowds. Some said, "He is a good man," [while] others said, "No; on the contrary, he misleads the crowd." ¹³Still, no one spoke openly about him because they were afraid of the Jews.ⁱ

**The First Dialogue.**§§ ¹⁴When the feast was already half over, Jesus went up into the temple area and began to teach. ¹⁵¶¶The Jews were amazed and said, "How does he know scripture without having studied?" ¹⁶Jesus answered them and said, "My teaching is not my own but is from

---

¶[7–8] These chapters contain events about the feast of Tabernacles (Sukkoth, Ingathering: Ex 23:16; Tents, Booths: Dt 16:13–16), with its symbols of booths (originally built to shelter harvesters), rain (water from Siloam poured on the temple altar), and lights (illumination of the four torches in the Court of the Women). They continue the theme of the replacement of feasts (Passover, Jn 2:13; 6:4; Hanukkah, Jn 10:22; Pentecost, Jn 5:1), here accomplished by Jesus as the Living Water. These chapters comprise seven miscellaneous controversies and dialogues. There is a literary inclusion with Jesus in hiding in Jn 7:4, 10; 8:59. There are frequent references to attempts on his life: Jn 7:1, 13, 19, 25, 30, 32, 44; 8:37, 40, 59.

**[7:3] **Brothers:** these relatives (cf. Jn 2:12 and see note on Mk 6:3) are never portrayed as disciples until after the resurrection (Acts 1:14). Mt 13:55 and Mk 6:3 give the names of four of them. Jesus has already performed works/signs in Judea; cf. Jn 2:23; 3:2; 4:45; 5:8.

††[7:6] **Time:** the Greek word means "opportune time," here a synonym for Jesus' "hour" (see note on Jn 2:4), his death and resurrection. In the wordplay, any time is suitable for Jesus' brothers, because they are not dependent on God's will.

‡‡[7:8] **I am not going up:** an early attested reading "not yet" seems a correction, since Jesus in the story does go up to the feast. "Go up," in a play on words, refers not only to going up to Jerusalem but also to exaltation at the cross, resurrection, and ascension; cf. Jn 3:14; 6:62; 20:17.

§§[7:14–31] Jesus teaches in the temple; debate with the Jews.

¶¶[7:15] **Without having studied:** literally, "How does he know letters without having learned?" Children were taught to read and write by means of the scriptures. But here more than Jesus' literacy is being discussed; the people are wondering how he can teach like a rabbi. Rabbis were trained by other rabbis and traditionally quoted their teachers.

e. [7:1] 5:18; 8:37, 40.   f. [7:2] Ex 23:16; Lv 23:34; Nm 29:12; Dt 16:13–16; Zec 14:16–19.   g. [7:4] 14:22.   h. [7:7] 15:18.   i. [7:13] 9:22; 19:38; 20:19.   j. [7:15] Lk 2:47.

the one who sent me. [17]Whoever chooses to do his will[*] shall know whether my teaching is from God or whether I speak on my own.[k] [18]Whoever speaks on his own seeks his own glory, but whoever seeks the glory of the one who sent him is truthful, and there is no wrong in him. [19]Did not Moses give you the law? Yet none of you keeps the law. Why are you trying to kill me?"[l] [20]The crowd answered, "You are possessed![†] Who is trying to kill you?"[m] [21]Jesus answered and said to them, "I performed one work[‡] and all of you are amazed[n] [22]because of it. Moses gave you circumcision—not that it came from Moses but rather from the patriarchs—and you circumcise a man on the sabbath.[o] [23]If a man can receive circumcision on a sabbath so that the law of Moses may not be broken, are you angry with me because I made a whole person well on a sabbath?[p] [24]Stop judging by appearances, but judge justly."[q]

[25]So some of the inhabitants of Jerusalem said, "Is he not the one they are trying to kill? [26]And look, he is speaking openly and they say nothing to him. Could the authorities[§] have realized that he is the Messiah? [27]But we know where he is from. When the Messiah comes, no one will know where he is from."[r] [28]So Jesus cried out in the temple area as he was teaching and said, "You know me and also know where I am from. Yet I did not come on my own, but the one who sent me, whom you do not know, is true.[s] [29]I know him, because I am from him, and he sent me."[t] [30]So they tried to arrest him, but no one laid a hand upon him, because his hour had not yet come.[u] [31]But many of the crowd began to believe in him, and said, "When the Messiah comes, will he perform more signs than this man has done?"[v]

**Officers Sent to Arrest Jesus.**[¶] [32]The Pharisees heard the crowd murmuring about him to this effect, and the chief priests and the Pharisees sent guards to arrest him. [33]So Jesus said, "I will be with you only a little while longer, and then I will go to the one who sent me.[w] [34]You will look for me but not find [me], and where I am you cannot come."[x] [35]So the Jews said to one another,

"Where is he going that we will not find him? Surely he is not going to the dispersion[**] among the Greeks to teach the Greeks, is he? [36]What is the meaning of his saying, 'You will look for me and not find [me], and where I am you cannot come'?"

**Rivers of Living Water.**[††] [37]On the last and greatest day of the feast, Jesus stood up and exclaimed, "Let anyone who thirsts come to me and drink.[y] [38]Whoever believes in me, as scripture says:

'Rivers of living water[‡‡] will flow from within him.'"[z]

[39]He said this in reference to the Spirit that those who came to believe in him were to receive. There was, of course, no Spirit yet,[§§] because Jesus had not yet been glorified.[a]

**Discussion About the Origins of the Messiah.**[¶¶] [40]Some in the crowd who heard these words said, "This is truly the Prophet."[b] [41]Others said, "This is the Messiah." But others said, "The Messiah will not come from Galilee, will he? [42]Does not scripture say that the Messiah will be of David's family and come from Bethlehem, the village where David lived?"[c] [43]So a division occurred in the crowd because of him. [44]Some of them even wanted to arrest him, but no one laid hands on him.

[45]So the guards went to the chief priests and Pharisees, who asked them, "Why did you not bring him?" [46]The guards answered, "Never before has anyone spoken like this one." [47]So the Pharisees answered them, "Have you also been deceived? [48]Have any of the authorities or the Pharisees believed in him?[d] [49]But this crowd, which does not know the law, is accursed." [50]Nicodemus, one of their members who had come to him earlier, said to them,[e] [51]"Does our law condemn a person before it first hears him and finds out what he is doing?"[f] [52]They answered and said to him, "You are not from Galilee also, are you? Look and see that no prophet arises from Galilee."

---

*[7:17] **To do his will**: presumably a reference back to the "work" of Jn 6:29: belief in the one whom God has sent.

†[7:20] **You are possessed**: literally, "You have a demon." The insane were thought to be possessed by a demoniacal spirit.

‡[7:21] **One work**: the cure of the paralytic (Jn 5:1–9) because of the reference to the sabbath (Jn 7:22; 5:9–10).

§[7:26] **The authorities**: the members of the Sanhedrin (same term as Jn 3:1).

¶[7:32–36] Jesus announces his approaching departure (cf. also Jn 8:21; 12:36; 13:33) and complete control over his destiny.

**[7:35] **Dispersion**: or "diaspora": Jews living outside Palestine. **Greeks**: probably refers to the Gentiles in the Mediterranean area; cf. Jn 12:20.

††[7:37, 39] Promise of living water through the Spirit.

‡‡[7:38] **Living water**: not an exact quotation from any Old Testament passage; in the gospel context the gift of the Spirit is meant; cf. Jn 3:5. **From within him**: either Jesus or the believer; if Jesus, it continues the Jesus-Moses motif (water from the rock, Ex 17:6; Nm 20:11) as well as Jesus as the new temple (cf. Ez 47:1). Grammatically, it goes better with the believer.

§§[7:39] **No Spirit yet**: Codex Vaticanus and early Latin, Syriac, and Coptic versions add "given." In this gospel, the sending of the Spirit cannot take place until Jesus' glorification through his death, resurrection, and ascension; cf. Jn 20:22.

¶¶[7:40–53] Discussion of the Davidic lineage of the Messiah.

---

k. [7:17] 6:29.  l. [7:19] Acts 7:53.  m. [7:20] 8:48–49; 10:20.  n. [7:21] 5:1–9.  o. [7:22] Gn 17:10; Lv 12:3.  p. [7:23] 5:2–9, 16; Mt 12:11–12; Lk 14:5.  q. [7:24] 8:15; Lv 19:15; Is 11:3–4.  r. [7:27] Heb 7:3.  s. [7:28] 8:19.  t. [7:29] 6:46; 8:55.  u. [7:30] 7:44; 8:20; Lk 4:29–30.  v. [7:31] 2:11; 10:42; 11:45.  w. [7:33] 13:33; 16:16.  x. [7:34] 8:21; 12:36; 13:33, 36; 16:5; Dt 4:29; Prv 1:28; Is 55:6; Hos 5:6.

y. [7:37] Rev 21:6.  z. [7:38] 4:10, 14; 19:34; Is 12:3; Ez 47:1.  a. [7:39] 16:7.  b. [7:40] Dt 18:15, 18.  c. [7:42] 2 Sm 7:12–14; Ps 89:3–4; 132:11; Mi 5:1; Mt 2:5–6.  d. [7:48] 12:42.  e. [7:50] 3:1; 19:39.  f. [7:51] Dt 1:16–17.

## CHAPTER 8

**A Woman Caught in Adultery.**[*] [[7:53]]Then each went to his own house, [1]while Jesus went to the Mount of Olives.[†g] [2]But early in the morning he arrived again in the temple area, and all the people started coming to him, and he sat down and taught them. [3]Then the scribes and the Pharisees brought a woman who had been caught in adultery and made her stand in the middle. [4]They said to him, "Teacher, this woman was caught in the very act of committing adultery. [5]Now in the law, Moses commanded us to stone such women.[‡] So what do you say?"[h] [6]They said this to test him, so that they could have some charge to bring against him. Jesus bent down and began to write on the ground with his finger.[§] [7]But when they continued asking him, he straightened up and said to them,[i] "Let the one among you who is without sin be the first to throw a stone at her." [8]Again he bent down and wrote on the ground. [9]And in response, they went away one by one, beginning with the elders. So he was left alone with the woman before him. [10]Then Jesus straightened up and said to her, "Woman, where are they? Has no one condemned you?"[j] [11]She replied, "No one, sir." Then Jesus said, "Neither do I condemn you. Go, [and] from now on do not sin any more."[k]

**The Light of the World.**[*] [12]Jesus spoke to them again, saying, "I am the light of the world. Whoever follows me will not walk in darkness, but will have the light of life."[l] [13]So the Pharisees said to him, "You testify on your own behalf, so your testimony cannot be verified." [14]Jesus answered and said to them, "Even if I do testify on my own behalf, my testimony can be verified,[††] because I know where I came from and where I am going. But you do not know where I come from or where I am going.[m] [15]You judge by appearances,[‡‡] but I do not judge anyone.[n] [16]And even if I should judge, my judgment is valid, because I am not alone, but it is I and the Father who sent me.[o] [17]Even in your law[§§] it is written that the testimony of two men can be verified.[p] [18]I testify on my behalf and so does the Father who sent me."[q] [19]So they said to him, "Where is your father?" Jesus answered, "You know neither me nor my Father. If you knew me, you would know my Father also."[r] [20]He spoke these words while teaching in the treasury in the temple area. But no one arrested him, because his hour had not yet come.[s]

**Jesus, the Father's Ambassador.**[¶¶] [21]He said to them again, "I am going away and you will look for me, but you will die in your sin."[***] Where I am going you cannot come."[22†††]So the Jews said, "He is not going to kill himself, is he, because he said, 'Where I am going you cannot come'?" [23]He said to them, "You belong to what is below, I belong to what is above. You belong to this world, but I do not belong to this world.[u] [24]That is why I told you that you will die in your sins. For if you do not believe that I AM,[‡‡‡] you will die in your sins."[v] [25]So they said to him, "Who are you?"[w] Jesus said to them, "What I told you from the beginning. [26]I have much to say about you in condemnation. But the one who sent me is true, and what I heard from him I tell the world."[x] [27]They did not realize that he was speaking to them of the Father. [28]So Jesus said [to them], "When you lift up the Son of Man, then you will realize that I AM, and that I do nothing on my own, but I say only what the Father taught me."[y] [29]The one who sent me is with me. He has not left me alone, because I always do what is pleasing to

---

[*][7:53–8:11] The story of the woman caught in adultery is a later insertion here, missing from all early Greek manuscripts. A Western text-type insertion, attested mainly in Old Latin translations, it is found in different places in different manuscripts: here, or after Jn 7:36 or at the end of this gospel, or after Lk 21:38, or at the end of that gospel. There are many non-Johannine features in the language, and there are also many doubtful readings within the passage. The style and motifs are similar to those of Luke, and it fits better with the general situation at the end of Lk 21, but it was probably inserted here because of the allusion to Jer 17:13 (cf. note on Jn 8:6) and the statement, "I do not judge anyone," in Jn 8:15. The Catholic Church accepts this passage as canonical scripture.

[†][8:1] **Mount of Olives:** not mentioned elsewhere in the gospel tradition outside of passion week.

[‡][8:5] Lv 20:10 and Dt 22:22 mention only death, but Dt 22:23–24 prescribes stoning for a betrothed virgin.

[§][8:6] Cf. Jer 17:13 (RSV): "Those who turn away from thee shall be written in the earth, for they have forsaken the LORD, the fountain of living water"; cf. Jn 7:38.

[¶][8:7] The first stones were to be thrown by the witnesses (Dt 17:7).

[**][8:12–20] Jesus the light of the world. Jesus replaces the four torches of the illumination of the temple as the light of joy.

[††][8:14] **My testimony can be verified:** this seems to contradict Jn 5:31, but the emphasis here is on Jesus' origin from the Father and his divine destiny. **Where I am going:** indicates Jesus' passion and glorification.

[‡‡][8:15] **By appearances:** literally, "according to the flesh." **I do not judge anyone:** superficial contradiction of Jn 5:22, 27, 30; here the emphasis is that the judgment is not by material standards.

[§§][8:17] **Your law:** a reflection of later controversy between church and synagogue.

[¶¶][8:21–30] He whose ambassador I am is with me. Jesus' origin is from God; he can reveal God.

[***][8:21] **You will die in your sin:** i.e., of disbelief; cf. Jn 8:24. **Where I am going you cannot come:** except through faith in Jesus' passion-resurrection.

[†††][8:22] The Jews suspect that he is referring to his death. Johannine irony is apparent here; Jesus' death will not be self-inflicted but destined by God.

[‡‡‡][8:24, 28] **I AM:** an expression that late Jewish tradition understood as Yahweh's own self-designation (Is 43:10); see note on Jn 4:26. Jesus is here placed on a par with Yahweh.

[§§§][8:25] **What I told you from the beginning:** this verse seems textually corrupt, with several other possible translations: "(I am) what I say to you"; "Why do I speak to you at all?" The earliest attested reading (Bodmer Papyrus P⁶⁶) has (in a second hand), "I told you at the beginning what I am also telling you (now)." The answer here (cf. Prv 8:22) seems to hinge on a misunderstanding of Jn 8:24 "*that* I AM" as "*what* I am."

---

g. [8:1–2] Lk 21:37–38. h. [8:5] Lv 20:10; Dt 22:22–29. i. [8:7] Dt 17:7. j. [8:10] Ez 33:11. k. [8:11] 5:14. l. [8:12] 1:4–5, 9; 12:46; Ex 13:22; Is 42:6; Zec 14:8.

m. [8:14] 5:31. n. [8:15] 12:47; 1 Sm 16:7. o. [8:16] 5:30. p. [8:17] Dt 17:6; 19:15; Nm 35:30. q. [8:18] 5:23, 37. r. [8:19] 7:28; 14:7; 15:21. s. [8:20] 7:30. t. [8:21] 7:34; 13:33. u. [8:23] 3:31; 17:14; 18:36. v. [8:24] Ex 3:14; Dt 32:39; Is 43:10. w. [8:25] 10:24. x. [8:26] 12:44–50. y. [8:28] 3:14; 12:32, 34.

him." ³⁰Because he spoke this way, many came to believe in him.

**Jesus and Abraham.**˙ ³¹Jesus then said to those Jews who believed in him,† "If you remain in my word, you will truly be my disciples, ³²and you will know the truth, and the truth will set you free."ᶻ ³³They answered him, "We are descendants of Abraham and have never been enslaved to anyone.‡ How can you say, 'You will become free'?"ᵃ ³⁴Jesus answered them, "Amen, amen, I say to you, everyone who commits sin is a slave of sin.ᵇ ³⁵A slave does not remain in a household forever, but a son§ always remains.ᶜ ³⁶So if a son frees you, then you will truly be free. ³⁷I know that you are descendants of Abraham. But you are trying to kill me, because my word has no room among you. ³⁸ᵈI tell you what I have seen in the Father's presence; then do what you have heard from the Father."

³⁹***They answered and said to him, "Our father is Abraham." Jesus said to them,ᵈ "If you were Abraham's children, you would be doing the works of Abraham. ⁴⁰But now you are trying to kill me, a man who has told you the truth that I heard from God; Abraham did not do this. ⁴¹You are doing the works of your father!" [So] they said to him, "We are not illegitimate. We have one Father, God."ᵉ ⁴²Jesus said to them, "If God were your Father, you would love me, for I came from God and am here; I did not come on my own, but he sent me.ᶠ ⁴³Why do you not understand what I am saying? Because you cannot bear to hear my word. ⁴⁴You belong to your father the devil and you willingly carry out your father's desires. He was a murderer from the beginning and does not stand in truth, because there is no truth in him. When he tells a lie, he speaks in character, because he is a liar and the father of lies.ᵍ ⁴⁵But because I speak the truth, you do not believe me. ⁴⁶Can any of you charge me with sin? If I am telling the truth, why do you not believe me?ʰ ⁴⁷Whoever belongs to God

hears the words of God; for this reason you do not listen, because you do not belong to God."ⁱ

⁴⁸The Jews answered and said to him, "Are we not right in saying that you are a Samaritan†† and are possessed?" ⁴⁹Jesus answered, "I am not possessed; I honor my Father, but you dishonor me. ⁵⁰I do not seek my own glory; there is one who seeks it and he is the one who judges.ʲ ⁵¹Amen, amen, I say to you, whoever keeps my word will never see death."ᵏ ⁵²[So] the Jews said to him, "Now we are sure that you are possessed. Abraham died, as did the prophets, yet you say, 'Whoever keeps my word will never taste death.' ⁵³Are you greater than our father Abraham,‡‡ who died? Or the prophets, who died? Who do you make yourself out to be?"ˡ ⁵⁴Jesus answered, "If I glorify myself, my glory is worth nothing; but it is my Father who glorifies me, of whom you say, 'He is our God.' ⁵⁵You do not know him, but I know him. And if I should say that I do not know him, I would be like you a liar. But I do know him and I keep his word.ᵐ ⁵⁶Abraham your father rejoiced to see my day; he saw it§§ and was glad.ⁿ ⁵⁷So the Jews said to him, "You are not yet fifty years old and you have seen Abraham?"¶¶ ⁵⁸***Jesus said to them,ᵒ "Amen, amen, I say to you, before Abraham came to be, I AM." ⁵⁹So they picked up stones to throw at him; but Jesus hid and went out of the temple area.ᵖ

## CHAPTER 9

**The Man Born Blind.** ¹†††As he passed by he saw a man blind from birth.�q ²‡‡‡His disciples asked him,ʳ "Rabbi, who sinned, this man or his parents, that he was born blind?" ³Jesus answered, "Neither he nor his parents sinned; it is so that the works of God might be made visible through him.ˢ ⁴We have to do the works of the one who

---

††[8:48] **Samaritan**: therefore interested in magical powers; cf. Acts 7:14–24.

‡‡[8:53] **Are you greater than our father Abraham?**: cf. Jn 4:12.

§§[8:56] **He saw it**: this seems a reference to the birth of Isaac (Gn 17:7; 21:6), the beginning of the fulfillment of promises about Abraham's seed.

¶¶[8:57] The evidence of the third-century Bodmer Papyrus P⁷⁵ and the first hand of Codex Sinaiticus indicates that the text originally read: "How can Abraham have seen you?"

***[8:58] **Came to be, I AM**: the Greek word used for "came to be" is the one used of all creation in the prologue, while the word used for "am" is the one reserved for the Logos.

†††[9:1–10:21] Sabbath healing of the man born blind. This sixth sign is introduced to illustrate the saying, "I am the light of the world" (Jn 8:12; 9:5). The narrative of conflict about Jesus contrasts Jesus (light) with the Jews (blindness, Jn 9:39–41). The theme of water is reintroduced in the reference to the pool of Siloam. Ironically, Jesus is being judged by the Jews, yet the Jews are judged by the Light of the world; cf. Jn 3:19–21.

‡‡‡[9:2] See note on Jn 5:14, and Ex 20:5, that parents' sins were visited upon their children. Jesus denies such a cause and emphasizes the purpose: the infirmity was providential.

---

*[8:31–59] Jesus' origin ("before Abraham") and destiny are developed; the truth will free them from sin (Jn 8:34) and death (Jn 8:51).

†[8:31] **Those Jews who believed in him**: a rough editorial suture, since in Jn 8:37 they are described as trying to kill Jesus.

‡[8:33] **Have never been enslaved to anyone**: since, historically, the Jews were enslaved almost continuously, this verse is probably Johannine irony, about slavery to sin.

§[8:35] **A slave . . . a son**: an allusion to Ishmael and Isaac (Gn 16; 21), or to the release of a slave after six years (Ex 21:2; Dt 15:12).

¶[8:38] **The Father**: i.e., God. It is also possible, however, to understand the second part of the verse as a sarcastic reference to descent of the Jews from the devil (Jn 8:44), "You do what you have heard from [your] father."

**[8:39] **The works of Abraham**: Abraham believed; cf. Rom 4:11–17; Jas 2:21–23.

---

z. [8:32] Is 42:7; Gal 4:31.   a. [8:33] Mt 3:9.   b. [8:34] Rom 6:16–17.   c. [8:35] Gn 21:10; Gal 4:30; Heb 3:5–6.   d. [8:39] Gn 26:5; Rom 4:11–17; Jas 2:21–23.   e. [8:41] Mal 2:10.   f. [8:42] 1 Jn 5:1.   g. [8:44] Gn 3:4; Wis 1:13; 2:24; Acts 13:10; 1 Jn 3:8–15.   h. [8:46] Heb 4:15; 1 Pt 2:22; 1 Jn 3:5.

i. [8:47] 10:26; 1 Jn 4:6.   j. [8:50] 7:18.   k. [8:51] 5:24–29; 6:40, 47; 11:25–26.   l. [8:53] 4:12.   m. [8:55] 7:28–29.   n. [8:56] Gn 17:17; Mt 13:17; Lk 17:22.   o. [8:58] 1:30; 17:5.   p. [8:59] 10:31, 39; 11:8; Lk 4:29–30.   q. [9:1–2] Is 42:7.   r. [9:2] Ex 20:5; Ez 18:20; Lk 13:2.   s. [9:3] 5:14; 11:4.

sent me while it is day. Night is coming when no one can work.[t] [5]While I am in the world, I am the light of the world."[u] [6]When he had said this, he spat on the ground and made clay with the saliva, and smeared the clay on his eyes,[v] [7]and said to him, "Go wash[*] in the Pool of Siloam" (which means Sent). So he went and washed, and came back able to see.[w]

[8]His neighbors and those who had seen him earlier as a beggar said, "Isn't this the one who used to sit and beg?" [9]Some said, "It is," but others said, "No, he just looks like him." He said, "I am." [10]So they said to him, "[So] how were your eyes opened?" [11]He replied, "The man called Jesus made clay and anointed my eyes and told me, 'Go to Siloam and wash.' So I went there and washed and was able to see." [12]And they said to him, "Where is he?" He said, "I don't know."

[13]They brought the one who was once blind to the Pharisees. [14]Now Jesus had made clay[†] and opened his eyes on a sabbath.[x] [15]So then the Pharisees also asked him how he was able to see. He said to them, "He put clay on my eyes, and I washed, and now I can see." [16]So some of the Pharisees said, "This man is not from God, because he does not keep the sabbath." [But] others said, "How can a sinful man do such signs?" And there was a division among them.[y] [17]So they said to the blind man again, "What do you have to say about him, since he opened your eyes?" He said, "He is a prophet."[z]

[18]Now the Jews did not believe that he had been blind and gained his sight until they summoned the parents of the one who had gained his sight. [19]They asked them, "Is this your son, who you say was born blind? How does he now see?" [20]His parents answered and said, "We know that this is our son and that he was born blind. [21]We do not know how he sees now, nor do we know who opened his eyes. Ask him, he is of age; he can speak for himself." [22a]His parents said this because they were afraid of the Jews, for the Jews had already agreed that if anyone acknowledged him as the Messiah, he would be expelled from the synagogue. [23]For this reason his parents said, "He is of age; question him."[b]

[24]So a second time they called the man who had been blind and said to him, "Give God the praise![§] We know that this man is a sinner."[c] [25]He replied, "If he is a sinner, I do not know. One thing I do know is that I was blind and now I see." [26]So they said to him, "What did he do to you? How did he open your eyes?" [27]He answered them, "I told you already and you did not listen. Why do you want to hear it again? Do you want to become his disciples, too?" [28]They ridiculed him and said, "You are that man's disciple; we are disciples of Moses! [29]We know that God spoke to Moses, but we do not know where this one is from."[d] [30]The man answered and said to them, "This is what is so amazing, that you do not know where he is from, yet he opened my eyes. [31]We know that God does not listen to sinners, but if one is devout and does his will, he listens to him.[e] [32a]It is unheard of that anyone ever opened the eyes of a person born blind. [33]If this man were not from God, he would not be able to do anything."[f] [34]They answered and said to him, "You were born totally in sin, and are you trying to teach us?" Then they threw him out.

[35]When Jesus heard that they had thrown him out, he found him and said, "Do you believe in the Son of Man?" [36]He answered and said, "Who is he, sir, that I may believe in him?" [37]Jesus said to him, "You have seen him and the one speaking with you is he."[g] [38]He said, "I do believe, Lord," and he worshiped him. [39]**Then Jesus said, "I came into this world for judgment, so that those who do not see might see, and those who do see might become blind."[h]

[40]Some of the Pharisees who were with him heard this and said to him, "Surely we are not also blind, are we?"[i] [41]Jesus said to them, "If you were blind, you would have no sin; but now you are saying, 'We see,' so your sin remains.[j]

# CHAPTER 10

**The Good Shepherd.** [1††]"Amen, amen, I say to you,[k] whoever does not enter a sheepfold[‡‡] through the gate but climbs over elsewhere is a thief and a robber. [2]But whoever enters through the gate is the shepherd of the sheep. [3]The gatekeeper opens it for him, and the sheep hear his

---

§[9:24] **Give God the praise!:** an Old Testament formula of adjuration to tell the truth; cf. Jos 7:19; 1 Sm 6:5 LXX. Cf. Jn 5:41.

¶[9:32] **A person born blind:** the only Old Testament cure from blindness is found in Tobit (cf. Tb 7:7; 11:7–13; 14:1–2), but Tobit was not born blind.

**[9:39–41] These verses spell out the symbolic meaning of the cure; the Pharisees are not the innocent blind, willing to accept the testimony of others.

††[10:1–21] The good shepherd discourse continues the theme of attack on the Pharisees that ends Jn 9. The figure is allegorical: the hired hands are the Pharisees who excommunicated the cured blind man. It serves as a commentary on Jn 9. For the shepherd motif, used of Yahweh in the Old Testament, cf. Ex 34; Gn 48:15; 49:24; Mi 7:14; Ps 23:1–4; 80:1.

‡‡[10:1] **Sheepfold:** a low stone wall open to the sky.

---

*[9:7] **Go wash:** perhaps a test of faith; cf. 2 Kgs 5:10–14. The water tunnel Siloam (= Sent) is used as a symbol of Jesus, sent by his Father.

†[9:14] In using spittle, kneading clay, and healing, Jesus had broken the sabbath rules laid down by Jewish tradition.

‡[9:22] This comment of the evangelist (in terms used again in Jn 12:42; 16:2) envisages a situation after Jesus' ministry. Rejection/excommunication from the synagogue of Jews who confessed Jesus as Messiah seems to have begun ca. A.D. 85, when the curse against the *mînîm* or heretics was introduced into the "Eighteen Benedictions."

---

t. [9:4] 11:9–10; 12:35–36. u. [9:5] 8:12. v. [9:6] 5:11; Mk 7:33; 8:23. w. [9:7] 2 Kgs 5:10–14. x. [9:14] 5:9. y. [9:16] 3:2; Mt 12:10–11; Lk 13:10–11; 14:1–4. z. [9:17] 4:19. a. [9:22] 7:13; 12:42; 16:2; 19:38. b. [9:23] 12:42.

c. [9:24] Jos 7:19; 1 Sm 6:5 LXX. d. [9:29] Ex 33:11. e. [9:31] 10:21; Ps 34:16; 66:18; Prv 15:29; Is 1:15. f. [9:33] 3:2. g. [9:37] 4:26; Dn 7:13. h. [9:39] Mt 13:33–35. i. [9:40] Mt 15:14; 23:26; Rom 2:19. j. [9:41] 15:22. k. [10:1–5] Gn 48:15; 49:24; Ps 23:1–4; 80:2; Jer 23:1–4; Ez 34:1–31; Mi 7:14.

voice, as he calls his own sheep by name and leads them out. [4]When he has driven out all his own, he walks ahead of them, and the sheep follow him,[i] because they recognize his voice. [5]But they will not follow a stranger; they will run away from him, because they do not recognize the voice of strangers." [6]Although Jesus used this figure of speech,[†] they did not realize what he was trying to tell them.

[7]So Jesus said again, "Amen, amen, I say to you, I am the gate for the sheep. [8]All who came [before me] are thieves and robbers, but the sheep did not listen to them. [9]I am the gate. Whoever enters through me will be saved, and will come in and go out and find pasture. [10]A thief comes only to steal and slaughter and destroy; I came so that they might have life and have it more abundantly. [11]I am the good shepherd. A good shepherd lays down his life for the sheep.[m] [12]A hired man, who is not a shepherd and whose sheep are not his own, sees a wolf coming and leaves the sheep and runs away, and the wolf catches and scatters them.[n] [13]This is because he works for pay and has no concern for the sheep. [14]I am the good shepherd, and I know mine and mine know me, [15]just as the Father knows me and I know the Father; and I will lay down my life for the sheep.[o] [16]I have other sheep[¶] that do not belong to this fold. These also I must lead, and they will hear my voice, and there will be one flock, one shepherd.[p] [17]This is why the Father loves me, because I lay down my life in order to take it up again.[q] [18]No one takes it from me, but I lay it down on my own. I have power to lay it down, and power to take it up again.[**] This command I have received from my Father."[r]

[19]Again there was a division among the Jews because of these words.[s] [20]Many of them said, "He is possessed and out of his mind; why listen to him?"[t] [21]Others said, "These are not the words of one possessed; surely a demon cannot open the eyes of the blind, can he?"[u]

## Feast of the Dedication.

[22]The feast of the Dedication[††] was then taking place in Jerusalem. It was winter.[v] [23]And Jesus walked about in the temple area on the Portico of Solomon. [24]So the Jews gathered around him and said to him, "How long are you going to keep us in suspense?[§§] If you are the Messiah, tell us plainly."[w] [25]Jesus answered them, "I told you[¶¶] and you do not believe. The works I do in my Father's name testify to me.[x] [26]But you do not believe, because you are not among my sheep.[y] [27]My sheep hear my voice; I know them, and they follow me. [28]I give them eternal life, and they shall never perish. No one can take them out of my hand.[z] [29]My Father, who has given them to me, is greater than all,[***] and no one can take them out of the Father's hand.[a] [30]The Father and I are one."[b]

[31]The Jews again picked up rocks to stone him.[c] [32]Jesus answered them, "I have shown you many good works from my Father. For which of these are you trying to stone me?" [33]The Jews answered him, "We are not stoning you for a good work but for blasphemy. You, a man, are making yourself God."[d] [34]Jesus answered them,[e] "Is it not written in your law, 'I said, "You are gods"'? [35]If it calls them gods to whom the word of God came, and scripture cannot be set aside, [36]can you say that the one whom the Father has consecrated[§§§] and sent into the world blasphemes because I said, 'I am the Son of God'?[f] [37]If I do not perform my Father's works, do not believe me; [38]but if I perform them, even if you do not believe me, believe the works, so that you may realize [and understand] that the Father is in me and I am in the Father."[g] [39][Then] they

---

*[10:4] **Recognize his voice:** the Pharisees do not recognize Jesus, but the people of God, symbolized by the blind man, do.

†[10:6] **Figure of speech:** John uses a different word for illustrative speech than the "parable" of the synoptics, but the idea is similar.

‡[10:7–10] In Jn 10:7–8, the figure is of a gate for the shepherd to come to the sheep; in Jn 10:9–10, the figure is of a gate for the sheep to **come in and go out.**

§[10:8] **[Before me]:** these words are omitted in many good early manuscripts and versions.

¶[10:16] **Other sheep:** the Gentiles, possibly a reference to "God's dispersed children" of Jn 11:52 destined to be gathered into one, or "apostolic Christians" at odds with the community of the beloved disciple.

**[10:18] **Power to take it up again:** contrast the role of the Father as the efficient cause of the resurrection in Acts 2:24; 4:10; etc.; Rom 1:4; 4:24. Yet even here is added: **This command I have received from my Father.**

l. [10:4] Mi 2:12–13.  m. [10:11] Ps 23:1–4; Is 40:11; 49:9–10; Heb 13:20; Rev 7:17.  n. [10:12] Zec 11:17.  o. [10:15] 15:13; 1 Jn 3:16.  p. [10:16] 11:52; Is 56:8; Jer 23:3; Ez 34:23; 37:24; Mi 2:12.  q. [10:17] Heb 10:10.  r. [10:18] 19:11.  s. [10:19] 7:43; 9:16.  t. [10:20] 7:20; 8:48.  u. [10:21] 3:2.

††[10:22] **Feast of the Dedication:** an eight-day festival of lights (Hebrew, Hanukkah) held in December, three months after the feast of Tabernacles (Jn 7:2), to celebrate the Maccabees' rededication of the altar and reconsecration of the temple in 164 B.C., after their desecration by Antiochus IV Epiphanes (Dn 8:13; 9:27; cf. 1 Mc 4:36–59; 2 Mc 1:18–2:19; 10:1–8).

‡‡[10:23] **Portico of Solomon:** on the east side of the temple area, offering protection against the cold winds from the desert.

§§[10:24] **Keep us in suspense:** literally, "How long will you take away our life?" Cf. Jn 11:48–50. **If you are the Messiah, tell us plainly:** cf. Lk 22:67. This is the climax of Jesus' encounters with the Jewish authorities. There has never yet been an open confession before them.

¶¶[10:25] **I told you:** probably at Jn 8:25 which was an evasive answer.

***[10:29] The textual evidence for the first clause is very divided; it may also be translated: "As for the Father, what he has given me is greater than all," or "My Father is greater than all, in what he has given me."

†††[10:30] This is justification for Jn 10:29; it asserts unity of power and reveals that the words and deeds of Jesus are the words and deeds of God.

‡‡‡[10:34] This is a reference to the judges of Israel who, since they exercised the divine prerogative to judge (Dt 1:17), were called "gods"; cf. Ex 21:6, besides Ps 82:6, from which the quotation comes.

§§§[10:36] **Consecrated:** this may be a reference to the rededicated altar at the Hanukkah feast; see note on Jn 10:22.

v. [10:22] 1 Mc 4:54, 59.  w. [10:24] Lk 22:67.  x. [10:25] 8:25 / 5:36; 10:38.  y. [10:26] 8:45, 47.  z. [10:28] Dt 32:39.  a. [10:29] Wis 3:1; Is 43:13.  b. [10:30] 1:1; 12:45; 14:9; 17:21.  c. [10:31] 8:59.  d. [10:33] 5:18; 19:7; Lv 24:16.  e. [10:34] Ps 82:6.  f. [10:36] 5:18.  g. [10:38] 14:10–11, 20.

tried again to arrest him; but he escaped from their power.

⁴⁰He went back across the Jordan to the place where John first baptized, and there he remained.ʰ ⁴¹Many came to him and said, "John performed no sign," but everything John said about this man was true." ⁴²And many there began to believe in him.ⁱ

## CHAPTER 11

**The Raising of Lazarus.**† ¹Now a man was ill, Lazarus from Bethany,ʲ the village of Mary and her sister Martha. ²Mary was the one who had anointed the Lord with perfumed oil and dried his feet with her hair; it was her brother Lazarus who was ill. ³So the sisters sent word to him, saying, "Master, the one you love is ill." ⁴When Jesus heard this he said, "This illness is not to end in death,‡ but is for the glory of God, that the Son of God may be glorified through it."ᵏ ⁵Now Jesus loved Martha and her sister and Lazarus. ⁶So when he heard that he was ill, he remained for two days in the place where he was. ⁷Then after this he said to his disciples, "Let us go back to Judea." ⁸The disciples said to him, "Rabbi, the Jews were just trying to stone you, and you want to go back there?"ˡ ⁹Jesus answered, "Are there not twelve hours in a day? If one walks during the day,ᵐ he does not stumble, because he sees the light of this world.ⁿ ¹⁰But if one walks at night, he stumbles, because the light is not in him."§ ¹¹He said this, and then told them, "Our friend Lazarus is asleep, but I am going to awaken him." ¹²So the disciples said to him, "Master, if he is asleep, he will be saved." ¹³But Jesus was talking about his death, while they thought that he meant ordinary sleep.° ¹⁴So then Jesus said to them clearly, "Lazarus has died.

¹⁵And I am glad for you that I was not there, that you may believe. Let us go to him." ¹⁶So Thomas, called Didymus,¶ said to his fellow disciples, "Let us also go to die with him."ᵖ

¹⁷When Jesus arrived, he found that Lazarus had already been in the tomb for four days. ¹⁸Now Bethany was near Jerusalem, only about two miles** away. ¹⁹And many of the Jews had come to Martha and Mary to comfort* them about their brother.ᑫ ²⁰When Martha heard that Jesus was coming, she went to meet him; but Mary sat at home. ²¹Martha said to Jesus, "Lord, if you had been here, my brother would not have died.ʳ ²²[But] even now I know that whatever you ask of God, God will give you." ²³Jesus said to her, "Your brother will rise." ²⁴Martha said to him, "I know he will rise, in the resurrection on the last day."ˢ ²⁵Jesus told her, "I am the resurrection and the life; whoever believes in me, even if he dies, will live,ᵗ ²⁶and everyone who lives and believes in me will never die. Do you believe this?" ²⁷††ᵘShe said to him, "Yes, Lord. I have come to believe that you are the Messiah, the Son of God, the one who is coming into the world."

²⁸When she had said this, she went and called her sister Mary secretly, saying, "The teacher is here and is asking for you." ²⁹As soon as she heard this, she rose quickly and went to him. ³⁰For Jesus had not yet come into the village, but was still where Martha had met him. ³¹So when the Jews who were with her in the house comforting her saw Mary get up quickly and go out, they followed her, presuming that she was going to the tomb to weep there. ³²When Mary came to where Jesus was and saw him, she fell at his feet and said to him, "Lord, if you had been here, my brother would not have died." ³³When Jesus saw her weeping and the Jews who had come with her weeping, he became perturbed‡‡ and deeply troubled, ³⁴and said, "Where have you laid him?" They said to him, "Sir, come and see." ³⁵And Jesus wept.ᵛ ³⁶So the Jews said, "See how he loved him." ³⁷But some of them said, "Could not the one who opened the eyes of the blind man have done something so that this man would not have died?"

³⁸So Jesus, perturbed again, came to the tomb. It was a cave, and a stone lay across it. ³⁹Jesus said, "Take away the stone." Martha, the

---

*[10:41] **Performed no sign**: this is to stress the inferior role of John the Baptist. The Transjordan topography recalls the great witness of John the Baptist to Jesus, as opposed to the hostility of the authorities in Jerusalem.

†[11:1–44] The raising of Lazarus, the longest continuous narrative in John outside of the passion account, is the climax of the signs. It leads directly to the decision of the Sanhedrin to kill Jesus. The theme of life predominates. Lazarus is a token of the real life that Jesus gives dead and raised will give to all who believe in him. Johannine irony is found in the fact that Jesus' gift of life leads to his own death. The story is not found in the synoptics, but cf. Mk 5:21 and parallels; Lk 7:11–17. There are also parallels between this story and Luke's parable of the rich man and poor Lazarus (Lk 16:19–31). In both a man named Lazarus dies; in Luke, there is a request that he return to convince his contemporaries of the need for faith and repentance, while in John, Lazarus does return and some believe but others do not.

‡[11:4] **Not to end in death**: this is misunderstood by the disciples as referring to physical death, but it is meant as spiritual death.

§[11:10] **The light is not in him**: the ancients apparently did not grasp clearly the entry of light *through* the eye; they seem to have thought of it as being *in* the eye; cf. Lk 11:34; Mt 6:23.

¶[11:16] **Called Didymus**: Didymus is the Greek word for twin. Thomas is derived from the Aramaic word for twin; in an ancient Syriac version and in the Gospel of Thomas (80:11–12) his given name, Judas, is supplied.

**[11:18] **About two miles**: literally, "about fifteen stades"; a stade was 607 feet.

††[11:27] The titles here are a summary of titles given to Jesus earlier in the gospel.

‡‡[11:33] **Became perturbed**: a startling phrase in Greek, literally, "He snorted in spirit," perhaps in anger at the presence of evil (death).

---

h. [10:40] 1:28.  i. [10:42] 2:23; 7:31; 8:30.  j. [11:1–2] 12:1–8; Lk 10:38–42; 16:19–31.  k. [11:4] 9:3, 24.  l. [11:8] 8:59; 10:31.  m. [11:9–10] 12:35; 1 Jn 2:10.  n. [11:9] 8:12; 9:4.  o. [11:13] Mt 9:24.

p. [11:16] 14:5, 22.  q. [11:19] 12:9, 17–18.  r. [11:21] 11:32.  s. [11:24] 5:29; 6:39–40, 44, 54; 12:48; Is 2:2; Mi 4:1; Acts 23:8; 24:15.  t. [11:25] 5:24; 8:51; 14:6; Dn 12:2.  u. [11:27] 1:9; 6:69.  v. [11:35] Lk 19:41.

dead man's sister, said to him, "Lord, by now there will be a stench; he has been dead for four days." ⁴⁰Jesus said to her, "Did I not tell you that if you believe you will see the glory of God?" ⁴¹So they took away the stone. And Jesus raised his eyes and said, "Father,* I thank you for hearing me. ⁴²I know that you always hear me; but because of the crowd here I have said this, that they may believe that you sent me."ʷ ⁴³And when he had said this, he cried out in a loud voice,† "Lazarus, come out!" ⁴⁴The dead man came out, tied hand and foot with burial bands, and his face was wrapped in a cloth. So Jesus said to them, "Untie him and let him go."

**Session of the Sanhedrin.** ⁴⁵Now many of the Jews who had come to Mary and seen what he had done began to believe in him.ˣ ⁴⁶But some of them went to the Pharisees and told them what Jesus had done. ⁴⁷So the chief priests and the Pharisees convened the Sanhedrin and said, "What are we going to do? This man is performing many signs.ʸ ⁴⁸If we leave him alone, all will believe in him, and the Romans will come‡ and take away both our land and our nation." ⁴⁹ᶻBut one of them, Caiaphas, who was high priest that year,§ said to them, "You know nothing, ⁵⁰nor do you consider that it is better for you that one man should die instead of the people, so that the whole nation may not perish." ⁵¹He did not say this on his own, but since he was high priest for that year, he prophesied that Jesus was going to die for the nation, ⁵²and not only for the nation, but also to gather into one the dispersed children of God.¶ ⁵³So from that day on they planned to kill him.ᵃ

⁵⁴So Jesus no longer walked about in public among the Jews, but he left for the region near the desert, to a town called Ephraim,** and there he remained with his disciples.

**The Last Passover.** ⁵⁵Now the Passover of the Jews was near, and many went up from the country to Jerusalem before Passover to purify†† themselves.ᵇ ⁵⁶They looked for Jesus and said to one another as they were in the temple area, "What do you think? That he will not come to

the feast?" ⁵⁷For the chief priests and the Pharisees had given orders that if anyone knew where he was, he should inform them, so that they might arrest him.

# CHAPTER 12

**The Anointing at Bethany.**ᶜ ¹‡Six days before Passover Jesus came to Bethany, where Lazarus was, whom Jesus had raised from the dead.ᵈ ²They gave a dinner for him there, and Martha served, while Lazarus was one of those reclining at table with him.ᵉ ³Mary took a liter of costly perfumed oil made from genuine aromatic nard and anointed the feet of Jesus§§ and dried them with her hair; the house was filled with the fragrance of the oil.ᶠ ⁴Then Judas the Iscariot, one [of] his disciples, and the one who would betray him, said, ⁵"Why was this oil not sold for three hundred days' wages¶¶ and given to the poor?". ⁶He said this not because he cared about the poor but because he was a thief and held the money bag and used to steal the contributions.ᵍ ⁷So Jesus said, "Leave her alone. Let her keep this for the day of my burial.*** ⁸You always have the poor with you, but you do not always have me."ʰ

⁹[The] large crowd of the Jews found out that he was there and came, not only because of Jesus, but also to see Lazarus, whom he had raised from the dead.ⁱ ¹⁰And the chief priests plotted to kill Lazarus too, ¹¹because many of the Jews were turning away and believing in Jesus because of him.ʲ

**The Entry into Jerusalem.**††† ¹²ᵏOn the next day, when the great crowd that had come to the feast heard that Jesus was coming to Jerusalem, ¹³they took palm branches‡‡‡ and went out to meet him, and cried out:

---

‡‡[12:1–8] This is probably the same scene of anointing found in Mk 14:3–9 (see note there) and Mt 26:6–13. The anointing by a penitent woman in Lk 7:36–38 is different. Details from these various episodes have become interchanged.

§§[12:3] **The feet of Jesus:** so Mk 14:3; but in Mt 26:6, Mary anoints Jesus' head as a sign of regal, messianic anointing.

¶¶[12:5] **Days' wages:** literally, "denarii." A denarius is a day's wage in Mt 20:2; see note on Jn 6:7.

***[12:7] Jesus' response reflects the rabbinical discussion of what was the greatest act of mercy, almsgiving or burying the dead. Those who favored proper burial of the dead thought it an essential condition for sharing in the resurrection.

†††[12:12–19] In John, the entry into Jerusalem follows the anointing whereas in the synoptics it precedes. In John, the crowd, not the disciples, are responsible for the triumphal procession.

‡‡‡[12:13] **Palm branches:** used to welcome great conquerors; cf. 1 Mc 13:51; 2 Mc 10:7. They may be related to the lûlāb, the twig bundles used at the feast of Tabernacles. **Hosanna:** see Ps 118:25–26. The Hebrew word means: "(O Lord), grant salvation." In Ps 118:26 to a pilgrim entering the temple gates, but here a title for Jesus (see notes on Mt 11:3 and Jn 6:14; 11:27). The **king of Israel:** perhaps from Zep 3:14–15, in connection with the next quotation from Zec 9:9.

---

*[11:41] **Father:** in Aramaic, *'abbā'*. See note on Mk 14:36.

†[11:43] **Cried out in a loud voice:** a dramatization of Jn 5:28; "the hour is coming when all who are in the tombs will hear his voice."

‡[11:48] **The Romans will come:** Johannine irony; this is precisely what happened after Jesus' death.

§[11:49] **That year:** emphasizes the conjunction of the office and the year. Actually, Caiaphas was high priest A.D. 18–36. The Jews attributed a gift of prophecy, sometimes unconscious, to the high priest.

¶[11:52] **Dispersed children of God:** perhaps the "other sheep" of Jn 10:16.

**[11:54] Ephraim is usually located about twelve miles northeast of Jerusalem, where the mountains descend into the Jordan valley.

††[11:55] **Purify:** prescriptions for purity were based on Ex 19:10–11, 15; Nm 9:6–14; 2 Chr 30:1–3, 15–18.

---

w. [11:42] 12:30.   x. [11:45] Lk 16:31.   y. [11:47] 12:19; Mt 26:3–5; Lk 22:2; Acts 4:16.   z. [11:49–50] 18:13–14.   a. [11:53] 5:18; 7:1; Mt 12:14.   b. [11:55] 2:13; 5:1; 6:4; 18:28; Ex 9:10–11, 15; Nm 9:6–14; 19:12; Dt 16:6; 2 Chr 30:1–3, 15–18.

c. [12:1–11] Mt 26:6–13; Mk 14:3–9.   d. [12:1–2] 11:1.   e. [12:2] Lk 10:38–42.   f. [12:3] 11:2.   g. [12:6] 13:29.   h. [12:8] Dt 15:11.   i. [12:9] 11:19.   j. [12:11] 11:45.   k. [12:12–19] Mt 21:1–16; Mk 11:1–10; Lk 19:28–40.

"Hosanna!
Blessed is he who comes in the name of
the Lord,
[even] the king of Israel."*l*

14Jesus found an ass and sat upon it, as is written:

15 "Fear no more, O daughter Zion;*
see, your king comes, seated upon
an ass's colt."*m*

16His disciples did not understand this at first, but when Jesus had been glorified they remembered that these things were written about him and that they had done this† for him.*n* 17‡So the crowd that was with him when he called Lazarus from the tomb and raised him from death continued to testify. 18This was [also] why the crowd went to meet him, because they heard that he had done this sign. 19So the Pharisees said to one another, "You see that you are gaining nothing. Look, the whole world§ has gone after him."*o*

**The Coming of Jesus' Hour.**¶ 20Now there were some Greeks** among those who had come up to worship at the feast.*p* 21††They came to Philip, who was from Bethsaida in Galilee, and asked him, "Sir, we would like to see Jesus."*q* 22Philip went and told Andrew; then Andrew and Philip went and told Jesus.*r* 23‡‡Jesus answered them,* "The hour has come for the Son of Man to be glorified. 24§§Amen, amen, I say to you, unless a grain of wheat falls to the ground and dies, it remains just a grain of wheat;*t* but if it dies, it produces much fruit. 25Whoever loves his life¶¶ loses it, and

whoever hates his life in this world will preserve it for eternal life.*u* 26Whoever serves me must follow me, and where I am, there also will my servant be. The Father will honor whoever serves me.*v*

27"I am troubled*** now. Yet what should I say? 'Father, save me from this hour'? But it was for this purpose that I came to this hour.*w* 28Father, glorify your name." Then a voice came from heaven, "I have glorified it and will glorify it again."*x* 29The crowd there heard it and said it was thunder; but others said, "An angel has spoken to him."*y* 30Jesus answered and said, "This voice did not come for my sake but for yours.*z* 31Now is the time of judgment on this world; now the ruler of this world††† will be driven out.*a* 32And when I am lifted up from the earth, I will draw everyone to myself."*b* 33He said this indicating the kind of death he would die. 34So the crowd answered him, "We have heard from the law that the Messiah remains forever.‡‡‡ Then how can you say that the Son of Man must be lifted up? Who is this Son of Man?"*c* 35Jesus said to them, "The light will be among you only a little while. Walk while you have the light, so that darkness may not overcome you. Whoever walks in the dark does not know where he is going.*d* 36While you have the light, believe in the light, so that you may become children of the light."*e*

**Unbelief and Belief Among the Jews.** After he had said this, Jesus left and hid from them. 37§§§Although he had performed so many signs in their presence they did not believe in him, 38¶¶¶in order that the word which Isaiah the prophet spoke might be fulfilled:

"Lord, who has believed our preaching,
to whom has the might of the Lord
been revealed?"*g*

39For this reason they could not believe, because again Isaiah said:

---

*[12:15] **Daughter Zion**: Jerusalem. **Ass's colt**: symbol of peace, as opposed to the war horse.
†[12:16] **They had done this**: the antecedent of **they** is ambiguous.
‡[12:17–18] There seem to be two different crowds in these verses. There are some good witnesses to the text that have another reading for Jn 12:17: "Then the crowd that was with him began to testify that he had called Lazarus out of the tomb and raised him from the dead."
§[12:19] **The whole world**: the sense is that everyone is following Jesus, but John has an ironic play on **world**; he alludes to the universality of salvation (Jn 3:17; 4:42).
¶[12:20–36] This announcement of glorification by death is an illustration of "the whole world" (Jn 12:19) going after him.
**[12:20] **Greeks**: not used here in a nationalistic sense. These are probably Gentile proselytes to Judaism; cf. Jn 7:35.
††[12:21–22] **Philip . . . Andrew**: the approach is made through disciples who have distinctly Greek names, suggesting that access to Jesus was mediated to the Greek world through his disciples. Philip and Andrew were from Bethsaida (Jn 1:44); Galileans were mostly bilingual. **See**: here seems to mean "have an interview with."
‡‡[12:23] Jesus' response suggests that only after the crucifixion could the gospel encompass both Jew and Gentile.
§§[12:24] This verse implies that through his death Jesus will be accessible to all. **It remains just a grain of wheat**: this saying is found in the synoptic triple and double traditions (Mk 8:35; Mt 16:25; Lk 9:24; Mt 10:39; Lk 17:33). John adds the phrases (Jn 12:25) **in this world** and **for eternal life**.
¶¶[12:25] **His life**: the Greek word *psychē* refers to a person's natural life. It does not mean "soul," for Hebrew anthropol-

ogy did not postulate body/soul dualism in the way that is familiar to us.
***[12:27] **I am troubled**: perhaps an allusion to the Gethsemane agony scene of the synoptics.
†††[12:31] **Ruler of this world**: Satan.
‡‡‡[12:34] There is no passage in the Old Testament that states precisely that the **Messiah remains forever**. Perhaps the closest is Ps 89:37.
§§§[12:37–50] These verses, on unbelief of the Jews, provide an epilogue to the Book of Signs.
¶¶¶[12:38–41] John gives a historical explanation of the disbelief of the Jewish people, not a psychological one. The Old Testament had to be fulfilled; the disbelief that met Isaiah's message was a foreshadowing of the disbelief that Jesus encountered. In Jn 12:42 and also in Jn 3:20 we see that there is no negation of freedom.

u. [12:25] Mt 10:39; 16:25; Mk 8:35; Lk 9:24; 17:33.   v. [12:26] 14:3; 17:24; Mt 16:24; Mk 8:34; Lk 9:23.   w. [12:27] 6:38; 18:11; Mt 26:38–39; Mk 14:34–36; Lk 22:42; Heb 5:7–8.   x. [12:28] 2:11; 17:5; Dn 4:31, 34.   y. [12:29] Ex 9:28; 2 Sm 22:14; Jb 37:4; Ps 29:3; Lk 22:43; Acts 23:9.   z. [12:30] 11:42; Lk 16:11; Lk 10:18; Rev 12:9.   b. [12:32] 3:14; 8:28; Is 52:13.   c. [12:34] Ps 89:5; 110:4; Is 9:7; Dn 7:13–14; Rev 20:1–6.   d. [12:35] 9:4; 11:10; Jb 5:14.   e. [12:36] Eph 5:8.   f. [12:37–43] Dt 29:2–4; Mk 4:11–12; Rom 9–11.   g. [12:38] Is 53:1; Rom 10:16.

---

l. [12:13] 1:49; Lv 23:40; 1 Mc 13:51; 2 Mc 10:7; Rev 7:9.   m. [12:15] Is 40:9; Zec 9:9.   n. [12:16] 2:22.   o. [12:19] 11:47–48.   p. [12:20] Acts 10:2.   q. [12:21] 1:44.   r. [12:22] 1:40.   s. [12:23] 2:4.   t. [12:24] Is 53:10–12; 1 Cor 15:36.

[40] "He blinded their eyes
    and hardened their heart,
so that they might not see with their eyes
    and understand with their heart and
    be converted,
and I would heal them."[h]

[41]Isaiah said this because he saw his glory* and spoke about him.[i] [42]Nevertheless, many, even among the authorities, believed in him, but because of the Pharisees they did not acknowledge it openly in order not to be expelled from the synagogue.[j] [43]For they preferred human praise to the glory of God.[k]

**Recapitulation.** [44]Jesus cried out and said, "Whoever believes in me believes not only in me but also in the one who sent me,[l] [45]and whoever sees me sees the one who sent me.[m] [46]I came into the world as light, so that everyone who believes in me might not remain in darkness.[n] [47]And if anyone hears my words and does not observe them, I do not condemn him, for I did not come to condemn the world but to save the world.[o] [48]Whoever rejects me and does not accept my words has something to judge him: the word that I spoke, it will condemn him on the last day,[p] [49]because I did not speak on my own, but the Father who sent me commanded me what to say and speak.[q] [50]And I know that his commandment is eternal life. So what I say, I say as the Father told me."

## III. THE BOOK OF GLORY[†]

## CHAPTER 13

**The Washing of the Disciples' Feet.**[‡] [1]Before the feast of Passover,[§] Jesus knew that his hour had come to pass from this world to the Father. He loved his own in the world and he loved them to the end.[r] [2]The devil had already induced[¶]

Judas, son of Simon the Iscariot, to hand him over. So, during supper,[s] [3]fully aware that the Father had put everything into his power and that he had come from God and was returning to God,[t] [4]he rose from supper and took off his outer garments. He took a towel and tied it around his waist. [5]**Then he poured water into a basin and began to wash the disciples' feet[u] and dry them with the towel around his waist. [6]He came to Simon Peter, who said to him, "Master, are you going to wash my feet?" [7]Jesus answered and said to him, "What I am doing, you do not understand now, but you will understand later." [8]Peter said to him, "You will never wash my feet." Jesus answered him, "Unless I wash you, you will have no inheritance with me."[v] [9]Simon Peter said to him, "Master, then not only my feet, but my hands and head as well." [10]Jesus said to him, "Whoever has bathed[††] has no need except to have his feet washed, for he is clean all over; so you are clean, but not all."[w] [11]For he knew who would betray him; for this reason, he said, "Not all of you are clean."[x]

[12]So when he had washed their feet [and] put his garments back on and reclined at table again, he said to them, "Do you realize what I have done for you? [13]You call me 'teacher' and 'master,' and rightly so, for indeed I am.[y] [14]If I, therefore, the master and teacher, have washed your feet, you ought to wash one another's feet. [15]I have given you a model to follow, so that as I have done for you, you should also do.[z] [16]Amen, amen, I say to you, no slave is greater than his master nor any messenger[‡‡] greater than the one who sent him.[a] [17]If you understand this, blessed are you if you do it. [18]I am not speaking of all of you. I know those whom I have chosen. But so that the scripture might be fulfilled, 'The one who ate my food has raised his heel against me.'[b] [19]From now on I am telling you before it happens, so that when it happens you may believe that I AM. [20]Amen, amen, I say to you, whoever receives the one I send receives me, and whoever receives me receives the one who sent me."[c]

**Announcement of Judas's Betrayal.**[d] [21]When he had said this, Jesus was deeply troubled and testified, "Amen, amen, I say to you, one of you will betray me." [22]The disciples looked at one

---

*[12:41] **His glory**: Isaiah saw the glory of Yahweh enthroned in the heavenly temple, but in John the antecedent of **his** is Jesus.

†[13:1–19:42] The Book of Glory. There is a major break here; the word "sign" is used again only in Jn 20:30. In this phase of Jesus' return to the Father, the discourses (Jn 13–17) precede the traditional narrative of the passion (Jn 18–20) to interpret them for the Christian reader. This is the only extended example of esoteric teaching of disciples in John.

‡[13:1–20] Washing of the disciples' feet. This episode occurs in John at the place of the narration of the institution of the Eucharist in the synoptics. It may be a dramatization of Lk 22:27—"I am your servant." It is presented as a "model" ("pattern") of the crucifixion. It symbolizes cleansing from sin by sacrificial death.

§[13:1] **Before the feast of Passover**: this would be Thursday evening, before the day of preparation; in the synoptics, the Last Supper is a Passover meal taking place, in John's chronology, on Friday evening. **To the end**: or, "completely."

¶[13:2] **Induced**: literally, "The devil put into the heart that Judas should hand him over."

---

**[13:5] The act of washing another's feet was one that could not be required of the lowliest Jewish slave. It is an allusion to the humiliating death of the crucifixion.

††[13:10] **Bathed**: many have suggested that this passage is a symbolic reference to baptism. The Greek root involved is used in baptismal contexts in 1 Cor 6:11; Eph 5:26; Ti 3:5; Heb 10:22.

‡‡[13:16] **Messenger**: the Greek has *apostolos*, the only occurrence of the term in John. It is not used in the technical sense here.

---

h. [12:40] Is 6:9–10; Mt 13:13–15; Mk 4:12.   i. [12:41] 5:39; Is 6:1, 4.   j. [12:42] 9:22.   k. [12:43] 5:44.   l. [12:44] 13:20; 14:1.   m. [12:45] 14:7–9.   n. [12:46] 1:9; 8:12.   o. [12:47] 3:17.   p. [12:48] Lk 10:16; Heb 4:12.   q. [12:49] 14:10, 31; Dt 18:18–19.   r. [13:1] 2:4; 7:30; 8:20; Mt 26:17, 45; Mk 14:12, 41; Lk 22:7.

s. [13:2] 6:71; 17:12; Mt 26:20–21; Mk 14:17–18; Lk 22:3.   t. [13:3] 3:35.   u. [13:5] 1 Sm 25:41.   v. [13:8] 2 Sm 20:1.   w. [13:10] 15:3.   x. [13:11] 6:70.   y. [13:13] Mt 23:8, 10.   z. [13:15] Lk 22:27; 1 Pt 2:21.   a. [13:16] 15:20; Mt 10:24; Lk 6:40.   b. [13:18] Ps 41:10.   c. [13:20] Mt 10:40; Mk 9:37; Lk 9:48.   d. [13:21–30] Mt 26:21–25; Mk 14:18–21; Lk 22:21–23.

another, at a loss as to whom he meant. [23]One of his disciples, the one whom Jesus loved,* was reclining at Jesus' side.[e] [24]So Simon Peter nodded to him to find out whom he meant. [25]He leaned back against Jesus' chest and said to him, "Master, who is it?"[f] [26]Jesus answered, "It is the one to whom I hand the morsel[†] after I have dipped it." So he dipped the morsel and [took it and] handed it to Judas, son of Simon the Iscariot. [27]After he took the morsel, Satan entered him. So Jesus said to him, "What you are going to do, do quickly."[g] [28][Now] none of those reclining at table realized why he said this to him. [29]Some thought that since Judas kept the money bag, Jesus had told him, "Buy what we need for the feast," or to give something to the poor.[h] [30]So he took the morsel and left at once. And it was night.

**The New Commandment.** [31‡]When he had left, Jesus said,[§] "Now is the Son of Man glorified, and God is glorified in him. [32][If God is glorified in him,] God will also glorify him in himself, and he will glorify him at once.[i] [33]My children, I will be with you only a little while longer. You will look for me, and as I told the Jews, 'Where I go you cannot come,' so now I say it to you.[j] [34]I give you a new commandment:[¶] love one another. As I have loved you, so you also should love one another.[k] [35]This is how all will know that you are my disciples, if you have love for one another."

**Peter's Denial Predicted.** [36]Simon Peter said to him, "Master, where are you going?" Jesus answered [him], "Where I am going, you cannot follow me now, though you will follow later."[l] [37]Peter said to him, "Master, why can't I follow you now? I will lay down my life for you." [38]Jesus answered, "Will you lay down your life for me? Amen, amen, I say to you, the cock will not crow before you deny me three times."[m]

# CHAPTER 14

**Last Supper Discourses.** [1**]"Do not let your hearts be troubled. You have faith[††] in God; have faith also in me. [2]In my Father's house there are many dwelling places. If there were not, would I have told you that I am going to prepare a place for you? [3‡‡]And if I go and prepare a place for you, I will come back again and take you to myself, so that where I am you also may be.[n] [4]Where [I] am going you know the way."[§§] [5]Thomas said to him, "Master, we do not know where you are going; how can we know the way?" [6]Jesus said to him, "I am the way and the truth[¶¶] and the life. No one comes to the Father except through me.[o] [7]If you know me, then you will also know my Father.*** From now on you do know him and have seen him."[p] [8]Philip said to him, "Master, show us the Father,[†††] and that will be enough for us."[q] [9]Jesus said to him, "Have I been with you for so long a time and you still do not know me, Philip? Whoever has seen me has seen the Father. How can you say, 'Show us the Father'?[r] [10]Do you not believe that I am in the Father and the Father is in me? The words that I speak to you I do not speak on my own. The Father who dwells in me is doing his works.[s] [11]Believe me that I am in the Father and the Father is in me, or else, believe because of the works themselves.[t] [12]Amen, amen, I say to you, whoever believes in me will do the works that I do, and will do greater ones than these, because I am going to the Father.[u] [13]And whatever you ask in my name, I will do, so that the Father may be glorified in the Son.[v] [14]If you ask anything of me in my name, I will do it.

**The Advocate.** [15]"If you love me, you will keep my commandments.[w] [16]And I will ask the Father, and he will give you another Advocate[‡‡‡]

*[13:23] **The one whom Jesus loved:** also mentioned in Jn 19:26; 20:2; 21:7. A disciple, called "another disciple" or "the other disciple," is mentioned in Jn 18:15 and Jn 20:2; in the latter reference he is identified with the disciple whom Jesus loved. There is also an unnamed disciple in Jn 1:35–40; see note on Jn 1:37.

†[13:26] **Morsel:** probably the bitter herb dipped in salt water.

‡[13:31–17:26] Two farewell discourses and a prayer. These seem to be Johannine compositions, including sayings of Jesus at the Last Supper and on other occasions, modeled on similar farewell discourses in Greek literature and the Old Testament (of Moses, Joshua, David).

§[13:31–38] Introduction: departure and return. Terms of coming and going predominate. These verses form an introduction to the last discourse of Jesus, which extends through Jn 14–17. In it John has collected Jesus' words to his own (Jn 13:1). There are indications that several speeches have been fused together, e.g., in Jn 14:31 and Jn 17:1.

¶[13:34] **I give you a new commandment:** this puts Jesus on a par with Yahweh. The commandment itself is not new; cf. Lv 19:18 and note there.

**[14:1–31] Jesus' departure and return. This section is a dialogue marked off by a literary inclusion in Jn 14:1, 27: "Do not let your hearts be troubled."

††[14:1] **You have faith:** could also be imperative: "Have faith."

‡‡[14:3] **Come back again:** a rare Johannine reference to the parousia; cf. 1 Jn 2:28.

§§[14:4] **The way:** here, of Jesus himself; also a designation of Christianity in Acts 9:2; 19:9, 23; 22:4; 24:14, 22.

¶¶[14:6] **The truth:** in John, the divinely revealed reality of the Father manifested in the person and works of Jesus. The possession of truth confers knowledge and liberation from sin (Jn 8:32).

***[14:7] An alternative reading, "If you knew me, then you would have known my Father also," would be a rebuke, as in Jn 8:19.

†††[14:8] **Show us the Father:** Philip is pictured asking for a theophany like Ex 24:9–10; 33:18.

‡‡‡[14:16] **Another Advocate:** Jesus is the first advocate (*paraclete*); see 1 Jn 2:1, where Jesus is an advocate in the sense of intercessor in heaven. The Greek term derives from legal terminology for an advocate or defense attorney, and can mean spokesman, mediator, intercessor, comforter, consoler, although no one of these terms encompasses the meaning in John. The Paraclete in John is a teacher, a witness to Jesus,

e. [13:23] 19:26; 20:2; 21:7,20; Mt 10:37.  f. [13:25] 21:20.  g. [13:27] 13:2; Lk 22:3.  h. [13:29] 12:5–6.  i. [13:32] 17:1–5.  j. [13:33] 7:33; 8:21.  k. [13:34] 15:12–13, 17; Lv 19:18; 1 Thes 4:9; 1 Jn 2:7–10; 3:23; 2 Jn 5.  l. [13:36] Mk 14:27; Lk 22:23.  m. [13:38] 18:27; Mt 26:33–35; Mk 14:29–31; Lk 22:33–34.

n. [14:3] 12:26; 17:24; 1 Jn 2:28.  o. [14:6] 8:31–47.  p. [14:7] 8:19; 12:45.  q. [14:8] Ex 24:9–10; 33:18.  r. [14:9] 1:18; 10:30; 12:45; 2 Cor 4:4; Col 1:15; Heb 1:3.  s. [14:10] 1:1; 10:37–38; 12:49.  t. [14:11] 10:38.  u. [14:12] 1:50; 5:20.  v. [14:13] 15:7, 16; 16:23–24; Mt 7:7–11.  w. [14:15] 15:10; Dt 6:4–9; Ps 119; Wis 6:18; 1 Jn 5:3; 2 Jn 6.

to be with you always,[x] [17]the Spirit of truth,* which the world cannot accept, because it neither sees nor knows it. But you know it, because it remains with you, and will be in you.[y] [18]I will not leave you orphans; I will come to you.[†] [19]In a little while the world will no longer see me, but you will see me, because I live and you will live.[z] [20]On that day you will realize that I am in my Father and you are in me and I in you.[a] [21]Whoever has my commandments and observes them is the one who loves me. And whoever loves me will be loved by my Father, and I will love him and reveal myself to him.[b] [22]Judas, not the Iscariot,[‡] said to him, "Master, [then] what happened that you will reveal yourself to us and not to the world?"[c] [23]Jesus answered and said to him, "Whoever loves me will keep my word, and my Father will love him, and we will come to him and make our dwelling with him.[d] [24]Whoever does not love me does not keep my words; yet the word you hear is not mine but that of the Father who sent me.

[25]"I have told you this while I am with you. [26]The Advocate, the holy Spirit that the Father will send in my name—he will teach you everything and remind you of all that [I] told you.[e] [27]Peace[§] I leave with you; my peace I give to you. Not as the world gives do I give it to you. Do not let your hearts be troubled or afraid.[f] [28]You heard me tell you, 'I am going away and I will come back to you.'[g] If you loved me, you would rejoice that I am going to the Father; for the Father is greater than I. [29]And now I have told you this before it happens, so that when it happens you may believe.[h] [30]I will no longer speak much with you, for the ruler of the world* is coming. He has no power over me, [31]but the world must know that I love the Father and that

I do just as the Father has commanded me. Get up, let us go.[i]

## CHAPTER 15

**The Vine and the Branches.** [††]"I am the true vine,[‡‡] and my Father is the vine grower.[j] [2]He takes away every branch in me that does not bear fruit, and every one that does he prunes[§§] so that it bears more fruit. [3]You are already pruned because of the word that I spoke to you.[k] [4]Remain in me, as I remain in you. Just as a branch cannot bear fruit on its own unless it remains on the vine, so neither can you unless you remain in me. [5]I am the vine, you are the branches. Whoever remains in me and I in him will bear much fruit, because without me you can do nothing. [6]¶¶Anyone who does not remain in me will be thrown out like a branch and wither; people will gather them and throw them into a fire and they will be burned. [7]If you remain in me and my words remain in you, ask for whatever you want and it will be done for you.[m] [8]By this is my Father glorified, that you bear much fruit and become my disciples.[n] [9]As the Father loves me, so I also love you. Remain in my love.[o] [10]If you keep my commandments, you will remain in my love, just as I have kept my Father's commandments and remain in his love.[p]

[11]"I have told you this so that my joy may be in you and your joy may be complete.[q] [12]This is my commandment: love one another as I love you.[r] [13]***No one has greater love than this,[s] to lay down one's life for one's friends. [14]You are my friends if you do what I command you. [15]I no longer call you slaves, because a slave does not know what his master is doing. I have called you friends,[†††] because I have told you everything I have heard

---

and a prosecutor of the world, who represents the continued presence on earth of the Jesus who has returned to the Father.

*[14:17] **The Spirit of truth:** this term is also used at Qumran, where it is a moral force put into a person by God, as opposed to the spirit of perversity. It is more personal in John; it will teach the realities of the new order (Jn 14:26), and testify to the truth (Jn 14:6). While it has been customary to use masculine personal pronouns in English for the Advocate, the Greek word for "spirit" is neuter, and the Greek text and manuscript variants fluctuate between masculine and neuter pronouns.

†[14:18] **I will come to you:** indwelling, not parousia.

‡[14:22] **Judas, not the Iscariot:** probably not the brother of Jesus in Mk 6:3 // Mt 13:55 or the apostle named Jude in Lk 6:16, but Thomas (see note on Jn 11:16), although other readings have "Judas the Cananean."

§[14:27] **Peace:** the traditional Hebrew salutation *šālôm*; but Jesus' "Shalom" is a gift of salvation, connoting the bounty of messianic blessing.

¶[14:28] **The Father is greater than I:** because he **sent, gave,** etc., and Jesus is "a man who has told you the truth that I heard from God" (Jn 8:40).

**[14:30] **The ruler of the world:** Satan; cf. Jn 12:31; 16:11.

††[15:1–16:4] Discourse on the union of Jesus with his disciples. His words become a monologue and go beyond the immediate crisis of the departure of Jesus.

‡‡[15:1–17] Like Jn 10:1–5, this passage resembles a parable. Israel is spoken of as a vineyard at Is 5:1–7; Mt 21:33–46 and as a vine at Ps 80:9–17; Jer 2:21; Ez 15:2; 17:5–10; 19:10; Hos 10:1. The identification of the vine as the Son of Man in Ps 80:15 and Wisdom's description of herself as a vine in Sir 24:17 are further background for portrayal of Jesus by this figure. There may be secondary eucharistic symbolism here; cf. Mk 14:25, "the fruit of the vine."

§§[15:2] **Takes away . . . prunes:** in Greek there is a play on two related verbs.

¶¶[15:6] Branches were cut off and dried on the wall of the vineyard for later use as fuel.

***[15:13] **For one's friends:** or: "those whom one loves." In Jn 15:9–13a, the words for love are related to the Greek *agapaō*. In Jn 15:13b–15, the words for love are related to the Greek *phileō*. For John, the two roots seem synonymous and mean "to love"; cf. also Jn 21:15–17. The word *philos* is used here.

†††[15:15] **Slaves . . . friends:** in the Old Testament, Moses (Dt 34:5), Joshua (Jos 24:29), and David (Ps 89:21) were called "servants" or "slaves of Yahweh"; only Abraham (Is 41:8; 2 Chr 20:7; cf. Jas 2:23) was called a "friend of God."

---

x. [14:16] 15:26; Lk 24:49; 1 Jn 2:1.   y. [14:17] 16:13; Mt 28:20; 2 Jn 1–2.   z. [14:19] 16:16.   a. [14:20] 10:38; 17:21; Is 2:17; 4:2–3.   b. [14:21] 16:27; 1 Jn 2:5; 3:24.   c. [14:22] 7:4; Acts 10:40–41.   d. [14:23] Rev 3:20.   e. [14:26] 15:26; 16:7, 13–14; Ps 51:13; Is 63:10.   f. [14:27] 16:33; Eph 2:14–18.   g. [14:28] 8:40.   h. [14:29] 13:19; 16:4.

i. [14:31] 6:38.   j. [15:1] Ps 80:9–17; Is 5:1–7; Jer 2:21; Ez 15:2; 17:5–10; 19:10; 13:10.   k. [15:3] 13:10.   l. [15:6] Ez 15:6–7; 19:10–14.   m. [15:7] 14:13; Mt 7:7; Mk 11:24; 1 Jn 5:14.   n. [15:8] Mt 5:16.   o. [15:9] 17:23.   p. [15:10] 8:29; 14:15.   q. [15:11] 16:22; 17:13.   r. [15:12] 13:34.   s. [15:13] Rom 5:6–8; 1 Jn 3:16.

from my Father.[t] [16]It was not you who chose me, but I who chose you and appointed you to go and bear fruit that will remain, so that whatever you ask the Father in my name he may give you.[u] [17]This I command you: love one another.[v]

**The World's Hatred.**[*] [18]"If the world hates you, realize that it hated me first.[w] [19]If you belonged to the world, the world would love its own; but because you do not belong to the world, and I have chosen you out of the world, the world hates you.[x] [20]Remember the word I spoke to you,[†] 'No slave is greater than his master.' If they persecuted me, they will also persecute you. If they kept my word, they will also keep yours.[y] [21]And they will do all these things to you on account of my name,[‡] because they do not know the one who sent me.[z] [22]If I had not come and spoken[§] to them, they would have no sin; but as it is they have no excuse for their sin.[b] [23]Whoever hates me also hates my Father.[b] [24]If I had not done works among them that no one else ever did, they would not have sin; but as it is, they have seen and hated both me and my Father.[c] [25]But in order that the word written in their law[¶] might be fulfilled, 'They hated me without cause.'[d]

[26]"When the Advocate comes whom I will send[**] you from the Father, the Spirit of truth that proceeds from the Father, he will testify to me.[e] [27]And you also testify, because you have been with me from the beginning.[f]

### CHAPTER 16

[1]"I have told you this so that you may not fall away. [2]They will expel you from the synagogues; in fact, the hour[††] is coming when everyone who kills you will think he is offering worship to God.[g] [3]They will do this because they have not known either the Father or me.[h] [4]I have told you this so that when their hour comes you may remember that I told you.[i]

**Jesus' Departure; Coming of the Advocate.**[‡‡] "I did not tell you this from the beginning, because I was with you. [5]But now I am going to the one who sent me, and not one of you asks me,[§§] 'Where are you going?'[i] [6]But because I told you this, grief has filled your hearts. [7]But I tell you the truth, it is better for you that I go. For if I do not go, the Advocate will not come to you.[k] But if I go, I will send him to you. [8][¶¶]And when he comes he will convict the world in regard to sin and righteousness and condemnation: [9]sin, because they do not believe in me;[l] [10]righteousness, because I am going to the Father and you will no longer see me; [11]condemnation, because the ruler of this world has been condemned.[m]

[12]"I have much more to tell you, but you cannot bear it now. [13][***]But when he comes, the Spirit of truth, he will guide you to all truth.[n] He will not speak on his own, but he will speak what he hears, and will declare to you the things that are coming. [14]He will glorify me, because he will take from what is mine and declare it to you. [15]Everything that the Father has is mine; for this reason I told you that he will take from what is mine and declare it to you.

[16]"A little while and you will no longer see me, and again a little while later and you will see me."[o] [17]So some of his disciples said to one another, "What does this mean that he is saying to us, 'A little while and you will not see me, and again a little while and you will see me,' and 'Because I am going to the Father'?" [18]So they said, "What is this 'little while' [of which he speaks]? We do not know what he means." [19]Jesus knew that they wanted to ask him, so he said to them, "Are you discussing with one another what I said, 'A little while and you will not see me, and again a little while and you will see me'? [20]Amen, amen, I say to you, you will weep and mourn, while the world rejoices; you will grieve, but your grief will become joy.[p]

---

*[15:18–16:4] The hostile reaction of the world. There are synoptic parallels, predicting persecution, especially at Mt 10:17–25; 24:9–10.

†[15:20] **The word I spoke to you:** a reference to Jn 13:16.

‡[15:21] **On account of my name:** the idea of persecution for Jesus' name is frequent in the New Testament (Mt 10:22; 24:9; Acts 9:14). For John, association with Jesus' name implies union with Jesus.

§[15:22, 24] Jesus' words (**spoken**) and deeds (**works**) are the great motives of credibility. **They have seen and hated:** probably means that they have seen his works and still have hated; but the Greek can be read: "have seen both me and my Father and still have hated both me and my Father." **Works . . . that no one else ever did:** so Yahweh in Dt 4:32–33.

¶[15:25] **In their law:** law is here used as a larger concept than the Pentateuch, for the reference is to Ps 35:19 or Ps 69:5. See notes on Jn 10:34; 12:34. **Their** law reflects the argument of the church with the synagogue.

**[15:26] **Whom I will send:** in Jn 14:16, 26, the Paraclete is to be sent by the Father, at the request of Jesus. Here the Spirit comes from both Jesus and the Father in mission; there is no reference here to the eternal procession of the Spirit.

††[16:2] **Hour:** of persecution, not Jesus' "hour" (see note on Jn 2:4).

‡‡[16:4b–33] A duplicate of Jn 14:1–31 on departure and return.

§§[16:5] **Not one of you asks me:** the difficulty of reconciling this with Simon Peter's question in Jn 13:36 and Thomas' words in Jn 14:5 strengthens the supposition that the last discourse has been made up of several collections of Johannine material.

¶¶[16:8–11] These verses illustrate the forensic character of the Paraclete's role: in the forum of the disciples' conscience he prosecutes the world. He leads believers to see (a) that the basic sin was and is refusal to believe in Jesus; (b) that, although Jesus was found guilty and apparently died in disgrace, in reality righteousness has triumphed, for Jesus has returned to his Father; (c) finally, that it is the ruler of this world, Satan, who has been condemned through Jesus' death (Jn 12:32).

***[16:13] **Declare to you the things that are coming:** not a reference to new predictions about the future, but interpretation of what has already occurred or been said.

---

t. [15:15] Dt 34:5; Jos 24:29; 2 Chr 20:7; Ps 89:21; Is 41:8; Rom 8:15; Gal 4:7; Jas 2:23.   u. [15:16] 14:13; Dt 7:6.   v. [15:17] 13:34; 1 Jn 3:23; 4:21.   w. [15:18] 7:7; 14:17; Mt 10:22; 24:9; Mk 13:13; Lk 6:22; 1 Jn 3:13.   x. [15:19] 17:14–16; 1 Jn 4:5.   y. [15:20] 13:16; Mt 10:24.   z. [15:21] 8:19; 16:3.   a. [15:22] 8:21, 24; 9:41.   b. [15:23] 5:23; Lk 10:16; 1 Jn 2:23.   c. [15:24] 3:2; 9:32; Dt 4:32–33.   d. [15:25] Ps 35:19; 69:4.   e. [15:26] 14:16, 26; Mt 10:19–20.   f. [15:27] Lk 1:2; Acts 1:8.

g. [16:2] 9:22; 12:42; Mt 10:17; Lk 21:12; Acts 26:11.   h. [16:3] 15:21.   i. [16:4] 13:19; 14:29.   j. [16:5] 7:33; 13:36; 14:5.   k. [16:7] 7:39; 14:16–17, 26; 15:26.   l. [16:9] 8:21–24; 15:22.   m. [16:11] 12:31.   n. [16:13] 14:17, 26; 15:26; Ps 25:5; 143:10; 1 Jn 2:27; Rev 7:17.   o. [16:16] 7:33; 14:19.   p. [16:20] Ps 126:6.

²¹When a woman is in labor, she is in anguish because her hour has arrived; but when she has given birth to a child, she no longer remembers the pain because of her joy that a child has been born into the world.�q ²²So you also are now in anguish. But I will see you again, and your hearts will rejoice, and no one will take your joy away from you.ʳ ²³On that day you will not question me about anything. Amen, amen, I say to you, whatever you ask the Father in my name he will give you.ˢ ²⁴Until now you have not asked anything in my name; ask and you will receive, so that your joy may be complete.

²⁵*ˮI have told you this in figures of speech. The hour is coming when I will no longer speak to you in figures but I will tell you clearly about the Father. ²⁶On that day you will ask in my name, and I do not tell you that I will ask the Father for you.ᵘ ²⁷For the Father himself loves you, because you have loved me and have come to believe that I came from God. ²⁸I came from the Father and have come into the world. Now I am leaving the world and going back to the Father.ᵛ ²⁹His disciples said, "Now you are talking plainly, and not in any figure of speech. ³⁰Now we realize that you know everything and that you do not need to have anyone question you. Because of this we believe that you came from God."† ³¹Jesus answered them, "Do you believe now? ³²Behold, the hour is coming and has arrived when each of you will be scattered‡ to his own home and you will leave me alone. But I am not alone, because the Father is with me.ʷ ³³I have told you this so that you might have peace in me. In the world you will have trouble, but take courage, I have conquered the world."ˣ

## CHAPTER 17

**The Prayer of Jesus.**§ ¹When Jesus had said this, he raised his eyes to heaven¶ and said, "Father,

the hour has come. Give glory to your son, so that your son may glorify you,ʸ ²**just as you gave him authority over all people,ᶻ so that he may give eternal life to all you gave him. ³††Now this is eternal life,ᵃ that they should know you, the only true God, and the one whom you sent, Jesus Christ. ⁴I glorified you on earth by accomplishing the work that you gave me to do. ⁵Now glorify me, Father, with you, with the glory that I had with you before the world began.ᵇ

⁶"I revealed your name‡‡ to those whom you gave me out of the world. They belonged to you, and you gave them to me, and they have kept your word. ⁷Now they know that everything you gave me is from you, ⁸because the words you gave to me I have given to them, and they accepted them and truly understood that I came from you, and they have believed that you sent me. ⁹I pray for them. I do not pray for the world but for the ones you have given me, because they are yours,ᶜ ¹⁰and everything of mine is yours and everything of yours is mine, and I have been glorified in them.ᵈ ¹¹And now I will no longer be in the world, but they are in the world, while I am coming to you. Holy Father, keep them in your name that you have given me, so that they may be one just as we are. ¹²When I was with them I protected them in your name that you gave me, and I guarded them, and none of them was lost except the son of destruction, in order that the scripture might be fulfilled.ᵉ ¹³But now I am coming to you. I speak this in the world so that they may share my joy completely.ᶠ ¹⁴I gave them your word, and the world hated them, because they do not belong to the world any more than I belong to the world.ᵍ ¹⁵§§I do not ask that you take them out of the worldʰ but that you keep them from the evil one. ¹⁶They do not belong to the world any more than I belong to the world. ¹⁷Consecrate them in the truth. Your word is truth.ⁱ ¹⁸As you sent me into the world, so I sent them into the world.ʲ ¹⁹And I consecrate myself for them, so that they also may be consecrated in truth.

²⁰"I pray not only for them, but also for those who will believe in me through their word, ²¹so

---

*[16:25] See note on Jn 10:6. Here, possibly a reference to Jn 15:1–16 or Jn 16:21.

†[16:30] The reference is seemingly to the fact that Jesus could anticipate their question in Jn 16:19. The disciples naively think they have the full understanding that is the climax of "the hour" of Jesus' death, resurrection, and ascension (Jn 16:25), but the only part of the hour that is at hand for them is their share in the passion (Jn 16:32).

‡[16:32] **You will be scattered**: cf. Mk 14:27 and Mt 26:31, where both cite Zec 13:7 about the sheep being dispersed.

§[17:1–26] Climax of the last discourse(s). Since the sixteenth century, this chapter has been called the "high priestly prayer" of Jesus. He speaks as intercessor, with words addressed directly to the Father and not to the disciples, who supposedly only overhear. Yet the prayer is one of petition, for immediate (Jn 17:6–19) and future (Jn 17:20–21) disciples. Many phrases reminiscent of the Lord's Prayer occur. Although still in the world (Jn 17:13), Jesus looks on his earthly ministry as a thing of the past (Jn 17:4, 12). Whereas Jesus has up to this time stated that the disciples could follow him (Jn 13:33, 36), now he wishes them to be with him in union with the Father (Jn 17:12–14).

¶[17:1] The action of looking up to heaven and the address Father are typical of Jesus at prayer; cf. Jn 11:41 and Lk 11:2.

**[17:2] Another possible interpretation is to treat the first line of the verse as parenthetical and the second as an appositive to the clause that ends v 1: **so that your son may glorify you (just as . . . all people), so that he may give eternal life** . . . .

††[17:3] This verse was clearly added in the editing of the gospel as a reflection on the preceding verse; Jesus nowhere else refers to himself as Jesus Christ.

‡‡[17:6] **I revealed your name**: perhaps the name **I AM**; cf. Jn 8:24, 28, 58; 13:19.

§§[17:15] Note the resemblance to the petition of the Lord's Prayer, "deliver us from the evil one." Both probably refer to the devil rather than to abstract evil.

---

q. [16:21] Is 26:17–18; Jer 31:13; Mi 4:9.  r. [16:22] 14:19; 15:11; 20:20.  s. [16:23] 14:13.  t. [16:25] Mt 13:34–35.  u. [16:26] 14:13.  v. [16:28] 1:1.  w. [16:32] 8:29; Zec 13:7; Mt 26:31; Mk 14:27.  x. [16:33] 14:27.

y. [17:1] 13:31.  z. [17:2] 3:35; Mt 28:18.  a. [17:3] 1:17; Wis 14:7; 15:3; 1 Jn 5:20.  b. [17:5] 1:1, 2; 12:28; Phil 2:6, 9–11.  c. [17:9] 17:20.  d. [17:10] 16:15; 2 Thes 1:10, 12.  e. [17:12] 13:18; 18:9; Ps 41:10; Mt 26:24; Acts 1:16.  f. [17:13] 15:11.  g. [17:14] 15:19.  h. [17:15] Mt 6:13; 2 Thes 3:3; 1 Jn 5:18.  i. [17:17] 1 Pt 1:22  j. [17:18] 20:21–22.

that they may all be one, as you, Father, are in me and I in you, that they also may be in us, that the world may believe that you sent me.[k] [22]And I have given them the glory you gave me, so that they may be one, as we are one, [23]I in them and you in me, that they may be brought to perfection as one, that the world may know that you sent me, and that you loved them even as you loved me. [24]Father, they are your gift to me. I wish that where I am* they also may be with me, that they may see my glory that you gave me, because you loved me before the foundation of the world.[l] [25]Righteous Father, the world also does not know you, but I know you, and they know that you sent me.[m] [26]I made known to them your name and I will make it known,† that the love with which you loved me may be in them and I in them."

## CHAPTER 18

**Jesus Arrested.**‡ [1]When he had said this, Jesus went out§ with his disciples across the Kidron valley to where there was a garden, into which he and his disciples entered.[n] [2]Judas his betrayer also knew the place, because Jesus had often met there with his disciples. [3]So Judas got a band of soldiers¶ and guards from the chief priests and the Pharisees and went there with lanterns, torches, and weapons.[o] [4]Jesus, knowing everything that was going to happen to him, went out and said to them, "Whom are you looking for?" [5]They answered him, "Jesus the Nazorean."** He said to them, "I AM." Judas his betrayer was also with them. [6]When he said to them, "I AM," they turned away and fell to the ground. [7]So he again asked them, "Whom are you looking for?" They said, "Jesus the Nazorean." [8]Jesus answered, "I told you that I AM. So if you are looking for me, let these men go." [9]†[p]This was to fulfill what he had said, "I have not lost any of those you gave me."

[10]Then Simon Peter, who had a sword, drew it, struck the high priest's slave, and cut off his right ear. The slave's name was Malchus.‡‡ [11]Jesus said to Peter, "Put your sword into its scabbard. Shall I not drink the cup§§ that the Father gave me?"[q]

[12]So the band of soldiers, the tribune, and the Jewish guards seized Jesus, bound him, [13]and brought him to Annas¶¶ first. He was the father-in-law of Caiaphas, who was high priest that year.[s] [14]It was Caiaphas who had counseled the Jews that it was better that one man should die rather than the people.[t]

**Peter's First Denial.**[u] [15]Simon Peter and another disciple*** followed Jesus. Now the other disciple was known to the high priest, and he entered the courtyard of the high priest with Jesus. [16]But Peter stood at the gate outside. So the other disciple, the acquaintance of the high priest, went out and spoke to the gatekeeper and brought Peter in. [17]Then the maid who was the gatekeeper said to Peter, "You are not one of this man's disciples, are you?" He said, "I am not." [18]Now the slaves and the guards were standing around a charcoal fire that they had made, because it was cold, and were warming themselves. Peter was also standing there keeping warm.

**The Inquiry Before Annas.**[v] [19]The high priest questioned Jesus about his disciples and about his doctrine. [20]Jesus answered him, "I have spoken publicly to the world. I have always taught in a synagogue or in the temple area††† where all the Jews gather, and in secret I have said nothing.[w] [21]Why ask me? Ask those who heard me what I said to them. They know what I said." [22]When he had said this, one of the temple guards standing there struck Jesus and said, "Is this the way you answer the high priest?"[x] [23]Jesus answered him, "If I have spoken wrongly, testify to the wrong; but if I have spoken rightly, why do you strike me?" [24]Then Annas sent him bound to Caiaphas‡‡‡ the high priest.[y]

**Peter Denies Jesus Again.**[z] [25]Now Simon Peter was standing there keeping warm. And they

---

*[17:24] **Where I am**: Jesus prays for the believers ultimately to join him in heaven. Then they will not see his glory as in a mirror but clearly (2 Cor 3:18; 1 Jn 3:2).

†[17:26] **I will make it known**: through the Advocate.

‡[18:1–14] John does not mention the agony in the garden and the kiss of Judas, nor does he identify the place as Gethsemane or the Mount of Olives.

§[18:1] **Jesus went out**: see Jn 14:31, where it seems he is leaving the supper room. **Kidron valley**: literally, "the winter-flowing Kidron"; this wadi has water only during the winter rains.

¶[18:3] **Band of soldiers**: seems to refer to Roman troops, either the full cohort of 600 men (1/10 of a legion), or more likely the maniple of 200 under their tribune (Jn 18:12). In this case, John is hinting at Roman collusion in the action against Jesus before he was brought to Pilate. The lanterns and torches may be symbolic of the hour of darkness.

**[18:5] **Nazorean**: the form found in Mt 26:71 (see note on Mt 2:23) is here used, not **Nazarene** of Mark. **I AM**: or "I am he," but probably intended by the evangelist as an expression of divinity (cf. their appropriate response in Jn 18:6); see note on Jn 8:24. John sets the confusion of the arresting party against the background of Jesus' divine majesty.

††[18:9] The citation may refer to Jn 6:39; 10:28; or 17:12.

‡‡[18:10] Only John gives the names of the two antagonists; both John and Luke mention the right ear.

§§[18:11] The theme of the cup is found in the synoptic account of the agony (Mk 14:36 and parallels).

¶¶[18:13] **Annas**: only John mentions an inquiry before Annas; cf. Jn 18:16, 19–24; see note on Lk 3:2. It is unlikely that this nighttime interrogation before Annas is the same as the trial before Caiaphas placed by Matthew and Mark at night and by Luke in the morning.

***[18:15–16] **Another disciple . . . the other disciple**: see note on Jn 13:23.

†††[18:20] **I have always taught . . . in the temple area**: cf. Mk 14:49 for a similar statement.

‡‡‡[18:24] **Caiaphas**: see Mt 26:3, 57; Lk 3:2; and the notes there. John may leave room here for the trial before Caiaphas described in the synoptic gospels.

---

k. [17:21] 10:30; 14:10–11, 20.   l. [17:24] 14:3; 1 Thes 4:17.   m. [17:25] 1:10.   n. [18:1] 2 Sm 15:23; Mt 26:30, 36; Mk 14:26, 32; Lk 22:39.   o. [18:3] Mt 26:47–51; Mk 14:43–44; Lk 22:47.   p. [18:9] 6:39; 10:28; 17:12.   q. [18:11] Mt 20:22; 26:39; Mk 10:38; Lk 22:42.   r. [18:12–14] Mt 26:57–58; Mk 14:53–54; Lk 22:54–55.   s. [18:13] Lk 3:2.   t. [18:14] 11:49–50.   u. [18:15–18] Mt 26:58, 69–70; Mk 14:54, 66–68; Lk 22:54–57.   v. [18:19–24] Mt 26:59–66; Mk 14:55–64; Lk 22:66–71.   w. [18:20] 6:59; 7:14, 26; Is 48:16; Mt 26:55; Mk 4:23; Lk 19:47; 22:53.   x. [18:22] Acts 23:2.   y. [18:24] Mt 26:57.   z. [18:25–27] Mt 26:71–75; Mk 14:69–72; Lk 22:58–62.

said to him, "You are not one of his disciples, are you?" He denied it and said, "I am not." ²⁶One of the slaves of the high priest, a relative of the one whose ear Peter had cut off, said, "Didn't I see you in the garden with him?" ²⁷Again Peter denied it. And immediately the cock crowed.*

**The Trial Before Pilate.** ²⁸ᵃThen they brought Jesus from Caiaphas to the praetorium.† It was morning. And they themselves did not enter the praetorium, in order not to be defiled so that they could eat the Passover. ²⁹So Pilate came out to them and said, "What charge do you bring [against] this man?" ³⁰They answered and said to him, "If he were not a criminal, we would not have handed him over to you." ³¹At this, Pilate said to them, "Take him yourselves, and judge him according to your law." The Jews answered him, "We do not have the right to execute anyone."‡ ³²§in order that the word of Jesus might be fulfilled that he said indicating the kind of death*ᵇ* he would die. ³³So Pilate went back into the praetorium and summoned Jesus and said to him, "Are you the King of the Jews?" ³⁴Jesus answered, "Do you say this on your own or have others told you about me?" ³⁵Pilate answered, "I am not a Jew, am I? Your own nation and the chief priests handed you over to me. What have you done?"*ᶜ* ³⁶Jesus answered, "My kingdom does not belong to this world. If my kingdom did belong to this world, my attendants [would] be fighting to keep me from being handed over to the Jews. But as it is, my kingdom is not here."*ᵈ* ³⁷So Pilate said to him, "Then you are a king?" Jesus answered, "You say I am a king.⁕ For this I was born and for this I came into the world, to testify to the truth. Everyone who belongs to the truth listens to my voice."*ᵉ* ³⁸Pilate said to him, "What is truth?"*ᶠ*

When he had said this, he again went out to the Jews and said to them, "I find no guilt in him. ³⁹But you have a custom that I release one prisoner to you at Passover.** Do you want me to release to you the King of the Jews?" ⁴⁰They

cried out again, "Not this one but Barabbas!"†† Now Barabbas was a revolutionary.

## CHAPTER 19

¹‡‡ᵍThen Pilate took Jesus and had him scourged. ²And the soldiers wove a crown out of thorns and placed it on his head, and clothed him in a purple cloak, ³and they came to him and said, "Hail, King of the Jews!" And they struck him repeatedly. ⁴Once more Pilate went out and said to them, "Look, I am bringing him out to you, so that you may know that I find no guilt in him."*ʰ* ⁵So Jesus came out, wearing the crown of thorns and the purple cloak. And he said to them, "Behold, the man!"*ⁱ* ⁶When the chief priests and the guards saw him they cried out, "Crucify him, crucify him!" Pilate said to them, "Take him yourselves and crucify him. I find no guilt in him."*ʲ* ⁷§§The Jews answered,*ᵏ* "We have a law, and according to that law he ought to die, because he made himself the Son of God." ⁸Now when Pilate heard this statement, he became even more afraid, ⁹and went back into the praetorium and said to Jesus, "Where are you from?" Jesus did not answer him.*ˡ* ¹⁰So Pilate said to him, "Do you not speak to me? Do you not know that I have power to release you and I have power to crucify you?" ¹¹Jesus answered [him], "You would have no power over me if it had not been given to you from above. For this reason the one who handed me over to you has the greater sin."*ᵐ* ¹²Consequently, Pilate tried to release him; but the Jews cried out, "If you release him, you are not a Friend of Caesar.⁕⁕ Everyone who makes himself a king opposes Caesar."*ⁿ*

¹³When Pilate heard these words he brought Jesus out and seated him*** on the judge's bench in the place called Stone Pavement, in Hebrew, Gabbatha. ¹⁴It was preparation day for Passover, and it was about noon.††† And he said to the Jews,

---

*[18:27] Cockcrow was the third Roman division of the night, lasting from midnight to 3 a.m.

†[18:28] **Praetorium:** see note on Mt 27:27. **Morning:** literally, "the early hour," or fourth Roman division of the night, 3 to 6 a.m. **The Passover:** the synoptic gospels give the impression that the Thursday night supper was the Passover meal (Mk 14:12); for John that meal is still to be eaten Friday night.

‡[18:31] **We do not have the right to execute anyone:** only John gives this reason for their bringing Jesus to Pilate. Jewish sources are not clear on the competence of the Sanhedrin at this period to sentence and to execute for political crimes.

§[18:32] The Jewish punishment for blasphemy was stoning (Lv 24:16). In coming to the Romans to ensure that Jesus would be crucified, the Jewish authorities fulfilled his prophecy that he would be exalted (Jn 3:14; 12:32–33). There is some historical evidence, however, for Jews crucifying Jews.

⁕[18:37] **You say I am a king:** see Mt 26:64 for a similar response to the high priest. It is at best a reluctant affirmative.

**[18:39] See note on Mt 27:15.

††[18:40] **Barabbas:** see note on Mt 27:16–17. **Revolutionary:** a guerrilla warrior fighting for nationalistic aims, though the term can also denote a robber. See note on Mt 27:38.

‡‡[19:1] Luke places the mockery of Jesus at the midpoint in the trial when Jesus was sent to Herod. Mark and Matthew place the scourging and mockery at the end of the trial after the sentence of death. Scourging was an integral part of the crucifixion penalty.

§§[19:7] **Made himself the Son of God:** this question was not raised in John's account of the Jewish interrogations of Jesus as it was in the synoptic account. Nevertheless, see Jn 5:18; 8:53; 10:36.

⁕⁕[19:12] **Friend of Caesar:** a Roman honorific title bestowed upon high-ranking officials for merit.

***[19:13] **Seated him:** others translate "(Pilate) sat down." In John's thought, Jesus is the real judge of the world, and John may here be portraying him seated on the judgment bench. **Stone Pavement:** in Greek *lithostrotos*; under the fortress Antonia, one of the conjectured locations of the praetorium, a massive stone pavement has been excavated. **Gabbatha** (Aramaic rather than Hebrew) probably means "ridge, elevation."

†††[19:14] **Noon:** Mk 15:25 has Jesus crucified "at the third hour," which means either 9 a.m. or the period from 9 to 12

a. [18:28–38a] Mt 27:1–2, 11–25; Mk 15:1–5; Lk 23:1–5.   b. [18:32] 3:14;   8:28;   12:32–33.   c. [18:35]   1:11.   d. [18:36]   1:10; 8:23.   e. [18:37] 8:47; 1 Tm 6:13.   f. [18:38b–40] Mt 27:15–26; Mk 15:6–15; Lk 23:18–25; Acts 3:14.

g. [19:1–16] Mt 27:27–31; Mk 15:16–20; Lk 23:13–25.   h. [19:4] 18:38.   i. [19:5] Is 52:14.   j. [19:6] 18:31; 19:15.   k. [19:7] 10:33–36; Lv 24:16.   l. [19:9] 7:28.   m. [19:11] 3:27; 10:18; Rom 13:1.   n. [19:12] Acts 17:7.

"Behold, your king!" [15]They cried out, "Take him away, take him away! Crucify him!" Pilate said to them, "Shall I crucify your king?" The chief priests answered, "We have no king but Caesar." [16]Then he handed him over to them to be crucified.[*]

**The Crucifixion of Jesus.** So they took Jesus, [17o]and carrying the cross himself[†] he went out to what is called the Place of the Skull, in Hebrew, Golgotha. [18]There they crucified him, and with him two others, one on either side, with Jesus in the middle. [19‡]Pilate also had an inscription written and put on the cross. It read, "Jesus the Nazorean, the King of the Jews." [20]Now many of the Jews read this inscription, because the place where Jesus was crucified was near the city; and it was written in Hebrew, Latin, and Greek. [21]So the chief priests of the Jews said to Pilate, "Do not write 'The King of the Jews,' but that he said, 'I am the King of the Jews.'"[p] [22]Pilate answered, "What I have written, I have written."

[23§]When the soldiers had crucified Jesus,[q] they took his clothes and divided them into four shares, a share for each soldier.[r] They also took his tunic, but the tunic was seamless, woven in one piece from the top down. [24]So they said to one another, "Let's not tear it, but cast lots for it to see whose it will be," in order that the passage of scripture might be fulfilled [that says]:

"They divided my garments among them,
        and for my vesture they cast lots."

This is what the soldiers did. [25¶]Standing by the cross of Jesus were his mother and his mother's sister, Mary the wife of Clopas, and Mary of Magdala. [26]When Jesus saw his mother[**] and the disciple there whom he loved, he said to his mother, "Woman, behold, your son."[t] [27]Then he said to the disciple, "Behold, your mother." And from that hour the disciple took her into his home.

[28]After this, aware that everything was now finished, in order that the scripture might be fulfilled,[††] Jesus said, "I thirst."[v] [29]There was a vessel filled with common wine.[‡‡] So they put a sponge soaked in wine on a sprig of hyssop and put it up to his mouth. [30§§]When Jesus had taken the wine, he said, "It is finished."[w] And bowing his head, he handed over the spirit.

**The Blood and Water.** [31]Now since it was preparation day, in order that the bodies might not remain on the cross on the sabbath, for the sabbath day of that week was a solemn one, the Jews asked Pilate that their legs be broken and they be taken down.[x] [32]So the soldiers came and broke the legs of the first and then of the other one who was crucified with Jesus. [33]But when they came to Jesus and saw that he was already dead, they did not break his legs, [34¶¶]but one soldier thrust his lance into his side, and immediately blood and water flowed out. [35]An eyewitness has testified, and his testimony is true; he knows[***] that he is speaking the truth, so that you

---

noon, the time when, according to John, Jesus was sentenced to death, was the hour at which the priests began to slaughter Passover lambs in the temple; see Jn 1:29.

*[19:16] **He handed him over to them to be crucified**: in context this would seem to mean "handed him over to the chief priests." Lk 23:25 has a similar ambiguity. There is a polemic tendency in the gospels to place the guilt of the crucifixion on the Jewish authorities and to exonerate the Romans from blame. But John later mentions the Roman soldiers (Jn 19:23), and it was to these soldiers that Pilate handed Jesus over.

†[19:17] **Carrying the cross himself**: a different picture from that of the synoptics, especially Lk 23:26, where Simon of Cyrene is made to carry the cross, walking behind Jesus. In John's theology, Jesus remained in complete control and master of his destiny (cf. Jn 10:18). **Place of the Skull**: the Latin word for skull is *Calvaria*; hence "Calvary." **Golgotha** is actually an Aramaic rather than a Hebrew word.

‡[19:19] The inscription differs with slightly different words in each of the four gospels. John's form is fullest and gives the equivalent of the Latin *INRI = Iesus Nazarenus Rex Iudaeorum*. Only John mentions its polyglot character (Jn 19:20) and Pilate's part in keeping the title unchanged (Jn 19:21–22).

§[19:23–25a] While all four gospels describe the soldiers casting lots to divide Jesus' garments (see note on Mt 27:35), only John quotes the underlying passage from Ps 22:19, and only John sees each line of the poetic parallelism literally carried out in two separate actions (Jn 19:23–24).

¶[19:25] It is not clear whether four women are meant, or three (i.e., **Mary the wife of Cl[e]opas** [cf. Lk 24:18] is in apposition with **his mother's sister**) or two (his mother

and his mother's sister, i.e., Mary of Cl[e]opas and Mary of Magdala). Only John mentions the mother of Jesus here. The synoptics have a group of women looking on from a distance at the cross (Mk 15:40).

**[19:26–27] This scene has been interpreted literally, of Jesus' concern for his mother; and symbolically, e.g., in the light of the Cana story in Jn 2 (the presence of the mother of Jesus, the address **woman**, and the mention of the **hour**) and of the upper room in Jn 13 (the presence of the beloved disciple; the **hour**). Now that the hour has come (Jn 19:28), Mary (a symbol of the church?) is given a role as the mother of Christians (personified by the beloved disciple); or, as a representative of those seeking salvation, she is supported by the disciple who interprets Jesus' revelation; or Jewish and Gentile Christianity (or Israel and the Christian community) are reconciled.

††[19:28] **The scripture . . . fulfilled**: either in the scene of Jn 19:25–27, or in the **I thirst** of Jn 19:28. If the latter, Ps 22:16; 69:22 deserve consideration.

‡‡[19:29] **Wine**: John does not mention the drugged wine, a narcotic that Jesus refused as the crucifixion began (Mk 15:23), but only this final gesture of kindness at the end (Mk 15:36). **Hyssop**, a small plant, is scarcely suitable for carrying a sponge (Mark mentions a reed) and may be a symbolic reference to the hyssop used to daub the blood of the paschal lamb on the doorpost of the Hebrews (Ex 12:22).

§§[19:30] **Handed over the spirit**: there is a double nuance of dying (giving up the last breath or spirit) and that of passing on the holy Spirit; see Jn 7:39, which connects the giving of the Spirit with Jesus' glorious return to the Father, and Jn 20:22, where the author portrays the conferral of the Spirit.

¶¶[19:34–35] John probably emphasizes these verses to show the reality of Jesus' death, against the docetic heretics. In the blood and water there may also be a symbolic reference to the Eucharist and baptism.

***[19:35] **He knows**: it is not certain from the Greek that this **he** is the **eyewitness** of the first part of the sentence. **May [come to] believe**: see note on Jn 20:31.

---

o. [19:17–22] Mt 27:32–37; Mk 15:21–26; Lk 23:26–35.    p. [19:21] 18:33; Lk 19:14.    q. [19:23–27] Mt 27:38–44; Mk 15:27–32; Lk 23:36–43.    r. [19:23–24] Ps 22:19; Mt 27:35; Mk 15:24; Lk 23:34.    s. [19:25] Mt 27:55; Mk 15:40–41; Lk 8:2; 23:49.

t. [19:26] 13:23.    u. [19:28–30] Mt 27:45–56; Mk 15:33–41; Lk 23:44–49.    v. [19:28] Ps 22:16; 69:22.    w. [19:30] 4:34; 10:18; 17:4; Lk 23:46.    x. [19:31] Ex 12:16; Dt 21:23.    y. [19:34] Nm 20:11; 1 Jn 5:6.

also may [come to] believe.[z] [36]For this happened so that the scripture passage might be fulfilled:

"Not a bone of it will be broken."[a]

[37]And again another passage says:

"They will look upon him whom they have pierced."[b]

**The Burial of Jesus.**[*] [38c]After this, Joseph of Arimathea, secretly a disciple of Jesus for fear of the Jews, asked Pilate if he could remove the body of Jesus. And Pilate permitted it. So he came and took his body. [39]Nicodemus, the one who had first come to him at night, also came bringing a mixture of myrrh and aloes weighing about one hundred pounds.[d] [40]They took the body of Jesus and bound it with burial cloths along with the spices, according to the Jewish burial custom. [41]Now in the place where he had been crucified there was a garden, and in the garden a new tomb, in which no one had yet been buried. [42]So they laid Jesus there because of the Jewish preparation day; for the tomb was close by.

## CHAPTER 20[†]
**The Empty Tomb.**[‡] [1]On the first day of the week,[e] Mary of Magdala came to the tomb early in the morning, while it was still dark,[§] and saw the stone removed from the tomb. [f] [2]So she ran[¶] and went to Simon Peter and to the other disciple whom Jesus loved, and told them, "They have taken the Lord from the tomb, and we don't know where they put him." [3][**]So Peter and the other disciple went out and came to the tomb. [4]They both ran, but the other disciple ran faster than Peter and arrived at the tomb first; [5]he bent down and saw the burial cloths there, but did not go in. [6§]When Simon Peter arrived

after him, he went into the tomb and saw the burial cloths[††] there, [7]and the cloth that had covered his head, not with the burial cloths but rolled up in a separate place.[h] [8]Then the other disciple also went in, the one who had arrived at the tomb first, and he saw and believed. [9‡‡]For they did not yet understand the scripture that he had to rise from the dead. [10]Then the disciples returned home.

**The Appearance to Mary of Magdala.**[§§] [11]But Mary stayed outside the tomb weeping.[j] And as she wept, she bent over into the tomb [12]and saw two angels in white sitting there, one at the head and one at the feet where the body of Jesus had been. [13]And they said to her, "Woman, why are you weeping?" She said to them, "They have taken my Lord, and I don't know where they laid him." [14]When she had said this, she turned around and saw Jesus there, but did not know it was Jesus.[k] [15]Jesus said to her, "Woman, why are you weeping? Whom are you looking for?"[l] She thought it was the gardener and said to him, "Sir, if you carried him away, tell me where you laid him, and I will take him." [16]Jesus said to her, "Mary!" She turned and said to him in Hebrew, "Rabbouni,"[¶¶] which means Teacher. [17]Jesus said to her, "Stop holding on to me,[***] for I have not yet ascended to the Father. But go to my brothers and tell them, 'I am going to my Father and your Father, to my God and your God.'"[m] [18]Mary of Magdala went and announced to the disciples, "I have seen the Lord," and what he told her.

**Appearance to the Disciples.**[†††] [19]On the evening of that first day of the week,[n] when the doors

---

[††][20:6–8] Some special feature about the state of the burial cloths caused the beloved disciple to believe. Perhaps the details emphasized that the grave had not been robbed.

[‡‡][20:9] Probably a general reference to the scriptures is intended, as in Lk 24:26 and 1 Cor 15:4. Some individual Old Testament passages suggested are Ps 16:10; Hos 6:2; Jon 2:1, 2, 10.

[§§][20:11–18] This appearance to Mary is found only in John, but cf. Mt 28:8–10 and Mk 16:9–11.

[¶¶][20:16] **Rabbouni**: Hebrew or Aramaic for "my master."

[***][20:17] **Stop holding on to me**: see Mt 28:9, where the women take hold of his feet. **I have not yet ascended**: for John and many of the New Testament writers, the ascension in the theological sense of going to the Father to be glorified took place with the resurrection as one action. This scene in John dramatizes such an understanding, for by Easter night Jesus is glorified and can give the Spirit. Therefore his ascension takes place immediately after he has talked to Mary. In such a view, the ascension after forty days described in Acts 1:1–11 would be simply a termination of earthly appearances or, perhaps better, an introduction to the conferral of the Spirit upon the early church, modeled on Elisha's being able to have a (double) share in the spirit of Elijah if he saw him being taken up (same verb as ascending) into heaven (2 Kgs 2:9–12). **To my Father and your Father, to my God and your God**: this echoes Ru 1:16: "Your people shall be my people, and your God my God." The Father of Jesus will now become the Father of the disciples because, once ascended, Jesus can give them the Spirit that comes from the Father and they can be reborn as God's children (Jn 3:5). That is why he calls them **my brothers**.

[†††][20:19–29] The appearances to the disciples, without or with Thomas (cf. Jn 11:16; 14:5), have rough parallels in

---

*[19:38–42] In the first three gospels there is no anointing on Friday. In Matthew and Luke the women come to the tomb on Sunday morning precisely to anoint Jesus.

†[20:1–31] The risen Jesus reveals his glory and confers the Spirit. This story fulfills the basic need for testimony to the resurrection. What we have here is not a record but a series of single stories.

‡[20:1–10] The story of the empty tomb is found in both the Matthean and the Lucan traditions; John's version seems to be a fusion of the two.

§[20:1] **Still dark**: according to Mark the sun had risen, Matthew describes it as "dawning," and Luke refers to early dawn. Mary sees the stone removed, not the empty tomb.

¶[20:2] Mary runs away, not directed by an angel/young man as in the synoptic accounts. The plural "we" in the second part of her statement might reflect a tradition of more women going to the tomb.

**[20:3–10] The basic narrative is told of Peter alone in Lk 24:12, a verse missing in important manuscripts and which may be borrowed from tradition similar to John. Cf. also Lk 24:24.

---

z. [19:35] 7:37–39; 21:24.   a. [19:36] Ex 12:46; Nm 9:12; Ps 34:21.   b. [19:37] Nm 21:9; Zec 12:10; Rev 1:7.   c. [19:38–42] Mt 27:57–60; Mk 15:42–46; Lk 23:46–49.   d. [19:39] 3:1–2; 7:50; Ps 45:9.   e. [20:1–10] Mt 28:1–10; Mk 16:1–11; Lk 24:1–12.   f. [20:1] 19:25.   g. [20:6] Lk 24:12.

h. [20:7] 11:44; 19:40.   i. [20:9] Acts 2:26–27; 1 Cor 15:4.   j. [20:11–18] Mk 16:9–11.   k. [20:14] 21:4; Mk 16:12; Lk 24:16; 1 Cor 15:43–44.   l. [20:15–17] Mt 28:9–10.   m. [20:17] Acts 1:9.   n. [20:19–23] Mt 28:16–20; Mk 16:14–18; Lk 24:36–44.

were locked, where the disciples' were, for fear of the Jews, Jesus came and stood in their midst and said to them, "Peace be with you." [20]When he had said this, he showed them his hands and his side.[†] The disciples rejoiced when they saw the Lord.[o] [21‡][Jesus] said to them again,[p] "Peace be with you. As the Father has sent me, so I send you." [22§]And when he had said this, he breathed on them and said to them,[q] "Receive the holy Spirit. [23¶]Whose sins you forgive are forgiven them, and whose sins you retain are retained."

**Thomas.** [24]Thomas, called Didymus, one of the Twelve, was not with them when Jesus came. [25]So the other disciples said to him, "We have seen the Lord." But he said to them, "Unless I see the mark of the nails in his hands and put my finger into the nailmarks and put my hand into his side, I will not believe."[s] [26]Now a week later his disciples were again inside and Thomas was with them. Jesus came, although the doors were locked, and stood in their midst and said, "Peace be with you."[t] [27]Then he said to Thomas, "Put your finger here and see my hands, and bring your hand and put it into my side, and do not be unbelieving, but believe." [28**]Thomas answered and said to him, "My Lord and my God!" [29††]Jesus said to him, "Have you come to believe because you have seen me?[v] Blessed are those who have not seen and have believed."

**Conclusion.**[‡‡] [30]Now Jesus did many other signs in the presence of [his] disciples that are not written in this book.[w] [31]But these are written that you may [come to] believe that Jesus is the Messiah, the Son of God, and that through this belief you may have life in his name.[x]

## IV. EPILOGUE: THE RESURRECTION APPEARANCE IN GALILEE

## CHAPTER 21

**The Appearance to the Seven Disciples.** [1§§]After this, Jesus revealed himself again to his disciples at the Sea of Tiberias. He revealed himself in this way.[y] [2]Together were Simon Peter, Thomas called Didymus, Nathanael from Cana in Galilee, Zebedee's sons,[¶¶] and two others of his disciples. [3***]Simon Peter said to them, "I am going fishing." They said to him, "We also will come with you." So they went out and got into the boat, but that night they caught nothing.[z] [4]When it was already dawn, Jesus was standing on the shore; but the disciples did not realize that it was Jesus.[a] [5]Jesus said to them, "Children, have you caught anything to eat?" They answered him, "No."[b] [6]So he said to them, "Cast the net over the right side of the boat and you will find something." So they cast it, and were not able to pull it in because of the number of fish. [7]So the disciple whom Jesus loved said to Peter, "It is the Lord." When Simon Peter heard that it was the Lord, he tucked in his garment, for he was lightly clad, and jumped into the sea. [8]The other disciples came in the boat, for they were not far from shore, only about a hundred yards, dragging the net with the fish. [9†††]When they climbed out on shore, they saw a charcoal fire with fish on it and bread. [10]Jesus said to them, "Bring some of the fish you just caught." [11]So Simon Peter went over and dragged the net ashore full of one hundred fifty-three[‡‡‡] large fish. Even though there were so

the other gospels only for Jn 20:19–23; cf. Lk 24:36–39; Mk 16:14–18.

*[20:19] **The disciples**: by implication from Jn 20:24 this means ten of the Twelve, presumably in Jerusalem. **Peace be with you**: although this could be an ordinary greeting, John intends here to echo Jn 14:27. The theme of rejoicing in Jn 20:20 echoes Jn 16:22.

†[20:20] **Hands and . . . side**: Lk 24:39–40 mentions "hands and feet," based on Ps 22:17.

‡[20:21] By means of this sending, the Eleven were made apostles, that is, "those sent" (cf. Jn 17:18), though John does not use the noun in reference to them (see note on Jn 13:16). A solemn mission or "sending" is also the subject of the post-resurrection appearances to the Eleven in Mt 28:19; Lk 24:47; Mk 16:15.

§[20:22] This action recalls Gn 2:7, where God breathed on the first man and gave him life; just as Adam's life came from God, so now the disciples' new spiritual life comes from Jesus. Cf. also the revivification of the dry bones in Ez 37. This is the author's version of Pentecost. Cf. also the note on Jn 19:30.

¶[20:23] The Council of Trent defined that this power to forgive sins is exercised in the sacrament of penance. See Mt 16:19; 18:18.

**[20:28] **My Lord and my God**: this forms a literary inclusion with the first verse of the gospel: "and the Word was God."

††[20:29] This verse is a beatitude on future generations; faith, not sight, matters.

‡‡[20:30–31] These verses are clearly a conclusion to the gospel and express its purpose. While many manuscripts read **come to believe**, possibly implying a missionary purpose for John's gospel, a small number of quite early ones read "continue to believe," suggesting that the audience consists of Christians whose faith is to be deepened by the book; cf. Jn 19:35.

§§[21:1–23] There are many non-Johannine peculiarities in this chapter, some suggesting Lucan Greek style; yet this passage is closer to John than Jn 7:53–8:11. There are many Johannine features as well. Its closest parallels in the synoptic gospels are found in Lk 5:1–11 and Mt 14:28–31. Perhaps the tradition was ultimately derived from John but preserved by some disciple other than the writer of the rest of the gospel. The appearances narrated seem to be independent of those in Jn 20. Even if a later addition, the chapter was added before publication of the gospel, for it appears in all manuscripts.

¶¶[21:2] **Zebedee's sons**: the only reference to James and John in this gospel (but see note on Jn 1:37). Perhaps the phrase was originally a gloss to identify, among the five, the **two others of his disciples**. The anonymity of the latter phrase is more Johannine (Jn 1:35). The total of seven may suggest the community of the disciples in its fullness.

***[21:3–6] This may be a variant of Luke's account of the catch of fish; see note on Lk 5:1–11.

†††[21:9, 12–13] It is strange that Jesus already has fish since none have yet been brought ashore. This meal may have had eucharistic significance for early Christians since Jn 21:13 recalls Jn 6:11 which uses the vocabulary of Jesus' action at the Last Supper; but see also note on Mt 14:19.

‡‡‡[21:11] The exact number 153 is probably meant to have a symbolic meaning in relation to the apostles' universal

o. [20:20] 14:27.   p. [20:21] 17:18; Mt 28:19; Mk 16:15; Lk 24:47–48.   q. [20:22] Gn 2:7; Ez 37:9; 1 Cor 15:45.   r. [20:23] Mt 16:19; 18:18.   s. [20:25] 1 Jn 1:1.   t. [20:26] 21:14.   u. [20:28] 1:1.   v. [20:29] 4:48; Lk 1:45; 1 Pt 1:8.   w. [20:30] 21:25.

x. [20:31] 3:14, 15; 1 Jn 5:13.   y. [21:1] Mt 26:32; 28:7.   z. [21:3] Mt 4:18; Lk 5:4–10.   a. [21:4] 20:14; Mt 28:17; Lk 24:16.   b. [21:5] Lk 24:41.   c. [21:9] Lk 24:41–43.

many, the net was not torn.*d* ¹²Jesus said to them, "Come, have breakfast." And none of the disciples dared to ask him," "Who are you?" because they realized it was the Lord. ¹³Jesus came over and took the bread and gave it to them, and in like manner the fish.*e* ¹⁴†This was now the third time*f* Jesus was revealed to his disciples after being raised from the dead.

**Jesus and Peter.**‡ ¹⁵When they had finished breakfast, Jesus said to Simon Peter,§ "Simon, son of John, do you love me more than these?"¶ He said to him, "Yes, Lord, you know that I love you." He said to him, "Feed my lambs." ¹⁶He then said to him a second time, "Simon, son of John, do you love me?" He said to him, "Yes, Lord, you know that I love you." He said to him, "Tend my sheep." ¹⁷He said to him the third time, "Simon, son of John, do you love me?" Peter was distressed that he had said to him a third time, "Do you love me?" and he said to him, "Lord, you know everything; you know that I love you." [Jesus] said to him, "Feed my sheep.*g* ¹⁸**"Amen,

amen, I say to you,*h* when you were younger, you used to dress yourself and go where you wanted; but when you grow old, you will stretch out your hands, and someone else will dress you and lead you where you do not want to go." ¹⁹He said this signifying by what kind of death he would glorify God. And when he had said this, he said to him, "Follow me."*i*

**The Beloved Disciple.** ²⁰Peter turned and saw the disciple following whom Jesus loved, the one who had also reclined upon his chest during the supper and had said, "Master, who is the one who will betray you?"*j* ²¹When Peter saw him, he said to Jesus, "Lord, what about him?" ²²Jesus said to him, "What if I want him to remain until I come?†† What concern is it of yours? You follow me."*k* ²³‡‡So the word spread among the brothers that that disciple would not die. But Jesus had not told him that he would not die, just "What if I want him to remain until I come? [What concern is it of yours?]"

**Conclusion.** ²⁴It is this disciple who testifies to these things and has written them,§§ and we know that his testimony is true.*l* ²⁵There are also many other things that Jesus did, but if these were to be described individually, I do not think the whole world would contain the books that would be written.*m*

---

mission; Jerome claims that Greek zoologists catalogued 153 species of fish. Or 153 is the sum of the numbers from 1 to 17. Others invoke Ez 47:10.

*[21:12] **None . . . dared to ask him:** is Jesus' appearance strange to them? Cf. Lk 24:16; Mk 16:12; Jn 20:14. The disciples do, however, recognize Jesus **before** the breaking of the bread (opposed to Lk 24:35).

†[21:14] This verse connects Jn 20 and 21; cf. Jn 20:19, 26.

‡[21:15–23] This section constitutes Peter's rehabilitation and emphasizes his role in the church.

§[21:15–17] In these three verses there is a remarkable variety of synonyms: two different Greek verbs for **love** (see note on Jn 15:13); two verbs for **feed/tend**; two nouns for **sheep**; two verbs for **know**. But apparently there is no difference of meaning. The threefold confession of Peter is meant to counteract his earlier threefold denial (Jn 18:17, 25, 27). The First Vatican Council cited these verses in defining that Jesus after his resurrection gave Peter the jurisdiction of supreme shepherd and ruler over the whole flock.

¶[21:15] **More than these:** probably "more than these disciples do" rather than "more than you love them" or "more than you love these things (fishing, etc.)."

**[21:18] Originally probably a proverb about old age, now used as a figurative reference to the crucifixion of Peter.

††[21:22] **Until I come:** a reference to the parousia.

‡‡[21:23] This whole scene takes on more significance if the disciple is already dead. The death of the apostolic generation caused problems in the church because of a belief that Jesus was to have returned first. Loss of faith sometimes resulted; cf. 2 Pt 3:4.

§§[21:24] **Who . . . has written them:** this does not necessarily mean he wrote them with his own hand. The same expression is used in Jn 19:22 of Pilate, who certainly would not have written the inscription himself. **We know:** i.e., the Christian community; cf. Jn 1:14, 16.

---

d. [21:11] 2 Chr 2:16.　e. [21:13] Lk 24:42.　f. [21:14] 20:19, 26. g. [21:17] 13:37–38; 18:15–18, 25–27; Mt 26:69–75; Mk 14:66–72; Lk 22:55–62.

h. [21:18] Acts 21:11, 14; 2 Pt 1:14.　i. [21:19] 13:36.　j. [21:20] 13:25. k. [21:22] Mt 16:28.　l. [21:24] 19:35.　m. [21:25] 20:30.

# THE ACTS OF THE
## APOSTLES

~~~

The Acts of the Apostles, the second volume of Luke's two-volume work, continues Luke's presentation of biblical history, describing how the salvation promised to Israel in the Old Testament and accomplished by Jesus has now under the guidance of the holy Spirit been extended to the Gentiles. This was accomplished through the divinely chosen representatives (Acts 10:41) whom Jesus prepared during his historical ministry (Acts 1:21–22) and commissioned after his resurrection as witnesses to all that he taught (Acts 1:8; 10:37–43; Lk 24:48). Luke's preoccupation with the Christian community as the Spirit-guided bearer of the word of salvation rules out of his book detailed histories of the activity of most of the preachers. Only the main lines of the roles of Peter and Paul serve Luke's interest.

Peter was the leading member of the Twelve (Acts 1:13, 15), a miracle worker like Jesus in the gospel (Acts 3:1–10; 5:1–11, 15; 9:32–35, 36–42), the object of divine care (Acts 5:17–21; 12:6–11), and the spokesman for the Christian community (Acts 2:14–36; 3:12–26; 4:8–12; 5:29–32; 10:34–43; 15:7–11), who, according to Luke, was largely responsible for the growth of the community in the early days (Acts 2:4; 4:4). Paul eventually joined the community at Antioch (Acts 11:25–26), which subsequently commissioned him and Barnabas to undertake the spread of the gospel to Asia Minor. This missionary venture generally failed to win the Jews of the diaspora to the gospel but enjoyed success among the Gentiles (Acts 13:14–14:27).

Paul's refusal to impose the Mosaic law upon his Gentile converts provoked very strong objection among the Jewish Christians of Jerusalem (Acts 15:1), but both Peter and James supported his position (Acts 15:6–21). Paul's second and third missionary journeys (Acts 16:36–21:16) resulted in the same pattern of failure among the Jews generally but of some success among the Gentiles. Paul, like Peter, is presented as a miracle worker (Acts 14:8–18; 19:12; 20:7–12; 28:7–10) and the object of divine care (Acts 16:25–31).

In Acts, Luke has provided a broad survey of the church's development from the resurrection of Jesus to Paul's first Roman imprisonment, the point at which the book ends. In telling this story, Luke describes the emergence of Christianity from its origins in Judaism to its position as a religion of worldwide status and appeal. Originally a Jewish Christian community in Jerusalem, the church was placed in circumstances impelling it to include within its membership people of other cultures: the Samaritans (Acts 8:4–25), at first an occasional Gentile (Acts 8:26–30; 10:1–48), and finally the Gentiles on principle (Acts 11:20–21). Fear on the part of the Jewish people that Christianity, particularly as preached to the Gentiles, threatened their own cultural heritage caused them to be suspicious of Paul's gospel (Acts 13:42–45; 15:1–5; 28:17–24). The inability of Christian missionaries to allay this apprehension inevitably created a situation in which the gospel was preached more and more to the Gentiles. Toward the end of Paul's career, the Christian communities, with the exception of those in Palestine itself (Acts 9:31), were mainly of Gentile membership. In tracing the emergence of Christianity from Judaism, Luke is insistent upon the prominence of Israel in the divine plan of salvation (see note on Acts 1:26; see also Acts 2:5–6; 3:13–15; 10:36; 13:16–41; 24:14–15) and that the extension of salvation to the Gentiles has been a part of the divine plan from the beginning (see Acts 15:13–18; 26:22–23).

In the development of the church from a Jewish Christian origin in Jerusalem, with its roots in Jewish religious tradition, to a series of Christian communities among the Gentiles of the Roman empire, Luke perceives the action of God in history laying open the heart of all humanity to the divine message of salvation. His approach to the history of the church is motivated by his theological interests. His history of the apostolic church is the story of a Spirit-guided community and a Spirit-guided spread of the Word of God (Acts 1:8). The travels of Peter and Paul are in reality the travels of the Word of God as it spreads from Jerusalem, the city of destiny for Jesus, to Rome, the capital of the civilized world of Luke's day. Nonetheless, the historical data he utilizes are of value for the understanding of the church's early life and development and as general background to the Pauline epistles. In the interpretation of Acts, care must be exercised to determine Luke's theological aims and interests and to evaluate his historical data without either exaggerating their literal accuracy or underestimating their factual worth.

Finally, an apologetic concern is evident throughout Acts. By stressing the continuity between Judaism and Christianity (Acts 13:16–41; 23:6–9; 24:10–21; 26:2–23), Luke argues that Christianity is deserving of the same toleration accorded Judaism by Rome. Part of Paul's defense before Roman authorities is to show that Christianity is not a disturber of the peace of the Roman Empire (Acts 24:5, 12–13; 25:7–8). Moreover, when he stands before Roman authorities, he is declared innocent of any crime against the empire (Acts 18:13–15; 23:29; 25:25–27; 26:31–32). Luke tells his story with the hope that Christianity will be treated as fairly.

Concerning the date of Acts, see the Introduction to the Gospel according to Luke.

The principal divisions of the Acts of the Apostles are the following:

I. The Preparation for the Christian Mission (1:1–2:13)
II. The Mission in Jerusalem (2:14–8:3)
III. The Mission in Judea and Samaria (8:4–9:43)
IV. The Inauguration of the Gentile Mission (10:1–15:35)
V. The Mission of Paul to the Ends of the Earth (15:36–28:31)

## I. THE PREPARATION FOR THE CHRISTIAN MISSION

### CHAPTER 1*

**The Promise of the Spirit.** ¹In the first book,ᵃ Theophilus, I dealt with all that Jesus did and taught ²until the day he was taken up, after giving instructions through the holy Spirit to the apostles whom he had chosen.ᵇ ³He presented himself alive to them by many proofs after he had suffered, appearing to them during forty daysᵗ and speaking about the kingdom of God.ᶜ

⁴While meeting with them, he enjoined them not to depart from Jerusalem, but to wait for "the promise of the Fatherᵗ about which you have heard me speak;ᵈ ⁵for John baptized with water, but in a few days you will be baptized with the holy Spirit."ᵉ

**The Ascension of Jesus.** ⁶When they had gathered together they asked him, "Lord, are you at this time going§ to restore the kingdom to Israel?" ⁷*He answered them,ᶠ "It is not for you to know the times or seasons that the Father

*[1:1–26] This introductory material (Acts 1:1–2) connects Acts with the Gospel of Luke, shows that the apostles were instructed by the risen Jesus (Acts 1:3–5), points out that the parousia or second coming in glory of Jesus will occur as certainly as his ascension occurred (Acts 1:6–11), and lists the members of the Twelve, stressing their role as a body of divinely mandated witnesses to his life, teaching, and resurrection (Acts 1:12–26).

†[1:3] **Appearing to them during forty days:** Luke considered especially sacred the interval in which the appearances and instructions of the risen Jesus occurred and expressed it therefore in terms of the sacred number forty (cf. Dt 8:2). In his gospel, however, Luke connects the ascension of Jesus with the resurrection by describing the ascension on Easter Sunday evening (Lk 24:50–53). What should probably be understood as one event (resurrection, glorification, ascension, sending of the Spirit—the paschal mystery) has been historicized by Luke when he writes of a visible ascension of Jesus after forty

days and the descent of the Spirit at Pentecost. For Luke, the ascension marks the end of the appearances of Jesus except for the extraordinary appearance to Paul. With regard to Luke's understanding of salvation history, the ascension also marks the end of the time of Jesus (Lk 24:50–53) and signals the beginning of the time of the church.

‡[1:4] **The promise of the Father:** the holy Spirit, as is clear from the next verse. This gift of the Spirit was first promised in Jesus' final instructions to his chosen witnesses in Luke's gospel (Lk 24:49) and formed part of the continuing instructions of the risen Jesus on the kingdom of God, of which Luke speaks in Acts 1:3.

§[1:6] The question of the disciples implies that in believing Jesus to be the Christ (see note on Lk 2:11) they had expected him to be a political leader who would restore self-rule to Israel during his historical ministry. When this had not taken place, they ask if it is to take place at this time, the period of the church.

¶[1:7] This verse echoes the tradition that the precise time of the parousia is not revealed to human beings; cf. Mk 13:32; 1 Thes 5:1–3.

a. [1:1] Lk 1:1–4. b. [1:2] Mt 28:19–20; Lk 24:44–49; Jn 20:22; 1 Tm 3:16. c. [1:3] 10:41; 13:31.

d. [1:4] Jn 14:16, 17, 26. e. [1:5] 11:16; Mt 3:11; Mk 1:8; Lk 3:16; Jn 1:26; Eph 1:13. f. [1:7] Mt 24:36; 1 Thes 5:1–2.

has established by his own authority. [8]"But you will receive power when the holy Spirit comes upon you,[g] and you will be my witnesses in Jerusalem, throughout Judea and Samaria, and to the ends of the earth." [9]When he had said this, as they were looking on, he was lifted up, and a cloud took him from their sight.[h] [10]While they were looking intently at the sky as he was going, suddenly two men dressed in white garments stood beside them.[i] [11]They said, "Men of Galilee, why are you standing there looking at the sky? This Jesus who has been taken up from you into heaven will return in the same way as you have seen him going into heaven."[j] [12k]Then they returned to Jerusalem from the mount called Olivet, which is near Jerusalem, a sabbath day's journey away.

**The First Community in Jerusalem.** [13]When they entered the city they went to the upper room where they were staying, Peter and John and James and Andrew, Philip and Thomas, Bartholomew and Matthew, James son of Alphaeus, Simon the Zealot, and Judas son of James. [14]All these devoted themselves with one accord to prayer, together with some women, and Mary the mother of Jesus, and his brothers.[l]

**The Choice of Judas's Successor.** [15]During those days Peter stood up in the midst of the brothers (there was a group of about one hundred and twenty persons in the one place). He said, [16]"My brothers, the scripture had to be fulfilled which the holy Spirit spoke beforehand through the mouth of David, concerning Judas, who was the guide for those who arrested Jesus.[m] [17]He was numbered among us and was allotted a share in this ministry. [18n]He bought a parcel of land with the wages of his iniquity, and falling headlong, he burst open in the middle, and all his insides spilled out.[†] [19]This became known to everyone who lived in Jerusalem, so that the parcel of land was called in their language 'Akeldama,' that is, Field of Blood. [20]For it is written in the Book of Psalms:

'Let his encampment become desolate,
    and may no one dwell in it.'

And:

'May another take his office.'[o]

[21]Therefore, it is necessary that one of the men who accompanied us the whole time the Lord Jesus came and went among us, [22]beginning from the baptism of John until the day on which he was taken up from us, become with us a witness to his resurrection."[p] [23]So they proposed two, Joseph called Barsabbas, who was also known as Justus, and Matthias. [24]Then they prayed, "You, Lord, who know the hearts of all, show which one of these two you have chosen [25]to take the place in this apostolic ministry from which Judas turned away to go to his own place." [26‡]Then they gave lots to them, and the lot fell upon Matthias, and he was counted with the eleven apostles.

# CHAPTER 2

**The Coming of the Spirit.** [1§]When the time for Pentecost was fulfilled, they were all in one place together.[r] [2]And suddenly there came from the sky a noise like a strong driving wind,[¶] and it filled the entire house in which they were.[s] [3]Then there appeared to them tongues as of fire,[**] which parted and came to rest on each one of them.[t] [4]And they were all filled with the holy Spirit and began to speak in different tongues,[††] as the Spirit enabled them to proclaim.[u]

[5]Now there were devout Jews from every nation under heaven staying in Jerusalem. [6]At this sound, they gathered in a large crowd, but they were confused because each one heard them speaking in his own language. [7]They were

---

‡[1:26] The need to replace Judas was probably dictated by the symbolism of the number twelve, recalling the twelve tribes of Israel. This symbolism also indicates that for Luke (see Lk 22:30) the Christian church is a reconstituted Israel.

§[2:1–41] Luke's pentecostal narrative consists of an introduction (Acts 2:1–13), a speech ascribed to Peter declaring the resurrection of Jesus and its messianic significance (Acts 2:14–36), and a favorable response from the audience (Acts 2:37–41). It is likely that the narrative telescopes events that took place over a period of time and on a less dramatic scale. The Twelve were not originally in a position to proclaim publicly the messianic office of Jesus without incurring immediate reprisal from those religious authorities in Jerusalem who had brought about Jesus' death precisely to stem the rising tide in his favor.

¶[2:2] **There came from the sky a noise like a strong driving wind:** wind and spirit are associated in Jn 3:8. The sound of a great rush of wind would herald a new action of God in the history of salvation.

**[2:3] **Tongues as of fire:** see Ex 19:18 where fire symbolizes the presence of God to initiate the covenant on Sinai. Here the holy Spirit acts upon the apostles, preparing them to proclaim the new covenant with its unique gift of the Spirit (Acts 2:38).

††[2:4] **To speak in different tongues:** ecstatic prayer in praise of God, interpreted in Acts 2:6, 11 as speaking in foreign languages, symbolizing the worldwide mission of the church.

---

*[1:8] Just as Jerusalem was the city of destiny in the Gospel of Luke (the place where salvation was accomplished), so here at the beginning of Acts, Jerusalem occupies a central position. It is the starting point for the mission of the Christian disciples to "the ends of the earth," the place where the apostles were situated and the doctrinal focal point in the early days of the community (Acts 15:2, 6). **The ends of the earth:** for Luke, this means Rome.

†[1:18] Luke records a popular tradition about the death of Judas that differs from the one in Mt 27:5, according to which Judas hanged himself. Here, although the text is not certain, Judas is depicted as purchasing a piece of property with the betrayal money and being killed on it in a fall.

---

g. [1:8] 2:1–13; 10:39; Is 43:10; Mt 28:19; Lk 24:47–48.  h. [1:9] 2 Kgs 2:11; Mk 16:19; Lk 24:51.  i. [1:10] Jn 20:17.  j. [1:11] Lk 24:51; Eph 4:8–10; 1 Pt 3:22; Rev 1:7.  k. [1:12–14] Lk 6:14–16.  l. [1:14] Lk 23:49.  m. [1:16] Ps 41:10; Lk 22:47.  n. [1:18] Mt 27:3–10.

o. [1:20] Ps 69:26; 109:8; Jn 17:12.  p. [1:22] 1:8–9; 10:39.  q. [1:26] Prv 16:33.  r. [2:1] Lv 23:15–21; Dt 16:9–11.  s. [2:2–3] Jn 3:8.  t. [2:3] Lk 3:16.  u. [2:4] 1:5; 4:31; 8:15, 17; 10:44; 11:15–16; 15:8; 19:6; Ps 104:30; Jn 20:33.

astounded, and in amazement they asked, "Are not all these people who are speaking Galileans?"[v] [8]Then how does each of us hear them in his own native language? [9]We are Parthians, Medes, and Elamites, inhabitants of Mesopotamia, Judea and Cappadocia, Pontus and Asia, [10]Phrygia and Pamphylia, Egypt and the districts of Libya near Cyrene, as well as travelers from Rome, [11]both Jews and converts to Judaism, Cretans and Arabs, yet we hear them speaking in our own tongues of the mighty acts of God."[w] [12]They were all astounded and bewildered, and said to one another, "What does this mean?" [13]But others said, scoffing, "They have had too much new wine."[x]

## II. THE MISSION IN JERUSALEM

**Peter's Speech at Pentecost.** [14]Then Peter stood[*] up with the Eleven, raised his voice, and proclaimed to them, "You who are Jews, indeed all of you staying in Jerusalem. Let this be known to you, and listen to my words. [15]These people are not drunk, as you suppose, for it is only nine o'clock in the morning. [16]No, this is what was spoken through the prophet Joel:

[17] 'It will come to pass in the last days,' God says,
        'that I will pour out a portion of my
            spirit upon all flesh.
    Your sons and your daughters shall
            prophesy,
        your young men shall see visions,
        your old men shall dream dreams.[y]
[18] Indeed, upon my servants and my handmaids
        I will pour out a portion of my spirit
            in those days,
        and they shall prophesy.
[19] And I will work wonders in the heavens
            above
        and signs on the earth below:
        blood, fire, and a cloud of
            smoke.
[20] The sun shall be turned to darkness,
        and the moon to blood,
            before the coming of the great
            and splendid day of the Lord,
[21] and it shall be that everyone shall be
            saved who calls on the name of
            the Lord.'[z]

[22]You who are Israelites, hear these words. Jesus the Nazorean was a man commended to you by God with mighty deeds, wonders, and signs, which God worked through him in your midst, as you yourselves know.[a] [23]This man, delivered up by the set plan and foreknowledge of God, you killed, using lawless men to crucify him.[b] [24]But God raised him up, releasing him from the throes of death, because it was impossible for him to be held by it.[c] [25]For David says of him:

    'I saw the Lord ever before me,[d]
        with him at my right hand I shall
            not be disturbed.
[26] Therefore my heart has been glad and my
            tongue has exulted;
        my flesh, too, will dwell in hope,
[27] because you will not abandon my soul to
            the netherworld,
        nor will you suffer your holy one to
            see corruption.[e]
[28] You have made known to me the paths of
            life;
        you will fill me with joy in your
            presence.'

[29]My brothers, one can confidently say to you about the patriarch David that he died and was buried, and his tomb is in our midst to this day. [30]But since he was a prophet and knew that God had sworn an oath to him that he would set one of his descendants upon his throne,[f] [31]he foresaw and spoke of the resurrection of the Messiah, that neither was he abandoned to the netherworld nor did his flesh see corruption.[g] [32]God raised this Jesus; of this we are all witnesses. [33]Exalted at the right hand of God,[†] he received the promise of the holy Spirit from the Father and poured it forth, as you [both] see and hear.[h] [34]For David did not go up into heaven, but he himself said:

    'The Lord said to my Lord,
        "Sit at my right hand[i]
[35]        until I make your enemies your
            footstool."'

[36]Therefore let the whole house of Israel know for certain that God has made him both Lord and Messiah, this Jesus whom you crucified."[j] [37]Now when they heard this, they were cut to the heart, and they asked Peter and the other apostles, "What are we to do, my brothers?"[k] [38]Peter [said] to them, "Repent and be baptized,[‡]

---

†[2:33] **At the right hand of God:** or "by the right hand of God."

‡[2:38] **Repent and be baptized:** repentance is a positive concept, a change of mind and heart toward God reflected in the actual goodness of one's life. It is in accord with the apostolic teaching derived from Jesus (Acts 2:42) and ultimately recorded in the four gospels. Luke presents baptism in Acts as the expected response to the apostolic preaching about Jesus

---

*[2:14–36] The first of six discourses in Acts (along with Acts 3:12–26; 4:8–12; 5:29–32; 10:34–43; 13:16–41) dealing with the resurrection of Jesus and its messianic import. Five of these are attributed to Peter, the final one to Paul. Modern scholars term these discourses in Acts the "kerygma," the Greek word for proclamation (cf. 1 Cor 15:11).

v. [2:7] 1:11.   w. [2:11] 10:46.   x. [2:13] 1 Cor 14:23.   y. [2:17] Is 2:2; 44:3; Jl 3:1–5.   z. [2:21] Rom 10:13.

a. [2:22] 10:38; Lk 24:19.   b. [2:23] 1 Thes 2:15.   c. [2:24] 13:34.   d. [2:25–28] Ps 16:8–11.   e. [2:27] 13:35.   f. [2:30] 2 Sm 7:12; Ps 132:11.   g. [2:31] 13:35; Ps 16:10.   h. [2:33] 1:4–5.   i. [2:34–35] Ps 110:1.   j. [2:36] 9:22; Rom 10:9; Phil 2:11.   k. [2:37] Lk 3:10.

every one of you, in the name of Jesus Christ for the forgiveness of your sins; and you will receive the gift of the holy Spirit.[l] [39]For the promise is made to you and to your children and to all those far off, whomever the Lord our God will call."[m] [40]He testified with many other arguments, and was exhorting them, "Save yourselves from this corrupt generation."[n] [41]Those who accepted his message were baptized, and about three thousand persons were added that day.[o]

**Communal Life.**[*] [42p]They devoted themselves to the teaching of the apostles and to the communal life, to the breaking of the bread and to the prayers.[q] [43]Awe came upon everyone, and many wonders and signs were done through the apostles.[r] [44]All who believed were together and had all things in common;[s] [45]they would sell their property and possessions and divide them among all according to each one's need. [46]Every day they devoted themselves to meeting together in the temple area and to breaking bread in their homes. They ate their meals with exultation and sincerity of heart, [47]praising God and enjoying favor with all the people. And every day the Lord added to their number those who were being saved.

## CHAPTER 3

**Cure of a Crippled Beggar.** [1†]Now Peter and John were going up to the temple area for the three o'clock hour of prayer.[‡] [2t]And a man crippled

from birth was carried and placed at the gate of the temple called "the Beautiful Gate" every day to beg for alms from the people who entered the temple. [3]When he saw Peter and John about to go into the temple, he asked for alms. [4]But Peter looked intently at him, as did John, and said, "Look at us." [5]He paid attention to them, expecting to receive something from them. [6§]Peter said, "I have neither silver nor gold, but what I do have I give you: in the name of Jesus Christ the Nazorean, [rise and] walk."[u] [7]Then Peter took him by the right hand and raised him up, and immediately his feet and ankles grew strong. [8]He leaped up, stood, and walked around, and went into the temple with them, walking and jumping and praising God.[v] [9]When all the people saw him walking and praising God, [10]they recognized him as the one who used to sit begging at the Beautiful Gate of the temple, and they were filled with amazement and astonishment at what had happened to him.

**Peter's Speech.** [11]As he clung to Peter and John, all the people hurried in amazement toward them in the portico called "Solomon's Portico."[w] [12]When Peter saw this, he addressed the people, "You Israelites, why are you amazed at this, and why do you look so intently at us as if we had made him walk by our own power or piety?[x] [13]The God of Abraham, [the God] of Isaac, and [the God] of Jacob, the God of our ancestors, has glorified[†] his servant Jesus whom you handed over and denied in Pilate's presence, when he had decided to release him.[y] [14]You denied the Holy and Righteous One[**] and asked that a murderer be released to you.[z] [15††]The author of life you put to death, but God raised him from the dead; of this we are witnesses.[a] [16]And by faith in his name, this man, whom you see and know, his name has made strong, and the faith that comes through it has given him this perfect health, in the presence of all of you. [17]Now I know, brothers, that you acted

and associates it with the conferring of the Spirit (Acts 1:5; 10:44–48; 11:16).

*[2:42–47] The first of three summary passages (along with Acts 4:32–37; 5:12–16) that outline, somewhat idyllically, the chief characteristics of the Jerusalem community: adherence to the teachings of the Twelve and the centering of its religious life in the eucharistic liturgy (Acts 2:42); a system of distribution of goods that led wealthier Christians to sell their possessions when the needs of the community's poor required it (Acts 2:44 and the note on Acts 4:32–37); and continued attendance at the temple, since in this initial stage there was little or no thought of any dividing line between Christianity and Judaism (Acts 2:46).

†[3:1–4:31] This section presents a series of related events: the dramatic cure of a lame beggar (Acts 3:1–10) produces a large audience for the kerygmatic discourse of Peter (Acts 3:11–26). The Sadducees, taking exception to the doctrine of resurrection, have Peter, John, and apparently the beggar as well, arrested (Acts 4:1–4) and brought to trial before the Sanhedrin. The issue concerns the authority by which Peter and John publicly teach religious doctrine in the temple (Acts 4:5–7). Peter replies with a brief summary of the kerygma, implying that his authority is prophetic (Acts 4:8–12). The court warns the apostles to abandon their practice of invoking prophetic authority in the name of Jesus (Acts 4:13–18). When Peter and John reply that the prophetic role cannot be abandoned to satisfy human objections, the court nevertheless releases them, afraid to do otherwise since the beggar, lame from birth and over forty years old, is a well-known figure in Jerusalem and the facts of his cure are common property (Acts 4:19–22). The narrative concludes with a prayer of the Christian community imploring divine aid against threats of persecution (Acts 4:23–31).

‡[3:1] For the three o'clock hour of prayer: literally, "at the ninth hour of prayer." With the day beginning at 6 a.m., the ninth hour would be 3 p.m.

§[3:6–10] The miracle has a dramatic cast; it symbolizes the saving power of Christ and leads the beggar to enter the temple, where he hears Peter's proclamation of salvation through Jesus.

¶[3:13] Has glorified: through the resurrection and ascension of Jesus, God reversed the judgment against him on the occasion of his trial. Servant: the Greek word can also be rendered as "son" or even "child" here and also in Acts 3:26; 4:25 (applied to David); Acts 4:27; and Acts 4:30. Scholars are of the opinion, however, that the original concept reflected in the words identified Jesus with the suffering Servant of the Lord of Is 52:13–53:12.

**[3:14] The Holy and Righteous One: so designating Jesus emphasizes his special relationship to the Father (see Lk 1:35; 4:34) and emphasizes his sinlessness and religious dignity that are placed in sharp contrast with the guilt of those who rejected him in favor of Barabbas.

††[3:15] The author of life: other possible translations of the Greek title are "leader of life" or "pioneer of life." The title clearly points to Jesus as the source and originator of salvation.

l. [2:38] 3:19; 16:31; Lk 3:3.　m. [2:39] Is 57:19; Jl 3:5; Eph 2:17. n. [2:40] Dt 32:5; Ps 78:8; Lk 9:41; Phil 2:15.　o. [2:41] 2:47; 4:4; 5:14; 6:7; 11:21, 24; 21:20.　p. [2:42–47] 4:32–35.　q. [2:42] 1:14; 6:4. r. [2:43] 5:12–16.　s. [2:44] 4:32, 34–35.　t. [3:2–8] 14:8–10.

u. [3:6] 4:10.　v. [3:8] Is 35:6; Lk 7:22.　w. [3:11] 5:12; Jn 10:23. x. [3:12] 14:15.　y. [3:13] Ex 3:6, 15; Is 52:13; Lk 23:14–25. z. [3:14] Mt 27:20–21; Mk 15:11; Lk 23:18; Jn 18:40.　a. [3:15] 4:10; 5:31 / 1:8; 2:32.

out of ignorance,* just as your leaders did;*b 18but God has thus brought to fulfillment what he had announced beforehand through the mouth of all the prophets,† that his Messiah would suffer.c 19Repent, therefore, and be converted, that your sins may be wiped away,d 20and that the Lord may grant you times of refreshment and send you the Messiah already appointed for you, Jesus,‡ 21whom heaven must receive until the times of universal restoration§ of which God spoke through the mouth of his holy prophets from of old. 22For Moses said:¶

'A prophet like me will the Lord, your
    God, raise up for you
    from among your own kinsmen;
to him you shall listen in all that he may
    say to you.*
23 Everyone who does not listen to that
    prophet
    will be cut off from the people.'f

24Moreover, all the prophets who spoke, from Samuel and those afterwards, also announced these days. 25You are the children of the prophets and of the covenant that God made with your ancestors when he said to Abraham, 'In your offspring all the families of the earth shall be blessed.'g 26For you first, God raised up his servant and sent him to bless you by turning each of you from your evil ways."h

*[3:17] **Ignorance**: a Lucan motif, explaining away the actions not only of the people but also of their leaders in crucifying Jesus. On this basis the presbyters in Acts could continue to appeal to the Jews in Jerusalem to believe in Jesus, even while affirming their involvement in his death because they were unaware of his messianic dignity. See also Acts 13:27 and Lk 23:34.

†[3:18] **Through the mouth of all the prophets**: Christian prophetic insight into the Old Testament saw the crucifixion and death of Jesus as the main import of messianic prophecy. The Jews themselves did not anticipate a suffering Messiah; they usually understood the Servant Song in Is 52:13–53:12 to signify their own suffering as a people. In his typical fashion (cf. Lk 18:31; 24:25, 27, 44), Luke does not specify the particular Old Testament prophecies that were fulfilled by Jesus. See also note on Lk 24:26.

‡[3:20] **The Lord . . . and send you the Messiah already appointed for you, Jesus**: an allusion to the parousia or second coming of Christ, judged to be imminent in the apostolic age. This reference to its nearness is the only explicit one in Acts. Some scholars believe that this verse preserves a very early christology, in which the title "Messiah" (Greek "Christ") is applied to him as of his parousia, his second coming (contrast Acts 2:36). This view of a future messiahship of Jesus is not found elsewhere in the New Testament.

§[3:21] **The times of universal restoration**: like "the times of refreshment" (Acts 3:20), an apocalyptic designation of the messianic age, fitting in with the christology of Acts 3:20 that associates the messiahship of Jesus with his future coming.

¶[3:22] A loose citation of Dt 18:15, which teaches that the Israelites are to learn the will of Yahweh from no one but their prophets. At the time of Jesus, some Jews expected a unique prophet to come in fulfillment of this text. Early Christianity applied this tradition and text to Jesus and used them especially in defense of the divergence of Christian teaching from traditional Judaism.

b. [3:17] 13:27; Lk 23:34; 1 Cor 2:8; 1 Tm 1:13.   c. [3:18] Lk 18:31.
d. [3:19] 2:38.   e. [3:22] 7:37; Dt 18:15, 18.   f. [3:23] Lv 23:29; Dt 18:19.   g. [3:25] Gn 12:3; 18:18; 22:18; Sir 44:19–21; Gal 3:8–9.
h. [3:26] 13:46; Rom 1:16.

## CHAPTER 4

1While they were still speaking to the people, the priests, the captain of the temple guard, and the Sadducees** confronted them, 2disturbed that they were teaching the people and proclaiming in Jesus the resurrection of the dead.i 3They laid hands on them and put them in custody until the next day, since it was already evening. 4But many of those who heard the word came to believe and [the] number of men grew to [about] five thousand.

**Before the Sanhedrin.** 5On the next day, their leaders, elders, and scribes were assembled in Jerusalem, 6with Annas the high priest, Caiaphas, John, Alexander, and all who were of the high-priestly class. 7They brought them into their presence and questioned them, "By what power or by what name have you done this?" 8Then Peter, filled with the holy Spirit, answered them, "Leaders of the people and elders:j 9If we are being examined today about a good deed done to a cripple, namely, by what means he was saved, 10then all of you and all the people of Israel should know that it was in the name of Jesus Christ the Nazorean whom you crucified, whom God raised from the dead; in his name this man stands before you healed. 11kHe is 'the stone rejected by you,'†† the builders, which has become the cornerstone.' 12‡‡There is no salvation through anyone else, nor is there any other name under heaven given to the human race by which we are to be saved."

13Observing the boldness of Peter and John and perceiving them to be uneducated, ordinary men, they were amazed, and they recognized them as the companions of Jesus. 14Then when they saw the man who had been cured standing there with them, they could say nothing in reply. 15So they ordered them to leave the Sanhedrin, and conferred with one another, saying, 16"What are we to do with these men? Everyone living in Jerusalem knows that a remarkable sign was done through them, and we cannot deny it. 17But so that it may not be spread any further among the people, let us give them a stern warning never again to speak to anyone in this name."m 18So they called them back and ordered them not to speak or teach at all in the name of Jesus.

**[4:1] The priests, the captain of the temple guard, and the Sadducees**: the priests performed the temple liturgy; the temple guard was composed of Levites, whose captain ranked next after the high priest. The Sadducees, a party within Judaism at this time, rejected those doctrines, including bodily resurrection, which they believed alien to the ancient Mosaic religion. The Sadducees were drawn from priestly families and from the lay aristocracy.

††[4:11] Early Christianity applied this citation from Ps 118:22 to Jesus; cf. Mk 12:10; 1 Pt 2:7.

‡‡[4:12] In the Roman world of Luke's day, salvation was often attributed to the emperor who was hailed as "savior" and "god." Luke, in the words of Peter, denies that deliverance comes through anyone other than Jesus.

i. [4:2] 23:6–8; 24:21.   j. [4:8] Mt 10:20.   k. [4:11] Ps 118:22; Is 28:16; Mt 21:42; Mk 12:10; Lk 20:17; Rom 9:33; 1 Pt 2:7.   l. [4:12] Mt 1:21; 1 Cor 3:11.   m. [4:17] 5:28.

¹⁹Peter and John, however, said to them in reply, "Whether it is right in the sight of God for us to obey you rather than God, you be the judges." ²⁰It is impossible for us not to speak about what we have seen and heard." ²¹After threatening them further, they released them, finding no way to punish them, on account of the people who were all praising God for what had happened. ²²For the man on whom this sign of healing had been done was over forty years old.

**Prayer of the Community.** ²³After their release they went back to their own people and reported what the chief priests and elders had told them. ²⁴And when they heard it, they raised their voices to God with one accord and said, "Sovereign Lord, maker of heaven and earth and the sea and all that is in them, ²⁵you said by the holy Spirit through the mouth of our father David, your servant:

'Why did the Gentiles rage
    and the peoples entertain folly?
²⁶ The kings of the earth took their stand
    and the princes gathered together
        against the Lord and against his
            anointed.'

²⁷Indeed they gathered in this city against your holy servant Jesus whom you anointed, Herod and Pontius Pilate, together with the Gentiles and the peoples of Israel, ²⁸to do what your hand and [your] will had long ago planned to take place. ²⁹And now, Lord, take note of their threats, and enable your servants to speak your word with all boldness, ³⁰as you stretch forth [your] hand to heal, and signs and wonders are done through the name of your holy servant Jesus." ³¹As they prayed, the place where they were gathered shook, and they were all filled with the holy Spirit and continued to speak the word of God with boldness.

**Life in the Christian Community.** ³²The community of believers was of one heart and mind, and no one claimed that any of his possessions was his own, but they had everything in common. ³³With great power the apostles bore witness to the resurrection of the Lord Jesus, and great favor was accorded them all. ³⁴There was no needy person among them, for those who owned property or houses would sell them, bring the proceeds of the sale, ³⁵and put them at the feet of the apostles, and they were distributed to each according to need.

³⁶Thus Joseph, also named by the apostles Barnabas (which is translated "son of encouragement"), a Levite, a Cypriot by birth, ³⁷sold a piece of property that he owned, then brought the money and put it at the feet of the apostles.

## CHAPTER 5

**Ananias and Sapphira.** ¹A man named Ananias, however, with his wife Sapphira, sold a piece of property. ²He retained for himself, with his wife's knowledge, some of the purchase price, took the remainder, and put it at the feet of the apostles. ³But Peter said, "Ananias, why has Satan filled your heart so that you lied to the holy Spirit and retained part of the price of the land? ⁴While it remained unsold, did it not remain yours? And when it was sold, was it not still under your control? Why did you contrive this deed? You have lied not to human beings, but to God." ⁵When Ananias heard these words, he fell down and breathed his last, and great fear came upon all who heard of it. ⁶The young men came and wrapped him up, then carried him out and buried him.

⁷After an interval of about three hours, his wife came in, unaware of what had happened. ⁸Peter said to her, "Tell me, did you sell the land for this amount?" She answered, "Yes, for that amount." ⁹Then Peter said to her, "Why did you agree to test the Spirit of the Lord? Listen, the footsteps of those who have buried your husband are at the door, and they will carry you out." ¹⁰At once, she fell down at his feet and breathed her last. When the young men entered they found her dead, so they carried her out and buried her beside her husband. ¹¹And great fear came upon the whole church and upon all who heard of these things.

**Signs and Wonders of the Apostles.** ¹²Many signs and wonders were done among the people at the hands of the apostles. They were all together in Solomon's portico. ¹³None of the others dared

*[4:27] **Herod:** Herod Antipas, ruler of Galilee and Perea from 4 B.C. to A.D. 39, who executed John the Baptist and before whom Jesus was arraigned; cf. Lk 23:6–12.

†[4:31] **The place . . . shook:** the earthquake is used as a sign of the divine presence in Ex 19:18; Is 6:4. Here the shaking of the building symbolizes God's favorable response to their prayer. Luke may have had as an additional reason for using the symbol in this sense the fact that it was familiar in the Hellenistic world. Ovid and Virgil also employ it.

‡[4:32–37] This is the second summary characterizing the Jerusalem community (see note on Acts 2:42–47). It emphasizes the system of the distribution of goods and introduces Barnabas, who appears later in Acts as the friend and companion of Paul, and who, as noted here (Acts 4:37), endeared himself to the community by a donation of money through the sale of property. This sharing of material possessions continues a practice that Luke describes during the historical ministry of Jesus (Lk 8:3) and is in accord with the sayings of Jesus in Luke's gospel (Lk 12:33; 16:9, 11, 13).

§[5:1–11] The sin of Ananias and Sapphira did not consist in the withholding of part of the money but in their deception of the community. Their deaths are ascribed to a lie to the holy Spirit (Acts 5:3, 9), i.e., they accepted the honor accorded them by the community for their generosity, but in reality they were not deserving of it.

¶[5:12–16] This, the third summary portraying the Jerusalem community, underscores the Twelve as its bulwark, especially because of their charismatic power to heal the sick; cf. Acts 2:42–47; 4:32–37.

n. [4:19] 5:29–32. o. [4:25–26] Ps 2:1–2. p. [4:27] Lk 23:12–13. q. [4:31] 2:4.

r. [4:34–35] 2:44–45. s. [4:36–37] 9:27; 11:22, 30; 12:25; 13:15; 1 Cor 9:6; Gal 2:1, 9, 13; Col 4:10. t. [5:3] Lk 22:3; Jn 13:2. u. [5:11] 2:43; 5:5; 19:17. v. [5:12] 2:43; 6:8; 14:3; 15:12.

to join them, but the people esteemed them. [14]Yet more than ever, believers in the Lord, great numbers of men and women, were added to them. [15]Thus they even carried the sick out into the streets and laid them on cots and mats so that when Peter came by, at least his shadow might fall on one or another of them.[w] [16]A large number of people from the towns in the vicinity of Jerusalem also gathered, bringing the sick and those disturbed by unclean spirits, and they were all cured.

**Trial Before the Sanhedrin.**[*] [17]Then the high priest rose up and all his companions, that is, the party of the Sadducees, and, filled with jealousy,[x] [18]laid hands upon the apostles and put them in the public jail. [19]But during the night, the angel of the Lord opened the doors of the prison, led them out, and said,[y] [20]"Go and take your place in the temple area, and tell the people everything about this life." [21]When they heard this, they went to the temple early in the morning and taught. When the high priest and his companions arrived, they convened the Sanhedrin, the full senate of the Israelites, and sent to the jail to have them brought in. [22]But the court officers who went did not find them in the prison, so they came back and reported, [23]"We found the jail securely locked and the guards stationed outside the doors, but when we opened them, we found no one inside." [24]When they heard this report, the captain of the temple guard and the chief priests were at a loss about them, as to what this would come to. [25]Then someone came in and reported to them, "The men whom you put in prison are in the temple area and are teaching the people." [26]Then the captain and the court officers went and brought them in, but without force, because they were afraid of being stoned by the people.[z]

[27]When they had brought them in and made them stand before the Sanhedrin, the high priest questioned them, [28]"We gave you strict orders [did we not?] to stop teaching in that name. Yet you have filled Jerusalem with your teaching and want to bring this man's blood upon us."[a] [29]But

Peter and the apostles said in reply, "We must obey God rather than men.[b] [30]†The God of our ancestors raised Jesus,[c] though you had him killed by hanging him on a tree. [31]God exalted him at his right hand‡ as leader and savior to grant Israel repentance and forgiveness of sins.[d] [32]We are witnesses of these things, as is the holy Spirit that God has given to those who obey him."[e]

[33]When they heard this, they became infuriated and wanted to put them to death. [34]But a Pharisee in the Sanhedrin named Gamaliel, a teacher of the law, respected by all the people, stood up, ordered the men to be put outside for a short time,[f] [35]and said to them, "Fellow Israelites, be careful what you are about to do to these men. [36]¶Some time ago, Theudas appeared, claiming to be someone important, and about four hundred men joined him, but he was killed, and all those who were loyal to him were disbanded and came to nothing. [37]After him came Judas the Galilean at the time of the census. He also drew people after him, but he too perished and all who were loyal to him were scattered. [38]So now I tell you, have nothing to do with these men, and let them go. For if this endeavor or this activity is of human origin, it will destroy itself. [39]But if it comes from God, you will not be able to destroy them; you may even find yourselves fighting against God." They were persuaded by him. [40]After recalling the apostles, they had them flogged, ordered them to stop speaking in the name of Jesus, and dismissed them.[g] [41]So they left the presence of the Sanhedrin, rejoicing that they had been found worthy to suffer dishonor for the sake of the name.[h] [42]And all day long, both at the temple and in their homes, they did not stop teaching and proclaiming the Messiah, Jesus.[i]

## CHAPTER 6
**The Need for Assistants.** [1]**At that time, as the number of disciples continued to grow, the

---

*[5:17–42] A second action against the community is taken by the Sanhedrin in the arrest and trial of the Twelve; cf. Acts 4:1–3. The motive is the jealousy of the religious authorities over the popularity of the apostles (Acts 5:17) who are now charged with the defiance of the Sanhedrin's previous order to them to abandon their prophetic role (Acts 5:28; cf. Acts 4:18). In this crisis the apostles are favored by a miraculous release from prison (Acts 5:18–24). (For similar incidents involving Peter and Paul, see Acts 12:6–11; 16:25–29.) The real significance of such an event, however, would be manifest only to people of faith, not to unbelievers; since the Sanhedrin already judged the Twelve to be inauthentic prophets, it could disregard reports of their miracles. When the Twelve immediately resumed public teaching, the Sanhedrin determined to invoke upon them the penalty of death (Acts 5:33) prescribed in Dt 13:6–10. Gamaliel's advice against this course finally prevailed, but it did not save the Twelve from the punishment of scourging (Acts 5:40) in a last endeavor to shake their conviction of their prophetic mission.

†[5:30] **Hanging him on a tree:** that is, crucifying him (cf. also Gal 3:13).

‡[5:31] **At his right hand:** see note on Acts 2:33.

§[5:34] **Gamaliel:** in Acts 22:3, Paul identifies himself as a disciple of this Rabbi Gamaliel I who flourished in Jerusalem between A.D. 25 and 50.

¶[5:36–37] Gamaliel offers examples of unsuccessful contemporary movements to argue that if God is not the origin of this movement preached by the apostles it will perish by itself. The movement initiated by Theudas actually occurred when C. Cuspius Fadus was governor, A.D. 44–46. Luke's placing of Judas the Galilean after Theudas and at the time of the census (see note on Lk 2:1–2) is an indication of the vagueness of his knowledge of these events.

**[6:1–7] The Hellenists . . . the Hebrews:** the Hellenists were not necessarily Jews from the diaspora, but were more probably Palestinian Jews who spoke only Greek. The Hebrews were Palestinian Jews who spoke Hebrew or Aramaic and who may also have spoken Greek. Both groups belong to the Jerusalem Jewish Christian community. The

---

w. [5:15] 19:11–12; Mk 6:56.   x. [5:17] 4:1–3, 6.   y. [5:19] 12:7–10; 16:25–26.   z. [5:26] Lk 20:19.   a. [5:28] Mt 27:25.

b. [5:29] 4:19.   c. [5:30] 2:23–24.   d. [5:31] 2:38.   e. [5:32] Lk 24:48; Jn 15:26.   f. [5:34] 22:3.   g. [5:40] Mt 10:17; Acts 4:17–18.   h. [5:41] Mt 5:10–11; 1 Pt 4:13.   i. [5:42] 2:46; 5:20–21, 25; 8:35; 17:3; 18:5, 28; 19:4–5.

Hellenists complained against the Hebrews because their widows were being neglected in the daily distribution.$^j$ $^2$So the Twelve called together the community of the disciples and said, "It is not right for us to neglect the word of God to serve at table.$^†$ $^3$Brothers, select from among you seven reputable men, filled with the Spirit and wisdom, whom we shall appoint to this task, $^4$whereas we shall devote ourselves to prayer and to the ministry of the word." $^5$The proposal was acceptable to the whole community, so they chose Stephen, a man filled with faith and the holy Spirit, also Philip, Prochorus, Nicanor, Timon, Parmenas, and Nicholas of Antioch, a convert to Judaism. $^{6k}$They presented these men to the apostles who prayed and laid hands on them.$^‡$ $^7$The word of God continued to spread, and the number of the disciples in Jerusalem increased greatly; even a large group of priests were becoming obedient to the faith.$^l$

**Accusation Against Stephen.** $^{8§}$Now Stephen, filled with grace and power, was working great wonders and signs among the people. $^9$Certain members of the so-called Synagogue of Freedmen, Cyrenians, and Alexandrians, and people from Cilicia and Asia, came forward and debated with Stephen, $^{10}$but they could not withstand the wisdom and the spirit with which he spoke.$^m$ $^{11}$Then they instigated some men

to say, "We have heard him speaking blasphemous words against Moses and God."$^n$ $^{12}$They stirred up the people, the elders, and the scribes, accosted him, seized him, and brought him before the Sanhedrin. $^{13}$They presented false witnesses$^¶$ who testified, "This man never stops saying things against [this] holy place and the law. $^{14}$For we have heard him claim that this Jesus the Nazorean will destroy this place and change the customs that Moses handed down to us."$^o$ $^{15}$All those who sat in the Sanhedrin looked intently at him and saw that his face was like the face of an angel.

## CHAPTER 7

**Stephen's Discourses.** $^1$Then the high priest asked, "Is this so?" $^{2p}$And he replied,$^{**}$ "My brothers and fathers, listen. The God of glory appeared to our father Abraham while he was in Mesopotamia,$^{††}$ before he had settled in Haran, $^3$and said to him, 'Go forth from your land and [from] your kinsfolk to the land that I will show you.'$^q$ $^4$So he went forth from the land of the Chaldeans and settled in Haran. And from there, after his father died, he made him migrate to this land where you now dwell.$^r$ $^5$Yet he gave him no inheritance in it, not even a foot's length, but he did promise to give it to him and his descendants as a possession, even though he was childless.$^s$ $^6$And God spoke thus,$^t$ 'His descendants shall be aliens in a land not their own, where they shall be enslaved and oppressed for four hundred years; $^7$but I will bring judgment on the nation they serve,' God said, 'and after that they will come out and worship me in this place.'$^u$ $^8$Then he gave him the covenant of circumcision, and so he became the father of Isaac, and circumcised him on the eighth day, as Isaac did Jacob, and Jacob the twelve patriarchs.$^v$

$^9$"And the patriarchs, jealous of Joseph, sold him into slavery in Egypt; but God was with him$^w$ $^{10}$and rescued him from all his afflictions.

conflict between them leads to a restructuring of the community that will better serve the community's needs. The real purpose of the whole episode, however, is to introduce Stephen as a prominent figure in the community whose long speech and martyrdom will be recounted in Acts 7.

*[6:2–4] The essential function of the Twelve is the "service of the word," including development of the kerygma by formulation of the teachings of Jesus.

†[6:2] **To serve at table:** some commentators think that it is not the serving of food that is described here but rather the keeping of the accounts that recorded the distribution of food to the needy members of the community. In any case, after Stephen and the others are chosen, they are never presented carrying out the task for which they were appointed (Acts 6:2–3). Rather, two of their number, Stephen and Philip, are presented as preachers of the Christian message. They, the Hellenist counterpart of the Twelve, are active in the ministry of the word.

‡[6:6] **They . . . laid hands on them:** the customary Jewish way of designating persons for a task and invoking upon them the divine blessing and power to perform it.

§[6:8–8:1] The summary (Acts 6:7) on the progress of the Jerusalem community, illustrated by the conversion of the priests, is followed by a lengthy narrative regarding Stephen. Stephen's defense is not a response to the charges made against him but takes the form of a discourse that reviews the fortunes of God's word to Israel and leads to a prophetic declaration: a plea for the hearing of that word as announced by Christ and now possessed by the Christian community.

The charges that Stephen depreciated the importance of the temple and the Mosaic law and elevated Jesus to a stature above Moses (Acts 6:13–14) were in fact true. Before the Sanhedrin, no defense against them was possible. With Stephen, who thus perceived the fuller implications of the teachings of Jesus, the differences between Judaism and Christianity began to appear. Luke's account of Stephen's martyrdom and its aftermath shows how the major impetus behind the Christian movement passed from Jerusalem, where the temple and law prevailed, to Antioch in Syria, where these influences were less pressing.

¶[6:13] **False witnesses:** here, and in his account of Stephen's execution (Acts 7:54–60), Luke parallels the martyrdom of Stephen with the death of Jesus.

**[7:2–53] Stephen's speech represents Luke's description of Christianity's break from its Jewish matrix. Two motifs become prominent in the speech: (1) Israel's reaction to God's chosen leaders in the past reveals that the people have consistently rejected them; and (2) Israel has misunderstood God's choice of the Jerusalem temple as the place where he is to be worshiped.

††[7:2] **God . . . appeared to our father Abraham . . . in Mesopotamia:** the first of a number of minor discrepancies between the data of the Old Testament and the data of Stephen's discourse. According to Gn 12:1, God first spoke to Abraham in Haran. The main discrepancies are these: in Acts 7:16 it is said that Jacob was buried in Shechem, whereas Gn 50:13 says he was buried at Hebron; in the same verse it is said that the tomb was purchased by Abraham, but in Gn 33:19 and Jos 24:32 the purchase is attributed to Jacob himself.

n. [6:11] Mt 26:59–61; Mk 14:55–58; Acts 21:21.  o. [6:14] Mt 26:59–61; 27:40; Jn 2:19.  p. [7:2] Gn 11:31; 12:1; Ps 29:3.  q. [7:3] Gn 12:1.  r. [7:4] Gn 12:5; 15:7.  s. [7:5] Gn 12:7; 13:15; 15:2; 16:1; Dt 2:5.  t. [7:6–7] Gn 15:13–14.  u. [7:7] Ex 3:12.  v. [7:8] Gn 17:10–14; 21:2–4.  w. [7:9] Gn 37:11, 28; 39:2, 3, 21, 23.

j. [6:1] 2:45; 4:34–35.  k. [6:6] 1:24; 13:3; 14:23.  l. [6:7] 9:31; 12:24; 16:5; 19:20; 28:30–31.  m. [6:10] Lk 21:15.

He granted him favor and wisdom before Pharaoh, the king of Egypt, who put him in charge of Egypt and [of] his entire household.[x] [11]Then a famine and great affliction struck all Egypt and Canaan, and our ancestors could find no food;[y] [12]but when Jacob heard that there was grain in Egypt, he sent our ancestors there a first time.[z] [13]The second time, Joseph made himself known to his brothers, and Joseph's family became known to Pharaoh.[a] [14]Then Joseph sent for his father Jacob, inviting him and his whole clan, seventy-five persons;[b] [15]and Jacob went down to Egypt. And he and our ancestors died[c] [16]and were brought back to Shechem and placed in the tomb that Abraham had purchased for a sum of money from the sons of Hamor at Shechem.[d]

[17]"When the time drew near for the fulfillment of the promise that God pledged to Abraham, the people had increased and become very numerous in Egypt,[e] [18]until another king who knew nothing of Joseph came to power [in Egypt].[f] [19]He dealt shrewdly with our people and oppressed [our] ancestors by forcing them to expose their infants, that they might not survive. [20]At this time Moses was born, and he was extremely beautiful. For three months he was nursed in his father's house;[g] [21]but when he was exposed, Pharaoh's daughter adopted him and brought him up as her own son.[h] [22]Moses was educated [in] all the wisdom of the Egyptians and was powerful in his words and deeds.

[23]"When he was forty years old, he decided to visit his kinsfolk, the Israelites. [24]When he saw one of them treated unjustly, he defended and avenged the oppressed man by striking down the Egyptian. [25]He assumed [his] kinsfolk would understand that God was offering them deliverance through him, but they did not understand. [26]The next day he appeared to them as they were fighting and tried to reconcile them peacefully, saying, 'Men, you are brothers. Why are you harming one another?' [27]Then the one who was harming his neighbor pushed him aside, saying, 'Who appointed you ruler and judge over us? [28]Are you thinking of killing me as you killed the Egyptian yesterday?' [29]Moses fled when he heard this and settled as an alien in the land of Midian, where he became the father of two sons.[k]

[30]"Forty years later, an angel appeared to him in the desert near Mount Sinai in the flame of a burning bush. [31]When Moses saw it, he was amazed at the sight, and as he drew near to look at it, the voice of the Lord came, [32]'I am the God of your fathers, the God of Abraham, of Isaac, and of Jacob.' Then Moses, trembling, did not dare to look at it. [33]But the Lord said to him, 'Remove the sandals from your feet, for the place where you stand is holy ground. [34]I have witnessed the affliction of my people in Egypt and have heard their groaning, and I have come down to rescue them. Come now, I will send you to Egypt.' [35]This Moses, whom they had rejected with the words, 'Who appointed you ruler and judge?' God sent as [both] ruler and deliverer, through the angel who appeared to him in the bush.[m] [36]This man led them out, performing wonders and signs in the land of Egypt, at the Red Sea, and in the desert for forty years.[n] [37]It was this Moses who said to the Israelites, 'God will raise up for you, from among your own kinsfolk, a prophet like me.'[o] [38]It was he who, in the assembly in the desert, was with the angel who spoke to him on Mount Sinai and with our ancestors, and he received living utterances to hand on to us.[p]

[39]"Our ancestors were unwilling to obey him; instead, they pushed him aside and in their hearts turned back to Egypt,[q] [40]saying to Aaron, 'Make us gods who will be our leaders. As for that Moses who led us out of the land of Egypt, we do not know what has happened to him.'[r] [41]So they made a calf in those days, offered sacrifice to the idol, and reveled in the works of their hands. [42]Then God turned and handed them over to worship the host of heaven, as it is written in the book of the prophets:[s]

'Did you bring me sacrifices and offerings
　　for forty years in the desert, O house
　　　　of Israel?[u]
[43]　No, you took up the tent of Moloch
　　　and the star of [your] god Rephan,
　　　　the images that you made to
　　　　　worship.
So I shall take you into exile beyond
　　Babylon.'

[44]"Our ancestors had the tent of testimony in the desert just as the One who spoke to Moses directed him to make it according to the pattern he had seen.[v] [45]Our ancestors who inherited it brought it with Joshua when they dispossessed the nations that God drove out from before our ancestors, up to the time of David,[w] [46]who found favor in the sight of God and asked that he might find a dwelling place for the house of Jacob.[x] [47]But Solomon built a house for him.[y] [48]Yet the Most High does not dwell in houses made by human hands. As the prophet says:[z]

[49]　'The heavens are my throne,
　　　the earth is my footstool.

x. [7:10] Gn 41:37–43; Ps 105:21; Wis 10:13–14.　y. [7:11] Gn 41:54–57; 42:5.　z. [7:12] Gn 42:1–2.　a. [7:13] Gn 45:3–4, 16.　b. [7:14] Gn 45:9–11, 18–19; 46:27; Ex 1:5 LXX; Dt 10:22.　c. [7:15] Gn 46:5–6; 49:33.　d. [7:16] Gn 23:3–20; 33:19; 49:29–30; 50:13; Jos 24:32.　e. [7:17] Ex 1:7.　f. [7:18] Ex 1:8.　g. [7:20] Ex 2:2; Heb 11:23.　h. [7:21] Ex 2:3–10.　i. [7:23–24] Ex 2:11–12.　j. [7:26–28] Ex 2:13–14.　k. [7:29] Ex 2:15, 21–22; 18:3–4.　l. [7:30–34] Ex 3:2–3.

m. [7:35] Ex 2:14.　n. [7:36] Ex 7:3, 10; 14:21; Nm 14:33.　o. [7:37] Dt 18:15; Acts 3:22.　p. [7:38] Ex 19:3; 20:1–17; Dt 5:4–22; 6:4–25.　q. [7:39] Nm 14:3.　r. [7:40] Ex 32:1, 23.　s. [7:41] Ex 32:4–6.　t. [7:42–43] Am 5:25–27.　u. [7:42] Jer 7:18; 8:2; 19:13.　v. [7:44] Ex 25:9, 40.　w. [7:45] Jos 3:14–17; 18:1; 2 Sm 7:5–7.　x. [7:46] 2 Sm 7:1–2; 1 Kgs 8:17; Ps 132:1–5.　y. [7:47] 1 Kgs 6:1; 1 Chr 17:12.　z. [7:48] 17:24.

What kind of house can you build for me?
      says the Lord,
   or what is to be my resting place?[a]
[50] Did not my hand make all these things?'

**Conclusion.** [51]"You stiff-necked people, uncircumcised in heart and ears, you always oppose the holy Spirit; you are just like your ancestors. [52]Which of the prophets did your ancestors not persecute? They put to death those who foretold the coming of the righteous one, whose betrayers and murderers you have now become.[b] [53]You received the law as transmitted by angels, but you did not observe it."[c]

**Stephen's Martyrdom.** [54]When they heard this, they were infuriated, and they ground their teeth at him. [55d]But he, filled with the holy Spirit, looked up intently to heaven and saw the glory of God and Jesus standing at the right hand of God,[*] [56]and he said, "Behold, I see the heavens opened and the Son of Man standing at the right hand of God." [57]But they cried out in a loud voice, covered their ears,[†] and rushed upon him together. [58]They threw him out of the city, and began to stone him. The witnesses laid down their cloaks at the feet of a young man named Saul.[e] [59]As they were stoning Stephen,[f] he called out, "Lord Jesus, receive my spirit."[‡] [60]Then he fell to his knees and cried out in a loud voice, "Lord, do not hold this sin against them"; and when he said this, he fell asleep.[g]

## CHAPTER 8

[1]Now Saul was consenting to his execution.[h]

**Persecution of the Church.** On that day, there broke out a severe persecution[§] of the church in Jerusalem, and all were scattered throughout the countryside of Judea and Samaria, except the apostles.[¶] [2]Devout men buried Stephen and made a loud lament over him. [3]Saul, meanwhile, was trying to destroy the church;[**] entering house after house and dragging out men and women, he handed them over for imprisonment.[i]

## III. THE MISSION IN JUDEA AND SAMARIA

**Philip in Samaria.** [4]Now those who had been scattered went about preaching the word.[j] [5]Thus Philip went down to [the] city of Samaria and proclaimed the Messiah to them.[k] [6]With one accord, the crowds paid attention to what was said by Philip when they heard it and saw the signs he was doing. [7]For unclean spirits, crying out in a loud voice, came out of many possessed people, and many paralyzed and crippled people were cured.[l] [8]There was great joy in that city.

**Simon the Magician.** [9]A man named Simon used to practice magic[††] in the city and astounded the people of Samaria, claiming to be someone great. [10]All of them, from the least to the greatest, paid attention to him, saying, "This man is the 'Power of God' that is called 'Great.'" [11]They paid attention to him because he had astounded them by his magic for a long time, [12]but once they began to believe Philip as he preached the good news about the kingdom of God and the name of Jesus Christ, men and women alike were baptized.[m] [13]Even Simon himself believed and, after being baptized, became devoted to Philip; and when he saw the signs and mighty deeds that were occurring, he was astounded.

[14]Now when the apostles in Jerusalem heard that Samaria had accepted the word of God, they sent them Peter and John, [15]who went down and prayed for them, that they might receive the holy Spirit, [16]for it had not yet fallen upon any of them; they had only been baptized in the name of the Lord Jesus.[‡‡] [17]Then they laid hands on them and they received the holy Spirit.[n]

---

*[7:55] **He . . . saw . . . Jesus standing at the right hand of God**: Stephen affirms to the Sanhedrin that the prophecy Jesus made before him has been fulfilled (Mk 14:62).

†[7:57] **Covered their ears**: Stephen's declaration, like that of Jesus, is a scandal to the court, which regards it as blasphemy.

‡[7:59] Compare Lk 23:34, 46.

§[8:1–40] Some idea of the severity of the persecution that now breaks out against the Jerusalem community can be gathered from Acts 22:4 and Acts 26:9–11. Luke, however, concentrates on the fortunes of the word of God among people, indicating how the dispersal of the Jewish community resulted in the conversion of the Samaritans (Acts 8:4–17, 25). His narrative is further expanded to include the account of Philip's acceptance of an Ethiopian (Acts 8:26–39).

¶[8:1] **All were scattered . . . except the apostles**: this observation leads some modern scholars to conclude that the persecution was limited to the Hellenist Christians and that the Hebrew Christians were not molested, perhaps because their attitude toward the law and temple was still more in line with that of their fellow Jews (see the charge leveled against the Hellenist Stephen in Acts 6:13–14). Whatever the facts, it appears that the Twelve took no public stand regarding Ste-

phen's position, choosing, instead, to await the development of events.

**[8:3] **Saul . . . was trying to destroy the church**: like Stephen, Saul was able to perceive that the Christian movement contained the seeds of doctrinal divergence from Judaism. A pupil of Gamaliel, according to Acts 22:3, and totally dedicated to the law as the way of salvation (Gal 1:13–14), Saul accepted the task of crushing the Christian movement, at least insofar as it detracted from the importance of the temple and the law. His vehement opposition to Christianity reveals how difficult it was for a Jew of his time to accept a messianism that differed so greatly from the general expectation.

††[8:9–13, 18–24] Sorcerers were well known in the ancient world. Probably the incident involving Simon and his altercation with Peter is introduced to show that the miraculous charisms possessed by members of the Christian community (Acts 8:6–7) were not to be confused with the magic of sorcerers.

‡‡[8:16] Here and in Acts 10:44–48 and Acts 19:1–6, Luke distinguishes between baptism in the name of the Lord Jesus and the reception of the Spirit. In each case, the Spirit is conferred through members of the Twelve (Peter and John) or their representative (Paul). This may be Luke's way of describing the role of the church in the bestowal of the Spirit. Elsewhere in Acts, baptism and the Spirit are more closely related (Acts 1:5; 11:16).

---

a. [7:49] Is 66:1–2.   b. [7:52] 2 Chr 36:16; Mt 23:31, 34.   c. [7:53] Gal 3:19; Heb 2:2.   d. [7:55–56] Mt 26:64; Mk 14:62; Lk 22:69; Acts 2:34.   e. [7:58] 22:20.   f. [7:59] Ps 31:6; Lk 23:46.   g. [7:60] Mt 27:46, 50; Mk 15:34; Lk 23:46.   h. [8:1] 22:20.

i. [8:3] 9:1, 13; 22:4; 26:9–11; 1 Cor 5:9; Gal 1:13.   j. [8:4] 11:19.   k. [8:5] 6:5; 21:8–9.   l. [8:7] Mk 16:17.   m. [8:12] 1:3; 19:8; 28:23, 31.   n. [8:17] 2:4; 4:31; 10:44–47; 15:8–9; 19:2, 6.

<sup>18</sup>*When Simon saw that the Spirit was conferred by the laying on of the apostles' hands, he offered them money <sup>19</sup>and said, "Give me this power too, so that anyone upon whom I lay my hands may receive the holy Spirit." <sup>20</sup>But Peter said to him, "May your money perish with you, because you thought that you could buy the gift of God with money. <sup>21</sup>You have no share or lot in this matter, for your heart is not upright before God. <sup>22</sup>Repent of this wickedness of yours and pray to the Lord that, if possible, your intention may be forgiven. <sup>23</sup>For I see that you are filled with bitter gall and are in the bonds of iniquity." <sup>24</sup>Simon said in reply, "Pray for me to the Lord, that nothing of what you have said may come upon me." <sup>25</sup>So when they had testified and proclaimed the word of the Lord, they returned to Jerusalem and preached the good news to many Samaritan villages.

**Philip and the Ethiopian.**† <sup>26</sup>Then the angel of the Lord spoke to Philip, "Get up and head south on the road that goes down from Jerusalem to Gaza, the desert route." <sup>27</sup>So he got up and set out. Now there was an Ethiopian eunuch, a court official of the Candace,‡ that is, the queen of the Ethiopians, in charge of her entire treasury, who had come to Jerusalem to worship,<sup>o</sup> <sup>28</sup>and was returning home. Seated in his chariot, he was reading the prophet Isaiah. <sup>29</sup>The Spirit said to Philip, "Go and join up with that chariot." <sup>30</sup>§Philip ran up and heard him reading Isaiah the prophet and said, "Do you understand what you are reading?" <sup>31</sup>He replied, "How can I, unless someone instructs me?" So he invited Philip to get in and sit with him.<sup>p</sup> <sup>32</sup>This was the scripture passage he was reading:<sup>q</sup>

"Like a sheep he was led to the slaughter,
    and as a lamb before its shearer is
        silent,
        so he opened not his mouth.
<sup>33</sup>  In [his] humiliation justice was denied
        him.

Who will tell of his posterity?
    For his life is taken from the
        earth."

<sup>34</sup>Then the eunuch said to Philip in reply, "I beg you, about whom is the prophet saying this? About himself, or about someone else?" <sup>35</sup>Then Philip opened his mouth and, beginning with this scripture passage, he proclaimed Jesus to him. <sup>36</sup>*As they traveled along the road they came to some water, and the eunuch said, "Look, there is water. What is to prevent my being baptized?" [<sup>37</sup>]¶ <sup>38</sup>Then he ordered the chariot to stop, and Philip and the eunuch both went down into the water, and he baptized him. <sup>39</sup>When they came out of the water, the Spirit of the Lord snatched Philip away, and the eunuch saw him no more, but continued on his way rejoicing.<sup>s</sup> <sup>40</sup>Philip came to Azotus, and went about proclaiming the good news to all the towns until he reached Caesarea.<sup>t</sup>

## CHAPTER 9

**Saul's Conversion.** <sup>1</sup>**Now Saul, still breathing murderous threats against the disciples of the Lord,<sup>u</sup> went to the high priest <sup>v</sup> <sup>2</sup>and asked him for letters to the synagogues in Damascus, that, if he should find any men or women who belonged to the Way,†† he might bring them back to Jerusalem in chains. <sup>3</sup>On his journey, as he was nearing Damascus, a light from the sky suddenly flashed around him.<sup>w</sup> <sup>4</sup>He fell to the ground and heard a voice saying to him, "Saul, Saul, why are you persecuting me?"<sup>x</sup> <sup>5</sup>He said, "Who are you, sir?" The reply came, "I am Jesus, whom you are persecuting.<sup>y</sup> <sup>6</sup>Now get up and go into the city and you will be told what you must do."<sup>z</sup> <sup>7</sup>The men who were traveling with

¶ [8:37] The oldest and best manuscripts of Acts omit this verse, which is a Western text reading: "And Philip said, 'If you believe with all your heart, you may.' And he said in reply, 'I believe that Jesus Christ is the Son of God.'"

** [9:1–19] This is the first of three accounts of Paul's conversion (with Acts 22:3–16 and Acts 26:2–18) with some differences of detail owing to Luke's use of different sources. Paul's experience was not visionary but was precipitated by the appearance of Jesus, as he insists in 1 Cor 15:8. The words of Jesus, "Saul, Saul, why are you persecuting me?" related by Luke with no variation in all three accounts, exerted a profound and lasting influence on the thought of Paul. Under the influence of this experience he gradually developed his understanding of justification by faith (see the letters to the Galatians and Romans) and of the identification of the Christian community with Jesus Christ (see 1 Cor 12:27). That Luke would narrate this conversion three times is testimony to the importance he attaches to it. This first account occurs when the word is first spread to the Gentiles. At this point, the conversion of the hero of the Gentile mission is recounted. The emphasis in the account is on Paul as a divinely chosen instrument (Acts 9:15).

†† [9:2] The Way: a name used by the early Christian community for itself (Acts 18:26; 19:9, 23; 22:4; 24:14, 22). The Essene community at Qumran used the same designation to describe its mode of life.

---

* [8:18–20] Simon attempts to buy the gift of God (Acts 8:20) with money. Peter's cursing of Simon's attempt so to use his money expresses a typically Lucan attitude toward material wealth (cf. Lk 6:24; 12:16–21; 16:13).

† [8:26–40] In the account of the conversion of the Ethiopian eunuch, Luke adduces additional evidence to show that the spread of Christianity outside the confines of Judaism itself was in accord with the plan of God. He does not make clear whether the Ethiopian was originally a convert to Judaism or, as is more probable, a "God-fearer" (Acts 10:1), i.e., one who accepted Jewish monotheism and ethic and attended the synagogue but did not consider himself bound by other regulations such as circumcision and observance of the dietary laws. The story of his conversion to Christianity is given a strong supernatural cast by the introduction of an angel (Acts 8:26), instruction from the holy Spirit (Acts 8:29), and the strange removal of Philip from the scene (8:39).

‡ [8:27] The Candace: Candace is not a proper name here but the title of a Nubian queen.

§ [8:30–34] Philip is brought alongside the carriage at the very moment when the Ethiopian is pondering the meaning of Is 53:7–8, a passage that Christianity, from its earliest origins, has applied to Jesus; cf. note on Acts 3:13.

o. [8:27] Is 56:3–5.   p. [8:31] Jn 16:13.   q. [8:32–33] Is 53:7–8 LXX.

r. [8:36] 10:47.   s. [8:39] 1 Kgs 18:12.   t. [8:40] 21:8.   u. [9:1] 8:3; 9:13; 22:4; 1 Cor 15:9; Gal 1:13–14.   v. [9:1–2] 9:14; 26:10.   w. [9:3] 1 Cor 9:1; 15:8; Gal 1:16.   x. [9:4] 22:6; 26:14.   y. [9:5] 22:8; 26:15; Mt 25:40.   z. [9:6] 22:10; 26:16.

him stood speechless, for they heard the voice but could see no one.[a] [8]Saul got up from the ground, but when he opened his eyes he could see nothing;[*] so they led him by the hand and brought him to Damascus.[b] [9]For three days he was unable to see, and he neither ate nor drank.

**Saul's Baptism.** [10c]There was a disciple in Damascus named Ananias, and the Lord said to him in a vision, "Ananias." He answered, "Here I am, Lord." [11]The Lord said to him, "Get up and go to the street called Straight and ask at the house of Judas for a man from Tarsus named Saul. He is there praying,[d] [12]and [in a vision] he has seen a man named Ananias come in and lay [his] hands on him, that he may regain his sight." [13]But Ananias replied, "Lord, I have heard from many sources about this man, what evil things he has done to your holy ones[†] in Jerusalem.[e] [14]And here he has authority from the chief priests to imprison all who call upon your name."[f] [15]But the Lord said to him, "Go, for this man is a chosen instrument of mine to carry my name before Gentiles, kings, and Israelites,[g] [16]and I will show him what he will have to suffer for my name." [17]So Ananias went and entered the house; laying his hands on him, he said, "Saul, my brother, the Lord has sent me, Jesus who appeared to you on the way by which you came, that you may regain your sight and be filled with the holy Spirit." [18]Immediately things like scales fell from his eyes and he regained his sight. He got up and was baptized, [19]and when he had eaten, he recovered his strength.[‡]

**Saul Preaches in Damascus.** He stayed some days with the disciples in Damascus, [20]and he began at once to proclaim Jesus in the synagogues, that he is the Son of God.[§] [21]All who heard him were astounded and said, "Is not this the man who in Jerusalem ravaged those who call upon this name, and came here expressly to take them back in chains to the chief priests?" [22]But Saul grew all the stronger and confounded [the] Jews who lived in Damascus, proving that this is the Messiah.

**Saul Visits Jerusalem.** [23]After a long time had passed, the Jews conspired to kill him, [24h]but their plot became known to Saul. Now they were keeping watch on the gates day and night

so as to kill him, [25]but his disciples took him one night and let him down through an opening in the wall, lowering him in a basket.

[26]When he arrived in Jerusalem[¶] he tried to join the disciples, but they were all afraid of him, not believing that he was a disciple. [27]Then Barnabas took charge of him and brought him to the apostles, and he reported to them how on the way he had seen the Lord and that he had spoken to him, and how in Damascus he had spoken out boldly in the name of Jesus. [28]He moved about freely with them in Jerusalem, and spoke out boldly in the name of the Lord. [29]He also spoke and debated with the Hellenists,[**] but they tried to kill him. [30]And when the brothers learned of this, they took him down to Caesarea and sent him on his way to Tarsus.[j]

**The Church at Peace.** [31††]The church throughout all Judea, Galilee, and Samaria was at peace. It was being built up and walked in the fear of the Lord, and with the consolation of the holy Spirit it grew in numbers.

**Peter Heals Aeneas at Lydda.** [32]As Peter was passing through every region, he went down to the holy ones living in Lydda. [33]There he found a man named Aeneas, who had been confined to bed for eight years, for he was paralyzed. [34]Peter said to him, "Aeneas, Jesus Christ heals you. Get up and make your bed." He got up at once. [35]And all the inhabitants of Lydda and Sharon saw him, and they turned to the Lord.

**Peter Restores Tabitha to Life.** [36]Now in Joppa there was a disciple named Tabitha (which translated means Dorcas).[‡‡] She was completely occupied with good deeds and almsgiving. [37]Now during those days she fell sick and died, so after washing her, they laid [her] out in a room upstairs. [38]Since Lydda was near Joppa, the disciples, hearing that Peter was there, sent two men to him with the request, "Please come to us without delay." [39]So Peter got up and went with them. When he arrived, they took him to the room upstairs where all the widows came to him weeping and showing him the tunics and cloaks that Dorcas had made while she was with them. [40]Peter sent them all out and knelt down and prayed. Then he turned to her body and said, "Tabitha, rise up." She opened her eyes, saw Peter, and sat up.[k] [41]He gave her his hand and raised her up, and when he had called

---

[*] [9:8] **He could see nothing**: a temporary blindness (Acts 9:18) symbolizing the religious blindness of Saul as persecutor (cf. Acts 26:18).

[†] [9:13] **Your holy ones**: literally, "your saints."

[‡] [9:19–30] This is a brief resume of Paul's initial experience as an apostolic preacher. At first he found himself in the position of being regarded as an apostate by the Jews and suspect by the Christian community of Jerusalem. His acceptance by the latter was finally brought about through his friendship with Barnabas (Acts 9:27).

[§] [9:20] **Son of God**: the title "Son of God" occurs in Acts only here, but cf. the citation of Ps 2:7 in Paul's speech at Antioch in Pisidia (Acts 13:33).

a. [9:7] 22:9; 26:13–14.  b. [9:8] 22:11.  c. [9:10–19] 22:12–16.  d. [9:11] 21:39.  e. [9:13] 8:3; 9:1.  f. [9:14] 9:1–2; 26:10; 1 Cor 1:2; 2 Tm 2:22.  g. [9:15] 22:15; 26:1; 27:24.  h. [9:24–25] 2 Cor 11:32–33.

[¶] [9:26] This visit of Paul to Jerusalem is mentioned by Paul in Gal 1:18.

[**] [9:29] **Hellenists**: see note on Acts 6:1–7.

[††] [9:31–43] In the context of the period of peace enjoyed by the community through the cessation of Paul's activities against it, Luke introduces two traditions concerning the miraculous power exercised by Peter as he was making a tour of places where the Christian message had already been preached. The towns of Lydda, Sharon, and Joppa were populated by both Jews and Gentiles and their Christian communities may well have been mixed.

[‡‡] [9:36] **Tabitha (Dorcas)**, respectively the Aramaic and Greek words for "gazelle," exemplifies the right attitude toward material possessions expressed by Jesus in the Lucan Gospel (Lk 6:30; 11:41; 12:33; 18:22; 19:8).

i. [9:26–27] Gal 1:18.  j. [9:30] 11:25.  k. [9:40] Mk 5:40–41.

the holy ones and the widows, he presented her alive. ⁴²This became known all over Joppa, and many came to believe in the Lord. ⁴³ᵗAnd he stayed a long time in Joppa with Simon, a tanner.

## IV. THE INAUGURATION OF THE GENTILE MISSION

### CHAPTER 10

**The Vision of Cornelius.**ᵐ ¹ᵗNow in Caesarea there was a man named Cornelius, a centurion of the Cohort called the Italica,‡ ²devout and God-fearing along with his whole household, who used to give alms generously§ to the Jewish people and pray to God constantly. ³One afternoon about three o'clock,¶ he saw plainly in a vision an angel of God come in to him and say to him, "Cornelius." ⁴He looked intently at him and, seized with fear, said, "What is it, sir?" He said to him, "Your prayers and almsgiving have ascended as a memorial offering before God. ⁵Now send some men to Joppa and summon one Simon who is called Peter. ⁶He is staying with another Simon, a tanner, who has a house by the sea."ⁿ ⁷When the angel who spoke to him had left, he called two of his servants and a devout soldier** from his staff, ⁸explained everything to them, and sent them to Joppa.

**The Vision of Peter.** ⁹††The next day, while they were on their way and nearing the city, Peter went up to the roof terrace to pray at about noontime.‡‡ ¹⁰He was hungry and wished to eat, and while they were making preparations

he fell into a trance. ¹¹ᵒHe saw heaven opened and something resembling a large sheet coming down, lowered to the ground by its four corners. ¹²In it were all the earth's four-legged animals and reptiles and the birds of the sky. ¹³A voice said to him, "Get up, Peter. Slaughter and eat." ¹⁴But Peter said, "Certainly not, sir. For never have I eaten anything profane and unclean."ᵖ ¹⁵The voice spoke to him again, a second time, "What God has made clean, you are not to call profane."ᵠ ¹⁶This happened three times, and then the object was taken up into the sky.

¹⁷§§While Peter was in doubt about the meaning of the vision he had seen, the men sent by Cornelius asked for Simon's house and arrived at the entrance. ¹⁸They called out inquiring whether Simon, who is called Peter, was staying there. ¹⁹As Peter was pondering the vision, the Spirit said [to him], "There are three men here looking for you.ʳ ²⁰So get up, go downstairs, and accompany them without hesitation, because I have sent them." ²¹Then Peter went down to the men and said, "I am the one you are looking for. What is the reason for your being here?" ²²They answered, "Cornelius, a centurion, an upright and God-fearing man, respected by the whole Jewish nation, was directed by a holy angel to summon you to his house and to hear what you have to say."ˢ ²³So he invited them in and showed them hospitality.

The next day he got up and went with them, and some of the brothers from Joppa went with him. ²⁴¶¶On the following day he entered Caesarea. Cornelius was expecting them and had called together his relatives and close friends. ²⁵ʳWhen Peter entered, Cornelius met him and, falling at his feet, paid him homage. ²⁶Peter, however, raised him up, saying, "Get up. I myself am also a human being." ²⁷While he conversed with him, he went in and found many people gathered together ²⁸ᵘand said to them, "You know that it is unlawful for a Jewish man to associate with, or visit, a Gentile, but God has shown me that I should not call any person profane or unclean.*** ²⁹And that is why I came without objection when sent for. May I ask, then, why you summoned me?"

³⁰Cornelius replied, "Four days ago††† at this hour, three o'clock in the afternoon, I was at

---

*[9:43] The fact that Peter lodged with a tanner would have been significant to both the Gentile and Jewish Christians, for Judaism considered the tanning occupation unclean.

†[10:1–48] The narrative centers on the conversion of Cornelius, a Gentile and a "God-fearer" (see note on Acts 8:26–40). Luke considers the event of great importance, as is evident from his long treatment of it. The incident is again related in Acts 11:1–18 where Peter is forced to justify his actions before the Jerusalem community and alluded to in Acts 15:7–11 where at the Jerusalem "Council" Peter supports Paul's missionary activity among the Gentiles. The narrative divides itself into a series of distinct episodes, concluding with Peter's presentation of the Christian kerygma (Acts 10:4–43) and a pentecostal experience undergone by Cornelius' household preceding their reception of baptism (Acts 10:44–48).

‡[10:1] The Cohort called the Italica: this battalion was an auxiliary unit of archers formed originally in Italy but transferred to Syria shortly before A.D. 69.

§[10:2] Used to give alms generously: like Tabitha (Acts 9:36), Cornelius exemplifies the proper attitude toward wealth (see note on Acts 9:36).

¶[10:3] About three o'clock: literally, "about the ninth hour." See note on Acts 3:1.

**[10:7] A devout soldier: by using this adjective, Luke probably intends to classify him as a "God-fearer" (see note on Acts 8:26–40).

††[10:9–16] The vision is intended to prepare Peter to share the food of Cornelius' household without qualms of conscience (Acts 10:48). The necessity of such instructions to Peter reveals that at first not even the apostles fully grasped the implications of Jesus' teaching on the law. In Acts, the initial insight belongs to Stephen.

‡‡[10:9] At about noontime: literally, "about the sixth hour."

§§[10:17–23] The arrival of the Gentile emissaries with their account of the angelic apparition illuminates Peter's vision: he is to be prepared to admit Gentiles, who were considered unclean like the animals of his vision, into the Christian community.

¶¶[10:24–27] So impressed is Cornelius with the apparition that he invites close personal friends to join him in his meeting with Peter. But his understanding of the person he is about to meet is not devoid of superstition, suggested by his falling down before him. For a similar experience of Paul and Barnabas, see Acts 14:11–18.

***[10:28] Peter now fully understands the meaning of his vision; see note on Acts 10:17–23.

†††[10:30] Four days ago: literally, "from the fourth day up to this hour."

---

o. [10:11–20] 11:5–12.   p. [10:14] Lv 11:1–47; Ez 4:14.   q. [10:15] Mk 7:15–19; Gal 2:12.   r. [10:19] 13:2.   s. [10:22] Lk 7:4–5. t. [10:25–26] 14:13–15; Rev 19:10.   u. [10:28] Gal 2:11–16.

l. [9:43] 10:6.   m. [10:1–8] 10:30–33.   n. [10:6] 9:43.

prayer in my house when suddenly a man in dazzling robes stood before me and said, ³¹"Cornelius, your prayer has been heard and your almsgiving remembered before God. ³²Send therefore to Joppa and summon Simon, who is called Peter. He is a guest in the house of Simon, a tanner, by the sea.' ³³So I sent for you immediately, and you were kind enough to come. Now therefore we are all here in the presence of God to listen to all that you have been commanded by the Lord."

**Peter's Speech.**` ³⁴Then Peter proceeded to speak and said,† "In truth, I see that God shows no partiality.ᵛ ³⁵Rather, in every nation whoever fears him and acts uprightly is acceptable to him. ³⁶‡You know the word [that] he sent to the Israelites§ as he proclaimed peace through Jesus Christ, who is Lord of all,ʷ ³⁷what has happened all over Judea, beginning in Galilee after the baptism that John preached,ˣ ³⁸how God anointed Jesus of Nazareth¶ with the holy Spirit and power. He went about doing good and healing all those oppressed by the devil, for God was with him.ʸ ³⁹We are witnesses** of all that he did both in the country of the Jews and [in] Jerusalem. They put him to death by hanging him on a tree. ⁴⁰This man God raised [on] the third day and granted that he be visible, ⁴¹not to all the people, but to us, the witnesses chosen by God in advance, who ate and drank with him after he rose from the dead.ᶻ ⁴²He commissioned usᵃ to preach to the people and testify that he is the one appointed by God as judge of the living and

the dead.†† ⁴³To him all the prophets bear witness, that everyone who believes in him will receive forgiveness of sins through his name."

**The Baptism of Cornelius.** ⁴⁴ᵇWhile Peter was still speaking these things, the holy Spirit fell upon all who were listening to the word.‡‡ ⁴⁵The circumcised believers who had accompanied Peter were astounded that the gift of the holy Spirit should have been poured out on the Gentiles also, ⁴⁶for they could hear them speaking in tongues and glorifying God. Then Peter responded, ⁴⁷"Can anyone withhold the water for baptizing these people, who have received the holy Spirit even as we have?"ᶜ ⁴⁸He ordered them to be baptized in the name of Jesus Christ. ⁴⁹Then they invited him to stay for a few days.

## CHAPTER 11

**The Baptism of the Gentiles Explained.**§§ ¹Now the apostles and the brothers who were in Judea heard that the Gentiles too had accepted the word of God. ²So when Peter went up to Jerusalem the circumcised believers confronted him, ³saying, "You entered¶¶ the house of uncircumcised people and ate with them." ⁴Peter began and explained it to them step by step, saying, ⁵ᵈ"I was at prayer in the city of Joppa when in a trance I had a vision, something resembling a large sheet coming down, lowered from the sky by its four corners, and it came to me. ⁶Looking intently into it, I observed and saw the four-legged animals of the earth, the wild beasts, the reptiles, and the birds of the sky. ⁷I also heard a voice say to me, 'Get up, Peter. Slaughter and eat.' ⁸But I said, 'Certainly not, sir, because nothing profane or unclean has ever entered my mouth.' ⁹But a second time a voice from heaven answered, 'What God has made clean, you are not to call profane.' ¹⁰This happened three times, and then everything was drawn up again into the sky. ¹¹Just then three men appeared at the house where we were, who had been sent to me from Caesarea. ¹²The Spirit told me to accompany them without discriminating. These six brothers*** also went with me, and we entered the

---

*[10:34–43] Peter's speech to the household of Cornelius typifies early Christian preaching to Gentiles.

†[10:34–35] The revelation of God's choice of Israel to be the people of God did not mean he withheld the divine favor from other people.

‡[10:36–43] These words are more directed to Luke's Christian readers than to the household of Cornelius, as indicated by the opening words, "You know." They trace the continuity between the preaching and teaching of Jesus of Nazareth and the proclamation of Jesus by the early community. The emphasis on this divinely ordained continuity (Acts 10:41) is meant to assure Luke's readers of the fidelity of Christian tradition to the words and deeds of Jesus.

§[10:36] **To the Israelites:** Luke, in the words of Peter, speaks of the prominent position occupied by Israel in the history of salvation.

¶[10:38] **Jesus of Nazareth:** God's revelation of his plan for the destiny of humanity through Israel culminated in Jesus of Nazareth. Consequently, the ministry of Jesus is an integral part of God's revelation. This viewpoint explains why the early Christian communities were interested in conserving the historical substance of the ministry of Jesus, a tradition leading to the production of the four gospels.

**[10:39] **We are witnesses:** the apostolic testimony was not restricted to the resurrection of Jesus but also included his historical ministry. This witness, however, was theological in character; the Twelve, divinely mandated as prophets, were empowered to interpret his sayings and deeds in the light of his redemptive death and resurrection. The meaning of these words and deeds was to be made clear to the developing Christian community as the word of salvation (cf. Acts 1:21–26). **Hanging him on a tree:** see note on Acts 5:30.

††[10:42] **As judge of the living and the dead:** the apostolic preaching to the Jews appealed to their messianic hope, while the preaching to Gentiles stressed the coming divine judgment; cf. 1 Thes 1:10.

‡‡[10:44] Just as the Jewish Christians received the gift of the Spirit, so too do the Gentiles.

§§[11:1–18] The Jewish Christians of Jerusalem were scandalized to learn of Peter's sojourn in the house of the Gentile Cornelius. Nonetheless, they had to accept the divine directions given to both Peter and Cornelius. They concluded that the setting aside of the legal barriers between Jew and Gentile was an exceptional ordinance of God to indicate that the apostolic kerygma was also to be directed to the Gentiles. Only in Acts 15 at the "Council" in Jerusalem does the evangelization of the Gentiles become the official position of the church leadership in Jerusalem.

¶¶[11:3] **You entered . . . :** alternatively, this could be punctuated as a question.

***[11:12] **These six brothers:** companions from the Christian community of Joppa (see Acts 10:23).

---

v. [10:34] Dt 10:17; 2 Chr 19:7; Jb 34:19; Wis 6:7; Rom 2:11; Gal 2:6; Eph 6:9; 1 Pt 1:17.   w. [10:36] Is 52:7; Na 2:1.   x. [10:37] Mt 4:12; Mk 1:14; Lk 4:14.   y. [10:38] Is 61:1; Lk 4:18.   z. [10:41] Lk 24:41–43.   a. [10:42] 1:8; 3:15; 17:31; Lk 24:48; Rom 14:9; 2 Tm 4:1.

b. [10:44] 11:15; 15:8.   c. [10:47] 8:36.   d. [11:5–12] 10:11–20.

man's house. [13]He related to us how he had seen [the] angel standing in his house, saying, 'Send someone to Joppa and summon Simon, who is called Peter,[e] [14]who will speak words to you by which you and all your household will be saved.' [15]As I began to speak, the holy Spirit fell upon them as it had upon us at the beginning,[f] [16]and I remembered the word of the Lord, how he had said, 'John baptized with water but you will be baptized with the holy Spirit.'[g] [17]If then God gave them the same gift he gave to us when we came to believe in the Lord Jesus Christ, who was I to be able to hinder God?"[h] [18]When they heard this, they stopped objecting and glorified God, saying, "God has then granted life-giving repentance to the Gentiles too."

**The Church at Antioch.**[*] [19]Now those who had been scattered by the persecution that arose because of Stephen went as far as Phoenicia, Cyprus, and Antioch, preaching the word to no one but Jews.[i] [20]There were some Cypriots and Cyrenians among them, however, who came to Antioch and began to speak to the Greeks as well, proclaiming the Lord Jesus. [21]The hand of the Lord was with them and a great number who believed turned to the Lord. [22]The news about them reached the ears of the church in Jerusalem, and they sent Barnabas [to go] to Antioch. [23]When he arrived and saw the grace of God, he rejoiced and encouraged them all to remain faithful to the Lord in firmness of heart, [24]for he was a good man, filled with the holy Spirit and faith. And a large number of people was added to the Lord. [25]Then he went to Tarsus to look for Saul, [26]and when he had found him he brought him to Antioch. For a whole year they met with the church and taught a large number of people, and it was in Antioch that the disciples were first called Christians.[†]

**The Prediction of Agabus.**[‡] [27]At that time some prophets came down from Jerusalem to Antioch, [28]and one of them named Agabus stood up and predicted by the Spirit that there would be a severe famine all over the world, and it happened under Claudius.[j] [29]So the disciples determined that, according to ability,[k] each should send relief to the brothers who lived in Judea. [30]This they did, sending it to the presbyters in care of Barnabas and Saul.

## CHAPTER 12

**Herod's Persecution of the Christians.**[¶] [1]About that time King Herod laid hands upon some members of the church to harm them. [2]He had James, the brother of John,[**] killed by the sword, [3]††and when he saw that this was pleasing to the Jews he proceeded to arrest Peter also. (It was [the] feast of Unleavened Bread.) [4]He had him taken into custody and put in prison under the guard of four squads of four soldiers each. He intended to bring him before the people after Passover. [5]Peter thus was being kept in prison, but prayer by the church was fervently being made to God on his behalf.[l]

[6]On the very night before Herod was to bring him to trial, Peter, secured by double chains, was sleeping between two soldiers, while outside the door guards kept watch on the prison. [7]Suddenly the angel of the Lord stood by him and a light shone in the cell. He tapped Peter on the side and awakened him, saying, "Get up quickly." The chains fell from his wrists. [8]The angel said to him, "Put on your belt and your sandals." He did so. Then he said to him, "Put on your cloak and follow me." [9]So he followed him out, not realizing that what was happening through the angel was real; he thought he was seeing a vision. [10]They passed the first guard, then the second, and came to the iron gate leading out to the city, which opened for them by itself. They emerged and made their way down an alley, and suddenly the angel left him. [11]Then Peter recovered his senses and said, "Now I know for certain that [the] Lord sent his angel and rescued me from the hand of Herod and from all that the Jewish people had been expecting." [12]When he realized this, he went to the house of Mary, the mother of John who is called Mark, where there were many people gathered in prayer.[m] [13]When he knocked on the gateway door, a maid

---

*[11:19–26] The Jewish Christian antipathy to the mixed community was reflected by the early missionaries generally. The few among them who entertained a different view succeeded in introducing Gentiles into the community at Antioch (in Syria). When the disconcerted Jerusalem community sent Barnabas to investigate, he was so favorably impressed by what he observed that he persuaded his friend Saul to participate in the Antioch mission.

†[11:26] **Christians:** "Christians" is first applied to the members of the community at Antioch because the Gentile members of the community enable it to stand out clearly from Judaism.

‡[11:27–30] It is not clear whether the prophets from Jerusalem came to Antioch to request help in view of the coming famine or whether they received this insight during their visit there. The former supposition seems more likely. Suetonius and Tacitus speak of famines during the reign of Claudius (A.D. 41–54), while the Jewish historian Josephus mentions a famine in Judea in A.D. 46–48. Luke is interested, rather, in showing the charity of the Antiochene community toward the Jewish Christians of Jerusalem despite their differences on mixed communities.

§[11:30] **Presbyters:** this is the same Greek word that elsewhere is translated "elders," primarily in reference to the Jewish community.

¶[12:1–19] Herod Agrippa ruled Judea A.D. 41–44. While Luke does not assign a motive for his execution of James and his intended execution of Peter, the broad background lies in Herod's support of Pharisaic Judaism. The Jewish Christians had lost the popularity they had had in Jerusalem (Acts 2:47), perhaps because of suspicions against them traceable to the teaching of Stephen.

**[12:2] **James, the brother of John:** this James, the son of Zebedee, was beheaded by Herod Agrippa ca. A.D. 44.

††[12:3–4] **Feast of Unleavened Bread . . . Passover:** see note on Lk 22:1.

---

e. [11:13] 10:3–5, 22, 30–32.   f. [11:15] 10:44.   g. [11:16] 1:5; 19:4; Lk 3:16.   h. [11:17] 15:8–9.   i. [11:19] 8:1–4.

j. [11:28] 21:10.   k. [11:29–30] 12:25.   l. [12:5] Jas 5:16.   m. [12:12] 12:25; 15:37.

named Rhoda came to answer it. [14]She was so overjoyed when she recognized Peter's voice that, instead of opening the gate, she ran in and announced that Peter was standing at the gate. [15]They told her, "You are out of your mind," but she insisted that it was so. But they kept saying, "It is his angel." [16]But Peter continued to knock, and when they opened it, they saw him and were astounded. [17]He motioned to them with his hand to be quiet and explained [to them] how the Lord had led him out of the prison, and said, "Report this to James[*] and the brothers." Then he left and went to another place. [18]At daybreak there was no small commotion among the soldiers over what had become of Peter.[n] [19]Herod, after instituting a search but not finding him, ordered the guards tried and executed. Then he left Judea to spend some time in Caesarea.

**Herod's Death.** [20†]He had long been very angry with the people of Tyre and Sidon, who now came to him in a body. After winning over Blastus, the king's chamberlain, they sued for peace because their country was supplied with food from the king's territory. [21]On an appointed day, Herod, attired in royal robes, [and] seated on the rostrum, addressed them publicly. [22]The assembled crowd cried out, "This is the voice of a god, not of a man." [23]At once the angel of the Lord struck him down because he did not ascribe the honor to God, and he was eaten by worms and breathed his last. [24]But the word of God continued to spread and grow.[o]

**Mission of Barnabas and Saul.** [25]After Barnabas and Saul completed their relief mission, they returned to Jerusalem,[‡] taking with them John, who is called Mark.[p]

## CHAPTER 13

[1§]Now there were in the church at Antioch prophets and teachers: Barnabas, Symeon who was called Niger, Lucius of Cyrene, Manaen

who was a close friend of Herod the tetrarch, and Saul. [2]While they were worshiping the Lord and fasting, the holy Spirit said, "Set apart for me Barnabas and Saul for the work to which I have called them." [3]Then, completing their fasting and prayer, they laid hands on them and sent them off.

**First Mission Begins in Cyprus.** [4]So they, sent forth by the holy Spirit, went down to Seleucia and from there sailed to Cyprus. [5]When they arrived in Salamis, they proclaimed the word of God in the Jewish synagogues. They had John[**] also as their assistant. [6]When they had traveled through the whole island as far as Paphos, they met a magician named Bar-Jesus who was a Jewish false prophet.[††] [7]He was with the proconsul Sergius Paulus, a man of intelligence, who had summoned Barnabas and Saul and wanted to hear the word of God. [8]But Elymas the magician (for that is what his name means) opposed them in an attempt to turn the proconsul away from the faith. [9]But Saul, also known as Paul,[‡‡] filled with the holy Spirit, looked intently at him [10]and said, "You son of the devil, you enemy of all that is right, full of every sort of deceit and fraud. Will you not stop twisting the straight paths of [the] Lord? [11]Even now the hand of the Lord is upon you. You will be blind, and unable to see the sun for a time." Immediately a dark mist fell upon him, and he went about seeking people to lead him by the hand. [12]When the proconsul saw what had happened, he came to believe, for he was astonished by the teaching about the Lord.

**Paul's Arrival at Antioch in Pisidia.** [13]From Paphos, Paul and his companions set sail and arrived at Perga in Pamphylia. But John left them and returned to Jerusalem.[q] [14]They continued on from Perga and reached Antioch in Pisidia. On the sabbath they entered [into] the synagogue and took their seats. [15]After the reading of the law and the prophets, the synagogue officials sent word to them, "My brothers, if one

---

*[12:17] **To James:** this James is not the son of Zebedee mentioned in Acts 12:2, but is James, the "brother of the Lord" (Gal 1:19), who in Acts 15; 21 is presented as leader of the Jerusalem Christian community. **He left and went to another place:** the conjecture that Peter left for Rome at this time has nothing to recommend it. His chief responsibility was still the leadership of the Jewish Christian community in Palestine (see Gal 2:7). The concept of the great missionary effort of the church was yet to come (see Acts 13:1–3).

†[12:20–23] Josephus gives a similar account of the Antiochene death that occurred in A.D. 44. Early Christian tradition considered the manner of it to be a divine punishment upon his evil life. See 2 Kgs 19:35 for the figure of the angel of the Lord in such a context.

‡[12:25] **They returned to Jerusalem:** many manuscripts read "from Jerusalem," since Acts 11:30 implies that Paul and Barnabas are already in Jerusalem. This present verse could refer to a return visit or subsequent relief mission.

§[13:1–3] The impulse for the first missionary effort in Asia Minor is ascribed to the prophets of the Antiochene community, under the inspiration of the holy Spirit. Just as the Jerusalem community had earlier been the center of missionary activity, so too Antioch becomes the center from which the missionaries Barnabas and Saul are sent out.

§[13:4–14:27] The key event in Luke's account of the first missionary journey is the experience of Paul and Barnabas at Pisidian Antioch (Acts 13:14–52). The Christian kerygma proclaimed by Paul in the synagogue was favorably received. Some Jews and "God-fearers" (see note on Acts 8:26–40) became interested and invited the missionaries to speak again on the following sabbath (Acts 13:42). By that time, however, the appearance of a large number of Gentiles from the city had so disconcerted the Jews that they became hostile toward the apostles (Acts 13:44–50). This hostility of theirs appears in all three accounts of Paul's missionary journeys in Acts, the Jews of Iconium (Acts 14:1–2) and Beroea (Acts 17:11) being notable exceptions.

**[13:5] **John:** that is, John Mark (see Acts 12:12, 25).

††[13:6] **A magician named Bar-Jesus who was a Jewish false prophet:** that is, he posed as a prophet. Again Luke takes the opportunity to dissociate Christianity from the magical acts of the time (Acts 13:7–11); see also Acts 8:18–24.

‡‡[13:9] **Saul, also known as Paul:** there is no reason to believe that his name was changed from Saul to Paul upon his conversion. The use of a double name, one Semitic (Saul), the other Greco-Roman (Paul), is well attested (cf, Acts 1:23, Joseph Justus; Acts 12:12, 25, John Mark).

of you has a word of exhortation for the people, please speak."

**Paul's Address in the Synagogue.** [16]So Paul got up, motioned with his hand, and said, "Fellow Israelites and you others who are God-fearing,[†] listen. [17]The God of this people Israel chose our ancestors and exalted the people during their sojourn in the land of Egypt.[r] With uplifted arm he led them out of it [18]and for about forty years he put up with[‡] them in the desert.[s] [19]When he had destroyed seven nations in the land of Canaan, he gave them their land as an inheritance[t] [20]at the end of about four hundred and fifty years.[§] After these things he provided judges up to Samuel [the] prophet.[u] [21]Then they asked for a king. God gave them Saul, son of Kish, a man from the tribe of Benjamin, for forty years.[v] [22]Then he removed him and raised up David as their king; of him he testified, 'I have found David, son of Jesse, a man after my own heart; he will carry out my every wish.'[w] [23]From this man's descendants God, according to his promise, has brought to Israel a savior, Jesus.[x] [24]John heralded his coming by proclaiming a baptism of repentance to all the people of Israel;[y] [25]and as John was completing his course, he would say, 'What do you suppose that I am? I am not he. Behold, one is coming after me; I am not worthy to unfasten the sandals of his feet.'[z]

[26]"My brothers, children of the family of Abraham, and those others among you who are God-fearing, to us this word of salvation has been sent. [27]The inhabitants of Jerusalem and their leaders failed to recognize him, and by condemning him they fulfilled the oracles of the prophets that are read sabbath after sabbath. [28]For even though they found no grounds for a death sentence, they asked Pilate to have him put to death,[a] [29]and when they had accomplished all that was written about him, they took him down from the tree and placed him in a tomb.[b] [30]But God raised him from the dead,[c] [31]and for many days he appeared to those who had come up with him from Galilee to Jerusalem.[d] These are [now] his witnesses before the people.[¶] [32]We ourselves are proclaiming this good news to you that what God promised our ancestors [33]he has brought to fulfillment for us, [their] children, by raising up Jesus, as it is written in the second psalm, 'You are my son; this day I have begotten you.'[e] [34]And that he raised him from the dead never to return to corruption he declared in this way, 'I shall give you the benefits assured to David.'[f] [35]That is why he also says in another psalm, 'You will not suffer your holy one to see corruption.'[g] [36]Now David, after he had served the will of God in his lifetime, fell asleep, was gathered to his ancestors, and did see corruption.[h] [37]But the one whom God raised up did not see corruption. [38]You must know, my brothers, that through him forgiveness of sins is being proclaimed to you, [and] in regard to everything from which you could not be justified[**] under the law of Moses, [39]in him every believer is justified.[i] [40]Be careful, then, that what was said in the prophets not come about:

[41]   'Look on, you scoffers,
           be amazed and disappear.
      For I am doing a work in your days,
           a work that you will never believe
                even if someone tells you.'"[j]

[42]As they were leaving, they invited them to speak on these subjects the following sabbath. [43]After the congregation had dispersed, many Jews and worshipers who were converts to Judaism followed Paul and Barnabas, who spoke to them and urged them to remain faithful to the grace of God.

**Address to the Gentiles.** [44]On the following sabbath almost the whole city gathered to hear the word of the Lord. [45]When the Jews saw the crowds, they were filled with jealousy and with violent abuse contradicted what Paul said. [46]Both Paul and Barnabas spoke out boldly and said, "It was necessary that the word of God be spoken to you first, but since you reject it and condemn yourselves as unworthy of eternal life,

---

*[13:16–41] This is the first of several speeches of Paul to Jews proclaiming that the Christian church is the logical development of Pharisaic Judaism (see also Acts 24:10–21; 26:2–23).

†[13:16] **Who are God-fearing**: see note on Acts 8:26–40.

‡[13:18] **Put up with**: some manuscripts read "sustained."

§[13:20] **At the end of about four hundred and fifty years**: the manuscript tradition makes it uncertain whether the mention of four hundred and fifty years refers to the sojourn in Egypt before the Exodus, the wilderness period and the time of the conquest (see Ex 12:40–41), as the translation here suggests, or to the time between the conquest and the time of Samuel, the period of the judges, if the text is read, "After these things, for about four hundred and fifty years, he provided judges."

¶[13:31] The theme of the Galilean witnesses is a major one in the Gospel of Luke and in Acts and is used to signify the continuity between the teachings of Jesus and the teachings of the church and to guarantee the fidelity of the church's teachings to the words of Jesus.

**[13:38–39] **Justified**: the verb is the same as that used in Paul's letters to speak of the experience of justification and, as in Paul, is here connected with the term "to have faith" ("every believer"). But this seems the only passage about Paul in Acts where justification is mentioned. In Lucan fashion it is paralleled with "forgiveness of sins" (a theme at Acts 2:38; 3:19; 5:31; 10:43) based on Jesus' resurrection (Acts 13:37) rather than his cross, and is put negatively (Acts 13:38). Therefore, some would translate, "in regard to everything from which you could not be acquitted . . . every believer is acquitted."

---

r. [13:17]Ex 6:1,6; 12:51.   s. [13:18]Ex 16:1,35; Nm 14:34.   t. [13:19] Dt 7:1; Jos 14:1–2.   u. [13:20] Jgs 2:16; 1 Sm 3:20.   v. [13:21] 1 Sm 8:5, 19; 9:16; 10:1, 20–21, 24; 11:15.   w. [13:22] 1 Sm 13:14; 16:12–13; Ps 89:20–21.   x. [13:23] Is 11:1.   y. [13:24] Mt 3:1–2; Mk 1:4–5; Lk 3:2–3.   z. [13:25] Mt 3:11; Mk 1:7; Lk 3:16; Jn 1:20, 27.   a. [13:28] Mt 27:20, 22–23; Mk 15:13–14; Lk 23:4, 14–15, 21–23; Jn 19:4–6, 15.   b. [13:29] Mt 27:59–60; Mk 15:46; Lk 23:53; Jn 19:38, 41–42.   c. [13:30] 2:24, 32; 3:15; 4:10; 17:31.

d. [13:31] 1:3, 8; 10:39, 41; Mt 28:8–10, 16–20; Mk 16:9, 12–20; Lk 24:13–53; Jn 20:11–29; 21:1–23.   e. [13:33] Ps 2:7.   f. [13:34] Is 55:3.   g. [13:35] Ps 16:10.   h. [13:36] 2:29; 1 Kgs 2:10.   i. [13:39] Rom 3:20.   j. [13:41] Heb 1:5.   k. [13:46] 3:26; Rom 1:16.

we now turn to the Gentiles.' ⁴⁷For so the Lord has commanded us, 'I have made you a light to the Gentiles, that you may be an instrument of salvation to the ends of the earth.'"*ˡ

⁴⁸The Gentiles were delighted when they heard this and glorified the word of the Lord. All who were destined for eternal life came to believe, ⁴⁹and the word of the Lord continued to spread through the whole region. ⁵⁰The Jews, however, incited the women of prominence who were worshipers and the leading men of the city, stirred up a persecution against Paul and Barnabas, and expelled them from their territory. ⁵¹ᵐSo they shook the dust from their feet in protest against them and went to Iconium.† ⁵²The disciples were filled with joy and the holy Spirit.

## CHAPTER 14

**Paul and Barnabas at Iconium.** ¹In Iconium they entered the Jewish synagogue together and spoke in such a way that a great number of both Jews and Greeks came to believe, ²although the disbelieving Jews stirred up and poisoned the minds of the Gentiles against the brothers. ³So they stayed for a considerable period, speaking out boldly for the Lord, who confirmed the word about his grace by granting signs and wonders to occur through their hands.ⁿ ⁴The people of the city were divided: some were with the Jews; others, with the apostles. ⁵When there was an attempt by both the Gentiles and the Jews, together with their leaders, to attack and stone them,° ⁶they realized it and fled to the Lycaonian cities of Lystra and Derbe and to the surrounding countryside, ⁷where they continued to proclaim the good news.

**Paul and Barnabas at Lystra.** ⁸‡At Lystra there was a crippled man, lame from birth, who had never walked. ⁹He listened to Paul speaking, who looked intently at him, saw that he had the faith to be healed, ¹⁰and called out in a loud voice, "Stand up straight on your feet." He jumped up and began to walk about. ¹¹When the crowds saw what Paul had done, they cried out in Lycaonian, "The gods have come down to us in human form."ᵖ ¹²They called Barnabas "Zeus"§ and Paul "Hermes," because he was the

chief speaker. ¹³And the priest of Zeus, whose temple was at the entrance to the city, brought oxen and garlands to the gates, for he together with the people intended to offer sacrifice.

¹⁴The apostles Barnabas and Paul tore their garments¶ when they heard this and rushed out into the crowd, shouting, ¹⁵**"Men, why are you doing this? We are of the same nature as you, human beings. We proclaim to you good news that you should turn from these idols to the living God, 'who made heaven and earth and sea and all that is in them.'�q ¹⁶In past generations he allowed all Gentiles to go their own ways;ʳ ¹⁷yet, in bestowing his goodness, he did not leave himself without witness, for he gave you rains from heaven and fruitful seasons, and filled you with nourishment and gladness for your hearts."ˢ ¹⁸Even with these words, they scarcely restrained the crowds from offering sacrifice to them.

¹⁹ᵗHowever, some Jews from Antioch and Iconium arrived and won over the crowds. They stoned Paul and dragged him out of the city, supposing that he was dead. ²⁰But when the disciples gathered around him, he got up and entered the city. On the following day he left with Barnabas for Derbe.

**End of the First Mission.** ²¹After they had proclaimed the good news to that city and made a considerable number of disciples, they returned to Lystra and to Iconium and to Antioch. ²²They strengthened the spirits of the disciples and exhorted them to persevere in the faith, saying, "It is necessary for us to undergo many hardships to enter the kingdom of God."ᵘ ²³They appointed presbyters†† for them in each church and, with prayer and fasting, commended them to the Lord in whom they had put their faith. ²⁴Then they traveled through Pisidia and reached Pamphylia. ²⁵After proclaiming the word at Perga they went down to Attalia. ²⁶From there they sailed to Antioch, where they had been commended to the grace of God for the work they had now accomplished.ᵛ ²⁷And when they arrived, they called the church together and reported what God had done with them and how he had opened the door of faith to the Gentiles. ²⁸Then they spent no little time with the disciples.

---

*[13:46] The refusal to believe frustrates God's plan for his chosen people; however, no adverse judgment is made here concerning their ultimate destiny. Again, Luke, in the words of Paul, speaks of the priority of Israel in the plan for salvation (see Acts 10:36).

†[13:51] See note on Lk 9:5.

‡[14:8–18] In an effort to convince his hearers that the divine power works through his word, Paul cures the cripple. However, the pagan tradition of the occasional appearance of gods among human beings leads the people astray in interpreting the miracle. The incident reveals the cultural difficulties with which the church had to cope. Note the similarity of the miracle worked here by Paul to the one performed by Peter in Acts 3:2–10.

§[14:12] **Zeus . . . Hermes:** in Greek religion, Zeus was the chief of the Olympian gods, the "father of gods and men";

Hermes was a son of Zeus and was usually identified as the herald and messenger of the gods.

¶[14:14] **Tore their garments:** a gesture of protest.

**[14:15–17] This is the first speech of Paul to Gentiles recorded by Luke in Acts (cf. Acts 17:22–31). Rather than showing how Christianity is the logical outgrowth of Judaism, as he does in speeches before Jews, Luke says that God excuses past Gentile ignorance and then presents a natural theology arguing for the recognition of God's existence and presence through his activity in natural phenomena.

††[14:23] **They appointed presbyters:** the communities are given their own religious leaders by the traveling missionaries. The structure in these churches is patterned on the model of the Jerusalem community (Acts 11:30; 15:2, 5, 22; 21:18).

---

l. [13:47] Is 49:6.   m. [13:51] Mt 10:14; Mk 6:11; Lk 9:5; 10:11. n. [14:3] Mk 16:17–20.   o. [14:5] 2 Tm 3:11.   p. [14:11] 28:6.

q. [14:15] 3:12; 10:26; Ex 20:11; Ps 146:6.   r. [14:16] 17:30.   s. [14:17] Wis 13:1.   t. [14:19–20] 2 Cor 11:25; 2 Tm 3:11.   u. [14:22] 1 Thes 3:3. v. [14:26] 13:1–3.

## CHAPTER 15

**Council of Jerusalem.** [1]Some who had come down from Judea were instructing the brothers,[w] "Unless you are circumcised according to the Mosaic practice,[x] you cannot be saved."[†] [2]Because there arose no little dissension and debate by Paul and Barnabas with them, it was decided that Paul, Barnabas, and some of the others should go up to Jerusalem to the apostles and presbyters about this question. [3]They were sent on their journey by the church, and passed through Phoenicia and Samaria telling of the conversion of the Gentiles, and brought great joy to all the brothers. [4]When they arrived in Jerusalem, they were welcomed by the church, as well as by the apostles and the presbyters, and they reported what God had done with them. [5]But some from the party of the Pharisees who had become believers stood up and said, "It is necessary to circumcise them and direct them to observe the Mosaic law."

[6†]The apostles and the presbyters met together to see about this matter. [7§]After much debate had taken place, Peter got up and said to them, "My brothers, you are well aware that from early days God made his choice among you that through my mouth the Gentiles would hear the word of the gospel and believe.[y] [8]And God, who knows the heart, bore witness by granting them the holy Spirit just as he did us.[z] [9]He made no distinction between us and them, for by faith he purified their hearts.[a] [10]Why, then, are you now putting God to the test by placing on the shoulders of the disciples a yoke that neither our ancestors nor we have been able to bear?[b] [11]On the contrary, we believe that we are saved through the grace of the Lord Jesus,[c] in the same way as they."[¶] [12]The whole assembly fell silent, and they listened while Paul and Barnabas described the signs and wonders God had worked among the Gentiles through them.

**James on Dietary Law.** [13**]After they had fallen silent, James responded, "My brothers, listen to me. [14]Symeon[††] has described how God first concerned himself with acquiring from among the Gentiles a people for his name. [15]The words of the prophets agree with this, as is written:

[16] 'After this I shall return[d]
and rebuild the fallen hut of David;
from its ruins I shall rebuild it
and raise it up again,
[17] so that the rest of humanity may seek out
the Lord,
even all the Gentiles on whom my
name is invoked.
Thus says the Lord who accomplishes
these things,
[18] known from of old.'

[19e]It is my judgment, therefore, that we ought to stop troubling the Gentiles who turn to God, [20]but tell them by letter to avoid pollution from idols, unlawful marriage, the meat of strangled animals, and blood.[f] [21]For Moses, for generations now, has had those who proclaim him in every town, as he has been read in the synagogues every sabbath."

**Letter of the Apostles.** [22]Then the apostles and presbyters, in agreement with the whole church, decided to choose representatives and to send them to Antioch with Paul and Barnabas. The ones chosen were Judas, who was called Barsabbas, and Silas, leaders among the brothers. [23]This is the letter delivered by them: "The apostles and the presbyters, your brothers, to the brothers in Antioch, Syria, and Cilicia of Gentile origin: greetings. [24]Since we have heard that some of our number [who went out] without

---

*[15:1–35] The Jerusalem "Council" marks the official rejection of the rigid view that Gentile converts were obliged to observe the Mosaic law completely. From here to the end of Acts, Paul and the Gentile mission become the focus of Luke's writing.

†[15:1–5] When some of the converted Pharisees of Jerusalem discover the results of the first missionary journey of Paul, they urge that the Gentiles be taught to follow the Mosaic law. Recognizing the authority of the Jerusalem church, Paul and Barnabas go there to settle the question of whether Gentiles can embrace a form of Christianity that does not include this obligation.

‡[15:6–12] The gathering is possibly the same as that recalled by Paul in Gal 2:1–10. Note that in Acts 15:2 it is only the apostles and presbyters, a small group, with whom Paul and Barnabas are to meet. Here Luke gives the meeting a public character because he wishes to emphasize its doctrinal significance (see Acts 15:22).

§[15:7–11] Paul's refusal to impose the Mosaic law on the Gentile Christians is supported by Peter on the ground that within his own experience God bestowed the holy Spirit upon Cornelius and his household without preconditions concerning the adoption of the Mosaic law (see Acts 10:44–47).

¶[15:11] In support of Paul, Peter formulates the fundamental meaning of the gospel: that all are invited to be saved through faith in the power of Christ.

**[15:13–35] Some scholars think that this apostolic decree suggested by James, the immediate leader of the Jerusalem community, derives from another historical occasion than the meeting in question. This seems to be the case if the meeting is the same as the one related in Gal 2:1–10. According to that account, nothing was imposed upon Gentile Christians in respect to Mosaic law; whereas the decree instructs Gentile Christians of mixed communities to abstain from meats sacrificed to idols and from blood-meats, and to avoid marriage within forbidden degrees of consanguinity and affinity (Lv 18), all of which practices were especially abhorrent to Jews. Luke seems to have telescoped two originally independent incidents here: the first a Jerusalem "Council" that dealt with the question of circumcision, and the second a Jerusalem decree dealing mainly with Gentile observance of dietary laws (see Acts 21:25 where Paul seems to be learning of the decree for the first time).

††[15:14] Symeon: elsewhere in Acts he is called either Peter or Simon. The presence of the name Symeon here suggests that, in the source Luke is using for this part of the Jerusalem "Council" incident, the name may have originally referred to someone other than Peter (see Acts 13:1 where the Antiochene Symeon Niger is mentioned). As the text now stands, however, it is undoubtedly a reference to Simon Peter (Acts 15:7).

---

w. [15:1–4] Gal 2:1–9.   x. [15:1] Lv 12:3; Gal 5:2.   y. [15:7] 10:27–43.   z. [15:8] 10:44–48.   a. [15:9] 10:34–35.   b. [15:10] Mt 23:4; Gal 5:1.   c. [15:11] Gal 2:16; 3:11; Eph 2:5–8.

d. [15:16–17] Am 9:11–12.   e. [15:19–20] 15:28–29; 21:25.   f. [15:20] Gn 9:4; Lv 3:17; 17:10–14.

any mandate from us have upset you with their teachings and disturbed your peace of mind, [25]we have with one accord decided to choose representatives and to send them to you along with our beloved Barnabas and Paul, [26]who have dedicated their lives to the name of our Lord Jesus Christ. [27]So we are sending Judas and Silas who will also convey this same message by word of mouth: [28]g"It is the decision of the holy Spirit and of us not to place on you any burden beyond these necessities, [29]namely, to abstain from meat sacrificed to idols, from blood, from meats of strangled animals, and from unlawful marriage. If you keep free of these, you will be doing what is right. Farewell.'"h

**Delegates at Antioch.** [30]And so they were sent on their journey. Upon their arrival in Antioch they called the assembly together and delivered the letter. [31]When the people read it, they were delighted with the exhortation. [32]Judas and Silas, who were themselves prophets, exhorted and strengthened the brothers with many words. [33]After they had spent some time there, they were sent off with greetings of peace from the brothers to those who had commissioned them. [[34]]* [35]But Paul and Barnabas remained in Antioch, teaching and proclaiming with many others the word of the Lord.

## V. THE MISSION OF PAUL TO THE ENDS OF THE EARTH

**Paul and Barnabas Separate.** [36]†After some time, Paul said to Barnabas, "Come, let us make a return visit to see how the brothers are getting on in all the cities where we proclaimed the word of the Lord." [37]Barnabas wanted to take with them also John, who was called Mark, [38]but Paul insisted that they should not take with them someone who had deserted them at Pamphylia and who had not continued with them in their work.i [39]So sharp was their disagreement that they separated. Barnabas took Mark and sailed to Cyprus. [40]But Paul chose Silas and departed after being commended by the brothers to the

grace of the Lord. [41]He traveled through Syria and Cilicia bringing strength to the churches.

## CHAPTER 16

**Paul in Lycaonia: Timothy.** [1]He reached [also] Derbe and Lystra where there was a disciple named Timothy, the son of a Jewish woman who was a believer, but his father was a Greek.j [2]The brothers in Lystra and Iconium spoke highly of him,k [3]and Paul wanted him to come along with him. On account of the Jews of that region, Paul had him circumcised,‡ for they all knew that his father was a Greek. [4]As they traveled from city to city, they handed on to the people for observance the decisions reached by the apostles and presbyters in Jerusalem. [5]Day after day the churches grew stronger in faith and increased in number.

**Through Asia Minor.** [6]They traveled through the Phrygian and Galatian territory because they had been prevented by the holy Spirit from preaching the message in the province of Asia. [7]When they came to Mysia, they tried to go on into Bithynia, but the Spirit of Jesus§ did not allow them, [8]so they crossed through Mysia and came down to Troas. [9]During [the] night Paul had a vision. A Macedonian stood before him and implored him with these words, "Come over to Macedonia and help us." [10]When he had seen the vision, we¶ sought passage to Macedonia at once, concluding that God had called us to proclaim the good news to them.

**Into Europe.** [11]**We set sail from Troas, making a straight run for Samothrace, and on the next day to Neapolis, [12]and from there to Philippi, a leading city in that district of Macedonia and a Roman colony. We spent some time in that city. [13]On the sabbath we went outside the city gate along the river where we thought there would be a place of prayer. We sat and spoke with the women who had gathered there. [14]One of them, a woman named Lydia, a dealer in purple cloth, from the city of Thyatira, a worshiper of

---

*[15:34] Some manuscripts add, in various wordings, "But Silas decided to remain there."

†[15:36–18:22] This continuous narrative recounts Paul's second missionary journey. On the internal evidence of the Lucan account, it lasted about three years. Paul first visited the communities he had established on his first journey (Acts 16:1–5), then pushed on into Macedonia, where he established communities at Philippi, Thessalonica, and Beroea (Acts 16:7–17:5). To escape the hostility of the Jews of Thessalonica, he left for Greece and while resident in Athens attempted, without success, to establish an effective Christian community there. From Athens he proceeded to Corinth and, after a stay of a year and a half, returned to Antioch by way of Ephesus and Jerusalem (Acts 17:16–18:22). Luke does not concern himself with the structure or statistics of the communities but aims to show the general progress of the gospel in the Gentile world as well as its continued failure to take root in the Jewish community.

‡[16:3] **Paul had him circumcised:** he did this in order that Timothy might be able to associate with the Jews and so perform a ministry among them. Paul did not object to the Jewish Christians' adherence to the law. But he insisted that the law could not be imposed on the Gentiles. Paul himself lived in accordance with the law, or as exempt from the law, according to particular circumstances (see 1 Cor 9:19–23).

§[16:7] **The Spirit of Jesus:** this is an unusual formulation in Luke's writings. The parallelism with Acts 16:6 indicates its meaning, the holy Spirit.

¶[16:10–17] This is the first of the so-called "we-sections" in Acts, where Luke writes as one of Paul's companions. The other passages are Acts 20:5–15; 21:1–18; 27:1–28:16. Scholars debate whether Luke may not have used the first person plural simply as a literary device to lend color to the narrative. The realism of the narrative, however, lends weight to the argument that the "we" includes Luke or another companion of Paul whose data Luke used as a source.

**[16:11–40] The church at Philippi became a flourishing community to which Paul addressed one of his letters (see Introduction to the Letter to the Philippians).

---

g. [15:28–29] 15:19–20.  h. [15:29] Gn 9:4; Lv 3:17; 17:10–14.
i. [15:38] 13:13.

j. [16:1] 1 Tm 1:2; 2 Tm 1:5.   k. [16:2] Phil 2:20.

God,* listened, and the Lord opened her heart to pay attention to what Paul was saying. ¹⁵After she and her household had been baptized, she offered us an invitation, "If you consider me a believer in the Lord, come and stay at my home," and she prevailed on us.

**Imprisonment at Philippi.** ¹⁶As we were going to the place of prayer, we met a slave girl with an oracular spirit,† who used to bring a large profit to her owners through her fortune-telling. ¹⁷She began to follow Paul and us, shouting, "These people are slaves of the Most High God, who proclaim to you a way of salvation." ¹⁸She did this for many days. Paul became annoyed, turned, and said to the spirit, "I command you in the name of Jesus Christ to come out of her." Then it came out at that moment.

¹⁹When her owners saw that their hope of profit was gone, they seized Paul and Silas and dragged them to the public square before the local authorities. ²⁰They brought them before the magistrates‡ and said, "These people are Jews and are disturbing our city ²¹and are advocating customs that are not lawful for us Romans to adopt or practice." ²²ˡThe crowd joined in the attack on them, and the magistrates had them stripped and ordered them to be beaten with rods. ²³After inflicting many blows on them, they threw them into prison and instructed the jailer to guard them securely. ²⁴When he received these instructions, he put them in the innermost cell and secured their feet to a stake.

**Deliverance from Prison.** ²⁵About midnight, while Paul and Silas were praying and singing hymns to God as the prisoners listened, ²⁶there was suddenly such a severe earthquake that the foundations of the jail shook; all the doors flew open, and the chains of all were pulled loose. ²⁷When the jailer woke up and saw the prison doors wide open, he drew [his] sword and was about to kill himself, thinking that the prisoners had escaped. ²⁸But Paul shouted out in a loud voice, "Do no harm to yourself; we are all here." ²⁹He asked for a light and rushed in and, trembling with fear, he fell down before Paul and Silas. ³⁰Then he brought them out and said, "Sirs, what must I do to be saved?" ³¹And they said, "Believe in the Lord Jesus and you and your household will be saved." ³²So they spoke the word of the Lord to him and to everyone in his house. ³³He took them in at that hour of the night and bathed their wounds; then he and all

his family were baptized at once. ³⁴He brought them up into his house and provided a meal and with his household rejoiced at having come to faith in God.

³⁵But when it was day, the magistrates sent the lictors§ with the order, "Release those men." ³⁶The jailer reported the[se] words to Paul, "The magistrates have sent orders that you be released. Now, then, come out and go in peace." ³⁷But Paul said to them, "They have beaten us publicly, even though we are Roman citizens and have not been tried, and have thrown us into prison.ᵐ And now, are they going to release us secretly? By no means. Let them come themselves and lead us out."¶ ³⁸The lictors reported these words to the magistrates, and they became alarmed when they heard that they were Roman citizens.ⁿ ³⁹So they came and placated them, and led them out and asked that they leave the city. ⁴⁰When they had come out of the prison, they went to Lydia's house where they saw and encouraged the brothers, and then they left.

## CHAPTER 17

**Paul in Thessalonica.** ¹When they took the road through Amphipolis and Apollonia, they reached Thessalonica, where there was a synagogue of the Jews.º ²Following his usual custom, Paul joined them, and for three sabbaths he entered into discussions with them from the scriptures, ³expounding and demonstrating that the Messiah had to suffer and rise from the dead, and that "This is the Messiah, Jesus, whom I proclaim to you."ᵖ ⁴Some of them were convinced and joined Paul and Silas; so, too, a great number of Greeks who were worshipers, and not a few of the prominent women. ⁵But the Jews became jealous and recruited some worthless men loitering in the public square, formed a mob, and set the city in turmoil. They marched on the house of Jason,�q intending to bring them before the people's assembly. ⁶When they could not find them, they dragged Jason and some of the brothers before the city magistrates, shouting, "These people who have been creating a disturbance all over the world have now come here, ⁷and Jason has welcomed them.ʳ They all act in opposition to the decrees of Caesar and claim instead that there is another king, Jesus."††

---

§[16:35] **The lictors:** the equivalent of police officers, among whose duties were the apprehension and punishment of criminals.

¶[16:37] Paul's Roman citizenship granted him special privileges in regard to criminal process. Roman law forbade under severe penalty the beating of Roman citizens (see also Acts 22:25).

**[17:6–7] The accusations against Paul and his companions echo the charges brought against Jesus in Lk 23:2.

††[17:7] **There is another king, Jesus:** a distortion into a political sense of the apostolic proclamation of Jesus and the kingdom of God (see Acts 8:12).

---

*[16:14] **A worshiper of God:** a "God-fearer." See note on Acts 8:26–40.

†[16:16] **With an oracular spirit:** literally, "with a Python spirit." The Python was the serpent or dragon that guarded the Delphic oracle. It later came to designate a "spirit that pronounced oracles" and also a ventriloquist who, it was thought, had such a spirit in the belly.

‡[16:20] **Magistrates:** in Greek, *stratēgoi,* the popular designation of the *duoviri,* the highest officials of the Roman colony of Philippi.

---

l. [16:22–23] 2 Cor 11:25; Phil 1:30; 1 Thes 2:2.

---

m. [16:37] 22:25.   n. [16:38] 22:29.   o. [17:1] 1 Thes 2:1–2.   p. [17:3] 3:18; Lk 24:25–26, 46.   q. [17:5] Rom 16:21.   r. [17:7] Lk 23:2; Jn 19:12–15.

[8]They stirred up the crowd and the city magistrates who, upon hearing these charges, [9]took a surety payment from Jason and the others before releasing them.

**Paul in Beroea.** [10]The brothers immediately sent Paul and Silas to Beroea during the night. Upon arrival they went to the synagogue of the Jews. [11]These Jews were more fair-minded than those in Thessalonica, for they received the word with all willingness and examined the scriptures daily to determine whether these things were so.[s] [12]Many of them became believers, as did not a few of the influential Greek women and men. [13]But when the Jews of Thessalonica learned that the word of God had now been proclaimed by Paul in Beroea also, they came there too to cause a commotion and stir up the crowds. [14]So the brothers at once sent Paul on his way to the seacoast, while Silas and Timothy remained behind.[t] [15]After Paul's escorts had taken him to Athens, they came away with instructions for Silas and Timothy to join him as soon as possible.

**Paul in Athens.*** [16]While Paul was waiting for them in Athens, he grew exasperated at the sight of the city full of idols. [17]So he debated in the synagogue with the Jews and with the worshipers, and daily in the public square with whoever happened to be there. [18]Even some of the Epicurean and Stoic philosophers[†] engaged him in discussion. Some asked, "What is this scavenger trying to say?" Others said, "He sounds like a promoter of foreign deities," because he was preaching about 'Jesus' and 'Resurrection.' [19]They took him and led him to the Areopagus[‡] and said, "May we learn what this new teaching is that you speak of?[u] [20]For you bring some strange notions to our ears; we should like to know what these things mean." [21]Now all the Athenians as well as the foreigners residing

there used their time for nothing else but telling or hearing something new.

**Paul's Speech at the Areopagus.** [22]Then Paul stood up at the Areopagus and said:[§]

"You Athenians, I see that in every respect you are very religious. [23]For as I walked around looking carefully at your shrines, I even discovered an altar inscribed, 'To an Unknown God.'[¶] What therefore you unknowingly worship, I proclaim to you. [24]The God who made the world and all that is in it, the Lord of heaven and earth, does not dwell in sanctuaries made by human hands,[v] [25]nor is he served by human hands because he needs anything. Rather it is he who gives to everyone life and breath and everything. [26]He made from one** the whole human race to dwell on the entire surface of the earth, and he fixed the ordered seasons and the boundaries of their regions, [27]so that people might seek God, even perhaps grope for him and find him, though indeed he is not far from any one of us.[w] [28]For 'In him we live and move and have our being,'[††] as even some of your poets have said, 'For we too are his offspring.' [29]Since therefore we are the offspring of God, we ought not to think that the divinity is like an image fashioned from gold, silver, or stone by human art and imagination.[x] [30]God has overlooked the times of ignorance, but now he demands that all people everywhere repent [31]because he has established a day on which he will 'judge the world with justice' through a man he has appointed, and he has provided confirmation for all by raising him from the dead."[y]

[32]When they heard about resurrection of the dead, some began to scoff, but others said, "We should like to hear you on this some other time." [33]And so Paul left them. [34]But some did join him, and became believers. Among them were Dionysius, a member of the Court of the

---

*[17:16–21] Paul's presence in Athens sets the stage for the great discourse before a Gentile audience in Acts 17:22–31. Although Athens was a politically insignificant city at this period, it still lived on the glories of its past and represented the center of Greek culture. The setting describes the conflict between Christian preaching and Hellenistic philosophy.

†[17:18] **Epicurean and Stoic philosophers**: for the followers of Epicurus (342–271 B.C.), the goal of life was happiness attained through sober reasoning and the searching out of motives for all choice and avoidance. The Stoics were followers of Zeno, a younger contemporary of Alexander the Great. Zeno and his followers believed in a type of pantheism that held that the spark of divinity was present in all reality and that, in order to be free, each person must live "according to nature." **This scavenger**: literally, "seed-picker," as of a bird that picks up grain. The word is later used of scrap collectors and of people who take other people's ideas and propagate them as if they were their own. **Promoter of foreign deities**: according to Xenophon, Socrates was accused of promoting new deities. The accusation against Paul echoes the charge against Socrates. **'Jesus' and 'Resurrection'**: the Athenians are presented as misunderstanding Paul from the outset; they think he is preaching about Jesus and a goddess named *Anastasis*, i.e., Resurrection.

‡[17:19] **To the Areopagus**: the "Areopagus" refers either to the Hill of Ares west of the Acropolis or to the Council of Athens, which at one time met on the hill but which at this time assembled in the Royal Colonnade (**Stoa Basileios**).

s. [17:11] Jn 5:39.  t. [17:14] 1 Thes 3:1–2.  u. [17:19] 1 Cor 1:22.

§[17:22–31] In Paul's appearance at the Areopagus he preaches his climactic speech to Gentiles in the cultural center of the ancient world. The speech is more theological than christological. Paul's discourse appeals to the Greek world's belief in divinity as responsible for the origin and existence of the universe. It contests the common belief in a multiplicity of gods supposedly exerting their powers through their images. It acknowledges that the attempt to find God is a constant human endeavor. It declares, further, that God is the judge of the human race, that the time of the judgment has been determined, and that it will be executed through a man whom God raised from the dead. The speech reflects sympathy with pagan religiosity, handles the subject of idol worship gently, and appeals for a new examination of divinity, not from the standpoint of creation but from the standpoint of judgment.

¶[17:23] **'To an Unknown God'**: ancient authors such as Pausanias, Philostratus, and Tertullian speak of Athenian altars with no specific dedication as altars of "unknown gods" or "nameless altars."

**[17:26] **From one**: many manuscripts read "from one blood." **Fixed . . . seasons**: or "fixed limits to the epochs."

††[17:28] **'In him we live and move and have our being'**: some scholars understand this saying to be based on an earlier saying of Epimenides of Knossos (6th century B.C.). **'For we too are his offspring'**: here Paul is quoting Aratus of Soli, a third-century B.C. poet from Cilicia.

v. [17:24] 7:48–50; Gn 1:1; 1 Kgs 8:27; Is 42:5.  w. [17:27] Jer 23:23; Wis 13:6; Rom 1:19.  x. [17:29] 19:26; Is 40:18–20; 44:10–17; Rom 1:22–23.  y. [17:31] 10:42.

Areopagus, a woman named Damaris, and others with them.

## CHAPTER 18

**Paul in Corinth.** ¹After this he left Athens and went to Corinth. ²There he met a Jew named Aquila,ᶻ a native of Pontus, who had recently come from Italy with his wife Priscilla* because Claudius had ordered all the Jews to leave Rome. He went to visit them ³and, because he practiced the same trade, stayed with them and worked, for they were tentmakers by trade. ⁴Every sabbath, he entered into discussions in the synagogue, attempting to convince both Jews and Greeks.

⁵When Silas and Timothy came down from Macedonia, Paul began to occupy himself totally with preaching the word, testifying to the Jews that the Messiah was Jesus. ⁶When they opposed him and reviled him, he shook out his garments† and said to them, "Your blood be on your heads! I am clear of responsibility. From now on I will go to the Gentiles."ᵃ ⁷So he left there and went to a house belonging to a man named Titus Justus, a worshiper of God;‡ his house was next to a synagogue.ᵇ ⁸Crispus,§ the synagogue official,ᶜ came to believe in the Lord along with his entire household, and many of the Corinthians who heard believed and were baptized. ⁹ᵈOne night in a vision the Lord said to Paul, "Do not be afraid. Go on speaking, and do not be silent, ¹⁰for I am with you. No one will attack and harm you, for I have many people in this city." ¹¹He settled there for a year and a half and taught the word of God among them.

**Accusations Before Gallio.** ¹²But when Gallio was proconsul of Achaia,¶ the Jews rose up together against Paul and brought him to the tribunal, ¹³saying, "This man is inducing people to worship God contrary to the law."** ¹⁴When Paul was about to reply, Gallio spoke to the Jews, "If it were a matter of some crime or malicious fraud, I should with reason hear the complaint of you Jews; ¹⁵but since it is a question of arguments over doctrine and titles and your own law, see to it yourselves. I do not wish to be a judge of such matters." ¹⁶And he drove them away from the tribunal. ¹⁷They all seized Sosthenes, the synagogue official, and beat him in full view of the tribunal. But none of this was of concern to Gallio.

**Return to Syrian Antioch.** ¹⁸Paul remained for quite some time, and after saying farewell to the brothers he sailed for Syria, together with Priscilla and Aquila. At Cenchreae he had his hair cutᵉ because he had taken a vow.†† ¹⁹When they reached Ephesus, he left them there, while he entered the synagogue and held discussions with the Jews. ²⁰Although they asked him to stay for a longer time, he did not consent, ²¹but as he said farewell he promised, "I shall come back to you again, God willing." Then he set sail from Ephesus. ²²Upon landing at Caesarea, he went up and greeted the church‡‡ and then went down to Antioch. ²³§§After staying there some time, he left and traveled in orderly sequence through the Galatian country and Phrygia, bringing strength to all the disciples.

**Apollos.** ²⁴A Jew named Apollos,ᶠ a native of Alexandria, an eloquent speaker, arrived in Ephesus. He was an authority on the scriptures.¶¶ ²⁵He had been instructed in the Way of the Lord and, with ardent spirit, spoke and taught accurately about Jesus, although he knew only the baptism of John. ²⁶He began to speak boldly in the synagogue; but when Priscilla and Aquila heard him, they took him aside and explained to him the Way [of God]*** more accurately. ²⁷And when he wanted to cross to Achaia, the brothers encouraged him and wrote to the disciples there to welcome him. After his arrival he gave great assistance to those who had come to believe through grace. ²⁸He vigorously refuted the Jews in public, establishing from the scriptures that the Messiah is Jesus.

## CHAPTER 19

**Paul in Ephesus.** ¹†††While Apollos was in Corinth, Paul traveled through the interior of

---

*[18:2] **Aquila . . . Priscilla**: both may already have been Christians at the time of their arrival in Corinth (see Acts 18:26). According to 1 Cor 16:19, their home became a meeting place for Christians. **Claudius**: the Emperor Claudius expelled the Jews from Rome ca. A.D. 49. The Roman historian Suetonius gives as reason for the expulsion disturbances among the Jews "at the instigation of Chrestos," probably meaning disputes about the messiahship of Jesus.

†[18:6] **Shook out his garments**: a gesture indicating Paul's repudiation of his mission to the Jews there; cf. Acts 28:17–31.

‡[18:7] **A worshiper of God**: see note on Acts 8:26–40.

§[18:8] **Crispus**: in 1 Cor 1:14 Paul mentions that Crispus was one of the few he himself baptized at Corinth.

¶[18:12] **When Gallio was proconsul of Achaia**: Gallio's proconsulship in Achaia is dated to A.D. 51–52 from an inscription discovered at Delphi. This has become an important date in establishing a chronology of the life and missionary work of Paul.

**[18:13] **Contrary to the law**: Gallio (Acts 18:15) understands this to be a problem of Jewish, not Roman, law.

††[18:18] **He had his hair cut because he had taken a vow**: a reference to a Nazirite vow (see Nm 6:1–21, especially Nm 6:18) taken by Paul (see also Acts 21:23–27).

‡‡[18:22] **He went up and greeted the church**: "going up" suggests a visit to the church in Jerusalem.

§§[18:23–21:16] Luke's account of Paul's third missionary journey devotes itself mainly to his work at Ephesus (Acts 19:1–20:1). There is a certain restiveness on Paul's part and a growing conviction that the Spirit bids him return to Jerusalem and prepare to go to Rome (Acts 19:21).

¶¶[18:24–25] Apollos appears as a preacher who knows the teaching of Jesus in the context of John's baptism of repentance. Aquila and Priscilla instruct him more fully. He is referred to in 1 Cor 1:12; 3:5–6, 22.

***[18:26] **The Way [of God]**: for the Way, see note on Acts 9:2. Other manuscripts here read "the Way of the Lord," "the word of the Lord," or simply "the Way."

†††[19:1–6] Upon his arrival in Ephesus, Paul discovers other people at the same religious stage as Apollos, though they seem to have considered themselves followers of Christ,

---

z. [18:2] Rom 16:3.  a. [18:6] 13:51; Mt 10:14; 27:24–25; Mk 6:11; Lk 9:5; 10:10–11.  b. [18:7] 13:46–47; 28:28.  c. [18:8] 1 Cor 1:14. d. [18:9–10] Jer 1:8.

e. [18:18] 21:24; Nm 6:18.  f. [18:24] 1 Cor 1:12.

the country and came [down] to Ephesus where he found some disciples. ²He said to them, "Did you receive the holy Spirit when you became believers?" They answered him, "We have never even heard that there is a holy Spirit." ³He said, "How were you baptized?" They replied, "With the baptism of John." ⁴Paul then said, "John baptized with a baptism of repentance, telling the people to believe in the one who was to come after him, that is, in Jesus."ᵍ ⁵When they heard this, they were baptized in the name of the Lord Jesus. ⁶And when Paul laid [his] hands on them, the holy Spirit came upon them, and they spoke in tongues and prophesied.ʰ ⁷Altogether there were about twelve men.

⁸He entered the synagogue, and for three months debated boldly with persuasive arguments about the kingdom of God. ⁹But when some in their obstinacy and disbelief disparaged the Way before the assembly, he withdrew and took his disciples with him and began to hold daily discussions in the lecture hall of Tyrannus. ¹⁰This continued for two years with the result that all the inhabitants of the province of Asia heard the word of the Lord, Jews and Greeks alike. ¹¹So extraordinary were the mighty deeds God accomplished at the hands of Paul ¹²that when face cloths or aprons that touched his skin were applied to the sick, their diseases left them and the evil spirits came out of them.ⁱ

**The Jewish Exorcists.** ¹³Then some itinerant Jewish exorcists tried to invoke the name of the Lord Jesus over those with evil spirits, saying, "I adjure you by the Jesus whom Paul preaches." ¹⁴When the seven sons of Sceva, a Jewish high priest, tried to do this, ¹⁵the evil spirit said to them in reply, "Jesus I recognize, Paul I know, but who are you?" ¹⁶The person with the evil spirit then sprang at them and subdued them all. He so overpowered them that they fled naked and wounded from that house. ¹⁷When this became known to all the Jews and Greeks who lived in Ephesus, fear fell upon them all, and the name of the Lord Jesus was held in great esteem. ¹⁸Many of those who had become believers came forward and openly acknowledged their former practices. ¹⁹Moreover, a large number of those who had practiced magic collected their books and burned them in public. They calculated their value and found it to be fifty thousand silver pieces. ²⁰Thus did the word of the Lord continue to spread with influence and power.

**Paul's Plans.** ²¹When this was concluded, Paul made up his mind to travel through Macedonia and Achaia, and then to go on to Jerusalem, saying, "After I have been there, I must visit Rome also."ʲ ²²Then he sent to Macedonia two of his assistants, Timothy and Erastus, while he himself stayed for a while in the province of Asia.

**The Riot of the Silversmiths.** ²³About that time a serious disturbance broke out concerning the Way. ²⁴There was a silversmith named Demetrius who made miniature silver shrines of Artemis* and provided no little work for the craftsmen. ²⁵He called a meeting of these and other workers in related crafts and said, "Men, you know well that our prosperity derives from this work. ²⁶As you can now see and hear, not only in Ephesus but throughout most of the province of Asia this Paul has persuaded and misled a great number of people by saying that gods made by hands are not gods at all.ᵏ ²⁷The danger grows, not only that our business will be discredited, but also that the temple of the great goddess Artemis will be of no account, and that she whom the whole province of Asia and all the world worship will be stripped of her magnificence."

²⁸When they heard this, they were filled with fury and began to shout, "Great is Artemis of the Ephesians!" ²⁹The city was filled with confusion, and the people rushed with one accord into the theater, seizing Gaius and Aristarchus, the Macedonians, Paul's traveling companions.ˡ ³⁰Paul wanted to go before the crowd, but the disciples would not let him, ³¹and even some of the Asiarchs† who were friends of his sent word to him advising him not to venture into the theater. ³²Meanwhile, some were shouting one thing, others something else; the assembly was in chaos, and most of the people had no idea why they had come together. ³³Some of the crowd prompted Alexander, as the Jews pushed him forward, and Alexander signaled with his hand that he wished to explain something to the gathering. ³⁴But when they recognized that he was a Jew, they all shouted in unison, for about two hours, "Great is Artemis of the Ephesians!" ³⁵Finally the town clerk restrained the crowd and said, "You Ephesians, what person is there who does not know that the city of the Ephesians is the guardian of the temple‡ of the great Artemis and of her image that fell from the sky? ³⁶Since these things are undeniable, you must

---

not of the Baptist. On the relation between baptism and the reception of the Spirit, see note on Acts 8:16.

g. [19:4] 1:5; 11:16; 13:24–25; Mt 3:11; Mk 1:8; Lk 3:16.  h. [19:6] 8:15–17; 10:44, 46.  i. [19:12] 5:15–16; Lk 8:44–47.  j. [19:21] 23:11; Rom 1:13; 15:22–32.

*[19:24] **Miniature silver shrines of Artemis**: the temple of Artemis at Ephesus was one of the seven wonders of the ancient world. Artemis, originally the Olympian virgin hunter, moon goddess, and goddess of wild nature, was worshiped at Ephesus as an Asian mother goddess and goddess of fertility. She was one of the most widely worshiped female deities in the Hellenistic world (see Acts 18:27).

†[19:31] **Asiarchs**: the precise status and role of the Asiarchs is disputed. They appear to have been people of wealth and influence who promoted the Roman imperial cult and who may also have been political representatives in a league of cities in the Roman province of Asia.

‡[19:35] **Guardian of the temple**: this title was accorded by Rome to cities that provided a temple for the imperial cult. Inscriptional evidence indicates that Ephesus was acknowledged as the temple keeper of Artemis and of the imperial cult. **That fell from the sky**: many scholars think that this refers to a meteorite that was worshiped as an image of the goddess.

k. [19:26] 17:29.  l. [19:29] Col 4:10.

calm yourselves and not do anything rash. [37]The men you brought here are not temple robbers, nor have they insulted our goddess. [38]If Demetrius and his fellow craftsmen have a complaint against anyone, courts are in session, and there are proconsuls. Let them bring charges against one another. [39]If you have anything further to investigate, let the matter be settled in the lawful assembly, [40]for, as it is, we are in danger of being charged with rioting because of today's conduct. There is no cause for it. We shall [not]* be able to give a reason for this demonstration." With these words he dismissed the assembly.

## CHAPTER 20

**Journey to Macedonia and Greece.** [1]When the disturbance was over, Paul had the disciples summoned and, after encouraging them, he bade them farewell and set out on his journey to Macedonia.[m] [2]As he traveled throughout those regions, he provided many words of encouragement for them. Then he arrived in Greece, [3]where he stayed for three months. But when a plot was made against him by the Jews as he was about to set sail for Syria, he decided to return by way of Macedonia.

**Return to Troas.** [4n]Sopater, the son of Pyrrhus, from Beroea, accompanied him, as did Aristarchus and Secundus from Thessalonica, Gaius from Derbe, Timothy, and Tychicus and Trophimus from Asia [5]who went on ahead and waited for us† at Troas.[o] [6]We sailed from Philippi after the feast of Unleavened Bread,‡ and rejoined them five days later in Troas, where we spent a week.

**Eutychus Restored to Life.** [7]On the first day of the week§ when we gathered to break bread, Paul spoke to them because he was going to leave on the next day, and he kept on speaking until midnight. [8]There were many lamps in the upstairs room where we were gathered, [9]and a young man named Eutychus who was sitting on the window sill was sinking into a deep sleep as Paul talked on and on. Once overcome by sleep, he fell down from the third story and when he was picked up, he was dead. [10p]Paul went down,¶ threw himself upon him, and said as he embraced him, "Don't be alarmed; there is

life in him." [11]Then he returned upstairs, broke the bread, and ate; after a long conversation that lasted until daybreak, he departed. [12]And they took the boy away alive and were immeasurably comforted.

**Journey to Miletus.** [13]We went ahead to the ship and set sail for Assos where we were to take Paul on board, as he had arranged, since he was going overland. [14]When he met us in Assos, we took him aboard and went on to Mitylene. [15]We sailed away from there on the next day and reached a point off Chios, and a day later we reached Samos, and on the following day we arrived at Miletus. [16**]Paul had decided to sail past Ephesus in order not to lose time in the province of Asia, for he was hurrying to be in Jerusalem, if at all possible, for the day of Pentecost.

**Paul's Farewell Speech at Miletus.** [17]From Miletus he had the presbyters of the church at Ephesus summoned. [18]When they came to him, he addressed them, "You know how I lived among you the whole time from the day I first came to the province of Asia. [19]I served the Lord with all humility and with the tears and trials that came to me because of the plots of the Jews, [20]and I did not at all shrink from telling you what was for your benefit, or from teaching you in public or in your homes. [21]I earnestly bore witness for both Jews and Greeks to repentance before God and to faith in our Lord Jesus. [22]But now, compelled by the Spirit, I am going to Jerusalem. What will happen to me there I do not know, [23]except that in one city after another the holy Spirit has been warning me that imprisonment and hardships await me.[q] [24]Yet I consider life of no importance to me, if only I may finish my course and the ministry that I received from the Lord Jesus, to bear witness to the gospel of God's grace.[r]

[25]"But now I know that none of you to whom I preached the kingdom during my travels will ever see my face again. [26]And so I solemnly declare to you this day that I am not responsible for the blood of any of you, [27]for I did not shrink from proclaiming to you the entire plan of God. [28s]Keep watch over yourselves and over the whole flock of which the holy Spirit has appointed you overseers,†† in which you tend the church of God

---

*[19:40] Some manuscripts omit the negative in [**not**] **be able**, making the meaning, "There is no cause for which we shall be able to give a reason for this demonstration."

†[20:5] The second "we-section" of Acts begins here. See note on Acts 16:10–17.

‡[20:6] **Feast of Unleavened Bread:** see note on Lk 22:1.

§[20:7] **The first day of the week:** the day after the sabbath and the first day of the Jewish week, apparently chosen originally by the Jerusalem community for the celebration of the liturgy of the Eucharist in order to relate it to the resurrection of Christ.

¶[20:10] The action of Paul in throwing himself upon the dead boy recalls that of Elijah in 1 Kgs 17:21 where the son of the widow of Zarephath is revived and that of Elisha in 2 Kgs 4:34 where the Shunamite woman's son is restored to life.

m. [20:1] 1 Cor 16:1.   n. [20:4] Rom 16:21.   o. [20:5] 21:29; 2 Tm 4:20.
p. [20:10] 1 Kgs 17:17–24; 2 Kgs 4:30–37; Mt 9:24; Mk 5:39; Lk 8:52.

**[20:16–35] Apparently aware of difficulties at Ephesus and neighboring areas, Paul calls the presbyters together at Miletus, about thirty miles from Ephesus. He reminds them of his dedication to the gospel (Acts 20:18–21), speaks of what he is about to suffer for the gospel (Acts 20:22–27), and admonishes them to guard the community against false prophets, sure to arise upon his departure (Acts 20:28–31). He concludes by citing a saying of Jesus (Acts 20:35) not recorded in the gospel tradition. Luke presents this farewell to the Ephesian presbyters as Paul's last will and testament.

††[20:28] **Overseers:** see note on Phil 1:1. **The church of God:** because the clause "that he acquired with his own blood" following "the church of God" suggests that "his own blood" refers to God's blood, some early copyists changed "the church of God" to "the church of the Lord." Some prefer the translation "acquired with the blood of his own," i.e., Christ.

q. [20:23] 9:16.   r. [20:24] 2 Tm 4:7.   s. [20:28] Jn 21:15–17; 1 Pt 5:2.

that he acquired with his own blood. [29]I know that after my departure savage wolves will come among you, and they will not spare the flock.[t] [30]And from your own group, men will come forward perverting the truth to draw the disciples away after them.[u] [31]So be vigilant and remember that for three years, night and day, I unceasingly admonished each of you with tears.[v] [32]And now I commend you to God and to that gracious word of his that can build you up and give you the inheritance among all who are consecrated. [33]I have never wanted anyone's silver or gold or clothing. [34]You know well that these very hands have served my needs and my companions.[w] [35]In every way I have shown you that by hard work of that sort we must help the weak, and keep in mind the words of the Lord Jesus who himself said, 'It is more blessed to give than to receive.'"[x]

[36]When he had finished speaking he knelt down and prayed with them all. [37]They were all weeping loudly as they threw their arms around Paul and kissed him, [38]for they were deeply distressed that he had said that they would never see his face again. Then they escorted him to the ship.

## CHAPTER 21

**Arrival at Tyre.** [1*]When we had taken leave of them we set sail, made a straight run for Cos, and on the next day for Rhodes, and from there to Patara. [2]Finding a ship crossing to Phoenicia, we went on board and put out to sea. [3]We caught sight of Cyprus but passed by it on our left and sailed on toward Syria and put in at Tyre where the ship was to unload cargo. [4]There we sought out the disciples and stayed for a week. They kept telling Paul through the Spirit not to embark for Jerusalem. [5]At the end of our stay we left and resumed our journey. All of them, women and children included, escorted us out of the city, and after kneeling on the beach to pray, [6]we bade farewell to one another. Then we boarded the ship, and they returned home.

**Arrival at Ptolemais and Caesarea.** [7]We continued the voyage and came from Tyre to Ptolemais, where we greeted the brothers and stayed a day with them. [8]On the next day we resumed the trip and came to Caesarea, where we went to the house of Philip the evangelist, who was one of the Seven,[†] and stayed with him.[y] [9]He had four virgin daughters gifted with prophecy. [10]We had been there several days when a prophet named Agabus[‡] came down from Judea. [11]He came up to us, took Paul's belt, bound

his own feet and hands with it, and said, "Thus says the holy Spirit: This is the way the Jews will bind the owner of this belt in Jerusalem, and they will hand him over to the Gentiles."[§] [12]When we heard this, we and the local residents begged him not to go up to Jerusalem. [13]Then Paul replied, "What are you doing, weeping and breaking my heart? I am prepared not only to be bound but even to die in Jerusalem for the name of the Lord Jesus." [14a]Since he would not be dissuaded we let the matter rest, saying,[b] "The Lord's will be done."[¶]

**Paul and James in Jerusalem.** [15]After these days we made preparations for our journey, then went up to Jerusalem. [16]Some of the disciples from Caesarea came along to lead us to the house of Mnason, a Cypriot, a disciple of long standing, with whom we were to stay. [17**]When we reached Jerusalem the brothers welcomed us warmly. [18]The next day, Paul accompanied us on a visit to James, and all the presbyters were present. [19]He greeted them, then proceeded to tell them in detail what God had accomplished among the Gentiles through his ministry. [20]They praised God when they heard it but said to him, "Brother, you see how many thousands of believers there are from among the Jews, and they are all zealous observers of the law. [21]They have been informed that you are teaching all the Jews who live among the Gentiles to abandon Moses and that you are telling them not to circumcise their children or to observe their customary practices. [22]What is to be done? They will surely hear that you have arrived. [23†]So do what we tell you. We have four men who have taken a vow.[c] [24]Take these men and purify yourself with them, and pay their expenses[‡‡] that they may have their heads shaved. In this way everyone will know that there is nothing to the reports they have been given about you but that you yourself live in observance of the law.

§[21:11] The symbolic act of Agabus recalls those of Old Testament prophets. Compare Is 20:2; Ez 4:1; Jer 13:1.

¶[21:14] The Christian disciples' attitude reflects that of Jesus (see Lk 22:42).

**[21:17–26] The leaders of the Jewish Christians of Jerusalem inform Paul that the Jews there believe he has encouraged the Jews of the diaspora to abandon the Mosaic law. According to Acts, Paul had no objection to the retention of the law by the Jewish Christians of Jerusalem and left the Jews of the diaspora who accepted Christianity free to follow the same practice.

††[21:23–26] The leaders of the community suggest that Paul, on behalf of four members of the Jerusalem community, make the customary payment for the sacrifices offered at the termination of the Nazirite vow (see Nm 6:1–24) in order to impress favorably the Jewish Christians in Jerusalem with his high regard for the Mosaic law. Since Paul himself had once made this vow (Acts 18:18), his respect for the law would be on public record.

‡‡[21:24] **Pay their expenses:** according to Nm 6:14–15 the Nazirite had to present a yearling lamb for a holocaust, a yearling ewe lamb for a sin offering, and a ram for a peace offering, along with food and drink offerings, upon completion of the period of the vow.

---

*[21:1–18] The third "we-section" of Acts (see note on Acts 16:10–17).

†[21:8] **One of the Seven:** see note on Acts 6:2–4.

‡[21:10] **Agabus:** mentioned in Acts 11:28 as the prophet who predicted the famine that occurred when Claudius was emperor.

---

t. [20:29] Jn 10:12.   u. [20:30] Mt 7:15; 2 Pt 2:1–3; 1 Jn 2:18–19.
v. [20:31] 1 Thes 2:11.   w. [20:34] 1 Cor 4:12; 1 Thes 2:9; 2 Thes 3:8.
x. [20:35] Sir 4:31.   y. [21:8] 6:5; 8:5–6.   z. [21:11] 11:28; 20:23.

a. [21:14]  19:15–16.   b. [21:14]  Mt 6:10;  26:39;  Mk 14:36; Lk 22:42.   c. [21:23–27] 18:18; Nm 6:1–21.

²⁵ᵈAs for the Gentiles who have come to believe, we sent them our decision that they abstain from meat sacrificed to idols, from blood, from the meat of strangled animals, and from unlawful marriage." ²⁶So Paul took the men, and on the next day after purifying himself together with them entered the temple to give notice of the day when the purification would be completed and the offering made for each of them.ᵉ

**Paul's Arrest.** ²⁷When the seven days were nearly completed, the Jews from the province of Asia noticed him in the temple, stirred up the whole crowd, and laid hands on him, ²⁸/shouting, "Fellow Israelites, help us. This is the man who is teaching everyone everywhere against the people and the law and this place, and what is more, he has even brought Greeks into the temple and defiled this sacred place."† ²⁹For they had previously seen Trophimus the Ephesian in the city with him and supposed that Paul had brought him into the temple. ³⁰The whole city was in turmoil with people rushing together. They seized Paul and dragged him out of the temple, and immediately the gates were closed. ³¹While they were trying to kill him, a report reached the cohort commander‡ that all Jerusalem was rioting. ³²He immediately took soldiers and centurions and charged down on them. When they saw the commander and the soldiers they stopped beating Paul. ³³The cohort commander came forward, arrested him, and ordered him to be secured with two chains; he tried to find out who he might be and what he had done. ³⁴Some in the mob shouted one thing, others something else; so, since he was unable to ascertain the truth because of the uproar, he ordered Paul to be brought into the compound. ³⁵When he reached the steps, he was carried by the soldiers because of the violence of the mob, ³⁶⁸for a crowd of people followed and shouted, "Away with him!"

³⁷Just as Paul was about to be taken into the compound, he said to the cohort commander, "May I say something to you?" He replied, "Do you speak Greek? ³⁸So then you are not the Egyptian¶ who started a revolt some time ago and led the four thousand assassins into the desert?"ʰ ³⁹Paul answered, "I am a Jew, of Tarsus in Cilicia, a citizen of no mean city; I request you to permit me to speak to the people." ⁴⁰When he had given his permission, Paul stood on the steps and motioned with his hand to the people; and when all was quiet he addressed them in Hebrew.**

## CHAPTER 22

**Paul's Defense Before the Jerusalem Jews.**††
¹"My brothers and fathers, listen to what I am about to say to you in my defense." ²When they heard him addressing them in Hebrew they became all the more quiet. And he continued, ³"I am a Jew, born in Tarsus in Cilicia, but brought up in this city. At the feet of Gamaliel I was educated strictly in our ancestral law and was zealous for God, just as all of you are today.ⁱ ⁴I persecuted this Way to death, binding both men and women and delivering them to prison.ʲ ⁵Even the high priest and the whole council of elders can testify on my behalf. For from them I even received letters to the brothers and set out for Damascus to bring back to Jerusalem in chains for punishment those there as well.

⁶"On that journey as I drew near to Damascus, about noon a great light from the sky suddenly shone around me.ᵏ ⁷I fell to the ground and heard a voice saying to me, 'Saul, Saul, why are you persecuting me?'ˡ ⁸I replied, 'Who are you, sir?' And he said to me, 'I am Jesus the Nazorean whom you are persecuting.'ᵐ ⁹My companions saw the light but did not hear the voice of the one who spoke to me.ⁿ ¹⁰I asked, 'What shall I do, sir?' The Lord answered me, 'Get up and go into Damascus, and there you will be told about everything appointed for you to do.'ᵒ ¹¹Since I could see nothing because of the brightness of that light, I was led by hand by my companions and entered Damascus.ᵖ

¹²ᑫ"A certain Ananias, a devout observer of the law, and highly spoken of by all the Jews who

---

\*[21:25] Paul is informed about the apostolic decree, seemingly for the first time (see note on Acts 15:13–35). The allusion to the decree was probably introduced here by Luke to remind his readers that the Gentile Christians themselves were asked to respect certain Jewish practices deriving from the law.

†[21:28] The charges against Paul by the diaspora Jews are identical to the charges brought against Stephen by diaspora Jews in Acts 6:13. **Brought Greeks into the temple:** non-Jews were forbidden, under penalty of death, to go beyond the Court of the Gentiles. Inscriptions in Greek and Latin on a stone balustrade marked off the prohibited area.

‡[21:31] **Cohort commander:** literally, "the leader of a thousand in a cohort." At this period the Roman cohort commander usually led six hundred soldiers, a tenth of a legion; but the number in a cohort varied.

§[21:36] **"Away with him!":** at the trial of Jesus before Pilate in Lk 23:18, the people similarly shout, "Away with this man."

¶[21:38] **The Egyptian:** according to the Jewish historian Josephus, an Egyptian gathered a large crowd on the Mount of Olives to witness the destruction of the walls of Jerusalem that would fall at the Egyptian "prophet's" word. The commotion was put down by the Roman authorities and the Egyptian escaped, but only after thousands had been killed. **Four thousand assassins:** literally, *sicarii*. According to Josephus, these were political nationalists who removed their opponents by assassination with a short dagger, called in Latin a *sica*.

\*\*[21:40] **In Hebrew:** meaning, perhaps, in Aramaic, which at this time was the Semitic tongue in common use.

††[22:1–21] Paul's first defense speech is presented to the Jerusalem crowds. Luke here presents Paul as a devout Jew (Acts 22:3) and zealous persecutor of the Christian community (Acts 22:4–5), and then recounts the conversion of Paul for the second time in Acts (see note on Acts 9:1–19).

h. [21:38] 5:36–37.   i. [22:3] 5:34; 26:4–5; 2 Cor 11:22; Gal 1:13–14; Phil 3:5–6.   j. [22:4] 8:3; 9:1–2; 22:19; 26:9–11; Phil 3:6.   k. [22:6] 9:3; 26:13; 1 Cor 15:8.   l. [22:7] 9:4; 26:14.   m. [22:8] 9:5; 26:15; Mt 25:40.   n. [22:9] 9:7; 26:13–14.   o. [22:10] 9:6; 26:16.   p. [22:11] 9:8.   q. [22:12–16] 9:10–19.

d. [21:25] 15:19–20, 28–29.   e. [21:26] 1 Cor 9:20.   f. [21:28] Rom 15:31.   g. [21:36] 22:22; Lk 23:18; Jn 19:15.

lived there, [13]came to me and stood there and said, 'Saul, my brother, regain your sight.' And at that very moment I regained my sight and saw him. [14]Then he said, 'The God of our ancestors designated you to know his will, to see the Righteous One, and to hear the sound of his voice; [15]for you will be his witness* before all to what you have seen and heard. [16]Now, why delay? Get up and have yourself baptized and your sins washed away, calling upon his name.'

[17]"After I had returned to Jerusalem and while I was praying in the temple, I fell into a trance [18]and saw the Lord saying to me, 'Hurry, leave Jerusalem at once, because they will not accept your testimony about me.' [19]But I replied, 'Lord, they themselves know that from synagogue to synagogue I used to imprison and beat those who believed in you.[r] [20]And when the blood of your witness Stephen was being shed, I myself stood by giving my approval and keeping guard over the cloaks of his murderers.'[s] [21]Then he said to me,[t] 'Go, I shall send you far away to the Gentiles.'"†

**Paul Imprisoned.** [22u]They listened to him until he said this, but then they raised their voices and shouted, "Take such a one as this away from the earth. It is not right that he should live."‡ [23]And as they were yelling and throwing off their cloaks and flinging dust into the air, [24]the cohort commander ordered him to be brought into the compound and gave instruction that he be interrogated under the lash to determine the reason why they were making such an outcry against him. [25v]But when they had stretched him out for the whips, Paul said to the centurion on duty, "Is it lawful for you to scourge a man who is a Roman citizen and has not been tried?"§ [26]When the centurion heard this, he went to the cohort commander and reported it, saying, "What are you going to do? This man is a Roman citizen." [27]Then the commander came and said to him, "Tell me, are you a Roman citizen?" "Yes," he answered. [28]The commander replied, "I acquired this citizenship for a large sum of money." Paul said, "But I was born one." [29]At once those who were going to interrogate him backed away from him, and the commander became alarmed

when he realized that he was a Roman citizen and that he had had him bound.

**Paul Before the Sanhedrin.** [30]The next day, wishing to determine the truth about why he was being accused by the Jews, he freed him and ordered the chief priests and the whole Sanhedrin to convene. Then he brought Paul down and made him stand before them.

## CHAPTER 23

[1]Paul looked intently at the Sanhedrin and said, "My brothers, I have conducted myself with a perfectly clear conscience before God to this day."[w] [2]The high priest Ananias¶ ordered his attendants to strike his mouth. [3]Then Paul said to him, "God will strike you," you whitewashed wall. Do you indeed sit in judgment upon me according to the law and yet in violation of the law order me to be struck?"[x] [4]The attendants said, "Would you revile God's high priest?" [5]Paul answered, "Brothers, I did not realize he was the high priest. For it is written,[y] 'You shall not curse a ruler of your people.'"††

[6]Paul was aware that some were Sadducees and some Pharisees, so he called out before the Sanhedrin, "My brothers, I am a Pharisee, the son of Pharisees; [I] am on trial for hope in the resurrection of the dead."[z] [7]When he said this, a dispute broke out between the Pharisees and Sadducees, and the group became divided. [8]For the Sadducees say that there is no resurrection or angels or spirits, while the Pharisees acknowledge all three.[a] [9]A great uproar occurred, and some scribes belonging to the Pharisee party stood up and sharply argued, "We find nothing wrong with this man. Suppose a spirit or an angel has spoken to him?" [10]The dispute was so serious that the commander, afraid that Paul would be torn to pieces by them, ordered his troops to go down and rescue him from their midst and take him into the compound. [11‡‡b]The following night the Lord stood by him and said, "Take courage. For just as you have borne witness to my cause in Jerusalem, so you must also bear witness in Rome."

**Transfer to Caesarea.** [12]When day came, the Jews made a plot and bound themselves by oath

---

*[22:15] **His witness**: like the Galilean followers during the historical ministry of Jesus, Paul too, through his experience of the risen Christ, is to be a witness to the resurrection (compare Acts 1:8; 10:39–41; Lk 24:48).

†[22:21] Paul endeavors to explain that his position on the law has not been identical with that of his audience because it has been his prophetic mission to preach to the Gentiles to whom the law was not addressed and who had no faith in it as a way of salvation.

‡[22:22] Paul's suggestion that his prophetic mission to the Gentiles did not involve his imposing the law on them provokes the same opposition as occurred in Pisidian Antioch (Acts 13:45).

§[22:25] **Is it lawful for you to scourge a man who is a Roman citizen and has not been tried?**: see note on Acts 16:37.

¶[23:2] **The high priest Ananias**: Ananias, son of Nedebaeus, was high priest from A.D. 47 to 59.

**[23:3] **God will strike you**: Josephus reports that Ananias was later assassinated in A.D. 66 at the beginning of the First Revolt.

††[23:5] Luke portrays Paul as a model of one who is obedient to the Mosaic law. Paul, because of his reverence for the law (Ex 22:27), withdraws his accusation of hypocrisy, "whitewashed wall" (cf. Mt 23:27), when he is told Ananias is the high priest.

‡‡[23:11] The occurrence of the vision of Christ consoling Paul and assuring him that he will be his witness in Rome prepares the reader for the final section of Acts: the journey of Paul and the word he preaches to Rome under the protection of the Romans.

---

r. [22:19] 8:3; 9:1–2; 22:4–5; 26:9–11. s. [22:20] 7:58; 8:1. t. [22:21] 9:15; Gal 2:7–9. u. [22:22] 21:36; Lk 23:18; Jn 19:15. v. [22:25] 16:37.

w. [23:1] 24:16. x. [23:3] Ez 13:10–15; Mt 23:27. y. [23:5] Ex 22:27. z. [23:6] 24:15, 21; 26:5; Phil 3:5. a. [23:8] Mt 22:23; Lk 20:27. b. [23:11] 19:21.

not to eat or drink until they had killed Paul. [13]There were more than forty who formed this conspiracy. [14]They went to the chief priests and elders and said, "We have bound ourselves by a solemn oath to taste nothing until we have killed Paul. [15]You, together with the Sanhedrin, must now make an official request to the commander to have him bring him down to you, as though you meant to investigate his case more thoroughly. We on our part are prepared to kill him before he arrives." [16]The son of Paul's sister, however, heard about the ambush; so he went and entered the compound and reported it to Paul. [17]Paul then called one of the centurions* and requested, "Take this young man to the commander; he has something to report to him." [18]So he took him and brought him to the commander and explained, "The prisoner Paul called me and asked that I bring this young man to you; he has something to say to you." [19]The commander took him by the hand, drew him aside, and asked him privately, "What is it you have to report to me?" [20]He replied, "The Jews have conspired to ask you to bring Paul down to the Sanhedrin tomorrow, as though they meant to inquire about him more thoroughly, [21]but do not believe them. More than forty of them are lying in wait for him; they have bound themselves by oath not to eat or drink until they have killed him. They are now ready and only wait for your consent." [22]As the commander dismissed the young man he directed him, "Tell no one that you gave me this information."

[23]Then he summoned two of the centurions and said, "Get two hundred soldiers ready to go to Caesarea by nine o'clock tonight,† along with seventy horsemen and two hundred auxiliaries. [24]Provide mounts for Paul to ride and give him safe conduct to Felix the governor." [25]Then he wrote a letter with this content: [26]*"Claudius Lysias to his excellency the governor Felix, greetings.§ [27]This man, seized by the Jews and about to be murdered by them, I rescued after intervening with my troops when I learned that he was a Roman citizen.c [28]I wanted to learn the reason for their accusations against him

so I brought him down to their Sanhedrin. [29]I discovered that he was accused in matters of controversial questions of their law and not of any charge deserving death or imprisonment.d [30]Since it was brought to my attention that there will be a plot against the man, I am sending him to you at once, and have also notified his accusers to state [their case] against him before you."

[31]So the soldiers, according to their orders, took Paul and escorted him by night to Antipatris. [32]The next day they re turned to the compound, leaving the horsemen to complete the journey with him. [33]When they arrived in Caesarea they delivered the letter to the governor and presented Paul to him. [34]When he had read it and asked to what province he belonged, and learned that he was from Cilicia, [35]he said, "I shall hear your case when your accusers arrive." Then he ordered that he be held in custody in Herod's praetorium.

## CHAPTER 24

**Trial Before Felix.** [1]Five days later the high priest Ananias came down with some elders and an advocate, a certain Tertullus, and they presented formal charges against Paul to the governor. [2]When he was called, Tertullus began to accuse him, saying, "Since we have attained much peace through you, and reforms have been accomplished in this nation through your provident care, [3]we acknowledge this in every way and everywhere, most excellent Felix, with all gratitude. [4]But in order not to detain you further, I ask you to give us a brief hearing with your customary graciousness. [5]eWe found this man to be a pest; he creates dissension among Jews all over the world and is a ringleader of the sect of the Nazoreans.¶ [6]He even tried to desecrate our temple, but we arrested him.f [?]" [8]If you examine him you will be able to learn from him for yourself about everything of which we are accusing him." [9]The Jews also joined in the attack and asserted that these things were so.

[10]††Then the governor motioned to him to speak and Paul replied, "I know that you have been a judge over this nation for many years and so I am pleased to make my defense before you. [11]As you can verify, not more than twelve days have passed since I went up to Jerusalem to worship. [12]Neither in the temple, nor in the

---

*[23:17] **Centurions:** a centurion was a military officer in charge of one hundred soldiers.

†[23:23] **By nine o'clock tonight:** literally, "by the third hour of the night." The night hours began at 6 p.m. **Two hundred auxiliaries:** the meaning of the Greek is not certain. It seems to refer to spearmen from the local police force and not from the cohort of soldiers, which would have numbered only 500–1000 men.

‡[23:26–30] The letter emphasizes the fact that Paul is a Roman citizen and asserts the lack of evidence that he is guilty of a crime against the empire. The tone of the letter implies that the commander became initially involved in Paul's case because of his Roman citizenship, but this is not an exact description of what really happened (see Acts 21:31–33; 22:25–29).

§[23:26] M. Antonius Felix was procurator of Judea from A.D. 52 to 60. His procuratorship was marked by cruelty toward and oppression of his Jewish subjects.

¶[24:5] **Nazoreans:** that is, followers of Jesus of Nazareth.

**[24:7] The Western text has added here a verse (really Acts 24:6b–8a) that is not found in the best Greek manuscripts. It reads, "and would have judged him according to our own law, but our cohort commander Lysias came and violently took him out of our hands and ordered his accusers to come before you."

††[24:10–21] Whereas the advocate Tertullus referred to Paul's activities on his missionary journeys, the apostle narrowed the charges down to the riot connected with the incident in the temple (see Acts 21:27–30; 24:17–20). In his defense, Paul stresses the continuity between Christianity and Judaism.

---

c. [23:27] 21:30–34; 22:27.

d. [23:29] 18:14–15; 25:18–19.   e. [24:5] 24:14; Lk 23:2.   f. [24:6] 21:28.

synagogues, nor anywhere in the city did they find me arguing with anyone or instigating a riot among the people. ¹³Nor can they prove to you the accusations they are now making against me. ¹⁴But this I do admit to you, that according to the Way, which they call a sect, I worship the God of our ancestors and I believe everything that is in accordance with the law and written in the prophets.<sup>g</sup> ¹⁵I have the same hope in God as they themselves have that there will be a resurrection of the righteous and the unrighteous.<sup>h</sup> ¹⁶Because of this, I always strive to keep my conscience clear before God and man.<sup>i</sup> ¹⁷After many years, I came to bring alms for my nation and offerings.<sup>j</sup> ¹⁸While I was so engaged, they found me, after my purification, in the temple without a crowd or disturbance.<sup>k</sup> ¹⁹But some Jews from the province of Asia, who should be here before you to make whatever accusation they might have against me— ²⁰or let these men themselves state what crime they discovered when I stood before the Sanhedrin, ²¹unless it was my one outcry as I stood among them, that 'I am on trial before you today for the resurrection of the dead.'"<sup>l</sup>

²²Then Felix, who was accurately informed about the Way, postponed the trial, saying, "When Lysias the commander comes down, I shall decide your case." ²³He gave orders to the centurion that he should be kept in custody but have some liberty, and that he should not prevent any of his friends from caring for his needs.

**Captivity in Caesarea.** ²⁴*Several days later Felix came with his wife Drusilla, who was Jewish. He had Paul summoned and listened to him speak about faith in Christ Jesus. ²⁵But as he spoke about righteousness and self-restraint and the coming judgment, Felix became frightened and said, "You may go for now; when I find an opportunity I shall summon you again." ²⁶At the same time he hoped that a bribe would be offered him by Paul, and so he sent for him very often and conversed with him.

²⁷Two years passed and Felix was succeeded by Porcius Festus. Wishing to ingratiate himself with the Jews, Felix left Paul in prison.<sup>†</sup>

## CHAPTER 25

**Appeal to Caesar.** ¹Three days after his arrival in the province, Festus went up from Caesarea to Jerusalem ²where the chief priests and Jewish leaders presented him their formal charges

against Paul.<sup>‡</sup> They asked him ³as a favor to have him sent to Jerusalem, for they were plotting to kill him along the way. ⁴Festus replied that Paul was being held in custody in Caesarea and that he himself would be returning there shortly. ⁵He said, "Let your authorities come down with me, and if this man has done something improper, let them accuse him."

⁶After spending no more than eight or ten days with them, he went down to Caesarea, and on the following day took his seat on the tribunal and ordered that Paul be brought in. ⁷When he appeared, the Jews who had come down from Jerusalem surrounded him and brought many serious charges against him, which they were unable to prove. ⁸In defending himself Paul said, "I have committed no crime either against the Jewish law or against the temple or against Caesar." ⁹§Then Festus, wishing to ingratiate himself with the Jews, said to Paul in reply, "Are you willing to go up to Jerusalem and there stand trial before me on these charges?" ¹⁰Paul answered, "I am standing before the tribunal of Caesar; this is where I should be tried. I have committed no crime against the Jews, as you very well know. ¹¹If I have committed a crime or done anything deserving death, I do not seek to escape the death penalty; but if there is no substance to the charges they are bringing against me, then no one has the right to hand me over to them. I appeal to Caesar." ¹²Then Festus, after conferring with his council, replied, "You have appealed to Caesar. To Caesar you will go."

**Paul Before King Agrippa.** ¹³When a few days had passed, King Agrippa and Bernice<sup>¶</sup> arrived in Caesarea on a visit to Festus. ¹⁴Since they spent several days there, Festus referred Paul's case to the king, saying, "There is a man here left in custody by Felix.<sup>m</sup> ¹⁵When I was in Jerusalem the chief priests and the elders of the Jews brought charges against him and demanded his condemnation. ¹⁶I answered them that it was not Roman practice to hand over an accused person before he has faced his accusers and had the opportunity to defend himself against their charge. ¹⁷So when [they] came together here, I made no delay; the next day I took my seat on the tribunal and ordered the man to be brought in. ¹⁸ⁿHis accusers stood around him, but did

---

\*[24:24–25] The way of Christian discipleship greatly disquiets Felix, who has entered into an adulterous marriage with Drusilla, daughter of Herod Agrippa I. This marriage provides the background for the topics Paul speaks about and about which Felix does not want to hear.

†[24:27] Very little is known of Porcius Festus who was a procurator of Judea from A.D. 60 to 62.

‡[25:2] Even after two years the animosity toward Paul in Jerusalem had not subsided (see Acts 24:27).

§[25:9–12] Paul refuses to acknowledge that the Sanhedrin in Jerusalem has any jurisdiction over him now (Acts 25:11). Paul uses his right as a Roman citizen to appeal his case to the jurisdiction of the Emperor (Nero, ca. A.D. 60) (Acts 25:12). This move broke the deadlock between Roman protective custody of Paul and the plan of his enemies to kill him (25:3).

¶[25:13] **King Agrippa and Bernice**: brother and sister, children of Herod Agrippa I whose activities against the Jerusalem community are mentioned in Acts 12:1–19. Agrippa II was a petty ruler over small areas in northern Palestine and some villages in Perea. His influence on the Jewish population of Palestine was insignificant.

g. [24:14] 24:5.  h. [24:15] Dn 12:2; Jn 5:28–29.  i. [24:16] 23:1.
j. [24:17] Rom 15:25–26; Gal 2:10.  k. [24:18–19] 21:26–30.
l. [24:21] 23:6; 24:15.

m. [25:14] 24:27.  n. [25:18–19] 18:14–15; 23:29.

not charge him with any of the crimes I suspected. [19]Instead they had some issues with him about their own religion and about a certain Jesus who had died but who Paul claimed was alive. [20]Since I was at a loss how to investigate this controversy, I asked if he were willing to go to Jerusalem and there stand trial on these charges. [21]And when Paul appealed that he be held in custody for the Emperor's decision, I ordered him held until I could send him to Caesar." [22]Agrippa said to Festus, "I too should like to hear this man." He replied, "Tomorrow you will hear him."

[23]The next day Agrippa and Bernice came with great ceremony and entered the audience hall in the company of cohort commanders and the prominent men of the city and, by command of Festus, Paul was brought in. [24]And Festus said, "King Agrippa and all you here present with us, look at this man about whom the whole Jewish populace petitioned me here and in Jerusalem, clamoring that he should live no longer. [25]I found, however, that he had done nothing deserving death, and so when he appealed to the Emperor, I decided to send him. [26]But I have nothing definite to write about him to our sovereign; therefore I have brought him before all of you, and particularly before you, King Agrippa, so that I may have something to write as a result of this investigation. [27]For it seems senseless to me to send up a prisoner without indicating the charges against him."

## CHAPTER 26

**King Agrippa Hears Paul.** [1]Then Agrippa said to Paul, "You may now speak on your own behalf." So Paul stretched out his hand and began his defense. [2]*"I count myself fortunate, King Agrippa, that I am to defend myself before you today against all the charges made against me by the Jews, [3]especially since you are an expert in all the Jewish customs and controversies. And therefore I beg you to listen patiently. [4]My manner of living from my youth, a life spent from the beginning among my people[†] and in Jerusalem, all [the] Jews know. [5]*They have known about me from the start, if they are willing to testify, that I have lived my life as a Pharisee, the strictest party of our religion. [6]*But now I am standing trial because of my hope in the promise made by God to our ancestors. [7]Our twelve tribes hope to attain to that promise as they fervently worship God day and night; and

on account of this hope I am accused by Jews, O king. [8]Why is it thought unbelievable among you that God raises the dead? [9]*I myself once thought that I had to do many things against the name of Jesus the Nazorean, [10]and I did so in Jerusalem. I imprisoned many of the holy ones with the authorization I received from the chief priests, and when they were to be put to death I cast my vote against them.[r] [11]Many times, in synagogue after synagogue, I punished them in an attempt to force them to blaspheme; I was so enraged against them that I pursued them even to foreign cities.

[12]"On one such occasion I was traveling to Damascus with the authorization and commission of the chief priests. [13]*At midday, along the way, O king, I saw a light from the sky, brighter than the sun, shining around me and my traveling companions.[t] [14]We all fell to the ground and I heard a voice saying to me in Hebrew, 'Saul, Saul, why are you persecuting me?[u] It is hard for you to kick against the goad.'[‡] [15]And I said, 'Who are you, sir?' And the Lord replied, 'I am Jesus whom you are persecuting.[v] [16]Get up now, and stand on your feet.[w] I have appeared to you for this purpose, to appoint you as a servant and witness of what you have seen [of me] and what you will be shown.[§] [17]I shall deliver you from this people and from the Gentiles to whom I send you,[x] [18]to open their eyes[¶] that they may turn from darkness to light and from the power of Satan to God, so that they may obtain forgiveness of sins and an inheritance among those who have been consecrated by faith in me.'[y]

[19]"And so, King Agrippa, I was not disobedient to the heavenly vision. [20]On the contrary, first to those in Damascus and in Jerusalem and throughout the whole country of Judea, and then to the Gentiles, I preached the need to repent and turn to God, and to do works giving evidence of repentance. [21]*That is why the Jews seized me [when I was] in the temple and tried to kill me. [22]*But I have enjoyed God's help to this very day, and so I stand here testifying to small and great alike, saying nothing different

---

‡[26:14] **In Hebrew:** see note on Acts 21:40. **It is hard for you to kick against the goad:** this proverb is commonly found in Greek literature and in this context signifies the senselessness and ineffectiveness of any opposition to the divine influence in his life.

§[26:16] The words of Jesus directed to Paul here reflect the dialogues between Christ and Ananias (Acts 9:15) and between Ananias and Paul (Acts 22:14–15) in the two previous accounts of Paul's conversion.

¶[26:18] **To open their eyes:** though no mention is made of Paul's blindness in this account (cf. Acts 9:8–9, 12, 18; 22:11–13), the task he is commissioned to perform is the removal of other people's spiritual blindness.

---

*[26:2–23] Paul's final defense speech in Acts is now made before a king (see Acts 9:15). In the speech Paul presents himself as a zealous Pharisee and Christianity as the logical development of Pharisaic Judaism. The story of his conversion is recounted for the third time in Acts in this speech (see note on Acts 9:1–19).

†[26:4] **Among my people:** that is, among the Jews.

---

o. [26:5] Phil 3:5–6; Gal 1:13–14; 2 Cor 11:22.   p. [26:6–8] 23:6; 24:15, 21; 28:20.

q. [26:9–11] 8:3; 9:1–2; 22:19; Phil 3:6.   r. [26:10] 9:14.   s. [26:13–14] 9:7.   t. [26:13] 9:3; 22:6.   u. [26:14] 9:4; 22:7.   v. [26:15] 9:5; 22:8; Mt 25:40.   w. [26:16] 9:6; 22:10; Ez 2:1.   x. [26:17] Jer 1:7.   y. [26:18] Is 42:7, 16; 61:1 LXX; Col 1:13.   z. [26:21] 21:31.   a. [26:22–23] 3:18; Lk 24:26–27, 44–47.

from what the prophets and Moses foretold,* ²³that the Messiah must suffer† and that, as the first to rise from the dead, he would proclaim light both to our people and to the Gentiles."ᵇ

**Reactions to Paul's Speech.** ²⁴While Paul was so speaking in his defense, Festus said in a loud voice, "You are mad, Paul; much learning is driving you mad." ²⁵But Paul replied, "I am not mad, most excellent Festus; I am speaking words of truth and reason. ²⁶The king knows about these matters and to him I speak boldly, for I cannot believe that [any] of this has escaped his notice; this was not done in a corner.‡ ²⁷King Agrippa, do you believe the prophets?§ I know you believe." ²⁸Then Agrippa said to Paul, "You will soon persuade me to play the Christian." ²⁹Paul replied, "I would pray to God that sooner or later not only you but all who listen to me today might become as I am except for these chains."

³⁰Then the king rose, and with him the governor and Bernice and the others who sat with them. ³¹And after they had withdrawn they said to one another, "This man is doing nothing [at all] that deserves death or imprisonment." ³²And Agrippa said to Festus, "This man could have been set free if he had not appealed to Caesar."ᶜ

## CHAPTER 27

**Departure for Rome.** ¹**When it was decided that we should sail to Italy, they handed Paul and some other prisoners over to a centurion named Julius of the Cohort Augusta.†† ²We went on board a ship from Adramyttium bound for ports in the province of Asia and set sail. Aristarchus, a Macedonian from Thessalonica, was with us.ᵈ ³On the following day we put in at Sidon where Julius was kind enough to allow Paul to visit his friends who took care of him. ⁴From there we put out to sea and sailed around the sheltered side of Cyprus because of the headwinds, ⁵and crossing the open sea off the coast of Cilicia and Pamphylia we came to Myra in Lycia.

**Storm and Shipwreck.** ⁶There the centurion found an Alexandrian ship that was sailing to Italy and put us on board. ⁷For many days we made little headway, arriving at Cnidus only with difficulty, and because the wind would not permit us to continue our course we sailed for the sheltered side of Crete off Salmone. ⁸We sailed past it with difficulty and reached a place called Fair Havens, near which was the city of Lasea.

⁹Much time had now passed and sailing had become hazardous because the time of the fast‡‡ had already gone by, so Paul warned them,ᵉ ¹⁰"Men, I can see that this voyage will result in severe damage and heavy loss not only to the cargo and the ship, but also to our lives." ¹¹The centurion, however, paid more attention to the pilot and to the owner of the ship than to what Paul said. ¹²Since the harbor was unfavorably situated for spending the winter, the majority planned to put out to sea from there in the hope of reaching Phoenix, a port in Crete facing westnorthwest, there to spend the winter.

¹³A south wind blew gently, and thinking they had attained their objective, they weighed anchor and sailed along close to the coast of Crete. ¹⁴Before long an offshore wind of hurricane force called a "Northeaster" struck. ¹⁵Since the ship was caught up in it and could not head into the wind we gave way and let ourselves be driven. ¹⁶We passed along the sheltered side of an island named Cauda and managed only with difficulty to get the dinghy under control. ¹⁷They hoisted it aboard, then used cables to undergird the ship. Because of their fear that they would run aground on the shoal of Syrtis, they lowered the drift anchor and were carried along in this way. ¹⁸We were being pounded by the storm so violently that the next day they jettisoned some cargo, ¹⁹and on the third day with their own hands they threw even the ship's tackle overboard. ²⁰Neither the sun nor the stars were visible for many days, and no small storm raged. Finally, all hope of our surviving was taken away.

²¹When many would no longer eat, Paul stood among them and said, "Men, you should have taken my advice and not have set sail from Crete and you would have avoided this disastrous loss. ²²I urge you now to keep up your courage; not one of you will be lost, only the ship. ²³For last night an angel of the God to whom [I] belong and whom I serve stood by

---

* [26:22] **Saying nothing different from what the prophets and Moses foretold:** see note on Lk 18:31.

† [26:23] **That the Messiah must suffer:** see note on Lk 24:26.

‡ [26:26] **Not done in a corner:** for Luke, this Greek proverb expresses his belief that he is presenting a story about Jesus and the church that is already well known. As such, the entire history of Christianity is public knowledge and incontestable. Luke presents his story in this way to provide "certainty" to his readers about the instructions they have received (Lk 1:4).

§ [26:27,28] If the Christian missionaries proclaim nothing different from what the Old Testament prophets had proclaimed (Acts 26:22–23), then the logical outcome for the believing Jew, according to Luke, is to become a Christian.

¶ [26:31–32] In recording the episode of Paul's appearance before Agrippa, Luke wishes to show that, when Paul's case was judged impartially, no grounds for legal action against him were found (see Acts 23:29; 25:25).

** [27:1–28:16] Here Luke has written a stirring account of adventure on the high seas, incidental to his main purpose of showing how well Paul got along with his captors and how his prophetic influence saved the lives of all on board. The recital also establishes the existence of Christian communities in Puteoli and Rome. This account of the voyage and shipwreck also constitutes the final "we-section" in Acts (see note on Acts 16:10–17).

†† [27:1] **Cohort Augusta:** the presence of a Cohort Augusta in Syria during the first century A.D. is attested in inscriptions. Whatever the historical background to this information given by Luke may be, the name Augusta serves to increase the prominence and prestige of the prisoner Paul whose custodians bear so important a Roman name.

‡‡ [27:9] **The time of the fast:** the fast kept on the occasion of the Day of Atonement (Lv 16:29–31), which occurred in late September or early October.

---

b. [26:23] Is 42:6; 49:6; Lk 2:32; 1 Cor 15:20–23.    c. [26:32] 25:11–12.    d. [27:2] 19:29; 20:4.

e. [27:9] Lv 16:29–31.

me [24]and said, 'Do not be afraid, Paul. You are destined to stand before Caesar; and behold, for your sake, God has granted safety to all who are sailing with you.'[f] [25]Therefore, keep up your courage, men; I trust in God that it will turn out as I have been told. [26]We are destined to run aground on some island."

[27]On the fourteenth night, as we were still being driven about on the Adriatic Sea, toward midnight the sailors began to suspect that they were nearing land. [28]They took soundings and found twenty fathoms; a little farther on, they again took soundings and found fifteen fathoms. [29]Fearing that we would run aground on a rocky coast, they dropped four anchors from the stern and prayed for day to come. [30]The sailors then tried to abandon ship; they lowered the dinghy to the sea on the pretext of going to lay out anchors from the bow. [31]But Paul said to the centurion and the soldiers, "Unless these men stay with the ship, you cannot be saved." [32]So the soldiers cut the ropes of the dinghy and set it adrift.

[33]Until the day began to dawn, Paul kept urging all to take some food. He said, "Today is the fourteenth day that you have been waiting, going hungry and eating nothing. [34]I urge you, therefore, to take some food; it will help you survive. Not a hair of the head of anyone of you will be lost." [35]When he said this, he took bread,[*] gave thanks to God in front of them all, broke it, and began to eat.[g] [36]They were all encouraged, and took some food themselves. [37]In all, there were two hundred seventy-six of us on the ship. [38]After they had eaten enough, they lightened the ship by throwing the wheat into the sea.

[39]When day came they did not recognize the land, but made out a bay with a beach. They planned to run the ship ashore on it, if they could. [40]So they cast off the anchors and abandoned them to the sea, and at the same time they unfastened the lines of the rudders, and hoisting the foresail into the wind, they made for the beach. [41]But they struck a sandbar and ran the ship aground. The bow was wedged in and could not be moved, but the stern began to break up under the pounding [of the waves]. [42]The soldiers planned to kill the prisoners so that none might swim away and escape, [43]but the centurion wanted to save Paul and so kept them from carrying out their plan. He ordered those who could swim to jump overboard first and get to the shore, [44]and then the rest, some on planks, others on debris from the ship. In this way, all reached shore safely.

## CHAPTER 28

**Winter in Malta.** [1]Once we had reached safety we learned that the island was called Malta. [2]The natives showed us extraordinary hospitality; they lit a fire and welcomed all of us because it had begun to rain and was cold. [3]Paul had gathered a bundle of brushwood and was putting it on the fire when a viper, escaping from the heat, fastened on his hand. [4]When the natives saw the snake hanging from his hand, they said to one another, "This man must certainly be a murderer; though he escaped the sea, Justice[†] has not let him remain alive." [5]But he shook the snake off into the fire and suffered no harm. [6]They were expecting him to swell up or suddenly to fall down dead but, after waiting a long time and seeing nothing unusual happen to him, they changed their minds and began to say that he was a god.[h] [7]In the vicinity of that place were lands belonging to a man named Publius, the chief of the island. He welcomed us and received us cordially as his guests for three days. [8]It so happened that the father of Publius was sick with a fever and dysentery. Paul visited him and, after praying, laid his hands on him and healed him. [9]After this had taken place, the rest of the sick on the island came to Paul and were cured. [10]They paid us great honor and when we eventually set sail they brought us the provisions we needed.

**Arrival in Rome.** [11]Three months later we set sail on a ship that had wintered at the island. It was an Alexandrian ship with the Dioscuri[‡] as its figurehead. [12]We put in at Syracuse and stayed there three days, [13]and from there we sailed round the coast and arrived at Rhegium. After a day, a south wind came up and in two days we reached Puteoli. [14]There we found some brothers and were urged to stay with them for seven days. And thus we came to Rome. [15]The brothers from there heard about us and came as far as the Forum of Appius and Three Taverns to meet us. On seeing them, Paul gave thanks to God and took courage. [16]When he entered Rome,[§] Paul was allowed to live by himself, with the soldier who was guarding him.

**Testimony to Jews in Rome.** [17]¶Three days later he called together the leaders of the Jews. When they had gathered he said to them, "My brothers, although I had done nothing against our people or our ancestral customs, I was handed over to the Romans as a prisoner from Jerusalem.[i]

---

†[28:4] **Justice**: in Greek mythology, the pursuing goddess of vengeance and justice.

‡[28:11] **Dioscuri**: that is, the Twin Brothers, Castor and Pollux, the sons of Zeus and the patrons of the sailors.

§[28:16] With Paul's arrival in Rome, the programmatic spread of the word of the Lord to "the ends of the earth" (Acts 1:8) is accomplished. In Rome, Paul is placed under house arrest, and under this mild form of custody he is allowed to proclaim the word in the capital of the civilized world of his day.

¶[28:17–22] Paul's first act in Rome is to learn from the leaders of the Jewish community whether the Jews of Jerusalem plan to pursue their case against him before the Roman jurisdiction. He is informed that no such plan is afoot, but that the Jews of Rome have heard the Christian teaching denounced. Paul's offer to explain it to them is readily accepted.

---

*[27:35] **He took bread . . .**: the words recall the traditional language of the celebration of the Eucharist (see Lk 22:19).

f. [27:24] 23:11.  g. [27:35] Mt 15:36; Mk 6:41; 8:6; Lk 22:19; 1 Cor 11:23–24.

h. [28:6] 14:11.  i. [28:17] 24:12–13; 25:8.

[18]After trying my case the Romans wanted to release me, because they found nothing against me deserving the death penalty.[j] [19]But when the Jews objected, I was obliged to appeal to Caesar, even though I had no accusation to make against my own nation.[k] [20]This is the reason, then, I have requested to see you and to speak with you, for it is on account of the hope of Israel* that I wear these chains."[l] [21]They answered him, "We have received no letters from Judea about you, nor has any of the brothers arrived with a damaging report or rumor about you. [22]But we should like to hear you present your views, for we know that this sect is denounced everywhere."[m]

[23]So they arranged a day with him and came to his lodgings in great numbers. From early morning until evening, he expounded his position to them, bearing witness to the kingdom of God and trying to convince them about Jesus from the law of Moses and the prophets. [24]Some were convinced by what he had said, while others did not believe. [25]†Without reaching any agreement among themselves they began

to leave; then Paul made one final statement. "Well did the holy Spirit speak to your ancestors through the prophet Isaiah, saying:

[26] 'Go to this people and say:"
    You shall indeed hear but not understand.
        You shall indeed look but never see.
[27] Gross is the heart of this people;
        they will not hear with their ears;
            they have closed their eyes,
    so they may not see with their eyes
        and hear with their ears
    and understand with their heart and be
            converted,
        and I heal them.'

[28]Let it be known to you that this salvation of God has been sent to the Gentiles; they will listen."[29]‡

[30]§He remained for two full years in his lodgings. He received all who came to him, [31]and with complete assurance and without hindrance he proclaimed the kingdom of God and taught about the Lord Jesus Christ.

---

*[28:20] **The hope of Israel**: in the words of Paul (Acts 23:6), Luke has identified this hope as hope in the resurrection of the dead.

†[28:25–28] Paul's final words in Acts reflect a major concern of Luke's writings: how the salvation promised in the Old Testament, accomplished by Jesus, and offered first to Israel (Acts 13:26), has now been offered to and accepted by the Gentiles. Quoting Is 6:9–10, Paul presents the scriptural support for his indictment of his fellow Jews who refuse to accept the message he proclaims. Their rejection leads to its proclamation among the Gentiles.

‡[28:29] The Western text has added here a verse that is not found in the best Greek manuscripts: "And when he had said this, the Jews left, seriously arguing among themselves."

§[28:30–31] Although the ending of Acts may seem to be abrupt, Luke has now completed his story with the establishment of Paul and the proclamation of Christianity in Rome. Paul's confident and unhindered proclamation of the gospel in Rome forms the climax to the story whose outline was provided in Acts 1:8—"You will be my witnesses in Jerusalem . . . and to the ends of the earth."

---

j. [28:18] 23:29; 25:25; 26:31–32.   k. [28:19] 25:11.   l. [28:20] 23:6; 24:15, 21; 26:6–8.   m. [28:22] 24:5, 14.

n. [28:26] Is 6:9–10; Mt 13:14–15; Mk 4:12; Lk 8:10; Jn 12:40; Rom 11:8.   o. [28:28] 13:46; 18:6; Ps 67:2; Is 40:5 LXX; Lk 3:6.

# NEW TESTAMENT LETTERS

In the New Testament canon, between the Acts of the Apostles and Revelation, there are twenty-one documents that take the form of letters or epistles. Most of these are actual letters, but some are more like treatises in the guise of letters. In a few cases even some of the more obvious elements of the letter form are absent; see the Introductions to Hebrews and to 1 John.

The virtually standard form found in these documents, though with some variation, is dependent upon the conventions of letter writing common in the ancient world, but these were modified to suit the purposes of Christian writers. The New Testament letters usually begin with a greeting including an identification of the sender or senders and of the recipients. Next comes a prayer, usually in the form of a thanksgiving. The body of the letter provides an exposition of Christian teaching, usually provoked by concrete circumstances, and generally also draws conclusions regarding ethical behavior. There often follows a discussion of practical matters, such as the writer's travel plans, and the letter concludes with further advice and a formula of farewell.

Fourteen of the twenty-one letters have been traditionally attributed to Paul. One of these, the Letter to the Hebrews, does not itself claim to be the work of Paul; when it was accepted into the canon after much discussion, it was attached at the very end of the Pauline corpus. The other thirteen identify Paul as their author, but most scholars believe that some of them were actually written by his disciples; see the Introductions to Ephesians, Colossians, 2 Thessalonians, and 1 Timothy.

Four of the letters in the Pauline corpus (Ephesians, Philippians, Colossians, and Philemon) are called the "Captivity Epistles" because in each of them the author speaks of being in prison at the time of writing. Three others (1–2 Timothy and Titus) are known as the "Pastoral Epistles" because, addressed to individuals rather than communities, they give advice to disciples about caring for the flock. The letters of the Pauline corpus are arranged in roughly descending order of length from Romans to Philemon, with Hebrews added at the end.

The other seven letters of the New Testament that follow the Pauline corpus are collectively referred to as the "Catholic Epistles." This term, which means "universal," refers to the fact that most of them are directed not to a single Christian community, as are most of the Pauline letters, but to a wider audience; see the Introduction to the catholic letters. Three of them (1–2–3 John) are closely related to the fourth gospel and thus belong to the Johannine corpus. The catholic letters, like those of the Pauline corpus, are also arranged in roughly descending order of length, but the three Johannine letters are kept together and Jude is placed at the end.

The genuine letters of Paul are earlier in date than any of our written gospels. The dates of the other New Testament letters are more difficult to determine, but for the most part they belong to the second and third Christian generations rather than to the first.

# THE LETTER TO THE
# ROMANS

Of all the letters of Paul, that to the Christians at Rome has long held pride of place. It is the longest and most systematic unfolding of the apostle's thought, expounding the gospel of God's righteousness that saves all who believe (Rom 1:16–17); it reflects a universal outlook, with special implications for Israel's relation to the church (Rom 9–11). Yet, like all Paul's letters, Romans too arose out of a specific situation, when the apostle wrote from Greece, likely Corinth, between A.D. 56 and 58 (cf. Acts 20:2–3).

Paul at that time was about to leave for Jerusalem with a collection of funds for the impoverished Jewish Christian believers there, taken up from his predominantly Gentile congregations (Rom 15:25–27). He planned then to travel on to Rome and to enlist support there for a mission to Spain (Rom 15:24, 28). Such a journey had long been on his mind (Rom 1:9–13; 15:23). Now, with much missionary preaching successfully accomplished in the East (Rom 15:19), he sought new opportunities in the West (Rom 15:20–21), in order to complete the divine plan of evangelization in the Roman world. Yet he recognized that the visit to Jerusalem would be hazardous (Rom 15:30–32), and we know from Acts that Paul was arrested there and came to Rome only in chains, as a prisoner (Acts 21–28, especially Acts 21:30–33 and Acts 28:14, 30–31).

The existence of a Christian community in Rome antedates Paul's letter there. When it arose, likely within the sizable Jewish population at Rome, and how, we do not know. The Roman historian Suetonius mentions an edict of the Emperor Claudius about A.D. 49 ordering the expulsion of Jews from Rome in connection with a certain "Chrestus," probably involving a dispute in the Jewish community over Jesus as the Messiah ("Christus"). According to Acts 18:2, Aquila and Priscilla (or Prisca, as in Rom 16:3) were among those driven out; from them, in Corinth, Paul may have learned about conditions in the church at Rome.

Opinions vary as to whether Jewish or Gentile Christians predominated in the house churches (cf. Rom 16:5) in the capital city of the empire at the time Paul wrote. Perhaps already by then Gentile Christians were in the majority. Paul speaks in Romans of both Jews and Gentiles (Rom 3:9, 29; see note on Rom 1:14). The letter also refers to those "weak in faith" (Rom 14:1) and those "who are strong" (Rom 15:1); this terminology may reflect not so much differences between believers of Jewish and of Gentile background, respectively, as an ascetic tendency in some converts (Rom 14:2) combined with Jewish laws about clean and unclean foods (Rom 14:14, 20). The issues were similar to problems that Paul had faced in Corinth (1 Cor 8). If Rom 16 is part of the letter to Rome (see note on Rom 16:1–23), then Paul had considerable information about conditions in Rome through all these people there whom he knew, and our letter does not just reflect a generalized picture of an earlier situation in Corinth.

In any case, Paul writes to introduce himself and his message to the Christians at Rome, seeking to enlist their support for the proposed mission to Spain. He therefore employs formulations likely familiar to the Christians at Rome; see note on the confessional material at Rom 1:3–4 and compare Rom 3:25–26; 4:25. He cites the Old Testament frequently (Rom 1:17; 3:10–18; 4; 9:7, 12–13, 15, 17, 25–29, 33; 10:5–13, 15–21; 15:9–12). The gospel Paul presents is meant to be a familiar one to those in Rome, even though they heard it first from other preachers.

As the outline below shows, this gospel of Paul (see Rom 16:25) finds its center in salvation and justification through faith in Christ (Rom 1:16–17). While God's wrath is revealed against all sin and wickedness of Gentile and Jew alike (Rom 1:18–3:20), God's power to save by divine righteous or justifying action in Christ is also revealed (Rom 1:16–17; 3:21–5:21). The consequences and implications for those who believe are set forth (Rom 6:1–8:39), as are results for those in Israel (Rom 9–11) who, to Paul's great sorrow (Rom 9:1–5), disbelieve. The apostle's hope is that, just as rejection of the gospel by some in Israel has led to a ministry of salvation for non-Jews, so one day, in God's mercy, "all Israel" will be saved (Rom 11:11–15, 25–29, 30–32). The fuller ethical response of believers is also drawn out, both with reference to life in Christ's body (Rom 12) and with regard to the world (Rom 13:1–7), on the basis of the eschatological situation (Rom 13:11–14) and conditions in the community (Rom 14:1–15:13).

Others have viewed Romans more in the light of Paul's earlier, quite polemical Letter to the Galatians and so see the theme as the relationship between Judaism and Christianity, a topic judged to be much in the minds of the Roman Christians. Each of these religious faiths claimed to be the way of salvation based upon a covenant between God and a people chosen and made the beneficiary of divine gifts. But Christianity regarded itself as the prophetic development and fulfillment of the faith of the Old Testament, declaring that the preparatory Mosaic covenant must now give way to the new and more perfect covenant in Jesus Christ. Paul himself had been the implacable advocate of freedom of Gentiles from the laws of the Mosaic covenant and, especially in Galatia, had refused to allow attempts to impose them on Gentile converts to the gospel. He had witnessed the personal hostilities that developed between the adherents of the two faiths and had written his strongly worded Letter to the Galatians against those Jewish Christians who were seeking to persuade Gentile Christians to adopt the religious practices of Judaism. For him, the purity of the religious understanding of Jesus as the source of salvation would be seriously impaired if Gentile Christians were obligated to amalgamate the two religious faiths.

Still others find the theme of Israel and the church as expressed in Rom 9–11 to be the heart of Romans. Then the implication of Paul's exposition of justification by faith rather than by means of law is that the divine plan of salvation works itself out on a broad theological plane to include the whole of humanity, despite the differences in the content of the given religious system to which a human culture is heir. Romans presents a plan of salvation stretching from Adam through Abraham and Moses to Christ (Rom 4; 5) and on to the future revelation at Christ's parousia (Rom 8:18–25). Its outlook is universal.

Paul's Letter to the Romans is a powerful exposition of the doctrine of the supremacy of Christ and of faith in Christ as the source of salvation. It is an implicit plea to the Christians at Rome, and to all Christians, to hold fast to that faith. They are to resist any pressure put on them to accept a doctrine of salvation through works of the law (see note on Rom 10:4). At the same time they are not to exaggerate Christian freedom as an abdication of responsibility for others (Rom 12:1–2) or as a repudiation of God's law and will (see notes on Rom 3:9–26; 3:31; 7:7–12, 13–25).

The principal divisions of the Letter to the Romans are the following:

   I.  Address (1:1–15)
  II.  Humanity Lost Without the Gospel (1:16–3:20)
 III.  Justification Through Faith in Christ (3:21–5:21)
 IV.  Justification and the Christian Life (6:1–8:39)
  V.  Jews and Gentiles in God's Plan (9:1–11:36)
 VI.  The Duties of Christians (12:1–15:13)
VII.  Conclusion (15:14–16:27)

# I. ADDRESS

## CHAPTER 1

**Greeting.**[*] [1]Paul, a slave of Christ Jesus,[†] called to be an apostle and set apart for the gospel of God,[a] [2]which he promised previously through his prophets in the holy scriptures,[b] [3‡]the gospel about his Son, descended from David according to the flesh,[c] [4]but established as Son of God in power according to the spirit of holiness through resurrection from the dead, Jesus Christ our Lord.[d] [5§]Through him we have received the grace of apostleship, to bring about the obedience of faith, for the sake of his name, among all the Gentiles,[e] [6]among whom are you also, who are called to belong to Jesus Christ;[f] [7]to all the beloved of God in Rome, called to be holy.[¶] Grace to you and peace from God our Father and the Lord Jesus Christ.[g]

**Thanksgiving.** [8]First, I give thanks[**] to my God through Jesus Christ for all of you, because your faith is heralded throughout the world.[h] [9]God is my witness, whom I serve with my spirit in proclaiming the gospel of his Son, that I remember you constantly,[i] [10††]always asking in my prayers that somehow by God's will I may at last find my way clear to come to you.[j] [11]For I long to see you, that I may share with you some spiritual gift so that you may be strengthened,[k] [12]that is, that you and I may be mutually encouraged by one another's faith, yours and mine. [13]I do not want you to be unaware, brothers,[‡‡] that I often planned to come to you, though I was prevented until now, that I might harvest some fruit among you, too, as among the rest of the Gentiles.[l] [14]To Greeks[§§] and non-Greeks alike, to the wise and the ignorant, I am under obligation; [15]that is why I am eager to preach the gospel also to you in Rome.[m]

# II. HUMANITY LOST WITHOUT THE GOSPEL

**God's Power for Salvation.**[¶¶] [16]For I am not ashamed of the gospel. It is the power of God for the salvation of everyone who believes: for Jew first, and then Greek.[n] [17]For in it is revealed

---

*[1:1–7] In Paul's letters the greeting or *praescriptio* follows a standard form, though with variations. It is based upon the common Greco-Roman epistolary practice, but with the addition of Semitic and specifically Christian elements. The three basic components are: name of sender; name of addressee; greeting. In identifying himself, Paul often adds phrases to describe his apostolic mission; this element is more developed in Romans than in any other letter. Elsewhere he associates co-workers with himself in the greeting: Sosthenes (1 Corinthians), Timothy (2 Corinthians; Philippians; Philemon) Silvanus (1 Thessalonians–2 Thessalonians). The standard secular greeting was the infinitive *chairein*, "greetings." Paul uses instead the similar-sounding *charis*, "grace," together with the Semitic greeting *šālôm* (Greek *eirēnē*), "peace." These gifts, foreshadowed in God's dealings with Israel (see Nm 6:24–26), have been poured out abundantly in Christ, and Paul wishes them to his readers. In Romans the Pauline *praescriptio* is expanded and expressed in a formal tone; it emphasizes Paul's office as apostle to the Gentiles. Rom 1:3–4 stress the gospel or *kerygma*, Rom 1:2 the fulfillment of God's promise, and Rom 1:1, 5 Paul's office. On his call, see Gal 1:15–16; 1 Cor 9:1; 15:8–10; Acts 9:1–22; 22:3–16; 26:4–18.

†[1:1] **Slave of Christ Jesus:** Paul applies the term slave to himself in order to express his undivided allegiance to the Lord of the church, the Master of all, including slaves and masters. "No one can serve (i.e., be a slave to) two masters," said Jesus (Mt 6:24). It is this aspect of the slave-master relationship rather than its degrading implications that Paul emphasizes when he discusses Christian commitment.

‡[1:3–4] Paul here cites an early confession that proclaims Jesus' sonship as messianic descendant of David (cf. Mt 22:42; 2 Tm 2:8; Rev 22:16) and as Son of God by the resurrection. As "life-giving spirit" (1 Cor 15:45), Jesus Christ is able to communicate the Spirit to those who believe in him.

§[1:5] Paul recalls his apostolic office, implying that the Romans know something of his history. **The obedience of faith:** as Paul will show at length in chaps. 6–8 and 12–15, faith in God's justifying action in Jesus Christ relates one to God's gift of the new life that is made possible through the death and resurrection of Jesus Christ and the activity of the holy Spirit (see especially Rom 8:1–11).

¶[1:7] **Called to be holy:** Paul often refers to Christians as "the holy ones" or "the saints." The Israelite community was called a "holy assembly" because they had been separated for the worship and service of the Lord (see Lv 11:44; 23:1–44). The Christian community regarded its members as sanctified by baptism (Rom 6:22; 15:16; 1 Cor 6:11; Eph 5:26–27). Christians are called to holiness (1 Cor 1:2; 1 Thes 4:7), that

is, they are called to make their lives conform to the gift they have already received.

**[1:8] In Greco-Roman letters, the greeting was customarily followed by a prayer. The Pauline letters usually include this element (except Gal and 1 and 2 Timothy) expressed in Christian thanksgiving formulas and usually stating the principal theme of the letter. In 2 Corinthians the thanksgiving becomes a blessing, and in Ephesians it is preceded by a lengthy blessing. Sometimes the thanksgiving is blended into the body of the letter, especially in 1 Thessalonians. In Romans it is stated briefly.

††[1:10–12] Paul lays the groundwork for his more detailed statement in Rom 15:22–24 about his projected visit to Rome.

‡‡[1:13] **Brothers** is idiomatic for all Paul's "kin in Christ," all those who believe in the gospel; it includes women as well as men (cf. Rom 4:3).

§§[1:14] **Greeks and non-Greeks:** literally, "Greeks and barbarians." As a result of Alexander's conquests, Greek became the standard international language of the Mediterranean world. **Greeks** in Paul's statement therefore means people who know Greek or who have been influenced by Greek culture. **Non-Greeks** were people whose cultures remained substantially unaffected by Greek influences. Greeks called such people "barbarians" (cf. Acts 28:2), meaning people whose speech was foreign. Roman citizens would scarcely classify themselves as such, and Nero, who was reigning when Paul wrote this letter, prided himself on his admiration for Greek culture. **Under obligation:** Paul will expand on the theme of obligation in Rom 13:8; 15:1, 27.

¶¶[1:16–17] The principal theme of the letter is salvation through faith. **I am not ashamed of the gospel:** Paul is not ashamed to proclaim the gospel, despite the criticism that Jews and Gentiles leveled against the proclamation of the crucified savior; cf. 1 Cor 1:23–24. Paul affirms, however, that it is precisely through the crucifixion and resurrection of Jesus that God's saving will and power become manifest. **Jew first** (cf. Rom 2:9–10) means that Jews especially, in view of the example of Abraham (Rom 4), ought to be the leaders in the response of faith.

---

a. [1:1] Gal 1:10; Phil 1:1; Jas 1:1 / Acts 9:15; 13:2; 1 Cor 1:1; Gal 1:15; Ti 1:1.  b. [1:2] 16:25–26; Ti 1:2.  c. [1:3] 9:5; 2 Sm 7:12; Mt 1:1; Mk 12:35; Jn 7:42; Acts 13:22–23; 2 Tm 2:8; Rev 22:16.  d. [1:4] 10:9; Acts 13:33; Phil 3:10.  e. [1:5] 15:15; Gal 2:7, 9 / 15:18; Acts 9:15; 26:16–18; Gal 1:16; 2:7, 9.  f. [1:6] 1 Cor 1:9.  g. [1:7] Nm 6:25–26; 1 Cor 1:2–3; 2 Cor 1:1–2.

h. [1:8] 16:19; 1 Thes 1:8.  i. [1:9] 2 Cor 1:23; Eph 1:16; Phil 1:8; 1 Thes 1:2; 2:5, 10; 2 Tm 1:3.  j. [1:10] 15:23, 32; Acts 18:21; 1 Cor 4:19; 1 Thes 2:17.  k. [1:11] 1 Thes 2:17; 3:10.  l. [1:13] 15:22; Jn 15:16; Acts 19:21.  m. [1:15] Acts 28:30–31.  n. [1:16] Ps 119:46; 1 Cor 1:18, 24 / Rom 2:9; Acts 3:26; 13:46.

the righteousness of God from faith to faith;* as it is written, "The one who is righteous by faith will live."°

**Punishment of Idolaters.** ¹⁸†The wrath‡ of God§ is indeed being revealed from heaven against every impiety and wickedness^p of those who suppress the truth by their wickedness. ¹⁹For what can be known about God is evident to them, because God made it evident to them.^q ²⁰Ever since the creation of the world, his invisible attributes of eternal power and divinity have been able to be understood and perceived in what he has made.^r As a result, they have no excuse; ²¹for although they knew God they did not accord him glory as God or give him thanks. Instead, they became vain in their reasoning, and their senseless minds were darkened.^s ²²While claiming to be wise,^t they became fools ²³and exchanged the glory of the immortal God for the likeness of an image of mortal man or of birds or of four-legged animals or of snakes.^u

²⁴Therefore, God handed them over to impurity through the lusts of their hearts¶ for the mutual degradation of their bodies.^v ²⁵They exchanged the truth of God for a lie and revered and worshiped the creature rather than the creator, who is blessed forever. Amen.^w ²⁶Therefore, God handed them over to degrading passions. Their females exchanged natural relations for unnatural, ²⁷and the males likewise gave up natural relations with females and burned with lust for one another. Males did shameful things with males and thus received in their own persons the due penalty for their perversity.^x ²⁸And since they did not see fit to acknowledge God, God handed them over to their undiscerning mind to do what is improper. ²⁹yThey are filled with every form of wickedness, evil, greed, and malice; full of envy, murder, rivalry, treachery, and spite. They are gossips ³⁰and scandalmongers and they hate God. They are insolent, haughty, boastful, ingenious in their wickedness, and rebellious toward their parents. ³¹They are senseless, faithless, heartless, ruthless. ³²Although they know the just decree of God that all who practice such things deserve death, they not only do them but give approval to those who practice them.^z

## CHAPTER 2

**God's Just Judgment.** ¹**"Therefore, you are without excuse,^a every one of you who passes judgment.†† For by the standard by which you judge another you condemn yourself, since you, the judge, do the very same things. ²We know that the judgment of God on those who do such things is true. ³Do you suppose, then, you who judge those who engage in such things and yet do them yourself, that you will escape the judgment of God?^b ⁴Or do you hold his priceless kindness, forbearance, and patience in low esteem, unaware that the kindness of God would lead you to repentance?^c ⁵By your stubbornness and impenitent heart,^d you are storing up wrath for yourself for the day of wrath and revelation of the just judgment of God, ⁶^ewho will repay

---

*[1:17] **In it is revealed the righteousness of God from faith to faith**: the gospel centers in Jesus Christ, in whom God's saving presence and righteousness in history have been made known. Faith is affirmation of the basic purpose and meaning of the Old Testament as proclamation of divine promise (Rom 1:2; 4:13) and exposure of the inability of humanity to effect its salvation even through covenant law. Faith is the gift of the holy Spirit and denotes acceptance of salvation as God's righteousness, that is, God's gift of a renewed relationship in forgiveness and power for a new life. Faith is response to God's total claim on people and their destiny. **The one who is righteous by faith will live**: see note on Heb 2:4.

†[1:18–3:20] Paul aims to show that all humanity is in a desperate plight and requires God's special intervention if it is to be saved.

‡[1:18–32] In this passage Paul uses themes and rhetoric common in Jewish-Hellenistic mission proclamation (cf. Wis 13:1–14:31) to indict especially the non-Jewish world. The close association of idolatry and immorality is basic, but the generalization needs in all fairness to be balanced against the fact that non-Jewish Christian society on many levels displayed moral attitudes and performance whose quality would challenge much of contemporary Christian culture. Romans themselves expressed abhorrence over devotion accorded to animals in Egypt. Paul's main point is that the wrath of God does not await the end of the world but goes into action at each present moment in humanity's history when misdirected piety serves as a facade for self-interest.

§[1:18] **The wrath of God**: God's reaction to human sinfulness, an Old Testament phrase that expresses the irreconcilable opposition between God and evil (see Is 9:11, 16, 18, 20; 10:4; 30:27). It is not contrary to God's universal love for his creatures, but condemns Israel's turning aside from the covenant obligations. Hosea depicts Yahweh as suffering intensely at the thought of having to punish Israel (Hos 11:8–9). God's wrath was to be poured forth especially on the "Day of Yahweh" and thus took on an eschatological connotation (see Zep 1:15).

¶[1:24] In order to expose the depth of humanity's rebellion against the Creator, **God handed them over to impurity through the lusts of their hearts**. Instead of curbing people's evil interests, God abandoned them to self-indulgence, thereby removing the facade of apparent conformity to the divine will. Subsequently Paul will show that the Mosaic law produces the same effect; cf. Rom 5:20; 7:13–24. The divine judgment expressed here is related to the theme of hardness of heart described in Rom 9:17–18.

**[2:1–3:20] After his general indictment of the Gentile, Paul shows that in spite of special revelation Jews enjoy no advantage in moral status before God (Rom 3:1–8). With the entire human race now declared guilty before God (Rom 3:9–20), Paul will then be able to display the solution for the total problem: salvation through God's redemptive work that is revealed in Christ Jesus for all who believe (Rom 3:21–31).

††[2:1–11] As a first step in his demonstration that Jews enjoy no real moral supremacy over Gentiles, Paul explains that the final judgment will be a review of performance, not of privilege. From this perspective Gentiles stand on an equal footing with Jews, and Jews cannot condemn the sins of Gentiles without condemning themselves.

---

o. [1:17] 3:21–22; Heb 2:4; Gal 3:11; Heb 10:38.   p. [1:18] 2:5, 8–9; Is 66:15; Eph 5:6; Col 3:6.   q. [1:19–32] Wis 13–19; Acts 14:15–17; 17:23–29.   r. [1:20] Jb 12:7–9; Ps 8:4; 19:2; Sir 17:7–9; Is 40:26; Acts 14:17; 17:25–28.   s. [1:21] Eph 4:17–18.   t. [1:22] Wis 13:1–9; Is 5:21; Jer 10:14; Acts 17:29–30; 1 Cor 1:19–21.   u. [1:23] Dt 4:15–19; Ps 106:20; Wis 11:15; 12:24; 13:10–19; Jer 2:11.

v. [1:24] Wis 12:25; 14:22–31; Acts 7:41–42; Eph 4:19.   w. [1:25] 9:5; Jer 13:25–27.   x. [1:27] Lv 18:22; 20:13; Wis 14:26; 1 Cor 6:9; 1 Tm 1:10.   y. [1:29–31] 13:13; Mt 15:19; Mk 7:21–22; Gal 5:19–21; 2 Tm 3:2–4.   z. [1:32] Acts 8:1; 2 Thes 2:12.   a. [2:1] Mt 7:1–2.   b. [2:3] Wis 16:15–16.   c. [2:4] 3:25–26; 9:22; Wis 11:23; 15:1; 2 Pt 3:9, 15.   d. [2:5] Ex 33:3; Acts 7:51; Rev 6:17; 11:18.   e. [2:6] Ps 62:12; Prv 24:12; Sir 16:14; Mt 16:27; Jn 5:29; 2 Cor 5:10.

everyone according to his works:* ⁷eternal life to those who seek glory, honor, and immortality through perseverance in good works, ⁸but wrath and fury to those who selfishly disobey the truth and obey wickedness.ʲ ⁹Yes, affliction and distress will come upon every human being who does evil, Jew first and then Greek. ¹⁰ᵍBut there will be glory, honor, and peace for everyone who does good, Jew first and then Greek. ¹¹ʰThere is no partiality with God.

**Judgment by the Interior Law.**† ¹²All who sin outside the law will also perish without reference to it, and all who sin under the law will be judged in accordance with it.ⁱ ¹³For it is not those who hear the law who are just in the sight of God; rather, those who observe the law will be justified.ʲ ¹⁴For when the Gentiles who do not have the law by nature observe the prescriptions of the law, they are a law for themselves even though they do not have the law.ᵏ ¹⁵They show that the demands of the law are written in their hearts,§ while their conscience also bears witness and their conflicting thoughts accuse or even defend them ¹⁶on the day when, according to my gospel, God will judge people's hidden works through Christ Jesus.ˡ

**Judgment by the Mosaic Law.**¶ ¹⁷Now if you call yourself a Jew and rely on the law and boast of Godᵐ ¹⁸and know his will and are able to discern what is important since you are instructed from the law,ⁿ ¹⁹and if you are confident that you are a guide for the blind and a light for those in darkness,ᵒ ²⁰that you are a trainer of the foolish and teacher of the simple,ᵖ because in the law you have the formulation of knowledge and truth— ²¹then you who teach another, are you failing to teach yourself? You who preach against stealing, do you steal?�q ²²You who forbid adultery, do you commit adultery? You who detest idols, do you rob temples? ²³You who boast of the law, do you dishonor God by breaking the law? ²⁴For, as it is written, "Because of you the name of God is reviled among the Gentiles."**

²⁵"Circumcision, to be sure, has value if you observe the law; but if you break the law, your circumcision has become uncircumcision.ʳ ²⁶Again, if an uncircumcised man keeps the precepts of the law, will he not be considered circumcised?ᵘ ²⁷Indeed, those who are physically uncircumcised but carry out the law will pass judgment on you, with your written law and circumcision, who break the law. ²⁸One is not a Jew outwardly. True circumcision is not outward, in the flesh.ᵛ ²⁹Rather, one is a Jew inwardly, and circumcision is of the heart, in the spirit, not the letter; his praise is not from human beings but from God.ʷ

## CHAPTER 3

**Answers to Objections.** ¹††What advantage is there then in being a Jew? Or what is the value of circumcision? ²Much, in every respect. [For] in the first place, they were entrusted with the utterances of God.ˣ ³What if some were unfaithful? Will their infidelity nullify the fidelity of God?ʸ ⁴Of course not! God must be true, though every human being is a liar,‡‡ as it is written:

"'That you may be justified in your words,
    and conquer when you are judged.'"ᶻ

⁵But if our wickedness provides proof of God's righteousness, what can we say? Is God unjust, humanly speaking, to inflict his wrath?ᵃ ⁶Of course not! For how else is God to judge the world? ⁷But if God's truth redounds to his glory through my falsehood, why am I still being condemned as a sinner? ⁸And why not say—as we are accused and as some claim we say—that we should do evil that good may come of it? Their penalty is what they deserve.ᵇ

**Universal Bondage to Sin.**§§ ⁹Well, then, are we better off? Not entirely, for we have already

---

*[2:6] **Will repay everyone according to his works:** Paul reproduces the Septuagint text of Ps 62:12 and Prv 24:12.

†[2:11] **No partiality with God:** this sentence is not at variance with the statements in Rom 2:9–10. Since Jews are the first to go under indictment, it is only fair that they be given first consideration in the distribution of blessings. Basic, of course, is the understanding that God accepts no bribes (Dt 10:17).

‡[2:12–16] Jews cannot reasonably demand from Gentiles the standard of conduct inculcated in the Old Testament since God did not address its revelation to them. Rather, God made it possible for Gentiles to know instinctively the difference between right and wrong. But, as Paul explained in Rom 1:18–32, humanity misread the evidence of God's existence, power, and divinity, and "while claiming to be wise, they became fools" (Rom 1:22).

§[2:15] Paul expands on the thought of Jer 31:33; Wis 17:11.

¶[2:17–29] Mere possession of laws is no evidence of virtue. By eliminating circumcision as an elitist moral sign, Paul clears away the last obstacle to his presentation of justification through faith without claims based on the receipt of circumcision and its attendant legal obligations.

**[2:24] According to Is 52:5 the suffering of Israel prompts her enemies to revile God. Paul uses the passage in support of his point that the present immorality of Israelites is the cause of such defamation.

††[3:1–4] In keeping with the popular style of diatribe, Paul responds to the objection that his teaching on the sinfulness of all humanity detracts from the religious prerogatives of Israel. He stresses that Jews have remained the vehicle of God's revelation despite their sins, though this depends on the fidelity of God.

‡‡[3:4] **Though every human being is a liar:** these words reproduce the Greek text of Ps 116:11. The rest of the verse is from Ps 51:6.

§§[3:9–20] **Well, then, are we better off?:** this phrase can also be translated "Are we at a disadvantage?" but the latter

---

f. [2:8] 2 Thes 1:8.  g. [2:10] 1:16; 3:9.  h. [2:11] Dt 10:17; 2 Chr 19:7; Sir 35:12–13; Acts 10:34; Gal 2:6; Eph 6:9; Col 3:25; 1 Pt 1:17. i. [2:12] 3:19.  j. [2:13] Mt 7:21; Lk 6:46–49; 8:21; Jas 1:22–25; 1 Jn 3:7.  k. [2:14] Acts 10:35.  l. [2:16] Acts 10:42; 17:31.  m. [2:17] Is 48:1–2; Mi 3:11; Phil 3:4–6.  n. [2:18] Phil 1:10.  o. [2:19] Mt 15:14; Lk 6:39.  p. [2:20] 2 Tm 3:15.  q. [2:21] Ps 50:16–21; Mt 23:3–4.

r. [2:24] Is 52:5; Ez 36:20; 2 Pt 2:2.  s. [2:25–29] Jer 4:4; 9:24–25.  t. [2:25] 1 Cor 7:19; Gal 5:6.  u. [2:26] Gal 5:6.  v. [2:28] Jn 7:24; 8:15, 39.  w. [2:29] Dt 30:6; Jer 4:4; 9:25; Col 2:11 / 1 Cor 4:5; 2 Cor 10:18.  x. [3:2] 9:4; Dt 4:7–8; Ps 103:7; 147:19–20.  y. [3:3] 9:6; 11:1, 29; Ps 89:30–37; 2 Tm 2:13.  z. [3:4] Ps 116:11 / Ps 51:6. a. [3:5] 9:14; Jb 34:12–17.  b. [3:8] 6:1.

brought the charge against Jews and Greeks alike that they are all under the domination of sin,ᶜ ¹⁰as it is written:ᵈ

"There is no one just, not one,
¹¹     there is no one who understands,
          there is no one who seeks God.
¹²  All have gone astray; all alike are worthless;
        there is not one who does good,
        [there is not] even one.
¹³  Their throats are open graves;
        they deceive with their tongues;
    the venom of asps is on their lips;ᵉ
¹⁴        their mouths are full of bitter
               cursing.ᶠ
¹⁵  Their feet are quick to shed blood;ᵍ
¹⁶        ruin and misery are in their ways,
¹⁷  and the way of peace they know not.
¹⁸        There is no fear of God before their
               eyes."ʰ

¹⁹Now we know that what the law* says is addressed to those under the law, so that every mouth may be silenced and the whole world stand accountable to God,ⁱ ²⁰since no human being will be justified in his sight† by observing the law; for through the law comes consciousness of sin.ʲ

### III. JUSTIFICATION THROUGH FAITH IN CHRIST

**Justification Apart from the Law.**‡ ²¹But now§ the righteousness of God has been manifested apart from the law, though testified to by the law

and the prophets,ᵏ ²²the righteousness of God through faith in Jesus Christ for all who believe. For there is no distinction;ˡ ²³all have sinned and are deprived of the glory of God.ᵐ ²⁴They are justified freely by his grace through the redemption in Christ Jesus,ⁿ ²⁵whom God set forth as an expiation,§ through faith, by his blood, to prove his righteousness because of the forgiveness of sins previously committed,ᵒ ²⁶through the forbearance of God—to prove his righteousness in the present time, that he might be righteous and justify the one who has faith in Jesus.

²⁷ᵖWhat occasion is there then for boasting?** It is ruled out. On what principle, that of works? No, rather on the principle of faith.†† ²⁸For we consider that a person is justified by faith apart from works of the law.�q ²⁹Does God belong to Jews alone? Does he not belong to Gentiles, too? Yes, also to Gentiles,ʳ ³⁰for God is one and will justify the circumcised on the basis of faith and the uncircumcised through faith.ˢ ³¹Are we then annulling the law by this faith? Of course not!ᵗ On the contrary, we are supporting the law.‡‡

### CHAPTER 4§§
**Abraham Justified by Faith.** ¹What then can we say that Abraham found, our ancestor according to the flesh?ᵘ ²¶¶Indeed, if Abraham was justified

---

version does not substantially change the overall meaning of the passage. Having explained that Israel's privileged status is guaranteed by God's fidelity, Paul now demonstrates the infidelity of the Jews by a citation of citations from scripture, possibly derived from an existing collection of *testimonia*. These texts show that all human beings share the common burden of sin. They are linked together by mention of organs of the body: throat, tongue, lips, mouth, feet, eyes.

*[3:19] **The law**: Paul here uses the term in its broadest sense to mean all of the scriptures; none of the preceding texts is from the Torah or Pentateuch.

†[3:20] **No human being will be justified in his sight**: these words are freely cited from Ps 143:2. In place of the psalmist's "no living person," Paul substitutes "no human being" (literally "no flesh," a Hebraism), and he adds "by observing the law."

‡[3:21–31] These verses provide a clear statement of Paul's "gospel," i.e., the principle of justification by faith in Christ. God has found a means of rescuing humanity from its desperate plight: Paul's general term for this divine initiative is the righteousness of God (Rom 3:21). Divine mercy declares the guilty innocent and makes them so. God does this not as a result of the law but apart from it (Rom 3:21), and not because of any merit in human beings but through forgiveness of their sins (Rom 3:24), in virtue of the redemption wrought in Christ Jesus for all who believe (Rom 3:22, 24–25). God has manifested his righteousness in the coming of Jesus Christ, whose saving activity inaugurates a new era in human history.

§[3:21] **But now**: Paul adopts a common phrase used by Greek authors to describe movement from disaster to prosperity. The

expressions indicate that Rom 3:21–26 are the consolatory answer to Rom 3:9–20.

¶[3:25] **Expiation**: this rendering is preferable to "propitiation," which suggests hostility on the part of God toward sinners. As Paul will be at pains to point out (Rom 5:8–10), it is humanity that is hostile to God.

**[3:27–31] People cannot boast of their own holiness, since it is God's free gift (Rom 3:27), both to the Jew who practices circumcision out of faith and to the Gentile who accepts faith without the Old Testament religious culture symbolized by circumcision (Rom 3:29–30).

††[3:27] **Principle of faith**: literally, "law of faith." Paul is fond of wordplay involving the term "law"; cf. Rom 7:21, 23; 8:2. Since "law" in Greek may also connote "custom" or "principle," his readers and hearers would have sensed no contradiction in the use of the term after the negative statement concerning law in Rom 3:20.

‡‡[3:31] **We are supporting the law**: giving priority to God's intentions. God is the ultimate source of law, and the essence of law is fairness. On the basis of the Mosaic covenant, God's justice is in question if those who sinned against the law are permitted to go free (see Rom 3:23–26). In order to rescue all humanity rather than condemn it, God thinks of an alternative: the law or "principle" of faith (Rom 3:27). What can be more fair than to admit everyone into the divine presence on the basis of forgiveness grasped by faith? Indeed, this principle of faith antedates the Mosaic law, as Paul will demonstrate in Rom 4, and does not therefore mark a change in divine policy.

§§[4:1–25] This is an expanded treatment of the significance of Abraham's faith, which Paul discusses in Gal 3:6–18; see notes there.

¶¶[4:2–5] Rom 4:2 corresponds to Rom 4:4, and Rom 4:3–5. The Greek term here rendered **credited** means "made an entry." The context determines whether it is credit or debit. Rom 4:8 speaks of "recording sin" as a debit. Paul's repeated use of accountants' terminology in this and other passages can

---

c. [3:9] 1:18–2:25; 3:23; Sir 8:5.   d. [3:10–11] Ps 14:1–3; 53:2–4; Eccl 7:20.   e. [3:13] Ps 5:10; 140:4.   f. [3:14] Ps 10:7.   g. [3:15–17] Prv 1:16; Is 59:7–8.   h. [3:18] Ps 36:2.   i. [3:19] 7:7.   j. [3:20] Ps 143:2; Gal 2:16 / 7:7.

k. [3:21] Is 51:6–8; Acts 10:43.   l. [3:22] 1:17; Gal 2:16; Phil 3:9.   m. [3:23] 3:9; 5:12.   n. [3:24] Eph 2:8; Ti 3:7 / Rom 5:1–2; Eph 1:7.   o. [3:25] Lv 16:12–15; Acts 17:31; 1 Jn 4:10.   p. [3:27] 8:2; 1 Cor 1:29–31.   q. [3:28] 5:1; Gal 2:16.   r. [3:29] 10:12.   s. [3:30] Dt 6:4; Gal 3:20; Jas 2:19 / Rom 4:11–12.   t. [3:31] 8:4; Mt 5:17.   u. [4:1] Gal 3:6–9.

on the basis of his works, he has reason to boast; but this was not so in the sight of God. [3v]For what does the scripture say? "Abraham believed God, and it was credited to him as righteousness." [4]A worker's wage is credited not as a gift, but as something due.[w] [5]But when one does not work, yet believes in the one who justifies the ungodly, his faith is credited as righteousness. [6]So also David declares the blessedness of the person to whom God credits righteousness apart from works:

7    "Blessed are they whose iniquities are
      forgiven[x]
      and whose sins are covered.
8    Blessed is the man whose sin the Lord
      does not record."

[9]Does this blessedness[†] apply only to the circumcised, or to the uncircumcised as well? Now we assert that "faith was credited to Abraham as righteousness."[y] [10]Under what circumstances was it credited? Was he circumcised or not? He was not circumcised, but uncircumcised. [11]And he received the sign of circumcision as a seal on the righteousness received through faith while he was uncircumcised. Thus he was to be the father of all the uncircumcised who believe, so that to them [also] righteousness might be credited,[z] [12]as well as the father of the circumcised who not only are circumcised but also follow the path of faith that our father Abraham walked while still uncircumcised.

**Inheritance Through Faith.** [13]It was not through the law that the promise was made to Abraham and his descendants that he would inherit the world, but through the righteousness that comes from faith.[a] [14]For if those who adhere to the law are the heirs, faith is null and the promise is void.[b] [15]For the law produces wrath;[c] but where there is no law, neither is there violation.[‡] [16]For this reason, it depends on faith, so that it may be a gift, and the promise may be guaranteed to all his descendants, not to those who only adhere to

the law but to those who follow the faith of Abraham, who is the father of all of us,[d] [17]as it is written, "I have made you father of many nations." He is our father in the sight of God, in whom he believed, who gives life to the dead and calls into being what does not exist.[e] [18]He believed, hoping against hope,[f] that he would become "the father of many nations," according to what was said, "Thus shall your descendants be." [19g]He did not weaken in faith when he considered his own body as [already] dead (for he was almost a hundred years old) and the dead womb of Sarah. [20]He did not doubt God's promise in unbelief;[§] rather, he was empowered by faith and gave glory to God [21]and was fully convinced that what he had promised he was also able to do.[h] [22]That is why "it was credited to him as righteousness."[i] [23]But it was not for him alone that it was written that "it was credited to him"; [24]it was also for us, to whom it will be credited, who believe in the one who raised Jesus our Lord from the dead,[j] [25]who was handed over for our transgressions and was raised for our justification.[k]

## CHAPTER 5

**Faith, Hope, and Love.[5]** [1]Therefore, since we have been justified by faith, we have peace[**] with God through our Lord Jesus Christ,[l] [2]through whom we have gained access [by faith] to this grace in which we stand, and we boast in hope of the glory of God.[m] [3]Not only that, but we even boast of our afflictions, knowing that affliction produces endurance, [4]and endurance, proven character, and proven character, hope,[n] [5]and hope

§[4:20] **He did not doubt God's promise in unbelief:** any doubts Abraham might have had were resolved in commitment to God's promise. Heb 11:8–12 emphasizes the faith of Abraham and Sarah.

¶[5:1–11] Popular piety frequently construed reverses and troubles as punishment for sin; cf. Jn 9:2. Paul therefore assures believers that God's justifying action in Jesus Christ is a declaration of peace. The crucifixion of Jesus Christ displays God's initiative in certifying humanity for unimpeded access into the divine presence. Reconciliation is God's gift of pardon for the entire human race. Through faith one benefits personally from this pardon or, in Paul's term, is justified. The ultimate aim of God is to liberate believers from the pre-Christian self as described in Rom 1–3. Since this liberation will first find completion in the believer's resurrection, salvation is described as future in Rom 5:10. Because this fullness of salvation belongs to the future it is called the Christian hope. Paul's Greek term for hope does not, however, suggest a note of uncertainty, to the effect: "I wonder whether God really means it." Rather, God's promise in the gospel fills believers with expectation and anticipation for the climactic gift of unalloyed commitment in the holy Spirit to the performance of the will of God. The persecutions that attend Christian commitment are to teach believers patience and to strengthen this hope, which will not disappoint them because the holy Spirit dwells in their hearts and imbues them with God's love (Rom 5:5).

**\*\*[5:1] We have peace:** a number of manuscripts, versions, and church Fathers read "Let us have peace"; cf. Rom 14:19.

be traced both to the Old Testament texts he quotes and to his business activity as a tentmaker. The commercial term in Gn 15:6, "attributed to him," reminds Paul in Rom 4:7–8 of Ps 32:2, in which the same term is used and applied to forgiveness of sins. Thus Paul is able to argue that Abraham's faith involved receipt of forgiveness of sins and that all believers benefit as he did through faith.

\*[4:3] Jas 2:24 appears to conflict with Paul's statement. However, James combats the error of extremists who used the doctrine of justification through faith as a screen for moral self-determination. Paul discusses the subject of holiness in greater detail than does James and beginning with Rom 6 shows how justification through faith introduces one to the gift of a new life in Christ through the power of the holy Spirit.

†[4:9] **Blessedness:** evidence of divine favor.

‡[4:15] Law has the negative function of bringing the deep-seated rebellion against God to the surface in specific sins; see note on Rom 1:18–32.

v. [4:3] Gn 15:6; Gal 3:6; Jas 2:14, 20–24.   w. [4:4] 11:6.   x. [4:7–8] Ps 32:1–2.   y. [4:9] 4:3.   z. [4:11] Gn 17:10–11; Gal 3:6–8.   a. [4:13] Gn 12:7; 18:18; 22:17–18; Sir 44:21; Gal 3:16–18, 29.   b. [4:14] Gal 3:18.   c. [4:15] 3:20; 5:13; 7:8; Gal 3:19.

d. [4:16] Sir 44:19; Gal 3:7–9.   e. [4:17] Gn 17:5; Heb 11:19 / Is 48:13.   f. [4:18] Gn 15:5.   g. [4:19–20] Gn 17:17; Heb 11:11.   h. [4:21] Gn 18:14; Lk 1:37.   i. [4:22] Gn 15:6.   j. [4:24] 10:9; 1 Pt 1:21.   k. [4:25] Is 53:4–5, 12; 1 Cor 15:17; 1 Pt 1:3 / 8:11.   l. [5:1] 3:24–28; Gal 2:16. m. [5:2] Eph 2:18; 3:12.   n. [5:4] 2 Cor 12:9–10; Jas 1:2–4; 1 Pt 1:5–7; 4:12–14.

does not disappoint, because the love of God has been poured out into our hearts through the holy Spirit that has been given to us.° ⁶For Christ, while we were still helpless, yet died at the appointed time for the ungodly. ⁷Indeed, only with difficulty does one die for a just person, though perhaps for a good person one might even find courage to die.* ⁸But God proves his love for us in that while we were still sinners Christ died for us.ᵖ ⁹How much more then, since we are now justified by his blood, will we be saved through him from the wrath.�q ¹⁰Indeed, if, while we were enemies, we were reconciled to God through the death of his Son, how much more, once reconciled, will we be saved by his life.ʳ ¹¹Not only that, but we also boast of God through our Lord Jesus Christ, through whom we have now received reconciliation.

**Humanity's Sin Through Adam.** ¹²†Therefore, just as through one person sin entered the world,ˢ and through sin, death, and thus death came to all, inasmuch as all sinned‡— ¹³for up to the time of the law, sin was in the world, though sin is not accounted when there is no law.ᵗ ¹⁴But death reigned from Adam to Moses, even over those who did not sin after the pattern of the trespass of Adam, who is the type of the one who was to come.ᵘ

**Grace and Life Through Christ.** ¹⁵But the gift is not like the transgression. For if by that one person's transgression the many died, how much more did the grace of God and the gracious gift of the one person Jesus Christ overflow for the many. ¹⁶And the gift is not like the result of the one person's sinning. For after one sin there was the judgment that brought condemnation; but the gift, after many transgressions, brought acquittal. ¹⁷For if, by the transgression of one person, death came to reign through that one, how much more will those who receive the abundance of grace and of the gift of justification come to reign in life through the one

person Jesus Christ. ¹⁸In conclusion, just as through one transgression condemnation came upon all, so through one righteous act acquittal and life came to all.ᵛ ¹⁹For just as through the disobedience of one person the many were made sinners, so through the obedience of one the many will be made righteous.ʷ ²⁰The law entered inˢ so that transgression might increase but, where sin increased, grace overflowed all the more,ˣ ²¹so that, as sin reigned in death, grace also might reign through justification for eternal life through Jesus Christ our Lord.ʸ

## IV. JUSTIFICATION AND THE CHRISTIAN LIFE

### CHAPTER 6

**Freedom from Sin; Life in God.** ¹ᵃWhat then shall we say? Shall we persist in sin that grace may abound? Of course not!ᶻ ²How can we who died to sin yet live in it?ᵃ ³Or are you unaware that we who were baptized into Christ Jesus were baptized into his death?ᵇ ⁴We were indeed buried with him through baptism into death, so that, just as Christ was raised from the dead by the glory of the Father, we too might live in newness of life.ᶜ

⁵For if we have grown into union with him through a death like his, we shall also be united with him in the resurrection.ᵈ ⁶We know that our old self was crucified with him, so that our sinful body might be done away with, that we might no longer be in slavery to sin.ᵉ ⁷For a dead person has been absolved from sin. ⁸If, then, we have died with Christ, we believe that we shall also live with him.ᶠ ⁹We know that Christ, raised from the dead, dies no more; death no longer has power over him.ᵍ ¹⁰As to his death, he died to sin once and for all; as to his life, he lives for God.ʰ ¹¹Consequently, you too must think of

---

*[5:7] In the world of Paul's time the **good person** is especially one who is magnanimous to others.

†[5:12–21] Paul reflects on the sin of Adam (Gn 3:1–13) in the light of the redemptive mystery of Christ. Sin, as used in the singular by Paul, refers to the dreadful power that has gripped humanity, which is now in revolt against the Creator and engaged in the exaltation of its own desires and interests. But no one has a right to say, "Adam made me do it," for all are culpable (Rom 5:12): Gentiles under the demands of the law written in their hearts (Rom 2:14–15), and Jews under the Mosaic covenant. Through the Old Testament law, the sinfulness of humanity that was operative from the beginning (Rom 5:13) found further stimulation, with the result that sins were generated in even greater abundance. According to Rom 5:15–21, God's act in Christ is in total contrast to the disastrous effects of the virus of sin that invaded humanity through Adam's crime.

‡[5:12] **Inasmuch as all sinned:** others translate "because all sinned," and understand Rom 5:13 as a parenthetical remark. Unlike Wis 2:24, Paul does not ascribe the entry of death to the devil.

§[5:20] **The law entered in:** sin had made its entrance (Rom 5:12); now the law comes in alongside sin. See notes on Rom 1:18–32; 5:12–21. **Where sin increased, grace overflowed all the more:** Paul declares that grace outmatches the productivity of sin.

¶[6:1–11] To defend the gospel against the charge that it promotes moral laxity (cf. Rom 3:5–8), Paul expresses himself in the typical style of spirited diatribe. God's display of generosity or grace is not evoked by sin but, as stated in Rom 5:8 is the expression of God's love, and this love pledges eternal life to all believers (Rom 5:21). Paul views the present conduct of the believers from the perspective of God's completed salvation when the body is resurrected and directed totally by the holy Spirit. Through baptism believers share the death of Christ and thereby escape from the grip of sin. Through the resurrection of Christ the power to live anew becomes reality for them, but the fullness of participation in Christ's resurrection still lies in the future. But life that is lived in dedication to God now is part and parcel of that future. Hence anyone who sincerely claims to be interested in that future will scarcely be able to say, "Let us sin so that grace may prosper" (cf. Rom 6:1).

---

o. [5:5] 8:14–16; Ps 22:5–6; 25:20.   p. [5:8] Jn 3:16; 1 Jn 4:10, 19.   q. [5:9] 1:18; 1 Thes 1:10.   r. [5:10] 8:7–8; 2 Cor 5:18; Col 1:21–22.   s. [5:12] Gn 2:17; 3:1–19; Wis 2:24 / Rom 3:19, 23.   t. [5:13] 4:15.   u. [5:14] 1 Cor 15:21.

v. [5:18] 1 Cor 15:21–22.   w. [5:19] Is 53:11; Phil 2:8–9.   x. [5:20] 4:15;7:7–8;Gal3:19.   y. [5:21]6:23.   z. [6:1]3:5–8.   a. [6:2]1Pt4:1.   b. [6:3] Gal 3:27.   c. [6:4] Col 2:12; 1 Pt 3:21–22.   d. [6:5] Phil 3:10–11; 2 Tm 2:11.   e. [6:6] Gal 5:24; 6:14; Eph 4:22–23.   f. [6:8] 1 Thes 4:17.   g. [6:9] Acts 13:34; 1 Cor 15:26; 2 Tm 1:10; Rev 1:18.   h. [6:10] Heb 9:26–28; 1 Pt 3:18.

yourselves as [being] dead to sin and living for God in Christ Jesus.*

¹²"Therefore, sin must not reign over your mortal bodies so that you obey their desires.* ¹³And do not present the parts of your bodies to sin as weapons for wickedness, but present yourselves to God as raised from the dead to life and the parts of your bodies to God as weapons for righteousness.* ¹⁴For sin is not to have any power over you, since you are not under the law but under grace.*

¹⁵What then? Shall we sin because we are not under the law but under grace? Of course not!* ¹⁶Do you not know that if you present yourselves to someone as obedient slaves,* you are slaves of the one you obey, either of sin, which leads to death, or of obedience, which leads to righteousness?* ¹⁷But thanks be to God that, although you were once slaves of sin, you have become obedient from the heart to the pattern of teaching to which you were entrusted.† ¹⁸Freed from sin, you have become slaves of righteousness. ¹⁹I am speaking in human terms because of the weakness of your nature. For just as you presented the parts of your bodies as slaves to impurity and to lawlessness for lawlessness, so now present them as slaves to righteousness for sanctification. ²⁰ᵖFor when you were slaves of sin, you were free from righteousness.‡ ²¹But what profit did you get then from the things of which you are now ashamed? For the end of those things is death.�q ²²But now that you have been freed from sin and have become slaves of God, the benefit that you have leads to sanctification,§ and its end is eternal life.ʳ ²³For the wages of sin is death, but the gift of God is eternal life in Christ Jesus our Lord.ˢ

## CHAPTER 7
**Freedom from the Law.**§ ¹Are you unaware, brothers (for I am speaking to people who know

the law), that the law has jurisdiction over one as long as one lives? ²Thus a married woman is bound by law to her living husband; but if her husband dies, she is released from the law in respect to her husband.ᵗ ³Consequently, while her husband is alive she will be called an adulteress if she consorts with another man. But if her husband dies she is free from that law, and she is not an adulteress if she consorts with another man.

⁴In the same way, my brothers, you also were put to death to the law through the body of Christ, so that you might belong to another, to the one who was raised from the dead in order that we might bear fruit for God. ⁵For when we were in the flesh, our sinful passions, awakened by the law, worked in our members to bear fruit for death.ᵘ ⁶But now we are released from the law, dead to what held us captive, so that we may serve in the newness of the spirit and not under the obsolete letter.ᵛ

**Acquaintance with Sin Through the Law.** ⁷**What then can we say? That the law is sin? Of course not!†† Yet I did not know sin except through the law, and I did not know what it is to covet except that the law said, "You shall not covet."ʷ ⁸But sin, finding an opportunity in the commandment, produced in me every kind of covetousness. Apart from the law sin is dead.ˣ ⁹I once lived outside the law, but when the commandment came, sin became alive; ¹⁰then I died, and the commandment that was for life turned out to be death for me.ʸ ¹¹For sin, seizing an opportunity in the commandment, deceived me and through it put me to death.ᶻ ¹²So then the law is holy, and the commandment is holy and righteous and good.ᵃ **Sin and Death.**‡‡ ¹³Did the good, then, become death for me? Of course not! Sin, in order that

---

*[6:12–19] Christians have been released from the grip of sin, but sin endeavors to reclaim its victims. The antidote is constant remembrance that divine grace has claimed them and identifies them as people who are alive only for God's interests.

†[6:17] In contrast to humanity, which was handed over to self-indulgence (Rom 1:24–32), believers are **entrusted** ("handed over") to God's **pattern of teaching**, that is, the new life God aims to develop in Christians through the productivity of the holy Spirit. Throughout this passage Paul uses the slave-master model in order to emphasize the fact that one cannot give allegiance to both God and sin.

‡[6:20] **You were free from righteousness**: expressed ironically, for such freedom is really tyranny. The commercial metaphors in Rom 6:21–23 add up only one way: sin is a bad bargain.

§[6:22] **Sanctification**: or holiness.

¶[7:1–6] Paul reflects on the fact that Christians have a different understanding of the law because of their faith in Christ. Law binds the living, not the dead, as exemplified in

marriage, which binds in life but is dissolved through death. Similarly, Christians who through baptism have died with Christ to sin (cf. Rom 6:2–4) are freed from the law that occasioned transgressions, which in turn were productive of death. Now that Christians are joined to Christ, the power of Christ's resurrection makes it possible for them to bear the fruit of newness of life for God.

**[7:7–25] In this passage Paul uses the first person singular in the style of diatribe for the sake of argument. He aims to depict the disastrous consequences when a Christian reintroduces the law as a means to attain the objective of holiness pronounced in Rom 6:22.

††[7:7–12] The apostle defends himself against the charge of identifying the law with sin. Sin does not exist in law but in human beings, whose sinful inclinations are not overcome by the proclamation of law.

‡‡[7:13–25] Far from improving the sinner, law encourages sin to expose itself in transgressions or violations of specific commandments (see Rom 1:24; 5:20). Thus persons who do not experience the justifying grace of God, and Christians who revert to dependence on law as the criterion for their relationship with God, will recognize a rift between their reasoned desire for the goodness of the law and their actual performance that is contrary to the law. Unable to free themselves from the slavery of sin and the power of death, they can only be rescued from defeat in the conflict by the power of God's grace working through Jesus Christ.

---

i. [6:11] 2 Cor 5:15; 1 Pt 2:24.   j. [6:12] Gn 4:7.   k. [6:13] 12:1; Eph 2:5; 5:14 / Col 3:5.   l. [6:14] Gal 5:18; 1 Jn 3:6.   m. [6:15] 5:17, 21.   n. [6:16–18] Jn 8:32–36.   o. [6:16] Jn 8:31–34; 2 Pt 2:19.   p. [6:20] Jn 8:34.   q. [6:21] 8:6, 13; Prv 12:28; Ez 16:61, 63.   r. [6:22] 1 Pt 1:9.   s. [6:23] Gn 2:17; Gal 6:7–9; Jas 1:15.

t. [7:2] 1 Cor 7:39.   u. [7:5] 6:21; 8:6, 13.   v. [7:6] 8:2; 2 Cor 3:6.   w. [7:7] 3:20;Ex20:17;Dt5:21.   x. [7:8] 5:13,20;1Cor15:56 / Rom4:15.   y. [7:10] Lv 18:5.   z. [7:11] Gn 3:13; Heb 3:13.   a. [7:12] 1 Tm 1:8.

it might be shown to be sin, worked death in me through the good, so that sin might become sinful beyond measure through the commandment.[b] [14]We know that the law is spiritual; but I am carnal, sold into slavery to sin.[c] [15]What I do, I do not understand. For I do not do what I want, but I do what I hate. [16]Now if I do what I do not want, I concur that the law is good. [17]So now it is no longer I who do it, but sin that dwells in me. [18]For I know that good does not dwell in me, that is, in my flesh. The willing is ready at hand, but doing the good is not.[d] [19]For I do not do the good I want, but I do the evil I do not want. [20]Now if [I] do what I do not want, it is no longer I who do it, but sin that dwells in me. [21]So, then, I discover the principle that when I want to do right, evil is at hand. [22]For I take delight in the law of God, in my inner self, [23e]but I see in my members another principle at war with the law of my mind, taking me captive to the law of sin that dwells in my members.* [24]Miserable one that I am! Who will deliver me from this mortal body? [25]Thanks be to God through Jesus Christ our Lord. Therefore, I myself, with my mind, serve the law of God but, with my flesh, the law of sin.[f]

## CHAPTER 8

**The Flesh and the Spirit.**[†] [1]Hence, now there is no condemnation for those who are in Christ Jesus. [2]For the law of the spirit of life in Christ Jesus has freed you from the law of sin and death.[g] [3]For what the law, weakened by the flesh, was powerless to do, this God has done: by sending his own Son in the likeness of sinful flesh and for the sake of sin, he condemned sin in the flesh,[h] [4]so that the righteous decree of the law might be fulfilled in us, who live not according to the flesh but according to the spirit.[i] [5]For those who live according to the flesh are concerned with the things of the flesh, but those who live according to the spirit with the things of the spirit. [6]The concern of the flesh is death, but the concern of the spirit is life and peace.[j] [7]For the concern of the flesh is hostility toward God; it does not submit to the law of God, nor can it;[k] [8]and those who are in the flesh cannot please God.[l] [9]But you are not in the flesh; on the contrary, you are in the spirit, if only the Spirit of God dwells in you. Whoever does not have the Spirit of Christ does not belong to him.[m] [10]But if Christ is in you, although the body is dead because of sin, the spirit is alive because of righteousness.[n] [11]If the Spirit of the one who raised Jesus from the dead dwells in you, the one who raised Christ from the dead will give life to your mortal bodies also, through his Spirit that dwells in you. [12]Consequently, brothers, we are not debtors to the flesh, to live according to the flesh. [13]For if you live according to the flesh, you will die, but if by the spirit you put to death the deeds of the body, you will live.[o]

**Children of God Through Adoption.**[‡] [14]For those who are led by the Spirit of God are children of God.[p] [15]For you did not receive a spirit of slavery to fall back into fear, but you received a spirit of adoption, through which we cry, "Abba,[§] Father!"[q] [16]The Spirit itself bears witness with our spirit that we are children of God,[r] [17]and if children, then heirs, heirs of God and joint heirs with Christ, if only we suffer with him so that we may also be glorified with him.[s]

**Destiny of Glory.**[¶] [18]I consider that the sufferings of this present time are as nothing compared with the glory to be revealed for us.[t] [19]For creation awaits with eager expectation the revelation of the children of God; [20]for creation was made subject to futility, not of its own accord but because of the one who subjected it,[u] in hope [21]that creation itself would be set free from slavery to corruption and share in the glorious freedom of the children of God.[v] [22]We know that all creation is groaning in labor pains even until

---

*[7:23] As in Rom 3:27, Paul plays on the term **law**, which in Greek can connote custom, system, or **principle**.

†[8:1–13] After his warning in Rom 7 against the wrong route to fulfillment of the objective of holiness expressed in Rom 6:22, Paul points his addressees to the correct way. Through the redemptive work of Christ, Christians have been liberated from the terrible forces of sin and death. Holiness was impossible so long as the **flesh** (or our "old self"), that is, self-interested hostility toward God (Rom 8:7), frustrated the divine objectives expressed in the law. What is worse, sin used the law to break forth into all manner of lawlessness (Rom 8:8). All this is now changed. At the cross God broke the power of sin and pronounced sentence on it (Rom 8:3). Christians still retain the flesh, but it is alien to their new being, which is life in the spirit, namely the new self, governed by the holy Spirit. Under the direction of the holy Spirit Christians are able to fulfill the divine will that formerly found expression in the law (Rom 8:4). The same Spirit who enlivens Christians for holiness will also resurrect their bodies at the last day (Rom 8:11). Christian life is therefore the experience of a constant challenge to put to death the evil deeds of the body through life of the spirit (Rom 8:13).

‡[8:14–17] Christians, by reason of the Spirit's presence within them, enjoy not only new life but also a new relationship to God, that of adopted children and heirs through Christ, whose sufferings and glory they share.

§[8:15] **Abba:** see note on Mk 14:36.

¶[8:18–27] The glory that believers are destined to share with Christ far exceeds the sufferings of the present life. Paul considers the destiny of the created world to be linked with the future that belongs to the believers. As it shares in the penalty of corruption brought about by sin, so also will it share in the benefits of redemption and future glory that comprise the ultimate liberation of God's people (Rom 8:19–22). After patient endurance in steadfast expectation, the full harvest of the Spirit's presence will be realized. On earth believers enjoy the firstfruits, i.e., the Spirit, as a guarantee of the total liberation of their bodies from the influence of the rebellious old self (Rom 8:23).

---

b. [7:13] 4:15; 5:20.  c. [7:14] 8:7–8; Ps 51:7.  d. [7:18] Gn 6:5; 8:21; Phil 2:13.  e. [7:23] Gal 5:17; 1 Pt 2:11.  f. [7:25] 1 Cor 15:57.  g. [8:2] 7:23–24; 2 Cor 3:17.  h. [8:3] Acts 13:38; 15:10 / Jn 3:16–17; 2 Cor 5:21; Gal 3:13; 4:4; Phil 2:7; Col 1:22; Heb 2:17; 4:15; 1 Jn 4:9.  i. [8:4] Gal 5:16–25.

j. [8:6] 6:21; 7:5; 8:13; Gal 6:8.  k. [8:7] 5:10; Jas 4:4.  l. [8:8] 1 Jn 2:16.  m. [8:9] 1 Cor 3:16.  n. [8:10] Gal 2:20; 1 Pt 4:6.  o. [8:13] Gal 5:24; 6:8; Eph 4:22–24.  p. [8:14] Gal 5:18.  q. [8:15] Mk 14:36; Gal 4:5–6; 2 Tm 1:7.  r. [8:16] Jn 1:12; Gal 3:26–29.  s. [8:17] Gal 4:7; 1 Pt 4:13; 5:1.  t. [8:18] 2 Cor 4:17.  u. [8:20] Gn 3:17–19.  v. [8:21] 2 Pt 3:12–13; Rev 21:1.

now;[w] [23]and not only that, but we ourselves, who have the firstfruits of the Spirit, we also groan within ourselves as we wait for adoption, the redemption of our bodies.[x] [24]For in hope we were saved. Now hope that sees for itself is not hope. For who hopes for what one sees?[y] [25]But if we hope for what we do not see, we wait with endurance.

[26]In the same way, the Spirit too comes to the aid of our weakness; for we do not know how to pray as we ought, but the Spirit itself intercedes with inexpressible groanings. [27]And the one who searches hearts knows what is the intention of the Spirit, because it intercedes for the holy ones according to God's will.[z]

**God's Indomitable Love in Christ.** [28]*We know that all things work for good for those who love God,[†] who are called according to his purpose.[a] [29]*For those he foreknew he also predestined to be conformed to the image of his Son, so that he might be the firstborn among many brothers.[b] [30]And those he predestined he also called; and those he called he also justified; and those he justified he also glorified.[c]

[31]§What then shall we say to this? If God is for us, who can be against us?[d] [32]He who did not spare his own Son but handed him over for us all, how will he not also give us everything else along with him?[e] [33]Who will bring a charge against God's chosen ones? It is God who acquits us.[f] [34]Who will condemn? It is Christ [Jesus] who died, rather, was raised, who also is at the right hand of God, who indeed intercedes for us.[g] [35]What will separate us from the love of Christ? Will anguish, or distress, or persecution, or famine, or nakedness, or peril, or the sword? [36]As it is written:[h]

"For your sake we are being slain all the
        day;
    we are looked upon as sheep to be
        slaughtered."

[37]No, in all these things we conquer overwhelmingly through him who loved us.[i] [38]For I am convinced that neither death, nor life, nor angels, nor principalities, nor present things,[¶] nor future things, nor powers,[j] [39]nor height, nor depth,[**] nor any other creature will be able to separate us from the love of God in Christ Jesus our Lord.

## V. JEWS AND GENTILES IN GOD'S PLAN[††]

## CHAPTER 9

**Paul's Love for Israel.**[‡‡] [1]I speak the truth in Christ, I do not lie; my conscience joins with the holy Spirit in bearing me witness[k] [2]that I have great sorrow and constant anguish in my heart. [3]For I could wish that I myself were accursed and separated from Christ for the sake of my brothers, my kin according to the flesh.[l] [4]They are Israelites; theirs the adoption, the glory, the covenants, the giving of the law, the worship, and the promises;[m] [5]theirs the patriarchs, and from them, according to the flesh, is the Messiah. God who is over all[§§] be blessed forever. Amen.[n]

**God's Free Choice.** [6]But it is not that the word of God has failed. For not all who are of Israel

---

[¶][8:38] **Present things** and **future things** may refer to astrological data. Paul appears to be saying that the gospel liberates believers from dependence on astrologers.

[**][8:39] **Height, depth** may refer to positions in the zodiac, positions of heavenly bodies relative to the horizon. In astrological documents the term for "height" means "exaltation" or the position of greatest influence exerted by a planet. Since hostile spirits were associated with the planets and stars, Paul includes **powers** (Rom 8:38) in his list of malevolent forces.

[††][9:1–11:36] Israel's unbelief and its rejection of Jesus as savior astonished and puzzled Christians. It constituted a serious problem for them in view of God's specific preparation of Israel for the advent of the Messiah. Paul addresses himself here to the essential question of how the divine plan could be frustrated by Israel's unbelief. At the same time, he discourages both complacency and anxiety on the part of Gentiles. To those who might boast of their superior advantage over Jews, he warns that their enjoyment of the blessings assigned to Israel can be terminated. To those who might anxiously ask, "How can we be sure that Israel's fate will not be ours?" he replies that only unbelief can deprive one of salvation.

[‡‡][9:1–5] The apostle speaks in strong terms of the depth of his grief over the unbelief of his own people. He would willingly undergo a curse himself for the sake of their coming to the knowledge of Christ (Rom 9:3; cf. Lv 27:28–29). His love for them derives from God's continuing choice of them and from the spiritual benefits that God bestows on them and through them on all of humanity (Rom 9:4–5).

[§§][9:5] Some editors punctuate this verse differently and prefer the translation, "Of whom is Christ according to the flesh, who is God over all." However, Paul's point is that God **who is over all** aimed to use Israel, which had been entrusted with every privilege, in outreach to the entire world through the Messiah.

---

*[8:28–30] These verses outline the Christian vocation as it was designed by God: **to be conformed to the image of his Son**, who is to **be the firstborn among many brothers** (Rom 8:29). God's redemptive action on behalf of the believers has been in process before the beginning of the world. Those whom God chooses are **those he foreknew** (Rom 8:29) or elected. Those who are **called** (Rom 8:30) are **predestined** or predetermined. These expressions do not mean that God is arbitrary. Rather, Paul uses them to emphasize the thought and care that God has taken for the Christian's salvation.

[†][8:28] **We know that all things work for good for those who love God**: a few ancient authorities have God as the subject of the verb, and some translators render: "We know that God makes everything work for good for those who love God . . . ."

[‡][8:29] **Image**: while man and woman were originally created in God's image (Gn 1:26–27), it is through baptism into Christ, the image of God (2 Cor 4:4; Col 1:15), that we are renewed according to the image of the Creator (Col 3:10).

[§][8:31–39] The all-conquering power of God's love has overcome every obstacle to Christians' salvation and every threat to separate them from God. That power manifested itself fully when God's own Son was delivered up to death for their salvation. Through him Christians can overcome all their afflictions and trials.

---

w. [8:22] 2 Cor 5:2–5.   x. [8:23] 2 Cor 1:22; Gal 5:5.   y. [8:24] 2 Cor 5:7; Heb 11:1.   z. [8:27] Ps 139:1; 1 Cor 4:5.   a. [8:28–29] Eph 1:4–14; 3:11.   b. [8:29] Eph 1:5; 1 Pt 1:2.   c. [8:30] Is 45:25; 2 Thes 2:13–14.   d. [8:31] Ps 118:6; Heb 13:6.   e. [8:32] Jn 3:16. f. [8:33–34] Is 50:8.   g. [8:34] Ps 110:1; Heb 7:25; 1 Jn 2:1.   h. [8:36] Ps 44:23; 1 Cor 4:9; 15:30; 2 Cor 4:11; 2 Tm 3:12.

i. [8:37] 1 Jn 5:4.   j. [8:38–39] 1 Cor 3:22; Eph 1:21; 1 Pt 3:22. k. [9:1] 2 Cor 11:31; 1 Tm 2:7.   l. [9:3] Ex 32:32.   m. [9:4–5] 3:2; Ex 4:22; Dt 7:6; 14:1–2.   n. [9:5] Mt 1:1–16; Lk 3:23–38 / Rom 1:25; Ps 41:14.

are Israel,[o] [7]nor are they all children of Abraham because they are his descendants; but "It is through Isaac that descendants shall bear your name."[p] [8]This means that it is not the children of the flesh who are the children of God, but the children of the promise are counted as descendants.[q] [9]For this is the wording of the promise, "About this time I shall return and Sarah will have a son."[r] [10]And not only that,[s] but also when Rebecca had conceived children by one husband, our father Isaac[*]—[11]before they had yet been born or had done anything, good or bad, in order that God's elective plan might continue, [12]not by works but by his call—she was told, "The older shall serve the younger."[t] [13]As it is written:[u]

"I loved Jacob
    but hated Esau."[†]

[14‡]What then are we to say? Is there injustice on the part of God? Of course not![v] [15]For he says to Moses:

"I will show mercy to whom I will,
    I will take pity on whom I will."[w]

[16]So it depends not upon a person's will or exertion, but upon God, who shows mercy.[x] [17]For the scripture says to Pharaoh, "This is why I have raised you up, to show my power through you that my name may be proclaimed throughout the earth."[y] [18]Consequently, he has mercy upon whom he wills,[z] and he hardens whom he wills.[§]

[19‡]"You will say to me then, "Why [then] does he still find fault? For who can oppose his will?"[a] [20]But who indeed are you, a human being, to talk back to God?[b] Will what is made say to its maker, "Why have you created me so?" [21]Or does not the potter have a right over the clay, to make out of the same lump one vessel for a noble purpose and another for an ignoble one? [22]What if God, wishing to show his wrath and make known his power, has endured with much patience the vessels of wrath made for destruction?[c] [23]This was to make known the riches of his glory to the vessels of mercy, which he has prepared previously for glory, [24]namely, us whom he has called, not only from the Jews but also from the Gentiles.

**Witness of the Prophets.** [25]As indeed he says in Hosea:

"Those who were not my people I will call
        'my people,'
    and her who was not beloved[**] I will
        call 'beloved.'[d]
[26] And in the very place where it was said to
        them, 'You are not my people,'
    there they shall be called children of
        the living God."[e]

[27f]And Isaiah cries out concerning Israel, "Though the number of the Israelites were like the sand of the sea, only a remnant will be saved; [28]for decisively and quickly will the Lord execute sentence upon the earth." [29]And as Isaiah predicted:

"Unless the Lord of hosts had left us
        descendants,
    we would have become like Sodom
        and have been made like
            Gomorrah."[g]

**Righteousness Based on Faith.**[††] [30]What then shall we say? That Gentiles, who did not pursue

---

*[9:10] **Children by one husband, our father Isaac:** Abraham had two children, Ishmael and Isaac, by two wives, Hagar and Sarah, respectively. In that instance Isaac, although born later than Ishmael, became the bearer of the messianic promise. In the case of twins born to Rebecca, God's elective procedure is seen even more dramatically, and again the younger, contrary to Semitic custom, is given the preference.

†[9:13] The literal rendering, **"Jacob I loved, but Esau I hated,"** suggests an attitude of divine hostility that is not implied in Paul's statement. In Semitic usage "hate" means to love less; cf. Lk 14:26 with Mt 10:37. Israel's unbelief reflects the mystery of the divine election that is always operative within it. Mere natural descent from Abraham does not ensure the full possession of the divine gifts; it is God's sovereign prerogative to bestow this fullness upon, or to withhold it from, whomsoever he wishes; cf. Mt 3:9; Jn 8:39. The choice of Jacob over Esau is a case in point.

‡[9:14–18] The principle of divine election does not invite Christians to theoretical inquiry concerning the nonelected, nor does this principle mean that God is unfair in his dealings with humanity. The instruction concerning divine election is a part of the gospel and reveals that the gift of faith is the enactment of God's mercy (Rom 9:16). God raised up Moses to display that mercy, and Pharaoh to display severity in punishing those who obstinately oppose their Creator.

§[9:18] The basic biblical principle is: those who will not see or hear *shall* not see or hear. On the other hand, the same God who thus makes stubborn or hardens the heart can reconstruct it through the work of the holy Spirit.

¶[9:19–29] The apostle responds to the objection that if God rules over faith through the principle of divine election, God cannot then accuse unbelievers of sin (Rom 9:19). For Paul, this objection is in the last analysis a manifestation of human insolence, and his "answer" is less an explanation of God's ways than the rejection of an argument that places humanity on a level with God. At the same time, Paul shows that God is far less arbitrary than appearances suggest, for God endures **with much patience** (Rom 9:22) a person like the Pharaoh of the Exodus.

**[9:25] **Beloved:** in Semitic discourse means "preferred" or "favorite" (cf. Rom 9:13). See Hos 2:1.

††[9:30–33] In the conversion of the Gentiles and, by contrast, of relatively few Jews, the Old Testament prophecies are seen to be fulfilled; cf. Rom 9:25–29. Israel feared that the doctrine of justification through faith would jeopardize the validity of the Mosaic law, and so they never reached their goal of righteousness that they had sought to attain through meticulous observance of the law (Rom 9:31). Since Gentiles, including especially Greeks and Romans, had a great regard

o. [9:6] Nm 23:19 / Mt 3:9.   p. [9:7] Gn 21:12; Gal 3:29.   q. [9:8] Gal 4:23,28.   r. [9:9] Gn 18:10,14.   s. [9:10] Gn 25:21.   t. [9:12] 11:5–6 / Gn 25:23–24.   u. [9:13] Mal 1:3.   v. [9:14] Dt 32:4.   w. [9:15] Ex 33:19.   x. [9:16] Eph 2:8; Ti 3:5.   y. [9:17] Ex 9:16.   z. [9:18] 11:30–32; Ex 4:21; 7:3.

a. [9:19] 3:7; Wis 12:12.   b. [9:20–21] Wis 15:7; Is 29:16; 45:9; Jer 18:6.   c. [9:22] 2:4; Wis 12:20–21; Jer 50:25.   d. [9:25] Hos 2:25.   e. [9:26] Hos 2:1.   f. [9:27–28] Is 10:22–23; Hos 2:1 / Rom 11:5 / Is 28:22.   g. [9:29] Is 1:9; Mt 10:15.

righteousness, have achieved it, that is, righteousness that comes from faith;[h] [31]but that Israel, who pursued the law of righteousness, did not attain to that law?[i] [32]Why not? Because they did it not by faith, but as if it could be done by works.[j] They stumbled over the stone that causes stumbling,[ ] [33]as it is written:

"Behold, I am laying a stone in Zion
    that will make people stumble
and a rock that will make them fall,
and whoever believes in him shall not be
    put to shame."[k]

## CHAPTER 10

[1]Brothers, my heart's desire and prayer to God on their behalf is for salvation.[l] [2]I testify with regard to them that they have zeal for God, but it is not discerning.[m] [3]For, in their unawareness of the righteousness that comes from God and their attempt to establish their own [righteousness], they did not submit to the righteousness of God.[n] [4]For Christ is the end[‡] of the law for the justification of everyone who has faith.[o]

[5§]Moses writes about the righteousness that comes from [the] law, "The one who does these things will live by them."[p] [6]But the righteousness that comes from faith says,[q] "Do not say in your heart, 'Who will go up into heaven?' (that is, to bring Christ down) [7•]or 'Who will go down into the abyss?' (that is, to bring Christ up from the dead)."[r] [8]But what does it say?

"The word is near you,
    in your mouth and in your heart"[s]

---

for righteousness, Paul's statement concerning Gentiles in Rom 9:30 is to be understood from a Jewish perspective: quite evidently they had not been interested in "God's" righteousness, for it had not been revealed to them; but now in response to the proclamation of the gospel they respond in faith.

*[9:32] Paul discusses Israel as a whole from the perspective of contemporary Jewish rejection of Jesus as Messiah. The Old Testament and much of Jewish noncanonical literature in fact reflect a fervent faith in divine mercy.

†[10:1–13] Despite Israel's lack of faith in God's act in Christ, Paul does not abandon hope for her salvation (Rom 10:1). However, Israel must recognize that the Messiah's arrival in the person of Jesus Christ means the termination of the Mosaic law as the criterion for understanding oneself in a valid relationship to God. Faith in God's saving action in Jesus Christ takes precedence over any such legal claim (Rom 10:6).

‡[10:4] The Mosaic legislation has been superseded by God's action in Jesus Christ. Others understand end here in the sense that Christ is the goal of the law, i.e., the true meaning of the Mosaic law, which cannot be correctly understood apart from him. Still others believe that both meanings are intended.

§[10:5–6] The subject of the verb says (Rom 10:6) is righteousness personified. Both of the statements in Rom 10:5–6 derive from Moses, but Paul wishes to contrast the language of law and the language of faith.

¶[10:7] Here Paul blends Dt 30:13 and Ps 107:26.

(that is, the word of faith that we preach), [9]for, if you confess** with your mouth that Jesus is Lord and believe in your heart that God raised him from the dead, you will be saved.[t] [10]For one believes with the heart and so is justified, and one confesses with the mouth and so is saved. [11]For the scripture says, "No one who believes in him will be put to shame."[u] [12]For there is no distinction between Jew and Greek; the same Lord is Lord of all, enriching all who call upon him.[v] [13]For "everyone who calls on the name of the Lord will be saved."[w]

[14††]But how can they call on him in whom they have not believed? And how can they believe in him of whom they have not heard? And how can they hear without someone to preach?[x] [15]And how can people preach unless they are sent? As it is written,[y] "How beautiful are the feet of those who bring [the] good news!"[‡‡] [16]But not everyone has heeded the good news; for Isaiah says, "Lord, who has believed what was heard from us?"[z] [17]Thus faith comes from what is heard, and what is heard comes through the word of Christ.[a] [18]But I ask, did they not hear? Certainly they did; for

"Their voice has gone forth to all the earth,
    and their words to the ends of the
        world."[b]

[19]But I ask, did not Israel understand?[c] First Moses says:

"I will make you jealous of those who are
        not a nation;
    with a senseless nation I will make
        you angry."

[20d]Then Isaiah speaks boldly and says:

"I was found [by] those who were not
        seeking me;
    I revealed myself to those who were
        not asking for me."

---

**[10:9–11] To confess Jesus as Lord was frequently quite hazardous in the first century (cf. Mt 10:18; 1 Thes 2:2; 1 Pt 2:18–21; 3:14). For a Jew it could mean disruption of normal familial and other social relationships, including great economic sacrifice. In the face of penalties imposed by the secular world, Christians are assured that **no one who believes in Jesus will be put to shame** (Rom 10:11).

††[10:14–21] The gospel has been sufficiently proclaimed to Israel, and Israel has adequately understood God's plan for the messianic age, which would see the gospel brought to the uttermost parts of the earth. As often in the past, Israel has not accepted the prophetic message; cf. Acts 7:51–53.

‡‡[10:15] **How beautiful are the feet of those who bring [the] good news:** in Semitic fashion, the parts of the body that bring the messenger with welcome news are praised; cf. Lk 11:27.

---

h. [9:30] 10:4, 20. i. [9:31] 10:3. j. [9:32] Is 8:14. k. [9:33] Is 28:16; 1 Pt 2:6–8. l. [10:1] 9:1, 3. m. [10:2] Acts 22:3. n. [10:3] 9:31–32; Phil 3:9. o. [10:4] Acts 13:38–39; 2 Cor 3:14; Heb 8:13. p. [10:5] Lv 18:5; Gal 3:12. q. [10:6] Dt 9:4; 30:12. r. [10:7] Dt 30:13; 1 Pt 3:19. s. [10:8] Dt 30:14.

t. [10:9] 1 Cor 12:3. u. [10:11] 9:33; Is 28:16. v. [10:12] 1:16; 3:22, 29; Acts 10:34; 15:9, 11; Gal 3:28; Eph 2:14. w. [10:13] Jl 3:5; Acts 2:21. x. [10:14] Acts 8:31. y. [10:15] Is 52:7; Na 2:1; Eph 6:15. z. [10:16] Is 53:1; Jn 12:38. a. [10:17] Jn 17:20. b. [10:18] Ps 19:5; Mt 24:14. c. [10:19] 11:11, 14; Dt 32:21. d. [10:20–21] 9:30; Is 65:1–2.

²¹But regarding Israel he says, "All day long I stretched out my hands to a disobedient and contentious people."

## CHAPTER 11

**The Remnant of Israel.**\* ¹I ask, then, has God rejected his people? Of course not!ᵉ For I too am an Israelite, a descendant of Abraham, of the tribe of Benjamin.ᶠ ²God has not rejected his people whom he foreknew. Do you not know what the scripture says about Elijah, how he pleads with God against Israel? ³"Lord, they have killed your prophets, they have torn down your altars, and I alone am left, and they are seeking my life."ᵍ ⁴But what is God's response to him? "I have left for myself seven thousand men who have not knelt to Baal."ʰ ⁵So also at the present time there is a remnant, chosen by grace.ⁱ ⁶But if by grace, it is no longer because of works; otherwise grace would no longer be grace.ʲ ⁷What then? What Israel was seeking it did not attain, but the elect attained it; the rest were hardened,ᵏ ⁸as it is written:

"God gave them a spirit of deep sleep,
　　eyes that should not see
　　and ears that should not hear,
down to this very day."ˡ

⁹And David says:ᵐ

"Let their table become a snare and a trap,
　　a stumbling block and a retribution
　　　for them;
¹⁰　let their eyes grow dim so that they may
　　　not see,
　　and keep their backs bent forever."

**The Gentiles' Salvation.** ¹¹†Hence I ask, did they stumble so as to fall? Of course not! But through their transgression salvation has come to the Gentiles, so as to make them jealous.ⁿ ¹²Now if their transgression is enrichment for the world, and if their diminished number is enrichment for the Gentiles, how much more their full number.

¹³Now I am speaking to you Gentiles. Inasmuch then as I am the apostle to the Gentiles, I glory in my ministryᵒ ¹⁴in order to make my race jealous and thus save some of them. ¹⁵For if their rejection is the reconciliation of the world, what will their acceptance be but life from the dead? ¹⁶‡If the firstfruits are holy, so is the whole batch of dough; and if the root is holy, so are the branches.ᵖ

¹⁷But if some of the branches were broken off, and you, a wild olive shoot, were grafted in their place and have come to share in the rich root of the olive tree,�q ¹⁸do not boast against the branches. If you do boast, consider that you do not support the root; the root supports you.ʳ ¹⁹Indeed you will say, "Branches were broken off so that I might be grafted in." ²⁰That is so. They were broken off because of unbelief, but you are there because of faith. So do not become haughty, but stand in awe.ˢ ²¹For if God did not spare the natural branches, [perhaps] he will not spare you either.ᵗ ²²See, then, the kindness and severity of God: severity toward those who fell, but God's kindness to you, provided you remain in his kindness; otherwise you too will be cut off.ᵘ ²³And they also, if they do not remain in unbelief, will be grafted in, for God is able to graft them in again.ᵛ ²⁴For if you were cut from what is by nature a wild olive tree, and grafted, contrary to nature, into a cultivated one, how much more will they who belong to it by nature be grafted back into their own olive tree.

**God's Irrevocable Call.** §²⁵I do not want you to be unaware of this mystery, brothers, so that you will not become wise [in] your own estimation: a hardening has come upon Israel in part, until the full number of the Gentiles comes in,ʷ ²⁶and thus all Israel will be saved,ˣ as it is written:ʸ

"The deliverer will come out of Zion,
　　he will turn away godlessness from
　　　Jacob;
²⁷　and this is my covenant with them
　　when I take away their sins."ᶻ

---

\*[11:1–10] Although Israel has been unfaithful to the prophetic message of the gospel (Rom 10:14–21), God remains faithful to Israel. Proof of the divine fidelity lies in the existence of Jewish Christians like Paul himself. The unbelieving Jews, says Paul, have been blinded by the Christian teaching concerning the Messiah.

†[11:11–15] The unbelief of the Jews has paved the way for the preaching of the gospel to the Gentiles and for their easier acceptance of it outside the context of Jewish culture. Through his mission to the Gentiles Paul also hopes to fill his fellow Jews with jealousy. Hence he hastens to fill the entire Mediterranean world with the gospel. Once all the Gentile nations have heard the gospel, Israel as a whole is expected to embrace it. This will be tantamount to resurrection of the dead, that is, the reappearance of Jesus Christ with all the believers at the end of time.

‡[11:16–24] Israel remains holy in the eyes of God and stands as a witness to the faith described in the Old Testament because of **the firstfruits** (or the first piece baked) (Rom 11:16), that is, the converted remnant, and **the root** that is holy, that is, the patriarchs (Rom 11:16). The Jews' failure to believe in Christ is a warning to Gentile Christians to be on guard against any semblance of anti-Jewish arrogance, that is, failure to recognize their total dependence on divine grace.

§[11:25–29] In God's design, Israel's unbelief is being used to grant the light of faith to the Gentiles. Meanwhile, Israel remains dear to God (cf. Rom 9:13), still the object of special providence, the mystery of which will one day be revealed.

e. [11:1–2] 1 Sm 12:22; Ps 94:14.　f. [11:1] 2 Cor 11:22; Phil 3:5.
g. [11:3] 1 Kgs 19:10, 14.　h. [11:4] 1 Kgs 19:18.　i. [11:5] 9:27.
j. [11:6] 4:4; Gal 3:18.　k. [11:7] 9:31.　l. [11:8] Dt 29:3; Is 29:10;
Mt 13:13–15; Acts 28:26–27.　m. [11:9–10] Ps 69:23–24; 35:8.
n. [11:11] Acts 13:46; 18:6; 28:28 / Rom 10:19; Dt 32:21.

o. [11:13] 1:5.　p. [11:16] Nm 15:17–21; Ez 44:30; Neh 10:36–38.
q. [11:17] Eph 2:11–19.　r. [11:18] 1 Cor 1:31.　s. [11:20] 12:16.
t. [11:21] 1 Cor 10:12.　u. [11:22] Jn 15:2, 4; Heb 3:14.　v. [11:23]
2 Cor 3:16.　w. [11:25] Prv 3:7 / Rom 12:16; Mk 13:10; Lk 21:24;
Jn 10:16.　x. [11:26–27] Ps 14:7; Is 59:20–21.　y. [11:26] Mt
23:39.　z. [11:27] Is 27:9; Jer 31:33–34.

²⁸In respect to the gospel, they are enemies on your account; but in respect to election, they are beloved because of the patriarchs.ᵃ ²⁹For the gifts and the call of God are irrevocable.ᵇ

**Triumph of God's Mercy.** ³⁰*Just as you once disobeyed God but have now received mercy because of their disobedience, ³¹so they have now disobeyed in order that, by virtue of the mercy shown to you, they too may [now] receive mercy. ³²For God delivered all to disobedience, that he might have mercy upon all.ᶜ

³³†Oh, the depth of the riches and wisdom and knowledge of God! How inscrutable are his judgments and how unsearchable his ways!ᵈ

³⁴ "For who has known the mind of the
   Lord‡
   or who has been his counselor?"ᵉ
³⁵ §"Or who has given him anythingᶠ
   that he may be repaid?"

³⁶For from him and through him and for him are all things. To him be glory forever. Amen.ᵍ

## VI. THE DUTIES OF CHRISTIANS¶

### CHAPTER 12

**Sacrifice of Body and Mind.** ¹**I urge you therefore, brothers, by the mercies of God,** to offer your bodies as a living sacrifice, holy and pleasing to God, your spiritual worship.ʰ ²Do not conform yourselves to this age but be transformed by the renewal of your mind, that you may discern what is the will of God, what is good and pleasing and perfect.ⁱ

**Many Parts in One Body.** ³ʲFor by the grace given to me I tell everyone among you not to think of himself more highly than one ought to think, but to think soberly, each according to the measure of faith that God has apportioned. ⁴ᵏFor as in one body we have many parts, and all the parts do not have the same function, ⁵so we, though many, are one body in Christⁱ and individually parts of one another. ⁶ⁱSince we have gifts that differ according to the grace given to us, let us exercise them:‡‡ if prophecy, in proportion to the faith; ⁷if ministry, in ministering; if one is a teacher, in teaching; ⁸if one exhorts, in exhortation; if one contributes, in generosity; if one is over others,§§ with diligence; if one does acts of mercy, with cheerfulness.

**Mutual Love.** ⁹Let love be sincere; hate what is evil, hold on to what is good;ᵐ ¹⁰love one another with mutual affection; anticipate one another in showing honor.ⁿ ¹¹Do not grow slack in zeal, be fervent in spirit, serve the Lord.ᵒ ¹²Rejoice in hope, endure in affliction, persevere in prayer.ᵖ ¹³Contribute to the needs of the holy ones,�q exercise hospitality. ¹⁴¶¶Bless those who persecute [you],ʳ bless and do not curse them.ˢ ¹⁵Rejoice with those who rejoice, weep with those who weep.ᵗ ¹⁶Have the same regard for one another; do not be haughty but associate with the lowly;

---

*[11:30–32] Israel, together with the Gentiles who have been handed over to all manner of vices (Rom 1), **has been delivered . . . to disobedience**. The conclusion of Rom 11:32 repeats the thought of Rom 5:20, "Where sin increased, grace overflowed all the more."

†[11:33–36] This final reflection celebrates the wisdom of God's plan of salvation. As Paul has indicated throughout these chapters, both Jew and Gentile, despite the religious recalcitrance of each, have received the gift of faith. The methods used by God in making this outreach to the world stagger human comprehension but are at the same time a dazzling invitation to abiding faith.

‡[11:34] The citation is from the Greek text of Is 40:13. Paul does not explicitly mention Isaiah in this verse, nor Job in Rom 11:35.

§[11:35] Paul quotes from an old Greek version of Jb 41:3a, which differs from the Hebrew text (Jb 41:11a).

¶[12:1–13:14] Since Christ marks the termination of the Mosaic law as the primary source of guidance for God's people (Rom 10:4), the apostle explains how Christians can function, in the light of the gift of justification through faith, in their relation to one another and the state.

**[12:1–8] The Mosaic code included elaborate directions on sacrifices and other cultic observances. The gospel, however, invites believers to present their **bodies as a living sacrifice** (Rom 12:1). Instead of being limited by specific legal maxims, Christians are liberated for the exercise of good judgment as they are confronted with the many and varied decisions required in the course of daily life. To assist them, God distributes a variety of gifts to the fellowship of believers, including those of prophecy, teaching, and exhortation (Rom 12:6–8). Prophets assist the community to understand the will of God as it applies to the present situation (Rom 12:6). Teachers help people to understand themselves and their responsibilities in relation to others (Rom 12:7). One who exhorts

offers encouragement to the community to exercise their faith in the performance of all that is pleasing to God (Rom 12:8). Indeed, this very section, beginning with Rom 12:1, is a specimen of Paul's own style of exhortation.

††[12:5] **One body in Christ**: on the church as the body of Christ, see 1 Cor 12:12–27.

‡‡[12:6] Everyone has some gift that can be used for the benefit of the community. When the instruction on justification through faith is correctly grasped, the possessor of a gift will understand that it is not an instrument of self-aggrandizement. Possession of a gift is not an index to quality of faith. Rather, the gift is a challenge to faithful use.

§§[12:8] **Over others**: usually taken to mean "rule over" but possibly "serve as a patron." Wealthier members in Greco-Roman communities were frequently asked to assist in public service projects. In view of the references to contributing **in generosity** and to **acts of mercy**, Paul may have in mind people like Phoebe (Rom 16:1–2), who is called a **benefactor** (or "patron") because of the services she rendered to many Christians, including Paul.

¶¶[12:14–21] Since God has justified the believers, it is not necessary for them to take justice into their own hands by taking vengeance. God will ultimately deal justly with all, including those who inflict injury on the believers. This question of personal rights as a matter of justice prepares the way for more detailed consideration of the state as adjudicator.

---

h. [12:1] 2 Cor 1:3 / Rom 6:13; 1 Pt 2:5. i. [12:2] Eph 4:17, 22–23; 1 Pt 1:14 / Eph 5:10, 17; Phil 1:10. j. [12:3] 15:15 / Phil 2:3 / 1 Cor 12:11; Eph 4:7. k. [12:4–5] 1 Cor 12:12, 27; Eph 4:25. l. [12:6–8] 1 Cor 12:4–11, 28–31; Eph 4:7–12; 1 Pt 4:10–11 / 2 Cor 9:7. m. [12:9] Am 5:15 / Am 4:15. n. [12:10] Jn 13:34; 1 Thes 4:9; 1 Pt 2:17; 2 Pt 1:7 / Phil 2:3. o. [12:11] Acts 18:25. p. [12:12] 5:2–3; Col 4:2; 1 Thes 5:17. q. [12:13] Heb 13:2; 1 Pt 4:9. r. [12:14–21] Mt 5:38–48; 1 Cor 4:12; 1 Pt 3:9. s. [12:14] Lk 6:27–28. t. [12:15] Ps 35:13; Sir 7:34; 1 Cor 12:26.

a. [11:28] 15:8; 1 Thes 2:15–16. b. [11:29] 9:6; Nm 23:19; Is 54:10. c. [11:32] Gal 3:22; 1 Tm 2:4. d. [11:33] Jb 11:7–8; Ps 139:6, 17–18; Wis 17:1; Is 55:8–9. e. [11:34] Jb 15:8; Wis 9:13; Is 40:13; Jer 23:18; 1 Cor 2:11–16. f. [11:35] Jb 41:3; Is 40:14. g. [11:36] 1 Cor 8:6; Col 1:16–17.

do not be wise in your own estimation.[u] [17]Do not repay anyone evil for evil; be concerned for what is noble in the sight of all.[v] [18]If possible, on your part, live at peace with all.[w] [19]Beloved, do not look for revenge but leave room for the wrath; for it is written, "Vengeance is mine, I will repay, says the Lord."[x] [20]Rather, "if your enemy is hungry, feed him; if he is thirsty, give him something to drink; for by so doing you will heap burning coals upon his head."[y] [21]Do not be conquered by evil but conquer evil with good.

## CHAPTER 13

**Obedience to Authority.**[*] [1]Let every person be subordinate to the higher authorities, for there is no authority except from God, and those that exist have been established by God.[z] [2]Therefore, whoever resists authority opposes what God has appointed, and those who oppose it will bring judgment upon themselves. [3]For rulers are not a cause of fear to good conduct, but to evil.[a] Do you wish to have no fear of authority? Then do what is good and you will receive approval from it, [4]for it is a servant of God for your good. But if you do evil, be afraid, for it does not bear the sword without purpose; it is the servant of God to inflict wrath on the evildoer.[b] [5]Therefore, it is necessary to be subject not only because of the wrath but also because of conscience.[c] [6]This is why you also pay taxes, for the authorities are ministers of God, devoting themselves to this very thing. [7]Pay to all their dues, taxes to whom taxes are due, toll to whom toll is due, respect to whom respect is due, honor to whom honor is due.[d]

**Love Fulfills the Law.**[†] [8]Owe nothing to anyone, except to love one another; for the one who loves another has fulfilled the law.[e] [9]The commandments, "You shall not commit adultery; you shall not kill; you shall not steal; you shall not covet," and whatever other commandment there may be, are summed up in this saying, [namely] "You shall love your neighbor as yourself."[f] [10]Love does no evil to the neighbor; hence, love is the fulfillment of the law.[g]

**Awareness of the End of Time.**[‡] [11]And do this because you know the time; it is the hour now for you to awake from sleep. For our salvation is nearer now than when we first believed;[h] [12]the night is advanced, the day is at hand. Let us then throw off the works of darkness [and] put on the armor of light;[i] [13]let us conduct ourselves properly as in the day,[§] not in orgies and drunkenness, not in promiscuity and licentiousness, not in rivalry and jealousy.[j] [14]But put on the Lord Jesus Christ, and make no provision for the desires of the flesh.[k]

## CHAPTER 14

**To Live and Die for Christ.**[¶] [1]Welcome anyone who is weak in faith,[l] but not for disputes over opinions.[m] [2]One person believes that one may eat anything, while the weak person eats only vegetables.[n] [3]The one who eats must not despise the one who abstains, and the one who abstains must not pass judgment on the one who eats; for God has welcomed him.[o] [4]Who are you to pass judgment on someone else's servant? Before his own master he stands or falls. And he will be upheld, for the Lord is able to make him stand.[p] [5][For] one person considers one day more important than another, while another person considers all days alike.[q] Let everyone be fully persuaded in his own mind.[**] [6]Whoever observes the day, observes it for the Lord. Also

*[13:1–7] Paul must come to grips with the problem raised by a message that declares people free from the law. How are they to relate to Roman authority? The problem was exacerbated by the fact that imperial protocol was interwoven with devotion to various deities. Paul builds on the traditional instruction exhibited in Wis 6:1–3, according to which kings and magistrates rule by consent of God. From this perspective, then, believers who render obedience to the governing authorities are obeying the one who is highest in command. At the same time, it is recognized that Caesar has the responsibility to make just ordinances and to commend uprightness; cf. Wis 6:4–21. That Caesar is not entitled to obedience when such obedience would nullify God's prior claim to the believers' moral decision becomes clear in the light of the following verses.

†[13:8–10] When love directs the Christian's moral decisions, the interest of law in basic concerns, such as familial relationships, sanctity of life, and security of property, is safeguarded (Rom 13:9). Indeed, says Paul, the same applies to any **other commandment** (Rom 13:9), whether one in the Mosaic code or one drawn up by local magistrates under imperial authority. Love anticipates the purpose of public legislation, namely, to secure the best interests of the citizenry. Since Caesar's obligation is to punish the wrongdoer (Rom 13:4), the Christian who acts in love is free from all legitimate indictment.

‡[13:11–14] These verses provide the motivation for the love that is encouraged in Rom 13:8–10.

§[13:13] **Let us conduct ourselves properly as in the day**: the behavior described in Rom 1:29–30 is now to be reversed. Secular moralists were fond of making references to people who could not wait for nightfall to do their carousing. Paul says that Christians claim to be people of the new day that will dawn with the return of Christ. Instead of planning for nighttime behavior they should be concentrating on conduct that is consonant with avowed interest in the Lord's return.

¶[14:1–15:6] Since Christ spells termination of the law, which included observance of specific days and festivals as well as dietary instruction, the jettisoning of long-practiced customs was traumatic for many Christians brought up under the Mosaic code. Although Paul acknowledges that in principle no food is a source of moral contamination (Rom 14:14), he recommends that the consciences of Christians who are scrupulous in this regard be respected by other Christians (Rom 14:21). On the other hand, those who have scruples are not to sit in judgment on those who know that the gospel has liberated them from such ordinances (Rom 14:10). See 1 Cor 8; 10.

**[14:5] Since the problem to be overcome was humanity's perverted mind or judgment (Rom 1:28), Paul indicates

u. [12:16] 15:5; Phil 2:2–3 / Rom 11:20; Prv 3:7; Is 5:21.   v. [12:17] Prv 3:4; 1 Thes 5:15; 1 Pt 3:9.   w. [12:18] Heb 12:14.   x. [12:19] Lv 19:18; Dt 32:35, 41; Mt 5:39; 1 Cor 6:6–7; Heb 10:30.   y. [12:20] Prv 25:21–22; Mt 5:44.   z. [13:1] Prv 8:15–16; Wis 6:3; Jn 19:11; 1 Pt 2:13–17; Ti 3:1.   a. [13:3] 1 Pt 2:13–14; 3:13.   b. [13:4] 12:19.   c. [13:5] 1 Pt 2:19.   d. [13:7] Mt 22:21; Mk 12:17; Lk 20:25.   e. [13:8] Jn 13:34; Gal 5:14.

f. [13:9] Ex 20:13–17 / Lv 19:18; Dt 5:17–21; Mt 5:43–44; 19:18–19; 22:39; Mk 12:31; Lk 10:27; Gal 5:14; Jas 2:8.   g. [13:10] Mt 22:40; 1 Cor 13:4–7.   h. [13:11] Eph 5:8–16; 1 Thes 5:5–7.   i. [13:12] Jn 8:12; 1 Thes 5:4–8; 1 Jn 2:8 / 2 Cor 6:7; 10:4; Eph 5:11; 6:13–17.   j. [13:13] Lk 21:34; Eph 5:18.   k. [13:14] Gal 3:27; 5:16; Eph 4:24; 6:11.   l. [14:1–23] 1 Cor 8:1–13.   m. [14:1] 15:1, 7; 1 Cor 9:22.   n. [14:2] Gn 1:29; 9:3; 1 Cor 8:1–13; 10:14–33.   o. [14:3] Col 2:16.   p. [14:4] 2:1; Mt 7:11; Jas 4:11–12.   q. [14:5] Gal 4:10.

whoever eats, eats for the Lord, since he gives thanks to God; while whoever abstains, abstains for the Lord and gives thanks to God. [7]None of us lives for oneself, and no one dies for oneself. [8]For if we live, we live for the Lord,* and if we die, we die for the Lord; so then, whether we live or die, we are the Lord's.[r] [9]For this is why Christ died and came to life, that he might be Lord of both the dead and the living.[s] [10]Why then do you judge your brother? Or you, why do you look down on your brother? For we shall all stand before the judgment seat of God;[t] [11]for it is written:

"As I live, says the Lord, every knee shall
    bend before me,
and every tongue shall give praise
    to God."[u]

[12]So [then] each of us shall give an account of himself [to God].[v]

**Consideration for the Weak Conscience.** [13]Then let us no longer judge one another, but rather resolve never to put a stumbling block or hindrance in the way of a brother.[w] [14]I know and am convinced in the Lord Jesus that nothing is unclean in itself; still, it is unclean for someone who thinks it unclean.[x] [15]If your brother is being hurt by what you eat, your conduct is no longer in accord with love. Do not because of your food destroy him for whom Christ died.[y] [16]So do not let your good be reviled.[z] [17]For the kingdom of God is not a matter of food and drink, but of righteousness, peace, and joy in the holy Spirit;[a] [18]whoever serves Christ in this way is pleasing to God and approved by others. [19]Let us[†] then pursue what leads to peace and to building up one another.[b] [20]For the sake of food, do not destroy the work of God.[c] Everything is indeed clean, but it is wrong for anyone to become a stumbling block by eating; [21]it is good not to eat meat or drink wine or do anything that causes your brother to stumble. [22]Keep the faith [that] you have to yourself in the presence of God; blessed is the one who does not condemn himself for what he approves. [23d]But whoever has doubts is condemned if he eats, because this is not from faith; for whatever is not from faith is sin.[‡]

## CHAPTER 15

**Patience and Self-Denial.** [1]We who are strong ought to put up with the failings of the weak and not to please ourselves;[e] [2]let each of us please our neighbor for the good, for building up.[f] [3]For Christ did not please himself; but, as it is written,[g] "The insults of those who insult you fall upon me."[§] [4]For whatever was written previously was written for our instruction, that by endurance and by the encouragement of the scriptures we might have hope.[h] [5]May the God of endurance and encouragement grant you to think in harmony[¶] with one another, in keeping with Christ Jesus;[i] [6]that with one accord you may with one voice glorify the God and Father of our Lord Jesus Christ.

**God's Fidelity and Mercy.**[**] [7]Welcome one another, then, as Christ welcomed you, for the glory of God.[j] [8]For I say that Christ became a minister of the circumcised to show God's truthfulness, to confirm the promises to the patriarchs,[k] [9]but so that the Gentiles might glorify God for his mercy. As it is written:

"Therefore, I will praise you among the
    Gentiles
and sing praises to your name."[l]

[10]And again it says:[m]

"Rejoice, O Gentiles, with his people."[††]

[11]And again:

"Praise the Lord, all you Gentiles,
    and let all the peoples praise him."[n]

[12]And again Isaiah says:

"The root of Jesse shall come,
    raised up to rule the Gentiles;
in him shall the Gentiles hope."[o]

himself to the question of intracommunity living. **Sin** in the singular is the dreadful power described in Rom 5:12–14.

§[15:3] Liberation from the law of Moses does not make the scriptures of the old covenant irrelevant. Much consolation and motivation for Christian living can be derived from the Old Testament, as in the citation from Ps 69:10. Because this psalm is quoted several times in the New Testament, it has been called indirectly messianic.

¶[15:5] **Think in harmony**: a Greco-Roman ideal. Not rigid uniformity of thought and expression but thoughtful consideration of other people's views finds expression here.

**[15:7–13] True oneness of mind is found in pondering the ultimate mission of the church: to bring it about that God's name be glorified throughout the world and that Jesus Christ be universally recognized as God's gift to all humanity. Paul here prepares his addressees for the climactic appeal he is about to make.

††[15:10] Paul's citation of Dt 32:43 follows the Greek version.

---

that the **mind** of the Christian is now able to function with appropriate discrimination (cf. Rom 12:2).

*[14:8] **The Lord**: Jesus, our Master. The same Greek word, *kyrios*, was applied to both rulers and holders of slaves. Throughout the Letter to the Romans Paul emphasizes God's total claim on the believer; see note on Rom 1:1.

†[14:19] Some manuscripts, versions, and church Fathers read, "We then pursue . . ."; cf. Rom 5:1.

‡[14:23] **Whatever is not from faith is sin**: Paul does not mean that all the actions of unbelievers are sinful. He addresses

---

r. [14:8] Lk 20:38; 2 Cor 5:15; Gal 2:20; 1 Thes 5:10.   s. [14:9] Acts 10:42.   t. [14:10] Acts 17:31; 2 Cor 5:10.   u. [14:11] Is 49:18 / Is 45:23; Phil 2:10–11.   v. [14:12] Gal 6:5.   w. [14:13] 1 Cor 8:9, 13.   x. [14:14] Mk 7:5, 20; Acts 10:15; 1 Cor 10:25–27; 1 Tm 4:4.   y. [14:15] 1 Cor 8:11–13.   z. [14:16] 2:24; Ti 2:5.   a. [14:17] 1 Cor 8:8.   b. [14:19] 12:18 / 15:2.   c. [14:20–21] 1 Cor 8:11–13; 10:28–29; Ti 1:15.   d. [14:23] Ti 1:15; Jas 4:17.

e. [15:1] 14:1–2.   f. [15:2] 14:1, 19; 1 Cor 9:19; 10:24, 33.   g. [15:3] Ps 69:10.   h. [15:4] 4:23–24; 1 Mc 12:9; 1 Cor 10:11; 2 Tm 3:16.   i. [15:5] 12:16; Phil 2:2; 4:2.   j. [15:7] 14:1.   k. [15:8] Mt 15:24 / Mi 7:20; Acts 3:25.   l. [15:9] 11:30 / 2 Sm 22:50; Ps 18:50.   m. [15:10] Dt 32:43.   n. [15:11] Ps 117:1.   o. [15:12] Is 11:10; Rev 5:5; 22:16.

¹³May the God of hope fill you with all joy and peace in believing, so that you may abound in hope by the power of the holy Spirit.ᵖ

## VII. CONCLUSION

**Apostle to the Gentiles.** ¹⁴*I myself am convinced about you, my brothers,† that you yourselves are full of goodness,† filled with all knowledge, and able to admonish one another. ¹⁵But I have written to you rather boldly in some respects to remind you, because of the grace given me by Godᑫ ¹⁶to be a minister of Christ Jesus to the Gentiles in performing the priestly service of the gospel of God, so that the offering up of the Gentiles may be acceptable, sanctified by the holy Spirit.ʳ ¹⁷In Christ Jesus, then, I have reason to boast in what pertains to God. ¹⁸For I will not dare to speak of anything except what Christ has accomplished through me to lead the Gentiles to obedience by word and deed,ˢ ¹⁹by the power of signs and wonders, by the power of the Spirit [of God], so that from Jerusalem all the way around to Illyricum‡ I have finished preaching the gospel of Christ. ²⁰Thus I aspire§ to proclaim the gospel not where Christ has already been named, so that I do not build on another's foundation,ᵗ ²¹but as it is written:ᵘ

"Those who have never been told of him
        shall see,
    and those who have never heard of
        him shall understand."¶

**Paul's Plans; Need for Prayers.** ²²That is why I have so often been prevented from coming to you. ²³But now, since I no longer have any opportunity in these regions and since I have desired to come to you for many years,ᵛ

²⁴I hope to see you in passing as I go to Spain and to be sent on my way there by you, after I have enjoyed being with you for a time.ʷ ²⁵**Now, however, I am going to Jerusalem to minister to the holy ones.ˣ ²⁶For Macedonia and Achaia†† have decided to make some contribution for the poor among the holy ones in Jerusalem;ʸ ²⁷they decided to do it, and in fact they are indebted to them, for if the Gentiles have come to share in their spiritual blessings, they ought also to serve them in material blessings.ᶻ ²⁸So when I have completed this and safely handed over this contribution to them, I shall set out by way of you to Spain; ²⁹and I know that in coming to you I shall come in the fullness of Christ's blessing.

³⁰I urge you, [brothers,] by our Lord Jesus Christ and by the love of the Spirit, to join me in the struggle by your prayers to God on my behalf,ᵃ ³¹that I may be delivered from the disobedient in Judea, and that my ministry for Jerusalem may be acceptable to the holy ones, ³²so that I may come to you with joy by the will of God and be refreshed together with you. ³³The God of peace be with all of you. Amen.ᵇ

## CHAPTER 16

**Phoebe Commended.** ¹‡‡I commend to you Phoebe our sister, who is [also] a minister§§ of the church at Cenchreae,ᶜ ²that you may receive her in the Lord in a manner worthy of the holy ones, and help her in whatever she may need from you, for she has been a benefactor to many and to me as well.

**Paul's Greetings.** ³Greet Prisca and Aquila,¶¶ my co-workers in Christ Jesus,ᵈ ⁴who risked their necks for my life, to whom not only I am grateful but also all the churches of the Gentiles; ⁵greet also the church at their house.*** Greet my beloved Epaenetus, who was the firstfruits in

---

*[15:14–33] Paul sees himself as apostle and benefactor in the priestly service of the gospel and so sketches plans for a mission in Spain, supported by those in Rome.

†[15:14] **Full of goodness:** the opposite of what humanity was filled with according to Rom 1:29–30.

‡[15:19] **Illyricum:** Roman province northwest of Greece on the eastern shore of the Adriatic.

§[15:20] **I aspire:** Paul uses terminology customarily applied to philanthropists. Unlike some philanthropists of his time, Paul does not engage in cheap competition for public acclaim. This explanation of his missionary policy is to assure the Christians in Rome that he is also not planning to remain in that city and build on other people's foundations (cf. 2 Cor 10:12–18). However, he does solicit their help in sending him on his way to Spain, which was considered the limit of the western world. Thus Paul's addressees realize that evangelization may be understood in the broader sense of mission or, as in Rom 1:15, of instruction within the Christian community that derives from the gospel.

¶[15:21] The citation from Is 52:15 concerns the Servant of the Lord. According to Isaiah, the Servant is first of all Israel, which was to bring the knowledge of Yahweh to all nations. In Rom 9–11 Paul showed how Israel failed in this mission. Therefore, he himself undertakes almost singlehandedly Israel's responsibility as the Servant and moves as quickly as possible with the gospel through the Roman empire.

**[15:25–27] Paul may have viewed the contribution he was gathering from Gentile Christians for the poor in Jerusalem (cf. 2 Cor 8–9) as a fulfillment of the vision of Is 60:5–6. In confidence that the messianic fulfillment was taking place, Paul stresses in Rom 14–16 the importance of harmonious relationships between Jews and Gentiles.

††[15:26] **Achaia:** the Roman province of southern Greece.

‡‡[16:1–23] Some authorities regard these verses as a later addition to the letter, but in general the evidence favors the view that they were included in the original. Paul endeavors through the long list of greetings (Rom 16:3–16, 21–23) to establish strong personal contact with congregations that he has not personally encountered before. The combination of Jewish and Gentile names dramatically attests the unity in the gospel that transcends previous barriers of nationality, religious ceremony, or racial status.

§§[16:1] **Minister:** in Greek, *diakonos;* see note on Phil 1:1.

¶¶[16:3] **Prisca and Aquila:** presumably the couple mentioned at Acts 18:2; 1 Cor 16:19; 2 Tm 4:19.

***[16:5] **The church at their house:** i.e., that meets there. Such local assemblies (cf. 1 Cor 16:19; Col 4:15; Phlm 2) might consist of only one or two dozen Christians each. It is understandable, therefore, that such smaller groups might

p. [15:13] 5:1–2.   q. [15:15] 1:5; 12:3.   r. [15:16] 11:13; Phil 2:17.   s. [15:18] Acts 15:12; 2 Cor 12:12.   t. [15:20] 2 Cor 10:13–18.   u. [15:21] Is 52:15.   v. [15:23] 1:10–13; Acts 19:21–22.

w. [15:24] 1 Cor 16:6.   x. [15:25] Acts 19:21; 20:22.   y. [15:26] 1 Cor 16:1; 2 Cor 8:1–4; 9:2, 12.   z. [15:27] 9:4 / 1 Cor 9:11.   a. [15:30] 2 Cor 1:11; Phil 1:27; Col 4:3; 2 Thes 3:1.   b. [15:33] 16:20; 2 Cor 13:11; Phil 4:9; 1 Thes 5:23; 2 Thes 3:16; Heb 13:20.   c. [16:1] Acts 18:18.   d. [16:3] Acts 18:2, 18–26; 1 Cor 16:19; 2 Tm 4:19.

Asia for Christ.ᵉ ⁶Greet Mary, who has worked hard for you. ⁷Greet Andronicus and Junia,* my relatives and my fellow prisoners; they are prominent among the apostles and they were in Christ before me. ⁸Greet Ampliatus, my beloved in the Lord. ⁹Greet Urbanus, our co-worker in Christ, and my beloved Stachys. ¹⁰Greet Apelles, who is approved in Christ. Greet those who belong to the family of Aristobulus. ¹¹Greet my relative Herodion. Greet those in the Lord who belong to the family of Narcissus. ¹²Greet those workers in the Lord, Tryphaena and Tryphosa. Greet the beloved Persis, who has worked hard in the Lord. ¹³Greet Rufus,† chosen in the Lord, and his mother and mine.ᶠ ¹⁴Greet Asyncritus, Phlegon, Hermes, Patrobas, Hermas, and the brothers who are with them. ¹⁵Greet Philologus, Julia, Nereus and his sister, and Olympas, and all the holy ones who are with them. ¹⁶Greet one another with a holy kiss. All the churches of Christ greet you.ᵍ

**Against Factions.** ¹⁷‡I urge you, brothers, to watch out for those who create dissensions and obstacles, in opposition to the teaching that you learned; avoid them.ʰ ¹⁸For such people do not serve our Lord Christ but their own appetites, and by fair and flattering speech they deceive the hearts of the innocent.ⁱ ¹⁹For while your obedience is known to all, so that I rejoice over you, I want you to be wise as to what is good, and simple as to what is evil;ʲ ²⁰then the God of peace will quickly crush Satan§ under your feet. The grace of our Lord Jesus be with you.ᵏ

**Greetings from Corinth.** ²¹Timothy, my co-worker, greets you; so do Lucius and Jason and Sosipater, my relatives.ˡ ²²I, Tertius, the writer of this letter, greet you in the Lord. ²³ᵐGaius, who is host to me and to the whole church, greets you. Erastus,¶ the city treasurer, and our brother Quartus greet you. [²⁴]**

**Doxology.**†† [²⁵Now to him who can strengthen you, according to my gospel and the proclamation of Jesus Christ,ⁿ according to the revelation of the mystery kept secret for long ages‡‡ ²⁶but now manifested through the prophetic writings and, according to the command of the eternal God, made known to all nations to bring about the obedience of faith,ᵒ ²⁷to the only wise God, through Jesus Christ be glory forever and ever. Amen.]ᵖ

---

§[16:20] This verse contains the only mention of Satan in Romans.

¶[16:23] This Erastus is not necessarily to be identified with the Erastus of Acts 19:22 or of 2 Tm 4:20.

**[16:24] Some manuscripts add, similarly to Rom 16:20, "The grace of our Lord Jesus Christ be with you all. Amen."

††[16:25–27] This doxology is assigned variously to the end of Rom 14; 15; 16 in the manuscript tradition. Some manuscripts omit it entirely. Whether written by Paul or not, it forms an admirable conclusion to the letter at this point.

‡‡[16:25] Paul's gospel reveals **the mystery kept secret for long ages**: justification and salvation through faith, with all the implications for Jews and Gentiles that Paul has developed in the letter.

---

experience difficulty in relating to one another on certain issues. **Firstfruits:** cf. Rom 8:23; 11:16; 1 Cor 16:15.

*[16:7] The name Junia is a woman's name. One ancient Greek manuscript and a number of ancient versions read the name "Julia." Most editors have interpreted it as a man's name, Junias.

†[16:13] This Rufus cannot be identified to any degree of certainty with the Rufus of Mk 15:21.

‡[16:17–18] Paul displays genuine concern for the congregations in Rome by warning them against self-seeking teachers. It would be a great loss, he intimates, if their obedience, which is known to all (cf. Rom 1:8), would be diluted.

---

e. [16:5] 1 Cor 16:19; Col 4:15; Phlm 2 / 1 Cor 16:15.    f. [16:13] Mk 15:21.    g. [16:16] 1 Cor 16:20; 2 Cor 13:12; 1 Thes 5:26; 1 Pt 5:14.    h. [16:17] Mt 7:15; Ti 3:10.

i. [16:18] Phil 3:18–19; Col 2:4; 2 Pt 2:3.    j. [16:19] 1:8; Mt 10:16; 1 Cor 14:20.    k. [16:20] 15:33; Gn 3:15; Lk 10:19 / 1 Cor 16:23; 1 Thes 5:28; 2 Thes 3:18.    l. [16:21] Acts 16:1–2; 19:22; 20:4; 1 Cor 4:17; 16:10; Phil 2:19–22; Heb 13:23.    m. [16:23] Acts 19:29; 1 Cor 1:14 / 2 Tm 4:20.    n. [16:25] 1 Cor 2:7; Eph 1:9; 3:3–9; Col 1:26.    o. [16:26] 2 Tm 1:10 / Rom 1:5; Eph 3:4–5, 9; 1 Pt 1:20.    p. [16:27] 11:36; Gal 1:5; Eph 3:20–21; Phil 4:20; 1 Tm 1:17; 2 Tm 4:18; Heb 13:21; 1 Pt 4:11; 2 Pt 3:18; Jude 25; Rev 1:6.

# THE FIRST LETTER TO THE

# CORINTHIANS

~∞~

Paul's first letter to the church of Corinth provides us with a fuller insight into the life of an early Christian community of the first generation than any other book of the New Testament. Through it we can glimpse both the strengths and the weaknesses of this small group in a great city of the ancient world, men and women who had accepted the good news of Christ and were now trying to realize in their lives the implications of their baptism. Paul, who had founded the community and continued to look after it as a father, responds both to questions addressed to him and to situations of which he had been informed. In doing so, he reveals much about himself, his teaching, and the way in which he conducted his work of apostleship. Some things are puzzling because we have the correspondence only in one direction. For the person studying this letter, it seems to raise as many questions as it answers, but without it our knowledge of church life in the middle of the first century would be much poorer.

Paul established a Christian community in Corinth about the year 51, on his second missionary journey. The city, a commercial crossroads, was a melting pot full of devotees of various pagan cults and marked by a measure of moral depravity not unusual in a great seaport. The Acts of the Apostles suggests that moderate success attended Paul's efforts among the Jews in Corinth at first, but that they soon turned against him (Acts 18:1–8). More fruitful was his year and a half spent among the Gentiles (Acts 18:11), which won to the faith many of the city's poor and underprivileged (1 Cor 1:26). After his departure the eloquent Apollos, an Alexandrian Jewish Christian, rendered great service to the community, expounding "from the scriptures that the Messiah is Jesus" (Acts 18:24–28).

While Paul was in Ephesus on his third journey (1 Cor 16:8; Acts 19:1–20), he received disquieting news about Corinth. The community there was displaying open factionalism, as certain members were identifying themselves exclusively with individual Christian leaders and interpreting Christian teaching as a superior wisdom for the initiated few (1 Cor 1:10–4:21). The community lacked the decisiveness to take appropriate action against one of its members who was living publicly in an incestuous union (1 Cor 5:1–13). Other members engaged in legal conflicts in pagan courts of law (1 Cor 6:1–11); still others may have participated in religious prostitution (1 Cor 6:12–20) or temple sacrifices (1 Cor 10:14–22).

The community's ills were reflected in its liturgy. In the celebration of the Eucharist certain members discriminated against others, drank too freely at the agape, or fellowship meal, and denied Christian social courtesies to the poor among the membership (1 Cor 11:17–22). Charisms such as ecstatic prayer, attributed freely to the impulse of the holy Spirit, were more highly prized than works of charity (1 Cor 13:1–2, 8), and were used at times in a disorderly way (1 Cor 14:1–40). Women appeared at the assembly without the customary head-covering (1 Cor 11:3–16), and perhaps were quarreling over their right to address the assembly (1 Cor 14:34–35).

Still other problems with which Paul had to deal concerned matters of conscience discussed among the faithful members of the community: the eating of meat that had been sacrificed to idols (1 Cor 8:1–13), the use of sex in marriage (1 Cor 7:1–7); and the attitude to be taken by the unmarried toward marriage in view of the possible proximity of Christ's second coming (1 Cor 7:25–40). There was also a doctrinal matter that called for Paul's attention, for some members of the community, despite their belief in the resurrection of Christ, were denying the possibility of general bodily resurrection.

To treat this wide spectrum of questions, Paul wrote this letter from Ephesus about the year A.D. 56. The majority of the Corinthian Christians may well have been quite faithful. Paul writes on their behalf to guard against the threats posed to the community by the views and conduct of various minorities. He writes with confidence in the authority of his apostolic mission, and he presumes that the Corinthians, despite their deficiencies, will recognize and accept it. On the other hand, he does not hesitate to exercise his authority as his judgment dictates in each situation, even going so far as to promise a direct confrontation with recalcitrants, should the abuses he scores remain uncorrected (1 Cor 4:18–21).

The letter illustrates well the mind and character of Paul. Although he is impelled to insist on his office as founder of the community, he recognizes that he is only one servant of God among many and generously acknowledges the labors of Apollos (1 Cor 3:5–8). He provides us in this letter with many valuable examples of his method of theological reflection and exposition. He always treats the questions at issue on the level of the purity of Christian teaching and conduct. Certain passages of the letter are of the greatest importance for the understanding of early Christian teaching on the Eucharist (1 Cor 10:14–22; 11:17–34) and on the resurrection of the body (1 Cor 15:1–58).

Paul's authorship of 1 Corinthians, apart from a few verses that some regard as later interpolations, has never been seriously questioned. Some scholars have proposed, however, that the letter as we have it contains portions of more than one original Pauline letter. We know that Paul wrote at least two other letters to Corinth (see 1 Cor 5:9; 2 Cor 2:3–4) in addition to the two that we now have; this theory holds that the additional letters are actually contained within the two canonical ones. Most commentators, however, find 1 Corinthians quite understandable as a single coherent work.

The principal divisions of the First Letter to the Corinthians are the following:

I. Address (1:1–9)
II. Disorders in the Corinthian Community (1:10–6:20)
    A. Divisions in the Church (1:10–4:21)
    B. Moral Disorders (5:1–6:20)
III. Answers to the Corinthians' Questions (7:1–11:1)
    A. Marriage and Virginity (7:1–40)
    B. Offerings to Idols (8:1–11:1)
IV. Problems in Liturgical Assemblies (11:2–14:40)
    A. Women's Headdresses (11:3–16)
    B. The Lord's Supper (11:17–34)
    C. Spiritual Gifts (12:1–14:40)
V. The Resurrection (15:1–58)
    A. The Resurrection of Christ (15:1–11)
    B. The Resurrection of the Dead (15:12–34)
    C. The Manner of the Resurrection (15:35–58)
VI. Conclusion (16:1–24)

## I. ADDRESS*

### CHAPTER 1

**Greeting.** ¹Paul, called to be an apostle of Christ Jesus by the will of God,† and Sosthenes our brother,ᵃ ²to the church of God that is in Corinth, to you who have been sanctified in Christ Jesus, called to be holy, with all those everywhere who call upon the name of our Lord Jesus Christ, their Lord and ours.ᵇ ³Grace to you and peace from God our Father and the Lord Jesus Christ.

**Thanksgiving.** ⁴I give thanks to my God always on your account for the grace of God bestowed on you in Christ Jesus, ⁵that in him you were enriched in every way, with all discourse and all knowledge, ⁶as the testimony‡ to Christ was confirmed among you, ⁷so that you are not lacking in any spiritual gift as you wait for the revelation of our Lord Jesus Christ.ᶜ ⁸He will keep you firm

---

*[1:1–9] Paul follows the conventional form for the opening of a Hellenistic letter (cf. Rom 1:1–7), but expands the opening with details carefully chosen to remind the readers of their situation and to suggest some of the issues the letter will discuss.

†[1:1] **Called . . . by the will of God:** Paul's mission and the church's existence are grounded in God's initiative. God's call, grace, and fidelity are central ideas in this introduction, emphasized by repetition and wordplays in the Greek.

‡[1:6] **The testimony:** this defines the purpose of Paul's mission (see also 1 Cor 15:15 and the note on 1 Cor 2:1). The forms of his testimony include oral preaching and instruction, his letters, and the life he leads as an apostle.

---

a. [1:1] Rom 1:1.

b. [1:2] Acts 18:1–11.  c. [1:7] Ti 2:13.

to the end, irreproachable on the day of our Lord Jesus [Christ].*d* *9*God is faithful, and by him you were called to fellowship with his Son, Jesus Christ our Lord.*e*

## II. DISORDERS IN THE CORINTHIAN COMMUNITY*

### A. Divisions in the Church*

**Groups and Slogans.** *10*I urge you, brothers, in the name of our Lord Jesus Christ, that all of you agree in what you say, and that there be no divisions among you, but that you be united in the same mind and in the same purpose.*f* *11*For it has been reported to me about you, my brothers, by Chloe's people, that there are rivalries among you. *12*I mean that each of you is saying, "I belong to*†* Paul," or "I belong to Apollos," or "I belong to Cephas," or "I belong to Christ."*g* *13‡*Is Christ divided? Was Paul crucified for you? Or were you baptized in the name of Paul? *14*I give thanks [to God] that I baptized none of you except Crispus and Gaius,*h* *15*so that no one can say you were baptized in my name. *16*(I baptized the household of Stephanas also; beyond that I do not know whether I baptized anyone else.)*i* *17§*For Christ did not send me to baptize but to preach the gospel, and not with the wisdom of human eloquence,*¶* so that the cross of Christ might not be emptied of its meaning.*j*

---

*[1:10–4:21] The first problem Paul addresses is that of divisions within the community. Although we are unable to reconstruct the situation in Corinth completely, Paul clearly traces the divisions back to a false self-image on the part of the Corinthians, coupled with a false understanding of the apostles who preached to them (cf. 1 Cor 4:6, 9; 9:1–5) and of the Christian message itself. In these chapters he attempts to deal with those underlying factors and to bring the Corinthians back to a more correct perspective.

†[1:12] **I belong to**: the activities of Paul and Apollos in Corinth are described in Acts 18. **Cephas** (i.e., "the Rock," a name by which Paul designates Peter also in 1 Cor 3:22; 9:5; 15:5 and in Gal 1:18; 2:9, 11, 14) may well have passed through Corinth; he could have baptized some members of the community either there or elsewhere. The reference to **Christ** may be intended ironically.

‡[1:13–17] The reference to baptism and the contrast with preaching the gospel in v 17a suggest that some Corinthians were paying special allegiance to the individuals who initiated them into the community.

§[1:17b–18] The basic theme of 1 Cor 1–4 is announced. Adherence to individual leaders has something to do with differences in rhetorical ability and also with certain presuppositions regarding wisdom, eloquence, and effectiveness (power), which Paul judges to be in conflict with the gospel and the cross.

¶[1:17b] **Not with the wisdom of human eloquence**: both of the nouns employed here involve several levels of meaning, on which Paul deliberately plays as his thought unfolds. **Wisdom** (*sophia*) may be philosophical and speculative, but in biblical usage the term primarily denotes practical knowledge such as is demonstrated in the choice and effective application of means to achieve an end. The same term can designate the arts of building (cf. 1 Cor 3:10) or of persuasive speaking (cf. 1 Cor 2:4) or effectiveness in achieving salvation. **Eloquence** (*logos*): this translation emphasizes one possible meaning of the term *logos* (cf. the references to rhetorical style and persuasiveness in 1 Cor 2:1, 4). But the term itself may denote an internal reasoning process,

---

**Paradox of the Cross.** *18*The message of the cross is foolishness to those who are perishing, but to us who are being saved it is the power of God.*k* *19*For it is written:

> "I will destroy the wisdom of the wise,
>> and the learning of the learned I will set aside."*l*

*20*Where is the wise one? Where is the scribe? Where is the debater of this age? Has not God made the wisdom of the world foolish?*m* *21**For since in the wisdom of God the world did not come to know God through wisdom, it was the will of God through the foolishness of the proclamation to save those who have faith. *22*For Jews demand signs and Greeks look for wisdom,*n* *23*but we proclaim Christ crucified, a stumbling block to Jews and foolishness to Gentiles,*o* *24*but to those who are called, Jews and Greeks alike, Christ the power of God and the wisdom of God. *25*For the foolishness of God is wiser than human wisdom, and the weakness of God is stronger than human strength.

**The Corinthians and Paul.***††* *26*Consider your own calling, brothers. Not many of you were wise by human standards, not many were powerful, not many were of noble birth. *27*Rather, God chose the foolish of the world to shame the wise, and God chose the weak of the world to shame the strong,*p* *28*and God chose the lowly and despised of the world, those who count for nothing, to reduce to nothing those who are something, *29*so that no human being might boast*‡‡* before God.*q* *30*It is due to him that you are in Christ Jesus, who became for us wisdom from God, as well as righteousness, sanctification, and redemption,*r* *31*so that, as it is written, "Whoever boasts, should boast in the Lord."*s*

---

plan, or intention, as well as an external word, speech, or message. So by his expression *ouk en sophia logou* in the context of gospel preaching, Paul may intend to exclude both human ways of reasoning or thinking about things and human rhetorical technique. **Human**: this adjective does not stand in the Greek text but is supplied from the context. Paul will begin immediately to distinguish between *sophia* and *logos* from their divine counterparts and play them off against each other.

**[1:21–25] True wisdom and power are to be found paradoxically where one would least expect them, in the place of their apparent negation. To human eyes the crucified Christ symbolizes impotence and absurdity.

††[1:26–2:5] The pattern of God's wisdom and power is exemplified in their own experience, if they interpret it rightly (1 Cor 1:26–31), and can also be read in their experience of Paul as he first appeared among them preaching the gospel (1 Cor 2:1–5).

‡‡[1:29–31] "Boasting (about oneself)" is a Pauline expression for the radical sin, the claim to autonomy on the part of a creature, the illusion that we live and are saved by our own resources. "Boasting in the Lord" (1 Cor 1:31), on the other hand, is the acknowledgment that we live only from God and for God.

---

k. [1:18] 2:14 / Rom 1:16.  l. [1:19] Is 29:14.  m. [1:20] Is 19:12. n. [1:22] Mt 12:38; 16:1 / Acts 17:18–21.  o. [1:23] 2:2; Gal 3:1 / Gal 5:11.  p. [1:27] Jas 2:5.  q. [1:29] Eph 2:9.  r. [1:30] Rom 4:17 / 6:11; Rom 3:24–26; 2 Cor 5:21 / Eph 1:7; Col 1:14; 1 Thes 5:23.  s. [1:31] Jer 9:23; 2 Cor 10:17.

d. [1:8] Phil 1:6.  e. [1:9] 1 Jn 1:3.  f. [1:10] Phil 2:2.  g. [1:12] 3:4, 22; 16:12; Acts 18:24–28.  h. [1:14] Acts 18:8 / Rom 16:23.  i. [1:16] 16:15–17.  j. [1:17] 2:1, 4.

## CHAPTER 2

¹When I came to you, brothers, proclaiming the mystery of God,* I did not come with sublimity of words or of wisdom.ᵗ ²For I resolved to know nothing while I was with you except Jesus Christ, and him crucified.ᵘ ³I came to you in weakness† and fear and much trembling, ⁴and my message and my proclamation were not with persuasive [words of] wisdom,‡ but with a demonstration of spirit and power,ᵛ ⁵so that your faith might rest not on human wisdom but on the power of God.ʷ

**The True Wisdom.**§ ⁶Yet we do speak a wisdom to those who are mature, but not a wisdom of this age, nor of the rulers of this age who are passing away. ⁷Rather, we speak God's wisdom,⁵ mysterious, hidden, which God predetermined before the ages for our glory, ⁸and which none of the rulers of this age** knew; for if they had known it, they would not have crucified the Lord of glory. ⁹But as it is written:

> "What eye has not seen, and ear has not
>     heard,
>   and what has not entered the human
>       heart,
>   what God has prepared for those
>     who love him,"ˣ

---

*[2:1] **The mystery of God:** God's secret, known only to himself, is his plan for the salvation of his people; it is clear from 1 Cor 1:18–25; 2:2, 8–10 that this secret involves Jesus and the cross. In place of **mystery,** other good manuscripts read "testimony" (cf. 1 Cor 1:6).

†[2:3] The **weakness** of the crucified Jesus is reflected in Paul's own bearing (cf. 2 Cor 10–13). **Fear and much trembling:** reverential fear based on a sense of God's transcendence permeates Paul's existence and preaching. Compare his advice to the Philippians to work out their salvation with "fear and trembling" (Phil 2:12), because God is at work in them just as his exalting power was paradoxically at work in the emptying, humiliation, and obedience of Jesus to death on the cross (Phil 2:6–11).

‡[2:4] Among many manuscript readings here the best is either "not with the persuasion of wisdom" or "not with persuasive words of wisdom," which differ only by a nuance. Whichever reading is accepted, the inefficacy of human wisdom for salvation is contrasted with the power of the cross.

§[2:6–3:4] Paul now asserts paradoxically what he has previously been denying. To the Greeks who "are looking for wisdom" (1 Cor 1:22), he does indeed bring a wisdom, but of a higher order and an entirely different quality, the only wisdom really worthy of the name. The Corinthians should be able to grasp Paul's preaching as wisdom and enter into a wisdom-conversation with him if they were more open to the Spirit and receptive to the new insight and language that the Spirit teaches.

⁵[2:7–10a] **God's wisdom:** his plan for our salvation. This was his own eternal secret that no one else could fathom, but in this new age of salvation he has graciously revealed it to us. For the pattern of God's secret, hidden to others and now revealed to the Church, see also Rom 11:25–36; 16:25–27; Eph 1:3–10; 3:3–11; Col 1:25–28.

**[2:8] **The rulers of this age:** this suggests not only the political leaders of the Jews and Romans under whom Jesus was crucified (cf. Acts 4:25–28) but also the cosmic powers behind them (cf. Eph 1:20–23; 3:10). **They would not have crucified the Lord of glory:** they became the unwitting executors of God's plan, which will paradoxically bring about their own conquest and submission (1 Cor 15:24–28).

---

t. [2:1] 1:17.  u. [2:2] 1:23; Gal 6:14.  v. [2:4] 4:20; Rom 15:19; 1 Thes 1:5.  w. [2:5] 2 Cor 4:7.  x. [2:9] Is 64:3.

---

¹⁰ʸthis God has revealed to us through the Spirit. For the Spirit scrutinizes everything, even the depths of God. ¹¹Among human beings, who knows what pertains to a person except the spirit of the person that is within? Similarly, no one knows what pertains to God except the Spirit of God. ¹²We have not received the spirit of the world but the Spirit that is from God, so that we may understand the things freely given us by God. ¹³And we speak about them not with words taught by human wisdom, but with words taught by the Spirit, describing spiritual realities in spiritual terms.††

¹⁴Now the natural person‡‡ does not accept what pertains to the Spirit of God, for to him it is foolishness, and he cannot understand it, because it is judged spiritually. ¹⁵The spiritual person, however, can judge everything but is not subject to judgment§§ by anyone.

¹⁶For "who has known the mind of the Lord, so as to counsel him?" But we have the mind of Christ.ᶻ

## CHAPTER 3

¹⁵⁵Brothers, I could not talk to you as spiritual people, but as fleshly people,*** as infants in Christ. ²I fed you milk, not solid food, because you were unable to take it. Indeed, you are still not able, even now,ᵃ ³for you are still of the flesh. While there is jealousy and rivalry among you,†††

---

††[2:13] **In spiritual terms:** the Spirit teaches spiritual people a new mode of perception (1 Cor 2:12) and an appropriate language by which they can share their self-understanding, their knowledge about what God has done in them. The final phrase in 1 Cor 2:13 can also be translated "describing spiritual realities to spiritual people," in which case it prepares for 1 Cor 2:14–16.

‡‡[2:14] **The natural person:** see note on 1 Cor 3:1.

§§[2:15] **The spiritual person . . . is not subject to judgment:** since spiritual persons have been given knowledge of what pertains to God (1 Cor 2:11–12), they share in God's own capacity to judge. One to whom the mind of the Lord (and of Christ) is revealed (1 Cor 2:16) can be said to share in some sense in God's exemption from counseling and criticism.

⁵⁵[3:1–4] The Corinthians desire a sort of wisdom dialogue or colloquy with Paul; they are looking for solid, adult food, and he appears to disappoint their expectations. Paul counters: if such a dialogue has not yet taken place, the reason is that they are still at an immature stage of development (cf. 1 Cor 2:6).

***[3:1] **Spiritual people . . . fleshly people:** Paul employs two clusters of concepts and terms to distinguish what later theology will call the "natural" and the "supernatural." (1) The natural person (1 Cor 2:14) is one whose existence, perceptions, and behavior are determined by purely natural principles, the *psychē* (1 Cor 2:14) and the *sarx* (flesh, a biblical term that connotes creatureliness, 1 Cor 3:1, 3). Such persons are only infants (1 Cor 3:1); they remain on a purely human level (*anthrōpoi,* 1 Cor 3:4). (2) On the other hand, they are called to be animated by a higher principle, the *pneuma,* God's spirit. They are to become spiritual (*pneumatikoi,* 1 Cor 3:1) and mature (1 Cor 2:6) in their perceptions and behavior (cf. Gal 5:16–26). The culmination of existence in the Spirit is described in 1 Cor 15:44–49.

†††[3:3–4] Jealousy, rivalry, and divisions in the community are symptoms of their arrested development; they reveal the immaturity both of their self-understanding (1 Cor 3:4) and of the judgments about their apostles (1 Cor 3:21).

---

y. [2:10] Mt 11:25; 13:11; 16:17.  z. [2:16] Wis 9:13; Is 40:13; Rom 11:34.  a. [3:2] Heb 5:12–14.

are you not of the flesh and behaving in an ordinary human way?[b] [4]Whenever someone says, "I belong to Paul," and another, "I belong to Apollos," are you not merely human?[c]

**The Role of God's Ministers.*** [5]What is Apollos, after all, and what is Paul? Ministers[†] through whom you became believers, just as the Lord assigned each one. [6]I planted, Apollos watered, but God caused the growth.[d] [7]Therefore, neither the one who plants nor the one who waters is anything, but only God, who causes the growth. [8]The one who plants and the one who waters are equal, and each will receive wages in proportion to his labor. [9]For we are God's co-workers; you are God's field, God's building.[e]

[10‡]According to the grace of God given to me, like a wise master builder I laid a foundation, and another is building upon it. But each one must be careful how he builds upon it, [11]for no one can lay a foundation other than the one that is there, namely, Jesus Christ. [12]If anyone builds on this foundation with gold, silver, precious stones, wood, hay, or straw, [13]the work of each will come to light, for the Day[§] will disclose it. It will be revealed with fire, and the fire [itself] will test the quality of each one's work.[f] [14]If the work stands that someone built upon the foundation, that person will receive a wage. [15]But if someone's work is burned up, that one will suffer loss; the person will be saved,[¶] but only as through fire. [16]Do you not know that you are the temple of God, and that the Spirit of God dwells in you?[g] [17]If anyone destroys God's temple, God will destroy that person; for the temple of God, which you are, is holy.[**]

[18]Let no one deceive himself. If anyone among you considers himself wise in this age, let him become a fool so as to become wise.[h] [19]For the wisdom of this world is foolishness in the eyes of God, for it is written:[i]

"He catches the wise in their own ruses,"

[20]and again:

"The Lord knows the thoughts of the wise, that they are vain."[j]

[21††]So let no one boast about human beings, for everything belongs to you,[k] [22]Paul or Apollos or Cephas, or the world or life or death, or the present or the future: all belong to you, [23]and you to Christ, and Christ to God.

## CHAPTER 4

[1]Thus should one regard us: as servants of Christ and stewards of the mysteries of God.[l] [2]Now it is of course required of stewards that they be found trustworthy. [3]It does not concern me in the least that I be judged by you or any human tribunal; I do not even pass judgment on myself; [4]I am not conscious of anything against me, but I do not thereby stand acquitted; the one who judges me is the Lord.[m] [5]Therefore, do not make any judgment before the appointed time, until the Lord comes, for he will bring to light what is hidden in darkness and will manifest the motives of our hearts, and then everyone will receive praise from God.

**Paul's Life as Pattern.[‡‡]** [6]I have applied these things to myself and Apollos for your benefit, brothers, so that you may learn from us not to go beyond what is written,[§§] so that none of you

---

*[3:5–4:5] The Corinthians tend to evaluate their leaders by the criteria of human wisdom and to exaggerate their importance. Paul views the role of the apostles in the light of his theology of spiritual gifts (cf. 1 Cor 12–14, where the charism of the apostle heads the lists). The essential aspects of all spiritual gifts (1 Cor 12:4–6 presents them as gifts of grace, as services, and as modes of activity) are exemplified by the apostolate, which is a gift of grace (1 Cor 3:10) through which God works (1 Cor 3:9) and a form of service (1 Cor 3:5) for the common good (elsewhere expressed by the verb "build up," suggested here by the image of the building, 1 Cor 3:9). The apostles serve the church, but their accountability is to God and to Christ (1 Cor 4:1–5).

†[3:5] **Ministers:** for other expressions of Paul's understanding of himself as minister or steward to the church, cf. 1 Cor 4:1; 9:17, 19–27; 2 Cor 3:6–9; 4:1; 5:18; 6:3–4; and 2 Cor 11:23 (the climax of Paul's defense).

‡[3:10–11] There are diverse functions in the service of the community, but each individual's task is serious, and each will stand accountable for the quality of his contribution.

§[3:13] **The Day:** the great day of Yahweh, the day of judgment, which can be a time of either gloom or joy. **Fire** both destroys and purifies.

¶[3:15] **Will be saved:** although Paul can envision very harsh divine punishment (cf. 1 Cor 3:17), he appears optimistic about the success of divine corrective means both here and elsewhere (cf. 1 Cor 5:5; 11:32 [discipline]). The text of 1 Cor 3:15 has sometimes been used to support the notion of purgatory, though it does not envisage this.

**[3:17] **Holy:** i.e., "belonging to God." The cultic sanctity of the community is a fundamental theological reality to which Paul frequently alludes (cf. 1 Cor 1:2, 30; 6:11; 7:14).

††[3:21–23] These verses pick up the line of thought of 1 Cor 1:10–13. If the Corinthians were genuinely wise (1 Cor 3:18–20), their perceptions would be reversed, and they would see everything in the world and all those with whom they exist in the church in their true relations with one another. Paul assigns all the persons involved in the theological universe a position on a scale: God, Christ, church members, church leaders. Read from top to bottom, the scale expresses ownership; read from bottom to top, the obligation to serve. This picture should be complemented by similar statements such as those in 1 Cor 8:6 and 1 Cor 15:20–28.

‡‡[4:6–21] This is an emotionally charged peroration to the discussion about divisions. It contains several exhortations and statements of Paul's purpose in writing (cf. 1 Cor 4:6, 14–17, 21) that counterbalance the initial exhortation at 1 Cor 1:10.

§§[4:6] **That you may learn from us not to go beyond what is written:** the words "to go" are not in the Greek, but have here been added as the minimum necessary to elicit sense from this difficult passage. It probably means that the Corinthians should avoid the false wisdom of vain speculation, contenting themselves with Paul's proclamation of the cross, which is the fulfillment of God's promises in the Old Testament (what is written). **Inflated with pride:** literally, "puffed up," i.e., arrogant, filled with a sense of self-importance. The term is particularly Pauline, found in the New

---

b. [3:3] Jas 3:13–16.　c. [3:4] 1:12.　d. [3:6] Acts 18:1–11, 24–28.
e. [3:9] Eph 2:20–22; 1 Pt 2:5.　f. [3:13] Mt 3:11–12; 2 Thes 1:7–10.
g. [3:16] 6:19; 2 Cor 6:16; Eph 2:20–22.

h. [3:18] 8:2; Is 5:21; Gal 6:3.　i. [3:19] 1:20 / Jb 5:13.　j. [3:20] Ps 94:11.　k. [3:21] 4:6 / Rom 8:32.　l. [4:1] Ti 1:7; 1 Pt 4:10.　m. [4:4] 2 Cor 1:12 / Rom 2:16; 2 Cor 5:10.

will be inflated with pride in favor of one person over against another. ⁷Who confers distinction upon you? What do you possess that you have not received? But if you have received it, why are you boasting as if you did not receive it? ⁸You are already satisfied; you have already grown rich; you have become kings* without us! Indeed, I wish that you had become kings, so that we also might become kings with you.

⁹†For as I see it, God has exhibited us apostles as the last of all, like people sentenced to death, since we have become a spectacle to the world, to angels and human beings alike.ⁿ ¹⁰We are fools on Christ's account, but you are wise in Christ; we are weak, but you are strong; you are held in honor, but we in disrepute.ᵒ ¹¹To this very hour we go hungry and thirsty, we are poorly clad and roughly treated, we wander about homelessᵖ ¹²and we toil, working with our own hands. When ridiculed, we bless; when persecuted, we endure;�q ¹³when slandered, we respond gently. We have become like the world's rubbish, the scum of all, to this very moment.

¹⁴I am writing you this not to shame you, but to admonish you as my beloved children.‡ ¹⁵Even if you should have countless guides to Christ, yet you do not have many fathers, for I became your father in Christ Jesus through the gospel.ʳ ¹⁶Therefore, I urge you, be imitators of me.ˢ ¹⁷For this reason I am sending you Timothy,

who is my beloved and faithful son in the Lord; he will remind you of my ways in Christ [Jesus], just as I teach them everywhere in every church.ᵗ

¹⁸ˢSome have become inflated with pride, as if I were not coming to you. ¹⁹But I will come to you soon, if the Lord is willing, and I shall ascertain not the talk of these inflated people but their power. ²⁰For the kingdom of God is not a matter of talk but of power.ᵘ ²¹Which do you prefer? Shall I come to you with a rod, or with love and a gentle spirit?ᵛ

*B. Moral Disorders¶*

## CHAPTER 5

**A Case of Incest.**** ¹It is widely reported that there is immorality among you, and immorality of a kind not found even among pagans— a man living with his father's wife.ʷ ²And you are inflated with pride.†† Should you not rather have been sorrowful? The one who did this deed should be expelled from your midst. ³I, for my part, although absent in body but present in spirit, have already, as if present, pronounced judgment on the one who has committed this deed,ˣ ⁴in the name of [our] Lord Jesus: when you have gathered together and I am with you in spirit with the power of the Lord Jesus, ⁵you are to deliver this man to Satan‡‡ for the destruction of his flesh, so that his spirit may be saved on the day of the Lord.ʸ

⁶ᶻYour boasting is not appropriate. Do you not know that a little yeast§§ leavens all the

---

Testament only in 1 Cor 4:6, 18–19; 5:2; 8:1; 13:4; Col 2:18 (cf. the related noun at 2 Cor 12:20). It sometimes occurs in conjunction with the theme of "boasting," as in 1 Cor 4:6–7 here.

*[4:8] **Satisfied . . . rich . . . kings:** these three statements could also be punctuated as questions continuing the series begun in v 7. In any case these expressions reflect a tendency at Corinth toward an overrealized eschatology, a form of self-deception that draws Paul's irony. The underlying attitude has implications for the Corinthians' thinking about other issues, notably morality and the resurrection, that Paul will address later in the letter.

†[4:9–13] A rhetorically effective catalogue of the circumstances of apostolic existence, in the course of which Paul ironically contrasts his own sufferings with the Corinthians' illusion that they have passed beyond the folly of the passion and have already reached the condition of glory. His language echoes that of the beatitudes and woes, which assert a future reversal of present conditions. Their present sufferings ("to this very hour," 11) place the apostles in the class of those to whom the beatitudes promise future relief (Mt 5:3–11; Lk 6:20–23); whereas the Corinthians' image of themselves as "already" filled, rich, ruling (1 Cor 4:8), as wise, strong, and honored (1 Cor 4:10) places them paradoxically in the position of those whom the woes threaten with future undoing (Lk 6:24–26). They have lost sight of the fact that the reversal is predicted for the future.

‡[4:14–17] **My beloved children:** the close of the argument is dominated by the tender metaphor of the father who not only gives his children life but also educates them. Once he has begotten them through his preaching, Paul continues to present the gospel to them existentially, by his life as well as by his word, and they are to learn, as children do, by imitating their parents (1 Cor 4:16). The reference to the **rod** in 1 Cor 4:21 belongs to the same image-complex. So does the image of the **ways** in 1 Cor 4:17: the ways that Paul teaches everywhere, "his ways in Christ Jesus," mean a behavior pattern quite different from the human ways along which the Corinthians are walking (1 Cor 3:3).

§[4:18–21] 1 Cor 4:20 picks up the contrast between a certain kind of talk (*logos*) and true power (*dynamis*) from 1 Cor 1:17–18 and 1 Cor 2:4–5. The kingdom, which many of them imagine to be fully present in their lives (1 Cor 4:8), will be rather unexpectedly disclosed in the strength of Paul's encounter with them, if they make a powerful intervention on his part necessary. Compare the similar ending to an argument in 2 Cor 13:1–4, 10.

¶[5:1–6:20] Paul now takes up a number of other matters that require regulation. These have come to his attention by hearsay (1 Cor 5:1), probably in reports brought by "Chloe's people" (1 Cor 1:11).

**[5:1–13] Paul first deals with the incestuous union of a man with his stepmother (1 Cor 5:1–8) and then attempts to clarify general admonitions he has given about associating with fellow Christians guilty of immorality (1 Cor 5:9–13). Each of these three brief paragraphs expresses the same idea: the need of separation between the holy and the unholy.

††[5:2] **Inflated with pride:** this remark and the reference to **boasting** in 1 Cor 5:6 suggest that they are proud of themselves despite the infection in their midst, tolerating and possibly even approving the situation. The attitude expressed in 1 Cor 6:2, 13 may be influencing their thinking in this case.

‡‡[5:5] **Deliver this man to Satan:** once the sinner is expelled from the church, the sphere of Jesus' lordship and victory over sin, he will be in the region outside over which Satan is still master. **For the destruction of his flesh:** the purpose of the penalty is medicinal: through affliction, sin's grip over him may be destroyed and the path to repentance and reunion laid open. With Paul's instructions for an excommunication ceremony here, contrast his recommendations for the reconciliation of a sinner in 2 Cor 2:5–11.

§§[5:6] **A little yeast:** yeast, which induces fermentation, is a natural symbol for a source of corruption that becomes all-pervasive. The expression is proverbial.

---

n. [4:9] 15:31; Rom 8:36; 2 Cor 4:8–12; 11:23 / Heb 10:33.   o. [4:10] 1:18; 3:18; 2 Cor 11:19 / 1 Cor 2:3; 2 Cor 13:9.   p. [4:11] Rom 8:35; 2 Cor 11:23–27.   q. [4:12] Acts 9:6–14; 18:3; 20:34; 1 Thes 2:9 / 1 Pt 3:9.   r. [4:15] Gal 4:19; Phlm 10.   s. [4:16] 11:1; Phil 3:17; 4:9; 1 Thes 1:6; 2 Thes 3:7, 9.

t. [4:17] 16:10; Acts 19:22.   u. [4:20] 2:4; 1 Thes 1:5.   v. [4:21] 2 Cor 1:23; 10:2.   w. [5:1] Lv 18:7–8; 20:11; Dt 27:20.   x. [5:3] Col 2:5.   y. [5:5] 1 Tm 1:20.   z. [5:6] Gal 5:9.

dough? [7]*Clear out the old yeast, so that you may become a fresh batch of dough, inasmuch as you are unleavened. For our paschal lamb, Christ, has been sacrificed.[a] [8]Therefore, let us celebrate the feast, not with the old yeast, the yeast of malice and wickedness, but with the unleavened bread of sincerity and truth.[b]

[9]†I wrote you in my letter not to associate with immoral people, [10]not at all referring to the immoral of this world or the greedy and robbers or idolaters; for you would then have to leave the world.[c] [11]But I now write to you not to associate with anyone named a brother, if he is immoral, greedy, an idolater, a slanderer, a drunkard, or a robber, not even to eat with such a person.[d] [12]For why should I be judging outsiders? Is it not your business to judge those within? [13]God will judge those outside. "Purge the evil person from your midst."[e]

## CHAPTER 6

**Lawsuits Before Unbelievers.**‡ [1]How can any one of you with a case against another dare to bring it to the unjust for judgment instead of to the holy ones? [2]§§Do you not know that the holy ones will judge the world? If the world is to be judged by you, are you unqualified for the lowest law courts?[f] [3]Do you not know that we will judge angels? Then why not everyday matters? [4]If, therefore, you have courts for everyday matters, do you seat as judges people of no standing in the church? [5]I say this to shame you. Can it be that there is not one among you wise enough to be able to settle a case between brothers? [6]But rather brother goes to court against brother, and that before unbelievers?

[7]Now indeed [then] it is, in any case, a failure on your part that you have lawsuits against one another. Why not rather put up with injustice? Why not rather let yourselves be cheated?[g] [8]Instead, you inflict injustice and cheat, and this to brothers. [9]Do you not know that the unjust will not inherit the kingdom of God? Do not be deceived; neither fornicators nor idolaters nor adulterers nor boy prostitutes' nor sodomites[h] [10]nor thieves nor the greedy nor drunkards nor slanderers nor robbers will inherit the kingdom of God. [11]That is what some of you used to be; but now you have had yourselves washed, you were sanctified, you were justified in the name of the Lord Jesus Christ and in the Spirit of our God.[i]

**Sexual Immorality.**** [12]"Everything is lawful for me,"†† but not everything is beneficial. "Everything is lawful for me," but I will not let myself be dominated by anything.[j] [13]"Food for the stomach and the stomach for food," but God will do away with both the one and the other. The body, however, is not for immorality, but for the Lord, and the Lord is for the body; [14]God raised the Lord and will also raise us by his power.[k]

[15]Do you not know that your bodies are members of Christ? Shall I then take Christ's members and make them the members of a prostitute?‡‡ Of course not![l] [16][Or] do you not

§[6:9–10] A catalogue of typical vices that exclude from the kingdom of God and that should be excluded from God's church. Such lists (cf. 1 Cor 5:10) reflect the common moral sensibility of the New Testament period.

¶[6:9] The Greek word translated as **boy prostitutes** may refer to catamites, i.e., boys or young men who were kept for purposes of prostitution, a practice not uncommon in the Greco-Roman world. In Greek mythology this was the function of Ganymede, the "cupbearer of the gods," whose Latin name was Catamitus. The term translated **sodomites** refers to adult males who indulged in homosexual practices with such boys. See similar condemnations of such practices in Rom 1:26–27; 1 Tm 1:10.

**[6:12–20] Paul now turns to the opinion of some Corinthians that sexuality is a morally indifferent area (1 Cor 6:12–13). This leads him to explain the mutual relation between the Lord Jesus and our bodies (1 Cor 6:13b) in a densely packed paragraph that contains elements of a profound theology of sexuality (1 Cor 6:15–20).

††[6:12–13] **Everything is lawful for me**: the Corinthians may have derived this slogan from Paul's preaching about Christian freedom, but they mean something different by it: they consider sexual satisfaction a matter as indifferent as food, and they attribute no lasting significance to bodily functions (1 Cor 6:13a). Paul begins to deal with the slogan by two qualifications, which suggest principles for judging sexual activity. **Not everything is beneficial**: cf. 1 Cor 10:23, and the whole argument of 1 Cor 8–10 on the finality of freedom and moral activity. **Not let myself be dominated**: certain apparently free actions may involve in fact a secret servitude in conflict with the lordship of Jesus.

‡‡[6:15b–16] **A prostitute**: the reference may be specifically to religious prostitution, an accepted part of pagan culture at Corinth and elsewhere; but the prostitute also serves as a symbol for any sexual relationship that conflicts with Christ's claim over us individually. **The two . . . will become one flesh**: the text of Gn 2:24 is applied positively to human marriage in Matthew and Mark, and in Eph 5:29–32: love of husband and wife reflect the love of Christ for his church. The application of the text to union with a prostitute is jarring, for such a union is a parody, an antitype of marriage, which does conflict with Christ's claim over us. This explains the horror expressed in 1 Cor 6:15b.

*[5:7–8] In the Jewish calendar, Passover was followed immediately by the festival of Unleavened Bread. In preparation for this feast all traces of old bread were removed from the house, and during the festival only unleavened bread was eaten. The sequence of these two feasts provides Paul with an image of Christian existence: Christ's death (the true Passover celebration) is followed by the life of the Christian community, marked by newness, purity, and integrity (a perpetual feast of unleavened bread). Paul may have been writing around Passover time (cf. 1 Cor 16:5); this is a little Easter homily, the earliest in Christian literature.

†[5:9–13] Paul here corrects a misunderstanding of his earlier directives against associating with immoral fellow Christians. He concedes the impossibility of avoiding contact with sinners in society at large but urges the Corinthians to maintain the inner purity of their own community.

‡[6:1–11] Christians at Corinth are suing one another before pagan judges in Roman courts. A barrage of rhetorical questions (1 Cor 6:1–9) betrays Paul's indignation over this practice, which he sees as an infringement upon the holiness of the Christian community.

§§[6:2–3] The principle to which Paul appeals is an eschatological prerogative promised to Christians: they are to share with Christ the judgment of the world (cf. Dn 7:22, 27). Hence they ought to be able to settle minor disputes within the community.

a. [5:7] Ex 12:1–13; Dt 16:1–2; 1 Pt 1:19.   b. [5:8] Ex 12:15–20; 13:7; Dt 16:3.   c. [5:10] 10:27; Jn 17:15.   d. [5:11] Mt 18:17; 2 Thes 3:6, 14; 2 Jn 10.   e. [5:13] Dt 13:6; 17:7; 22:24.   f. [6:2] Wis 3:8; Mt 19:28; Rev 20:4.

g. [6:7] Mt 5:38–42; Rom 12:17–21; 1 Thes 5:15.   h. [6:9] 15:50; Gal 5:19–21; Eph 5:5.   i. [6:11] Ti 3:3–7.   j. [6:12] 10:23.   k. [6:14] Rom 8:11; 2 Cor 4:14.   l. [6:15] 12:27; Rom 6:12–13; 12:5; Eph 5:30.

know that anyone who joins himself to a prostitute becomes one body with her? For "the two," it says, "will become one flesh."[m] [17]But whoever is joined to the Lord becomes one spirit with him.[n] [18]Avoid immorality. Every other sin a person commits is outside the body, but the immoral person sins against his own body.[*] [19]Do you not know that your body is a temple[†] of the holy Spirit within you, whom you have from God, and that you are not your own?[o] [20]For you have been purchased at a price. Therefore glorify God in your body.[p]

## III. ANSWERS TO THE CORINTHIANS' QUESTIONS

### A. Marriage and Virginity[‡]

## CHAPTER 7

**Advice to the Married.**[§] [1]Now in regard to the matters about which you wrote: "It is a good thing for a man not to touch a woman,"[¶] [2]but because of cases of immorality every man should have his own wife, and every woman her own husband. [3]The husband should fulfill his duty toward his wife, and likewise the wife toward her husband. [4]A wife does not have authority over her own body, but rather her husband, and

---

[*][6:18] **Against his own body**: expresses the intimacy and depth of sexual disorder, which violates the very orientation of our bodies.

[†][6:19–20] Paul's vision becomes trinitarian. **A temple**: sacred by reason of God's gift, his indwelling Spirit. **Not your own**: but "for the Lord," who acquires ownership by the act of redemption. **Glorify God in your body**: the argument concludes with a positive imperative to supplement the negative "avoid immorality" of 1 Cor 6:18. Far from being a terrain that is morally indifferent, the area of sexuality is one in which our relationship with God (and his Christ and his Spirit) is very intimately expressed: he is either highly glorified or deeply offended.

[‡][7:1–40] Paul now begins to answer questions addressed to him by the Corinthians (1 Cor 7:1–11:1). The first of these concerns marriage. This chapter contains advice both to the married (1–16) and to the unmarried (1 Cor 7:25–38) or widowed (1 Cor 7:39–40); these two parts are separated by 1 Cor 7:17–24, which enunciate a principle applicable to both.

[§][7:1–16] It seems that some Christians in Corinth were advocating asceticism in sexual matters. The pattern **it is a good thing . . . , but** occurs twice (1 Cor 7:1–2, 8–9; cf. 1 Cor 7:26), suggesting that in this matter as in others the Corinthians have seized upon a genuine value but are exaggerating or distorting it in some way. Once again Paul calls them to a more correct perspective and a better sense of their own limitations. The phrase it is a **good thing** (1 Cor 7:1) may have been the slogan of the ascetic party at Corinth.

[¶][7:1–7] References to Paul's own behavior (1 Cor 7:7–8) suggest that his celibate way of life and his preaching to the unmarried (cf. 1 Cor 7:25–35) have given some the impression that asceticism within marriage, i.e., suspension of normal sexual relations, would be a laudable ideal. Paul points to their experience of widespread immorality to caution them against overestimating their own strength (1 Cor 7:2); as individuals they may not have the particular gift that makes such asceticism feasible (1 Cor 7:7) and hence are to abide by the principle to be explained in 1 Cor 7:17–24.

---

m. [6:16] Gn 2:24; Mt 19:5; Mk 10:8; Eph 5:31.  n. [6:17] Rom 8:9–10; 2 Cor 3:17.  o. [6:19] 3:16–17; Rom 5:5.  p. [6:20] 3:23; 7:23; Acts 20:28 / Rom 12:1; Phil 1:20.

similarly a husband does not have authority over his own body, but rather his wife. [5]Do not deprive each other, except perhaps by mutual consent for a time, to be free for prayer, but then return to one another, so that Satan may not tempt you through your lack of self-control. [6]This I say by way of concession,[**] however, not as a command. [7]Indeed, I wish everyone to be as I am, but each has a particular gift from God,[††] one of one kind and one of another.[q]

[8][*]Now to the unmarried and to widows I say: it is a good thing for them to remain as they are, as I do, [9]but if they cannot exercise self-control they should marry, for it is better to marry than to be on fire. [10][*]To the married, however, I give this instruction (not I, but the Lord):[§§] A wife should not separate from her husband [11]— and if she does separate she must either remain single or become reconciled to her husband— and a husband should not divorce his wife.

[12]To the rest[¶¶] I say (not the Lord): if any brother has a wife who is an unbeliever, and she is willing to go on living with him, he should not divorce her; [13]and if any woman has a husband who is an unbeliever, and he is willing to go on living with her, she should not divorce her husband. [14]For the unbelieving husband is made holy through his wife, and the unbelieving wife is made holy through the brother. Otherwise your children would be unclean, whereas in fact they are holy.[r]

[15]If the unbeliever separates,[***] however, let him separate. The brother or sister is not bound in such cases; God has called you to peace. [16]For how do you know, wife, whether you will save your husband; or how do you know, husband, whether you will save your wife?

**The Life That the Lord Has Assigned.**[†††] [17]Only, everyone should live as the Lord has assigned,

---

[**][7:6] **By way of concession**: this refers most likely to the concession mentioned in 1 Cor 7:5a: temporary interruption of relations for a legitimate purpose.

[††][7:7] **A particular gift from God**: use of the term *charisma* suggests that marriage and celibacy may be viewed in the light of Paul's theology of spiritual gifts (1 Cor 12–14).

[‡‡][7:8] Paul was obviously unmarried when he wrote this verse. Some interpreters believe that he had previously been married and widowed; there is no clear evidence either for or against this view, which was expressed already at the end of the second century by Clement of Alexandria.

[§§][7:10–11] (**Not I, but the Lord**): Paul reminds the married of Jesus' principle of nonseparation (Mk 10:9). This is one of his rare specific references to the teaching of Jesus.

[¶¶][7:12–14] **To the rest**: marriages in which only one partner is a baptized Christian. Jesus' prohibition against divorce is not addressed to them, but Paul extends the principle of nonseparation to such unions, provided they are marked by peacefulness and shared sanctification.

[***][7:15–16] **If the unbeliever separates**: the basis of the "Pauline privilege" in Catholic marriage legislation.

[†††][7:17–24] On the ground that distinct human conditions are less significant than the whole new existence opened up by God's call, Paul urges them to be less concerned with changing their states of life than with answering God's call where it finds them. The principle applies both to the married state (1 Cor 7:1–16) and to the unmarried (1 Cor 7:25–38).

---

q. [7:7] Mt 19:11–12.  r. [7:8] 1 Tm 5:11–16 / 9:5.  s. [7:10–11] Mt 5:32; 19:9.  t. [7:14] Rom 11:16.

just as God called each one. I give this order in all the churches. [18]Was someone called after he had been circumcised? He should not try to undo his circumcision. Was an uncircumcised person called? He should not be circumcised.[u] [19]Circumcision means nothing, and uncircumcision means nothing; what matters is keeping God's commandments.[v] [20]Everyone should remain in the state in which he was called.

[21]Were you a slave when you were called? Do not be concerned but, even if you can gain your freedom, make the most of it. [22]For the slave called in the Lord is a freed person in the Lord, just as the free person who has been called is a slave of Christ.[w] [23]You have been purchased at a price. Do not become slaves to human beings.[x] [24]Brothers, everyone should continue before God in the state in which he was called.

**Advice to Virgins and Widows.** [25]Now in regard to virgins I have no commandment from the Lord,[*] but I give my opinion as one who by the Lord's mercy is trustworthy. [26]So this is what I think best because of the present distress: that it is a good thing for a person to remain as he is.[y] [27]Are you bound to a wife? Do not seek a separation. Are you free of a wife? Then do not look for a wife. [28]If you marry, however, you do not sin, nor does an unmarried woman sin if she marries; but such people will experience affliction in their earthly life, and I would like to spare you that.

[29]I tell you, brothers, the time is running out. From now on, let those having wives act as not having them,[z] [30]those weeping as not weeping, those rejoicing as not rejoicing, those buying as not owning, [31]those using the world as not using it fully. For the world in its present form is passing away.

[32]I should like you to be free of anxieties. An unmarried man is anxious about the things of the Lord, how he may please the Lord. [33]But a married man is anxious about the things of the world, how he may please his wife,[a] [34]and he is divided. An unmarried woman or a virgin is anxious about the things of the Lord, so that she may be holy in both body and spirit. A married woman, on the other hand, is anxious about the things of the world, how she may please her husband.[b] [35]I am telling you this for your own benefit, not to impose a restraint upon you, but for the sake of propriety and adherence to the Lord without distraction.[c]

[36]If anyone thinks he is behaving improperly toward his virgin, and if a critical moment has come[§] and so it has to be, let him do as he wishes. He is committing no sin; let them get married. [37]The one who stands firm in his resolve, however, who is not under compulsion but has power over his own will, and has made up his mind to keep his virgin, will be doing well. [38]So then, the one who marries his virgin does well; the one who does not marry her will do better.

[39]A wife is bound to her husband as long as he lives. But if her husband dies, she is free to be married to whomever she wishes, provided that it be in the Lord.[d] [40]She is more blessed, though, in my opinion, if she remains as she is, and I think that I too have the Spirit of God.[e]

*B. Offerings to Idols[**]*

## CHAPTER 8

**Knowledge Insufficient.** [1]Now in regard to meat sacrificed to idols:[††] we realize that "all of us have knowledge"; knowledge inflates with pride, but love builds up.[f] [2]If anyone supposes he knows something, he does not yet know as he ought to know. [3]But if one loves God, one is known by him.[g]

---

‡[7:36–38] The passage is difficult to interpret, because it is unclear whether Paul is thinking of a father and his unmarried daughter (or slave), or of a couple engaged in a betrothal or spiritual marriage. The general principles already enunciated apply: there is no question of sin, even if they should marry, but staying as they are is "better" (for the reasons mentioned in 1 Cor 7:28–35). Once again the *charisma* of 1 Cor 7:7 which applies also to the unmarried (1 Cor 7:8–9), is to be presupposed.

§[7:36] **A critical moment has come:** either because the woman will soon be beyond marriageable age, or because their passions are becoming uncontrollable (cf. 1 Cor 7:9).

¶[7:39–40] Application of the principles to the case of widows. If they do choose to remarry, they ought to prefer Christian husbands.

**[8:1–11:1] The Corinthians' second question concerns meat that has been sacrificed to idols; in this area they were exhibiting a disordered sense of liberation that Paul here tries to rectify. These chapters contain a sustained and unified argument that illustrates Paul's method of theological reflection on a moral dilemma. Although the problem with which he is dealing is dated, the guidelines for moral decisions that he offers are of lasting validity. Essentially Paul urges them to take a communitarian rather than an individualistic view of their Christian freedom. Many decisions that they consider pertinent only to their private relationship with God have, in fact, social consequences. Nor can moral decisions be determined by merely theoretical considerations; they must be based on concrete circumstances, specifically on the value and needs of other individuals and on mutual responsibility within the community. Paul here introduces the theme of "building up" (*oikodomē*), i.e., of contributing by individual action to the welfare and growth of the community. This theme will be further developed in 1 Cor 14; see note on 1 Cor 14:3b–5. Several years later Paul would again deal with the problem of meat sacrificed to idols in Rom 14:1–15:6.

††[8:1a] **Meat sacrificed to idols:** much of the food consumed in the city could have passed through pagan religious ceremonies before finding its way into markets and homes. **"All of us have knowledge":** a slogan, similar to 1 Cor 6:12, which reveals the self-image of the Corinthians. 1 Cor 8:4 will specify the content of this knowledge.

---

*[7:25–28] Paul is careful to explain that the principle of 1 Cor 7:17 does not bind under sin but that present earthly conditions make it advantageous for the unmarried to remain as they are (1 Cor 7:28). These remarks must be complemented by the statement about "particular gifts" from 1 Cor 7:7.

†[7:29–31] **The world . . . is passing away:** Paul advises Christians to go about the ordinary activities of life in a manner different from those who are totally immersed in them and unaware of their transitoriness.

---

u. [7:18] 1 Mc 1:15 / Acts 15:1–2.   v. [7:19] Rom 2:25, 29; Gal 5:6; 6:15.   w. [7:22] Eph 6:5–9; Col 3:11; Phlm 16.   x. [7:23] 6:20. y. [7:26] 7:8.   z. [7:29] Rom 13:11.   a. [7:33] Lk 14:20.   b. [7:34] 1 Tm 5:5.   c. [7:35] Lk 10:39–42.

d. [7:39] Rom 7:2.   e. [7:40] 7:25.   f. [8:1] Rom 15:14 / 1 Cor 13:1–13; Rom 14:15, 19.   g. [8:3] Rom 8:29; Gal 4:9.

⁴So about the eating of meat sacrificed to idols: we know that "there is no idol in the world," and that "there is no God but one."ʰ ⁵Indeed, even though there are so-called gods in heaven and on earth (there are, to be sure, many "gods" and many "lords"), ⁶yet for us there is

one God, the Father,
    from whom all things are and for
        whom we exist,
and one Lord, Jesus Christ,
    through whom all things are and
        through whom we exist.ⁱ

**Practical Rules.** ⁷But not all have this knowledge. There are some who have been so used to idolatry up until now that, when they eat meat sacrificed to idols, their conscience, which is weak, is defiled.ʲ

⁸†Now food will not bring us closer to God. We are no worse off if we do not eat, nor are we better off if we do.ᵏ ⁹But make sure that this liberty of yours in no way becomes a stumbling block to the weak.ˡ ¹⁰If someone sees you, with your knowledge, reclining at table in the temple of an idol, may not his conscience too, weak as it is, be "built up" to eat the meat sacrificed to idols? ¹¹Thus through your knowledge, the weak person is brought to destruction, the brother for whom Christ died.ᵐ ¹²When you sin in this way against your brothers and wound their consciences, weak as they are, you are sinning against Christ. ¹³ᵐTherefore, if food causes my brother to sin, I will never eat meat again, so that I may not cause my brother to sin.

**CHAPTER 9**§

**Paul's Rights as an Apostle.** ¹Am I not free? Am I not an apostle? Have I not seen Jesus our Lord?

Are you not my work in the Lord?ᵒ ²Although I may not be an apostle for others, certainly I am for you, for you are the seal of my apostleship in the Lord.

³My defense against those who would pass judgment on me¶ is this. ⁴"Do we not have the right to eat and drink? ⁵Do we not have the right to take along a Christian wife, as do the rest of the apostles, and the brothers of the Lord, and Cephas? ⁶Or is it only myself and Barnabas who do not have the right not to work?ᵖ ⁷Who ever serves as a soldier at his own expense? Who plants a vineyard without eating its produce? Or who shepherds a flock without using some of the milk from the flock?�q ⁸Am I saying this on human authority, or does not the law also speak of these things? ⁹It is written in the law of Moses, "You shall not muzzle an ox while it is treading out the grain."ʳ Is God concerned about oxen, ¹⁰or is he not really speaking for our sake? It was written for our sake, because the plowman should plow in hope, and the thresher in hope of receiving a share.ˢ ¹¹If we have sown spiritual seed for you, is it a great thing that we reap a material harvest from you?ᵗ ¹²If others share this rightful claim on you, do not we still more?ᵘ **Reason for Not Using His Rights.** Yet we have not used this right.†† On the contrary, we endure everything so as not to place an obstacle to the gospel of Christ. ¹³‡‡Do you not know that those

and his apostleship (1 Cor 9:1), themes that the chapter will develop in reverse order, 1 Cor 9:1–18 treating the question of his apostleship and the rights that flow from it, and 1 Cor 9:19–27 exploring dialectically the nature of Paul's freedom. The language is highly rhetorical, abounding in questions, wordplays, paradoxes, images, and appeals to authority and experience. The argument is unified by repetitions; its articulations are highlighted by inclusions and transitional verses.

¶ [9:3] **My defense against those who would pass judgment on me:** the reference to a defense (*apologia*) is surprising, and suggests that Paul is incorporating some material here that he has previously used in another context. The defense will touch on two points: the fact of Paul's rights as an apostle (1 Cor 9:4–12a and 1 Cor 9:13–14) and his nonuse of those rights (1 Cor 9:12b and 1 Cor 9:15–18).

** [9:4–12a] Apparently some believe that Paul is not equal to the other apostles and therefore does not enjoy equal privileges. His defense on this point (here and in 1 Cor 9:13–14) reinforces the assertion of his apostolic character in 1 Cor 9:2. It consists of a series of analogies from natural equity (1 Cor 9:7) and religious custom (1 Cor 9:13) designed to establish his equal right to support from the churches (1 Cor 9:4–6, 11–12a); these analogies are confirmed by the authority of the law (1 Cor 9:8–10) and of Jesus himself (1 Cor 9:14).

†† [9:12b] It appears, too, that suspicion or misunderstanding has been created by Paul's practice of not living from his preaching. The first reason he asserts in defense of this practice is an entirely apostolic one; it anticipates the developments to follow in 1 Cor 9:19–22. He will give a second reason in 1 Cor 9:15÷18.

‡‡ [9:13–14] The position of these verses produces an interlocking of the two points of Paul's defense. These arguments by analogy (1 Cor 9:13) and from authority (1 Cor 9:14) belong with those of 1 Cor 9:7–10 and ground the first point. But Paul defers them until he has had a chance to mention "the gospel of Christ" (1 Cor 9:12b), after which it is more appropriate to mention Jesus' injunction to his preachers and to argue by

*[8:6] This verse rephrases the monotheistic confession of 1 Cor 8:4 in such a way as to contrast it with polytheism (1 Cor 8:5) and to express our relationship with the one God in concrete, i.e., in personal and Christian terms. **And for whom we exist:** since the Greek contains no verb here and the action intended must be inferred from the preposition *eis*, another translation is equally possible: "toward whom we return." **Through whom all things:** the earliest reference in the New Testament to Jesus' role in creation.

†[8:8–9] Although the food in itself is morally neutral, extrinsic circumstances may make the eating of it harmful. **A stumbling block:** the image is that of tripping or causing someone to fall (cf. 1 Cor 8:13; 9:12; 10:12, 32; 2 Cor 6:3; Rom 14:13, 20–1). This is a basic moral imperative for Paul, a counterpart to the positive imperative to "build one another up"; compare the expression "giving offense" as opposed to "pleasing" in 1 Cor 10:32–33.

‡[8:13] His own course is clear: he will avoid any action that might harm another Christian. This statement prepares for the paradigmatic development in 1 Cor 9.

§[9:1–27] This chapter is an emotionally charged expansion of Paul's appeal to his own example in 1 Cor 8:13; its purpose is to reinforce the exhortation of 1 Cor 8:9. The two opening questions introduce the themes of Paul's freedom

h. [8:4] 10:19; Dt 6:4.   i. [8:6] Mal 2:10 / Rom 11:36; Eph 4:5–6 / 1 Cor 1:2–3 / Jn 1:3; Col 1:16.   j. [8:7] 10:28; Rom 14:23 / Rom 14:1; 15:1.   k. [8:8] Rom 14:17.   l. [8:9] Rom 14:13, 20–21.   m. [8:11] Rom 14:15, 20.   n. [8:13] Mt 18:6; Rom 14:20–21.

o. [9:1] 1 Cor 9:19 / 2 Cor 12:12 / 1 Cor 15:8–9 / Acts 9:17; 26:16.   p. [9:6] Acts 4:36–37; 13:1–2; Gal 2:1, 9, 13; Col 4:10.   q. [9:7] 2 Tm 2:3–4.   r. [9:9] Dt 25:4; 1 Tm 5:18.   s. [9:10] 2 Tm 2:6.   t. [9:11] Rom 15:27.   u. [9:12] 2 Cor 11:7–12; 12:13–18; 2 Thes 3:6–12.

who perform the temple services eat [what] belongs to the temple, and those who minister at the altar share in the sacrificial offerings?$^v$ $^{14}$In the same way, the Lord ordered that those who preach the gospel should live by the gospel.$^w$

$^{15}$I have not used any of these rights, however, nor do I write this that it be done so in my case. I would rather die. Certainly no one is going to nullify my boast.$^x$ $^{16}$If I preach the gospel, this is no reason for me to boast, for an obligation has been imposed on me, and woe to me if I do not preach it!$^y$ $^{17}$If I do so willingly, I have a recompense, but if unwillingly, then I have been entrusted with a stewardship.$^z$ $^{18}$What then is my recompense? That, when I preach, I offer the gospel free of charge so as not to make full use of my right in the gospel.$^a$

**All Things to All.** $^{19†}$Although I am free in regard to all, I have made myself a slave to all so as to win over as many as possible.$^b$ $^{20}$To the Jews I became like a Jew to win over Jews; to those under the law I became like one under the law—though I myself am not under the law—to win over those under the law. $^{21}$To those outside the law I became like one outside the law—though I am not outside God's law but within the law of Christ—to win over those outside the law. $^{22}$To the weak I became weak, to win over the weak. I have become all things to all, to save at least some.$^c$ $^{23}$All this I do for the sake of the gospel, so that I too may have a share in it.

$^{24‡}$Do you not know that the runners in the stadium all run in the race, but only one wins the prize? Run so as to win.$^d$ $^{25}$Every athlete exercises discipline in every way. They do it to win a perishable crown, but we an imperishable one.$^e$ $^{26}$Thus I do not run aimlessly; I do not fight as if I were shadowboxing. $^{27}$No, I drive my body and train it, for fear that, after having preached to others, I myself should be disqualified.$^§$

## CHAPTER 10

**Warning Against Overconfidence.** $^{1*}$I do not want you to be unaware, brothers, that our ancestors were all under the cloud and all passed through the sea,$^f$ $^2$and all of them were baptized into Moses in the cloud and in the sea.$^g$ $^3$All ate the same spiritual food, $^4$and all drank the same spiritual drink, for they drank from a spiritual rock that followed them,$^{**}$ and the rock was the Christ.$^h$ $^5$Yet God was not pleased with most of them, for they were struck down in the desert.$^i$

$^{6††}$These things happened as examples for us, so that we might not desire evil things, as they did.$^j$ $^7$And do not become idolaters, as some of them did, as it is written, "The people sat down to eat and drink, and rose up to revel."$^k$ $^8$Let us not indulge in immorality as some of them did, and twenty-three thousand fell within a single day.$^l$ $^9$Let us not test Christ$^{‡‡}$ as some of them did, and suffered death by serpents.$^m$ $^{10}$Do not grumble as some of them did, and suffered death by the destroyer.$^n$ $^{11}$These things happened to them as an example, and they have been written down as a warning to us, upon whom the end of the ages has come.$^{§§}$ $^{12}$Therefore, whoever thinks he is standing secure should take care not to fall.$^{¶¶}$ $^{13}$No trial has come to you but what is human. God is faithful and will not let you be tried beyond your strength; but with the trial he will also provide a way out, so that you may be able to bear it.$^o$

---

they are, 1 Cor 9:19–22), and finally is seen to be necessary for his own salvation (1 Cor 9:23–27). Mention of the possibility of disqualification provides a transition to 1 Cor 10.

¶[10:1–5] Paul embarks unexpectedly upon a panoramic survey of the events of the Exodus period. The privileges of Israel in the wilderness are described in terms that apply strictly only to the realities of the new covenant ("baptism," "spiritual food and drink"); interpreted in this way they point forward to the Christian experience (1 Cor 10:1–4). But those privileges did not guarantee God's permanent pleasure (1 Cor 10:5).

**[10:4] A spiritual rock that followed them**: the Torah speaks only about a rock from which water issued, but rabbinic legend amplified this into a spring that followed the Israelites throughout their migration. Paul uses this legend as a literary type: he makes the rock itself accompany the Israelites, and he gives it a spiritual sense. **The rock was the Christ**: in the Old Testament, Yahweh is the Rock of his people (cf. Dt 32, Moses' song to Yahweh the Rock). Paul now applies this image to the Christ, the source of the living water, the true Rock that accompanied Israel, guiding their experiences in the desert.

††[10:6–13] This section explicitates the typological value of these Old Testament events: the desert experiences of the Israelites are examples, meant as warnings, to deter us from similar sins (idolatry, immorality, etc.) and from a similar fate.

‡‡[10:9] **Christ**: to avoid Paul's concept of Christ present in the wilderness events, some manuscripts read "the Lord."

§§[10:11] **Upon whom the end of the ages has come**: it is our period in time toward which past ages have been moving and in which they arrive at their goal.

¶¶[10:12–13] **Take care not to fall**: the point of the whole comparison with Israel is to caution against overconfidence, a sense of complete security (1 Cor 10:12). This warning is immediately balanced by a reassurance, based, however, on God (1 Cor 10:13).

---

analogy from the sacred temple service to his own liturgical service, the preaching of the gospel (cf. Rom 1:9; 15:16).

*[9:15–18] Paul now assigns a more personal motive to his nonuse of his right to support. His preaching is not a service spontaneously undertaken on his part but a stewardship imposed by a sort of divine compulsion. Yet to merit any reward he must bring some spontaneous quality to his service, and this he does by freely renouncing his right to support. The material here is quite similar to that contained in Paul's "defense" at 2 Cor 11:5–12; 12:11–18.

†[9:19–23] In a rhetorically balanced series of statements Paul expands and generalizes the picture of his behavior and explores the paradox of apostolic freedom. It is not essentially freedom from restraint but freedom for service—a possibility of constructive activity.

‡[9:24–27] A series of miniparables from sports, appealing to readers familiar with Greek gymnasia and the nearby Isthmian games.

§[9:27] **For fear that . . . I myself should be disqualified**: a final paradoxical turn to the argument: what appears at first a free, spontaneous renunciation of rights (1 Cor 9:12–18) seems subsequently to be required for fulfillment of Paul's stewardship (to preach effectively he must reach his hearers wherever

---

v. [9:13] Nm 18:8, 31; Dt 18:1–5. w. [9:14] Mt 10:10; Lk 10:7–8. x. [9:15] 2 Cor 11:9–10. y. [9:16] Acts 26:14–18. z. [9:17] 4:1; Gal 2:7. a. [9:18] 2 Cor 11:7–12. b. [9:19] Mt 20:26–27. c. [9:22] 10:33; Rom 15:1; 2 Cor 11:29. d. [9:24] Heb 12:1. e. [9:25] 2 Tm 2:5 / 2 Tm 4:7–8; Jas 1:12; 1 Pt 5:4.

f. [10:1] Ex 13:21–22; 14:19–20 / Ex 14:21–22, 26–30. g. [10:2] Rom 6:3; Gal 3:27 / Ex 16:4–35. h. [10:4] Ex 17:1–7; Nm 20:7–11; Dt 8:15. i. [10:5] Nm 14:28–38; Jude 5. j. [10:6] Nm 11:4, 34. k. [10:7] Ex 32:6. l. [10:8] Nm 25:1–9. m. [10:9] Nm 21:5–9. n. [10:10] Nm 14:2–37; 16:1–35. o. [10:13] Mt 6:13; Jas 1:13–14 / 1 Cor 1:9.

**Warning Against Idolatry.** [*] [14]Therefore, my beloved, avoid idolatry.[p] [15]I am speaking as to sensible people; judge for yourselves what I am saying. [16]The cup of blessing that we bless, is it not a participation in the blood of Christ? The bread that we break, is it not a participation in the body of Christ?[q] [17]Because the loaf of bread is one, we, though many, are one body, for we all partake of the one loaf.[r]

[18]Look at Israel according to the flesh; are not those who eat the sacrifices participants in the altar?[s] [19]So what am I saying? That meat sacrificed to idols is anything? Or that an idol is anything? [20]No, I mean that what they sacrifice, [they sacrifice] to demons,[†] not to God, and I do not want you to become participants with demons.[t] [21]You cannot drink the cup of the Lord and also the cup of demons. You cannot partake of the table of the Lord and of the table of demons.[u] [22]Or are we provoking the Lord to jealous anger? Are we stronger than he?[v]

**Seek the Good of Others.** [‡] [23]"Everything is lawful," but not everything is beneficial.[§] "Everything is lawful," but not everything builds up.[w] [24]No one should seek his own advantage, but that of his neighbor.[x] [25]*Eat anything sold in the market, without raising questions on grounds of conscience, [26]for "the earth and its fullness are the Lord's."[y] [27]If an unbeliever invites you and you want to go, eat whatever is placed before you, without raising questions on grounds of conscience. [28]But if someone says to you, "This was offered in sacrifice," do not eat it on account of the one who called attention to it and on account of conscience; [29]I mean not your own conscience, but the other's. For why should my freedom be determined by someone else's conscience? [30]If I partake thankfully, why am I reviled for that over which I give thanks?[z]

[31]So whether you eat or drink, or whatever you do, do everything for the glory of God. [32]*Avoid giving offense, whether to Jews or Greeks or the church of God, [33]just as I try to please everyone in every way, not seeking my own benefit but that of the many, that they may be saved.[a]

## CHAPTER 11

[1]Be imitators of me, as I am of Christ.[b]

## IV. PROBLEMS IN LITURGICAL ASSEMBLIES[††]

[2]I praise you because you remember me in everything and hold fast to the traditions, just as I handed them on to you.[c]

### A. Women's Headdresses[‡‡]

**Man and Woman.** [3]But I want you to know that Christ is the head of every man, and a husband the head of his wife,[§§] and God the head

---

*[10:14–22] The warning against idolatry from 1 Cor 10:7 is now repeated (1 Cor 10:14) and explained in terms of the effect of sacrifices: all sacrifices, Christian (1 Cor 10:16–17), Jewish (1 Cor 10:18), or pagan (1 Cor 10:20), establish communion. But communion with Christ is exclusive, incompatible with any other such communion (1 Cor 10:21). Compare the line of reasoning at 1 Cor 6:15.

†[10:20] **To demons:** although Jews denied divinity to pagan gods, they often believed that there was some nondivine reality behind the idols, such as the dead, or angels, or demons. The explanation Paul offers in 1 Cor 10:20 is drawn from Dt 32:17: the power behind the idols, with which the pagans commune, consists of demonic powers hostile to God.

‡[10:23–11:1] By way of peroration Paul returns to the opening situation (1 Cor 8) and draws conclusions based on the intervening considerations (1 Cor 9–10).

§[10:23–24] He repeats in the context of this new problem the slogans of liberty from 1 Cor 6:12, with similar qualifications. Liberty is not merely an individual perfection, nor an end in itself, but is to be used for the common good. The language of 1 Cor 10:24 recalls the descriptions of Jesus' self-emptying in Phil 2.

¶[10:25–30] A summary of specific situations in which the eating of meat sacrificed to idols could present problems of conscience. Three cases are considered. In the first (the marketplace, 1 Cor 10:25–26) and the second (at table, 1 Cor 10:27), there is no need to be concerned with whether food has passed through a pagan sacrifice or not, for the principle of 1 Cor 8:4–6 still stands, and the whole creation belongs to the one God. But in the third case (1 Cor 10:28), the situation changes if someone present explicitly raises the question of the sacrificial origin of the food; eating in such circumstances may be subject to various interpretations, some of which could be harmful to individuals. Paul is at pains to insist that the enlightened Christian conscience need not change its judgment about the neutrality, even the goodness, of the food in itself (1 Cor 10:29–30); yet the total situation is altered to the extent that others are potentially endangered, and this calls for a different response, for the sake of others.

**[10:32–11:1] In summary, the general rule of mutually responsible use of their Christian freedom is enjoined first negatively (1 Cor 10:32), then positively, as exemplified in Paul (1 Cor 10:33), and finally grounded in Christ, the pattern for Paul's behavior and theirs (1 Cor 11:1; cf. Rom 15:1–3).

††[11:2–14:40] This section of the letter is devoted to regulation of conduct at the liturgy. The problems Paul handles have to do with the dress of women in the assembly (1 Cor 11:3–16), improprieties in the celebration of community meals (1 Cor 11:17–34), and the use of charisms or spiritual gifts (1 Cor 12:1–14:40). The statement in 1 Cor 11:2 introduces all of these discussions, but applies more appropriately to the second (cf. the mention of praise in 1 Cor 11:17 and of tradition in 1 Cor 11:23).

‡‡[11:3–16] Women have been participating in worship at Corinth without the head-covering normal in Greek society of the period. Paul's stated goal is to bring them back into conformity with contemporary practice and propriety. In his desire to convince, he reaches for arguments from a variety of sources, though he has space to develop them only sketchily and is perhaps aware that they differ greatly in persuasiveness.

§§[11:3] **A husband the head of his wife:** the specific problem suggests to Paul the model of the head as a device for clarifying relations within a hierarchical structure. The model is similar to that developed later in greater detail and nuance in Eph 5:21–33. It is a hybrid model, for it grafts onto a strictly theological scale of existence (cf. 1 Cor 3:21–23) the hierarchy of sociosexual relations prevalent in the ancient world: men, dominant, reflect the active function of Christ in relation to his church; women, submissive, reflect the passive role of the church with respect to its savior. This gives us the functional scale: God, Christ, man, woman.

---

p. [10:14] 1 Jn 5:21.   q. [10:16] Mt 26:26–29; Acts 2:42.   r. [10:17] Rom 12:5; Eph 4:4.   s. [10:18] Lv 7:6.   t. [10:20] Dt 32:17.   u. [10:21] 2 Cor 6:14–18.   v. [10:22] Dt 32:21 / Eccl 6:10.   w. [10:23] 6:12.   x. [10:24] Rom 15:2; Phil 2:4, 21.

y. [10:26] Ps 24:1; 50:12. z. [10:30] Rom 14:6; 1 Tm 4:3–4. a. [10:33] 9:22; Rom 15:2.   b. [11:1] 4:16; Phil 3:17.   c. [11:2] 15:3; 2 Thes 2:15.

of Christ.*d* *4†*Any man who prays or prophesies with his head covered brings shame upon his head. *5*But any woman who prays or prophesies with her head unveiled brings shame upon her head, for it is one and the same thing as if she had had her head shaved. *6*For if a woman does not have her head veiled, she may as well have her hair cut off. But if it is shameful for a woman to have her hair cut off or her head shaved, then she should wear a veil.

*7†*A man, on the other hand, should not cover his head, because he is the image and glory of God, but woman is the glory of man.*e* *8*For man did not come from woman, but woman from man;*f* *9*nor was man created for woman, but woman for man;*g* *10*for this reason a woman should have a sign of authority‡ on her head, because of the angels. *11§*Woman is not independent of man or man of woman in the Lord.*h* *12*For just as woman came from man, so man is born of woman; but all things are from God.*i*

*13¶*Judge for yourselves: is it proper for a woman to pray to God with her head unveiled? *14*Does not nature itself teach you that if a man wears his hair long it is a disgrace to him, *15*whereas if a woman has long hair it is her glory, because long hair has been given [her]

for a covering? *16*But if anyone is inclined to be argumentative, we do not have such a custom, nor do the churches of God.

### B. The Lord's Supper**

**An Abuse at Corinth.** *17*In giving this instruction, I do not praise the fact that your meetings are doing more harm than good. *18*First of all, I hear that when you meet as a church there are divisions among you, and to a degree I believe it;*j* *19*there have to be factions among you in order that [also] those who are approved among you may become known.†† *20*When you meet in one place, then, it is not to eat the Lord's supper, *21*for in eating, each one goes ahead with his own supper, and one goes hungry while another gets drunk. *22*Do you not have houses in which you can eat and drink? Or do you show contempt for the church of God and make those who have nothing feel ashamed? What can I say to you? Shall I praise you? In this matter I do not praise you.*k*

**Tradition of the Institution.** *23‡‡*For I received from the Lord what I also handed on to you,*l* that the Lord Jesus, on the night he was handed over, took bread, *24*and, after he had given thanks, broke it and said, "This is my body that is for you. Do this in remembrance of me." *25*In the same way also the cup, after supper, saying, "This cup is the new covenant in my blood. Do this, as often as you drink it, in remembrance of me."*m* *26*For as often as you eat this bread and drink the cup, you proclaim the death of the Lord until he comes.

*27*Therefore whoever eats the bread or drinks the cup of the Lord unworthily will have to answer for the body and blood of the Lord.§§ *28*A person should examine himself,¶¶ and so eat the

---

*[11:4–6] From man's direct relation to Christ, Paul infers that his head should not be covered. But woman, related not directly to Christ on the scale but to her husband, requires a covering as a sign of that relationship. **Shameful . . . to have her hair cut off**: certain less honored classes in society, such as lesbians and prostitutes, are thought to have worn their hair close-cropped.

†[11:7–9] The hierarchy of v 3 is now expressed in other metaphors: the image (*eikōn*) and the reflected glory (*doxa*). Paul is alluding basically to the text of Gn 1:27, in which mankind as a whole, the male-female couple, is created in God's image and given the command to multiply and together dominate the lower creation. But Gn 1:24 is interpreted here in the light of the second creation narrative in Gn 2, in which each of the sexes is created separately (first the man and then the woman from man and for him, to be his helpmate, Gn 2:20–23), and under the influence of the story of the fall, as a result of which the husband rules over the woman (Gn 3:16). This interpretation splits the single image of God into two, at different degrees of closeness.

‡[11:10] **A sign of authority**: "authority" (*exousia*) may possibly be due to mistranslation of an Aramaic word for "veil"; in any case, the connection with 1 Cor 11:9 indicates that the covering is a sign of woman's subordination. **Because of the angels**: a surprising additional reason, which the context does not clarify. Presumably the reference is to cosmic powers who might inflict harm on women or whose function is to watch over women or the cult.

§[11:11–12] These parenthetical remarks relativize the argument from Gn 2–3. **In the Lord**: in the Christian economy the relation between the sexes is characterized by a mutual dependence, which is not further specified. And even in the natural order conditions have changed: the mode of origin described in Gn 2 has been reversed (1 Cor 11:12a). But the ultimately significant fact is the origin that all things have in common (1 Cor 11:12b).

¶[11:13–16] The argument for conformity to common church practice is summed up and pressed home. 1 Cor 11:14–15 contain a final appeal to the sense of propriety that contemporary Greek society would consider "natural" (cf. 1 Cor 11:5–6).

**[11:17–34] Paul turns to another abuse connected with the liturgy, and a more serious one, for it involves neglect of basic Christian tradition concerning the meaning of the Lord's Supper. Paul recalls that tradition for them and reminds them of its implications.

††[11:19] **That . . . those who are approved among you may become known**: Paul situates their divisions within the context of the eschatological separation of the authentic from the inauthentic and the final revelation of the difference. The notion of authenticity-testing recurs in the injunction to self-examination in view of present and future judgment (1 Cor 11:28–32).

‡‡[11:23–25] This is the earliest written account of the institution of the Lord's Supper in the New Testament. The narrative emphasizes Jesus' action of self-giving (expressed in the words over the bread and the cup) and his double command to repeat his own action.

§§[11:27] It follows that the only proper way to celebrate the Eucharist is one that corresponds to Jesus' intention, which fits with the meaning of his command to reproduce his action in the proper spirit. If the Corinthians eat and drink unworthily, i.e., without having grasped and internalized the meaning of his death for them, **they will have to answer for the body and blood**, i.e., will be guilty of a sin against the Lord himself (cf. 1 Cor 8:12).

¶¶[11:28] **Examine himself**: the Greek word is similar to that for "approved" in 1 Cor 11:19, which means "having been

---

d. [11:3] Eph 5:23.  e. [11:7] Gn 1:26–27; 5:1.  f. [11:8] Gn 2:21–23.  g. [11:9] Gn 2:18.  h. [11:11] Gal 3:27–28.  i. [11:12] 8:6; Rom 11:36.

j. [11:18] 1:10–12; Gal 5:20.  k. [11:22] Jas 2:1–7.  l. [11:23] 11:2; 15:3 / 10:16–17; Mt 26:26–29; Mk 14:22–25; Lk 22:14–20.  m. [11:25] Ex 24:8; 2 Cor 3:6; Heb 8:6–13.

bread and drink the cup. [29]For anyone who eats and drinks without discerning the body, eats and drinks judgment* on himself. [30]That is why many among you are ill and infirm, and a considerable number are dying. [31]If we discerned ourselves, we would not be under judgment; [32]but since we are judged by [the] Lord, we are being disciplined so that we may not be condemned along with the world.[n]

[33]Therefore, my brothers, when you come together to eat, wait for one another. [34]If anyone is hungry, he should eat at home, so that your meetings may not result in judgment. The other matters I shall set in order when I come.

*C. Spiritual Gifts[t]*

## CHAPTER 12

**Unity and Variety.** [1]Now in regard to spiritual gifts, brothers, I do not want you to be unaware. [2]*You know how, when you were pagans, you were constantly attracted and led away to mute idols.[o] [3]Therefore, I tell you that nobody speaking by the spirit of God says, "Jesus be accursed." And no one can say, "Jesus is Lord," except by the holy Spirit.[p]

[4§]There are different kinds of spiritual gifts but the same Spirit;[q] [5]there are different forms of service but the same Lord; [6]there are different

workings but the same God who produces all of them in everyone. [7]To each individual the manifestation of the Spirit is given for some benefit. [8]To one is given through the Spirit the expression of wisdom; to another the expression of knowledge according to the same Spirit;[r] [9]to another faith by the same Spirit; to another gifts of healing by the one Spirit; [10]to another mighty deeds; to another prophecy; to another discernment of spirits; to another varieties of tongues; to another interpretation of tongues.[s] [11]But one and the same Spirit produces all of these, distributing them individually to each person as he wishes.[t]

**One Body, Many Parts.[§]** [12]As a body is one though it has many parts, and all the parts of the body, though many, are one body, so also Christ.[u] [13]For in one Spirit we were all baptized into one body, whether Jews or Greeks, slaves or free persons, and we were all given to drink of one Spirit.[v]

[14]Now the body is not a single part, but many. [15]If a foot should say, "Because I am not a hand I do not belong to the body," it does not for this reason belong any less to the body. [16]Or if an ear should say, "Because I am not an eye I do not belong to the body," it does not for this reason belong any less to the body. [17]If the whole body were an eye, where would the hearing be? If the whole body were hearing, where would the sense of smell be? [18]But as it is, God placed the parts, each one of them, in the body as he intended. [19]If they were all one part, where would the body be? [20]But as it is, there are many parts, yet one body. [21]The eye cannot say to the hand, "I do not need you," nor again the head to the feet, "I do not need you." [22]Indeed, the parts of the body that seem to be weaker are all the more necessary, [23]and those parts of the body that we consider less honorable we surround with greater honor, and our less presentable parts are treated with greater propriety, [24]whereas our more presentable parts do not need this. But God has so constructed the body as to give greater honor to a part that is without it, [25]so that there may be no division in the body, but that the parts may have the same concern for one another. [26]If [one] part suffers, all the parts suffer with it; if one part is honored, all the parts share its joy.

**Application to Christ.[**]** [27]Now you are Christ's body, and individually parts of it.[w] [28]Some

---

tested and found true." The self-testing required for proper eating involves **discerning the body** (1 Cor 11:29), which, from the context, must mean understanding the sense of Jesus' death (1 Cor 11:26), perceiving the imperative to unity that follows from the fact that Jesus gives himself to all and requires us to repeat his sacrifice in the same spirit (1 Cor 11:18–25).

*[11:29–32] **Judgment**: there is a series of wordplays in these verses that would be awkward to translate literally into English; it includes all the references to judgment (*krima*, 1 Cor 11:29, 34; *krinō*, 1 Cor 11:31, 32) discernment (*diakrinō*, 1 Cor 11:29, 31), and condemnation (*katakrinō*, 1 Cor 11:32). The judgment is concretely described as the illness, infirmity, and death that have visited the community. These are signs that the power of Jesus' death is not yet completely recognized and experienced. Yet even the judgment incurred is an expression of God's concern; it is a medicinal measure meant to rescue us from condemnation with God's enemies.

†[12:1–14:40] Ecstatic and charismatic activity were common in early Christian experience, as they were in other ancient religions. But the Corinthians seem to have developed a disproportionate esteem for certain phenomena, especially tongues, to the detriment of order in the liturgy. Paul's response to this development provides us with the fullest exposition we have of his theology of the charisms.

‡[12:2–3] There is experience of the Spirit and an understanding of ecstatic phenomena that are specifically Christian and that differ, despite apparent similarities, from those of the pagans. It is necessary to discern which spirit is leading one; ecstatic phenomena must be judged by their effect (1 Cor 12:2). 1 Cor 12:3 illustrates this by an example: power to confess Jesus as Lord can come only from the Spirit, and it is inconceivable that the Spirit would move anyone to curse the Lord.

§[12:4–6] There are some features common to all charisms, despite their diversity: all are **gifts** (*charismata*), grace from outside ourselves; all are **forms of service** (*diakoniai*), an expression of their purpose and effect; and all are workings (*energēmata*), in which God is at work. Paul associates each

of these aspects with what later theology will call one of the persons of the Trinity, an early example of "appropriation."

¶[12:12–26] The image of **a body** is introduced to explain Christ's relationship with believers (1 Cor 12:12). 1 Cor 12:13 applies this model to the church: by baptism all, despite diversity of ethnic or social origins, are integrated into one organism. 1 Cor 12:14–26 then develop the need for diversity of function among the parts of a body without threat to its unity.

**[12:27–30] Paul now applies the image again to the church as a whole and its members (1 Cor 12:27). The lists

n. [11:32] Dt 8:5; Heb 12:5–11.   o. [12:2] Eph 2:11–18.   p. [12:3] Rom 10:9; 1 Jn 4:2–3.   q. [12:4] Rom 12:6; Eph 4:7, 11.

r. [12:8] 2:6–13.   s. [12:10] 14:5, 26, 39; Acts 2:4.   t. [12:11] 7:7; Eph 4:7.   u. [12:12] 10:17; Rom 12:4–5; Eph 2:16; Col 3:15.   v. [12:13] Gal 3:28; Eph 2:13–18; Col 3:11 / Jn 7:37–39.   w. [12:27] Rom 12:5–8; Eph 1:23; 4:12; 5:30; Col 1:18, 24.

people God has designated in the church to be, first, apostles;* second, prophets; third, teachers; then, mighty deeds; then gifts of healing, assistance, administration, and varieties of tongues.[x] [29]Are all apostles? Are all prophets? Are all teachers? Do all work mighty deeds? [30]Do all have gifts of healing? Do all speak in tongues? Do all interpret? [31]Strive eagerly for the greatest spiritual gifts.

**The Way of Love.** But I shall show you a still more excellent way.

## CHAPTER 13[†]

[1]If I speak in human and angelic tongues[‡] but do not have love, I am a resounding gong or a clashing cymbal.[y] [2]And if I have the gift of prophecy and comprehend all mysteries and all knowledge; if I have all faith so as to move mountains but do not have love, I am nothing.[z] [3]If I give away everything I own, and if I hand my body over so that I may boast but do not have love, I gain nothing.[a]

[4]Love is patient, love is kind. It is not jealous, [love] is not pompous, it is not inflated,[b] [5]it is not rude, it does not seek its own interests, it is not quick-tempered, it does not brood over injury,[c] [6]it does not rejoice over wrongdoing but rejoices with the truth. [7]It bears all things, believes all things, hopes all things, endures all things.[d]

[8]Love never fails. If there are prophecies, they will be brought to nothing; if tongues, they

will cease; if knowledge, it will be brought to nothing. [9]For we know partially and we prophesy partially, [10]but when the perfect comes, the partial will pass away. [11]When I was a child, I used to talk as a child, think as a child, reason as a child; when I became a man, I put aside childish things. [12]At present we see indistinctly, as in a mirror, but then face to face. At present I know partially; then I shall know fully, as I am fully known.[e] [13]*So faith, hope, love remain, these three;[f] but the greatest of these is love.

## CHAPTER 14

**Prophecy Greater than Tongues.** [†]Pursue love, but strive eagerly for the spiritual gifts, above all that you may prophesy.[g] [2‡]For one who speaks in a tongue does not speak to human beings but to God, for no one listens; he utters mysteries in spirit. [3]On the other hand, one who prophesies does speak to human beings, for their building up,[§] encouragement, and solace.[h] [4]Whoever speaks in a tongue builds himself up, but whoever prophesies builds up the church. [5]Now I should like all of you to speak in tongues, but even more to prophesy. One who prophesies is greater than one who speaks in tongues, unless he interprets, so that the church may be built up.

[6*]Now, brothers, if I should come to you speaking in tongues, what good will I do you if I do not speak to you by way of revelation, or

---

in 1 Cor 12:28–30 spell out the parallelism by specifying the diversity of functions found in the church (cf. Rom 12:6–8; Eph 4:11).

\*[12:28] **First, apostles**: apostleship was not mentioned in 1 Cor 12:8–10, nor is it at issue in these chapters, but Paul gives it pride of place in his listing. It is not just one gift among others but a prior and fuller gift that includes the others. They are all demonstrated in Paul's apostolate, but he may have developed his theology of charisms by reflecting first of all on his own grace of apostleship (cf. 1 Cor 3:5–4:14; 9:1–27; 2 Cor 2:14–6:13; 10:1–13:30, esp. 1 Cor 11:23 and 12:12).

†[13:1–13] This chapter involves a shift of perspective and a new point. All or part of the material may once have been an independent piece in the style of Hellenistic eulogies of virtues, but it is now integrated, by editing, into the context of 1 Cor 12–14 (cf. the reference to tongues and prophecy) and into the letter as a whole (cf. the references to knowledge and to behavior). The function of 1 Cor 13 within the discussion of spiritual gifts is to relativize all the charisms by contrasting them with the more basic, pervasive, and enduring value that gives them their purpose and their effectiveness. The rhetoric of this chapter is striking.

‡[13:1–3] An inventory of gifts, arranged in careful gradation: neither tongues (on the lowest rung), nor prophecy, knowledge, or faith, nor even self-sacrifice has value unless informed by love.

§[13:4–7] This paragraph is developed by personification and enumeration, defining love by what it does or does not do. The Greek contains fifteen verbs; it is natural to translate many of them by adjectives in English.

¶[13:8–13] The final paragraph announces its topic, **Love never fails** (1 Cor 13:8), then develops the permanence of love in contrast to the charisms (1 Cor 13:9–12), and finally asserts

love's superiority even over the other "theological virtues" (1 Cor 13:13).

\*\*[13:13] In speaking of love, Paul is led by spontaneous association to mention faith and hope as well. They are already a well-known triad (cf. 1 Thes 1:3), three interrelated (cf. 1 Cor 13:7) features of Christian life, more fundamental than any particular charism. **The greatest . . . is love**: love is operative even within the other members of the triad (1 Cor 13:7), so that it has a certain primacy among them. Or, if the perspective is temporal, love will remain (cf. "never fails," 1 Cor 13:8) even when faith has yielded to sight and hope to possession.

††[14:1–5] 1 Cor 14:1b returns to the thought of 1 Cor 12:31a and reveals Paul's primary concern. The series of contrasts in 1 Cor 14:2–5 discloses the problem at Corinth: a disproportionate interest in tongues, with a corresponding failure to appreciate the worth of prophecy. Paul attempts to clarify the relative values of those gifts by indicating the kind of communication achieved in each and the kind of effect each produces.

‡‡[14:2–3a] They involve two kinds of communication: tongues, private speech toward God in inarticulate terms that need interpretation to be intelligible to others (see 1 Cor 14:27–28); prophecy, communication with others in the community.

§§[14:3b–5] They produce two kinds of effect. One who speaks in tongues **builds himself up**; it is a matter of individual experience and personal perfection, which inevitably recalls Paul's previous remarks about being inflated, seeking one's own good, pleasing oneself. But a prophet **builds up the church**: the theme of "building up" or "edifying" others, the main theme of the letter, comes to clearest expression in this chapter (1 Cor 14:3; 4, 5, 12, 17). It has been anticipated at 1 Cor 8:1 and 1 Cor 10:23, and by the related concept of "the beneficial" in 1 Cor 6:12; 10:23; 12:7; etc.

¶¶[14:6–12] Sound, in order to be useful, must be intelligible. This principle is illustrated by a series of analogies from music (1 Cor 14:7–8) and from ordinary human speech (1 Cor 14:10–11); it is applied to the case at hand in 1 Cor 14:9, 12.

---

x. [12:28] Eph 2:20; 3:5; 4:11.   y. [13:1] 8:1; 16:14; Rom 12:9–10; 13:8–10.   z. [13:2] 4:1; 14:2 / 1:5; 8:1–3; 12:8 / Mt 17:20; 21:21; Col 2:3.   a. [13:3] Mt 6:2.   b. [13:4] Eph 4:2 / 1 Cor 4:6, 18; 5:2; 8:1.   c. [13:5] 10:24, 33; Phil 2:4, 21; 1 Thes 5:15.   d. [13:7] Prv 10:12; 1 Pt 4:8.

e. [13:12] 2 Cor 5:7; Heb 11:1 / 2 Tm 2:19; 1 Jn 3:2.   f. [13:13] Col 1:4; 1 Thes 1:3; 5:8.   g. [14:1] 14:5, 12, 39.   h. [14:3] 14:4–5, 12, 17, 26; 3:9; 8:1, 10; 10:23.

knowledge, or prophecy, or instruction? [7]Likewise, if inanimate things that produce sound, such as flute or harp, do not give out the tones distinctly, how will what is being played on flute or harp be recognized? [8]And if the bugle gives an indistinct sound, who will get ready for battle? [9]Similarly, if you, because of speaking in tongues, do not utter intelligible speech, how will anyone know what is being said? For you will be talking to the air. [10]It happens that there are many different languages in the world, and none is meaningless; [11]but if I do not know the meaning of a language, I shall be a foreigner to one who speaks it, and one who speaks it a foreigner to me. [12]So with yourselves: since you strive eagerly for spirits, seek to have an abundance of them for building up the church.

**Need for Interpretation.**[*] [13]Therefore, one who speaks in a tongue should pray to be able to interpret. [14][For] if I pray in a tongue, my spirit[†] is at prayer but my mind is unproductive. [15]So what is to be done? I will pray with the spirit, but I will also pray with the mind. I will sing praise with the spirit, but I will also sing praise with the mind.[i] [16]Otherwise, if you pronounce a blessing [with] the spirit, how shall one who holds the place of the uninstructed say the "Amen" to your thanksgiving, since he does not know what you are saying? [17]For you may be giving thanks very well, but the other is not built up. [18]I give thanks to God that I speak in tongues more than any of you, [19]but in the church I would rather speak five words with my mind, so as to instruct others also, than ten thousand words in a tongue.

**Functions of These Gifts.** [20][‡]Brothers, stop being childish in your thinking. In respect to evil be like infants, but in your thinking be mature.[j] [21]It is written in the law:

"By people speaking strange tongues
　　and by the lips of foreigners
I will speak to this people,
　　and even so they will not listen to me,[k]

says the Lord." [22]Thus, tongues are a sign not for those who believe but for unbelievers, whereas prophecy is not for unbelievers but for those who believe.

[23][§]So if the whole church meets in one place and everyone speaks in tongues, and then uninstructed people or unbelievers should come in, will they not say that you are out of your minds?[l] [24]But if everyone is prophesying, and an unbeliever or uninstructed person should come in, he will be convinced by everyone and judged by everyone, [25]and the secrets of his heart will be disclosed, and so he will fall down and worship God, declaring, "God is really in your midst."[m]

**Rules of Order.** [26][¶]So what is to be done, brothers? When you assemble, one has a psalm, another an instruction, a revelation, a tongue, or an interpretation. Everything should be done for building up.[n] [27]If anyone speaks in a tongue, let it be two or at most three, and each in turn, and one should interpret. [28]But if there is no interpreter, the person should keep silent in the church and speak to himself and to God.

[29]Two or three prophets should speak, and the others discern. [30]But if a revelation is given to another person sitting there, the first one should be silent. [31]For you can all prophesy one by one, so that all may learn and all be encouraged. [32]Indeed, the spirits of prophets are under the prophets' control, [33]since he is not the God of disorder but of peace.

As in all the churches of the holy ones,[**] [34]women should keep silent in the churches, for they are not allowed to speak, but should be

---

*[14:13–19] The charism of interpretation lifts tongues to the level of intelligibility, enabling them to produce the same effect as prophecy (cf. 1 Cor 14:5, 26–28).

†[14:14–15] **My spirit:** Paul emphasizes the exclusively ecstatic, nonrational quality of tongues. The tongues at Pentecost are also described as an ecstatic experience (Acts 2:4, 12–13), though Luke superimposes further interpretations of his own. **My mind:** the ecstatic element, dominant in earliest Old Testament prophecy as depicted in 1 Sm 10:5–13; 19:20–24, seems entirely absent from Paul's notion of prophecy and completely relegated to tongues. He emphasizes the role of reason when he specifies instruction as a function of prophecy (1 Cor 14:6, 19, 31). But he does not exclude intuition and emotion; cf. references to encouragement and consolation (1 Cor 14:3, 31) and the scene describing the ideal exercise of prophecy (1 Cor 14:24–25).

‡[14:20–22] The Corinthians pride themselves on tongues as a sign of God's favor, a means of direct communication with him (2:28). To challenge them to a more mature appraisal, Paul draws from scripture a less flattering explanation of what speaking in tongues may signify. Isaiah threatened the people that if they failed to listen to their prophets, the Lord would speak to them (in punishment) through the lips of Assyrian conquerors (Is 28:11–12). Paul compresses Isaiah's text and makes God address his people directly. Equating tongues with foreign languages (cf. 1 Cor 14:10–11), Paul concludes from Isaiah that **tongues are a sign not for those who believe,** i.e., not a mark of God's pleasure for those who listen to him but a mark of his displeasure with those in the community who are faithless, who have not heeded the message that he has sent through the prophets.

§[14:23–25] Paul projects the possible missionary effect of two hypothetical liturgical experiences, one consisting wholly of tongues, the other entirely of prophecy. **Uninstructed** (*idiōtai*): the term may simply mean people who do not speak or understand tongues, as in 1 Cor 14:16, where it seems to designate Christians. But coupled with the term "unbelievers" it may be another way of designating those who have not been initiated into the community of faith; some believe it denotes a special class of non-Christians who are close to the community, such as catechumens. **Unbelievers** (*apistoi*): he has shifted from the inner-community perspective of 1 Cor 14:22; the term here designates non-Christians (cf. 1 Cor 6:6; 7:15; 10:27).

¶[14:26–33a] Paul concludes with specific directives regarding exercise of the gifts in their assemblies. Verse 26 enunciates the basic criterion in the use of any gift: it must contribute to "building up."

**[14:33b–36] Verse 33b may belong with what precedes, so that the new paragraph would begin only with 1 Cor 14:34. 1 Cor 14:34–35 change the subject. These two verses have the theme of submission in common with 1 Cor 14:11 despite differences in vocabulary, and a concern with what is or is not becoming; but it is difficult to harmonize the injunction to silence here with 1 Cor 11 which appears to take it for granted that women do pray and prophesy aloud in the assembly (cf. 1 Cor 11:5, 13). Hence the verses are often considered an interpolation, reflecting the discipline of later churches; such an interpolation would have to have antedated our manuscripts,

---

i. [14:15] Eph 5:19; Col 3:16.　j. [14:20] Mt 10:16; Rom 16:19; Eph 4:14.

k. [14:21] Is 28:11–12; Dt 28:49.　l. [14:23] Acts 2:6, 13.　m. [14:25] 4:5 / Is 45:14; Zec 8:23.　n. [14:26] Eph 4:12.

subordinate, as even the law says.º ³⁵But if they want to learn anything, they should ask their husbands at home. For it is improper for a woman to speak in the church. ³⁶Did the word of God go forth from you? Or has it come to you alone?

³⁷If anyone thinks that he is a prophet or a spiritual person, he should recognize that what I am writing to you is a commandment of the Lord. ³⁸If anyone does not acknowledge this, he is not acknowledged. ³⁹So, [my] brothers, strive eagerly to prophesy, and do not forbid speaking in tongues, ⁴⁰but everything must be done properly and in order.

## V. THE RESURRECTION

### A. The Resurrection of Christ

### CHAPTER 15*

**The Gospel Teaching.†** ¹Now I am reminding you, brothers, of the gospel I preached to you, which you indeed received and in which you also stand. ²Through it you are also being saved, if you hold fast to the word I preached to you, unless you believed in vain. ³‡For I handed on to you as of first importance what I also received: that Christ died for our sins in accordance with the scriptures;ᵖ ⁴that he was buried; that he was raised on the third day in accordance with scriptures;�q ⁵that he appeared to Cephas, then to the Twelve.ʳ ⁶After that, he appeared to more

than five hundred brothers at once, most of whom are still living, though some have fallen asleep. ⁷After that he appeared to James, then to all the apostles. ⁸Last of all, as to one born abnormally, he appeared to me.ˢ ⁹For I am the least⁹ of the apostles, not fit to be called an apostle, because I persecuted the church of God.ᵗ ¹⁰But by the grace of God I am what I am, and his grace to me has not been ineffective. Indeed, I have toiled harder than all of them; not I, however, but the grace of God [that is] with me. ¹¹Therefore, whether it be I or they, so we preach and so you believed.

### B. The Resurrection of the Dead

**Results of Denial.⁹** ¹²But if Christ is preached as raised from the dead, how can some among you say there is no resurrection of the dead? ¹³If there is no resurrection of the dead, then neither has Christ been raised.ᵘ ¹⁴And if Christ has not been raised, then empty [too] is our preaching; empty, too, your faith. ¹⁵Then we are also false witnesses to God, because we testified against God that he raised Christ, whom he did not raise if in fact the dead are not raised.ᵛ ¹⁶For if the dead are not raised, neither has Christ been raised, ¹⁷and if Christ has not been raised,** your faith is vain; you are still in your sins. ¹⁸Then those who have fallen asleep in Christ have perished. ¹⁹If for this life only we have hoped in Christ, we are the most pitiable people of all. **Christ the Firstfruits.††** ²⁰ᵂBut now Christ has been raised from the dead, the firstfruits‡‡ of those who have fallen asleep. ²¹§§For since death

---

all of which contain them, though some transpose them to the very end of the chapter.

*[15:1–58] Some consider this chapter an earlier Pauline composition inserted into the present letter. The problem that Paul treats is clear to a degree: some of the Corinthians are denying the resurrection of the dead (1 Cor 15:12), apparently because of their inability to imagine how any kind of bodily existence could be possible after death (1 Cor 15:35). It is plausibly supposed that their attitude stems from Greek anthropology, which looks with contempt upon matter and would be content with the survival of the soul, and perhaps also from an overrealized eschatology of gnostic coloration, such as that reflected in 2 Tm 2:18, which considers the resurrection a purely spiritual experience already achieved in baptism and in the forgiveness of sins. Paul, on the other hand, will affirm both the essential corporeity of the resurrection and its futurity. His response moves through three steps: a recall of the basic kerygma about Jesus' resurrection (1 Cor 15:1–11), an assertion of the logical inconsistencies involved in denial of the resurrection (1 Cor 15:12–34), and an attempt to perceive theologically what the properties of the resurrected body must be (1 Cor 15:35–58).

†[15:1–11] Paul recalls the tradition (1 Cor 15:3–7), which he can presuppose as common ground and which provides a starting point for his argument. This is the fundamental content of all Christian preaching and belief (1 Cor 15:1–2, 11).

‡[15:3–7] The language by which Paul expresses the essence of the "gospel" (1 Cor 15:1) is not his own but is drawn from older credal formulas. This credo highlights Jesus' death for our sins (confirmed by his burial) and Jesus' resurrection (confirmed by his appearances) and presents both of them as fulfillment of prophecy. **In accordance with the scriptures**: conformity of Jesus' passion with the scriptures is asserted in Mt 16:1; Lk 24:25–27, 32, 44–46. Application of some Old Testament texts (Ps 2:7; 16:8–11) to his resurrection is illustrated by Acts 2:27–31; 13:29–39; and Is 52:13–53:12 and Hos 6:2 may also have been envisaged.

§[15:9–11] A persecutor may have appeared disqualified (*ouk . . . hikanos*) from apostleship, but in fact God's grace has qualified him. Cf. the remarks in 2 Corinthians about his qualifications (2 Cor 2:16; 3:5) and his greater labors (2 Cor 11:23). These verses are parenthetical, but a nerve has been touched (the references to his abnormal birth and his activity as a persecutor may echo taunts from Paul's opponents), and he is instinctively moved to self-defense.

¶[15:12–19] Denial of the resurrection (1 Cor 15:12) involves logical inconsistencies. The basic one, stated twice (1 Cor 15:13, 16), is that if there is no such thing as (bodily) resurrection, then it has not taken place even in Christ's case.

**[15:17–18] The consequences for the Corinthians are grave: both forgiveness of sins and salvation are an illusion, despite their strong convictions about both. Unless Christ is risen, their faith does not save.

††[15:20–28] After a triumphant assertion of the reality of Christ's resurrection (1 Cor 15:20a), Paul explains its positive implications and consequences. As a soteriological event of both human (1 Cor 15:20–23) and cosmic (1 Cor 15:24–28) dimensions, Jesus' resurrection logically and necessarily involves ours as well.

‡‡[15:20] **The firstfruits**: the portion of the harvest offered in thanksgiving to God implies the consecration of the entire harvest to come. Christ's resurrection is not an end in itself; its finality lies in the whole harvest, ourselves.

§§[15:21–22] Our human existence, both natural and supernatural, is corporate, involves solidarity. **In Adam . . . in Christ**: the Hebrew word *ādām* in Genesis is both a common noun for mankind and a proper noun for the first man. Paul here presents Adam as at least a literary type of Christ; the

---

o. [14:34] 1 Tm 2:11–15; 1 Pt 3:1.    p. [15:3] 11:23 / 1 Pt 2:24; 3:18 / Is 53:4–12.    q. [15:4] Acts 2:23–24 / Ps 16:8–11; Hos 6:1–2; Jon 2:1.    r. [15:5] Mk 16:14; Mt 28:16–17; Lk 24:36; Jn 20:19.

s. [15:8] 9:1; Acts 9:3–6; Gal 1:16.    t. [15:9] Acts 8:3; 9:1–2; Gal 1:23; Eph 3:8; 1 Tm 1:15.    u. [15:13] 1 Thes 4:14.    v. [15:15] Acts 5:32.    w. [15:20] Rom 8:11; Col 1:18; 1 Thes 4:14.

came through a human being, the resurrection of the dead came also through a human being. [22]For just as in Adam all die, so too in Christ shall all be brought to life,[x] [23]but each one in proper order: Christ the firstfruits; then, at his coming, those who belong to Christ;[y] [24]then comes the end,[*] when he hands over the kingdom to his God and Father, when he has destroyed every sovereignty and every authority and power.[z] [25]For he must reign until he has put all his enemies under his feet.[a] [26†]The last enemy[b] to be destroyed is death, [27†]for "he subjected everything under his feet."[c] But when it says that everything has been subjected, it is clear that it excludes the one who subjected everything to him. [28]When everything is subjected to him, then the Son himself will [also] be subjected to the one who subjected everything to him, so that God may be all in all.[d]

**Practical Arguments.**[§] [29]Otherwise, what will people accomplish by having themselves baptized for the dead?[¶] If the dead are not raised at all, then why are they having themselves baptized for them?

[30**]Moreover, why are we endangering ourselves all the time?[e] [31]Every day I face death; I swear it by the pride in you [brothers] that I have in Christ Jesus our Lord.[f] [32]If at Ephesus I fought with beasts, so to speak, what benefit was it to me? If the dead are not raised:

> "Let us eat and drink,
> for tomorrow we die."[g]

[33]Do not be led astray:

> "Bad company corrupts good morals."

[34]Become sober as you ought and stop sinning. For some have no knowledge of God; I say this to your shame.[h]

### C. The Manner of the Resurrection[††]

[35‡‡]But someone may say, "How are the dead raised? With what kind of body will they come back?"

**The Resurrection Body.** [36§§]You fool! What you sow is not brought to life unless it dies.[i] [37]And what you sow is not the body that is to be but a bare kernel of wheat, perhaps, or of some other kind; [38¶]but God gives it a body as he chooses, and to each of the seeds its own body. [39¶¶]Not all flesh is the same, but there is one kind for human beings, another kind of flesh for animals, another kind of flesh for birds, and another for fish. [40]There are both heavenly bodies and earthly bodies, but the brightness of the heavenly is one kind and that of the earthly another. [41]The brightness of the sun is one kind, the brightness of the moon another, and the brightness of the stars another. For star differs from star in brightness.

[42***]So also is the resurrection of the dead. It is sown corruptible; it is raised incorruptible. [43]It

---

parallelism and contrast between them will be developed further in 1 Cor 15:45–49 and in Rom 5:12–21.

*[15:24–28] Paul's perspective expands to cosmic dimensions, as he describes the climax of history, **the end**. His viewpoint is still christological, as in 1 Cor 15:20–23. 1 Cor 15:24, 28 describe Christ's final relations to his enemies and his Father in language that is both royal and military; 1 Cor 15:25–28 insert a proof from scripture (Ps 110:1; 8:6) into this description. But the viewpoint is also theological, for God is the ultimate agent and end, and likewise soteriological, for we are the beneficiaries of all the action.

†[15:26] **The last enemy . . . is death**: a parenthesis that specifies the final fulfillment of the two Old Testament texts just referred to, Ps 110:1 and Ps 8:7. Death is not just one cosmic power among many, but the ultimate effect of sin in the universe (cf. 1 Cor 15:56; Rom 5:12). Christ defeats death where it prevails, in our bodies. The destruction of the last enemy is concretely the "coming to life" (1 Cor 15:22) of "those who belong to Christ" (1 Cor 15:23).

‡[15:27b–28] **The one who subjected everything to him**: the Father is the ultimate agent in the drama, and the final end of the process, to whom the Son and everything else is ordered (1 Cor 15:24, 28). **That God may be all in all**: his reign is a dynamic exercise of creative power, an outpouring of life and energy through the universe, with no further resistance. This is the supremely positive meaning of "subjection": that God may fully be God.

§[15:29–34] Paul concludes his treatment of logical inconsistencies with a listing of miscellaneous Christian practices that would be meaningless if the resurrection were not a fact.

¶[15:29] **Baptized for the dead**: this practice is not further explained here, nor is it necessarily mentioned with approval, but Paul cites it as something in their experience that attests in one more way to belief in the resurrection.

**[15:30–34] A life of sacrifice, such as Paul describes in 1 Cor 4:9–13 and 2 Corinthians, would be pointless without the prospect of resurrection; a life of pleasure, such as that expressed in the Epicurean slogan of 1 Cor 15:32, would be far more consistent. **I fought with beasts**: since Paul does not elsewhere mention a combat with beasts at Ephesus, he may be speaking figuratively about struggles with adversaries.

††[15:35–58] Paul imagines two objections that the Corinthians could raise: one concerning the manner of the resurrection (**how?**), the other pertaining to the qualities of the risen body (**what kind?**). These questions probably lie behind their denial of the resurrection (1 Cor 15:12), and seem to reflect the presumption that no kind of body other than the one we now possess would be possible. Paul deals with these objections in inverse order, in 1 Cor 15:36–49 and 1 Cor 15:50–58. His argument is fundamentally theological and its appeal is to the understanding.

‡‡[15:35–49] Paul approaches the question of the nature of the risen body (**what kind of body?**) by means of two analogies: the seed (1 Cor 15:36–44) and the first man, Adam (1 Cor 15:45–49).

§§[15:36–38] The analogy of the seed: there is a change of attributes from seed to plant; the old life-form must be lost for the new to emerge. By speaking about the seed as a **body** that dies and comes to life, Paul keeps the point of the analogy before the reader's mind.

¶¶[15:39–41] The expression "its own body" (1 Cor 15:38) leads to a development on the marvelous diversity evident in bodily life.

***[15:42–44] The principles of qualitative difference before and after death (1 Cor 15:36–38) and of diversity on different levels of creation (1 Cor 15:39–41) are now applied to the human body. Before: a body animated by a lower, natural life-principle (*psychē*) and endowed with the properties of natural

---

x. [15:22] Gn 3:17–19; Rom 5:12–19.   y. [15:23] 1 Thes 4:15–17.
z. [15:24] Eph 1:22.   a. [15:25] Ps 110:1.   b. [15:26] Rom 6:9;
2 Tm 1:10; Rev 20:14; 21:4.   c. [15:27] Ps 8:7; Eph 1:22; Phil 3:21.
d. [15:28] Eph 4:6; Col 3:11.   e. [15:30] 2 Cor 4:8–12; 11:23–27.

f. [15:31] Ps 44:23; Rom 8:36.   g. [15:32] 4:9; 2 Cor 4:10–11 / Wis
2:5–7; Is 22:13.   h. [15:34] Mt 22:29; Mk 12:24.   i. [15:36] Jn
12:24.   j. [15:38] Gn 1:11.

is sown dishonorable; it is raised glorious. It is sown weak; it is raised powerful.[k] [44]It is sown a natural body; it is raised a spiritual body. If there is a natural body, there is also a spiritual one.

[45]So, too, it is written, "The first man, Adam,* became a living being," the last Adam a life-giving spirit.[l] [46]But the spiritual was not first; rather the natural and then the spiritual. [47]The first man was from the earth, earthly; the second man, from heaven. [48]As was the earthly one, so also are the earthly, and as is the heavenly one, so also are the heavenly. [49]Just as we have borne the image of the earthly one, we shall also bear the image[†] of the heavenly one.[m]

**The Resurrection Event.** [50‡]This I declare, brothers: flesh and blood cannot inherit the kingdom of God, nor does corruption[§] inherit incorruption.[n] [51§]Behold, I tell you a mystery. We shall not all fall asleep, but we will all be changed,[o] [52]in an instant, in the blink of an eye, at the last trumpet. For the trumpet will sound, the dead will be raised incorruptible, and we shall be changed.[p] [53]For that which is corruptible must clothe itself with incorruptibility, and that which is mortal must clothe itself with immortality.[q] [54**]And when this which is corruptible clothes itself with incorruptibility and this which is mortal clothes itself with immortality, then the word that is written shall come about:[r]

"Death is swallowed up in victory.
[55] Where, O death, is your victory?
   Where, O death, is your sting?"[s]

[56]The sting of death is sin,[††] and the power of sin is the law.[t] [57]But thanks be to God who gives us the victory through our Lord Jesus Christ.[u]

[58]Therefore, my beloved brothers, be firm, steadfast, always fully devoted to the work of the Lord, knowing that in the Lord your labor is not in vain.

## VI. CONCLUSION

## CHAPTER 16

**The Collection.**[‡‡] [1]Now in regard to the collection[§§] for the holy ones, you also should do as I ordered the churches of Galatia.[v] [2]On the first day of the week each of you should set aside and save whatever he can afford, so that collections will not be going on when I come. [3]And when I arrive, I shall send those whom you have approved with letters of recommendation to take your gracious gift to Jerusalem. [4]If it seems fitting that I should go also,[¶¶] they will go with me. **Paul's Travel Plans.**[***] [5]I shall come to you after I pass through Macedonia (for I am going to pass through Macedonia),[w] [6]and perhaps I shall stay or even spend the winter with you, so that you may send me on my way wherever I may go. [7]For I do not wish to see you now just in passing, but I hope to spend some time with you, if the Lord permits.[x] [8†††]I shall stay in Ephesus[y]

---

existence (corruptibility, lack of glory, weakness). After: a body animated by a higher life-principle (*pneuma*; cf. 1 Cor 15:45) and endowed with other qualities (incorruptibility, glory, power, spirituality), which are properties of God himself.

*[15:45] The analogy of **the first man, Adam**, is introduced by a citation from Gn 2:7. Paul alters the text slightly, adding the adjective **first**, and translating the Hebrew *ādām* twice, so as to give it its value both as a common noun (**man**) and as a proper name (**Adam**). 1 Cor 15:45b then specifies similarities and differences between the two Adams. **The last Adam**, Christ (cf. 1 Cor 15:21–22) has become **a . . . spirit** (*pneuma*), a life-principle transcendent with respect to the natural soul (*psychē*) of the first Adam (on the terminology here, cf. note on 1 Cor 3:1). Further, he is not just alive, but life-giving, a source of life for others.

†[15:49] **We shall also bear the image**: although it has less manuscript support, this reading better fits the context's emphasis on futurity and the transforming action of God; on future transformation as conformity to the image of the Son, cf. Rom 8:29; Phil 3:21. The majority reading, "let us bear the image," suggests that the image of the heavenly man is already present and exhorts us to conform to it.

‡[15:50–57] These verses, an answer to the first question of 1 Cor 15:35, explain theologically how the change of properties from one image to another will take place: God has the power to transform, and he will exercise it.

§[15:50–53] **Flesh and blood . . . corruption**: living persons and the corpses of the dead, respectively. In both cases, the gulf between creatures and God is too wide to be bridged unless God himself transforms us.

¶[15:51–52] **A mystery**: the last moment in God's plan is disclosed; cf. notes on 1 Cor 2:1, 7–10a. The final trumpet and the awakening of the dead are stock details of the apocalyptic scenario. **We shall not all fall asleep**: Paul expected that some of his contemporaries might still be alive at Christ's return; after the death of Paul and his whole generation, copyists altered this statement in various ways. **We will all be changed**: the statement extends to all Christians, for Paul is not directly speaking about anyone else. Whether they have died before the end or happen still to be alive, all must be transformed.

**[15:54–55] **Death is swallowed up in victory**: scripture itself predicts death's overthrow. **O death**: in his prophetic

vision Paul may be making Hosea's words his own, or imagining this cry of triumph on the lips of the risen church.

††[15:56] **The sting of death is sin**: an explanation of Hosea's metaphor. Death, scorpion-like, is equipped with a sting, sin, by which it injects its poison. Christ defeats sin, the cause of death (Gn 3:19; Rom 5:12).

‡‡[16:1–4] This paragraph contains our earliest evidence for a project that became a major undertaking of Paul's ministry. The collection for the church at Jerusalem was a symbol in his mind for the unity of Jewish and Gentile Christianity. Cf. Gal 2:10; Rom 15:25–29; 2 Cor 8–9 and the notes to this last passage.

§§[16:1] **In regard to the collection**: it has already begun in Galatia and Macedonia (cf. 2 Cor 8), and presumably he has already instructed the Corinthians about its purpose.

¶¶[16:4] **That I should go also**: presumably Paul delivered the collection on his final visit to Jerusalem; cf. Rom 15:25–32; Acts 24:14.

***[16:5–12] The travel plans outlined here may not have materialized precisely as Paul intended; cf. 2 Cor 1:8–2:13; 7:4–16.

†††[16:8] **In Ephesus until Pentecost**: this tells us the place from which he wrote the letter and suggests he may have composed it about Easter time (cf. 1 Cor 5:7–8).

r. [15:54] Is 25:8; 2 Cor 5:4; 2 Tm 1:10; Heb 2:14–15.   s. [15:55] Hos 13:14.   t. [15:56] Rom 4:15; 7:7, 13.   u. [15:57] Jn 16:33; 1 Jn 5:4.   v. [16:1] Acts 24:17; Rom 15:25–32; 2 Cor 8–9; Gal 2:10.   w. [16:5] Acts 19:21; Rom 15:26; 2 Cor 1:15–16.   x. [16:7] Acts 18:21.   y. [16:8] 15:32; Acts 18:19; 19:1–10.

---

k. [15:43] Phil 3:20–21; Col 3:4.   l. [15:45] Gn 2:7 / Jn 5:21–29; 2 Cor 3:6, 17.   m. [15:49] Gn 5:3 / Rom 8:29; Phil 3:21.   n. [15:50] Jn 3:3–6.   o. [15:51] 1 Thes 4:14–17.   p. [15:52] Jl 2:1; Zec 9:14; Mt 24:31; Rev 11:15–18.   q. [15:53] 2 Cor 5:2–4.

until Pentecost, [9]because a door has opened for me wide and productive for work, but there are many opponents.[z]

[10]If Timothy comes, see that he is without fear in your company, for he is doing the work of the Lord just as I am.[a] [11]Therefore, no one should disdain him. Rather, send him on his way in peace that he may come to me, for I am expecting him with the brothers. [12]Now in regard to our brother Apollos, I urged him strongly to go to you with the brothers, but it was not at all his will that he go now. He will go when he has an opportunity.[b]

**Exhortation and Greetings.** [13]Be on your guard, stand firm in the faith, be courageous, be strong. [14]Your every act should be done with love.

[15]I urge you, brothers—you know that the household of Stephanas[c] is the firstfruits of Achaia and that they have devoted themselves to the service of the holy ones— [16]be subordinate to such people and to everyone who works and toils with them. [17]I rejoice in the arrival of Stephanas, Fortunatus, and Achaicus, because they made up for your absence, [18]for they refreshed my spirit as well as yours. So give recognition to such people.[d]

[19]The churches of Asia send you greetings. Aquila and Prisca together with the church at their house send you many greetings in the Lord.[e] [20]All the brothers greet you. Greet one another with a holy kiss.[f]

[21]I, Paul, write you this greeting in my own hand.[g] [22]If anyone does not love the Lord, let him be accursed.[†] *Marana tha.*[h] [23]The grace of the Lord Jesus be with you.[i] [24]My love to all of you in Christ Jesus.

---

*[16:19–24] These paragraphs conform to the normal epistolary conclusion, but their language is overlaid with liturgical coloration as well. The greetings of the Asian churches are probably to be read, along with the letter, in the liturgy at Corinth, and the union of the church is to be expressed by a holy kiss (1 Cor 16:19–20). Paul adds to this his own greeting (1 Cor 16:21) and blessings (1 Cor 16:23–24).

†[16:22] **Accursed**: literally, "anathema." This expression (cf. 1 Cor 12:3) is a formula for exclusion from the community; it may imply here a call to self-examination before celebration of the Eucharist, in preparation for the Lord's coming and judgment (cf. 1 Cor 11:17–34). **Marana tha**: an Aramaic expression, probably used in the early Christian liturgy. As understood here ("O Lord, come!"), it is a prayer for the early return of Christ. If the Aramaic words are divided differently (*Maran atha*, "Our Lord has come"), it becomes a credal declaration. The former interpretation is supported by what appears to be a Greek equivalent of this acclamation in Rev 22:20 "Amen. Come, Lord Jesus!"

---

z. [16:9] Acts 14:27; 2 Cor 2:12.   a. [16:10] 4:17; Acts 16:1; 19:22; Phil 2:19–23.   b. [16:12] 1:12; 3:4–6, 22; Acts 18:24–28.   c. [16:15] 1:16.   d. [16:18] 1 Thes 5:12–13.

e. [16:19] Acts 18:2, 18, 26; Rom 16:3–5.   f. [16:20] Rom 16:16; 2 Cor 13:12; 1 Thes 5:26; 1 Pt 5:14.   g. [16:21] Gal 6:11; Col 4:18; 2 Thes 3:17.   h. [16:22] 12:3; Rom 9:3; Gal 1:8–9; Rev 22:20.   i. [16:23] Rom 16:20.

# THE SECOND LETTER TO THE
# CORINTHIANS

The Second Letter to the Corinthians is the most personal of all of Paul's extant writings, and it reveals much about his character. In it he deals with one or more crises that have arisen in the Corinthian church. The confrontation with these problems caused him to reflect deeply on his relationship with the community and to speak about it frankly. One moment he is venting his feelings of frustration and uncertainty, the next he is pouring out his relief and affection. The importance of the issues at stake between them calls forth from him an enormous effort of personal persuasion, as well as doctrinal considerations that are of great value for us. Paul's ability to produce profound theological foundations for what may at first sight appear to be rather commonplace circumstances is perhaps nowhere better exemplified than in Second Corinthians. The emotional tone of the letter, its lack of order, and our ignorance of some of its background do not make it easy to follow, but it amply repays the effort required of the reader.

Second Corinthians is rich and varied in content. The interpretation of Exodus in chapter 3, for instance, offers a striking example of early apologetic use of the Old Testament. Paul's discussion of the collection in chaps. 8–9 contains a theology of sharing of possessions, of community of goods among Christian churches, which is both balanced and sensitive. Furthermore, the closing chapters provide an illustration of early Christian invective and polemic, because the conflict with intruders forces Paul to assert his authority. But in those same chapters Paul articulates the vision and sense of values that animate his own apostolate, revealing his faith that Jesus' passion and resurrection are the pattern for all Christian life and expressing a spirituality of ministry unsurpassed in the New Testament.

The letter is remarkable for its rhetoric. Paul falls naturally into the style and argumentation of contemporary philosophic preachers, employing with ease the stock devices of the "diatribe." By a barrage of questions, by challenges both serious and ironic, by paradox heaped upon paradox, even by insults hurled at his opponents, he strives to awaken in his hearers a true sense of values and an appropriate response. All his argument centers on the destiny of Jesus, in which a paradoxical reversal of values is revealed. But Paul appeals to his own personal experience as well. In passages of great rhetorical power (2 Cor 4:7–15; 6:3–10; 11:21–29; 12:5–10; 13:3–4) he enumerates the circumstances of his ministry and the tribulations he has had to endure for Jesus and the gospel, in the hope of illustrating the pattern of Jesus' existence in his own and of drawing the Corinthians into a reappraisal of the values they cherish. Similar passages in the same style in his other letters (cf. especially Rom 8:31–39; 1 Cor 1:26–31; 4:6–21; 9:1–27; 13:1–13; Phil 4:10–19) confirm Paul's familiarity with contemporary rhetoric and demonstrate how effectively it served to express his vision of Christian life and ministry.

Second Corinthians was occasioned by events and problems that developed after Paul's first letter reached Corinth. We have no information about these circumstances except what is contained in the letter itself, which of course supposes that they are known to the readers. Consequently the reconstruction of the letter's background is an uncertain enterprise about which there is not complete agreement.

The letter deals principally with these three topics: (1) a crisis between Paul and the Corinthians, occasioned at least partially by changes in his travel plans (2 Cor 1:12–2:13), and the successful resolution of that crisis (2 Cor 7:5–16); (2) further directives and encouragement in regard to the collection for the church in Jerusalem (2 Cor 8:1–9:15); (3) the definition and defense of Paul's ministry as an apostle. Paul's reflections on this matter are occasioned by visitors from other churches who passed through Corinth, missionaries who differed from Paul in a variety of ways, both in theory and in practice. Those differences led to comparisons. Either the visitors themselves or some of the local church members appear to have sown confusion among the Corinthians with regard to Paul's authority or his style, or both. Paul deals at length with aspects of this situation in 2 Cor 2:14–7:4 and again in 2 Cor 10:1–13:10, though the manner of treatment and the thrust of the argument differ in each of these sections.

Scholars have noticed a lack of continuity in this document. For example, the long section of 2 Cor 2:14–7:4 seems abruptly spliced into the narrative of a crisis and its resolution. Identical or similar topics, moreover, seem to be treated several times during the letter (compare 2 Cor 2:14–7:4 with 2 Cor 10:1–13:10, and 2 Cor 8:1–24 with 2 Cor 9:1–15). Many judge, therefore, that this letter as it stands incorporates several briefer letters sent to Corinth over a certain span of time. If this is so, then Paul himself or, more likely, some other editor clearly took care to gather those letters together and impose some literary unity upon the collection, thus producing the document that has come down to us as the Second Letter to the Corinthians. Others continue to regard it as a single letter, attributing its inconsistencies to changes of perspective in Paul that may have been occasioned by the arrival of fresh news from Corinth during its composition. The letter, or at least some sections of it, appears to have been composed in Macedonia (2 Cor 2:12–13; 7:5–6; 8:1–4; 9:2–4). It is generally dated about the autumn of A.D. 57; if it is a compilation, of course, the various parts may have been separated by intervals of at least some months.

The principal divisions of the Second Letter to the Corinthians are the following:

I.  Address (1:1–11)
II.  The Crisis Between Paul and the Corinthians (1:12–7:16)
        A. Past Relationships (1:12–2:13)
        B. Paul's Ministry (2:14–7:4)
        C. Resolution of the Crisis (7:5–16)
III.  The Collection for Jerusalem (8:1–9:15)
IV.  Paul's Defense of His Ministry (10:1–13:10)
V.  Conclusion (13:11–13)

## I. ADDRESS

### CHAPTER 1

**Greeting.** [1]Paul, an apostle of Christ Jesus by the will of God, and Timothy our brother, to the church of God that is in Corinth, with all the holy ones throughout Achaia:[a] [2]grace to you and peace from God our Father and the Lord Jesus Christ.

**Thanksgiving.** [3b]Blessed be the God and Father of our Lord Jesus Christ, the Father of compassion and God of all encouragement,[†] [4]who encourages us in our every affliction, so that we may be able to encourage those who are in any affliction with the encouragement with which we ourselves are encouraged by God.[c] [5]For as Christ's sufferings overflow to us, so through Christ[‡] does our encouragement also overflow. [6]If we are afflicted, it is for your encouragement and salvation; if we are encouraged, it is for your encouragement, which enables you to endure the same sufferings that we suffer. [7]Our hope for you is firm, for we know that as you share in the sufferings, you also share in the encouragement.[§]

[8]We do not want you to be unaware, brothers, of the affliction that came to us in the province of Asia;[¶] we were utterly weighed down beyond our strength, so that we despaired even of life.[d] [9]Indeed, we had accepted within ourselves the

---

*[1:1–11] The opening follows the usual Pauline form, except that the thanksgiving takes the form of a doxology or glorification of God (2 Cor 1:3). This introduces a meditation on the experience of suffering and encouragement shared by Paul and the Corinthians (2 Cor 1:4–7), drawn, at least in part, from Paul's reflections on a recent affliction (2 Cor 1:8–10). The section ends with a modified and delayed allusion to thanksgiving (2 Cor 1:11).

†[1:3] **God of all encouragement**: Paul expands a standard Jewish blessing so as to state the theme of the paragraph. The theme of "encouragement" or "consolation" (*paraklēsis*) occurs ten times in this opening, against a background formed by multiple references to "affliction" and "suffering."

‡[1:5] **Through Christ**: the Father of compassion is the Father of our Lord Jesus (2 Cor 1:3); Paul's sufferings and encouragement (or "consolation") are experienced in union with Christ. Cf. Lk 2:25: the "consolation of Israel" is Jesus himself.

§[1:7] **You also share in the encouragement**: the eschatological reversal of affliction and encouragement that Christians expect (cf. Mt 5:4; Lk 6:24) permits some present experience of reversal in the Corinthians' case, as in Paul's.

¶[1:8] **Asia**: a Roman province in western Asia Minor, the capital of which was Ephesus.

---

a. [1:1] Eph 1:1; Col 1:1 / 2 Cor 1:19; Acts 16 / Rom 1:7; 1 Cor 1:2.   b. [1:3] 1 Cor 15:24; Eph 1:3; 1 Pt 1:3 / Rom 15:5.

c. [1:4] 7:6–7, 13; 1 Thes 3:6–8; 2 Thes 2:16.   d. [1:8] Acts 20:18–19; 1 Cor 15:32.

sentence of death,* that we might trust not in ourselves but in God who raises the dead.ᵉ ¹⁰He rescued us from such great danger of death, and he will continue to rescue us; in him we have put our hope [that] he will also rescue us again,ᶠ ¹¹as you help us with prayer, so that thanks may be given by many on our behalf for the gift granted us through the prayers of many.ᵍ

## II. THE CRISIS BETWEEN PAUL AND THE CORINTHIANS

### A. Past Relationships†

**Paul's Sincerity and Constancy.** ¹²‡For our boast is this, the testimony of our conscience that we have conducted ourselves in the world, and especially toward you, with the simplicity and sincerity of God, [and] not by human wisdom but by the grace of God. ¹³For we write you nothing but what you can read and understand, and I hope that you will understand completely, ¹⁴as you have come to understand us partially, that we are your boast as you also are ours, on the day of [our] Lord Jesus.ʰ

¹⁵With this confidence I formerly intended to come§ to you so that you might receive a double favor, ¹⁶namely, to go by way of you to Macedonia, and then to come to you again on my return from Macedonia, and have you send me on my way to Judea.ⁱ ¹⁷So when I intended this, did I act lightly?¶ Or do I make my plans according to human considerations, so that

with me it is "yes, yes" and "no, no"?ʲ ¹⁸As God is faithful,** our word to you is not "yes" and "no." ¹⁹For the Son of God, Jesus Christ, who was proclaimed to you by us, Silvanus and Timothy and me, was not "yes" and "no," but "yes" has been in him.ᵏ ²⁰For however many are the promises of God, their Yes is in him; therefore, the Amen from us also goes through him to God for glory.ˡ ²¹††But the one who gives us security with you in Christ and who anointed us is God;ᵐ ²²he has also put his seal upon us and given the Spirit in our hearts as a first installment.ⁿ

**Paul's Change of Plan.** ²³ᵒBut I call upon God as witness, on my life, that it is to spare you that I have not yet gone to Corinth.‡‡ ²⁴Not that we lord it over your faith; rather, we work together for your joy, for you stand firm in the faith.

## CHAPTER 2

¹For I decided not to come to you again in painful circumstances. ²For if I inflict pain upon you, then who is there to cheer me except the one pained by me? ³And I wrote as I did§§ so that when I came I might not be pained by those in whom I should have rejoiced, confident about all of you that my joy is that of all of you. ⁴For

---

*[1:9–10] **The sentence of death**: it is unclear whether Paul is alluding to a physical illness or to an external threat to life. The result of the situation was to produce an attitude of faith in God alone. **God who raises the dead**: rescue is the constant pattern of God's activity; his final act of encouragement is the resurrection.

†[1:12–2:13] The autobiographical remarks about the crisis in Asia Minor lead into consideration of a crisis that has arisen between Paul and the Corinthians. Paul will return to this question, after a long digression, in 2 Cor 7:5–16. Both of these sections deal with travel plans Paul had made, changes in the plans, alternative measures adopted, a breach that opened between him and the community, and finally a reconciliation between them.

‡[1:12–14] Since Paul's own conduct will be under discussion here, he prefaces the section with a statement about his habitual behavior and attitude toward the community. He protests his openness, single-mindedness, and conformity to God's grace; he hopes that his relationship with them will be marked by mutual understanding and pride, which will constantly increase until it reaches its climax at the judgment. Two references to boasting frame this paragraph (2 Cor 1:12, 14), the first appearances of a theme that will be important in the letter, especially in 2 Cor 10–13; the term is used in a positive sense here (cf. note on 1 Cor 1:29–31).

§[1:15] **I formerly intended to come**: this plan reads like a revision of the one mentioned in 1 Cor 16:5. Not until 2 Cor 1:23–2:1 will Paul tell us something his original readers already knew, that he has canceled one or the other of these projected visits.

¶[1:17] **Did I act lightly?**: the subsequent change of plans casts suspicion on the original intention, creating the impression that Paul is vacillating and inconsistent or that **human considerations** keep dictating shifts in his goals and projects (cf. the counterclaim of 2 Cor 1:12). **"Yes, yes" and "no, no"**: stating something and denying it in the same or the next breath; being of two minds at once, or from one moment to the next.

**[1:18–22] **As God is faithful**: unable to deny the change in plans, Paul nonetheless asserts the firmness of the original plan and claims a profound constancy in his life and work. He grounds his defense in God himself, who is firm and reliable; this quality can also be predicated in various ways of those who are associated with him. Christ, Paul, and the Corinthians all participate in analogous ways in the constancy of God. A number of the terms here, which appear related only conceptually in Greek or English, would be variations of the same root, *'mn*, in a Semitic language, and thus naturally associated in a Semitic mind, such as Paul's. These include the words **yes** (2 Cor 1:17–20), **faithful** (2 Cor 1:18), **Amen** (2 Cor 1:20), **gives us security** (2 Cor 1:21), **faith, stand firm** (2 Cor 1:24).

††[1:21–22] The commercial terms **gives us security, seal, first installment** are here used analogously to refer to the process of initiation into the Christian life, perhaps specifically to baptism. The passage is clearly trinitarian. The Spirit is the **first installment** or "down payment" of the full messianic benefits that God guarantees to Christians. Cf. Eph 1:13–14.

‡‡[1:23–24] **I have not yet gone to Corinth**: some suppose that Paul received word of some affair in Corinth, which he decided to regulate by letter even before the first of his projected visits (cf. 2 Cor 1:16). Others conjecture that he did pay the first visit, was offended there (cf. 2 Cor 2:5), returned to Ephesus, and sent a letter (2 Cor 2:3–9) in place of the second visit. The expressions **to spare you** (2 Cor 1:23) and **work together for your joy** (2 Cor 1:24) introduce the major themes of the next two paragraphs, which are remarkable for insistent repetition of key words and ideas. These form two clusters of terms in the English translation: (1) cheer, rejoice, encourage, joy; (2) pain, affliction, anguish. These clusters reappear when Paul resumes treatment of this subject in 2 Cor 7:5–16.

§§[2:3–4] **I wrote as I did**: we learn for the first time about the sending of a letter in place of the proposed visit. Paul mentions the letter in passing, but emphasizes his motivation in sending it: to avoid being saddened by them (cf. 1 Cor 2:1), and to help them realize the depth of his love. Another motive will be added in 2 Cor 7:12: to bring to light their own concern for him. **With many tears**: it has been suggested that we may have all or part of this "tearful letter" somewhere in the Corinthian correspondence, either in 1 Cor 5 (the case of the incestuous man), or in 1 Corinthians as a whole, or in 2 Cor 2:10–13. None of these hypotheses is entirely convincing. See note on 2 Cor 13:1.

---

e. [1:9] 4:7–11; Rom 4:17.　f. [1:10] 2 Tm 4:18.　g. [1:11] 4:15; 9:12.
h. [1:14] Phil 2:16; 1 Thes 2:19–20.　i. [1:16] 1 Cor 16:5–9; Acts 19:21.
j. [1:17] Mt 5:37; Jas 5:12.　k. [1:19] Acts 16:1–3; 1 Thes 1:1; 2 Thes 1:1.　l. [1:20] 1 Cor 14:16; Rev 3:14.　m. [1:21] 1 Jn 2:20, 27.　n. [1:22] Eph 1:13–14; 4:30 / 2 Cor 5:5; Rom 5:5; 8:16, 23.　o. [1:23] 13:2.

out of much affliction and anguish of heart I wrote to you with many tears, not that you might be pained but that you might know the abundant love I have for you.

**The Offender.** [*] [5]If anyone has caused pain, he has caused it not to me, but in some measure (not to exaggerate) to all of you. [6]This punishment by the majority is enough for such a person, [7]so that on the contrary you should forgive and encourage him instead, or else the person may be overwhelmed by excessive pain. [p] [8]Therefore, I urge you to reaffirm your love for him. [9]For this is why I wrote, to know your proven character, whether you were obedient in everything. [q] [10]Whomever you forgive anything, so do I. For indeed what I have forgiven, if I have forgiven anything, has been for you in the presence of Christ, [11]so that we might not be taken advantage of by Satan, for we are not unaware of his purposes. [r]

**Paul's Anxiety.** [†] [12]When I went to Troas for the gospel of Christ, although a door was opened for me in the Lord, [s] [13]I had no relief in my spirit because I did not find my brother Titus. [t] So I took leave of them and went on to Macedonia.

### B. Paul's Ministry [§]

**Ministers of a New Covenant.** [14]But thanks be to God, [u] who always leads us in triumph in

Christ [††] and manifests through us the odor of the knowledge of him [‡‡] in every place. [15]For we are the aroma of Christ for God among those who are being saved and among those who are perishing, [u] [16]to the latter an odor of death that leads to death, to the former an odor of life that leads to life. Who is qualified [§§] for this? [17]For we are not like the many who trade on the word of God; but as out of sincerity, indeed as from God and in the presence of God, we speak in Christ. [v]

## CHAPTER 3

[¶¶w]Are we beginning to commend ourselves again? Or do we need, as some do, letters of recommendation to you or from you? [2]You are our letter, [***] written on our hearts, known and read by all, [3†††x]shown to be a letter of Christ administered

[††][2:14a] **Leads us in triumph in Christ**: this metaphor of a festive parade in honor of a conquering military hero can suggest either a positive sharing in Christ's triumph or an experience of defeat, being led in captivity and submission (cf. 2 Cor 4:8–11; 1 Cor 4:9). Paul is probably aware of the ambiguity, as he is in the case of the next metaphor.

[‡‡][2:14b–16a] **The odor of the knowledge of him**: incense was commonly used in triumphal processions. The metaphor suggests the gradual diffusion of the knowledge of God through the apostolic preaching. **The aroma of Christ**: the image shifts from the fragrance Paul diffuses to the aroma that he is. Paul is probably thinking of the "sweet odor" of the sacrifices in the Old Testament (e.g., Gn 8:21; Ex 29:18) and perhaps of the metaphor of wisdom as a sweet odor (Sir 24:15). **Death . . . life**: the aroma of Christ that comes to them through Paul is perceived differently by various classes of people. To some his preaching and his life (cf. 1 Cor 1:17–2:6) are perceived as death, and the effect is death for them; others perceive him, despite appearances, as **life**, and the effect is life for them. This fragrance thus produces a separation and a judgment (cf. the function of the "light" in John's gospel).

[§§][2:16b–17] **Qualified**: Paul may be echoing either the self-satisfied claims of other preachers or their charges about Paul's deficiencies. No one is really qualified, but the apostle contrasts himself with those who dilute or falsify the preaching for personal advantage and insists on his totally good conscience: his ministry is from God, and he has exercised it with fidelity and integrity (cf. 2 Cor 3:5–6).

[¶¶][3:1] Paul seems to allude to certain preachers who pride themselves on their written credentials. Presumably they reproach him for not possessing similar credentials and compel him to spell out his own qualifications (2 Cor 4:2; 5:12; 6:4). The Corinthians themselves should have performed this function for Paul (2 Cor 5:12; cf. 2 Cor 12:11). Since he is forced to find something that can recommend him, he points to them: their very existence constitutes his **letter** of recommendation (2 Cor 3:1–2). Others who engage in self-commendation will also be mentioned in 2 Cor 10:12–18.

[***][3:2–3] Mention of "letters of recommendation" generates a series of metaphors in which Paul plays on the word "letter": (1) the community is Paul's letter of recommendation (2 Cor 3:2a); (2) they are a letter engraved on his affections for all to see and read (2 Cor 3:2b); (3) they are a letter from Christ that Paul merely delivers (2 Cor 3:3a); (4) they are a letter written by the Spirit on the tablets of human hearts (2 Cor 3:3b). One image dissolves into another.

[†††][3:3b] This verse contrasts Paul's letter with those **written . . . in ink** (like the credentials of other preachers) and those **written . . . on tablets of stone** (like the law of Moses). These contrasts suggest that the other preachers may have claimed special relationship with Moses. If they were Judaizers zealous for the Mosaic law, that would explain the detailed contrast between the old and the new covenants (2 Cor 3:6; 4:7–6:10). If they were charismatics who claimed Moses as

[*][2:5–11] The nature of the **pain** (2 Cor 2:5) is unclear, though some believe an individual at Corinth rejected Paul's authority, thereby scandalizing many in the community. In any case, action has been taken, and Paul judges the measures adequate to right the situation (2 Cor 2:6). The follow-up directives he now gives are entirely positive: forgive, encourage, love. **Overwhelmed** (2 Cor 2:7): a vivid metaphor (literally "swallowed") that Paul employs positively at 2 Cor 5:4 and in 1 Cor 15:54 (2 Cor 2:7). It is often used to describe satanic activity (cf. 1 Pt 5:8); note the reference to Satan here in 2 Cor 2:11.

[†][2:12–13] **I had no relief**: Paul does not explain the reason for his anxiety until he resumes the thread of his narrative at 2 Cor 7:5: he was waiting to hear how the Corinthians would respond to his letter. Since 2 Cor 7:5–16 describes their response in entirely positive terms, we never learn in detail why he found it necessary to defend and justify his change of plans, as in 2 Cor 1:15–24. Was this portion of the letter written before the arrival of Titus with his good news (2 Cor 7:6–7)?

[‡][2:13] **Macedonia**: a Roman province in northern Greece.

[§][2:14–7:4] This section constitutes a digression within the narrative of the crisis and its resolution (2 Cor 1:12–2:13 and 2 Cor 7:5–16). The main component (2 Cor 2:14–6:10) treats the nature of Paul's ministry and his qualifications for it; this material bears some similarity to the defense of his ministry in chaps. 10–13, but it may well come from a period close to the crisis. This is followed by a supplementary block of material quite different in character and tone (2 Cor 6:14–7:1). These materials may have been brought together into their present position during final editing of the letter; appeals to the Corinthians link them to one another (2 Cor 6:11–13) and lead back to the interrupted narrative (2 Cor 7:2–4).

[¶][2:14–6:10] The question of Paul's adequacy (2 Cor 2:16; cf. 2 Cor 3:5) and his credentials (2 Cor 3:1–2) has been raised. Paul responds by an extended treatment of the nature of his ministry. It is a ministry of glory (2 Cor 3:7–4:6), of life (2 Cor 4:7–5:10), of reconciliation (2 Cor 5:11–6:10).

[**][2:14–16a] The initial statement plunges us abruptly into another train of thought. Paul describes his personal existence and his function as a preacher in two powerful images (2 Cor 2:14) that constitute a prelude to the development to follow.

p. [2:7] Col 3:13.    q. [2:9] 7:15.    r. [2:11] Eph 4:27.    s. [2:12] Acts 16:8.    t. [2:13] 7:6; 1 Tm 1:3.

u. [2:15] 4:3; 1 Cor 1:18.    v. [2:17] 4:2; 1 Cor 5:8.    w. [3:1] Acts 18:27; Rom 16:1; 1 Cor 16:3.    x. [3:3] Ex 24:12; 31:18; 32:15–19 / Jer 31:33; Ez 11:19; 36:26–27.

by us, written not in ink but by the Spirit of the living God, not on tablets of stone but on tablets that are hearts of flesh.

[4]*Such confidence we have through Christ toward God. [5]Not that of ourselves we are qualified to take credit for anything as coming from us; rather, our qualification comes from God,[y] [6]who has indeed qualified us as ministers of a new covenant, not of letter but of spirit;[z] for the letter brings death, but the Spirit gives life.[†]

**Contrast with the Old Covenant.** [7]‡Now if the ministry of death,[§] carved in letters on stone, was so glorious that the Israelites could not look intently at the face of Moses because of its glory that was going to fade,[a] [8]how much more[¶] will the ministry of the Spirit be glorious? [9]For if the ministry of condemnation was glorious, the ministry of righteousness will abound much more in glory. [10]Indeed, what was endowed with glory has come to have no glory in this respect because of the glory that surpasses it. [11]For if what was going to fade was glorious, how much more will what endures be glorious.

[12]Therefore, since we have such hope,** we act very boldly [13]and not like Moses,[††] who put a veil over his face so that the Israelites could not look intently at the cessation of what was fading. [14]Rather, their thoughts were rendered dull, for to this present day[‡‡] the same veil remains unlifted when they read the old covenant, because through Christ it is taken away. [15]To this day, in fact, whenever Moses is read, a veil lies over their hearts,[b] [16]but whenever a person turns to the Lord the veil is removed.[c] [17]Now the Lord is the Spirit,[§§] and where the Spirit of the Lord is, there is freedom. [18]¶¶All of us, gazing with unveiled face on the glory of the Lord, are being transformed into the same image from glory to glory, as from the Lord who is the Spirit.[d]

# CHAPTER 4

**Integrity in the Ministry.** [1]***Therefore, since we have this ministry through the mercy shown us, we are not discouraged. [2]Rather, we have renounced shameful, hidden things; not acting deceitfully or falsifying the word of God, but by

---

their model, that would explain the extended treatment of Moses himself and his glory (2 Cor 3:7–4:6). **Hearts of flesh:** cf. Ezekiel's contrast between the heart of flesh that the Spirit gives and the heart of stone that it replaces (Ez 36:26); the context is covenant renewal and purification that makes observance of the law possible.

*[3:4–6] These verses resume 2 Cor 2:1–3:3. Paul's confidence (2 Cor 3:4) is grounded in his sense of God-given mission (2 Cor 2:17), the specifics of which are described in 2 Cor 3:1–3. 2 Cor 3:5–6 return to the question of his qualifications (2 Cor 2:16), attributing them entirely to God. 2 Cor 3:6 further spells out the situation described in 2 Cor 3:3b and "names" it: Paul is writing within a **new covenant**, characterized by the Spirit, which **gives life**. The usage of a **new covenant** is derived from Jer 31:31–33 a passage that also speaks of writing on the heart; cf. 2 Cor 3:2.

†[3:6b] This verse serves as a topic sentence for 2 Cor 3:7–6:10. For the contrast between **letter** and **spirit,** cf. Rom 2:29; 7:5–6.

‡[3:7–4:6] Paul now develops the contrast enunciated in 2 Cor 3:6b in terms of the relative glory of the two covenants, insisting on the greater glory of the new. His polemic seems directed against individuals who appeal to the glorious Moses and fail to perceive any comparable glory either in Paul's life as an apostle or in the gospel he preaches. He asserts in response that Christians have a glory of their own that far surpasses that of Moses.

§[3:7] **The ministry of death:** from his very first words, Paul describes the Mosaic covenant and ministry from the viewpoint of their limitations. They lead to **death** rather than life (2 Cor 3:6–7; cf. 2 Cor 4:7–5:10), to **condemnation** rather than reconciliation (2 Cor 3:9; cf. 2 Cor 5:11–6:10). **Was so glorious:** the basic text to which Paul alludes is Ex 34:29–35 to which his opponents have undoubtedly laid claim. **Going to fade:** Paul concedes the glory of Moses' covenant and ministry, but grants them only temporary significance.

¶[3:8–11] **How much more:** the argument "from the less to the greater" is repeated three times (2 Cor 3:8, 9, 11). 2 Cor 3:10 expresses another point of view: the difference in glory is so great that only the new covenant and ministry can properly be called "glorious" at all.

**[3:12] **Such hope:** the glory is not yet an object of experience, but that does not lessen Paul's confidence. **Boldly:** the term *parrēsia* expresses outspoken declaration of Christian conviction (cf. 2 Cor 4:1–2). Paul has nothing to hide and no reason for timidity.

††[3:13–14a] **Not like Moses:** in Exodus Moses veiled his face to protect the Israelites from God's reflected glory.

Without impugning Moses' sincerity, Paul attributes another effect to the veil. Since it lies between God's glory and the Israelites, it explains how they could fail to notice the glory disappearing. **Their thoughts were rendered dull:** the problem lay with their understanding. This will be expressed in 2 Cor 3:14b–16 by a shift in the place of the veil: it is no longer over Moses' face but over their perception.

‡‡[3:14b–16] The parallelism in these verses makes it necessary to interpret corresponding parts in relation to one another. **To this present day:** this signals the shift of Paul's attention to his contemporaries; his argument is typological, as in 1 Cor 10. The Israelites of Moses' time typify the Jews of Paul's time, and perhaps also Christians of Jewish origin or mentality who may not recognize the temporary character of Moses' glory. **When they read the old covenant:** the lasting dullness prevents proper appraisal of Moses' person and covenant. When his writings are read in the synagogue, a veil still impedes their understanding. **Through Christ:** i.e., in the new covenant. **Whenever a person turns to the Lord:** Moses in Exodus appeared before God without the veil and gazed on his face unprotected. Paul applies that passage to converts to Christianity: when they turn to the Lord fully and authentically, the impediment to their understanding is removed.

§§[3:17] **The Lord is the Spirit:** the "Lord" to whom the Christian turns (2 Cor 3:16) is the Spirit of whom Paul has been speaking, the life-giving Spirit of the living God (2 Cor 3:6, 8), the inaugurator of the new covenant and ministry, who is also the Spirit of Christ. **The Spirit of the Lord:** the Lord here is the living God (2 Cor 3:3), but there may also be an allusion to Christ as Lord (2 Cor 3:14, 16). **Freedom:** i.e., from the ministry of death (2 Cor 3:7) and the covenant that condemned (2 Cor 3:9).

¶¶[3:18] Another application of the veil image. **All of us . . . with unveiled face:** Christians (Israelites from whom the veil has been removed) are like Moses, standing in God's presence, beholding and reflecting his glory. **Gazing:** the verb may also be translated "contemplating as in a mirror"; 2 Cor 4:6 would suggest that the mirror is Christ himself. **Are being transformed:** elsewhere Paul speaks of transformation, conformity to Jesus, God's image, as a reality of the end time, and even 2 Cor 3:12 speaks of the glory as an object of hope. But the life-giving Spirit, the distinctive gift of the new covenant, is already present in the community (cf. 2 Cor 1:22, the "first installment"), and the process of transformation has already begun. **Into the same image:** into the image of God, which is Christ (2 Cor 4:4).

***[4:1–2] A ministry of this sort generates confidence and forthrightness; cf. 2 Cor 1:12–14; 2:17.

---

y. [3:5] Jn 3:27.   z. [3:6] Eph 3:7 / Jer 31:31–34.   a. [3:7] Ex 34:29–35.

b. [3:15] Rom 11:7–10.   c. [3:16] Ex 34:34.   d. [3:18] Rom 8:29–30; 12:2; Gal 4:19; Phil 3:10, 20–21 / 2 Cor 4:4–6; 1 Cor 15:49; Col 1:15; 3:9–11; 1 Jn 3:2.

the open declaration of the truth we commend ourselves to everyone's conscience in the sight of God.$^e$ $^3$And even though our gospel is veiled,$^*$ it is veiled for those who are perishing,$^f$ $^4$in whose case the god of this age has blinded the minds of the unbelievers, so that they may not see the light of the gospel of the glory of Christ, who is the image of God.$^g$ $^5$For we do not preach ourselves$^†$ but Jesus Christ as Lord, and ourselves as your slaves for the sake of Jesus. $^6$‡For God who said, "Let light shine out of darkness," has shone in our hearts to bring to light the knowledge of the glory of God on the face of [Jesus] Christ.$^h$

**The Paradox of the Ministry.** $^7$§But we hold this treasure$^¶$ in earthen vessels, that the surpassing power may be of God and not from us. $^8$**We are afflicted in every way, but not constrained; perplexed, but not driven to despair;$^i$ $^9$persecuted, but not abandoned; struck down, but not destroyed; $^{10}$††always carrying about in the body the dying of Jesus, so that the life of Jesus may also be manifested in our body. $^{11}$For we who live are constantly being given up to death for

the sake of Jesus, so that the life of Jesus may be manifested in our mortal flesh.$^k$

$^{12}$‡‡So death is at work in us, but life in you. $^{13}$§§Since, then, we have the same spirit of faith, according to what is written, "I believed, therefore I spoke," we too believe and therefore speak,$^l$ $^{14}$knowing that the one who raised the Lord Jesus will raise us also with Jesus and place us with you in his presence.$^m$ $^{15}$Everything indeed is for you, so that the grace bestowed in abundance on more and more people may cause the thanksgiving to overflow for the glory of God.$^n$

$^{16}$¶¶Therefore, we are not discouraged;*** rather, although our outer self is wasting away, our inner self is being renewed day by day.$^o$ $^{17}$For this momentary light affliction is producing for us an eternal weight of glory beyond all comparison,$^p$ $^{18}$as we look not to what is seen but to what is unseen; for what is seen is transitory, but what is unseen is eternal.$^q$

## CHAPTER 5

**Our Future Destiny.** $^1$For we know that if our earthly dwelling,$^{†††}$ a tent, should be destroyed, we have a building from God, a dwelling not made with hands, eternal in heaven. $^2$‡‡‡For in

---

$^*$[4:3–4] **Though our gospel is veiled**: the final application of the image. Paul has been reproached either for obscurity in his preaching or for his manner of presenting the gospel. But he confidently asserts that there is no veil over his gospel. If some fail to perceive its light, that is because of unbelief. The veil lies over their eyes (2 Cor 3:14), a blindness induced by Satan, and a sign that they are headed for destruction (cf. 2 Cor 2:15).

$^†$[4:5] **We do not preach ourselves**: the light seen in his gospel is the glory of Christ (2 Cor 4:4). Far from preaching himself, the preacher should be a transparent medium through whom Jesus is perceived (cf. 2 Cor 4:10–11). **Your slaves**: Paul draws attention away from individuals as such and toward their role in relation to God, Christ, and the community; cf. 1 Cor 3:5; 2 Cor 4:1.

$^‡$[4:6] Autobiographical allusion to the episode at Damascus clarifies the origin and nature of Paul's service; cf. Acts 9:1–19; 22:3–16; 26:2–18. **"Let light shine out of darkness"**: Paul seems to be thinking of Gn 1:3 and presenting his apostolic ministry as a new creation. There may also be an allusion to Is 9:1 suggesting his prophetic calling as servant of the Lord and light to the nations; cf. Is 42:6, 16; 49:6; 60:1–2, and the use of light imagery in Acts 26:13–23. **To bring to light the knowledge**: Paul's role in the process of revelation, expressed at the beginning under the image of the odor and aroma (2 Cor 2:14–15), is restated now, at the end of this first moment of the development, in the imagery of light and glory (2 Cor 4:3–6).

$^§$[4:7–5:10] Paul now confronts the difficulty that his present existence does not appear glorious at all; it is marked instead by suffering and death. He deals with this by developing the topic already announced in 2 Cor 3:3, 6, asserting his faith in the presence and ultimate triumph of life, in his own and every Christian existence, despite the experience of death.

$^¶$[4:7] **This treasure**: the glory that he preaches and into which they are being transformed. **In earthen vessels**: the instruments God uses are human and fragile; some imagine small terracotta lamps in which light is carried.

$^{**}$[4:8–9] A catalogue of his apostolic trials and afflictions. Yet in these the negative never completely prevails; there is always some experience of rescue, of salvation.

$^{††}$[4:10–11] Both the negative and the positive sides of the experience are grounded christologically. The logic is similar to that of 2 Cor 1:3–11. His sufferings are connected with Christ's, and his deliverance is a sign that he is to share in Jesus' resurrection.

$^{‡‡}$[4:12–15] His experience does not terminate in himself, but in others (2 Cor 4:12, 15; cf. 2 Cor 1:4–5). Ultimately, everything is ordered even beyond the community, toward God (2 Cor 4:15; cf. 2 Cor 1:11).

$^{§§}$[4:13–14] Like the psalmist, Paul clearly proclaims his faith, affirming life within himself despite death (2 Cor 4:10–11) and the life-giving effect of his experience upon the church (2 Cor 4:12, 14–15). **And place us with you in his presence**: Paul imagines God presenting him and them to Jesus at the parousia and the judgment; cf. 2 Cor 11:2; Rom 14:10.

$^{¶¶}$[4:16–18] In a series of contrasts Paul explains the extent of his faith in life. Life is not only already present and revealing itself (2 Cor 4:8–11, 16) but will outlast his experience of affliction and dying: it is eternal (2 Cor 4:17–18).

$^{***}$[4:16] **Not discouraged**: i.e., despite the experience of death. Paul is still speaking of himself personally, but he assumes his faith and attitude will be shared by all Christians. **Our outer self**: the individual subject of ordinary perception and observation, in contrast to the interior and hidden self, which undergoes renewal. **Is being renewed day by day**: this suggests a process that has already begun; cf. 2 Cor 3:18. The renewal already taking place even in Paul's dying is a share in the life of Jesus, but this is recognized only by faith (2 Cor 4:13, 18; 2 Cor 5:7).

$^{†††}$[5:1] **Our earthly dwelling**: the same contrast is restated in the imagery of a dwelling. The language recalls Jesus' saying about the destruction of the temple and the construction of another building **not made with hands** (Mk 14:58), a prediction later applied to Jesus' own body (Jn 2:20).

$^{‡‡‡}$[5:2–5] 2 Cor 5:2–3 and 4 are largely parallel in structure. **We groan, longing**: see note on 2 Cor 5:5. **Clothed with our heavenly habitation**: Paul mixes his metaphors, adding the image of the garment to that of the building. **Further clothed**: the verb means strictly "to put one garment on over another." Paul may desire to put the resurrection body on over his mortal body, without dying; 2 Cor 5:2, 4 permit this meaning but do not impose it. Or perhaps he imagines the resurrection body as a garment put on over the Christ-garment first received in baptism (Gal 3:27) and preserved by moral behavior (Rom 13:12–14; Col 3:12; cf. Mt 22:11–13). Some support for this interpretation may be found in the context; cf. the

---

e. [4:2] 2:17; 1 Thes 2:4–7.   f. [4:3] 2:15–16; 2 Thes 2:10.   g. [4:4] Jn 12;31–36 / 1 Tm 1:11.   h. [4:6] Gn 1:3; Is 9:1; Acts 26:13–23; Gal 1:15–16 / Jn 8:12; Heb 1:3.   i. [4:8] 6:4–10; 1 Cor 4:9–13.   j. [4:10] Col 1:24.

k. [4:11] Rom 8:36; 1 Cor 15:31.   l. [4:13] Ps 116:10.   m. [4:14] Rom 4:24–25; 8:11; 1 Cor 6:14; 1 Thes 4:14.   n. [4:15] 1:11.   o. [4:16] 4:1. p. [4:17] Mt 5:11–12; Rom 8:18.   q. [4:18] Rom 8:24–25; Heb 11:1.   r. [5:1] Is 38:12 / Col 3:1–4 / Mk 14:58; Col 2:11; Heb 9:11, 24.

this tent we groan, longing to be further clothed with our heavenly habitation[s] [3]if indeed, when we have taken it off,[*] we shall not be found naked. [4]For while we are in this tent we groan and are weighed down, because we do not wish to be unclothed[†] but to be further clothed, so that what is mortal may be swallowed up by life.[t] [5]Now the one who has prepared us for this very thing is God,[u] who has given us the Spirit as a first installment.[‡]

[6]So we are always courageous, although we know that while we are at home in the body we are away from the Lord, [7]for we walk by faith, not by sight. [8]Yet we are courageous, and we would rather leave the body and go home to the Lord.[v] [9]Therefore, we aspire to please him, whether we are at home or away. [10]For we must all appear[¶] before the judgment seat of Christ, so that each one may receive recompense, according to what he did in the body, whether good or evil.[w]

**The Ministry of Reconciliation.** [11]***Therefore, since we know the fear of the Lord, we try to

persuade others; but we are clearly apparent to God, and I hope we are also apparent to your consciousness.[x] [12]We are not commending ourselves to you again but giving you an opportunity to boast of us, so that you may have something to say to those who boast of external appearance rather than of the heart.[y] [13]For if we are out of our minds,[††] it is for God; if we are rational, it is for you. [14‡‡]For the love of Christ impels us, once we have come to the conviction that one died for all; therefore, all have died.[z] [15]He indeed died for all, so that those who live might no longer live for themselves but for him who for their sake died and was raised.[a]

[16]Consequently,[§§] from now on we regard no one according to the flesh; even if we once knew Christ according to the flesh, yet now we know him so no longer. [17b]So whoever is in Christ is a new creation: the old things have passed away; behold, new things have come. [18¶¶]And all this is from God, who has reconciled us to himself through Christ and given us the ministry of reconciliation, [19]namely, God was reconciling the world to himself in Christ, not counting their trespasses against them and entrusting to us the message of reconciliation.[c] [20]So we are ambassadors for Christ, as if God were appealing through us. We implore you on behalf of Christ, be reconciled to God.[d] [21]***For our sake he made

references to baptism (2 Cor 5:5), to judgment according to works (2 Cor 5:10), and to present renewal (2 Cor 4:16), an idea elsewhere combined with the image of "putting on" a new nature (Eph 4:22–24; Col 3:1–5, 9–10).

*[5:3] **When we have taken it off**: the majority of witnesses read "when we have put it on," i.e., when we have been clothed (in the resurrection body), then we shall not be without a body (naked). This seems tautology, though some understand it to mean: whether we are "found" (by God at the judgment) clothed or naked depends upon whether we have preserved or lost our original investiture in Christ (cf. the previous note). In this case to "put it on" does not refer to the resurrection body, but to keeping intact the Christ-garment of baptism. The translation follows the western reading (Codex Bezae, Tertullian), the sense of which is clear: to "take it off" is to shed our mortal body in death, after which we shall be clothed in the resurrection body and hence not "naked" (cf. 1 Cor 15:51–53).

†[5:4] **We do not wish to be unclothed**: a clear allusion to physical death (2 Cor 4:16; 5:1). Unlike the Greeks, who found dissolution of the body desirable (cf. Socrates), Paul has a Jewish horror of it. He seems to be thinking of the "intermediate period," an interval between death and resurrection. **Swallowed up by life**: cf. 1 Cor 15:54.

‡[5:5] God has created us for resurrected bodily life and already prepares us for it by the gift of the Spirit in baptism. **The Spirit as a first installment**: the striking parallel to 2 Cor 5:1–5 in Rom 8:17–30 describes Christians who have received the "firstfruits" (cf. "first installment" here) of the Spirit as "groaning" (cf. 2 Cor 5:2, 4 here) for the resurrection, the complete redemption of their bodies. In place of clothing and building, Rom 8 uses other images for the resurrection: adoption and conformity to the image of the Son.

§[5:6–9] Tension between present and future is expressed by another spatial image, the metaphor of the country and its citizens. At present we are like citizens in exile or far away from home. The Lord is the distant homeland, believed in but unseen (2 Cor 5:7).

¶[5:10] **We must all appear**: the verb is ambiguous: we are scheduled to "appear" for judgment, at which we will be "revealed" as we are (cf. 2 Cor 11; 2:14; 4:10–11).

**[5:11–15] This paragraph is transitional. Paul sums up much that has gone before. Still playing on the term "appearance," he reasserts his transparency before God and the Corinthians, in contrast to the self-commendation, boasting, and preoccupation with externals that characterize some others (cf. 2 Cor 1:12–14; 2:14; 3:1; 3:7–4:6). 2 Cor 5:14 recalls 2 Cor 3:7–4:6, and sums up 2 Cor 4:7–5:10.

††[5:13] **Out of our minds**: this verse confirms that a concern for ecstasy and charismatic experience may lie behind the discussion about "glory" in 2 Cor 3:7–4:6. Paul also enjoys such experiences but, unlike others, does not make a public display of them or consider them ends in themselves. **Rational**: the Greek virtue *sōphrosynē*, to which Paul alludes, implies reasonableness, moderation, good judgment, self-control.

‡‡[5:14–15] These verses echo 2 Cor 4:14 and resume the treatment of "life despite death" from 2 Cor 4:7–5:10.

§§[5:16–17] **Consequently**: the death of Christ described in 2 Cor 5:14–15 produces a whole new order (2 Cor 5:17) and a new mode of perception (2 Cor 5:16). **According to the flesh**: the natural mode of perception, characterized as "fleshly," is replaced by a mode of perception proper to the Spirit. Elsewhere Paul contrasts what Christ looks like according to the old criteria (weakness, powerlessness, death) and according to the new (wisdom, power, life); cf. 2 Cor 5:15, 21; 1 Cor 1:17–3:3. Similarly, he describes the paradoxical nature of Christian existence, e.g., in 2 Cor 4:10–11, 14. **A new creation**: rabbis used this expression to describe the effect of the entrance of a proselyte or convert into Judaism or of the remission of sins on the Day of Atonement. The new order created in Christ is the new covenant (2 Cor 3:6).

¶¶[5:18–21] Paul attempts to explain the meaning of God's action by a variety of different categories; his attention keeps moving rapidly back and forth from God's act to his own ministry as well. **Who has reconciled us to himself**: i.e., he has brought all into oneness. **Not counting their trespasses**: the reconciliation is described as an act of justification (cf. "righteousness," 2 Cor 5:21); this contrasts with the covenant that condemned (2 Cor 3:8). **The ministry of reconciliation**: Paul's role in the wider picture is described: entrusted with the message of reconciliation (2 Cor 5:19), he is Christ's ambassador, through whom God appeals (2 Cor 5:20a). In v 20b Paul acts in the capacity just described.

***[5:21] This is a statement of God's purpose, expressed paradoxically in terms of sharing and exchange of attributes.

s. [5:2] Rom 8:23 / 1 Cor 15:51–54.　t. [5:4] Is 25:8; 1 Cor 15:54.
u. [5:5] 1:22.　v. [5:8] Phil 1:21–23.　w. [5:10] Mt 16:27; 25:31–46;
Rom 2:16; 14:10–11.

x. [5:11] 1:12–14.　y. [5:12] 3:1 / 2 Cor 1:14; Phil 1:26.　z. [5:14]
Rom 6:1–6.　a. [5:15] Rom 4:25; 6:4–11; 14:9; Col 3:3–4.　b. [5:17]
Gal 6:15; Eph 2:15 / Is 43:18–21; Rev 21:5.　c. [5:19] Rom 5:10–11;
Col 1:20.　d. [5:20] Eph 6:20; Phlm 9.

him to be sin who did not know sin,[e] so that we might become the righteousness of God in him.

## CHAPTER 6

**The Experience of the Ministry.** [*]Working together,[f] then, we appeal to you not to receive the grace of God in vain.[†] [2]For he says:

"In an acceptable time[‡] I heard you,
    and on the day of salvation I helped you."[g]

Behold, now is a very acceptable time; behold, now is the day of salvation. [3h]We cause no one to stumble[§] in anything, in order that no fault may be found with our ministry; [4i]on the contrary, in everything we commend ourselves as ministers of God, through much endurance,[**] in afflictions, hardships, constraints,[i] [5]beatings, imprisonments, riots, labors, vigils, fasts;[j] [6††]by purity, knowledge, patience, kindness, in a holy spirit, in unfeigned love,[k] [7]in truthful speech, in the power of God; with weapons of righteousness at the right and at the left;[l] [8]through glory and dishonor, insult and praise. We are treated as deceivers and yet are truthful;[‡‡] [9]as unrec-

ognized and yet acknowledged; as dying and behold we live; as chastised and yet not put to death;[m] [10]as sorrowful yet always rejoicing; as poor yet enriching many; as having nothing and yet possessing all things.[n]

[11§§]We have spoken frankly to you, Corinthians; our heart is open wide. [12]You are not constrained by us; you are constrained by your own affections.[o] [13]As recompense in kind (I speak as to my children), be open yourselves.[p]

**Call to Holiness.** [14¶¶]Do not be yoked with those who are different, with unbelievers.[***] For what partnership do righteousness and lawlessness have? Or what fellowship does light have with darkness? [15]What accord has Christ with Beliar? Or what has a believer in common with an unbeliever? [16q]What agreement has the temple of God with idols? For we are the temple of the living God; as God said:

"I will live with them and move among them,[†††]
    and I will be their God
    and they shall be my people.
[17] Therefore, come forth from them
    and be separate," says the Lord,
"and touch nothing unclean;
    then I will receive you[r]
[18] and I will be a father to you,

---

As Christ became our righteousness (1 Cor 1:30), we become God's righteousness (cf. 2 Cor 5:14–15).

*[6:1–10] This paragraph is a single long sentence in the Greek, interrupted by the parenthesis of 2 Cor 5:2. The one main verb is "we appeal." In this paragraph Paul both exercises his ministry of reconciliation (cf. 2 Cor 5:20) and describes how his ministry is exercised: the "message of reconciliation" (2 Cor 5:19) is lived existentially in his apostolic experience.

†[6:1] **Not to receive . . . in vain:** i.e., conform to the gift of justification and new creation. The context indicates how this can be done concretely: become God's righteousness (2 Cor 5:21), not live for oneself (2 Cor 5:15) or be reconciled with Paul (2 Cor 6:11–13; 7:2–3).

‡[6:2] **In an acceptable time:** Paul cites the Septuagint text of Is 49:8; the Hebrew reads "in a time of favor"; it is parallel to "on the day of salvation." **Now:** God is bestowing favor and salvation at this very moment, as Paul is addressing his letter to them.

§[6:3] **Cause no one to stumble:** the language echoes that of 1 Cor 8–10 as does the expression "no longer live for themselves" in 2 Cor 5:15. **That no fault may be found:** i.e., at the eschatological judgment (cf. 1 Cor 4:2–5).

¶[6:4a] This is the central assertion, the topic statement for the catalogue that follows. **We commend ourselves:** Paul's self-commendation is ironical (with an eye on the charges mentioned in 2 Cor 3:1–3) and paradoxical (pointing mostly to experiences that would not normally be considered points of pride but are perceived as such by faith). Cf. also the self-commendation in 2 Cor 11:23–29. **As ministers of God:** the same Greek word, *diakonos*, means "minister" and "servant"; cf. 2 Cor 11:23, the central assertion in a similar context, and 1 Cor 3:5.

**[6:4b–5] **Through much endurance:** this phrase functions as a subtitle; it is followed by an enumeration of nine specific types of trials endured.

††[6:6–7a] A list of virtuous qualities in two groups of four, the second fuller than the first.

‡‡[6:8b–10] A series of seven rhetorically effective antitheses, contrasting negative external impressions with positive inner reality. Paul perceives his existence as a reflection of

Jesus' own and affirms an inner reversal that escapes outward observation. The final two members illustrate two distinct kinds of paradox or apparent contradiction that are characteristic of apostolic experience.

§§[6:11–13] Paul's tone becomes quieter, but his appeal for acceptance and affection is emotionally charged. References to the heart and their mutual relations bring the development begun in 2 Cor 2:14–3:3 to an effective conclusion.

¶¶[6:14–7:1] Language and thought shift noticeably here. Suddenly we are in a different atmosphere, dealing with a quite different problem. Both the vocabulary and the thought, with their contrast between good and evil, are more characteristic of Qumran documents or the Book of Revelation than they are of Paul. Hence, critics suspect that this section was inserted by another hand.

***[6:14–16a] The opening injunction to separate from unbelievers is reinforced by five rhetorical questions to make the point that Christianity is not compatible with paganism. Their opposition is emphasized also by the accumulation of five distinct designations for each group. These verses are a powerful statement of God's holiness and the exclusiveness of his claims.

†††[6:16c–18] This is a chain of scriptural citations carefully woven together. God's covenant relation to his people and his presence among them (2 Cor 6:16) is seen as conditioned on cultic separation from the profane and cultically impure (2 Cor 6:17); that relation is translated into the personal language of the parent-child relationship, an extension to the community of the language of 2 Sm 7:14 (2 Cor 6:18). Some remarkable parallels to this chain are found in the final chapters of Revelation. God's presence among his people (Rev 21:22) is expressed there, too, by applying 2 Sm 7:14 to the community (Rev 21:7). There is a call to separation (Rev 18:4) and exclusion of the unclean from the community and its liturgy (Rev 21:27). The title "Lord Almighty" (*Pantokratōr*) occurs in the New Testament only here in 2 Cor 6:18 and nine times in Revelation.

---

e. [5:21] Is 53:6–9; Gal 3:13 / Rom 3:24–26; 1 Cor 1:30; 1 Pt 2:24; 1 Jn 3:5–8.   f. [6:1] 1 Cor 3:9; 1 Thes 3:2.   g. [6:2] Is 49:8.   h. [6:3] 1 Cor 9:12; 10:32 / 2 Cor 8:20–21.   i. [6:4] 4:8–11; 11:23–27; 1 Cor 4:9–13. j. [6:5] Acts 16:23.   k. [6:6] Gal 5:22–23.   l. [6:7] 10:4; Rom 13:12; Eph 6:11–17.

m. [6:9] 4:10–11; Rom 8:36.   n. [6:10] Rom 8:32; 1 Cor 3:21. o. [6:12] 7:3.   p. [6:13] Gal 4:19.   q. [6:16] 1 Cor 10:20–21 / 1 Cor 3:16–17; 6:19 / Ex 25:8; 29:45; Lv 26:12; Jer 31:1; 32:38; Ez 37:27.   r. [6:17] Is 52:11; Ez 20:34, 41; Rev 18:4; 21:27.

and you shall be sons and daughters
to me,
says the Lord Almighty."ˢ

## CHAPTER 7

¹Since we have these promises, beloved, let us cleanse ourselves from every defilement of flesh and spirit, making holiness perfect in the fear of God.

²*Make room for us; we have not wronged anyone, or ruined anyone, or taken advantage of anyone. ³I do not say this in condemnation, for I have already said that you are in our hearts, that we may die together and live together.ᵗ ⁴I have great confidence in you, I have great pride in you; I am filled with encouragement, I am overflowing with joy all the more because of all our affliction.

### C. Resolution of the Crisis†

**Paul's Joy in Macedonia.** ⁵‡For even when we came into Macedonia,§ our flesh had no rest, but we were afflicted in every way—external conflicts, internal fears.ᵘ ⁶But God, who encourages the downcast, encouraged us by the arrival of Titus,ᵛ ⁷and not only by his arrival but also by the encouragement with which he was encouraged in regard to you, as he told us of your yearning, your lament, your zeal for me, so that I rejoiced even more. ⁸For even if I saddened you by my letter, I do not regret it; and if I did regret it ([for] I see that that letter saddened you, if only for a while),ʷ ⁹I rejoice now, not because you were saddened, but because you were saddened into repentance; for you were saddened

in a godly way, so that you did not suffer loss in anything because of us. ¹⁰For godly sorrow produces a salutary repentance without regret, but worldly sorrow produces death. ¹¹For behold what earnestness this godly sorrow has produced for you, as well as readiness for a defense, and indignation, and fear, and yearning, and zeal, and punishment. In every way you have shown yourselves to be innocent in the matter. ¹²So then even though I wrote to you, it was not on account of the one who did the wrong, or on account of the one who suffered the wrong, but in order that your concern for us might be made plain to you in the sight of God.ˣ ¹³For this reason we are encouraged.

And besides our encouragement,** we rejoice even more because of the joy of Titus, since his spirit has been refreshed by all of you. ¹⁴For if I have boasted to him about you, I was not put to shame. No, just as everything we said to you was true, so our boasting before Titus proved to be the truth. ¹⁵And his heart goes out to you all the more, as he remembers the obedience of all of you, when you received him with fear and trembling.ʸ ¹⁶I rejoice, because I have confidence in you in every respect.

## III. THE COLLECTION FOR JERUSALEM††

## CHAPTER 8

**Generosity in Giving.** ¹‡‡We want you to know, brothers,§§ of the grace of God¶¶ that has been

---

*[7:2–4] These verses continue the thought of 2 Cor 6:11–13, before the interruption of 2 Cor 6:14–7:1. 2 Cor 7:4 serves as a transition to the next section: the four themes it introduces (confidence; pride or "boasting"; encouragement; joy in affliction) are developed in 2 Cor 7:5–16. All have appeared previously in the letter.

†[7:5–16] This section functions as a peroration or formal summing up of the whole first part of the letter, 2 Cor 1–7. It deals with the restoration of right relations between Paul and the Corinthians, and it is marked by fullness and intensity of emotion.

‡[7:5–7] Paul picks up the thread of the narrative interrupted at 2 Cor 2:13 (2 Cor 7:5) and describes the resolution of the tense situation there depicted (2 Cor 7:6–7). Finally Titus arrives and his coming puts an end to Paul's restlessness (2 Cor 2:13; 2 Cor 7:5), casts out his fears, and reverses his mood. The theme of encouragement and affliction is reintroduced (cf. 2 Cor 1:3–11); here, too, encouragement is traced back to God and is described as contagious (2 Cor 7:6). The language of joy and sorrow also reappears in 2 Cor 7:7 (cf. 2 Cor 1:23–2:1 and the note on 2 Cor 1:23–24).

§[7:5] **Macedonia:** see note on 2 Cor 2:13.

¶[7:8–12] Paul looks back on the episode from the viewpoint of its ending. The goal of their common activity, promotion of their joy (2 Cor 1:24), has been achieved, despite and because of the sorrow they felt. That sorrow was God-given. Its salutary effects are enumerated fully and impressively in 2 Cor 7:10–11; not the least important of these is that it has revealed to them the attachment they have to Paul.

**[7:13–16] Paul summarizes the effect of the experience on Titus: encouragement, joy, love, relief. Finally, he describes its effects on himself: encouragement, joy, confidence, pride or "boasting" (i.e., the satisfaction resulting from a boast that proves well-founded; cf. 2 Cor 7:4; 1:12, 14).

††[8:1–9:15] Paul turns to a new topic, the collection for the church in Jerusalem. There is an early precedent for this project in the agreement mentioned in Gal 2:6–10. According to Acts, the church at Antioch had sent Saul and Barnabas to Jerusalem with relief (Acts 11:27–30). Subsequently Paul organized a project of relief for Jerusalem among his own churches. Our earliest evidence for it comes in 1 Cor 16:1–4—after it had already begun (see notes there); by the time Paul wrote Rom 15:25–28 the collection was completed and ready for delivery. 2 Cor 8–9 contain what appear to be two letters on the subject. In them Paul gives us his fullest exposition of the meaning he sees in the enterprise, presenting it as an act of Christian charity and as an expression of the unity of the church, both present and eschatological. These chapters are especially rich in the recurrence of key words, on which Paul plays; it is usually impossible to do justice to these wordplays in the translation.

‡‡[8:1–24] This is a letter of recommendation for Titus and two unnamed companions, written from Macedonia probably at least a year later than 1 Cor 16. The recommendation proper is prefaced by remarks about the ideals of sharing and equality within the Christian community (2 Cor 8:1–15). Phil 4:10–20 shows that Paul has reflected on his personal experience of need and relief in his relations with the community at Philippi; he now develops his reflections on the larger scale of relations between his Gentile churches and the mother church in Jerusalem.

§§[8:1–5] The example of the Macedonians, a model of what ought to be happening at Corinth, provides Paul with the occasion for expounding his theology of "giving."

¶¶[8:1] **The grace of God:** the fundamental theme is expressed by the Greek noun *charis,* which will be variously

---

s. [6:18] 2 Sm 7:14; Ps 2:7; Is 43:6; Jer 31:9; Rev 21:7 / Rev 4:8; 11:17; 15:3;21:22.   t. [7:3]6:11–13.   u. [7:5]2:13.   v. [7:6]7:13–14;1 Thes 3:6–8.   w. [7:8] 2:2–4; Heb 12:11.

x. [7:12] 2:3, 9; 7:8.   y. [7:15] 2:9.

given to the churches of Macedonia;[z] [2]for in a severe test of affliction, the abundance of their joy and their profound poverty overflowed in a wealth of generosity on their part. [3†]For according to their means, I can testify, and beyond their means, spontaneously, [4]they begged us insistently for the favor of taking part in the service to the holy ones,[a] [5]and this, not as we expected, but they gave themselves first to the Lord and to us[‡] through the will of God, [6]so that we urged Titus[§] that, as he had already begun, he should also complete for you this gracious act also.[b] [7†]Now as you excel in every respect, in faith, discourse, knowledge, all earnestness, and in the love we have for you,[c] may you excel in this gracious act also.

[8]I say this not by way of command, but to test the genuineness of your love by your concern for others. [9]*[d]For you know the gracious act of our Lord Jesus Christ, that for your sake he became poor although he was rich, so that by his poverty you might become rich. [10]And I am giving counsel in this matter, for it is appropriate for you who began not only to act but to act willingly last year:[e] [11]complete it now, so that your eager[††] willingness may be matched by your completion of it out of what you have. [12‡‡]For if the eagerness is there, it is acceptable according to what one has, not according to what one does not have; [13]not that others should have relief while you are burdened, but that as a matter of equality [14]your surplus at the present time should supply their needs, so that their surplus may also supply your needs, that there may be equality. [15]As it is written:

> "Whoever had much did not have more,
> and whoever had little did not have
> less."[f]

## Titus and His Collaborators.[§§] [16]But thanks be to God who put the same concern for you into the heart of Titus, [17]for he not only welcomed our appeal but, since he is very concerned, he has gone to you of his own accord. [18]With him we have sent the brother[¶¶] who is praised in all the churches for his preaching of the gospel.[g] [19]And not only that, but he has also been appointed our traveling companion by the churches in this gracious work administered by us for the glory of the Lord [himself] and for the expression of our eagerness.[h] [20]This we desire to avoid, that anyone blame us[***] about this lavish gift administered by us, [21]for we are concerned for what is honorable not only in the sight of the Lord but also in the sight of others.[i] [22]And with them we have sent our brother whom we often tested in many ways and found earnest, but who is now much more earnest because of his great confidence in you. [23]As for Titus, he is my partner and co-worker for you; as for our brothers, they are apostles of the churches, the glory of Christ.

---

translated throughout these chapters as "grace" (2 Cor 8:1; 9:8, 14), "favor" (2 Cor 8:4), "gracious act" (2 Cor 8:6, 7, 9) or "gracious work" (2 Cor 8:19), to be compared to "gracious gift" (1 Cor 16:3). The related term, *eucharistia*, "thanksgiving," also occurs in 2 Cor 9:11, 12. The wordplay is not superficial; various mutations of the same root signal inner connection between aspects of a single reality, and Paul consciously exploits the similarities in vocabulary to highlight that connection.

*[8:2] Three more terms are now introduced. **Test** (*dokimē*): the same root is translated as "to test" (2 Cor 8:8) and "evidence" (2 Cor 9:13); it means to be tried and found genuine. **Abundance**: variations on the same root lie behind "overflow" (2 Cor 8:2; 9:12), "excel" (2 Cor 8:7), "surplus" (2 Cor 8:14), "superfluous" (2 Cor 9:1) "make abundant" and "have an abundance" (2 Cor 9:8). These expressions of fullness contrast with references to need (2 Cor 8:14; 9:12). **Generosity**: the word *haplotēs* has nuances of both simplicity and sincerity; here and in 2 Cor 9:11, 13 it designates the singleness of purpose that manifests itself in generous giving.

†[8:3–4] Paul emphasizes the spontaneity of the Macedonians and the nature of their action. **They begged us insistently**: the same root is translated as "urge," "appeal," "encourage" (2 Cor 8:6, 17; 9:5). **Taking part**: the same word is translated "contribution" in 2 Cor 9:13 and a related term as "partner" in 2 Cor 8:23. **Service** (*diakonia*): this word occurs also in 2 Cor 9:1, 13 as "service"; in 2 Cor 9:12 it is translated "administration," and in 2 Cor 8:19, 20 the corresponding verb is rendered "administer."

‡[8:5] **They gave themselves . . . to the Lord and to us**: on its deepest level their attitude is one of self-giving.

§[8:6] **Titus**: 1 Cor 16 seemed to leave the organization up to the Corinthians, but apparently Paul has sent Titus to initiate the collection as well; 2 Cor 8:16–17 will describe Titus' attitude as one of shared concern and cooperation.

¶[8:7] The charitable service Paul is promoting is seen briefly and in passing within the perspective of Paul's theology of the charisms. **Earnestness** (*spoudē*): this or related terms occur also in 2 Cor 8:22 ("earnest") and 2 Cor 8:8, 16, 17 ("concern").

**[8:9] The dialectic of Jesus' experience, expressed earlier in terms of life and death (2 Cor 5:15), sin and righteousness (2 Cor 5:21), is now rephrased in terms of poverty and wealth. Many scholars think this is a reference to Jesus' preexistence with God (his "wealth") and to his incarnation and death (his "poverty"), and they point to the similarity between this verse and Phil 2:6–8. Others interpret the wealth and poverty as succeeding phases of Jesus' earthly existence, e.g., his sense of intimacy with God and then the desolation and the feeling of abandonment by God in his death (cf. Mk 15:34).

††[8:11] **Eager**: the word *prothymia* also occurs in 2 Cor 8:12, 19; 9:2.

‡‡[8:12–15] Paul introduces the principle of **equality** into the discussion. The goal is not impoverishment but sharing of resources; balance is achieved at least over the course of time. In 2 Cor 8:15 Paul grounds his argument unexpectedly in the experience of Israel gathering manna in the desert: equality was achieved, independently of personal exertion, by God, who gave with an even hand according to need. Paul touches briefly here on the theme of "living from God."

§§[8:16–24] In recommending Titus and his companions, Paul stresses their personal and apostolic qualities, their good dispositions toward the Corinthians, and their authority as messengers of the churches and representatives of Christ.

¶¶[8:18] **The brother**: we do not know the identity of this co-worker of Paul, nor of the third companion mentioned below in 2 Cor 8:22.

***[8:20–22] **That anyone blame us**: 2 Cor 12:16–18 suggests that misunderstandings may indeed have arisen concerning Paul's management of the collection through the messengers mentioned here, but those same verses seem to imply that the Corinthians by and large would recognize the honesty of Paul's conduct in this area as in others (cf. 2 Cor 6:3).

---

z. [8:1] 11:9; Rom 15:26.  a. [8:4] Acts 24:17; Rom 15:31.  b. [8:6] 2:13; 7:6–7, 13–14; 8:16, 23; 12:18.  c. [8:7] 1 Cor 1:5.  d. [8:9] 6:10; Phil 2:6–8.

e. [8:10] 9:2; 1 Cor 16:1–4.  f. [8:15] Ex 16:18.  g. [8:18] 12:18.  h. [8:19] 1 Cor 16:3–4.  i. [8:21] Rom 12:17.

²⁴So give proof before the churches of your love and of our boasting about you to them.*

## CHAPTER 9

**God's Indescribable Gift.**† ¹Now about the service to the holy ones, it is superfluous for me to write to you, ²for I know your eagerness, about which I boast of you to the Macedonians, that Achaia‡ has been ready since last year; and your zeal has stirred up most of them.ʲ ³Nonetheless, I sent the brothers⁵ so that our boast about you might not prove empty in this case, so that you might be ready, as I said, ⁴for fear that if any Macedonians come with me and find you not ready we might be put to shame (to say nothing of you) in this conviction. ⁵So I thought it necessary to encourage the brothers to go on ahead to you and arrange in advance for your promised gift, so that in this way it might be ready as a bountiful gift and not as an exaction.

⁶Consider this: whoever sows sparingly will also reap sparingly, and whoever sows bountifully will also reap bountifully.ᵏ ⁷Each must do as already determined, without sadness or compulsion, for God loves a cheerful giver.ˡ ⁸Moreover, God is able to make every grace abundant for you, so that in all things, always having all you need, you may have an abundance for every good work. ⁹As it is written:

"He scatters abroad, he gives to the poor;
    his righteousness endures forever."ᵐ

¹⁰The one who supplies seed to the sower and bread for food will supply and multiply your seed and increase the harvest of your righteousness.ⁿ

¹¹""You are being enriched in every way for all generosity, which through us produces thanksgiving to God, ¹²for the administration of this public service is not only supplying the needs of the holy ones but is also overflowing in many acts of thanksgiving to God. ¹³Through the evidence of this service, you are glorifying God for your obedient confession of the gospel of Christ and the generosity of your contribution to them and to all others,ᵒ ¹⁴while in prayer on your behalf they long for you, because of the surpassing grace of God upon you. ¹⁵Thanks be to God for his indescribable gift!ᵖ

## IV. PAUL'S DEFENSE OF HIS MINISTRY††

## CHAPTER 10

**Accusation of Weakness.**‡‡ ¹Now I myself, Paul, urge you through the gentleness and clemency of Christ,§§ I who am humble when face to face with you, but brave toward you when absent, ²⁵⁵¶I

---

liturgically colored and conveys a sense of fullness. With a final play on the words *charis* and *eucharistia* (see note on 2 Cor 8:1), he describes a circle that closes on itself: the movement of grace overflowing from God to them and handed on from them through Paul to others is completed by the prayer of praise and thanksgiving raised on their behalf to God.

††[10:1–13:10] These final chapters have their own unity of structure and theme and could well have formed the body of a separate letter. They constitute an *apologia* on Paul's part, i.e., a legal defense of his behavior and his ministry; the writing is emotionally charged and highly rhetorical. In the central section (2 Cor 11:16–12:10), the *apologia* takes the form of a boast. This section is prepared for by a prologue (2 Cor 11:1–15) and followed by an epilogue (2 Cor 12:11–18), which are similar in content and structure. These sections, in turn, are framed by an introduction (2 Cor 10:1–18) and a conclusion (2 Cor 12:19–13:10), both of which assert Paul's apostolic authority and confidence and define the purpose of the letter. The structure that results from this disposition of the material is chiastic, i.e., the first element corresponds to the last, the second to the second last, etc., following the pattern a b c b¹, a¹.

‡‡[10:1–18] Paul asserts his apostolic authority and expresses the confidence this generates in him. He writes in response to certain opinions that have arisen in the community and certain charges raised against him and in preparation for a forthcoming visit in which he intends to set things in order. This section gives us an initial glimpse of the situation in Corinth that Paul must address; much of its thematic material will be taken up again in the finale (2 Cor 12:19–13:10).

§§[10:1–2] A strong opening plunges us straight into the conflict. Contrasts dominate here: presence versus absence, gentleness-clemency-humility versus boldness-confidence-bravery. **Through the gentleness and clemency of Christ**: the figure of the gentle Christ, presented in a significant position before any specifics of the situation are suggested, forms a striking contrast to the picture of the bold and militant Paul (2 Cor 10:2–6); this tension is finally resolved in 2 Cor 13:3–4. **Absent . . . present**: this same contrast, with a restatement of the purpose of the letter, recurs in 2 Cor 13:10, which forms an inclusion with 2 Cor 10:1–2.

¶¶[10:2b–4a] **Flesh**: the Greek word *sarx* can express both the physical life of the body without any pejorative overtones (as in "we are in the flesh," 3) and our natural life insofar as it is marked by limitation and weakness (as in the other expressions) in contrast to the higher life and power conferred by the Spirit; cf. note on 1 Cor 3:1. The wordplay is intended to express the paradoxical situation of a life already taken over by the Spirit but not yet seen as such except by faith. Lack of empirical evidence of the Spirit permits misunderstanding and misjudgment, but Paul resolutely denies that his behavior and effectiveness are as limited as some suppose.

---

*[8:24] As Paul began by holding up the Macedonians as examples to be imitated, he closes by exhorting the Corinthians to show their love (by accepting the envoys and by cooperating as the Macedonians do), thus justifying the pride Paul demonstrates because of them before other churches.

†[9:1–15] Quite possibly this was originally an independent letter, though it deals with the same subject and continues many of the same themes. In that case, it may have been written a few weeks later than 2 Cor 8, while the delegation there mentioned was still on its way.

‡[9:2] **Achaia**: see note on Rom 15:26.

§[9:3] **I sent the brothers**: the Greek aorist tense here could be epistolary, referring to the present; in that case Paul would be sending them now, and 2 Cor 9 would merely conclude the letter of recommendation begun in 2 Cor 8. But the aorist may also refer to a sending that is past as Paul writes; then 2 Cor 9, with its apparently fresh beginning, is a follow-up message entrusted to another carrier.

¶[9:8–10] The behavior to which he exhorts them is grounded in God's own pattern of behavior. God is capable of overwhelming generosity, as scripture itself attests (2 Cor 9:9), so that they need not fear being short. He will provide in abundance, both supplying their natural needs and increasing their righteousness. Paul challenges them to godlike generosity and reminds them of the fundamental motive for encouragement: God himself cannot be outdone.

**[9:11–15] Paul's vision broadens to take in all the interested parties in one dynamic picture. His language becomes

---

j. [9:2] 8:10; Rom 15:26.  k. [9:6] Prv 11:24–25.  l. [9:7] Prv 22:8 LXX.  m. [9:9] Ps 112:9.  n. [9:10] Is 55:10.

o. [9:13] 8:4; Rom 15:31.  p. [9:15] Rom 5:15–16.  q. [10:2] 13:2, 10; 1 Cor 4:21.

beg you that, when present, I may not have to be brave with that confidence with which I intend to act boldly against some who consider us as acting according to the flesh. ³For, although we are in the flesh, we do not battle according to the flesh,* ⁴for the weapons of our battle are not of flesh but are enormously powerful, capable of destroying fortresses. We destroy arguments* ⁵and every pretension raising itself against the knowledge of God, and take every thought captive in obedience to Christ, ⁶and we are ready to punish every disobedience, once your obedience is complete.*

⁷Look at what confronts you. Whoever is confident of belonging to Christ should consider that as he belongs to Christ, so do we.† ⁸ᵘAnd even if I should boast a little too much of our authority, which the Lord gave for building you up and not for tearing you down, I shall not be put to shame. ⁹May I not seem as one frightening you through letters. ¹⁰For someone will say, "His letters are severe and forceful, but his bodily presence is weak, and his speech contemptible."ᵛ ¹¹Such a person must understand that what we are in word through letters when absent, that we also are in action when present.ʷ

¹²Not that we dare to class or compare ourselves with some of those who recommend themselves. But when they measure themselves by one another and compare themselves with one another, they are without understanding.ˣ ¹³But we will not boast beyond measure but will keep to the limits¶ God has apportioned us, namely, to reach even to you. ¹⁴For we are not overreaching ourselves, as though we did not reach you; we indeed first came to you with the gospel of Christ. ¹⁵We are not boasting beyond measure, in other people's labors; yet our hope is that, as your faith increases, our influence among you may be greatly enlarged, within our proper limits, ¹⁶so that we may preach the gospel even beyond you, not boasting of work already done in another's sphere.ʸ ¹⁷"Whoever boasts, should boast in the Lord."** ¹⁸For it is not the one who recommends himself who is approved,†† but the one whom the Lord recommends.ᵃ

## CHAPTER 11

**Preaching Without Charge.**‡‡ ¹If only you would put up with a little foolishness from me!§§ Please put up with me.ᵇ ²For I am jealous of you with the jealousy of God, since I betrothed you to one husband to present you as a chaste virgin to Christ.ᶜ ³But I am afraid that, as the serpent deceived Eve*** by his cunning, your thoughts may be corrupted from a sincere [and pure] commitment to Christ.ᵈ ⁴For if someone comes and preaches another Jesus††† than the one we preached,ᵉ or if you receive a different spirit

---

*[10:3b–6] Paul is involved in combat. The strong military language and imagery are both an assertion of his confidence in the divine power at his disposal and a declaration of war against those who underestimate his resources. The threat is echoed in 2 Cor 13:2–3.

†[10:7–8] **Belonging to Christ . . . so do we**: these phrases already announce the pattern of Paul's boast in 2 Cor 11:21b–29, especially 2 Cor 11:22–23. **For building you up and not for tearing you down**: Paul draws on the language by which Jeremiah described the purpose of the prophetic power the Lord gave to him (Jer 1:9–10; 12:16–17; 24:6). Though Paul's power may have destructive effects on others (2 Cor 10:2–6), its intended effect on the community is entirely constructive (cf. 2 Cor 13:10). **I shall not be put to shame**: his assertions will not be refuted; they will be revealed as true at the judgment.

‡[10:9–10] Paul cites the complaints of some who find him lacking in personal forcefulness and holds out the threat of a personal *parousia* (both "return" and "presence") that will be forceful, indeed will be a demonstration of Christ's own power (cf. 2 Cor 13:2–4).

§[10:12–18] Paul now qualifies his claim to boldness, indicating its limits. He distinguishes his own behavior from that of others, revealing those "others" as they appear to him: as self-recommending, immoderately boastful, encroaching on territory not assigned to them, and claiming credit not due to them.

¶[10:13] **Will keep to the limits**: the notion of proper limits is expressed here by two terms with overlapping meanings, *metron* and *kanōn*, which are played off against several expressions denoting overreaching or expansion beyond a legitimate sphere.

**[10:17] **Boast in the Lord**: there is a legitimate boasting, in contrast to the immoderate boasting to which 2 Cor 10:13, 15 allude. God's work through Paul in the community is the object of his boast (2 Cor 10:13–16; 2 Cor 1:12–14) and constitutes his recommendation (2 Cor 3:1–3). Cf. notes on 2 Cor 1:12–14 and 1 Cor 1:29–31.

††[10:18] **Approved**: to be approved is to come successfully through the process of testing for authenticity (cf. 2 Cor 13:3–7 and the note on 2 Cor 8:2). **Whom the Lord recommends**: self-commendation is a premature and unwarranted anticipation of the final judgment, which the Lord alone will pass (cf. 1 Cor 4:3–5). Paul alludes to this judgment throughout 2 Cor 10–13, frequently in final or transitional positions; cf. 2 Cor 11:15; 12:19a; 13:5–7.

‡‡[11:1–15] Although these verses continue to reveal information about Paul's opponents and the differences he perceives between them and himself, 2 Cor 11:1 signals a turn in Paul's thought. This section constitutes a prologue to the boasting that he will undertake in 2 Cor 11:16–12:10, and it bears remarkable similarities to the section that follows the central boast, 2 Cor 12:11–18.

§§[11:1] **Put up with a little foolishness from me**: this verse indicates more clearly than the general statement of intent in 2 Cor 10:13 the nature of the project Paul is about to undertake. He alludes ironically to the Corinthians' toleration for others. **Foolishness**: Paul qualifies his project as folly from beginning to end; see note on 2 Cor 11:16–12:10.

¶¶[11:2] Paul gives us a sudden glimpse of the theological values that are at stake. **The jealousy of God**: the perspective is that of the covenant, described in imagery of love and marriage, as in the prophets; cf. 1 Cor 10:22. **I betrothed you**: Paul, like a father (cf. 2 Cor 12:14), betroths the community to Christ as his bride (cf. Eph 5:21–33) and will present her to him at his second coming. Cf. Mt 25:1–13 and the nuptial imagery in Rev 21.

***[11:3] **As the serpent deceived Eve**: before Christ can return for the community Paul fears a repetition of the primal drama of seduction. Corruption of minds is satanic activity (see 2 Cor 2:11; 4:4). Satanic imagery recurs in 2 Cor 11:13–15, 20; 12:7b, 16–17; see notes on these passages.

†††[11:4] **Preaches another Jesus**: the danger is specified, and Paul's opponents are identified with the cunning serpent. The battle for minds has to do with the understanding of Jesus, the Spirit, the gospel; the Corinthians have flirted with another understanding than the one that Paul handed on to them as traditional and normative.

---

r. [10:4] 6:7; 13:2–3; 1 Cor 1:25; Eph 6:10–14.　s. [10:6] 2:9.
t. [10:7] 1 Cor 1:12.　u. [10:8] 13:10.　v. [10:10] 1 Cor 2:3.
w. [10:11] 13:1–2.　x. [10:12] 3:1–2; 4:2; 5:12; 6:4; 10:18; 12:11.

y. [10:16] Rom 15:20–21.　z. [10:17] Jer 9:22–23; 1 Cor 1:31.
a. [10:18] 13:3–9.　b. [11:1] 11:21; 12:11.　c. [11:2] Hos 2:21–22;
Eph 5:26–27.　d. [11:3] Gn 3:1–6.　e. [11:4] Gal 1:6–9.

from the one you received or a different gospel from the one you accepted, you put up with it well enough. 5ªFor I think that I am not in any way inferior to these "superapostles." 6Even if I am untrained in speaking, I am not so in knowledge;ᵍ in every way we have made this plain to you in all things.†

7ªDid I make a mistake when I humbled myself so that you might be exalted, because I preached the gospel of God to you without charge?ʰ 8I plundered other churches by accepting from them in order to minister to you. 9And when I was with you and in need, I did not burden anyone, for the brothers who came from Macedonia supplied my needs. So I refrained and will refrain from burdening you in any way.ⁱ 10By the truth of Christ in me, this boast of mine shall not be silenced in the regions of Achaia.ʲ 11ªAnd why? Because I do not love you? God knows I do!ᵏ

12And what I do I will continue to do, in order to end this pretext of those who seek a pretext for being regarded as we are in the mission of which they boast. 13ªFor such people are

false apostles, deceitful workers, who masquerade as apostles of Christ. 14And no wonder, for even Satan masquerades as an angel of light. 15So it is not strange that his ministers also masquerade as ministers of righteousness. Their end will correspond to their deeds.

**Paul's Boast: His Labors.** 16ªªI repeat, no one should consider me foolish;†† but if you do, accept me as a fool, so that I too may boast a little.‡‡ 17What I am saying I am not saying according to the Lord but as in foolishness, in this boastful state. 18Since many boast according to the flesh, I too will boast. 19For you gladly put up with fools, since you are wise yourselves. 20§§For you put up with it if someone enslaves you, or devours you, or gets the better of you, or puts on airs, or slaps you in the face. 21To my shame I say that we were too weak!¶¶

But what anyone dares to boast of (I am speaking in foolishness) I also dare. 22ªªªAre they Hebrews? So am I. Are they Israelites? So am I. Are they descendants of Abraham? So am I.ˡ 23†††Are they ministers of Christ? (I am talking like an insane person.)ᵐ I am still more,‡‡‡ with

*[11:5] **These "superapostles"**: this term, employed again in 2 Cor 12:11b, designates the opponents of whom Paul has spoken in 2 Cor 10 and again in 2 Cor 11:4. They appear to be intruders at Corinth. Their preaching is marked at least by a different emphasis and style, and they do not hesitate to accept support from the community. Perhaps these itinerants appeal to the authority of church leaders in Jerusalem and even carry letters of recommendation from them. But it is not those distant leaders whom Paul is attacking here. The intruders are "superapostles" not in the sense of the "pillars" at Jerusalem (Gal 2), but in their own estimation. They consider themselves superior to Paul as apostles and ministers of Christ, and they are obviously enjoying some success among the Corinthians. Paul rejects their claim to be apostles in any superlative sense (*hyperlian*), judging them bluntly as "false apostles," ministers of Satan masquerading as apostles of Christ (2 Cor 11:13–15). On the contrary, he himself will claim to be a superminister of Christ (*hyper egō*, 2 Cor 11:23).

†[11:6] Apparently found deficient in both rhetorical ability (cf. 2 Cor 10:10) and knowledge (cf. 2 Cor 10:5), Paul concedes the former charge but not the latter. **In every way**: in all their contacts with him revelation has been taking place. Paul, through whom God reveals the knowledge of himself (2 Cor 2:14), and in whom the death and life of Jesus are revealed (2 Cor 4:10–11; cf. 2 Cor 6:4), also demonstrates his own role as the bearer of true knowledge. Cf. 1 Cor 1:18–2:16.

‡[11:7–10] Abruptly Paul passes to another reason for complaints: his practice of preaching without remuneration (cf. 1 Cor 9:3–18). He deftly defends his practice by situating it from the start within the pattern of Christ's own self-humiliation (cf. 2 Cor 10:1) and reduces objections to absurdity by rhetorical questions (cf. 2 Cor 12:13).

§[11:11–12] Paul rejects lack of affection as his motive (possibly imputed to him by his opponents) and states his real motive, a desire to emphasize the disparity between himself and the others (cf. 2 Cor 11:19–21). The topic of his gratuitous service will be taken up once more in 2 Cor 12:13–18. 1 Cor 9:15–18 gives a different but complementary explanation of his motivation.

¶[11:13–15] Paul picks up again the imagery of 2 Cor 11:3 and applies it to the opponents: they are false apostles of Christ, really serving another master. **Deceitful . . . masquerade**: deception and simulation, like cunning (2 Cor 11:3), are marks of the satanic. **Angel of light**: recalls the contrast between light and darkness, Christ and Beliar at 2 Cor 6:14–15. **Ministers of righteousness**: recalls the earlier contrast between the

ministry of condemnation and that of righteousness (2 Cor 3:9). **Their end**: the section closes with another allusion to the judgment, when all participants in the final conflict will be revealed or unmasked and dealt with as they deserve.

**[11:16–12:10] Paul now accepts the challenge of his opponents and indulges in boasting similar to theirs, but with differences that he has already signaled in 2 Cor 10:12–18 and that become clearer as he proceeds. He defines the nature of his project and unmistakably labels it as folly at the beginning and the end (2 Cor 11:16–23; 12:11). Yet his boast does not spring from ignorance (2 Cor 11:21; 12:6) nor is it concerned merely with human distinctions (2 Cor 11:18). Paul boasts "in moderation" (2 Cor 10:13, 15) and "in the Lord" (2 Cor 10:17).

††[11:16–29] The first part of Paul's boast focuses on labors and afflictions, in which authentic service of Christ consists.

‡‡[11:16–21] These verses recapitulate remarks already made about the foolishness of boasting and the excessive toleration of the Corinthians. They form a prelude to the boast proper.

§§[11:20] Paul describes the activities of the "others" in terms that fill out the picture drawn in vv 3–4, 13–15. Much of the vocabulary suggests fleshly or even satanic activity. **Enslaves**: cf. Gal 2:4. **Devours**: cf. 1 Pt 5:8. **Gets the better**: the verb *lambanō* means "to take," but is used in a variety of senses; here it may imply financial advantage, as in the English colloquialism "to take someone." It is similarly used at 2 Cor 12:16 and is there connected with cunning and deceit. **Puts on airs**: the same verb is rendered "raise oneself" (2 Cor 10:5) and "be too elated" (2 Cor 12:7).

¶¶[11:21] Paul ironically concedes the charge of personal weakness from 2 Cor 10:1–18 but will refute the other charge there mentioned, that of lack of boldness, accepting the challenge to demonstrate it by his boast.

***[11:22] The opponents apparently pride themselves on their "Jewishness." Paul, too, can claim to be a Jew by race, religion, and promise. **Descendants of Abraham**: elsewhere Paul distinguishes authentic from inauthentic heirs of Abraham and the promise (Rom 4:13–18; 9:7–13; 11:1; Gal 3:9, 27–29; cf. Jn 8:33–47). Here he grants his opponents this title in order to concentrate on the principal claim that follows.

†††[11:23a] **Ministers of Christ . . . I am still more**: the central point of the boast (cf. note on 2 Cor 11:5). **Like an insane person**: the climax of his folly.

‡‡‡[11:23b–29] Service of the humiliated and crucified Christ is demonstrated by trials endured for him. This rhetorically impressive catalogue enumerates many of the labors and perils Paul encountered on his missionary journeys.

f. [11:5] 12:11.  g. [11:6] 1 Cor 1:5, 17; 2:1–5.  h. [11:7] 12:13–18; Acts 18:3; 1 Cor 9:6–18.  i. [11:9] Phil 4:15, 18.  j. [11:10] 1 Cor 9:15.  k. [11:11] 12:15.

l. [11:22] Acts 22:3 / Rom 11:1; Phil 3:5–6.  m. [11:23] 6:5; Acts 16:22–24; 1 Cor 15:31–32.

far greater labors, far more imprisonments, far worse beatings, and numerous brushes with death. [24]Five times at the hands of the Jews I received forty lashes minus one.[n] [25]Three times I was beaten with rods, once I was stoned, three times I was shipwrecked, I passed a night and a day on the deep;[o] [26]on frequent journeys, in dangers from rivers, dangers from robbers, dangers from my own race, dangers from Gentiles, dangers in the city, dangers in the wilderness, dangers at sea, dangers among false brothers; [27]in toil and hardship, through many sleepless nights, through hunger and thirst, through frequent fastings, through cold and exposure.[p] [28]And apart from these things, there is the daily pressure upon me of my anxiety for all the churches. [29]Who is weak, and I am not weak? Who is led to sin, and I am not indignant?[q]

**Paul's Boast: His Weakness.**[*] [30]If I must boast, I will boast of the things that show my weakness. [31†]The God and Father of the Lord Jesus knows, he who is blessed forever, that I do not lie. [32]At Damascus, the governor under King Aretas guarded the city of Damascus, in order to seize me, [33]but I was lowered in a basket through a window in the wall and escaped his hands.[r]

## CHAPTER 12

[1‡]I must boast; not that it is profitable, but I will go on to visions and revelations of the Lord. [2]I know someone in Christ who, fourteen years ago (whether in the body or out of the body I do not know, God knows), was caught up to the third heaven. [3]And I know that this person (whether in the body or out of the body I do not know, God knows) [4]was caught up into Paradise and heard ineffable things, which no one may utter.[s] [5]About this person I will boast,

but about myself I will not boast, except about my weaknesses. [6]Although if I should wish to boast, I would not be foolish, for I would be telling the truth. But I refrain, so that no one may think more of me than what he sees in me or hears from me [7]because of the abundance of the revelations. Therefore, that I might not become too elated,[§] a thorn in the flesh was given to me, an angel of Satan, to beat me, to keep me from being too elated.[t] [8]Three times¶ I begged the Lord about this, that it might leave me,[u] [9††]but he said to me, "My grace is sufficient for you, for power is made perfect in weakness." I will rather boast most gladly of my weaknesses,[‡‡] in order that the power of Christ may dwell with me.[v] [10]Therefore, I am content with weaknesses, insults, hardships, persecutions, and constraints, for the sake of Christ;[w] for when I am weak, then I am strong.[§§]

**Selfless Concern for the Church.**[¶¶] [11]I have been foolish. You compelled me, for I ought to have

---

revelations were not a personal achievement, nor were they meant to draw attention to any quality of his own.

¶ [12:7] **That I might not become too elated**: God assures that there is a negative component to his experience, so that he cannot lose proper perspective; cf. 2 Cor 1:9; 4:7–11. A **thorn in the flesh**: variously interpreted as a sickness or physical disability, a temptation, or a handicap connected with his apostolic activity. But since Hebrew "thorn in the flesh," like English "thorn in my side," refers to persons (cf. Nm 33:55; Ez 28:24), Paul may be referring to some especially persistent and obnoxious opponent. The language of 2 Cor 12:7–8 permits this interpretation. If this is correct, the frequent appearance of singular pronouns in depicting the opposition may not be merely a stylistic variation; the singular may be provoked and accompanied by the image of one individual in whom criticism of Paul's preaching, way of life, and apostolic consciousness is concentrated, and who embodies all the qualities Paul attributes to the group. **An angel of Satan**: a personal messenger from Satan; cf. the satanic language already applied to the opponents in 2 Cor 11:3, 13–15, 20.

** [12:8] **Three times**: his prayer was insistent, like that of Jesus in Gethsemane, a sign of how intolerable he felt the thorn to be.

†† [12:9] **But he said to me**: Paul's petition is denied; release and healing are withheld for a higher purpose. The Greek perfect tense indicates that Jesus' earlier response still holds at the time of writing. **My grace is sufficient for you**: this is not a statement about the sufficiency of grace in general. Jesus speaks directly to Paul's situation. **Is made perfect**: i.e., is given most fully and manifests itself fully.

‡‡ [12:9b–10a] Paul draws the conclusion from the autobiographical anecdote and integrates it into the subject of this part of the boast. **Weaknesses**: the apostolic hardships he must endure, including active personal hostility, as specified in a final catalogue (2 Cor 12:10a). **That the power of Christ may dwell with me**: Paul pinpoints the ground for the paradoxical strategy he has adopted in his self-defense.

§§ [12:10] **When I am weak, then I am strong**: Paul recognizes a twofold pattern in the resolution of the weakness-power (and death-life) dialectic, each of which looks to Jesus as the model and is experienced in him. The first is personal, involving a reversal in oneself (Jesus, 2 Cor 13:4a; Paul, 2 Cor 1:9–10; 4:10–11; 6:9). The second is apostolic, involving an effect on others (Jesus, 2 Cor 5:14–15; Paul, 2 Cor 1:6; 4:12; 13:9). The specific kind of "effectiveness in ministry" that Paul promises to demonstrate on his arrival (2 Cor 13:4b; cf. 2 Cor 10:1–11) involves elements of both; this, too, will be modeled on Jesus' experience and a participation in that experience (2 Cor 9; 13:3b).

¶¶ [12:11–18] This brief section forms an epilogue or concluding observation to Paul's boast, corresponding to the prologue in 2 Cor 11:1–15. A four-step sequence of ideas is

---

* [11:30–12:10] The second part of Paul's boast, marked by a change of style and a shift in focus. After recalling the project in which he is engaged, he states a new topic: his weaknesses as matter for boasting. Everything in this section, even the discussion of privileges and distinctions, will be integrated into this perspective.

† [11:31–32] The episode at Damascus is symbolic. It aptly illustrates Paul's weakness but ends in deliverance (cf. 2 Cor 4:7–11).

‡ [12:1–4] **In the body or out of the body**: he seemed no longer confined to bodily conditions, but he does not claim to understand the mechanics of the experience. **Caught up**: i.e., in ecstasy. **The third heaven . . . Paradise**: ancient cosmologies depicted a multitiered universe. Jewish intertestamental literature contains much speculation about the number of heavens. Seven is the number usually mentioned, but the Testament of Levi (2:7–10; 3:1–4) speaks of three; God himself dwelt in the third of these. Without giving us any clear picture of the cosmos, Paul indicates a mental journey to a nonearthly space, set apart by God, in which secrets were revealed to him. **Ineffable things**: i.e., privileged knowledge, which it was not possible or permitted to divulge.

§ [12:5–7] **This person**: the indirect way of referring to himself has the effect of emphasizing the distance between that experience and his everyday life, just as the indirect **someone in Christ** (2 Cor 12:2) and all the passive verbs emphasize his passivity and receptivity in the experience. The

---

n. [11:24] Dt 25:2–3.  o. [11:25] Acts 14:19; 27:43–44.  p. [11:27] 1 Cor 4:11.  q. [11:29] 1 Cor 9:22.  r. [11:33] Acts 9:23–25.  s. [12:4] Lk 23:43; Rev 2:7.

t. [12:7] Nm 33:55; Jos 23:13; Ez 28:24.  u. [12:8] Mt 26:39–44.  v. [12:9] 4:7.  w. [12:10] 6:4–5; Rom 5:3 / Phil 4:13.

been commended by you. For I am in no way inferior to these "superapostles,"ˣ even though I am nothing. ¹²˟The signs of an apostle were performed among you with all endurance, signs and wonders, and mighty deeds.ʸ ¹³˟In what way were you less privileged than the rest of the churches, except that on my part I did not burden you? Forgive me this wrong!ᶻ

¹⁴Now I am ready to come to you this third time. And I will not be a burden, for I want not what is yours, but you. Children ought not to save for their parents, but parents for their children. ¹⁵I will most gladly spend and be utterly spent for your sakes. If I love you more, am I to be loved less? ¹⁶But granted that I myself did not burden you, yet I was crafty and got the better of you by deceit.ᵃ ¹⁷Did I take advantage of you through any of those I sent to you? ¹⁸I urged Titus to go and sent the brother with him. Did Titus take advantage of you? Did we not walk in the same spirit? And in the same steps?ᵇ

**Final Warnings and Appeals.**‡ ¹⁹Have you been thinking all along that we are defending§ ourselves before you? In the sight of God we are speaking in Christ, and all for building you up, beloved. ²⁰For I fear that⁴ when I come I may find you not such as I wish, and that you may find me not as you wish; that there may be rivalry, jealousy, fury, selfishness, slander, gossip, conceit, and disorder.ᶜ ²¹I fear that when I

come again** my God may humiliate me before you, and I may have to mourn over many of those who sinned earlier and have not repented of the impurity, immorality, and licentiousness they practiced.

## CHAPTER 13

¹This third time I am coming†† to you. "On the testimony of two or three witnesses a fact shall be established."ᵈ ²I warned those who sinned earlier‡‡ and all the others, and I warn them now while absent, as I did when present on my second visit, that if I come again I will not be lenient, ³§§since you are looking for proof of Christ speaking in me. He is not weak toward you but powerful in you. ⁴For indeed he was crucified out of weakness, but he lives by the power of God. So also we are weak in him, but toward you we shall live with him by the power of God.

⁵¶¶Examine yourselves to see whether you are living in faith. Test yourselves. Do you not

---

common to these two sections: Paul qualifies his boast as folly (2 Cor 11:1; 12:11a), asserts his noninferiority to the "superapostles" (2 Cor 11:5; 12:11b), exemplifies this by allusion to charismatic endowments (2 Cor 11:6; 12:12), and finally denies that he has been a financial burden to the community (2 Cor 11:7–12; 12:13–18).

\*[12:12] Despite weakness and affliction (suggested by the mention of **endurance**), his ministry has been accompanied by demonstrations of power (cf. 1 Cor 2:3–4). **Signs of an apostle**: visible proof of belonging to Christ and of mediating Christ's power, which the opponents require as touchstones of apostleship (2 Cor 12:11; cf. 2 Cor 13:3).

†[12:13–18] Paul insists on his intention to continue refusing support from the community (cf. 2 Cor 11:8–12). In defending his practice and his motivation, he once more protests his love (cf. 2 Cor 11:11) and rejects the suggestion of secret self-enrichment. He has recourse here again to language applied to his opponents earlier: "cunning" (2 Cor 11:3), "deceit" (2 Cor 11:13), "got the better of you" (see note on 2 Cor 11:20), "take advantage" (2 Cor 2:11).

‡[12:19–13:10] This concludes the development begun in 2 Cor 10. In the chiastic arrangement of the material (see note on 2 Cor 10:1–13:10), this final part corresponds to the opening; there are important similarities of content between the two sections as well.

§[12:19] This verse looks back at the previous chapters and calls them by their proper name, a defense, an *apologia* (cf. 1 Cor 9:3). Yet Paul insists on an important distinction: he has indeed been speaking for their benefit, but the ultimate judgment to which he submits is God's (cf. 1 Cor 4:3–5). This verse also leads into the final section, announcing two of its themes: judgment and building up.

¶[12:20] **I fear that . . .** : earlier Paul expressed fear that the Corinthians were being victimized, exploited, seduced from right thinking by his opponents (2 Cor 11:3–4, 19–21). Here he alludes unexpectedly to moral disorders among the Corinthians themselves. The catalogue suggests the effects of factions that have grown up around rival apostles.

\*\*[12:21] **Again**: one can also translate, "I fear that when I come my God may again humiliate me." Paul's allusion to the humiliation and mourning that may await him recall the mood he described in 2 Cor 2:1–4, but there is no reference here to any individual such as there is in 2 Cor 2:5–11. The crisis of 2 Cor 2 has happily been resolved by integration of the offender and repentance (2 Cor 7:4–16), whereas 2 Cor 12:21 is preoccupied with still unrepentant sinners. The sexual sins recall 1 Cor 5–7.

††[13:1] **This third time I am coming**: designation of the forthcoming visit as the "third" (cf. 2 Cor 12:14) may indicate that, in addition to his founding sojourn in Corinth, Paul had already made the first of two visits mentioned as planned in 2 Cor 1:15, and the next visit will be the long-postponed second of these. If so, the materials in 2 Cor 1:12–2:13 plus 2 Cor 7:4–16 and 2 Cor 10–13 may date from the same period of time, presumably of some duration, between Paul's second and third visit, though it is not clear that they are addressing the same crisis. The chronology is too unsure and the relations between sections of 2 Corinthians too unclear to yield any certainty. The hypothesis that 2 Cor 10–13 are themselves the "tearful letter" mentioned at 2 Cor 2:3–4 creates more problems than it solves.

‡‡[13:2] **I warned those who sinned earlier**: mention of unrepentant sinners (2 Cor 12:21 and here) and of an oral admonition given them on an earlier visit complicates the picture at the very end of Paul's development. It provides, in fact, a second explanation for the show of power that has been threatened from the beginning (2 Cor 10:1–6), but a different reason for it, quite unsuspected until now. It is not clear whether Paul is merely alluding to a dimension of the situation that he has not previously had occasion to mention, or whether some other community crisis, not directly connected with that behind 2 Cor 10–13, has influenced the final editing. **I will not be lenient**: contrast Paul's hesitation and reluctance to inflict pain in 2 Cor 1:23 and 2 Cor 2:1–4. The next visit will bring the showdown.

§§[13:3–4] Paul now gives another motive for severity when he comes, the charge of weakness leveled against him as an apostle. The motive echoes more closely the opening section (2 Cor 10:1–18) and the intervening development (especially 2 Cor 11:30–12:10). **Proof of Christ speaking in me**: the threat of 2 Cor 10:1–2 is reworded to recall Paul's conformity with the pattern of Christ, his insertion into the interplay of death and life, weakness and power (cf. note on 2 Cor 12:10b).

¶¶[13:5–9] Paul turns the challenge mentioned in 2 Cor 13:3 on them: they are to put themselves to the test to demonstrate whether Christ is in them. These verses involve a complicated series of plays on the theme of *dokimē* (testing, proof,

---

x. [12:11] 11:5.   y. [12:12] Rom 15:19; 1 Thes 1:5.   z. [12:13] 11:9–12.
a. [12:16] 11:3, 13.   b. [12:18] 2:13; 8:16, 23.   c. [12:20] 1 Cor 1:11; 3:3.

d. [13:1] Dt 19:15; Mt 18:16; Jn 8:17; Heb 10:28.

realize that Jesus Christ is in you?—unless, of course, you fail the test. [6]I hope you will discover that we have not failed. [7]But we pray to God that you may not do evil, not that we may appear to have passed the test but that you may do what is right, even though we may seem to have failed. [8]For we cannot do anything against the truth, but only for the truth. [9]For we rejoice when we are weak but you are strong. What we pray for is your improvement.

[10]*[e]I am writing this while I am away, so that when I come I may not have to be severe in virtue of the authority that the Lord has given me to build up and not to tear down.

## V. CONCLUSION[†]

[11]Finally, brothers, rejoice. Mend your ways, encourage one another, agree with one another, live in peace, and the God of love and peace will be with you. [12]Greet one another with a holy kiss. All the holy ones greet you.[f]

[13]The grace of the Lord Jesus Christ and the love of God and the fellowship of the holy Spirit be with all of you.[g]

---

passing and failing a test). Behind this stands the familiar distinction between present human judgment and final divine judgment. This is the final appearance of the theme (cf. 2 Cor 10:18; 11:15; 12:19).

*[13:10] **Authority . . . to build up and not to tear down**: Paul restates the purpose of his letter in language that echoes 2 Cor 10:2, 8, emphasizing the positive purpose of his authority in their regard. This verse forms an inclusion with the topic sentence of the section (2 Cor 12:19), as well as with the opening of this entire portion of the letter (2 Cor 10:1–2).

e. [13:10] 10:8.

---

†[13:11–13] These verses may have originally concluded 2 Cor 10–13, but they have nothing specifically to do with the material of that section. It is also possible to consider them a conclusion to the whole of 2 Corinthians in its present edited form. The exhortations are general, including a final appeal for peace in the community. The letter ends calmly, after its many storms, with the prospect of ecclesial unity and divine blessing. The final verse is one of the clearest trinitarian passages in the New Testament.

f. [13:12] Rom 16:16; 1 Cor 16:20 / Phil 4:22; 1 Thes 5:26; 1 Pt 5:14.   g. [13:13] Rom 16:20; 1 Cor 16:23.

# THE LETTER TO THE
# GALATIANS

၁၉

The Galatians to whom the letter is addressed were Paul's converts, most likely among the descendants of Celts who had invaded western and central Asia Minor in the third century B.C. and had settled in the territory around Ancyra (modern Ankara, Turkey). Paul had passed through this area on his second missionary journey (Acts 16:6) and again on his third (Acts 18:23). It is less likely that the recipients of this letter were Paul's churches in the southern regions of Pisidia, Lycaonia, and Pamphylia where he had preached earlier in the Hellenized cities of Perge, Iconium, Pisidian Antioch, Lystra, and Derbe (Acts 13:13–14:27); this area was part of the Roman province of Galatia, and some scholars think that South Galatia was the destination of this letter.

If it is addressed to the Galatians in the north, the letter was probably written around A.D. 54 or 55, most likely from Ephesus after Paul's arrival there for a stay of several years on his third missionary journey (Acts 19; 20:31). On the South Galatian theory, the date would be earlier, perhaps A.D. 48–50. Involved is the question of how one relates the events of Gal 2:1–10 to the "Council of Jerusalem" described in Acts 15 (see notes on each passage).

In any case, the new Christians whom Paul is addressing were converts from paganism (Gal 4:8–9) who were now being enticed by other missionaries to add the observances of the Jewish law, including the rite of circumcision, to the cross of Christ as a means of salvation. For, since Paul's visit, some other interpretation of Christianity had been brought to these neophytes, probably by converts from Judaism (the name "Judaizers" is sometimes applied to them); it has specifically been suggested that they were Jewish Christians who had come from the austere Essene sect.

These interlopers insisted on the necessity of following certain precepts of the Mosaic law along with faith in Christ. They were undermining Paul's authority also, asserting that he had not been trained by Jesus himself, that his gospel did not agree with that of the original and true apostles in Jerusalem, that he had kept from his converts in Galatia the necessity of accepting circumcision and other key obligations of the Jewish law, in order more easily to win them to Christ, and that his gospel was thus not the full and authentic one held by "those of repute" in Jerusalem (Gal 2:2). Some scholars also see in Galatians 5; 6 another set of opponents against whom Paul writes, people who in their emphasis on the Spirit set aside all norms for conduct and became libertines in practice.

When Paul learned of the situation, he wrote this defense of his apostolic authority and of the correct understanding of the faith. He set forth the unique importance of Christ and his redemptive sacrifice on the cross, the freedom that Christians enjoy from the old burdens of the law, the total sufficiency of Christ and of faith in Christ as the way to God and to eternal life, and the beauty of the new life of the Spirit. Galatians is thus a summary of basic Pauline theology. Its themes were more fully and less polemically developed in the Letter to the Romans.

Autobiographically, the letter gives us Paul's own accounts of how he came to faith (Gal 1:15–24), the agreement in "the truth of the gospel" (Gal 2:5, 14) that he shared with the Jewish Christian leaders in Jerusalem, James, Cephas, and John (Gal 2:1–10), and the rebuke he had to deliver to Cephas in Antioch for inconsistency, contrary to the gospel, on the issue of table fellowship in the racially mixed church of Jewish and Gentile Christians in Antioch (Gal 2:11–14; cf. Gal 2:15–21). At the conclusion of the letter (Gal 6:11–18), Paul wrote in his own hand (cf. 2 Thes 3:17–18) a vivid summary of the message to the Galatians.

In his vigorous emphasis on the absolute preeminence of Christ and his cross as God's way to salvation and holiness, Paul stresses Christian freedom and the ineffectiveness of the Mosaic law for gaining divine favor and blessings (Gal 3:19–29). The pious Jew saw in the law a way established by God to win divine approval by a life of meticulous observance of ritual, social, and moral regulations. But Paul's profound insight into the higher designs of God in Christ led him to understand and welcome the priority of promise and faith (shown in the experience of Abraham, Gal 3:6–18) and the supernatural gifts of the Spirit (Gal 3:2–5; 5:16–6:10). His enthusiasm for this new vision of the life of grace in Christ and of the uniquely salvific role of Christ's redemptive death on the cross shines through this whole letter.

The principal divisions of the Letter to the Galatians are the following:

I. Address (1:1–5)
II. Loyalty to the Gospel (1:6–10)
III. Paul's Defense of His Gospel and His Authority (1:11–2:21)
IV. Faith and Liberty (3:1–4:31)
V. Exhortation to Christian Living (5:1–6:10)
VI. Conclusion (6:11–18)

## I. ADDRESS

### CHAPTER 1

**Greeting.**[*] [1a]Paul, an apostle[†] not from human beings nor through a human being but through Jesus Christ and God the Father who raised him from the dead,[b] [2a]and all the brothers who are with me, to the churches of Galatia: [3]grace to you and peace from God our Father and the Lord Jesus Christ, [4b]who gave himself for our sins that he might rescue us from the present evil age in accord with the will of our God and Father,[c] [5]to whom be glory forever and ever. Amen.[d]

### II. LOYALTY TO THE GOSPEL[ʃ]

[6e]I am amazed that you are so quickly forsaking the one who called you[**] by [the] grace [of Christ] for a different gospel [7](not that there is another). But there are some who are disturbing you and wish to pervert the gospel of Christ.

[8/]But even if we or an angel from heaven should preach [to you] a gospel other than the one that we preached to you, let that one be accursed![††] [9]As we have said before, and now I say again, if anyone preaches to you a gospel other than the one that you received, let that one be accursed!

[10g]Am I now currying favor with human beings or God? Or am I seeking to please people? If I were still trying to please people, I would not be a slave of Christ.[‡‡]

### III. PAUL'S DEFENSE OF HIS GOSPEL AND HIS AUTHORITY[§§]

**His Call by Christ.** [11h]Now I want you to know, brothers, that the gospel preached by me is not of human origin. [12]For I did not receive it from a human being, nor was I taught it, but it came through a revelation of Jesus Christ.[¶¶]

---

*[1:1–5] See note on Rom 1:1–7, concerning the greeting.
†[1:1] **Apostle**: because of attacks on his authority in Galatia, Paul defends his apostleship. He is not an apostle commissioned by a congregation (Phil 2:25; 2 Cor 8:23) or even by prophets (1 Tm 1:18; 4:14) but **through Jesus Christ and God the Father**.
‡[1:2] **All the brothers**: fellow believers in Christ, male and female; cf. Gal 3:27–28. Paul usually mentions the co-sender(s) at the start of a letter, but the use of **all** is unique, adding weight to the letter. **Galatia**: central Turkey more likely than the Roman province of Galatia; see Introduction.
§[1:4] The greeting in Gal 1:3 is expanded by a christological formula that stresses deliverance through the Lord Jesus from a world dominated by Satan; cf. 2 Cor 4:4; Eph 2:2; 6:12.
ʃ[1:6–10] In place of the usual thanksgiving (see note on Rom 1:8), Paul, with little to be thankful for in the Galatian situation, expresses amazement at the way his converts are deserting the gospel of Christ for a perverted message. He reasserts the one gospel he has preached (Gal 1:7–9) and begins to defend himself (Gal 1:10).
**[1:6] **The one who called you**: God or Christ, though in actuality Paul was the divine instrument to call the Galatians.

a. [1:1–3] Rom 1:1–7; 1 Cor 1:1–3. b. [1:1] 1:11–12. c. [1:4] 2:20; Eph 5:2; 1 Tm 2:6 / 1 Jn 5:19 / Rom 12:2; Eph 5:16; Heb 10:10. d. [1:5] Rom 16:27; 2 Tm 4:18. e. [1:6–7] 5:8, 10; Acts 15:1, 24; 2 Cor 11:4.

††[1:8] **Accursed**: in Greek, *anathema*; cf. Rom 9:3; 1 Cor 12:3; 16:22.
‡‡[1:10] This charge by Paul's opponents, that he sought to conciliate people with flattery and to curry favor with God, might refer to his mission practices (cf. 1 Cor 9:19–23) but the word **still** suggests it refers to his pre-Christian days (cf. Gal 1:14; Phil 3:6). The self-description **slave of Christ** is one Paul often uses in a greeting (Rom 1:1).
§§[1:11–2:21] Paul's presentation on behalf of his message and of his apostleship reflects rhetorical forms of his day: he first narrates the facts about certain past events (Gal 1:12–2:14) and then states his contention regarding justification by faith as the gospel message (Gal 2:15–21). Further arguments follow from both experience and scripture in Galatians 3; 4, before he draws out the ethical consequences (Gal 5:1–6:10). The specific facts that he takes up here to show that his gospel is not a human invention (Gal 1:11) but **came through a revelation of Jesus Christ** (Gal 1:12) deal with his own calling as a Christian missionary (Gal 1:13–17), his initial relations with the apostles in Jerusalem (Gal 1:18–24), a later journey to Jerusalem (Gal 2:1–10), and an incident in Antioch involving Cephas and persons from James (Gal 2:11–14). The content of Paul's revealed gospel is then set forth in the heart of the letter (Gal 2:15–21).
¶¶[1:12] Although Paul received his gospel **through a revelation** from Christ, this did not exclude his use of early Christian confessional formulations. See note on Gal 1:4.

f. [1:8–9] 1 Cor 16:22 / Gal 5:3, 21; 2 Cor 13:2. g. [1:10] 2 Cor 5:11 / 1 Thes 2:4. h. [1:11–12] 1 Cor 15:1 / Gal 1:1; Eph 3:3.

¹³°For you heard of my former way of life in Judaism, how I persecuted the church of God beyond measure and tried to destroy it,ⁱ ¹⁴and progressed in Judaism beyond many of my contemporaries among my race, since I was even more a zealot for my ancestral traditions.ʲ ¹⁵But when [God], who from my mother's womb had set me apart and called me through his grace, was pleasedᵏ ¹⁶to reveal his Son to me,ˡ so that I might proclaim him to the Gentiles, I did not immediately consult flesh and blood,† ¹⁷nor did I go up to Jerusalem to those who were apostles before me; rather, I went into Arabia‡ and then returned to Damascus.

¹⁸°Then after three years⁵ I went up to Jerusalem to confer with Cephas and remained with him for fifteen days.ᵐ ¹⁹But I did not see any other of the apostles,ⁿ only James the brother of the Lord.⁺ ²⁰(As to what I am writing to you, behold, before God, I am not lying.)ᵒ ²¹Then I went into the regions of Syria and Cilicia.ᵖ ²²And I was unknown personally to the churches of Judea that are in Christ; ²³they only kept hearing that "the one who once was persecuting us is now preaching the faith he once tried to destroy."�q ²⁴So they glorified God because of me.

## CHAPTER 2

**The Council of Jerusalem.**†† ¹Then after fourteen years I again went up to Jerusalem with Barnabas,‡‡ taking Titus along also.ʳ ²I went up in accord with a revelation,§§ and I presented to them the gospel that I preach to the Gentiles—but privately to those of repute—so that I might not be running, or have run, in vain.ˢ ³Moreover, not even⁵⁵ Titus, who was with me, although he was a Greek, was compelled to be circumcised,ᵗ ⁴but because of the false brothers*** secretly brought in, who slipped in to spy on our freedom that we have in Christ Jesus,ᵘ that they might enslave us— ⁵to them we did not submit even for a moment, so that the truth of the gospel††† might remain intact for you.ᵛ ⁶But from those who were reputed to be important (what they once were makes no difference to me; God shows no partiality)—those of repute made me add nothing.ʷ ⁷‡‡‡On the contrary, when they saw that I had been entrusted with the gospel to the uncircumcised, just as Peter to the circumcised,ˣ ⁸for the one who worked in Peter for an apostolate to the circumcised worked also in me for the Gentiles, ⁹and when they recognized the grace bestowed upon me, James and Cephas and

*[1:13–17] Along with Phil 3:4–11, which also moves from autobiography to its climax in a discussion on justification by faith (cf. Gal 2:15–21), this passage is Paul's chief account of the change from his **former way of life** (Gal 1:13) to service as a Christian missionary (Gal 1:16); cf. Acts 9:1–22; 22:4–16; 26:9–18. Paul himself does not use the term "conversion" but stresses revelation (Gal 1:12, 16). In Gal 1:15 his language echoes the Old Testament prophetic call of Jeremiah. Unlike the account in Acts (cf. Acts 22:4–16), the calling of Paul here includes the mission to proclaim Christ **to the Gentiles** (Gal 1:16).

†[1:16] **Flesh and blood**: human authorities (cf. Mt 16:17; 1 Cor 15:50). Paul's apostleship comes from God (Gal 1:1).

‡[1:17] **Arabia**: probably the region of the Nabataean Arabs, east and south of Damascus.

§[1:18–24] Paul's first journey to Jerusalem as a Christian, according to Galatians (cf. Acts 9:23–31 and the note on Acts 12:25). He is quite explicit about contacts there, testifying under oath (Gal 1:20). On returning to **Syria** (perhaps specifically Damascus, cf. Gal 1:17) **and Cilicia** (including his home town Tarsus, cf. Acts 9:30; 22:3), Paul most likely engaged in missionary work. He underscores the fact that Christians in Judea knew of him only by reputation.

¶[1:18] **After three years**: two years and more, since Paul's call. To **confer with** Cephas may mean simply "pay a visit" or more specifically "get information from" him about Jesus, over a two-week period. **Cephas**: Aramaic name of Simon (Peter); cf. Mt 16:16–18 and the notes there.

**[1:19] **James the brother of the Lord**: not one of the Twelve, but a brother of Jesus (see note on Mk 6:3). He played an important role in the Jerusalem church (see note on Gal 2:9), the leadership of which he took over from Peter (Acts 12:17). Paul may have regarded James as an apostle.

††[2:1–10] Paul's second journey to Jerusalem, according to Galatians, involved a private meeting with **those of repute** (Gal 2:2). At issue was a Gentile, Titus, and the question

of circumcision, which **false brothers** (Gal 2:4) evidently demanded for him. Paul insists that the gospel he preaches (Gal 2:2; cf. Gal 1:9, 11) remained intact with no addition by those of repute (Gal 2:6); that Titus was not **compelled** to accept circumcision (Gal 2:3); and that he and the reputed **pillars** in Jerusalem agreed on how each would advance the missionary task (Gal 1:7–10). Usually, Gal 1:1–10 is equated with the "Council of Jerusalem," as it is called, described in Acts 15. See notes on Acts 15:6–12, 13–35, the latter concerning the "decree" that Paul does not mention.

‡‡[2:1] **After fourteen years**: thirteen or more years, probably reckoned from the return to Syria and Cilicia (Gal 1:21), though possibly from Paul's calling as a Christian (Gal 1:15). **Barnabas**: cf. Gal 2:9, 13; 1 Cor 9:6. A Jewish Christian missionary, with whom Paul worked (Acts 4:36–37; 11:22, 25, 30; 12:25; 13:1–3; 15:2). **Titus**: a missionary companion of Paul (2 Cor 2:13; 7:6, 13–15; 8:6, 16, 23; 12:18), non-Jewish (Gal 2:3), never mentioned in Acts.

§§[2:2] **A revelation**: cf. Gal 1:1, 12. Paul emphasizes it was God's will, not Jerusalem authority, that led to the journey. Acts 15:2 states that the church in Antioch appointed Paul and Barnabas for the task. **Those of repute**: leaders of the Jerusalem church; the term, while positive, may be slightly ironic (cf. Gal 1:6, 9). **Run, in vain**: while Paul presents a positive picture in what follows, his missionary work in Galatia would have been to no purpose if his opponents were correct that circumcision is needed for complete faith in Christ.

¶¶[2:3] **Not even** a Gentile Christian like Titus was compelled to receive the rite of circumcision. The Greek text could be interpreted that he voluntarily accepted circumcision, but this is unlikely in the overall argument.

***[2:4] **False brothers**: Jewish Christians who took the position that Gentile Christians must first become Jews through circumcision and observance of the Mosaic law in order to become Christians; cf. Acts 15:1.

†††[2:5] **The truth of the gospel**: the true gospel, in contrast to the false one of the opponents (Gal 1:6–9); the gospel of grace, used as a norm (Gal 2:14).

‡‡‡[2:7–9] Some think that actual "minutes" of the meeting are here quoted. Paul's apostleship to the Gentiles (Gal 1:16) is recognized alongside that of Peter to the Jews. Moreover, the right to proclaim the gospel without requiring circumcision and the Jewish law is sealed by a handshake. That Paul and colleagues **should go to the Gentiles** did not exclude his preaching to the Jews as well (Rom 1:13–16) or Cephas to Gentile areas.

i. [1:13] Acts 8:1–3; 9:1–2; 1 Cor 15:9.   j. [1:14] Acts 26:4–5.   k. [1:15] Is 49:1; Jer 1:4.   l. [1:16] 1:11–12; Rom 1:5; 1 Cor 15:10; Acts 9:3–9 / Gal 2:2, 7 / Mt 16:17.   m. [1:18] Acts 9:26–30 / Jn 1:42.   n. [1:19] 2:9; Mt 13:55; Acts 12:17.   o. [1:20] Rom 9:1; 2 Cor 11:31.   p. [1:21] Acts 9:30.   q. [1:23] 1:13.

r. [2:1] Acts 15:2.   s. [2:2] 1:11–12, 16 / 1:16 / Phil 2:16.   t. [2:3] 2 Cor 2:13; 7:6–7; 8:16–17; 12:18; Ti 1:4 / Gal 2:14; 6:12.   u. [2:4] 5:1; Acts 15:1, 24.   v. [2:5] 2:14; 4:16.   w. [2:6] Dt 10:17; Rom 2:11.   x. [2:7] 1:15–16; Acts 9:15; 15:12; 22:21; Rom 1:5.

John,* who were reputed to be pillars, gave me and Barnabas their right hands in partnership, that we should go to the Gentiles and they to the circumcised.^y ¹⁰Only, we were to be mindful of the poor,† which is the very thing I was eager to do.^z

**Peter's Inconsistency at Antioch.**‡ ¹¹ᵃAnd when Cephas came to Antioch, I opposed him to his face because he clearly was wrong.^§ ¹²For, until some people came from James,¶ he used to eat with the Gentiles; but when they came, he began to draw back and separated himself, because he was afraid of the circumcised.^b ¹³And the rest of the Jews** [also] acted hypocritically along with him, with the result that even Barnabas was carried away by their hypocrisy.^c ¹⁴But when I saw that they were not on the right road in line with the truth of the gospel, I said to Cephas in front of all,^d "If you, though a Jew, are living like a Gentile and not like a Jew, how can you compel the Gentiles to live like Jews?"††

**Faith and Works.**‡‡ ¹⁵We, who are Jews by nature and not sinners from among the Gentiles, ¹⁶ᵉ[yet]

who know that a person is not justified by works of the law but through faith in Jesus Christ, even we have believed in Christ Jesus that we may be justified by faith in Christ and not by works of the law, because by works of the law no one will be justified.^§§ ¹⁷But if, in seeking to be justified in Christ, we ourselves are found to be sinners, is Christ then a minister of sin?¶¶ Of course not! ¹⁸But if I am building up again those things that I tore down, then I show myself to be a transgressor.*** ¹⁹For through the law I died to the law,††† that I might live for God. I have been crucified with Christ;^f ²⁰yet I live, no longer I, but Christ lives in me; insofar as I now live in the flesh, I live by faith in the Son of God who has loved me and given himself up for me.^g ²¹I do not nullify the grace of God; for if justification comes through the law, then Christ died for nothing.^h

## IV. FAITH AND LIBERTY

### CHAPTER 3

**Justification by Faith.**‡‡‡ ¹O stupid§§§ Galatians! Who has bewitched you, before whose eyes Jesus Christ was publicly portrayed as crucified?^i ²I want to learn only this from you:^j did you receive the Spirit from works of the law, or from faith in what you heard?¶¶¶ ³Are you so stupid?^k After beginning with the Spirit, are you now ending with the flesh?**** ⁴Did you experience so

*[2:9] **James and Cephas and John:** see notes on Gal 1:18, 19; on Peter and John as leaders in the Jerusalem church, cf. Acts 3:1 and 8:14. The order here, with James first, may reflect his prominence in Jerusalem after Peter (Cephas) departed (Acts 12:17).

†[2:10] **The poor:** Jerusalem Christians or a group within the church there (cf. Rom 15:26). The collection for them was extremely important in Paul's thought and labor (cf. Rom 15:25–28; 1 Cor 16:1–4; 2 Cor 8–9).

‡[2:11–14] The decision reached in Jerusalem (Gal 2:3–7) recognized the freedom of Gentile Christians from the Jewish law. But the problem of table fellowship between Jewish Christians, who possibly still kept kosher food regulations, and Gentile believers was not yet settled. When Cephas first came to the racially mixed community of Jewish and Gentile Christians in Antioch (Gal 2:12), he ate with non-Jews. Pressure from persons arriving later from Jerusalem caused him and Barnabas to draw back. Paul therefore publicly rebuked Peter's inconsistency toward the gospel (Gal 2:14). Some think that what Paul said on that occasion extends through Gal 2:16 or 2:21.

§[2:11] **Clearly was wrong:** literally, "stood condemned," by himself and also by Paul. His action in breaking table fellowship was especially grievous if the eating involved the meal at the Lord's supper (cf. 1 Cor 11:17–25).

¶[2:12] **Some people came from James:** strict Jewish Christians (cf. Acts 15:1, 5; 21:20–21), either sent by James (Gal 1:19; 2:9) or claiming to be from the leader of the Jerusalem church. **The circumcised:** presumably Jewish Christians, not Jews.

**[2:13] **The Jews:** Jewish Christians, like Barnabas. **Hypocrisy:** literally, "pretense," "play-acting"; moral insincerity.

††[2:14] **Compel the Gentiles to live like Jews:** that is, conform to Jewish practices, such as circumcision (Gal 2:3–5) or regulations about food (Gal 2:12).

‡‡[2:15–21] Following on the series of incidents cited above, Paul's argument, whether spoken to Cephas at Antioch or only now articulated, is pertinent to the Galatian situation, where believers were having themselves circumcised (Gal 6:12–13) and obeying other aspects of Jewish law (Gal 4:9–10; 5:1–4). He insists that salvation is by faith in Christ, not by works of the law. His teaching on the gospel concerns justification by faith (Gal 2:16) in relation to sin (Gal 2:17), law (Gal 2:19), life in Christ (Gal 2:19–20), and grace (Gal 2:21).

§§[2:16] **No one will be justified:** Ps 143:2 is reflected.

¶¶[2:17] **A minister of sin:** literally, "a servant of sin" (cf. Rom 15:8), an agent of sin, one who promotes it. This is possibly a claim by opponents that justification on the basis of faith in Christ makes Christ an abettor of sin when Christians **are found to be sinners.** Paul denies the conclusion (cf. Rom 6:1–4).

***[2:18] To return to observance of the law as the means to salvation would entangle one not only in inevitable transgressions of it but also in the admission that it was wrong to have abandoned the law in the first place.

†††[2:19] **Through the law I died to the law:** this is variously explained: the law revealed sin (Rom 7:7–9) and led to death and then to belief in Christ; or, the law itself brought the insight that law cannot justify (Gal 2:16; Ps 143:2); or, the "law of Christ" (Gal 6:2) led to abandoning the Mosaic law; or, the law put Christ to death (cf. Gal 3:13) and so provided a way to our salvation, through baptism into Christ, through which we die (**crucified with Christ;** see Rom 6:6). Cf. also Gal 3:19–25 on the role of the law in reference to salvation.

‡‡‡[3:1–14] Paul's contention that justification comes not through the law or the works of the law but by faith in Christ and in his death (Gal 2:16, 21) is supported by appeals to Christian experience (Gal 3:1–5) and to scripture (Gal 3:6–14). The gift of God's Spirit to the Galatians came from the gospel received in faith, not from doing what the law enjoins. The story of Abraham shows that faith in God brings **righteousness** (Gal 3:6; Gn 15:6). The promise to Abraham (Gal 3:8; Gn 12:3) extends to the Gentiles (Gal 3:14)

§§§[3:1] **Stupid:** not just senseless, for they were in danger of deserting their salvation.

¶¶¶[3:2] **Faith in what you heard:** Paul's message received with faith. The Greek can also mean "the proclamation of the faith" or "a hearing that comes from faith."

****[3:3] On the contrast of **Spirit** and **flesh,** cf. Rom 8:1–11. Having received the Spirit, they need not be circumcised now.

y. [2:9] Rom 15:15 / Gal 1:18–19; Jn 1:42; Acts 12:17 / Gal 2:1.
z. [2:10] Acts 11:29–30; Rom 15:25–28; 1 Cor 16:1–4; 2 Cor 8:9.  a. [2:11] 1:18 / Acts 11:19–30; 15:1–2.  b. [2:12] Acts 10:15, 28; 11:3.  c. [2:13] 2:1, 9.  d. [2:14] 2:5 / 1:18; 2:9 / 2:3.  e. [2:16] 3:2, 11; Ps 143:1–2; Rom 3:20, 28; 4:5; 11:6; Eph 2:8–9; Phil 3:9.

f. [2:19] 6:14; Rom 6:6, 8, 10; 7:6.  g. [2:20] 1:4; Rom 8:10–11; Col 3:3–4.  h. [2:21] 5:2.  i. [3:1] 5:7; 1 Cor 1:23.  j. [3:2] 2:16 / 3:14; Rom 10:17.  k. [3:3] 5:16–18.

many things* in vain?—if indeed it was in vain. [5]Does, then, the one who supplies the Spirit to you and works mighty deeds among you do so from works of the law or from faith in what you heard?[l] [6]Thus Abraham "believed God,"[m] and it was credited to him as righteousness."[t]

[7‡]Realize then that it is those who have faith who are children of Abraham.[n] [8]Scripture, which saw in advance that God would justify the Gentiles by faith, foretold the good news to Abraham, saying, "Through you shall all the nations be blessed."[o] [9]Consequently, those who have faith are blessed along with Abraham who had faith.[p] [10§]For all who depend on works of the law are under a curse; for it is written, "Cursed be everyone who does not persevere in doing all the things written in the book of the law."[q] [11]And that no one is justified before God by the law is clear, for "the one who is righteous by faith will live."[r] [12]But the law does not depend on faith; rather, "the one who does these things will live by them."[s] [13]Christ ransomed us from the curse of the law by becoming a curse for us, for it is written, "Cursed be everyone who hangs on a tree,"[t] [14]that the blessing of Abraham might be extended to the Gentiles through Christ Jesus, so that we might receive the promise of the Spirit through faith.[u]

**The Law Did Not Nullify the Promise.** [15¶]Brothers, in human terms I say that no one can annul or amend even a human will once ratified.[v] [16]Now the promises were made to Abraham and to his descendant.[**] It does not say, "And to descendants," as referring to many, but as referring to one, "And to your descendant," who is Christ.[w] [17]This is what I mean: the law, which came four hundred and thirty years afterward,[††] does not annul a covenant previously ratified by God, so as to cancel the promise.[x] [18]For if the inheritance comes from the law,[y] it is no longer from a promise; but God bestowed it on Abraham through a promise.[‡‡]

[19§§]Why, then, the law? It was added for transgressions, until the descendant[¶¶] came to whom the promise had been made; it was promulgated by angels at the hand of a mediator.[z] [20]Now there is no mediator when only one party is involved, and God is one.[a] [21]Is the law then opposed to the promises [of God]? Of course not! For if a law had been given that could bring life, then righteousness would in reality come from the law.[b] [22]But scripture confined all things under the power of sin, that through faith in Jesus Christ the promise might be given to those who believe.[c] **What Faith Has Brought Us.**[***] [23]Before faith came, we were held in custody under law, confined for the faith that was to be revealed.[d]

---

*[3:4] **Experience so many things**: probably the **mighty deeds** of Gal 1:5 but possibly the experience of sufferings.

†[3:6] **Abraham . . . righteousness**: see Gn 15:6; Rom 4:3. The Galatians like Abraham heard with faith and experienced justification. This first argument forms the basis for the further scriptural evidence that follows.

‡[3:7–9] **Faith** is what matters, for **Abraham** and the **children of Abraham**, in contrast to the claims of the opponents that circumcision and observance of the law are needed to bring the promised blessing of Gn 12:3; cf. Gn 18:18; Sir 44:21; Acts 3:25.

§[3:10–14] Those **who depend** not on promise and faith **but on works of the law are under a curse** because they do **not persevere in doing all the things written in the book of the law** (Gal 3:10; Dt 27:26) in order to gain life (Gal 3:12; Lv 18:5; cf. Rom 10:5). But scripture teaches that **no one is justified before God by the law** (Gal 3:11; Heb 2:4, adapted from the Greek version of Habakkuk; cf. Rom 1:17; Heb 10:38). Salvation, then, depends on faith in Christ who died on the cross (Gal 3:13), taking upon himself a curse found in Dt 21:23 (about executed criminals hanged in public view), to free us from **the curse of the law** (Gal 3:13). That the Gentile Galatians have received the promised Spirit (Gal 3:14) by faith and in no other way returns the argument to the experience cited in Gal 3:1–5.

¶[3:15–18] A third argument to support Paul's position that salvation is not through the law but by promise (Gal 3:1–14) comes from legal practice and scriptural history. A legal agreement or **human will**, duly **ratified**, is unalterable (Gal 3:15). God's **covenant** with **Abraham** and its repeated promises (Gn 12:2–3, 7; 13:15; 17:7–8; 22:16–18; 24:7) is not superseded by **the law**, which came much later, in the time of Moses. **The inheritance** (of the Spirit and the blessings) is by promise, not by law (Gal 3:18). Paul's argument hinges on

the fact that the same Greek word, *diathēkē*, can be rendered as **will** or testament (Gal 3:15) and as **covenant** (Gal 3:17).

**[3:16] **Descendant**: literally, "and to his seed." The Hebrew, as in Gn 12:7; 15:18; 22:17–18, is a collective singular, traditionally rendered as a plural, **descendants**, but taken by Paul in its literal number to refer to **Christ** as descendant of Abraham.

††[3:17] **Four hundred and thirty years afterward**: follows Ex 12:40 in the Greek (Septuagint) version, in contrast to Gn 15:13 and Acts 7:6, for chronology.

‡‡[3:18] This refutes the opponents' contention that the promises of God are fulfilled only as a reward for human observance of the law.

§§[3:19–22] A digression: if the Mosaic law, then, does not save or **bring life**, why was it given? Elsewhere, Paul says the law served to show what sin is (Rom 3:20; 7:7–8). Here the further implication is that the law in effect served to produce transgressions. Moreover, it was received at second hand **by angels**, through a **mediator**, not directly from God (Gal 3:19). The law does not, however, oppose God's purposes, for it carries out its function (Gal 3:22), so that **righteousness** comes by **faith** and **promise**, not by human works of the law.

¶¶[3:19] **The descendant**: Christ (Gal 3:16). **By angels**: Dt 33:2–4 stressed their presence as enhancing the importance of the law; Paul uses their role to diminish its significance (cf. Acts 7:38, 53). **A mediator**: Moses. But in a covenant of promise, where all depends on the one God, no mediator is needed (Gal 3:20).

***[3:23–29] Paul adds a further argument in support of righteousness or justification by faith and through God's promise rather than by observance of the law (Gal 2:16; 3:22): as **children of God, baptized into Christ**, the Galatians are all **Abraham's descendant** and **heirs of the promise** to Abraham (Gal 3:8, 14, 16–18, 29). The teaching in Gal 3:23–25, that since **faith** (Christianity) **has come, we are no longer under** the law, could be taken with the previous paragraph on the role of the Mosaic law, but it also fits here as a contrast between the situation **before faith** (Gal 3:23) and the results after faith has come (Gal 3:25–29).

---

l. [3:5] 2:16.   m. [3:6] Gn 15:6; Rom 4:3; Jas 2:23.   n. [3:7] 3:29; Rom 4:11–12 / Sir 44:19–21.   o. [3:8] Gn 12:3; 18:17–19; Acts 3:25.   p. [3:9] Rom 4:16.   q. [3:10] Dt 27:26; Jas 2:10.   r. [3:11] 2:16; Heb 2:4; Rom 1:17.   s. [3:12] Lv 18:5; Rom 10:5.   t. [3:13] Dt 21:23; Rom 8:3; 2 Cor 5:21.   u. [3:14] Gn 3:2–3, 5; Is 44:3; Jl 3:1–2; Acts 2:33.

v. [3:15] Rom 3:5 / Heb 9:16–17.   w. [3:16] Gn 12:7; 13:15; 17:8; 22:17; 24:7; Mt 1:1.   x. [3:17] Ex 12:40.   y. [3:18] Rom 4:16; 11:6.   z. [3:19] Rom 4:15; 5:20; 7:7, 13 / Acts 7:38, 53.   a. [3:20] Dt 6:4.   b. [3:21] Rom 7:7, 10; 8:2–4.   c. [3:22] Rom 3:9–20, 23; 11:32.   d. [3:23] 4:3–5; 5:18.

²⁴Consequently, the law was our disciplinarian* for Christ, that we might be justified by faith.ᵉ ²⁵But now that faith has come, we are no longer under a disciplinarian.ᶠ ²⁶For through faith you are all children of God† in Christ Jesus.ᵍ ²⁷‡For all of you who were baptized into Christʰ have clothed yourselves with Christ.§ ²⁸There is neither Jew nor Greek, there is neither slave nor free person, there is not male and female; for you are all one in Christ Jesus.ⁱ ²⁹And if you belong to Christ, then you are Abraham's descendant, heirs according to the promise.ʲ

## CHAPTER 4

**God's Free Children in Christ.**¶ ¹I mean that as long as the heir is not of age,** he is no different from a slave, although he is the owner of everything, ²but he is under the supervision of guardians and administrators until the date set by his father. ³ᵃIn the same way we also, when we were not of age, were enslaved to the elemental powers of the world.†† ⁴But when the fullness of time had come, God sent his Son, born of a woman, born under the law,ˡ ⁵to ransom those under the law, so that we might receive adoption.ᵐ ⁶As proof that you are children,‡‡ God sent the spirit of his Son into our hearts, crying out, "Abba, Father!"ⁿ ⁷So you are no longer a slave but a child, and if a child then also an heir, through God.ᵒ

**Do Not Throw This Freedom Away.**§§ ⁸ᵖAt a time when you did not know God, you became slaves to things that by nature are not gods;¶¶ ⁹but now that you have come to know God, or rather to be known by God, how can you turn back again to the weak and destitute elemental powers? Do you want to be slaves to them all over again?�q ¹⁰You are observing days,ʳ months, seasons, and years.*** ¹¹I am afraid on your account that perhaps I have labored for you in vain.†††

**Appeal to Former Loyalty.**‡‡‡ ¹²I implore you, brothers, be as I am, because I have also become as you are.§§§ You did me no wrong;ˢ ¹³you know that it was because of a physical illness¶¶¶ that I originally preached the gospel to you, ¹⁴and you did not show disdain or contempt because of the trial caused you by my physical condition, but rather you received me as an angel of God, as Christ Jesus. ¹⁵Where now is that blessedness of yours?**** Indeed, I can testify to you that, if it had been possible, you would have torn out your eyes and given them to me. ¹⁶So now have I become your enemy by telling you the truth? ¹⁷They show interest in you, but not in a good way; they want to isolate you,†††† so that you may show interest in them.ᵗ ¹⁸Now it is good to be shown interest for good reason at all times, and not only when I am with you. ¹⁹My children, for whom I am again in labor until Christ be formed in you!ᵘ ²⁰I would like to be with you now and to change my tone, for I am perplexed because of you.

---

*[3:24–25] **Disciplinarian**: the Greek *paidagōgos* referred to a slave who escorted a child to school but did not teach or tutor; hence, a guardian or monitor. Applying this to the law fits the role of the law described in Gal 3:19–25.

†[3:26] **Children of God**: literally "sons," in contrast to the young child under the disciplinarian in Gal 3:24–25. The term includes males and females (Gal 3:28).

‡[3:27–28] Likely a formula used at baptism that expresses racial, social-economic, and sexual equality in Christ (cf. Col 3:11).

§[3:27] **Clothed yourselves with Christ**: literally, "have put on Christ"; cf. Rom 13:14; Eph 4:24; Col 3:10. Baptismal imagery, traceable to the Old Testament (Jb 29:14; Is 59:17) but also found in pagan mystery cults.

¶[4:1–7] What Paul has argued in Gal 3:26–29 is now elaborated in terms of the Christian as **the heir** (Gal 4:1, 7; cf. Gal 3:18, 29) freed from control by others. Again, as in Gal 3:2–5, the proof that Christians are children of God is the gift of the Spirit of Christ relating them intimately to God.

**[4:1, 3] **Not of age**: an infant or minor.

††[4:3] **The elemental powers of the world**: while the term can refer to the "elements" like earth, air, fire, and water or to elementary forms of religion, the sense here is more likely that of celestial beings that were thought in pagan circles to control the world; cf. Gal 4:8; Col 2:8, 20.

‡‡[4:6] **Children**: see note on Gal 3:26; here in contrast to the infant or young person **not of age** (Gal 3:1, 3). **Abba**: cf. Mk 14:36 and the note; Rom 8:15.

§§[4:8–11] On the basis of the arguments advanced from Gal 3:1 through Gal 4:7, Paul now launches his appeal to the Galatians with the question, **how can you turn back** to the slavery of the law (Gal 4:9)? The question is posed with

reference to bondage to the **elemental powers** (see note on Gal 4:3) because the Galatians had originally been converted to Christianity from paganism, not Judaism (Gal 4:8). The use of the direct question is like Gal 3:3–5.

¶¶[4:8] **Things that by nature are not gods**: or "gods that by nature do not exist."

***[4:10] This is likely a reference to ritual observances from the Old Testament, promoted by opponents: sabbaths or Yom Kippur, new moon, Passover or Pentecost, sabbatical years.

†††[4:11] Cf. Gal 2:2. If the Galatians become **slaves . . . all over again** to the law (Gal 4:9), Paul will have worked in vain among them.

‡‡‡[4:12–20] A strongly personal section. Paul appeals to past ties between the Galatians and himself. He speaks sharply of the opponents (Gal 4:17–18) and pastorally to the Galatians (Gal 4:19–20).

§§§[4:12] **Because I have also become as you are**: a terse phrase in Greek, meaning "Be as I, Paul, am," i.e., living by faith, independent of the law, for, in spite of my background in Judaism (Gal 1:13), I have become as you Galatians are now, a brother in Christ.

¶¶¶[4:13] **Physical illness**: because its nature is not described, some assume an eye disease (Gal 4:15); others, epilepsy; some relate it to 2 Cor 12:7–9. **Originally**: this may also be translated "formerly" or "on the first (of two) visit(s)"; cf. Acts 16:6; 18:23.

****[4:15] **That blessedness of yours**: possibly a reference to the Galatians' initial happy reception of Paul (Gal 4:14) and of his gospel (Gal 1:6; 3:1–4) and their felicitation at such blessedness, but the phrase could also refer ironically to earlier praise by Paul of the Galatians, no longer possible when they turn from the gospel to the claims of the opponents (Gal 4:17–18; 1:7). If the word is a more literal reference to a beatitude, Gal 3:26–28 may be in view.

††††[4:17] **Isolate you**: that is, from the blessings of the gospel and/or from Paul.

---

e. [3:24] 2:16.  f. [3:25] Rom 10:4.  g. [3:26] 4:5–7; Jn 1:12; Rom 8:14–17.  h. [3:27] Rom 6:3; 13:14; Eph 4:24.  i. [3:28] Rom 10:12; 1 Cor 12:13; Col 3:11.  j. [3:29] 3:7, 14, 16, 18; Rom 4:16–17; 9:7 / Gal 4:1, 7; Rom 4:13–14; 8:17; Heb 6:12; Jas 2:5.  k. [4:3] 3:23 / 4:9; Col 2:20.  l. [4:4] Mk 1:15.  m. [4:5] 3:13, 26.  n. [4:6] 3:26; Rom 8:15.  o. [4:7] 3:29; Rom 8:16–17.  p. [4:8] 1 Cor 12:2.

q. [4:9] 4:3; Col 2:20.  r. [4:10] Col 2:16–20.  s. [4:12] 1 Cor 11:1.  t. [4:17] 1:7; 6:12; Acts 20:30.  u. [4:19] 1 Cor 4:14–15; 2 Cor 6:13; 1 Thes 2:7–8.

**An Allegory on Christian Freedom.*** <sup>21</sup>Tell me, you who want to be under the law, do you not listen to the law? <sup>22</sup>For it is written that Abraham had two sons, one by the slave woman and the other by the freeborn woman.<sup>v</sup> <sup>23</sup>The son of the slave woman was born naturally, the son of the freeborn through a promise.<sup>w</sup> <sup>24</sup>Now this is an allegory. These women represent two covenants. One was from Mount Sinai, bearing children for slavery; this is Hagar.<sup>x</sup> <sup>25</sup>Hagar represents Sinai,† a mountain in Arabia; it corresponds to the present Jerusalem, for she is in slavery along with her children. <sup>26</sup>But the Jerusalem above is freeborn, and she is our mother.<sup>y</sup> <sup>27</sup>For it is written:

> "Rejoice, you barren one who bore no
>     children;‡
> break forth and shout, you who were
>     not in labor;
> for more numerous are the children of the
>     deserted one
>     than of her who has a husband."‡

<sup>28</sup>Now you, brothers, like Isaac, are children of the promise.<sup>a</sup> <sup>29</sup>But just as then the child of the flesh persecuted the child of the spirit, it is the same now. <sup>30</sup>But what does the scripture say?

> "Drive out the slave woman and her son!
>     For the son of the slave woman shall
>         not share the inheritance with
>         the son"<sup>b</sup>

of the freeborn. <sup>31</sup>Therefore, brothers, we are children not of the slave woman but of the free-born woman.<sup>c</sup>

## V. EXHORTATION TO CHRISTIAN LIVING

## CHAPTER 5

**The Importance of Faith.**§ <sup>1</sup>For freedom¶ Christ set us free; so stand firm and do not submit again to the yoke of slavery.<sup>d</sup>

<sup>2</sup>It is I, Paul, who am telling you that if you have yourselves circumcised, Christ will be of no benefit to you.<sup>e</sup> <sup>3</sup>Once again I declare to every man who has himself circumcised<sup>f</sup> that he is bound to observe the entire law.** <sup>4</sup>You are separated from Christ, you who are trying to be justified by law; you have fallen from grace. <sup>5</sup>gFor through the Spirit, by faith, we await the hope of righteousness. <sup>6</sup>hFor in Christ Jesus, neither circumcision nor uncircumcision counts for anything, but only faith working through love.††

**Be Not Misled.**‡‡ <sup>7</sup>You were running well;§§ who hindered you from following [the] truth? <sup>8</sup>¶¶That enticement does not come from the one who called you.¶¶ <sup>9</sup>A little yeast leavens the whole batch of dough.<sup>j</sup> <sup>10</sup>I am confident of you in the Lord that you will not take a different view, and that the one who is troubling you will bear the condemnation, whoever he may be.<sup>k</sup> <sup>11</sup>As for me, brothers, if I am still preaching circumcision,*** why am I still being persecuted? In that case, the stumbling block of the cross has been abolished.<sup>l</sup> <sup>12</sup>Would that those who are upsetting you might also castrate themselves!†††

**Freedom for Service.**‡‡‡ <sup>13</sup>For you were called for freedom, brothers.<sup>m</sup> But do not use this freedom

---

*[4:21–31] Paul supports his appeal for the gospel (Gal 4:9; 1:6–9; 2:16; 3:2) by a further argument from scripture (cf. Gal 3:6–18). It involves the relationship of **Abraham** (Gal 3:6–16) to his wife, Sarah, the **freeborn woman**, and to Hagar, **the slave woman**, and the contrast between the sons born to each, **Isaac**, child of promise, and Ishmael, son of Hagar (Gn 16; 21). Only through Isaac is the promise of God preserved. This **allegory** (Gal 4:24), with its equation of the Sinai covenant and Mosaic law with slavery and of the promise of God with freedom, Paul uses only in light of previous arguments. His quotation of Gn 21:10 at Gal 4:30 suggests on a scriptural basis that the Galatians should expel those who are troubling them (Gal 1:7).

†[4:25] **Hagar represents Sinai** . . . : some manuscripts have what seems a geographical note, "For Sinai is a mountain in Arabia."

‡[4:27] Is 54:1 in the Septuagint translation is applied to Sarah as the **barren one** (in Gn 15) who ultimately becomes the mother not only of Isaac but now of numerous children, i.e., of all those who believe, the **children of the promise** (Gal 4:28).

§[5:1–6] Paul begins the exhortations, continuing through Gal 6:10, with an appeal to the Galatians to side with freedom instead of slavery (Gal 5:1). He reiterates his message of justification or righteousness by faith instead of law and circumcision (Gal 5:2–5); cf. Gal 2:16; 3:3. Faith, not circumcision, is what counts (Gal 5:6).

¶[5:1] **Freedom**: Paul stresses as the conclusion from the allegory in Gal 4:21–31 this result of Christ's work for us. It is a principle previously mentioned (Gal 2:4), the responsible use of which Gal 5:13 will emphasize.

**[5:3] Cf. Gal 3:10–12. Just as those who seek to live by the law must carry out all its contents, so those who have faith and live by promise must stand firm in their freedom (Gal 5:1, 13).

††[5:6] Cf. Rom 2:25–26; 1 Cor 7:19; Gal 6:15. The Greek for **faith working through love** or "faith expressing itself through love" can also be rendered as "faith energized by (God's) love."

‡‡[5:7–12] Paul addresses the Galatians directly: with questions (Gal 5:7, 11), a proverb (Gal 5:9), a statement (Gal 5:8), and biting sarcasm (Gal 5:12), seeking to persuade the Galatians to break with those trying to add law and circumcision to Christ as a basis for salvation.

§§[5:7] **Running well**: as in an athletic contest; cf. Gal 2:2; 1 Cor 9:24–26; Phil 2:16; 3:14.

¶¶[5:8] **The one who called you**: see note on Gal 1:6.

***[5:11] **Preaching circumcision**: this could refer to Paul's pre-Christian period (possibly as a missionary for Judaism); more probably it arose as a charge from opponents, based perhaps on the story in Acts 16:1–3 that Paul had circumcised Timothy "on account of the Jews." Unlike the Gentile Titus in Gal 2:3, Timothy was the son of a Jewish mother. The **stumbling block of the cross**: cf. 1 Cor 1:23.

†††[5:12] A sarcastic half-wish that their knife would go beyond mere circumcision; cf. Phil 3:2 and the note there.

‡‡‡[5:13–26] In light of another reminder of the freedom of the gospel (Gal 5:13; cf. Gal 5:1), Paul elaborates on what

---

v. [4:22] Gn 16:15; 21:2–3.   w. [4:23] Gn 17:16; Rom 4:19–20; 9:7–9.
x. [4:24] 3:17 / Ex 19:20 / Gn 16:1.   y. [4:26] Heb 12:22; Rev 21:2.
z. [4:27] Is 54:1.   a. [4:28] Rom 9:8.   b. [4:30] Gn 21:10.   c. [4:31]
3:29; Jn 8:35.

d. [5:1] 2:4; 4:5, 9; Jn 8:32, 36.   e. [5:2] 2:21; Acts 15:1–29.   f. [5:3]
3:10; Rom 2:25; Jas 2:10.   g. [5:5] Rom 8:23, 25.   h. [5:6] 3:28;
6:15; 1 Cor 7:19.   i. [5:8] 1:6.   j. [5:9] 1 Cor 5:6.   k. [5:10] 1:7.
l. [5:11] 6:12, 14; 1 Cor 1:23.   m. [5:13] 5:1 / Rom 6:18; 1 Cor 8:9;
1 Pt 2:16.

as an opportunity for the flesh; rather, serve* one another through love. ¹⁴For the whole law" is fulfilled in one statement, namely, "You shall love your neighbor as yourself."† ¹⁵But if you go on biting and devouring one another, beware that you are not consumed by one another.

¹⁶oI say, then: live by the Spirit and you will certainly not gratify the desire of the flesh.‡ ¹⁷For the flesh has desires against the Spirit, and the Spirit against the flesh; these are opposed to each other, so that you may not do what you want.ᵖ ¹⁸But if you are guided by the Spirit, you are not under the law.�q ¹⁹sNow the works of the flesh are obvious: immorality, impurity, licentiousness,ʳ ²⁰idolatry, sorcery, hatreds, rivalry, jealousy, outbursts of fury, acts of selfishness, dissensions, factions,ˢ ²¹occasions of envy,ᵗ drinking bouts, orgies, and the like. I warn you, as I warned you before, that those who do such things will not inherit the kingdom of God. ²²In contrast, the fruit of the Spirit is love, joy, peace, patience, kindness, generosity, faithfulness,ᵗ ²³gentleness, self-control. Against such there is no law.ᵘ ²⁴Now those who belong to Christ [Jesus] have crucified their flesh with its passions and desires.ᵛ ²⁵If we live in the Spirit, let us also follow the Spirit.ʷ ²⁶Let us not be conceited, provoking one another, envious of one another.ˣ

### CHAPTER 6

**Life in the Community of Christ.**** ¹Brothers, even if a person is caught in some transgression, you who are spiritual should correct that one in a gentle spirit, looking to yourself, so that you also may not be tempted.ʸ ²Bear one another's burdens,ᶻ and so you will fulfill the law of

Christ.†† ³ᵃFor if anyone thinks he is something when he is nothing, he is deluding himself. ⁴‡‡Each one must examine his own work, and then he will have reason to boast with regard to himself alone, and not with regard to someone else; ⁵for each will bear his own load.ᵇ

⁶§§One who is being instructed in the word should share all good things with his instructor.§§ ⁷Make no mistake: God is not mocked, for a person will reap only what he sows, ⁸because the one who sows for his flesh will reap corruption from the flesh, but the one who sows for the spirit will reap eternal life from the spirit.ᵈ ⁹Let us not grow tired of doing good, for in due time we shall reap our harvest, if we do not give up.ᵉ ¹⁰So then, while we have the opportunity, let us do good to all,ᶠ but especially to those who belong to the family of the faith.⁵⁵

## VI. CONCLUSION

**Final Appeal.***** ¹¹See with what large letters††† I am writing to you in my own hand!ᵍ ¹²‡‡‡It is those who want to make a good appearance in the flesh who are trying to compel you to have yourselves circumcised, only that they may not be persecuted for the cross of Christ.ʰ ¹³Not even those having themselves circumcised§§§ observe the law themselves; they only want you to be circumcised so that they may boast of your flesh.

---

††[6:2] **The law of Christ:** cf. Rom 8:2; 1 Cor 9:21; Gal 5:14. The principle of love for others is meant. To **bear one another's burdens** is to "serve one another through love" (Gal 5:13).

‡‡[6:4–5] Self-examination is the cure for self-deception. Compare what you are with what you were before, and give the glory to God; cf. Rom 6:19–22. **Load:** used elsewhere of a soldier's pack. Correcting one's own conduct avoids burdening others with it.

§§[6:6] Implies oral instruction in the faith by catechists; these are to be remunerated for their service; cf. Rom 15:27.

¶¶[6:10] **The family of the faith:** the Christian household or church. Doing good has a universal object (**to all**), but the local community makes specific the reality of those to be served.

***[6:11–18] A postscript in Paul's own hand, as was his practice (see 1 Cor 16:21; 2 Thes 3:17). Paul summarizes his appeal against his opponents (Gal 6:12–13), then returns to his message of glorying in the cross, not in circumcision, as the means of salvation (Gal 6:14–15; cf. Gal 5:11). A benediction follows at Gal 6:16. In the polemical spirit that the attack on his apostleship called forth (Gal 1:11–2:21), Paul reasserts his missionary credentials (Gal 6:17) before giving a final benediction (Gal 6:18).

†††[6:11] **Large letters:** in contrast to the finer hand of the scribe who wrote the letter up to this point. The larger Greek letters make Paul's message even more emphatic. Some find a hint of poor eyesight on Paul's part. See note on Gal 4:13.

‡‡‡[6:12–15] The Jewish Christian opponents wished **not** to be **persecuted,** possibly by Jews. But since Judaism seems to have had a privileged status as a religion in the Roman empire, circumcised Christians might, if taken as Jews, thereby avoid persecution from the Romans. In any case, Paul instead stresses conformity with **the cross of our Lord Jesus Christ;** cf. Gal 2:19–21; 5:11.

§§§[6:13] **Those having themselves circumcised:** other manuscripts read, "those who have had themselves circumcised."

---

believers are called to do and be: they fulfill the law by love of neighbor (Gal 5:14–15), walking in the Spirit (Gal 5:16–26), as is illustrated by concrete **fruit of the Spirit** in their lives.

*[5:13] **Serve . . . through love:** cf. Gal 5:6.

†[5:14] Lv 19:18, emphasized by Jesus (Mt 22:39; Lk 10:27); cf. Rom 13:8–10.

‡[5:16–25] **Spirit . . . flesh:** cf. Gal 3:3 and the note on Rom 8:1–13.

§[5:19–23] Such lists of vices and virtues (cf. Rom 1:29–31; 1 Cor 6:9–10) were common in the ancient world. Paul contrasts **works of the flesh** (Gal 5:19) with **fruit** (not "works" or **the Spirit** (Gal 5:22). Not law, but the Spirit, leads to such traits.

¶[5:21] **Occasions of envy:** after the Greek word *phthonoi,* "envies," some manuscripts add a similar sounding one, *phonoi,* "murders."

**[6:1–10] The ethical exhortations begun at Gal 5:1 continue with a variety of admonitions to the community (**brothers:** see note on Gal 1:2). Nearly every sentence contains a separate item of practical advice; the faith and freedom of the gospel underlie each maxim. Tensions and temptation within communal life have previously been addressed in Gal 5:15, 26, and Gal 6:1 continues with a case in which a **person is caught in some transgression** such as those in Gal 5:19–21; cf. Gal 2:17.

n. [5:14] Lv 19:18; Mt 22:39; Rom 13:8–10.  o. [5:16] 5:24–25; Rom 8:5.  p. [5:17] Rom 7:15, 23; 8:6.  q. [5:18] Rom 6:14; 8:14.  r. [5:19–21] Rom 1:29–31; 1 Cor 6:9–10; Col 3:5–6, 8.  s. [5:20] Rev 22:15.  t. [5:22] Eph 5:9 / 1 Cor 13:4–7; 2 Cor 6:6; 1 Tm 4:12; 2 Pt 1:6.  u. [5:23] 1 Tm 1:9.  v. [5:24] 2:19; Rom 6:6; 8:13.  w. [5:25] 5:16.  x. [5:26] Phil 2:3.  y. [6:1] Mt 18:15; Jas 5:19 / 1 Cor 10:12–13.  z. [6:2] Col 3:13 / 1 Cor 9:21.

a. [6:3–4] 1 Cor 3:18; 8:2; 2 Cor 12:11.  b. [6:5] Rom 14:12.  c. [6:6] 1 Cor 9:14.  d. [6:8] Prv 11:18; Rom 8:6, 13.  e. [6:9] 2 Thes 3:13; Heb 12:1–3.  f. [6:10] 1 Thes 5:15.  g. [6:11] 1 Cor 16:21.  h. [6:12] 5:2, 11.

[14] But may I never boast except in the cross of our Lord Jesus Christ, through which[*] the world has been crucified to me, and I to the world.[i] [15] For neither does circumcision mean anything, nor does uncircumcision,[j] but only a new creation.[†] [16] Peace and mercy be to all who follow this rule[‡] and to the Israel of God.[k]

[17] From now on, let no one make troubles for me; for I bear the marks of Jesus[§] on my body.[l] [18] The grace of our Lord Jesus Christ be with your spirit, brothers. Amen.[m]

---

[*][6:14] **Through which**: or "through whom."
[†][6:15] **New creation**: or "new creature"; cf. 2 Cor 5:17.
[‡][6:16] **This rule**: the principle in Gal 6:14–15. **The Israel of God**: while the church may be meant (the phrase can be translated "to all who follow this rule, even the Israel of God";

cf. Gal 6:10; 1 Cor 10:18), the reference may also be to God's ancient people, Israel; cf. Ps 125:5; 128:6.
§[6:17] **The marks of Jesus**: slaves were often branded by marks (stigmata) burned into their flesh to show to whom they belonged; so also were devotees of pagan gods. Paul implies that instead of outdated circumcision, his body bears the scars of his apostolic labors (2 Cor 11:22–31), such as floggings (Acts 16:22; 2 Cor 11:25) and stonings (Acts 14:19), that mark him as belonging to the Christ who suffered (cf. Rom 6:3; 2 Cor 4:10; Col 1:24) and will protect his own.

i. [6:14] 2:20; 1 Cor 2:2.   j. [6:15] 5:6; 1 Cor 7:19 / 2 Cor 5:17.   k. [6:16] Ps 125:5; 128:6.

l. [6:17] 2 Cor 4:10.   m. [6:18] Phil 4:23; 2 Tm 4:22; Phlm 25.

# THE LETTER TO THE
# EPHESIANS

༄

Ephesians is the great Pauline letter about the church. It deals, however, not so much with a congregation in the city of Ephesus in Asia Minor as with the worldwide church, the head of which is Christ (Eph 4:15), the purpose of which is to be the instrument for making God's plan of salvation known throughout the universe (Eph 3:9–10). Yet this ecclesiology is anchored in God's saving love, shown in Jesus Christ (Eph 2:4–10), and the whole of redemption is rooted in the plan and accomplishment of the triune God (Eph 1:3–14). The language is often that of doxology (Eph 1:3–14) and prayer (cf. Eph 1:15–23; 3:14–19), indeed of liturgy and hymns (Eph 3:20–21; 5:14).

The majestic chapters of Ephesians emphasize the unity in the church of Christ that has come about for both Jews and Gentiles within God's household (Eph 1:15–2:22, especially Eph 2:11–22) and indeed the "seven unities" of church, Spirit, hope; one Lord, faith, and baptism; and the one God (Eph 4:4–6). Yet the concern is not with the church for its own sake but rather as the means for mission in the world (Eph 3:1–4:24). The gifts Christ gives its members are to lead to growth and renewal (Eph 4:7–24). Ethical admonition is not lacking either; all aspects of human life and relationships are illumined by the light of Christ (Eph 4:25–6:20).

The letter is seemingly addressed by Paul to Christians in Ephesus (Eph 1:1), a place where the apostle labored for well over two years (Acts 19:10). Yet there is a curiously impersonal tone to the writing for a community with which Paul was so intimately acquainted (cf. Eph 3:2 and Eph 4:21). There are no personal greetings (cf. Eph 6:23). More significantly, important early manuscripts omit the words "in Ephesus" (see note on Eph 1:1). Many therefore regard the letter as an encyclical or "circular letter" sent to a number of churches in Asia Minor, the addressees to be designated in each place by its bearer, Tychicus (Eph 6:21–22). Others think that Ephesians is the letter referred to in Col 4:16 as "to the Laodiceans."

Paul, who is designated as the sole author at Eph 1:1, is described in almost unparalleled terms with regard to the significant role he has in God's plan for bringing the Gentiles to faith in Christ (Eph 3:1–12). Yet at the time of writing he is clearly in prison (Eph 3:1; 4:1; 6:20), suffering afflictions (Eph 3:13). Traditionally this "Captivity Epistle" has, along with Colossians, Philippians, and Philemon, been dated to an imprisonment in Rome, likely in A.D. 61–63. Others appeal to an earlier imprisonment, perhaps in Caesarea (Acts 23:27–27:2). Since the early nineteenth century, however, much of critical scholarship has considered the letter's style and use of words (especially when compared with Colossians), its concept of the church, and other points of doctrine put forward by the writer as grounds for serious doubt about authorship by Paul. The letter may then be the work of a secretary writing at the apostle's direction or of a later disciple who sought to develop Paul's ideas for a new situation around A.D. 80–100.

The principal divisions of the Letter to the Ephesians are the following:

I. Address (1:1–14)
II. Unity of the Church in Christ (1:15–2:22)
III. World Mission of the Church (3:1–4:24)
IV. Daily Conduct, an Expression of Unity (4:25–6:20)
V. Conclusion (6:21–24)

## I. ADDRESS

## CHAPTER 1

**Greeting.**[*] [1:1]Paul, an apostle of Christ Jesus by the will of God, to the holy ones who are [in Ephesus][†] faithful in Christ Jesus:[a] [2]grace to you and peace from God our Father and the Lord Jesus Christ.[b]

**The Father's Plan of Salvation.** [3][‡]Blessed be the God and Father of our Lord Jesus Christ,[c] who has blessed us in Christ with every spiritual blessing in the heavens,[§] [4]as he chose us in him, before the foundation of the world, to be holy and without blemish before him.[d] In love [5]he destined us for adoption to himself through Jesus Christ, in accord with the favor of his will,[e] [6]for the praise of the glory of his grace that he granted us in the beloved.[f]

**Fulfillment Through Christ.** [7]In him we have redemption by his blood, the forgiveness of transgressions, in accord with the riches of his grace[g] [8]that he lavished upon us. In all wisdom and insight,[h] [9]he has made known to us the mystery[ı] of his will in accord with his favor that he

set forth in him[i] [10]as a plan for the fullness of times, to sum up all things in Christ, in heaven and on earth.[j]

**Inheritance Through the Spirit.** [11]In him we were also chosen, destined in accord with the purpose of the One who accomplishes all things according to the intention of his will,[k] [12]so that we might exist for the praise of his glory, we who first hoped[**] in Christ. [13]In him you also, who have heard the word of truth, the gospel of your salvation, and have believed in him, were sealed[††] with the promised holy Spirit,[l] [14]which is the first installment[‡‡] of our inheritance toward redemption as God's possession, to the praise of his glory.[m]

## II. UNITY OF THE CHURCH IN CHRIST

**The Church as Christ's Body.**[§§] [15]Therefore, I, too, hearing of your faith in the Lord Jesus and of your love[¶¶] for all the holy ones,[n] [16]do not cease giving thanks for you, remembering you in my prayers,[o] [17]that the God of our Lord Jesus Christ, the Father of glory, may give you a spirit of wisdom and revelation resulting in knowledge of him.[p] [18]May the eyes of [your] hearts be enlightened, that you may know what is the hope that belongs to his call, what are the riches of glory in his inheritance among the holy ones,[q] [19]and what is the surpassing greatness of his power for us who believe, in accord with the exercise of his great might,[r] [20]which he worked in Christ, raising him from the dead and seating him at his right hand in the heavens,[s] [21]far above every principality, authority, power, and dominion, and every name that is named not only in this age but also in the one to come.[t] [22]And he put all things beneath his feet and gave him as head

---

*[1:1–2] For the epistolary form used at the beginning of letters, see note on Rom 1:1–7. Twenty-two of the thirty Greek words in Eph 1:1–2 also occur in Col 1:1–2.

†[1:1] **[In Ephesus]**: the phrase is lacking in important early witnesses such as P[46] (3rd cent.), and Sinaiticus and Vaticanus (4th cent.), appearing in the latter two as a fifth-century addition. Basil and Origen mention its absence from manuscripts. See Introduction. Without the phrase, the Greek can be rendered, as in Col 1:2, "to the holy ones and faithful brothers in Christ."

‡[1:3–14] While a Pauline letter usually continues after the greeting with a prayer of thanksgiving, as in Eph 1:15–23 below, Ephesians first inserts a blessing of God for the blessings Christians have experienced, as in 2 Cor 1:3–4 and 1 Pt 1:3–12. The blessing here, akin to a Jewish *berakah*, is rich in images almost certainly drawn from hymns and liturgy. Many ideas here are also found in Col 1:3–23. Certain phrases are frequently repeated, such as **in Christ** (Eph 1:3, 10, 12) or **in him** (Eph 1:4, 7, 9, 11, 13) or **in the beloved** (Eph 1:6) and **(for) the praise of his) glory** (Eph 1:6, 12, 14). Some terms like **chose** (Eph 1:4) and **destined** (Eph 1:5) reflect Old Testament theology (Dt 7:7; 9:4–6; 23:5) or Pauline themes (**redemption**, Eph 1:7, 14; **grace**, Eph 1:6, 7) or specific emphases in Colossians (**forgiveness**, Col 1:14). A triadic structure is discernible in Eph 1:3–14: **God the Father** (Eph 1:3–6, 8, 11), **Christ** (Eph 1:3, 5, 7–10, 12), and the **Spirit** (Eph 1:13–14). The spiritual blessings Christians have received through Christ (Eph 1:3) are gratefully enumerated: the call to holiness (Eph 1:4; cf. Col 1:22); the gift of divine **adoption** establishing a unique spiritual relationship with God the Father through Christ (Eph 1:5; cf. Gal 4:5); liberation from sin through Christ's sacrificial death (Eph 1:7); revelation of God's plan of salvation in Christ (Eph 1:9; cf. Eph 3:3–4; Rom 16:25); the gift of election and faith in Christ bestowed upon Jewish Christians (see note on Eph 1:12, **we who first hoped in Christ**); and finally, the same gift granted to Gentiles (Eph 1:13, **you also**). In the Christ-centered faith and existence of the Christian communities the apostle sees the predetermined **plan** of God to bring all creation under the final rule of Christ (Eph 1:4–5, 9–10) being **made known** (Eph 1:9) and carried through, to God's **glory** (Eph 1:6, 12, 14).

§[1:3] **In the heavens**: literally, "in the heavenlies" or "in the heavenly places," a term in Ephesians for the divine realm.

¶[1:9] **Mystery**: as in Rom 16:25; Col 1:26–27 and elsewhere, a secret of God now revealed in the **plan** to save and **sum up all things in Christ** (Eph 1:10); cf. Eph 3:3–6.

**[1:12] **We who first hoped**: probably Jewish Christians (contrast Eph 1:13, **you**, the Gentiles); possibly the people of Israel, "we who already enjoyed the hope of Christ," or perhaps present hope in contrast to future redemption (cf. Eph 1:14).

††[1:13] **Sealed**: by God, in baptism; cf. Eph 4:30; 2 Cor 1:22.

‡‡[1:14] **First installment**: down payment by God on full salvation, as at 2 Cor 1:22.

§§[1:15–23] See note on Rom 1:8 for the thanksgiving form in a letter. Much of the content parallels thoughts in Col 1:3–20. The prayer moves from God and Christ (Eph 1:17, 20–21) to the Ephesians (Eph 1:17–19) and the church (Eph 1:22–23). Paul asks that the blessing imparted by God the Father (Eph 1:3) to the Ephesians will be strengthened in them through the message of the gospel (Eph 1:13, 17–19). Those blessings are seen in the context of God's **might** in establishing the sovereignty of Christ over all other creatures (Eph 1:19–21) and in appointing him **head** of the church (Eph 1:22–23). For the allusion to angelic spirits in Eph 1:21, see Rom 8:38 and Col 1:16. Here, as in 1 Cor 15:24–25 and Col 2:15, every such **principality** and **power** is made subject to Christ.

¶¶[1:15] **Your faith . . . your love**: some manuscripts omit the latter phrase, but cf. Col 1:4.

---

a. [1:1] Rom 1:7; 1 Cor 1:1–2; Col 1:1.   b. [1:2] Col 1:2.   c. [1:3] 2:6; 2 Cor 1:3.   d. [1:4] 5:27; Jn 15:16; 17:24; Rom 8:29; 2 Thes 2:13.   e. [1:5] Jn 1:12; 1 Jn 3:1.   f. [1:6] Mt 3:17; Col 1:13.   g. [1:7] 2:7–13; Rom 3:24; Col 1:14, 20.   h. [1:8] Col 1:9.

i. [1:9] 3:3, 9; Rom 16:25.   j. [1:10] Gal 4:4; Col 1:16, 20.   k. [1:11] Is 46:10; Rom 8:28; Col 1:12; Rev 4:11.   l. [1:13] 4:30; Acts 2:33; Col 1:5–6.   m. [1:14] 2 Cor 1:22; 5:5.   n. [1:15] Col 1:3–4; Phlm 4–5.   o. [1:16] Col 1:3, 9.   p. [1:17] 3:14, 16; Col 1:9–10; 1 Jn 5:20.   q. [1:18] 4:4; Col 1:12, 27.   r. [1:19] 2 Cor 13:4; Col 1:11; 2:12.   s. [1:20] Ps 110:1; Heb 1:3.   t. [1:21] Phil 2:9; Col 1:16; 1 Pt 3:22.

over all things to the church,ᵘ ²³which is his body,ˣ the fullness of the one who fills all things in every way.ᵛ

## CHAPTER 2†

**Generosity of God's Plan.**‡ ¹ᵂYou were dead in your transgressions and sins§ ²in which you once lived following the age of this world,ˢ following the ruler of the power of the air, the spirit that is now at work in the disobedient.ˣ ³All of us once lived among them in the desires of our flesh, following the wishes of the flesh and the impulses, and we were by nature children of wrath, like the rest.ʸ ⁴But God, who is rich in mercy, because of the great love he had for us, ⁵·even when we were dead in our transgressions, brought us to life with Christ** (by grace you have been saved),

⁶raised us up with him, and seated us with him in the heavens in Christ Jesus,ᵃ ⁷that in the ages to come he might show the immeasurable riches of his grace in his kindness to us in Christ Jesus.ᵇ ⁸For by grace you have been saved through faith, and this is not from you; it is the gift of God;ᶜ ⁹it is not from works, so no one may boast.ᵈ ¹⁰For we are his handiwork, created in Christ Jesus for the good works that God has prepared in advance, that we should live in them.ᵉ

**One in Christ.**†† ¹¹Therefore, remember that at one time you, Gentiles in the flesh, called the uncircumcision by those called the circumcision, which is done in the flesh by human hands, ¹²were at that time without Christ, alienated from the community of Israel‡‡ and strangers to the covenants of promise, without hope and without God in the world.ᶠ ¹³But now in Christ Jesus you who once were far off have become near by the blood of Christ.ᵍ

¹⁴·§§For he is our peace, he who made both one and broke down the dividing wall of enmity, through his flesh,ʰ ¹⁵abolishing the law with its commandments and legal claims, that he might create in himself one new person¶¶ in place of the two, thus establishing peace,ⁱ ¹⁶and might reconcile both with God, in one body, through the cross, putting that enmity to death by it.ʲ ¹⁷He came and preached peace to you who were far off and peace to those who were near,ᵏ ¹⁸for through him we both have access in one Spirit to the Father.ˡ

¹⁹So then you are no longer strangers and sojourners, but you are fellow citizens with the holy ones and members of the household of God,ᵐ ²⁰built upon the foundation of the

---

*[1:23] **His body**: the church (Eph 1:22); cf. note on Col 1:18. Only in Ephesians and Colossians is Christ the **head** of the **body**, in contrast to the view in 1 Cor 12 and Rom 12:4–8 where Christ is equated with the entire body or community. **Fullness**: see note on Col 1:19. Some take **the one who fills** as God, others as Christ (cf. Eph 4:10). If in Christ "dwells the fullness of the deity bodily" (Col 2:9), then, as God "fills" Christ, Christ in turn fills the church and the believer (Eph 3:19; 5:18). But the difficult phrases here may also allow the church to be viewed as the "complement" of Christ who is "being filled" as God's plan for the universe is carried out through the church (cf. Eph 3:9–10).

†[2:1–22] The gospel of **salvation** (Eph 1:13) that God **worked in Christ** (Eph 1:20) is reiterated in terms of what God's **great love** (Eph 2:4), expressed in Christ, means for us. The passage sometimes addresses **you**, Gentiles (Eph 2:1–2, 8, 11–13, 19, 22), but other times speaks of **all of us** who believe (Eph 2:3–7, 10, 14, 18). In urging people to **remember** their grim past when they were **dead** in sins (Eph 2:1–3, 11–12) and what they are **now in Christ** (Eph 2:4–10, 13), the author sees both Jew and Gentile reconciled with God, now **one new person**, a new humanity, **one body, the household of God**, a **temple** and **dwelling place** of God's Spirit (Eph 2:15–16, 19–22). The presentation falls into two parts, the second stressing more the meaning for the church.

‡[2:1–10] The recipients of Paul's letter have experienced, in their redemption from **transgressions and sins**, the effect of Christ's supremacy over the power of the devil (Eph 2:1–2; cf. Eph 6:11–12), who rules not from the netherworld but from the **air** between Our God in heaven and human beings on earth. Both Jew and Gentile have experienced, through Christ, God's free gift of salvation that already marks them for a future heavenly destiny (Eph 2:3–7). The language **dead**, **raised us up**, and **seated us . . . in the heavens** closely parallels Jesus' own passion and Easter experience. The terms in Eph 2:8–9 describe salvation in the way Paul elsewhere speaks of justification: **by grace**, **through faith**, **the gift of God**, **not from works**; cf. Gal 2:16–21; Rom 3:24–28. Christians are a newly created people in Christ, fashioned by God for a life of goodness (Eph 2:10).

§[2:1–7] These verses comprise one long sentence in Greek, the main verb coming in Eph 2:5, God **brought us to life**, the object you/us **dead in . . . transgressions** being repeated in Eph 2:1, 5; cf. Col 2:13.

¶[2:2] **Age of this world**: or "aeon," a term found in gnostic thought, possibly synonymous with the **rulers of this world**, but also reflecting the Jewish idea of "two ages," this present evil age and "the age to come"; cf. 1 Cor 3:19; 5:10; 7:31; Gal 1:4; Ti 2:12. **The disobedient**: literally, "the sons of disobedience," a Semitism as at Is 30:9.

**[2:5] Our relation through baptism **with Christ**, the risen Lord, is depicted in terms of realized eschatology, as already exaltation, though Eph 2:7 brings in the future aspect too.

††[2:11–22] The Gentiles lacked Israel's messianic expectation, lacked the various **covenants** God made with **Israel**, lacked **hope** of salvation and knowledge of the true **God** (Eph 2:11–12); but through Christ all these religious barriers between Jew and Gentile have been transcended (Eph 2:13–14) by the abolition of the Mosaic covenant-law (Eph 2:15) for the sake of uniting Jew and Gentile into a single religious community (Eph 2:15–16), imbued with the same holy **Spirit** and worshiping the same **Father** (Eph 2:18). The Gentiles are now included in God's **household** (Eph 2:19) as it arises upon the **foundation** of **apostles** assisted by those endowed with the prophetic gift (Eph 3:5), the preachers of Christ (Eph 2:20; cf. 1 Cor 12:28). With Christ as the **capstone** (Eph 2:20; cf. Is 28:16; Mt 21:42), they are being built into the holy **temple** of God's people where the divine presence dwells (Eph 2:21–22).

‡‡[2:12] **The community of Israel**: or "commonwealth"; cf. Eph 4:18. **The covenants**: cf. Rom 9:4: with Abraham, with Moses, with David.

§§[2:14–16] The elaborate imagery here combines pictures of Christ as **our peace** (Is 9:5), his crucifixion, the ending of the Mosaic law (cf. Col 2:14), reconciliation (2 Cor 5:18–21), and the destruction of **the dividing wall** such as kept people from God in the temple or a barrier in the heavens.

¶¶[2:15] **One new person**: a corporate body, the Christian community, made up of Jews and Gentiles, replacing ancient divisions; cf. Rom 1:16.

a. [2:6] Rom 8:10–11; Phil 3:20; Col 2:12.   b. [2:7] 1:7.   c. [2:8] Rom 3:24; Gal 2:16.   d. [2:9] 1 Cor 1:29.   e. [2:10] 4:24; Ti 2:14.   f. [2:12] Rom 9:4; Col 1:21, 27.   g. [2:13] 2:17; Is 57:19; Col 1:20.   h. [2:14] Gal 3:28.   i. [2:15] 2 Cor 5:17; Col 2:14.   j. [2:16] Col 1:20, 22.   k. [2:17] Is 57:19; Zec 9:10.   l. [2:18] 3:12.   m. [2:19] Heb 12:22–23.

---

u. [1:22] 4:15; Ps 8:7; Mt 28:18; Col 1:18.   v. [1:23] 4:10, 12; Rom 12:5; 1 Cor 12:27; Col 1:19.   w. [2:1] Col 1:21; 2:13.   x. [2:2] 6:12; Jn 12:31; Col 1:13.   y. [2:3] Col 3:6–7.   z. [2:5] Rom 5:8; 6:13; Col 2:13.

apostles and prophets,[n] with Christ Jesus himself as the capstone.[*] [21]Through him the whole structure is held together and grows into a temple sacred in the Lord;[o] [22]in him you also are being built together into a dwelling place of God in the Spirit.[p]

## III. WORLD MISSION OF THE CHURCH

### CHAPTER 3

**Commission to Preach God's Plan.**[†] [1]Because of this,[q] I, Paul, a prisoner of Christ[‡] [Jesus] for you Gentiles— [2]if, as I suppose, you have heard of the stewardship[§] of God's grace that was given to me for your benefit,[r] [3][namely, that] the mystery[¶] was made known to me by revelation, as I have written briefly earlier.[s] [4]When you read this you can understand my insight into the mystery of Christ, [5]which was not made known to human beings in other generations as it has now been revealed to his holy apostles and prophets by the Spirit,[t] [6]that the Gentiles are coheirs, members of the same body, and copartners in the promise in Christ Jesus through the gospel.[u]

[7]Of this I became a minister by the gift of God's grace that was granted me in accord with the exercise of his power.[v] [8]To me, the very least of all the holy ones, this grace was given, to preach to the Gentiles the inscrutable riches of Christ,[w] [9]and to bring to light [for all][**] what is the plan of the mystery hidden from ages past in God who

created all things,[x] [10]so that the manifold wisdom of God might now be made known through the church to the principalities and authorities[††] in the heavens.[y] [11]This was according to the eternal purpose that he accomplished in Christ Jesus our Lord, [12]in whom we have boldness of speech and confidence of access through faith in him.[z] [13]So I ask you not to lose heart over my afflictions for you; this is your glory.[a]

**Prayer for the Readers.**[‡‡] [14]For this reason I kneel before the Father, [15]from whom every family[§§] in heaven and on earth is named, [16]that he may grant you in accord with the riches of his glory to be strengthened with power through his Spirit in the inner self,[b] [17]and that Christ may dwell in your hearts through faith; that you, rooted and grounded in love,[c] [18]may have strength to comprehend with all the holy ones what is the breadth and length and height and depth,[d] [19]and to know the love of Christ that surpasses knowledge, so that you may be filled with all the fullness of God.[e]

[20]Now to him who is able to accomplish far more than all we ask or imagine, by the power at work within us,[f] [21]to him be glory in the church and in Christ Jesus to all generations, forever and ever. Amen.

### CHAPTER 4

**Unity in the Body.**[¶¶] [1]I, then, a prisoner for the Lord, urge you to live in a manner worthy of

---

*[2:20] **Capstone**: the Greek can also mean cornerstone or keystone.

†[3:1–13] Paul reflects on his mission to the Gentiles. He alludes to his call and appointment to the apostolic office (Eph 3:2–3) and how his **insight** through revelation, as well as that of the other apostles and charismatic prophets in the church (Eph 3:4–5), has deepened understanding of God's plan of salvation in Christ. Paul is the special herald (Eph 3:7) of a new **promise** to the **Gentiles** (Eph 3:6): that the divine plan includes them in the spiritual benefits promised to Israel. Not only is this unique apostolic role his; Paul also has been given the task of explaining to all the divine **plan** of salvation (Eph 3:8–9), once **hidden**. Through **the church**, God's plan to save through Christ is becoming manifest to angelic beings (Eph 3:10; cf. Eph 1:21), in accord with God's **purpose** (Eph 3:11). The fulfillment of the plan in Christ gives the whole church more **confidence** through **faith** in God (Eph 3:12). The readers of this letter are also thereby encouraged to greater confidence despite Paul's imprisonment (Eph 3:13).

‡[3:1] **A prisoner of Christ**: see Introduction. Paul abruptly departs from his train of thought at the end of Eph 3:1, leaving an incomplete sentence.

§[3:2] **Stewardship**: the Greek is the same term employed at Eph 1:10 for the **plan** that God administers (Col 1:25) and in which Paul plays a key role.

¶[3:3–4] **The mystery**: God's resolve to deliver Gentiles along with Israel through Christ; cf. notes on Eph 1:10; 3:9.

**[3:9] **[For all]**: while some think this phrase was added so as to yield the sense "to enlighten all about the plan . . . ," it is more likely that some manuscripts and Fathers omitted it accidentally or to avoid the idea that **all** conflicted with Paul's assignment to preach to **the Gentiles** (Eph 3:8) specifically.

††[3:10] **Principalities and authorities**: see note on Eph 1:15–23 regarding Eph 3:21.

‡‡[3:14–21] The apostle prays that those he is addressing may, like the rest of the church, deepen their understanding of God's plan of salvation in Christ. It is a plan that affects the whole universe (Eph 3:15) with **the breadth and length and height and depth** of God's love in Christ (Eph 3:18) or possibly the universe in all its dimensions. The apostle prays that they may perceive the redemptive love of Christ for them and be completely immersed in the fullness of God (Eph 3:19). The prayer concludes with a doxology to God (Eph 3:20–21).

§§[3:14–15] **Every family**: in the Greek there is wordplay on the word for **the Father** (*patria, patēr*). The phrase could also mean "God's whole family" (cf. Eph 2:21).

¶¶[4:1–16] A general plea for unity in the church. Christians have been fashioned through the **Spirit** into a single harmonious religious community (**one body**, Eph 4:4, 12; cf. Eph 4:16), belonging to a single **Lord** (in contrast to the many gods of the pagan world), and by one way of salvation through **faith**, brought out especially by the significance of **baptism** (Eph 4:1–6; cf. Rom 6:1–11). But Christian unity is more than adherence to a common belief. It is manifested in the exalted Christ's gifts to individuals to serve so as to make the community more Christlike (Eph 4:11–16). This teaching on Christ as the source of the gifts is introduced in Eph 4:8 by a citation of Ps 68:18, which depicts Yahweh triumphantly leading Israel to salvation in Jerusalem. It is here understood of Christ, ascending **above all the heavens**, the **head** of the church; through his redemptive death, resurrection, and ascension he has become the source of the church's spiritual gifts. The "descent" of Christ (Eph 4:9–10) refers more probably to the incarnation (cf. Phil 2:6–8) than to Christ's presence after his death in the world of the dead (cf. 1 Pt 3:19).

---

n. [2:20] Is 28:16; Rev 21:14.   o. [2:21] 1 Cor 3:16; Col 2:19. p. [2:22] 1 Pt 2:5.   q. [3:1] Phil 1:7, 13; Col 1:24–29; 4:18; Phlm 9; 2 Tm 2:9.   r. [3:2] Col 1:25.   s. [3:3] 1:9–10; Col 1:26.   t. [3:5] Col 1:26.   u. [3:6] 2:13, 18–19.   v. [3:7] Rom 15:15; Col 1:25, 29. w. [3:8] 1 Cor 15:8–10; Gal 1:16; 2:7–9.

x. [3:9] Rom 16:25; Col 1:26–27.   y. [3:10] 1 Pt 1:12.   z. [3:12] Rom 5:1–2; Heb 4:16.   a. [3:13] Col 1:22, 24; 2 Tm 2:10.   b. [3:16] 6:10; Rom 7:22; 2 Cor 4:16; Col 1:11.   c. [3:17] Jn 14:23; Col 1:23; 2:7.   d. [3:18] Col 2:2.   e. [3:19] Col 2:3, 9.   f. [3:20] Rom 16:25–27; Col 1:29.

the call you have received,[g] [2]with all humility and gentleness, with patience, bearing with one another through love,[h] [3]striving to preserve the unity of the spirit through the bond of peace:[i] [4]one body and one Spirit, as you were also called to the one hope of your call;[j] [5]one Lord, one faith, one baptism;[k] [6]one God and Father of all, who is over all and through all and in all.[l]

**Diversity of Gifts.** [7]But grace was given to each of us according to the measure of Christ's gift.[m] [8]Therefore, it says:

"He ascended[†] on high and took prisoners captive;
he gave gifts to men."[n]

[9]What does "he ascended" mean except that he also descended into the lower [regions] of the earth? [10]The one who descended is also the one who ascended far above all the heavens, that he might fill all things.

[11][‡]And he gave some as apostles, others as prophets, others as evangelists, others as pastors and teachers,[o] [12]to equip the holy ones for the work of ministry,[§] for building up the body of Christ, [13]until we all attain to the unity of faith and knowledge of the Son of God, to mature manhood,[¶] to the extent of the full stature of Christ,[p] [14]so that we may no longer be infants, tossed by waves and swept along by every wind of teaching arising from human trickery, from their cunning in the interests of deceitful scheming.[q] [15]Rather, living the truth in love, we should grow in every way into him who is the head,[r] Christ,[**] [16]from whom the whole body, joined and held together by every supporting ligament, with the proper functioning of each

part, brings about the body's growth and builds itself up in love.[s]

**Renewal in Christ.**[††] [17]So I declare and testify in the Lord that you must no longer live as the Gentiles do, in the futility of their minds;[t] [18]darkened in understanding, alienated from the life of God because of their ignorance, because of their hardness of heart,[u] [19]they have become callous and have handed themselves over to licentiousness for the practice of every kind of impurity to excess.[v] [20]That is not how you learned Christ, [21]assuming that you have heard of him and were taught in him, as truth is in Jesus, [22]that you should put away the old self of your former way of life, corrupted through deceitful desires,[w] [23]and be renewed in the spirit of your minds,[x] [24]and put on[‡‡] the new self, created in God's way in righteousness and holiness of truth.[y]

## IV. DAILY CONDUCT, AN EXPRESSION OF UNITY[§§]

**Rules for the New Life.** [25]Therefore, putting away falsehood, speak the truth, each one to his neighbor, for we are members one of another.[z] [26]Be angry but do not sin;[a] do not let the sun set on your anger,[¶¶] [27]and do not leave room for the devil.[b] [28]The thief must no longer steal, but rather labor, doing honest work[***] with his [own] hands, so that he may have something to share with one in need.[c] [29]No foul language should come out of your mouths, but only such as is good for needed edification, that it may impart grace to those who hear.[d] [30]And do not grieve the holy Spirit of God, with which you were sealed for the day of redemption.[†††] [31]All bitterness, fury, anger, shouting, and reviling must be removed from you, along with all malice.[e] [32][And] be kind to one another, compassionate, forgiving one another as God has forgiven you in Christ.[f]

## CHAPTER 5
[1]So be imitators of God,[‡‡‡] as beloved children,[g] [2]and live in love, as Christ loved us and handed

---

*[4:4–6] The "seven unities" (church, **Spirit**, **hope**; **Lord**, **faith** in Christ [Eph 1:13], **baptism; one God**) reflect the triune structure of later creeds in reverse.

†[4:8–10] While the emphasis is on an ascension and gift-giving by Christ, there is also a reference in taking **prisoners captive** to the aeons and powers mentioned at Eph 1:21; 2:2; 3:10; 6:12.

‡[4:11] Concerning this list of ministers, cf. 1 Cor 12:28 and Rom 12:6–8. **Evangelists:** missionary preachers (cf. Acts 21:8; 2 Tm 4:5), not those who wrote gospels. **Pastors and teachers:** a single group in the Greek, shepherding congregations.

§[4:12] The ministerial leaders in Eph 4:11 are to equip the whole people of God for their **work of ministry**.

¶[4:13] **Mature manhood:** literally, "a perfect man" (cf. Col 1:28), possibly the "one new person" of Eph 2:15, though there *anthrōpos* suggests humanity, while here *anēr* is the term for male. This personage becomes visible in the church's growing to its fullness in the unity of those who believe in Christ.

**[4:15–16] The head, Christ:** cf. Col 1:18 and contrast 1 Cor 12:12–27 and Rom 12:4–5 where Christ is identified with the whole body, including the head. The imagery may derive from ancient views in medicine, the **head** coordinating and caring for the body, each **ligament** (perhaps the ministers of Eph 4:11) supporting the whole. But as at Eph 2:19–22, where the temple is depicted as a growing organism, there may also be the idea here of growing toward the capstone, Christ.

††[4:17–24] Paul begins to indicate how the new life in Christ contrasts with the Gentiles' old way of existence. Literally, **the old self** (Eph 4:22) and **the new self** (Eph 4:24) are "the old man" and "the new man" (*anthrōpos*, person), as at Eph 2:15; cf. note on Eph 4:13.

‡‡[4:24] **Put on:** in baptism. See note on Gal 3:27.

§§[4:25–6:20] For similar exhortations to a morally good life in response to God's gift of faith, see notes on Rom 12:1–13:14 and Gal 5:13–26.

¶¶[4:26] If angry, seek reconciliation that day, not giving the devil (Eph 6:11) opportunity to lead into sin.

***[4:28] **Honest work:** literally, "the good." **His [own] hands:** some manuscripts have the full phrase as in 1 Cor 4:12.

†††[4:30] See note on Eph 1:13.

‡‡‡[5:1] **Imitators of God:** in forgiving (Eph 4:32) and in loving (as exhibited in how **Christ loved us**).

---

g. [4:1] 3:1; Col 1:10.   h. [4:2] Col 3:12–13.   i. [4:3] Col 3:14–15. j. [4:4] Rom 12:5; 1 Cor 10:17; 12:12–13.   k. [4:5] 1 Cor 8:6.   l. [4:6] 1 Cor 12:6.   m. [4:7] Rom 12:3, 6; 1 Cor 12:28.   n. [4:8] Ps 68:19; Col 2:15.   o. [4:11] 1 Cor 12:28.   p. [4:13] Col 1:28.   q. [4:14] 1 Cor 14:20; Col 2:4, 8; Heb 13:9; Jas 1:6.   r. [4:15] 1 Cor 11:3; Col 1:18; 2:19.

s. [4:16] Col 2:19.   t. [4:17] Rom 1:21.   u. [4:18] Col 1:21; 1 Pt 1:14. v. [4:19] Col 3:5.   w. [4:22] Rom 8:13; Gal 6:8; Col 3:9.   x. [4:23] Rom 12:2.   y. [4:24] Gn 1:26–27; Col 3:10.   z. [4:25] Zec 8:16.   a. [4:26] Ps 4:5 LXX; Mt 5:22.   b. [4:27] 2 Cor 2:11.   c. [4:28] 1 Thes 4:11.   d. [4:29] 5:4; Col 3:16; 4:6.   e. [4:31] Col 3:8.   f. [4:32] Mt 6:14; Col 3:12–13.   g. [5:1] Mt 5:45, 48.

himself over for us as a sacrificial offering to God for a fragrant aroma.[h] [3]Immorality or any impurity or greed must not even be mentioned among you, as is fitting among holy ones,[i] [4]no obscenity or silly or suggestive talk, which is out of place, but instead, thanksgiving.[j] [5]Be sure of this, that no immoral or impure or greedy person, that is, an idolater, has any inheritance in the kingdom of Christ and of God.[k]

**Duty to Live in the Light.** [6]Let no one deceive you with empty arguments, for because of these things the wrath of God is coming upon the disobedient.[*] [7]So do not be associated with them. [8]For you were once darkness, but now you are light in the Lord. Live as children of light,[m] [9]for light produces every kind of goodness and righteousness and truth.[n] [10]Try to learn what is pleasing to the Lord.[o] [11]Take no part in the fruitless works of darkness; rather expose them;[p] [12]for it is shameful even to mention the things done by them in secret; [13]but everything exposed by the light becomes visible,[q] [14]for everything that becomes visible is light. Therefore, it says:[r]

"Awake, O sleeper,
    and arise from the dead,
and Christ will give you light."[†]

[15†]Watch carefully then how you live, not as foolish persons but as wise,[s] [16]making the most of the opportunity, because the days are evil. [17]Therefore, do not continue in ignorance, but try to understand what is the will of the Lord. [18]And do not get drunk on wine, in which lies debauchery, but be filled with the Spirit,[t] [19]addressing one another [in] psalms and hymns and spiritual songs, singing and playing to the Lord in your hearts,[u] [20]giving thanks always and for everything in the name of our Lord Jesus Christ to God the Father.[v]

**Wives and Husbands.** [21§]Be subordinate to one another[w] out of reverence for Christ.[¶] [22]Wives should be subordinate to their husbands as to the Lord.[x] [23]For the husband is head of his wife just as Christ is head of the church, he himself the savior of the body.[y] [24]As the church is subordinate to Christ, so wives should be subordinate to their husbands in everything. [25]Husbands, love your wives, even as Christ loved the church and handed himself over for her[z] [26]to sanctify her, cleansing her by the bath of water with the word,[a] [27]that he might present to himself the church in splendor, without spot or wrinkle or any such thing, that she might be holy and without blemish.[b] [28]So [also] husbands should love their wives as their own bodies. He who loves his wife loves himself. [29]For no one hates his own flesh but rather nourishes and cherishes it, even as Christ does the church, [30]because we are members of his body.[c]

[31] "For this reason a man shall leave [his]
        father and [his] mother
    and be joined to his wife,
    and the two shall become one flesh."[d]

[32]This is a great mystery, but I speak in reference to Christ and the church.[e] [33]In any case, each one of you should love his wife as himself, and the wife should respect her husband.

## CHAPTER 6

**Children and Parents.** [1]Children, obey your parents [in the Lord], for this is right.[f] [2]"Honor your father and mother."[g] This is the first commandment with a promise, [3]"that it may go well with you and that you may have a long life on earth." [4]Fathers, do not provoke your children to anger, but bring them up with the training and instruction of the Lord.[h]

**Slaves and Masters.** [5]Slaves, be obedient to your human masters with fear and trembling, in sincerity of heart, as to Christ,[i] [6]not only when being watched, as currying favor, but as slaves of Christ, doing the will of God from the heart,[j] [7]willingly serving the Lord and not human beings, [8]knowing that each will be requited from

---

*[5:6] See note on Eph 2:2.

†[5:14] An early Christian hymn, possibly from a baptismal liturgy. For the content compare Eph 2:5–6; 3:9 and Is 60:1.

‡[5:15–16, 19–20] The wording is similar to Col 4:5 and Eph 3:16–17.

§[5:21–6:9] Cf. notes on Col 3:18–4:1 and 1 Pt 2:18–3:7 for a similar listing of household duties where the inferior is admonished first (**wives**, Eph 5:22; **children**, Eph 6:1; **slaves**, Eph 6:5), then the superior (**husbands**, Eph 5:25; **fathers**, Eph 6:4; **masters**, Eph 6:9). Paul varies this pattern by an emphasis on mutuality (see Eph 5:20); use of Old Testament material about **father and mother** in Eph 6:2; the judgment to come for slave-owners.(**you have a Master in heaven**, Eph 6:9); and above all the initial principle of subordination **to one another** under **Christ**, thus effectively undermining exclusive claims to domination by one party. Into the section on **wives** and **husbands** an elaborate teaching on **Christ** and **the church** has been woven (Eph 5:22–33).

¶[5:21–33] The apostle exhorts married Christians to a strong mutual love. Holding with Gn 2:24 that marriage is a divine institution (Eph 5:31), Paul sees Christian marriage as taking on a new meaning symbolic of the intimate relationship of love between Christ and the church. The wife should serve her husband in the same spirit as that of the church's service to Christ (Eph 5:22, 24), and the husband should care for his wife with the devotion of Christ to the church (Eph 5:25–30). Paul gives to the Genesis passage its highest meaning in the light of the union of Christ and the church, of which Christlike loyalty and devotion in Christian marriage are a clear reflection (Eph 5:31–33).

h. [5:2] Ex 29:18; Ps 40:7; Gal 2:20; 1 Jn 3:16.   i. [5:3] Gal 5:19; Col 3:5.
j. [5:4] 4:29; Col 3:8.   k. [5:5] 1 Cor 6:9–10; Gal 5:21; Col 3:5.
l. [5:6] Rom 1:18; Col 2:4, 8.   m. [5:8] 2:11–13; Jn 12:36; Col 1:12–13.
n. [5:9] Gal 5:22.   o. [5:10] Rom 12:2.   p. [5:11] Rom 13:12.
q. [5:13] Jn 3:20–21.   r. [5:14] Is 26:19; 60:1.   s. [5:15–16] Col 4:5.
t. [5:18] Prv 23:31 LXX; Lk 21:34.   u. [5:19] Ps 33:2–3; Col 3:16.
v. [5:20] Col 3:17.

w. [5:21] 1 Pt 5:5.   x. [5:22] Col 3:18–4:1; 1 Pt 3:1–7.   y. [5:23] 1 Cor 11:3; Col 1:18.   z. [5:25] Col 3:19; 1 Tm 2:6.   a. [5:26] Rom 6:4; Ti 3:5–7.   b. [5:27] 2 Cor 11:2; Col 1:22.   c. [5:30] Rom 12:5; 1 Cor 6:15.   d. [5:31] Gn 2:24; Mt 19:5; Mk 10:7–8.   e. [5:32] Rev 19:7.   f. [6:1] Prv 6:20; Sir 3:1–6; Col 3:20.   g. [6:2–3] Ex 20:12; Dt 5:16.   h. [6:4] Col 3:21–22.   i. [6:5] Col 3:22–25; 1 Tm 6:1–2; Ti 2:9–10.   j. [6:6] 1 Pt 2:18.

the Lord for whatever good he does, whether he is slave or free. [9]Masters, act in the same way toward them, and stop bullying, knowing that both they and you have a Master in heaven and that with him there is no partiality.[k]

**Battle Against Evil.** [10*]Finally, draw your strength from the Lord and from his mighty power. [11]Put on the armor of God so that you may be able to stand firm against the tactics of the devil.[l] [12]For our struggle is not with flesh and blood but with the principalities, with the powers, with the world rulers of this present darkness, with the evil spirits in the heavens.[m] [13]Therefore, put on the armor of God, that you may be able to resist on the evil day and, having done everything, to hold your ground.[n] [14]So stand fast with your loins girded in truth, clothed with righteousness as a breastplate,[o] [15]and your feet shod in readiness for the gospel of peace.[p] [16]In all circumstances, hold faith as a shield, to quench all [the] flaming arrows of the evil one.[q] [17]And take the helmet of salvation and the sword of the Spirit, which is the word of God.[r]

**Constant Prayer.** [18]With all prayer and supplication, pray at every opportunity in the Spirit. To that end, be watchful with all perseverance and supplication for all the holy ones[s] [19]and also for me, that speech may be given me to open my mouth, to make known with boldness the mystery of the gospel[t] [20]for which I am an ambassador in chains, so that I may have the courage to speak as I must.[u]

## V. CONCLUSION

**A Final Message.**[†] [21]So that you also may have news of me and of what I am doing, Tychicus, my beloved brother and trustworthy minister in the Lord, will tell you everything.[v] [22]I am sending him to you for this very purpose, so that you may know about us and that he may encourage your hearts.[w]

[23]Peace be to the brothers, and love with faith, from God the Father and the Lord Jesus Christ. [24]Grace be with all who love our Lord Jesus Christ in immortality.[x]

---

*[6:10–20] A general exhortation to courage and prayer. Drawing upon the imagery and ideas of Is 11:5; 59:16–17; and Wis 5:17–23, Paul describes the Christian in terms of the dress and equipment of Roman soldiers. He observes, however, that the Christian's readiness for combat is not directed against human beings but against the spiritual powers of evil (Eph 6:10–17; cf. Eph 1:21; 2:2; 3:10). Unique importance is placed upon prayer (Eph 6:18–20).

k. [6:9] Col 4:1.  l. [6:11] Rom 13:12; 2 Cor 6:7; 10:4; Jas 4:7.
m. [6:12] 1:21; 2:2; Col 1:13.  n. [6:13] Rom 13:12.  o. [6:14] Wis 5:17–20; Is 11:5; Lk 12:35; 1 Thes 5:8.  p. [6:15] Is 52:7.  q. [6:16] 1 Pt 5:9.

†[6:21–24] **Tychicus**: the bearer of the letter; see note on Col 4:7. Eph 6:21–22 parallel Col 4:7–8, often word for word. If Ephesians is addressed to several Christian communities (see Introduction), it is understandable that no greetings to individual members of these communities should have been included in it.

r. [6:17] Is 59:17; 1 Thes 5:8.  s. [6:18] Mt 26:41; Col 4:2–3.
t. [6:19] Acts 4:29; Col 4:3; 2 Thes 3:1.  u. [6:20] 2 Cor 5:20; Col 4:4.
v. [6:21] Acts 20:4; Col 4:7; 2 Tm 4:12.  w. [6:22] Col 4:8.  x. [6:24] 1 Pt 1:8.

# THE LETTER TO THE
# PHILIPPIANS

Philippi, in northeastern Greece, was a city of some importance in the Roman province of Macedonia. Lying on the great road from the Adriatic coast to Byzantium, the Via Egnatia, and in the midst of rich agricultural plains near the gold deposits of Mt. Pangaeus, it was in Paul's day a Roman town (Acts 16:21), with a Greek-Macedonian population and a small group of Jews (see Acts 16:13). Originally founded in the sixth century B.C. as Krenides by the Thracians, the town was taken over after 360 B.C. by Philip II of Macedon, the father of Alexander the Great, and was renamed for himself, "Philip's City." The area became Roman in the second century B.C. On the plains near Philippi in October 42 B.C., Antony and Octavian decisively defeated the forces of Brutus and Cassius, the slayers of Julius Caesar. Octavian (Augustus) later made Philippi a Roman colony and settled many veterans of the Roman armies there.

Paul, according to Acts (Acts 16:9–40), established at Philippi the first Christian community in Europe. He came to Philippi, via its harbor town of Neapolis (modern Kavalla), on his second missionary journey, probably in A.D. 49 or 50, accompanied by Silas and Timothy (Acts 15:40; 16:3; cf. Phil 1:1) and Luke, if he is to be included in the "we" references of Acts 16:10–17. The Acts account tells of the conversion of a business woman, Lydia; the exorcism of a slave girl; and, after an earthquake, while Paul and Silas were imprisoned in Philippi, the faith and baptism of a jailer and his family. None of these persons, however, is directly mentioned in Philippians (cf. the notes on Phil 4:2 and Phil 4:3). Acts 16 concludes its account by describing how Paul (and Silas), asked by the magistrates to leave Philippi, went on to Thessalonica (Acts 17:1–10), where several times his loyal Philippians continued to support him with financial aid (Phil 4:16). Later, Paul may have passed through Philippi on his way from Ephesus to Greece (Acts 20:1–2), and he definitely stopped there on his fateful trip to Jerusalem (Acts 20:6).

Paul's letter to the Christians at Philippi was written while he was in a prison somewhere (Phil 1:7, 13, 14, 17), indeed in danger of death (Phil 1:20–23). Although under guard for preaching Christ, Paul rejoices at the continuing progress of the gospel (Phil 1:12–26) and expresses gratitude for the Philippians' renewed concern and help in an expression of thanks most clearly found at Phil 4:10–20. Much of the letter is devoted to instruction about unity and humility within the Christian community at Philippi (Phil 1:27–2:18) and exhortations to growth, joy, and peace in their life together (Phil 4:1–9). The letter seems to be drawing to a close at the end of what we number as Phil 2, as Paul reports the plans of his helper Timothy and of Epaphroditus (whom the Philippians had sent to aid Paul) to come to Philippi (Phil 2:19–3:1), and even Paul's own expectation that he will go free and come to Philippi (Phil 1:25–26; 2:24). Yet quite abruptly at Phil 3:2, Paul erupts into warnings against false teachers who threaten to impose on the Philippians the burdens of the Mosaic law, including circumcision. The section that follows, Phil 3:2–21, is a vigorous attack on these Judaizers (cf. Gal 2:11–3:29) or Jewish Christian teachers (cf. 2 Cor 11:12–23), giving us insights into Paul's own life story (Phil 3:4–6) and into the doctrine of justification, the Christian life, and ultimate hope (Phil 3:7–21).

The location of Paul's imprisonment when he wrote to the Philippians, and thus the date of the letter, are uncertain. The traditional view has been that it stems from Paul's confinement in Rome, between A.D. 59 and 63 (cf. Acts 28:14–31). One modern view suggests the period when he was imprisoned at Caesarea, on the coast of Palestine, A.D. 57 or 58 (Acts 23:23–26:32); another suggests Corinth (cf. 2 Cor 11:9). Much recent scholarship favors Ephesus, around A.D. 55, a situation referred to in 2 Cor 1:8 concerning "the affliction that came to us" in Asia Minor (cf. also 1 Cor 15:32). The reference at Phil 1:13 to the "praetorium" (cf. also Phil 4:22) can be understood to mean the imperial guard or government house at Ephesus (or Caesarea), or the praetorian camp in Rome. Involved in a decision are the several journeys back and forth between Philippi and wherever Paul is imprisoned, mentioned in the letter (Phil 2:25–28; 4:14); this factor causes many to prefer Ephesus because of its proximity to Philippi. The Ephesian hypothesis dates the composition of Philippians to the mid-50s when most of Paul's major letters were written.

There is also a likelihood, according to some scholars, that the letter as we have it is a composite from parts of three letters by Paul to the Philippians. Seemingly Phil 4:10–20 is a brief note of appreciation for help sent through Epaphroditus. The long section from Phil 1:3 to Phil 3:1 is then another letter, with news of Paul's imprisonment and reports on Timothy and Epaphroditus (who has fallen ill while with Paul), along with exhortations to the Philippians about Christian conduct; and Phil 3:2–21 a third communication warning about threats to Philippian Christianity. The other verses in Phil 4 and Phil 1:1–2, are variously assigned by critics to these three underlying letters, which an editor presumably put together to produce a picture of Paul writing earnestly from prison (Phil 1–2), facing opponents of the faith (Phil 3), and with serene joy advising and thanking his Philippians (Phil 4). If all four chapters were originally a unity, then one must assume that a break occurred between the writing of Phil 3:1 and Phil 3:2, possibly involving the receipt of bad news from Philippi, and that Paul had some reasons for delaying his words of thanks for the aid brought by Epaphroditus till the end of his letter.

This beautiful letter is rich in insights into Paul's theology and his apostolic love and concern for the gospel and his converts. In Philippians, Paul reveals his human sensitivity and tenderness, his enthusiasm for Christ as the key to life and death (Phil 1:21), and his deep feeling for those in Christ who dwell in Philippi. With them he shares his hopes and convictions, his anxieties and fears, revealing the total confidence in Christ that constitutes faith (Phil 3:8–10). The letter incorporates a hymn about the salvation that God has brought about through Christ (Phil 2:6–11), applied by Paul to the relations of Christians with one another (Phil 2:1–5). Philippians has been termed "the letter of joy" (Phil 4:4, 10). It is the rejoicing of faith, based on true understanding of Christ's unique role in the salvation of all who profess his lordship (Phil 2:11; 3:8–12, 14, 20–21).

The principal divisions of the Letter to the Philippians are the following:

    I. Address (1:1–11)
    II. Progress of the Gospel (1:12–26)
   III. Instructions for the Community (1:27–2:18)
   IV. Travel Plans of Paul and His Assistants (2:19–3:1)
    V. Polemic: Righteousness and the Goal in Christ (3:2–21)
   VI. Instructions for the Community (4:1–9)
  VII. Gratitude for the Philippians' Generosity (4:10–20)
VIII. Farewell (4:21–23)

## I. ADDRESS

### CHAPTER 1

**Greeting.**[*] [1]Paul and Timothy, slaves[†] of Christ Jesus, to all the holy ones in Christ Jesus who are in Philippi, with the overseers and ministers:[a] [2b]grace to you and peace from God our Father and the Lord Jesus Christ.[‡]

**Thanksgiving.**[§] [3]I give thanks to my God at every remembrance of you,[c] [4]praying always with joy in my every prayer for all of you, [5]because of your partnership for the gospel from the first day until now. [6d]I am confident of this, that the one who began a good work in you will continue to complete it until the day of Christ Jesus.[ſ] [7]It is right that I should think this way about all of you, because I hold you in my heart, you who are all partners with me in grace, both in my imprisonment and in the defense and confirmation of the gospel. [8]For God is my witness, how I long for all of you with the affection of Christ Jesus.[e] [9]And this is my prayer: that your love may increase ever more and more in knowledge and every kind of perception,[f] [10]to discern what is of value, so that you may be pure and blameless for the day of Christ,[g] [11]filled with the fruit of righteousness that comes through Jesus Christ for the glory and praise of God.[h]

## II. PROGRESS OF THE GOSPEL[**]

[12]I want you to know, brothers, that my situation has turned out rather to advance the gospel, [13]so that my imprisonment has become well known in Christ throughout the whole praetorium[††] and to all the rest,[i] [14‡‡]and so that the majority of the brothers, having taken encouragement in the Lord from my imprisonment, dare more than ever to proclaim the word fearlessly.

[15]Of course, some preach Christ from envy and rivalry, others from good will. [16]The latter act out of love, aware that I am here for the defense of the gospel; [17]the former proclaim Christ out of selfish ambition, not from pure motives, thinking that they will cause me trouble in my imprisonment. [18]What difference does it make, as long as in every way, whether in pretense or in truth, Christ is being proclaimed?[k] And in that I rejoice.[§§]

Indeed I shall continue to rejoice, [19¶¶]for I know that this will result in deliverance for me[***] through your prayers and support from the Spirit of Jesus Christ.[l] [20]My eager expectation and hope is that I shall not be put to shame in any way, but that with all boldness, now as always, Christ will be magnified in my body, whether by life or by death.[m] [21]For to me life is

---

[*][1:1–2] See note on Rom 1:1–7, concerning the greeting.

[†][1:1] **Slaves:** Paul usually refers to himself at the start of a letter as an apostle. Here he substitutes a term suggesting the unconditional obligation of himself and Timothy to the service of Christ, probably because, in view of the good relationship with the Philippians, he wishes to stress his status as a co-servant rather than emphasize his apostolic authority. Reference to Timothy is a courtesy: Paul alone writes the letter, as the singular verb throughout shows (Phil 1:3–26), and the reference (Phil 2:19–24) to Timothy in the third person. **Overseers:** the Greek term *episkopos* literally means "one who oversees" or "one who supervises," but since the second century it has come to designate the "bishop," the official who heads a local church. In New Testament times this office had not yet developed into the form that it later assumed, though it seems to be well on the way to such development in the Pastorals; see 1 Tm 3:2 and Ti 1:7, where it is translated bishop. At Philippi, however (and at Ephesus, according to Acts 20:28), there was more than one *episkopos*, and the precise function of these officials is uncertain. In order to distinguish this office from the later stages into which it developed, the term is here translated as **overseers**. **Ministers:** the Greek term *diakonoi* is used frequently in the New Testament to designate "servants," "attendants," or "ministers." Paul refers to himself and to other apostles as "ministers of God" (2 Cor 6:4) or "ministers of Christ" (2 Cor 11:23). In the Pastorals (1 Tm 3:8, 12) the *diakonos* has become an established official in the local church; hence the term is there translated as **deacon**. The *diakonoi* at Philippi seem to represent an earlier stage of development of the office; we are uncertain about their precise functions. Hence the term is here translated as **ministers**. See Rom 16:1, where Phoebe is described as a *diakonos* (minister) of the church of Cenchreae.

[‡][1:2] The gifts come **from** Christ the Lord, not simply through him from the Father; compare the christology in Phil 2:6–11.

[§][1:3–11] As in Rom 1:8–15 and all the Pauline letters except Galatians, a thanksgiving follows, including a direct prayer for the Philippians (Phil 1:9–11); see note on Rom 1:8. On their **partnership for the gospel** (Phil 1:5), cf. Phil 1:29–30; 4:10–20. Their devotion to the faith and to Paul made them his pride and joy (Phil 4:1). The characteristics thus manifested are evidence of the community's continuing preparation for the Lord's parousia (Phil 1:6, 10). Paul's especially warm relationship with the Philippians is suggested here (Phil 1:7–8) as elsewhere in the letter. The eschatology serves to underscore a concern for ethical growth (Eph 1:9–11), which appears throughout the letter.

[ſ][1:6] **The day of Christ Jesus:** the parousia or triumphant return of Christ, when those loyal to him will be with him and share in his eternal glory; cf. Phil 1:10; 2:16; 3:20–21; 1 Thes 4:17; 5:10; 2 Thes 1:10; 1 Cor 1:8.

[**][1:12–26] The body of the letter begins with an account of Paul's present **situation**, i.e., his **imprisonment** (Phil 1:12–13; see Introduction), and then goes on with advice for the Philippians (Phil 1:27–2:18). The **advance** of **the gospel** (Phil 1:12) and the **progress** of the Philippians **in the faith** (Phil 1:25) frame what is said.

[††][1:13] **Praetorium:** either the praetorian guard in the city where Paul was imprisoned or the governor's official residence in a Roman province (cf. Mk 15:16; Acts 23:35). See Introduction on possible sites.

[‡‡][1:14–18] Although Paul is imprisoned, Christians there nonetheless go on preaching Christ. But they do so with varied motives, **some** with personal hostility toward Paul, others out of personal ambition.

[§§][1:18] **Rejoice:** a major theme in the letter; see Introduction.

[¶¶][1:19–25] Paul earnestly debates his prospects of martyrdom or continued missionary labor. While he may **long to depart this life** and thus **be with Christ** (Phil 1:23), his overall and final expectation is that he will be delivered from this imprisonment and **continue in the service** of the Philippians and of others (Phil 1:19, 25; Phil 2:24). In either case, Christ is central (Phil 1:20–21); if to live means Christ for Paul, death means to be united with Christ in a deeper sense.

[***][1:19] **Result in deliverance for me:** an echo of Jb 13:16, hoping that God will turn suffering to ultimate good and deliverance from evil.

---

e. [1:8] Rom 1:9; 2 Cor 1:23; 1 Thes 2:5.  f. [1:9] Eph 3:14–19; Col 1:9–10; Phlm 6.  g. [1:10] Rom 2:18; 12:2 / 1:6.  h. [1:11] Jn 15:8.  i. [1:12–13] Eph 3:1; 6:20; 2 Tm 2:9; Phlm 9.  j. [1:13] 4:22.  k. [1:18] 4:10.  l. [1:19] Jb 13:16 / 2 Cor 1:11.  m. [1:20] 1 Cor 6:20; 1 Pt 4:16.

---

a. [1:1] Rom 1:1; 2 Cor 1:1; 1 Thes 1:1; Phlm 1 / 1 Tm 3:1–13.
b. [1:2] Rom 1:7; Gal 1:3; Phlm 3.  c. [1:3] Rom 1:8; 1 Cor 1:4; 1 Thes 1:2.  d. [1:6] 2:13 / 1:10; 2:16; 1 Cor 1:8.

Christ, and death is gain.*n* *22*If I go on living in the flesh, that means fruitful labor for me. And I do not know which I shall choose.*o* *23*I am caught between the two. I long to depart this life and be with Christ, [for] that is far better.*p* *24*Yet that I remain [in] the flesh is more necessary for your benefit. *25*And this I know with confidence, that I shall remain and continue in the service of all of you for your progress and joy in the faith, *26*so that your boasting in Christ Jesus may abound on account of me when I come to you again.

### III. INSTRUCTIONS
### FOR THE COMMUNITY

**Steadfastness in Faith.** *27*Only, conduct your-selves in a way worthy of the gospel of Christ, so that, whether I come and see you or am absent, I may hear news of you, that you are standing firm in one spirit, with one mind struggling together for the faith of the gospel,*q* *28*not intimidated in any way by your opponents. This is proof to them of destruction, but of your salvation. And this is God's doing. *29*For to you has been granted, for the sake of Christ, not only to believe in him but also to suffer for him.*r* *30*Yours is the same strug-gle*s* as you saw in me and now hear about me.*t*

### CHAPTER 2
**Plea for Unity and Humility.** *1*If there is any encouragement in Christ, any solace in love, any participation in the Spirit, any compassion and mercy, *2*complete my joy by being of the same mind, with the same love, united in heart, think-ing one thing.*t* *3*Do nothing out of selfishness or out of vainglory; rather, humbly regard others as more important than yourselves,*u* *4*each looking out not for his own interests, but [also] everyone for those of others.*v*

*5*Have among yourselves the same attitude that is also yours in Christ Jesus,*§*

---

*6* Who,¶ though he was in the form of God,*w*
did not regard equality with God
something to be grasped.**

*7* Rather, he emptied himself,
taking the form of a slave,
coming in human likeness;††
and found human in appearance,*x*

*8* he humbled himself,*y*
becoming obedient to death,
even death on a cross.‡‡

*9* Because of this, God greatly exalted him
and bestowed on him the name§§
that is above every name,*z*

*10* that at the name of Jesus
every knee should bend,¶¶
of those in heaven and on earth and
under the earth,*a*

*11* and every tongue confess that
Jesus Christ is Lord,***
to the glory of God the Father.*b*

**Obedience and Service in the World.**††† *12c*So then, my beloved, obedient as you have always

---

held that Christ here functions as a model for moral imitation, it is not the historical Jesus but the entire Christ event that Phil 2:6–11 depict. Therefore, the appeal is to have in relations among yourselves that same relationship you have in Jesus Christ, i.e., serving one another as you serve Christ (Phil 2:4).

¶[2:6–11] Perhaps an early Christian hymn quoted here by Paul. The short rhythmic lines fall into two parts, Phil 2:6–8 where the subject of every verb is Christ, and Phil 2:9–11 where the subject is God. The general pattern is thus of Christ's humili-ation and then exaltation. More precise analyses propose a divi-sion into six three-line stanzas (Phil 2:6; 7abc, 7d–8, 9, 10, 11) or into three stanzas (Phil 2:6–7ab, 7cd–8, 9–11). Phrases such as **even death on a cross** (Phil 2:8c) are considered by some to be additions (by Paul) to the hymn, as are Phil 2:10c, 11c.

**[2:6] Either a reference to Christ's preexistence and those aspects of divinity that he was willing to give up in order to serve in human form, or to what the man Jesus refused to grasp at to attain divinity. Many see an allusion to the Genesis story: unlike Adam, Jesus, **though . . . in the form of God** (Gn 1:26–27), did not reach out for **equality with God**, in contrast with the first Adam in Gn 3:5–6.

††[2:7] **Taking the form of a slave, coming in human like-ness:** or ". . . taking the form of a slave. // Coming in human likeness, and found human in appearance." While it is common to take Phil 2:6–7 as dealing with Christ's preexistence and Phil 2:8 with his incarnate life, so that lines Phil 2:7b–7c are parallel, it is also possible to interpret so as to exclude any reference to preexistence (see note on Phil 2:6) and to take Phil 2:6–8 as pre-senting two parallel stanzas about Jesus' human state (Phil 2:6–7b; 7cd–8); in the latter alternative, **coming in human likeness** begins the second stanza and parallels Phil 2:6a to some extent.

‡‡[2:8] There may be reflected here language about the ser-vant of the Lord, Is 52:13–53:12 especially Is 53:12.

§§[2:9] **The name:** "Lord" (Phil 2:11), revealing the true nature of the one who is named.

¶¶[2:10–11] **Every knee should bend . . . every tongue confess:** into this language of Is 45:23 there has been inserted a reference to the three levels in the universe, according to ancient thought, **heaven, earth, under the earth.**

***[2:11] **Jesus Christ is Lord:** a common early Christian accla-mation; cf. 1 Cor 12:3; Rom 10:9. But doxology to God the Father is not overlooked here (Phil 2:11c) in the final version of the hymn.

†††[2:12–18] Paul goes on to draw out further ethical impli-cations for daily life (Phil 2:14–18) from the salvation God works in Christ.

---

*[1:27–30] Ethical admonition begins at this early point in the letter, emphasizing steadfastness and congregational unity in the face of possible suffering. The **opponents** (Phil 1:28) are those in Philippi, probably pagans, who oppose the gospel cause. **This is proof . . .** (Phil 1:28) may refer to the whole out-look and conduct of the Philippians, turning out for their salva-tion but to the judgment of the opponents (cf. 2 Cor 2:15–16), or possibly the sentence refers to the opinion of the opponents, who hold that the obstinacy of the Christians points to the destruction of such people as defy Roman authority (though in reality, Paul holds, such faithfulness leads to salvation).

†[1:30] A reference to Paul's earlier imprisonment in Philippi (Acts 16:19–24; 1 Thes 2:2) and to his present confinement.

‡[2:1–11] The admonition to likemindedness and unity (Phil 2:2–5) is based on the believers' threefold experience with Christ, God's love, and the Spirit. The appeal to humility (Phil 2:3) and to obedience (Phil 2:12) is rooted in christology, spe-cifically in a statement about Christ Jesus (Phil 2:6–11) and his humbling of self and obedience to the point of death (Phil 2:8).

§[2:5] **Have . . . the same attitude that is also yours in Christ Jesus:** or, "that also Christ Jesus had." While it is often

---

n. [1:21] Gal 2:20.  o. [1:22] Rom 1:13.  p. [1:23] 2 Cor 5:8.  q. [1:27] Eph 4:1; Col 1:10; 1 Thes 2:12 / 4:3.  r. [1:29] Mt 5:10; 10:38; Mk 8:34; Acts 5:41.  s. [1:30] 1:13; Acts 16:22–24.  t. [2:2] Rom 15:5; 1 Cor 1:10.  u. [2:3] Rom 12:3, 10; Gal 5:26.  v. [2:4] 1 Cor 10:24, 33; 13:5.

w. [2:6] Jn 1:1–2; 17:5; Col 2:9; Heb 1:3.  x. [2:7] Is 53:3, 11; Jn 1:14; Rom 8:3; 2 Cor 8:9; Gal 4:4; Heb 2:14, 17.  y. [2:8] Mt 26:39; Jn 10:17; Heb 5:8; 12:2.  z. [2:9] Acts 2:33; Mt 23:12; Eph 1:20–21; Heb 1:3–4.  a. [2:10] Is 45:23; Jn 5:23; Rom 14:11; Rev 5:13.  b. [2:11] Acts 2:36; Rom 10:9; 1 Cor 12:3.  c. [2:12] Ps 2:11; 1 Cor 2:3; 2 Cor 7:15.

been, not only when I am present but all the more now when I am absent, work out your salvation with fear and trembling.* ¹³For God is the one who, for his good purpose, works in you both to desire and to work.ᵈ ¹⁴Do everything without grumbling or questioning,ᵉ ¹⁵that you may be blameless and innocent, children of God without blemish in the midst of a crooked and perverse generation,† among whom you shine like lights in the world,ᶠ ¹⁶as you hold on to the word of life, so that my boast for the day of Christ may be that I did not run in vain or labor in vain.ᵍ ¹⁷But, even if I am poured out as a libation‡ upon the sacrificial service of your faith, I rejoice and share my joy with all of you.ʰ ¹⁸In the same way you also should rejoice and share your joy with me.ⁱ

### IV. TRAVEL PLANS OF PAUL AND HIS ASSISTANTS§

**Timothy and Paul.** ¹⁹I hope, in the Lord Jesus, to send Timothyˢ to you soon, so that I too may be heartened by hearing news of you.ʲ ²⁰For I have no one comparable to him for genuine interest in whatever concerns you. ²¹For they all seek their own interests, not those of Jesus Christ.ᵏ ²²But you know his worth, how as a child with a father he served along with me in the cause of the gospel. ²³He it is, then, whom I hope to send as soon as I see how things go with me, ²⁴but I am confident in the Lord that I myself will also come soon.**

**Epaphroditus.** ²⁵With regard to Epaphroditus,†† my brother and co-worker and fellow soldier, your messenger and minister in my need, I consider it necessary to send him to you.ˡ ²⁶For he has been longing for all of you and was distressed because you heard that he was ill. ²⁷He was indeed ill, close to death; but God had mercy on him, not just on him but also on me, so that I might not have sorrow upon sorrow. ²⁸I

send him therefore with the greater eagerness, so that, on seeing him, you may rejoice again, and I may have less anxiety. ²⁹Welcome him then in the Lord with all joy and hold such people in esteem,ᵐ ³⁰because for the sake of the work of Christ he came close to death, risking his life to make up for those services to me that you could not perform.

### CHAPTER 3
**Concluding Admonitions.** ¹Finally, my brothers, rejoice‡‡ in the Lord. Writing the same things to you is no burden for me but is a safeguard for you.ⁿ

### V. POLEMIC: RIGHTEOUSNESS AND THE GOAL IN CHRIST§§

**Against Legalistic Teachers.** ²§§Beware of the dogs! Beware of the evil-workers!ᵒ Beware of the mutilation!*** ³For we are the circumcision,††† we who worship through the Spirit of God, who boast in Christ Jesus and do not put our confidence in flesh,ᵖ ⁴although I myself have grounds for confidence even in the flesh.ۡ�q
**Paul's Autobiography.** If anyone else thinks he can be confident in flesh, all the more can I.

*[2:12]* **Fear and trembling:** a common Old Testament expression indicating awe and seriousness in the service of God (cf. Ex 15:16; Jdt 2:28; Ps 2:11; Is 19:16).

†[2:15–16]* **Generation . . . as you hold on to . . . :** or ". . . generation. Among them shine like lights in the world because you hold the word of life. . . ."

‡[2:17]* **Libation:** in ancient religious ritual, the pouring out on the ground of a liquid offering as a sacrifice. Paul means that he may be facing death.

§[2:19–3:1]* The plans of Paul and his assistants for future travel are regularly a part of a Pauline letter near its conclusion; cf. Rom 15:22–29; 1 Cor 16:5–12.

¶[2:19]* **Timothy:** already known to the Philippians (Acts 16:1–15; cf. 1 Cor 4:17; 16:10).

**[2:24]* **I myself will also come soon:** cf. Phil 1:19–25 for the significance of this statement.

††[2:25]* **Epaphroditus:** sent by the Philippians as their messenger (literally, "apostle") to aid Paul in his imprisonment, he had fallen seriously ill; Paul commends him as he sends him back to Philippi.

‡‡[3:1]* **Finally . . . rejoice:** the adverb often signals the close of a letter; cf. Phil 4:8; 2 Cor 13:11. While the verb could also be translated "good-bye" or "farewell," although it is never so used in Greek epistolography, the theme of joy has been frequent in the letter (Phil 1:18; 2:2, 18); note also Phil 4:4 and the addition of "always" there as evidence for the meaning "rejoice." To write **the same things** may refer to what Paul has previously taught in Philippi or to what he has just written or to what follows.

§§[3:2–21]* An abrupt change in content and tone, either because Paul at this point responds to disturbing news he has just heard about a threat to the faith of the Philippians in the form of false teachers, or because part of another Pauline letter was inserted here; see Introduction. The chapter describes these teachers in strong terms as **dogs.** The persons meant are evidently different from the rival preachers of Phil 1:14–18 and the opponents of Phil 1:28. Since Phil 3:2–4 emphasize Jewish terms like **circumcision** (Phil 3:2–3, 5), some relate them to the "Judaizers" of the Letter to the Galatians. Other phrases make them appear more like the false teachers of 2 Cor 11:12–15, the **evil-workers.** The latter part of the chapter depicts the **many** who are **enemies** of Christ's cross in terms that may sound more Gentile or even "gnostic" than Jewish (Phil 3:18–19). Accordingly, some see two groups of false teachers in Phil 3, others one group characterized by a claim of having attained "perfect maturity" (Phil 3:12–15).

§§[3:2–11]* Paul sets forth the Christian claim, especially using personal, autobiographical terms that are appropriate to the situation. He presents his own experience in coming to know Christ Jesus in terms of **righteousness** or justification (cf. Rom 1:16–17; 3:21–5:11; Gal 2:5–11), contrasting the **righteousness from God** through faith and that of one's own **based on the law** as two exclusive ways of pleasing God.

***[3:2]* **Beware of the mutilation:** literally, "incision," an ironic wordplay on "circumcision"; cf. Gal 5:12. There may be an association with the self-inflicted mutilations of the prophets of Baal (1 Kgs 18:28) and of devotees of Cybele who slashed themselves in religious frenzy.

†††[3:3]* **We are the circumcision:** the true people of God, seed and offspring of Abraham (Gal 3:7, 29; 6:15). **Spirit of God:** some manuscripts read "worship God by the Spirit."

d. [2:13] 1:6; 1 Cor 12:6; 15:10; 2 Cor 3:5.   e. [2:14] 1 Cor 10:10; 1 Pt 4:9.   f. [2:15] 1 Thes 3:13 / Dt 32:5; Mt 10:16; Acts 2:40 / Dn 12:3; Mt 5:14, 16; Eph 5:8.   g. [2:16] 1 Thes 2:19 / Is 49:4; 65:23; Gal 2:2.   h. [2:17] Rom 15:16; 2 Tm 4:6.   i. [2:18] 3:1; 4:4.   j. [2:19] Acts 16:1–3; 17:14–15; 1 Cor 4:17; 16:10.   k. [2:21] 1 Cor 13:5; 2 Tm 4:10.   l. [2:25] 4:10–11, 15–16, 18.

m. [2:29] 1 Cor 16:18.   n. [3:1] 2:18; 4:4.   o. [3:2] Ps 22:17, 21; Rev 22:15 / 2 Cor 11:13 / Gal 5:6, 12.   p. [3:3] Rom 2:28–29; Col 2:11.   q. [3:4] 2 Cor 11:18, 21–23.

⁵Circumcised on the eighth day,* of the race of Israel, of the tribe of Benjamin, a Hebrew of Hebrew parentage, in observance of the law a Pharisee,ʳ ⁶in zeal I persecuted the church, in righteousness based on the law I was blameless.ˢ **Righteousness from God.** ⁷[But] whatever gains I had, these I have come to consider a loss† because of Christ.ᵗ ⁸More than that, I even consider everything as a loss because of the supreme good of knowing Christ Jesus my Lord. For his sake I have accepted the loss of all things and I consider them so much rubbish, that I may gain Christ ⁹and be found in him, not having any righteousness of my own based on the law but that which comes through faith in Christ,ᵘ the righteousness from God, depending on faith ¹⁰to know him and the power of his resurrection and [the] sharing of his sufferings by being conformed to his death,ᵛ ¹¹if somehow I may attain the resurrection from the dead.ʷ

**Forward in Christ.** ‡ ¹²ᵡIt is not that I have already taken hold of it or have already attained perfect maturity,§ but I continue my pursuit in hope that I may possess it, since I have indeed been taken possession of by Christ [Jesus]. ¹³Brothers, I for my part do not consider myself to have taken possession. Just one thing: forgetting what lies behind but straining forward to what lies ahead, ¹⁴I continue my pursuit toward the goal, the prize of God's upward calling, in Christ Jesus.ʸ ¹⁵Let us, then, who are "perfectly mature" adopt this attitude. And if you have a different attitude, this too God will reveal to you. ¹⁶Only, with regard to what we have attained, continue on the same course.¶

**Wrong Conduct and Our Goal.** ** ¹⁷Join with others in being imitators of me,†† brothers, and observe those who thus conduct themselves according to the model you have in us.ᶻ ¹⁸For

many, as I have often told you and now tell you even in tears, conduct themselves as enemies of the cross of Christ.ᵃ ¹⁹Their end is destruction. Their God is their stomach; their glory is in their "shame." Their minds are occupied with earthly things.ᵇ ²⁰But our citizenship‡‡ is in heaven, and from it we also await a savior, the Lord Jesus Christ.ᶜ ²¹He will change our lowly body to conform with his glorified body by the power that enables him also to bring all things into subjection to himself.ᵈ

## VI. INSTRUCTIONS FOR THE COMMUNITY§§

### CHAPTER 4

**Live in Concord.** ¹Therefore, my brothers, whom I love and long for, my joy and crown, in this way stand firm in the Lord, beloved.ᵉ

²I urge Euodia and I urge Syntyche¶¶ to come to a mutual understanding in the Lord. ³Yes, and I ask you also, my true yokemate,*** to help them, for they have struggled at my side in promoting the gospel, along with Clement and my other co-workers, whose names are in the book of life.ᶠ **Joy and Peace.** ⁴Rejoice††† in the Lord always. I shall say it again: rejoice!ᵍ ⁵Your kindness‡‡‡ should be known to all. The Lord is near.ʰ ⁶Have no anxiety at all, but in everything, by prayer and petition, with thanksgiving, make your requests known to God.ⁱ ⁷Then the peace of God that surpasses all understanding will guard your hearts and minds in Christ Jesus.ʲ

⁸ᵏFinally, brothers, whatever is true, whatever is honorable, whatever is just, whatever is pure, whatever is lovely, whatever is gracious, if there is any excellence and if there is anything worthy of praise, think about these things.§§§

---

*[3:5] **Circumcised on the eighth day**: as the law required (Gn 17:12; Lv 12:3).

†[3:7] **Loss**: his knowledge of Christ led Paul to reassess the ways of truly pleasing and serving God. His reevaluation indicates the profound and lasting effect of his experience of the meaning of Christ on the way to Damascus some twenty years before (Gal 1:15–16; Acts 9:1–22).

‡[3:12–16] To be **taken possession of by Christ** does not mean that one has already arrived at perfect spiritual maturity. Paul and the Philippians instead press on, trusting in God.

§[3:12] **Attained perfect maturity**: possibly an echo of the concept in the mystery religions of being an initiate, admitted to divine secrets.

¶[3:16] Some manuscripts add, probably to explain Paul's cryptic phrase, "thinking alike."

**[3:17–21] Paul and those who live a life centered in Christ, envisaging both his suffering and resurrection, provide a model that is the opposite of opponents who reject Christ's cross (cf. 1 Cor 1:23).

††[3:17] **Being imitators of me**: not arrogance, but humble simplicity, since all his converts know that Paul is wholly dedicated to imitating Christ (1 Cor 11:1; cf. also Phil 4:9; 1 Thes 1:6; 2 Thes 3:7, 9; 1 Cor 4:6).

‡‡[3:20] **Citizenship**: Christians constitute a colony of heaven, as Philippi was a *colonia* of Rome (Acts 16:12). The hope Paul expresses involves the final coming of Christ, not a status already attained, such as the opponents claim.

§§[4:1–9] This series of ethical admonitions rests especially on the view of Christ and his coming (cf. Phil 4:5) in Phil 3:20–21. Paul's instructions touch on unity within the congregation, joy, prayer, and the Christian outlook on life.

¶¶[4:2] **Euodia . . . Syntyche**: two otherwise unknown women in the Philippian congregation; on the advice to them, cf. Phil 2:2–4.

***[4:3] **Yokemate**: or "comrade," although the Greek *syzygos* could also be a proper name. **Clement**: otherwise unknown, although later writers sought to identify him with Clement, bishop of Rome (Eusebius, *Ecclesiastical History* 3.15.1).

†††[4:4] **Rejoice**: see note on Phil 3:1.

‡‡‡[4:5] **Kindness**: considerateness, forbearance, fairness. **The Lord is near**: most likely a reference to Christ's parousia (Phil 1:6, 10; 3:20–21; 1 Cor 16:22), although some sense an echo of Ps 119:151 and the perpetual presence of the Lord.

§§§[4:8] The language employs terms from Roman Stoic thought.

---

r. [3:5] Lk 1:59; 2:21 / Acts 22:3; 23:6; 26:5.    s. [3:6] Acts 8:3; 22:4; 26:9–11.    t. [3:7] Mt 13:44, 46; Lk 14:33.    u. [3:9] Rom 3:21–22.    v. [3:10] Rom 6:3–5; 8:17; Gal 6:17.    w. [3:11] Jn 11:23–26; Acts 4:2; Rev 20:5–6.    x. [3:12] 1 Tm 6:12, 19.    y. [3:14] 1 Cor 9:24–25; 2 Tm 4:7.    z. [3:17] 1 Cor 4:16; 11:1; 1 Thes 1:7; 1 Pt 5:3.

a. [3:18] 1 Cor 1:17, 23; Gal 6:12.    b. [3:19] Rom 8:5–6; 16:18.    c. [3:20] Eph 2:6, 19; Col 3:1–3; Heb 12:22.    d. [3:21] Rom 8:23, 29; 1 Cor 15:42–57; 2 Cor 3:18; 5:1–5 / 1 Cor 15:27–28.    e. [4:1] 1 Thes 2:19–20.    f. [4:3] Ex 32:32–33; Ps 69:29; Dn 12:1; Lk 10:20; Rev 3:5; 13:8; 17:8; 20:12, 15; 21:27.    g. [4:4] 2:18; 3:1.    h. [4:5] Ti 3:2 / Ps 145:18; Heb 10:37; Jas 5:8–9.    i. [4:6] Mt 6:25–34; 1 Pt 5:7 / Col 4:2.    j. [4:7] Jn 14:27; Col 3:15.    k. [4:8] Rom 12:17.

⁹Keep on doing what you have learned and received and heard and seen in me.ˡ Then the God of peace will be with you.⃰

## VII. GRATITUDE FOR THE PHILIPPIANS' GENEROSITY†

¹⁰I rejoice greatly in the Lord that now at last you revived your concern for me. You were, of course, concerned about me but lacked an opportunity.ᵐ ¹¹Not that I say this because of need, for I have learned, in whatever situation I find myself, to be self-sufficient.ⁿ ¹²I know indeed how to live in humble circumstances; I know also how to live with abundance. In every circumstance and in all things I have learned the secret of being well fed and of going hungry, of living in abundance and of being in need. ¹³I have the strength for everything through him who empowers me.ᵒ ¹⁴Still, it was kind of you to share in my distress.

¹⁵You Philippians indeed know that at the beginning of the gospel,‡ when I left Macedonia, not a single church shared with me in an account of giving and receiving, except you alone. ¹⁶For even when I was at Thessalonica you sent me something for my needs, not only once but more than once. ¹⁷It is not that I am eager for the gift; rather, I am eager for the profit that accrues to your account. ¹⁸I have received full payment and I abound. I am very well supplied because of what I received from you through Epaphroditus, "a fragrant aroma," an acceptable sacrifice,§ pleasing to God.ᵖ ¹⁹My God will fully supply whatever you need, in accord with his glorious riches in Christ Jesus.�q ²⁰To our God and Father, glory forever and ever. Amen.ʳ

## VIII. FAREWELLˢ

²¹Give my greetings to every holy one in Christ Jesus. The brothers who are with me send you their greetings; ²²all the holy ones send you their greetings, especially those of Caesar's household."⃰ ²³The grace of the Lord Jesus Christ be with your spirit.

---

⃰ [4:9] Cf. note on Phil 3:17.

† [4:10–20] Paul, more directly than anywhere else in the letter (cf. Phil 1:3–5), here thanks the Philippians for their gift of money sent through Epaphroditus (Phil 2:25). Paul's own policy was **to be self-sufficient** as a missionary, supporting himself by his own labor (1 Thes 2:5–9; 1 Cor 9:15–18; cf. Acts 18:2–3). In spite of this reliance on self and on God to provide (Phil 4:11–13) Paul accepted gifts from the Philippians **not only once but more than once** (Phil 4:16) when he was in Thessalonica (Acts 17:1–9), as he does now, in prison (**my distress**, Phil 4:14). While commercial terms appear in the passage, like **an account of giving and receiving** (Phil 4:15) and **received full payment** (Phil 4:18), Paul is most concerned about the spiritual growth of the Philippians (Phil 4:10, 17, 19); he emphasizes that God will care for their needs, through Christ.

l. [4:9] 1 Thes 4:1 / Rom 15:33; 16:20; 1 Cor 14:33; 1 Thes 5:23. m. [4:10] 1:18; 2:25; 1 Cor 9:11; 2 Cor 11:9. n. [4:11–12] 1 Cor 4:11; 2 Cor 6:10; 11:27 / 2 Cor 12:9–10. o. [4:13] Col 1:29; 2 Tm 4:17.

‡ [4:15] **The beginning of the gospel**: it was at Philippi that Paul first preached Christ in Europe, going on from there to Thessalonica and Beroea (Acts 16:9–17:14).

§ [4:18] **Aroma . . . sacrifice**: Old Testament cultic language (cf. Gn 8:21; Ex 29:18, 25, 41; Lv 1:9, 13; Ez 20:41) applied to the Philippians' gift; cf. Eph 5:2; 2 Cor 2:14–16.

¶ [4:21–23] On the usual greetings at the conclusion of a letter, see note on 1 Cor 16:19–24. Inclusion of greetings from **all the holy ones** in the place from which Paul writes would involve even the Christians of Phil 1:14–18 who had their differences with Paul.

⃰⃰ [4:22] **Those of Caesar's household**: minor officials or even slaves and freedmen, found in Ephesus or Rome, among other places.

p. [4:18] Gn 8:21; Ex 29:18; Eph 5:2; Heb 13:16. q. [4:19] 1 Thes 3:11, 13. r. [4:20] Rom 16:27; Eph 5:20. s. [4:22] 1:13.

# THE LETTER TO THE
# COLOSSIANS

This letter is addressed to a congregation at Colossae in the Lycus Valley in Asia Minor, east of Ephesus. At the time of writing, Paul had not visited there, the letter says (Col 1:4; 2:1). The community had apparently been established by Epaphras of Colossae (Col 1:7; 4:12; Phlm 23). Problems, however, had arisen, brought on by teachers who emphasized Christ's relation to the universe (cosmos). Their teachings stressed angels (Col 2:18; "principalities and powers," Col 2:15), which were connected with astral powers and cultic practices (see note on Col 2:16) and rules about food and drink and ascetical disciplines (Col 2:16, 18). These teachings, Paul insists, detract from the person and work of Christ for salvation as set forth magnificently in a hymnic passage at Col 1:15–20 and reiterated throughout the letter. Such teachings are but "shadows"; Christ is "reality" (Col 2:17).

For help in dealing with these problems that the new teachers posed at Colossae, Epaphras sought out Paul, who was then imprisoned (Col 4:10, 18) at a place that the letter does not mention. Paul, without entering into debate over the existence of angelic spirits or their function, simply affirms that Christ possesses the sum total of redemptive power (Col 1:19) and that the spiritual renewal of the human person occurs through contact in baptism with the person of Christ, who died and rose again (Col 2:9–14). It is unnecessary for the Christian to be concerned about placating spirits (Col 2:15) or avoiding imagined defilement through ascetical practices in regard to food and drink (Col 2:20–23). True Christian asceticism consists in the conquering of personal sins (Col 3:5–10) and the practice of love of neighbor in accordance with the standard set by Christ (Col 3:12–16).

Paul commends the community as a whole (Col 1:3–8); this seems to indicate that, though the Colossians have been under pressure to adopt the false doctrines, they have not yet succumbed. The apostle expresses his prayerful concern for them (Col 1:9–14). His preaching has cost him persecution, suffering, and imprisonment, but he regards these as reflective of the sufferings of Christ, a required discipline for the sake of the gospel (see note on 1:24; cf. 1:29; 2:1). His instructions to the Christian family and to slaves and masters require a new spirit of reflection and action. Love, obedience, and service are to be rendered "in the Lord" (Col 3:18–4:1).

Colossians follows the outline of a typical Pauline letter. It is distinguished by the poetic lines in Col 1:15–20 concerning who Christ is and what Christ means in creation and redemption. This hymn may be compared with similar passages in Phil 2:6–11; 1 Tm 3:16; and Jn 1:1–18. It was apparently familiar liturgical material to the author, the audience, and the false teachers. In Col 1:21–2:7, however, Paul interprets the relation between the body of Christ, which he insists is the church (Col 1:18), and the world or cosmos to be one not simply of Christ's preexistence and rule but one of missionary advance into the world by the spreading of the word (Col 1:25, 28). In this labor of the missionary body of Christ, Paul as a minister plays a prime part in bringing Christ and the gospel as hope to the Gentiles (Col 1:23, 25, 27). To "every creature under heaven" the word is to be proclaimed, so that everyone receives Christ, is established in faith, and walks in Christ (Col 1:28; 2:6, 7).

Paul wrote the Letter to the Colossians while in prison, but his several imprisonments leave the specific place and date of composition uncertain. On this point the same problem exists as with Ephesians and Philippians (see the Introductions to these letters). Traditionally the house arrest at Rome, in which Paul enjoyed a certain restricted freedom in preaching (see Acts 28:16–28), or a second Roman imprisonment has been claimed as the setting. Others suggest a still earlier imprisonment at Caesarea (see Acts 23:12–27:1) or in Ephesus (see Acts 19). Still others regard the letter as the work of some pupil or follower of Paul, writing in his name. In any case, the contents are often closely paralleled by thoughts in Ephesians.

The principal divisions of the Letter to the Colossians are the following:

I.   Address (1:1–14)
II.  The Preeminence of Christ (1:15–2:3)
III. Warnings Against False Teachers (2:4–23)
IV.  The Ideal Christian Life in the World (3:1–4:6)
V.   Conclusion (4:7–18)

## I. ADDRESS

### CHAPTER 1

**Greeting.**\* ¹Paul, an apostle of Christ Jesus by the will of God, and Timothy our brother,ᵃ ²to the holy ones and faithful brothers in Christ in Colossae: grace to you and peace from God our Father.

**Thanksgiving.**† ³We always give thanks to God, the Father of our Lord Jesus Christ, when we pray for you,ᵇ ⁴for we have heard of your faith in Christ Jesus and the love that you have for all the holy ones ⁵because of the hope reserved for you in heaven. Of this you have already heard through the word of truth, the gospel,ᶜ ⁶that has come to you. Just as in the whole world it is bearing fruit and growing, so also among you, from the day you heard it and came to know the grace of God in truth, ⁷ᵈas you learned it from Epaphras‡ our beloved fellow slave, who is a trustworthy minister of Christ on your behalf ⁸and who also told us of your love in the Spirit.

**Prayer for Continued Progress.**§ ⁹Therefore, from the day we heard this, we do not cease praying for you and asking that you may be filled with the knowledge of his will through all spiritual wisdom and understandingᵉ ¹⁰to live in a manner worthy of the Lord, so as to be fully pleasing, in every good work bearing fruit and growing in the knowledge of God, ¹¹strengthened with every power, in accord with his glorious might, for all endurance and patience, with joy ¹²⁵giving thanks to the Father, who has made you fit to share in the inheritance of the holy ones in light.ᶠ ¹³He delivered us from the power of darkness and transferred us to the kingdom of his beloved Son, ¹⁴in whom we have redemption, the forgiveness of sins.ᵍ

## II. THE PREEMINENCE OF CHRIST

### His Person and Work

¹⁵ \*\*"He is the image†† of the invisible God,
    the firstborn of all creation.ʰ
¹⁶ For in him‡‡ were created all things in
        heaven and on earth,
    the visible and the invisible,
    whether thrones or dominions or
        principalities or powers;

---

\*[1:1–2] For the epistolary form used by Paul at the beginning of his letters, see note on Rom 1:1–7. On **holy ones** or "God's people," see note on Rom 1:7. Awareness of their calling helps this group to be **faithful brothers** and sisters in Christ, i.e., dedicated to the tasks implied in their calling.

†[1:3–8] On thanksgiving at the start of a letter, see note on Rom 1:8. The apostle, recalling his own prayers for them and the good report about them he has received (Col 1:3–4), congratulates the Colossians upon their acceptance of Christ and their faithful efforts to live the gospel (Col 3:6–8). To encourage them he mentions the success of the gospel elsewhere (Col 1:6) and assures them that his knowledge of their community is accurate, since he has been in personal contact with Epaphras (Col 1:7–8), who likely had evangelized Colossae and other cities in the Lycus Valley of Asia Minor (cf. Col 4:12, 13; Phlm 23). On **faith, love,** and **hope** (Col 1:4, 5, 8), see note on 1 Cor 13:13; cf. 1 Thes 1:3; 5:8.

‡[1:7] **Epaphras:** now with Paul but a Colossian, founder of the church there.

§[1:9–14] Moved by Epaphras' account, the apostle has prayed and continues to pray fervently for the Colossians that, in their response to the gospel, they **may be filled with the knowledge of** God's will (Col 1:9; cf. Col 3:10). Paul expects a mutual interaction between their life according to the gospel and this knowledge (Col 1:10), yielding results (**fruit,** Col 1:10; cf. Col 1:6) **in every good work:** growth, strength, **endurance, patience, with joy** (Col 1:11), and the further giving of thanks (Col 1:12).

¶[1:12–14] A summary about **redemption** by **the Father** precedes the statement in Col 1:15–20 about the **beloved Son** who is God's love in person (Col 1:13). Christians share **the inheritance . . . in light** with **the holy ones,** here probably the angels (Col 1:12). The imagery reflects the Exodus (**delivered . . . transferred**) and Jesus' theme of the **kingdom.** Redemption is explained as **forgiveness of sins** (cf. Acts 2:38; Rom 3:24–25; Eph 1:7).

\*\*[1:15–20] As the poetic arrangement indicates, these lines are probably an early Christian hymn, known to the Colossians and taken up into the letter from liturgical use (cf. Phil 2:6–11; 1 Tm 3:16). They present Christ as the mediator of creation (Col 1:15–18a) and of redemption (Col 1:18b–20). There is a parallelism between **firstborn of all creation** (Col 1:15) and **firstborn from the dead** (Col 1:18). While many of the phrases were at home in Greek philosophical use and even in gnosticism, the basic ideas also reflect Old Testament themes about Wisdom found in Prv 8:22–31; Wis 7:22–8:1; and Sir 1:4. See also notes on what is possibly a hymn in Jn 1:1–18.

††[1:15] **Image:** cf. Gn 1:27. Whereas the man and the woman were originally created in the image and likeness of God (see also Gn 1:26), Christ as image (2 Cor 4:4) of the **invisible God** (Jn 1:18) now shares this new nature in baptism with those redeemed (cf. Col 3:10–11).

‡‡[1:16–17] Christ (though not mentioned by name) is preeminent and supreme as God's agent in the creation of **all things** (cf. Jn 1:3), as prior to **all things** (Col 1:17; cf. Heb 1:3).

---

a. [1:1] Eph 1:1.   b. [1:3] Eph 1:15–16; Phlm 4–5.   c. [1:5] Eph 1:13, 18; 1 Pt 1:4.   d. [1:7] Phlm 23.

e. [1:9] Eph 1:15–17; 5:17; Phil 1:9.   f. [1:12] 3:17; Jn 8:12; Acts 26:18; 1 Tm 6:16; 1 Pt 2:9.   g. [1:14] Eph 1:7.   h. [1:15] Ps 89:28; Jn 1:3, 18; 2 Cor 4:4.

all things were created through him
and for him.[i]

17 He is before all things,
and in him all things hold together.
18 He is the head of the body, the church.[*]
He is the beginning, the firstborn from
the dead,
that in all things he himself might be
preeminent.[j]
19 For in him all the fullness[†] was pleased to
dwell,
20 and through him to reconcile all
things for him,
making peace by the blood of his
cross[‡]
[through him], whether those on
earth or those in heaven.[k]

21§And you who once were alienated and hostile in mind because of evil deeds[l] 22he has now reconciled in his fleshly body through his death, to present you holy, without blemish, and irreproachable before him, 23provided that you persevere in the faith, firmly grounded, stable, and not shifting from the hope of the gospel that you heard, which has been preached to every creature under heaven, of which I, Paul, am a minister. **Christ in Us.**[¶] 24Now I rejoice in my sufferings for your sake, and in my flesh I am filling

up what is lacking[**] in the afflictions of Christ on behalf of his body, which is the church, 25of which I am a minister in accordance with God's stewardship given to me to bring to completion for you the word of God, 26the mystery hidden from ages and from generations past. But now it has been manifested to his holy ones,[m] 27to whom God chose to make known the riches of the glory of this mystery among the Gentiles; it is Christ in you, the hope for glory.[n] 28It is he whom we proclaim, admonishing everyone and teaching everyone with all wisdom, that we may present everyone perfect in Christ.[o] 29For this I labor and struggle, in accord with the exercise of his power working within me.[p]

## CHAPTER 2

1For I want you to know how great a struggle I am having for you and for those in Laodicea[††] and all who have not seen me face to face, 2that their hearts may be encouraged as they are brought together in love, to have all the richness of fully assured understanding, for the knowledge of the mystery of God, Christ,[q] 3in whom are hidden all the treasures of wisdom and knowledge.[r]

### III. WARNINGS AGAINST FALSE TEACHERS[‡‡]

*[1:18] **Church:** such a reference seemingly belongs under "redemption" in the following lines, not under the "creation" section of the hymn. Stoic thought sometimes referred to the world as "the body of Zeus." Pauline usage is to speak of the church as the body of Christ (1 Cor 12:12–27; Rom 12:4–5). Some think that the author of Colossians has inserted the reference to the church here so as to define "head of the body" in Paul's customary way. See Col 1:24. **Preeminent:** when Christ was raised by God as **firstborn from the dead** (cf. Acts 26:23; Rev 1:5), he was placed over the community, the church, that he had brought into being, but he is also indicated as crown of the whole new creation, over **all things.** His further role is to **reconcile all things** (Col 1:20) for God or possibly "to himself."

†[1:19] **Fullness:** in gnostic usage this term referred to a spiritual world of beings above, between God and the world; many later interpreters take it to refer to **the fullness of the deity** (Col 2:9); the reference could also be to the fullness of grace (cf. Jn 1:16).

‡[1:20] **The blood of his cross:** the most specific reference in the hymn to redemption through Christ's death, a central theme in Paul; cf. Col 2:14–15; 1 Cor 1:17, 18, 23. [**Through him**]: the phrase, lacking in some manuscripts, seems superfluous but parallels the reference to reconciliation through Christ earlier in the verse.

§[1:21–23] Paul, in applying this hymn to the Colossians, reminds them that they have experienced the reconciling effect of Christ's death. He sees the effects of the cross in the redemption of human beings, not of cosmic powers such as those referred to in Col 1:16, 20 (**all things**). Paul also urges adherence to Christ in faith and begins to point to his own role as minister (Col 1:23), sufferer (Col 1:24), and proclaimer (Col 1:27–28) of this gospel.

¶[1:24–2:3] As the community at Colossae was not personally known to Paul (see Introduction), he here invests his teaching with greater authority by presenting a brief sketch of his apostolic ministry and sufferings as they reflect those of Christ on behalf of the church (Col 1:24). The preaching of God's word (Col 1:25) carries out the divine plan (**the mystery,** Col 1:26) to make Christ known to the Gentiles (Col

1:27). It teaches the God-given wisdom about Christ (Col 1:28), whose power works mightily in the apostle (Col 1:29). Even in those communities that do not know him personally (Col 2:1), he can increase the perception of God in Christ, unite the faithful more firmly in love, and so bring encouragement to them (Col 2:2). He hopes that his apostolic authority will make the Colossians perceive more readily the defects in the teaching of others who have sought to delude them, the next concern in the letter.

**[1:24] **What is lacking:** although variously interpreted, this phrase does not imply that Christ's atoning death on the cross was defective. It may refer to the apocalyptic concept of a quota of "messianic woes" to be endured before the end comes; cf. Mk 13:8, 19–20, 24 and the note on Mt 23:29–32. Others suggest that Paul's mystical unity with Christ allowed him to call his own **sufferings the afflictions of Christ.**

††[2:1] **Laodicea:** chief city in Phrygia, northwest of Colossae; cf. Col 4:13, 16; Rev 3:14–22.

‡‡[2:4–23] In face of the threat posed by false teachers (Col 2:4), the Colossians are admonished to adhere to the gospel as it was first preached to them (Col 2:6), steeping themselves in it with grateful hearts (Col 2:7). They must reject religious teachings originating in any source except the gospel (Col 2:8) because in Christ alone will they have access to God, **the deity** (Col 2:9). So fully has Christ enlightened them that they need no other source of religious knowledge or virtue (Col 2:10). They do not require **circumcision** (Col 2:11), for **in baptism** their whole being has been affected by Christ (Col 2:12) through forgiveness of sin and resurrection to a new life (Col 2:13; cf. Col 3:1 and Rom 6:1–11).

On the cross Christ canceled the record of the debt that stood against us with all its claims (Col 2:14), i.e., he eliminated the law (cf. Eph 2:15) that human beings could not observe— and that could not save them. He forgave sins against the law (Col 2:14) and exposed as false and misleading (Col 2:15) all other powers (cf. Col 1:16) that purport to offer salvation. Therefore, the Colossians are not to accept judgments from such teachers on **food and drink** or to keep certain religious festivals or engage in certain cultic practices (Col 2:16), for the Colossians would thereby risk severing themselves from

i. [1:16] 1 Cor 8:6; Eph 1:10, 21. j. [1:18] 1 Cor 11:3; 12:12, 27; 15:20; Eph 1:22–23; Rev 1:5. k. [1:20] 2 Cor 5:18–19; Eph 1:10. l. [1:21] Eph 2:14–16.

m. [1:26] Rom 16:25–26; 1 Cor 2:7; Eph 3:3, 9. n. [1:27] 3:4; Rom 8:10. o. [1:28] Eph 4:13. p. [1:29] 2:1; 4:12; Phil 4:13. q. [2:2] 1:26–27; Eph 3:18–19. r. [2:3] Prv 2:4–5; Is 45:3; Rom 11:33; 1 Cor 1:30.

**A General Admonition.** [4]I say this so that no one may deceive you by specious arguments.[s] [5]For even if I am absent in the flesh, yet I am with you in spirit, rejoicing as I observe your good order and the firmness of your faith in Christ.[t] [6]So, as you received Christ Jesus the Lord, walk in him, [7]rooted in him and built upon him and established in the faith as you were taught, abounding in thanksgiving.[u] [8]See to it that no one captivate you with an empty, seductive philosophy according to human tradition, according to the elemental powers of the world[*] and not according to Christ.[v]

**Sovereign Role of Christ.** [9]*For in him dwells the whole fullness of the deity[†] bodily, [10]and you share in this fullness in him, who is the head of every principality and power. [11]*In him[‡] you were also circumcised with a circumcision not administered by hand, by stripping off the carnal body, with the circumcision of Christ. [12]You were buried with him in baptism, in which you were also raised with him through faith in the power of God, who raised him from the dead.[y] [13]*And even when you were dead [in] transgressions and the uncircumcision of your flesh, he brought you to life along with him, having forgiven us all our transgressions; [14]*obliterating the bond against us, with its legal claims, which was opposed to us, he also removed it from our midst, nailing it to the cross;[a] [15]despoiling the principalities and the powers, he made a public spectacle of them,[b] leading them away in triumph by it.[¶]

**Practices Contrary to Faith.** [16]*Let no one, then, pass judgment on you in matters of food and drink or with regard to a festival or new moon or sabbath.[**] [17]These are shadows of things to come; the reality belongs to Christ.[d] [18]Let no one disqualify you, delighting in self-abasement and worship of angels, taking his stand on visions,[††] inflated without reason by his fleshly mind,[e] [19]and not holding closely to the head, from whom the whole body, supported and held together by its ligaments and bonds, achieves the growth that comes from God.[f]

[20]If you died with Christ to the elemental powers of the world, why do you submit to regulations as if you were still living in the world? [21]"Do not handle! Do not taste! Do not touch!" [22]These are all things destined to perish with use; they accord with human precepts and teachings.[g] [23]While they have a semblance of wisdom in rigor of devotion and self-abasement [and] severity to the body, they are of no value against gratification of the flesh.

## IV. THE IDEAL CHRISTIAN LIFE IN THE WORLD

### CHAPTER 3

**Mystical Death and Resurrection.**[‡‡] [1]If then you were raised with Christ, seek what is above, where Christ is seated at the right hand of God.[h] [2]Think of what is above, not of what is on earth. [3]For you have died, and your life is hidden with Christ in God.[i] [4]When Christ your life appears, then you too will appear with him in glory.

**Renunciation of Vice.**[§§] [5]Put to death, then, the parts of you that are earthly:[j] immorality, impurity, passion, evil desire, and the greed that is idolatry.[¶¶] [6]Because of these the wrath of God[***] is coming [upon the disobedient].[k] [7]By these you too once conducted yourselves, when you lived in that way. [8]But now you must put them all away:[†††] anger, fury, malice, slander, and obscene language out of your mouths.[l] [9]Stop lying to one another, since you have taken off the old self with its practices[m] [10]‡‡‡and have put on the new

Christ (Col 2:19). If, when they accepted the gospel, they believed in Christ as their savior, they must be convinced that their salvation cannot be achieved by appeasing ruling spirits through dietary practices or through a wisdom gained simply by means of harsh asceticism (Col 2:20–23).

[*][2:8] **Elemental powers of the world:** see note on Gal 4:3.

[†][2:9] **Fullness of the deity:** the divine nature, not just attributes; see note on Col 1:19.

[‡][2:11] A description of baptism (Col 2:12) in symbolic terms of the Old Testament rite for entry into the community. The false teachers may have demanded physical circumcision of the Colossians.

[§][2:14] The elaborate metaphor here about how God canceled the legal claims against us through Christ's cross depicts not Christ being nailed to the cross by men but the **bond . . . with its legal claims** being nailed to the cross by God.

[¶][2:15] The picture derives from the **public spectacle** and **triumph** of a Roman emperor's victory parade, where captives marched in subjection. **The principalities and the powers** are here conquered, not reconciled (cf. Col 1:16, 20). An alternate rendering for **by it** (the cross) is "by him" (Christ).

[**][2:16] **Festival or new moon or sabbath:** yearly, monthly, and weekly observances determined by religious powers associated with a calendar set by the heavenly bodies, sun, moon, and stars (cf. Col 2:8).

[††][2:18] Ascetic practices encouraged by the false teachers included subjection of self humbly to their rules, worship of angels, and cultivation of visions, though exact details are unclear.

[‡‡][3:1–4] By retaining the message of the gospel that the risen, living Christ is the source of their salvation, the Colossians will be free from false religious evaluations of the things of the world (Col 3:1–2). They have died to these; but one day **when Christ . . . appears**, they will live with Christ in the presence of God (Col 3:3–4).

[§§][3:5–17] In lieu of false asceticism and superstitious festivals, the apostle reminds the Colossians of the moral life that is to characterize their response to God through Christ. He urges their participation in the liturgical hymns and prayers that center upon God's plan of salvation in Christ (Col 3:16).

[¶¶][3:5, 8] The two lists of five vices each are similar to enumerations at Rom 1:29–31 and Gal 5:19–21.

[***][3:6] **The wrath of God:** see note on Rom 1:18. Many manuscripts add, as at Eph 5:6, "upon the disobedient."

[†††][3:8–10] Put . . . away; have taken off; have put on: the terms may reflect baptismal practice, taking off garments and putting on new ones after being united with Christ; here translated into ethical terms.

[‡‡‡][3:10] **Image:** see note on Col 1:15.

s. [2:4] Eph 4:14.    t. [2:5] 1 Cor 5:3; Phil 1:27.    u. [2:7] Eph 2:20–22; 3:17.    v. [2:8] Gal 4:3; Eph 5:6.    w. [2:9] 1:19; Eph 3:19.    x. [2:11] 1:22; Jer 4:4; Rom 2:25–29; Phil 3:3.    y. [2:12] Rom 6:3–4.    z. [2:13] Eph 2:1, 5.    a. [2:14] Eph 2:14–15.    b. [2:15] 1:16, 20; 2 Cor 2:14; Eph 1:21.    c. [2:16] Rom 14:3–4; 1 Tm 4:3.    d. [2:17] Heb 8:5; 10:1.

e. [2:18] 2:23; Mt 24:4.    f. [2:19] Eph 2:21–22; 4:16.    g. [2:22] Is 29:13.    h. [3:1] 2:12; Ps 110:1; Phil 3:20; Eph 2:6.    i. [3:3] Rom 6:2–5.    j. [3:5] Mt 15:19; Rom 1:29–30; Gal 5:19–21; Eph 5:3, 5.    k. [3:6] Rom 1:18.    l. [3:8] Eph 4:22, 25, 31.    m. [3:9] Rom 6:4, 6; Eph 4:22–25; Heb 12:1; 1 Pt 2:1; 4:2.

self, which is being renewed, for knowledge, in the image of its creator.ⁿ ¹¹Here there is not Greek and Jew, circumcision and uncircumcision, barbarian, Scythian,* slave, free; but Christ is all and in all.º

¹²Put on then, as God's chosen ones, holy and beloved, heartfelt compassion, kindness, humility, gentleness, and patience,ᵖ ¹³bearing with one another and forgiving one another, if one has a grievance against another; as the Lord has forgiven you, so must you also do.�q ¹⁴And over all these put on love, that is, the bond of perfection.ʳ ¹⁵And let the peace of Christ control your hearts, the peace into which you were also called in one body. And be thankful.ˢ ¹⁶Let the word of Christ dwell in you richly, as in all wisdom you teach and admonish one another, singing psalms, hymns, and spiritual songs with gratitude in your hearts to God.ᵗ ¹⁷And whatever you do, in word or in deed, do everything in the name of the Lord Jesus, giving thanks to God the Father through him.ᵘ

**The Christian Family.** ¹⁸†Wives, be subordinate to your husbands, as is proper in the Lord.ᵛ ¹⁹Husbands, love your wives, and avoid any bitterness toward them. ²⁰Children, obey your parents in everything, for this is pleasing to the Lord.ʷ ²¹Fathers, do not provoke your children, so they may not become discouraged.ˣ

**Slaves and Masters.** ²²Slaves,‡ obey your human masters in everything, not only when being watched, as currying favor, but in simplicity of heart, fearing the Lord.ʸ ²³Whatever you do, do from the heart, as for the Lord and not for others, ²⁴knowing that you will receive from the Lord the due payment of the inheritance; be slaves of the Lord Christ. ²⁵For the wrongdoer will receive recompense for the wrong he committed, and there is no partiality.ᶻ

### CHAPTER 4

¹Masters, treat your slaves justly and fairly, realizing that you too have a Master in heaven.

---

*[3:11] **Scythian:** a barbarous people from north of the Black Sea.

†[3:18–4:6] After general recommendations that connect family life and the social condition of slavery with the service of Christ (Col 3:18–4:1), Paul requests prayers for himself, especially in view of his imprisonment (Col 3:2–3), and recommends friendly relations and meaningful discussions of Christian teaching with **outsiders**, i.e., non-Christians (Col 3:5–6). See note on Eph 5:21–6:9.

‡[3:22–25] **Slaves:** within this table of duties in family and societal relations, involving wives and husbands, children and parents (Col 3:18–21), such as also appears in Eph 5:22–6:9, slaves here receive special attention because of the case of Onesimus the slave returning to his master (Col 4:9; Phlm 10–12).

---

n. [3:10] Gn 1:26–27.  o. [3:11] 1 Cor 12:13; Gal 3:27–28.  p. [3:12] Eph 4:1–2, 32; 1 Thes 5:15.  q. [3:13] Mt 6:14; 18:21–35; Eph 4:32.  r. [3:14] Rom 13:8–10.  s. [3:15] Rom 12:5; 1 Cor 12:12; Eph 2:16; 4:3–4; Phil 4:7.  t. [3:16] Eph 5:19–20.  u. [3:17] 1 Cor 10:31.  v. [3:18] Eph 5:22; Ti 2:5; 1 Pt 3:1.  w. [3:20] Eph 6:1.  x. [3:21] Eph 6:4.  y. [3:22] Eph 6:5; 1 Tm 6:1; Ti 2:9–10; 1 Pt 2:18.  z. [3:25] Rom 2:11.

**Prayer and Apostolic Spirit.** ²Persevere in prayer, being watchful in it with thanksgiving;ᵃ ³at the same time, pray for us, too, that God may open a door to us for the word, to speak of the mystery of Christ, for which I am in prison,ᵇ ⁴that I may make it clear, as I must speak. ⁵Conduct yourselves wisely toward outsiders, making the most of the opportunity.ᶜ ⁶Let your speech always be gracious, seasoned with salt, so that you know how you should respond to each one.

### V. CONCLUSION§

**Tychicus and Onesimus.** ⁷Tychicus,¶ my beloved brother, trustworthy minister, and fellow slave in the Lord, will tell you all the news of me.ᵈ ⁸I am sending him to you for this very purpose, so that you may know about us and that he may encourage your hearts, ⁹together with Onesimus, a trustworthy and beloved brother, who is one of you. They will tell you about everything here.ᵉ

**From Paul's Co-Workers.** ¹⁰Aristarchus,** my fellow prisoner, sends you greetings, as does Mark the cousin of Barnabas (concerning whom you have received instructions; if he comes to you, receive him),ᶠ ¹¹and Jesus,†† who is called Justus, who are of the circumcision; these alone are my co-workers for the kingdom of God, and they have been a comfort to me. ¹²Epaphras‡‡ sends you greetings; he is one of you, a slave of Christ [Jesus], always striving for you in his prayers so that you may be perfect and fully assured in all the will of God.ᵍ ¹³For I can testify that he works very hard for you and for those in Laodicea§§ and those in Hierapolis. ¹⁴Luke¶¶ the beloved physician sends greetings, as does Demas.ʰ

**A Message for the Laodiceans.** ¹⁵Give greetings to the brothers in Laodicea and to Nympha and to the church in her house.*** ¹⁶And when this

---

§[4:7–18] Paul concludes with greetings and information concerning various Christians known to the Colossians.

¶[4:7] **Tychicus:** Acts 20:4 mentions his role in the collection for Jerusalem; Eph 6:21 repeats what is said here; see also 2 Tm 4:12; Ti 3:12.

**[4:10] **Aristarchus:** a Thessalonian who was with Paul at Ephesus and Caesarea and on the voyage to Rome (Acts 19:29; 20:4; 27:2). **Mark:** also referred to at Phlm 24 and 2 Tm 4:11 and, as "John Mark," in Acts (Acts 12:12, 25; 13:13; 15:37–40). See also 1 Pt 5:13 and the note there. Traditionally the author of the second gospel.

††[4:11] **Jesus:** a then common Jewish name, the Greek form of Joshua.

‡‡[4:12] **Epaphras:** see notes on Col 1:3–8 and Col 1:7.

§§[4:13] **Laodicea:** see note on Col 2:1. **Hierapolis:** a city northeast of Laodicea and northwest of Colossae.

¶¶[4:14] **Luke:** only here described as a medical doctor; cf. Phlm 24 and 2 Tm 4:11. Traditionally the author of the third gospel. **Demas:** cf. Phlm 24; he later deserted Paul (2 Tm 4:10).

***[4:15] **Nympha and . . . her house:** some manuscripts read a masculine for the house-church leader, "Nymphas and . . . his house."

---

a. [4:2] Lk 18:1; Rom 12:12; Eph 6:18–20; 1 Thes 5:17.  b. [4:3] Rom 15:30; 1 Cor 16:9; Eph 6:19; 2 Thes 3:1.  c. [4:5] Eph 5:15–16.  d. [4:7] Acts 20:4; Eph 6:21–22; Phil 1:12.  e. [4:9] Phlm 10–11.  f. [4:10] Acts 19:29; 20:4; 27:2 / Acts 12:12, 25; 13:13; 15:37, 40; 2 Tm 4:11; Phlm 24; 1 Pt 5:13.  g. [4:12] 1:7; Rom 15:30.  h. [4:14] Phlm 24; 2 Tm 4:10–11.

letter is read before you, have it read also in the church of the Laodiceans, and you yourselves read the one from Laodicea.* 17And tell Archippus, "See that you fulfill the ministry[†] that you received in the Lord."i

18The greeting is in my own hand,[‡] Paul's. Remember my chains. Grace be with you.j

---

\*[4:16] **The one from Laodicea**: either a letter by Paul that has been lost or the Letter to the Ephesians (cf. note on Eph 1:1 **in Ephesus**).

†[4:17] **Fulfill the ministry**: usually taken to mean that **Archippus**, the son of Philemon and Apphia (Phlm 1–2),

is "pastor" at Colossae. An alternate interpretation is that Archippus, not Philemon, is the owner of the slave Onesimus and that Paul is asking Archippus to complete the service he has received in the Lord by sending Onesimus back to minister to Paul in his captivity (cf. Phlm 20).

‡[4:18] **My own hand**: a postscript in Paul's own hand was his custom; cf. Gal 6:11–18 and 2 Thes 3:17–18.

---

i. [4:17] Phlm 2.

j. [4:18] 1 Cor 16:21; Gal 6:11; Eph 3:1; 2 Thes 3:17.

# THE FIRST LETTER TO THE
# THESSALONIANS

～✦～

When Paul parted from Barnabas (Acts 15:36–41) at the beginning of what is called his second missionary journey, he chose Silvanus (Silas) as his traveling companion. Soon afterwards he took Timothy along with him (Acts 16:1–3). Paul was now clearly at the head of his own missionary band. About A.D. 50, he arrived in Greece for the first time. In making converts in Philippi and, soon afterwards, in Thessalonica, he was beset by persecution from Jews and Gentiles alike. Moving on to Beroea, he was again harassed by enemies from Thessalonica and hurriedly left for Athens (Acts 16:11–17:15). Silvanus and Timothy remained behind for a while. Paul soon sent Timothy back to Thessalonica to strengthen that community in its trials (1 Thes 3:1–5). Timothy and Silvanus finally returned to Paul when he reached Corinth (Acts 18:1–18), probably in the early summer of A.D. 51. Timothy's return with a report on conditions at Thessalonica served as the occasion for Paul's first letter (1 Thes 3:6–8).

The letter begins with a brief address (1 Thes 1:1) and concludes with a greeting (1 Thes 5:26–28). The body of the letter consists of two major parts. The first (1 Thes 1:2–3:13) is a set of three sections of thanksgiving connected by two *apologiae* (defenses) dealing, respectively, with the missionaries' previous conduct and their current concerns. Paul's thankful optimism regarding the Thessalonians' spiritual welfare is tempered by his insistence on their recognition of the selfless love shown by the missionaries. In an age of itinerant peddlers of new religions, Paul found it necessary to emphasize not only the content of his gospel but also his manner of presenting it, for both attested to God's grace as freely bestowed and powerfully effected.

The second part of the letter (1 Thes 4:1–5:25) is specifically hortatory or parenetic. The superabundant love for which Paul has just prayed (1 Thes 3:12–13) is to be shown practically by living out the norms of conduct that he has communicated to them. Specific "imperatives" of Christian life, principles for acting morally, stem from the "indicative" of one's relationship to God through Christ by the sending of the holy Spirit. Thus, moral conduct is the practical, personal expression of one's Christian faith, love, and hope.

The principal divisions of the First Letter to the Thessalonians are the following:

I. Address (1:1–10)
II. Previous Relations with the Thessalonians (2:1–3:13)
III. Specific Exhortations (4:1–5:25)
IV. Final Greeting (5:26–28)

## I. ADDRESS

### CHAPTER 1

**Greeting.** [1] [a]Paul, Silvanus, and Timothy to the church of the Thessalonians in God the Father and the Lord Jesus Christ: grace to you and peace.

**Thanksgiving for Their Faith.** [2]We give thanks to God always for all of you, remembering you in our prayers, unceasingly[b] [3]calling to mind your work of faith and labor of love and endurance in hope[†] of our Lord Jesus Christ, before our God and Father, [4]knowing, brothers loved by God, how you were chosen.[c] [5]For our gospel did not come to you in word alone, but also in power and in the holy Spirit and [with] much conviction. You know what sort of people we were [among] you for your sake.[d] [6]And you

---

*[1:1] On the address, see note on Rom 1:1–7.

a. [1:1] Acts 15:40; 16:1–3, 19; 17:14–15; 2 Thes 1:1–2.   b. [1:2] 2 Thes 1:3.

†[1:3] **Faith . . . love . . . hope:** this, along with 1 Thes 5:8, is the earliest mention in Christian literature of the three "theological virtues" (see 1 Cor 13:13). The order here stresses eschatological hope, in line with the letter's emphasis on the Lord's second, triumphal coming, or parousia (1 Thes 1:10; 2:12, 19; 3:13; 4:13–5:11; 5:23).

c. [1:4] 2 Thes 2:13.   d. [1:5] Acts 13:52; 17:1–9.

became imitators' of us and of the Lord, receiving the word in great affliction, with joy from the holy Spirit, [7]so that you became a model for all the believers in Macedonia and in Achaia.[e] [8]For from you the word of the Lord has sounded forth not only in Macedonia and [in] Achaia, but in every place your faith in God has gone forth, so that we have no need to say anything.[f] [9]For they themselves openly declare about us what sort of reception we had among you, and how you turned to God from idols to serve the living and true God[g] [10]and to await his Son from heaven, whom he raised from [the] dead, Jesus, who delivers us from the coming wrath.[h]

## II. PREVIOUS RELATIONS WITH THE THESSALONIANS

### CHAPTER 2

**Paul's Ministry Among Them.** [1]For you yourselves know, brothers, that our reception among you was not without effect. [2]Rather, after we had suffered and been insolently treated, as you know, in Philippi, we drew courage through our God to speak to you the gospel of God with much struggle.[i] [3]Our exhortation was not from delusion or impure motives, nor did it work through deception. [4]But as we were judged worthy[†] by God to be entrusted with the gospel, that is how we speak, not as trying to please human beings, but rather God, who judges our hearts.[j] [5]Nor, indeed, did we ever appear with flattering speech, as you know, or with a pretext for greed—God is witness— [6]nor did we seek praise from human beings, either from you or from others,[k] [7]although we were able to impose our weight as apostles of Christ. Rather, we were gentle[‡] among you, as a nursing mother cares for her children. [8]With such affection for you, we were determined to share with you not only the gospel of God, but our very selves as well, so dearly beloved had you become to us. [9]You recall, brothers, our toil and drudgery. Working night and day in order not to burden any of you, we proclaimed to you the gospel of God.[l] [10]You are witnesses, and so is God, how devoutly and justly and blamelessly we behaved toward you believers. [11]As you know, we treated each one of you as a father treats his children,[m] [12]exhorting and encouraging you and insisting that you conduct yourselves as worthy of the God who calls you into his kingdom and glory.[n]

**Further Thanksgiving.** [13]And for this reason we too give thanks to God unceasingly, that, in receiving the word of God from hearing us, you received not a human word but, as it truly is, the word of God, which is now at work in you who believe. [14]For you, brothers, have become imitators of the churches of God that are in Judea in Christ Jesus. For you suffer the same things from your compatriots as they did from the Jews, [15]who killed both the Lord Jesus and the prophets and persecuted us; they do not please God, and are opposed to everyone,[o] [16]trying to prevent us from speaking to the Gentiles that they may be saved, thus constantly filling up the measure of their sins. But the wrath of God has finally begun to come upon them.[p]

**Paul's Recent Travel Plans.** [17]Brothers, when we were bereft of you for a short time, in person, not in heart, we were all the more eager in our great desire to see you in person.[q] [18]We decided to go to you—I, Paul, not only once but more than once—yet Satan thwarted us.[r] [19]For what is our hope or joy or crown to boast of in the presence of our Lord Jesus at his coming if not you yourselves? [20]For you are our glory and joy.

### CHAPTER 3

[1]That is why, when we could bear it no longer, we decided to remain alone in Athens[s] [2]and sent Timothy, our brother and co-worker for God in the gospel of Christ, to strengthen and encourage you in your faith,[u] [3]so that no one be disturbed in these afflictions. For you yourselves know that we are destined[**] for this. [4]For even when we were among you, we used to warn you in advance that we would undergo affliction,

§[2:14] Luke's picture of the persecutions at Philippi (by Gentiles) and in Thessalonica and Beroea (by Jews) seems to be considerably schematized (Acts 16:11–40; 17:1–15). Paul pictures the Thessalonian community as composed of converts from paganism (1 Thes 1:9) and speaks here of persecution by their (pagan) compatriots rather than by Jews.

¶[2:15–16] Paul is speaking of historical opposition on the part of Palestinian Jews in particular and does so only some twenty years after Jesus' crucifixion. Even so, he quickly proceeds to depict the persecutors typologically, in apocalyptic terms. His remarks give no grounds for anti-Semitism to those willing to understand him, especially in view of Paul's pride in his own ethnic and religious background (Rom 9:1–5; 10:1; 11:1–3; Phil 3:4–6). Sinful conduct (1 Thes 2:16) is itself an anticipation of the ultimate wrath or judgment of God (Rom 1:18–2:5), whether or not it is perceived as such.

**[3:3] We are destined: the Greek phraseology and the context suggest Paul's concern to alert his readers to difficulties he knew they would necessarily face and to enable them to see their present experience in the light of what he warned them would happen in the future. This line of thought is followed in 2 Thes 2:1–15.

---

*[1:6] **Imitators:** the Pauline theme of "imitation" (see 1 Thes 2:14; 1 Cor 4:16; 11:1; 2 Thes 3:9) is rooted in Paul's view of solidarity in Christ through sharing in Jesus' cross and in the Spirit of the risen Lord.

†[2:4] **Judged worthy:** Paul regards "worthiness" not as grounded in one's own talent or moral self-righteousness but in God's discernment of genuinely selfless attitudes and actions (see 2 Cor 10:17–18).

‡[2:7] **Gentle:** many excellent manuscripts read "infants" (*nēpioi*), but "gentle" (*ēpioi*) better suits the context here.

e. [1:7] 2 Thes 1:4; 1 Cor 4:16; 11:1 / 2:14; Phil 3:17.  f. [1:8] Rom 1:8.  g. [1:9] Acts 14:15; Gal 4:8 / 4:5.  h. [1:10] Rom 2:1–16; 5:9; 13:4 / 5:9.  i. [2:2] Acts 16:19–17:10.  j. [2:4] Gal 1:10.  k. [2:6] Jn 5:41, 44; 1 Cor 10:31; 2 Cor 4:17.  l. [2:9] Acts 20:34; 1 Cor 4:12; 9:3–18; 2 Thes 3:7–9.

m. [2:11] Acts 20:31.  n. [2:12] 1 Pt 5:10 / 4:7; 2 Thes 2:14.  o. [2:15] Acts 2:23; 7:52.  p. [2:16] Gn 15:16; 2 Mc 6:14 / Rom 1:18; 2:5–6.  q. [2:17] 3:10; Rom 1:10–11.  r. [2:18] Rom 15:22.  s. [2:19] 2 Cor 1:14; Phil 2:16; 4:1.  t. [3:1] Acts 17:14.  u. [3:2] Acts 16:1–2; 1 Cor 3:5–9.

just as has happened, as you know.$^v$ $^5$For this reason, when I too could bear it no longer, I sent to learn about your faith, for fear that somehow the tempter had put you to the test and our toil might come to nothing.

$^6$But just now Timothy has returned to us from you, bringing us the good news of your faith and love, and that you always think kindly of us and long to see us as we long to see you. $^7$Because of this, we have been reassured about you, brothers, in our every distress and affliction, through your faith. $^8$For we now live, if you stand firm in the Lord.

**Concluding Thanksgiving and Prayer.** $^9$What thanksgiving, then, can we render to God for you, for all the joy we feel on your account before our God? $^{10}$Night and day we pray beyond measure to see you in person and to remedy the deficiencies of your faith. $^{11}$Now may God himself, our Father, and our Lord Jesus direct our way to you, $^{12}$and may the Lord make you increase and abound in love for one another and for all, just as we have for you,$^w$ $^{13}$so as to strengthen your hearts, to be blameless in holiness before our God and Father at the coming of our Lord Jesus with all his holy ones. [Amen.]$^x$

## III. SPECIFIC EXHORTATIONS

### CHAPTER 4

**General Exhortations.** $^1$Finally, brothers, we earnestly ask and exhort you in the Lord Jesus that, as you received from us how you should conduct yourselves to please God—and as you are conducting yourselves—you do so even more. $^2$For you know what instructions$^†$ we gave you through the Lord Jesus.

**Holiness in Sexual Conduct.**$^‡$ $^3$This is the will of God, your holiness: that you refrain from immorality, $^4$that each of you know how to acquire a wife for himself in holiness and honor, $^5$not in lustful passion as do the Gentiles who do not know God;$^y$ $^6$not to take advantage of or exploit a brother in this matter, for the Lord is an avenger in all these things, as we told you before and solemnly affirmed. $^7$For God did not call us to impurity but to holiness. $^8$Therefore, whoever disregards this, disregards not a human being but God, who [also] gives his holy Spirit to you.$^z$

**Mutual Charity.** $^9$On the subject of mutual charity you have no need for anyone to write you, for you yourselves have been taught by God to love one another.$^a$ $^{10}$Indeed, you do this for all the brothers throughout Macedonia. Nevertheless we urge you, brothers, to progress even more,$^b$ $^{11}$and to aspire to live a tranquil life, to mind your own affairs, and to work with your [own] hands, as we instructed you, $^{12}$that you may conduct yourselves properly toward outsiders and not depend on anyone.

**Hope for the Christian Dead.** $^{13}$We do not want you to be unaware, brothers, about those who have fallen asleep, so that you may not grieve like the rest, who have no hope. $^{14}$For if we believe that Jesus died and rose, so too will God, through Jesus, bring with him those who have fallen asleep.$^c$ $^{15}$Indeed, we tell you this, on the word of the Lord, that we who are alive, who are left until the coming of the Lord,$^§$ will surely not precede those who have fallen asleep.$^d$ $^{16}$For the Lord himself, with a word of command, with the voice of an archangel and with the trumpet of God, will come down from heaven, and the dead in Christ will rise first.$^e$ $^{17}$Then we who are alive, who are left, will be caught up together$^¶$ with them in the clouds to meet the Lord in the air. Thus we shall always be with the Lord. $^{18}$Therefore, console one another with these words.

### CHAPTER 5

**Vigilance.** $^1$Concerning times and seasons, brothers, you have no need for anything to be written to you.$^f$ $^2$For you yourselves know very well that the day of the Lord will come like a thief at night.$^g$ $^3$When people are saying, "Peace

---

*[3:9–10] The tension between Paul's optimism concerning the Thessalonians' faith and his worries about their perseverance remains unresolved. Perhaps this is accounted for not only by the continuing harassment but also by the shortness of his own stay in Thessalonica (even if that were over twice as long as the conventional three weeks that Luke assigns to it, Acts 17:2).

†[4:2] **Instructions**: these include specific guidelines on the basis of the Lord's authority, not necessarily sayings Jesus actually uttered. More profoundly, as 1 Thes 4:8 implies, the instructions are practical principles that Paul worked out in accordance with his understanding of the role of the Spirit.

‡[4:3–8] Many think that this passage deals with a variety of moral regulations (fornication, adultery, sharp business practices). It can be more specifically interpreted as bringing general norms to bear on a specific problem, namely, marriage within degrees of consanguinity (as between uncle and niece) forbidden in Jewish law but allowed according to a Greek heiress law, which would insure retention of an inheritance within the family and perhaps thereby occasion divorce. In that case, "immorality" (1 Thes 4:3) should be rendered as "unlawful marriage" and "this matter" (1 Thes 4:6) as "a lawsuit." The phrase in 1 Thes 4:4, "acquire a wife for himself," has often been interpreted to mean "control one's body."

§[4:15] **Coming of the Lord**: Paul here assumes that the second coming, or parousia, will occur within his own lifetime but insists that the time or season is unknown (1 Thes 5:1–2). Nevertheless, the most important aspect of the parousia for him was the fulfillment of union with Christ. His pastoral exhortation focuses first on hope for the departed faithful, then (1 Thes 5:1–3) on the need of preparedness for those who have to achieve their goal.

¶[4:17] **Will be caught up together**: literally, snatched up, carried off; cf. 2 Cor 12:2; Rev 12:5. From the Latin verb here used, *rapiemur*, has come the idea of "the rapture," when believers will be transported away from the woes of the world; this construction combines this verse with Mt 24:40–41 (see note there) // Lk 17:34–35 and passages from Revelation in a scheme of millennial dispensationalism.

---

v. [3:4] Acts 14:22; 2 Thes 2:5–7; 2 Tm 3:12.   w. [3:12] 4:9–10; 2 Thes 1:3.   x. [3:13] 5:23; 1 Cor 1:8.

y. [4:5] Ps 79:6; Jer 10:25; 2 Thes 1:8; 1 Pt 3:7.   z. [4:8] Lk 10:16.   a. [4:9] Jn 6:45; 13:34; 1 Jn 2:20–21, 27; 4:7.   b. [4:10] 2 Thes 3:6–12.   c. [4:14] 1 Cor 15:3–4, 12, 20.   d. [4:15] 1 Cor 15:51; Rev 14:13; 20:4–6.   e. [4:16] Mt 24:31; 1 Cor 15:23, 52.   f. [5:1] Mt 24:36–45.   g. [5:2] 2 Pt 3:10.

and security," then sudden disaster comes upon them, like labor pains upon a pregnant woman, and they will not escape.

⁴But you, brothers, are not in darkness, for that day to overtake you like a thief.ʰ ⁵For all of you are children of the light* and children of the day. We are not of the night or of darkness. ⁶Therefore, let us not sleep as the rest do,' but let us stay alert and sober.ⁱ ⁷Those who sleep go to sleep at night, and those who are drunk get drunk at night. ⁸But since we are of the day, let us be sober, putting on the breastplate of faith and love and the helmet that is hope for salvation.ʲ ⁹For God did not destine us for wrath, but to gain salvation through our Lord Jesus Christ, ¹⁰who died for us, so that whether we are awake or asleep we may live together with him.†

¹¹Therefore, encourage one another and build one another up, as indeed you do.ᵏ

**Church Order.** ¹²We ask you, brothers, to respect those who are laboring among you and who are over you in the Lord and who admonish you, ¹³and to show esteem for them with special love on account of their work. Be at peace among yourselves.

¹⁴We urge you, brothers, admonish the idle, cheer the fainthearted, support the weak, be patient with all. ¹⁵See that no one returns evil for evil; rather, always seek what is good [both] for each other and for all.ˡ ¹⁶Rejoice always. ¹⁷Pray without ceasing. ¹⁸In all circumstances give thanks, for this is the will of God for you in Christ Jesus.ᵐ ¹⁹†Do not quench the Spirit. ²⁰Do not despise prophetic utterances. ²¹Test everything; retain what is good. ²²Refrain from every kind of evil.

**Concluding Prayer.** ²³§May the God of peace himself make you perfectly holy and may you entirely, spirit, soul, and body, be preserved blameless for the coming of our Lord Jesus Christ.ⁿ ²⁴The one who calls you is faithful, and he will also accomplish it. ²⁵Brothers, pray for us [too].

## IV. FINAL GREETING

²⁶Greet all the brothers with a holy kiss.⁵ ²⁷I adjure you by the Lord that this letter be read to all the brothers. ²⁸The grace of our Lord Jesus Christ be with you.

---

*[5:5] **Children of the light:** that is, belonging to the daylight of God's personal revelation and expected to achieve it (an analogous development of imagery that appears in Jn 12:36).

†[5:10] Characteristically, Paul plays on words suggesting ultimate and anticipated death and life. Union with the crucified and risen Lord at his parousia is anticipated in some measure in contrasted states of our temporal life. The essential element he urges is our indestructible personal union in Christ's own life (see Rom 5:1–10).

‡[5:19–21] Paul's buoyant encouragement of charismatic freedom sometimes occasioned excesses that he or others had to remedy (see 1 Cor 14; 2 Thes 2:1–15; 2 Pt 3:1–16).

§[5:23] Another possible translation is, "May the God of peace himself make you perfectly holy and sanctify your spirit fully, and may both soul and body be preserved blameless for the coming of our Lord Jesus Christ." In either case, Paul is not offering an anthropological or philosophical analysis of human nature. Rather, he looks to the wholeness of what may be called the supernatural and natural aspects of a person's service of God.

¶[5:26] **Kiss:** the holy embrace (see Rom 16:16; 1 Cor 16:20; 2 Cor 13:12; 1 Pt 5:14) was a greeting of respect and affection, perhaps given during a liturgy at which Paul's letter would have been read.

---

h. [5:4] Eph 5:8–9.   i. [5:6] Mt 24:42; Rom 13:12–13; 1 Pt 5:8.   j. [5:8] Is 59:17; Rom 13:11–14; Eph 6:11, 14–17.   k. [5:11] Rom 15:2; 1 Cor 8:1; 14:12, 26; Eph 4:29.

l. [5:15] Prv 20:22; Mt 5:38–42; Rom 12:17.   m. [5:18] Eph 5:20.   n. [5:23] 2 Thes 3:16.

# THE SECOND LETTER TO THE
# THESSALONIANS

This letter is addressed to the same church as the letter that precedes it in the canon and contains many expressions parallel to those in the First Letter to the Thessalonians, indeed verbatim with them. Yet other aspects of the contents of the Second Letter to the Thessalonians suggest a more impersonal tone and changed circumstances in the situation at Thessalonica.

The letter begins with an address (2 Thes 1:1–2) that expands only slightly on that of 1 Thes 1:1. It ends with a greeting insisting on its Pauline authority in the face of false claims made in Paul's name (see note on 2 Thes 2:2). The body of the letter falls into three short parts, of which the second is notoriously difficult (2 Thes 2).

The opening thanksgiving and prayer (2 Thes 1:3–12) speak of the Thessalonians' increasing faith and love in the face of outside persecution. God's eventual judgment against persecutors and his salvation for the faithful are already evidenced by the very fact of persecution. The second part (2 Thes 2:1–17), the heart of the letter, deals with a problem threatening the faith of the community. A message involving a prophetic oracle and apparently a forged letter, possibly presented at a liturgical gathering (cf. 2 Thes 2:2 and 1 Cor 14:26–33), to the effect that the day of the Lord and all that it means have already come, has upset the life of the Thessalonian church.

The writer counters their preoccupation with the date of the parousia (or coming again of the Lord Jesus from heaven, 2 Thes 2:1) by recalling Paul's teaching concerning what must happen first and by going on to describe what will happen at the Lord's coming (2 Thes 2:8); he indicates the twofold process by which the "activity of Satan" and God's actions (2 Thes 2:9–11) are working out, namely, a growing division between believers and those who succumb to false prophecy and "the lie." He concludes by insisting on Pauline traditions and by praying for divine strength (2 Thes 2:13–17). The closing part of the letter (2 Thes 3:1–16) deals in particular with the apostle's directives and model style of life and with correction of disorderly elements within the community.

Traditional opinion holds that this letter was written shortly after 1 Thessalonians. Occasionally it has been argued that 2 Thessalonians was written first or that the two letters are addressed to different segments within the church at Thessalonica (2 Thessalonians being directed to the Jewish Christians there) or even that 2 Thessalonians was originally written to some other nearby place where Paul carried out mission work, such as Philippi or Beroea. Increasingly in recent times, however, the opinion has been advanced that 2 Thessalonians is a pseudepigraph, that is, a letter written authoritatively in Paul's name, to maintain apostolic traditions in a later period, perhaps during the last two decades of the first century.

In any case, the presumed audience of Second Thessalonians and certain features of its style and content require that it be read and studied in a Pauline context, particularly that provided by 1 Thessalonians. At the same time, and especially if the letter is regarded as not by Paul himself, its apocalyptic presentation of preconditions for the parousia (2 Thes 2:1–12) may profit from and require recourse to a wider biblical basis for interpretation, namely Old Testament books such as Daniel and Isaiah and especially, in the New Testament, the synoptic apocalyptic discourse (Mk 13; Mt 24–25; Lk 21:5–36) and the Book of Revelation.

The principal divisions of the Second Letter to the Thessalonians are the following:

I. Address (1:1–12)
II. Warning Against Deception Concerning the Parousia (2:1–17)
III. Concluding Exhortations (3:1–16)
IV. Final Greetings (3:17–18)

## I. ADDRESS

### CHAPTER 1

**Greeting.**[*] [1]Paul, Silvanus, and Timothy to the church of the Thessalonians in God our Father and the Lord Jesus Christ:[a] [2]grace to you and peace from God [our] Father and the Lord Jesus Christ.

**Thanksgiving.** [3†]We ought to thank God always for you, brothers, as is fitting, because your faith flourishes ever more, and the love of every one of you for one another grows ever greater.[b] [4]Accordingly, we ourselves boast of you in the churches of God regarding your endurance and faith in all your persecutions and the afflictions you endure.

[5]This is evidence of the just judgment of God, so that you may be considered worthy of the kingdom of God for which you are suffering.[c] [6]For it is surely just on God's part to repay with afflictions those who are afflicting you, [7]and to grant rest along with us to you who are undergoing afflictions, at the revelation of the Lord Jesus from heaven with his mighty angels, [8]in blazing fire, inflicting punishment on those who do not acknowledge God and on those who do not obey the gospel of our Lord Jesus.[d] [9]These will pay the penalty of eternal ruin, separated from the presence of the Lord and from the glory of his power,[e] [10]when he comes to be glorified among his holy ones‡ and to be marveled at on that day among all who have believed, for our testimony to you was believed.[f]

**Prayer.** [11]To this end, we always pray for you, that our God may make you worthy of his calling and powerfully bring to fulfillment every good purpose and every effort of faith,[g] [12§]that the name of our Lord Jesus may be glorified in you, and you in him,[h] in accord with the grace of our God and Lord Jesus Christ.

## II. WARNING AGAINST DECEPTION CONCERNING THE PAROUSIA

### CHAPTER 2

**Christ and the Lawless One.**¶ [1]We ask you, brothers, with regard to the coming of our Lord Jesus Christ and our assembling with him,[i] [2]not to be shaken out of your minds suddenly, or to be alarmed either by a "spirit,"** or by an oral statement, or by a letter allegedly from us to the effect that the day of the Lord is at hand.[j] [3]Let no one deceive you in any way. For unless the apostasy comes first and the lawless one is revealed,†† the one doomed to perdition, [4k]who opposes and exalts himself above every so-called god and object of worship, so as to seat himself in the temple of God,‡‡ claiming that he

---

¶[2:1–17] The Thessalonians have been **shaken** by a message purporting to come from Paul himself that **the day of the Lord** is already present. He warns against this deception in eschatology by citing a scenario of events that must first occur (2 Thes 2:3–12) before the end will come. The overall point Paul makes is the need to reject such lies as Satan sends; he also reaffirms the Thessalonians in their calling (2 Thes 2:13–14). They are to uphold what Paul himself has taught (2 Thes 2:15). There is a concluding prayer for their strengthening (2 Thes 2:16–17). As in 2 Thes 1:8–10, the Old Testament provides a good deal of coloring; cf. especially Is 14:13–14; 66:15, 18–21; Ez 28:2–9; Dn 11:36–37. The contents of 2 Thes 2:3b–8 may come from a previously existing apocalypse. The details have been variously interpreted.

An alternative to the possibilities noted below understands that an oracular utterance, supposedly coming from a prophetic spirit (2 Thes 2:2–3a), has so disrupted the community's thinking that its effects may be compared to those of the mania connected with the worship of the Greek god Dionysus. On this view, the writer seems to allude in 2 Thes 2:6–8 to Dionysiac "seizure," although, of course, ironically, somewhat as Paul alludes to witchcraft ("an evil eye") in Gal 3:1 in speaking of the threat to faith posed by those disturbing the Galatians (Gal 1:6–7; 5:10b). On this view of 2 Thes 2, the Greek participles *katechon* (rendered above as **what is restraining**) and *katechōn* (**the one who restrains**) are to be translated "the seizing power" in 2 Thes 2:6 and "the seizer" in 2 Thes 2:7. They then allude to a pseudocharismatic force or spirit of Dionysiac character that has suddenly taken hold of the Thessalonian community (see 2 Thes 2:2). The addressees **know** (2 Thes 2:6) this force or spirit because of the problem it is causing. This pseudocharismatic force or spirit is a kind of anticipation and advance proof of the ultimate, climactic figure (**the lawless one** or the rebel, 2 Thes 2:3), of which the community has been warned (see note on 1 Thes 3:3). It is, however, only the beginning of the end that the latter's manifestation entails; the end is not yet. For in the course of the **mystery of lawlessness** (2 Thes 2:7), false prophetism, after it ceases in the Thessalonian community, will be manifested in the world at large (2 Thes 2:8–12), where it will also be eliminated in turn by the Lord Jesus.

**[2:2] "Spirit":** a Spirit-inspired utterance or ecstatic revelation. **An oral statement:** literally, a "word" or pronouncement, not necessarily of ecstatic origin. **A letter allegedly sent by us:** possibly a forged letter, so that Paul calls attention in 2 Thes 3:17 to his practice of concluding a genuine letter with a summary note or greeting in his own hand, as at Gal 6:11–18 and elsewhere.

††[2:3b–5] This incomplete sentence (anacoluthon, 2 Thes 2:4) recalls what the Thessalonians had already been taught, an apocalyptic scenario depicting, in terms borrowed especially from Dn 11:36–37 and related verses, human self-assertiveness against God in **the temple of God** itself. **The lawless one** represents the climax of such activity in this account.

‡‡[2:4] **Seat himself in the temple of God:** a reflection of the language in Dn 7:23–25; 8:9–12; 9:27; 11:36–37; 12:11 about the attempt of Antiochus IV Epiphanes to set up a statue of Zeus in the Jerusalem temple and possibly of the Roman emperor Caligula to do a similar thing (Mk 13:14). Here the imagery suggests an attempt to install someone in the place of

---

*[1:1–2] On the address, see note on Rom 1:1–7 and cf. 1 Thes 1:1.

†[1:3–12] On the thanksgiving, see note on Rom 1:8 and cf. 1 Thes 1:2–10. Paul's gratitude to God for the faith and love of the Thessalonians (2 Thes 1:3) and his Christian pride in their faithful endurance (2 Thes 1:4–5) contrast with the condemnation announced for those who afflict them, a judgment to be carried out at the parousia (2 Thes 1:6–10), which is described in vivid language drawn from Old Testament apocalyptic. A prayer for the fulfillment of God's purpose in the Thessalonians (2 Thes 1:11–12) completes the section, as is customary in a Pauline letter (cf. 1 Thes 1:2–3).

‡[1:10] **Among his holy ones:** in the Old Testament, this term can refer to an angelic throng (cf. also Jude 14), but here, in parallel with **among all who have believed,** it can refer to the triumphant people of God.

§[1:12] **The grace of our God and Lord Jesus Christ:** the Greek can also be translated, "the grace of our God and of the Lord Jesus Christ."

---

a. [1:1] 1 Thes 1:1.  b. [1:3] 1 Cor 1:4; 1 Thes 1:2; 3:12.  c. [1:5] Phil 1:28; 1 Thes 2:12.  d. [1:8] Ps 79:5–6; Is 66:15; Jer 10:25.  e. [1:9] Is 2:10, 19, 21.  f. [1:10] Ps 89:8; Dn 7:18–22, 27; 1 Thes 3:13.  g. [1:11] 1 Thes 1:2–3.  h. [1:12] Is 66:5.

i. [2:1] 1 Thes 4:13–17.  j. [2:2] Mt 24:6; 1 Cor 14:26, 32–33; 1 Thes 5:1–2.  k. [2:4] Dn 11:36–37; Ez 28:2.

is a god— [5]do you not recall that while I was still with you I told you these things? [6]And now you know what is restraining,[*] that he may be revealed in his time. [7][†]For the mystery of lawlessness is already at work. But the one who restrains is to do so only for the present, until he is removed from the scene.[l] [8]And then the lawless one will be revealed, whom the Lord [Jesus] will kill with the breath of his mouth and render powerless by the manifestation of his coming,[m] [9]the one whose coming springs from the power of Satan in every mighty deed and in signs and wonders that lie,[n] [10]and in every wicked deceit for those who are perishing because they have not accepted the love of truth so that they may be saved. [11]Therefore, God is sending them a deceiving power so that they may believe the lie, [12]that all who have not believed the truth but have approved wrongdoing may be condemned.

[13]But we ought to give thanks to God for you always, brothers loved by the Lord, because God chose you as the firstfruits[‡] for salvation through sanctification by the Spirit and belief in truth.[o] [14]To this end he has [also] called you through our gospel to possess the glory of our Lord Jesus Christ.[p] [15]Therefore, brothers, stand firm and hold fast to the traditions that you were taught, either by an oral statement or by a letter of ours.[§]

[16]May our Lord Jesus Christ himself and God our Father, who has loved us and given us everlasting encouragement and good hope through his grace, [17]encourage your hearts and strengthen them in every good deed and word.

## III. CONCLUDING EXHORTATIONS

### CHAPTER 3[*]

**Request for Prayers.** [1]Finally, brothers, pray for us, so that the word of the Lord may speed forward and be glorified, as it did among you,[q] [2]and that we may be delivered from perverse and wicked people, for not all have faith. [3]But the Lord is faithful; he will strengthen you and guard you from the evil one.[r] [4]We are confident of you in the Lord that what we instruct you, you [both] are doing and will continue to do.[s] [5]May the Lord direct your hearts to the love of God and to the endurance of Christ.

**Neglect of Work.** [6]We instruct you, brothers, in the name of [our] Lord Jesus Christ, to shun any brother who conducts himself in a disorderly way and not according to the tradition they received from us.[**] [7]For you know how one must imitate us. For we did not act in a disorderly way among you, [8]nor did we eat food received free from anyone. On the contrary, in toil and drudgery, night and day we worked, so as not to burden any of you.[t] [9]Not that we do not have the right. Rather, we wanted to present ourselves as a model for you, so that you might imitate us.[u] [10]In fact, when we were with you, we instructed you that if anyone was unwilling to work, neither should that one eat.[v] [11]We hear that some are conducting themselves among you in a disorderly way, by not keeping busy but minding the business of others.[w] [12]Such people we instruct and urge in the Lord Jesus Christ to work quietly and to eat their own food. [13]But

God, **claiming that he is a god** (cf. Ez 28:2). Usually, it is the Jerusalem temple that is assumed to be meant; on the alternative view sketched above (see note on 2 Thes 2:1–17), **the temple** refers to the Christian community.

*[2:6–7] **What is restraining . . . the one who restrains**: neuter and masculine, respectively, of a force and person holding back the lawless one. The Thessalonians know what is meant (2 Thes 2:6), but the terms, seemingly found only in this passage and in writings dependent on it, have been variously interpreted. Traditionally, 2 Thes 2:6 has been applied to the Roman empire and 2 Thes 2:7 to the Roman emperor (in Paul's day, Nero) as bulwarks holding back chaos (cf. Rom 13:1–7). A second interpretation suggests that cosmic or angelic powers are binding Satan (2 Thes 2:9) and so restraining him; some relate this to an anti-Christ figure (1 Jn 2:18) or to Michael the archangel (Rev 12:7–9; 20:1–3). A more recent view suggests that it is the preaching of the Christian gospel that restrains the end, for in God's plan the end cannot come until the gospel is preached to all nations (Mk 13:10); in that case, Paul as missionary preacher par excellence is "the one who restrains," whose removal (death) will bring the end (2 Thes 2:7). On the alternative view (see note on 2 Thes 2:1–17), the phrases should be referred to that which and to him who seizes (a prophet) in ecstasy so as to have him speak pseudo-oracles.

†[2:7–12] **The lawless one** and **the one who restrains** are involved in an activity or process, **the mystery of lawlessness**, behind which **Satan** stands (2 Thes 2:9). The action of the **Lord [Jesus]** in overcoming the lawless one is described in Old Testament language (**with the breath of his mouth**; cf. Is 11:4; Jb 4:9; Rev 19:15). His **coming** is literally the Lord's "parousia." The biblical concept of the "holy war," eschatologically conceived, may underlie the imagery.

‡[2:13] **As the firstfruits**: there is also strong manuscript evidence for the reading, "God chose you from the beginning," thus providing a focus on God's activity from beginning to end; **firstfruits** is a Pauline term, however; cf. Rom 8:23; 11:16; 16:5 among other references.

§[2:15] Reference to **an oral statement** and a **letter** (2 Thes 2:2) and the content here, including a formula of conclusion

(cf. 1 Cor 16:13; Gal 5:1), suggest that 2 Thes 2:1–15 or even 2 Thes 2:1–17 are to be taken as a literary unit, notwithstanding the incidental thanksgiving formula in 2 Thes 2:13.

¶[3:1–18] The final chapter urges the Thessalonians to pray for Paul and his colleagues (2 Thes 3:1–2) and reiterates confidence in the Thessalonians (2 Thes 3:3–5), while admonishing them about a specific problem in their community that has grown out of the intense eschatological speculation, namely, not to work but to become instead disorderly busybodies (2 Thes 3:6–15). A benediction (2 Thes 3:16) and postscript in Paul's own hand round out the letter. On 2 Thes 3:17–18, cf. note on 2 Thes 2:2.

**[3:6] Some members of the community, probably because they regarded the parousia as imminent or the new age of the Lord to be already here (2 Thes 2:2), had apparently ceased to work for a living. The disciplinary problem they posed could be rooted in distorted thinking about Paul's own teaching (cf. 1 Thes 2:16; 3:3–4; 5:4–5) or, more likely, in a forged letter (2 Thes 2:2) and the type of teaching dealt with in 2 Thes 2:1–15. The apostle's own moral teaching, reflected in his selfless labors for others, was rooted in a deep doctrinal concern for the gospel message (cf. 1 Thes 2:3–10).

l. [2:7] Mt 13:36–43; Acts 20:29; Gal 5:10; 2 Pt 2:1; Rev 22:11. m. [2:8] Is 11:4; Rev 19:15.   n. [2:9] Mt 24:24; Rev 13:13.   o. [2:13] 1 Thes 2:13; 5:9.   p. [2:14] Rom 5:1–10; 8:29–30; 1 Thes 4:7; 5:9.

q. [3:1] Eph 6:19; Col 4:3.   r. [3:3] 1 Thes 5:24 / 1 Cor 16:13 / Mt 6:13. s. [3:4] 2 Cor 7:16; 1 Thes 4:1–2.   t. [3:8] 1 Thes 2:9.   u. [3:9] Mt 10:10; Phil 3:17.   v. [3:10] 1 Thes 4:11.   w. [3:11] 1 Thes 5:14.

you, brothers, do not be remiss in doing good. [14]If anyone does not obey our word as expressed in this letter, take note of this person not to associate with him, that he may be put to shame. [15]Do not regard him as an enemy but admonish him as a brother.[x] [16]May the Lord of peace himself give you peace at all times and in every way. The Lord be with all of you.[y]

## IV. FINAL GREETINGS

[17]This greeting is in my own hand, Paul's. This is the sign in every letter; this is how I write.[z] [18]The grace of our Lord Jesus Christ be with all of you.

---

x. [3:15] 2 Cor 2:7; Gal 6:1.　y. [3:16] Jn 14:27; Rom 15:33.

z. [3:17] 1 Cor 16:21; Gal 6:11.

# THE FIRST LETTER TO
# TIMOTHY

The three letters, First and Second Timothy and Titus, form a distinct group within the Pauline corpus. In the collection of letters by the Apostle to the Gentiles, they differ from the others in form and contents. All three suggest they were written late in Paul's career. The opponents are not "Judaizers" as in Galatians but false teachers stressing "knowledge" (*gnōsis*; see note on 1 Tm 6:20–21). Attention is given especially to correct doctrine and church organization. Jesus' second coming recedes into the background compared to references in Paul's earlier letters (though not Colossians and Ephesians). The three letters are addressed not to congregations but to those who shepherd congregations (Latin, *pastores*). These letters were first named "Pastoral Epistles" in the eighteenth century because they all are concerned with the work of a pastor in caring for the community or communities under his charge.

The first of the Pastorals, 1 Timothy, is presented as having been written from Macedonia. Timothy, whom Paul converted, was of mixed Jewish and Gentile parentage (Acts 16:1–3). He was the apostle's companion on both the second and the third missionary journeys (Acts 16:3; 19:22) and was often sent by him on special missions (Acts 19:22; 1 Cor 4:17; 1 Thes 3:2). In 1 Timothy (1 Tm 1:3), he is described as the administrator of the entire Ephesian community.

The letter instructs Timothy on his duty to restrain false and useless teaching (1 Tm 1:3–11; 4:1–5; 6:3–16) and proposes principles pertaining to his relationship with the older members of the community (1 Tm 5:1–2) and with the presbyters (1 Tm 5:17–22). It gives rules for aid to widows (1 Tm 5:3–8) and their selection for charitable ministrations (1 Tm 5:9–16) and also deals with liturgical celebrations (1 Tm 2:1–15), selections for the offices of bishop and deacon (1 Tm 3:1–13), relation of slaves with their masters (1 Tm 6:1–2), and obligations of the wealthier members of the community (1 Tm 6:17–19). This letter also reminds Timothy of the prophetic character of his office (1 Tm 1:12–20) and encourages him in his exercise of it (1 Tm 4:6–16). The central passage of the letter (1 Tm 3:14–16) expresses the principal motive that should guide the conduct of Timothy—preservation of the purity of the church's doctrine against false teaching. On this same note the letter concludes (1 Tm 6:20–21).

From the late second century to the nineteenth, Pauline authorship of the three Pastoral Epistles went unchallenged. Since then, the attribution of these letters to Paul has been questioned. Most scholars are convinced that Paul could not have been responsible for the vocabulary and style, the concept of church organization, or the theological expressions found in these letters. A second group believes, on the basis of statistical evidence, that the vocabulary and style are Pauline, even if at first sight the contrary seems to be the case. They state that the concept of church organization in the letters is not as advanced as the questioners of Pauline authorship hold since the notion of hierarchical order in a religious community existed in Israel before the time of Christ, as evidenced in the Dead Sea Scrolls. Finally, this group sees affinities between the theological thought of the Pastorals and that of the unquestionably genuine letters of Paul. Other scholars, while conceding a degree of validity to the positions mentioned above, suggest that the apostle made use of a secretary who was responsible for the composition of the letters. A fourth group of scholars believes that these letters are the work of a compiler, that they are based on traditions about Paul in his later years, and that they include, in varying amounts, actual fragments of genuine Pauline correspondence.

If Paul is considered the more immediate author, the Pastorals are to be dated between the end of his first Roman imprisonment (Acts 28:16) and his execution under Nero (A.D. 63–67); if they are regarded as only more remotely Pauline, their date may be as late as the early second century. In spite of these problems of authorship and dating, the Pastorals are illustrative of early Christian life and remain an important element of canonical scripture.

The principal divisions of the First Letter to Timothy are the following:

I.   Address (1:1–2)
II.  Sound Teaching (1:3–20)
III. Problems of Discipline (2:1–4:16)
IV.  Duties Toward Others (5:1–6:2a)
V.   False Teaching and True Wealth (6:2b–19)
VI.  Final Recommendation and Warning (6:20–21)

## I. ADDRESS

## CHAPTER 1

**Greeting.**[*] [1]Paul, an apostle of Christ Jesus by command of God our savior and of Christ Jesus our hope,[a] [2]to Timothy, my true child in faith: grace, mercy, and peace from God the Father and Christ Jesus our Lord.[b]

## II. SOUND TEACHING

**Warning Against False Doctrine.**[†] [3]I repeat the request I made of you when I was on my way to Macedonia,[c] that you stay in Ephesus to instruct certain people not to teach false doctrines [4]or to concern themselves with myths and endless genealogies, which promote speculations rather than the plan of God that is to be received by faith.[d] [5]The aim of this instruction is love from a pure heart, a good conscience, and a sincere faith.[e] [6]Some people have deviated from these and turned to meaningless talk,[f] [7]wanting to be teachers of the law, but without understanding either what they are saying or what they assert with such assurance.

[8]We know that the law is good, provided that one uses it as law,[g] [9]with the understanding that law is meant not for a righteous person but for the lawless and unruly, the godless and sinful, the unholy and profane, those who kill their fathers or mothers, murderers, [10]the unchaste,

sodomites,[¶] kidnappers, liars, perjurers, and whatever else is opposed to sound teaching,[h] [11]according to the glorious gospel of the blessed God, with which I have been entrusted.[i]

**Gratitude for God's Mercy.**[**] [12]I am grateful to him who has strengthened me, Christ Jesus our Lord, because he considered me trustworthy in appointing me to the ministry.[j] [13]I was once a blasphemer and a persecutor and an arrogant man, but I have been mercifully treated because I acted out of ignorance in my unbelief.[k] [14]Indeed, the grace of our Lord has been abundant, along with the faith and love that are in Christ Jesus.[l] [15]This saying is trustworthy[††] and deserves full acceptance: Christ Jesus came into the world to save sinners. Of these I am the foremost.[m] [16]But for that reason I was mercifully treated, so that in me, as the foremost, Christ Jesus might display all his patience as an example for those who would come to believe in him for everlasting life. [17]To the king of ages,[‡‡] incorruptible, invisible, the only God, honor and glory forever and ever. Amen.[n]

**Responsibility of Timothy.**[§§] [18]I entrust this charge to you, Timothy, my child, in accordance

---

[¶][1:10] **Sodomites:** see 1 Cor 6:9 and the note there.

[**][1:12–17] Present gratitude for the Christian apostleship leads Paul to recall an earlier time when he had been a fierce persecutor of the Christian communities (cf. Acts 26:9–11) until his conversion by intervention of divine mercy through the appearance of Jesus. This and his subsequent apostolic experience testify to the saving purpose of Jesus' incarnation. The fact of his former ignorance of the truth has not kept the apostle from regarding himself as having been the worst of sinners (1 Tm 1:15). Yet he was chosen to be an apostle, that God might manifest his firm will to save sinful humanity through Jesus Christ (1 Tm 1:16). The recounting of so great a mystery leads to a spontaneous outpouring of adoration (1 Tm 1:17).

[††][1:15] **This saying is trustworthy:** this phrase regularly introduces in the Pastorals a basic truth of early Christian faith; cf. 1 Tm 3:1; 4:9; 2 Tm 2:11; Ti 3:8.

[‡‡][1:17] **King of ages:** through Semitic influence, the Greek expression could mean "everlasting king"; it could also mean "king of the universe."

[§§][1:18–20] Timothy is to be mindful of his calling, which is here compared to the way Barnabas and Saul were designated by Christ as prophets for missionary service; cf. Acts 13:1–3. Such is probably the sense of the allusion to the prophetic words (1 Tm 1:18). His task is not to yield, whether in doctrine or in conduct, to erroneous opinions, taking warning

---

[*][1:1–2] For the Pauline use of the conventional epistolary form, see note on Rom 1:1–7.

[†][1:3–7] Here Timothy's initial task **in Ephesus** (cf. Acts 20:17–35) is outlined: to suppress the idle religious speculations, probably about Old Testament figures (1 Tm 1:3–4, but see note on 1 Tm 6:20–21), which do not contribute to the development of love within the community (1 Tm 1:5) but rather encourage similar useless conjectures (1 Tm 1:6–7).

[‡][1:4] The **plan of God that is to be received by faith:** the Greek may also possibly mean "God's trustworthy plan" or "the training in faith that God requires."

[§][1:8–11] Those responsible for the speculations that are to be suppressed by Timothy do not present the Old Testament from the Christian viewpoint. The Christian values the Old Testament not as a system of law but as the first stage in God's revelation of his saving plan, which is brought to fulfillment in the good news of salvation through faith in Jesus Christ.

---

a. [1:1] 2:3; Lk 1:47; Ti 1:3; 2:10 / Col 1:27.   b. [1:2] 2 Tm 1:2; Ti 1:4.   c. [1:3] Acts 20:1.   d. [1:4] 4:7; Ti 1:14; 3:9; 2 Pt 1:16.   e. [1:5] Rom 13:10.   f. [1:6] 6:4, 20; Ti 1:10.   g. [1:8] Rom 7:12, 16.

h. [1:10] 4:6; 6:3; 2 Tm 4:3; Ti 1:9; 2:1.   i. [1:11] Ti 1:3.   j. [1:12] Phil 4:13 / Acts 9:15; Gal 1:15–16.   k. [1:13] Acts 8:3; 9:1–2; 1 Cor 15:9; Gal 1:13.   l. [1:14] Rom 5:20; 2 Tm 1:13.   m. [1:15] Lk 15:2; 19:10.   n. [1:17] Rom 16:27.

with the prophetic words once spoken about you.⁺ Through them may you fight a good fight° ¹⁹by having faith and a good conscience. Some, by rejecting conscience, have made a shipwreck of their faith,ᵖ ²⁰among them Hymenaeus† and Alexander, whom I have handed over to Satan to be taught not to blaspheme.�q

## III. PROBLEMS OF DISCIPLINE

### CHAPTER 2

**Prayer and Conduct.** ‡¹First of all, then, I ask that supplications, prayers, petitions, and thanksgivings be offered for everyone,ʳ ²for kings and for all in authority, that we may lead a quiet and tranquil life in all devotion and dignity. ³This is good and pleasing to God our savior,ˢ ⁴who wills everyone to be saved and to come to knowledge of the truth.ᵗ

⁵ For there is one God.
    There is also one mediator between God
        and the human race,
    Christ Jesus, himself human,ᵘ
⁶ who gave himself as ransom for all.

This was the testimony§ at the proper time.ᵛ ⁷For this I was appointed preacher and apostle (I am speaking the truth, I am not lying), teacher of the Gentiles in faith and truth.ʷ

⁸⁺It is my wish, then, that in every place the men should pray, lifting up holy hands, without anger or argument. ⁹Similarly, [too,] women should adorn themselves with proper conduct, with modesty and self-control, not with braided hairstyles and gold ornaments, or pearls, or expensive clothes,ˣ ¹⁰but rather, as befits women who profess reverence for God, with good deeds.ʸ ¹¹A woman must receive instruction silently and under complete control.ᶻ ¹²I do not permit a woman to teach or to have authority over a man.⁺⁺ She must be quiet. ¹³For Adam was formed first, then Eve.ᵃ ¹⁴Further, Adam was not deceived, but the woman was deceived and transgressed.ᵇ ¹⁵But she will be saved through motherhood, provided women persevere in faith and love and holiness, with self-control.ᶜ

### CHAPTER 3

**Qualifications of Various Ministers.** ¹⁺⁺This saying is trustworthy:‡‡ whoever aspires to the office of bishop desires a noble task.ᵈ ²Therefore, a bishop must be irreproachable, married only once, temperate, self-controlled, decent, hospitable, able to teach, ³not a drunkard, not aggressive, but gentle, not contentious, not a lover of money.ᵉ ⁴He must manage his own household well, keeping his children under control with perfect dignity; ⁵for if a man does not know how to manage his own household, how can he take care of the church of God? ⁶He should not be a recent convert, so that he may not become

---

from what has already happened at Ephesus in the case of Hymenaeus and Alexander (1 Tm 1:19–20).

*[1:18] **The prophetic words once spoken about you:** the Greek may also be translated, "the prophecies that led (me) to you." It probably refers to testimonies given by charismatic figures in the Christian communities. **Fight a good fight:** this translation preserves the play on words in Greek. The Greek terms imply a lengthy engagement in battle and might well be translated "wage a good campaign."

†[1:20] **Hymenaeus:** mentioned in 2 Tm 2:17 as saying that the resurrection has already taken place (in baptism). **Alexander:** probably the Alexander mentioned in 2 Tm 4:14 as the coppersmith who "did me a great deal of harm." **Whom I have handed over to Satan:** the same terms are used in the condemnation of the incestuous man in 1 Cor 5:5.

‡[2:1–7] This marked insistence that the liturgical prayer of the community concern itself with the needs of all, whether Christian or not, and especially of those in authority, may imply that a disposition existed at Ephesus to refuse prayer for pagans. In actuality, such prayer aids the community to achieve peaceful relationships with non-Christians (1 Tm 2:2) and contributes to salvation, since it derives its value from the presence within the community of Christ, who is the one and only savior of all (1 Tm 2:3–6). The vital apostolic mission to the Gentiles (1 Tm 2:7) reflects Christ's purpose of universal salvation. 1 Tm 2:5 contains what may well have been a very primitive creed. Some interpreters have called it a Christian version of the Jewish *shema*: "Hear, O Israel! The LORD is our God, the LORD alone . . ." (Dt 6:4–5). The assertion in 1 Tm 2:7, "I am speaking the truth, I am not lying," reminds one of similar affirmations in Rom 9:1; 2 Cor 11:31; and Gal 1:20.

§[2:6] **The testimony:** to make sense of this overly concise phrase, many manuscripts supply "to which" (or "to whom"); two others add "was given." The translation has supplied "This was."

¶[2:8–15] The prayer of the community should be unmarred by internal dissension (1 Tm 2:8); cf. Mt 5:21–26; 6:14; Mk 11:25. At the liturgical assembly the dress of women should be appropriate to the occasion (1 Tm 2:9); their chief adornment is to be reputation for good works (1 Tm 2:10). Women are not to take part in the charismatic activity of the assembly (1 Tm 2:11–12; cf. 1 Cor 14:34) or exercise authority; their conduct there should reflect the role of man's helpmate (1 Tm 2:13; cf. Gn 2:18) and not the later relationship of Eve to Adam (1 Tm 2:14; cf. Gn 3:6–7). As long as women perform their role as wives and mothers in faith and love, their salvation is assured (1 Tm 2:15).

**[2:12] **A man:** this could also mean "her husband."

††[3:1–7] The passage begins by commending those who aspire to the office of bishop (*episkopos*; see note on Phil 1:1) within the community, but this first sentence (1 Tm 3:1) may also imply a warning about the great responsibilities involved. The writer proceeds to list the qualifications required: personal stability and graciousness; talent for teaching (1 Tm 3:2); moderation in habits and temperament (1 Tm 3:3); managerial ability (1 Tm 3:4); and experience in Christian living (1 Tm 3:5–6). Moreover, the candidate's previous life should provide no grounds for the charge that he did not previously practice what he now preaches. No list of qualifications for presbyters appears in 1 Timothy. The presbyter-bishops here and in Titus (see note on Ti 1:5–9) lack certain functions reserved here for Paul and Timothy.

‡‡[3:1] **This saying is trustworthy:** the saying introduced is so unlike others after this phrase that some later Western manuscripts read, "This saying is popular." It is understood by some interpreters as concluding the preceding section (1 Tm 2:8–15). **Bishop:** literally, "overseer"; see note on Phil 1:1.

---

o. [1:18] 4:14 / 6:12; 2 Tm 4:7; Jude 3.  p. [1:19] 3:9.  q. [1:20] 2 Tm 2:17; 4:14 / 1 Cor 5:5.  r. [2:1] Eph 6:18; Phil 4:6.  s. [2:3] 1:1; 4:10.  t. [2:4] 2 Tm 3:7; 2 Pt 3:9.  u. [2:5] 1 Cor 8:6; Heb 8:6; 9:15; 12:24 / Rom 5:15.  v. [2:6] Mk 10:45; Gal 1:4; 2:20; Eph 5:25; Ti 2:14.  w. [2:7] Acts 9:15; 1 Cor 9:1; Gal 2:7–8.

x. [2:9] 1 Pt 3:3–5.  y. [2:10] 5:10; 1 Pt 3:1.  z. [2:11–12] 1 Cor 14:34–35.  a. [2:13] Gn 1:27; 2:7, 22; 1 Cor 11:8–9.  b. [2:14] Gn 3:6, 13; 2 Cor 11:3.  c. [2:15] 5:14.  d. [3:1–7] Ti 1:6–9.  e. [3:3] Heb 13:5.

conceited and thus incur the devil's punishment.* [7]He must also have a good reputation among outsiders, so that he may not fall into disgrace, the devil's trap.[f]

[8†]Similarly, deacons must be dignified, not deceitful, not addicted to drink, not greedy for sordid gain, [9]holding fast to the mystery of the faith with a clear conscience. [10]Moreover, they should be tested first; then, if there is nothing against them, let them serve as deacons. [11]Women,[‡] similarly, should be dignified, not slanderers, but temperate and faithful in everything.[g] [12]Deacons may be married only once and must manage their children and their households well. [13]Thus those who serve well as deacons gain good standing and much confidence in their faith in Christ Jesus.

**The Mystery of Our Religion.**[§] [14]I am writing you about these matters, although I hope to visit you soon. [15]But if I should be delayed, you should know how to behave in the household of God, which is the church of the living God, the pillar and foundation of truth.[h] [16]Undeniably great is the mystery of devotion,

Who[r] was manifested in the flesh,
    vindicated in the spirit,

seen by angels,
    proclaimed to the Gentiles,
believed in throughout the world,
    taken up in glory.[i]

## CHAPTER 4

**False Asceticism.**[**] [1]Now the Spirit explicitly says that in the last times some will turn away from the faith by paying attention to deceitful spirits and demonic instructions[j] [2]through the hypocrisy of liars with branded consciences. [3]They forbid marriage and require abstinence from foods that God created to be received with thanksgiving by those who believe and know the truth.[k] [4]For everything created by God is good, and nothing is to be rejected when received with thanksgiving,[l] [5]for it is made holy by the invocation of God in prayer.[††]

**Counsel to Timothy.** [6‡‡]If you will give these instructions to the brothers, you will be a good minister of Christ Jesus, nourished on the words of the faith and of the sound teaching you have followed. [7]Avoid profane and silly myths. Train yourself for devotion,[m] [8]for, while physical training is of limited value, devotion is valuable in every respect, since it holds a promise of life both for the present and for the future.[n] [9]This saying is trustworthy and deserves full acceptance.[o] [10]For this we toil and struggle,[§§] because we have set our hope on the living God, who is the savior of all, especially of those who believe.[p]

[11§§]Command and teach these things. [12]Let no one have contempt for your youth,[***] but set an example for those who believe, in speech, conduct, love, faith, and purity.[q] [13]Until I arrive, attend to the reading,[†††] exhortation, and teaching. [14]Do not neglect the gift you have, which

---

*[3:6] **The devil's punishment:** this phrase could mean the punishment once incurred by the devil (objective genitive) or a punishment brought about by the devil (subjective genitive).

†[3:8–13] Deacons, besides possessing the virtue of moderation (1 Tm 3:8), are to be outstanding for their faith (1 Tm 3:9) and well respected within the community (1 Tm 3:10). Women in the same role, although some interpreters take them to mean wives of deacons, must be dignified, temperate, dedicated, and not given to malicious talebearing (1 Tm 3:11). Deacons must have shown stability in marriage and have a good record with their families (1 Tm 3:12), for such experience prepares them well for the exercise of their ministry on behalf of the community (1 Tm 3:13). See further the note on Phil 1:1.

‡[3:11] **Women:** this seems to refer to women deacons but may possibly mean wives of deacons. The former is preferred because the word is used absolutely; if deacons' wives were meant, a possessive "their" would be expected. Moreover, they are also introduced by the word "similarly," as in 1 Tm 3:8; this parallel suggests that they too exercised ecclesiastical functions.

§[3:14–16] In case there is some delay in the visit to Timothy at Ephesus planned for the near future, the present letter is being sent on ahead to arm and enlighten him in his task of preserving sound Christian conduct in the Ephesian church. The care he must exercise over this community is required by the profound nature of Christianity. It centers in Christ, appearing in human flesh, vindicated by the holy Spirit; the mystery of his person was revealed to the angels, announced to the Gentiles, and accepted by them in faith. He himself was taken up (through his resurrection and ascension) to the divine glory (1 Tm 3:16). This passage apparently includes part of a liturgical hymn used among the Christian communities in and around Ephesus. It consists of three couplets in typical Hebrew balance: flesh-spirit (contrast), seen-proclaimed (complementary), world-glory (contrast).

¶[3:16] **Who:** the reference is to Christ, who is himself "the mystery of our devotion." Some predominantly Western manuscripts read "which," harmonizing the gender of the pronoun with that of the Greek word for mystery; many later (eighth/ninth century on), predominantly Byzantine manuscripts read "God," possibly for theological reasons.

**[4:1–5] Doctrinal deviations from the true Christian message within the church have been prophesied, though the origin of the prophecy is not specified (1 Tm 4:1–2); cf. Acts 20:29–30. The letter warns against a false asceticism that prohibits marriage and regards certain foods as forbidden, though they are part of God's good creation (1 Tm 4:3).

††[4:5] **The invocation of God in prayer:** literally, "the word of God and petition." The use of "word of God" without an article in Greek suggests that it refers to the name of God being invoked in blessing rather than to the "word of God" proclaimed to the community.

‡‡[4:6–10] Timothy is urged to be faithful, both in his teaching and in his own life, as he looks only to God for salvation.

§§[4:10] **Struggle:** other manuscripts and patristic witnesses read "suffer reproach."

¶¶[4:11–16] Timothy is urged to preach and teach with confidence, relying on the gifts and the mission that God has bestowed on him.

***[4:12] **Youth:** some commentators find this reference a sign of pseudepigraphy. Timothy had joined Paul as a missionary already in A.D. 49, some fifteen years before the earliest supposed date of composition.

†††[4:13] **Reading:** the Greek word refers to private or public reading. Here, it probably designates the public reading of scripture in the Christian assembly.

---

i. [3:16] Jn 1:14; Rom 1:3–4.   j. [4:1] 1 Tm 3:1; 4:3; 2 Pt 3:3; Jude 18.   k. [4:3] Gn 9:3; Rom 14:6; 1 Cor 10:30–31.   l. [4:4] Gn 1:31; Acts 10:15.   m. [4:7] 1:4; 2 Tm 2:16; Ti 1:14.   n. [4:8] 6:6.   o. [4:9] 1:15; 2 Tm 2:11; Ti 3:8.   p. [4:10] 2:4; Ti 2:11.   q. [4:12] 1 Cor 16:11; Ti 2:15 / Phil 3:17.

---

f. [3:7] 2 Cor 8:21; 2 Tm 2:26.   g. [3:11] Ti 2:3.   h. [3:15] Eph 2:19–22.

was conferred on you through the prophetic word[*] with the imposition of hands of the presbyterate.[r] [15]Be diligent in these matters, be absorbed in them, so that your progress may be evident to everyone. [16]Attend to yourself and to your teaching; persevere in both tasks, for by doing so you will save both yourself and those who listen to you.

## IV. DUTIES TOWARD OTHERS

### CHAPTER 5

[1†]Do not rebuke an older man, but appeal to him as a father. Treat younger men as brothers,[s] [2]older women as mothers, and younger women as sisters with complete purity.

**Rules for Widows.** [3]Honor widows who are truly widows. [4]But if a widow has children or grandchildren, let these first learn to perform their religious duty to their own family and to make recompense to their parents, for this is pleasing to God. [5]The real widow, who is all alone, has set her hope on God and continues in supplications and prayers night and day.[t] [6]But the one who is self-indulgent is dead while she lives. [7]Command this, so that they may be irreproachable. [8]And whoever does not provide for relatives and especially family members has denied the faith and is worse than an unbeliever.

[9]Let a widow be enrolled if she is not less than sixty years old, married only once, [10]with a reputation for good works, namely, that she has raised children, practiced hospitality, washed the feet of the holy ones, helped those in distress, involved herself in every good work.[u] [11]But exclude younger widows, for when their sensuality estranges them from Christ, they want to marry [12]and will incur condemnation for

breaking their first pledge. [13]And furthermore, they learn to be idlers, going about from house to house, and not only idlers but gossips and busybodies as well, talking about things that ought not to be mentioned.[v] [14]So I would like younger widows to marry, have children, and manage a home, so as to give the adversary no pretext for maligning us.[w] [15]For some have already turned away to follow Satan. [16]If any woman believer[‡] has widowed relatives, she must assist them; the church is not to be burdened, so that it will be able to help those who are truly widows.

**Rules for Presbyters.**[§] [17]Presbyters who preside well deserve double honor, especially those who toil in preaching and teaching.[x] [18]For the scripture says, "You shall not muzzle an ox when it is threshing," and, "A worker deserves his pay."[y] [19]Do not accept an accusation against a presbyter unless it is supported by two or three witnesses.[z] [20]Reprimand publicly those who do sin, so that the rest also will be afraid.[a] [21]I charge you before God and Christ Jesus and the elect angels to keep these rules without prejudice, doing nothing out of favoritism. [22]Do not lay hands too readily on anyone, and do not share in another's sins. Keep yourself pure.[b] [23]Stop drinking only water, but have a little wine for the sake of your stomach and your frequent illnesses.

[24]Some people's sins are public, preceding them to judgment; but other people are followed by their sins. [25]Similarly, good works are also public; and even those that are not cannot remain hidden.

### CHAPTER 6

**Rules for Slaves.** [1†]Those who are under the yoke of slavery must regard their masters as worthy

---

*[4:14] **Prophetic word:** this may mean the utterance of a Christian prophet designating the candidate or a prayer of blessing accompanying the rite. **Imposition of hands:** this gesture was used in the Old Testament to signify the transmission of authority from Moses to Joshua (Nm 27:18–23; Dt 34:9). The early Christian community used it as a symbol of installation into an office: the Seven (Acts 6:6) and Paul and Barnabas (Acts 13:3). **Of the presbyterate:** this would mean that each member of the college of presbyters imposed hands and appears to contradict 2 Tm 1:6, in which Paul says that he imposed hands on Timothy. This latter text, however, does not exclude participation by others in the rite. Some prefer to translate "for the presbyterate," and thus understand it to designate the office into which Timothy was installed rather than the agents who installed him.

†[5:1–16] After a few words of general advice based on common sense (1 Tm 5:1–2), the letter takes up, in its several aspects, the subject of widows. The first responsibility for their care belongs to the family circle, not to the Christian community as such (1 Tm 5:3–4, 16). The widow left without the aid of relatives may benefit the community by her prayer, and the community should consider her material sustenance its responsibility (1 Tm 5:5–8). Widows who wish to work directly for the Christian community should not be accepted unless they are well beyond the probability of marriage, i.e., sixty years of age, married only once, and with a reputation for good works (1 Tm 5:9–10). Younger widows are apt to be troublesome and should be encouraged to remarry (1 Tm 5:11–15).

‡[5:16] **Woman believer:** some early Latin manuscripts and Fathers have a masculine here, while most later manuscripts and patristic quotations conflate the two readings, perhaps to avoid unfair restriction to women.

§[5:17–25] The function of presbyters is not exactly the same as that of the *episkopos*, "bishop" (1 Tm 3:1); in fact, the relation of the two at the time of this letter is obscure (but cf. note on Ti 1:5–9). The Pastorals seem to reflect a transitional stage that developed in many regions of the church into the monarchical episcopate of the second and third centuries. The presbyters possess the responsibility of preaching and teaching, for which functions they are supported by the community (1 Tm 5:17–18). The realization that their position subjects them to adverse criticism is implied in the direction to Timothy (1 Tm 5:19–20) to make sure of the truth of any accusation against them before public reproof is given. He must be as objective as possible in weighing charges against presbyters (1 Tm 5:21), learning from his experience to take care in selecting them (1 Tm 5:22). Some scholars take 1 Tm 5:22 as a reference not to ordination of presbyters but to reconciliation of public sinners. The letter now sounds an informal note of personal concern in its advice to Timothy not to be so ascetic that he even avoids wine (1 Tm 5:23). Judgment concerning the fitness of candidates to serve as presbyters is easy with persons of open conduct, more difficult and prolonged with those of greater reserve (1 Tm 5:24–25).

¶[6:1–2] Compare the tables for household duties, such as that of Col 3:18–4:1. Domestic relationships derive new meaning from the Christian faith.

---

r. [4:14] 5:22; Acts 6:6; 8:17; 2 Tm 1:6.   s. [5:1] Lv 19:32; Ti 2:2.   t. [5:5] Jer 49:11; Lk 2:37; 18:7.   u. [5:10] Jn 13:14; Heb 13:2.

v. [5:13] 2 Thes 3:11.   w. [5:14] 1 Cor 7:9.   x. [5:17] 1 Cor 16:18; Phil 2:29.   y. [5:18] Dt 25:4; 1 Cor 9:8 / Mt 10:10; Lk 10:7.   z. [5:19] Dt 17:6; 19:15; Mt 18:16; 2 Cor 13:1.   a. [5:20] Gal 2:14; Eph 5:11; 2 Tm 4:2; Ti 1:9, 13.   b. [5:22] 4:14; 2 Tm 1:6.

of full respect, so that the name of God and our teaching[*] may not suffer abuse.[c] [21]Those whose masters are believers must not take advantage of them because they are brothers but must give better service because those who will profit from their work are believers and are beloved.[d]

## V. FALSE TEACHING AND TRUE WEALTH

Teach and urge these things. [3]Whoever teaches something different and does not agree with the sound words of our Lord Jesus Christ and the religious teaching[e] [4]is conceited, understanding nothing, and has a morbid disposition for arguments and verbal disputes. From these come envy, rivalry, insults, evil suspicions, [5]and mutual friction among people with corrupted minds, who are deprived of the truth, supposing religion to be a means of gain.[f] [6†]Indeed, religion with contentment is a great gain.[g] [7]For we brought nothing into the world, just as we shall not be able to take anything out of it.[h] [8]If we have food and clothing, we shall be content with that.[i] [9]Those who want to be rich are falling into temptation and into a trap and into many foolish and harmful desires, which plunge them into ruin and destruction.[j] [10]For the love of money is the root of all evils, and some people in their desire for it have strayed from the faith and have pierced themselves with many pains.
**Exhortations to Timothy.**[§] [11]But you, man of God,[‡] avoid all this. Instead, pursue righteousness,

devotion, faith, love, patience, and gentleness.[k] [12]Compete well for the faith. Lay hold of eternal life, to which you were called when you made the noble confession in the presence of many witnesses.[l] [13]I charge [you] before God, who gives life to all things, and before Christ Jesus, who gave testimony under Pontius Pilate for the noble confession,[m] [14]to keep the commandment without stain or reproach until the appearance of our Lord Jesus Christ [15]that the blessed and only ruler will make manifest at the proper time, the King of kings and Lord of lords,[n] [16]who alone has immortality, who dwells in unapproachable light, and whom no human being has seen or can see. To him be honor and eternal power. Amen.[o]
**Right Use of Wealth.**[**] [17]Tell the rich in the present age not to be proud and not to rely on so uncertain a thing as wealth but rather on God, who richly provides us with all things for our enjoyment.[p] [18]Tell them to do good, to be rich in good works, to be generous, ready to share, [19]thus accumulating as treasure a good foundation for the future, so as to win the life that is true life.[q]

## VI. FINAL RECOMMENDATION AND WARNING[††]

[20]O Timothy, guard what has been entrusted to you. Avoid profane babbling and the absurdities of so-called knowledge.[r] [21]By professing it, some people have deviated from the faith.
Grace be with all of you.[s]

---

*[6:1] **Our teaching**: this refers to the teaching of the Christian community.

†[6:2b–10] Timothy is exhorted to maintain steadfastly the position outlined in this letter, not allowing himself to be pressured into any other course. He must realize that false teachers can be discerned by their pride, envy, quarrelsomeness, and greed for material gain. 1 Tm 6:6 is rather obscure and is interpreted, and therefore translated, variously. The suggestion seems to be that the important gain that religion brings is spiritual, but that there is material gain, too, up to the point of what is needed for physical sustenance (cf. 1 Tm 6:17–19).

‡[6:6] **Contentment**: the word *autarkeia* is a technical Greek philosophical term for the virtue of independence from material goods (Aristotle, Cynics, Stoics).

§[6:11–16] Timothy's position demands total dedication to God and faultless witness to Christ (1 Tm 6:11–14) operating from an awareness, through faith, of the coming revelation in Jesus of the invisible God (1 Tm 6:15–16).

¶[6:11] **Man of God**: a title applied to Moses and the prophets (Dt 33:1; 1 Sm 2:27; 1 Kgs 12:22; 13:1; etc.).

**[6:17–19] Timothy is directed to instruct the rich, advising them to make good use of their wealth by aiding the poor.

††[6:20–21] A final solemn warning against the heretical teachers, with what seems to be a specific reference to gnosticism, the great rival and enemy of the church for two centuries and more (the Greek word for "knowledge" is *gnōsis*). If gnosticism is being referred to here, it is probable that the warnings against "speculations" and "myths and genealogies" (cf. especially 1 Tm 1:4; Ti 3:9) involve allusions to that same kind of heresy. Characteristic of the various gnostic systems of speculation was an elaborate mythology of innumerable superhuman intermediaries, on a descending scale ("genealogies"), between God and the world. Thus would be explained the emphasis upon Christ's being the one mediator (as in 1 Tm 2:5). Although fully developed gnosticism belonged to the second and later centuries, there are signs that incipient forms of it belonged to Paul's own period.

---

c. [6:1] Eph 6:5; Ti 2:9–10.   d. [6:2] Phlm 16.   e. [6:3] Gal 1:6–9; 2 Tm 1:13; Ti 1:1.   f. [6:5] 2 Tm 3:8; 4:4; Ti 1:14.   g. [6:6] 4:8; Phil 4:11–12; Heb 13:5.   h. [6:7] Jb 1:21; Eccl 5:14.   i. [6:8] Prv 30:8.   j. [6:9] Prv 23:4; 28:22.

k. [6:11] 2 Tm 2:22.   l. [6:12] 1 Cor 9:26; 2 Tm 4:7.   m. [6:13] Jn 18:36–37; 19:11.   n. [6:15] 2 Mc 13:4; Rev 17:14.   o. [6:16] Ex 33:20; Ps 104:2.   p. [6:17] Ps 62:11; Lk 12:20.   q. [6:19] Mt 6:20.   r. [6:20] 2 Tm 1:14 / 1 Tm 4:7.   s. [6:21] 1:6; 2 Tm 2:18.

# THE SECOND LETTER TO
# TIMOTHY

The authorship and date of this letter, as one of the Pastoral Epistles, are discussed in the Introduction to the First Letter to Timothy.

The tone here is more personal than in First Timothy, for this letter addresses Timothy in vivid terms (2 Tm 1:6–14; 2:1–13) and depicts Paul's courage and hope in the face of discouragements late in the course of his apostolic ministry (2 Tm 1:15–18; 3:10–17; 4:9–18). Indeed, the letter takes on the character of a final exhortation and testament from Paul to the younger Timothy (2 Tm 4:1–8). Paul is portrayed as a prisoner (2 Tm 1:8, 16; 2:9) in Rome (2 Tm 1:17), and there is a hint that Timothy may be in Ephesus (2 Tm 2:17). The letter reveals that, with rare exceptions, Christians have not rallied to Paul's support (2 Tm 1:15–18) and takes a pessimistic view of the outcome of his case (2 Tm 4:6). It describes Paul as fully aware of what impends, looking to God, not to human beings, for his deliverance (2 Tm 4:3–8, 18). It recalls his mission days with Timothy (2 Tm 1:3–5; cf. Acts 16:1–4). It points to his preaching of the gospel as the reason for his imprisonment and offers Timothy, as a motive for steadfastness, his own example of firmness in faith despite adverse circumstances (2 Tm 1:6–14). The letter suggests that Timothy should prepare others to replace himself as Paul has prepared Timothy to replace him (2 Tm 2:1–2). Paul urges him not to desist out of fear from preserving and spreading the Christian message (2 Tm 2:3–7). It presents the resurrection of Jesus and his messianic role as the heart of the gospel for which Paul has been ready to lay down his life (2 Tm 2:8–9) and thus not only to express his own conviction fully but to support the conviction of others (2 Tm 2:10–13).

This letter, like the preceding one, urges Timothy to protect the community from the inevitable impact of false teaching (2 Tm 2:14–3:9), without fear of the personal attacks that may result (2 Tm 3:10–13). It recommends that he rely on the power of the scriptures, on proclamation of the word, and on sound doctrine (2 Tm 3:14–4:2), without being troubled by those who do not accept him (2 Tm 4:3–5). The letter poignantly observes in passing that Paul has need of his reading materials and his cloak (2 Tm 4:13) and, what will be best of all, a visit from Timothy.

On the theory of authorship by Paul himself, Second Timothy appears to be the last of the three Pastoral Epistles. The many scholars who argue that the Pastorals are products of the Pauline school often incline toward Second Timothy as the earliest of the three and the one most likely to have actual fragments of material from Paul himself.

The principal divisions of the Second Letter to Timothy are the following:

I. Address (1:1–5)
II. Exhortations to Timothy (1:6–2:13)
III. Instructions Concerning False Teaching (2:14–4:8)
IV. Personal Requests and Final Greetings (4:9–22)

## I. ADDRESS

### CHAPTER 1

**Greeting.** *¹Paul, an apostle of Christ Jesus by the will of God[a] for the promise of life in Christ Jesus,† ²to Timothy, my dear child: grace, mercy, and peace from God the Father and Christ Jesus our Lord.

**Thanksgiving.** ³[b]I am grateful to God, whom I worship with a clear conscience as my ancestors

---

*[1:1–2] For the formula of address and greeting, see note on Rom 1:1–7.

a. [1:1] 1 Tm 4:8.

†[1:1] **The promise of life in Christ Jesus**: that God grants through union with Christ in faith and love; cf. Col 3:4; 1 Tm 4:8.

b. [1:3] 1 Tm 3:9 / Phil 3:5.

did,* as I remember you constantly in my prayers, night and day. ⁴I yearn to see you again, recalling your tears, so that I may be filled with joy, ⁵as I recall your sincere faith that first lived in your grandmother Lois and in your mother Eunice and that I am confident lives also in you.ᶜ

## II. EXHORTATIONS TO TIMOTHY

**The Gifts Timothy Has Received.** ⁶For this reason, I remind you to stir into flame the gift of Godᵍ that you have through the imposition of my hands.ᵈ ⁷For God did not give us a spirit of cowardice but rather of power and love and self-control.ᵉ ⁸So do not be ashamed of your testimony to our Lord,§ nor of me, a prisoner for his sake; but bear your share of hardship for the gospel with the strength that comes from God.ᶠ

⁹¶He saved us and called us to a holy life, not according to our works but according to his own design and the grace bestowed on us in Christ Jesus before time began,ᵍ ¹⁰but now made manifest through the appearance of our savior Christ Jesus, who destroyed death and brought life and immortality to light through the gospel,ʰ ¹¹**for which I was appointed preacher and apostleⁱ and teacher. ¹²††On this account I am suffering these things; but I am not ashamed,ʲ for I know him in whom I have believed and am confident that he is able to guard what has been entrusted to me until that day. ¹³Take as your norm the sound words that you heard from me, in the faith and love that are in Christ Jesus.ᵏ ¹⁴Guard this rich trust with the help of the holy Spirit that dwells within us.ˡ

**Paul's Suffering.** ¹⁵‡‡ᵐYou know that everyone in Asia deserted me, including Phygelus and Hermogenes. ¹⁶§§May the Lord grant mercy to the family of Onesiphorusⁿ because he often gave me new heart and was not ashamed of my chains. ¹⁷But when he came to Rome, he promptly searched for me and found me. ¹⁸May the Lord grant him to find mercy from the Lord¶¶ on that day. And you know very well the services he rendered in Ephesus.ᵒ

## CHAPTER 2

**Timothy's Conduct.** ¹***So you, my child, be strong in the grace that is in Christ Jesus. ²And what you heard from me through many witnesses entrust to faithful people who will have the ability to teach others as well. ³Bear your share of hardship along with me like a good soldier of Christ Jesus.ᵖ ⁴To satisfy the one who recruited him, a soldier does not become entangled in the business affairs of life.�q ⁵Similarly, an athlete cannot receive the winner's crown except by competing according to the rules.ʳ ⁶The hard-working farmer ought to have the first share of the crop.ˢ ⁷Reflect on what I am saying, for the Lord will give you understanding in everything.ᵗ

⁸†††Remember Jesus Christ, raised from the dead, a descendant of David: such is my gospel,ᵘ ⁹for which I am suffering, even to the point of chains, like a criminal. But the word of God is not chained.ᵛ ¹⁰Therefore, I bear with everything for the sake of those who are chosen, so

---

§§[1:16–18] **The family of Onesiphorus because he . . . of my chains:** Onesiphorus seems to have died before this letter was written. His family is mentioned twice (here and in 2 Tm 4:19), though it was Onesiphorus himself who was helpful to Paul in prison and rendered much service to the community of Ephesus. Because the apostle complains of abandonment by all in Asia during his second imprisonment and trial, the assistance of Onesiphorus seems to have been given to Paul during his first Roman imprisonment (A.D. 61–63).

¶¶[1:18] **Lord . . . Lord:** the first "Lord" here seems to refer to Christ, the second "Lord" to the Father.

***[2:1–7] This passage manifests a characteristic deep concern for safeguarding the faith and faithfully transmitting it through trustworthy people (2 Tm 2:1–2; cf. 2 Tm 1:14; 1 Tm 6:20; Ti 1:9). Comparisons to the soldier's detachment, the athlete's sportsmanship, and the farmer's arduous work as the price of recompense (2 Tm 2:4–6) emphasize the need of singleness of purpose in preaching the word, even at the cost of hardship, for the sake of Christ (2 Tm 2:3).

†††[2:8–13] The section begins with a sloganlike summary of Paul's gospel about Christ (2 Tm 2:8) and concludes with what may be part of an early Christian hymn (2 Tm 2:11b–12a; most exegetes include the rest of 2 Tm 2:12 and all of 2 Tm 2:13 as part of the quotation). The poetic lines suggest that through baptism Christians die spiritually with Christ and hope to live with him and reign with him forever, but the Christian life includes endurance, witness, and even suffering, as the final judgment will show and as Paul's own case makes clear; while he is imprisoned for preaching the gospel (2 Tm 2:9), his sufferings are helpful to the elect for obtaining the salvation and glory available in Christ (2 Tm 2:10), who will be true to those who are faithful and will disown those who deny him (2 Tm 2:12–13).

---

*[1:3] **As my ancestors did:** this emphasizes the continuity of Judaism and Christianity; for a similar view, see Rom 9:3–5; Phil 3:4–6.

†[1:4–5] Purportedly written from prison in Rome (2 Tm 1:8, 17; 4:6–8) shortly before the writer's death, the letter recalls the earlier sorrowful parting from Timothy, commending him for his faith and expressing the longing to see him again.

‡[1:6] **The gift of God:** the grace resulting from the conferral of an ecclesiastical office. **The imposition of my hands:** see note on 1 Tm 4:14.

§[1:8] **Do not be ashamed of your testimony to our Lord:** i.e., of preaching and suffering for the sake of the gospel.

¶[1:9–10] Redemption from sin and the call to holiness of life are not won by personal deeds but are freely and graciously bestowed according to God's eternal plan; cf. Eph 1:4.

**[1:11] **Teacher:** the overwhelming majority of manuscripts and Fathers read "teacher of the nations," undoubtedly a harmonization with 1 Tm 2:7.

††[1:12] **He is able to guard . . . until that day:** the intervening words can also be translated "what I have entrusted to him" (i.e., the fruit of his ministry) as well as "what has been entrusted to me" (i.e., the faith). The same difficult term occurs in 2 Tm 1:14, where it is modified by the adjective "rich" and used without a possessive.

‡‡[1:15] Keen disappointment is expressed, here and later (2 Tm 4:16), that the Christians of the province of Asia,

should have abandoned the writer and done nothing to defend his case in court.

---

c. [1:5] 1 Tm 1:5 / Acts 16:1.   d. [1:6] 1 Tm 4:14; 5:22 / Acts 6:6; 8:17.   e. [1:7] Rom 5:5; 8:15; 1 Cor 2:4.   f. [1:8] 2:3, 15; Rom 1:16.   g. [1:9] Eph 2:8–9; Ti 3:5 / Eph 1:4; Ti 1:2.   h. [1:10] Rom 16:26; 1 Pt 1:20 / 1 Tm 6:14 / Phil 3:20; Ti 1:4; 2:13; 2 Pt 1:11 / 1 Cor 15:54–55; Heb 2:14 / 1 Cor 15:53–54.   i. [1:11] 1 Tm 2:7.   j. [1:12] 1 Pt 4:16 / 1 Tm 1:10–11.   k. [1:13] 1 Tm 1:14.   l. [1:14] 1 Tm 6:20 / Rom 8:11.

m. [1:15] 4:16.   n. [1:16] 4:19.   o. [1:18] Jude 21.   p. [2:3] 1:8; 4:5; Phlm 2.   q. [2:4] 1 Cor 9:6.   r. [2:5] 1 Cor 9:25.   s. [2:6] 1 Cor 9:7–10.   t. [2:7] Prv 2:6.   u. [2:8] Rom 1:3; 1 Cor 15:4, 20 / Rom 2:16; Gal 1:11; 2:2.   v. [2:9] Phil 1:12–14.

that they too may obtain the salvation that is in Christ Jesus, together with eternal glory.[w] [11]This saying is trustworthy:

> If we have died with him
>> we shall also live with him;[x]
> [12] if we persevere
>> we shall also reign with him.
> But if we deny him
>> he will deny us.[y]
> [13] If we are unfaithful
>> he remains faithful,
>> for he cannot deny himself.[z]

## III. INSTRUCTIONS CONCERNING FALSE TEACHING

**Warning Against Useless Disputes.** [14*]Remind people of these things and charge them before God[†] to stop disputing about words. This serves no useful purpose since it harms those who listen.[a] [15]Be eager to present yourself as acceptable to God, a workman who causes no disgrace, imparting the word of truth without deviation.[b] [16]Avoid profane, idle talk, for such people will become more and more godless,[c] [17]and their teaching will spread like gangrene. Among them are Hymenaeus and Philetus,[d] [18]who have deviated from the truth by saying that [the] resurrection has already taken place and are upsetting the faith of some.[e] [19]Nevertheless, God's solid foundation stands, bearing this inscription, "The Lord knows those who are his"; and, "Let everyone who calls upon the name of the Lord avoid evil."[f]

[20]In a large household there are vessels not only of gold and silver but also of wood and clay, some for lofty and others for humble use. [21]If anyone cleanses himself of these things, he will be a vessel for lofty use, dedicated, beneficial to the master of the house, ready for every good work.[g] [22]So turn from youthful desires and pursue righteousness, faith, love, and peace, along with those who call on the Lord[‡] with purity of heart.[h] [23]Avoid foolish and ignorant debates, for

you know that they breed quarrels.[i] [24]A slave of the Lord should not quarrel, but should be gentle with everyone, able to teach, tolerant,[j] [25]correcting opponents with kindness. It may be that God will grant them repentance that leads to knowledge of the truth,[k] [26§]and that they may return to their senses out of the devil's snare,[l] where they are entrapped by him, for his will.

## CHAPTER 3

**The Dangers of the Last Days.[¶]** [1]But understand this: there will be terrifying times in the last days.[m] [2]People will be self-centered and lovers of money, proud, haughty, abusive, disobedient to their parents, ungrateful, irreligious,[n] [3]callous, implacable, slanderous, licentious, brutal, hating what is good, [4]traitors, reckless, conceited, lovers of pleasure rather than lovers of God, [5]as they make a pretense of religion but deny its power. Reject them.[o] [6]For some of these slip into homes and make captives of women weighed down by sins, led by various desires,[p] [7]always trying to learn but never able to reach a knowledge of the truth.[q] [8]Just as Jannes and Jambres opposed Moses, so they also oppose the truth—people of depraved mind, unqualified in the faith.[r] [9]But they will not make further progress, for their foolishness will be plain to all, as it was with those two.

**Paul's Example and Teaching.[**]** [10]You have followed my teaching, way of life, purpose, faith, patience, love, endurance, [11]persecutions, and sufferings, such as happened to me in Antioch, Iconium, and Lystra, persecutions that I endured. Yet from all these things the Lord delivered me.[s] [12]In fact, all who want to live religiously in Christ Jesus will be persecuted.[t] [13]But wicked people and charlatans will go from bad to worse, deceivers and deceived. [14]But you, remain faithful to what you have learned and believed,

20–21; Rom 10:12–13; cf. 2 Tm 2:19, literally, "Everyone who names the name of the Lord").

§[2:26] Some interpreters would render this passage, "Thus they may come to their senses and, forced to do his (i.e., God's) will, may escape the devil's trap." This interpretation of the Greek is possible, but the one accepted in the text seems more likely.

¶[3:1–9] The moral depravity and false teaching that will be rampant in the last days are already at work (2 Tm 3:1–5). The frivolous and superficial, too, devoid of the true spirit of religion, will be easy victims of those who pervert them by falsifying the truth (2 Tm 3:6–8), just as Jannes and Jambres, Pharaoh's magicians of Egypt (Ex 7:11–12, 22), discredited the truth in Moses' time. Exodus does not name the magicians, but the two names are widely found in much later Jewish, Christian, and even pagan writings. Their origins are legendary.

**[3:10–17] Paul's example for Timothy includes persecution, a frequent emphasis in the Pastorals. Timothy is to be steadfast to what he has been taught and to scripture. The scriptures are the source of wisdom, i.e., of belief in and loving fulfillment of God's word revealed in Christ, through whom salvation is given.

---

*[2:14–19] For those who dispute about mere words (cf. 2 Tm 2:23–24) and indulge in irreligious talk to the detriment of their listeners (2 Tm 2:16–19), see notes on 1 Tm 1:3–7; 6:20–21. Hymenaeus and Philetus (2 Tm 2:17), while accepting the Christian's mystical death and resurrection in Christ through baptism, claimed that baptized Christians are already risen with Christ in this life and thus that there is no future bodily resurrection or eternal glory to come. The first quotation in 2 Tm 2:19 is from Nm 16:5; the other quotation is from some unidentified Jewish or Christian writing.

†[2:14] **Before God:** many ancient manuscripts read "before the Lord."

‡[2:22] **Those who call on the Lord:** those who believe in Christ and worship him as Lord, i.e., Christians (Acts 9:14–16,

w. [2:10] Col 1:24; 1 Tm 1:15.   x. [2:11] Rom 6:8.   y. [2:12] Mt 10:22, 33; Lk 12:9.   z. [2:13] Nm 23:19; Rom 3:3–4; 1 Cor 10:13; Ti 1:2.   a. [2:14] 1 Tm 6:4.   b. [2:15] 1:8; 2 Cor 6:7; Eph 1:13; Col 1:5.   c. [2:16] 1 Tm 4:7.   d. [2:17] 1 Tm 1:20.   e. [2:18] 2 Thes 2:2.   f. [2:19] Is 28:16; 1 Cor 3:10–15 / Nm 16:5; Jn 10:14.   g. [2:21] 3:17.   h. [2:22] Gal 5:22; 1 Tm 6:11 / Rom 10:13; 1 Cor 1:2.

i. [2:23] 1 Tm 1:4; 4:7; 6:4; Ti 3:9.   j. [2:24] 1 Tm 3:2–3.   k. [2:25] 3:7; 1 Tm 2:4.   l. [2:26] 1 Tm 3:7.   m. [3:1] 1 Tm 4:1; 2 Pt 3:3; Jude 18.   n. [3:2–4] Rom 1:29–31.   o. [3:5] Rom 2:20–22; Ti 1:16.   p. [3:6] Ti 1:11.   q. [3:7] 2:25.   r. [3:8] Ex 7:11, 22; 1 Tm 6:5.   s. [3:11] Acts 13:50; 14:5, 19 / Ps 34:20.   t. [3:12] Jn 15:20; Acts 14:22.

because you know from whom you learned it,[u] [15]and that from infancy you have known [the] sacred scriptures, which are capable of giving you wisdom for salvation through faith in Christ Jesus.[v] [16]*All scripture[w] is inspired by God and is useful for teaching, for refutation, for correction, and for training in righteousness,[†] [17]so that one who belongs to God may be competent, equipped for every good work.[x]

## CHAPTER 4

**Solemn Charge.**[‡] [1]I charge you in the presence of God and of Christ Jesus, who will judge the living and the dead, and by his appearing and his kingly power:[y] [2]proclaim the word; be persistent whether it is convenient or inconvenient; convince, reprimand, encourage through all patience and teaching.[z] [3]For the time will come when people will not tolerate sound doctrine but, following their own desires and insatiable curiosity,[§] will accumulate teachers[a] [4]and will stop listening to the truth and will be diverted to myths.[b] [5]But you, be self-possessed in all circumstances; put up with hardship; perform the work of an evangelist; fulfill your ministry.

**Reward for Fidelity.** [6]¶For I am already being poured out like a libation, and the time of my departure is at hand. [7]**I have competed well; I have finished the race;[d] I have kept the faith. [8]††From now on the crown of righteousness awaits me, which the Lord, the just judge, will award to me on that day,[e] and not only to me, but to all who have longed for his appearance.

## IV. PERSONAL REQUESTS AND FINAL GREETINGS

**Paul's Loneliness.** [9]‡‡Try to join me soon, [10]for Demas, enamored of the present world, deserted me and went to Thessalonica, Crescens to Galatia,[§§] and Titus to Dalmatia.[f] [11]Luke is the only one with me. Get Mark and bring him with you, for he is helpful to me in the ministry.[g] [12]I have sent Tychicus to Ephesus.[h] [13]When you come, bring the cloak I left with Carpus in Troas, the papyrus rolls, and especially the parchments.[i]

[14]Alexander[¶¶] the coppersmith did me a great deal of harm; the Lord will repay him according to his deeds.[j] [15]You too be on guard against him, for he has strongly resisted our preaching.

[16]At my first defense no one appeared on my behalf, but everyone deserted me. May it not be held against them![k] [17]But the Lord stood by me and gave me strength, so that through me the proclamation might be completed and all the Gentiles might hear it. And I was rescued from the lion's mouth.[l] [18]The Lord will rescue me from every evil threat and will bring me safe to his heavenly kingdom. To him be glory forever and ever. Amen.[m]

**Final Greeting.** [19]Greet Prisca and Aquila[***] and the family of Onesiphorus.[n] [20]Erastus[†††] remained in Corinth, while I left Trophimus sick at Miletus.[o] [21]Try to get here before winter. Eubulus, Pudens, Linus,[‡‡‡] Claudia, and all the brothers send greetings.

[22]The Lord be with your spirit. Grace be with all of you.[p]

---

*[3:16–17] **Useful for teaching . . . every good work**: because as God's word the scriptures share his divine authority. It is exercised through those who are ministers of that authority.

†[3:16] **All scripture is inspired by God**: this could possibly also be translated, "All scripture inspired by God is useful for . . . ." In this classic reference to inspiration, God is its principal author, with the writer as the human collaborator. Thus the scriptures are the word of God in human language. See also 2 Pt 1:20–21.

‡[4:1–5] The gravity of the obligation incumbent on Timothy to preach the word can be gauged from the solemn adjuration: in the presence of God, and of Christ coming as universal judge, and by his appearance and **his kingly power** (2 Tm 4:1). Patience, courage, constancy, and endurance are required despite the opposition, hostility, indifference, and defection of many to whom the truth has been preached (2 Tm 4:2–5).

§[4:3] **Insatiable curiosity**: literally, "with itching ears."

¶[4:6] The apostle recognizes his death through martyrdom to be imminent. He regards it as an act of worship in which his blood will be poured out in sacrifice; cf. Ex 29:38–40; Phil 2:17.

**[4:7] At the close of his life Paul could testify to the accomplishment of what Christ himself foretold concerning him at the time of his conversion, "I will show him what he will have to suffer for my name" (Acts 9:16).

††[4:8] When the world is judged at the parousia, all who have eagerly looked for the Lord's appearing and have sought to live according to his teachings will be rewarded. The crown is a reference to the laurel wreath placed on the heads of victorious athletes and conquerors in war; cf. 2 Tm 2:5; 1 Cor 9:25.

‡‡[4:9–13] Demas either abandoned the work of the ministry for worldly affairs or, perhaps, gave up the faith itself (2 Tm 4:10). Luke (2 Tm 4:11) may have accompanied Paul on parts of his second and third missionary journeys (Acts 16:10–12; 20:5–7). Notice the presence of the first personal pronoun "we" in these Acts passages, suggesting to some that Luke (or at least some traveling companion of Paul's) was the author of Acts. Mark, once rejected by Paul (Acts 13:13; 15:39), is now to render him a great service (2 Tm 4:11); cf. Col 4:10; Phlm 24. For Tychicus, see Eph 6:21; cf. also Acts 20:4; Col 4:7.

§§[4:10] **Galatia**: some manuscripts read "Gaul" or "Gallia."

¶¶[4:14–18] **Alexander**: an opponent of Paul's preaching (2 Tm 4:14–15), perhaps the one who is mentioned in 1 Tm 1:20. Despite Paul's abandonment by his friends in the province of Asia (cf. 2 Tm 1:15–16), the divine assistance brought this first trial to a successful issue, even to the point of making the gospel message known to those who participated in or witnessed the trial (2 Tm 4:16–17).

***[4:19] **Prisca and Aquila**: they assisted Paul in his ministry in Corinth (Acts 18:2–3) and Ephesus (Acts 18:19, 26; 1 Cor 16:19). They risked death to save his life, and all the Gentile communities are indebted to them (Rom 16:3–5).

†††[4:20] **Erastus**: he was the treasurer of the city of Corinth (Rom 16:24); cf. also Acts 19:22. **Trophimus**: from the province of Asia, he accompanied Paul from Greece to Troas (Acts 20:4–5).

‡‡‡[4:21] **Linus**: Western tradition sometimes identified this Linus with the supposed successor of Peter as bishop of Rome, and Claudia as the mother of Linus (*Apostolic Constitutions*, fourth century).

---

f. [4:10] Col 4:14; Phlm 24 / 2 Cor 2:13; 7:6–7; 8:23; Gal 2:3; Ti 1:4.  g. [4:11] Col 4:14; Phlm 24 / Col 4:10; Phlm 24.  h. [4:12] Acts 20:4; Eph 6:21; Col 4:7.  i. [4:13] Acts 16:8; 20:6.  j. [4:14] 1 Tm 1:20 / 2 Sm 3:39; Ps 28:4; 62:12; Prv 24:12; Rom 2:6.  k. [4:16] 1:15.  l. [4:17] Acts 23:11; 27:23; Phil 4:13 / 1 Mc 2:60; Ps 22:22; Dn 6:23.  m. [4:18] 2 Cor 1:10 / Rom 16:27.  n. [4:19] Acts 18:2; Rom 16:3; 1 Cor 16:19 / 2 Tm 1:16.  o. [4:20] Acts 19:22; Rom 16:24 / Acts 20:4; 21:29.  p. [4:22] Gal 6:18; Phil 4:23; Col 4:18; 1 Tm 6:21; Ti 3:15.

u. [3:14] 2:2.  v. [3:15] Jn 5:39.  w. [3:16] Rom 15:4; 2 Pt 1:19–21.  x. [3:17] 2:21.  y. [4:1] 1 Tm 5:21; 6:14 / Acts 10:42; Rom 14:9–10; 1 Pt 4:5.  z. [4:2] Acts 20:20, 31; 1 Tm 5:20.  a. [4:3] 1 Tm 4:1.  b. [4:4] 1 Tm 1:4; 4:7; Ti 1:14.  c. [4:6] Phil 2:17.  d. [4:7] 1 Tm 1:18; 6:12; Jude 3 / Acts 20:24; 1 Cor 9:24; Heb 12:1.  e. [4:8] 2:5; Wis 5:16; 1 Cor 9:25; Phil 3:14; Jas 1:12; 1 Pt 5:4; Rev 2:10.

# THE LETTER TO
# TITUS

꧁꧂

The third of the Pastoral Epistles in the New Testament is addressed to a different co-worker of Paul than are First and Second Timothy. The situation is different, too, for Titus is addressed as the person in charge of developing the church on the large Mediterranean island of Crete (Ti 1:5), a place Paul had never, according to the New Testament, visited. The tone is closer to that of First Timothy as three topics of church life and structure are discussed: presbyter-bishops (see note on Ti 1:5–9), groups with which one must work in the church (Ti 2:1–10), and admonitions for conduct based on the grace and love of God that appeared in Jesus Christ (Ti 2:11–3:10). The warmer personal tone of Second Timothy is replaced by emphasis on church office and on living in the society of the day, in which deceivers and heretics abound (Ti 1:10–16; 3:9–10).

The Pauline assistant who is addressed, Titus, was a Gentile Christian, but we are nowhere informed of his place of birth or residence. He went from Antioch with Paul and Barnabas to Jerusalem (Gal 2:1; cf. Acts 15:2). According to 2 Corinthians (2 Cor 2:13; 7:6, 13–14), he was with Paul on his third missionary journey; his name, however, does not appear in Acts. Besides being the bearer of Paul's severe letter to the Corinthians (2 Cor 7:6–8), he had the responsibility of taking up the collection in Corinth for the Christian community of Jerusalem (2 Cor 8:6, 16–19, 23). In the present letter (Ti 1:5), he is mentioned as the administrator of the Christian community in Crete, charged with the task of organizing it through the appointment of presbyters and bishops (Ti 1:5–9; here the two terms refer to the same personages).

The letter instructs Titus about the character of the assistants he is to choose in view of the pastoral difficulties peculiar to Crete (Ti 1:5–16). It suggests the special individual and social virtues that the various age groups and classes in the Christian community should be encouraged to acquire (Ti 2:1–10). The motivation for transformation of their lives comes from christology, especially the redemptive sacrifice of Christ and his future coming, as applied through baptism and justification (Ti 2:11–14; 3:4–8). The community is to serve as a leaven for Christianizing the social world about it (Ti 3:1–3). Good works are to be the evidence of their faith in God (Ti 3:8); those who engage in religious controversy are, after suitable warning, to be ignored (Ti 3:9–11).

The authorship and date of the Letter to Titus are discussed in the Introduction to 1 Timothy. Those who assume authorship by Paul himself usually place Titus after 1 Timothy and before 2 Timothy. Others see it as closely related to 1 Timothy, in a growing emphasis on church structure and opposition to heresy, later than the letters of Paul himself and 2 Timothy. It has also been suggested that, if the three Pastorals once circulated as a literary unit, Titus was meant to be read ahead of 1 and 2 Timothy.

The principal divisions of the Letter to Titus are the following:

I. Address (1:1–4)
II. Pastoral Charge (1:5–16)
III. Teaching the Christian Life (2:1–3:15)

## I. ADDRESS

### CHAPTER 1

**Greeting.**\* [1]Paul, a slave of God and apostle of Jesus Christ for the sake of the faith of God's chosen ones and the recognition of religious truth,[a] [2]in the hope of eternal life that God, who does not lie, promised before time began,[b] [3]who indeed at the proper time revealed his word in the proclamation with which I was entrusted by the command of God our savior,[c] [4]to Titus, my true child in our common faith: grace and peace from God the Father and Christ Jesus our savior.[d]

## II. PASTORAL CHARGE

**Titus in Crete.** [5†]For this reason I left you in Crete so that you might set right what remains to be done and appoint presbyters in every town, as I directed you, [6†]on condition that a man be blameless, married only once, with believing children who are not accused of licentiousness or rebellious. [7]For a bishop as God's steward must be blameless, not arrogant, not irritable, not a drunkard, not aggressive, not greedy for sordid gain, [8]but hospitable, a lover of goodness, temperate, just, holy, and self-controlled, [9]holding fast to the true message as taught so that he will be able both to exhort with sound doctrine and to refute opponents.[f] [10†]For there are also many rebels, idle talkers and deceivers, especially the Jewish Christians.[§] [11]It is imperative to silence them, as they are upsetting whole families by teaching for sordid gain what they should not. [12]One of them, a prophet of their own, once said, "Cretans have always been liars, vicious beasts, and lazy gluttons."[¶] [13]That testimony is true. Therefore, admonish them sharply, so that they may be sound in the faith,[g] [14]instead of paying attention to Jewish myths and regulations of people who have repudiated

the truth.[h] [15]To the clean all things are clean, but to those who are defiled and unbelieving nothing is clean; in fact, both their minds and their consciences are tainted.[i] [16]They claim to know God, but by their deeds they deny him. They are vile and disobedient and unqualified for any good deed.

## III. TEACHING THE CHRISTIAN LIFE

### CHAPTER 2

**Christian Behavior.**\*\* [1]As for yourself, you must say what is consistent with sound doctrine, namely,[j] [2]that older men should be temperate, dignified, self-controlled, sound in faith, love, and endurance. [3]Similarly, older women should be reverent in their behavior, not slanderers, not addicted to drink, teaching what is good, [4]so that they may train younger women to love their husbands and children, [5]to be self-controlled, chaste, good homemakers, under the control of their husbands, so that the word of God may not be discredited.[k]

[6]Urge the younger men, similarly, to control themselves, [7]showing yourself as a model of good deeds in every respect, with integrity in your teaching, dignity, [8]and sound speech that cannot be criticized, so that the opponent will be put to shame without anything bad to say about us.

[9]Slaves are to be under the control of their masters in all respects, giving them satisfaction, not talking back to them[l] [10]or stealing from them, but exhibiting complete good faith, so as to adorn the doctrine of God our savior in every way.[m]

**Transformation of Life.** [11††]For the grace of God has appeared, saving all[n] [12]and training us to reject godless ways and worldly desires and to live temperately, justly, and devoutly in this age, [13]as we await the blessed hope, the appearance[‡‡] of the glory of the great God and of our savior Jesus Christ,[o] [14]who gave himself for us to

---

\*[1:1–4] On the epistolary form, see note on Rom 1:1–7. The apostolate is the divinely appointed mission to lead others to the true faith and through it to eternal salvation (Ti 1:1–3).

†[1:5–9] This instruction on the selection and appointment of presbyters, substantially identical with that in 1 Tm 3:1–7 on a bishop (see note there), was aimed at strengthening the authority of Titus by apostolic mandate; cf. Ti 2:15. In Ti 1:5, 7 and Acts 20:17, 28, the terms *episkopos* and *presbyteros* ("bishop" and "presbyter") refer to the same persons. Deacons are not mentioned in Titus. See also note on Phil 1:1.

‡[1:10–16] This adverse criticism of the defects within the community is directed especially against certain Jewish Christians, who busy themselves with useless speculations over persons mentioned in the Old Testament, insist on the observance of Jewish ritual purity regulations, and thus upset whole families by teaching things they have no right to teach; cf. Ti 3:9; 1 Tm 1:3–10.

§[1:10] **Jewish Christians:** literally, "those of the circumcision."

¶[1:12] **Cretans . . . gluttons:** quoted from Epimenides, a Cretan poet of the sixth century B.C.

\*\*[2:1–10] One of Titus' main tasks in Crete is to become acquainted with the character of the Cretans and thereby learn to cope with its deficiencies (see Ti 1:12). The counsel is not only for Titus himself but for various classes of people with whom he must deal: older men and women (Ti 2:2–4), younger women and men (Ti 2:4–7), and slaves (Ti 2:9–10); cf. Eph 6:1–9; Col 3:18–4:1.

††[2:11–15] Underlying the admonitions for moral improvement in Ti 2:1–10 as the moving force is the constant appeal to God's revelation of salvation in Christ, with its demand for transformation of life.

‡‡[2:13] **The blessed hope, the appearance:** literally, "the blessed hope and appearance," but the use of a single article in Greek strongly suggests an epexegetical, i.e., explanatory sense. **Of the great God and of our savior Jesus Christ:** another possible translation is "of our great God and savior Jesus Christ."

h. [1:14] 3:9; 1 Tm 1:4; 4:7; 2 Tm 4:4; 2 Pt 1:16.   i. [1:15] Mk 7:18–23; Acts 10:15; Rom 14:14–23.   j. [2:1] 1:9, 13; 2:8; 1 Tm 1:10; 6:3; 2 Tm 1:13; 4:3.   k. [2:5] 1 Cor 11:3; 14:34; Eph 5:22–24; Col 3:18; 1 Tm 2:11–15; 1 Pt 3:1–6.   l. [2:9] 1 Cor 7:21–22; Eph 6:5–8; Col 3:22–25; 1 Tm 6:1–2; 1 Pt 2:18.   m. [2:10] 1:3; 3:4; Ps 24:5; 1 Tm 1:1; 2:3; 4:10; Jude 25.   n. [2:11] 1 Tm 2:4; 4:10.   o. [2:13] 1 Cor 1:7; Phil 3:20; 1 Thes 1:10 / 2 Tm 1:10 / Ti 1:4; 3:6; 2 Pt 1:11; 2:20; 3:2, 18.

a. [1:1] 1 Tm 2:4; 4:3; 2 Tm 2:25; 3:7; Heb 10:26.   b. [1:2] 3:7; 2 Tm 1:1; 1 Jn 2:25.   c. [1:3] 2:10; 3:4; Ps 24:5; 1 Tm 1:1; 2:3; 4:10; Jude 25.   d. [1:4] 2:13; 3:6; Phil 3:20; 2 Tm 1:10; 2 Pt 1:1, 11; 2:20; 3:2, 18.   e. [1:6–7] 1 Tm 3:2–7; 2 Tm 2:24–26.   f. [1:9] 1:13; 2:1–2, 8; 1 Tm 1:10; 6:3; 2 Tm 1:13; 4:3.   g. [1:13] 1:9.

deliver us from all lawlessness and to cleanse for himself a people as his own, eager to do what is good.*p*

¹⁵Say these things. Exhort and correct with all authority. Let no one look down on you.*q*

## CHAPTER 3

¹*Remind them to be under the control of magistrates and authorities,† to be obedient, to be open to every good enterprise.*r* ²They are to slander no one, to be peaceable, considerate, exercising all graciousness toward everyone. ³For we ourselves were once foolish, disobedient, deluded, slaves to various desires and pleasures, living in malice and envy, hateful ourselves and hating one another.*s*

⁴ But when the kindness and generous love
   of God our savior appeared,*t*
⁵ not because of any righteous deeds we
      had done
   but because of his mercy,
   he saved us through the bath of rebirth
      and renewal by the holy Spirit,*u*
⁶ whom he richly poured out on us

through Jesus Christ our savior,*v*
⁷ so that we might be justified by his grace
   and become heirs in hope of eternal
      life.*w*

⁸This saying is trustworthy.

**Advice to Titus.**‡ I want you to insist on these points, that those who have believed in God be careful to devote themselves to good works; these are excellent and beneficial to others.*x* ⁹ᵇAvoid foolish arguments, genealogies, rivalries, and quarrels about the law,*y* for they are useless and futile. ¹⁰After a first and second warning, break off contact with a heretic,*z* ¹¹realizing that such a person is perverted and sinful and stands self-condemned.

**Directives, Greetings, and Blessing.**¶ ¹²When I send Artemas to you, or Tychicus, try to join me at Nicopolis, where I have decided to spend the winter.*a* ¹³Send Zenas the lawyer and Apollos on their journey soon, and see to it that they have everything they need.*b* ¹⁴But let our people, too, learn to devote themselves to good works to supply urgent needs, so that they may not be unproductive.*c*

¹⁵All who are with me send you greetings. Greet those who love us in the faith.

Grace be with all of you.*d*

---

*[3:1–8] The list of Christian duties continues from Ti 2:9–10, undergirded again as in Ti 2:11–13 by appeal to what God in Christ has done (Ti 2:4–7; cf. Ti 2:11–14). The spiritual renewal of the Cretans, signified in God's merciful gift of baptism (Ti 3:4–7), should be reflected in their improved attitude toward civil authority and in their Christian relationship with all (Ti 3:1–3).

†[3:1] **Magistrates and authorities**: some interpreters understand these terms as referring to the principalities and powers of the heavenly hierarchy. **To be open to every good enterprise**: this implies being good citizens. It could also be translated "ready to do every sort of good work" (as Christians); cf. Ti 3:14.

p. [2:14] Gal 1:4; 2:20; Eph 5:2, 25; 1 Tm 2:6; 1 Pt 1:18–19 / Ps 130:8.   q. [2:15] 1 Tm 4:12.   r. [3:1] Rom 13:1–7; 1 Tm 2:1–2; 1 Pt 2:13–14.   s. [3:3] 1 Cor 6:9–11; Eph 2:1–3; 5:8; Col 3:5–7; 1 Pt 4:3.   t. [3:4] 1:3; 2:10; Ps 24:5; 1 Tm 1:1; 2:3; 4:10; Jude 25.   u. [3:5] Dt 9:5; Eph 2:4–5, 8–9; 2 Tm 1:9.

‡[3:8–11] In matters of good conduct and religious doctrine, Titus is to stand firm.

§[3:9] See note on 1 Tm 6:20–21.

¶[3:12–15] **Artemas** or **Tychicus** (2 Tm 4:12) is to replace Titus, who will join Paul in his winter sojourn at Nicopolis in Epirus, on the western coast of Greece.

v. [3:6] 1:4; 2:13; Phil 3:20; 2 Tm 1:10; 2 Pt 1:1, 11; 2:20; 3:2, 18.   w. [3:7] 1:2; 2 Tm 1:1; 1 Jn 2:25.   x. [3:8] 1 Tm 1:15; 3:1; 4:9; 2 Tm 2:11.   y. [3:9] 1 Tm 1:4; 4:7; 2 Tm 2:23.   z. [3:10] Mt 18:15–18; Rom 16:17; 1 Cor 5:11; 2 Thes 3:6, 14–15.   a. [3:12] Acts 20:4; Eph 6:21; Col 4:7; 2 Tm 4:12.   b. [3:13] Acts 18:24–26; 1 Cor 1:12; 3:4–6, 22; 4:6; 16:12.   c. [3:14] 2:14; 3:8; Heb 10:24; 1 Pt 3:13.   d. [3:15] Heb 13:25.

# THE LETTER TO
# PHILEMON

~~~

This short letter addressed to three specific individuals was written by Paul during an imprisonment, perhaps in Rome between A.D. 61 and 63 (see the Introduction to Colossians for other possible sites). It concerns Onesimus, a slave from Colossae (Col 4:9), who had run away from his master, perhaps guilty of theft in the process (Phlm 18). Onesimus was converted to Christ by Paul (Phlm 10). Paul sends him back to his master (Phlm 12) with this letter asking that he be welcomed willingly by his old master (Phlm 8–10, 14, 17) not just as a slave but as a brother in Christ (Phlm 16). Paul uses very strong arguments (especially Phlm 19) in his touching appeal on behalf of Onesimus. It is unlikely that Paul is subtly hinting that he would like to retain Onesimus as his own slave, lent to Paul by his master. Rather, he suggests he would like to have Onesimus work with him for the gospel (Phlm 13, 20–21). There is, however, little evidence connecting this Onesimus with a bishop of Ephesus of the same name mentioned by Ignatius of Antioch (ca. A.D. 110).

Paul's letter deals with an accepted institution of antiquity, human slavery. But Paul breathes into this letter the spirit of Christ and of equality within the Christian community. He does not attack slavery directly, for this is something the Christian communities of the first century were in no position to do, and the expectation that Christ would soon come again militated against social reforms. Yet Paul, by presenting Onesimus as "brother, beloved . . . to me, but even more so to you" (Phlm 16), voiced an idea revolutionary in that day and destined to break down worldly barriers of division "in the Lord."

**Address and Greeting.** [1*]Paul, a prisoner for Christ Jesus, and Timothy our brother, to Philemon, our beloved and our co-worker,[a] [2]to Apphia our sister,[†] to Archippus our fellow soldier, and to the church at your house.[b] [3]Grace to you and peace[‡] from God our Father and the Lord Jesus Christ.[c]

**Thanksgiving.** [4§d]I give thanks to my God always, remembering you in my prayers, [5]as I hear of the love and the faith you have in the Lord Jesus and for all the holy ones,[¶] [6]so that your partnership in the faith may become effective in recognizing every good there is in us[**] that leads to Christ.[e]

**Plea for Onesimus.** [7]For I have experienced much joy and encouragement[††] from your love, because the hearts of the holy ones have been refreshed by you, brother.[f] [8]Therefore, although I have the full right[‡‡] in Christ to order you to do what is proper, [9]I rather urge you out of love, being as I am, Paul, an old man,[§§] and now also a prisoner for Christ Jesus.[g] [10]I urge you on behalf of my child Onesimus, whose father I have become in my imprisonment,[h] [11]who was once

*[1] **Prisoner**: as often elsewhere (cf. Romans, 1 Corinthians, Galatians especially), the second word in Greek enunciates the theme and sets the tone of the letter. Here it is the prisoner appealing rather than the apostle commanding.

†[2] **Apphia our sister**: sister is here used (like brother) to indicate a fellow Christian. **The church at your house**: your here is singular. It more likely refers to Philemon than to the last one named, Archippus; Philemon is then the owner of the slave Onesimus (Phlm 10). An alternate view is that the actual master of the slave is Archippus and that the one to whom the letter is addressed, Philemon, is the most prominent Christian there; see note on Col 4:17.

‡[3] **Grace . . . and peace**: for this greeting, which may be a combination of Greek and Aramaic epistolary formulae, see note on Rom 1:1–7.

§[4] **In my prayers**: literally, "at the time of my prayers."

¶[5] **Holy ones**: a common term for members of the Christian community (so also Phlm 7).

**[6] **In us**: some good ancient manuscripts have in you (plural). **That leads to Christ: leads to** translates the Greek preposition *eis*, indicating direction or purpose.

††[7] **Encouragement**: the Greek word *paraklēsis* is cognate with the verb translated "urge" in Phlm 9–10, and serves as an introduction to Paul's plea. **Hearts**: literally, "bowels," expressing in Semitic fashion the seat of the emotions, one's "inmost self." The same Greek word is used in Phlm 12 and again in Phlm 20, where it forms a literary inclusion marking off the body of the letter.

‡‡[8] **Full right**: often translated "boldness," the Greek word *parrēsia* connotes the full franchise of speech, as the right of a citizen to speak before the body politic, claimed by the Athenians as their privilege (Euripides).

§§[9] **Old man**: some editors conjecture that Paul here used a similar Greek word meaning "ambassador" (cf. Eph 6:20). This conjecture heightens the contrast with "prisoner" but is totally without manuscript support.

a. [1] 9; Eph 3:1; 4:1; Phil 1:7, 13.   b. [2] Col 4:17.   c. [3] Rom 1:7; Gal 1:3; Phil 1:2.   d. [4–5] Rom 1:8–9; Eph 1:15–16.

e. [6] Phil 1:9; Col 1:9.   f. [7] 2 Cor 7:4.   g. [9] 1; Eph 3:1; 4:1; Phil 1:7, 13.   h. [10] 1 Cor 4:14–15; Gal 4:19; Col 4:9.

useless to you but is now useful* to [both] you and me. [12]I am sending him, that is, my own heart, back to you. [13]I should have liked to retain him for myself, so that he might serve† me on your behalf in my imprisonment for the gospel,$^i$ [14]but I did not want to do anything without your consent, so that the good you do might not be forced but voluntary.$^j$ [15]Perhaps this is why he was away from‡ you for a while, that you might have him back forever, [16]no longer as a slave but more than a slave, a brother, beloved especially to me, but even more so to you, as a man§ and in the Lord.$^k$ [17]So if you regard me as a partner, welcome him as you would me. [18]And if he has done you any injustice or owes you anything, charge it to me. [19]I, Paul, write this in my own hand: I will pay. May I not tell you that you owe me your very self.$^l$ [20]Yes, brother, may I profit from you in the Lord. Refresh my heart in Christ.

[21]With trust in your compliance I write to you, knowing that you will do even more than I say. [22]At the same time prepare a guest room for me, for I hope to be granted to you through your prayers.$^m$

**Final Greetings.** [23]Epaphras,** my fellow prisoner in Christ Jesus, greets you,$^n$ [24]as well as Mark, Aristarchus, Demas, and Luke, my coworkers. [25]The grace of the Lord Jesus Christ be with your spirit.$^o$

---

*[11] **Useless . . . useful**: here Paul plays on the name Onesimus, which means "useful" or "beneficial." The verb translated "profit" in Phlm 20 is cognate.

†[13] **Serve**: the Greek *diakoneō* could connote a ministry.

‡[15] **Was away from**: literally, "was separated from," but the same verb means simply "left" in Acts 18:1. It is a euphemism for his running away.

§[16] **As a man**: literally, "in the flesh." With this and the following phrase, Paul describes the natural and spiritual orders.

¶[18–19] **Charge it to me . . . I will pay**: technical legal and commercial terms in account keeping and acknowledgment of indebtedness.

i. [13] Phil 2:30.   j. [14] 2 Cor 9:7; 1 Pt 5:2.   k. [16] 1 Tm 6:2.

**[23–24] **Epaphras**: a Colossian who founded the church there (Col 1:7) and perhaps also in Laodicea and Hierapolis (Col 2:1; 4:12–13). **Aristarchus**: a native of Thessalonica and fellow worker of Paul (Acts 19:29; 20:4; 27:2). For Mark, Demas, and Luke, see 2 Tm 4:9–13 and the note there.

l. [19] Gal 6:11; 2 Thes 3:17.   m. [22] Heb 13:19.   n. [23] Col 1:7; 4:12–13.   o. [25] Acts 12:12, 15; 13:13; 15:37–39; 19:29; 20:4; 27:2; Col 4:10, 14; 2 Tm 4:10–13.

# THE LETTER TO THE
# HEBREWS

‿⁀

As early as the second century, this treatise, which is of great rhetorical power and force in its admonition to faithful pilgrimage under Christ's leadership, bore the title "To the Hebrews." It was assumed to be directed to Jewish Christians. Usually Hebrews was attached in Greek manuscripts to the collection of letters by Paul. Although no author is mentioned (for there is no address), a reference to Timothy (Heb 13:23) suggested connections to the circle of Paul and his assistants. Yet the exact audience, the author, and even whether Hebrews is a letter have long been disputed.

The author saw the addressees in danger of apostasy from their Christian faith. This danger was due not to any persecution from outsiders but to a weariness with the demands of Christian life and a growing indifference to their calling (Heb 2:1; 4:14; 6:1–12; 10:23–32). The author's main theme, the priesthood and sacrifice of Jesus (Heb 3–10), is not developed for its own sake but as a means of restoring their lost fervor and strengthening them in their faith. Another important theme of the letter is that of the pilgrimage of the people of God to the heavenly Jerusalem (Heb 11:10; 12:1–3, 18–29; 13:14). This theme is intimately connected with that of Jesus' ministry in the heavenly sanctuary (Heb 9:11–10:22).

The author calls this work a "message of encouragement" (Heb 13:22), a designation that is given to a synagogue sermon in Acts 13:15. Hebrews is probably therefore a written homily, to which the author gave an epistolary ending (Heb 13:22–25).

The author begins with a reminder of the preexistence, incarnation, and exaltation of Jesus (Heb 1:3) that proclaimed him the climax of God's word to humanity (Heb 1:1–3). He dwells upon the dignity of the person of Christ, superior to the angels (Heb 1:4–2:2). Christ is God's final word of salvation communicated (in association with accredited witnesses to his teaching: cf. Heb 2:3–4) not merely by word but through his suffering in the humanity common to him and to all others (Heb 2:5–16). This enactment of salvation went beyond the pattern known to Moses, faithful prophet of God's word though he was, for Jesus as high priest expiated sin and was faithful to God with the faithfulness of God's own Son (Heb 2:17–3:6).

Just as the infidelity of the people thwarted Moses' efforts to save them, so the infidelity of any Christian may thwart God's plan in Christ (Heb 3:6–4:13). Christians are to reflect that it is their humanity that Jesus took upon himself, with all its defects save sinfulness, and that he bore the burden of it until death out of obedience to God. God declared this work of his Son to be the cause of salvation for all (Heb 4:14–5:10). Although Christians recognize this fundamental teaching, they may grow weary of it and of its implications, and therefore require other reflections to stimulate their faith (Heb 5:11–6:20).

Therefore, the author presents to the readers for their reflection the everlasting priesthood of Christ (Heb 7:1–28), a priesthood that fulfills the promise of the Old Testament (Heb 8:1–13). It also provides the meaning God ultimately intended in the sacrifices of the Old Testament (Heb 9:1–28): these pointed to the unique sacrifice of Christ, which alone obtains forgiveness of sins (Heb 10:1–18). The trial of faith experienced by the readers should resolve itself through their consideration of Christ's ministry in the heavenly sanctuary and his perpetual intercession there on their behalf (Heb 7:25; 8:1–13). They should also be strengthened by the assurance of his foreordained parousia, and by the fruits of faith that they have already enjoyed (Heb 10:19–39).

It is in the nature of faith to recognize the reality of what is not yet seen and is the object of hope, and the saints of the Old Testament give striking example of that faith (Heb 11:1–40). The perseverance to which the author exhorts the readers is shown forth in the early life of Jesus. Despite the afflictions of his ministry and the supreme trial of his suffering and death, he remained confident of the triumph that God would bring him (Heb 12:1–3). The difficulties of human life have meaning when they are accepted as God's discipline (Heb 12:4–13), and if Christians persevere in fidelity to the word in which they have believed, they are assured of possessing forever the unshakable kingdom of God (Heb 12:14–29).

The letter concludes with specific moral commandments (Heb 13:1–17), in the course of which the author recalls again his central theme of the sacrifice of Jesus and the courage needed to associate oneself with it in faith (Heb 13:9–16).

As early as the end of the second century, the church of Alexandria in Egypt accepted Hebrews as a letter of Paul, and that became the view commonly held in the East. Pauline authorship was contested in the West into the fourth century, but then accepted. In the sixteenth century, doubts about that position were again raised, and the modern consensus is that the letter was not written by Paul. There is, however, no widespread agreement on any of the other suggested authors, e.g., Barnabas, Apollos, or Prisc(ill)a and Aquila. The document itself has no statement about its author.

Among the reasons why Pauline authorship has been abandoned are the great difference of vocabulary and style between Hebrews and Paul's letters, the alternation of doctrinal teaching with moral exhortation, the different manner of citing the Old Testament, and the resemblance between the thought of Hebrews and that of Alexandrian Judaism. The Greek of the letter is in many ways the best in the New Testament.

Since the letter of Clement of Rome to the Corinthians, written about A.D. 96, most probably cites Hebrews, the upper limit for the date of composition is reasonably certain. While the letter's references in the present tense to the Old Testament sacrificial worship do not necessarily show that temple worship was still going on, many older commentators and a growing number of recent ones favor the view that it was and that the author wrote before the destruction of the temple of Jerusalem in A.D. 70. In that case, the argument of the letter is more easily explained as directed toward Jewish Christians rather than those of Gentile origin, and the persecutions they have suffered in the past (cf. Heb 10:32–34) may have been connected with the disturbances that preceded the expulsion of the Jews from Rome in A.D. 49 under the emperor Claudius. These were probably caused by disputes between Jews who accepted Jesus as the Messiah and those who did not.

The principal divisions of the Letter to the Hebrews are the following:

   I. Introduction (1:1–4)
  II. The Son Higher Than the Angels (1:5–2:18)
 III. Jesus, Faithful and Compassionate High Priest (3:1–5:10)
 IV. Jesus' Eternal Priesthood and Eternal Sacrifice (5:11–10:39)
  V. Examples, Discipline, Disobedience (11:1–12:29)
 VI. Final Exhortation, Blessing, Greetings (13:1–25)

## I. INTRODUCTION*

### CHAPTER 1

¹In times past, God spoke in partial and various ways to our ancestors through the prophets; ²in these last days, he spoke to us through a son, whom he made heir of all things and through whom he created the universe,ᵃ

³ who is the refulgence of his glory,
    the very imprint of his being,
and who sustains all things by his mighty
        word.
When he had accomplished purification
        from sins,
he took his seat at the right hand of the
        Majesty on high,ᵇ
⁴ as far superior to the angels
as the name he has inherited is more
        excellent than theirs.ᶜ

## II. THE SON HIGHER THAN THE ANGELS

**Messianic Enthronement.**† ⁵For to which of the angels did God ever say:

---

*[1:1–4] The letter opens with an introduction consisting of a reflection on the climax of God's revelation to the human race in his Son. The divine communication was initiated and maintained during Old Testament times in fragmentary and varied ways through **the prophets** (Heb 1:1), including Abraham, Moses, and all through whom God spoke. But now in **these last days** (Heb 1:2) the final age, God's revelation of his saving purpose is achieved **through a son**, i.e., one who is Son, whose role is redeemer and mediator of creation. He was made **heir of all things** through his death and exaltation to glory, yet he existed before he appeared as man; through him God **created the universe**. Heb 1:3–4, which may be based upon a liturgical hymn, assimilate the Son to the personified Wisdom of the Old Testament as **refulgence of** God's **glory** and **imprint of his being** (Heb 1:3; cf. Wis 7:26). These same terms are used of the Logos in Philo. The author now turns from the cosmological role of the preexistent Son to the redemptive work of Jesus: he brought about purification from sins and has been exalted to the right hand of God (see Ps 110:1). The once-humiliated and crucified Jesus has been declared God's Son, and this name shows his superiority to the angels. The reason for the author's insistence on that superiority is, among other things, that in some Jewish traditions angels were mediators of the old covenant (see Acts 7:53; Gal 3:19). Finally, Jesus' superiority to the angels emphasizes the superiority of the new covenant to the old because of the heavenly priesthood of Jesus.

†[1:5–14] Jesus' superiority to the angels is now demonstrated by a series of seven Old Testament texts. Some scholars see in the stages of Jesus' exaltation an order corresponding to that of enthronement ceremonies in the ancient Near East, especially in Egypt, namely, elevation to divine status (Heb 1:5–6); presentation to the angels and proclamation of everlasting lordship (Heb 1:7–12); enthronement and conferral of royal power (Heb 1:13). The citations from the Psalms in Heb 1:5, 13 were traditionally used of Jesus' messianic sonship (cf. Acts 13:33) through his resurrection and exaltation (cf. Acts 2:33–35); those in Heb 1:8, 10–12 are concerned with his divine kingship and his creative function. The central quotation in Heb 1:7 serves to contrast the angels with the Son. The author quotes it according to the Septuagint translation, which is quite different in meaning from that of the Hebrew

---

a. [1:2] Is 2:2; Jer 23:20; Ez 38:16; Dn 10:14 / Jn 3:17; Rom 8:3; Gal 4:4 / Prv 8:30; Wis 7:22; Jn 1:3; 1 Cor 8:6; Col 1:16.    b. [1:3] Wis 7:26; 2 Cor 4:4; Col 1:15 / Heb 8:1; 10:12; 12:2; Mk 16:19; Acts 2:33; 7:55–56; Rom 8:34; Eph 1:20; Col 3:1; 1 Pt 3:22.    c. [1:4] Eph 1:21; Phil 2:9–11.

---

"You are my son; this day I have begotten
        you"?ᵈ

Or again:

"I will be a father to him, and he shall be a
        son to me"?

⁶And again, when he leads‡ the first-born into the world, he says:

"Let all the angels of God worship him."ᵉ

⁷Of the angels he says:

"He makes his angels winds
        and his ministers a fiery flame";ᶠ

⁸but of the Son:

"Your throne, O God,§ stands forever and
        ever;
and a righteous scepter is the scepter
        of your kingdom.ᵍ
⁹ You loved justice and hated wickedness;
        therefore God, your God, anointed
            you
with the oil of gladness above your
        companions";

¹⁰and:

"At the beginning, O Lord, you
        established the earth,ʰ
and the heavens are the works of
        your hands.
¹¹ They will perish, but you remain;
        and they will all grow old like a
            garment.
¹² You will roll them up like a cloak,
        and like a garment they will be
            changed.
But you are the same, and your years will
        have no end."

¹³But to which of the angels has he ever said:

"Sit at my right hand
        until I make your enemies your
            footstool"?ⁱ

---

("You make the winds your messengers, and flaming fire your ministers"). The angels are only **sent to serve . . . those who are to inherit salvation** (Heb 1:14).

‡[1:6] **And again, when he leads**: the Greek could also be translated "And when he again leads" in reference to the parousia.

§[1:8–12] **O God**: the application of the name "God" to the Son derives from the preexistence mentioned in Heb 1:2–3; the psalmist had already used it of the Hebrew king in the court style of the original. See note on Ps 45:7. It is also important for the author's christology that in Heb 1:10–12 an Old Testament passage addressed to God is redirected to Jesus.

---

d. [1:5] Ps 2:7 / 2 Sm 7:14.    e. [1:6] Dt 32:43 LXX; Ps 97:7.    f. [1:7] Ps 104:4 LXX.    g. [1:8] Ps 45:7–8.    h. [1:10–12] Ps 102:26–28. i. [1:13] Ps 110:1.

[14]Are they not all ministering spirits sent to serve, for the sake of those who are to inherit salvation?[j]

## CHAPTER 2

### Exhortation to Faithfulness.[*]
[1]Therefore, we must attend all the more to what we have heard, so that we may not be carried away. [2]For if the word announced through angels proved firm, and every transgression and disobedience received its just recompense,[k] [3]how shall we escape if we ignore so great a salvation? Announced originally through the Lord, it was confirmed for us by those who had heard.[l] [4]God added his testimony by signs, wonders, various acts of power, and distribution of the gifts of the holy Spirit according to his will.[m]

### Exaltation Through Abasement.[†]
[5]For it was not to angels that he subjected the world to come, of which we are speaking. [6]Instead, someone has testified somewhere:

"What is man that you are mindful of
　　him,
　　　or the son of man that you care for
　　　　him?"[n]
[7]　You made him for a little while lower than
　　　the angels;
　　　you crowned him with glory and
　　　　honor,
[8]　　　subjecting all things under his feet."

In "subjecting" all things [to him], he left nothing not "subject to him." Yet at present we do not see "all things subject to him,"[o] [9]but we do see Jesus "crowned with glory and honor" because he suffered death, he who "for a little while" was made "lower than the angels," that by the grace of God he might taste death for everyone.[p]

[10]For it was fitting that he, for whom and through whom all things exist, in bringing many children to glory, should make the leader to their salvation perfect through suffering.[q] [11]He who consecrates and those who are being consecrated all have one origin. Therefore, he is not ashamed to call them "brothers," [12]saying:

"I will proclaim your name to my
　　brothers,
　　　in the midst of the assembly I will
　　　　praise you";[r]

[13]and again:

"I will put my trust in him";

and again:

"Behold, I and the children God has given
　　me."[s]

[14]Now since the children share in blood and flesh, he likewise shared in them, that through death he might destroy the one who has the power of death, that is, the devil,[t] [15]and free those who through fear of death had been subject to slavery all their life. [16]Surely he did not help angels but rather the descendants of Abraham; [17]therefore, he had to become like his brothers in every way, that he might be a merciful and faithful high priest before God to expiate the sins of the people.[u] [18]Because he himself was tested through what he suffered, he is able to help those who are being tested.

---

*[2:1–4] The author now makes a transition into exhortation, using an a fortiori argument (as at Heb 7:21–22; 9:13–14; 10:28–29; 12:25). The **word announced through angels** (Heb 2:2), the Mosaic law, is contrasted with the more powerful word that Christians have received (Heb 2:3–4). Christ's supremacy strengthens Christians against being **carried away** from their faith.

†[2:5–18] The humanity and the suffering of Jesus do not constitute a valid reason for relinquishing the Christian faith. Ps 8:6–7 is also applied to Jesus in 1 Cor 15:27; Eph 1:22; and probably 1 Pt 3:22. This christological interpretation, therefore, probably reflects a common early Christian tradition, which may have originated in the expression **the son of man** (Heb 2:6). The psalm contrasts God's greatness with man's relative insignificance but also stresses the superiority of man to the rest of creation, of which he is lord. Hebrews applies this christologically: Jesus lived a truly human existence, **lower than the angels**, in the days of his earthly life, particularly in his suffering and death; now, **crowned with glory and honor**, he is raised above all creation. The author considers all things as already **subject to him** because of his exaltation (Heb 2:8–9), though **we do not see** this yet. The reference to Jesus as **leader** (Heb 2:10) sounds the first note of an important leitmotif in Hebrews: the journey of the people of God to the sabbath rest (Heb 4:9), the heavenly sanctuary, following Jesus, their "forerunner" (Heb 6:20). It was fitting that God should make him **perfect through suffering**, consecrated by obedient suffering. Because he is perfected as high priest, Jesus is then able to consecrate his people (Heb 2:11); access to God is made possible by each of these two consecrations. If Jesus is able to help human beings, it is because he has become one of us; we are his "brothers." The author then cites three Old Testament texts as proofs of this unity between ourselves and the Son. Ps 22:23 is interpreted so as to make Jesus the singer of this lament, which ends with joyful praise of the Lord in the assembly of "brothers." The other two texts are from Is 8:17–18. The first of these seems intended to display in Jesus an example of the trust in God that his followers should emulate. The second curiously calls these followers "children"; probably this is to be understood to mean children of Adam, but the point is our solidarity with Jesus. By sharing human nature, including the ban on death, Jesus broke the power of the devil over death (Heb 2:14); the author shares the view of Hellenistic Judaism that death was not intended by God and that it had been introduced into the world by the devil. The **fear of death** (Heb 2:15) is a religious fear based on the false conception that death marks the end of a person's relations with God (cf. Ps 115:17–18; Is 38:18). Jesus deliberately allied himself with the **descendants of Abraham** (Heb 2:16) in order to be a **merciful and faithful high priest**. This is the first appearance of the central theme of Hebrews, Jesus the great high priest expiating the **sins of the people** (Heb 2:17), as one who experienced the same tests as they (Heb 2:18).

---

j. [1:14] Ps 91:11; Dn 7:10.　k. [2:2] Acts 7:38, 53; Gal 3:19.　l. [2:3] 10:29; 12:25.　m. [2:4] Mk 16:20; Acts 14:3; 19:11.

n. [2:6] Ps 8:5–7.　o. [2:8] Mt 28:18; 1 Cor 15:25–28; Eph 1:20–23; Phil 3:21; 1 Pt 3:22.　p. [2:9] Phil 2:6–11.　q. [2:10] 12:2; Is 53:4 / Rom 11:36; 1 Cor 8:6.　r. [2:12] Ps 22:23.　s. [2:13] Is 8:17, 18.　t. [2:14] Is 25:8; Hos 13:14; Jn 12:31; Rom 6:9; 1 Cor 15:54–55; 2 Tm 1:10; Rev 12:10.　u. [2:17] 4:15; 5:1–3.

## III. JESUS, FAITHFUL AND COMPASSIONATE HIGH PRIEST

### CHAPTER 3

**Jesus, Superior to Moses.**[*] [1]Therefore, holy "brothers," sharing in a heavenly calling, reflect on Jesus, the apostle and high priest of our confession, [2]who was faithful to the one who appointed him, just as Moses was "faithful in [all] his house."[v] [3]But he is worthy of more "glory" than Moses, as the founder of a house has more "honor" than the house itself.[w] [4]Every house is founded by someone, but the founder of all is God. [5]Moses was "faithful in all his house" as a "servant" to testify to what would be spoken, [6†x]but Christ was faithful as a son placed over his house. We are his house, if [only] we hold fast to our confidence and pride in our hope.

**Israel's Infidelity a Warning.** [7‡]Therefore, as the holy Spirit says:

"Oh, that today you would hear his voice,[y]

[8]    'Harden not your hearts as at the rebellion
        in the day of testing in the desert,

[9]    where your ancestors tested and
            tried me
        and saw my works[z] [10]for forty
            years.
    Because of this I was provoked with
        that generation
        and I said, "They have always
            been of erring heart,
        and they do not know my ways."

[11]    As I swore in my wrath,
        "They shall not enter into my
            rest."'"

[12]Take care, brothers, that none of you may have an evil and unfaithful heart, so as to forsake the living God. [13]Encourage yourselves daily while it is still "today," so that none of you may grow hardened by the deceit of sin. [14]We have become partners of Christ if only we hold the beginning of the reality firm until the end,[a] [15]for it is said:

"Oh, that today you would hear his voice:
    'Harden not your hearts as at the rebellion.'"[b]

[16c]Who were those who rebelled when they heard? Was it not all those who came out of Egypt under Moses? [17]With whom was he "provoked for forty years"? Was it not those who had sinned, whose corpses fell in the desert?[d] [18]And to whom did he "swear that they should not enter into his rest," if not to those who were disobedient?[e] [19]And we see that they could not enter for lack of faith.

### CHAPTER 4

**The Sabbath Rest.** [1]Therefore, let us be on our guard while the promise of entering into his rest remains, that none of you seem to have failed. [2]For in fact we have received the good news just as they did. But the word that they heard did not profit them, for they were not united in faith with those who listened. [3]For we who believed enter into [that] rest, just as he has said:[f]

"As I swore in my wrath,
    'They shall not enter into my rest,'"

and yet his works were accomplished at the foundation of the world. [4]For he has spoken somewhere about the seventh day in this manner,

---

*[3:1–6] The author now takes up the two qualities of Jesus mentioned in Heb 2:17, but in inverse order: faithfulness (Heb 3:1–4:13) and mercy (Heb 4:14–5:10). Christians are called **holy "brothers"** because of their common relation to him (Heb 2:11), **the apostle**, a designation for Jesus used only here in the New Testament (cf. Jn 13:16; 17:3), meaning one sent as God's final word to us (Heb 1:2). He is compared with Moses probably because he is seen as mediator of the new covenant (Heb 9:15) just as Moses was of the old (Heb 9:19–22, including his sacrifice). But when the author of Hebrews speaks of Jesus' sacrifice, he does not consider Moses as the Old Testament antitype, but rather the high priest on the Day of Atonement (Heb 9:6–15). Moses' faithfulness **in [all] his house** refers back to Nm 12:7, on which this section is a midrashic commentary. In Heb 3:3–6, the author does not indicate that he thinks of either Moses or Christ as the founder of the household. **His house** (Heb 3:2, 5, 6) means God's house, not that of Moses or Christ; in the case of Christ, compare Heb 3:6 with Heb 10:21. The **house** of Heb 3:6 is the Christian community; the author suggests its continuity with Israel by speaking not of two houses but of only one. Heb 3:6 brings out the reason why Jesus is superior to Moses: the latter was the faithful **servant** laboring **in** the house founded by God, but Jesus is God's **son**, placed over the house.

†[3:6] The majority of manuscripts add "firm to the end," but these words are not found in the three earliest and best witnesses and are probably an interpolation derived from Heb 3:14.

‡[3:7–4:13] The author appeals for steadfastness of faith in Jesus, basing his warning on the experience of Israel during the Exodus. In the Old Testament the Exodus had been invoked as a symbol of the return of Israel from the Babylonian exile (Is 42:9; 43:16–21; 51:9–11). In the New Testament the redemption was similarly understood as a new exodus, both in the experience of Jesus himself (Lk 9:31) and in that of his followers (1 Cor 10:1–4). The author cites Ps 95:7–11, a salutary example of hardness of heart, as a warning against the danger of growing weary and giving up the journey. To call God **living** (Heb 3:12) means that he reveals himself in his works (cf. Jos 3:10; Jer 10:11). The **rest** (Heb 3:11) into which Israel was to enter was only a foreshadowing of that rest to which Christians are called. They are to remember the example of Israel's revolt in the desert that cost a whole generation the loss of the promised land (Heb 3:15–19; cf. Nm 14:20–29). In Heb 4:1–11, the symbol of **rest** is seen in deeper dimension: because the promise to the ancient Hebrews foreshadowed that given to Christians, it is **good news**; and because the promised land was the place of rest that God provided for his people, it was a share in his own rest, which he enjoyed after he had finished his creative work (Heb 3:3–4; cf. Gn 2:2). The author attempts to read this meaning of God's rest into Ps 95:7–11 (Heb 3:6–9). The Greek form of the name of Joshua, who led Israel into the promised land, is Jesus (Heb 3:8). The author plays upon the name but stresses the superiority of

Jesus, who leads his followers into heavenly rest. Heb 3:12–13 are meant as a continuation of the warning, for the word of God brings judgment as well as salvation. Some would capitalize **the word of God** and see it as a personal title of Jesus, comparable to that of Jn 1:1–18.

y. [3:7–11] Ps 95:7–11.  z. [3:9] Ex 17:7; Nm 20:2–5.  a. [3:14] Rom 8:17.  b. [3:15] Ps 95:7–8.  c. [3:16–19] Nm 14:1–38; Dt 1:19–40.  d. [3:17] Nm 14:29.  e. [3:18] Nm 14:22–23; Dt 1:35.  f. [4:3] 3:11; Ps 95:11.

v. [3:2] Nm 12:7.  w. [3:3] 2 Cor 3:7–8.  x. [3:6] 10:21; Eph 2:19; 1 Tm 3:15; 1 Pt 4:17.

"And God rested on the seventh day from all his works";[g] [5]and again, in the previously mentioned place, "They shall not enter into my rest."[h] [6]Therefore, since it remains that some will enter into it, and those who formerly received the good news did not enter because of disobedience, [7]he once more set a day, "today," when long afterwards he spoke through David, as already quoted:[i]

"Oh, that today you would hear his voice:
'Harden not your hearts.'"

[8]Now if Joshua had given them rest, he would not have spoken afterwards of another day.[j] [9]Therefore, a sabbath rest still remains for the people of God. [10]And whoever enters into God's rest, rests from his own works as God did from his. [11]Therefore, let us strive to enter into that rest, so that no one may fall after the same example of disobedience.

[12]Indeed, the word of God is living and effective, sharper than any two-edged sword, penetrating even between soul and spirit, joints and marrow, and able to discern reflections and thoughts of the heart.[k] [13]No creature is concealed from him, but everything is naked and exposed to the eyes of him to whom we must render an account.[l]

**Jesus, Compassionate High Priest.** [14]Therefore, since we have a great high priest who has passed through the heavens, Jesus, the Son of God, let us hold fast to our confession.[m] [15]For we do not have a high priest who is unable to sympathize with our weaknesses, but one who has similarly been tested in every way, yet without sin.[n] [16]So let us confidently approach the throne of grace to receive mercy and to find grace for timely help.[o]

## CHAPTER 5

[1]Every high priest is taken from among men and made their representative before God, to offer gifts and sacrifices for sins.‡ [2]He is able to deal patiently§ with the ignorant and erring, for he himself is beset by weakness [3]and so, for this reason, must make sin offerings for himself as well as for the people.[p] [4]No one takes this honor upon himself but only when called by God, just as Aaron was.[q] [5]In the same way, it was not Christ who glorified himself in becoming high priest, but rather the one who said to him:

"You are my son;
    this day I have begotten you";[r]

[6]just as he says in another place:¶

"You are a priest forever
    according to the order of
        Melchizedek."[s]

[7]In the days when he was in the flesh, he offered prayers and supplications with loud cries and tears to the one who was able to save him from death,** and he was heard because of his reverence.[t] [8]Son though he was,†† he learned obedience from what he suffered;[u] [9]and when he was made perfect, he became the source of eternal salvation for all who obey him,[v] [10]declared by God high priest according to the order of Melchizedek.[w]

## IV. JESUS' ETERNAL PRIESTHOOD AND ETERNAL SACRIFICE

**Exhortation to Spiritual Renewal.** [11]‡‡About this we have much to say, and it is difficult

was of divine appointment (Heb 5:4), as was also the case with the sinless Christ (Heb 5:5). For Heb 5:6, see note on Ps 110:4. Although Jesus was Son of God, he was destined as a human being to learn obedience by accepting the suffering he had to endure (Heb 5:8). Because of his perfection through this experience of human suffering, he is the cause of salvation for all (Heb 5:9), a **high priest according to the order of Melchizedek** (Heb 5:10; cf. Heb 5:6 and Heb 7:3).

‡[5:1] **To offer gifts and sacrifices for sins:** the author is thinking principally of the Day of Atonement rite, as is clear from Heb 9:7. This ritual was celebrated to atone for "all the sins of the Israelites" (Lv 16:34).

§[5:2] **Deal patiently:** the Greek word *metriopathein* occurs only here in the Bible; this term was used by the Stoics to designate the golden mean between excess and defect of passion. Here it means rather the ability to sympathize.

¶[5:6–8] The author of Hebrews is the only New Testament writer to cite Ps 110:4, here and in Heb 7:17, 21, to show that Jesus has been called by God to his role as priest. Heb 5:7–8 deal with his ability to sympathize with sinners, because of his own experience of the trials and weakness of human nature, especially fear of death. In his present exalted state, weakness is foreign to him, but he understands what we suffer because of his previous earthly experience.

**[5:7] **He offered prayers . . . to the one who was able to save him from death:** at Gethsemane (cf. Mk 14:35), though some see a broader reference (see note on Jn 12:27).

††[5:8] **Son though he was:** two different though not incompatible views of Jesus' sonship coexist in Hebrews, one associating it with his exaltation, the other with his preexistence. The former view is the older one (cf. Rom 1:4).

‡‡[5:11–6:20] The central section of Hebrews (5:11–10:39) opens with a reprimand and an appeal. Those to whom the author directs his teaching about Jesus' priesthood, which is

*[4:14–16] These verses, which return to the theme first sounded in Heb 2:16–3:1, serve as an introduction to the section that follows. The author here alone calls Jesus **a great high priest** (Heb 4:14), a designation used by Philo for the Logos; perhaps he does so in order to emphasize Jesus' superiority over the Jewish high priest. He has **been tested in every way, yet without sin** (Heb 4:15); this indicates an acquaintance with the tradition of Jesus' temptations, not only at the beginning (as in Mk 1:13) but throughout his public life (cf. Lk 22:28). Although the reign of the exalted Jesus is a theme that occurs elsewhere in Hebrews, and Jesus' throne is mentioned in Heb 1:8, **the throne of grace** (Heb 4:16) refers to the throne of God. The similarity of Heb 4:16 to Heb 10:19–22 indicates that the author is thinking of our confident access to God, made possible by the priestly work of Jesus.

†[5:1–10] The true humanity of Jesus (see note on Heb 2:5–18) makes him a more rather than a less effective high priest to the Christian community. In Old Testament tradition, the high priest was identified with the people, guilty of personal sin just as they were (Heb 5:1–3). Even so, the office

g. [4:4] Gn 2:2.    h. [4:5] Ps 95:11.    i. [4:7] 3:7–8, 15; Ps 95:7–8.
j. [4:8] Dt 31:7; Jos 22:4.    k. [4:12] Wis 18:15–16; Is 49:2; Eph 6:17;
Rev 1:16; 2:12.    l. [4:13] Jb 34:21–22; Ps 90:8; 139:2–4.    m. [4:14]
9:11, 24.    n. [4:15] 2:17–18; 5:2.    o. [4:16] 8:1; 10:19, 22, 35; 12:2;
Eph 3:12.

p. [5:3] Lv 9:7; 16:15–17, 30, 34.    q. [5:4] Ex 28:1.    r. [5:5] Ps 2:7.
s. [5:6] Ps 110:4.    t. [5:7] Mt 26:38–44; Mk 14:34–40; Lk 22:41–
46; Jn 12:27.    u. [5:8] Rom 5:19; Phil 2:8.    v. [5:9] 7:24–25, 28.
w. [5:10] 6:20; Ps 110:4.

to explain, for you have become sluggish in hearing. [12]Although you should be teachers by this time, you need to have someone teach you again the basic elements of the utterances of God. You need milk, [and] not solid food.[x] [13]Everyone who lives on milk lacks experience of the word of righteousness, for he is a child. [14]But solid food is for the mature, for those whose faculties are trained by practice to discern good and evil.

## CHAPTER 6

[1]Therefore, let us leave behind the basic teaching about Christ and advance to maturity, without laying the foundation all over again: repentance from dead works and faith in God,[y] [2]instruction about baptisms[*] and laying on of hands, resurrection of the dead and eternal judgment.[z] [3]And we shall do this, if only God permits. [4]For it is impossible in the case of those who have once been enlightened and tasted the heavenly gift[†] and shared in the holy Spirit[a] [5]and tasted the good word of God and the powers of the age to come,[‡] [6]and then have fallen away, to bring them to repentance again, since they are recrucifying the Son of God for themselves[§] and holding him up to contempt.[b] [7]Ground that has absorbed the rain falling upon it repeatedly and brings forth crops useful to those for whom it is cultivated receives a blessing from God.[c] [8]But if it produces

thorns and thistles, it is rejected; it will soon be cursed and finally burned.[d]

[9]But we are sure in your regard, beloved, of better things related to salvation, even though we speak in this way. [10]For God is not unjust so as to overlook your work and the love you have demonstrated for his name by having served and continuing to serve the holy ones. [11]We earnestly desire each of you to demonstrate the same eagerness for the fulfillment of hope until the end,[e] [12]so that you may not become sluggish, but imitators of those who, through faith and patience,[f] are inheriting the promises.[¶]

**God's Promise Immutable.** [13**,g]When God made the promise to Abraham, since he had no one greater by whom to swear, "he swore by himself," [14]and said, "I will indeed bless you and multiply" you.[h] [15]And so, after patient waiting,[i] he obtained the promise.[††] [16]Human beings swear by someone greater than themselves; for them an oath serves as a guarantee and puts an end to all argument. [17]So when God wanted to give the heirs of his promise an even clearer demonstration of the immutability of his purpose, he intervened with an oath,[j] [18]so that by two immutable things,[‡‡] in which it was impossible for God to lie, we who have taken refuge might be strongly encouraged to hold fast to the hope that lies before us.[k] [19]This we have as an anchor of the soul,[l] sure and firm, which reaches into the interior behind the veil,[§§] [20]where Jesus has entered on our behalf as forerunner, becoming high priest forever according to the order of Melchizedek.[m]

## CHAPTER 7

**Melchizedek, a Type of Christ.** [1**]This "Melchizedek, king of Salem and priest of God Most

**difficult to explain**, have become **sluggish in hearing** and forgetful of even **the basic elements** (Heb 5:12). But rather than treating of basic teachings, the author apparently believes that the challenge of more advanced ones may shake them out of their inertia (**therefore**, Heb 6:1). The six examples of **basic teaching** in Heb 6:1–3 are probably derived from a traditional catechetical list. No effort is made to address apostates, for their very hostility to the Christian message cuts them off completely from Christ (Heb 6:4–8). This harsh statement seems to rule out repentance after apostasy, but perhaps the author deliberately uses hyperbole in order to stress the seriousness of abandoning Christ. With Heb 6:9 a milder tone is introduced, and the criticism of the community (Heb 6:1–3, 9) is now balanced by an expression of confidence that its members are living truly Christian lives, and that God will justly reward their efforts (Heb 6:10). The author is concerned especially about their persevering (Heb 6:11–12), citing in this regard the achievement of Abraham, who relied on God's promise and on God's oath (Heb 6:13–18; cf. Gn 22:16), and proposes to them as a firm anchor of Christian hope the high priesthood of Christ, who is now living with God (Heb 6:19–20).

*[6:2] **Instruction about baptisms**: not simply about Christian baptism but about the difference between it and similar Jewish rites, such as proselyte baptism, John's baptism, and the washings of the Qumran sectaries. **Laying on of hands**: in Acts 8:17; 19:6 this rite effects the infusion of the holy Spirit; in Acts 6:6; 13:3; 1 Tm 4:14; 5:22; 2 Tm 1:6 it is a means of conferring some ministry or mission in the early Christian community.

†[6:4] **Enlightened and tasted the heavenly gift**: this may refer to baptism and the Eucharist, respectively, but more probably means the neophytes' enlightenment by faith and their experience of salvation.

‡[6:5] **Tasted the good word of God and the powers of the age to come**: the proclamation of the **word of God** was accompanied by signs of the Spirit's power (1 Thes 1:5; 1 Cor 2:4).

§[6:6] **They are recrucifying the Son of God for themselves**: a colorful description of the malice of apostasy, which is portrayed as again crucifying and deriding the Son of God.

¶[6:12] **Imitators of those . . . inheriting the promises**: the author urges the addressees to imitate the faith of the holy people of the Old Testament, who now possess the promised goods of which they lived in hope. This theme will be treated fully in Heb 6:11.

**[6:13] **He swore by himself**: God's promise to Abraham, which he confirmed by an oath ("I swear by myself," Gn 22:16) was the basis for the hope of all Abraham's descendants.

††[6:15] **He obtained the promise**: this probably refers not to Abraham's temporary possession of the land but to the eschatological blessings that Abraham and the other patriarchs have now come to possess.

‡‡[6:18] **Two immutable things**: the promise and the oath, both made by God.

§§[6:19] **Anchor . . . into the interior behind the veil**: a mixed metaphor. The Holy of Holies, beyond the veil that separates it from the Holy Place (Ex 26:31–33), is seen as the earthly counterpart of the heavenly abode of God. This theme will be developed in Heb 9.

¶¶[7:1–3] Recalling the meeting between Melchizedek and Abraham described in Gn 14:17–20, the author enhances the significance of this priest by providing the popular etymological meaning of his name and that of the city over which he ruled (Heb 7:2). Since Genesis gives no information on the parentage or the death of Melchizedek, he is seen here as a

x. [5:12] 1 Cor 3:1–3.   y. [6:1] 9:14.   z. [6:2] 9:10; Mk 7:4 / Acts 6:6; 8:17; 13:3; 19:6; 1 Tm 4:14; 5:22; 2 Tm 1:6.   a. [6:4] 10:26, 32; Ps 34:6; 2 Cor 4:6.   b. [6:6] 2 Pt 2:21.   c. [6:7] Gn 1:11–12; Dt 11:11.

d. [6:8] Gn 3:17–18; Mt 7:16; 13:7; Mk 4:7; Lk 8:7.   e. [6:11] 3:14.   f. [6:12] 5:11; Gal 3:14; Eph 1:13–14.   g. [6:13] Gn 22:16.   h. [6:14] Gn 22:17.   i. [6:15] 6:12; Rom 4:20.   j. [6:17] 6:12.   k. [6:18] Nm 23:19; 1 Sm 15:29; Jn 8:17; 2 Tm 2:13.   l. [6:19] 10:20; Ex 26:31–33; Lv 16:2.   m. [6:20] 5:10; Ps 110:4.

High,"" "met Abraham as he returned from his defeat of the kings" and "blessed him."[n] [2]And Abraham apportioned to him "a tenth of everything." His name first means righteous king, and he was also "king of Salem," that is, king of peace. [3]Without father, mother, or ancestry, without beginning of days or end of life,[‡] thus made to resemble the Son of God, he remains a priest forever.[o]

[4][5]See how great he is to whom the patriarch "Abraham [indeed] gave a tenth" of his spoils.[p] [5]The descendants of Levi who receive the office of priesthood have a commandment according to the law to exact tithes from the people, that is, from their brothers, although they also have come from the loins of Abraham.[q] [6]But he who was not of their ancestry received tithes from Abraham and blessed him who had received the promises. [7]Unquestionably, a lesser person is blessed by a greater.[¶] [8]In the one case, mortal men receive tithes; in the other, a man of whom it is testified that he lives on. [9]One might even say that Levi[**] himself, who receives tithes, was tithed through Abraham, [10]for he was still in his father's loins when Melchizedek met him.

[11][††]If, then, perfection came through the levitical priesthood, on the basis of which the people received the law, what need would there still have been for another priest to arise according to the order of Melchizedek, and not reckoned according to the order of Aaron?[r] [12]When there is a change of priesthood, there is necessarily a change of law as well. [13]Now he of whom these things are said[‡‡] belonged to a different tribe, of which no member ever officiated at the altar. [14]It is clear that our Lord arose from Judah,[§§] and in regard to that tribe Moses said nothing about priests.[s] [15][¶¶]It is even more obvious if another priest is raised up after the likeness of Melchizedek, [16]who has become so, not by a law expressed in a commandment concerning physical descent but by the power of a life that cannot be destroyed.[***] [17]For it is testified:

"You are a priest forever
    according to the order of
        Melchizedek."[t]

[18]On the one hand, a former commandment is annulled because of its weakness and uselessness,[u] [19]for the law brought nothing to perfection; on the other hand, a better hope[†††] is introduced, through which we draw near to God. [20][‡‡‡]And to the degree that this happened

---

type of Christ, representing a priesthood that is unique and eternal (Heb 7:3).

*[7:1] The author here assumes that Melchizedek was a priest of the God of Israel (cf. Gn 14:22 and the note there).

†[7:2] In Gn 14, the Hebrew text does not state explicitly who gave tithes to whom. The author of Hebrews supplies Abraham as the subject, according to a contemporary interpretation of the passage. This supports the argument of the midrash and makes it possible to see in Melchizedek a type of Jesus. The messianic blessings of righteousness and peace are foreshadowed in the names "Melchizedek" and "Salem."

‡[7:3] **Without father, mother, or ancestry, without beginning of days or end of life:** this is perhaps a quotation from a hymn about Melchizedek. The rabbis maintained that anything not mentioned in the Torah does not exist. Consequently, since the Old Testament nowhere mentions Melchizedek's ancestry, birth, or death, the conclusion can be drawn that he remains . . . forever.

§[7:4–10] The tithe that Abraham gave to Melchizedek (Heb 7:4), a practice later followed by the levitical priesthood (Heb 7:5), was a gift (Heb 7:6) acknowledging a certain superiority in Melchizedek, the foreign priest (Heb 7:7). This is further indicated by the fact that the institution of the levitical priesthood was sustained by hereditary succession in the tribe of Levi, whereas the absence of any mention of Melchizedek's death in Genesis implies that his personal priesthood is permanent (Heb 7:8). The levitical priesthood itself, through Abraham, its ancestor, paid tithes to Melchizedek, thus acknowledging the superiority of his priesthood over its own (Heb 7:9–10).

¶[7:7] **A lesser person is blessed by a greater:** though this sounds like a principle, there are some examples in the Old Testament that do not support it (cf. 2 Sm 14:22; Jb 31:20). The author may intend it as a statement of a liturgical rule.

**[7:9] Levi:** for the author this name designates not only the son of Jacob mentioned in Genesis but the priestly tribe that was thought to be descended from him.

††[7:11–14] The levitical priesthood was not typified by the priesthood of Melchizedek, for Ps 110:4 speaks of a priesthood of a new order, the order of Melchizedek, to arise in messianic times (Heb 7:11). Since the levitical priesthood served the Mosaic law, a new priesthood (Heb 7:12) would

not come into being without a change in the law itself. Thus Jesus was not associated with the Old Testament priesthood, for he was a descendant of the tribe of Judah, which had never exercised the priesthood (Heb 7:13–14).

‡‡[7:13] **He of whom these things are said:** Jesus, the priest "according to the order of Melchizedek." According to the author's interpretation, Ps 110 spoke prophetically of Jesus.

§§[7:14] **Judah:** the author accepts the early Christian tradition that Jesus was descended from the family of David (cf. Mt 1:1–2, 16, 20; Lk 1:27; 2:4; Rom 1:3). The Qumran community expected two Messiahs, one descended from Aaron and one from David; Hebrews shows no awareness of this view or at least does not accept it. Our author's view is not attested in contemporaneous Judaism.

¶¶[7:15–19] Jesus does not exercise a priesthood through family lineage but through his immortal existence (Heb 7:15–16), fulfilling Ps 110:4 (Heb 7:17; cf. Heb 7:3). Thus he abolishes forever both the levitical priesthood and the law it serves, because neither could effectively sanctify people (Heb 7:18) by leading them into direct communication with God (Heb 7:19).

***[7:16] **A life that cannot be destroyed:** the life to which Jesus has attained by virtue of his resurrection; it is his exaltation rather than his divine nature that makes him priest. The Old Testament speaks of the Aaronic priesthood as eternal (see Ex 40:15); our author does not explicitly consider this possible objection to his argument but implicitly refutes it in Heb 7:23–24.

†††[7:19] **A better hope:** this hope depends upon the sacrifice of the Son of God; through it we "approach the throne of grace" (Heb 4:16); cf. Heb 6:19, 20.

‡‡‡[7:20–25] As was the case with the promise to Abraham (Heb 6:13), though not with the levitical priesthood, the eternal priesthood of the order of Melchizedek was confirmed by God's oath (Heb 7:20–21); cf. Ps 110:4. Thus Jesus becomes the guarantee of a permanent covenant (Heb 7:22) that does not require a succession of priests as did the levitical priesthood (Heb 7:23) because his high priesthood is eternal and unchangeable (Heb 7:24). Consequently, Jesus is able to save all who draw near to God through him since he is their ever-living intercessor (Heb 7:25).

---

n. [7:1] Gn 14:17–20.   o. [7:3] 4:14; 6:6; 10:29.   p. [7:4] Gn 14:20.   q. [7:5] Nm 18:21 / Gn 35:11.

r. [7:11] 5:6; Ps 110:4.   s. [7:14] Gn 49:10; Is 11:1; Mt 1:1–2, 16, 20; 2:6; Lk 1:27; 2:4; Rom 1:3; Rev 5:5.   t. [7:17] 5:6; Ps 110:4.   u. [7:18] 10:1.

not without the taking of an oath*—for others became priests without an oath, <sup>21</sup>but he with an oath, through the one who said to him:

"The Lord has sworn, and he will not
        repent:<sup>v</sup>
    'You are a priest forever'"—

<sup>22w</sup>to that same degree has Jesus [also] become the guarantee of an [even] better covenant.<sup>†</sup> <sup>23</sup>Those priests were many because they were prevented by death from remaining in office, <sup>24</sup>but he, because he remains forever, has a priesthood that does not pass away.<sup>x</sup> <sup>25‡</sup>Therefore, he is always able to save those who approach God through him, since he lives forever to make intercession for them.<sup>y</sup>

<sup>26z</sup>It was fitting that we should have such a high priest:<sup>§</sup> holy, innocent, undefiled, separated from sinners, higher than the heavens.<sup>¶</sup> <sup>27</sup>He has no need, as did the high priests, to offer sacrifice day after day,**<sup>a</sup> first for his own sins and then for those of the people; he did that once for all when he offered himself. <sup>28</sup>For the law appoints men subject to weakness to be high priests, but the word of the oath, which was taken after the law, appoints a son, who has been made perfect forever.<sup>b</sup>

## CHAPTER 8

**Heavenly Priesthood of Jesus.**<sup>††</sup> <sup>1</sup>The main point of what has been said is this: we have such a

---

high priest, who has taken his seat at the right hand of the throne of the Majesty in heaven,<sup>c</sup> <sup>2</sup>a minister of the sanctuary<sup>‡‡</sup> and of the true tabernacle that the Lord, not man, set up.<sup>d</sup> <sup>3</sup>Now every high priest is appointed to offer gifts and sacrifices; thus the necessity for this one also to have something to offer.<sup>e</sup> <sup>4</sup>If then he were on earth, he would not be a priest, since there are those who offer gifts according to the law.<sup>f</sup> <sup>5</sup>They worship in a copy and shadow of the heavenly sanctuary, as Moses was warned when he was about to erect the tabernacle. For he says, "See that you make everything according to the pattern shown you on the mountain."<sup>g</sup> <sup>6</sup>Now he has obtained so much more excellent a ministry as he is mediator of a better covenant, enacted on better promises.<sup>h</sup>

**Old and New Covenants.**<sup>§§</sup> <sup>7</sup>For if that first covenant had been faultless, no place would have been sought for a second one. <sup>8</sup>But he finds fault with them and says:<sup>¶¶</sup>

"Behold, the days are coming, says the
        Lord,<sup>i</sup>
    when I will conclude a new covenant
        with the house of Israel and
        the house of Judah.
<sup>9</sup>  It will not be like the covenant I made
        with their fathers
    the day I took them by the hand to
        lead them forth from the land
        of Egypt;
    for they did not stand by my covenant
        and I ignored them, says the Lord.
<sup>10</sup>  But this is the covenant I will establish
        with the house of Israel
    after those days, says the Lord:

---

*[7:20] **An oath:** God's oath in Ps 110:4.

†[7:22] **An [even] better covenant:** better than the Mosaic covenant because it will be eternal, like the priesthood of Jesus upon which it is based. Heb 7:12 argued that a change of priesthood involves a change of law; since "law" and "covenant" are used correlatively, a new covenant is likewise instituted.

‡[7:25] **To make intercession:** the intercession of the exalted Jesus, not the sequel to his completed sacrifice but its eternal presence in heaven; cf. Rom 8:34.

§[7:26] This verse with its list of attributes is reminiscent of Heb 7:3 and is perhaps a hymnic counterpart to it, contrasting the exalted Jesus with Melchizedek.

¶[7:26–28] Jesus is precisely the high priest whom the human race requires, holy and sinless, installed far above humanity (Heb 7:26); one having no need to offer sacrifice daily for sins but making a single offering of himself (Heb 7:27) once for all. The law could only appoint high priests with human limitations, but the fulfillment of God's oath regarding the priesthood of Melchizedek (Ps 110:4) makes the Son of God the perfect priest forever (Heb 7:28).

**[7:27] Such daily sacrifice is nowhere mentioned in the Mosaic law; only on the Day of Atonement is it prescribed that the high priest must **offer sacrifice . . . for his own sins and then for those of the people** (Lv 16:11–19). **Once for all:** this translates the Greek words *ephapax/hapax* that occur eleven times in Hebrews.

††[8:1–6] The Christian community has in Jesus the kind of high priest described in Heb 7:26–28. In virtue of his ascension Jesus has taken his place at God's right hand in accordance with Ps 110:1 (Heb 8:1), where he presides over the heavenly sanctuary established by God himself (Heb 8:2). Like every high priest, he has his offering to make (Heb 8:3; cf. Heb 9:12, 14), but it differs from that of the levitical

v. [7:21] Ps 110:4.   w. [7:22] 8:6–10; 9:15–20; 10:29; 12:24; 13:20.
x. [7:24] 5:6; 13:8.   y. [7:25] Rom 8:34; 1 Jn 2:1; Rev 1:18.   z. [7:26] 4:14, 15.   a. [7:27] 5:3; 9:12, 25–28; 10:11–14; Ex 29:38–39; Lv 16:6, 11, 15–17; Nm 28:3–4; Is 53:10; Rom 6:10.   b. [7:28] 5:1–2, 9.

---

priesthood in which he had no share (Heb 8:4) and which was in any case but a shadowy reflection of the true offering in the heavenly sanctuary (Heb 8:5). But Jesus' ministry in the heavenly sanctuary is that of mediator of a superior covenant that accomplishes what it signifies (Heb 8:6).

‡‡[8:2] **The sanctuary:** the Greek term could also mean "holy things" but bears the meaning "sanctuary" elsewhere in Hebrews (Heb 9:8, 12, 24, 25; 10:19; 13:11). **The true tabernacle that the Lord . . . set up** is contrasted with the earthly tabernacle that Moses set up in the desert. **True** means "real" in contradistinction to a mere "copy and shadow" (Heb 8:5); compare the Johannine usage (e.g., Jn 1:9; 6:32; 15:1). The idea that the earthly sanctuary is a reflection of a heavenly model may be based upon Ex 25:9, but probably also derives from the Platonic concept of a real world of which our observable world is merely a shadow.

§§[8:7–13] Since the first covenant was deficient in accomplishing what it signified, it had to be replaced (Heb 8:7), as Jeremiah (Jer 31:31–34) had prophesied (Heb 8:8–12). Even in the time of Jeremiah, the first covenant was antiquated (Heb 8:13). In Heb 7:22–24, the superiority of the new covenant was seen in the permanence of its priesthood; here the superiority is based on better promises, made explicit in the citation of Jer 31:31–34 (LXX: 38), namely, in the immediacy of the people's knowledge of God (Heb 8:11) and in the forgiveness of sin (Heb 8:12).

¶¶[8:8–12] In citing Jeremiah the author follows the Septuagint; some apparent departures from it may be the result of a different Septuagintal text rather than changes deliberately introduced.

c. [8:1] 1:3; 4:14; 7:26–28.   d. [8:2] 9:11; Ex 33:7; Nm 24:6 LXX.
e. [8:3] 5:1.   f. [8:4] 7:13.   g. [8:5] 9:23; Ex 25:40; Acts 7:44; Col 2:17.   h. [8:6] 7:22; 9:15.   i. [8:8] Jer 31:31–34.

I will put my laws in their minds
  and I will write them upon their
    hearts.
I will be their God,
  and they shall be my people.[j]
[11] And they shall not teach, each one his
    fellow citizen
  and kinsman, saying, 'Know the Lord,'
for all shall know me,
  from least to greatest.
[12] For I will forgive their evildoing
  and remember their sins no more."

[13][k]When he speaks of a "new" covenant, he declares the first one obsolete. And what has become obsolete and has grown old is close to disappearing.

## CHAPTER 9

### The Worship of the First Covenant.[†] [1]Now [even] the first covenant had regulations for worship and an earthly sanctuary. [2]For a tabernacle was constructed, the outer one,[‡] in which were the lampstand, the table, and the bread of offering; this is called the Holy Place.[l] [3§]Behind the second veil was the tabernacle called the Holy of Holies,[m] [4]in which were the gold altar of incense[¶] and the ark of the covenant entirely covered with gold. In it were the gold jar containing the manna, the staff of Aaron that had sprouted, and the tablets of the covenant.[n] [5**]Above it were the cherubim of glory overshadowing the place of expiation. Now is not the time to speak of these in detail.[o]

[6]With these arrangements for worship, the priests, in performing their service,[††] go into the outer tabernacle repeatedly,[p] [7]but the high priest alone goes into the inner one once a year, not without blood[‡‡] that he offers for himself and for the sins of the people.[q] [8]In this way the holy Spirit shows that the way into the sanctuary had not yet been revealed while the outer tabernacle still had its place. [9]This is a symbol of the present time,[§§] in which gifts and sacrifices are offered that cannot perfect the worshiper in conscience [10]but only in matters of food and drink and various ritual washings: regulations concerning the flesh, imposed until the time of the new order.[r]

### Sacrifice of Jesus. [11¶¶]But when Christ came as high priest of the good things that have come to be,[***] passing through the greater and more perfect tabernacle not made by hands, that is, not belonging to this creation,[s] [12]he entered once for all into the sanctuary, not with the blood of goats and calves but with his own blood, thus obtaining eternal redemption.[t] [13]For if the blood of goats and bulls and the sprinkling of a heifer's ashes[†††] can sanctify those who are defiled so that their flesh is cleansed,[u] [14]how much more will the blood of Christ, who through the eternal spirit[‡‡‡] offered himself unblemished to God, cleanse our consciences from dead works to worship the living God.[v]

---

*[8:13] **Close to disappearing**: from the prophet's perspective, not that of the author of Hebrews.

†[9:1–10] The regulations for worship under the old covenant permitted all the priests to enter the Holy Place (Heb 2:6), but only the high priest to enter the Holy of Holies and then only once a year (Heb 9:3–5, 7). The description of the sanctuary and its furnishings is taken essentially from Ex 25–26. This exclusion of the people from the Holy of Holies signified that they were not allowed to stand in God's presence (Heb 9:8) because their offerings and sacrifices, which were merely symbols of their need of spiritual renewal (Heb 9:10), could not obtain forgiveness of sins (Heb 9:9).

‡[9:2] **The outer one**: the author speaks of the **outer tabernacle** (Heb 9:6) and the **inner one** (Heb 9:7) rather than of one Mosaic tabernacle divided into two parts or sections.

§[9:3] **The second veil**: what is meant is the veil that divided the Holy Place from the Holy of Holies. It is here called **the second**, because there was another veil at the entrance to the Holy Place, or "outer tabernacle" (Ex 26:36).

¶[9:4] **The gold altar of incense**: Ex 30:6 locates this altar in the Holy Place, i.e., the first tabernacle, rather than in the Holy of Holies. Neither is there any Old Testament support for the assertion that the jar of manna and the staff of Aaron were in the ark of the covenant. For the tablets of the covenant, see Ex 25:16.

**[9:5] **The place of expiation**: the gold "mercy seat" (Greek *hilastērion*, as in Rom 3:25), where the blood of the sacrificial animals was sprinkled on the Day of Atonement (Lv 16:14–15). This rite achieved "expiation" or atonement for the sins of the preceding year.

††[9:6] **In performing their service**: the priestly services that had to be performed regularly in the Holy Place or **outer tabernacle** included burning incense on the incense altar twice each day (Ex 30:7), replacing the loaves on the table of the bread of offering once each week (Lv 24:8), and constantly caring for the lamps on the lampstand (Ex 27:21).

‡‡[9:7] **Not without blood**: blood was essential to Old Testament sacrifice because it was believed that life was located in the blood. Hence blood was especially sacred, and its outpouring functioned as a meaningful symbol of cleansing from sin and reconciliation with God. Unlike Hebrews, the Old Testament never says that the blood is "offered." The author is perhaps retrojecting into his description of Mosaic ritual a concept that belongs to the New Testament antitype, as Paul does when he speaks of the Israelites' passage through the sea as a "baptism" (1 Cor 10:2).

§§[9:9] **The present time**: this expression is equivalent to the "present age," used in contradistinction to the "age to come."

¶¶[9:11–14] Christ, the high priest of the spiritual blessings foreshadowed in the Old Testament sanctuary, has actually entered the true sanctuary of heaven that is not of human making (Heb 9:11). His place there is permanent, and his offering is his own blood that won eternal redemption (Heb 9:12). If the sacrifice of animals could bestow legal purification (Heb 9:13), how much more effective is the blood of the sinless, divine Christ who spontaneously offered himself to purge the human race of sin and render it fit for the service of God (Heb 9:14).

***[9:11] **The good things that have come to be**: the majority of later manuscripts here read "the good things to come"; cf. Heb 10:1.

†††[9:13] **A heifer's ashes**: ashes from a red heifer that had been burned were mixed with water and used for the cleansing of those who had become ritually defiled by touching a corpse; see Nm 19:9, 14–21.

‡‡‡[9:14] **Through the eternal spirit**: this expression does not refer either to the holy Spirit or to the divine nature of Jesus but to the life of the risen Christ, "a life that cannot be destroyed" (Heb 7:16).

---

j. [8:10] 10:16–17. k. [8:13] Rom 10:4. l. [9:2] Ex 25:23–30. m. [9:3] Ex 26:31–34. n. [9:4] Ex 16:32–34; 25:10, 16, 21; 30:1–10; Lv 16:12–13; Nm 17:2–7, 16–26. o. [9:5] Ex 25:16–22; 26:34; Lv 16:14–15.

p. [9:6] Ex 27:21; 30:7; Lv 24:8. q. [9:7] Ex 30:10; Lv 16:1–14. r. [9:10] 13:9; Lv 11; 14:8; Nm 19:11–21; Col 2:16. s. [9:11] 4:14; 10:1, 20. t. [9:12] 7:27; Mt 26:28. u. [9:13] 10:4; Lv 16:6–16; Nm 19:9, 14–21. v. [9:14] 10:10; Rom 5:9; 1 Tm 3:9; Ti 2:14; 1 Pt 1:18–19; 1 Jn 1:7; Rev 1:5.

[9:15]*For this reason he is mediator of a new covenant: since a death has taken place for deliverance from transgressions under the first covenant, those who are called may receive the promised eternal inheritance.[w] [16†]Now where there is a will, the death of the testator must be established. [17]For a will takes effect only at death; it has no force while the testator is alive. [18]Thus not even the first covenant was inaugurated without blood. [19‡]When every commandment had been proclaimed by Moses to all the people according to the law, he took the blood of calves [and goats], together with water and crimson wool and hyssop, and sprinkled both the book itself and all the people,[x] [20]saying, "This is 'the blood of the covenant which God has enjoined upon you.'"[y] [21]In the same way, he sprinkled also the tabernacle[§] and all the vessels of worship with blood.[z] [22§]According to the law almost everything is purified by blood,[a] and without the shedding of blood there is no forgiveness.

[23***]Therefore, it was necessary for the copies of the heavenly things to be purified by these rites, but the heavenly things themselves by better sacrifices than these.[b] [24]For Christ did not enter into a sanctuary made by hands, a copy of the true one, but heaven itself, that he might now appear before God on our behalf.[c] [25]Not that he might offer himself repeatedly, as the high priest enters each year into the sanctuary with blood that is not his own; [26]if that were so, he would have had to suffer repeatedly from the foundation of the world. But now once for all he has appeared at the end of the ages[††] to take away sin by his sacrifice.[d] [27]Just as it is appointed that human beings die once, and after this the judgment,[e] [28]so also Christ, offered once to take away the sins of many,[‡‡] will appear a second time, not to take away sin but to bring salvation to those who eagerly await him.[f]

## CHAPTER 10

**One Sacrifice Instead of Many.** [1§§]Since the law has only a shadow of the good things to come,[¶¶] and not the very image of them, it can never make perfect those who come to worship by the same sacrifices that they offer continually each year.[g] [2]Otherwise, would not the sacrifices have

---

*[9:15–22] Jesus' role as **mediator of the new covenant** is based upon his sacrificial **death** (cf. Heb 8:6). His death has effected **deliverance from transgressions**, i.e., deliverance from sins committed under the old covenant, which the Mosaic sacrifices were incapable of effacing. Until this happened, the **eternal inheritance** promised by God could not be obtained (Heb 9:15). This effect of his work follows the human pattern by which a last will and testament becomes effective only with the death of the testator (Heb 9:16–17). The Mosaic covenant was also associated with death, for Moses made use of blood to seal the pact between God and the people (Heb 9:18–21). In Old Testament tradition, guilt could normally not be remitted without the use of blood (Heb 9:22; cf. Lv 17:11).

†[9:16–17] **A will . . . death of the testator**: the same Greek word *diathēkē*, meaning "covenant" in Heb 9:15, 18, is used here with the meaning **will**. The new covenant, unlike the old, is at the same time a will that requires the **death of the testator**. Jesus as eternal Son is the one who established the new covenant together with his Father, author of both covenants; at the same time he is the testator whose death puts his **will** into effect.

‡[9:19–20] A number of details here are different from the description of this covenant rite in Ex 24:5–8. Exodus mentions only calves ("young bulls," NAB), not goats (but this addition in Hebrews is of doubtful authenticity), says nothing of the use of **water and crimson wool and hyssop** (these features probably came from a different rite; cf. Lv 14:3–7; Nm 19:6–18), and describes Moses as splashing blood on the altar, whereas Hebrews says he sprinkled it on the book (but both book and altar are meant to symbolize the agreement of God). The words of Moses are also slightly different from those in Exodus and are closer to the words of Jesus at the Last Supper in Mk 14:24 // Mt 26:28.

§[9:21] According to Exodus, the tabernacle did not yet exist at the time of the covenant rite. Moreover, nothing is said of sprinkling it with blood at its subsequent dedication (Ex 40:9–11).

¶[9:22] **Without the shedding of blood there is no forgiveness**: in fact, ancient Israel did envisage other means of obtaining forgiveness; the Old Testament mentions contrition of heart (Ps 51:17), fasting (Jl 2:12), and almsgiving (Sir 3:29). The author is limiting his horizon to the sacrificial cult, which did always involve the shedding of blood for its expiatory and unitive value.

**[9:23–28] Since the blood of animals became a cleansing symbol among Old Testament prefigurements, it was necessary that the realities foreshadowed be brought into being by a

shedding of blood that was infinitely more effective by reason of its worth (Heb 9:23). Christ did not simply prefigure the heavenly realities (Heb 9:24) by performing an annual sacrifice with a blood not his own (Heb 9:25); he offered the single sacrifice of himself as the final annulment of sin (Heb 9:26). Just as death is the unrepeatable act that ends a person's life, so Christ's offering of himself for all is the unrepeatable sacrifice that has once for all achieved redemption (Heb 9:27–28).

††[9:26] **At the end of the ages**: the use of expressions such as this shows that the author of Hebrews, despite his interest in the Platonic concept of an eternal world above superior to temporal reality here below, nevertheless still clings to the Jewish Christian eschatology with its sequence of "the present age" and "the age to come."

‡‡[9:28] **To take away the sins of many**: the reference is to Is 53:12. Since the Greek verb *anapherō* can mean both "to take away" and "to bear," the author no doubt intended to play upon both senses: Jesus took away sin by bearing it himself. See the similar wordplay in Jn 1:29. **Many** is used in the Semitic meaning of "all" in the inclusive sense, as in Mk 14:24. **To those who eagerly await him**: Jesus will appear a **second time** at the parousia, as the high priest reappeared on the Day of Atonement, emerging from the Holy of Holies, which he had entered to **take away sin**. This dramatic scene is described in Sir 50:5–11.

§§[10:1–10] Christian faith now realizes that the Old Testament sacrifices did not effect the spiritual benefits to come but only prefigured them (Heb 10:1). For if the sacrifices had actually effected the forgiveness of sin, there would have been no reason for their constant repetition (Heb 10:2). They were rather a continual reminder of the people's sins (Heb 10:3). It is not reasonable to suppose that human sins could be removed by the blood of animal sacrifices (Heb 10:4). Christ, therefore, is here shown to understand his mission in terms of Ps 40:6–8, cited according to the Septuagint (Heb 10:5–7). Jesus acknowledged that the Old Testament sacrifices did not remit the sins of the people and so, perceiving the will of God, offered his own body for this purpose (Heb 10:8–10).

¶¶[10:1] **A shadow of the good things to come**: the term **shadow** was used in Heb 8:5 to signify the earthly counterpart of the Platonic heavenly reality. But here it means a prefiguration of what is to come in Christ, as it is used in the Pauline literature; cf. Col 2:17.

---

w. [9:15] 1 Tm 2:5.    x. [9:19] 9:12–13.    y. [9:20] Ex 24:3–8; Mt 26:28; Mk 14:24.    z. [9:21] Ex 40:9; Lv 8:15, 19.    a. [9:22] Lv 17:11.

b. [9:23] Jb 15:15.    c. [9:24] 7:25; Rom 8:34; 1 Jn 2:1–2.    d. [9:26] 7:27; Jn 1:29; Gal 4:4.    e. [9:27] Gn 3:19.    f. [9:28] 10:10; Is 53:12.    g. [10:1] 8:5; Col 2:17.

ceased to be offered, since the worshipers, once cleansed, would no longer have had any consciousness of sins? ³But in those sacrifices there is only a yearly remembrance of sins,ʰ ⁴for it is impossible that the blood of bulls and goats take away sins.ⁱ ⁵For this reason, when he came into the world, he said:*

"Sacrifice and offering you did not desire,ʲ
     but a body you prepared for me;
⁶ holocausts and sin offerings you took no
          delight in.
⁷ Then I said, 'As is written of me in the
          scroll,
     Behold, I come to do your will,
          O God.'"

⁸First he says, "Sacrifices and offerings, holocausts and sin offerings,† you neither desired nor delighted in." These are offered according to the law.ᵏ ⁹Then he says, "Behold, I come to do your will." He takes away the first to establish the second.ˡ ¹⁰By this "will," we have been consecrated through the offering of the body of Jesus Christ once for all.ᵐ

¹¹‡Every priest stands daily at his ministry, offering frequently those same sacrifices that can never take away sins.ⁿ ¹²But this one offered one sacrifice for sins, and took his seat forever at the right hand of God;ᵒ ¹³§now he waits until his enemies are made his footstool. ¹⁴For by one offering he has made perfect forever those who are being consecrated.ᵖ ¹⁵¶The holy Spirit also testifies to us, for after saying:

¹⁶ "This is the covenant I will establish with
          them after those days, says the
          Lord:
     'I will put my laws in their hearts,
     and I will write them upon their
          minds,'"�q

¹⁷he also says:**

"Their sins and their evildoing
     I will remember no more."ʳ

¹⁸Where there is forgiveness of these, there is no longer offering for sin.

**Recalling the Past.**†† ¹⁹Therefore, brothers, since through the blood of Jesus we have confidence of entrance into the sanctuaryˢ ²⁰‡‡by the new and living way he opened for us through the veil,ᵗ that is, his flesh, ²¹§§ᵘand since we have "a great priest over the house of God," ²²let us approach with a sincere heart and in absolute trust, with our hearts sprinkled clean from an evil conscience¶¶ and our bodies washed in pure water.ᵛ

---

*[10:5–7] A passage from Ps 40:7–9 is placed in the mouth of the Son at his incarnation. As usual, the author follows the Septuagint text. There is a notable difference in Heb 10:5 (Ps 40:7b), where the Masoretic text reads "ears you have dug for me" ("ears open to obedience you gave me," NAB), but most Septuagint manuscripts have "a body you prepared for me," a reading obviously more suited to the interpretation of Hebrews.

†[10:8] **Sacrifices and offerings, holocausts and sin offerings**: these four terms taken from the preceding passage of Ps 40 (with the first two changed to plural forms) are probably intended as equivalents to the four principal types of Old Testament sacrifices: peace offerings (Lv 3, here called **sacrifices**); cereal offerings (Lv 2, here called **offerings**); holocausts (Lv 1); and **sin offerings** (Lv 4–5). This last category includes the guilt offerings of Lv 5:14–19.

‡[10:11–18] Whereas the levitical priesthood offered daily sacrifices that were ineffectual in remitting sin (Heb 10:11), Jesus offered a single sacrifice that won him a permanent place at God's right hand. There he has only to await the final outcome of his work (Heb 10:12–13; cf. Ps 110:1). Thus he has brought into being in his own person the new covenant prophesied by Jeremiah (Jer 31:33–34) that has rendered meaningless all other offerings for sin (Heb 10:14–18).

§[10:13] **Until his enemies are made his footstool**: Ps 110:1 is again used; the reference here is to the period of time between the enthronement of Jesus and his second coming. The identity of the **enemies** is not specified; cf. 1 Cor 15:25–27.

¶[10:15–17] The testimony of the scriptures is here invoked to support what has just preceded. The passage cited

is a portion of the new covenant prophecy of Jer 31:31–34, which the author previously used in Heb 8:8–12.

**[10:17] **He also says**: these words are not in the Greek text, which has only *kai*, "also," but the expression **"after saying"** in Heb 10:15 seems to require such a phrase to divide the Jeremiah text into two sayings. Others understand "the Lord says" of Heb 10:16 (here rendered **says the Lord**) as outside the quotation and consider Heb 10:16b as part of the second saying. Two ancient versions and a number of minuscules introduce the words "then he said" or a similar expression at the beginning of Heb 10:17.

††[10:19–39] Practical consequences from these reflections on the priesthood and the sacrifice of Christ should make it clear that Christians may now have direct and confident access to God through the person of Jesus (Heb 10:19–20), who rules God's house as high priest (Heb 10:21). They should approach God with sincerity and faith, in the knowledge that through baptism their sins have been remitted (Heb 10:22), mindful themselves of the hope they expressed in Christ at that event (Heb 10:23). They are to encourage one another to Christian love and activity (Heb 10:24), not refusing, no matter what the reason, to participate in the community's assembly, especially in view of the parousia (Heb 10:25; cf. 1 Thes 4:13–18). If refusal to participate in the assembly indicates rejection of Christ, no realistic exists to obtain forgiveness for so great a sin (Heb 10:26); only the dreadful judgment of God remains (Heb 10:27). For if violation of the Mosaic law could be punished by death, how much worse will be the punishment of those who have turned their backs on Christ by despising his sacrifice and disregarding the gifts of the holy Spirit (Heb 10:28–29). Judgment belongs to the Lord, and he enacts it by his living presence (Heb 10:30–31). There was a time when the spirit of their community caused them to welcome and share their sufferings (Heb 10:32–34). To revitalize that spirit is to share in the courage of the Old Testament prophets (cf. Is 26:20; Heb 2:3–4), the kind of courage that must distinguish the faith of the Christian (Heb 10:35–39).

‡‡[10:20] **Through the veil, that is, his flesh**: the term **flesh** is used pejoratively. As the temple veil kept people from entering the Holy of Holies (it was rent at Christ's death, Mk 15:38), so the flesh of Jesus constituted an obstacle to approaching God.

§§[10:21] **The house of God**: this refers back to Heb 3:6, "we are his house."

¶¶[10:22] **With our hearts sprinkled clean from an evil conscience**: as in Heb 9:13 (see note there), the sprinkling

---

h. [10:3] Lv 16:21; Nm 5:15 LXX.   i. [10:4] Is 1:11; Mi 6:6–8.   j. [10:5–7] Ps 40:7–9.   k. [10:8] 10:5–6; Ps 40:7.   l. [10:9] 7; Ps 40:8; Mt 26:39; Mk 14:36; Lk 22:42; Jn 6:38.   m. [10:10] 9:12, 14.   n. [10:11] 7:27; Dt 10:8;18:7.   o. [10:12–13] Ps 110:1.   p. [10:14] 9:28.

q. [10:16] 8:10; Jer 31:33.   r. [10:17] 8:12; Jer 31:34.   s. [10:19] 3:6; 4:16; 6:19–20; Eph 1:7; 3:12.   t. [10:20] Jn 14:6 / Heb 6:19–20; 9:8, 11–12; Mt 27:51; Mk 15:38; Lk 23:45.   u. [10:21] 3:6.   v. [10:22] 9:13–14; Ez 36:25; 1 Cor 6:11; Ti 3:5; 1 Pt 3:21.

<sup>23</sup>Let us hold unwaveringly to our confession that gives us hope, for he who made the promise is trustworthy.<sup>w</sup> <sup>24</sup>We must consider how to rouse one another to love and good works. <sup>25</sup>We should not stay away from our assembly,<sup>*</sup> as is the custom of some, but encourage one another, and this all the more as you see the day drawing near.<sup>x</sup>

<sup>26†</sup>If we sin deliberately after receiving knowledge of the truth, there no longer remains sacrifice for sins <sup>27</sup>but a fearful prospect of judgment and a flaming fire that is going to consume the adversaries.<sup>z</sup> <sup>28</sup>Anyone who rejects the law of Moses<sup>‡</sup> is put to death without pity on the testimony of two or three witnesses.<sup>a</sup> <sup>29</sup>Do you not think that a much worse punishment is due the one who has contempt for the Son of God, considers unclean the covenant-blood by which he was consecrated, and insults the spirit of grace?<sup>b</sup> <sup>30</sup>We know the one who said:

"Vengeance is mine; I will repay,"

and again:

"The Lord will judge his people."<sup>c</sup>

<sup>31</sup>It is a fearful thing to fall into the hands of the living God.<sup>d</sup>

<sup>32</sup>Remember the days past when, after you had been enlightened,<sup>§</sup> you endured a great contest of suffering.<sup>e</sup> <sup>33</sup>At times you were publicly exposed to abuse and affliction; at other times you associated yourselves with those so treated.<sup>f</sup> <sup>34</sup>You even joined in the sufferings of those in prison and joyfully accepted the confiscation of your property, knowing that you had a better and lasting possession.<sup>g</sup> <sup>35</sup>Therefore, do not throw away your confidence; it will have great recompense.<sup>h</sup> <sup>36</sup>You need endurance to do the will of God and receive what he has promised.<sup>i</sup>

<sup>37</sup> "For, after just a brief moment,<sup>¶</sup>
 he who is to come shall come;
 he shall not delay.<sup>j</sup>
<sup>38</sup> But my just one shall live by faith,
 and if he draws back I take no
  pleasure in him."<sup>k</sup>

<sup>39</sup>We are not among those who draw back and perish, but among those who have faith and will possess life.

## V. EXAMPLES, DISCIPLINE, DISOBEDIENCE

### CHAPTER 11**

**Faith of the Ancients.** <sup>1</sup>Faith is the realization of what is hoped for and evidence<sup>††</sup> of things not seen.<sup>l</sup> <sup>2</sup>Because of it the ancients were well attested. <sup>3m</sup>By faith we understand that the universe was ordered by the word of God,<sup>‡‡</sup> so that what is visible came into being through the invisible. <sup>4§§</sup>By faith Abel offered to God a

---

motif refers to the Mosaic rite of cleansing from ritual impurity. This could produce only an external purification, whereas sprinkling with the blood of Christ (Heb 9:14) cleanses the **conscience. Washed in pure water**: baptism is elsewhere referred to as a washing; cf. 1 Cor 6:11; Eph 5:26.

*[10:25] **Our assembly**: the liturgical **assembly** of the Christian community, probably for the celebration of the Eucharist. **The day**: this designation for the parousia also occurs in the Pauline letters, e.g., Rom 2:16; 1 Cor 3:13; 1 Thes 5:2.

†[10:26] **If we sin deliberately**: verse 29 indicates that the author is here thinking of apostasy; cf. Heb 3:12; 6:4–8.

‡[10:28] **Rejects the law of Moses**: evidently not any sin against the law, but idolatry. Dt 17:2–7 prescribed capital punishment for idolaters who were convicted on the testimony of two or three witnesses.

§[10:32] **After you had been enlightened**: "enlightenment" is an ancient metaphor for baptism (cf. Eph 5:14; Jn 9:11), but see Heb 6:4 and the note there.

¶[10:37–38] In support of his argument, the author uses Hb 2:3–4 in a wording almost identical with the text of the Codex Alexandrinus of the Septuagint but with the first and second lines of Heb 10:4 inverted. He introduces it with a few words from Is 26:20: **after just a brief moment**. Note the Pauline usage of Hb 2:4 in Rom 1:17; Gal 3:11.

**[11:1–40] This chapter draws upon the people and events of the Old Testament to paint an inspiring portrait of religious faith, firm and unyielding in the face of any obstacles that confront it. These pages rank among the most eloquent and lofty to be found in the Bible. They expand the theme announced in Heb 6:12, to which the author now returns (Heb 10:39). The material of this chapter is developed chronologically. Heb 11:3–7 draw upon the first nine chapters of Genesis (Gn 1–9); Heb 11:8–22, upon the period of the patriarchs; Heb 11:23–31, upon the time of Moses; Heb 11:32–38, upon the history of the judges, the prophets, and the Maccabean martyrs. The author gives the most extensive description of faith provided in the New Testament, though his interest does not lie in a technical, theological definition. In view of the needs of his audience he describes what authentic faith does, not what it is in itself. Through faith God guarantees the blessings to be hoped for from him, providing evidence in the gift of faith that what he promises will eventually come to pass (Heb 11:1). Because they accepted in faith God's guarantee of the future, the biblical personages discussed in Heb 11:3–38 were themselves commended by God (Heb 11:2). Christians have even greater reason to remain firm in faith since they, unlike the Old Testament men and women of faith, have perceived the beginning of God's fulfillment of his messianic promises (Heb 11:39–40).

††[11:1] **Faith is the realization . . . evidence**: the author is not attempting a precise definition. There is dispute about the meaning of the Greek words *hypostasis* and *elenchos*, here translated **realization** and **evidence**, respectively. *Hypostasis* usually means "substance," "being" (as translated in Heb 1:3), or "reality" (as translated in Heb 3:14); here it connotes something more subjective, and so **realization** has been chosen rather than "assurance" (RSV). *Elenchos*, usually "proof," is used here in an objective sense and so translated **evidence** rather than the transferred sense of "(inner) conviction" (RSV).

‡‡[11:3] **By faith . . . God**: this verse does not speak of the faith of the Old Testament men and women but is in the first person plural. Hence it seems out of place in the sequence of thought.

§§[11:4] The "Praise of the Ancestors" in Sir 44:1–50:21 gives a similar list of heroes. The Cain and Abel narrative in Gn 4:1–16 does not mention Abel's faith. It says, however, that

---

w. [10:23] 3:1, 6; 4:14; 1 Cor 10:13.   x. [10:25] Rom 13:12; 1 Cor 3:13.   y. [10:26] 3:12; 6:4–8.   z. [10:27] 10:31; 9:27; Is 26:11 LXX; Zep 1:18.   a. [10:28] Dt 17:6.   b. [10:29] 6:6.   c. [10:30] Dt 32:35, 36; Rom 12:19.   d. [10:31] 10:27; Mt 10:28; Lk 12:4–5.   e. [10:32] 6:4.   f. [10:33] 1 Cor 4:9.   g. [10:34] 13:3; Mt 6:19–20; Lk 12:33–34.   h. [10:35] 4:16.   i. [10:36] Lk 21:19.

j. [10:37] Is 26:20; Heb 2:3.   k. [10:38] Heb 2:4; Rom 1:17; Gal 3:11.   l. [11:1] 1:3; 3:14; Rom 8:24; 2 Cor 4:18.   m. [11:3] Gn 1:3; Ps 33:6; Wis 9:1; Jn 1:3.

sacrifice greater than Cain's. Through this he was attested to be righteous, God bearing witness to his gifts, and through this, though dead, he still speaks.[n] [5]By faith Enoch was taken up so that he should not see death, and "he was found no more because God had taken him." Before he was taken up, he was attested to have pleased God.[o] [6]But without faith it is impossible to please him,[p] for anyone who approaches God must believe that he exists and that he rewards those who seek him. [7]By faith Noah, warned about what was not yet seen, with reverence built an ark for the salvation of his household. Through this he condemned the world and inherited the righteousness that comes through faith.[q]

[8]By faith Abraham obeyed when he was called to go out to a place that he was to receive as an inheritance; he went out, not knowing where he was to go.[r] [9]By faith he sojourned in the promised land as in a foreign country, dwelling in tents with Isaac and Jacob, heirs of the same promise;[s] [10]for he was looking forward to the city with foundations, whose architect and maker is God.[t] [11]By faith he received power to generate, even though he was past the normal age—and Sarah herself was sterile—for he thought that the one who had made the promise was trustworthy.[u] [12]So it was that there came forth from one man, himself as good as dead, descendants as numerous as the stars in the sky and as countless as the sands on the seashore.[v]

[13]All these died in faith. They did not receive what had been promised but saw it and greeted it from afar and acknowledged themselves to be strangers and aliens on earth,[w] [14]for those who speak thus show that they are seeking a homeland. [15]If they had been thinking of the land from which they had come, they would have had opportunity to return. [16]But now they desire a better homeland, a heavenly one. Therefore, God is not ashamed to be called their God, for he has prepared a city for them.[x]

[17]By faith Abraham, when put to the test, offered up Isaac, and he who had received the promises was ready to offer his only son,[y] [18]of whom it was said, "Through Isaac descendants

shall bear your name."[z] [19†]He reasoned that God was able to raise even from the dead,[a] and he received Isaac back as a symbol. [20]By faith regarding things still to come Isaac‡ blessed Jacob and Esau.[b] [21]By faith Jacob, when dying, blessed each of the sons of Joseph and "bowed in worship, leaning on the top of his staff."[c] [22]By faith Joseph, near the end of his life, spoke of the Exodus of the Israelites and gave instructions about his bones.[d]

[23§]By faith Moses was hidden by his parents for three months after his birth, because they saw that he was a beautiful child, and they were not afraid of the king's edict. [24§]By faith Moses, when he had grown up, refused to be known as the son of Pharaoh's daughter;[f] [25]he chose to be ill-treated along with the people of God rather than enjoy the fleeting pleasure of sin. [26]He considered the reproach of the Anointed greater wealth than the treasures of Egypt, for he was looking to the recompense. [27]By faith he left Egypt, not fearing the king's fury, for he persevered as if seeing the one who is invisible.[g] [28]By faith he kept the Passover and sprinkled the blood, that the Destroyer of the firstborn might not touch them.[h] [29]By faith they crossed the Red Sea as if it were dry land, but when the Egyptians attempted it they were drowned.[i] [30]By faith the walls of Jericho fell after being encircled for seven days.[j] [31]By faith Rahab the harlot did not perish with the disobedient, for she had received the spies in peace.[k]

[32]What more shall I say? I have not time to tell of Gideon, Barak, Samson, Jephthah, of David and Samuel and the prophets,[l] [33]who by faith conquered kingdoms, did what was righteous, obtained the promises; they closed the mouths of lions,[m] [34]put out raging fires, escaped the devouring sword; out of weakness they were made powerful, became strong in battle, and turned back foreign invaders.[n] [35]Women received back their dead through resurrection. Some were tortured and would not accept deliverance, in order to obtain a better resurrection.[o]

---

†[11:19] **As a symbol:** Isaac's "return from death" is seen as a **symbol** of Christ's resurrection. Others understand the words *en parabolē* to mean "in figure," i.e., the word **dead** is used figuratively of Isaac, since he did not really die. But in the one other place that *parabolē* occurs in Hebrews, it means symbol (Heb 9:9).

‡[11:20–22] Each of these three patriarchs, Isaac, Jacob, and Joseph, had faith in the future fulfillment of God's promise and renewed this faith when near death.

§[11:24–27] The reason given for Moses' departure from Egypt differs from the account in Ex 2:11–15. The author also gives a christological interpretation of his decision to share the trials of his people.

God "looked with favor on Abel and his offering" (Gn 4:4); in view of Heb 11:6 the author probably understood God's favor to have been activated by Abel's faith. **Though dead, he still speaks:** possibly because his blood "cries out to me from the soil" (Gn 4:10), but more probably a way of saying that the repeated story of Abel provides ongoing witness to faith.

*[11:6] One must believe not only that God *exists* but that he is concerned about human conduct; the Old Testament defines folly as the denial of this truth; cf. Ps 52:2.

n. [11:4] 12:24; Gn 4:4, 10. o. [11:5] Gn 5:24; Sir 44:16. p. [11:6] Wis 4:10. q. [11:7] Gn 6:8–22; Sir 44:17–18; Mt 24:37–39; Lk 17:26–27; 1 Pt 3:20; 2 Pt 2:5. r. [11:8] Gn 12:1–4; 15:7–21; Sir 44:19–22; Acts 7:2–8; Rom 4:16–22. s. [11:9] Gn 12:8; 13:12; 23:4; 26:3; 35:27. t. [11:10] 12:22; 13:14; Rev 21:10–22. u. [11:11] Gn 17:19; 21:2; Rom 4:19–21 / 1 Cor 10:13. v. [11:12] Gn 15:5; 22:17; 32:13; Ex 32:13; Dt 10:22; Dn 3:36 LXX. w. [11:13] Gn 23:4; Ps 39:13. x. [11:16] 13:14; Ex 3:6. y. [11:17] Gn 22:1–10; Sir 44:20; 1 Mc 2:52; Jas 2:21.

z. [11:18] Gn 21:12 LXX; Rom 9:7. a. [11:19] Rom 4:16–22. b. [11:20] Gn 27:27–40. c. [11:21] Gn 27:38–40; 47:31 LXX; 48:15–16. d. [11:22] Gn 50:24–25. e. [11:23] Ex 2:2; Acts 7:20. f. [11:24–25] Ex 2:10–15; Acts 7:23–29. g. [11:27] Ex 2:15; Acts 7:29. h. [11:28] Ex 12:21–23; Wis 18:25; 1 Cor 10:10. i. [11:29] Ex 14:22–28. j. [11:30] Jos 6:12–21. k. [11:31] Jos 2:1–21; 6:22–25; Jas 2:25. l. [11:32] Jgs 4:6–22; 6:11–8:32; 11:1–12:7. m. [11:33] Dn 6:23. n. [11:34] Dn 3:22–25, 49–50. o. [11:35] 1 Kgs 17:17–24; 2 Kgs 4:18–37; 2 Mc 6:18–7:42.

³⁶Others endured mockery, scourging, even chains and imprisonment.ᵖ ³⁷They were stoned, sawed in two, put to death at sword's point; they went about in skins of sheep or goats, needy, afflicted, tormented.�q ³⁸The world was not worthy of them. They wandered about in deserts and on mountains, in caves and in crevices in the earth.ʳ

³⁹Yet all these, though approved because of their faith, did not receive what had been promised. ⁴⁰God had foreseen something better for us, so that without us they should not be made perfect.ˢ

## CHAPTER 12

**God Our Father.**† ¹Therefore, since we are surrounded by so great a cloud of witnesses, let us rid ourselves of every burden and sin that clings to us‡ and persevere in running the race that lies before us ²while keeping our eyes fixed on Jesus, the leader and perfecter of faith. For the sake of the joy that lay before him he endured the cross, despising its shame, and has taken his seat at the right of the throne of God.ˢ ³Consider how he endured such opposition from sinners, in order that you may not grow weary and lose heart. ⁴In your struggle against sin you have not yet resisted to the point of shedding blood. ⁵You have also forgotten the exhortation addressed to you as sons:

"My son, do not disdain the discipline of
    the Lordᵗ
    or lose heart when reproved by him;
⁶ for whom the Lord loves, he disciplines;
    he scourges every son he
        acknowledges."

⁷Endure your trials as "discipline"; God treats you as sons. For what "son" is there whom his father does not discipline?ᵘ ⁸If you are without discipline, in which all have shared, you are not sons but bastards. ⁹Besides this, we have had our earthly fathers to discipline us, and we respected them. Should we not [then] submit all the more to the Father of spirits and live?ᵛ ¹⁰They disciplined us for a short time as seemed right to them, but he does so for our benefit, in order that we may share his holiness. ¹¹At the time, all discipline seems a cause not for joy but for pain, yet later it brings the peaceful fruit of righteousness to those who are trained by it.ʷ

¹²So strengthen your drooping hands and your weak knees.ˣ ¹³Make straight paths for your feet, that what is lame may not be dislocated but healed.ʸ

**Penalties of Disobedience.** ¹⁴Strive for peace with everyone, and for that holiness without which no one will see the Lord. ¹⁵See to it that no one be deprived of the grace of God, that no bitter root spring up and cause trouble, through which many may become defiled,ᵃ ¹⁶that no one be an immoral or profane person like Esau, who sold his birthright for a single meal.ᵇ ¹⁷For you know that later, when he wanted to inherit his father's blessing, he was rejected because he found no opportunity to change his mind, even though he sought the blessing with tears.ᶜ

¹⁸You have not approached that which could be touched**ᵈ and a blazing fire and gloomy darkness and storm ¹⁹and a trumpet blast and a voice speaking words such that those who heard begged that no message be further addressed to them,ᵉ ²⁰for they could not bear to hear the command: "If even an animal touches the mountain, it shall be stoned."ᶠ ²¹Indeed, so fearful was the spectacle that Moses said, "I am terrified and trembling."ᵍ ²²No, you have approached Mount Zion and the city of the living God, the

---

*[11:40] **So that without us they should not be made perfect**: the heroes of the Old Testament obtained their recompense only after the saving work of Christ had been accomplished. Thus they already enjoy what Christians who are still struggling do not yet possess in its fullness.

†[12:1–13] Christian life is to be inspired not only by the Old Testament men and women of faith (Heb 12:1) but above all by Jesus. As the architect of Christian faith, he had himself to endure the cross before receiving the glory of his triumph (Heb 12:2). Reflection on his sufferings should give his followers courage to continue the struggle, if necessary even to the shedding of blood (Heb 12:3–4). Christians should regard their own sufferings as the affectionate correction of the Lord, who loves them as a father loves his children.

‡[12:1] **That clings to us**: the meaning is uncertain, since the Greek word *euperistatos*, translated **cling**, occurs only here. The papyrus P⁴⁶ and one minuscule read *euperispastos*, "easily distracting," which also makes good sense.

§[12:15–17] Esau serves as an example in two ways: his **profane** attitude illustrates the danger of apostasy, and his inability to secure a blessing afterward illustrates the impossibility of repenting after falling away (see Heb 6:4–6).

¶[12:18–29] As a final appeal for adherence to Christian teaching, the two covenants, of Moses and of Christ, are compared. The Mosaic covenant, the author argues, is shown to have originated in fear of God and threats of divine punishment (Heb 12:18–21). The covenant in Christ gives us direct access to God (Heb 12:22), makes us members of the Christian community, God's children, a sanctified people (Heb 12:23), who have Jesus as mediator to speak for us (Heb 12:24). Not to heed the voice of the risen Christ is a graver sin than the rejection of the word of Moses (Heb 12:25–26). Though Christians fall away, God's kingdom in Christ will remain and his justice will punish those guilty of deserting it (Heb 12:28–29).

**[12:18] This remarkably beautiful passage contrasts two great assemblies of people: that of the Israelites gathered at Mount Sinai for the sealing of the old covenant and the promulgation of the Mosaic law, and that of the followers of Jesus gathered at **Mount Zion, the heavenly Jerusalem**, the assembly of the **new covenant**. This latter scene, marked by the presence of **countless angels** and of **Jesus** with his redeeming **blood**, is reminiscent of the celestial liturgies of the Book of Revelation.

---

p. [11:36] 2 Chr 36:16; Jer 20:2; 37:15. q. [11:37] 2 Chr 24:21.
r. [11:38] 1 Mc 2:28–30. s. [12:2] 2:10; Ps 110:1; Phil 2:6–8. t. [12:5–6] Prv 3:11–12 / Dt 8:5; 1 Cor 11:32. u. [12:7] Prv 13:24; Sir 30:1.

v. [12:9] Nm 16:22; 27:16 LXX. w. [12:11] 2 Cor 4:17; Phil 1:11; Jas 3:18. x. [12:12] Is 35:3; Sir 25:23; Jb 4:3–4. y. [12:13] Prv 4:26 LXX. z. [12:14] Rom 12:18; 14:19. a. [12:15] Dt 29:18 (17 LXX). b. [12:16] Gn 25:33. c. [12:17] Gn 27:34–38. d. [12:18] Ex 19:12–14; Dt 4:11; 5:22–23. e. [12:19] Ex 19:16, 19; 20:18–19. f. [12:20] Ex 19:12–13. g. [12:21] Dt 9:19.

heavenly Jerusalem, and countless angels in festal gathering,[h] [23]and the assembly of the first-born enrolled in heaven,[*] and God the judge of all, and the spirits of the just made perfect,[i] [24]and Jesus, the mediator of a new covenant, and the sprinkled blood that speaks more eloquently[†] than that of Abel.[j]

[25]See that you do not reject the one who speaks. For if they did not escape when they refused the one who warned them on earth, how much more in our case if we turn away from the one who warns from heaven.[k] [26]His voice shook the earth at that time, but now he has promised, "I will once more shake not only earth but heaven."[l] [27]That phrase, "once more," points to [the] removal of shaken, created things, so that what is unshaken may remain.[m] [28]Therefore, we who are receiving the unshakable kingdom should have gratitude, with which we should offer worship pleasing to God in reverence and awe.[n] [29]For our God is a consuming fire.[o]

## VI. FINAL EXHORTATION, BLESSING, GREETINGS

### CHAPTER 13

[1]Let mutual love continue. [2]Do not neglect hospitality, for through it some have unknowingly entertained angels.[p] [3]Be mindful of prisoners as if sharing their imprisonment, and of the ill-treated as of yourselves, for you also are in the body.[q] [4]Let marriage be honored among all and the marriage bed be kept undefiled, for God will judge the immoral and adulterers.[r] [5]Let your life be free from love of money but be content with what you have, for he has said, "I will never forsake you or abandon you."[s] [6]Thus we may say with confidence:

"The Lord is my helper,
[and] I will not be afraid.
What can anyone do to me?"[t]

[7]Remember your leaders who spoke the word of God to you. Consider the outcome of their way of life and imitate their faith. [8]Jesus Christ is the same yesterday, today, and forever.[u]

[9]Do not be carried away by all kinds of strange teaching.[§] It is good to have our hearts strengthened by grace and not by foods, which do not benefit those who live by them.[v] [10]We have an altar[¶] from which those who serve the tabernacle have no right to eat. [11]The bodies of the animals whose blood the high priest brings into the sanctuary as a sin offering are burned outside the camp.[w] [12]Therefore, Jesus also suffered outside the gate, to consecrate the people by his own blood.[x] [13]Let us then go to him outside the camp, bearing the reproach that he bore. [14]For here we have no lasting city, but we seek the one that is to come.[y] [15]Through him [then] let us continually offer God a sacrifice of praise, that is, the fruit of lips that confess his name.[z] [16]Do not neglect to do good and to share what you have; God is pleased by sacrifices of that kind.[a]

[17]"Obey your leaders and defer to them, for they keep watch over you and will have to give an account, that they may fulfill their task with joy and not with sorrow, for that would be of no advantage to you.

[18]Pray for us, for we are confident that we have a clear conscience, wishing to act rightly in every respect. [19]I especially ask for your prayers that I may be restored to you very soon.

[20][††]May the God of peace, who brought up from the dead the great shepherd of the sheep by the blood of the eternal covenant, Jesus our Lord,[b] [21]furnish you with all that is good, that you may do his will. May he carry out in you what is pleasing to him through Jesus Christ, to whom be glory forever [and ever]. Amen.

---

* [12:23] **The assembly of the firstborn enrolled in heaven**: this expression may refer to the angels of Heb 12:22, or to the heroes of the Old Testament (see Heb 11), or to the entire assembly of the new covenant.

† [12:24] **Speaks more eloquently**: the blood of Abel, the first human blood to be shed, is contrasted with that of Jesus. Abel's blood cried out from the earth for vengeance, but the blood of Jesus has opened the way for everyone, providing cleansing and access to God (Heb 10:19).

‡ [13:1–16] After recommendations on social and moral matters (Heb 13:1–6), the letter turns to doctrinal issues. The fact that the original leaders are dead should not cause the recipients of this letter to lose their faith (Heb 13:7), for Christ still lives and he remains always the same (Heb 13:8). They must not rely for their personal sanctification on regulations concerning foods (Heb 13:9), nor should they entertain the notion that Judaism and Christianity can be intermingled (Heb 13:10; cf. notes on Gal 2:11–14; 2:15–21). As Jesus died separated from his own people, so must the Christian community remain apart from the religious doctrines of Judaism (Heb 13:11–14). Christ must be the heart and center of the community (Heb 13:15–16).

§ [13:9] **Strange teaching**: this doctrine about **foods** probably refers to the Jewish food laws; in view of Heb 13:10, however, the author may be thinking of the Mosaic sacrificial banquets.

¶ [13:10] **We have an altar**: this does not refer to the Eucharist, which is never clearly mentioned in Hebrews, but to the sacrifice of Christ.

** [13:17–25] Recommending obedience to the leaders of the community, the author asks for prayers (Heb 13:17–19). The letter concludes with a blessing (Heb 13:20–21), a final request for the acceptance of its message (Heb 13:22), information regarding Timothy (Heb 13:23), and general greetings (Heb 13:24–25).

†† [13:20–21] These verses constitute one of the most beautiful blessings in the New Testament. The resurrection of Jesus is presupposed throughout Hebrews, since it is included in the author's frequently expressed idea of his exaltation, but this is the only place where it is explicitly mentioned.

---

h. [12:22] Gal 4:26; Rev 21:2.   i. [12:23] Lk 10:20; Rev 5:11.   j. [12:24] 7:22; 8:6; 9:15 / 11:4; Gn 4:10.   k. [12:25] Ex 20:19.   l. [12:26] Ex 19:18; Jgs 5:4–5; Ps 68:9; Hg 2:6.   m. [12:27] Is 66:22; Mt 24:35; Mk 13:31; Lk 21:33.   n. [12:28] Dn 7:14, 18 / Rom 1:9.   o. [12:29] Dt 4:24; Is 33:14.   p. [13:2] Gn 18:3; 19:2–3; Jgs 6:11–22; Tb 5:4.   q. [13:3] Mt 25:36.   r. [13:4] 1 Cor 5:13; Eph 5:5.   s. [13:5] Dt 31:6, 8; Jos 1:5.

t. [13:6] Ps 27:1–3; 118:6.   u. [13:8] 1:12; 7:24; Rev 1:17.   v. [13:9] Rom 14:17; 1 Cor 8:8; Eph 4:14; Col 2:16.   w. [13:11] Ex 29:14; Lv 16:27.   x. [13:12] Mt 21:39; Mk 12:8; Lk 20:15; Jn 19:17.   y. [13:14] 11:10, 14.   z. [13:15] Hos 14:3.   a. [13:16] Phil 4:18.   b. [13:20] Is 63:11; Zec 9:11; Jn 10:11; Acts 2:24; Rom 15:33.

²²Brothers, I ask you to bear with this message of encouragement, for I have written to you rather briefly. ²³I must let you know that our brother Timothy has been set free. If he comes soon, I shall see you together with him.ᶜ

²⁴Greetings to all your leaders and to all the holy ones. Those from Italy send you greetings. ²⁵Grace be with all of you.ᵈ

c. [13:23] Acts 16:1.

d. [13:25] Ti 3:15.

# THE
# CATHOLIC LETTERS

In addition to the thirteen letters attributed to Paul and the Letter to the Hebrews, the New Testament contains seven other letters. Three of these are attributed to John, two to Peter, and one each to James and Jude, all personages of the apostolic age. The term "catholic letter" first appears, with reference only to 1 John, in the writings of Apollonius of Ephesus, a second-century apologist, known only from a citation in Eusebius's *Ecclesiastical History*. Eusebius himself (A.D. 260–340) used the term to refer to all seven letters.

The reason for the term "catholic," which means "universal," was the perception that these letters, unlike those of Paul, which were directed to a particular local church, were apparently addressed more generally to the universal church. This designation is not entirely accurate, however. On the one hand, Hebrews has no specifically identified addressees, and originally this was probably true of Ephesians as well. On the other hand, 3 John is addressed to a named individual, 2 John to a specific, though unnamed, community, and 1 Peter to a number of churches that are specified as being located in Asia Minor.

While all seven of these writings begin with an epistolary formula, several of them do not appear to be real letters in the modern sense of the term. In the ancient world it was not unusual to cast an exhortation in the form of a letter for literary effect, a phenomenon comparable to the "open letter" that is sometimes used today.

With the exception of 1 Peter and 1 John, the ancient church showed reluctance to include the catholic letters in the New Testament canon. The reason for this was widespread doubt whether they had actually been written by the apostolic figures to whom they are attributed. The early Christians saw the New Testament as the depository of apostolic faith; therefore, they wished to include only the testimony of apostles. Today we distinguish more clearly between the authorship of a work and its canonicity: even though written by other, later witnesses than those whose names they bear, these writings nevertheless testify to the apostolic faith and constitute canonical scripture. By the late fourth or early fifth centuries, most objections had been overcome in both the Greek and Latin churches (though not in the Syriac), and all seven of the catholic letters have since been acknowledged as canonical.

# THE LETTER OF
# JAMES

~~∽~~

The person to whom this letter is ascribed can scarcely be one of the two members of the Twelve who bore the name James (see Mt 10:2–3; Mk 3:17–18; Lk 6:14–15), for he is not identified as an apostle but only as "slave of God and of the Lord Jesus Christ" (Jas 1:1). This designation most probably refers to the third New Testament personage named James, a relative of Jesus who is usually called "brother of the Lord" (see Mt 13:55; Mk 6:3). He was the leader of the Jewish Christian community in Jerusalem whom Paul acknowledged as one of the "pillars" (Gal 2:9). In Acts he appears as the authorized spokesman for the Jewish Christian position in the early Church (Acts 12:17; 15:13–21). According to the Jewish historian Josephus (*Antiquities* 20:201–203), he was stoned to death by the Jews under the high priest Ananus II in A.D. 62.

The letter is addressed to "the twelve tribes in the dispersion." In Old Testament terminology the term "twelve tribes" designates the people of Israel; the "dispersion" or "diaspora" refers to the non-Palestinian Jews who had settled throughout the Greco-Roman world (see Jn 7:35). Since in Christian thought the church is the new Israel, the address probably designates the Jewish Christian churches located in Palestine, Syria, and elsewhere. Or perhaps the letter is meant more generally for all Christian communities, and the "dispersion" has the symbolic meaning of exile from our true home, as it has in the address of 1 Peter (1 Pt 1:1). The letter is so markedly Jewish in character that some scholars have regarded it as a Jewish document subsequently "baptized" by a few Christian insertions, but such an origin is scarcely tenable in view of the numerous contacts discernible between the Letter of James and other New Testament literature.

From the viewpoint of its literary form, James is a letter only in the most conventional sense; it has none of the characteristic features of a real letter except the address. It belongs rather to the genre of parenesis or exhortation and is concerned almost exclusively with ethical conduct. It therefore falls within the tradition of Jewish wisdom literature, such as can be found in the Old Testament (Proverbs, Sirach) and in the extracanonical Jewish literature (Testaments of the Twelve Patriarchs, the Books of Enoch, the Manual of Discipline found at Qumran). More specifically, it consists of sequences of didactic proverbs, comparable to Tb 4:5–19, to many passages in Sirach, and to sequences of sayings in the synoptic gospels. Numerous passages in James treat of subjects that also appear in the synoptic sayings of Jesus, especially in Matthew's Sermon on the Mount, but the correspondences are too general to establish any literary dependence. James represents a type of early Christianity that emphasized sound teaching and responsible moral behavior. Ethical norms are derived not primarily from christology, as in Paul, but from a concept of salvation that involves conversion, baptism, forgiveness of sin, and expectation of judgment (Jas 1:17; 4:12).

Paradoxically, this very Jewish work is written in an excellent Greek style, which ranks among the best in the New Testament and appears to be the work of a trained Hellenistic writer. Those who continue to regard James of Jerusalem as its author are therefore obliged to suppose that a secretary must have put the letter into its present literary form. This assumption is not implausible in the light of ancient practice. Some regard the letter as one of the earliest writings in the New Testament and feel that its content accurately reflects what we would expect of the leader of Jewish Christianity. Moreover, they argue that the type of Jewish Christianity reflected in the letter cannot be situated historically after the fall of Jerusalem in A.D. 70.

Others, however, believe it more likely that James is a pseudonymous work of a later period. In addition to its Greek style, they observe further that (a) the prestige that the writer is assumed to enjoy points to the later legendary reputation of James; (b) the discussion of the importance of good works seems to presuppose a debate subsequent to that in Paul's own day; (c) the author does not rely upon prescriptions of the Mosaic law, as we would expect from the historical James; (d) the letter contains no allusions to James's own history and to his relationship with Jesus or to the early Christian community of Jerusalem. For these reasons, many recent interpreters assign James to the period A.D. 90–100.

The principal divisions of the Letter of James are the following:

I. Address (1:1)
II. The Value of Trials and Temptation (1:2–18)
III. Exhortations and Warnings (1:19–5:12)
IV. The Power of Prayer (5:13–20)

## I. ADDRESS

## CHAPTER 1

[1]James, a slave of God and of the Lord Jesus Christ, to the twelve tribes in the dispersion, greetings.[a]

## II. THE VALUE OF TRIALS AND TEMPTATION

**Perseverance in Trial.** [2b]Consider it all joy, my brothers, when you encounter various trials,[†] [3]for you know that the testing[‡] of your faith produces perseverance. [4]And let perseverance be perfect, so that you may be perfect and complete, lacking in nothing. [5]But if any of you lacks wisdom,[§] he should ask God who gives to all generously and ungrudgingly, and he will be given it.[c] [6]But he should ask in faith, not doubting, for the one who doubts is like a wave of the sea that is driven and tossed about by the wind.[d] [7]For that person must not suppose that he will receive anything from the Lord, [8]since he is a man of two minds, unstable in all his ways.

[9]The brother in lowly circumstances[e] should take pride in his high standing,[e] [10]and the rich one in his lowliness, for he will pass away "like the flower of the field."[f] [11]For the sun comes up with its scorching heat and dries up the grass, its flower droops, and the beauty of its appearance vanishes. So will the rich person fade away in the midst of his pursuits.

**Temptation.** [12g]Blessed is the man who perseveres in temptation,[**] for when he has been proved he will receive the crown of life that he promised to those who love him. [13†]No one experiencing temptation should say, "I am being tempted by God"; for God is not subject to temptation to evil, and he himself tempts no one.[h] [14]Rather, each person is tempted when he is lured and enticed by his own desire. [15]Then desire conceives and brings forth sin, and when sin reaches maturity it gives birth to death.

[16‡‡]Do not be deceived, my beloved brothers: [17]all good giving and every perfect gift[§§] is from above, coming down from the Father of lights, with whom there is no alteration or shadow caused by change. [18]He willed to give us birth by the word of truth that we may be a kind of firstfruits of his creatures.[¶¶]

---

** [1:12] **Temptation**: the Greek word used here is the same one used for "trials" in Jas 1:2. **The crown of life**: in ancient Palestine, crowns or wreaths of flowers were worn at festive occasions as signs of joy and honor. In the Hellenistic world, wreaths were given as a reward to great statesmen, soldiers, athletes. **Life**: here means eternal life. **He promised**: some manuscripts read "God" or "the Lord," while the best witnesses do not specify the subject of "promised."

†† [1:13–15] It is contrary to what we know of God for God to be the author of human temptation (Jas 1:13). In the commission of a sinful act, one is first beguiled by passion (Jas 1:14), then consent is given, which in turn causes the sinful act. When sin permeates the entire person, it incurs the ultimate penalty of death (Jas 1:15).

‡‡ [1:16–18] The author here stresses that God is the source of all good and of good alone, and the evil of temptation does not come from him.

§§ [1:17] **All good giving and every perfect gift** may be a proverb written in hexameter. **Father of lights**: God is here called the Father of the heavenly luminaries, i.e., the stars, sun, and moon that he created (Gn 1:14–18). Unlike orbs moving from nadir to zenith, he never changes or diminishes in brightness.

¶¶ [1:18] Acceptance of the gospel message, **the word of truth**, constitutes new birth (Jn 3:5–6) and makes the recipient the firstfruits (i.e., the cultic offering of the earliest grains, symbolizing the beginning of an abundant harvest) of a new creation; cf. 1 Cor 15:20; Rom 8:23.

---

\* [1:1] **James, a slave of God and of the Lord Jesus Christ**: a declaration of the writer's authority for instructing the Christian communities; cf. Rom 1:1. Regarding the identity of the author, see Introduction. **Dispersion**: see Introduction.

† [1:2] **Consider it all joy . . . various trials**: a frequent teaching of the New Testament derived from the words and sufferings of Jesus (Mt 5:10–12; Jn 10:11; Acts 5:41).

‡ [1:3–8] The sequence of testing, perseverance, and being perfect and complete indicates the manner of attaining spiritual maturity and full preparedness for the coming of Christ (Jas 5:7–12; cf. 1 Pt 1:6–7; Rom 5:3–5). These steps require wisdom (Jas 1:5).

§ [1:5] **Wisdom**: a gift that God readily grants to all who ask in faith and that sustains the Christian in times of trial. It is a kind of knowledge or understanding not accessible to the unbeliever or those who doubt, which gives the recipient an understanding of the real importance of events. In this way a Christian can deal with adversity with great calm and hope (cf. 1 Cor 2:6–12).

¶ [1:9–11] Throughout his letter (see Jas 2:5; 4:10, 13–16; 5:1–6), the author reaffirms the teaching of Jesus that worldly prosperity is not necessarily a sign of God's favor but can even be a hindrance to proper humility before God (cf. Lk 6:20–25; 12:16–21; 16:19–31).

---

a. [1:1] Jn 7:35; 1 Pt 1:1. b. [1:2] Rom 5:3–5; 1 Pt 1:6; 4:13–16. c. [1:5] Prv 2:2–6; Wis 9:4, 9–12. d. [1:6] Mt 7:7; Mk 11:24. e. [1:9] 2:5.

f. [1:10] Is 40:6–7. g. [1:12] 1 Cor 9:25; 2 Tm 4:8; 1 Pt 5:4; Rev 2:10. h. [1:13] Sir 15:11–20; 1 Cor 10:13. i. [1:18] Jn 1:12–13; 1 Pt 1:23.

## III. EXHORTATIONS AND WARNINGS

**Doers of the Word.** [19]Know this, my dear brothers: everyone should be quick to hear,* slow to speak, slow to wrath,ʲ [20]for the wrath of a man does not accomplish the righteousness of God.ᵏ [21]Therefore, put away all filth and evil excess and humbly welcome the word that has been planted in you and is able to save your souls.ˡ

[22]Be doers of the word and not hearers only, deluding yourselves.ᵐ [23]For if anyone is a hearer of the word and not a doer, he is like a man who looks at his own face in a mirror. [24]He sees himself, then goes off and promptly forgets what he looked like. [25]But the one who peers into the perfect law† of freedom and perseveres, and is not a hearer who forgets but a doer who acts, such a one shall be blessed in what he does.ⁿ

[26‡]If anyone thinks he is religious and does not bridle his tongue§ but deceives his heart, his religion is vain.ᵒ [27]Religion that is pure and undefiled before God and the Father is this: to care for orphans and widows¶ in their affliction and to keep oneself unstained by the world.ᵖ

## CHAPTER 2

**Sin of Partiality.**** [1]My brothers, show no partiality as you adhere to the faith in our glorious Lord Jesus Christ. [2]For if a man with gold rings on his fingers and in fine clothes comes into your assembly, and a poor person in shabby clothes also comes in, [3]and you pay attention to the one wearing the fine clothes and say, "Sit here, please," while you say to the poor one, "Stand there," or "Sit at my feet," [4]have you not made distinctions among yourselves and become judges with evil designs?††

[5]Listen, my beloved brothers. Did not God choose those who are poor‡‡ in the world to be rich in faith and heirs of the kingdom that he promised to those who love him?�q [6]But you dishonored the poor person. Are not the rich oppressing you? And do they themselves not haul you off to court? [7]Is it not they who blaspheme the noble name that was invoked over you?ʳ [8]However, if you fulfill the royal§§ law according to the scripture, "You shall love your neighbor as yourself," you are doing well.ˢ [9]But if you show partiality, you commit sin, and are convicted by the law as transgressors.ᵗ [10]For whoever keeps the whole law, but falls short in one particular, has become guilty in respect to all of it.ᵘ [11]For he who said, "You shall not commit adultery," also said, "You shall not kill."ᵛ Even if you do not commit adultery but kill, you have become a transgressor of the law. [12¶¶]So speak and so act as people who will be judged by the law of freedom. [13]For the judgment is merciless to one who has not shown mercy; mercy triumphs over judgment.ˣ

**Faith and Works.**** [14]What good is it, my brothers, if someone says he has faith but does not have works? Can that faith save him?ʸ [15]If a brother or sister has nothing to wear and has no food for the day, [16]and one of you says to them, "Go in peace, keep warm, and eat well," but you do not give them the necessities of the body, what good is it?ᶻ [17]So also faith of itself, if it does not have works, is dead.

[18]Indeed someone may say, "You have faith and I have works." Demonstrate your faith to me without works, and I will demonstrate my faith to you from my works. [19]You believe that God is

---

*[1:19–25] To **be quick to hear** the gospel is to accept it readily and to act in conformity with it, removing from one's soul whatever is opposed to it, so that it may take root and effect salvation (Jas 1:19–21). To listen to the gospel message but not practice it is failure to improve oneself (Jas 1:22–24). Only conformity of life to the perfect law of true freedom brings happiness (Jas 1:25).

†[1:25] **Peers into the perfect law**: the image of a person doing this is paralleled to that of hearing God's word. The **perfect law** applies the Old Testament description of the Mosaic law to the gospel of Jesus Christ that brings freedom.

‡[1:26–27] A practical application of Jas 1:22 is now made.

§[1:26] For control of the tongue, see note on Jas 3:1–12.

¶[1:27] In the Old Testament, orphans and widows are classical examples of the defenseless and oppressed.

**[2:1–13] In the Christian community there must be no discrimination or favoritism based on status or wealth (Jas 2:2–4; cf. Mt 5:3; 11:5; 23:6; 1 Cor 1:27–29). Divine favor rather consists in God's election and promises (Jas 2:5). The rich who oppress the poor blaspheme the name of Christ (Jas 2:6–7). By violating one law of love of neighbor, they offend against the whole law (Jas 2:8–11). On the other hand, conscious awareness of the final judgment helps the faithful to fulfill the whole law (Jas 2:12).

††[2:4] When Christians show favoritism to the rich they are guilty of the worst kind of prejudice and discrimination. The author says that such Christians set themselves up as judges who judge not by divine law but by the basest, self-serving motives.

‡‡[2:5] The poor, "God's poor" of the Old Testament, were seen by Jesus as particularly open to God for belief in and reliance on him alone (Lk 6:20). God's law cannot tolerate their oppression in any way (Jas 2:9).

§§[2:8] **Royal**: literally, "kingly"; because the Mosaic law came from God, the universal king. There may be an allusion to Jesus' uses of this commandment in his preaching of the kingdom of God (Mt 22:39; Mk 12:31; Lk 10:27).

¶¶[2:12–13] The law upon which the last judgment will be based is the law of freedom. As Jesus taught, mercy (which participates in God's own loving mercy) includes forgiveness of those who wrong us (see Mt 6:12, 14–15).

***[2:14–26] The theme of these verses is the relationship of faith and works (deeds). It has been argued that the teaching here contradicts that of Paul (see especially Rom 4:5–6). The problem can only be understood if the different viewpoints of the two authors are seen. Paul argues against those who claim to participate in God's salvation because of their good deeds as well as because they have committed themselves to trust in God through Jesus Christ (Paul's concept of faith). Paul certainly understands, however, the implications of true faith for a life of love and generosity (see Gal 5:6, 13–15). The author of James is well aware that proper conduct can only come about with an authentic commitment to God in faith (Jas 2:18, 26). Many think he was seeking to correct a misunderstanding of Paul's view.

---

j. [1:19] Prv 14:17; Sir 5:11.   k. [1:20] Eph 4:26.   l. [1:21] Col 3:8.   m. [1:22] Mt 7:26; Rom 2:13.   n. [1:25] 2:12; Ps 19:8; Rom 8:2.   o. [1:26] 3:2; Ps 34:14.   p. [1:27] Ex 22:21.

q. [2:5] 1 Cor 1:26–28; Rev 2:9.   r. [2:7] 1 Pt 4:4.   s. [2:8] Lv 19:18; Mt 22:39; Rom 13:9.   t. [2:9] Dt 1:17.   u. [2:10] Gal 3:10.   v. [2:11] Ex 20:13–14; Dt 5:17–18.   w. [2:12] 1:25; Rom 8:2.   x. [2:13] Mt 5:7; 6:14–15; 18:32–33.   y. [2:14] Mt 25:31–46; Gal 5:6.   z. [2:16] 1 Jn 3:17.

one. You do well. Even the demons believe that and tremble. ²⁰Do you want proof, you ignoramus, that faith without works is useless? ²¹Was not Abraham our father justified by works when he offered his son Isaac upon the altar?ᵃ ²²You see that faith was active along with his works, and faith was completed by the works. ²³Thus the scripture was fulfilled that says, "Abraham believed God, and it was credited to him as righteousness," and he was called "the friend of God."ᵇ ²⁴See how a person is justified by works and not by faith alone. ²⁵And in the same way, was not Rahab the harlot also justified by works when she welcomed the messengers and sent them out by a different route?ᶜ ²⁶For just as a body without a spirit is dead, so also faith without works is dead.

## CHAPTER 3

**Power of the Tongue.**˙ ¹Not many of you should become teachers, my brothers, for you realize that we will be judged more strictly, ²for we all fall short in many respects. If anyone does not fall short in speech, he is a perfect man, able to bridle his whole body also.ᵈ ³If we put bits into the mouths of horses to make them obey us, we also guide their whole bodies. ⁴It is the same with ships: even though they are so large and driven by fierce winds, they are steered by a very small rudder wherever the pilot's inclination wishes. ⁵In the same way the tongue is a small member and yet has great pretensions.

Consider how small a fire can set a huge forest ablaze. ⁶The tongue is also a fire. It exists among our members as a world of malice, defiling the whole body and setting the entire course of our lives on fire, itself set on fire by Gehenna. ⁷For every kind of beast and bird, of reptile and sea creature, can be tamed and has been tamed by the human species, ⁸but no human being can tame the tongue. It is a restless evil, full of deadly poison.ᵉ ⁹With it we bless the Lord and Father, and with it we curse human beings who are made in the likeness of God. ¹⁰From the same mouth come blessing and cursing. This need not be so, my brothers. ¹¹Does a spring gush forth from the same opening both pure and brackish water? ¹²Can a fig tree, my brothers, produce olives, or a grapevine figs? Neither can salt water yield fresh.ᶠ **True Wisdom.**† ¹³Who among you is wise and understanding? Let him show his works by

a good life in the humility that comes from wisdom.ᵍ ¹⁴But if you have bitter jealousy and selfish ambition in your hearts, do not boast and be false to the truth. ¹⁵Wisdom of this kind does not come down from above but is earthly, unspiritual, demonic. ¹⁶For where jealousy and selfish ambition exist, there is disorder and every foul practice. ¹⁷But the wisdom from above is first of all pure, then peaceable, gentle, compliant, full of mercy and good fruits, without inconstancy or insincerity.ʰ ¹⁸And the fruit of righteousness is sown in peace for those who cultivate peace.ⁱ

## CHAPTER 4

**Causes of Division.**‡ ¹Where do the wars and where do the conflicts among you come from? Is it not from your passions§ that make war within your members?ʲ ²You covet but do not possess. You kill and envy but you cannot obtain; you fight and wage war. You do not possess because you do not ask. ³You ask but do not receive, because you ask wrongly, to spend it on your passions. ⁴Adulterers!§ Do you not know that to be a lover of the world means enmity with God? Therefore, whoever wants to be a lover of the world makes himself an enemy of God.ᵏ ⁵Or do you suppose that the scripture speaks without meaning when it says, "The spirit that he has made to dwell in us tends toward jealousy"?** ⁶But he bestows a greater grace; therefore, it says:ˡ

"God resists the proud,
        but gives grace to the humble."††

‡[4:1–12] The concern here is with the origin of conflicts in the Christian community. These are occasioned by love **of the world,** which **means enmity with God** (Jas 4:4). Further, the conflicts are bound up with failure to pray properly (cf. Mt 7:7–11; Jn 14:13; 15:7; 16:23), that is, not asking God at all or using God's kindness only for one's pleasure (Jas 4:2–3). In contrast, the proper dispositions are submission to God, repentance, humility, and resistance to evil (Jas 4:7–10).

§[4:1–3] **Passions:** the Greek word here (literally, "pleasures") does not indicate that pleasure is evil. Rather, as the text points out (Jas 4:2–3), it is the manner in which one deals with needs and desires that determines good or bad. The motivation for any action can be wrong, especially if one does not pray properly but seeks only selfish enjoyment (Jas 4:3).

¶[4:4] **Adulterers:** a common biblical image for the covenant between God and his people is the marriage bond. In this image, breaking the covenant with God is likened to the unfaithfulness of adultery.

**[4:5] The meaning of this saying is difficult because the author of James cites, probably from memory, a passage that is not in any extant manuscript of the Bible. Other translations of the text with a completely different meaning are possible: "The Spirit that he (God) made to dwell in us yearns (for us) jealously," or, "He (God) yearns jealously for the spirit that he has made to dwell in us." If this last translation is correct, the author perhaps had in mind an apocryphal religious text that echoes the idea that God is zealous for his creatures; cf. Ex 20:5; Dt 4:24; Zec 8:2.

††[4:6] The point of this whole argument is that God wants the happiness of all, but that selfishness and pride can make that impossible. We must work with him in humility (Jas 4:10).

---

*[3:1–12] The use and abuse of the important role of teaching in the church (Jas 3:1) are here related to the good and bad use of the tongue (Jas 3:9–12), the instrument through which teaching was chiefly conveyed (see Sir 5:11–6:1; 28:12–26).

†[3:13–18] This discussion of true wisdom is related to the previous reflection on the role of the teacher as one who is in control of his speech. The qualities of the wise man endowed from above are detailed (Jas 3:17–18; cf. Gal 5:22–23), in contrast to the qualities of earthbound wisdom (Jas 3:14–16; cf. 2 Cor 12:20).

---

a. [2:21] Gn 22:9–12; Heb 11:17.   b. [2:23] Gn 15:6; Rom 4:3; Gal 3:6 / 2 Chr 20:7; Is 41:8.   c. [2:25] Jos 2:1–21.   d. [3:2] 1:26; Prv 13:3; Sir 28:12–26.   e. [3:8] Ps 140:4.   f. [3:12] Mt 7:16–17.

g. [3:13] Eph 4:1–2.   h. [3:17] 1:17; Wis 7:22–23.   i. [3:18] Mt 5:9.   j. [4:1] Rom 7:23; 1 Pt 2:11.   k. [4:4] Mt 6:24; Lk 16:13; Rom 8:7; 1 Jn 2:15–16.   l. [4:6] Jb 22:29; Prv 3:34; Mt 23:12; 1 Pt 5:5.

⁷So submit yourselves to God. Resist the devil, and he will flee from you.ᵐ ⁸Draw near to God, and he will draw near to you. Cleanse your hands, you sinners, and purify your hearts, you of two minds.ⁿ ⁹Begin to lament, to mourn, to weep. Let your laughter be turned into mourning and your joy into dejection. ¹⁰Humble yourselves before the Lord and he will exalt you.ᵒ

¹¹Do not speak evil of one another, brothers. Whoever speaks evil of a brother or judges his brother speaks evil of the law and judges the law.* If you judge the law, you are not a doer of the law but a judge. ¹²There is one lawgiver and judge who is able to save or to destroy. Who then are you to judge your neighbor?ᵖ

**Warning Against Presumption.**† ¹³Come now, you who say, "Today or tomorrow we shall go into such and such a town, spend a year there doing business, and make a profit"— ¹⁴you have no idea what your life will be like tomorrow.‡ You are a puff of smoke that appears briefly and then disappears.�q ¹⁵Instead you should say, "If the Lord wills it,§ we shall live to do this or that." ¹⁶But now you are boasting in your arrogance. All such boasting is evil. ¹⁷So for one who knows the right thing to do and does not do it, it is a sin.ˢ

### CHAPTER 5
**Warning to the Rich.**** ¹Come now, you rich, weep and wail over your impending miseries.ᵗ ²Your wealth has rotted away, your clothes have become moth-eaten,ᵗ ³your gold and silver have corroded, and that corrosion will be a testimony against you; it will devour your flesh like a fire. You have stored up treasure for the last days.ᵘ ⁴Behold, the wages you withheld from the workers who harvested your fields are crying aloud, and the cries of the harvesters have reached the

ears of the Lord of hosts.ᵛ ⁵You have lived on earth in luxury and pleasure; you have fattened your hearts for the day of slaughter.ʷ ⁶You have condemned; you have murdered the righteous one;ˣ he offers you no resistance.††

**Patience and Oaths.** ⁷‡‡Be patient, therefore, brothers, until the coming of the Lord. See how the farmer waits for the precious fruit of the earth, being patient with it until it receives the early and the late rains.§§ ⁸You too must be patient. Make your hearts firm, because the coming of the Lord is at hand.ʸ ⁹Do not complain, brothers, about one another, that you may not be judged. Behold, the Judge is standing before the gates. ¹⁰Take as an example of hardship and patience, brothers, the prophets who spoke in the name of the Lord. ¹¹Indeed we call blessed those who have persevered. You have heard of the perseverance of Job, and you have seen the purpose of the Lord, because "the Lord is compassionate and merciful."ᶻ

¹²ᵃBut above all, my brothers, do not swear, either by heaven or by earth or with any other oath, but let your "Yes" mean "Yes" and your "No" mean "No," that you may not incur condemnation.¶¶

### IV. THE POWER OF PRAYER

**Anointing of the Sick.** ¹³Is anyone among you suffering? He should pray. Is anyone in good spirits? He should sing praise. ¹⁴Is anyone among you sick?*** He should summon the presbyters of the church, and they should pray over him and anoint [him] with oil in the name of the Lord,ᵇ ¹⁵and the prayer of faith will save the sick person, and the Lord will raise him up. If he has committed any sins, he will be forgiven.†††

---

\* [4:11] Slander of a fellow Christian does not break just one commandment but makes mockery of the authority of law in general and therefore of God.

† [4:13–17] The uncertainty of life (Jas 4:14), its complete dependence on God, and the necessity of submitting to God's will (Jas 4:15) all help one know and do what is right (Jas 4:17). To disregard this is to live in pride and arrogance (Jas 4:16); failure to do what is right is a sin (Jas 4:17).

‡ [4:14] Some important Greek manuscripts here have, "You who have no idea what tomorrow will bring. Why, what is your life?"

§ [4:15] **If the Lord wills it**: often in piety referred to as the "*conditio Jacobaea*," the condition James says we should employ to qualify all our plans.

¶ [4:17] **It is a sin**: those who live arrogantly, forgetting the contingency of life and our dependence on God (Jas 4:13–16), are guilty of sin.

** [5:1–6] Continuing with the theme of the transitory character of life on earth, the author points out the impending ruin of the godless. He denounces the unjust rich, whose victims cry to heaven for judgment on their exploiters (Jas 5:4–6). The decay and corrosion of the costly garments and metals, which symbolize wealth, prove them worthless and portend the destruction of their possessors (Jas 5:2–3).

†† [5:6] The author does not have in mind any specific crime in his readers' communities but rather echoes the Old Testament theme of the harsh oppression of the righteous poor (see Prv 1:11; Wis 2:10, 12, 20).

‡‡ [5:7–11] Those oppressed by the unjust rich are reminded of the need for patience, both in bearing the sufferings of human life (Jas 5:9) and in their expectation of the coming of the Lord. It is then that they will receive their reward (Jas 5:7–8, 10–11; cf. Heb 10:25; 1 Jn 2:18).

§§ [5:7] **The early and the late rains**: an expression related to the agricultural season in ancient Palestine (see Dt 11:14; Jer 5:24; Jl 2:23).

¶¶ [5:12] This is the threat of condemnation for the abuse of swearing oaths (cf. Mt 5:33–37). **By heaven or by earth**: these words were substitutes for the original form of an oath, to circumvent its binding force and to avoid pronouncing the holy name of God (see Ex 22:10).

*** [5:14] In case of sickness a Christian should ask for the presbyters of the church, i.e., those who have authority in the church (cf. Acts 15:2, 22–23; 1 Tm 5:17; Ti 1:5). They are to pray over the person and anoint with oil; oil was used for medicinal purposes in the ancient world (see Is 1:6; Lk 10:34). In Mk 6:13, the Twelve anoint the sick with oil on their missionary journey. **In the name of the Lord**: by the power of Jesus Christ.

††† [5:15] The results of the prayer and anointing are physical health and forgiveness of sins. The Roman Catholic

---

m. [4:7] 1 Pt 5:8–9.   n. [4:8] Zec 1:3; Mal 3:7.   o. [4:10] Jb 5:11; Mt 23:12; Lk 14:11; 18:14; 1 Pt 5:6.   p. [4:12] Mt 7:1; Rom 2:1; 14:4.   q. [4:14] Prv 27:1 / Ps 39:6–7.   r. [4:17] Lk 12:47.   s. [5:1] Lk 6:24.   t. [5:2] Mt 6:19.   u. [5:3] Ps 21:10; Prv 11:4; Jdt 16:17.

v. [5:4] Lv 19:13; Dt 24:14–15; Mal 3:5.   w. [5:5] Jer 12:3; Lk 16:19–25.   x. [5:6] Wis 2:10–20.   y. [5:8] Lk 21:19; Heb 10:36 / Heb 10:25; 1 Pt 4:7.   z. [5:11] Ex 34:6; Ps 103:8.   a. [5:12] Mt 5:34–37.   b. [5:14] Mk 6:13.

**Confession and Intercession.** [16]Therefore, confess your sins to one another and pray for one another, that you may be healed. The fervent prayer of a righteous person is very powerful. [17]Elijah was a human being like us; yet he prayed earnestly that it might not rain, and for three years and six months it did not rain upon the land.[c] [18]Then he prayed again, and the sky gave rain and the earth produced its fruit.[d]

**Conversion of Sinners.** [19e]My brothers, if anyone among you should stray from the truth and someone bring him back, [20]he should know that whoever brings back a sinner from the error of his way will save his soul from death and will cover a multitude of sins.[*]

---

Church (Council of Trent, Session 14) declared that this anointing of the sick is a sacrament "instituted by Christ and promulgated by blessed James the apostle."

*[5:20] When a Christian is instrumental in the conversion of a sinner, the result is forgiveness of sins and a reinstatement of the sinner to the life of grace.

c. [5:17] 1 Kgs 17:1; Lk 4:25.   d. [5:18] 1 Kgs 18:45.

e. [5:19] Mt 18:15; Gal 6:1.   f. [5:20] Prv 10:12; 1 Pt 4:8.

# THE FIRST LETTER OF
# PETER

This letter begins with an address by Peter to Christian communities located in five provinces of Asia Minor (1 Pt 1:1), including areas evangelized by Paul (Acts 16:6–7; 18:23). Christians there are encouraged to remain faithful to their standards of belief and conduct in spite of threats of persecution. Numerous allusions in the letter suggest that the churches addressed were largely of Gentile composition (1 Pt 1:14, 18; 2:9–10; 4:3–4), though considerable use is made of the Old Testament (1 Pt 1:24; 2:6–7, 9–10, 22; 3:10–12).

The contents following the address both inspire and admonish these "chosen sojourners" (1 Pt 1:1) who, in seeking to live as God's people, feel an alienation from their previous religious roots and the society around them. Appeal is made to Christ's resurrection and the future hope it provides (1 Pt 1:3–5) and to the experience of baptism as new birth (1 Pt 1:3, 23–25; 3:21). The suffering and death of Christ serve as both source of salvation and example (1 Pt 1:19; 2:21–25; 3:18). What Christians are in Christ, as a people who have received mercy and are to proclaim and live according to God's call (1 Pt 2:9–10), is repeatedly spelled out for all sorts of situations in society (1 Pt 2:11–17), work (even as slaves, 1 Pt 2:18–20), the home (1 Pt 3:1–7), and general conduct (1 Pt 3:8–12; 4:1–11). But over all hangs the possibility of suffering as a Christian (1 Pt 3:13–17). In 1 Pt 4:12–19 persecution is described as already occurring, so that some have supposed the letter was addressed both to places where such a "trial by fire" was already present and to places where it might break out.

The letter constantly mingles moral exhortation (*paraklēsis*) with its catechetical summaries of mercies in Christ. Encouragement to fidelity in spite of suffering is based upon a vision of the meaning of Christian existence. The emphasis on baptism and allusions to various features of the baptismal liturgy suggest that the author has incorporated into his exposition numerous homiletic, credal, hymnic, and sacramental elements of the baptismal rite that had become traditional at an early date.

From Irenaeus in the late second century until modern times, Christian tradition regarded Peter the apostle as author of this document. Since he was martyred at Rome during the persecution of Nero between A.D. 64 and 67, it was supposed that the letter was written from Rome shortly before his death. This is supported by its reference to "Babylon" (1 Pt 5:13), a code name for Rome in the early church.

Some modern scholars, however, on the basis of a number of features that they consider incompatible with Petrine authenticity, regard the letter as the work of a later Christian writer. Such features include the cultivated Greek in which it is written, difficult to attribute to a Galilean fisherman, together with its use of the Greek Septuagint translation when citing the Old Testament; the similarity in both thought and expression to the Pauline literature; and the allusions to widespread persecution of Christians, which did not occur until at least the reign of Domitian (A.D. 81–96). In this view the letter would date from the end of the first century or even the beginning of the second, when there is evidence for persecution of Christians in Asia Minor (the letter of Pliny the Younger to Trajan, A.D. 111–12).

Other scholars believe, however, that these objections can be met by appeal to use of a secretary, Silvanus, mentioned in 1 Pt 5:12. Such secretaries often gave literary expression to the author's thoughts in their own style and language. The persecutions may refer to local harassment rather than to systematic repression by the state. Hence there is nothing in the document incompatible with Petrine authorship in the 60s.

Still other scholars take a middle position. The many literary contacts with the Pauline literature, James, and 1 John suggest a common fund of traditional formulations rather than direct dependence upon Paul. Such liturgical and catechetical traditions must have been very ancient and in some cases of Palestinian origin.

Yet it is unlikely that Peter addressed a letter to the Gentile churches of Asia Minor while Paul was still alive. This suggests a period after the death of the two apostles, perhaps A.D. 70–90. The author would be a disciple of Peter in Rome, representing a Petrine group that served as a bridge between the Palestinian origins of Christianity and its flowering in the Gentile world. The problem addressed would not be official persecution but the difficulty of living the Christian life in a hostile, secular environment that espoused different values and subjected the Christian minority to ridicule and oppression.

The principal divisions of the First Letter of Peter are the following:

I. Address (1:1–2)

II. The Gift and Call of God in Baptism (1:3–2:10)

III. The Christian in a Hostile World (2:11–4:11)

IV. Advice to the Persecuted (4:12–5:11)

V. Conclusion (5:12–14)

## I. ADDRESS

### CHAPTER 1

**Greeting.**[*] ¹Peter, an apostle of Jesus Christ, to the chosen sojourners of the dispersion[†] in Pontus, Galatia, Cappadocia, Asia, and Bithynia,[*a] ²in the foreknowledge of God the Father, through sanctification by the Spirit, for obedience and sprinkling with the blood of Jesus Christ: may grace and peace be yours in abundance.[b]

### II. THE GIFT AND CALL OF GOD IN BAPTISM

**Blessing.** ³[‡]Blessed be the God and Father of our Lord Jesus Christ, who in his great mercy gave us a new birth to a living hope through the resurrection of Jesus Christ from the dead,[c] ⁴to an inheritance that is imperishable, undefiled, and unfading, kept in heaven for you[d] ⁵who by the power of God are safeguarded through faith, to a salvation that is ready to be revealed in the final time. ⁶[§]In this you rejoice, although now

for a little while you may have to suffer through various trials,[e] ⁷so that the genuineness of your faith, more precious than gold that is perishable even though tested by fire, may prove to be for praise, glory, and honor at the revelation of Jesus Christ.[f] ⁸Although you have not seen him you love him; even though you do not see him now yet believe in him, you rejoice with an indescribable and glorious joy,[g] ⁹as you attain the goal of [your] faith, the salvation of your souls.

¹⁰¶Concerning this salvation, prophets who prophesied about the grace that was to be yours searched and investigated it, ¹¹investigating the time and circumstances that the Spirit of Christ within them indicated when it testified in advance to the sufferings destined for Christ and the glories to follow them.[h] ¹²It was revealed to them that they were serving not themselves but you with regard to the things that have now been announced to you by those who preached the good news to you [through] the holy Spirit sent from heaven, things into which angels longed to look.

**Obedience.** ¹³**Therefore, gird up the loins of your mind,[††] live soberly, and set your hopes

---

*[1:1–2] The introductory formula names **Peter** as the writer (but see Introduction). In his comments to the presbyters (1 Pt 5:1), the author calls himself a "fellow presbyter." He addresses himself to the Gentile converts of Asia Minor. Their privileged status as a **chosen** and sanctified people makes them worthy of God's **grace** and **peace.** In contrast is their actual existence as aliens and **sojourners,** scattered among pagans, far from their true country.

†[1:1] **Dispersion:** literally, diaspora; see Jas 1:1 and Introduction to that letter. **Pontus . . . Bithynia:** five provinces in Asia Minor, listed in clockwise order from the north, perhaps in the sequence in which a messenger might deliver the letter.

‡[1:3–5] A prayer of praise and thanksgiving to God who bestows the gift of new life and hope in baptism (**new birth,** 1 Pt 1:3) **through the resurrection of Jesus Christ from the dead.** The new birth is a sign of an **imperishable inheritance** (1 Pt 1:4), of **salvation** that is still in the future (**to be revealed in the final time,** 1 Pt 1:5).

§[1:6–9] As the glory of Christ's resurrection was preceded by his sufferings and death, the new life of faith that it bestows

is to be subjected to many **trials** (1 Pt 1:6) while achieving its goal: the glory of the fullness of **salvation** (1 Pt 1:9) at the coming of Christ (1 Pt 1:7).

¶[1:10–12] The **Spirit of Christ** (1 Pt 1:11) is here shown to have been present in the prophets, moving them to search, investigate, and prophesy about the **grace** of **salvation** that was to come (1 Pt 1:10), and in the apostles impelling them to preach the fulfillment of salvation in the message of Christ's sufferings and glory (1 Pt 1:12).

**[1:13–25] These verses are concerned with the call of God's people to holiness and to mutual love by reason of their redemption through the blood of Christ (1 Pt 1:18–21).

††[1:13] **Gird up the loins of your mind:** a figure reminiscent of the rite of Passover when the Israelites were in flight from their oppressors (Ex 12:11), and also suggesting the vigilance of the Christian people in expectation of the parousia of Christ (Lk 12:35).

---

a. [1:1] Jas 1:1.   b. [1:2] Rom 8:29.   c. [1:3] Ti 3:5.   d. [1:4] Mt 6:19–20.

e. [1:6] Jas 1:2–3.   f. [1:7] 1 Cor 3:13.   g. [1:8] 2 Cor 5:6–7.   h. [1:11] Is 52:13–53:12; Dn 9:24.

completely on the grace to be brought to you at the revelation of Jesus Christ. [14]Like obedient children, do not act in compliance with the desires of your former ignorance* [15]but, as he who called you is holy, be holy yourselves in every aspect of your conduct,[i] [16]for it is written, "Be holy because I [am] holy."[j]

**Reverence.** [17]Now if you invoke as Father him who judges impartially according to each one's works, conduct yourselves with reverence during the time of your sojourning,[k] [18]realizing that you were ransomed from your futile conduct, handed on by your ancestors, not with perishable things like silver or gold[l] [19]but with the precious blood of Christ[m] as of a spotless unblemished lamb.[†] [20]He was known before the foundation of the world but revealed in the final time for you, [21]who through him believe in God who raised him from the dead and gave him glory, so that your faith and hope are in God.

**Mutual Love.**[‡] [22]Since you have purified yourselves by obedience to the truth for sincere mutual love, love one another intensely from a [pure] heart.[n] [23]You have been born anew,[o] not from perishable but from imperishable seed, through the living and abiding word of God,[§] [24]for:

"All flesh is like grass,
      and all its glory like the flower of
            the field;
the grass withers,
      and the flower wilts;[p]
[25]  but the word of the Lord remains forever."

This is the word that has been proclaimed to you.

## CHAPTER 2

**God's House and People.** [1]Rid yourselves of all malice and all deceit, insincerity, envy, and all slander;[q] [2]like newborn infants, long for pure spiritual milk so that through it you may grow into salvation, [3]for you have tasted that the Lord

is good." [4]Come to him, a living stone,[††] rejected by human beings but chosen and precious in the sight of God,[s] [5]and, like living stones, let yourselves be built[‡‡] into a spiritual house to be a holy priesthood to offer spiritual sacrifices acceptable to God through Jesus Christ.[t] [6]For it says in scripture:

"Behold, I am laying a stone in Zion,
      a cornerstone, chosen and precious,
and whoever believes in it shall not be put
            to shame."[u]

[7]Therefore, its value is for you who have faith, but for those without faith:

"The stone which the builders rejected
      has become the cornerstone,"[v]

[8]and

"A stone that will make people stumble,
      and a rock that will make them fall."

They stumble by disobeying the word, as is their destiny.[w]

[9]§§But you are "a chosen race, a royal priesthood, a holy nation, a people of his own, so that you may announce the praises" of him who called you out of darkness into his wonderful light.[x]

[10]  Once you were "no people"
            but now you are God's people;
      you "had not received mercy"
            but now you have received mercy.[y]

## III. THE CHRISTIAN IN A HOSTILE WORLD

**Christian Examples.** [11]¶¶Beloved, I urge you as

---

*[1:14–16] The **ignorance** here referred to (1 Pt 1:14) was their former lack of knowledge of God, leading inevitably to godless conduct. Holiness (1 Pt 1:15–16), on the contrary, is the result of their call to the knowledge and love of God.

†[1:19] Christians have received the redemption prophesied by Isaiah (Is 52:3), through the blood (Jewish symbol of life) of the spotless lamb (Is 53:7, 10; Jn 1:29; Rom 3:24–25; cf. 1 Cor 6:20).

‡[1:22–25] The new birth of Christians (1 Pt 1:23) derives from Christ, the **imperishable seed** or sowing that produces a new and lasting existence in those who accept the gospel (1 Pt 1:24–25), with the consequent duty of loving **one another** (1 Pt 1:22).

§[1:23] **The living and abiding word of God:** or, "the word of the living and abiding God."

¶[2:1–3] Growth toward salvation is seen here as two steps: first, stripping away all that is contrary to the new life in Christ; second, the nourishment (**pure spiritual milk**) that the newly baptized have received.

**[2:3] **Tasted that the Lord is good:** cf. Ps 34:9.

††[2:4–8] Christ is the cornerstone (cf. Is 28:16) that is the foundation of the spiritual edifice of the Christian community (1 Pt 2:5). To unbelievers, Christ is an obstacle and a stumbling block on which they are destined to fall (1 Pt 2:8); cf. Rom 11:11.

‡‡[2:5] **Let yourselves be built:** the form of the Greek verb could also be indicative passive, "you are being built" (cf. 1 Pt 2:9).

§§[2:9–10] The prerogatives of ancient Israel mentioned here are now more fully and fittingly applied to the Christian people: "a chosen race" (cf. Is 43:20–21) indicates their divine election (Eph 1:4–6); "a royal priesthood" (cf. Ex 19:6) to serve and worship God in Christ, thus continuing the priestly functions of his life, passion, and resurrection; "a holy nation" (Ex 19:6) reserved for God, a people he claims for his own (cf. Mal 3:17) in virtue of their baptism into his death and resurrection. This transcends all natural and national divisions and unites the people into one community to glorify the one who led them from the darkness of paganism to the light of faith in Christ. From being "no people" deprived of all mercy, they have become the very people of God, the chosen recipients of his mercy (cf. Hos 1:9; 2:25).

¶¶[2:11–3:12] After explaining the doctrinal basis for the Christian community, the author makes practical applications in terms of the virtues that should prevail in all the social relationships of the members of the community: good example to Gentile neighbors (1 Pt 2:11–12); respect for human authority (1 Pt 2:13–17); obedience, patience, and endurance of hardship in domestic relations (1 Pt 2:18–25); Christian

---

i. [1:15] Mt 5:48; 1 Jn 3:3.   j. [1:16] Lv 11:44; 19:2.   k. [1:17] 2:11.
l. [1:18] Is 52:3; 1 Cor 6:20.   m. [1:19] Ex 12:5; Jn 1:29; Heb 9:14.
n. [1:22] Rom 12:10.   o. [1:23] 1 Jn 3:9.   p. [1:24] Is 40:6–8.   q. [2:1–2] Jas 1:21.   r. [2:3] Ps 34:9.

s. [2:4] Ps 118:22; Mt 21:42; Acts 4:11.   t. [2:5] Eph 2:21–22.
u. [2:6] Is 28:16.   v. [2:7] Ps 118:22; Mt 21:42; Lk 20:17; Acts 4:11.
w. [2:8] Is 8:14; Rom 9:33.   x. [2:9] Ex 19:6; Is 61:6; Rev 1:6; 20:6.
y. [2:10] Hos 1:9; 2:25 / Hos 1:6.

aliens and sojourners* to keep away from worldly desires that wage war against the soul.ᶻ ¹²Maintain good conduct among the Gentiles, so that if they speak of you as evildoers, they may observe your good works and glorify God on the day of visitation.

**Christian Citizens.†** ¹³Be subject to every human institution for the Lord's sake, whether it be to the king as supremeᵃ ¹⁴or to governors as sent by him for the punishment of evildoers and the approval of those who do good. ¹⁵For it is the will of God that by doing good you may silence the ignorance of foolish people. ¹⁶Be free, yet without using freedom as a pretext for evil, but as slaves of God.ᵇ ¹⁷Give honor to all, love the community, fear God, honor the king.ᶜ

**Christian Slaves.** ¹⁸‡Slaves, be subject to your masters with all reverence, not only to those who are good and equitable but also to those who are perverse.ᵈ ¹⁹For whenever anyone bears the pain of unjust suffering because of consciousness of God, that is a grace. ²⁰But what credit is there if you are patient when beaten for doing wrong? But if you are patient when you suffer for doing what is good, this is a grace before God. ²¹For to this you have been called, because Christ also suffered§ for you, leaving you an example that you should follow in his footsteps.ᵉ

²² "He committed no sin,ᶠ
and no deceit was found in his
mouth."¶

²³When he was insulted, he returned no insult; when he suffered, he did not threaten; instead, he handed himself over to the one who judges justly.ᵍ ²⁴He himself bore our sins in his body upon the cross, so that, free from sin, we might live for righteousness. By his wounds you have been healed.ʰ ²⁵For you had gone astray like sheep,ⁱ but you have now returned to the shepherd and guardian of your souls.**

## CHAPTER 3

**Christian Spouses.** ††¹Likewise, you wives should be subordinate to your husbands so that, even if some disobey the word, they may be won over without a word by their wives' conduct ²when they observe your reverent and chaste behavior.ʲ ³Your adornment should not be an external one: braiding the hair, wearing gold jewelry, or dressing in fine clothes,ᵏ ⁴but rather the hidden character of the heart, expressed in the imperishable beauty of a gentle and calm disposition, which is precious in the sight of God. ⁵For this is also how the holy women who hoped in God once used to adorn themselves and were subordinate to their husbands; ⁶thus Sarah obeyed Abraham, calling him "lord." You are her children when you do what is good and fear no intimidation.

⁷Likewise, you husbands should live with your wives in understanding, showing honor to the weaker female sex, since we are joint heirs of the gift of life, so that your prayers may not be hindered.‡‡

**Christian Conduct.§§** ⁸Finally, all of you, be of one mind, sympathetic, loving toward one another, compassionate, humble. ⁹Do not return evil for evil, or insult for insult; but, on the contrary, a blessing, because to this you were called, that you might inherit a blessing.ᵐ ¹⁰For:

---

behavior of husbands and wives (1 Pt 3:1–7); mutual charity (1 Pt 3:8–12).

*[2:11] **Aliens and sojourners**: no longer signifying absence from one's native land (Gn 23:4), this image denotes rather their estrangement from the world during their earthly pilgrimage (see also 1 Pt 1:1, 17).

†[2:13–17] True Christian freedom is the result of being servants of God (1 Pt 2:16; see note on 1 Pt 2:18–23). It includes reverence for God, esteem for every individual, and committed love for fellow Christians (1 Pt 2:17). Although persecution may threaten, subjection to human government is urged (1 Pt 2:13, 17) and concern for the impact of Christians' conduct on those who are not Christians (1 Pt 2:12, 15).

‡[2:18–21] Most of the labor in the commercial cities of first-century Asia Minor was performed by a working class of slaves. The sense of freedom contained in the gospel undoubtedly caused great tension among Christian slaves: witness the special advice given concerning them here and in 1 Cor 7:21–24; Eph 6:5–8; Col 3:22–25; Phlm. The point made here does not have so much to do with the institution of slavery, which the author does not challenge, but with the nonviolent reaction (1 Pt 2:20) of slaves to unjust treatment. Their patient suffering is compared to that of Jesus (1 Pt 2:21), which won righteousness for all humanity.

§[2:21] **Suffered**: some ancient manuscripts and versions read "died" (cf. 1 Pt 3:18).

¶[2:22–25] After the quotation of Is 53:9b, the passage describes Jesus' passion with phrases concerning the Suffering Servant from Is 53:4–12, perhaps as employed in an early Christian confession of faith; cf. 1 Pt 1:18–21 and 1 Pt 3:18–22.

**[2:25] **The shepherd and guardian of your souls**: the familiar shepherd and flock figures express the care, vigilance, and love of God for his people in the Old Testament (Ps 23; Is 40:11; Jer 23:4–5; Ez 34:11–16) and of Jesus for all humanity in the New Testament (Mt 18:10–14; Lk 15:4–7; Jn 10:1–16; Heb 13:20).

††[3:1–6] The typical marital virtues of women of the ancient world, obedience, reverence, and chastity (1 Pt 3:1–2), are outlined here by the author, who gives them an entirely new motivation: Christian wives are to be virtuous so that they may be instrumental in the conversion of their husbands. In imitation of **holy women** in the past (1 Pt 3:5) they are to cultivate the interior life (1 Pt 3:4) instead of excessive concern with their appearance (1 Pt 3:3).

‡‡[3:7] Husbands who do not respect their wives will have as little success in prayer as those who, according to Paul, have no love: their prayers will be "a resounding gong or a clashing cymbal" (1 Cor 13:1). Consideration for others is shown as a prerequisite for effective prayer also in Mt 5:23–24; 1 Cor 11:20–22; Jas 4:3. After all, whatever the social position of women in the world and in the family, they are equal recipients of the gift of God's salvation. Paul is very clear on this point, too (see 1 Cor 11:11–12; Gal 3:28).

§§[3:8–12] For the proper ordering of Christian life in its various aspects as described in 1 Pt 2:11–3:9, there is promised the blessing expressed in Ps 34:13–17. In the Old Testament this refers to longevity and prosperity; here, it also refers to eternal life.

---

z. [2:11] Gal 5:24.   a. [2:13] Rom 13:1–7.   b. [2:16] Gal 5:13. c. [2:17] Prv 24:21; Mt 22:21.   d. [2:18] Eph 6:5.   e. [2:21] Mt 16:24. f. [2:22] Is 53:9.

g. [2:23] Mt 5:39.   h. [2:24] Is 53:4, 12 / Is 53:5.   i. [2:25] Is 53:6. j. [3:2] 1 Cor 7:12–16; Eph 5:22–24; Col 3:18; 1 Tm 2:9–15.   k. [3:3] 1 Tm 2:9–10.   l. [3:7] Eph 5:25–33; Col 3:19.   m. [3:9] Mt 5:44; Lk 6:28; Rom 12:14.

"Whoever would love life"
and see good days
must keep the tongue from evil
and the lips from speaking deceit,
[11] must turn from evil and do good,
seek peace and follow after it.
[12] For the eyes of the Lord are on the righteous
and his ears turned to their prayer,
but the face of the Lord is against evildoers."

**Christian Suffering.**[*] [13]Now who is going to harm you if you are enthusiastic for what is good? [14]But even if you should suffer because of righteousness, blessed are you. Do not be afraid or terrified with fear of them, [15]but sanctify Christ as Lord in your hearts. Always be ready to give an explanation to anyone who asks you for a reason for your hope,[o] [16]but do it with gentleness and reverence, keeping your conscience clear, so that, when you are maligned, those who defame your good conduct in Christ may themselves be put to shame. [17]For it is better to suffer for doing good, if that be the will of God, than for doing evil.

[18]For Christ also suffered[†] for sins once, the righteous for the sake of the unrighteous, that he might lead you to God. Put to death in the flesh, he was brought to life in the spirit.[p] [19]In it he also went to preach to the spirits in prison,[‡] [20]who had once been disobedient while God patiently waited in the days of Noah during the building of the ark, in which a few persons, eight in all, were saved through water.[q] [21]This prefigured baptism, which saves you now. It is not a removal of dirt from the body but an appeal to God[§] for a clear conscience, through the resurrection of Jesus Christ,[r] [22]who has gone into heaven and is at the right hand of God, with angels, authorities, and powers subject to him.[s]

**CHAPTER 4**

**Christian Restraint.**[¶] [1]Therefore, since Christ suffered in the flesh, arm yourselves also with the same attitude (for whoever suffers in the flesh has broken with sin), [2]so as not to spend what remains of one's life in the flesh on human desires, but on the will of God. [3]For the time that has passed is sufficient for doing what the Gentiles like to do: living in debauchery, evil desires, drunkenness, orgies, carousing, and wanton idolatry.[t] [4]They are surprised that you do not plunge into the same swamp of profligacy, and they vilify you; [5]but they will give an account to him who stands ready to judge the living and the dead.[u] [6]For this is why the gospel was preached even to the dead[**] that, though condemned in the flesh in human estimation, they might live in the spirit in the estimation of God.

**Christian Charity.**[††] [7]The end of all things is at hand. Therefore, be serious and sober for prayers. [8]Above all, let your love for one another be intense, because love covers a multitude of sins.[‡‡] [9]Be hospitable to one another without complaining.[w] [10]As each one has received a gift, use it to serve one another as good stewards of God's varied grace.[x] [11]Whoever preaches, let it be with the words of God; whoever serves, let it be with the strength that God supplies, so that in all things God may be glorified through Jesus Christ,[y] to whom belong glory and dominion forever and ever. Amen.[§§]

**IV. ADVICE TO THE PERSECUTED**

**Trial of Persecution.**[¶¶] [12]Beloved, do not be surprised that a trial by fire is occurring among you, as if something strange were happening to

---

*[3:13–22] This exposition, centering on 1 Pt 3:17, runs as follows: by his suffering and death Christ the righteous one saved the unrighteous (1 Pt 3:18); by his resurrection he received new life in the spirit, which he communicates to believers through the baptismal bath that cleanses their consciences from sin. As Noah's family was saved **through water**, so Christians are saved through the waters of baptism (1 Pt 3:19–22). Hence they need not share the fear of sinners; they should rather rejoice in suffering because of their hope in Christ. Thus their innocence disappoints their accusers (1 Pt 3:13–16; cf. Mt 10:28; Rom 8:35–39).

†[3:18] **Suffered**: very many ancient manuscripts and versions read "died." **Put to death in the flesh**: affirms that Jesus truly died as a human being. **Brought to life in the spirit**: that is, in the new and transformed existence freed from the limitations and weaknesses of natural human life (cf. 1 Cor 15:45).

‡[3:19] **The spirits in prison**: it is not clear just who these spirits are. They may be the spirits of the sinners who died in the flood, or angelic powers, hostile to God, who have been overcome by Christ (cf. 1 Pt 3:22; Gn 6:4; Enoch 6–36, especially 21:6; 2 Enoch 7:1–5).

§[3:21] **Appeal to God**: this could also be translated "pledge," that is, a promise on the part of Christians to live with a good conscience before God, or a pledge from God of forgiveness and therefore a good conscience for us.

¶[4:1–6] Willingness to suffer with Christ equips the Christian with the power to conquer sin (1 Pt 4:1). Christ is here portrayed as the judge to whom those guilty of pagan vices must render an account (1 Pt 4:5; cf. Jn 5:22–27; Acts 10:42; 2 Tm 4:1).

**[4:6] **The dead**: these may be the sinners of the flood generation who possibly referred to in 1 Pt 3:19. But many scholars think that there is no connection between these two verses, and that the **dead** here are Christians who have died since hearing the preaching of the gospel.

††[4:7–11] The inner life of the eschatological community is outlined as the **end** (the parousia of Christ) and the judgment draws near in terms of seriousness, sobriety, prayer, and love expressed through hospitality and the use of one's gifts for the glory of God and of Christ.

‡‡[4:8] **Love covers a multitude of sins**: a maxim based on Prv 10:12; see also Ps 32:1; Jas 5:20.

§§[4:11] Some scholars feel that this doxology concludes the part of the homily addressed specifically to the newly baptized, begun in 1 Pt 1:3; others that it concludes a baptismal liturgy. Such doxologies do occur within a New Testament letter, e.g., Rom 9:5. Some propose that 1 Pt 4:11 was an alternate ending, with 1 Pt 4:12–5:14 being read in places where persecution was more pressing. But such doxologies usually do not occur at the end of letters (the only examples are 2 Pt 3:18, Jude 25, and Rom 16:27, the last probably a liturgical insertion).

¶¶[4:12–19] The suffering to which the author has already frequently referred is presented in more severe terms. This has led some scholars to see these verses as referring to an actual persecution. Others see the heightening of the language

---

n. [3:10–12] Ps 34:13–17.   o. [3:15] Is 8:12.   p. [3:18] 1 Cor 15:45.
q. [3:20] Gn 7:7, 17; 2 Pt 2:5.   r. [3:21] Eph 5:26; Heb 10:22.
s. [3:22] Eph 1:20–21.

t. [4:3] Eph 2:2–3; 4:17–19; Col 3:7; Ti 3:3.   u. [4:5] Acts 10:42; 2 Tm 4:1.   v. [4:8] Prv 10:12; Jas 5:20.   w. [4:9] Heb 13:2.   x. [4:10] Rom 12:6–8; 1 Cor 12:4–11.   y. [4:11] 1 Cor 10:31.

you.[z] [13]But rejoice to the extent that you share in the sufferings of Christ, so that when his glory is revealed you may also rejoice exultantly.[a] [14]If you are insulted for the name of Christ, blessed are you, for the Spirit of glory and of God rests upon you.[b] [15]But let no one among you be made to suffer as a murderer, a thief, an evildoer, or as an intriguer. [16]But whoever is made to suffer as a Christian should not be ashamed but glorify God because of the name. [17]For it is time for the judgment to begin with the household of God; if it begins with us, how will it end for those who fail to obey the gospel of God?[c]

[18] "And if the righteous one is barely saved,
where will the godless and the
sinner appear?"[d]

[19]As a result, those who suffer in accord with God's will hand their souls over to a faithful creator as they do good.

### CHAPTER 5

**Advice to Presbyters.**[*] [1]So I exhort the presbyters[†] among you, as a fellow presbyter and witness to the sufferings of Christ and one who has a share in the glory to be revealed. [2]Tend the flock of God in your midst, [overseeing] not by constraint but willingly, as God would have it, not for shameful profit but eagerly.[e] [3]Do not lord it over those assigned to you, but be examples to the flock. [4]And when the chief Shepherd is revealed, you will receive the unfading crown of glory.[‡]

**Advice to the Community.**[§] [5]Likewise, you younger members,[¶] be subject to the presbyters.

---

as only a rhetorical device used at the end of the letter to emphasize the suffering motif.

*[5:1–4] In imitation of Christ, the chief shepherd, those entrusted with a pastoral office are to tend the flock by their care and example.

†[5:1] **Presbyters**: the officially appointed leaders and teachers of the Christian community (cf. 1 Tm 5:17–18; Ti 1:5–8; Jas 5:14).

‡[5:4] See note on 1 Pt 2:25.

§[5:5–11] The community is to be subject to the presbyters and to show humility toward one another and trust in God's love and care (1 Pt 5:5–7). With sobriety, alertness, and steadfast faith they must resist the evil one; their sufferings are shared with Christians everywhere (1 Pt 5:8–9). They will be strengthened and called to eternal glory (1 Pt 5:10–11).

¶[5:5] **Younger members**: this may be a designation for office-holders of lesser rank.

---

z. [4:12] 1:6–7; 3:14, 17.   a. [4:13] Rom 5:3–5; 8:17; 2 Tm 2:12. b. [4:14] Acts 5:41 / Is 11:2.   c. [4:17] Lk 23:31; 2 Thes 1:8. d. [4:18] Prv 11:31 LXX.   e. [5:2] Acts 20:28; Ti 1:7.   f. [5:4] Wis 5:15–16; 1 Cor 9:25; 2 Tm 4:8; Jas 1:12.

---

And all of you, clothe yourselves with humility in your dealings with one another, for:

"God opposes the proud
but bestows favor on the humble."[g]

[6]So humble yourselves under the mighty hand of God, that he may exalt you in due time.[h] [7]Cast all your worries upon him because he cares for you.[i]

[8]Be sober and vigilant. Your opponent the devil is prowling around like a roaring lion looking for [someone] to devour.[j] [9]Resist him, steadfast in faith, knowing that your fellow believers throughout the world undergo the same sufferings. [10]The God of all grace who called you to his eternal glory through Christ [Jesus] will himself restore, confirm, strengthen, and establish you after you have suffered a little.[k] [11]To him be dominion forever. Amen.

### V. CONCLUSION

[12]I write you this briefly through Silvanus,[**] whom I consider a faithful brother, exhorting you and testifying that this is the true grace of God. Remain firm in it. [13]The chosen one[††] at Babylon sends you greeting, as does Mark, my son. [14]Greet one another with a loving kiss. Peace to all of you who are in Christ.[l]

---

**[5:12] **Silvanus**: the companion of Paul (see 2 Cor 1:19; 1 Thes 1:1; 2 Thes 1:1). Jews and Jewish Christians, like Paul, often had a Hebrew name (Saoul, Silas) and a Greek or Latin name (Paul, Silvanus). On Silvanus's possible role as amanuensis, see Introduction.

††[5:13] **The chosen one**: feminine, referring to the Christian community (*ekklēsia*) at **Babylon**, the code name for Rome in Rev 14:8; 17:5; 18:2. **Mark, my son**: traditionally a prominent disciple of Peter and co-worker at the church in Rome, perhaps the John Mark referred to in Acts 12:12, 25; 13:5, 13; and in Acts 15:37–39, a companion of Barnabas. Perhaps this is the same Mark mentioned as Barnabas's cousin in Col 4:10, a co-worker with Paul in Phlm 24 (see also 2 Tm 4:11).

---

g. [5:5] Prv 3:34.   h. [5:6] Jb 22:29; Jas 4:10.   i. [5:7] Ps 55:23; Mt 6:25–33; Lk 12:22–31; Phil 4:6.   j. [5:8] 1 Thes 5:6.   k. [5:10] Rom 8:18; 2 Cor 4:17.   l. [5:14] Rom 16:16; 1 Cor 16:20; 2 Cor 13:12.

# THE SECOND LETTER OF
# PETER

This letter can be appreciated both for its positive teachings and for its earnest warnings. It seeks to strengthen readers in faith (2 Pt 1:1), hope for the future (2 Pt 3:1–10), knowledge (2 Pt 1:2, 6, 8), love (2 Pt 1:7), and other virtues (2 Pt 1:5–6). This aim is carried out especially by warning against false teachers, the condemnation of whom occupies the long central section of the letter (2 Pt 2:1–22). A particular crisis is the claim by "scoffers" that there will be no second coming of Jesus, a doctrine that the author vigorously affirms (2 Pt 3:1–10). The concept of God's "promises" is particularly precious in the theology of 2 Peter (2 Pt 1:4; 3:4, 9, 13). Closing comments at 2 Pt 3:17–18 well sum up the twin concerns: that you not "be led into" error and "fall" but instead "grow in grace" and "knowledge" of Jesus Christ.

Second Peter is clearly structured in its presentation of these points. It reminds its readers of the divine authenticity of Christ's teaching (2 Pt 1:3–4), continues with reflections on Christian conduct (2 Pt 1:5–15), then returns to the exalted dignity of Jesus by incorporating into the text the apostolic witness to his transfiguration (2 Pt 1:16–18). It takes up the question of the interpretation of scripture by pointing out that it is possible to misunderstand the sacred writings (2 Pt 1:19–21) and that divine punishment will overtake false teachers (2 Pt 2:1–22). It proclaims that the parousia is the teaching of the Lord and of the apostles and is therefore an eventual certainty (2 Pt 3:1–13). At the same time, it warns that the meaning of Paul's writings on this question should not be distorted (2 Pt 3:14–18).

In both content and style this letter is very different from 1 Peter, which immediately precedes it in the canon. The opening verse attributes it to "Symeon Peter, a slave and apostle of Jesus Christ." Moreover, the author in 2 Pt 3:1 calls his work a "second letter," referring probably to 1 Peter as his first, and in 2 Pt 1:18 counts himself among those present at the transfiguration of Jesus.

Nevertheless, acceptance of 2 Peter into the New Testament canon met with great resistance in the early church. The oldest certain reference to it comes from Origen in the early third century. While he himself accepted both Petrine letters as canonical, he testifies that others rejected 2 Peter. As late as the fifth century some local churches still excluded it from the canon, but eventually it was universally adopted. The principal reason for the long delay was the persistent doubt that the letter stemmed from the apostle Peter.

Among modern scholars there is wide agreement that 2 Peter is a pseudonymous work, i.e., one written by a later author who attributed it to Peter according to a literary convention popular at the time. It gives the impression of being more remote in time from the apostolic period than 1 Peter; indeed, many think it is the latest work in the New Testament and assign it to the first or even the second quarter of the second century.

The principal reasons for this view are the following. The author refers to the apostles and "our ancestors" as belonging to a previous generation, now dead (2 Pt 3:2–4). A collection of Paul's letters exists and appears to be well known, but disputes have arisen about the interpretation of them (2 Pt 3:14–16). The passage about false teachers (2 Pt 2:1–18) contains a number of literary contacts with Jude 4–16, and it is generally agreed that 2 Peter depends upon Jude, not vice versa. Finally, the principal problem exercising the author is the false teaching of "scoffers" who have concluded from the delay of the parousia that the Lord is not going to return. This could scarcely have been an issue during the lifetime of Simon Peter.

The Christians to whom the letter is addressed are not identified, though it may be the intent of 2 Pt 3:1 to identify them with the churches of Asia Minor to which 1 Peter was sent. Except for the epistolary greeting in 2 Pt 1:1–2, 2 Peter does not have the features of a genuine letter at all, but is rather a general exhortation cast in the form of a letter. The author must have been a Jewish Christian of the dispersion for, while his Jewish heritage is evident in various features of his thought and style, he writes in the rather stilted literary Greek of the Hellenistic period. He appeals to tradition against the twin threat of doctrinal error and moral laxity, which appear to reflect an early stage of what later developed into full-blown gnosticism. Thus he forms a link between the apostolic period and the church of subsequent ages.

The principal divisions of the Second Letter of Peter are the following:

I. Address (1:1–2)
II. Exhortation to Christian Virtue (1:3–21)
III. Condemnation of the False Teachers (2:1–22)
IV. The Delay of the Second Coming (3:1–16)
V. Final Exhortation and Doxology (3:17–18)

## I. ADDRESS

### CHAPTER 1

**Greeting.** [1]"Symeon Peter, a slave and apostle of Jesus Christ, to those who have received a faith of equal value to ours through the righteousness of our God and savior Jesus Christ: [2]may grace and peace be yours in abundance through knowledge[†] of God and of Jesus our Lord.

## II. EXHORTATION TO CHRISTIAN VIRTUE

**The Power of God's Promise.**[‡] [3]His divine power has bestowed on us everything that makes for life and devotion, through the knowledge of him[a] who called us by his own glory and power.[§] [4]Through these, he has bestowed on us the precious and very great promises, so that through them you may come to share in the divine nature, after escaping from the corruption that is in the world because of evil desire.[b] [5]For this

very reason, make every effort to supplement your faith with virtue, virtue with knowledge,[c] [6]knowledge with self-control, self-control with endurance, endurance with devotion, [7]devotion with mutual affection, mutual affection with love. [8]If these are yours and increase in abundance, they will keep you from being idle or unfruitful in the knowledge of our Lord Jesus Christ. [9d]Anyone who lacks them is blind and shortsighted, forgetful of the cleansing of his past sins. [10**]Therefore, brothers, be all the more eager to make your call and election firm, for, in doing so, you will never stumble. [11]For, in this way, entry into the eternal kingdom of our Lord and savior Jesus Christ will be richly provided for you.

**Apostolic Witness.** [12††]Therefore, I will always remind you of these things, even though you already know them and are established in the truth you have. [13]I think it right, as long as I am in this "tent,"[‡‡] to stir you up by a reminder, [14]since I know that I will soon have to put it aside, as indeed our Lord Jesus Christ has shown me.[e] [15]I shall also make every effort to enable you always to remember these things after my departure.

[16]We did not follow cleverly devised myths when we made known to you the power and coming[§§] of our Lord Jesus Christ, but we had

---

*[1:1] **Symeon Peter**: on the authorship of 2 Peter, see Introduction; on the spelling here of the Hebrew name *Simʿōn*, cf. Acts 15:14. The greeting is especially similar to those in 1 Peter and Jude. The words translated **our God and savior Jesus Christ** could also be rendered "our God and the savior Jesus Christ"; cf. 2 Pt 1:11; 2:20; 3:2, 18.

†[1:2] **Knowledge**: a key term in the letter (2 Pt 1:3, 8; 2:20; 3:18), perhaps used as a Christian emphasis against gnostic claims.

‡[1:3–4] Christian life in its fullness is a gift of divine power effecting a knowledge of Christ and the bestowal of divine promises (2 Pt 3:4, 9). **To share in the divine nature**, escaping from a corrupt world, is a thought found elsewhere in the Bible but expressed only here in such Hellenistic terms, since it is said to be accomplished through knowledge (2 Pt 1:3); cf. 2 Pt 1:2; 2:20; but see also Jn 15:4; 17:22–23; Rom 8:14–17; Heb 3:14; 1 Jn 1:3; 3:2.

§[1:3] **By his own glory and power**: the most ancient papyrus and the best codex read "through glory and power."

¶[1:5–9] Note the climactic gradation of qualities (2 Pt 1:5–7), beginning with faith and leading to the fullness of Christian life, which is love; cf. Rom 5:3–4; Gal 5:6, 22 for a similar series of "virtues," though the program and sense here are different than in Paul. The fruit of these is knowledge of Christ (2 Pt 1:8) referred to in 2 Pt 1:3; their absence is spiritual blindness (2 Pt 1:9).

**[1:10–11] Perseverance in the Christian vocation is the best preventative against losing it and the safest provision for attaining its goal, the kingdom. **Kingdom of . . . Christ**, instead of "God," is unusual; cf. Col 1:13 and Mt 13:41, as well as the **righteousness of . . . Christ** (2 Pt 1:1).

††[1:12–19] The purpose in writing is to call to mind the apostle's witness to the truth, even as he faces the end of his life (2 Pt 1:12–15), his eyewitness testimony to Christ (1 Pt 1:16–18), and the true prophetic message (2 Pt 1:19) through the Spirit in scripture (2 Pt 1:20–21), in contrast to what false teachers are setting forth (2 Pt 2).

‡‡[1:13] **Tent**: a biblical image for transitory human life (Is 38:12), here combined with a verb that suggests not folding or packing up a tent but its being discarded in death (cf. 2 Cor 5:1–4).

§§[1:16] **Coming**: in Greek *parousia*, used at 2 Pt 3:4, 12 of the second coming of Christ. The word was used in the

---

a. [1:3] 2 Cor 4:6; 1 Pt 2:9.   b. [1:4] 2 Cor 7:1; 1 Jn 2:15.

c. [1:5–7] Gal 5:22–23.   d. [1:9] 1 Jn 2:9, 11.   e. [1:14] Is 38:12; Jn 21:18–19.

been eyewitnesses of his majesty.*f* 17For he received honor and glory from God the Father* when that unique declaration came to him from the majestic glory, "This is my Son, my beloved, with whom I am well pleased."*g* 18We† ourselves heard this voice come from heaven while we were with him on the holy mountain. 19h*Moreover, we possess the prophetic message that is altogether reliable. You will do well to be attentive to it, as to a lamp shining in a dark place, until day dawns and the morning star rises in your hearts. 20‡Know this first of all, that there is no prophecy of scripture that is a matter of personal interpretation, 21for no prophecy ever came through human will; but rather human beings moved by the holy Spirit spoke under the influence of God.

## III. CONDEMNATION OF THE FALSE TEACHERS

### CHAPTER 2

**False Teachers.**§ 1There were also false prophets among the people, just as there will be false teachers among you, who will introduce destructive heresies and even deny the Master who ransomed them, bringing swift destruction on themselves.*i* 2Many will follow their licentious ways, and because of them the way of truth will be reviled.*j* 3In their greed they will exploit you with fabrications, but from of old their condemnation has not been idle and their destruction does not sleep.*k*

**Lessons from the Past.** 4For if God did not spare the angels when they sinned, but condemned them to the chains of Tartarus** and handed them over to be kept for judgment;*l* 5††and if he did not spare the ancient world, even though he preserved Noah, a herald of righteousness, together with seven others, when he brought a flood upon the godless world;*m* 6and if he condemned the cities of Sodom and Gomorrah [to destruction], reducing them to ashes, making them an example for the godless [people] of what is coming;*n* 7and if he rescued Lot, a righteous man oppressed by the licentious conduct of unprincipled people 8(for day after day that righteous man living among them was tormented in his righteous soul at the lawless deeds that he saw and heard), 9then the Lord knows how to rescue the devout from trial and to keep the unrighteous under punishment for the day of judgment,*o* 10and especially those who follow the flesh with its depraved desire and show contempt for lordship.*p*

**False Teachers Denounced.**‡‡ Bold and arrogant, they are not afraid to revile glorious beings,§§ 11¶¶whereas angels,*q* despite their superior strength and power, do not bring a reviling judgment against them from the Lord. 12But these people, like irrational animals born by nature for capture and destruction, revile things that they do not understand, and in their destruction they will also be destroyed,*r* 13suffering wrong*** as payment

§ [2:4–6] The false teachers will be punished just as surely and as severely as were the fallen **angels** (2 Pt 2:4; cf. Jude 6; Gn 6:1–4), the sinners of Noah's day (2 Pt 2:5; Gn 7:21–23), and the inhabitants of the cities of the Plain (2 Pt 2:6; Jude 7; Gn 19:25). Whereas there are three examples in Jude 5–7 (Exodus and wilderness; rebellious angels; Sodom and Gomorrah), 2 Peter omitted the first of these, has inserted a new illustration about Noah (2 Pt 2:5) between Jude's second and third examples, and listed the resulting three examples in their Old Testament order (Gn 6; 7; 19).

** [2:4] **Chains of Tartarus**: cf. Jude 6; some manuscripts in 2 Peter read "pits of Tartarus." **Tartarus**: a term borrowed from Greek mythology to indicate the infernal regions.

†† [2:5–10a] Although God did not spare the sinful, he kept and saved the righteous, such as **Noah** (2 Pt 2:5) and **Lot** (2 Pt 2:7), and **he knows how to rescue the devout** (2 Pt 2:9), who are contrasted with the false teachers of the author's day. On Noah, cf. Gn 5:32–9:29, especially 7:1. On Lot, cf. Gn 13 and 19.

‡‡ [2:10b–22] Some take 2 Pt 2:10b, 11 with the preceding paragraph. Others begin the new paragraph with 2 Pt 2:10a, supplying from 2 Pt 2:9 **The Lord knows how . . . to keep . . . under punishment**, with reference to God and probably specifically Christ (2 Pt 2:1). The conduct of the false teachers is described and condemned in language similar to that of Jude 8–16. This arrogance knows no bounds; animallike, they are due to be caught and destroyed. They seduce even those who have knowledge of Christ (2 Pt 2:20).

§§ [2:11] **Glorious beings**: literally, "glories"; cf. Jude 8. While some think that illustrious personages are meant or even political officials behind whom (fallen) angels stand, it is more likely that the reference is to glorious angelic beings (cf. Jude 8).

¶¶ [2:11] **From the Lord**: some manuscripts read "before the Lord"; cf. Jude 9.

*** [2:13] **Suffering wrong**: some manuscripts read "receiving a reward." **In their deceits**: some manuscripts read "in their love feasts" (Jude 12).

extrabiblical writings for the visitation of someone in authority; in Greek cult and Hellenistic Judaism it was used for the manifestation of the divine presence. That the apostles **made known** has been interpreted to refer to Jesus' transfiguration (2 Pt 1:17) or to his entire first coming or to his future coming in power (2 Pt 3).

* [1:17] The author assures the readers of the reliability of the apostolic message (including Jesus' power, glory, and coming; cf. note on 2 Pt 1:16) by appeal to the transfiguration of Jesus in glory (cf. Mt 17:1–8 and parallels) and by appeal to the prophetic message (2 Pt 1:19; perhaps Nm 24:17). Here, as elsewhere, the New Testament insists on continued reminders as necessary to preserve the historical facts about Jesus and the truths of the faith; cf. 2 Pt 3:1–2; 1 Cor 11:2; 15:1–3. **My Son, my beloved**: or, "my beloved Son."

† [1:18] **We**: at Jesus' transfiguration, referring to Peter, James, and John (Mt 17:1).

‡ [1:20–21] Often cited, along with 2 Tm 3:16, on the "inspiration" of scripture or against private interpretation, these verses in context are directed against the false teachers of 2 Pt 2 and clever tales (2 Pt 1:16). The prophetic word in scripture comes admittedly through **human beings** (2 Pt 1:21), but **moved by the holy Spirit**, not from their own interpretation, and is a matter of what the author and Spirit intended, not the **personal interpretation** of false teachers. Instead of **under the influence of God**, some manuscripts read "holy ones of God."

§ [2:1–3] The pattern of **false prophets** among the Old Testament people of God will recur through **false teachers** in the church. Such destructive opinions of heretical sects bring loss of faith in Christ, contempt for the way of salvation (cf. 2 Pt 2:21), and immorality.

f. [1:16] Lk 9:28–36; Jn 1:14.   g. [1:17] Ps 2:7; Mt 17:4–6.   h. [1:19] Lk 1:78–79; Rev 2:28.   i. [2:1] Mt 24:11, 24; 1 Tm 4:1; Jude 4.   j. [2:2] Is 52:5.   k. [2:3] Rom 16:18.

l. [2:4] Jude 6.   m. [2:5] Gn 8:15–19; Heb 11:7.   n. [2:6] Gn 19:24–25; Jude 7.   o. [2:9] 1 Cor 10:13; Rev 3:10.   p. [2:10] Jude 8.   q. [2:11] Jude 9.   r. [2:12] Ps 49:13–15; Jude 10.

for wrongdoing. Thinking daytime revelry a delight, they are stains and defilements as they revel in their deceits while carousing with you.[s] [14]Their eyes are full of adultery and insatiable for sin. They seduce unstable people, and their hearts are trained in greed. Accursed children! [15]Abandoning the straight road, they have gone astray, following the road of Balaam, the son of Bosor,[*] who loved payment for wrongdoing,[t] [16]but he received a rebuke for his own crime: a mute beast spoke with a human voice and restrained the prophet's madness.[u]

[17]These people are waterless springs and mists driven by a gale; for them the gloom of darkness has been reserved.[v] [18]For, talking empty bombast, they seduce with licentious desires of the flesh those who have barely escaped[†] from people who live in error.[w] [19]They promise them freedom, though they themselves are slaves of corruption, for a person is a slave of whatever overcomes him.[x] [20]For if they, having escaped the defilements of the world through the knowledge of [our] Lord and savior Jesus Christ, again become entangled and overcome by them, their last condition is worse than their first.[y] [21]For it would have been better for them not to have known the way of righteousness than after knowing it to turn back from the holy commandment handed down[‡] to them.[z] [22]§What is expressed in the true proverb has happened to them,[a] "The dog returns to its own vomit," and "A bathed sow returns to wallowing in the mire."

## IV. THE DELAY OF THE SECOND COMING

### CHAPTER 3

**Denial of the Parousia.** [1]§This is now, beloved, the second letter I am writing to you; through them by way of reminder I am trying to stir up your sincere disposition, [2]to recall the words previously spoken by the holy prophets and the commandment of the Lord and savior through your apostles.[b] [3]Know this first of all, that in the last days scoffers[**] will come [to] scoff, living according to their own desires[c] [4]and saying, "Where is the promise of his coming?[††] From the time when our ancestors fell asleep, everything has remained as it was from the beginning of creation."[d] [5]They deliberately ignore the fact that the heavens existed of old and earth was formed out of water and through water[‡‡] by the word of God;[e] [6]through these the world that then existed was destroyed,[f] deluged with water.[§§] [7]The present heavens and earth have been reserved by the same word for fire, kept for the day of judgment and of destruction of the godless.[g]

[8]¶But do not ignore this one fact, beloved, that with the Lord one day is like a thousand years[***] and a thousand years like one day.[h] [9]The Lord does not delay his promise, as some regard "delay," but he is patient with you, not wishing that any should perish but that all should come to repentance.[i] [10]But the day of the Lord will come like a thief,[†††] and then the heavens will pass away with a mighty roar and the elements will be dissolved by fire, and the earth and everything done on it will be found out.[j]

**Exhortation to Preparedness.**[‡‡‡] [11]Since everything is to be dissolved in this way, what sort

---

*[2:15] **Balaam, the son of Bosor**: in Nm 22:5, Balaam is said to be the son of Beor, and it is this name that turns up in a few ancient Greek manuscripts by way of "correction" of the text. Balaam is not portrayed in such a bad light in Nm 22. His evil reputation and his **madness** (2 Pt 2:16), and possibly his surname Bosor, may have come from a Jewish tradition about him in the first/second century, of which we no longer have any knowledge.

†[2:18] **Barely escaped**: some manuscripts read "really escaped."

‡[2:21] **Commandment handed down**: cf. 2 Pt 3:2 and Jude 3.

§[2:22] The second proverb is of unknown origin, while the first appears in Prv 26:11.

¶[3:1–4] The false teachers not only flout Christian morality (cf. Jude 8–19); they also deny the second coming of Christ and the judgment (2 Pt 3:4; cf. 2 Pt 3:7). They seek to justify their licentiousness by arguing that the promised return of Christ has not been realized and the world is the same, no better than it was before (2 Pt 3:3–4). The author wishes to strengthen the faithful against such errors by reminding them in this **second letter** of the instruction in 1 Peter and the teaching of the **prophets** and of Christ, conveyed through

the **apostles** (2 Pt 3:1–2; cf. Jude 17); cf. 1 Pt 1:10–12, 16–21, especially 16–21; Eph 2:20.

**[3:3] **Scoffers**: cf. Jude 18, where, however, only the passions of the scoffers are mentioned, not a denial on their part of Jesus' parousia.

††[3:4–7] The false teachers tried to justify their immorality by pointing out that the promised **coming** (parousia) of the Lord has not yet occurred, even though early Christians expected it in their day. They thus insinuate that God is not guiding the world's history anymore, since nothing has changed and the first generation of Christians, **our ancestors** (2 Pt 3:4), has all died by this time. The author replies that, just as God destroyed the earth by water in the flood (2 Pt 3:5–6, cf. 2 Pt 2:5), so he will destroy it along with the false teachers on judgment day (2 Pt 3:7). **The word of God**, which called the world into being (Gn 1; Ps 33:6) and **destroyed** it by the waters of a flood, will destroy it again by fire on **the day of judgment** (2 Pt 3:5–7).

‡‡[3:5] **Formed out of water and through water**: Gn 1:2, 6–8 is reflected as well as Greek views that water was the basic element from which all is derived.

§§[3:6] **Destroyed, deluged with water**: cf. 2 Pt 2:5; Gn 7:11–8:2.

¶¶[3:8–10] The scoffers' objection (2 Pt 3:4) is refuted also by showing that **delay** of the Lord's second coming is not a failure to fulfill his word but rather a sign of his patience: God is giving time for repentance before the final judgment (cf. Wis 11:23–26; Ez 18:23; 33:11).

***[3:8] Cf. Ps 90:4.

†††[3:10] **Like a thief**: Mt 24:43; 1 Thes 5:2; Rev 3:3. **Will be found out**: cf. 1 Cor 3:13–15. Some few versions read, as the sense may demand, "will not be found out"; many manuscripts read "will be burned up"; there are further variants in other manuscripts, versions, and Fathers. Total destruction is assumed (2 Pt 3:11).

‡‡‡[3:11–16] The second coming of Christ and the judgment of the world are the doctrinal bases for the moral

---

s. [2:13] Jude 12.   t. [2:15] Nm 31:16; Jude 11.   u. [2:16] Nm 22:28–33.   v. [2:17] Jude 12–13.   w. [2:18] Jude 16.   x. [2:19] Jn 8:34; Rom 6:16–17.   y. [2:20] Mt 12:45.   z. [2:21] Ez 3:20.   a. [2:22] Prv 26:11.

b. [3:2] Jude 17.   c. [3:3] 1 Tm 4:1; 2 Tm 3:1; Jude 18.   d. [3:4] Is 5:19.   e. [3:5] Gn 1:2, 6, 8; Ps 24:2.   f. [3:6] Gn 7:21.   g. [3:7] Is 51:6; Mt 3:12.   h. [3:8] Ps 90:4.   i. [3:9] Ez 18:23; 1 Tm 2:4.   j. [3:10] Is 66:15–16; Mt 24:29.

of persons ought [you] to be, conducting yourselves in holiness and devotion,[k] [12]waiting for and hastening the coming of the day of God,[l] because of which the heavens will be dissolved in flames and the elements melted by fire. [13]But according to his promise we await new heavens and a new earth[†] in which righteousness dwells.[m]

[14]Therefore, beloved, since you await these things, be eager to be found without spot or blemish before him, at peace. [15]And consider the patience of our Lord as salvation, as our beloved brother Paul, according to the wisdom

given to him, also wrote to you,[n] [16]speaking of these things[‡] as he does in all his letters. In them there are some things hard to understand that the ignorant and unstable distort to their own destruction, just as they do the other scriptures.

## V. FINAL EXHORTATION AND DOXOLOGY[§]

[17]Therefore, beloved, since you are forewarned, be on your guard not to be led into the error of the unprincipled and to fall from your own stability.[o] [18]But grow in grace and in the knowledge of our Lord and savior Jesus Christ. To him be glory now and to the day of eternity. [Amen.][p]

---

exhortation to readiness through vigilance and a virtuous life; cf. Mt 24:42, 50–51; Lk 12:40; 1 Thes 5:1–11; Jude 20–21.

*[3:12] **Flames . . . fire**: although this is the only New Testament passage about a final conflagration, the idea was common in apocalyptic and Greco-Roman thought. **Hastening**: eschatology is here used to motivate ethics (2 Pt 3:11), as elsewhere in the New Testament. Jewish sources and Acts 3:19–20 assume that proper ethical conduct can help bring the promised day of the Lord; cf. 2 Pt 3:9. Some render the phrase, however, "desiring it earnestly."

†[3:13] **New heavens and a new earth**: cf. Is 65:17; 66:22. The divine promises will be fulfilled after the day of judgment will have passed. The universe will be transformed by the reign of God's **righteousness** or justice; cf. Is 65:17–18; Acts 3:21; Rom 8:18–25; Rev 21:1.

‡[3:16] **These things**: the teachings of this letter find parallels in Paul, e.g., God's will to save (Rom 2:4; 9:22–23; 1 Cor 1:7–8), the coming of Christ (1 Thes 4:16–17; 1 Cor 15:23–52), and preparedness for the judgment (Col 1:22–23; Eph 1:4–14; 4:30; 5:5–14). **Other scriptures**: used to guide the faith and life of the Christian community. The letters of Paul are thus here placed on the same level as books of the Old Testament. Possibly other New Testament writings could also be included.

§[3:17–18] To avoid the dangers **of error** and loss of **stability**, Christians are **forewarned** to be **on guard** and to **grow in grace and knowledge** (2 Pt 1:2) of Christ. The doxology (2 Pt 3:18) recalls 1 Pt 4:11. Some manuscripts add **Amen**.

---

k. [3:11] Acts 3:19–21.   l. [3:12] Is 34:4; Heb 10:27.   m. [3:13] Is 65:17; 66:22; Rom 8:21; Rev 21:1, 27.

n. [3:15] Rom 8:19; Jude 24.   o. [3:17] Mk 13:5; Heb 2:1.   p. [3:18] Rom 16:27.

# THE FIRST LETTER OF
# JOHN

Early Christian tradition identified this work as a letter of John the apostle. Because of its resemblance to the fourth gospel in style, vocabulary, and ideas, it is generally agreed that both works are the product of the same school of Johannine Christianity. The terminology and the presence or absence of certain theological ideas in 1 John suggest that it was written after the gospel; it may have been composed as a short treatise on ideas that were developed more fully in the fourth gospel. To others, the evidence suggests that 1 John was written after the fourth gospel as part of a debate on the proper interpretation of that gospel. Whatever its relation to the gospel, 1 John may be dated toward the end of the first century. Unlike 2 and 3 John, it lacks in form the salutation and epistolary conclusion of a letter. These features, its prologue, and its emphasis on doctrinal teaching make it more akin to a theological treatise than to most other New Testament letters.

The purpose of the letter is to combat certain false ideas, especially about Jesus, and to deepen the spiritual and social awareness of the Christian community (1 Jn 3:17). Some former members (1 Jn 2:19) of the community refused to acknowledge Jesus as the Christ (1 Jn 2:22) and denied that he was a true man (1 Jn 4:2). The specific heresy described in this letter cannot be identified exactly, but it is a form of docetism or gnosticism; the former doctrine denied the humanity of Christ to insure that his divinity was untainted, and the latter viewed the appearance of Christ as a mere stepping-stone to higher knowledge of God. These theological errors are rejected by an appeal to the reality and continuity of the apostolic witness to Jesus. The author affirms that authentic Christian love, ethics, and faith take place only within the historical revelation and sacrifice of Jesus Christ. The fullness of Christian life as fellowship with the Father must be based on true belief and result in charitable living; knowledge of God and love for one another are inseparable, and error in one area inevitably affects the other. Although the author recognizes that Christian doctrine presents intangible mysteries of faith about Christ, he insists that the concrete Christian life brings to light the deeper realities of the gospel.

The structure and language of the letter are straightforward yet repetitious. The author sets forth the striking contrasts between light and darkness, Christians and the world, and truth and error to illustrate the threats and responsibilities of Christian life. The result is not one of theological argument but one of intense religious conviction expressed in simple truths. The letter is of particular value for its declaration of the humanity and divinity of Christ as an apostolic teaching and for its development of the intrinsic connection between Christian moral conduct and Christian doctrine.

The principal divisions of the First Letter of John are the following:

I. Prologue (1:1–4)
II. God as Light (1:5–3:10)
III. Love for One Another (3:11–5:12)
IV. Epilogue (5:13–21)

## I. PROLOGUE

## CHAPTER 1
### The Word of Life*

1 What was from the beginning,
    what we have heard,
    what we have seen with our eyes,
    what we looked upon
    and touched with our hands
    concerns the Word of life—*a*

2 for the life was made visible;
    we have seen it and testify to it
    and proclaim to you the eternal life
    that was with the Father and was
        made visible to us—*b*

3 what we have seen and heard
    we proclaim now to you,
    so that you too may have fellowship
        with us;
    for our fellowship is with the Father
    and with his Son, Jesus Christ.*c*

4 We are writing this so that our joy may be
    complete.*d*

## II. GOD AS LIGHT

**God Is Light.** 5Now this is the message that we
have heard from him and proclaim to you: God
is light,† and in him there is no darkness at all.
6If we say, "We have fellowship with him," while
we continue to walk in darkness, we lie and do
not act in truth.*e* 7But if we walk in the light as he
is in the light, then we have fellowship with one
another, and the blood of his Son Jesus cleanses
us from all sin.*f* 8If we say, "We are without sin,"
we deceive ourselves,‡ and the truth is not in
us.*g* 9If we acknowledge our sins, he is faithful
and just and will forgive our sins and cleanse us
from every wrongdoing.*h* 10If we say, "We have

not sinned," we make him a liar, and his word
is not in us.*i*

## CHAPTER 2
**Christ and His Commandments.** 1My children,§
I am writing this to you so that you may not commit sin. But if anyone does sin, we have an Advocate with the Father, Jesus Christ the righteous
one.*j* 2He is expiation for our sins, and not for our
sins only but for those of the whole world.*k* 3The
way we may be sure¶ that we know him is to keep
his commandments.*l* 4Whoever says, "I know
him," but does not keep his commandments is
a liar, and the truth is not in him.*m* 5But whoever
keeps his word, the love of God is truly perfected
in him. This is the way we may know that we are
in union with him:*n* 6whoever claims to abide in
him ought to live [just] as he lived.
**The New Commandment.**** 7Beloved, I am writing no new commandment to you but an old
commandment that you had from the beginning. The old commandment is the word that
you have heard.*o* 8And yet I do write a new commandment to you, which holds true in him and
among you,†† for the darkness is passing away,
and the true light is already shining.*p* 9Whoever
says he is in the light, yet hates his brother, is still
in the darkness.*q* 10Whoever loves his brother
remains in the light, and there is nothing in him
to cause a fall.*r* 11Whoever hates his brother is
in darkness; he walks in darkness and does not
know where he is going because the darkness
has blinded his eyes.
**Members of the Community.**‡‡ 12I am writing to
you, children, because your sins have been forgiven*s* for his name's sake.§§

---

§[2:1] **Children:** like the term "beloved," this is an expression of pastoral love (cf. Jn 13:33; 21:5; 1 Cor 4:14). **Advocate:** for the use of the term, see Jn 14:16. Forgiveness of sin is
assured through Christ's intercession and expiation or "offering"; the death of Christ effected the removal of sin.
¶[2:3–6] **The way we may be sure:** to those who claim,
"I have known Christ and therefore I know him," our author
insists on not mere intellectual knowledge but obedience to
God's commandments in a life conformed to the example of
Christ; this confirms our knowledge of him and is **the love of
God . . . perfected.** Disparity between moral life and the commandments proves improper belief.
**[2:7–11] The author expresses the continuity and fresh-
ness of mutual charity in Christian experience. Through
Christ the commandment of love has become the **light** defeating the **darkness** of evil in a new age. All hatred as darkness
is incompatible with the light and Christian life. Note also the
characteristic Johannine polemic in which a positive assertion
is emphasized by the negative statement of its opposite.
††[2:8] **Which holds true in him and among you:** literally,
"a thing that holds true in him and in you."
‡‡[2:12–17] The Christian community that has experienced the grace of God through forgiveness of sin and knowledge of Christ is armed against the evil one.
§§[2:12] **For his name's sake:** because of Christ our sins are
forgiven.

---

*[1:1–4] There is a striking parallel to the prologue of the
gospel of John (Jn 1:1–18), but the emphasis here is not on
the preexistent Word but rather on the apostles' witness to the
incarnation of life by their experience of the historical Jesus.
He is **the Word of life** (1 Jn 1:1; cf. Jn 1:4), **the eternal life
that was with the Father and was made visible** (1 Jn 1:2; cf.
Jn 1:14), and was **heard, seen, looked upon,** and **touched** by
the apostles. The purpose of their teaching is to share their
life, called **fellowship . . . with the Father and with his Son,
Jesus Christ,** with those who receive their witness (1 Jn 1:3;
Jn 1:14, 16).
†[1:5–7] **Light** is to be understood here as truth and goodness; **darkness** here is error and depravity (cf. Jn 3:19–21;
17:17; Eph 5:8). To **walk** in light or darkness is to live according to truth or error, not merely intellectual but moral as well.
Fellowship with God and with one another consists in a life
according to the truth as found in God and in Christ.
‡[1:8–10] Denial of the condition of sin is self-deception
and even contradictory of divine revelation; there is also
the continual possibility of sin's recurrence. Forgiveness and
deliverance from sin through Christ are assured through
acknowledgment of them and repentance.

---

a. [1:1] 2:13; Jn 1:1, 14; 20:20, 25, 27.  b. [1:2] Jn 15:27; 17:5.
c. [1:3] Jn 17:21; Acts 4:20.  d. [1:4] Jn 15:11; 2 Jn 12.  e. [1:6] Jn
12:35.  f. [1:7] Mt 26:28; Rom 3:24–25; Heb 9:14; 1 Pt 1:19; Rev
1:5.  g. [1:8] 2 Chr 6:36; Prv 20:9.  h. [1:9] Prv 28:13; Jas 5:16.

i. [1:10] 5:10.  j. [2:1] Jn 14:16; Heb 7:25.  k. [2:2] 4:10.  l. [2:3] Jn
14:15; 15:10.  m. [2:4] 4:20.  n. [2:5] Jn 14:23.  o. [2:7] 3:11; Dt
6:5; Mt 22:37–40.  p. [2:8] Jn 13:34 / Jn 1:5; Rom 13:12.  q. [2:9] Jn
8:12.  r. [2:10] Eccl 2:14; Jn 11:10.  s. [2:12] 1 Cor 6:11.

[13]I am writing to you, fathers, because you know him who is from the beginning.

I am writing to you, young men, because you have conquered the evil one.[t]

[14]I write to you, children, because you know the Father.

I write to you, fathers, because you know him who is from the beginning.

I write to you, young men, because you are strong and the word of God remains in you, and you have conquered the evil one.

[15]Do not love the world or the things of the world.[*] If anyone loves the world, the love of the Father is not in him.[u] [16]For all that is in the world, sensual lust,[†] enticement for the eyes, and a pretentious life, is not from the Father but is from the world. [17]Yet the world and its enticement are passing away. But whoever does the will of God remains forever.[v]

**Antichrists.** [18]Children, it is the last hour;[‡] and just as you heard that the antichrist was coming, so now many antichrists have appeared. Thus we know this is the last hour.[w] [19]They went out from us, but they were not really of our number;[§] if they had been, they would have remained with us. Their desertion shows that none of them was of our number. [20]But you have the anointing that comes from the holy one,[¶] and you all have knowledge.[x] [21]I write to you not because you do not know the truth but because you do, and because every lie is alien to the truth.[y] [22]**Who is the liar? Whoever denies that Jesus is the Christ. Whoever denies the Father and the Son, this is the antichrist.[z] [23]No one who denies the Son has the Father, but whoever confesses the Son has the Father as well.[a]

**Life from God's Anointing.** [24b]Let what you heard from the beginning remain in you. If what you heard from the beginning remains in you, then you will remain in the Son and in the Father.[††] [25]And this is the promise that he made us: eternal life.[c] [26]I write you these things about those who would deceive you. [27]As for you, the anointing that you received from him remains in you, so that you do not need anyone to teach you. But his anointing teaches you about everything and is true and not false; just as it taught you, remain in him.

**Children of God.** [28‡‡]And now, children, remain in him, so that when he appears we may have confidence and not be put to shame by him at his coming. [29]If you consider that he is righteous, you also know that everyone who acts in righteousness is begotten by him.

## CHAPTER 3

[1§§]See what love the Father has bestowed on us that we may be called the children of God. Yet so we are. The reason the world does not know us is that it did not know him.[d] [2]Beloved, we are God's children now; what we shall be has not yet been revealed. We do know that when it is revealed[¶¶] we shall be like him, for we shall see him as he is.[e] [3]Everyone who has this hope based on him makes himself pure, as he is pure.[f]

**Avoiding Sin.** [4]Everyone who commits sin commits lawlessness, for sin is lawlessness.[***] [5]You know that he was revealed to take away sins, and in him there is no sin.[g] [6]No one who remains in him sins; no one who sins has seen him or known him. [7]Children, let no one deceive you. The person who acts in righteousness is righteous, just as he is righteous. [8]Whoever sins belongs to the devil, because the devil has sinned from the beginning. Indeed, the Son of God was revealed to destroy the works of the devil.[h] [9]No one who is begotten by God commits sin, because God's seed remains in him; he cannot

---

*[2:15] **The world**: all that is hostile toward God and alienated from him. Love of the **world** and love of God are thus mutually exclusive; cf. Jas 4:4.

†[2:16] **Sensual lust**: literally, "the lust of the flesh," inordinate desire for physical gratification. **Enticement for the eyes**: literally, "the lust of the eyes," avarice or covetousness; the eyes are regarded as the windows of the soul. **Pretentious life**: literally, "pride of life," arrogance or ostentation in one's earthly style of life that reflects a willful independence from God and others.

‡[2:18] **It is the last hour**: literally, "a last hour," the period between the death and resurrection of Christ and his second coming. **The antichrist**: opponent or adversary of Christ; the term appears only in 1 John–2 John, but "pseudochrists" (translated "false messiahs") in Mt 24:24 and Mk 13:22, and Paul's "lawless one" in 2 Thes 2:3, are similar figures. **Many antichrists**: Matthew, Mark, and Revelation seem to indicate a collectivity of persons, here related to the false teachers.

§[2:19] **Not really of our number**: the apostate teachers only proved their lack of faith by leaving the community.

¶[2:20] **The anointing that comes from the holy one**: this anointing is in the Old Testament sense of receiving the Spirit of God. The **holy one** probably refers to Christ. True knowledge is the gift of the Spirit (cf. Is 11:2), and the function of the Spirit is to lead Christians to the truth (Jn 14:17, 26; 16:13).

**[2:22–23] Certain gnostics denied that the earthly Jesus was the Christ; to deny knowledge of the Son is to deny the Father, since only through the Son has God been fully revealed (Jn 1:18; 14:8–9).

††[2:24] Continuity with the apostolic witness as proclaimed in the prologue is the safeguard of right belief.

‡‡[2:28–29] Our confidence at his judgment is based on the daily assurance of salvation. Our actions reflect our true relation to him.

§§[3:1–3] The greatest sign of God's love is the gift of his Son (Jn 3:16) that has made Christians true children of God. This relationship is a present reality and also part of the life to come; true knowledge of God will ultimately be gained, and Christians prepare themselves now by virtuous lives in imitation of the Son.

¶¶[3:2] **When it is revealed**: or "when he is revealed" (the subject of the verb could be Christ).

***[3:4] **Lawlessness**: a reference to the activity of the antichrist, so it is expressed as hostility toward God and a rejection of Christ. The author goes on to contrast the states of sin and righteousness. Christians do not escape sin but realize that when they sin they cease to have fellowship with God. Virtue and sin distinguish the children of God from the children of the devil.

---

t. [2:13] 1:1; Jn 1:1.   u. [2:15] Rom 8:7–8; Jas 4:4; 2 Pt 1:4.   v. [2:17] Is 40:8; Mt 7:21; 1 Cor 7:31; 1 Pt 4:2.   w. [2:18] 1 Tm 4:1.   x. [2:20] Jn 14:26.   y. [2:21] 3:19; 2 Pt 1:12.   z. [2:22] 2 Thes 2:4.   a. [2:23] Jn 14:7–9.

b. [2:24] Jn 14:23.   c. [2:25] Jn 5:24; 10:28; 17:2.   d. [3:1] Jn 1:12; Eph 1:5 / Jn 15:21; 17:25.   e. [3:2] Phil 3:21.   f. [3:3] 2:6.   g. [3:5] Is 53:9; Jn 1:29; 8:46; 1 Pt 2:22.   h. [3:8] Jn 8:44; 12:31–32.

sin because he is begotten by God.* [10]In this way, the children of God and the children of the devil are made plain; no one who fails to act in righteousness belongs to God, nor anyone who does not love his brother.

## III. LOVE FOR ONE ANOTHER

[11†]For this is the message you have heard from the beginning: we should love one another,[i] [12]unlike Cain who belonged to the evil one and slaughtered his brother. Why did he slaughter him? Because his own works were evil, and those of his brother righteous.[j] [13]Do not be amazed, [then,] brothers, if the world hates you.[k] [14]We know that we have passed from death to life because we love our brothers. Whoever does not love remains in death.[l] [15]Everyone who hates his brother is a murderer, and you know that no murderer has eternal life remaining in him.[m] [16]The way we came to know love was that he laid down his life for us; so we ought to lay down our lives for our brothers.[n] [17]If someone who has worldly means sees a brother in need and refuses him compassion, how can the love of God remain in him?[o] [18]Children, let us love not in word or speech but in deed and truth.[p]

**Confidence Before God.**[‡] [19][Now] this is how we shall know that we[§] belong to the truth and reassure our hearts before him [20]in whatever our hearts condemn, for God is greater than our hearts and knows everything. [21]Beloved, if [our] hearts do not condemn us, we have confidence in God [22]and receive from him whatever we ask, because we keep his commandments and do what pleases him.[q] [23]And his commandment is this: we should believe in the name of his Son, Jesus Christ, and love one another just as he commanded us.[r] [24]Those who keep his commandments remain in him, and he in them, and the way we know that he remains in us is from the Spirit that he gave us.[s]

## CHAPTER 4

**Testing the Spirits.**[¶] [1]Beloved, do not trust every spirit but test the spirits to see whether they belong to God, because many false prophets have gone out into the world.[t] [2]This is how you can know the Spirit of God: every spirit that acknowledges Jesus Christ come in the flesh belongs to God,[u] [3]and every spirit that does not acknowledge Jesus** does not belong to God. This is the spirit of the antichrist that, as you heard, is to come, but in fact is already in the world.[v] [4]You belong to God, children, and you have conquered them, for the one who is in you is greater than the one who is in the world. [5]They belong to the world; accordingly, their teaching belongs to the world, and the world listens to them.[w] [6]We belong to God, and anyone who knows God listens to us, while anyone who does not belong to God refuses to hear us. This is how we know the spirit of truth and the spirit of deceit.[x]

**God's Love and Christian Life.**[7††]Beloved, let us love one another, because love is of God; everyone who loves is begotten by God and knows God. [8]Whoever is without love does not know God, for God is love. [9]In this way the love of God was revealed to us: God sent his only Son into the world so that we might have life through him.[y] [10]In this is love: not that we have loved God, but that he loved us and sent his Son as expiation for our sins.[z] [11]Beloved, if God so loved us, we also must love one another. [12]No one has ever seen God. Yet, if we love one another, God remains in us, and his love is brought to perfection in us.[a]

[13‡‡]This is how we know that we remain in him and he in us, that he has given us of his Spirit. [14]Moreover, we have seen and testify that the Father sent his Son as savior of the world.

---

*[3:9] A habitual sinner is a child of the devil, while a child of God, who by definition is in fellowship with God, cannot sin. **Seed:** Christ or the Spirit who shares the nature of God with the Christian.

†[3:11–18] Love, even to the point of self-sacrifice, is the point of the commandment. The story of Cain and Abel (1 Jn 3:12–15; Gn 4:1–16) presents the rivalry of two brothers, in a contrast of evil and righteousness, where envy led to murder. For Christians, proof of deliverance is love toward others, after the example of Christ. This includes concrete acts of charity, out of our material abundance.

‡[3:19–24] Living a life of faith in Jesus and of Christian love assures us of abiding in God no matter what our feelings may at times tell us. Our obedience gives us confidence in prayer and trust in God's judgment. This obedience includes our belief in Christ and love for one another.

§[3:19b–20] This difficult passage may also be translated "we shall be at peace before him in whatever our hearts condemn, for . . ." or "and before God we shall convince our hearts, if our hearts condemn us, that God is greater than our hearts."

¶[4:1–6] Deception is possible in spiritual phenomena and may be tested by its relation to Christian doctrine (cf. 1 Cor 12:3): those who fail to acknowledge Jesus Christ in the flesh are false prophets and belong to the antichrist. Even though these false prophets are well received in the world, the Christian who belongs to God has a greater power in the truth.

**[4:3] Does not acknowledge Jesus:** some ancient manuscripts add "Christ" and/or "to have come in the flesh" (cf. 1 Jn 4:2), and others read "every spirit that annuls (or severs) Jesus."

††[4:7–12] Love as we share in it testifies to the nature of God and to his presence in our lives. One who loves shows that one is a child of God and knows God, for God's very being is love; one without love is without God. The revelation of the nature of God's love is found in the free gift of his Son to us, so that we may share life with God and be delivered from our sins. The love we have for one another must be of the same sort: authentic, merciful; this unique Christian love is our proof that we know God and can "see" the invisible God.

‡‡[4:13–21] The testimony of the Spirit and that of faith join the testimony of love to confirm our knowledge of God. Our love is grounded in the confession of Jesus as the Son of God and the example of God's love for us. Christian life is founded on the knowledge of God as love and on his continuing presence that relieves us from fear of judgment (1 Jn 4:16–18). What Christ gives us confidence, even as we live and love in this world. Yet Christian love is not abstract but lived in the concrete manner of love for one another.

---

i. [3:11] 2:7; Jn 13:34; 15:12, 17.    j. [3:12] Gn 4:8; Jude 11.    k. [3:13] Mt 24:9; Jn 15:18; 17:14.    l. [3:14] Lv 19:17; Jn 5:24.    m. [3:15] Jn 8:44.    n. [3:16] Mt 20:28; Jn 10:11; 15:13.    o. [3:17] Dt 15:7, 11; Jas 2:15–16.    p. [3:18] Jas 1:22.    q. [3:22] 5:15; Mt 7:7–11; 21:22; Jn 14:13–14.    r. [3:23] Jn 13:34; 15:17.    s. [3:24] 4:13; Jn 14:21–23.

t. [4:1] 2:18; Mt 24:24.    u. [4:2] 1 Cor 12:3; 1 Thes 5:21.    v. [4:3] 3:22.    w. [4:5] Jn 15:19.    x. [4:6] Jn 8:47; 10:16.    y. [4:9] Jn 3:16.    z. [4:10] Rom 5:8.    a. [4:12] Jn 1:18; 1 Tm 6:16.

[15]Whoever acknowledges that Jesus is the Son of God, God remains in him and he in God. [16]We have come to know and to believe in the love God has for us.

God is love, and whoever remains in love remains in God and God in him. [17]In this is love brought to perfection among us, that we have confidence on the day of judgment because as he is, so are we in this world.[b] [18]There is no fear in love, but perfect love drives out fear because fear has to do with punishment, and so one who fears is not yet perfect in love. [19]We love because he first loved us. [20]If anyone says, "I love God," but hates his brother, he is a liar; for whoever does not love a brother whom he has seen cannot love God* whom he has not seen.[c] [21]This is the commandment we have from him: whoever loves God must also love his brother.[d]

### CHAPTER 5

**Faith Is Victory over the World.** [1†]Everyone who believes that Jesus is the Christ is begotten by God, and everyone who loves the father loves [also] the one begotten by him.[e] [2]In this way we know that we love the children of God when we love God and obey his commandments. [3]For the love of God is this, that we keep his commandments. And his commandments are not burdensome,[f] [4]for whoever is begotten by God conquers the world. And the victory that conquers the world is our faith.[g] [5]Who [indeed] is the victor over the world but the one who believes that Jesus is the Son of God?[h]

[6]This is the one who came through water and blood,[‡] Jesus Christ, not by water alone, but by water and blood. The Spirit is the one that testifies, and the Spirit is truth.[i] [7]So there are three that testify, [8]the Spirit, the water, and the blood, and the three are of one accord.[j] [9]If we accept human testimony, the testimony of God is surely greater. Now the testimony of God is this, that he has testified on behalf of his Son.[k] [10]Whoever believes in the Son of God has this testimony within himself. Whoever does not believe God has made him a liar by not believing the testimony God has given about his Son.[l] [11]And this is the testimony: God gave us eternal life, and this life is in his Son.[m] [12]Whoever possesses the Son has life; whoever does not possess the Son of God does not have life.

## IV. EPILOGUE[§]

**Prayer for Sinners.** [13]I write these things to you so that you may know that you have eternal life, you who believe in the name of the Son of God.[n] [14]And we have this confidence in him, that if we ask anything according to his will, he hears us.[o] [15]And if we know that he hears us in regard to whatever we ask, we know that what we have asked him for is ours. [16]If anyone sees his brother sinning, if the sin is not deadly, he should pray to God and he will give him life. This is only for those whose sin is not deadly. There is such a thing as deadly sin, about which I do not say that you should pray.[p] [17]All wrongdoing is sin, but there is sin that is not deadly.

[18]We know that no one begotten by God sins; but the one begotten by God he protects, and the evil one cannot touch him. [19]We know that we belong to God, and the whole world is under the power of the evil one. [20]We also know that the Son of God has come and has given us discernment to know the one who is true. And we are in the one who is true, in his Son Jesus Christ. He is the true God and eternal life.[q] [21]Children, be on your guard against idols.

---

*[4:20] **Cannot love God**: some ancient manuscripts read "how can he love . . . ?"

†[5:1–5] **Children of God** are identified not only by their love for others (1 Jn 4:7–9) and for God (1 Jn 5:1–2) but by their belief in the divine sonship of Jesus Christ. Faith, the acceptance of Jesus in his true character and the obedience in love to God's commands (1 Jn 5:3), is the source of the Christian's power in the world and conquers the world of evil (1 Jn 5:4–5), even as Christ overcame the world (Jn 16:33).

‡[5:6–12] **Water and blood** (1 Jn 5:6) refers to Christ's baptism (Mt 3:16–17) and to the shedding of his blood on the cross (Jn 19:34). **The Spirit** was present at the baptism (Mt 3:16; Mk 1:10; Lk 3:22; Jn 1:32, 34). **The testimony** to Christ as the Son of God is confirmed by divine witness (1 Jn 5:7–9), greater by far than the two legally required human witnesses (Dt 17:6). To deny this is to deny God's truth; cf. Jn 8:17–18. The gist of the divine witness or **testimony** is that **eternal life** (1 Jn 5:11–12) is given in Christ and nowhere else. To **possess the Son** is not acceptance of a doctrine but of a person who lives now and provides life.

§[5:13–21] As children of God we have confidence in prayer because of our intimate relationship with him (1 Jn 5:14–15). In love, we pray (1 Jn 5:16–17) for those who are **in sin**, but not in **deadly sin** (literally, "sin unto death"), probably referring to apostasy or activities brought on under the antichrist; cf. Mk 3:29; Heb 6:4–6; 10:26–31. Even in the latter case, however, prayer, while not enjoined, is not forbidden. The letter concludes with a summary of the themes of the letter (1 Jn 5:18–20). There is a sharp antithesis between the children of God and those belonging to the world and to the evil one. The Son reveals the God of truth; Christians dwell in the true God, **in his Son**, and have eternal life. The final verse (1 Jn 5:21) voices a perennial warning about **idols**, any type of rival to God.

---

b. [4:17] 2:28.　c. [4:20] 2:4.　d. [4:21] Jn 13:34; 14:15, 21; 15:17.　e. [5:1] Jn 8:42; 1 Pt 1:23.　f. [5:3] Jn 14:15.　g. [5:4] Jn 16:33.　h. [5:5] 1 Cor 15:57.　i. [5:6] Jn 15:26; 19:34.

j. [5:8] Jn 5:32, 36; 15:26.　k. [5:9] Jn 5:32, 37.　l. [5:10] Jn 3:33.　m. [5:11] 1:2; Jn 1:4; 5:21, 26; 17:3.　n. [5:13] Jn 1:12; 20:31.　o. [5:14] 3:21–22; Mt 7:7; Jn 14:13–14.　p. [5:16] Mt 12:31.　q. [5:20] Jer 24:7; Jn 17:3; Eph 1:17.

# THE SECOND LETTER OF
# JOHN

~☙~

Written in response to similar problems, the Second and Third Letters of John are of the same length, perhaps determined by the practical consideration of the writing space on one piece of papyrus. In each letter the writer calls himself "the Presbyter," and their common authorship is further evidenced by internal similarities in style and wording, especially in the introductions and conclusions. The literary considerations that link 2 John and 3 John also link them with the First Letter and the Gospel of John. The concern with "truth," christology, mutual love, the new commandment, antichrist, and the integrity of witness to the earthly Jesus mark these works as products of the Johannine school. The identity of the Presbyter is problematic. The use of the title implies more than age, and refers to his position of leadership in the early church. The absence of a proper name indicates that he was well known and acknowledged in authority by the communities to which he writes. Although traditionally attributed to John the apostle, these letters were probably written by a disciple or scribe of an apostle. The traditional place and date of composition, Ephesus at the end of the first century, are plausible for both letters.

The Second Letter is addressed to "the chosen Lady" and "to her children." This literary image of a particular Christian community reflects the specific destination and purpose of the letter. Unlike 1 John, this brief letter is not a theological treatise but a reply to problems within the church. The Johannine themes of love and truth are used to support practical advice on Christian living. The Presbyter encourages community members to show their Christianity by adhering to the great commandment of mutual love and to the historical truth about Jesus. The false teaching present among them is a spiritualizing christology that may tempt some members to discount teachings about the incarnation and death of Jesus the Christ; cf. 1 Jn 4:2. For their protection the Presbyter forbids hospitality toward unknown or "progressive" Christians to prevent their infiltration of the community. The Second Letter preserves the Johannine concerns of doctrinal purity and active love in the form of pastoral advice to a threatened community.

---

1[a]The Presbyter to the chosen Lady and to her children whom I love in truth—and not only I but also all who know the truth— 2because of the truth that dwells in us and will be with us forever. 3Grace, mercy, and peace† will be with us from God the Father and from Jesus Christ the Father's Son in truth and love.

4I rejoiced greatly to find some of your children‡ walking in the truth just as we were commanded by the Father.[b] 5But now, Lady, I ask you, not as though I were writing a new commandment but the one we have had from the beginning: let us love one another.[c] 6For this is love, that we walk according to his commandments;§ this is the commandment, as you heard from the beginning, in which you should walk.[d]

7Many deceivers have gone out into the world, those who do not acknowledge Jesus

---

*[1] **The chosen Lady**: literally, "elected"; this could also be translated "Kyria (a woman's name) chosen (by God)" or "the lady Electa" or "Electa Kyria." The adjective "chosen" is applied to all Christians at the beginning of other New Testament letters (1 Pt 1:1; Ti 1:1). The description is of a specific community with "children" who are its members. **The truth**: the affirmation of Jesus in the flesh and in contrast to false teaching (2 Jn 7).

†[3] **Grace, mercy, and peace**: like 1 Timothy; 2 Timothy this letter adds **mercy** to the terms used frequently in a salutation to describe Christian blessing; it appears only here in the Johannine writings. The author also puts the blessing in relation to **truth** and **love**, the watchwords of the Johannine teaching. **The Father's Son**: the title that affirms the close relationship of Christ to God; similar variations of this title occur elsewhere (Jn 1:14; 3:35), but the precise wording is not found elsewhere in the New Testament.

‡[4] **Some of your children**: this refers to those whom the Presbyter has recently encountered, but it may also indicate the presence of false doctrine in the community: the Presbyter encourages those who have remained faithful. **Walking in the truth**: an expression used in the Johannine writings to describe a way of living in which the Christian faith is visibly expressed; cf. 1 Jn 1:6–7; 2:6, 11; 3 Jn 3.

§[6] **His commandments**: cf. 1 Jn 3:23; 2:7–8; 4:21; obedience to the commandment of faith and love includes all others.

---

a. [1] Jn 8:32; 3 Jn 1.

b. [4] 3 Jn 3.   c. [5] Jn 13:34; 15:12; 1 Jn 4:7.   d. [6] Jn 13:34; 14:15; 1 Jn 5:3.   e. [7] 1 Jn 2:22; 4:2.

Christ as coming in the flesh; such is the deceit-ful one and the antichrist.* ⁸Look to yourselves that you† do not lose what we worked for but may receive a full recompense. ⁹Anyone who is so "progressive"‡ as not to remain in the teach-ing of the Christ does not have God; whoever remains in the teaching has the Father and the Son. ¹⁰§If anyone comes to you and does not bring this doctrine, do not receive him in your house or even greet him;ᵍ ¹¹for whoever greets him shares in his evil works.

¹²¶Although I have much to write to you, I do not intend to use paper and ink. Instead, I hope to visit you and to speak face to face so that our joy may be complete.ʰ ¹³The children of your chosen sister** send you greetings.

---

*[7] **The antichrist:** see 1 Jn 2:18–19, 22; 4:3.

†[8] **You** (plural): it is not certain whether this means the Christians addressed or includes the Presbyter, since some of the ancient Greek manuscripts and Greek Fathers have "we."

‡[9] **Anyone who is so "progressive"**: literally, "Anyone who goes ahead." Some gnostic groups held the doctrine of the Christ come in the flesh to be a first step in belief, which the more advanced and spiritual believer surpassed and abandoned in his knowledge of the spiritual Christ. The author affirms that fellowship with God may be gained only by holding to the com-plete doctrine of Jesus Christ (1 Jn 2:22–23; 4:2; 5:5–6).

§[10–11] At this time false teachers were considered so dangerous and divisive as to be shunned completely. From this description they seem to be wandering preachers. We see here a natural suspicion of early Christians concerning such itinerants and can envisage the problems faced by missionar-ies such as those mentioned in 3 Jn 10.

¶[12] **Our joy:** a number of other Greek manuscripts read "your joy."

**[13] **Chosen sister:** the community of which the Presby-ter is now a part greets you (singular), the community of the Lady addressed.

---

f. [9] Jn 8:31; 1 Jn 2:23; 4:15.

g. [10] Rom 16:17; 2 Thes 3:6.   h. [12] Jn 15:11; 1 Jn 1:4; 3 Jn 13.

# THE THIRD LETTER OF
# JOHN

~~~

The Third Letter of John preserves a brief glimpse into the problems of missionary activity and local autonomy in the early church. In contrast to the other two letters of John, this work was addressed to a specific individual, Gaius. This letter is less theological in content and purpose. The author's goal was to secure hospitality and material support for his missionaries, and the Presbyter is writing to another member of the church who has welcomed missionaries in the past. The Presbyter commends Gaius for his hospitality and encourages his future help. He indicates he may come to challenge the policy of Diotrephes that is based on evil gossip.

The problems of the Presbyter in this short letter provide us with valuable evidence of the flexible and personal nature of authority in the early church. The Presbyter writes to Gaius, whom perhaps he had converted or instructed, on the basis of their personal links. The brothers have also confirmed him as a loyal Christian in action and belief. Gaius accepted the missionaries from the Presbyter and presumably will accept Demetrius on the Presbyter's recommendation. In contrast, Diotrephes refuses to receive either letters or friends of the Presbyter. Although he is portrayed as ambitious and hostile, he perhaps exemplifies the cautious and sectarian nature of early Christianity; for its own protection the local community mistrusted missionaries as false teachers. Most interestingly, Diotrephes seems comfortable in ignoring the requests of the Presbyter. The Presbyter seems to acknowledge that only a personal confrontation with Diotrephes will remedy the situation (3 Jn 10). The division, however, may also rest on doctrinal disagreement in which Gaius and the other "friends" accept the teaching of the Presbyter, and Diotrephes does not; the missionaries are not received for suspicion of theological error. Diotrephes has thus been viewed by some as an overly ambitious local upstart trying to thwart the advance of orthodox Christianity, by others as an orthodox church official suspicious of the teachings of the Presbyter and those in the Johannine school who think as he does, or by still others as a local leader anxious to keep the debates in the Johannine community out of his own congregation.

This brief letter and the situation that it mirrors show us how little we know about some details of early development in the church: schools of opinion existed around which questions of faith and life were discussed, and personal ties as well as doctrine and authority played a role in what happened amid divisions and unity.

---

[1] ¹The Presbyter to the beloved Gaius whom I love in truth.ᵃ

²Beloved, I hope you are prospering in every respect and are in good health, just as your soul is prospering. ³I rejoiced greatly when some of the brothers† came and testified to how truly you walk in the truth.ᵇ ⁴Nothing gives me greater joy than to hear that my children are walking in the truth.ᶜ

⁵Beloved, you are faithful in all you do‡ for the brothers, especially for strangers;ᵈ ⁶they have testified to your love before the church.ᵉ Please help them in a way worthy of God to continue their journey.§ ⁷For they have set out for the sake of the Name¶ and are accepting nothing from

---

*[1] **Beloved Gaius**: a frequent form of address for fellow Christians in New Testament epistolary literature.

†[3] **The brothers**: in this letter, the term may refer to Christians who have been missionaries and received hospitality from Gaius (3 Jn 5–6). **Walk in the truth**: the common Johannine term to describe Christian living; this description presents Gaius as following the teachings of the Presbyter in contrast to Diotrephes.

‡[5] **You are faithful in all you do**: Gaius's aid to the missionaries is a manifestation of his true Christian faith.

§[6] **Help them . . . to continue their journey**: the Presbyter asks Gaius not only to continue to welcome the missionaries to his community but also to equip them for further travels.

¶[7] **The Name**: of Jesus Christ (cf. Acts 5:41; 1 Jn 2:12; 3:23; 5:13). **Accepting nothing**: not expecting support from the pagans to whom they preach the gospel, so that they will not be considered as beggars; they required support from

---

a. [1] 2 Jn 1.   b. [3] 5; Gal 6:10; 2 Jn 4.   c. [4] 1 Thes 2:11–12; 1 Tm 1:2; 2 Tm 1:2; 1 Jn 2:1; 2 Jn 4.

d. [5] Rom 12:13; Gal 6:10; Heb 13:2.   e. [6] Acts 15:3; Col 1:10; 1 Thes 2:12.

the pagans. [8]Therefore, we ought to support such persons, so that we may be co-workers in the truth.

[9]I wrote to the church, but Diotrephes, who loves to dominate,* does not acknowledge us. [10]Therefore, if I come,† I will draw attention to what he is doing, spreading evil nonsense about us. And not content with that, he will not receive the brothers, hindering those who wish to do so and expelling them from the church.

[11]Beloved, do not imitate evil‡ but imitate good. Whoever does what is good is of God;

whoever does what is evil has never seen God.[f] [12]Demetrius§ receives a good report from all, even from the truth itself. We give our testimonial as well, and you know our testimony is true.[g]

[13]I have much to write to you, but I do not wish to write with pen and ink.[h] [14]Instead, I hope to see you soon, when we can talk face to face. [15]Peace be with you. The friends greet you; greet the friends¶ there each by name.[i]

---

other Christians; cf. Paul's complaints to the Corinthians (1 Cor 9:3–12).

*[9] **Who loves to dominate**: the Presbyter does not deny Diotrephes' place as leader but indicates that his ambition may have caused him to disregard his letter and his influence.

†[10] **If I come**: the Presbyter may visit the community to challenge the actions of Diotrephes toward himself and the missionaries. **Will not receive the brothers**: Diotrephes may have been critical of the teachings of the Presbyter and sought to maintain doctrinal purity; cf. 1 Jn 2:19 and 2 Jn 10–11.

‡[11] **Do not imitate evil**: Gaius should not be influenced by the behavior of Diotrephes.

§[12] **Demetrius**: because of the fear of false teachers, Demetrius, perhaps the bearer of the letter, is provided with a recommendation from the Presbyter; cf. 2 Cor 3:1; Rom 16:1. **Even from the truth itself**: this refers probably to the manner of Demetrius's life that testifies to his true belief; cf. Gaius above (3 Jn 3).

¶[15] **Friends**: although a Johannine term for Christians (Jn 15:15), the word here may refer to those in the community loyal to the Presbyter and to Gaius.

---

f. [11] 1 Jn 2:29; 3:6, 10.   g. [12] Jn 19:35; 21:24; 1 Tm 3:7.   h. [13] 2 Jn 12.   i. [15] Jn 20:19, 21, 26; Eph 6:23; 1 Pt 5:14.

# THE LETTER OF
# JUDE

~~~

This letter is by its address attributed to "Jude, a slave of Jesus Christ and brother of James" (Jude 1). Since he is not identified as an apostle, this designation can hardly be meant to refer to the Jude or Judas who is listed as one of the Twelve (Lk 6:16; Acts 1:13; cf. Jn 14:22). The person intended is almost certainly the other Jude, named in the gospels among the relatives of Jesus (Mt 13:55; Mk 6:3), and the James who is listed there as his brother is the one to whom the Letter of James is attributed (see the Introduction to James). Nothing else is known of this Jude, and the apparent need to identify him by reference to his better-known brother indicates that he was a rather obscure personage in the early church.

The letter is addressed in the most general terms to "those who are called, beloved in God the Father and kept safe for Jesus Christ" (Jude 1), hence apparently to all Christians. But since its purpose is to warn the addressees against false teachers, the author must have had in mind one or more specific Christian communities located in the unidentified region where the errors in question constituted a danger. While the letter contains some Semitic features, there is nothing to identify the addressees specifically as Jewish Christians; indeed, the errors envisaged seem to reflect an early form of gnosticism, opposed to law, that points rather to the cultural context of the Gentile world. Like James and 2 Peter, the Letter of Jude manifests none of the typical features of the letter form except the address.

There is so much similarity between Jude and 2 Peter, especially Jude 4–16 and 2 Pt 2:1–18, that there must be a literary relationship between them. Since there is no evidence for the view that both authors borrowed from the same source, it is usually supposed that one of them borrowed from the other. Most scholars believe that Jude is the earlier of the two, principally because he quotes two apocryphal Jewish works, the Assumption of Moses (Jude 9) and the Book of Enoch (Jude 14–15) as part of his structured argument, whereas 2 Peter omits both references. Since there was controversy in the early church about the propriety of citing noncanonical literature that included legendary material, it is more probable that a later writer would omit such references than that he would add them.

Many interpreters today consider Jude a pseudonymous work dating from the end of the first century or even later. In support of this view they adduce the following arguments: (a) the apostles are referred to as belonging to an age that has receded into the past (Jude 17–18); (b) faith is understood as a body of doctrine handed down by a process of tradition (Jude 3); (c) the author's competent Greek style shows that he must have had a Hellenistic cultural formation; (d) the gnostic character of the errors envisaged fits better into the early second century than into a period several decades earlier. While impressive, these arguments are not entirely compelling and do not completely rule out the possibility of composition around the year A.D. 80, when the historical Jude may still have been alive.

This little letter is an urgent note by an author who intended to write more fully about salvation to an unknown group of readers, but who was forced by dangers from false teachers worming their way into the community (Jude 3–4) to dash off a warning against them (Jude 5–16) and to deliver some pressing Christian admonitions (Jude 17–23). The letter is justly famous for its majestic closing doxology (Jude 24–25).

**Address and Greeting.** [1*]Jude, a slave of Jesus Christ and brother of James, to those who are called, beloved in God the Father and kept safe for Jesus Christ:[a] [2]may mercy, peace, and love be yours in abundance.[b]

**Occasion for Writing.** [3]Beloved, although I was making every effort to write to you about our common salvation,[†] I now feel a need to write to encourage you to contend for the faith that was once for all handed down to the holy ones.[c] [4]For there have been some intruders, who long ago were designated for this condemnation, godless persons, who pervert the grace of our God into licentiousness and who deny our only Master and Lord, Jesus Christ.[d]

**The False Teachers.** [5]I wish to remind you, although you know all things, that [the] Lord who once saved a people from the land of Egypt later destroyed those who did not believe.[‡] [6*]The angels too, who did not keep to their own domain but deserted their proper dwelling, he has kept in eternal chains, in gloom, for the judgment of the great day.[§] [7]Likewise, Sodom, Gomorrah, and the surrounding towns, which, in the same manner as they, indulged in sexual promiscuity and practiced unnatural vice,[¶] serve as an example by undergoing a punishment of eternal fire.[g]

[8]Similarly, these dreamers** nevertheless also defile the flesh, scorn lordship, and revile glorious beings. [9]Yet the archangel Michael, when he argued with the devil in a dispute over the body of Moses, did not venture to pronounce a reviling judgment[††] upon him but said, "May the Lord rebuke you!"[h] [10]But these people revile what they do not understand and are destroyed by what they know by nature like irrational animals.[i] [11]Woe to them![j] They followed the way of Cain, abandoned themselves to Balaam's error for the sake of gain, and perished in the rebellion of Korah.[‡‡] [12]These are blemishes on your love feasts,[§§] as they carouse fearlessly and look after themselves. They are waterless clouds blown about by winds, fruitless trees in late autumn, twice dead and uprooted.[k] [13]They are like wild waves of the sea, foaming up their shameless deeds, wandering stars for whom the gloom of darkness has been reserved forever.

[14¶¶]Enoch, of the seventh generation from Adam, prophesied also about them when he said,[l] "Behold, the Lord has come with his countless holy ones [15]to execute judgment on all and to convict everyone for all the godless deeds that they committed and for all the harsh words godless sinners have uttered against him." [16]These people are complainers, disgruntled ones who live by their desires; their mouths utter bombast as they fawn over people to gain advantage.[m]

**Exhortations.** [17]But you, beloved, remember the words spoken beforehand by the apostles of our Lord Jesus Christ,[n] [18]for they told you,[o] "In [the] last time there will be scoffers who will live according to their own godless desires."[***] [19]These are the ones who cause divisions; they live on the natural plane, devoid of the Spirit.[p] [20]But you, beloved, build yourselves up in your most holy faith; pray in the holy Spirit.[q] [21]Keep

---

*[1] **Jude . . . brother of James:** for the identity of the author of this letter, see Introduction. **To those who are called:** the vocation to the Christian faith is God's free gift to those whom he loves and whom he safely protects in Christ until the Lord's second coming.

†[3–4] **Our common salvation:** the teachings of the Christian faith derived from the apostolic preaching and to be kept by the Christian community.

‡[5] For this first example of divine punishment on those who had been saved but did not then keep faith, see Nm 14:28–29 and the note there. Some manuscripts have the word "once" (*hapax* as at Jude 3) after "you know"; some commentators have suggested that it means "knowing one thing" or "you know all things once for all." Instead of "[the] Lord" manuscripts vary, having "Jesus," "God," or no subject stated.

§[6] This second example draws on Gn 6:1–4 as elaborated in the apocryphal Book of Enoch (cf. Jude 14): heavenly beings came to earth and had sexual intercourse with women. God punished them by casting them out of heaven into darkness and bondage.

¶[7] **Practiced unnatural vice:** literally, "went after alien flesh." This example derives from Gn 19:1–25, especially 4–11, when the townsmen of Sodom violated both hospitality and morality by demanding that Lot's two visitors (really messengers of Yahweh) be handed over to them so that they could abuse them sexually. **Unnatural vice:** this refers to the desire for intimacies by human beings with angels (the reverse of the example in Jude 6). Sodom (whence "sodomy") and Gomorrah became proverbial as object lessons for God's punishment on sin (Is 1:9; Jer 50:40; Am 4:11; Mt 10:15; 2 Pt 2:6).

**[8] **Dreamers:** the writer returns to the false teachers of Jude 4, applying charges from the three examples in Jude 5, 6, 7. This may apply to claims they make for revelations they have received by night (to the author, hallucinations). **Defile the flesh:** this may mean bodily pollutions from the erotic dreams of sexual license (Jude 7). **Lordship . . . glorious beings:** these may reflect the Lord (Jude 5; Jesus, Jude 4)

whom they spurn and the angels (Jude 6; cf. note on 2 Pt 2:10, here, as there, literally, "glories").

††[9] **The archangel Michael . . . judgment:** a reference to an incident in the apocryphal Assumption of Moses. Dt 34:6 had said of Moses, literally in Greek, "they buried him" or "he (God?) buried him" (taken to mean "he was buried"). The later account tells how Michael, who was sent to bury him, was challenged by the devil's interest in the body. Our author draws out the point that if an archangel refrained from reviling even the devil, how wrong it is for mere human beings to revile glorious beings (angels).

‡‡[11] **Cain . . . Balaam . . . Korah:** examples of rebellious men and of the punishment their conduct incurred; cf. Gn 4:8–16; Nm 31:1–35; 31:16. See note on 2 Pt 2:15.

§§[12] **Blemishes on your love feasts:** or "hidden rocks" or "submerged reefs" (cf. Jude 13). The opponents engaged in scandalous conduct in connection with community gatherings called **love feasts** (agape meals), which were associated with eucharistic celebrations at certain stages of early Christian practice; cf. 1 Cor 11:18–34 and the note on 2 Pt 2:13.

¶¶[14–15] Cited from the apocryphal Book of Enoch 1:9.

***[18] This is the substance of much early Christian preaching rather than a direct quotation of any of the various New Testament passages on this theme (see Mk 13:22; Acts 20:30; 1 Tm 4:1–3; 2 Pt 3:3).

---

h. [9] Dn 10:21; 12:1. i. [10] 2 Pt 2:12. j. [11] Gn 4:8–16; 1 Jn 3:12 / Nm 31:15–16; 2 Pt 2:15; Rev 2:14 / Nm 16:19–35. k. [12] 2 Pt 2:13, 17. l. [14–15] Mt 16:27; Heb 12:22–23. m. [16] 18; 1 Cor 10:10; 2 Pt 2:10, 18. n. [17] Heb 2:3; 2 Pt 3:2. o. [18] 1 Tm 4:1; 2 Tm 3:1–5; 2 Pt 3:3. p. [19] 1 Cor 2:14; Jas 3:15. q. [20] 2; Eph 6:18; Col 2:7.

---

a. [1] Mt 13:55; Mk 6:3; Acts 12:17; Rom 1:7. b. [2] Gal 6:16; 1 Tm 1:2; 2 Pt 1:2. c. [3] 17, 20; 1 Tm 6:12. d. [4] Gal 2:4; 2 Tm 3:6; 2 Pt 2:1. e. [5] Nm 14:35; 1 Cor 10:5; Heb 3:16, 17. f. [6] 2 Pt 2:4, 9. g. [7] Dt 29:22–24; Mt 25:41; 2 Thes 1:8–9; 2 Pt 2:6; 3:7.

yourselves in the love of God and wait for the mercy of our Lord Jesus Christ that leads to eternal life.[r] [22]On those who waver, have mercy;[*] [23]save others by snatching them out of the fire; on others have mercy with fear,[†] abhorring even the outer garment stained by the flesh.

**Doxology.**[‡] [24]To the one who is able to keep you from stumbling and to present you unblemished and exultant, in the presence of his glory,[s] [25]to the only God, our savior, through Jesus Christ our Lord be glory, majesty, power, and authority from ages past, now, and for ages to come. Amen.[t]

---

*[22] **Have mercy**: some manuscripts read "convince," "confute," or "reprove." Others have "even though you waver" or "doubt" instead of **who waver**.

†[23] **With fear**: some manuscripts connect the phrase "with fear" with the imperative "save" or with the participle "snatching." Other manuscripts omit the phrase "on others have mercy," so that only two groups are envisioned. Rescue of those led astray and caution in the endeavor are both

enjoined. **Outer garment stained by the flesh**: the imagery may come from Zec 3:3–5, just as that of **snatching . . . out of the fire** comes from Zec 3:2; the very garments of the godless are to be abhorred because of their contagion.

‡[24–25] With this liturgical statement about the power of God to keep the faithful from stumbling, and praise to him through Jesus Christ, the letter reaches its conclusion by returning to the themes with which it began (Jude 1–2).

r. [21] Ti 2:13.

s. [24] 2 Cor 4:14; 1 Pt 4:13.    t. [25] Rom 11:36; 1 Tm 1:17.

# THE BOOK OF
# REVELATION

The Apocalypse, or Revelation to John, the last book of the Bible, is one of the most difficult to understand because it abounds in unfamiliar and extravagant symbolism, which at best appears unusual to the modern reader. Symbolic language, however, is one of the chief characteristics of apocalyptic literature, of which this book is an outstanding example. Such literature enjoyed wide popularity in both Jewish and Christian circles from ca. 200 B.C. to A.D. 200.

This book contains an account of visions in symbolic and allegorical language borrowed extensively from the Old Testament, especially Ezekiel, Zechariah, and Daniel. Whether or not these visions were real experiences of the author or simply literary conventions employed by him is an open question.

This much, however, is certain: symbolic descriptions are not to be taken as literal descriptions, nor is the symbolism meant to be pictured realistically. One would find it difficult and repulsive to visualize a lamb with seven horns and seven eyes; yet Jesus Christ is described in precisely such words (Rev 5:6). The author used these images to suggest Christ's universal (seven) power (horns) and knowledge (eyes). A significant feature of apocalyptic writing is the use of symbolic colors, metals, garments (Rev 1:13–16; 3:18; 4:4; 6:1–8; 17:4; 19:8), and numbers (*four* signifies the world, *six* imperfection, *seven* totality or perfection, *twelve* Israel's tribes or the apostles, *one thousand* immensity). Finally the vindictive language in the book (Rev 6:9–10; 18:1–19:4) is also to be understood symbolically and not literally. The cries for vengeance on the lips of Christian martyrs that sound so harsh are in fact literary devices the author employed to evoke in the reader and hearer a feeling of horror for apostasy and rebellion that will be severely punished by God.

The lurid descriptions of the punishment of Jezebel (Rev 2:22) and of the destruction of the great harlot, Babylon (Rev 16:9–19:2), are likewise literary devices. The metaphor of Babylon as harlot would be wrongly construed if interpreted literally. On the other hand, the stylized figure of the woman clothed with the sun (Rev 12:1–6), depicting the New Israel, may seem to be a negative stereotype. It is necessary to look beyond the literal meaning to see that these images mean to convey a sense of God's wrath at sin in the former case and trust in God's providential care over the church in the latter.

The Book of Revelation cannot be adequately understood except against the historical background that occasioned its writing. Like Daniel and other apocalypses, it was composed as resistance literature to meet a crisis. The book itself suggests that the crisis was ruthless persecution of the early church by the Roman authorities; the harlot Babylon symbolizes pagan Rome, the city on seven hills (Rev 17:9). The book is, then, an exhortation and admonition to Christians of the first century to stand firm in the faith and to avoid compromise with paganism, despite the threat of adversity and martyrdom; they are to await patiently the fulfillment of God's mighty promises. The triumph of God in the world of men and women remains a mystery, to be accepted in faith and longed for in hope. It is a triumph that unfolded in the history of Jesus of Nazareth and continues to unfold in the history of the individual Christian who follows the way of the cross, even, if necessary, to a martyr's death.

Though the perspective is eschatological—ultimate salvation and victory are said to take place at the end of the present age when Christ will come in glory at the parousia—the book presents the decisive struggle of Christ and his followers against Satan and his cohorts as already over. Christ's overwhelming defeat of the kingdom of Satan ushered in the everlasting reign of God (Rev 11:15; 12:10). Even the forces of evil unwittingly carry out the divine plan (Rev 17:17), for God is the sovereign Lord of history.

The Book of Revelation had its origin in a time of crisis, but it remains valid and meaningful for Christians of all time. In the face of apparently insuperable evil, either from within or from without, all Christians are called to trust in Jesus' promise, "Behold, I am with you always, until the end of the age" (Mt 28:20). Those who remain steadfast in their faith and confidence in the risen Lord need have no fear. Suffering, persecution, even death by martyrdom, though remaining impenetrable mysteries of evil, do not comprise an absurd dead end. No matter what adversity or sacrifice Christians may endure, they will in the end triumph over Satan and his forces because of their fidelity to Christ the victor. This is the enduring message of the book; it is a message of hope and consolation and challenge for all who dare to believe.

The author of the book calls himself John (Rev 1:1, 4, 9; 22:8), who because of his Christian faith has been exiled to the rocky island of Patmos, a Roman penal colony. Although he never claims to be John the apostle, whose name is attached to the fourth gospel, he was so identified by several of the early church Fathers, including Justin, Irenaeus, Clement of Alexandria, Tertullian, Cyprian, and Hippolytus. This identification, however, was denied by other Fathers, including Denis of Alexandria, Eusebius of Caesarea, Cyril of Jerusalem, Gregory Nazianzen, and John Chrysostom. Indeed, vocabulary, grammar, and style make it doubtful that the book could have been put into its present form by the same person(s) responsible for the fourth gospel. Nevertheless, there are definite linguistic and theological affinities between the two books. The tone of the letters to the seven churches (Rev 1:4–3:22) is indicative of the great authority the author enjoyed over the Christian communities in Asia. It is possible, therefore, that he was a disciple of John the apostle, who is traditionally associated with that part of the world. The date of the book in its present form is probably near the end of the reign of Domitian (A.D. 81–96), a fierce persecutor of the Christians.

The principal divisions of the Book of Revelation are the following:

I. Prologue (1:1–3)

II. Letters to the Churches of Asia (1:4–3:22)

III. God and the Lamb in Heaven (4:1–5:14)

IV. The Seven Seals, Trumpets, and Plagues, with Interludes (6:1–16:21)

V. The Punishment of Babylon and the Destruction of Pagan Nations (17:1–20:15)

VI. The New Creation (21:1–22:5)

VII. Epilogue (22:6–21)

## I. PROLOGUE[*]

### CHAPTER 1

[1]The revelation of Jesus Christ, which God gave to him, to show his servants what must happen soon. He made it known by sending his angel to his servant John,[a] [2]who gives witness to the word of God and to the testimony of Jesus Christ by reporting what he saw. [3]Blessed is the one[†] who reads aloud and blessed are those who listen to this prophetic message and heed what is written in it, for the appointed time is near.[b]

---

[*][1:1-3] This prologue describes the source, contents, and audience of the book and forms an inclusion with the epilogue (Rev 22:6–21), with its similar themes and expressions.

[†][1:3] **Blessed is the one:** this is the first of seven beatitudes in this book; the others are in Rev 14:13; 16:15; 19:9; 20:6; 22:7, 14. **This prophetic message:** literally, "the words of the prophecy"; so Rev 22:7, 10, 18, 19 by inclusion. **The appointed time:** when Jesus will return in glory; cf. Rev 1:7; 3:11; 22:7, 10, 12, 20.

---

a. [1:1] 22:6–8, 20; Dn 2:28 / Rev 19:10.   b. [1:3] 22:7 / Lk 11:28.

## II. LETTERS TO THE CHURCHES OF ASIA

**Greeting.**[‡] [4]John, to the seven churches in Asia:[§] grace to you and peace from him who is and who was and who is to come, and from the seven spirits before his throne,[c] [5]and from Jesus Christ, the faithful witness, the firstborn of the dead and ruler of the kings of the earth. To him who loves us and has freed us[¶] from our sins by

---

[‡][1:4–8] Although Revelation begins and ends (Rev 22:21) with Christian epistolary formulae, there is nothing between Rev 4; 22 resembling a letter. The author here employs the standard word order for greetings in Greek letter writing: "N. to N., greetings . . ."; see note on Rom 1:1.

[§][1:4] **Seven churches in Asia:** Asia refers to the Roman province of that name in western Asia Minor (modern Turkey); these representative churches are mentioned by name in Rev 1:11, and each is the recipient of a message (Rev 2:1–3:22). **Seven** is the biblical number suggesting fullness and completeness; thus the seer is writing for the whole church.

[¶][1:5] **Freed us:** the majority of Greek manuscripts and several early versions read "washed us"; but "freed us" is supported by the best manuscripts and fits well with Old Testament imagery, e.g., Is 40:2.

---

c. [1:4] 8; 4:8; 11:17; 16:5; Ex 3:14.

his blood,[d] [6]who has made us into a kingdom, priests for his God and Father, to him be glory and power forever [and ever]. Amen.[e]

[7] Behold, he is coming amid the clouds,
    and every eye will see him,
    even those who pierced him.
All the peoples of the earth will lament
    him.
    Yes. Amen.[f]

[8]"I am the Alpha and the Omega,"* says the Lord God, "the one who is and who was and who is to come, the almighty."[g]
**The First Vision.**[†] [9]I, John, your brother, who share with you the distress, the kingdom, and the endurance we have in Jesus, found myself on the island called Patmos[‡] because I proclaimed God's word and gave testimony to Jesus. [10]I was caught up in spirit on the Lord's day[§] and heard behind me a voice as loud as a trumpet, [11]which said, "Write on a scroll[¶] what you see and send it to the seven churches: to Ephesus, Smyrna, Pergamum, Thyatira, Sardis, Philadelphia, and Laodicea." [12]"Then I turned to see whose voice it was that spoke to me, and when I turned, I saw seven gold lampstands [13]and in the midst of the lampstands one like a son of man,[††] wearing an ankle-length robe, with a gold sash around his chest.[h] [14]The hair of his head was as white as white wool or as snow,[‡‡] and his eyes were like a fiery flame. [15]His feet were like polished brass refined in a furnace,[§§] and his voice was like

the sound of rushing water. [16]In his right hand he held seven stars.[¶¶] A sharp two-edged sword came out of his mouth, and his face shone like the sun at its brightest.[i]

[17]When I caught sight of him, I fell down at his feet as though dead.*** He touched me with his right hand and said, "Do not be afraid. I am the first and the last,[j] [18]the one who lives. Once I was dead, but now I am alive forever and ever. I hold the keys to death and the netherworld.[†††] [19]Write down, therefore, what you have seen, and what is happening, and what will happen afterwards.[‡‡‡] [20]This is the secret meaning[§§§] of the seven stars you saw in my right hand, and of the seven gold lampstands: the seven stars are the angels of the seven churches, and the seven lampstands are the seven churches.

## CHAPTER 2

**To Ephesus.** [¶¶¶]"To the angel of the church**** in Ephesus,[††††] write this:
"'The one who holds the seven stars in his right hand and walks in the midst of the seven gold lampstands says this: [2]"I know your works,

---

*[1:8] **The Alpha and the Omega**: the first and last letters of the Greek alphabet. In Rev 22:13 the same words occur together with the expressions "the First and the Last, the Beginning and the End"; cf. Rev 1:17; 2:8; 21:6; Is 41:4; 44:6.

†[1:9–20] In this first vision, the seer is commanded to write what he sees to the seven churches (Rev 1:9–11). He sees Christ in glory, whom he depicts in stock apocalyptic imagery (Rev 1:12–16), and hears him describe himself in terms meant to encourage Christians by emphasizing his victory over death (Rev 1:17–20).

‡[1:9] **Island called Patmos**: one of the Sporades islands in the Aegean Sea, some fifty miles south of Ephesus, used by the Romans as a penal colony. **Because I proclaimed God's word**: literally, "on account of God's word."

§[1:10] **The Lord's day**: Sunday. **As loud as a trumpet**: the imagery is derived from the theophany at Sinai (Ex 19:16, 19; cf. Heb 12:19 and the trumpet in other eschatological settings in Is 27:13; Jl 2:1; Mt 24:31; 1 Cor 15:52; 1 Thes 4:16).

¶[1:11] **Scroll**: a papyrus roll.

**[1:12–16] A symbolic description of Christ in glory. The metaphorical language is not to be understood literally; cf. Introduction.

††[1:13] **Son of man**: see note on Mk 8:31. **Ankle-length robe**: Christ is priest; cf. Ex 28:4; 29:5; Wis 18:24; Zec 3:4. **Gold sash**: Christ is king; cf. Ex 28:4; 1 Mc 10:89; 11:58; Dn 10:5.

‡‡[1:14] **Hair . . . as white as white wool or as snow**: Christ is eternal, clothed with the dignity that belonged to the "Ancient of Days"; cf. Rev 1:18; Dn 7:9. **His eyes were like a fiery flame**: Christ is portrayed as all-knowing; cf. Rev 2:23; Ps 7:10; Jer 17:10; and similar expressions in Rev 2:18; 19:12; Dn 10:6.

§§[1:15] **His feet** . . . **furnace**: Christ is depicted as unchangeable; cf. Ez 1:27; Dn 10:6. The Greek word translated

"refined" is unconnected grammatically with any other word in the sentence. **His voice . . . water**: Christ speaks with divine authority; cf. Ez 1:24.

¶¶[1:16] **Seven stars**: in the pagan world, Mithras and the Caesars were represented with seven stars in their right hand, symbolizing their universal dominion. **A sharp two-edged sword**: this refers to the word of God (cf. Eph 6:17; Heb 4:12) that will destroy unrepentant sinners; cf. Rev 2:16; 19:15; Wis 18:15; Is 11:4; 49:2. **His face . . . brightest**: this symbolizes the divine majesty of Christ; cf. Rev 10:1; 21:23; Jgs 5:31; Is 60:19; Mt 17:2.

***[1:17] It was an Old Testament belief that for sinful human beings to see God was to die; cf. Ex 19:21; 33:20; Jgs 6:22–23; Is 6:5.

†††[1:18] **Netherworld**: Greek Hades, Hebrew Sheol, the abode of the dead; cf. Rev 20:13–14; Nm 16:33.

‡‡‡[1:19] **What you have seen, and what is happening, and what will happen afterwards**: the three parts of the Book of Revelation, the vision (Rev 1:10–20), the situation in the seven churches (Rev 2–3), and the events of Rev 6–22.

§§§[1:20] **Secret meaning**: literally, "mystery." **Angels**: these are the presiding spirits of the seven churches. Angels were thought to be in charge of the physical world (cf. Rev 7:1; 14:18; 16:5) and of nations (Dn 10:13; 12:1), communities (the seven churches), and individuals (Mt 18:10; Acts 12:15). Some have seen in the "angel" of each of the seven churches its pastor or a personification of the spirit of the congregation.

¶¶¶[2:1–3:22] Each of the seven letters follows the same pattern: address; description of the exalted Christ; blame and/or praise for the church addressed; threat and/or admonition; final exhortation and promise to all Christians.

****[2:1–7] The letter to Ephesus praises the members of the church there for their works and virtues, including discerning false teachers (Rev 2:2–3), but admonishes them to repent and return to their former devotion (Rev 2:4–5). It concludes with a reference to the Nicolaitans (see note on Rev 2:6) and a promise that the victor will have access to eternal life (Rev 2:7).

††††[2:1] **Ephesus**: this great ancient city had a population of ca. 250,000; it was the capital of the Roman province of Asia and the commercial, cultural, and religious center of Asia. The other six churches were located in the same province, situated roughly in a circle; they were selected for geographical reasons rather than for the size of their Christian communities. **Walks in the midst of the seven gold lampstands**: this signifies that Christ is always present in the church; see note on Rev 1:4.

---

d. [1:5] 3:14; 1 Cor 15:20; Col 1:18 / Heb 9:14; 1 Pt 1:19; 1 Jn 1:7.   e. [1:6] Ex 19:6; 1 Pt 2:9.   f. [1:7] Dn 7:13 / Zec 12:10; Mt 24:30; Jn 19:37.   g. [1:8] 17; 21:6; 22:13; Is 41:4; 44:6; 48:12.   h. [1:13] Dn 7:13; 10:5.

i. [1:16] Heb 4:12.   j. [1:17] Dn 8:18 / Rev 1:8.

your labor, and your endurance, and that you cannot tolerate the wicked; you have tested those who call themselves apostles but are not, and discovered that they are impostors.* ³Moreover, you have endurance and have suffered for my name, and you have not grown weary. ⁴Yet I hold this against you: you have lost the love you had at first. ⁵Realize how far you have fallen. Repent, and do the works you did at first. Otherwise, I will come to you and remove your lampstand from its place, unless you repent. ⁶But you have this in your favor: you hate the works of the Nicolaitans,† which I also hate.

⁷"Whoever has ears ought to hear what the Spirit says to the churches. To the victor‡ I will give the right to eat from the tree of life that is in the garden of God."ᵏ

**To Smyrna.**§ ⁸"To the angel of the church in Smyrna,ⁿ write this:

"'The first and the last, who once died but came to life, says this: ⁹"I know your tribulation and poverty, but you are rich."** I know the slander of those who claim to be Jews and are not, but rather are members of the assembly of Satan.ˡ ¹⁰Do not be afraid of anything that you are going to suffer. Indeed, the devil will throw some of you into prison, that you may be tested, and you will face an ordeal for ten days. Remain faithful until death, and I will give you the crown of life.

¹¹"Whoever has ears ought to hear what the Spirit says to the churches.ᵐ The victor shall not be harmed by the second death.'"††

**To Pergamum.**‡‡ ¹²"To the angel of the church in Pergamum,§§ write this:

"'The one with the sharp two-edged sword says this: ¹³"I know that you live where Satan's throne¶¶ is, and yet you hold fast to my name and have not denied your faith in me, not even in the days of Antipas, my faithful witness, who was martyred among you, where Satan lives. ¹⁴"Yet I have a few things against you. You have some people there who hold to the teaching of Balaam, who instructed Balak to put a stumbling block before the Israelites: to eat food sacrificed to idols and to play the harlot.ⁿ ¹⁵Likewise, you also have some people who hold to the teaching of [the] Nicolaitans. ¹⁶Therefore, repent. Otherwise, I will come to you quickly and wage war against them with the sword of my mouth.

¹⁷"Whoever has ears ought to hear what the Spirit says to the churches. To the victor I shall give some of the hidden manna;††† I shall also give a white amulet upon which is inscribed a new name, which no one knows except the one who receives it.'"ᵒ

**To Thyatira.**‡‡‡ ¹⁸"To the angel of the church in Thyatira,§§§ write this:

"'The Son of God, whose eyes are like a fiery flame and whose feet are like polished brass,

---

‡‡[2:12–17] The letter to Pergamum praises the members of the church for persevering in their faith in Christ even in the midst of a pagan setting and in face of persecution and martyrdom (Rev 2:13). But it admonishes them about members who advocate an unprincipled morality (Rev 2:14; cf. 2 Pt 2:15; Jude 11) and others who follow the teaching of the Nicolaitans (Rev 2:15; see note there). It urges them to repent (Rev 2:16) and promises them the hidden manna and Christ's amulet (Rev 2:17).

§§[2:12] **Pergamum:** modern Bergama, ca. forty-five miles northeast of Smyrna, a center for various kinds of pagan worship. It also had an outstanding library (the word *parchment* is derived from its name).

¶¶[2:13] **Satan's throne:** the reference is to emperor worship and other pagan practices that flourished in Pergamum, perhaps specifically to the white marble altar erected and dedicated to Zeus by Eumenes II (197–160 B.C.).

***[2:14–15] Like Balaam, the biblical prototype of the religious compromiser (cf. Nm 25:1–3; 31:16; 2 Pt 2:15; Jude 11), the Nicolaitans in Pergamum and Ephesus (Rev 2:6) accommodated their Christian faith to paganism. They abused the principle of liberty enunciated by Paul (1 Cor 9:19–23).

†††[2:17] **The hidden manna:** this is the food of life; cf. Ps 78:24–25. **White amulet:** literally, "white stone," on which was written a magical name, whose power could be tapped by one who knew the secret name. It is used here as a symbol of victory and joy; cf. Rev 3:4–5. **New name:** this is a reference to the Christian's rebirth in Christ; cf. Rev 3:12; 19:12; Is 62:2; 65:15.

‡‡‡[2:18–29] The letter to Thyatira praises the progress in virtue of this small Christian community (Rev 2:19) but admonishes them for tolerating a false prophet who leads them astray (Rev 2:20). Her fate is sealed, but there is hope of repentance for her followers (Rev 2:21–22). Otherwise, they too shall die (Rev 2:23). They are warned against Satanic power or knowledge (Rev 2:24–25). Those who remain faithful will share in the messianic reign, having authority over nations (Rev 2:26–27), and will in fact possess Christ himself (Rev 2:8).

§§§[2:18] **Thyatira:** modern Akhisar, ca. forty miles southeast of Pergamum, a frontier town famous for its workers' guilds (cf. Acts 16:14), membership in which may have involved festal meals in pagan temples.

---

*[2:2] **Who call themselves . . . impostors:** this refers to unauthorized and perverse missionaries; cf. Acts 20:29–30.

†[2:6] **Nicolaitans:** these are perhaps the impostors of Rev 2:2; see note on Rev 2:14–15. There is little evidence for connecting this group with Nicolaus, the proselyte from Antioch, mentioned in Acts 6:5.

‡[2:7] **Victor:** referring to any Christian individual who holds fast to the faith and does God's will in the face of persecution. **The tree of life that is in the garden of God:** this is a reference to the tree in the primeval paradise (Gn 2:9); cf. Rev 22:2, 14, 19. The decree excluding humanity from the tree of life has been revoked by Christ.

§[2:8–11] The letter to Smyrna encourages the Christians in this important commercial center by telling them that although they are impoverished, they are nevertheless rich, and calls those Jews who are slandering them members of the assembly of Satan (Rev 2:9). There is no admonition; rather, the Christians are told that they will suffer much, even death, but the time of tribulation will be short compared to their eternal reward (Rev 2:10), and they will thus escape final damnation (Rev 2:11).

¶[2:8] **Smyrna:** modern Izmir, ca. thirty miles north of Ephesus, and the chief city of Lydia, with a temple to the goddess Roma. It was renowned for its loyalty to Rome, and it also had a large Jewish community very hostile toward Christians.

**[2:9–10] The church in Smyrna was materially poor but spiritually rich. Accusations made by Jewish brethren occasioned the persecution of Christians; cf. Acts 14:2, 19; 17:5, 13.

††[2:11] **The second death:** this refers to the eternal death, when sinners will receive their final punishment; cf. Rev 20:6, 14–15; 21:8.

---

k. [2:7] 11, 17, 29; 3:6, 13, 22; 13:9; Mt 11:15.   l. [2:9] Jas 2:5.
m. [2:11] 20:6, 14; 21:8.

n. [2:14] Nm 22–24; 25:1–3; 31:16; 2 Pt 2:15; Jude 11.   o. [2:17] Is 62:2; 65:15.

says this: ¹⁹"I know your works, your love, faith, service, and endurance, and that your last works are greater than the first. ²⁰Yet I hold this against you, that you tolerate the woman Jezebel, who calls herself a prophetess, who teaches and misleads my servants to play the harlot and to eat food sacrificed to idols.* ²¹I have given her time to repent, but she refuses to repent of her harlotry. ²²So I will cast her on a sickbed and plunge those who commit adultery with her into intense suffering unless they repent of her works. ²³I will also put her children† to death. Thus shall all the churches come to know that I am the searcher of hearts and minds and that I will give each of you what your works deserve.ᵖ ²⁴But I say to the rest of you in Thyatira, who do not uphold this teaching and know nothing of the so-called deep secrets of Satan:‡ on you I will place no further burden, ²⁵except that you must hold fast to what you have until I come.

²⁶ "'"To the victor,§ who keeps to my ways'
        until the end,
    I will give authority over the
        nations.�q
²⁷ He will rule them with an iron rod.
    Like clay vessels will they be
        smashed,

²⁸just as I received authority from my Father. And to him I will give the morning star. ²⁹"'"Whoever has ears ought to hear what the Spirit says to the churches.'"

### CHAPTER 3
**To Sardis.**" ¹"To the angel of the church in Sardis,†† write this:

"'The one who has the seven spirits of God and the seven stars says this: "I know your works, that you have the reputation of being alive, but you are dead. ²Be watchful and strengthen what

is left, which is going to die, for I have not found your works complete in the sight of my God. ³Remember then how you accepted and heard; keep it, and repent. If you are not watchful, I will come like a thief, and you will never know at what hour I will come upon you.ʳ ⁴However, you have a few people in Sardis who have not soiled their garments; they will walk with me dressed in white, because they are worthy.ˢ

⁵"'"The victor will thus be dressed in white,‡‡ and I will never erase his name from the book of life but will acknowledge his name in the presence of my Father and of his angels.ᵗ

⁶"'"Whoever has ears ought to hear what the Spirit says to the churches.'"

**To Philadelphia.**§§ ⁷"To the angel of the church in Philadelphia,¶¶ write this:

"'The holy one, the true,
    who holds the key of David,
    who opens and no one shall close,
    who closes and no one shall open,ᵘ

says this:
⁸"'"I know your works (behold, I have left an open door"" before you, which no one can close). You have limited strength, and yet you have kept my word and have not denied my name. ⁹Behold, I will make those of the assembly of Satan who claim to be Jews and are not, but are lying, behold I will make them come and fall prostrate at your feet, and they will realize that I love you.ᵛ ¹⁰Because you have kept my message of endurance,††† I will keep you safe in the time of trial that is going to come to the whole world to test the inhabitants of the earth. ¹¹I am coming

---

*[2:20] The scheming and treacherous Jezebel of old (cf. 1 Kgs 19:1–2; 21:1–14; 2 Kgs 9:22, 30–34) introduced pagan customs into the religion of Israel; this new Jezebel was doing the same to Christianity.

†[2:23] **Children**: spiritual descendants.

‡[2:24] **The so-called deep secrets of Satan**: literally, "the deep things of Satan," a scathing reference to the perverse teaching of the Nicolaitans (Rev 2:15).

§[2:26–28] The Christian who perseveres in faith will share in Christ's messianic authority (cf. Ps 2:8–9) and resurrection victory over death, symbolized by the morning star; cf. Rev 22:16.

¶[2:26] **Who keeps to my ways**: literally, "who keeps my works."

**[3:1–6] The letter to Sardis does not praise the community but admonishes its members to watchfulness, mutual support, and repentance (Rev 3:2–3). The few who have remained pure and faithful will share Christ's victory and will be inscribed in the book of life (Rev 3:4–5).

††[3:1] **Sardis**: this city, located ca. thirty miles southeast of Thyatira, was once the capital of Lydia, known for its wealth at the time of Croesus (6th century B.C.). Its citadel, reputed to be unassailable, was captured by surprise, first by Cyrus and later by Antiochus. The church is therefore warned to be on guard.

‡‡[3:5] **In white**: white is a sign of victory and joy as well as resurrection; see note on Rev 2:17. **The book of life**: the roll in which the names of the redeemed are kept; cf. Rev 13:8; 17:8; 20:12, 15; 21:27; Phil 4:3; Dn 12:1. They will be acknowledged by Christ in heaven; cf. Mt 10:32.

§§[3:7–13] The letter to Philadelphia praises the Christians there for remaining faithful even with their limited strength (Rev 3:8). Members of the assembly of Satan are again singled out (Rev 3:9; see Rev 2:9). There is no admonition; rather, the letter promises that they will be kept safe at the great trial (Rev 3:10–11) and that the victors will become pillars of the heavenly temple, upon which three names will be inscribed: God, Jerusalem, and Christ (Rev 3:12).

¶¶[3:7] **Philadelphia**: modern Alasehir, ca. thirty miles southeast of Sardis, founded by Attalus II Philadelphus of Pergamum to be an "open door" (Rev 3:8) for Greek culture; it was destroyed by an earthquake in A.D. 17. Rebuilt by money from the Emperor Tiberius, the city was renamed Neo-Caesarea; this may explain the allusions to "name" in Rev 3:12. **Key of David**: to the heavenly city of David (cf. Is 22:22), "the new Jerusalem" (Rev 3:12), over which Christ has supreme authority.

***[3:8] **An open door**: opportunities for sharing and proclaiming the faith; cf. Acts 14:27; 1 Cor 16:9; 2 Cor 2:12.

†††[3:10] **My message of endurance**: this does not refer to a saying of Jesus about patience but to the example of Christ's patient endurance. **The inhabitants of the earth**: literally, "those who live on the earth." This expression, which also occurs in Rev 6:10; 8:13; 11:10; 13:8, 12, 14; 17:2, 8, always refers to the pagan world.

---

p. [2:23] 1 Sm 16:7; Jer 11:20; 17:10.   q. [2:26] 12:5; Ps 2:8–9.

r. [3:3] Mt 24:42–44; Mk 13:33; 1 Thes 5:2; 2 Pt 3:10.   s. [3:4] 7:13–14.   t. [3:5] Ps 69:29; Dn 12:1 / Mt 10:32.   u. [3:7] Is 22:22; Mt 16:19.   v. [3:9] 2:9 / Is 45:14; 60:14.

quickly. Hold fast to what you have, so that no one may take your crown.ʷ

¹²"""The victor I will make into a pillar* in the temple of my God, and he will never leave it again. On him I will inscribe the name of my God and the name of the city of my God, the new Jerusalem, which comes down out of heaven from my God, as well as my new name.ˣ

¹³"""Whoever has ears ought to hear what the Spirit says to the churches.""

**To Laodicea.**† ¹⁴"To the angel of the church in Laodicea,‡ write this:

""The Amen, the faithful and true witness, the source of God's creation, says this:ʸ ¹⁵"I know your works; I know that you are neither cold nor hot.ˢ I wish you were either cold or hot. ¹⁶"So, because you are lukewarm, neither hot nor cold, I will spit you out of my mouth. ¹⁷"*ᶻFor you say, 'I am rich and affluent and have no need of anything,' and yet do not realize that you are wretched, pitiable, poor, blind, and naked. ¹⁸I advise you to buy from me gold refined by fire†† so that you may be rich, and white garments to put on so that your shameful nakedness may not be exposed, and buy ointment to smear on your eyes so that you may see. ¹⁹Those whom I love, I reprove and chastise. Be earnest, therefore, and repent.ᵃ

²⁰"""Behold, I stand at the door and knock. If anyone hears my voice and opens the door, [then] I will enter his house and dine with him,

and he with me.‡‡ ²¹I will give the victor the right to sit with me on my throne, as I myself first won the victory and sit with my Father on his throne.ᵇ

²²"""Whoever has ears ought to hear what the Spirit says to the churches."""

## III. GOD AND THE LAMB IN HEAVEN

### CHAPTER 4
**Vision of Heavenly Worship.**§§ ¹After this I had a vision of an open door§§ to heaven, and I heard the trumpetlike voice that had spoken to me before, saying, "Come up here and I will show you what must happen afterwards." ²"At once I was caught up in spirit.ᶜ A throne was there in heaven, and on the throne sat ³one whose appearance sparkled like jasper and carnelian. Around the throne was a halo as brilliant as an emerald. ⁴Surrounding the throne I saw twenty-four other thrones on which twenty-four elders††† sat, dressed in white garments and with gold crowns on their heads.ᵈ ⁵From the throne came flashes of lightning, rumblings, and peals of thunder.‡‡‡ Seven flaming torches burned in front of the throne, which are the seven spirits of God. ⁶"In front of the throne was something that resembled a sea of glass like crystal.§§§

In the center and around the throne, there were four living creatures covered with eyes in front and in back. ⁷The first creature resembled a lion, the second was like a calf, the third had a face like that of a human being, and the fourth looked like an eagle¶¶¶ in flight. ⁸The four living

---

*[3:12] **Pillar**: this may be an allusion to the rebuilding of the city; see note on v 7. **New Jerusalem**: it is described in Rev 21:10–22:5.

†[3:14–22] The letter to Laodicea reprimands the community for being lukewarm (Rev 3:15–16), but no particular faults are singled out. Their material prosperity is contrasted with their spiritual poverty, the violet tunics that were the source of their wealth with the white robe of baptism, and their famous eye ointment with true spiritual perception (Rev 3:17–18). But Christ's chastisement is inspired by love and a desire to be allowed to share the messianic banquet with his followers in the heavenly kingdom (Rev 3:9–21).

‡[3:14] **Laodicea**: ca. forty miles southeast of Philadelphia and ca. eighty miles east of Ephesus, a wealthy industrial and commercial center, with a renowned medical school. It exported fine woolen garments and was famous for its eye salves. It was so wealthy that it was proudly rebuilt without outside aid after the devastating earthquake of A.D. 60/61. **The Amen**: this is a divine title (cf. Hebrew text of Is 65:16) applied to Christ; cf, 2 Cor 1:20. **Source of God's creation**: literally, "the beginning of God's creation," a concept found also in Jn 1:3; Col 1:16–17; Heb 1:2; cf. Prv 8:22–31; Wis 9:1–2.

§[3:15–16] Halfhearted commitment to the faith is nauseating to Christ; cf. Rom 12:11.

¶[3:16] **Spit**: literally, "vomit." The image is that of a beverage that should be either hot or cold. Perhaps there is an allusion to the hot springs of Hierapolis across the Lycus river from Laodicea, which would have been lukewarm by the time they reached Laodicea.

**[3:17] Economic prosperity occasioned spiritual bankruptcy.

††[3:18] **Gold . . . fire**: God's grace. **White garments**: symbol of an upright life; the city was noted for its violet/purple cloth. **Ointment . . . eyes**: to remove spiritual blindness; one of the city's exports was eye ointment (see note on Rev 3:14).

‡‡[3:20] Christ invites all to the messianic banquet in heaven; cf. Is 25:6; Lk 14:15; 22:30.

§§[4:1–11] The seer now describes a vision of the heavenly court in worship of God enthroned. He reverently avoids naming or describing God but pictures twenty-four elders in priestly and regal attire (Rev 4:4) and God's throne and its surroundings made of precious gems and other symbols that traditionally express the majesty of God (Rev 4:5–6). Universal creation is represented by the four living creatures (Rev 4:6–7). Along with the twenty-four elders, they praise God unceasingly in humble adoration (Rev 4:8–11).

¶¶[4:1] The ancients viewed heaven as a solid vault, entered by way of actual doors.

***[4:2–8] Much of the imagery here is taken from Ez 1; 10.

†††[4:4] **Twenty-four elders**: these represent the twelve tribes of Israel and the twelve apostles; cf. Rev 21:12–14.

‡‡‡[4:5] **Flashes of lightning, rumblings, and peals of thunder**: as in other descriptions of God's appearance or activity; cf. Rev 8:5; 11:19; 16:18; Ex 19:16; Ez 1:4, 13. **The seven spirits of God**: the seven "angels of the presence" as in Rev 8:2 and Tb 12:15.

§§§[4:6] **A sea of glass like crystal**: an image adapted from Ez 1:22–26. **Four living creatures**: these are symbols taken from Ez 1:5–21; they are identified as cherubim in Ez 10:20. **Covered with eyes**: these suggest God's knowledge and concern.

¶¶¶[4:7] **Lion . . . calf . . . human being . . . eagle**: these symbolize, respectively, what is noblest, strongest, wisest, and swiftest in creation. **Calf**: traditionally translated "ox," the Greek word refers to a heifer or young bull. Since the second century, these four creatures have been used as symbols of the evangelists Mark, Luke, Matthew, and John, respectively.

---

w. [3:11] 2:25; 22:7, 20.   x. [3:12] 21:2–3; Ez 48:35 / Rev 19:13.
y. [3:14] 1:5.   z. [3:17] Prv 13:7; Lk 12:21.   a. [3:19] Prv 3:11–12;
1 Cor 11:32; Heb 12:5–11.

b. [3:21] Lk 22:28–30; Mt 19:28.   c. [4:2–3] Is 6:1 / Ez 1:26–28.
d. [4:4] Is 24:23.   e. [4:6] Ex 24:10.

creatures, each of them with six wings,* were covered with eyes inside and out. Day and night they do not stop exclaiming:

> "Holy, holy, holy is the Lord God
>     almighty,
>     who was, and who is, and who is to
>         come."*f*

⁹Whenever the living creatures give glory and honor and thanks to the one who sits on the throne, who lives forever and ever, ¹⁰the twenty-four elders fall down before the one who sits on the throne and worship him, who lives forever and ever. They throw down their crowns before the throne, exclaiming:

> ¹¹ "Worthy are you, Lord our God,
>     to receive glory and honor and
>         power,
>   for you created all things;
>         because of your will they came to be
>             and were created."*g*

## CHAPTER 5

**The Scroll and the Lamb.**† ¹I saw a scroll‡ in the right hand of the one who sat on the throne. It had writing on both sides and was sealed with seven seals.*h* ²Then I saw a mighty angel who proclaimed in a loud voice, "Who is worthy to open the scroll and break its seals?" ³But no one in heaven or on earth or under the earth was able to open the scroll or to examine it. ⁴I shed many tears because no one was found worthy to open the scroll or to examine it. ⁵One of the elders said to me, "Do not weep. The lion of the tribe of Judah, the root of David,§ has triumphed, enabling him to open the scroll and its seven seals."*i*

⁶Then I saw standing in the midst of the throne and the four living creatures and the elders a Lamb¶ that seemed to have been slain. He had seven horns and seven eyes; these are the [seven] spirits of God sent out into the whole world.*j* ⁷He came and received the scroll from the right hand of the one who sat on the throne. ⁸When he took it, the four living creatures and the twenty-four elders fell down before the Lamb. Each of the elders held a harp and gold bowls filled with incense, which are the prayers of the holy ones. ⁹They sang a new hymn:

> "Worthy are you to receive the scroll
>     and to break open its seals,
>   for you were slain and with your
>         blood you purchased for God
>   those from every tribe and tongue,
>         people and nation.
> ¹⁰ You made them a kingdom and priests for
>         our God,
>     and they will reign on earth."*k*

¹¹I looked again and heard the voices of many angels who surrounded the throne and the living creatures and the elders. They were countless** in number,*l* ¹²and they cried out in a loud voice:

> "Worthy is the Lamb that was slain
>     to receive power and riches, wisdom
>         and strength,
>     honor and glory and blessing."

¹³Then I heard every creature in heaven and on earth and under the earth and in the sea, everything in the universe, cry out:

> "To the one who sits on the throne and to
>         the Lamb
>     be blessing and honor, glory and
>         might,
>   forever and ever."

¹⁴The four living creatures answered, "Amen," and the elders fell down and worshiped.

## IV. THE SEVEN SEALS, TRUMPETS, AND PLAGUES, WITH INTERLUDES††

---

\* [4:8] **Six wings:** like the seraphim of Is 6:2.

† [5:1–14] The seer now describes a papyrus roll in God's right hand (Rev 5:1) with seven seals indicating the importance of the message. A mighty angel asks who is worthy to open the scroll, i.e., who can accomplish God's salvific plan (Rev 5:2). There is despair at first when no one in creation can do it (Rev 5:3–4). But the seer is comforted by an elder who tells him that Christ, called the lion of the tribe of Judah, has won the right to open it (Rev 5:5). Christ then appears as a Lamb, coming to receive the scroll from God (Rev 5:6–7), for which he is acclaimed as at a coronation (Rev 5:8–10). This is followed by a doxology of the angels (Rev 5:11–12) and then finally by the heavenly church united with all of creation (Rev 5:13–14).

‡ [5:1] **A scroll:** a papyrus roll possibly containing a list of afflictions for sinners (cf. Ez 2:9–10) or God's plan for the world. **Sealed with seven seals:** it is totally hidden from all but God. Only the Lamb (Rev 5:7–9) has the right to carry out the divine plan.

§ [5:5] **The lion of the tribe of Judah, the root of David:** these are the messianic titles applied to Christ to symbolize his victory; cf. Rev 22:16; Gn 49:9; Is 11:1, 10; Mt 1:1.

¶ [5:6] Christ is the Paschal Lamb without blemish, whose blood saved the new Israel from sin and death; cf. Ex 12; Is 53:7; Jn 1:29, 36; Acts 8:32; 1 Pt 1:18–19. This is the main title for Christ in Revelation, used twenty-eight times. **Seven horns and seven eyes:** Christ has the fullness (see note on Rev 1:4) of power (horns) and knowledge (eyes); cf. Zec 4:7. **[Seven] spirits:** as in Rev 1:4; 3:1; 4:5.

** [5:11] **Countless:** literally, "100,000,000 plus 1,000,000," used by the author to express infinity.

†† [6:1–16:21] A series of seven disasters now begins as each seal is broken (Rev 6:1–8:1), followed by a similar series as seven trumpets sound (Rev 8:2–11:19) and as seven angels pour bowls on the earth causing plagues (Rev 15:1–16:21). These gloomy sequences are interrupted by longer or shorter

---

f. [4:8] Is 6:2–3 / Rev 1:4, 8; 11:17; 16:5.   g. [4:11] Rom 4:17; 16:27.   h. [5:1] Is 29:11.   i. [5:5] Is 11:1, 10; Rom 15:12.

j. [5:6] Jn 1:29.   k. [5:10] 1:6; Ex 19:6; Is 61:6.   l. [5:11] Dn 7:10; Jude 14–15.

## CHAPTER 6[*]

**The First Six Seals.** [1†]Then I watched while the Lamb broke open the first of the seven seals, and I heard one of the four living creatures cry out in a voice like thunder, "Come forward." [2]I looked, and there was a white horse, and its rider had a bow.[‡] He was given a crown, and he rode forth victorious to further his victories.[m]

[3]When he broke open the second seal, I heard the second living creature cry out, "Come forward." [4§n]Another horse came out, a red one. Its rider was given power to take peace away from the earth, so that people would slaughter one another. And he was given a huge sword.

[5]When he broke open the third seal, I heard the third living creature cry out, "Come forward." I looked, and there was a black horse,[¶] and its rider held a scale in his hand. [6]I heard what seemed to be a voice in the midst of the four living creatures. It said, "A ration of wheat costs a day's pay,[**] and three rations of barley cost a day's pay. But do not damage the olive oil or the wine."[o]

[7]When he broke open the fourth living creature cry out, "Come forward." [8]I looked, and there was a pale green[††] horse. Its rider was named Death, and Hades accompanied him. They were given authority over a quarter of the earth, to kill with sword, famine, and plague, and by means of the beasts of the earth.[p]

[9]When he broke open the fifth seal, I saw underneath the altar[‡‡] the souls of those who had been slaughtered because of the witness they bore to the word of God. [10]They cried out in a loud voice, "How long will it be, holy and true master,[§§] before you sit in judgment and avenge our blood on the inhabitants of the earth?" [11]Each of them was given a white robe, and they were told to be patient a little while longer until the number was filled of their fellow servants and brothers who were going to be killed as they had been.

[12¶¶]Then I watched while he broke open the sixth seal, and there was a great earthquake; the sun turned as black as dark sackcloth[***] and the whole moon became like blood.[q] [13]The stars in the sky fell to the earth like unripe figs[†††] shaken loose from the tree in a strong wind. [14]Then the sky was divided[‡‡‡] like a torn scroll curling up, and every mountain and island was moved from its place.[r] [15]The kings of the earth, the nobles,[§§§] the military officers, the rich, the powerful, and every slave and free person hid themselves in caves and among mountain crags. [16]They cried out to the mountains and the rocks, "Fall on us and hide us from the face of the one who sits on the throne and from the wrath of the Lamb,[s] [17]because the great day of their[¶¶¶] wrath has come and who can withstand it?"

## CHAPTER 7[****]

**The 144,000 Sealed.** [1]After this I saw four angels

---

scenes suggesting the triumph of God and his witnesses (e.g., Rev 7; 10; 11; 12; 13; 14).

*[6:1–17] This chapter provides a symbolic description of the contents of the sealed scroll. The breaking of the first four seals reveals four riders. The first rider (of a white horse) is a conquering power (Rev 6:1–2), the second (red horse) a symbol of bloody war (Rev 6:3–4), the third (black horse) a symbol of famine (Rev 6:5–6), the fourth (pale green horse) a symbol of Death himself, accompanied by Hades (the netherworld) as his page (Rev 6:7–8). Rev 6:8b summarizes the role of all four riders. The breaking of the fifth seal reveals Christian martyrs in an attitude of sacrifice as blood poured out at the foot of an altar begging God for vindication, which will come only when their quota is filled; but they are given a white robe symbolic of victory (Rev 6:9–11). The breaking of the sixth seal reveals typical apocalyptic signs in the sky and the sheer terror of all people at the imminent divine judgment (Rev 6:12–17).

†[6:1–8] The imagery is adapted from Zec 1:8–10; 6:1–8.

‡[6:2] White horse . . . bow: this may perhaps allude specifically to the Parthians on the eastern border of the Roman empire. Expert in the use of the bow, they constantly harassed the Romans and won a major victory in A.D. 62; see note on Rev 9:13–21. But the Old Testament imagery typifies the history of oppression of God's people at all times.

§[6:4] Huge sword: this is a symbol of war and violence; cf. Ez 21:14–17.

¶[6:5] Black horse: this is a symbol of famine, the usual accompaniment of war in antiquity; cf. Lv 26:26; Ez 4:12–13. The scale is a symbol of shortage of food with a corresponding rise in price.

**[6:6] A day's pay: literally, "a denarius," a Roman silver coin that constitutes a day's wage in Mt 20:2. Because of the famine, food was rationed and sold at an exorbitant price. A liter of flour was considered a day's ration in the Greek historians Herodotus and Diogenes Laertius. Barley: food of the poor (Jn 6:9, 13; cf. 2 Kgs 7:1, 16, 18); it was also used to feed animals; cf. 1 Kgs 5:8. Do not damage: the olive and the vine are to be used more sparingly in time of famine.

††[6:8] Pale green: symbol of death and decay; cf. Ez 14:21.

‡‡[6:9] The altar: this altar corresponds to the altar of holocausts in the temple in Jerusalem; see also Rev 11:1. Because of the witness . . . word of God: literally, "because of the word of God and the witness they had borne."

§§[6:10] Holy and true master: Old Testament usage as well as the context indicates that this is addressed to God rather than to Christ.

¶¶[6:12–14] Symbolic rather than literal description of the cosmic upheavals attending the day of the Lord when the martyrs' prayer for vindication (Rev 6:10) would be answered; cf. Am 8:8–9; Is 34:4; 50:3; Jl 2:10; 3:3–4; Mt 24:4–36; Mk 13:5–37; Lk 21:8–36.

***[6:12] Dark sackcloth: for mourning, sackcloth was made from the skin of a black goat.

†††[6:13] Unripe figs: literally, "summer (or winter) fruit."

‡‡‡[6:14] Was divided: literally, "was split," like a broken papyrus roll torn in two, each half then curling up to form a roll on either side.

§§§[6:15] Nobles: literally, "courtiers," "grandees." Military officers: literally, "commanders of 1,000 men," used in Josephus and other Greek authors as the equivalent of the Roman tribunus militum. The listing of various ranks of society represents the universality of terror at the impending doom.

¶¶¶[6:17] Their: this reading is attested in the best manuscripts, but the vast majority read "his" in reference to the wrath of the Lamb in the preceding verse.

****[7:1–17] An interlude of two visions precedes the breaking of the seventh seal, just as two more will separate the sixth and seventh trumpets (Rev 10). In the first vision (Rev 7:1–8), the elect receive the seal of the living God as protection against the coming cataclysm; cf. Rev 14:1; Ez 9:4–6; 2 Cor 1:22; Eph 1:13; 4:30. The second vision (Rev 7:9–17) portrays the faithful Christians before God's throne to encourage those on earth to persevere to the end, even to death.

m. [6:2] Zec 1:8–10; 6:1–3.　n. [6:4] Ez 21:14–16.　o. [6:6] Lv 26:26; Ez 4:16–17.

p. [6:8] Ez 14:21.　q. [6:12] Jl 3:4; Mt 24:29.　r. [6:14] Is 34:4 / Rev 16:20.　s. [6:16] Is 2:19; Hos 10:8; Lk 23:30.

standing at the four corners of the earth,* holding back the four winds of the earth so that no wind could blow on land or sea or against any tree.[t] [2]Then I saw another angel come up from the East,[†] holding the seal of the living God. He cried out in a loud voice to the four angels who were given power to damage the land and the sea, [3]"Do not damage the land or the sea or the trees until we put the seal on the foreheads of the servants of our God."[u] [4]I heard the number of those who had been marked with the seal, one hundred and forty-four thousand marked[‡] from every tribe of the Israelites:[v] [5]twelve thousand were marked from the tribe of Judah,[§] twelve thousand from the tribe of Reuben, twelve thousand from the tribe of Gad, [6]twelve thousand from the tribe of Asher, twelve thousand from the tribe of Naphtali, twelve thousand from the tribe of Manasseh, [7]twelve thousand from the tribe of Simeon, twelve thousand from the tribe of Levi, twelve thousand from the tribe of Issachar, [8]twelve thousand from the tribe of Zebulun, twelve thousand from the tribe of Joseph, and twelve thousand were marked from the tribe of Benjamin.

**Triumph of the Elect.** [9]After this I had a vision of a great multitude, which no one could count, from every nation, race, people, and tongue. They stood before the throne and before the Lamb, wearing white robes and holding palm branches[¶] in their hands. [10]They cried out in a loud voice:

"Salvation comes from[**] our God, who is seated on the throne, and from the Lamb."

[11]All the angels stood around the throne and around the elders and the four living creatures. They prostrated themselves before the throne, worshiped God, [12]and exclaimed:

"Amen. Blessing and glory, wisdom and thanksgiving, honor, power, and might

be to our God forever and ever. Amen."

[13]Then one of the elders spoke up and said to me, "Who are these wearing white robes, and where did they come from?" [14]I said to him, "My lord, you are the one who knows." He said to me, "These are the ones who have survived the time of great distress;[††] they have washed their robes and made them white in the blood of the Lamb.[w]

[15] "For this reason they stand before God's throne and worship him day and night in his temple. The one who sits on the throne will shelter them.
[16] They will not hunger or thirst anymore, nor will the sun or any heat strike them.[x]
[17] For the Lamb who is in the center of the throne will shepherd them and lead them to springs of life-giving water,[‡‡] and God will wipe away every tear from their eyes."[y]

## CHAPTER 8[§§]

**The Seven Trumpets.** [1]When he broke open the seventh seal, there was silence in heaven[¶¶] for about half an hour.[z] [2]And I saw that the seven angels who stood before God were given seven trumpets.[a]

**The Gold Censer.** [3]Another angel came and stood at the altar,[***] holding a gold censer. He was given a great quantity of incense to offer, along with the prayers of all the holy ones, on the gold altar that was before the throne.[b] [4]The smoke of the incense along with the prayers of the holy ones went up before God from the hand of the angel. [5]Then the angel took the censer, filled it with burning coals from the altar, and

---

*[7:1] **The four corners of the earth**: the earth is seen as a table or rectangular surface.

†[7:2] **East**: literally, "rising of the sun." The east was considered the source of light and the place of paradise (Gn 2:8). **Seal**: whatever was marked by the impression of one's signet ring belonged to that person and was under his protection.

‡[7:4–9] **One hundred and forty-four thousand**: the square of twelve (the number of Israel's tribes) multiplied by a thousand, symbolic of the new Israel (cf. Rev 14:1–5; Gal 6:16; Jas 1:1) that embraces people **from every nation, race, people, and tongue** (Rev 7:9).

§[7:5–8] Judah is placed first because of Christ; cf. "the Lion of the tribe of Judah" (Rev 5:5). Dan is omitted because of a later tradition that the antichrist would arise from it.

¶[7:9] **White robes . . . palm branches**: symbols of joy and victory; see note on Rev 3:5.

**[7:10] **Salvation comes from**: literally, "(let) salvation be ascribed) to." A similar hymn of praise is found at the fall of the dragon (Rev 12:10) and of Babylon (Rev 19:1).

††[7:14] **Time of great distress**: fierce persecution by the Romans; cf. Introduction.

‡‡[7:17] **Life-giving water**: literally, "the water of life," God's grace, which flows from Christ; cf. Rev 21:6; 22:1, 17; Jn 4:10, 14.

§§[8:1–13] The breaking of the seventh seal produces at first silence and then seven symbolic disasters, each announced by a trumpet blast, of which the first four form a unit as did the first four seals. A minor liturgy (Rev 8:3–5) is enclosed by a vision of seven angels (Rev 8:2, 6). Then follow the first four trumpet blasts, each heralding catastrophes modeled on the plagues of Egypt affecting the traditional prophetic third (cf. Ez 5:12) of the earth, sea, fresh water, and stars (Rev 8:7–12). Finally, there is a vision of an eagle warning of the last three trumpet blasts (Rev 8:13).

¶¶[8:1] **Silence in heaven**: as in Zep 1:7, a prelude to the eschatological woes that are to follow; cf. Introduction.

***[8:3] **Altar**: there seems to be only one altar in the heavenly temple, corresponding to the altar of holocausts in Rev 6:9, and here to the altar of incense in Jerusalem; cf. also Rev 9:13; 11:1; 14:18; 16:7.

---

t. [7:1] Jer 49:36; Zec 6:5.   u. [7:3] Ex 7:2–14; Ez 9:4; 2 Cor 1:22; Eph 1:13; 4:30.   v. [7:4] 14:1.

w. [7:14] Mt 24:21.   x. [7:16] Is 49:10.   y. [7:17] 21:4; Is 25:8. z. [8:1] Heb 2:20; Zep 1:7; Zec 2:17.   a. [8:2] 4:5; Tb 12:15.   b. [8:3] Ps 141:2; Tb 12:12.

hurled it down to the earth. There were peals of thunder, rumblings, flashes of lightning, and an earthquake.[c]

**The First Four Trumpets.** [6]The seven angels who were holding the seven trumpets prepared to blow them.[d]

[7]When the first one blew his trumpet, there came hail and fire mixed with blood, which was hurled down to the earth. A third of the land was burned up, along with a third of the trees and all green grass.[*]

[8][†]When the second angel blew his trumpet, something like a large burning mountain was hurled into the sea. A third of the sea turned to blood,[e] [9]a third of the creatures living in the sea[‡] died, and a third of the ships were wrecked.

[10]When the third angel blew his trumpet, a large star burning like a torch fell from the sky. It fell on a third of the rivers and on the springs of water.[f] [11]The star was called "Wormwood,"[§] and a third of all the water turned to wormwood. Many people died from this water, because it was made bitter.[g]

[12]When the fourth angel blew his trumpet, a third of the sun, a third of the moon, and a third of the stars were struck, so that a third of them became dark. The day lost its light for a third of the time, as did the night.[h]

[13]Then I looked again and heard an eagle flying high overhead cry out in a loud voice, "Woe! Woe! Woe[¶] to the inhabitants of the earth from the rest of the trumpet blasts that the three angels are about to blow!"

## CHAPTER 9

**The Fifth Trumpet.**[**] [1]Then the fifth angel blew his trumpet, and I saw a star[††] that had fallen from the sky to the earth. It was given the key for the passage to the abyss. [2]It opened the passage to the abyss,[i] and smoke came up out of the passage like smoke from a huge furnace. The sun and the air were darkened by the smoke from the passage.[j] [3]Locusts came out of the smoke onto the land, and they were given the same power as scorpions[‡‡] of the earth.[k] [4]They were told not to harm the grass of the earth or any plant or any tree, but only those people who did not have the seal of God on their foreheads. [5]They were not allowed to kill them but only to torment them for five months;[§§] the torment they inflicted was like that of a scorpion when it stings a person. [6]During that time these people will seek death but will not find it, and they will long to die but death will escape them.[l]

[7][¶¶]The appearance of the locusts was like that of horses ready for battle. On their heads they wore what looked like crowns of gold; their faces were like human faces,[m] [8]and they had hair like women's hair. Their teeth were like lions' teeth,[n] [9]and they had chests like iron breastplates. The sound of their wings was like the sound of many horse-drawn chariots racing into battle. [10]They had tails like scorpions, with stingers; with their tails they had power to harm people for five months. [11]They had as their king the angel of the abyss, whose name in Hebrew is Abaddon[***] and in Greek Apollyon.

[12]The first woe has passed, but there are two more to come.

**The Sixth Trumpet.**[†††] [13]Then the sixth angel blew his trumpet, and I heard a voice coming from the [four][‡‡‡] horns of the gold altar before God,[o] [14]telling the sixth angel who held the trumpet, "Release the four angels[§§§] who are bound at the banks of the great river Euphrates." [15]So the four angels were released, who were prepared for this hour, day, month, and year to kill a third of the human race. [16]The number of cavalry troops was two hundred million; I heard their number. [17]Now in my vision this is how I saw the horses and their riders. They wore red,

---

[*][8:7] This woe resembles the seventh plague of Egypt (Ex 9:23–24); cf. Jl 3:3.

[†][8:8–11] The background of these two woes is the first plague of Egypt (Ex 7:20–21).

[‡][8:9] **Creatures living in the sea:** literally, "creatures in the sea that had souls."

[§][8:11] **Wormwood:** an extremely bitter and malignant plant symbolizing the punishment God inflicts on the ungodly; cf. Jer 9:12–14; 23:15.

[¶][8:13] **Woe! Woe! Woe:** each of the three woes pronounced by the angel represents a separate disaster; cf. Rev 9:12; 11:14. The final woe, released by the seventh trumpet blast, includes the plagues of Rev 16.

[**][9:1–12] The fifth trumpet heralds a woe containing elements from the eighth and ninth plagues of Egypt (Ex 10:12–15, 21–23) but specifically reminiscent of the invasion of locusts in Jl 1:4–2:10.

[††][9:1] **A star:** late Judaism represented fallen powers as stars (Is 14:12–15; Lk 10:18; Jude 13), but a comparison with Rev 1:20 and Rev 20:1 suggests that here it means an angel. **The passage to the abyss:** referring to Sheol, the netherworld, where Satan and the fallen angels are kept for a thousand years, to be cast afterwards into the pool of fire; cf. Rev 20:7–10. The abyss was conceived of as a vast subterranean cavern full of fire. Its only link with the earth was a kind of passage or mine shaft, which was kept locked.

[‡‡][9:3] **Scorpions:** their poisonous sting was proverbial; Ez 2:6; Lk 11:12.

[§§][9:5] **For five months:** more or less corresponding to the life-span of locusts.

[¶¶][9:7–10] Eight characteristics are listed to show the eschatological and diabolical nature of these locusts.

[***][9:11] **Abaddon:** Hebrew (more precisely, Aramaic) for destruction or ruin. **Apollyon:** Greek for the "Destroyer."

[†††][9:13–21] The sixth trumpet heralds a woe representing another diabolical attack symbolized by an invasion by the Parthians living east of the Euphrates; see note on Rev 6:2. At the appointed time (Rev 9:15), the frightful horses act as God's agents of judgment. The imaginative details are not to be taken literally; see Introduction and the note on Rev 6:12–14.

[‡‡‡][9:13] **[Four]:** many Greek manuscripts and versions omit the word. The horns were situated at the four corners of the altar (Ex 27:2; 30:2–3); see note on Rev 8:3.

[§§§][9:14–15] **The four angels:** they are symbolic of the destructive activity that will be extended throughout the universe.

---

c. [8:5] Ez 10:2; Ps 11:6 / Rev 4:5; 11:19; 16:18.    d. [8:6] 16:1–21.    e. [8:8] Ex 7:20.    f. [8:10] Is 14:12.    g. [8:11] Jer 9:14.    h. [8:12] Ex 10:21–23.

i. [9:2] 20:1.    j. [9:2] Gn 19:28.    k. [9:3] Ex 10:12–15; Wis 16:9.    l. [9:6] Jb 3:21.    m. [9:7] Jl 2:4.    n. [9:8] Jl 1:6.    o. [9:13] Ex 30:1–3.

blue, and yellow breastplates,* and the horses' heads were like heads of lions, and out of their mouths came fire, smoke, and sulfur.ᵖ ¹⁸By these three plagues of fire, smoke, and sulfur that came out of their mouths a third of the human race was killed. ¹⁹For the power of the horses is in their mouths and in their tails; for their tails are like snakes, with heads that inflict harm.

²⁰The rest of the human race, who were not killed by these plagues, did not repent of the works of their hands,† to give up the worship of demons and idols made from gold, silver, bronze, stone, and wood, which cannot see or hear or walk.�q ²¹Nor did they repent of their murders, their magic potions, their unchastity, or their robberies.

## CHAPTER 10

**The Angel with the Small Scroll.** ¹‡Then I saw another mighty angel come down from heaven wrapped in a cloud, with a halo around his head; his face was like the sun and his feet were like pillars of fire. ²In his hand he held a small scroll that had been opened. He placed his right foot on the sea and his left foot on the land,§ ³and then he cried out in a loud voice as a lion roars. When he cried out, the seven thunders¶ raised their voices, too.ʳ ⁴When the seven thunders had spoken, I was about to write it down; but I heard a voice from heaven say, "Seal up what the seven thunders have spoken, but do not write it down." ⁵Then the angel I saw standing on the sea and on the land raised his right hand to heaven ⁶and swore by the one who lives forever and ever, who created heaven and earth and sea** and all that is in them, "There shall be no more delay.ˢ ⁷At the time when you hear the seventh angel blow his trumpet, the mysterious plan of God††

shall be fulfilled, as he promised to his servants the prophets."ᵗ

⁸Then the voice that I had heard from heaven spoke to me again and said, "Go, take the scroll that lies open in the hand of the angel who is standing on the sea and on the land." ⁹So I went up to the angel and told him to give me the small scroll. He said to me, "Take and swallow it. It will turn your stomach sour, but in your mouth it will taste as sweet‡‡ as honey." ¹⁰I took the small scroll from the angel's hand and swallowed it. In my mouth it was like sweet honey, but when I had eaten it, my stomach turned sour.ᵘ ¹¹Then someone said to me, "You must prophesy again about many peoples, nations, tongues, and kings."§§

## CHAPTER 11

**The Two Witnesses.** ¹¶ᵛThen I was given a measuring rod like a staff and I was told, "Come and measure the temple of God and the altar, and count those who are worshiping in it. ²But exclude the outer court*** of the temple; do not measure it, for it has been handed over to the Gentiles, who will trample the holy city for forty-two months. ³I will commission my two witnesses††† to prophesy for those twelve hundred and sixty days, wearing sackcloth." ⁴ʷThese are the two olive trees and the two lampstands‡‡‡ that stand before the Lord of the earth. ⁵§§§§If anyone wants to harm them, fire comes out of their mouths and devours their enemies. In this way, anyone wanting to harm them is sure to be slain. ⁶They have the power to close up the sky so that no rain can fall during the time of

---

‡‡[10:9–10] The small scroll was sweet because it predicted the final victory of God's people; it was sour because it also announced their sufferings. Cf. Ez 3:1–3.

§§[10:11] This further prophecy is contained in chaps. 12–22.

¶¶[11:1] The temple and altar symbolize the new Israel; see note on Rev 7:4–9. The worshipers represent Christians. The measuring of the temple (cf. Ez 40:3–42:20; 47:1–12; Zec 2:5–6) suggests that God will preserve the faithful remnant (cf. Is 4:2–3) who remain true to Christ (Rev 14:1–5).

***[11:2] The outer court: the Court of the Gentiles. Trample . . . forty-two months: the duration of the vicious persecution of the Jews by Antiochus IV Epiphanes (Dn 7:25; 12:7); this persecution of three and a half years (half of seven, counted as 1260 days in Rev 11:3; 12:6) became the prototype of periods of trial for God's people; cf. Lk 4:25; Jas 5:17. The reference here is to the persecution by the Romans; cf. Introduction.

†††[11:3] The two witnesses, wearing sackcloth symbolizing lamentation and repentance, cannot readily be identified. Do they represent Moses and Elijah, or the Law and the Prophets, or Peter and Paul? Most probably they refer to the universal church, especially the Christian martyrs, fulfilling the office of witness (two because of Dt 19:15; cf. Mk 6:7; Jn 8:17).

‡‡‡[11:4] The two olive trees and the two lampstands: the martyrs who stand in the presence of the Lord; the imagery is taken from Zec 4:8–14, where the olive trees refer to Zerubbabel and Joshua.

§§§[11:5–6] These details are derived from stories of Moses, who turned **water into blood** (Ex 7:17–20), and of Elijah, who called down fire from heaven (1 Kgs 18:36–40; 2 Kgs 1:10) and closed up the sky for three years (1 Kgs 17:1; cf. 18:1).

---

*[9:17] **Blue**: literally, "hyacinth-colored." **Yellow**: literally, "sulfurous."

†[9:20] **The works of their hands**: i.e., the gods their hands had made.

‡[10:1–11:14] An interlude in two scenes (Rev 10:1–11 and Rev 11:1–14) precedes the sounding of the seventh trumpet; cf. Rev 7:1–17. The first vision describes an angel astride sea and land like a colossus, with a small scroll open, the contents of which indicate that the end is imminent (Rev 10). The second vision is of the measuring of the temple and of two witnesses, whose martyrdom means that the kingdom of God is about to be inaugurated.

§[10:2] **He placed . . . on the land**: this symbolizes the universality of the angel's message, as does the figure of the small scroll open to be read.

¶[10:3] **The seven thunders**: God's voice announcing judgment and doom; cf. Ps 29:3–9, where thunder, as the voice of Yahweh, is praised seven times.

**[10:6] **Heaven and earth and sea**: the three parts of the universe. **No more delay**: cf. Dn 12:7; Heb 2:3.

††[10:7] **The mysterious plan of God**: literally, "the mystery of God," the end of the present age when the forces of evil will be put down (Rev 17:1–19:4, 11–21; 20:7–10; cf. 2 Thes 2:6–12; Rom 16:25–26), and the establishment of the reign of God when all creation will be made new (Rev 21:1–22:5).

---

p. [9:17] Jb 41:10–13.  q. [9:20] Ps 135:15–17; Is 17:8; Dn 5:4.  r. [10:3] Ps 29:3–9; Jer 25:30; Am 3:8.  s. [10:6] Dt 32:40; Dn 12:7 / Ez 12:28.

t. [10:7] Am 3:7.  u. [10:10] Ez 3:1–3.  v. [11:1] Ez 40:3–5 / Zec 2:5–9.  w. [11:4] Zec 4:3, 14.

their prophesying. They also have power to turn water into blood and to afflict the earth with any plague as often as they wish.[x]

[7]When they have finished their testimony, the beast that comes up from the abyss[*] will wage war against them and conquer them and kill them.[y] [8]Their corpses will lie in the main street of the great city,[†] which has the symbolic names "Sodom" and "Egypt," where indeed their Lord was crucified. [9‡]Those from every people, tribe, tongue, and nation will gaze on their corpses for three and a half days, and they will not allow their corpses to be buried. [10]The inhabitants of the earth will gloat over them and be glad and exchange gifts because these two prophets tormented the inhabitants of the earth. [11]But after the three and a half days, a breath of life from God entered them. When they stood on their feet, great fear fell on those who saw them.[z] [12]Then they heard a loud voice from heaven say to them, "Come up here." So they went up to heaven in a cloud as their enemies looked on.[a] [13]At that moment there was a great earthquake, and a tenth of the city fell in ruins. Seven thousand people[§] were killed during the earthquake; the rest were terrified and gave glory to the God of heaven.

[14]The second woe has passed, but the third is coming soon.

**The Seventh Trumpet.**[¶] [15]Then the seventh angel blew his trumpet. There were loud voices in heaven, saying, "The kingdom of the world now belongs to our Lord and to his Anointed, and he will reign forever and ever." [16]The twenty-four elders who sat on their thrones before God prostrated themselves and worshiped God [17]and said:

"We give thanks to you, Lord God
        almighty,
    who are and who were.
For you have assumed your great power
    and have established your reign.

[18] The nations raged,
        but your wrath has come,
        and the time for the dead to be
            judged,
    and to recompense your servants, the
            prophets,
        and the holy ones and those who
            fear your name,
        the small and the great alike,
    and to destroy those who destroy the
            earth."[b]

[19]Then God's temple in heaven was opened, and the ark of his covenant could be seen in the temple. There were flashes of lightning, rumblings, and peals of thunder, an earthquake, and a violent hailstorm.

# CHAPTER 12

**The Woman and the Dragon.** [1**]A great sign appeared in the sky, a woman[††] clothed with the sun, with the moon under her feet, and on her head a crown of twelve stars.[c] [2]She was with child and wailed aloud in pain as she labored to give birth.[‡‡] [3]Then another sign appeared in the sky; it was a huge red dragon,[§§] with seven heads and ten horns, and on its heads were seven diadems.[d] [4]Its tail swept away a third of the stars in the sky and hurled them down to the earth. Then the dragon stood before the woman about to give birth, to devour her child when she gave birth.[e] [5]She gave birth to a son, a male child,

---

[*][11:7] **The beast . . . from the abyss:** the Roman emperor Nero, who symbolizes the forces of evil, or the antichrist (Rev 13:1, 8; 17:8); cf. Dn 7:2–8, 11–12, 19–22 and Introduction.

[†][11:8] **The great city:** this expression is used constantly in Revelation for Babylon, i.e., Rome; cf. Rev 14:8; 16:19; 17:18; 18:2, 10, 21. **"Sodom" and "Egypt":** symbols of immorality (cf. Is 1:10) and oppression of God's people (cf. Ex 1:11–14). **Where indeed their Lord was crucified:** not the geographical but the symbolic Jerusalem that rejects God and his witnesses, i.e., Rome, called Babylon in Rev 16–18; see note on Rev 17:9 and Introduction.

[‡][11:9–12] Over the martyrdom (Rev 11:7) of the two witnesses, now called prophets, the ungodly rejoice **for three and a half days,** a symbolic period of time; see note on Rev 11:2. Afterwards they go in triumph to heaven, as did Elijah (2 Kgs 2:11).

[§][11:13] **Seven thousand people:** a symbolic sum to represent all social classes (seven) and large numbers (thousands); cf. Introduction.

[¶][11:15–19] The seventh trumpet proclaims the coming of God's reign after the victory over diabolical powers; see note on Rev 10:7.

[**][12:1–14:20] This central section of Revelation portrays the power of evil, represented by a dragon, in opposition to God and his people. First, the dragon pursues the woman about to give birth, but her son is saved and "caught up to God and his throne" (Rev 12:5). Then Michael and his angels cast the dragon and his angels out of heaven (Rev 12:7–9). After this, the dragon tries to attack the boy indirectly by attacking members of his church (Rev 12:13–17). A beast, symbolizing the Roman empire, then becomes the dragon's agent, mortally wounded but restored to life and worshiped by all the world (Rev 13:1–10). A second beast arises from the land, symbolizing the antichrist, which leads people astray by its prodigies to idolize the first beast (Rev 13:11–18). This is followed by a vision of the Lamb and his faithful ones, and the proclamation of imminent judgment upon the world in terms of the wine of God's wrath (Rev 14:1–20).

[††][12:1–6] The woman adorned with the sun, the moon, and the stars (images taken from Gn 37:9–10) symbolizes God's people in the Old and the New Testament. The Israel of old gave birth to the Messiah (Rev 12:5) and then became the new Israel, the church, which suffers persecution by the dragon (Rev 12:6, 13–17); cf. Is 50:1; 66:7; Jer 50:12. This corresponds to a widespread myth throughout the ancient world that a goddess pregnant with a savior was pursued by a horrible monster; by miraculous intervention, she bore a son who then killed the monster.

[‡‡][12:2] Because of Eve's sin, the woman gives birth in distress and pain (Gn 3:16; cf. Is 66:7–14).

[§§][12:3] **Huge red dragon:** the Devil or Satan (cf. Rev 12:9; 20:2), symbol of the forces of evil, a mythical monster known also as Leviathan (Ps 74:13–14) or Rahab (Jb 26:12–13; Ps 89:11). **Seven diadems:** these are symbolic of the fullness of the dragon's sovereignty over the kingdoms of this world; cf. Christ with many diadems (Rev 19:12).

---

x. [11:6] Ex 7:17.   y. [11:7] Dn 7:21.   z. [11:11] Ez 37:5, 10.   a. [11:12] 2 Kgs 2:11.

b. [11:18] Ps 2:1, 5 / Am 3:7.   c. [12:1] Gn 37:9.   d. [12:3] Dn 7:7.   e. [12:4] Dn 8:10.

destined to rule all the nations with an iron rod.* Her child was caught up to God and his throne.ʲ ⁶The woman herself fled into the desert where she had a place prepared by God, that there she might be taken care of for twelve hundred and sixty days.†

⁷*Then war broke out in heaven; Michael§ and his angels battled against the dragon. The dragon and its angels fought back, ⁸but they did not prevail and there was no longer any place for them in heaven. ⁹The huge dragon, the ancient serpent,¶ who is called the Devil and Satan, who deceived the whole world, was thrown down to earth, and its angels were thrown down with it.ᵍ

¹⁰Then I heard a loud voice in heaven say:

"Now have salvation and power come,
    and the kingdom of our God
    and the authority of his Anointed.
For the accuser** of our brothers is cast
        out,
    who accuses them before our God
        day and night.
¹¹ They conquered him by the blood of the
        Lamb
    and by the word of their testimony;
    love for life did not deter them from
        death.
¹² Therefore, rejoice, you heavens,
    and you who dwell in them.
But woe to you, earth and sea,
    for the Devil has come down to you
        in great fury,
    for he knows he has but a short
        time."

¹³When the dragon saw that it had been thrown down to the earth, it pursued the woman who had given birth to the male child.ʰ ¹⁴But the woman was given the two wings of the great eagle,†† so that she could fly to her place in the desert, where, far from the serpent, she was taken care of for a year, two years, and a half-year.ⁱ ¹⁵The

serpent,‡‡ however, spewed a torrent of water out of his mouth after the woman to sweep her away with the current. ¹⁶But the earth helped the woman and opened its mouth and swallowed the flood that the dragon spewed out of its mouth. ¹⁷Then the dragon became angry with the woman and went off to wage war against the rest of her offspring, those who keep God's commandments and bear witness to Jesus.§§ ¹⁸It took its position¶¶ on the sand of the sea.ʲ

## CHAPTER 13

**The First Beast.**\*** ¹Then I saw a beast come out of the sea with ten horns and seven heads; on its horns were ten diadems, and on its heads blasphemous name[s].ᵏ ²The beast I saw was like a leopard, but it had feet like a bear's, and its mouth was like the mouth of a lion.†††ˡ To it the dragon gave its own power and throne, along with great authority. ³I saw that one of its heads seemed to have been mortally wounded, but this mortal wound was healed.‡‡‡ Fascinated, the whole world followed after the beast. ⁴They worshiped the dragon because it gave its authority to the beast; they also worshiped the beast§§§ and said, "Who can compare with the beast or who can fight against it?"

⁵¶¶¶The beast was given a mouth uttering proud boasts and blasphemies,ᵐ and it was given authority to act for forty-two months.**** ⁶It opened its mouth to utter blasphemies against God, blaspheming his name and his dwelling and those who dwell in heaven. ⁷It was also allowed to wage war against the holy ones and conquer them, and it was granted authority over every tribe, people, tongue, and nation.ⁿ ⁸All

‡‡[12:15] The serpent is depicted as the sea monster; cf. Rev 13:1; Is 27:1; Ez 32:2; Ps 74:13–14.

§§[12:17] Although the church is protected by God's special providence (Rev 12:16), the individual Christian is to expect persecution and suffering.

¶¶[12:18] **It took its position:** many later manuscripts and versions read "I took my position," thus connecting the sentence to the following paragraph.

***[13:1–10] This wild beast, combining features of the four beasts in Dn 7:2–28, symbolizes the Roman empire; the seven heads represent the emperors; see notes on Rev 17:10 and Rev 17:12–14. The blasphemous names are the divine titles assumed by the emperors.

†††[13:2] Satan (Rev 12:9), the prince of this world (Jn 12:31), commissioned the beast to persecute the church (Rev 13:5–7).

‡‡‡[13:3] This may be a reference to the popular legend that Nero would come back to life and rule again after his death (which occurred in A.D. 68 from a self-inflicted stab wound in the throat); cf. Rev 13:14; Rev 17:8. Domitian (A.D. 81–96) embodied all the cruelty and impiety of Nero. Cf. Introduction.

§§§[13:4] **Worshiped the beast:** allusion to emperor worship, which Domitian insisted upon and ruthlessly enforced. **Who can compare with the beast:** perhaps a deliberate parody of the name Michael; see note on Rev 12:7.

¶¶¶[13:5–6] Domitian, like Antiochus IV Epiphanes (Dn 7:8, 11, 25), demanded that he be called by divine titles such as "our lord and god" and "Jupiter." See note on Rev 11:2.

****[13:5] **Forty-two months:** this is the same duration as the profanation of the holy city (Rev 11:2), the prophetic mission of the two witnesses (Rev 11:3), and the retreat of the woman into the desert (Rev 12:6, 14).

---

*[12:5] **Rule . . . iron rod:** fulfilled in Rev 19:15; cf. Ps 2:9. **Was caught up to God:** reference to Christ's ascension.

†[12:6] God protects the persecuted church in the desert, the traditional Old Testament place of refuge for the afflicted, according to the typology of the Exodus; see note on Rev 11:2.

‡[12:7–12] Michael, mentioned only here in Revelation, wins a victory over the dragon. A hymn of praise follows.

§[12:7] **Michael:** the archangel, guardian and champion of Israel; cf. Dn 10:13, 21; 12:1; Jude 9. In Hebrew, the name Michael means "Who can compare with God?"; cf. Rev 13:4.

¶[12:9] **The ancient serpent:** who seduced Eve (Gn 3:1–6), mother of the human race; cf. Rev 20:2; Eph 6:11–12. **Was thrown down:** allusion to the expulsion of Satan from heaven; cf. Lk 10:18.

**[12:10] **The accuser:** the meaning of the Hebrew word "Satan," found in Rev 12:9; Zec 3:1; 1 Chr 21:1; he continues to accuse Christ's disciples.

††[12:14] **Great eagle:** symbol of the power and swiftness of divine help; cf. Ex 19:4; Dt 32:11; Is 40:31.

f. [12:5] Is 66:7 / Ps 2:9.   g. [12:9] Gn 3:1–4; Lk 10:18.   h. [12:13] Gn 3:15.   i. [12:14] Ex 19:4; Dn 7:25; 12:7.

j. [12:18] Gn 3:15.   k. [13:1] 2 Thes 2:3–12.   l. [13:2] Dn 7:3–6.   m. [13:5] Dn 7:8, 11, 25; 8:14; 9:27; 11:36; 12:7.   n. [13:7] Dn 7:21.

the inhabitants of the earth will worship it, all whose names were not written from the foundation of the world in the book of life, which belongs to the Lamb who was slain.°

9　Whoever has ears ought to hear these words.ᵖ
10　Anyone destined for captivity goes into captivity.
　　Anyone destined to be slain by the sword shall be slain by the sword.�q

Such is the faithful endurance of the holy ones.
**The Second Beast.*** ¹¹Then I saw another beast come up out of the earth; it had two horns like a lamb's but spoke like a dragon. ¹²It wielded all the authority of the first beast in its sight and made the earth and its inhabitants worship the first beast, whose mortal wound had been healed. ¹³It performed great signs, even making fire come down from heaven to earth in the sight of everyone.ʳ ¹⁴It deceived the inhabitants of the earth with the signs it was allowed to perform in the sight of the first beast, telling them to make an image for the beast who had been wounded by the sword and revived. ¹⁵It was then permitted to breathe life into the beast's image, so that the beast's image could speak and [could] have anyone who did not worship it put to death.ˢ ¹⁶It forced all the people, small and great, rich and poor, free and slave, to be given a stamped image on their right hands or their foreheads,ᵗ ¹⁷so that no one could buy or sell except one who had the stamped image of the beast's name or the number that stood for its name.

¹⁸ᵘWisdom is needed here; one who understands can calculate the number of the beast, for it is a number that stands for a person. His number is six hundred and sixty-six.

## CHAPTER 14

**The Lamb's Companions.‡** ¹Then I looked and there was the Lamb standing on Mount Zion,§

and with him a hundred and forty-four thousand who had his name and his Father's name written on their foreheads.ᵛ ²I heard a sound from heaven like the sound of rushing water or a loud peal of thunder. The sound I heard was like that of harpists playing their harps. ³They were singing [what seemed to be] a new hymn before the throne, before the four living creatures and the elders. No one could learn this hymn except the hundred and forty-four thousand who had been ransomed from the earth.ʷ ⁴These are they who were not defiled with women; they are virginsᵗ and these are the ones who follow the Lamb wherever he goes. They have been ransomed as the firstfruits of the human race for God and the Lamb.ˣ ⁵On their lips no deceit** has been found; they are unblemished.ʸ

**The Three Angels.††** ⁶Then I saw another angel flying high overhead, with everlasting good news‡‡ to announce to those who dwell on earth, to every nation, tribe, tongue, and people. ⁷He said in a loud voice, "Fear God and give him glory, for his time has come to sit in judgment. Worship him who made heaven and earth and sea and springs of water."ᶻ

⁸A second angel followed, saying:

"Fallen, fallen is Babylon the great,ᵃ
　that made all the nations drink
　the wine of her licentious passion."§§

⁹A third angel followed them and said in a loud voice, "Anyone who worships the beast or its image, or accepts its mark on forehead or hand, ¹⁰will also drink the wine of God's fury,¶¶ poured

---

4:6–8; Zep 3:12–20. **A hundred and forty-four thousand:** see note on Rev 7:4–9. **His Father's name . . . foreheads:** in contrast to the pagans who were marked with the name or number of the beast (Rev 13:16–17).

¶[14:4] **Virgins:** metaphorically, because they never indulged in any idolatrous practices, which are considered in the Old Testament to be adultery and fornication (Rev 2:14–15, 20–22; 17:1–6; cf. Ez 16:1–58; 23:1–49). The parallel passages (Rev 7:3; 22:4) indicate that the 144,000 whose foreheads are sealed represent all Christian people.

**[14:5] **No deceit:** because they did not deny Christ or do homage to the beast. Lying is characteristic of the opponents of Christ (Jn 8:44), but the Suffering Servant spoke no falsehood (Is 53:9; 1 Pt 2:22). **Unblemished:** a cultic term taken from the vocabulary of sacrificial ritual.

††[14:6–13] Three angels proclaim imminent judgment on the pagan world, calling all peoples to worship God the creator. Babylon (Rome) will fall, and its supporters will be tormented forever.

‡‡[14:6] **Everlasting good news:** that God's eternal reign is about to begin; see note on Rev 10:7.

§§[14:8] This verse anticipates the lengthy dirge over Babylon (Rome) in Rev 18:1–19:4. The oracle of Is 21:9 to Babylon is applied here.

¶¶[14:10–11] **The wine of God's fury:** image taken from Is 51:17; Jer 25:15–16; 49:12; 51:7; Ez 23:31–34. Eternal punishment in the fiery pool of burning sulfur (or "fire and brimstone"; cf. Gn 19:24) is also reserved for the Devil, the beast, and the false prophet (Rev 19:20; 20:10; 21:8).

---

\*[13:11–18] The second beast is described in terms of the false prophets (cf. Rev 16:13; 19:20; 20:10) who accompany the false messiahs (the first beast); cf. Mt 24:24; Mk 13:22; 2 Thes 2:9; cf. also Dt 13:2–4. Christians had either to worship the emperor and his image or to suffer martyrdom.

†[13:18] Each of the letters of the alphabet in Hebrew as well as in Greek has a numerical value. Many possible combinations of letters will add up to 666, and many candidates have been nominated for this infamous number. The most likely is the emperor Caesar Nero (see note on Rev 13:3), the Greek form of whose name in Hebrew letters gives the required sum. (The Latin form of this name equals 616, which is the reading of a few manuscripts.) Nero personifies the emperors who viciously persecuted the church. It has also been observed that "6" represents imperfection, falling short of the perfect number "7," and is represented here in a triple or superlative form.

‡[14:1–5] Now follows a tender and consoling vision of the Lamb and his companions.

§§[14:1] **Mount Zion:** in Jerusalem, the traditional place where the true remnant, the Israel of faith, is to be gathered in the messianic reign; cf. 2 Kgs 19:30–31; Jl 3:5; Ob 17; Mi

---

o. [13:8] 3:5; 17:8; 20:12.　p. [13:9] Mt 13:9.　q. [13:10] Jer 15:2.
r. [13:13] Dt 13:2–4; Mt 24:24; 2 Thes 2:9–10.　s. [13:15] Dn 3:5–7, 15.　t. [13:16] 14:9; 16:2; 19:20; 20:4.　u. [13:18] 17:9.

v. [14:1] Jl 3:5; Ob 17; Acts 2:21.　w. [14:3] Ps 33:3; 96:1; 98:1; Is 42:10.　x. [14:4] Jer 2:2; Jas 1:18.　y. [14:5] Zep 3:13.　z. [14:7] 2:10; Mt 10:28.　a. [14:8] 18:2–3; Is 21:9; Jer 51:8 / Is 51:17; Jer 25:15–17.

full strength into the cup of his wrath, and will be tormented in burning sulfur before the holy angels and before the Lamb. [11]The smoke of the fire that torments them will rise forever and ever, and there will be no relief day or night for those who worship the beast or its image or accept the mark of its name."[b] [12]Here is what sustains the holy ones who keep God's commandments[c] and their faith in Jesus.[*]

[13d]I heard a voice from heaven say, "Write this: Blessed are the dead who die in the Lord from now on." "Yes," said the Spirit, "let them find rest from their labors, for their works accompany them."[†]

**The Harvest of the Earth.**[‡] [14]Then I looked and there was a white cloud, and sitting on the cloud one who looked like a son of man, with a gold crown on his head and a sharp sickle in his hand.[e] [15]Another angel came out of the temple, crying out in a loud voice to the one sitting on the cloud, "Use your sickle and reap the harvest, for the time to reap has come, because the earth's harvest is fully ripe."[f] [16]So the one who was sitting on the cloud swung his sickle over the earth, and the earth was harvested.

[17]Then another angel came out of the temple in heaven who also had a sharp sickle. [18]Then another angel [came] from the altar,[§] [who] was in charge of the fire, and cried out in a loud voice to the one who had the sharp sickle, "Use your sharp sickle and cut the clusters from the earth's vines, for its grapes are ripe." [19]So the angel swung his sickle over the earth and cut the earth's vintage. He threw it into the great wine press of God's fury.[g] [20]The wine press was trodden outside the city and blood poured out of the wine press to the height of a horse's bridle for two hundred miles.[¶]

## CHAPTER 15

**The Seven Last Plagues.** [1]**Then I saw in heaven another sign,[††] great and awe-inspiring: seven

angels with the seven last plagues, for through them God's fury is accomplished.

[2]Then I saw something like a sea of glass mingled with fire.[‡‡] On the sea of glass were standing those who had won the victory over the beast and its image and the number that signified its name. They were holding God's harps,[h] [3]and they sang the song of Moses,[§§] the servant of God, and the song of the Lamb:

"Great and wonderful are your works,
    Lord God almighty.
Just and true are your ways,
    O king of the nations.[i]
[4] Who will not fear you, Lord,
    or glorify your name?
For you alone are holy.
    All the nations will come
    and worship before you,
    for your righteous acts have been
        revealed."[j]

[5]After this I had another vision. The temple that is the heavenly tent of testimony[***] opened, [6]and the seven angels with the seven plagues came out of the temple. They were dressed in clean white linen, with a gold sash around their chests.[k] [7]One of the four living creatures gave the seven angels seven gold bowls filled with the fury of God, who lives forever and ever. [8]Then the temple became so filled with the smoke from God's glory and might that no one could enter it until the seven plagues of the seven angels had been accomplished.[l]

## CHAPTER 16

**The Seven Bowls.**[†††] [1]I heard a loud voice speaking from the temple to the seven angels, "Go and pour out the seven bowls of God's fury upon the earth."

[2]The first angel went and poured out his bowl on the earth. Festering and ugly sores broke out on those who had the mark of the beast or worshiped its image.[‡‡‡]

---

*[14:12] In addition to **faith in Jesus**, the seer insists upon the necessity and value of works, as in Rev 2:23; 20:12–13; 22:12; cf. Mt 16:27; Rom 2:6.

†[14:13] See note on Rev 1:3. According to Jewish thought, people's actions followed them as witnesses before the court of God.

‡[14:14–20] The reaping of the harvest symbolizes the gathering of the elect in the final judgment, while the reaping and treading of the grapes symbolizes the doom of the ungodly (cf. Jl 4:12–13; Is 63:1–6) that will come in Rev 19:11–21.

§[14:18] **Altar:** there was only one altar in the heavenly temple; see notes above on Rev 6:9; 8:3; 11:1.

¶[14:20] **Two hundred miles:** literally sixteen hundred stades. The *stadion*, a Greek unit of measurement, was about 607 feet in length, approximately the length of a furlong.

**[15:1–16:21] The seven bowls, the third and last group of seven after the seven seals and the seven trumpets, foreshadow the final cataclysm. Again, the series is introduced by a heavenly prelude, in which the victors over the beast sing the canticle of Moses (Rev 15:2–4).

††[15:1–4] A vision of the victorious martyrs precedes the vision of woe in Rev 15:5–16:21; cf. Rev 7:9–12.

‡‡[15:2] **Mingled with fire:** fire symbolizes the sanctity involved in facing God, reflected in the trials that have prepared the victorious Christians or in God's wrath.

§§[15:3] **The song of Moses:** the song that Moses and the Israelites sang after their escape from the oppression of Egypt (Ex 15:1–18). The martyrs have escaped from the oppression of the Devil. **Nations:** many other Greek manuscripts and versions read "ages."

¶¶[15:5–8] Seven angels receive the bowls of God's wrath.

***[15:5] **Tent of testimony:** the name of the meeting tent in the Greek text of Ex 40. Cf. 2 Mc 2:4–7.

†††[16:1–21] These seven bowls, like the seven seals (Rev 6:1–17; 8:1) and the seven trumpets (Rev 8:2–9:21; 11:15–19), bring on a succession of disasters modeled in part on the plagues of Egypt (Ex 7–12). See note on Rev 6:12–14.

‡‡‡[16:2] Like the sixth Egyptian plague (Ex 9:8–11).

---

b. [14:11] 19:3.   c. [14:12] 12:17.   d. [14:13] Mt 11:28–29; 2 Thes 1:7; Heb 4:10.   e. [14:14] 1:7; Dn 7:13.   f. [14:15] Jl 4:13; Mt 13:36–43.   g. [14:19] 19:15; Is 63:1–6.

h. [15:2] 7:9, 14; 13:15–18.   i. [15:3] Ps 92:6; 98:1 / Dt 32:4; Ps 145:17.   j. [15:4] Ps 86:9–10; Jer 10:7.   k. [15:6] 19:8.   l. [15:8] 1 Kgs 8:10; Is 6:4.

³The second angel poured out his bowl on the sea. The sea turned to blood like that from a corpse; every creature living in the sea died. ⁴The third angel poured out his bowl on the rivers and springs of water. These also turned to blood.ᵐ ⁵Then I heard the angel in charge of the waters say:

"You are just, O Holy One,
  who are and who were,
    in passing this sentence."ⁿ
⁶ For they have shed the blood of the holy
      ones and the prophets,
    and you [have] given them blood
      to drink;
    it is what they deserve."ᵒ

⁷Then I heard the altar cry out,

"Yes, Lord God almighty,
  your judgments are true and just."ᵖ

⁸The fourth angel poured out his bowl on the sun. It was given the power to burn people with fire. ⁹People were burned by the scorching heat and blasphemed the name of God who had power over these plagues, but they did not repent or give him glory.�q

¹⁰The fifth angel poured out his bowl on the throne of the beast.† Its kingdom was plunged into darkness, and people bit their tongues in pain ¹¹and blasphemed the God of heaven because of their pains and sores. But they did not repent of their works.ˢ

¹²The sixth angel emptied his bowl on the great river Euphrates. Its water was dried up to prepare the way for the kings of the East.‡ ¹³I saw three unclean spirits like frogs§ come from the mouth of the dragon, from the mouth of the beast, and from the mouth of the false prophet.ᵗ ¹⁴These were demonic spirits who performed signs. They went out to the kings of the whole world to assemble them for the battle on the great day of God the almighty.ᵘ ¹⁵("Behold, I am coming like a thief.¶ Blessed is the one who watches and keeps his clothes ready, so that he may not go naked and people see him exposed.)ᵛ ¹⁶They then

assembled the kings in the place that is named Armageddon** in Hebrew.

¹⁷The seventh angel poured out his bowl into the air. A loud voice came out of the temple from the throne, saying, "It is done."ʷ ¹⁸Then there were lightning flashes, rumblings, and peals of thunder, and a great earthquake. It was such a violent earthquake that there has never been one like it since the human race began on earth.ˣ ¹⁹The great city†† was split into three parts, and the gentile cities fell. But God remembered great Babylon, giving it the cup filled with the wine of his fury and wrath. ²⁰‡‡Every island fled, and mountains disappeared. ²¹Large hailstones like huge weights came down from the sky on people, and they blasphemed God for the plague of hail because this plague was so severe.ʸ

## V. THE PUNISHMENT OF BABYLON AND THE DESTRUCTION OF PAGAN NATIONS

### CHAPTER 17

**Babylon the Great.** ¹§§Then one of the seven angels who were holding the seven bowls came and said to me, "Come here. I will show you the judgment on the great harlot¶¶ who lives near the many waters.ᶻ ²***The kings of the earth have had intercourse with her,ᵃ and the inhabitants of the earth became drunk on the wine of her harlotry." ³Then he carried me away in spirit to a deserted place where I saw a woman seated on a scarlet beast††† that was covered with blasphemous names, with seven heads and ten horns.ᵇ ⁴The woman was wearing purple and scarlet and adorned with gold, precious stones, and pearls.ᶜ She held in her hand a gold cup that was filled with the abominable and sordid deeds of her harlotry. ⁵On her forehead was written a name, which is a mystery, "Babylon the great, the mother of harlots and of the abominations

---

*[16:3–4] Like the first Egyptian plague (Ex 7:20–21). The same woe followed the blowing of the second trumpet (Rev 8:8–9).

†[16:10] **The throne of the beast:** symbol of the forces of evil. **Darkness:** like the ninth Egyptian plague (Ex 10:21–23); cf. Rev 9:2.

‡[16:12] **The kings of the East:** Parthians; see notes on Rev 6:2 and Rev 17:12–13. **East:** literally, "rising of the sun," as in Rev 7:2.

§[16:13] **Frogs:** possibly an allusion to the second Egyptian plague (Ex 7:26–8:11). **The false prophet:** identified with the two-horned second beast (Rev 13:11–18 and the note there).

¶[16:15] **Like a thief:** as in Rev 3:3 (cf. Mt 24:42–44; 1 Thes 5:2). **Blessed:** see note on Rev 1:3.

m. [16:4] Ex 7:14–24.   n. [16:5] 1:4.   o. [16:6] Ez 35:6; Mt 23:34–35.
p. [16:7] Dn 3:27; Tb 3:2.   q. [16:9] Am 4:6.   r. [16:10] Ex 10:21–23.
s. [16:11] Ex 9:8–11 / Jer 5:3.   t. [16:13] Ex 8:2–3.   u. [16:14] 1 Cor 1:8.   v. [16:15] Mt 24:42–44 / 3:17.

**[16:16] **Armageddon:** in Hebrew, this means "Mountain of Megiddo." Since Megiddo was the scene of many decisive battles in antiquity (Jgs 5:19–20; 2 Kgs 9:27; 2 Chr 35:20–24), the town became the symbol of the final disastrous rout of the forces of evil.

††[16:19] **The great city:** Rome and the empire.

‡‡[16:20–21] See note on Rev 6:12–14. **Hailstones:** as in the seventh Egyptian plague (Ex 9:23–24); cf. Rev 8:7. **Like huge weights:** literally, "weighing a talent," about one hundred pounds.

§§[17:1–19:10] The punishment of Babylon is now described as a past event and, metaphorically, under the image of the great harlot who leads people astray into idolatry.

¶¶[17:1–6] Babylon, the symbolic name (Rev 17:5) of Rome, is graphically described as "the great harlot."

***[17:2] **Intercourse . . . harlotry:** see note on Rev 14:4. The pagan kings subject to Rome adopted the cult of the emperor.

†††[17:3] **Scarlet beast:** see note on Rev 13:1–10. **Blasphemous names:** divine titles assumed by the Roman emperors; see note on Rev 13:5–6.

w. [16:17] Is 66:6.   x. [16:18] Mk 13:19.   y. [16:21] Ex 9:22–26.
z. [17:1] Jer 50:38; 51:13.   a. [17:2] Jer 51:7.   b. [17:3] 13:1.   c. [17:4] 18:16.

of the earth." ⁶'I saw that the woman was drunk on the blood of the holy ones and on the blood of the witnesses to Jesus.

**Meaning of the Beast and Harlot.**† When I saw her I was greatly amazed. ⁷The angel said to me, "Why are you amazed? I will explain to you the mystery of the woman and of the beast that carries her, the beast with the seven heads and the ten horns. ⁸ᵃᵈThe beast that you saw existed once but now exists no longer. It will come up from the abyss and is headed for destruction. The inhabitants of the earth whose names have not been written in the book of life from the foundation of the world shall be amazed when they see the beast, because it existed once but exists no longer, and yet it will come again. ⁹Here is a clue§ for one who has wisdom. The seven heads represent seven hills upon which the woman sits. They also represent seven kings:ᵉ ¹⁰five have already fallen, one still lives, and the last has not yet come,¶ and when he comes he must remain only a short while. ¹¹The beast** that existed once but exists no longer is an eighth king, but really belongs to the seven and is headed for destruction. ¹²The ten horns that you saw represent ten kings who have not yet been crowned;†† they will receive royal authority along with the beast for one hour.ᶠ ¹³They are of one mind and will give their power and authority to the beast. ¹⁴They will fight with the Lamb, but the Lamb will conquer them, for he is Lord of lords and king of kings, and those with him are called, chosen, and faithful."ᵍ

¹⁵Then he said to me, "The waters that you saw where the harlot lives represent large numbers of peoples, nations, and tongues. ¹⁶The ten horns‡‡ that you saw and the beast will hate the harlot; they will leave her desolate and naked; they will eat her flesh and consume her with fire.ʰ ¹⁷For God has put it into their minds to carry out his purpose and to make them come to an agreement to give their kingdom to the beast until the words of God are accomplished. ¹⁸The

woman whom you saw represents the great city that has sovereignty over the kings of the earth."

## CHAPTER 18

**The Fall of Babylon.**§§ ¹After this I saw another angel coming down from heaven, having great authority, and the earth became illumined by his splendor.ⁱ ²⁵⁵He cried out in a mighty voice:

"Fallen, fallen is Babylon the great.ʲ
　　She has become a haunt for demons.
She is a cage for every unclean spirit,
　　a cage for every unclean bird,
　　[a cage for every unclean] and
　　　disgusting [beast].
³　For all the nations have drunk***
　　the wine of her licentious passion.
The kings of the earth had intercourse
　　with her,
　　and the merchants of the earth
　　　grew rich from her drive for
　　　luxury."ᵏ

⁴Then I heard another voice from heaven say:

"Depart from her,††† my people,
　　so as not to take part in her sins
　　and receive a share in her plagues,ˡ
⁵　for her sins are piled up to the sky,
　　and God remembers her crimes.ᵐ
⁶　Pay her back as she has paid others.
　　Pay her back double for her deeds.
　　Into her cup pour double what she
　　　poured.ⁿ
⁷　To the measure of her boasting and
　　　wantonness
　　repay her in torment and grief;
for she said to herself,
　　'I sit enthroned as queen;
　　I am no widow,
　　and I will never know grief.'ᵒ
⁸　Therefore, her plagues will come in one
　　　day,
　　pestilence, grief, and famine;
　　she will be consumed by fire.

---

*[17:6] Reference to the great wealth and idolatrous cults of Rome.

†[17:6b–18] An interpretation of the vision is here given.

‡[17:8] Allusion to the belief that the dead Nero would return to power (Rev 17:11); see note on Rev 13:3.

§[17:9] **Here is a clue:** literally, "Here a mind that has wisdom." **Seven hills:** of Rome.

¶[17:10] There is little agreement as to the identity of the Roman emperors alluded to here. The number seven (Rev 17:9) suggests that all the emperors are meant; see note on Rev 1:4.

**[17:11] **The beast:** Nero; see note on Rev 17:8.

††[17:12–13] **Ten kings who have not yet been crowned:** perhaps Parthian satraps who are to accompany the revived Nero (the beast) in his march on Rome to regain power; see note on Rev 13:3. In Rev 19:11–21, the Lamb and his companions will conquer them.

‡‡[17:16–18] **The ten horns:** the ten pagan kings (Rev 17:12) who unwittingly fulfill God's will against harlot Rome, the great city; cf. Ez 16:37.

§§[18:1–19:4] A stirring dirge over the fall of Babylon-Rome. The perspective is prophetic, as if the fall of Rome had already taken place. The imagery here, as elsewhere in this book, is not to be taken literally. The vindictiveness of some of the language, borrowed from the scathing Old Testament prophecies against Babylon, Tyre, and Nineveh (Is 23; 24; 27; Jer 50–51; Ez 26–27), is meant to portray symbolically the inexorable demands of God's holiness and justice; cf. Introduction. The section concludes with a joyous canticle on the future glory of heaven.

¶¶[18:2] Many Greek manuscripts and versions omit **a cage for every unclean . . . beast.**

***[18:3–24] Rome is condemned for her immorality, symbol of idolatry (see note on Rev 14:4), and for persecuting the church; cf. Rev 19:2.

†††[18:4] **Depart from her:** not evacuation of the city but separation from sinners, as always in apocalyptic literature.

---

d. [17:8] 13:3–4 / 3:5; 13:8; 20:12.　e. [17:9] 13:18.　f. [17:12] Dn 7:24.　g. [17:14] 19:11–21; 2 Mc 13:4; 1 Tm 6:15 / Rom 1:6; 1 Pt 2:9; Jude 1.　h. [17:16] Ez 16:37–41; 23:25–29.

i. [18:1] Ez 43:2.　j. [18:2] 14:8; Is 21:9; Jer 50:2–3; 51:8.　k. [18:3] 17:2; Jer 51:7.　l. [18:4] Is 48:20; Jer 50:8.　m. [18:5] Jer 51:9.　n. [18:6] Jer 50:15 / Jer 16:18.　o. [18:7] Is 47:8–9.

For mighty is the Lord God who judges
    her.""

⁹The kings of the earth who had intercourse
with her in their wantonness will weep and
mourn over her when they see the smoke of her
pyre. ¹⁰They will keep their distance for fear of
the torment inflicted on her, and they will say:

"Alas, alas, great city,
    Babylon, mighty city.
    In one hour your judgment has come."

¹¹The merchants of the earth will weep and
mourn for her, because there will be no more
markets' for their cargo: ¹²their cargo of gold,
silver, precious stones, and pearls; fine linen,
purple silk, and scarlet cloth; fragrant wood of
every kind, all articles of ivory and all articles
of the most expensive wood, bronze, iron, and
marble; ¹³cinnamon, spice,† incense, myrrh,
and frankincense; wine, olive oil, fine flour, and
wheat; cattle and sheep, horses and chariots, and
slaves, that is, human beings.

¹⁴ "The fruit you craved
        has left you.
    All your luxury and splendor are gone,
        never again will one find them."ᵖ

¹⁵The merchants who deal in these goods, who
grew rich from her, will keep their distance for
fear of the torment inflicted on her. Weeping
and mourning, ¹⁶they cry out:

"Alas, alas, great city,
    wearing fine linen, purple and scarlet,
    adorned [in] gold, precious stones,
        and pearls.�q
¹⁷ In one hour this great wealth has been
        ruined."

Every captain of a ship, every traveler at sea, sailors, and seafaring merchants stood at a distance
¹⁸and cried out when they saw the smoke of her
pyre, "What city could compare with the great
city?" ¹⁹They threw dust on their heads and
cried out, weeping and mourning:

"Alas, alas, great city,
    in which all who had ships at sea
        grew rich from her wealth.
    In one hour she has been ruined."
²⁰ Rejoice over her, heaven,
        you holy ones, apostles, and
            prophets.

---

*[18:11] Ironically, the merchants weep not so much for
Babylon-Rome, but for their lost markets; cf. Ez 27:36.

†[18:13] **Spice**: an unidentified spice plant called in Greek
*amōmon*.

p. [18:14] Hos 10:5 / Am 6:7.    q. [18:16] 17:4.    r. [18:19] Ez 27:27–32.

---

For God has judged your case against her.""ˢ

²¹A mighty angel picked up a stone like a huge
millstone and threw it into the sea and said:

"With such force will Babylon the great
        city be thrown down,
    and will never be found again.ᵗ
²² No melodies of harpists and musicians,
        flutists and trumpeters,
    will ever be heard in you again.
    No craftsmen in any trade
        will ever be found in you again.
    No sound of the millstone
        will ever be heard in you again.ᵘ
²³ No light from a lamp
        will ever be seen in you again.
    No voices of bride and groom
        will ever be heard in you again.
    Because your merchants were the great
        ones of the world,
    all nations were led astray by your
        magic potion.ᵛ
²⁴ In her was found the blood of prophets
        and holy ones
    and all who have been slain on the
        earth."ʷ

## CHAPTER 19

¹After this I heard what sounded like the loud
voice of a great multitude in heaven, saying:

"Alleluia!‡
Salvation, glory, and might belong to our
        God,
²        for true and just are his judgments.
    He has condemned the great harlot
        who corrupted the earth with her
            harlotry.
    He has avenged on her the blood of his
        servants."ˣ

³They said a second time:

"Alleluia! Smoke will rise from her forever
        and ever."ʸ

⁴The twenty-four elders and the four living creatures fell down and worshiped God who sat on
the throne, saying, "Amen. Alleluia."
**The Victory Song.**§ ⁵A voice coming from the
throne said:

---

‡[19:1, 3, 4, 6] **Alleluia**: found only here in the New Testament, this frequent exclamation of praise in the Hebrew
psalms was important in Jewish liturgy.

§[19:5–10] A victory song follows, sung by the entire
church, celebrating the marriage of the Lamb, the union of
the Messiah with the community of the elect.

s. [18:20] 19:1–2; Dt 32:43.    t. [18:21] Jer 51:63–64; Ez 26:21.
u. [18:22] Is 24:8; Ez 26:13.    v. [18:23] Jer 7:34; 16:9; 25:10.
w. [18:24] 16:6.    x. [19:2] Dn 3:27 / Jer 51:48–49.    y. [19:3] 14:11;
Is 34:10.

"Praise our God, all you his servants,
    [and] you who revere him, small
      and great."ᶻ

⁶Then I heard something like the sound of a great multitude or the sound of rushing water or mighty peals of thunder, as they said:

"Alleluia!
The Lord has established his reign,
    [our] God, the almighty.
⁷ Let us rejoice and be glad
    and give him glory.
For the wedding day of the Lamb* has
      come,
    his bride has made herself ready.ᵃ
⁸ She was allowed to wear
    a bright, clean linen garment."ᵇ

(The linen represents the righteous deeds of the holy ones.)†

⁹Then the angel said to me, "Write this: Blessed‡ are those who have been called to the wedding feast of the Lamb." And he said to me, "These words are true; they come from God."ᶜ ¹⁰I fell at his feet to worship him. But he said to me, "Don't! I am a fellow servant of yours and of your brothers who bear witness to Jesus. Worship God.ᵈ Witness to Jesus is the spirit of prophecy."§

**The King of Kings.** ¹¹¶Then I saw the heavens opened, and there was a white horse; its rider was [called] "Faithful and True." He judges and wages war in righteousness.ᵉ ¹²His eyes were [like] a fiery flame, and on his head were many diadems. He had a name** inscribed that no one knows except himself.ᶠ ¹³He wore a cloak that had been dipped in†† blood, and his name was called the Word of God.ᵍ ¹⁴The armies of heaven followed him, mounted on white horses and wearing clean white linen.ʰ ¹⁵Out of his mouth

came a sharp sword to strike the nations. He will rule them with an iron rod, and he himself will tread out in the wine press‡‡ the wine of the fury and wrath of God the almighty.ⁱ ¹⁶He has a name written on his cloak and on his thigh, "King of kings and Lord of lords."ʲ

¹⁷§§Then I saw an angel standing on the sun. He cried out [in] a loud voice to all the birds flying high overhead, "Come here. Gather for God's great feast, ¹⁸to eat the flesh of kings, the flesh of military officers, and the flesh of warriors, the flesh of horses and of their riders, and the flesh of all, free and slave, small and great."ᵏ ¹⁹Then I saw the beast and the kings of the earth and their armies gathered to fight against the one riding the horse and against his army. ²⁰The beast was caught and with it the false prophet¶¶ who had performed in its sight the signs by which he led astray those who had accepted the mark of the beast and those who had worshiped its image. The two were thrown alive into the fiery pool burning with sulfur.ˡ ²¹The rest were killed by the sword that came out of the mouth of the one riding the horse, and all the birds gorged themselves on their flesh.

## CHAPTER 20
**The Thousand-year Reign.** ¹***Then I saw an angel come down from heaven, holding in his hand the key to the abyss††† and a heavy chain.ᵐ ²He seized the dragon, the ancient serpent, which is the Devil or Satan,‡‡‡ and tied it up for a thousand yearsⁿ ³and threw it into the abyss, which he locked over it and sealed, so that it could no longer lead the nations astray until the thousand years are completed. After this, it is to be released for a short time.

⁴Then I saw thrones; those who sat on them were entrusted with judgment. I also saw the souls of those who had been beheaded for their witness to Jesus and for the word of God, and who had not worshiped the beast or its image

---

*[19:7] **The wedding day of the Lamb**: symbol of God's reign about to begin (Rev 21:1–22:5); see note on Rev 10:7. **His bride**: the church; cf. 2 Cor 11:2; Eph 5:22–27. Marriage is one of the biblical metaphors used to describe the covenant relationship between God and his people; cf. Hos 2:16–22; Is 54:5–6; 62:5; Ez 16:6–14. Hence, idolatry and apostasy are viewed as adultery and harlotry (Hos 2:4–15; Ez 16:15–63); see note on Rev 14:4.
†[19:8] See note on Rev 14:12.
‡[19:9] **Blessed**: see note on Rev 1:3.
§[19:10] **The spirit of prophecy**: as the prophets were inspired to proclaim God's word, so the Christian is called to give witness to the Word of God (Rev 19:13) made flesh; cf. Rev 1:2; 6:9; 12:17.
¶[19:11–16] Symbolic description of the exalted Christ (cf. Rev 1:13–16) who together with the armies of heaven overcomes the beast and its followers; cf. Rev 17:14.
**[19:12] **A name**: in Semitic thought, the name conveyed the reality of the person; cf. Mt 11:27; Lk 10:22.
††[19:13] **Had been dipped in**: other Greek manuscripts and versions read "had been sprinkled with"; cf. Rev 19:15. **The Word of God**: Christ is the revelation of the Father; cf. Jn 1:1, 14; 1 Jn 2:14.

‡‡[19:15] The treading of the wine press is a prophetic symbol used to describe the destruction of God's enemies; cf. Is 63:1–6; Jl 4:13.
§§[19:17–21] The certainty of Christ's victory is proclaimed by an angel, followed by a reference to the mustering of enemy forces and a fearsome description of their annihilation. The gruesome imagery is borrowed from Ez 39:4, 17–20.
¶¶[19:20] **Beast . . . false prophet**: see notes on Rev 13. **The fiery pool . . . sulfur**: symbol of God's punishment (Rev 14:10; 20:10, 14–15), different from the abyss; see note on Rev 9:1.
***[20:1–6] Like the other numerical values in this book, the thousand years are not to be taken literally; they symbolize the long period of time between the chaining up of Satan (a symbol for Christ's resurrection-victory over death and the forces of evil) and the end of the world. During this time God's people share in the glorious reign of God that is present to them by virtue of their baptismal victory over death and sin; cf. Rom 6:1–8; Jn 5:24–25; 16:33; 1 Jn 3:14; Eph 2:1.
†††[20:1] **Abyss**: see note on Rev 9:1.
‡‡‡[20:2] **Dragon . . . serpent . . . Satan**: see notes on Rev 12:3, 9, 10, 15.

---

z. [19:5] 11:18; Ps 115:13.  a. [19:7] Mt 22:9; Eph 5:27.  b. [19:8] 15:6; Is 61:10; Mt 22:11–12.  c. [19:9] Mt 8:11; Lk 14:15.  d. [19:10] 22:8–9.  e. [19:11] Is 11:4.  f. [19:12] 1:14–16; 2:18 / Lk 10:22.  g. [19:13] Is 63:1 / Jn 1:1.  h. [19:14] 15:6; 19:8.

i. [19:15] 14:20; Is 63:3.  j. [19:16] 17:14; 2 Mc 13:4.  k. [19:18] Ez 39:17–20.  l. [19:20] 14:10.  m. [20:1] 9:1.  n. [20:2] Gn 3:1.

nor had accepted its mark* on their foreheads or hands. They came to life and they reigned with Christ for a thousand years.*o* *5*The rest of the dead did not come to life until the thousand years were over. This is the first resurrection. *6*Blessed† and holy is the one who shares in the first resurrection. The second death has no power over these; they will be priests of God and of Christ, and they will reign with him for [the] thousand years.

*7‡*When the thousand years are completed, Satan will be released from his prison. *8*He will go out to deceive the nations at the four corners of the earth, Gog and Magog,§ to gather them for battle; their number is like the sand of the sea.*p* *9*They invaded the breadth of the earth¶ and surrounded the camp of the holy ones and the beloved city. But fire came down from heaven and consumed them.*q* *10*The Devil who had led them astray was thrown into the pool of fire and sulfur, where the beast and the false prophet were. There they will be tormented day and night forever and ever.

**The Large White Throne.** ** *11*Next I saw a large white throne and the one who was sitting on it. The earth and the sky fled from his presence and there was no place for them.*r* *12*I saw the dead, the great and the lowly, standing before the throne, and scrolls were opened. Then another scroll was opened, the book of life.†† The dead were judged according to their deeds, by what was written in the scrolls.*s* *13*The sea gave up its dead; then Death and Hades‡‡ gave up their dead. All the dead were judged according to their deeds. *14t*Then Death and Hades were thrown into the pool of fire. (This pool of fire is the second death.§§) *15*Anyone whose name was not found written in the book of life was thrown into the pool of fire.

## VI. THE NEW CREATION¶¶

### CHAPTER 21

**The New Heaven and the New Earth.** *1u*Then I saw a new heaven and a new earth. The former

heaven and the former earth had passed away, and the sea was no more.*** *2*I also saw the holy city, a new Jerusalem,††† coming down out of heaven from God, prepared as a bride adorned for her husband.*v* *3*I heard a loud voice from the throne saying, "Behold, God's dwelling is with the human race.*w* He will dwell with them and they will be his people‡‡‡ and God himself will always be with them [as their God].§§§ *4*He will wipe every tear from their eyes, and there shall be no more death or mourning, wailing or pain, [for] the old order has passed away."*x*

*5*The one who sat on the throne¶¶¶ said, "Behold, I make all things new." Then he said, "Write these words down, for they are trustworthy and true."*y* *6*He said to me, "They are accomplished.**** I [am] the Alpha and the Omega, the beginning and the end. To the thirsty I will give a gift from the spring of life-giving water.*z* *7*The victor†††† will inherit these gifts, and I shall be his God, and he will be my son.*a* *8*But as for cowards,‡‡‡‡ the unfaithful, the depraved, murderers, the unchaste, sorcerers, idol-worshipers, and deceivers of every sort, their lot is in the burning pool of fire and sulfur, which is the second death."*b*

**The New Jerusalem.**§§§§ *9*One of the seven angels who held the seven bowls filled with the seven last plagues came and said to me, "Come here. I will show you the bride, the wife of the Lamb."¶¶¶¶ *10*He took me in spirit to a great, high mountain and showed me the holy city Jerusalem coming down out of heaven from God.*c* *11*It gleamed with the splendor of God. Its radiance was like that of a precious stone, like jasper, clear as crystal.*d* *12*It had a massive, high wall, with twelve gates where twelve angels were stationed and on which names were inscribed, [the names] of the twelve tribes of the Israelites. *13*There were

---

*[20:4] **Beast . . . mark**: see Rev 13 and its notes.

†[20:6] **Blessed**: see note on Rev 1:3. **Second death**: see note on Rev 2:11. **Priests**: as in Rev 1:6; 5:10; cf. 1 Pt 2:9.

‡[20:7–10] A description of the symbolic battle to take place when Satan is released at the end of time, when the thousand years are over; see note on Rev 20:1–6.

§[20:8] **Gog and Magog**: symbols of all pagan nations; the names are taken from Ez 38:1–39:20.

¶[20:9] **The breadth of the earth**: Palestine. **The beloved city**: Jerusalem; see note on Rev 14:1.

**[20:11–15] A description of the final judgment. After the intermediate reign of Christ, all the dead are raised and judged, thus inaugurating the new age.

††[20:12] **The book of life**: see note on Rev 3:5. **Judged . . . scrolls**: see note on Rev 14:12.

‡‡[20:13] **Hades**: the netherworld; see note on Rev 1:18.

§§[20:14] **Second death**: see note on Rev 2:11.

¶¶[21:1–22:5] A description of God's eternal kingdom in heaven under the symbols of a new heaven and a new earth; cf. Is 65:17–25; 66:22; Mt 19:28.

***[21:1] **Sea . . . no more**: because as home of the dragon it was doomed to disappear; cf. Jb 7:12.

†††[21:2] **New Jerusalem . . . bride**: symbol of the church (Gal 4:26); see note on Rev 19:7.

‡‡‡[21:3–4] Language taken from Ez 37:27; Is 25:8; 35:10; cf. Rev 7:17.

§§§[21:3] **People**: other ancient manuscripts read a plural, "peoples."

¶¶¶[21:5] **The one . . . on the throne**: God himself; cf. Rev 4:1–11.

****[21:6] **They are accomplished**: God's reign has already begun; see note on Rev 20:1–6. **Alpha . . . Omega**: see note on Rev 1:8. **Life-giving water**: see note on Rev 7:17.

††††[21:7] **The victor**: over the forces of evil; see the conclusions of the seven letters (Rev 2:7, 11, 17, 26; 3:5, 12, 21). **He will be my son**: the victorious Christian enjoys divine affiliation by adoption (Gal 4:4–7; Rom 8:14–17); see note on Rev 2:26–28.

‡‡‡‡[21:8] **Cowards**: their conviction is so weak that they deny Christ in time of trial and become traitors. **Second death**: see note on Rev 2:11.

§§§§[21:9–22:5] Symbolic descriptions of the new Jerusalem, the church. Most of the images are borrowed from Ez 40–48.

¶¶¶¶[21:9] **The bride, the wife of the Lamb**: the church (Rev 21:2), the new Jerusalem (Rev 21:10); cf. 2 Cor 11:2.

v. [21:2] 19:7–9.   w. [21:3] Ez 37:27.   x. [21:4] 7:17; Is 25:8; 35:10.
y. [21:5] Is 43:19; 2 Cor 5:17.   z. [21:6] 22:17; Ps 36:8–9; Is 55:1.
a. [21:7] 2 Sm 7:14.   b. [21:8] 22:15; Rom 1:29–32.   c. [21:10] Ez 40:2.   d. [21:11] Heb 11:10.

o. [20:4] Mt 19:28.   p. [20:8] Ez 38:2, 9, 16.   q. [20:9] Ez 38:22.
r. [20:11] 2 Pt 3:7, 10, 12.   s. [20:12] Rom 2:6.   t. [20:14] 1 Cor 15:26, 54–55.   u. [21:1] Is 65:17; 66:22; Rom 8:19–23; 2 Pt 3:13.

three gates facing east, three north, three south, and three west.ᵉ ¹⁴The wall of the city had twelve courses of stones as its foundation, on which were inscribed the twelve names of the twelve apostles* of the Lamb.ᶠ

¹⁵†The one who spoke to me held a gold measuring rod to measure the city, its gates, and its wall. ¹⁶The city was square, its length the same as [also] its width. He measured the city with the rod and found it fifteen hundred miles‡ in length and width and height. ¹⁷He also measured its wall: one hundred and forty-four cubits§ according to the standard unit of measurement the angel used. ¹⁸¶The wall was constructed of jasper, while the city was pure gold, clear as glass. ¹⁹The foundations of the city wall were decorated with every precious stone; the first course of stones was jasper, the second sapphire, the third chalcedony, the fourth emerald,ᵍ ²⁰the fifth sardonyx, the sixth carnelian, the seventh chrysolite, the eighth beryl, the ninth topaz, the tenth chrysoprase, the eleventh hyacinth, and the twelfth amethyst. ²¹The twelve gates were twelve pearls, each of the gates made from a single pearl; and the street of the city was of pure gold, transparent as glass.

²²**ʰI saw no temple in the city, for its temple is the Lord God almighty and the Lamb. ²³††The city had no need of sun or moon to shine on it,ⁱ for the glory of God gave it light, and its lamp was the Lamb. ²⁴The nations will walk by its light,‡‡ and to it the kings of the earth will bring their treasure.ʲ ²⁵During the day its gates will never be shut, and there will be no night there. ²⁶The treasure and wealth of the nations will be brought there, ²⁷but nothing unclean will enter it, nor any[one] who does abominable things or tells lies. Only those will enter whose names are written in the Lamb's book of life.ᵏ

---

*[21:14] **Courses of stones . . . apostles**: literally, "twelve foundations"; cf. Eph 2:19–20.

†[21:15–17] The city is shaped like a gigantic cube, a symbol of perfection (cf. 1 Kgs 6:19–20). The measurements of the city and its wall are multiples of the symbolic number twelve; see note on Rev 7:4–9.

‡[21:16] **Fifteen hundred miles**: literally, twelve thousand stades, about 12,000 furlongs (see note on Rev 14:20); the number is symbolic: twelve (the apostles as leaders of the new Israel) multiplied by 1,000 (the immensity of Christians); cf. Introduction. **In length and width and height**: literally, "its length and width and height are the same."

§[21:17] **One hundred and forty-four cubits**: the cubit was about eighteen inches in length. **Standard unit of measurement the angel used**: literally, "by a human measure, i.e., an angel's."

¶[21:18–21] The gold and precious gems symbolize the beauty and excellence of the church; cf. Ex 28:15–21; Tb 13:16–17; Is 54:11–12.

**[21:22] Christ is present throughout the church; hence, no temple is needed as an earthly dwelling for God; cf. Mt 18:20; 28:20; Jn 4:21.

††[21:23] **Lamp . . . Lamb**: cf. Jn 8:12.

‡‡[21:24–27] All men and women of good will are welcome in the church; cf. Is 60:1, 3, 5, 11. **The . . . book of life**: see note on Rev 3:5.

---

## CHAPTER 22

¹Then the angel showed me the river of life-giving water,§§ sparkling like crystal, flowing from the throne of God and of the Lambˡ ²down the middle of its street. On either side of the river grew the tree of life¶¶ that produces fruit twelve times a year, once each month; the leaves of the trees serve as medicine for the nations. ³Nothing accursed will be found there anymore. The throne of God and of the Lamb will be in it, and his servants will worship him. ⁴They will look upon his face,*** and his name will be on their foreheads. ⁵Night will be no more, nor will they need light from lamp or sun, for the Lord God shall give them light, and they shall reign forever and ever.ᵐ

## VII. EPILOGUE†††

⁶And he said to me, "These words are trustworthy and true, and the Lord, the God of prophetic spirits, sent his angel to show his servants what must happen soon."ⁿ ⁷‡‡‡"Behold, I am coming soon."§§§ Blessed is the one who keeps the prophetic message of this book.ᵒ

⁸It is I, John, who heard and saw these things, and when I heard and saw them I fell down to worship at the feet of the angel who showed them to me. ⁹But he said to me, "Don't! I am a fellow servant of yours and of your brothers the prophets and of those who keep the message of this book. Worship God."ᵖ

¹⁰Then he said to me, "Do not seal up the prophetic words of this book, for the appointed time¶¶¶ is near. ¹¹Let the wicked still act wickedly, and the filthy still be filthy. The righteous must still do right, and the holy still be holy."

¹²"Behold, I am coming soon. I bring with me the recompense I will give to each according to his deeds.�q ¹³I am the Alpha and the Omega,ʳ the first and the last, the beginning and the end."****

¹⁴Blessed are they who wash their robes so as to have the right to the tree of life and enter the city†††† through its gates.ˢ ¹⁵Outside are the dogs, the sorcerers, the unchaste, the murderers, the

---

§§[22:1, 17] **Life-giving water**: see note on Rev 7:17.

¶¶[22:2] **The tree of life**: cf. Rev 22:14; see note on Rev 2:7. **Fruit . . . medicine**: cf. Ez 47:12.

***[22:4] **Look upon his face**: cf. Mt 5:8; 1 Cor 13:12; 1 Jn 3:2.

†††[22:6–21] The book ends with an epilogue consisting of a series of warnings and exhortations and forming an inclusion with the prologue by resuming its themes and expressions; see note on Rev 1:1–3.

‡‡‡[22:7, 12, 20] **I am coming soon**: Christ is the speaker; see note on Rev 1:3.

§§§[22:7, 14] **Blessed**: see note on Rev 1:3.

¶¶¶[22:10] **The appointed time**: see note on Rev 1:3.

****[22:13] Christ applies to himself words used by God in Rev 1:8.

††††[22:14] **The city**: heavenly Jerusalem; see note on Rev 21:2.

---

e. [21:13] Ez 48:31–35.   f. [21:14] Eph 2:20.   g. [21:19] Is 54:11–12.   h. [21:22] Jn 2:19–20.   i. [21:23] Is 60:1–2, 19–20.   j. [21:24] Is 60:11.   k. [21:27] Is 35:8; 52:1; Zec 13:2 / Rev 3:5; 20:12.

l. [22:1] Ez 47:1–12.   m. [22:5] Is 60:20.   n. [22:6] 1:1.   o. [22:7] 12, 20 / 1:3.   p. [22:9] 19:10.   q. [22:12] 7, 20 / Ps 62:12; 2 Tm 4:14.   r. [22:13] 1:8; 21:6; Is 41:4; 44:6.   s. [22:14] 7:14–15; 22:2.

idol-worshipers, and all who love and practice deceit.ᵗ

¹⁶"I, Jesus, sent my angel to give you this testimony for the churches. I am the root and offspring of David,* the bright morning star."ᵘ

¹⁷The Spirit and the bride† say, "Come." Let the hearer say, "Come." Let the one who thirsts come forward, and the one who wants it receive the gift of life-giving water.ᵛ

¹⁸I warn everyone who hears the prophetic words in this book: if anyone adds to them, God will add to him the plagues described in this book, ¹⁹and if anyone takes away from the words in this prophetic book, God will take away his share in the tree of life and in the holy city described in this book.ʷ

²⁰ˣThe one who gives this testimony says, "Yes, I am coming soon." Amen! Come, Lord Jesus!

²¹The grace of the Lord Jesus be with all.

---

*[22:16] **The root . . . of David**: see note on Rev 5:5. **Morning star**: see note on Rev 2:26–28.
†[22:17] **Bride**: the church; see note on Rev 21:2.

t. [22:15] 21:8; Rom 1:29–32. u. [22:16] 1:1, 11–12; 22:6 / 2:28. v. [22:17] 21:6; Is 55:1.

---

‡[22:20] **Come, Lord Jesus**: a liturgical refrain, similar to the Aramaic expression *Marana tha*—"Our Lord, come!"—in 1 Cor 16:22; cf. note there. It was a prayer for the coming of Christ in glory at the parousia; see note on Rev 1:3.

w. [22:19] Dt 4:2.   x. [22:20] 7, 12 / Acts 3:20–21; 1 Cor 15:23; 16:22.

# CALENDAR OF
# READINGS

~e~2~

## THE 3-YEAR CYCLE OF READINGS FOR SUNDAY MASS

The readings you hear at Mass on Sundays follow a three-year cycle. Year A is keyed to the Gospel according to Matthew, Year B to the Gospel according to Mark, and Year C to the Gospel according to Luke. Some portion of the Gospel according to John is read every year, mostly during the Easter season.

The Church Year begins with Advent, the period immediately preceding Christmas. Most of the Church Year, however, falls in the calendar year following Christmas. For reference purposes, the years shown in this chart refer to the calendar year that follows Advent and Christmas. The readings for that Church Year, therefore, begin with the first Sunday of Advent in the previous calendar year.

| Cycle A | 2011 | 2014 | 2017 | 2020 | 2023 | 2026 | 2029 | 2032 | 2035 | 2038 | 2041 |
| Cycle B | 2012 | 2015 | 2018 | 2021 | 2024 | 2027 | 2030 | 2033 | 2036 | 2039 | 2042 |
| Cycle C | 2013 | 2016 | 2019 | 2022 | 2025 | 2028 | 2031 | 2034 | 2037 | 2040 | 2043 |

Another way to identify which cycle is to be followed in a particular year is to add up all the digits for any given year; if the resulting sum is divisible by three, the assigned cycle for that year is C. If the digits do not add up to a number divisible by three, perform the same exercise on the years immediately preceding and following the one you want to know about. Once you have found the nearest C year, you can easily figure out the letter of the years just before and just after it.

To determine where the current Sunday falls within the current liturgical year, contact your local parish or consult a church bulletin, missal, or Roman Catholic lectionary website.

For each Sunday, three readings are listed. These will be read in the order shown. The first reading is typically from the Old Testament; the second is usually from a letter in the New Testament; the third and final reading is from one of the appointed Gospels. When one of the Major Feasts of the Year falls on Sunday, the readings for the Sunday Mass are displaced by readings more appropriate for the feast day. For these readings, see page 1434.

The Weekday Lectionary showing the daily readings for Monday through Saturday begins on page 1435. See the instructions there for identifying the correct readings for the different days.

**Year A** (go to p. 1428)          **Year B** (go to p. 1430)          **Year C** (go to p. 1432)

**1** refers to First Reading          **2** refers to Second Reading          **3** refers to Gospel

## YEAR A

### ADVENT SEASON

#### 1st Sunday of Advent
1 Is 2:1-5
2 Rom 13:11-14
3 Mt 24:37-44

#### 2nd Sunday of Advent
1 Is 11:1-10
2 Rom 15:4-9
3 Mt 3:1-12

#### 3rd Sunday of Advent
1 Is 35:1-6a, 10
2 Jas 5:7-10
3 Mt 11:2-11

#### 4th Sunday of Advent
1 Is 7:10-14
2 Rom 1:1-7
3 Mt 1:18-24

### CHRISTMAS SEASON

#### Christmas Vigil
1 Is 62:1-5
2 Acts 13:16-17, 22-25
3 Mt 1:1-25

#### Christmas (At Midnight)
1 Is 9:1-6
2 Ti 2:11-14
3 Lk 2:1-14

#### Christmas (At Dawn)
1 Is 62:11-12
2 Ti 3:4-7
3 Lk 2:15-20

#### Christmas (During the Day)
1 Is 52:7-10
2 Heb 1:1-6
3 Jn 1:1-18

#### Sunday After Christmas (Holy Family)
1 Sir 3:3-7, 14-17a
2 Col 3:12-21
3 Mt 2:13-15, 19-23

#### January 1 (Solemnity of Mary, Mother of God)
1 Nm 6:22-27
2 Gal 4:4-7
3 Lk 2:16-21

#### 2nd Sunday After Christmas
1 Sir 24:1-4, 12-16

2 Eph 1:3-6, 15-18
3 Jn 1:1-18

#### Epiphany
1 Is 60:1-6
2 Eph 3:2-3a, 5-6
3 Mt 2:1-12

#### Sunday After Epiphany (Baptism of the Lord)
1 Is 42:1-4, 6-7
2 Acts 10:34-38
3 Mt 3:13-17

### LENTEN SEASON

#### Ash Wednesday
1 Jl 2:12-18
2 2 Cor 5:20—6:2
3 Mt 6:1-6, 16-18

#### 1st Sunday of Lent
1 Gn 2:7-9; 3:1-7
2 Rom 5:12-19
3 Mt 4:1-11

#### 2nd Sunday of Lent
1 Gn 12:1-4a
2 2 Tm 1:8b-10
3 Mt 17:1-9

#### 3rd Sunday of Lent
1 Ex 17:3-7
2 Rom 5:1-2, 5-8
3 Jn 4:5-42

#### 4th Sunday of Lent
1 1 Sm 16:1b, 6-7, 10-13a
2 Eph 5:8-14
3 Jn 9:1-41

#### 5th Sunday of Lent
1 Ez 37:12-14
2 Rom 8:8-11
3 Jn 11:1-45

#### Passion Sunday (Palm Sunday)
Procession: Mt 21:1-11
1 Is 50:4-7
2 Phil 2:6-11
3 Mt 26:14-27, 66

### EASTER TRIDUUM AND EASTER SEASON

#### Mass of Lord's Supper
1 Ex 12:1-8, 11-14
2 1 Cor 11:23-26
3 Jn 13:1-15

#### Good Friday
1 Is 52:13—53:12
2 Heb 4:14-16; 5:7-9
3 Jn 18:1—19:42

#### Easter Vigil
1 Gn 1:1—2:2
  Gn 22:1-18
  Ex 14:15—15:1
  Is 54:5-14
  Is 55:1-11
  Bar 3:9-15, 32-44
  Ez 36:16-17a, 18-28
2 Rom 6:3-11
3 Mt 28:1-10

#### Easter Sunday
1 Acts 10:34a, 37-43
2 Col 3:1-4
  or 1 Cor 5:6b-8
3 Jn 20:1-9
  or Mt 28:1-10

*Evening:*
3 Lk 24:13-35

#### 2nd Sunday of Easter
1 Acts 2:42-47
2 1 Pt 1:3-9
3 Jn 20:19-31

#### 3rd Sunday of Easter
1 Acts 2:14, 22-33
2 1 Pt 1:17-21
3 Lk 24:13-35

#### 4th Sunday of Easter
1 Acts 2:14a, 36-41
2 1 Pt 2:20b-25
3 Jn 10:1-10

#### 5th Sunday of Easter
1 Acts 6:1-7
2 1 Pt 2:4-9
3 Jn 14:1-12

#### 6th Sunday of Easter
1 Acts 8:5-8, 14-17
2 1 Pt 3:15-18
3 Jn 14:15-21

#### Ascension of Our Lord
1 Acts 1:1-11
2 Eph 1:17-23
3 Mt 28:16-20

#### 7th Sunday of Easter
1 Acts 1:12-14
2 1 Pt 4:13-16
3 Jn 17:1-11a

### Pentecost Vigil
1 Gn 11:1-9
 or Ex 19:3-8a, 16-20b
 or Ez 37:1-14
 or Jl 3:1-5
2 Rom 8:22-27
3 Jn 7:37-39

### Mass of the Day
1 Acts 2:1-11
2 1 Cor 12:3b-7, 12-13
3 Jn 20:19-23

## SOLEMNITIES OF THE LORD DURING ORDINARY TIME

### Trinity Sunday
### (Sunday after Pentecost)
1 Ex 34:4b-6, 8-9
2 2 Cor 13:11-13
3 Jn 3:16-18

### Corpus Christi
1 Dt 8:2-3, 14b, 16a
2 1 Cor 10:16-17
3 Jn 6:51-58

### Sacred Heart of Jesus
1 Dt 7:6-11
2 1 Jn 4:7-16
3 Mt 11:25-30

## ORDINARY TIME

### 1st Sunday
*(See Baptism of the Lord, above)*

### 2nd Sunday
1 Is 49:3, 5-6
2 1 Cor 1:1-3
3 Jn 1:29-34

### 3rd Sunday
1 Is 8:23b—9:3
2 1 Cor 1:10-13, 17
3 Mt 4:12-23

### 4th Sunday
1 Zep 2:3; 3:12-13
2 1 Cor 1:26-31
3 Mt 5:1-12a

### 5th Sunday
1 Is 58:7-10
2 1 Cor 2:1-5
3 Mt 5:13-16

### 6th Sunday
1 Sir 15:16-21
2 1 Cor 2:6-10
3 Mt 5:17-37

### 7th Sunday
1 Lv 19:1-2, 17-18
2 1 Cor 3:16-23
3 Mt 5:38-48

### 8th Sunday
1 Is 49:14-15
2 1 Cor 4:1-5
3 Mt 6:24-34

### 9th Sunday
1 Dt 11:18, 26-28, 32
2 Rom 3:21-25a, 28
3 Mt 7:21-27

### 10th Sunday
1 Hos 6:3-6
2 Rom 4:18-25
3 Mt 9:9-13

### 11th Sunday
1 Ex 19:2-6a
2 Rom 5:6-11
3 Mt 9:36—10:8

### 12th Sunday
1 Jer 20:10-13
2 Rom 5:12-15
3 Mt 10:26-33

### 13th Sunday
1 2 Kgs 4:8-11, 14-16a
2 Rom 6:3-4, 8-11
3 Mt 10:37-42

### 14th Sunday
1 Zec 9:9-10
2 Rom 8:9, 11-13
3 Mt 11:25-30

### 15th Sunday
1 Is 55:10-11
2 Rom 8:18-23
3 Mt 13:1-23

### 16th Sunday
1 Wis 12:13, 16-19
2 Rom 8:26-27
3 Mt 13:24-43

### 17th Sunday
1 1 Kgs 3:5, 7-12
2 Rom 8:28-30
3 Mt 13:44-52

### 18th Sunday
1 Is 55:1-3

2 Rom 8:35, 37-39
3 Mt 14:13-21

### 19th Sunday
1 1 Kgs 19:9a, 11-13a
2 Rom 9:1-5
3 Mt 14:22-33

### 20th Sunday
1 Is 56:1, 6-7
2 Rom 11:13-15, 29-32
3 Mt 15:21-28

### 21st Sunday
1 Is 22:19-23
2 Rom 11:33-36
3 Mt 16:13-20

### 22nd Sunday
1 Jer 20:7-9
2 Rom 12:1-2
3 Mt 16:21-27

### 23rd Sunday
1 Ez 33:7-9
2 Rom 13:8-10
3 Mt 18:15-20

### 24th Sunday
1 Sir 27:30—28:7
2 Rom 14:7-9
3 Mt 18:21-35

### 25th Sunday
1 Is 55:6-9
2 Phil 1:20c-24, 27a
3 Mt 20:1-16a

### 26th Sunday
1 Ez 18:25-28
2 Phil 2:1-11
3 Mt 21:28-32

### 27th Sunday
1 Is 5:1-7
2 Phil 4:6-9
3 Mt 21:33-43

### 28th Sunday
1 Is 25:6-10a
2 Phil 4:12-14, 19-20
3 Mt 22:1-14

### 29th Sunday
1 Is 45:1, 4-6
2 1 Thes 1:1-5b
3 Mt 22:15-21

### 30th Sunday
1 Ex 22:20-26
2 1 Thes 1:5c-10
3 Mt 22:34-40

### 31st Sunday
1 Mal 1:14b-2:2b, 8-10
2 1 Thes 2:7b-9, 13
3 Mt 23:1-12

### 32nd Sunday
1 Wis 6:12-16
2 1 Thes 4:13-18
3 Mt 25:1-13

### 33rd Sunday
1 Prv 31:10-13, 19-20, 30-31
2 1 Thes 5:1-6
3 Mt 25:14-30

### 34th Sunday
### (Christ the King)
1 Ez 34:11-12, 15-17
2 1 Cor 15:20-26, 28
3 Mt 25:31-46

## YEAR B

## ADVENT SEASON

### 1st Sunday of Advent
1 Is 63:16b-17,19b; 64:2b-7
2 1 Cor 1:3-9
3 Mk 13:33-37

### 2nd Sunday of Advent
1 Is 40:1-5, 9-11
2 2 Pt 3:8-14
3 Mk 1:1-8

### 3rd Sunday of Advent
1 Is 61:1-2a, 10-11
2 1 Thes 5:16-24
3 Jn 1:6-8, 19-28

### 4th Sunday of Advent
1 2 Sm 7:1-5, 8b-12, 14a, 16
2 Rom 16:25-27
3 Lk 1:26-38

## CHRISTMAS SEASON

### Christmas Vigil
1 Is 62:1-5
2 Acts 13:16-17, 22-25
3 Mt 1:1-25

### Christmas (At Midnight)
1 Is 9:1-6
2 Ti 2:11-14
3 Lk 2:1-14

### Christmas (At Dawn)
1 Is 62:11-12
2 Ti 3:4-7
3 Lk 2:15-20

### Christmas (During the Day)
1 Is 52:7-10
2 Heb 1:1-6
3 Jn 1:1-18

### Sunday After Christmas
### (Holy Family)
1 Gn 15:1-6; 21:1-3
2 Heb 11:8, 11-12, 17-19
3 Lk 2:22-40 or 22, 39-40

### January 1 (Solemnity of
### Mary, Mother of God)
1 Nm 6:22-27
2 Gal 4:4-7
3 Lk 2:16-21

### 2nd Sunday After Christmas
1 Sir 24:1-2, 8-12
2 Eph 1:3-6, 15-18
3 Jn 1:1-18

### Epiphany
1 Is 60:1-6
2 Eph 3:2-3a, 5-6
3 Mt 2:1-12

### Sunday After Epiphany
### (Baptism of the Lord)
1 Is 55:1-11
2 1 Jn 5:1-9
3 Mk 1:7-11

## LENTEN SEASON

### Ash Wednesday
1 Jl 2:12-18
2 2 Cor 5:20—6:2
3 Mt 6:1-6, 16-18

### 1st Sunday of Lent
1 Gn 9:8-15
2 1 Pt 3:18-22
3 Mk 1:12-15

### 2nd Sunday of Lent
1 Gn 22:1-2, 9a, 10-13, 15-18
2 Rom 8:31b-34
3 Mk 9:2-10

### 3rd Sunday of Lent
1 Ex 20:1-17
2 1 Cor 1:22-25
3 Jn 2:13-25

### 4th Sunday of Lent
1 2 Chr 36:14-16, 19-23
2 Eph 2:4-10
3 Jn 3:14-21

### 5th Sunday of Lent
1 Jer 31:31-34
2 Heb 5:7-9
3 Jn 12:20-33

### Passion Sunday
### (Palm Sunday)
Procession: Mk 11:1-10 or
Jn 12:12-16
1 Is 50:4-7
2 Phil 2:6-11
3 Mk 14:1—15:47

## EASTER TRIDUUM
## AND EASTER SEASON

### Mass of Lord's Supper
1 Ex 12:1-8, 11-14
2 1 Cor 11:23-26
3 Jn 13:1-15

### Good Friday
1 Is 52:13—53:12
2 Heb 4:14-16; 5:7-9
3 Jn 18:1—19:42

### Easter Vigil
1 Gn 1:1—2:2
Gn 22:1-18
Ex 14:15—15:1
Is 54:5-14
Is 55:1-11
Bar 3:9-15, 32—4:4
Ez 36:16-28
2 Rom 6:3-11
3 Mk 16:1-7

### Easter Sunday
1 Acts 10:34a, 37-43
2 Col 3:1-4
or 1 Cor 5:6b-8
3 Jn 20:1-9
or Mk 16:1-8

*Evening:*
3 Lk 24:13-35

### 2nd Sunday of Easter
1 Acts 4:32-35
2 1 Jn 5:1-6
3 Jn 20:19-31

### 3rd Sunday of Easter
1 Acts 3:13-15, 17-19
2 1 Jn 2:1-5a
3 Lk 24:35-48

### 4th Sunday of Easter
1 Acts 4:8-12
2 1 Jn 3:1-2
3 Jn 10:11-18

### 5th Sunday of Easter
1 Acts 9:26-31
2 1 Jn 3:18-24
3 Jn 15:1-8

### 6th Sunday of Easter
1 Acts 10:25-26, 34-35, 44-48
2 1 Jn 4:7-10
3 Jn 15:9-17

### Ascension of Our Lord
1 Acts 1:1-11
2 Eph 1:17-23 or 4:1-13
3 Mk 16:15-20

### 7th Sunday of Easter
1 Acts 1:15-17, 20a, 20c-26
2 1 Jn 4:11-16
3 Jn 17:11b-19

### Pentecost Vigil
1 Gn 11:1-9
  or Ex 19:3-8a, 16-20b
  or Ez 37:1-14
  or Jl 3:1-5
2 Rom 8:22-27
3 Jn 7:37-39

### Mass of the Day
1 Acts 2:1-11
2 1 Cor 12:3b-7, 12-13
3 Jn 20:19-23

### Pentecost - Optional
2 Gal 5:16-25
3 Jn 15:26-27; 16:12-15

## SOLEMNITIES OF THE LORD DURING ORDINARY TIME

### Trinity Sunday
(Sunday After Pentecost)
1 Dt 4:32-34, 39-40
2 Rom 8:14-17
3 Mt 28:16-20

### Corpus Christi
1 Ex 24:3-8
2 Heb 9:11-15
3 Mk 14:12-16, 22-26

### Sacred Heart of Jesus
1 Hos 11:1, 3-4, 8c-9
2 Eph 3:8-12, 14-19
3 Jn 19:31-37

## ORDINARY TIME

### 1st Sunday
(See Baptism of the Lord, above)

### 2nd Sunday
1 1 Sm 3:3b-10, 19
2 1 Cor 6:13c-15a, 17-20
3 Jn 1:35-42

### 3rd Sunday
1 Jon 3:1-5, 10
2 1 Cor 7:29-31
3 Mk 1:14-20

### 4th Sunday
1 Dt 18:15-20
2 1 Cor 7:32-35
3 Mk 1:21-28

### 5th Sunday
1 Jb 7:1-4, 6-7
2 1 Cor 9:16-19, 22-23
3 Mk 1:29-39

### 6th Sunday
1 Lv 13:1-2, 45-46
2 1 Cor 10:31—11:1
3 Mk 1:40-45

### 7th Sunday
1 Is 43:18-19, 21-22, 24b-25
2 2 Cor 1:18-22
3 Mk 2:1-12

### 8th Sunday
1 Hos 2:16b, 17b, 21-22
2 2 Cor 3:1b-6
3 Mk 2:18-22

### 9th Sunday
1 Dt 5:12-15
2 2 Cor 4:6-11
3 Mk 2:23—3:6

### 10th Sunday
1 Gn 3:9-15
2 2 Cor 4:13—5:1
3 Mk 3:20-35

### 11th Sunday
1 Ez 17:22-24
2 2 Cor 5:6-10
3 Mk 4:26-34

### 12th Sunday
1 Jb 38:1, 8-11
2 2 Cor 5:14-17
3 Mk 4:35-41

### 13th Sunday
1 Wis 1:13-15; 2:23-24

2 2 Cor 8:7, 9, 13-15
3 Mk 5:21-43

### 14th Sunday
1 Ez 2:2-5
2 2 Cor 12:7-10
3 Mk 6:1-6

### 15th Sunday
1 Am 7:12-15
2 Eph 1:3-14
3 Mk 6:7-13

### 16th Sunday
1 Jer 23:1-6
2 Eph 2:13-18
3 Mk 6:30-34

### 17th Sunday
1 2 Kgs 4:42-44
2 Eph 4:1-6
3 Jn 6:1-15

### 18th Sunday
1 Ex 16:2-4, 12-15
2 Eph 4:17, 20-24
3 Jn 6:24-35

### 19th Sunday
1 1 Kgs 19:4-8
2 Eph 4:30—5:2
3 Jn 6:41-51

### 20th Sunday
1 Prv 9:1-6
2 Eph 5:15-20
3 Jn 6:51-58

### 21st Sunday
1 Jos 24:1-2a, 15-17, 18b
2 Eph 5:21-32
3 Jn 6:60-69

### 22nd Sunday
1 Dt 4:1-2, 6-8
2 Jas 1:17-18, 21b-22, 27
3 Mk 7:1-8, 14-15, 21-23

### 23rd Sunday
1 Is 35:4-7a
2 Jas 2:1-5
3 Mk 7:31-37

### 24th Sunday
1 Is 50:5-9a
2 Jas 2:14-18
3 Mk 8:27-35

### 25th Sunday
1 Wis 2:12, 17-20
2 Jas 3:16—4:3
3 Mk 9:30-37

**26th Sunday**
1 Nm 11:25-29
2 Jas 5:1-6
3 Mk 9:38-43, 45, 47-48

**27th Sunday**
1 Gn 2:18-24
2 Heb 2:9-11
3 Mk 10:2-16

**28th Sunday**
1 Wis 7:7-11
2 Heb 4:12-13
3 Mk 10:17-30

**29th Sunday**
1 Is 53:10-11
2 Heb 4:14-16
3 Mk 10:35-45

**30th Sunday**
1 Jer 31:7-9
2 Heb 5:1-6
3 Mk 10:46-52

**31st Sunday**
1 Dt 6:2-6
2 Heb 7:23-28
3 Mk 12:28b-34

**32nd Sunday**
1 1 Kgs 17:10-16
2 Heb 9:24-28
3 Mk 12:38-44

**33rd Sunday**
1 Dn 12:1-3
2 Heb 10:11-14, 18
3 Mk 13:24-32

**34th Sunday**
**(Christ the King)**
1 Dn 7:13-14
2 Rev 1:5-8
3 Jn 18:33b-37

### YEAR C

## ADVENT SEASON

**1st Sunday of Advent**
1 Jer 33:14-16
2 1 Thes 3:12—4:2
3 Lk 21:25-28, 34-36

**2nd Sunday of Advent**
1 Bar 5:1-9
2 Phil 1:4-6, 8-11
3 Lk 3:1-6

**3rd Sunday of Advent**
1 Zep 3:14-18a
2 Phil 4:4-7
3 Lk 3:10-18

**4th Sunday of Advent**
1 Mi 5:1-4a
2 Heb 10:5-10
3 Lk 1:39-45

## CHRISTMAS SEASON

**Christmas Vigil**
1 Is 62:1-6
2 Acts 13:16-17, 22-25
3 Mt 1:1-25

**Christmas (At Midnight)**
1 Is 9:1-6
2 Ti 2:11-14
3 Lk 2:1-14

**Christmas (At Dawn)**
1 Is 62:11-12
2 Ti 3:4-7
3 Lk 2:15-20

**Christmas (During the Day)**
1 Is 57:7-10
2 Heb 1:1-6
3 Jn 1:1-18

**Sunday After Christmas**
**(Holy Family)**
1 1 Sam 1:20-22, 24-28
2 1 Jn 3:1-2, 21-24
3 Lk 2:41-52

**January 1 (Solemnity of Mary, Mother of God)**
1 Nm 6:22-27
2 Gal 4:4-7
3 Lk 2:16-21

**2nd Sunday After Christmas**
1 Sir 24:1-2, 8-12
2 Eph 1:3-6, 15-18
3 Jn 1:1-18

**Epiphany**
1 Is 60:1-6
2 Eph 3:2-3a, 5-6
3 Mt 2:1-12

**Sunday After Epiphany**
**(Baptism of the Lord)**
1 Is 40:1-5, 9-11
2 Ti 2:11-14; 3:4-7
3 Lk 3:15-16, 21-22

## LENTEN SEASON

**Ash Wednesday**
1 Jl 2:12-18
2 2 Cor 5:20—6:2
3 Mt 6:1-6, 16-18

**1st Sunday of Lent**
1 Dt 26:4-10
2 Rom 10:8-13
3 Lk 4:1-13

**2nd Sunday of Lent**
1 Gn 15:5-12, 17-18
2 Phil 3:17—4:1
3 Lk 9:28b-36

**3rd Sunday of Lent**
1 Ex 3:1-8a, 13-15
2 1 Cor 10:1-6, 10-12
3 Lk 13:1-9

**4th Sunday of Lent**
1 Jos 5:9a, 10-12
2 2 Cor 5:17-21
3 Lk 15:1-3, 11-32

**5th Sunday of Lent**
1 Is 43:16-21
2 Phil 3:8-14
3 Jn 8:1-11

**Passion Sunday**
**(Palm Sunday)**
Procession: Lk 19:28-40
1 Is 50:4-7
2 Phil 2:6-11
3 Lk 22:14—23:56

## EASTER TRIDUUM AND EASTER SEASON

**Mass of Lord's Supper**
1 Ex 12:1-8, 11-14
2 1 Cor 11:23-26
3 Jn 13:1-15

**Good Friday**
1 Is 52:13—53:12
2 Heb 4:14-16; 5:7-9
3 Jn 18:1—19:42

**Easter Vigil**
1 Gn 1:1—2:2
  Gn 22:1-18
  Ex 14:15—15:1
  Is 54:5-14
  Is 55:1-11
  Bar 3:9-15, 32—4:4
  Ez 36:16-28

2 Rom 6:3-11
3 Lk 24:1-12

**Easter Sunday**
1 Acts 10:34a, 37-43
2 Col 3:1-4
  or 1 Cor 5:6b-8
3 Jn 20:1-9
  or Lk 24:1-12

*Evening:*
3 Lk 24:13-35

**2nd Sunday of Easter**
1 Acts 5:12-16
2 Rev 1:9-11a, 12-13, 17-19
3 Jn 20:19-31

**3rd Sunday of Easter**
1 Acts 5:27b-32, 40b-41
2 Rev 5:11-14
3 Jn 21:1-19 or 1-14

**4th Sunday of Easter**
1 Acts 13:14, 43-52
2 Rev 7:9, 14b-17
3 Jn 10:27-30

**5th Sunday of Easter**
1 Acts 14:21b-27
2 Rev 21:1-5a
3 Jn 13:31-33a, 34-35

**6th Sunday of Easter**
1 Acts 15:1-2, 22-29
2 Rev 21:10-14, 22-23
3 Jn 14:23-29

**Ascension of the Lord**
1 Acts 1:1-11
2 Eph 1:17-23
  or Heb 9:24-28; 10:19-23
3 Lk 24:46-53

**7th Sunday of Easter**
1 Acts 7:55-60
2 Rev 22:12-14, 16-17, 20
3 Jn 17:20-26

**Pentecost Vigil**
1 Gn 11:1-9
  or Ex 19:3-8a, 16-20b
  or Ez 37:1-14
  or Jn 3:1-5
2 Rom 8:22-27
3 Jn 7:37-39

**Mass of the Day**
1 Acts 2:1-11
2 1 Cor 12:3b-7, 12-13
  or Rom 8:8-27

3 Jn 20:19-23
  or Jn 14:15-16, 23b-26

# SOLEMNITIES OF THE LORD DURING ORDINARY TIME

**Trinity Sunday**
(Sunday after Pentecost)
1 Prv 8:22-31
2 Rom 5:1-5
3 Jn 16:12-15

**Corpus Christi**
1 Gn 14:18-20
2 1 Cor 11:23-26
3 Lk 9:11b-17

**Sacred Heart of Jesus**
1 Ez 34:11-16
2 Rom 5:5b-11
3 Lk 15:3-7

# ORDINARY TIME

**1st Sunday**
*(See Baptism of the Lord, above)*

**2nd Sunday**
1 Is 62:1-5
2 1 Cor 12:4-11
3 Jn 2:1-12

**3rd Sunday**
1 Neh 8:2-4a, 5-6, 8-10
2 1 Cor 12:12-30
3 Lk 1:1-4; 4:14-21

**4th Sunday**
1 Jer 1:4-5, 17-19
2 1 Cor 12:31—13:13
3 Lk 4:21-30

**5th Sunday**
1 Is 6:1-2a, 3-8
2 1 Cor 15:1-11
3 Lk 5:1-11

**6th Sunday**
1 Jer 17:5-8
2 1 Cor 15:12, 16-20
3 Lk 6:17, 20-26

**7th Sunday**
1 1 Sm 26:2, 7-9, 12-13, 22-23
2 1 Cor 15:45-49
3 Lk 6:27-38

**8th Sunday**
1 Sir 27:4-7
2 1 Cor 15:54-58
3 Lk 6:39-45

**9th Sunday**
1 1 Kgs 8:41-43
2 Gal 1:1-2, 6-10
3 Lk 7:1-10

**10th Sunday**
1 1 Kgs 17:17-24
2 Gal 1:11-19
3 Lk 7:11-17

**11th Sunday**
1 2 Sm 12:7-10, 13
2 Gal 2:16, 19-21
3 Lk 7:36—8:3

**12th Sunday**
1 Zec 12:10-11
2 Gal 3:26-29
3 Lk 9:18-24

**13th Sunday**
1 1 Kgs 19:16b, 19-21
2 Gal 5:1, 13-18
3 Lk 9:51-62

**14th Sunday**
1 Is 66:10-14c
2 Gal 6:14-18
3 Lk 10:1-12, 17-20

**15th Sunday**
1 Dt 30:10-14
2 Col 1:15-20
3 Lk 10:25-37

**16th Sunday**
1 Gn 18:1-10a
2 Col 1:24-28
3 Lk 10:38-42

**17th Sunday**
1 Gn 18:20-32
2 Col 2:12-14
3 Lk 11:1-13

**18th Sunday**
1 Eccl 1:2; 2:21-23
2 Col 3:1-5, 9-11
3 Lk 12:13-31

**19th Sunday**
1 Wis 18:6-9
2 Heb 11:1-2, 8-19
3 Lk 12:32-48

**20th Sunday**
1 Jer 38:4-6, 8-10

2  Heb 12:1-4
3  Lk 12:49-53

### 21st Sunday
1  Is 66:18-21
2  Heb 12:5-7, 11-13
3  Lk 13:22-30

### 22nd Sunday
1  Sir 3:19-21, 30-31
2  Heb 12:18-19, 22-24a
3  Lk 14:1, 7-14

### 23rd Sunday
1  Wis 9:13-19
2  Phlm 9b-10, 12-17
3  Lk 14:25-33

### 24th Sunday
1  Ex 32:7-11, 13-14
2  1 Tm 1:12-17
3  Lk 15:1-32

### 25th Sunday
1  Am 8:4-7
2  1 Tm 2:1-8
3  Lk 16:1-13

### 26th Sunday
1  Am 6:1a, 4-7
2  1 Tm 6:11-16
3  Lk 16:19-31

### 27th Sunday
1  Hb 1:2-3; 2:2-4
2  2 Tim 1:6-8, 13-14
3  Lk 17:5-10

### 28th Sunday
1  2 Kgs 5:14-17
2  2 Tm 2:8-13
3  Lk 17:11-19

### 29th Sunday
1  Ex 17:8-13
2  2 Tm 3:14—4:2
3  Lk 18:1-8

### 30th Sunday
1  Sir 35:15b-17, 20-22a
2  2 Tm 4:6-8, 16-18
3  Lk 18:9-14

### 31st Sunday
1  Wis 11:23—12:2
2  2 Thes 1:11—2:2
3  Lk 19:1-10

### 32nd Sunday
1  2 Mc 7:1-2, 9-14

2  2 Thes 2:16—3:5
3  Lk 20:27-38

### 33rd Sunday
1  Mal 3:19-20a
2  2 Thes 3:7-12
3  Lk 21:5-19

### 34th Sunday
### (Christ the King)
1  2 Sm 5:1-3
2  Col 1:12-20
3  Lk 23:35-43

## READINGS FOR THE MAJOR FEASTS OF THE YEAR

### Feb. 2: Presentation of the Lord
1  Mal 3:1-4
2  Heb 2:14-18
3  Lk 2:22-40

### Mar. 19: Joseph, Husband of Mary
1  2 Sm 7:4-5a, 12-14a, 16
2  Rom 4:13, 16-18, 22
3  Mt 1:16, 18-21, 24a
   or Lk 2:41-51a

### Mar. 25: Annunciation
1  Is 7:10-14
2  Heb 10:4-10
3  Lk 1:26-28

### June 24: John the Baptist Vigil
1  Jer 1:4-10
2  1 Pt 1:8-12
3  Lk 1:5-17

### Mass of the Day
1  Is 49:1-6
2  Acts 13:22-26
3  Lk 1:57-66, 80

### June 29: Peter and Paul Vigil
1  Acts 3:1-10
2  Gal 1:11-20
3  Jn 21:15-19

### Mass of the Day
1  Acts 12:1-11
2  2 Tm 4:6-8, 17-18
3  Mt 16:13-19

### Aug. 6: Transfiguration
1  Dn 7:9-10, 13-14
2  2 Pt 1:16-19
3  (A) Mt 7:1-9
   (B) Mk 9:2-10
   (C) Lk 9:28b-36

### Aug. 15: Assumption Vigil
1  1 Chr 15:3-4, 15; 16:1-2
2  1 Cor 15:54-57
3  Lk 11:27-28

### Mass of the Day
1  Rev 11:19a; 12:1-6a, 10ab
2  1 Cor 15:20-26
3  Lk 1:39-56

### Sept. 14: Triumph of the Cross
1  Nm 21:4-9
2  Phil 2:6-11
3  Jn 3:13-17

### Nov. 1: All Saints
1  Rev 7:2-4, 9-14
2  1 Jn 3:1-3
3  Mt 5:1-12a

### Nov. 2: All Souls First Mass
1  Jb 19:1, 23-27
2  1 Cor 15:51-57
3  Jn 6:37-40

### Second Mass
1  Wis 3:1-9
2  Phil 3:20-21
3  Jn 11:17-27

### Third Mass
1  2 Mc 12:43-46
2  Rev 14:13
3  Jn 14:1-6
*(Other Readings may be chosen)*

### Nov. 9: Dedication of St. John Lateran
1  2 Chr 5:6-10, 13—6:2
2  1 Cor 3:9-13, 16-17
3  Lk 19:1-10
*(Other Readings may be chosen)*

### Dec. 8: Immaculate Conception
1  Gn 3:9-15, 20
2  Eph 1:3-6, 11-12
3  Lk 1:26-38

# WEEKDAY LECTIONARY

Only two readings are appointed each day in the Weekday Lectionary. Unlike the Readings for Sunday Mass, the list of Weekday Readings is not separated into three cycles. During the Advent, Christmas, Lenten, and Easter Seasons the same texts are assigned for reading every year. During the Season of the Year (Ordinary Time), however, the first readings differ for odd years (Year I) and even years (Year II). The Gospel readings listed are to be read in both Year I and Year II.

## ADVENT SEASON

### 1st Week of Advent
Monday: Is 2:1-5 (Year A Is 4:2-6); Mt 8:5-11
Tuesday: Is 11:1-10; Lk 10:21-24
Wednesday: Is 25:6-10a; Mt 15:29-37
Thursday: Is 26:1-6; Mt 7:21, 24-27
Friday: Is 29:17-24; Mt 9:27-31
Saturday: Is 30:19-21, 23-26; Mt 9:35—10:1, 6-8

### 2nd Week of Advent
Monday: Is 35:1-10; Lk 5:17-26
Tuesday: Is 40:1-11; Mt 18:12-14
Wednesday: Is 40:25-31; Mt 11:28-30
Thursday: Is 41:13-20; Mt 11:11-15
Friday: Is 48:17-19; Mt 11:16-19
Saturday: Sir 48:1-4, 9-11; Mt 17:10-13

### 3rd Week of Advent
Monday: Num 24:2-7, 15-17a; Mt 21:23-27
Tuesday: Zep 3:1-2, 9-13; Mt 21:28-32
Wednesday: Is 45:6b-8, 18, 21b-25; Lk 7:18b-23
Thursday: Is 54:1-10; Lk 7:24-30
Friday: Is 56:1-3a, 6-8; Jn 5:33-36

December 17: Gn 49:2, 8-10; Mt 1:1-17
December 18: Jer 23:5-8; Mt 1:18-24
December 19: Jgs 13:2-7, 24-25a; Lk 1:5-25
December 20: Is 7:10-14; Lk 1:26-38
December 21: Sg 2:8-14 or Zep 3:14-18a; Lk 1:39-45
December 22: 1 Sm 1:24-28; Lk 1:46-56
December 23: Mal 3:1-4, 23-24; Lk 1:57-66
December 24: 2 Sm 7:1-5, 8b-11, 16; Lk 1:67-79

## CHRISTMAS SEASON

### Octave of Christmas
Second day (St. Stephen): Acts 6:8-10; 7:54-59; Mt 10:17-22
Third day (St. John): 1 Jn 1:1-4; Jn 20:2-8
Fourth day (Holy Innocents): 1 Jn 1:5—2:2; Mt 2:13-18
Fifth day: 1 Jn 2:3-11; Lk 2:22-35
Sixth day: 1 Jn 2:12-17; Lk 2:36-40
Seventh day: 1 Jn 2:18-21; Jn 1:1-18

January 2: 1 Jn 2:22-28; Jn 1:19-28
January 3: 1 Jn 2:29—3:6; Jn 1:29-34

January 4: 1 Jn 3:7-10; Jn 1:35-42
January 5: 1 Jn 3:11-21; Jn 1:43-51
January 6 (if Epiphany not celebrated): 1 Jn 5:5-13; Mk 1:6b-11
*(Readings may vary slightly depending on when Epiphany is celebrated)*

### Week after Epiphany
Monday after Epiphany: 1 Jn 3:22—4:6; Mt 4:12-17, 23-25
Tuesday after Epiphany: 1 Jn 4:7-10; Mk 6:34-44
Wednesday after Epiphany: 1 Jn 4:11-18; Mk 6:45-52
Thursday after Epiphany: 1 Jn 4:19—5:4; Lk 4:14-22a
Friday after Epiphany: 1 Jn 5:5-13; Lk 5:12-16
Saturday after Epiphany: 1 Jn 5:14-21; Jn 3:22-30

## LENTEN SEASON

Ash Wednesday: Jl 2:12-18; 2 Cor 5:20—6:2; Mt 6:1-6, 16-18
Thursday after Ash Wednesday: Dt 30:15-20; Lk 9:22-25
Friday after Ash Wednesday: Is 58:1-9a; Mt 9:14-15
Saturday after Ash Wednesday: Is 58:9b-14; Lk 5:27-32

### First Week of Lent
Monday: Lv 19:1-2, 11-18; Mt 25:31-46
Tuesday: Is 55:10-11; Mt 6:7-15
Wednesday: Jon 3:1-10; Lk 11:29-32
Thursday: Est C:12, 14-16, 23-25; Mt 7:7-12
Friday: Ez 18:21-28; Mt 5:20-26
Saturday: Dt 26:16-19; Mt 5:43-48

### Second Week of Lent
Monday: Dn 9:4b-10; Lk 6:36-38
Tuesday: Is 1:10, 16-20; Mt 23:1-12
Wednesday: Jer 18:18-20; Mt 20:17-28
Thursday: Jer 17:5-10; Lk 16:19-31
Friday: Gn 37:3-4, 12-13a, 17b-28; Mt 21:33-43, 45-46
Saturday: Mi 7:14-15, 18-20; Lk 15:1-3, 11-32

### Third Week of Lent
Monday: 2 Kgs 5:1-15a; Lk 4:24-30
Tuesday: Dn 3:25, 34-43; Mt 18:21-35

Wednesday: Dt 4:1, 5-9; Mt 5:17-19
Thursday: Jer 7:23-28; Lk 11:14-23
Friday: Hos 14:2-10; Mk 12:28b-34
Saturday: Hos 6:1-6; Lk 18:19-24

### Fourth Week of Lent

Monday: Is 65:17-21; Jn 4:43-54
Tuesday: Ez 47:1-9, 12; Jn 5:1-3a, 5-16
Wednesday: Is 49:8-15; Jn 5:17-30
Thursday: Ex 32:7-14; Jn 5:31-47
Friday: Wis 2:1a, 12-22; Jn 7:1-2, 10, 25-30
Saturday: Jer 11:18-20; Jn 7:40-53

### Fifth Week of Lent

Monday: Dn 13:1-9, 15-17, 19-30, 33-62; Jn
8:1-11 (Year C: Jn 8:12-20)
Tuesday: Nm 21:4-9; Jn 8:21-30
Wednesday: Dn 3:14-20, 91-92, 95; Jn 8:31-42
Thursday: Gn 17:3-9; Jn 8:51-59
Friday: Jer 20:10-13; Jn 10:31-42
Saturday: Ez 37:21-28; Jn 11:45-56

### Holy Week

Monday: Is 42:1-7; Jn 12:1-11
Tuesday: Is 49:1-6; Jn 13:21-33, 36-38
Wednesday: Is 50:4-9a; Mt 26:14-25
Thursday Chrism Mass: Is 61:1-3a, 6a, 8b-9;
Rev 1:5-8; Lk 4:16-21

## EASTER SEASON

### Octave of Easter

Monday: Acts 2:14, 22-32; Mt 28:8-15
Tuesday: Acts 2:36-41; Jn 20:11-18
Wednesday: Acts 3:1-10; Lk 24:13-35
Thursday: Acts 3:11-26; Lk 24:35-48
Friday: Acts 4:1-12; Jn 21:1-14
Saturday: Acts 4:13-21; Mk 16:9-15

### Second Week of Easter

Monday: Acts 4:23-31; Jn 3:1-8
Tuesday: Acts 4:32-37; Jn 3:7-15
Wednesday: Acts 5:17-26; Jn 3:16-21
Thursday: Acts 5:27-33; Jn 3:31-36
Friday: Acts 5:34-42; Jn 6:1-15
Saturday: Acts 6:1-7; Jn 6:16-21

### Third Week of Easter

Monday: Acts 6:8-15; Jn 6:22-29
Tuesday: Acts 7:51—8:1a; Jn 6:30-35
Wednesday: Acts 8:1b-8; Jn 6:35-40
Thursday: Acts 8:26-40; Jn 6:44-51
Friday: Acts 9:1-20; Jn 6:52-59
Saturday: Acts 9:31-42; Jn 6:60-69

### Fourth Week of Easter

Monday: Acts 11:1-18; Jn 10:1-10
(Year A: Jn 10:11-18)
Tuesday: Acts 11:19-26; Jn 10:22-30
Wednesday: Acts 12:24—13:5a; Jn 12:44-50
Thursday: Acts 13:13-25; Jn 13:16-20

Friday: Acts 13:26-33; Jn 14:1-6
Saturday: Acts 13:44-52; Jn 14:7-14

### Fifth Week of Easter

Monday: Acts 14:5-18; Jn 14:21-26
Tuesday: Acts 14:19-28; Jn 14:27-31a
Wednesday: Acts 15:1-6; Jn 15:1-8
Thursday: Acts 15:7-21; Jn 15:9-11
Friday: Acts 15:22-31; Jn 15:12-17
Saturday: Acts 16:1-10; Jn 15:18-21

### Sixth Week of Easter

Monday: Acts 16:11-15; Jn 15:26—16:4a
Tuesday: Acts 16:22-34; Jn 16:5-11
Wednesday: Acts 17:15, 22—18:1; Jn 16:12-15
Thursday: Acts 18:1-8; Jn 16:16-20
Friday: Acts 18:9-18; Jn 16:20-23a
Saturday: Acts 18:23-28; Jn 16:23b-28

### Seventh Week of Easter

Monday: Acts 19:1-8; Jn 16:29-33
Tuesday: Acts 20:17-27; Jn 17:1-11a
Wednesday: Acts 20:28-38; Jn 17:11b-19
Thursday: Acts 22:30; 23:6-11; Jn 17:20-26
Friday: Acts 25:13-21; Jn 21:15-19
Saturday: Acts 28:16-20, 30-31; Jn 21:20-25

## SEASON OF THE YEAR

*(I indicates the Year I reading; II indicates the
Year II reading; the Gospel is the same each year)*

### Week One

Monday: I - Heb 1:1-6; II - 1 Sm 1:1-8;
Mk 1:14-20
Tuesday: I - Heb 2:5-12; II - 1 Sm 1:9-20;
Mk 1:21-28
Wednesday: I - Heb 2:14-18; II - 1 Sm 3:1-10,
19-20; Mk 1:29-39
Thursday: I - Heb 3:7-14; II - 1 Sm 4:1-11;
Mk 1:40-45
Friday: I - Heb 4:1-5, 11; II - 1 Sm 8:4-7, 10-22a;
Mk 2:1-12
Saturday: I - Heb 4:12-16; II - 1 Sm 9:1-14, 17-19;
10:1a; Mk 2:13-17

### Week Two

Monday: I - Heb 5:1-10; II - 1 Sm 15:16-23;
Mk 2:18-22
Tuesday: I - Heb 6:10-20; II - 1 Sm 16:1-13;
Mk 2:23-28
Wednesday: I - Heb 7:1-3, 15-17; II - 1 Sm 17:32-
33, 37, 40-51; Mk 3:1-6
Thursday: I - Heb 7:25—8:6; II - 1 Sm 18:6-9;
19:1-7; Mk 3:7-12
Friday: I - Heb 8:6-13; II - 1 Sm 24:3-21;
Mk 3:13-19
Saturday: I - Heb 9:2-3, 11-14; II - 2 Sm 1:1-4,
11-12, 19, 23-27; Mk 3:20-21

## Week Three

Monday: I - Heb 9:15, 24-28; II - 2 Sm 5:1-7, 10; Mk 3:22-30

Tuesday: I - Heb 10:1-10; II - 2 Sm 6:12b-15, 17-19; Mk 3:31-35

Wednesday: I - Heb 10:11-18; II - 2 Sm 7:4-17; Mk 4:1-20

Thursday: I - Heb 10:19-25; II - 2 Sm 7:18-19, 24-29; Mk 4:21-25

Friday: I - Heb 10:32-39; II - 2 Sm 11:1-4a, 5-10a, 13-17; Mk 4:26-34

Saturday: I - Heb 11:1-2, 8-9; II - 2 Sm 12:1-7a, 10-17; Mk 4:35-41

## Week Four

Monday: I - Heb 11:32-40; II - 2 Sm 15:13-14, 30; 16:5-13; Mk 5:1-20

Tuesday: I - Heb 12:1-4; II - 2 Sm 18:9-10, 14b, 24-25a, 30—19:3; Mk 5:21-43

Wednesday: I - Heb 12:4-7, 11-15; II - 2 Sm 24:2, 9-17; Mk 6:1-6

Thursday: I - Heb 12:18-19, 21-24; II - 1 Kgs 2:1-4, 10-12; Mk 6:7-13

Friday: I - Heb 13:1-8; II - Sir 47:2-11; Mk 6:14-29

Saturday: I - Heb 13:15-17, 20-21; II - 1 Kgs 3:4-13; Mk 6:30-34

## Week Five

Monday: I - Gn 1:1-19; II - 1 Kgs 8:1-7, 9-13; Mk 6:53-56

Tuesday: I - Gn 1:20—2:4a; II - 1 Kgs 8:22-23, 27-30; Mk 7:1-13

Wednesday: I - Gn 2:4b-9, 15-17; II - 1 Kgs 10:1-10; Mk 7:14-23

Thursday: I - Gn 2:18-25; II - 1 Kgs 11:4-13; Mk 7:24-30

Friday: I - Gn 3:1-8; II - 1 Kgs 11:29-32; 12:19; Mk 7:31-37

Saturday: I - Gn 3:9-24; II - 1 Kgs 12:26-32; 13:33-34; Mk 8:1-10

## Week Six

Monday: I - Gn 4:1-15, 25; II - Jas 1:1-11; Mk 8:11-13

Tuesday: I - Gn 6:5-8; 7:1-5, 10; II - Jas 1:12-18; Mk 8:14-21

Wednesday: I - Gn 8:6-13, 20-22; II - Jas 1:19-27; Mk 8:22-26

Thursday: I - Gn 9:1-13; II - Jas 2:1-9; Mk 8:27-33

Friday: I - Gn 11:1-9; II - Jas 2:14-24, 26; Mk 8:34—9:1

Saturday: I - Heb 11:1-7; II - Jas 3:1-10; Mk 9:2-13

## Week Seven

Monday: I - Sir 1:1-10; II - Jas 3:13-18; Mk 9:14-29

Tuesday: I - Sir 2:1-11; II - Jas 4:1-10; Mk 9:30-37

Wednesday: I - Sir 4:11-19; II - Jas 4:13-17; Mk 9:38-40

Thursday: I - Sir 5:1-8; II - Jas 5:1-6; Mk 9:41-50

Friday: I - Sir 6:5-17; II - Jas 5:9-12; Mk 10:1-12

Saturday: I - Sir 17:1-15; II - Jas 5:13-20; Mk 10:13-16

## Week Eight

Monday: I - Sir 17:19-27; II - 1 Pt 1:3-9; Mk 10:17-27

Tuesday: I - Sir 35:1-12; II - 1 Pt 1:10-16; Mk 10:28-31

Wednesday: I - Sir 36:1, 5-6, 10-17; II - 1 Pt 1:18-25; Mk 10:32-45

Thursday: I - Sir 42:15-25; II - 1 Pt 2:2-5, 9-12; Mk 10:46-52

Friday: I - Sir 44:1, 9-13; II - 1 Pt 4:7-13; Mk 11:11-26

Saturday: I - Sir 51:12b-20; II - Jude 17, 20b-25; Mk 11:27-33

## Week Nine

Monday: I - Tb 1:3; 2:1-8; II - 2 Pt 1:2-7; Mk 12:1-12

Tuesday: I - Tb 2:9-14; II - 2 Pt 3:12-15a, 17-18; Mk 12:13-17

Wednesday: I - Tb 3:1-11a, 16; II - 2 Tm 1:1-3, 6-12; Mk 12:18-27

Thursday: I - Tb 6:10-11; 7:1, 9-17; 8:4-7; II - 2 Tm 2:8-15; Mk 12:28-34

Friday: I - Tb 11:5-17; II - 2 Tm 3:10-17; Mk 12:35-37

Saturday: I - Tb 12:1, 5-15, 20; II - 2 Tm 4:1-8; Mk 12:38-44

## Week Ten

Monday: I - 2 Cor 1:1-7; II - 1 Kgs 17:1-6; Mt 5:1-12

Tuesday: I - 2 Cor 1:18-22; II - 1 Kgs 17:7-16; Mt 5:13-16

Wednesday: I - 2 Cor 3:4-11; II - 1 Kgs 18:20-39; Mt 5:17-19

Thursday: I - 2 Cor 3:15—4:1, 3-6; II - 1 Kgs 18:41-46; Mt 5:20-26

Friday: I - 2 Cor 4:7-15; II - 1 Kgs 19:9a, 11-16; Mt 5:27-32

Saturday: I - 2 Cor 5:14-21; II - 1 Kgs 19:19-21; Mt 5:33-37

## Week Eleven

Monday: I - 2 Cor 6:1-10; II - 1 Kgs 21:1-16; Mt 5:38-42

Tuesday: I - 2 Cor 8:1-9; II - 1 Kgs 21:17-29; Mt 5:43-48

Wednesday: I - 2 Cor 9:6-11; II - 1 Kgs 2:1, 6-14; Mt 6:1-6, 16-18

Thursday: I - 2 Cor 11:1-11; II - Sir 48:1-14; Mt 6:7-15

Friday: I - 2 Cor 11:18, 21b-30; II - 2 Kgs 11:1-4, 9-18, 20; Mt 6:19-23

Saturday: I - 2 Cor 12:1-10; II - 2 Chr 24:17-25; Mt 6:24-34

### Week Twelve

Monday: I - Gn 12:1-9; II - 2 Kgs 17:5-8, 13-15a, 18; Mt 7:1-5

Tuesday: I - Gn 13:2, 5-18; II - 2 Kgs 19:9b-11, 14-21, 31-35a, 36; Mt 7:6, 12-14

Wednesday: I - Gn 15:1-12, 17-18; II - 2 Kgs 22:8-13; 23:1-3; Mt 7:15-20

Thursday: I - Gn 16:1-12, 15-16; II - 2 Kgs 24:8-17; Mt 7:21-29

Friday: I - Gn 17:1, 9-10, 15-22; II - 2 Kgs 25:1-12; Mt 8:1-4

Saturday: I - Gn 18:1-15; II - Lam 2:2, 10-14, 18-19; Mt 8:5-17

### Week Thirteen

Monday: I - Gn 18:16-33; II - Am 2:6-10, 13-16; Mt 8:18-22

Tuesday: I - Gn 19:15-29; II - Am 3:1-8; 4:11-12; Mt 8:23-27

Wednesday: I - Gn 21:5, 8-20a; II - Am 5:14-15, 21-24; Mt 8:28-34

Thursday: I - Gn 22:1-19; II - Am 7:10-17; Mt 9:1-8

Friday: I - Gn 23:1-4, 19; 24:1-8, 62-67; II - Am 8:4-6, 9-12; Mt 9:9-13

Saturday: I - Gn 27:1-5, 15-29; II - Am 9:11-15; Mt 9:14-17

### Week Fourteen

Monday: I - Gn 28:10-22a; II - Hos 2:16, 17b-18, 21-22; Mt 9:18-26

Tuesday: I - Gn 32:22-33; II - Hos 8:4-7, 11-13; Mt 9:32-38

Wednesday: I - Gn 41:55-57; 42:5-7a, 17-24a; II - Hos 10:1-3, 7-8, 12; Mt 10:1-7

Thursday: I - Gn 44:18-21, 23b-29; 45:1-5; II - Hos 11:1-4, 8c-9; Mt 10:7-15

Friday: I - Gn 46:1-7, 28-30; II - Hos 14:2-10; Mt 10:16-23

Saturday: I - Gn 49:29-33; 50:15-24; II - Is 6:1-8; Mt 10:24-33

### Week Fifteen

Monday: I - Ex 1:8-14, 22; II - Is 1:10-17; Mt 10:34—11:1

Tuesday: I - Ex 2:1-15a; II - Is 7:1-9; Mt 11:20-24

Wednesday: I - Ex 3:1-6, 9-12; II - Is 10:5-7, 13b-16; Mt 11:25-27

Thursday: I - Ex 3:13-20; II - Is 26:7-9, 12, 16-19; Mt 11:28-30

Friday: I - Ex 11:10-12, 14; II - Is 38:1-6, 21-22, 7-8; Mt 12:1-8

Saturday: I - Ex 12:37-42; II - Mi 2:1-5; Mt 12:14-21

### Week Sixteen

Monday: I - Ex 14:5-18; II - Mi 6:1-4, 6-8; Mt 12:38-42

Tuesday: I - Ex 14:21—15:1; II - Mi 7:14-15, 18-20; Mt 12:46-50

Wednesday: I - Ex 16:1-5, 9-15; II - Jer 1:1, 4-10; Mt 13:1-9

Thursday: I - Ex 19:1-2, 9-11, 16-20b; II - Jer 2:1-3, 7-8, 12-13; Mt 13:10-17

Friday: I - Ex 20:1-17; II - Jer 3:14-17; Mt 13:18-23

Saturday: I - Ex 24:3-8; II - Jer 7:1-11; Mt 13:24-30

### Week Seventeen

Monday: I - Ex 32:15-24, 30-34; II - Jer 13:1-11; Mt 13:31-35

Tuesday: I - Ex 33:7-11; 34:5b-9, 28; II - Jer 14:17-22; Mt 13:36-43

Wednesday: I - Ex 34:29-34; II - Jer 15:10, 16-21; Mt 13:44-46

Thursday: I - Ex 40:16-21, 34-38; II - Jer 18:1-6; Mt 13:47-53

Friday: I - Lv 23:1, 4-11, 15-16, 27, 34b-37; II - Jer 26:1-9; Mt 13:54-58

Saturday: I - Lv 25:1, 8-17; II - Jer 26:11-16, 24; Mt 14:1-12

### Week Eighteen

Monday: I - Nm 11:4b-15; II - Jer 28:1-17; Mt 14:13-21 or Mt 14:22-36

Tuesday: I - Nm 12:1-13; II - Jer 30:1-2, 12-15, 18-22; Mt 14:22-36 or Mt 15:1-2, 10-14

Wednesday: I - Nm 13:1-2a, 25—14:1, 26-29a, 34-35; II - Jer 31:1-7; Mt 15:21-28

Thursday: I - Nm 20:1-13; II - Jer 31:31-34; Mt 16:13-23

Friday: I - Dt 4:32-40; II - Na 2:1, 3; 3:1-3, 6-7; Mt 16:24-28

Saturday: I - Dt 6:4-13; II - Hb 1:12—2:4; Mt 17:14-20

### Week Nineteen

Monday: I - Dt 10:12-22; II - Ez 1:2-5, 24-28c; Mt 17:22-27

Tuesday: I - Dt 31:1-8; II - Ez 2:8—3:4; Mt 18:1-5, 10, 12-14

Wednesday: I - Dt 34:1-12; II - Ez 9:1-7; 10:18-22; Mt 18:15-20

Thursday: I - Jos 3:7-10a, 11, 13-17; II - Ez 12:1-12; Mt 18:21—19:1

Friday: I - Jos 24:1-13; II - Ez 16:1-15, 60, 63; Mt 19:3-12

Saturday: I - Jos 24:14-29; II - Ez 18:1-10, 13b, 30-32; Mt 19:13-15

### Week Twenty

Monday: I - Jgs 2:11-19; II - Ez 24:15-24; Mt 19:16-22

Tuesday: I - Jgs 6:11-24a; II - Ez 28:1-10; Mt 19:23-30

Wednesday: I - Jgs 9:6-15; II - Ez 34:1-11; Mt 20:1-16a

Thursday: I - Jgs 11:29-39a; II - Ez 36:23-28; Mt 22:1-14

Friday: I - Ru 1:1, 3-6, 14b-16, 22; II - Ez 37:1-14; Mt 22:34-40

Saturday: I - Ru 2:1-3, 8-11; 4:13-17; II - Ez 43:1-7a; Mt 23:1-12

## Week Twenty-one

Monday: I - 1 Thes 1:1-5, 8b-10; II - 2 Thes 1:1-5, 11b-12; Mt 23:13-22

Tuesday: I - 1 Thes 2:1-18; II - 2 Thes 2:1-3a, 13-17; Mt 23:23-26

Wednesday: I - 1 Thes 2:9-13; II - 2 Thes 3:6-10, 16-18; Mt 23:27-32

Thursday: I - 1 Thes 3:7-13; II - 1 Cor 1:1-9; Mt 24:42-51

Friday: I - 1 Thes 4:1-8; II - 1 Cor 1:17-25; Mt 25:1-13

Saturday: I - 1 Thes 4:9-12; II - 1 Cor 1:26-31; Mt 25:14-30

## Week Twenty-two

Monday: I - 1 Thes 4:13-18; II - 1 Cor 2:1-5; Lk 4:16-30

Tuesday: I - 1 Thes 5:1-6, 9-11; II - 1 Cor 2:10b-16; Lk 4:31-37

Wednesday: I - Col 1:1-8; II - 1 Cor 3:1-9; Lk 4:38-44

Thursday: I - Col 1:9-14; II - 1 Cor 3:18-23; Lk 5:1-11

Friday: I - Col 1:15-20; II - 1 Cor 4:1-5; Lk 5:33-39

Saturday: I - Col 1:21-23; II - 1 Cor 4:9-15; Lk 6:1-5

## Week Twenty-three

Monday: I - Col 1:24—2:3; II - 1 Cor 5:1-8; Lk 6:6-11

Tuesday: I - Col 2:6-15; II - 1 Cor 6:1-11; Lk 6:12-19

Wednesday: I - Col 3:1-11; II - 1 Cor 7:25-31; Lk 6:20-26

Thursday: I - Col 3:12-17; II - 1 Cor 8:1b-7, 11-13; Lk 6:27-38

Friday: I - 1 Tm 1:1-2, 12-14; II - 1 Cor 9:16-19, 22b-27; Lk 6:39-42

Saturday: I - 1 Tm 1:15-17; II - 1 Cor 10:14-22a; Lk 6:43-49

## Week Twenty-four

Monday: I - 1 Tm 2:1-8; II - 1 Cor 11:17-26, 33; Lk 7:1-10

Tuesday: I - 1 Tm 3:1-13; II - 1 Cor 12:12-14, 27-31a; Lk 7:11-17

Wednesday: I - 1 Tm 3:14-16; II - 1 Cor 12:31—13:13; Lk 7:31-35

Thursday: I - 1 Tm 4:12-16; II - 1 Cor 15:1-11; Lk 7:36-50

Friday: I - 1 Tm 6:2c-12; II - 1 Cor 15:12-20; Lk 8:1-3

Saturday: I - 1 Tm 6:13-16; II - 1 Cor 15:36-37, 42-49; Lk 8:4-15

## Week Twenty-five

Monday: I - Ezr 1:1-6; II – Prv 3:27-34; Lk 8:16-18

Tuesday: I - Ezr 6:7-8, 12b, 14-20; II - Prv 21:1-6, 10-13; Lk 8:19-21

Wednesday: I - Ezr 9:5-9; II - Prv 30:5-9; Lk 9:1-6

Thursday: I - Hg 1:1-8; II - Eccl 1:2-11; Lk 9:7-9

Friday: I - Hg 1:15b—2:9; II - Eccl 3:1-11; Lk 9:18-22

Saturday: I - Zec 2:5-9a, 14-15a; II - Eccl 11:9—12:8; Lk 9:43b-45

## Week Twenty-six

Monday: I - Zec 8:1-8; II - Jb 1:6-22; Lk 9:46-50

Tuesday: I - Zec 8:20-23; II - Jb 3:1-3, 11-17, 20-23; Lk 9:51-56

Wednesday: I - Neh 2:1-8; II - Jb 9:1-12, 14-16; Lk 9:57-62

Thursday: I - Neh 8:1-4a, 5-6, 7b-12; II - Jb 19:12-27; Lk 10:1-12

Friday: I - Bar 1:15-22; II - Jb 38:1, 12-21; 40:3-5; Lk 10:13-16

Saturday: I - Bar 4:5-12, 27-29; II - Jb 42:1-3, 5-6, 12-17; Lk 10:17-24

## Week Twenty-seven

Monday: I - Jon 1:1—2:1, 11; II - Gal 1:6-12; Lk 10:25-37

Tuesday: I - Jon 3:1-10; II - Gal 1:13-24; Lk 10:38-42

Wednesday: I - Jon 4:1-11; II - Gal 2:1-2, 7-14; Lk 11:1-4

Thursday: I - Mal 3:13-20a; II - Gal 3:1-5; Lk 11:5-13

Friday: I - Jl 1:13-15; 2:1-2; II - Gal 3:7-14; Lk 11:15-26

Saturday: I - Jl 4:12-21; II - Gal 3:22-29; Lk 11:27-28

## Week Twenty-eight

Monday: I - Rom 1:1-7; II - Gal 4:22-24, 26-27, 31; Lk 11:29-32

Tuesday: I - Rom 1:16-25; II - Gal 5:1-6; Lk 11:37-41

Wednesday: I - Rom 2:1-11; II - Gal 5:18-25; Lk 11:42-46

Thursday: I - Rom 3:21-29; II - Eph 1:3-10; Lk 11:47-54

Friday: I - Rom 4:1-8; II - Eph 1:11-14; Lk 12:1-7

Saturday: I - Rom 4:13, 16-18; II - Eph 1:15-23; Lk 12:8-12

## Week Twenty-nine

Monday: I - Rom 4:20-25; II - Eph 2:1-10; Lk 12:13-21

Tuesday: I - Rom 5:12, 15b, 17-19, 20b-21; II - Eph 2:12-22; Lk 12:35-38

Wednesday: I - Rom 6:12-18; II - Eph 3:2-12; Lk 12:39-48

Thursday: I - Rom 6:19-23; II - Eph 3:14-21; Lk 12:49-53

Friday: I - Rom 7:18-25a; II - Eph 4:1-6; Lk 12:54-59

Saturday: I - Rom 8:1-11; II - Eph 4:7-16;
Lk 13:1-9

### Week Thirty

Monday: I - Rom 8:12-17; II - Eph 4:32—5:8;
Lk 13:10-17
Tuesday: I - Rom 8:18-25; II - Eph 5:21-33;
Lk 13:18-21
Wednesday: I - Rom 8:26-30; II - Eph 6:1-9;
Lk 13:22-30
Thursday: I - Rom 3:31b-39; II - Eph 6:10-20;
Lk 13:31-35
Friday: I - Rom 9:1-5; II - Phil 1:1-11; Lk 14:1-6
Saturday: I - Rom 11:1-2a, 11-12; 25-29;
II - Phil 1:18b-26; Lk 14:1, 7-11

### Week Thirty-one

Monday: I - Rom 11:29-36; II - Phil 2:1-4;
Lk 14:12-14
Tuesday: I - Rom 12:5-16a; II - Phil 2:5-11;
Lk 14:15-24
Wednesday: I - Rom 13:8-10; II - Phil 2:12-18;
Lk 14:25-33
Thursday: I - Rom 14:7-12; II - Phil 3:3-8a;
Lk 15:1-10
Friday: I - Rom 15:14-21; II - Phil 3:17—4:1;
Lk 16:1-8
Saturday: I - Rom 16:3-9, 16, 22-27; II - Phil
4:10-19; Lk 16:9-15

### Week Thirty-two

Monday: I - Wis 1:1-7; II - Ti 1:1-9; Lk 17:1-6
Tuesday: I - Wis 2:23—3:9; II - Ti 2:1-8, 11-14;
Lk 17:7-10
Wednesday: I - Wis 6:1-11; II - Ti 3:1-7;
Lk 17:11-19

Thursday: I - Wis 7:22b—8:1; II - Phlm 7-20;
Lk 17:20-25
Friday: I - Wis 13:1-9; II - 2 Jn 4-9; Lk 17:26-37
Saturday: I - Wis 18:14-16; 19:6-9; II - 3 Jn 5-8;
Lk 18:1-8

### Week Thirty-three

Monday: I - 1 Mc 1:10-15, 41-43, 54-57, 62-63;
II - Rev 1:1-4; 2:1-5a; Lk 18:35-43
Tuesday: I - 2 Mc 6:18-31; II - Rev 3:1-6, 14-22;
Lk 19:1-10
Wednesday: I - 2 Mc 7:1, 20-31; II - Rev 4:1-11;
Lk 19:11-28
Thursday: I - 1 Mc 2:15-29; II - Rev 5:1-10;
Lk 19:41-44
Friday: I - 1 Mc 4:36-37, 52-59; II - Rev 10:8-11;
Lk 19:45-48
Saturday: I - 1 Mc 6:1-13; II - Rev 11:4-12;
Lk 20:27-40

### Week Thirty-four

Monday: I - Dn 1:1-6, 8-20; II - Rev 14:1-3,
4b-5; Lk 21:1-4
Tuesday: I - Dn 2:31-45; II - Rev 14:14-19;
Lk 21:5-11
Wednesday: I - Dn 5:1-6, 13-14, 16-17, 23-28;
II - Rev 15:1-4; Lk 21:12-19
Thursday: I - Dn 6:11-28; II - Rev 18:1-2, 21-23;
19:1-3, 9a; Lk 21:20-28
Friday: I - Dn 7:2-14; II - Rev 20:1-4,
11-15—21:1-2; Lk 21:29-33
Saturday: I - Dn 7:15-27; II - Rev 22:1-7;
Lk 21:34-36

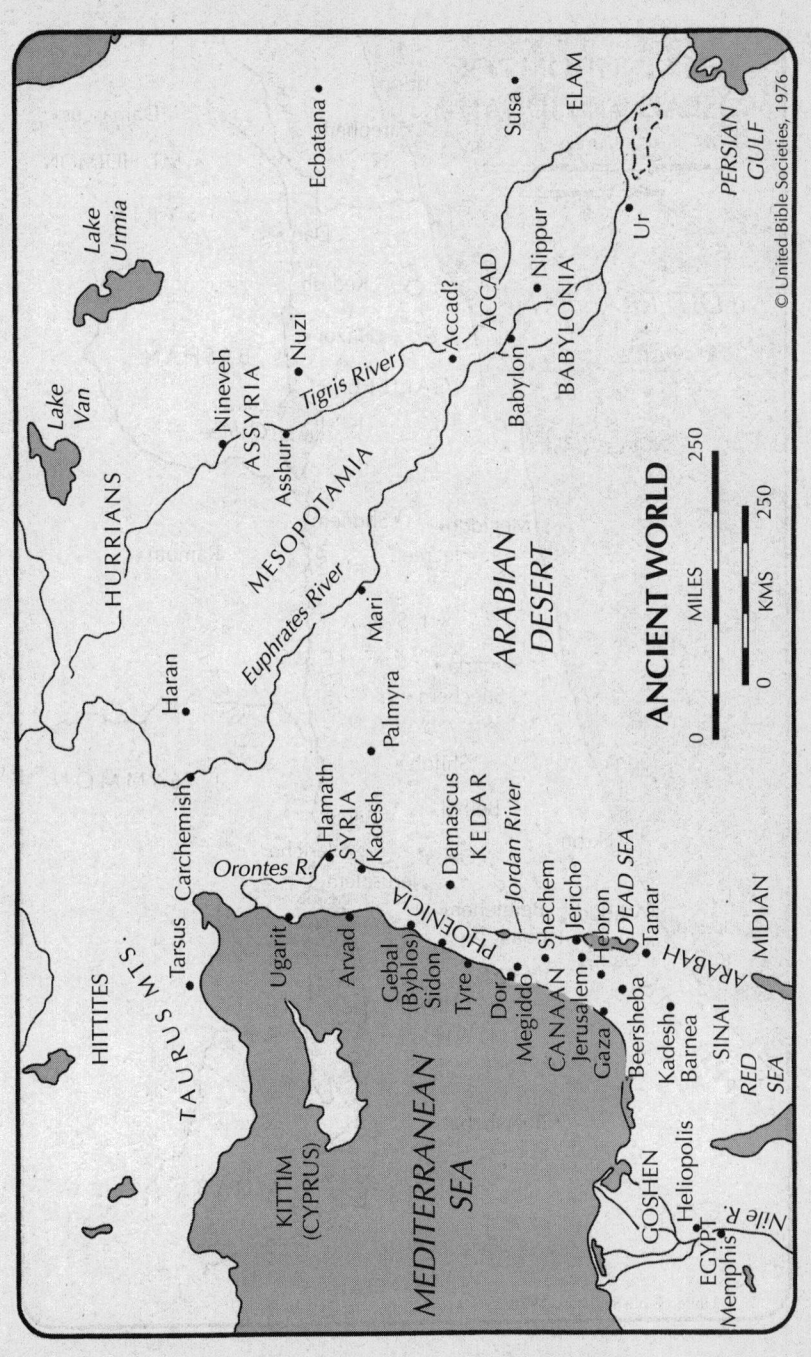

ANCIENT WORLD

© United Bible Societies, 1976

THE KINGDOMS OF
ISRAEL AND JUDAH

MILES
0          40

KMS
0          40

MEDITERRANEAN
SEA

Sidon

Zarephath

LEBANON MTS.

Damascus

MT. HERMON

SYRIA

Tyre

PHOENICIA

Dan

Kedesh

Hazor

BASHAN

GALILEE

Lake
Galilee

MT. CARMEL

Megiddo        Shunem

Jezreel

Ramoth

ISRAEL

Jordan River

GILEAD

AMMON

Samaria

Shechem

Joppa

Shiloh

Bethel

Gilgal

Geba        Jericho

Ekron        Jerusalem

Ashkelon        Ashdod        Bethlehem

Libnah

Gath?        Lachish

Gaza        Hebron

PHILISTIA        JUDAH

Gath?        Dead Sea

Beersheba

MOAB

EDOM

© United Bible Societies, 1978

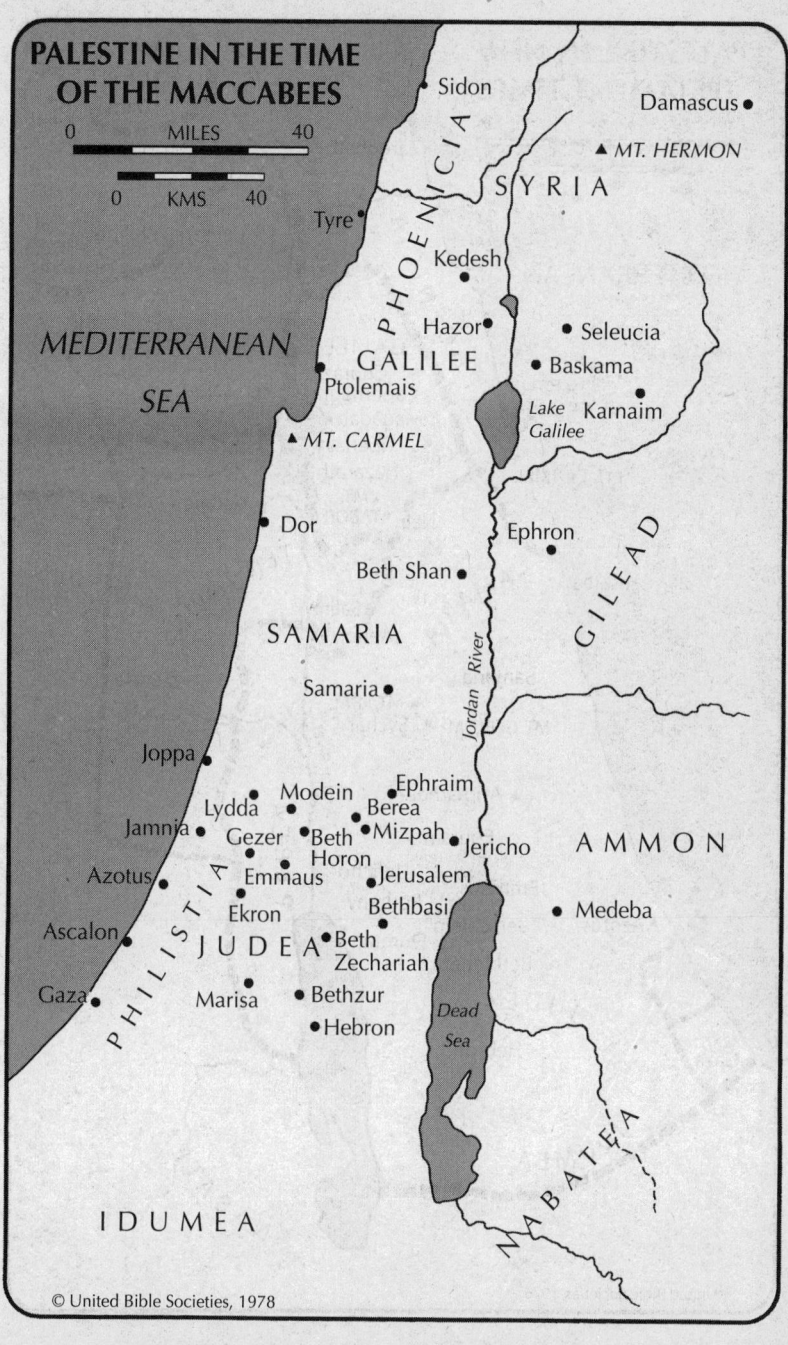

# PALESTINE IN THE TIME OF THE MACCABEES

MILES 0 — 40

KMS 0 — 40

MEDITERRANEAN SEA

Sidon

Damascus

▲ MT. HERMON

S Y R I A

PHOENICIA

Tyre

Kedesh

Hazor

GALILEE

Ptolemais

Seleucia

Baskama

Lake Galilee

Karnaim

▲ MT. CARMEL

Dor

Ephron

GILEAD

Beth Shan

Jordan River

SAMARIA

Samaria

Joppa

Modein

Ephraim

Lydda

Berea

Jamnia

Gezer

Beth Horon

Mizpah

Jericho

AMMON

Azotus

Emmaus

Jerusalem

Medeba

Ascalon

Ekron

Bethbasi

Gaza

JUDEA

Beth Zechariah

PHILISTIA

Marisa

Bethzur

Dead Sea

Hebron

NABATEA

IDUMEA

© United Bible Societies, 1978

# PALESTINE IN NEW TESTAMENT TIMES

MILES
0          40

KMS
0          40

MEDITERRANEAN

SEA

Sidon

ABILENE

Abila

Damascus

Zarephath

LEBANON MTS.

SYRIA

▲ MT. HERMON

Tyre

PHOENICIA

Caesarea Philippi

GALILEE

Ptolemais

Chorazin

Capernaum

Bethsaida

Magadan

Lake

Cana

Tiberias

Galilee

MT. CARMEL ▲

Nazareth

▲ MT. TABOR

Nain

Gadara

TEN TOWNS

Caesarea

SAMARIA

Salim

Aenon

Samaria

▲ MT. EBAL

Gerasa

MT. GERIZIM ▲ Sychar

Joppa

Arimathea?

Jordan River

Ephraim

PEREA

Jericho

Emmaus

Bethany

Azotus

Jerusalem

Qumran

Ascalon

Bethlehem

JUDEA

Gaza

Hebron

Dead
Sea

IDUMEA

NABATEA

© United Bible Societies, 1976